# DICTIONARY
# OF
# INTERNATIONAL
# BIOGRAPHY

## 2005/06

### 32nd Edition

All communications to: International Biographical Centre
St Thomas' Place, ELY, CB7 4GG, GREAT BRITAIN

## PUBLISHER
Nicholas S. Law

## EDITOR IN CHIEF
Sara Rains

## PRODUCTION/DESIGN
Scott Gwinnett

## EDITORIAL ASSISTANTS
Ann Dewison
Rebecca Partner

## ISBN: 1 903986 19 2

Printed and bound in the United Kingdom by:
Antony Rowe Limited, Bumper's Farm Industrial Estate,
Chippenham, Wiltshire, SN14 6LH, England

# FOREWORD BY THE DIRECTOR GENERAL

I am delighted to offer the Thirty Second Edition of the Dictionary of International Biography, the flagship publication of the International Biographical Centre of Cambridge, England, to its many readers or 'users' throughout the world.

The Dictionary of International Biography attempts to reflect contemporary achievement in every profession and field of interest within as many countries as possible. It is an ever growing reference source since very few biographical entries are repeated from one edition to the next and only then when they have been updated with relevant new material. In this way each new Edition adds thousands of new biographies to those already published in the series; to date more than 220,000 biographies have been presented from information supplied and checked by those individuals who are featured.

I am often asked how we select individuals for inclusion in the Dictionary of International Biography and for that matter other titles published by the IBC. Readers and researchers should know that we publish only information which has been provided by those listed and in every case we have had their permission to publish it. Selection is made on the grounds of achievement and contribution on a professional, occupational, national or international level, as well as interest to the reader. An additional intention is to provide librarians of major libraries with a cumulative reference work consisting of Volumes published annually.

It cannot be emphasised too strongly that there is no charge or fee of any kind for inclusion in the Dictionary. Every entrant was sent at least one typescript for approval before publication in order to eliminate errors and to ensure accuracy and relevance. While great care has been taken by our Editors it is always possible that in a work of this size a few errors may have been made. If this is the case, my apologies in advance.

I would be grateful to hear from readers and researchers who feel that particular individuals should appear in future Volumes of the Dictionary of International Biography or any other relevant IBC works of reference. Such recommendations may be sent to the IBC's Research Department. Since our researchers have great difficulty in contacting some important figures it is always helpful to us to have addresses.

**Nicholas S. Law**
**Director General**
**International Biographical Centre**
**Cambridge**

**November 2005**

# INTERNATIONAL BIOGRAPHICAL CENTRE
# RANGE OF REFERENCE TITLES

From one of the widest ranges of contemporary biographical reference works published under any one imprint, some IBC titles date back to the 1930's. Each edition is compiled from information supplied by those listed, who include leading personalities of particular countries or professions. Information offered usually includes date and place of birth; family details; qualifications; career histories; awards and honours received; books published or other creative work; other relevant information including postal address. Naturally there is no charge or fee for inclusion. New editions are freshly compiled and contain on average 80-90% new information. New titles are regularly added to the IBC reference library.
Titles include:

2000 Eminent Scientists of Today
Dictionary of International Biography
Outstanding People of the 21st Century
Who's Who in the 21st Century
2000 Outstanding Scientists of the 21st Century
2000 Outstanding Scholars of the 21st Century
2000 Outstanding Intellectuals of the 21st Century
Living Science

Enquiries to:
**International Biographical Centre**
**St Thomas' Place, ELY**
**CB7 4GG, GREAT BRITAIN**

# CONTENTS

**Foreword by the Director General**                                      III

**Range of IBC Titles**                                                   IV

**Biographies**                                                     1 - 1084

**20th Century Honours List**                                  1085 - 1105

**21st Century Honours List**                                  1107 - 1123

# BIOGRAPHIES

BIOGRAPHIES

# DICTIONARY OF INTERNATIONAL BIOGRAPHY

## A

**AAKER Everett,** b. 20 April 1954, Wigan, Lancashire, England. Author. Education: HNC, Business Studies, Wirral College of Technology. 1982-86. Appointments: Professional career in business in England; Feature Writer, TV Scene Magazine, 1987-90. Publication: Television Western Players of the Fifties: A Biographical Encyclopaedia of All Regular Cast Members in Western Series, 1949-59, 1997; Television Crime Busters of the Fifties: A Biographical Encyclopaedia of All Regular Cast Members in Crime and Mystery Series 1948-59, 2005. Honour: Associate, London Academy of Music and Dramatic Art, 1977. Membership: Institute of Purchasing and Supply, 1987. Address: c/o McFarland & Co, PO Box 611, Jefferson, North Carolina 28640, USA.

**AARÅS Arne,** b. 7 March 1937, Holla, Norway. Physician. m. Astrid, 1 son, 2 daughters. Education: Graduate, Medical School, 1964, PhD, 1987, University of Oslo; Hospital training in Ear, Nose and Throat, Gynaecology, Geriatric Medicine, Surgery, Internal Medicine; Occupational Medicine Courses: Arbetsmedisinske Institutet, Karolinska Institutet, Stockholm, Sweden, 1971, Norwegian Employer Federation and Johns Hopkins Hospital, Baltimore, USA, 1987-88. Appointments: District Doctor in Sweden, 3 years; Concurrently, Occupational Physician with a large packaging company; Occupational Doctor, Centre for Occupational Medicine, Sweden, 5 years; Co-ordinator for Occupational Medicine, Standard Telefon og Kabelfabrikk A/S (ITT Norway, later, Alcatel STK A/S), 1974-; Co-operator with Work Physiology Institute in Oslo, 1977-; Associate Chairman, Work Inspectorate, Oslo, 10 years; Co-ordinator for an international study of musculoskeletal, visual and psychosocial stress for VDU workers with 5 participating countries, 1990-; Professor, Department of Optometry and Visual Sciences, Buskerud University College. Publications: Approximately 90 papers. Honours: Award, Nordic Ergonomic Society, 1995; Distinguished International Colleague Award, Human Factors and Ergonomics Society, 1999. Memberships: International Committee of Occupational Medicine; Norwegian Research Council (5 years); Ergonomic Society, UK. Address: Finstadkroken 12, 1475 Finstadjordet, Norway. E-mail: arne.aaras@alcatel.no

**AARONSON Edward John (Jack),** b. 16 August 1918. Company Director. m. Marian Davies, 2 sons. Education: CFS, London. Career: RA, Palestine to Tunisia, 1940-44, India, 1945-46, W/S Captain; Articled, Jackson Pixley & Co, 1946-49; Founder, General Secretary, The Anglo Israel Chamber of Commerce, 1950-53; Economic Advisor (Export), GEC, 1954-61, later General Manager Overseas Operations, 1961-63; Economic Advisor, Celmac Ltd, 1964-65; Deputy Chairman and part-time Chief Executive, The Steel Barrel Scammells & Associated Engineers Ltd, later Anthony Carrimore Ltd, 1965-68; Industrial Advisor, later Director, Armitage Industrial Holdings Ltd, 1965-68, Director, later Chairman, George Turton Platt, 1966-68; Director, E R & F Turner Ltd, 1967-68; Chairman Br Northrop Ltd, 1968-73; Chairman and Chief Executive, Scheme Manager and Creditors Committee Chairman, The G R A Property Trust Ltd, 1975-83; Non-Executive Chairman, Wand FC Bonham & Sons Ltd, 1981-89; Non-Executive Director, Camlab Ltd, 1982-89; Non-Executive Chairman, The Reject Shop plc, 1985-90. Memberships: FBI Standing Committees on overseas credit and overseas investment from inception, 1958-63; Council, The Export Group for the Construction Industries, 1960-63; Member, British Greyhound Racing Board, 1975-83; Chairman, NGRC Race Course Promoters Association, 1978-83; FCA, 1960; FInstD, 1980; Member General Committee,

1976-79, 1980-83, Chairman Pension Fund Trustees, 1985-, Reform Club. Address: 2 The Paddock, The Street, Bishops Cannings, Devizes SN10 2LD, England.

**AARONSON Michael John (Mike),** b. 8 September 1947, London, England. Director General. m. Andrene Margaret Dundas Sutherland, 2 sons, 1 daughter. Education: MA (Hons), Philosophy and Psychology, St John's College, Oxford, 1969. Appointments: Relief Co-ordinator, Save the Children Fund, Nigeria, 1969-71; HM Diplomatic Service, 1972-88: Third rising to First Secretary, HM Embassy Paris, 1973-77; British High Commission, Lagos, 1981-83; HM Embassy, Rangoon, 1987-88; Overseas Director, 1988-95, Director General, 1995-, Save the Children Fund; Governor, Westminster Foundation for Democracy, 2001-; Chair of the Board, Centre for Humanitarian Dialogue, Geneva, 2001-; Visiting Fellow, Nuffield College, Oxford, 2004-; Member of Council, Royal Society of Arts, Manufacturing and Commerce, 2004-. Honours: Freeman City of London, Worshipful Company of Merchant Taylors, CBE, 2000. Memberships: Royal Society of Arts, Manufactures and Commerce; MCC. Address: Save the Children Fund, 1 St John's Lane, London EC1M 4AR, England. E-mail: m.aaronson@savet hechildren.org.uk Website: www.savethechildren.org.uk

**AARSETH Sverre Johannes,** b. 20 July 1934, Steinkjer, Norway. Astronomer. Education: BSc, Oslo, 1959; PhD, Cantab, 1963. Appointments: Research Scientist, Institute of Astronomy, University of Cambridge, 1967-2001; Retired, 2001. Publications: Over 100 research papers in dynamical astronomy; Gravitational N-Body Simulations, 2003. Honours: Dirk Brouwer Award, American Astronomical Society; Asteroid #9836 named Aarseth. Memberships: Royal Astronomical Society; Royal Geographical Society; Alpine Club. Address: Institute of Astronomy, Madingley Road, Cambridge CB3 0HA, England. Website: www.ast.cam.ac.uk/~sverre

**ABADIR Karim Maher,** b. 6 January 1964, Egypt. Professor of Econometrics and Statistics. Education: Bachelor of Arts, Economics, Master of Arts, Economics, The American University in Cairo; DPhil, Economics, Oxford University, England. Appointments: Lecturer, Economics, Lincoln College, Oxford, England, 1988-92; Research Fellow, Economics, American University in Cairo, 1992-93; Senior Lecturer, Statistics and Econometrics, 1993-94, Reader, Econometrics, 1994-96, University of Exeter, England; Professor, Econometrics and Statistics, Departments of Mathematics and Economics, University of York, England, 1996-. Publications: Numerous publications in professional journals and books; Numerous papers presented at national and international conferences. Honours: Invited lecturer at many conferences; ESRC Grants, 1996-1998, 2001-2004, 2003-2006; Multa Scripsit Award, 1997; University of York Grant, 1998; Plura Scripsit Award, 2001. Memberships: Econometric Society; Institute of Mathematical Statistics; Fellow, Royal Statistical Society; European Science Foundation's Network on Econometric Methods for the Modelling of Nonstationary Data, Policy Analysis and Forecasting; Professional Association of Diving Instructors; Founder and Director, various undergraduate and graduate degrees; Editor of various journals. Address: Department of Economics, University of York, Heslington, York YO10 5DD, England. E-mail: kma4@york.ac.uk

**ABADJIEV Valentin Ivanov,** b. 8 September 1946, Razgrad, Bulgaria. Associate Professor in Applied Mechanics. m. Evdokia Nikolova, 1 daughter. Education: MSc, Mechanical Engineering, University of Rousse, Rousse, 1970; PhD, Applied Mechanics, Bulgarian Academy of Sciences, Sofia, 1985. Appointments: Research Fellow, Institute Motors/Cars, Sofia,

1972-83; Assistant Professor, 1983-88, Associate Professor, 1988-, Institute of Mechanics, Bulgarian Academy of Sciences; Chairman of Board of Directors, Education/Science Co, Sofia, 1997-2000. Publications: Author, co-author, over 70 scientific publications of applied mechanics; 1 book; 19 Bulgarian patents. Honours: National Medal for Inventions, State Committee of Science, 1987; 3rd Competitive Session Science Award, Ministry of Education and Science, 1997. Memberships: Steering Committee of Bulgarian Union of Standardization, 2001-; National Technical Committee Standardization, 1993-; Science Council Institute Mechanics, 1993-; Regional Municipal Council, Sofia, 1994-99; High Testimonial Committee, Special Science Council, 1998-; Board of Directors, Education/Science Co, 1997-2002. Address: Institute of Mechanics, Bulgarian Academy of Sciences, Academic G Bonchev Str, Bl 4, 1113 Sofia, Bulgaria. E-mail: abadjiev@imbm.bas.bg

**ABALA Felipe C,** b. 15 September 1964, Ekiran, Alangalang, Leyte, Philippines. Information Technology Professional; Industrial Engineer. Education: BSc, Industrial Engineering, Leyte Institute of Technology (now Eastern Visayas State University), Philippines, 1987; MBA, Columbia Southern University, Alabama, USA, 2004; Incorporated Engineer, UK (in progress); Chartered IT Professional, UK; Information Systems Professional of Canada; Certified Manufacturing Engineer, USA; Certified Computing Professional, USA; Certified Information Technology Project Manager, USA; Certified Internet Professional, USA; IT Management Proficiency, USA. Appointments: Production Supervisor, Fashion'e Fabric Inc, Pasig City, Philippines, 1987-89; Industrial Engineer, Cinderella Dresses Inc, Quezon City, Philippines, 1989-90; Education Program Specialist II, Department of Education of the Republic of the Philippines, 1990-91; Production Controller, EPIC Electronics Industries Inc, Taguig City, Philippines, 1991; Production Controller, 1992-93, Local Area Network Administrator and Systems Developer, 1993-98, Information Technology Project Teams Manager, 1998-, Defence Force's Maintenance, Repair and Overhaul Operations, General Maintenance Directorate, Abu Dhabi, United Arab Emirates. Honours: One of Top Ten Students, Leyte Institute of Technology College of Engineering; Educational Grant for BSc Degree Program; Listed in Who's Who publications and biographical dictionaries. Memberships include: Chartered Member, British Computer Society; IEE; Senior Member, IIE, USA; Senior Member, Society of Manufacturing Engineers, USA; Senior Member, IEEE and IEEE Computer Society; IT Co-ordinator, Professional Chartered Engineers, United Arab Emirates; Certified Member, Canadian Information Processing Society; Australian Computer Society. Address: PO Box 51683, Abu Dhabi, United Arab Emirates. Website: www.pca64.com

**ABBADO Claudio,** b. 26 June 1933, Milan, Italy. Conductor. Education: Giuseppe Verdi Conservatory, Milan; Academy of Music, Vienna, with Hans Swabarowsky. Debut: La Scala, Milan, 1960, in concert celebrating tercentenary of A Scarlatti; Salzburg Festival, 1965, local premiere of G Manzoni's opera Atomtod. Career: Conducted opening of La Scala season, 1967; Music Director, La Scala, 1968-86; Covent Garden debut, 1968 (Don Carlos); Has conducted the Vienna Philharmonic Orchestra from 1972; Tour of USA with Cleveland and Philadelphia Orchestras, 1972; Tour with La Scala company to Munich, 1972; USSR, 1974; London 1976 (Simon Boccanegra); USA, 1976; Japan, 1981; Tour with the Vienna Philharmonic to Japan and China, 1973; Founder, European Community Youth Orchestra, 1978; Musical Director, London Symphony Orchestra, 1979-88 (series of concerts, Mahler, Vienna and the 20th Century, 1985); Principal Conductor, Chamber Orchestra of Europe, 1981; Founder of La Filharmonica della Scala, 1982;

Principal Guest Conductor of Chicago Symphony Orchestra, 1982-85; Debut at the Vienna State Opera, 1984; Director, 1986-91; Founder, Gustav Mahler Jugendorchester, Vienna, 1986; Conductor, New Year's Eve concerts, Vienna, 1988 and 1990; Appointed Musical Director and Principal Conductor, Berlin Philharmonic Orchestra, 1989-2002; Promenade Concerts, London, 1991, with the Gustav Mahler Jugendorchester (5th Symphony) and the Berlin Philharmonic (Brahms 2nd Piano Concerto and Mahler 4); Conductor, The House of the Dead, Salzburg Festival, 1992; Bruckner's 5th Symphony with the Gustav Mahler Youth Orchestra, Promenade Concerts, 1993; La Scala, 1994, Il Barbiere di Siviglia; Artistic Director, Salzburg Easter Festival, 1994; Engaged to conduct Tristan und Isolde at Salzburg, 1999; Founder, Lucern Festival Orchestra, 2001. Recordings include: Operas by Rossini and Verdi, Mussorgsky, Berg, Schubert (Fierabras); Music by Berg and Nono; Complete Symphonies of Mahler, Schubert, Mendelssohn, Beethoven and Tchaikovsky; Mozart Piano Concertos with Rudolf Serkin; Brahms Piano Concerto No 1, with Brendel and Vivaldi's Four Seasons, with Viktoria Mullova; Works of Haydn and Prokofiev, Bartók, Ravel, Debussy; currently working on cycle of complete Bruckner symphonies. Publication: La Casa Del Suoni: Book for Children about Music; Musica sopra Berlino, 1998, 2001; Suite Concertante from the Ballet Hawaii, 2000. Honours include: Mozart Medaille; Premio Abbiati; Officier of the French Légion d'Honneur; Koussevitzky Prize (Tanglewood); Winner, Mitropoulos Conducting Competition; Conductor of the Year, Opernwelt Review, 2000; Oscar della Lirica, 2001. Address: Berliner Philharmonisches Orchester, Matthäikirchstrasse 1, 10785 Berlin, Germany.

**ABBOTT Gerry,** b. 13 February 1935, Bow, London, England. University Teacher. m. Khin-Thant Han, 1 son, 2 daughters. Education: BA Honours, English, University College, London, 1958; PGCE with TEFL, Institute of Education, London, 1959; PhD, Education, University of Manchester, 1998. Appointments: National Service, 1953-55; Commissioned, 1955; Lecturer, College of Education, Bangkok, 1959-63; British Council Education Officer, Jordan, 1963-65; Lecturer, Teaching of English Overseas, Manchester University including numerous postings in Asia and Africa, 1965-92; Honorary Fellow, Manchester University, 1992-. Publications: Relative Clauses, 1969; Conditionals, 1970; Question-Word Questions, 1970; The Teaching of English as an International Language (with Peter Wingard), 1981; Back to Mandalay, 1990; Traveller's History of Burma, 1998; Numerous articles. Honours: 1st Prize, English Speaking Union Essay Competition, 1978; Appointed Honorary Fellow, Manchester University, 1992. Memberships: IATEFL; Amnesty International; Friends of the Earth; World Development Movement; Britain-Burma Society. Address: 16 Manor Drive, Manchester M21 7GQ, England.

**ABBOTT-JOHNSON Winsome Joy,** b. 17 September 1947, Australia. Dietician; Nutritionist. Widow, 1 son, 1 daughter. Education: Dip. Science, 1968; BSc, 1969; Dip. Nutrition and Dietetics, 1971; MApplSc, 1995. Appointments: Dietician, Sydney Adventist Hospital, 1971; Locum Dietician, 1979-81, Dietician, 1981-90, Senior Dietician, 1990-98, Senior Advanced Level Dietician, 1998-, Princess Alexandra Hospital, Brisbane, Australia.; Private Practice, 1998-; Part-time Lecturer, Queensland University of Technology, 1988-2002. Publications: Articles in medical journals as author and co-author include most recently: Child-Pugh class, nutritional indicators and early liver transplant outcomes, 2001; Growth hormone treatment in adults with chronic liver disease: a randomized, double-blind placebo-controlled, cross-over study, 2002; Contributing author: Tomorrow's Nutrition Today, Australian Seventh-day Adventist Dietetic Association, 1975. Honours:

# DICTIONARY OF INTERNATIONAL BIOGRAPHY

Princess Alexandra Hospital Week Prize (jointly), 1994; Bob McMahon Scientific Prize (jointly), 1990, David Russell Clinical Prize (jointly), 1994, Australian Society of Parenteral and Enteral Nutrition. Memberships: Chairperson, Adventist Health Association, Queensland, 1994-95; Vice-Chairperson, Nutrition Society of Australia, Queensland Branch, 1996-97; American Overseas Dietetic Association; Dietetic Association of Australia; Australian Society of Parenteral and Enteral Nutrition; Transplant Society of Australia and New Zealand. Address: 29 Brooke St, Crestmead, QLD 4132, Australia. E-mail: winsome@universal.net.au

**ABBS Peter Francis,** b. 22 February 1942, Cromer, Norfolk, England. Author; Lecturer. m. Barbara Beazeley, 10 June 1963, 1 son, 2 daughters. Education: BA, University of Bristol, England; DPhil, University of Sussex, England. Appointments: Lecturer, Senior Lecturer, Reader, Professor of Creative Writing, 1999-, University of Sussex, England. Publications: Poetry: For Man and Islands; Songs of a New Taliesin; Icons of Time; Personae; Love After Sappho, 2000; Viva la Vada, 2005; Non-Fiction: English for Diversity; Root and Blossom - The Philosophy, Practice and Politics of English Teaching; English Within the Arts; The Forms of Poetry; The Forms of Narrative; Autobiography in Education; Proposal for a New College (with Graham Carey); Reclamations - Essays on Culture, Mass-Culture and the Curriculum; A is for Aesthetic - Essays on Creative and Aesthetic Education; The Educational Imperative; The Polemics of Education; Editor, The Black Rainbow - Essays on the Present Breakdown of Culture; Living Powers - The Arts in Education; The Symbolic Order - A Contemporary Reader on the Arts Debate; The Polemics of Imagination: Essays on Art, Culture and Society; Against the Flow: Education, the Arts and Postmodern Culture, 2004. Contributions to: Times Higher Education Supplement; Agenda; Independent; Acumen; Stand; Daily Telegraph. Membership: Founding Member, New Metaphysical Art. Address: Graduate Research Centre in the Humanities, University of Sussex, Falmer, Brighton BN1 9RG, England.

**ABBUD-FILHO Mario,** b. 15 December 1952, Taquaritinga, Brazil. Physician. m. Patricia Abbud, 2 sons. Education: Medical Degree, 1975; Master in Medicine, 1980; Research Fellow, Paris V University, France, 1981-82; Research Fellow, Harvard Medical School, Boston, USA, 1983-84. Appointments: Director, Transplantation Laboratory of Institute of Urology and Nephrology, 1985-; Associate Professor of Medicine, Division of Nephrology Medical School, Rio Preto, 1992-; Head, Interdepartmental Transplantation Center (CINTRANS), Medical School of Rio Preto, 1997-; President, Brazilian Transplantation Society, 1991-92; Editor-in-Chief, Brazilian Transplantation Journal; Editor, HB Scientifica; President, Medical Society of Sao Jose do Rio Preto. Publications: Numerous articles for professional scientific medical journals. Honours: Certificate of Relevant Work as Physician to the City of Sao Jose do Rio Preto. Memberships: American Transplantation Society; International Transplantation Society; International Society of Nephrology; Brazilian Transplantation Society; Brazilian Society of Nephrology. Address: Rua Voluntarios de Sao Paulo #3826, 15015-200 Sao Jose de Rio Preto, SP, Brazil. E-mail: mabbud@terra.com.br

**ABD AL-MEGUID Ahmed Esmat,** b. 22 March 1923, Alexandria, Egypt. Diplomatist. m. Eglal Abou-Hamda, 1950, 3 sons. Education: Faculty of Law, Alexandria; University of Paris; PhD. Appointments: Attaché, Secretary, Egyptian Embassy, London; Head, British Desk, 1954-56, Assistant Director, Legal Department, 1961-63, Head, Cultural and Technical Assistance Department, 1967-68, Ministry of Foreign Affairs, Cairo;

Counsellor, Permanent Mission to United Nations European Office, Geneva, 1957-61; Minister Counsellor, Egyptian Embassy, Paris, 1963-67; Official Spokesman of Government and Head of Information Department, 1968-69; Ambassador to France, 1969-70; Minister of State for Cabinet Affairs, 1970-72; Head, Permanent Delegation to United Nations, 1972-82; Chairman, Cairo Preparatory Conference for Geneva Peace Conference, 1977; Minister of Foreign Affairs, 1984-91; Deputy Prime Minister, 1985-91; Secretary-General, League of Arab States, 1991-2001; Private law practice, 2001-; Director, Cairo International Arbitration Centre; Participant, United Nations Conferences on Law of the Sea, 1959, Consular Relations, 1963, Law of Treaties, 1969. Publications: Several articles in Revue Egyptienne de Droit International. Honours: Decorated, 1967, Grand Croix, 1971, Ordre National du Mérite, Egypt; First Class Decoration, Arab Republic of Egypt, 1970; Numerous foreign decorations. Memberships: Politbureau; National Democratic Party; International Law Association; Advisory Council, Institute for International Studies. Address: 78 El Nile Street, Apt 23, Giza, Egypt.

**ABD-ELMOTAAL Hussein,** b. 7 October 1960, Cairo, Egypt. Professor. m. R Abd-Elkader, 1 son, 1 daughter. Education: BSc, Ain Shams University, Egypt, 1983; MSc, Ain Shams University, Egypt, 1987; PhD, Graz University of Technology, Austria, 1991. Appointments: Professor of Surveying and Geodesy, Head of Civil Engineering Department, Faculty of Engineering, Minia University. Honours: International Association of Geodesy, Best Paper Award, 1993; State Prize in Engineering Sciences, Egyptian Ministry for Scientific Research, 2003. Membership: Member, International Association of Geodesy. Address: Civil Engineering Department, Faculty of Engineering, Minia University, 61111 Minia, Egypt.

**ABDOULAYE Souley,** Politician; Business Executive. Appointments: Formerly Banker; Minister of Commerce, Transport and Tourism, Niger, 1993-94; Prime Minister of Niger, 1994-95; Minister of Transport, 1996. Memberships: Convention Démocratique et Social-Rahana. Address: c/o Ministry of Transport, Niamey, Niger.

**ABDUL Paula,** b. 19 June 1963, Los Angeles, California, USA. Singer; Dancer; Choreographer. Education: Television and Radio Studies, Cal State, Northridge College. Musical Education: Studied jazz and tap dance. Career: Choreographer, LA Laker basketball cheerleaders; Scenes in films: Bull Durham; Coming To America; The Waiting Game; Appeared in a Saturday Night Live sketch with David Duchovny. Choreographer, pop videos including: The Jacksons and Mick Jagger: Torture; George Michael: Monkey; with Janet Jackson: Nasty; When I Think Of You; What Have You Done For Me Lately; Fitness video, Cardio Dance. Worldwide performances as singer include: Tours throughout US, UK, Japan and Far East; Prince's Trust Rock Gala, London Palladium, 1989; America Has Heart (earthquake and hurricane benefit concert), 1989; LIFEbeat's Counteraid (AIDS benefit concert), 1993; Own dance company, Co Dance; Judge, American Idol, 2002-03. Recordings: Solo albums: Forever Your Girl (Number 1, US), 1989; Shut Up And Dance (The Dance Mixes), 1990; Spellbound (Number 1, US), 1991; Head Over Heels, 1995; Contributor, Disney charity album For Our Children, 1991; Greatest Hits, 2000; US Number 1 singles include: Straight Up; Forever Your Girl; Cold Hearted; Opposites Attract; Rush Rush; The Promise Of A New Day. Honours: MTV Video Award, Best Choreography, Janet Jackson's Nasty, 1987; Emmy, Best Choreography, for Tracey Ullman Show, 1989; Rolling Stone Awards, including Best Female Singer, 1989; American Music Awards include: Favourite Pop/Rock Female Vocalist, 1989,

1992; Billboard Magazine, Top Female Pop Album, 1990; Grammy, Best Music Video, Opposites Attract, 1991; Star on Hollywood Walk Of Fame, 1993; Humanitarian of the Year, Starlight Foundation, Los Angeles, 1992; Numerous Gold and Platinum discs. Address: Third Rail Entertainment, Tri-Star Bldg, 10202 W Washington Avenue, Suite 26, Culver City, CA 90232, USA.

**ABDULLAH IBN AL HUSSEIN (HM King)**, b. 30 January 1962, Amman. King of Jordan; Head of State; Army Officer. m. Rania Yassin, 1993, 1 son, 1 daughter. Education: Islamic Education College; St Edmund's School, Surrey, England; Deerfield Academy, USA; Sandhurst Military Academy; Oxford University; Advanced Study, International Affairs, School of Foreign Service, Georgetown University, Washington, 1987-88; Attended Command and Staff College, Camberley, England, 1990. Appointments: Commissioned 2nd Lieutenant, 1981; Reconnaissance Troup Leader, 13th/18th Bn, Royal Hussars (British Army), Federal Republic of Germany and England; Rank of 1st Lieutenant, 1984; Platoon Commander and Co second-in-Command, 40th Armoured Brigade, Jordan; Commander, Tank Co 91st Armoured Brigade 1985-86 (rank of Captain); Tactics Instructor, Helicopter Anti-Tank Wing, 1986-87; Commander, Co 17th Tank Battalion, 2nd Guards Brigade then Battalion 2nd in Command (rank of Major), 1989; Armour Rep, Office of the Inspector General, 1991; Commander, 2nd Armoured Car Regiment, 40th Brigade (rank of Lieutenant Colonel), 1992; Rank of Colonel, 1993; Deputy Commander, Jordanian Special Forces, 1994; Rank of Brigadier, 1994; Assumed Command of Royal Jordanian Special Forces; Commander, Special Operations Command, 1997-; President, Jordan National Football Federation; President, International Tourism Golden Rudder Society; Head, National for Committee for Tourism and Archaeological Film Production, 1997-; Succeeded to the throne 7 February 1999. Address: Royal Hashemite Court, Amman, Jordan.

**ABDULLAHI Onimisi Ekuh**, b. 25 December 1954, Okene, Nigeria. Educator. m. Salamatu Abdullahi, 3 sons, 3 daughters. Education: Grade II Teachers' Certificate, Ochaja Teachers' College, Ochaja, 1969-73 Nigeria Certificate in Education, Advanced Teachers' College, Zaria (affiliated to ABU, Zaria), 1974-77; BA, Geography, Education, 1978-81, MEd, Psychology, 1981-82, Bayero University, Kano; PhD, Educational Psychology, University of Ilorin, 1986-88, MEd, Guidance and Counselling, University of Ibadan, 1988-89. Appointments: Primary School Teacher, 1973-74; Tutor, Teachers' College, 1977-78; Lecturer II, 1983-85, Head, Department of Educational Psychology, 1986-91, Senior Lecturer, 1987-89, Principal Lecturer, 1989-91, College of Education, Jalingo; Lecturer II, 1991-93, Lecturer I, 1993-95, Senior Lecturer, 1995-2002, Co-ordinator, Postgraduate Studies, Department of Educational Foundations, 1997-2004, Assistant Hall Master, 2000-2002, Member University Senate, 2001-2002, Head of Department, Department of Educational Foundations, 2000-2002, Associate Professor, 2002-, Deputy Dean, Faculty of Education, 2001-2003, University of Ilorin; External Examiner (Teaching Practice), 1997-2000, Provost, Federal College of Education, Okene, Nigeria, 2004-. Publications: Book chapters: Typology of Research, 1995; Raising Research Questions, 1995; The Professional Consultancy Function of Counsellors, 1997; Perspectives on History of Education in Nigeria; 19 articles in professional journals; Numerous papers presented at conferences. Honours: Best Student in Mathematics, 1969, Best Student in Mathematics and Geography, 1970-72, Ochaja Teacher's College; Certificate of Merit, Ochaja Old Boys' Association, 1993; Merit Award, Rotary Club of Okene, 2004; Fellow, Senior Staff Union of Colleges of Education in

Nigeria, 2005. Memberships: Nigerian Academy of Education; Nigerian Association of Educational Psychologists; Counselling Association of Nigeria; International Association for Cross-Cultural Psychology; Nigerian Psychological Association; National Association of Educational Researchers and Evaluation. Address: Federal College of Education, PMB 1026, Okene, Kogi State, Nigeria.

**ABE Fujio**, b. 4 July 1949, Sukagawa, Fukushima, Japan. Metallurgist. m. Rie Abe, 1 son, 1 daughter. Education: Bachelor of Engineering, Metallurgy, Iwate University, 1972; Master of Engineering, Materials Science, 1974, Doctor of Engineering, Materials Science, 1977, Tohoku University. Appointments: Researcher, Japan Society for the Promotion of Science, 1977-78; Researcher, 1978-, Director of Heat Resistant Design Group, National Institute for Materials Science (formerly National Research Institute for Metals). Publications: Articles in scientific journals include: Low-activation Materials for Fusion Reactors, 2001; Creep-Resistant Steels, 2001; Creep-strengthening of steel at high temperatures using nano-sized carbonitride dispersions, 2003; Baitinic and martensitic creep-resistant steels, 2004. Honours: Nishiyama Memorial Award, The Iron and Steel Institute of Japan, 1998; Best Paper Awards: The Iron and Steel Institute of Japan, 2000, 7th Liege Conference on Materials for Advanced Power Engineering 2002, Belgium, 2002, 6th International Charles Parsons Turbine Conference, Dublin, Ireland, 2003. Memberships: The Iron and Steel Institute of Japan; The Japan Institute of Metals; The Japan Pressure Vessel Research Council. Address: National Institute for Materials Science, 1-2-1 Sengen Tsukuba 305-0047, Japan. E-mail: abe.fujio@nims.go.jp

**ABLE Graham George**, b. 28 July 1947, Norwich, England. School Principal. m. Mary Susan Munro, 1 son, 1 daughter. Education: BA (later MA), Natural Sciences, 1968, PGCE, 1969, Trinity College, Cambridge; MA (by research and thesis), Social Sciences, Durham University, 1983. Appointments: Teacher of Chemistry, 1969-83, Housemaster (Boarding), 1976-83, Sutton Valence School; Second Master, Barnard Castle School, 1983-88; Headmaster, Hampton School, 1988-96; Master (Principal), Dulwich College, London, 1997-; Chairman, Dulwich College Enterprises Ltd, 1997-; Chairman, Total Science Solutions, 2004-. Publications: MA Thesis on boarding education, 1983; Head to Head (co-author), 1992; Various newspaper and magazine articles. Memberships: Chairman, Academic Policy, 1998-2001, Chairman, 2003, Headmasters and Headmistresses Conference; Vice-President, 2004-, International Boy's School Coalition; Member of Council, Imperial College, 1999-; Member of Council, Roedean School, 2000-. Address: Dulwich College, London SE21 7LD, England. E-mail: the.master@du lwich.org.uk

**ABRAHAM F Murray**, b. 24 October 1939, Pittsburgh, Pennsylvania, USA. Actor. m. Kate Hannan, 1962, 2 children. Education: Texas University. Career: Professor, Brooklyn College, 1985-; Director, No Smoking Please; Appeared in numerous Broadway plays, musicals, on television, also films including: Amadeus, 1985; The Name of the Rose, Russicum, Slipstream, Hard Rain, Personal Choice, Eye of the Widow, 1989; An Innocent Man, 1990; Mobsters, 1991; Bonfire of the Vanities, 1991; By The Sword, 1992; Last Action Hero, 1993; Surviving the Game, Nostradamus, 1994; Mighty Aphrodite, 1995; Children of the Revolution, 1996; Mimic, 1997; Star Trek IX, 1998; Falcone, Esther, 1999; Finding Forrester, 2000; I cavaleieri che fecero l'impresa, 2001; 13 Ghosts, 2001; Joshua, 2002. Narrator, Herman Melville, Damned in Paradise, 1985. Honours: Obie Award, for Uncle Vanya, 1984; Golden Globe Award, 1985; Los Angeles Film Critics Award, 1985; Academy

Award, for Amadeus, 1985. Address: c/o Paradigm, Santa Monica Boulevard # 2500, Los Angeles, CA 90067, USA.

**ABRAMSKY Jennifer,** b. 7 October 1946. Radio Producer and Editor. m. Alasdair Liddell, 1976, 1 son, 1 daughter. Education: BA, University of East Anglia. Appointments: Programme Operations Assistant, 1969, Producer, The World at One, 1973, Editor, PM, 1978, Producer, Radio Four Budget Programmes, 1979-86, Editor, Today Programme, 1986-87, Editor, News and Current Affairs Radio, 1987-93, established Radio Four News FM, 1991, Controller, Radio Five Live, 1993-96, Director, Continuous News, including Radio Five Live, BBC News 24, BBC World, BBC News Online, Ceefax, and Director, 1998-2000, BBC Radio and Music, 2000-, BBC Radio: News International Visiting Professor of Broadcast Media, 2002. Honours: Woman of Distinction, Jewish Care, 1990; Honorary Professor, Thames Valley University, 1994; Sony Radio Academy Award, 1995; Honorary MA, Salford University, 1997; Royal Academy Fellowship, 1998. Memberships: Member, Economic and Social Research Council, 1992-96; Editorial Board, British Journalism Review, 1993-; Member, Board of Governors, BFI, 2000-. Address: BBC, Broadcasting House, Portland Place, London W1A 1AA, England.

**ABSE Dannie,** b. 22 September 1923, Cardiff, Glamorgan, Wales. Physician; Poet; Writer; Dramatist. m. Joan Mercer, 4 August 1951, 1 son, 2 daughters. Education: St Illtyd's College, Cardiff; University of South Wales and Monmouthshire, Cardiff; King's College, London; MD, Westminster Hospital, London, 1950. Appointments: Manager, Chest Clinic, Central Medical Establishment, London, 1954-82; Senior Fellow in Humanities, Princeton University, New Jersey, 1973-74. Publications: Poetry: Funland and Other Poems, 1973; Lunchtime, 1974; Way Out in the Centre, 1981; White Coat, Purple Coat: Collected Poems, 1948-88, 1989; Remembrance of Crimes Past, 1990; On the Evening Road, 1994; Intermittent Journals, 1994; Twentieth-Century Anglo-Welsh Poetry, 1997; A Welsh Retrospective, 1997; Arcadia, One Mile, 1998; Goodbye Twentieth Century, 2001; New and Collected Poems, 2002, many others. Editor: The Music Lover's Literary Companion, 1988; The Hutchinson Book of Post-War British Poets, 1989. Fiction: Ash on a Young Man's Sleeve, 1954; Some Corner of an English Field, 1956; O Jones, O Jones, 1970; Voices in the Gallery, 1986. Contributions to: BBC and various publications in UK and USA. Honours: Foyle Award, 1960; Welsh Arts Council Literature Prizes, 1971, 1987; Cholmondeley Award, 1985. Memberships: Poetry Society, President, 1979-92; Royal Society of Literature, Fellow, 1983; Welsh Academy, Fellow, 1990, President, 1995. Address: c/o Shiel Land Associates Ltd, 43 Doughty Street, London WC1N 2LF, England.

**ABUBAKAR Abdulsalami (General),** b. 13 June 1942, Minna, Nigeria. Head of State; Army Officer. Education: Kaduna. Appointments: Joined, 1963, with United Nations Peacekeeping Force, Lebanon, 1978-79, Chief of Defence Staff, Chairman, Joint Chiefs of Staff of the Armed Forces, 1993-98, Commander-in-Chief, 1998, Nigerian Army; Formerly active, Committee of West African Chiefs of Staff; Head of Nigerian Government, 1998-99; Appointed UN Special Envoy to Democratic Republic of the Congo, 2000; Head of Commonwealth Observer Mission to Oversee Zimbabwe's Parliamentary Elections, 2000; Mission to Monitor Presidential Elections in Zimbabwe, March 2002. Address: c/o UN Mission in the Democratic Republic of the Congo, United Nations Plaza, New York, NY 10017, USA.

**ABUSITTA Yousif Ahmed,** b. 4 January 1954, Elobeid, Sudan. Engineer. m. Magda Hago Ahmed. Education: BSc (Hons) Mechanical Engineering, University of Khartoum, 1973-78; Graduate Diploma, Management Studies, University of Dublin, 1984-85. Appointments: Mill Engineer, 1980-83, Chief Maintenance Engineer, 1983-85, Chief Engineer, 1985-90, Deputy Factory Manager, 1990-93, Projects and Investment Manager, 1994-97, Factory Manager, 1997-2004, General Manager, Training Department, 2004-, Kenana Sugar Company, Sudan. Publications: Co-author, Development of Production and Manufacturing of Sugar Crops in Arab World, 1997. Honours: Chartered Engineer, Engineering Council, UK; European Engineer, European Federation of National Engineering Associations. Memberships: Institution of Mechanical Engineers; Sudan Engineering Society; American Society of Mechanical Engineers; Institute of Management. Address: Kenana Sugar Company, 39 Fitzroy Square, London W1T 6EZ, England. E-mail: yabusitta@hotmail.com

**ABUSSUUD Abdulaziz,** b. 5 August, 1940, Qatif, Saudi Arabia. Company Executive. m. Sabiha Al-Sinan, 3 sons. Education: Bachelor of Business Administration, American University of Beirut, 1971; Various Diplomas in Management and Insurance. Appointments: Various positions in Arab Commercial Enterprises (Group of Companies), 1961-86; Senior Vice-President, Gulf and Eastern Province of Saudi Arabia, 1986-88, Senior Group Vice-President, 1988-89, President and Chief Executive Officer, 1989-, Arab Commercial Enterprises. Memberships: Chartered Insurance Institute, London; Board of Directors, Amex (Saudi Arabia) Ltd; Vice-Chairman, National Committee for Insurance Services, Riyadh, Saudi Arabia. Address: Arab Commercial Enterprises, PO Box 667, Riyadh 11421, Saudi Arabia. E-mail: aaa@ace-ins.com Website: www.ace-ins.com

**ACCARDO Salvatore,** b. 26 September 1941, Turin, Italy. Violinist; Conductor. Education: Studied with Luigi d' Ambrosio at Naples Conservatory, diploma in 1956; Postgraduate study with Yvonne Astruc at the Accademia Chigiana, Sienna. Career: Has toured extensively as solo violinist and latterly as conductor in Europe and America; Founded the Turin L'Orchestra da Camera Italiana in 1968; Soloist with the ensemble Musici, 1972-77 and Semaines Musicales of Chamber Music at Naples; Repertory includes Bach, Vivaldi and Paganini; Works composed for him include Fantasia for Violin and Orchestra by Walter Piston, Argot for Solo Violin by Franco Donatoni, and Dikhtas by Iannis Xenakis, 1980; Conducted Rossini's opera L'Occasione fa il Ladro at the 1987 Pesaro Festival; Plays several Stradivarius violins and a Guarnerius del Gesu o 1733; Took part in a performance of Schoenberg's String Trio at the Elizabeth Hall in London in 1990; Recordings include: Paganini's 24 Caprices and the Six Concertos. Publications: L'Arte del Violino, 1987; Edn Paganini Sixth Concerto, Paganini; Variations on "Carmagnola". Address: c/o Agenzia Resia Srl Rappresentanze e Segreterie Internazionali Artistiche, Via Manzoni 31, 20121 Milan, Italy.

**ACEVEDO BLANCO Manuel,** b. 17 December 1962, San José, Costa Rica. Medical Doctor. m. Sylvia Araya, 3 sons. Education: Bachelor in Medical Sciences, Cum Laude Probatus, 1983; Licensed in Medical Sciences, Cum Laude Probatus, 1984; Doctor in Medical Sciences, Bene Probatus, 1985; Specialist in Internal Medicine, 1990. Appointments: Founder and Chief of Pain Management Clinic and Palliative Care, Cañas, Guanacaste, Costa Rica (also known as Cañas Pain Clinic); Chief of Epidemiology Program, Cañas Clinic (an institutional, non-private clinic), Guanacaste, Costa Rica. Publications: Papers presented at congresses: Endoscopic Diagnosis of Whipple Disease (Case Report); Co-Morbid Factors in Cancer Patients; General Guidelines for Management of Symptoms and Complication of the Untreatable and/or

Terminal Patient, 2001. Honour: Distinguished Leadership Award, American Biographical Institute; International Man of the Year, IBC, 2001. Memberships: International Association for the Study of Pain; Vice-President, Costa Rica Association for the Study of Pain; International Association for Hospice and Palliative Care. Address: Tilarán, Guanacaste, Costa Rica, Central America. E-mail: maceblanc@racsa.co.cr

**ACHEBE (Albert) Chinua (lumogu),** b. 16 November 1930, Ogidi, Nigeria. Writer; Poet; Editor; Professor. m. Christie Okoli, 10 September 1961, 2 sons, 2 daughters. Education: University College, Ibadan, 1948-53; BA, London University, 1953; Received training in broadcasting, BBC, London, 1956. Appointments: Producer, 1954-58, Controller, Eastern Region, Enugu, Nigeria, 1958-61, Founder-Director, Voice of Nigeria, 1961-66, Nigerian Broadcasting Corp, Lagos; Senior Research Fellow, 1967-72, Professor of English, 1976-81, Professor Emeritus, 1985-, University of Nigeria, Nsukka; Founding Editor, Okike: A Nigerian Journal of New Writing, 1971-; Professor of English, University of Massachusetts, 1972-75; Director, Okike Arts Centre, Nsukka, 1984-; Founder-Publisher, Uwa Ndi Igbo: A Bilingual Journal of Igbo Life and Arts, 1984-; Pro-Chancellor and Chairman of the Council, Anambra State University of Technology, Enugu, 1986-88; Charles P Stevenson Professor, Bard College, New York, 1990-; Visiting Professor and Lecturer at universities in Canada and the US; Goodwill Ambassador, UN Population Fund, 1998-. Publications: Novels: Things Fall Apart, 1958; No Longer at Ease, 1960; Arrow of God, 1964; A Man of the People, 1966; Anthills of the Savannah, 1987. Other Fiction: The Sacrificial Egg and Other Stories, 1962; Girls at War (short stories), 1973. Juvenile Fiction: Chike and the River, 1966; How the Leopard Got His Claws (with John Iroaganachi), 1972; The Flute, 1978; The Drum, 1978. Poetry: Beware, Soul-Brother and Other Poems, 1971; Christmas in Biafra and Other Poems, 1973. Essays: Morning Yet on Creation Day, 1975; The Trouble With Nigeria, 1983; Hopes and Impediments, 1988; Editor: Don't Let Him Die: An Anthology of Memorial Poems for Christopher Okigbo (with Dubem Okafor), 1978; Aka Weta: An Anthology of Igbo Poetry (with Obiora Udechukwu), 1982; African Short Stories (with C L Innes), 1984; The Heinemann Book of Contemporary African Short Stories (with C L Innes), 1992; Another Africa (with R Lyons), 1998; Home and Exile, autobiographical essay, 2000. Contributions to: Periodicals. Honours: Margaret Wrong Memorial Prize, 1959; Nigerian National Trophy, 1961; Jock Campbell/New Statesman Award, 1965; Commonwealth Poetry Prize, 1972; Neil Gunn International Fellow, Scottish Arts Council, 1975; Lotus Award for Afro-Asian Writers, 1975; Nigerian National Order of Merit, 1979; Order of the Federal Republic of Nigeria, 1979; Commonwealth Foundation Senior Visiting Practitioner Award, 1984; Booker Prize Nomination, 1987; 30 honorary doctorates, 1972-99; Campion Medal, 1996; National Creativity Award, Nigeria, 1999. Memberships: American Academy of Arts and Letters, honorary member; American Academy of Arts and Sciences, foreign honorary member; Association of Nigerian Authors, founder and president, 1981-86; Vice-president, Royal African Society, London, 1988; Commonwealth Arts Organization; Modern Language Association of America, honorary fellow; Royal Society of Literature, fellow, London, 1981; Writers and Scholars Educational Trust, London; Writers and Scholars International, London; Nigerian Academy of Letters, 1999. Address: Bard College, PO Box 41, Annandale-on-Hudson, NY 12504, USA.

**ACHIDI ACHU Simon,** b. 1934, Santa Mbu, Cameroon. Politician. Education: Yaoundé; University of Besançon, France; National School of Magistracy, Yaoundé. Appointments: Agricultural Assistant, Cameroon Development Corporation; Interpreter for Presidency, Yaoundé, Chief Accountant, Widikum Council, President, North-West Provincial Co-operative Union Ltd; Minister-delegate in charge of State Reforms, 1971; Minister of Justice, Keeper of the Seals, 1972-75; Private business, 1975-88; Elected Member of Parliament for Cameroon People's Democratic Movement, 1988; Prime Minister of Cameroon, 1992-96. Address: c/o Prime Minister's Office, Yaoundé, Cameroon.

**ACKLAND Sidney Edmond Jocelyn (Joss),** b. 29 February 1928, London, England. Actor. m. Rosemary Kirkcaldy, 18 August 1951, 2 sons, 1 deceased, 5 daughters. Education: Dame Alice Owens School; Central School of Speech Training and Dramatic Art. Career includes: Theatre work, 1945-; Member, Old Vic Theatre Company, 1958-61; Parts include: Toby Belch, Caliban, Pistol, Falstaff in Henry IV Part 1 and Merry Wives of Windsor; Artistic Director, Mermaid Theatre, 1961-63; West End Theatre roles include: Come as You Are; Hotel in Amsterdam; Clarence Darrow in Never the Sinner; Falstaff in Henry IV Parts 1 and 2; Captain Hook and Mr Darling in Peter Pan, Barbican Theatre; Sam in The Collaborators; Mitch in A Streetcar Named Desire; National tours include: Petruchio in The Taming of the Shrew; Sir in The Dresser; W End Musicals include: Justice Squeezum in Lock Up Your Daughters; Jorrocks in Jorrocks; Frederik in A Little Night Music; Peron in Evita; Captain Hook and Mr Darling in Peter Pan - The Musical; Chichester Festival Theatre, Ill in The Visit; John Tarleton in Misalliance; Over 300 TV appearances include: Barrett in The Barrets of Wimpole Street; C S Lewis in Shadowlands; Herman Goering in The Man Who Lived at the Ritz; Alan Holly in First and Last; Isaac in The Bible; Onassis in A Woman Named Jackie; The Captain in Deadly Voyage; Van de Furst in Heat of the Sun; Films include: Seven Days to Noon; The House That Dripped Blood; England Made Me; Royal Flash; A Zed and Two Noughts; The Godfather in The Sicilian; Broughton in White Mischief; Lethal Weapon 2; The Hunt for Red October; The Palermo Connection; Nowhere to Run; Object of Beauty; Miracle on 34th Street; Lord Clare in Firelight; The Monseigneur in My Giant; Gerald Carmody in Daisies in December; King Arthur in A Kid at King Arthur's Court; Mighty Ducks 1 and 3; Matisse in Surviving Picasso; Swaffer in Swept from the Sea; Mumbo Jumbo, 2000; Painting Faces, 2001; Othello, 2001; K19: The Widowmaker, 2001; No Good Deed, 2001; The House on Turk Street, 2002; I'll Be There, 2003. Publication: I Must Be in There Somewhere, autobiography, 1989. Memberships: Drug Helpline; Amnesty International; Covent Garden Community Association. Address: c/o Jonathan Altaras Associates, 2nd Floor, 13 Shorts Gardens, London, EC2H 9AT, England.

**ACKMAN Robert George,** b. 27 September 1927, Dorchester, New Brunswick, Canada. Chemist. m. Catherine Isobel McKinnon, 2 daughters. Education: BA, University of Toronto, 1950; MSc, Dalhousie University, Halifax, Nova Scotia, Canada, 1952; PhD, University of London, DIC, Imperial College of Science and Technology, London, 1956; LLD Dalhousie University, 2000. Appointments: Fisheries Research Board of Canada, 1950, 1956, rose to Director, Marine Lipids, 1972-79; Full Professor, Nova Scotia Technical College, Department of Food Science and Technology, 1980-90; Research Professor, 1990-94, Professor Emeritus, 1995-, Dalhousie University/ Canadian Institute of Fisheries Technology; Retired 2004. Publications: Over 600 on marine lipids, gas chromatography, thin-layer chromatography with FID readout; Low erucic acid rapeseed oil; Specialty long-chain omega-3 polyunsaturated fatty acids; Fish and marine invertebrate fatty acids; Editor: Marine Biogenic Lipids, 2 volumes. Honours: Fellow, Chemical Institute of Canada, 1972; H P Kaufman Medal International Society of Fat Research, 1980; Supelco-AOCS Award, 1994;

Officer, Order of Canada, 2001; LL.D honoris causa, Dalhousie University, 2003. Memberships: CIC; AOCS; AOAC; Nova Scotia Institute of Science; Original Member ISI Highly Cited Researcher's Database. Address: Canadian Institute of Fisheries Technology, Dalhousie University, PO Box 1000, Halifax, NS, B3J 2X4 Canada. E-mail: robert.ackman@dal.ca

**ADAM Gottfried W J,** b. 1 December 1939, Treysa, Germany. Professor. 3 sons. Education: Dr Theol, University of Bonn, 1968; Dr Theol, Habil, University of Marburg, 1975. Appointments: Assistant, Theology Faculty, University of Bonn, 1966-67; Assistant, 1968-75, Lecturer, Professor, Practical Theology, 1976-77, 1980, University of Marburg; Professor, University of Goettingen, 1978-79; Professor, Protestant Theology, Chair, Philosophy Faculty, University of Wuerzburg, 1981-92; Professor, Religious Education, Chair, Faculty of Protestant Theology, Vienna, 1992; Dean, Faculty of Protestant Theology, University of Vienna, 1999. Publications: Author: 6 books; Editor, Co-editor: 20 books; 3 periodicals; 3 book series; 400 articles on theological and religious educational questions. Honours: Diploma of Theology, honoris causa, Sibiu, Romania, 1996; Károli Gáspár Református University, Budapest, Hungary, 2000. Memberships: Wissenschaftliche Gesellschaft für Theologie; Rudolf-Bultmann-Gesellschaft für Hermenentische Theologie; Arbeitskreis für Religionspaedagogik; Religious Education Association, USA. Address: Chair of Religious Education, Faculty of Protestant Theology, Rooseveltplatz 10, A-1010 Wien, Austria. E-mail: gottfried.adam@univie.ac.at

**ADAM Theo,** b. 1 August 1926, Dresden, Germany. Singer (Bass Baritone); Producer. Education: Sang in Dresden Kreuzchor and studied with Rudolf Dietrich in Dresden and in Weimar. Debut: Dresden in 1949 as the Hermit in Der Freischütz. Career includes: Berlin State Opera from 1952; Bayreuth debut in 1952 as Ortel in Meistersinger, later sang Wotan, Gurnemanz, King Henry, Pogner, Sachs and Amfortas; Covent Garden debut in 1967 as Wotan, Metropolitan Opera debut in 1969 as Sachs; Guest appearances include Hamburg, Vienna, Budapest and Chicago with roles including Berg's Wozzeck and Verdi's King Philip; Sang in and produced the premiere production of Dessau's Einstein at Berlin State Opera in 1974; Sang at Salzburg Festival, 1981, 1984 in premieres of Cerha's Baal and Berio's Un Re in Ascolto; In 1985 sang at reopened Semper Opera House, Dresden, in Der Freischütz and as Ochs in Der Rosenkavalier; Sang Don Alfonso at Tokyo in 1988 and La Roche in Capriccio at Munich Festival, 1990; Staged Graun's Cesare e Cleopatra for the 250th Anniversary of the Berlin State Opera, 1992; Sang Schigolch in Lulu at the Festival Hall in London, 1994 and at the Berlin Staatsoper, 1997; Sang in Henze's Bassarids at Dresden, 1997. Publication: Seht, hier ist Tinte, Feder, Papier..., autobiography, 1983. Recordings: Bach Cantatas; Freischütz; Parsifal; Meistersinger; Die Zauberflöte; Così fan tutte; Der Ring des Nibelungen; St Matthew Passion; Fidelio; Krenek's Karl V; Baal; Dantons Tod; Rosenkavalier; Die schweigsame Frau. Address: Schillerstrasse 14, 01326 Dresden, Germany.

**ADAMS Anna Theresa, (Theresa Butt, Anna Butt as painter),** b. 9 March 1926, London, England. Writer; Artist. m. Norman Adams, 18 January 1947, 2 sons. Education: NDD Painting, Harrow School of Art, 1945; NDD, Sculpture, Hornsey College of Art, 1950. Appointments: Teaching at various schools; Designer, Chelsea Pottery, 1953-55; Part-time Art Teacher, Manchester, 1966-70; Art Teacher, Settle High School, 1971-74; Poetry Editor, Green Book, 1989-92. Publications: Journey Through Winter, 1969; Rainbow Plantation, 1971; Memorial Tree, 1972; A Reply to Intercepted Mail, 1979; Brother Fox, 1983; Trees in Sheep Country, 1986; Dear Vincent,

1986; Six Legs Good, 1987; Angels of Soho, 1988; Nobodies, 1990; Island Chapters, 1991; Life on Limestone, 1994; Green Resistance: Selected and New Poems, 1996; A Paper Ark, 1996; The Thames: Anthology of River Poems, 1999; London in Verse & Prose, 2002; Flying Underwater, 2004. Contributions to: Poetry Review; P N Review; The Countryman; 10th Muse; Country Life; Yorkshire Life; Dalesman; Pennine Platform; Western Mail; Stand; Sunday Telegraph; Poetry Durham; Poetry Canada; Poetry Nottingham; Poetry Matters; Encounter; Spokes; Meridian; Acumen; Aquarius; Orbis; Spectator; The North; Yorkshire Journal; Rialto; Scintilla; The Interpreter's House. Honours: 1st Prize, Yorkshire Poets, 1974, 1976, 1977; 1st Prize, Arnold Vincent Bowen, 1976; Several Prizes, Lancaster Festival Poetry Competition; 1st Prize, Lincoln Open, 1984; 1st Prize, Rhyme International, 1986; 2nd Prize, Cardiff Festival Poetry Competition, 1987. Memberships: Poetry Society, London; Committee, Piccadilly Poets. Address: 6 Gainsborough Road, Chiswick, London W4 1NJ, England.

**ADAMS Bryan,** b. 5 November 1959, Kingston, Ontario, Canada. Singer; Songwriter; Musician. Career: International Recording Artist; Signed contract with A&M Records, 1979; 45 million albums sold world-wide, 1995; Numerous worldwide tours. Creative Works: Albums: Bryan Adams; Cuts Like A Knife, 1983; You Want It You Got It; Reckless, 1984; Into The Fire, 1987; Waking Up The Neighbours, 1991; Live! Live! Live!; 18 'Til I Die, 1996; The Best of Me, 2000. Singles: Kids Wanna Rock; Summer of 69; Heaven; Run To You; Can't Stop This Thing We've Started; It's Only Love; Everything I Do, I Do It For You; Have You Ever Really Loved A Woman; I Finally Found Someone; Soundtrack: Spirit: Stallion of the Cimarron. Photography exhibitions: Toronto; Montreal; Saatchi Gallery, London; Royal Jubilee Exhibition, Windsor Castle, 2002. Publications: Bryan Adams: The Officials Biography, 1995; Made in Canada; Photographs by Bryan Adams. Honour: Longest Standing No 1 in UK Singles Charts, 16 weeks, 1994; Diamond Sales Award; 12 Juno Awards; Recording Artist of the Decade; Order of Canada; Order of British Columbia. Address: c/o Press Department, A&M Records, 136-144 New King's Road, London, SW6 4LZ, England.

**ADAMS Gerard (Gerry),** b. 6 October 1948, Belfast, Ireland. Politician; Writer. m. Colette McArdle, 1971, 1 son. Appointments: Founder Member, Northern Ireland Civil Rights Association; Elected to Northern Ireland Assembly, 1982; MP, Sinn Fein, West Belfast, 1983-92, 1997-; Vice-President, Sinn Fein, 1978-83; President, Sinn Fein, 1983-; Member, for Belfast West, Northern Ireland Assembly, 1998-2000. Publications: Books: Falls Memory, Politics of Irish Freedom; Pathway to Peace, 1988; Cage 11 (autobiography), 1990; The Street and Other Stories, 1992; Selected Writings, 1994; Our Day Will Come (autobiography), 1996; Before the Dawn (autobiography), 1996, An Irish Voice, 1997; An Irish Journal, 2001. Memberships: PEN; West Belfast Festival. Address: 51-55 Falls Road, Belfast, BT12 4PD, Northern Ireland.

**ADAMS Jad,** b. 27 November 1954, London, England. Writer; TV Producer. Education: BA, University of Sussex, 1976; MA, University of London Birkbeck College, 1982; Fellow of the Royal Historical Society, 1997. Appointments: Television Professional, 1982-; Currently series producer; Councillor, London Borough of Lewisham, 1978-86; Chair, Nightwatch (homeless charity), 1992-. Publications: Tony Benn: A Biography, 1992; The Dynasty: The Nehru-Gandhi Story, 1997; Madder Music, Stranger Wine: The Life of Ernest Dowson, 2000; Pankhurst, 2003; Hideous Absinthe, 2004. Honour: Young Journalist of the Year, British Press Awards, 1977; Best International Current Affairs Documentary, Royal Television

Society, 1987. Membership: Institute of Historical Research. Address: 2 Kings Garth, 29 London Road, London SE23 3TT, England. E-mail: jadadams@btinternet.com Website: www.jadadams.co.uk

**ADAMS Mac,** b. 15 April 1943, Brynmawr, South Wales (US citizen). Professor; Artist. m. Barbara, 1 daughter. Education: NDD, 1966, ATD, 1967, Cardiff College of Art, Wales; Master of Fine Arts, Rutgers University, USA, 1969. Appointments: Professor, State University of New York at Old Westbury, New York, 1988-; As an artist and sculptor: one man and group exhibitions in USA and Europe; Works held in public collections. Honours: National Endowment Fellowship for the Arts, 1976, 1980 and 1982; Berlin Deutscher Akademischer Austauschdienst Berliner Kunstleprogram, 1981; New York State Fellowship for the Arts, 1988; New York State University Chancellors Research Award, 2002. Address: 18 Llewellyn Road, Montclair, New Jersey 07042, USA. E-mail: mbadams2@aol.com

**ADAMS Richard,** b. 9 May 1920. Author. m. Barbara Elizabeth Acland, 26 September 1949, 2 daughters. Education: Bradfield College, Berkshire, 1938; Worcester College, Oxford, 1938; MA, Modern History, Oxford University, 1948. Appointments: Army service, 1940-46; Civil Servant, 1948-74; Assistant Secretary, Department of the Environment, 1974; Writer-in-Residence, University of Florida, 1975; Writer-in-Residence, Hollins College, VA, 1976. Publications: Watership Down, 1972, 2nd edition, 1982; Shardik, 1974; Nature Through the Seasons, co-author Max Hooper, 1975; The Tyger Voyage (narrative poem), 1976; The Ship's Cat (narrative poem), 1977; The Plague Dogs, 1977; Nature Day and Night, (co-author Max Hooper), 1978; The Girl in a Swing, 1980; The Iron Wolf (short stories), 1980; Voyage Through the Antarctic (co-author Ronald Lockley), 1982; Maia, 1984; The Bureaucats, 1985; A Nature Diary, 1985; Occasional Poets, anthology, 1986; The Legend of Te Tuna, narrative poem, 1986; Traveller, 1988; The Day Gone By, autobiography, 1990; Tales from Watership Down, 1996; The Outlandish Knight, 2000. Honours: Carnegie Medal for Watership Down, 1972; Guardian Award for Children's Fiction for Watership Down, 1972. Memberships: President, RSPCA, 1980-82. Address: 26 Church Street, Whitchurch, Hampshire RG28 7AR, England.

**ADAMSON Donald,** b. 30 March 1939, Culcheth, Cheshire, England. Critic; Biographer; Historian. m. Helen Freda Griffiths, 24 September 1966, 2 sons. Education: Magdalen College, Oxford, England, 1956-59; University of Paris, France, 1960-61; MA, MLitt, DPhil (Oxon). Appointment: Visiting Fellow, Wolfson College, Cambridge. Publications: T S Eliot: A Memoir, 1971; The House of Nell Gwyn, jointly, 1974; Les Romantiques Français Devant La Peinture Espagnole, 1989; Blaise Pascal: Mathematician, Physicist, And Thinker About God, 1995; Rides Round Britain, The Travel Journals of John Byng, 5th Viscount Torrington, 1996; The Curriers' Company: A Modern History, 2000; various translations of Balzac and Maupassant. Honour: JP, Cornwall, England, 1993. Membership: FSA, 1979; FRSL, 1983; FIL, 1989; KSTJ, 1998. Address: Dodmore House, Meopham, Kent, DA13 0AJ, England. E-mail Address: aimsworthy@aol.com

**ADCOCK Fleur,** b. 10 February 1934, Papakura, New Zealand. Poet. Education: MA Victoria University of Wellington, 1955. Publications: The Eye of the Hurricane, 1964; Tigers, 1967; High Tide in the Garden, 1971; The Scenic Route, 1974; The Inner Harbour, 1979; Below Loughrigg, 1979; Selected Poems, 1983; The Virgin and the Nightingale, 1983; The Incident Book, 1986; Time Zones, 1991; Looking Back, 1997; Poems

1960-2000, 2000; Editor: The Oxford Book of Contemporary New Zealand Poetry, 1982; The Faber Book of 20th Century Women's Poetry, 1987; Translator and Editor: Hugh Primas and the Archpoet, 1994. Honour: Order of the British Empire, 1996. Membership: Fellow, Royal Society of Literature. Address: 14 Lincoln Road, London N2 9DL, England.

**ADDIS Richard James,** b. 23 August 1956. Journalist. m. Eunice Minogue, 1983, 1 son, 2 daughters. Education: MA Cantab, Downing College, Cambridge. Appointments: With Evening Standard, 1985-89; Deputy Editor, Sunday Telegraph, 1989-91; Executive Editor, Daily Mail, 1991-95; Editor, The Express on Sunday, 1996-98; Consultant Editor, Mail on Sunday, 1998-99; Editor, The Globe and Mail, Toronto, Ontario, Canada, 1999-2002; Assistant Editor, Design Editor, Financial Times, 2002-; Appointed Honorary Governor, York University, Canada, 2002. Address: Financial Times, One Southwark Bridge, London SE1 9HL, England. Website: www.ft.com

**ADDISON Mark Eric,** b. 22 January 1956. Civil Servant. m. Lucinda Clare Booth, 1987. Education: St John's College, Cambridge; City University; Imperial College, London; MA Cantab; MSc; PhD. Appointments: With Department of Employment, 1978-95, including Private Secretary to Parliamentary Under-Secretary of State, 1982, Private Secretary to Prime Minister, 1985, Regional Director, London Training Agency, 1988-91, Director of Finance and Resource Management, 1991-94; Director of Safety Policy, Health and Safety Executive, 1994-98; Chief Executive, Crown Prosecution Service, 1998-2001; Director General, Operations and Service Delivery, Department for Environment, Food and Rural Affairs, 2001-. Address: Department for Environment, Food and Rural Affairs, 1a Page Street, London SW1P 4PQ, England. Website: www.defra.gov.uk

**ADEDAPO Adeolu Alex,** b. Nigeria. Educator; Veterinarian. Education: DVM, 1988, MSc, Veterinary Pharmacology, 1995, PhD, 2002, University of Ibadan, Nigeria. Appointments: Niger Feeds and Agricultural Operations Ltd, Ile-Ife, Nigeria, 1988-89; Veterinarian, Private Veterinary Consultancy Services, Lagos, Nigeria, 1990-92; Manager, GLIF Veterinary Ventures, Lagos; Lecturer II, 1995-99, Frontline Clinician at the Teaching Hospital, 1997-2002; Sub-Dean, Undergraduate, Faculty of Veterinary Medicine, 1999-2003, Lecturer I, 1999-2002, Senior Lecturer, 2002, Consultant, Pharmacology and Toxicology, Veterinary Teaching Hospital, 2002-, University of Ibadan, Ibadan, Nigeria. Publications: Numerous articles in scientific journals as co-author include most recently: Effects of corticosteroid administration on the infectivity of Trypanosoma brucei brucei 8/18 in Nigerian domestic chickens, 2004; Effects of chromatographic fractions of Euphorbia hirta on the haematological parameters of rats, 2004; Phytochemical analysis of the leaves of Phyllanthus amarus and Euphorbia hirta, 2004; Effects of dexamethasone on the infectivity of Trypanosoma vivax &486 and the serum biochemistry changes in Nigerian domestic chickens (Gallus gallus domesticus), 2004; Effects of dexamethasone on the pathogenicity of Trypanosoma congolese and the haematological changes in two and four weeks old Nigerian domestic chickens (Gallus gallus domesticus), 2004. Honours: OMPADEC Professional Postgraduate Scholarship, Nigeria; Basir-Thomas Biomedical Foundation Award, Nigeria; 2002 Staff of the Year Award, Association of Veterinary Medical Students, University of Ibadan. Address: Department of Veterinary Physiology and Pharmacology, University of Ibadan, Ibadan, Nigeria. E-mail: uivetmed@steineng.net

**ADELMAN Saul Joseph,** b. 18 November 1944, Atlantic City, New York, USA. Astronomer; College Professor. m. Carol, 3

sons. Education: BS, Physics, University of Maryland, 1966; PhD, Astronomy, California Institute of Technology, 1972. Appointments: Postdoctorate, NASA Space Flight Center, 1972-74, 1984-86; Assistant Astronomer, Boston University, 1974-78; Assistant Professor, Associate Professor, Professor, The Citadel, 1978-. Publications: 310 papers; 5 articles; 1 book. Honours: Phi Beta Kappa; Phi Kappa Phi; Sigma Pi Sigma; Sigma Xi. Memberships: International Astronomical Union; American Astronomical Society; Astronomical Society of the Pacific; Canadian Astronomical Society. Address: The Citadel Department of Physics, 171 Moultrie St, Charleston, SC 29409, USA.

**ADER Robert,** b. 20 February 1932, New York, USA. Psychologist. m. Gayle Simon, 4 daughters. Education: BS, Tulane University, New Orleans, USA, 1953; PhD, Cornell University, Ithaca, New York, USA, 1957. Appointments: Teaching and Research Assistantships, Department of Psychology, Cornell University, 1953-57; Research Instructor, Psychiatry, University of Rochester School of Medicine and Dentistry, 1957-59; Research Senior Instructor, 1959-61; Research Assistant Professor, 1961-64; Associate Professor, 1964-68; Professor, Department of Psychiatry, University of Rochester, 1968-; Visiting Professor, Rudolf Magnus Institute for Pharmacology, University of Utrecht, The Netherlands, 1970-71; Dean's Professor, University of Rochester School of Medicine and Dentistry, 1982-83; Professor of Medicine, 1983-; George L Engel Professor, Psychosocial Medicine, 1983-2002; Distinguished University Professor, 2002-; Fellow, Centre for Advanced Study in the Behavioural Sciences, 1992-93. Publications: Behaviourally conditioned immunosuppression; Behaviour and the Immune System; Psychoneuroimmunology; The role of conditioning in pharmacotherapy; Many other publications. Honours: Research Scientist Award; Institutional Training Grant; Editor-in-Chief, Brain Behaviour and Immunity; Honorary MD; Honorary ScD; Many other honours. Memberships: Academy of Behavioural Medicine Research, President, 1984-85; American Psychosomatic Society, President, 1979-80; International Society for Developmental Psychobiology, President, 1981-82; Psychoneuroimmunology Research Society, Founding President, 1993-94; Many other memberships. Address: 7 Moss Creek Ct, Pittsford, NY 14534-1071, USA.

**ADETILOYE Philip Omoniyi,** b. 18 October 1952, Ise-Ekiti, Nigeria. Agronomist. m. Catherine, 5 sons. Education: BSc Plant Soil Science, 1976, PhD Crop Science, 1980, University of Nigeria, Nsukka. Appointments: Research Fellow, IITA, 1977-80; Lecturer O A, University of Ile-Ife, 1981-89; Visiting Scientist, USDA, 1992-93; Senior Lecturer, 1990-2001, Associate Professor, 2002-, University of Agriculture, Abeokuta; Visiting Scientist, Igbinedion University, Okada, 2003-. Publications: Several articles in professional journals; Author, Humankind, Religion, Science and the Future, 1996; Geometric Art for Creative Thinking, 1996. Honours: Federal Government of Nigeria Scholar, 1973-76; Ford Foundation Fellow, 1977-80; Grantee Federal Ministry Award, 1984, 1996; USAID, 1992. Memberships: Agriculture Society of Nigeria; African Crop Science Association; Society for Scientific Exploration, USA. Address: College of Plant Science and Crop Production, University of Agriculture, Abeokuta. E-mail: poadetiloye@yahoo.com

**ADETUNJI Nasiru Adewale,** b. 10 February 1970, Abeokuta, Nigeria. Chemist. m. Rasidat Sade Akintunde, 1 son, 1 daughter. Education: Final Diploma in Science Laboratory Technology, Chemistry/Biochemistry Option, 1998; MBA, 2001; PGD, Analytical/Environmental Chemistry, 2002. Appointments:

Laboratory Assistant, 1990-94, Laboratory Technician, 1995-98, Quality Control Supervisor, 1998-2000, Assistant Manager, Quality Control, 2001-, IPI (Nig.) Ltd; Quality Control Supervisor, 1998-2000. Publications: Comparative Studies of the Composition of Detergent in Nigerian Market, 1998; Financing Small and Medium Scale Enterprises in Nigeria, 2001; Physico-Chemical Properties and Antimicrobial Activities of Mondora Myristica (Calabash Nutmeg) Oil Extract, 2002. Honour: Commendation on Installation and Commissioning of Sulphonation Plant of Tudab Engineering (Nigeria), Limited. Memberships: Nigerian Institute of Science Technology; American Chemical Society. Address: 4 Sanni Street, Off Araromi Ayetoro Road, PO Box 3482, Abeokuta, Ogun State, Nigeria. E-mail: naadetunji2@yahoo.com

**ADEY Christopher,** b. 1943, Essex, England. Conductor. Education: Royal Academy of Music, London, principally as violinist with Manoug Parikian. Career: Violinist until 1973 mainly with Halle and London Philharmonic Orchestras; Debut as Conductor in 1973; Became Associate Conductor for BBC Scottish Symphony Orchestra, 1973-76; Frequent guest appearances throughout Britain and with the leading London orchestras; Associate Conductor with Ulster Orchestra, 1981-84; Has worked in most European countries, Middle and Far East, Canada and USA; Frequent broadcasts for BBC and abroad; Extensive repertoire covering symphonic and chamber orchestra works of all periods and including choral works and opera; Professor of Conducting at Royal College of Music, 1979-92; Orchestral Trainer in demand at conservatoires throughout Britain and maintains a large commitment to guest conducting with county, national and international youth orchestras; Cycle of the complete Martinu symphonies for BBC, 1992. Honours include: ARAM, 1979; Commemorative Medal of Czech Government, 1986; FRCM, 1989. Address: 137 Ansden Road, Willesden Green, London NW2 4AH, England.

**ADIE Kathryn (Kate)** b. 19 September 1945, England. Television News Correspondent. Education: Newcastle University. Appointments: Technician and Producer, BBC Radio, 1969-76; Reporter, BBC TVS, 1977-79; BBC TV News, 1979-81; Correspondent, 1982-; Chief Correspondent, 1989-2003; Freelance Journalist, Broadcaster and TV Presenter, 2003-. Publication: The Kindness of Strangers, autobiography, 2002. Honours: RTS News Award, 1981, 1987; Monte Carlo International News Award, 1981, 1990; Honorary MA, Bath University, 1987; BAFTA Richard Dimbleby Award, 1989; Honorary DLitt, City University, 1989; Honorary MA, Newcastle University, 1990; Freeman of Sunderland, 1990; Honorary DLitt, Sunderland University, 1991; Loughborough University, 1991; Honorary Professor, Sunderland University, 1995. Address: c/o BBC Television, Wood Lane, London W12 7RJ, England.

**ADJANI Isabelle,** b. 27 June 1955, France. Actress. Education: Lycée de Courbevoie. Appointment: President, Commission d'avances sur recettes, 1986-88. Career: Films include: Faustine et le bel été, 1972, Barocco, 1977; Nosferatu, 1978; Possession, 1980; Quartet, 1981; l'Eté Meurtrier, 1983; Camille Claudel, 1988; La Reine Margot, 1994; Diabolique, 1996. Theatre includes: La Maison de Bernada Alba, 1970; l'Avare, 1972-73 Port-Royal, 1973; Ondine, 1974; TV includes: Le Petit Bougnat, 1969; l'Ecole des Femmes, 1973; Top á Sacha Distel, 1974; Princesse aux Petit Pois, 1986. Honours: Best Actress, Cannes, Possession, 1981; Best Actress, Cannes, Quartet, 1982; Best Actress César, Best Actress Award, Berlin Film Festival, Camille Claudel, 1989; Best Actress César, La Reine Margot, 1995. Address: c/o Phonogram, 89 Boulevard Auguste Blanqui, 75013 Paris, France.

# DICTIONARY OF INTERNATIONAL BIOGRAPHY

**ADJI Boukary,** b. Niger. Politician; Economist. Appointments: Minister of Finance, Niger, 1983-87; Deputy Governor, Central Bank of West African States, to 1996, 1997-; Prime Minister of Niger, 1996. Address: Banque Centrale des Etats de l'Afrique de l'Ouest, avenue Abdoulaye Fadiga, BP 3108, Dakar, Senegal. E-mail: webmaster@bceao.int Website: www.bceao.int

**ADLER-KARLSSON Gunnar,** b. 6 March 1933, Karlshamn, Sweden. Professor. m. Marianne Ehrnford. Education: Studies at Harvard University and Berkeley University, 1961-62; Dr of Law, 1962; Dr of Economics, 1968. Appointments: Collaborator of Gunnar Myrdal, Stockholm University, 1962-68; Professor, University of Roskilde, 1974-89; Director, Capri Institute for International Social Philosophy, 1979-; Opened Europe's first Philosophical Park in Capri, 2000. Publications: 15 books on social problems and numerous articles in professional journals. Memberships: Numerous. Address: Box 79, I-80071, Anacapri, Italy. E-mail: adler.karlsson@capri.it Website: www.capriinstitute.org and www.wwwgak.org

**ADLERSHTEYN Leon,** b. 28 October 1925, St Petersburg, Russia. Naval Architect; Researcher; Educator. m. Irina Bereznaya. Education: MS, Shipbuilding Institute, St Petersburg, Russia 1945-51; DSc, Central Research Institute for Shipbuilding Technology, St Petersburg, Russia, 1970. Appointments: Private, Soviet Army, 1943-45; Foreman, Deputy Chief, Hull Shop, Baltic Shipyard, St Petersburg, Russia, 1951-63; Chief Technologist, Team Leader, 1963-74, Chief Researcher, 1993-94, Central Research Institute for Shipbuilding Technology; Head of the Chair, Professor, Shipbuilding Academy, 1974-94; Retired 1994. Publications: Author or co-author of 11 books which include: Accuracy in Ship Hull Manufacturing; Mechanisation and Automation of Ship Manufacturing; Modular Shipbuilding; Ship Examiner (2 editions); Handbook of Ship Marking and Examining Works and over 160 brochures and scientific articles; 9 Russian Patents. Honours: Order of the Patriotic War, 1st Class; 13 Russian Military Medals; 3 Medals of American Legion; Medals of Russian Industrial Exhibition; Listed in numerous Who's Who and biographical publications. Memberships: Fellow, Institute of Marine Engineering, Science and Technology, UK; Society of Naval Architects and Marine Engineers, USA; American Association of Invalids and Veterans of WWII from the former Soviet Union. Address: 72 Montgomery Street, Apt 1510, Jersey City, NJ 07302-3827, USA. E-mail: berez@aol.com

**ADOBOLI Eugène Koffi,** b. 1934. Politician. Appointments: Formerly with Mission to United Nations; Prime Minister of Togo, 1999-2000. Address: c/o Office of the Prime Minister, Lomé, Togo.

**ADRIANO Dino,** b. 24 April 1943. Company Executive. m. Susan Rivett, 1996, 2 daughters. Education: Highgate College. Appointments: Articled clerk, George W Spencer & Co, 1959-64; Trainee, Accounting department, J Sainsbury plc, 1964-65; Financial Accounts Department, 1965-73, Branch Financial Control Manager, 1973-80, Area Director, Sainsbury's Central and Western Area, 1986-89, Assistant Managing Director, 1995-96, Deputy Chief Executive, 1996-97, Joint Group Chief Executive, 1997-98, Group Chief Executive, 1998-2000, Chair, Chief Executive, 1997-2000, Sainsbury's Supermarkets Ltd; General Manager, 1981-86, Managing Director, 1989-95, Deputy Chief Executive, 1996-97, Homebase; Director, Laura Ashley plc, 1996-98; Trustee, 1990-96, Adviser on Retail Matters, 1996-, Vice Chair, 2001-, Oxfam; Trustee, Women's Royal Voluntary Service, 2001-. Address: Stamford House, Stamford Street, London SE1 9LL, England.

**ADUJA Peter,** b. 19 October 1920, Vigan, Philippines. Attorney. m. Melodie Cabalowa, 1 son, 1 daughter. Education: Bachelor of Arts, University of Hawaii,1944; Juris Doctor Degree, Boston University School of Law, 1951. Appointments: WWII US Army Service, 1944-46; Attorney-at-Law, Hawaii.; Secretary, Hilo Girls Home Advisory Board, Director of Finance and Chairman, Honolulu Adult Rehabilitation Center Board, 1992-, Lifetime Member of the Board, 1998-; Associate Editor, Hakalau Community Newspaper; Vice-Commander and Judge Advocate, American Legion Post No 3, Hilo; Senior Vice-Commander Department of Hawaii, 1980-; Commander and Judge Advocate of Post No 15 and Member of Department Executive Committee. Executive Secretary, Philippine Chamber of Commerce; President, Oahu Filipino Council; Director, Legislative Chair and President, Oahu Health Council; Member, Adult Education Advisory Board; Director: Philippines Veterans Band, American Red Cross, Hawaii Chapter, Big Brothers of Hawaii, Health and Community Service of Hawaii; Director and President, Haiku Plantation Community Association; Member, Hawaii Legislature, 1954-56, 1966-74; Delegate, Hawaii Constitutional Convention, 1968; Legal Advisor to the Ilocos Surian Association and the Vigan Association of Hawaii, 1985-; Member, Kualoa Master Plan Advisory Council, 1993-. Honours: Award for Outstanding Service to the Big Brothers of Hawaii, 1963-68; Award of Merit, Chamber of Commerce of Hawaii, 1986; National Commanders Team Plaque, 1986; Member of the Order of International Fellowship, International Biographical Centre. Memberships include: Eagle Scout, Life Scout, Star Scout, Patrol Leader, Senior Patrol Leader, Junior Assistant Scout Master, Assistant Scout Master, Scout Master, Boy Scouts of America; Secretary, Hilo Senior Baseball League; Parliamentarian Waiakea Parent Teachers Association; President, Maharlikan Club; President, Mililani Torchbearers of Hilo; President, US and Filipino Veterans Association, 1980-. Address:47-315 Kamehanena Hwy, Kaneohe, HI 96744, USA

**ADVANI Chanderban Ghanshamdas,** b. 23 July 1924, Hyderbad Sind, India. Businessman. m. Veena Chandru, 1 son, 1 daughter. Education: BA. Appointments: Manager, Narain Advani & Co, Karachi; Manager, French Drugs Co, Karachi; Manager, Indo-French Traders, Pondicherry; General Manager, L L Mohnani & Co, Yokohama, Japan; Chief Executive Officer, Nephews' International Inc. Yokohama, Japan; Proprietor, Nephews' Commercial Corporation, Karachi, India. Publications: Articles to various magazines and newspapers including Bharat Ratna, Hong Kong; Indian, Hong Kong. Honours: Medals, Citations, Mayors of Mumbai (India), Yokohama (Japan), Key to Yokohama from the Mayor of Yokohama. Memberships: Indian Chamber of Commerce, Japan; Indian Merchants Association of Yokohama; Foreign Correspondents Club of Japan; India International Centre, New Delhi; Yokohama Chamber of Commerce and Industry, Yokohama; Sinnim Lodge, Shriners Club, Tokyo. Address: 502, New Port Building, 25/16 Yamashita Cho, Naka Ku, Port PO Box 216, Yokohama 231-86-91, Japan. E-mail: nephewsjapan@yahoo.com

**AFFLECK Ben,** b. 15 August 1972, Berkeley, California, USA. Actor. Career: Appeared in films including School Ties, 1992, Buffy the Vampire Slayer, 1995, Dazed and Confused, 1995, Mallrats, 1995, Glory Daze, 1997, Office Killer, 1997, Chasing Amy, 1997, Going All the Way, 1997, Good Will Hunting, film and screenplay, 1997, Phantoms, 1998, Armageddon, 1998, Shakespeare in Love, 1998, Reindeer Games, 1999, Forces of Nature, 1999, Dogma, 1999, Daddy and Them, 1999, The Boiler Room, 1999, 200 Cigarettes, 1999; Bounce, 2000; The Third Wheel (also producer), 2000; Pearl Harbor, 2001; The Sum of All Fear, 2002; Changing Lanes, 2002; Daredevil, 2003.

Television appearances include: Voyage of the Mimi, Against the Grain, Lifetstories: Family in Crisis, Hands of a Stranger, Daddy. Honours: Academy Award for Good Will Hunting, 1997; Golden Globe for Best Original Screenplay, 1997. Address: c/o Creative Artists Agency, 9830 Wilshire Boulevard, Beverly Hills, CA 90212, USA.

**AFSHINNIA Farsad,** b. 16 March 1970, Tehran, Iran. Physician. m. Parisa Jahanbani. Education: MD, Isfahan University of Medical Sciences, Iran, 1988-95; Speciality in Internal Medicine, Brookdale University Hospital and Medical Center, New York, USA, 2002-2005. Appointments: Physician, VA Hospital of Janbazan Foundation, Iran, 1995-97; Physician, Private Practice, Iran, 1997-99; Researcher and Methodologist, Isfahan University of Medical Sciences, Iran, 1998-2000; Physician, Group Practice in Private Sector, Iran, 1999-2000; Physician, Resident of Internal Medicine, Brookdale Hospital, USA, 2002-2005; Attending Physician, Jersey Shore University Hospital, Neptune, New Jersey, USA, 2005-. Publications: Book: Applied Data Analysis, 2nd edition, 2005; Article: Relation of left ventricular geometry and renal function in hypertensive patients with diastolic heart failure, 2005. Honours: Best Researcher of Isfahan University of Medical Sciences, 1994; Certificates of Merit, American College of Physicians, 2003, 2004, 2005; Award Winner, American College of Physicians, 2005; Man of the Year, 2005. Memberships: American College of Physicians; American Medical Association; American Heart Association; American Diabetes Association. Address: 33F Woodbridge Terrace, Woodbridge, NJ 07095, USA.

**AGA KHAN IV Karim (HH Prince),** b. 13 December 1936, Creux-de-Genthod, Geneva, Switzerland. Spiritual Leader and Imam of Ismaili Muslims. m. (1) Sarah Frances Croker-Poole, 1969, div. 1995, 2 sons, 1 daughter, (2) Princess Gabriele zu Leiningen, 1998. Education: BA, Harvard University. Career: Became Aga Khan IV on death of Aga Khan III, 1957; Granted title of His Highness by Queen Elizabeth II, 1957, title of His Royal Highness by the Shah of Iran, 1959; Founder, Chairman, Aga Khan Foundation, 1967, Aga Khan Award for Architecture, 1977-, Institute of Ismailim Studies, 1977-; Founder, Chancellor, Aga Khan University, Pakisitan, 1983; Founder, Chairman, Aga Khan Trust for Culturre, 1988; Founder and Chancellor, University of Central Asia, 2001. Honours: Commandeur, Ordre du Mérite Mauritanien, 1960; Grand Croix, Ordre du Prince Henry du Gouvernement Portugais, 1960, Ordre National de la Côte d'Ivoire, 1965, Ordre de la Haute-Volta, 1965, Ordre National Malagache, 1966, Ordre du Croissant Vert des Comores, 1966; Grand Cordon, Ordre du Tadj de l'Empire d'Iran, 1967; Honorary LLD, Peshawar University, 1967, University of Sind, 1970; Grand Cordon, Nishan-i-Imtiaz, Pakistan, 1970; Cavaliere di Gran Croce, Ordine al Merito della Repubblica, Italy, 1977; Grand Officier, Ordre National du Lion, Senegal, 1982; Nishan-e-Pakistan, 1983; Honorary LLD, McGill University, Montreal, 1983; Thomas Jefferson Memorial Foundation Medal in Architecture, University of Virginia, 1984; Honor Award, American Institute of Architects, 1984; Grand Cordon of Ouissam-al Arch, Morocco, 1986; Gold Medal, Consejo Superior de Colegios de Arquitectos, Spain, 1987; Honorary LLD, McMaster University, 1987; Cavaliere del Lavaro, Italy, 1988; Honorary DLitt, London University, 1989; Commandeur, Légion d'Honneur, France, 1990; Gran Cruz, Orden del Mérito Civil, Spain, 1991; Silver Medal, Académie d'Architecture, Paris, 1991; Huésped de Honor de Granada, Spain, 1991; Honorary LLD, University of Wales, 1993, Brown University, 1996; Hadrian Award, World Monuments Fund, USA, 1996; Grand Croix, Order of Merit, Portugal, 1998, Order of Friendship, Tajikistan, 1998; Gold Medal, City of Granada, Spain, 1998; Insignia of Honour, Union Internationale

des Architectes, 2001. Memberships: Royal Yacht Squadron, 1982-; Honorary Fellow, Royal Institute of British Architects, 1991; Honorary Member, American Institute of Architects, 1992; Founder President, Costa Smeralda Yacht Club, Sardinia. Address: Aiglemont, 60270 Gouvieux, France.

**AGASSI Andre,** b. 29 April 1970, Las Vegas, USA. Tennis Player. m. (1) Brooke Shields, 1997, divorced 1999; (2) Steffi Graf, 1 son. Education: Coached from age of 13 by Nick Bolletteri; Strength coach Gil Reyes. Appointments: Semi Finalist, French Open, 1988; US Open, 1988, 1989; Member, US Team which defeated Australia in Davis Cup Final, 1990; Defeated Stefan Edberg to win inaugural ATP World Championships, Frankfurt, 1991; Finalist, French Open, 1990, 1991; US Open, 1990, 1995; Australian Open, 1994; Wimbledon, 1999; Men's Singles Wimbledon Champion, 1992; Won, US Open, 1994; Canadian Open, 1995; Australian Open, 1995, 2000, 2001, 2003; Winner, Olympic Games Tennis Tournament, 1996; Association of Tennis Professionals World Champion, 1990. Address: International Management Group, 1 Brieview Plaza, Suite 1300, Cleveland, OH 44114, USA.

**AGBA Emmanuel Hemen,** b. 20 July 1962, Benue, Nigeria. Physicist; Lecturer. m. Pamela Mbanan, 2 sons. Education: WASCE, Division One, 1979; BSc (Hons) Applied Physics, Benin, 1984; MSc Physics, Biophysics, Benin, 1990; PhD Physics, Medical Physics, Benin, 1999. Appointments: Senior Lecturer in Physics, College of Education, K/Ala, Benue State, 1990-92; Lecturer II in Physics, 1992-95, Lecturer I in Physics, 1995-2002; Head of Department of Physics, 1998-2004, Senior Lecturer in Physics, 2002-, Co-ordinator, Remedial Studies, 2004-, Benue State University, Makurdi. Publications: More than 10 journal articles in reputable international and local journals. Honours: Best Graduating Award Winner in Chemistry and Biology, Bristow Secondary School, Gboko, 1979; Benue State Government Undergraduate Scholarship, 1979-84; Benue State Government Postgraduate Scholarship, 1986-87; Federal Government Postgraduate Scholarship, 1987-88; Benue State University Staff Fellowship Award, 1995-98; First PhD Graduate in Physics, University of Benin, 1999; Merit Award for Administrative Excellence, Nigerian Association of Science Students, 2000. Memberships: Nigerian Institute of Physics; International Radiation Physics Society; Nigerian Institute for Biomedical Engineering. Address: Department of Physics, Benue State University, PMB 102119, Makurdi, Nigeria. E-mail: hemenagba@yahoo.com

**AGEE William J,** b. 5 January 1938, Boise, Idaho, USA. m. (1) Diane Weaver, 1957, 1 son, 2 daughters, (2) Mary Cunningham, 1982, 1 daughter. Education: Stanford University; University of Idaho; Harvard University. Appointments: Boise Cascade Corporation, 1963-72; Senior Vice-President, Chief Financial Officer, 1972-76, President and COO, 1976-77, Chair and Chief Executive Officer, 1977-83, President, 1977-79, Bendix Corporation; Chief Executive Officer, 1983-; Chair, President, Chief Executive Officer, Morrison Knudsen Corporation, 1988-95, Semper Enterprises Inc, Massachusetts; Director, ASARCO, Equitable Life Assurance Society of US, Dow Jones & Co Inc, Economic Club of Detroit, Detroit Renaissance Inc, National Council for US-China Trade, General Foods Corporation, Detroit Economic Growth Corporation, 1978-, United Foundation, National Council for US-China Trade. Honours: Numerous honorary degrees. Memberships: Conference Board, Council on Foreign Relations, Business Roundtable, American and other institutes of CPAs, Board of Directors, Associates of Harvard Business School, 1977-; United Negroes College Fund, 1977; Chair, Governor's Higher Education Capital Investment Advisory Committee; President's Industrial Advisory Sub

Committee on Economy and Trade Policy, 1978-79; Advisory Council, Cranbrook Educational Community, 1978; Trustee, 1978; Trustee, Urban Institute, Committee for Economic Development, 1977; Citizen Research Council, Michigan, 1977.

**AGIS Derya Fazila,** b. 4 May 1977, Ankara, Turkey. Linguist; Philologist. Education: BA (honours), Italian Language and Literature, Ankara University, 1995-99; Graduate specialisation course in translation studies with literary emphasis: French/Italian, Italian/French, University of Bari, Italy, 2001-2002; Special Student, Department of Psychology, 2002-2003, MS, Department of Cognitive Sciences, 2003-, Middle East Technical University, Ankara, Turkey; MA Student, Department of English Linguistics, Hacettepe University, 2005-. Appointments: Ongoing Research Student, Middle East Technical University and Hacettepe University, 2003-, 2005-; Research Fellowship, Brown University, USA, 2000-2001; Research into Theology and Biblical Studies, Val D'Itria Cultural Centre, Bari, Italy, 2002; Part-time work experience: Translator, Bilge, Candost, Efe and Gursoy Translation Offices, Ankara, Turkey, 1996-2005; Translator, Inlingua Translation Office, Bari, Italy, 2002; Private Teacher, English, French and Italian, 1999-2003; Internship training as a tourist guide, Cruise & Shipping Travel Agency, Bari, Italy, 2002. Publications: Papers presented at symposia include: The Interlanguage Transitions Reinforcement Method for Teaching French to Turkish Children, 2004; Discovering the Kantian Origins of Cognitive Linguistics, 2005; Poems and articles. Honours: Global Citizenship, Finnish U N Association, 1995; Summer Course Fellowship, University of Milan, 1999; Kenyon Fellowship, Brown University, USA; Turkish and Italian Friendship Association, Fellowship, 2001; Leading Educators of the World, IBC, 2005. Memberships: MLA, 2000-2001; International Pragmatics Association, 2004. Address: Ozveren Sokak No 38-7, Ulku Apt, TR-06570 Maltepe, Ankara, Turkey. E-mail: deryaagis@yahoo.com

**AGNEW John Broughton,** b. 27 October 1933, Sydney, Australia. Chemical Engineer. m. Elizabeth, 3 sons. Education: BE, Sydney, 1955; PhD, Monash, 1966. Appointments: BP, 1955-61; University of Melbourne, 1961-64; Monash University, 1964-83; University of Adelaide, 1983-98. Publications: 120 papers in professional journals and conference proceedings. Honours: Chemeca Medal; Centenary Medal; ICI Award of Excellence; Emeritus Professor, Adelaide University; John A Brodie Medal; Honorary Fellow IE Australia; Fellow Australian Academy of Technological Sciences and Engineering. Memberships: Several. Address: 12 Fowlers Road, Glen Osmond, SA 5064, Australia.

**AGNEW Jonathan Geoffrey William,** b. 30 July 1941, Windsor, England. Investment Banker. m. (1) Honourable Joanna Campbell, 1966, divorced 1985, 1 son, 2 daughters, (2) Marie-Claire Dreesmann, 1990, 1 son, 1 daughter. Education: ; MA Cantab, Trinity College, Cambridge. Appointments: With The Economist, 1964-65, IBRD, 1965-67; Positions, 1967-73; Director, 1971, Hill Samuel and Co; Non-Executive Director, Thos Agnew and Sons Ltd, 1969-; Positions, 1973-82, Managing Director, 1977, Morgan Stanley and Co; With J G W Agnew and Co, 1983-86; Chief Executive, ISRO, 1986; Positions, 1987-93, Chief Executive, 1989-93, Kleinwort Benson Group PLC; Chairman, Limit PLC, 1993-; Member, Council, Lloyd's, 1995-98; Chairman, Henderson Geared Income and Growth Trust, PLC, 1995-2003; Non-Executive Director, 1997, Deputy Chairman, 1999-2002, Chair, 2002-, Nationwide Building Society; Chairman, Gerrard Group PLC, 1998-; Non Executive Director, Beazley Group PLC, 2002-; Director, Soditic Ltd,

2001-. Address: Flat E, 51 Eaton Square, London SW1W 9BE, England. E-mail: jonathan.agnew@limit.com.uk

**AGNEW Morland Herbert Julian,** b. 20 September 1943, London, England. Art Dealer. m. (1) Elizabeth Margaret Moncrieff Mitchell, 1973, divorced 1992, 1 son, 2 daughters. (2) Victoria Burn Callander, 1993, 1 son. Education: MA Cantab, Trinity College, Cambridge. Appointments: Joined, 1965, Director, 1968, Managing Director, 1987-92, Chairman, 1992-, Thos Agnew and Sons Ltd. Memberships: President, British Antique Dealers Association, 1079-81; Chairman, Society of London Art Dealers, 1986-90. Address: Egmere Farm House, Egmere, Nr Walsingham, Norfolk, England. E-mail: julianagnew@agnewsgallery.co.uk Website: www.agnewsgallery.co.uk

**AGNEW Una Brigid,** b. 29 November 1937, Rassan, Dundalk, Eire. Lecturer in Spirituality. Education: BA, Honours, English and Irish, 1961-64; H. Dip. in Ed., 1964-65, University College, Dublin; MA, Formative Spirituality, Duquesne University, Pittsburgh, USA; PhD, University College, Dublin, 1985-91. Appointments: Teacher, 2nd level, Ireland, France and California, 1970-71; Part-time Lecturer in Spirituality: Mater Dei Institute, Dublin, 1975-80, Kimmage Manor, Dublin, 1975-89; Part-time Lecturer, Theology Department, St Patrick's College, National University of Ireland, Maynooth, 1992-96; Lecturer, Notre Dame University, Keough Centre, Dublin, 1998-2000; Lecturer in Spirituality, Formation Programme, Irish Missionary Union, 1976-80, 1983-2003; Director of Spiritual Studies Programme, 1985-89, Senior Lecturer, 1995-99, Associate Professor, 1999, Head of Department of Spirituality, 2005, Milltown Institute; Lecturer on topics relating to Patrick Kavanagh's life and works, Rural and Literary Centre, Inniskeen, Co Monaghan, 1989-; Guest Lecturer throughout Ireland on Spirituality in the works of Patrick Kavanagh. Publications: Word Made Flesh: The Spiritual Dimension of the work of Patrick Kavanagh (PhD thesis), 1991; Book: The Mystical Imagination of Patrick Kavanagh: A Buttonhole in Heaven, 1998; Book chapters: The Poet and the Word: Spirituality in the Work of Patrick Kavanagh, in Neglected Wells, 1996; History of Shelagh Chapel and A Brief History of the Local Schools in The Shelagh Book: History Naomh Malachi's GAA Football Club, 1994; Two Account Books from the Hearth of the Kavanagh Household in The Clogher Record Vol XXV, 2004; Articles and book reviews in learned journals. Honours: Founder Member, Board of Directors, 2003, Company Secretary, 2005-, All Ireland Spiritual Guidance Association; Guest Speaker at Kavanagh Centenary Celebrations at Inniskeen (the poet's place of birth) and at NCH Dublin, 2004. Memberships: Irish Theological Association; All Ireland Spiritual Guidance Association; Accredited Member, Kavanagh Society, Inniskeen, County Monaghan. Address: 7 Grosvenor Road, Rathmines, Dublin 6, Eire. E-mail: uagnew@milltown-institute.ei

**AGUIRRE SALA Jorge Francisco,** b. 13 October 1960, Mexico. Philosopher; Psychologist. m. Martha Heckel, 1 son, 1 daughter. Education: Honour Degree, 1978-82, PhD, 1988-94, Philosophy, Specialisation, Psychotherapeutic Psychology, 1997-2002, Universidad Iberoamericana. Appointments: Philosophy Teacher, Universidad Nacional Autonoma de Mexico, 1984-86; Philosopher; Psychologist. Publications: 4 articles in professional journals. Honours: Diploma Mejor Estudiante de la Generacion, Otorgado por la Universidad Iberoamericana, 1982; Diploma al Mejor Estudiante de México Otorgado por el Diario de México, 1982; Mención Honorífica, Otorgado por la Universidad Iberoamericana el 8-11-85, por Estudios de Licenciatura; Mención Honorífica, Otorgado por la Universidad Iberoamericana el 10-11-94, por Estudios de Doctorado; Diploma al Merito Universitario, Universidad

Iberoamericana, 2000. Memberships: National System of Researchers; American Association of Collegiate Registrars and Admission Officers; Mexican Association of Philosophy; International Platonic Society; International Society for Neoplatonic Studies. Address: Ave Ignacio Morones Prieto 4500 CP 66238, San Pedro Garza Garcia, Nuevo Leon, Mexico. E-mail: joaguirre@udem.net

**AGUTTER Jenny,** b. 20 December 1952, Taunton, Somerset, England. Actress; Dancer. m. Johan Tham, 1990, 1 son. Education: Elmhurst Ballet School. Career: Film debut East of Sudan, 1964; Appeared in numerous films for both cinema and TV, dramas, plays and series on stage; Plays include: Spring Awakening; Tempest; Betrayal; Breaking the Code; Love's Labour's Lost; Peter Pan, 1997-98; Films include: Ballerina, 1964; The Railway Children, 1969; Logan's Run, 1975; Equus, 1975; The Eagle has Landed, Sweet William, 1980; An American Werewolf in London, 1981; Secret Places, 1983; Dark Tower, 1987; King of the Wind, 1989; Child's Play 2, 1991; Freddie as Fro 7, 1993; Blue Juice, 1995; English Places, English Faces, 1996; TV includes: Amy, 1980; Not a Penny More, Not a Penny Less, 1990; The Good Guys, 1991; Love Hurts, Heartbreak, 1994; The Buccaneers, 1995; And the Beat Goes On, 1996; A Respectable Trade, 1997; Bramwell, 1998; The Railway Children, 2000; Spooks, 2002. Publication: Snap, 1983. Honour: BAFTA Award for Equus. Address: c/o Marmont Management, Langham House, 308 Regent Street, London W1B 3AT, England.

**AGYEMAN Edward Dua,** b. 22 November 1939, Kumasi, Ghana. Chartered Accountant. m. Agnes Agyeman, 3 daughters. Education: BA (Hons), Business Studies, Middlesex University, Enfield, England, 1973; Certificate of Education, Garnet College, University of London, 1975; Diploma in Management and Finance, City University Business School, London, 1976; Professional Accountancy Qualification (ACCA), 1977. Appointments: Accounting Officer, London Borough of Islington, London, 1968-73; Lecturer, Accounting and Taxation, Redbridge Technical College, Romford, Essex, 1973-76; Examiner in Accounting, London Chamber of Commerce and Industry, 1974-76; Lecturer, Accountancy and Taxation, Emile Woolf College of Accountancy, London, 1977-78; First Director of Education and Training, Institute of Chartered Accountants, Ghana, 1978-82; First Executive Director, Liberian Institute of Certified Public Accountants, Monrovia, Liberia, 1982-83; First Director of Training, West African Region, Pannell Kerr Forster (Chartered Accountants), 1984-87; Deputy Auditor-General, Audit Service of Ghana, 1987-90; Chairman, Committee of Enquiry into the Financial Administration of New Times Corporation, 1988; Director of Administration, Non-Performing Assets Recovery Trust, Ghana, 1990-93; Tax Consultant, Trades Union Congress of Ghana, 1993-94; Associate Consultant, PAB Consult, Ghana, 1993-95; Programme Co-ordinator, European Union Human Resources Development Programme, Ministry of Local Government and Rural Development, Ghana, 1995-97; Tax and Investigations Consultant, Edward Agyeman Consult, 1997-2001; Acting Auditor-General, Audit Service of Ghana, 2001-2003; Member, 2002, Chairman, 2004, AFROSAI-E Regional Training Committee; Auditor-General of Ghana, 2003-. Publications: 9 books include: Principle and Practice of Nigeria Taxation, 1987; Accounting and Disclosure Requirements for Companies in Ghana, 1992; PAYE Deduction Tables, 1st edition, 1994, 2nd edition, 1995, 3rd edition, 1998; Income Tax, Gift Tax and Capital Gains Tax, 2004. Memberships: Fellow, Association of Chartered Certified Accountants, 1982; Associate, Institute of Arbitrators, 2004. Address: King Edward Plaza, PO Box TN366, Teshie Nungua Estates, Accra, Ghana.

**AHARONI Herzl,** b. 18 December 1937, Haifa, Israel. Professor. m. Miriam, 2 sons, 2 daughters. Education: BSc, 1964, MSc, 1967, Dip Ing, 1970, DSc, 1972, Electrical Engineering Faculty, Technion, Israel Institute of Technology, Haifa, Israel; Research on Semiconductor devices breakdown mechanisms and C.V.D of Si-Ge hetroepitaxial layers. Appointments: Professor, Department of Electrical and Computer Engineering, specialising in new processing development in microelectrics, Ben Gurion University, 1973-; Sabbatical activities include: Visiting Associate Professor, University of California at San Diego, lectures on semiconductor technology and circuit analysis, 1978-79; Advanced Photovoltaic Development Group Jet Propulsion Laboratory, Pasadena, California, 1979-80; ITO/InP photovoltaic devices, Solar Energy Research Institute, Golden, Colorado, 1984-86; Light emission from Si devices, University of Pretoria, Pretoria, South Africa, 1993-94; Low temperature Si devices processing, Tohoku University, Sendai, Japan, 1994-96, 1999-2001. Publications: 10 patents which include: Indirect Bandgap Semiconductor Optoelectronic Device; Optoelectronic Device with Separately Controllable Injection Means; Over 190 scientific publications including 4 conference invited papers and a plenary paper: Temperature Dependence of Surface Morphology of Chemical Vapor Deposition Grown Ge on Ge Substrates, 1990; In-Situ Measurement of Crystalline-Amorphous Transition in single crystal Si Substrates During Ion Implantation, 1992; In-Situ Computerized Optical Reflectivity Measurement System for Ion Implantation, 1993; Visible Light From Guardring Avalanche Silicon Photodiodes at Different Current Levels, 1993; The Spatial Distribution of Light From Silicon LED's, 1996; Analysis of n+p Silicon Junctions with Varying Substrate Doping Concentrations Made Under Ultraclean Processing Technology, 1997; Thin Inter-Polyoxide Films for Flash Memories Grown at low Temperature ($400^{\circ}$C) by Oxygen Radicals, 2001; Highly Reliable Gate Oxidation Using Ctalytic Water Vapor Generator for MOS Device Fabrication, 2002; Silicon LED's Fabricated in Standard VLSI Technology as Components for All Silicon Monolithic Optoelectronic Systems, 2002; Low Operating Voltage Integrated Silicon Light Emitting Devices, 2004; Two and Multiterminal Silicon Light Emitting Devices in Standard CMOS/BiCMOS IC Technology, 2004; Low Temperature Growth ($400^{\circ}$C) of High Integrity Thin Silicon Oxynitride Films by Microwave Excited High Density Plasma, 2004; Two and Multiterminal CMOS/BiCHOS Si LEDs, 2005. Poetry: Poems in the Rain, 1989; Poems From Heaven and Earth, 1993. Honours: Award for Research at the Jet Propulsion Laboratory, Research Associateship by NASA, National Research Council, USA, 1979; Faculty of Engineering Best Teacher Awards, Ben Gurion University, 1987, 1988; Esteemed Teacher Citation, Student Association, Ben Gurion University, 1988-89; Distinguished Research Professor, Rand Afrikaans University, Johannesburg, South Africa, 1990; Ben-Gurion University Annual Prize in Applied Electronics, awarded by the Polish Jewish Ex-Servicemen's Association of London, 1998; Supervised and co-authored a student conference paper which received the Young Researcher Award, SSDM, 2001; Fellow, IEE, 2003; Distinguished Lecturer, IEEE, 2003; Ben-Gurion University Outstanding Teaching Award, 2005; Fellow, Institute of Physics, 2005. Memberships: Senior Member, IEEE; Member of the American Physical Society; Israel Association of Crystal Growth; The Israel Vacuum Society; The Israel Physical Society. Address: Department of Electrical & Computer Engineering, Ben Gurion University of the Negev, PO Box 653, Beer Sheva 84105, Israel.

**AHERN Bertie,** b. 12 September 1951, Dublin, Ireland. Prime Minister of the Republic of Ireland. m. Miriam Patricia Kelly, 1975, separated, 2 daughters. Education: Dublin Institute of Technology, Rathmines; University College, Dublin.

Appointments: Elected to Dáil, 1977; Assistant Chief Whip, 1980-81; Spokeman Youth Affairs, 1981; Government Chief Whip, Minister of State, Department of Taoiseach and of Defence, 1982; Lord Mayor, 1986-87; Minister for Labour, 1987-91; Minister for Finance, 1991-94; Membe, Board of Governors, IMF, 1991-94; World Bank; Chairman, EIB, 1991-92; Leader of the Opposition, 1994-97; Prime Minister and Leader of Fianna Fáil, 1997-; President, European Council, 2004; Former Member, Board of Governors, UCD, Dublin Port & Docks Board, Eastern Health Board, Dublin Chamber of Commerce. Honours: Grand Cross, Order of Merit with Star and Sash, Germany, 1991; The Stara Planina, Bulgaria, 2005. Memberships: Chairman, Dublin Millennium Committee. Address: Department of the Taoiseach, Government Buildings, Upper Merrion Street, Dublin 2, Republic of Ireland.

**AHLSEN Leopold,** b. 12 January 1927, Munich, Germany. Author. m. Ruth Gehwald, 1964, 1 son, 1 daughter. Publications: 13 plays, 23 radio plays, 68 television plays, 7 novels. Honours: Gerhart Hauptmann Prize; Schiller-Förderungspreis; Goldener Bildschirm; Hörspielpreis der Kriegsblinden; Silver Nymph of Monte Carlo; Bundesverdienstkreuz. Address: Waldschulstrasse 58, 81827 Munich, Germany.

**AHLSKOG J Eric,** b. 14 September 1945, Chicago, Illinois, USA. Neurologist. m. Faye Wayland, 3 sons. Education: BA, Michigan State University, 1967; PhD, Princeton University, 1973; MD, Dartmouth Medical School, 1976. Appointments: Instructor of Neurology, 1981-86, Assistant Professor of Neurology, 1986-93, Associate Professor of Neurology, 1993-98, Professor of Neurology, 1998-, Mayo Medical School, Rochester; Chair, Division of Movement Disorders, Department of Neurology, Rochester, 1992-2001; Consultant and Chair, Section of Movement Disorders, Mayo Clinic, Rochester, 2002-. Publications: Numerous articles in professional journals. Honours: Honors College, Michigan State University, 1967; Alpha Omega Alpha, Dartmouth Medical School, 1975. Memberships: American Academy of Neurology; Movement Disorder Society. Address: Department of Neurology, Mayo Clinic, 200 First St SW, Rochester, MN 55905, USA.

**AHMAD Aqueil,** b. India. Professor. m. Joyce L Ahmad, 1 son, 1 daughter. Education: MSc, Psychology, 1956; PhD, Psychology, 1963. Appointments: Senior Associate, Southern Technology Council, Southern Growth Policies Board; Founding Chairman, Professor, Center for Science Policy and Management of Research, Administrative Staff College of India, Hyderabad; Assistant to Associate Professor of Sociology, University of North Dakota; Senior Scientist, Planning Division, Council of Scientific and Industrial Research, New Delhi; Visiting Professor, Scholar at numerous institutions including: Moorhead State University, Minnesota; Research Policy Institute, University of Lund, Sweden; East West Centre, Honolulu; Beijing National University, China; Wuhan Institute of Management, China; Center for the Interdisciplinary Study of Science and Technology, Northwestern University, Evanston, Illinois; Adjunct Professor at numerous schools and universities; Currently Sociology Professor, University of North Carolina-Greensboro, USA. Publications: 5 books; 56 journal articles; 10 contributions to books; 16 monographs and project reports; 13 book reviews; 50 conference papers; over 75 special lectures. Honours: Outstanding Educators of America Citations, 1971 and 1973; American Men and Women Science, citation, 1973. Memberships: American Sociological Association; Southern Sociological Society; Humanist Sociology. Address: 7504 Dodsons Crossroads, Hillsborough, NC 27278, USA. E-mail: aahmad@unc.edu

**AHMED Mohammed Mujtaba,** b. 15 February 1951, Sokoto, Nigeria. Civil Servant. m. Maryam M Ahmed, 2 sons, 4 daughters. Education: Diploma in Journalism, London Film and Journalism School, London, England, 1972-74; BSc, Political Science, 1975-77, Masters in Public Administration, 1977-78, Ohio University, USA. Appointments: Press Officer, 1970, Head, Film Unit Department, 1973, Ministry of Information, Sokoto; Administrative Officer, Executive Office of the Governor, Sokoto, 1978; Principal Assistant Secretary, Ministry of Trade and Industry, Sokoto, 1978; Under Secretary, Ministry of Agriculture and Forestry, Sokoto, 1980; Under Secretary Finance, Ministry of Finance, Sokoto, 1980-82; Deputy Permanent Secretary, Acting Secretary, Government and Constitutional Matters, Governor's Office Sokoto, 1982-84; Secretary, State Hotels Management and Tourism Development Board, Sokoto, 1984-85; Secretary, 1985-88, Director, 1988, Sokoto State Executive Council; Director General, Government House, Sokoto, 1988-89; Comptroller of Customs, 1989, Comptroller Promotion, 1989-91, Customs Area Controller, Yobe State Area Command, 1991-98; Comptroller, Federal Operations Unit, 1998-99; Deputy Comptroller General of Customs, Excise and Industrial Incentive, 1999-2001; Deputy Comptroller General, Enforcement and Drugs Department, 2001-, Nigeria Customs Service. Publications: The Role of Nigeria Customs Service in the Manufacture-in-Bond Scheme; Restoration of excise duty on 1996/1997 de-excised goods - confectioneries and other selected luxury goods in the next millennium; The challenges on Nigeria customs in the next millennium; The imperative for the restoration of excise duty on luxury goods. Memberships: Current memberships include: National Committee on the Proliferation and Illicit Trafficking in Small and Light Weapons, 2001; Sub-committee on All African Games Sub-committee on Security. Address: Nigeria Customs Service, Abidjan Street, Wuse, Zone 3, Abuja, Nigeria. E-mail: ahmedmm@nigeriacustoms.org

**AHN Yong,** b. 24 August 1966, Daejeon, Korea. Medical Doctor; Neurosurgeon. m. Hwayoung Kim, 1 daughter. Education: MD, Seoul National University College of Medicine, 1985-71, Intern and Resident, Department of Neurosurgery, Seoul National University Hospital, 1991-96; Master's Degree, Seoul National University College of Medicine, 1999-2001. Appointments: Head of Neurosurgery, Chungpyung Army Hospital, 1996-99; Clinical Fellow, Department of Neurosurgery, Seoul National University Hospital, 1999-2000; Fellowship, American Board of Minimally Invasive Spinal Surgery, 2000-2001; Fellowship, Royal College of Surgeons; Currently, Chief, Department of Neurosurgery, Wooridul Spine Hospital. Publications: Posterolateral percutaneous endoscopic lumbar feraminotomy for L4-S1, 2003; Percutaneous endoscopic lumbar dissectomy for recurrent disc herniation, 2004; Factors predicting excellent outcome of percutaneous cervical discectomy, 2004; Percutaneous ventral decompression for L4-L5 degenerative spondylolisthesis in medically compromised elderly patients, 2004. Address: 47-4 Chungdam-dong, Gangnam-gu, Seoul, Korea. E-mail: ns-ay@wooridul.co.kr

**AHRENDS Peter,** b. 30 April 1933, Berlin, Germany. Architect. m. Elizabeth Robertson, 1954, 2 daughters. Education: AA (Hons) School of Architecture; ARIBA. Appointments: Denys Lasdun and Partners, 1959-60; Teacher, Architectural Association School of Architecture, 1960-61; Partner, Director, Ahrends, Burton and Koralek architectural practice, London, 1961-; Professor, Bartlett School of Architecture and Planning, University College, London, 1987-90; Chair, Architects Support Group South Africa; Chair Camden Design Advisory Group; Member, RIBA Annual Awards Group; Principal projects include most recently New British Embassy, Moscow, 2000

# DICTIONARY OF INTERNATIONAL BIOGRAPHY

Dublin Corporation Convent Lands Master Plan, 2000; Dublin Corporation/NEIC Civic Centre, 2001; Great Egyptian Museum Competition Entry, 2002; Whitworth Art Gallery Development Plan Review, 2002; Designs on Democracy Stockport winning competition entry, 2002; Riverside Building, London Docklands, 2003; Bexhill Town Centre, 2004. Publications: Ahrends, Burton and Koralek (monograph), 1991; Collaborations: The Architecture of ABK, August/Birkhäuser; Numerous articles in professional journals. Honours: Good Design in Housing Award, 1977, Architecture Awards, 1978, 1993, 1996, 1999, Structural Steel Design Award, 1980, Structural Steel Commendation, 1993; Gulbenkian Museum of the Year Award, 1999. Memberships: Royal Institute of British Architects; Design Council; Chairman, UK Architects Against Apartheid, 1988-93. Address: 16 Rochester Road, London NW1 9JH, England. E-mail: abk@abklondon.com Website: www.abk.co.uk

**AHTIALA Pekka,** b. 12 June 1935, Helsinki, Finland. m. Anna-Maija, 1 son, 2 daughters. Education: BBA, 1956, MBA, 1958, Helsinki School of Economics and Administration; PhD, Harvard University, USA, 1964. Appointments: Teaching Fellow, Instructor, Harvard, early 1960s; Professor of Economics, 1965-99, Dean, Faculty of Economics and Administration, 1969-71, University of Tampere; Minister of the Chancery responsible for Economic Policy, Finnish Government; Visiting Professor of Economics, Northwestern University and Princeton University. Publications: 4 books; Articles in several professional journals. Honours: Blue Cross of Finland; Earhart Prize, Harvard University; Knight Commander of the Order of the Lion of Finland; World Culture Prize; Statue of Victory, Centro Studi e Ricerche Delle Nazioni, Italy, 1985; Best Paper Award, Multinational Finance Journal, 1999; Honorary Member, Junior Chamber International; Honorary Member, Omicron Delta Epsilon. Memberships: Nomination College of the Nobel Prize Committee on Economics; Finnish Economic Association; American Economic Association; European Economic Association. Address: Liutunkuja 3, 36240 Kangasala, Finland.

**AIBONI Sam Amaize,** b. 17 July 1941, Warri, Delta State of Nigeria. Lecturer; Barrister; Solicitor. m. Vicky F, 2 sons, 2 daughters. Education: LLM, Moscow, 1971; MA, 1972; LLB, Cantab, 1973; LLD, Uppsala, Sweden, 1978; (BL) Barrister at Law. Appointments: Regional Director, International University Exchange Fund, Geneva, Switzerland and Lusaka, Zambia; Company Secretary, Niger Agencies, Holborn, London, England; Legal Expert, Council of Europe, Strasbourg, France; Research Fellow, Swedish Institute of International Law, Uppsala, Sweden; Dean of Law, University of Jos, Bendel State University, Ekpoma, Nigeria. Publication: Protection of Refugees in Africa. Honours: Visiting Professor, Osgoode Hall Law School, York University, Toronto, Canada; Fellow, Institute of Economic and Social Research (ISESR), Memorial University, St Johns, Newfoundland, Canada; Professor of Law, College of Law, Igbinelyon University, Okada, Edo State, Nigeria; Federal Government of Nigeria Scholar; Scholar, Cambridge University, UK; Edvard Cassel Foundation Scholar, Uppsala University, Uppsala, Sweden. Memberships: Nigeria Bar Association; Association of Law Teachers of Nigeria; International Law Association; Nigerian Society of International Law. Address: PO Box 4829, Benin City, Nigeria.

**AICHINGER Ilse,** b. 1 November 1921, Vienna, Austria. Novelist; Playwright. Education: University of Vienna, 1945-48. Appointment: Member of Grupe 47, 1951-. Publications: Die Grössere Hoffnung, 1948; Rede Unter dem Galgen, 1953; Eliza, Eliza, 1965; Selected Short Stories and Dialogue, 1966; Nachricht und Tag: Erzählungen, 1970; Schlechte Worter, 1976;

Meine Sprache und Ich Erzählungen, 1978; Spiegelsichte: Erzählungen und Dialoge, 1979. Plays, Zu Keiner Stunde, 1957, 1980; Besuch im Pfarrhaus, 1961; Auckland: 4 Horspiele, 1969; Knopfe, 1978; Weisse Chrysanthemum, 1979; Radio Plays, Selected Poetry and Prose of Ilse Aichinger, 1983; Collected Works, 8 volumes, 1991. Honours: Belgian Europe Festival Prize, 1987; Town of Solothurn Prize, 1991. Address: c/o Fischer Verlag, Postfach 700480, 6000 Frankfurt, Germany.

**AIELLO Danny,** b. 20 May 1933, New York City, New York, USA. Actor. m. Sandy Cohen, 1955, 3 sons, 1 daughter. Career: Numerous film appearances including Bang the Drum Slowly, 1973; The Godfather II, 1976; Once Upon a Time in America, 1984; The Purple Rose of Cairo, 1985; Moonstruck, 1987, Do the Right Thing, 1989, Harlem Nights, 1989, Jacob's Ladder, 1990, Once Around, 1991, Hudson Hawk, 1991, The Closer, 1991, 29th Street, 1991, Mistress, 1992, Ruby, 1992, The Pickle, 1992, The Cemetery Club, 1992, The Professional, 1994, Prêt-à-Porter, 1994, Léon, 1994, City Hall, 1995, Power of Attorney, 1995, Two Days in the Valley, 1996, Mojave Moon, 1996, Two Much, 1996, A Brooklyn State of Mind, 1997, Bring Me the Head of Mavis Davis, 1998, Dust, 1999, Prince of Central Park, 2000, Dinner Rush, 2000, Off Key, 2001, The Russian Job, 2002, Marcus Timberwolf, 2002, The Last Request, 2002; Theatre appearances including Lamppost Reunion, 1975, Gemini, 1977, Hurlyburly, 1985; Appeared in TV films including The Preppie Murder, 1989, A Family of Strangers, 1993, The Last Don, mini-series, 1997, Dellaventura, series, 1997, The Last Don II, mini-series, 1998. Honours: Theatre World Award for Lamppost Reunion, 1975; Obie Award for Gemini, 1977; Boston Critics Award, Chicago Critics Award, Los Angeles Critics Award, all for Best Supporting Actor in Do the Right Thing, 1989; Emmy Award for A Family of Strangers, 1993. Address: William Morris Agency, 151 South El Camino Drive, Beverly Hills, CA 90212, USA.

**AIMÉE Anouk, (Françoise Dreyfus),** b. 27 April 1932, Paris, France. Actress. m. (2) Nico Papatakis, 1951, 1 daughter, (3) Pierre Barouh, 1966, (4) Albert Finney, 1970, divorced 1978. Education: Institut de Megève; Cours Bauer-Therond. Career: Theatre appearances include Sud, 1954, Love Letters, 1990, 1994; Appeared in films including Les mauvaises rencontres, 1955, Tous peuvent me tuer, Pot bouille and Montparnasse 19, 1957, La tête contre les murs, 1958, Les drageurs, 1959, La dolce vita, Le farceur, Lola, Les amours de Paris, L'imprévu, Quai Notre Dame, 1960, Le jugement dernier, Sodome et Gomorrhe, 1961; Les grands Chemins, Education sentimentale, Huit et demi, 1962, Un homme et une femme, 1966, Un soir un train, 1967, The Appointment Shop, Model Shop, Justine, 1968, Si c'était à refaire, 1976, Mon premier amour, 1978, Salto nel vuoto, 1979, La tragédie d'un homme ridicule, 1981, Qu'est-ce qui fait courir David?, 1982, Le Général de l'armée morte, 1983, Vive la Vie, Le succès à tout prix, 1984, Un homme et une femme: vingt ans déjà, 1986, Docteur Norman Bethune, 1992, Les Marmottes, 1993, Les Cents et Une Nuits, 1995, Prêt-à-porter, 1995; Appeared on television in Une page d'amour, 1979, Des voix dans le jardin. Honours: Commandeur des Arts et des Lettres. Address: Bureau Georges Beaume, 3 Quai Malaquais, 75006 Paris, France.

**AINSWORTH Cynthea L,** b. 6 September 1953, St Joseph, Missouri, USA. Consultant on Alaskan History. m. James N Ainsworth. Education: BA, Classical Studies, 1981, MA, Teaching English and Literature, 1989, University of Missouri at Columbia; PhD, Folklore, Indiana University, 1997. Appointments: Adjunct Faculty Teacher of English Literature, Composition and History, University of Missouri, 1981-84; University of Alaska, 1986-; Linguistic Anthropology, 1992-;

Owner of Consulting Business Moon Magic Studio, 1991-; Director of Native Language Archives and Film Production Manager, 1995-. Publications; Author, 1 book, 3 articles on Alaskan natives and History; Videographer and Director, 7 documentary films on Alaskan native culture and history; Co-editor of 8 books for teaching Ahtna Indian language; 4 government reports on Alaskan anthropology; Author/Contributor to 3 encyclopaedias on American folklore. Honour: Achievement in Science Award, IBC 2005. Memberships: American Folklore Society; Alaskan Anthropology Association. Address: SR 560, Gakona, AK 99586, USA.

**AITMATOV Chingiz Torekulovich,** b. 12 December 1928, Sheker Villaga, Kirghizia, USSR. Writer; Diplomat. m. Maria Urmatova, 1974, 3 sons, 1 daughter. Education: Kirghiz Agricultural Institute. Appointments: Writer, 1952-; Former Correspondent, Pravda; Member, Soviet Union Communist Party, 1959-91; First Secretary, 1964-69, Chairman, 1969-86, Cinema Union of Kirghiz SSR; Deputy to USSR Supreme Soviet, 1966-89; Candidate Member, 1969-71, Member, 1971-90, Central Committee, Kirghiz SSR Communist Party; Vice-Chairman, Committee of Solidarity with Peoples of Asian and African Countries, 1974-89; Chairman, Union of Writers of Kyrgyzstan, 1986-; Chief Editor, Innostrannaya Literatura, 1988-90; People's Deputy of the USSR, 1989-91; Member, Presidential Council, 1990-91; USSR Ambassador to Luxembourg, 1990-92; Kyrgyzstan Ambassador to Belgium and Luxembourg, 1992-. Publications include: Short stories, novels; Djamilya, 1959; Mr Poplar in a Red Kerchief, 1960; Face to Face, Short Stories, Melody, 1961; Tales of the Hills and the Steppes, 1963; Camel's Eye, The First Teacher, Farewell Gulsary, Mother Earth, 1963; Stories, 1967; The White Steamship, English translation, 1972; The Lament of the Migrating Bird, English translation, 1972; The Ascent of Mount Fuji, co-author, 1973; Earth and Water, co-author, 1978; Works, 3 volumes, 1978; Early Storks, 1979; Stories, 1979; Piebald Dog, Running Along the Sea Shore, The Day Lasts More Than a Hundred Years, 1980; Executioner's Block, 1986, English translation, 1987; Mother Earth and Other Stories, 1989; The Place of the Skull, The White Cloud of Chingiz Khan, 1991; A Conversation at the Foothill of Fujiyama Mountain, co-author, 1992; The Brand of Cassandra, 1994. Honours: Lenin Prize for Tales of the Hills and the Steppes, 1963; People's Writer of Kirghiz SSR, 1968; State Prize in Literature, 1968, 1977, 1983; Hero of Socialist Labour, 1978; Austrian State Prize for European Literature, 1994; Others from Germany, India, Turkey, USA. Memberships: Kirghiz Academy of Science, 1974; European Academy of Arts, Science and Humanity, 1983; Chairman, Issyk-Kul Forum, 1986-; World Academy of Art and Science, 1987. Address: Toktogul str 98, Apt 9, 720000 Bishkek, Kyrgyzstan.

**AJANI Janet Abiodun Ajoke,** b. 24 December 1964, Igede-Ekiti, Ekiti State, Nigeria. m. O Ajani, 1 daughter. Education: Commercial Certificate, 1977; Teacher's Grade 2 Certificate, 1982; National Diploma in Business Administration and Management, 1988; Higher National Diploma in Business and Management, 1996; Master Degree, in view. Appointments: Secretary, Igede-Ekiti, 1978; Teacher, Eko-Ende, via Ikirun, Osun State, 1982-84; Audit Department, Obafemi Awolowo University, Ile-Ife, 1988-92; Head, Internal Audit, Federal College of Agriculture, Akure, 1992-. Publications: Audit Guide and Procedure. Honours: Fellowship and Certified Professional Audit Manager, 2004; National Merit Award for Probity and Accountability, 2004; PhD, Accounting and Auditing, Irish University Business School, London, 2005. Memberships: Fellowship Member, The Nigerian Institute of Internal Auditors. Address: International Audit Department, Federal College of Agriculture, Akure, Ondo State, Nigeria. E-mail: janetajani@yahoo.com

**AJMAL Ibrahim Hussain,** b. 15 May 1935, Palayamkottai, Tamil Nadu (British citizen). Engineering Manager. 2 sons. Education: BE, Civil Engineering, UNI, Madras, 1955; Diploma, Imperial College, London, 1964; MBA, Cranfield, 1973; Chartered Engineer, 1962. Appointments: Assistant Engineer, Kymore Cement Works Associate Cement Companies Ltd, Bombay, 1956-57; Training with Sir William Halcrow & Partners, London, 1957-60; Civil Engineer, Designer, Nuclear Power Division, Simon Carves Ltd, London, 1960-61; Design Engineer, L G Mouchel & Partners, London, 1962-63; Engineer, Senior Engineer, Bertlin & Partners, London, Bombay, 1963-69; Senior Assistant Engineer, London Borough, Hillingdon, 1969-71; Senior Engineer, Project Manager, Peter Fraenkel & Partners, London, 1973-75; Senior Resident Engineer, Halcrow Group, London, Al Jubail, 1976-80; Site Engineer, Dar Al Handasah, Noble Associates, London Underground, Luanda, London, 1980-82; Senior Engineer, Construction projects and Maintenance Directorate, Ministry Works, Power and Water, Bahrain, 1983-85; Support to Associate Consultant on Planning Applications, Roughton & Partners for the Maidstone Borough Council, 1985-86; Noro Project Manager/Co-ordinator, SIG Ministry of Transport Works and Utilities, Honiara Solomon Islands (seconded as technical co-operation officer by ODA, Glasgow) 1987-89; Freelance Engineer, Scott Wilson Associates, Fluor Daniel and others, 1990-95; Structural Engineer/Design Group Advisor, Devonport Management Ltd, Plymouth, 1996-2000; Project Manager, Hyder Consulting, London, 2000; Associate Consultant, Advisory Service to Peter Fraenkel Maritime Ltd, Dorking, London Borough of Hounslow and others, 2001-. Memberships: English Bridge Union. Address: 3 Chase Court, Wimbledon Chase, London SW20 9ER, England. E-mail: ajmalih@hotmail.com Website: www.professionalassociates.com

**AKALE Matt Alfa Gordon,** b. 5 April 1947, Atte, Nigeria. Science Educator. m. Christine Zuyeali Funmi, 3 sons, 2 daughters. Education: Federal College of Education, Zaria, Nigeria, 1967-70; B Ed, M Ed, PhD, Ahmadu Bello University, Zaria, 1974-87; Institute of Education, University of London, London, England, 1982 King's College, London, 1990, 1994. Appointments: Senior Lecturer, Ahmadu Bello University Institute of Education; Chief Programmes Officer, National Commission for Colleges of Education; Director, Academic Programmes. National Commission for Colleges of Education, Abuja, Nigeria. Publications: Articles in professional journals include: Design, Organisation and Administration of Science Laboratory, 1981; Relationship between Psycho-Social Environment and Cognitive Achievement in Science, 1998; Funding Teacher Education, 2002. Honour: Fellow, Science Teachers' Association of Nigeria. Memberships: Science Teachers' Association of Nigeria; Nigeria Academy of Education. Address: c/o National Commission for Colleges of Education, Ralph Shodeinde Street, Cadastral Zone AO1, Garki, PMB 0394, Abuja, Nigeria. E-mail: info@ncce.edu.ng

**AKASHI Yasushi,** b. 19 January 1931, Akita, Japan. Head of Research Institute. m. Itsuko Akashi, 1 son, 1 daughter. Education: BA, University of Tokyo, 1954; MA, University of Virginia, 1956; Fletcher School of Law and Diplomacy, 1956-57; PhD, Ritsumeikan University, 1998. Appointments: Under-Secretary- General of the UN, 1979-92; Special Representative of the UN Secretary-General for Cambodia, 1992-93; Special Representative of the UN Secretary-General for the former Yugoslavia, 1994-95; Under-Secretary-General of the UN, 1996-97; President, Hiroshima Peace Institute,

1998-99; Chairman, The Japan Centre for Conflict Prevention, 1999-; Representative of the Government of Japan for Peace-Building in Sri Lanka, 2002-. Publications: The United Nations, 1965, revised, 1975, 1985; The World Seen From the United Nations, 1992; An Agenda for Hope, 1993; Perseverance and Hope – 560 Days in Cambodia, 1995. Honours: New York Japanese Chamber of Commerce Annual Award, 1994; The Yomiuri International Co-operation Award, 1996; Foreign Minister's Commendation, 1998. Memberships: President, The Japan Association for United Nations Studies; Chairman, City Club of Tokyo; Board Member, International Olympic Truce Foundation. Address: 106, 5-15-21 Roppong, Minato-ken, Tokyo 106 0032, Japan.

**AKERS-JONES David (Sir)**, b. 14 April 1927. Civil Servant. m. Jane Spickernell, deceased 2002, 1 son, deceased, 1 daughter. Education: MA Oxon, Brasenose College, Oxford. Appointments: British India Steam Navigation Co, 1945-49; Malayan Civil Service, 1954-57; Hong Kong Civil Service, 1957-86, including Secretary for New Territories and for District Administration, 1973-85, Chief Secretary, 1985-86, Hong Kong Government; Acting Governor, Hong Kong, 1986-87; Chairman, National Mutual Asia Hong Kong, now AXA China Region, 1987-, Hong Kong Housing Authority, 1988-93, AXA Life Advisory Board, 2001-, Global Asset Management, Hong Kong; Hong Kong Affairs Advisor to China, 1993-97; Director, Sime Darby Hong Kong, Hysan Development Co Ltd, The Mingly Corporation Ltd, Shui On Properties Ltd; Member, Council, Australian National Gallery. Honours: Knight Commander, Order of the British Empire; Companion, Order of St Michael and St George; Honorary Member, Royal Institute of Civil Servants; Honorary DCL, Kent University, 1987; Honorary LLD, Chinese University of Hong Kong, 1988; Honorary DScS, City University, Hong Kong, 1993. Memberships: President, Outward Bound Trust, Hong Kong, 1986; Vice-President, World Wildlife Fund Hong Kong, 1995-. Address: Dragon View, 128 Castle Peak Road, Tsing Lung Tau, New Territories, Hong Kong Special Administrative Region, China. E-mail:akersjon@pacific.net.hk

**AKIHITO Emperor**, b. 23 December 1933, Tokyo, Japan. Emperor of Japan. m. Michiko Shoda, 10 April 1959, 2 sons, 1 daughter. Education: Private Tutors; Graduate, Gakushin University, 1956. Appointments: Invested, Crown Prince of Japan, 1952; Succeeded late father Emperor Hirohito, 1989; Crowned Emperor of Japan, 1990-; Honorary President: 3rd Asian Games, 1958; International Sports Games for the Disabled, 1964; 11th Pacific Scientific Congress, 1966; University of Tokyo, 1967; Japan World Exhibition, Osaka, 1970; 2nd International Conference on Indo-Pacific Fish, 1985. Publications: Co-author, Fish of the Japanese Archipelago; Contributor, numerous articles to professional journals including 25 papers in journal of Ichthyological Society of Japan. Honours include: Collar of the Superior Order of the Chrysanthemum, 1989. Memberships: Ichthyological Society of Japan; Linnean Society of London (Honorary); Research Association of Austin Museum (Honorary). Address: The Imperial Palace, 1-1 Chiyoda, Chiyoda-ku, Tokyo 100, Japan.

**AKINADE Emmanuel Aderemi**, b. 22 June 1947, Ibadan, Nigeria. University Teacher; Researcher. m. Folake Folarin, 2 sons, 1 daughter. Education: BSc (Hons), Biology, University of Lagos, 1973; PGDE, 1980, MEd, Guidance and Counselling, 1982, PhD, Counselling Psychology, 1988, University of Ibadan. Appointments: Education Officer II, 1974, to Assistant Chief Education Officer, FME, 1990; Senior Lecturer, 1990-2000, Associate Professor, 2000-04, Professor of Counselling Psychology, 2004, Lagos State University, Lagos, Nigeria;

Head of Department, Educational Foundations, 1992-94, 2002-04; Visiting Counselling Psychologist and Senior Lecturer in Psychology, University of Botswana, Gaborone, 1998-2002; Professor of Counselling Psychology, -2004. Publications: Modern Concise Dictionary of Psychology, 2001; Psychology of Human Learning, 2002; A Concise Counselling Practicum, 2003; Evaluation of Guidance and Counselling, 2004; Sexuality Education and Couple Guidance, 2005; Dictionary of Counselling Psychology (Guidance and Counselling), 2005; Dozens of book chapters and articles in refereed journals; Retirement and Marital Counselling Consultant. Honours: Nigeria Police Scholarship, 1961-65; Federal Government of Nigeria Scholarship, 1970-73; Oyo State Graduate Scholarship, 1980-82. Memberships: Counselling Association of Nigeria, 1982-; Editor, The Counsellor, and Eko Journal of Education. Address: Faculty of Education, Lagos State University, PMB 1087 Apapa, Lagos, Nigeria. E-mail: emanuelalasu@yahoo.com

**AKINPELUMI Matthew Akinlolu**, b. 17 May 1959, Ondo State, Nigeria. Management Consultant. m. 2 sons, 2 daughters. Education: Salesmanship Courses, Professional Diploma, Institute of Commerce, London, 1980, Rapid Results College (Correspondence Institute), London; Professional Diploma in Marketing, Adetitun Professional Education Centre, 1978-80; Graduate Diploma, 1983, Postgraduate Diploma, 1986, Association of Business Executives of Nigeria; Postgraduate Diploma, Mass Communication, Polytechnic, Ibadan, 1992. Appointments: Market Research Officer, Epiro International Management Consultants Ibadan, 1980-86; Established St Matthews Management Consultants which was appointed by Managing and Marketing Sales Association, UK, Studentaid Publications Ltd, UK and the Society of Sales Management Administrators, London as Nigerian representatives, 1986-; Founder, Leadership Trust Foundation (NGO), 1999; Founder, Certified Institute of Management, 2004-; Established St Matthews Farm (palm producing farm), Ondo State, Nigeria, 2004. Publications: Building Leadership in Fear of God; Exploration in Management Talents: The Versatile Manager: A Grid Profile. Honours: Manager of the Year 1999, Association of Business Executives of Nigeria; Honorary Doctorate, All Saints University, USA; Honorary Chieftancy Titles: Gbobaniyi of Ola Land; Bobaselu of Agbowa-Ikosi Land; Bobajiro of Iju Land; Orunba Maiyegun of Ijesamosu-ekiti Land; Bobadara of Erunwon Ijebu; Shettima of Damaturu; Iya of Mafara; Lisa-Jigan of Ondo Kingdom; Citizenship Merit Award Winner, Igbara Oke Land; Patron: Ekimogun Students Adssociation; Adeyemi College of Education, University of Ado-Ekiti. Memberships include: Institute of Commercial Management, UK; British Institute of Supervisory Management; Association of Business Executives. Address: PO Box 1567, Ile-Ife, Osun State, Nigeria, West Africa.

**AKRAM Wasim**, b. 3 June 1966, Lahore, Pakistan. Cricketer. Education: Islamia College. Appointments: Left-Hand Mid-Order Batsman, Left-Arm Fast Bowler; Played for Pakistan Automobile Corporation, 1984-85, Lahore, 1985-86, Lancashire, 1988-98 (Captain 1998); only bowler to have captured more than 400 wickets in both Test and one-day cricket; played in 104 Tests for Pakistan, 1984-85 to 2003, 25 as Captain, scoring 2,898 runs (average 22.64) including 3 hundreds and taking 414 wickets (average 23.6); Has scored 7,106 runs (7 hundreds) and taken 1,022 wickets in first class cricket to 2001; Toured England, 1987, 1992, 1996 (Captain); 350 limited-overs internationals (109 as Captain) taking record 490 wickets to 2003; Wisden Cricketer of the Year, 1993. Publication: Wasim, autobiography. Address: c/o Pakistan Cricket Board, Gaddafi Stadium, Ferozepur Road, Lahore 54600, Pakistan.

**AL ABOUD Khalid Mohammad Owain,** b. 13 May 1970, Makkah, Saudi Arabia. Dermatologist. m. Samiah Al Nofie, 1 son. Education: MBBS, College of Medicine, King Abdul Aziz University, Jeddah, 1993; Arab Board in Dermatology, 1999; Jordanian Board in Dermatology, 2000; Saudi Board in Dermatology, 2001. Appointments: Internship, Al Noor Specialist Hospital, Makkah, Saudi Arabia; General Practitioner, King Faisal Hospital, Taif, Saudi Arabia, 1995; Arab Board Training Programme in Assir Central Hospital, Abha, 1995-99; Dermatology Specialist, King Faisal Hospital, Taif, Saudi Arabia, 1999-; Medical Director and Assistant Director, Taif Maternity Hospital, Taif, Saudi Arabia, 2000-; Scientific collaboration with Department of Medical Genetics, Antwerp, Belgium and with Dr Ervin Epstein, University of California, USA. Publications: 10 articles in international medical journals as author include most recently: Ectopic respiratory mucous in the skin associated with skeletal malformation and polydactyly, 2001; Vaginitis Emphysematosa, 2002; Contributions to dermatology web sites; Contributions to newspapers and magazines; Papers presented at national and international conferences. Memberships: Saudi Society of Dermatology; Society of Pediatric Dermatology; American Academy of Dermatology. Address: PO Box No 5440, Makkah, Saudi Arabia. E-mail: amoa65@hotmail.com

**AL-ABDULMUNIM Abdulmunim Ibrahim,** b. 11 May 1962, Buridah, Al-Qassim, Saudi Arabia. Professor. m. Al-Rabdi Amal, 3 sons, 1 daughter. Education: BSc, Economics, King Saud University, Saudi Arabia, 1984; MA, Economics, University of Arizona, USA, 1989; PhD, Economics, Strathclyde University, Scotland, 1995. Appointments include: Demonstrator, 1983-95, Assistant Professor, 1995-99, Associate Professor, 1999-, Head of Department of Economics, 1996-99, Vice-Dean, 1998-2000, Dean, 2000-, College of Business and Economics, King Saud University, Al-Qasssim Branch; Other University appointments include: Member of the Council of the College of Business and Economics, 1995-; Member, Students' Fund Directors Board, King Saud University, 1996-99; Director of Research and Human Resources Development Centre, 1996-98; Supervisor of Student Affairs Unit, 1995-2000; Member of the Permanent Committee, Prince Abdullah Institute for Researches and Consultative Studies, King Saud University, Riyadh, 1998-; Supervisor of Exams Committees, College of Business and Economics, 1997-; Member, Industrial Committee Commerce Chamber in Al-Qassim, 1996-; Member, Higher Studies Programme Committee, 1997-; Chairman of the academic committee for the economic dimension proceeded from the International Conference on Celebration of the 20th anniversary of the Custodian of the Two Holy Mosques, King Fahd Bin Abduaziz's reign of the Kingdom, College of Business and Economics, King Saud University Al-Qassim Branch. Publications include: Articles: Econometrics of human development in the Kingdom of Saudi Arabia, 2002; Taxation incentives to fight the environment pollution with a proposed plan for application in the Kingdom of Saudi Arabia, 2002; Estimation of CES Production Function Model for Saudi Economy, 2003; Resources specification for financing health services in the Kingdom of Saudi Arabia, 2004; The Industrial Economics (textbook), 2001; 10 papers presented at symposia and conferences. Honour: The British Cultural Council Scholarship for Summer Research – Postdoctoral, 1998. Memberships: Saudi Economic Association; Scottish Economic Union; International Economic Development Association in Scotland; British Economic Royal Association; American Western International Economic Association. Address: College of Business and Economics, Al-Qassim University, Buridah, PO Box 6033, Saudi Arabia. E-mail: alabdulmunim@yahoo.com

**AL-ARRAYED Jalil Ebrahim,** b. 26 January 1933. Emeritus Professor; University Administrator. Education: BA, Chemistry, American University, Beirut, Lebanon, 1954; MEd, Science Education, Leicester University, England, 1964; PhD, Comparative Science Education and Management of Curriculum Development, Bath University, England, 1974. Appointments: Teacher, Sciences, Maths, 1954-59, Science Inspector, 1959-66, Bahrain Government Department of Education; Principal, Bahrain Men's Teachers Training College, 1966-72; Under-Secretary, Bahrain Ministry of Education, 1974-82; Executive Council Member (Bahrain Rep), 1975-82, Deputy Chairman, 1978-79; Chairman, 1979-80, Arab Bureau of Education for the Gulf States; Member, Bahrain Representative, Council for Higher Education in the Gulf States, 1976-92; Member, Board of Trustees, Bahrain University College of Arts, Science and Education, 1979-86; Member Founding Committee, Arabian Gulf University, 1980-85; Member, IIEP Council of Consultant Fellows, Paris, 1984-92; Rector, Bahrain University College of Arts, Science and Education, 1982-87; Professor of Education, Vice President, Academic Affairs, University of Bahrain, 1987-91, Acting President, 1991; Participant, various regional and international conferences on education reform, and Chair, several committees. Publications: Author of books: A Critical Analysis of Arab School Science Teaching, 1980, Development and Evaluation of University Faculty in Arab Gulf States, 1994, Some Aspects of Contemporary Management Thought, 1996; More than 50 articles on educational issues in general and science education in particular, 1956-78. Honours: Gold Medal for Academic Achievement, Bahrain Government Department of Education, 1969; Prize for Academic Achievement, Bahrain Ministry of Education, 1975; American Biographical Institute Commemorative Medal of Honour, 1988; State Award for Outstanding Citizens, Government of Bahrain, 1992; International Association of University Presidents Certificate for Outstanding Contributions, 1996. Memberships: Life Fellow, International Biographical Association; Life Member, Indian Institute of Public Administration; Various organizations including: Chartered Management Institute; Institute of Administrative Management, UK; International Association of University Presidents; Royal Society of Chemistry (UK); Listed in numerous biographical dictionaries. Address: PO Box 26165, Adlia, Manama, Bahrain.

**AL-KODMANI Nasser,** b. 1 January 1961, Damascus, Syria, Civil Engineer. m. Rima Haj Ibrahim, 2 sons. Education: First Certificate in English, Cambridge University, British Council, Damascus, 1980; Test of English as a Foreign Language, Princeton University, USA, TOEFL, American Cultural Centre, Damascus, 1984; Bachelor of Science in Civil Engineering, Damascus University, Syria, 1985; Course in project evaluation and visibility study, Damascus, 1990; Course in Construction Management, Abu-Dhabi, UAE, 1993. Appointments: Lieutenant, Syrian Armed Forces; Site Engineer, General Company for Building, Presidential Palace project, Damascus, Syria, 1985-86; Structural Engineer, General Company for Engineering and Consulting, Damascus, Syria, 1986-91; Construction Manager, A. C. C., Abu-Dhabi, UAE, 1991-; Carried out projects HE Sheikh Mohammed Bin Khalifah Tower, Citi Bank Tower; HE Sheikh Surour City Complex, Liwa Center; HE Dr Manae Saeed Al-Otaiba Palace; Commercial building for HE Sheikh Nahyan Bin Hamdan al Nahyan; Lulu Island Development; Shuweihat Power and Water Project and lot-D; Captital Plaza Development, Abu-Dhabi Publications: Earthquake Effects on Soil – Foundation Systems. Honours: Listed in several biographical publications. Membership: Syrian Engineers Syndicate, 1986-; American Society of Civil Engineers, 1992-; UAE Society of Civil Engineers, 1992-.

Address: P O Box 2113, Abu Dhabi, United Arab Emirates. E-mail: kodmani@hotmail.com Website: www.accsal.com

**AL-MARAYATI Abid A,** b. 14 October 1931, Iraq. Professor. Education: BA, 1952, MA, 1954, Bradley University; PhD, New York University, 1959. Appointments: Instructor, Department of Government, University of Massachusetts, 1960; Technical Assistance Officer, International Atomic Energy Agency, Austria, 1960-62; Associate Professor, State University College of New York, 1962-64; Research Fellow, Harvard University, 1964-65; Associate Professor, Arizona State University, 1965-68; Professor and Former Director, Center for International Studies, Department of Political Science, University of Toledo, 1968-; Visiting Professor, University of Kuwait, 1982-83; Visiting Professor, Institute for Public Administration, Riyadh, Saudi Arabia, 1985-86; Visiting Professor, Beijing Foreign Studies University, 1991; Asylum Officer, Immigration and Naturalization Service, Justice Department, 1998; Distinguished Scholar, National Endowment for the Humanities, Hawaii Pacific University, 2002-03. Publications: 5 books; Over 20 articles and papers; Reviews of books and articles; Research proposals. Memberships: International Studies Association; American Political Science Association; The Middle East Institute; The Middle East Studies Association of North America; Phi Kappa Phi. Address: University of Toledo, 2109 Terrace View West, Toledo, OH 43607, USA. E-mail: a_almarayati@yahoo.com

**AL-RAHMAH Abdullah Nasser,** b. 20 December 1943, Al-Rass, Qassim. Saudi Arabia. Professor. m. Fatimah Abbas Al-Amoudi, 3 sons, 7 daughters. Education: BSc, King Saud University, 1969; PhD, Mycology, Glasgow University, 1975. Appointments: Demonstrator, Botany and Microbiology Department, 1969-71, Assistant Professor, 1975-77, Associate Professor, 1977-86, Vice Dean of University Library, 1978-80, Professor, 1986-, Head of Department, King Saud University. Publications: Over 45 research papers in professional journals. Honours: Award, 14th Kuwaiti Exhibition Book in the Field of Scientific Book Authoring, 1988. Memberships: British Mycological Society; Arabian Plant Protection Society; Saudi Biological Society. Address: Department of Botany and Microbiology, College of Science, King Saud University, PO Box 2455, Riyadh 11451, Saudi Arabia.

**AL-RASHED Abdallah Mohammed,** b. 2 October 1954, Riyadh, Saudi Arabia. Professor of Mathematics. Education: BS, University of Petroleum and Minerals, Dhahran, 1976; MS, 1978, PhD, 1981, Colorado State University, USA. Appointments: Faculty Member, 1981, Director of Research Centre, 1984, Chairman, Mathematics Department, 1985, Dean of Graduate Studies, 1994, King Saud University Riyadh; Currently, President, King Khalid University; Committee Member, 1981, Deputy Minister, 1994 Ministry of Education, Riyadh; Consultant, Saudi Arabian National Centre for Science and Technology, Riyadh, 1985-. Publications: Books: Integral Calculus, 1985; Real Analysis, 1985; Numerous articles in professional journals. Memberships: American Mathematics Society; Mathematics Association of America; London Mathematics Society. Address: President's Office, King Khalid University, PO Box 418, Abha, Saudi Arabia.

**AL SOFI Mohammad Abdul-Kareem,** b. 11 June 1945, Saudi Arabia. Consultancy Vice-Chairman. m. Fathalla Mohammad Fawziah, 1 son, 3 daughters. Education: College of Petroleum and Minerals, Dharan, Saudi Arabia, 1964-67; BSc, Chemical and Petroleum Refining Engineering, Colorado School of Mines, USA, 1967-70; Higher Diploma in Desalination and Mechanical Engineering, University of Glasgow, Scotland, 1977-78. Appointments: Process Engineer, 1970-73, Operation Supervisor,

1973-76, Petroleum Refineries; Operation Supervisor, 1976; Deputy Plant Manager, 1976-77, Operation and Maintenance Company for Desalination and Electricity (in house production); Technical Director, 1979, Vice-President, Operations, 1980, Senior Vice-President Operations, 1981, Local and International Joint Venture Management in Olayan Financing Company; Plant Manager, 1981-82, Plants General Manager, 1982-83, Director General of Research, 1983-84, O&M Technical Advisor, 1984-87, Research and Development Technical Advisor, 1987-2001, Saline Water Conversion Corporation; Independent Consultant, 2001-2002; Vice-Chairman, Arabian Consulting Engineering Centre, 2002-; Participant in desalination and power production research and development, surveys, studies, projects, proposals and reports as principal or co-investigator; Participant in numerous national and international conferences. Publications: 10 papers on heat exchanger scale control; 5 papers on energy and electricity; 5 papers on desalination feed water treatment; 5 papers on water and power production economics; 5 papers on strategies, planning and process of water and power production and consumption; Introduction to Arabic Encyclopaedia of Desalination and Water Reuse; 1 patent application; Member of Editorial Board of Desalination Journal. Honours: Best paper Award, WSTA Conference, 1994; Principal Author of Best Paper Award, IDA Conference, 1999; 2 Awards as Co-worker in distinguished research work, MAREI/KACST, 2001-2002; Title of Professor earned from the Institute of Mechanical Engineering for applied engineering work, 2004 Memberships: International Desalination Association, former Board Member; Founding Member, Water Science and Technology Association, President, 1995-97, Secretary General, 1997-99. Address: Arabian Consulting Engineering Centre, PO Box 3790, Al-Khobar 31952, Kingdom of Saudi Arabia. E-mail: maks@acec-sa.com

**ALAGNA Roberto,** b. 7 June 1963, Clichy-sur-Bois, France. Singer (Tenor). m. (2) Angela Gheorghiu, 1996. Education: Studied in France and Italy. Debut: Plymouth, 1988, as Alfredo in La Traviata for Glyndebourne Touring Opera. Career: Sang Rodolfo at Covent Garden (1990) and has returned for Gounod's Roméo and Don Carlos, 1994-96; sang Donizetti's Roberto Devereux at Monte Carlo (1992) and the Duke of Mantua at the Vienna Staatsoper (1995); Sang Don Carlos at the Théâtre du Châtelet, Paris, 1996; American appearances at Chicago and New York (debut at Met 1996, as Rodolfo); Alfredo at La Scala, Milan. Recordings include: video of Gounod's Roméo et Juliette (Pioneer); La Traviata, from La Scala (Sony) and Don Carlos, Paris; Duets and Arias (with Angela Gheorghiu), La Boheme 1996, Don Carlos 1996, La Rondine 1997. Honours include: Winner, Pavarotti Competition, 1988; Chevalier des Arts et des Lettres; Personalite Musicale de l'Annee, 1994; Laurence Olivier Award for Outstanding Achievement in Opera, 1995; Victor Award for Best Singer, 1997. Address: c/o Lévon Sayan, 9 chemin de Plonjon, Geneva, Switzerland.

**ALAHUHTA Eila Marjatta,** b. 23 September 1926, Mikkeli, Finland. Special Needs Educator; Professor Emerita; Consultant, Alahuta Consulting. 2 sons, 3 daughters, 1 deceased. Education: MA; DPhil; Training as Special Teacher. Appointments: Teacher in Primary School and School for the Handicapped, 1948-73; Chief Teacher, Finnish College of Speech, 1973-80; Associate Professor of Special Pedagogy, University of Jyväskylä, 1977-83; Academic Docent, Special Education, University of Helsinki, 1979-90; Professor of Logopedics, University of Oulu, 1983-93, Dean and Vice Dean, Faculty of Humanities, University of Oulu, 1988-90; Adjunct Professor of Speech Pathology, Faculty of Liberal Arts, Wayne State University, USA, 1989-92. Publications: On the Defects of Perception, Reasoning and Spatial Orientation Ability in Linguistically Handicapped

Children, 1976; I Play and I Talk, I Move and I Read, 1990, 1995. Honours: Order of the White Rose of Finland, First Class, 1990; Finnish RA Prize, 1991; Corporation of the Union of Finnish Towns, Medal of Merit, 1993; IOM, International Order of Merit, 1994; Deputy Director General, 1994; International Woman of the Year, 1995-96; International Sash of Academia, 1997; Most Admired Woman of the Decade, 1998; World Who's Who Hall of Fame, 1999; Outstanding Woman of the 21st Century, 2000; The First Five Hundred at the New Millennium, 2000; Order of International Fellowship, ABI, 2001; Life Patron IBA, 2001; Lifetime Achievement Award, IBC, 2002; Adviser to the Director General, IBC, 2002; Vice Consul, IBC, 2002; The American Medal of Honor, 2002; Companion of Honour, IBC, 2003; World Laureate of Finland, 2003; International Ambassador of Goodwill, IBC, 2003; International Medal of Honour, IBC, 2003; Ambassador of Grand Eminence, ABI, 2004; DDG Innercircle Award, IBC, 2004; World Academy of Letters, Chair of Philosophy and Humanities for Achievement in Education, ABI, 2004; WPDF Membership Document, IBC, 2004; Governor's Passport, IBC, 2004; International Order of Distinction, IBC, 2004. Memberships include: World Association for Education Research; Nordic Association for the Study of Child Language; Member of the Academic Counsel, London Diplomatic Academy. Address: Koivuhovintie 6A, FIN-02700 Kauniainen, Finland.

**ALAINI Mohsen Ahmed al-,** b. 20 October 1932, Bani Bahloul, North Yemen. Politician; Diplomat. m. Aziza Abulahom, 1962, 2 sons, 2 daughters. Education: Faculty of Law, Cairo University; Sorbonne, Paris. Appointments: Schoolteacher, Aden, 1958-60; International Confederation of Arab Trade Unions, 1960-62; Minister of Foreign Affairs, Yemeni Republic, September-December 1962, May-July 1965, 1974-80; Permanent Representative to United Nations, 1962-65, 1965-66, 1967-69, 1980-81; Prime Minister, November-December 1967, 1974-80; Ambassador to USSR, 1968-70; Prime Minister, Minister of Foreign Affairs, February 1971, September 1971-December 1972, June 1974-January 1975; Ambassador to UK, 1973-74; Ambassador to France, August-September 1974, 1975-76; Ambassador to Federal Republic of Germany, 1981-84; Ambassador to USA, 1984- 97; Deputy Chair, Consultative Council, 1997-. Publications: Battles and Conspiracies against Yemen, 1957; Fifty Years of Mounting Sands, autobiography, 2000. Address: PO Box 7922, San'a, Yemen.

**ALARCON RIVERA Fabián Ernesto,** b. 1947, Quito, Ecuador. Politician. m. Lucía Peña, 2 sons, 1 daughter. Education: Pontifical Catholic University. Appointments: Councillor, Quito, 1969; Former Prefect of Pinchincha Province; Former Deputy to Congress (three times); Formerly Speaker of Congress (three times), Ecuador; Acting President of Ecuador, 6-10 February 1997; President of Ecuador, 1997-98; Arrested on charges of illegally hiring personnel, March 1999. Memberships: Frente Radical Alfarista. Address: c/o Office of the President, Palacio Nacional, García Moreno 1043, Quito, Ecuador.

**ALBARN Damon,** b. 23 March 1968, Whitechapel, London, England. Singer; Songwriter. Education: Drama School, Stratford East, 1 year. Musical Education: Part-time Music course, Goldsmith's College. Career: First solo concerts, Colchester Arts Centre; Member, Blur; Numerous television and radio appearances, include: Later With Jools Holland; Top Of The Pops; Loose Ends, Radio 4; Later With... Britpop Now; Extensive tours, include: Alexandra Palace, Reading Festival, 1993; Glastonbury, 1994; Mile End, 1995; V97, 1997; UK Arena Tour, 1997; Glastonbury, 1998; T in the Park, 1999; Reading and Leeds Festival, 1999; Actor, film, Face, 1997; Score for Ravenous, 1998; Score for Ordinary Decent Criminal,

1999; score for 101 Reykjavik (with Einar Benediktsson), 2000. Recordings: Albums: with Blur: Leisure, 1991; Modern Life Is Rubbish, 1993; Parklife, 1994; The Great Escape, 1995; Blur, 1997; 13, 1999; Best of 2000; (with Gorillaz) Gorillaz, 2001; G-Slides, 2002; Phase One Celebrity Take Down, 2002; Singles: She's So High, 1990; There's No Other Way, 1991; Bang, 1991; Popscene, 1992; For Tomorrow, 1993; Chemical World, 1993; Sunday Sunday, 1993; Girls And Boys, 1994; To The End, 1994; Parklife, 1994; End Of A Century, 1994; Country House, 1995; The Universal, 1995; Stereotypes, 1996; Beetlebum, 1997; Song 2, 1997; On Your Own, 1997; MOR, 1997; Tender, 1999; Coffee and TV, 1999; No Distance Left To Run, 1999; Music is My Radar, 2000; (with Gorillaz) Clint Eastwood, 2000; 19-2000, 2001; Rock the House, 2001; Tomorrow Comes Today, 2002; Solo: Original score for film Ravenous, directed by Antonia Bird, with Michael Nyman, 1998; Score for film Ordinary Decent Criminal, directed by Thasseus O'Sullivan, 1999; Mali Music, various contributors, 2002. Honours: Mercury Prize Nomination; Platinum album, Parklife; BRIT Awards: Best Single, Video, Album and Band, 1995; Q Awards, Best Album, 1994, 1995; Mercury Music Prize nomination, 1999; Platinum albums. Current Management: CMO Management, Unit 32, Ransome Dock, 35-37 Parkgate Road, London SW11 4NP, England.

**ALBEE Edward (Franklin III),** b. 12 March 1928, Virginia, USA. Playwright. Education: Trinity College, Hartford, Connecticut, 1946-47. Appointments: Lecturer at various US colleges and universities. Publications: Plays: The Zoo Story, 1958; The Death of Bessie Smith, 1959; The Sandbox, 1959; The American Dream, 1960; Who's Afraid of Virginia Woolf?, 1962; Tiny Alice, 1963; A Delicate Balance, 1966; Box, 1970; Quotations from Chairman Mao, 1970; All Over, 1971; Seascape, 1975; Counting the Ways, 1976; Listening, 1977; The Lady from Dubuque, 1979; Finding the Sun, 1982; The Man Who Had Three Arms, 1983; Marriage Play, 1987; Three Tall Women, 1991; Fragments, 1993; The Play about the Baby, 1996; The Goat, or, Who is Sylvia? 2000; Occupant, 2001. Adaptions of: Carson McCuller's The Ballad of the Sad Café, 1963; James Purdy's Malcolm, 1965; Giles Cooper's Everything in the Garden, 1967; Vladimir Nabokov's Lolita, 1980. Honours: Pulitzer Prizes in Drama, 1967, 1975, 1994; American Academy and Institute of Arts and Letters Gold Medal, 1980; Theater Hall of Fame, 1985. Memberships: Dramatists Guild Council; Edward F Albee Foundation, president. Address: 14 Harrison Street, New York, NY 10013, USA.

**ALBERT II,** b. 6 June 1934, Belgium. King of Belgium. m. Donna Paola Ruffo Di Calabria, 1959, 2 sons, 1 daughter. Appointments: Formerly Prince of Liege; Former Vice Admiral of Navy; President, Caisse d'Epargne et de Retraite, 1954-92; President, Belgian Red Cross, 1958-93; President, Belgian Office of Foreign Trade, 1962; Appointed by Council of Europe as President of Conference of European Ministers responsible for protection of Cultural and Architectural Heritage, 1969; Participant in Numerous Conferences on environment including UN Conference, Stockholm, 1972; Chair, Belgian Olympic and Interfed Committee; Succeeded to the throne 9 August 1993 following death of his brother King Baudouin I. Address: Cabinet of the King, The Royal Place, rue Bréderode, 1000 Brussels, Belgium.

**ALBERTI Kurt George Matthew Mayer (Sir),** b. 27 September 1937, Germany. Professor of Medicine. m.(1) 1964, 3 sons, (2) Stephanie Amiel, 1988. Education: Balliol College, Oxford; MA; DPhil; FRCP; FRCPath; FRCPEd; FRCPGlas; FRCPI. Appointments: Research Fellow, Harvard University, USA, 1966-69; Research Officer, Oxford University, England,

1969-73; Professor of Chemical Pathology, Southampton University, 1973-78; Professor of Clinical Biochemistry, 1978-85, Professor of Medicine, 1985-2002, Dean of Medicine, 1995-97, University of Newcastle; Director of Research and Development, Northern and Yorkshire Region, 1992-95; President, Royal College of Physicians, 1997-2002; Professor of Metabolic Medicine, Imperial College, London, 1999-2002; Senior Research Fellow, London, 2002-; National Director for Emergency Access, Department of Health, 2002-. Publications: International Textbook of Diabetes Mellitus, 1st and 2nd editions, co-editor; Diabetes Annual, volumes 1-6, co-editor; Over 1,000 papers, reviews and edited books. Honours: Honorary MD, University of Aarhus, Denmark, 1998; Honorary Fellow, Balliol College, Oxford, 1999; DMed hc (University of Aarhus), (Southampton), 2000; Fellow, Academy of Medicine, Singapore, Hong Kong; Fellow, College of Physicians, Sri Lanka, Thailand. Address: Royal College of Physicians, 11 St Andrew's Place, Regents Park, London NW1 4LE, England. E-mail: professor.alberti@rcplondon.ac.uk

**ALBRIGHT Carol Rausch,** b. 20 March 1936, Evergreen Park, Illinois, USA. Writer; Editor; Retired Foundation Administrator. m. (1) Saul Gorski, 2 July 1961, deceased 22 June 1983, (2) John Albright, 26 October 1991, 2 sons. Education: BA, Augustana College, Rock Island, Illinois, 1956; Graduate Study, Lutheran Schools of Theology, Chicago, Berkeley, Washington University, St Louis. Appointments: Director, Lutheran Campus Ministry, Oregon State University, 1958-61; Publishing Consultant, 1966-70; Assistant Editor, World Book Encyclopaedia , 1970-75; Publishing Consultant, 1975-98; Contributing Editor, Doctor I've Read...., 1983-93; Executive Editor, Zygon: Journal of Religion and Science, 1989-98; Managing Editor, Science and Religion South, 1995-99; Publisher, Bridge Building, 1999; Co-Director, John Templeton Foundation Science and Religion Course Programme, Southern US, 1995-99; Co-Director, CTNS Science and Religion course programme, Midwestern US,1999-2001. Publications: Beginning with the end; The Humanizing Brain; Where God Lives in the Human Brain; Growing in the Image of God; NeuroTheology. Honours: Academic Achievement Award, Institute for Religion in an Age of Science; Phi Beta Kappa; Chicago Women in Publishing: Award for Excellence in Periodical Writing. Memberships: Treasurer, Centre for Advanced Study in Religion and Science; Executive Council, American Theological Society, Midwest Division; Vice President for Religion, Institute for Religion in an Age of Science; Augustana Lutheran Church of Hyde Park; European Society for the study of Science and Theologgi; Society of Midland Authors. Address: 5415 S Hyde Park Blvd, Chicago, IL 60615, USA.

**ALBRIGHT Jack Lawrence,** b. 14 March 1930, San Francisco, California. Educator, Professor Emeritus. m. Lorraine A Hughes, August 1957, 2 daughters. Education: BS, with honours, California Polytechnic State University, San Luis Obispo, 1952; MS, Dairy Science, Washington State University, 1954; PhD, Animal Science, Washington State University, 1957; Certificate in Animal Behaviour, Michigan State University, 1964. Appointments: Various positions including: Professor, Animal Science, Purdue University 1966-96; Professor of Animal Management and Behaviour, School of Veterinary Medicine, Purdue University 1974-96; Professor Emeritus of Animal Science and Veterinary Medicine, Purdue University, 1996-. Publications: Authored or co-authored 131 refereed research publications: 116 scientific abstracts; 89 books, books chapters, reviews and bound proceedings; 247 invited research lectures; 264 popular articles; 34 extension bulletins; 323 extension publications, talks, radio and TV interviews. Honours include: Fellow, American Association for the Advancement

of Science, 1963; Fellow, Indiana Academy of Science, 1983; Fellow, American Dairy Science Association, 1997; Paso Robles High School, California First Inaugural Academic Hall of Fame 1998; Honorary Member of Los Lecheros Dairy Club, California Polytechnic State University, 1999; Tablet of Honor, Kiwanis International Foundation, 2000; Listed in Who's Who and biographical publications. Memberships: Life Member, American Dairy Science Association; Life Member, American Society of Animal Science; International Society for Applied Ethology; Universities Federation of Animal Welfare and Humane Slaughter Association, UK; Hoofed Animal Humane Association, USA; Council for Agriculture Science and Technology, USA. Address: Purdue University, West Lafayette, IN 47907, USA. E-mail: jla9@juno.com

**ALBRIGHT Madeleine Korbel,** b. 1938, Czechoslovakia. American Politician; Professor of International Affairs. m. Joseph Albright, divorced, 3 daughters. Education: Wellesley College; Columbia University. Appointments: Professor, International Affairs, Georgetown University, 1982-83; Head, Centre for National Policy, 1985-93; Former Legislative Aide to Democratic Senator Edmund Muskie; Former Member, National Security Council Staff in Carter Administration; Advisor, Democratic candidates, Geraldine Ferraro, 1984, Michael Dukakis, 1988; Permanent Representative to United Nations, 1993-97; Secretary of State, 1997-2001; Co-founder, The Albright Group, 2001-; Chair, National Democratic Institute, Washington DC, 2001-. Publications: Poland: the Role of the Press in Political Change, 1983; numerous articles. Memberships: Council on Foreign Relations; American Political Science Association; American Association for Advancement of Slavic Studies. Address: 901 15th Street, NW, Suite 1000, Washington, DC 20005, USA.

**ALCARAZ Jose Luis,** b. 3 July 1963, Hellin, Albacete, Spain. Engineering University Professor. Education: Bachelor, Murcia, Spain, 1981; Graduated in Industrial Engineering, Valencia, Spain, 1988; Doctor in Industrial Engineering, San Sebastian, Spain, 1993. Assistant Lecturer, Valencia, Spain, 1988-89, San Sebastian, Spain, 1989-93, Bilbao, Spain, 1993-94; Full Professor, Bilbao, Spain, 1994-. Publications: Books: Theory of Plasticity and Applications, 1993; Elasticity and Strength of Materials, 1995; Contributed papers to international journals. Honour: Graduation Special Award, 1988. Memberships: European Mechanics Society; New York Academy of Sciences; Spanish Association for Mechanical Engineering. Address: Dep Ingenieria Mecánica, Escuela Superior de Ingenieros, Alameda Urquijo, s/n, 48013 Bilbao, Spain.

**ALDA Alan,** b. 28 January 1936, New York, USA. Actor. m. Arlene Weiss, 3 daughters. Education: Fordham University. Appointments: Performed with Second City, 1963; Broadway roles in The Owl and the Pussycat, Purlie Victorious, Fair Game of Lovers, The Apple Tree, Our Town, London, 1991, Jake's Women, 1992. Creative Works: Films include: Gone are the Days, 1963; Paper Lion, 1968; The Extraordinary Seaman, 1968; The Moonshine War, 1970; Jenny, 1970; The Mephisto Waltz, 1971; To Kill a Clown, 1972; California Suite, 1978; Same Time Next Year, 1978; The Seduction of Joe Tynan, also wrote screenplay, 1979; Four Seasons, 1981; Sweet Liberty, 1986; A New Life, 1987; Crimes and Misdemeanours, 1989; Betsy's Wedding, 1990; Whispers in the Dark, 1992; And the Band Played On, 1993; Manhattan Murder Mystery, 1993; White Mile, 1994; Canadian Bacon, 1995; Everybody Says I Love You, 1996; Murder at 1600, 1997; Mad City, 1997; The Object of My Affection, 1998; Numerous TV includes: The Glass House, 1972; MASH, 1972-83. Honours: Theatre World Award; 5 Emmy Awards; 2 Directors Guild Awards; Writers

Guild Award; 7 Peoples Choice Awards; Humanities Award for Writing; 5 Golden Globe Awards. Memberships: Trustee, Museum of TV and Radio; Rockefeller Foundation; President, National Commission for Observance of International Women's Year, 1976; Co-chair, National ERA Countdown Campaign, 1982. Address: c/o Martin Bregman Productions, 641 Lexington Avenue, NY 10022, USA.

**ALDINGTON Charles Harold Stuart Low (Lord),** b. 22 June 1948, London, England. Investment Banker. m. Regine von Csongrady-Schopf, 1989, 1 son, 2 daughters. Education: BA honours, New College, Oxford. Appointments: Citibank NA, New York , Hong Kong and Dusseldorf, 1971-77; Head of Ship Finance, Head of UK Corporate Lending, Director, Continental Europe, Grindlays Bank, 1978-86; Deutsche Bank AG: Director, Duisburg Branch, 1986-87; Managing Director, London, 1988-96; Managing Director, Investment Banking, 1996-; Chairman: European Vocational College, 1991-96; CENTEC, subsequently FOCUS Central London, Central London TEC, 1995-99; Council Member, British-German Chamber of Commerce and Industry, 1995. Memberships: Oxford University Court of Benefactors, 1990-; Trustee, English International, 1979-86; Trustee, Whitechapel Art Gallery Foundation, 1991-96. Address: 59 Warwick Square, SW1V 2AL, London, England.

**ALDISS Brian Wilson,** b. 18 August 1925, East Dereham, England. Literary Editor; Writer; Critic. m. (2) Margaret Manson, 11 December 1965, 2 sons, 2 daughters. Appointments: President, British Science Fiction Association, 1960-64; Guest of Honour at World Science Fiction Convention; London, 1965, World Science Fiction Convention Brighton, 1979; Chairman, Committee of Management, Society of Authors, 1977-78; Arts Council Literature Panel, 1978-80; Booker McConnell Prize Judge, 1981; Fellow, Royal Society of Literature, 1990; Prix Utopia, 1999; Grand Master of Science Fiction, 2000. Publications: Novels include: Hothouse, 1962; Frankenstein Unbound, 1973; The Malacia Tapestry, 1976; Life in the West, 1980; The Helliconia Trilogy, 1982, 1983, 1985, 1996; Forgotten Life, 1988; Dracula Unbound, 1991; Remembrance Day, 1993; Somewhere East of Life, 1994; Story collections include: Seasons in Flight, 1984; Best SF Stories of Brian W Aldiss, 1988; A Romance of the Equator, Best Fantasy Stories, 1989; A Tupolev Too Far, 1993; The Secret of This book, 1995. Non-Fiction includes: Cities and Stones: A Traveller's Jugoslavia, 1966; Bury My Heart Heart at W H Smith's: A Writing Life, 1990; The Detached Retina (essays), 1995; At the Caligula Hotel (collected poems), 1995; Songs From the Steppes of Central Asia, 1996; The Twinkling of an Eye, My Life as a Englishman, 1998; When the Feast is Finished, 1998; White Mars (with Roger Penrose), 1999; Supertoys Last All Summer Long, 2001; The Cretan Teat, 2001; Super-State, 2002; Researches and Churches in Serbia, 2002; The Dark Sun Rises, poems, 2002; Affairs in Hampden Ferrers, 2003. Contributions to: Times Literary Supplement; Nature. Honours: Hugo Awards, 1962, 1987; Nebula Award, 1965; various British Science Fiction Association awards; Ferara Cometa d'Argento, 1977; Prix Jules Verne, Sweden, 1977; Science Fiction Research Association Pilgrim Awards, 1978; First International Association of the Fantastic in the Arts Distinguished Scholarship Award, 1986; J Lloyd Eaton Award, 1988; World Science Fiction President's Award, 1988. Hugo Nomination, 1991. Membership: Royal Society of Literature, fellow, honorary DLitt, 2000. Address: Hambleden, 39 St Andrews Road, Old Headington, Oxford OX3 9DL, England.

**ALDRICH Christiaan,** b. 7 July 1960, Bloemfontein, South Africa. Chemical Engineer. m. Annemarie Aldrich, 1 daughter. Education: BEng (Chem), 1982; MEng (Metall) 1985; PhD

(Engineering) 1993. Appointments: Process Engineer, Sasol, 1985-87; Senior Researcher, 1992-93, Senior Lecturer, 1994-95, Associate Professor, 1996-98, Professor, Process Engineering, 1999-, University of Stellenbosch; Director of Institute for Mineral Processing and Intelligent Process Systems, 1999-. Publications: Over 80 peer reviewed papers in international journals since 1994; Numerous contributions to the proceedings of international conferences, symposia and workshops. Honours: British Association Silver ($S_2A_3$) Medal, 2000; FRD President's Award, 1996. Memberships: MSAIMM, MAAS, MIEE. Address: Department of Process Engineering, University of Stellenbosch, Private Bag X1, Matieland, 7602, Stellenbosch, South Africa. E-mail: ca1@sun.ac.za

**ALDRIDGE (Harold Edward) James,** b. 10 July 1918, England. Author; Journalist. m. Dina Mitchnik, 1942, 2 sons. Appointments: with Herald and Sun, Melbourne, Australia, 1937-38; Daily Sketch and Sunday Dispatch, London, 1939; Australian Newspaper Service, North American Newspaper Alliance (as war correspondent), Finland, Norway, Middle East, Greece, USSR, 1939-45; Correspondent, Time and Life, Tehran, 1944. Plays: 49th State, 1947; One Last Glimpse, 1981. Publications: Signed with Their Honour, 1942; The Sea Eagle, 1944; Of Many Men, 1946; The Diplomat. 1950; The Hunter, 1951; Heroes of the Empty View, 1954; Underwater Hunting for Inexperienced Englishmen, 1955; I Wish He Would Not Die, 1958; Gold and Sand, short stories, 1960; The Last Exile, 1961; A Captive in the Land, 1962; The Statesman's Game, 1966; My Brother Tom, 1966; The Flying 19, 1966; Living Egypt, with Paul Strand, 1969; Cairo: Biography of a City, 1970; A Sporting Proposition, 1973; The Marvellous Mongolian, 1974; Mockery in Arms, 1974; The Untouchable Juli, 1975; One Last Glimpse, 1977; Goodbye Un-America, 1979; The Broken Saddle, 1982; The True Story of Lilli Stubek, 1984; The True Story of Spit Mac Phee, 1985; The True Story of Lola MacKellar, 1993. Honours: Rhys Memorial Award, 1945; Lenin Peace Prize, 1972; Australian Childrens Book of the Year, 1985; Guardian Children's Fiction Prize. Address: c/o Curtis Brown, 28/29 Haymarket, London, SW1Y 4SP, England.

**ALDRIN Buzz,** b. 20 January 1930, Montclair, New Jersey. American Astronaut. m. (1) divorced 1978, (2) Lois Driggs-Cannon, 1988, 2 sons, 1 daughter. Education: US Military Academy; MA Institute of Technology. Appointments: Former Member, US Air Force; Completed Pilot Training, 1952; Flew Combat Mission during Korean War; Aerial Gunnery Instructor, Nellis Air Force Base, Nevada; Attended Squadron Officers School, Air University, Maswell Air Force Base, Alabama; Flight Commander, 36th Tectical Fighter Wing, Bitburg, Germany; Completed Astronautics Studies, MIT, 1963; Selected by NASA as Astronaut, 1963; Later assigned to Manned Spacecraft Centre, Houston, Texas; Pilot of Backup Crew for Gemini IX Mission, 1966; Pilot, Gemini XII, 1966; Backup Command module pilot for Apollo VIII; Lunar Module Pilot for Apollo XI; Landed on the moon, 20 July 1969; Commandant Aerospace Research Pilot School, 1971-72; Scientific Consultant, Beverly Hills Oil Co, Los Angeles; Chair, Starcraft Enterprises; Fellow, American Institute of Aeronautics and Astronautics; Retired from USAF, 1972; President, Research and Engineering Consultants Inc, 1972-; Consultant, JRW Jet Propulsion Laboratory. Publications: First on the Moon: A Voyage with Neil Armstrong, 1970; Return to Earth, 1973; Men from Earth, 1989; Encounter with the Tiber, 1996; Encounter with the Tiber – the Return, 2000. Honours: Honorary Member, Royal Astronautical Society; Several Honorary Degrees; Numerous Decorations and Awards. Address: 233 Emerald Bay, Laguna Beach, CA 92651, USA.

**ALEKSANDROV Aleksandr Pavlovich,** b. 20 February 1943, Moscow, Russia. Cosmonaut; Pilot. m. Natalia Valentinovna Aleksandrova, 1 son, 1 daughter. Education: Baumann Technical Institute, Moscow; PhD. Appointments: Served in Soviet Army; Space Programme, 1964-; Participant, elaboration of control system of spacecraft, Cosmonaut, from 1978; Participant, Soyuz-T and Salyut programmes; Successful completion of 149-day flight to Salyut-T orbital station, 1983; Spacewalk, July 1987; Return to Earth, 1987; Completed 160-day flight on Mir Space Station; Chief, Department of Crew Training and Extra Vehicular Activity, Energya design and production firm; Member, Extra Vehicular Activity Committee, IAF, 1994-. Honours: Hero of Soviet Union, 1983, 1987; Hero of Syria. Memberships: Academician, International Informatization Academy, 1997. Address: Khovanskaya Str 3-27, 129515 Moscow, Russia.

**ALEKSIN Anatoliy,** b. 3 August 1924, Moscow, Russia. Writer. m. Tatyana Alexina, 1 son, 1 daughter. Education: Moscow Institute of Oriental Studies, 1950. Career: Writer, 1951-; Playwright; Scriptwriter; Member, Russian Academy of Education, 1982-; Secretary, Union of the Writers of Russia, 1970-89; President of the Association, Peace to the Children of the World, 1986-90; Chairman, Council of Children's and Youth Literature of Russia, 1970-90; Host of monthly TV show, Friend's Faces, 1971-86; Writer of film, television scripts and numerous plays, staged in Russia and abroad. Publications: More than 200 books translated into 48 languages (over 100 million printed copies); Collected works published in 3 volumes, 1979-81, 5 volumes, 1998-99, 9 volumes, 2000-2001; More than 800 magazine articles; Editorial Board, Yunost Magazine, 1973-93. Honours: Mildred Batchelder Award Nomination for A Late Born Child, Association of American Libraries, USA, 1973; Russian Government Award, 1974; USSR Government Award, 1978; Two Orders of the Labour Banner; Included in Hans Christian Andersen Awards; IBBY Honour List; The International Board on Books for Young People; Chosen as an Outstanding Example of Literature with International Importance, 1976; International European Maxim Gorky Award, 1980; Award of Federations of Unions of Writers of Israel, 1999; Jubilee Medal, 200th Anniversary of A S Pushkin, 1999; Compassion Award for Assistance to People Suffering from Cancer, 1998, 2000; Title: Man of Legend, 2004. Memberships: Writers Union of Moscow; International PEN Club; Russian Writers Union of Israel; Russian Academy of Education. Address: Rubinstein Street 39/17, Tel-Aviv, Jaffo-Dalet 68212, Tel Aviv, Israel.

**ALEKSOVSKI Dusko,** b. 10 January 1948, Topolovik, Macedonia. Rock Art Researcher. m. Bogorotka Ampova, 1 son, 2 daughters. Education: Faculty of Filology, 1970; Doctorate, 1981; Appointments: Redactor in Chief to the Review, Voice of Osogovo; President, Macedonian Rock Art Research Centre; President, Organising Committee of the World Rock Art Congress, Macedonia, 2002; President, Enterprising Committee for establishment of World Rock Art Academy; President, World Academy of Rock Art. Publications: 8 books. Honours: Honorary Diploma; Special Diploma; 4 Gold Medals. Memberships: Macedonian Rock Art Research Centre; Centro Studi e Museo d'Arte Preistorica, Pinerolo, Italy; One of seven members of the World Consortium for Studying World Prehistoric Writing, Rome, Italy. E-mail: karpumet@mt.net.mk Website: www.unet.com.mk/rockart/

**ALEMÁN LACAYO Arnoldo,** b. 23 January 1946, Managua, Nicaragua. Politician. Education: National Autonomous University. Appointments: Former Leader, Pro-Somoza Liberal Student Youth Organization, 1960s; Imprisoned for alleged counter-revolutionary activity, 1980; Placed under house arrest, 1989; Mayor of Managua, 1990; President, Federation of Central American Municipalities, 1993-95; Leader, Liberal Party Alliance, 1996; President of Nicaragua, 1997-2001. Address: Oficina del Presidente, Managua, Nicaragua.

**ALESSENDRE Angelina,** b. 3 November 1946, Beaconsfield, Buckinghamshire, England. Ballet Dancer; Dance Teacher. 1 son, 1 daughter. Education: French Institute, Budapest, 1959; Trained as a dancer under Miss Ballantyne, Betty Haines, Dr Ronald Heavey MBE. Career: Professional Ballet Dancer; Performances in England and Italy including The Scala and the Cambridge Theatres, London; Became interested in teaching dance to children with learning difficulties in 1990; Founded the Alessendre Special Needs Dance School, 1992; Won international recognition for uncovering latent talents in people with special needs and helping them to develop into well adjusted and confident individuals more able to lead active, happy and fulfilled lives; Developed an innovative curriculum able to suit all sorts of learning difficulties including children with Down's Syndrome; The Larondina Dance Company (established in 1992) acts as a showcase for the School's work; Pupils have performed with great success in London's West End and in Moscow; Performances in France, Ecuador and Nigeria are planned. Publications: Articles in Moscow Times, local papers and educational magazines. Membership: British Theatre Dance Association. Address: 17 Whistlers Avenue, Battersea, London SW11 3TS, England. E-mail: info@asneeds.org.uk Website: www.asneeds.org.uk

**ALESSI Dario Renato,** b. 23 December 1967, Strasbourg, France (British and Italian citizen). Education: BSc in Biochemistry, 1988, PhD in Biochemistry, 1991, University of Birmingham, School of Biochemistry; Postdoctoral research, MRC Protein Phosphorylation Unit, University of Dundee, 1996. Appointments: Principal Investigator, MRC Protein Phosphorylation Unit, 1997-, Honorary Reader, 2001, Honorary Professor, 2003, University of Dundee. Publications: Over 100 articles in professional scientific journals. Honours: Colworth Medal, Biochemical Society, 1999; Eppendorf Young European Investigator Award, 2000; Fellow, Royal Society of Edinburgh, 2002; Morgagni Young Investigator Prize, Italy, 2002; Pfizer Academic Award for Europe, 2002; Royal Society of Edinburgh Makdougall Brisbane Prize, 2002; Philip Leverhulme Prize, 2002; FEBS Anniversary Prize, Gesellschaft für Biochemie un Molekularbiologie, 2003; T D Lawrence Lecture of Diabetes, UK, 2004. Address: University of Dundee, MRC Protein Phosphorylation Unit, School of Life Sciences, MSI/WTB Complex, Dow Street, Dundee DD1 5EH, Scotland. E-mail: c.chapman@dundee.ac.uk

**ALEXANDER (Robert) McNeill,** b. 7 July 1934, Lisburn, Northern Ireland. Emeritus Professor of Zoology. m. Ann Elizabeth Coulton, 1 son, 1 daughter. Education: BA, 1955, PhD, 1958, MA, 1959, Cambridge University; DSc, University of Wales, 1969. Appointments: Assistant Lecturer, 1958-61, Lecturer, 1961-68, Senior Lecturer, 1968-69, University College of North Wales; Professor of Zoology, 1969-99, Emeritus Professor and Research Professor, 1999-, University of Leeds; Editor: Proceedings of the Royal Society B, 1998-2004. Publications: Books: Functional Design in Fishes, 1967; Animal Mechanics, 1968, 1983; Size and Shape, 1971; The Chordates, 1975, 1981; Biomechanics, 1975; The Invertebrates, 1979; Locomotion of Animals, 1982; Optima for Animals, 1982, 1996; Elastic Mechanisms for Animal Movement, 1988; Dynamics of Dinosaurs and other Extinct Giants, 1989; Animals, 1990; The Human Machine, 1992; Exploring Biomechanics: Animals in Motion, 1992; Bones, 1994; How Animals Move ( a multimedia

CD-ROM), 1995; Energy for Animal Life, 1999; Principles of Animal Locomotion, 2003; Human Bones, 2004; About 270 scientific papers most of them on human and animal biomechanics. Honours include: Scientific Medal, Zoological Society of London, 1969; Linnean Medal for Zoology, Linnean Society of London, 1979; Fellow of the Royal Society, 1987; Muybridge Medal, International Society for Biomechanics, 1991; Member, Academia Europaea, 1996; CBE, 2000; Honorary DSc, University of Aberdeen, 2002; Honorary Doctor, University of Wageningen, 2003; Honorary Fellow, Zoological Society of London, 2003; Borelli Award, American Society of Biomechanics, 2004; Member, European Academy of Sciences, 2004. Memberships: Royal Society; Zoological Society of London, Secretary, 1992-99; Society for Experimental Biology, President, 1995-97; Honorary Member, Society for Integrative and Comparative Biology; International Society for Vertebrate Morphology, President, 1997-2001; Foreign Honorary Member, American Academy of Arts and Sciences; International Society for Biomechanics. Address: School of Biology, University of Leeds, Leeds LS2 9JT, England. E-mail: r.m.alexander@leeds.ac.uk

**ALEXANDER Bill,** b. 23 February 1948, Hunstanton, Norfolk, England. Theatre Director. m. Juliet Harmer, 1978, 2 daughters. Education: Keele University. Appointments: Directed Shakespeare and classical and contemporary drama, Bristol Old Vic; Joined, 1977, Associate Director, 1984-91, Artistic Director, 1991-, Royal Shakespeare Company, productions including Tartuffe, Richard III, 1984, Volpone, The Accrington Pals, Clay, Captain Swing, School of Night, A Midsummer Night's Dream, The Merry Wives of Windsor; Other theatre work, Nottingham Playhouse, Royal Court Theatre, Victory Theatre, New York and Shakespeare Theatre, Washington DC; Artistic Director, Birmingham Repertory Company, 1993-2000, productions including Othello, The Snowman, Macbeth, Dr Jekyll and Mr Hyde, The Alchemist, Awake and Sing, The Way of the World, Divine Right, The Merchant of Venice, Old Times, Frozen, Hamlet, The Tempest, The Four Alice Bakers, Jumpers, Nativity, 1999; Quarantine, 2000; Twelfth Night, 2000; An Enemy of the People, 2002; Frozen, 2002; Mappa Mundi, 2002; The Importance of Being Ernest, 2002. Publications: Film, The Snowman, 1998. Honours: Olivier Award for Director of the Year, 1986. Address: Rose Cottage, Tunley, Gloucestershire GL7 6LP, England.

**ALEXIOU Georgia (Gorgo),** b. 25 November 1951, Mercada, Ftiotida, Greece. Professor of Gymnastics. Education: Diploma (University Grade), National Gymnastic Academy, Thessaloniki, Greece. Appointments: Secondary School Gymnastics Professor, Thessaloniki area, 1973-; Assistant Headmistress, 2nd Gymnasium Malakopis, 2 years; Environmental Professor, teaching programmes prepared in collaboration with the students; Participant in several educational seminars on gymnastics, athletics and the environment; Organiser of archaeological, ecological and environmental excursions. Publications: The Logic of the Sixth Sense (poetry), 1996, 2nd and 3rd editions, 1997, bilingual edition Greek and Albanian, 2004; Drosostalides (Cool Drops) (poetry), 1996, 2nd edition 1997; The Last Smile (poetry), 1997; Heliotropes (Sunflowers) (poetry), Greek edition 1997, Greek-English Edition, 2000; Megalinaria (Exalting Hymns) (poetry), 1998; Matomenos Dromos (Bleeding Road) (poetry), 1998; Autumn Leaves (poetry), 1999; Dancing with the Flames (poetry), 1999; The Pale Queen, parallel title, Chlorida's Mourning (historical novel), 2004; Poems, narratives and essays included in several newspapers, magazines and anthologies. Honours include: Silver Medal, the White Dove of Peace, Poetical Society, Melbourne Australia; Sappho's Prize, Speech Art and Greek Culture Association, Bavaria, Germany;

Honour Certificate, Academy of Greek Language and Culture, Voopertal, Germany. Memberships include: Makednos Pan-Hellenic Society; Board Member, Hellenic Amphictionism Association; Defkalion Society; Panhellenic Association for Environmental Education; Panhellenic Association of Greek Writers; Literature Association of North Greece; Organisation for the Internationalisation of the Greek Language; Musical Association of North Greece; Home of Europe Society; Global Academy of Arts and Education, USA. Address: K Varnali 4 (Constantinupoliton), 54352 Thessaloniki, Greece.

**ALI Abid,** b. 25 April 1965, Lahore, Pakistan. Business Manager. m. Saima Abid, 1 son, 2 daughters. Education: Associate Cost and Management Accountant. MBA; PhD; Certified Business Manager; Chartered Business Administrator. Appointments: Costing Manager, Service Industries Limited; Site Finance Manager, Site Knowledge Manager, Site Operational Excellence Champion, Glaxo SmithKline, Ltd. Publications: Completed research on implementation of Lean Sign in Pharmaceutical Industry. Honours: Listed in Who's Who publications and biographical dictionaries. Memberships: Institute of Management Accountants, USA; Institute of Cost and Management Accountants of Pakistan. Address: 347 A/3 Gulberg III, Lahore, Pakistan. E-mail: abid.ali@gsk.com

**ALI Muhammad,** b. 17 January 1942, Louisville, Kentucky. American Boxer. m. (1) Sonji Roi, divorced, (2) Belinda Boyd, divorced, (3) Veronica Porche, 1977, divorced, (4) Yolanda Williams, 2 sons, 7 daughters. Education: Louisville. Appointments: Amateur Boxer, 1954-60; Olympic Games Light-Heavyweight Champion, 1960; Professional Boxer, 1960-; Won World heavyweight title, 1964; Stripped of title after refusing to be drafted into US Army, 1967; Returned to Professional Boxing, 1970; Regained World Heavyweight, 1974; Lost Title to Leon Spinks, 1978; Regained Title, Spinks, 1978; 56 victories in 61 fights, 1981; Lost to Larry Holmes, 1980; Acted in films, The Greatest; Freedom Road. Publications: The Greatest: My Own Story, 1975; Healing, 1996; More Than a Hero (with Hana Ali), 2000. Honours: Names Messenger of Peace, UN; Athlete of the Century, GQ Magazine; Lifetime Achievement Award, Amnesty International; Hon Consu General for Bangladesh in Chicago; named Messenger of Peace, UN, 1999. Memberships: Black Muslim Movement; Peace Corps Advisory Council. Address: P O Box 160, Berrien Springs, MI 49103, USA.

**ALLADIN Saleh Mohammed,** b. 3 March 1931, Secunderabad, India. Retired Professor of Astronomy. m. Farhat Akhtar, 2 sons, 3 daughters. Education: St Patrick's High School Senior, Cambridge, 1948; BSc, Nizam College, 1953; MSc, Physics, Osmania University, 1955; PhD, Astronomy and Astrophysics, University of Chicago, 1963. Appointments: Research Scholar, Osmania University, 1955-59; Research Assistant, Yerkes Observatory, USA, 1960-63; Lecturer, 1964-65; Senior Research Fellow, 1965-68, Reader, 1968-78, Professor, 1978-91, Osmania University; Senior Associate Inter University Centre for Astronomy and Astrophysics, Pune, 1990-96. Publications: Articles on: The Dynamics of Colliding Galaxies, 1965; Gravitational Interactions between Galaxies, with Narasimhan, 1982; Views of Scientists on the Existence of God, 1991. Honours: Senior Visiting Fellow at the Universities of Oxford and Cambridge, 1980; Meghnad Saha Award for the Year 1981; University Grants Commission, India; Man of the Year, 2000; Listed in several biographical publications. Memberships: International Astronomical Union; Astronomical Society of India. Address: Alladin Building, 72 Sarojini Devi Road, Secunderabad 500 003, A P India.

**ALLAIN Hervé,** b. 11 February 1950, St Brieuc, France. Professor of Medicine. m. Nicole Döé de Maindreville, 3 sons, 1 daughter. Education: Master in Biology, 1975; Doctor in Medicine, 1977; Degree in Neurology, 1977; Degree in Pharmacology, 1979. Appointments: Professor of Medicine, University of Rennes I, France, 1982; Head, Department of Experimental and Clinical Pharmacology, Rennes University and Medical School, 1992-2005. Publications: 500 papers and book chapters; 190 citations in Medline. Memberships: Societé Francaise de Neurologie; Societé Francaise de Pharmacologie. Address: Laboratoire de Pharmacologie, University of Rennes I, 2 Av-Pr Léon Bernard, 35043 Rennes, France. E-mail: herve.allain@univ-rennes1.fr

**ALLAN Andrew Norman,** b. 26 September 1943, Newcastle upon Tyne, England. Television Executive. m. (1) 2 daughters, (2) Joanna Forrest, 1978, 2 sons, 1 daughter. Education: BA, Birmingham University. Appointments: Presenter, ABC Television, 1965-66; Producer, Thames TV, 1966-69, 1971-75; Head of News, 1976-78; Producer, ITN, 1970; Director of Programmes, 1978-83, Deputy Managing Director, 1982-83, Managing Director, 1983-84, Tyne Tees TV; Director of Programmes, 1984-90, Managing Director, 1993-94, Central Independent TV; Managing Director, Central Broadcasting, 1990-93; Chief Executive, 1994-95, Director of Programmes, 1996-98, Carlton TV; Director, TV12, 1999-; Media Consultant, 1998-; Chair, Birmingham Repertory, 2000-; Chair, Route 4 PLC, 2001. Memberships: Fellow, Royal Television Society. Address: Wardington Lodge, Wardington, Banbury, Oxon OX17 1SE, England.

**ALLASON Rupert William Simon,** b. 8 November 1951, London, England. Author. m. Nicole Van Moppes, 15 June 1979, dissolved 1996, 1 son, 1 daughter. Education: Downside School, Bath, England; University of Grenoble, France; University of London, England. Appointments: Member of Parliament (Conservative) for Torbay, 1987-97; Editor, World Intelligence Review, 1985-. Publications: SPY! (with Richard Deacon), 1980; British Security Service Operations 1909-45, 1981; A Matter of Trust: MI5 1945-72, 1982; MI6: British Secret Intelligence Service Operations 1909-45, 1983; The Branch: A History of the Metropolitan Police Special Branch, 1983; Unreliable Witness: Espionage Myths of the Second World War, 1984; GARBO (co-authored with Juan Pjujol), 1985; GCHQ: The Secret Wireless War, 1986; Molehunt, 1987; The Friends: Britain's Postwar Secret Intelligence Operations, 1988; Games of Intelligence, 1989; Seven Spies Who Changed the World, 1991; Secret War: The Story of SOE, 1992; The Faber Book of Espionage, 1993; The Illegals, 1993; The Faber Book of Treachery, 1995; The Secret War for the Falklands, 1997; Counterfeit Spies, 1998; Crown Jewels, 1998; Venona, 1999; The Third Secret, 2000; Mortal Crimes, 2004; The Guy Liddell Diaries (editor), 2005; The Historical Dictionary of British Intelligence. Address: PO Box 2, Goring on Thames, RG8 9SB, England.

**ALLEN Blair H,** b. 2 July 1933, Los Angeles, California, USA. Writer; Poet; Editor; Artist. m. Juanita Aguilar Raya, 27 January 1968, 1 son, 1 daughter. Education: AA, San Diego City College, 1964; University of Washington, 1965-66; BA, San Diego State University, 1970. Appointments: Book Reviewer, Los Angeles Times, 1977-78; Special Feature Editor, Cerulean Press and Kent Publications, 1982-. Publications: Televisual Poems for Bloodshot Eyeballs, 1973; Malice in Blunderland, 1974; N/Z, 1979; The Atlantis Trilogy, 1982; Dreamwish of the Magician, 1983; Right Through the Silver Lined 1984 Looking Glass, 1984; The Magical World of David Cole (editor), 1984; Snow Summits in the Sun (anthology, editor), 1988; Trapped in a Cold War Travelogue, 1991; May Burning into August, 1992; The Subway Poems, 1993; Bonfire on the Beach, by John Brander (editor), 1993; The Cerulean Anthology of Sci-Fi/Outer Space/Fantasy/Poetry and Prose Poems (anthology, editor), 1995; When the Ghost of Cassandra Whispers in My Ears, 1996; Ashes Ashes All Fall Down, 1997; Around the World in 56 Days, 1998; Thunderclouds from the Door, 1999; Jabberbunglemerkeltoy, 1999; The Athens Café, 2000; The Day of the Jamberee Call, 2001; Assembled I Stand, 2002; Wine of Starlight, 2002; Snow Birds in Cloud Hands (anthology, editor), 2003; Trek into Yellowstone's Cascade Corner Wilderness, 2003; Hour of Iced Wheels, 2003; Light in the Crossroads, 2004. Contributions to: Numerous periodicals and 14 anthologies. Honours: Nominated for "Pushcart Prize", for Poetry, 1982; 1st Prize for Poetry, Pacificus Foundation Competition, 1992; Pacificus Foundation Literary Prize for Lifetime Achievement in Poetry, 2003; Various other honours and awards. Memberships: The Academy of American Poets; Association for Applied Poetry; Beyond Baroque Foundation; California State Poetry Society; Medina Foundation. Address: PO Box 162, 264 W. E. Street, Colton, CA 92324, USA.

**ALLEN Geoffrey (Sir),** b. 29 October 1928, Clay Cross, Derbyshire, England. Polymer Scientist; Administrator. m. Valerie Frances Duckworth, 1972, 1 daughter. Education: PhD, University of Leeds. Appointments: Postdoctoral Fellow, National Research Council, Canada, 1952-54; Lecturer, 1955-65, Professor of Chemical Physics, 1965-75, University of Manchester Institute of Science and Technology; Professor of Polymer Science, 1975-76, Professor of Chemical Technology, 1976-81, Imperial College of Science and Technology, University of London; Chair, Science Research Council, 1977-81; Visiting Fellow, Robinson College, Cambridge, 1980-; Head of Research, 1981-90, Director for Research and Engineering, 1982-90; Unilever PLC, 1981-90; Non-Executive Director, Courtaulds, 1987-93; President, Plastics and Rubber Institute, 1990-92; Executive Adviser, Kobe Steel Ltd, 1990-2000; Member, National Consumer Council, 1993-; Chancellor, University of East Anglia, 1994-. Honours: Honorary MSc, Manchester; Dr hc, Open University; Honorary DSc, Durham, East Anglia, 1984, Bath, Bradford, Keele, Loughborough, 1985, Essex, Leeds, 1986, Cranfield, 1988, Surrey, 1989, North London, 1999. Memberships: Fellow, Royal Society, Vice-President, 1991-93; Fellow, Institute of Physics; Fellow, Plastics and Rubber Institute. Address: 18 Oxford House, 52 Parkside, London SW19 5NE, England.

**ALLEN Keith William,** b. 9 April 1926, Reading, England. Retired University Don. m. Marguerite Florence Woods, 1 son, 4 daughters. Education: BSc, University of Reading, 1949; MSc, University of London, 1958; DSc, City University, 1994; Chartered Scientist, Chemist and Physicist. Appointments: Lecturer in Chemistry, 1949-83, Director of Adhesion Studies, 1982-92, City University; Visiting Professor, Oxford Brookes University, England, 1998-. Publications: Editor, Adhesion 1 – Adhesion 15 book series; Approximately 80 papers in refereed journals. Honours: Fulbright Scholar, 1961-62; Ellinger-Gardonyl and Wake Medals, 1999; Honorary Fellowship of the University, Oxford Brookes University, 2002. Memberships: Fellow, Royal Society of Chemistry; Fellow, Institute of Materials. Address: Ranworth, Tydehams, Newbury, RG14 6JT, England.

**ALLEN Thomas (Sir),** b. 10 September 1944, Seaham, County Durham, England. m. (1) Margaret Holley, 1968, divorced 1986, 1 son, (2) Jeannie Gordon Lascelles, 1988, 1 stepson, 1 stepdaughter. Education: Royal College of Music. Appointments: Principal Baritone: Welsh National Opera, 1968-

72; Royal Opera House, Covent Garden, 1972-78; Glyndebourne Opera, 1973; Performances include: Die Zauberflote, 1973; Le Nozze di Figaro, 1974; Cosi fan Tutte, 1975; Don Giovanni, 1977; The Cunning Little Vixen, 1977; Simon Boccanegra, Billy Budd, La Boheme, L'Elisir d'Amore, Faust, Albert Herring, Die Fledermause, La Traviata, A Midsummer Night's Dream, Beckmesser, etc. Publications: Foreign Parts: A Singer's Journal, 1993; Art Exhibitions: Chelsea Festival, 2001; Salisbury Playhouse, 2001. Honours: Honorary Fellow, University of Sunderland; Queen's Prize, 1967; Gulbenkian Fellow, 1968; MA Hon, Newcastle, 1984; RAM Hon, 1988; DMus Hon, Durham, 1988. Address: c/o Askonas Holt Ltd, Lonsdale Chambers, 27 Chancery Lane, London WC2A 1PF, England.

**ALLEN Tim,** b. 13 June 1953, Denver, USA. Education: West Michigan University; University of Detroit. Career: Creative Director, advertising agency; Comedian, Showtime Comedy Club All Stars, 1988; TV series include: Tim Allen: Men are Pigs, 1990; Home Improvement, 1991-; Tim Allen Rewrites America; Films include: Comedy's Dirtiest Dozen; The Santa Clause, 1994; Toy Story, 1995; Meet Wally Sparks, 1997; Jungle 2 Jungle, 1997; For Richer for Poorer, 1997; Galaxy Quest, 1999; Toy Story 2, 2000; Buzz Lightyear of Star Command: the Adventure Begins, 2000; Who is Cletis Tout?, 2001; Joe Somebody, 2001; Big Trouble, 2002; The Santa Clause 2, 2002. Publications: Don't Stand Too Close to a Naked Man, 1994; I'm Not Really Here, 1996. Honours: Favourite Comedy Actor, People's Choice Award, 1995, 1997-99. Address: c/o Commercial Unlimited, 8883 Wilshire Boulevard, Suite 850, Beverly Hills, CA 90211, USA.

**ALLEN William Anthony,** b. 13 May 1949, Croydon, Surrey, England. Economist. m. Rosemary Margaret, 1 son, 2 daughters. Education: BA, 1st Class Honours, Mathematics, Balliol College, Oxford, 1967-70; MSc, with distinction, Economics, London School of Economics, 1970-72. Appointments: Bank of England, 1972-2004: Head of Money Market Operations Division, 1986-90; Head of Foreign Exchange Division, 1990-94; Deputy Director for Monetary Analysis, 1994-98; Deputy Director for Market Operations, 1999-2002; Director for Europe, 2002-2004; Economic Adviser, Brevan Howard Asset Management LLP, 2004-. Publications: Numerous articles in economics journals and Central Bank bulletins. Membership: Guild of International Bankers. Address: Brevan Howard Asset Management LLP, Almack House, 28 King Street, London SW1Y 6XA, England. E-mail: bill.allen@brevanhoward.com

**ALLEN William Richard (Twink),** b. 29 August 1940, Auckland, New Zealand. Veterinary Scientist. m. Diana Margaret, 1 son, 2 daughters. Education: Medical Intermediate, Auckland University, 1960; BVSc, Sydney University, 1965; PhD, Cambridge University, 1970; MRCVS, 1966; DESM, 1986; DSc hc, Krakow, 1986; ScD, 1995; CBiol, FIBiol, 1996; DipECAR, 2003. Appointments: Veterinary Practice, Kaitaia, New Zealand, 1965-66; Graduate Student, Cambridge Veterinary School, 1966-70; Post Doctoral Researcher, AFRC Animal Research Station, Cambridge, 1970-72; Scientific Officer, Director, Thoroughbred Breeders' Association Equine Fertility Unit, 1972-; Jim Joel Professor of Equine Reproduction, Cambridge, 1995-.Publications: 250 scientific refereed papers and book chapters on various aspects of Equine, Camelid and Elephant Reproductive Physiology. Honours: CBE, 2001. Memberships: Professorial Fellow, Robinson College, Cambridge; Society for Study of Fertility; Endocrine Society; British Equine Veterinary Association; European Society for Domestic Animal Reproduction. Address: University of Cambridge Equine Fertility Unit, Mertoun Paddocks, Woodditton Road, Newmarket, Suffolk, CB8 9BH, England.

**ALLEN Woody (Allen Stewart Konigsberg),** b. 1 December 1935, Brooklyn, New York. American Actor; Writer. m. (1) Harlene Rosen, divorced, (2) Louise Lasser, divorced, 1 son with Mia Farrow, (3) Soon-Yi Previn, 2 adopted daughters. Education: City College, New York; New York University. Career: Wrote for TV Performers: Herb Shriner, 1953; Sid Caesar, 1957; Art Carney, 1958-59; Jack Parr and Carol Channing; Also wrote for Tonight Show and the Gary Moore Show; Debut performance, Duplex, Greenwich Village, 1961; Performed in a variety of nightclubs across the US; Plays: Play It Again Sam; Don't Drink the Water, 1966; The Floating Light Bulb, 1981; Death Defying Acts, 1995; Films Include: What's New Pussycat?, 1965; Casino Royale, 1967; What's Up, Tiger Lily?, 1967; Take the Money and Run, 1969; Bananas, 1971; Everything You Always Wanted to Know About Sex, 1972; Play it Again Sam, 1972; Sleeper, 1973; Love and Death, 1976; The Front, 1976; Annie Hall, 1977; Interiors, 1978; Manhattan, 1979; Stardust Memories, 1980; A Midsummer Night's Sex Comedy, 1982; Zelig, 1983; Broadway Danny Rose, 1984; The Purple Rose of Cairo, 1985; Hannah and her Sister, 1985; Radio Days, 1987; September, 1987; Another Woman, 1988; Oedipus Wrecks, 1989; Crimes and Misdemeanors, 1989; Alice, 1990; Scenes from a Mall, Shadows and Fog, 1991; Husbands and Wives, 1992; Manhattan Murder Mystery, 1993; Bullets Over Broadway, 1995; Mighty Aphrodite, 1995; Everybody Says I Love You, 1997; Deconstructing Harry, 1997; Celebrity, 1998; Wild Man Blues, 1998; Stuck on You, 1998; Company Men, 1999; Sweet and Lowdown, 1999; Small Town Crooks, 2000; The Curse of the Jade Scorpion, 2001; Hail Sid Caesar! 2001; Hollywood Ending, 2002. Publications: Getting Even, 1971; Without Feathers, 1975; Side Effects, 1980; The Complete Prose, 1994; Contributions to Playboy and New Yorker. Honours: Academy Award for Best Director; Best Writer; D W Griffith Award, 1996. Address: 930 Fifth Avenue, New York, NY 10021, USA.

**ALLENDE Isabel,** b. 2 August 1942, Lima, Peru. Writer. m. (1) Miguel Frias, 1962, 1 son, 1 daughter, (2) William C Gordon, 17 July 1988. Appointments: Journalist, Paula Magazine, 1967-74, Mampato Magazine, 1969-74; Channel 13 World Hunger Campaign, 1964; Channel 7, various humourous programmes, 1970-74; Maga-Cine-Ellas, 1973; Administrator, Marroco School, Caracas, 1978-82; Freelance journalist, El Nacional newspaper, Caracas, 1976-83; Visiting teacher, Montclair State College, New Jersey, 1985, University of Virginia, Charlottesville, 1988, University of California, Berkeley, 1989; Writer, 1981-. Publications: The House of the Spirits, 1982; Of Love and Shadows, 1984; La Gorda de Porcelana, 1984; Eva Luna, 1989; Tales of Eva Luna, 1990; The Infinite Plan, 1992; Paula, 1995; Aphrodite, a memoir of the senses, 1998; Daughter of Fortune, 1999; Portrait in Sepia, 2000. Honours: Novel of the Year, Panorama Literario, Chile, 1983; Point de Mire, Belgium, 1985; Author of the Year and Book of the Year, Germany, 1984; Grand Prix d'Evasion, France, 1984; Colima for Best Novel, Mexico, 1985; Author of the Year, Germany, 1986; Mulheres Best Novel, Portugal, 1987; Dorothy and Jillian Gish Prize, 1998; Sara Lee Frontrunner Award, 1998; GEMS Women of the Year Award, 1999; Donna Dell'Anno Award, Italy, 1999; Plays: Paula; Stories of Eva Luna; The House of the Spirits; Eva Luna. Address: 116 Caledonia Street, Sausalito, CA 94965, USA.

**ALLEY Kirstie,** b. Wichita, Kansas, USA. Actress. m. Parker Stevenson, 1 son, 1 daughter. Education: University of Kansas. Appointments: Stage appearances include: Cat on a Hot Tin Roof; Answers; Regular TV Show Cheers, 1987-93; Other appearances in TV films and series: Star Trek II, The Wrath of Khan, 1982; One More Chance, Blind Date, Champions, 1983; Runaway, 1984; Summer School, 1987; Look Who's Talking Too, 1990; Madhouse, 1990; Look Who's Talking Now, 1993; David's Mother (TV Film), 1994; Village of the Damned, 1995; It Takes Two, 1995; Sticks and Stones, 1996; Nevada, 1996; For Richer or Poorer, 1997; Victoria's Closet, 1997; Deconstructing Harry, 1997; Toothless, 1997; Drop Dead Gorgeous, 1999; The Mao Game, 1999; Blonde, 2001; Salem Witch Trials, 2002; Back By Midnight, 2002. Address: Jason Weinberg and Associates, 122 East 25th Street, 2nd Floor, New York, NY 10010, USA.

**ALLEYNE George (Sir),** b. 7 October 1932, Barbados. Physician. m. Sylvan I Chen, 1958, 2 sons, 1 daughter. Education: MD, University of West Indies; Senior Resident, University Hospital of West Indies, 1963; FRCP. Appointments: Tropical Metabolism Research Unit, Jamaica, 1964-72; Professor of Medicine, 1972-81, Chair, Department of Medicine, 1976-81, University of West Indies; Head of Research Unit, 1981-83, Director of Health Programmes, 1982-90, Assistant Director, 1990-95, Director, 1995-, Pan American Health Organization, Washington DC, USA. Publications include: The Importance of Health: A Caribbean Perspective, 1989; Public Health for All, 1991; Health and Tourism, 1992; Over 100 articles in major scientific research journals. Honours: Honorary DSc, West Indies University, 1988; Order of the Caribbean Community, 2001. Address: Pan American Health Organization, 525 23rd Street NW, Washington, DC 20037, USA.

**ALLI Waheed (Baron of Norbury in the London Borough of Croydon),** b. 16 November 1964. Business Executive. Appointments: Co-Founder, Joint Managing Director, Planet 24 Productions Ltd, formerly 24 Hour Productions, 1992-99; Managing Director, Production, Carlton Productions, 1988-2000; Director, Carlton TV, 1998-2000; Director, Chorion, 2002-. Memberships: Member, Teacher Training Agency, 1997-98; Panel 2000, Creative Industry Taskforce; Board member, English National Ballet, 2001-; Director, Shine Entertainment Ltd; Shine M; Castaway TV; Digital Radio Group Ltd. Address: House of Lords, London SW1A 0PW, England.

**ALLIANCE David (Sir),** b. June 1932. Business Executive. Appointments: 1st acquisition, Thomas Hoghton, Oswaldtwistle, 1956; Chair, N Brown Group, 1968-; Acquired Spirella, 1968, Vantona Ltd to form Vantona Group, 1975; Group Chief Executive, 1975-90, Chair, 1989-99, Coats Viyella; Acquired Carrington Viyella to form Vantona Viyella, 1983, Carrington Viyella to form Vantona Viyella, 1983, Nottingham Manufacturing, 1985, Coats Patons to form Coats Viyella, 1986; Chair, Tootal Group PLC, 1991-99. Honours: Commander, Order of the British Empire; Honorary Fellow, University of Manchester Institute of Science and Technology; Honorary LLD, Manchester, 1989; Honorary FCGI, 1991; Honorary DSc, Heriot-Watt, 1991; Honorary LLD, Liverpool, 1996. Memberships: Fellow, Royal Society of Arts; Companion, British Institute of Management. Address: N Brown Group, 53 Dale Street, Manchester M60 6ES, England.

**ALLISON John William Francis,** b. 31 March 1962, Durban, South Africa. Lecturer in Law. Education: BA, 1982, LLB, 1984, University of Stellenbosch; LLM, 1986, M Phil, 1987, PhD, 1992, Cambridge University. Appointments: Junior Lecturer, University of Stellenbosch, 1985; Bigelow Fellow and Lecturer in Law, University of Chicago Law School, USA, 1987-88; Lecturer, Queen Mary College, University of London, 1989-91; Research Fellow, Queens' College, University of Cambridge, 1991-94; Senior Lecturer, Department of Roman

and Comparative Law, University of Cape Town, South Africa, 1994-95; University Lecturer, 1995-2001, University Senior Lecturer, 2001-, University of Cambridge. Publications include: The Procedural Reason for Judicial Restraint (journal article), 1994; A Continental Distinction in the Common Law: A Historical and Comparative Perspective on English Public Law (book), 1996; Parliamentary Sovereignty, Europe and the Economy of Common Law in M Andenas (editor), Liber Amicorum in Honour of Lord Slynn of Hadley: Judicial Review in International perspective, 2000; The Historical English Constitution in Europe (book), in progress. Honours: Jubilee Scholarship, Rondebosch Boys' High School, 1985-87; Elsie Ballot Scholarship, 1985-87; W M Tapp Studentship, Gonville and Caius College, Cambridge, 1988-89, 1990-91; Yorke Prize, Cambridge Law Faculty, 1993. Memberships: Fellow of Queens' College; European Group of Public Law. Address: Queens' College, Cambridge CB3 9ET, England.

**ALLISON Roderick Stuart,** b. 28 November 1936, Norwich, Norfolk, England. Civil Servant. m. Anne, 1 son, 1 daughter. Education: Manchester Grammar School, 1948-49, 1951-55; Dumfries Academy, 1949-51; Balliol College, Oxford, 1955-59. Appointments: Director of Personnel, Department of Employment, 1980-85; Head of Industrial Relations Policy, Department of Employment, 1985-89; Director of Safety Policy, 1989-94; Chief Executive Offshore Safety, 1994-96; Member, Health & Safety Executive, 1995-96; UK Chairman, Channel Tunnel Safety Authority, 1997-2003. Honours: CB, 1994. Address: Channel Tunnel Safety Authority, c/o Health & Safety Executive, 2 Southwark Bridge, London SE1 9HS, England.

**ALMODÓVAR Pedro,** b. 25 September 1951, La Mancha, Spain. Film Director. Career: Fronted a rock band; Worked at Telefónica, 10 years; Started film career with full-length super-8 films; Made 16mm short films, 1978-83, including Salome; Other films including Pepe, Luci, Bom y otras montón, Laberinto de pasiones, 1980, Dark Habits, 1983, What Have I Done to Deserve This?, 1985, Matador, 1986, Law of Desire, 1987, Women on the Verge of a Nervous Breakdown, 1988, Tie Me Up, Tie Me Down, 1990, Tacones Lejanos, 1991, Kika, 1993, The Flower of My Secret, 1996, Live Flesh, 1997, All About My Mother, 1991; Talk to Her, 2002. Publications: Fuego en las entrañas, 1982; The Patty Diphusa Stories and Other Writings, 1992. Honours: Felix Award, 1988; Academy Award for Best Foreign Language Film, 1999; BAFTA Award for Best Film not in the English Language, 2003; Academy Award for Best Original Screenplay, 2003. Address: c/o El Deseo SA, Ruiz Perelló 15, Madrid 28028, Spain.

**ALON Azaria,** b. 15 November 1918, Wollodarsk, Ukraine. In Israel since 1925. Biologist. m. Ruth Diamant, 2 sons, 1 daughter. Appointments: Member of Kibbutz Beit-Hashitta, 1938-; Agricultural Worker; Youth Movement Leader; Educator; Teacher of Biology; One of Founders of Society for the Protection of Nature in Israel, 1951, General Secretary, 1969-77, Publication Editor; Played major part in campaign to save the wild flowers of Israel, 1964-; Created Governmental Nature Reserves Authority, Board Member, 1964-76; Mapping nature reserves and national parks of Israel, 1951-65; Numerous campaigns to save wildlife and environment; Created Field Study Centres; Took part in Stockholm Convention, 1972 and IUCN conferences, 1963-90; Writer, Lecturer, Broadcaster on conservation of nature and the environment, 1951-; Senior Lecturer on Landscape, Technion, Haifa, Israel, 1992-. Publications: Hundreds of articles in daily papers, periodicals on nature, environment and conservation; 33 books: 8 books on flowers and trees; 3 books on Sinai and Israel's deserts; 5 books on landscape and animals; 3 books on environmental education;

7 books on plants and animals for children; 2 guidebooks to nature trails in Israel; Numerous booklets and brochures; Editor, Encyclopaedia of Plant and Animal Life of Israel, 12 volumes; Nature and landscape photographs: More than 1000 published in books and papers; Radio programme, The Landscape of Our Country, over 2,400 programmes broadcast. Honours: Kol Israel (Israel Radio) Prize, 1962; Zimerman Prize for Environmental Activity, 1977; Israel Prize, co-winner, 1980; Knesset (Israel Parliament) Prize for Environmental Activity, 1984; 500 Global Role of Honor, UNEP, 1987; Dr Honoris Causa, Weizman Institute, 1991; Yigal Alon Prize for Life Activity, 1994; Lions Israel Honour Roll for Life Activity, 2004. Memberships: Society for the Protection of Nature in Israel; Life & Environment. Address: Beit Hashitta, Israel 18910. E-mail: azaralon@bethashita.org.il

**ALPERT Herb,** b. 31 March 1935, Los Angeles, California, USA. Musician (trumpet); Songwriter; Arranger; Record Company Executive. m. Lani Hall, 1 son, 2 daughters. Education: University of Southern California. Career: 3 television specials; Leader, own group Tijuana Brass; Multiple world tours; Owner, Dore Records; Manager, Jan And Dean; Co-founder with Jerry Moss, A&M Records (formerly Carnival), 1962-89; Artists have included: The Carpenters; Captain And Tennille; Carole King; Cat Stevens; The Police; Squeeze; Joe Jackson; Bryan Adams. Compositions include: Wonderful World, Sam Cooke (co-writer with Lou Adler). Recordings: The Lonely Bull; A Taste Of Honey; Spanish Flea; Tijuana Taxi; Casino Royale; This Guy's In Love With You (Number 1, UK and US), 1968; Rise (Number 1, US), 1979; Albums include: The Lonely Bull, 1963; Tijuana Brass, 1963; Tijuana Brass Vol 2, 1964; South Of The Border, 1965; Whipped Cream And Other Delights, 1965; Going Places, 1966; SRO, 1967; Sounds Like Us, 1967; Herb Alpert's 9th, 1968; The Best Of The Brass, 1968; Warm, 1969; Rise, 1979; Keep Your Eyes On Me, 1979; Magic Man, 1981; My Abstract Heart, 1989; Midnight Sun, 1992; Second Wind, 1996; Passion Dance, 1997; Colors, 1999. Honours: Numerous Grammy Awards. Address: c/o Kip Cohen, La Brea Tours, Inc., 1414 Sixth Street, Santa Monica, CA 90401, USA.

**ALSOP William Allen,** b. 12 December 1947, Nottingham, England. Architect. m. Sheila Bean, 1972, 2 sons, 1 daughter. Education: Architectural Association. Career: Teacher of Sculpture, St Martin's College; Worked with Cedric Price; In practice with John Lyall; Designed ferry terminal, Hamburg; Design work on Cardiff barrage; Feasibility studies to recycle former De Lorean factory, Belfast; Designed government building, Marseilles; Established own practice, collaborates with Bruce Maclelan in producing architectural drawings; Principal, Alsop and Störmer Architects, 1979-2000; Principal, Director and Chair, Alsop Architects, 2001; Chair, Architecture Foundation, 2001-; Projects include: North Greenwich Station, 2000; Peckham Library and Media Centre, 2000; Commissioned to design Fourth Grace, Liverpool, 2002-. Publications: City of Objects, 1992; William Alsop Buildings and Projects, 1992; William Alsop Architect: Four Projects, 1993; Will Alsop and Jan Störmer, Architects, 1993; Le Grand Bleu-Marseille, 1994; Alsop and Störmer: Selected and Current Works. Honours: Officer, Order of the British Empire; Honorary LLD, Leicester; Stirling Prize, 2000. Memberships: Fellow, Royal Society of Arts. Address: 72 Pembroke Road, London W8 6NX, England. E-mail: walsop@alsopandstormer.co.uk Website: www.alsopandstormer.com

**ALTARAC Silvio,** b. 30 December 1958, Zagreb, Croatia. Urological Surgeon. m. Lidija Lopičić, 1 son, 1 daughter. Education: MD, 1983, PhD, 1989, School of Medicine, Zagreb. Appointments: Teaching Assistant, Department of Physiology and Immunology, Zagreb, 1985-89; Clinical Research Fellow, University Hospital Pittsburgh, 1990, Royal Hallamshire Hospital, Sheffield, 1993-94, University Hospital Innsbruck, 1995, Brigham and Women's Hospital, Harvard University, Boston, 1995-96. Publications: Numerous articles in professional journals; Expert columnist, Salud (i) Ciencia, Buenos Aires, Argentina; Citations, Campbell's Urology, Smith's General Urology; European Association of Urology: Guidelines on Urological Trauma; Reviewer, Croatian Medical Journal. Honours: Academician Drago Perović's Medal; Rector's Award for academic excellence; Listing in numerous biographical publications. Memberships: European Association of Urology; American Urological Association. Address: Bukovačka cesta 229C, 10 000 Zagreb, Croatia.

**ALTHER Lisa,** b. 23 July 1944, Tennessee, USA. Writer; Reviewer; University Professor. m. Richard Alther, 26 August 1966, divorced, 1 daughter. Education: BA, Wellesley College, 1966. Appointments: Staff Member, Atheneum Publishers, New York City, 1967-68; Freelance writer, 1968-; Lecturer, St Michael's College, Winooski, Vermont, 1980-81; Professor and Basler Chair, East Tennessee State University, 1999. Publications: Kinflicks, 1975; Original Sins, 1980; Other Women, 1984; Bedrock, 1990; Birdman and the Dancer, 1993; Five Minutes in Heaven, 1995. Contributions to: New York Times Magazine; New York Times Book Review; Natural History; New Society; Arts and Antiques; Boston Globe; Washington Post; Los Angeles Times; San Francisco Chronicle; Southern Living. Memberships: Authors Guild; National Writers Union; PEN. E-mail: lalther@aol.com

**ALTON Roger Martin,** b. 20 December 1947, Oxford, England. Journalist. Divorced, 1 daughter. Education: Exeter College, Oxford. Appointments: Graduate Trainee, then General Reporter and Deputy Features Editor, Liverpool Post, 1969-73; Sub-Editor, News, 1973-76, Chief Sub-Editor, News, 1976-81, Deputy Sports Editor, 1981-85, Arts Editor, 1985-90, Weekend Magazine Editor, 1990-93, Features Editor, 1993-96, Assistant Editor, 1996-98, The Guardian; Editor, The Observer, 1998-. Honours: Editor of the Year, What the Papers Say Awards, 2000. Address: Office of the Editor, The Observer, 119 Farringdon Road, London EC1R 3ER, England. E-mail: editor@observer.co.uk Website: www.observer.co.uk

**ALWALEED (HRH Prince Alwaleed Bin Talal Bin AbdulAziz Alsaud),** b. March 1955, Riyadh, Saudi Arabia. Private Entrepreneur; International Investor. Education: BSc, Business Administration, magna cum laude, Menlo College, California, 1970; MA, Social Science, with honours, Syracuse University, 1985. Honours: Recent recognitions include: Muhammad Islamic Foundation Trophy, 2004; Entertainment Personality of the Year, 2004; Lifetime Achievement Award, Arabian Hotel Investment Conference, Dubai, 2005; Damascus Award, Tourism Investment Forum in Damascus, 2005; Legend of Economic Achievement, Alasdaf magazine, 2005; Global Achievement Award, American-Arab Anti Discrimination Committee, USA, 2005; Recent honours include: The Insignia of Grand Officer, President of Gambia, 2005; The Commander of the National Order, President of Mali, 2005; The Star of Africa with Grade of Grand Band, President of Liberia, 2005; Grand Officer of the National Order, President of Benin, 2005; The Distinguished Order of the Crested Crane First Class, President of Uganda, 2005; The Order of the Golden Heart of Kenya, President of Kenya, 2005; Honorary degrees: Doctorate of Humane Letters, honoris causa, University of New Haven, 1992; Doctorate in Business Management, Kyungwon University, Korea, 1998; Doctorate in Law, Syracuse University, 1999; Doctorate in Law, Exeter University, 2002; Doctorate in Law,

# DICTIONARY OF INTERNATIONAL BIOGRAPHY

American University in Cairo, 2002; Doctorate in Humanities, AlAqsa University, Gaza, 2004; Doctorate of Letters, honoris causa, University for Developmental Studies, Ghana, 2004; Honorary Doctorate of Letters, The Islamic University, Uganda, 2005. Address: Corporate Communications Department, Kingdom Holding Company, Kingdom Center, Floor 66 PO Box 1, Riyadh 11321, Saudi Arabia.

**AMANPOUR Christiane,** b. 12 January 1958, London, England. Broadcasting Correspondent. m. James Rubin, 1998, 1 son. Education: New Hall, Cambridge; University of Rhode Island, USA. Appointments: Radio Producer and Research Assistant, BBC Radio, London, 1980-82; Radio Reporter, WBRU, Brown University, USA, 1981-83; Electronic Graphics Designer, WJAR, Providence, Rhode Island, 1983; Assistant, CNN International Assignment Desk, Atlanta, Georgia, 1983; News Writer, CNN, Atlanta, 1984-86; Reporter, Producer, CNN, New York, 1987-90; International Correspondent, 1990, Senior International Correspondent, 1994, Chief International Correspondent, 1996, CNN; Assignments include Gulf War coverage, 1990-91, USSR break-up and subsequent war in Tbilisi, 1991, extensive reports on conflict in former Yugoslavia and civil unrest and crises coverage, Haiti, Algeria, Somalia and Rwanda. Honours: Dr hc, Rhode Island; 3 Dupont-Columbia Awards, 1986-96; 2 News and Documentary Emmy Awards, 1999; George Foster Peabody Award, 1999; George Polk Award, 1999; University of Missouri Award for Distinguished Service to Journalism, 1999. Memberships: Fellow, Society of Professional Journalists. Address: c/o CNN International, CNN House, 19-22 Rathbone Place, London W1P 1DF, England.

**AMATO Giuliano,** b. 13 May 1938, Turin, Italy. Appointments: Joined Italian Socialist Party, 1958; Member, Central Committee, 1978-; Assistant Secretary; elected Deputy for Turin-Novara-Vercelli, 1983, 1987; Former Under-Secretary of State; President and Vice-President, Council of Ministers; Minister of the Treasury, 1987-89; Professor, Italian and Comparative Constitutional Law, University of Rome; National Deputy Secretary, Italian Socialist Party, 1988-92; Foreign debt negotiator for Albanian government, 1991-92, Prime Minister of Italy, 1992-93, 2000-01; Minister for Treasury, 1999-2001; Vice President, EU Special Convention on a Pan-European Constitution, 2001-. Address: Special Convention on a European Constitution, European Union, 200 rue de la Loi, 1049 Brussels, Belgium.

**AMAYA Kazuo,** b. 1 March 1928, Tokyo, Japan. Consultant; Company Director. m. Hiroko Amaya, 2 sons. Education: Graduate, Department of Chemistry, Faculty of Science, 1951, Doctor of Science, 1961, University of Tokyo, Japan. Appointments: Assistant and Lecturer, Kobe University, 1951-58; Chief Researcher, National Chemical Laboratory for Industry, 1958-88; Professor, Gunma University, 1988-93; Consultant, JBI Company, 1993-; Director, Tsukuba-Soken, 1993; President, Clean Energy Forum, 2003-. Publications: The Molecular Anvil Model of an Enzyme Taking into Consideration the Flexibility of Enzyme, 1987; Contribution of mutagenic and non-mutagenic substances to carcinogenesis, 1989; The present state of various simple methods of analysing air and water pollutants, 1991; The present global environmental problems have to be recognised as global cancer caused by mankind, 1997. Honour: Mikami Award for researches on various simple methods of measuring environmental pollution, 1991. Memberships: Chemical Society of Japan; Japan Society of Calorimetry and Thermal Analysis; Japan Society for Atmospheric Environment; President, Japanese Research Society of Detergents and Environmental Science. Address:

3-15-5 Okusawa Setagaya-ku, Tokyo 158-0083, Japan. E-mail: qwr05136@nifty.ne.jp

**AMBRUS Julian L,** b. 29 November 1924, Budapest. Physician; University Professor. m. Clara M Ambrus, 4 sons, 3 daughters. Education: MD, 1949; PhD, 1954; ScD (hc); FACP. Appointments: Professor of Internal Medicine, School of Medicine, State University of New York at Buffalo, New York, 1955-; Director of Cancer Research, Roswell Park, Memorial Cancer Institute, 1955-92; Chairman, Department of Experimental Pathology, State University of New York at Buffalo, RPC, 1982-92. Publications: Over 500 publications; 67 books or book chapters. Honours include: ScD, honoris causa, Niagara University, 1987; Distinguished Alumnus Award, Jefferson Medical College, 1990; Knight Commander of the Holy Sepulchre, Vatican, 1991; Foreign Member, National Academy of Science, Hungary, 1993. Memberships: Fellow, American College of Physicians; Member, American Society for Cancer Research. Address: Buffalo General Hospital, Kaleida Health System, State University of New York at Buffalo, 100 High Street, Buffalo, NY 14203, USA.

**AMEKURA Hiroshi,** b. 6 November 1964, Tokyo, Japan. Physicist. Education: BSc, 1989; MSc, 1991; PhD, 1999. Appointments: Researcher, 1991-99, Senior Researcher, 1999-2000, National Research Institute for Metals; Guest Scientist, Forschungszentrum, Jülich, Germany, 1997-98; Assistant Director of Nanotechnology Policy, Cabinet Office, Japanese Government, temporary post, 2001; Senior Researcher, National Institute for Materials Science, 2001-. Publications: More than 70 papers in reputable scientific journals. Honour: Young Scientist Award, 12th International Conference on Ion Implantation Technology, 1998. Membership: Japan Society of Applied Physics; The Japan Institute of Metals; MRS - Japan. Address: National Institute for Materials Science, 3-13 Sakura, Tsukuba, Ibaraki 305-0003, Japan. E-mail: amekura.hiroshi@nims.go.jp

**AMELING Elly,** b. 1938, Rotterdam, Netherlands. Opera Singer. m. Arnold W Beider, 1964. Education: Studied Singing with Jo Bollekamp, Jacoba and Sam Dresden, Bodi Rapp; Studied French Art Song with Pierre Bernac. Career: Recitals, Europe, South Africa, Japan; US debut, 1968; Annual tours, USA and Canada, 1968-; Has sung with Concertgebouw, New Philharmonic Orchestra, BBC Symphony Orchestra, Berlin Philharmonic, Cincinnati Symphony, San Francisco Symphony, Toronto Symphony, Chicago Symphony; Appeared in Mozart Festival, Washington DC, 1974, Caramoor Festival, 1974, Art Song Festival, Princeton, New Jersey, 1974. Publications: Recordings including Mozart Concert; Handel Concert; Bach Cantatas; Wolf's Mörike Lieder; Aimez-vous Handel?; Aimez-vous Mozart?; Bach's Christmas Oratorio; Mahler's Symphony No 2; Bruckner's Te Deum; Wolf's Italienisches Liederbuch. Honours: 1st Prize, Concours International de Musique, Geneva; Grand Prix du Disque; Edison Prize; Preis der Deutschen Schallplattenkritik; Stereo Review Record of the Year Award; Knight, Order of Orange-Nassau.

**AMES Lloyd Leroy,** b. 23 August 1927, Norwich, Connecticut, USA. Staff Scientist. m. Joan Nilsine Romstad, 10 June 1953, 1 son, 3 daughters. Education: BA, Geology, University of New Mexico, 1952; MS, Mineralogy, University of Utah, 1955; PhD, 1956; Post PhD, 1957. Appointments: Staff Scientist, Geochemistry Section Environmental Science Department. Publications: Many journal articles and annual reports. Memberships: American Mineralogy Society; Mineralogical Association of Canada. Address: 43703 East Austin Ct, West Richland, WA 99353, USA.

**AMIN DADA Idi (Field Marshal),** b. 1925, Kakwa Region, West Nile. Ugandan Former Head of State and Army Officer. Appointments: Joined King's African Rifles, 1946; Corporal, 1959, Major, 1963, Colonel, 1964; Deputy Commander, Ugandan Army, 1964; Commander, Uganda Army and Air Force, 1966-70; Brigadier-General, 1967, Major-General, 1968, Field Marshal, 1975; President, Chief of Armed Forces, 1971-79; Minister of Defence, 1971-75; Chair, Defence Council, 1972-79; Minister of Internal Affairs, 1973, 1978-79, of Information and Broadcasting, 1973, of Foreign Affairs, 1974-75, 1978, of Health, 1977-79, of Information, Broadcasting and Tourism, Game and Wildlife, 1978-79; Chief of Staff, Ugandan Army, 1974-79; Chair, OAU Association of Heads of State, 1975-76, presided Kampala Summit, 1975, Addis Ababa Summit, 1976. Honours: Heavyweight Boxing Champion of Uganda, 1951-60; 8 highest military decorations, Uganda; Honorary LLD, Kampala, 1976.

**AMIRALI Evangelia-Lila,** b. 28 November 1962. Medical Doctor; Psychiatrist. m. J Hadjinicolaou, 4 sons. Education: MD, University of Athens, Greece, 1986; MSc, in progress; Candidate, Canadian Institute of Psychoanalysis. Appointments: Research Fellow, McGill University, 1988-90, Clinical Fellow, 1990-92; Psychiatrist, Child Psychiatrist, 2001, Universite de Montreal. Honours: A S Onassis Scholarship, 1990-92; Berta Mizne Award, 1988-90; Best Promising Clinician Prize, Department of Psychiatry, McGill University, 1999-2000; American Psychiatric Association Women Fellowship, 2001. Memberships: APA; CPA; QMA; AMPQ. Address: 2875 Douglas Avenue, Montreal, QC H3R 2C7, Canada.

**AMIS Martin Louis,** b. 25 August 1949, Oxford, England. Author. m. (1) Antonia Phillips, 2 sons (2) Isabel Fonseca, 3 daughters. Education: BA, Exeter College, Oxford. Appointments: Fiction and Poetry Editor, Times Literary Supplement, 1974; Literary Editor, New Statesman, 1977-79; Special Writer, Observer Newspaper, 1980-. Publications: The Rachel Papers, 1973; Dead Babies, 1975; Success, 1978; Other People: A Mystery Story, 1981; Invasion of the Space Invaders, 1982; Money: A Suicide Note, 1984; The Moronic Inferno and Other Visits to America, 1986; Einstein's Monsters: Five Stories, 1987; London Fields, 1989; Time's Arrow, 1991; Visiting Mrs Nabokov and Other Excursions,1993; The Information, 1995; Night Train, 1997; Heavy Water and Other Stories, 1999; Experience, 2000; The War Against Cliché, 2001; Koba the Dread: Laughter and the Twenty Million, 2002; Yellow Dog, 2003. Honours: Somerset Maugham Award, 1974; James Tait Black Memorial Prize, 2000. Address: c/o Wylie Agency (UK), 17 Bedford Square, London WC1B 3JA, England. E-mail: mail: wylieagency.co.uk

**AMLIE Jan Peder,** b. 23 September 1940, Bøverbru, V Toten, Norway. Physician. m. May Lisbet, 1 son, 2 daughters. Education: Cand Med, 1965, Dr Med, 1981, Oslo University; Speciality Internal Medicine and Cardiology, Sweden and Norway, 1973; Professor in Cardiology, 1991. Appointments: Assistant Doctor, Sweden, 1966-73; University Lecturer, 1973-75, Research Fellow, 1975-80, Cardiologist, 1981-89, Professor, 1990-, Rikshospitalet, Oslo, Norway. Publications: 115 papers in medical journals and conference proceedings include: Prolonged Ventricular Repolarization, 1983; Dispension of Repolarization, 2000. Honour: President, UEMS, Cardiology Section. Memberships: Norwegian Society of Cardiology, President, 1987-91; FESC, 1989. Address: Risbakken 10, Oslo 0374, Norway.

**AMMANN Jean-Christophe,** b. 14 Janaury 1939, Berlin, Germany. Art Director. m. Judith. Education: PhD, University Fribourg, Switzerland, 1966. Appointments: Professor, University Frankfurt/M and Giessen, 1992-; University of Heidelberg Lecturer, 2001-02. Publications: Articles in professional journals. Honours: Decorated Officier des Arts and des Lettres, 2000; Wormland Foundation Culture Award, 2001; Decorated Goethe-Medal, City of Frankfurt/M, 2003. Address: Klettenbergstrasse 11, D-60322, Frankfurt/M, Germany.

**AMOROSO Santi,** b. 17 June 1925, Italy. Physician. m Gabriella Malanga, 3 sons, 1 daughter. Education: Graduate, 1949, Specialist in Pulmonary Diseases, 1951, Medical School, University "La Sapienza", Rome Italy; Licensed to practice medicine in Italy, Maryland, USA, Virginia, USA, 1959; Certified by ABFP, USA, 1978. Appointments: Internship and Residency, St Mary's Memorial Hospital, Knoxville, Tennessee, 1953-59; General Practitioner, Overlea Medical Group, Baltimore, Maryland, 1959-62; General Practitioner, Perry Hall Medical Group, Baltimore, Maryland, 1962-64; Private Practice, Rome Italy, 1964-. Publications: 2 medical articles in an Italian medical journal; Book of poetry, Gocciole di Rugiada (Dewdrops). Honours: 2nd Place, Poetry Competition sponsored by Association of Italian Physicians Writers, 1996. Memberships: Former Member, AMA and AAFP; Member, Italian Medical Association. Address: Via Villa Belardi 24, 00154 Rome, Italy. E-mail: santi.amoroso@libero.it

**AMOYAL Pierre Alain Wilfred,** b. 22 June 1949, Paris, France. Violinist. Education: Studied at the Paris Conservatoire and with Jascha Heifetz between 1966 and 1971. Debut: Paris 1971, in the Berg Concerto, with the Orchestre de Paris. Career: Appearances with the BBC Symphony Orchestra, Hallé Orchestra, London Philharmonic, Philharmonia, Berlin Philharmonic, Boston Symphony, Cleveland Orchestra, Philadelphia Orchestra and Orchestras in Canada and France; Conductors include Karajan, Ozawa, Boulez, Dutoit, Sanderling, Maazel, Solti, Prêtre, Masur and Rozhdestvensky; Plays Concertos by Berg, Schoenberg and Dutilleux, in addition to the standard repertory; Played Brahms Concerto with the Royal Philharmonic Orchestra, 1995; Artist in Residence at Beaumaris Festival in Wales, 1995; Recitals at St John's Smith Square for the BBC; New York Carnegie Hall debut 1985; Professor at the Paris Conservatoire from 1977; Currently Professor at the Lausanne Conservatoire. Recordings: Concertos by Dutilleux, Respighi and Saint Saëns with the Orchestre National conducted by Charles Dutoit; Chamber music (sonatas by Brahms, Fauré and Franck) with Pascal Rogé; Schoenberg Concerto with the London Symphony Orchestra conducted by Boulez. Honours include: Ginette Neveu Prize, 1963; Paganini Prize, 1964; Enescu Prize, 1970. Address: c/o Jacques Thelen, 252 rue du Faubourg Saint-Honoré, 75008 Paris, France.

**AMY Jean-Jacques,** b. 20 September 1940, Antwerp. Medical Doctor. 2 sons. Education: MD, Université Libre de Bruxelles, 1965; Degree in Tropical Medicine, Institute of Tropical Medicine, Antwerp, 1966. Appointments: Resident, The Mount Sinai Hospital, New York, 1967-71; Lecturer, Makerere University Medical School, Kampala, Uganda, 1971-73; Research Associate, University Hospital, Ghent, 1973-75; Attending Obstetrician and Gynaecologist, University Hospital, St Pierre, Brussels, 1975-78; Professor and Head of Department, University Hospital AZ-VUB, Brussels, 1979-. Publications: 286 scientific publications in obstetrics and gynaecology; Editor of 15 books. Honours: Distinguished Humanist Award. Memberships: Royal Belgian Society of Gynaecology and Obstetrics, Past President; Flemish Society of Obstetrics and Gynaecology, Past President. Address: Department of Gynaecology, Andrology and Obstetrics, Academisch Ziekenhuis V U B, Laarbeeklaan 101 B 1090, Brussels, Belgium.

# DICTIONARY OF INTERNATIONAL BIOGRAPHY

**AN Seongsu,** b. 22 October 1969, Ahndong, Korea. Researcher. Education: BA, Physics, 1997, MA, Solid State Physics, 1999, Dongguk University; PhD, Nuclear Engineering, Purdue University, 2005. Appointments: Research Assistant, 2000-03, Teaching Assistant, 2003-05, Purdue University, USA. Publication: ICF Target Applications of Strongly Coupled Dense Plasmas to Plasma Heating (PhD Dissertation). Honours: The Chancellor's List, 2004-05; Estus H and Vashti L Magoon Award, Purdue University, 2004 and 2005; Man of the Year 2005, ABI; Professional Award, ABI, 2005; Listed in national and international biographical dictionaries. Memberships: ANS (Fusion Energy Division, Aerospace Nuclear Science of Technology); APS (DCMP, DPP, DCOMP, GSNP). Address: 144 Halsey Dr, Apt 07, West Lafayette, IN 47906-3320, USA. E-mail: san@ecn.purdue.edu

**ANAND Mulk Raj,** b. 12 December 1905, Peshawar, India. Novelist; University Teacher. m. (2) Shirin Vajifdar, 1950, 1 daughter. Education: BA (Hons), Punjab University, 1924; PhD, University College, University of London, 1929; Cambridge University, 1929-30. Appointments: Director, Kutub publishers, Bombay, 1946-; Teacher, Universities of Punjab, Benares, and Rajasthan, Jaipur, 1948-66. Publications: Untouchable, 1935 The Coolie, 1936; Two Leaves and a Bud, 1937; The Village, 1939; Lament on the Death of a Master of Arts, 1939; Across the Black Waters, 1940; The Sword and the Sickle, 1942; The Big Heart, 1945; Seven Summers: The Story of an Indian Childhood, 1951; Private Life of an Indian Prince, 1953; The Old Woman and the Cow, 1960; The Road, 1961; Morning Face, 1968; Confession of a Lover, 1976; The Bubble, 1984; Death of a Hero, 1995; Also: Various short stories and other works. Honours: Padma Bhushan, 1967; Sahitya Academy Award, 1974; Fellow, National Academy of Art, New Delhi; Hon DLitt, Delhi, Benares, Andhra, Patiala, Shantiniketan; Laureate of International Peace Prize. Address: Jassim House, 25 Cuffe Parade, Colaba, Mumbai 400005, India.

**ANCONA Leonardo,** b. 2 May 1922, Milan, Italy. Psychiatrist; Psychoanalyst; Group Analyst. m. Angiola M Mangiarotti, 2 sons, 1 daughter. Education: MD, 1946; Psychiatry, 1951; Psychoanalysis, 1975; Group Analyst, 1978. Appointments: Full Professor, Psychology, Catholic University, Milan, 1951; Psychiatry, Catholic University, Rome, 1978; Director, Post Graduate School in Psychiatry, Institute of Psychiatry, Catholic University, Rome, 1973-92; Emeritus in Psychiatry, 1998. Publications: 10 books, 405 articles in professional journals. Honours: Rockefeller Fellow, New York; Aquinas Fund Fellow, Montreal; Member, Royal College of Psychiatrists; CMIL (Lourdes); Honorary President of IL CERCHIO; Honorary President, AIEMPR. Memberships: SPI; IPA; IAGP; AIEMPR; SIPS. Address: Via Nemea 21, 00194 Roma, Italy.

**ANCRAM Earl of, Michael Andrew Foster Jude Kerr, 13th Marquis of Lothian,** b. 7 July 1945. Politician. m. Lady Jane Fitzalan-Howard, 1975, 2 daughters. Education: Ampleforth; Christ Church College, Oxford; Edinburgh University. Appointments: Formerly in business; Columnist, Daily Telegraph (Manchester edition); Partner, Tenanted Arable Farm; Called to Scottish Bar, 1970; Practised Law, 1970-79; MP, Berwickshire and East Lothian, 1974; Edinburgh South, 1979-87; Devizes, 1992-; Parliamentary, Under-Secretary of State, Scottish Office, 1983-87; Parliamentary, Under-Secretary, Northern Ireland Office, 1993-94; Minister of State, 1994-96; Shadow Cabinet Spokesman for Constitutional Affairs, 1997-98; Chair, Conservative Party, 1998-2001; Vice Chair, 1975-80, Chair, 1980-83, Conservative Party, Scotland; Chair, North Corporate Communications, 1989-91; Director, CSM Parliamentary Consultants, 1988-92; Member of Board Scottish Homes, 1988-90; D L Roxburgh, Ettrick and Lauderdale, 1990; Privy Counsellor, 1996; Queen's Counsel, 1996. Memberships: House of Commons Energy Select Committee, 1979-83. Address: House of Commons, London, SW1A 0AA, England.

**ANDERSLAND Orlando B,** b. 15 August 1929, Albert Lea, Minnesota, USA. Civil Engineering Educator. m. Phyllis Burgess, 2 sons, 1 daughter. Education: BCE, University of Minnesota, 1952; MSCE, 1956, PhD, 1960, Purdue University at West Lafayette, Indiana. Appointments: 1st Lieutenant, US Army Corps of Engineers, 1952-55; Staff Engineer, National Academy of Science, American Association of State Highway Officials Road Test, Ottawa, Illinois, 1956-57; Research Engineer, Purdue University, 1957-59; Faculty, 1960, Professor, 1968, Professor Emeritus, 1994-, Michigan State University. Publications: Co-author, Frozen Ground Engineering, 1994, 2nd edition, 2004; Co-editor, Contributor, Geotechnical Engineering for Cold Regions, 1978; Chapter in Ground Engineers Handbook, 1987; Numerous articles in professional journals; Co-author, Geotechnical Engineering and Soil Testing, 1992; Patentee in field. Honours: Distinguished Faculty Award, Michigan State University, 1979; Norwegian Postdoctoral Fellowship, 1966; Best Paper Award, ASCE Journal of Cold Regions Engineering, 1991; Proceedings of the Association Asphalt Paving Technologists, 1956; National Defence Service Medal; United Nations Service Medal; Korean Service Medal. Memberships: Fellow, American Society of Civil Engineers; American Society for Testing Materials; International Society for Soil Mechanics and Foundation Engineering; American Society for Engineering Education; Chi Epsilon; Tau Beta Pi; Sigma Xi. Address: Department of Civil and Environmental Engineering, Michigan State University, East Lansing, MI 48824, USA.

**ANDERSON Elizabeth Lang,** b. 3 March 1960, Orange, New Jersey, USA. Composer; Professor. m. David S Baltuch. Education: BA, Music, Gettysburg College, Gettysburg, Pennsylvania, 1982; Master of Music in Composition, Peabody Institute, Baltimore, Maryland, 1987; Certificate, Composition, Royal Conservatory of Brussels, 1990; Diploma, Electronic Music Composition, Royal Conservatory, Antwerp, 1993; Premier Prix in Electroacoustic Music Composition, Royal Conservatory of Mons, 1997; Superior Diploma In Electroacoustic Music Composition, Royal Conservatory of Mons, 1998; PhD, Electroacoustic Music Composition, in progress, City University, London, 1998-. Appointments: Instructor of Musicianship (Creative Music Theory), Peabody Preparatory, Baltimore, Maryland, 1985-87; Professor, Electroacoustic Music Composition, Academy of Soignies, Belgium, 1994-2002; Appointed to the Faculty of the Electroacoustic Music Department, Royal Conservatory of Mons, 2003-. Publications: Perception in Electroacoustic Music: A Preliminary Investigation and Expansion of the Reception Behaviours Devised by François Delalande, to be published. Honours: Music honoured in several competitions specialising in electroacoustic music including: Ascap/Seamus, Bourges, Metamorphoses, Noroit, Sao Paulo, Stockholm; Commissions from Musiques & Recherches, Belgium and La Chambre d'Ecoute, Belgium; Numerous works frequently performed at international festivals; Overseas Research Students Award Scheme Grant funded by the Committee of Vice-Chancellors and Principals of the Universities of the United Kingdom; Grant, British Federation of Women Graduates Charitable Foundation; Grant, Foundation SPES. Memberships: International Computer Music Association; International Alliance for Women in Music; Sonic Arts Network; Society for Electro-Acoustic Music in the United States. Address: Avenue de Monte Carlo, 11, 1190 Brussels, Belgium. E-mail: e.anderson@skynet.be

**ANDERSON Gerry,** b. 14 April 1929, England. Film Maker. m. (1) Betty Wrightman, 1952, 2 daughters, (2) Sylvia Thamm, 1961, divorced, 1 son, (3), Mary Robbins, 1981, 1 son. Appointments: Trainee, Colonial Film Unit, 1943; Assistant Editor, Gainsborough Pictures, 1945-47; Dubbing Editor, 1949-53; Film Director, Polytechnic Films, 1954-55; Co-founder: Pentagon Films, 1955, AP Films, 1956, AP Merchandising, 1961; Director of TV commercials, 1961, 1988-92; Chair, Century 21 Organisation, 1966-75. TV Series Include: Adventure of Twizzle (52 shows), 1956; Torchy the Battery Boy (26 shows), 1957; Four Feather Falls (52 shows), 1958; Supercar (39 shows), 1959; Fireball XL5 (39 shows), 1961; Stingray (39 shows), 1962-63; Thunderbirds (32 shows screened in 20 countries), 1964-66; Captain Scarlet (32 shows), 1967; Joe 90 (30 shows), 1968; The Secret Service (13 shows), 1968; UFO (26 shows), 1969-70; The Protectors (52 shows), 1971-72; Space 1999 (48 shows), 1973-76; Terrahawks (39 shows), 1982-83; Dick Spanner (26 shows), 1987; Space Precinct, 1993-95; Lavender Castle, 1997; Firestorm, 2002; Numerous TV commercials; Films: Thunderbirds are Go, 1966; Thunderbird 6, 1968; Doppelganger, 1969. Honours: Honorary Fellow, British Kinematograph Sound and TV Society; President, Thames Valley and Chiltern Air Ambulance; Silver Arrow Award.

**ANDERSON Gillian,** b. 9 August 1968, Chicago, USA. Actress. m. Errol Clyde Klotz, divorced, 1 daughter. Education: DePaul University, Chicago; Goodman Theatre School, Chicago. Appointments: Worked at National Theatre, London; Appeared in two off-broadway productions; Best Known Role as Special Agent Dana Scully in TV Series, The X Files (Feature Film 1998); Film, The House of Mirth, 2000; Plays include: Absent Friends, Manhattan Theater Club, 1991; The Philanthropist, Along Wharf Theater, 1992; What the Night is For, Comedy Theatre, London, 2002; TV Films include, Home Fire Burning, 1992; When Planes Go Down, 1996; Presenter, Future Fantastic, BBC TV. Honours: Golden Globe Awards, 1995, 1997; Screen Actors' Guild Awards, 1996, 1997; Emmy Award, 1997. Address: William Morris Agency, 151 El Camino Drive, Beverly Hills, CA 90212, USA. Website: www.gilliananderson.ws

**ANDERSON John Anthony (Sir),** b. 2 August 1945, Wellington, New Zealand. Banker. m. Carol M Anderson, 1970, 2 sons, 1 daughter. Education: Christ's College; Victoria University of Wellington; FCA. Appointments: Deloitte Haskins and Sells chartered accountants, Wellington, 1962-69; Guest and Bell sharebrokers, Melbourne, Victoria, Australia, 1969-72; Joined, 1972, Chief Executive, Director, 1979, South Pacific Merchant Finance Ltd, Wellington; Deputy Chief Executive, 1988, Chief Executive, Director, 1990-2003, National Bank of New Zealand; Chair, Petroleum Corporation of New Zealand Ltd, 1986-88; Director, New Zealand Steel Ltd, 1986-87, Lloyds Merchant Bank, London, 1986-92, Lloyds Bank NZA, Australia, 1989-97; New Zealand Bankers' Association, 1991-92, 1999-2000; President, New Zealand Bankers Institute, 1990-2001; Chair, New Zealand Cricket Board, 1995-, New Zealand Sports Foundation Inc, 1999-2002; Managing Director, ANZ National Bank Ltd, 2003-; Other professional and public appointments. Honours: Knight Commander, Order of the British Empire; 1990 Commemoration Medal. Memberships: Chair, New Zealand Merchant Banks Association, 1982-89; Chair, New Zealand Bankers Association, 1992-. Address: 5 Fancourt Street, Karori, Wellington 5, New Zealand.

**ANDERSON Katrina Marysia Tomaszewska,** b. 7 December 1947, Springfield by Cupar, Fife, Scotland. Community Educator. m. William Anderson, 1 son, 2 daughters. Education: Master of Arts, English Literature (Honours), University of Dundee, 1999; Open University Postgraduate Diploma in Community Education, Northern College, Dundee, 2001. Appointments: Personal Assistant to husband in the family business, 1986-; Community Educator; Member, Volunteer, Tracing and Message Co-ordinator, Public Speaker, British Red Cross. Publications: Numerous poems published by International Society of Poets, 1998, 2000; Triumph House, 1997-2001; Brownstone Books, 1997. Honours: Cultural Relations Officer to Scotland, HRP (Title: The Hon); Medal, HRP, 1998; Honoured Poet, 1998; One of the Best Poets of the 20th Century; Listed in Who's Who publications and biographical dictionaries. Memberships: International Society of Poets; University of Dundee Alumni; British Red Cross; Lifetime Partronage, Hutt River Province, Australia. Address: 31 Clyde Court, Rimbleton, Glenrothes, Fife KY6 2BN, Scotland.

**ANDERSON Michael,** b. 30 January 1920, London, England. Film Director. 1 son. Education: France. Appointments: Co-Director with Peter Ustinov, film, Private Angelo, 1949; Director, films: Waterfront, 1950; Hell Is Sold Out, 1952; Night Was Our Friend; Dial 17; Will Any Gentleman?; The House of the Arrow, 1952; The Dam Busters, 1954; Around the World in Eighty Days, 1956; Yangtse Incident, 1957; Chase a Crooked Shadow, 1957; Shake Hands with the Devil, 1958; Wreck of the Mary Deare, 1959-60; All the Fine Young Cannibals, 1960; The Naked Edge, 1961; Flight from Ashiya, in Japan, 1962; Operation Crossbow, 1964; The Quiller Memorandum, 1966; Shoes of The Fisherman, 1969; Pope Joan, 1970-71; Doc Savage, in Hollywood, 1973; Conduct Unbecoming, 1974; Logan's Run, MGM Hollywood, 1975; Orca - Killer Whale, 1976; Dominique, 1977; The Martian Chronicles, 1978; Bells, 1979-80; Millenium; Murder by Phone; Second Time Lucky; Separate Vacations; Sword of Gideon; Jeweller's Shop; Young Catherine; Millennium; Summer of the Monkeys. Address: c/o Film Rights Ltd, 113-117 Wardour Street, London W1, England.

**ANDERSON (Göran) Patrik,** b. 16 September 1963, Uddevalla, Sweden. Physician. 2 daughters. Education: MD, University of Gothenburg, Sweden, 1988; Authorised Physician, Swedish Board of Health and Welfare, 1991; Certified Specialist of Internal Medicine, 1998; Certified Specialist of Haematology, 2001. Appointments: Assisting Researcher, Department of Lung Pharmacology, Faculty of Medicine University of Gothenburg, Sweden, 1992-93; Consultant, Haematology Department, Sahlgrenska University Hospital/Östra, Gothenburg, Sweden, 1998-2002; Senior Physician, Department of Internal Medicine, Hospital of Southern Älvsborg, Skene, Sweden, 2002-. Publications: Articles in medical journals including: Lung, 1996; American Journal of Hematology, 2003. Memberships: European Hematology Association; Swedish Society of Medicine; Swedish Medical Association; Swedish Society of Palliative Medicine; Gothenburg Society of Medicine; Swedish Society of Hematology; Swedish Society of the History of Medicine; American Society of Hematology; Swedish Society of Internal Medicine. Address: Department of Internal Medicine, Hospital of Southern Älvsborg, Skene, SE-51181, Sweden. E-mail: phacit@yahoo.com

**ANDERSON Robert Geoffrey William,** b. 2 May 1944, London, England. Museum Director. m. Margaret Elizabeth Callis Lea, 1973, 2 sons. Education: St John's College, Oxford; MA, Oxon; DPhil. Appointments: Keeper, Science Museum, London, 1980-84; Director, Royal Scottish Museum, 1984-85; National Museums of Scotland, 1985-92, British Museum, London, 1992-; Curator, School of Advanced Study, University of London, 1994-. Publications: The Playfair Collection, 1978; Science in India, 1982; Science, Medicine and Dissent, editor,

1987; A New Museum for Scotland, editor, 1990; Joseph Black: a Bibliography, co-editor, 1992; Making Instruments Count, joint editor, 1993; The Great Court at the British Museum, 2000. Honours: Dexter Award, American Chemical Society, 1986; Honorary Fellow, Society of Antiquaries, Scotland, 1991; Honorary DSc, Edinburgh, 1995; Honorary DSc, Durham, 1998. Memberships: Fellow, Royal Society of Edinburgh; President, British Society for the History of Science, 1988-80; President, Scientific Instrument Committee, International Union of History and Philosophy of Science, 1982-97; President, British Society for the History of Science, 1988-90; Board, Boerhaave Museum, Leiden, Netherlands, 1995-99. Address: The British Museum, London WC1B 3DSG, England.

**ANDERSON William Robert,** b. 26 January 1929, Kittanning, Pennsylvania, USA. Physician; Pathologist. m. Carol J Tammen, 1 son, 1 daughter. Education: BA, University of Rochester, 1951; MD, University of Pennsylvania School of Medicine, 1958; Anatomic and Clinical Pathology Residencies, New York Hospital, Cornell Medical Centre, 1958-69, New York VA Hospital, 1960-62. Appointments: Neuropathology Fellowship, Duke University, 1962-64; Director, Anatomic Pathology, Hennepin County Medical Centre, 1967-97; Chief of Pathology, 1984-95; Professor, Department of Laboratory Medicine and Pathology, University of Minnesota School of Medicine, 1975-. Publications: Numerous scientific publications in national and international pathology journals. Honours: Phi Beta Kappa, University of Rochester, 1951; Sigma Xi, Duke University, 1963; Mentor Recognition, University of Minnesota, 1989. Memberships: College of American Pathologists; International Academy of Pathology; Society for Ultrastructural Pathology; President, Minnesota Society of Pathologists, 1980-81. Address: 5725 Merry Lane, Excelsior, MN 55331, USA.

**ANDO Nisuke,** b. 6 August 1935, Kyoto, Japan. Professor of International Law. m. Noriko Fujimoto, 1 son, 2 daughters. Education: LLB, 1959, LLM, 1961, Kyoto University; PhD, Fletcher School of Law and Diplomacy, 1971. Appointments: Lecturer and Associate Professor, 1965-68, 1968-81, Kyoto University; Professor, 1981-90, Kobe University; Professor, Kyoto University, 1990-98; Professor, Doshisha University, 1998-. Publications: Surrender, Occupation and Private Property in International Law, 1991; Japan and International Law - Past, Present and Future, editor, 1999; Liber Amicorum Judge Shigeru Oda, co-editor, 2002; Towards Implementing Universal Human Rights, editor, 2004. Honours: Fulbright Graduate Scholar, 1962-64; Fulbright Research Fellow, 1969-70; British Council Fellow, 1976-78; Fulbright 50th Anniversary Distinguished Fellow, 1996. Memberships: Human Rights Committee under the International Covenant on Civil and Political Rights, 1987-; Judge, Administrative Tribunal of the International Monetary Fund, 1994-; Judge, Permanent Court of Arbitration, 2001-. Address: 922-66 Kokubu 2-chome, Otsu-Shi, Shiga-ken 520-0844, Japan.

**ANDRÉ Maurice,** b. 21 May 1933, Alès, Gard, France. Trumpeter. Education: Studied with his father and with Sabarich at the Paris Conservatoire. Career: Soloist with the Concerts Lamoureuz, 1953-60, L'Orchestre Philharmonique of ORTF (French Radio), 1953-62, and the orchestra of the Operé-Comique, Paris, 1962-67; Many concert performances in Europe; North American Professor at the Paris Conservatoire, 1967-78; Composers who have written for him include Boris Blacher (Concerto 1971), Charles Chaynes, Marcel Landowski, Jean-Claude Eloy, Harold Genzmer, Bernhard Krol, Jean Langlais (Chorals for trumpet and organ), Henri Tomasi and André Jolivet (Arioso barocco, 1968). Honours: Chevalier de la Légion d'honneur; Commandeur des Arts et des Lettres;

First Prize, Geneva International Competition, 1955, Munich International Competition, 1963, Schallplattenpreis, Berlin, 1970, Victoire de la musique, 1987.

**ANDREEV Rumen Dimov,** b. 20 March 1955, Sofia, Bulgaria. Engineer. Education: Master of Science, 1980, PhD, 1987, Sofia Technical University, Sofia, Bulgaria. Appointments: Constructor, Institute of Computer Technique, 1980-82; Research Fellow, Central Institute of Computer Technique and Technology, 1982-88; Research Associate, Central Laboratory of Automation and Scientific Instrumentation, 1988-93; Associate Professor, Institute of Computer and Communication Systems, Bulgarian Academy of Sciences, 1994-. Publications: Monograph: Graphics Systems: Architecture and Realization, 1993; Articles in scientific journals including: Computer Graphics Forum; Computers and Graphics; Interacting with Computers. Honours: Medal, Ministry of Defence, Republic of Bulgaria, 1974; Listed in Who's Who publications and biographical dictionaries. Memberships: Bulgarian Union of Automation and Informatics, British Computer Society; New York Academy of Sciences. Address: Institute of Computer and Communication Systems, Bulgarian Academy of Sciences, str Acad. G Bonchev Bl 2, 1113 Sofia, Bulgaria. E-mail: rumen@agatha.iac.bg

**ANDRES-BARQUIN Pedro Jose,** b. 9 January 1964, Zaragoza, Spain. Neuroscientist; Veterinarian. m. Maria Clemencia Hernandez, 2 daughters. Education: DVM, 1987, PhD, 1992, University of Zaragoza, Spain; MPH, Spanish National School of Public Health, Spain, 1993. Appointments: Fellow: University of Zaragoza, 1982-92, INSERM, France, 1990-91, University of California, San Francisco, 1994-98; Head of Laboratory, F Hoffmann-La Roche, Basel, Switzerland, 2000-. Publications: Contributor of articles to professional journals in the field of biomedical research and education. Honours: CAI Degree Prize, 1987, National Degree Prize, 1988, Spanish Ministry of Education and Science; Gold Medal Prize, Veterinary Medicine, Official Association of Veterinary Surgeons of Malaga, 2004; Albeiter Gold Medal Prize, Offical Association of Veterinary Surgeons of Murcia, 2004; International Health Professional of the Year, IBC, Cambridge, England, 2004. Memberships: Society for Neuroscience; American Society for Cell Biology; Spanish Society for Biochemistry and Molecular Biology. Address: Claragraben 117, Basel 4057, Switzerland. E-mail: pjandres@datacomm.ch

**ANDRETTI Mario Gabriele,** b. 28 February 1940, Montona, Italy. Racing Driver. m. Dee Ann Hoch, 1961, 2 sons, 1 daughter. Appointments: Began midget car racing in US, graduating to US Auto Club National Formula; Indy Car National Champion, 1965, 1966, 1969, 1984; USAC Champion, 1965, 1966, 1969, 1974; Winner, Indianapolis 500 Miles, 1969; Winner, Daytona 500 Miles NASCAR Stock Car Race, 1967; Began Formula 1 Racing in 1968; World Champion, 1978; Third, 1977; Winner, International Race of Champions, 1979; President, MA 500 Inc, 1968-; Newman/Haas Racing, 1983; Honours: Driver of the Year, 1967, 1978, 1984; Driver of the Quarter Century, 1992; Driver of the Century, 1999-2000; All Time Indy Car Lap Leader (7587); Grand Prix Wins: South African (Ferrari); Japanese (Lotus Ford), 1976; US (Lotus Ford), 1977; Spanish (Lotus Ford), 1977; French (Lotus Ford), 1977; Italian (Lotus Ford), 1977; Argentine (Lotus Ford), 1978; Belgian (Lotus Ford), 1978; Spanish (Lotus Ford), 1978; French (Lotus Ford), 1978; German (Lotus Ford), 1978; Dutch (Lotus Ford), 1978. Address: 475 Rose Inn Avenue, Nazareth, PA 18064, USA.

**ANDREW Christopher Robert,** b. 18 February 1963, Richmond, Yorks. Rugby Football Player. m. Sara, 3 daughters.

Education: Cambridge University. Appointments: Chartered Surveyor; Fly-half; Former Member, Middlesbrough, Cambridge University, Nottingham, Gordon, Sydney, Australia clubs; Member, 1987-91, 1992-96, Captain, 1989-90, Wasps Club; Toulouse, 1991-92; Barbarians, Newcastle, 1996-; International debut England versus Romania, 1985; Five nations debut, England Versus France, 1985; Captain, England Team, England versus Romania, Bucharest, 1989; Retired from International Rugby, 1995; Director of Rugby, Newcastle Rugby Football Club, 1995-. Publications: A Game and a Half, 1995. Honours: Record Holder for Drop Goals in Internationals. Memberships: Grand Slam Winning Team. Address: c/o Newcastle Rugby Ltd, Newcastle upon Tyne, NE13 8AF, England.

**ANDREWS Anthony,** b. 1 December 1948, Hampstead, London, England. Actor. m. Georgina Simpson, 1 son, 2 daughters. Career: Started acting, 1967; TV appearances include Doomwatch, Woodstock, 1972, A Day Out, Follyfoot, Fortunes of Nigel, 1973, The Pallisers, David Copperfield, 1974, Upstairs Downstairs, 1975, French Without Tears, The Country Wife, Much Ado About Nothing, 1977, Danger UXB, 1978, Romeo and Juliet, 1979, Brideshead Revisited, 1980, Ivanhoe, 1982, The Scarlet Pimpernel, 1983, Colombo, 1988, The Strange Case of Dr Jekyll and Mr Hyde, 1989, Hands of a Murderer, 1990, Lost in Siberia, 1990, The Law Lord, 1991, Jewels, 1992, Ruth Rendell's Heartstones, Mothertime; Films include The Scarlet Pimpernel, Under the Volcano, A War of the Children, Take Me High, 1973, Operation Daybreak, 1975, Les Adolescents, 1976, The Holcroft Covenant, 1986, Second Victory, 1987, Woman He Loved, 1988, The Lighthorsemen, 1988, Hannah's War, 1988, Lost in Siberia, as actor and producer, 1990, Haunted, as actor and producer, 1995; Appeared in plays, 40 Years On, A Midsummer Night's Dream, Romeo and Juliet, One of Us, 1986, Coming into Land, 1986, Dragon Variation, Tima and the Conways. Address: c/o Peters Fraser and Dunlop Ltd, 503 The Chambers, Chelsea Harbour, London SW10 0XF, England.

**ANDREWS Julie (Dame),** b. 1 October 1935, Walton-on-Thames, Surrey, England. Singer; Actress. m. (1) Tony Walton, 10 May 1959, divorced, 1 daughter; (2) Blake Edwards, 1969. Musical Education: Voice lessons with Lillian Stiles-Allen. Career: As actress: Debut, Starlight Roof, London Hippodrome, 1947; Appeared: Royal Command Performance, 1948; Broadway production, The Boy Friend, NYC, 1954; My Fair Lady, 1956-60; Camelot, 1960-62; Putting It Together, 1993; Film appearances include: Mary Poppins, 1964; The Americanization Of Emily, 1964; Torn Curtain, 1966; The Sound Of Music, 1966; Hawaii, 1966; Thoroughly Modern Millie, 1967; Stark, 1968; Darling Lili, 1970; The Tamarind Seed, 1973; 10, 1979; Little Miss Marker, 1980; S.O.B., 1981; Victor/Victoria, 1982; The Man Who Loved Women, 1983; That's Life!, 1986; Duet For One, 1986; The Sound of Christmas, TV, 1987; Relative Values, 1999; The Princess Diaries, 2001; Television debut, 1956; Host, The Julie Andrews Hour, 1972-73; Julie (comedy series), ABC-TV, 1992; Television films include Our Sons, 1991. Recordings: Albums: A Christmas Treasure, 1968; The Secret Of Christmas, 1977; Love Me Tender, 1983; Broadway's Fair, 1984; Love Julie, 1989; Broadway: The Music Of Richard Rogers, 1994; Here I'll Stay, 1996; Nobody Sings It Better, 1996; with Carol Burnett: Julie And Carol At Carnegie Hall, 1962; At The Lincoln Center, 1989; Cast and film soundtacks: My Fair Lady (Broadway cast), 1956; Camelot (Broadway cast), 1961; Mary Poppins (film soundtrack), 1964; The Sound Of Music (film soundtrack), 1965; The King And I (studio cast), 1992. Publications: Mandy (as Julie Edwards), 1971; The Last Of The Really Great Whangdoodles, 1974. Honours: Oscar, Mary Poppins, 1964; Golden Globe Awards, Hollywood Foreign Press Association, 1964, 1965; BAFTA Silver Mask,

1989; Kennedy Center Honor, 2001. Address: c/o Triad Artists, 10100 Santa Monica Boulevard, 16th Floor, Los Angeles, CA 90067, USA.

**ANDREWS Lyman Henry,** b. 2 April 1938, Denver, Colorado, USA. Writer. Education: BA, Brandeis University, 1960. Appointments: Assistant Lecturer, University of Wales, Swansea, 1964-65; Lecturer, University of Leicester, 1965-88; Poetry Critic, Sunday Times, 1969-78; Visiting Professor, Indiana University, 1978-79. Publications: Ash Flowers; Fugitive Visions; The Death of Mayakovsky; Kaleidoscope. Contributions to: Times; Sunday Times; Times Higher Educational Supplement; British Book News; San Francisco Examiner; Denver Post; Partisan Review; Encounter; El Corno Empumado; Les Lettres Nouvelles; New Mexico Quarterly; Carolina Quarterly; Transatlantic Review; Anglo Welsh Review; Poetry Quarterly; Root and Branch; Evergreen Review. Honours: Fulbright Fellowship; James Phelan Travelling Fellowship; Woodrow Wilson National Fellowship. Address: Flat 4-32, Victoria Centre, Nottingham, NG1 3PA, England.

**ANDREWS Marcia Gladys Tricker,** b. 7 February 1923, London, England. Painter. m. Edward Philip Andrews, 1 son, 1 daughter. Education: St Andrews School, London; New City, London; Various educational institutions. Career: Painter in oils; Exhibitions include: Medway Maritime Hospital, Healing Arts Programme Initiative; Brook Theatre Gallery; Usher Gallery, Lincoln; Tunbridge Wells Museum and Art Gallery; University of Surrey; De La Warr Pavilion; Mall Galleries; Libraries in Gillingham and, Strood; Central Library, Uxbridge; The Barbican; Institute of Art, London; Mexico City; Museum of Modern Art, Morelia; Leek Gallery; The Maltings, Farnham; Stables Gallery, Hastings; The Turret Gallery, London; Easthampstead Education Centre; St Martins-in-the-Fields; Work in collections: University of Surrey; Medway Council Library Loan Service; Private collections at home and abroad. Membership: Life Member, International Art Association. Address: 40 Robin Hood Lane, Walderslade, Chatham, Kent ME5 9LD, England.

**ANDREWS Richard Nigel Lyon,** b. 6 December 1944, Newport, Rhode Island, USA. Professor. m. Hannah Page Wheeler, 1 son, 1 daughter. Education: AB, Yale University, 1966; MRP, University of North Carolina, Chapel Hill, 1970; PhD, University of North Carolina, 1972. Appointments: Peace Corps Volunteer, 1966-68; Natural Resource Planner Aid, New York State Department of Conservation, 1969; Budget Examiner, Water Resources Branch, US Office of Management and Budget, 1970-72; Research Associate, University of North Carolina, 1972; Assistant Professor, Natural Resource Policy, University of Michigan, Ann Arbor, 1972-75; Assistant Professor, Urban and Regional Planning, 1974-75; Associate Professor, Natural Resource Policy, Urban and Regional Planning, 1975-81; Acting Chairman, Regional Planning Curriculum, 1975-76; Chairman, Resource Policy, Management Program, 1978-81; Professor of Environmental Policy, University of North Carolina, 1981-; Director, Institute for Environmental Studies, 1981-91; Director, Environmental Management and Policy Program, 1990-94; Chair of the Faculty, 1997-2000; Thomas Willis Lambeth Distinguished Professor of Public Policy, 2004-. Publications: 5 Books; Numerous Articles. Honours: Honorary Member, Golden Key National Honour Society; Fellow, National Academy of Public Administration; Fellow, American Association for the Advancement of Science; Member, Sigma Xi; Member, Delta Omega. Memberships: American Association for the Advancement of Science; Association for Public Policy Analysis and Management;

Society for Policy Sciences. Address: 298 Azalea Drive, Chapel Hill, NC 27517, USA.

**ANDRONACHE Daniel-Costel,** b. 2 May 1961, Deva, Hunedoara County, Romania. Mining Engineer. m. Daniela Oniţa. Education: Graduate, Mine Specialisation, The Institute of Mining, Petroşani, 1986. Appointments: Mining Engineer, "Moldova Novà" Mining (subsidiary of "Minevest" S. A. Deva Romania), 1986-87; Manager, Chief Engineer, Engineer, "Certej" Mining (subsidiary of "Minevest" S. A. Deva, Romania), 1987-2001; General Manager, C.N.C.A.F. "Minvest" S.A. Deva, Romania (National Copper Gold and Iron Company), 2001-. Publications: Articles in professional journals include: System regarding the leading of mining in open-pit for useful non-ferrous minerals, 2002; Synthesis of the C.N.C.A.F. "Minvest" S.A. Deva's reform program beginning with 1990 and strategical ways for reorganisation until 2007, 2004. Honours: Diploma of Excellence Prod-Min first edition, University of Bucharest for production research and marketing activity of "Minvest" S.A. Deva; Diploma of Excellence Prod-Min first edition, National Agency for Mineral Resources for presentation of C.N.C.A.F "Minvest" S.A. Deva's activity and the beauty of the samples exhibited, 2002; Certificate of Invention conferred by University of Petroşani for "Theoretical and experimental researches regarding the reduction of refractivity influence of some gold ores from operating mineral deposits upon the degree of recovery of the precious metals", 2003. Memberships: President, Board of Administration of C.N.C.A.F "Minvest" S.A. Deva; Vice-President of the Board of Administration of two joint ventures: S.C. "Rosia Montana Gold Corporation" S.A and "Devagold" S.A. Address: Deva, Hunedoara County, Romania. E-mail: andronache@xnet.com

**ANDSNES Leif Ove,** b. 7 April 1970, Karmoy, Norway. Pianist. Education: Studied at the Music Conservatory of Bergen with Jiri Hlinka. Debut: Oslo, 1987; British debut, Edinburgh Festival with the Oslo Philharmonic, Mariss Jansons, 1989; US Debut, Cleveland Symphony, Neeme Järvi. Career: Appearances include: Schleswig-Holstein Festival and with orchestras such as Los Angeles Philharmonic, Japan Philharmonic, Berlin Philharmonic, London Philharmonic, Philharmonia, City of Birmingham Symphony Orchestra, Royal Scottish National Orchestra, BBC Philharmonic Orchestra for his debut at the Proms, 1992 and Chicago Symphony Orchestra; Soloist, Last Night of the Proms, 2002; Artistic Director, Risor Festival; Recitals at Teatro Communale, Bologna, Wigmore Hall, Barbican Hall, London, Herkulesaal, Munich, Concertgebouw, Amsterdam, Konzerthaus Vienna and Glasgow Royal Concert Hall. Recordings include: Grieg: A Minor and Liszt A Major concerti; Grieg: Lyric Pieces; Janacek, Solo Piano Music; Chopin, Sonatas and Grieg, Solo Piano Music; Brahmns and Schumann works for piano and viola with Lars Anders Tomter. Honours include: First Prize, Hindemith Competition, Frankfurt am Main; Levin Prize, Bergen, 1999; Norwegian Music Critics' Prize, 1988; Grieg Prize, Bergen, 1990; Dorothy B Chandler Performing Art Award, Los Angeles, 1992; Gilmore Prize, 1997; Instrumentalist Award, Royal Philharmonic Society, 2000; Gramophone Award, Best Concerto Recording, 2000; Best Instrumental Recording, 2002; Commander, Royal Norwegian Order of St Olav, 2002. Address: c/o Kathryn Enticott, IMG Artists (Europe), Lovell House, 616 Chiswick High Road, London W4 5RX, England.

**ANEER Gunnar,** Environmentalist. Education: Undergraduate courses in Statistics, Botany, Zoology, Filosofie Kandidat Degree, 1969, PhD, Department of Zoology, 1979; Docent (Associate Professor), Zoology, Marine Ecology, 1984, University of Stockholm, Sweden. Appointments: Third Amanuensis, 1969, First Amanuensis, 1969-70, Department of Zoology, Research Associate, 1972-73, 1973-79, 1979-83, 1983-90, Askö Laboratory, Department of Zoology, University of Stockholm, Sweden; Environmental Investigator, County Administrative Board of Stockholm, 1990-; In charge of Information Office for the Baltic Proper, 1992-; Several consultancy positions in Sweden and abroad include: Swedish Expert in a Helsinki Commission Working Group, Baltic Early Warning Event Reporting System, 1998-; Marine Monitoring Expert in the preparation group of the Svealand Coastal Water Association, 1999-. Publications: Over 20 articles in scientific journals as author and co-author include most recently: Between-reader variation in herring otolith ages and effects on estimated population parameters, 2000; A Tagging experiment on spring-spawning Baltic herring (Clupea harengus membras) in Southwest Finland in 1990-98, 2001; 9 scientific reports; 8 conference papers; 13 popular science papers. Address: County Administrative Board of Stockholm, Section for Environmental Information, Box 22067, S-104 22 Stockholm, Sweden. E-mail: gunnar.aneer@ab.lst.se

**ANG Hooi Hoon,** b. 11 January 1964, Ipoh Perak. Lecturer; Researcher. Education: BPharm (Hons), 1988, PhD, 1993, University of Science, Malaysia; Admitted to PHP Institute, awarded Gold Medal, Doctoral Fellow, PHP Institute of Asia, Japan, 1995. Appointments: Graduate Assistant, School of Pharmaceutical Sciences, University of Science, Malaysia, 1988-90; Assistant Quality Control Manager, private pharmaceutical company, Ipoh Perak, 1992-93; Lecturer, 1994-2002, Associate Professor, 2002-, School of Pharmaceutical Sciences, University of Science, Malaysia. Publications: total of 300 publications. Honours: Awards from scientific institutions, fellowships, grants include: Third World Academy of Science, Trieste and Chinese Academy of Science Visiting Professorship, Beijing, February to April 1998; Awards: Young Investigator, European Societies of Chemotherapy, Stockholm, Sweden, 1998; Young Investigator, Science Council of Japan and Japanese Society of Parasitology, 1998; UNESCO Regional Office of Southeast Asia, Jakarta, 1998; Young Scientist and Technologist, ASEAN Committee of Science and Technology, Vietnam, 1998; Gold Star Award, Certificate of Achievement, International Woman of the Year Award, International Biographical Centre, England, 1998; International Woman of the Millennium, IBC, Cambridge, 1999; Postdoctoral Fellowship for Foreign Researchers Awardee, Japan Society for the Promotion of Science, 1999-2000; American Medal of Honor, ABI, 2003. Memberships: Vice-Chairman, 1994-95, Honorary Secretary, 1995-, Malaysian Pharmaceutical Society, Penang; Malaysian Society of Parasitology and Tropical Medicine; Malaysian Microbiology Society; Japanese Society of Parasitology; Third World Academy of Science, Trieste; Institute of Biology, Queensberry, UK, 1998-. Address: School of Pharmaceutical Sciences, University of Science, Malaysia, Minden 11800, Penang, Malaysia.

**ANG Lee,** b. 1954, Taipei, Taiwan. Film Director. m. Jane Lin. Education: New York University. Moved to USA 1978. Films: Pushing Hands, 1992; The Wedding Banquet, 1993; Eat Drink Man Woman, 1995; Sense and Sensibility, 1996; The Ice Storm, 1998; Ride with the Devil, 1998; Crouching Tiger, Hidden Dragon, 1999; Chosen, 2001. Honours: Winner, National Script Writing Contest, Taiwanese Government, 1990; Academy Award for Best Foreign Film, 1999; David Lean Award for Best Director; BAFTA, 2001; Golden Globe for Best Director, 2001

**ANGELI Giuliana,** b. Gaeta, Umbria, Italy. Painter; Poet. Education: Graduate in Pedagogy, Specialization in Psychology, University of Naples. Appointments: Lecturer, University of

Urbino; Journalist: Messaggero, Doxa and Rai Tv; Exhibitions as an artist: Foligno, Macerata, Trevi, Florence, Biarritz, Spoleto, Chianciano, Rome, Civitanova Marche, Milan, Recanati, Parigi, New York, Salsomaggiore, Jesi, Terni, Malta, London, Tangier, Ferrara; Participated in meetings: Biennale di Brescia, Rassegna Itinerante '84, Biennale of Waterbury and la Spezia, Collettiva 1986 (Rome), Salon des Nation (Parigi) and Festive of Due Mondi (Spoleto). Publications: Contributions to literary magazines such as Mondo Libero (Italian-American magazine); Works collected in Golden Book, Centre of International Studies with UNESCO, 1961. Honours: Many prestigious prizes for her artistic works and literary activities including: Award of the Prime Minister, 1965 and 1968; Title of Cavaliere of Italian Republic, 1982; Golden Campidoglio, 1975; Leonardo da Vinci, 1978; Dante Aligheri, 1979; Soverato, 1985; Brugnato, 1988; Fano, 1989; Sutri, 1990; Firenze, 1991; Catania, 1998; Many works in private and public collections around the world. Address: Via F Ili Cervi, 8 – Macerata, Italy.

**ANGELIDIS Angel,** b. 28 October 1946, Alexandroupolis, Greece; Engineer; Economist. Education: MSc, Agricultural University of Athens, Greece; PhD, Polytechnic University of Madrid, Spain; PhD, University of Montpellier, France. Appointments: Director, Ministry of Co-ordination, Athens, Greece; Member of the Cabinet of a Commissioner, EU Commission, Brussels, Belgium; Head of Division, European Parliament, Luxembourg; Advisor, European Parliament, Luxembourg. Publications: EU and the Forests; The EU Rural Development Policy; The Agricultural Agreement of the Uruguay Round of GATT; Manual of the Common Fisheries Policy of the EU; The New Reform of the Common Agricultural Policy of the EU; Actions in Favour of the Ultra-Peripheral Regions of the EU. Honours: Vice-President of the Agricultural Economic Society of Greece; Orden de Merito Agricola, Spain; Orden Isabela Catolica (in course), Spain. Address: 23 rue J P Sauvage, L-2514 Luxembourg. E-mail: aangelidis@europarl.eu.int

**ANGELOU Maya,** b. 4 April 1928, St Louis, Missouri, USA. Author. Appointments: Associate editor, Arab Observer, 1961-62; Assistant administrator, teacher, School of Music and Drama, University of Ghana, 1963-66; Feature editor, African Review, Accra, 1964-66; Reynolds Professor of American Studies, Wake Forest University, 1981-; Teacher of modern dance, Rome Opera House, Hambina Theatre, Tel Aviv; Member, Board of Governors, Maya Angelou Institute for the Improvement of Child and Family Education, Winston-Salem State University, North Carolina, 1998-; Theatre appearances include: Porgy and Bess, 1954-55; Calypso, 1957; The Blacks, 1960; Mother Courage, 1964; Look Away, 1973; Roots, 1977; How to Make an American Quilt, 1995; Plays: Cabaret for Freedom, 1960; The Least of These, 1966; Getting' Up Stayed On My Mind, 1967; Ajax, 1974; And Still I Rise, 1976; Moon On a Rainbow Shawl (producer), 1988. Film: Down in the Delta (director), 1998. Publications include: I Know Why the Caged Bird Sings, 1970; Just Give Me A Cool Drink of Water 'Fore I Die, 1971; Georgia, Georgia (screenplay), 1972; Oh Pray My Wings Are Gonna Fit Me Well, 1975; Singin' and Swingin' and Gettin' Merry Like Christmas, 1976; And Still I Rise, 1976; The Heart of a Woman, 1981; Shaker, Why Don't You Sing, 1983; All God's Children Need Travelling Shoes, 1986; Now Sheba Sings the Song, 1987; I Shall Not Be Moved, 1990; Gathered Together in My Name, 1991; Wouldn't Take Nothing for my Journey Now, 1993; Life Doesn't Frighten Me, 1993; Collected Poems, 1994; My Painted House, My Friendly Chicken and Me, 1994; Phenomenal Woman, 1995; Kofi and His Magic, 1996; Even the Stars Look Lonesome, 1997; Making Magic in the World, 1998. Honours: Horatios Alger Award, 1992; Grammy Award Best Spoken

Word or Non-Traditional Album, 1994; Honorary Ambassador to UNICEF, 1996-; Lifetime Achievement Award for Literature, 1999; National Medal of Arts; Distinguished visiting professor at several universities; Chubb Fellowship Award, Yale University; Nominated, National Book Award, I Know Why the Caged Bird Sings; Tony Award Nomination, Performances in Look Away; Honorary degrees, Smith College, Lawrence University; Golden Eagle Award; First Reynolds Professor; The Matrix Award; American Academy of Achievements Golden Plate Award; Distinguished Woman of North Carolina; Essence Woman of the Year; Many others. Memberships: The Directors Guild of America; Equity; AFTRA; Woman's Prison Association; Harlem Writers Guild; Horatio Alger Association of Distinguished Americans; National Society for the Prevention of Cruelty to Children. Address: Care Dave La Camera, Lordly and Dame Inc, 51 Church Street, Boston, MA 02116-5417, USA.

**ANGUS Beverley Margaret,** b. 18 November 1934, Lautoka, Fiji. Parasitologist. m. James Robert Angus, 1 son, 1 daughter. Education: BSc, 1979, PhD, 1994, University of Queensland, Australia; Graduate Diploma, Education, Queensland University of Technology, Australia. Appointments: Scientific Researcher, 1980-; Research Associate and Honorary Consultant, Queensland Museum, Australia, 1997-. Publications: Books: Tick Fever and Cattle Tick in Australia 1829-1996, 1998; Parasitology and the Queensland Museum. Memberships: Australian Society for Parasitology; Australian Society for History of Medicine; Australian Veterinary History Society; Professional Historians' Association of Australia, Queensland. Address: 96 Mallawa Drive, Palm Beach, Queensland 4221, Australia. E-mail: bmangus@bigpond.net.au

**ANGUS Kenneth William, (Ken Angus),** b. 13 August 1930, Rhu, Dunbartonshire, Scotland. Veterinary Pathologist. m. Marna Renwick Redpath, 4 November 1977, 1 son. Education: BVMS, Glasgow, 1955; FRCVS, 1976; DVM, Glasgow, 1985. Publications: Scotchpotch, 1995; Eechtie-Peechtie-Pandy, 1996; Wrack and Pinion, 1997; Breakfast with Kilroy, 2000; Only the Sound of Sparrows, 2001; Conversations with Hamsters, 2002; A Little Overnight Rain, 2004. Contributions to: New Writing Scotland; First Time; Cencrastus; Orbis; Poetry Scotland; Poetry Monthly; Poetry Life; Scarp (University of Wollongong, Berrima, Australia); Staple. Honours: Scottish International Poetry Competition, 1998. Memberships: Scottish Poetry Library; Poetry Association of Scotland. Address: 12 Temple Village, Gorebridge, Midlothian EH23 4SQ, Scotland.

**ANGUS Michael Richardson (Sir),** b. 5 May 1930, Ashford, Kent, England. Company Director. m. Eileen Isabel May Elliott, 1952, 2 sons, 1 daughter. Education: BSc, Bristol University. Appointments: Served RAF, 1951-54; Joined Unilever PLC, 1954; Marketing Director, 1962-65, Managing Director, Research Bureau, 1965-67, Thibaud Gibbs, Paris, France, 1962-65; Sales Director, Lever Brothers, UK, 1967-70; Director, Unilever PLC and Unilever NV, 1970-92, Toilet Preparations Co-ordinator, 1970-76, Chemicals Co-ordinator, 1976-80, Regional Director, North America, 1979-84, Chair, Chief Executive Officer, Unilever United States Inc, New York, 1980-84, Chair, Chief Executive Officer, Lever Brothers Co, New York, 1980-84, Vice-Chair, 1984-86, Chair, 1986-92, Unilever PLC, Vice-Chair, Unilever NV, 1986-92; Governor, 1974, Chair of Governors, 1991-2002, Ashridge Management College; Joint Chair, 1984-89, President, 1990-94, Netherlands British Chamber of Commerce; Director, Leverhulme Trust, 1984-; Member of Council, 1986-, President, 1998, British Executive Service Overseas; Non-Executive Director, 1986-, Deputy Chair, 1992, Chair, 1992-99, Whitbread PLC; Non-Executive

Director, Thorn EMI PLC, 1988-93; Non-Executive Director, 1988-2000, Deputy Chair, 1989-2000, British Airways PLC; Director, 1991-, Deputy Chair, 1991-94, National Westminster Bank PLC; Deputy President, 1991-92, 1994-95, President, 1992-94, Confederation of British Industry; Chair of Governors, Royal Agricultural College, Cirencester, 1992-; Director, 1994-2000, Chair, 1994-98, Deputy Chair, 1998-2000, The Boots Co PLC; Member, Council of Management, Ditchley Foundation, 1994-; D L Gloucestershire, 1997; Chair, RAC Holdings Ltd, 1999-. Honours: Holland Trade Award, 1990; Honorary DSc, Bristol, 1990; Knight Bachelor, 1990; Commander, Order of Orange Nassau, 1992; Honorary DSc, Buckingham, 1994; Honorary LLD, Nottingham, 1996. Memberships: Companion, Institute of Management. Address: Cerney House, North Cerney, Cirencester, Gloucestershire GL7 7BX, England.

**ANIE Sylvia Josephine.** Director of Policy Planning, Research, Monitoring and Evaluation. Education: BSc, 1st Class Honours, Applied Chemistry, University of Greenwich, England, 1982-86; PhD, Medical School, University of Manchester, England, 1986-90; Professional Certificate in Management, Open University Business School, England, 1995; Certificate, Principles and Practices of Behaviour Change Communication, Family Health International, 2001; Certificate, Strengthening Monitoring and Evaluation of National HIV/AIDS Programmes in the Context of the Expanded Response, MEASURE Evaluation, 2001; Certificate, Evaluation of AIDS Programmes, Makerere University, Uganda, 2002; Diploma: HIV and AIDS Prevention, College of Venereal Disease Prevention, London, 2004. Appointments: Junior Analyst, Drug Control and teaching Centre, Kings College, University of London, 1986; Teaching Assistant, Department of Pharmacy, University of Manchester, England, 1986-89; Postdoctoral Researcher, University College London/Institute of Neurology, University of London, 1990; Medical and Scientific Research Advisor, The Spastics Society, England, 1991-96; Deputy Chief Executive, Korle Bu Teaching Hospital, Ghana, 1997-2001; Director of Policy Planning, Research, Monitoring, Evaluation, Ghana AIDS Commission, Ghana, 2001-; Current Consultancies: World Bank; UNDP; Danida-Danish AID Programme; USAID Partners for Health Reformplus; UNDP-GOG; UNAIDS; IBIS NGO. Articles in scientific journals and reports as co-author include: Mutual health Organisations: A Quality Information Survey in Ghana, 2002; Contributor to: HIV/AIDS related knowledge, attitudes and behaviour. Demographic and Health Survey, Ghana, 2003; Balancing science, pragmatics and the need for collaboration in Ghana: How to be strategic in planning a national M/E system, 2004. Memberships: Fellow, Society of Medicine, UK; Professional Member and Chartered Chemist, Royal Society of Chemistry, UK; International Society of Magnetic Resonance in Medicine. Address: Ghana AIDS Commission, PO Box CT 5169, Accra, Ghana. E-mail: dranie@africaonline.com.gh

**ANIKPO Daniel,** b, 1 January 1948, Ivory Coast. Consultant. m. Emilienne N'Tame Anikpo, 1 son, 2 daughters. Education: Master's Degree in Economics, 1974; Postgraduate Degree in Agro-Economics, 1975; Postgraduate Degree in Economics, 1975. Appointments: Head Manager, Engineers and Technicians Council; Minister of Trade, Ivory Coast; Freelance Consultant, Geneva, Switzerland. Publications: Books: Du Défi au pari africain, Le Projet de Société de Consensus et de participation; La Mega-Economie, Revoir le Developpement. Honours: Man of the Year, American Biographical Institute, 2005; Listed as one of the 1000 Great Minds of the 21st Century, American Biographical Institute; Listed as one of the 2000 Outstanding Intellectuals of the 21st Century, International Biographical Centre, England. Memberships: Black Educated Urban Professionals, Geneva. Address: 213 Route de Malangou,

1224 Chene-Bougeries, Geneva, Switzerland. E-mail: anikpodaniel@mega-economie.li

**ANISTON Jennifer,** b. 11 February 1969, Sherman Oaks, California, USA. Actress. m. Brad Pitt, 2000. Education: New York High School of the Performing Arts. Appointments: Theatre includes: For Dear Life; Dancing on Checker's Grave; Films include: Leprechaun, 1993; She's The One, 1996; Dream for an Insomniac, 1996; 'Til There Was You, 1996; Picture Perfect, 1997; The Object of My Affection, 1998; Office Space, 1999; The Iron Giant, 1999; Rock Star, 2001; The Good Girl, 2002; TV includes, Molloy (series), 1989; The Edge; Ferris Bueller; Herman's Head; Friends, 1994-2004. Honours: Emmy Award for Best Actress, 2002; Golden Globe for Best TV Actress in a Comedy, 2003. Address: c/o CAA, 9830 Wilshire Boulevard, Beverly Hills, CA 90212, USA.

**ANN-MARGARET,** b. 1941, Stockholm, Sweden. Actress; Singer; Dancer. m. Roger Smith, 1967. Appointments: Film Debut, Pocketful of Miracles, 1961; Films include: State Fair; Bye Bye Birdie; Once a Thief; The Cincinnati Kid; Stagecoach; Murderer's Row; C C & Co; Carnal Knowledge; RPM; Train Robbers; Tommy; The Twist; Joseph Andrews; Last Remark of Beau Geste; Magic; Middle Age Crazy; Return of the Soldier; I Ought to be in Pictures; Looking to Get Out; Twice in a Lifetime; 52 Pick-Up, 1987; New Life, 1988; Something More; Newsies, 1992; Grumpy Old Men, 1993; Grumpier Old Men, 1995; Any Given Sunday, 1999; The Last Producer, 2000; A Woman's a Helluva Thing, 2000; TV includes: Who Will Love My Children?, 1983; A Streetcar Named Desire, 1984; The Two Mrs Grenvilles, 1987; Our Sons, 1991; Nobody's Children, 1994; Following her Heart; Seduced by Madness; The Diana Borchardt Story, 1996; Blue Rodeo, 1996; Pamela Hanniman, 1999; Happy Face Murders, 1999; Perfect Murder, Perfect Town, 2000; The Tenth Kingdom, 2000; Also appears in cabaret. Publications: (with Todd Gold) Ann-Margaret: My Story, 1994. Honours: Five Golden Globe Awards; Three Female Star of the Year Awards. Address: William Morris Agency, 151 S, El Camino Drive, Beverly Hills, CA 90212, USA.

**ANNADURAI S,** b. 13 July 1967, Vellore, Tamilnadu, India. Pharmacist; Teacher; Researcher. m. I A Tamizharas, 1 daughter. Education: DPharm, Christian Medical College, Vellore, 1986; BPharm, Madras Medical College, Madras, 1990; MPharm, 1993, PhD (Pharmacy), 1998, Jadavpur University, Calcutta. Appointments: Pharmacy Intern, Christian Medical College, 1986; Graduate Apprentice, Indian Drugs and Pharmaceuticals Ltd, Madras, 1991; Junior Research Fellow, UGC at Jadavpur University, 1991-93; Lecturer in Pharmacy, S B College of Pharmacy, Sivakasi, 1993-94; Senior Research Fellow, CSIR at Jadavpur University, 1994-97; Lecturer, 1998-2002, Central and State Government Approved Formulation and Manufacturing Chemist, 1999-, Senior Lecturer, PhD grade, 2002-, Reader in Pharmacy, 2004, Department of Pharmacy, Christian Medical College. Publications: Original scientific research papers in many national and international conferences; Articles in peer-reviewed journals, 8 international and 2 national; Co-author, text book. Honours: First Class First in Order of Merit; Gold Medals in DPharm and MPharm; University Rank holder in BPharm; Junior Research Fellowship, UGC; Senior Research Fellowship, CSIR. Memberships: Indian Pharmaceutical Association; Indian Graduates Pharmacy Association; Association of Pharmacy Teachers of India; Indian Institute of Chemists; State Pharmacy Council of India; Life Fellow Institution of Chemists (India), 2003-; Man of the Year Commemorative Award, 2005; Adviser, International Research Board; Member, American Biographical Institute, USA, 2005. Address: Department of Pharmacy, Christian Medical College and Hospital, Ida Scudder Road,

Vellore 632 004, Vellore District, Tamilnadu State, India. E-mail: annadurai36@hotmail.com

**ANNAN Henry George**, b. 23 October 1945, Accra, Ghana. Consultant Obstetrician and Gynaecologist. m. Zetha Melanie, 4 sons, 1 daughter. Education: Cambridge University and St Bartholomew's Hospital, 1966-73; MA (Cantab) MB B Chir, 1973; MRCOG, 1978; FRCOG, 1992; MEWI, 1996; FICS, 2003; FGCPS, 2004; FFFP, 2005. Appointments: Consultant Obstetrician and Gynaecologist, Whipps Cross University Hospital, 1986-; Recognised Clinical Teacher and Honorary Senior Lecturer, University of London, 1991-; Clinical Director, 1995-98; Examiner for RCOG, GMC (PLAB) and MBBS; RCOG College Tutor and Preceptor in Minimal Access Surgery, 1997-; Council Member, Obstetrics and Gynaecology Section, RSM, 1987-90; RCOG Hospital Recognition Committee, 1997-2000; Member, International Editorial Advisory Board for Obstetrics and Gynaecology Today, 2001-. Publications: Many publications in medical journals, 1980-2004; Presentations and lectures to healthcare professionals at local, regional, national and international meetings. Honours: Vice Chair, African Caribbean Medical Society, 1991-93; Justice of the Peace, 1996-2001; Governor, Epping Forest College, Freeman of the City of London, 1999; Professional Achievers Award for Medicine, Innovation and Dedication, 2002; Gathering of Africa's Best Award for Achievement, 2003. Memberships: British Society of Gynaecological Endoscopy; American Association of Gynecological Laparoscopists; International Continence Society; Royal Society of Medicine; Worshipful Society of Apothecaries of London; Founder Member, Expert Witness Institute; MCC; Guards Polo Club; ROSL; Oxford and Cambridge Club; Fellow, Atlantic Council of UK. Address: Bachelors Hall, York Hill, Loughton, Essex IG10 1HZ, England. E-mail: henrygannan@hotmail.com

**ANNAUD Jean-Jacques**, b. 1 October 1943, Juvisy, Orge, France. Film Director. m. (1) Monique Rossignol, 1970, divorced, 1980, 1 daughter, (2) Laurence Duval, 1982, 1 daughter. Education: Institut des Hautes Etudes Cinématographiques, Paris; L-ès-L, Sorbonne, University of Paris. Career: Freelance Commercial Film Director, 500 films, 1966-75; Director, feature films including Black and White in Colour, 1976; Hot Head, 1979; Quest for Fire, 1981; Name of the Rose, 1988; The Bear, 1988; The Lover, 1992; Wings of Courage, 1994; Seven years in Tibet, 1997; Enemy at the Gates, 2001. Honours: Academy Award for Best Foreign Film, 1976; César Award, 1981; 2 César Awards, 1988. Address: 9 rue Guénégard, 75006 Paris, France.

**ANNEAR Jeremy**, b. 18 February 1949, Exeter, Devon, England. Artist. m. Judy Buxton, 2 sons, 3 daughters. Education: Shebbear College, UK, 1960-65; Exeter College of Art, UK, 1966-69; BEd, Rolle College/Exeter University, 1973-76. Appointments: Assistant Director, Dyrons Arts Centre, 1976-84; Lecturer, South Devon College, 1982-84; Director, Ryders Gallery/Art Centre, 1984-86; Visiting Lecturer, Cheltenham College of Art, 1997-98; Established reputation with many national and international solo and mixed exhibitions. Publications: Catalogue forward: Norbert Lynton & John Russell Taylor, Messums Fine Art, 1997/98 and 2000; Galleries Magazine review, 2001; Catching the Wave : Contemporary Art & Artists in Cornwall, 2002. Honours: Work in public collections: Lazard Bros, UK; Ionian Trust, UK; The Royal Holloway Collection, UK; The Royal West of England Academy, UK. Memberships: Elected Member, Penwith Society of Artists, 1988; Elected Member, Newlyn Society of Artists, 1989; Elected Committee, Newlyn Society of Artists, 1993; Elected Council of Management, Newlyn Art Gallery, 1993.

Address: Chapel House, Garras, Helston, Cornwall, TR12 6LN, England. E-mail: jeremy-annear@tiscali.co.uk

**ANNESLEY Hugh (Sir)**, b. 22 June 1939, Dublin, Ireland. Police Officer. m. Elizabeth Ann MacPherson, 1970, 1 son, 1 daughter. Appointments: Joined Metropolitan Police, 1958; Assistant Chief Constable of Sussex with special responsibility for personnel and training, 1976; Deputy Assistant Commissioner, Assistant Commissioner, 1985, Metropolitan Police; Head, Operations Department, Scotland Yard, 1987-89; Chief Constable, Royal Ulster Constabulary, 1989-96. Honours: Queen's Police Medal. Memberships: National Executive Institute, Federal Bureau of Investigation, 1986; Executive Committee, Interpol, British Representative, 1987-90, 1993-94; Member, 1997, Chair, 2000-, Board of Governors, Hill School for Girls. Address: c/o Brooklyn, Knock Road, Belfast BT5 6LE, Northern Ireland.

**ANNIS Francesca**, b. 1945, Actress. 1 son, 2 daughters. Appointments: with Royal Shakespeare Company, 1975-78; Plays include: The Tempest; The Passion Flower Hotel; Hamlet; Troilus and Cressida; Comedy of Errors; The Heretic; Mrs Klein; Rosmersholm; Lady Windermere's Fan; Hamlet; Films include: Cleopatra; Saturday Night Out; Murder Most Foul; The Pleasure Girls; Run With the Wind; The Sky Pirates; The Walking Stick; Penny Gold; Macbeth; Krull; Dune; Under the Cherry Moon; Golden River; El Rio de Oro; The Debt Collector; the End of the Affair; TV includes: Great Expectations; Children in Uniform; Love Story; Danger Man; The Human Jungle; Lily Langtry (role of Lily); Madam Bovary; Partners in Crime; Coming Out of Ice; Why Didn't They Ask Evans?; Magnum PI; Inside Story; Onassis - The Richest Man in the World, 1990; Parnell and the Englishwoman, 1991; Absolute Hell, 1991; The Gravy Train, 1991; Weep No More My Lady, 1991; Between the Lines, 1993; Reckless, 1997; Deadly Summer, 1997; Wives and Daughters, 1999; Milk, 1999; Deceit, 2000. Address: c/o ICM, 76 Oxford Street, London, W1N 0AX, England.

**ANOMOHANRAN Ochuko**, b. 10 May 1967, Eku, Nigeria. Lecturer. m. Eguono Anomohanran, 1 daughter. Education: BSc, Physics, Bendel State University, Ekpoma, Nigeria, 1990; MSc, Geophysics, Ambrose Alli University, Ekpoma, Nigeria, 1996. Appointments: Physics Lecturer, Bauchi State Polytechnic, Nigeria, 1990-91; Physics and Mathematics Tutor, Ziks Grammar School, Sapele, Nigeria, 1991-92; Physics Lecturer, Delta State University, Abraka, Nigeria, 1992-. Publications: A survey of x-ray diagnostic services in Delta State Nigeria; The effect of gamma irradiation on the germination and growth of certain Nigerian agricultural crops; Comparative study of environmental noise in parts of Delta State, Nigeria; The use of 3rd degree polynomal for accurate conversion of time to depth; Energy generation, uses and distribution; The sky and its content. Honour: Outstanding Scientist of the 21st Century. Memberships: Institute of Physics, London; Science Association of Nigeria; Nigeria Institute of Physics. Address: Physics Department, Delta State University, PMB 1, Abraka, Delta State, Nigeria. E-mail: mrochuko@yahoo.com

**ANONGBA Patrick Norbert B**, b. 3 February 1960, Abidjan, Cote D'Ivoire. Physicist; Educator. m. Maria Teresa Varela, 2 sons, 1 daughter. Education: Physical Engineer, Department of Physics, 1985, DSc, 1989, Ecole Polytechnique Fédérale de Lausanne. Appointments: Assistant, Ecole Polytechnique Fédérale de Lausanne, 1985-90; Postdoctoral Research Associate, Institut de Physique Expérimentale, Université de Lausanne, 1990-92; Research Associate, Max-Planck-Institut für Metallforschung, Stuttgart, Germany, 1992-94; Assistant Professor, 1995-97, Associate Professor, 1997-, UFR Sciences des Structures de la Matière et de Technologie, Université de Cocody, Cote d'Ivoire. Publications: Several articles in professional journals. Honours include: Research Fellow, Max-Planck-Institut-Gesellschaft, 1992-94, Japan Society for the Promotion of Science, 1996-97; Fulbright Research Fellow, Department of Materials, Science and Engineering, University of Pennsylvania, 2000-01; Visiting Professor, Universidad Politécnica de Cataluña, Spain, 2002-2003. Memberships: Swiss Physical Society; New York Academy of Sciences; Japan Society for the Promotion of Science. Address: UFR Sciences des Structures de la Matière et de Technologie, Université de Cocody, Cote d'Ivoire. E-mail: anongba@yahoo.fr

**ANOSOV Dmitry Victorovich,** b. 30 November 1936, Moscow. Mathematician. m. Lidia Ivanovna Kramarenko, 1 daughter. Education: Department of Mathematics and Mechanics, Moscow State University, 1953-58; Postgraduate Courses, Steklov Maths Institute, 1958-61. Appointments: Professor, Moscow State University, 1968-73, 1996-; Professor, Independent Moscow University, 1993-; Various Positions, Steklov Maths Institute, 1961- up to Chief of Department, Differential Equations, 1997-; Chief of the Chair, Dynamical Systems, 2000-. Publications: About 55 papers including: Geodesic Flows on Closed Riemanian Manifolds with Negative Curvature; The Riemann-Hillbert Problem (co-author). Honours: Prize, Moscow Mathematics Society; State Prize of USSR; Humboldt Prize; Lyapunov Prize of Russian Academy of Science (jointly with A I Neistadt), 2001; Honourable Professor, Moscow State University. Memberships: Presidium Member, Moscow Mathematics Society; Russian Academy of Science; Former Associate Member, Academy of Sciences, USSR. Address: Steklov Mathematical Institute, Gubkina Str 8, 119991 Moscow GSP 1, Russia.

**ANSTEE Margaret Joan (Dame),** b. 25 June 1926, Writtle, Essex, England. United Nations Official; Lecturer; Consultant; Author. Education: Modern and Medieval Languages, Newnham College, Cambridge, 1944-47; MA, Newnham College, 1955; BSc, Economics, London University, 1964. Appointments: Lecturer in Spanish, Queen's University, Belfast, 1947-48; Third Secretary, Foreign Office, 1948-52; Administrative Officer, UN Technical Assistance Board, Manila, 1952-54; Spanish Supervisor, University of Cambridge, 1955-56; Officer-in-Charge, UN Technical Assistance Board, Bogota, 1956-57, Resident Representative, Uruguay, 1957-59, Bolivia, 1960-65; Resident Representative, UNDP Ethiopia and UNDP Liaison Officer, ECA, 1965-67; Senior Economic Adviser, Office of Prime Minister, London, 1967-68; Senior Assistant to Commissioner in charge of study of Capacity of UN Development System, 1968-69; Resident Representative, UNDP, Morocco, 1969-72, Chile (also UNDP Liaison Officer with ECLA) 1972-74; Deputy to UN Under Secretary General in charge of UN Relief Operation to Bangladesh and Deputy Co-ordinator of UN Emergency Assistance to Zambia, 1973; Deputy Regional Director for Latin America, UNDP, New York, 1974-78; Deputy Assistant Administrator and Head, UNDP Administrator's Special Unit, 1975-77; Assistant Secretary-General of UN, Department of Technical Co-operation for Development), 1978-87; Special Representative of Secretary-General to Bolivia, 1982-92, for co-ordination of earthquake relief assistance to Mexico, 1985-87; Under Secretary-General, UN, 1987-93, Director-General of UN office at Vienna, Head of Centre for Social Development and Humanitarian Affairs, 1987-92, Special Representative of Secretary-General for Angola and Head of Angolan Verification Mission, 1992-93; Adviser to UN Secretary-General on peacekeeping, post-conflict peacebuilding and training troops for UN peacekeeping missions, 1994-; Chair, Advisory Group of Lessons Learned Unit, Department

of Peacekeeping Operations, UN, 1996-2002; Co-ordinator of UN Drug Control Related Activities, 1987-90, of International Co-operation for Chernobyl, 1991-92; Secretary-General, 8th UN Congress on Prevention of Crime and Treatment of Offenders, August 1990; Writer, lecturer, consultant and adviser (ad honorem) to Bolivian Government, 1993-97, 2002-. Publications: The Administration of International Development Aid, 1969; Gate of the Sun: A Prospect of Bolivia, 1970; Africa and the World, 1970; Orphan of the Cold War: The Inside Story of the Collapse of the Angolan Peace Process, 1992-93, 1996; Never Learn to Type: A woman at the United Nations, 2003, 2nd edition, 2004. Memberships: Member, Advisory Board, UN Studies at Yale University, 1996-; Member, Advisory Council, Oxford Research Group, 1997-; Member, Advisory Board, UN Intellectual History Project, 1999-; Trustee, Helpage International, 1994-97; Patron and Board Member, British Angola Forum, 1998-; Member, President Carter's International Council for Conflict Resolution, 2001-; Vice President, UK UN Association, 2002-. Honours: Honorary Fellow, Newnham College, Cambridge, 1991; Dr h c (Essex), 1994; Honorary LLD (Westminster), 1996; Honorary DSc (Economics) (London), 1998; Hon LLD, (Cambridge) 2004; Reves Peace Prize, William & Mary College, USA, 1993; Commander, Ouissam Alaouite, Morocco, 1972; Dama Gran Cruz Condor of the Andes, Bolivia, 1986; Grosse Goldene Ehrenzeichen am Bande, Austria, 1993; Dame Commander of the Most Distinguished Order of St Michael and St George, 1994. Address: c/o PNUD, Casilla 9072, La Paz, Bolivia; c/o The Walled Garden, Knill, Nr Presteigne, Powys LD8 2PR, United Kingdom.

**ANTE (Nadia Pešautová),** b. 18 August 1951, Krnov, Czech Republic. Artist; Painter. m. Vratislav Paur, 2 daughters. Education: Charles University, Prague, 1988-91; Drawing, painting and restoration with Mr M Hladky and Professor Vojkovsky. Career: Professional artist; Owner, Archa-Art-Gallery, Prague; Organiser of exhibitions to introduce new artists from the Czech Republic and overseas; Solo exhibitions include: Czech Republic: The Prague House of Culture; The Green House Gallery, Prague; P+P Kobylka Gallery, Prague; Gallery JCM, Dobris; Volvo Salon, Prague; Hotel Hoffmeister, Prague; Studio Mobilizer Design, Prague; On-going exhibition at Archa-Art-Gallery, Prague; Abroad: Gallery Nievergelt, Zurich Switzerland; Gallery Millennium, Paris France; Lion Club, Paris, France; Studio Mobilizer Design, Bratislava, Slovak Republic; Joint exhibitions: Czech Republic: The Green House Gallery, Prague; The Dobris Chateau; Deslo Studio, Prague; European Property Development, Prague; Abroad: Stylusart, Barcelona, Spain; Gallery Keller, Geneva, Switzerland; Centre Culturel C Peugeot, Paris, France; Works in public collections: Museum of Modern Art, Monaco; The Dobris Chateau, Czech Republic; The Bechyne Chateau, Czech Republic; The City of Prague Collection; Gallery Nievergelt, Zurich, Switzerland; Gallery Millennium, Paris; Lion Club, Paris; DaVinci Strategic Advisors, Colorado Springs, USA; Works in private collections world-wide. Honours: Toile D'Or de L'Année 2002-2003, French Cultural Solidarity, 2003, Créateur d'Aujourd'hui, 2004, Federation National de La Culture Française; European Medal of Franz Kafka, European Circle of Franz Kafka, Prague, 2004; European Prize for Fine Arts, European Union of Arts, 2004; Listed in Who's Who publications and biographical and artistic dictionaries. Memberships: Patron, Sue Ryder Foundation; Member, European Art Group. Address: Prague, Czech Republic. E-mail: antepraha@seznam.cz

**ANTONIONI Michelangelo,** b. 29 September 1913, Ferrara, Italy. Film Director. m. (1) Letizia, 1942, (2) Enrica Fico, 1986. Education: University of Bologna. Appointments: Films include: Gente del Po, 1943-47; Amorosa Menzogna, 1949; NU, 1948;

Sette Canne un Vestito; La Villa dei Mostri; Superstizione, 1949; Documentaries: Cronaca di un Amore, 1950; La Signora Senza Camelie, 1951-52; I Vinti, 1952; Amore in Citta, 1953; Le Amiche, 1955; Il Grido, 1957; L'Avventura, 1959; La Notte, 1961; L'Eclisse, 1962; Il Deserto Rosso, 1964; Blow Up, 1966; Zabriskie Point, 1970; Chung Kuo-China, 1972; The Passenger, 1974; Il Mistero di Oberwald, 1979; Identificazione di una Donna, 1982; Fumbha Mela, 1989; Roma 90, 1989; Beyond the Clouds, 1995. Honours: City of Munich Prize; Critics Award, Cannes, 1960; Silver Bear, Berlin Film Festival, 1961; Golden Lion, XXV Venice Film Festival, 1964; Golden Palm, Cannes Film Festival, 1967; Best Director, Annual Awards, National Society of Film Critics; Grand Prix, Cannes Film Festival, 1982; Knight Grand Cross; Order of Merit; Commander, Ordre des Arts et des Lettres, 1992; Legion d'honneur. Address: Via Flemming III, 00191, Rome, Italy.

**ANTZELEVITCH Charles,** b. 25 March 1951, Israel. Executive Director. m. Brenda, 24 June 1973, 1 son, 1 daughter. Education: BA, Queens College, City University of New York, Flushing, 1973; PhD, University of New York at Syracuse, 1978. Appointments: Postdoctoral Fellow, Experimental Cardiology Department, Masonic Medical Research Laboratory, Utica, New York, 1977-80; Assistant Professor, Pharmacology Department, SUNY Health Science Centre, Syracuse, 1980-83; Research Scientist, Experimental Cardiology, Masonic Medical Research Laboratory, 1980-83; Associate Professor, Pharmacology Department, SUNY Health Science Centre, 1983-86; Senior Research Scientist, Experimental Cardiology, Masonic Medical Research Laboratory, 1984; Executive Director, Director of Research, 1984-, Gordon K Moe Scholar, 1987-, Masonic Medical Research Laboratory; Professor of Pharmacology, SUNY Health Science Centre, 1995-. Publications: Numerous articles in professional journals. Honours include: Distinguished Service Award, RAM Medical Research Foundation, 1994; Charles Henry Johnson Medal, Grand Lodge F and AM, NYS, 1996; Distinguished Scientist Award, NASPE, 2002; Excellence in Cardiovascular Science Award, NE Affiliate AHA, 2003. Memberships: AHA; Association for the Advancement of Science; FASEB; APS; Cardiac Electrophysiology Society; Upstate New York Cardiac Electrophysiology Society; New York Academy of Sciences; North American Society for Pacing and Electrophysiology; ISHR; ISCE. Address: Masonic Medical Research Laboratory, 2150 Bleecker Street, Utica, NY 13501, USA.

**AP-THOMAS Ifan,** b. 27 July 1917, Manchester, England. Retired Radiologist; Poet. m. Beti Robinson Owen, 29 Mar 1958, 1 son, 1 daughter. Education: MB, University of Edinburgh, 1939. Publications: Journey to the Silverless Island; The Oakwoods of Love. Address: 7 Bryn Estyn Road, Wrexham LL13 9ND, Wales.

**APASOV M Alexander,** b. 13 June 1950, Gorno-Altaisk, Russia. Physicist; Educator. m. Galina Vasilyevna Yemets, 1 son. Education: Engineer-Physicist, Tomsk Polytechnical Institute, 1967-73; Postgraduate, 1981-85; Candidate of Science, 1991; Associate Professor, 2000; Doctor of Science, 2002. Appointments: Laboratory Assistant, Joint Institute for Nuclear Research, Dubna, USSR, 1971-73; Senior Laboratory Assistant, Physical Energetic Institute, Obninsk, 1973-75; Engineer-Designer, Bolshevik Works, Leningrad, 1975-77; Chief of the Laboratory, Machine Works, Yurga, 1977-92; Chief of the Office, Abrasive Works, Yurga, 1992-95; Department Head, Dean, Tomsk Polytechnic University Branch, Yurga, Russia, 1995-2004. Publications: Welding Destruction (monograph), 2002; Special Electometallurgy (textbook), 2003; Physical Foundation of Non-Destructive

Testing During Welding (monograph), 2004; Materials Sciences (textbook), 2005; Method to Analyse Failure of Welded Joints (Certificate); Method of Non-Melting Revealing (patent); Other patents and articles. Honours: Prize-Winner (Laureate) Nuclear Physics, Obninsk, 1974; Prize-Winner (Laureate), Technical Physics, Yurga, 1980; Tomsk Polytechnic University, Associate Professor of the Year Contest Winner, 2003. Memberships: Deputy, Town Soviet of People's Deputies, 1990-95, 1997-99; First Lieutenant, Russian Military. Address: Moskovskay str. 26, Apart. 4, Yurga, Kemerovo Region, Russia 652050. E-mail: mchm@ud.tpu.edu.ru

**APPIAH James Peter King,** b. 16 February 1951, Baman, Kumasi, Ghana. Writer; Apostle. m. Angela Mabel Asare, 1 daughter. Education: Unesco Certificate in Writing and Publishing, 1972; Certificate of Completion, Morris Cerullo School of Ministry, San Diego, 1981; BA, Literary Studies, Pacific Western University, 1990; Diploma in Journalism, Story Writing, ICS Scranton, 1993; PhD, English Grade A, Washington International University, USA, 2001; Masters Degree in Biblical Studies, Dec.2004, Grade A, Florida Christian University, Orlando, FL. U.S.A. Appointments: Library Assistant, Ghana Library, 1973-76; Founder, President, Followers of Christ International Church, FOCIC, 1974; Director, Adonten Literary Works, Kumasi, 1976-95; Ordained Bishop, Universal Ministries, 1980 President, Founder, Director, Editor in Chief, Appiah Esthermat Ltd, 1995; Feed the Poor and Preach the Gospel Ministries, 2002. Publications: The Lord of Praise, 1988; Prayer, The Key to a Triumphant Christian Living, 1992; Overcomers in the Blood, 1995; The Meaning of Pentecost, 1995; Ode to the Dead, Dedicated to the Princess of the People, 1998; Many other publications. Honours: Mondello Poetry International Award, First Prize, 1987; Honoured, City of Palermo (Unione Quartieri), 1988; Deputy Governor, ABI, 1999; Appointed to Research Board of Advisors, ABI, 2002; Selected among 500 Leading Intellectuals of the World and Great Minds of the Century, ABI, 2002. Memberships: Morris Cerullo World Evangelism, Italy 1995-; United Christians Association in Italy, 1996; United Christians Association, 1998-; Ghana Young Pioneers; Ghana Youth Club; Ghana Association of Writers; United Christian Association; Christian Writers Forum; Member of the Adonten Royal Family of Asante, Mansa Nana. Address: Via Michele Fusco 95/2, 41100 Modena, Italy.

**APPLEBY Malcolm Arthur,** b. 6 January 1946, Beckenham, Kent, England. Artist. m. Philippa Swann, 1 daughter. Education: Beckenham School of Art; Ravensbourne College of Art; Central School of Arts and Crafts; Sir John Cass School of Art; Royal College of Art. Career: Artist, Designer and Engraver; Held one-man art exhibition, Aberdeen Art Gallery, 1998. Honours: Littledale Scholar, 1969; Liveryman, Worshipful Company of Goldsmiths, 1991; Hon D Litt, Heriot-Watt, 2000. Address: Aultbeag, Grandtully, by Aberfeldy, Perthshire PH15 2QU, Scotland.

**APPLEYARD Sir Raymond K,** b. 5 October 1922, Birtley, England. Scientist. m. Joan Greenwood, 1947, 1 son, 1 daughter. Education: Trinity College, Cambridge. Appointments: Instructor, Physics and Biophysics, Tale University, 1949-51; Fellow, Natural Sciences, Rockerfeller Foundation, 1951-53; Associate Research Officer, Atomic Energy of Canada Ltd, 1953-56; Secretary, UN Science Committee on the Effects of Atomic Radiation, 1957-61; Director, Biology Services, European Atomic Energy Community (EURATOM), 1961-73; Executive Secretary, European Molecular Biology Organisation, 1965-73; Secretary, European Molecular Biology Conference, 1969-73; Director General, Science and Technical Information and Information Management Commission of European

# DICTIONARY OF INTERNATIONAL BIOGRAPHY

Communities, 1973-81; Information Market and Innovation, 1981-86; President, Institute of Information Sciences, 1981-82; Institute of Translation and Interpreting, 1989-94; Honorary Doctor of Medicine (Ulm), 1977.

**APROBERTS Ruth,** b. 14 November 1919, Vancouver, British Columbia, Canada. University Professor of English. m. Robert P apRoberts, 1 son, 3 daughters. Education: BA, University of British Columbia, 1941; MA, University of California, Berkeley, 1950; PhD, University of California, Los Angeles, 1966. Appointments: Lecturer, UC, Los Angeles; Lecturer, Haceteppe University, Ankara, Turkey, 1969-70; Assistant Professor, 1971, Full Professor, 1978, Professor Emeritus, 1991-, University of California, Riverside. Publications: Trollope, Artist and Moralist, 1971; Arnold and God, 1984; The Ancient Dialect: Carlyle and Comparative Religion, 1988; The Biblical Web, 1994; Many articles and reviews. Honours: Outstanding Teacher, UCR, 1977; Guggenheim Fellow, 1978-79; Arnold and God, Outstanding Academic Book, Choice, 1984; Outstanding Emeritus, 1993. Memberships: MLA, Tyndale Society; Association of Literary Scholars and Critics; Walter Pater Society; William Morris Society; Trollope Society; Jane Austen Society. Address: 5970 Lincoln Avenue, Riverside, Lincoln, CA 92506, USA.

**APTED Michael,** b. 10 February 1941, Aylesbury, England. Film Director. Education: Cambridge University. Career: Researcher, Granada TV, 1963; Investigative Reporter, World in Action; Director debut as feature film director, The Triple Echo, 1972; Other films include Stardust, 1975; The Squeeze, 1977; Agatha, 1979; Coal Miner's Daughter, 1980; Continental Divide, 1981; P'TangYang Kipperbang, Gorky Park, 1983; Firstborn, 1984; Critical Condition, Gorillas in the Mist, 1988; Class Action, 1990; Incident at Oglala, Thunderheart, 1992; Blink, Moving the Mountain, 1993; Nell, 1994; Extreme Measures, 1996; Enigma, 2001; Enough, 2002; Television direction includes Coronation Street episodes, The Lovers comedy series, Folly Foot children's series, Another Sunday and Sweet F A, Kisses at Fifty, Poor Girl, Jack Point, UP document series including 28 UP, 35 UP, 42 UP; Always Outnumbered. Address: Michael Apted Film Co, 1901 Avenue of the Stars, Suite 1245, Los Angeles, CA 90067, USA.

**AQUINO Corazon (Cory),** b. 25 January 1933. Politician. m. Benigno S Aquino Jnr, 1954, assassinated 1983, 1 son, 4 daughter. Education: Mount St Vincent College, New York; Lived in USA in exile with husband, 1980-83. Appointments: President, Philippines, post-Marcos, 1986-92. Membership: United Nationalist Democratic Organization, 1985-; William Fulbright Prize for International Peace, 1996; Ramon Magsaysay Award for International Understanding, 1998. Address: 25 Times Street, Quezon City, Philippines.

**ARAGALL GARRIGA Giacomo (Jaime),** b. 6 June 1939, Barcelona, Spain. Tenor. Education: Studied with Francesco Puig in Barcelona and with Vladimir Badiali in Milan. Debut: La Fenice, Venice, 1963 in the first modern performance of Verdi's Jerusalem. Career: La Scala Milan in 1963 as Mascagni's Fritz; In 1965 sang in Haydn's Le Pescatrici with Netherlands Opera and at the Edinburgh Festival; Vienna Staatsoper debut in 1966 as Rodolfo in La Bohème; Covent Garden debut in 1966 as the Duke of Mantua; Metropolitan Opera debut in 1968; Guest appearances in Berlin, Italy, San Francisco and at the Lyric Opera Chicago; Sang at San Carlo Opera Naples in 1972 in a revival of Donizetti's Caterina Cornaro; Festival appearances at Bregenz and Orange in 1984 as Cavaradossi and Don Carlos; Sang Gabriele Adorno at Barcelona in 1990 and Don Carlos at the Orange Festival in 1990; Sang Rodolfo at Barcelona in

1991 and Don Carlos at the Deutsche Opera Berlin, 1992; Sang Cavaradossi at the Opéra Bastille, 1994. Other roles include Pinkerton, Romeo in I Capuleti e i Montecchi, Werther and Gennaro in Lucrezia Borgia. Recordings: La Traviata; Lucrezia Borgia; Faust; Rigoletto; Simon Boccanegra; Madama Butterfly. Address: c/o Stafford Law Associates, 6 Barham Close, Weybridge, Surrey KT13 9PR, England.

**ARAKAWA Hiroaki,** b. 18 August 1960, Akita, Japan. Medical Doctor; Radiologist. m. Kyoko Aoki, 2 daughters. Education: Bachelor of Science, Kyoko University, 1983; Graduate, Tohoku Medical School, 1989; Visiting Scholarship, Department of Radiology, University of California, San Francisco, 1996-97; Medical Doctor, St Marianna University School of Medicine, 1998. Appointments: Intern, Nakadori Hospital, 1989-91; Resident in Radiology, St Marianna University School of Medicine, 1991-96; Fellow, Department of Radiology, St Marianna University Hospital, 1997-2000; Assistant Professor, Department of Radiology, Dokkyo Medical School, 2000-. Publications: Books: Medical Radiology volume on Imaging of Occupational and Environmental Disorders; International Classification of HCRT for Occupational Lung Diseases, 2005; Articles in medical journals: Inhomogeneous lung attenuation at thin-section CT, 1998; Nonspecific Interstitial Pneumonia Associated with Polymyositis and Dermomyositis, 2003. Memberships: Japan Radiological Society; Radiologic Society of North America; Japanese Society of Thoracic Radiology. Address: 880 Kita-Kobayashi, Miba, Tochigi, 321-0293 Japan.

**ARAYA Negusse,** b. 16 August 1950, Eritrea. Educationalist. m. Gabriela, 3 sons, 1 daughter. Education: BA (Hons), Educational Administration, Addis Ababa University, Ethiopia, 1978-82; MA, International Education, 1985-87, PhD, Teacher Education, 1988-90, Humboldt University of Berlin, Germany. Appointments: Country Director, British Council, Eritrea, 1994-; Resident Representative, British Executive Services Overseas, 1995-; Chairman, Board of Directors of Haben (local NGO working in relief, rehabilitation and development programmes), 2000-. Publications: The status of co-curricular activities in selected secondary schools in Addis Ababa, Ethiopia, 1981; Progress and problems of Government Education in Ethiopia, 1987; Tasks and problems in the professional qualification of secondary teachers in Ethiopia taking into special consideration the programme of Asmara University, 1990. Membership: Family Reproductive Health Association of Eritrea. Address: PO Box 9217, Asmara, Eritrea.

**ARBNORI Pjeter,** b. 18 January 1935, Durrës, Albania. Academician; Writer; Member of International Informatization Academy in General Consultative Status of United Nations, New York, Geneve; Member of Parliament. m. Suzana Gjeluci, 16 June 1991, 1 son, 1 daughter. Education: Degree, Philology, 1960. Appointments: Teacher, 1953; Teacher of Literature, 1960-61; Founder, Social Democratic (illegal) Party, 1960; Sentenced to death and imprisoned, 28 years, 1961-89; Carpenter, 1989; Founder, Chairman, Democratic Party of Shkodra, 1990; MP, 1991; MP, Speaker of Parliament, 1992; MP, Speaker, 1996; MP, 1997 Commission on Human Rights; MP, 2001 Commission on Human Rights, 1997; Hunger strike, 20 days, August-September 1997; Supporter of Access of Opposition Parties in Electric Media, 1997. Publications include: Novels: Long Stories: Kur dynden vikingët; Bukuroshja me Hijen; Mugujt e Mesjetës; E bardha dhe e zeza; E panjohura; Vdekja e Gebelsit; Shtëpia e mbetur përgjysmë; Vorbulla; Nga jeta në burgjet komuniste; Letter from Prison; The Fight to Remain a Man: 10300 days and nights in the Prisons of Communism; The Martyrs, I Martiri, The New Martyrs in Albania (English); Translations: Histoire d'Angleterre, Andre Maurois; The Rise and Fall of the Third

Reich, Willam Shirer. Honours: People's Teacher; Torch of Democracy; Grand Officier de L'Ordre de Pleiade; The Pride of Scutari; Citizen of Honor of Vaudejës; President of the Board, Institute for Political Research "Alcide De Gasperi". Address: Rruga "Emin Duraku", Pallati 10/b, Tirana, Albania.

**ARBUTHNOTT Robert,** b. 28 September 1936, Kuala Lumpur, Malaysia. British Council Officer. m. (Sophie) Robina Axford, 1 son, 2 daughters. Education: BA, MA, Modern Languages, Emmanuel College, Cambridge, 1957-60; Institute of Education, London and School of Oriental and African Studies, 1972-73; Royal College of Defence Studies, 1986. Appointments: Military Service, 2nd Lieutenant The Black Watch, 1955-57; British Council Service, 1960-94: Karachi, Lahore, 1960-64, London, 1964-67, Representative, Nepal, 1967-72, Representative, Malaysia, 1973-76, Director, Educational Contracts, 1977-78, Controller Personnel, 1978-81, Representative, Germany, 1981-85; Minister (Cultural Affairs), British High Commission and Director British Council in India, 1988-93. Honours: Exhibitioner, Emmanuel College, Cambridge; CBE, 1991. Memberships: Fellow, Royal Asiatic Society; Member, Royal Society for Asian Affairs; Oxford-Cambridge Club. Address: Woodfield, Maplehurst, Horsham, West Sussex, RH13 6QY, England.

**ARCHANGELSKY Sergio,** b. 27 March 1931, Morocco. Palaeontologist. m. Jos Ballester, 1 son, 1 daughter. Education: PhD, Natural Sciences, Buenos Aires University, 1957. Appointments: Professor, La Plata University, 1961-78; Superior Researcher, National Research Council, Argentina, 1985-; Head, Paleobotany Division, Argentine Museum of Natural History, 1985-. Publications: Fundamentals of Palaeobotany, 1970; Fossil Flora of the Baqueró Group, Cretaceous, Patagonia, 2003. Honours: Visiting Professor, Ohio State University, USA, 1984; Corresponding Member, Botanical Society America, 1975; Academician, National Academy Sciences, Cordoba, 1990; Honorary Vice-President, XVI International Botanical Congress, St Louis, USA, 1999. Memberships: Argentine Geological Society; Argentine Palaeontological Society; British Palaeontological Association; Fellow, Paleobotanical Society, India. Address: Urquiza 1132 Vicente, Lopez B1638BWJ, Buenos Aires, Argentina.

**ARCHER Jeffrey Howard (Lord Archer of Weston-Super-Mare),** b. 15 April 1940, Mark, Somerset, England. Author; Politician. m. Mary Weeden, 2 sons. Education: Brasenose College, Oxford. Appointments: Member, GLC for Havering, 1966-70; Member of Parliament for Louth (Conservative), 1969-74; Deputy Chair, Conservative Party, 1985-86; Served two years of a four year prison sentence for perjury and perverting the course of justice, 2001. Publications: Not a Penny More, Not a Penny Less, 1975; Shall We Tell the President?, 1977; Kane & Abel, 1979; A Quiver Full of Arrows (short stories), 1980; The Prodigal Daughter, 1982; First Among Equals, 1984; A Matter of Honour, 1986; A Twist in the Tale (short stories), 1988; As The Crow Flies, 1991; Honour Among Thieves, 1993; Twelve Red Herrings (short stories), 1994; The Fourth Estate, 1995; Collected Short Stories, 1997; The Eleventh Commandment, 1998; To Cut a Long Story Short (short stories), 2000; A Prison Diary, Volumes I, II and III, 2003; Sons of Fortune, 2003; Plays: Beyond Reasonable Doubt, 1987; Exclusive, 1989; The Accused, 2000. Honours: Queen's Birthday Honours, 1992; Lord Archer of Western super Mare. Address: Peninsula Heights, 93 Albert Embankment, London SE1 7TY, England.

**ARCHER Richard Donald,** b. 3 July 1947, Leicester, England. School Teacher. Education: BA, University of Durham, 1965-69; PGCE, University of Liverpool, 1969-70; Mus B, Trinity College Dublin; M Mus, University of Sheffield; M Phil, University of East Anglia; FRCO; FTCL (Organ); LRAM (Piano Accompaniment)l ARCM (Organ); ADCM. Appointments: Head of Modern Languages, Stoneygate School, Leicester, 1989-; Conductor, Hinckley Choral Union, 1979-; Organist, Leicester Philharmonic Society Concerts, 1980-; Director of Music, St John the Baptist, Leicester, 1993-; Conductor, City of Leicester Singers, 1994-; Organist at Local Concerts; Guest Conductor; Accompanist. Compositions: Works for local choirs in manuscript including 2 sonnets; Fire of the Spirit; Recording: Fire of the Spirit. Honours: First Prize, Organ Playing Competition, Southport, 1976; Other organ playing competitions. Memberships: Incorporated Society of Musicians; Musicians Union; Royal College of Organists; Association of Teachers and Lecturers; Hymn Society of Great Britain and Ireland; Methodist Church Music Society. Address: 11 Frampton Avenue, Leicester LE3 0SG, England.

**ARCHER OF SANDWELL, Baron of Sandwell in the West Midlands; Peter Kingsley Archer,** b. 20 November 1926, Wednesbury, England. Barrister; MP (Retired). m. Margaret Irene, 1 son. Education: London School of Economics, 1948-50; University College, London, 1950-52; LLB (External, London), 1947; LLM, London, 1950; BA, Philosophy, London, 1952. Appointments: Barrister, 1954; QC, 1971; Retired, 1994; Recorder, 1980-96; Member of Parliament, 1966; Solicitor General, 1974-79; Shadow Cabinet: Legal Affairs, 1979-82, Trade, 1982-83, Northern Ireland, 1983-87; Member House of Lords, 1992; Chairman, Council on Tribunals, 1992-99; Chairman, Enemy Property Compensation Assessment Panel, 1999-. Publications: The Queen's Courts, 1956; Social Welfare and the Citizen, 1957; Communism and the Law, 1963; Freedom at Stake, 1966; Human Rights, 1969; Purpose in Socialism (Symposium), 1973. Honours: Privy Councillor, 1977; Honorary Fellow, University College London, 1976; Honorary LLD, University of Wolverhampton, 1999. Memberships: President, Fabian Society; President, World Disarmament; President, One World Trust. Address: House of Lords, London, SW1 0PW, England.

**ARCULUS Ronald (Sir),** b. 11 February 1923, Birmingham, England. Retired Diplomat and Company Director. Education: MA, Exeter College, Oxford, 1941, 1945-47. Appointments: 4th Queen's Own Hussars, 1942-45; HM Diplomatic Service, 1947-83; Ambassador to Italy, 1979-83; Director, Trustee and Consultant, Glaxo Holdings, 1983-92. Honours: KCMG; KCVO; Knight Grand Cross, Italian Order of Merit. Memberships: Army and Navy Club; Cowdray Park Polo Club; Hurlingham Club. Address: 20 Kensington Court Gardens, London W8 5QF, England.

**ARDEN John,** b. 26 Oct 1930, Barnsley, Yorkshire, England. Playwright. m. Margaretta Ruth D'Arcy, 4 sons, 1 dec. Education: King's College, Cambridge; Edinburgh College of Art. Publications include: Fiction: Silence Among the Weapons, 1982; Books of Bale, 1988; Cogs Tyrannic, 1991; Jack Juggler and the Emperor's Whore, 1995; The Stealing Steps, 2003. Essays: To Present the Pretence, 1977; Awkward Corners (with M D'Arcy), 1988. Plays produced include: All Fall Down, 1955; The Life of Man, 1956; The Waters of Babylon, 1957; Live Like Pigs, 1958; Serjeant Musgrave's Dance, 1959; Soldier Soldier, 1960; Wet Fish, 1961; The Workhouse Donkey, 1963; Ironhand, 1963; Armstrong's Last Goodnight, 1964; Left-Handed Liberty, 1965; Squire Jonathan, 1968; The Bagman, 1970; Pearl, 1978; Don Quixote, 1980; Garland for a Hoar Head, 1982; The Old Man Sleeps Alone, 1982; The Little Novels of Wilkie Collins, 1998; Woe alas, the Fatal Cashbox, 2000; Wild Ride to Dublin, 2003; Poor Tom, thy Horn is Dry, 2003. With M D'Arcy: The

Happy Haven, 1960; The Business of Good Government, 1960; Ars Longa Vita Brevis, 1964; The Royal Pardon, 1966; Friday's Hiding, 1966; Harold Muggins is a Martyr, 1968; The Hero Rises Up, 1968; The Ballygombeen Bequest, 1972; The Island of the Mighty, 1972; The Non-Stop Connolly Show, 1975; Vandaleur's Folly, 1978; The Manchester Enthusiasts, 1984; Whose is the Kingdom?, 1988; A Suburban Suicide, 1994. Address: c/o Casarotto Ramsay Ltd, National House, 60-66 Wardour Street, London W1V 3HP, England.

**ARDEN-GRIFFITH Paul,** b. 18 January 1952, Stockport, England. Opera, Oratorio and Concert Singer. Education: GRSM (Teachers), ARMCM (Teachers), pianoforte and singing, ARMCM (Performers), Singing, Royal Northern College of Music, Manchester. Career: A Midsummer Night's Dream, Sadlers Wells Theatre, 1973; The Merry Widow, English National Opera, 1975; Paul Bunyan, Aldeburgh Festival, 1976; We Come To the River, Royal Opera Covent Garden, 1976; Of Mice and Men, Wexford Festival Opera, Eire, 1980; Carmina Burana, Singapore Festival of the Arts, Singapore, 1984; Phantom of the Opera, Her Majesty's Theatre, 1986; The Duenna, Wexford Festival Opera, Eire, 1989; The Legendary Lanza, Wexford Festival Opera, Eire, 1989; The Barber of Seville, Opera East, UK Tour, 1992; Sunset Boulevard, Rhein-Main Theatre, Frankfurt, Germany, 1998; Sweeney Todd, Royal Opera Covent Garden, London, 2003; Die Fledermaus, Opera Holland Park, London, 2004. Recordings: Paul Arden-Griffith – The Song Is You, 1986; Phantom of the Opera (Original Cast Album), 1987; An Evening with Alan Jay Lerner, 1987; Minstrel Magic (Black & White Minstrel Cast Album), 1993; A Minstrel on Broadway, 1994; Encore! – Paul Arden Griffith in Concert, 1995; The Classic Collection, 1995; Accolade!, 1996. Honours: Gwilym, Gwalchmai Jones Scholarship for Singing; Listed in several Who's Who and biographical publications. Memberships: British Actors Equity Association; Musicians' Union; PAMRA; Concert Artistes' Association. Address: c/o Ken Spencer Personal Management, 138 Sandy Hill Road, London SE 18 7BA, England. E-mail: pagtenor@onetel.net.uk

**AREM Joel Edward,** b. 28 December 1943, New York, USA. Mineralogist; Gemologist. m. Deborah, 1 son, 1 daughter. Education: BS, Geology, Brooklyn College, 1964; MA, Geology, Harvard University, 1967; PhD, Mineralogy, 1970. Appointments include: Consultant, US Department of Commerce, 1975-76; Consultant, Encyclopaedia Britannica Educational Corp, 1975-76; Consultant, Jewellers Circular-Keystone, 1978-85; President, Accredited Gemologists Association, 1977-79; Co-Founder, Editorial Board, PreciouStones Newsletter, 1978-84. Publications: Crystal Chemistry and Structure of Idocrase, PhD Dissertation, 1970; Man-Made Crystals, 1973; Rocks and Minerals, 1973; Gems and Jewelry, 1975, 2nd edition, 1992; Color Encyclopedia of Gemstones, 1977, 2nd edition, 1987; Discovering Rocks and Minerals, 1991. Honours include: Harvard University Scholarships, 1964-66; National Science Foundation Scholarships, 1966-68; Sigma Xi; Phi Beta Kappa. Memberships: Fellow, Gemmological Association of Great Britain; Fellow, Canadian Gemmological Association; Mineralogical Society of America; American Association for Crystal Growth; Mineral Museums Advisory Council; Friends of Mineralogy. Address: PO 5056, Laytonsville, MD 20882, USA.

**ARKHIPOV Andrei,** b. 8 September 1946, Karaganda, Kazakhstan, USSR. Physicist. 2 sons. Education: Graduate, Leningrad State University, Russia, 1970; PhD, 1973, DSc, 1993, Institute of High Energy Physics, Russia. Appointments: Scientist of Theoretical Physics Division, 1973-1985, Senior Scientist, 1985-95, Principal Researcher, 1995-, Institute of

High Energy Physics, Russia; Lecturer, Physics, Moscow State University, 1978-98. Publications: Articles in scientific journals including: Soviet Journal of Theoretical and Mathematical Physics, 1990; Nuclear Physics, 2001; Hadron Spectroscopy, 2002. Honours: Nominated for International Scientist of the Year, 2003; Inaugural Member, Leading Scientists of the World, 2005; Nominated as inaugural member of the Leading Scientist of the World 2005. Address: Theoretical Physics Division, Institute for High Energy Physics, 142280 Protvino, Moscow Region, Russia. E-mail: arkhipov@mx.ihep.su

**ARKIN Alan Wolf,** b. 26 March 1934, USA. Actor; Director. m. (1) 2 sons, (2) Barbara Dana, 1 son. Education: Los Angeles City College; Los Angeles State Col; Bennington College, Appointments: Made professional theatre debut with the Compass Players, St Louis, 1959; Joined 2nd City Group, Chicago, 1960; NY debut, Roy, Revue from the 2nd city, 1961; Played David Kolvitz, Enter Laughing, 1963-64; Appeared, Revue A View Under The Bridge, 1964; Harry Berline, Luv; Director, Eh?, Circle in the Square, 1966; Hail Scrawdyke, 1966; Little Murders, 1969; White House Murder Case, 1970; Director, The Sunshine Boys, Eh?, 1972; Director, Molly, 1973; Joan Lorraine, 1974; Films Include: The Heart is a Lonely Hunter, 1968; Popi, 1969; Catch 22, 1970; Little Murders (also director), 1971; Last of the Red Hot Lovers, 1972; Freebie and the Bean, 1974; Rafferty and the Gold Dust Twins, 1975; Hearts of the W, 1975; The In-laws, 1979; The Magician of Lublin, 1979; Simon, 1980; Chu Chu and the Philly Flash, 1981; The Last Unicorn, 1982; Joshua Then and Now (also director), 1985; Coupe de Ville, 1989; Havana, 1990; Edward Scissorhands, 1990; The Rocketeer, 1990; Glengarry Glen Ross, 1992; Indian Summer, 1993; So I Married an Axe Murderer, 1993; Steal Big, Steal Little, 1995; Mother Night, 1995; Grosse Point Blank, 1997; Gattaca, 1998; The Slums of Beverly Hills, 1998; Jakob the Liar, 1999; Arigo, 2000; America's Sweethearts, 2001; Thirteen Conversations About One Thing, 2001; Counting Sheep, 2002. TV Appearances Include: The Other Side of Hell, 1978; The Defection of Simas Kudirka, 1978; Captain Kangaroo, A Deadly Business, 1986; Escape from Sobibor, Necessary Parties; Cooperstown; Taking the Heat; Doomsday Gun. Publications: Tony's Hard Work Day; The Lemming Condition; Halfway Through the Door; The Clearing, 1986; Some Fine Grampha, 1995. Honours: Theatre World Award; Award Best Supporting Actor. Address: c/o William Morris Agency, 151 El Camino Drive, Beverly Hills, CA 90212, USA.

**ARMANI Giorgio,** b. 11 July 1934, Piacenza, Italy. Fashion Designer. Education: University of Milan. Appointments: Window dresser; Assistant buyer for La Rinascente, Milan, 1957-64; Designer and Product Developer, Hitman (menswear co of Cerruti Group), 1964-70; Freelance designer for several firms, 1970; founded Giorgio Armani SpA with Sergio Galeotti, 1975; Appeared on cover of Time, 1982. Honours: Dr hc (Royal College of Art), 1991; Numerous awards including Cutty Sark, 1980, 1981, 1984, 1986, 1987; First Designer Laureate, 1985; Ambrogino D'Oro, Milan, 1982; International Designer Award, Council of Fashion Designer of America, 1983; L'Pacchio D'Oro, 1984, 1986, 1987, 1988; L'Occhiolino D'Oro, 1984, 1986, 1987, 1988; Time-Life Achievement Award, 1987; Cristobal Balenciaga Award, 1988; Woolmark Award, New York, 1989, 1992; Senken Award, Japan, 1989; Award from People for the Ethical Treatment of Animals, USA, 1990; Fiorino d'Oro, Florence, for promoting Made in Italy image, 1992; Honorary Nomination from Brera Academy, Milan, 1993; Aguja de Oro Award, Spain, for best International Designer, 1993; Grand'Uffciale dell'ordine al merito, 1986; Gran Cavaliere, 1987. Address: Via Borgonuovo 21, 20121, Milan, Italy.

**ARMATRADING Joan** b. 9 December 1950, Basseterre, St Kitts, West Indies. Singer; Songwriter; Musician (guitar). Musical Education: Self-taught piano and guitar. Career: Songwriting, performing partnership, with Pam Nestor, 1969-73; Solo artiste, 1973-; Appearances include: Regular international tours; Concerts include: Prince's Trust Gala, Wembley Arena, 1986; Nelson Mandela's 70th Birthday Tribute, Wembley Stadium, 1988; Numerous world tours, 1973-96. Compositions include: Down To Zero; Willow, 1977. Recordings: Singles: Love And Affection, 1976; Rosie, 1980; Me Myself I, 1980; All The Way From America, 1980; I'm Lucky, 1981; Drop The Pilot, 1983; Perfect Day, 1997; Albums include: Whatever's For Us, 1973; Joan Armatrading, 1976; Show Some Emotion, 1977; Stepping Out, 1979; Me Myself I, 1980; Walk Under Ladders, 1981; The Key, 1983; Track Record, 1983; The Shouting Stage, 1988; The Very Best Of..., 1991; What's Inside, 1995; Living For You; Greatest Hits, 1996; Love And Affection, 1997; Lover Speak, 2003; Also appears on: Listen To The Music: 70's Females, 1996; Carols Of Christmas Vol 2, 1997; Prince's Trust 10th Anniversary Birthday, 1997; Film soundtrack, The Wild Geese, 1978. Honour: BASCA Ivor Novello Award for Outstanding Contemporary Collection, 1996; MBE, 2001. Membership: President, Women of the Year, UK. Address: c/o F Winter and Co, Ramillies House, 2 Ramillies Street, London W1F 7LN, England.

**ARMOUR James (Sir),** b. 17 September 1929, Basra, Iraq. Academic Veterinarian. m. Christine Strickland, 2 sons, 2 daughters. Education: MRCVS, PhD, University of Glasgow, 1947-52. Appointments: Veterinary Officer, Veterinary Research Officer, Colonial Service, Nigeria, 1952-60; Research Scientist, Cooper McDougall, Robertson, 1960-63; Lecturer, Senior Lecturer, Reader, Veterinary Parasitology, 1963-75; Professor in Veterinary Parasitology, 1975-96, Dean of the Veterinary School, 1984-91, Vice Principal, 1991-96, University of Glasgow; Chairman Veterinary Products Committee (Part of Medicines Commission), 1988-97; Chairman, Glasgow Hospitals NHS Dental Trust, 1995-99; Chairman, Moredun Foundation, 2000-2004; Chairman, St Andrew's Clinics for Children in Africa. Publications: 150 articles on veterinary parasitology: Pathogenesis, immunology and control of internal parasites of livestock; Joint author of textbook on veterinary parasitology, translated into Spanish, Portuguese, Italian, Arabic and Russian. Honours: CBE, 1989; Kt, 1995; Honorary Degrees: Dr h.c., Utrecht, DVM&S, Edinburgh, DU, Glasgow; Fellow, Royal Society of Edinburgh; Fellow, Academy of Medical Sciences; Honorary Fellow, Royal College of Veterinary Surgeons; Honorary Fellow, Institute of Biology. Memberships: Royal College of Veterinary Surgeons; British Veterinary Association; World Association for Advancement of Veterinary Parasitology; British Association for Veterinary Parasitology. Address: Flat 4, Mokoia, 11 Crosbie Road, Troon, KA10 6HE, Scotland. E-mail: jarmour@amserve.net

**ARMSTRONG Hilary Jane,** b. 30 November 1945, Sunderland, England. Member of Parliament. m. Paul Corrigan. Education: BSc Sociology, West Ham College of Technology, 1964-67; Diploma in Social Work, Birmingham University, 1969-70. Appointments: VSO (Voluntary Service Overseas), Murray Girls High School, Kenya, 1967-69; Social Worker, Newcastle Social Services Department, 1970-73; Community Worker, Southwick Neighbourhood Action Project, 1973-75; Lecturer in Community and Youth Work, Sunderland Polytechnic, 1975-86; Member of Parliament, North West Durham, 1987-; Minister of State, Local Government and Housing, 1997-99; Minister of State, Local Government and Regions, 1999-2001; Government Chief Whip, 2001-. Honours: Privy Councillor, 2000. Address: House of Commons, London SW1A 0AA, England.

**ARMSTRONG Isobel Mair,** b. 25 March 1937, London, England. Emeritus Professor of English. m. John Michael Armstrong, 2 sons, 1 daughter. Education: BA, PhD, University of Leicester. Appointments: Assistant Lecturer then Lecturer, University College London, 1963-70; Lecturer then Senior Lecturer, University of Leicester, 1971-79; Professor of English, University of Southampton, 1979-89; Professor of English, Birkbeck College, University of London, 1989-2002. Publications: The Major Victorian Poets, 1969; Victorian Scrutinies, 1972; Language as Living Form in Nineteenth Century Poetry, 1982; Victorian Poetry: Poetry, Poetics and Politics, 1993; Nineteenth Century Women Poets (co-editor), 1996; The Radical Aesthetic, 2000. Honours: Fellow, British Academy, 2003; Hon DLitt, University of Leicester, 2004. Memberships: President, British Association of Victorian Studies, 2003; Senior Research Fellow Institute of English Studies, 2002. Address: School of English and Humanities, Birkbeck College, Malet Street, London WC1E 7HX, England.

**ARMSTRONG Neil A,** b. 5 August 1930, Wapakoneta, Ohio, USA. Astronaut; Professor of Engineering. m. Janet Shearon, 2 sons. Education: Purdue University; University of South California. Appointments: Naval Aviator, 1949-52; Flew combat missions during Korean War; Joined NASA Lewis Flight Propulsion Laboratory, 1955; Transferred to NASA High Speed Flight Station, Edwards, California; Aeronautical Research Pilot, X-15 Project Pilot Flying to over 200,000 ft and at approximately 4,000 mph; Other Flight Test Work Including X-1 Rocket Research Plane; F-100, F-101, F-104, F5D, B-47 and the Paraglider; Selected as Astronaut by NASA, 1962; Command Pilot for Gemini VIII, 1966; Backup Pilot for Gemini V, 1965; Flew to moon, Apollo XI, 1969; First man to set foot on the moon, 1969; Chair, Peace Corps, National Advisory Council, 1969; Deputy Associate Administrator, Aeronautics, NASA, Washington, 1970-71; Professor of Engineering, University of Cincinnati, 1971-79; Chair, Cardwell International Ltd, 1979-81; Chair, CTA Inc, 1982-92; AIL Systems Inc, 1989-; Director of numerous companies. Honours: Honorary Member, International Academy of Astronautics; Honorary Fellow, International Astronomical Federation; Numerous decorations and awards from 17 countries; Presidential Medal of Freedom, NASA Exceptional Service Award; Royal Geographic Society, Gold Medal and Harmon International Aviation Trophy, 1970. Memberships: President's Commission on Space Shuttle, 1986; National Commission on Space, 1985-86; National Academy of Engineering; Fellow, Society of Experimental Test Pilots; American Institute of Aeronautics and Astronautics; Royal Astronautical Society. Address: EDO Corporation, 60 East 42nd Street, Suite 5010, New York, NY 10165, USA.

**ARNAUT Luk Raf Remi,** b. 8 March 1966, Gent, Belgium. Research Scientist. m. Maria V Tsiplakova. Education: "First Prize" Degree in Music Theory and Solfège, Royal Conservatoire of Music, Gent, Belgium, 1982; Degree in Applied Physics and Electrical Engineering, University of Gent, Gent, Belgium, 1989; MSc, Communication Engineering and Digital Electronics, 1991; PhD, Electrical Engineering, 1994, UMIST, Manchester, England. Appointments: Research Associate of Electrical Engineering, UMIST, Manchester, 1991-94; Postdoctoral Research Scientist, QinetiQ, Farnborough, England, 1994-95; Visiting Scientist, Naval Research Laboratories, Washington DC, USA, 1995; Consultant, Technical Manager, Russtech Project, BAE Systems, Bristol UK, 1995-96; Senior Research Scientist, Technical Manager, Complex Electromagnetics Team, Key Advisor to Centre for Mathematical Modelling National Physical Laboratory, Teddington, England, 1996-. Publications: Principal author of over 40 articles in professional journals including, Proceedings of IEE (SMT), IEEE Transactions on Electromagnetic Compatibility, IEEE Transactions on Antennas and Propagation; Archiv für Elektronik und Übertragungstechnik; Radio Science; Journal of Electromagnetic Waves and Applications; Numerous conference proceedings; Book Chapters: Progress in Electromagnetics Research, 1997; Advances in Complex Electromagnetic Materials, 1997; Advances in Electromagnetics of Complex Materials and Metamaterials, 2003; 2 patents. Honours: Erasmus Scholarship, European Union, 1990; Peter Allen Scholarship, 1994; Numerous invited presentations at conferences and symposia on advanced electromagnetic materials and reverberation processes; Invited Lecturer, Southampton University, 1995; Winner Rayleigh Award, 2002 (runner-up 2001); Honorary Professional Membership: Fellow, IEE, Senior Member, IEEE, Chartered Engineer. Address: National Physical Laboratory, Division of Enabling Metrology, F2-A11, Teddington, TW11 0LW, England.

**ARNOLD David Charles**, b. 30 December 1941, Atlanta, Georgia, USA. Opera and Concert Singer. Education: BA, MA, Indiana University, Bloomington, Indiana; Artist's Diploma, New England Conservatory of Music, Boston, Massachusetts. Appointments: Metropolitan Opera, New York City Opera Company, English National Opera; Komische Oper, Berlin; International Festivals: Spoleto in Italy and USA; Concertgebouw, The Netherlands; Significant associations: Performing as soloist with Sir Georg Solti and the Chicago Symphony; Leonard Bernstein in premiere of David Diamond's 9th Symphony; André Previn and the Pittsburgh Symphony; James Levine with the Metropolitan Opera. Honours: National Opera Institute Career Grant; New York City Opera Gold Debut Award, Sullivan Foundation Award; Shoshana Foundation Award; Invited to sing at: White House on 2 occasions. Address: Grant House, 309 Wood Street, Burlington, NJ 08016, USA.

**ARNOLD David Michael**, b. 21 April 1958, Maidstone, Kent, England. Singer; Composer; Artist; Writer; Poet. 1 son. Education: Technical School; Music, Hackney & Hastings Colleges. Appointments: Various radio appearances, 1980-94; Founder, Own Record Label; Meridian TV, 1993, 1995. Creative Works: Recordings: High Upon the Rhythm; Hallelujah; Valentine; National Health Tender. Publications: Various. Memberships: PRS; MCPS. Address: 3B Castledown Avenue, Hastings, East Sussex TN34 3RJ, England. E-mail: vibezone@excite.com Website: www.vibezone.co.uk

**ARNOLD Graham**, b. 24 May 1932, Sydenham, England. Artist. m. Ann Telfer. Education: Beckenham School of Art, 1947-52; Royal College of Art, 1955-58; Further studies in Rome, Italy. Appointments: Painter in Residence, Digswell House, Hertfordshire, 1960-63; Senior Lecturer in Fine Art, Kingston Poly, 1963-72; Visiting Tutor in Fine Art, Westminster School, 1961-65, The Royal Academy Schools, 1966-71; Founder Member, The Brotherhood of Ruralists, with Ann Arnold, David Inshaw, Peter Blake, Jann Howarth, Graham Ovenden and Annie Ovenden, 1975; Work in public collections including: Royal Academy of Arts; Bristol City Art Gallery; Contemporary Arts Society; University of Liverpool Gallery; National Gallery of New Zealand; The British Museum; Southport Museum and Art Gallery; Many private collections. Publications: Illustrations for numerous books. Honours: ARCA, 1958; Rome Scholarship, Royal College of Art, 1958-60; RAS West Arts Academy. Memberships: Arts Club, London. Address: Caractacus, Chapel Lawn, Bucknell, Shropshire SY7 0BW, England.

**ARNOLD Thomas Richard (Sir)**, b. 25 January 1947, London, England. Theatre Producer; Publisher; Consultant. m. Elizabeth Jane, dissolved 1993, 1 daughter. Education:

MA, Pembroke College, Oxford. Appointments: Member of Parliament (Conservative), Hazel Grove, Manchester, 1974-97; Parliamentary Private Secretary to Secretary of State for Northern Ireland, 1979-81; Parliamentary Private Secretary to Lord Privy Seal, Foreign and Commonwealth Office, 1981-82; Vice-Chairman, Conservative Party, 1983-92, Member, 1992-94, Chairman, 1994-97, Treasury and Civil Service Select Committees. Honours: Freeman of the City of London (Baker's Company), 1969; Knighted, 1990. Address: 19 Ordnance Hill, London NW8 6PR, England.

**ARORA Yogesh**, b. 6 September 1970, Muzaffarnagar (UP), India. Chef. Education: Institute of Hotel Management, Pusa, New Delhi, India, 1987-90; Bachelor of Commerce, University of Delhi, New Delhi, India, 1988-91. Appointments: Chef Trainee, 1990-92, Demi Chef de Partie, 1992-94, Holiday Inn Crowne Plaza, New Delhi, India; Sous Chef, Khazana Restaurant, Singapore, 1994-96; Junior Sous Chef, 1996-99, Sous Chef, Tiffin Room, 1999-2003, Chef de Cuisine, Tiffin Room, 2003-, Raffles Hotel, Singapore; Conducted a number of culinary demonstrations at the Raffles Culinary Academy. Publications: Work featured in numerous newspapers and magazines and on many national and international television programmes. Honours: Bronze Medal, 13th Food & Hotel Asia, 2002; Raffles Hotel Food Promotion, Hotel Vier Jahreszeiten, Hamburg Germany, 2002; Tiffin Room Awarded Singapore's Finest Restaurant, Wine and Dine Magazine, 1998-2004; Awarded 2 Stars, Wine and Dine Food Guide, 2003; Excellent Service Award (Silver) Singapore Hotel Association, 2003; Silver Medal, 14th Food & Hotel Asia, 2004; Raffles Hotel Tiffin Room Food Promotion Swissotel, Osaka, Japan, 2004. Address: Raffles Hotel, 1 Beach Road, Singapore 189673. E-mail: yogesh arora1970@yahoo.com Website: www.raffleshotel.com

**ARQUETTE Patricia**, b. 8 April 1968. Actress. m. Nicholas Cage, divorced. Appointments: Films Include: Pretty Smart, 1986; A Nightmare on Elm Street 3: Dream Warriors, 1987; Time Out, 1988; Far North, 1988; The Indian Runner, 1991; Prayer of the Rollerboys, 1991; Ethan Frome, 1993; Trouble Bound, 1993; Inside Monkey Zetterland, 1993; True Romance, 1993; Holy Matrimony, 1994; Ed Wood, 1994; Beyond Infinity, 1995; Infinity, 1995; Flirting with Disaster, 1996; The Secret Agent, 1996; Lost Highway, 1997; Nightwatch, 1998; In the Boom Boom Room, 1999; Goodbye Lover, 1999; Stigmata, 1999; Bringing Out the Dead, 1999; Little Nicky, 2000; Human Nature, 2001; Films for TV Include: Daddy, 1987; Dillinger, 1991; Wildflower, 1991; Betrayed by Love, 1994; Toby's Story, 1998; The Hi -Lo Country, 1998; The Badge, 2002. Address: c/o UTA, 9560 Wilshire Blvd, 5th Floor, Beverley Hills, CA 90212, USA.

**ARQUETTE Rosanna**, b. 10 August 1959, New York, USA. Actress. m. (1) divorced, (2) James N Howard, divorced, (3) John Sidel, 1993. Appointments: Actress; Founder, Flower Child Productions; Films include: Gorp, 1980; SOB, 1981; Off The Wall, 1983; The Aviator, 1985; Desperately Seeking Susan, 1985; 8 Million Ways to Die, 1986; After Hours, 1986; Nobody's Fool, 1986; The Big Blue, 1988; Life Lessons, Black Rainbow, 1989; Wendy Cracked a Walnut, 1989; Sweet Revenge, 1990; Baby, It's You, 1990; Flight of the Intruder, 1990; The Linguini Incident, 1992; Fathers and Sons, 1992; Nowhere to Run, 1993; Pulp Fiction, 1994; Search and Destroy, 1995; Crash, 1996; Liar, 1997; Gone Fishin', 1997; Buffalo '66, 1997; Palmer's Pick Up, 1998; I'm Losing You, 1998; Homeslice, 1998; Floating Away, 1998; Hope Floats, 1998; Fait Accompli, 1998; Sugar Town, 1999; Palmer's Pick Up, 1999; Pigeonholed, 1999; Interview with a Dead Man, 1999; The Whole Nine Yards, 2000; Too Much Flesh, 2000; Things Behind the Sun, 2001; Big Bad

Love, 2001; Good Advice, 2001; Diary of a Sex Addict, 2001. TV Films include: Harvest Home; The Wall; The Long Way Home; The Executioner's Song; One Cooks, the Other Doesn't; The Parade; Survival Guide; A Family Tree; Promised a Miracle; Sweet Revenge; Separation; The Wrong Man; Nowhere to Hide; I Know What You Did. Address: 8033 West Sunset Boulevard, #16, Los Angeles, CA 90046, USA.

**ARSENJEV Serghey,** b. 3 December 1937, Tiraspol Town, Moldova. Mechanical Engineer. m. Victoria Arsenjeva, 1 son, 1 daughter. Education: Masters Degree of Engineering for Lifting and Transporting Machines and Equipment, Polytechnic Institute of Odessa, USSR, 1958-63. Appointments: Principal Investigator, The Fundaments of Liquid and Gas Motion Physics, Physical Technical Group, Pavlograd, Ukraine, 1990-. Publications: 28 articles, More than 200 of R&D accounts, reports, methods, 25 author's certificates and patents. Address: Physical Technical Group, Dobroljubova Street, 2, 29; Pavlograd Town, 51400 Ukraine. E-mail: loz@inbox.ru Website: www.lozik.h1.ru

**ARTHUR Sir Gavyn Farr,** b. 13 September 1951, Africa. Barrister; Chairman, Arab Financial Forum. Education: Harrow School; BA Hons (Jurisprudence), 1974; MA, Christ Church, Oxford, 1979. Appointments: Called to the Bar, 1974; Joined Harcourt Chambers (now Senior Member), 1977; SCL Children Law Committee, 1981-86; Member, Western Circuit Committee, 1986; Chairman, Research Committee on Child Care Proceedings, 1987; Member, Midland Circuit, 1988; Member, Ward of Farringdon Without, 1988-91; Alderman of the City of London, 1991; President, Cripplegate Ward Club, 1991; Sheriff of the City of London, 1998-99; Bencher, Hon Society of the Middle Temple, 2001; Recorder, Crown Court, 2002; Chancellor, City University, 2002; Admiral of Port of London, 2002; Lord Mayor of London, 2002-03. Honours: Freeman of the City of London, 1979; Vice President, British Red Cross, 1993; Officer, 2000, Knight of Grace, 2002, Knight of Justice, 2003, Order of St John; Knight Bachelor, 2003; Doctor of Civil Laws, City University, 2002; Order of Honour of Republic of Georgia, 2003; Governor, The Honourable Irish Society, 2004; Companion, Order of Mercy, 2004; Member, H M Lieutenancy for City of London. Memberships: Anglo-Austrian Society; British Lebanese Society; British Ukrainian Law Association; British Tunisia Society; The Pilgrims; The Cook Society. Address: Guildhall, London EC4Y 9DB, England. E-mail: garthur@harcourtchambers.law.co.uk

**ARTHUR Rasjid Arthur James,** b. 7 June 1928, Stirling, Scotland. Journalist. Education: MA, Honours, English, Edinburgh University, 1950. Appointments: National Service, RAF, 1950-52; Local Reporter, Stirling, 1952-54; Sub Editor, 1954-55, Leader Writer, 1955-64, The Scotsman; Features Editor, News Editor and Writer, Central Office of Information, London, 1965-78; Freelance Writer on environment, development and related topics, 1978-. Publications: Many articles on environmental subjects for British and international magazines and for the London Press Service of the Press Association. Membership: Chartered Institute of Journalists. Address: 32 Midway, Middleton Cheney, Banbury OX17 2 QW, England. E-mail: raj@rasjid.fsnet.co.uk

**AS-SALAAM Jamaal (William L Williams Jr),** b. 20 April 1955, Albany, New York, USA. Actor; Writer; Poet; Director; Producer. m. (1) Veronica Foster, divorced, 1 son, 1 daughter, (2) Arlene Hooks, divorced, 1 son, (3) Terisita Ann Lopez, divorced, 1 daughter. Education: State University of New York, Film History, 1972-76; University of Northern Colorado, Accounting, 1984-86; National University, Encino,

California, 1990-92; California Arts Partnership, 1995-98; MCSE, Ednet Career Institute, 1998. Appointments: Track Labourer, Burlington No RR, 1978-85; Computer Specialist, Denver Public School, 1980-86; Saks Consultant, Tom Hopkins Sales Training, Denver, 1984-86; Technical Support, Teleoptics, Los Angeles, 1988-94; Computer Technician, Los Angeles County Schools, California, 1987-94; Digital Video Editor, California Arts Community Partners, Los Angeles, 1994-99; Researcher, Sales Inc, Beverley Hills, California, 1996-97; Producer, Mile High Cable Co, Denver, 1983-86; Radio Announcer, Station KUVO, Denver, 1984-85; Actor; Director; Writer; Producer. Publications: Facing East, 1995; Portraits of Life, 1997. Memberships: Inner City Cultural Center; Denver Black Arts Theater Company; Win/Win Business Forum, Denver; Telepoetics; Los Angeles in Support of Gang Truce; Black Radical Congress. Honours: California Arts Community Project Award, California Institute of Arts; 1st prize, Upstate Photography, New York. Address: PO Box 815, Englewood, CO 80042-1072, USA. E-mail: jamaal21@hotmail.com

**ASCHERI Mario,** b. 7 February 1944, Ventimiglia, Italy. Professor of Legal History. m. Cecilia Papi, 2 sons. Education: Law Degree, Siena, 1967. Appointments: Professor, University of Siena, 1971-; Professor, University of Sassari, 1972-76; Professor of Legal History, University of Rome 3 and Siena, 2002-. Publications include: Books: Istituzioni medievali, 1999; I diritti del Medioevo italiano (secoli XI-XV), 2000; Siena nella storia, 2000; Lo spazio storico di Siena, 2001; Introduzione storica al diritto moderno e contemporaneo, 2003. Honours: Doctor honoris causa, Université d'Auvergne, Clermont-Ferrand, France, 2001; Beirat Max-Planck-Institut für europäische Rechtsgeschichte, Frankfurt/Main, Germany; Consiglio Direttivo Deputazione di Storia patria per la Toscana, Florence; Direttore Sezione di Storia Accademia Senese degli Intronati, Siena; Premio della Città di Siena (Mangia d'oro), 2003; Premio della Città di Ventimiglia (San Segundin), 2003. Memberships: Editorial Member of historical periodicals published in Florence, Turin, Siena, Saragoza, Madrid. Address: Via G Duprè 99, I-53100 Siena, Italy. E-mail: ascheri@uniroma3.it

**ASH William,** b. 30 November 1917, Dallas, Texas, USA. Author; Radio Drama Script Editor. m. Ranjana, 1 son, 1 daughter. Education: University of Texas, Austin, Texas; MA, Modern Greats, Balliol College, Oxford. Appointments: Fighter Pilot, Royal Canadian Airforce, WWII; Prisoner of War, 1942-45; Representative, India and Pakistan, BBC, External Services; Script Editor, BBC Radio Drama Department; Literary Manager, Soho Poly Theatre; Chairman, Writers' Guild of Great Britain; Lecturer and Workshop Presenter. Publications: Fiction: The Lotus in the Sky, 1961; Choice of Arms, 1962; The Longest Way Round, 1963; Ride a Paper Tiger, 1968; Take-Off, 1969; Incorporated, 1980; Right Side Up, 1984; She? 1986; Bold Riot, 1992; What's the Big Idea, 1993; But My Fist Is Free, 1997; Rise Like Lions, 1998; Non-fiction: Marxism and Moral Concepts, 1964; Pickaxe and Rifle: The Story of the Albanian People, 1974; Morals and Politics: The Ethics of Revolution, 1977; A Red Square: The Autobiography of an Unconventional Revolutionary, 1978; The Way to Write Radio Drama, 1985; Marxist Morality, 1997. Honour: MBE (Military Division). Memberships: Writer's Guild; NATFHE. Address: Flat 9, 43 Moscow Road, London W2 4AH, England.

**ASHCROFT Richard.** Vocalist; Songwriter; Musician (guitar). Career: Vocalist, The Verve; Concerts include: Lollaplooza Tour, US, 1994; UK tours, 1994-95; Support to Oasis, Paris, 1995; Glastonbury Festival, 1995. Compositions include: On Your Own; Drive You Home; History; No Knock On My Door. Recordings: Albums: A Storm In Heaven, 1993; A Northern

Soul, 1995; Urban Hymns, 1997; Singles: This Is Music, 1995; On Your Own, 1995, 1995; History, 1995; Bitter Sweet Symphony, 1997; The Drugs Don't Work, 1997; Sonnet, 1998; Lucky Man, 1998. Current Management: Larrikin Management, 8391 Beverly Blvd #298, Los Angeles, CA 90048, USA.

**ASHDOWN Sir Jeremy John Durham (Paddy), Baron Ashdown of Norton Sub-Hamdon,** b. 27 February 1941, New Delhi, India. Member of Parliament. m. Jane Courtenay, 1962, 1 son, 1 daughter. Appointments: Served RM and 42 Commando, 1959-71; Commanded 2 Special Boat Section; Captain, Royal Marines; HM Diplomatic Service, 1st Secretary, UK Mission to United Nations, Geneva, 1971-76; Commercial Managers Department, Westlands Group, 1976-78; Senior Manager, Morlands Ltd, 1978-81; Liberal Candidate, 1979; Dorset County Council, 1982-83, Spokesman for Trade and Industry, 1983-86; Liberal Member of Parliament for Yeovil, 1983-88; Liberal/SDP Alliance Spokesman on Education and Science, 1987; Liberal Democrat Member of Parliament for Yeovil, 1988-2001; Liberal Democrat Spokesman on Northern Ireland, 1988-; Leader, Liberal Democrats, 1988-99; Appointed Privy Counsellor, 1989; Appointed Non-Executive Director of Time Companies Ltd and Independent Newspapers Ltd, 1999; UN International High Representative to Bosnia and Herzegovina, 2002-. Publications: Citizen's Britain: A Radical Agenda for the 1990s, 1989; Beyond Westminster, 1994; Making Change our Ally, 1994; The Ashdown Diaries 1988-97, 2000; The Ashdown Diaries Vol II, 1997-99, 2001.

**ASHE Geoffrey Thomas,** b. 29 March 1923, London, England. Writer; Lecturer. m. (1) Dorothy Irene Train, 3 May 1946, deceased, 4 sons, 1 daughter, (2) Maxine Lefever, 8 December 1992, divorced, (3) Patricia Chandler, 3 April 1998. Education: BA, University of British Columbia, Canada, 1943; BA, Trinity College, Cambridge University, 1948. Appointment: Associate Editor, Arthurian Encyclopaedia, 1986. Publications: King Arthur's Avalon, 1957; From Caesar to Arthur, 1960; Land to the West, 1962; The Land and the Book, 1965; Gandhi, 1968; The Quest for Arthur's Britain, 1968; Camelot and the Vision of Albion, 1971; The Art of Writing Made Simple, 1972; The Finger and the Moon, 1973; The Virgin, 1976; The Ancient Wisdom, 1977; Miracles, 1978; Guidebook to Arthurian Britain, 1980; Kings and Queens of Early Britain, 1982; Avalonian Quest, 1982; The Discovery of King Arthur, 1985; Landscape of King Arthur, 1987; Mythology of the British Isles, 1990; King Arthur: The Dream of a Golden Age, 1990; Dawn Behind the Dawn, 1992; Atlantis, 1992; The Traveller's Guide to Arthurian Britain, 1997; The Book of Prophecy, 1999; The Hell-Fire Clubs, 2000. Contributions to: Numerous magazines and journals. Honour: Fellow, Royal Society of Literature, 1963. Memberships: Medieval Academy of America; Camelot Research Committee, secretary. Address: Chalice Orchard, Well House Lane, Glastonbury, Somerset BA6 8BJ, England.

**ASHER Jane,** b. 5 April 1946. Actress; Author; Businesswoman. m. Gerald Scarfe, 2 sons, 1 daughter. Career: As Cook: Owner Jane Asher's Party Cake Shop and Sugarcraft, 1990-; Cake Designer and Consultant for Sainsbury's, 1992-99; Actress: Films include: Greengage Summer; Masque of the Red Death; Alfie; Dreamchild; Tirant Lo Blanc, 2005; TV Appearances include: Brideshead Revisited, 1981; Murder Most Horrid, 1991; The Choir, 1995; Good Living, 1997-99; Tricks Of The Trade, 1999; Crossroads, 2003; Murder at the Vicarage, 2004; New Tricks, 2005; Stage Appearances include: Making it Better, Hampstead and Criterion Theatres, 1992; Things We Do for Love, Yvonne Arnaud and Gielgud Theatres, 1998; Is Everybody Happy, 2000; House and Garden, Royal National Theatre, 2000; What the Butler Saw, National Tour 2001;

Festen, Almeida Theatre, 2004; Festen, Lyric Theatre, London, 2004-05. Publications include: The Moppy Stories, 1987, 2005; Calendar of Cakes, 1989; Eats for Treats, 1990; Time to Play, 1993; Jane Asher's Book of Cake Decorating Ideas, 1993; The Longing (novel), 1996; The Question (novel), 1998; Losing It (novel), 2002; Cakes for Fun, 2005. Honour: Honorary LLD, Bristol University, 2001. Memberships: BAFTA; FORUM UK; Associate, RADA; Fellow, Royal Society of Arts; Charity Work: President: National Autistic Society, Arthritis Care, West London Family Service Unit; Vice-President: Child Accident Prevention Trust, Mobility Trust, National Deaf Children's Society. Address: c/o Actual Management, 7 Great Russell Street, London, WC1B 3NH, England.

**ASHER Ronald E,** b. 23 July 1926, Gringley-on-the-Hill, Nottinghamshire, England. University Professor. 2 sons. Education: BA, University of London, 1950; Certificate in Phonetics of French, University College London, 1951; PhD, University of London, 1955; DLitt, University of Edinburgh, 1993. Appointments: Lecturer, Linguistics, 1953-57, Lecturer in Tamil, 1957-65, School of Oriental and African Studies, University of London; Visiting Professor of Linguistics, University of Chicago, 1961-62; Senior Lecturer, 1965-70, Reader, 1970-77, Professor of Linguistics, 1977-93, Vice-Principal, 1990-93, Honorary Fellow, Faculty of Arts/School of Humanities and Social Sciences, 1993-99, 2001-, University of Edinburgh; Visiting Professor of Linguistics and International Communication, International Christian University, Tokyo, 1994-95; First occupant of Vaikom Muhammad Basheer Chair, Mahatma Gandhi University, Kottayam, Kerala, India, 1995-96. Publications: Books include most recently: Critical essays on the novels and stories of Vaikom Muhammad Basheer, 1999; Colloquial Tamil (joint author), 2002; What the Sufi said (Translation from the Malayalam of novel by K P Ramanunni; joint translator), 2002; Wind Flowers: Contemporary Short Fiction from Kerala (joint editor and translator), 2004. Address: Theoretical and Applied Linguistics, The University of Edinburgh, Adam Ferguson Building, George Square, Edinburgh EH8 9LL, Scotland.

**ASHKENAZY Vladimir,** b. 6 July 1937, Gorky, USSR. Musician. m. Thorunn Sofia Johannsdottir, 2 sons, 3 daughters. Education: Central School of Music, Moscow, 1945-55; Moscow Conservatory, 1955-62. Appointments: Conductor, Philharmonia Orchestra, Royal Philharmonic Orchestra, Cleveland Orchestra, Deutsches Symphonie-Orchester Berlin; Guest conductor, Berlin Philharmonic, Boston Symphony, Los Angeles Philharmonic, San Francisco Symphony, Philadelphia and Concertgebouw Orchestras; Chief Conductor of the Czech Philharmonic Orchestra, 1998-2003; Conductor Laureate, Philharmonia Orchestra; Music Director, NHK Symphony Orchestra, 2004-05; Music Director, European Union Youth Orchestra; Conductor Laureate, Iceland Symphony Orchestra. Honours: 2nd prize, Chopin Competition, Warsaw, 1955; 1st prize, Queen Elisabeth Competition, Brussels, 1956; 1st prize, Tchaikovsky Competition, Moscow, 1962; Six Grammy awards, -1999; Order of the Falcon, highest civil decoration of Iceland. Address: Savinka, Kappelistrasse 15, 6045 Meggen, Switzerland.

**ASHLEY Bernard,** b. 2 April 1935, London, England. Writer. Education: Teachers Certificate; Advanced Diploma, Cambridge Institute of Education. Publications: The Trouble with Donovan Croft, 1974; Terry on the Fence, 1975; All My Men, 1977; A Kind of Wild Justice, 1978; Break in the Sun, 1980; Dinner Ladies Don't Count, 1981; Dodgem, 1982; High Pavement Blues, 1983; Janey, 1985; Running Scared, 1986; Bad Blood, 1988; The Country Boy, 1989; The Secret of Theodore

Brown, 1989; Clipper Street, 1990; Seeing off Uncle Jack, 1992; Cleversticks, 1993; Three Seven Eleven, 1993; Johnnie's Blitz, 1995; I Forgot, Said Troy, 1996; A Present for Paul, 1996; City Limits, 1997; Tiger Without Teeth, 1998; Growing Good, 1999; Little Soldier, 1999; Revenge House, 2002; Freedom Flight, 2003; Ten Days to Zero, 2005. Contributions to: Books for Your Children; Junior Education; Books for Keeps; Times Educational Supplement; School Librarian. Honours: The Other Award, 1976; Runner Up, Carnegie Medal, 1979, 1986; Royal TV Society Best Children's Entertainment Programme, 1993; Runner Up, Guardian Award, 2000; Honorary Doctorate in Education, Greenwich University, 2003; Honorary Doctorate in Letters, Leicester University, 2004. Memberships: Writers Guild; Board of Governors, Greenwich Theatre; Children's Committee, BAFTA. Address: 128 Heathwood Gardens, London SE7 8ER, England.

**ASHLEY Leonard (Raymond Nelligan),** b. 5 December 1928, Miami, Florida, USA. Professor Emeritus of English; Author; Editor. Education: BA, 1949, MA, 1950, McGill University; AM, 1953, PhD, 1956, Princeton University. Appointments: Instructor, University of Utah, 1953-56; Assistant to the Air Historian, Royal Canadian Air Force, 1956-58; Instructor, University of Rochester, 1958-61; Faculty, New School for Social Research (part-time), 1962-72; Faculty, Brooklyn College of the City University, New York, 1961-95; Professor Emeritus, 1995-. Publications: What's in a Name?; Elizabethan Popular Culture; George Peele: The Man and His Work; Colley Cibber; Nineteenth-Century British Drama; Authorship and Evidence in Renaissance Drama; Mirrors for Man; Other People's Lives; The Complete Book of Superstition, Prophecy and Luck; The Complete Book of Magic and Witchcraft; The Complete Book of Devils and Demons; The Complete Book of the Devil's Disciples; The Complete Book of Spells, Curses and Magical Recipes; The Complete Book of Vampires; The Complete Book of Ghosts and Poltergeists; The Complete Book of Werewolves; The Complete Book of Dreams; The Complete Book of Sex Magic; The Complete Book of Numerology; What I Know About You; Ripley's Believe It Or Not Book of the Military; The Air Defence of North America; George Alfred Henty and the Victorian Mind; Turkey: Names and Naming Practices; A Military History of Modern China (collaborator); Shakespeare's Jest Book (editor); Phantasms of the Living (editor); Ballad Poetry of Ireland (editor); Relics of Irish Poetry (editor); Language in Contemporary Society (co-editor); Language in The Era of Globalization (co-editor); Language and Identity (co-editor); Geolinguistic Perspectives (co-editor); Phantasms of the Living (editor); Language in Modern Society; Regular reviewer in Bibliotheque d'Humanisme et Renaissance, etc. Contributions to: Anthologies such as Modern American Drama: The Female Canon and Art, Glitter and Glitz, its Mainstream Playwrights... 1920s America; Reference books such as: Great Writers of the English Language; History of the Theater; Encyclopaedias (US and abroad); DLB; New DNB; Numerous works on names and naming including: Names of Places, Names in Literature, Names in Popular Culture, Art Attack: Essays on Names in Satire, Cornish Names; Over 150 articles in periodicals and scholarly journals; Poetry in over 60 publications. Honours: Shakespeare Gold Medal, 1949; LHD (Columbia Theological) honoris causa, 1998; American Name Society Best Article Award; Fellowships and grants; American Name Society, president 1979, 1987, long-time member editorial board, executive board; International Linguistics Association, Secretary, 1980-82; American Association of University Professors, former president, Brooklyn College Chapter; McGill Graduates Society of New York, President, 1970-75; American Society of Geolinguistics, president 1991-; Princeton Club of New York; New York Academy of Sciences; Modern Language Association; American Dialect Society. Address: Library Technical Services, Brooklyn College of the City University of New York, Brooklyn, NY 11210, USA.

**ASHTON Robert,** b. 21 July 1924, Chester, England. Retired University Professor. m. Margaret Alice Sedgwick, 30 August 1946, 2 daughters. Education: Magdalen College School, Oxford, 1938-40; University College, Southampton, 1946-49; BA, First Class Honours, London, 1949; PhD, London School of Economics, 1953. Appointments: Assistant Lecturer, Lecturer, Senior Lecturer, Nottingham University, 1952-63; Visiting Associate Professor, University of California, Berkeley, 1962-63; Professor, 1963-89, Emeritus Professor, 1989-, University of East Anglia; Visiting Fellow, All Souls College, Oxford, 1974-75, 1987; James Ford Special Lecturer in History, University of Oxford, 1982. Publications: The English Civil War: Conservatism and Revolution 1603-49, 1978, 2nd edition, 1989; The Crown and the Money Market 1603-40, 1960; James I by his Contemporaries, 1969; The City and the Court 1603-1643, 1979; Reformation and Revolution, 1558-1660, 1984; Counter Revolution: The Second Civil War and its Origins 1646-1648, 1994. Contributions to: Economic History Review; Bulletin of Institute of Historical Research; Past and Present; Historical Journal. Membership: Royal Historical Society, fellow 1961-, vice-president, 1983-84. Address: The Manor House, Brundall, Norwich NR13 5JY, England.

**ASHWORTH Anne,** b. 24 July 1931, Blackpool, England. Librarian; Poet. m. 3 April 1957, 1 son. Education: BA, Open University; ALA, Associate of the Library Association. Appointment: Librarian, Blackpool Sixth Form College, 1971-92. Publications: Mirrorwork, 1989; The Girl Who Runs Backwards, 1997; The Oblique Light, 1998; The Verb to be is Everywhere Irregular, 2003. Contributions to: Poetry Review; Orbis; Rialto; Staple; Writing Women; Envoi; Iota; Pennine Platform; Other Poetry; Reform; and others. Address: 2 Belle Vue Place, Blackpool, Lancashire FY3 9EG, England.

**ASIKAINEN Ilmari,** b. 5 April 1941, Somero, Finland. Neurology Specialist. m. Ulla Paavilainen, 1 son, 2 daughters. Education: MD, University of Bern, Switzerland, 1969; Specialist in Neurology, University of Helsinki, Finland, 1979; Dr, Medical Science, 2000. Appointments: Ward Physician in Charge, Mikkeli Central Hospital, Mikkeli, 1970-72; General Practitioner, Lahti, 1972-75; Assistant Physician in Neurology, Helsinki University Central Hospital, 1975-78; Specialist in Neurology, Kotka Central Hospital, Kotka, 1979-80, Kauniala Hospital, Kauniala, 1980-. Publications: Articles in the field of traumatic brain injury, in international medical journals. Honour: Recipient, Diploma and Gold Medal, Finnish Health Care and Social Security Federation, 1998. Memberships: American Association for the Advancement of Science; Finnish Medical Association; Finnish Federation of Neurology. Address: Vanha Turuntie 36, 02700 Kauniainen, Finland.

**ASKEW Reginald James Albert,** b. 16 May 1928, Aberdeen, Scotland. Clerk in Holy Orders. m. Kate Wigley, 1 son, 2 daughters. Education: BA, 1951, MA, 1956, Corpus Christi College, Cambridge; Scholae Cancelarii, Lincoln, 1955-57; King's College London, 1957-61. Appointments: Ordained Deacon, Church of England, 1957; Ordained Priest, 1958; Curate of Highgate, 1957-61; Lecturer and Vice-Principal, Wells Theological College, 1961-69; Priest Vicar, Wells Cathedral, 1961-69; Vicar, Christ Church, Lancaster Gate, 1969-73; Principal, Salisbury and Wells Theological College, 1973-87; Dean, King's College London, 1987-93; Retired, 1993. Publications: The Tree of Noah, 1971; Muskets and Altars, Jeremy Taylor and the Last of the Anglicans, 1997; Contributor:

The Reality of God, 1986. Honours: Pilkington Prize, 1957, 1958; Canon, 1975-87, Canon Emeritus, 1988-, Salisbury Cathedral; Chaplain, Worshipful Company of Merchant Taylors, 1996-97. Memberships: Corrymeela Community, 1971-; President, Bath and Wells Clerical Society, 1996-. Address: Carters Cottage, North Wootton, Shepton Mallet, Somerset BA4 4AF, England. E-mail: reginald.askew@virgin.net

**ASKEY Thelma J.** Director of Trade and Development Agency. Education: BA, Tennessee Technological University, 1970. Appointments: Minority Trade Counsel, 1985-94, Staff Director, 1995-98, Trade Subcommittee, Committee on Ways and Means, US House of Representatives, Washington, DC; Commissioner, International Trade Commission, Washington, DC, 1998-2001; Director of Trade and Development Agency, 2001-. Address: Trade and Development Agency US, 1000 Wilson Boulevard Suite 1600, Arlington, VA 22209-3901, USA.

**ASNAFI Nader,** b. 9 January 1960, Tehran, Iran. Manager. m. Maria Dahlberg, 2 sons. Education: MSc, 1987; Licentiate, 1990; PhD, 1997; Associate Professor, 2002. Appointments: Esselte Dymo, Tore, Sweden, 1984-85; Department of Materials Science and Production Technology, Luleå University of Technology, Sweden, 1985-91; Swedish Institute for Metals Research, 1991-98; Project Leader, Industrial Development Centre, Olofström, Sweden, 1998-99; Manager, Sapa Technology, 1999-2001; Manager, Advanced Engineering, Product Design and Technology Development, Volvo Cars Body Components, Olofström, 2001-. Address: Jupitervägen 5, 29170 Kristianstad, Sweden. E-mail: nasnafi@volvocars.com

**ASPLUND Olle Olof Arne,** b. 11 March 1943, Stockholm, Sweden. Consultant Plastic Surgeon. m. Franziska, 3 sons. Education: Medical Licentiate, Karolinska Hospital, Stockholm, Sweden, 1970; Specialisation in Plastic Surgery, Stockholm, 1978; Dr. Med. Scis. Korolinska Institute, Stockholm, 1984. Appointments: Danderyd Hospital, Stockholm, 1970-74; Karolinska Hospital, Stockholm, 1975-84; Charing Cross Hospital, 1991-2002; Consultant Plastic Surgeon, Charing Cross Hospital, 2002-. Publications: Numerous articles in medical journals include: Breast reconstruction after mastectomy (Dr. Med. Scis. Thesis), 1984; Vertical scar breast reduction, 1996. Honour: Barrons Prize, British Association of Plastic Surgeons, 1995. Memberships: British Association of Aesthetic Plastic Surgeons; British Association of Plastic Surgeons; Swedish and Nordic Association of Plastic Surgeons; European Section of International Confederation for Plastic, Reconstructive and Aesthetic Surgery. Address: Charing Cross Hospital, Department of Plastic Surgery, Fulham Place Road, London W6 8RF, England.

**ASSUMPCÃO Francisco B Jr,** b. 7 September 1951, São Paulo, Brazil. Psychiatrist. 2 daughters. Education: MD, Medical School FUABC, S Andre, Brazil, 1974; Doctor, Psychology PUC, São Paulo, Brazil, 1988; Professor, Child Psychiatry, Medicine School, Universidade De São Paulo, Brazil, 1993. Publications: Child and Adolescent Psychiatry Handbook; Psychology and Comics; Psiquiatria Infantil Brasileira; Psiquiatria da Infância e Adolescência; Autismo; Adolescência Normal e Patologica; Semiologia em Psiquiatria da Infância e da Adolescência. Honour: Colar Gran Cruz Merito Da Medicina; Medal for Science and Peace. Memberships: Brazilian Psychiatry Society; APAL; Brazilian Child Psychiatry Association. Address: Al Lorena 105 ap 83, J Paulista, São Paulo, Brazil, CEP 01424-002. E-mail: cassiterides@bol.com.br

**ASTRAUSKAS Rimantas,** b. 9 April 1954, Kaunas, Lithuania. Ethnomusicologist; Producer. Education: MA, Lithuanian State Conservatoire, 1978; Doctor of Humanities, Musicology, Lithuanian Academy of Music, 1993; Probations: St Peters College, University of Oxford, 1995; Danish Folk Song Archives, Copenhagen, 1995; Bergen University, 1995; University of Tampere, 2002, 2004. Career: Producer, Lithuanian State TV and Radio Committee, 1978-88; Lecturer, Lithuanian Academy of Music, 1988-; Associate Professor of Ethnomusicology, 1993-; Chairman, Council for Support of Ethnic Culture, Parliament of the Republic of Lithuania,2000-2002; Head of the department of Ethnomusicology, Lithuanian Academy of Music and Theatre, 1995-2001. Publications: Typological Classification of Tunes (editor), 1996; Ritual and Music (editor), 1999; Folk Cultures at the Beginning of the 3rd Millennium (editor), 2001; Ethnic Relations and Musical Folklore (editor), 2002; Over 30 articles on Lithuanian traditional music. Honour: Special Award, Best Broadcast at International Contest of Musical Broadcasts in Kishinev, 1982. Memberships: Presidium Member, International Organisation of Folk Art; Deputy Chairman, Lithuanian Committee, International Council for Traditional Music; CORD Member, European Seminar in Ethnomusicology; Lithuanian Composers' Union. Address: V.Grybo 1/29-11, LT-10313, Vilnius 55, Lithuania. E-mail: astram@delfi.lt

**ÅSTRÖM (Hans) Gustaf (Erik),** b. 11 September 1918, Högsjö, Sweden. Managing Director. 1 son, 1 daughter. Education: Engineering Special Student at the University of Technology Stockholm, 1949-51. Appointments: Repairman, Engineering Workshop, Utansjö Cellulosa AB, Sweden, 1933-39; Chief Engineer for Methods and Manufacturing, Swedish Air Force, Malmslätt, Sweden, 1943-59; Director, Sundsvalls Verkstäder AB, Örebro, 1959-65; Travelling as a Managing Director and Rationalisation Expert for several Swedish companies, 1966-68; Director, Sundsvalls Verkstäder AB, Örebro, 1969-83; Managing Director, Emhart Singapore Pte Ltd, 1983-86 (The company made big losses and a risk was taken to move Örebro Plant to Singapore. However, after 3½ years Mr Åström had turned over the Singapore losses to profit, and the manufacturing in Örebro could be kept in Sweden). Publications: Several books on genealogical research. Honours: Chairman and Secretary, Sweden's Association of Manufacturing Companies, Örebro, 1959-82; Representative, Örebro Administrative Province, His Majesty the King's Swedish Education Department, 1963-76; Member, Örebro County School Officers, 1970-76 Managing Director, Örebro Health Care AB, 1974-80; Ministry of Justices Member of the County Court, Örebro Administrative Province, 1981-83. Memberships: Honorary Member, Örebro Technical Museum Society; Rotary, 1962-; Nordic Union Society; Honorary Member, Genealogical Research Association of Ådalen; Permanent Member, Society of Friends of the Mining Industry; Örebro Pistol Shooting Club. Address: Karlsgatan 32 P, 703 41 Örebro, Sweden.

**ASTROM Paul Fredrik Karl,** b. 15 January 1929, Sundsvall, Vaesternld, Sweden. Archaeologist; Publisher. m. (1) Lena Soderhjelm, 1957, divorced 1974, 2 sons, (2) Inez Elisabet Mossberg, 1974, 1 son. Education: BA, University of Uppsala, Sweden, 1950; MA, 1951, BLic, 1957, University of Lund; PhD, University of Lund, 1958, University of Vienna, 1994, University of Athens, 1995, Joannina, 2001. Appointments: 1st amanuensis, Museum of Antiquities, University of Lund, 1951-55; Assistant Professor, University of Lund, 1957-69; Cultural Attaché, Royal Swedish Embassy, Athens, 1958-63; Director, Swedish Institute in Athens, 1958-63, Swedish Institute in Rome, 1967-69; Visiting Assistant Professor, University of Missouri, Columbia, 1963-64; Professor, Goteborg (Sweden) University, 1969-93; Publisher, Studies in Mediterranean Archaeology; others. Publications: Author: The Middle Cypriote

Bronze Age, 1957; The Cuirass Tomb, Parts I and II, 1977, 1981; Gunnar Ekelof och antiken, 1992; others; Author/Editor: Hala Sultan Tekke 1-11, 1975-2001. Honours: Faxe Prize for Best Dissertation, University of Lund, 1958; Knight, Royal Order of the North Star, 1974; Prize, Swedish Academy, 1992; Grand Commander, Order of the Merit of Cyprus, 2005. Memberships: Fellow, Explorers Club; Member: Royal Society of Humanities and Sciences, Lund; Royal Society of Letters, Gothenburg; Society of Letters, Lund; Austrian Archaeological Institute; Royal Academy of Letters; Honorary Member: Archaeological Society, Athens; Society of Cypriote Studies; Corresponding Member, Institut de France. Address: Mimersvaegen 44, SE-43364 Saevedalen, Sweden. E-mail: paul.astrom@bredband.net

**ATA Atef Abdel-Moneim,** b. 28 May 1962, Egypt. Assistant Professor. m. Education: BSc (Hons), Mechanical Engineering, 1985, MSc, Engineering Mathematics, 1990, Alexandria University, Egypt; PhD, joint-venture, Alexandria University, Egypt and University of Miami, Florida, USA, 1996. Appointments: Assistant Lecturer, 1987-90, Lecturer, 1990-96, Assistant Professor, 1996-2001, Associate Professor, 2005-, Faculty of Engineering, Alexandria University, Egypt; Assistant Professor, Mechatronics Engineering Department, Faculty of Engineering, International Islamic University Malaysia, 2001-05. Publications: 11 articles in scientific journals include most recently: Transverse Vibration of Trapezoidal Plate Having Some Combinations of Clamped and Simply Supported Edge Conditions, 2001; Dynamic Analysis of a Rigid-Flexible Manipulator Constrained by Arbitrary Shaped Surfaces, 2003; 12 papers presented at international conferences. Honours: Phi Beta Kappa, University of Miami Chapter, USA, 1996; Listed in Who's Who publications and biographical dictionaries. Memberships: IEEE Robotics and Automation Society; Egyptian Engineering Syndicate. Address: Mechatronics Engineering Department, Faculty of Engineering, International Islamic University Malaysia, Kuala Lumpur 53100, Malaysia. E-mail: atef@iiu.edu.my

**ATHAR Husain,** b. 20 September 1968, Rawalpindi, Pakistan. Physicist. m. Sara Hashmi. Education: MSc, Physics, Quaid-i-Azam University, Islamabad, Pakistan, 1988-90; ICTP Diploma in High Energy Physics, ICTP, Trieste, Italy, 1992-93; PhD, Physics, Quaid-i-Azam University, Islamabad, Pakistan, 1996. Appointments: Post Doctoral Fellow, Santiago de Compostela University, Spain, 1997-99; Post Doctoral fellow, Tokyo Metropolitan University, Japan, 2000; Post Doctoral Fellow, 2001, Staff Scientist, 2002- Physics Division, NCTS, Taiwan. Publications: Research articles in scientific journals: Physical Review D; Physics Letters B; Astroparticle Physics; Co-editor, Proceedings of 1st NCTS Astroparticle Physics Workshop, Taiwan, 2001. Honours: WL Fellow, Islamabad, Pakistan, 1992-96; President Talent Scholarship for MSc, Islamabad, Pakistan, 1988-90. Memberships: Life Member, Pakistan Physical Society; Life Member, Pakistan Institute of Physics. Institute of Physics, National Chiao-Tung University, 1001 Ta Hsueh Road, Hsinchu 300, Taiwan. E-mail: athar.husain@cern.ch

**ATHERTON Michael Andrew,** b. 23 March 1968, Manchester, England. Cricketer. Education: Manchester Grammar School; Downing College, Cambridge. Appointments: Right Hand Opening Batsman; Leg Spin Bowler; Played for Cambridge University, 1987-89 (captain 1988-89); Lancashire, 1987-2001; England debut, 1989; 115 tests to May 2000, 54 as captain; (England record) Scoring 7,728 runs (average 37.69) including 16 centuries (to 1 January 2002); Has scored 18,349 first class runs (47 centuries) to end of 2000-01 season, including 1,193 in debut season; Toured Australia, 1990-91, 1994-95 (captain); 54 limited-overs internationals (43 as captain), to 20 August

1998; Toured South Africa, 1995-96, Zimbabwe and New Zealand, 1996-97, West Indies, 1998; Member, touring team in Australia, 1998-99, South Africa, 1999-2000, Pakistan and Sri Lanka, 2000-01; Retired, 2001; Cricket Commentator for Channel 4. Publications: A Test of Cricket, 1995; Opening Up (autobiography), 2002. Address: c/o Lancashire County Cricket Club, Old Trafford, Manchester, M16 0PX, England.

**ATKINSON Rowan Sebastian,** b. 6 January 1955, Newcastle-upon-Tyne, England. Actor; Author. m. Sunetra Sastry, 1990. Education: Universities of Newcastle and Oxford. Appointments: Stage Appearances include: Beyond a Joke, Hampstead, 1978; Oxford University, Revues at Edinburgh Fringe, One Man Show, London, 1981; The Nerd, 1985; The New Revue, 1986; The Sneeze, 1988; TV Appearances: Not the Nine O'Clock News, 1979-82; Blackadder, 1983; Blackadder II, 1985; Blackadder the Third, 1987; Blackadder Goes Forth, 1989; Mr Bean (13 episodes), 1990-96; Rowan Atkinson on Location in Boston, 1993; Full Throttle, 1994; The Thin Blue Line, 1995; Films Include: Never Say Never Again; The Tall Guy, 1989; The Appointments of Dennis Jennings, 1989; The Witches, 1990; Four Weddings and a Funeral, 1994; Hot Shots - Part Deux, 1994; Bean: The Ultimate Disaster Movie, 1997; Blackadder – Back and Forth, 2000; Maybe Baby, 2000; Rat Race, 2002; Scooby Doo, 2002; Johnny English, 2003; Love Actually, 2003; Keeping Mum, 2006. Address: c/o PBJ Management Ltd, 7 Soho Street, London W1D 3DQ, England. E-mail: general@pbjmgt.co.uk

**ATTENBOROUGH David Frederick,** b. 8 May 1926, London, England. Naturalist; Film-Maker; Author. Education: Zoology, Clare College, Cambridge, England. Appointments: Military Service, Royal Navy, 1947-49; Editorial Assistant, educational publishing; Joined BBC Television, Trainee Producer, 1952; First expedition to West Africa, 1954; Many trips to study wildlife and human cultures, 1954-64; TV series, Zoo Quest; Controller, BBC2, 1965-68; Director of Television Programmes, BBC, 1969-72; Member, Board of Management; TV Series include: Life on Earth, 1979, The Living Planet, 1983, The Trials of Life, 1990; The Private Life of Plants, 1995; The Life of Birds, 1998; Life of Mammals, 2002. Publications: Zoo Quest to Guiana, 1956; Zoo Quest for a Dragon, 1957; Zoo Quest in Paraguay, 1959; Quest in Paradise, 1960; Zoo Quest to Madagascar, 1961; Quest under Capricorn, 1963; The Tribal Eye, 1976; Life on Earth, 1979; The Living Planet, 1984; The First Eden, 1987; The Trials of Life, 1990; The Private Life of Plants, 1994; The Life of Birds, 1998; The Life of Mammals, 2002; Life on Air, autobiography, 2002. Honours include: Silver Medal, Zoological Society of London, 1966; Gold Medal Royal Geographical Society; Kalinga Prize, UNESCO; Honorary Degrees: Leicester, London, Birmingham, Liverpool, Heriot-Watt, Sussex, Bath, Ulster, Durham, Bristol, Glasgow, Essex, Cambridge, Oxford; Knighted, 1985; Encyclopaedia Britannica Award, 1987; Edinburgh Medal, Edinburgh Science Festival, 1998; BP Natural World Book Prize, 1998. Memberships include: Fellow, Royal Society, Honorary Fellow, British Academy of Film and Television Arts. Address: 5 Park Road, Richmond, Surrey, England.

**ATTENBOROUGH Richard (Baron Attenborough of Richmond-upon-Thames),** b. 29 August 1923, Cambridge, England. Actor; Producer; Director. m. Sheila Beryl Grant Sim, 1945, 1 son, 2 daughters. Education: Royal Academy of Dramatic Art, London. Appointments: First Stage Appearance as Richard Miller in Ah! Wilderness, Palmers Green 1941; West End Debut, Awake and Sing, 1942; First Film Appearance, In Which We Serve, 1942; Joined RAF, 1943; Seconded to RAF Film Unit for Journey Together, 1944; Demobilised, 1946;

Returned to Stage, 1949; Formed Beaver Films, with Bryan Forbes, 1959; Allied Film Makers, 1960; Goodwill Ambassador for UNICEF, 1987-; Director, Chelsea Football Club, 1969-82; Many stage appearances; Film Appearances: School for Secrets; The Man Within; Dancing With Crime; Brighton Rock; London Belongs to Me; The Guinea Pig; The Lost People; Boys in Brown; Morning Departure; The Magic Box; The Great Escape; Dr Doolittle; David Copperfield; Jurassic Park; Miracle on 34th Street; The Lost World: Jurassic Park; Elizabeth; Puckoon; Many others; Produced: Whistle Down the Wind, 1961; The L Shaped Room; Directed: Young Winston, 1972; A Bridge Too Far, 1976; Magic, 1978; A Chorus Line, 1985; Grey Owl, 2000; Produced and Directed: Oh! What a Lovely War, 1968; Gandhi, 1981; Cry Freedom!, 1987; Chaplin, 1992; Shadowlands, 1993; In Love and War, 1997; Grey Owl, 1998. Publications: In Search of Gandhi, 1982; Richard Attenborough's Chorus Line, 1986; Cry Freedom, A Pictorial Record, 1987. Honours: 8 Oscars; 5 BAFTA Awards; 5 Hollywood Golden Globes; Directors Guild of America Award; others. Memberships: Tate Foundation; Royal Academy of Dramatic Arts; Help a London Child; Others. Address: Old Friars, Richmond Green, Surrey, TW9 1NQ, England.

**ATWOOD Margaret (Eleanor),** b. 18 November 1939, Ottawa, Ontario, Canada. Poet; Author; Critic. m. Graeme Gibson, 1 daughter. Education: BA, Victoria College, University of Toronto, 1961; AM, Radcliffe College, Cambridge, Massachusetts, 1962; Harvard University, 1962-63, 1965-67. Appointments: Teacher, University of British Columbia, 1964-65, Sir George Williams University, Montreal, 1967-68, University of Alberta, 1969-70, York University, 1971-72; Writer-in-Residence, University of Toronto, 1972-73, University of Alabama, Tuscaloosa, 1985, Macquarie University, Australia, 1987; Berg Chair, New York University, 1986. Publications: Poetry: Double Persephone, 1961; The Circle Game, 1964; Kaleidoscopes Baroque, 1965; Talismans for Children, 1965; Speeches for Doctor Frankenstein, 1966; The Animals in That Country, 1968; The Journals of Susanna Moodie, 1970; Procedures for Underground, 1970; Oratorio for Sasquatch, Man and Two Androids, 1970; Power Politics, 1971; You Are Happy, 1974; Selected Poems, 1976; Marsh Hawk, 1977; Two-Headed Poems, 1978; True Stories, 1981; Notes Towards a Poem That Can Never Be Written, 1981; Snake Poems, 1983; Interlunar, 1984; Selected Poems II: Poems Selected and New, 1976-1986, 1986; Selected Poems 1966-1984, 1990; Margaret Atwood Poems 1965-1975, 1991; Morning in the Burned House, 1995. Fiction: The Edible Woman, 1969; Surfacing, 1972; Lady Oracle, 1976; Dancing Girls, 1977; Life Before Man, 1979; Bodily Harm, 1981; Encounters With the Element Man, 1982; Murder in the Dark, 1983; Bluebeard's Egg, 1983; Unearthing Suite, 1983; The Handmaid's Tale, 1985; Cat's Eye, 1988; Wilderness Tips, 1991; Good Bones, 1992; The Robber Bride, 1993; Alias Grace, 1996; The Blind Assassin, 2000; Oryx and Crake, 2003. Non-Fiction: Survival: A Thematic Guide to Canadian Literature, 1972; Days of The Rebels 1815-1840, 1977; Second Words: Selected Critical Prose, 1982; The Oxford Book of Canadian Verse in English (editor), 1982; The Best American Short Stories (editor with Shannon Ravenel), 1989; Strange Things: The Malevolent North in Canadian Literature, 1995; Negotiating with the Dead, 2002. Contributions to: Books in Canada; Canadian Literature; Globe and Mail; Harvard Educational Review; The Nation; New York Times Book Review; Washington Post. Honours: Guggenheim Fellowship, 1981; Companion of the Order of Canada, 1981; Fellow, Royal Society of Canada; Foreign Honorary Member, American Academy of Arts and Sciences, 1988; Order of Ontario, 1990; Centennial Medal, Harvard University, 1990; Commemorative Medal, 125th Anniversary of Canadian Confederation, 1992;

Giller Prize, 1996; Author of the Year, Canadian Book Industry Award, 1997; Marian McFadden Memorial Lecturer, Indianapolis-Marion County Public Library Foundation, 1998; Booker Prize, 2000; Honorary degrees. Memberships: Writers Union of Canada, president, 1981-82; PEN International, president, 1985-86. Address: McClelland & Stewart, 481 University Ave, Suite 900, Toronto, Ontario, Canada M5G 2E9.

**AUGSBACH Linda Jean Keller,** b. 7 June 1951, Glendale, West Virginia, USA. Elementary School Teacher. m. Charles William Augsbach. Education: AA Degree, Minnesota Bible College; Postgraduate studies, Kentucky Christian College, 1973-74; BS Degree, Malone College, Canton, Ohio, 1975. Appointments: Grades 1-8 Tutor, Minerva Local School, Ohio, 1976-77; Grades 1 and 2 Teacher, Christian School of Cinncinnati, Ohio, 1977-78; Substitute Teacher, Canton (Ohio) City School, 1978-82; Substitute Teacher, Pasco County School, Florida, 1982-83; Grade 6 Teacher, Dade City, Florida, 1983-87; Grade 4 Teacher, New Port Richey, Florida, 1987-88; Grade 6 Teacher, 1988-91, Grade 4 Teacher, 1991-96, alternately Grade 4 and Grade 5 Teacher, 1996-99, alternately Grade 4 and Grade 5 Teacher, 2000-, Mittye P. Locke Elementary, Elfers, Florida. Publications: Article in Learning Magazine, 1991; Copyright secured, 1999, for large curriculum: Learning: It's Just a Game – Science, History, Word Structure, Grammar, Writing and More, All Rolled Into One Exciting Unit, currently preparing for publication. Honours: The Best Teachers in America Selected by the Best Students, 1996; Selected attendee of Governor Bush's Second Annual Educators' Leadership Summit, 2002; Listed in Who's Who publications and biographical dictionaries. Membership: Christian Educators' Association International. Address: 1441 Wegman Drive, Tarpon Springs, FL 34689, USA.

**AUGUSTYN Józef,** b. 21 March 1950, Olpiny, Poland. Jesuit; Theologian. Education: BA Philosophical Studies, Jesuit School of Philosophy, Krakow, Poland, 1971-73; Theological Studies, Jesuit School of Theology, Warsaw, Poland, 1973-76; Graduate Studies, ThL, Religious Education, ATK University, Warsaw; Christian Spirituality, Gregorian University Rome, 1981-82; Research, The Center of Ignatian Spirituality, Quebec, Canada, 1989; PhD, Theology, Catholic University, Warsaw, 1994. Appointments: Professor, University School of Philosophy and Education "Ignatianum", Krakow, Poland; Editor, Pastores, 1996-2001; Currently Editor, Spiritual Life; Advisor, Polish Government, Department of Education, 1996-; Reviewer of Textbooks on sexual education and family values and public health and education, 1997-2000. Publications: 40 books and over 200 articles in the fields of spiritual life, Christian education, psychology and religion include: A Practice of Spiritual Direction, 1993; Sexual Integration. A Guidebook for discovering and maturing human sexuality, 1994; Homosexuality and Love, 1996; Sexual education in schools and families, 1997; Fatherhood: Pedagogical and spiritual dimensions, 1999; Know Yourself, 1999; Celibacy: Pedagogical and spiritual dimensions, 1999; Meditations based on the Spiritual Exercises of St Ignatius Loyola, 6 volumes, 2001. Honour: Award from the journal Powsciagliwosc I Praca, 1991. Memberships: Fellow of the State Committee, Department of Education, responsible for creating and implementing the school subject, Human Development and Sexuality, 1998; Advisor, Committee for Christian Education, Polish Conference of Catholic Bishops. Address: ul Kopernika 26, PL-31-501 Cracow, Poland.

**AUSTIN-COOPER Richard Arthur,** b. 21 February 1932. International Banking Personnel Manager (Retired). m. (1) Sylvia Anne Shirley Berringer; (2) Valerie Georgina Drage, 1 son, 1 daughter; (3) Mariola Danuta Sikorska; (4) Rosemary

Swaisland (née Gillespie). Education: Wellingborough Grammar School; Tottenham Grammar School. Appointments: Served RA, 1950-52 and TAVR in the RA, Intelligence Corps, 21 SAS Regt (Artist's Rifles), Essex ACF, 1952-68 and the Hon Artillery Co, 1978-79 (Commissioned 2 Lt TAVR 1968), OC ACF Canvey Island; With Barclays Bank, 1948-60; Head Cashier, Bank of Baroda, 1960-63, Lloyd's Bank, 1963-69; Deputy Head, Stocks and Shares Department, Banque de Paris et des Pays Bas, 1969-74; Assistant Manager, Banking Division, Brook Street Bureau of Mayfair Ltd, 1974-75; Chief Custodian and London Registrar, Canadian Imperial Bank of Commerce and Registrar in Britain for Angostura Bitters Ltd, 1975-78; Personnel Officer, Deutsche Bank AG London Branch, 1978-85; Senior Manager, Head of Human Resources, Deutsche Bank Capital Markets Ltd, 1985-90; Partner Charsby Associates Recruitment Consultants, London, 1989-91; Retired, 1991. Publications: Books: Butterhill and Beyond, 1991; The Beavers of Barnack, 1995; The de Gidlow Family of Ince, 1996; The Peisley Family of Clifton Hampden, Oxon, 1996. Honours: Prizes for: Athletics, Operatic Singing (Tenor), Painting; Freeman, City of London, 1964; Hon LLD, Hon MA (USA), FHG, 1965; FRSA, 1974; FRSAIre, 1980, FCIB, 1987. Memberships: Founder Fellow, Institute of Heraldic and Genealogical Studies; Treasurer, Irish Genealogical Research Society; Irish Peers Association, 1964-; Life Governor Sherriff's and Recorder's Fund at the Old Bailey, 1979-; Vice-President, Bourne Lincs Family History Society, 1993-; Chairman, Arthritis Care, Stamford, Lincolnshire, 1993-94; Chairman, Eastbourne Branch, British Cardiac Patients Association, 2003-; Vice-Chairman, Trustee and Member Executive Committee, Friends of Eastbourne Hospitals, 2003-; Governor, American College in Oxford; Governor, City of London School for Girls; Governor, Freeman's School; Governor, Lansbury Adult Education Institute; Representative, City of London Corporation on the Greater London Arts Council; Trustee, City of London Imperial Volunteers; Member, City of London-TAVR Association; Coal, Corn and Rates Committee; A Manager, Barbican School of Music and Drama; Member, City of London Mayor's Court of Common Council for Cripplegate Ward, 1978-81; SAS Regimental Association; Intelligence Corps OCA; Artists Rifles Association. Address: 2 Lea House, 1 Mill Road, Eastbourne, East Sussex BN21 2LY, England.

**AVAKYAN Sergei Vazgenovitch,** b. 2 April 1943, Yerevan, Armenia. Physicist. m. Baranova Lubov Alexandrovna, 2 October 1967, 1 daughter. Education: Diploma, Leningrad State University, 1965; PhD, 1975; Senior Scientific Worker in Optics, 1978; Doctor of Science, Physics and Mathematics, 1987. Appointments: Scientific Worker, A F Ioffe Physiko-Technical Institute, 1966-70; Scientific Worker, 1971-77, Senior Scientific Worker, 1977-95, Leading Scientific Worker 1995-96, Head of Laboratory of Aerospace Physical Optics, 1996-, Chief-constructor of Space Instrumentation, 2002-, S I Vavilov State Optical Institute. Publications: 5 book and 3 handbooks. Honours: Labour Heroism, 1977; Yuri Gagarin Diploma, 1982. Memberships: Problem Council, Physics of Collision; Russian Academy of Science; Physical Society of St Petersburg; International Society of Optical Engineering; D S Rogdenstvensky Russian Optical Society; Scientific-Technical Council of the Russian Aerospace Agency. Address: Kurchatov Str 4, apt 75, St Petersburg, 194223 Russia. E-mail: avak@soi.spb.ru

**AVEDON Richard,** b. 15 May 1923, New York, USA. Photographer. m. (1) Dorcas Nowell, 1944, (2) Evelyn Franklin, 1951, 1 son, 1 daughter. Education: Columbia. Appointments: Staff Photographer, Harper's Bazaar, 1945-65; Member, Editorial Staff Theatre Arts Magazine, 1952-53; Vogue magazine, 1966-90; Photographer, New Yorker, 1992-; One Man Exhibitions: Smithsonian Institute, 1962; Minneapolis Institute of Arts, 1970; Museum of Modern Art, 1974; Marlborough Gallery, New York, 1975; Metropolitan Museum of Art New York, 1978; University of Art Museum, Berkeley, California, 1980; Amon Carter Museum, Fort Worth, TX, 1985; American Tour, Retrospective Richard Avedon Evidence, 1944-94; Whitney Museum of American Art, New York, 1994; Visiting Artist, Harvard University, 1986-87. Publications: Observations, 1959; Nothing Personal, 1964; Alice in Wonderland, 1973; Portraits, 1976; Rolling Stones Magazine, The Family, 1976; Avedon, Photographs, 19447-77; In the American West, 1985; An Autobiography, 1993; Evidence. Honours: Fellow, Timothy Dwight College, Yale University, 1975; President's Fellow, Rhode Island School of Design, 1978; Highest Achievement Medal Awards, Art Directors Show, 1950; Popular Photography World's 10 Greatest Photographers; National Magazine Award for Visual Excellence; Citation of Dedication to Fashion Photography, Pratt Institute; Chans Citation, University of California; Art Directors Club Hall of Fame; American Society of Magazine Photographers Photographer of the Year; Best Photography Book of the Year Award; Maine Photography Workshop; Director of the Year, Adweek magazines; Dr hc; Lifetime Achievement Award, Council of Fashion Designers of America; Harvard University Certificate of Recognition, Priz Nadar. Mental Health Association of New York City Human Award; Lifetime Achievement Award, Columbia University Graduate School of Journalism, 2000; Berlin Photography Prize, Deutsches Centrum for Photography, 2000. Address: 407 East 75th Street, New York, NY 10021, USA.

**AVERY Bryan,** b. 2 January 1944, Aston Tirrold, Berkshire, England. Architect. 1 daughter. Education: Dip Arch, Department of Architecture, Leicester College of Art & Design, 1962-68; MA, History and Theory of Architecture, Faculty of Fine Art, Essex University, 1969-70. Appointments: Founding Director, Avery Associates Architects: projects include: The Museum of the Moving Image, London, 1984-88; National Film Theatre, London, 1984-99; The British Film Institute's London Imax, 1990-99; The Royal Academy of Dramatic Art, London, 1981-2001; The Commonwealth Institute, Kensington, 2001-02; Oakham School, Music Department and Concert Hall, Rutland, 2001-; London's Transport Museum, Covent Garden, 2001-. Publications: Works much published in UK and abroad. Honours: PA Award for Innovation, 1988; UNISCO Award, 1984; City Heritage Award, 1992; Aluminium Imagination Award, 1997; Glassex Award (Best Building), 1997; British Construction Industry Award, 1997, 1999; British Council for Offices Award, 1998; Millennium Products Award x 2, 1999; Comedia Creative City Award for Urban Innovation, 2000; Civic Trust Award – for years 1989, 1998, 2000, 2002; British Institute of Architectural Technologists Award, 2002; United States Institute of Theatre & Technicians Award, 2003; Royal Institute of British Architects Award, 2001. Memberships: Royal Institute of British Architects; Fellow, Royal Society of Arts; The Architecture Club. Address: Avery Associates Architects, 270 Vauxhall Bridge Road, London, SW1V 1BB, England. E-mail: enquiries@avery-architects.co.uk Website: avery-architects.co.uk

**AVERY Charles Henry Francis,** b. 26 December 1940, London, England. Fine Art Consultant. m. (Kathleen) Mary, 3 daughters (triplets). Education: MA, PhD, St John's College, Cambridge; Academic Diploma, Courtauld Institute of Art, London. Appointments: Deputy Keeper of Sculpture, Victoria and Albert Museum, 1965-69; Director, Sculpture Department, Christie's, 1979-90; Currently, Independent Fine Art Consultant. Publications: Books: Florentine Renaissance

Sculpture, 1970; Studies in European Sculpture, 1981, 1987; Giambologna the Complete Sculpture, 1987l Renaissance and Baroque Bronzes in the Frick Art Museum, 1993; Donatello: An Introduction, 1994; David Le Marchand (1674-1726). An Ingenious Man for Carving in Ivory, 1996; Bernini, Genius of the Baroque, 1997; Studies in Italian Sculpture, 2001. Honours: Cavaliere Dell'ordine Al Merito della Repubblica Italiana, 1979; Medal of the Ministry of Culture, Poland; FSA, 1985; Leverhulme Research Fellow, 1997-99. Memberships: United Oxford and Cambridge; Beckenham Tennis Club. Address: Holly Tree House, 20 Southend Road, Beckenham, Kent BR3 1SD, England.

**AWABI Hazim Bashir,** b. 1 July 1945, Mosul, Iraq. Academic Engineer. 4 daughters. Education: BSc, Mechanical Engineering, 1967, MSc, Heat Transfer, 1969, University of Manchester; PhD, Industrial Aerodynamics, Nottingham Trent University, 1974. Appointments: Engineer, Engineering Sciences Data Unit International, London, 1974-75; Lecturer, Mechanical Engineering Department, Baghdad University of Technology, Iraq, 1975-81; Head of the Air Distribution Section, Building Services Research and Information Association, Bracknell, England, 1981-93; Lecturer, Department of Mechanical, Manufacturing and Software Engineering, Napier University, Edinburgh, 1983-90; Senior Lecturer, School of Construction Management and Engineering, University of Reading, 1990-. Publications: Author of the computational fluid dynamics code VORTEX© for simulating the airflow and heat transfer in and around buildings; Book: Ventilation of Buildings (2 editions); Contributor to 3 books; Over 120 scientific articles in journals and conference proceedings. Honours: Numerous research grants from UK and European funding agencies; Honorary Professor, Department of Architecture and Urban Planning, Chongqing University, China, 1994; Visiting Professor, Department of Civil Engineering, University of Technology, Lisbon, Portugal, 1999-2001. Memberships: Institution of Mechanical Engineers, London, 1977-; Royal Aeronautical Society, London, 1978-95; Chartered Institute of Building Services Engineers, London, 1989-; American Society of Heating, Refrigeration and Air-Conditioning Engineers, 1998-; Board of Trustees, World Renewable Energy Network, 1992-2005; Editorial Board, 1995-2005, Associate Editor, 2005, International Journal of Renewable Energy; Editorial Board, International Journal of Ventilation, 2002-; Chairman and Organiser, Seventh International Conference on Air Distribution in Rooms (ROOMVENT 2000), Reading, 2000; Member, International Committees of numerous conferences in indoor environment and energy; Reviewer for many scientific journals; Assessor for research funding agencies in various countries. Address: Indoor Environment and Energy Research Group, School of Construction Management and Engineering, University of Reading, Reading RG6 6AW, England. E-mail: h.b.awabi@reading.ac.uk

**AWADALLAH Bassem,** b. 21 December 1964, Jerusalem, Israel. Minister of Planning and International Co-operation. Education: BSc, (Hons), Foreign Service, International Economics, International Finance and Commerce, Georgetown University, School of Foreign Service, Washington DC, USA, 1981-84; MSc, (Hons), Economics, 1984-85, PhD, Economics, 1985-88, London School of Economics, University of London; Training courses, Nomura Securities, Daiwa Securities and Schroeder Warburg, 1986, 1988. Appointments: Finance Manager, EDGO Group of Companies, London, 1988-90; Finance and Project Development Manager, New Work Co Ltd, Amman, Jordan, 1990-91; Economic Advisor to the Prime Minister of the Hashemite Kingdom of Jordan, The Prime Ministry, Amman: Duties including: Director of the Economic Department at the Prime Ministry, Senior Co-ordinator and Rapporteur of the Ministerial Economic Council, Co-ordinator of the Joint Jordanian-Israeli Higher Committee for the implementation of the Treaty of Peace between Jordan and Israel, Senior Member, Jordanian-Israeli and Jordanian-Palestine Economic Committees, Member of the Board of Directors: National Electricity and Power Company, Arab Potash Company, Hydro-Agri Jordan, Holy Land Hotels Company, 1991-99; Economic Adviser to His Majesty the King, Director of the Economic Department, The Royal Hashemite Court, Amman, Jordan, 1999-2001; Minister of Planning, 2001-2003, Minister of Planning and International Co-operation, 2003-, Hashemite Kingdom of Jordan. Publications: The economic liberalization "infitah" policy in Egypt; a case study in the inter-relation of external and internal factors, 1985; The Political Economy of the West Bank of Jordan (1972-1986), (doctoral dissertation). Honours: Al Hussein Medal for Distinguished Service; Al Kawkab Decoration of the First Order of the Hashemite Kingdom of Jordan; The Royal Hashemite Award for distinguished service at the MENA Summit in Amman; Al Istiqlal Decoration of the First Order of the Hashemite Kingdom of Jordan. Address: Ministry of Planning and International Co-operation, PO Box 555, Amman, 11118 Jordan. E-mail: bassem@go.com.jo

**AWDRY Christopher Vere,** b. 2 July 1940, Devizes, Wiltshire, England. Writer; Author. 1 son, 1 daughter. Education: Worksop College, 1954-58. Appointments: Printing and publishing, 1958-67; Civil Service, 1967-87; Columnist, Cambs, Hunts and Peterborough Life, 1978-83; Writer, The Railway Series (Thomas the Tank Engine), 1983-; Lecturer, WEA, 1992-. Publications: Numerous titles in The Railway Series, 1983-; Encyclopaedia of British Railway Companies, 1990; Brunel's Broad Gauge Railway, 1992; Contributions to: Little Railways of Britain, 1992; Encyclopaedia of the GWR, 1993; Over the Summit, 1993; Foreword to Explore Britain's Steam Railways, 1995; Awdry's Steam Railways, 1995; Railways Galore, 1996; Volume in the Past and Present Series: Blisworth-Peterborough Branch Line, 2001; Numerous articles in newspapers, journals and magazines. Memberships: President: Talyllyn Railway Preservation Society, Corris Railway Society, Forest of Dean Railway Society, Barrow-in-Furness Model Railway Society; Patron: Joe Homan Charity, Wensleydale Railway; Railway and Canal Historical Society. Address: 1 Hutton Close, Clay Lake, Spalding, Lincolnshire PE12 6UY, England.

**AYATOLLAHI Seyyed Mohammad Taghi,** b. 6 January 1953, Shiraz, Iran. Professor. m. Sareh, 1 daughter. Education: BSc, Statistics, Shiraz University, School of Arts and Sciences, 1970-76; MSc, Biostatistics, School of Graduate Studies, 1976-78; MS, Biostatistics, Columbia University, School of Public Health, 1978-80; PhD, Medical Statistics, London University, School of Hygiene and Tropical Medicine, 1989-91; PDRA; FSS; CStat, Medical Statistics, Epidemiology, Newcastle University, The Medical School, UK, 1992-94. Appointments: Technician, 1975-76; Senior Teacher, High Schools of Shiraz; Statistician, Programmer, Shiraz University, 1976-78; Lecturer, Head, Department of Biostatistics, 1982-89; Associate Dean, School of Medicine, 1983-84; Chairman, Educational Planning Bureau, 1984-85; Vice Chancellor, Shiraz University, 1984-88; Chairman, Secretary, Cultural Council, Shiraz University of Medical Sciences, 1988-89; Visiting Lecturer, London School of Hygiene and Tropical Medicine, 1990-91; Computer Programmer, University College of London, 1990-91; Statistical Programmer, Oxford University, 1991-92; Research Associate, Newcastle University, 1992-94; Professor, Shiraz University of Medical Sciences, 1994-; Dean, School of Graduate Studies, Shiraz University of Medical Sciences, 1996-2000; Dean,

# DICTIONARY OF INTERNATIONAL BIOGRAPHY

School of Public Health, Shiraz University of Medical Sciences, 1998-2003. Publications: over 170 papers and 18 books published. Honours: Distinguished Graduate Student; Fellow, Royal Statistical Society; Chartered Statistician; International Man of the Year; Noble Prize Winner, 2001; many others. Memberships: New York Academy of Sciences; Society for the Study of Human Biology; Iran Statistical Society; others. Address: Department of Biostatistics and Epidemiology, P O Box 71345-1874, Shiraz, Islamic Republic, Iran.

**AYCKBOURN Alan (Sir),** b. 12 April 1939, London, England. Theatre Director; Playwright; Artistic Director. Plays: Mr Whatnot, 1963; Relatively Speaking, 1965; How The Other Half Loves, 1969; Time And Time Again, 1971; Absurd Person Singular, 1972; The Norman Conquests, 1973; Absent Friends, 1974; Confusions, 1974; Bedroom Farce, 1975; Just Between Ourselves, 1976; Ten Times Table, 1977; Joking Apart, 1978; Sisterly Feelings, 1979; Taking Steps, 1979; Season's Greetings, 1980; Way Upstream, 1981; Intimate Exchanges, 1982; A Chorus Of Disapproval, 1984; Woman In Mind, 1985; A Small Family Business, 1987; Henceforward..., 1987; Man Of The Moment, 1988; Mr A's Amazing Maze Plays, 1988; The Revengers' Comedies, 1989; Invisible Friends, 1989; Body Language, 1990; Wildest Dreams, 1991; Time Of My Life, 1992; Dreams From A Summer House, (music by John Pattison), 1992; Communicating Doors, 1994; Haunting Julia, 1994; By Jeeves (with Andrew Lloyd Webber), 1996; The Champion Of Paribanou, 1996; Things We Do For Love, 1997; Comic Potential, 1998; The Boy Who Fell Into A Book, 1998; House & Garden, 1999; Callisto #7, 1999; Whenever, 2000; GamePlan, 2001; FlatSpin, 2001; RolePlay (aka Damsels In Distress Trilogy), 2001; Snake In The Grass, 2002; The Jollies, 2002; Sugar Daddies, 2003; Orvin – Champion Of Champions, 2003; My Sister Sadie, 2003; Drowning On Dry Land, 2004; Private Fears In Public Places, 2004; Miss Yesterday, 2004; Improbable Fiction, 2005. Honours: Hon DLitt, Hull, 1981, Keele, 1987, Leeds, 1987, York, 1992, Bradford, 1994, Cardiff University of Wales, 1996, Open University, 1998, Manchester, 2003; Commander of the Order of the British Empire, 1987; Cameron Mackintosh Professor of Contemporary Theatre, 1992; Knighthood, 1997. Memberships: Fellow, Royal Society of Arts. Address: c/o Casarotto Ramsay and Associates Ltd, National House, 60-66 Wardour Street, London W1V 4ND, England. Website: www.alanayckbourn.net

**AYKROYD Daniel Edward,** b. 1 July 1952, Ottawa, Canada. Actor. m. (1) Maureen Lewis, 1974, divorced, 3 sons, (2) Donna Dixon, 1984, 2 daughters. Education: Carleton University, Ottawa. Appointments: Started as stand up comedian and worked on Saturday Night Live, 1975-79; Created and performed as the Blues Brothers; Albums include: Made in America; Films include: 1941, 1979; Mr Mike's Mondo Video, 1979; The Blues Brothers, 1980; Neighbors, 1981; Doctor Detroit, 1983; Trading Places, 1983; Twilight Zone, 1983; Ghostbusters, 1984; Nothing Lasts for Ever, 1984; Into the Night, 1985; Spies Like Us, 1985; Dragnet, 1987; Caddyshack II, 1988; The Great Outdoors, 1988; My Stepmother is an Alien, 1988; Ghostbusters II, 1989; Driving Miss Daisy, 1990; My Girl; Loose Cannons; Valkemania; Nothing But Trouble, 1991; Coneheads, 1993; My Girl II, 1994; North; Casper, 1995; Sergeant Bilko, 1996; Grosse Point Blank, 1997; Blues Brothers 2000, 1997; The Arrow, 1997; Susan's Plan, 1998; Antz, 1999; Diamonds, 1999; The House of Mirth, 2000; Stardom, 2000; Dying to Get Rich, 2000; The Devil and Daniel Webster, Not A Girl, Pearl Harbour, 2001; Evolution, 2001; Crossroads, 2002; Who Shot Victor Fox, 2002; The Curse of the Jade Scorpion, 2002. Honours: Emmy Award, 1976-77. Address: c/o CAA, 9830 Wilshire Boulevard, Beverly Hills, CA 90212, USA.

**AYLMER Gerald Edward,** b. 30 April 1926, England. Historian. Education: BA, 1950, MA, 1951, PhD, 1955, Oxford University. Appointments: J E Proctor Visiting Fellow, Princeton University, New Jersey, 1950-51; Junior Research Fellow, Balliol College, Oxford, 1951-54; Assistant Lecturer, 1954-57, Lecturer, 1957-62, University of Manchester; Professor and Head of Department, University of York, 1963-78; Master, St Peter's College, Oxford, 1978-91, Honorary Fellow, 1991; Editorial Board, 1968-98, Chairman, 1989-98, History of Parliament; Member, 1978-, Chairman, 1989-94, Royal Commission on Historical Manuscripts. Publications: The King's Servants, 1625-1642, 1961; The Diary of William Lawrence, 1961; The Struggle for the Constitution 1603-1689, 1963; The Interregnum 1646-1660, 1972; The State's Servants, 1649-1660, 1973; The Levellers in the English Revolution, 1975; A History of York Minster, 1977; Rebellion or Revolution 1640-1660, 1986; Hereford Cathedral: A History (editor with D Tiller), 2000; The Crown's Servants 1660-1685, 2002. Honour: Fellow, British Academy, 1976; Honorary Degrees, Exeter University, Manchester University, 1991. Memberships: Royal Historical Society, vice president, 1973-77, president, 1984-88, honorary vice president, 1988; Historical Association, honorary vice president, 1992-. Address: 18 Albert Street, Jericho, Oxford OX2 6AZ, England.

**AZAB Hassan Ahmed,** b. 16 June 1950, Ismailia, Egypt. Professor of Chemistry. m. Naima Fouad, 1 son, 1 daughter. Education: BSc, Chemistry, 1972; MSc, Chemistry, 1976; PhD, Chemistry, 1983. Appointments: Professor of Analytical and Inorganic Chemistry, Head of Chemistry Department, Vice-Dean, Faculty of Science, Suez Canal University, Ismailia, Egypt. Publications: More than 70 international publications in the field of analytical and inorganic chemistry; Recent publication on biologically important DNA-protein-metal ions systems. Honours: TWAS Award, 1989; Peaceful Fellowship, 1990 DAAD Award, 1996, 2003; DGF Award, 2000; EV (NATO) Award, 2004; Senior Visiting Award, WOU, 2005. Memberships: American Chemical Society; American Association for the Advancement of Science. Address: Faculty of Science, Chemistry Department, Suez Canal University, Ismailia, Egypt. E-mail: azab2@yahoo.com

**AZINGER Paul William,** b. 6 January 1960, Holyoke, Massachusetts, USA. Golfer. m. Toni, 2 daughters. Education: Florida State University. Appointments: Started playing golf aged 5; Turned professional, 1981; Won Phoenix Open, 1987; Herz Bay Hill Classic, 1988; Canon Greater Hartford Open, 1989; MONY Tournament of Champions, 1990; AT and T Pebble Beach National Pro Am, 1991; TOUR Championship, 1992; BMW International Open, 1990; Memorial Tournament, New England Classic, PGA Championship, Inverness, 1993; GWAA Ben Hogan Trophy, 1995; Member, US Ryder Cup Team, 1989, 1991, 1993, 2001; Broadcasting debut as reporter for NBC, 1995; Ryder Cup. Publications: Zinger. Honours: PGA Tour Player of the Year, 1987. Address: PGA Tour, 112 Tpc Boulevard, Ponte Vedra Beach, FL 33082, USA.

**AZNAR José Maria,** b. 25 February 1953, Madrid, Spain. Lawyer; Politician. m. 3 children. Education: Licence in Law, Complutense University of Madrid. Appointments: State Finance Inspector; Secretary General, Logrono Popular Alliance Party, 1979; Secretary General, Popular Alliance Party, 1982-87; Avila Delegate, 1982-87; Castilla y León Regional President, Popular Alliance Party; National Vice-President, Popular Party, 1989; President, Autonomous Community of Castilla y León's Popular Alliance, 1987-89; Popular Party's Elected Candidate for Presidency of Government, 1989; National Delegate for Madrid in the 4th, 5th and 6th Legislature;

President of the Popular Parliamentarian Group in the Congress of Delegates, 1991; Vice President, European Popular Party; Vice President International Democratic Union; Vice President, European Democratic Union; Invested President of Government of Spain (Prime Minister), 1996-2004; President, International Democratic Centre (IDC), 2001. Address: Partido Popular, Genova 13, Madrid, Spain.

# B

**BABAN Serwan M J,** b. 23 April 1958, Kirkuk, Iraq. University Professor. m. Judith Anne, 2 daughters. Education: BSc, Geology, 1980, MSc, Geophysics, 1983, University of Baghdad, Iraq; PhD, Environmental Remote Sensing, University of East Anglia, UK, 1991. Appointments: Research Associate, Senior Research Associate, University of East Anglia, UK; Lecturer, Senior Lecturer, Coventry University, UK; Professor of Surveying and Land Information, 2000-, Chairman, School of Graduate Studies and Research, 2004-, The University of the West Indies, Trinidad and Tobago. Publications: Over 80 articles in international and national journals, international conference proceedings, chapters in books as well as consultancy reports including most recently: Modelling Sites for Reservoirs in Tropical Environments, 2003; Responding to the Effects of Climate Change, 2003; Flooding and Landslides in the West Indies, 2004; Information Poverty and Decision-Making, 2004; Mapping Landslide Susceptibility in the Tropics, 2004, 2005; Examining land use changes due to irrigated agriculture in Jordan using Geoinformatics, 2005; Evaluating Water Circulation and Contaminant Transport Models for the Intra-American Seas, 2005; Accomplishing Sustainable Development in Southern Kurdistan Using Geoinformatics, 2005. Memberships: Fellow, Royal Geographical Society, 1999-; Remote Sensing Society Council, 1999-2001; Fellow, Geological Society, 2000-; Fellow, Remote Sensing and Photogrammetry Society, 2001; Visiting Fellow, School of Environmental Sciences, University of East Anglia, UK, 2002-; Member and National Representative, International Association of Hydrological Sciences. Address: Department of Surveying and Land Information, University of the West Indies, St Augustine, Trinidad and Tobago, West Indies.

**BABATUNDE Bukola Bunmi,** b. 19 February 1965, Ikirun, Nigeria. Researcher and Lecturer in Animal Nutrition. m. Isaac Aderemilekun Babatunde. Education: BSc, Agriculture, 1987, MSc, Agricultural Biochemistry and Nutrition, 1990, PhD, Animal Nutrition, 1989, University of Ibadan, Nigeria. Appointments: Junior Research Fellow, 1990-92, Livestock Feed Analyst and Consultant, 1990-92; Lecturer III and Researcher, 1992-94, Lecturer II and Researcher, 1994-97, Lecturer I and Researcher, 1997-2000, Senior Lecturer and Researcher, 2000-, Federal College of Animal Health and Production Technology, Institute of Agricultural Research and Training, Apata, Ibadan, Nigeria; Currently working on a Research programme in Dairy Calves Immunity, La Trobe University, Bundoora, Australia. Publications: Article as co-author, Comparative utilization of three commonly used fibrous ingredients in maize-soyabean meal-fish meal diets by broiler chicks, 2000; Other articles in journals including: Journal of Biological Wastes, 1988; Journal of Agricultural Research, 2002; Journal of Pure and Applied Science, 2003; Nigerian Poultry Science Journal, 2004. Honours: Admitted to Role of Honour, Nigerian Society for Animal Production, 2001; Honorary Appointment, Research Board of Advisors, American Biographical Institute; La Trobe University Research Scholarship in the Year 2004; Listed in Who's Who publications and biographical dictionaries. Memberships: New York Academy of Sciences; World Poultry Science Association; Animal Science Association of Nigeria; Nigerian Society of Animal Production. Address: Department of Agricultural Sciences, La Trobe University, Bundoora Campus, Vic 3086, Australia. E-mail: buki9465@yahoo.com

**BABICH Alexander,** b. 12 November 1952, Donetsk, Ukraine. Metallurgist; Educator. m. Eugenia Goldstein, 1 son. Education: Metallurgy Engineering, Donetsk Polytechnic Institute, 1974; PhD (Tech), 1984; Associate Professor, 1989. Appointments: Furnace Worker, Foreman, Donetsk Steel Plant, 1974-76; Engineer, Scientific worker, Donetsk Polytechnic Institute, 1978-85; Associate Professor, Donetsk State University of Technology, 1985-96; Visiting Researcher, National Centre for Metallurgical Investigation, Madrid, 1997-98; Researcher, Aachen University of Technology, 1998-. Publications: Over 130 publications including a monograph, a textbook and 13 patents. Honours: Grant, Ministry of Education and Science, Spain; Who's Who in the World Diploma, 1999; Listed in several biographical publications, Address: Hauptstr 78, 52066 Aachen, Germany. E-mail: babich@iehk.rwth-aachen.de

**BABINEAU Jean Joseph,** b. 10 August 1952, Moncton, New Brunswick, Canada. Teacher; Writer. m. Gisèle Ouellette, 27 August 1993, 1 son. Education: BA, 1977; BA, French, 1981; BEd, 1985; MA, French, 2002. Publication: Bloupe, 1993; Gîte, 1998; Vortex, 2003. Contributions to: Éloizes; Mots en Volet; Littéréalité; Satellite; Nouvelles d'Amerique; Virages; Le Front Moebius. Honour: Canada Council Exploration Grant, 1989; New Brunswick Arts Branch Creation Grant, 1998, 2002; Prix litteraire Antoinese-Maillet Acadie Vie, 2004. Membership: AAAPNB. Address: 12 allée Gite Lane, Grand-Barachois, New Brunswick, E4P 7N9, Canada.

**BABITSKY Vladimir,** b. 4 April 1938, Gomel, USSR. Mechanical Engineer. m. Eleonora Lublina, 1 son. Education: MSc Mechanical Engineering, Moscow State Technological University, 1960; PhD, 1964, DSc, 1973, USSR Academy of Sciences. Appointments: Engineer, 1960-61, Research Assistant, 1961-67, Senior Research Assistant and a Head of a research group, 1967-87, Founder and Head, Vibrations Systems Laboratory, 1987-91, Institute for Machine Studies, USSR Academy of Sciences; Guest Professor, Institute B for Mechanics, Munich, Germany, 1990; Consultant, HILTI AG, 1992-95; Professor of Dynamics, Loughborough University, England, 1995-. Books: Theory of vibro-impact systems and applications, 1998 (translation from Russian 1978); Vibration of strongly nonlinear discontinuous systems (co-author), 2001 (translation from Russian, 1985); Dynamics and Control of Machines (co-author), 2000; Resonant Robotic Systems (co-author), 2003. Memberships: Euromech; FICoVIS; IFAC. Address: Wolfson School of Mechanical and Manufacturing Engineering, Loughborough University, Loughborough LE11 3TU, England. E-mail: v.i.babitsky@lboro.ac.uk

**BABU Yallapragada Ramesh,** b. 14 January 1952, Bhattiprolu, India. Engineer. Education: Graduate, Mechanical Department, College of Engineering, Jawaharlal Nehru Technological University, 1975; MEng, Industrial Engineering, College of Engineering, Sri Venkateswara University, 1979; PhD, Mechanical Department, College of Engineering, Andhra University, 1993. Appointments: Lecturer, Mechanical Department, Bapatla Engineering College, 1982-86; Faculty, College of Engineering, Gandhi Institute of Technology and Management, Visakhapatnam, 1986-. Publications: Several articles in professional journals. Honours: World Lifetime Achievement Award, 1997; 20th Century Award for Achievement, 1998; 2000 Millennium Medal of Honour, 1998; International Man of the Millennium, 1999; Outstanding Man of the 20th Century, 1999; International Personality of the Year 2001; International Scientist of the Year, 2001; International Man of the Year 2000-2001; Great Minds of the 21st Century; International Book of Honor; International Who's Who of Twentieth Century Achievement; 2000 Outstanding Scientists of the 20th Century; 2000 Outstanding Scientists of the 21st Century. Memberships: Indian Institution of Industrial Engineering; Institution of Engineers, India; Research Board of

Advisors, ABI, USA; Advisory Council IBC, England; Listed in numerous biographical publications including Five Hundred Leaders of Influence. Address: Mechanical Department, College of Engineering, Gandhi Institute of Technology and Management, Visakhapatnam 530045, Andhra Pradesh, India.

**BACALL Lauren,** b. 16 September 1924, New York, USA. Actress. m. (1) Humphrey Bogart, 1945, died 1957, (2) Jason Robards, 1961, divorced, 2 sons, 1 daughter. Career: Films include: Two Guys from Milwaukee, 1946; The Big Sleep; Young Man with a Horn; How to Marry a Millionaire; Blood Alley, Sex and the Single Girl; Murder on the Orient Express, 1974; Appointment with Death, 1988; Misery, 1990; All I Want for Christmas, 1991; The Field, 1993; Pret á Porter, 1995. Publications: Lauren Bacall by Myself, 1978; Lauren Bacall Now, 1994. Honours: 2 Tony Awards, 1970, 1981; Woman of the Year Award, 1981. Address: c/o Johnnies Planco, William Morris Agency, 1325 Avenue of the Americas, New York, NY 10019, USA.

**BACHARACH Burt,** b. 12 May 1928, Kansas City, Missouri, USA. Composer; Arranger; Conductor; Musician (piano). m. (1) Paula Stewart, (2) Angie Dickinson, (3) Carole Bayer Sager, 1982, 1 son, 1 daughter. Musical Education: Composition and Theory, McGill University, Montreal; Music Academy West, Santa Barbara. Career: Jazz musician, 1940s; Accompanist, arranger, conductor, various artists including Vic Damone; Marlene Dietrich; Joel Gray; Steve Lawrence. Compositions: Popular songs, film music and stage musicals; Regular collaborations with Hal David, 1962-70; Carole Bayer Sager, 1981-; Numerous hit songs as co-writer include: with Hal David: The Story Of My Life, Marty Robbins; Magic Moments, Perry Como; Tower Of Strength, Frankie Vaughan; Wives And Lovers, Jack Jones; 24 Hours From Tulsa, Gene Pitney; What The World Needs Now Is Love, Jackie DeShannon; Walk On By; Trains And Boats And Planes; Do You Know The Way To San Jose?; Alfie (all by Dionne Warwick); Anyone Who Had A Heart, Cilla Black; There's Always Something There To Remind Me, Sandie Shaw; Make It Easy On Yourself, Walker Brothers; What's New Pussycat?, Tom Jones; This Guy's In Love With You, Herb Alpert; Raindrops Keep Fallin' On My Head, Sacha Distel; Close To You, The Carpenters; Numerous film scores include: The Man Who Shot Liberty Valence; Wives And Lovers; What's New Pussycat?; Alfie; Casino Royale; Butch Cassidy And The Sundance Kid; with Carole Bayer Sager: Making Love, Roberta Flack; Heartlight, Neil Diamond; That's What Friends Are For, Dionne Warwick And Friends (AIDs charity record); On My Own, Patti Labelle and Michael McDonald; with Carole Bayer Sager, Peter Allen and Christopher Cross: Arthur's Theme, Christopher Cross. Recordings: Albums include: Hit Maker, 1965; Reach Out, 1967; Make It Easy On Yourself, 1969; Burt Bacharach, 1971; Portrait In Music, 1971; Living Together, 1973; Greatest Hits, 1974; Futures, 1977, 1999; Woman, 1979; Walk On By, 1989; Butch Cassidy And The Sundance Kid, 1989; Publications: Numerous songbooks. Honours: Entertainers of the Year, with Hal David, Cue Magazine, 1969; 3 Academy Awards; Several Academy Award Nominations; 4 Grammy Awards; 2 Emmy Awards; 1 Tony Award. Address: c/o McMullen And Co, Hollywood, CA, USA.

**BACHTA Abdelkader,** b. 5 July 1945, Tozeur, Tunisia. Professor of Philosophy and History of Science. m. Hafida, 3 sons. Education: Tunisian General Certificate of Education, 1966; French General Certificate of Education, 1968; Professorship of French Literature, 1968; Bachelor's Degree of Philosophy, Tunisia, 1972; Master of Philosophy, Tunisia, 1976; Highest grade of doctorate in France, Philosophy, Paris,

1983. Appointments: Professor of French in Secondary School; Professor of Philosophy in Secondary School, Tunisia; Seaker, at France, Philosophy, Paris X; Professor of Philosophy in University EAU; Professor of Philosophy in Tunis (the highest grade). Publications: Books include: (in French) L'espace et le temps chez Newton et Kant, 1991; (Arabic) What is the Epistemology?, 1995; Méthods in Islamic Science; Articles in journals on philosophy and history of science in Arabic and French. Honours: Memberships: Vice President, Arabic Society of Philosophy; CTHS French Section History of Science; Society of 18c S Grench; Society of History of Science, French. Address: BP 390 Pupliposte Nassr 1, Rianna 2037, Tunisia.

**BACK Lloyd,** b. 13 February 1933, San Francisco, USA. Mechanical Engineer. m. Carol Peterson, 1 son, 2 daughters. Education: BS, 1959, PhD, 1962, University of California at Berkeley. Appointments: Supervisor, Fluid Dynamics, Reactive Processes and Biomedical Research, Jet Propulsion Laboratory, California Institute of Technology, Pasadena, 1962-92; Clinical Assistant Professor of Medicine, University of Southern California, 1974-92; Volunteer Faculty Member, School of Medicine, University of Southern California, Los Angeles, 1992-. Publications: Over 150 experimental and analytical publications in technical journals including investigations in rocket propulsion and blood flow through diseased arteries. Honours: Exceptional Service Award, NASA, 1979; ASME Fellow, Heat Transfer Division; Distinguished Service Award, 1987; 50th Anniversary Award, 1988. Memberships: ASME; AIAA. Address: 16 Rushingwind, Irvine, CA 92614-7409, USA.

**BACKLEY Steve,** b. 12 February 1969, Sidcup, Kent, England. Athelete. Career: Specialist in Javelin; Coached by John Trower; Commonwealth record holder, 1992 (91,46m); Gold Medal European Junior Championships, 1987; Silver Medal, World Junior Championships, 1988; Gold Medal European Cup, 1989, 1997; Bronze Medal, 1995; Gold Medal World Student Games, 1989, 1991; Gold Medal World Cup, 1989, 1994, 1998; Gold Medal Commonwealth Games, 1990, 1994, 2002; Silver Medal, 1998; Gold Medal European Championships, 1990, 1994, 1998, 2002; Bronze Medal Olympic Games, 1992; Silver Medal, 1996, 2000; Silver Medal World Championships, 1995, 1997; Athlete of the Year, UK Athletics, 2000. Publication: The Winning Mind.

**BACON Kevin,** b. 8 July 1958, Philadelphia. American Actor. m. Kyra Sedgewick, 1 son, 1 daughter. Education: Manning St Actor's Theatre. Appointments: Stage appearances include: Getting On, 1978; Glad Tidings, 1979-80; Mary Barnes, 1980; Album, 1980; Forty-Deuce, 1981; Flux, 1982; Poor Little Lambs, 1982; Slab Boys, 1983; Men Without Dates, 1985; Loot, 1986; Loot, 1986; Road; Spike Heels; TV appearances include: The Gift, 1979; Enormous Changes at the Last Minute, 1982; The Demon Murder Case, 1983; Tender Age, Lemon Sky; Frasier; Happy Birthday Elizabeth: A Celebration of Life, 1997; Film appearances include: National Lampoon's Animal House, 1978; Starting Over, 1979; Hero at Large, 1980; Friday the 13th, 1980; Only When I Laugh, 1981; Diner, 1982; Footloose, 1984; Quicksilver, 1985; White Water Summer, 1987; Planes, Trains and Automobiles, 1987; End of the Line, 1988; She's having A Baby, 1988; Criminal Law, 1989; The Big Picture, 1989; Tremors, 1990; Flatliners, 1990; Queens Logic, 1991; He Said/She Said, 1991; Pyrates, 1991; JFK, 1992; A Few Good Men, 1992; The Air Up There, 1994; The River Wild, 1994; Murder in the First, 1995; Apollo 13, 1995; Sleepers, 1996; Telling Lies in America, 1997; Picture Perfect, 1997; Digging to China, 1997; Wild Things, 1998; My Dog Skip, 1999; The Hollow Man, 1999; Stir of Echoes, 1999; Novocain, 2000; We

Married Margo, 2000; 24 Hours, 2001; Trapped, 2002. Address: c/o Kevin Huvane, Creative Artists Agency, 9830 Wilshire Boulevard, Beverley Hills, CA 90212, USA.

**BADAWI Mohamed Mustafa,** b. 10 June 1925, Alexandria, Egypt. Lecturer; Writer. Education: BA, Alexandria University, 1946; BA, 1950, PhD, 1954, London University. Appointments: Research Fellow, 1947-54, Lecturer, 1954-60, Assistant Professor, 1960-64, Alexandria University, Egypt; Lecturer, Oxford University, and Brasenose College, 1964-92; Fellow, St Antony's College, Oxford, 1967-; Editor, Journal of Arabic Literature, Leiden, 1970; Advisory Board Member, Cambridge History of Arabic Literature. Publications: An Anthology of Modern Arabic Verse, 1970; Coleridge as Critic of Shakespeare, 1973; A Critical Introduction to Modern Arabic Poetry, 1975; Background to Shakespeare, 1981; Modern Arabic Literature and the West, 1985; Modern Arabic Drama in Egypt, 1987; Early Arabic Drama, 1988; Modern Arabic Literature: Cambridge History of Arabic literature (editor), 1992; A Short History of Modern Arabic Literature, 1993; Several books and volumes of verse in Arabic. Honour: King Faisal International Prize for Arabic Literature. Memberships: Ministry of Culture, Egypt; Unesco Expert on Modern Arabic Culture. Address: St Antony's College, Oxford, England.

**BADMAN May Edith, (May Ivimy),** b. 10 November 1912, Greenwich, London, England. Retired Local Government Officer; Poet. m. Raymond Frank Badman, 19 October 1968, 1 son, 1 daughter. Appointments: Former Council Member and Honorary Treasurer, The Poetry Society; Founder-Organiser, Ver Poets, 1966-. Publications: Night is Another World, 1964; Midway This Path, 1966; Late Swings, 1980; Prayer Sticks, 1980; Parting the Leaves, 1984; Strawberries in the Salad, 1992; The Best Part of the Day, 1992. Contributions to: Many anthologies, magazines, and radio. Honours: Dorothy Tutin Award, 1983; Howard Sergeant Memorial Award, 1990. Memberships: Poetry Society; Royal Society of Literature; St Albans Art Society; Society of Women Writers and Journalists. Address: Haycroft, 61/63 Chiswell Green Lane, St Albans, Hertfordshire, AL2 3AL, England.

**BAEDECKER Philip Ackerman,** b. 19 December 1939, East Orange, New Jersey, USA. Research Chemist. m. Mary Jo LaFuze, 1 daughter. Education: BS, Chemistry, Ohio University, Athens, Ohio, 1957-61; MS, Chemistry, University of Kentucky, Lexington, Kentucky, 1964; PhD, Chemistry, 1967. Appointments: Research Associate, Massachusetts Institute of Technology, 1967-68; Assistant Professor, 1970-71, Assistant Research Chemist, 1968-73, University of California, Los Angeles; Research Chemist, Branch of Analytical Laboratories, 1974-81, Chief, 1981-86, Research Chemist,1986-96, Branch of Geochemistry, US Geological Survey. Publications: Published reports, abstracts. Honours: Haggin Fellow; Paul I Murrill Fellow; Tennessee Eastman Fellow; NSF Fellow; NASA Citatation; NAPAP Citation. Memberships: American Chemical Society; Meteoritical Society; American Association for the Advancement of Science; Sigma Xi; Geological Society of Washington. Address: 2221 Terra Ridge Drive, Vienna, VA 22181-3276, USA.

**BAGAYEV Sergei Nikolayevich,** b. 9 September 1941, Novosibirsk, Russia. Scientist. 1 son. Education: Graduate, Physical Department, Novosibirsk University, 1964. Appointments: Director, Institute of Laser Physics; Director General, Siberian Laser Center; Professor, Moscow Physicotechnical Institute, Moscow, 1994-. Publications: Over 300 scientific papers in professional journals. Honour: State Prize of the Russian Federation, 1998; Order of Friendship,

1999; Medal For Strengthening Military Co-operation, Ministry of Defence of the Russian Federation, 1999; VA Koptyug Prize, SB RAS and Belarus National Academy of Sciences, 1999; Cavalier of the Legion of Honour, France, 2004. Memberships include: Optical Society of America; Academician of Russian Academy of Sciences; Vice President, International Union of Pure and Applied Physics; International Committee on Quantum Electronics; Vice-President, United Physical Society of the Russian Federation, 1998-; Presidium, Russian Academy of Sciences; President "Znaniye" Society, Russia, 2004-; Editorial Boards of the journals: Kvantovaya Elektronika, Applied Physics B, Laser Physics. Address: Institute of Laser Physics, Siberian Division of Russian Academy of Sciences, Prospekt Lavrentyeva 13/3, Novosibirsk 630090, Russia.

**BAGG Charles,** b. 7 May 1920, London, England. Physician (Retired). m. Diana Ovenden, deceased, 1980, 2 daughters. Education: MA (Camb), MRCS, LRCP, 1946; DPM, 1951; MRCPsych, 1971; FRCPsych, 1983; Cambridge University, Westminster Hospital Medical School; Postgraduate Courses, Neurology, Queen's Square, London. Appointments: Various junior hospital appointments; Consultant Psychiatrist, Samaritans, Chilterns Branch, Buckinghamshire; Address to Samaritans National Conference; Regional Tutor, Marriage Guidance Council, Hertfordshire; Lecturer in Psychiatry, High Wycombe and Amersham School of Midwifery; Consultant Psychiatrist, St John's Hospital, Aylesbury, appointed by the Oxford Regional Health Board; Clinical Director, Amersham Child and Family Guidance Clinic; Consultant in Preventive Psychiatry, Buckinghamshire County Council; Deputy Director General, International Biographical Centre (Inner Circle). Publications: Handbook of Psychiatry for Social Workers and Health Visitors; Palmar Digital Sweating in Women Suffering from Depression; Responses of Neonates to Noise in Relation to Personalities of their Parents; Senile Dementia and Psychiatric Problems of the Aged; Rare Pre-Senile Dementia Associated with Cortical Blindness; How Does Electoplexy Work?; Chapters in Samaritans books; Reviews of psychiatric articles in Occupational Therapy: Current Themes in Psychiatry; Behaviour Modification for the Mentally Handicapped; Community Care for the Mentally Disabled; Series of articles in British Medicine. Honours: DSc (Honoris Causa), MGS International University Foundation; Bronze Medal, Albert Einstein International Academy; Mitchell Memorial Prize for Music in Hospitals (Jointly); Silver Medal, IBC; Gold Medal, ABI. Memberships: Fellow, IBA; Fellow World Literary Academy; Member, Poetry Society supported by the Arts Council, England. Address: 20A Westgate, Chichester, West Sussex PO19 3EU, England.

**BAGGIO Roberto,** b. 18 February 1967, Caldogno, Italy. Footballer. m. Andreina Fabbri, 2 daughters. Appointments: Vicenza, 1985; Florentina, 1985-90; Juventus, 1990-95; Milan, 1995-97; Bologna, 1997-98; Inter Milan, 1998-2000; Brescia, 2000-; 300 career goals to 15 December 2002; Played for Italian National Team in 1990, 1994 and 1998 World Cups. Honours: Golden Ball Award, France, 1993; FIFA World Player of the Year, 1993; European Footballer of the Year, 1993; European Player of the Year, 1994; World Player of the Year, 1994. Address: Bologna FC, Via Casteldebole 10, 40132 Bologna, Italy.

**BAGHEBO Michael,** b. 23 March 1963, Foropa Town, Nigeria. Chartered Tax and Management Practitioner. m. Timipa Michael, 3 sons, 2 daughters. Education: NCE, Economics and Political Science, River State College of Education, Port Harcourt, 1985-88; BSc Honours, Education Economics, 2nd Class Upper Division, 1990-93, MSc, Economics, 1998-2001, University of Port Harcourt; Doctorate Degree, Public

Administration, All Saint University of America, New York, 2003; PhD (Hons), Finance, Marlborough University, USA, 2003. Appointments: Accountant, Economic and Mathematics Teacher, Osalees International School, Effurun, Nigeria, 1989-90; Mathematics, Economics and Government Teacher, CSS Famgbe, Attissa, Nigeria, 1990-96; Teacher on transfer to St Judes Girls Secondary School, Amarata, Nigeria, 1996-98; Transport/Advances Officer, 1998-99, PRO/Information Officer, 1999-2001, National Orientation Agency; Lecturer in then Satellite University Campus of Futo, UNICAL and OAU, Yenagoa; Secretary/General Administration, Bayelsa State Board of Internal Revenue, 2001-02, Executive Chairman, 2002-03, Bayelsa State Board of Internal Revenue, Yenagoa, Nigeria. Publications: Poverty Alleviation and Economic Development in Nigeria (MSc thesis); Bsc(Ed) Project on Problems and Prospects of 6-3-3-4 Education Policy in Nigeria; Multiplier Effect of Poverty; Dynamism in Governance; Stable Environment for Sustainable Development. Honours include: DOC Degree in Public Administration; PhD, Finance; Distinguished Public Service Medal; Award for Excellence in Public Revenue Administration; Award for Excellence in Nigerian Public Service; Certified Distinguished Administrator; Chieftancy Title of Gbadero of Ifetedo Land, Osun State, Nigeria; Distinguished Leadership Award. Memberships: Honorary Senior Fellowship, Institute of Internal Auditors of Nigeria; Fellow, Chartered Institute of Public Administrators of Nigeria; Fellow, Marlborough University Graduate Association; Fellow, Certified Institute of Management; Associate Member, Chartered Institute of Taxation of Nigeria; Member, Nigerian Institute of Public Relations. Address: Edepie-Epie, PO Box 1147, Yenagoa, Bayelsa State, Nigeria.

**BAGNALL Sir Anthony John Crowther,** b. 8 June 1945, Urmston, Lancashire, England. Royal Air Force Pilot. m. Pamela Diane Wilson, 1 son, 2 daughters. Education: Stretford Grammar School; RAF College, Cranwell. Appointments: Advanced Staff College, 1978; Squadron Commander 43 Squadron, 1983; Director, Air Staff Briefing and Co-ordination, 1985-87; Station Commander, RAF Leuchars, 1987-90; RCDS, 1990; Director, Air Force Staff Duties, 1991; Assistant Chief of the Air Staff, 1992-94; AOC II Group, 1994-96; Deputy Commander-in-Chief, Allied Forces Central Europe, 1996-98; Air Member for Personnel and Air Officer Commanding Personnel and Training Command, 1998-2000; Commander in Chief, Strike Command, 2000-01; Vice Chief of the Defence Staff, 2001-. Honours: OBE, 1982; CB, 1994; KCB, 1998; GBE, 2003. Memberships: President, RAF Rowing Club. Address: c/o Lloyds TSB, 53 King Street, Manchester M60 2ES, England.

**BAHK Jaewan,** b. 24 January 1955, Masan, Korea. Member of National Assembly of Korea. m. Moon Oak Oh, 1 son, 1 daughter. Education: BA, Economics, Seoul National University, 1977; MPP, 1988, PhD in Public Policy, 1992, Harvard University. Appointments: Assistant Director, National Security Council, 1980-83; Assistant Director, Board of Audit & Inspection, Korea, 1983-92; Deputy Director, Ministry of Finance, Korea, 1992-94; Assistant Chief Secretary, Office of the President of Korea, 1994-96; Professor, Sungkyunkwan University, 1996-2004; Chairman of National Council on Brain Korea 21 projects, 2002; Professor, University of California at San Diego, 2002-03. Publications: Numerous articles published in professional journals. Honours: Presidential Award for Best Academic Article, Seoul National University, 1974; Government Fellowship for Overseas Study, 1986; SBS Fellowship for Overseas Research, 2002. Memberships: International Institute of Public Finance; Many other associations. Address: #702 National Assembly Members Bldg, #1 Youido-dong, Seoul, Korea 150-702. E-mail: jbahk@assembly.go.kr Website: http://www.jll.org

**BAIK Yung Hong,** b. 11 May 1944, Chonnam, Korea. Professor. m. Young Myo Ko, 2 daughters. Education: MD, Chonnam National University Medical School, 1970; PhD, Pharmacology, Graduate School, Chonnam National University. Appointments: President, Korean Society of Pharmacology, 1992; Director, Research Institute of Medical Sciences, 1994-96; Currently, Professor, Dean, 1996-98, Chonnam National University Medical School; Dean of Academic Affairs, Chonnam National University, 2002-2004; Delegate of Korea, IUPHAR, 2003. Publications: Pharmacology, 3rd edition, 2004; Articles in medical journals including: Journal of Cardiovascular Pharmacology, 1994; European Journal of Pharmacology, 1999; BBRC, 2003, 2004. Honours: Prize of High Scholarship, The Chief of the Army, Korea; Scientific Prize, Gwangju Medical Association. Memberships: Trustee, Korean Society of Pharmacology and Circulation, 1980; Active Member, New York Academy of Sciences, 1998. Address: Department of Pharmacology, Chonnam National University Medical School, 5 Hakdong Dongku Gwangju, South Korea 501-746. E-mail: yhbaik@chonnam.ac.kr

**BAILEY Cecil Dewitt,** b. 25 October 1921, Zama, Southeast Attala County, Mississippi, USA. Engineer; Educator. m. Myrtis Taylor, 3 daughters, 2 deceased. Education: Bachelor of Science, Aeronautical Engineering, Mississippi State University, 1950; Master of Science, Aeronautical Engineering, 1954, PhD, 1962, Purdue University. Appointments: Pilot, Various USAF Aircraft, World War II, 1943-47; Pilot, B-47 Six Engine Jet Powered Bomber and Instructor, High Speed Aerodynamics, McConnell Air Force Base, Kansas, USA, 1950-52; Assistant Professor, Air Force Institute of Technology, Wright-Patterson Air Force Base, Ohio, 1954-58; Chief, Air Force Systems Command Office, NASA Langley Research Center, Hampton, Virginia, 1959-63; Staff Engineer, Headquarters, Air Force Systems Command, Andrews Air Force Base, Maryland, 1963-65; Associate Professor, Air Force Institute of Technology, Wright-Patterson Air Force Base, Ohio, 1965-67; Professor, The Ohio State University, Columbus, Ohio, 1967-85; Professor Emeritus, 1985-. Publications: More than 20 technical papers in 8 archival journals include: A New Look at Hamilton's Principle, 1975; Vibration and Stability of Non-conservative Follower Force Systems, 1981; Further Remarks on the Law of Varying Action and Symbol , 1989; The Unifying Laws of Classical Mechanics, 2002; Hamilton and the Law of Varying Action Revisited, 2004. Honours: Commendation Medal, USAF Air Force Systems Command, 1962; Commendation Medal, USAF Institute of Technology, 1976; Charles E MacQuigg Award for Outstanding Teaching, 1976. Address: 4176 Ashmore Road, Columbus, Ohio 43220, USA. E-mail: cecildbailey@aol.com

**BAILEY Colin B,** b. 20 October 1955, London, England. Art Historian; Curator. Education: BA (Hons), Brasenose College, 1975-78, Diploma in the History of Art, 1978-79, D Phil, 1979-85, Oxford University. Appointments: Assistant Curator of European Painting, Philadelphia Museum of Art, USA,1985-89; Curator of European Painting and Sculpture, 1989-90; Senior Curator, 1990-94, Kimbell Art Museum, Fort Worth, Texas, USA; Chief Curator, 1995-98, Deputy Director and Chief Curator, 1998-2000, National Gallery of Canada; Chief Curator, The Frick Collection, New York, New York, USA, 2000-. Publications: Books: Masterpieces of Impressionism and Post Impressionism: The Annenberg Collection (co-author with Joseph J Rishel), 1989; The Loves of the Gods: Mythological Painting from Watteau to David, 1991-92; Renoir's Portraits: Impressions of an Age, 1997; Jean-Baptiste Greuze, The

Laundress, 2000; Gustav Klimt (1862-1918): Modernism in the Making (General editor of the catalogue and curator of the exhibition), 2001; Patriotic Taste: Collecting Modern Art in Pre-Revolutionary Paris, 2002; The Age of Watteau, Chardin and Fragonard: Masterpieces of French Eighteenth-Century Genre Painting, 2003; Numerous articles and essays in learned journals. Honours: Chevalier de l'Ordre des Arts et des Lettres, 1994; Paul Mellon Senior Visiting Fellow, CASVA, National Gallery of Art, Washington DC, 1994; Clark Fellow, Sterling and Francine Clark Institute, Williamstown, Massachusetts, 1999; Mitchell Prize (for best book in art history 2002-03), 2004. Memberships: Arts Correspondent, CBC Midday, 1995-2000; Trustee and Vice-President, The American Association of Museum Curators, 2001-. Address: The Frick Collection, 1 East 70th Street, New York, NY 10021, USA.

**BAILEY David,** b. 2 January 1938, London, England. Photographer; Film Director. m. (1) Rosemary Bramble, 1960, (2) Catherine Deneuve, 1965; (3) Marie Helvin, divorced, (4) Catherine Dyer, 1986, 2 sons, 1 daughter. Appointments: Self taught photographer for Vogue, UK, USA, France, Italy; Advertising Photography, 1959-; Director, Commercials, 1966-; TV Documentaries, 1968-; Exhibition National Portrait Gallery, 1971; Photographers Gallery, 1973; Olympus Gallery, 1980, 1982, 1983; Victoria and Albert Museum, 1983; International Centre of Photography, New York, 1984; Hamilton Gallery, 1990, 1992; Director, Producer, TV Film Who Dealt?, 1993; Documentary: Models Close Up, 1998; Director, feature film, The Intruder, 1999. Publications: Box of Pinups, 1964; Goodbye Baby and Amen, 1969; Warhol, 1974; Beady Minces, 1974; Mixed Moments, 1976; Trouble and Strife, 1980; NW1, 1982; Black and White Memories, 1983; Nudes, 1981-84, 1984; Imagine, 1985; The Naked Eye: Great Photographers of the Nude (with Martin Harrison), 1988; If We Shadows, 1992; The Lady is a Tramp, 1995; Rock and Roll Heroes, 1997; Archive, 1999; Chasing Rainbows, 2001. Honours: Dr hc, Bradford University, 2001. Address: c/o Robert Montgomery and Partners, 3 Junction Mews, Sale Place, London, W2, England.

**BAILEY D(avid) R(oy) Shackleton,** b. 10 December 1917, Lancaster, England. Pope Professor Emeritus of Latin Language and Literature; Writer; Editor; Translator. m. (1) Hilary Ann Bardwell, 1967, dissolved 1974, (2) Kristine Zvirbulis, 1994. Education: BA, 1939, MA, 1943, LittD, 1957, Cambridge University. Appointments: Fellow, 1944-55, Praelector, 1954-55, Fellow and Deputy Bursar, 1964, Senior Bursar, 1965-68, Gonville and Caius College, Cambridge; University Lecturer in Tibetan, Cambridge University, 1948-68; Fellow and Director of Studies in Classics, Jesus College, Cambridge, 1955-64; Visiting Lecturer in Classics, Harvard College, 1963; Professor of Latin, 1968-74, Adjunct Professor, 1989-, University of Michigan; Andrew V Raymond Visiting Professor, State University of New York at Buffalo, 1973-74; Professor of Greek and Latin, 1975-82, Pope Professor of Latin Language and Literature, 1982-88, Professor Emeritus, 1988-, Harvard University; Editor, Harvard Studies in Classical Philology, 1978-84; Visiting Professor, Peterhouse, Cambridge, 1980-81. Publications: The Sátapañcasátka of Matrceta, 1951; Propertiana, 1956; Towards a Text of Cicero ad Atticum, 1960; Ciceronis Epistulae ad Atticum IX-XVI, 1961; Cicero's Letters to Atticus, vols I and II, 1965, vol V, 1966, vol VI, 1967, vols III and IV, 1968, vol VII, 1970; Cicero, 1971; Two Studies in Roman Nomenclature, 1976; Cicero: Epistulae ad Familiares, 2 volumes, 1977; Cicero's Letters to Atticus, 1978; Cicero's Letters to His Friends, 2 volumes, 1978; Towards a Text of Anthologia Latina, 1979; Selected Letters of Cicero, 1980; Cicero: Epistulae ad Q Fratrem et M Brutum, 1981; Profile of Horace, 1982; Anthologia Latina I.1, 1982; Horatius, 1985; Cicero: Philippics, 1986; Ciceronis

Epistulae, 4 volumes, 1987-88; Lucanus, 1988; Onomasticon to Cicero's Speeches, 1988; Quintilianus: Declamationes minores, 1989; Martialis, 1990; Back from Exile, 1991; Martial, 3 volumes, 1993; Homoeoteleuton in Latin Dactylic Verse, 1994; Onomasticon to Cicero's Letters, 1995; Onomasticon to Cicero's Treatises, 1996; Selected Classical Papers, 1997; Cicero: Letters to Atticus, 1999; Valerius Maximus, 2000; Cicero's Letters to Friends, 2000; Cicero's Letters to Quintus and Brutus, 2002; Statius Silvae, 2003; and others. Contributions to: Scholarly periodicals. Honours: Charles Goodwin Prize, American Philological Association, 1978; National Endowment for the Humanities Fellowship, 1980-81; Hon LittD, University of Dublin, 1984; Kenyon Medal, British Academy, 1985; Honorary Member, Society for Roman Studies, 1999; Honorary Fellow, Gonville and Caius College, 2000. Memberships: American Academy of Arts and Science, fellow, 1979-; American Philosophical Society; British Academy, fellow. Address: 303 North Division, Ann Arbor, MI 48104, USA.

**BAILEY Donovan,** b. 16 December 1967, Manchester, Jamaica. Canadian Athlete; Marketing Consultant. 1 daughter. Emigrated to Canada in 1981. Appointments: Member, Canada's Winning 4 x 100m team, Commonwealth Games, 1994; Olympic Games, 1996; World Indoor record holder for 50m, 1996; Canadian 100m record holder, 1995, 1996; World Commonwealth and Olympic 100m record holder, 1996; Retired from athletics, 2001; Founder, Donovan Bailey Foundation to assist Canadian amateur athletes. Honour: Sprinter of the Decade, Track and Field News, 1999. Address: c/o Flynn Sports Management, 606-1185, Eglinton Avenue East, Toronto, Ontario, M3C 3C6, Canada.

**BAILYN Bernard,** b. 10 September 1922, Hartford, Connecticut, USA. Professor Emeritus of History; Writer. m. Lotte Lazarsfeld, 18 June 1952, 2 sons. Education: AB, Williams College, 1945; MA, 1947, PhD, 1953, Harvard University. Appointments: Instructor, 1953-54, Assistant Professor, 1954-58, Associate Professor, 1958-61, Professor of History, 1961-66, Winthrop Professor of History, 1966-81, Adams University Professor, 1981-93, Director, Charles Warren Center for Studies in American History, 1983-94, James Duncan Phillips Professor of Early American History, 1991-93, Professor Emeritus, 1993-, Harvard University; Trevelyan Lecturer, 1971, Pitt Professor of American History, 1986-87, Cambridge University; Fellow, British Academy, and Christ's College, Cambridge, 1991. Publications: The New England Merchants in the Seventeenth Century, 1955; Massachusetts Shipping, 1697-1714: A Statistical Study (with Lotte Bailyn), 1959; Education in the Forming of American Society: Needs and Opportunities for Study, 1960; Pamphlets of the American Revolution, 1750-1776, Vol 1 (editor), 1965; The Apologia of Robert Keayne: The Self-Portrait of a Puritan Merchant (editor), 1965; The Ideological Origins of the American Revolution, 1967, new edition, 1992; The Origins of American Politics, 1968; The Intellectual Migration: Europe and America, 1930-1960 (editor with Donald Fleming), 1969; Religion and Revolution: Three Biographical Studies, 1970; Law in American History (editor with Donald Fleming), 1972; The Ordeal of Thomas Hutchinson, 1974; The Great Republic: A History of the American People (with others), 1977, 4th edition, 1992; The Press and the American Revolution (editor with John B Hench), 1980; The Peopling of British North America: An Introduction, 1986; Voyagers to the West: A Passage in the Peopling of America on the Eve of the Revolution, 1986; Faces of Revolution: Personalities and Themes in the Struggle for American Independence, 1990; Strangers within the Realm: Cultural Margins of the First British Empire (editor with Philip B Morgan), 1991; The Debate on the Constitution: Federalist and Antifederalist Speeches, Articles and Letters during the Struggle over Ratification, 2 volumes, 1993. Contributions to: Scholarly journals. Honours: Bancroft Prize, 1968; Pulitzer Prizes in History, 1968, 1987; National Book Award in History, 1975; Thomas Jefferson Medal, American Philosophical Society, 1993; Honorary doctorates; Catton Prize, Society of American Historians, 2000. Memberships: American Academy of Arts and Sciences; American Historical Association, president, 1981; American Philosophical Society; National Academy of Education; Royal Historical Society. Address: 170 Clifton Street, Belmont, MA 02178, USA.

**BAINBRIDGE Beryl Margaret (Dame),** b. 21 November 1934, Liverpool, England. Author. Appointments: Actress, Repertory Theatres in UK, 1949-60; Clerk, Gerald Duckworth & Co Ltd, London, 1971-73. Publications: A Weekend with Claude, 1967; Another Part of the Wood, 1968; Harriet Said, 1972; The Dressmaker, 1973; The Bottle Factory Outing, 1974; Sweet William, 1975; A Quiet Life, Injury Time, 1976; Young Adolf, 1978; Winter Garden, 1980; English Journey or the Road to Milton Keynes, 1984; Watson's Apology, 1984; Mum & Mr Amitage, 1985; Forever England, 1986; Filthy Lucre, 1986; An Awfully Big Adventure, 1989; The Birthday Boys, 1991; Every Man For Himself, 1996; Master Georgie, 1998 According to Queeney, 2001. Honours: Guardian Fiction Award, 1974; Whitbread Award, 1977; Fellow, Royal Society of Literature, 1978; DLitt, University of Liverpool, 1986; Whitbread Award, 1997; James Tate Black Award, 1998; W H Smith Fiction Award, 1998; Dame Commander of the Order of the British Empire, 2000; David Cohen Prize, 2003. Address: 42 Albert Street, London NW1 7NU, England.

**BAKDASH Mohammed Hisham,** b. 9 August 1934, Damascus, Syria. Physician. m. Mary Anne Robinson, 1 son, 1 daughter. Education: Certificate in Science, Damascus University, 1953; MD, 1959; ECFMG, USA, 1964; American Board of Neurosurgery, 1969; Intern, St Joseph Hospital, New York City, 1963; Resident in General Surgery, St Joseph's Infirmary, Atlanta, 1964; Resident in Neurosurgery, Barrow Neurology Institute, Phoenix, 1965-66; Harbor General Hospital, Torrence, 1967; Fellow, Chief Resident in Neurosurgery, University of California Los Angeles, 1968-69. Appointments: Assistant Professor, 1969-74, Associate Professor, 1974-79, Professor, 1979-99, Chairman of Department, 1969-99, Professor Emeritus, 2000-, Neurosurgery, Damascus University College of Medicine; Chief Examiner in Neurosurgery, Syrian Ministry of Health, 1969-2000; Chief of Neurosurgery, Muassat University Hospital, Damascus, 1969-99; Secretary, Arab Board of Neurosurgeons, 1995-99. Publications: Author of numerous articles in professional medical journals. Honours: Citation of Merit, Syrian Supreme Council of Sciences, 1987; Syrian Medical Association, 1991; Certificate of Appreciation, Pan Arab Association of Surgeons, 1994. Memberships: American Association of Neurological Surgeons; Fellow, ACS; Syrian Society of Neuroscientists. Address: Jisr Abiad, Damascus, Syria.

**BAKER Alan,** b. 19 August 1939, London, England. Mathematician. Education: BSc, Mathematics, University of London, 1961; PhD, Cambridge University, 1964. Appointments: Research Fellow, 1964-68, Director of Studies, Mathematics, 1968-74, Trinity College, Cambridge; Professor of Pure Mathematics, Cambridge University, 1974; Numerous Visiting Professorships in the USA and Europe; First Turán Lecturer, János Bolyai Mathematical Society, Hungary, 1978; Research into transcendental numbers. Publications: Numerous papers; Transcendental Number Theory, 1975; A Concise Introduction to the Theory of Numbers, 1984; New Advances in Transcendence Theory, as editor, 1988. Memberships: Fellow,

Royal Society, 1973; Honorary Fellow, Indian National Science Academy, 1980; European Academy, 1998; Doctor Honoris Causa, University of Louis Pasteur, Strasbourg, 1998; Honorary Member, Hungarian Academy of Sciences, 2001. Address: Department of Pure Mathematics and Mathematical Statistics, 16 Mill Lane, Cambridge, CB2 1SB, England.

**BAKER Norman,** b. 1957, Aberdeen, Scotland. Member of Parliament. Education: Degree in German, London University. Appointments include: Regional Executive Director, Our Price Records; Clerk, Hornsey Railway Station; Manager of a wine shop; Teacher of English as a Foreign Language; Liberal Democrats Environment Campaigner, House of Commons, 1989-90; Constituency Organiser, Liberal Democrat MP for Eastbourne, 1991; Member, Lewes District Council, 1987-99, Leader, 1991-97; Chair, Economic Development and Public Transport sub-committees, East Sussex County Council, 1993-97; Member of Parliament for Lewes Constituency, 1997-. Honours: Best Newcomer MP Award, 1997; Runner Up, Best Questioner, Runner Up, Best Opposition MP, Channel 4 Awards; Inquisitor of the Year, Zurich/Spectator Parliamentarian of the Year Awards, 2001; Winner, Opposition MP of the Year Award, Channel 4, 2002; RSPCA Lord Erskine Award, 2003. Address: 204 High Street, Lewes, East Sussex, BN7 2NS, England.

**BAKER Reginald Arthur,** b. 28 March 1933, Carshalton, Surrey, England. Local Government Officer; Concert Pianist and Organist. Education: General education, fragmentary because of World War II; Musical Education: Trinity College of Music, London; Privately with several teachers including Frank Merrick and Reginald Jevons (who was himself a past pupil of John Ireland and Vaughan Williams). Appointments: Several years as Arts Officer to Westminster City Council, responsible for music, the visual arts and some special services at Westminster Abbey and Westminster Cathedral; Recitalist in London, Edinburgh and Berlin as well as local events in Sutton and Croydon; Now retired. Publications: Compositions in manuscript awaiting a publisher. Membership: Incorporated Society of Musicians. Address: 30 White Lodge Close, Christchurch Park, Sutton, SM2 5TQ, England.

**BAKER William,** b. 6 July 1944, Shipston, Warwickshire, England. Professor. m. 16 November 1969, 2 daughters. Education: BA Hons, Sussex University, 1963-66; MPhil, London University, 1966-69; PhD, 1974; MLS, Loughborough, 1986. Appointments: Lecturer; Thurrock Technical College, 1969-71; Ben-Gurion University, 1971-77; University of Kent, 1977-78; West Midlands College, 1978-85; Professor, Pitzer College, Claremont, California, 1981-82; Housemaster, Clifton College, 1986-89; Professor, Northern Illinois University, 1989-; Presidential Research Professor (Distinguished Professor), Northern Illinois University, 2003-; Editor, The Year's Work in English Studies, 2000-; George Eliot – G.H. Lewes Studies, 1981-. Publications: Harold Pinter, 1973; George Eliot and Judaism, 1975; The Early History of the London Library, 1992; Literary Theories: A Case Study in Critical Performance, 1996; Nineteenth Century British Book Collectors and Bibliographers, 1997; Twentieth Century British Book Collectors and Bibliographers, 1999; Pre-Nineteenth Century British Book Collectors and Bibliographers, 1999; The Letters of Wilkie Collins, 1999; Twentieth Century Bibliography and Textual Criticism, 2000; George Eliot: A Bibliographical History, 2002. Other: Editions of letters by George Henry Lewes, George Eliot, and Wilkie Collins, 2000-. Honours: Ball Brothers Foundation Fellowship, Lilly Library, Indiana University, 1993; Bibliographical Society of America, Fellowship, 1994-95; American Philosophical Society Grant, 1997; Choice Outstanding Academic Book of the Year Award, 2000; National

Endowment for the Humanities Senior Fellowship, 2002-03. Memberships: Bibliographical Society of America; ALA; MLA; SHARP. Address: Department of English, Northern Illinois University, DeKalb, Illinois, USA.

**BAKEWELL Joan Dawson,** b. 16 April 1933, Stockport. Broadcaster; Writer. m. (1)Michael Bakewell, 1955, 1 son, 1 daughter, (2) Jack Emery, 1975. Education: Newnham College, Cambridge. Appointments: TV Critic, The Times, 1978-81; Columnist, Sunday Times, 1988-90; Associate, Newnham College, Cambridge, 1980-91; Associate Fellow, 1984-87; Gov BFI, 1994-99; Chair, 1999-2003; TV Includes: Sunday Break, 1962; Home at 4.30 (writer and producer), 1964; Meeting Point, The Second Sex, 1964; Late Night Line Up, 1965-72; The Youthful Eve, 1968; Moviemakers, National Film Theatre, 1971; Film 72; Film 73; Holiday, 74, 75, 76, 77, 78 (series); Reports Action (series) 1976-78; Arts UK:OK?, 1980; Heart of the Matter, 1988-2000; My Generation, 2000; One Foot in the Past, 2000; Taboo (series), 2001; Radio includes: Artist of the Week, 1998-99; The Brains Trust, 1999-; Belief, 2000. Publications; The New Priesthood: British Television Today, 1970; A Fine and Private Place, 1977; The Complete Traveller, 1977; The Heart of the Heart of the Matter, 1996; Contributions to journals. Address: c/o Knight Ayton Management, 10 Argyll Street, London, W1V 1AB, England.

**BALA'ZS András,** b. 15 November 1949, Budapest, Hungary. Biophysicist. m. Mária Majoros, 1 son. Education: BA, Biology, 1974, MA, Theoretical Chemistry, 1976, Eötvös L University; PhD (Candidate) Biology, Hungarian Academy of Sciences. Appointments: Research Assistant, 1974-81, Research Worker, 1981-95, Consultant, 1995-, Eötvös L University, Theoretical Chemistry Group, Departments of Atomic/Biological Physics. Publications: In professional journals. Honours: Listed in biographical publications. Memberships: European Cell Biology Organisation; Union of Hungarian Chemists; Hungarian Biochemical Society; Hungarian Theoretical Biological Society; Molecular Electronics and Biocomputing Society; Vienna Freud Museum; World Wild Fund. Address: Department of Biological Physics, Eötvös L University, Pa'zmány Sétány 1, H-1117 Budapest, Hungary.

**BALAKIRSKY Vladimir,** b. 2 October 1957, St Petersburg, Russia. Mathematician. m. Anahit Ghazaryan. Education: Masters Degree, 1980, PhD, 1987, Leningrad Aircraft Instrumentation Institute. Appointments: Engineer, LOMO, 1980-90; Engineer, Pargolovsky Zaved, 1992-93; Researcher, University of Lund, Sweden, 1993-94; Researcher, University of Bielefeld, Germany, 1995-98; Researcher, University of Eindhoven, The Netherlands, 1999-. Publications: Numerous papers published in journals, Problems of Information Transmission and IEEE Transactions in Information Theory. Memberships: Data Security Association Confident; IEEE. Address: Grazhdansky Prospekt, D104, Korp 4, Kv 21, 195267 St Petersburg, Russia. E-mail: v.b.balakirsky@tue.nl

**BALASA Sabin,** b. 17 June 1932, Dobriceni, Olt, Romania. Painter; Film Author; Writer. m. Melania, 2 sons. Education: Fine Arts Institute, Bucharest, Romania; Additional studies at Sienna and Perugia, Italy. Appointments: Painter; Freelancer; Author of cartoons; 12 films of animated paintings; 25 murals: 21 at A I Cuza University, Iasi, Romania, 2 at Galati University, Romania, 1 at Bucharest Hotel, Bucharest, Romania, 2 at Agricola International Bacau, Romania; Solo exhibitions: Rome, Italy, 1978 and 1980; Stockholm-Sweden, 1982; Bucharest, Romania, 1982, 1992; Kerkera, Greece, 1985; Moscow; Tbilisi, Georgia, 1988; Israel, 1994; "Top Business Art Gallery" World Trade Centre, Bucharest, Romania, 2000; "Top Business Art

Gallery" A I Cuza University, Iasi, Romania, 2002; Works in museums and private collections in Italy, France, Sweden, Germany, USA, Israel, Norway, Canada, Australia including Picasso d'Antibes Museum; The White House. Publications: The Blue Desert (novel), 1996; Exodus towards the Light (novel), 2002. Honours: Gold Medal, European Painting Competition, Italy, 1965; Silver Pelican, Cartoons International Festival Mamaia, Romania, 1966; Accademico d'Italia con Medaglia d'Oro, Salsomaggiore, Italy, 1980; Diploma de Maestro di Pittara Honoris Causa, Italy, 1982; Gold Medal, International Parliament, USA, 1982; Accademico delle Nazioni, Italy, 1983; Grand Premio delle Nazioni, Italy, 1983; Statue of Victory, Italy, 1983; Cavalier of the Arts, Italy, 1985; Palma d'Oro d'Europa, Italy, 1986; Honorary Doctorate, USA, 1988; Albert Einstein Bronze Medal, USA, 1989; Honorary Diploma and Medal "Pro Amicitia-Pro Fidelitate", Iasi City Hall; National Award Magic Romania, Top Business; Listed in Who's Who publications and biographical dictionaries. Address: 14 Kiseleff St, Sect.1,71269 Bucharest, Romania. E-mail: contact@sabinbalasa.com Website: www.sabinbalasa.com

**BALASUBRAMANIAN Vengatesan,** b. 4 June 1962, Villupuram, India. Materials Scientist. m. Kusuma, 1 son, 1 daughter. Education: BSc, 1982; MSc, 1984; PhD, 1990. Appointments: Researcher, 1984-89; Lecturer, Anna University, 1989-93; Research and Development Manager, 1993-2002, Deputy Director, NanoTech Laboratory, 2002-, Canare Electric Co Ltd, Japan. Publications: Several research papers in international reputed journals. Honours: Numerous national and international awards. Memberships: IEEE, USA; IEE, UK. Address: Canare Electric Co Ltd, NanoTech Laboratory, 2888-1 Rikka, Kumabari, Nagakute-cho, Aichi-gun, Aichi-ken, 480-1101, Japan. E-mail: cbsvenki@canare.co.jp

**BALDINI Edoardo,** b. 22 December 1962, Piacenza, Italy. Surgeon. m. Paola Pareti. Education: Diploma di Maturita Scientifica, 1981; Diploma di Laurea in Medicina e Chirurgia, 1987; Specialisation in General Surgery, 1992; Diplome Universitaire de Laparoscopie Appliquee a La Chirurgie Digestive, Nice, Paris, 1994; Diplome Etudes Approfondies in Surgical Sciences, 1999. Appointments: Physician, Piacenza Military Hospital, 1988-90, Civil Hospital Guastalla, 1990, Civil Hospital Aosta, 1990-91; Surgeon, Centre Hospitalier Universitaire de Nice, France, 1991-99; Surgeon, G Da Saliceto Hospital, Piacenza, Italy, 2000-. Publications: Articles concerning liver transplantation, hepatobiliary surgery and laparoscopic surgery. Memberships: New York Academy of Sciences; European Association for Endoscopic Surgery; Association Française de Chirurgie. Address: Via Ricci Oddi 23, 29100 Piacenza, Italy. E-mail: ebaldini@inwind.it

**BALDWIN Alec (Alexander Rae Baldwin III),** b. 3 April 1958, Masapequa, New York, USA. Actor. m. Kim Basinger, 1993, 1 daughter. Education: George Washington University; New York University; Lee Strasberg Theatre Institute; Studied with Mira Rostova and Elaine Aiken. Appointments: Stage Appearances Include: Loot, 1986; Serious Money, 1988; Prelude to a Kiss, 1990; A Streetcar named Desire, 1992; TV Appearances Include: The Doctors, 1980-82; Cutter to Houston, 1982; Knot's Landing, 1984-85; Love on the Run, 1985; A Dress Gray, 1986; The Alamo: 13 Days to Glory, 1986; Sweet Revenge, 1990; Nuremberg, 2000; Path to War, 2000; Second Nature, 2002; Film Appearances Include: Forever Lulu, 1987; She's Having A baby, 1987; Beetlejuice, 1988; Married to the Mob, 1988; Talk Radio, 1988; Working Girl, 1988; Great Balls of Fire, 1989; The Hunt for Red October, 1990; Miami Blues, 1990; Alice, 1990; The Marrying Man, 1991; Prelude to a Kiss, 1992; Glengarry Glen Ross, 1992; Malice, 1993; The Getaway,

1994; The Shadow, 1994; Heaven's Prisoners, 1995; Looking for Richard, 1996; The Juror, 1996; Ghosts of Mississippi, 1996; Bookworm, 1997; The Edge, 1997; Thick as Thieves, 1998; Outside Providence, 1998; Mercury Rising (producer), 1998; The Confession, 1999; Notting Hill, 1999; Thomas and the Magic Railroad, 2000; State and Main, 2000; Pearl Harbor, 2001; Final Fantasy: The Spirit's Within, 2001; The Royal Tenenbaums, 2001; The Devil and Daniel Webster, 2001; Path to War, 2002; Dr Seuss' The Cat in the Hat, 2003; The Cooler, 2003; Along Came Polly, 2004. Honours: The World Award, 1986. Memberships: Screen Actors Guild; American Federation of TV and Radio Artists; Actors Equity Association.

**BALDWIN Mark,** b. 29 July 1944, Simla, India. Publisher; Author. m. Myfanwy Dundas, 2 July 1977, 3 sons. Education: BA, MA, St Catharine's College, Cambridge, 1962-65; MSc, DIC, PhD, Imperial College, 1970-86. Appointments: Engineer with Mott Hay & Anderson, 1965-70; Lecturer, Imperial College, London, England, 1971-86; Publisher & Bookseller, 1986-. Publications: British Freight Waterways Today and Tomorrow, 1980; Canals - A New Look, 1984; Canal Books, 1984; Simon Evans - His Life and Later Work, 1992; Cleobury 2000, 1999. Contributions to: Proc Institution Civil Engineers; Waterways World; Canal and Riverboat, Antiquarian Book Monthly Review, Book and Magazine Collector; Lecturer on Second World War Codebreaking. Address: 24 High Street, Cleobury Mortimer, Kidderminster DY14 8BY, England.

**BALDWIN Michael,** b. 1 May 1930, Gravesend, Kent, England. Author; Poet. Education: Open Scholar, 1949, Senior Scholar, 1953, St Edmund Hall, Oxford, 1950-55. Appointments: Assistant Master, St Clement Danes Grammar School, 1955-59; Lecturer, Senior Lecturer, Principal Lecturer, Head of English and Drama Department, Whitelands College, 1959-78. Publications: Poetry: The Silent Mirror, 1951; Voyage From Spring, 1956; Death on a Live Wire, 1962; How Chas Egget Lost His Way in a Creation Myth, 1967; Hob, 1972; Buried God, 1973; Snook, 1980; King Horn, 1983; Fiction includes: Grandad with Snails, 1960; Miraclejack, 1963; Sebastian, 1967; Underneath and Other Situations, 1968; There's a War On, 1970; The Gamecock, 1980; The Rape of Oc, 1993. The First Mrs Wordsworth, 1996; Dark Lady, 1998. Contributions to: Listener; Encounter; New Statesman; Texas Review; BBC Wildlife Magazine; Outposts. Honours: Rediffusion Prize, 1970; Cholmondeley Award, 1984; Fellow, Royal Society of Literature, 1985. Memberships: Vice Chairman, Arvon Foundation, 1974-90; Chairman, Arvon Foundation at Lumb Bank, 1980-89; Crime Writer's Association; The Colony Room. Address: 35 Gilbert Road, Bromley, Kent BR1 3QP, England; The Athenaeum, Pall Mall, London, England.

**BALDWIN William,** b. 7 August 1948, Bolton, England. Clerk in Holy Orders. m. Sheila Margaret, 1 son, 1 daughter. Education: Bolton Technical College (part-time student), 1965-68; Nursing and Midwifery Council State Registration (General and Psychiatric Nursing), Bolton School of Nursing (Royal Bolton Hospital) and Whittingham Hospital, Preston, 1968-73; Further Education Teacher's Certificate/Registered Clinical Nurse Tutor, 1974-75; Examiners Qualification, Royal College of Nursing Study Centre, Birmingham, 1996; North West Ordination Course, General Ministry Examination, 1975-78; B Th (Hons), MA, Church History, PhD, Greenwich School of Theology (distance learning student), 1991-97. Appointments include: Various NHS appointments, 1968-78; Ordained Deacon, 1978; Ordained Priest, 1979; Assistant Curate, St Anne Royton, 1978-82; Vicar, St Thomas Halliwell, 1982-87; Rector of Atherton Team Ministry, 1987-2002; Team Vicar of Atherton and Hindsford with Howe Bridge St Michael, 2002-;

Area Dean of Leigh, 2001-; Part-time Chaplain to: Oldham General Hospital/Kershaw's Cottage Hospital, 1978-82; Royal Bolton Hospital, 1983-87; Royal Naval Association/White Ensign Association, 1987-2002; Advisor on healing to the Lord Bishop of Manchester, 1991-2001; Tutor for distance learning students, Greenwich School of Theology, 1996-; Personal Tutor, Manchester, Ordained Local Ministry Course; Member, Manchester Diocesan Synod, 1982-97, 2001-; Member, Wigan Metropolitan Borough Council's Faith Forum, 2001; Board Member SRB5 (single regeneration budget board) Atherton Building Communities Partnership, 2001-; Board Member, Leigh Primary Care Group, 1998-2002; Non-Executive Director, 5 Boroughs NHS Trust, 2002-; Mental Health Act Manager, 2002-. Publications include: Booklets: Agape: A Devotion on 1 Corinthians 13, 1987; Christian Discipleship and the Created Order; Recognising Holiness in the Ordinary, 2000; Pastoral Letters of a Parish Priest, 2002; Poetry Address Book, 2003; Book: The Doctrine of Humanity Revisited, 2003; Several religious and secular poems published in anthologies. Honours: Elected Fellow of the Royal Society of Health, 1983; Awarded Serving Brother of the Order of St John of Jerusalem for service to humanity by H M the Queen, 1988. Memberships: Associate, St George's House, Windsor Castle; Friend of St George's Chapel; Institute of Advanced Motorists. Address: Atherton Rectory, Bee Fold Lane, Atherton, Manchester M46 0BL, England. E-mail: frbill@fsmail.net

**BALL Michael Thomas,** b. 14 February 1932, Eastbourne, England. Retired Bishop. Education: Queens' College, Cambridge; Wells Theological College. Appointments: Schoolmaster, 1955-76; Co-founder, Community of the Glorious Ascension (religious community for men and women), 1960; Curate, Stroud, 1971-76; Senior Anglican Chaplain, Sussex University and Parish Priest of Stanmer with Falmer, 1976-80; Bishop of Jarrow, 1980-90; Bishop of Truro, 1990-97. Publications: So There We Are, 1996; The Foolish Risks of God, 2003; Articles to various magazines. Address: Manor Lodge, Aller, Langport, Somerset TA10 0QN, England.

**BALLANTYNE Colin Kerr,** b. 7 June 1951, Glasgow, Scotland. University Professor. m. Rebecca Trengove, 1 son, 1 daughter. Education: MA, University of Glasgow, 1973; MSc, McMaster University, Canada, 1975; PhD, University of Edinburgh; DSc, University of St Andrews, 2000. Appointments: Lecturer, Geography, 1980-89, Warden of McIntosh Hall, 1985-95, Senior Lecturer in Geography and Geology, 1989-94, Professor in Physical Geography, 1994-, University of St Andrews; Visiting Professor, UNIS, Svalbard, Norway, 1998-; Visiting Erskine Fellow, University of Christchurch, New Zealand, 2003. Publications: 130 scientific papers; Books include: The Quarternary of the Isle of Skye, 1991; The Periglaciation of Great Britain, 1994; Classic Landforms of the Isle of Skye, 2000; Paraglacial Geomorphology, 2002. Honours: Fellow, Royal Geographical Society, 1983; Warwick Award, British Geomorphological Research Group, 1987; President's Medal, Royal Scottish Geographical Society, 1991; Newbigin Prize, Royal Scottish Geographical Society, 1992; Fellow, Royal Society of Edinburgh, 1996; Scottish Science Award, Saltire Society, 1996; Fellow, Royal Society of Arts, 1996; Wiley Award, British Geomorphological Research Group, 1999. Memberships: Quarternary Research Association; British Geomorphological Research Group; Royal Scottish Geographical Society; International Permafrost Association; Edinburgh Geological Society. Address: School of Geography and Geosciences, University of St Andrews, Fife KY16 9AL, Scotland. E-mail: ckb@St-and.ac.uk

**BALLARD James Graham,** b. 15 November 1930, Shanghai, China; British Novelist; Short Story Writer. m. Helen Mary Mathews, 1954, deceased 1964, 1 son, 2 daughters. Education: King's College, Cambridge. Publications: The Drowned World, 1963; The 4 Dimensional Nightmare, 1963; The Terminal Beach, 1964; The Drought, 1965; The Crystal World, 1966; The Disaster Area, 1967; The Atrocity Exhibition, 1970; Crash, 1973; Vermilion Sands, 1973; Concrete Island, 1974; High Rise, 1975; Low Flying Aircraft, 1976; The Unlimited Dream Company, 1979; Myths of the Near Future, 1982; Empire of the Sun, 1984; The Venus Hunters, 1986; The Day of Creation, 1987; Running Wild, 1988; Memories of the Space Age, 1988; War Fever, 1990; The Kindness of Women, 1991; The Terminal Beach (short stories), 1992; Rushing to Paradise, 1994; A User's Guide to the Millennium, 1996; Cocaine Nights, 1996; Super-Cannes, 2000; The Complete Short Stories, 2001. Address: 36 Old Charlton Road, Shepperton, Middx, TW17 8AT, England.

**BALLESTEROS Severiano,** b. 9 April 1957, Santander, Spain. Golfer. m. Carmen Botin, 1988, 2 sons, 1 daughter. Career: Professional Golfer, 1974-; Spanish Young Professional title, 1975, 1978; French Open, 1977, 1982, 1985, 1986; Japan Open, 1977, 1978; Swiss Open, 1977, 1978, 1989; German Open, 1978, 1988; Open Championship, Lytham St Anne's, 1979, 1988; St Andrews, 1984; US Masters, 1980, 1983; World Matchplay Championship, Wentworth, 1981, 1982, 1984, 1985; Australian PGA Championship, 1981; Spanish Open, 1985; Dutch Open, 1986; British Masters, 1991; PGA Championship, 1991; International Open, 1994; Numerous other titles in Europe, US, Australia; Member, Ryder Cup team 1979, 1983, 1985, 1987, 1989, 1995. Publication: Trouble Shooting, 1996. Honours: Prince of Asturias Prize for sport, 1989. Address: Fairway SA, Pasaje de Pena 2-4, 39008 Santander, Spain.

**BALLS Edward Michael,** b. 25 February 1967. Chief Economic Adviser to the Treasury. m. Yvette Cooper, 1 son, 1 daughter. Education: BA, Economics, Keble College, Oxford University; MPA, Economics, Harvard University, USA. Appointments: Economics Leader Writer and Columnist, Financial Times, 1990-94; Economic Adviser to Gordon Brown as Shadow Chancellor of the Exchequer, 1994-97; Chancellor of the Exchequer's Economic Adviser, 1997-99; Chancellor's Representative at the G20; Chief Economic Adviser to the Treasury, 1999-. Publications: Principal Editor, 1995 World Banking Development Report – Workers in an Integrating World; Contributions to learned journals including: Scottish Journal of Political Economy; World Economics; Reports published by the Fabian Society, Social Justice Commission, Smith Institute; Reforming Britain's Macroeconomic Policy (co-editor), 2001; Microeconomic Reform in Britain (co-editor), 2004. Honour: Honorary Doctorate of Law, Nottingham University, 2003. Memberships: Chair, IMF Deputies Committee; Treasury Management Board; Prime Minister's Strategy Unit Steering Board; Northern Way Steering Group. Address: H M Treasury, 1 Horse Guards Road, London SW1A 2HQ, England.

**BALNAVE Derick,** b. 17 June 1941, Lisburn, Northern Ireland. Academic. m. Maureen Dawson, 1 son, 1 daughter. Education: BSc, 1963, PhD, 1966, DSc, 1983, Queen's University, Belfast, Northern Ireland. Appointments: Scientific, 1966-69, Senior Scientific, 1969-73, Principal Scientific, 1973-77, Officer, Department of Agriculture, Northern Ireland; Assistant Lecturer, 1967-71, Lecturer, 1971-75, Senior Lecturer, 1975-77, Reader, 1977, Queen's University, Belfast; Senior Lecturer, 1978-81, Associate Professor, 1981-2001, University of Sydney, Australia; Research Director, Poultry Research Foundation, University of Sydney, 1978-2001; Honorary Governor, Poultry Research Foundation, University of Sydney, 2001-; Adjunct

Professor, North Carolina State University, 1995-; Visiting Fellow, Cornell University, 1989. Publications: Approximately 150 scientific papers in professional journals; Over 200 conference and trade publications. Honours: Recipient, World's Poultry Science Association Australia Poultry Award, 1998. Memberships: Fellow, Royal Society of Chemistry; World's Poultry Science Association; Poultry Science Association Inc. Address: 26 Valley View Drive, Narellan, New South Wales, 2567 Australia. E-mail: derick.balnave@bigpond.com

**BALTAS Nicholas Constantinos,** b. 20 August 1946, Kastania, Evrytania, Greece. Professor of Economics. m. Maria (Tsamboula) Balta, 1 son, 1 daughter. Education: Athens School of Economics and Business Science, Department of Economics, 1965-70; MSoc Sc, 1970-72, PhD, 1972-74, University of Birmingham. Appointments: Research Assistant, Department of Econometrics and Social Statistics, University of Birmingham, 1972; Lecturer, Economics, British Institute of Marketing, 1975-76; Lecturer, Econometrics, Department of Economics, Aristotelion University of Thessaloniki, 1976-79; Senior Economist, Research and Planning Division, Agricultural Bank of Greece, 1976-1986; Associate Professor of Economics, 1985-90, Professor of Economics, 1990-, Head of Department, 1999-2003, Athens University of Economics and Business, Department of Economics; Expert, Ministry of Agriculture, Greece, 2002-03; Expert, European Commission (DGRTD and DG TREN), 2002-03; Expert, Economic and Social Committee, Greece, 2003 and 2004. Publications include: Books and Research Monographs: The Role of State Intervention in Fruit Production, 1977; Financing Investment in the Agricultural Sector, 1983; Topics of Economic Policy of the European Communities, 1989; A Short Run Model for the Poultry Sector in Greece, 1991; Incorporating Environmental Valuation into Policy Analysis, 1996; Economic Interdependence and Cooperation in Europe, 1998; Development Strategy and Investment in the Processing and Marketing of Agricultural Products, 2001; Numerous journals, book and conference proceedings and articles including: Private Investment and the Demand for Loanable Funds in the Greek Agricultural Sector, 1999; Common Agricultural Policy: Past, Present and Future, 2001; Modelling Farmers Land Use Decisions, 2002; The Welfare Effects of the Berlin CAP Agreement on Greek Agriculture, 2002; The Economy of the European Union, 2004; Book review: The Greek Economy: Sources of Growth in the Postwar Era, 1993. Honours: Fulbright Scholarship, 1991; British Council Scholarship, 1993; Jean Monnet Chair: EU Institutions and Economic Policy, 1999. Memberships include: Hellenic University Association for European Studies, President, 1999-2000 and 2002-03; European Community Studies Association; The Agricultural Economics Society; Greek Agricultural Economic Society; Hellenic Economic Association, Hellenic Operational Research Society. Address: Athens University of Economics and Business, 76 Patission Str, 104 34 Athens, Greece. E-mail: baltas@aueb.gr

**BALTAZZI Evan Serge,** b. 11 April 1921, Smyrna, USA. Director of Basic Sciences Research; Professor of Research. m. Nellie D Biorlaro, 1 son, 2 daughters. Education: DSc, Paris, 1949; DPhil, Oxon, 1954. Appointments: Senior Scientist; Professor of Research; Director of Research; President Consulting Firm; Served on 10 member committee on US currency, National Academy of Sciences, 1985-87. Publications: 42 publications (36 US and foreign); 6 books; Patents; Numerous articles. Honours: Citizen of the Year, 1964; Distinguished Service Award, 1965; Fellow, Chemical Society; American Chemical Society; SPSE, Chair, Gordon Research Conference and other international conferences and symposia. Address: 825 Greengate Oval, Sagamore Hills, OH 44067, USA.

# DICTIONARY OF INTERNATIONAL BIOGRAPHY

**BAMBER Juliette Madeleine,** b. 21 August 1930, Tidworth, England. Occupational Therapist; Counsellor. m. Donald Liddle, 1957, divorced 1995, 2 sons. Education: Art School, Foundation Course, 1947-49 Psychology, Honours, Birkbeck College, 1957-60. Publications: Breathing Space, 1991; On the Edge, 1993; Altered States, 1996; Touch Paper, 1996; The Ring of Words, 1996; The Wasting Game, 1997; The Long Pale Corridor, 1998; Flying Blind, 2000. Honours: 1st Prize, London Writers; 1st Prize, National Poetry Foundation; A Blue Nose Poet of the Year, 1998; Commended in Houseman Prize, 2000. Address: 9 Western Road, East Finchley, London N2 9JB, England.

**BAMHRAH Charan Singh,** b. 17 May 1932, Howrah, India. Retired Lecturer. m. Amrit Kaur. Education: ISc, 1951; Sahitya Ratna, 1952; City and Guilds, 1978-79; Certificate in Education, 1979-80. Appointments: English Teacher, South Vietnam, 1959-75; Lecturer in UK, 1977-92; P/T Lecturer, Lancaster University, 1992-97. Publication: In Search of Employment and Training. Honours: Best Orator in Banares District, India; Best Teacher in South Vietnam. Address: 80 St Michael's Close, Feniscowles, Blackburn, Lancashire BB2 5DL, England.

**BANARASI Das,** b. 16 October 1955, Akorhi, Mirzapur, India. Teacher; Poet. m. Vimala Devi, 10 March 1972, 1 son. Education: Sahityacharya (Equivalent to MA in Sanskrit), 1982; BTC, 1988; MA, Hindi Literature, 1993. Appointments: Assistant Teacher, Government Basic School, Mirzapur, India. Publications: Srihanumadvandana, 1982; Srivindhya vasinicharitamrit, 1989; Sriashtabhujakathamanjari, 1991; Paryavarankaumudi in Sanskrit, Hindi, English, 1993; Utsarg, 1995; Hymn to Lord (Hanuman), 1995; Gandhari, 1996; Silver Poems, 1998. Contributions to: Poet International, Anthologised in Poems 96, World Poetry, 1996-2000. Honours: Sanskrit Literature Award, Uttar Pradesh Government Sanskrit Academy, 1995; Gram Ratna Award by Gram Panchayat Akorhi, Mirzapur, 1996; Winged Word Award, International Socio-Literary Foundation, 1997. Address: s/o Srimolai, Village-Post Akorhi, District, Mirzapur 231307, UP, India.

**BANAT Mohamed,** b. 15 July 1949, Algeria. Company Vice-President; Scientific Consultant; Professor. m. Yoko Matsuda, 2 sons. Education: Bachelor's Degree, Physics, University of Algiers, 1972; DEA's Degree, Physics, University of Toulouse, France, 1973; PhD, Physics, with special honours, University Paul Sabatier, Toulouse, France, 1975; DSc, with special honours, National Polytechnic Institute, Toulouse, France, 1985. Appointments: Researcher Scientist, IMFT/CNRS, Toulouse, France, 1980-85, Tokyo Institute of Technology, Japan, 1986-87; Consultant Scientist, Tokyo, Japan, 1987-88; Visiting Scientist, Tsukuba University, Japan, 1988-90; Senior Consultant Scientist, R&D Project Leader, Tokyo, 1990-99; R&D Project Supervisor, Riken/Science and Technology Agency, Japan, 1999-2000; Vice-President, Bell-Consulting Ltd, Tokyo, 1999-; R&D Consultant to numerous companies and institutions including: Mitsubishi-Atomic-Power-Industry, Japan Gasoline Corporation, Nuclear Fuel Industry. Publications include: Original Results related to the interfacial-turbulence physical phenomenon (in the physics of fluids), 1992; Discovery of the mechanism of the void-drift phenomena in thermalhydraulics with the down stream applications for the power and process industries, 1995. Honours: Special Honours PhD and DSc; Visiting Scientist, Long Term Invited Distinguished Scientists Programme, Tsukuba University, Japan, 1988-90; Listed in Who's Who publications and biographical dictionaries. Memberships: American Society of Mechanical Engineers; Japan Society of Mechanical Engineers. E-mail: tykam@k4.dion.ne.jp

**BANATVALA Jangu,** b. 7 January 1934, London. Doctor of Medicine. m. Roshan Mugaseth, 3 sons, 1 daughter, deceased. Education: Gonville and Caius College, Cambridge; The London Hospital Medical College; Fulbright Fellow, Department of Epidemiology and Health, Yale University, USA. Appointments: Polio Fund Research Fellow, Department of Pathology, University of Cambridge, 1961-64; Research Fellow, Department of Epidemiology and Health, University of Yale, 1964-65; Senior Lecturer and Reader, 1965-75, Professor, Clinical Virology, Honorary Consultant to the Hospitals (NHS trusts), 1975-99, St Thomas' Hospital Medical School later United Medical and Dental Schools of Guy's and St Thomas' Hospitals; Registrar, 1985-87, Vice President, 1987-90, Royal College of Pathologists; Honorary Consultant Microbiologist to the Army, 1992-97; Chairman, Department of Health Advisory Group on Hepatitis, 1990-98; Emeritus Professor, Clinical Virology, Guy's King's and St Thomas' School of Medicine and Dentistry, 1999-. Publications include: About 230 peer reviewed original papers published in General Medical journals and specialist Medical Journals; 50 Editorials for Lancet and BMJ; 30 Chapters in books; Editor, 3 books including Editions 1-5 of Principles and Practice of Clinical Virology (joint editor); Various reports on blood borne virus infections for Royal Colleges of Pathologists, Senate of Surgery, Cl Br Ireland and Royal College of Surgeons and Obstetrics in Gynaecology. Honours: Lionel Whitby Medal, University of Cambridge, 1964; Founder Member, Academy of Medical Sciences, 1998; CBE, 1999. Memberships: Council of Governors, Forrest School, London, Mill Hill School, London; President, European Association Against Virus Diseases, 1981-83; Freeman, City of London, 1987; Council of the Medical Defence Union, 1987-2003; Liveryman, Society of Apothecaries, 1986; Athenaeum; MCC; Leander, Henley on Thames; Honorary member, Hawks, Cambridge. Address: Church End, Henham, Bishops Stortford, Hertfordshire, CM22 6AN, England. E-mail: jangu@church-end-henham.co.uk

**BANDERAS Antonio,** b. 1960, Malaga, Spain. Film Actor. m. (1) Anna Banderas, (2) Melanie Griffith, 1996, 1 child. Appointments: Began Acting aged 14; Performed with National Theatre, Madrid, 6 Years; Films Include: Labyrinth of Passion; El Senor Galindez; El Caso Almeria; The Stilts; 27 Hours; Law of Desire; Matador; Tie Me Up! Tie Me Down!; Woman on the Verge of a Nervous Breakdown; The House of Spirits; Interviews with the Vampire; Philadelphia; The Mambo King; Love and Shadow; Miami Rhapsody; Young Mussolini; Return of Mariaolu; Assassins; Desperado; Evita; Never Talk to Strangers; Crazy in Alabama (director); The 13th Warrior; Dancing in the Dark, 2000; The Body, 2000; Spy Kids, 2001; Femme Fatale, 2002; Frida, 2002; Spy Kids 2: Island of Lost Dreams, 2002; Spy Kids 3-D: Game Over, 2003; Once Upon a Time in Mexico, 2003; Imagining Argentina, 2003. Address: c/o CAA, 9830 Wilshire Boulevard, Beverley Hills, CA 90212, USA.

**BANDYOPADHYAY Prayag, (B Prayag),** b. 19 April 1945, India. m. Mitali, 16 April 1984, 1 daughter. Education: MA. Appointments: Lecturer, 1969-74; Senior Assistant Professor, 1974-. Publications: Prelude; Summer Thoughts; Shadows in a Subway; Selected Poems; The Highway Penguins; The Blue Threads; The Voice of a Terror; The Words Upside Down. Contributions to: Youth Times; Illustrated Weekly of India; Asian Modern Poetry, 1982, 1984, 1988; Li Poetry, Taiwan, 1989. Honours: 1st Prize, 5th World Congress of Poets, 1981; Mentioned as Poet Extraordinary in Tokyo; Honorary DLitt. Membership: Asian Poetry Centre, chairman. Address: 357/1/12/1, Prince Anwar Shah Road, Calcutta 68, India. E-mail: sachinky@hotmail.com

**BANERJEE Kishore Kumar,** b. 4 January 1960, Calcutta, India. Researcher. m. Sujata, 1 son. Education: PhD, Sciences, Jadavpur University. Appointments: Faculty Member, Department of Occupational Health, All India Institute of Hygiene and Public Health, India; Senior Chemist (R&D), Albert David Ltd, Calcutta, India. Publication: Evaluation of benzene exposure in an automobile repairing workshop, 2001. Honour: Australian Postgraduate Award. Memberships: Global Environmental Technology Network (WHO), Geneva; Medical/ Scientific Member, The Asthma and Allergy Research Institute, Australia. Address: 8/5 Barry Road, Oaklands Park, SA 5046, Australia. E-mail: kkb90@hotmail.com

**BANERJEE Lakshmi Narayan,** b. 4 May 1949, Bhaga, Bihar, India. Scientist; General Manager. m. Pratima, 1974, 1 son, 1 daughter. Education: MSc, Inorganic Chemistry, Intheye, 1970; AMII, Ceramic Engineering. Appointments: M/S National Reractories Salanpur, 1970-72; M/S Simon Carves India Ltd, 1972-74; Assistant Manager, M/S Kumardhubi Firecly SILICA Works Ltd, 1974-89; Manager, R&D, M/S Indoflogates Ltd, 1989-98; General Manager, M/S Orient Abrasives Ltd, 1998-. Publications: Many papers in national and international journals; 8 booklets for ISI on chemical analysis of refractory materials and instrumental methods of analysis; Development and use of zero cement castable in UNIT, 1995; High Alu Chrome base castable in Indian Ceramic Science, 1996; The Use of Furnace Gate Valve to Produce Clean and Slag-free Steel at USA in UNITCER, 1997; The use of Baffle in Tundish in IREFRON, 1998. Honours: AMII degree in Ceramics Science, 1989. Memberships: Life Member, Indian Ceramic Society; Member, American Ceramic Society; Member of ISI Governing Body. Address: Orient Abrasives Ltd, SP 148A, RIICO Industrial State, Bhiwadi, Alwar (Ratasthan) India.

**BANERJI Prasanta,** b. 17 October 1933, Jamalpur, India. Homeopathic Doctor. m. Krishna Chatterji, 1 son, 1 daughter. Education: Intermediate in Science, Calcutta University, 1951; Registered Homeopathic Physician, India. Appointments: Medical Consultant, Examiner, Hospital, Mihijam College of Homeopathy, India, 1956-60; Homeopathic Physician, Charitable Dispensary of the late Dr Pareshnath Banerji, Bihar, India, 1956-60; Private Practice, Homeopathic Medicine, Calcutta, India, 1961-; Managing Trustee, P.B. Homeopathic Research Foundation, Calcutta, India, 1992; Lecturer in field to various conferences; Research into the treatment of diseases including: various types of cancer, tumours of the brain, osteomyelitis, osteosarcoma, acromegaly, renal failures, nephritis. Publications: Contributor of articles to professional journals. Honour: Fellow, Mihijam Institute of Homeopathy, 1956; Honorary Adviser to Honorable Minister of Health and Family Welfare, Government of India. Memberships: Member, Key Advisory Group of Experts to Honorable Minister of Health and Family Welfare, Government of India; Member, Programme Advisory Committee for National Cancer Control Programme, Government of India; American Association for the Advancement of Science; New York Academy of Sciences; Calcutta Club; Tollygunge Club. Address: 10/3/1 Elgin Road, Kolkata 700020, India. E-mail: pbhrf@vsnl.com

**BANG Oh Young,** b. 17 June 1967, Seoul, South Korea. Neurologist. m. Sarah Yoon, 2 sons. Education: Bachelor's Degree, 1992, Master's Degree, 1996, Yonsei University, Seoul, South Korea; Doctoral Degree, Ajou University, Suwon, South Korea 2001. Appointments: Resident, Yonsei University, 1993-97; Assistant Professor, Ajou University, 2002-. Publications: Articles in medical journals including: Annals of Neurology, 2003; Neurobiology of Aging, 2003; Neurology, 2004; Stroke, 2004; Neurobiology of Diseases, 2004; Journal of Neurology,

Neurosurgery, Psychiatry, 2004, 2005. Honours: Grants: Korean Research Foundation, 2003 Ministry of Health and Welfare, 2004-2009. Membership: Korean Neurology Association, 1998-. Address: Department of Neurology, School of Medicine, Ajou University, San 5, Woncheon-Dong, Yeongtong-Gu, Gyeonggi-Do, Suwon 442-749, Republic of Korea. E-mail: nmboy@unitel.co.kr

**BANGERTER Michael,** b. Brighton, England. Actor; Playwright; Lecturer, Tutor, Open College of the Arts; Poet. m. Katya Wyeth, 8 May 1971, 1 son, 1 daughter. Education: Graduate Diploma, RADA, Teaching Certificate, Certificate in Advanced Writing; MA, Lancaster. Appointments: Actor in many television, film and theatre prooductions; Playwright in theatre and radio; Reviewer. Eyelines, 2002. CD; Dancing Bears, 2002 (Poetry and Music). Publications: A Far Line of Hills, 1996; Freezing the Frame, 2001. Contributions to: Envoi; Pause; Iota; Blithe Spirit; Pennine Platform; New Hope International Writing; Others. Honour: Award Winner, Kent and Sussex National Open Competition, 1991. Memberships: Association of University Teachers; British Haiku Society. Address: Botriphnie Stables, Drummuir, Keith, Banffshire AB55 5JE, England.

**BANISTER Judith,** b. 10 September 1943, Washington DC, USA. Demographer. m. Kim Woodard, 1 son, 1 daughter. Education: BA, Swarthmore College, 1965; PhD, Stanford University, 1978. Appointments: Postdoctoral Research Fellow, East West Population Institute, 1978-80; Analyst, US Bureau of the Census, 1980-82; Adjunct Professor, George Washington University, 1981-91; Chief, China Branch, US Bureau of the Census, 1982-92; Chief, Center for International Research, US Bureau of the Census, 1992-94; Chief, International Programs Center, US Bureau of the Census, 1994-97; Professor, Hong Kong University of Science And Technology, 1997-2001; Senior Consultant, Javelin Investments, 2001-; Honorary Professor, Hong Kong University, 2002-. Publications: China's Changing Population, 1987; Vietnam Population Dynamics and Prospects, 1993; Articles, Conference Papers on China, Korea, Indochina, South Asia. Memberships: International Union for the Scientific Study of Population; Population Association of America; Association of Asian Studies; American Chamber of Commerce, Beijing. Address: Beijing Javelin Investment Consulting Company, Guan Cheng Yuan (Citichamp Place), Building 16, Suite 21-A, Madian, Haidian District, Beijing 100088, China.

**BANKS Brian (Robert),** b. 4 October 1956, Carshalton, Surrey, England. Teacher; Writer; Poet. 2 sons, 2 daughters. Education: Westminster College; Middlesex Polytechnic. Publications: The Image of J-K Huysmans, 1990; Phantoms of the Belle Epoque, 1993; Atmosphere and Attitudes, 1993; Muse & Messiah: The Life, Imagination and Legacy of Bruno Schilz, 1994; Contributions to: Books and journals. Memberships: Société de J-K Huysmans, Paris; 1890's Society. Address: c/o 4 Meretune Court, Martin Way, Morden, Surrey SM4 4AN, England. E-mail: love4muza@hotmail.com

**BANKS Iain,** b. 1954, Fife, Scotland. Author. Education: Stirling University. Appointments: Technician, British Steel, 1976; IBM, Greenock, 1978. Publications: The Wasp Factory, 1984; Walking on Glass, 1985; The Bridge, 1986; Espedair Street, 1987; Canal Dreams, 1989; The Crow Road (adapted as TV series, 1996), 1992; Complicity, 1993; Whit, 1995; Science Fiction: Consider Phlebas, 1987; The Player of Games, 1988; Use of Weapons, 1990; The State of the Art, 1991; Against a Dark Background, 1993; Feersum Endjinn, 1994; Excession, 1996; A Song of Stone, 1998; Inversions, 1998; The Business,

1999; Windward, 2000; Dead Air, 2002. Address: c/o Little, Brown, Brettenham House, Lancaster Place, London, WC2E 7EN, England.

**BANKS Russell,** b. 28 March 1940, Barnstead. Author. m. (1) Darlene Bennett, divorced, 1962, 1 daughter, (2) Mary Gunst, divorced 1977, 3 daughters, (3) Kathy Walton, divorced 1988, (4) Chase Twichell. Education: Colgate University; University of North Carolina, Chapel Hill. Appointments: Teacher, Creative Writing, Emerson College, Boston; University of New Hampshire, Durham; University of Alabama; New England College; Teacher, Creative Writing, Princeton University, 1982-. Publications: Waiting to Freeze, 1967; 30/6, 1969; Snow; Meditation of a Cautious Man in Winter, 1974; Novels: Family Life, 1975; Hamilton Stark, 1978; The Book of Jamaica, 1980; The Relation of My Imprisonment, 1984; Continental Drift, 1985; Affliction, 1989; The Sweet Hereafter, 1991; Rule of the Bone, 1995; Cloudsplitter, 1998; The Angel on the Roof, 2000; Collected Short Stories; Searching for Survivors, 1975; The New World, 1978; Trailerpark, 1981; Success Stories, 1986; Short Stories in literary magazines. Honours: Fels Award for Fiction, 1974; John Dos Passos Award; American Academy of Arts and Letters Award, 1985. Address: 1000 Park Avenue, New York, NY 10028, USA.

**BANNISTER Matthew,** b. 16 March 1957. Broadcasting Executive. m. (1) Amanda Gerrard Walker, 1984, deceased 1988, 1 daughter, (2) Shelagh Margaret Mcleod, 1989, 1 son. Education: Nottingham University. Appointments: Presenter, BBC Radio Nottingham, 1978-81; Reporter, Presenter, Capital Radio, London, 1981-83; Deputy Head, News and Talks, 1985-87; Head, 1987-88; Newsbeat, BBC Radio 1, 1983-85; Managing Editor, BBC Greater London Radio, 1988-91; Project Co-ordinator, BBC Charter Renewal, 1991-93; Controller, BBC Radio 1, 1993-96; Director, BBC Radio, 1996-98; Head of Productions, BBC TV, 1999-2000; Director, Marketing and Communications Association, 2000; Chair, Trust the DJ, 2001-; Presenter, BBC Radio 5 Live, 2002-. Membership: Board, Chichester Festival Theatre, 1999-. Address: Trust the DJ, Units 13-14, Barley Shotts Business Park, Acklam Road, London, W10 5YG, England. E-mail: contact@trustthedj.com Website: www.trustthedj.com

**BANNISTER Roger G (Sir),** b. 23 March 1929, London. Athlete; Consultant Physician; Neurologist; University Administrator. m. Moyra Elver Jacobsson, 2 sons, 2 daughters. Education: University College School Exeter; Merton College; Oxford St Mary's Hospital, Medical School, London. Appointments: Winner, Oxford and Cambridge Mile, 1947-50; President, Oxford University, Athletic Club, 1948; British Mile Champion, 1951, 1953, 1954; World Record One Mile, 1954; First Sub Four Minute Mile, 1954; Master Pembroke College, Oxford, 1985-93; Honorary Consultant Neurologist, St Mary's Hospital, Medical School, National Hospital for Neurology and Neurosurgery, London (non-executive director); London and Oxford District and Region; Chair, St Mary's Hospital Development Trust; Chair, Government Working Group on Sport in the Universities, 1995-97; Chair, Clinical Autonomic Research Society, 1982-84. Publications: First Four Minutes, 1955 (republished as 5oth Anniversary Edition, 2004); Editor, Brain and Bannister's Clinical Neurology, 1992; Autonomic Faliure (co-editor), 1993; Various Medical Articles on Physiology and Neurology. Honours: Honorary Fellow, Exeter College, Oxford, 1950; Merton College, Oxford, 1986; Honorary Fellow, UMIST, 1974; Honorary LLD, Liverpool, 1972; Honorary DSc, Sheffield, 1978; Grinnell, 1984; Bath, 1984; Rochester, 1986; Williams, 1987; Dr hc, Jvvaskyla, Finland; Honorary MD, Pavia, 1986; Honorary DL, University of Victoria, Canada,

1994; University of Wales, Cardiff, 1995; Loughborough, 1996; University of East Anglia, 1997; Hans-Heinrich Siegbert Prize, 1977. Memberships: Physiological Society; Medical Research Society; Association of British Neurologists; Fellow, Imperial College; Leeds Castle Foundation, 1988-; St Mary's Hospital Medical School Trust, 1994-; First Lifetime Award, American Academy of Neurology, 2005. Address: 21 Bardwell Road, Oxford, OX2 6SU, England.

**BAR-COHEN Yoseph,** b. 3 September 1947, Baghdad, Iraq. Physicist. m. Yardena, 1 son, 1 daughter. Education: BSc, Physics, 1971, MSc, Materials Science, 1973, PhD, Physics, 1979, Hebrew University, Jerusalem, Israel. Appointments: Senior NDE Specialist, Israel Aircraft Industry, 1971-79; Postdoctorate, National Research Council, 1979-80; Senior Physicist, Systems Research Laboratory, Dayton, Ohio, 1980-83; Principal Specialist, McDonnell Douglas Corporation, Long Beach, California, 1983-91; Senior Research Scientist and Group Supervisor, Advanced Technologies, Jet Propulsion Laboratory, Pasadena, California, 1991-. Publications: over 260 journals and proceedings papers and 3 edited books; 16 patents. Honours: National Research Council Fellowship Award, 1979; Nova Award, Outstanding Achievement in Technology, 1996; Nova Award, Technical Innovation and Leadership, 1998; Two SPIE Lifetime Achievement Award, 2001 and 2005; NASA Exceptional Engineering Achievement Medal, 2001. Memberships: Fellow, American Society for Non-destructive Testing; Fellow, International Society for Optical Engineering. Address: Jet Propulsion Laboratory, MS-125-224, 4800 Oak Grove Drive, Pasadena, CA 91109-8099, USA.

**BAR-TAL Daniel,** b. 31 January 1946, Russia. Professor of Social Psychology. m. Svetlana, 1 son, 2 daughters. Education: BA, Psychology and Sociology, Tel Aviv University, 1970; MS, Social Psychology, 1973, PhD, Social Psychology, 1974, University of Pittsburgh. Appointments: Lecturer, 1975-79, Senior Lecturer, 1979-83, School of Education, Tel Aviv University; Visiting Associate Professor, Department of Psychology, Vanderbilt University, 1981-82, Brandeis University, 1987-88, Ecole des Hautes Etudes en Sciences Sociales, Paris, 1991-, Department of Psychology, University of Maryland, 1995, Department of Psychology, University of Muenster, Germany, 1997; NIAS, Holland, 2000-2001; Fellow Professor, 1983-89; Professor of Social Psychology, School of Education, Tel Aviv University, 1989-. Publications include: Stereotypes and Prejudice: Changing Conceptions, 1990; Patriotism in the Life of Individuals and Nations, 1997; Security Concerns: Insights From the Israeli Experience, 1998; How Children Understand War and Peace, 1999; Patriotism, 2004; Stereotypes and Prejudice in Conflict, 2005; Shared Beliefs in a Society, 2000. Honours: Otto Klineberg Intercultural and International Relations Prize, SPSSI, 1991; President, International Society of Political Psychology, 1999-2000; Golestan Fellowship, NIAS, 2000-2001. Memberships: American Psychological Association; European Association of Experimental Social Psychology; International Society of Political Psychology; Society for the Advancement of Social Psychology; Society for the Psychological Study of Social Issues; Society for Experimental Psychology. Address: School of Education, Tel Aviv University, Tel Aviv 69978, Israel.

**BARBARA John Anthony James,** b. 2 April 1946, Cairo, Egypt (British). Transfusion Microbiologist. m. Gillian, 1 son, 1 daughter. Education: BA (Hons) Natural Sciences, Trinity College, Cambridge, 1968; MSc, Medical School, Birmingham University, 1969; MA, Cantab, PhD, Department of Microbiology, Reading University, 1972. Appointments: Lecturer, Department of Virology, Reading University, 1972-

74; Examiner, Oxford University, GCE A Level Biology, 1974-85; Head of Microbiology, North London Blood Transfusion Centre, 1974-96; Honorary Associate Research Fellow, Brunel University, Middlesex, 1984-90; Open University Research Student Supervisor, 1988-99; Lead Scientist in Microbiology, London and South East Zone, 1996-2000; Principal, Transfusion Microbiology National Laboratories and Microbiology Consultant, National Blood Authority, 2000-; External Examiner, Bristol University, 2003-; Visiting Professor, University of West of England, 2004. Publications: Over 300 papers, chapters, abstracts and reviews. Honours: Hong Kong Red Cross Foundation Lecturer, 1996; Kenneth Goldsmith memorial prize of the BBTS, 1991; Iain Cook Memorial Award of the SNBTS, 2002; Gold Medal of the BBTS, 2003; Oliver Memorial Award, 2003. Memberships: Institute of Biology; Past President, British Blood Transfusion Society; American Association of Blood Banks; Past Vice President, International Society of Blood Transfusion; Royal College of Pathologists; Association of Clinical Microbiologists. Address: National Transfusion Microbiology Laboratories, National Blood Service, North London, Colindale Avenue, London NW9 5BG, England. E-mail: john.barbara@nbs.nhs.uk Website: www.blood.co.uk

**BARBER Benjamin R,** Political Scientist; Writer. m. Leah Kreutzer. Education: Certificate, London School of Economics and Political Science; MA, PhD, Department of Government, Harvard University. Appointments include: Walt Whitman Professor of Political Science, Director, Walt Whitman Center for the Culture and Politics of Democracy, Rutgers University, New Brunswick, New Jersey, 1969-2001; Chairman, Chief Strategic Officer, Bodies Electric, software company; Gershon and Carrol Kekst Professorship of Civil Society, University of Maryland, 2001-; Principal of the New Democracy Collaborative, offices in New York, Washington and University of Maryland, 2001-. Publications: Books including: Marriage Voices, novel, 1981; Strong Democracy, 1984; Jihad vs McWorld, 1995, translated into 10 languages; A Passion for Democracy, Collected American Essays, 1999; The Truth of Power: Intellectual Affairs in the Clinton White House, 2001; Fear's Empire, 2004; Frequent contributor to Harper's Magazine, The New York Times, The Atlantic, The Nation, Le Nouvel Observateur, Die Zeit, many other scholarly and popular American and European publications; Founding editor, former editor-in-chief, Political Theory international quarterly; Television work including: Co-author, 10-part series The Struggle for Democracy, and companion book, 1988, and contributions to Greek Fire series, UK, The American Promise series, USA, many other educational documentaries; Stage works include Home and the River (libretto); KASPAR (co-creator with Leah Kreutzer); several off-Broadway and regional productions. Honours include: The John Dewey Prize, 2003; Guggenheim, Fulbright and Social Science Research Fellowships; Honorary Doctorates, Connecticut College, Monmouth University, Grinnell College, Member Council on Foreign Relations, 2000-; Palmes Academiques (Chevalier) of the French Government, 2001; The Berlin Prize of the American Academy of Berlin, 2002. Address: Department of Government and Politics, 3140 Tydings Hall, Room 1143, University of Maryland, College Park, MD 20742-8227, USA. Email: bbarber@gvpt.umd.edu

**BARBER Francis,** b. 13 May 1957, Wolverhampton, England. Actress. Education: Bangor University; Cardiff University. Appointments: Hull Truck Theatre Company; Glasgow Citizens Theatre; Tricycle Theatre; RSC; TV Appearances include: Clem Jack Story; Home Sweet Home; Flame to the Phoenix; Reilly; Ace of Spies; Those Glory Glory Days; Hard Feelings; Behaving Badly; The Nightmare Year; Film Appearances include:

The Missionary, 1982; A Zed and Two Noughts; White City Castaway; Prick Up Your Ears; Sammy and Rosie Get Laid; We Think the World of You; The Grasscutter; Separate Bedrooms; Young Soul Rebels; Secret Friends; The Lake; Soft Top, Hard Shoulder; The Fish Tale; Three Steps to Heaven; Photographing Fairies; Shiner; Still Crazy; Esther Kahn; Mauvaise passe; Stage Appearances include: Night of the Iguana; Pygmalion; Closer; Uncle Vanya.

**BARBIROLLI Evelyn (Lady),** b. 24 November 1911, Wallingford, England. Musician; Solo Oboist. m. Sir John Barbirolli. Education: Royal College of Music, London. Career: Freelance Oboe Player; Member, London Symphony Orchestra; Principal, Glyndebourne Opera Orchestra, 1934-40. Publication: Book: Life with Glorious John. Honours: OBE; FRCM; FRAM; FTCL; FNCM; Honorary DMus, Durham University; Honorary MA, Leeds University. Address: 15A Buckland Crescent, London NW3 5DH, England.

**BARBOSA Pedro,** b. 12 May 1948, Porto, Portugal. Writer; Professor; Researcher. 1 daughter. Education: BA, Romance Philology, Universidade de Coimbra, 1974; MA, Semiotics, Université Louis Pasteur, Strasbourg, France, 1988; PhD, Communication Sciences, Universidade Nova Lisboa, 1993. Appointments: Coordinator Professor, Instituto Politécnico do Porto; Visiting Scholar, PUC de São Paulo, Brazil; Researcher, Universidade Nova de Lisboa, Portugal; Researcher, Université Artois, France; Lecturer, University of Siena, Italy. Publications: Essay: Teoria do Teatro Moderno, 1982; Aspectos da Renovação Dramatúrgica na Trilogia do Teatro-no-Teatro de Pirandello, 1993; Metamorfoses do Real: arte, imaginário e conhecimento estético, 1995; A Ciberliteratura: criação literária e cumputador, 1996; Arte, Comunição & Semiótica, 2002; Theatre: Eróstrato, 1984; Anticleia ou os Chapéus-de-Chuva do Sonho, 1992; PortoMetropolitanoLento, 1993; PortoImaginárioLento, 2001; Alletsator – XPTO.Kosmos.2001, 2001; Fiction: O Guardador de Retretes, 1976, 1978, 1980; Histórias da Menina Minhó-Minhó, 1988; Prefácio para uma Personagem Só, 1993; Cyberliterature includes: Teoria do Homem Sentado, 1996; O Motor Textual, 2001. Honours: Essay Prize, Association of Portuguese Writers, 1982. Memberships: Association of Portuguese Authors; Association of Portuguese Writers. Address: Rua Andresas, 412 6 E, 4100, Porto, Portugal. E-mail: pedrobarbosa@netcabo.pt Website: www.pedrobarbosa.net

**BARCLAY Linwood L,** b. 20 March 1955, New Haven, Connecticut, USA. Journalist; Author. m. Neetha, 1 son, 1 daughter. Education: BA (Hons), English, Trent University, Peterborough, Ontario, Canada. Appointments: Journalist, 1981, Columnist, 1993-, Toronto Star, Toronto, Canada; Public Speaker. Publications: Father Knows Zilch, 1996; This House is Nuts, 1997; Mike Harris Made Me Eat My Dog, 1998; Last Resort, 2000; Bad Move, 2004; Bad Guys, 2005. Honours: Best Columnist Award, Canadian Community Newspaper Association, 1981; Stephen Leacock Award of Merit (and Finalist for Stephen Leacock Award for Humour) for Book "Last Resort", 2001. Memberships: Writers Union of Canada; Canadian Journalists for Freedom of Expression; Southern Ontario Newspaper Guild; Crime Writers of Canada; Mystery Writers of America. Address: Burlington, Ontario, Canada. E-mail: lbarclay@thestar.ca

**BARDOT Brigitte,** b. 28 September 1934, Paris, France. Actress and Animal Rights Campaigner. m. (4) Bernard D'Ormale, 1992. Education: Paris Conservatoire. Career: Films include: Manina: La fille sans voile; Futures vedettes; Le grandes manouveures; En effueillent la marguerite; Une parisienne; En case de malheur; Voulez-vous danser avec moi?; Please not now?; Viva Maria; Les femmes, 1969; Don Juan, 1973. Publications: Initiales BB, 1996; Le Carré de Pluton, 1999. Memberships: President Fondation Brigitte Bardot. Honours: Etoile de Cristal, Academy of Cinema, 1966; Chevalier Légion d'honneur. Address: Fondation Brigitte Bardot, 45 rue Vineuse, 75016 Paris, France. E-mail: fbb@fondationbrigittebardot.fr

**BARKE Hemchandra Chandrabhan,** b. 27 October 1975, Mumbai, India. Insurance Manager. m. Poonam, 1 son. Education: General Insurance Corporation, Specialised Insurance Course, 1992-93; Associate, 1992, Fellow, 1995, Insurance Institute of India; B Com, University of Bombay, 1996; Postgraduate, Marketing Management, Institute of Management Development and Research, Bombay, 1996; LLB, Government Law College, Bombay, 1997; Associate, Institute of Risk Management, London, 1997; Associate, Chartered Insurance Institute, London, 1999; Chartered Property Casualty Underwriter, 2001, Associate in Reinsurance, 2002, Associate in Marine Insurance Management, 2002, Associate in Claims, American Institute of Chartered Property Casualty Underwriters, USA. Appointments: Trainee, The New India Assurance Company Ltd, Bombay, India, 1992; Officer, National Insurance Company Ltd, Bombay, India, 1995-98; Technical Manager, Arab Commercial Enterprises (Associates of Sedgwicks UK, now Marsh), Kuwait, 1998-99; Manager, Tata Aig Risk Management Services Ltd, Bombay, India, 1999; Manager, Underwriting and Risk Management, The Tokio Marine and Fire Insurance Co Ltd, Dubai, United Arab Emirates, 2000-. Publications: Contributor of several articles in press and professional publications. Honours: Certificate, International Who's Who Historical Society, USA; Certificate, for participation and contributing to management Development Seminar 2003 with focus on strategies for expansion in international markets, The Tokio Marine and Fire Insurance Co Ltd, Japan. Memberships include: American Institute of Chartered Property Casualty Underwriters, USA; Chartered Insurance Institute, London; Institute of Risk Management, London; Insurance Institute of India; Indian Institute of Insurance and Risk Management; College of Insurance, India; Loss Prevention Association of India; Indian Institute of Packaging; Emirates Insurance Association, United Arab Emirates; Education Committee, Logistics and Supply Chain Management Group of UAE. Address: The Tokio Marine and Fire Insurance Co Ltd, Office Block, 3rd Floor, Deira City Centre, Dubai, United Arab Emirates. E-mail: barke@tokiomarine.ae

**BARKER Dennis (Malcolm),** b. 21 June 1929, Lowestoft, England. Journalist; Novelist. m. Sarah Katherine Alwyn, 1 daughter. Education: National Diploma in Journalism, 1959. Appointments: Reporter and Sub-Editor, Suffolk Chronicle & Mercury, Ipswich, 1947-48; Reporter, Feature Writer, Theatre and Film Critic, 1948-58, East Anglian Daily Times; Estates and Property Editor 1958-63, also Theatre Critic, 1960-63, Express & Star, Wolverhampton; Midlands Correspondent, 1963-67, Reporter, Feature Writer, Columnist, The Guardian, 1967-91 (contributor). Publications: Novels: Candidate of Promise, 1969; The Scandalisers, 1974; Winston Three Three Three, 1987; Non-fiction: The People of the Forces Trilogy (Soldiering On, 1981, Ruling the Waves, 1986, Guarding the Skies, 1989); One Man's Estate, 1983; Parian Ware, 1985; Fresh Start, 1990; The Craft of the Media Interview, 1998; How to Deal with the Media (2000); Seize the Day (contributor), 2001; The Guardian Book of Obituaries (contributor), 2003; Oxford Dictionary of National Biography (contributor), 2004. Contributions to: BBC; Punch; East Anglian Architecture & Building Review (editor and editorial director, 1956-58); The Guardian, 1991-. Memberships: National Union of Journalists, Secretary, Suffolk Branch, 1953-58, Chairman 1958; Chairman, Home Counties District Council,

1956-57; Life Member, 1991; Life Member, Newspaper Press Fund; Writers Guild of Great Britain; Broadcasting Press Guild; Society of Authors. Address: 67 Speldhurst Road, London W4 1BY, England.

**BARKER Elspeth,** b. 16 November 1940, Edinburgh, Scotland. Writer. m. George Granville Barker, 29 July 1989, 3 sons, 2 daughters. Education: St Leonards School, Scotland, 1953-57; Oxford University, England, 1958-61. Publications: O Caledonia, 1991; Anthology of Loss, 1997. Contributions to: Independent on Sunday; Guardian; Harpers & Queen; TLS; Vogue; Big Issue; Sunday Times; Observer; Daily Mail. Honours: David Higham Award, Scottish Arts Council; Angel Literary Award; Royal Society of Literature Winifred Holtby Award. Address: Bintry House, Ittenigham, Aylsham, Norfolk NR11 7AT, England.

**BARKER Ralph Hammond,** b. 21 October 1917, Feltham, Middlesex, England. Author. m. (1) Joan Muriel Harris, deceased, (2) Diana Darvey, deceased, 1 adopted daughter. Education: Hounslow College, Hounslow, Middlesex, 1926-34. Career: Journalist, Sporting Life, London, 1935; Wartime Service RAF, 1940-46; Post-war Service RAF, 1949-61; Freelance contributor under contract to the Sunday Express, London, 1955-88; Full-time Author, 1961-. Publications: Books: Down in the Drink, 1955; The Ship-Busters, 1957; The Last Blue Mountain, 1959; Strike Hard, Strike Sure, 1963, 2003; Ten Great Innings, 1964; The Thousand Plan, 1965, 1975; Great Mysteries of the Air, 1966; Ten Great Bowlers, 1967; Aviator Extraordinary, 1969; Test Cricket, England v Australia (with Irving Rosenwater), 1969; Verdict on a Lost Flyer, 1969; The RAF at War, 1970; The Schneider Trophy Races, 1971, 1981; Against the Sea, 1972; One Man's Jungle, 1975; Survival in the Sky, 1975; The Blockade Busters, 1976; The Cricketing Family Edrich, 1976; The Hurricats, 1978, 2000; Not Here, But in Another Place, 1980; Innings of a Lifetime, 1982; Goodnight, Sorry for Sinking You, 1984; Purple Patches, 1987; That Eternal Summer, 1990; The Royal Flying Corps, Parts I and II, 1994, 1995; A Brief History of The Royal Flying Corps in World War I, 2002; Men of the Bombers, forthcoming 2005; Articles: Over 250 main feature articles for the Sunday Express; Contributor to The Cricketer International and The Cricket Society Journal. Honour: Buchpreis des Deutschen Alpenvereins, 1982. Memberships: Society of Authors; Authors' Licensing and Collecting Society; NUJ; RAF Association; RAF Club; MCC; Savage Club; Cricket Society. Address: Old Timbers, 16 Aldercombe Lane, Caterham, Surrey CR3 6ED, England.

**BARKIN Ellen,** b. 16 April 1955, New York, USA. Actress. m. Gabriel Byrne, 1988, 1 son. Education: City University of New York; Hunter College, Indiana. Appointments: Stage Appearances include: Shout Across the River, 1980; Killings on the Last Line, 1980; Extremities, 1982; Eden Court; TV Appearances include: Search for Tomorrow, Kent State, 1981; We're Fighting Back, 1981; Terrible Joe Moran, 1984; Before Women Has Wings, 1998. Films include: Diner, 1982; Daniel, 1983; Tender Mercies, 1983; Eddie and the Cruisers, 1983; The Adventures of Buckaroo Banzai, 1984; Harry and Son, 1984; Enormous Changes at the Last Minute, 1985; Down by Law, 1986; The Big Easy, 1987; Siesta, 1987; Sea of Love, 1989; Johnny Handsome; Switch; Man Trouble, 1992; Mac, 2993; This Boy's Life, 1993; Into the West, 1993; Bad Company, 1995; Wild Bill, 1995; Mad Dog Times, 1996; The Fan, 1996; Fear and Loathing in Las Vegas; Popcorn; Drop Dead Gorgeous; The White River Kid, 1999; Crime and Punishment in Suburbia, 2000; Mercy, 2000; Someone Like You, 2001. Honour: Emmy Award. Address: c/o CAA, 9830 Wilshire Boulevard, Beverly Hills, CA 90212, USA.

# DICTIONARY OF INTERNATIONAL BIOGRAPHY

**BARLOW Matthew B,** b. 30 January 1935, Carlisle, England. Senior Project Manager. m. Mary Alice Jenkins, 1 son. Education: BA, Ealing College; BSc, University of Petroleum and Minerals, Dhahran, Saudi Arabia, 1978; BS, University of Oriental African Studies, Lagos, Nigeria, 1981; MSc, Aston University, Birmingham, England, 1986. Appointments: Departmental Managing Director, Finance and Administration, National Bank of Nigeria, Lagos, 1979-82; Project Manager, Chemsult, Sacramento, California and Johannesburg, South Africa, 1978-91; Loss Leaders Representative, Arabian Oil, Saudi Arabia, 1977-97; From Assistant Superintendent to Superintendent, Complant International, Saudi Arabia, 1989-; Associate Assistant, Life Insurance Pension Service, Gloucester, England, 1979-; General Manager, Western Executive, Cheltenham, England, 1986-; Technical Manager, Wescott Freight, Gloucestershire, 1990-; Chartered Accountant, PES Middleborough, Lucern, Switzerland, 1977-97. Memberships: Fellow: Institute of International Accountants, Royal Institute of British Architects, British Institute of Management, Institute of Cost and Management Accountants, Institute of Accountants, American Institute of Cost and Consulting Engineers; Member, New York Academy of Sciences. Address: 12 The Springs, Lydney, Gloucestershire, GL5 5NF, England.

**BARNABY (Charles) Frank,** b. 27 September 1927, Andover, Hampshire, England. Physicist; Author. m. 19 December 1972, 1 son, 1 daughter. Education: BSc, 1951, MSc, 1954, PhD, 1960, London University. Appointments: Physicist, UK Atomic Energy Authority, 1950-57; Member, Senior Scientific Staff, Medical Research Council, University College Medical School, 1957-68; Executive Secretary, Pugwash Conferences on Science and World Affairs, 1968-70; Director, Stockholm International Peace Research Institute (SIPRI), 1971-81; Professor of Peace Studies, Frei University, Amsterdam, 1981-85; Director, World Disarmament Campaign (UK), 1982-; Chair, Just Defence, 1982-; Consultant, Oxford Research Group, 1998-; Editor, International Journal of Human Rights. Publications: Man and the Atom, 1971; Disarmament and Arms Control, 1973; Nuclear Energy, 1975; The Nuclear Age, 1976; Prospects for Peace, 1980; Future Warfare, 1983; The Automated Battlefield, 1986; Star Wars Brought Down to Earth, 1986; The Invisible Bomb, 1989; The Gaia Peace Atlas, 1989; The Role and Control of Arms in the 1990's, 1992; How Nuclear Weapons Spread, 1993; Instruments of Terror, 1997; How to Build a Nuclear Bomb ad Other Weapons of Mass Destruction, 2003. Contributions to: Ambio; New Scientist; Technology Review. Honour: Honorary Doctorates, Frei University, Amsterdam, 1982, University of Southampton, 1996. Address: Brandreth, Station Road, Chilbolton, Stockbridge, Hampshire SO20 6HW, England.

**BARNARD Robert,** b. 23 November 1936, Burnham on Crouch, Essex, England. Crime Writer. m. Mary Louise Tabor, 7 February 1963. Education: Balliol College, Oxford, 1956-59; Dr Phil, University of Bergen, Norway, 1972. Publications: Death of an Old Goat, 1974; Sheer Torture, 1981; A Corpse in a Gilded Cage, 1984; Out of the Blackout, 1985; Skeleton in the Grass, 1987; At Death's Door, 1988; Death and the Chaste Apprentice, 1989; Masters of the House, 1994; A Cry in the Dark, 2003. As Bernard Bastable: Dead, Mr Mozart, 1995; Too Many Notes, Mr Mozart, 1995. Honours: Seven Times Nominated for Edgar Awards; Recipient of Diamond Dagger for Lifetime's Achievement in Crime Fiction, 2003. Memberships: Crime Writers Association; Chairman, Brontë Society, 1996-99, 2002-2005; Society of Authors. Address: Hazeldene, Houghley Lane, Leeds LS13 2DT, England.

**BARNES Clive (Alexander),** b. 13 May 1927, London, England. Journalist; Dance and Theatre Critic. m. (2) Patricia Amy Evelyn Winckley, 26 June 1958, 1 son, 1 daughter. Education: King's College, London; BA, St Catherine's College, Oxford, 1951. Appointments: Co-Editor, Arabesque, 1950; Assistant Editor, 1950-58, Associate Editor, 1958-61, Executive Editor, 1961-65, Dance and Dancers; Administrative Officer in Town Planning, London County Council, 1952-61; Chief Dance Critic, 1961-65, New York Correspondent, 1970-, The Times, London; Dance Critic, 1965-78, Drama Critic, 1967-78, New York Times; Associate Editor and Chief Dance and Drama Critic, New York Post, 1978-. Publications: Ballet in Britain Since the War, 1953; Frederick Ashton and His Ballets, 1961; Ballet Here and Now (with A V Coton and Frank Jackson), 1961; Ballett, 1965: Chronik und Bilanz des Ballettjahres (editor with Horst Koegler), 1965; Ballett 1966: Chronik und Bilanz des Ballettjahres (editor with Horst Koegler), 1966; Fifty Best Plays of the American Theatre from 1787 to the Present (editor), 4 volumes, 1969; Best American Plays: Sixth Series, 1963-1967 (editor with John Gassner), 1971; Best American Plays: Seventh Series (editor), 1975; Inside American Ballet Theatre, 1977; Nureyev, 1982; Best American Plays: Eighth Series, 1974-1982 (editor), 1983; Best American Plays: Ninth Series, 1983-1992 (editor), 1993. Contributions to: Many periodicals. Honours: Knight of the Order of Dannebrog, Denmark, 1972; Commander of the Order of the British Empire, 1975. Address: c/o New York Post, 210 South Street, New York, NY 10002, USA.

**BARNES David Michael William,** b. 16 July 1943, Cardiff, Wales. Barrister. m. Susan, 2 sons. Education: 1st Class Degree, Jurisprudence, Wadham College, Oxford. Appointments: Called to Bar, 1965; Honorary Research Fellow, Lady Margaret Hall, Oxford, 1979; Queen's Counsel, 1981; Recorder of Crown Court, 1984; Bencher, Middle Temple, 1989; Visiting Fellow, University of Auckland, New Zealand, 1994. Publications: Editor, Hill & Redman's Law of Landlord and Tenant, 1971-81; Guide to the Law of Rent Reviews, 2001. Membership: Beefsteak Club. Address: Wilberforce Chambers, 8 New Square, Lincoln's Inn, London, WC2A 3QP.

**BARNES Richard John Black,** b. 13 August 1950, Nyasaland, Malawi. Editor. m. Lucette Aylmer, 21 June 1975, 1 son, 1 daughter. Education: Stonyhurst College, 1959-68; Royal College of Agriculture, 1970-72; Polytechnic of Central London, 1972-75. Publications: The Sun in the East, 1983; Eye on the Hill - Horse Travels in Britain, 1987; John Bell, Sculptor, 1999; The Year of Public Sculpture, 2001; The Obelisk - A Monumental Feature in Britain, 2004; Memberships: Fellow of the Royal Geographical Society; Fellow of the Royal Society of Arts. Address: c/o Frontier Publishing, Windetts Farm, Long Lane, Kirstead, Norwich NR15 1EG, England.

**BARNETT Anthony (Peter John),** b. 10 September 1941, London, England. Author; Publisher. Education: MA, University of Essex. Appointment: Editorial Director, Allardyce, Barnett, Publishers. Publications: Poetry: Blood Flow, 1975; Fear and Misadventure, 1977; The Resting Bell, Collected Poems, 1987. Prose and Poetry: Carp and Rubato, 1995; Anti-Beauty, 1999; Miscanthus: Selected & New Poems, 2005. Critical and Biographical: The Poetry of Anthony Barnett, 1993. Music Biography: Desert Sands, The Recordings and Performances of Stuff Smith, 1995; Black Gypsy, The Recordings of Eddie South, 1999; Selected Poems, 2004. Contributions to: Anthologies, journals and periodicals. Address: c/o Allardyce, Barnett, Publishers, 14 Mount Street, Lewes, East Sussex BN7 1HL, England. Website: www.abar.net

**BARNETT Correlli (Douglas),** b. 28 June 1927, Norbury, Surrey, England. Author. m. Ruth Murby, 28 December 1950, 2 daughters. Education: BA, 1951, MA, 1955, Exeter College,

Oxford. Appointments: Keeper of the Churchill Archives Centre and Fellow, Churchill College, 1977-95; Defence Lecturer, Cambridge University, 1980-84; Development Fellow, Churchill College, 1997-. Publications: The Hump Organisation, 1957; The Channel Tunnel (co-author), 1958; The Desert Generals, 1960, new enlarged edition 1984; The Swordbearers, 1963; The Great War (co-author), 1964; The Lost Peace (co-author), 1966; Britain and Her Army, 1970; The Collapse of British Power, 1972; The Commanders, 1973; Marlborough, 1974; Strategy and Society, 1975; Bonaparte, 1978; The Great War, 1979; The Audit of War, 1986; Engage the Enemy More Closely: The Royal Navy in the Second World War, 1991; The Lost Victory: British Dreams, British Realities 1945-1950, 1995; The Verdict of Peace: Britain Between Her Yesterday and the Future, 2001. Honours: Best Television Documentary Script Award, Screenwriter's Guild, 1964; Royal Society of Literature Award, 1970; Chesney Gold Medal, Royal United Services Institute for Defence Studies, 1991; Yorkshire Post Book of the Year Award, 1991; DSc Honoris Causa, Cranfield University, 1993; CBE, 1997. Address: Catbridge House, East Carleton, Norwich NR14 8JX, England.

**BARNIE John Edward,** b. 27 March 1941, Abergavenny, Gwent, Wales. Editor; Writer; Poet. m. Helle Michelsen, 28 October 1980, 1 son. Education: BA, Honours, 1963, MA, 1966, PhD, 1971, Birmingham University; Dip Ed, Nottingham University, 1964. Appointments: Lecturer, English Literature, University of Copenhagen, 1969-82; Assistant, then Editor, Planet: The Welsh International, 1985-. Publications: Borderland, 1984; Lightning Country, 1987; Clay, 1989; The Confirmation, 1992; Y Felan a Finnau, 1992; The City, 1993; Heroes, 1996; No Hiding Place, 1996; The Wine Bird, 1998; Ice, 2001; At the Salt Hotel, 2003. Contributions to: American Poetry Review; Critical Quarterly; Poetry Wales; New Welsh Review; Anglo-Welsh Review; Kunapipi; Juke Blues. Honour: Welsh Arts Council Prize for Literature, 1990. Memberships: Yr Academi Gymreig; Harry Martinson-Sällskapet. Address: Greenfields, Comins Coch, Aberystwyth, SY23 3BG, Ceredigion, Wales.

**BARON Jeremy Hugh,** b. 25 April 1931, London, England. Gastroenterologist (retired). m. (1) Wendy Dimson, 1 son, 1 daughter, (2) Carla Lord. Education: University College School, 1942-48; MA, DM, Queen's College, Oxford, 1948-52; Middlesex Hospital Medical School, 1952-54. Appointments: Consultant Physician, Tottenham Hospitals, London, 1968-71; Consultant Physician, St Charles Hospital, London, 1971-94; Sub Dean, 1983-87, Consultant Physician and Gastroenterologist, 1988-96, St Mary's Hospital Medical School; Senior Lecturer, Royal Postgraduate Medical School, Hammersmith Hospital, London, 1968-96; Honorary Senior Lecturer/Consultant, Imperial College, Faculty of Medicine, London, 1996-; Honorary Professorial Lecturer, Mt Sinai School of Medicine, New York, USA, 1996-. Publications: 7 books; Articles contributed to professional journals. Honours: Honorary membership, medals and prizes from gastroenterologists in Argentina, Denmark, Finland, France and Germany; Hunterian Professor, Royal College of Surgeons of England. Memberships: FRCP (London); FRCS (England), FRCP (Glasgow); British Medical Association; Royal Society of Medicine; Society of Authors; British Society of Gastroenterology; Society of Apothecaries; Oxford and Cambridge Club. Address: Thomas Hunt Gastroenterology Unit, St Mary's Hospital, London W2 1NY, England.

**BARR Geoffrey Samuel,** b. 1 November 1952, Liverpool, England. Head and Neck Surgeon. m. Rowena M Bickerton, 5 May 1984, 2 sons, 1 daughter. Education: Queen's College, University of St Andrews, 1971-77. Appointments: Department of Head and Neck Surgery, University of Liverpool, 1980-84; Department of Head and Neck Surgery, University of Dundee, 1984-93; Department of Head and Neck Surgery, University of Birmingham, 1989-93; Consultant Otolaryngologist, Head and Neck Surgeon, Gwynedd Hospital, 1993-; Part time advisor to National Health Service Executive on Medical Research and Computing. Publications: Over 50 articles in peer reviewed medical and surgical journals. Honours: MBChB, University of Dundee, 1977; Fellow, Royal College of Surgeons, 1984; Master of Surgery, University of Dundee, 1989; Honorary Member, Oriole Society; Honorary Archivist, Schofield Statistical Society. Memberships: Royal Society of Medicine; Royal College of Surgeons; British Association of Otolaryngology, Head and Neck Surgery; British Association of Head and Neck Oncologists; Hospital Consultants and Specialists Association. Address: Department of Head and Neck Surgery, Gwynedd Hospital, Bangor, Gwynedd LL57 2PW, Wales, United Kingdom. E-mail: geoffrey.barr@nww-tr.wales.nhs.uk

**BARR Patricia Miriam,** b. 25 April 1934, Norwich, Norfolk, England. Writer. Education: BA, University of Birmingham; MA, University College, London. Publications: The Coming of the Barbarians, 1967; The Deer Cry Pavilion, 1968; A Curious Life for a Lady, 1970; To China with Love, 1972; The Memsahibs, 1976; Taming the Jungle, 1978; Chinese Alice, 1981; Uncut Jade, 1983; Kenjiro, 1985; Coromandel, 1988; The Dust in the Balance, 1989. Honour: Winston Churchill Fellowship for Historical Biography, 1972. Membership: Society of Authors. Address: 6 Mount Pleasant, Norwich NR2 2DG, England.

**BARRETT Bernard (Barney),** b. 3 May 1944, Pensacola, Florida, USA. Plastic Surgeon. 1 son, 3 daughters. Education: Tulane University, New Orleans, Louisiana, 1962-65; Diplomate American Board of Plastic Surgery, 1977; Fellow, American College of Surgeons, 1978. Appointments: Clinical Associate, Plastic Surgery, University of Texas Medical School, Houston, Texas, 1976-; Associate Chief of Plastic Surgery, St Luke's Episcopal Hospital, Houston, Texas, 1991-; Plastic Surgeon, Clinical Professor of Surgery, Baylor College of Medicine, Houston, Texas, 1997-. Publications: Manual of Patient Care in Plastic Surgery, 1st and 2nd editions; An Experimental method of segmental pancreatic transplantation in surgery; Treatment of full thickness abdominal and chest wall losses with split-thickness skin grafting; Rotation-advancement technique for cleft lip closure. Honours: Outstanding Teaching Plastic Surgeon at St Luke's Episcopal Hospital; Presidential Appointment, Federal Council on Aging, appointed by President George Bush. Memberships: American College of Surgeons, 1978-; American Society of Plastic Surgeons, 1979-; American Association of Plastic Surgeons, 1998-. Address: 6624 Fannin St, Ste 2200, Houston, TX 77030, USA.

**BARRETT Charles Kingsley,** b. 4 May 1917, Salford, England. Retired University Professor. m. Margaret E Heap, 16 Aug 1944, 1 son, 1 daughter. Education: BA, 1938, MA, 1942, BD, 1948, DD, 1956, Cambridge University, England. Appointments: Lecturer, 1945-58, Professor, 1958-82, University of Durham. Publications: The Holy Spirit and the Gospel Tradition, 1947; The Epistle to the Romans, 1957, new edition, 1991; From First Adam to Last, 1962; The First Epistle to the Corinthians, 1968; The Signs of an Apostle, 1970; The Second Epistle to the Corinthians, 1973; The Gospel According to St John, 1955, new edition, 1978; Freedom and Obligation, 1985; Paul: An Introduction to His Thought, 1994; The Acts of the Apostles, Volume 1, 1994, Volume 2, 1998; Jesus and the Word, 1996. Contributions to: Many learned journals. Honours: Fellow, British Academy, 1961; Burkitt Medal for Biblical

Studies, 1966; Honorary DD, Hull University, 1970; Aberdeen University, 1972; DTheol, Hamburg University, 1981; Honorary Fellow, Pembroke College, Cambridge, 1995. Memberships: Studiorum Novi Testamenti Societas, president, 1973-74; Society for Old Testament Study; Royal Norwegian Society of Sciences and Letters, 1991; Honorary Member, Society of Biblical Literature (USA). Address: 22 Rosemount, Pity Me, Durham DH1 5GA, England.

**BARRETT Edwin Radford, (Ted Barrett),** b. 26 Mar 1929, Southampton, England. Sports Journalist. m. Patricia Shuttleworth, 28 Sept 1957, 1 son, 1 daughter. Education: BSc, Econ, Lond, 1950. Appointments: Reporter, Northern Daily Telegraph, 1952-56; Sub Editor, Press Association, 1956-59; Sub Editor, Reporter, Daily Telegraph, 1959-79; Sports Editor, 1979-88. Publications: Golf Chronicle/Daily Telegraph, 1994, revised edition, 2000; The Ultimate Encyclopaedia of Golf, with Michael Hobbs, 1995, revised edition as Complete Book of Golf, 1998. Contributions to: Golf Weekly; Amateur Golf; the Lady Magazine, Daily Telegraph and provincial newspapers. Address: 12 Oak Avenue, Upminster, Essex RM14 2LB, England.

**BARRON Christine Angela,** b. 9 May 1949, Birmingham, England. Composer; Musician; Author; Adjudicator; Music Teacher. Education: Moseley School of Art, Birmingham. Musical Education: School of Contemporary Pop and Jazz; University of Leeds. Career: Began as freelance percussionist, including work with Birmingham Symphony Orchestra; Theatre, cabaret musician with top entertainers including: Bruce Forsyth; Des O'Connor; Leslie Crowther; Val Doonican. Part-time lecturer, percussion and composition; North Warwickshire and Hinkley College of Technology and Art, Nuneaton, Warwickshire; Well known in the UK for innovative percussion workshops and master classes featuring percussion; Adjudicator and Member, British and International Federation of Festivals for Music, Dance and Speech. Compositions include: Television signature tunes: Shut That Door (also released as single); Where Are They Now; Commissioned by Chappell Music Library for album, short pieces as jingles, theme, incidental music for television, radio, films (distributed worldwide); Collaboration with Boosey and Hawkes Music Publishers on albums, including album recorded by Royal Philharmonic Orchestra; Also wrote for their educational catalogue under pseudonyms: Chris Barron, Christine Barron. Publications: 2 comprehensive tutors with cassette for Learn As You Play series: Learn As You Play Drums; Learn As You Play Tuned Percussion and Timpani; Learn As You Play Drums Cassette. Memberships: The British Academy of Composers and Songwriters; British and International Federation of Festivals for Music, Dance and Speech. Address: 27 Madeira Croft, Coventry, Warwickshire CV5 8NX, England.

**BARRYMORE Drew,** b. 22 February 1975, Los Angeles, USA. Film Actress. m. (1) Jeremy Thomas, 1994, divorced, (2) Tom Green, 2001, divorced 2002. Appointments: Appeared in Dog Food Commercial, 1976; Film debut in TV Movie Suddenly Love, 1978; Films include: Altered States, 1980; ET, The Extra Terrestrial, 1982; Irreconcilable Differences, 1984; Firestarter, 1984; Cat's Eye, 1985; See You in the Morning, 1988; Guncrazy, 992; Poison Ivy, 1992; Beyond Control: The Amy Fisher Story, 1992; Wayne's World 2, 1993; Bad Girls, 1994; Boys in the Side, 1995; Batman Forever, 1995; Mad Love, 1995; Scream, 1996; Everyone Says I Love you, 1996; All She Wanted, 1997; Best Men, 1997; Never Been Kissed, 1998; Home Fries, 1998; The Wedding Singer, 1998; Ever After, 1998; Charlie's Angels (also producer), 2000; Donnie Darko (also producer), 2001; Riding in Cars With Boys, 2001; Confessions of a Dangerous Mind, 2002; Duplex (also producer); So Love Returns (also producer); Charlie's Angels: Full Throttle (also producer), 2003; Duplex, 2003; 50 First Dates, 2004. Address: c/o EMA, 9025 Wilshire Boulevard, Suite 450, Beverly Hills, CA 90211, USA

**BARSZCZ Anna Maria,** b. 22 July 1948, Miechów, Poland. Academic Teacher. m. Joseph, 1 son, 1 daughter. Education: MSc, 1971, Doctor, 1982, Habilitation, 1995, Forestry, Agricultural University of Kraków. Appointments: Assistant Lecturer, 1971; Lecturer, 1982; University Professor, 2002. Publications: 50 articles and creative works: timber quality, wood defects, standards for timber quality classification, non-wood forest products. Honours: 5 awards of the President of the Agricultural University, Kraków. Membership: Polish Forestry Association. Address: Department of Forest and Wood Utilisation, 29 Listopada 46, 31-425 Kraków, Poland. E-mail: rlbarszc@cyf-kr.edu.pl

**BARTHA Géza,** b. 9 February 1973, Budapest, Hungary. Civil Engineer. m. Tunde Barthane Toth. Education: Civil Engineer, Technical University of Budapest, 1997. Appointments: PhD Student, Department of Highway and Railway Engineering, Technical University of Budapest, Hungary, 1997-2001; Technologist, Vegyepszer Co Ltd, Budapest, 2001-2003; Technologist, Maépteszt Ltd (Vegyepszer-Group), Budapest, 2004-. Publications: Numerous articles in scientific journals and presented at conferences include: Besteht ein Zusammenhang zwischen den erweiterten Eignungsprüfungen von Asphalt? 2001; Temperature changes in Asphalt Pavements in Summer, 2002. Membership: Hungarian Road Society. Address: Alsó u. 97/4, Érd, H-2030 Hungary. E-mail: bartha.geza@vegyepszer.hu

**BARTHOLD Kenneth Van,** b. 10 December 1927, Surabaya, Java, Indonesia. Concert Pianist; Teacher. m. (1) Prudence C M (2) Sarianne MC (3) Gillian R. 2 sons, 2 daughters. Education: Music Scholar, Bryanston School; British and French Government Scholar, Paris National Conservatoire of Music, Laureat du Conservatoire National du Musique; LRAM. Career: Debut: Bournemouth Municipal Orchestra, 1944; Wigmore Hall, 1956; Frequent recitals in London Piano Series, Queen Elizabeth Hall and throughout the UK; Concerts in Canada, France, Israel and Eire including broadcasts; Concerto appearances with many orchestras including London Symphony Orchestra, English Chamber Orchestra, London Classical Players, Polyphonia under such conductors as: Sir Adrian Boult, Raymond Leppard, Sir Roger Norrington, Bryan Fairfax; Teaching: Director of Studies, Victoria College of Music, 1953-59; Professor of Piano, Trinity College of Music, 1959-65; Head of Music, City Literary Institute, 1960-83; Edinburgh University Annual Master Classes during the International Festival, 1968-; Senior Piano Tutor, ILEA, 1983-90; Lecturer on 19th and 20th Century Opera, Wimbledon College of Art, 1983-94; Master Classes in Israel, Canada and throughout the UK; International Juror in France and Canada; Wrote and presented 21 hour-long documentaries on television including the first ever full length studio documentary, BBC, 1964; Further frequent appearances interviewing, linking, profiling and performing on BBC and ITV. Recordings: Decca/Argo-Mozart Recital; Chopin Recital; Schumann Recital; Chopin Compilation; Darmo-Chopin/Liszt; Hommage à Pierre Max Dubois; Publications: Co-author, The Story of the Piano, 1976; Reviewer BBC Music Magazine; Various articles. Honour: Critics Award (television), 1972. Address: Arvensis, Stour Lane, Stour Row, Shaftesbury, Dorset SP7 0QL, England. E-mail: kvanbarthold@aol.com

**BARTLETT Neil,** b. 15 September 1932, Newcastle upon Tyne, England. Chemist. m. Christina Isabel Cross, 1952, 3 sons, 1 daughter. Education: PhD, University of Durham,

1957. Appointments: University of British Columbia, Canada, 1958-66; Professor of Chemistry, Princeton University, USA, 1966-69; Scientist, Bell Telephone Laboratories, Murray Hill, New Jersey, 1966-69; Professor of Chemistry, University of California at Berkeley, 1969-94; Principal Investigator; Lawrence Berkeley Laboratory, 1969-; Professor Emeritus, 1994-; Carried out research on compounds of rare gases. Publications include: The Oxidation of Oxygen and Related Chemistry, 2001; Over 160 scientific papers and reports. Honours: Honorary doctorates from several universities; Research Corporation Award, 1965; Dannie Heineman Prize, 1971; Robert A Welch Award, 1976; W H Nichols Medal, USA, 1983; Moissan Fluorine Centennial Medal, Paris, 1986; Prix Moissan, 1988; American Chemical Society Award for Distinguished Service to Inorganic Chemistry, 1989; Pauling Medal, American Chemical Society, 1989; Award for Creative Work in Fluorine Chemistry, American Chemical Society, 1992; Bonner Chemiepreis, 1992; Foreign Fellow, Royal Society of Canada, 2001; Honorary FRSC, 2002; Royal Society (London) Davy Medal, 2002. Memberships: Leopoldina Academy, Halle, 1969; Corresponding member, Göttingen Academy, 1977; American Academy of Arts and Sciences, 1977; National Academy of Sciences, 1979; Associé Etranger, Academie des Sciences, France, 1989. Address: Department of Chemistry, University of California, Berkeley, CA 94720, USA.

**BARTON John,** b. 1928. Theatre Director. m. Anne. Education: King's College, Cambridge. Appointments: Dean, King's College, Cambridge; Assistant Director, Associate Director, 1959-89, Advisory Director, 1989-, Royal Shakespeare Company; Shakespeare workshops and masterclasses in Europe and America. Publications: Adapted works: The Hollow Crown, 1961; The Wars of the Roses, with Peter Hall, 1963; The Greeks, 1980; Morte D'Arthur, 1983; Tantalus, 2000. Address: 14 De Walden Ct, 85 New Cavendish Street, London W1W 6XD, England. E-mail: tantalus@rsc.org.uk

**BARTON Matthias,** b. 6 August 1964, Wolfsburg, Germany. Physician. Education: MD, 1994, Dr. med., 1994, University of Hannover Medical School, Germany; PD (Associate Professor) in Cardiology, University of Zurich School of Medicine, Switzerland, 2001. Appointments: Fellow, Internal Medicine/ Cardiology, Hannover Medical School, 1994-95; Fellow, Cardiology, University Hospital, Bern, 1995-97; Fellow, Cardiology, 1997-99, Attending Physician, Internal Medicine, 2000-, Director of Research, Medical Policlinic, Internal Medicine, 2001-, University Hospital, Zurich. Publications: Book chapter: Estrogen and apoptosis in atherosclerosis, in Midlife Health – Current concepts and challenges for the future (editors, G Samsioe and S Skouby), 2002; Journal articles as author include: Angiotensin II increases vascular and renal endothelin converting enzyme activity in vivo: Role of $ET_A$-receptors for endothelin regulation, 1997; Salt Wars. On "The (Political Science of Salt)", 1998; Endothelin$_A$ receptor blockade restores NO-mediated endothelial dysfunction and inhibits atherosclerosis in apoE-deficient mice, 1998; Postmenopausal hormone-replacement therapy, 2002; Role of podocytes for reversal of glomerulosclerosis and proteinuria in the aging kidney after endothelin inhibition, 2004. Honours include: DAAD Scholarship for Clinical Training Abroad, 1993; Hannover Medical School, DFG Research Fellowship Award, 1995; Adumed Foundation Fellowship Award, 1997; Cardio-Vascular Biology Prize, Swiss Society of Cardiology, 1999; SCORE Career Development Award, Swiss National Science Foundation, 2000; Swiss Cardiology Fellowship Award, 2000; Finalist, Silver Medal of the Ludwig Heilmeyer Society, 2000; Young Investigator Award, 2000, 2001; Fellow, Council on Arteriosclerosis, Thrombosis and Vascular Biology,

2001, Fellow Council for High Blood Pressure Research, 2002, American Heart Association. Memberships: German and Swiss Medical Associations; German and European Societies of Cardiology; American Heart Association; European Council for Blood Pressure and Cardiovascular Research; International and European Atherosclerosis Societies; North American Association for the Study of Obesity; American Diabetes Association. Address: Medical Policlinic, Department of Internal Medicine, University Hospital Zurich, Ramistrasse 100, 8091 Zurich, Switzerland. E-mail: barton@usz.ch

**BARTOSCH Thorsten,** b. 28 February 1966, Erlangen, Germany. Education: Studies Electrical Engineering, 1987-93, Diploma, 1993, Friedrich-Alexander University, Erlangen-Nuremberg, Germany. Thesis, 2000. Appointments: Researcher, Friedrich-Alexander University, 1993-94; Researcher, Institute of Telecommunications, Friedrich-Alexander University, 1994-98; Trader in Nepalese Textiles and Ornaments, private business, 1993-96; System Engineer Smart Cards Division, Giesecke & Devrient, Germany, 1998-99; Engineer, Electric/ Electronic Department, 1999-2003, Team leader for HW and SW, Transfer Case Development Project, 2003-; Team Leader, Advance Development, Vehicle Acoustics, 2003-, Magna Steyr Engineering, Austria. Publications: 1 in $CO_2$ laser development, 5 in volcano seismology and signal processing, 3 in high-frequency vibro-acoustics. Address: Weizbergstr. 34/8, 8160 Weiz, Austria. E-mail: thorsten.bartosch@nt.e-technik.uni-erlangen.de

**BARTZATT Ronald,** b. 18 December 1953, Lincoln, Nebraska, USA. Research Chemist. Education: Medical Technology, 1976; BSc, 1978, MSc, 1980, PhD, 1982, University of Nebraska. Appointments: Medical Laboratory Technician, 1973-76; Research Chemist, 1976-84; Research Biochemist, 1984-89; Research Chemist, Educator, University of Nebraska, 1989-. Publications: Several articles in professional journals including: Analytical Letters, Bioscience Reports, Virus Research, Medical Science Research, Journal of Pharmacy and Pharmacology; Journal of Pharmaceutical and Biomedical Analysis; Journal of Biochemical and Biophysical Methods. Memberships: American Chemical Society ASCP, Nebraska Academy of Science; Nebraska Association of Science Teachers; Eppley Institute; ACS. Address: University of Nebraska, College of Arts and Sciences, Chemistry Department, Medical Chemistry Laboratory, Omaha, NE 68182, USA. E-mail: bartzatt@mail.u nomaha.edu

**BARYSHNIKOV Mikhail,** b. 28 January 1948, Riga, latvia. Ballet Dancer. 1 daughter. Education: Riga Ballet School; Kirov Ballet School, Leningrad. Career: Member, Kirov Ballet Company, 1969-74; Guest Artist with many leading ballet companies, including American Ballet Theatre, National Ballet of Canada; Royal Ballet; Hamburg Ballet; Federal Republic of Germany; Ballet Victoria, Australia; Stuttgart Ballet, Federal Republic of Germany; Alvin Ailey Co, USA, 1974-; Joined New York City Ballet Company, 1978, resigned 1979; Artistic Director, American Ballet Theatre, 1980-90; Co-Founder, White Oak Dance Project, 1990-; Stage debut in Metamorphosis, 1989; Launched perfume Misha, 1989; Ballets (world premieres) Vestris, 1969; Medea, 1975; Push Comes to Shove, 1976; Hamlet Connotations, 1976; Other Dances, 1976; Pas de Duke, 1976; La Dame de Pique, 1978' L'Apres-midi d'un Faune, 1978; Santa Fe Saga, 1978; Opus 19, 1979; Rhapsody, 1980; Films: The Turning Point, 1977; White Nights, 1985; Giselle, 1987; Dancers, 1987; Dinosaurs, 1991; Choreography: Nutcracker, 1976; Don Quixote, 1978; Cinderella, 1984. Publications: Baryshnikov at Work, 1977. Address: c/o Vincent & Farrell

# DICTIONARY OF INTERNATIONAL BIOGRAPHY

Associates, 481 Eighth Avenue, Suite 740, New York, NY 10001, USA.

**BASINGER Kim,** b. 8 December 1953, Athens, Georgia, USA. Actress. m. (1) Ron Britton, divorced, (2) Alec Baldwin, divorced, 1 daughter. Career: Model, 1971-76; As actress, films include: Never Say Never Again, 1982; The Man Who Loved Women, 1983; 9 1/2 Weeks, 1985; Batman, 1989; Too Hot to Handle, 1991; The Real McCoy, 1993; Wayne's World, 1994; The Getaway, 1994; Prêt-à-Porter, 1994; LA Confidential, 1997; I Dreamed of Africa, 2000; Bless the Child, 2000; 8 Mile, 2002; People I Know, 2002. Honours: Oscar, 1983; Academy Award and Golden Globe for Best Supporting Actress, 1997. Address: 3960 Laurel Canyon Boulevard, #414, Studio City, CA 91604, USA.

**BASMAJIAN John V,** b. 21 June 1921, Constantinople. Medical Scientist. m. Dora Lucas, 1 son, 2 daughters. Education: MD, Honours, University of Toronto, 1945; Fellowships, honours, Royal College of Physicians of Canada, Glasgow, Edinburgh, Australia, 1977-99; Honorary LLD, Queen's University, 1999; Honorary DSc, McMaster University, 2001; Honorary Diploma, St Lawrence College. Appointments: Hospital residencies, 1946-49; Lecturer to Full Professor of University of Toronto, 1949-56; Professor and Head, Anatomy, Queen's University, Canada, 1956-69; Professor and Director, Emory University Rehabilitation Research and Training Centre, Atlanta, 1969-77; Professor then Professor Emeritus, McMaster University, Canada, 1977-. Publications: Medical books on medical science in several languages; 400 articles, 5 medical movies. Honour: Officer of the Order of Canada, 1995, and Ontario, 1991. Memberships: Honorary Member of many associations and institutions; former President, three scientific bodies, international and North American. Address: 9-210 Fiddlers Green Road, Hamilton, Ontario L9G 1W6, Canada.

**BASNET Narayan Bahadur,** b. 25 August 1960, Sotang Village, Solukhumbu, Nepal. Paediatrician; Researcher. m. Sangeeta B Basnet, 1 son, 1 daughter. Education: Certificate in General Medicine, 1979; Diploma in Public Administration, 1981; Master degree, Public Administration, 1985; MBBS, 1990; PhD, 2000. Appointments: House Officer, Medical Instructor, 1991-93; Medical Officer, Co-investigator, ARI Project, Kathmandu, Nepal; Medical Co-ordinator, Association of Medical Doctors of Asia, 1994-95; Visiting Researcher, Department of Paediatrics, University of Tokyo, Japan, 2000-2001; Postdoctoral Fellow, Japan Society for the Promotion of Science, 2001-2003; Pediatric Cardiologist, Kanti Children's Hospital, Kathmandu, Nepal, June 2004-; Research Collaborator on "cross-cultural study of feeding/weaning in Asia", sponsored by Japanese Government, Professor Y Konishi, 2004. Publications: Articles in medical journals including: Journal of the Nepal Medical Association, 1995; Asian Medical Journal, 1998; International Medical Journal, 1998; Heart Vessels, 2000; Pediatric Cardiology, 2001 Indian Pediatrics, 2001; Journal of Pediatric Nursing, 2004; Children and CHILDREN, NESAJ Online, 2004; Several international conference abstracts and papers in Nepali; Book: Nepal at the Dawn of the 21st Century: General Health and Medical Information, 2001. Honours: Research Awards, The Graduate School of Medicine University of Tokyo, Japan, 1999, 2001; Mahendra Vidyabhusan, MOE, HMG, Nepal, 2005. Memberships: Life Member, Nepal Paediatric Society; Life Member, Nepal Medical Association; Life Member, Nepal Family Planning Association; Life Member, Cardiological Society of India; World Federation for Mental Health; AMDA; Japan Pediatric Society; AAAS. Address: PO Box 1563, Kathmandu, Nepal. E-mail: nbbasnet777@hotmail.com

**BASSETT John Walden Jr,** b. 21 March 1938, Roswell, New Mexico, USA. Attorney. m. Nolana Knight, 1 son, 1 daughter. Education: AB, Economics, Stanford University, 1960; JD with Honors, University of Texas School of Law, 1964. Appointments: Special Assistant to Attorney General of US, White House Fellow, 1967; New Mexico State Board of Education, 1987-1991. Publications: Associate Editor, University of Texas Law Review. Honors: Order of Coif, University of Texas School of Law, 1964; White House Fellow, 1967; Paul Harris Award, Rotary Club. Address: 5060 Bright Sky Road, Roswell, New Mexico, 88201, USA.

**BASSEY Shirley,** b. 8 January 1937, Tiger Bay, Cardiff, Wales. Singer; Entertainer. m. (1) Kenneth Hume, divorced 1965, deceased, (2) Sergio Novak, 1971, divorced 1981, 1 daughter, deceased, one adopted son. Appointments: Variety and Revue Singer, 1950s; Concerts and TV appearances world-wide; Semi-Retired, 1981-. Creative Works: I'm In the Mood For Love, 1981; Love Songs, 1982; All By Myself, 1984; I Am What I Am, 1984; Playing Solitaire, 1985; I've Got You Under My Skin, 1985; Sings The Songs From The Shows, 1986; Born To Sing the Blues, 1987; Let Me Sing And I'm Happy, 1988; Her Favourite Songs, 1988; Keep The Music Playing, 1991; Great Shirley Bassey (album), 1999; Various compilations. Honours: CBE; 20 Gold Discs; 14 Silver Discs; TV Times Award, Best Female Singer, 1972; Britannia Award, Best Female Solo Singer in the Last 50 years, 1977; American Guild of Variety Artists Award, Best Female Entertainer, 1976. Address: c/o CSS Stellar Management, Drury House, 34-43 Russell Street, London, WC2B 5HA, England.

**BASSIL Andrea, (Anna Nilsen)** b. 16 September 1948, Manchester, England. Children's Book Author/Illustrator; Games Devisor. Education: Eastbourne School of Art, 1966-67; Dip AD, Edinburgh College of Art, 1967-72; SCSE, Moray House College of Education, 1972-73. Appointments: Full Time Assistant Teacher of Art, Mussleburgh Grammar School, 1973-74, St Margaret's School Edinburgh, 1974-85; ND and HND Course Director, Natural History Illustration, Bournemouth and Poole College of Art and Design, 1985-90; Head of Graphic Arts and Illustration, Anglia Polytechnic University, 1990-95; Children's Author/Illustrator, 1995-; Games Consultant, EFL CD Rom, Oxford University Press, 1996; Concept Designer and Illustrator, Falcon Games Ltd, 2004; Concept Devisor and Illustrator, Gibsons Amazeing Puzzles, 2004. Publications under pseudonym Anna Nilsen include: Terrormazia, 1995; Percy the Park Keeper Activity Book, 1996; Fairy Tales, 1996; Where is Percy's Dinner?, 1996; Ble Mae Cinio Bonso?, 1996; Follow the Kite, 1997; In the Jungle, 1998; On the Farm, 1998; People in My Neighborhood, 1998; Follow the Kite, 1998; I Can Spell Three Letter Words, 1998; Let's all Dig and Burrow, 1998; Let's all Hang and Dangle, 1998; Let's all Swim and Dive, 1999; Let's all Leap and Jump, 1999; Lego Puzzle Books: Spycatcher, Treasure Smuggler, Gold Robber, Jewel Thief, Insectoid Invasion, 1998; I Can Count from 1 – 10, 1999; I Can Count From 1 – 20, 1999; I Can Add, 2000; I Can Subtract, 2000; I Can Multiply, 2001; Magnificent Mazes (author and illustrator), 2001; Art Fraud Detective, 2000; The Great Art Scandal, 2003; Tip Truck! Tip!, 2004; Wave Baby! Wave!, 2004; Robotic Maths Games and Puzzles, 2004 My Best Dad, 2004; Bella's Mid-summer Secret, 2005; Peepers Jungle, 2005, Peepers People, 2005; Peepers, 2005; Art Auction Mystery, 2005. Honours: Goldsmith's Hall, Travelling Scholarship, 1981; Several Literary Awards for Art Fraud Detective, 2001-2003. Memberships: Society of Authors; Cambridge Illustration Group; Authors Licensing and Collecting Society; Children's Book Circle. Address: 16, Emery Street, Cambridge, Cambridgeshire CB1 2AX, England.

**BATCHELOR John Barham,** b. 15 March 1942, Farnborough, England. Professor of English Literature; Writer; Editor. m. Henrietta Jane Letts, 14 September 1968, 2 sons, 1 daughter. Education: MA, 1964, PhD, 1969, Magdalene College, Cambridge; MA, University of New Brunswick, 1965. Appointments: Lecturer in English, Birmingham University, 1968-76; Fellow and Tutor, New College, Oxford, 1976-90; Joseph Cowen Professor of English Literature, University of Newcastle upon Tyne, 1990-; Adjunct Professor, University of Lancaster, 2001-. Publications: Mervyn Peake, 1974; Breathless Hush (novel), 1974; The Edwardian Novelists, 1982; H G Wells, 1985; Virginia Woolf, 1991; The Life of Joseph Conrad: A Critical Biography, 1994; The Art of Literary Biography (editor), 1995; Shakespearean Continuities (joint editor), 1997; John Ruskin: No Wealth But Life, 2000. Contributions to: Dictionary of National Biography; Times Literary Supplement; Observer; Economist; Articles in English, Yearbook of English Studies; Review of English Studies. Membership: International Association of Professors of English; English Association; MHRA. Address: Department of English, University of Newcastle, Newcastle upon Tyne NE1 7RU, England.

**BATCHELOR Ronald Ernest,** b. 15 July 1934, Southampton, England. Retired University Teacher. m. Patricia Anne, 1 son, 1 daughter. Education: Graduated French, Spanish, Latin (Hons), 1953-56, Certificate of Education, 1956-57, MA, thesis on the novels of Julian Green, 1958-61, University of Southampton; PhD Thesis, La Francophobie de Miguel de Unamuno, University of Nottingham, 1962-67. Appointments: Lecturer, University of Besançon, France, 1957-59; Teacher of English, S. Sebastián, Spain, 1959-61; Teacher of French, Spanish, Southampton, 1961-62; Lecturer in French, 1962-67, Senior Lecturer in French, 1967-97, University of Nottingham. Publications: Unamuno Novelist A European Perspective, 1972; Using French A Guide to Contemporary Usage (co-author), 1982; Using Spanish A Guide to Contemporary Usage (co-author), 1992; Using French Synonyms (co-author), 1993; Using Spanish Synonyms, 1994; French for Marketing The Language of Media and Communications (co-author), 1997; Usage pratique et courant des synonymes anglais (co-author), 1998; Using Spanish Vocabulary (co-author), 2003; A Student Grammar of Spanish, 2005; Vocabulaire de la langue anglaise, ongoing; Numerous articles in learned journals on literary, philosophical and historical topics. Honours: Listed in several biographical dictionaries; Member of advisory board of Anales de la Literatura Española Contemporánea, University of Colorado. Address: 20 Moor Lane, Bramcote, Nottingham NG9 3FH, England. E-mail: ronald@ronald48.fsnet.co.uk

**BATE (Andrew) Jonathan,** b. 26 June 1958, Sevenoaks, Kent, England. Professor of English Literature; Critic; Novelist. m. (1) Hilary Gaskin, 1984, divorced 1995, (2) Paula Byrne, 1996, 1 son, 1 daughter. Education: MA, 1980, PhD, 1984, St Catharine's College, Cambridge. Appointments: Harkness Fellow, Harvard University, 1980-81; Research Fellow, St Catharine's College, Cambridge, 1983-85; Fellow, Trinity Hall, and Lecturer, Trinity Hall and Girton College, Cambridge, 1985-90; Visiting Associate Professor, University of California at Los Angeles, 1989; King Alfred Professor of English Literature, 1991-, Leverhulme Personal Research Professor, 1999-, University of Liverpool; Research Reader, British Academy, 1994-96. Publications: Shakespeare and the English Romantic Imagination, 1986; Charles Lamb: Essays of Elia (editor), 1987; Shakespearean Constitutions: Politics, Theatre, Criticism 1730-1830, 1989; Romantic Ecology: Wordsworth and the Environmental Tradition, 1991; The Romantics on Shakespeare (editor), 1992; Shakespeare and Ovid, 1993; The Arden Shakespeare: Titus Andronicus (editor), 1995; Shakespeare:

An Illustrated Stage History (editor), 1996; The Genius of Shakespeare, 1997; The Cure for Love, 1998; The Song of the Earth, 2000. Contributions to: Scholarly publications. Honours: Calvin and Rose Hoffman Prize, 1996; FBA, 1999; Honorary Fellow, St Catherine's College, Cambridge, 2000. Literary Agent: David Godwin Associates. Address: c/o Department of English, University of Liverpool, PO Box 147, Liverpool L69 3BX, England.

**BATEMAN Robert McLellan,** b. 1930, Toronto, Canada. Artist. m. (1) Suzanne Bowerman, 1961, 2 sons, 1 daughter, (2) Birgit Ilse Freybe, 1975, 2 sons. Education: BA, University of Toronto, 1954; Ontario College of Education, 1955. Appointments: High School Art Teacher, Nelson High School, Burlington, Ontario, 1958-63, 1965-69, Government College, Umuahia, Nigeria, 1963-65, Lord Elgin High School, 1970-76; Lecturer, Resource Person in Art, Photography, Nature and Conservation. Creative Works: Major Exhibitions: Tryon Gallery, London, 1975, 1979; Beckett Gallery, Hamilton, Ontario, 1978, 1987; 1991; Images of the Wild, National Museum of Natural Sciences, Ottawa, 1981-82; Joslyn Art Museum, Omaha, Nebraska, 1987; Leigh Yawkey Woodson Art Museum, Wausau, Wisconsin, 1986-97; Smithsonian Institute, Museum of Natural History, Washington, 1987; Frye Art Museum, Seattle, Washington, 1988; Colorado Springs Fine Arts Museum, 1991; Carnegie Museum of Natural History, 1991; Canadian Embassy, Tokyo, 1992; Suntory Museum, Osaka and Tokyo, 1995-96; National Museum of Wildlife Art, 1997; Everard Read Gallery, Johannesburg, South Africa, 2000; Beckett Fine Art Gallery, Toronto, 2002; Gerald Peters Gallery, Santa Fe, New Mexico, 2004; Several works in permanent collections. Publications: Books: The Art of Robert Bateman, 1981; The World of Robert Bateman, 1985; Robert Bateman: Artist in Nature, 1990; Robert Bateman,: Natural Worlds, 1996; Thinking Like a Mountain, 2000; Birds, 2002; Backyard Birds, 2005. Honours include: Queen Elizabeth Silver Jubilee Medal, 1977; Master Artist, Leigh Yawkey Woodson Art Museum, 1982; Officer of the Order of Canada, 1984; Governor General's Award for Conservation, Quebec City, 1987; Society of Animal Artists Award of Excellence, 1979, 1980, 1986, 1990; Rachel Carson Award, Society of Environmental Toxicology and Chemistry, 1996; Golden Plate Award, American Academy for Achievement, 1998; Order of British Columbia, 2001; Awards include 10 honorary doctorates. Memberships include: Royal Canadian Academy of Arts; Elsa Wild Animal Appeal; Sierra Club; Harmony Foundation, Ottawa; Jane Goodall Institute, Canada; Ecotrust; Kenya Wildlife Fund; Audubon Society; Sierra Legal Defense League. Address: PO Box 115, Fulford Harbour, Salt Spring Island, BC V8K 2P2, Canada.

**BATES Kathy,** b. 28 June 1948, Memphis, Tennessee, USA. Actress. m. Tony Campisi, 1991, divorced. Education: Southern Methodist University. Career: Various jobs before acting; Theatre includes: Varieties, 1976; Chocolate Cake, 1980; 'night Mother, 1983; Rain of Terror, 1985; Films include: Taking Off, 1971; Arthur 2: On the Rocks, 1988; High Stakes, 1989; Dick Tracy, 1990; Misery, 1990; Prelude to a Kiss, 1991; Fried Green Tomatoes at the Whistle Stop Café, 1991; North, 1994; Diabolique, 1996; The War at Home, 1996; Primary Colors, 1998; Titanic, 1998; A Civil Action, 1999; Dash and Lilly, 1999; My Life as a Dog, 1999; Bruno, 2000; Rat Race, 2001; American Outlaws, 2001; About Schmidt, 2002; Love Liza, 2002; Evelyn, 2003; The Ingrate, 2004; Around the World in 80 Days, 2004; The Bridge of San Luis Rey, 2004. TV Films and Appearances include: No Place Like Home; Murder Ordained; The Love Boat; St Elsewhere; LA Law; Cagney & Lacey; Annie, 1999; My Sister's Keeper, 2002. Honours: Pulitzer Prize (Crimes of the Heart, 1981); Outer Circle Critic's Award ('night Mother, 1983); Obie Award (Frankie and Johnny in the Claire de Lune,

1987); Academy Award for Best Actress and Golden Globe (Misery, 1990). Address: c/o Susan Smith Associates, 121 N San Vincente Boulevard, Beverly Hills, CA 90211-2303, USA.

**BATSTONE Patricia, (Annette Collins),** b. 8 July 1941, West Hartlepool, England. Freelance Writer. m. Geoffrey Batstone, 2 sons. Education: BA in Theology; MEd, RE and Literature, PGCE, University of Hull; University of Exeter; PhD, RE and Literature. Career: Proprietor of Cottage Books, which became Patricia Batestone Publications, 2000. Publications: Messages of Devon, 1991; Farewell to Wincolmlee, 1994; Time and the Gospel, 1995; A World of Love, 1996; Memo to God, and Other Lenten Messages, 1998; Still Dancing, Thoughts on Spirituality, 1998; Candles in the Darkness, 1998; In Debt to C. S. Lewis, 1999; Meeting Jesus, 2000; Candles in Draughty Spaces, Meditations for the Millennium, 2000; Penitential Tears; Happy in Hospital? – An Anthology of Experiences by Patients for Patients, editor, 2000; Fifty Days – Reflections for Lent and Beyond, 2001; Lenten Light – A Study of Mark 9:1-29 for Lent and Eastertide, 2001; and prose devotional books; IBRA Notes for 1999 and 2001; Fishcakes and Fantasy: Getting the Message Across Creatively, 1996 (original text of the Winterton Memorial Lecture, UK Alliance); Tolkien's Moral Universe, paper in Canadian, C S Lewis Journal; Contributions to: Springboard; Dial 174; Areopagus; One; Triumph Herald; Poetry Church Anthology; Feather Books; The Dictionary of Methodism; Shafts of Light, the LPMA Millennium Prayer Book, 2000; The Methodist Recorder, articles and correspondence; The Expository Times – sermons; Daughters of Eve – Characterisation, Authenticity and Poetic Licence in Bible-based Narrative Poetry, Feather Books Christianity and Literature Series, No 4, 2001; Retired from publishing 2001. Honour: Areopagus Open, 1996; Highly Commended, Julia Carns Poetry Competition, 1998; Shortlisted, Association of Christian Writers' Annual Anthology Competition; Joint Second, Kestrel Open Competitions, both classes; Shortlisted, Wendy Webb Davidian Competition, 2002-03; Second prizewinner, Spring Davidian. Memberships: Society of Women Writers and Journalists; Wesley Historical Society; Editor, The Methodist Retreat and Spirituality Network; Administrator, Editor, Association of Teetotallers in Methodism; Former Deputy Editor, Areopagus; Formerly Controlling Editor, Miscellany Postal Workshops, 1990-95; Retired from publishing, 2001. Address: 5 Foxglove Close, Dunkeswell, Devon EX14 4QE, England.

**BATT Jürgen Otto Helmut,** b. 18 August 1933, Gumbinnen, Germany. Professor of Mathematics. m. Hannelore Ulbricht, 2 daughters. Education: State Examination for Gymnasium Teachers, 1959; Dr. rer.nat. Technical College, Aachen, Germany, 1962; Habilitation, University of Munich, 1969. Appointments: Assistant, Nuclear Centre, Jülich, 1962-64; Assistant, Heidelberg University, 1964-66; Visiting Professor, 1967-68, Associate Professor, 1970-71, Kent State University, USA; Supernumerary Professor, 1974, Full Professor, Applied Mathematics, 1976-99, Dean of the Faculty of Mathematics, 1977-79, University of Munich. Publications: Many scientific articles in the area of differential equations and functional analysis in professional journals. Honours: Member of the University Senate, 1986-88; Member of the Assembly, 1988-98; Scholarly invitations to the following countries: Romania, USA, Switzerland, France, Austria, Italy, Netherlands, Australia, Brazil, India, Spain, Canada, China, Bulgaria, Czechoslovakia, Israel and Russia. Memberships: Deutsche Mathematiker-Vereinigung; American Mathematical Society; International Federation of Nonlinear Analysts. Address: Bauschneiderstrasse 11, 81241 Munich, Germany. E-mail: batt@rz.mathematik.uni-muenchen.de

**BATTEN John Randolph,** b. 29 July 1947, London, England. Education and Development Consultant. m. Ruth Neri Villanueva, 2 daughters. Education: MA, Education, Western Carolina University, USA, 1975; PhD, Educational Supervision and Administration, The University of Alabama, USA, 1978. Appointments: Secondary Teacher, Alperton High School, London, UK, 1969-70; Director of Students and Head of Mathematics Department, Priory Adult College of Education, Kingston, Jamaica, 1970-77; Graduate intern, The University of Alabama, USA, 1977-78; Director, Education and Culture Group, Director of International Training, IIRR, Philippines, 1978-86; Regional Technical Adviser, CARE, Nairobi, Kenya, 1986-89; Country Director, Action Aid Kenya, Nairobi, 1989-95; Chief Executive Officer, Action Aid, London, 1995-98; Director General, African Medical Research Foundation, Nairobi, 1998-2001; Founding Director, The Poverty Eradication Network, Nairobi, 2001-. Honours: Ramon Magsaysay Award for International Training, 1984; MBE, 1975; Conrad Hilton Award, 1999; Chairman, The Resource Alliance, 2001-. Address: PO Box 47074, Nairobi, Kenya. E-mail: jrbatten@africaonline.co.ke

**BATTERHAM Robin John,** b. 3 April 1941, Brighton, Victoria, Australia. Chief Scientist of Australia; Chief Technologist, Rio Tinto P/L. Education: BE, University of Melbourne; LLD (Hon), PhD, AMusA, Post Nominals, AO, FAA, FTSE, FREng, CE, CPE, CSci, FNAE, FAusIMM, FISS, FIChemE; FIEAust; FICD; FAIM. Appointments: Chief, CSIRO Division of Mineral Engineering, 1984-88; Vice President, Resource & Processing Development CRA Ltd, 1988-94; Cr Academy of Technical Science, 1988-93; President, International Mineral Processing Congress, 1989-; Deputy-Chair, Co-op Research Centres, 1992-; G K William Co-op Research Centre, 1993-99; Chair, Australian IMM Proceedings Committee, 1995-99; Deputy Director, Music, Scot's Church, Melbourne; Chairman, International Network for Acid Prevention, 1998-; Chief Scientist of Australia, 1999-; Member, Major National Research Facilities Commission, 2001-; Australia Research Council Member, 1999-; President, Institution of Chemical Engineers, 2004-. Publications: 77 refereed papers in international journals and conferences. Honours: Officer of the Order of Australia; Presidents Medal, Australian Society of Sugar Cane Technologists; Fellow, Academy of Technology and Engineering Sciences; Fellow, Australian Academy of Science; Foreign Fellow, National Academy of Engineering, USA; Foreign Fellow, Swiss Academy of Engineering Sciences; CSIRO Postdoctorate Award; Esso Award of Excellence in Chemical Engineering, 1992; Distinguished Lecturer, University of British Columbia, University of Waterloo, University of California, Berkeley, University of Utah; Kernot Medal, University of Melbourne, 1996; Chemeca Medal, 2003; Centenary Medal of Australia, 2003; Australasian Institute of Mining and Metallurgy Medal, 2004. Memberships: Fellow, Iron Steel Society, America; Fellow, Australia Institute of Mining Metallurgy; Fellow, Institution of Chemical Engineers; Fellow, Institute of Australian Engineers; Fellow, Australian Institute of Management; Fellow, Australian Academy of Sciences; Fellow, Australian Academy of Technological Sciences and Engineering; Fellow, Royal Academy of Engineering. Address: 153 Park Drive, Parkville, Vic 3052, Australia.

**BAUGH Lisa Saunders,** b. August 27 1969, Houston, Texas, USA. Research Chemist. m. Simon David Peter Baugh. Education: BS Chemistry (High Honours), University of Texas, 1991; PhD Polymer Chemistry, University of California at Berkeley, 1996. Appointments: Visiting Scholar, Polymer Science and Engineering Department, University of Massachusetts at Amherst, 1994-96; Senior Research Chemist,

Air Products and Chemicals, Allentown, Pennsylvania, 1996-97; Senior Chemist, 1997-2005, Research Associate, 2005-, ExxonMobil Research and Engineering, Annandale, New Jersey; Guest Lecturer, Various Colleges and Universities, 1997- ; College/High School Textbook Essayist, Saunders College/HBJ and Holt, Rinehart and Winston, 1990-; Professional Classical Violinist and Violist, 1987-. Publications: Editor, Transition Metal Catalysts in Macromolecular Design, 2000; Editor, Late Transition Metal Polymerisation Catalysts, 2003; Author of articles in scientific journals including: Macromolecules, Chemical Reviews, Journal of the American Chemical Society; Patentee in the field of polymer chemistry. Honours: National Science Foundation Predoctoral Fellow; National Merit Scholar, Deans Honoured Graduate, Merck Index Award, University of Texas. Memberships: American Chemical Society; Catalysis and Surface Science Secretariat, Secretary General/Program Chair 2001, Polymeric Materials Science and Engineering Division, Member at Large, 2000-, Awards Judge, 1999-, Membership Chair, 2004-, Women Chemists Committee, Committee Associate 2002-04; Editorial Advisory Board, Chemistry Magazine, 2003-; Alpha Chi Sigma Fraternity (Beta Theta Chapter); Phi Beta Kappa; Phi Kappa Phi. Address: ExxonMobil Research and Engineering, Route 22 East, Annandale, New Jersey, 08801, USA.

**BAUMAN Frank Anthony**, b. 10 June 1921, Portland, Oregon, USA. Lawyer (Inactive). m. (1) Mildred Inez Packer, 9 September 1950, deceased 1997, 1 son, 2 daughters, (2) Divorced. Education: US Naval Japanese Language School, University of Colorado, 1943-44; AB, Stanford University, 1944; JD, Yale University, 1949, Co-Chairman Class of 1949 Reunion, 2004; Postgraduate, International Law, University of London, 1951-52. Appointments: Member, Oregon US District Court; US Supreme Court; Private Practice, Portland, 1950-71: Wilbur Beckett Oppenheimer Mautz & Souther, Veatch Bauman Lovett, Keane Haessler Bauman & Harper; Lawyers Commission for Civil Rights Under Law, Mississippi, 1969; Representative, UN Australia and New Zealand, 1971-76; Papua New Guinea, 1971-73; Private Practice, Portland, 1978-91; Adjunct Professor of Law, Lewis and Clark Law School, 1978-80; Advisor Lillian Baumann Fund, 1985-; Co-Trustee Mildred P Bauman Trust, 1997-. Publications: The Prospects for International Law, 1973; Can a World Court be Made to Work, 1973; The Promise of the United Nations, 1973. Honours: Recipient, World Peace Award Assembly of the Bahais, Portland, 1985; E B MacNaughton Civil Liberties Award, ACLU, 1998. Memberships include: Member and Past Trustee, President, World Affairs Council of Oregon, 1954-; Member and Past Chairman, Portland Committee on Foreign Relations, 1978-; Past Director and President, Oregon UN Association, 1977-92; Past Director and President, English Speaking Union, Portland, 1992-98; Director, Member, Executive Committee, English Speaking Union, US, New York, 1997-2003; Member, American Bar Association, ABA; Patron, American Society of International Law; International Law Association, American branch; UN Association, USA; Arlington Club; Yale Club of New York City. Address: The Ladd Carriage House, 1331 S W Broadway, Portland, OR 97201, USA. E-mail: FABEsquire@aol.com

**BAUMAN Janina**, b. 18 August 1926, Warsaw, Poland. Writer. m. Zygmunt Bauman, 18 August 1948, 3 daughters. Education: Academy of Social Sciences, 1951; University of Warsaw, 1959. Appointments: Script Editor, Polish Film, 1948-68. Publications: Winter in the Morning: A Dream of Belonging; Various other books and short stories published in Poland since 1990. Contributions to: Jewish Quarterly; Oral History; Polin; British Journal of Holocaust Education; Thesis Eleven.

Honour: Award by Polityka Weekly, Poland, 1991. Address: 1 Lawnswood Gardens, Leeds, Yorkshire LS16 6HF, England.

**BAUMAN Robert Patten**, b. 27 March 1931. Business Executive. m. Patricia Hughes Jones, 1961, 1 son, 1 daughter. Education: Ohio Wesleyan University; Harvard School of Business. Appointments: Joined Gen Foods Corporation, 1958; Corporation Vice President, 1968; Group Vice President, 1970; Executive Vice President, Corporation 1972-81; Director, Avco Corporation, 1980; Chair, CEO, 1981-85; Vice Chair, Director, Textron Inc, 1985-86; Chair, Chief Executive, Beecham Group, 1986-89; CEO, SmithKline Beecham, 1989-94; Chair, British Aerospace PLC, 1994-98; BTR PLC, London, 1998-99; Non-Executive Director, Bolero.net, 2001-; Director, Cap Cities/ABC Inc; Union Pacific Corporation; Trustee, Ohio Wesleyan University. Publications: Plants as Pets, 1982; From Promise to Performance, 1997. E-mail: RPBauman@aol.com

**BAUMAN Zygmunt**, b. 19 November 1925, Poznan, Poland. Sociologist. m. Janina Bauman, 18 August 1948, 3 daughters. Education: MA, 1954; PhD, 1956. Appointments: Warsaw University, 1953-68; Tel Aviv University, 1968-75; University of Leeds, 1971-91. Publications: Modernity and the Holocaust; Legislators and Interpreters; Intimations of Postmodernity; Thinking Sociologically; Modernity and Ambivalence; Freedom; Memories of Class; Culture as Praxis; Between Class and Elite; Mortality, Immortality and Other Life Strategies; Postmodernity and its Discontents, 1997; In Search of Politics, 1999; Liquid Modernity, 2000; Individualized Society, 2000; Community: Seeking Safety in an Uncertain World, 2001; Society Under Siege, 2002; Liquid Love: On the Frailty of Human Bonds, 2003; Society Under Siege, 2002; Liquid Life, 2005; Wasted lives, 2004. Contributions to: Times Literary Supplement; New Statesman; Professional Periodicals. Honour: Amalfi European Prize for Sociology; Theodor Adorno Prize, 1998; Dr honoris causa: Oslo, 1997, Lapland, 1999, Uppsala, 2000, West of England, 2001, London, 2002, Sofia, 2002, Charles University, Prague, 2002, Copenhagen, 2002, University of Leeds, 2004. Memberships: British Sociological Association; Polish Sociological Association. Address: 1 Lawnswood Gardens, Leeds LS16 6HF, England.

**BAUROV Yuriy Alexeevich**, b. 14 March 1947, Russia. Physicist. m. 2 sons. Education: Moscow Aviation Institute, 1972; PhD, 1978. Appointments: Chief of Laboratory, Central Research Institute of Machine Building; Presidency of Council of Directors, Closed Joint-Stock Company, Research Institute of Cosmic Physics. Publications: Books: On the Structure of Physical Vacuum and a New Interaction in Nature (Theory, Experiment, Applications), 2000; Global Anisotropy of Physical Space, Experimental and Theoretical Basis, Nova Science, New York, 2004; Several articles in professional journals. Honour: Diplôme 26 Salon International des Inventions, Genève, 1998. Membership: New York Academy of Sciences, 1994-98. Address: Central Research Institute for Machine Building, 141070, Korolovov, Moscow Region, Pionerskaya 4, Russia.

**BAXTER Myrtle M (Bobbi)**, b. 10 November 1928, Weableau, Missouri, USA. Artist; Homemaker. m. Clarence E Baxter, 2 sons, 1 deceased, 1 daughter. Education: College Degree, Nevada Beauty College; College Degree, American School of Art, 1995; Studied portrait painting with Harry Fredman, Kansas City, Missouri for 3 years; Studies at Jewish Community Center with Hallmark Artist Charles Vault, 2 years; Many private art classes. Career: Donated 26 paintings to Bates County Museum; President, Vice-President and Show Chairman: many art meetings; Nominated to induct others into offices; Taught art to children and adults for 25 years; Owner of art gallery; Beautician, owner of 3 beauty shops; Hairdresser, 18 years; Member of several art organisations; Art exhibited at many art shows. Publications: Articles in Xchange Newspaper, Osage Valley Magazine; Appearances on Butler Radio; Poems published in poetry book, Memories; Member of Wings of Poetry. Honours: Numerous awards for art; 5 awards for poetry; Listed in Who's Who publications and biographical dictionaries. Memberships: Bates County Fine Arts League; Bates County Museum; Butler Art Club; 1st Baptist Church; Baptist Ladies Organisation. Address: RR5 Box 65, Butler, MO 64730, USA. E-mail: lonestar@iland.net Website: lonestarmasterpiecehorizons.net

**BAYAZID Hakam,** b. 29 April 1941, Damascus, Syria. Civil Engineer. m. Hadba Sabbagh, 2 sons, 2 daughters. Education: BSCE, Purdue University, 1964; MSCE, University of Missouri, 1969; PhD, University of Missouri, 1972; MBA Work, Indiana University at South Bend, 1975-78. Appointments: Senior Civil Engineer, Ball Corporation, Broomfield, Colorado, USA, 1978-80; Assistant Professor of Civil Engineering, King Abdul Aziz University, Jeddah; Project Manager, Saud Consult, Riyadh, 1982-93; Senior Civil Engineer, Saudi Oger Ltd, 1993-. Publications: Author and co-author, Another Look at Buckling of Circular Arches, 1978. Honours: Charter Member, Structural Engineering Institute; Life Member, Society of Sigma Xi, Post Doctoral Fellowship, University of Missouri, 1972; Listed in biographical publications. Membership: Fellow, American Society of Civil Engineers. Address: GPC Division, Saudi Oger, P O Box 1449, Riyadh 11431, Saudi Arabia. E-mail: hbayazid@saudioger.com

**BAYLEY Peter (Charles),** b. 25 January 1921, Gloucester, England. Professor Emeritus; Writer. Education: Crypt School, Gloucester; Exhibitioner, University College, Oxford, 1940-41; MA (first class), English Language and Literature, Oxford University, 1947. Appointments: War Service, Royal Artillery, Far East, 1941-46; Fellow, University College, 1947-72; Praelector in English, 1949-72, University Lecturer, 1952-72, Oxford University; Master, Collingwood College, University of Durham, 1972-78; Berry Professor and Head of English Department, 1978-85, Berry Professor Emeritus, 1985-, University of St Andrews, Fife. Publications: Edmund Spenser, Prince of Poets, 1971; Poems of Milton, 1982; An ABC of Shakespeare, 1985; Editor: The Faerie Queene, by Spenser, Book II, 1965, Book 1, 1966, 1970; Loves and Deaths, 1972. Contributions to: Patterns of Love and Courtesy, 1966; Oxford Bibliographical Guides, 1971; A Casebook on Spenser's The Faerie Queene, 1977; C S Lewis at the Breakfast Table, 1979; The Encyclopedia of Oxford, 1988; Sir William Jones 1746-94, 1998. Address: 63 Oxford Street, Woodstock, Oxford OX20 1TJ, England.

**BAYLIS Robert Goodwin,** b. 29 November 1925, Luton, Bedfordshire, England. Consulting Engineer. 2 sons, 1 daughter. Education: Highgate School; Trinity College, Cambridge. Appointments: Royal Navy; Director, Scientific Defense Management; Director, Hare Carding PR; Chairman, Nuffield Theatre; Director, BMT Reliability Consultants. Honours: CB; OBE. Memberships: Fellow, Institution of Electrical Engineers; Member, Royal Aeronautical Society. Address: Broadwaters, 4 Cliff Road, Hill Head, PO14 3JS, England. E-mail: gowith.theflow@ntlworld.com

**BAYLISS Peter,** b. 1 September 1936, Luton, England. Mineralogist. m. Daphne Phyllis Webb. Education: BE, 1959, MSc, 1962, PhD, 1967, University of New South Wales, Australia. Appointments: Professor, University of Calgary, Calgary, Alta, Canada, 1967-92; Professor Emeritus,

1992-. Publications: 101 papers; 15 monographs; Over 33 book reviews; 61 X-ray powder diffraction data. Honours: University Soccer Blue, 1961; Commonwealth Scholarship, 1964; Fellow, Mineralogical Society of America, 1970; Killam Fellowship, 1981; New mineral named peterbaylissite, 1995; Fellow, International Centre Diffraction Data, 2000; Fellow, Mineralogical Society, Great Britain, 2000. Memberships: Mineralogical Association of Canada; Association Internationale pour l'Etude des Argiles. Address: Department of Mineralogy, Australian Museum, 6 College Street, Sydney, NSW 2010, Australia.

**BAYRAKÇEKEN Fuat,** b. 26 October 1936, Tokat, Turkey. Professor; Dr Engineering; Spectroscopist. m. Aysun, 1 son, 1 daughter. Education: BSEng, Engineering Physics, 1960, MSEE, Electronics, 1962, BS, Applied Mathematics, 1964, Ankara University; PhD, London University, 1969. Appointments: Teaching, Research positions: Suffolk University, Texas University; University Notre Dame; University of Helsinki; University of London; Royal Society of London; Boston College; Amherst College; US Army Research and Development Command; Max-Planck Institute for Spectroscopy; Max-Planck Institute for Photochemistry; Middle East Technical University; Ankara University; MIT, University of Massachusetts; Yeditepe University. Publications: Numerous papers and articles for journals. Honours: Fulbright Teaching Award, USA; Pre-doctoral and Post-doctoral Research and Teaching Awards. Memberships: Optical Society of America; American Society for Photobiology; Sigma X, USA; Spectroscopy Society. Address: Yeditepe University, Department of Electronics Engineering, Kayişdaği, 34755 Istanbul, Turkey. E-mail: fubay@yeditepe.edu.tr

**BEALE Alfred James,** b. 12 July 1935, Edinburgh, Scotland. Management Consultant. m. Kathleen, 1 son, 1 daughter. Education: George Heriot's School, Edinburgh, 1941-53; MA (Hons), University of Edinburgh, 1957. Appointments: Commissioned Officer, 1st Battalion The Royal Scots, 1957-59; Salesman, Brand Manager in Advertising Department, Procter & Gamble, 1959-64; Operating level, 1964-68, supervisor capacity, 1968-72, diagnostic survey work, 1972-77, Director, North East England, 1978-81, PA Consulting Group; Chief Executive, PA Cambridge Economic Consultants, -1993; Retired, 1993. Publications: Irish Salesmen Under the Microscope, 1971. Honours: OBE, 1997. Memberships: Honorary Fellow, Charted Institute of Marketing; Fellow, Chartered Management Institute; Fellow, Institute of Management Consultancy; Fellow, Institute of Directors; Fellow, Royal Society of Arts. Address: Hallbankfield, Newcastle Road, Corbridge, Northumberland NE45 5LN, England.

**BEALE Geoffrey Herbert,** b. 11 June 1913, Wandsworth, London, England. Research Scientist. 3 sons. Education: Imperial College of Science and Technology, London, 1931-35. Appointments: Research Scientist, John Innes Horticulture Institute, Merton, London, 1935-40; Intelligence Corps, British Army, 1941-46; Scientific Worker, Cold Spring Harbor, New York, USA, 1947; Rockefeller Fellow, Indiana University, USA, 1947-48; Lecturer, Senior Lecturer, 1948-63, Royal Society Research Professor, 1963-78, Edinburgh University. Publications: Numerous articles on genetics of paramecium and malaria parasites and plants; Books: Genetics of Paramecium Aurelia, 1954; Extranuclear Genetics (with J Knowles), 1978; Malaria Parasites (with S Thaithong), 1992. Honours: MBE, 1946, FRS, 1959; FRSE, 1966; Honorary DSc, Chulalongkorn University, Bangkok, Thailand, 1996. Memberships: Royal Society, London; Royal Society, Edinburgh; Genetical Society.

# DICTIONARY OF INTERNATIONAL BIOGRAPHY

Address: 23 Royal Terrace, Edinburgh EH7 5AH, Scotland. E-mail: g.beale@ed.ac.uk

**BEALE Hugh Gurney,** b. 4 May 1948. Professor of Law. m. Jane Wilson Cox, 2 sons, 1 daughter. Education: BA (Hons), Jurisprudence, Exeter College, Oxford. Appointments: Lecturer, Law, University of Connecticut, 1969-71; Lecturer, Law, University College of Wales, Aberystwyth, 1971-73; Lecturer, Law, 1973-86, Reader, Law, 1986-87, University of Bristol; Professor of Law, University of Warwick, 1987-; Law Commissioner, 2000-. Publications: Remedies for Breach of Contract, 1980; Principles of European Contract Law: Parts I & II, joint editor with Ole Lando, 2000; Contract cases and materials, joint editor, 4th edition, 2001; Casebooks on the Common Law of Europe: Contract Law, joint editor, 2002; Chitty on Contracts, general editor, 29th edition, 2004. Honours: Honorary Bencher, Lincoln's Inn, 1999; Honorary QC, 2002; Fellow, British Academy, 2004. Membership: Commission on European Contract Law. Address: Law Commission, Conquest House, 37/38 John Street, London, WC1N 2BQ. E-mail: hugh.b eale@lawcommission.gsi.gov.uk

**BEALE Jack Gordon (Honourable),** b. 17 July 1917, Sydney, Australia. Environmental and Water Resource Scientist. m. Stephanie, 2 sons. Education: Diploma, honours, Mechanical Engineering, Sydney Technical College, 1939; MEng, University of New South Wales, 1964; DSc, University of New South Wales, 1997. Appointments include: Principal, J G Beale & Associates, Consulting Chartered Engineers, 1942-; Member of Parliament, New South Wales, 1942-73; Executive Chairman, Water Research Foundation of Australia, 1956-; Chairman, Zenith Group, 1956-; Australian Water Resources Council, 1965-71; Australian Agricultural Council, 1967-71; Australian Environment Council, 1971-73; Member, Queen's New South Wales Executive Council, 1965-73; New South Wales Minister for Conservation, 1965-71 and for Environment, 1971-73; Senior Advisor, UNEP, UNDP, 1974-77; Chairman, Green Australia Ltd, 1985-. Publications include: National Conifer Planting, 1960; Australian Forestry Council, 1961; Soil Erosion Classification in New South Wales, 1966; Guidelines for Environmental Impact Assosment, 1971; Environmental Policy, Legislative and Administrative Initiatives, 1972; Flood Mapping and Flood Risk, 1973; Sustainable Development of Whole River Valley, 1973; Protection and Management of the Thailand Environment, 1975; Environmental Management of the Venezuela Environment, 1976; Environmental Management in the Philippines: Policy, Legal and Administrative Initiatives, 1977; The Manager and the Environment, 1980; Brown Australia: Degraded Landscape, 1981; Green Australia: Water, Soil and Vegetation Program to Rejuvenate the Australian Landscape, 1981; Response to Climate Change, 1985; Droughtproof Climatically Distributed Network of Hydropower Stations, 1987; Efficacy of Hydroelectricity Generation in Reduction of Greenhouse Gas Emissions, 1989; Honours: Honorary Fellow, Institution of Engineers, Australia, 1998; LLD, Australian National University, 1999; Order of Australia, 1999; Biographical listings in many Who's Who publications. Memberships: Institution of Engineers, Australia; Member, Advisory Committee, Centre for Resource and Environment Studies, Australian National University; Several Leading International Institutes and Associations in Engineering and Biological Systems. Address: 12/93 Elizabeth Bay Road, Elizabeth Bay, NSW 2011, Australia.

**BEALE Peter John (Sir),** b. 18 March 1934, Essex, England. Medical Practitioner. m. (1) Julia, deceased 2000, 4 sons, 2 daughters, 1 deceased; (2) Mary, 2 December 2001. Education: Gonville and Caius College, Cambridge, 1952-55; Westminster Hospital, 1955-58; BA; MB BChir, 1958; FRCP, 1979; FFCM, 1992; FFOM, 1993. Appointments: Army Doctor, 1960-94; Surgeon General, UK Armed Forces, 1991-94; Chief Medical Adviser, British Red Cross, 1994-2000; Governor, Yehudi Menuhin School. Publications: Medical articles on military matters Honour: KBE, 1991. Memberships: President, Tedworth Golf Club, 1999-2003; President, Army Officer's Golf Society, 2001-05. Address: The Old Bakery, Avebury, Wiltshire SN8 1RF. E-mail: peter.beale1@virgin.net

**BEALE Philippa,** b. 17 January 1946, Winchester, Hampshire, England. Sculptor; Painter; Teacher. m. Christopher Allan Plato, 1 son. Education: NDD, Winchester School of Art, 1964-65; BA (Hons), Goldsmith's College, London, 1965-69; Postgraduate Diploma, Psychology and Philosophy of Further and Technical Education, University of Reading, 1969-70; MFA, Fine Art, Goldsmith's College (part-time), 1985-87; Candidate for PhD, Open University, 2000-. Appointments: Art Teacher, Elliot Comprehensive School, London, 1970-72; Art Teacher, Eastleigh Technical College, Hampshire, 1971-73; Visiting Tutor, Hornsea College of Art, 1973-76; Senior Lecturer, Design Department, 1975-77, Head of Foundation, 1977-81, Lecturer in Fine Art, 1981-82, Course Administrator, 1984-85 Advanced Typographic Design, Course Leader, 1985-88, Postgraduate Diploma in Design and Media Technology, London College of Printing; Course Leader, Foundation and Continuing Studies, 1988-89, Dean for School of Art, 1993-94, Head of Fine Art, 1995-96, Director of Studies, Principal Lecturer, 1997-, Central St Martins College of Art and Design, London; Selector (with Ann Jones) for the exhibition at the Museum of Women's Art called Women at Work, 1998; Moderator to Access Course, Greenwich Community College, 2000; Validation Member of CLDT Validation Panel for Cert FE Course, 2002; Most recent personal exhibitions include: From Wilson to Callaghan, Posterstudio, London, 1997, video viewing ICA, London, 1998; Visions, Key London Ltd, London, 2001; St Sebastian, Chelsea Arts Club, London, 2003; Most recent group exhibitions include: Art and the Spirit, The Stations of the Cross, St Pancras Church, London, 2002; Strike, Wolverhampton Art Gallery, 2002; Voyage, New Flowers East Gallery, London; 90th Anniversary Exhibition, The Cork Street Gallery, London, 2003; Flowers West, New York, 2003; Meunier Gallery, London, 2004; Flower Central, London, 2004; Works in permanent collections: Victoria and Albert National Art Archive; Southampton Art Gallery; Jan Van Eyck Academy, Holland; Arts Council, United Kingdom. Memberships: The London Group, President, 1995-99; Royal Society of Arts; Chelsea Arts Club; Chartered Institute of Managers. Address: Foundation Studies, Central Saint Martins College of Art and Design, Saffron House, 10 Back Hill, London EC1R 5LQ; E-mail: p.beale@csm.art.ac.uk Website: www.thelondongroup.com

**BEALES Derek (Edward Dawson),** b. 12 June 1931, Felixstowe, England. Emeritus Professor of Modern History; Writer. Education: BA, 1953, MA, PhD, 1957, Sidney Sussex College, Cambridge University. Appointments: Research Fellow, 1955-58, Fellow, 1958-, Tutor, 1961-70, Vice Master, 1973-75, Sidney Sussex College, Cambridge University; Assistant Lecturer, 1962-65, Lecturer, 1965-80, Chairman, Faculty Board of History, 1979-81, Professor of Modern History, 1980-97, Emeritus Professor, 1997-, Sidney Sussex College, Cambridge University; Editor, Historical Journal, 1971-75; Member of Council, Royal Historical Society, 1984-87; British Academy Representative, Standing Committee for Humanities, European Science Foundation, 1993-99; Recurring Visiting Professor, Central European University, Budapest, 1995-. Publications: England and Italy 1859-60, 1961; From Castlereagh to Gladstone 1815-85, 1969; The Risorgimento and the Unification of Italy, 1971, 2nd edition, with E F Biagini, 2002; History and Biography, 1981; History, Society and the Churches: Essays in Honour of Owen Chadwick (editor with G F A Best), 1985; Joseph II: In the Shadow of Maria Theresa 1741-80, 1987; Mozart and the Habsburgs, 1993; Sidney Sussex College Quatercentenary Essays, (editor with H B Nisbet), 1996; Prosperity and Plunder: European Catholic Monasteries in the Age of Revolution, 1650-1815, 2003; Enlightenment and Reform in the Eighteenth Century, 2005. Honours: Prince Consort Prize, 1960; Doctor of Letters, 1988; Fellow, British Academy, 1989; Stenton Lecturer, University of Reading, 1992; Birkbeck Lecturer, Trinity College, Cambridge, 1993; Leverhulme 2000 Emeritus Fellowship, 2001-2003; Paolucci/ Bagchot Prize, Intercollegiate Studies Institute, Wilmington, Delaware, USA, 2004. Memberships: Fellow, Royal Historical Society; Member, Athenaeum. Address: Sidney Sussex College, Cambridge CB2 3HU, England. E-mail: deb1000@cam.ac.uk

**BEAN Sean,** b. 17 April 1958, Sheffield, Yorkshire, England. Actor. m. (1) Debra James, 1981, divorced, (2) Melanie Hill, 1991, divorced 1997, 2 children, (3) Abigail Cruttenden, 1997, divorced 2000, 1 child. Education: Royal Academy of Dramatic Art. Creative Works: Appearances include: the Last Days of Mankind and Der Rosenkavalier at Citizen's Theatre, Glasgow, Who Knew Mackenzie? and Gone, Theatre Upstairs, Roy Court, Romeo in Romeo and Juliet, RSC, Stratford-upon-Avon, 1986, Captain Spencer in The Fair Maid of the West, RSC, London; TV Appearances include: Clarissa; Fool's Gold; Role of Mellors in BBC Dramatization of Lady Chatterley's Lover; Inspector Morse; Role Sharpe in TV Series; A Woman's Guide to Adultery; Jacob; Bravo Two Zero; Extremely Dangerous; Films: Caravaggio, Stormy Monday, War Requiem, The Field, Patriot Games, Gone With the Wind, Goldeneye, When Saturday Comes, Anna Karenina, Ronin; The Lord of the Rings: The Fellowship of the Ring; Don't Say a Word; Equilibrium; Tom and Thomas; The Big Empty; Windprints; Essex Boys; Troy, 2004. Address: c/o ICM Ltd, Oxford House, London W1R 1RB, England.

**BEAR Carolyn Ann, (Chlöe Rayban),** b. 10 April 1944, Exeter, England. Author. m. Peter Julian Bear, 2 daughters. Education: University of Western Australia (1 year); University of Newcastle upon Tyne; BA Hons, Philosophy. Publications: Under Different Stars, 1988; Wild Child, 1991; Virtual Sexual Reality, 1994; Love in Cyberia, 1996; Screen Kiss, 1997; Clash on the Catwalk, 1997; Havana to Hollywood, 1997; Street to Stardom, 1997; Models Move On, 1998; Terminal Chic, 2000. Honours: Shortlisted for Guardian Children's Fiction Prize, 1995; Shortlisted for Guardian Children's Fiction Prize, 1996; Shortlisted for Carnegie Medal Fiction Prize, 1996. Address: 17 Alwyne Villas, London N1 2HG, England.

**BEAR Isabel Joy,** b. 4 January 1927, Camperdown, Victoria, Australia. Research Scientist. Education: Associate Diploma in Applied Chemistry, MTC, 1950; Associate Diploma in Applied Science, 1950; Fellowship Diploma Applied Chemistry, RMIT 1972; D App Sc, 1978. Appointments: Experimental Scientist, AERE Harwell, 1950-51; Research Assistant, University of Birmingham, UK, 1951-53; Experimental Scientist, CSIRO Division of Industrial Chemistry/Mineral Chemistry, 1953-67; Senior Research Scientist, CSIRO Division of Mineral Chemistry/Products, 1967-72; Principal Research Scientist, 1972-79; Senior Principal Research Scientist, 1979-92; Honorary Fellow, 1992-97. Publications: More than 70 refereed papers in scientific journals; Co-author: Alumina to Zirconia – The History of the CSIRO Division of Mineral Chemistry, 2001. Honours: Appointed, Member of the Order of Australia for Services to Science; Leighton Medallist, Royal Australian

Chemical Institute; Listed on the Victorian Honour Roll of Women, 2005. Memberships: Royal Australian Chemical Institute; Australasian Institute of Mining and Metallurgy. Address: 2/750 Waverley Road, Glen Waverley, VIC 3150, Australia.

**BEASLEY John David, (David Sellers),** b. 26 October 1944, Hornsea, Yorkshire, England. Social Worker. m. Marian Ruth Orford, 15 Mar 1969, 1 son, 2 daughters. Education: London University Diploma in Sociology; Certificate of Qualification in Social Work, Polytechnic of North London, England. Appointments: United Kingdom Band of Hope Union, 1960-70; Social Worker, London Borough of Tower Hamlets, 1970-94. Publications: Who Was Who in Peckham, 1985; The Bitter Cry Heard and Heeded, 1989; 500 Quotes and Anecdotes, 1992; Origin of Names in Peckham and Nunhead, 1993; Peckham and Nunhead Churches, 1995; Peckham Rye Park Centenary, 1995; Peckham and Nunhead, 1995; Another 500 Quotes and Anecdotes, 1996; Transport in Peckham and Nunhead, 1997; East Dulwich, 1998; The Story of Peckham and Nunhead, 1999; Peckham and Nunhead Remembered, 2000; Southwark Remembered, 2001; East Dulwich Remembered, 2002; Southwark Revisited, 2004; Contributions to: Challenge; South London Press. Honour: Southwark Civic Award, 1997. Membership: Society of Authors. Address: South Riding, 6 Everthorpe Road, London SE15 4DA, England.

**BEASLEY William Gerald,** b. 22 December 1919, Hanwell, Middlesex, England. Professor Emeritus; Writer. m. Hazel Polwin, 1 son. Education: BA, 1940, PhD, 1950, University of London. Appointment: Professor of History of the Far East, School of Oriental and African Studies, 1954-83, Professor Emeritus, 1983-, University of London. Publications: Great Britain and the Opening of Japan 1833-1858, 1951; Select Documents on Japanese Foreign Policy 1853-1868 (editor and translator), 1955; Historians of China and Japan (editor with E G Pulleyblank), 1961; The Modern History of Japan, 1963, 3rd edition, 1981; The Meiji Restoration, 1972; Modern Japan: Aspects of History, Literature and Society (editor), 1975; Japanese Imperialism 1894-1945, 1987; The Rise of Modern Japan, 1990; Japan Encounters the Barbarian: Japanese Travellers in America and Europe, 1995; The Japanese Experience: A Short History of Japan, 1999. Honours: Honorary D Litt, University of Hong Kong, 1978; CBE, 1980; Order of the Rising Sun, 1981; Professor Emeritus, 1983; Honorary Fellow of SOAS; Japan Foundation Award, 2001. Memberships: Fellow, British Academy, 1967; Honorary Member, Japan Academy, 1984. Address: 172 Hampton Road, Twickenham TW2 5NJ, England.

**BEASON Fedlyn Arthniel,** b. 6 December 1941, Jamaica. Minister of Religion. m. Esmine James, 1 son, 1 daughter. Education: AA, Bible Knowledge, Christian Bible Institute, Cleveland, Tennessee, USA, 1973; Advanced Teacher's Certificate, Evangelical Teacher Training Association, USA, 1977; B Th, School of Religion, Pacific Western University, 1981; Doctor of Divinity, 1995, M Litt, 1995, Doctor of Philosophy, 1999, Doctor of Religious Education, 2003, European Theological Seminary. Appointments: Religious service includes: Pastor and District Overseer, New Testament Church of God, Jamaica, 1963-90; Chairman, Bethel Bible College Board of Directors, 1990-98; Administrative Bishop, New Testament Church of God, Jamaica and Grand Cayman, 1990-98; Member, Caribbean Executive Council, 1980-98, Member International Advisory Council, 1990-, World Missions Council, 1994-98, Caribbean Field Director World Mission, 1998-, Member International Executive Council, Church of God; Public service includes: Civil Service, Public

Works, St Elizabeth, Jamaica, 1967-72; Road and Works Contractor, Public Works Department, Government of Jamaica, 1967-71; President, JAMAL, Peckham, Clarendon, Jamaica; Chairman, Portland Ministers Fraternal, Jamaica, 1976-79; Chairman, Board of Management, Portland and St Thomas Regional Government Hospitals, 1977-79; Chairman, Board of Management, Spring Bank All Age School, 1976-80, Port Antonio Secondary School, 1980-98; Founder and Chairman, James Brown Health Clinic, Kingston, Jamaica, 1982-98; Lay Magistrate, Justice of the Peace. Publications: Articles in religious journals include: How to develop and manage a church, 1990 Aids (HIV): a Biblical Perspective, 1993; The Christian's Stance and Politics and Civic Responsibilities, 1997; Who Cares for the Children, 1998. Honours: Numerous honours and awards include: National Award for Outstanding Community Service, Prime Minister of Jamaica, 1983; Church of God, Distinguished Leadership Awards; Commander Club Award (Gold Leader), Disabled American Veterans, 2000; Fraternal Order of Police District No 5, Certificate of Appreciation, 2004. Address: 16501 SW 18 Street, Miramar, FL 33027, USA. E-mail: cogcarib@aol.com

**BEATRICE Pier Franco,** b. 29 June 1948, Padua. University Professor. m. Paola Isaia, 2 sons. Education: Degree in Arts, University of Padua, 1970; PhD, Early Christian Studies, Catholic University of Milan, 1978. Appointments: Professor, Early Christian Literature, University of Padua, 1979-; Visiting Professor, History of Religions, University of Liège, 1996; Visiting Professor, Patristic Theology, Boston College, 1998-99; Visiting Professor, University of Malta, 2004. Publications: Tradux Peccati; La Lavanda Dei Piedi; L'Eredità Delle Origini; L'Intolleranza Cristiana; Anonymi Monophysitae Theosophia. Honours: Various Who's Who Entries and International Awards. Memberships: North American Patristics Society; International Association of Patristic Studies; Studiorum Novi Testamenti Societas; International Association for the History of Religions. Address: Via Metastasio 16, I-35125, Padova, Italy.

**BEATRIX Wilhelmina Armgard (Queen of the Netherlands),** b. 31 January 1938, Baarn, The Netherlands. m. Claus George Willem Otto Frederik Geert von Amsberb, 10 March 1966, 3 sons. Education: Leiden State University. Honour: Hon K.G. Address: c/o Government Information Service, Press & Publicity Department, Binnenhof 19, 2513 AA The Hague, The Netherlands.

**BEATTIE Ann,** b. 7 September 1947, Washington, District of Columbia, USA. Writer; Poet. m. Lincoln Perry. Education: BA, American University, Washington, DC, 1969; MA, University of Connecticut, 1970. Appointments: Visiting Assistant Professor, 1976-77, Visiting Writer, 1980, University of Virginia, Charlottesville; Briggs Copeland Lecturer in English, Harvard University, 1977; Guggenheim Fellow, 1977. Publications: Secrets and Surprises, 1978; Where You'll Find the Other Stories, 1986; What Was Mine and Other Stories, 1991; With This Ring, 1997; My Life, Starring Dara Falcon, 1998; Park City: New and Selected Stories, 1998; New and Selected Poems, 1999; Perfect Recall, 2000. Contributions to: Various publications. Memberships: American Academy and Institute of Arts and Letters; PEN; Authors' Guild. Honours: Award in literature, 1980; Hon LHD, American University. Address: c/o Janklow and Nesbit, 598 Madison Avenue, New York, NY 10022, USA.

**BEATTY Warren,** b. 30 March 1937, Richmond, Virginia, USA. Actor. m. Annette Bening, 1992, 4 children. Education: Stella Adler Theatre School. Creative Works: Film Appearances include: Splendor in the Grass, 1961; Roman Spring of Mrs

Stone, 1961; All Fall Down, 1962; Lilith, 1965; Mickey One, 1965; Promise Her Anything, 1966; Kaleidoscope, 1966; Bonnie and Clyde, 1967; The Only Game in Town, 1969; McCabe and Mrs Miller, 1971; Dollars, 1972; The Parallax View, 1974; Shampoo, 1975; The Fortune, 1976; Heaven Can Wait, 1978; Reds, 1981; Ishtar, 1987; Dick Tracy, 1989; Bugsy, 1991; Love Affair, Bulworth, 1998; Town and Country, 2001. TV Appearances include: Studio One; Playhouse 90; A Salute to Dustin Hoffman, 1999. Theatre Roles include: A Loss of Roses, 1960. Honours include: Academy Award, Best Director, 1981; Commander, Ordre des Art.s et des Lettres. Address: CAA, 9830 Wilshire Boulevard, Beverly Hills, CA 90212, USA.

**BEAVEN Freda,** b. 30 July 1923, Croydon, Surrey. Musician; Singer; Accompanist. m. C H J Beaven, 18 August 1945, 1 son. Education: Piano tuition from childhood; Private singing tuition, 1940-, later with Henry Cummings FRAM. Career: LRAM Teacher, 1967; LRAM Performer, 1968; Choral Experience at BBC, 1963-70; Recitals in London, 1968-; Director, The Lindsey Singers, Madrigals, 1970-74; Private Teaching, Singing, Piano and Theory, 1967-; Professional Choralist, London, 1970-74; Voice Tutor and Accompanist, Westwood Centre, Oldham, 1980-88; Singing and Theory Specialist; Voice and Language Tutor, Oldham Further Education College, 1980-88; Currently gives specialist voice training and advanced coaching to the singers of the English Song, French Song, Italian and German Lieder repertories, Southport. Publications: Music Theory Makes Sense, textbook, 1985; Established Roselle Publications, 1985; Contributions to: Singing, publication of the Association of Teachers of Singing. Honours: LRAM Diploma Performer; LRAM Diploma. Memberships: Royal Society of Musicians; Association of Teachers of Singing. Address: Southport, Merseyside PR8 2AF, England.

**BEAVEN Johnson A, III,** b. 12 November 1958, Indianapolis, Indiana, USA. Clergyman; Educator. 1 son. Education: BSc, Ball State University, Muncie, Indiana, 1981; Biblical Studies Program, Moody Bible Institute, Chicago, Illinois, 1987-1992; Biblical Language Studies, Simmons Bible College, Louisville, Kentucky, 2004-05; Continuing Education, Christian Theological Seminary, Fuller Theological Seminary, Louisville Theological Seminary; MA, Religion, Trinity Evangelical Divinity School, Deerfield, Illinois. Appointments: Pastor, Citadel of Faith Church Inc, 1984-; Regional Manager and Regional Vice President, Primerica Financial Services, 1988-91; National Adjutant 1991-99, First Jurisdiction of Indiana Executive Board Secretary, Church of God In Christ Inc, 2005-; Community Liaison, IPS Thomas Edison Middle School, 1991-93; Pension Administrator, Indiana State Teachers' Retirement Fund, 1994-96; Regional Training Director, Excel Communications, 1995-97; President/Owner, Beaven Real Estate Inc, 1996-98; Community-Based Family Resources and Support Federal Grant Network Steering Committee, State of Indiana Family and Social Services Administration, 1998-2002; Seminar Presenter, IMPACTraining, 1999-; Adjunct Instructor, C H Mason Institute of All Saints Bible College, 2000-; Simmons Bible College, 2003-; Area Director, International Bible Institute/IBI Publishers, 2005-. Memberships: American Academy of Religion; Evangelical Homiletics and Theological Societies; Society for Pentecostal Studies. Address: 1005 Loughery Lane, Indianapolis, Indiana 46228-1322, USA. E-mail: jbeaveniii@aol.com

**BECK Matthias,** b. 27 November 1956, Hannover, Germany. Assistant Professor of Medical Ethics and Interdisciplinary Research. Education: Mag. Pharm. University of Münster, Germany, 1982; MD, University of Munich, Germany, 1988; BA, Philosophy, Jesuit University of Philosophy, Munich, 1989;

Dr. theol., University of Freiburg, Germany. Appointments: Current position: Assistant Professor of Medical Ethics and Interdisciplinary Research, University of Vienna, Austria; Scientific Research Projects: Medical College, Srinagar, India, 1985; Aims of Medicine, 1999-2000, Psychooncology: psychological, philosophical and theological aspects of cancer, 2000-2001, University of Vienna, Institute of Ethics and Law in Medicine; Lectures, 2000-: Anthropological background of psychosomatic medicine. "Soul" in psychology, philosophy and theology/body-mind-problem; Psychooncology: anthropological and ethical perspectives; Ethical questions concerning in-vitro-fertilisation, cloning (research and reproductive cloning), embryonic and adult stem cells; Euthanasia, brain-death-definition, organ transplantation; PGD, patentability of genes; gene-diagnosis and gene-therapy; Interpretation of sickness viewing aspects of science, psychosomatics, philosophy and theology; Medical ethics in different religions. Publications: Books: Hippokrates am Scheideweg. Medizin zwischen naturwissenschaftlichem Materialismus und ethischer Verantwortung, 2001; Seele und Krankheit. Psychosomatische Medizin und theologische Anthropologie, 3rd edition, 2003; Der Krebs und die Seele. Gen-Geist-Gehirn-Gott, 2004; Many articles about preimplantation-genetic-diagnosis (PGD), pre-natal-diagnosis (PND), embryonic/adult stem cell research, euthanasia, body-mind-problem, interpretation of sickness viewing aspects of science, psychosomatics, philosophy and theology. Honours: Man of the Year 2005, American Biographical Institute; Man of Achievement, ABI, 2005; Order of International Ambassadors; Outstanding Professional Award, ABI; Listed in Who's Who publications and biographical dictionaries. Memberships: European Academy of Sciences and Arts; Academy of Ethics in Medicine, Göttingen, Germany; Life Fellowship, International Biographical Association, Cambridge, England; Member, ABI's Research Board of Advisors, USA; Scientific Advisory Board, Austria GenAu-Program. Address: Institute of Ethics and Law in Medicine, University of Vienna, Spitalgasse 2-4/Hof2.8, A-1090 Vienna, Austria. E-mail: matth ias.beck@univie.ac.at

**BECKER Boris,** b. 22 November 1967, Leimen, Germany. Tennis Player. m. Barbara Feltus, divorced, 2001, 1 son. Appointments: Started playing tennis at Blau-Weiss Club, Leimen; Won W German Junior Championship, 1983; Runner-up, US Junior Championship; Coached by Ion Tiriac, 1984-; Quarter Finalist, Australia Championship; Winner, Young Masters Tournament, Birmingham, England, 1985; Grand Prix Tournament, Queen's, 1985; Won Men's Singles Championship, Wimbledon, 1985, 1986, 1989, Finalist, 1988, 1990, 1991, 1995; Finalist, Benson & Hedges Championship, Wembley, London, 1985; Masters Champion, 1988, Finalist, 1989; US Open Champion, 1989; Semi Finalist, French Open, 1989; Winner, Davis Cup, 1989, Australian Open Championship, 1991, 1996, IBM/ATP Tour Championship, 1992, 1995, Grand Slam Cup, 1996. Honours: Sportsman of the Year, 1985; Hon Citizen of Leimen, 1986; Named World Champion, 1991; 64 titles (49 singles). Memberships: Board member, Bayern Munich Football Club, 2001-; Chair, Laurens Sport for Good Foundation, 2002-. Address: Nusslocher Strasse 51, 69181 Leimen, Baden, Germany.

**BECKERT Thomas E (Berhard),** b. 22 August 1966, Kempten, Germany. Pharmacist. m. Katrin Buszello, 1 son, 1 daughter. Education: Courses in Pharmacy, 1986-91, Registration as Pharmacist, 1991, Albert-Ludwigs University, Freiburg; Courses in Political Economy, 1992-93, Dr rer nat, Doctor of Natural Sciences, Pharmaceutical Technology, 1992-95, Eberhard-Karls University, Tübingen. Appointments include: Scientific Assistant, Department of Pharmaceutical

Technology, Eberhard-Karls University, Tübingen, 1992-95; Manager, Apotheke Diezenhalde, Böblingen, 1993-95; Business (marketing), Tübingen and Ulm, 1995-96; Military Service, Military Hospital, Ulm, 1995-96; Head, Technical Customer Service, Pharma Polymers Division, Röhm, GmbH, Darmstadt, Germany, 1996-2001; Member of Board, Dr Rentschler Arzneimittel GmbH, Laupheim, Germany, 2002-. Publications: 2 books and book chapters; Author or co-author, 7 scientific papers in professional journals; 13 poster research presentations at scientific conferences; 8 patents. Honours include: Award for best Abitur in Chemistry, 1986; Scholarship holder Konrad-Adenauer-Stiftung, 1987-90; Member of Town Parliament, 1997; Manuscript Reviewer for scientific journals, 1997-; Adjunct Assistant Professor, University of Rhode Island, USA, 2003. Memberships: Arbeitsgemeinschaft für Pharmazeutische Verfahrenstechnik; Deutsche Pharmazeutischen Gesellschaft; Christian Democratic Union; Controlled Release Society; BPI, Working Group Pharmacy. Address: Anton-Braith-Weg 30, 88447 Warthausen, Germany. E-mail: tombeckert@t-online.de

**BECKET Michael Ivan H,** b. 11 September 1938, Budapest, Hungary. Freelance Writer. m. Kay. Education: Open University. Appointments: Exhibition Organiser, Shell International Petroleum, 1959-61; Journalist, Electrical and Radio Trading, 1961; Market Researcher, Young & Rubicam, 1962; Civil Service: Board of Trade, National Board for Prices and Incomes, National Development Office, 1962-68; Daily Telegraph, 1968-2003. Publications: Books: Computer by the Tail, 1972; Economic Alphabet, 1976, 2nd edition, 1981; Bluff Your Way in Finance, 1990; Office Warfare: An Executive Survival Guide, 1993; An A-Z of Finance, 1999; Stakeholder Pensions, 2001; How the Stock Market Works, 2002; Starting Your Own Business, 2003. Address: 9 Kensington Park Gardens, London W11 3HB, England

**BECKETT Kenneth Albert,** b. 12 January 1929, Brighton, Sussex, England. Horticulturist; Technical Advisor; Editor. m. Gillian Tuck, 1 August 1973, 1 son. Education: Diploma, Horticulture, Royal Horticultural Society. Appointments: Technical Editor, Gardener's Chronicle, Reader's Digest. Retired. Publications: The Love of Trees, 1975; Illustrated Dictionary of Botany, 1977; Concise Encyclopaedia of Garden Plants, 1978; Amateur Greenhouse Gardening, 1979; Growing Under Glass, 1981; Complete Book of Evergreens, 1981; Growing Hardy Perennials, 1981; Climbing Plants, 1983; The Garden Library, 4 volumes: Flowering House Plants, Annuals and Biennials, Roses, Herbs, 1984; The RHS Encyclopaedia of House Plants, 1987; Evergreens, 1990; Alpine Garden Society Encyclopaedia of Alpines, 2 volumes, 1993-94. Contributions to: The Garden; The Plantsman. Honours: Veitch Memorial Medal, Royal Horticultural Society, 1987; Lyttel Trophy, 1995 and Clarence Elliott Memorial Award, 1995, Alpine Garden Society. Memberships: The Royal Horticultural Society; The Wild Plant Conservation Charity; Botanical Society of the British Isles; Plantsman; International Dendrology Society; Alpine Garden Society. Address: Bramley Cottage, Docking Road, Stanhoe, King's Lynn, Norfolk PE31 8QF, England.

**BECKETT Margaret Mary,** b. 15 January 1943, Ashton-under-Lyne, Lancashire, England. Politician. m. Leo Beckett, 2 step-sons. Education: Manchester College of Science and Technology, John Dalton Polytechnic. Appointments: Engineering Apprentice, Association of Electrical Industries, Manchester; Experimental Officer, University of Manchester; Researcher, Labour Party Headquarters; Special Adviser at ODA February-October 1974; Parliamentary Private Secretary, Minister for Overseas Development, 1974-75; Assistant Government Whip, 1975-76; Minister, Department of

Education, 1976-79; Labour MP Lincoln, 1974-79; Sponsored by TGWU, 1977-; Principal Researcher, Granada TV, 1979-83; Labour Party National Executive Committee, 1980-97; MP, Derby South, 1983-; Opposition Spokesperson, Social Security, 1984-89; Shadow Chief Secretary, 1989-92; Shadow Leader of the House, Campaigns Coordinator, Deputy Leader of the Opposition, 1992-94; Appointed to Privy Council, 1993; Leader of the Opposition, 1994; Shadow Secretary of State for Health, 1994-95; Shadow President, 1995-97, President, 1997-98, Board of Trade, President of Privy Council, Leader, House of Commons, 1998-2001; Secretary of State, Department of Environment, Food and Rural Affairs, 2001-. Publications: The Need for Consumer Protection, 1972; The National Enterprise Board; The Nationalisation of Shipbuilding, Shiprepair and Marine Engineering; Relevant Sections of Labour's Programme, 1972, 1973; Renewing the NHS, 1995; Vision for Growth - A New Industrial Strategy for Britain, 1996. Memberships: Transport and General Workers' Union, Parliamentary Labour Party Group, National Executive Committee, 1988-98; National Union of Journalists; BECTU; Fabian Society; Tribune Group; Socialist Education Committee; Labour Women's Action Committee; Derby Co-op Party; Socialist Environment and Resources Association; Amnesty International; Council of St George's College, Windsor, 1976-1982. Address: House of Commons, London SW1A 0AA, England.

**BECKHAM David Robert Joseph,** b. 2 May 1975, Leytonstone, London. Footballer. m. Victoria Adams, 4 July 1999, 3 sons. Career: Player with Manchester United, trainee, 1991, team debut, 1992, league debut, 1995, 325 appearances, 78 goals, December 2002; 7 caps for England Under 21s, represented England 1996-, Captain, 2000-, 58 caps, 9 goals December 2002; Joined Real Madrid, 2003-. Publication: David Beckham: My World, 2001. Honours: Bobby Charlton Skills Award, 1987; Manchester United Player of the Year, 1996-97; Young Player of the Year Professional Football Association, 1996-97; Sky Football Personality of the Year, 1997; 5 Premiership Medals; 2 Football Association Medals; European Cup Medal; 2 Charity Shield Winner Medals. Address: SFX Sports Group Europe Ltd, Priest House, 1624 High Street, Knowle, West Midlands, B93 0JU, England. Website: www.manutd.com

**BECKHAM Victoria, (Posh Spice),** b. 7 April 1975, Cuffley, England. Vocalist. m. David Beckham, 4 July 1999, 3 sons. Career: Member, Spice Girls; Numerous TV and radio appearances, magazine interviews; Film, Spiceworld: The Movie, 1997; World tour including dates in UK, Europe, India and USA. Recordings: Singles: Wannabe, 1996; Say You'll Be There, 1996; 2 Become 1, 1996; Mama/ Who Do You Think You Are, 1997; Step To Me, 1997; Spice Up Your Life, 1997; Too Much, 1997; Stop, 1998; (How Does It Feel To Be) On Top of the World, with England United, 1998; Move Over/Generation Next, 1998; Viva Forever, 1998; Goodbye, 1998; Holler/Let Love Lead the Way, 2000; Out of Your Mind, 2000; Not Such an Innocent Girl, 2001; A Mind of Its Own, 2002; Albums: Spice, 1996; Spiceworld, 1997; Forever, 2001. Honours: Best Video (Say You'll Be There), Best Single (Wannebe), Brit Awards, 1997; 2 Ivor Novello song writing awards, 1997; Best Band, Smash Hits Award, 1997; 3 American Music Awards, 1998; Special Award for International Sales, Brit Awards, 1998. Publications: Learning to Fly, autobiography, 2001. Address: c/o Lee & Thompson, Green Garden House, 15-22 St Christopher's Place, London, W1M 5HE, England. Website: c3.vmg.co.uk/spicegirls

**BECKINSALE Kate,** b. 26 July 1973, London, England. Actress. 1 daughter with Micheal Sheen. Education: French and Russian Literature, New College, Oxford University, 1991-94. Career: TV includes: One Against the Wind, 1991; Cold Comfort Farm, 1995; Films include: Much Ado About Nothing, 1993; Haunted, 1995; Emma, 1997; Shooting Fish, 1997; The Golden Bowl, 2000; Pearl Harbor, 2001; Serendipity, 2001; Laurel Canyon, 2002; Underworld, 2003; Tiptoes, 2003; Van Helsing, 2004.

**BECKLES WILLSON Robina Elizabeth,** b. 26 September 1930, London, England. Writer. m. Anthony Beckles Willson, 1 son, 1 daughter, Education: BA, 1948, MA, 1952, University of Liverpool. Appointments: Teacher, Liverpool School of Art, 1952-56; Ballet Rambert Educational School, London, 1956-58. Publications: Leopards on the Loire, 1961; A Time to Dance, 1962; Musical Instruments, 1964; A Reflection of Rachel, 1967; The Leader of the Band, 1967; Roundabout Ride, 1968; Dancing Day, 1971; The Last Harper, 1972; The Shell on Your Back, 1972; What a Noise, 1974; The Voice of Music, 1975; Musical Merry-go-Round, 1977; The Beaver Book of Ballet, 1979; Eyes Wide Open, 1981; Anna Pavlova: A Legend Among Dancers, 1981; Pocket Book of Ballet, 1982; Secret Witch, 1982; Square Bear, 1 983; Merry Christmas, 1983; Holiday Witch, 1983; Sophie and Nicky series, 2 volumes, Hungry Witch, 1984; Music Maker, 1986; Sporty Witch, 1986; The Haunting Music, 1987; Mozart's Story, 1991; Just Imagine, 1993; Harry Stories in Animal World, 1996; Ambulance!, 1996; Very Best Friend, 1998; The King Who Had Dirty Feet, 2000; The Emperor's New Clothes, 2000. Address: 44 Popes Avenue, Twickenham, Middlesex TW2 5TL, England.

**BEDDINGTON John Richard,** b. 15 September 1942, Haslemere, Surrey, England. Sports Manager. m. Roseann Madden, 11 July 1972, 2 sons. Education: Eton College, 1956-60; Goethe Institute, 1960-61; College of Law, 1962-65. Appointments: Articled Clerk, Birkbeck, Julius, Coburn and Broad, 1962-65; Marketing Department, BP Chemicals (UK) Ltd, 1966-72; European Director, Grand Prix Tennis Circuit, 1972-77; Vice President, International Management Group, 1977-82; Chairman, Chief Executive Officer, Beddington Sports Management Inc, Toronto, Canada, 1982-; Executive Vice President, Tennis Canada, 1983-95; Tournament Director, Chairman, Canadian Open Tennis Championships, Toronto and Montreal, 1979-95; Chairman, Canadian Open Squash Championships, 1985-95; Group Managing Director, Masters International Ltd, 1995-97; Consultant, Tennis Canada, 1995-98; Chairman, Chief Executive Officer, Beddington Sports Management Ltd, 1997-; Chairman, Canadian Corporate Golf Challenge, 1997-; Tournament Director, The Masters Tennis, Royal Albert Hall, 1997-; Consultant, Squash Rackets Association, 1997-99; Chairman, British Open Squash Championships, 2003-. Publications include: Play Better Squash, 1974; Several articles in a wide variety of sports publications. Honours: Several organisation awards for sports events; Listed in several Who's Who publications. Memberships: Director, WTA Tour, 1993-98; Duke of Edinburgh Award, Toronto, 1990-95; Professional Squash Association, 1998-2000; Cambridge Club, Toronto; All England Lawn Tennis Club; Fellow, Royal Geographical Society; Lambton Leisure. Address: The Old School House, Hook End, Checkendon, Oxon RG8 0UL, England. E-mail: jrbeddington@btinternet.com

**BEDFORD William,** b. 9 December 1943, Grantham, Lincolnshire, England. Writer. m. Fiona Mary White, 1 son, 1 daughter. Education: BA (Hons), 1976, PhD, 1980, University of Sheffield. Appointments: Lloyd's Broker, City of London, 1961-71; Postgraduate Tutor, University of Sheffield, 1977-79; Lecturer, Middlesex Polytechnic, 1980-81; Freelance Feature Writer with Punch, Harper's, Independent, Telegraph, Catholic Herald, London Review of Books, Washington

Times and others, 1978-; Editor, Delta, 1978-79; Occasional Editor, Agenda, 1980, 1988, 1989; Full-time writer, 1984-. Publications: The Hollow Landscapes, 1977; Journeys, 1988; Happiland, 1990; Golden Gallopers, 1991; All Shook Up, 1992; Nightworld, 1992; Catwalking, 1993; Imaginary Republics, 1993; The Lost Mariner, 1995; Jacob's Ladder, 1996; The Freedom Tree, 1997; The Joyriders, 1998; Esme's Owl, 1999; The Stowaway, 2001; Great Expectations: a retelling, 2002; Whitemen, 2003; The Piano Player (radio drama), 2003; Dotheboys Hall (dramatisation), 2004; Theseus and the Minotaur: a retelling, 2004; The Glow-worm Who Lost Her Glow, 2004; Contributions to Annual Bibliography of English Language and Literature, 1974, 1975, 1976. Honours: Moore Smith Prize, Gibbons Prize, University of Sheffield; Arts Council Major Bursary, 1978; Runner-up, Guardian Fiction Prize, 1990; Society of Authors Fiction Prize, 1993; Yorkshire and Humberside Arts Award, 1993. Address: Rogers, Coleridge & White, 20 Powis Mews, London W11 1JN, England.

**BEDI Raman,** b. 20 May 1953, India. Chief Dental Officer - England. m. Kathryn, 3 sons. Education: Bachelor of Dental Surgery, University of Bristol, 1976; Diploma in Higher Education (Theology), Trinity College, Bristol, 1979; Fellowship in Dental Surgery, Royal College of Surgeons of Edinburgh, 1982; MSc, Health Education, University of Manchester, 1986; Doctor of Dental Surgery, University of Bristol, 1993; Fellowship of Dental Surgery, Royal College of Surgeons of England, 2002; Doctor of Science, University of Bristol, 2003; Fellowship of the Faculty of Public Health, 2003; Fellowship of the Faculty of Dental Practice, Royal College of Surgeons of England, 2004. Appointments: Lecturer, Paediatric Dentistry, University of Manchester, 1979-82; Clinical Lecturer in Children's Dentistry and Orthodontics, University of Hong Kong, 1983-86; Clinical Lecturer in Preventive Dentistry, University of Edinburgh, 1988-91; Senior Lecturer in Paediatric Dentistry, University of Birmingham, 1991-96; Co-Director, WHO Collaborating Centre for Oral Health, Disability and Culture, 1996-; Professor Transcultural Oral Health, Honorary Consultant in Paediatric Dentistry and Specialist in Dental Public Health, Eastman Dental Institute, University College London, 1996-2002; King's College London, 2002-; Chief Dental Officer England, Department of Health, 2002-. Publications: Over 180 refereed articles. Honours: George Fawn Prize in Children's Dentistry and Orthodontics, University of Bristol, 1976; Sir Patrick Forrest Travelling Scholarship, 1988; The Asian Guild Award (Community Service), 2003; The Asian Jewel Award, 2003. Memberships: Anglo-Asian Odontological Group; British Association for the Study of Community Dentistry; British Dental Association; British Society for the Study of Paediatric Dentistry; British Society for Disability and Oral Health; Christian Dental Fellowship; European Association of Dental Public Health; International Association for Dentistry for Children; International Association for Dental Research; Overseas Doctors Association; Royal College of Surgeons of Edinburgh; Royal College of Surgeons of England; Faculty of Public Health; Faculty of General Dental Practitioners, Royal College of Surgeons of England; Association of Professors of Dentistry. Address: 11/053, New King's Beam House, 22 Upper Ground, London SE1 9BW, England. E-mail: raman.bedi@dh.gsi.gov.uk

**BEDRITSKY Alexander Ivanovich,** b. 10 July 1947, Tashkent district, Uzbekistan, USSR. Hydrometeorologist. m. 3 children. Education: Diploma, Tashkent Electro-Technical Institute of Telecommunication, 1966-75; PhD in Geography, 2000. Appointments: Senior Engineer, Computer Center of the WWW Regional Center, Tashkent, 1969-77; Chief Engineer, Middle Asian Regional Scientific Research Hydrometeorological Institute, 1977-80; Deputy Chief of Uzbek Republican Administration for Hydrometeorology, 1980-92, USSR Committee for Hydrometeorology, Tashkent; First Deputy Chairman, Committee for Hydrometeorology and Environmental Monitoring, Russian Federation Ministry for Ecology and Natural Resources, Moscow, 1992-93; Head, Russian Federal Service for Hydrometeorology and Environmental Monitoring, Moscow, 1993-. Honours: Russian Government's Prize, 1999. Memberships: Intergovernmental Council for Hydrometeorology; WMO Executive Council; President, World Meteorological Organization, XIV World Meteorological Congress, 2003. Address: Roshydromet, Novovagan'kovsky Street 12, 123995, Moscow, Russia.

**BEERBAUM Frederik (Freek),** b. 1942, Hilversum, The Netherlands. Artist. Education: Graduate, Gerrit Rietveld Academy, Amsterdam, 1969. Career: Artist living and working in The Netherlands and Portugal; Exhibitions from 1971 include more recently: SBK Leeuwarden, Internal Dialogue 65, improvisations, solo, 1990; Drents Museum, Assen, Goed Bekeken 3, Contemporary Art from Drenthe, 1991; NAM, Dutch Petroleum Company, organised by Arts Council, Drenthe, solo, 1992; 24 Drawings, Arti et Amicitiae, Amsterdam, solo, 1995; At Sea Everything is Possible, Arts Centre Zaabstad, Zaandam, solo, 1996; Arundel Festival, Arundel, West Sussex, England, 1997; Mirror Image, portraits, Arti et Amicitiae, Amsterdam, 1998; Drenthe by the Sea, Veere and Drents Museum, 1999; Millennium Exhibition Arts Centre (SBK), Amsterdam, solo, 2000; Where No Birds Sing, Town Hall, Aljezur, Portugal, solo, 2003; Hogeschool, Utrecht, 2003; "Eros and Thanatos" 733 drawings, slide show, DVD, Arti et Amicitiae, Amsterdam, 2005; Works in collections: Stedelijk Museum for Modern and Contemporary Art, Amsterdam; Amsterdam Council; Arts Council Drenthe; NAM (Dutch Petroleum Company); Ericsson Holland, Enschede, Amsterdam; Slotervaart Hospital, Amsterdam; Insurance Company "Het Groene Land", Lelystad; SBK: Amsterdam, Assen, Leeuwarden, Hilversum, Tilburg, Arnhem, Maastricht, Utrecht; Hogeschool van Utrecht. Publications: Works featured in newspapers and magazines; Exhibition catalogues; Book cover, Children, Problems at School and Stress, 1991; Book cover and 24 drawings, Silent Terror, 1995; Book Cover, Stress theoretical aspects of remedial education, 1999; 12 paintings commissioned by the Hogeschool van Utrecht for a book, In het hoofd van de meester (In the Mind of the Teacher). Membership: Arti et Amicitiae, 1978-. Address: CP 1366 Azenha, 8670-115 Aljezur, Algarve, Portugal; Kerkstraatt 167, 1017 GH Amsterdam, The Netherlands. Website: www.beerbaumart.com

**BEERE Susan,** b. 26 April 1951, Virginia, USA. Ceramic Tile Artist. m. Hugh L Wilkerson. Education: Palomar Junior College, 1970; Mesa College, 1987. Appointments: Taught children, Del Mar Shores Elementary, 1977-; Private Teacher, 1985-2001. Publications: Many articles in local papers and magazines. Commissions and Creative Works: Numerous commissions including, Nancy Hayward, 1975-2004, Candace Gietzen, 1978-2001; Dr A J Foster, Del Mar Medical Clinic, 1980-83; Richard Reilly, Curator Emeritus of the James S Copley Library, La Jolla, 1991; Del Mar Library, Historic Room, 1984-; Gerhard Design Group, 1998-2000; Georgiana G Rodiger, 1986-2004; Shiela Cameron, 1979-99, Maxine Edwards, 1980-84; Joyce Klein, 1981. Honours: Superior Achievement, Art Competition, 1970; Second Prize, Sculptor, 1971; Competitive Bid Winner, Fine Arts Association, 1979; Award of Merit, San Angelo Museum of Art, 1991; Chosen for cover and in Handmade Tiles by Frank Giorgini, 2nd edition, 1995. Address: PO Box 70, Del Mar, CA 92014, USA. E-mail: susan@susanbeere.com Website: www.susanbeere.com

**BEEVOR Antony,** b. 14 December 1946, London, England. Historian; Novelist. m. Artemis Cooper, 2 February 1986, 1 son, 1 daughter. Education: Winchester College; Grenoble University; Royal Military Academy, Sandhurst. Appointments: Executive Council French Theatre Season, 1997; Chairman, Society of Authors, 2003-. Publications: The Spanish Civil War, 1982; The Enchantment of Christina Von Retzen (novel), 1988; Inside the British Army, 1990; Crete: The Battle and the Resistance, 1991; Paris After the Liberation 1944-49, 1994; Stalingrad, 1998; Berlin – The Downfall 1945, 2002; The Mystery of Olga Chekhova, 2004; A Writer at War. Vasily Grossman with the Red Army 1941-1945 (editor), 2005. Contributions to: Times Literary Supplement; Times; Telegraph; Independent, New York Times, Spectator. Honours: Runciman Award, 1992; Chevalier de l'Ordre des Arts et Lettres, (French Government), 1997; Fellow, Royal Society of Literature, 1999; D. Litt., University of Kent, 2004; Samuel Johnson Prize for Non-Fiction, 1999; Wolfson Prize for History, 1999; Hawthornden Prize, 1999. Memberships: Society of Authors; Royal Geographical Society; Anglo Hellenic League; Friends of the British Libraries. Address: 54 Saint Maur Road, London SW6 4DP, England.

**BEG Muhammad Abdul Jabbar,** b. 10 October 1944, Dinajpur, East Bengal, India. Academic Scholar. m. S Nahar, 1 son, 1 daughter. Education: BA, Honours, Islamic History, 1965, MA, 1966, University of Rajshahi, East Pakistan; PhD, Middle Eastern History, Faculty of Oriental Studies, University of Cambridge, 1971. Appointments: Education Officer (temporary), Pakistan High Commission, London, 1971; Language Specialist (temporary), British Museum, 1972; Lecturer, Islamic History, Universiti Kebangsaan, Malaysia, 1974-76; Lecturer, History and Civilisation of Islam, National University of Malaysia, 1977-78; Associate Professor, National University of Malaysia, 1979-85; Associate Professor of History, University Brunei Darussalam, 1986-89; Associate Professor, Markfield Institute of Higher Education, Leicester, UK, 2001. Publications: Books: Islamic and Western Concepts of Civilisation, 1980, 3rd edition, 1982; Social Mobility in Islamic Civilisation – the classical period, 1981; Fine Arts in Islamic Civilisation (edited), 1981; Arabic Loan-words in Malay: a comparative study, 1983; Historic Cities of Asia (edited), 1986; Brief Lives of the Companions of the Prophet Muhammad, 2003; Articles to learned journals and the Encyclopaedia of Islam. Memberships: The Cambridge Society; Royal Asiatic Society of England and Ireland; Middle East Institute, Washington DC; MESA, USA. Address: 237 Colhams Lane, Cambridge CB1 3HY, England. E-mail: majbeg@hotmail.com

**BELAFONTE Harry,** b. 1 March 1927, New York, USA. Singer. m. (2) Julie Robinson, 1957, 1 son, 3 daughters. Education: Jamaica, 1935-39. Appointments: US Navy, 1943-45; American Negro Theatre; President, Belafonte Enterprises include: Goodwill Ambossador for UNICEF, 1987; Host, Nelson Mandela Birthday Concert, Wembley, 1988. Creative Works: European Tours, 1958, 1976, 1981, 1983, 1988; Broadway appearances: Three For Tonight; Almanac; Belafonte At The Palace; Films: Bright Road; Carmen Jones, 1952; Island in the Sun, 1957; The World, the Flesh and the Devil, 1958; Odds Against Tomorrow, 1959; The Angel Levine, 1969; Grambling's White Tiger, 1981; White Man's Burden; Buck and the Preacher, 1971; Uptown Saturday Night, 1974; Concerts in USA, Europe, 1989, Canada, 1990, USA and Canada, 1991, North America, Europe and Far East, 1996. Honours include: Golden Acord Award, Bronx Community College, 1989; Mandela Courage Award, 1990; National Medal of the Arts, 1994; New York Arts and Business Council Award, 1997; Distinguished American Award, John F Kennedy Library,

Boston, 2002; Several honorary doctorates. Membership: Board Member, New York State Martin Luther King JR Institute for Non-violence, 1989-.

**BELENKY Alexander Solomonovich,** b. 16 March 1946, Moscow, USSR. Strategic Management Consultant. Education: Piano studies, music school, 1958-61; Engineering, Moscow Institute of Chemical Engineering, 1962-67; Student of Professor Theodor Gutman, Gnesyn's College of Music, Moscow, 1963-68; Student, Gnesyn's Musical Institute, Moscow, 1968-70; Mathematician, summa cum laude diploma, Mechanics-Mathematical Faculty at Moscow State University, 1970-74; PhD in Mathematics, USSR Academy of Sciences, 1981; DSc in Applications of Mathematical Methods, Russian Academy of Sciences, 1995. Appointments: Head of a group, development of control systems for the USSR refinery industry, 1968-1976, Senior Researcher, development of control systems for transportation, 1977-93, Institute of Control Sciences, USSR Academy of Sciences; Visiting Scientist, Operation Research Centre, Massachusetts Institute of Technology, 1991-92, 1993-94. Publications: 6 books, including: Operations Research in Transportation Systems: Ideas and Schemes of Optimization Methods for Strategic Planning and Operations Management, 1998; Extreme Outcomes of US Presidential Elections, 2003; Winning the US Presidency: Rules of the Game and Playing by the Rules, 2004; 5 brochures; Over 85 articles in the field of operations research and its applications. Honours: Professor of Applications of Mathematical Methods, Russian Academy of Sciences, 1997. Memberships: Moscow House of Scientists, 1981; Russian Academy of Transport, 1996. Address: PO Box 1314, Brookline, MA 02446, USA.

**BELHOCINE Tarik-Zine,** b. 8 August 1967, Algiers, Algeria. Nuclear Physician; Researcher. Education: MD, Medicine, 1993, Doctor Diploma in Nuclear Medicine, 1998, University of Algiers, Algeria. Appointments: Fellowship from the International Atomic Energy Agency, 1998-99, PhD Thesis in Nuclear Oncology, 1999-2003, University of Liège, Belgium. Publications: Book chapters in Nuclear Oncology as co-author: Positron Emission Tomography Imaging in Genitourinary Carcinoma, 2001; Apoptosis 2003: From Signalling Pathways to Therapeutic Tools, 2003; Tc99m-Annexin V Uptake and Imaging to Monitor Chemosensitivity, 2004; [18]FDG PET for Metabolic Monitoring of Chemosensitivity, 2004; [18]FDG PET and PET/CT in Uterine Cancers, 2005; Articles in scientific journals as author and co-author include most recently: Early detection of relapse by whole- body positron emission tomography in the follow-up of patients with Hodgkin's disease, 2003; An appraisal of [18]F-FDG PET imaging in post-therapy surveillance of uterine cancers: Clinical evidence and a research proposal, 2003; Staging of primary cervical cancers: the role of nuclear medicine, 2003; Imaging of large vessel vasculitis with [18]FDG PET: Illusion or reality? 2003; The Imaging of Apoptosis with the Radiolabeled annexin V: Optimal Timing for Clinical Feasibility, 2004; Nuclear Medicine in the Era of Genomics and Proteomics: Lessons from Annexin V, 2004; A Plea for the Elective Inclusion of the Brain in Routine Whole-Body [18]FDG PET, 2005. Honours: Scientist of the Year, 2004; Member of Gerson Lehrhan Group's Council of Advisors; Listed in Who's Who publications and biographical dictionaries. Memberships: European Association of Nuclear Medicine; American Society of Nuclear Medicine; French Society of Biophysics and Nuclear Medicine; Belgian Society of Nuclear Medicine; American Association for the Advancement of Science; Advisory Board of The Scientist; European Society of Urogenital Radiology; International Federation of Gynaecology and Obstetrics; European Society of Cardiology.

Address: 48 Boulevard Mohamed V, Algiers, Algeria. E-mail: tarikbelhocine@yahoo.fr

**BELKIN Boris David,** b. 26 January 1948, Sverdlovsk, Russia. Violinist. m. Dominique, 1 son, 1 daughter. Education: Began violin studies aged 6; Central Music School, Moscow; Moscow Conservatory with Yankelevitz and Andrievsky. Career: Public appearances from 1955; Debut in West, 1974 with Zubin Mehta and the Israel Philharmonic; Performances with Berlin Philharmonic, Concertgebouw, IPO, Los Angeles Philharmonic, Philadelphia, Cleveland, Season 1987-88; Pittsburgh, Royal Philharmonic and Tokyo Philharmonic Orchestras. Recordings: Paganini Concerto No 1 with the Israel Philharmonic; Tchaikovsky and Sibelius Concertos with the Philharmonia Orchestra; Prokofiev's Concertos with the Zurich Tonhalle Orchestra; Brahms Concerto with the London Symphony; Glazunov and Shostakovich Concerto No 1 with the Royal Philharmonic; Brahms Sonatas with Dalberto. Honour: Won Soviet National Competition for Violinists, 1972. Address: c/o Terry Harrison Artists Management, The Orchard, Market Street, Charlbury, Oxon OX7 3PJ, England.

**BELL Edward (Eddie),** b. 2 August 1949, Airdrie, Scotland. Chairman; Director. m. Junette Bannatyne, 1 son, 2 daughters. Education: Airdrie High School. Appointments: Hodder & Stoughton, 1970-85, latterly Deputy Managing Director; Managing Director, Collins General Division, 1985-89; Deputy Managing Director, Fontana William Collins, 1985; Founder, Harper Paperbacks USA, 1989-90; Deputy Chief Executive and Publisher, 1990-91, Chief Executive and Publisher, 1991-92, Executive Chairman and Publisher, 1992-2000, Harper Collins; Non Executive Director, beCogent Ltd, 2000-; Non Executive Director, Haynes Publishing Ltd, 2000-; Non Executive Director, Management Diagnostics Ltd, 2001; Chairman, Those Who Can Ltd, 2001-; Non Executive Chairman OAG Worldwide Ltd, 2001; Partner Bell Lomax Literary and Sport Agency, 2002-. Memberships: RAC; Annabels; Autowink (Epsom); The Savage; Mannings Heath Club; The Addington Golf Club. Address: The Bell Lomax Agency, James House, 1 Babmaes Street, London SW1Y 6HF, England.

**BELL (John) Robin (Sinclair),** b. 28 February 1933, Edinburgh, Scotland. Writer to the Signet. m. Patricia Upton, 4 sons, 1 deceased. Education: BA, Worcester College, Oxford; LLB, Edinburgh University. Appointments: National Service: Commissioned, The Royal Scots (Berlin), 1951-53; Captain, Territorial Army, 1953-63; Solicitor, Coward Chance, London, 1961-62; Solicitor, 1963-94, Partner, 1963, Senior Partner, 1987-94, Tods Murray WS, Edinburgh; Member, Company Law Committee of Council of Bars and Law Societies of European Union, 1976-94; Council Member, 1975-78, Member, Company Law Committee, 1975-71, Law Society of Scotland; Non-Executive Director: Edinburgh Financial Trust plc, 1983-87, Upton and Southern Holdings plc, 1984-93, Citizens Advice Scotland, 1997-99, East of Scotland Water Authority, 1995-2002; Scottish Charities Nominee, 1995-2001. Honour: MBE, 1999; Memberships: New Club, Edinburgh; The Royal Scots Club, Edinburgh. Address: 29 Saxe Coburg Place, Edinburgh EH3 5BP, Scotland.

**BELL Martin,** b. 31 August 1938. Broadcaster. m. (1) Nelly Gourdon, 1971, 2 daughters, (2) Rebecca Sobel, 1983, (3) Fiona Goddard, 1998. Education: King's College, Cambridge. Appointments: Joined BBC, 1962; News Assistant, Norwich, 1962-64; General Reporter, London and Overseas, 1964-76; Diplomatic Correspondent, 1976-77; Chief, North American Correspondent, 1977-89; Berlin Correspondent, BBC TV News, 1989-93; Vienna Correspondent, 1993-94; Foreign Affairs Correspondent, 1994-96; Special Correspondent, Nine O'Clock News, 1997; Reported in over 70 countries, covered wars in Vietnam, Middle East, 1967, 1973, Angola, Rhodesia, Biafra, El Salvadore, Gulf, 1991, Nicaragua, Croatia, Bosnia; Independent Member of Parliament for Tatton, 1997-2001; Humanitarian Ambassador for UNICEF, 2001-. Publication: In Harms Way, 1995; An Accidental MP, 2000. Honours include: Royal TV Society Reporter of the Year, 1995; Institute of Public Relations President's Medal, 1996; Several honorary degrees. Address: 71 Denman Drive, London W11 6RA, England.

**BELL BURNELL (Susan) Jocelyn,** b. 15 July 1943, Belfast, Northern Ireland. Astronomer. m. Martin Burnell, (dissolved), 1 son. Education: BSc, University of Glasgow, 1965; PhD, Cambridge University, 1968. Appointments: Worked with Gamma-Ray Astronomy, University of Southampton, 1968; X-Ray Astronomy, Mullard Space Science Laboratory, 1974-82; Senior Research Fellow, Royal Observatory, Edinburgh; Scotland, 1982; Head, James Clerk Maxwell Telescope Section; Professor of Physics, Open University, Milton Keynes, England, 1991-99; Visiting Professor for Distinguished Teaching, Princeton University, 1999-2000; Dean of Science, University of Bath, 2001-; President, Royal Astronomical Society, 2002-04; Discovered first four pulsating radio stars (pulsars); Research contributions in the field of X-ray and gamma-ray astronomy; Frequent radio and TV broadcaster on science, on being a woman in science and on science and religion. Publications: 2 books; About 70 scientific papers and 35 Quaker publications. Honours: 14 honorary doctorates; Joseph Black Medal and Cowie Book Prize, Glasgow University, 1962; Michelson Medal, Franklin Institute, USA, 1973; J Robert Oppenheimer Memorial Prize, Center for Theoretical Studies, Florida, 1978; Beatrice M Tinsley Prize, American Astronomical Society, 1987; Herschel Medal, Royal Astronomical Society, 1989; Honorary Fellow, New Hall, Cambridge, 1996; CBE, 1999; Magellanic Premium, American Philosophical Society, 2000. Memberships: FRAS, 1969; International Astronomical Union, 1979; FInstP, 1992; American Astronomical Society, 1992; FRSA, 1999. Science Faculty Office, University of bath, Bath BA2 7AY, England.

**BELLAMY Matthew James,** b. 9 June 1978, Cambridge, England. Singer, pianist, songwriter, guitarist with band Muse. Albums (as Muse) include: Showbiz, 1999; Origin of Symmetry, 2001; Hullabaloo, 2002; Absolution, 2003. Hit Singles (as Muse) include; Muscle Museum, 1999; Uno, 1999; Unintended, 2000; Feelin' Good, 2001; New Born, 2001; Plug in Baby, 2001; Dead Star, 2002; Hysteria, 2003; Time is Running Out, 2003. TV Appearances include: Top of the Pops, 2001; Later With Jools Holland, 2001; Top of the Pops, 2002; CD:UK, 2003.

**BELLAMY David James,** b. 18 January 1933, England. Botanist; Writer. m. Rosemary Froy, 1959, 2 sons, 3 daughters. Education: Chelsea College of Science and Technology; PhD, Bedford College, London University. Appointments: Lecturer, Botany, 1960-68, Senior Lecturer, Botany, 1968-82, Honorary Professor, Adult Education, 1982-, University of Durham; Television and radio presenter, scriptwriter of series including: Bellamy's New World, 1983; Seaside Safari, 1985; The End of the Rainbow Show, 1986; Bellamy on Top of the World, 1987; Turning the Tide, 1987; Bellamy's Bulge, 1987-88; Bellamy's Birds Eye View, 1988; Moa's Ark, 1989-90; Special Professor of Botany, University of Nottingham, 1987-; Visiting Professor, Natural Heritage Studies, Massey University, New Zealand, 1989-91; Director, Botanical Enterprises, David Bellamy Associates, National Heritage Conservation Fund, New Zealand, Conservation Foundation, London. Publications: The Great Seasons, 1981; Discovering the Countryside with

David Bellamy, 4 volumes, 1982-83; The Mouse Book, 1983; The Queen's Hidden Garden, 1984; Bellamy's Ireland, 1986; Bellamy's Changing World, 4 volumes, 1988; England's Last Wilderness, 1989; How Green are You?, 1991; Tomorrow's Earth, 1991; World Medicine, 1992; Poo, You and the Poteroo's Loo, 1997; Bellamy's Changing Countryside, 1998; The Glorious Trees of Great Britain, 2002; Jolly Green Giant, autobiography, 2002; The Bellamy Herbal, 2003; Various books connected with television series. Honours: Officer of the Order of the British Empire; Dutch Order of the Golden Ark; UNEP Global 500 Award; Duke of Edinburgh's Award for Underwater Research; British Academy of Film and Television Arts; BSAC Diver of the Year; Richard Dimbleby Award; Chartered Institute of Water and Environmental Management, fellow. Memberships: Fellow, Linnaean Society; Founder-Director, Conservation Foundation; President, WATCH, 1982-83; President, Youth Hostels Association, 1983; President, Population Concern; President, National Association of Environmental Education. Address: Mill House, Bedburn, Bishop Auckland, County Durham DL13 3NW, England.

**BELLAMY J Andrew,** b. 13 September 1963, Wurzburg, Germany. Producer. Education: BA, Business, Economics, Colorado College, Colorado Springs, USA, 1985; AAS, Advertising and Communications, Fashion Institute of Technology, New York, New York, USA, 1987. Appointments: Senior Producer, Style with Elsa Klensch, CNN, New York, New York, 1987-2001; Producer, Unaired Pilot, Food with Love, NINE, New York, New York, 2004; Currently unemployed. Honours: Life Member, American Biographical Institute Inc; Listed in Who's Who publications and biographical dictionaries. Membership: Producers Guild of America, 2002-. Address: PO Box 647, New York, NY 10113-0647, USA. E-mail: andy.bellamy@verizon.net

**BELLINI Anna Lisa,** b. 6 February 1967, Rome, Italy. Pianist. m. Marco Nieddu. Education: Graduate with highest honours, Piano with Giuliana Bordoni Brengola, Conservatory Santa Cecilia, Rome; Studies with Maria Tipa, Scuola di Musica di Fiesole; Chamber Music with Riccardo Brengola, Accademia Musicale Chigiana di Siena. Career: Concerts in Italian cities including: Florence, Naples, Ferrara, Pistoia, Mantova, Genoa, Rome, Parma, Sienna, Modena, also in Germany, Chile, Japan, France, Belgium, Switzerland; Invited to Okinawa Moon Beach Music Camp and Festival, Japan and played for the Japanese Emperor Akihito and his wife, Michico on the occasion of their visit to Italy; During 2003 played: Beethoven's Concerto No 4 to celebrate Maria Tipo's 70th Birthday in Florence, Mozart's Piano Concerto K467 in the Glocke Bremen Grosser Saal, Hindemith's Die Vier Temperamente for piano and string orchestra at the International Festival- Hinterzarten in the Black Forest, Beetohoven's Concerto No 5 in the Anfitcatro in Sutri for the Sutri Beethoven Festival and Beethoven's Tripolo Concerto for the inauguration of the Teatro Auditorium in Chicti; Pianist with Trio Reger. Publications: Numerous reviews in magazines and newspapers. Honours: Special Price, E Iacovelli-Marchi, Conservatorio Santa Cecilia; Diploma d'Onore, Accademia Musicale Chigiana; First Prize: Concorso Martha Del Vecchio, Arenzano; XXV Concorso Nazionale (La Specia); Coppa d'Italia Competition, Osimo; Second Prize and Special Prize, Robert Schumann, M Clementi-Kawai Competition in Florence; Third Prize: Ennio Porrino Competition, Cagliari; Alberto Mazzati Competition, Milan; European Competition of Contemporary Music, Bela Bartok, Rome. Memberships: President, Associazione "Amici dell Musica di Sutri", Italy; Art Director, Sutri Beethoven Festival, 2002-. Address: Via della Dodecapoli 21, Sutri (VT) I-01015 Italy. E-mail: info@annalisabellini.it

**BELSKI Alexey Ivanovich,** b. 18 March 1936, Kurganie, Russia. Medical Educator. m. Halina Pavlovna Gvozdeva, 1956, 2 sons. Education: Graduate, Agricultural College, 1955; Diploma, 1966, PhD, 1968, Moscow Agricultural Institute. Appointments: Technick Sta, Pochinok, Russia, 1955-60; Gargarin, Russia, 1960-61; Headmaster, Agricultural Sta, Pochinok, 1961-69; Magister, Milioration & Farming Institute, Kagul, Moldova, 1969-71; Agricultural Academy, Kastroma, Russia, 1971-78; Physician, Agricultural University, Sumy, Ukraine, 1978-2000; Science Sta, Gardening, Tukums, Latvia, 1982-89; Firm Rosko, Sochi, Russia, 1991-95. Publications: Fruit & Berries plants near the Dneiper, 1966; The Difference of Nature, 1974; Biolingeum of Cherry Trees in European Part of the USSR, 1978; Industrial Technology of a Cherry Tree, 1992; Editorial board, Magnitology, 1978-; Contributed nurmerous articles to scientific journals. Honours: Big Golden Medal, 1974; Big Silver Medal, 1976. Memberships: Regional Society of Political and Scientific Knowledge (master); Regional Society of Nature Protection (master); World Academy of Science (Eurasia); World Laser Association; World Society of Gardeners. Address: University Agricultural Administration, 160 Kiriv Str, Sumy 40021, Ukraine.

**BELYAVSKIY Evgeniy Danilovich,** b. 26 August 1940, Taganrog, USSR. Radio Physicist. m. Lyudmila, 2 sons. Education: Engineering Degree, USSR, 1964; PhD, Radiophysics, Saratov University, 1970; D of Physics, Maths Science, USSR, 1987. Appointments: Worker, Mechanical Plant, Poltava, USSR, 1957-59; Engineer, Orion Research Institute, Kiev, 1965-70; Researcher, 1970-71; Senior Researcher, 1971-89; Head of Laboratory, 1989-96; Professor, Physics, Kiev Politechnical Institute, Ukraine, 1996-. Publications: 97 articles to professional journals. Address: kv 212, Prospect Majokovskogo 79, 02232 Kiev, Ukraine.

**BENAUD Richard,** b. 6 October 1930. Cricketer. m. Daphne Elizabeth Surfleet, 1967, 2 sons. Appointments: Right-Hand Middle-Order Batsman and Right-Arm Leg-Break & Googly Bowler, Played for New South Wales, 1948-49 to 1963-64 (Captain, 1958-59, 1963); Played in 63 Tests for Australia, 1951-52 to 1963-64 as Captain, 28 as Captain, scoring 2,201 runs, including 3 hundreds, taking 248 wickets; First to score 2,000 runs and take 200 wickets in tests; Scored 11,719 runs and took 945 wickets in 1st Class Cricket; Toured England, 1953, 1956, 1961; International Sports Consultant; TV Commentator, BBC, 1960-99; Channel Nine, 1977-, Channel 4, 1999-2005. Publications: Way of Cricket, 1960; Tale of Two Tests, 1962; Spin Me A Spinner, 1963; The New Champions, 1965; Willow Patterns, 1972; Benaud on Reflection, 1984; The Appeal of Cricket, 1995; Anything But...An Autobiography, 1998. Honours: OBE; Wisden Cricketer of the Year, 1962. Address: 19/178 Beach Street, Coogee, New South Wales 2034, Australia.

**BENDON Christopher Graham (Chris),** b. 27 March 1950, Leeds, Yorkshire, England. Freelance Writer; Critic. m. Sue Moules, 30 August 1979, 1 daughter. Education: BA, English, St David's University College, Lampeter, 1980. Appointments: Editor, Spectrum Magazine, 1983-88. Publications: Books: In Praise of Low Music, 1981; Software, 1984; Matter, 1986; Cork Memory, 1987; Ridings Writings - Scottish Gothic, 1990; Constructions, 1991; Perspective Lessons, Virtual Lines..., 1992; Jewry, 1995; Crossover, 1996; Novella, 1997. Chapbooks: Testaments, 1983; Quanta, 1984; Aetat 23, 1985; The Posthumous Poem, 1988; A Dyfed Quartet, 1992. Contributions to: Anthologies, magazines and journals. Honours: Hugh MacDiarmid Memorial Trophy, 1st Prize, Scottish Open Poetry Competition, 1988; £1000 Prize, Guardian/WWF Poetry

Competition, 1989; several awards, Royal Literary Fund. Membership: The Welsh Academy. Address: 14 Maesyderi, Lampeter, Ceredigion SA48 7EP, Wales.

**BENECKE Mark,** b. Germany. Forensic Biologist; DNA Typing Expert; Forensic Entomologist; Invertebrate Zoologist; Criminalist. Education: Biologist Diploma, Zoology, Genetics, Psychology, theory, 1994; Biologist Diploma, DNA Typing of Nematode Strains, Grade A thesis, 1995; PhD, DNA Typing of Biological Stains, summa cum laude, 1997. Appointments: Institute for Zoology, 1995, 1999, Institute for Legal Medicine, 1996, University of Cologne; Consultant, 1997, Forensic Biologist, Criminalist II, 1998, Chief Medicine Examiner's Office, New York City, USA; International Forensic Research and Consulting, Germany, 2000; Scientific Consultant, Colombian Association of Legal Medicine, Institute for Legal Medicine Bogota, Natural Sciences Research Institute of University of Manila, Genetics Department of Odessa University; Trainer, several police academies; Guest, Federal Bureau of Investigation Academy, Quantico, Virginia, USA; Visiting Assistant Professor, Consultant, Molecular Biology Department, University of the Philippines, Diliman, Metro Manila, Philippines; Assistant Visiting Professor, Department of Molecular Biology and Cell Biology, University for Medicine and Pharmacy, Hochiminh City, Vietnam; Visiting Scientist, Instituto Nacional de Medicina Legal y Ciencias Forenses, Bogota, Visiting Scientist: University of Antoquia, Medellin, Columbia; Guest Lecturer, Columbia University, Chief Medical Examiner's Office, John Jay College for Criminal Justice, all New York City, Universities of Berlin, Kaiserslautern, Bonn, Essen, Freiburg, Cologne and Konstanz, Germany; Singapore; China, police academies. Publications: Articles and papers on forensic entomology, DNA and DNA typing, and zoological topics; 3 popular science books: Encyclopedia of Scientists and Inventors, 1997; The dream of eternal life. Biomedicine as a key to longevity, 1998, 2002; Forensic Biology, 1999, 2001 and 2006; Murderous Methods: Criminal Cases of the 20th Century – A Pitaval, 2002 (German) and 2005 (English); Co-editor, Annals of Improbable Research; Guest editor, Forensic Science International and guest editor for Aggrawal's Journal of Forensic Medicine and Toxicology. Honours: Fortüne Scholarship, North Rhine Westphalia. Memberships: Fellow, Linnean Society of London; American Academy of Forensic Sciences; German Society for Legal Medicine; German Zoological Society; Society of German Natural Scientists and Medical Doctors; International Academy of Legal Medicine; International Society of Forensic Genetics; Colombian Society for Legal Medicine; Guangzhou Society for Legal Medicine, China. Address: Postfach 250411, 50520 Köln, Germany. Website: www.benecke.com

**BENEDICT Stewart Hurd,** b. 27 December 1924, Mineola, New York, USA. Writer; Editor. Education: AB, summa cum laude, Drew University, 1944; MA, The Johns Hopkins University, 1945; Study at New York University, 1946-49, 1961-64. Appointments: Instructor in German New York University, 1946-49; Assistant Professor, Humanities, Michigan Technical University, 1951-54, 1955-61; Assistant Professor of English, New Jersey City State College, 1961-64; Adjunct Professor of English: City College of New York, Rutgers University, Hudson County Community College, Essex County Community College, 1964-95; Drama Reviewer: Jersey Journal, 1964-71; Michael's Thing , 1990-2000, Stage Press Weekly, 2002-2003; Book Reviewer for Publishers Weekly, 1970-98. Publications: Books include: Tales of Terror and Suspense, 1963; The Teacher's Guide to ..., several books in a series, 1966-73; The Literary Guide to the United States, 1981; Street Beat, 1982; Curtain Going Up, 2002 Numerous plays, 1967-2003, include most recently: The Robbery, 1996; Absolutely Fabulous Fairy Tales,

1996; Fancy Bread, 1996; Be Still My Liver, 1996; Yuletide Treasure, 1996; The Hero, 1999; Homicidal Murders, 2002; The Gap, 2003; Humanoids Using Goodness, 2003; Chapters in books; Periodical articles; Translations; Encyclopaedia articles. Honours: Various prizes, North Jersey Press Association. Memberships: Dramatists Guild; Communications Workers of America; Democratic Party. Address: Apt 4-A, 27 Washington Square N, New York, NY 10011-9165, USA.

**BENEDICT XVI, His Holiness Pope, (Joseph Ratzinger),** b. 1927, Bavaria, Germany. Head of the Roman Catholic Church. Education: Traunstein seminary; Ordained Priest, Freising, Southern Germany, 1951. Appointments: Lecturer, Theology, University of Tuebingen, 1966-69; Lecturer, Dean and Vice-president, Regensburg University, Bavaria, 1969; Cardinal of Munich, 1977; Head of the Congregation for the Doctrine of the Faith (formerly Holy Office of the Inquisition), 1981-2005-; Elected Pope Benedict XVI, 2005-. Address: Apostolic Palace, 00120 Vatican City, Rome, Italy.

**BENIGNI Roberto,** b. 27 October 1952, Misericordia, Tuscany. Actor; Director; Writer. Creative Works: Films include: Beliungua ti voglio bene, 1977; Down By Law, 1986; Tutto Benigni, 1986; Johnny Stecchino, Night on Earth, 1992; Son of the Pink Panther, 1993; Mostro, Life is Beautiful, 1998; Asterisk & Obelisk, 1999; Pinocchio, 2002; Coffee and Cigarettes, 2003. Honours include: Academy Award, Best Actor and Best Foreign Film, 1998.

**BENING Annette,** b. 29 May 1958, Topeka, USA. Actress. m. (1) Steven White, divorced, (2) Warren Beatty, 1992, 4 children. Creative Works: Stage appearances in works by Ibsen, Chekhov and Shakespeare in San Diego and San Francisco; Other roles in Coastal Disturbances, The Great Outdoors; Films: Valmont; The Grifters; Regarding Henry; Guilty By Suspicion; Bugsy; Love Affair; The American President; Richard III; Blue Vision; Mars Attacks!; Against All Enemies; The Siege; In Dreams; American Beauty; Forever Hollywood; What Planet Are You From?; Open Range, 2003. Address: c/o Kevin Huvane, CAA, 9830 Wilshire Boulevard, Beverly Hills, CA 90212, USA.

**BENJAMIN Alexander,** b. 1 June 1924, London, England. Orthopaedic Surgeon. m. Barbara Yates, 2 sons, 2 daughters. Education: MB, BS, London, 1946; FRCS, England, 1953. Appointments: Honorary Lecturer, Postgraduate Institute of Orthopaedics, 1961; Consultant Orthopaedic and Traumatic Surgeon, West Herts Hospital Trust, 1961-. Publications: Book: Surgical Repair & Reconstruction in Rheumatoid Disease, 1980, 2nd edition, 1981; Book chapters: Forearm Fractures in Watson Jones Fractures & Joint Injuries 5th edition, 1978, 6th edition, 1982; Shoulder Double Osteotomy in Operative Shoulder Surgery Stephen Copeland, 1995; Papers in international journals include: Double Osteotomy for Painful Knee in Rheumatoid and Osteoarthritis, 1969; Double Osteotomy of the Shoulder, 1974; Double Osteotomy in the Fingers, 1974. Honours: Charrington Prize in Practical Anatomy, 1946; Sir Frederick Treves Prize in Clinical Surgery, 1946; The Most Venerable Order of the Hospital of St John and Jerusalem, 2003. Memberships: Fellow of the Royal Society of Medicine; Founder Member, Cerebral Palsy Surgical Society; Founder and Secretary, Rheumatoid Arthritis Surgical Society; Founder Member, British Orthopaedic Foot Surgery Society; Emeritus Member, Sicot; British Society for Surgery of the Hand. Address: Fosse House, Brownlow Road, Berkhamsted, Herts HP4 1HD, England. E-mail: bobbie_Alec@benjamin1.me.uk

**BENJAMIN Ellen J,** b. Boston, Massachusetts, USA. Private and Public Policy Analyst. Education: BA, Social

Service Administration and Policy, Park College, Parkville, Missouri, USA, 1976; Graduate Credits, Political Science, Public Administration and Labour Market Analysis, University of New Hampshire; Urban Studies Graduate Level Public Administration and Policy, Portland State University, Portland, Oregon, 1991-93. Appointments: Director of Policy and Advisor to the President of the Council, New England Council Inc.; Senior Policy Analyst for the Council of the State Governments Northeastern Committee on Human Service, New York City; Policy Advisor to the President of the New Hampshire State Senate, Director of Research for the entire Senate, Legislative Analyst for the Legislative Committee on Review of Agencies and Programs (Sunset Committee), Research Assistant in the Office of Legislative Services, Concord, New Hampshire; Research Associate for the Small Business Development Program, University of New Hampshire, Durham, New Hampshire; Committee Assistant, Maine Legislative Committee on Health and Institutional Services, Augusta, Maine; Assistant Director, Grant Writer, York County Employment and Training Agency, York County, Maine; Assistant Director of Adult Education, South Berwick, Maine; Sole Assistant to the Director of Planning and Research for all the programs administered by the Missouri Department of Social Services, Jefferson City Missouri; Currently, Public, Private Policy Analyst working in an independent consultant basis, Los Angeles, California. Publications: Human Capital: The Key to New England's Increased Productivity and Competitiveness, CSG Government News and ERC Conference Report Articles; Proceedings on productions of DC Seminar on Health Care Cost Containment in 1985 NYC and 1986 Annual AIDS Sessions; The Benjamin Report, in publication. Honours: International Who's Who of Women, 1992; Great Minds of the 21st Century (and nominated to Dedication), 2004; Great Women of the 21st Century, Premier Edition, 2004; Woman of the Year 2004, nominated by The American Biographical Institute Board of International Research for Private/Public Policy, 2004; 2000 Outstanding Intellectuals of the 21st Century, 2004; Empire Who's Who Registry of Executives and Professionals "Honors Edition", 2004-2005. Website: www.benjaminreport.com

**BENN Christoph,** b. 2 March 1960, Lubeck, Germany. Medical Doctor. m. Elisabeth Benn, 1 son, 2 daughters. Education: MD, University of Göttingen, Germany, 1984; MA, Applied Theology, University of Leeds, England, 1985; DTM&H, University of Liverpool, England, 1988; Master of Public Health, Johns Hopkins University, Baltimore, Maryland, USA, 1998. Appointments: Medical Superintendent, Bulongwa Hospital, Tanzania, 1988-92; Moderator, Working Group HIV/AIDS, World Council of Churches, 1994-96; Deputy Director, German Institute for Medical Mission, Tübingen, Germany, 1998-2003; Member, Board of Directors, Global Fund to Fight AIDS, TB, Malaria, 2002-2003; Director of External Relations, The Global Fund to Fight AIDS, TB and Malaria, 2003-. Publications: Ethics, Medical Ethics and HIV/AIDS, 1996; Equity and Resource Allocation: Dialogue Between Islam and Christianity. Medicine Health Care and Philosophy, 2002; Influence of Cultural and Religious Frameworks on Future of HIV/AIDS, 2002. Honours: Warrington Yorck Medal, University of Liverpool, 1988; Carl Taylor Award in Bioethics and Internal Health, 1998. Memberships: International AIDS Society; International Association of Physicians in AIDS Care; Deutsche Tropen Medizinische Gesellschaft. Address: Paul-Lechler Strasse 24, D-72076 Tübingen, Germany. E-mail: chrbenn@aol.com

**BENNETT Alan,** b. 9 May 1934, Leeds, England. Dramatist. Education: BA, Modern History, Oxford, 1957. Career: Junior Lecturer, Modern History, Magdalen College, Oxford, 1960-

62; Co-author and Actor, Beyond the Fringe, Edinburgh, 1960, London, 1961, New York, 1962; Fellow, Royal Academy; Author and Actor, On the Margin, TV series, 1966, Forty Years On, play, 1968. Plays: Getting On, 1971; Habeas Corpus, 1973; The Old Country, 1977; Enjoy, 1980; Kafka's Dick, 1986; Single Spies, 1988; The Wind in the Willows, 1990; The Madness of King George II, 1991, film, 1995; The Lady in the Van, 1999; TV scripts: A Day Out, 1972; Sunset Across the Bay, 1975; A Little Outing, A Visit from Miss Prothero, 1977; Doris and Doreen, The Old Crowd, Me! I'm Afraid of Virginia Woolf, All Day on the Sands, Afternoon Off, One Fine Day, 1978-79; Intensive Care, Our Winnie, A Woman of No Importance, Rolling Home, Marks, Say Something Happened, An Englishman Abroad, 1982; The Insurance Man, 1986; 102 Boulevard Haussmann, 1991; A Question of Attribution, 1991; Talking Heads, 1992; Talking Heads 2, 1998; Films: A Private Function, 1984; Prick Up Your Ears, 1987; The Madness of King George, 1994; TV documentaries: Dinner at Noon, 1988; Poetry in Motion, 1990; Portrait or Bust, 1994; The Abbey, 1995; Telling Tales, 1999; Publications: Beyond the Fringe, 1962; Forty Years On, 1969; Getting On, 1972; Habeas Corpus, 1973; The Old Country, 1978; Enjoy, 1980; Office Suite, 1981; Objects of Affection, 1982; The Writer in Disguise, 1985; Two Kafka Plays, 1987; Talking Heads, 1988; Single Spies, 1989; The Lady in the Van, 1991; The Wind in the Willows, 1991; The Madness of King George III, 1992, screenplay, 1995; Writing Home, 1994; The Clothes They Stood Up In, 1998; Talking Heads 2, 1998; The Complete Talking Heads, 1998; A Box of Alan Bennett, 2000; The Laying on of Hands, 2001; regular contributions to London Review of Books. Screenplays: A Private Function, 1984; Prick Up Your Ears, 1987; The Madness of King George, 1995. Honours: Honorary Fellow, Exeter College, Oxford; Honorary DLitt, Leeds; Evening Standard Award, 1961, 1969; Hawthornden Prize, 1988; 2 Olivier Awards, 1993; Evening Standard Award, 1996; Lifetime Achievement Award, British Book Awards, 2003. Address: Peter, Fraser and Dunlop, The Chambers, Chelsea Harbour, London, SW10 0XF, England.

**BENNETT John Makepeace,** b. 31 July 1921, Warwick, Queensland, Australia. Retired Computer Scientist. m. Rosalind Mary, 1 son, 3 daughters. Education: Southport CEGS; Universities of Queensland, Sydney, Melbourne and Cambridge. Appointments: 4 years RAAF Radar; 6 years Computer Department, Software and Computer Design Groups (Manchester and London), Ferranti Ltd; 31 years University of Sydney; Governor, ICCC, 1980-. Publications: Over 100 reports and papers in professional journals. Honours: IFIP Vice-President 1975-77; IFIP Silver Core Award, 1977; ACS Chips Award, 1981; Fulbright Award, 1981; ANCCAC Medal, 1984; AO (Officer of the Order of Australia), 1983; Fellow, Australian Academy of Technological Sciences and Engineering; Centenary Medal, 2003. Memberships: Program and Organising Committees of 12 international conferences. Address: PO Box 22, 26 Beatty Street, Balgowlah, NSW 2093, Australia.

**BENNETT Tony (Anthony Dominick Benedetto),** b. 3 August 1926, Astoria, USA. Singer; Entertainer. m. (1) Patricia Beech, 1952, 2 children, (2) Sandra Grant, 1971, 2 daughters. Education: American Theatre Wing, New York; University Berkeley, California. Appointment: Owner, Improv Records. Creative Works: Paintings exhibited at Butler Institute of American Art, Youngstown, Ohio, 1994; Records include: The Art of Excellence, 1986; Bennett/Berlin, 1988; Astoria: Portrait of the Artist, 1990; Perfectly Frank, 1992; Steppin Out, 1993; The Essence of Tony Bennett, 1993; MTV Unplugged, 1994; Here's to the Ladies, 1995; The Playground, 1998; Cool, 1999; The Ultimate Tony, 2000. Publication: The Good Life:

The Autobiography of Tony Bennett. Honours include: Several Grammy Awards and Gold Records.

**BENNION Francis Alan Roscoe,** b. 2 January 1923, Wallasey, Cheshire, England. m. (1) Barbara Elisabeth Braendle, 28 July 1951, divorced 1975, 3 daughters, (2) Mary Anne Field, 2 November 1977. Education: St Andrews University, Scotland, 1941; Balliol College, Oxford, 1946-48; BA, Law, 1949, MA, 1951, University of Oxford, England; Called to the Bar by Middle Temple, Jan 1951. Appointments: Royal Air Force Volunteer Reserve, Commissioned Pilot, 1941-46; Editor, Halsbury's Statutes with Butterworths, 1948; Lecturer and Tutor in Law, St Edmund Hall, University of Oxford, 1951-53; Practice at the Bar of England and Wales, 1951-94; Parliamentary Counsel, 1953-68, 1973-75; Chief Executive, Royal Institution of Chartered Surveyors, Governor of College of Estate Management, 1965-68; Research Associate, University of Oxford Centre for Socio-Legal Studies, Member of Law Faculty, University of Oxford, 1984-; Chairman, Oxford City Football Club, 1988-89. Publications: The Constitutional Law of Ghana, 1962; Professional Ethics: The Consultant Professions and Their Code, 1969; Tangling with the Law: Reforms in Legal Process, 1970; Consumer Credit Control, 1976-2004; The Consumer Credit Act Manual 1978, 3rd edition, 1986; Statute Law, 1980, 3rd edition, 1990; Statutory Interpretation, 1984, 4th edition, 2002; Victorian Railway Days, 1989; The Sex Code: Morals for Moderns, 1991; Understanding Common Law Legislation, 2001. Contributions to: Annual Volumes of All England Law Reports Annual Review, 1985-; Information Sources in Law, editor R G Logan, 1986; The Law Commission and Law Reform, editor G Zellick, 1988; Reviewing Legal Education, editor P Birks, 1994; Halsbury's Laws of England, 1995. Honours: Gibbs Law Scholar, Oxford University; Jenkyns Law Prize, Younger Prize, Paton Memorial Studentship, Balliol College, Oxford; Harmsworth Scholarship, Middle Temple. Memberships: Society of Authors, 1971-; Defence of Literature and the Arts Society, 1971-91; Society of Legal Scholars, 1984-; International Committee for the Defence of Salman Rushdie and his Publishers, 1988-90. Address: 11 Blueberry Downs, Coastguard Road, Budleigh Salterton EX9 6NU, England. Website: www.francisbennion.com. E-mail: fbennion@aol.com

**BENSON Glenwyn,** b. 23 November 1947, Newcastle upon Tyne. Television Executive. m. Ian Benson. 1 son, 1 daughter. Education: MA, History, Girton College, Cambridge, 1967-70; Frank Knox Fellowship, Harvard University, USA 1970-71; Executive Programme, Stanford University, USA, 1998. Appointments: Local newspapers and television, 1972-85; Deputy Editor, Weekend World, ITV, 1987-88; Editor, On the Record, BBC, 1992-95; Editor, Panorama, BBC, 1992-94; Head of Science, BBC, 1997-99; Head of Specialist Factual, 1999-2002; Head of Factual TV Commissioning, BBC, 2002-. Honours: News and Current Affairs Award, Woman in Film and Television, 2004; Fellow, Royal Society of Arts. Memberships: Royal Television Society; Governor of National Film and Television School. Address: BBC White City, 201 Ward Lane, London, W12, England. E-mail: glenwyn.benson@bbc.co.uk

**BENSON Valerie A,** b. 11 August 1949. Freelance Journalist; Artist; Writer; Educator; Gourmet Cook. Education: BA, MA, Fine Arts and Languages (Italian, Thai, Sanskrit & French), Columbia Pacific University; Graduate, Guatemalan Airborne School, 1993. Appointments: Professor of Art History, Waubonsee Community College; Swedish/American Gourmet Cook and Cookbook Author; Make a Difference Day volunteer, Points of Light Foundation, 1998; Designed the City of Warrenville's Sesquicentennial Mural; Artwork displayed at Art Institute of Chicago and Campanile Galleries. Publications: I've

Never Been to Sweden Cookbook; Contributor to Static-Line Airborne Connection Magazine, FATE Magazine. Honours: Mentioned in Brad and Francie Steiger's Book, Star People; First Woman to jump with Elite Parachute Forces in Honduras, 1993; Listed in national and international biographical dictionaries. Memberships: Lifetime Member, Warrenville Historical Society; Vastergoland Society.

**BENYON William Richard (Sir),** b. 17 January 1930, London, England. Landowner. m. Elizabeth Hallifax, 2 sons, 3 daughters. Education: Royal Naval College Dartmouth. Appointments: Served Royal Navy, 1947-57; Courtaulds Ltd, 1957-64; Landowner, 1964-; MP (Conservative), Buckingham, 1970-83, Milton Keynes, 1983-92; Parliamentary Private Secretary to Paul Channon as Minister for Housing, 1972-74; Opposition Whip, 1974-77; Member of the Executive, 1922 Committee, 1982-89. Honours: JP, Berkshire, 1962-77; DL, 1970; Knight, 1994; Vice-Lord Lieutenant of Berkshire, 1994-2005; High Sheriff of Berkshire, 1995. Memberships: Chairman: Peabody Trust, 1992-98; Chairman, Ernest Cook Trust, 1992-2004; Clubs: Boodle's; Pratt's; Beefsteak. Address: Englefield House, Englefield, Reading, Berkshire RG7 5EN, England. E-mail: benyuon@englefield.co.uk

**BENZI Roberto,** b. 12 December 1937, Marseille, France. Conductor. m. Jane Rhodes. Education: Sorbonne; Private music studies; Conducting with André Clutyens, 1947. Career: International Conductor with orchestras including: Orchestre National de France; Nouvel Orchestre Philharmonique; Orchestre de Paris; Parisien Colonne and Lamoureux Orchestras; London Symphony; London Philharmonic; Royal Philharmonic; Philharmonia Orchestra; Stockholm Philharmonic; Orchestre de la Suisse Romande; Zurich Tonhalle; Accademia Santa Cecilia di Roma; Concertgebouw of Amsterdam; Wiener Symphoniker; Guzenich Orchestra of Cologne; NDR of Hamburg; Dresdener Staatskapelle, Leipzig Gewandhaus Orchestra; Czech Philharmonic; Leningrad Philharmonic; State Orchestra of the USSR; Moscow Philharmonic; Israel Philharmonic; Cleveland and Philadelphia Orchestras; Pittsburgh Symphony; Montreal Symphony; Founder and Director of Orchestre de Bordeaux-Aquitaine, 1973-87; Permanent Conductor, Arnhem Philharmonic Orchestra, The Netherlands, 1989-98; Musical Director, Dutch National Youth Orchestra, 1990-95. Publications: Orchestrations of: J Brahms op 23: Variations on a theme by R Schumann; J Brahms op 24: Variations and Fugue on a theme by Haendel; E Satie: Je te veux, valse; G Rossini: Prelude, Theme and Variations for Horn. Honours: Knight, French Legion d'Honneur; Knight, French Ordre National du Mérite; Knight, Palmes Académique; Knight, Royal Order of Orange-Nassau. Address: 12 Villa Sainte Foy, 92200 Neuilly sur Seine, France.

**BENZING Rosemary Anne,** b. 18 September 1945, South India. Teacher; Counsellor; Freelance Journalist; Poet. m. Richard Benzing, 5 April 1969, 1 son, 1 daughter. Education: BA, Honours, English and Philosophy, University College of North Wales, Bangor, 1968; Diploma in Education, 1969; Diploma in Counselling, 1990. Appointments: Teacher, Edward Shelley High School, Walsall, 1968-71; Supply Teacher, Shropshire LEA, 1980-; Counsellor, SRCC, 1988-98. Contributions to: Hybrid; Foolscap; Folded Sheets; Smoke; Borderlines; Envoi; First Time; Purple Patch; Shropshire Magazine; Plowman; White Rose; Poetry Nottingham; Symphony; Psycho Poetica; Third Half; Krax; Bare Wires; Housewife Writers' Forum. Honour: Anglo Welsh Poetry Competition, 1986. Membership: Poetry Society. Address: Roden House, Shawbury, Shrewsbury, Shropshire, England.

**BERASATEGUI Vicente Ernesto,** b. 13 May 1934, Argentina. Ambassador. m. Teresita Mazza. Education: Degree in Law, School of Law, University of Buenos Aires, Argentina; Master in International Relations and Organisation, American University, Washington DC, USA. Appointments: Argentine Foreign Service: Attaché, 1954, Third Secretary, 1959, Second Secretary, 1962, First Secretary, 1966, Second Counsellor, 1967, First Counsellor, 1970, Minister Plenipotentiary, Grade B, 1973, Grade A, 1975; Ambassador Extraordinary and Plenipotentiary, 1985; Head, OAS Division of the Foreign Ministry, 1960; Embassy of the United States of America, 1961-65; Secretary, Policy Making Committee of the Minister for Foreign Affairs, 1967-69; Deputy to the Director General for Political Affairs of the Foreign Ministry, 1970-72; Deputy Permanent Representative to the United Nations, Geneva, 1972-76; Representative to 58 international conferences and meetings, 11 as Head of Delegation, 1959-76; Member of delegations to meetings with Heads of State or Government: Bolivia, 1971, Chile, 1971, Austria, 1994, Spain, 1994, France, 1995, Ireland, 1995, Germany, 1996, Turkey, 1996; Director for Western European Affairs of the Foreign Ministry, 1994-96; Ambassador of the Argentine Republic to the Kingdom of Denmark, 1997-2000; Currently Ambassador of the Argentine Republic to the United Kingdom of Great Britain and Northern Ireland; Numerous positions in the field of disarmament include: Head of the Argentine Delegation to the Conference of the Committee on Disarmament, 1974-76; Observer, First Review Conference of the Treaty on the Non-Proliferation of Nuclear Weapons, 1975; United Nations positions include, Secretary of the First Committee of the General Assembly, Deputy Secretary, Committee on Disarmament, 1980; Representative of the Secretary General, 1992-93; Member of the Advisory Board of the Secretary General on Disarmament Matters, 2001-; Academic activities include: Professor of Foreign Policy, School of Law, University of Buenos Aires, 1971; Professor, Graduate Institute of International Studies, Geneva, 1987-93; Lecturer on International Relations at institutes of advanced studies in Argentina, France and USA. Honours: Grand Cross, Order of the Dannebrod, Denmark; Grand Officer, Order of Distinguished Services, Peru; Commander: Order of Bernardo O'Higgins, Chile, Order of the Condor of the Andes, Bolivia, Order of Civil Merit, Spain, Order of Merit, Italy and France. Memberships: Pi Gamma Mu; Argentine Council for International Relations; Royal Institute for International Affairs, UK; International Institute for Strategic Studies, UK. Address: 65 Brook Street, London, W1K 4AH, England.

**BERECZ Endre,** b. 10 January 1925, Csorna, Hungary. Professor Emeritus. m. Maria Illés, 1 son, 1 daughter. Education: Chemist, 1949; Candidate of Chemical Sciences, CSc, 1954; Dr rer nat, 1960; Doctor of Chemical Science, DSc, 1974; Doctor honoris causa, University of Miskolc, 1995. Appointments: Assistant, First Assistant, Assistant Professor, Eötvös L University, 1949-63; Full Professor, Head of Department of Physical Chemistry, Technical University of Heavy Industries, Miskolc, 1963-92; Dean of the Faculty of Metallurgy, 1965-68; University of Miskolc, 1990-. Publications: 283 science and professional articles; Monographs: 1 Hungarian, 1 English; 8 chapters in monographs; 13 textbooks for university students; 7 patents; 101 reports on research works sponsored by grants and state foundations. Honours: Outstanding Worker of Education, 1968, Metallurgy, 1972; Silver Class Medal of the Order of Labour, 1976; Medals for the Human Environment, 1982, 1989; A Szent-Györgyi Prize, 1995. Memberships: Science and Technology Advisory Committee, 1983-95; Board of Administration, European Federation of Corrosion 1995-2001; National Representative, 1.2 Committee of IUPAC, 1985-

97; President, Hungarian Corrosion Association, 1992-2004. Address: H-1025 Budapest, Zöldmáli lejtö 5, Hungary.

**BEREDER Frédéric Laurent,** b. 18 May 1960. Architect. m. Jin Wu, 1 son, 1 daughter. Education: Master in Architecture, France, 1986; Diploma, Tokyo Institute of Technology, Japan, 1991; First Class Architect and Building Engineer, Japan, 1997. Appointments: Director, Duct Sarl, 1986-89; Representative, Dumez Japan, 1991-93; Advisor, SE Corporation, 1993-96; President, Nichifutsu Sekkei KK, 1997-2003; Chairman, BEREDER Co Ltd (was Nichifutsu Sekkei KK), 2003-; Adviser, INGEROSEC, 2003-. Honours: 1st Prize Artificial Reefs, 1989; International Order of Merit, IBC; Listed in several biographical publications. Memberships: Ordre des Architects; College Architectural Expert; International College for Architect Experts; The Japan Institute of Architects; Tokyo Society of Architects and Building Engineers. Address: BEREDER Co Ltd, Kannai Keihin Bldg, 2-4-2 Ogi-Cho Naka-Ku, Yokohama 231-0027, Japan. Website: www.bereder-select.com

**BERESNEVICH Vitaly,** b. 14 August 1952, Belarus, Minsk. Scientist. m. Galina, 2 daughters. Education: Mechanical Engineer, Riga Polytechnical Institute, 1975; Candidate, Technical Sciences, 1984; Dr Sc Eng, 1992. Appointments: Assistant Doctoral Student, Riga Polytechnical Institute, 1975-80; Researcher, Riga Technical University, 1980-85; Senior Researcher, 1985-. Publications: 132 scientific publications; Non linear and parametric oscillations of technological vibromachines, 1991. Honours: Honorary Diploma, 1985; Silver Medal, Outstanding Scientists of the 20th Century, IBC, 1999; Listed in numerous Who's Who and other biographical publications. Memberships: New York Academy of Science, USA; Research Board of Advisors, ABI, 1999-. Address: Riga Technical University, 1 Kalku Street, Riga, LV-1658, Latvia. E-mail: vitalijs.beresnevics@rtu.lv

**BERESNIEWICZ Aleksander,** b. 5 April 1927, Lithuania. Research Chemist. m. Irene Corcoran, 5 sons. Education: PhD, Physical Chemistry, University of Illinois, USA, 1954. Appointments: Promoted to Research Fellow, 1983-, E I du Pont Nemours & Co; Retired, 1990. Publications: Several publications; 17 patents. Memberships: Sigma Xi; American Chemical Society; New York Academy of Sciences. Address: 2501 Elmdale Lane, Wilmington, DE 19810, USA.

**BERG Adrian,** b. 12 March 1929, London, England. Artist; Painter. Education: Gonville and Caius College, Cambridge; Trinity College, Dublin; St Martin's and Chelsea Schools of Art; Royal College of Art. Career: One-man exhibitions in London, Florence, Düsseldorf, Montreal, Toronto, Chicago; Arts Council, Serpentine Gallery; Paintings 1977-86, Piccadilly Gallery; Touring Exhibition, A Sense of Place, Barbican Centre, London, Bath, Plymouth, Gwent, Sheffield, Newcastle upon Tyne, Edinburgh, 1993-94; Royal Academy, 1992-94, watercolours, 1999; Work in Collections: Arts Council; British Museum; European Parliament; Government Picture Collections; Hiroshima City Museum of Contemporary Art; Tate Gallery, Tokyo Metropolitan Art Museum. Honours: Gold Medal, Florence Biennale, 1973; Major Prize, Tolly Cobbold Eastern Arts Association Exhibition, 1981; Third Prize, John Moores Liverpool Exhibition, 1982-83; First National Trust Foundation for Art Award, 1987; First Prize, RWS Open, 2001. Memberships: RA; Honorary Fellow RCA, 1994. Address: c/o Royal Academy of Arts, Burlington House, Piccadilly, London W1J 0BD, England.

**BERG Paul,** b. 30 June 1926, New York, New York, USA. Molecular Biologist. Education: Graduated, Pennsylvania State

University, 1948; Doctorate, Western Reserve University, 1952. Appointments: American Cancer Society Research Fellow, Institute of Cytophysiology, Copenhagen, School of Medicine, Washington University, St Louis, 1952-54; Several positions, Washington University, 1955-74; Assistant Professor, Associate Professor, Microbiology Department, School of Medicine, 1955-59, Professor of Microbiology, 1959-69, Chairman, Microbiology Department, 1969-74; Wilson Professor of Biochemistry, Medical Centre, Stanford University, 1970-94; Director, Beckman Center for Molecular and Genetic Medicine, 1985-2001; Chair, National Advisory Committee, Human Genome Project, 1990-92; Robert W Cahill Professor of Cancer Research, 1994-2000; Director, National Foundation for Biomedical Research, 1994-; Research in genetic engineering, particularly DNA recumbent techniques; Advocated restrictions on genetic engineering research. Publications: Genes and Genomes, 1991; Dealing with Genes: The Language of Heredity, 1992; Exploring Genetic Mechanisms, 1997. Honour: Nobel Prize for Chemistry (with Walter Gilbert and Frederick Sanger), 1980. Address: Stanford University School of Medicine, Beckman Center, B-062, Stanford, CA 94305, USA.

**BERGER André,** b. 30 July 1942, Acoz, Belgium. Professor. m. M A Lallemand, 3 daughters. Education: MS, Meteorology, MIT, 1971; DSc, Catholic University Louvain, Belgium, 1973; Dr Honoris Causa, University Aix-Marseille, France, 1989; Docteur honoris causa de l'Université Paul Sabatier, Toulouse, 2000; Dr honoris causa, Faculté Polytechnique de Mons, 2004. Appointments: Assistant, University Catholic Louvain, 1965-73, Suppléant, 1973-76, Chargé de Cours, 1976-84, Head Institute of Astronomy and Geophysics, 1978-2001, Professor, 1984-89, Ordinary Professor, 1989-; Visiting Professor, Vrij Universiteit, Brussels, 1982-92, maitre de conference, University Liège, Belgium, 1985-93; Chaire Francqui, 1989; Chairman, Panel Special Program on Science of Global Environment Change NATO, 1992-93; Chairman, Special Program Panel in Air-Sea Interactions, 1981; Chairman International Commission Climate, 1987-93; Chairman, Paleoclimate Commission International Quaternary Association, 1987-95; President of European Geophysical Society, 2000-02; Member, Hearings Board European Parliament and Belgium Ministry of Research; Member, Science Council Gaz de France, 1994-99, Member Environment Council Electricité de France, 1998-; Member of the Scientific Committee of European Environment Agency, 2002-; Member, Scientific Council of Meteo-France, 2001-; Vice Chairman, 1998-99, Chairman, 2000-03, Expert Advisory Group on Global Change, Climate and Biodiversity of the European Commission; Member, Scientific Council of Centre National de le Recherche Scientifique, France, 2002-04; Member, Comité d'Orientation Scientifique et Stratégique du Collège de France, 2003-. Publications: Le Climat de la Terre, un passé pour quel avenir?, 1992; Editor: Climatic Variations and Variability: Facts and Theories, 1981; Co-Editor: Milankovitch and Climate, Understanding the Response to Orbital Forcing, 1984; Understanding Climate Change, 1989; Contributor, research articles on climatic variations and climate modelling to professional journals. Honours: Recipient, Médaille d'Argent de Sa Sainteté, Pope Paul VI, Vatican, 1979; Prix de la première biennale Italian Society Physics, 1980; Prix Charles Lagrange, Classe des Sciences Academie Royale des Sciences, des Lettres et des Beaux-Arts de Belgique, 1984; Norbert Gerbier-Mumm International Award, World Meteorological Society; Golden Award of European Geophysical Society, 1989; Milutin Milankovitch Medal, 1994; Prix quinquennial du Fonds National de la Recherche Scientifique de Belgique, 1995; European Latsis Prize, 2001; Knighted, 1996; Academia Europaea, 1989, Council Member, 1993-99; Koninklijke Nederlandse Akademie van Wetenschappen, Foreign Member, 1997; Fellow of American Geophysical Union, 1999; Associate Foreign Member, Académie des Sciences, Paris, 2000; Member of the Royal Academy of Sciences, Letters and Arts Belgium, 2002; Associate, The Royal Astronomical Society, 2003; Honorary President of European Geo-Sciences Union; Chevalier de la Legíon d'Honneur in France, 2004. Memberships: International Union of Geodesy and Geophysics, Lecturer, 1987; World Institute Science; American Geophysical Union; American Meteorological Society; Royal Meteorological Society, Foreign Member. Address: Catholic University Louvain, Institute Astronomy and Geophysics G Lemaitre, 2 Chemin du Cyclotron, B-1348 Louvain-la-Neuve, Belgium. E-mail: berger@astr.ucl/ac/be

**BERGER John,** b. 5 November 1926, London, England. Author; Art Critic. Education: Central School of Art; Chelsea School of Art, London. Appointments: Painter, Teacher of Drawing; Visiting Fellow, BFI, 1990-; Numerous TV appearances and exhibitions. Publications include: Fiction: A Painter of Our Time, 1958; The Foot of Clive, 1962; Corker's Freedom, 1964; Pig Earth, 1979; Once in Europa, 1989; Lilac and Flag, 1991; To The Wedding, 1995; Photocopies, 1996; King: A Street Story, 1999; Non-fiction includes: About Looking, 1980; Another Way of Telling, 1982; And Our Faces; My Heart; Brief as Photos, 1984; The White Bird, 1985; Keeping a Rendezvous (essays and poems), 1992; Titian: Nymph and Shepherd, 1996; Steps Towards a Small Theory of the Visible, 1996; The Shape of a Pocket, 2001; John Berger Selected Essays, 2001; Radio: Will It Be A Likeness? 1996; Poetry and translations. Honours include: New York Critics Prize, Best Scenario of Year, 1976; George Orwell Memorial Prize, 1977; Prize, Best Reportage, Union of Journalists and Writers, Paris, 1977. Address: Quincy, Mieussy, 74440 Taninges, France.

**BERGER Thomas (Louis),** b. 20 July 1924, Cincinnati, Ohio, USA. Author. m. Jeanne Redpath, 12 June 1950. Education: BA, University of Cincinnati, 1948; Postgraduate Studies, Columbia University, 1950-51. Appointments: Librarian, Rand School of Social Science, New York City, 1948-51; Staff, New York Times Index, 1951-52; Associate Editor, Popular Science Monthly, 1952-53; Distinguished Visiting Professor, Southampton College, 1975-76; Visiting Lecturer, Yale University, 1981, 1982; Regent's Lecturer, University of California at Davis, 1982. Publications: Crazy in Berlin, 1958; Reinhart in Love, 1962; Little Big Man, 1964; Killing Time, 1967; Vital Parts, 1970; Regiment of Women, 1973; Sneaky People, 1975; Who is Teddy Villanova?, 1977; Arthur Rex, 1978; Neighbors, 1980; Reinhart's Women, 1981; The Feud, 1983; Nowhere, 1985; Being Invisible, 1987; The Houseguest, 1988; Changing the Past, 1989; Orrie's Story, 1990; Meeting Evil, 1992; Robert Crews, 1994; Suspects, 1996; The Return of Little Big Man, 1999; Best Friends, 2003; Adventures of the Artificial Woman, 2004. Other: Plays and screenplays: Other People, Stockbridge Theatre festival, 1970. Honours: Dial Fellow, 1962; Rosenthal Award, National Institute of Arts and Letters, 1965; Western Heritage Award, 1965; Ohiona Book Award, 1982; Pulitzer Prize Nomination, The Feud, 1984; LittD, Long Island University, 1986. Address: PO Box 11, Palisades, NY 10964, USA. E-mail: dca@doncongdon.com

**BERGKAMP Dennis,** b. 20 May 1969, Amsterdam, Netherlands. Footballer. m. Henrita Ruizendaal, 1 son, 1 daughter. Appointments: Striker, Played for Ajax Amsterdam 1986-92, Holland, 1990-2000, Inter Milan, 1992-95, Arsenal, London, England, 1995-; All-time leading scorer for Holland. Honours: Dutch Player of the Year, 1992, 1993; English Player of the Year, 1998; Football Writers' Player of the Year, 1998.

Address: c/o Arsenal F C, Arsenal Stadium, Avenell Road, London N5 1BU, England.

**BERGMAN Ingmar,** b. 14 July 1918, Uppsala, Sweden. Film Director; Theatre Producer. m. (1) Ingrid Karlebovon Rosen, 1971, deceased, 1995, 8 children. Education: Stockholm University. Career: Producer, Royal Theatre, Stockholm, 1940-42; Scriptwriter, Producer, Svensk Filmindustri, 1940-44; Theatre Director, Helsingborg, 1944-46; Gothenburg, 1946-49, Malmo, 1954-63; Leading Director, Royal Dramatic Theatre, Stockholm, 1963; Director, Mme de Sade Theatre, 1989; Chair, European Cinema Society, 1989-; Plays include: A Painting on Wood. The City, The Rite, The Lie, Scenes From a Marriage, To Damascus, 1974; The Merry Widow, Twelfth Night, 1975; Tartuffe, 1980; King Lear, 1985; John Gabriel Borkman, 1985; Miss Julie, 1986; Hamlet, 1986; Maria Stuart, 2000. Films include: Crisis, 1945; It Rains on Our Love, 1946; A Ship Bound for India, 1947; Music in Darkness, 1947; Port of Call, 1948; Prison, 1948; Thirst, 1949; To Joy, 1949; Summer Interlude, 1950; This Can't Happen Here, 1950; Waiting Women, 1952; Summer with Monika, 1952; Sawdust and Tinsel, 1953; A Lesson in Love, 1954; Journey into Autumn, 1955; Smiles of a Summer Night, 1955; The Touch, 1971; Cries and Whispers, 1972; Scenes From A Marriage, 1974; The Serpent's Egg, 1977; Fanny and Alexander, 1981; After the Rehearsal, 1984; Private Confessions, 1998; TV: Making Noise and Acting Up, 1996; Scriptwriter, The Best Intentions, 1991, Faithless, 2000. Publications: Four Stories, 1977; The Magic Lantern (autobiography), 1988; Fanny and Alexander, 1989; Images: My Life in Film, 1993; Sunday's Child, 1994; Private Confessions, 1997. Honours include: Erasmus Prize, 1965; Award, Best Director, National Society of Film Critics, 1970; Order of the Yugoslav Flag, 1971; Luigi Pirandello International Theatre Prize, 1971; Goethe Award, Frankfurt, 1976; Gold Medal, Swedish Academy, 1977; European Film Award, 1988; Le Prix Sonning, 1989; Praemium Imperiale Prize, Japan, 1991; Dorothy & Lilian Gish Prize, 1995. Membership: Swedish Academy of Letters.

**BERGR Věroslav,** b. 25 May 1928, Lomnice, Semily, Czech Republic. Painter; Sculptor; Graphic Artist; Illustrator. m. Zdenka Vovsová-Bergrová, 7 May 1952. Education: Student, Ukrainian Academy, Prague, 1950-58; Student, School of Plastic Arts, Prague, 1958-63. Career: Head of Research, Mechanical Workshop, Prague, 1960-89; Co-Author, Czechoslovak patentee #147719; Chief Illustrator, Světova Literatura periodical, 1975-. Publications: 2 monographs, 1992, 1996. Honours: Medal of Prague Uprising, 1945; Laureate of the Franz Kafka Award, 1998; State Medal of 55th Anniversary of the End of the Second World War, 2000. Memberships: Association of Painters. Commissions and Creative Works: 25 autonomous expositions, 1959-98; 45 collective expositions; Illustrator of 48 books, mostly poetry; Sculptor, memorial grave #74, Vyšehrad cemetery; Artwork represented in many galleries in Czech Republic and other countries. Address: Marie Cibulkové 30, CZ 14000 Prague 4, Czech Republic.

**BERGROVÁ Zdenka,** b. 10 March 1923, Prague, Czech Republic. Poet; Author; Translator. m. Věroslav Bergr, 7 May 1952. Education: PhD, Charles University, Prague, 1990. Publications: Author, A Fairy Tale in Verse, 1946; To The Sole Reader, Verses 1968-73, 1990; Fly, Ye Birds' Notes, Verses, 1990; Prague is a Seal, Verses, 1990; Words of a Night, Verses, 1996; Humour Has a Black Bottom, Verses, 1996; Shimmy and other monkey tales, 2002; Vortoj de la nokto, Esperanto verses, 2002; Translated and published 70,000 verses: Pushkin, Lermontov, Chevtchenko, N A Někrasov, Jesenin, Pasternak, Verlaine, Sonnets William Shakespeare and others, 1949-2005.

Honours: 1st place, Screenplay Competition, Prague, 1946; Medal of Barricade Fighters for Freedom Association, Prague, 1945; Medal for Translations from Chevtchenko, Kyiv, 1962; Laureate of the Franz Kafka Award, Prague, 1999; State Medal of 55th Anniversary of the End of the Second World War, Prague, 2000; Public acknowledgement from the Capital Prague for attendance at Prague rising in 1945, 2002; Diploma and T G Masaryk Medal (sculpted by Otakar Spaniel) for life-long literary work, Masaryk Academy of Arts, 2002; Josef Jungmann Medal for Literary work, Eastern Nations Friends Society, Czech Republic, 2003. Memberships: Society of Writers; Society of Translators. Address: Marie Cibulkové 30, CZ 14000 Prague 4, Czech Republic.

**BERGSJØ Per Bjarne,** b. 17 March 1932, Baerum, Norway. Professor Emeritus. m. Jenny Benjaminsen, 2 sons, 1 daughter. Education: MD, Faculty of Medicine, Oslo University, 1956; Residencies in surgery, obstetrics, gynaecology, gynaecological oncology, pathology and anaesthesiology, 1956-1969; Dr Med, University of Oslo, 1968; Specialist, Obstetrics and Gynaecology, Norway, 1969; ECFMG, 1969;. Appointments: Associate Professor, University of Bergen, Norway, 1971-72; Associate Professor, Faculty of Medicine, University of Oslo, 1973-80; Lectured, Johns Hopkins University, 1985; Head of Department, Gynaecology and Obstetrics, Akerhus Central Hospital, Norway, 1973-80; Professor I, Department of Obstetrics and Gynaecology, University of Bergen, Norway, 1980-1999; Consultant, The Norwegian System of Compensation to Patients, -2001. Guest scientist, Norwegian Institute of Public Health, Oslo, Norway, 2003-. Publications: 430 titles or articles in referred scientific journals, review and editorial articles, books and chapters in monographs and textbooks; Textbooks, monographs and special reports include: General plan of obstetrics and gynaecology in Norway, 3 volumes, 1976-78; Svangerskapsomsorg i allmennpraksis, 1985, revised 1991, 1998; Obstetrikk, 1987, revised 1993, 1998, 2000; Gynekologi, 1990, revised 1997, 2000; Obstetrikk og gynekologi, 2004. Author: Action against AIDS, The Mutan Report, 1996. Honours: The Schering Prize, Norwegian Gynaecological Society, 1992. Memberships include: The Norwegian Medical Association; The Federation of Scandinavian Societies of Obstetrics and Gynaecology; The Norwegian Gynaecological Society; The Norwegian Non-fiction Writers and Translators Association, 1989-; Society of Research Scientists, 1991-; Society of Senior Physicians, 2000-; Fellow, Royal Society of Medicine, UK. Address: Bergheimveien 11 C, N-1367 Snarøya, Norway. E-mail: p-bergsj@online.no. Office: Norwegian Institute of Public Health, Division of Epidemiology, P.O. BOX 4404 Nydalen, No – 0403 Oslo, Norway. E-mail: Per.Bergsjo@fhi.no

**BERGSTRÖM Lars Magnus,** b. 14 April 1966, Södertälje, Sweden. Scientist; Physical Chemistry. Education: MSc, 1990, PhD, 1995, Royal Institute of Technology, Stockholm. Appointments: Research and Teaching Assistant, Royal Institute of Technology, 1990-96; Postdoctoral Scientist, Riso National Laboratory, Condensed Matter Physics and Chemistry Department, Denmark, 1996-99; Associate Professor, Department of Chemistry, Surface Chemistry, Royal Institute of Technology, 1999-2004; Associate Professor, Department of Pharmacy, Pharmaceutical Physical Chemistry, Uppsala University, 2004-. Publications include: Fluctuations Promoting the Spontaneous Formation of Surfactant Micelles and Vesicles, 1995; Thermodynamics of Surfactant Micelles and Vesicles, 2001. Membership: European Colloid and Interface Society. Address: Department of Pharmacy, Pharmaceutical Physical Chemistry, Uppsala University, SE-75125, Uppsala, Sweden. E-mail: magnus.bergstrom@farmaci.uu.se

**BERKOFF Steven, b.** 3 August 1937, London, England. Writer; Director; Actor. m. (1) Alison Minto, 1970, (2) Shelley Lee, 1976, divorced. Education: Webber-Douglas Academy of Dramatic Art, London, 1958-59; École Jacques Lecoq, Paris, 1965. Appointments: Director of plays and actor in numerous plays, films and TV; Founding Director, London Theatre Group, 1973; Massage, performed at Edinburgh Festival, 1997; Shakespeare's Villains, Theatre Royal, Haymarket, UK and World Tour, 1998, 1999. Plays: In the Penal Colony, 1968; Metamorphosis, 1969; Agamemnon, 1973, 1984; The Fall of the House of Usher, 1974; The Trial, 1976; East, 1978; Hamlet, 1980, 2001; Greek, 1980; Decadence, 1981; West, 1983; Harry's Christmas, 1985; Kvetch and Acapulco, 1986; Sink the Belgrano!, 1986; With Massage, 1987; Lunch, Dog, actor, 1994; Brighton Beach Scumbags, 1994; Dahling You Were Marvellous, 1994; Coriolanus, 1996; Mermaid, 1996; Massage, 1997; Shakespeare's Villains, 1998; Messiah, 2000; Films include: Octopussy; First Blood 2; Beverley Hills Cop; Absolute Beginners; War and Remembrance; The Krays; Decadence. Publications: America, 1988; I am Hamlet, 1989; A Prisoner in Rio, 1989; The Theatre of Steven Berkoff: Photographic Record, 1992; Coriolanus in Deutschland, 1992; Overview, collected essays, 1994; Free Association, autobiography, 1996; Graft: Tales of an Actor, 1998; Shopping in the Santa Monica Mall, 2000; Ritual in Blood, 2000; Messiah, 2000; Oedipus, 2000; The Secret Love Life of Ophelia, 2001. Honours: Los Angeles Drama Critics Circle Award, 1983; Comedy of the Year Award, Evening Standard, 1991. Address: c/o Joanna Marston, Rosica Colin Ltd, 1 Clareville Grove Mews, London SW7 5AH, England.

**BERLIN Barry Adrian, b.** 9 October 1957, Aston, Birmingham. Barrister. m. Sally Louise Berlin. Barrister. Education: BSc, Law, Government, Policy and Modern History, 1980; Called to the Bar, Gray's Inn, 1981. Appointments: Practising Barrister, St Philips Chambers; Leader at the Bar (Consumer Law) – Chambers and Partners; Practice includes: Health and safety at work, trading standards, white collar fraud, environmental protection, food safety and licensing, for local authorities, multi-national companies and government agencies (including the Environment Agency); Appointed to the Attorney General's A-List for Crime, 2003; Appointed Recorder, Midlands Circuit, 2005. Publications: Section 80 of Environmental Protection Act, 1990; Regulation of Investigatory Powers Act, 2000; Human Rights Act, 1998; Criminal Justice Act, 2003; Guides to Local Authorities. Membership: Criminal Bar Association. Address: St Philips Chambers, 55 Temple Row, Birmingham B2 5LS, England. E-mail: bberlin@st-philips.co.uk

**BERLUSCONI Silvio, b.** 1936, Milan, Italy. Politician; Businessman. Education: University of Milan. Appointments: Owner, building and property development company, 1962-; Business interests include: Fininvest; Milan 2 Housing project, 1969; Canale 5 Network, 1980-; Owner, Italia 1 TV network, 1983; Owner, Rete 4 TV network, 1984; Stakeholder, La Cinq commercial TV network, 1985; Stakeholder, Chain, Cinema 5; Owner, Estudios Roma, 1986; Owner, Milan AC Football Club, 1986; Owner, La Standa department store, 1988; Chairman, Arnoldo Mondadori Editore SpA, 1990, half-share, 1991; Founder, President, Forza Italia political movement, 1993-; Full time political career, 1994-; Prime Minister of Italy, 1994, 2001-; MEP, 1999; Minister of Foreign Affairs, 2002; Stood trial on corruption charges. Address: Office of the Prime Minister, Palazzo Chigi Piazza Colonna 370, 00187 Rome, Italy.

**BERMAN Isaac b.** 1913, Russia, Israeli Citizen 1921. Barrister-at-Law; Politician. Education: Teachers Training College, Jerusalem; University College, London; Inner Temple, London.

Appointments: Served with British Army, WWII, 1943-45; Manager, Willis Overland & Kaizer Assembly Plant, Haifa, Israel, 1950-54; Private Law Practice, Tel-Aviv, 1954-; Served with IDF with rank of Major; Speaker of the Knessett, Israel, 1980-81; Minister of Energy and Infrastructure, Israel, 1981-82. Publications: Articles in Jerusalem Post, Haaretz, Maariv, Yediot Ahronot and periodicals. Address: PO Box 32351, Tel-Aviv 61322, Israel.

**BERNE Stanley, b.** 8 June 1923, Port Richmond, Staten Island, New York, USA. Research Professor; Writer. m. Arlene Zekowski, July 1952. Education: BS, Rutgers University, 1947; MA, New York University, 1950; Graduate Fellow, Louisiana State University, Baton Rouge, 1954-59; PhD, Marlborough University, 1990. Appointments: Associate Professor, English, 1960-80, Research Professor, English, 1980-, Eastern New Mexico University, Portales; Host, Co-Producer, TV series, Future Writing Today, KENW-TV, PBS, 1984-85. Publications: A First Book of the Neo-Narrative, 1954; Cardinals and Saints: On the aims and purposes of the arts in our time, 1958; The Dialogues, 1962; The Multiple Modern Gods and Other Stories, 1969; The New Rubaiyat of Stanley Berne (poetry), 1973; Future Language, 1976; The Great American Empire, 1981; Every Person's Little Book of P-L-U-T-O-N-I-U-M (with Arlene Zekowski), 1992; Alphabet Soup: A Dictionary of Ideas, 1993; To Hell with Optimism, 1996; Dictionary of the Avant-Gardes, 1998; Gravity Drag, 1998; The Living Underground, 1999; Swimming to Significance, 1999; Extremely Urgent Messages, 2000; Empire Sweets - or How I Learned to Live and Love in the Greatest Empire on Earth!; Legal Tender - or It's All About Money!; You and Me - or How to Survive in the Greatest Empire on Earth! Contributions to: Anthologies and other publications. Honours: Literary research awards, Eastern New Mexico University, 1966-76. Memberships: PEN; New England Small Press Association; Rio Grande Writers Association; Santa Fe Writers. Literary Agent: Pamela Tree, Rising Tide Press, PO Box 6136, Santa Fe, New Mexico. Address: Box 4595, Santa Fe, NM 87502, USA.

**BERNSTEIN Carl, b.** 14 February 1944, Washington, District of Columbia, USA. Journalist; Writer. m. Nora Ephron, 14 April 1976, divorced, 2 sons. Education: University of Maryland, 1961-64. Appointments: Copyboy to Reporter, Washington Star, 1960-65; Reporter, Elizabeth Journal, New Jersey, 1965-66, Washington Post, 1966-76; Washington Bureau Chief, 1979-81, Correspondent, 1981-84, ABC-TV; Correspondent, Contributor, Time magazine, 1990-91; Visiting Professor, New York University, 1992-93; Contributing Editor to Vanity Fair, 1997-; Executive Vice President and Executive Director, Voter.com, -2001. Publications: All the President's Men (with Bob Woodward), 1973; The Final Days (with Bob Woodward), 1976; Loyalties: A Son's Memoir, 1989; His Holiness (with Marco Politi), 1996. Honours: Drew Pearson Prize for Investigative Reporting, 1972; Pulitzer Prize Citation, 1972; Honorary LLD, Boston University, 1975. Address: c/o Janklow and Nesbit Associates, 598 Madison Avenue, New York, NY 10022, USA.

**BERNSTEIN Marcelle, b.** 14 June 1945, Manchester, England. Writer; Journalist. m. Eric Clark, 12 April 1972, 1 son, 2 daughters. Appointments: Staff, The Guardian, Daily Mirror, Observer. Publications: Nuns, 1976; Sadie, 1983; Salka, 1986; Lili, 1988; Body and Soul, (dramatised as a prizewinning 6 part television series), 1991; Sacred and Profane, 1995, (filmed as Le Pacte du Silence, 2003); Saints and Sinners, 1998. Contributions to: Numerous US and UK magazines. Honours: Arts Council Award, 1986; Helene Heroys Award, 1988. Memberships:

Society of Authors. Address: Carole Blake, Blake Friedmann Agency, 122 Arlington Road, London, NW1 7IIP, England.

**BERRY Chuck (Charles Edward Anderson Berry),** b. 18 October 1926, St Louis, USA. Singer; Composer. m. Thermetta Suggs, 1948, 4 children. Appointments: TV Appearances, 1955-. Creative Works: Albums: After School Sessions, 1958; One Dozen Berry's, 1958; New Juke Box Hits, 1960; Chuck Berry, 1960; More Chuck Berry, 1960; On Stage, 1960; You Can Never Tell, 1964; Greatest Hits, 1964; Two Great Guitars, 1964; Chuck Berry in London, 1965; Fresh Berrys, 1965; St Louis to Liverpool, 1966; Golden Hist, 1967; At the Fillmore, 1967; Medley, 1967; In Memphis, 1972; Concerto in B Goods, 1969; Home Again, 1971; The London Sessions, 1972; Golden Decade, 1972; St Louis to Frisco to Memphis, 1972; Let the Good Times Roll, 1973; Golden Decade vol II, 1973, vol V, 1974; Bio, 1973; Back in the USA, 1973; I'm a Rocker, 1975; Chuck Berry 75, 1975; Motovatin, 1976; Rockit, 1979; Chess Masters, 1983; The Chess Box, 1989; Missing Berries, 1990; Rarities, 1990; On the Blues Side, 1993. Films: Go, Johnny Go, Rock, Rock, Rock, 1956; Jazz on a Summer's Day, 1960; Let the Good Times Roll, 1973; Hail! Hail! Rock 'n' Roll, 1987. Publication: Chuck Berry: The Autobiography, 1987. Honours include: Grammy Award for Life Achievement, 1984. Address: Berry Park, 691 Buckner Road, Wentzville, MO 63385, USA.

**BERRY Francis,** b. 23 March 1915, Ipoh, Malaysia. Poet; Writer; Professor Emeritus. m. (1) Nancy Melloney Graham, 4 September 1947, 1 son, 1 daughter, (2) Eileen Marjorie Lear, 9 April 1970. Education: University College of the South West, 1937-39, 1946-47; BA, University of London, 1947; MA, University of Exeter, 1949. Appointments: Professor of English Literature, University of Sheffield, 1967-70; Professor of English, Royal Holloway, University of London, 1970-80. Publications: Gospel of Fire, 1933; Snake in the Moon, 1936; The Iron Christ, 1938; Fall of a Tower, 1943; The Galloping Centaur, 1952; Murdock and Other Poems, 1955; Poets' Grammar, 1958; Morant Bay and Other Poems, 1961; Poetry and the Physical Voice, 1962; Ghosts of Greenland, 1966; The Shakespeare Inset, 1966; I Tell of Greenland, 1977; From the Red Fort, 1984; Collected Poems, 1994. Contributions to: Periodicals; BBC; Observer; Notes and Queries. Membership: Fellow, Royal Society of Literature. Address: 4 Eastgate Street, Winchester, Hampshire SO23 8EB, England.

**BERRY Halle,** b. 14 August 1968, Cleveland, Ohio, USA. Actress; Model. m. (1) David Justice, 1993, divorced 1996, 1 daughter, (2) Eric Benet, 2001. Career: Numerous formal beauty contests in 1980s; TV and Film actress, 1989-; Films: Strictly Business, 1991; Jungle Fever, 1991; The Last Boy Scout, 1991; Boomerang, 1992; Father Hood, 1993; Alex Haley's Queen, 1993; The Program, 1993; The Flintstones, 1994; Losing Isaiah, 1995; The Rich Man's Wife, 1996; Executive Decision, 1996; Race the Sun, 1996; Girl 6, 1996; B.A.P.S, 1997; Why Do Fools Fall in Love, 1998; The Wedding, 1998; Bulworth, 1998; Victims of Fashion, 1999; Ringside, 1999; Introducing Dorothy Dandridge (also producer), 1999; X-Men, 2000; Swordfish, 2001; Monster's Ball, 2001; James Bond: Die Another Day, 2002; X-Men 2, 2003; Gothika, 2003; TV appearances: TV debut in sitcom Living Dolls, 1989; Knots Landing, 1991-92. Honours: Harvard Foundation for Intercultural and Race Relations Award; Golden Globe for Best Actress, Screen Actor's Guild Award, 1999; Academy Award, 2002; NAACP Award for Best Supporting Actress, 2003. Membership: National Breast Cancer Coalition. Address: c/o William Morris Agency, 151 South El Camino Drive, Beverly Hills, LA 90212, USA.

**BERRY Robert James,** b. 26 October 1934, Preston, England. University Teacher. m. Caroline, 1 son, 2 daughters. Education: Gonville and Caius College Cambridge; University College London. Appointments: Professor of Genetics, University College London, 1978-2000; President: Linnean Society, 1982-85, British Ecological Society, 1987-89, European Ecological Federation, 1990-92, Mammal Society, 1995-98. Publications: Books: Teach Yourself Genetics, 1965; Adam and the Ape, 1972, 1975; Inheritance and Natural History, 1977; Natural History of Shetland, 1980; Neo-Darwinism, 1982; Free to Be Different, 1984; Natural History of Orkney, 1985; God and Evolution, 1988, 2000; God and the Biologist, 1996; Science, Life and Christian Belief, 1998; Orkney Nature, 2000; God's Stewards, 2002; God's Book of Works, 2003; Editor of 10 books; About 200 papers in scientific and other journals. Honours: UK Templeton Award for long and distinguished advocacy of the Christian faith among scientists, 1996; Marsh Award for Ecology, 2001. Memberships: Natural Environment Research Council, 1981-87; Human Fertilisation and Embryology Authority, 1990-96; Trustee, National Museums and Galleries on Merseyside, 1985-94; Chairman, 1968-87, President, 1993-95, Christians in Science; General Synod of the Church of England, 1970-90; Moderator, Environmental Issues Network of Churches Together in Britain and Ireland, 1989-. Address: Quarfseter, Sackville Close, Sevenoaks, Kent TN13 3QD, England.

**BERRY Roger Julian,** b. 6 April 1935, New York, USA. Physician. m. (Joseline) Valerie (Joan) Butler. Education: BA, New York University, 1954; BSc, 1957, MD, 1958, Duke University, Durham, North Carolina; DPhil, 1967, MA, Magdalen College, Oxford; MRCP, 1971; FRCP; 1978; FRCR, 1979; Honorary FACR, 1983; MFOM, 1988; FFOM, 1993. Appointments: Head, Radiobiology Laboratory, Churchill Hospital, Oxford, 1969-74; Royal Naval Reserve, 1971-92, Principal Medical Officer (Reserves), 1987-88, Captain Medical Training (Reserves) on staff of Commander-in-Chief, Naval Home Command, 1988-90; Head, Neutrons and Therapeutic Effects Group, MRC Radiobiology Unit, Harwell, 1974-76; Sir Brian Windeyer Professor of Oncology, Middlesex Hospital School of Medicine (University of London), 1976-87; Director, Health Safety and Environmental Protection, British Nuclear Fuels plc, 1987-92; Director, Westlakes Research Institute, Cumbria, 1992-95; Commissioner, International Commission on Radiological Protection, 1985-89; Chairman, British Committee on Radiation Units and Measurements, 1995-2000; Visiting Professor, Institute of Environmental and Natural Sciences, Lancaster University, 1993-2003; Trustee, Bishop Barrow's Charity and Governor King William's College, 2000-. Publications: Book: Manual on Radiation Dosimetry (with N W Holm), 1970; Contributions to: Oxford Textbook of Medicine; Florey's Textbook of Pathology; Hunter's Diseases of Occupation; Over 190 scientific papers in medical journals. Honours include: Academic: Roentgen Prize, 1970, Silvanus Thompson Memorial Lecturer, 1991, British Institute of Radiology; Douglas Lea Memorial Lecturer, Institute of Physical Sciences in Medicine, 1993; Civil: Freeman of the City of London, 1982; Reserve Decoration, 1986; Honorary Physician to HM The Queen, 1987-90; OStJ, 1990. Memberships: President, 1986-87, British Institute of Radiology; Yeoman, 1981, Liveryman, 1984, Worshipful Society of Apothecaries of London; Fellow, Society for Radiological Protection, 1991-; Associate Member, The Nautical Institute, 1998-; Royal Overseas League; Royal Naval Sailing Association. Address: 109 Fairways Drive, Mount Murray, Santon, Douglas, Isle of Man IM4 2JE, United Kingdom. E-mail: r.j.b@advsys.co.uk

**BERTIE, His Most Eminent Highness Frà Andrew,** b. 15 May 1929, London, England. Head of State. Education: Ampleforth College, 1943-47; MA, Christ Church, Oxford, 1951-54; School of Oriental and African Studies, London University, 1959-60. Appointments: Lieutenant, Scots Guards, 1948-50; City Press, 1954-57; Ethicon, 1957-59; Worth School, 1960-83; Elected 78th Prince and Grand Master of the Sovereign Military Hopitaller Order of St John of Jerusalem of Rhodes and of Malta, 1988-. Address: Palazzo Malta, via Condotti 68, 00187 Rome, Italy.

**BERTOLAMI Orfeu,** b. 3 January 1959, São Paulo, Brazil. Physicist. m. M C Bento, October 1992, 1 daughter. Education: Graduate, Physics, São Paulo University, 1981; MSc, Inst Fís Teórica, São Paulo, 1983; Advanced Degree, Mathematics, University of Cambridge, England, 1984; PhD, Physics, University of Oxford, England, 1987. Appointments: Post-doctoral Positions; Institut für Theoretische Physik; University of Heidelberg, Germany, 1987-89; Instituto de Física and Mat, Lisbon, Portugal, 1989-91; Associate Professor, Departmento Física, Instituto Superior Técnico, Lisbon, 1991-; Scientific Associate, Theory Division, CERN, 1993-95; Research Associate, Istituto Nazionale Fisica Nucleare, Turim, 1994-95; Visiting Scholar, Physics Department, New York University, 1999. Publications: Over 115 Publications; 72 of which in specialised international Physics Journals. Honours: Honorary Mentions in the Essay Contest, Gravity Research Foundation, USA, 1995, 1997, 2001, 2003; Third Prize, 1999; Prémio União Latina (Latin America, Portugal), 2001. Memberships: Sociedade Portuguesa de Física; Sociedade Portuguesa de Astronomia. Address: Instituto Superior Técnico, Dept Física, Av Rovisco Pais, 1049-001, Lisboa, Portugal. E-mail: orfeu@cosmos.ist.utl.pt Website: http@//alfa.ist.utl.pt/~orfeu/homeorfeu.html

**BERTOLUCCI Bernardo,** b. 16 March 1940, Parma. Film Director. m. Clare Peploe, 1978. Creative Works: Director: La Commare Secca, 1962; Prima della Rivoluzione, 1964; Il Fico Infruttuoso in Vangelo 70, 1968; Partner, 1970; La Strategia del Ragno, 1970; Il Conformista, 1970; Last Tango in Paris, 1972; 1900, 1975; La Luna, 1979; Tragedy of a Ridiculous Man, 1981; The Last Emperor, 1986; The Sheltering Sky, 1989; Little Buddha, 1993; Stealing Beauty, 1995; I Dance Alone, 1996; Besieged, 1998. Publications: In cerca del mistero (poems), 1962; Paradiso e inferno (poems), 1999. Honours: Viareggio Prize, 1962; European Film Award, 1988. Address: c/o Jeff Berg, ICM, 8942 Wilshire Boulevard, Beverly Hills, CA 90211, USA.

**BERTRAND Bernard Marie Ghislain,** b. 28 June 1949, Saint Denis, Belgium. Otorhinolaryngologist. m. Christine Lamarque, 1 son, 1 daughter. Education: MD, Catholic University of Louvain, 1974; ORL, 1978;. Appointments: Resident, 1979; Adjunct Head of Clinic, 1982; Consultant Intern, Cliniques Universitaires St-Luc, Brussels; Associate Head of Clinic, 1989, Associate Head of Department, 1993. Head and Chairman of Department of ENT, Cliniques Universitaires, Catholic University of Louvain de Mont-Godinne, 1995; Professor, Catholic University of Louvain, 1995. Publications: Author and co-author of over 700 papers and communications presented at national and international conferences and symposia; Author and co-author of over 120 papers in scientific journals including most recently: Transnasal endoscopic orbital decompression and Graves' ophthalmopathy, 2000; Secondary ciliary dyskinesia in upper respiratory tract, 2000; Les manifestations allergiques de la spère ORL, 2001; La valve vestibulaire ou valve narinaire: concept et description, 2001; La polypose naso-sinusienne – Résultats à un an de la chirurgie endoscopique endosinusienne

suivie d'une corticothérapie topique chez 72 patients, 2001; Is septal deviation a risk factor for chronic sinusitis? Review of literature; Author and co-author of 17 books and book chapters. Honours: Glaxo Allen Award, 1995; Prix du meilleur poster, 1997; Prix Acta Medica, 1998; Glaxo Wellcome Award, 2000. Memberships include: European Rhinologic Society, 1983-; French and Belgian Societies of Otorhinolaryngology and Cervico Facial Surgery. 1984-; European Academy of Facial Plastic Surgery, 1985; International Member, American Academy of Facial Plastic and Reconstructive Surgery, 1985; American Rhinologic Society; International Society for Laser Surgery and Medicine, 1988; European Academy of Allergology and Clinical Immunology, 1992; Member of the Jury, Prix Acta Medica Belgica, 2001; President of the Jury, GlaxoSmithKline Awards in Rhinology, 2001. Address: ENT Department, Cliniques Universitaires de Mont-Godinne, Ave Dr Terasse-Yvoir, B5530 Belgium. E-mail: bernard.bertrand@orlo.ucl.ac.be

**BERWIND Robert T,** b. 1 August 1939, Mineapolis, Minnesota, USA. Physician; Minister. m. Alison Berwind. Education: BSc, Colgate University, Hamilton, New York, 1961; MD, 1965, Urology Residency, 1965-70, Jefferson Medical University, Philadelphia, Pennsylvania; DD, University of Liverpool, Liverpool, England, 1990; PhD, Theology, Trinity Seminary, 1996. Appointments: Missionary Doctor, Zimbabwe, Africa, 1975-90; Private Practice, Urology, Houson, Texas, 1990-. Address: PO Box 877, Coldspring, TX 77331. E-mail: rberwind@eastex.met

**BESSON Luc,** b. 18 March 1959, Paris, France. Film Director. 1 daughter. Appointments: Assistant, Films in Hollywood and Paris; 1st Assistant for several advertising films. Creative Works: Films directed and produced: Le Dernier Combat, 1982; Subway, 1984; The Big Blue, 1988; Nikita, 1990; Atlantis, 1991; The Professional, 1994; Leon, 1994; The Fifth Element, 1996; Joan of Arc, 1999; The Messenger, 1999; The Dancer, 2000; Exit, 2000; Yamakasi, 2001; Baiser mortel du dragon, 2001; Le Transporteur, 2002; Taxi 3, 2003; Tristan, 2003; Cheeky, 2003; Vice & Versa, 2003; Crimson Rivers 2: Angels of the Apocalypse, 2004.

**BEST George,** b. 22 May 1946. Footballer. m. (1) Angela Macdonald Janes, 1978, 1 son, (2) Alexandra Jane Pursey, 1995. Appointments: Joined Manchester United, 1963; 381 League Appearances (137 goals); 46 Football Association Cup Competition appearances (21 goals); 25 League Cup Competition appearances (9 goals); 34 European Competition Appearances (11 goals); Represented Northern Ireland 37 times; Sports Commentator, Sky TV. Honours: Irish Footballer of the Year, 1967; European Footballer of the Year, 1968; British Footballer of the Year, 1969, 1971; Sky TV Greatest Sportsman Award, 1995; Total Sport Magazine Greatest Sportsman of All Time; BBC Lifetime Achievement Award, 2002. Address: c/o British Sky Broadcasting Ltd, Grant Way, Middlesex TW7 5QD, England.

**BEST Keith Lander,** b. 10 June 1949, Brighton, England. Chief Executive; Barrister. m. Elizabeth Gibson, 2 daughters. Education: BA (Hons) Jurisprudence, MA, Keble College, Oxford. Appointments: Called to the Bar, 1971; Lecturer in Law, Central London Polytechnic, 1973; General common law practice as barrister, 1973-87; Brighton Borough Councillor, 1976-80: Chairman of Lands Committee; Member of Parliament, Anglesey/Ynys Môn, 1979-87; Parliamentary Private Secretary to Secretary of State for Wales, 1981-84; Chairman (voluntary, unpaid), Executive Committee, World Federalist Movement/Institute for Global Policy, 1987-;

Director, Prisoners Abroad (national charity), 1989-93; Chairman, Conservative Action for Electoral reforms, 1992- ; Chief Executive Immigration Advisory Service (national charity), 1993-; Chairman, Electronic Immigration Network (national charity), 1996-; Chairman, Electoral Reform Society, 1997-2003; Chairman, Association of Registered Immigration Advisers, 2003-; Trustee, Odyssey Trust, 2003-; Director of Electoral Reform International Services Ltd; Named on Society Guardian as one of the 100 Most Influential People in Public Services in the UK, September 2003; Served in airborne and commando forces leaving with the rank of Major, Territorial Army, 1967-87. Publications: Write Your Own Will, 1978; The Right Way to Prove a Will, 1981; Various articles in magazines, Wall Street Journal, newspapers; Former Deputy Editor District Council Revue. Honours: Territorial Decoration; Freeman of the City of London. Memberships include: management Committee, Brighton Housing Trust; Chairman, Vauxhall Conservative Association, 1997-98; Amnesty; FRSA. Address: 15 St Stephen's Terrace, London SW8 1DJ, England. E-mail: keith.best@iasuk.org

**BEST Ronald O'Neal,** b. 25 May 1957, London, England. Artist. Education: Byam Shaw School of Art; Croydon College of Art; RCA, London; Assistant to Winston Branch, painter. Career: Painter and printmaker, oils, etchings, watercolours; Teacher, Essendine Centre, 1989-91, Kensington and Chelsea College, 1994; Litho Teacher, Heatherley School of Fine Art, London, 1997-2001; Co-ordinator, Visual Arts, Portobello Festival; Founder, Chelsea Painters and Printmakers, 1999; Manager, Notting Hill Fine Art Gallery; Co-ordinator, Art for the Unemployed, Portobello Academy of Drawing. Exhibitions: Royal Institute of Oil Painters; New English Art Club; Pastel Society; Society of Graphic Art; Salon des National, Paris; Lynn Stern Young Artists, London; Eva Jekel Gallery; Twentieth Century British Art Fair; Royal College of Art, London; 1492-1992 Un Nouveau Regard sur les Caraibes, Paris; Art House, Amsterdam; Pall Mall Deposit Gallery; The Portobello Group; W11 Gallery; Gallery Café; Portobello Printmakers; Notting Hill Fine Art. Work in collections: Royal College of Art; Croydon College; Grange Museum, London. Address: 50 Berkhamsted Avenue, Wembley, Middlesex, England.

**BETHE Hans Albrecht,** b. 2 July 1906, Strasbourg, Germany (now France) (US Citizen). Physicist; Astronomer. Education: University of Frankfurt; PhD, University of Munich, 1928. Appointments: Instructor, Physics, University of Frankfurt, University of Stuttgart, 1928-29; Lecturer, Universities of Munich and Tübingen, 1930-33; Moved to Britain prior to World War II, 1933; University of Manchester, 1933-34; Assistant Professor, 1935, Professor, 1937-75; John Wendell Anderson Professor of Physics, Cornell University; Chief, Theoretical Physics Division, Los Alamos Science Laboratory, New Mexico, USA; Consultant, Los Alamos, 1947-. Honours: Morrison Prize, New York Academy of Sciences, 1938, 1940; American Medal of Merit, 1946; Draper Medal, National Academy of Sciences, 1948; Planck Medal, 1955, 1961; Nobel Prize for Physics, 1967; Fermi Award; National Medal of Science, 1976. Memberships: Fellow, American Physical Society, President, 1954; Foreign Member, Royal Society, 1957. Address: Newman Laboratory, Cornell University, Ithaca, NY 14853, USA.

**BETKE Klaus (Hermann),** b. 30 October 1914, München, Germany. Emeritus Professor of Paediatrics. m. (Gertrud) Katharine Hein, 5 sons, 2 daughters. Education: Medical Education, Universities of Freiburg, Königsberg, Berlin; Paediatric Training: University Children's Hospitals of Würzburg, Erlangen, Freiburg. Appointments: Professor of Paediatrics and Chairman of the Children's Hospitals:

Tübingen, 1961-67, München, 1967-83; Emeritus, 1983; Counsellor-at-Large, International Society of Haematology, 1972-91; Vice-President, Deutsche Akademie d. Naturforscher Leopoldina, 1980-90; Secretary General, UNESPA, 1976-83. Publications: Der menschliche rote Blutfarbstoff bei Fetus und reifem Organismus, 1954; Hämatologie der ersten Lebenszeit, 1958; Keller/Wiskott: Lehrbuch d. Kinderheilkunde (Editor 5th edition, 1984, 6th edition, 1991); Elementare Päiatrie (Editor, 1st edition 1973, 4th edition, 1991). Honours: Bayerischer Verdienstorden 1970; Bayerischer Orden für Wissenschaft und Kunst (Maximiliansorden), 1981; Otto-Heubner-Preis, 1983; Dr med. honoris causa, Bochum, 1987. Memberships: Deutsche Akademie d. Naturforscher Leopoldina; Finnische Akademie d. Wissenschaften; Bayerischer Akademie d. Wissenschaften. Address: An der Dornwiese 18, D-82166, Lochham, Germany.

**BETTON David John William,** b. 30 December 1947, Hammersmith, London. Barrister. m. Gillian Mary. 1 son, 3 daughters (from a previous marriage). Education: BA, MA, Law, Emmanuel College, Cambridge; College of Law. Appointments: Called to the Bar, 1972; Senior Legal Advisor, HM Customs and Excise, 1976-86; National Director of VAT, Clark Whitehill Chartered Accountants, 1986-91; Senior VAT Consultant, KPMG LLP Chartered Accountants, 1991-. Publications: VAT and Printing; VAT: A Guide for Practitioners. Honours: Freeman, City of London; Liveryman Worshipful Company of Plumbers. Membership: MCC. Address: c/o KPMG, PO Box 486, 1 Puddle Dock, London EC4V 3PD, England.

**BEWES Richard Thomas,** b. 1 December 1934, Nairobi, Kenya. Anglican Clergyman; Writer. m. Elisabeth Ingrid Jaques, 18 April 1964, 2 sons, 1 daughter. Education: Marlborough School, 1948-53; MA, Emmanuel College, Cambridge, 1954-57; Ridley Hall Theological College, Cambridge, 1957-59. Publications include: The Church Reaches Out, 1981; The Church Marches On, 1986; When God Surprises, 1986; A New Beginning, 1989; The Resurrection, 1989; Speaking in Public - Effectively, 1998; The Lamb Wins, 2000; Talking About Prayer, 2000; The Bible Truth Treasury, 2000; The Stone That Became a Mountain, 2001; Wesley Country, 2001; The Top 100 Questions, 2002; Words That Circled the World, 2002; Beginning the Christian Life, 2004; 150 Pocket Thoughts, 2004. Contributions to: Decision Magazine. Honours: OBE, 2005. Membership: Guild of British Songwriters. Address: 50 Curzon Road, Ealing, London W5 1NF, England.

**BEYER Rolf,** b. 27 May 1947, Wiesmoor, Ostfriesland, Germany. Writer. m. Marie-Martine Fillâtre. Education: Johannes Gutenberg University, Mainz, Germany; University of Heidelberg, Germany, 1968-72. Appointments: Teacher, Primary and Secondary Schools for the Handicapped, Mannheim, Germany, 1972-80; Lecturer, Internationales Studienzentrum, University of Heidelberg, 1980-; Staff Member, Weslyan University, Massachusetts, USA, 1982; Staff Member, Polytechnic of North London, England, 1983; Staff Member, Miami University, Ohio, USA, 1995; Guest Lecturer, International Education Centre, Shah Alam, Malaysia, 2002-. Publications: Author: Ideology and Illusions, 1981; Hegel as political thinker, 1983; The unbound Prometheus, 1985; Germany today. Politics-Economics-Society, 1986; The Queen of Sheba, 1987; Female mystics in Middle Ages, 1989; Visions and Ecstasies, 1993; King Solomon, 1993; Audiobooks: Ruins of Conscience - Hans Henny Jahnn, 1984; King Solomon, 1990; The dream of golden ages, 1990; The Mystery of Beauty, 1991; French Philosophers, 1992; Ancient Mystery Cults, 1993; Poems in World Literature, 1994; Violence, 1995; Marguerite Duras, 1995; Taboos - do we need them? 1996; Abbé Pierre, 1996; Marguerite Yourcenar, 1997; Roland Barthes, 1997; Culture of

Native people, 1997; The Goddesses in Us, 1998; Myths-Stories about our Origin, 1999; The Mystery of Religion, 1999; History of Betrayal, 2000; The Transcendent Voice, 2000; Philosophy Today, 2001; Philosophy of History, 2002; Waiting, 2002; Trust in Reason – Immanuel Kant, 2004; Friedrich Schiller, 2004. Honours: Included in Kuerschner's Book Calendar, 2003, 2004; Listed in Who's Who publications and biographical dictionaries. Address: Friedrich-Ebert-Strasse 25, D-69207 Sandhausen, Germany. E-mail: rolf.beyer@urz.uni-heidelberg.de

**BHANDARI Debkala,** b. 28 December 1957, Lumbini, Gulmi, Dhurkot Vastu-7, Nepal. Gynaecologist. m. Chandra Prasad Bhusal, 1 son. Education: SLC Board, Nepal; Certificate Level, Tribhuvan University; Bachelor, Medicine & Surgery, GA Medical College, Patna, India; Master's degree, Guyane Ayurved in BHU, India; PhD, Infertility, in progress. Appointments: Nursing; Medical practice, integration of Ayurvedic and Western medicines, 59 districts of Nepal, 27 years; Social Worker; Researcher; Government employee. Publications: Role of Daruharidra in yoni Vrana; Antimicrobial effect of Crude extract of B Asiatica; and others. Honours: Aiswarya Scholarship; Best Employer, Gorkha Dakshin Bahu; Good Administrator Award; Good Governance Award; Great Women of the 21st Century Award; and others. Address: Regional Ayurvedic Hospital, Dang, Vijauri, Nepal.

**BHARADWAJ Prem Datta,** b. 20 May 1931, Gorakhpur, Uttar Pradesh, India. Professor of Physics. m. Vidya Wati Sharma, 14 February 1949, 3 sons, 1 daughter. Education: BS, NREC College, Khurja, 1st class with Merit, Uttar Pradesh, India, 1950; MS, 1st class, 1st, Agra University, Agra, Uttar Pradesh, India, 1952; PhD, SUNY, Buffalo, New York, USA 1964. Appointments: Assistant Professor, Physics, B R College, Agra, India, 1952-54, 1959-60; Lecturer, Physics, Government Colleges, Uttar Pradesh Director of Education, India, 1954-59; Graduate Assistant, Department Physics, SUNY, Buffalo, New York, USA, 1960-62; Assistant Professor, Physics, 1962-64, Associate Professor, Physics, 1964-66, Professor, Physics, 1966-, Chairman, Physics Department, 1976-86, Niagara University, New York, USA; Honorary Consultant, NSF, USA, 1966-71; Visiting Professor, Department Crystallography, Roswell Park Cancer Institute, Buffalo, New York, USA, 1970-71; Honorary Reviewer, Physics, NYS Regents Examinations, 1976. Publications: Co-author, Intermediate Agriculture Physics and Climatology, book, 1954; Several publications in professional journals. Honours include: 1994 Hind Rattan (Jewel of India) Award for Outstanding Service, Achievements and Contributions among Non-Resident Indians, from Government of India, 1995; Rajiv Gandhi National Unity Award for excellence, from Government of India, 1995; Honoured for Outstanding Work in field of Education and Community Service, India Association Buffalo, 1997. Memberships: American Physical Society; India Association Buffalo, Co-Founder, 1961, Executive Committee Member, 1978; Sathya Sai Centre Buffalo, President, 1990-93; Hindi Samaj Greater Buffalo, Co-Founder, 1986, President, 1996-97; Hindu Cultural Society West New York, Trust Committee Member, 1999-2001. Address: 100 North Parrish Drive, Amherst, NY 14228-1477, USA.

**BHARGAVA Pushpa Mittra,** b. 22 February 1928, Rajasthan, India. Scientist; Writer; Consultant. m. Edith, 11 August 1958, 1 son, 1 daughter. Education: BSc, 1944; MSc, 1946; PhD, 1949. Appointments: Lecturer, Chemistry, Lucknow University; Research Fellow, National Institute of Sciences; Project Associate, McArdle Memorial Laboratory for Cancer Research, University of Wisconsin, USA; Special Wellcome Research Fellow, National Institute of Medical Research, London, UK, 1949-58; Appointed Scientist B, Regional Research Laboratory,

Hyderabad, India, 1958; Promoted to Scientist C, E and F; Scientist in Charge, Director, CCMB, Hyderabad, 1977-1990; CSIR Distinguished Fellow, 1990-93; Director, Anveshna Consultants, Hyderabad, 1993-. Publications: Over 125 major science publications; 400 articles; 4 books. Honours: Over 100 major national and international honours and awards; Padma Bhushan from the President of India; Chevalier de la Legion d'Honneur; Honorary DSc; National Citizen Award; Visiting Professorship, College de France; Life Fellow, Clare Hall, Cambridge; Wattumal Memorial Prize for Biochemistry; FICCI Award, Medical Sciences; Ranbaxy Award for Medical Sciences; SICO Award for Biotechnology; Goyal Prize; R D Birla Award for Medical Sciences. Memberships: President or Past President: Society of Biological Chemicals of India; Indian Academy of Social Sciences; Association for Promotion of DNA Fingerprinting and Other DNA Technologies; Society for Science Values; 125 major national and international standing committees. Address: Anveshna, Furqan Cottage, 12-13-100, Lane #1, Street #3, Tarnaka, Hyderabad 500 017, India. E-mail: chanchak@nettlinx.com

**BHARGAVA Samir,** b. 5 April 1965, Mumbai, India. Ear, Nose and Throat Surgeon. m. Shalini, 1 son, 1 daughter. Education: DORL, College of Physicians and Surgeons, 1990; Diplomate of National Board, Delhi, 1991; MS (ENT) University of Bombay, 1991; DLO, Royal College of Surgeons, London, UK, 1993. Appointments: Associate Professor, Ear, Nose and Throat, GS Medical College and KEM Hospital, -1997; Honorary Consultant, Sir Hurkisondas Hospital, Guru Nanak Hospital. Publications: Co-author: A Short Textbook of ENT Diseases; More than 20 articles in national and international journals and books. Honours: Homi Gandhi Research Scholarship; Dr Manubhai Mehta Prize, CPS, 1990; Seth Gagalbhai Nathubhai Prize, MS (ENT), 1991; Best Surgeon Award, All India Medical Professional, Delhi, 2001. Memberships: Association of Otolaryngologists of India; Indian Society of Otology; Indian Medical Association; Consultants' Association. Address: Bhargava Nursing Home, Gopal Bhuvan, Tagore Road, Santacruz (W), Mumbai 400 054, India. E-mail: bharsam@bom5.vsnl.net.in

**BHATT Huthi Venkatakrishna,** b. 11 August 1942, Sastav, Karnataka, India. Pharmacologist, Neurobehavioural Toxicologist. m. Geetha Devi. 2 daughters. Education: Bachelor of Science, Master of Science, Twice Doctorate, Doctor of Philosophy, in Physiology and Pharmacology, CSAV. CSSR and Guj. India; Diploma United Nations and International Understanding. Appointments: Research Scientist, 1965-72; Research Officer, 1972-79; Senior Research Officer, 1980-85; Assistant Director, 1986-92; Deputy Director, 1993-97; Senior Grade Deputy Director, 1998-, Research Centre, Indian Council of Medical Research, NIOH, Ahmedabad, India. Publications: 340 Research Communications; 100 in foreign journals. Honours: Numerous Awards including Archana Award, 1998; Harri Ohm Ashram Interuniversity Smark Trust Award, 1980-2001. Memberships: The New York Academy of Science, 1994; American Association for the Advancement of Science; International Brain Research Organization, Paris, 1997; International Commission on Occupational Health, Singapore, 1994; The National Academy of Medical Science, New Dehli, 1996; Fellowships: Institute of Chemists, 1977; Society of Toxicology, 1994; The Zoological Society, The Academy of Environmental Biology, 1993. Address: Block II Flat 13, Suramya Apartments, Sola Road, Ahmedaba-380063, Gujarat, India. E-mail: hvkbhatt@yahoo.co.in

**BHOPAL Rajinder S,** b. 10 April 1953, British citizen. Professor of Public Health. m. 4 children. Education: BSc

(Hons), Physiology, 1975, MBChB, 1978, MD, 1991, University of Edinburgh; MPH, Glasgow University, 1985. Appointments: Professor of Epidemiology and Public Health, Head of Department of Epidemiology and Public Health, University of Newcastle upon Tyne, 1991-99; Honorary Consultant, Public Health Medicine, 1991-99; Non-Executive Director, Newcastle and North Tyneside Health Authority, 1992-96; Visiting Professor, School of Public Health, North Carolina, USA, 1996-97; Non-Executive Director, Health Education Authority, 1998-99; Bruce and John Usher Chair of Public Health, University of Edinburgh, 1999-; Honorary Consultant in Public Health Medicine, Lothian Health Board, 1999-; Head of Department, Division of Community Health Services, University of Edinburgh, 2000-03. Publications: Around 150 articles in peer reviewed journals and chapters in books; 1 textbook, Concept of Epidemiology, 2002; and 2 edited volumes, Public Health: Past, Present and Future, and The Epidemic of Coronary Heart Disease in South Asian Populations. Honours: John Maddison Research Prize, 1992; J T Neech Prize, 1994; J W Starkey Silver Medal, 2000; CBE, 2001. Memberships: Royal College of Physicians (UK); Member, Fellow, Faculty of Public Health Medicine; Fellow, Royal College of Physicians. Address: Division of Community Health Sciences, Public Health Sciences, University of Edinburgh Medical School, Teviot Place, Edinburgh EH8 9AG, Scotland. E-mail: raj.bhopal@ed.ac.uk

**BHUMIBOL ADULYADEJ (King of Thailand),** b. 5 December 1927, Cambridge, USA. Education: Bangkok, Lausanne, Switzerland. m. Queen Sirikit, 28 April 1950, 1 son, 3 daughters. Address: Chitralada Villa, Bangkok, Thailand.

**BIDDISS Michael Denis,** b. 15 April 1942, Farnborough, Kent, England. Professor of History; Writer. m. Ruth Margaret Cartwright, 8 April 1967, 4 daughters. Education: MA, PhD, Queens' College, Cambridge, 1961-66; Centre des Hautes Etudes Européennes, University of Strasbourg, 1965-66. Appointments: Fellow in History, Downing College, Cambridge, 1966-73; Lecturer/Reader in History, University of Leicester, 1973-79; Professor of History, University of Reading, 1979-2004, Emeritus Professor, 2004-. Publications: Father of Racist Ideology, 1970; Gobineau: Selected Political Writings (editor), 1970; Disease and History (co-author), 1972, new edition, 2000; The Age of the Masses, 1977; Images of Race (editor), 1979; Thatchersim: Personality and Politics (co-editor), 1987; The Nuremberg Trial and the Third Reich, 1992; The Uses and Abuses of Antiquity (co-editor), 1999; The Humanities in the New Millennium (co-editor), 2000. Memberships: Historical Association, president, 1991-94; Faculty, History and Philosophy of Medicine, Society of Apothecaries, London, president, 1994-98; Royal Historical Society, joint vice president, 1995-99. Address: c/o School of History, University of Reading, Whiteknights, Reading RG6 6AA, England.

**BIELBY John Nicholas Lyne,** b. 4 June 1939, London, England. Lecturer; Poet; Writer. m. Sheila Marland, 22 August 1964, 1 son, 1 daughter. Education: BA, 1961; MA, 1983; Diploma Primary Education, 1972; Diploma Psychology and Sociology of Education, 1973. Appointments: Lecturer, St John's College, Agra, India; Teacher, Bradley Junior School, Huddersfield; Lecturer, Senior Lecturer, Bradford and Ilkley Community College; Lecturer, Leeds University. Publications: Three Early Tudor Poets, 1976; An Invitation to Supper, 1978; Making Sense of Reading, 1994; How to Teach Reading, 1998; Teaching Reading at Key Stage 2, 1999; Remember Wyatt, 1999. Contributions to: Contributor to Perspectives on the Teaching and Learning of Phonics, 2002. Poetry Reviewing, Times Educational Supplement. Honours: Awards from New Poetry, Lancaster (3 times) and Yorkshire Open; Rhyme

International, 1989; Runner-up, Arvon, 1991; Editor, Pennine Platform. Memberships: Pennine Poets; Bradford Poetry Society. Address: Frizingley Hall, Frizinghall Road, Bradford BD9 4LD, West Yorkshire, England.

**BIER Werner Philipp,** b. 30 September 1956, Birkenfeld, Germany. Economist. m. Birgit Bier. Education: Studies in Economics and Business Administration, University of Saarland, 1975-80; Master's Degree in Economics, 1980. Appointments: Research Assistant and Lecturer, Economics, University of Saarland, 1980-89; Economist, Deutsche Bundesbank, 1989-90; Administrator of the European Commission, Statistical Office of the European Communities, 1991-94; Senior Economist Statistician and Head of Unit, General Economic and Financial Statistics, European Monetary Institute, 1995-98; Head of Division, Euro Area Accounts and Economic Statistics, 1998-2004, Deputy Director General, Statistics, 2004-, European Central Bank. Publications: Les critères de déficit et de dette publics dans le cadre de l'UEM: approche statistique, 1994; Measurement of Inflation: The Choice of the European Central Bank, 2001; Extended Statistics for the Support of the Stability and Growth Pact, 2004. Address: Kaiserstrasse 29, D-60311 Frankfurt am Main, Germany. E-mail: werner.bier@ecb.int

**BIKAUSKIENĖ-JAKUBAUSKAITĖ Jūratė** b. 23 August 1955, Kvitikas, Šiauliai, Lithuania. Primary Education Teacher. m. Audrius Bilevičius, 2 sons. Education: Master's Degree, Primary Education Pedagogics and Methods, Šiauliai Pedagogical Institute, 1981. Appointments: Primary Education Teacher, Šiauliai 5th Secondary School (Didždvaris Gymansium), 1981-2004; Primary Education Teacher "Šeltinis" General Education School, 2004-; Consultant of quality evaluation of primary education changes, Centre of Pedagogues' Professional Development of the Republic of Lithuania. Publications: Co-author, Integrated Education and Self-education in First Grade, 1997; Created a system of criterion evaluation by ideographic principle of individual advance and 1st-2nd and 3rd -4th year pupils' Achievement Books applied to this system, 1998; Created first level (primary) daybook suitable for ideographic evaluation that is used currently in Lithuania as an official document, 1999; Prepared and published, Integrated Education and Self-education in the Second Grade, 2002; Gives consultations in periodicals. Honours: Teacher of the Year, 1999 and awarded a National Premium; Title of Primary Education Teacher Expert, 1999. Memberships: Lithuanian Association of Primary Education Pedagogues; Independent Experts of the Ministry of Science and Education; President, Šiauliai Group of Lithuanian Association of Primary Education Pedagogues. Address: Spindulio 6-7, Šiauliai, LT-76174, Lithuania. E-mail: selitinis@takas.ly

**BIKBULATOV Igor,** b. 19 October 1941, Buribye, Bashkortostan, Russia. Scientist. m. Nina Muravyova, 3 daughters. Education: Bachelor of Technical Sciences, 1963, Doctor of Chemical Sciences, 1970, Professor of Faculty of General Chemical Technologies, 1985, Ufa Oil Institute. Appointments: Operator, chemical plant producing chemical rubber, Research Laboratory Engineer, Head of Laboratory, Head of the Sterlitamak Branch, Head of the Faculty of Ecology and Rational Use of Nature, Ufa Oil University, Sterlitamak, Bashkortostan, Russia. Publications: Wasteless production of chlorohydrins; Microwave radiation and intensification of chemical processes; Polymeric covering for isolating the surfaces of open reservoirs; Capsule of a pipeline; A building for placing chemical productions; Chrolohydrins I. Obtaining chloric acid in saturated chloride-ion solution. Honours: Inventor of the USSR; Honoured Higher School Worker of the Russian Federation; Honoured Worker of Science of Bashkortostan.

Memberships: Academician, International Academy of Science of Pedagogical Education; Scientific Society of Ufa State Oil Technical University. Address: October Avenue 2, Sterlitamark, Bashkortostan, Russia. E-mail: infor@sfugntu.bashnet.ru

**BILEVIČIENĖ-JAKUBAUSKAITĖ Zita,** b. 23 August 1955, Kvitokas, Taishet District, Russia. Primary Education Teacher. m. Audrius Bilevičius, 1 daughter. Education: Master's Degree, Primary Education Pedagogics and Methods, Šiauliai Pedagogical Institute, 1973-77. Appointments: Primary Education Teacher, Šiauliai 2nd 8-year School, 1977-79; Primary Education Teacher, Šiauliai 5th Secondary School (Didždvaris Gymnasium), 1979-2001; Primary Education Teacher, "Šėltinis" General Education School, 2004-. Publications: Co-author, Integrated Education and Self-education in First Grade, 1997; Created a system of criterion evaluation by ideographic principle of individual advance and 1st-2nd and 3rd –4th year pupils' Achievement Books applied to this system, 1998; Created first level (primary) daybook suitable for ideographic evaluation that is used currently in Lithuania as an official document, 1999; Prepared and published, Integrated Education and Self-education in the Second Grade, 2002; Gives consultations in periodicals. Honours: Teacher of the Year, 1999 and awarded a National Premium; Title of Primary Education Teacher Expert, 1999. Memberships: Lithuanian Association of Primary Education Pedagogues; Independent Experts of the Ministry of Science and Education; Consultant of quality evaluation of primary education changes, Centre of Pedagogues' Professional Development of the Republic of Lithuania. Address: Vandentieko 3, Šiauliai, LT-76225, Lithuania. E-mail: seltinis@takas.lt

**BILIMORIA Karan,** b. 26 November 1961, India (British National). Chief Executive. m. Heather Walker, 2 sons, 2 daughters. Education: B Com (Hons), Indian Institute of Management and Commerce, Osmania University, Hyderabad, India, 1978-81; Diploma in Accounting, London Metropolitan University, 1981-82; ACA (England and Wales), 1982-86; MA Law, Sidney Sussex College, Cambridge University, 1986-88; Business Growth Programme, Cranfield University, 1998; FCA (England and Wales), 2002. Appointments include: Ernst and Young, 1987-87; Consulting Accountant, Cresvale Ltd, London, 1988; Sales and Marketing Director, European Accounting Focus Magazine, 1989; Founder and Chief Executive, Cobra Beer Ltd, Founder of General Bilimoria Wines, Founder and Chairman of Cobrabyte Technologies, 1989-; Member: National Employment Panel, Department for Work and Pensions, Chairman, Small and Medium Size Enterprise Board; Neighbourhood Renewal Private Sector Panel, Office of the Deputy Prime Minister; New Deal Taskforce, Department for Education and Employment, 1999-2001; Board Member and Charter Member, The Indus Entrepreneurs (TiE) UK; Member, UK India Consultative Group, Foreign and Commonwealth Office, 2002-2003; Mentor, Metropolitan Police Joint Mentoring Initiative, 2002-2004; Founding President, UK Zoroastrian Chamber of Commerce; Council Member and Honorary Life Fellow, RSA, 2004-; Patron, RSA India; Visiting Entrepreneur, Centre for Entrepreneurial Learning, University of Cambridge; Ambassador, London 2012 Olympic Bid; Chancellor, Thames Valley University; Governor, Thames Valley University, 2001-04; Representative Deputy Lieutenant, London Borough of Hounslow; Non-Executive Director, Brake Bros Ltd; Chairman, Advisory Board, Shrimati Pushpa Wati Loomba Memorial Trust. Honours: Non-Resident Indian Millennium Honour, India, 2001; Outstanding Achievement Award, Executives Association of Great Britain, 2002; Asian of the Year, 2002; London Entrepreneur of the Year, 2003; Entrepreneur of the Year, Asian Achievement Awards, 2003; Business of the Year (Cobra Beer Ltd), Asian

Business Awards, 2003; International Envoy for London; Entrepreneur of the Year, London Chamber of Commerce and Industry, 2003; Excellence Award, Non-Resident Indian Institute, 2003; CBE, 2004; Pride of India Award, Non-Resident Indian Institute, 2004; RSA Albert Medal, 2004; Monde Selection Awards for Cobra Beer Ltd: Gold Medal, 2001, 2002, 2003, International High Quality Trophy, 2003, 2 Grand Gold Medals and 4 Gold Medals, 2004 2 Grand Gold Medals and 9 Gold Medals, 2005; Honorary Member, Cranfield Management Association; Outstanding Achievement Award, Institute of Chartered Accountants in England and Wales; National Champion, National Council for Graduate Entrepreneurship. Memberships include: Governor, Ditchley Foundation; Champion, Roko Cancer Appeal; Member, Young Presidents' Organisation, Chairman, London Chapter, 2004-05; Fellow, Institute of Directors; Founding Patron, Oxford Entrepreneurs; Vice President, Cambridge Union, 1988; Member, Cambridge University Polo Team (Indian Tour Captain), 1988; Patron, Rethink Mental Illness; Patron, Thare Mache Starfish Initiative; Patron, Thames Community Foundation; Patron, St Andrew's University Cricket Club; Member, Tyson Task Force on the Recruitment and Development of Non-Executive Directors; Vice Patron, Memorial Gates Trust, 1999-2004; Chairman, Memorial Gates Committee; Vice Chairman, Asian Business Association; UK Chairman, Indo British Partnership; Member, Presidents Committee, London First; Honorary President, Training for Life; Fellow, Chartered Accountant; Companion, Chartered Management Institute; FRIMA Golf Club, Dehra Dun; Kelvin Grove Club, Cape Town; Member, The Drapers' Company; Freeman, City of London; Ambassador, Interactive University. Address: Cobra Beer Ltd, Alexander House, 14-16 Peterborough Road, London SW6 3BN, England. E-mail: kfbilimoria@cobrabeer.com

**BILIŪTĖ-ALEKNAVIČIENĖ Elvyra,** b. 26 September 1948, Tolkūnai Village, Alytus District, Lithuania. Teacher of Lithuanian Language and Literature. m. Juozas Aleknavičius, 1 daughter. Education: Diploma of Philology, Lithuanian Literature and Language Teaching, Vilnius State University, 1967-72. Appointments: Methodologist, Alytus Evening Secondary School N1, 1973-79; Lecturer, Alytus Vocational School N54, 1979-95; Inspector, Alytus Municipality Education Department, 1996-. Publications: Books about Lithuanian education history, monographs about distinguished teachers and writers: Light of Kindness, 1996; Wings of Eternity, 1997; Love Song, 1999; Cradle of Life, 2000; Angel of Hope, 2002; Development of Primary School Teachers Training and Education System in Lithuania in 1940-57, 2004; Co-author, Historic Development of Alytus, 2004; Articles on pedagogical topics. Honours: Honorary Diploma, Central Board of Lithuanian Catholic Science Academy, 1995; Gratitude Paper, Ministry of Education, 1996; Gratitude Paper, Lithuanian Parliament, 2001; Gratitude Papers, Mayor of Alytus, 2001, 2004; 21st Century Award for Achievement, 2004. Memberships: Chairwoman, Lithuanian Language and Literature Teachers' Union, Alytus Division; Lithuanian Beekeepers' Union; Lithuanian Florists' Union, Alytus Division. Address: Zuvinto Str 13-89, LT-62354 Alytus, Lithuania.

**BILK Acker (Bernard Stanley),** b. 28 January 1929, Pensford, Somerset, England. Musician (clarinet); Composer; Bandleader. m. Jean, 1 son, 1 daughter. Career: Began playing clarinet in Royal Engineers, 1948; Clarinet, Ken Colyer's Band; Formed Bristol Paramount Jazz Band; Currently freelance artiste; Guest musician on numerous records; Tours world-wide with Paramount Jazz Band; Played with Reunion Paramount Jazz Band, Isle of Bute Jazz Festival, 1995; Performed with Van Morrison, Prague, 2004, Oxford, 2005. Recordings with Van

Morrison, 2001, 2001; 3B Concerts reuniting Acker and his Band with the Big Chris Barber Band and Kenny Ball and his Jazzmen, 2004; Giants of Jazz Concerts with Humphrey Lyttelton and George Melly, 2004; Owner of publishing company. Recordings: Singles include: Somerset; Aria; Stranger On The Shore (Number 1, US and UK, 1961); Albums include: The One For Me; Sheer Magic; Evergreen; Chalumeau-That's My Home; Three In The Morning (with Humphrey Lyttelton, John Barnes, Dave Green, Dave Cliff, Bobby Worth); Giants Of Jazz (with Paramount Jazz Band, Kenny Ball and his Jazzmen, Kenny Baker Don Lusher All Stars); Chris Barber and Acker Bilk, That's It Then!; Clarinet Moods, Acker Bilk, with string orchestra; Acker Bilk - The Oscars; Clarinet Moods with Acker Bilk; All the Hits and More; The Christmas Album; Acker Bilk And His Paramount Jazz Band; Acker Bilk In Holland; It Looks Like A Big Time Tonight; Hits Blues And Class; Great Moments; Best of Acker Bilk; As Time Goes By, 2004. Honour: MBE, 2001; BMI Award, London, 2004; Honorary Degree of Master of the Arts, University of Bristol, 2005. Address: c/o Acker's Agency, 53 Cambridge Mansions, Cambridge Road, London SW11 4RX, England.

**BILLINGS Stephen Alec**, b. 14 August 1951, Staffordshire, England. Professor of Signal Processing and Complex Systems. m. Catherine Grant Billings, 1 son, 1 daughter. Education: First Class Honours Degree, Electrical Engineering, Liverpool University, 1969-72; PhD, Control Systems, Sheffield University, 1972-75. Appointments: Lecturer, 1975-83, Senior Lecturer, 1983-85, Department of Control Engineering, Reader, 1985-90, Professor of Signal Processing and Complex Systems, 1990-, Department of Automatic Control and Systems Engineering, University of Sheffield. Publications: Over 200 journal articles and over 50 conference papers. Honours: Honoured by the Institute of Scientific Information (ISA), USA as one of the worlds most highly cited researchers in all branches of engineering, 1980-2000; Awarded D. Eng., Liverpool University, 1990. Memberships: Fellow, Institute of Electrical Engineers (UK); Chartered Engineer and Chartered Scientist; Fellow, Institute of Mathematics and its Applications; Chartered Mathematician. Address: Department of Automatic Control and Systems Engineering, University of Sheffield, Mappin Street, Sheffield S1 3JD, England. E-mail: s.billings@sheffield.ac.uk

**BILLINGTON Rachel (Mary)**, b. 11 May 1942, Oxford, England. Writer. m. 16 December 1967, 2 sons, 2 daughters. Education: BA, English, London University. Publications: Over 20 books, including: Loving Attitudes, 1988; Theo and Matilda, 1990; The First Miracles, 1990; Bodily Harm, 1992; The Family Year, 1992; The Great Umbilical, 1994; Magic and Fate, 1996; The Life of Jesus (for children), 1996; Perfect Happiness, 1996; The Tiger Sky, 1998; The Life of St Francis (for children), 1999; A Woman's Life, 2002; Far Out! (for children), 2002; The Space Between, 2004. Contributions to: Reviewer, Columnist and short story writer for various publications; 2 plays for BBC TV; 4 plays for Radio. Memberships: Society of Authors; President, PEN, 1997-. Address: The Court House, Poyntington, Near Sherborne, Dorset DT9 4LF, England.

**BILLINGTON Sandra**, b. 10 September 1943, Eccles, England. Self-Employed Writer. Education: Guildhall School of Music and Drama, 1961-63; RADA, 1965-67; BA (Cantab), 1975, PhD (Cantab), 1980, Lucy Cavendish College, Cambridge. Appointments: Actress, BBC Radio Manchester, 1955-59; Theatre/Film, 1967-72; Lecturer, 1979-92, Reader, 1992-2003, Department of Theatre, Film and TV, University of Glasgow; Writer, 2003-. Publications: A Social History of the Fool, 1984; Mock Kings in Medieval Society and Renaissance Drama, 1991; The Concept of the Goddess (co-editor), 1996;

Midsummer: A Cultural sub-text from Chrétien de Troyes to Jean Michel, 2000; Between Worlds, 2005; Midsummer's Imprint: British Celt to Anglo-Norman, forthcoming. Honours: Katharine Briggs Prize for Folklore, 1984; Michaelis Jena Ratcliff Prize for Folklore, 1991; FRSE, 1998. Membership: Traditional Cosmology Society. Address: 4 Doune Quadrant, Glasgow, G20 6DL, England.

**BILLIS David**, b. 10 April 1934. Voluntary Sector Specialist. m. Jacqueline Nahoma Ludwig, 2 sons. Education: BSc (Econ), PhD, London School of Economics. Appointments include: In Charge of Finance and Accounts, Kibbutz Zikkim, 1957-66; Founder and Director, Programme of Research and Training into Voluntary Action, Brunel University; Reader in Social Service Organisation and Founder Director, Centre for Voluntary Organisation, currently Emeritus Reader, London School of Economics; Visiting Professor, Imperial College School of Management, 1998-2001; Director, Worklevels Ltd; Co-Founder, Nonprofit Management and Leadership. Publications: Books include: Welfare Bureaucracies, 1984; Organisational Design (with R W Rowbottom), 1987; Organising Public and Voluntary Agencies, 1993; Voluntary Agencies (with M Harris), 1996. Honour: Distinguished Lifetime Achievement Award, American Association for Research on Nonprofit Organizations and Voluntary Action, 1995. Memberships: Association for Research on Non Profit Organisations and Voluntary Action, 1985-. Address: 19 Cranbourne Road, London N10 2BT, England. E-mail: worklevels@blueyonder.co.uk

**BIMBERG ZU LENNINGHAUSEN Guido von**, b. 14 March 1954, Halle, Germany (US national, 1997). Musicologist and Entertainment Business Executive. m. Christiane Bimberg, 11 April 1981, 1 son. Education: Studied Musicology, Music Education, Piano, Literature, Art History, Theatre (Halle, Berlin, Munich, Tashkent, Moscow, Harvard and Stanford); Business Administration (Schwyz, Lausanne, Harvard); PhD, 1979; MBA, Schwyz-Lausanne and Harvard, 1979; Research Fellowship, Baltic, Central Asian, Caucasian, Russian, Siberian and Ukrainian Archives, 1979-80; Habilitation, 1981, PhD in Business Administration, Lausanne and Harvard, 1982. Appointments: Founder of several rock bands, 1970-82; Founder, 1973, Chairman, 1979-86, German Society of Music Agencies and Discjockeys; Manager, German, Russian, Caribbean and USA popstars; Creator, TV show formats; Copyright counsellor; Lyricist and Composer, charts and musicals; Associate Professor, Music History, Halle, 1979-83; Chair Professor of Musicology, Dresden; Chair Professor Musicology, Martin Luther University, Halle, 1983-95; Chair Professor Musicology, Music Academy of Dortmund, 1995-; Chair Professor, Music and Interdisciplinary Studies, 1983-86, Havanna University, 1990-; Fellow Chair of Entertainment and Media Business, Washington University, 1992-, German Academy of Humanities, 1992-; Chair Professor, Entertainment and Media Business, Central University of California, Los Angeles, 1995-; Professor, Honorary Senator, Moscow University, 1995-; Chair Professor, Entertainment Business, International School of Business Administration, Academy of Sciences, Berlin, 1997-; Numerous visiting professorships and Permanent University Fellowships in Europe, America, Africa, Asia and Australia; Senior Consultant, 1991-, Supervisory Board, 2001-, MRI Inc; Co-director, 1994-, CCO, 2000-, Music Tourist Agency, Nashville; Vice President, Media Science Inc, 2000-; CEO, Music and Media Business Inc, Los Angeles, 2001-; Board of Directors: Digital Media Corporation, 2000-; Entertainment Network Inc, 2001-; Congress and Festival Director, Werckmeister Festival, Alicante Festival, Singapore Music Festival, Tokyo Classics, Broadway Summit, Los Angeles Hit Factory, Nashville Music Contest and International Musical Congress and Festival ICMF New

# DICTIONARY OF INTERNATIONAL BIOGRAPHY

York; Honorary Consul, Russian Federation, 2002; Director, Co-Director, several music congresses and festivals, including: Fasch Festival, Werckmeister Festival, Alicante Festival, Singapore Music Festival, Tokyo Classics, Los Angeles Hit Factory, Nashville Music Contest; Senator, German Academy of Sciences and Arts, Westphalian Music Academy; President: German Academy of the Humanities, Bonn, 1998-; International Entertainment Business Society; German Music Research Foundation; German Handel Society; Vice President: German Musicological Society; German Fasch Society; Werckmeister Society; Member, Board of Directors, International Society for Music Education; Member of Council, American Musicological Society; Member, Association Board, College Music Society; Member, International Musicological Society; Royal Music Association, Japanese Musicological Society. Publications: Over 20 scholarly books including: Opera in 18th-century Russia, 1981, 3rd edition, 2003; Dramaturgy of the Handel Operas, 1985, 2nd edition, 2003; Anatolij Lunacharsky: Essays in music, 1985, 2nd edition, 2001; The Wonderful Sound, German, 1985-2002, million copies in many countries; Schütz-Bach-Händel, 1989; Mozarts Entführung aus dem Serail, 1990; Music of Russian and German Composers, 1990; Fasch and Music in 18th Century Europe, 1995; Andreas Werckmeister, Die musicalische Temperatur, co-author, 1996; Denkmäler der Musik in Mitteldeutschland, co-editor, 1996-; General education and thematic catalogue of Fasch works, co-editor, 1996; Music in the 18th Century European Society, 1997, 2nd edition, 2002; Perspectives in Musicology and Music Education for the 21st Century, 1997, 2nd edition, 2002; Music in Canada/La Musique au Canada, 1997, 2nd edition, 2002; Music Sources from the Westphalian Music Archive, 1997; Denkmäler der Musik in Westfalen, 1997; International Studies Women in Music, 1999; Women in Music in Westphalia, 1999, Broadway on the Ruhr: The Musical Comedy in the New Millennium, co-editor, 2000; Music Technology, 2001; Digital Music Business, 2001; Leni Timmermann, 2002; Introducing Music, 2002; Musicology and Entertainment Business, 2002; Baroque Music Recovered by the Telemann Orchestra Tradition, (co-author), 2002; Eitelfriedrich Thom – Great Germans in Theory and Practice of Music, co-author, 2003; La musique en activité, 2004; Music books for children. Contributions: over 200 articles to professional international journals. Honours: Modest Musorgsky Prize, 1990; American Musicology Award, 1992; Canadian Culture Prize, 1992; Guido Adler Prize of German Musicology, 1994; Gold Crown Medal Hong Kong Music Association, 1995; Prize Musica Westphalia, 1997; Bundesverdienstkreuz, 1998; German Handel Prize, 1998; German National Prize for Music and Musicology, 2000; Innovation Prize for music and media technology, 2000; Grosses Bundes-Verdienstkreuz des Verdienstordens, 2002; Knight of the Empire, 2003; Dr hc, Universities of Moscow, 2003, and New York, 2003; Books in commemoration of 50th Birthday: No Limits (edited by Professor Dr Hiroshi Watanabe), 2004; Festschrift Guido Bimberg/RuedigerPfeiffer (edited by Dr Ching-Wah Wang), 2004. Address: German Academy for Humanities, Postfach 550133, D-44209 Dortmund, Germany. E-mail: prof.dr.bimberg@crossoverstudies.com

BINCHY Maeve, b. 28 May 1940, Dublin, Ireland. Writer. m. Gordon Thomas Snell, 29 January 1977. Education: BA, University College, Dublin, 1960. Appointments: Teacher, History and French, Pembroke School, Dublin, 1961-68; Columnist, Irish Times, London, 1968-2000; Writer. Publications: My First Book, 1976; The Central Line: Stories of Big City Life, 1978; Maeve's Diary, 1979; Victoria Line, 1980; Light a Penny Candle, 1982; Maeve Binchy's Dublin Four, 1982; The Lilac Bus, 1984; Echoes, 1985; Firefly Summer, 1987; Silver Wedding, 1988; Circle of Friends, 1991; The Copper Beech, 1992; The Glass Lake, 1995; Evening Class, 1996; Tara Road, 1999; Scarlet Feather, 2000; Aches and Pains, 2000; Quentins, 2002. Honours: International TV Festival Golden Prague Award, Czech TV, 1979; Jacobs Award, 1979; Hon DLit, National University of Ireland, 1990, Queen's Belfast, 1998. Address: Dalkey, Co. Dublin, Ireland.

BINJI Aishatu Muhammad, b. 2 March 1954, Kano, Nigeria. Accountant. m. Muhammad H Binji, 2 sons, 2 daughters. Education: BSc, Accounting, 1st class honours, Institute of Administration ABU Zaria, 1974-77; Strathclyde University Glasgow, Scotland, 1987. Appointments: Accountant, Gwandu Rice Scheme, 1977-78; Accountant GII, Ministry of Finance, Treasury Division, Sokoto, 1978-79; Accountant in charge of store, 1979-80, Agricultural Chief Accountant, 1980-82, Gusau Agricultural Development Project; Chief Accountant, SADP Headquarters, 1982-84; Head, Accounts Department, Sokoto Agricultural Development Project, 1984-88; Financial Controller, Farmers Agricultural Supply Company, 1988-95; Accountant General, Ministry of Finance, Sokoto, 1995-. Publications: Yara Mu Karanta; Simple Maths; Read and Write the Arabic Alphabets; My A B C D Writing Book. Honours: Member, Federal Republic of Nigeria, 2001; National Productivity Order of Merit Award, 1999-2000; Merit Award, Madrasatul Ihyaul Islam Sokoto; Merit Award, Sokoto Medical Students Association, UDUS Chapter; Merit Award, Sokoto Medical and Veterinary Students Association, UDUS Chapter. Memberships: Institute of Corporate Executives of Nigeria. Address: Ministry of Finance, Sokoto, Nigeria.

BINOCHE Juliette, b. 9 March 1964, Paris, France. Actress. 1 son, 1 daughter. Education: National Conservatory of Drama; Private Theatrical Studies. Creative Works: Films include: Les nanas; La vie de famille; Rouge Baiser; Rendez-Vous; Mon beau-frère a tué ma soeur; Mauvais Sang; Un tour de manège; Les amants du Pont-Neuf; The Unbearable Lightness of Being; Wuthering Heights, 1992; Damage, 1992; Trois Couleurs: Bleu, 1993; Le Hussard sur le Toit, 1995; The English Patient, 1996; Alice et Martin, 1999; Les Enfants du Siècle, 1999; La Veuve de Saint-Pierre, 2000; Chocolat, 2001; Code Unknown, 2001; Décalage horaire, 2002; Country of My Skull, 2004; Play: Naked, 1998. Honours: Academy Award, Best Supporting Actress, 1996; Berlin Film Festival Award, 1996; BAFTA Award, 1997. Address: c/o UTA, 9560 Wilshire Boulevard, Floor 5, Beverly Hills, CA 90212, USA.

BIRCH Clive Francis William, b. 22 December 1931, Edgware, Middlesex, England. Publisher; Author. Education: Uppingham School. Appointments: RAF National Service, 1950; Office Junior, Stretford Telegraph, 1952; Reporter, Stockport Express, 1954; Editor, Bucks Examiner, 1956; Public Relations Officer, Frigidaire Division, General Motors, 1958; Product Development, Metro-Cammell Weymann Ltd, 1959; Group Advertisement Manager, Modern Transport Publishing Company Ltd, 1965; Manager, Electrical Press Ltd, 1966; Director, Illustrated Newspapers Ltd, 1969 (including, Editor, Illustrated London News, 1970); Director, Northwood Publications Ltd, 1971; Managing Director designate, Textile Trade Publications Ltd, 1972; Publishing Director, Mercury House Ltd, 1973; Chairman, Barracuda Books Ltd, 1974-92; Managing Director, Quotes Ltd, 1985-97; Principal, Radmore Birch Associates (including Baron Books), 1991-; Visiting Tutor, RCA Vehicle Design Department, 2004-; Publishing Consultant, Boltneck Publications, 2005-. Publications: Book of Chesham; Book of Amersham (co-author) Book of Aylesbury; Book of Beaconsfield (co-author); Yesterday's Town : Chesham; Yesterday's Town: Amersham (co-author); Maps of Bucks (editor); Chesham Century (co-author); Remember Chesham; In Camera Series - Vale of Aylesbury; Buckingham; Chesham;

Chiltern Thames; Milton Keynes (2); The Missendens; Chalfont St Giles; Chorleywood & Chenies; Wish you were here series – Buckingham; Chesham; The Freedom - City of London (co-author); On the Move - Road Haulage Association (co-author); Carr and Carman - London's Transport. Honours: Honorary Life Member, Chiltern Car Club, 1956; Fellow, Royal Society of Arts, 1980; Fellow, Society of Antiquaries of London, 1981; Honorary Life Member, Institution of the Royal Corps of Transport, 1985; MBE, 2000. Memberships include: Founder Chairman, Buckingham and District Chamber of Trade, Commerce and Industry, 1983-87; Founder and Chairman, Buckingham Heritage Trust, 1985-97; Freeman City of London, 1960; Liveryman, Worshipful Company of Carmen, 1960, Court of Assistants, 1966, Master 1984-85; Founder Chairman, Carmen's Ball, 1985; Deputy Master, 1988-89; Chairman RSA Carmen Lectures, 1991-; Chairman, Carmen Marketing and Media, 1994-; Chairman, Carmen Awards Committee, 1999-; Founder Carmen Research Fellowship, 2001; Honorary Editor, 2002-; Chairman Carmen Past Masters, 2004-; Senior Past Master, Carmen, 2005-; Chevalier de la Confrerie des Chevaliers du Trou Normand, 1991. Address: King's Cote, Valley Road, Finmere, Oxon MK18 4AL, England.

**BIRCHER Andrea U,** b. 6 March 1928, Bern, Switzerland. Nursing Professor Emeritus. Education: Nursing Diploma, Knapp College of Nursing, 1957; BS, Nursing, 1961, MS, Psychiatric Nursing, 1962, University of California, San Francisco; PhD, Adult Education and Psychiatric Nursing, University of California, Berkeley, 1966. Appointments: Staff, Head Nurse, Cottage Hospital, Santa Barbara, 1957-58; Junior and Senior Psychiatric Nurse, Langley Porter Neuropsychiatric Institute, San Francisco, 1958-66; Assistant Professor, University of Illinois College of Nursing, 1966-72; Professor, 1972-93, University of Oklahoma College of Nursing; Professor Emeritus, 1993-. Publications: Several articles in professional journals. Memberships: American Nurses Association; American Nurses Association of California; AAUP. Address: 1161 Cypress Point Lane, Apt 201, Ventura, CA 93003-6074, USA.

**BIRD Harold Dennis (Dickie),** b. 19 April 1933, Barnsley, Yorkshire, England. County Test Cricket Umpire. Education: MCC Advanced Cricket Coach. Appointments: Umpired 159 international matches including 68 Test Matches, World Cup Matches, One Day International matches; Umpired 3 World Cup Finals; Umpired 4 World Cup Tournaments; Umpired Queen's Silver Jubilee Test Match, 1977, Centenary Test Match, 1980-. Women's World Cup, Women's World Cup Final, New Zealand, 1982; Umpired 32 major cup finals at Lord's including: Gillette Cup Finals, Nat West Cup Finals, Benson & Hedges Cup, Rothmans Cup, Sharjah, United Arab Emirates and the Final; Umpire, Asia Cup, Sharjah, 1984; Umpire, Rothmans Cup, Sharjah, 1985; Umpire, Asia Cup, Sri Lanka and Final, 1985; Umpire, Champion's Cup, Sharjah, 1986; Umpire, all major cup quarter-finals, semi-finals, England; Played County Cricket for Yorkshire County Cricket Club, Leicestershire County Cricket Club; Umpire, Bicentenary Test Match, England, 1987; Umpire, 3 test matches, Zimbabwe v India, 1992; Zimbabwe v New Zealand, 2 tests, Zimbabwe, 1992; West Indies v Pakistan test series, 3 matches, 1993; Umpire 60th Diamond Test Match, Pakistan v Australia, Karachi, 1994; West Indies Test Match, Kampur, 1994; 3 test matches in New Zealand, New Zealand v Pakistan, 1994; Umpire, 2 test matches in Australia, Australia v Pakistan, 1995. Publications: Not Out; That's Out; From the Pavilion End; Dickie Bird, My Autobiography, 1997; White Cap and Bails, 1999; Dickie Bird's Britain, 2002. Honours: Voted Yorkshire Personality of Year, 1977; Reception to meet HM Queen Mother, Clarence House, London, 1977; MBE, 1986;

World Record, umpiring 67 Test Matches; World Record, Umpire 92 One-Day International Matches; Met numerous celebrities including HM the Queen, 17 times including private lunch, Buckingham Palace, 1991, PM John Major, 1991, Ex-PM Margaret Thatcher, 1981; Radio: Guest on Down Your Way with Brian Johnston, 1975; TV appearances: Parkinson, 1979, Through the Keyhole, 1990, This is Your Life, 1992; Breakfast with Frost, 1996, Clive James, 1996; BBC Documentary of his life, 1996; Guest, Desert Island Discs with Sue Lawley, 1996; Clive Anderson TV Show, 1998; Gloria Hunniford, 1998, Trevor Macdonald Show, 1999; World Panel Test Umpires, 1992; Honorary Life Member, Yorkshire County Cricket Club, 1994; Honorary Life Member, MCC, 1996; Life Long Achievement Award, 1996; Honorary Life Member, Leicestershire County Cricket Club, 1996; Honorary Member, Cambridge University Cricket Club; Honorary Doctorate, Sheffield Hallam University, 1996, Yorkshire Man of Year, 1996; People of Year Award, 1996; Variety Club of Great Britain Award; Honorary LLD, Leeds University, 1997; Freeman of the Borough of Barnsley, 2000; Barnsley Millennium Award of Merit for outstanding service to the community, 2000; Dinner with Tony Blair at Chequers, 2001; Appeared on John Inverdale Show, On-side, BBC1, 2001; Guest on A Question of Sport, 4 times; Founder, Dickie Bird Foundation for underprivileged children to help with grants to buy sports equipment nationwide. Memberships: MCC; Lord's Taverners; World Cup Panel of Umpires, 1987. Address: White Rose Cottage, 40 Paddock Road, Staincross, Barnsley, South Yorkshire S75 6LE, England.

**BIRLEY Julia (Davies),** b. 13 May 1928, London, England. Writer. m. 12 September 1954, 1 son, 3 daughters. Education: BA, Classics, Oxon. Publications: Novels: The Children on the Shore; The Time of the Cuckoo; When You Were There; A Serpent's Egg; Dr Spicer; Short Stories. Contributions to: Guardian. Memberships: PEN; Charlotte Yonge Society. Address: Upper Bryn, Longtown, Hereford HR2 0NA, England.

**BIRNBAUM Edwin,** b. 18 February 1961, Antwerp, Belgium. Consultant. Education: MSc, Commercial Engineer, SOLVAY, Free University, Brussels, 1984; MBA, Catholic University of Louvain, 1987. Appointments: Brand Manager, P & G Benelux, 1984-88; Strategy Consultant, Bain & Company, 1989-91; Marketing Director, Dixons, 1991-93; Marketing Director to Chief Executive Officer, Wickes, 1993-97; Managing Director, MaxiGB/Carrefour, 1997-98; International Vice President, CHEP, 1998-2003; Established pallet business, Israel; Launched largest global RFID pilot, USA; Board Member, Board of Overseers and Advisory Committee, Auto Id Center, 2001-; Chief Executive Officer, Clarity, 2003-. Address: Clarity, Dennenlaan 20, B-2020 Antwerpen, Belgium. E-mail: edwin@c larityadvisers.com Website: www.clarityadvisers.com

**BIRO Leonida Lucien,** b. 22 December 1949, Bucharest, Romania. Engineer. m. Adriana Biro, 1 son, 2 daughters. Education: Engineering Diploma, Polytechnic Institute of Bucharest, Nuclear Power Plants Section, 1967-72; PhD, Nuclear Reactors Technology, Nuclear Safety, Institute for Physics and Nuclear Engineering, Bucharest, 1978-83. Appointments: Senior Engineer, Head of Thermohydraulics Calculations Branch, Institute for Nuclear Power Reactors, 1976-90; Director General, 1990-2000, President, State Secretary, 2001, National Commission for Nuclear Activities Control (CNCAN), Bucharest; Deputy Director General, National Company "Nuclearelectrica", 2002. Publications: Over 150 technical papers published in international and domestic journals or presented in international and national conferences. Honours: Chairman of Working Group III – Energy Related Equipment, Conference of Energy Charter Treaty; IAEA expert for the new IAEA Workshop on Safety Evaluation for Akkuyu NPP, Ankara, Turkey, 1998; President, Advisory Security Group of the Director General of the International Atomic Energy Agency. Memberships: Technical Advisor Group for the CNCAN - Romania/AECB - Canada co-operation; CNCAN Representative for the Nuclear Safety Convention as national co-ordinator; Romanian Representative, CONCERT Group Meeting. Address: National Commission for Nuclear Activities Control, Blvd Libertatii 14, PO Box 42-2, Bucharest 5, Romania 761061. E-mail: lucian.biro@cncan.ro

**BIRT John, Baron of Liverpool,** b. 10 December 1944, Liverpool, England. Broadcasting Executive. m. Jane Frances Lake, 1965, 1 son, 1 daughter. Education: St Mary's College, Liverpool; St Catherine's College, Oxford. Appointments: TV Producer, Nice Time, 1968-69; Joint Editor, World in Action, 1969-70; Producer, The Frost Programme, 1971-72; Executive Producer, Weekend World, 1972-74; Head, Current Affairs, London Weekend TV, 1974-77; Co-Producer, The Nixon Interviews, 1977; Controller, Features and Current Affairs, LWT, 1977-81; Director of Programmes, 1982-87; Deputy Director General, 1987-92, Director General, 1992-2000, BBC; Vice President, Royal TV Society, 1994-2000; Adviser to Prime Minister on criminal justice, 2000-01, Strategy Adviser, 2001-; Adviser to McKinsey and Co Inc; Chair, Capital Ventures Fund, 2000. Publications: The Harder Path – The Autobiography. Honours: Visiting Fellow, Nuffield College, Oxford, 1991-99; Honorary Fellow: University of Wales, Cardiff, 1997; St Catherine's College, Oxford, 1992; Hon DLitt, Liverpool John Moores, 1992; City, 1998; Bradford, 1999; Emmy Award, US National Academy of Television, Arts and Sciences; Life Peerage, 2000. Memberships: Media Law Group, 1983-94; Working Party on New Technologies, 1981-83; Broadcasting Research Unit, Executive Committee, 1983-87; International Museum of TV and Radio, New York, 1994-2000; Opportunity 2000 Target Team, Business in the Community, 1991-98. Address: House of Lords, London SW1A 0PW, England.

**BIRTS Peter William,** b. 9 February 1946, Brighton, England. Barrister. m. Angela, 1 son, 2 daughters. Education: Lancing College, Sussex; MA, St John's College, Cambridge. Appointments: Called to the Bar, 1968; Recorder, 1989; Queen's Counsel, 1990; Judicial Studies Board, 1992-96; Chairman, Mental Health Tribunal, 1994-; Queen's Counsel Northern Ireland, 1996; Deputy High Court Judge, 2000. Publications: Trespass – Summary Procedure for Possession of Land, 1987; Remedies for Trespass, 1990; Contributed to Butterworths Costs Service, 2000-; Articles in various journals on countryside law and civil procedure. Honours: Choral Scholarship to St John's College, Cambridge, 1964; MA (Cantab), 1973. Memberships: London and Common Law Bar Association; Bencher of Gray's Inn, 1998-. Address: Pump Court Chambers, 3 Pump Court, London EC4Y 7AJ, England. E-mail: pb@3pumpcourt.com

**BISHOP James Drew,** b. 18 June 1929, London, England. Journalist. m. 5 June 1959, 2 sons. Education: BA, History, Corpus Christi College, Cambridge, 1953. Appointments: Foreign Correspondent, 1957-64, Foreign News Editor, 1964-66, Features Editor, 1966-70, The Times; Editor, 1971-87, Editor-in-Chief, 1987-94, The Illustrated London News. Publications: Social History of Edwardian Britain, 1977; Social History of the First World War, 1982; The Story of The Times (with Oliver Woods), 1983; Illustrated Counties of England, editor, 1985; The Sedgwick Story, 1998. Contributions to: Books, newspapers and magazines. Membership: Association of British Editors, chairman, 1987-96; Chairman, National Heritage, 1998-. Address: Black Fen, Stoke By Nayland, Suffolk, CO6 4QD, England.

**BJÖRK (Björk Godmunsdottir),** b. 21 November 1965. Reykjavik, Iceland. Singer. 1 son, 1 daughter. Career: Solo release, aged 11; Singer, various Icelandic groups include: Exodus; Tappi Tikarras; Kukl; Singer, The Sugarcubes, 1987-92; Solo artiste, 1992-; Recent appearances include Reading Festival, 1995. Recordings: Solo albums: Björk, 1977; Debut, 1993; Post, 1995; Telegram, 1996; Homogenic, 1997; Vespertine, 2001; Hit singles: with The Sugarcubes: Birthday; Solo singles: Venus As A Boy; Violently Happy; Human Behaviour; Big Time Sensuality; Play Dead; Army Of Me; Isobel; It's Oh So Quiet; Possibly Maybe; I Miss You/Cover Me; Hyperballad; Hunter; Bachelorette; All Is Full Of Love; Alarm Call; Selmasongs, 2000; Other recordings: Gling-Go, Trio Gudmundar Ingolfssonar, 1990; Ex-El, Graham Massey, 1991; Tank Girl, 1995; Mission Impossible, 1996; Nearly God, 1996; Archive, 1997; Tibetan Freedom Concert, 1997; Not For Threes, 1998; Great Crossover Potential, 1998; Y2K Beat The Clock Version 1, 1999; Film: Dancer in the Dark, 2000. Honours: BRIT Award, Best International Female Artist, 1996; Platinum and Gold records. Address: One Little Indian, 250 York Road, London SW11 3SJ, England.

**BJÖRNSSON Ólafur Grímur,** b. 6 January 1944, Iceland. Senior Investigator; Physician. Education: Cand real, College of Reykjavík, 1964; Cand phil, 1965; Cand mag (part I of II), 1966, MD 1973, University of Iceland; PhD, University of London, England, 1982; Diploma in Clinical Biochemistry and Clinical Physiology, Iceland, 1984. Appointments: Intern at various hospitals affiliated with the University of Iceland, 1973-75; Medical Resident, Department of Clinical Biochemistry, University Hospital of Iceland, 1975-77; Research Fellow, Hammersmith Hospital, University of London, 1977-82; Senior Research Fellow, Medical Research Council Lipid Metabolic Unit, London, 1982-84; Research Associate, Department of Biochemistry and Biophysics, University of Pennsylvania, USA, 1984-89; Research Associate, Metabolic Research Laboratory, University of Oxford, England, 1989-94. Publications: Numerous articles in professional scientific medical journals; Editor of a Festschrift to Professor Emeritus David Davidsson, University of Iceland; Collaboration work, National Energy Authority, National Museum of Iceland, Department of Clinical Biochemistry, University Hospital of Iceland, University of Akureyri; Project Grantee, Icelandic Government, Icelandic Science Foundation and University Hospital of Iceland. Honour: Listed in Who's Who publications. Memberships: American Society of Biochemistry and Molecular Biology; Biophysical Society, USA; European Society for Clinical Investigation; The Icelandic Society London. Address: Department of Physiology, University of Iceland, Vatnsmýrarvegur 16, 101 Reykjavík, Iceland.

**BLACK Peter Mclaren,** b. 23 May 1944, Calgary, Canada. Neurosurgeon. m. Katharine, 2 sons, 3 daughters. Education: AB, Harvard College, 1966; MD, McGill University, 1970; PhD, Georgetown University, 1978. Appointments: Assistant Professor of Surgery, 1980-84, Associate Professor, 1984-87, Harvard Medical School; Franc D Ingraham Professor of Neurosurgery, Harvard Medical School, 1987-; Senior Surgeon the Active Staff, Brigham and Women's Hospital, Boston, Massachusetts, 1998-. Publications: Numerous articles in professional medical journals. Honours include: J Francis Williams Prize in Medicine, McGill University, 1970; Teacher-Investigator Award, NINDS, 1973-78; Distinguished Service Award, American Association of Neurological Surgeons and Congress of Neurological Surgeons, 1995. Memberships include: American Medical Association; Society for Health and Human Values; Research Society of Neurological Surgeons; Congress of Neurological Surgeons; New England Neurosurgical

Society; New York Academy of Sciences; Society for Biological Psychiatry; Society of University Neurosurgeons; American Academy of Neurological Surgeons; American College of Surgeons; International Society of Pituitary Surgeons. Address: Department of Neurosurgery, Brigham and Womens Hospital, 75 Francis Street, Boston, MA 02115, USA.

**BLACKBURN Julia Karen Eugenie,** b. 12 August 1948, London, England. Writer. m. (1) May 1978, divorced 1995, 1 son, 1 daughter, (2) December 1999. Education: BA Hons, English Literature, York University. Publications: The White Men, 1978; Charles Waterton, 1989; The Emperor's Last Island, 1991; Daisy Bates in the Desert, 1994; The Book of Colour, 1995; The Leper's Companions, 1999; For a Child: A Selection of the Poems of Thomas Blackburn, 1999; Old Man Goya, 2002; With Billie, 2005. Memberships: Society of Authors; PEN; Fellow, Royal Society of Literature, 2003. Address: c/o Toby Eady, Third Floor, 9 Orme Court, London W2 4RL, England.

**BLACKMAN Honor,** b. 22 August 1926, London. Actress. Creative Works: Films include: Fame is the Spur, 1947; Green Grow the Rushes, 1951; Come Die My Love, 1952; The Rainbow Jacket, 1953; The Glass Cage, 1954; Dead Man's Evidence, 1955; A Matter of Who, 1961; Goldfinger, 1964; Life at the Top, 1965; Twist of Sand, 1967; The Virgin and the Gipsy, 1970; To the Devil a Daughter, 1975; Summer Rain, 1976; The Cat and the Canary, 1977; Talos - The Mummy; To Walk with Lions; Bridget Jones's Diary, 2001; Plays include: Madamoiselle Colombe, 2000; TV appearances include: Four Just Men, 1959; Man of Honour, 1960; Ghost Squad, 1961; Top Secret, 1962; The Avengers, 1962-64; The Explorer, 1968; Visit From a Stranger, 1970; Out Damned Spot, 1972; Wind of Change, 1977; Robin's Nest, 1982; Never the Twain, 1982; The Secret Adversary, 1983; Lace, 1985; The First Modern Olympics, 1986; Minder on the Orient Express, 1986; Dr Who, 1986; William Tell, 1986; The Upper Hand (TV series). Address: c/o Jean Diamond, London Management, 2-4 Noel Street, London W1V 3RB, England.

**BLACKWELL Colin Roy,** b. 4 September 1927, South Molton, Devon, England. Consulting Engineer. m. Susan Elizabeth Hunt. Education: BSc, Honours, Civil Engineering, University of Bristol, 1959-51. Appointments: Commissioned 83 LAA Regiment Royal Artillery, served Middle East, 1946-48; Joined, 1951, Site Engineer, Gold Coast (later Ghana), 1955-57, Senior Engineer, 1957-68, Principal Engineer, 1969-82, Freeman Fox & Partners, Consulting Engineers; Director, Freeman Fox Ltd, 1983-87; Consultant on telescopes and observatories to Hyder Consulting Ltd (formerly Acer Consultants Ltd, formerly Acer Freeman Fox), 1987-; Member, CIRIA Research Committee, 1976-79; Member, British Council Mission to Saudi Arabia, 1985; BSI CSB Committee, 1986-91. Publications: Das 64m Radioteleskop in Parkes (Australien), 1966; The reflector dishes of the 210 ft radio telescope at Parkes, Australia and the 150 ft diameter radio telescope at Lake Transverse, Ontario, 1966. Memberships: Fellow, Institution of Civil Engineers; Fellow, American Society of Civil Engineers; Fellow Royal Astronomical Society. Address: 34 Drayton Gardens, London SW10 9SA, England.

**BLAINEY Geoffrey Norman,** b. 11 March 1930, Melbourne, Victoria, Australia. Writer. Education: Wesley College, Melbourne; Queen's College, University of Melbourne. Publications: The Peaks of Lyell, 1954; A Centenary History of the University of Melbourne, 1957; Gold and Paper, 1958; Mines in the Spinifex, 1960; The Rush That Never Ended, 1963; A History of Camberwell, 1965; If I Remember Rightly: The Memoirs of W S Robinson, 1966; Wesley College: The First Hundred Years (co-author and editor), 1967; The Tyranny of Distance, 1966; Across a Red World, 1968; The Rise of Broken Hill, 1968; The Steel Master, 1971; The Causes of War, 1973; Triumph of the Nomads, 1975; A Land Half Won, 1980; The Blainey View, 1982; Our Side of the Country, 1984; All for Australia, 1984; The Great Seesaw, 1988; A Game of our Own: The Origins of Australian Football, 1990; Odd Fellows, 1991; Eye on Australia, 1991; Jumping Over the Wheel, 1993; The Golden Mile, 1993; A Shorter History of Australia, 1994; White Gold, 1997; A History of the AMP, 1999; In Our Time, 1999; A History of the World, 2000; This Land is All Horizons, 2002; Black Kettle and Full Moon, 2003; A Very Short History of the World, 2004-. Honours: Gold Medal, Australian Literature Society, 1963; Encyclopaedia Britannica Gold Award, New York, 1988. Memberships: Australia Council, chairman, 1977-81; Commonwealth Literary Fund, chairman, 1971-73; Professor of Economic History and History, University of Melbourne, 1968-88; Inaugural Chancellor of University of Ballarat, 1994-98; Chairman, National Council for Centenary of Federation, 2001. Address: PO Box 257, East Melbourne, Victoria 3002, Australia.

**BLAIR Anna Dempster,** b. 12 February 1927, Glasgow, Scotland. Author. m. Matthew Blair, 13 June 1952, 1 son, 1 daughter. Education: Dunfermline College, Graduated 1947. Appointment: Teacher, Glasgow Education Authority, 1947-52, 1965-75. Publications: A Tree in the West; The Rowan on the Ridge, 1980; Historical Novels: Tales of Ayrshire (Traditional Tales Retold), 1993; Tea at Miss Cranston's Reminiscences/Social History, 1985; Croft and Creel, 1987; Scottish Tales, 1987; The Goose-Girl of Eriska, 1989; Traditional Tales: More Tea at Miss Cranston's, 1991; Seed Corn, 1989. Contributions to: Old Giffnock (local history); Various others. Address: 20 Barrland Drive, Giffnock, Glasgow G46 7QD, Scotland.

**BLAIR Anthony Charles Lynton (Tony),** b. 6 May 1953, Edinburgh, Scotland. Member of Parliament; Politician. m. Cherie Booth, 1980, 3 sons, 1 daughter. Education: Fettes College, Edinburgh; St Johns College, Oxford. Appointments: Barrister, Trade Union and Employment Law; MP, Sedgefield, 1983-; Shadow Treasury Spokesman, 1984-87, Trade and Industry Spokesman, 1987-88, Energy Spokesman, 1988-89, Employment Spokesman, 1989-92, Home Affairs Spokesman, 1992-94; Leader, Labour Party, 1994-, Prime Minister, First Lord of the Treasury and Minister for the Civil Service, 1997-. Publication: New Britain: My Vision of a Young Country, 1996; The Third Way, 1998. Honours: Honorary Bencher, Lincolns Inn, 1994; Honorary LLD, Northumbria; Charlemagne Prize, 1999. Address: 10 Downing Street, London SW1A 2AA, England.

**BLAIR Claude,** b. 30 Nov 1922, Manchester, England. Antiquary; Art Historian. Education: BA, 1950, MA, 1963, University of Manchester. Appointments: Assistant, Tower of London Armouries, 1951-56; Honorary Editor, Journal of Arms and Armour Society, 1953-77; Assistant Keeper, 1956-72, Deputy Keeper, 1966-72, Keeper, 1972-82, Metalwork, Victoria and Albert Museum, London; Consultant, Christie's, London, 1982-2004; Bonham's, London, 2005-. Publications: European Armour, 1958; European and American Arms, 1962; Pistols of the World, 1968; Three Presentation Swords in the Victoria and Albert Museum, 1972; The James A de Rothschild Collection at Waddesdon Manor: Arms, Armour and Base-Metalwork, 1974; Pollard's History of Firearms, 1983; A History of Silver, 1987; General Editor and contributor to The Crown Jewels, 1998. Honours: FSA, 1956; OBE, 1994; Gold Medal of the Society of Antiquaries, 1998; LittD (Honoris causa), Manchester

University, 2004; CVO, 2005. Address: 90 Links Road, Ashtead, Surrey KT21 2HW, England.

**BLAIR David Chalmers Leslie Jr,** b. 8 April 1951, Long Beach, California, USA. Alternative Rock Artist; Composer; Artist; Author. Education: BA, French, ESL certificate, California State University at Long Beach, 1979; Postgraduate Studies, Université de Provence, Aix-en-Provence, France, 1979-80. Publications: Novels: Death of an Artist, 1982; Vive la France, 1993; Death of America, 1994; Mother, 1998; Evening in Wisconsin, 2001; The Girls (and Women) I Have Known, 2001; A Small Snack Shop in Stockholm, Sweden, 2002; Composer, Writer and Recorder of 108 albums including: Her Garden of Earthly Delights; Sir Blair of Rothes; Europe; St Luke Passion. Membership: Libertarian Party, USA. Address: 19331 105th Avenue, Cadott, WI 54727, USA. Website: www.booklocker.com(mother)

**BLAIR John Samuel Greene,** b. 31 December 1928, Wormit, Fife, Scotland. Medical Historian; Former Surgeon. m. Ailsa Jean Bowes, 2 sons, 1 daughter. Education: High School of Dundee, Harris Gold Medal for Dux of School, Dux in English, 1946; Harkness Scholar, St Andrews University 1946-50; MB ChB, 1951; ChM, 1961; Clinical part of MD, St Andrews, 1953; D (Obst) RCOG, 1952; FRCS (Ed), 1958; FICS, 1983; BA (External), London, 1955. Appointments include: RAMC service 1952-55; Joined TA via St Andrews OTC (CO, 1967-71); Commanded RAMC and other Reserve Units, retired as Honorary Colonel, 225 (Highland) Field Ambulance, RAMC; Served at Musgrave Park Military Hospital as Consultant Surgeon on 2 tours during 1975-76, part of Security Forces Northern Ireland Command; Consultant Surgeon, Perth Royal Infirmary, 1965-90; Honorary Senior Lecturer in Surgery, Dundee University, Postgraduate Clinical Tutor, Perth, 1966-1971; Honorary Senior Lecturer, 1990-97, Reader, 1997-2001, History of Medicine, University of St Andrews; Current appointment: Honorary Senior Teaching Fellow, Medical History, Faculty of Medicine, University of Dundee. Publications: 14 articles in medical and surgical journals; 12 major historical articles; Books include: History of St Andrews OTC, 1982; History of Medicine in St Andrews University, 1987; Ten Tayside Doctors, 1988; History of the Bridge of Earn Hospital 1940-1990, 1990; History of the Royal Perth Golfing Society and County and City Club, 1997; In Arduis Fidelis. Definitive Centenary History of the Royal Army Medical Corps, 1989-1998, 1998, second edition, 2001; The Conscript Doctors: Memories of National Service, 2001; History of Tayforth Officers Training Corps, 2003; Numerous invited lectures. Honours include: OBE (Military), 1974; Doctor of Letters, honoris causa, St Andrews, 1991; John Blair Fund set up by British Society for the History of Medicine, 1996; Honorary Fellow, Royal College of Physicians of Edinburgh, 2000; Fellow, Society of Antiquaries (Scotland), 1997; Fellow Royal Historical Society, 2001; Honorary Member, SSHM, 2003. Memberships: Fellow BMA, 1993; Knight of St John - Hospitaller, Priory of Scotland, 1992-2000; President, Scottish Society of the History of Medicine, 1991-94; President, British Society for the History of Medicine, 1993-95; Apothecaries Lecturer, Worshipful Society of Apothecaries, London, 1994-; Ostler Club of London, 1996; Vice-President, International Society for the History of Medicine, 2000-; American Ostler Society, 2002. Address: "The Brae", 143 Glasgow Road, Perth PH2 0LX, Scotland. E-mail: jgb143@aol.com

**BLAKE Quentin Saxby,** b. 16 December 1932, Sidcup, Kent, England. Artist; Illustrator; Teacher. Education: Downing College, Cambridge; London Institute of Education; Chelsea School of Art. Appointments: Freelance Illustrator, 1957-; Tutor, Royal College of Art, 1965-86, Head, Illustration Department, 1978-86, Visiting Professor, 1989-, Senior Fellow, 1988; Children's Laureate, 1999. Publications: Illustrations for over 250 works for children and adults, including collaborations with Roald Dahl, Russell Hoban, Joan Aiken, Michael Rosen, John Yeoman; Non-fiction: La Vie de la Page, 1995; Quentin Blake: Words and Pictures, 2000; Tell Me a Picture, 2001; Laureate's Progress, 2002. Honours: Honorary Fellow: Brighton University, 1996; Downing College, Cambridge, 2000; Honorary RA; Chevalier des Arts et des Lettres, 2002; Dr hc: London Institute, 2000, Northumbria, 2001, RCA, 2001; Cambridge University, 2004; CBE, 2005. Address: Flat 8, 30 Bramham Gardens, London SW5 0HF, England.

**BLAKEMORE Colin,** b. 1 June 1944, Stratford-on-Avon, England. Neurophysiologist; Professor of Physiology. m. Andree Elizabeth Washbourne, 1965, 3 daughters. Education: Natural Sciences, Corpus Christi College, Cambridge, 1965; PhD, Physiological Optics, Neurosensory Laboratory, University of California at Berkeley, 1968. Appointments: Demonstrator, Physiological Laboratory, Cambridge University, 1968-72; Lecturer in Physiology, Cambridge, 1972-79; Fellow and Director of Medical Studies, Downing College, 1971-79; Professorial Fellow of Magdalen College, Oxford, 1979-; Waynflete Professor of Physiology, Oxford University, 1979-; Chief Executive European Dana Alliance for the Brain, 1996-; President, 1997-98, Vice President, 1990-, British Association for the Advancement of Science; President, British Neuroscience Association, 1997-2000; Director, McDonnell-Pew Centre for Cognitive Neuroscience, Oxford, 1990-2003; Director, MRC Interdisciplinary Research Centre for Cognitive Neuroscience, Oxford, 1996-2003; Chief Executive Medical Research Council; Associate Director, MRC Research Centre in Brain and Behaviour, Oxford, 1990-;. Publications: Editor, Handbook of Psychobiology, 1975; Mechanics of the Mind, 1977; Editor, Mindwaves, 1987; The Mind Machine, 1988, Editor, Images and Understanding, 1990; Vision: Coding and Efficiency, 1990; Sex and Society, 1999; Oxford Companion to the Body, 2001; Contributions to: Constraints on Learning, 1973; Illusion in Art and Nature, 1973; The Neurosciences Third Study Program, 1974; and to professional journals. Honours: Robert Bing Prize, 1975; Man of the Year, 1978; Christmas Lectures for Young People, Royal Institute, 1982; John Locke Medal, 1983; Netter Prize, 1984; Bertram Louis Abrahams Lecture, 1986; Cairns Memorial Lecture and Medal, 1986; Norman McAllister Gregg Lecture and Medal, 1988; Royal Society Michael Faraday Medal, 1989; Robert Doyne Medal, 1989; John P McGovern Science and Society Lecture and Medal, 1990; Montgomery Medal, 1991; Sir Douglas Robb Lectures, 1991; Honorary DSc, Aston, 1992; Honorary Osler Medal, 1993; Ellison-Cliffe Medal, 1993; DSc, Salford, 1994; Charles F Prentice Award, 1994; Annual Review Prize Lecture, 1995; Century Lecture, 1996; Alcon Prize, 1996; Newton Lecture, 1997; Cockcroft Lecture, 1997; Memorial Medal, 1998; Alfred Meyer Award, 2001; British Neuroscience Association Outstanding Contribution to Neuroscience, 2001. Memberships: Editorial Board, Perception, 1971; Behavioural and Brain Sciences, 1977; Journal of Developmental Physiology, 1978-86; Experimental Brain Research, 1979-89; Language and Communication, 1979; Reviews in the Neurosciences, 1984-; News in Physiological Sciences, 1985; Clinical Vision Sciences, 1986; Chinese Journal of Physiological Sciences, 1988; Advances in Neuroscience, 1989-; Vision Research, 1993-; Honorary Member, Physiological Society, 1998; Associate Editor, NeuroReport, 1989-; Honorary Associate, Rationalist Press Association, 1986-; Editor-in-Chief, IBRO News, 1986-; Leverhulme Fellowship, 1974-75; BBC Reith Lecturer, 1976; Lethaby Professor, RCA, London, 1978; Storer Lecturer, University of California at Davis, 1980; Regents' Professor, 1995-96; Macallum Lecturer, University of Toronto, 1984; Fellow, World Economic Forum, 1994-98; Honorary Fellow, Corpus Christi College, Cambridge, 1994-; Founder, Fellow, Academy of Medical Sciences, 1998-; Foreign Member, Royal Netherlands Academy of Arts and Sciences, 1993; Member, Worshipful Company of Spectacle Makers and Freemen of the City of London, 1997; Member, Livery, 1998; Patron and Member, Professional Advisory Panel Headway (National Head Injuries Association), 1997-; Patron, Association for Art, Science, Engineering and Technology, 1997- Address: Medical Research Council, 20 Park Crescent, London W1B 1AL, England

**BLANCHETT Cate,** b. 1969, Australia. Actress. m. Andrew Upton, 1997, 1 son. Education: Melbourne University, National Institute of Dramatic Art. Appointments: Plays include: Top Girls; Kafka Dances; Oleanna; Hamlet; Sweet Phoebe; The Tempest; The Blind Giant is Dancing; Plenty. Films include: Parkland; Paradise Road, 1997; Thank God He Met Lizzie, 1997; Oscar and Lucinda, 1997; Elizabeth, 1998; Dreamtime Alice, also co-producer; The Talented Mr Ripley; An Ideal Husband; Pushing Tin, 1999; Bandit, 2000; The Man Who Cried, 2000; The Gift, 2000; Bandits, 2000; Heaven, 2001; The Lord of the Rings: The Fellowship of the Ring, 2001; Charlotte Gray, 2001; The Shipping News, 2002; The Lord of the Rings: The Two Towers, 2002; The Lord of the Rings: The Return of the King, 2003; TV includes: Heartland, 1994; GP Police Rescue. Honours: Newcomer Award, 1993; Rosemont Best Actress Award; Golden Globe Award, 1998; BAFTA Award for Best Actress, 1999; Best Actress, National Board of Review, 2001; Golden Camera Award, 2001. Address: c/o Robyn Gardiner, PO Box 128, Surry Hill, 2010 NSW, Australia.

**BLANKHOLM Hans Peter,** b. 17 November 1952, Kolding, Denmark. Professor of Archaeology. m. Karen Marie Christensen, 2 sons. Education: Cand. Phil, 1978, Magister (Mag.Art), 1981, Dr. Phil., 1991, University of Århus, Denmark. Appointments: Professor of Archaeology, University of Tromsø, Norway. Research in hunter-gatherer archaeology of the temperate and arctic areas, and in analytical methodology, including multivariate statistics, spatial analysis and geographical information systems (GIS). Publications: Intrasite spatial analysis in theory and practice, 1991; On the track of a prehistoric economy: Maglemosian subsistence in early prehistoric south Scandinavia, 1996; Earliest Mesolithic site in northern Norway? A reassessment of Sarnes By, 2004. Honours: Listed in Who's Who publications and biographical dictionaries. Memberships: European Academy of Sciences; Union International des Sciences Pré- et Pròtohistòriques. Address: Department of Archaeology, University of Tromsø, 9037 Tromsø, Norway. E-mail: hanspb@sv.uit.no

**BLASHFORD-SNELL John Nicholas,** b, 22 October 1936, Hereford, England. Colonel; Royal Engineers; Explorer; Author. m. Judith, 2 daughters. Education: Victoria College, Jersey, Channel Islands; RMA Sandhurst; The Staff College, Camberley. Appointments: Various military postings and commands, and leader of numerous scientific, military and youth development expeditions; Instructor and Adventure Training Officer, RMA Sandhurst, 1963-66; Leader, Great Abbai, Blue Nile Expedition, 1968; Chairman, Scientific Exploration Society, 1969-; Commander, Operation Drake, 1978-81; Director-General, Operation Raleigh, 1984-91; Lecturer, Ministry of Defence, 1991-; Chairman, The Starting Point Appeal, The Merseyside Youth Association, 1993-2001; Chairman, The Liverpool Construction Crafts Guild, 2001-; Appeal Director, The Trinity Sailing Trust, 2004-. Publications: Books, including Weapons and Tactics, (co-author), 1972; Where the Trails Run Out, 1974; In the Steps of Stanley, 1975;

In the Wake of Drake, (co-author), 1980; Operation Drake, (co-author), 1981; 3 titles co-authored with Ann Tweedy, documenting the story of Operation Raleigh; Mammoth Hunt, (co-author), 1996; Kota Mama, (co-author), 2000; East to the Amazon (with Richard Snailham), 2002. Honours: MBE; OBE; Selgrave Trophy, 1975; Freeman of the City of Hereford, 1984; Honorary DEng, University of Bournemouth, 1997; Honorary DSc, Durham University, 1986; Darien Medal, Colombia, 1972; Livingstone Medal, Royal Scottish Geographical Society, 1975; Patron's Medal, Royal Geographical Society, 1993; Paul Harris Fellow, Rotary International, 1981; Gold Medal, Institute of Royal Engineers, 1994; La Paz Medal, Bolivia, 2001; President, Just a Drop Charity, 2002-. Memberships: President, Galley Hill Gun Club; President, The Centre for Fortean Zoology; The Vole Club; Trustee, Operation New World, 1996-. Address: Scientific Exploration Society, Expedition Base, Motcombe, Dorset, SP7 9PB, England. E-mail: jbs@ses-explore.org

**BLATNÝ Pavel,** b. 14 September 1931, Brno, Czech Republic. m. Danuse Spirková, 19 June 1982, 1 son, 1 daughter. Education: Studied Piano, Conducting and Composition; Musicology, University of Brno, 1958; Berklee School of Music, Boston, USA, 1968. Career: Composer; Conductor; Pianist; Chief, Music Department, Czech Television, to 1992; Professor, Janácek's Academy, Brno, to 1990. Compositions include: Concerto for Jazz Orchestra, 1962-64; Roll-call; Willow; Christmas Eve; Noonday Witch; Bells; Twelfth Night, based on Shakespeare's play, 1975; Full-length Musical for Children, Dilia, 1979; Two Movements for brasses, 1982; Signals for jazz orchestra, 1985; Prologue for mixed choir and jazz orchestra, 1984; Per organo e big band, 1983; Ring a Ring o' Roses, for solo piano, 1984; Symphony "Erbeniada" written for the festival "Prague Spring", world premier, 2004. Honours: Prize of Leos Jánácek, 1984; Antiteatro D'Argento for the Life's Work, Italy, 1988; Award for Life's Work, City of Brno, 2004. Membership: President, Club of Moravian Composers. Address: Absolonova 35, 62400 Brno. Czech Republic.

**BLAU Joseph Norman,** b. 5 October 1928, Berlin, Germany. Consultant Neurological Physician. m. Jill Seligman, 2 sons, 1 daughter. Education: St Bartholomew's Medical College, London; Army (RAMC) Head Injury Hospital, Wheatley, Oxfordshire; Neurological Registrar to Sir Russell (later Lord) Brain, The London Hospital, Whitechapel; Research Fellow, Neurology Department (Immunology), Massachusetts General Hospital, USA; Degrees: MD, FRCP; FRCPath. Appointments: Formerly: Consultant Neurologist: Northwick Park Hospital and Research Centre, Harrow Middlesex, Royal National Throat, Nose and Ear Hospital, Gray's Inn Road, London, National Hospital for Neurology and Neurosurgery, Queen Square, London; Currently: Recognised Teacher in Neurology, University of London Institute of Neurology, Queen Square, London; Consultant Neurologist, St Luke's Hospital for the Clergy, Honorary Director and Honorary Consultant Neurologist, City of London Migraine Clinic, London. Publications: Books: The Headache and Migraine Handbook, 1986; Migraine - Clinical, Therapeutic, Conceptual and Research Aspects (editor and contributor), 1987; Understanding Headaches and Migraine, 1991; Book Chapter: Cervicogenetic Headache (with H Merskey), 2002; Articles: Life long migraine without headache (with SI Cohen), 2003; Harold G Woolf. The man and his migraine, 2004; Water deprivation headache (with Kell and Sperling), 2004; Ponytail Headache, 2004. Honours: Open Science Scholarship, St Bartholomew's Hospital Medical College; Nuffield Medical Research Fellowship; Research Fellow, Harvard University. Memberships: Fellow and Councillor, Medical Society of London; Life Fellow, Royal Society of Medicine; Member and Past Chairman,

British Association for the Study of Headache; Life Fellow, Past Councillor, Anglo-Dutch Migraine Association; Member, Association of British Neurologists; Member, International Headache Society; Honorary Medical Advisor, Migraine Action Association; Honorary Medical Advisor, British Society for Music Therapy; London Medical Orchestra (Cellist). Address: 5 Marlborough Hill, London NW8 0NN, England.

**BLEASDALE Alan,** b. 23 March 1946. Playwright; Novelist. m. Julia Moses, 1970, 2 sons, 1 daughter. Education: Teachers Certificate, Padgate Teachers Training College. Publications: Scully, 1975; Who's Been Sleeping in My Bed, 1977; No More Sitting on the Old School Bench, 1979; Boys From the Blackstuff (televised), 1982; Are You Lonesome Tonight?, 1985; No Surrender, 1986; Having a Ball, 1986; It's A Madhouse, 1986; The Monocled Mutineer (televised), 1986; GBH (TV series), 1992; On the Ledge, 1993; Jake's Progress (TV), 1995; Oliver Twist, 1999. Honours: BAFTA Writer's Award, 1982; RTS Writer's Award, 1982; Broadcasting Press Guild TV Award for Best Series, 1982; Best Musical, London Stand Drama Awards, 1985; Hon DLitt, Liverpool Polytechnic, 1991; Best Writer, Monte Carlo International TV Festival, 1996; Best Drama Series, TV and Radio Industries Club, 2000. Address: c/o Harvey Unna and Stephen Durbridge Ltd, 24 Pottery Lane, Holland Park, London, W11 4LZ, England.

**BLEASDALE Cyril,** b. 8 July 1934, Liverpool, England. Director General. m. Catherine, 2 daughters. Education: Executive Programme, Stanford University, California, 1977. Appointments: Managing Director, Freightliner, 1975-82; Director, British Rail Intercity, 1982-86; General Manager, British Rail LM, 1986-89; Director, Scotrail, 1990-94; Chairman, Management Transport Consultancy, 1994-; Managing Director, Rail News, 1997-; Deputy Chairman, International Air Rail Organisation; Director General, Chartered Institute of Logistics and Transport, 1999-; Chairman, Herts Business Initiative, 2002-; Deputy Chairman, Transaid World-wide (Charity). Publications: Various on transport related issues. Honours: OBE, 1988; FCILT. Membership: RAC Club, London. Address: 40 Grieve Croft, Glasgow G71 8LU, Scotland.

**BLESSED Brian,** b. 9 October 1936, Mexborough, South Yorkshire, England. Actor. m. Hildegard Zimmerman, 1978, 1 daughter. Education: Bristol Old Vic. Appointments: Repertory companies in Nottingham and Birmingham; Stage appearances: Hamlet; Richard III; Henry V; State of Revolution; Metropolis; Cats; The Lion in Winter; Hard Times; One man show, An Evening with Brian Blessed; Chitty Chitty Bang Bang, 2002-03; Films include: Flash Gordon; Return to Treasure Island; Trojan Women; Man of La Mancha; Henry V; War and Remembrance; Robin Hood Prince of Thieves; Prisoners of Honour; Much Ado About Nothing; Hamlet; King Lear; Tarzan; Star Wars – The Phantom Menace; Mumbo Jumbo; TV includes: Z Cars; The Three Musketeers; I, Claudius; My Family and Other Animals; Blackadder; Tom Jones. Publications: The Turquoise Mountain; The Dynamite Kid; Nothing's Impossible; Blessed Everest; Quest to the Lost World. Address: c/o Derek Webster, AIM, Nederlander House, 7 Great Russell Street, London WC1B 3NH, England. E-mail: info@aim.demon.co.uk Website: www.a-i-m.net

**BLETHYN Brenda Anne,** b. 20 February 1946, Ramsgate, Kent, England. Actress. Partner, Michael Mayhew, 1977. Education: Thanet Technical College; Guildford School of Acting. Creative Works: Theatre appearances include: Mysteries, 1979; Steaming, 1981; Double Dealer, 1982; Benefactors, 1984; Dalliance, 1987; A Doll's House, 1987; Born Yesterday, 1988; The Beaux' Stratagem, 1989; An Ideal Husband, 1992; Wildest

Dreams, 1993; The Bed Before Yesterday, 1994; Habeas Corpus, 1996; Absent Friends, 1996; Mrs Warren's Profession, 2002-03. Films: The Witches, A River Runs Through It, 1992; Secrets and Lies, 1996; Remember Me, 1996; Music From Another Room, 1997; Girls' Night, 1997; Little Voice, 1999; Night Train, 1999; Daddy and Them, 1999; RKO 281, 1999; Saving Grace, 2000; On the Nose, In the Winter Dark, 1999; The Sleeping Dictionary, 2000; Yellow Bird, Pumpkin, 2000; Anne Frank – The Whole Story, 2001; Lovely and Amazing, 2001; Plots with a View, 2000; Sonny, 2002; Blizzard, 2002; Piccadilly Jim, 2004; Beyond the Sea, 2004; A Way of Life, 2004; On a Clear Day, 2005; Pooh's Heffalump Movie, 2005; Pride and Prejudice, 2005. TV includes: Henry VI (Part I), 1981; King Lear, 1983; Chance in a Million, 1983-85; The Labours of Erica, 1987; The Bullion Boys, 1993; The Buddah of Suburbia, 1993; Sleeping with Mickey, 1993; Outside Edge, 1994-96; First Signs of Madness, 1996; Belonging, 2004. Honours include: Best Actress Award, Cannes Film Festival, 1996; Boston Film Critics Award, 1997; LA Film Critics Award, 1997; Golden Globe, 1997; London Film Critics Award, 1997; BAFTA, 1997; Honorary Dr of Letters, 1999. Membership: Poetry Society, 1976-. Address: c/o ICM, 76 Oxford Street, London W1N 0AX, England.

**BLETSKAN Dmitry Ivanovich,** b. 7 November 1946, Goliatin, Mezhgorsky district, Transcarpathian region, Ukraine. Physicist. m. Elena Balazh, 1 son. Education: Higher Education, Uzhgorod State University, 1967; Candidate of Physico-Mathematical Sciences, 1973; PhD, 1985. Appointments: Assistant Professor, Chair of Semiconductors, 1970-88, Professor, 1988-, Uzhgorod National University. Director, R&P Company "Technocrystal", 1991-. Publications: More than 150 scientific articles; More than 200 inventions and patents; Monograph: Crystalline and glass-like chalcogenides of Si, Ge, Sn and alloys based on them. Textbooks for students: Electric measurements and measuring instruments; Practical works (electrics and magnetics). Honour: Ukraine State Prize-Winner in the field of science and engineering, 1989. Memberships: Academic Council on Theses for Scientific Degree, Uzhgorod National University; Academician, Academy of Engineering Sciences of the Russian Federation. E-mail: kan@interlan.ru

**BLETSKAN Mikhail Ivanovich,** b. 3 November 1939, Goliatin, Mezhgorsky district, Transcarpathian region, Ukraine. Philosopher; Professor. m. Emma Shvab, 2 daughters. Education: Higher Education, Philological Faculty, Uzhgorod State University, 1961; Candidate of Philosophy, 1968; PhD, 1990. Appointments: Senior Teacher of Philosophy, 1968-72, Assistant Professor, 1972-85, Chief of Chair, 1985-, Professor of Philosophy, 1990-, Uzhgorod National University. Publications: 48 Scientific publications: Monographs: Dialectics of scientific abstract formation; History of Ukrainian Philosophy; Social and political ideas in Ukraine at the end of XIX and in XX Centuries; Historical and philosophical prerequisites; Logics; History of Russian Philosophy. Honours: Medal of Ukraine "For Labour Valour", 1977; Title Honourable Labourer of Popular Schooling of Ukraine; Premium for textbooks for Uzhgorod University. Memberships: Corresponding Member of the Ukrainian Academy of Political Sciences, 1995; Academician of Academy of Higher School, 2005. E-mail: bletskan@iss.univ.uzhgorod.ua

**BLETSKAN Nikolay Ivanovich,** b. 22 July 1938, Goliatin, Mazhgorsky region, Ukraine. Physicist. m. Liudmila V Tereschenkova, 2 daughters. Education: Graduated, Uzhgorod State University, 1963; Candidate of Technical Science, 1970; Major Researcher, 1978; Assistant Professor, Moscow Institute of Electronic Engineering, 1983; Doctor of Technical Science, 1985; Professor, MIEE, 1987. Appointments: President,

Sapphire, Joint Stock Company Research and Production Centre. Publications: 125 articles and publications; 117 patents and inventions; 2 monographs: Oxygen in Silicon Single Crystals; Processes of Real Crystals Growing. Honours: Award, Council of Ministers, USSR, 1983; Order of Honour, USSR, 1986. Membership: Corresponding Member, Academy of Engineering Sciences, 1992; Person of the Year, 1999; Academician, 2003. Address: 42F 59, Str Letchika Babushkina, 129281 Moscow, Russia.

**BLIGE Mary J,** b. 11 January 1971, New York, USA. Singer. Career: Solo recording artiste; Support to Jodeci, UK tour, 1995. Recordings: Albums: What's The 411, 1992; My Life, 1994; Mary Jane, 1995; Share My World, 1997; The Tour, 1998; Mary, 1999; No More Drama, 2001; Ballads, 2001; Singles: What's The 411, 1992; Sweet Thing, 1993; My Love, 1994; You Bring Me Joy, 1995; All Night Long, 1995; Not Gon' Cry, 1996; Love Is All We Need, 1997; Everything, 1997; Seven Days, 1999; All That I Can Say, 1999; As, with George Michael, 1999; Also appears on: Father's Day, 1990; Changes, 1992; Close To You, 1992; Panther, 1995; Show, 1995; MTV Party To Go, 1995; Waiting To Exhale, 1995; Nutty Professor, 1996; Case, 1996; Ironman, 1996; Love And Consequences, 1998; Miseducation Of Lauryn Hill, 1998; Nu Nation Project, 1998. Address: Steve Lucas Associates, 156 W 56th Street, New York, NY 10019, USA.

**BLOCK William Charles,** b. 22 February 1937, Lowestoft, Suffolk, England. Research Scientist; Biologist. m. Flora May Watt, 2 sons, 1 daughter. Education: St Cuthberts Society, University of Durham, 1956-63; BSc (Honours), Zoology, University of Durham, 1960; CBiol, MIBiol – Chartered Biologist, 1961, Fellow, 1981, Institute of Biology; PhD, Animal Ecology, University of Durham, 1963; MA, University of Cambridge, 1966; DSc, University of Durham, 1986. Appointments include: Assistant Lecturer, Lecturer, Zoology, Makerere University College, University of East Africa, Kampala, Uganda, 1963-66; University Demonstrator in Entomology, University of Cambridge, 1966-67; Lecturer in Zoology, University of Leicester, 1967-76; Leverhulme Research Fellow, Senior Visiting Scientist, British Antarctic Survey, Signy Island and South Georgia, 1971-72; Principal Scientific Officer, Head of Terrestrial Biology Section, 1976-82, Individual Merit Post (Grade 6), Head of Terrestrial Biology Section and Fellfield Ecology Research Programme Leader, 1982-9, Individual Merit Post (Grade 5), leader of BAS Survival Strategies Programme, 1991-97, Senior Research Associate, Biological Sciences Division, 1997-2002, Emeritus Fellow, Biological Sciences Division, 2002-, British Antarctic Survey; Honorary Professor: School for Biological Science, University of Birmingham, 1997-2002, School of Science and Engineering, University of Abertay, Dundee, 1997-, School of Environmental Sciences, 1998-, University of East Anglia; Numerous fieldwork expeditions to Antarctica, 1971-96. Publications: 245 scientific publications: 158 articles in refereed journals, 8 book chapters, 1 book, 78 reports, book reviews and abstracts. Honour: Polar Medal, 1989. Memberships (Current): British Ecological Society; Fellow, Institute of Biology; Fellow, Royal Entomological Society of London, 1964; Senior Member, Wolfson College, Cambridge; Honorary Member, Society for Low Temperature Biology; Cyroletters Limited Liability Partnership. Address: British Antarctic Survey, High Cross, Madingley Road, Cambridge CB3 0ET, England. E-mail: wcb@bas.ac.uk

**BLONDEL Jean Fernand Pierre,** b. 26 October 1929, Toulon, France. University Professor; Writer. m. (1) Michele Hadet, 1954, divorced, (2) Teresa Ashton, 1982, 2 daughters.

Education: Diploma, Institut Études Politiques, Paris, 1953; BLitt, Oxford, England, 1955. Publications: Voters, Parties and Leaders, 1963; An Introduction to Conservative Government, 1969; Comparative Legislatures, 1973; Political Parties, 1978; World Leaders, 1980; The Discipline of Politics, 1982; The Organisation of Governments, 1982; Government Ministers in the Contemporary World, 1985; Political Leadership, 1987; Governing Together, co-editor, 1993; Comparative Government, 1995; Party and Government (co-editor), 1996; People and Parliament in the European Union (joint-author), 1998; Democracy, Governance and Economic Performance (co-editor), 1999. Contributions to: European Journal of Political Research. Honours: Honorary Doctorates, University of Salford, 1990, University of Essex, 1992, Catholic University of Louvain, 1992, University of Turku, 1995; Skytte Prize in Political Science, 2004. Memberships: Royal Swedish Academy of Sciences; American Political Science Association; British Political Studies Association; Association Française de Science Politique. Address: 15 Marloes Road, London W8 6LQ, England.

**BLOOM Arthur David,** b. 4 October 1934, Boston, Massachusetts, USA. Physician; Biomedical Scientist. m. Deborah Schwarz, 2 sons, 2 daughters. Education: AB, Harvard College, cum laude, 1956; MD, New York University School of Medicine, 1960. Appointments: Assistant and Associate Professor, Genetics and Pediatrics, University of Michigan, 1968-74; Professor of Human Genetics and Pediatrics, Columbia University, New York, 1974-88; President, Conte Institute for Environmental Health, 1986-93; President, Comité International de Scientifiques sur la Santé et l'Environnement, Paris, France, 1993-98; Professor, University of Vermont College of Medicine, USA, 1995-2001. Publications: 102 publications in scientific literature including 8 books; Tales of An American Emigré in Paris, 2000; Citron's Sonata, 2004. Memberships: Board of Directors, American Society Human Genetics; Society for Pediatric Research; AAAS; Director, Environmental Mutagenesis Society; Harvard Club of France; Executive Committee, American Club of Paris. Address: 17 rue des Coches, 78100 Saint Germain en Laye, France.

**BLOOM Claire,** b. 15 February 1931, London, England. Actress. m. (1) Rod Steiger, 1959, 1 daughter. (2) 1969, (3) Philip Roth, 1990, divorced 1995. Education: London, Bristol and New York. Appointments: Oxford Repertory Theatre, 1946; Stratford-on-Avon, 1948. Creative Works: Performances include: Mary, Queen of Scots in Vivat, Vivat Regina!, New York, 1972; A Streetcare Named Desire, London, 1974; The Innocents, USA, 1976; Rosmersholm, London, 1977; The Cherry Orchard, Chichester Festival, 1981; When We Dead Awaken, 1990; The Cherry Orchard, USA, 1994; Long Day's Journey into Night, USA, 1996; Electra, New York, 1998; Conversations after a Burial, London, 2000; A Little Night Music, 2003. Films include: A Doll's House, 1973; Islands in the Stream, 1975; The Clash of the Titans, 1979; Always, 1984; Sammy and Rosie Get Laid, 1987; Brothers, 1988; Crimes and Misdemeanours, 1989; Mighty Aphrodite, 1994; Daylight, 1995; Shakespeare's Women and Claire Bloom; The Book of Eve, 2001; Imagining Argentina, 2002. TV appreances include: A Shadow in the Sun, 1988; The Camomile Lawn, 1991; The Mirror Crack'd From Side to Side, 1992; Remember, 1993; A Village Affair, 1994; Family Money, 1996; The Lady in Question; Love and Murder; Yesterday's Children; One woman shows: Enter the Actress; These are the Women: A Portrait of Shakespeare's Heroines. Publications: Limelight and After, 1982; Leaving a Doll's House, 1996. Honours include: Evening Standard Drama Award for Best Actress, 1974. Address: c/o Jeremy Conway, 18-21 Jermyn Street, London SW1Y 6HB, England.

**BLOOM Orlando,** b. 13 January 1977, Canterbury, Kent, England. Actor. Education: National Youth Theatre, London; Scholarship, British American Drama Academy; Guildhall School of Music and Drama, 3 years. Career: Assistant, shooting club. Film appearances include: Wilde, 1997; The Lord of the Rings: The Fellowship of the Ring, 2001; The Lord of the Rings: The Two Towers, 2002; The Lord of the Rings: The Return of the King, 2003; Pirates of the Carribean: Curse of the Black Pearl, 2003; Troy, 2004; The Calcium Kid, 2004. TV appearances include: TV series "Casualty"; Midsomer Murders, 2000; Smack The Pony, 2000; The Saturday Show, 2001; So Graham Norton, 2002; The Tonight Show with Jay Leno, 2003; Primetime Live, 2003; V Graham Norton, 2003; V Graham Norton, 2003; The Brendan Leanard Show, 2003; Access Hollywood, 2003; GMTV, 2004; T4, 2004. Honours: Internet Movie Awards, 2002; Empire Award, 2002; MTV Movie Awards, 2002; Hollywood Discovery Awards; MTV Movie Awards, 2004.

**BLOOM Stephen,** b. 24 October 1942, Maidstone, Kent, England. Professor of Medicine; Head of Division. m. Margaret Janet Sturrock, 2 sons, 2 daughters. Education: MB BChir, 1967; MA, 1968; FRCP, 1978; MD, 1979; DSc, 1982; FRCPath, 1993; FMedSci, 1997. Appointments: Professor of Medicine (Consultant Physician), Imperial College London and Hammersmith Hospital, 1982-; Director of Endocrinology, 1982-, Director, Chemical Pathology, 1994, Clinical Director, Pathology and Therapy Services, 1996-, Hammersmith Hospital Trust; Head of Division of Investigative Science, Imperial College, 1997-. Publications: Co-edited books include: Gastrointestinal and Related Hormones, 1979; Radioimmunoassay of Gut Regulatory peptides, 1981; Basic Science in Gastroenterology, 1982; Gastrointestinal and Hepatobiliary Cancer, 1983; Systemic Role of Regulatory Peptides, 1982; Endocrine Tumours, 1985; Peptides: A Target for New Drug Development, 1991; Surgical Endocrinology, 1993; Numerous articles in major scientific and medical journals. Honours include: Walter Knox Chemistry Prize, 1962; Bacteriology Prize, 1965; Ophthalmology Prize, 1966; Radiotherapy and Radiology Prize, 1967; British Society of Gastroenterology Research Medal, 1977; Copp Lecturer, American Diabetic Association, 1978; Goulstonian Lecturer, Royal College of Physicians, 1979; Prossor White Oration, 1981; Eric-Sharpe Prize for Oncology, 1987; Arnold Bloom Lecture British Diabetic Association, 1995; Dale Medal, Society for Endocrinology, 2003. Memberships: Association of Physicians; Physiological Society; British Diabetic Association; Endocrine Society (British and American); Society of Gastroenterology (British and American); Medical Research Society; Bayliss & Starling Society; Royal Society of Medicine; European Association for the Study of Diabetes; American Diabetic Association; European Neuroscience Association. Address: Department of Metabolic Medicine, Imperial College London, 6th Floor, Commonwealth Building; Hammersmith Campus, Du Cane Road, London W12 0NN, England. Website: www.imperial.ac.uk

**BLOW DARLINGTON Joyce,** b. 4 May 1929, Morecambe, England. Retired. m. J A B Darlington. Education: MA, University of Edinburgh. Appointments: Council of Industrial Design, 1953-63; Publicity and Advertising Manager, Heal & Son Ltd, 1963-65; Board of Trade, 1965-67; Monopolies Commission, 1967-70; Assistant Secretary, Department of Trade & Industry, 1970-72; Assistant Secretary, Department of Prices and Consumer Protection, 1972-74; Under-Secretary, Office of Fair Trading, 1977-80; Under Secretary, Department of Trade and Industry, 1980-84; Vice-President, Trading Standard Institute, 1985-; Chairman, Mail Order Publishers

Authority, 1985-92; Chairman, Direct Marketing Association Authority, 1992-97; Board Member, 1987-97, Chairman, Consumer Policy Committee, 1987-93, British Standards Institution; Trustee, University of Edinburgh Development Trust, 1990-94; Chairman, East Sussex Family Health Services Authority, 1990-96; President, Association for Quality in Healthcare, 1991-94; Chairman, Public Relations Education Trust, 1992-97; Chairman, Child Accident Prevention Trust, 1996-2002. Publication: Consumers and International Trade: A Handbook, 1987. Honours: Freeman City of London, 1984; OBE, 1994. Memberships: Hon FCIPR; FCMI; FRSA. Address: 17 Fentiman Road, London SW8 1LD, England

**BLUM Igor Robert,** b. 24 October 1969, Frankfurt am Main, Germany. Dentist; Researcher, Educator. Education: DDS, Dental Surgery, Semmelweis University, Budapest, Hungary, 1990-95; MSc, Oral Surgery, 1995-97, PhD, Restorative Dentistry, 1998-2002, University of Manchester, UK; Dr Med Dent, (Magna cum laude), Dental Medicine, Goethe University of Frankfurt, Germany, 2000-2002. Appointments: Associate Clinician in Dental Implantology, 1998-2001, Associate Clinician in Oral Medicine, 1998-2001, University of Manchester, UK; Founder and Chief Executive Officer, Globaldentistry, 2002; Clinical Teacher in Oral Surgery, 2004-05, Clinical Teacher in Prosthodontics, 2004-05, University of Manchester, UK; Lecturer at international conferences; Lecturer in Restorative Dentistry, University of Bristol, England, 2005-. Publications: Numerous articles in scientific dental journals as author, first author and co-author include most recently: Contemporary views on dry socket (alveolar osteitis): A clinical appraisal of standardisation, aetiopathogenesis and management: a critical review, 2002; The teaching of the repair of direct composite restorations, 2002; The repair of direct composite restorations: an international survey of the teaching of operative techniques and materials, 2003; Defective direct composite restorations – replace or repair? A Comparison of teaching between Scandinavian dental schools, 2003. Honours: First Class Achievement for Oral Health Sciences Thesis, National Institute of Dentistry, 1995; Achievement in introducing a standardised definition for alveolar osteitis (dry socket) to the dental profession. Listed in Who's Who publications and biographical dictionaries. Memberships: Postgraduate Membership in Oral Surgery; Postgraduate Membership in Prosthodontics; General Dental Council, England; Hessian Dental Chamber of Germany; British Dental Association; Royal College of Surgeons of England; Royal College of Surgeons of Edinburgh; European Association of Osseointegration; Association of Dental Educators in Europe; International Association for Dental Research. Address: 109 Pinkers Mead, Emersons Green, Bristol BS16 7EJ, England.

**BLUNKETT Rt Hon David,** b. 6 June 1947, England. Politician. 3 sons. Education: Sheffield University. Appointments: Worker, East Midlands Gas Board; Teacher, Industrial Relations and Politics, Barnsley College of Technology; Joined Labour Party, 1963; Member, Sheffield City Council, 1970-87, Leader, 1980-87; Member, South Yorkshire County Council, 1973-77; MP for Sheffield Brightside, 1987-; National Executive Committee (NEC) of Labour Party, 1983; Chair, NEC Local Government Committee, 1984; Local Government Front Bench Spokesman in Opposition's Environment Team, 1988-92; Shadow Secretary of State for Health, 1992-94, for Education, 1994-95, for Education and Employment, 1995-97; Secretary of State for Education and Employment, 1997-2001, for the Home Department, 2001-04. Publications: Local Enterprise and Workers' Plans, 1981; Building From the Bottom: The Sheffield Experience, 1983; Democracy in Crisis: The Town Halls Respond, 1987; On a

Clear Day (autobiography), 1995; Politics and Progress, 2001. Address: House of Commons, London SW1A 0AA, England.

**BLYTHE Ronald George,** b. 6 November 1922, Acton, Suffolk, England. Author. Appointments: Associate Editor, New Wessex Edition of the Works of Thomas Hardy, 1978. Publications: A Treasonable Growth, 1960; Immediate Possession, 1961; The Age of Illusion, 1963; Akenfield, 1969; William Hazlett: Selected Writings, editor, 1970; The View in Winter, 1979; From the Headlands, 1982; The Stories of Ronald Blythe, 1985; Divine Landscapes, 1986; Each Returning Day, 1989; Private Words, 1991; Word from Wormingford, 1997; First Friends, 1998; Going to meet George, 1998; Talking About John Clare, 1999; Out of the Valley, 2000; The Circling Year, 2001; Talking to the Neighbours, 2002; The Assassin, 2004; Borderland, 2005; Critical Studies of Jane Austen, Thomas Hardy, Leo Tolstoy, Literature of the Second World War, Henry James. Contributions to: Observer; Sunday Times; New York Times; Listener; Atlantic Monthly; London Magazine; Tablet; New Statesman; Bottegue Oscure; Guardian. Honours: Heinemann Award, 1969; Society of Authors Travel Scholarship, 1970; Angel Prize for Literature, 1986; Honorary MA, University of East Anglia, 1991; Hon DLitt, Anglia Polytechnic University, 2001; MLitt, Lambeth; Hon DLitt, University of Essex, 2002; Lay Canon, St Edmundsbury Cathedral, 2003. Memberships: Royal Society of Literature, fellow; Society of Authors; The John Clare Society, president; Fabian Society. Address: Bottengoms Farm, Wormingford, Colchester, Essex, England.

**BNINSKI Kazimierz Andrzej,** b. 28 February 1939, Gdynia, Poland. Physician in General Practice. m. Teresa Maria de Gallen Bisping, 2 July 1988, 2 sons, 1 daughter. Education: MD, University of Gdansk, Poland, 1964. Appointments: Senior House Officer, Nelson Hospital, London, England, 1967; Senior House Officer, St Mary Abbots Hospital, London, England, 1968; Registrar in Medicine, St Mary's Hospital, 1972-77; Physician, 7th US Army, Germany, 1977-81; Junior Partner, General Practice, 1981-87; Senior Doctor, Director-in-Charge Polish Clinic, London, 1988-. Address: 131 Harley Street, London W1G 6BB, England.

**BOARDMAN Christopher Miles,** b. 26 August 1968, England. Cyclist. m. Sally-Anne Edwards, 1988, 3 sons, 1 daughter. Education: Withens College. Appointments: Competed in 9 World Championships; Holder of various national records and 20 national titles; Individual Pursuit, Olympic Games, Barcelona, 1992, Double World Champion, 1997, 1998; World Record for Distance Cycled in 1 hour, 1993, 1996; Won, World 4,000m Cycling Championships, Broke his own world record, 1996; Retired, 2001. Honours include: Bronze Medal, Commonwealth Games, Edinburgh, 1986; 2 Bronze Medals, Commonwealth Games, Auckland, 1990; Gold Medal, Olympic Games, Barcelona, 1992; Winner, Tour de France Prologue and holder, Yellow Jersey, 1994. Address: c/o Beyond Level Four Ltd, Lindfield House, Station Approach, Meols, Wirral L47 8XA, England.

**BOBIER Claude-Abel,** b. 18 March 1934, France. m. Manissier Arlette, 4 September 1959, 3 daughters. Education: BS, 1953; ENS St Cloud, 1956-60; Agreg SN, 1960; Doctor, 1971. Appointments: University of Paris VI, 1960-75; Professor, University of Tunis, 1975-86; MC University of Bordeaux I, 1986-99; Retired as Consultant, 1999. Publications include: Les éléments structuraux recents essentiels de la Tunisie nord-orientale, 1983; Morphologie de la marge Caraibe Colombienne: Relation avec la structure et la sedimentation, 1991; The Post-Triassic Sedimentary Cover of Tunisa: Seismic Sequences and Structure, 1991; Apports de l'analyse morphostructurale dans la connaissance de la physiographie du golfe de Tehuantepec (Mexique est-pacifique), 1993; Sequence stratigraphy, Basin dynamics and Petroleum geology of the Miocene from Eastern Tunisia, 1996; Recent tectonic activity in the South Barbados Prism. Deep towed side scan sonar imagery, 1998; Distribution des sédiments sur la marge du Golfe de Tehuantepec (Pacifique oriental). Example d'interaction tectonique-eustatisme, 2000; Rôle de l'halocinese dans l'evolution du Bassin d'Essaouira/ Sud Ouest Morocain), 2004; Rôle du systeme de failles E-W dans l'evolution geódynamique de l'Avant Pays de la chaîne alpine de Tunisie. Example de l'accident de Sbiba-Cherishira Tunisie Centrale. Honour: International Ambassador's Order, 1998. Memberships: American Association of Petrololeum Geololgists; American Geophysical Union; New York Academy of Sciences. Address: 6 Square du Gue, F-33170 Gradignan, France.

**BOBKO Nataliya Andreyevna,** b. 30 November 1960, Kiev, Ukraine. Psychophysiologist. Education: Biologist-Physiologist of Humans and Animals, Teacher of Biology and Chemistry (MSc equivalent), Biological Department, Kiev State University, 1982; Candidate of Biological Science, Hygiene (PhD equivalent), Kiev Research Institute of Labour Hygiene and Occupational Diseases, 1992. Appointments: Senior High-Educated Laboratory Assistant, 1982-84, Junior Research Scientist, 1984-85, Laboratory of Mental Labour Physiology, Junior Research Scientist, 1985-91, Research Scientist, Laboratory of Labour Physiology of Process Operators, 1991-92, Senior Research Scientist, Laboratory of Chronobiology Problems in Labour, 1992-95, Senior Research Scientist, Laboratory of Mental Labour Physiology, 1995-, Department of Labour Physiology, Institute for Occupational Health, Kiev, Ukraine (before 1992, Kiev Research Institute of Labour Hygiene and Occupational Diseases). Publications: Over 110 publications in national and international peer reviewed journals, collections and presented at conferences as author and co-author include most recently: Cognitive performance and its psycholphysiological maintenance in operative personnel at Chernobyl NPP control rooms: effect of professional duties differences and workplace environment, 2004; Long-term effects of cosmoheliogeophysical factors on cardiovascular system work in human-operators of round-the-clock industry, 2004. Honours: 12 travel grants to attend international congresses, symposiums and conferences, 1995-2005; Title: Senior Research Scientist, Institute for Occupational Health, Kiev, Ukraine, 1994. Memberships: International Commission on Occupational Health, 2001-, National Secretary to Ukraine, Member of the Joint Board of Shiftwork Committee and Working Time Society, Member of the Scientific Committee on Neurotoxicology and Psychophysiology; Member of Sigma Xi, The Scientific Research Society, USA, 2002-; Patents: 2001, 2003, 2004. Address: Institute for Occupational Health, Saksagansky St 75, Kiev, 01033 Ukraine. E-mail: natalia@ioh .freenet.kiev.ua

**BOBROVSKAYA Nataliya I,** b. 12 November 1939, Khatinnach, Khabarovskii Region, Russia. Eco-Physiologist; Geobotanist. Education: Diploma, Leningrad State University, 1961; Diploma, Doctor of Philosophy, 1973; Diploma, Doctor of Sciences, 1991; Diploma of Correspondence, Russian Academy of Ecology, 1998. Appointments: Junior Scientific Worker, 1961-74, Senior Scientific Worker, 1974-91, Chief, Laboratory of Steppe Vegetation, 1991-, Komarov Botanical Institute, St Peterburg, Russia. Publications: 2 monographs: Water relations in trees and shrubs of desert, 1985; Water relations of steppe and desert plants of Mongolia, 1991; 51 articles in scientific journals. Honours: Honours of Presidents of Academy of sciences, USSR; Bronze Medal of the Central Committee of VDNH, URSS.

Membership: Russian Academy of Ecology. Address: Komarov Botanical Institute, ul. Prof. Popova 2, St Petersburg, Russia 197276. E-mail: cinadmin@ok3277spb.edu

**BOCHAROV Yury,** b. 30 July 1928, Moscow Region, Russia. University Professor. m. Valentina Bocharova, 2 daughters. Education: Graduate, Engineering, Bauman Higher Technology School, Moscow, Russia, 1953; Mechanical Engineering Researcher, University of California, Berkeley, USA, 1960; Candidate of Engineering Science (PhD), 1961, Doctor of Science, Engineering, 1972, Bauman Higher Technology School, Moscow, Russia; Academician (Full Member), Russian Academy for Natural Science. Appointments: Design Engineer, Metal Forming, 1953-56; PhD Student, 1956-60; Assistant Professor, 1957, Associate Professor, 1964, Professor, 1974-, Dean of Mechanical Engineering, 1974-76, 1979-81, Vice Rector, 1981-85, Head of Department, 1985-91, Bauman Higher Technology School (since 1991, Baumann State Technical University), Moscow, Russia; Technical Advisor, Bahr-Dar Polytechnic, Ethiopia, 1967-69; UNESCO Expert, Mechanical Engineering Design, University of Moratuwa, Sri Lanka, 1976-79. Publications: 9 books and text books; More than 300 articles; More than 100 patents and invention certificates; Latest publication: Metal Forming Machinery. Mechanical Engineering Encyclopedia Vol IV.4 (author, editor-in-chief), 2005. Honours: State Award for Professional Excellence, 1980; Russian Academy for Natural Science Award for Science and Economy Development, 2000; State Honours for Science Development, 2003. Memberships: IACEE; ASEE; RANS. Address: Khokhlovsky Per 10-50, Moscow 109028, Russia. E-mail: yuri9310@yandex.ru

**BOE Grethe,** b. 11 March 1958, Oslo, Norway. Computer Engineer; Website Co-Editor. m. Oyvind K Myhre, 1 son, 1 daughter. Education: BA, English (major), Political Science, Astronomy, University of Oslo, 1982. Appointments: Systems Engineer, IBM, Norway, 1983-92; Freelance Computer Consultant, 1992-; Editor and Technical Advisor at http: //www.harrisonfordmedia.com, 2002-. Publications: Articles on website. Honours: IBM Professional Excellence Award, 1986; IBM Professional Marketing Award, 1988, 1990; Life Fellow of the International Biographical Association, 2005; Member of the Order of International Fellowship, 2005; Deputy Director General of the IBC, 2005; International Order of Merit, 2005; International Professional of the Year, 2005; Outstanding Female Executive Award, 2005; Order of International Ambassadors, ABI, 2005; International Medal of Vision, 2005; Life Achievement Award, IBC, 2005; World Congress of Arts, Sciences and Communication, Lifetime Achievement Award, 2005; Listed in various Who's Who publications and biographical dictionaries. Address: Skolebakken 5, 2750 Gran, Norway. E-mail: gboee@online.no Website: www.harrisonfordmedia.com

**BOEV Zlatozar Nikolaev,** b. 20 October 1955, Sofia, Bulgaria. Zoologist; Ornithologist. m. Education: Graduate, Department of Zoology of the Vertebrate Animal, Faculty of Biology, University of Sofia, 1975-80; Postgraduate, Zoology Department, National Museum of Natural History, 1984-86. Appointments: Doctor of Philosophy, 1986; Associate Professor, 1992; Doctor of Sciences, 1999; Professor of Zoology, 2001. Publications: Over 170 papers in scientific journals chiefly on fossil and sub-fossil birds; Over 255 articles in popular science journals; 5 textbooks; 12 popular books; 14 countries in Europe, North America and Asia. Memberships include: Society of Avian Palaeontology and Evolution; International Council for Archaeology; Society of European Avian Curators; Association for Environmental Archaeology and others. Address: National

Museum of Natural History, Bulgarian Academy of Sciences, 1 Blvd Tsar Osvoboditel, 1000 Sofia, Bulgaria. E-mail: boev@nmnh.bas.bg

**BOGDANOFF Stewart R,** b. 16 August 1940, London, England. Educator. m. Eileen Dolan, 1 son, 2 daughters. Education: BSc, Kings College, Briarcliff Manor, New York, 1963; MA and Professional Degree, New York University, 1965; Graduate Work NYU, SUNY New Platz, Harvard University, 1972-; Certificate in Administration and Supervision, 1988. Appointments: Coach, intramural director, curriculum writer, fundraiser Thomas Jefferson Elementary School, Lakeland School District, 1965-96; Physical Education Teacher, Lakeland School District, 1965-96; Head Teacher, Thomas Jefferson Elementary School, Lakeland School District, 1984-96; Acting Principal, Thomas Jefferson Elementary School, 1985-86; Educational Consultant, Speaker, Writer, 1996-. Honours include: New York State Teacher of Year, honoured at White House by President Reagan, 1983; Project Inspiration Award, National Association for Sport and Physical Education, 1992; Point of Light Award, President Bush, 1992; International Man of Year Award and Men of Achievement Award, International Biographical Centre, England, 1993; 1st teacher from NYS inducted into National Teachers Hall of Fame, Emporia, Kansas, honoured by President Clinton at Rose Garden ceremony, Scholarship in name of Stewart Bogdanoff established by Servicemaster, 1993; Founders 2000 Award from American Alliance for Health, Physical Education Recreation and Dance with room dedicated in his honour, National Center in Reston, Virginia, 1995; J C Penny Golden Rule Award, Westchester County United Way Volunteer of Year, 1995; Inducted into Briarcliff High School Hall of Distinguished Alumni, 1995; Golden Years Award, New York State Association for Health, Physical Education, Recreation and Dance; Selected as one of the Fifty Most Influential People in Westchester and Putnam Counties during the 20th Century, Journal News; American Medal of Honor, ABI, 2003; Listed in numerous Who's Who and biographical publications including: Who's Who in American Education; Contemporary Who's Who, ABI, 2003; Great Minds of the 21st Century, ABI, 2003-04. Memberships include: Kappa Delta Pi; New York State Teachers of the Year; Harvard Principals Center, others. Address: 588 Heritage Hills of Westchester, Unit A, Somers, NY 10589, USA.

**BOGDANOV Michael,** b. 15 December 1938. Film, Television and Theatre Director. Education: University of Dublin, Trinity College; Munich and Sorbonne. Appointments include: Director, Producer, Writer, TV in England and Ireland; Producer, Director, Radio Telefis Eireann, 1966-69; Own TV Series, Broad And Narrow, ATV; Director, The Bourgeois Gentilhomme, Oxford Playhouse, 1969; Assistant Director, Royal Shakespeare Co; Peter Brook's Associate, A Midsummer Night's Dream, Stratford and World Tour; Associate Director, Tyneside Theatre Co, 1971; Associate Director, Leicester Haymarket Theatre Trust, Artistic Director, Phoenix Theatre, 1973; Artistic Director, Young Vic Theatre, 1978; Director, Royal Shakespeare Co, 1979; Associate Director, Royal National Theatre, 1980-88; Co-Founder, Joint Artistic Director, English Shakespeare Co, 1986; Intendant, Deutsches Schauspielhaus, Hamburg, 1989-92.; Worked as a director in theatres throughout England, Wales, Denmark, Germany, USA, Hong Kong, Australia; Formed The Wales Theatre Company, 2003; TV work: Shakespeare on the Estate, BBC, 1994; The Tempest in Butetown, BBC, Break My Heart, HTV, 1996; Macbeth, Granada, 1997; A Light in the Valley, BBC Wales, 1998; Voices of a Nation, BBC, 1999; A Light on the Hill, BBC Wales, 1999; A Light in the City, BBC Wales, 2000; The Welsh in Shakespeare, BBC, 2002. Publications: The English Shakespeare Company - The Story of the Wars of the Roses; Reineke Fuchs; Hiawatha; The Ancient Mariner; Sir Gawain and the Green Knight; Beowulf; Shakespeare in a Multi-Cultural Society. Honours: Numerous theatre awards including SWET; Olivier Director of the Year, 1979, 1989; TV and film awards, and nominations including: Best Arts Documentary, Royal Television Society, 1995; Best Drama Documentary, Banff Film Festival, 1995; Best Regional Film, Royal Television Society, 1999. Memberships: Founder Member, Vice Chairman, Directors Guild of GB; Patron, Swansea Arts Festival, Playbox Theatre Co, New Vic Theatre Co, Sherman Theatre Cardiff, Theatrebox; Chair, Welsh Arts Awards; Board Member, Royal Academy of Dramatic Art, Theatre Royal, Bath; MCC.

**BOGDANOVICH Peter,** b. 30 July 1939, Kingston, New York, USA. Film Director; Writer; Producer; Actor. m. (1) Polly Platt, 1962, divorced 1970, 2 daughters, (2) L B Straten, 1988. Appointments: Film Feature-Writer, Esquire, New York Times, Village Voice, Cahiers du Cinema, Los Angeles Times, New York Magazine, Vogue, Variety and others, 1961-.Publications: The Cinema of Orson Welles, 1961; The Cinema of Howard Hawks, 1962; The Cinema of Alfred Hitchcock, 1963; John Ford, 1968; Fritz Lang in America, 1969; Allan Dwan: The Last Pioneer, 1971; Pieces of Time: Peter Bogdanovich on the Movies (in UK as Picture Shows), 1961, enlarged edition, 1985; The Killing of the Unicorn: Dorothy Stratten (1960-1980), 1984; A Year and a Day Calendar (editor), 1991; This is Orson Welles, 1992; Who the Devil Made It, 1997. Films: The Wild Angels, 1966; Targets, 1968; The Last Picture Show, 1971; What's Up Doc?, 1972; Paper Moon, 1973; Daisy Miller, 1974; At Long Last Love, 1975; Nickelodeon, 1976; Saint Jack, 1979; They All Laughed, 1981; Mask, 1985; Illegally Yours, 1988; Texasville, 1990; Noises Off, 1992; The Thing Called Love, 1993; Who The Devil Made It (director), 1997; Mr Jealousy, 1997; Highball, 1997; Coming Soon, 1999; Rated X, 2000; The Independent, 2000 The Cat's Meow (director), 2001. Honours: New York Film Critics' Award for Best Screenplay, British Academy Award for Best Screenplay, 1971; Writer's Guild of America Award for Best Screenplay, 1972; Silver Shell, Mar del Plata, Spain, 1973; Best Director, Brussels Festival, 1974; Pasinetti Award, Critic Prize, Venice Festival, 1979. Memberships: Directors Guild of America; Writer's Guild of America; Academy of Motion Picture Arts and Sciences. Address: c/o William Pfeiffer, 30 Lane of Acres, Haddonfield, NJ 08033, USA.

**BOGLE Joanna Margaret, (Julia Blythe),** b. 7 September 1952, Carshalton, Surrey, England. Author; Journalist. m. James Stewart Lockhart Bogle, 20 September 1980. Appointments: Local Borough Councillor, London Borough of Sutton, 1974-81; Governor, London Oratory School, 1976-86. Publications: A Book of Feasts and Seasons, 1986; When the Summer Ended (with Cecylia Wolkowinska), 1991; A Heart for Europe (with James Bogle), 1992; Caroline Chisholm, 1993; Come On In - It's Awful!, editor, 1994; We Didn't Mean to Start a School, 1998. Contributions to: local newspapers, 1970-74; South London News, 1984-86; Catholic Times, 1994-; various national newspapers, 1980-. Address: Christian Projects, PO Box 44741, London SWIP 2XA, England.

**BOGOMOLOV Edward A,** b. 19 September 1940, Leningrad, USSR. Physicist. m. Galina (Stratilova) Bogomolova, 1 daughter. Education: Graduate, Physics, Leningrad State University, 1963; PhD, Astrophysics, 1984, Diploma of Senior Scientist, 1988, Dr of Sciences (Physics and Mathematics), in Astrophysics, 2004, Ioffe Physico-Technical Institute, St Petersburg. Appointments: Practical Researcher, 1963-65, Scientist, 1965-86, Senior Scientist, 1986-99, Head of the Cosmic Spectrometry Laboratory, 1999-, Ioffe Physico-Technical Institute, Russian Academy of Sciences. Publications:

75 scientific works in journals, books and the proceedings of 8 international cosmic ray conferences. Honours: Grantee: Soros Foundation, 1992, INTAS, 1997; Russian Foundation for Basic research Grants, 1997, 2000; Many Medals. Memberships: Space Council of the Russian Academy of Sciences (RAS), Section of Cosmic Ray Physics, 1997; Scientific Council of the RAS on Complex Cosmic Ray Problems, 1999-; PAMELA (international space experiment) collaboration, 1996-. Address: Ioffe Physico-Technical Institute, Politekhnicheskaya 26, 194021 St Petersburg, Russia. E-mail: edward.bogomolov@p op.ioffe.rssi.ru

**BOHR Aage Niels,** b. 19 June 1922, Copenhagen, Denmark. Physicist. m. (1) Marietta Bettina, deceased, 1978, 2 sons, 1 daughter, (2) Bente Scharff, 1981. Education: Graduated, University of Copenhagen. Appointments: Associate, Department of Science and Industrial Research, London, 1943-45; Research Assistant, Institute of Theoretical Physics, Copenhagen, 1946; Professor of Physics, University of Copenhagen, 1956-; Director, Niels Bohr Institute, 1963-70; Director, Nordita (Nordic Institute of Theoretical Physics), 1975-81. Memberships: Danish, Norwegian, Pontifical, Swedish, Polish, Finnish, Yugoslav Academies of Science; National Academy of Sciences, USA; American Academy of Arts and Sciences; American Philosophical Society; Royal Physiograph Society, Lund, Sweden; Academy of Technical Sciences, Copenhagen; Deutsche Academie der Naturforsche Lepoldina. Publications: Rotational States of Atomic Nuclei, 1954; Co-author, Nuclear Structure, Vol I, 1969, Vol II, 1975. Honours: Honorary PhD, Oslo, Heidelberg, Trondheim, Manchester, Uppsala; Dannie Heineman Prize, 1960; Pius XI Medal, 1963; Atoms for Peace Award, 1969; Ørsted Medal, 1970; Rutherford Medal, 1972; John Price Wetherill Medal, 1974; Nobel Prize for Physics, 1975; Ole Rømer Medal , 1976. Address: c/o Niels Bohr Institute, Blegdamsvej 15-17, 2100 Copenhagen, Denmark.

**BOICE Martha Hibbert,** b. 1 October 1931, Toledo, Ohio, USA. Writer; Publisher. m. William V Boice, 1 son, 2 daughters. Education: BA, Ohio Wesleyan University, 1953; MSW, University of Michigan School of Social Work, 1955. Appointments: Caseworker, Travelers Aid, Toledo, Ohio, 1955-57; Publisher, Knot Garden Press, Dayton, Ohio, 1986-. Publications: Organiser, compiler, A Sense of Place, 1977; Author, compiler, Shaker Herbal Fare, 1985; The Wreath Maker, 1987; The Herbal Rosa, 1990; Maps of the Shaker West, 1997; Columnist, Centerville-Bellbrook Times, 1984. Honours: Distinguished Service Award, National Association of Monnett Clubs, Ohio Wesleyan University, 1974; Volunteer of the Year, Dayton-Montgomery County Park District, 1985; Centerville, Ohio' Mayor's Award for Community Service, 1988; Award of Excellence, OAHSM, 1998; Listed in biographical publications. Memberships: Phi Beta Kappa; Centerville-Washington Township Historical Society, Landmark Chair, 1972-78, 1980-84, 1997-2000; Landmarks Foundation of Centerville-Washington Township, Chair, 1997-2001; Herb Society of America; Library Committee Chain, 1988-1991; Western Shaker Study Group, Secretary, 2001-; Program Chain, 2003 and 2004, Trustee, Friends of White Water Shaker Village, 2002-. Address: 7712 Eagle Creek Drive, Dayton, OH 45459, USA. E-mail: marthabolce@aol.com

**BOJKOV Vassil Kroumov,** b. 29 July 1956, Velingrad, Bulgaria. Economist. m. Maia Bojkova, 1 son. Education: MSc Mathematics, Sofia University "Kliment Ohridsky, 1981; MSc, Economy, University of National and World Economy, 1998; Management, Marketing and Control in Tourism, Institute for Postgraduate Studies, 2000. Appointments: Chairman, Board of Directors, Nove Holding; President, Bulgarian Shooting Federation; President of the Professional Football Club, CSKA; President, Bulgarian Chess Federation Founder of Bulgarian Business Club "Vuzrajdane" and Tracia Foundation. Honours: Nominee, MR Economics Awards, Bulgaria; Listed in Who's Who publications and biographical dictionaries. Membership: New York Academy of Sciences. Address: 43, Moskovska Str, 1000 Sofia, Bulgaria. E-mail: vb@nove.bg Website: www.nove.bg

**BOKSENBERG Alexander,** b. 18 March 1936. Astronomer. m. Adella Coren, 1960, 1 son, 1 daughter. Education: BSc, Physics, University of London; PhD, 1961. Appointments: SRC Research Assistant, Department of Physics and Astronomy, University College London, 1960-65; Lecturer in Physics, 1965-75; Head of Optical and Ultraviolet Astronomy Research Group, 1969-81; Reader in Physics, 1975-78; SRC Senior Fellow, 1976-81; Professor of Physics and Astronomy, 1978-81; Sherman Fairchild Distinguished Scholar, California Institute of Technology, 1981-82; Director, Royal Greenwich Observatory, 1981-93; Royal Observatories, 1993-96; Research Professor, University of Cambridge and PPARC Senior Research Fellow, Universities of Cambridge and London, 1996-; Extraordinary Fellow, Churchill College, Cambridge, 1996-. Honours: Chair, New Industrial Concepts Ltd, 1969-81; President, West London Astronomical Society, 1978-; Chair, SRC Astronomy Committee, 1980-81; Numerous other committees on astronomy, 1980-; Visiting Professor, Department of Physics and Astronomy, University College, London, 1981-, Astronomy Center, University of Sussex, 1981-89; Honorary Doctorate, Paris Observatory, 1982; Asteroid (3205) named Boksenberg, 1988; Honorary Professor of Experimental Astronomy, University of Cambridge, 1991-; Hon DSc (Sussex), 1991; Executive Editor, Experimental Astronomy, 1995-; Honorary President, Astronomical Society of Glasgow; Hannah Jackson Medal, 1998. Membership: Past member of over 30 other councils, boards, committees, etc, 1970-; ESA Hubble Space Telescope Instrument Definition Team, 1973-; Fellow, Royal Society, 1978; SA Astronomical Observatory Advisory Committee, 1978-85; Freeman, Clockmakers Co, 1984; British Council Science Advisory Committee, 1987-91; Liveryman, 1989; Fachbeirat of Max Planck Institut für Astronomie, 1991-95; Fellow, University College, London, 1991-; Member of Court, 1994. Address: University of Cambridge, Institute of Astronomy, The Observatories, Madingley Road, Cambridge, CB3 0HA, England.

**BOLAND Janet Miriam,** b. 6 December 1923, Kitchener, Ontario, Canada. Lawyer; Justice Supreme Court. m. (1) John Boland, (2) Taylor Statten, 3 sons. Education: BA, University of Western Ontario, 1946; Law Degree, Osgoode Hall Law School, 1950; Called to the Bar, 1950. Appointments: Private Practice, 1950-58; Associate, White, Bristol, Beck & Phillips, Toronto, 1958-68; Partner, Lang, Mitchener, Farquharson, Cranston & Wright, Toronto, 1968; Appointed Queen's Counsel, 1966; Instructed in real estate and landlord and tenant law, Bar Admissions Course, 1967-72; Appointed County Court Judge, County of York, 1972; Appointed to Trial Division, Supreme Court of Ontario, 1976-98; Retired from Supreme Court, 1998; Member, Canada Pension Appeals Board, 1989-. Publications: Many judgements in civil and criminal trials. Honours: QC, 1966; Honorary Doctorate of Law, Sir Wilfred Laurier University, 1976. Memberships: President, Canadian Women's Senior Golf Association; Honorary President, Junior League of Toronto; Hamilton Golf and Country Club. Address: # 1605 33 Harbour Square, Toronto, Ontario, Canada M5J 2G2.

**BOLDON Ato,** b. 30 December 1973, Port of Spain, Trinidad (resident of USA, 1988-). Athlete. Education: University of California, Los Angeles. Appointments: Coached by John Smith; Central American and Caribbean Record Holder at 60m indoors (6.49 secs), 100m (9.86 secs) and 200m (19.77 secs). Honours: Gold Medal, World Junior Championships 100m and 200m, 1992; 4th, Commonwealth Games 100m, 1994; Bronze Medal, World Championships 100m, 1995; Gold Medal, NCAA Championships, 1996; Bronze Medals, Olympic Games 100m and 200m, 1996; 100m World Champion, 1997, 1999; Gold Medal, World Championships 200m, 1997; Gold Medal, Goodwill Games, New York, 200m, 1998; Gold Medal, Commonwealth Games 100m, 1998; Silver Medal, 100m, Bronze Medal, 200m, Olympic Games, 2000; Youngest sprinter ever to run under 10 seconds in the 100m and under 20 seconds in the 200m (at end of 2001). Website: www.atoboldon.com

**BOLDYREV Alexander Alexandrovitch,** b. 5 September 1940, Arkhangelsk City, Russia. Biologist; Professor of Biochemistry. m. Valeria Maltseva, 28 September 1963, 2 daughters. Education: MSc, 1963, PhD, 1967, M V Lomonosov Moscow State University; DSc, Leningrad State University, 1977; Postdoctoral Fellow, University Aarhus, Denmark, 1973-74. Appointments: Senior Science Researcher, Moscow State University, 1975-87; Visiting Professor, King's College London, England, 1982, 1986; Visiting Professor, Waseda University, Tokyo, Japan, 1990, 1993; Head, Laboratory of Clinical Neurochemistry, Institute of Neurology, Moscow, 1993-. Publications: More than 300 science articles and reviews in Russian and international journals; Several textbooks and monographs including: Carnosine and protection of tissues against oxidative stress, 1999. Honours: V S Gulevitch Prize, Russian Academy of Medical Sciences; Honorable Professor, International Albert Schweizer University; Honorable Professor, King's College, London; Meritorious Science Worker, Russia. Memberships include: International Society for Neurochemistry; Society for Neuroscience; The European Peptide Club; New York Academy of Sciences; London Diplomatic Academy, UK; International Academy of Scientific Discovers and Inventors, Russia; American Association for the Advancement of Sciences, USA. Address: Department of Biochemistry, M V Lomonosov Moscow State University, School of Biology, Room 141, Lenin's Hills 119992, Moscow, Russia. E-mail: aaboldyrev@mail.ru

**BOLES Timothy Coleridge,** b. 27 November 1958, United Kingdom. Managing Director. m. Deborah Clare Lewis, 2 sons. Education: Royal Military College, Sandhurst. Appointments: Commissioned into RHG/D (Blues and Royals); Captain, 1982-86; Special Reserve Commission, 1987-2000; Sedgwick Underwriting Agencies, 1986-88; Director: Gardner Mountain and Capel Cure Agencies Ltd, 1989-94, Harrison Brothers, 1994-99, Managing Director, Simcocks Pensions Ltd, 2003-; Chairman: Everitt Boles Motorsport Insurance Management, 1999-2002, AKG Group, 1999-. Honours: GSM, Northern Ireland; UN Peacekeeping Medal, 1982; FRGS, 1983; MSI, 2004. Memberships: Chartered Insurance Institute, 1988; Securities & Investment Institute, 1998. Address: Glen Wyllin Lodge, Kirk Michael, Isle of Man, IM6 1AN, United Kingdom.

**BOLGER Dermot,** b. 6 February 1959, Finglas, Ireland. Novelist; Dramatist; Poet; Editor. m. Bernadette Clifton, 1988, 2 sons. Education: Finglas and Benevin College, Finglas. Appointments: Factory hand, library assistant, professor author; Founder and Editor, Raven Arts Press, 1979-92; Founder and Executive Editor, New Island Books, Dublin, 1992-. Publications: Novels: Night Shift, 1985; The Woman's Daughter, 1987, augmented edition, 1991; The Journey Home,

1990; Emily's Shoes, 1992; A Second Life, 1994; Father's Music, 1997; Finbar's Hotel (collaborative novel), 1997; Ladies Night at Finbar's Hotel (collaborative novel), 1999; Temptation, 2000; The Valparaiso Voyage, 2001. Plays: The Lament for Arthur Cleary, 1989; Blinded by the Light, 1990; In High Germany, 1990; The Holy Ground, 1990; One Last White Horse, 1991; The Dublin Bloom, 1994; April Bright, 1995; The Passion of Jerome, 1999; Consenting Adults, 2000. Poetry: The Habit of Flesh, 1979; Finglas Lilies, 1980; No Waiting America, 1981; Internal Exiles, 1986; Leinster Street Ghosts, 1989; Taking My Letters Back: New and Selected Poems, 1998. Editor: The Dolmen Book of Irish Christmas Stories, 1986; The Bright Wave: Poetry in Irish Now, 1986; 16 on 16: Irish Writers on the Easter Rising, 1988; Invisible Cities: The New Dubliners: A Journey through Unofficial Dublin, 1988; Invisible Dublin: A Journey through Its Writers, 1992; The Picador Book of Contemporary Irish Fiction, 1993; 12 Bar Blues (with Aidan Murphy), 1993; The New Picador Book of Contemporary Irish Fiction, 2000; Druids, Dudes and Beauty Queens: The Changing Face of Irish Theatre, 2001. Contributions to: Anthologies. Honours: A E Memorial Prize, 1986; Macauley Fellowship, 1987; A Z Whitehead Prize, 1987; Samuel Beckett Award, 1991; Edinburgh Fringe First Award, 1991, 1995; Stewart Parker BBC Award, 1991; Playwright in Association, Abbey Theatre, Dublin, 1998. Address: c/o A P Watt, 20 John Street, London WC1N 2DR, England.

**BOLGER Leslie,** b. 11 August 1947, Liverpool, England. Musician (guitarist); Lecturer. m. Claire Holland, 3 daughters. Education: Certificate in Education (with distinction), University of Manchester. Musical Education: Studied with world renowned jazz guitarist George Gola, Australia. Career: Jazz performances with artistes including: Martin Taylor; Louis Stewart; Ike Isaacs; Gary Potter; Kenny Baker; Don Rendel; Many television and radio broadcasts; Arranger, Music Adviser, Granada Television; Session guitarist, Arranger, Piccadilly Radio; Backing guitarist for many top cabaret artists including: Russ Abbott; Joe Longthorne; Bob Monkhouse; Matt Monro; Vince Hill. Publications: Many publications include Fretwire magazine. Honours: Many first places with honours or distinction for Les Bolger Jazz Guitar Ensemble. Membership: Musicians' Union. Address: 12 Firbank Close, Daresbury View, Runcorn, Cheshire WA7 6NR, England.

**BOLKIAH, HRH Prince Jefri,** b. Brunei. Politician. Appointments: Minister of Culture, Youth and Sports; Deputy Minister of Finance; Minister of Finance, 1988-97; Former chair, Royal Brunei Airlines; Chair, Brunei Investment Agency; Former proprietor, Asprey & Garrad. Address: c/o Ministry of Finance, Bandar Seri Begawan, Brunei. Address: c/o Ministry of Finance, Bandar Seri Begawan, Brunei.

**BOLKIAH HRH, Prince Mohamed,** b. 27 August 1947, Brunei. Politician. Education: Royal Military Academy, Sandhurst, England. Appointment: Ministry of Foreign Affairs, 1984-. Address: Ministry of Foreign Affairs, Jalan Subok, Bandar Seri Begawan, Brunei.

**BOLKIAH MU'IZUDDIN WADDAULAH, HM Sultan Sir Muda Hassanal,** b. 15 July 1946, Brunei. m. (1) Rajah Isteri Anak Saleha, 1965, 1 son, 5 daughters, (2) Pengiran Isteri Hajjah Mariam, divorced 2003, 2 sons, 2 daughters. Education: Victoria Institute, Kuala Lumpur, Malaysia; Royal Military Academy, Sandhurst, England. Appointments: Crown Prince and Heir Apparent, 1961; Ruler of State of Brunei, 1967-; Prime Minister of Brunei, 1984-; Minister of Finance and Home Affairs, 1984-86, of Defence, 1986-, also Finance and Law. Honours include: Honorary Captain, Coldstream Guards, 1968; Honorary

Marshall, RAF, 1992; Sovereign and Chief of Royal Orders, Sultans of Brunei. Address: Istana Darul Hana, Bandar Seri Begawan, BA 1000, Brunei. E-mail: pro@jpm.gov.bn

**BOLLAND Alexander,** b. 21 November 1950, Kilmarnock, Scotland. Queen's Counsel. m. Agnes H P Moffat, 1 son, 2 daughters. Education: University of St Andrews, 1969-74; University of Glasgow, 1974-77. Appointments: Admitted Faculty of Advocates, 1978; Captain, Directorate of Army Legal Services, 1978-80; Standing Junior Counsel, Department of Employment, 1988-92; Temporary Sheriff, 1989-99; Queens' Counsel, 1992-; Part Time Chairman, Employment Tribunals, 1993-. Memberships: New Club, Edinburgh; Naval and Military, London. Address: 60 North Street, St Andrews, Fife, Scotland.

**BOLLENGIER Francine,** b. 12 July 1940, Antwerp, Belgium. Professor; Senior Scientist. Education: Masters Degree, Sciences, cum laude, Université Libre de Bruxelles, 1962; Masters Degree, Biomedical Sciences, summa cum laude, 1975, Doctor of Sciences, summa cum laude, 1976, Vrije Universiteit Brussel; Clinical Biologist, Medical Chemistry, nomination by the Belgian Government, 1976; Appointments: Scientific Collaborator, Department of Enzymology, 1963-65, Scientific Collaborator, Department of Human Reproduction, 1965-71, Université Libre de Bruxelles; Assistant, 1971-76, Principal Assistant, 1976-78, Assistant Professor, 1978-85, Department of Physiopathology of the Nervous System, Assistant Professor, 1986-91, Associate Professor, 1992-2003, Department of Pharmacology, Vrije Universiteit Brussel; Retired, Honorary Associate Professor, 2004-. Publications: 50 scientific articles of which 40 in international journals. Honours: Jean Stas Prize, Koninkijke Academie voor Wetenschappen en Letteren, België; Referee for National Alliance for Research on Schizophrenia and Depression, USA. Memberships: 3 national and 4 international societies. Address: Italielei, 171, PB 11, 2000 Antwerpen, Belgium.

**BON JOVI Jon (John Bongiovi),** b. 2 March 1962, Sayreville, New Jersey, USA. Vocalist; Songwriter; Musician (guitar). m. Dorothea Hurley, May 1989, 1 son, 1 daughter. Career: Singer, local bands: Raze; Atlantic City Expressway; Singer, founder member, US rock group Bon Jovi, 1984-; 40 million albums sold worldwide to date; Numerous worldwide tours, including US, UK, Europe, USSR, South America, Australia, Japan, 1984-; Support tours with Kiss; Scorpions; .38 Special; Headliners, Donington Monsters Of Rock Festival, 1987; Moscow Music Peace Festival, 1989; Numerous television, radio and video appearances worldwide; Own management company, BJM; Own record label Jambco. Recordings: US Number 1 singles include: You Give Love A Bad Name, 1986; Living On A Prayer, 1987; Bad Medicine, 1988; I'll Be There For You, 1989; Solo: Blaze Of Glory, 1990; Destination Anywhere, 1997; Midnight In Chelsea Pt 1, 1997; Real Life Pt 1, 1999; Real Life Pt 2, 1999; Numerous other hits include: Wanted Dead Or Alive; Lay Your Hands On Me; Living In Sin; Born To Be My Baby; Keep The Faith; In These Arms; I'll Sleep When I'm Dead; Bed Of Roses; Always; I Believe; Someday I'll Be Saturday Night; This Ain't A Love Song; Lie To Me; These Days; Hey God; One Road Man; Albums: Bon Jovi, 1984; 7800° Fahrenheit, 1985; Slippery When Wet (13 million copies sold), 1986; New Jersey, 1988; Keep The Faith, 1991; Crossroad (Best Of), 1994; These Days, 1995; Solo album: Blaze Of Glory (film soundtrack, Young Guns II); Contributor, Stairway To Heaven/Highway To Hell charity record, 1989; Two Rooms (Elton John/Bernie Taupin tribute album), 1991. Honours: American Music Awards, Favourite Pop/Rock Band, 1988; Favourite Pop/Rock Single, 1991; Bon Jovi Day, Sayreville, 1989; Silver Clef, Nordoff-Robbins Music Therapy, 1990; All albums Gold or Platinum status; Golden Globe, Best Original Song, Blaze Of Glory, 1991; Oscar Nomination, Blaze Of Glory; Best Selling Album Of Year, Crossroad, 1994; BRIT Award, Best International Group, 1996. Current Management: c/o BJM, 809 Elder Circle, Austin, TX 78733, USA.

**BOND Brian James,** b. 17 April 1936, Marlow, Buckinghamshire, England. Military Historian. m. Madeleine Carr. Education: BA, History, Worcester College, Oxford, 1959; MA, King's College, London, 1962; MA, All Souls College, Oxford, 2000. Appointments: Lecturer, 1966, Reader, 1977, Professor, 1986, Department of War Studies, King's College, London; Retired 2001. Publications: Books include: The Pursuit of Victory: From Napoleon to Saddam Hussein, 1996; The Unquiet Western Front, 2002. Honours: Fellow of King's College, London; President, British Commission for Military History, 1986-. Memberships: Royal United Services Institute; Royal Over-Seas League. Address: Olmeda, Ferry Lane, Medmenham, Marlow, Bucks SL7 2EZ, England.

**BOND (Thomas) Michael,** b. 13 January 1926, Newbury, Berkshire, England. Author. m. (1) Brenda May Johnson, 29 June 1950, divorced 1981, 1 son, 1 daughter, (2) Susan Marfrey Rogers, 1981. Education: Presentation College, 1934-40. Publications: Children's Books: A Bear Called Paddington, 1958; More About Paddington, 1959; Paddington Helps Out, 1960; Paddington Abroad, 1961; Paddington at Large, 1962; Paddington Marches On, 1964; Paddington at Work, 1966; Here Comes Thursday, 1966; Thursday Rides Again, 1968; Paddington Goes to Town, 1968; Thursday Ahoy, 1969; Parsley's Tail, 1969; Parsley's Good Deed, 1969; Parsley's Problem Present, 1970; Parsley's Last Stand, 1970; Paddington Takes the Air, 1970; Thursday in Paris, 1970; Michael Bond's Book of Bears, 1971; Michael Bond's Book of Mice, 1971; The Day the Animals Went on Strike, 1972; Paddington Bear, 1972; Paddington's Garden, 1972; Parsley Parade, 1972; The Tales of Olga de Polga, 1972; Olga Meets Her Match, 1973; Paddington's Blue Peter Story Book, 1973; Paddington at the Circus, 1973; Paddington Goes Shopping, 1973; Paddington at the Seaside, 1974; Paddington at the Tower, 1974; Paddington on Top, 1974; Windmill, 1975; How to Make Flying Things, 1975; Eight Olga Readers, 1975; Paddington's Cartoon Book, 1979; J D Polson and the Dillogate Affair, 1981; Paddington on Screen, 1981; Olga Takes Charge, 1982; The Caravan Puppets, 1983; Paddington at the Zoo, 1984; Paddington's Painting Exhibition, 1985; Elephant, 1985; Paddington Minds the House, 1986; Paddington at the Palace, 1986; Paddington's Busy Day, 1987; Paddington and the Magical Maze, 1987; Paddington and the Christmas Surprise, 1997; Paddington at the Carnival, 1998; Paddington Bear, 1998. Adult Books: Monsieur Pamplemousse, 1983; Monsieur Pamplemousse and the Secret Mission, 1984; Monsieur Pamplemousse Takes the Cure, 1987; The Pleasures of Paris, Guide Book, 1987; Monsieur Pamplemousse Aloft, 1989; Monsieur Pamplemousse Investigates, 1990; Monsieur Pamplemousse Rests His Case, 1991; Monsieur Pamplemousse Stands Firm, 1992; Monsieur Pamplemousse on Location, 1992; Monsieur Pamplemousse Takes the Train, 1993; Bears and Forebears (autobiography), 1996; Monsieur Pamplemousse Afloat, 1998; Monsieur Pamplemousse on Probation, 2000; Monsieur Pamplemousse on Vacation, 2002; Monsieur Pamplemousse Hits the Headlines, 2003. Honour: Officer of the Order of the British Empire, 1997. Address: The Agency, 24 Pottery Lane, Holland Park, London W11 4LZ, England.

**BONDI Hermann (Sir),** b. 1 November 1919, Vienna, Austria (British Citizen). Mathematician. m. Christine M Stockman, 1947, 2 sons, 3 daughters. Education: BA, Mathematics, Cambridge University, 1940; Research Student, 1941.

Appointments: Naval Radar Work, British Admiralty, 1942; Fellowship, Trinity College, 1943; Assistant Lecturer, 1945-48; Visiting Professor, Cornell University, 1951, Harvard University, 1953; Chair of Applied Mathematics, King's College, London; Advisory Posts, Ministry of Defence, National Space Committee, European Space Organization, Department of Energy, National Environment Research Council. Publications: Cosmology, 1960; The University at Large, 1961; Relativity and Common Sense, 1964; Assumption and Myth in Physical Theory, 1967; Science, Churchill and Me (autobiography), 1990; Numerous books on cosmology and related subjects. Honour: Knighted, 1973; Honorary Fellow: Regent's College, 1988, Institute of Physics, 1992, Institute of Mathematics and its Applications, 1993, Indian Academy of Sciences, 1996; Honorary DSc: Sussex, Bath, Surrey, 1974, York, 1980, Southampton, 1981, Salford, 1982, Birmingham, 1984, St Andrews, 1985, Vienna, 1993, Plymouth, 1995; Gold Medal, Institute of Mathematics and its Applications, 1988; GD Birla International Award for Humanism, 1990; Planetary Award, Association of Space Explorers, 1993; President's Decoration for Science and Arts, Austria, 1997; Gold Medal, Royal Astronomical Society, 2001. Membership: Fellow of the Royal Society, 1959. Address: Churchill College, Cambridge, CB3 0DS, England.

**BONDS Georgia Anna Arnett,** b. 30 December 1917, New York, USA. Writer; Lecturer. m. Alfred Bryan Bonds, 2 sons, 2 daughters. Education: BA, University of North Carolina, 1938; MA, Louisiana State University, 1941; Post Graduate Work, University of North Carolina, 1941-42; Baldwin Wallace College, 1960-. Appointments: Editorial Assistant, The Southern Review; Editorial Assistant Public School Curriculum of Louisiana; Editor of English version of Wheat Growing In Egypt; First Lady of Baldwin Wallace College; Volunteer, World Association of Girl Guides And Girl Scouts; Worked world-wide for peace through international understanding. Publications: The Lake Erie Girl Scout Council, the First Seventy Five Years; First two chapters of A Promise Kept, 1912-2002, ninety years of helping girls succeed; Novel, Who Killed Bob Lawson?, 2003; Numerous articles in popular magazines. Honours: World Friendship and Understanding Through Girl Scouting; Thanks Badges, 1971, 1997. Memberships: Phi Beta Kappa; United Methodist Church; YWCA; AAUW; Eastern Star; AARP. Address: PO Box 768, Berea, OH, USA.

**BONHAM CARTER Helena,** b. 26 May 1966, Golders Green, London, England. Actress. 1 son. Career: Films include: Lady Jane; A Room with a View; Maurice; Francesco; The Mask; Getting it Right; Hamlet; Where Angels Fear to Tread; Howard's End, 1991; A Dark Adapted Eye (TV), 1994; Mary Shelley's Frankenstein, 1994; The Glace Bay Miners' Museum, 1994; A Little Loving, 1995; Mighty Aphrodite, 1995; Twelfth Night, 1996; Margaret's Museum, 1996; Parti Chinois, 1996; The Theory of Flight, 1997; Keep the Aspidistra Flying, 1997; The Wings of the Dove, 1998; The Revengers' Comedies, 1998; Women Talking Dirty, 1999; Fight Club, 1999; Until Human Voices Wake Us, 2000; Planet of the Apes, 2002; The Heart of Me, 2002; Novocaine, 2002; Till Human Voices Wake Us, 2003; Charlie and the Chocolate Factory, 2005. Television appearances include: A Pattern of Roses; Miami Vice; A Hazard of Hearts; The Vision; Arms and the Man; Beatrix Potter. Address: c/o Conway van Gelder Limited, 18/21 Jermyn Street, London, SW1Y 6HP, England.

**BONNEAU Guy,** b. 14 July 1967, Chicoutimi, Quebec, Canada. University Professor. m. Angélique Brazeau-Bonneau, 1 son, 1 daughter. Education: MA, 1991, Theology, Biblical Studies, PhD, Theology, Biblical Studies, 1995, University of Montreal,

Canada. Appointments: Research Assistant, 1989, Research and Teaching Assistant, 1991, Faculty of Theology, University of Montreal; Lecturer, University of Montreal, University of Sherbrooke, University of Quebec at Chicoutimi, University of Quebec at Trois Rivières, Canada, 1992-96; Adjunct Professor, 1996-2001, Chair, 1999-2002, Associate Professor, 2001, Religious Studies Department, University of Sudbury, Canada; Responsible for development of a new undergraduate programme in Theology, University of Sudbury, 2001-2002. Publications: 12 books include most recently: L'espérance du Royaume. Clés de lecture l'évangile de Marc, 2003; San Marcos Nuevas lecturas, 2003; Profetismo e instituçāo no christianismo primitivo, 2003; Paul et les Corinthiens I: La première lettre, 2004; Paul et les Corinthiens II: La seconde lettre, 2004; 9 research papers. Memberships: Stodiurum Novi Testamenti Societas; Société Canadienne de Théologie; Association Catholique des Études Bibliques au Canada. Address: University of Sudbury, Sudbury, Ontario P3E 2C6, Canada. E-mail: gbonneau@hotmail.com

**BONNER Gerald**, b. 18 June 1926, London, England. Retired Academic m. Priscilla Jane Hodgson, 1 son, 1 daughter. Education: First Class Honours, School of Modern History, 1952, Wadham College, Oxford, 1949-53; MA, 1956. Appointments: Military Service, 1944-48; Assistant Keeper, Department of Manuscripts, British Museum, 1953-64; Lecturer, Reader in Theology, University of Durham, 1964-89; Distinguished Professor, Early Christian Studies, Catholic University of America, Washington DC, 1990, 1991-94; Visiting Professor, Augustinian Studies, Villanova University, 1999. Publications: St Augustine of Hippo: Life and Controversies, 1963, 3rd edition, 2002; God's Decree and Man's Destiny, 1987; Church and Faith in the Patristic Tradition, 1996; Augustine of Hippo: The Monastic Rules, with a commentary by Gerald Bonner, 2004; Articles in the Augustinus Lexicon, 1986-2002; Augustine Through the Ages: An Encyclopaedia, 1999 and in learned journals. Honour: Johannes Quasten Medal, School of Religious Studies, Catholic University of America. Memberships: Fellow, Society of Antiquaries of London. Address: 7 Victoria Terrace, Durham DH1 4RW, England.

**BONNEVIE Mai-Bente**, b. 15 May 1936, Oslo, Norway. Artist; Painter; Teacher. Divorced, 3 sons. Education: School of Arts and Crafts, Oslo, 1957-58; John Cass Art School, London, 1963; Bachelor's Degree, History of Art, University of Oslo, 1974; The Academy of Art, Oslo, 1980-84. Career: Lecturer in University of Texas, University of Tacoma, Pacific Lutheran University, USA, 1988; Lecturer in Art History, Oslo Drawing & Painting School and other art schools, University of Oslo, colleges and art associations, 1980-99; Solo exhibitions: Ministry of Foreign Affairs, New York, USA, 1988; Gallery LNM, 1991; "Of Earth", Nordic House, Reykjavik, Iceland, 1993; Risør Art Association, 1995; Lillesand Art Association, 1997; "Sun in Earth" Gallery, Hå-Jæren, Norway, 1997; Denmark Region Gallery, 1999; Gallery Allmenningen, Bergen, 2003; Gallery A, Oslo, 2004; Laesø, Denmark, 2005; Group exhibitions include most recently: Hommage à Rian, Norabakken, 1998; Roskilde Kunstforening, Denmark, 1998; Farge, Stavanger Kunstforening, 2000; Galleri LNM, 2000; Galleri Voss, 2002; Springside Exhibition, Philadelphia, USA, 2004. Publications: "Another Language", anthology on Norwegian Women Writers and Poets a Feminist Project – PAX, 1977; Co-editor, Sirene, feminist periodical, 1970s; Several articles on art and feminism; Several book covers and scenery commission. Honours: The Artists Association Blom Scholarship, 1987-97; Ingrid Lindbäck Langaard Fund, 1988-93; The State of Norway's Yearly Scholarship for Artists, 1990-; The City of Oslo's Cultural Prize, 1998; Norwegian Visual Artists Fund, 1998-; The Fund of Visual Artists, 2003-05. Memberships: Norwegian Association

of Visual Artists, NBK; National Union of Artists, LNM; Young Artists Association, UKS; Artist Association; Board Member, Nansen School, Lillehammer Humanistic Academy, Norway; Board Member, Hans Christian Ostrø's Memory Prize, Oslo; Board Member, The Prize of Zola, Oslo. Address: Stensgaten 24A, 0358 Oslo, Norway.

**BONNEY George L W**, b. 10 January 1920, London, England. Surgeon; Author. m. Margaret, 2 daughters. Education: Scholar, Eton College; Scholar, St Mary's Hospital Medical School, University of London; MS, University of London, 1947. Appointments: Surgeon-Lieutenant, Royal Naval Volunteer Reserve; Research Assistant, Institute of Orthopaedics, London; Consultant Orthopaedic Surgeon, Southend Group of Hospitals; Consultant Orthopaedic Surgeon, St Mary's Hospital, Paddington, London; Member of Council, Medical Defence Union, London; Honorary Consultant Orthopaedic Surgeon, St Mary's Hospital, London. Publications: Surgical Disorders of the Peripheral Nerves (jointly), 1998; The Battle of Jutland 1916, 2002; Articles in various journals, chapters in books on medical negligence, lesions of nerves, disorders of the cervical spine. Honours: Travelling Fellowship, British Postgraduate Medical Federation; Watson-Jones Lecturer, Royal College of Surgeons; Henry Floyd Lecturer, Institute of Orthopaedics. Memberships: Society of Authors; Fellow, Royal Society of Medicine; Life Member, British Medical Association; Senior Fellow, British Orthopaedic Association; Honorary Fellow, Medical Defence Union; Leander Club, Henley-on-Thames; Member, Past President, Old Etonian Medical Society. Address: 6 Wooburn Grange, Grange Drive, Wooburn Green, Bucks HP10 0QU, England.

**BONO (Paul Hewson)**, 10 May 1960, Dublin, Ireland. Singer; Lyricist. m. Alison, 2 daughters, 1 son. Career: Founder member, lead singer, rock group U2, 1978-; Regular national, international and worldwide tours; Major concerts include: US Festival, 1983; The Longest Day, Milton Keynes Bowl, 1985; Live Aid, Wembley, 1985; Self Aid, Ireland, 1986; A Conspiracy Of Hope (Amnesty International US tour), 1986; Smile Jamaica (hurricane relief concert), 1988; Very Special Arts Festival, White House, 1988; New Year's Eve Concert, Dublin (televised throughout Europe), 1989; Yankee Stadium, New York (second concert ever), 1992; Group established own record company, Mother Records. Compositions include: Co-writer, Jah Love, Neville Brothers; Lyrics, Misere, Zucchero and Pavarotti; Screenplay, Million Dollar Hotel. Recordings: Albums: with U2: Boy, 1980; October, 1981; War (Number 1, UK), 1983; Under A Blood Red Sky, 1983; The Unforgettable Fire (Number 1, UK), 1984; Wide Awake In America, 1985; The Joshua Tree (Number 1, UK and US), 1987; Rattle And Hum, also film (Number 1, US), 1988; Achtung Baby (Number 1, US), 1991; Zooropa (Number 1, UK and US), 1993; Passengers (film soundtrack), with Brian Eno, 1995; Pop, 1997; All Than You Can't Leave Behind, 2000; Hit singles include: Out Of Control (Number 1, Ireland), 1979; Another Day (Number 1, Ireland), 1980; New Year's Day, 1983; Two Hearts Beat As One, 1983; Pride (In The Name Of Love), 1984; The Unforgettable Fire, 1985; With Or Without You (Number 1, US), 1987; I Still Haven't Found What I'm Looking For (Number 1, US), 1987; Where The Streets Have No Name, 1987; Desire (Number 1, UK), 1988; Angel Of Harlem, 1988; When Love Comes To Town, with B B King, 1989; All I Want Is You, 1989; The Fly (Number 1, UK), 1991; Mysterious Ways, 1992; One, 1992; Even Better Than The Real Thing, 1992; Who's Gonna Ride Your Wild Horses, 1992; Stay, 1993; Hold Me, Thrill Me, Kiss Me (from film soundtrack Batman Forever), 1995; Discotheque, 1997; If God Will Send His Angels, 1998; Sweetest Thing, 1998; Contributor, Do They Know It's Christmas?, Band Aid, 1985;

# DICTIONARY OF INTERNATIONAL BIOGRAPHY

Sun City, Little Steven, 1985; In A Lifetime, Clannad, 1986; Mystery Girl, Roy Orbison, 1988; Special Christmas, charity album, 1987; Folkways - A Vision Shared (Woody Guthrie tribute), 1988; Live For Ireland, 1989; Red Hot + Blue (Cole Porter tribute), 1990; Tower Of Song (Leonard Cohen tribute), 1995; Pavarotti And Friends, 1996; Forces Of Nature, 1999. Honours: Grammy Awards: Album Of The Year, Best Rock Performance, The Joshua Tree, 1987; Best Rock Performance, Desire, 1989; Best Rock Vocal, 1993; BRIT Awards: Best International Group,1988-90; Best Live Act, 1993; World Music Award, Irish Artist Of The Year, 1993; Juno Award, International Entertainer Of The Year, 1993; Q Awards: Best Act In The World, 1990, 1992, 1993; Merit Award, 1994; Best International Group and Award for Outstanding Contribution to the Music Industry, Brit Awards, 2001; Numerous poll wins and awards, Billboard and Rolling Stone magazines; Gold and Platinum discs. Current Management: Principle Management, 30-32 Sir John Rogersons Quay, Dublin 2, Ireland.

**BONSU Benjamin Daniel,** b. 21 May 1933, Daaman, Mampon-Asante, Ghana. Catechist; Herbalist. m. 29 October 1956, 5 sons, 2 daughters. Education: Office Supervision, 1971; Office Management, 1972; Personnel Management, 1980. Appointments: Teacher, 1953-67; Mill Operator, Gihoc Fibre, 1968-78; Assistant Personnel Officer, Gihoc Fibre, 1979-83; Personnel Officer, Gihoc Farms, 1984; Service Manager, Gihoc Fibre, 1985-87; Catechist, PCG, 1956-67, 1975-; Herbalist, Federation of Traditional Healers, 1958-. Publications: Several articles in professional journals; Awaree Eye Onyankopon Nhyehee, 1986. Honours: Gihoc Fibre Products Co Ltd 10 years Service Award, 1968-78, 1986, 15 years Service Award, 1968-83, 1986. Memberships: Traditional Medicine Practitioners Association, Ghana; Ghana Institute of Personnel Management; Federation of Traditional Healers. Address: Sankofa Herbal Store & Clinic, PO Box 8224, Ahensan-Kumasi, Ghana.

**BONTING Sjoerd Lieuwe,** b. 6 October 1924, Amsterdam, The Netherlands. Biochemist; Anglican Priest-Theologian. m. (1) Susan Maarsen, deceased, 2 sons, 2 daughters, (2) Erica Schotman. Education: BSc, Chemistry, 1944, MSc, cum laude, Biochemistry, 1950, PhD, Biochemistry, 1952, University of Amsterdam; Ordained Priest, Episcopal Church, Washington, 1964. Appointments: Research Associate, University of Iowa, 1952-55; Assistant Professor, University of Minnesota, 1955-56; Assistant Professor, Biochemistry, University of Illinois, Chicago, USA, 1956-60; Section Chief, National Institute of Health, Bethesda, Maryland, 1960-65; Professor, Head, Department of Biochemistry, University of Nymegen, Netherlands, 1965-85; Scientific Consultant, NASA-Ames Research Centre, Moffett Field, 1985-93; Assistant Priest, St Thomas Episcopal Church, Sunnyvale, USA, 1985-90; Assistant Priest, St Mark's Episcopal Church, Palo Alto, California, 1990-93; Anglican Chaplain, Church of England, Netherlands, 1965-85, 1993-. Publications: Scientific publications: 363 articles, 9 books including: Transmitters in the Visual Process, 1976; Membrane Transport, 1981; Advances in Space Biology and Medicine, vols 1-7, 1989-99; Theological publications: 63 articles, 7 books including: Evolution and Creation, 1978; Word and World, 1989; Creation and Evolution, 1996, 2nd edition, 1997; Humanity, Chaos, Reconciliation, 1998; Belief and Unbelief, 2000; Chaos Theology, a Revised Creation Theology, 2002; Creation and Double Chaos, 2005. Honours: Rudolf Lehmann Scholar, Amsterdam, 1941-46; Postdoctoral Fellowship, USPHS, Iowa City, USA, 1952-54; Fight for Sight Citation, National Council to Combat Blindness and Association for Research in Ophthalmology, 1961, 1962; Arthur S Flemming Award, Jaycees, Washington DC, USA, 1964; Prize for Enzymology on Leucocytes, Karger Foundation,

Basel, Switzerland, 1964; Honorary Licentiate in Theology, St Mark's Institute of Theology, London, 1975; Citation by Archbishop of Canterbury for 20 years chaplaincy work in the Netherlands, 1985. Memberships: Sigma Xi, 1955-; American Society of Biology Chemists, 1958-; AAAS, 1960-; American Society of Cell Biology, 1960-; Netherlands Biochemical Society, 1965-; Board of Directors, Multidisciplinary Center for Church and Society, The Netherlands, 1981-85; Society of Ordained Scientists, 1989-. Address: Specreyse 12, 7471 TH Goor, The Netherlands. E-mail: s.l.bonting@wxs.nl Website: www.chaostheologie.nl

**BOORSTIN Daniel J(oseph),** b. 1 October 1914, Atlanta, Georgia, USA. Historian; Librarian of Congress Emeritus. m. Ruth Carolyn Frankel, 9 April 1941, 3 sons. Education: AB, summa cum laude, Harvard University, 1934; BA, 1st class honours, Rhodes Scholar, 1936, BCL, 1st class honours, 1937, Balliol College, Oxford, 1937; Postgraduate Studies, Inner Temple, London, 1934-37; JSD, Sterling Fellow, Yale University, 1940. Appointments: Instructor, Tutor in History and Literature, Harvard University and Radcliffe College, 1938-42; Lecturer in Legal History, Harvard Law School, 1939-42; Assistant Professor of History, Swarthmore College, 1942-44; Assistant Professor, 1944-49, Professor, 1949-56, Professor of American History, 1956-64, Preston and Sterling Morton Distinguished Service Professor, 1964-69, University of Chicago; Fulbright Visiting Lecturer in American History, University of Rome, 1950-51, Kyoto University, 1957; 1st Incumbent of Chair in American History, University of Paris, 1961-62; Pitt Professor of American History and Institutions, Cambridge University, 1964-65; Director, 1969-73, Senior Historian, 1973-75, National Museum of History and Technology, Smithsonian Institution, Washington, DC; Shelby and Kathryn Cullom Davis Lecturer, Graduate Institute of International Studies, Geneva, 1973-74; Librarian of Congress, 1975-87, Librarian of Congress Emeritus, 1987-, Washington, DC. Publications: The Mysterious Science of the Law, 1941; Delaware Cases, 1792-1830, 1943; The Lost World of Thomas Jefferson, 1948; The Genius of American Politics, 1953; The Americans: The Colonial Experience, 1958; America and the Image of Europe, 1960; The Image or What Happened to the American Dream, 1962; The Americans: The National Experience, 1965; The Landmark History of the American People, 1968, new edition, 1987; The Decline of Radicalism, 1969; The Sociology of the Absurd, 1970; The Americans: The Democratic Experience, 1973; Democracy and Its Discontents, 1974; The Exploring Spirit, 1976; The Republic of Technology, 1978; A History of the United States (with Brooks M Kelley), 1980, new edition, 1991; The Discoverers, 1983; Hidden History, 1987; The Creators, 1992; Cleopatra's Nose: Essays on the Unexpected, 1994; The Daniel J Boorstin Reader, 1995; The Seekers, 1998. Honours: Bancroft Award, 1959; Francis Parkman Prize, 1966; Pulitzer Prize in History, 1974; Dexter Prize, 1974; Watson-Davis Prize, 1986; Charles Frankel Prize, 1989; National Book Award, 1989; Many other honours, including numerous honorary doctorates. Memberships: American Academy of Arts and Sciences; American Antiquarian Society; American Philosophical Society; American Studies Association, president, 1969-71; Organization of American Historians; Royal Historical Society, corresponding member. Address: 3541 Ordway Street North West, Washington, DC 20016, USA.

**BOOTH Cherie,** b. 23 September 1954, Bury, Lancashire, England. Barrister. m. A C L (Tony) Blair, 1980, 3 sons, 1 daughter. Education: London School of Economics. Appointments: Lincoln's Inn Bar, 1976; In Practice, 1976-77; New Court Chambers, 1977-91; Gray's Inn Square Chambers, 1991-2000; Queens Council, 1995; Assistant Recorder, 1996-

99; Governor, London School of Economics, 1998-; Recorder, 1999-; Matrix Chambers, 2000-. Publication: Contributor, Education Law, 1997. Honours: FJMU; FRSA; Fellow, John Moores University, Liverpool, Chancellor, 1998-; Patron, CLIC-Sargent Cancer Care for Children, 1998-; Patron, Breast Cancer Care, 1997-; Islington Music Centre, 1999-; Honorary Degree, Open University, 1999; Honorary LLD, Westminster University; Fellow of LSE; Fellow of International Society of Lawyers in Public Service. Memberships: Fellow, Institute of Advisory Legal Studies. Address: Matrix Chambers, Griffin Building, Grays Inn, London WC1R 5LN, England.

**BOOTHROYD Christine,** b. 31 March 1934, Batley, Yorkshire, England. Linguist; Poet. m. Don Brinkley, 10 April 1982, 1 stepson, 1 stepdaughter. Education: Leeds College of Commerce, 1951-52; Teachers Certificate, University College of Wales, Aberystwyth, 1966; Diplomas in Italian, Perugia and Florence. Appointments: Teacher of French/Italian, Leeds, 1963-65; Lecturer in charge of Modern Languages, North Oxfordshire Technical College, 1966-77; Part-time Lecturer, French/Italian, Banbury and Harrogate. Publications: The Floating World, 1975; The Snow Island, 1982; The Lost Moon, 1992. Contributions to: Arts Council Anthology 3; Workshop New Poetry; Orbis; Glasgow Magazine; Writers in Concert; Doors; Krax; Moorlands Review; Envoi; Penniless Press; Links; Dalesman; Poetry Nottingham; Yorkshire Journal. Membership: Harrogate Writers' Circle; Italian Cultural Institute. Address: 35 St George's Road, Harrogate, North Yorkshire HG2 9BP, England.

**BORG Björn Rune,** b. 6 June 1956, Sodertalje, Sweden. Tennis Player; Business Executive. m. (1) Mariana Simionescu, 1980, divorced 1984, 1 son by Jannike Bjorling, (2) Loredana Berte, 1989, divorced 1992. Appointments: Professional Player, 1972-; Italian Champion, 1974, 1978; French Champion, 1974, 1975, 1978, 1979, 1980, 1981; Wimbledon Champion, 1976, 1977, 1978, 1979, 1980 (runner-up 1981); WCT Champion, 1976; Grand Prix Masters Champion, 1980, 1981; World Champion, 1979, 1980; Winner, Stockholm Open, 1980; Retired, 1983, returned, 1984, 1992; Founder, Björn Borg Enterprises Ltd. Publication: Björn Borg - My Life and Game (with Eugene Scott), 1980. Honours: Sweden's Sportsperson of the Century; Voted second-best tennis player ever, Sports Illustrated and l'Equipe newspaper. Address: c/o International Management Group, The Pier House, Strand on the Green, Chiswick, London W4 3NN, England.

**BORGIOTTI Giorgio V,** b. 23 November 1932, Rome, Italy. Scientist; Professor. m. Janet Sexton, 2 sons. Education: Dr Ing Degree, University of Rome, Italy, 1957. Appointments: Technical Staff Member, Jet Propulsion Laboratory, 1976-77; Research Staff Member, Institute for Defense Analysis, 1980-83; Operation Chief Scientist, Science Appl IntCorp, 1983-88; Professor, School of Engineering and Applied Sciences, George Washington University, 1988-96. Publications: More than 30 papers on applied electromagnetics, radar and antennae; More than 20 papers on structural acoustics. Memberships: IEEE, Fellow; URSI; Sigma Xi; Cosmos Club. Address: 5822 Highland Drive, Chevy Chase, MD 20815, USA.

**BORN Anne,** b. 9 July 1930, Cooden Beach, Sussex, England. Poet; Reviewer; Translator. m. Povl Born, 1 June 1950, 3 sons, 1 daughter. Education: MA, Copenhagen, 1955; MLitt, Oxford, 1976. Appointments: Writer-in-Residence: Barnstaple, 1983-85; Kingsbridge, 1985-87; Buckinghamshire, January-February, 1996. Publications: 13 Collections of Poetry; 4 History books; 35 translated books, novels and poetry. Contributions to: Poems in: Times Literary Supplement; Ambit; The Rialto; Green

Book; Scratch; Cimarron Review; Tears in the Fence; The Frogmore Papers, Seam, South, Salzburg Poetry Review, Poetry Cornwall, The Interpreter's House, Acumen, Linus, Oasis; many published articles and reviews. Honours: Over 20 prizes and commendations; Freeman of the City of London. Memberships: Society of Authors; Translators Association, Chair, 1987, 1993-95; University Women's Club; Fellow of Hawthornden Castle; Vice Chair, Devonshire Association. Address: Oversteps, Froude Road, Salcombe, South Devon TQ8 8LH, England. E-mail: anne@oversteps.fsnet.co.uk

**BORN Gustav Victor Rudolf,** b. 29 July 1921. Professor Emeritus. m. (1) Wilfreda Ann Plowden-Wardlaw 2 sons, 1 daughter, (2) Faith Elizabeth Maurice-Williams, 1 son, 1 daughter. Education: Vans Dunlop Scholar, MB, ChB, University of Edinburgh, 1943; DPhil (Oxford), 1951, MA, 1956. Appointments include: Medical Officer, RAMC, 1943-47; Member, Scientific Staff, Medical Research Council, 1952-53, Research Officer, Nuffield Institute for Medical Research, 1953-60, Departmental Demonstrator in Pharmacology, 1956-60, University of Oxford; Vandervell Professor of Pharmacology, RCS and University of London, 1960-73; Sheild Professor of Pharmacology, University of Cambridge and Fellow, Gonville and Caius College, Cambridge, 1973-78; Professor of Pharmacology, King's College, University of London, 1978-86, Professor Emeritus, 1986-; Research Director, The William Harvey Research Institute, St Bartholomew's Hospital Medical College, 1989-; Visiting Professor in Chemistry, Northwestern University, Illinois, 1970; William S Creasey Visiting Professor in Clinical Pharmacology, Brown University, 1977; Professor of Fondation de France, Paris, 1982-84; Honorary Director, Medical Research Council Thrombosis Research Group, 1964-73; Scientific Advisor, Vandervell Foundation, 1967-2001; President, International Society on Thrombosis and Haemostasis, 1977-79; Adviser, Heineman Medical Research Center, Charlotte, North Carolina, USA, 1981-; Kuratorium, Shakespeare Prize, Hamburg, 1991-98; Forensic Science Advisory Group, Home Office; Numerous invited lectures. Publications: Articles in scientific journals and books. Honours include: FRS, 1972; FRCP, 1976; Hon FRCS, 2002; FKC, 1988; Honorary Fellow, St Peter's College, Oxford, 1972; Nine Honorary Degrees; Albrecht von Haller Medal, Göttingen University, 1979; Chevalier de l'Ordre National de Mérite, France, 1980; Auenbrugger Medal, Graz University, 1984; Royal Medal, Royal Society, 1987; Alexander von Humboldt Award, 1995; Gold Medal for Medicine, Ermst Jung Foundation, Hamburg, 2001. Memberships include: Honorary Life Member, New York Academy of Sciences; Akademia Leopoldina; Honorary Member German Physiological Society; Corresponding Member, German Pharmacological Society; Royal Belgian Academy of Medicine. Address: 5 Walden Lodge, 48 Wood Lane, Highgate, London N6 5UU, England.

**BÖRNER Klaus,** b. 22 June 1929, Senftenberg, Germany. Musician; Pianist; University Professor; Conductor; Composer. m. Helga Kibat, 1 son, 1 daughter. Education: Academy of Music Weimar, 1946-50; Piano, Conducting, Musicology; Exam for Piano Teaching, 1949; Conservatoire de Lausanne, 1950-52; Exam de virtuosité, 1952; Master Classes with Alfred Cortot, Edwin Fischer, Wilhelm Kempff. Career: Concerts as Pianist around the world, 70 countries; Solo recitals and soloist with orchestra, chamber music, accompanying singers; Radio, TV in four continents; piano teaching; Conservatory Dusseldorf, 1956-69; Professor, University Mainz 1969-97; Guest Professor: Several times in New Zealand, Hong Kong, Japan, Indonesia; Founder and Director of International Music Summer Camp SYLT, Germany, 1959-89. Publications: Original version of Beethoven Waldstein Sonata; Schumann Papillons: Teaching

Experience and Students Reaction; Chance and Dilemma of the Urtext; Fingerings in Piano Sonatas by C. Ph. E. Bach, Henle edition; Piano Duet Repertoire, 2004; Compositions: Trio for horn, violin, piano; Lieder; Fantasy for piano duet; Quartet for 4 bassoons. Honours: Prize of Young Soloists, Weimar 1950; 1st Prize, International Piano Competition, Barcelona 1956 ; Other National Awards. Memberships: Jeunesses Musicales of Germany, 1953-, including a term as Vice-President; Tonkünstlerverband (Association of German Musicians); European Piano Teachers' Association, German Section; Address: Nibelungenstr 38, D-41462 Neuss, Germany.

**BORST Arno, b.** 8 May 1925, Alzenau, Germany. University Professor Emeritus. m. Gudrun Witzig, 2 sons, 2 daughters. Education: Graduate, Universities of Göttingen and Munich, 1945-50; Dr Phil, Göttingen University, 1951. Appointments: Assistant, Münster University, 1951-57; Professor, Erlangen University, 1962-68; Professor, Konstanz University, 1968-90. Publications: The Cathari, 1953; The Tower of Babel, 6 volumes, 1957-63; Ways of Life in the Middle Ages, 1973; Monks at the Lake of Konstanz, 1978; The Medieval Game of Dueling Numbers, 1986; Barbarians, Heretics and Artists, 1988; Computus, 1990; The Book of Natural History, 1994; The Carolingian Calendar, 3 volumes, 2001. Honours include: Award, German Research Community, 1956; Award, Historical College, 1986; Premio Balzan, 1996. Memberships: Academies of Science at Heidelberg, Munich and Braunschweig. Address: Laengerbohlstr. 42, D-78467, Germany.

**BOTTOMLEY OF NETTLESTONE Rt Hon Baroness, Virginia Hilda Brunette Maxwell, b.** 12 March 1948. Politician. m. Peter Bottomley, 1967, 1 son, 2 daughters. Education: London School Economics. Appointments: Various positions before election as Conservative MP for Surrey South, 1984-2005; Parliamentary Private Secretary to Chris Patten, 1985-87; Parliamentary Private Secretary for Foreign and Commonwealth Affairs Sir Geoffrey Howe QC MP, 1987-88; Parliament Under-Secretary, Department of the Environment, 1988-89; Ministry for Health, 1989-92; Secretary of State, Department of Health, 1992-95, with responsibility for family policy, 1994-95; Chairman, Millennium Commission, 1995-97; Secretary of State, Department of National Heritage, 1995-97; Vice Chairman, British Council, 1997-2000; House of Commons Select Committee on Foreign Affairs, 1997-99; Supervisory Board, Akzo Nobel, NV; Executive Director, Odger Ray and Berndtson; President, Abbeyfield Society; Council Member, Ditchley Foundation; Governor, London School of Economics, London University of the Arts; UK Advisory Council; International Chamber of Commerce; Advisory Council, Cambridge University Judge School of Management Studies. Address: House of Lords, London SW1A 0PW, England.

**BOUDON Raymond, b.** 27 January 1934, Paris, France. Professor. m. Rose Marie Riessner, 1 son. Appointments: Invited Professor, University of Geneva, Harvard University, University of Bocconi of Bologna, Oxford University, University of Chicago and University of Stockholm; Professor, University of Bordeaux; Professor, University of Paris-Sorbonne, Paris, 1967-; Editor, Annee Sociologique; Editor, Sociologies series. Publications: 13 books; Numerous articles in professional journals. Honours: Invited lecturer at: Lazarsfeld Lecture, Columbia University; Patten Foundation Lecture, Indiana University; Lurçy Lecture, University of Chicago; Sidney Ball Lecture, Oxford University; Fulvio Guerrini Lecture, University of Turin; Eilert Sund Lecture, University of Oslo; Wei Lun Lecture, Chinese University of Hong Kong; Doctor honoris causa, University of Cluj, University of Antwerp; Prix Girardeau, Académie des sciences morales et politiques; Grand

Prix Moron, Académie française; Prix Futuribles, European Price Amalfi for the Social Sciences, Grand Prix des Sciences Humaines de la Ville de Paris. Memberships: National Center for Scientific Research; Institut de France; Academia Europea; British Academy; American Academy of Arts and Sciences; Royal Society of Canada; Central European Academy of Art and Science; International Academy of Human Sciences of St Petersburg; European Academy of Sociology; Fellow, Centre for Advanced Study in the Behavioural Sciences; Editorial Board Member, Theory and Decision, Epistémè. Address: 51 avenue Trudaine, 75009 Paris, France.

**BOULAUD Denis, b.** 15 January 1947, Villeparisis, France. Research Director. m. Sophie Payet, 1 son, 1 daughter. Education: PhD, Geophysics, 1974, PhD, Physics (State Doctorate), University of Paris. Appointments: Assistant Professor, University of Paris, 1977-81; Assistant Head of Laboratory, 1981-84, Head of Laboratory, 1984-98, Research Director, 1996-, Head of Service, 1998-2003, Atomic Energy Commission, Scientific Director, 2003, Institute for Radiological Protection and Nuclear Safety. Publications: Book: Aerosols: physics and measurement techniques; 8 book chapters; 55 papers in journals with reviewers; 185 communications in different conferences and congresses. Honour: Chevalier de l'ordre des Palmes Académiques, 2000; Award, International Aerosol Fellow, 2002. Memberships: President, French Association on Aerosol Research; General Secretary, European Aerosol Assembly, 1998-2000. Address: 6, allée de l'étang, F 91190 Gif/Yvette, France.

**BOULIER Jean François, b.** 14 March 1956, Caen, France. Executive. m. Marianne, 1 son, 2 daughters. Education: Ecole Polytechnique, 1977-80; ENGREF, 1980-82; Doctorate in Fluid Mechanics, Grenoble University, 1985. Appointments: Researcher, CNRS, 1985-87; Head of Quantative Analysis, Credit Commercial de France, 1987-89; Head of Research and Innovation, 89-99, Head of Market Risk Management, 1996-99, CCF; Chief Investment Officer, President, Sinopia Asset Management, 1999-2002; Professor of Finance, University Paris Dauphine, 2000-03; Head of Euro Fixed Income and Credits, Credit Aquicole Asset Management, 2004-; Associate Professor, Paris Dauphine University, 2000-; Deputy Chief Investment Officer, Head of Fixed Income, Credit Lyonnais Asset Management, 2002-. Publications: Numerous articles and reports in professional journals; Editor, Creator, Quants, quarterly journal of CCF; editor, Banque et Marchés, journal of the French Finance Association. Honour: Institute of Quantative Investment Research award, 1993. Listed in numerous publications. Memberships: Honorary Chairman, French Finance Association; Honorary Chairman, French Asset and Liability Managers' Association; Board Member, French Pension Fund Association; Chairman, Research Committee of INQUIRE, Europe; Chairman of the Asset Management Technical Committee of the French Fund Manager's Association, AFG; Secretary, Board of AMTE, the Euro Bond Market Association, 2004-. Address: 5 quai de l'Orme de Sully, 78230 Le Pecq, France. E-mail: jean-francois.boulier@ca-assetmanagement.fr

**BOULOS Alkiviadis, b.** 11 December 1975, Greece. Systems Engineer. Education: English Academy Foundation Course MIS, Athens, Greece, 1993-94; BEng, Electrical Power Engineering, University of Glasgow, Scotland, 1994-98; MSc, Drives and Power Engineering, Heriot-Watt University, Edinburgh, Scotland, 1998-99; MSc by Research, Control Engineering, 2000-2001, PhD (part-time basis), Control Theory and Applications, 2002-, Coventry University, Coventry, England; NVQ, Management Level 4, 2001-2003. Appointments:

Student Trainee, Public Power Corporation, Lavrion Steam Electric Station, Greece, 1995-98; Part-time Lecturer, Coventry University, School of Mathematical and Information Sciences, 2001; Senior Engineer, Electrical Department, Jaguar Cars, 2001-2002; Jaguar Research Specialist, Jaguar Land Rover, Research and Development Department, 2002-2004; Senior Engineer, Jaguar Land Rover, Electrical Department, 2005-. Publications: Articles in professional journals and conference proceedings as co-author include: Accommodating thermal stress in combined cycle power plants start-up phase, 2000; Fuzzy logic supervisory controller for combined cycle power plant in start-up phase, 2001; A comparison of fixed PID, Fuzzy Logic and Fuzzy PID supervisory control strategy for combined cycle power plant, 2001; Fuzzy logic approach to accommodate thermal stress and improve the start-up phase in combined cycle power plants, 2002; Development of a thermal model to accommodate thermal effects during charging cycles in lead-acid (SLI) batteries, 2003; Validation of battery-alternator model against experimental data-A first step towards developing a future power supply system, 2004. Memberships: Institute of Electrical Engineers; Coventry Hellenic Club. Address: 209 Humber Avenue, Stoke, Coventry CV1 2AQ, England. E-mail: aboulos@jaguar.com

**BOULTON James Thompson,** b. 17 February 1924, Pickering, Yorkshire, England. Emeritus Professor of English Studies. m. Margaret Helen Leary, 6 August 1949, 1 son, 1 daughter. Education: BA, University College, University of Durham, 1948; BLitt, Lincoln College, University of Oxford, 1952; PhD, University of Nottingham, 1960. Appointments: Lecturer, Senior Lecturer, Reader in English Literature, 1951-63, Professor, 1964-75, Dean of Faculty of Arts, 1970-73, University of Nottingham; Professor of English Studies and Head of Department, 1975-88, Dean of Faculty of Arts, 1981-84, Public Orator, 1984-88, Director of Institute for Advanced Research in Arts and Social Sciences, 1987-99, Deputy Director, 1999-, Emeritus Professor, 1989-, University of Birmingham. Publications: Edmund Burke: Sublime and Beautiful (editor), 1958, 3rd edition, 1987; The Language of Politics in the Age of Wilkes and Burke, 1963; Samuel Johnson: The Critical Heritage, 1971; Defoe: Memoirs of a Cavalier (editor), 1972; The Letters of D H Lawrence (editor), 8 volumes, 1979-00; Selected letters of D H Lawrence (editor), 1997; Volume I, The Early Writings: The Writings and Speeches of Edmund Burke (co-editor), 1997; D H Lawrence: Late Essays and Articles (editor), 2004; James Boswell: An Account of Corsica (co-editor), 2005. Honours: Fellow, Royal Society of Literature, 1968; Hon DLitt, Durham University, 1991, Nottingham University, 2003; Fellow, British Academy, 1994. Address: Institute for Advanced Research in Arts and Social Sciences, University of Birmingham, Edgbaston, Birmingham B15 2TT, England.

**BOUMA Arnold Heiko,** b. 5 September 1932, Groningen, The Netherlands. Professor. m. Mechelina Helena Kampers, 3 sons. Education: BS, Geology, University of Groningen, Netherlands, 1956; MS, 1959; PhD, University of Utrecht, 1961; Fulbright Post-doctoral Fellowship, Scripps Institute of Oceanography, California, USA, 1962-63. Appointments: Lecturer, University of Utrecht, 1963-66; Associate Professor, Professor, Marine Geology, Texas A&M University, 1966-75; Research Scientist, Geologist in Charge, US Geological Survey, 1975-81; Senior Scientist, Manager, Vice President, Gulf Oil Company, 1981-85; Senior Research Associate, Chevron Oil Company, 1985-88; McCord Endowed Professor, Oil-related Sedimentary Geology, Louisiana State University, 1988-. Publications: 3 books; Co-editor, 9 books; 132 papers in refereed journals; 122 other papers; 58 abstracts; 33 book reviews; 48 reports. Honours: F P Shepard Award for Excellence in Marine Geology,

1982; Best Papers Awards; Teaching Awards; Invited Keynote Speaker; Distinguished Research Master of Engineering, Science and Technology, Louisiana State University, 2004. Memberships: Society for Sedimentary Geology; American Association Petroleum Geologists; International Association Sedimentologists; Dutch Geological and Mining Society; Local Geological Societies. Address: Department of Geology and Geophysics, Louisiana State University, Baton Rouge, Louisiana 70803, USA.

**BOUND John Pascoe,** b.13 November 1920, Redhill, Surrey, England. Paediatrician, Consultant (Retired). m. Gwendoline, deceased 1998, 2 daughters. Education: MB, BS, DCH, 1943, MD, 1950, University College, London and University College Hospital Medical School; MRCP (Lond), 1950; FRCP, 1971; FRCPCH, 1997. Appointments: House Physician, University College Hospital, 1943; Assistant Medical Officer, Alder Hey Children's Hospital, Liverpool, 1943-44; RAMC, 1944-47; Member, Sprue Research Team, Poona, India for 1 year; House Physician, North Middlesex Hospital, 1947; Paediatric Registrar and Senior Registrar, Hillingdon Hospital, Middlesex, 1948-53; Paediatric Registrar, 1953-54, First Assistant, Department of Paediatrics, 1954-56, University College Hospital, London; Consultant Paediatrician, Victoria Hospital, Blackpool, Lancashire, 1956-83. Publications: Articles on neonatal conditions and perinatal mortality; Articles on congenital malformations including: Incidence of congenital heart disease in the Fylde of Lancashire 1957-71; Seasonal prevalence of major congenital malformations, 1957-81; Neural tube defects, maternal cohorts and age: a pointer to aetiology; Down's Syndrome: prevalence and ionising radiation in an area of North West England, 1957-91; Involvement of deprivation and environmental lead in neural tube defects, 1957-81; Book, Borrowdale Beauty. Honour: International Medal of Honour, International Biographical Centre, Cambridge, 2003. Memberships: British Medical Association, 1943-; Expert Group on Special Care for Babies, Department of Health and Social Security, London, 1969-70; British Paediatric Association, 1960-97, Academic Board, 1972-75. Address: 48, St Annes Road East, Lytham St Annes, Lancs FY8 1UR, England.

**BOUND Sally Anne,** b. 7 September 1956, Hobart, Australia. Research Horticulturist. m. Chris White, 2 daughters. Education: BSc Botany and Zoology, University of Tasmania, 1979; Certificate in Horticulture, Hobart Technical College, 1981; Graduate Diploma of Science, University of Tasmania, 1993; PhD Agricultural Science, in progress. Appointments: Research Assistant, Botany Department, University of Tasmania, 1978-80; Part-time Teacher, Examiner and Moderator, Syllabus Writer, Education Department, Hobart Technical College, 1980-89; Technical Assistant, Research Clerk, Acting Senior Technical Officer, Technical Officer, Acting Manager, Senior Agricultural Research Officer, Department of Primary Industry and Fisheries, 1980-98; Senior Research Horticulturist, Acting Group Research Leader, Tasmanian Institute of Agricultural Research, 1998-. Publications: Numerous articles in refereed journals and popular press; Books and book chapters; Conference and Symposium papers and presentations. Honours: Nominated, Tasmanian Rural Woman of the Year, 1997; Listed in international biographical publications. Memberships: Australian Institute of Agricultural Science and Technology; International Society for Horticultural Science; American Society for Horticultural Science; Australia Pacific Extension Network; International Dwarf Fruit Tree Association; Life Member, Scientific Faculty, IBC. Address: Tasmanian Institute of Agricultural Research, 13 St Johns Avenue, New Town, Tasmania 7008, Australia. E-mail: sally.bound@dpiwe.tas.gov.au

**BOURNE Malcolm Cornelius,** b. 18 May 1926, Moonta, Australia. Professor of Food Science; Active Emeritus. m. Elizabeth Schumacher, 3 sons, 2 daughters. Education: BSc, Chemistry, University of Adelaide, 1950; MS, Food Science, 1961, PhD, Agricultural Chemistry, 1962, University of California, Davis, USA. Appointments: Chief Chemist, Brookers (Australia) Ltd, 1949-58; Research Assistant, University California, Davis, 1958-62; Professor, Food Science, 1962-95, Emeritus Professor, Food Science, 1995-, Cornell University. Publications: Many publications in refereed journals; Author, Food Texture and Viscosity, 1982, reprinted, 1994, second edition, 2002; Editor in Chief, Journal of Texture Studies, 1980-. Honours: Fellow, Institute of Food Science and Technology, UK, 1966; Fellow, Institute of Food Technologists and International Award; Inaugural Fellow, 1998, Vice President, 2001-03, President, 2003-2006, International Academy Food Science and Technology; Honorary Fellow, Australian Institute of Food Science and Technology, 1999; Fellow, Royal Australian Chemical Institute, 2003. Address: NYSAES, Cornell University, Geneva, NY 14456, USA.

**BOUTROS-GHALI Boutros,** b. 14 November 1922, Cairo, Egypt. Former Secretary General, United Nations. m. Maria Leia Nadler. Education: LLB, Cairo University, 1946; PhD, Paris University, 1949. Appointments: Professor, International Law and International Relations, Head, Department of Political Sciences, Cairo University, 1949-77; Founder, Editor, Al Ahram Iktisadi, 1960-75; Ministry of State, Foreign Affairs, Egypt, 1977-91; Member, UN Commission of International Law, 1979-92; Member, Secretariat, National Democratic Party, 1980-92; MP, 1987-92; Deputy PM, Foreign Affairs, 1991-92; Secretary-General, UN, 1992-96; Secretary-General, Organisations Internationales de la Francophonie. Publications: Contribution a l'étude des ententes régionales, 1949; Cours de diplomatie et de droit diplomatique et consulaire, 1951; Le problème du Canal de Suez (jtly), 1957; Egypt and the United Nations (jtly), 1957; Le principe d'égalité des états et les organisations internationales, 1961; Contribution a une théorie générale des Alliances, 1963; Foreign Policies in a World of Change, 1963; L'Organisation de l'unité africaine, 1969; Le mouvement Afro-Asiatique, 1969; Les difficultés institutionelles du panafricanisme, 1971; La ligue des états arabes, 1972; Les Conflits de frontières en Afrique, 1973; Numerous books in Arabic and contributions to periodicals. Address: 2 Av El Nil Giza, Cairo, Egypt.

**BOWIE David (David Jones),** b. 8 January 1947, Brixton, London, England. Singer; Actor. (1) Angela Barnet, divorced, 1 son, (2) Iman Abdul Majid, 1992, 1 daughter. Career: Solo recording artist, 1970-; Lead singer, Tin Machine, 1989-91; Actor, films, 1976-; World tours, concerts, television and radio appearances, many as Ziggy Stardust and Aladdin Sane; Performances include: Live Aid, Wembley, 1985; Glass Spider Tour, 1987; ICA ' Intruders at the Palace'; Sound and Vision Tour, 1990; Dodger Stadium, Los Angeles, 1990; Morrissey World Tour, 1991; A Concert For Life (Freddie Mercury Tribute), 1992; Wembley Arena, 1993; USA East Coast Ballroom Tour, 1996; 50th Birthday Benefit Show, 1997; Hammersmith Ballroom, 1998; Docklands Arena, 1999; Placebo US Tour, 1999; 'Hours' Promotional Tour, 1999. Film appearances include: The Man Who Fell To Earth, 1976; Christiane F, 1980; Just A Gigolo, 1981; Cat People, 1982; The Hunger, 1983; Merry Christmas Mr Lawrence, 1983; Ziggy Stardust and The Spiders from Mars, 1983; Labyrinth, 1986; Absolute Beginners, 1986; The Last Temptation Of Christ, 1988; The Linguini Incident, 1990; Basquiat, 1996; Trainspotting, 1996; Il Mio West, 1998; Everybody Loves Sunshine, 1999; Mr Rices Secret, 2000. Theatre includes: The Elephant Man, 1980. Recordings: Numerous solo albums include: The Rise And Fall

Of Ziggy Stardust..., 1972; Aladdin Sane, 1973; Diamond Dogs, 1974; David Live, 1974; Young Americans, 1975; Station To Station, 1976; Low, Heroes, 1977; Let's Dance, 1983; Ziggy Stardust - The Motion Picture, 1983; Scary Monsters and Super Creeps, 1980; Black Tie White Noise, 1993; Outside, 1995; Earthling, 1997; David Bowie, 1998; Hours, 1999; Numerous solo hit singles include: Absolute Beginners; Ashes To Ashes; Blue Jean; China Girl; Diamond Dogs; Fashion; Jean Genie; Life On Mars; Rebel Rebel; Space Oddity; Growin' Up; Fame 90; Heart's Filthy Lesson; Hallo Spaceboy; Little Wonder; I Can't Read; with Bing Crosby: Peace On Earth/Little Drummer Boy; with Mick Jagger: Dancing In The Street; with Queen: Under Pressure; Other projects include: Theme for When The Wind Blows, 1986. Honours include: Grammy Awards, 1984; Music Video Awards; Silver Clef Award for Outstanding Achievement, 1987; Ivor Novello Awards include: Outstanding Contribution to British Music, 1990; Q Magazine Inspiration Award (with Brian Eno), 1995; BRIT Award, Outstanding Contribution to Music, 1996; BMI Pop Awards, 1999; MTV Video Music Awards (China Girl), 1984, (Dancing in the Streets), 1986; Rock and Rolls Hall of Fame, 1996; Q Awards, 1995. Address: Isolar Enterprises, 641 5th Avenue, Ste 22Q, New York, NY 10022, USA.

**BOWLER John Vaughan,** b. 22 March 1959. Education: King George V School, Hong Kong, 1971-75; Worksop College, Nottinghamshire, England, 1975-77; BSc (London) (1st Class Honours) in Basic Medical Sciences and Physiology, 1981, MB BS (London) (with Distinction) in Pathology, Medicine and Surgery, 1984, St Thomas' Hospital Medical School, University of London; MRCP (UK), 1987; MD (London), 1993; Certificate of Completion of Specialist Training, 1997; FRCP, 2001. Appointments: House Surgeon, St Helier Hospital, Surrey, 1984-85; House Physician, Department of Medicine, 1985, Senior House Officer, Intensive Therapy, 1985-86, St Thomas' Hospital; Senior House Officer in Neurology, Hammersmith Hospital, 1986; Senior House Officer in Cardiology, National Heart Hospital, 1986-87; Registrar in General Medicine, Queen Mary's Hospital, Kent, 1987; Registrar in Neurology, Atkinson Morley's Hospital, 1987-88; Chest Heart and Stroke Association Research Fellow in Neurology, Charing Cross and Westminster Medical School, 1988-90; Registrar in Neurology, Charing Cross Hospital, 1991-92; Clinical Fellow in Neurology, University of Western Ontario, Canada, 1992-95; Lecturer (Honorary Senior Registrar) in Clinical Neurology, Charing Cross and Westminster Medical School, 1995-98; Consultant Neurologist and Honorary Senior Lecturer in Neurology, Royal Free Hospital, Royal Free and University College Medical School and the North Middlesex Hospital, 1998-. Publications: Numerous articles in professional scientific journals; Abstracts, posters and chapters in books. Honours: The Cochrane Prize, 1978; MRC Scholarship to read for the Intercalated BSc, 1980; The Third Beaney Prize, 1983; The Mead Medal and Perkins Prize, 1984. Memberships: Fellow, Royal College of Physicians; Member, Association of British Neurologists; Corresponding Associate Member, American Academy of Neurology; International Fellow, Stroke Council, American Stroke Association; Fellow, American Heart Association; Founder Member, The International Society for Vascular Behavioural and Cognitive Disorders. Address: Department of Neurology, Royal Free Hospital, Pond Street, London NW3 2QG, England. E-mail: john.bowler@ucl.ac.uk

**BOWRING Peter,** b. 22 April 1923, Bromborough, England. Company Director. m. (1) Barbara Ekaterina Brewis, 1946, divorced, 1 son, 1 daughter. (2) Carol Gillian Hutchings, 1979, divorced. (3) Carole Mary Dear, 1986. Education: Shrewsbury School. Appointments: Commissioned Rifle Brigade, 1942, served in Egypt, North Africa, Italy and Austria, mentioned in dispatches; Director, C T Bowring & Co Ltd, 1956; Chair, C T Bowring Trading (Holdings) Ltd, 1967; Deputy Chair, C T Bowring and Co Ltd, 1973; Chair: Bowmaker (Plant) Ltd, 1972-83, C T Bowring & Co Ltd, 1978-82; Director, 1980-82, Vice Chair, 1982-84, Marsh and McLennan Companies Inc.; Director, 1975-79, Chair, 1982-89, Vice-President, 1991- Aldebridge Foundation; Chair, 1977-87, President, 1987-2000, Help the Aged Ltd; Chair, Inter-Action Social Enterprise Trust Ltd, 1989-91; Chair, Wakefield (Tower Hill, Trinity Square) Trust, 2002-; Master, Worshipful Company of World Traders, 1989-90; Trustee: Zoological Society Development Trust, 1987-90, Ironbridge Gorge Museum Development Trust, 1987-93, 1987-93 (Companion 1993), Upper Severn Navigation Trust (now Spry Trust Ltd), 1987-; Director, Independent and Secondary Education Trust, 1986-, Centre for Policy Studies, 1983-88, City Arts Trust, 1984-94, International Human Assistance Programs Inc., 1985-89, Rhein Chemie Holding GmbH, 1968-. Publication: The Last Minute, 2000. Honour: CBE, 1993. Memberships: Lloyds, 1968-98; Worshipful Company of Insurers; Company of Watermen and Lightermen; Freeman City of London; Board of Governors, 1974-94, Chair, 1977-90 (Companion, 1998), St Dunstan's Educational Foundation; Board of Governors, Shrewsbury School, 1969-97; Fellowships: Institute of Directors, Royal Society of Arts, Zoological Society. Address: Flat 79, New Concordia Wharf, Mill Street, London SE1 2BB, England.

**BOYD Brandon**, b. 15 February 1976, Van Nuys, California, USA. Composer, singer for band Incubus. Education: Calabasas High School, 1994. Albums (as Incubus); Fungus Amongus, 1996; S.C.I.E.N.C.E., 1997; Enjoy Incubus, 1997; Make Youself, 1999; When Incubus Attacks, Vol 1, 2000; Morning View, 2001; A Crow Left of the Murder; 2004. Singles include: Stellar, Drive, Wish you were here, Are you In, Nice to know you, Talk Shows on Mute, Southern Girl, Here in my Room. Publications: White Fluffy Clouds, 2004. Concerts include: Le Plan Ris-Orangis 1998, House Of Blues, Los Angeles 1998, ATT Acoustic; Hammerstein Ballroom, New York City, NY, 2001, KROQ Mansion Concert, 2002; Lollapalooza, 2003.

**BOYD Graham**, b. 26 April 1928, Bristol, England. Artist. m. Pauline Lilian, 1 son, 1 daughter. Education: NDD, Watford School of Art, 1951; ATD, Institute of Education, London. Appointments: Army Service, 1946-48; Resident in Southern Rhodesia (Zimbabwe), 1953-55; Exchange Associate Professor, Plymouth State College, University of New Hampshire, USA, 1972-73; Visiting Artist, Reading University, 1975-83; Principal Lecturer in Fine Art, Head of Painting, Course Leader P/T BA/BA Honours Fine Art Degree Course, Herts College of Art & Design, St Albans/University of Hertfordshire, 1976-93; Participant in 2nd Triangle Workshop, New York, USA, 1983; Visiting Artist, Exeter College of Art and Design, 1983; Artists in Essex Exhibitions Selector, 1985; Guest Artist, Triangle Workshop, Barcelona, 1987; Anglo-Dutch Artists Workshop, Rounton, North Yorkshire, 1992; Guest Artist, International Multi-Media Symposium, Faial, Azores, 1995; Intuition and Reason Lecture to Tate Gallery Guides and Hertfordshire Visual Artists Forum, 2003; Exhibitions: Solo exhibitions, 1962 onwards include most recently: Colour Transactions, deli Art, Charterhouse Street, London, 1999; Graham Boyd – Disruptive Tendencies, University of Hertfordshire, 2001; The Energy of Colour, 2 person exhibition with Sheila Girling, Pilgrim Gallery, London, 2003; Striking Lights, Recent Painting, deli Art, 2004; The Long Haul, Bushey Museum and Art Gallery, 2004; The Alchemy of Colour, The Pavilion Gallery, Chenies Manor, Rickmansworth, 2004; Dancing with Colour, The Salt

Gallery, Hayle, Cornwall, 2004; Group Exhibitions, 1950 onwards include most recently: Driven to Abstraction, Bell Gallery, Winchester, 2000; deli Art in Bristol, The Crypt Gallery, Summer Exhibition, Lemon Street Gallery, Truro, 2002; Confluence, The Pilgrim Gallery, London, 2004; Summer Exhibition, The Salt Gallery, Hayle, 2004; Works in public and private collections. Publications: Works featured in numerous newspaper and journal articles and exhibition catalogues. Address: Blackapple, 54 Scatterdells Lane, Chipperfield, Herts WD4 9EX, England.

**BOYD Robert David Hugh (Sir)**, b. 14 May 1938, Cambridge, England. Physician. m. Meriel Cornelia Boyd, 1 son, 2 daughters. Education: Cambridge University; University College Hospital Medical School. Appointments: MRC Fellow, University of Colorado, USA, 1971-72; Senior Lecturer, University College Hospital Medical School, 1973-80; Professor of Child Health, 1981-96, Dean of the Medical Faculty, 1989-93, University of Manchester; Chair Manchester Health Authority, 1994-96; Principal, St George's Hospital Medical School, 1996-2003; Pro-Vice Chancellor, Medicine, University of London, 2001-2003; Chair, Council of Heads of UK Medical Schools, 2001-2003; Chair, Lloyds TSB Foundation for England and Wales, 2003-; Chair, Council for Assisting Refugee Academics, 2004-. Publications: Paediatric Problems in General Practice (Joint), 3rd edition, 1996; Scientific articles on placenta, foetus, childhood illness, medical education. Honours: KB; Honorary DSc, Kingston University; Hon DSc, Keele University; Hon FRCPCH; Honorary Fellow, St George's Hospital Medical School. Memberships: F Med Sci; FRCP (London); FFPH. Address: The Stone House, Adlington, Macclesfield, Cheshire, SK10 4NU, England.

**BOYDE Andreas**, b. 13 November 1967, Oschatz, Germany. Pianist. Education: Spezialschule and Musikhochschule, Dresden; Guildhall School of Music and Drama, London; Masterclasses, Musikfestwochen Luzern. Debut: With Berlin Symphony Orchestra, 1989. Career: Concerts with Dresden Philharmonic Orchestra, 1992, 1996; Recital, Munich Philharmonic Hall, Gasteig, 1992; Festival La Roque d'Antheron, France, 1993; Concert, Zurich Tonhalle with Zurich Chamber Orchestra, 1994; Concerts with Freiburg Philharmonic Orchestra, 1994, 1997, 1999; Dresden State Orchestra, 1994, 1995; Recitalist in Schumann Cycle Dusseldorf, 1995; South American debut, recital in Teatro Municipal Santiago, Chile, 1996; Concert, Munich Herkulessaal with Munich Symphony, 1997; Concert tour with Northwest German Philharmonic Orchestra, 1997; Recital, Munich Prinzregenten Theatre, 1997; Concert tour with Odessa Philharmonic Orchestra, including Cologne Philharmonic Hall and Stuttgart Liederhalle, 1997; Recital, Dresdner Musikfestspiele, 1998; Gave European premiere of Piano Concerto, Four Parables by Schoenfield with Dresdner Sinfoniker, 1998; Concerts with Halle Philharmonic, 1999, 2004; Schumann recital tour including own reconstruction of Schubert Variations in New York, Germany, London Wigmore Hall, 2000; World premiere of Piano Concerto by John Pickard with Dresdner Sinfoniker, 2000; Concerts, Konzertsaal KKL Lucerne with Lucerne Symphony Orchestra, 2000; Concerts with Bamberger Symphoniker, 2000, 2001; Concert tour with National Symphony Orchestra of Ukraine in the United Kingdom, 2001; Concert with Bournemouth Symphony Orchestra, 2001; Recital tour in the United Kingdom, 2001; Concerts with Israel Northern Symphony Orchestra, 2001; Beethoven Fest Bonn, 2001; Concert tour with Bolshoi Symphony Orchestra in the United Kingdom, 2001; Recital, London Wigmore Hall, 2001; Concerts with Bucharest Philharmonic Orchestra, 2002; Concerts with Slovak Philharmonic Orchestra, 2002; Concerts, London Royal Festival

Hall with London Philharmonic Orchestra, 2002; Concert, Manchester Bridgewater Hall with Hallé Orchestra, 2002, 2003; Concert tour with NYOS, including Birmingham Symphony Hall and Concertgebouw Amsterdam, 2002; Concert, Prague Autumn Festival with Prague Radio Orchestra in Prague Rudolfinum, 2003; Beethoven recital, Teatro Municipal Santiago, Chile, 2003; Concerts with Malaysian Philharmonic Orchestra, 2003; Concerts with London Mozart Players, 2004; Concert, Munich Prinzregenten Theatre, 2004. Publications: Schumann, Variationen über ein Thema von Schubert, reconstructed score by Andreas Boyde, 2000. Recordings: CD releases including works by Schumann, Tchaikovsky, Mussorgsky, Ravel, Dvorak, Schoenfeld, Brahms and Rachmaninoff; Frequent broadcasts with most German Radio Stations and the BBC. Address: Künstlersekretariat Astrid Schoerke, Grazer Strasse 30, 30519 Hannover, Germany.

**BOYKIN Lorraine S,** b. 2 January 1931, USA. Nutritionist. Memberships: Fellow of American College of Nutrition. Address: 771 Park Lane, East Meadow, New York 11554, USA.

**BOYLE Danny,** b. 20 October 1956, Bury, Lancashire, England. Film Director. Appointments: Artistic Director, Royal Court Theatre, 1982-87; Producer, Elephant, TV film, 1989; Director, The Greater Good, TV series, 1991, Mr Wroe's Virgins, TV, 1993, Not Even God is Wise Enough, TV, 1993; Executive Producer, Twin Town, 1996. Creative Works: Films: Shallow Grave, 1994; Trainspotting, 1996; A Life Less Ordinary, 1996; The Beach, 1999; Vacuuming Completely Nude in Paradise, 2001; Strumpet, 2001; Alien Love Triangle, 2002; 28 Days Later, 2002. Honour: Golden Ephebe Award, 1997. Address: c/o ICM, 6th Floor, 76 Oxford Street, London W1N 0AX, England.

**BRADFORD Barbara Taylor,** b. Leeds, Yorkshire, England. Journalist; Novelist. m. Robert Bradford, 1963. Appointments: Editor, Columnist, UK and US periodicals. Publications: Complete Encyclopedia of Homemaking Ideas, 1968; How to Be the Perfect Wife, 1969; Easy Steps to Successful Decorating, 1971; Making Space Grow, 1979; A Woman of Substance, 1979; Voice of the Heart, 1983; Hold the Dream, 1985; Act of Will, 1986; To Be the Best, 1988; The Women in His Life, 1990; Remember, 1991; Angel, 1993; Everything to Gain, 1994; Dangerous to Know, 1995; Love in Another Town, 1995; Her Own Rules, 1996; A Secret Affair, 1996; Power of a Woman, 1997; A Sudden Change of Heart, 1998; Where You Belong, 2000; The Triumph of Katie Byrne, 2001; Three Weeks in Paris, 2002; Emma's Secret, 2003; Unexpected Blessings, 2004-05; Just Rewards, 2006. Address: c/o Bradford Enterprises, 450 Park Avenue, Suite 1903, New York, NY 10022, USA.

**BRADFORD Sarah Mary Malet,** b. 3 September 1938, Bournemouth, England. Author; Journalist; Critic. m. (1) Anthony John Bradford, 31 April 1959, 1 son, 1 daughter (2) Viscount Bangor, 1 October 1976. Education: Lady Margaret Hall, Oxford, England, 1956-59. Appointment: Manuscript Expert, Christie's, 1975-78. Publications: The Story of Port, 1978, 1983; Portugal and Madeira, 1969; Portugal, 1973; Cesare Borgia, 1976; Disraeli, 1982; Princess Grace, 1984; King George VI, 1989; Elizabeth: A Biography of Her Majesty The Queen, 1996; America's Queen, The Life of Jacqueline Kennedy Onassis, 2000; Lucrezia Borgia, 2004. Contributions to: Reviews in Daily Telegraph, Sunday Telegraph, The Times, Sunday Times, Times Literary Supplement, Literary Review; Mail on Sunday; Daily Mail; Spectator. Address: c/o Gillon Aitken Associates, 18-21 Cavave Place, London SW10 9PT, England

**BRADING David Anthony,** b. 26 August 1936, Ilford, Essex, England. Academic. m. Celia Wu, 1 son. Education: BA, Pembroke College, Cambridge, 1960; Yale College, USA, 1961; PhD, University College London, 1965. Appointments: Assistant Professor, University of California at Berkeley, 1965-71; Associate Professor, Yale University, 1971-73; Lecturer in Latin American History, 1973-92; Reader, Latin American History, 1992-99, Professor of Mexican History, Cambridge, 1999-2003. Publications: Books and articles in professional journals. Honours: Litt D, Cambridge, 1991; Fellow, Academia Scientiarum et Artium Europaea, 1993; Fellow, British Academy, 1995; Order of Aztec Eagle, 2002. Address: 28 Storey's Way, Cambridge, CB3 0DT, England.

**BRADLEY Marjorie,** b. 22 May 1916, Portsmouth, Hampshire, England. Retired Civil Servant; Poet. m. Reuben Stephen Bradley, 22 June 1938, 3 sons. Education: Municipal College, Portsmouth. Appointments: Junior Clerk, 1933-37; Tax Officer, 1937-38; Secretary, West Riding County Council, 1951-58; Clerical Officer, Department of Health and Social Security, 1958-73. Publication: Coffee Spoons. Contributions to: Envoi; Writer; London Calling; Purple Patch; Civil Service Author; Focus; Weyfarers; Success Magazine. Honours: Civil Service Authors, Herbert Spencer Competition; Open Poetry Competition; Envoi Magazine Open Competition; Salopian Poetry Competition; Success and Springboard Magazine Competitions. Memberships: Society of Civil Service Authors; Patchway Writers Group. Address: 88 Oak Close, Little Stoke, Bristol BS12 6RD, England.

**BRAGG Melvyn,** b. 6 October 1939, Wigton, Cumbria, England. Author; Broadcaster. m. Cate Haste, 1 son, 2 daughters. Education: 2nd Class Honours, Modern History, Wadham College, Oxford, 1961. Appointments: General Trainee, BBC, 1961; Producer on Monitor, 1963; Director, films including portrait of Sir John Barbirolli, 1963; Writer, Debussy film for Ken Russell, 1963; Editor, for BBC2, New Release (Arts Magazine) which became Review, then Arena, 1964; Documentary, Writers World, 1964; Take It or Leave It (Literary Panel Game), 1964; Presenter, for Tyne Tees TV, In the Picture (local arts programme), 1971; Presenter/Producer, for BBC, Second House, 1974-8; Editor/Presenter, BBC, Read All About It, 1974-78; Interviewer for BBC, Tonight, 1974-78; Editor, Presenter, The South Bank Show, 1978; Head of Arts LWT, 1982-90; Programmes for Channel Four, 1982-90; Controller of Arts, LWT, 1990; Director, LWT Productions, 1992; Deputy Chairman, 1985-90, Chairman, 1990-95, Border TV, 1990-95; Governor LSE, 1997; Presenter, In Our Time, BBC Radio 4, 1998-. Publications: Books include: For Want of a Nail, 1965; The Second Inheritance, 1966; Without a City Wall, 1968; The Cumbrian Trilogy, 1984; The Christmas Child, 1984; Love and Glory, 1984; The Nerve, 1971; Josh Lawton, 1972; The Silken Net, 1974; Autumn Manoeuvres, 1978; A Time to Dance (BBC TV adaption 1992), 1991; Crystal Rooms, 1992; CREDO, 1996; The Sword and The Miracle (USA publication), 1997; The Soldier's Return, 1999; A Son of War, 2001; The Adventure of English (executive producer/presenter of television series), 2001; Crossing The Lines, 2003; Screenplays: Isadora; The Music Lovers; Jesus Christ Superstar; A Time to Dance, 1992; Musicals: Mardi Gras, 1976; The Hired Man, 1985; Play: King Lear In New York, 1992; Journalist in various newspapers. Honours include: Numerous for the South Bank Show, including 3 Prix Italias; Ivor Novello Award for Best Musical, 1985; Richard Dimbleby Award for Outstanding Contribution to TV, 1987; 2 TRIC Awards, 1990, 1994; Numerous honorary degrees. Memberships: President, MIND; President, The National Campaign for the Arts (NCA). Address: 12 Hampstead Hill Gardens, London, NW3 2PL, England

**BRAMALL, Field Marshal Baron, Edwin Noel Westby,** b. 18 December 1923, Tunbridge Wells, Kent. Army Officer; Lord Lieutenant of Greater London. m. Avril, The Lady Bramall, 1 son, 1 daughter. Education: Eton College, 1937-42; Student, Army Staff College, Camberley, 1952; Imperial Defence College, 1970. Appointments: Joined Army 1942; Commissioned into KRRC, 1943; Served in NW Europe, 1944-45; Occupation of Japan, 1946, War Office, 1947-48; Instructor, School of Infantry, 1949-51; PSC, 1952; Middle East, 1953-58; Instructor Staff College, 1958-61; Staff of Lord Mountbatten, Ministry of Defence, 1963-64; CO 2 Green Jackets, Malaysia, 1965-66; Command, 5 Airportable Brigade, 1967-69, IDC 1970; GOC, 1 Division BAOR, 1971-73; Lieutenant General, 1973; Commander, British Forces Hong Kong, 1973-76; General, 1976; Colonel Commandant 3 Battalion Royal Green Jackets, 1973-84; Colonel, 2 Gurkhas, 1976-86; Commander-in-Chief, UK Land Forces, 1976-78; Vice-Chief of Defence Staff, Personnel and Logistics, 1978-79; Chief of General Staff, 1979-82; ADC General to H M The Queen, 1979-82; Field Marshal, 1982; Chief of the Defence Staff, 1982-85. Publication: The Chiefs: The Story of the UK Chiefs of Staff (co-author). Honours: Lord Lieutenant of Greater London, 1986-98; KG; GCB; OBE; MC; JP. Memberships include: President, Gurkha Brigade Association, 1987-; President, Greater London Playing Fields Association, 1990-; President, MCC, 1988-89; Izingari Cricket Club; Free Foresters Cricket Club; Travellers; Army and Navy; Pratts. Address: House of Lords, Westminster, London SW1A 0PW, England.

**BRAMWELL Fitzgerald,** b. 16 May 1945, Brooklyn, New York, USA. Chemist. m. Charlott, 2 sons, 2 daughters. Education: BA, Chemistry, Columbia University, 1966; MS, 1967, PhD, 1970, Chemistry, University of Michigan. Appointments include: Dean, Graduate Studies and Research, Brooklyn College, CUNY, 1990-95; Executive Director, University of Kentucky Research Foundation, 1995-2001; Vice-President, Research and Graduate Studies, University of Kentucky, 1995-2001; Professor, Chemistry, University of Kentucky, 1995-. Publications include: Instructor's Guide for Investigations in General Chemistry Quantitative Techniques and Basic Principles, 1978; Instructor's Guide for Basic Laboratory Principles in General Chemistry with Quantitative Techniques, 1990; Basic Laboratory Principles in General Chemistry with Quantitative Techniques, 1990. Honours include: Distinguished Service Award, Brooklyn College Graduate Students Organization, 1994, 1995, Brooklyn Subsection of American Chemical Society, 1995; Department of Chemistry Alumni Excellence Award, University of Michigan, 1996; Lyman T Johnson Alumni Association Award, University of Kentucky, 1996; CCNY LSAMP Founders Award, 2000; Kentucky Geological Survey Outstanding Leadership Award, 2000; Claude Feuss Award, Phillips Academy, Andover, 2000; Omicron Delta Kappa, Nu Chapter, 2001. Memberships include: Kentucky Academy of Sciences, 1996-; American Association for the Advancement of Science, 1996-; American Institute of Chemists and Chemical Engineers, 1996-; Sigma Xi, 1971-; American Physical Society, 1967-95; American Chemical Society, 1966-. Address: Chemistry Department, University of Kentucky, Lexington, KY 40506-0055, USA.

**BRANAGH Kenneth,** b. 10 December 1960, Belfast, Northern Ireland. Actor; Director. m. (1) Emma Thompson, divorced, (2) Lindsay Brunnock. Education: Royal Academy of Dramatic Art. Appointments: Numerous Theatre and Radio Work. Creative Works: Films: High Season; A Month in the Country; Henry V, 1989; Dead Again, 1991; Peter's Friends, 1992; Swing Kids, 1992; Swan Song, 1992; Much Ado About Nothing, 1993; Mary Shelley's Frankenstein; Othello, 1995; In the Bleak Midwinter, 1995; Hamlet, 1996; The Theory of Flight, 1997; The Proposition, 1997; The Gingerbread Man, 1997; Celebrity, 1998; Wild, Wild West, 1998; Love's Labour's Lost, 2000; How to Kill Your Neighbor's Dog, 2002; Rabbit Proof Fence, 2002; Harry Potter and the Chamber of Secrets, 2002; Alien Love Triangle, 2002. Publications: Public Enemy (play), 1988; Beginning (memoirs), 1989; The Making of Mary Shelley's Frankenstein, 1994; In the Bleak Midwinter, 1995; Screenplays for Henry V, Much Ado About Nothing, Hamlet. Honours: Evening Standard Best Film Award; New York Film Critics Circle Best Director Award; Hon DLitt, Queens University, Belfast, 1990; BAFTA Award, Best Director, 1990. Address: Shepperton Studios, Studio Road, Shepperton, Middlesex TW17 0QD, England.

**BRANCH Michael Arthur,** b. 24 March 1940, Langley, Kent, England. Academic. m. Ritva-Riitta Hannele Kari, 3 daughters. Education: BA (Hons), Hungarian, School of Slavonic and East European Studies, 1959-63, PhD, Finno-Ulgrian Studies, School of Slavonic and East European Studies and University of Helsinki, 1964-67, University of London. Appointments: Assistant Lecturer, Lecturer, Hungarian and Finno-Ungrian Studies, 1967-71, Lecturer in Finnish, 1972-77, Reader in Finnish, 1977-85, Professor of Finnish, 1985-2001, Director, 1980-2001, School of Slavonic and Eastern European Studies, University of London; Fellow, University College London, 2001-; Leverhulme Emeritus Fellow, 2004-2006. Publications include: A J Sjögren – Studies of the North, 1973; Finnish Folk Poetry: Epic (with M Kuusi), 1977; Student Glossary of Finnish (co-author), 1980; The Great Bear (co-author), 1993; Uses of Tradition (co-editor), 1994; Finland and Poland in the Russian Empire (co-editor), 1995; National History and Identity (editor), 1999. Honours: Honorary Degree, University of Oulu, 1983; Commander of Finnish Lion, 1980; Polish Order of Merit, 1994; Estonian Order of Terra Mariana Cross, 2000; CMG, 2000; Order of the Lithuanian Grand Duke Gediminas, 2002. Memberships: Athenaeum; Latvian Academy of Sciences. Address: 33 St Donatt's Road, London SE14 6NU, England.

**BRAND Gregor,** b. 7 June 1957, Bettenfeld, Germany. Writer; Publisher. 2 daughters. Education: Assessor Iuris, Faculty of Law, University of Trier, Germany, 1983. Appointments: Research Fellow, University of Trier, Germany, 1983-85; Founder, Gregor Brand Verlag (Publishing House), 1985-. Publications: Books: Ausschaltversuche (poetry), 1985; Der Schwarze Drachen stuerzt ins Meer (poetry), 1987; Spätes Zweites Jahrtausend (poetry), 1998; Gesammelte Gedichte (collected poetry), 2000; Sefer Pralnik, 2001; More than 80 articles. Honours: Listed in more than 12 national and international lexica and encyclopaedias. Memberships include: Czechoslovak Society of Arts and Sciences. Address: Am Denkmal 4, 24793 Bargstedt, Germany. Website: http://www.gregorbrand.de.vu

**BRANDENBURG Stan C,** b. 3 January 1940. Corporate President. m. Ninitz Brandenburg, 1 son, 2 daughters. Education: BA, University of Arizona, 1966. Appointments: Enrolled Agent, enrolled to practice before IRS; Certified Tax Professional; Accredited in Federal Taxation; Registered Insurance and Financial Advisor; Accredited Accountant; President, Brandenburg Financial Incorporated, Agent Tax Firm, San Fernando, California, 1971-; President, Team Securities Corporation, Securities Exchange Firm, 1989-; General Partner, Brandenburg Insurance Service; previously Director of numerous companies in the financial and other sectors; Past President and Past Treasurer, San Fernando Chapter, California Society of Enrolled Agents affiliate of the National Association of Enrolled Agents, 1990-. Publications: Articles in professional journals. Honour: California Businessman of the Year. Memberships include: National Association of Enrolled Agents; National Association of Tax Consultants; American Institute of Tax Studies; National Society of Accountants; National Ethics Bureau. Address: 6812 Owensmouth Avenue #200, Canoga Park, CA 91303-2040, USA. Website: brandeburginc.com

**BRANDL Heinz G,** b. 29 June 1940, Znaim. Full University Professor. m. Annerose Brandl, 2 sons, 1 daughter. Education: Dipl-Ing (MSc), 1963; DrTechn, 1966; Habilitation (Associate Professor), 1971. Appointments: Head of Soil Laboratory, Vienna Technical University, 1969-72; Associate Professor, Head of Consulting Company, 1971-78; Full Professor and Head of Institutes for Soil and Rock Engineering, Geotechnics at Graz and Vienna Technical Universities, 1978-. Publications: Over 400 scientific publications including 18 books in 16 languages, covering whole field of geotechnics; About 450 invited scientific keynote lectures worldwide; Responsibly involved in more than 3500 engineering projects. Honours: Numerous scientific honours and awards from Austria and elsewhere; Honorary Doctorate. Memberships: Royal Academy of Sciences, Brussels; New York Academy of Sciences; Past President, ISSMGE-Europe (International Society for Geotechnics); President, Austrian Society of Engineers and Architects; Numerous international committees. Address: Nussbergg 7A/23, A-1190 Vienna, Austria.

**BRANDON Peter Samuel,** b. 4 June 1943, Writtle, Essex, England. Chartered Surveyor. m. Mary A E Canham, 1 son, 2 daughters. Education: MSc, Architecture, University of Bristol, 1978; DSc, Information Systems, University of Salford, 1996. Appointments: Surveyor, Surveying Practice, 1963-67; Surveyor, Local Government, 1968-70; Lecturer, 1969-73, Head of Surveying Department, 1981-85, Portsmouth Polytechnic; Principal Lecturer, Bristol Polytechnic, 1973-81; Head of Surveying Department, University of Salford 1985-93, Pro Vice Chancellor, 1993-2001, Director, Strategic Programmes and Public Orator, 2001-2003, University of Salford; Director of Strategic Programmes, School of Construction and Property Management, University of Salford, 2003-; Freelance Adviser on Research and Educational Matters, 2003-. Publications: Numerous articles including: Microcomputers in Building Appraisal (with G Moore), 1983; Computer Programs for Building Cost Appraisal (with G Moore and P Main), 1985; An Integrated Database for Quantity (with J Kirkham), 1989; Editor: Building, Cost Modelling and Computers, 1987; Quantity Surveying Techniques: New Direction, 1990; Investment, Procurement & Performance in Construction, 1991; Integrated Construction Information, 1995; Evaluation of the Built Environment for Sustainability, 1997; Cities & Sustainability: Sustaining Cultural Heritage, 2000; Evaluating Sustainable Development (co-author Patrizia Lombardi), 2005; Over 150 publications in more than 30 countries worldwide. Honour: Honorary Member, South African Association of Quantity Surveyors for services to Quantity Surveying worldwide, 1994. Membership: Fellow, Royal Institute of Chartered Surveyors. Address: 3 Woodland Drive, Lymm, Cheshire, WA13 0BL, England. E-mail: p.s.brandon@salford.ac.uk

**BRANFIELD John Charles,** b. 19 January 1931, Burrow Bridge, Somerset, England. Writer; Teacher. m. Kathleen Elizabeth Peplow, 2 sons, 2 daughters. Education: MA, Queens' College, Cambridge University; MEd, University of Exeter. Publications: Nancekuke,1972; Sugar Mouse, 1973; The Scillies Trip, 1975; Castle Minalto, 1979; The Fox in Winter, 1980; Brown Cow, 1983; Thin Ice, 1983; The Falklands Summer, 1987; The Day I Shot My Dad, 1989; Lanhydrock Days, 1991; A Breath of Fresh Air, 2001; Ella and Charles Naper: Life and Art at Lamorna, 2003; Charles Simpson: Painter of Animals and Birds, Coastline and Moorland, 2005. Address: Mingoose Villa, Mingoose, Mount Hawke, Truro, Cornwall TR4 8BX, England.

**BRANSON Richard Charles Nicholas,** b. 18 July 1950. Founder; Chairman; President. m. (1) 1969, dissolved, (2) Joan Templeman, 1989, 1 son, 1 daughter. Education: Stowe. Appointments: Editor, Student Magazine, 1968-69; Founder, Student Advisory Centre (now Help), 1970; Founder, Virgin Mail-Order Company, 1969, First Virgin record shop, 1971; Recording Company, 1973; Nightclub (The Venue), 1976; Virgin Atlantic Airways, 1984; Founder and Chairman, Virgin Retail Group, Virgin Communications, Virgin Travel Group, Voyager Group; Group also includes publishing, broadcasting, contraction, heating systems, holidays; Chairman, 1986-88, President, 1988-, UK 2000; Director, Intourist Moscow Ltd, 1988-90; Founder, The Healthcare Foundation, 1987; Founder, Virgin Radio, 1993; Founder, Virgin Rail Group Ltd, 1996; Launched Virgin Cola drink, 1994, Babylon Restaurant, 2001; Crossed Pacific in hot air balloon with Per Lindstrand, 1991. Honours: Blue Riband Title for Fastest Atlantic Crossing, 1986; Seagrave Trophy, 1987. Publication: Losing My Virginity, autobiography, 1998. Address: c/o Virgin Group PLC, 120 Campden Hill Road, London W8 7AR, England.

**BRASSEAUX Carl Anthony,** b. 19 August 1951, Opelousas, Louisiana, USA. Historian. m. Glenda, 21 July 1973, 2 sons, 1 daughter. Education: BA, Political Science, cum laude, University of the South West, Louisiana, 1974; MA, History, 1975; Doctorat de 3e cycle, University of Paris, 1982. Appointments: Assistant Director, Center for Louisiana Studies, 1975-2000; Professor, History and Geography Department, University of Louisiana, Lafayette, 1998-; Director, Center for Louisiana Studies, 2003-; Director, Center for Cultural and Eco-Tourism, University of Louisiana at Lafayette, 2001-; Director, Center for Louisiana Studies, 2004-. Publications: 102 scholarly publications in journals in North America and Europe; 33 book length works. Honours: Kemper Williams Prize, 1979; Robert L Brown Prize, 1980; President's Memorial Award, Louisiana Historical Association, 1986; Book Prize, French Colonial Historical Society, 1987; Chevalier, L'Ordre des Palmes Academiques, 1994; University Distinguished Professor, History, 1995; National Daughters of the American Revolution Award, 1995; Fellow, Louisiana Historical Association, 2000-; Louisiana Writer of the Year, 2003; Louisiana Humanist of the Year, 2005-. Membership: Louisiana Historical Association. Address: 201 Parliament Drive, Lafayette, LA 70506, USA.

**BRASSEUL Jacques Pierre,** b. 23 May 1946, Neuilly sur Seine, France. Professor. m. Claudia Korn, 1 son, 2 daughters. Education: Agregation, University of Paris, 1970; Doctorat d'Etat, University of Lyon, 1980. Appointments: Assistant Professor, University of Paris, France, 1973-80; Professor, University of Lyon, France, 1980-82; Professor, University of Dakar, Senegal, 1982-86; Professor, University of Toamasina, Madagascar, 1986-90; Professor, University of Lyon, France, 1990-93; Professor, University of La Reunion, Reunion Island, 1993-96; Professor, University of Toulon, France, 1996-. Publications: Histoire des faits économiques, 3 volumes, 1997, 1998, 2003; Introduction à l'économie du developpement, 1993; Les Nouveaux Pays Industrialisés, 1993; Amerique latine in Encyclopaedia Universalis, 1995; Petite histoire des faits économiques, 2001; Un monde meilleur?, 2005. Address: 10 allée Chevalier Paul, 83400 Hyères, France. E-mail: jacques@brasseul.com

**BRAUN Warren Lloyd,** b. 11 August 1922, Postville, Iowa, USA. Author; Retired Consulting Engineer. m. Lillian, 1

daughter. Education: BSEE, Valparasio Technical Institute, Indiana; Radio Engineering, Capital Radio Engineering Institute, DC; Business Administration, Alexander Hamilton Institute, New York. Appointments: Chief Engineer, WJMA (now WKEY), Covington, Virginia, 1941; Chief Engineer, 1941-45, Technical Director, 1946-58, WSVA Radio, Harrisonburg, Virginia; Designed and constructed: WTON, Staunton, Virginia, 1947; WJMA, Orange, Virginia, 1948; WSIR, Winter Haven, Florida, 1946; New WSVA building and broadcast plants, 1950, 1957; WSVA-FM, Harrisonburg, 1946; WJZ-TV, Baltimore, Maryland, 1948-49; WSVA-TV, Harrisonburg, 1953; Assistant General Manager, 1959-63; General Manager, 1964-65, WSVA AM-FM-TV, Harrisonburg; Consulting Engineer, 1957-; Chairman, Chief Executive Officer, 1972-90, Chairman Emeritus of the Board, 1990-, ComSonics Inc. Publications: Author of over 25 books and other papers; 10 patents. Honours: Jefferson David Medal, UDC, 1961; Honorary Member, Junior Chamber of Commerce, 1966; Man of the Year, Harrisonburg/Rockingham County Merchants Association; Engineer of the Year 1965; Elected Fellow, Audio Engineering Society, 1966; ASE International Award, 1969; E H Rietzke Award, 1972; Fellow, International Consular Academy, 1972; Distinguished Service Award, VSPE, 1974; Executive of the Year, Professional Secretaries International, 1983; Businessman of the Year, Harrisonburg-Rockingham County Chamber of Commerce, 1985; Honorary Doctor of Science, Shenandoah College and Conservatory, 1987; Hall of Fame Award, Virginia Cable Television Association, 2002. Memberships: Audio Engineering Society; International Broadcasters Society; American Institute of Electrical Engineers; Acoustical Society of America; National Society of Professional Engineers; Virginia Society of Professional Engineers; Society of Motion Pictures and Television Engineers; IEEE. Address: 680 New York Ave, Harrisonburg, VA 22801, USA. E-mail: wlb81110@ntelos.net

**BRAYDEN David James,** b. 8 January 1963, Dublin, Ireland. University Lecturer. m. Anne O'Loughlin, 2 daughters. Education: BSc, 1984, MSc, 1985, University College Dublin; M. Phil., 1986, PhD, 1989, University of Cambridge. Appointments: Postdoctoral Research Fellow, Stanford University, California, USA, 1989-91; Senior Scientist, Elan Corporation, Dublin, Ireland, 1991-2000; Senior Lecturer, University College Dublin and Principal Investigator, Conway Institute of Biotechnology, University College Dublin, 2001-. Publications: Pathogen invasion across the intestine (co-author), 2004; In vitro and ex vivo intestinal tissue models to measure mucoadhesion of poly(methacrylate) and N-trimetholated chitosan (co-author), 2005. Honours: Sir Patrick Dun Gold Medal for best paper at National Scientific Medical Meeting, 1994; PR Pharmaceuticals Prize for outstanding veterinary controlled release paper, 2004. Memberships: School of Veterinary Sciences, University College Dublin, Belfield, Dublin 2, Ireland. E-mail: david.brayden@ucd.ie Website: www.ucd.ie/conway/cv_526.html

**BRAZHNIKOV Andrey V,** b. 28 October 1959, Kostroma, Russia. Scientist; Educator. m. Elena S Karpenko, 1 daughter. Education: BS, Electrical Engineering, major in Automatics and Telemechanics, Honours Degree, cum laude, 1982; PhD, Electromechanics 1985. Appointments: Chief of Laboratory, Research Institute, Krasnoyarsk, 1987-88; Deputy Director, Educational Institute, Director of Educational Centre, 1997-2002; Chief of several scientific projects among them 2 international projects, 1991-. Publications: More than 60 scientific works include: Additional Resources of Control of Multiphase Inverter Drives, 1993; Prospects for the Use of Multiphase Electric Drives in the Field of Mining Machines, 1995; Improvement of Technical and Economic Characteristics of Drilling Rigs Owing

to the Use of Multiphase Electric Drives, 1996; Hydrodynamic Modelling of Force Fields, 1997. Honours: Annual Prizes for Scientific Work, Russian Research and Higher Educational Institutes, 1980-; Prizes for organising scientific work, Academy of Non-Ferrous Metals and Gold, Krasnoyarsk, Russia, 1997-; Listed in Who's Who publications and biographical dictionaries. Memberships: Institute of Electrical and Electronics Engineers; Research Board of Advisors, American Biographical Institute. Address: State University of Non-Ferrous Metals and Gold, 95 Krasnoyarsky Rabochy Avenue, 660025 Krasnoyarsk, Russia. E-mail: dnn@color.krasline.ru

**BREEZE David John,** b. 25 July 1944, Blackpool, England. Civil Servant. m. Pamela Diane Silvester, 2 sons. Education: BA, Honours, Modern History, 1965, PhD, 1970, University College, University of Durham. Appointments: Inspector of Ancient Monuments, 1969-89; Chief Inspector of Ancient Monuments, Scotland, 1989-2005. Publications: Books: The Northern Frontiers of Roman Britain, 1982; Roman Forts in Britain, 1983; A Queen's Progress, 1987; Roman Officers and Frontiers (with B Dobson), 1993; Roman Scotland: Frontier Country, 1996; The Stone of Destiny (with G Munro), 1997; Historic Scotland, 1998; Hadrian's Wall, 4th edition (with B Dobson), 2000; Historic Scotland, People and Places, 2002; The Antonine Wall, 2004; Frontiers of the Roman Empire (with S Jilek and A Thiel), 2005; Papers in British and foreign journals. Honours: Trustee, Senhouse Roman Museum, Maryport, 1985-; President, Society of Antiquaries of Scotland, 1987-90; Chairman, Hadrian's Wall Pilgrimages, 1989, 1999; Chairman, British Archaeological Awards, 1993-; Visiting Professor of Archaeology, University of Durham, 1994-; Honorary Professor, University of Edinburgh, 1996-; Honorary Professor, University of Newcastle, 2003-; Vice-President, Royal Archaeological Institute, 2002-; Vice-President, Cumberland and Westmorland Antiquarian and Archaeological Society, 2002-. Memberships: RSA, 1975; FSA Scot, 1970; FRSE, 1991; FRSA, 1999; MIFA, 1990; Corresponding Member, German Archaeological Institute; UK Representative, International Committee on Archaeological Heritage Management, 1998-; Member of the Council, Society of Antiquaries of Newcastle upon Tyne, 2002-. Address: Historic Scotland, Longmore House, Salisbury Place, Edinburgh EH9 1SH, Scotland. E-mail: david.breeze@scotland.gov.uk

**BREGU Eleonora (Lady of Soul),** b. 8 April 1953, Erseka, Albania. Head of the Holy Mission Eleonore. Divorced, 1 son, 3 daughters. Education: Graduate, Faculty of Law, University of Tirana, 2000. Appointments: Lady, 20 July 1987; Founder and Head of the Holy Mission Eleonore, 1987-; Dervishe, 3 November 1992; Nigjar, 8 October 1993; Lady of Soul, 8 October 1996; Scientific sessions: What is religion?, Erseka; What is Equilibrium?, Tirana; Who was born first, man or his belief?; The Origin of Communication, Florida, USA; Holy Mission Eleonore, The Greatest Space and Civilisation of The New Millennium, Lisbon, Portugal; Meetings: All in the contribution for national peace, 30 January 1996; What does say the Divine Connection for Albanians, 18 April 1997. Publications: Poetry book: Rowing in no Returning, 1996; Philosophical books: Man in front of his being, 1995; Cosmos and we, 2000; Argument with the Philosophers, 2002; Sacred Messages: Spiritual Contact with Saint Marie, 1997; Sacred Message for the Bulgarian People from contact with her Holiness Vanga of Petrovic, Sofia, 1998; Sacred Message for the Albanian People, Tirana, 1997, 1998; Sacred Message for the Kosovo People, Tirana, 1999; Spiritual activity of The Lady of Soul in collaboration with The Heavenly Levels including activation of the Cosmic-Energetic Centres for protection of Equilibrium: Typhoon in Florida, 1997; Eclipse of the sun, 1999; Earthquake in India, 2001; Earthquakes in The Balkans and Asia, 2000, 2001; Civil conflict in Albania, 1997-

98; War in Kosovo, 1999; Terrorist attack, USA, September 11 2001. Honours: Saintliness; The Title Lady of Soul; The nomination of Holy Mission named Eleonore; Diplomas from ABI, IBC; Devotion of 1,700,000 spiritual members; Lifetime Achievement Award; Woman of the Year, 1998; 2000 Millennium Medal of Honour; Gold Star Award. Memberships: Deputy Governor of the American Biographical Institute. International Order of Fellowship; Deputy Director General of the International Biographical Centre; IBC Millenium Time Capsule Commission; Member London Diplomatic Academy. Address: Holy Mission Eleonore, PO Box 7435, St "Muhamet Gjollesha", Tirana, Albania.

**BREMNER Rory Keith Ogilvy,** b. 6 April 1961, Edinburgh, Scotland. Impressionist; Satirist. m. Tessa Campbell Fraser, 2 daughters. Education: BA (Hons), French and German, Kings College, London, 1984. Career: TV series, BBC, 1985-92; TV series, Channel 4, 1993-; Translation, The Silver Lake, Weill, 1998; Translation, Bizet's Carmen, Broomhill Opera, 2000. Honours: BAFTA, 1994, 1995; RTS, 1994, 1998, 1999; British Comedy Award, 1992; Channel 4 Political Humourist of the Year, 1999, 2001. Address: The Richard Stone Partnership, 2 Henrietta Street, London WC2E 8PS, England.

**BRENNER Sydney,** b. 13 January 1927, Germiston, South Africa (British Citizen). Molecular Biologist. m. May Woolf Balkind, 3 sons, 1 stepson, 2 daughters. Education: MSc, 1947, MB, BCh, 1951, University of Witwatersrand, Johannesburg; PhD, Oxford University, 1954. Appointments: Virus Laboratory, University of California at Berkeley, 1954; Lecturer in Physiology, University of Witwatersrand, 1955-57; Researcher, 1957-79, Director, Molecular Biology Laboratory, 1979-86, Director, Molecular Genetics Unit, 1986-92, Medical Research Council, Cambridge; Member, Scripps Institute, La Jolla, California, 1992-94; Director, Molecular Sciences Institute, Berkeley, California, 1996-2001; Distinguished Research Professor, Salk Institute, La Jolla, California, 2001-. Honours: Honorary DSc: Dublin, Witwatersrand, Chicago, London, Leicester, Oxford; Honorary LLD, Glasgow, Cambridge; Honorary DLitt, Singapore; Warren Triennial Prize, 1968; William Bate Hardy Prize, Cambridge Philosophical Society, 1969; Gregor Mendel Medal of German Academy of Science Leopoldina, 1970; Albert Lasker Medical Research Award, 1971; Gairdner Foundation Annual Award, Canada, 1978; Royal Medal of Royal Society, 1974; Prix Charles Leopold Mayer, French Academy, 1975; Krebs Medal, Federation of European Biochemical Societies, 1980; Ciba Medal, Biochemical Society, 1981; Feldberg Foundation Prize, 1983; Neil Hamilton Fairley Medal, Royal College of Physicians, 1985; Croonian Lecturer, Royal Society of London, 1986; Rosenstiel Award, Brandeis University, 1986; Prix Louis Jeantet de Médecine, Switzerland, 1987; Genetics Society of America Medal, 1987; Harvey Prize, Israel Institute of Technology, 1987; Hughlings Jackson Medal, Royal Society of Medicine, 1987; Waterford Bio-Medical Science Award, The Research Institute of Scripps Clinic, 1988; Kyoto Prize, Inamori Foundation, 1990; Gairdner Foundation Award, Canada, 1991; Copley Medal, Royal Society, 1991; King Faisal International Prize for Science (King Faisal Foundation), 1992; Bristol-Myers Squibb Award for Distinguished Achievement in Neuroscience Research, 1992; Albert Lasker Award for Special Achievement, 2000; Nobel Prize for Physiology or Medicine, 2002. Memberships: Member, Medical Research Council, 1978-82, 1986-90; Fellow, King's College, Cambridge, 1959-; Honorary Professor of Genetic Medicine, University of Cambridge, Clinical School, 1989-; Foreign Associate, NAS, 1977; Foreign Member, American Philosophical Society, 1979; Foreign Member, Real Academia de Ciencias, 1985; External Scientific Member,

Max Planck Society, 1988; Member, Academy Europea, 1989; Corresponding Scientifique Emerite de l'INSERM, Associe Etranger Academie des Sciences, France; Fellow, American Academy of Microbiology; Foreign Honorary Member, American Academy of Arts and Sciences, 1965; Honorary Member, Deutsche Akademie der Natursforsche Leopoldina, 1975; Society for Biological Chemists, 1975; Honorary FRSE; Honorary Fellow, Indian Academy of Sciences, 1989; Honorary Member, Chinese Society of Genetics, 1989; Honorary Fellow, Royal College of Pathologists, 1990; Honorary Member, Associate of Physicians of GB and Ireland, 1991. Address: Kings College, Cambridge, CB2 1ST, England.

**BRENT William B,** b. 28 June 1924, Kentucky, USA. Geologist. Education: BA, University of Virginia, 1949; MA, 1952, PhD, 1955, Cornell University; JD, University of Virginia, 1966. Appointments: Assistant Professor, Geology, Oklahoma State University; Associate Professor of Geology, Louisiana Tech University; Visiting Associate Professor of Geology, University of Virginia; Chief Geologist, Tennessee Division of Geology; Consulting Geologist. Publications: Texts and maps on the geologic structure and stratigraphy of the Appalachian Valley. Membership: Fellow, Geological Society of America; Sigma Xi. Address: 3100 Shore Drive, Apt 1048, Virginia Beach, VA 23451, USA.

**BRESENHAM Jack E,** b. USA. Chief Technical Officer; Emeritus Professor of Computer Science. Education: BSEE, University of New Mexico, 1959; MSIE, 1960, PhD, 1964, Stanford University. Appointments: Senior Technical Staff Member, Manager, Engineer, Planner, Programmer, Analyst, IBM, 1960-87; Teacher, Professor of Computer Science, Winthrop University, 1987-2003; Chief Technical Officer, Bresenham Consulting. Publications include: Algorithm for computer control of a digital plotter, 1965, reprinted, 1980, reprinted, 1998; Pixel processing fundamentals, 1996; Teaching the graphics processing pipeline: cosmetic and geometric attribute implications, 2001; The Analysis and Statistics of Line Distribution, 2002; 9 US Patents. Honours include: IBM Outstanding Contribution Award, 1967 and 1984; Distinguished Citizen Award, Wofford College National Alumni Association, 1993; Honorary Director and Invited Lecturer, University of Cantabria, Santander, Spain, July 2000; Jury Member of habilitation a diriger les recherches panel, University of Paris-8 for Jean Jaques Bourdin, 2000; Golden Quill Award in recognition of work to improve writing skills among computer science students, Winthrop University, 2001; Honorary Chair, The 11th International Conference in Central Europe on Computer Graphics, Visualization and Computer Vision, 2003; Named Distinguished Alumnus, School of Engineering, University of New Mexico, 2003. Address: 1166 Wendy Road, Rock Hill, SC 29732, USA.

**BREWER Derek Stanley,** b. 13 July 1923, Cardiff, Wales. Writer; Editor; Emeritus Professor. m. Lucie Elisabeth Hoole, 3 sons, 2 daughters. Education: Magdalen College, Oxford, 1941-42, 1945-48; BA, MA (Oxon), 1948; PhD, Birmingham University, 1956; LittD, Cambridge University, 1980. Appointments: include Professor, International Christian University, Tokyo, 1956-58; Senior Lecturer, Birmingham, 1958-65; Fellow, 1965-90, Master, 1977-90, Professor, 1983-90, Life Fellow, 1990-, Emeritus Professor, 1990-, Emmanuel College, Cambridge; Editor, The Cambridge Review, 1981-86. Publications: Numerous contributions to specialist scholarly journals, and several books, mainly in the fields of medieval and later English literature, especially the works of Geoffrey Chaucer; Titles include, Chaucer, 1953; Proteus, 1958; The Parlement of Foulys, (editor), 1960; Chaucer: The Critical

Heritage, 1978; Chaucer and his World, 1978, reprinted, 1992; Symbolic Stories, 1980, reprinted, 1988; English Gothic Literature, 1983; Chaucer: An Introduction, 1984; Medieval Comic Tales (editor), 1996; A Companion to the Gawain-Poet, 1996, (editor); A New Introduction to Chaucer, 1998; Seatonian Exercises and Other Verses, 2000; The World of Chaucer, 2000. Honours: Honorary Doctorates from 7 Universities; Seatonian Prize Poem, 1969, 1972, 1979, 1980, 1983, 1986, 1988, 1992, 1994, 1999. Address: Emmanuel College, Cambridge, CB2 3AP, England. E-mail: dsb27@cam.ac.uk

**BRIDGEMAN, Viscountess Victoria Harriet Lucy,** b. 30 March 1942, Durham, England. Library Director; Writer. m. Viscount Bridgeman, 1966, 4 sons. Education: MA, Trinity College, Dublin, 1964. Appointment: Executive Editor, The Masters, 1965-69; Editor, Discovering Antiques, 1970-72; Established own company producing books and articles on fine and decorative arts; Founder and Managing Director, Bridgeman Art Library, London, New York, Paris and Berlin. Publications: An Encyclopaedia of Victoriana, 1974; An Illustrated History, The British Eccentric, 1975; Society Scandals, 1976; Beside the Seaside, 1976; A Guide to Gardens of Europe, 1979; The Last Word, 1983; 8 titles in Connoisseur's Library series. Honours: European Woman of the Year Award, Arts Section, 1997; FRSA. Address: 19 Chepstow Road, London W2 5BP, England.

**BRIDGES Jeff,** b. 4 December 1949, Los Angeles, USA. Actor. m. Susan Geston, 3 daughters. Creative Works: Films include: Halls of Anger, 1970; The Last Picture Show, 1971; Fat City, 1971; Bad Company, 1972; The Last American Hero, 1973; The Iceman Cometh, 1973; Thunderbolt and Lightfoot, 1974; Hearts of the West, 1975; Rancho Deluxe, 1975; King Kong, 1976; Stay Hungry, 1976; Somebody Killed Her Husband, 1978; Winter Kills, 1979; The American Success Company, 1980; Heaven's Gate, 1980; Cutter's Way, 1981; Tron, 1982; Kiss Me Goodbye, 1982; The Last Unicorn, 1982; Starman, 1984; Against All Odds, 1984; Jagged Edge, 1985; 8 Million Ways to Die, 1986; The Morning After, 1986; Nadine, 1987; Tucker, the Man and His Dream, 1988; See You in the Morning, 1990; Texasville, 1990; The Fabulous Baker Boys, 1990; The Fisher King, 1991; American Heart, The Vanishing, Blown Away, 1994; Fearless, 1994; Wild Bill, White Squall, 1995; The Mirror Has Two Faces, 1996; The Big Lebowski, 1997; Arlington Road, 1998; Simpatico, 1999; The Muse, 1999; The Contender, 2000; Raising the Hammoth (TV voice), 2000; K-Pax, 2002; Masked and Anonymous, 2003; Seabiscuit, 2003; The Door in the Floor, 2004. Address: c/o Creative Artists Agency, 9830 Wilshire Boulevard, Beverly Hills, CA 90212, USA.

**BRIERS Richard David,** b. 14 January 1934, Merton, England. Actor. m. Ann Davies, 1957, 2 daughters. Education: Royal Academy of Dramatic Art. Creative Works: Stage roles include: Arsenic and Old Lace, 1965; Relatively Speaking, 1966; The Real Inspector Hound, 1968; Cat Among the Pigeons, 1969; The Two of Us, 1970; Butley, 1972; Absurd Person Singular, 1973; Absent Friends, 1975; Middle Age Spread, 1979; The Wild Duck, 1980; Arms and the Man, 1981; Run for Your Wife, 1983; Why Me?, 1985; The Relapse, 1986; Twelfth Night, 1987; King Lear, 1990; Midsummer Night's Dream, 1990; Coriolanus, 1991; Uncle Vanya, 1991; Home, 1994; A Christmas Carol, 1996; The Chairs, 1997; Spike, 1999; Bedroom Farce, 2002. Films: Henry V, 1988; Much Ado About Nothing, 1992; Swan Song, 1993; Mary Shelley's Frankenstein, 1995; In the Bleak Midwinter, 1995; Hamlet, 1996; Love's Labours Lost, 1999; Unconditional Love, 2000; Television series include: Brother-in-Law; Marriage Lines; The Good Life; OneUpManShip; The Other One; Norman Conquests; Ever-Decreasing Circles; All in Good Faith,; Monarch of the Glen. Publications: Natter Natter,

1981; Coward and Company, 1987; A Little Light Weeding, 1993; A Taste of the Good Life, 1995. Address: Hamilton Asper Management, Ground Floor, 24 Hanway Street, London W1P 9DD, England.

**BRIGGS, Baron of Lewes in the County of Sussex; Asa Briggs,** b. 7 May 1921, Keighley, Yorkshire, England. Writer. m. Susan Anne Banwell, 1955, 2 sons, 2 daughters. Education: 1st Class History Tripos, Parts I and II, Sidney Sussex College, Cambridge, 1941; BSc, 1st Class (Economics), London, 1941. Publications: Victorian People, 1954; The Age of Improvement, 1959, new edition, 2000; History of Broadcasting in the United Kingdom, 5 volumes, 1961-95; Victorian Cities, 1963; A Social History of England, 1983, 3rd edition, 1999; Victorian Things, 1988. Honours: Marconi Medal for Communications History, 1975; Life Peerage, 1976; Medaille de Vermeil de la Formation, Foundation de l'Académie d'Architecture, 1979; Wolfson History Prize, 2000; 20 honorary degrees. Memberships: British Academy, fellow; American Academy of Arts and Sciences; Social History Society, president; Victorian Society, president Address: The Caprons, Keere Street, Lewes BN7 1TY, England.

**BRIGGS Raymond Redvers,** b. 18 January 1934, Wimbledon, London, England. Illustrator; Writer; Cartoonist. m. Jean T Clark, 1963, deceased 1973. Education: Wimbledon School of Art; Slade School of Fine Art, London, NDD; DFA (Lond); FSCD FRSL. Appointments: Freelance illustrator, 1957-; Children's author, 1961-. Publications: Midnight Adventure, 1961; Ring-a-Ring o'Roses, 1962; The Strange House, 1963; Sledges to the Rescue, 1963; The White Land, 1963; Fee Fi Fo Fum, 1964; The Mother Goose Treasury, 1966; Jim and the Beanstalk, 1970; The Fairy Tale Treasury, 1975; Fungus the Bogeyman, 1977; The Snowman, 1978; Gentleman Jim, 1980; When the Wind Blows, 1982, stage and radio versions, 1983; The Tinpot Foreign General & the Old Iron Woman, 1984; Unlucky Wally, 1987; Unlucky Wally, Twenty Years On, 1989; The Man, 1992; The Bear 1994; Ethel and Ernest, 1998. Honours: Kate Greenaway Medals, 1966, 1973; British Academy of Film and Television Arts Award; Francis Williams Illustration Awards, V & A Museum, 1982; Broadcasting Press Guild Radio Award, 1983; British Book Awards: Childrens' Author of the Year, 1992; Kurt Maschler Award, 1992; British Book Awards, Illustrated Book of the Year, 1998. Memberships: Royal Society of Literature; Society of Authors. Address: Weston, Underhill Lane, Westmeston, Near Hassocks, Sussex BN6 8XG, England.

**BRIGHOUSE OF BRIGHOUSE, David John, Lord,** b. 24 November 1931, Upton, Cheshire, England. Retired. m. Mary Irene Alice Barrett Arbasini-Bovary, Contessa della Torre dei Torti de San Pietro, 2 sons, 1 daughter. Education: ACMA, MBA, Oxbridge and Fundaçao Getulio Vargas, Brazil; IDOEF, Buenos Aires; RM (Retired). Appointments: Vestey Group, South American Division, 1958-91; Trustee and Treasurer, Kent Information Federation for the Disabled, 1996-2001; Councillor, Medway Council, 2000-2003; Member of the Kent Flood Defence Committee; School Governor, Gad's Hill School, Higham; Trustee, Foords Almshouses, Rochester. Honours: Order of St James, Spain; Environment Agency – Defenders of the South. Memberships: Catenian Association (Medway Circle); Gillingham Golf Club; Country Club UK. Address: Aurikberg, 130 Maidstone Road, Chatham, Kent ME4 6DX, England. E-mail: mary@brighouse.force9.co.uk

**BRIGHTMAN Sarah.** Singer; Actress. Career: Dancer with Hot Gossip and Pan's People; Stage roles include: Cats; Requiem; the Phantom of the Opera; Aspects of Love (all music by Andrew Lloyd Webber); I and Albert; The Nightingale; The Merry Widow; Trelawney of the Wells; Relative Values; Dangerous Obsession; The Innocents. Concerts include: Barcelona Olympic Games, 1992; Recordings include: 5 Top Ten singles; Eden, album, 1999. Address: c/o JAA, 2 Goodwins Court, London WC2N 4LL, England.

**BRINDLEY Lynne J**, b. 2 July 1950, United Kingdom. Librarian; Chief Executive. Education: BA, 1st Class Honours, Music, University of Reading, 1971; Diploma in Library and Information Studies, University College, London, 1975; MA, Library and Information Studies, University of London, 1975; Degree Module in Computers and Computing, Open University, 1978; Diploma in Management, Open University Business School, 1984-84. Appointments include: Head of Marketing and Support Group, Bibliographic Services Division, 1979-83, Head of Chief Executives Office, 1983-85 British Library; Director of Library and Information Services, 1985-90, Pro-Vice-Chancellor for Information Technology, 1987-90, Aston University, Birmingham; Management Consultant, then Principal Consultant, KPMG Management Consulting, 1991-92; Librarian and Director of Information Services, London School of Economics, 1992-97; University Librarian, 1997-2000, Pro-Vice-Chancellor, 1998-2000, University of Leeds; Chief Executive Officer, The British Library, 2000-; Advisory Council for Libraries and Information Resources, Stanford University, California, USA, 1999-; Chair of IT Sub-Group, Conference of European National Libraries, 2000-; Research Libraries Support Group, 2001-; Executive Committee, National Museum Directors Conference, 2001-; Member Board of Trustees, Ithaka Horbors Inc, 2004-05. Publications: Numerous publications in the field of knowledge management, information industry and digital libraries. Honours: Honorary D.Letters: Nottingham Trent University, 2001, University of Leicester, 2002, Guildhall University, London, 2002, University of Sheffield, 2004, University of Reading, 2004; UCL Fellowship, 2002; Honorary D.Litt, University of Oxford, 2002; Freeman of the City of London, 1989; Freeman of the Worshipful Company of Goldsmiths, 1989, Liveryman, 1993; Fellow, Royal Society of Arts; Companion Institute of Management, 2004. Memberships: Fellow, Institute of Information Scientists; Fellow, Library Association. Address: The British Library, 96 Euston Road, London NW1 2DB, England. E-mail: chief-executive@bl.uk

**BRINSMADE Akbar Fairchild**, b. 31 May 1917, Puebla, State of Puebla, Mexico. Chemical Engineer Consultant, PE. m. Juanita Phillips, 1 son, 2 daughters. Education: BS, Chemistry, University of Wisconsin, Madison, 1935-39; MS, Chemical Engineering Practice, Massachusetts Institute of Technology, Cambridge, Massachusetts, 1940-42; Postgraduate studies: University of Houston, 1943-44, Polytechnic Institute, Brooklyn, New York, 1945-46, New York University, 1947-49, Tulane University, 1967-73; Registered Professional Engineer, North Carolina, 1958, Louisiana, 1979. Appointments: General Manager, Cia Minera San Francisco y Anex, San Luis Potosi, Mexico 1939-40; Senior Research Engineer, Shell Oil Company, Houston and New York City, 1942-48; Project Manager, International Industrial Consultants, New York City and Caracas, Venezuela, 1949-50; Managing Director, Promotora Nacional de Industrias, Caracas, Venezuela, 1952-57; Research and Development Engineer, Hercules Powder Co, Rocket Center, West Virginia, 1959-64; Research Engineering Specialist, Chrysler Space Division, New Orleans, Louisiana, 1966-69; Chemical Engineer Consultant to major US and foreign corporations, 1969-. Publications: Book Chapters in Solid Rocket Technology, 1967, and Author, Travel to the Stars, 1996; Author: The Expansion of the Universe - Revisited, 2000; US Patent: Gravity Habitat Module for Space Vehicle,

2001. Honours: Phi Eta Sigma; Military ROTC Bombardiers, University of Oklahoma, 1935; Phi Lambda Upsilon, University of Wisconsin, 1937. Memberships (current): Fellow, American Institute of Chemists; American Institute of Chemical Engineers; American Chemical Society; National Society of Professional Engineers; Louisiana Engineering Society; Sigma Alpha Epsilon Fraternity. Address: 486 Channel Mark Drive, Biloxi, MS 39531, USA

**BROADBENT Dennis Elton**, b. 6 February 1945, Price, Utah, USA. Psychologist; Director. m. Helen McRae, 1 son, 4 daughters. Education: BS, Psychology, Brigham Young University, 1972; MS, Education and Developmental Psychology, Florida State University, 1973; PhD, Clinical and Behaviour Therapy, School Psychology, Florida State University, 1979; Diplomate Forensic, Clinical Psychology, American Board of Psychological Specialties, 1999; Diplomate, Mental Health, 2001; Fellow, American Association of Integrative Medicine, 2001. Appointments include: Publisher, Psychological and Family Health Notes, 1983-; Director, Psychological and Family Health Associates, 1980-; Adjunct Professor, Glendale Community College, Glendale, Arizona, 1980-84; Private Clinical, Counselling, Consultant and School Psychologist, Psychological and Family Health Associates, Phoenix, Arizona, 1980-; Executive Director, Family Resource Center, 1980-; Director, Family Resource Center Charities, 1993-96; Director, The Southwest Institute for Behavioral Studies, 1986-; General Partner, The Family Resource Center, 1983-. Publications include: The Great Plan of Happiness, submitted for review; Teaching Values in Arizona Schools, 1990; Behavioral Marriage, Family, and Sexual Counseling: Principles and Techniques, submitted for publication. Honours include: Full University Scholarship, College of Eastern Utah, Brigham Young University; Forensics and Music Awards; Magna Cum Laude, Brigham Young University. Memberships: American Psychological Association; National Council on Family Relations; American College of Forensic Examiners; American Association of Integrative Medicine. Address: 3101 W Peoria Avenue Ste B309, Phoenix, AZ 85029-5210, USA.

**BRODIE David**, b. 24 June 1946, United Kingdom. m. Megan, 1 son, 1 daughter. Education: Kings School, Worcester, 1957-64; Bromsgrove College of Further Education, 1964-65; Loughborough College of Education, 1964-69; Loughborough University of Technology, 1969-72, 1978-80; Salford University, 1973-77. Appointments: Director of Physical Education, Abingdon School, Berkshire, 1969-72; Lecturer in Physical Education, St Peter's College, Saltley, Birmingham, 1972-74; Senior Lecturer and Research Fellow, Carnegie School, Leeds Polytechnic, 1974-81; Director, Department of Movement Science and Physical Education, University of Liverpool, 1981-90; Professor and Head of Department of Movement Science and Physical Education, School of Health Sciences, Liverpool University, 1990-2000; Professor and Head of Department, Research Centre for Health Studies, Buckinghamshire Chilterns University College, 2001-. Publications: 7 books; 115 refereed journal papers. Honours: Emeritus Professor, University of Liverpool; Visiting Professor, Chester College. Memberships: British Cardiac Society; Physiological Society; British Association of Cardiac Rehabilitation. Address: Faculty of Health Studies, BCUC, Gorelands Lane, Chalfont-St-Giles, Bucks HP8 4AD, England. E-mail: david.brodie@bcuc.ac.uk

**BRODSKY Andrey Konstantinovich**, b. 19 April 1943, USSR. Biologist; Zoologist. m. Marina Losina, 1 son. Education: Dr Sci Biol, PhD, Professor, Department of Entomology, Leningrad State University. Appointments: Research Assistant, 1970-80, Associated Professor, 1980-86, Full Professor, Department of Invertebrate Zoology, 1986-, Director of Educational Programme, Biodiversity and Nature Conservation, St Petersburg State University; Expert on TACIS Project, Capacity Building in Business and Management Training in the Lake Baikal Region, Hochshule Bremen, 1997; Co-ordinator, Local Agenda 21 in LIFE Project, Coastal conservation and LA21 – pilot project for Russia, 1999; National Co-ordinator in BLAF21, 2000-. Publications: 74 scientific papers; 6 books; 3 text books; Numerous popular articles. Honour: VIP of St Petersburg for the 1990's. Memberships: Russian Entomology Society; Interdisciplinary Commission for Ecological Education in North West Russia. Address: ul Korablestroitelei 23-1-372 St Petersburg 199226, Russia. E-mail: brodsky@mail.bio.pu.ru

**BROMSEN Maury Austin,** b. 25 April 1919, New York, New York, USA. Bibliographer; Historian; Antiquarian Bookseller. Education: BSS Degree, cum laude with honours in History, College of the City of New York, 1939; MA, History, University of California, Berkeley, 1941; MA, Harvard University, 1945; Honorary LHD, Northeastern University, 1987. Appointments: Tutor, History Department, College of City of New York, 1941; Visiting Professor, Catholic University of Chile, 1952; Instructor, History, College of the City of New York, 1943-44; Editor and Director of Office of Bibliography, Pan American Union, (now OAS), 1950-53; Proprietor and Director, The Maury A Bromsen Company, Dealers in Rare Books, Manuscripts and Fine Arts, 1954-. Publications: Founding Editor, Inter-American Review of Bibliography, 1951-2001; José Toribio Medina: Humanist of the Americas, 1960, translated into Spanish 1968; Simon Bolivar: A Bicentennial Tribute, 1983. Honours: Phi Beta Kappa; Academia Nacional de la Historia, Argentina; Colonial Society of Massachusetts; Sociedad de Bibliofilos Argentinos; Sociedad de Bibliofilos Chilenos; Boston Public Library's Honorary Curator, Latin American Collections; Honorary Curator and Bibliographer of the John Carter Brown Library; The President's Medal, Brown University, 2003. Memberships: Antiquarian Booksellers Association of America; Endowed the Maury A Bromsen – Simon Bolivar Room, John Carter Brown Library, 1999; Bibliographical Society of America; Charter Member, Manuscript Society; Latin American Studies Association; Conference on Latin American History; Life Member, Filson Club; Member, Countway Library of Medicine's Rare Books and Special Collections Subcommittee, Harvard Medical School, 2003. Address: 770 Boylston Street, Suite 23-F, Boston MA 02199, USA.

**BRONKAR Eunice Dunalee (Connor),** b. 8 August 1934, New Lebanon, Ohio, USA. Visual Artist; Teacher. m. Charles William Bronkar, 1 daughter. Education: BFA, Wright State University, Dayton, Ohio, 1971; M Art Ed, with WSU and teacher certification, 1983; Additional studies, Dayton Art Institute, 1972, Wright State University, 1989; Participation in 12 workshops, 1972-93. Appointments: Part-time Teacher, Springfield Museum of Art, 1967-77; Education Chairman, 1973-74; Lead Teacher, Commercial Art Program, Clark State Community College, Springfield, Ohio, 1984-94; Assistant Professor Rank, 1989; Adjunct Instructor, 1974-84; Adjunct Assistant Professor, 1998-2000; Numerous solo exhibitions; Juried exhibitions: Over 100 national, regional, state and area shows; Cleaned and restored art collections: Seven public and numerous private collections; Advisory Board, Clark County Joint Vocational Commercial Art Program. Publications: Work featured in American Artist Renown, 1981; Catalogues and magazines. Honours: Teacher Excellence Award, Clark State community College, 1992; Over 50 art awards at exhibitions including 3 Best of Shows; 2 commissioned portraits, Continental Hall, Washington DC. Memberships include: Pastel Society of America; Allied Artists of America; National Museum of Women in the Arts; Ohio Watercolor Society; Portrait Society of America. Commissions and Creative Works: Work in public and private collections in Massachusetts, New Mexico, New York, Ohio and others, Athens, Greece, Jerusalem and Jaffa, Israel; Commissioned portraits.

**BROOKE Christopher Nugent Lawrence,** b. 23 June 1927, United Kingdom. Historian. m. Rosalind Beckford Clark, 3 sons, 1 deceased. Education: BA, MA, DLitt, Gonville and Caius College, Cambridge. Appointments: National Service, 1948-50; Fellow, Gonville and Caius College, 1949-56 and 1977-, Assistant Lecturer in History, 1953-54, Lecturer in History, 1965-56; Dixie Professor of Ecclesiastical History, 1977-94, University of Cambridge; Professor of Medieval History, University of Liverpool, 1956-67; Professor of History, Westfield College London, 1967-77. Publications: Books include: From Alfred to Henry III, 1961; The Saxon and Norman Kings, 1963, 3rd edition, 2001; Europe in the Central Middle Ages, 1964, 3rd edition, 2000; The Monastic World 1000-1300 (with Wim Swaan), 1974, 2nd edition as The Age of the Cloister, 2003; A History of Gonville and Caius College, 1985; Oxford and Cambridge (with Roger Highfield and Wim Swaan), 1988; The Medieval Idea of Marriage, 1989; A History of the University of Cambridge IV, 1870-1990, 1993; Jane Austen, Illusion and Reality, 1999; A History of Emmanuel College, Cambridge (with S Bendall and P Collinson), 1999; Churches and Churchmen in Medieval Europe, 1999; The Monastic Constitutions of Lanfranc (with D Knowles), 2002. Honours include: FSA, 1964; FBA, 1970; FRHistS; Fellow, Società di Studi Francescani (Assisi); Honorary DUniv York. Memberships include: Royal Commission on Historical Monuments, 1977-84; President, Society of Antiquaries, 1981-84; Vice-President, Cumberland and Westmorland Antiquarian and Archaeological Society, 1985-89; Northamptonshire Record Society, 1987-; CBE, 1995. Address: Gonville and Caius College, Cambridge CB2 1TA, England.

**BROOKE OF SUTTON MANDVILLE, Baron of Sutton Mandville in the County of Wiltshire; Peter Leonard Brooke,** b. 3 March 1934, London. Peer; Legislator. m. Lindsay Allinson, 3 sons (by first late wife). Education: MA (Oxon), Balliol College, Oxford, 1953-57; MBA, Harvard Business School. Appointments: Royal Engineers, 1952-53; Research Associate, IMEDE, Lausanne, Switzerland, 1960-61; Spencer Stuart Management Consultants, 1971-79 (Chairman, 1974-79); MP for the Cities of London and Westminster (Westminster South till 1997), 1977-2001; Government Whip and Assistant Government Whip, 1979-83; Parliamentary Secretary, Department of Education and Science, 1983-85, Minister of State, HM Treasury, 1985-87; Paymaster General, 1987-89; Chairman of the Conservative Party, 1987-89; Secretary of State for Northern Ireland, 1989-92; Secretary of State for National Heritage, 1992-94; Chairman, Select Committee on Northern Ireland Affairs, 1997-2001; Appointed to House of Lords in Dissolution Honours, 2001; Chairman, Association of Conservative Peers, 2004-. Honours: Senior Fellow, Royal College of Art, 1987; Member of the Privy Council, 1988; Presentation Fellow, King's College, London, 1989; Companion of Honour, 1992; Honorary Fellow, Queen Mary Westfield, 1996; Hon D Litt, University of Westminster, 1999; Hon D Litt, London Guildhall University, 2001; Trustee, 1974-2001, Fellow, 2002, The Wordsworth Trust. Memberships: Fellow of the Society of Antiquaries; President, British Antique Dealers Association, 1995-; President, British Art Market Federation, 1996-; Pro-Chancellor and Chairman, Council, of the University of London, 2002-. Address: House of Lords, London SW1A 0PW, England.

**BROOKE Rosalind Beckford**, b. 5 November 1925, United Kingdom. Historian. m. Christopher N L Brooke, 3 sons. Education: BA, 1946, MA, 1950, Girton College, Cambridge. Appointments: Temporary Senior History Mistress, Mitcham County Grammar School for Girls, 1949-50; Regular Supervisor of Cambridge undergraduates for the History Tripos for various colleges, 1951-56; Part-time History Mistress, Birkenhead High School, 1958-59; Lecturer, Palaeography, 1963, Tutorial Teacher, part-time, 1964-66, University of Liverpool; Lecturer, part-time, Medieval History, 1968-73, Honorary Research Fellow, 1973-77, University College, London; Regular Supervisor of Cambridge Undergraduates for History Tripos and Theology Tripos for various colleges, 1977-94; Approved course of lectures for the History Faculty, Cambridge University, 1978-81. Publications: Books: Early Franciscan Government: From Elias to Bonaventure, 1959, reprinted 2004; The Writings of Leo, Rufino and Angelo, Companions of St Francis (editor and translator), 1970, reprinted 1990; The Coming of the Friars, 1975; Popular Religion in the Middle Ages (with CNL Brooke), 1985; Contributions to learned journals and The Oxford Dictionary of National Biography, 2004. Honours: Exhibitioner, Girton College, Cambridge, 1943; Bryce-Tebb Scholarship, 1946-48; Old Girtonian's Studentship, 1948-49; Pennsylvania State International Fellowship (Paris and Normandy), International Federation of University Women, 1950-51; FRHistS, 1959; Fellow, Società Internazionale di Studi Francescani (Assisi), 1972; FSA, 1989. Memberships: Honorary Member, Lucy Cavendish College, 1977; Senior Member, Clare Hall, 1985. Address: The Old Vicarage, Ulpha, Broughton in Furness, Cumbria LA20 6DU, England.

**BROOKES Hugh Clive**, b. 21 April 1941, Cape Town, South Africa. Professor of Inorganic Chemistry. m. Bridget, 3 daughters. Education: BSc Hons, 1962, PhD, 1966, University of Cape Town. Appointments: Research Fellow, National Research Council, Canada, 1967-69; Lecturer, Professor, University of Natal, Durban, South Africa, 1969-. Publications: Widely published in peer-reviewed scientific journals, mainly in the field of electrochemistry. Honours: Fellow, National Research Council of Canada, 1967-69; Visiting Scientist, University of Southampton, UK, 1975; Visiting Scientist, Imperial College, London, 1983; Senior Fulbright Fellow, USA, 1992-93; Honorary Research Associate, University of Kwa-Zulu Natal, 2003-. Memberships: Royal Society of Chemistry, London; South African Chemical Institute. Address: School of Pure and Applied Chemistry, University of Kwa-Zulu Natal, Durban, 4041, South Africa. E-mail: brookes@ukzn.ac.za

**BROOKES John Andrew**, b. 11 October 1933, Durham, England. Education: Commercial Horticulture Durham County School of Horticulture; 3 Year Apprenticeship with Nottingham Corporation Parks Department; 1 Year Assistant to Brenda Colvin PPILA; Diploma, Landscape Design, University College, London; 3 Years Assistant to Dame Sylvia Crowe PPILA; 3 Years Assistant Editorial Architectural Design; Private Practice, 1964-; Fellow, Society of Garden Designers. Appointments: Lecturer in Landscape Design, Institute of Park Administration; Assistant Lecturer, Landscape Design, Regent Street Polytechnic; Lecturer, Landscape Design, Royal Botanical Gardens, Kew; Director, Inchbald School of Garden Design; Set up Inchbald School of Interior Design, Teheran, Iran, 1978; Founded Clock House School of Garden Design, 1980; Faculty Lecturer, Henry Clews Foundation, La Napoule, S France, 1986-95; Principal Lecturer, Garden Design School, Royal Botanic Gardens, Kew, 1990-95; Chairman, Society of Garden Designers, 1996. Publications include: Gardens of Paradise, 1987; The Country Garden, 1987; The Small Garden Book, 1989; John Brookes' Garden Design Book,

1991; Planting the Country Way, 1994; John Brookes' Garden Design Workbook, 1994; Home and Garden Style, 1996; John Brookes' The New Garden, 1998. Honour: MBE – Citation: Garden Designer. For Services to Horticulture in the UK and Overseas. Membership: External Review Group, National Botanical Institute, Kirstenbosch, South Africa, 1995. Address: Clock House, Denmans, Fontwell, Nr Arundel, West Sussex BN18 0SU, England.

**BROOKING Barry Alfred**, b. 2 February 1944. Chief Executive. Divorced. Education: Teacher's Certificate, University of Wales, 1962-65; Chartered Teacher's Certificate, College of Preceptors, 1970; BA, History and Education, Open University, 1974-76; Advanced Television Production Certificate, University of London, 1976; MA, Manpower Studies, University of London, 1978-80; Business Management Certificate, University of Westminster, 1981. Appointments: Commissioned Officer, retiring as Lieutenant Commander, 1965-81; Business Management Administrator, Medical Protection Society, 1981-92; Regional Director, St John Ambulance, 1992-95; Chief Executive, Parkinson's Disease Society of the United Kingdom, 1995-99; First Chief Executive, British Psychological Society, 2000-04. Memberships: Chartered Institute of Management; Royal Television Society; Chartered Institute of Personnel and Development. Address: 9 Hawkmoor Parke, Bovey Tracey, Devon TQ13 9NL, England.

**BROOKNER Anita**, b. 16 July 1928, London, England. Novelist; Art Historian. Education: BA, King's College, London; PhD, Courtauld Institute of Art, London. Appointments: Visiting Lecturer in Art History, University of Reading, 1959-64; Lecturer, 1964-77, Reader in Art History, 1977-88, Courtauld Institute of Art; Slade Professor of Art, Cambridge University, 1967-68. Publications: Fiction: A Start in Life, 1981; Providence, 1982; Look at Me, 1983; Hotel du Lac, 1984; Family and Friends, 1985; A Misalliance, 1986; A Friend from England, 1987; Latecomers, 1988; Lewis Percy, 1989; Brief Lives, 1990; A Closed Eye, 1991; Fraud, 1992; A Family Romance, 1993; A Private View, 1994; Incidents in the Rue Laugier, 1995; Visitors, 1998; Undue Influence, 1999; The Bay of Angels, 2000. Non-Fiction: An Iconography of Cecil Rhodes, 1956; J A Dominique Ingres, 1965; Watteau, 1968; The Genius of the Future: Studies in French Art Criticism, 1971; Greuze: The Rise and Fall of an Eighteenth-Century Phenomenon, 1972; Jacques-Louis David, a Personal Interpretation: Lecture on Aspects of Art, 1974; Jacques-Louis David, 1980, revised edition, 1987. Editor: The Stories of Edith Wharton, 2 volumes, 1988, 1989. Contributions to: Books and periodicals. Honours: Fellow, Royal Society of Literature, 1983; Booker McConnell Prize, National Book League, 1984; Commander of the Order of the British Empire, 1990. Address: 68 Elm Park Gardens, London SW10 9PB, England.

**BROOKS (Troyal) Garth**, b. 7 February 1962, Tulsa, Oklahoma, USA. Country Music Singer; Songwriter; Musician (guitar). m. Sandra Mahl, 1986, 2 daughters. Education: BS, Journalism and Advertising, Oklahoma State University, 1985. Career: Television specials include: This Is Garth Brooks, 1992; This Is Garth Brooks Too!, 1994; Garth Brooks - The Hits, 1995; Garth Brooks Live in Central Park, 1997; Best selling country album ever, No Fences (over 13 million copies). Recordings: Albums: Garth Brooks, 1989; No Fences, 1990; Ropin' The Wind, 1991; The Chase, 1992; Beyond The Season, 1992; In Pieces, 1993; The Hits, 1994; Fresh Horses, 1995; Sevens, 1997; In The Life Of Chris Gaines, 1999; The Colors Of Christmas, 1999; Scarcrow, 2001; Singles: If Tomorrow Never Comes, 1989; Tour EP, 1994; To Make You Feel My Love, 1998; One Heart At A Time, 1998; Lost In You, 1999. Honours: Grammy

Award; CMA Horizon Award, Video of the Year, 1990; CMA Awards: Best Single, Best Album 1991; Music City News/TNN Award, Video of Year, 1991; CMA Entertainer of the Year, 1991-92; Numerous ACM Awards include: Music Entertainer of the Year, 1991-94, Best Single 1991, Best Album 1991; ASCAP Voice of Music Award, 1992; 9 People's Choice Awards; Top-selling solo artist in American music history, RIAA. Memberships: Inducted into Grand Ole Opry; ASCAP; CMA; ACM. Current Management: c/o Scott Stern, GB Management Inc, 1111 17th Avenue South, Nashville, TN 37212, USA.

**BROOKS James,** b. 11 October 1938, West Cornforth, County Durham, UK. Consultant; Academic. m. Jan, 1 son, 1 daughter. Education: BTech(Hons), Applied Chemistry, 1964; MPhil, Analysis of wool wax and related products, 1966; PhD, chemical constituents of various plant spore walls, 1970; Fellow, Geological Society (FGS), 1974; Fellow, Royal Society of Chemistry, FRSC, 1976; Chartered Chemist (CChem), 1976; DSc, research work in chemistry, geology, petroleum sciences and the origin of life, 2001; Chartered Geologist (CGeol), 2001; Chartered Scientist (CSci), 2004. Appointments: Research Geochemist, BP Research Centre, British Petroleum, 1969-75; Senior Research Fellow, University of Bradford, 1975-77; Visiting Scientist, Norwegian Continental Shelf Institute, 1975-78; Research Associate, Exploration Co-ordinator, Senior Scientist, Section Head of Production Geology, British National Oil Corporation/Britoil, 1977-86; Visiting Lecturer, University of Glasgow, 1978-99; Technical Director, Sutherland Oil and Gas Investments, 1996-98; Brooks Associates, 1986-; Chairman/Director, Petroleum Geology '86 Ltd, 1986-99; Executive Member, Scottish Baptist College, 2001-; Myron Spurgeon Visiting Professor in Geological Sciences, Ohio University, Athens, Ohio, USA, 2003; Collaborative research, teaching, professional and conference activities at numerous universities and research institutes throughout the USA, Canada, Europe, Russia and parts of Asia. Publications include: 15 books as author or editor and over 90 scientific research papers published in peer-refereed journals including: Chemical Structure of the Exine of Pollen Walls and a new function for carotenoids in nature, 1968; Chemistry and Morphology of Precambrian Microorganisms, 1973; Origin and Development of Living Systems, 1973; A Critical Assessment of the Origin of Life, 1978; Biological Relationships of Test Structure and Models for calcification and test formation in the Globigerinacea, 1979; The Chemistry of Fossils: biochemical stratigraphy of fossil plants, 1980; Organic Matter in Meteorites and Precambrian Rocks - clues about the origin of life, 1981; Origin of Life: from the first moments of the universe to the beginning of life on earth, 1985; Tectonic Controls on Oil & Gas occurrences in the Northern North Sea, 1989; Classic Petroleum Source Rocks, 1990; Cosmochemistry and Human Significance, 1999. Honours include: UK Government Exchange Scientist to USSR, 1971; Royal Society Visiting Scientist to India, 1977 and to USSR, 1991; Vice-President, Geological Society, 1984-89; Geological Society Christmas Lecture on Origin of Life, 1983; Golden Medallion and Order of Merit for book Origin of Life, 1985; Secretary, Geological Society, 1988-92; Life Member, American Association of Petroleum Geologists, 1993-; Distinguished Achievement Award, AAPG, 1993; Distinguished Service Award, The Geological Society, 1999; President of the Baptist Union of Scotland, 2002; First holder of Myron Sturgeon Visiting Professor in Geological Sciences, Ohio University, 2003; Man of Achievement, American Biographical Institute, 2005. Memberships: International IPU Committee, 1972-81; NERC Higher Degrees Research Committee, 1981-84; UK Consultative Committee on Geological Sciences, 1987-92; External Examiner, University of London, 1992-97; Series Editor, Geological Special Publications, 1989-93;

International Editorial Board of Marine and Petroleum Geology, 1984-96; Council of Geological Society, 1984-92; Chairman, Shawlands Academy School Board, 1991-96; Board of Ministry of the Baptist Union of Scotland, 1998-. Address: 10 Langside Drive, Newlands, Glasgow, G43 2EE, UK. E-mail: jim_brooks@ntlworld.com

**BROOKS Mel (Melvin Kaminsky),** b. 1926, New York, USA. Actor; Writer; Producer; Director. m. (1) Florence Baum, 2 sons, 1 daughter, (2) Anne Bancroft, 1964, 1 son. Appointments: Script Writer, TV Series, Your Show of Shows, 1951-54, Caesar's Hour, 1954-57, Get Smart, 1965; Founder, Feature Film Production Company, Brooksfilms. Creative Works: Films include: The Critic (cartoon), 1963; The Producers, 1968; The Twelve Chairs, 1970; Blazing Saddles, 1974; Young Frankenstein, 1974; Silent Movie, 1976; High Anxiety, 1977; The Elephant Man (producer), 1980; History of the World Part I, 1981; My Favorite Year (producer), 1982; To Be or Not to Be (actor, producer), 1983; Fly I, 1986; Spaceballs, 1987; 84 Charing Cross Road, 1987; Fly II, 1989; Life Stinks (actor, director, producer), 1991; Robin Hood: Men in Tights, 1993; Dracula: Dead and Loving It, 1995; Svitati, 1999; It's A Very Merry Muppet Christmas Movie (Voice), 2002; Jakers! The Adventures of Piggley Winks (TV Series), 2003. Musical: The Producers: The New Mel Brooks Musical (producer, co-writer, composer), 2001. Honours: Academy Awards, 1964, 1968. Address: c/o The Culver Studios, 9336 West Washington Boulevard, Culver City, CA 90232, USA.

**BROSNAN Pierce,** b. 16 May 1953, Navan, County Meath, Ireland. Actor. m. (1) Cassandra Harris, deceased, 1 son, (2) Keely Shaye Smith, 2001, 2 sons. Education: Drama Centre. Creative Works: Stage appearances include: Wait Until Dark; The Red Devil; Sign; Filumenia. TV appearances include: Detective, Remington Steele (series); Noble House (NBC mini-series); Nancy Astor; Around the World in Eighty Days; The Heist; Murder 101; Victim of Love; Live Wire; Death Train; Robinson Crusoe, 1994; The James Bond Story, 1999. Films: The Mirror Crack'd; The Long Good Friday; Nomads; The Fourth Protocol; Taffin; The Deceivers; Mister Johnson; The Lawnmower Man; Mrs Doubtfire; Love Affair; Robinson Crusoe; Mars Attacks!; The Mirror Has Two Faces; Dante's Peak; The Nephew, 1998; The Thomas Crown Affair, 1999; Grey Owl, 2000; The Tailor of Panama, 2001; Evelyn, 2003; Law of Attraction, 2004; Role of James Bond in Goldeneye 1994, Tomorrow Never Dies 1997, The World is Not Enough 1999; Die Another Day, 2002

**BROUGHTON Peter,** b. 8 September 1944, Keighley, Yorkshire, England. Civil Engineer. m. Jan, 2 sons. Education: BSc, Hons, Civil Engineering, 1963-66, PhD, Structural Engineering, 1966-70, Manchester University; FREng; FICE; FIStructE; FRINA; FIMarEST. Appointments: Research Student, Research Assistant, Department of Civil Engineering, University of Manchester, 1966-71; Structural Engineering Surveyor, Lloyds Register of Shipping, London, 1971-74; Partner, Subsidiary Practice, Campbell Reith and Partner, 1974-75; Structural Engineer, Burmah Oil Trading Ltd, 1975-77; Supervising Structural Engineer, British National Oil Corporation, 1977-79; Senior Structural Engineer, 1979-82, Civil Engineering Supervisor, 1982-86, Project Manager, 1990-94, Project Manager, 1998-2003, Phillips Petroleum UK Ltd; Project Engineer, 1986-90, Project Manager, 1994-98, Phillips Petroleum Company Norway; Visiting Professor, Department of Civil Engineering, Imperial College, University of London, 1991-; Royal Academy of Engineering Visiting Professor, Department of Engineering Science, University of Oxford, 2004-; Consultant, Peter Fraenkel Maritime Ltd, 2003-.

Publications include: Book: The Analysis of Cable and Catenary Structures, 1994; Numerous articles in journals including: The Ekofisk Protective Barrier, 1992; Cast Steel Nodes for the Ekofisk 2/4J Jacket, 1997; The Effects of Subsidence on the Steel Jacket and Piled Foundations Design for the Ekofisk 2/4X and 2/4J Platforms, 1996; Foundation Design for the Refloat of the Maureen Steel Gravity Platform, 2002; The Refloat of the Maureen Steel Gravity Platform, 2002; Deconstruction and Partial Re-Use of the Maureen Steel Gravity Platform and Loading Column, 2004. Honours include: Stanley Grey Award, The Institute of Marine Engineers, 1992; The George Stephenson Medal, 1993; Bill Curtin Medal, 1997; Overseas Premium, 1998; David Hislop Award, 1999, Certificate for Contribution to Institution Activity, 2002, The Institution of Civil Engineers; Phillips Petroleum Presidential Shield Award, 2002. Address: Appletrees, 30 Portsmouth Road, Camberley, Surrey GU15 1JX, England.

**BROUWER Maria,** b. 25 January 1950, Leiden, The Netherlands. Economist. Education: MSc, 1975, D Phil, 1990, University of Amsterdam. Appointments: University of Nydenrode, 1975-77; Research Foundation, 1978-1980, Professor of Economics, 1980-, University of Amsterdam. Publications: Schumpeterian Puzzles, 1991; Weber, Schumpeter Knight, 2002; Small Business Economics, 1998, 2000. Honour: Award for best summary articles, Dutch Social Sciences, 1987. Membership: International J A Schumpeter Society. Address: Zeeburger Straat 72, 1018 AG Amsterdam, The Netherlands. E-mail: m.t.brouwen@uva.nl

**BROWN Ann Meriwether,** b. 23 February 1929, Birmingham, Alabama. Artist. m. 1951, 3 daughters. Education: A study of nude models with Dr Julius Delbos, extensive drawing and sketching; Graduate, Honourable Mention in Art, Mount Vernon College, Washington DC; Sculpture, University of Washington; Studied Business and Law, Massey Business College, Birmingham, Alabama; Studies in Advertising Design under Bell Comer, Birmingham, Alabama; Water colour painting and design with Dr Keiser and Harry Lowe, Auburn University; Attended classes in oil painting with Professor Lemuel McDaniels for 8 years; Attended classes with Professors Al Sellers, Howard Goodson and Max Hellman, Birmingham Museum of Art; Studies at South Eastern Bible College, Birmingham Alabama for 4 years. Career: Taught and studied at Studio One, Birmingham, Alabama, work shown twice a year at Studio One for 25 years; Instructed Artists in local studios; Held lectures and demonstrations at the Jewish Community Center, Roebuck and Vestavia Civic Centers; Instructed art at the Opportunity Center for the Service Guild, 7 years; Taught art at the Mercy Home for underprivileged children for Junior League, 4 years; Works shown in Jury Shows, Birmingham Museum of Art; Art Shows at various galleries in Birmingham and across the USA; Bible teacher all over the state of Alabama; Taught Bible in the local county jail; Speaker at banquets, Christian women's clubs, churches and homes; Past Board Member, Brother Bryan Mission. Memberships: Junior League of Birmingham; DAR John Parke Custis Society; Salvation Army; Birmingham Symphony Club Association; Arlington Historical Society; Briarwood Presbyterian Church; Service Guild; Opera Guild; Theta Kappa Delta Sorority; The Meriwether Society of America; The National Museum "Women in the Arts"; Birmingham Museum of Art; Birmingham Spinsters Club; Birmingham Country Club; The Holiday Assembly; Birmingham Ski Club; Shade Valley YMCA; World Thrust for Christ. Address: 2428 Park Lane, Birmingham, AL 35213, USA.

**BROWN B Marietta Craig,** b. 17 January 1953, North Carolina, USA. Accountant; Minister. m. Richard Brown,

deceased. Education: Accountancy Degree, 1973; Doctorate in Divinity, 1977. Appointments: Counsellor, 700 Club; Ordained, licensed minister, serving two pastors; Worked with inner-city projects; Ordained by Reverend Rod Parsley, 1997, and Dr Creflo Dollar, 1999; Travelled overseas with pastoral work. Publications: Articles in several local newspapers. Memberships: Founder, Restoring America's Families Ministries; Teen Zone; Agape Minister's Fellowship; Restoration Christian Academy; Angel Care Center; Pray Thru Ministries; National Pastor, World Harvest Ministerial Fellowship. Address: PO Box 2489, 210 S Market St Petersburg, VA 23804, USA. E-mail: restorefam@aol.com Website: www.restorefam.org

**BROWN James,** b. 3 May 1928, Barnwell, South Carolina, USA. Soul Singer; Broadcasting Executive. m. (1) Deidre Jenkins, (2) Adrienne Brown (deceased 1996). Career: Singer with, then leader of own backing group Famous Flames, 1956-68; Solo performer, recording artist, 1969-; President, JB Broadcasting Ltd, 1968-; James Brown Network, 1968-; Film appearances include: Ski Party, 1964; Come To The Table, 1974; The Blues Brothers, 1980; Concerts include: The Biggest Show Of Stars tour, 1963; The TAMI Show, 1964; Newport Jazz Festival, 1969; Festival Of Hope, Garden City, 1972; Grand Ole Opry, Nashville, 1979; Montreux Jazz Festival, 1981; Coca-Cola Music Festival, Essex, 1992; Pori Jazz, Finland, 1995; Owner, several US radio stations; Co-owner, Brown Stone Records, 1992-. Compositions include: Film scores: Black Caesar, 1972; Slaughter's Big Rip Off, 1972. Recordings: Over 75 albums include: Live At The Apollo, 1963; I Can't Stand Myself, 1968; Hot Pants, 1971; The Payback, 1974; I'm Real, 1988; Universal James, 1992; Hit singles include: Please, Please, Please, 1956; Out Of Sight, 1964; Poppa's Got A Brand New Bag, 1965; I Got You (I Feel Good), 1966; It's A Man's Man's Man's World, 1966; Cold Sweat, 1967; I Got The Feelin', 1968; Say It Loud, 1968; Give It Up Or Turn It Loose, 1969; Get Up, I Feel Like Being A Sex Machine, 1970; Super Bad, 1970; Get On The Good Foot, 1972; Get Up Offa That Thing, 1976; Living In America (used in film Rocky IV), 1986; I'm Real, 1988; Soul Jubilee, 1990; Love Over-Due, 1991; Love Power Peace, 1992; Funky Christmas, 1995; Hookedonbrown, 1996; Say It Live And Loud, 1998; On Stage Live, 1999. Honours: Inducted, Rock'n'Roll Hall Of Fame, 1986; Grammy Awards: Best R&B Recording, 1965; Best R&B Performance, 1987; 44 Gold discs; Award Of Merit, American Music Awards, 1992; NARAS Lifetime Achievement Award, 1992; Lifetime Achievement Trophy, Rhythm & Blues Foundation Pioneer Awards, 1993; Lifetime Achievement Award, National Association of Black Owned Broadcasters' Awards, 1993. Current Management: Brothers Management Associates. Address: 141 Dunbar Avenue, Fords, NJ 08863, USA.

**BROWN Olivia Parker,** b. 29 January 1934, Maryland, USA. Teacher. m. Leonard L Brown, 2 sons, 1 daughter. Education: Bachelor of Science, State Teachers' College, 1955; Master of Education, University of Maryland, 1962. Appointments: In Service Workshop Trainee; Special Drama and Speech Classes; Interim Building Supervisor; Curriculum Specialist; Use of Media (TV); Mentoring; Tutoring; Demonstration Lessons; English Department Head. Publication: Monthly Newsletter, ELC of Our Redeemer. Honours: Listed in Who's Who publications and biographical dictionaries. Memberships: AA County, Maryland Teachers Association; PC County, Maryland Teachers Association; United Federation of Teachers; Maryland State Teachers Association; Lutheran Church. Address: 4411 19th St NE, Washington, DC20019, USA.

**BROWN Ralph,** b. 30 June 1931, United Kingdom. Vicar General, Archdiocese of Westminster. Education: Licence in Canon Law, 1961, Doctorate, 1963, Pontifical Gregorian University, Rome. Appointments: Commissioned, Middlesex Regiment, 1949, Served in Korea, 1950; Ordained Priest, Westminster Cathedral, 1959; Diocese of Westminster: Vice Chancellor, Vice Officialis, 1964-69, Officialis, 1969-76 and 1987-, Vicar General, 1976-2000; Papal Chamberlain, 1972; Secretary, 1974-80 and 1986-89, President, 1980-86, Canon Law Society of Great Britain and Ireland; National Co-ordinator of Papal Visit to England and Wales, 1982; Canonical Advisor to British Military Ordinariate, 1987-; Prelate of Honour to His Holiness the Pope, 1987; Protonotary Apostolic, 1999. Publications: Marriage Annulment, 1969, 3rd edition, 1990; Matrimonial Decisions of Great Britain and Ireland (editor), 1969-; The Code of Canon Law in English Translation (co-translator), 1983; The Canon Law: Letter and Spirit (co-editor), 1995; Various articles in Heythrop Journal; Studia Canonica; Theological Digest; The Jurist. Honours: Knight of the Equestrian Order of the Holy Sepulchre, 1984, Commander, 1991; Silver Palm of Jerusalem, 1999; Prior Westminster Section, 1994; Cross Pro Piis Meritis, Order of Malta. Memberships: Honorary Member: Canon Law Society of Australia and New Zealand, Canadian Canon Law Society, Canon Law Society of America; Old Brotherhood of English Secular Clergy, Secretary, 1993-. Address: Flat 3, 8 Morpeth Terrace, London SW1P 1EQ, England.

**BROWN William Arthur,** b. 22 April 1945, Oxford, England. University Professor. m. Kim Brown, 2 step daughters. Education: BA, Wadham College, Oxford. Appointments: Director, SSRC Industrial Relations Research Unit, University of Warwick, 1980-85; Montague Burton Professor of Industrial Relations, University of Cambridge, 1985-; Master of Darwin College, Cambridge, 2000-. Publications: Piecework Bargaining, 1973; The Changing Contours of British Industrial Relations, 1981; The Individualisation of Employment Contracts in Great Britain, 1998. Honour: CBE. Memberships: Low Pay Commission, 1997-; ACAS Council, 1998-2004. Address: Darwin College, Silver Street, Cambridge CB3 9EU, England.

**BROWNE Jackson,** b. 9 October 1948, Heidelberg, Germany. Singer; Songwriter; Musician (guitar, piano). Career: Brief spell with Nitty Gritty Dirt Band, 1966; Solo singer, songwriter, musician, 1967-; Tours and concerts with Joni Mitchell; The Eagles; Bruce Springsteen; Neil Young; Major concerts include: Musicians United For Safe Energy (MUSE), Madison Square Garden (instigated by Browne and Bonnie Raitt), 1979; Glastonbury Festival, 1982; Montreux Jazz Festival, 1982; US Festival, 1982; Benefit concerts for: Amnesty International, Chile, 1990; Christie Institute, Los Angeles, 1990; Victims of Hurricane Inki, Hawaii, 1992; Various concerts for other environmental causes; Nelson Mandela Tributes, Wembley Stadium, 1988, 1990; Sang with Bonnie Raitt and Stevie Wonder, memorial service for Stevie Ray Vaughan, Dallas, Texas, 1990; Compositions: Songs recorded by Tom Rush; Nico; Linda Ronstadt; The Eagles; Co-writer with Glenn Frey, Take It Easy. Recordings: Albums: Jackson Browne, 1972; For Everyman, 1973; Late For The Sky, 1974; The Pretender, 1976; Running On Empty, 1978; Hold Out (Number 1, US), 1980; Lawyers In Love, 1983; Lives In The Balance, 1987; World In Motion, 1989; I'm Alive, 1993; Looking East, 1996; Also featured on No Nukes album, 1980; Sun City, Artists United Against Apartheid, 1985; For Our Children, Disney AIDS benefit album, 1991; The Next Voice You Hear: The Best of Jackson Browne, 1997; Singles include: Doctor My Eyes, 1972; Here Come Those Tears Again, 1977; Running On Empty, 1978; Stay, 1978; That Girl Could Sing, 1980; Somebody's Baby, used in film Fast Times At Ridgemont High, 1982; Tender Is The Night, 1983; You're A Friend Of Mine, with Clarence Clemons,

1986; For America, 1987. Current Management: Donald Miller, 12746 Kling Street, Studio City, CA 91604, USA.

**BROWNE Jimmie,** b. 3 January 1953, Galway, Ireland. Engineer. m. Maeve, 4 sons. Education: BE, 1974, M Eng Sc, 1978, National University of Ireland, Galway, Ireland; PhD, 1988, DSc, 1990, University of Manchester. Appointments: Engineer, Nortel Networks, 1974-76; Research Assistant, National University of Ireland, Galway, 1976-78; Research Associate, UMIST, Manchester, England, 1978-80; Senior Lecturer, 1980-89, Professor, 1990-, Dean of Engineering, 1995-2000, Registrar and Deputy President, 2001-, National University of Ireland, Galway. Publications: 5 books as co-author include: Queuing Theory in Manufacturing Systems Analysis and Design, 1993; Production Management Systems - An Integrated Perspective, 2nd edition, 1997; IT and Manufacturing Partnerships - Delivering the Promise, 1998; CAD/CAM Principles, Practice and Manufacturing Management, 2nd edition, 1998; Strategic Decision Making in Modern Manufacturing, 2004; 8 edited and co-edited books; Numerous articles in peer reviewed academic journals. Honours: Fellow, Institution of Engineers in Ireland; Fellow, Irish Academy of Engineering; Member, Royal Irish Academy. Memberships: Institution of Engineers of Ireland, Royal Irish Academy. Address: 17 College Road, Galway, Ireland. E-mail: jimmie.browne@niugalway.ie

**BROWNJOHN J(ohn Nevil) Maxwell,** b. Rickmansworth, Hertfordshire, England. Literary Translator; Screenwriter. Education: MA, Lincoln College, Oxford. Publications: Night of the Generals, 1962; Memories of Teilhard de Chardin, 1964; Klemperer Recollections, 1964; Brothers in Arms, 1965; Goya, 1965; Rodin, 1967; The Interpreter, 1967; Alexander the Great, 1968; The Poisoned Stream, 1969; The Human Animal, 1971; Hero in the Tower, 1972; Strength Through Joy, 1973; Madam Kitty, 1973; A Time for Truth, 1974; The Boat, 1974; A Direct Flight to Allah, 1975; The Manipulation Game, 1976; The Hittites, 1977; Willy Brandt Memoirs, 1978; Canaris, 1979; Life with the Enemy, 1979; A German Love Story, 1980; Richard Wagner, 1983; The Middle Kingdom, 1983; Solo Run, 1984; Momo, 1985; The Last Spring in Paris, 1985; Invisible Walls, 1986; Mirror in the Mirror, 1986; The Battle of Wagram, 1987; Assassin, 1987; Daddy, 1989; The Marquis of Bolibar, 1989; Eunuchs for Heaven, 1990; Little Apple, 1990; Jaguar, 1990; Siberian Transfer, 1992; The Swedish Cavalier, 1992; Infanta, 1992; The Survivor, 1994; Acts, 1994; Love Letters From Cell 92, 1994; Turlupin, 1995; Nostradamus, 1995; The Karnau Tapes, 1997; Heroes Like Us, 1998; The Photographer's Wife, 1999; Carl Haffner's Love of the Draw, 1999; Birds of Passage, 2000; Eduard's Homecoming, 2000; The 13 ½ Lives of Captain Bluebear, 2000; The Stone Flood, 2001; Libidissi, 2001; Where do We Go From Here?, 2001; The Alexandria Semaphore, 2001; Headhunters, 2002; Berlin Blues, 2003; The Russian Passenger, 2004; Rumo, 2004; The City of Dreaming Books, 2005; Mimus, 2005; Ice Moon, 2006; Screen Credits: Tess (with Roman Polanski), 1979; The Boat, 1981; Pirates, 1986; The Name of the Rose, 1986; The Bear, 1989; Bitter Moon (with Roman Polanski), 1992; The Ninth Gate (with Roman Polanski), 2000. Honours: Schlegel Tieck Special Award, 1979; US Pen Prize, 1981; Schlegel Tieck Prize, 1993, 1999; US Christopher Award, 1995; Helen and Kurt Wolff Award, US, 1998. Memberships: Translators Association; Society of Authors. Address: The Vine House, Nether Compton, Sherborne, Dorset DT9 4QA, England.

**BROWNLOW Bertrand (John),** b. 13 January 1929, Nazeing, Essex, England. Aviation Consultant. m. Kathleen Shannon, 2 sons, 1 deceased, 1 daughter. Education: Beaufort Lodge School; Royal Air Force. Appointments: Group Captain,

Defence and Air Attache, Sweden, 1969-71; Group Captain, Commanding Officer, Experimental Flying, RAF Farnborough, 1971-73; Air Commodore, Assistant Commandant, RAF College Cranwell, 1973-74; Air Commodore, Director of Flying (Research and Development), Ministry of Defence Procurement Executive, 1974-77; Air Commodore, Commandant, Aeroplane and Armament Experimental Establishment, 1977-80; Air Vice-Marshal, Commandant, RAF College Cranwell, 1980-82; Air Vice-Marshal, Director General, RAF Training, 1982-84; Director, Airport and Flight Operations, Marshall Aerospace, -1994; Non-Executive Director, Civil Aviation Authority Board, 1994-97; Aviation Consultant, 1994-. Publications: Articles in professional magazines and publications. Honours: Air Force Cross, 1961; OBE, 1966; CB, 1982; Royal Aero Club Silver Medal, 1983; Clark Trophy for Contribution to Air Safety, Popular Flying Association, 1996; Freeman of the City of London, 1997; Liveryman, The Guild of Air Pilots and Air Navigators, 1997; Sword of Honour, The Guild of Air Pilots and Air Navigators, 2000. Memberships: Fellow, Royal Aeronautical Society; Empire Test Pilots' School Association; Liveryman, The Guild of Air Pilots and Air Navigators; Popular Flying Association; General Aviation Confidential Incident Reporting Programme Advisory Board; CAA, General Aviation Safety Review Working Group; Governor, Papworth Foundation Hospital Trust. Address: Woodside, Abbotsley Road, Croxton, St Neots, Cambridgeshire PE19 6SZ, England. E-mail: jbrownav@compuserve.com

**BROWNLOW Kevin**, b. 2 June 1938, Crowborough, Sussex, England. Author; Film Director; Film Historian. Publications: The Parade's Gone By, 1968; How It Happened Here, 1968, 2005; Adventures with D W Griffith, (editor), 1973; Hollywood: The Pioneers, 1979; The War, the West, and the Wilderness, 1979; Napoleon: Abel Gance's Classic Film, 1983, 2004; Behind the Mask of Innocence, 1990; David Lean - A Biography, 1996; Mary Pickford Rediscovered, 1999. Address: c/o Photoplay, 21 Princess Road, London NW1 8JR, England.

**BRUDENELL Edmund Crispin Stephen James George**, b. 24 October 1928, London, England. Landowner. m. Marian Manningham-Buller, 2 sons, 1 daughter. Education: Royal Agricultural College, Cirencester. Appointments: High Sheriff of Leicestershire, 1969; Deputy Lieutenant of Northamptonshire, 1977; High Sheriff of Northamptonshire, 1987. Membership: Liveryman Worshipful Company of Fishmongers. Address: Deene Park, Corby, Northamptonshire, England.

**BRUN Henry**, b. 11 February 1940, New York, New York, USA. Publisher. m. Renée Brun, 1 son, 2 daughters. Education: BA, History, 1962, Post Graduate Studies, History, 1962-64, Brooklyn College, New York, New York, USA; MSc, Educational Administration, Pace University, New York, New York, USA, 1975. Appointments: Teacher, Executive Assistant to Superintendent of High Schools, Coordinator of Alternative High Schools, Assistant Principal, Principal, New York City Public School System, 1962-94; Chief Operating Officer, 1994-95, President, 1995-, AMSCO School Publications Inc. Publications: Textbooks: Women of the Ancient World; Retreat from Imperialism; Global Studies; The World Today; America Today; Global History and Geography. Honours: Association of Assistant Principals in New York City; Award for demonstrating the highest degree of scholarship, pedagogical skill and professionalism, 1999. Memberships: Society of Antiquaries of Newcastle upon Tyne; Council for British Archaeology; Friends of Vindolanda. Address: AMSCO School Publications, Inc. 315 Hudson Street, New York, New York 10013, USA. E-mail: hbpres@worldnet.att.net

**BRUNDA Daniel Donald**, b. 22 October 1930, Lansford, Pennsylvania, USA. Mechanical Engineer; Aerospace Engineer; Electromagnetics Scientist; Electromagnetic Powerline Radiation Engineer and Founder; Inventor; Author. Education: BSME, Lehigh University, 1952; MSME, 1953; Postgraduate, Johns Hopkins University, 1955, Princeton University, 1958-65, Drexel University, 1983. Appointments: Aerodynamicist, Bell Aircraft; Performance Engineer, Glenn L Martin, Baltimore; Aerospace Engineer, US Naval Air Propulsion Centre, Ewing, New Jersey, 1957-72, Local Manager, Independent Research and Development (IRAD), 1972-83; Consultant, Powerline Radiation Energy Engineer, Ewing, New Jersey, 1978-. Publications: Over 20 articles to professional journals; 1 patent; Powerline Radiation, Your Genes, copyrighted report, 2001, book published (by Xlibris) 2004; Control System for Adjusting the Amount of Low Frequency Electromagnetic Radiation of Power Transmission Lines, copyrighted report, 2001; The Design of Safe Electric Transmission and Distribution Lines, copyrighted book, 2001, published (by Xlibris), 2003. Honours: Lifetime Deputy Governor American Biographical Institute; Lifetime Deputy Director General in the Americas, International Biographical Centre; Member of Order of International Fellowship, 2001; Included in International Order of Merit, 2002; Certificate of Commendation for Services Rendered Since 1978, Mayor of Ewing Township, 2001; Work exhibited in IBA Gallery of Excellence, 2001; Scientific Faculty Member of the IBC, 2002; IBC On-Line Hall of Fame, 2002, (http://www.internationalbiographicalcentre.com); Scientific Advisor to the Director General, IBC, 2002; 2000 Outstanding Scientists of the 21st Century; The Lifetime of Achievement 100; IBC Ambassador of Goodwill and 1000 Greats, 2003; Living Science; Living Legends; Great Minds of the 21st Century, ABI, 2003; One Thousand Great Americans, 2003; Hall of Fame and Inner Circle, IBC, 2004; Greatest Living Legends, IBC, 2004; Genius Elite in Engineering and Science, 2004; Einsteinian Chair of Science, World Academy of Letters, ABI, 2004. Memberships: Associate Fellow, Bioelectromagnetic Society; Life Member, ASME; Senior Member, AIAA; Ambassador of Grand Eminence, ABI, 2002; Founding Cabinet Member, World Peace and Diplomacy Forum, IBC, 2003; Order of Distinction, IBC, 2004; Da Vinci Award, IBC, 2004. Address: 106 West Upper Ferry Road, Ewing, NJ 08628, USA.

**BRUNO Franklin Roy (Frank)**, b. 16 November 1961, London, England. Boxer. m. Laura Frances Mooney, 1990, divorced, 2001, 1 son, 2 daughters. Education: Oak Hall School, Sussex. Appointments: Began boxing with Wandsworth Boys' Club, London, 1970; Member, Sir Philip Game Amateur Boxing Club, 1977-80; Won 20 out of 21 contests as amateur; Professional Career, 1982-96; Won 38 out of 42 contests as professional, 1982-89; European Heavyweight Champion, 1985-86 (relinquished title); World heavyweight title challenges against Tim Witherspoon, 1986, Mike Tyson, 1989; Staged comeback, won 1st contest, 1991; Lost 4th World Title Challenge against Lennox Lewis, 1993; World Heavyweight Boxing Champion, 1995-96, lost title to Mike Tyson, 1996; Appearances in Pantomimes, 1990, 1991, 1996, 1997, 1999; Former presenter, BBC TV. Publication: Personality: From Zero to Hero (with Norman Giller), 1996. Honours: SOS Sports Personality of the Year, 1990; TV Times Sports Personality of the Year, 1990; Lifetime Achievement Award, BBC Sports Personality of the Year Awards, 1996. Address: c/o PO Box 2266, Brentwood, Essex CM15 0AQ, England.

**BRUTIAN Lilit**, b. 7 August 1953, Yerevan, Armenia. Professor of Linguistics and English. m. Leonid Zilfugarian, 1 son, 1 daughter. Education: MA with distinction, English Language and Literature, 1970-75, PhD, Philology, 1975-80,

Yerevan State University, Yerevan, Armenia; Certificate, International Summer Institute on Argumentation, University of Amsterdam, 1990; Doctor of Sciences in Philology, Institute of Linguistics, National Academy of Sciences, Yerevan, Armenia, 1984-92. Appointments: Assistant Professor, Chair of Foreign Languages, 1979-84, Associate Professor of English, Chair of English Philology and Chair of Foreign Languages, 1984-94, Professor of Linguistics and English, Chair of Linguistics, Chair of English Philology, 1994-, Yerevan State University; Senior Researcher, 1984-93, Principal Researcher, 1993-95, Institute of Linguistics, Head of Chair of Foreign Languages, 1994-96, National Academy of Sciences of Armenia; Visiting Professor, Institute for the Advancement of Philosophy for Children, Montclair State University, New Jersey, USA, 1994-95. Publications: 60 scientific publications, including 6 monographs include most recently: The Principles of the Theory of Implication, 2002; Teaching Place-Names as a Means of Intensification of Students' Knowledge, 2003; On David the Invincible's Linguistic Views, 2004; On the Pragmatics of Argumentative Discourse, in press. Memberships include: International Society for the Study of Argumentation, The Netherlands; International Pragmatics Association, Belgium; Scientific Council Awarding Scientific Degrees, Yerevan State University and National Academy of Sciences of Armenia; Committee granting PhD Degrees, Brusov Linguistic University; Council, Department of Romance and Germanic Philology, Yerevan State University; Terminological Committee Affiliated to the Government of the Republic of Armenia. Address: The 9th Street of Aigestan, 69/61, Yerevan, Armenia 375025. E-mail: lilit.brutian@gmail.com

**BRUTTON Philip John Anthony Forsyth-Forrest,** b. 27 February 1925, Newcastle upon Tyne, England. Retired. m. Moira Joan Penton, 1 son, (twin sons deceased), 1 daughter. Education: Durham School, Durham; Royal Military College, Sandhurst. Appointments: Regular Officer, Welsh Guards, 1943-50, Captain, 1st Guards Brigade, Palestine, 1946-48, retired with the rank of Captain; Regular Army Reserve of Officers, 1950-75; Journalist, Daily Mail, 1950-55; Banker, Heller & Partners, 1955-60; Advertising Executive, London Press Exchange, 1960-65; Property development in Knightsbridge and Paris, 1965-75; Divisional Director, Banque, Française du Commerce Extérieure, 1975-86; Author, 1992-2005. Publications: Ensign in Italy, 1992; A Captain's Mandate, Palestine 1946-48, 1995; Maggie's Foundation, 2004; Nine Lives or the Felix Factor, 2005; The Phoenix Factor, an Autobiography, 2005. Honours: Mentioned in Despatches; Cross of Officer, Pro Merito Melitensi with Swords (Cross of Officer Military Division with Swords for the Merit of Knights of Malta); Silver Medal, Hospitality of Lourdes. Memberships: Society of St Vincent de Paul, International Council, Paris, retired 2003; Member of Hospitality of Lourdes; Life Member, Catholic Union of Great Britain; Clubs: White's, Pratt's. Address: 10 rue de Dragon, 75006 Paris, France.

**BRUTUS Dennis,** b. 28 November 1924, Salisbury, Rhodesia. Educationist; Poet; Writer. m. May Jaggers, 14 May 1950, 4 sons, 4 daughters. Education: BA, University of the Witwatersrand, Johannesburg, South Africa, 1947. Appointments: Director, World Campaign for Release of South African Political Prisoners; International Defence and Aid Fund, formerly UN Representative; Director, Program on African and African-American Writing in Africa and the Diaspora, 1989-; Visiting Professor at universities in Amherst, Austin, Boston, Dartmouth, Denver, Evanstown, Pittsburgh. Publications: Sirens, Knuckles, Boots, 1963; Letters to Martha and Other Poems from a South African Prison, 1968; Poems from Algiers, 1970; Thoughts Abroad, 1970; A Simple Lust: Selected Poems,

1973; China Poems, 1975; Stubborn Hope, 1978; Strains, 1982; Salutes and Censures, 1984; Airs and Tributes, 1988; Still the Sirens, 1993. Contributions to: Periodicals. Honours: Mbari Prize for Poetry in Africa; Freedom Writers' Award, Kenneth David Kaunda Humanism Award; Academic Excellence Award, National Council for Black Studies, 1982; UN Human Rights Day Award, 1983; Paul Robeson Award; Langston Hughes Award. Memberships: President, South African Non-Racial Olympic Committee (SAN-ROC); Chair, International Campaign Against Racism in Sport (ICARIS), Africa Network, 1984-; ARENA (Institute for Study of Sport and Social Issues); African Literature Association; American Civil Liberties Union; Amnesty International; PEN; Union of Writers of African Peoples.

**BRYSON James Graeme,** b. 4 February 1913, Caerleon, Monmouthshire, England (now Gwent, Wales). Judge (Retired). m. Jean Glendinning, 2 sons and 1 son deceased, 4 daughters. Education: LLM, Liverpool University, 1935; BSc, Open University, 1984. Appointments: Solicitor, 1935-47; Commissioned Officer to Royal Artillery, 1936; War Service, 1939-45, Lieutenant Colonel, now Colonel; Commanded Artillery Regiments, 1947-55; Registrar and Deputy Judge and District Judge to High Court of Justice and Admiralty Registrar, 1947-79; Chairman, Medical Appeal Tribunal, 1978-86; Northwest Cancer Research Fund: Trustee, 1950-80, President, 1985-2001, Life President, 2001-. Publications: Books: Contributor to Halsbury's Laws of England, 1976; Shakespeare in Lancashire and the Gunpowder Plot, 1997; A Cathedral in my Time, 2003; A Century of Liverpool Lawyers, 2003; Poetry in My Veins, 2004. Honours: Territorial Decoration and two bars, 1952; OBE (Military), 1955; Queen's Commendation for Bravery, 1961; Her Majesty's Vice Lord Lieutenant of the County of Merseyside, 1979-89; County Life President, Royal British Legion; Fellow, Royal Society of Arts; Knight Commander, Order of St Gregory; Knight Commander, Knights of the Holy Sepulchre. Memberships: Life Member, Royal British Legion; Past President, Athenaeum (Liverpool); Honourable Society of Knights of the Round Table; Liverpool Law Society, President, 1970;Vice-Patron, Regular Forces Employment Association. Address: 2 Thirlmere Road, Hightown, Liverpool L38 3RQ, England.

**BUAQUIÑA Vaughn Sarigumba,** b. 6 October 1959, Oroquieta City, Philippines. Educator; University Professor; Academic Administrator. m. Verla Jean F, 3 daughters. Education: BSc, Mathematics, Mindanao State University, 1980; MBA-MIM, International Academy of Management and Economics, 1988; MS, Mathematics, MLQU, Manila, 1989; MS, Applied Mathematics, Ohio University, USA, 1991; Doctor of Mathematics, City University LA, California, USA, 1992; Bachelor of Laws, Philippine Law School, 1995. Appointments: Chairman, Mathematical Sciences & Computer Studies Department and Member, Presidential Advisory Board, Professor of Mathematics, De La Salle University, Cavite, 1988-89, 1992-93; Member of Board of Trustees, Board Secretary Pro-Tempoze, University Officer-in-Charge/Acting President, Adjunct Professor, Graduate School of Business/Public Health, 1992-95, 2002-03, Adventist University of the Philippines; Professor, 1993-, Dean, 1998-, Institute of Graduate Studies, Editor-in-Chief, college journals and gazettes, 1998-, Director, Center for Research, Planning and Development, 2004-, San Sebastian College-Recoletos, Manila; Associate Dean, 1994-95, Dean, 1995-98, Professor of Mathematics and Statistics and Operations Research, 1993-2002, Technological University of the Philippines Graduate School; VPAA & Chief Operating Officer, PHILSSEC Institute of Technology, 1999-2003; Professor of Mathematics/Statistics, 2000-03, Co-ordinator,

Research Centre School of CE-EnSE, 2001-02, Mapua Institute of Technology; Dean, Graduate School and Director, Research and Publication Center, Saint Jude College, Manila, 2001-02; Philippine Representative, Republic of the Philippines Educational Assistance Package for the Union of Myanmar/Burma; Chairman, Prince Hoedhiono Kadarisman Professorial Chair for Small & Medium Scale Industries. Publications: Several research papers published and presented at local conferences, American regional conferences and internationally. Honours: BSc-Cum Laude; Consistent University Full Scholar; Most Outstanding Graduate of the College of Arts and Sciences; Saber Medal Award for Leadership; Most Outstanding Graduate of the Year; Don Gonzalo Puyat Academic Excellence Award; Don Gonzalo Puyat Scholar; MBA-Summa Cum Laude; Hall of Fame, De La Salle University System; Plaque of Recognition for accomplishments and valued service as 2nd President of the De La Salle University (Cavite) Faculty Association, 1990; Gintong Sikap Award, 1995; Golden Leadership Award, 1996; Dr Jose P Rizal Immortal Award, 1996; Golden Scroll of Honour, 1997; Listed in biographical dictionaries; Resource and guest speaker at many international seminars and workshops. Memberships: Mathematical Association of America; American Statistical Association; Southeast Asian Mathematics Society; Operations Research Society of the Philippines; Graduate Education Association for Chartered Colleges and Universities – National Capital Region of the Philippines; Kiwanis Club International, 1983-; Tau Kappa Phi Fraternity, 1983-; Church Elder, 1988-present; Phi Delta Kappa International, 1992-present; North Philippine Union Mission Development Board, 1997-2001; Adviser, Adventist Ministry to Colleges and University Students; Technological University of the Philippines, 1997-2001; Philippine-Japan Fellows Association, 1997-; Founding Chairman, Board of Trustees, Light in the Prison Foundation, 1999-2001; Board of Trustees, Executive Committee, Central Luzon Conference of the Seventh-Day Adventist Church, 1999-2002; Head Elder and Vice Chairman, Aniban Seventh-Day Adventist Church, 1999-2002, 2005; Academy of Management, Briarcliff Manor, New York, 2000-; Amicus Adviser, Mapua Institute of Technology, Manila, 2001-03; Board of Trustees, Adventist Development & Relief Agency, Philippines, 2002-; Chairman, School Board, Christian Builder's School, 2003-; Asia Academy of Management, Hong Kong, 2004-. Address: L-2, B-18, Graszyo St, Ina Executive Homes, Valley-1, Paranague City, Philippines. E-mail: vaughn_elwyn@yahoo.com

**BUBKA Sergey Nazarovich,** b. 4 December 1963, Voroshilovgrad, Ukraine. Athlete. m. Lilya Tioutiounik, 1983, 2 sons. Appointments: World Champion Pole Vaulter, 1983; 16 World Records from 5-85m 1984 to 6.13m 1992, including world's first 6m jump, Paris, 1985; 18 World Indoor Records, from 5.81 1984 to 6.15 1993; Holder of indoors and outdoors world records, 2002; Now represents OSC Berlin. Honours include: Olympic Gold Medal, 1988. Memberships include: Member, IOC Executive Board, IOC Evaluation Commission for 2008; IOC Athletes' Commission; IAAF Council, 2001-; National Olympic Committee Board; Chairman, EOC Athletes; Commission; President, S Bubka Sports Club; Elected to Parliament, United Union Faction, 2002- Address: c/o State Committee of Physical Culture & Sport, 42 Esplanadnaya, 252023 Kiev, Ukraine.

**BUCHAN Vivian Eileen Eaton,** b. 19 May 1911, Eagle Grove, Iowa, USA. Freelance Writer; Poet. m. Warren Joseph Buchan, 4 September 1933. Education: BA, English, Coe College, 1933; MA, English, University of Illinois, 1958. Appointments: Teacher in Rhetoric Programme, University of Illinois, 1957-58; University of Iowa, 1959-67; Board of Directors, 1970-76, President, 1976, Iowa City Public Library. Publications: English

Compositions, manual, 1960; Bibliography: Sara Teasdale 1967-68; Sun Signs, 1979; Make Presentations with Confidence, 1991, translated into Portugese, Indonesian, Chinese, Japanese, Arabic. Contributions to: Approx 900 articles, essays, columns, poems in over 80 national and international publications. Honours: 2nd Place, Lyrical Iowa, 1964; 2nd Place, 1981, 3rd Place, 1987, 1st Place, 1995, 1996, editor: Iowa Poetry Association, 1970-84; International Woman of the Year, 1982-83; Merit Award, Coe College, 1983; Iowa City High School Hall of Fame, 1983; Friend of Education, Iowa City School Board, 1984; 4th Place, 1989, 2nd Place, 1989, 2 Grand Prizes, 1991, World of Poetry; President's Award for Highest Achievement in Liberal Arts Education, Coe College, 1992-93; Women's Inner Circle of Achievement, 1995; International Woman of the Year, 1995-96; Most Admired Woman of the Century, 1995-96; Most Admired Woman of the Decade, 1995-96; 20th Century Award of Achievement in Literature, Poetry and Art, 1997; Eaton-Buchan Art Gallery, Coe College, dedicated 1998; 1st place, Iowa Poetry Contest Sonnet Division (I Am the Wind), 2005; Listed in national and international biographical dictionaries. Address: 2423 Walden Road, #225, Iowa City, IA 52246-4104, USA.

**BUCHANAN Colin Ogilvie,** b. 9 Aug 1934, Croydon, Surrey, England. Church of England Clerk in Holy Orders. Education: BA, 1959, MA, 1962, Lincoln College, Oxford; Tyndale Hall, Bristol, 1959-61; DD, 1993. Appointments: Bishop of Woolwich, Diocese of Southwark, 1996-2004; Retired, 2004; Honorary Assistant Bishop, Diocese of Bradford, 2004-. Publications: Modern Anglican Liturgies, 1958-68, 1968; Further Anglican Liturgies, 1968-75, 1975; Editor, News of Liturgy Monthly, 1975-2003; Latest Anglican Liturgies, 1976-84, 1985; Modern Anglican Ordination Rites, 1987; The Bishop in Liturgy, 1988; Open to Others, 1992; Joint Author: Growing into Union, 1970; Anglican Worship Today, 1980; Reforming Infant Baptism, 1990; Sole Author: Infant Baptism and the Gospel, 1993; Cut the Connection: Disestablishment and the Church of England, 1994; Is the Church of England Biblical? 1998; Contributing Editor: Common Worship Today, 2000. Membership: House of Bishops of General Synod of the Church of England, 1990-2004; Church of England General Synod Council for Christian Unity, 1991-2001; Vice President, Electoral Reform Society. Address: c/o Bradford Diocesan Office, Kadugli House, Elmsley Street, Steeton, Keighley, BC20 6SE, England. E-mail: cobtalk@onetel.com.

**BUCHANAN Pat(rick Joseph),** b. 2 November 1938, Washington, District of Columbia, USA. American Government Official; Journalist. m. Shelley Ann Scarney, 8 May 1971. Education: AB, English, cum laude, Georgetown University, 1961; MS, Journalism, Columbia University, 1962. Appointments: Editorial Writer, 1962-64, Assistant Editorial Editor, 1964-66, St Louis Globe Democrat; Executive Assistant to Richard M Nixon, 1966-69; Special Assistant to President Richard M Nixon, 1969-73; Consultant to Presidents Richard M Nixon and Gerald R Ford, 1973-74; Syndicated Columnist, 1975-; Various radio and television broadcasts as commentator, panellist, moderator, etc, 1978-; Assistant to President Ronald Reagan and Director of Communications, White House, Washington DC, 1985-87; Candidate for the Republican Party Nomination for President of the US, 1992, 1996; Chairman, The American Cause, 1993-95, 1997-; Chairman, Pat Buchanan & Co, Mutual Broadcasting System, 1993-95. Publications: The New Majority, 1973; Conservative Votes, Liberal Victories, 1975; Right from the Beginning, 1988; Barry Goldwater, The Conscience of A Conservative, 1990; The Great Betrayal, 1998; A Republic, Not an Empire, 2000. Contributions to: Newspapers and periodicals. Honour: Knight of Malta, 1987. Memberships:

Republican Party; Roman Catholic Church. Address: 1017 Savile Lane, McLean, VA 22101, USA.

**BUCHINSKA Todorka Vassileva,** b. 28 June 1955, Blagoevgrad, Bulgaria. Chemical Engineer. m. Kalin Buchinski, 1 son. Education: ELC, American University in Bulgaria, Blagoevgrad, 1994; MS in Chemical Engineering, Higher Institute of Chemical Technology, Sofia, 1973-78; Concentration in Synthetic Organic Chemistry; US Accredited; CEC, Education Direct, Scranton, Pennsylvania, USA, 2004. Appointments: Chemical Engineer, Manager of Quality Control, Head of Chemical Laboratory, Oil Company, Blagoevgrad, 1978-86; Synthetic Organic Chemist, Institute of Molecular Biology, Sofia, 1986-87; Associate Organic Chemist, Senior Organic Chemist, Research Scientist, Head of Research Group, Leader of Scientific Project, Laboratory of Bio-organic Chemistry, Blagoevgrad, 1987-; Consultant, South West University, Blagoevgrad, 1990-93; Consultant, Regional Environmental Centre, Blagoevgrad, 1998-. Publications: Numerous articles in national and international scientific journals. Memberships: American Chemical Society; New York Academy of Sciences; Federation of American Societies for Experimental Biology. Address: Laboratory of Bio-organic Chemistry, Institute of Molecular Biology, PO Box 212, Blagoevgrad 2700, Bulgaria. E-mail: tbuchin@infonet.techno-link.com

**BUCHWALD Art,** b. 20 October 1925, Mt Vernon, New York, USA. Journalist; Author; Playwright. m. Ann McGarry, 11 October 1952, 1 son, 2 daughters. Education: University of Southern California, Los Angeles, 1945-48. Appointments: Syndicated columnist for newspapers around the world. Publications: Paris After Dark, 1950; Art Buchwald's Paris, 1954; The Brave Coward, 1957; More Caviar, 1958; Un Cadeau Pour le Patron, 1958; A Gift From the Boys, 1959; Don't Forget to Write, 1960; How Much is That in Dollars?, 1961; Is it Safe to Drink the Water?, 1962; Art Buchwald's Secret List to Paris, 1963; I Chose Capitol Punishment, 1963; And Then I Told the President, 1965; Son of the Great Society, 1966; Have I Ever Lied to You?, 1968; The Establishment is Alive and Well in Washington, 1969; Counting Sheep, 1970; Getting High in Government Circles, 1971; I Never Danced at the White House, 1973; The Bollo Caper, 1974; I Am Not a Crook, 1974; Irving's Delight, 1975; Washington is Leaking, 1976; Down the Seine and Up the Potomac, 1977; The Buchwald Stops Here, 1978; Laid Back in Washington, 1981; While Reagan Slept, 1983; You CAN Fool All of the People All of the Time, 1985; I Think I Don't Remember, 1987; Whose Rose Garden is it Anyway?, 1989; Lighten Up, George, 1991; Leaving Home: A Memoir, 1994; I'll Always Have Paris, 1996. Honours: Priz de la Bonne Humeur, 1958; Pulitzer Prize in Commentary, 1982. Memberships: American Academy of Arts and Sciences; American Academy of Humor Columnists. Address: Suite 3804, 540 Park Avenue, New York, NY 10021, USA.

**BUCK Karen,** b. 30 August 1958. Member of Parliament. Partner: Barrie Taylor, 1 son. Education: BSc, MSc, MA, London School of Economics. Appointments: Charity specialising in employment for disabled people; London Borough of Hackney; Policy Officer specialising in health, Labour Party Head Office; Labour Party's Campaigns Unit, 1992-97; Elected, Labour Member of Parliament for Regent's Park and Kensington North; Select Committee on Social Security, 1997-2001; Work and Pensions Select Committee, 2001-. Memberships: Chair, London Group of Labour MPs; Member, Mayor of London's Affordable Housing Commission; Board Member, Constituency SRB projects. Address: House of Commons, London SW1A 0AA, England. E-mail: k.buck@rpkn-labour.co.uk

**BUCKINGHAMSHIRE Earl of, Sir (George) Miles Hobart-Hampden,** b 15 December 1944, Madras, India. m. (1) Susan Jennifer Adams, dissolved, (2) Alison Wightman, 2 stepsons. Education: Clifton College, Bristol, 1958-63; BA, Honours, History, Exeter University, 1963-67; MA, Area Studies, History and Politics of the Commonwealth, Birkbeck College, London University, 1967-68. Appointments: Noble Lowndes & Partners Ltd, latterly Director of Scottish Pension Trustees, 1970-81; Director, HSBC Gibbs, 1981-86; Warldley Investment Services International (subsidiary of HSBC), 1986-91, Marketing Director and Managing Director, 1988-91; The Wyatt Company, 1991-95; Partner, Watson Wyatt LLP, Watson Wyatt Worldwide, 1996-2004; BESTrustees Plc, 2004-, Director, 2005; Sat in House of Lords, 1984-99; Member All Party Groups on Occupational Pensions and on ageing issues; Member of Select Committee of EC sub-committees on Social and Consumer Affairs, 1985-90, on Finance, Trade and External Relations, 1990-92; Honorary Trustee, Illinois Wesleyan University, USA, 1991-; President, Old Cliftonian Society, 2000-2003 and Governor of Clifton College, 1994-; Member of Council, 2000- Buckinghamshire Chilterns University College. Memberships: Affiliated Member, Institute of Actuaries, 2001-; Director, Hatfield Real Tennis Club, 2001-; Freeman, Cities of Glasgow and Geneva (Upper New York State USA); Director, Britain-Australia Society, 2004-; Patron: Sleep Apnoea Trust, Hobart Town (1804) Early Settlers Association (Tasmania), John Hampden Society; President, Friends of the Vale of Aylesbury; President, Downend Police and Community Amateur Boxing Club. Address: The Old Rectory, Church Lane, Edgcott, Aylesbury, Bucks HP18 0TU, England.

**BUCKLEY Richard Anthony,** b. 16 April 1947, Leicester, England. Legal Scholar. m. Alison Jones, 1 daughter. Education: BA (Oxford), Jurisprudence, 1968, Doctor of Philosophy, 1973, Merton College, Oxford. Appointments: Lecturer in Laws, King's College, London, 1970-75; Fellow and Tutor in Law, Mansfield College, Oxford, 1975-93; Professor of Law, University of Reading, 1993-. Publications: The Law of Nuisance, 1st edition, 1981, 2nd edition, 1996; The Modern Law of Negligence, 1st edition, 1988, 3rd edition, 1999; Illegality and Public Policy, 2002. Articles in legal periodicals. Honours: Leverhulme Research Fellow, 2001. Address: School of Law, University of Reading, PO Box 217, Reading, RG6 2AH, England.

**BUCKMAN James Cecil,** b. 4 August 1923, Croydon, Surrey, England. Teacher. m. Peggy Taylor. Education: Stanley Techynical School, 1936-39; City & Guilds Technical Electricity Grade 1, Borough Polytechnic, 1941; City & Guilds Telephony, Wimbledon Technical College, 1942; Course by correspondence with Wolsey Hall, Oxford, Royal Navy, 1945-46; Forces' Preliminary Exam, in lieu of London Matriculation, 1946; BSc, Geography and Geology, Bristol University, 1950; PGCE, School of Education, 1951; MSc, by research, 1973. Appointments: Workshop experience, Ellis Optical Company, 1939-40; Apprenticed as Youth in Training, Post Office Telecommunications, 1940-42; Unestablished Skilled Workman, 1942-43; Rating, Air Branch of the Royal Navy, 1943-46; Recommended three months accelerated advancement to Air Mechanic Electrics First Class, served on Staff of Admiral (Air), 1945-46; In Education: Supply teaching, Surrey, 1952; Appointed by Air Service Training Ltd of Hamble as member of Team to set up the Pakistan Air Force Pre Cadet College at Sargodha in the Punjab, Head of Department, Housemaster, Deputy Headmaster, 1952-59; Housemaster and Head of Department, Aitchison College, Lahore, 1959-63; Master on Supply, Hampton School, 1963; Assistant Master, Brighton, Hove & Sussex Grammar School, 1963-69; Head of Geography, De la Salle College, Hove, 1969-71; Bristol Cathedral School part-time 6th Form, (while on Sabbatical at University completing MSc thesis), 1971-72; Head of Geography, Alleyn's School, Dulwich 1972-83; Retired, 1983; Part time teaching at Shoreham College, Hurstpierpoint College and on Supply in West Sussex, 1983-93. Publications: Article in Geography, Resources of Natural Gas in East Pakistan (now Bangladesh), 1968; Book, The Steyning Line and Its Closure, 2002. Honours: 12+ examination for entry to Stanley Technical School, 1936; 1st Class Award for Swimming; Royal Society of Arts Grouped Course Certificate and First Prize in Geography, 1938. Memberships: Scouting: Started Senior Scouts section of 7th Sanderstead Group, 1943; Elected Life Fellow, Royal Geographical Society, 1955; Bristol University Convocation and as an elected Representative on University Court – completed 3 four-year terms; University of Bristol Boat Club Alumni; currently Royal British Legion; Independent, Schools Committee, 1973-83 and Chairman, Inner London Branch, 1975-78 of Assistant Masters' Association (now Association of Teachers & Lecturers, ATL); Affiliated, Charted Institute of Transport (now Logistics and Transport), 1975; Probus; Steyning Society, Sussex Wildlife Trust; Steyning Parish Councillor, 1987-89; Life Member, Cyclists Touring Club; Life Member, Youth Hostels Association; Sometime Parochial Church Council of Steyning & Deanery Synod. Address: 38 King's Stone Avenue, Steyning, West Sussex BN44 3FJ, England.

**BUCUR Constantin I,** b. 19 March 1923, Gura Vaii, Racová, Bacau, Romania. m. Brigitte Iorgovan, 1 son. Education: Ferdinand Boarding College, Bacau; D A Sturza Military College for Officers, Craiova, Romania; Cavalry College for Officers, Targoviste, Romania, 1941-43; MSc with Distinction, ANEF Bucharest, 1947-51; PhD, Université Libre de Bruxelles, Belgium, 1968; Dr honoris causa, University of Craiova, 1998. Appointments: Higher Education Inspector, Bucharest, 1951-53; Assistant Lecturer, Part-time, IEFS, Bucharest, 1951-53; Lecturer, 1953, Consultant, 1962, Professor, 1984, Traian Vuia Polytechnic and University of Timisoara-Romania; Organiser, Principal Researcher and Director, Physical Education Research Centre, 1953-84; Director, Sportforschung Zentrum, Mannheim, Germany, 1986-. Publications: 71 books and 600 booklets about sport research; 115 academic reports; Created own system in sport; Inventor of 45 sports testing apparatus prototypes; Organised 70 conferences in field. Honours: Wounded, WWII, awarded medals for bravery, Retired Brigadier General. Membership: Full Member, Professor Emeritus, American Romanian Academy of Arts and Sciences; Scientific Collaborator, Academia Română, Filiala Timişoara. Address: c/o Mariana Zavati Gardner, 14 Andrew Goodall Close, East Dereham, Norfolk, NR19 1SR, England.

**BUCUR Romulus Vasile,** b. 19 March 1928, Padova, Italy. Chemistry Researcher (Retired). m. Doina Rodica Motiu, 1 daughter. Education: Graduate, Chemistry, University of Cluj, Romania, 1955; PhD, Electrochemistry, University of Bucharest, Romania, 1970. Appointments: Head, Laboratory, Solvay Plant, Ocna Mures, Romania, 1955-56; Scientific Researcher, Institute of Atomic Physics, Cluj, Romania, 1956-58; Principal Scientific Researcher, 1958-87, Head, Laboratory, 1974-87, Institute of Isotopic and Molecular Technology, Cluj, Romania; Scientific Researcher, Inorganic Chemistry, Uppsala University, Sweden, 1988-93; Scientific Research Associate, Materials Chemistry Department, Ångström Laboratory, Uppsala University, Sweden, 1993-98. Publications: About 120 scientific papers in the field of analysis and separation of heavy water, solid state electrochemistry (metallic hydrides and sulphides), materials for hydrogen storage, and piezoelectric quartz crystal microbalance. Membership: Honorary Member, The International Association

for Hydrogen Energy, USA, 1983-. Address: Näktergalsv 5, SE-35242 Växjö, Sweden. E-mail: romulus.bucur@telia.com

**BUDAEV Vladimir Michailovich,** b. 25 October 1955, Moscow, Russia. Architect. 1 daughter. Education: Diploma in Architecture, Moscow Architectural Institute, 1984. Appointments: Head of the Project and Chief-Architect, Park Pobedy (Park of Victory Over Fascism in the Second World War) with the Memorial, Poklonnaya Gora, Moscow, 1985-98; Chief Architect, Central Museum of the Great Patriotic War, 1941-45, Central Obelisk (150m high), 1993-95; Chief Architect, Church of Georgiy Pobedonosetz (Church of Saint Georg, the first church built in Russia since 1917), 1993-95; Chief Architect, Synagogue-Memorial, with Museum of Holocaust in Park Pobedy, Moscow, 1996-98; Architect-constructor, Monument of Tsar Peter the Great, Moskva River, 1997; Architect-constructor, Zoo, Moscow, 1997; Architect of several multi-storey municipal buildings, 1998-2001; Head of Architectural and Artistic Planning Institute, Moscow, 1993-2001; Chief Architect, Central Scientific Kucherenko's Institute of Building Constructions, Moscow, 2003-. Publications: Several conceptual publications in professional journals. Honours: Winner, International Contest for the best project for Trinity Cathedral, Moscow commemorating the Millennium of Christening of Russia, 1990; Medal of Holy Sergiy Radonezsky, from Russian Orthodox Church, 1995; Certificate of Honour from President of Russia, 1995; Honoured Architect of Russia, 1996; Medal and Diploma, IBC, 1999; Synagogue-Memorial with Museum of Holocaust in Park Pobedy, Moscow qualified as one of the best in the world by the JOINT (International Jewish Congress); Listed in numerous international directories of biography. Membership: Union of Architects of Russia, FIBA; Corresponding Member of International Academy of Investment and Economy of Building, 2000. Address: Petrovka 26-28, 103051 Moscow, Russia.

**BUDENHOLZER Frank Edward,** b. 21 August 1945. Catholic Priest; Educator; Chemist. Education: BA, Divine Word College, Epworth, Iowa, 1967; BS, DePaul University, Chicago, Illinois, 1969; MA, Catholic Theological Union, Chicago, Illinois, 1974; PhD, University of Illinois, Chicago, 1977. Appointments: Teaching Assistant, University of Illinois, Chicago, 1972-76; Chinese Language Training, Hsinchu, Taiwan, 1978-80; Associate Professor, Chemistry, Fu Jen University, 1978-83; Professor, Chemistry, 1983-; Director, Graduate Institute of Chemistry, 1980-84; Dean, College of Science and Engineering, 1984-90; Vice-President, 1990-97; Visiting Scholar, Center for Theolology and the Natural Sciences; 1997-98; Visiting Scholar, University of California, 1997-98; Member, Board of Trustees, Fu Jen University, 1999-; Resident Trustee, Fu Jen University, 2001-, Academic Co-ordinator, Centre for the Study of Religion and Science, 2002-; Co-ordinator, Center for the Study of Science and Religion, 2001-. Publications: Religion and Science in Taiwan: Rethinking the Connection; Some Comments on the Problem of Reductionism; Classical Trajectory Study of the HFCO-HF+CO Reaction. Memberships: American Chemical Society; American Physical Society; Chinese Chemical Society; Chinese Physical Society; Institute for Religion in an Age of Science; Hastings Center; Institute for Theoretical Encounter with Science and Technology. Address: Department of Chemistry, Fu Jen Catholic University, Hsinchuang 242, Taiwan. E-mail: chem1003@mails.fju.edu.tw

**BUJAUSKAS Algimantas V,** b. 24 December 1932, Lithuania. Biologist. m. Janina Ivanauskaite, 6 March 1965, 1 son. Education: Diploma, Vilnius University, 1963; Dr.H. 1988; Professor, 1994. Appointments: Former Professor, Chief Scientific Worker, Lithuanian Institute of Agriculture.

Publications: Several articles in professional journals; Memoirs, 1998; 4 books of poetry, 1998, 1999, 2000; Monograph: Potato Breeding for Resistance to Potato Cyst Nematode and Meristemic Seed Production, 2000; Selected Works: Aurora Borealis, Memoirs and Poetry of a Deportee, 2002. Honour: National Award, 1996. Memberships: Catholic Academy of Sciences, Lithuania. Address: Traku Voke, Tishevich 13-3, LT-02231 Vilnius, Lithuania.

**BUKHARIN Oleg Valeryevich**, b. 1937, Russia. Director; Head of Department. Education: Chelyabinsk Medical Institution, 1960; Master of Medicine, 1963; MD, 1971. Appointments: Reader, 1969; Professor of Microbiology, 1972; Director, Institute for Cellular and Intracellular Symbiosis; Head, Department of Microbiology, Orenburg Medical Institute. Publications: Author of over 370 articles. Honours: 90 Author Certificates and Patents in Russia; Honoured Scientist of the Russian Soviet Federative Socialist Republic, 1979; 5 gold and silver medals, All-Union Agricultural Exhibition of the USSR; Order of Russian "Honour", 1996; Mechnikov Prise Laureate in biology from the Russian Academy of Sciences, 2002; Order of Russia "Great Services to Fatherland of IY Class", 2003; Government awards: Russian Governmental Prize Laureate in Science and Technology, 2004; Honourable Citizen of Orenburg. Memberships: Fellow, All-Russian Governing Board to Specialists in Microbiology, Epidemiology and Parasitology; Chairman, Academic Councils for awarding doctors' theses, Orenburg; Member, Editorial Board of the Journal of Microbiology, Epidemiology and Immunology; Member, Editorial Council of the Journal of Antibiotics and Chemotherapy; Deputy of the Supreme Soviet of Russia, 1975-80. Address: Institute for Cellular and Intracellular Symbiosis, No 11 Pionerskaya Str, Orenburg 460000, Russia.

**BULAKHOV Vladislav**, b. 25 March 1960, Irkutsk, Russia. Musician. m. Nadejda Kravchenko, 2 daughters. Education: Graduate, Violin, Krashodar Music College "N A Rimsky-Korsakov", 1979; Graduate, Violin, Gnessins Russian Academy of Music, 1984. Career: Artist of the re-established New Moscow Chamber Orchestra headed by Igor Zhukov, 1983-94; Organiser "The Seasons" Chamber Orchestra, Moscow, 1994; Artistic Director and Conductor, "The Seasons" Chamber Orchestra, Moscow, 1994-. Honour: Honoured Artist of Russia. Address: Moscow, Russia. E-mail: vbukhalov@mtu-net.ru

**BULLOCK Sandra**, b. 22 July 1966, USA. Actress. Education: East Carolina University. Creative Works: Off-Broadway Productions include: No Time Flat (WPA Theatre). TV Roles: The Preppy Murder (film); Lucky Chances (mini series); Working Girl (NBC series). Films: Love Potion 9; The Vanishing; The Thing Called Love; When The Party's Over; Demolition Man; Wrestling Ernest Hemingway; Speed; While You Were Sleeping; Two If By Sea; Moll Flanders; A Time To Kill; In Love and War; Practical Magic; Forces of Nature; Director, Making Sandwiches, 1996, Speed 2, 1997; Hope Floats (also executive producer), 1998; 28 Days, 2000; Famous, 2000; Miss Congeniality, 2000; Murder by Numbers, 2001; Exactly 3: 30, 2001; Divine Secrets of the Ya-Ya Sisterhood, 2002; Two Weeks' Notice, 2002; Loverboy, 2004. Address: CAA, 9830 Wilshire Boulevard, Beverly Hills, CA 90212, USA.

**BULSON Philip Stanley**, b. 21 April 1925, Yeovil, Somerset, England. Structural and Civil Engineer. Education: Plymouth and Devonport Technical College; BSc(Eng), DSc(Eng), University of London; PhD, University of Bristol. Appointments: Engineering Cadet (Army) and Commission in Royal Engineers, 1943-48; Senior and Principal Scientific Officer, Military Engineering, Design and Research, 1953-65, Senior Principal and Deputy Chief Scientific Officer (Individual Merit), 1965-74, Ministry of Defence; Head of Military Engineering Experimental Establishment, Christchurch (MEXE) also known as MVEE(c) and RARDE(c), 1974-85; Visiting Professor, University of Southampton, 1983-; Director, Special Services, Mott, Hay and Anderson, 1986-88; Consultant to Mott MacDonald Group (specialising in the effect of explosions on structures), 1989-2000. Publications: Books as sole author: The Stability of Flat Plates, 1970; Buried Structures, 1985; Explosive Loading of Engineering Structures, 1997; Books as co-author, contributor or editor: Background to Buckling, 1980; Engineering Structures, 1983; Structures Under Shock and Impact, 1989, 1992, 1994; The Future of Structural Testing, 1990; Rapidly Assembled Structures, 1991; Aluminium Structural Analysis, 1992; Research reports for the Ministry of Defence and numerous papers in professional journals. Honour: CBE, 1986. Memberships: Fellow of Royal Academy of Engineering; Fellow of the Institution of Structural Engineers; Fellow of the Institution of Civil Engineers; Fellow of the Institution of Mechanical Engineers; Liveryman, Worshipful Company of Engineers; Member, Athenaeum Club; Chairman, Committee on Structural Use of Aluminium, British Standards Institute. Address: Playford Rise, Sway, Lymington, Hampshire SO41 6DA, England.

**BUNTON Hope**, b. 11 January 1921, Willingham, Cambridgeshire, England. Teacher; Poet. m. John Bunton, 15 July 1961, divorced. Education: University of London, 1939-42; International Language School, London, 1971. Appointments: Our Lady's Convent, Brigg; Edmund Campion Comprehensive School; 6th Form College, Preston. Publications: Until All Is Silence; Beyond Silence; Through My Eyes. Contributions to: Envoi; Writer's Voice; Lancashire Life; Cambridgeshire Life; Lincolnshire Writers; Liverpool Echo; Viewpoint; Breakthru; Bedsitter; Lantern Light; Journal of Indian Writing in English; Anthology of Peace Poems for Lancashire Literature Festival; Haiku magazine; Radio Merseyside; Radio Lancashire; Poetry Now; New Hope International; Parnassus of World Poets; Darius Anthology; Railway Anthology, 1996; Countryside Tales; Acorn Magazine; Imagine Writing Group. Honours: 2nd Prize, Religious Section, 3rd Prize, Topical Section, Chorley Arts Poetry Competition. Address: 10 Clifton Street, Preston, Lancashire PR1 8EE, England.

**BURACAS Antanas**, b. 17 June 1939, Kaunas, Lithuania. Political and Financial Economist. m. Marija Regina Jovaisaite, 2 sons, 1 daughter. Education: Magister of Political Economy, 1962; Dr Political Economy, Institute of World Economy and International Relations, USSR Academy of Sciences, 1967; Dr hab in Political Economy, 1971; Center for Central Banking Studies, Bank of England, 1992. Appointments: Senior Researcher and Head, Departments of Social Infrastructure and Mathematical Modelling, Lithuanian Academy of Sciences 1967-91; Founding Vice Director, Scientific Center, Bank of Lithuania, 1991-92; Professor of Banking and Macroeconomics, Vytauti Magnus University 1991-2005; Intellectual Paradigmatics, 2000-; Chairman, State Nostrificat Commission in Social Sciences, 1994-; Associate Professor and Professor of Political Economy and Banking, Kaunas Polytechnic Institute and Vilnius University, 1962-75, 1995-99; Vice-Chairman, Editing Board, Lithuanian Universal Encyclopaedia, 1999- (now 7/20 vol). Publications include: 32 books including: Reference Dictionary of Banking and Commerce in 7 volumes, 1997-2006; Sacred Arts in Lithuania, 1999; The Old Types of the Grand Duchy of Lithuania, 2004. Honours: Elected Academician, Lithuanian Academy of Sciences, 1976-; Lithuanian Independence Medal, 2000; Honorary Chairman, Lithuanian Human Rights Association, 2000; Fellow, World Innovation

Foundation, 2001; Listed in international and national biographical publications. Memberships: Founding President, Lithuanian Association for Protection of Human Rights, 1989-94; Co-founding Member, Lithuanian Reform Movement Sajudis, 1988-94; Deputy of its I-II Seimas and Councils; President, Lithuanian Association of History and Philosophy of Science, 1986-92; International Sociological Association, 1982-86. Address: Lūkescių 15, Vilnius 2043, Lithuania 04125. E-mail: anbura@lrs.lt Website: www.buracas.com

**BURBIDGE Geoffrey,** b. 24 September 1925. Astrophysicist. m. Margaret Peachey, 1948, 1 daughter. Education: Graduated, Physics, Bristol University, 1946; PhD, University College, London; Agassiz Fellow, Harvard University. Appointments: Research Fellow, University of Chicago, 1952-53; Research Fellow, Cavendish Laboratories, Cambridge; Carnegie Fellow, Mount Wilson and Palomar University, Caltech, 1955-57; Assistant Professor, Department of Astronomy, University of Chicago, 1957; Associate Professor, 1962-63, Professor of Physics, 1963-88, Professor Emeritus, 1988, University of California at San Diego -; Director, Kitt Peak National Observatory, Arizona, 1978-84; Scientific editor, Astrophysics Journal, 1996-. Publications: Quasi-Stellar Objects, with Margaret Burbidge, 1967; A Different Approach to Cosmology, with F Moyle and J Narlikar, 2000; Astrophysics papers in scientific journals. Address: Department of Physics, Center for Astrophysics and Space Sciences, University of California, San Diego, La Jolla, CA 92093, USA.

**BURDA Renate Margarete,** b. 14 January 1960, Munich, Germany. Biologist. Education: Abitur, 1980; Diploma, Biology, Ludwig-Maximilian University, Munich, 1993. Appointments: Science Worker, Fluid Engineering, Technology University, Munich, 1985-2000; Laboratory Worker, Medical Care of Urology, Munich, 1995, 1998, 2000; Chief Assistant, Venomous Spider Working Group, Weissenburg, 1995-; Lector, Journal, Latrodecta, 1995-; Scientist, ABiTec, Munich, 2000-; Medical Information, Smith Kline Beecham, Munich, 1996-97, 2000; Medical Customer Care Center, GlaxoSmith Kline, 2001-; Medical Client Service, Bayer Diagnostics, Munich, 1999-2000. Publications: The Role of Web-Building Spiders; New Results Supporting the Theory that Cribra Orbitalia can be caused by iron deficiency anaemia; Electrophoresis of Scorpion Venoms; Die Rolle Radnetzbauender Spinnen in der Biologischen Schädlingsbekämpfung. Honours: Many exhibitions. Memberships: Judge of Trampoline Sports; Venomous Spider Working Group. Address: Eichenstr 17, 82054 Sauerlach, Germany.

**BURFORD Jeremy Michael Joseph,** b. 3 June 1942, Burnham, Buckinghamshire, England. Circuit Judge. Education: Diocesan College, Cape Town, South Africa; BA, University of Cape Town, 1962; MA, Emmanuel College, Cambridge; LL M, Harvard Law School, 1967. Appointments: Practice at the Bar, 1969-93; Queen's Counsel, 1987; Circuit Judge, 1993-. Honour: Kennedy Scholar, 1966. Address: Southampton Crown Court, London Road, Southampton, SO15 2XQ, England.

**BÜRGEL (Johann) Christoph,** b. 16 September 1931, Germany. Professor of Islamic Studies. m. Magdalena Kluike, deceased 7 November 1997, 2 sons. Education: PhD, 1960, Habilitation, 1968, University of Göttingen, Germany. Appointment: Professor of Islamic Studies, Head of the Institute of Islamic Studies, University of Bern, Switzerland, 1970; Retired 1995. Publications: Die Hofkorrespondenz ʿAdud ad-Daulas, 1965; Arerroes contra Galenum, 1968; The Feather of Simurgh, 1988; Allmacht und Mächtigkeit, 1991; Translations: 3 epics from Nizami (d. 1209), 1980, 1991, 1997; 2 anthologies

from the Diwan of Rumi, 1974, reprinted 2003, 1992; Hafiz, 1972, reprinted 1977; Two volumes of poetry (lyrics): Im Lichtnetz, 1983; Im Sog Deutsche Ghaselen, 2003; Some 130 contributions to books and journals and some 140 book reviews. Honours: Medal, Government of Pakistan; Rückert Prize from the Town of Schweinfurt, 1983 Literature Prize from the Town of Bern, 1993 both for his lyrics and his translations of poetry from Arabic, Persian and Urdu. Memberships: UEAI; IASTAM; Humboldt Society; Institute for Advanced Study, Princeton, 2002-. Address: Eichholzweg 28, CH 3024 Muri/BE, Switzerland. E-mail: johann.buergel@islam.unibe.ch

**BURGEN Arnold Stanley Vincent,** b. 20 March 1922, London, England. Scientist. m. Olga Kennard, 2 sons, 1 daughter. Education: MB, BS 1945, MD, 1949, London; Member, 1949, Fellow, Royal College of Physicians; Fellow, Royal Society, 1964. Appointments: Demonstrator, Assistant Lecturer, Middlesex Hospital Medical School, 1945-49; Professor, Physiology, McGill University, Montreal, 1949-62; Deputy Director, McGill University Medical Clinic, 1957-62; Professor, Pharmacology, Cambridge University, 1962-71; Director, National Institute for Medical Research, 1971-82; Master, Darwin College, Cambridge, 1982-89; Foreign Secretary, Royal Society, 1981-86. Honours: Honorary DSc, McGill University, Liverpool and Leeds; Honorary MD, Utrecht, Zurich; Honorary Fellow, Downing College, Darwin College, Cambridge, Wolfson College, Oxford. Knight Bachelor, 1976; Wellcome Gold Medal, 1999. Publications: Papers in journals of pharmacology and physiology. Memberships: Academia Europaea; Academy of Finland; American Association of Physicians; Foreign Member, US Academy of Sciences. Address: Keelson, 8A Hills Avenue, Cambridge, CB1 7XA, England.

**BURGON Geoffrey Alan,** b. 15 July, 1941, United Kingdom. Composer; Conductor. m. (1) Janice Elizabeth Garwood, divorced, 1 son, 1 daughter, (2) Jacqueline Louise Krofchak, 1 son. Career: Composer and conductor. Compositions: Dramatic works include: Joan of Arc, 1970; Orpheus, 1982; Hard Times, 1990; Orchestral music includes: Concerto for string orchestra, 1963; Gending, 1968; Trumpet Concerto, 1993; Piano Concerto, 1997; A Distant Dawn, 1999; Orchestral music with voices includes: Requiem, 1976; The World Again, 1983; Revelations, 1984; Mass 1984; Title Divine, 1986; A Vision, 1990; City Adventures (world premier BBC Proms), 1996; Merciless Beauty, 1996; Ballet music includes: The Golden Fish, 1964; Running Figures, 1975; Songs, Lamentations and Praises, 1979; The Trials of Prometheus, 1988; Choral music include: Three Elegies, 1964; Short Mass, 1965; Two Hymns to Mary, 1967; Mai Himama, 1970; A Prayer to the Trinity, 1972; The Fire of Heaven, 1973; Noche Oscura, 1974; Dos Coros, 1975; Nuni dimittis, 1979; Laudate Dominum, 1980; But Have Been Found Again, 1993; The Song of the Creatures, 1987; Four Sacred Pieces, 1999; Magic Words, 2000; Chamber music includes: Gloria, 1973; Six Studies, 1980; Chamber music with voices includes: Five Sonnets of John Donne, 1967; Worldes Blisse, 1971; Lunar Beauty, 1986; Clarinet Quintet, 1998; String Quartet, 1999; Heavenly Things; Film and TV scores include: The Changeling, 1973; Dr Who and the Terror of the Zygons, 1975; Monty Python's Life of Brian, 1979; Tinker Tailor Soldier Spy, 1979; The Dogs of War, 1980; Brideshead Revisited, 1981; Turtle Diary, 1985; The Death of the Heart, 1985; Bleak House, 1986; The Chronicles of Narnia, 1988; Children of the North, 1990; Robin Hood, 1991; The Agency, 1991; Martin Chuzzlewit, 1994; Silent Witness, 1996; Turning World, 1997; Cider with Rosie, 1998; When Trumpets Fade, 1998; Longitude, 1999; Labrynth, 2001; The Forsyte Saga, 2002. Address: c/o Chester Music, 8-9 Frith St, London W1V 5TZ, England

**BURKE John Frederick, (Owen Burke, Harriet Esmond, Jonathan George, Joanna Jones, Robert Miall, Sara Morris, Martin Sands),** b. 8 March 1922, Rye, England. Author. m. (1) Joan Morris, 13 September 1940, 5 daughters, (2) Jean Williams, 29 June 1963, 2 sons. Appointments: Production Manager, Museum Press; Editorial Manager, Paul Hamlyn Books for Pleasure Group; European Story Editor, 20th Century Fox Productions. Publications: Swift Summer, 1949; An Illustrated History of England, 1974; Dr Caspian Trilogy, 1976-78; Musical Landscapes, 1983; Illustrated Dictionary of Music, 1988; A Travellers History of Scotland, 1990; Bareback, 1998; Death by Marzipan, 1999; We've Been Waiting for You, 2000; Stalking Widow, 2000; The Second Strain, 2002; Wrong Turnings, 2004. Film and TV Novelisations. Contributions to: The Bookseller; Country Life; Denmark. Honour: Atlantic Award in Literature, 1948-49. Memberships: Society of Authors; Danish Club. Address: 5 Castle Gardens, Kirkcudbright, Dumfries & Galloway DG6 4JE, Scotland.

**BURKE Kathy,** b. London, England. Actress. Education: Anna Scher's Theatre School, London. Creative Works: TV include: Harry Enfield and Chums; Absolutely Fabulous; Common as Muck; Mr Wroes' Virgins; Tom Jones; Gimme Gimme Gimme. Films: Scrubbers; Nil By Mouth; Elizabeth, 1998; This Year's Love, 1999; Love, Honour and Obey, 2000; The Martins, 2001; Once Upon a Time in the Midlands, 2002; Anita and Me, 2002. Theatre includes: Mr Thomas, London; Boom Bang-a-Bang, London (director). Honours: Royal TV Society Award; Best Actress, Cannes Film Festival, 1997.

**BURKERT Andreas Michael,** b. 12 May 1959, Gangkofen, Germany. Astronomer. m. Inge C Burkert, 1 son. Education: Diploma in Physics, University of Munich, 1986; PhD, Astrophysics, 1989. Appointments: Research Associate, University of Illinois, 1989-90; Research Associate, University of California, 1990-91; Research Associate, Max Planck Institute for Astrophysics, 1991-94; Head, Theoretical Research Group, Max Planck Institute for Astronomy, 1995-2003; Promotion for a BAT Ib Position to a BAT Ia Position, 1996; Promotion for a BAT Ia Position to a C3 Position, 1997; Full Professor and Director of University Observatory, University Munich, 2003-. Honours: Student Fellowship from the German Government, 1984; Feodor Lynen Postdoctoral Fellowship, Humboldt Foundation; Award for the best PhD in Physics, University of Munich; Feodor Lynen Postdoctoral Fellowship, Humboldt Foundation; Ludwig Biermann Prize, German Astronomical Society. Memberships: German Astronomical Society; American Astronomical Society; German Physical Society; International Astronomical Union. Address: University Observatory Munich, Scheinerstr 1, D-81679 Munich, Germany. E-mail: burkert@usm.uni-muenchen.de

**BURKETT Mary Elizabeth,** b. 7 October 1924, Northumberland, England. Teacher; Museum Director. Education: BA, University of Durham. Appointments: Art Teacher, The Laurels School, Wroxall Abbey, 1949-53; Teacher of Art and Craft, Charlotte Mason College, Ambleside, 1954-62; Assistant then Director, Abbot Hall Art Gallery and Museums, Kendal, 1962-86; Director, Border TV, 1982-93; Member: North Western Area Museums and Art Gallery Services Area Council, 1975-86; Arts Council Fine Arts Committee, 1978-80; National Trust North Western Region Executive Committee, 1978-85; Judge: Scottish Museum of the Year Award, 1977-2000, English Museum of the Year Award, 1986-2000; Member, British Tourist Authority Museums Mission to USA, 1981. Publications: The Art of the Felt Maker, 1979; Kurt Schwitters (in the Lake District), 1979; William Green of Ambleside (with David Sloss), 1984; Monograph on Christopher Steele, 1987;

Read's Point of View (with David Sloss), 1995; Percy Kelly, A Cumbrian Artist (with V M Rickerby), 1996; Monograph of George Senhouse of Mayport, 1997. Honours: OBE, 1978; FMA, 1980; Leverhulme Fellowship for studies in Cumbrian portrait painting, 1986; Honorary MA, Lancaster University, 1997. Memberships: Friends of Abbot Hall Art Gallery Committee, 2000-; Trustee: Carlisle Cathedral Appeal, 1981-86, Armitt Trust, 1982-86, Senhouse Trust, 1985-; President: Feltmakers Association, 1984-, Executive Committee Lake District Art Gallery Trust, 1993-98, Carlisle Cathedral Fabric Committee, 1993-2001, Blencathra Appeal Committee, 1993-95; President Romney Society, 1999-; President, NADFAS, North Cumbria, 2003-. E-mail: m.e.burkett@amserve.net

**BURKHOLZ Herbert Laurence,** b. 9 December 1932, New York, New York, USA. Author. m. Susan Blaine, 1 November 1961, 2 sons. Education: BA, New York University, 1951. Appointment: Writer-in-Residence, College of William and Mary, 1975. Publications: Sister Bear, 1969; Spy, 1969; The Spanish Soldier, 1973; Mulligan's Seed, 1975; The Death Freak, 1978; The Sleeping Spy, 1983; The Snow Gods, 1985; The Sensitives, 1987; Strange Bedfellows, 1988; Brain Damage, 1992; Writer in Residence, 1992; The FDA Follies, 1994; Full Time Sinner, 2005. Contributions to: New York Times; Town & Country; Playboy; Penthouse; Longevity. Honour: Distinguished Scholar, 1976. Address: 4 Della Lane, Boonsboro, MD 21713, USA.

**BURMAN Peter Ashley Thomas Insull,** b. 15 September 1944, Solihull, England. Art and Architectural Historian. Education: Exhibitioner, BA, 1966, MA, 1970, Kings College Cambridge; Conservation Techniques and Philosophy, ICCROM, Rome, 1980. Appointments: Assistant Secretary, Deputy Secretary, Secretary (Chief Executive), Church of England, Council for the Care of Churches and the Cathedrals Fabric Commission for England, 1968-90; Director, Centre for Conservation Studies, University of York, 1990-2002; Director, Conservation and Property Services, The National Trust for Scotland, 2003-; Visiting Professor, Department of Fine Arts, University of Canterbury, Christchurch, New Zealand, 2002. Publications include: Books: Chapels and Churches: Who Cares?, 1977; St Paul's Cathedral, 1987; 6 book chapters; Refereed articles: Reflections on the Lime Revival, 1995; The Ethics of Using Traditional Building Materials, 1997; The Study and Conservation of Nineteenth Century Wall Paintings, 2003. Honours: Doctorate, honoris causa, Brandenburg Technical University, Cottbus, Germany; Fellow, Society of Antiquaries, 1973; MBE, 1990; Esher Award, SPAB, 2003. Memberships include: Chairman, Fabric Advisory Committee, St Paul's Cathedral; Historic Environment Advisory Council for Scotland; Council Member and Convenor, Glasite Meeting House Committee, Architectural Heritage Society of Scotland; Trustee, Greyfriars Kirkyard Trust, Edinburgh; Furniture History Society; Garden History Society; SPAB; Ancient Monuments Society; Georgian Group; Victorian Society; Twentieth Century Society. Address: The National Trust for Scotland, Wemyss House, 28 Charlotte Square, Edinburgh EH2 4ET, Scotland.

**BURNELL-NUGENT James Michael (Vice Admiral Sir),** b. 20 November 1949, Stutton, Nr Ipswich, Suffolk, England. Royal Navy Officer. m. Mary Woods, 1970-73, 3 sons, 1 daughter. Education: MA (Hons), Mathematics, Corpus Christi College, Cambridge, 1968-71. Appointments: Royal Navy: Joined 1971; Captain HMS Olympus (submarine), 1978; Captain, HMS Conqueror (submarine), 1984-86; Captain, 1990; Captain, Second Frigate Squadron and Captain HMS Brilliant (Bosnia), 1992-93; Commodore, 1994; Captain, HMS Invincible (Gulf, Kosovo), 1997-99; Rear Admiral, 1999; Assistant Chief of Naval Staff, 1999-2001; Member, Admiralty Board, 1999-2001 and 2003-; Commander UK Maritime Forces and ASW Striking Force (Operation Enduring Freedom), 2001-2002; Vice Admiral, 2003-; Second Sea Lord and Commander-in-Chief, Naval Home Command, 2003-; ADC to Her Majesty the Queen, 2003-. Honours: CBE, 1999; KCB, 2004; Queen's Gold Medal; Max Horton Prize; Freeman of the City of London, 1999; Younger Brother, Trinity House, 2004. Address: c/o The Naval Secretary, Victory Building, HM Naval Base, Portsmouth, England.

**BURNETT Alfred David,** b. 15 August 1937, Edinburgh, Scotland. University Librarian; Poet. Education: MA, Honours, English Language and Literature, University of Edinburgh, 1959; ALA, University of Strathclyde, 1964. Appointments: Library Assistant, Glasgow University Library, 1959-64; Assistant Librarian, Durham University Library, England, 1964-90. Publications: Mandala, 1967; Diversities, 1968; A Ballad Upon a Wedding, 1969; Columbaria, 1971; Shimabara, 1972; Fescennines, 1974; Thirty Snow Poems, 1973; Hero and Leander, 1975; The True Vine, 1975; He and She, 1976; The Heart's Undesign, 1977; Figures and Spaces, 1978; Jackdaw, 1980; Thais, 1981; Romans, 1983; Vines, 1984; Autolycus, 1987; Kantharos, 1989; Lesbos, 1990; Mirror and Pool, translations from Chinese (with John Cayley), 1992; Nine Poets, 1993; The Island, 1994, 2nd edition, 1996; Twelve Poems, 1994; Something of Myself, 1994; Six Poems, 1995; Transfusions, translations from French, 1995; Hokusai, 1996; Marina Tsvetaeva, 1997; Chesil Beach, 1997; Akhmatova, 1998; Cinara, 2001; Evergreens, 2002; Twelve Women, 2004; Editor, anthologies. Contributions to: Poetry Durham; Numerous professional and critical periodical contributions and monographs. Honours: Essay Prize, 1956, Patterson Bursary in Anglo-Saxon, 1958, University of Edinburgh; Kelso Memorial Prize, University of Strathclyde, 1964; Essay Prize, Library Association, 1966; Sevensma Prize, International Federation of Library Associations, 1971; Hawthornden Fellowships, 1988, 1992 and 2002; Panizzi Medal, British Library, 1991; Fellow, British Centre for Literary Translation, Norwich, 1994. Memberships: Poetry Book Society; Fine Press Book Association; Private Libraries Association. Address: 33 Hastings Avenue, Merry Oaks, Durham DH1 3QG, England.

**BURNS Jim,** b. 19 February 1936, Preston, Lancashire, England. Writer; Part-time Teacher. Education: BA Honours, Bolton Institute of Technology, 1980. Appointments: Editor, Move, 1964-68; Editor, Palantir, 1976-83; Jazz Editor, Beat Scene, 1990-. Publications: A Single Flower, 1972; The Goldfish Speaks from beyond the Grave, 1976; Fred Engels bei Woolworth, 1977; Internal Memorandum, 1982; Out of the Past: Selected Poems 1961-1986, 1987; Confessions of an Old Believer, 1996; The Five Senses, 1999; As Good a Reason As Any, 1999; Beats, Bohemians and Intellectuals, 2000; Take it Easy, 2003; Bopper, 2003. Contributions to: London Magazine; Stand; Ambit; Jazz Journal; Critical Survey; The Guardian; New Statesman; Tribune; New Society; Penniless Press; Prop; Verse; Others. Address: 11 Gatley Green, Gatley, Cheadle, Cheshire SK8 4NF, England.

**BURR Martin John,** b. 19 February 1953, Amersham, Buckinghamshire, England. Barrister. Education: MA, 1978, Diploma in Comparative Philology, 1977, Pembroke College, Oxford. Appointments: Called to the Bar by Middle Temple, 1978; Practising Barrister, 1979-; Joint Head of Chambers at 2 Temple Gardens, 1989-93; Sole Head of Chambers at Eldon Chambers, 1993-; Associate of the Chartered Institute of Arbitrators, 1990; Member of the Society of Trusts and Estates Practitioners, 1992. Publications: Books include: The Law and

Health Visitors, 1982; Chancery Practice, 1991-97; Taxation Recent Developments, 1999; Land Law, forthcoming. Numerous papers and poems published. Compositions: 39 Oratorios, 1981-2004. Honours: Freeman of the City of London; Secretary of the Guild Church Council at St Dunstan-in-the-West, Fleet Street, London; Member of the Council, Henry Bradshaw Society; Deputy Governor, American Biographical Institute; Lifetime Academy of Achievement, American Biographical Institute; Fellow, American Biographical Institute. Memberships: Middle Temple; Lincoln's Inn; Inner Temple; Sion College; Philological Society; Henry Sweet Society; International Arthurian Society; British Archaeological Association; Anglican and Eastern Churches Association; Henry Bradshaw Society; Society of Trust and Estate Practitioners; Ecclesiastical Law Society; Selden Society; Arthur Ransome Society. Address: First Floor, Temple Chambers, Temple Avenue, London, England EC4Y 0DA, England

**BURRELL Leroy,** b. 21 February 1967, Landsdowne, Philadelphia, USA. Athlete. m. Michelle Finn, 2 sons. Education: University of Houston, Texas. Appointments: Established 'Clean' World Record, Running 100m in 9.9 seconds at US Championships, New York, 1991; Established World Record 100m, 1994; Head Track and Field Coach, University of Houston, 1998-. Honour: Olympic Gold Medal, 4x100m relay, Barcelona, 1992. Address: USA Track & Field Press Information Department, 1 RCA Dome, Suite 140, Indianapolis, IN 46225, USA.

**BURRELL Mark William,** b. 9 April 1937, London, England. Businessman. m. Margot, 2 sons, 1 daughter. Education: Pembroke College, Cambridge University, 1957-59, Harvard Business School, 1974. Appointments: A Managing Director, Lazard Brothers, 1970-86; Executive Director, Pearson plc, 1986-97; Chairman, Millbank Financial Services, 1986-; Non-Executive Director, Research Machines plc, 1997-2001; Non-Executive Director, Chairman, Merlin Communications International Ltd, 1997-2001; Chairman, Conafex SA, 1999-; Chairman, Margaret Pyke Memorial Trust, 1997; Member of Court, University of Sussex, 1997-; High Sheriff of West Sussex, 2002-2003; Governor, Northbrook College, Sussex, 2004-. Memberships: Harvard Club Great Britain; Whites; Boodles; Knepp Castle Polo Club. Address: Bakers House, Bakers Lane, Shipley, Horsham, West Sussex RH13 8GJ, England.

**BURRELL Michael Philip,** b. 12 May 1937, Harrow, England. Actor; Playwright. Education: BA, MA (Cantab), Peterhouse, Cambridge, 1958-61. Career: Freelance actor since 1961, appearing in major British companies including, the Royal Shakespeare Company, the Chichester Festival Company and Stratford East; Numerous TV appearances; Over 25 feature films; Directing career since 1964, posts include, Associate Director, Royal Lyceum Theatre, Edinburgh 1966-68; Director, Angles Theatre, Wisbech, 1995-2001; Serves on various arts boards, including the Drama Panel of the Eastern Arts Association, 1981-86; King's Lynn Festival and Arts Centre, 1992-95; Theatre Royal, Bury St Edmunds, 1994-2000; Company Secretary, Tiebreak Touring Theatre Ltd, 1987-2004; Chairman, Wisbech Events Forum, 1998-; Chairman, Huntingdon Branch Liberal Democrats, 2003-; Chairman, Natural High Experience Ltd, 2004-. Publications: Over 17 plays including the multi-award winning Hess, 1978, 5 London productions, including one by the RSC at the Almeida; Borrowing Time; My Sister Next Door; The Man Who Lost America; Love Among the Butterflies; Lord of the Fens; Several articles; A current weekly column, In My View, in the Fenland Citizen newspaper. Honours: Obie Award, for Hess, 1980; Best Actor, Best Show, Edmonton Journal Awards, 1984, 1985;

Capital Critics Award for Best Actor, Ottawa, 1986; Bronze Award, New York Film Festival, 1988; Edmonton Journal Award for Best Show, for My Sister Next Door, 1989; Honorary President, Peterhouse Heywood Society, 2002-. Memberships: National Liberal Club, London. Address: c/o Richard Stone Partnership, 2 Henrietta Street, London WC2E 8PS, England. Website: www.michaelburrell.co.uk

**BURRILL Timothy,** b. 8 June 1931, St Asaph, North Wales, UK. m. (1) Philippa Hare, deceased, 1 daughter (2) Santa Raymond, divorced, 1 son, 2 daughters. Education: Sorbonne, Paris, France. Appointments: Entered film industry 1956; Joined Brookfield Productions, 1965; Managing Director, Burrill Productions, 1966-; Director, World Film Services, 1967-69; First Production Administrator, National Film and TV School, 1972; Managing Director: Allied Stars, responsible for Chariots of Fire, 1980-81, Pathé Productions Ltd, 1994-99; Director: Artistry Ltd, responsible for Superman and Supergirl films, 1982, Central Casting, 1988-92; Consultant: National Film Development Fund, 1980-81, The Really Useful Group, 1989-90; UK Film Industry Representative on Eurimages, 1994-96; Vice-Chairman, 1979-81 Chairman, 1980-83, BAFTA, Film Asset Development plc, 1987-94, First Film Foundation, 1989-98, Production Training Fund, 1993-2001; Executive Committee, 1990-2001, Vice-Chairman, 1993-94, The Producers' Association; Director, British Film Commission, 1997-99; Producer Member: Cinematograph Films Council, 1980-83; General Council ACTT, 175-76; Executive Committee, British Film and TV Producers' Association, 1981-90; Governor, National Film and TV School, 1981-92, Royal National Theatre, 1982-88; Member, UK Government's Middleton Committee on Film Finance, 1996; Le Club de Producteurs Européens; Board Member, International Federation of Film Producers Association, 1997-, UK Government's Film Policy Review, 1997-98, European Film Academy, 1997-. Films as Co-Producer include most recently: The Pianist, 2001-2002; Swimming Pool, 2002-2003; Blueberry, 2002-2003; Two Brothers, 2002; Les Anges de l'Apocalypse, 2003; Double Zero, 2003; San Antonio, 2003; Oliver Twist, 2004; Renaissance, 2004; Animal, 2004. Address: 19 Cranbury Road, London SW6 9NS, England. E-mail: timothy@timothyburrill.co.uk

**BURROUGHS Andrew,** b. 5 April 1958, United Kingdom. Journalist. m. Jacqueline Margaret Wylson, divorced, 1 son, 1 daughter. Education: Exhibitioner, MA, St Catharine's College Cambridge; Guildhall School of Music and Drama. Appointments: News Trainee, Westminster Press, 1979-82; Far East Broadcasting, Seychelles, 1982-84; BBC World Service, 1985-85; BBC Radio 4, 1985-86; Producer, BBC News and Current Affairs, 1986-88; Religion, Arts and Community Affairs Correspondent, 1988-94, Social Affairs Correspondent and Videojournalist (features), 1994-98, Social Affairs Unit BBC TV; Videojournalism Features Correspondent, BBC News, 1998-2001; Videojournalist Features Correspondent, BBC Europe Direct, 2001-; TV News Correspondent, BBC News 24 and BBC World, 2001-. Publication: Contributor: BBC Review of the Year, 1990, 1991. Honours: Highly Commended, BP Arts Journalism Award, 1991; TV Award Race in the Media, 1994. Membership: Wolfe Society (representative of descendant family General James Wolfe). Address: BBC Room 1634, Stage VI, Television Centre, Wood Lane, London W12 7RJ. E-mail: andrewburroughs@bbc.co.uk

**BURROW John Anthony,** b. 1932, Loughton, England. Professor; Writer. Education: BA, 1953, MA, 1955, Christ Church, Oxford. Appointments: Fellow, Jesus College, Oxford University, 1961-75; Winterstoke Professor, University of Bristol, 1976-98. Publications: A Reading of Sir Gawain and the

Green Knight, 1965; Geoffrey Chaucer: A Critical Anthology, 1969; Ricardian Poetry: Chaucer, Gower Langland and the Gawain Poet, 1971; Sir Gawain and the Green Knight, 1972; English Verse 1300-1500, 1977; Medieval Writers and Their Work, 1982; Essays on Medieval Literature, 1984; The Ages of Man, 1986; A Book of Middle English, 1992; Langlands Fictions, 1993; Thomas Hoccleve, 1994; Gestures and Looks in Medieval Narrative, 2002. Address: 9 The Polygon, Clifton, Bristol, England.

**BURROWAY Janet (Gay),** b. 21 September 1936, Tucson, Arizona, USA. Professor; Writer; Poet. m. (1) Walter Eysselinck, 1961, divorced 1973, 2 sons, (2) William Dean Humphries, 1978, divorced 1981, (3) Peter Ruppert, 1993, 1 stepdaughter. Education: University of Arizona, 1954-55; AB, Barnard College, 1958; BA, 1960, MA, 1965, Cambridge University; Yale School of Drama, 1960-61. Appointments: Instructor, Harpur College, Binghamton, New York, 1961-62; Lecturer, University of Sussex, 1965-70; Associate Professor, 1972-77, Professor, 1977-, MacKenzie Professor of English, 1989-95, Robert O Lawson Distinguished Professor, 1995-2002, Emerita, 2002-, Florida State University; Fiction Reviewer, Philadelphia Enquirer, 1986-90; Reviewer, New York Times Book Review, 1991-; Essay-Columnist, New Letters: A Magazine of Writing and Art, 1994-. Publications: Fiction: Descend Again, 1960; The Dancer From the Dance, 1965; Eyes, 1966; The Buzzards, 1969; The Truck on the Track, children's book, 1970; The Giant Jam Sandwich, children's book, 1972; Raw Silk, 1977; Opening Nights, 1985; Cutting Stone, 1992. Poetry: But to the Season, 1961; Material Goods, 1980; Essays: Embalming Mom, 2002. Other: Writing Fiction: A Guide to Narrative Craft, 1982, 6th edition, 2002; Imaginative Writing, 2002; Editor, From Where You Dream: The Process of Writing Fiction, by Robert Olem Butler. Contributions to: Numerous journals and periodicals. Honours: National Endowment for the Arts Fellowship, 1976; Yaddo Residency Fellowships, 1985, 1987; Lila Wallace-Reader's Digest Fellow, 1993-94; Carolyn Benton Cockefaire Distinguished Writer-in-Residence, University of Missouri, 1995; Woodrow Wilson Visiting Fellow, Furman University, Greenville, South Carolina, 1995; Erskine College, Due West, South Carolina, 1997; Drury College, Springfield, Illinois, 1999. Memberships: Associated Writing Programs, vice president, 1988-89; Authors Guild. Address: 240 De Soto Street, Tallahassee, FL 32303, USA. E-mail: jburroway@english.fsu.edu

**BURSHTEIN Sheldon,** b. 13 March 1952, Montreal, Quebec, Canada. Lawyer. Education: B(Civ)Eng, 1974, BCL, 1977, LLB, 1978, McGill University. Appointments: Admitted to Law Society of Upper Canada, 1980; Registered Professional Engineer, Ontario, 1980; Registered Trademark Agent, Canada, 1980; Lawyer, Patent Agent and Trademark Agent; Registered Trademark Agent, US (Canadian Applicants), 1982; Partner, Blake Cassels & Graydon, LLP, Toronto, Ontario, 1986-; Registered Patent Agent, Canada, 1987, US (Canadian Applicants), 1987; Certified Specialist, Intellectual Property (Patent, Trademark and Copyright) Law, Law Society of Upper Canada, 1994. Publications: Book, Patent Your Own Invention in Canada, 1991; Co-author, book, The Use of Another's Trademark, 1997; Author, book, Corporate Counsel Guide to Intellectual Property Law, 2000; Author, Domain Names and Trademark Issues on the Internet: Canadian Law & Practice, 2005; Author, numerous chapters in books on Intellectual Property, Licensing and related topics; Author of numerous contributions to journals, conferences on Patents, Trademarks, Copyright and Designs, Confidential Information, Electronic Commerce, Licensing and Franchising, Intellectual Property Aspects of Commercial Transactions, Intellectual Property and

Free Trade, Intellectual Property Management, Engineering. Honours: Marie F Morency Memorial Prize, Intellectual Property Institute of Canada, Highest National Standing in Patent Drafting Exam, 1987; Selected as one of the World's Leading Patent Law Experts, Managing Intellectual Property; World's Leading Trademark Law Experts and World's Top 50 Trademark Lawyers Managing Intellectual Property; Selected to appear in: "World's Leading Patent Law Experts", 2005; "World's Leading Trade Mark and Copyright Law Experts", 2005; and many others. Memberships: Editorial Advisory Board, The Licensing Journal; Advisory Board, Multimedia and Technology Licensing Law Report; Editorial Board, Laws of Com; Columnist, World Licensing Law Report, Pharmaceutical, Canada; Chairman and Former Chairman, Various Committees, Intellectual Property Institute of Canada and other organisations. Address: c/o Blake Cassels & Graydon, LLP, PO Box 25, Commerce Court West, Toronto, Ontario M5L 1A9, Canada.

**BURTON Anthony George Graham,** b. 24 December 1934, Thornaby, England. Writer; Broadcaster. m. 28 March 1959, 2 sons, 1 daughter. Publications: A Programmed Guide to Office Warfare, 1969; The Jones Report, 1970; The Canal Builders, 1972, 4th edition, 2005; The Reluctant Musketeer, 1973; Canals in Colour, 1974; Remains of a Revolution, 1975, 2001; The Master Idol, 1975; The Miners, 1976; The Navigators, 1976; Josiah Wedgwood, 1976; Canal, 1976; Back Door Britain, 1977; A Place to Stand, 1977; Industrial Archaeological Sites of Britain, 1977; The Green Bag Travellers, 1978; The Past At Work, 1980; The Rainhill Story, 1980; The Past Afloat, 1982; The Changing River, 1982; The Shell Book of Curious Britain, 1982; The National Trust Guide to Our Industrial Past, 1983; The Waterways of Britain, 1983; The Rise and Fall of King Cotton, 1984; Walking the Line, 1985; Wilderness Britain, 1985; Britain's Light Railways, 1985; The Shell Book of Undiscovered Britain and Ireland, 1986; Britain Revisited, 1986; Landscape Detective, 1986; Opening Time, 1987; Steaming Through Britain, 1987; Walk the South Downs, 1988; Walking Through History, 1988; The Great Days of the Canals, 1989; Cityscapes, 1990; Astonishing Britain, 1990; Slow Roads, 1991; The Railway Builders, 1992; Canal Mania, 1993; The Grand Union Canal Walk, 1993; The Railway Empire, 1994; The Rise and Fall of British Shipbuilding, 1994; The Cotswold Way, 1995; The Dales Way, 1995; The West Highland Way, 1996; The Southern Upland Way, 1997; William Cobbett: Englishman, 1997; The Wye Valley Walk, 1998; The Caledonian Canal, 1998; Best Foot Forward, 1998; The Cumbria Way, 1999; The Wessex Ridgeway, 1999. Thomas Telford, 1999; Weekend Walks: Dartmoor and Exmoor, 2000; Weekend Walks: The Yorkshire Dales, 2000; Traction Engines, 2000; Richard Trevithick, 2000; The Orient Express, 2001; Weekend Walks: The Peak District, 2001; The Anatomy of Canals: The Early Years, 2001; The Daily Telegraph Guide to Britain's Working Past, 2001; The Anatomy of Canals: The Nania Years, 2002; Hadrian's Wall Path, 2003; The Daily Telegraph Guide to Britain's Maritime Past, 2003; The Anatomy of Canals: Decline and Renewal, 2003; On the Rails, 2004; The Ridgeway, 2005. Membership: Outdoor Writers Guild. Address: c/o Sara Menguc, 4 Hatch Place, Kingston upon Thames KT2 5NB, England.

**BURTON Diane,** b. 26 July 1954, Johannesburg, South Africa. Managing Director. m. Andrew, 1 son, 1 daughter. Education: BA, English; PGCE; Diploma in Public Relations. Appointments: Account Executive, The Public Relations Company Ltd; Managing Director, Moss International Ltd; Senior Lecturer, Leeds Business School; Senior Lecturer, Trinity and All Saints, Leeds University; Managing Director Cicada Public Relations Ltd. Publications: Film Production in The South African Handbook of Public Relations, 1982; Promoting the Product or Service in Financing Growth, 1989; Cam Distance Learning Programme Module on Management and Strategy, 1994; IoD Masters in Company Direction chapter on Media, 1998. Honours: Shortlisted for Yorkshire Business Woman of the Year, 1998; Key Note Speaker, PRISA International Conference in Namibia, 2000; IPR Cream Awards for best issues and crisis management campaigns, 2001, 2002. Memberships: Honorary Fellow, Trinity and All Saints, Leeds University; Fellow Institute of Public Relations; Fellow, Chartered Institute of Personnel and Development; Fellow, Royal Society of Arts. Address: Cicada PR, 101 Station Parade, Harrogate HG1 1HB, England. E-mail: di@cicada-pr.com

**BURTON Gregory Keith,** b. 12 February 1956, Sydney, New South Wales, Australia. Barrister-at-Law; Senior Counsel. m. (1) Suzanne Louise Brandstater, 1994, 1 son, 1 daughter, (2) Penelope Josephine Whitehead, 2004, 2 sons, 3 daughters. Education: BCL, Oxon; BA Honours, LLB Honours, University of Sydney; Graded Arbitrator, Accredited Mediator, Conciliator and Evaluator; Associate, Institute Arbitrators and Mediators, Australia; Barrister, New South Wales, High Court and Federal Courts, Queensland, Ireland; Barrister and Solicitor, Victoria, Western Australia, ACT, Northern Territory. Appointments: Solicitor, Freehill Hollingdale and Page, 1980-83; Associate to Sir William Deane, High Court of Australia, 1984-85; Senior Adviser to Federal MP, 1986; Lecturer, Law, Australian National University, 1987-88; Bar, 1989-; Senior Counsel, 2004-. Publications: Australian Financial Transactions Law, 1991; Chapters and articles in, and editor of, journals, book and legal encyclopaedias; Directions in Finance Law, 1990; Weaver and Craigie's Banker and Customer in Australia (co-author). Honours: Dux, Trinity Grammar School, Sydney, 1968-73; University Medal, History, University of Sydney, 1978; Prizes in Equity, Commercial Law, Public Law, English, History, Government; Editorial Committee, Sydney Law Review, 1978-79. Memberships: NSW Bar Association; Business Law Section, Law Council of Australia; Banking and Financial Services Law Association; Commercial Law Association; Australian Institute Administrative Law; Various ADR Organizations; Centre International Legal Studies, Vienna; Centre Independent Studies; Institute of Public Affairs; Sydney Institute; Director, Australian Elizabethan Theatre Trust; Procurator, Presbyterian Church of Australia. Address: 5th Floor, Wentworth Chambers, 180 Phillip Street, Sydney, NSW, Australia 2000.

**BURTON, Hon Mr Justice; Hon Sir Michael John,** b. 12 November 1946, Manchester, England. High Court Judge. m. Corinne Ruth Cowan, deceased, 1992, 4 daughters. Education: Kings Scholar, Captain of School, Eton College, 1959-64; MA, Balliol College, Oxford, 1965-69 (JCR President of Balliol, First President, Oxford University Student Council). Appointments: Called to Bar, Gray's Inn, 1970; Barrister, 1970-98; Lecturer in Law, Balliol College, Oxford, 1970-73; Candidate (Labour), Kensington Council, 1971; Parliamentary Candidate (Labour), Stratford-on-Avon, 1974; Candidate (Social Democrat), GLC Putney, 1981; Queen's Counsel, 1984; Recorder of the Crown Court, 1989-98; Head of Chambers, 1991-98; Deputy Judge of the High Court, 1993-98; Judge of the High Court of Justice (Queen's Bench Division), 1998-; Judge of the Employment Appeal Tribunal, 2000-, President, 2002-; Chairman, Central Arbitration Committee, 2000-; President, Interception of Communications Tribunal, 2000-2001; Vice-President, Investigatory Powers Tribunal, 2000-; Member, Bar Council Legal Services Commission, 1995; Publication: Civil Appeals (editor) 2002. Honours: Queen's Counsel, 1984; Bencher of Gray's Inn, 1993; Knighted, 1998. Memberships: Honorary Fellow, 1999-, Member of Council, 2003-05, Goldsmith's

College London University; Fellow, Eton College, 2004-. Address: c/o Royal Courts of Justice, Strand, London WC2A 2RR, England.

**BURTON Tim,** b. 1958, Burbank, California, USA. Film Director. Education: California Arts Institute. Appointments: Animator, Walt Disney Studios, projects include: The Fox and the Hound, The Black Cauldron; Animator, Director, Vincent (short length film). Creative Works: Films director: Frankenweenie, 1984; Aladdin, 1985; Pee-wee's Big Adventure, 1985; Beetlejuice, 1988; Batman, 1989; Edward Scissorhands, 1991; Batman Returns, 1992; Ed Wood, 1994; Batman Forever, 1996; Mars Attacks!, 1996; Sleepy Hollow, 1999; Planet of the Apes, 2001; The Heart of Me, 2002; Big Fish, 2003; Producer, The Nightmare Before Christmas, 1993; Cabin Boy, 1994; James and the Giant Peach, 1996; Lost in Oz (TV), 2000. Publications: My Art and Films, 1993; The Melancholy Death of Oyster Boy and Other Stories, 1997. Honours include: 2 Awards, Chicago Film Festival. Address: Chapman, Bird & Grey, 1990 South Bundy Drive, Suite 200, Los Angeles, CA 90025, USA.

**BURTON Verona Devine,** b. 23 November 1922, Reading, Pennsylvania, USA. Botanist. m. Daniel, 1 son. Education: AB, Hunter College, City of New York, 1944; MA, University of Iowa, 1946; PhD, University of Iowa, 1948. Appointments: Professor, Biology, Minnesota State University, 1948-86; Professor Emeritus, 1987-. Publications: Publications in American Journals. Memberships: Iowa Academy of Sciences; International Society for Plant Morphology; AAAS; Midwest College Biology Teachers. Address: 512 Hickory Street, Mankato, MN 56001, USA.

**BURY Robert Frederick,** b. 10 August 1948, Finedon, Northamptonshire, England. Consultant Radiologist. m. Linda Joyce, 3 sons, 1 daughter. Education: BSc, 1970, MBBS, 1973, Middlesex Hospital Medical School, University of London; FRCS (London), 1978; FRCR, 1983. Appointments: Royal Air Force Medical Branch, 1973-87; Retired from Royal Air Force with rank of Wing Commander, 1988; Consultant Radiologist, Leeds Teaching Hospital Trust and Senior Clinical Lecturer in Radiology, Lecturer in Medical Physics, University of Leeds, 1988-. Publications: Books: Radiology: A Practical Guide, 1988; Imaging Strategy: a guide for clinicians (with R Fowler), 1992; Several book chapters; Over 30 articles in medical journals. Memberships: British Institute of Radiology; British Nuclear Medicine Society. Address: 3 Elmete Avenue, Leeds LS8 2JX, England. E-mail: bob.bury@ntlworld.com

**BUSCEMI Steve,** b. 13 December 1957, Brooklyn, New York, USA. m. Jo Andres, 1987, 1 son. Education: Graduated, Valley Stream Central High School, Valley Stream, New York, 1975; Career: Bartender; Ice-cream truck driver; Stand-up comedian; Firefighter; Actor. Films include: The Way It Is, 1984; Sleepwalk, 1986; New York Stories, 1989; Pulp Fiction, 1994; Reservoir Dogs, 1994; Desperado, 1995; Escape From L.A., 1996; Big Daddy, 1999; Ghost World, 2000; Domestic Disturbance, 2001; Mr. Deeds, 2002; Big Fish, 2003; Coffee and Cigarettes, 2003; Spy-Kids 3-D: Game Over, 2003; Home on The Range, voice, 2004; TV includes: Saturday Night Live, 1975; Miami Vice, 1984; The Equaliser, 1985; Crossbow, 1986; The Simpsons, 1989; In The Life, 1992; Mad About You, 1992; The Drew Carey Show, 1995; The Sopranos, 2004. Honours include: Independent Spirit Award, Best Supporting Male, 1993; Chicago Film Critics Association Award, Best Supporting Actor, 2002; Independent Spirit Award, Best Supporting Male, 2002; Kansas City Film Critics Circle Award, Best Supporting Actor, 2002; Las Vegas Film Critics Society Award, Best Supporting Actor, 2002; San Diego Film Critics Society Award, 1997.

**BUSH Barbara Pierce,** b. 8 June 1925, Rye, New York, USA. Former First Lady of USA. m. George Bush, 1945, 4 sons, 1 daughter. Education: Smith College. Appointments: Various committees and councils dealing with literature and cancer care; President, Ladies of the Senate, 1981-88; Member, Staff Office of George Bush, 1992-. Honours: Outstanding Mother of the Year, 1984; Numerous honours degrees, Distinguished Leadership, United Negro College Fund, 1986; Distinguished American Woman, Mount St Joseph College, 1987. Publication: Barbara Bush: A Memoir, 1994. Address: 490 E L'Enfant Plaza, SW, Room 6125, Washington, DC 20594, USA.

**BUSH Duncan (Eric),** b. 6 Apr 1946, Cardiff, Wales. Poet; Writer; Teacher. m. Annette Jane Weaver, 4 June 1981, 2 sons. Education: BA, 1st Class Honours, in English and European Literature, Warwick University, 1978; Exchange Scholarship, Duke University, USA, 1976-77; DPhil, Research in English Literature, Wadham College, Oxford, 1978-81. Appointments: European Editor, The Kansas Quarterly & Arkansas Review; Co-editor, The Amsterdam Review; Writing Tutor with various institutions. Publications: Aquarium, 1983; Salt, 1985; Black Faces, Red Mouths, 1986; The Genre of Silence, 1987; Glass Shot, 1991; Masks, 1994; The Hook, 1997; Midway, 1998. Editor: On Censorship, 1985. Contributions to: BBC and periodicals. Honours: Eric Gregory Award for Poetry, 1978; Barbara Campion Memorial Award for Poetry, 1982; Welsh Arts Council Prizes for Poetry, Arts Council of Wales Book of the Year, 1995, for Masks. Memberships: Welsh Academy; Society of Authors. Address: 15 Rue de Fischbach, Blaschette, L-7391, Luxembourg.

**BUSH George Herbert Walker,** b. 12 June 1924, Milton, USA. American Politician. m. Barbara Pierce, 1945, 4 sons, 1 daughter. Education: Phillips Academy, Andover, Massachusetts; Yale University. Appointments: Naval Carrier Pilot, 1942-45; Co-Founder, Director, Zapata Petroleum Corporation, 1953-59; Founder, President, Zapata Offshore Corporation, 1956-64, Chair, 1964-66; Member, House of Representatives, 7th District of Texas, 1967-71; Permanent Representative to UN, 1971-72; Chair, Republican National Committee, 1973-74; Head, US Liaison Office, Peking, 1974-75; Director, CIA, 1976-77; Vice President, USA, 1981-89, President, USA, 1989-93. Publications: Looking Forward: An Autobiography (with Victor Gold), 1988; A World Transformed (with Brent Scowcroft), 1998; All the Best, George Bush, 1999. Honours include: Several honorary degrees; Churchill Award, 1991; Honorary GCB, 1993. Address: Suite 900, 10000 Memorial Drive, Houston, TX 77024-3422, USA.

**BUSH George W,** b. 6 July 1946, USA. President of the United States of America. m. Laura Lane Welch, twin daughters. Education: Bachelor's Degree, History, Yale University; Master of Business Administration, Harvard University. Appointments: F-102 Pilot, Texas Air National Guard; Founder and Manager, Spectrum 7 Energy Corporation (merged with Harken Energy Corporation, 1986), Midland Texas; Director, Harken Energy Corporation; Professional Baseball Team Executive with Texas Rangers, 1989-94; Elected Governor of Texas, 1994; Re-elected, 1998; Elected President of the United States, 2001-2004, re-elected 2004-. Address: The White House, Washington, DC 20500, USA.

**BUSH Kate (Catherine),** b. 30 July 1958, Bexleyheath, Kent, England. Singer; Songwriter. Education: Voice, dance and mime lessons. Career: Limited live performances include: Tour Of Life, Europe, 1979; Secret Policeman's Third Ball, London, 1987; Television appearances include: Bringing It All Back Home documentary, 1991; Writer, director, actress, film The

Line, The Cross And The Curve, 1994. Recordings (mostly self-composed): Albums: The Kick Inside, 1978; Lionheart, 1978; Never For Ever (Number 1, UK), 1980; The Dreaming, 1982; Hounds Of Love (Number 1, UK), 1985; The Whole Story (Number 1, UK), 1987; The Sensual World (Number 2, UK), 1989; This Womans Work, 1990; The Red Shoes (Number 2, UK), 1993; Contributor, Games Without Frontiers, Peter Gabriel, 1980; Two Rooms - Celebrating The Songs Of Elton John And Bernie Taupin, 1991; Singles include: Wuthering Heights (Number 1, UK), 1978; The Man With The Child In His Eyes, 1978; Wow, 1979; Breathing, 1980; Babooshka, 1980; Army Dreamers, 1980; Sat In Your Lap, 1981; Running Up That Hill, 1985; Cloudbusting, 1985; Hounds Of Love, 1986; Experiment IV, 1986; Don't Give Up, duet with Peter Gabriel, 1986; This Woman's Work (from film soundtrack She's Having A Baby), 1988; The Sensual World, 1989; Moments Of Pleasure, 1993; Rubberband Girl, 1993; Man I Love, 1994; The Red Shoes, 1994. Honours: Ivor Novello Awards, Outstanding British Lyric, The Man With The Child In His Eyes, 1979; BRIT Award, Best British Female Artist, 1987. Address: PO Box 120, Welling, Kent, DA16 3DA, England.

**BUSH Laura Lane Welch,** b. 4 November 1986, Midland, Texas, USA. m. George W Bush, 1977, 2 Daughters, 1981.Education: Bachelor's degree, Education, Southern Methodist University, 1968; Masters degree, Library Science, University of Texas, Austin, 1973. Career: School Teacher; Librarian; First Lady, Texas; First Lady, United States, 2001-. TV Appeerences: A&E Biography: George W Bush - Son Also Rises, 2000; Express Yourself, 2001; Last Party, 2001; Intimate Portrait, 2003; Larry King Live, 2003; The Tonight Show with Jay Leno, 2004.

**BUSH Ronald,** b. 16 June 1946, Philadelphia, Pennsylvania, USA. Professor of American Literature; Writer. m. Marilyn Wolin, 14 December 1969, 1 son. Education: BA, University of Pennsylvania, 1968; BA, Cambridge University, 1970; PhD, Princeton University, 1974. Appointments: Assistant to Associate Professor, Harvard University, 1974-82; Associate Professor, 1982-85; Professor, 1985-97, California Institute of Technology; Visiting Fellow, Exeter College, Oxford, 1994-95; Drue Heinz Professor of American Literature, Oxford University, 1997-; Visiting Fellow, American Civilization Program, Harvard University, 2004. Publications: The Genesis of Ezra Pound's Cantos, 1976; T S Eliot: A Study in Character and Style, 1983; T S Eliot: The Modernist in History (editor), 1991; Prehistories of the Future: The Primitivist Project and the Culture of Modernism (co-editor), 1995; Claiming the Stones/ Naming the Bones: Cultural Property and the Negotiation of National and Ethnic Identity (co-editor), 2002. Contributions to: Scholarly books and journals. Honours: National Endowment for the Humanities fellowships, 1977-78, 1992-93. Address: St John's College, Oxford OX1 3JP, England.

**BUSH Stephen Frederick,** b. 6 May 1939, Bath, England. University Professor; Entrepreneur. m. Gillian Mary, 1 son, 1 daughter. Education: Senior Scholar, 1958, Starred First Class Honours in Engineering, 1960, Research Scholar, 1961, MA, PhD, 1965, Trinity College Cambridge; SM, Control Engineering, Massachusetts Institute of Technology, 1960-61; MSc, University of Manchester, 1979. Appointments: Technical Officer, Section Manager, Group Manager, Process Technology Group, ICI Corporate Laboratory, 1963-71; Head, Systems Technology Department, ICI Europa Ltd, 1971-79; Professor of Polymer Engineering, 1979-2003, Head of Centre for Manufacture, 2000-, Professor of Process Manufacture, 2004-, University of Manchester Institute of Science and Technology (UMIST); Consultant to many companies including: ICI,

Cookson Group (USA), United Biscuits, Terrys-Suchard, Lucas, Curver Ltd, Founder and Managing Director, Prosyma Research, 1987-; Executive Chairman, NEPPCO Ltd, 2000-; Director, Surgiplas Ltd, 2001-. Publications: About 200 papers and 20 granted patents on the science and economics of process manufacture include: Fibre Reinforced Polymer Compositions and Process and Apparatus for their production (patent), 1988; On the Importance of Manufacture to the Economy, 1999; Scale, Order and Complexity in Polymer Processing, 2000; Guest contributor to TV and Radio current affairs programmes including: Moral Maze, Straw Poll; Newsnight, Panorama and the Today programme. Honours include: Sir George Nelson Prize for Applied Mechanics, Cambridge; Senior Moulton Medal, Institution of Chemical Engineers, 1969; Sir George Beilby Medal and Prize, Royal Society of Chemistry and the Metals Society, 1979; Fellowships: Institution of Mechanical Engineers; Institution of Chemical Engineers; Plastics and Rubber Institute; Institute of Materials; Royal Society of Arts and Manufactures. Memberships: Council, Institution of Mechanical Engineers, 1978-81; Council of Plastics and Rubber Institute, 1985-87; Vice-Chairman, Campaign for an Independent Britain, 1990-98; Council, Manchester Statistical Society, 2001-. Address: Genval House, Millstone Close, Poynton, Cheshire SK12 1XS, England. E-mail: stephen.f.bush@umist.ac.uk

**BUSSARD Janice Wingeier,** b. 2 March 1925, Lowell, Michigan, USA. Retired Educator; Inventor. m. James W Bussard, 4 daughters. Education: BS, Western Michigan University, 1946; Certificate, Secondary Education Teacher, Michigan Education Teacher. Appointments: High School Teacher, 1946-86; Inventor in the area of holography with one Canadian patent and several US patents, 1989-98; Manufacturer of holographic labels for security, authentication and decoration for applications to any substrate. Address: 201 North Fruitport Road, Spring Lake, MI 49456, USA.

**BUSSELL Darcy,** b. 27 April 1969, London, England. Ballerina. m. Angus Forbes, 1997, 1 daughter. Education: Royal Ballet School. Career: Birmingham Royal Ballet, then Sadlers Wells, 1987; Soloist; Royal Ballet, 1988, first solo, 1989; Principal, 1989-. Appearances include: The Spirit of Fugue, created for her by David Bintley; Swan Lake; The Nutcracker; The Prince of the Pagodas; Cinderella; Sleeping Beauty; Bloodlines; Romeo and Juliet; Giselle; Raymonda; Numerous appearances on TV; Guest with other ballet companies in Paris, St Petersburg and New York. Publications: My Life in Dance, 1998; Favourite Ballet Stories; The Young Dancer. Honours: Prix de Lausanne, 1989; Dancer of the Year, Dance and Dancers Magazine, 1990; Sir James Garreras Award, Variety Club of Great Britain, 1991; Evening Standard Ballet Award, 1991; Cosmopolitan Achievement Award, 1991; OBE, 1995. Address: The Royal Opera House, Covent Garden, London, WC2E 9DD, England.

**BUTCHER Raymond Michael,** b. Portsmouth, England. Teacher; Jazz Musician. Education: BA (Hons) Music, Kingston University, 1992-95; PGCE (UCE), Music Secondary Teaching, 1998. Appointments: Teaching Posts: George Dixon School, Shenley Court, 2000-2003, Supply Teacher, 2003-; Music career: Played many jazz and blues festivals across Europe; Played for Diana, Princess of Wales, on her visit to Portsmouth; Trumpeter, National Youth Jazz Orchestra, 1995; Played with The Five Keys; Trumpeter, Show Band of cruise liner, Holland/ America Line, 1996; Trumpeter in touring band, King Pleasure and the Biscuit Boys; Jazz Musician, improviser and composer, worked with Steve Ajao, Andy Hamilton, Ron Kenoly, Adlan Cruz, Beverley Knight, Noel Richards Worship Band, Hyde Park March for Jesus, Angel Lee; First Trumpet, International

Christian Embassy of Jerusalem Orchestra. Recording: Currently working on album due for release 2004: War on the Saints, free jazz and own compositions with Raymond Butcher, trumpet; Miles Levin, drums; Peter Daly and Edgar Marcias, piano; Mike Green, bass; Chris Bowden and Simeon Murray, saxophones; Carina Round, The Disconnection CD; Solo trumpet, world premiere of Stephen Berkhoff's Requiem for Ground Zero. Honours: Played for Ariel Sharon, Israeli Prime Minister, Jerusalem, 2003. Address: 835 (b) Hagley Road West, Quinton, Birmingham B32 1AD, England.

**BUTLER (Frederick) Guy,** b. 21 January 1918, Cradock, Cape Province, South Africa. Retired Professor of English Literature; Poet; Writer; Dramatist. m. Jean Murray Satchwell, 7 December 1940, 4 children. Education: BA, 1938, MA, 1939, Rhodes University; BA, 1947, MA, 1951, Brasenose College, Oxford. Appointments: Schoolmaster, St John's College, Johannesburg, 1940; Lecturer, University of Witwatersrand, 1948-50; Senior Lecturer, 1951, Professor of English Literature, 1952-86, Rhodes University. Publications: Stranger to Europe 1939-49, 1952, with additional poems, 1960; A Book of South African Verse (editor), 1959; South of the Zambezi: Poems from South Africa, London and New York, 1966; On First Seeing Florence, 1968; Selected Poems, 1975, with additional poems, 1989; Songs and Ballads, 1978; Pilgrimage to Dias Cross, 1987; Out of the African Ark: Animal Poems (editor with David Butler), 1988; A Rackety Colt (novel), 1989; The Magic Tree: South African Stories in Verse (editor with Jeff Opland), 1989; Guy Butler: Essays and Lectures (edited by Stephen Watson), 1994; Collected Poems (edited by Lawrence Wright), 1999. The Prophetic Nun, 2000. Contributions to: Various publications. Honours: 1st Prize, 1949, 2nd Prize, 1953, for Poetry, South African Broadcasting Corporation; Honorary DLitt, University of Natal, 1970, University of Witwatersrand, 1984, Rhodes University, 1994; Central News Agency Award, 1976; Literary Award, Cape Tercentenary Foundation, 1981; Honorary DLitt et Phil, University of South Africa, 1989; Gold Medal, English Academy of South Africa, 1989; Lady Usher Prize for Literature, 1992; Freedom of the City of Grahamstown, 1994. Memberships: English Academy of South Africa, honorary life member; Shakespeare Society of South Africa, national president, 1985. Address: High Corner, 122 High Street, Grahamstown, Cape Province 0461, South Africa.

**BUTLER Michael Gregory,** b. 1 November 1935, Nottingham, England. Professor of Modern German Literature; Writer; Poet. m. Jean Mary Griffith, 31 December 1961, 1 son, 1 daughter. Education: BA, 1957, MA, 1960, Cambridge University; DipEd, Oxford University, 1958; FIL, 1967; PhD (CNAA), 1974; Litt.D., Cambridge University, 1998. Appointments: Assistant Master, King's School, Worcester, 1958-61, Reuchlin Gymnasium, Pforzheim, Germany, 1961-62; Head of German, Ipswich School, England, 1962-70; Lecturer in German, 1970-80, Senior Lecturer, 1980-86, Head, Department of German Studies, 1984, Professor of Modern German Literature, 1986-, Head, School of Modern Languages, 1988-93, Public Orator, 1997-2005, University of Birmingham. Publications: Nails and Other Poems, 1967; Samphire (co-editor), 3 volumes, 1968-83; The Novels of Max Frisch, 1975; Englische Lyrik der Gegenwart (editor with Ilsabe Arnold Dielewicz), 1981; The Plays of Max Frisch, 1985; Frisch: 'Andorra', 1985, revised edition, 1994; Rejection and Emancipation - Writing in German-speaking Switzerland 1945-1991 (editor with M Pender), 1991; The Narrative Fiction of Heinrich Böll, 1994; The Making of Modern Switzerland, 1948-1998 (ed.) 2000; The Challenge of German Culture (ed.), 2000. Contributions to: Migrant; Mica (California); Poetry Review; BBC; Sceptre Press; Vagabond (Munich); Universities Poetry; Many reviews in the Times

Literacy Supplement. Honour: Taras Schevchenko Memorial Prize, 1961; Cross of the Order of Merit, Federal Republic of Germany, 1999. Address: 45 Westfields, Catshill, Bromsgrove B61 9HJ, England.

**BUTLER (Sir) Richard Clive,** b. 12 January 1929, London, England. Retired Farmer and Company Director. m. Susan, 2 sons, 1 daughter. Education: Eton College; MA in Agriculture, Pembroke College, Cambridge. Appointments: Board Member, NFU Mutual Insurance Society, 1985-96; Main Board Non-Executive Director, NatWest Bank, 1986-96; Board Member, Avon Insurance, 1990-96. Honours: DL, Essex, 1972; KB, 1981; Master, Worshipful Company of Skinners, 1994-95; Master, Worshipful Company of Farmers, 1997-98; Trustee, The Butler Trust. Memberships: Life Member, Council of the National Farmers' Union for England and Wales. Address: Gladfen Hall, Halstead, Essex CO9 1RN, England.

**BUTLIN Ron,** b. 17 November 1949, Edinburgh, Scotland; Poet. Writer. m. Regula Staub (the writer Regi Claire), 18 June 1993. Education: MA, Dip CDAE, Edinburgh University. Appointments: Writer-in-Residence, Edinburgh University, 1983, 1985, Midlothian Region, 1990-91, Stirling University, 1993; Writer-in-Residence, The Craigmillar Literacy Trust, 1997-98; Examiner in Creative Writing, Stirling University, 1997-; Writer in Residence, St Andrews University, 1998-. Publications: Creatures Tamed by Cruelty, 1979; The Exquisite Instrument, 1982; The Tilting Room, 1984; Ragtime in Unfamiliar Bars, 1985; The Sound of My Voice, 1987; Histories of Desire, 1995; Night Visits, 1997; When We Jump We Jump High! (editor), 1998; Faber Book of Twentieth Century Scottish Poetry; Our Piece of Good Fortune, 2003; No More Angels, 2004; Vivaldi and the Number 3, 2004; Without a Backward Glance: New and Selected Poems 2005; Good Angel, Bad Angel (opera), 2005. Contributions to: Sunday Herald; Scotsman; Edinburgh Review; Poetry Review; Times Literary Supplement. Honours: Writing Bursaries, 1977, 1987, 1990, 1994, 2003; Scottish Arts Council Book Awards, 1982, 1984, 1985; Scottish Canadian Writing Fellow, 1984; Poetry Book Society Recommendation, 1985; Prix Millepages, 2004 (Best Foreign Novel); Prix Lucioles, 2005 (Best Foreign Novel). Membership: Scottish Arts Council, literature committee, 1995-96. Address: 7W Newington Place, Edinburgh EH9 1QT, Scotland.

**BUTTERWORTH Arthur Eckersley,** b. 4 August 1923, Manchester, England. Composer; Conductor. m. Diana Stewart, 2 daughters. Education: Royal Manchester College of Music. Career: Member Scottish National Orchestra, 1949-54; Member, Hallé Orchestra, 1955-61; Conductor, Huddersfield Philharmonic Orchestra, 1962-93; Teacher, Huddersfield School of Music. Compositions include: Symphony No 1 op 15, Cheltenham Festival, 1957 and BBC Proms, 1958; Symphony No 2 op 25, Bradford, 1965; Organ Concerto, 1973; Violin Concerto, 1978, Symphony No 3 op 52, Manchester, 1979; Piano Trio, Cheltenham Festival Commission, 1983; Symphony No 4 op 72, Manchester, 1986; Odin Symphony for Brass op 76, National Brass Band Festival London, 1989; Northern Light op 88, Leeds, 1991; Concerto alla Veneziana op 93, York, 1992; Viola Concerto op 82, Manchester, 1993; Mancunians op 96, Hallé Orchestra Commission, Manchester, 1995; 'Cello Concerto op 98, Huddersfield, 1994; Guitar Concerto op 109, Leeds, 2000; Symphony No 5 op 115, Manchester, 2003. Honour: MBE, 1995. Membership: Vice-President, British Music Society. Address: Pohjola, Dales Avenue, Embsay, Skipton, North Yorkshire, BD23 6PE, England.

**BUXTON Judy,** b. 16 December 1961, Sydney, Australia. Artist; Painter. m. Jeremy Annear, 2 daughters. Education:

Foundation Diploma, Art and Design, Torquay College, Devon, 1986-87; BA Hons, Fine Art (1st class), Falmouth College of Art, 1987-90; PG RA Dip, Royal Academy Schools, 1990-93. Appointments: Artist; Painter; Visiting Lecturer, Falmouth College of Arts, 1995; Established Chapel House studio courses, 1996. Publications: New Millennium Gallery Exhibition Catalogue, 2003; William Packer Review, Hunting Art Prizes, Royal College of Art, 2003; Living on the Edge, 2004; Pip Palmer Galleries, 2004; Catching the Wave, Art & Artists in Cornwall, Tom Cross, Halsgrove Press. Honours: Freedom of the City of London, 1993; Worshipful Company Painter-Stainers, 1993; Royal Water Colour Award, 1993; David Murray Travel Scholarship, 1993; Natwest Art Prize, 1997. Memberships: Newlyn Society of Artists; Royal Academy Schools Alumni. Address: Chapel House, Garras, Helston, Cornwall, TR12 6LN, England.

**BUZZONI Alberto,** b. 4 November 1958, Ro Di Ferrara, Italy. Astronomer. m. Claribel Garcia. Education: Doctor of Astronomy, University of Bologna, Italy, 1982. Appointments: Associate Professor, Bologna Astronomical Observatory, Italy; Tutor, 15 doctorate thesis in Astronomy, Physics and Philosophy of Science. Publications: 90 articles on international scientific reviews. Memberships: Italian Astronomical Society, 1985; International Astronomical Union, 1997. Address: Oss Astronomico di Bologna, Via Ranzani 1, I 40127 Bologna, Italy. Website: www.bo.astro.it/~eps/home.html

**BYATT Dame Antonia Susan,** b. 24 August 1936, England. Author. m. (1) Ian C R Byatt, 1959, dissolved 1969, 1 son (deceased), 1 daughter, (2) Peter J Duffy, 1969, 2 daughters. Education: The Mount School, York, Newnham College, Cambridge; Bryn Mawr College, USA; Somerville College, Oxford. Appointments: Westminster Tutors, 1962-65, Extra-Mural Lecturer, University of London, 1962-71; Part-time Lecturer, Department of Liberal Studies, Central School of Art and Design, 1965-69, Lecturer, 1972-81, Tutor of Admissions, 1980-82, Assistant Tutor, 1977-80, Senior Lecturer, 1981-83, Department of English, University College London; Associate, Newnham College, Cambridge, 1977-82; Full time writer, 1983-; External Assessor in Literature, Central School of Art and Design, External Examiner, UEA; Regular Reviewer and contributor to press, radio and TV. Publications: Shadow of the Sun, 1964, 1991; Degrees of Freedom, 1965, 1994; The Game, 1967; Wordsworth and Coleridge in Their Time, 1970, Unruly Times, 1989; The Virgin in the Garden, 1978; Still Life, 1985; Sugar and Other Stories, 1987; Possession: A Romance, 1990; George Eliot: The Mill on the Floss (editor), George Eliot: Selected Essays and Other Writings (editor), 1990; Passions of the Mind (essays), 1991; Angels and Insects, 1992; The Matisse Stories, 1993; The Djinn in the Nightingale's Eye: Five Fairy Stories, 1994; Imagining Characters (with Ignês Sodré), 1995; Babel Tower, 1996; The Oxford Book of English Short Stories (editor), 1998; Elementals: Stories of Fire and Ice, 1998; The Biographer's Tale, 2000; On Histories and Stories, 2000; Portraits in Fiction, 2001; Bird Hand Book (jointly), 2001; A Whistling Woman, 2002; Little Black Book of Stories (short stories), 2003; O Henry Prize Stories (contributed short story, The Thing in the Forest), 2003; Author of varied literary criticism, articles, reviews and broadcasts. Honours: PEN Macmillan Silver Pen of Fiction, 1985; Booker Prize for Fiction, 1990; Irish Times-Aer Lingus Literature Prize, 1990; CBE, 1990; Premio Malaparte Award, Capri, 1995; Mythopoeic Fantasy Award for Adult Literature, 1998; DBE, 1999; Toepfer Foundation Shakespeare Prize for contributions to British Culture, 2002; Chevalier de l'Ordre des Arts et des Lettres, France, 2003; Fellow, English Association, 2004; Hon DLitt: University of Bradford, 1987; University of Durham, 1991;

University of York, 1991; University of Nottingham, 1992; University of Liverpool, 1993; University of Portsmouth, 1994; University of London, 1995; University of Cambridge, 1999; University of Sheffield, 2000; Honorary Fellow: Newnham College, Cambridge, 1999; London Institute, 2000; UCL, 2004; University of Kent, 2004. Memberships: Panel of Judges, Hawthornden Prize, BBC's Social Effects of TV Advisory Group, 1974-77; Communications and Cultural Studies Board, CNAA, 1978-84; Committee of Management, Society of Authors, 1984-88 (Chair, 1986-88); Creative and Performing Arts Board, 1985-87; Kingman Committee on English Language, 1987-88; Advisory Board, Harold Hyam Wingate Fellowship, 1988-92; Member, Literary Advisory Panel British Council, 1990-98; London Library Committee, 1990-; Board British Council, 1993-98. Address: c/o Rogers, Coleridge & White, 20 Powis Mews, London W11 1JN, England.

**BYE Erik,** b. 13 September 1945, Oslo, Norway. Senior Scientist. m. Kirsten Offenberg, 2 daughters. Education: Cand real, Chemistry, 1972, Dr philos, 1976, University of Oslo. Appointments: Scientific Assistant in Chemistry, University of Oslo, 1972-78; Postdoctoral studies, ETH, Zurich, 1977; Scientist, Occupational Hygiene, National Institute of Occupational Health, 1979-; Guest Researcher, SINTEF, Oslo, 1987. Publications: Scientific publications in international journals of chemistry and occupational hygiene. Address: National Institute of Occupational Health, PO Box 8149 Dep, N-0033 Oslo, Norway. E-mail: erik.bye@stami.no

**BYKOV Anatoly,** b. 12 September 1946, Iskitim, Novosibirsk District, Russia. Artist; Painter. m. Irina, 1 son. Education: "I Repin" Institute of Painting, Sculpture and Architecture, Leningrad Department of Art, 1980. Career: Painter, USSR Artistic Fund, 1981-82; Participant in over 50 exhibitions including: Cologne, Germany, 1984; Central Exhibition Hall, Moscow, Russia, 1986; International Exhibition, Hanover, Germany, 1990; Personal Exhibition, Central House of Scientist, Moscow, 1992; Alta Norway, 1992; Several works acquired by Academy of Fine Arts, Artistic Fund of the USSR, Khimsky Art Gallery, Museum of Tobolsk; Many works purchased by galleries and private collectors in Norway, Japan, Austria, Germany. Publications include: Works featured in: Catalogues: 40 Anniversary of Great Victory, 1985; Poesy in Painting, 1994, Academy of Sciences Exhibition, 1996, Khimki Art Gallery, 1996; Newspapers: Moscow Artist, 1990, Altaposten, Norway, 1992, Culture, 1992, Rural Youth, 1993, Vremya, 2002, Vestnik intellektyalnoj sobstvennosti, 2003; Saur Allgemeines Kunstler-lexikon, Reference Book, 1997; Sokolniki Company Calendar, 2002; Book: The Academy of Arts, 1982. Honours: Honorary Diploma, Monuments Protection, 1989; Message of Thanks, President of the Academy of Science of Russia. Membership: Union of Artists, USSR, 1985-; Member, International Confederation of Artists, Moscow Union of Painters, Russia, 1994; Listed in The Contemporary Who's Who, ABI, 2003. Address: Bulv Donskogo Dom 9 Korp 1, Kv 307 Moscow 117216, Russia. E-mail: pavel-bykov@yandex.ru Website: www.chat.ru/~chamois

**BYRNE Gabriel,** b. 1950, Dublin, Ireland. Actor. m. Ellen Barken, 1988, divorced, 1 son, 1 daughter. Education: University College, Dublin. Appointments: Archaeologist; Teacher; Actor. Creative Works: Films include: Hanna K Gothic; Julia and Julia; Siesta; Miller's Crossing; Hakon Hakenson; Dark Obsession; Cool World; A Dangerous Woman; Little Women; Usual Suspects; Frankie Starlight; Dead Man; Last of the High Kings; Mad Dog Time; Somebody is Waiting; The End of Violence (director); Tony's Story; Polish Wedding; This is the Dead; The Man in the Iron Mask; Quest for Camelot; An Ideal Husband;

Enemy of the State; Stigmata; End of Days; Spider; Ghost Ship; Shade, 2003; Vanity Fair, 2004; Co-Producer, In the Name of the Father. Address: c/o ICM, 8942 Wilshire Boulevard, Beverly Hills, CA 96211, USA.

# C

**CAAN James,** b. 26 March 1940, Bronx, New York, USA. Actor; Director. m. (1) DeeJay Mathis, 1961, 1 daughter, (2) Sheila Ryan, 1976, 1 son, (3) Linda O'Gara, 1995, 2 children. Creative Works: Films include: Irma La Douce, 1963; Lady in a Cage, 1964; The Glory Guys, 1965; Countdown, 1967; Games, 1967; Eldorado, 1967; Journey to Shiloh, 1968; Submarine XI, 1968; Man Without Mercy, 1969; The Rain People, 1969; Rabbit Run, 1970; T R Baskin, 1971; The Godfather, 1972; Slither, 1973; Cinderella Liberty, 1975; Freebie and the Bean, 1975; The Gambler, 1975; Funny Lady, 1975; Rollerball, 1975; The Killer Elite, 1975; Harry and Walter Go to New York, 1976; Silent Movie, 1976; A Bridge Too Far, 1977; Another Man, Another Chance, 1977; Comes a Horseman, 1978; Chapter Two, 1980; Thief, 1982; Kiss Me Goodbye, 1983; Bolero, 1983; Gardens of Stone, 1988; Alien Nation, 1989; Dad, 1989; Dick Tracy, 1990; Misery, 1991; For the Boys, 1991; Dark Backward, 1991; Honeymoon in Vegas, 1992; Flesh and Bone, 1993; The Program, 1994; North Star, 1995; Boy Called Hate, 1995; Eraser, 1996; Bulletproof, 1996; Bottle Rocket, 1996; This Is My Father, 1997; Poodle Springs, 1997; Blue Eyes, 1998; The Yards, 1999; The Way of the Gun, 1999; In the Boom Boom Room, 2000; Luckytown, 2000; Viva Las Nowhere, 2000; In the Shadows, 2001; Night at the Golden Eagle, 2002; City of Ghosts, 2002; Dogville, 2003; Dallas 362, 2003; This Thing of Ours, 2003; Jericho Mansions, 2003; Elf, 2003; Director, Actor, Hide in Plain Sight, 1980; Director, Violent Streets, 1981; Starred in television movie, Brian's Song, 1971; The Warden, 2000; Numerous other TV appearances. Address: c/o Fred Specktor, Endeavor, 9701 Wilshire Boulevard, 10th Floor, Beverly Hills, CA 90212, USA.

**CABALLE Monserrat,** b. 12 April 1933, Barcelona, Spain. Soprano Opera Singer. m. Bernabé Marti, 1 son, 1 daughter. Education: Conservatorio del Liceo; Private studies. Appointments: North American Debut, Manon, Mexico City, 1964; US Debut, Carnegie Hall, 1965; Appearances in several opera houses and at numerous festivals. Creative Works: Lucrezia Borgia; La Traviata; Salome; Aida. Honours: Most Excellent and Illustrious Dobna and Cross of Isabella the Catholic; Commandeur des Arts et des Lettres, 1986; Numerous honorary degrees, awards and medals. Address: c/o Columbia Artists Management Inc, 165 West 57th Street, New York, NY 10019, USA.

**CABRERA Leticia,** b. 29 September 1954, Mexico City, Mexico. Plant Systematist. m. Gregg Dieringer, 2 sons. Education: BS, Science Faculty, National Autonomous University of Mexico, 1985; PhD, Department of Botany, University of Texas at Austin, USA, 1992. Appointments: Associate Investigator, National Institute for the Investigations of Biological Resources, Mexico City, 1986; Teaching Assistant, University of Texas at Austin, 1988-92; Biology Instructor, Austin Community College, 1991; Researcher, Institute of Ecology, Veracruz, Mexico, 1992-93; Assistant Professor, Western Illinois University, 1995-99; Assistant Professor, University of Texas at Brownsville, 1999-2003; Adjunct Professor, Northwest Missouri State University, Missouri, 2003-. Publications: Numerous professional and general publications, translations and presentations. Honours: Several grants and fellowships; Academic Scholarship, Consejo Nacional de Ciencia y Tecnologia, 1987-90; Walton Scholarship, University of Virginia, 1990; Memorial Fellowship for scholastic achievement, University of Texas at Austin, 1992; 2 Hispanic Scholarship, Latino Initiative Programs, 2000. Memberships: Botanical Society of America; American Society of Plant Taxonomists; Torrey Botanical Society. Address: Department of Biological Sciences, Northwest Missouri State University, 800 University Drive, Maryville MO 64468, USA. E-mail: cabrera@mail.nwmissouri.edu

**CABRIJAN Tomislav Viktor,** b. 22 October 1934. Professor of Internal Medicine. m. Ivanka Tusek, 1 son, 1 daughter. Education: MD, Zagreb, Croatia, 1959; Internal Medicine Specialist, University of Zagreb, 1968; PhD, University of Zagreb, 1975; Full Professor, Internal Medicine, 1987. Appointments: Ward Internist, Endocrinologist, Sisters of Mercy, University Hospital of Zagreb, 1968-70; Head, Center for Diabetes, Department of Endocrinology, 1970-90; Head, Department of Endocrinology Diabetes and Metabolic Diseases, 1990; Acting Director, Sisters of Mercy, University Hospital of Zagreb, 1990. Publications: Obesity and Apnea Syndrome, 1993; How to Care About Your Diabetes, 1995; Urgent States in Endocrinology, 1996; Rational Diagnosis and Therapy in Endocrinology, 2000. Honour: Fellowship, Alexander von Humboldt Foundation, Germany, 1972, 1975, 1978, 1982, 1989, 1998; Yearly Award for Science from the Parliament of the Republic of Croatia, 2000. Memberships: German Diabetes Association; Croatian Academy of Medical Sciences; European Association for the Study of Diabetes; American Endocrine Society; European Federation of Endocrine Societies. Address: Petrova 110, 10 000 Zagreb, Croatia.

**CACKOVIC Hinko,** b. Zagreb, Croatia. Resident in Berlin, Germany 1970-. Scientist; Physicist; Artist; Photographer (Art); Painter; Sculptor (mixed media, metalwork). m. Jasna Loboda-Cackovic. Education: Diploma, Physics, University of Zagreb, Croatia, 1962; MSc, Solid State Physics, University of Zagreb, 1964; PhD, Fritz-Haber Institut der Max-Planck-Gesellschaft, Berlin-Dahlem, Germany, and University of Zagreb, 1970. Appointments: Scientist, Institute of Physics, University of Zagreb, 1962-65; Scientist, Atom Institute Ruder Boskovic, Zagreb, 1967-71; Postdoctoral, 1970-72, Scientist, 1965-67, 1970-80, Fritz-Haber Institut der Max-Planck-Gesellschaft, Germany; Scientist, Technical University, Berlin, Germany, 1980-95. Publications: Over 55 scientific articles to professional journals, including: Physics of polymers; Synthetic and biological molecules; Polymer liquid crystals; Self-ordering of the matter; Memory of solid and fluid matter; Order/ disorder phenomena in the atomic, molecular and colloidal dimensions; Mutual dependence of order between atomic and colloidal entities; Development of small and wide angle x-rays scattering analysis and of broad line nuclear magnetic resonance analysis; Development of physical instruments; Works of Art in professional journals and books; Photographs cutting out parts of reality to change it; Creative activity in photography/ sculpturing and science (physics, chemistry) is influenced by literature music, astrophysics; New aesthetic spaces are forming, through the fusion of art and science, in sculptures built up by physical instruments and machines; Developing of Universal Art including mentioned multidisciplinary fields; Intention to contribute: to synthesis of science art and harmony, to the ethic and aesthetic part of human living and activity, to freedom in all its facets through culture in the widest sense; Photographs presented at numerous exhibitions in Germany, Austria, France, Switzerland, 1991- and in Internet galleries, 1998-; Innovative works, two-artist group JASHIN, with Jasna Loboda-Cackovic from 1997; Permanent art representations: Gallery Kleiner Prinz, Baden-Baden, Germany, 1991-; Cyber Museum at wwwARTchannel, www.art-channel.net, 1999-; Virtual Gallery of Forschungs-Institut Bildender Künste, Germany, www.artgala.de, 1999-; Permanent representation of art and science biography by Brigitte Schellmann Who's Who in German ® (www.whoswho-german.de). Honours:

Two Euro honorary Prizes, Exhibitions, Dresden and Baden-Baden, Germany, 1994, 1995; Prize, for photography, 5th Open Art Prize, Bad Neuheim, Germany, 1995 and prize "Phoenix", First, Second, Third and Fourth, Photography Prize at International Internet Art Competitions, 1998, 2000, 2001, 2003; Distinguished Leadership Award, ABI, 2000; Grants: Technical University Berlin, Germany, 1965-67; Alexander von Humboldt Stiftung, Bad Godesberg, Germany, 1970-72; Max-Planck-Gesellschaft, Fritz-Haber-Institut, Berlin-Dahlem, Germany, 1972-73. Memberships: Deutsche Physikalische Gesellschaft, 1972-95; International Biographical Association, 1998-; Virtual Gallery, Forschungs-Institut Bildender Künste, 1999-; Europäischer Kulturkreis Baden-Baden, 2002-. Address: Im Dol 60, 14195 Berlin, Germany.

**CADBURY (Nicholas) Dominic,** b. 12 May 1940. Business Executive. m. Cecilia Sarah Symes, 1972, 3 daughters. Education: Eton College; Trinity College, Cambridge; Stanford University, USA. Appointments: Chief Executive, Cadbury Schweppes PLC, 1984-93, Chair, 1993-2000; Director, Economic Group, 1990-2003, Chair, 1994-2003; Joint Deputy Chair, Guinness, 1994-97, Deputy Chair, 1996-97; Joint Deputy Chair, EMI Group PLC, 1999-2004; President, Food and Drink Federation, 1999; Chair, Wellcome Trust, 2000-; Chair, Transense Techs, 2000-03; Non-Executive Director, Misys PLC, 2000-; Chancellor, University of Birmingham, 2002-. Memberships: Royal Mint Advisory Committee, 1986-94; President, Committee CBI, 1989-94; Food Association, 1989-2000; Stanford Advisory Council, 1989-95. Address: The Wellcome Trust, 183 Euston Road, London, NW1, England.

**CAESAR Anthony Douglass,** b. 3 April 1924, Southampton, England. Clerk in Holy Orders. Education: MA, MusB, FRCO, Magdalene College, Cambridge; St Stephen's House, Oxford. Appointments: RAF, 1943-46; Assistant Music Master, Eton College, 1948-51; Precentor, Radley College, 1952-59; Assistant Curate, St Mary Abbots, Kensington, 1961-65; Priest-in-Ordinary to The Queen, 1968-70; Chaplain, Royal School of Church Music, 1965-70; Assistant Secretary, Advisory Council for the Church's Ministry, 1965-70; Resident Priest, St Stephen's Church, Bournemouth, 1970-73; Precentor and Sacrist, 1974-79, Honorary Canon, 1975-76, 1979-91, Residentiary Canon, 1976-79, Winchester Cathedral; Sub-Dean of HM Chapels Royal, Deputy Clerk of The Closet, Sub-Almoner and Domestic Chaplain to The Queen, 1979-91; Chaplain, St Cross Hospital, Winchester, 1991-93. Publications: Co-Editor, New English Hymnal 1986, Church Music. Honours: John Stewart of Rannoch Scholar in Sacred Music, 1943; LVO, 1987; CVO, 1991; Extra Chaplain to The Queen, Canon Emeritus, Winchester Cathedral, 1991-. Address: 2 Old Kiln, Yarbridge, Brading, Sandown, Isle of Wight, PO36 0BP, England.

**CAFFREY Idris,** b. 16 November 1949, Rhayader, Powys. Education: Swansea College of Education, 1968-71. Publications: Pacing Backwards, 1996; Pathways, 1997; Other Places, 1998; Warm Rain, 2000; Departures and Returns, 2002. Address: 5 Lyndale, Wilnecote, Tamworth, B77 5DX, England.

**CAGE Nicolas (Nicholas Coppla),** b. 7 January 1964, Long Beach, California, USA. Actor. m. 1 son with Kristina Fulton, (1) Patricia Arquette, 1995, divorced 2000, (2) Lisa Marie Presley, 2002, divorced 2002, (3) Alice Kim, 2004, 1 son. Creative Works: Films include: Valley Girl, 1983; Rumble Fish; Racing With the Moon; The Cotton Club; Birdy; The Boy in Blue; Raising Arizona; Peggy Sue Got Married; Moonstruck; Vampire's Kiss; Killing Time; The Short Cut; Queens Logic; Wild of Heart; Wings of the Apache; Zandalee; Red Rock West; Guarding Tess; Honeymoon in Vegas; It Could Happen to You; Kiss of Death; Leaving Las Vegas; The Rock, 1996; The Funeral, 1996; Con Air, 1997; Face Off, 1997; Eight Millimeter, 1999; Bringing Out the Dead, 1999; Gone in 60 Seconds, 2000; The Family Man, 2001; Captain Corelli's Mandolin, 2001; Christmas Carol: The Movie (voice), 2001; Windtalkers, 2002; Sonny, 2002; Adaptation, 2002; Matchstick Men, 2003; Producer, The Life of David Gale, 2003; National Treasure, 2004. Honours include: Golden Globe Award, Best Actor, 1996; Academy Award, Best Actor, 1996; Lifetime Achievement Award, 1996; P J Owens Award, 1998; Charles A Crain Desert Palm Award, 2001. Address: Saturn Films, 9000 West Sunset Boulevard, Suite 911, West Hollywood, CA 90069, USA.

**CAGLAR Mine,** b. 14 November 1967, Turkey. Applied Probabilist. m. Mehmet Caglar, 1 son, 1 daughter. Education: BS, Middle East Technical University, 1989; MS, Bilkent University, 1991. Appointments: Assistant in Instruction, Princeton University, USA, 1992-97; Research Scientist, Bellcore, 1997-98; Assistant Professor of Mathematics, Koc University, Istanbul, Turkey, 1999-. Publications: Articles in scientific journals include: A Long Range-Dependent Workload Model for Packet Data Traffic, 2004. Memberships: Sigma Xi; Informs; Bernoulli Society. Address: Koc University, College of Arts and Sciences, Sariyer, Istanbul, Turkey 34450. Website: http://home.ku.edu.tr/~mcaglar

**CAIMBEUL Maoilios MacAonghais,** b. 23 March 1944, Isle of Skye, Scotland. Writer; Poet. m. Margaret Hutchison, 2 December 1971, 1 son. Education: BA, Edinburgh University; Teaching Diploma, Jordanhill College, Glasgow, 1978. Appointments: Gaelic Teacher, Tobermory High School, 1978-84; Gaelic Development Officer, Highlands and Islands Development Board, 1984-87; Writer, 1987-. Publications: Eileanan, 1980; Bailtean, 1987; A Càradh an Rathaid, 1988; An Aghaidh na Sìorraidheachd, (anthology with 7 other Gaelic poets), 1991; Saoghal Ùr, 2003. Contributions to: Gairm; Lines Review; Chapman; Cencrastus; Orbis; Poetry Ireland Review; Comhar; Gairfish; Baragab; Weekend Scotsman; West Highland Free Press; Anthologies: Air Ghleus 2, 1989; Twenty of the Best, 1990; The Patched Fool, 1991; Somhairle, Dàin is Deilbh, 1991; An Tuil, 1999; An Leabhar Mòr, PNE, 2002. Honours: Award, Gaelic Books Council Poetry Competition, 1978-79; Poetry/Fiction Prize, Gaelic Books Council, 1982-83. Membership: Scottish PEN. Address: 12 Flodigarry, Staffin, Isle of Skye, Iv51 GHZ.

**CAINE Michael (Sir) CBE (Maurice Joseph Micklewhite),** b. 14 March 1933, London, England. m. (1) Patricia Haines, divorced, 1 daughter; (2) Shakira Khatoon Baksh, 1 daughter. Career: British Army service in Berlin and Korea, 1951-53; Repertory theatres, Horsham and Lowestoft, 1953-55; Theatre Workshop, London, 1955; Acted in: Over 100 TV plays 1957-63; Films include: A Hill in Korea, 1956; Zulu, 1964; The Ipcress File, 1965; Alfie, 1966; The Wrong Box, 1966; Gambit, 1966; Funeral in Berlin, 1966; Billion Dollar Brain, 1967; Woman Times Seven, 1967; Deadfall, 1967; The Magus, 1968; Battle of Britain, 1968; Play Dirty, 1968; The Italian Job, 1969; Too Late the Hero, 1970; The Last Valley, 1970; Kidnapped, 1971; Pulp, 1971; Get Carter, 1971; Zee and Co, 1972; Sleuth, 1973; The Wilby Conspiracy, 1974; The Eagle Has Landed, The Man Who Would be King, 1975; A Bridge Too Far, The Silver Bears, 1976; The Swarm, California Suite, 1977; Ashanti, 1978; Beyond the Poseidon Adventure, 1979; The Island, 1979; Deathtrap, 1981; The Hand, 1981; Educating Rita, 1982; Jigsaw Man, 1982; The Honorary Consul, 1982; Blame it on Rio, 1983; Water, 1984; The Holcroft Covenant, 1984; Sweet Liberty, 1985; Mona Lisa, 1985; The Whistle Blower, 1985; Half Moon Street, 1986; The Fourth Protocol, 1986; Hannah and

# DICTIONARY OF INTERNATIONAL BIOGRAPHY

her Sisters (Academy Award), 1986; Surrender, 1987; Without a Clue, 1988; Jack the Ripper (TV, Golden Globe Award), 1988; Dirty Rotten Scoundrels, 1988; A Shock to the System, 1989; Bullseye, 1989; Noises Off, 1991; Blue Ice, 1992; The Muppet Christmas Carol, 1992; On Deadly Ground, 1993; World War II Then There Were Giants, 1994; Bullet to Beijing, 1995; Blood and Wine, 1996; Mandela and de Klerk, 1996; 20,000 Leagues Under the Sea, 1997; Shadowrun, 1997; Little Voice, 1998; The Debtors, 1999; The Cider House Rules; Curtain Call, 1999; Quills, 1999; Get Carter, 2000; Shiner, 2000; Last Orders, 2001; Quick Sands, 2001; The Quiet American, 2002; The Actors, 2003; Secondhand Lions, 2003; The Statement, 2003; Around the Bend, 2004; The Weather Man, 2005; Batman Begins, 2005; Bewitched, 2005. Publications: Michael Caine's File of Facts, 1987; Not Many People Know This, 1988; What's It All About, 1992; Acting in Film, 1993. Honours: CBE, 1992; Knighted by HM Queen Elizabeth II, 2000; Numerous awards, nominations and citations from film and TV industry institutes, including several Golden Globe and Academy awards. Address: International Creative Management, Oxford House, 76 Oxford Road, London W1R 1RB, England.

**CAIRD George,** b. 30 August 1950, Montreal Canada. Musician. m. (1) Sarah Verney, 3 sons, 1 daughter, (2) Jane Salmon, 1 daughter. Education: National Youth Orchestra of Great Britain, 1967-69; Royal Academy of Music, 1969-72; Nordwestdeutsche Musikakademie, Detmold, 1972-73; BA (Hons) Music, MA, Peterhouse, Cambridge, 1973-76. Appointments: Teaching: Private Oboe and Ensemble Teaching, 1972-; Purcell School, 1976-84; Professor of Oboe and Head of Woodwind and Orchestral Studies, Royal Academy of Music, 1984-93; Principal, Birmingham Conservatoir, University of Central England, Birmingham, 1993-; Orchestral Work with BBC Symphony Orchestra, London Philharmonic, London Symphony Orchestra, Philharmonia Orchestra, City of London Sinfonia, BBC Welsh Symphony Orchestra, London Sinfonietta; English Music Theatre Company, 1974-76; Kent Opera, 1977-79; Opera 80, 1980-83; London Bach Orchestra, 1980-85; Academy of St Martin-in-the-Fields, 1984-92; Chamber Music: Vega Wind Quintet, 1971-89, Arcadia Trio, 1974-92; Albion Ensemble, 1976-; George Caird Oboe Quartet, 1978-88; Caird Oboe Quartet, 2003-: Musical Director, Harlow Youth Orchestra, 1984-89; Conductor and Director of Concerts with London Bach Orchestra, Academy of St Martin-in-the-Fields, Guernsey Youth Orchestra, Royal Academy of Music, Birmingham Conservatoire; Numerous Master Classes; Adjudicator for many UK and European competitions and conservatories. Publications: Articles in professional journals and chapters in textbooks. Recordings include most recently: Mississippi Five, twentieth century music for wind quintet, The Albion Ensemble, 1996; The Classical Harmonie, Wind Music by Hummel, Beethoven, Gluck, The Albion Ensemble; 20th Century Oboe Music for oboe and piano, George Caird and Malcolm Wilson,1999; An English Renaissance, English Music for oboe and strings, George Caird and Caird Oboe Quintet, 2004. Honours: FRAM, 1989; Professor, University of Central England, 1993; FRSA, 1994; FRCM, FLCM, 1999; FRNCM, 2004. Memberships include: Royal Society of Arts; Incorporated Society of Musicians; Music Education Council; Incorporated Society of Musicians; Association of European Conservatoires. Address: Birmingham Conservatoire, Paradise Place, Birmingham B3 3HG, England. E-mail: george.caird@uce.ac.uk

**CAIRNS David (Adam),** b. 8 June 1926, Loughton, Essex, England. Music Critic; Writer. m. Rosemary Goodwin, 19 December 1959, 3 sons. Education: Trinity College, Oxford. Appointments: Music Critic, Evening Standard, and Spectator,

1958-62, Financial Times, 1963-67, New Statesman, 1967-70, Sunday Times, 1973-; Classical Programme Co-ordinator, Philips Records, 1967-73; Distinguished Visiting Scholar, Getty Center for the History of Art and Humanities, 1992; Visiting Resident Fellow, Merton College, Oxford, 1993. Publications: The Memoirs of Hector Berlioz (editor and translator), 1969, 4th edition, 1990; Responses: Musical Essays and Reviews, 1973; The Magic Flute, 1980; Falstaff, 1982; Berlioz, 2 volumes, 1989, 2000; Berlioz Volume II: Servitude and Greatness, 1832-1869, 1999. Honours: Chevalier, 1975, Officier, 1991, de l'Ordre des Arts des Lettres, France; Derek Allen Memorial Prize, British Academy, 1990; Royal Philharmonic Society Award, 1990; Yorkshire Post Prize, 1990; Commander of the Order of the British Empire, 1997; Whitbread Biography Prize, 1999; Royal Philharmonic Society Award, 1999; Samuel Johnson Non-Fiction Prize, 2000. Address: 49 Amerland Road, London SW18 1QA, England.

**CAIRNS Hugh John Forster,** b. 21 November 1922. Professor of Microbiology. m. Elspeth Mary Forster, 1948, 2 sons, 1 daughter. Education: Medical Degree, Balliol College, Oxford, 1943. Appointments: Surgical Resident, Radcliffe Infirmary, Oxford, 1945; Various appointments in London, Newcastle, Oxford; Virologist, Hall Institute, Melbourne, Australia, 1950-51; Viruses Research Institute, Entebbe, Uganda, 1952-54; Director, Cold Spring Harbor Laboratory of Quantative Biology, New York, 1963-68; Professor, State University of New York, American Cancer Society; Head, Mill Hill Laboratories, Imperial Cancer Research Fund, London, 1973-81; Department of Microbiology, Harvard School of Public Health, Boston, 1982-91; Research work into penicillin-resistant staphylococci, influenza virus, E.coli and DNA replication in mammals. Address: Holly Grove House, Wilcote, Chipping Norton, Exon, OX7 3EA, England.

**CAITHNESS Peter Westmacott,** b. 25 May 1932, Cricklewood, London, England. Security Technologies Marketing Consultant. m. Claude-Noële Gauthier, 1 son, 2 daughters. Appointments: National Service, 2nd Lieutenant, Royal Artillery, 1950-52; Overseas Management Trainee, Hong Kong & Shanghai Banking Corporation, 1953-54; Overseas Sales Manager, Bradbury Wilkinson, 1954-70; Sales and Marketing Director, Aeroprint, 1970-85; Consultant, British American Banknote Corporation, 1986-96; Director, SATS (UK) Ltd, 1996-. Publications: Numerous articles about security printing in popular and professional journals. Honours: National Marketing Award, 1972; Queen's Award for Export, 1980. Memberships: Institute of Marketing. Address: Berriedale, 26 Baker's Orchard, Wooburn Green, Buckinghamshire, HP10 0LS, England.

**CALDER Nigel (David Ritchie),** b. 2 December 1931, London, England. Writer. m. Elisabeth Palmer, 22 May 1954, 2 sons, 3 daughters. Education: BA, 1954, MA, 1957, Sidney Sussex College, Cambridge. Appointments: Research Physicist, Mullard Research Laboratories, Redhill, Surrey, 1954-56; Staff Writer, 1956-60, Science Editor, 1960-62, Editor, 1962-66, New Scientist; Science Correspondent, New Statesman, 1959-62, 1966-71. Publications: The Environment Game, 1967, US edition as Eden Was No Garden: An Inquiry Into the Environment of Man, 1967; Technopolis: Social Control of the Uses of Science, 1969; Violent Universe: An Eyewitness Account of the New Astronomy, 1970; The Mind of Man: An Investigation into Current Research on the Brain and Human Nature, 1970; Restless Earth: A Report on the New Geology, 1972; The Life Game: Evolution and the New Biology, 1974; The Weather Machine: How Our Weather Works and Why It Is Changing, 1975; The Human Conspiracy, 1976; The Key to the

Universe: A Report on the New Physics, 1977; Spaceships of the Mind, 1978; Einstein's Universe, 1979; Nuclear Nightmares: An Investigation into Possible Wars, 1980; The Comet is Coming!: The Feverish Legacy of Mr Halley, 1981; Timescale: An Atlas of the Fourth Dimension, 1984; 1984 and Beyond: Nigel Calder Talks to His Computer About the Future, 1984; The English Channel, 1986; The Green Machines, 1986; Future Earth: Exploring the Frontiers of Science (editor with John Newell), 1989; Scientific Europe, 1990; Spaceship Earth, 1991; Giotto to the Comets, 1992; Beyond this World, 1995; The Manic Sun, 1997; Magic Universe: The Oxford Guide to Modern Science, 2003. Contributions to: Television documentaries; Numerous periodicals. Honours: UNESCO Kalinga Prize, 1972; AAAS, honorary fellow, 1986. Memberships: Association of British Science Writers, Chairman, 1960-62; Cruising Association, London, Vice President, 1982-85; Fellow, Royal Astronomical Society, Council, 2001-04; Fellow, Royal Geographical Society; Fellow, American Association for the Advancement of Science. Address: 26 Boundary Road, Crawley, West Sussex RH10 8BT, England. E-mail: nc@windstream.demon.co.uk

**CALLAHAN Lough,** b. 18 January 1948, Dayton, Ohio, USA. Investment Management Consultant. m. Mary Reilly Callahan, 5 May 1973, 1 son, 1 daughter, deceased 1996. Education: AB Honours, Holy Cross College, 1969; JD cum laude, Harvard Law School, 1972. Appointments: Lawyer, Davis Polk & Wardell, New York City, 1972-80; Investment Banker, S G Warburg Co Ltd and S G Warburg Securities, 1980-92; Director, 1983-92; Head of International Capital Markets, 1985-88; Joint Head of Fixed Interest Division, 1989-92; Fund Management, Mercury Asset Management Ltd, 1992-99; Director, 1992-99; Managing Director Closed-end Funds Division, 1992-99; Director, 1986-91, Vice Chairman, 1988-91, International Primary Markets Association; Director, Euroclear Clearance System S C 1991-93; Consultant, Ernst & Young, 1999-; Director, Tribune Trust plc, 1999-; Executive Committee and Director, Association of Investment Trust Companies, 2000-; Chairman, The European Technology and Income Company Limited, 2000-02. Membership: Chelsea Arts Club. Address: 7 Spencer Hill, London SW19 4PA, England.

**CALLOW Simon Philip Hugh,** b. 15 June 1949, England. Actor; Director; Writer. Education: Queen's University, Belfast; Drama Centre. Creative Works: Stage appearances include: Kiss of the Spider Woman, 1985; Faust, 1988; Single Spies, 1988, 1989; The Destiny of Me, 1993; The Alchemist, 1996; The Importance of Being Oscar, 1997; Chimes at Midnight, 1997; The Mystery of Charles Dickens, 2001-04; The Holy Terror, 2004; Films include: Four Weddings and A Funeral, 1994; Ace Ventura: When Nature Calls, 1995; James and the Giant Peach (voice), 1996; The Scarlet Tunic, 1996; Woman In White, 1997; Bedrooms and Hallways, 1997; Shakespeare in Love, 1997; Interview with a Dead Man, 1997; No Man's Land, 2000; Thunderpants, 2001; A Christmas Carol, 2001; The Civilization of Maxwell Bright, 2003; Bright Young Things, 2003; George and the Dragon, 2004; Phantom of the Opera, 2005; Bob the Butler, 2005; TV: Patriot Witness, 1989; Trial of Oz, 1991; Bye Bye Columbus, 1992; Femme Fatale, 1993; Little Napoleons, 1994; An Audience with Charles Dickens, 1996; A Christmas Dickens, 1997; The Woman in White, 1998; Trial-Retribution, 1999, 2000; Galileo's Daughter; The Mystery of Charles Dickens, 2002; Dr Who, 2005; Marple, 2005; Midsomer Murders, 2005. Director: Carmen Jones, 1994; Il Trittico, 1995; Les Enfants du Paradis, 1996; Stephen Oliver Trilogy, 1996; La Calisto, 1996; Il Turco in Italia, 1997; HRH, 1997; The Pajama Game, 1998; The Consul, 1999; Tomorrow Week (play for radio), 1999; Jus' Like That, 2003; Le Roi Malgré Lui, 2003; Several other radio broadcasts. Publications:

Being An Actor, 1984; A Difficult Actor: Charles Laughton, 1987; Shooting the Actor, or the Choreography of Confusion, 1990; Acting in Restoration Comedy, 1991; Orson Wells: The Road to Xanadu, 1995; Les Enfants du Paradis, 1996; Snowdon - On Stage, 1996; The National, 1997; Love is Where it Falls, 1999; Shakespeare on Love, 2000; Charles Laughton's the Night of the Hunter, 2000; Oscar Wilde and His Circle, 2000; The Nights of the Hunter, 2001; Dicken's Christmas, 2002; Henry IV Part One, 2002; Henry IV Part Two, 2003; Hello Americans, 2006; Several translations; Weekly columns in professional newspapers; Contributions to The Guardian, The Times, The Sunday Times, The Observer, Evening Standard and others. Honours: Laurence Olivier Theatre Award, 1992; Patricia Rothermere Award, 1999; CBE, 1999. Address: c/o BAT, 180 Wardour Street, London, W1V 3AA, England.

**CALNE Roy (Yorke) (Sir),** b. 30 December 1930. Professor of Surgery; Consultant Surgeon. m. Patricia Doreen Whelan, 1956, 2 sons, 4 daughters. Education: Guy's Hospital Medical School; MB, BS, Hons, London, 1953. Appointments: Guy's Hospital, 1953-54; RAMC, 1954-56; Departmental Anatomy Demonstrator, Oxford University, 1957-58; Senior House Officer, Nuffield Orthopaedic Centre, Oxford, 1958; Surgical Registrar, Royal Free Hospital, 1958-60; Harkness Fellow in Surgery, Peter Bent Brigham Hospital, Harvard Medical School, 1960-61; Lecturer in Surgery, St Mary's Hospital, London, 1961-62; Senior Lecturer and Consultant Surgeon, Westminster Hospital, 1962-65; Professor of Surgery, 1965-98, Emeritus Professor, 1998, University of Cambridge; Ghim Seng Professor of Surgery, National University of Singapore, 1998-. Publications include: Renal Transplantation, co-author, 1963; Lecture Notes in Surgery, 1965; A Gift of Life, 1970; Clinical Organ Transplantation, editor and contributor, 1971; Immunological Aspects of Transplantation Surgery, editor and contributor, 1973; Transplantation Immunology, 1984; Surgical Anatomy of the Abdomen in the Living Subject, 1988; Too Many People, 1994; Art Surgery and Transplantation, 1996; The Ultimate Gift, 1998; Numerous papers and book chapters. Honours include: Hallet Prize, 1957, Jacksonian Prize, 1961, Hunterian Professor, 1962, Cecil Joll Prize, 1966, Hunterian Orator, 1989, Royal College of Surgeons; Honorary MD, Oslo, 1986, Athens, 1990, Hanover, 1991, Thailand, 1993, Belfast, 1994, Edinburgh, 2001; Prix de la Société Internationale de Chirurgie, 1969; Fastin Medal, Finnish Surgical Society, 1977; Lister Medal, 1984; Knighted, 1986; Cameron Prize, Edinburgh University, 1990; Ellison-Cliffe Medal, 1990; The Medawar Prize, Transplantation Society, 1992; Honorary Fellow, Royal College of Surgeons of Thailand, 1992; Ernst Jung Prize, 1996; Gold Medal of the Catalan Transplantation Society, 1996; Grand Officer of the Republic of Italy, 2000; King Faisal International Prize for Medicine, 2001; Prince Mahidol Prize for Medicine, 2002. Memberships include: Fellow, Royal College of Surgeons; Fellow, Royal Society; Fellow, Association of Surgeons of Great Britain; European Society for Organ Transplantation, 1983-84; Corresponding Fellow, American Surgical Association. Address: 22 Barrow Road, Cambridge CB2 2AS, England.

**CALOGERO Francesco,** b. 6 February 1935, Fiesole, Italy. University Professor. m. Luisa La Malfa. 1 son, 1 daughter. Education: Laurea in Fisica, cum laude, Rome University, 1958. Appointments: Various positions, Rome University, 1958-; Professor of Theoretical Physics, Rome University La Sapienza, 1976-; Military service, 1959-60; two years in USA, 1961-63; three months in India, 1967; one year in Moscow, 1969-70; one year in London, 1979-80; Visiting Professor in Groningen, London, Montpellier, Hefei, Paris, Cuernavaca. Publications: Over 300 scientific papers published in international journals; 3 written books; 2 edited books; Over 400 publications on science and society (mainly arms control), including written and edited books and a regular column in the oldest popular science magazine in Italy; Member of several editorial boards. Honour: Accepted 1995 Nobel Peace Prize on behalf of the Pugwash Conferences on Science and World Affairs. Memberships: Member, 1987-90, Scientific Secretary, 1990-93, Chairman, 1993-96, Mathematical Physics Commission, International Union of Pure and Applied Physics; Secretary General, Pugwash Conferences, 1989-97; Chairman, Pugwash Council, 1997-2002; Scientific Council, Italian Union of Scientists for Disarmament; Committee on International Security and Arms Control of the Accademia dei Lincei. Address: Via Sant' Alberto Magno 1, 00153 Rome, Italy. E-mail: francesco.calogero@roma1.infn.it

**CALVIN Wyn (Wyndham Calvin-Thomas),** b. 28 August 1928, Narberth, Pembrokeshire, Wales. Actor. Education: Canton High School, Cardiff, Wales. Career: Non-stop career in Theatre, TV and Radio from 1945-. Publications: Numerous newspaper columns and magazine articles over many years. Honours: MBE; Officer of the Order of St John; Honorary Fellow, Royal Welsh College of Music and Drama; Liveryman, Wales Livery Guild; Freeman of the City of London; preceptor and past King Rat of the Grand Order of Water Rats (Britain's principle show-business fraternity and charity); Honorary Citizen , City of Macon, Georgia, USA. Memberships: Founder-Trustee Children's Hospital for Wales Appeal; Vice-president, London Welsh Male Choir; President, South Wales Massed Male Choirs; Executive Committee Member, Entertainment Artists Benevolent Fund. Address: 121 Cathedral Road, Cardiff CF11 9PH, Wales.

**CAMERON James,** b. 16 August 1954, Kapuskasing, Ontario, Canada. Director; Screenwriter. m. Linda Hamilton, 1966, 1 daughter. Education: Fullerton Junior College. Appointments: Founder, Lightstorm Entertainment, 1990, Head, 1992-; Chief Executive Officer, Digital Domain, 1993-. Creative Works: Films: Piranha II - The Spawning (director); The Terminator (director, and screenplay), 1984; The Abyss (director and screenplay), 1994; Terminator 2: Judgement Day (co-screenwriter, director, producer), 1994; Point Break (executive producer), 1994; True Lies; Strange Days; Titanic, 1996; Solaris (producer), 2002; Terminator 3: Rise of the Machines (writer), 2003. Honours include: Academy Award, Best Director; 11 Academy Awards. Address: Lightstorm Entertainment, 919 Santa Monica Boulevard, Santa Monica, CA 90401, USA.

**CAMERY John William,** b. 5 February 1951, Cincinnati, Ohio, USA. Computer Software Engineer. Education: BA (Honours) Mathematics, University of Cincinnati, 1972; MSc, Carnegie-Mellon University, 1974. Appointments: Mathematician, US Army Material Systems Analysis Agency, Maryland, 1973; Student Assistant Engineering, Spectrum Analysis Task Force, Federal Communications Commission, Park Ridge, Illinois, 1974; Mathematician, US Army Communications Electronics-Engineering Installation Agency, Washington DC, 1975-83; Mathematician, Defense Communications Agency, JDSSC, Washington DC, 1983-86; Programmer Analyst, General Sciences Corp, Laurel, Maryland, 1986-87; Software Engineer, Sygnetron Protection Systems, 1987-88; Consultant, Lockheed-Martin Ocean Systems, Operations, Glen Burnie, Maryland, 1988-89; Computer Software Engineer, RDA Logicon, Leavenworth, Kansas, 1989-2001; Senior Systems Analyst, Anteon Corporation, Wheeler Army Airfield, Hawaii, 2001-. Publications: Simulation Techniques for a Multiple CPU Military Communication System(co-author), 1976; Pentagon Consolidated Telecommunications Centers System (PCTCS), Video Subsystem Reference Manual, 1982; Tying Together New Technologies in Battle Simulation, 2003. Memberships:

American Mathematical Society, 1974-; Christian Church; European Math Society; Greater Cincinnati Amateur Radio Association (WA8WNR), 1967; Imperial Hawaii Vacation Club, 1981-; IEEE Computer Society; Republican Party; Société Mathematique de France. Address: 94-647 Kauakapuu Loop, Mililani, HI 96789-1832, USA.

**CAMPBELL Alastair John,** b. 25 May 1957, England; Civil Servant; Journalist. Partner, Fiona Miller, 2 sons, 1 daughter. Education: Gonville & Caius College, Cambridge. Appointments: Trainee Reporter, Tavistock Times, Sunday Independent, 1980-82; Freelance Reporter, 1982-83; Reporter, Daily Mirror, 1982-86, Political Editor, 1989-93; News Editor, Sunday Today, 1985-86; Political Correspondent, Sunday Mirror, 1986-87, Political Editor, 1987-89, Columnist, 1989-91; Assistant Editor, Columnist, Today, 1993-95; Press Secretary to Leader of the Opposition, 1994-97; Press Secretary to Prime Minister, 1997-2001; Director of Communications, 2001-. Membership: President, Keighley Branch, Burnley Football Supporters' Club. Address: Prime Minister's Office, 10 Downing Street, London SW1A 2AA, England.

**CAMPBELL Margaret,** b. London, England. Author; Lecturer on Musical Subjects. m. Richard Barrington Beare, deceased, 2 sons, 1 daughter. Education: Art Scholarship, London. Career: Talks and Interviews on BBC Radio; Cleveland Radio; Voice of America; USA; CBC Canada; BBC and Southern Television; Lectures at Cornell; Oberlin; Indiana; Oklahoma and Southern Methodist Universities; Manhattan School of Music, New York; Rice University; University of Texas at Austin; University of Southern California USA; Cambridge, Guildford and Bath Universities; Guildhall School of Music and Drama; Purcell School, England; Festivals at Bergen and Utrecht, Holland; Editor, Journal of British Music Therapy, 1974-90; Member of Jury, International Cello Competition at Spring Festival, Prague, Czech Republic, 1994; Lectures at the Conservatoire and University of Sofia, Bulgaria, 1996; Member of Council (ESTA), 1996; Lectures at Sibelius Academy of Music, Helsinki, Finland, 1998 Publications: Dolmetsch: The Man and His Work, London and USA in 1975; The Great Violinists, London and USA in 1981, Germany 1982; Japan 1983 and China, 1999; The Great Cellists, 1988, Japan, 1996, China, 1999; Henry Purcell: Glory of His Age, London 1993, paperback 1995; Married to Music. A Biography of Julian Lloyd Weber, 2001; The Great Violinists and The Great Cellists revised 2nd editions, 2004. Contributions: The New Grove Dictionary of Music, 1980; The Independent; The Strad; Cambridge Companion to the Cello, 1999; The New Grove Dictionary of Music & Musicians, 2nd edition, 2000. Honours: Winston Churchill Memorial Travelling Fellowship, 1971; Fellow of the Royal Society of Arts, 1991; Board of Governors, The Dolmetsch Foundation. Memberships: Society of Authors; Royal Society of Literature; Royal Society of Arts. Address: 71 Shrublands Avenue, Berkhamsted, Hertfordshire HP4 3JG, England.

**CAMPBELL Neve,** b. 3 October 1973, Guelph, Ontario, Canada. Actress. m. Jeff Colt, divorced 1998. Education: National Ballet School, Canada. Career: Dance: The Phantom of the Opera; The Nutcracker; Sleeping Beauty; Films include: Paint Cans, 1994; The Dark, 1994; Love Child, 1995; The Craft, 1996; Scream, 1996; A Time to Kill, 1996; Simba's Pride, 1997; Scream 2, 1997; Wild Things, 1998; Hairshirt, 1998; 54, 1998; Three to Tango, 1999; Scream 3, 2000; Investigating Sex, 2001; Last Call, 2002; The Company, 2003; Blind Horizon, 2004; TV includes: Catwalk, 1992-93; Web of Deceit, 1993; Baree, 1994; The Forget-Me-Not Murders, 1994; Party of Five, 1994-98; The Canterville Ghost, 1996. Honours: Saturn Award for Best Actress, 1996; MTV Movie Award for Best

Female Performance, 1996; Blockbuster Entertainment Award for Favourite Actress – Horror, 1997. Address: Creative Artists Agency, 9830 Wilshire Boulevard, Beverly Hills, CA 90212, USA.

**CAMPBELL Peter Walter,** b. 17 June 1926, Poole, England. University Teacher. Education: New College, Oxford, 1945-47; Nuffield College, Oxford, 1947-49. Appointments: Lecturer in Government, University of Manchester, 1949-60; Professor of Political Economy, 1960-64, Professor of Politics, 1964-91, University of Reading. Publications: Encyclopaedia of World Politics (with W Theimer), 1950; French Electoral Systems and Elections 1789-1957, 1958; The Constitution of the Fifth Republic (with B Chapman), 1958; Articles in British, French and New Zealand journals of politics and public administration; Editor, Political Studies, 1963-69. Membership: Political Studies Association of the UK. Address: 6 Treyarnon Court, 37 Eastern Avenue, Reading RG1 5RX, England.

**CAMPBELL Ramsey,** b. 4 January 1946, Liverpool, England. Writer; Film Reviewer. m. Jenny Chandler, 1 January 1971, 1 son, 1 daughter. Appointments: Film Reviewer, BBC Radio Merseyside, 1969-; Full-time Writer, 1973-. Publications: Novels: The Doll Who Ate His Mother, 1976; The Face That Must Die, 1979; The Parasite, 1980; The Nameless, 1981; Incarnate, 1983; The Claw, 1983, US edition as Night of the Claw; Obsession, 1985; The Hungry Moon, 1986; The Influence, 1988; Ancient Images, 1989; Midnight Sun, 1990; The Count of Eleven, 1991; The Long Lost, 1993; The One Safe Place, 1995; The House on Nazareth Hill, 1996; The Last Voice They Hear, 1998; Silent Children, 2000; Pact of the Fathers, 2001; The Darkest Part of the Woods, 2002; The Overnight (novel), 2004; Secret Stories (novel), 2005; Short stories: The Inhabitant of the Lake and Less Welcome Tenants, 1964; Demons by Daylight, 1973; The Height of the Scream, 1976; Dark Companions, 1982; Cold Print, 1985; Black Wine (with Charles L Grant), 1986; Night Visions 3 (with Clive Barker and Lisa Tuttle), 1986; Scared Stiff, 1987; Dark Feasts: The World of Ramsey Campbell, 1987; Waking Nightmares, 1991; Alone With The Horrors, 1993; Strange Things and Stranger Places, 1993; Ghosts and Grisly Things (short stories), 1998; Ramsey Campbell, Probably (non-fiction), 2002; Told by the Dead (short stories), 2003; Novella: Needing Ghosts, 1990. Honours: Liverpool Daily Post and Echo Award for Literature, 1993; World Fantasy Award, Bram Stoker Award, Best Collection, 1994; Best Novel, International Horror Guild, 1998; Grand Master, World Horror Convention, 1999; Lifetime Achievement Award, Horror Writers' Association, 1999; Many others. Memberships: British Fantasy Society, President; Society of Fantastic Films, President. Address: 31 Penkett Road, Wallasey CH45 7QF, Merseyside, England. Website: www.ramseycampbell.com

**CAMPBELL Robert Adair,** b. 14 March 1928, Bermuda. Retired Lieutenant Colonel Royal Marines. m. Norma Louie Tyler, 3 sons, 1 foster son, 3 daughters. Education: Ampleforth College, York, 1938-46. Appointments: Joined Royal Marines, 1946; Commissioned 1947; 45 Commando, Canal Zone and Malta, 1953-55; Captain, 1956; Captain of Marines, HMS Bermuda, 1957-59; Instructor, School of Infantry, Warminster, 1959-61; Staff of MGRM Portsmouth, 1961-63; 45 Commando, Aden and Radfan, commanding X Company, 1964-65; Major, 1964; OC Junior Wing, RM Deal, 1965-67; Staff of Supreme Allied Commander Atlantic, Norfolk, Virginia, USA, 1967-70; Joint Services Staff Course, Latimer, 1970-71; Lieutenant Colonel, 1971; Commanded 41 Commando Group, Malta and Mediterranean, 1971-73; Last Commanding Officer, RM Barracks Eastney, 1973; GI Staff of MGRM Portsmouth; Took early retirement to run family estate. Honours: Queen's

Commendation for Brave Conduct, Aden, 1965; Elected Knight of Honour and Devotion, British Association Sovereign Military Order of Malta, 1978; Pro Ecclesia et Ponticife (Papal Medal), 2004; Represented Royal Marines at the following sports: Cricket, 1948-74, Rugby, 1947-56, Athletics, 1948-50, Small bore shooting, 1953-73, Polo and other equestrian events, 1955-59. Memberships: Standing Committee, Dee Salmon Fishing Improvement Association, 1976-2005; RNLI North East Committee, 1976-86; Member, North East Scotland River Purification Board, 1977-89; Mandatory and Trustee, Atlantic Salmon Conservation Trust Scotland, 1986-94; Chairman, Dee Salmon Fishery Board, 1987-96; Council, Scottish District Salmon Fishery Boards, 1988-97; Member, Migratory Fish Committee, 1988-94, Chairman, 1992-94, Council and Executive Committee, 1988-94, Member, Scottish Council, 1978-94, Salmon & Trout Association; Committee, Atlantic Salmon Trust, 1988-97, 1999-2005; Trustee and Committee Member, Margaret Blackwood Homes, 1987-96; Director, North Atlantic Salmon Fund (UK), 1995-2005. Address: Altries, Maryculter, Aberdeen AB12 5GD, Scotland. E-mail: altries@btinternet.com

**CAMPBELL William Ian,** b. 30 May 1952, Belfast, Northern Ireland. Consultant in Anaesthesia and Pain Medicine. m. Elizabeth, 2 sons, 1 daughter. Education: MB BCh, 1976, MD, 1989, PhD, 1997, Queens University, Belfast; FFA RCSI, Royal College of Surgeons, Ireland, 1980; FRCA, Royal College of Anaesthetists, London, 1997; D Pain Medicine, Fac. Anaes, Royal College of Surgeons, Ireland, 2001. Appointments: Clinical Director, Anaesthesia and Intensive Care, 1990-95; Director, Intensive Care, 1996-99; Lead Clinician, Chronic Pain, 1996-; College Tutor to Ulster Community and Hospital Trust, 1996-99; Regional Advisor, Pain, to Royal College of Anaesthetists, London, 2003-; Examiner, Primary FFA RCSI, Dublin, 1993-; Vice-Chairman, 1998-2000, Chairman, 2000-2002, Medical Staff Committee, UCHT. Publications: Textbook of Clinical Pain Management (co-editor); Chapters in books: Physiology of Pain; Measurement of pain; Various publications on acute pain measurement and management; Chronic pain measurement and management; Anaesthetics and intensive care topics. Honours: Dundee Medal in Anaesthesia, 1983; Bronze Medallion, Community Medical Association Award, 1991. Memberships: British Medical Association; Fellow Royal Society of Medicine; Fellow, Ulster Medical Society; Fellow, Royal College of Anaesthetists, London and College of Anaesthetists, Royal College of Surgeons, Ireland; International Association for the Study of Pain; British Pain Society, Honorary Assistant Treasurer, 1999-2001, Honorary Treasurer, 2001-2003; Northern Ireland Pain Society, Founder, Convenor, 1988-95; Northern Ireland Society of Anaesthesia; Associate, Royal Photographic Society (Visual Art), 1999; Amateur Radio, full licence, 1985. Address: The Pain Clinic, The Ulster Hospital Dundonald, UCH Trust, Belfast BT16 1RH, Northern Ireland. E-mail: william.campbell@ucht.n-i.nhs.uk

**CAMPBELL OF ALLOWAY, Baron of Ayr in the District of Kyle and Carrick, Alan Robertson Campbell,** b. 24 May 1917, United Kingdom. Queen's Counsel. m. Vivien de Kantzow. Education: Trinity Hall Cambridge; Ecole des Sciences Politiques, Paris. Appointments: Sits as Conservative Peer in the House of Lords; Commissioned 2 Lt RA Supplementary Reserve, 1939, served in BEF France and Belgium, 1939-40, POW, 1940-45; Called to the Bar, Inner Temple, 1939, Bencher, 1972; Western Circuit, Recorder, Crown Court, 1976-89; Head of Chambers; Consultant to Sub-Committee of Legal Committee of Council of Europe on Industrial Espionage, 1965-74; Chairman, Legal Research Committee, Society of Conservative Lawyers, 1968-80; Member of House of Lords Select Committees on:

Murder and Life Imprisonment, 1988-89, Privileges, 1982-2000, Personal Bills, 1987-88, Joint Consolidation Bills, 2000; Member: House of Lords Ecclesiastical Committee, 2003-; Joint Committee on Human Rights; All Party Committees on Defence, and on Children. Honours: MA (Cantab); Emergency Reserve Decoration; QC, 1965. Memberships: Law Advisory Committee Bar Council, 1974-80; Management Committee, Association for European Law, 1975-90; Old Carlton Club Political Committee, 1967-79; Co-Patron, Inns of Court School of Law Conservatives, 1996-2000; President, Colditz Association, 1998-2004; Carlton; Pratt's; Beefsteak Clubs; Perennial Guest of Third Guards Club. Address: House of Lords, London SW1A 0PW, England.

**CAMPESE David Ian,** b. 21 October 1962, Queanbeyan, Australia. Rugby Football Player. m. Lara Berkenstein, 2003. Appointments: Partner, Campo's Sports Store; International Debut, Australia v New Zealand, 1982; Captain, Australian Team; Winner, World Cup, 1991; World's Leading Try Scorer with 64; Scored 310 points; Australian Most Capped Player (represented Australia 101 times); Director, David Campese Management Group, 1997-. Publication: On a Wing and a Prayer. Honours: Australian Writers Player of the Year, 1991; English Rugby Writers Player of the Year, 1991; International Rugby Hall of Fame, 2001; Order of Australia Medal, 2002. Address: David Campese Management Group, Suite 4, 870 Pacific Highway, Gordon, NSW 2072, Australia.

**CAMPION Jane,** b. 30 April 1954, Wellington, New Zealand. Film Director; Writer. Education: BA, Anthropology, Victoria University, Wellington; Diploma of Fine Arts, Chelsea School of Arts, London, completed at Sydney College of the Arts; Diploma in Direction, Australian Film & TV School, 1981-84. Career: Writer/Director, films: Peel, 1981-82; Passionless Moments, Mishaps of Seduction and Conquest, 1984-85; Girls Own Story, 1983-84; After Hours, 1984; Producer: I episode ABC TV drama series, Dancing Daze, 1986; Director, Two Friends, for ABC TV Drama, 1985-86; An Angel at My Table, 1989-90; Sweetie, 1988; Writer/Director, The Piano, 1993; Director, The Portrait of a Lady, 1997; Holy Smoke, 1999; In the Cut, 2003. Honours: Numerous awards include: for the Piano: Best Picture, 66th Academy Awards Nomination, Best Director, 66th Academy Awards Nomination, LA Film Critics Association, New York Film Critics Circle, Australia Film Critics, Director's Guild of America Nomination, BAFTA Nomination, AFI Awards, Producer, Producer's Guild of America, Best Screenplay, 66th Academy Awards, BAFTA Nomination, AFI Awards; For The Portrait of a Lady: Francesco Pasinetti Award, National Union of Film Journalists, 1996. Address: HLA Management Pty Ltd, 87 Pitt Street, Redfern, NSW 2016, Australia.

**CAMPTON David,** b. 5 June 1924, Leicester, England. Playwright; Children's Fiction Writer. Publications: On Stage: Containing 17 Sketches and 1 Monologue, 1964; Resting Place, 1964; The Manipulator, 1964; Split Down the Middle, 1965; Little Brother, Little Sister and Out of the Flying Pan, 1966; Two Leaves and a Stalk, 1967; Angel Unwilling, 1967; Ladies Night: 4 Plays for Women, 1967; More Sketches, 1967; Laughter and Fear, 9 One-Act Plays, 1969; The Right Place, 1969; On Stage Again: Containing 14 Sketches and 2 Monologues, 1969; Now and Then, 1970; The Life and Death of Almost Everybody, 1970; Timesneeze, 1970; Gulliver in Lilliput (reader), 1970; Gulliver in The Land of Giants (reader), 1970; The Wooden Horse of Troy (reader), 1970; Jonah, 1971; The Cagebirds, 1971; Us and Them, 1972; Carmilla, 1972; In Committee, 1972; Come Back Tomorrow, 1972; Three Gothic Plays, 1973; Modern Aesop (reader), 1976; One Possessed, 1977; What Are You Doing Here?, 1978; The Do-It-Yourself Frankenstein

Outfit, 1978; Zodiac, 1978; After Midnight: Before Dawn, 1978; Pieces of Campton, 1979; Parcel, 1979; Everybody's Friend, 1979; Who Calls?, 1980; Attitudes, 1980; Freedom Log, 1980; Dark Wings, 1981; Look-Sea, 1981; Great Whales, 1981; Who's a Hero, Then?, 1981; Dead and Alive, 1983; But Not Here, 1984; Singing in the Wilderness, 1986; Mrs Meadowsweet, 1986; The Vampyre (children's book), 1986; Our Branch in Brussels, 1986; Cards, Cups and Crystal Ball, 1986; Can You Hear the Music?, 1988; The Winter of 1917, 1989; Smile, 1990; Becoming a Playwright, 1992; The Evergreens, 1994; Permission to Cry, 1996. Contributions to: Amateur Stage; Writers News; Drama; Whispers. Address: 35 Liberty Road, Glenfield, Leicester LE3 8JF, England.

**CAMROSE (Viscount), Sir Adrian Michael Berry.** b. 15 June 1937, London, England. Writer; Journalist. Education: Christ Church, Oxford, 1959. Appointments: Correspondent, Time Magazine, New York City, 1965-67; Science Correspondent, 1977-96, Consulting Editor (Science), 1996-, Daily Telegraph, London. Publications: The Next Ten Thousand Years: A Vision of Man's Future in the Universe, 1974; The Iron Sun: Crossing the Universe Through Black Holes, 1977; From Apes to Astronauts, 1981; The Super Intelligent Machine, 1983; High Skies and Yellow Rain, 1983; Koyama's Diamond (fiction), 1984; Labyrinth of Lies (fiction), 1985; Ice With Your Evolution, 1986; Computer Software: The Kings and Queens of England, 1985; Harrap's Book of Scientific Anecdotes, 1989; The Next 500 Years, 1995; Galileo and the Dolphins, 1996; The Giant Leap, 1999. Honour: Royal Geographic Society, fellow, 1984-. Memberships: Royal Astronomical Society, London, Fellow, 1973-; British Interplanetary Society, Fellow, 1986-. Address: 11 Cottesmore Gardens, Kensington, London W8, England.

**CANNING Bernard John,** b. 30 March 1932, Derry, Ireland. Roman Catholic Priest. Education: St Columb's College, Derry; St Kieran's College, Kilkenny. Appointments: Ordained Priest for Diocese of Paisley, 1956; Assistant, St James's, Renfrew, 1956-68; Assistant, St Fergus, Paisley, 1968-74; Assistant, St Laurence's. Greenock, 1974-87; Parish Priest: Christ the King, Howwood and Our Lady of Fatima, Lochwinnoch, 1987-95, St James's, Paisley, 1995-96; St John the Baptist, Port Glasgow, 1996-99, St Thomas's, Neilston, 1999-; 1st Press officer of Paisley Diocese, 1962-88; Board of Governors, Catholic Press Office, 1968-87; First Archivist of the Diocese of Paisley, 1983-; Appointed as Full Canon of Paisley, 2001-. Publications: St James's, Renfrew 1903-1963 – Diamond Jubilee, 1963; Joy and Hope, St Fergus, Paisley, 1971; Glimpses of St Mary's, Paisley, 1976; A Building from God 1877-1997 – St James's, Renfrew; Padraig H Pearse and Scotland, 1979; Irish Born Secular Priests in Scotland 1829-1979; Adventure in Faith, St Ninian's, Gourock, 1880-1980; The Living Stone, St Aloysius, Springburn, 1882-1982; Instruments of His Work, 1884-1984 (Little Sisters of the Poor, Greenock), 1984; By Columb's Footsteps Trod, The Long Tower's Holy Dead 1784-1984; St Mungo's Ladyburn, Greenock 1935-1985; The Charleston Story, St Charles, Paisley, 1986; Bishops of Ireland 1870-1987; Combined Parish of Howwood and Lochwinnoch 1928-1988; St Fillan's, Houston 1841-1991; St Mary's, Paisley 1891-1991, 1991, Centenary, 1991; The Poor Sisters of Nazareth and Derry 1892-1992; Rosemount Primary School, Derry 1891-1991; St Colms' Church, Kilmalcolm, 1992; Bishop Neil Farren 1893-1980, Bishop of Derry, 1993; St John the Baptist (Parish) 1946-1996, 1996; Diocese of Paisley, 1947-1997, 2001; The Street That is Gone, But Lives On, 2001; Derry City Cemetery 1853-2003 – 150 Year, 2003; Numerous articles in journals and newspapers. Honour: Fellow of the Society of Antiquaries of

Scotland, 1989. Address: St Thomas's Presbytery, 70 Main Street, Neilston, Glasgow G78 3NJ, Scotland.

**CANNINGS Della M,** b. Exeter, Devon, England. Chief Constable. m. Michael Barker. Education: Graduate, Mathematical Studies, University of Bath; 17th Special Course as a Sergeant, 1979, Strategic Command Course as Chief Superintendent, 1999, Police Staff College. Appointments: Joined Devon and Cornwall Constabulary as a Graduate Entrant, served in Plymouth, Exeter, Torbay, Dartmoor and South and East Devon, attained rank of Chief Superintendent, gained experience as a hostage negotiator, firearms commander and commander of environmental protests, 1975-2000; Gold Control Commander for the Total Eclipse in Devon and Cornwall, 1999; Senior Police Adviser, Home Office, 1993-95; Assistant Chief Constable and Deputy Chief Constable of Cleveland Police, 2000-2002; Chief Constable, North Yorkshire Police, 2002-; Held ACPO portfolios on Safer and Healthier Policing and National Airwave Programme; Travelled extensively giving presentations to police and criminological conferences most recently in Iran, the Basque and Catalan regions of Spain, Hungary, Cyprus and Italy; Received Home Office funding for 2 projects: the use of lap top computers and the policing implications of the Single European Act, 1992. Honours: Harkness Fellow, USA; Award, Ernst and Young; Chief Constable's Commendation. Memberships: Chairman, ACPO Women's Forum; Institute of Directors; Chairman, North Yorkshire Prince's Trust Board. Address: Police Headquarters, Newby Wiske Hall, Northallerton, North Yorkshire DL7 9HA, England.

**CANNON Jack Philip,** b. 21 December 1929, Paris, France. Composer. m. Jane Dyson (Baroness Buijs van Schouwenburg). 1 daughter. Education: Dartington Hall, Devon; Royal College of Music, London. Appointments: Lecturer, Oxford Extramural Studies, 1950-58; Lecturer in Music, Sydney University, Australia, 1958-60; Deputy Professor of Composition, 1950-58; Professor of Composition, Royal College of Music, London, 1960-95. Publications: Many articles for music journals; 3 operas, chorus/orchestral works, orchestral works, choral works, chamber music, mostly commissioned by national and international bodies; Important historical commissions include: Symphony commissioned by the BBC to mark Britain's entry to the EC, 1972; Symphony commission by Radio France for première at a diplomatic occasion in Paris, 1972; Te Deum commissioned by and dedicated to H M The Queen of England for the Service of Thanksgiving at St George's Chapel, Windsor Castle, 1975. Honours: Grand Prix and Critics' Prize, Paris, 1965; Fellow of the Royal College of Music, 1971; Bard of Gorsedd Kernow, 1997. Memberships: Royal Philharmonic Society; British Academy of Composers and Songwriters; Savile; Chelsea Arts. Address: Elmdale Cottage, March, Aylesbury, Bucks HP17 8SP, England.

**CANTER Jean Mary,** b. 18 March 1943, Epsom, Surrey. Artist. Education: 13+ Art Award, Epsom School of Art, 1956-61; Major Art Award, Wimbledon School of Art, 1961-63. Career: Colourist, Baynton Williams Antique Prints; Part-time Tutor, Mid-Surrey Adult Education, 1972-; Freelance Artist; Exhibitions: London Royal Institute of Painters in Watercolours; Royal Watercolour Society; Society of Graphic Fine Art and many other society exhibitions; Medici Gallery; Llewellyn Alexander Gallery, London and many provincial galleries. Publications: Work reproduced and many demonstration for "How-to-do-it" Art Books; Several features for Artists and Illustrators Magazine; Regular contributor with The Drawing Class to Painting World Magazine, 1999-2001. Honours: Prizes: Society of Graphic Fine Art Exhibitions, Frisk Ltd, 1983, 1985,

Rexel Ltd, 1984, 1996, Daler-Rowney, 1990, Liquitex, 1993, 1997, Winsor and Newton, 1996; Commendation of Excellence. Llewellyn Alexander Gallery, 2004. Memberships: Elected to the Society of Graphic Fine Art, 1977, Vice President, 1987-90, 1993-94, President, 1994-99; UK Coloured Pencil Society, 2003. Address: 7 Cox Lane, Ewell, Epsom, Surrey KT19 9LR, England.

**CANTLIFFE Daniel J,** b. 31 October 1943, New York, USA. Professor of Horticulture. m. Elizabeth, 4 daughters. Education: BS, Delaware Valley College, 1965; MS, 1967, PhD, 1971, Purdue University. Appointments: Research Assistant, Purdue University, 1965-69; Research Associate, Cornell University, 1969-70; Research Scientist, Horticulture Research Institute of Ontario, 1970-74; Visiting Professor, Department of Horticulture, University of Hawaii, 1979-80; Assistant Professor, Assistant Horticulturist, 1974-76, Associate Professor, Associate Horticulturist, 1976-81, Professor, 1981-92, Vegetable Crops Department, Professor and Chairman, Horticultural Sciences Department, 1992-, University of Florida. Publications: 2 book editorships; 4 monographs; 1 bulletin; 18 book chapters; 622 publications. Honours include: Distinguished Agricultural Alumni Award, Purdue University, 1999; Best and Most Meritorious Paper, Vegetable Section, Florida State Horticultural Society, 1990, 1992, 1998, 2000, 2001, 2002, 2004; Southern Region, American Society for Horticultural Science Leadership and Administration Award, 2000; Professorial Salary Adjustment Program Award, 2001 and University of Florida Research Foundation Professorship, 2005-2007, University of Florida; Outstanding Graduate Educator, 1991, Outstanding Researcher, 1997, Outstanding International Horticulturist, 2001, American Society for Horticultural Science. Memberships include: American Society for Horticultural Science; American Society of Plant Biology; American Society of Agronomy; Crop Science Society of America; Florida State Horticultural Society; International Seed Science Society; International Society for Horticultural Science; Listed in national and international biographical dictionaries. Address: Horticultural Sciences Department, University of Florida, IFAS, PO Box 110690, Gainesville, FL 32611-0690, USA. E-mail: djc@ifas.ufl.edu

**CAO TRONG Thiem,** b. 1 April 1942, Thanh Phong, Thanh Liem, Ha Nam, Vietnam. Artist. m. Pham Thi Thinh, 1 son, 2 daughters. Education: Graduate, Porcelain Decoration Faculty, Hanoi Industrial Arts University, 1977; Graduate, Hanoi Fine Arts University, 1984; Graduate, High Ranking Political Theory School, 1985. Career: Composing and studying arts. Publications: Chief Author: Vietnamese Art Museum, 1999; Art Collection of Vietnamese Porcelain, 2000; Art Work – Collection of the Vietnamese Art Museum, 2002; Member of Editorial Council: Author, Vietnamese Industrial Art Works in 2nd half of XXth Century, 1999; Vietnamese National Museums, 2001; Vietnamese Propaganda Pictures 1945-2002, 2002; Selected Vietnamese Art in XXth Century, 2002; Articles include: Vietnamese Art Museum – a glorious stage, 2000; Vietnamese Art in XXth Century from the view of the collection of the art museum, 2001; 35 Years of the Vietnam Art Museum, 2002. Honours: Third Class Resistance War Honour; Third Class Labour Decoration. Memberships: Vietnamese Fine Arts Association; Hanoi Fine Arts Association. Address: No 3 Hoang Cau, Group 90, O Cho Dua, Dong Da District, Hanoi City, Vietnam.

**CAPUTO Daniel V,** b. New York City, USA. Psychologist; Professor. Education: PhD, Clinical Psychology, University of Illinois, 1961. Appointment: Professor, Psychology, Queens College, City University of New York; Professor Emeritus,

Psychology, 1998. Publications include: Multivariate Analysis of Type A Personality. Memberships: American Psychological Association; New York Academy of Sciences. Address: 16-07 150th Street, Whitestone, NY 11357-2545, USA.

**CARANI Dorothy Miriam Meyers,** b. 6 April 1927, Pittsburgh, Pennsylvania, USA. Author; Poet; Lyricist. m. Lee Carani, 2 sons, 3 daughters. Education: Self-trained Author. Appointments: Tenant Council President, Senior Apartment Building, College Park, Maryland, USA, 1998; Author. Publications: 15 Anthologies: Poetry Press, Yes Press, American Poetry, December Press, Illiad, Amherst, Sparrowgrass, National Library of Poetry, New Millennium, Famous Poets, Poetic Odyssey; 3 books in progress: Unto Me He Said (biblical); You Might Find it Here (humour); Great Men, Great Minds, Great Words (historical). Honours: American Presidential Eagle Award for contributions to literature, 1990; Silver Jubilee Album Award; England's White Rose Award; Lyndon B Weatherford/Homer Honor Society, International Poets. Memberships: ASCAP; Songwriters Club of America-Tin Pan Alley – Broadway Music; 100 Club; National Author's Registry. Address: 5320 Dorsey Hall Drive, Apt III, Ellicott City, MD 21042-7867, USA.

**CARDIN Pierre,** b. 2 July 1922, San Biagio di Callatla, Italy. Couturier. Appointments: Worker, Christian Dior; Founder, Own Fashion Houses, 1949; Founder, Espace Pierre Cardin (Theatre Group); Director, Ambassadeurs-Pierre Cardin Theatre (now Espace Pierre Cardin Theatre), 1970-; Manager, Société Pierre Cardin, 1973; Chair, Maxims, 1982-; Honorary UNESCO Ambassador, 1991. Creative Works: Exhibition at Victoria & Albert Museum, 1990. Publications: Fernand Léger, Sa vie, Son oeuvre, Son reve, 1971; Le Conte du Ver a Soie, 1992. Honours include: Grand Officer of Merit, Italy, 1988; Order of the Sacred Treasure (Gold & Silver Star), 1991. Address: 27 Avenue Marigny, 75008 Paris, France.

**CARDONA Manuel,** b. 7 September 1934, Barcelona, Spain. Physicist. m. Inge (Hecht), 2 sons, 1 daughter. Education: Licenciado, Physics, Barcelona University, 1955; DSc, Physics, University of Madrid, 1958; PhD, Applied Physics, 1959, Harvard University. Appointments include: Instructor, Electronics, University of Madrid, 1955-56; Research Assistant, Harvard University, 1956-59; Technical Staff, RCA Laboratories, Zurich, 1959-61; Princeton (New Jersey), 1961-64; Visiting Professor, University of Pennsylvania, Spring, 1964; Associate Professor, Physics, 1964-66, Professor, 1966-71, Brown University; Scientific Member and Director, Max-Planck Institute for Solid State Research, Stuttgart, 1971-2000; Business Managing Director, Max-Planck Institute, 1973-74; Chairman, Scientific Council, Paul Drude Institut, Berlin, 1993-98; Chairman, International Union of Pure Applied Physics (IUPAP) Semiconductor Commission, 1996-2002; Air New Zealand University, 2001; Adjunct Professor, Arizona State University, Arizona, USA, 2003. Publications: About 1200 scientific publications in international journals, 11 monographs on solid state physics; Textbook on semiconductors. Honours include: Grants, fellowships, honorary doctorates from universities of Madrid, Barcelona, Sherbrooke (Canada), Rome, Regensburg, Toulouse, Thessaloniki (Greece), Brno (Czechoslovakia), Valencia (Spain); Prizes include: ITALGAS Prize, 1992; Max Planck Prize (with E E Haller, U C Berkeley), 1994; John Wheatley Prize and Frank Isakson Prize, American Physical Society, 1985, 1997; Ernst Mach Medal, Czech Academy of Science, 1999; Nevill Mott Medal, British Institute of Physics, 2001 Miller Visiting Professor, University of California, Berkeley, 3 months, 2000; Fellow, Institute of Physics, 2001; Honorary Member, AF Ioffe

Institute, St Petersburg, 2003; Adjunct Professor, Arizona State University, 2003; Honorary Chairman, International Conference of Physics of Semiconductors, Flagstaff, Arizona, 2004; Blaise Pascal Medal, European Academy of Science, 2004; Matteucci Medal, Italian Academy of Science, 2004. Memberships include: Fellow, American Physical Society; Full Member, National Academy of Sciences of USA; Academia Europaea; Corresponding Member, Royal Academy of Sciences, Spain; Mexican Academy of Sciences; European Academy of Sciences; Academy of Sciences, Barcelona; Member, Global Photonics Advisory Board, CUNY, New York, 2004; Member, Advisory Board, Science Foundation of Ireland, 2003. Address: Max-Planck-Institut für Festkörperforschung, Heisenbergstr. 1, 70569, Stuttgart, Germany.

**CARDONE Fabio,** b. 10 October 1960, Chieti, Italy. Physicist. m. Aquilani Silvia, 1 daughter. Education: Classic Humanities Diploma, 1979; PhD, Physics, 1984; Ms Sc, Elementary Particle Physics, 1985. Appointments: Researcher, Physicist, University of Wisconsin, 1985-86; INFN, Rome, 1984-92; CERN, Geneva, 1989-92; Professor of Physics, Gregoriana University, Rome, 1992-96; St Thomas Angelicum University, Rome, 1993-97; Tuscia University, 1996-99; Danzig (Gdansk) University, 1999; L'Aquila University, 1999-2000; Rome I University, 2000-04; Messina University, 2001-02; Lecturer, MIT, 2002; Fellow, National Institute of Applied Optics, 2000-03; Fellow, National Institute of High Mathematics of Italy, 2000-; Adviser, Senate of Italian Republic, 1995-2001; Adviser, Rome Province Government, 2000-01; Adviser, European Parliament, 2002-04; Member, CNR National Council of Researches, 2003-; Adviser, Italian Army, 2004-. Publications: Articles and papers contributed to professional journals, mainly in the fields of theoretical, phenomenological and experimental physics; Several textbooks, including Radon, 1997 (co-authored); Radioattivita, 1998 (co-authored); Enrico Fermi e secchi della sora Cesarina, 2000; Energy and Geometry, 2004. Honours: Galilei Prize in Physics, 1985; Honor Prize for Research in Physics, Abruzzo Region, 1991; IBC Medal, 2001; Presidential Seal of Honour, ABI, 2002. Memberships: New York Academy of Sciences; American Association for Advancement of Sciences; Italian Physics Society (SIF); Italian Society of Applied Mathematics (SIMAI); International Society of Relativity and Gravitation (SIGRAV). Address: Via Villaggio Italia 5, I-67039, Sulmona, Italy.

**CAREY John,** b. 5 April 1934, London, England. University Professor. m. Gillian Booth, 13 August 1960, 2 sons. Education: Lambe Open Scholar, 1954-57; BA, 1957; D Phil, 1960, St John's College, Oxford. Publications: Milton, 1969; The Violent Effigy: A Study of Dickens' Imagination, 1973; Thackerary, Prodigal Genius, 1977; John Donne: Life, Mind and Art, 1981; Original Copy: Selected Reviews and Journalism, 1987; The Faber Book of Reportage, 1987; Donne, 1990; The Intellectuals and the Masses, 1992; The Faber Book of Science, 1995; The Faber Book of Utopias, 1999; Pure Pleasure, 2000; What Good Are the Arts? 2005. Contributions to: Principal Book Reviewer, Sunday Times. Honours: Fellow, Royal Society of Literature; Fellow, British Academy; Honorary Fellow, St John's College, 1991, Balliol College, 1992. Address: Merton College, Oxford OX1 4SD, England.

**CAREY Peter,** b. 7 May 1943, Bacchus March, Victoria, Australia. Author. m. (2) Alison Summers, 1985, 2 sons. Education: Monash University. Appointments: Partner, McSpedden Carey Advertising Consultants, Sydney; Teacher, Columbia University, Princeton University. Publications: The Fat Man in History (short stories), 1974; War Crimes (short stories), 1979; Bliss (novel), 1981; Illywhacker (novel), 1985;

Oscar and Lucinda, 1988; The Tax Inspector (novel), 1991; The Unusual Life of Tristan Smith (novel), 1994; Collected Stories, 1995; The Big Bazoohley (children's novel), 1995; Jack Maggs, 1997; The True History of the Kelly Gang, 2000; 30 Days in Sydney: A Wildly Distorted Account, 2001; My Life as a Fake, 2003; Wrong About Japan, 2005; Screenplays: Bliss; Until the End of the World; Film: Oscar and Lucinda, 1998. Honours include: Miles Franklin Award; National Council Award; Age Book of the Year Award. Address: c/o Amanda Urban, ICM, 40 West 57th Street, New York, NY 10019, USA.

**CAREY Peter Philip,** b. 7 May 1943, Bacchus Marsh, Australia. Novelist. m. Alison Summers, 16 March 1985, 2 sons. Education: Dr of Letters, University of Queensland, 1989. Appointment: Writer in Residence, New York University, 1990; Director, Graduate Writing Program, Hunter College, City University of New York, 2000. Publications: The Fat Man in History, 1974; War Crimes, 1979, 1981; Illywhacker, 1985; Oscar and Lucinda, 1989; Until the End of the World, 1990; The Tax Inspector, 1991; The Unusual Life of Tristan Smith, 1994; Collected Stories, 1995; Jack Maggs, 1997; True History of the Kelly Gang, 2000; My Life as a Fake, 2003; Wrong About Japan, 2005. Honours: New South Wales Premier's Literary Award; Miles Franklin Award; National Book Council Award; The Age Book of Year Award; Victorian Premier's Literary Award; Won the Booker Prize Twice, for Oscar & Lucinda and True History; True History Won the 2001 Commonwealth Prize for Best Book. Membership: Royal Society of Literature. Address: c/o Deborah Rogers, Rogers, Coleridge & White Ltd, 20 Powis Mews, London W11 1JN, England.

**CARINE James,** b. 14 September 1934, Isle of Man, United Kingdom. Retired. m. Carolyn Sally Taylor, 5 sons, 2 deceased, 1 daughter. Education: Royal Naval College, Dartmouth, 1951-52; Qualified Company Secretary (FCIS), 1970. Appointments: Royal Navy, 1951-91; Captain, Executive Assistant to Deputy Supreme Allied Command Atlantic, 1982-95; Captain, Chief Staff Officer (Personnel and Logistics), 1985-88; Commodore in Command of HMS Drake, Devonport Naval Barracks, 1988-89; Rear Admiral, Chief of Staff to Commander-in-Chief, 1989-91; Chief Executive of The Arab Horse Society, 1992-2000; Member, Copyright Tribunal, 1999-; Chairman, Wiltshire Ambulance Service NHS Trust, 2002-. Honours: Freedom of City of London, 1988; Master, Worshipful Company of Chartered Secretaries, 1997-98; Knight of the Order of St Gregory the Great, 1983. Memberships: Fellow Chartered Institute of Secretaries and Administrators, 1970; Admiralty Board nominated Trustee/Director and Executive and Investment Committees of the United Services Trustee (Quoted Unit Trusts), 1995-2005; Trustee/Director and Management and Financial Committees of the Ex-Services Mental Welfare Society (Combat Stress), 1997-2002; Governor St Antony's – Lewiston School, 1997-2005; Wiltshire Committee of the National Art Collections Fund, 2001-; Independent Chairman, Wiltshire and Swindon Fire Authority Standards Committee, 2001-; Independent Chairman, North Wiltshire District Council Standards Committee, 2002-; Chairman, Age Concern, Swindon, 2002-05. Address: 5 Little Sands, Yatton Keynell, Chippenham, Wiltshire SN14 7BA, England. E-mail: james@carine.demon.co.uk

**CARL XVI GUSTAF, (King of Sweden),** b. 30 April 1946. m. Silvia Sommerlath, 1976, 1 son, 2 daughters. Education: Sigtuna; University of Uppsala; University of Stockholm. Appointments: Created Duke of Jämtland; Became Crown Prince, 1950; Succeeded to the throne on death of his grandfather, King Gustaf VI Adolf, 1973. Honours: Dr hc, Swedish University of Agricultural Sciences, Stockholm Institute of Technology,

Abo Academy, Finland. Memberships: Chair, Swedish Branch, World Wide Fund for Nature; Honorary President, World Scout Foundation. Address: Royal Palace, 111 30 Stockholm, Sweden.

**CARLING William David Charles,** b. 12 December 1965, Bradford-on-Avon, England. Rugby Player. m. (1) Julia Carling, 1994, divorced 1996, (2) Lisa Cooke, 1999, 1 son, 1 step-son, 1 step-daughter. Education: Durham University. Appointments: Owner, Inspirational Horizons Co, Insights Ltd; Former Member, Durham University Club; Member, Harlequins Club; International Debut, England v France, 1988; Captain, England Team, 1988-96; Retired, International Rugby, 1997; Played 72 times for England, Captain 59 times (world record); Rugby Football Commentator, ITV, 1997-. Publications: Captain's Diary, 1991; Will Carling (autobiography), 1994; The Way to Win, 1995; My Autobiography, 1998. Address: c/o Mike Burton Management, Bastian House, Brunswick House, Brunswick Road, Gloucester, GL1 1JJ, England. E-mail: will@willcarling.com

**CARLTON-PORTER Robert William,** b. 29 November 1944, Lincolnshire, England. Treasurer. m. Angela, 1 son. Education: Nottingham University; Cranfield College. Appointments: Financial Director, Hoechst UK Ltd, 1973-83; Financial Director, English China Clays plc, 1983-92; Director of several unlisted companies; Director, Western Trust and Savings plc; Director, ARAM Resources plc; Chairman and Chief Executive Officer, Newport Holdings plc; Chairman Rok Property Solutions plc; Non-Executive Director, Michelmersh Brick Holdings plc. Honours: Associate, Chartered Institute of Bankers; Fellow, Chartered Management Institute; Foundation Fellow, Association of Corporate Treasurers; Member, Chartered Institute of Marketing. Memberships: Former Member, London Stock Exchange Pre-emption Committee; Former Chairman, 100 Group of Finance Directors Environmental Reporting Group; Chairman, Association of Corporate Treasurers, 1991-92; Governor and Treasurer, Kingswood School, Bath. Address: 4 Laggan House, College Road, Bath BA1 5RU, England.

**CARLYLE Robert,** b. 14 April 1961, Glasgow, Scotland. Actor. m. Anastasia Shirley, 1997, 2 children. Education: Royal Scottish Academy of Music & Drama. Appointments: Director, Rain Dog Theatre Company. Creative Works: Productions include: Wasted; One Flew Over the Cuckoo's Nest; Conquest of the South Pole; Macbeth; Stage appearances include: Twelfth Night; Dead Dad Dog; Nae Problem; City; No Mean City; Cuttin' a Rug; Othello; TV includes: Face; Go on Byrne'; Taggart; The Bill; Looking After Jo Jo, 1998; Hitler: The Rise of Evil, 2003; Gunpowder, Treason and Plot, 2004; Films include: The Full Monty; Carla's Song; Trainspotting; Priest; Marooned; Being Human; Riff Raff; Silent Scream; Apprentices; Plunkett and Macleane, 1999; The World is Not Enough, 1999; Angela's Ashes, 2000; The Beach, 2000; There's Only One Jimmy Grimble, 2000; To End All Wars, 2000; 51st State, 2001; Once Upon a Time in the Midlands, 2002; Black and White, 2002; Dead Fish, 2004; Marilyn Hotchkiss Ballroom Dancing of Charm School, 2005; The Mighty Celt, 2005. Honours include: Paper Boat Award, 1992; BAFTA Award, Best Actor; Salerno Film Festival Award, 1997; Evening Standard Outstanding British Actor Award, 1998; Bowmore Whiskey/Scottish Screen Award for Best Actor, 2001; David Puttnam Patrons Award. Address: c/o ICM, Oxford House, 76 Oxford Street, London, W1D 1BS, England.

**CARMEN Ira H,** b. 3 December 1934, Boston, Massachusetts, USA. College Professor. m. Lawrence Lowell Putnam, 2 daughters. Education: BA, University of New Hampshire, 1957;

MA, 1959, PhD, 1964, University of Michigan. Appointments: Member, Political Science Faculty, University of Illinois, 1968-; Member, Institute for Genomic Biology, University of Illinois, 2004-. Publications: Books, Movies, Censorship, and the Law, 1966; Power and Balance, 1978; Cloning and The Constitution, 1986; Politics in the Laboratory; The Constitution of Human Genomics, 2004. Honours: President George Bush's Educators Advisory Committee, 1989; Recipient of Six Awards for Teaching Excellence, University of Illinois. Memberships: Recombinant DNA Advisory Committee, National Institutes of Health, 1990-1994; Human Genome Organisation, elected 1996. Address: Department of Political Science, 361 Lincoln Hall, University of Illinois, Urbana, IL 61801, USA.

**CARPENTER Harry Leonard,** b. 17 October 1925, South London, England. TV Sports Commentator. m. Phyllis Barbara, 1 son. Appointments: Greyhound Express, 1941-43; Greyhound Owner, 1946-48; Speedway Gazette, 1948-50; Sporting Record, 1950-54; Sports Commentator, BBC TV, 1949-94; Daily Mail, 1954-62. Publications: Masters of Boxing, 1964; Illustrated History of Boxing, 1975; The Hardest Game, 1981; Where's Harry, 1992. Honours: Davi Award, Best Sports programme on video, 1983; American Sportcasters Award, International Sportscaster of Year, 1989; Tric Award, Sports Personality of the Year, 1989; OBE, 1991. Memberships: Royal and Ancient Golf Club of St Andrews; Royal St George's Golf Club, Sandwich; Boxing Writers' Club. Address: Sommerfield Ltd, 35 Queen Street, London, SW1H 9JD, England.

**CARPINTERI Alberto,** b. 23 December 1952, Bologna, Italy. Structural Engineer. Education: PhD, Nuclear Engineering cum laude, University of Bologna, Bologna, Italy, 1976; PhD, Mathematics cum laude, University of Bologna, 1981. Appointments include: Researcher, Consiglio Nazionale delle Ricerche, Bologna, Italy, 1978-80; Assistant Professor, University of Bologna, 1981-86; Professor of Structural Mechanics, Politecnico di Torino, Italy, 1986-; Founding Member and Director, Graduate School in Structural Engineering, Politecnico di Torino, Italy, 1990-; Director, Department Structural Engineering, Politecnico di Torino, 1989-95. Publications include: Localized Damage: Computer-Aided Assessment and Control, 1994; Advanced Technology for Design and Fabrication of Composite Materials and Structures, 1995; Structural Mechanics, 1997; Fractals and Fractional Calculus in Continuum Mechanics, 1998; Computational Fracture Mechanics in Concrete Technology, 1999. Honours include: Robert l'Hermite International Prize, 1982; JSME Medal, 1993; Doctor of Physics Honoris Causa, 1994; International Cultural Diploma of Honor, 1995; Honorary Professor, Nanjing Architectural and Civil Engineering Institute, Nanjing, China, 1996; Honorary Professor, Albert Schweitzer University, Geneva, Switzerland, 2000. Memberships: International Congress on Fracture, 1981-, Vice-President, 2005-2009; International Association of Fracture Mechanics for Concrete and Concrete Structures, 1992-, President, 2004-2007; Réunion Internationale des Laboratories d'Essais et de Recherches sur les Matériaux et les Constructions, 1982-; American Society of Civil Engineers, 1985-; European Structural Integrity Society, 1991-, President, 2002-2006-; European Mechanics Society, 1994-. Address: Chair of Structural Mechanics, Politecnico di Torino, 10129 Torino, Italy.

**CARR Peter Derek,** b. 12 July 1930, Mexborough, Yorkshire. Chairman. m. Geraldine Pamela, 1 son, 1 daughter. Education: Ruskin College, Oxford; Fircroft College, Birmingham; London University. Appointments: Director, Commission on Industrial Relations, 1969-74; Labour Counsellor, British Embassy, Washington, 1978-83; Regional Director, Department of

Employment, 1984-89; Chairman, Occupational Pensions Board, 1993-98; Chairman, Northern Screen Commission, 1992-2000; Chairman, County Durham Development Company, 1990-99; Company Chairman, Durham County Waste Management, 1990-; Chairman, Northumberland and Tyne & Wear Strategic Health Authority, 2002-; Chairman, Northern Assembly Health Forum, 2003-; Chairman, Northern Advisory Committee on Clinical Excellence Awards, 2003-. Publications: Industrial Relations in the National Newspapers; Worker Participation in Europe; It Occurred To Me, 2004; Various articles on Management Issues in several journals. Honours: CBE, 1989; Deputy Lieutenant; Honorary Degree, University of Northumbria; Member of Council, University of Newcastle, 2005-. Membership: Royal Overseas League. Address: 4 Corchester Towers; Corbridge, Northumberland, NE45 5NP, England. E-mail: petercarr@aol.com

**CARRERAS Jose,** b. 5 December 1947, Barcelona, Spain. Singer (Tenor). m. Ana Elisa, 1 son, 1 daughter. Appointments: Debut, Gennaro in Lucrezia Borgia, Liceo Opera House, Barcelona, 1970-71 Season; Appeared in La Boheme, Un Ballo in Maschera, I Lombardi alla Prima Crociata at Teatro Regio, Parm, Italy, 1972; US Debut as Pinkerton in Madame Butterfly with NYC Opera, 1972; Debut, Metro Opera as Cavaradossi, 1974; Debut, La Scala as Riccardo in Un Ballo in Maschera, 1975; Appeared in Film, Don Carlos, 1980, West Side Story (TV), 1985; Appeared at major opera houses and festivals including Teatro Colon, Buenos Aires, Covent Garden, London, Vienna Staatsoper, Easter Festival and Summer Festival, Salzburg, Lyric Opera of Chicago. Creative Works: Recordings include: Un Ballo in Maschera; La Battaglia di Legnano; Il Corsaro; Un Giorno di Regno; I Due Foscari; Simone Boccanegra; Macbeth; Don Carlos; Tosca; Thais; Aida; Cavalleria Rusticana; Pagliacci; Lucia di Lammermoor; Turandot; Elisabetta di Inghilterra; Otello (Rossini). Publication: Singing From the Soul, 1991. Honours: Grammy Award, 1991; Sir Lawrence Olivier Award, 1993; Gold Medal of City of Barcelona; Albert Schweizer Music Award, 1996; Commandeur des Arts et des Lettres; Chevalier Légion d'honneur and numerous other awards. Memberships: President, Jose Carreras International Leukaemia Foundation, 1988-; Honorary Member, Royal Academy of Music, 1990. Address: c/o FIJC, Muntaner 383, 2, 08021 Barcelona, Spain. E-mail: fundacio@fcarreras.es Website: www.fcarreras.es

**CARREY Jim,** b. 17 January 1962, Newmarket, Canada. Actor. m. (1) Melissa Worner, 1986, divorced, 1 daughter, (2) Lauren Holly, 2001. Appointments: Performed, Comedy Clubs, Toronto. Creative Works: Films include: Peggy Sue Got Married, 1986; The Dead Pool, 1988; Earth Girls Are Easy, 1989; Ace Ventura! Pet Detective; The Mask; Ace Ventura: When Nature Calls, 1995; Dumb and Dumber; Liar Liar, 1996; Batman Forever; The Cable Guy; The Truman Show, 1997; Man on the Moon; How the Grinch Stole Christmas, 2000; Me, Myself and Irene, 2000; The Majestic, 2001; Bruce Almighty, 2003; Pecan Pie, 2003; Eternal Sunshine of the Spotless Mind, 2004; Several TV appearances. Address: UTA, 9560 Wilshire Boulevard, 5th Floor, Beverly Hills, CA 90212, USA.

**CARRICK Roger John (Sir),** b. 13 October 1937. Diplomat (Retired); International Consultant; Deputy Chairman, the D Group. m. Hilary Elizabeth Blinman, 1 September 1962, 2 sons. Education: Joint Services School for Linguists, London University School for Slavonic and East European Studies. Appointments: Royal Navy, 1956-58; Diplomatic Service, 1956-97: Foreign Office, 1958-61; Third Secretary British Legation (later Embassy), Sofia, Bulgaria, 1962-65; Foreign Office, 1965-67; Second, later First Secretary (Economic), British Embassy,

Paris, 1967-71; Head of Chancery, British High Commission, Singapore, 1971-74; Foreign and Commonwealth Office, 1974-77; Visiting Fellow, University of California, Berkeley, 1977-78; Counsellor, British Embassy Washington, 1978-82; Head of Department, Foreign and Commonwealth Office, 1982-85; HM Consul-General, Chicago, 1985-88; Assistant Under-Secretary of State, Foreign and Commonwealth Office, 1988-90; HM Ambassador to Indonesia, 1990-94; British High Commission to Australia, 1994-97; Member, Board of Trustees, Chevening Estate, 1998-2003; Joint Founder, Worldwide Advice on Diplomatic Estates; Consultant, KPMG (Australia), 1998-2001; NED, Strategy International Ltd, 2001-. Publications: East-West Technology Transfer in Perspective, 1978; RolleroundOz, 1998. Honours: Lieutenant of the Royal Victorian Order, 1972; Companion, Order of St Michael and St George (CMG), 1983; Knight Commander (KCMG), 1995; Freeman of the City of London, 2002. Memberships: Royal Overseas League; Cook Society, Chairman, 2002; Pilgrims; Royal Society for Asian Affairs; Anglo-Indonesian Society; Primary Club; Vice President, Britain-Australia Society; Churchill Fellow, Westminster College, Fulton, Missouri. Address: Windhover, Wootton Courtenay, Minehead, Somerset TA24 8RD, England. E-mail: rjc@wcwh.freeserve.co.uk

**CARRINGTON 6th Baron (Peter Alexander Rupert Carrington)**, b. 6 June 1919. m. Iona, 1 son, 2 daughters. Education: Eton; RMC Sandhurst. Appointments: Major, Grenadier Guards, Northwest Europe; Justice of the Peace, Buckinghamshire, 1948, DL, 1951; Parliamentary Secretary, Ministry of Agriculture and Fisheries, 1951-54; MOD, 1954-56; High Commissioner, Australia, 1956-59; First Lord of Admiralty, 1959-63; Minister without portfolio and leader of House of Lords, 1963-64; Leader of Opposition, House of Lords, 1964-70, 1974-79; Secretary of State for Defence, 1970-74, Department of Energy, 1974; Minister of Aviation Supply, 1971-74; Secretary of State for Foreign and Commonwealth Affairs, and Minister of Overseas Development, 1979-82; Chairman, Conservative Party, 1972-74; Secretary General, NATO, 1984-88; Chariman, EC Peace Conference, Yugoslavia, 1991-92; Chairman, GEC, 1983-84 (director, 1982-84); Director, Christie's International plc, 1988-98 (chairman, 1988-93); Director, The Telegraph plc, 1990-; Non-Executive Director, Chime Communications, 1993-99; Non-Executive Director, Christie's Fine Art Ltd, 1998-. Publications: Reflect on Things Past: The Memoirs of Lord Carrington, 1988. Honours: Honorary Fellow, St Antony's College, Oxford, 1982; Honorary Bencher, Middle Temple, 1983; Honorary Elder, Brother Trinity House, 1984; Honorary LLD, universities of Leeds (1981), Cambridge (1981), Philippines (1982), South Carolina (1983), Aberdeen (1985), Harvard (1986), Sussex (1989), Reading (1989), Nottingham (1993), Birmingham (1993); Honorary DSc, Cranfield, 1983; Honorary DCL, University of Newcastle, 1998; Honorary Duniv, Essex; Liveryman, Worshipful Company of Clothworkers. Memberships: Fellow, Eton, 1966-81; Member, International Board, United World Colleges, 1982-84; Chairman, Board of Trustees V&A Museum, 1983-88; Chancellor: Order of St Michael and St George (1984-94), University of Reading (1992-), Order of the Garter (1994-); President: Pilgrims (1983-2002), VSO (1993-98). Address: 32A Ovington Square, London SW3 1LR, England.

**CARRINGTON Simon Robert,** b. 23 October 1942, Salisbury, UK. Conductor; University Professor; Freelance Choral Consultant. m. Hilary Stott, 1 son, 1 daughter. Education: MA, Cantab; Choral Scholar, King's College, Cambridge; Teaching Certificate, New College, Oxford. Appointments: Founder and Co-Director, The King's Singers, 1968-2001; Director, Choral Activities, University of Kansas, Lawrence, 1994-2001; Director,

Choral Activities, New England Conservatory, Boston, 2001-03; Professor of Choral Conducting, Conductor of the Yale Schola Cantorum, Yale School of Music, New Haven, 2005-; With the King's Singers: 3,000 concerts; 72 recordings, television and radio performances worldwide. Publications: Various choral arrangements. Honours: Grammy Nomination, 1986; Numerous awards and citations at choral festivals worldwide. Memberships: American Choral Directors Association; Association of British Choral Directors; Chorus America. Address: Yale School of Music, Yale Institute of Sacred Music, 409 Prospect Street, New Haven, CT 06511, USA. E-mail: simon.carrington@yale.edu Website: www.simoncarrington.com

**CARTER Jimmy (James Earl Jr),** b. 1 October 1924, Plains, Georgia, USA. Politician; Farmer. m. Rosalynn Smith, 1946, 3 sons, 1 daughter. Education: Georgia Southwest College; Georgia Institute of Technology; US Naval Academy. Appointments: US Navy, 1946-53; Peanut Farmer, Warehouseman, 1953-77; Busman, Carter Farms, Carter Warehouses, Georgia; State Senator, Georgia, 1962-66; Governor of Georgia, 1971-74; President of USA, 1977-81; Distinguished Professor, Emory University, Atlanta, 1982-; Leader, International Observer Teams, Panama, 1989, Nicaragua, 1990, Dominican Republic, 1990, Haiti, 1990; Host, Peace Negotiations, Ethiopia, 1989; Visitor, Korea, 1994; Negotiator, Haitian Crisis, 1994; Visitor, Bosnia, 1994. Publications: Why Not The Best?, 1975; A Government as Good as its People, 1977; Keeping Faith: Memoirs of a President, 1982; The Blood of Abraham: Insights into the Middle East, 1985; Everything to Gain: Making the Most of the Rest of Your Life, 1987; An Outdoor Journal, 1988; Turning Point: A Candidate, a State and a Nation Come of Age, 1992; Always a Reckoning (poems), 1995; Sources of Strength, 1997; The Virtues of Ageing, 1998; An Hour Before Daylight, 2001. Honours include: Onassis Foundation Award, 1991; Notre Dame University Award, 1992; Matsunaga Medal of Peace, 1993; J William Fulbright Prize for International Understanding, 1994. Address: The Carter Center, 453 Freedom Parkway, 1 Copenhill Avenue, North East Atlanta, GA 30307, USA.

**CARWARDINE Richard John,** b. 12 January 1947, Cardiff, Wales. University Professor. m. Linda Margaret Kirk, 17 May 1975. Education: BA, Oxford University, 1968; MA, 1972; DPhil, 1975. Appointments: Lecturer, Senior Lecturer, Reader, Professor, University of Sheffield, 1971-2002; Rhodes Professor of American History and Fellow of St Catherine's College, Oxford University, 2002- Visiting Professor, Syracuse University, New York, 1974-75; Visiting Fellow, University of North Carolina, Chapel Hill, 1989. Publications: Transatlantic Revivalism: Popular Evangelicalism in Britain and America 1790-1865, 1978; Evangelicals and Politics in Antebellum America, 1993; Lincoln, 2003. Address: c/o St Catherine's College, Oxford OX1 3UJ, England.

**CARY Phillip Scott,** b. 10 June 1958, USA. Professor. m. Nancy Hazle, 3 sons. Education: BA, English Literature and Philosophy, Washington University, St Louis, 1980; MA, Philosophy, 1989, PhD, Philosophy and Religious Studies, 1994, Yale University. Appointments: Teaching Assistant, Philosophy Department, Yale University, 1988-92; Adjunct Faculty, Philosophy Department, University of Connecticut, 1993; Adjunct Faculty, Hillier College, University of Hartford, 1993-94; Arthur J Ennis Postdoctoral Fellow, 1994-97, Rocco A and Gloria C Postdoctoral Fellow, 1997-98, Core Humanities Programme, Villanova University; Assistant Professor of Philosophy, 1998-2001, Associate Professor of Philosophy, 2001-, Scholar in Residence, Templeton Honors College, 1999-, Eastern University, St Davids. Publications: 1 book; 13 articles in professional journals. Honours: University Fellowship, Yale

University; Mylonas Scholarship, Freshman History Award, Phi Beta Kappa, Washington University; Listed in national and international biographical dictionaries. Memberships: APA; AAR; SCP. Address: Eastern University, 1300 Eagle Road, St Davids, PA 19087-3696, USA. E-mail: pcary@eastern.edu

**CASH Pat,** b. 27 May 1965, Australia. Tennis Player. m. Emily, 1 son, 1 daughter. Education: Whitefriars College. Appointments: Coached by Ian Barclay; Trainer, Anne Quinn; Winner, US Open Junior, 1982 Brisbane and in winning Australian Davis Cup team, 1983; Quarter-finals, Wimbledon, 1985, Finalist, Australian Open, 1987, 1988; Wimbledon Champion, 1987; Retired, 1997; Co-Established a tennis training and coaching centre, Queensland; Sports Commentator. Honour: Australian Tennis Hall of Fame. Address: c/o Pat Cash and Associates, PO Box 2238, Footscray, Victoria 3011, Australia.

**CASSIAN Nina,** b. 27 November 1924, Galati, Romania. Poet; Composer; Film Critic; Translator. Education: University of Bucharest and Conservatory of Music. Appointment: Visiting Professor, New York University, 1985-86. Publications: Verses: 50 books including: (in Romanian) At the Scale 1/1, 1947; Ages of the Year, 1957; The Dialogue of Wind and Sea, 1957; Outdoor Performance, 1961; Everyday Holidays, 1961; Gift Giving, 1963; The Discipline of the Harp, 1965; Blood, 1966; Parallel Destinies, 1967; Ambitus, 1968; Chronophagy 1944-69, 1969; The Big Conjugation, 1971; Requiem, 1971; Lotto Poems, 1974; 100 Poems, 1974; Suave, 1977; Mercy, 1981; Countdown, 1983; Arguing with Chaos, 1994; The Un-Making of the World, 1997; (in English) Lady of Miracles, 1982; Call Yourself Alive?, 1988; Life Sentence: Selected Poems, 1990; Cheer Leader for a Funeral, 1993;  Take My Word for It, 1998; Chapbook: Something Old, Something New, 2001. Other: Prose; children's plays and poetry. Honours: Writers Union of Romania Awards, 1967, 1984; Writers Association of Bucharest Award, 1981; Fulbright Grant, 1986; New York Public Library Literary Lion, 1994. Address: 555 Main Street, No 502, Roosevelt Island, New York, NY 10044, USA.

**CASTILLO Susan,** b. 15 March 1948, Jackson, Mississippi, USA. Professor of American Literature. 1 son, 1 daughter. Education, M Phil, 1980, PhD, 1989, Oporto University, Portugal. Appointments: Lecturer, Oporto University, 1978-96; Lecturer, Department of English Literature, 1996-99, Reader, Department of English Literature, 1999-2001, John Nichol Professor of American Literature, 2001-, Glasgow University. Publications: Notes from the Periphery, 1995; Native American Women in Literature and Culture, 1995; The Literatures of Colonial America: An Anthology, 2001; The Candlewoman's Trade (poetry), 2002; Engendering Identities, 1994; Over 50 articles in academic journals; Associate Editor, Journal of American Studies. Honours: Listed in Who's Who publications and biographical dictionaries. Memberships: Society of Early Americanists; Hakluyt Society; British Association for American Studies; European Association for American Studies. Address: Department of English Literature, Glasgow University, Glasgow G12 8QQ, Scotland.

**CASTLEDEN Rodney,** b. 23 March 1945, Worthing, Sussex, England. Teacher; Archaeologist; Writer. m. Sarah Dee, 29 July 1987. Education: BA, Geography, Hertford College, 1967, Dip Ed, 1968, MA, 1972, MSc, Geomorphology, 1980, Oxford University. Appointments: Assistant Geography Teacher, Wellingborough High School, 1968-74 and Wellingborough School, 1974-75; Acting Head of Geography, Overstone School, 1975-76; Assistant Geography Teacher, North London Collegiate School, 1976-79; Head of Geography Department, 1979-90, Head of Humanities Faculty, 1990-2001, Head of

Social Science Faculty, 2001-04, Roedean School. Publications include: Classic Landforms of the Sussex Coast, 1982; The Wilmington Giant: The Quest for a Lost Myth, 1983; The Stonehenge People: An Exploration of Life in Neolithic Britain, 1987; The Knossos Labyrinth, 1989; Minoans: Life in Bronze Age Crete, 1990; Book of British Dates, 1991; Neolithic Britain, 1992; The Making of Stonehenge, 1993; World History: a Chronological Dictionary of Dates, 1994; British History: A Chronological Dictionary of Dates, 1994; The Cerne Giant, 1996; Classic Landforms of the Sussex Coast, 2nd edition, 1996; Knossos, Temple of the Goddess, 1997; Atlantis Destroyed, 1998; Out in the Cold, 1998; The English Lake District, 1998; King Arthur: the Truth Behind the Legend, 1999; The Little Book of Kings and Queens, 1999; Ancient British Hill Figures, 2000; The History of World Events, 2003; The World's Most Evil People, 2004; Infamous Murderers, 2005; Serial Killers, 2005; Mycenaeans, 2005; Music: Cuckmere Suite, a suite for string orchestra, 1999; Winfrith, a chamber opera, 2000. Memberships: Society of Authors; Sussex Archaeological Society. Address: 15 Knepp Close, Brighton, Sussex, BN2 4LD, England.

**CASTONGUAY ROSATI Diane Claire,** b. 27 November 1941, Brooklyn, New York, USA. Artist. m. Vincent S Rosati, 1 son, 1 daughter. Education: BS, cum laude, Wagner College, 1976; MPH, Columbia University School of Public Health, 1980. Appointments: Nurse Epidemiologist, Doctors Hospital of Staten Island, 1977-80; Infection Control Coordinator, Staten Island Hospital, 1980-; Professional Artist; Curator. Publications: Several articles in professional journals. Commissions and Creative Works: Numerous exhibitions including: 10 solo shows, 1992-; Pen and Brush Annual Pastel Exhibition, 1992; Mixed Media Shows; Moorings Gallery, Nova Scotia Sign of the Whale Art Gallery, Nova Scotia, Canada, 1992; Silvermine Guild Art Centre, International Print Biennial, 1994, 1996; International Miniprint Exhibition, Conn Graphics Art Centre, 1997; Acadia University Exhibition, invitational 4 person show, Nova Scotia; Curator, Coastline Gallery, Nova Scotia; Works in private collections. Honours include: Gerald Mennin Award for Graphics, National Art Club 97th Annual Exhibiting Members Show, 1995; Honorable Mention, Salmagundi Spring Auction, 1996; Robert Brockman Award, Pen and Brush 15th Pastel Exhibition, 1996; Solo Show Awards in Mixed Media and Pastel, Pen and Brush, 1997; Philip Isenburg Award in Graphics, Pen and Brush, 1997; Dorothy Koatz Myers Award, Salmagundi Non Juried Summer Exhibition, 1997; Silver Medal of Honour, 56th Annual Audubon Artists Show, 1998; Gene Alden Walker Memorial Award, Pen and Brush Graphics Show, 1999. Memberships include: National Art Club; Print Club of Albany; Society of American Graphic Artists; Visual Arts of Nova Scotia; National Association of Woman Artists; The Pen and Brush; Audubon Pastel Society of Canada; Salmagundi Club. Address: 1618 McLean Lake Road, RR#2 Sable River, NS B0T 1V0, Canada.

**CATON-JONES Michael,** b. 15 October 1957, Broxburn, Scotland. Film Director. Education: National Film School. Appointments: Stagehand, London West End Theatres. Creative Works: Films: Liebe Mutter; The Making of Absolute Beginners; Scandal, 1989; Memphis Belle, 1990; Doc Hollywood, 1991; This Boy's Life, 1993; Rob Roy, 1994; The Jackal, 1997; City By The Sea, 2002. Honours: 1st Prize, European Film School Competition.

**CATOR Albemarle (Alby),** b. 23 August 1953, Norwich, Norfolk, England. Company Director. m. (1) Fiona, dissolved, (2) Victoria, 4 sons. Education: Harrow School. Appointments: Short Service Commission, Scotts Guards, 1971-75; Management Trainee in merchant banking disciplines, then

Manager, Samuel Montagu & Co Limited, 1975-84; Executive Director, Loan Syndication, 1984-86, Executive Director, Head of Distribution, 1986-88, Executive Director, Co-Head Banking and Corporate Finance, 1988-91, Chemical Bank International Limited; Executive Director, Loan Syndication and Debt Trading, 1991-94, Managing Director, European Primary Group, 1994-95, Managing Director Debt Markets Group, 1995-97, NatWest Markets; Founding Director and Principal Shareholder, AC European Finance Limited (now Westhall Capital Limited), 1998-2003; Director, ECU Group plc, 2004-; Securities and Futures Authority registered Director and General Representative. Address: Woodbastwick Hall, Woodbastwick, Norwich NR13 6HL, England. E-mail: actor@dircon.co.uk

**CAULFIELD Patrick,** b. 29 January 1936, London, England. Artist. m. (1) Pauline Jacobs, 1968, divorced, 3 sons, (2) Janet Nathan, 1999. Education: Chelsea School of Art; RCA. Appointments: Teacher, Chelsea College of Art. Creative Works: Exhibitions: FBA Galleries, 1961; Robert Fraser Gallery, London, 1965, 1967; Robert Elkon Gallery, New York, 1966, 1968; Waddington Galleries, 1969, 1971, 1973, 1975, 1979, 1981, 1985, 1997, 1998, 2002; Also in France, Belgium, Italy, Australia, USA, Japan; Retrospective Exhibition, Tate Gallery, London, 1981; Serpentine Gallery, London, 1992; Hayward Gallery, London, 1999; Numerous group exhibitions in England, Europe, New York; Design, for Ballet Party Game, Covent Garden, 1984; Public Collections include: Tate Gallery; Victoria & Albert Museum; Manchester City Art Gallery and other museums and galleries in England, USA, Australia, Germany, Japan. Honours: Elected, Senior Fellowship, RCA, 1993; Honorary Fellow, London Institute, 1996; CBE, 1996; Honorary Fellowship, Bolton Institute, 1999; Honorary Doctorate, University of Surrey, 2000; Honorary Doctorate, University of Portsmouth, 2002. Address: 19 Belsize Square, London NW3 4HT, England.

**CAUNA Nikolais,** b. 4 April 1914, Riga, Latvia. Scientist; Medical Educator. m. Dzidra Priede. Education: MD, University of Latvia, 1942; MSc, 1964, DSc, 1961, University of Durham, England. Appointments: Lecturer, Anatomy, University of Latvia, Riga, 1942-44; General Practice Medicine, Sarsted and Eschershausen, West Germany, 1944-46; Acting Chairman, Anatomy Department, Baltic University, Hamburg, Germany, 1946-48; Lecturer, Anatomy, Medical School, University of Durham, England, 1948-57; Reader, 1958-61, Professor of Anatomy, School of Medicine, University of Pittsburgh, 1961-75; Professor, Chairman, 1975-83; Professor Emeritus, 1984-. Publications: Numerous book chapters; Articles for professional journals. Honours: Golden Apple Award, University of Pittsburgh, 1964, 1967, 1973; Research Grant, Royal Society, England, 1958-60; American Cancer Grant, 1961; Camillo Golgi Medal, Italy, 1973; USPHS Grant, 1962-83. Memberships: Anatomy Society of Great Britain and Ireland; American Association of Anatomists; Royal Micros Society; Histochem Society; Member of Editorial Board of several journals. Address: 5850 Meridian Road, Apartment C-311 Gibsonia, Pennsylvania 15044, USA.

**CAUNT Lorna Margaret,** b. 30 November 1927. Teacher; Secretary; Laboratory Technician; Poet. m. Tony Caunt, 27 February 1954, 2 sons, 1 daughter. Education: BSc, Zoology, London University, 1949. Publications: Keeping Company, 1989; No Sense of Grandeur, 1991; No One About, 1993. Contributions to: Outposts; Envoi; Weyfarers; Iota; Staple; Pause; First Time; Doors; Poetry Nottingham; Poet's England; The Countryman; Spokes; Vision On (Ver); Ver Poets' Voices; Arcadian; Psychopoetica; Success Magazine. Honours: 2nd prize, Arts Council/David bookshops, 1985, 1987, 1988; Ver

Poets Internal Competitions, 1988 twice, 1990,1991, 1992 twice; Various mentions. Memberships: Ver Poets; Welwyn Garden City Literary Society; Ware Poetry Reading Group. Address: 1 Templewood, Welwyn Garden City, Hertfordshire AL8 7HT, England.

**CAUSLEY Charles (Stanley),** b. 24 August 1917, Launceston, Cornwall, England. Poet; Dramatist; Editor. Education: Launceston College. Appointment: Service in Royal Navy, 1940-46; Teacher, Cornwall, 1947-76. Publications: Survivors Leave, 1953; Union Street, 1957; Johnny Alleluia, 1961; Penguin Modern Poets 3, 1962; Underneath the Water, 1968; Pergamon Poets 10, 1970; Timothy Winters, 1970; Six Women, 1974; Ward 14, 1974; St Martha and the Dragon, 1978; Collected Poems, 1951-75, 1975; Secret Destinations, 1984; 21 Poems, 1986; The Young Man of Cury, 1991; Bring in the Holly, 1992; Collected Poems for Children, 1996; Penguin Modern Poets 6, 1996; Collected Poems, 1951-97, 1997; Collected Poems, 1951-2000, 2000. Other: Several plays: Libretto for William Mathias's opera Jonah, 1990. Contributions to: Various publications. Honours: Queen's Gold Medal for Poetry, 1967; Honorary DLitt, University of Exeter, 1977; Honorary MA, Open University, 1982; Commander of the Order of the British Empire, 1986; T S Eliot Award, Ingersoll Foundation, USA, 1990; Heywood Hill Literary Prize, 2000. Address: 2 Cyprus Well, Launceston, Cornwall, PL15 8BT, England.

**CAVE Philip,** b. 2 June 1949, Finedon, Northamptonshire, England. Landscape Architect. 1 son. Education: BSc, Honours, Plant Science, University of Newcastle upon Tyne, 1970; MA, Landscape Design, Sheffield University, 1973. Appointments: Landscape Architect, Nottinghamshire County Council, 1973-74; Landscape Architect, Norwich City Council, 1974-75; Study tour through Middle East, Asia, Far East and Japan, 1975-77; Landscape Architect, Mathews Ryan Partnership, 1978-79; Principal, Philip Cave Associates, Landscape Architects and Urban Designers, 1979-. Publications: Book: Creating Japanese Gardens, 1993; Section in book: Good Place Guide, 2003; Articles in Urban Design Quarterly, Landscape Design. Honours: Civic Trust Commendation, 2002; Bromley Environmental Award, 2002. Memberships: Landscape Institute, 1975; Urban Design Group, 1982. Address: 5 Dryden Street, Covent Garden, London WC2E 9NB, England. E-mail: principal@philipcave.com Website www.philipcave.com

**CAWS Ian,** b. 19 March 1945, Bramshott, Hants, England. Local Government Officer. m. Hilary Walsh, 20 June 1970, 3 sons, 2 daughters. Education: Certificate in Social Work, 1970; Certificate for Social Workers with the Deaf, 1973. Appointments: Senior Social Worker with the Deaf, 1974; County Team Leader of Deaf Services, 1986; Arts Development Officer, 1991. Publications: Looking for Bonfires, 1975; Bruised Madonna, 1979; Boy with a Kite, 1981; The Ragman Totts, 1990; Chamomile, 1994; The Feast of Fools, 1994; The Playing of the Easter Music (with Martin C Caseley and B L Pearce), 1996; Herrick's Women, 1996; Dialogues in Mask, 2000; Taro Fair, 2003. Contributions to: Acumen Magazine; London Magazine; New Welsh Review; Observer; Poetry Review; Scotsman; Spectator; Stand Magazine; Swansea Review. Honours: Eric Gregory Award, 1973; Poetry Book Society Recommendation, 1990. Membership: Poetry Society. Address: 9 Tennyson Avenue, Rustington, West Sussex BN16 2PB, England.

**CAYLEFF Susan Evelyn,** b. 3 April 1954, Boston, Massachusetts, USA. Professor; Department Chair. Education: BA, University of Massachusetts, Amherst, 1976; MA, Sarah Lawrence College, 1978; MA, 1979, PhD, 1983, Brown

University. Appointments: Teaching Associate, Brown University, 1979-83; Assistant Professor, The Medical Humanities, University of Texas, Medical Branch, Galveston, 1983-87; Professor, Chair, Department of Women's Studies, San Diego State University, 1987-97. Publications include: Babe: The Greatest All-Sport Athlete of All Time; Babe: The Life and Legend of Babe Didrikson Zaharias; Co-writer, Wings of Gauze: Women of Color and the Experience of Health and Illness; Wash and Be Healed: The Water-Cure Movement and Women's Health. Honour: Pulitzer Prize Nominee, 1995; Outstanding Book Award, Gay and Lesbian Alliance Against Defamation, 1996. Memberships: National Women's Studies Association; American Historical Association; Organization of American Historians; North American Society for Sport History; American Association for the History of Medicine; Co-ordinating Caucus of Women in the Historical Profession; Pacific Southwest Women's Studies Association. Address: Department of Women's Studies, San Diego State University, San Diego, CA 92182, USA.

**CAZAN Octavia,** b. 19 February 1933, Sacelu, Jud Gorj, Romania. Librarian; Artist. m. Nicolae Cazan, 1 son. Education: Librarianship courses, Tg-Jiu, Romania; Painting Classes, Plastic Arts School, Tg-Jiu, Romania. Career: Club Manager, Barseşti; Librarian, Painting Teacher, Industrial Secondary School Nr 2, Tg-Jiu; Organised Painting Club at the Secondary School; Many Solo Exhibitions; Collaborated with other painters in Group Exhibitions; Has painted over 985 works using different techniques including Water Colour, Oils, Guache, Wood; Works are recognised in 65 countries and in are many private and state collections. Publications: Works are reviewed in magazines and newspapers; Album Catalogue of her works produced with the help of her husband. Honours: Numerous prizes at exhibitions in 1976, 1989, 1988, 1999, 2002, 2003. Memberships: Bucharest Association of Artists, 1993; CIVA, Minneapolis, USA, 1994. Address: Comuna Sacelu, Jud Gorj COD 217410, Romania.

**CAZEAUX Isabelle Anne-Marie,** b. 24 February 1926, New York, USA. Professor Emeritus of Musicology. Education: BA, magna cum laude, Hunter College, 1945; MA, Smith College, 1946; Ecole normale de musique, Paris, Licence d'enseignement, 1950; Première médaille, Conservatoire National de Musique, Paris, 1950; MS in Library Science, Columbia University, 1959, PhD, 1961, Columbia University. Appointments: Music and phonorecords cataloguer, New York Public Library, 1957-63; Faculty of Musicology, Bryn Mawr College, 1963-92; Faculty of Musicology, Manhattan School of Music, 1969-82; A C Dickerman Professor and Chairman, Music Department, Bryn Mawr College; Visiting Professor, Douglass College, Rutgers University, 1978. Publications: Translations: The Memoirs of Philippe de Commynes, 2 vols, 1969-73; Editor: Claudin de Sermisy, Chansons, 2 vols, 1974; Author: French Music in the Fifteenth and Sixteenth Centuries, 1975; Articles. Honours: Libby van Arsdale Prize for Music, Hunter College, 1945; Fellowships and scholarships from Smith College, Columbia University, Institute of International Education, 1941-59; Grants from Martha Baird Rockefeller Fund for Music, 1971-72, Herman Goldman Foundation, 1980; Listed in New Grove Dictionary of Music and Musicians, 1980. Memberships: American Musicological Society; International Musicological Society; Société française de musicologie; National Opera Association. Address: 415 East 72nd Street, Apt 5FE, New York, NY 10021, USA.

**ČEKIĆ Smail,** b. 7 September 1953, Gusinje, Montenegro. Professor of History; Institute Director. m. Elmaza Čekić, 2 sons, 2 daughters. Education: Bachelor, School of Philosophy, University of Priština, 1976; Master's Degree, School of Philosophy, University of Belgrade, 1980; PhD, School of Philosophy, University of Split, 1990. Appointments: History Teacher, Secondary School, Prizren, 1976-78; Fellow Assistant, Institute for History of Montenegro, 1979-83; Fellow Assistant, 1985-90, Assistant Professor, Military History, 1990-94, Associate Professor, Political History, 1994-2001, Professor, History of Bosnia and Herzegovina, 2001-, Faculty of Political Sciences, University of Sarajevo; Director of the Institute for the Research of Crimes against Humanity and International Law, University of Sarajevo, 1992-. Publications include: Aggression on Bosnia and Genocide against Bosniacs in 1991-1993, 1994, English version, 1995; Causes, objectives and extent of the aggression against Bosnia and Herzegovina 1991-1995, 1995; Genocide on Bosniacs in the Second World War, Documents, 1996; History of Genocide on Bosniacs, 1997; Crimes against Bosniacs in Srebrenica during the Aggression on the Republic of Bosnia and Herzegovina, 1991-1995 (member of editorial board), 1999; Genocide in Srebrenica, UN "Safe Haven" in July 1995 (co-author), 2000; The Movement of Bagauda, 2002; The Revolutionary Work of the Communist Party of Yugoslavia in the Army of the Kingdom of Yugoslavia, 2004; Aggression of the Republic of Bosnia and Herzegovina – planning, preparation and execution, 2004; Numerous other scientific and professional works. Honour: Great Scholar of the 21st Century for Genocide and History Studies, American Biographical Institute, 2005. Memberships: Commission for the research of events in and around Srebrenica 10-15 July, 1995; World Victimology Society, 1996-; International Association of Genocide Scholars, 2002-. Address: Gajev Trg 4, Sarajevo 71000, Bosnia-Herzegovina. E-mail: intitut_zl@hotmail.com Website: www.inzl.unsa.ba

**CELA Camilo José,** b. 11 May 1916, Iria Flavia, La Coruña, Spain. Writer; Poet. m. (1) María del Rosario Conde Picavea, 12 March 1944, 1 son, (2) Marina Castano, 1991. Education: University of Madrid, 1933-36, 1939-43. Publications: Fiction: La Familia de Pascual Duarte, 1942, English translation as Pascual Duarte's Family, 1946; Pabellón de reposo, 1943, English translation as Rest Home, 1961; Nuevas andanzas y desventuras de Lazarillo de Tormes, 1944; Caminos inciertos: La colmena, 1951, English translation as The Hive, 1953; Santa Balbina 37: Gas en cada piso, 1952; Timoteo, el incomprendido, 1952; Mrs Caldwell habla con su hijo, 1953, English translation as Mrs Caldwell Speaks to Her Son, 1968; Café de artistas, 1955; Historias de Venezuela: La catira, 1955; Tobogán de hambrientos, 1962; Visperas, festividad y octava de San Camilo del año 1936 en Madrid, 1969; Oficio de tinieblas 5, o, Novela de tesis escrita para ser cantada por un de enfermos, 1973; Mazurca para doe muertos, 1983; Cristo versus Arizona, 1988; Madera de boj, 1999; Also many volumes of stories. Poetry: Pisando la dudosa luz del día, 1945; Reloj de Sangre, 1989. Non-Fiction: Diccionario Secreto, 2 volumes, 1968, 1971; Enciclopedia del Erotismo, 1976-77; Memorias, entendimientos y voluntades (memoirs), 1993. Other: Volumes of essays, travel books. Honours: Premio de la crítica, 1955; Spanish National Prize for Literature, 1984; Nobel Prize for Literature, 1989; Planeta Prize, 1994. Membership: Real Academia Espanola, 1957. Address: c/o Agencia Literaria Carmen Balcells, Diagonal 580, 08021 Barcelona, Spain.

**CERMAK Vladimir Vaclav Karel,** b. 17 May 1937, Praha, Czech Republic. Geophysicist. m. Marta Kozesnikova, 2 sons. Education: Prom fys (MSc), Charles University, Praha, 1960; RNDr (PhD), Geophysical Institute, Praha, 1967; Postdoctorate Fellow, Dominion Observatory, Ottawa, Canada, 1968-70; DrSc, Czechoslovak Academy of Sciences, 1981. Appointments: Director of Institute, Geophysical Institute, Czech Academy of Sciences, 1990-98; Member, Board of Directors, International Geothermal Association, 1993-98; Vice President, European

Geophysical Society, 1994-98; Chairman, International Heat Flow Commission of IASPEI, 1995-99; Chief Scientist, International Geological Correlation Programme, Project No 428 Borehole and Climate, 1999-2003; President, Czech National Committee for Geodesy and Geophysics, 1999-. Publications: 13 articles in professional scientific journals. Honours: Silver Medal for Merits in Physics, Czechoslovak Academy of Sciences, 1987; Edward A Flinn III Medal, American Geophysical Society, 1995; O Yu Schmidt Medal, Institute of Physics of the Earth, Russian Academy of Sciences, 1995; Patricius Plakette, Deutsche Geothermische Vereinband, 1998; Ernst Mach Medal for Merits in Physics, Academy of Sciences of the Czech Republic, 2003. Memberships: Academia Europea; American Geophysical Union; European Union of Geosciences; Deutsche Geophysikalische Gesselschaft; Editorial Boards of Geothermics, Tectonphysics, Studia Geoph et Geod. Address: c/o Geophysical Institute, Czech Academy of Sciences, 141-41 Praha 4, Czech Republic. E-mail: cermak@ig.cas.cz

**CERWENKA Herwig R,** b. 18 June 1964, Leoben, Austria. Surgeon; Researcher. m. Wilma Zinke-Cerwenka, 1 son, 2 daughters. Education: Matura Examination, 1982; Doctor of Medicine, 1988; ECFMG/FMGEMS, 1989; Ius practicandi, 1993; Diploma in Emergency Medicine; Diploma in Surgery. Appointment: Professor of Surgery, Researcher, Department of Visceral Surgery, Medical University, Graz, Austria. Publications: Numerous publications in scientific journals and contributions to books. Honours: Performance Grant, Karl-Franzens University; Numerous other grants and awards for congress contributions and publications. Memberships: International Society of Surgery; International Association of Surgeons and Gastroenterologists; Austrian Society of Surgery; Austrian Society of Surgical Research. Address: Department of Visceral Surgery, Medical University, Auenbruggerplatz 29, A-8036 Graz, Austria. E-mail: herwig.cerwenka@meduni-grat.at

**CHADWICK Peter,** b. 23 March 1931, Huddersfield, England. Retired. m. Sheila Salter, deceased 2004, 2 daughters. Education: Huddersfield College; BSc, University of Manchester, 1952; PhD, 1957, ScD, 1973, Pembroke College, Cambridge. Appointments: Scientific Officer, then Senior Scientific Officer, AWRE, Aldermaston, 1955-59; Lecturer, then Senior Lecturer in Applied Mathematics, University of Sheffield, 1959-65; Professor of Mathematics, 1965-91, Emeritus Professor of Mathematics, 1991-, Leverhulme Emeritus Fellow, 1991-93, University of East Anglia. Publications: Numerous papers and articles in learned journals and books; Continuum Mechanics, Concise Theory and Problems, 1976, 1999. Honours: FRS, 1977; Honorary DSc, University of Glasgow, 1991. Memberships: Fellow, Cambridge Philosophical Society; Honorary Member, British Society of Rheology. Address: 8 Stratford Crescent, Cringleford, Norwich NR4 7SF, England.

**CHADWICK Peter Kenneth,** 10 July 1946, Manchester, England. Writer; Psychologist. m. Rosemary Jill McMahon, 1983. Education: BSc, Geology, University College of Wales, Aberystwyth, 1967; BSc, Psychology, University of Bristol, 1975; MSc, DIC, Structural Geology and Rock Mechanics, Imperial College, London University, 1968; PhD, Structural Geology, University of Liverpool, 1971; PhD, Cognitive and Abnormal Psychology, Royal Holloway and Bedford New College, University of London, 1989 (careers in both geology and psychology). Appointments: Royal Society European Programme Research Fellow, Geology and Psychology, University of Uppsala, Sweden, 1972-73; Senior Demonstrator in Psychology, University of Liverpool, 1975-76; Lecturer in Psychology, University of Strathclyde, 1976-78; Lecturer in Motivation Psychology, Goldsmiths College, University of

London, 1984-85; Professor of Community Psychology, Boston University, 1991-94; Lecturer in Psychology, Birkbeck College, Faculty of Continuing Education, 1982-; Associate Lecturer in Psychology, Open University, London Region, 1982-98; Lecturer in Psychology, City Literary Institute, London, 1982-98; Associate Lecturer in Psychology, Open University, East of England Region, 1994-. Publications: Visual Illusions in Geology, 1976; Peak Preference and Waveform Perception, 1983; Borderline, 1992; Understanding Paranoia, 1995; Schizophrenia – The Positive Perspective, 1997; Personality as Art, 2001; Paranormal, Spiritual and Metaphysical Aspects of Psychosis, 2004; Publications mainly on human factors in science and on psychosis. Honours: Royal Society European Programme Research Fellowship, 1972-73; Bristol University Postgraduate Scholarship, 1975; British Medical Association Exhibition, 1985; Postdoctoral Award, British Gas Social Policy Unit, 1991; Royal Literary Fund Award, 1995. Memberships: Fellow, Geological Society of London, 1972-77; Honorary Member, Mizar Society for Social Responsibility in Science, University of Mississippi, 1975-; Associate Fellow, British Psychological Society, 1989-; Psychology and Psychotherapy Association, 1995-. Address: Psychology Division, Birkbeck College, Faculty of Continuing Education, University of London, School of Social and Natural Sciences, 26 Russell Square, Bloomsbury, London WC1B 5DQ, England.

**CHAKRABORTY Indra Nath,** b. 26 January 1957, Jamshedpur, India. Research and Development Materials Scientist. m. Kanchana Banerjee, 1 son. Education: BTech, Ceramic Engineering, Banaras Hindu University, India; MS, Glass Science, PhD, Ceramics, Alfred University, New York, USA. Appointments: Post Doctoral Fellow, University of Missouri-Rolla, USA; Research Officer, The Associated Cement Companies, India; Senior Manager, Research and Development, The Associated Cement Companies. Publications: Over 40 technical papers in the field of glass, cement and refractories; 4 Indian patents. Honours: ICI Award, Indian Chemical Society for Product Development; Academic Council Member of BHU. Memberships: Sigma Xi; Phi Kappa Phi; Fellow, Indian Ceramic Society; Council Member, Indian Ceramic Society. Address: 202, Omkar Tower, 18 Tikekar Road, Dhantoli, Nagpur 440012, India. E-mail: inc-refnagpur@acccement.com

**CHALFONT Baron, (Alun Arthur Gwynne Jones),** b. 5 December 1919, Llantarnam, Wales. Member, House of Lords; Writer. m. Mona Mitchell, 6 November 1948, 1 daughter, deceased. Education: West Monmouth, Wales. Appointments: Regular Officer, British Army, 1940-61; Broadcaster and Consultant on Foreign Affairs, BBC, 1961-64; Minister of State, Foreign and Commonwealth Office, 1964-70; Minister for Disarmament, 1964-67, 1969-70; Minister in charge of day-to-day negotiations for Britain's entry into Common Market, 1967-69; Permanent Representative, Western European Union, 1969-70; Foreign Editor, New Statesman, 1970-71; Chairman, Industrial Cleaning Papers, 1979-86, All Party Defence Group of the House of Lords, 1980-96, Peter Hamilton Security Consultants Ltd, 1984-86, VSEL Consortium, later VSEL plc, 1987-95, Radio Authority, 1991-94, Marlborough Stirling Group, 1994-; Director, W S Atkins International, 1979-83, IBM UK Ltd, 1973-90, Lazard Brothers & Company Ltd, 1983-90, Shandwick plc, 1985-95, Triangle Holdings, 1986-90, TV Corporation plc, 1996-; President, Abington Corporation Ltd, 1981-, Nottingham Building Society, 1983-90; All Party Defence Group House of Lords, 1996-. Publications: The Sword and the Spirit, 1963; The Great Commanders (editor), 1973; Montgomery of Alamein, 1976; Waterloo: Battle of Three Armies (editor), 1979; Star Wars: Suicide or Survival, 1985; Defence of the Realm, 1987; By God's Will: A Portrait of the Sultan of Brunei, 1989; The Shadow of My Hand, 2000. Contributions to: Periodicals and journals. Honours: Officer of the Order of the British Empire, 1961; Created a Life Peer, 1964; Honorary Fellow, University College of Wales, 1974; Liveryman, Worshipful Company of Paviors; Freeman of the City of London. Memberships: International Institute for Strategic Studies; Royal Institute of International Affairs; Royal Society of the Arts, fellow; United Nations Association, chairman, 1972-73. Address: House of Lords, London SW1A 0PW, England.

**CHALKLIN Christopher William,** b. 3 April 1933, London, England. University Teacher (Retired). m. Mavis, 1 son, 2 daughters. Education: BA, University of New Zealand, 1953; BA, 1955, MA, University of Oxford; B. Litt., University of Oxford, 1960; Litt.D., University of Canterbury, 1986. Appointments: Assistant Archivist, Kent County Council, 1958-62; Senior Fellow, University of Wales, 1963-65; Lecturer in History, 1965-75, Reader in History, 1975-93, University of Reading. Publications: Seventeenth century Kent: A Social and Economic History, 1965; The Provincial Towns of Georgian England: A Study of the Building Process, 1974; English Counties and Public Building 1650-1830, 1998. Address: 8 Tilehouse Road, Guildford, Surrey GU4 8AL, England.

**CHAMBERS Aidan,** b. 27 December 1934, Chester-le-Street, County Durham, England. Author; Publisher. m. Nancy Harris Lockwood, 30 March 1968. Education: Borough Road College, Isleworth, London University. Publications: The Reluctant Reader, 1969; Introducing Books to Children, 1973; Breaktime, 1978; Seal Secret, 1980; The Dream Cage, 1981; Dance on My Grave, 1982; The Present Takers, 1983; Booktalk, 1985; Now I Know, 1987; The Reading Environment, 1991; The Toll Bridge, 1992; Tell Me: Children, Reading and Talk, 1993; Only Once, 1998; Postcards From No Man's Land, 1999; Reading Talk, 2001; This Is All: The Pillow Book of Cordelia Kenn, 2005; Contributions to: Numerous magazines and journals. Honours: Children's Literature Award for Outstanding Criticism, 1978; Eleanor Farjeon Award, 1982; Silver Pencil Awards, 1985, 1986, 1994; Carnegie Medal, 1999; Stockport School Book Award KS4, 2000; Hans Christian Andersen Award, 2002; Michael L Printz Award, 2002; Honorary Doctorate, University of Umeå, Sweden, 2003; Honorary President, School Library Association, 2003-. Membership: Society of Authors. Address: Lockwood, Station Road, Woodchester, Stroud, Gloucestershire, GL5 5EQ, England.

**CHAMBERS Allan Anthony,** b. 14 July 1948, Liverpool, England. Investment Banker. m. Monica J Pope, 2 sons. Education: MSc, Cranfield University, 1969-71; SM, Massachusetts Institute of Technology, 1973-75; PMD, Harvard Business School, 1979. Appointments: Senior Manager, Commerzbank A G, 1982-84; AVP, Bankers Trust Company, 1979-82; Director, Commercial Union plc, 1984-89; Senior Executive Banker, Vice President, Merill Lynch Group, 1990-95; Director, Daiwa Asset Management, 1995-97; Adviser, Global Equities S.A., 1997-; Man Group plc; eK Transfer Ltd; EBM – Sustainability Ltd; ESSsa (GENEVA). Publications: Processes of Innovation; Hedge Fund Strategies, 1975. Honours: Travelling Fellow, City Livery, The Worshipful Company of Scientific Instrument Makers, 1973-75. Memberships: Freeman and Liveryman of the City of London; Fellow, The Royal Society of Arts; Member, Royal Society of St George. Address: Mount Shell Farm, Langford Road, Wickham Bishops, Essex, CM8 3JG, England. E-mail: allanachambers@aol.com

**CHAMBERS Guy,** Producer; Writer; Musician. Appointments: Jimmy Nail, Robbie Williams, World Party, The Waterboys,

Julian Cope, Lemon Trees. Creative Works: Recordings with Robbie Williams, Cathy Denis, World Party, Holly Johnson, Blast, Julian Cope, Fried, Lemon Trees. Memberships: Musicians Union; PRS. Address: One Management, 43 St Alban's Avenue, London W4 5JS, England.

**CHAN Eric Kwong Yuen,** b. 24 February 1958. Biomedical Engineer; Corporate Officer. Partner, Rebecca Young. Education: BSc, Electrical Engineering, Purdue University, 1982, MSc Engineering, 1984, PhD, Biomedical Engineering 1991, University of Texas at Austin; Global BioExecutive Certificate, University of california at Berkeley, 2005. Appointments: Development Engineer, Schlumberger-Austin Systems Center, Austin, Texas, 1986-86; Director of Engineering, 1991-93; Vice President, Engineering, 1993-98, Arrhythmia Research Technology Inc, Austin, Texas; Vice President, Product Development, CARDIMA Inc, Fremont, California, 1998-. Publications: Peer-reviewed book chapters and journal articles include most recently as co-author: Signal-averaged P-wave ECG discriminates between persistent and paroxysmal atrial fibrillation, 2001; New Concepts in Radiofrequency Energy Delivery and Coagulum Formation During Catheter Ablation. Energy Delivery Management and a Quantitative Measure for Estimating the Probability of Coagulum Formation During Radiofrequency Ablation, 2002; Characterization of Anatomically Compliant Linear Cardiac Lesions Created by the CARDIMA Radiofrequency Surgical Ablation System, 2004; Quadratic Model Predicts Lesion Outcome for the CARDIMA Cardiac Electrophysiology Radiofrequency Ablation System, 2005. Honours: Honourable Mention for Best Engineering Dissertation, University of Texas at Austin; Research Grant Scholarship, Professional Development Award, Graduate College, University of Texas at Austin; Elected Fellow, European Society of Cardiology, 2003; Listed in Who's Who publications and biographical dictionaries. Memberships: Senior Member, IEEE; Eta Kappa Nu; Phi Kappa Phi. Address: 93 Bayview Drive, San Carlos, CA 94070, USA. E-mail: ericchan@comcast.net

**CHAN Gary Yuk Fei,** b. 15 November 1962, Hong Kong. University Vice-President. m. Fok Wan Ching, 1 daughter. Education: BA, Simon Fraser University, 1986; MA, English, 1993, MBA, 1996, Doctor of Business Administration, 2002, Doctor of Psychology, 2003; Empresarial University; PhD, Psychology, Rutherford University, 2004; Fellow, American Board of Medical Psychotherapists and Psychodiagnosticians. Appointments: Director, University of Southern Queensland, Hong Kong and China Programme; Professor of Social Science in Psychology, 1999-, Professor of Business Administration, Vice-President, International Operations and Development, 2005-, Empresarial University. Publications: Business Diagnosis in Chinese Business Setting; Psychology of Chinese Business Operations. Honour: Kentucky Colonel (Highest honour given by the Governor of Kentucky), 2005. Membership: Commander, Sovereign Order of the Knights of Justice. Address: 192 Cypress Drive, Phase 1A, Palm Springs, Yuen Long, NT, Hong Kong. E-mail: garyprofessor@hotmail.com

**CHAN Nor Norman,** b. 27 May 1967, Hong Kong. Physician. Education: MB ChB, University of Liverpool, 1991; MRCP, London, 1994; Diploma of Child Health, London, 1995; Certificate of Completion of Specialist Training in Diabetes, Endocrinology and General Internal Medicine, UK 2001; MD, UK, 2002. Appointments: Specialist Registrar in Diabetes/Endocrinology: Hemel Hempstead General Hospital, Hertfordshire, 1995-96; Watford General Hospital, Hertfordshire, 1996-97; Chelsea and Westminster Hospital, London, 1997-98; Charing Cross Hospital, London, 1998;

University College London, 1998-2000; The Middlesex Hospital, London, 2000-01; Assistant Professor at the Prince of Wales Hospital, The Chinese University of Hong Kong, Hong Kong, 2002-2004; Clinical Director, Qualigenics Diabetes Centre, Hong Kong Resort International Limited, 2004-. Publications: Over 90 articles in professional medical journals. Honours: Junior Fellowship, British Heart Foundation, 1998. Memberships: Royal College of Physicians; British Endocrine Society; American Diabetes Association; Honorary Secretary, Hong Kong Atherosclerosis Society; Editorial Board, The Hong Kong Medical Diary. Address: A4 Solemar Villas, 15 Silver Cape Road, Clear Water Bay, Kowloon, Hong Kong.

**CHANG Chen-Yu,** b. 6 June 1969, Taipei, Taiwan. Lecturer. m. Hoi-Laam Karen Yu. Education: BSc, Civil Engineering, 1988-92, MSc, Construction Management, 1992-94, National Taiwan University; MPhil/PhD, Construction Economics and Management, University College London, University of London, England, 1997-2001. Appointments: Part-time Site Supervisor, construction project of NTU main library, 1992-94; Military Engineering Officer, construction project in Kaoshiung, 1994-96; Researcher, Century Development Corporation, 2002; Associate Researcher, Taiwan Construction Research Institute, 2002-04; Lecturer in Construction Economics, Bartlett School of Construction and Project Management, 2003-. Publications: 5 papers in professional journals; 10 conference papers; 8 magazine articles; 8 completed research papers. Honours: Book Scroll Award, National Taiwan University, 1988, 1989, 1990; Best Paper Award, Society of Chinese Engineers, 1991; Outstanding Compulsory Military Officer Certificate, Army of Taiwan, 1996; Ministry of Education Fellowship, Taiwan, 1996; Advanced Institute of Management Research (AIM) Scholar, 2004; Listed in national and international biographical dictionaries. Memberships: Associate Member, American Society of Civil Engineers; Member, Chinese Society of Civil and Hydraulic Engineers. Address: Wates House, The Bartlett, 22 Gordon Street, London WC1H 0QB, England. E-mail: chen-yu.chang@ucl.ac.uk

**CHANG David Dah-Chung,** b. 18 September 1954, Taiwan. Structural Engineer; Certified Building Official. Education: Bachelor of Science, 1972-76, Master of Science, 1976-78, National Cheng Kung University, Taiwan; Master of Science and Engineering, 1980-82, PhD Program, 1982-83, University of California, Los Angeles. Appointments: Plan Check Supervisor, Building and Safety Department, City of Los Angeles, 1983-; Vice-Chair, International Existing Building Code Committee, International Code Council, 1999-2004. Publications: Article in Structure Magazine about International Existing Building Code; Lecture publication for seminars of Structural Engineers Association. Honours: Honourable Speaker for Structural Engineers Association of Southern California, 7 times, 1997-2005. Memberships: American Society of Civil Engineers; American Concrete Institute; Structural Engineers of California, Applied Technology Council; Founder, North American Cheng Kung University Alumni Association, 1993; President, National Cheng Kung University Alumni Association, Southern California, 1993; President, National Cheng Kung University Alumni Association Foundation, Southern California, 1997. Address: 9746 Sunflower Street, Alta Loma, CA 91737, USA.

**CHANG Hyun Kyu,** b. 22 November 1959, Hoseong, Korea. Medical Doctor; Professor. m. Mee Young Kim, 1 son, 1 daughter. Education: Graduate, MS, Internal Medicine, PhD, Rheumatology, College of Medicine, Hanyang University, Korea. Appointments: Medical Specialist, Department of Internal Medicine, Hanyang University Medical Centre; Rheumatology Fellowship, Hanyang University Rheumatology Hospital; Fellowship, Department of Allergy and Immunology, University of Tennessee, USA; Associate Professor, Division of Rheumatology and Allergy, Ulsan University; Chief and Associate Professor, Division of Rheumatology, Dankook University. Publications: Articles in medical journals including: Annals of Rheumatic Diseases; Clinical and Experimental Rheumatology; Lupus; Journal of Korean Medical Sciences. Memberships: American College of Rheumatology; American Academy of Allergy, Asthma and Immunology; Korean Rheumatism Association. Address: Kolong Apt 504-301, Imae-dong, Bundang-gu, Seongnam-si, Gyeonggido, 463-949, South Korea. E-mail: hank22@naver.com Website: www.rheuma.or.kr

**CHANG Jung,** b. 25 March 1952, Yibin, China. Author. m. Jon Halliday. Education: University of York. Career: Full-time writer. Publication: Wild Swans: Three Daughters of China, 1991. Honours: NCR Book Award, UK, 1992; UK Writer's Guild Best Non-Fiction Book, 1992; Fawcett Society Book Award, UK, 1992; Book of the Year, UK, 1993; Golden Bookmark Award, Belgium, 1993, 1994; Best Book of 1993, Humo, Belgium; Bjørnsonordenen, Den Norske Orden for Literature, Norway, 1995; Doctor honoris causa: Buckingham, 1996, Warwick, York, 1997, Open University, 1998. Address: c/o Gillon Aitken Associates, 18-21 Cavaye Place, London SW10 9PT, England. E-mail: reception@gillonaitken.co.uk

**CHANG Michael,** b. 22 February 1972, Hoboken, New Jersey, USA. Tennis Player. Appointments: Aged 15 was youngest player since 1918 to compete in men's singles at US Open, 1987; Turned Professional, 1988; Played Wimbledon, 1988; Winner, French Open, 1989; Davis Cup Debut, 1989; Winner, Canadian Open, 1990; Semi-Finalist, US Open, 1992, Finalist, 1996; Finalist, French Open, 1995; Semi-Finalist, Australian Open, 1995, Finalist, 1996; Winner of 34 singles titles by end of 2002. Address: Advantage International, 1751 Pinnacle Drive, Suite 1500, McLean, VA 22102, USA.

**CHANG Shih-Lin,** b. 1 May 1946, Anhwei, China. Professor. m. Ling-Mei P Chang, 3 sons. Education: BS, Electrophysics, National Chiao Tung University, 1968; MS, Physics, Clemson University, USA, 1971; PhD, Physics, Polytechnic Institute of Brooklyn, USA, 1975. Appointments: Assistant Professor, 1975-78, Associate Professor, 1979-84, Professor, 1985, Solid State and Material Science, Universidade Estadual de Campinas, Brazil; Professor, Physics, 1985-, National Tsing Hua University, Taiwan; Head, Physics Department, National Tsing Hua University, 1987-90; Director General, Natural Science and Mathematics Department, National Science Council, Republic of China, 1993-94; Deputy Director, Synchrotron Radiation Research Centre, Republic of China, 1995; Dean of Research and Development, National Tsing Hua University, 1998-2004; Director, Joint Research Institute of ITRI/NYHU, 2003-2004. Publications: Over 100 scientific papers; 2 books; 1 monograph. Honours: Outstanding Research Award; Dr Sun Yat-Sen Academic Prize; Academic Prize in Natural Science; National Chair Professor in Natural Science (Ministry of Education); Tsing-Hua Chair Professor (Natural Science), 2004-; Elected member, Asian-Pacific Academy of Materials Science. Memberships: American Crystallographic Association; Asian Crystallographic Association; Physical Society of the Republic of China; American Physical Society. Address: 101, Section 2, Kuang Fu Road, Hsinchu, Taiwan, 300, Republic of China. E-mail: slchang@phys.nthu.edu.tw

**CHANG Shuenn-Yih,** b. 12 June 1958, Taiwan. Professor. m. Chiu-Li Huang, 2 daughters. Education: BS, 1977-81, MS, 1981-83, National Taiwan University; M Eng, University of

California, Berkeley, California, USA, 1988-92; PhD, University of Illinois, Urbana-Champaign, USA, 1992-94. Appointments: Engineer, Eastern International Engineers, 1985-87; Associate Research Fellow, National Center for Research on Earthquake Engineering, 1995-2002; Associate Professor, National Taipei University of Technology, 2002-. Publications: Application of the Momentum Equations of Motion to Pseudodynamic Testing, 2001; Explicit Pseudodynamic Algorithm with Unconditional Stability, 2002; Accuracy of Time History Analysis of Impulses, 2003; Nonlinear Error Propagation of Explicit Pseudodynamic Algorithm, 2003. Honours: Research Award, National Science Council, Taiwan, Republic of China; Research Award, Chinese Institute of Civil and Hydraulic Engineering. Memberships: Senior Member, Chinese Institute of Civil and Hydraulic Engineering; Chinese Institute of Earthquake Engineering. Address: National Taipei University of Technology, Department of Civil Engineering, #1 Section 3 Jungshiau East Road, Taipei, Taiwan, Republic of China. E-mail: changsy@ntut.edu.tw

**CHANG Yung-Hsien**, b. 27 October 1947, Taiwan. Professor; Medical Doctor. m. Yu-Ju Ho Chang, 1 son, 1 daughter. Education: MD, China Medical College, 1966-72; PhD, cum laude, Hamburg University, Germany, 1978-84. Appointments: Deputy Superintendent, China Medical University Hospital, 1992-2002; Founder President, China Medical Association of Acupuncture, 1997-2003; Professor, Graduate Institute of Integration Chinese and Western Medicine, China Medical University, 1997-; Vice-President, China Medical University, 1999; Specialist in Orthopaedics, Rehabilitation and Acupuncture. Publications: Books: An Internet Resource Guide to Traditional Chinese Medicine in Taiwan, 2004; Environment of Clinical Trial for Traditional Chinese Medicine and Regulation in Taiwan, 2004; Channel Medicine and Acupuncture Science, 2005; Papers: Effect of Acupuncture at Pai-Hui on the Deficit of Memory Storage in Rats, 1999; Development of Bioengineering Technology in the Diagnosis of Chinese Medicine, 2003; Clinical Evaluation of the Traditional Chinese Prescription for Dry Eye, 2005. Honours: Best Professor Award, Education Ministry, 1990; Special Contribution of Medical Profession, 1993; Honorary Professor, Fujian College of Traditional Chinese Medicine, 1999; Honorary Professor, London College of Traditional Chinese Medicine, 2004. Memberships: Founding Member, International Society for Chinese Medicine; Founding Member, Chinese Medical Association of Acupuncture. Address: China Medical University, 91 Hsueh Shih Rd, Taichung 40402, Taiwan. E-mail: yhchang@mail.cmu.edu.tw

**CHANNON Merlin George Charles**, b. 14 September 1924, St Johns Wood, London, England. Retired HM Inspector of Schools; Community Musician; Handelian. m. Ann Carew Robinson, 21 July 1951, 1 daughter. Education: Guildhall School of Music, College of St Mark and St John, 1943-45; BMus (London), Trinity College of Music, 1950-55; MA, Birmingham University, 1981-84; PhD, Open University, 1986-95. Appointments: Teacher, Middlesex and London schools, 1945-54; Director of Music, Woolverstone Hall School, Suffolk, 1955-62; Director of Music and Senior Lecturer, St Paul's College, Cheltenham, 1962-65; HM Inspector of Schools, Department of Education and Science, Midland and Eastern Divisions successively, 1965-84; Conductor of various amateur orchestral and choral societies including: Ipswich Orchestral Society, 1956-62; Ipswich Bach Choir, 1957-62, 1975-87; Dudley Choral Society, 1966-72; Clent Hills Choral Society and Clent Cantata Choir, 1968-72; Kidderminster Choral Society, 1970-72; Suffolk Singers, 1972-78; Stowmarket Choral Society, 1973-75; Eye Bach Choir, 1974-94. Publications: Handel's 'Judas Maccabaeus' in Music and Letters and in the New Novello Choral Edition. Honours: Vice President, Ipswich Bach Choir; Hon FTCL; Conductor Emeritus, Eye Bach Choir. Memberships: Royal Music Association; Incorporated Society of Musicians; MCC; Royal Overseas League. Address: 42 Church Street, Eye, Suffolk, IP23 7BD, England.

**CHAO Fu-Hou (Jacob)**, b. 8 March 1941, citizen of Taiwan. Adviser Mennonite Christian Hospital. m. Mary Ho, 2 daughters. Education: BS, Accounting, National Cheng-Chi University, Taiwan, 1968; MBA, Marketing, Tulane University, USA, 1994. Appointments: Cost Management and Analysis Analyst, China Airlines, 1968-70; Senior Accountant, Metropolitan Bank, Taipei, 1970-72; Senior Budget and Accounts Analyst, American Embassy AID, 1972; Supervisor, Financial Controls, Chase Manhattan Bank, Taipei, 1972-77; Manager, Administrations, Arnhold Trading Co, Ltd. (Taiwan), 1977-79; Country Manager, APA/Taiwan-Card, 1979-82, Country Manager, APA/Taiwan-CFSG, 1982-83, Director and Country Manager, APA/Taiwan-CFSG, 1983, Acting General Manager, APA/Taiwan-TRS, 1983, General Manager, APA/Taiwan-TRS, 1984-87; Vice President and General Manager, APA/Taiwan-TRS, 1987-90, Vice President and Deputy Chairman, Japan, East Asia/Taiwan-TRS, 1990-91, American Express International (Taiwan) Inc; Adviser, Mennonite, Christian Hospital, Taiwan, 1998-. Publication: Feasibility study for the card entry to Taiwanese market, 1981. Honours: Dean's Service Award, Tulane University, USA, 1994; President Awards, G1 Rating, American Express International Inc, Asia, Pacific and Australia, 1986-88; Launched the American Express New Taiwan Dollar Card in Taiwan, never seen before, an historical breakthrough, 1989; Great Minds of the 21st Century, ABI, 2004/05; World Lifetime Achievement Award, ABI, 2005. Memberships: Deputy Chairman of the Board, Mennonite Christian Hospital, 2 terms; Council Chairman, Deacons' Council, Mennonite Christian Church, Taipei, 4 terms. Address: 3F21, Lane 46, Ching Cheng Street, Taipei 105, Taiwan. E-mail: jacobchao@mch.org.tw

**CHAPMAN Allan**, b. 30 May 1946, Manchester, England. Historian of Science. m. Rachel Elizabeth Woodrow. Education: Cromwell Road Boy's Secondary Modern School, Manchester, 1958-62; BA in History (1st Class Honours), Lancaster University, 1972; MA, 1972, Doctor of Philosophy, 1978, Oxford University. Appointments: Self-funded Scholar; Member, Faculty of Modern History, Oxford University, 1983-; Member of Congregation, Oxford University; President, Society for the History of Astronomy; Vice President, William Hershal Society. Publications: 8 published books including: England's Leonardo, Robert Hooke and the Seventeenth Century Scientific Revolution, 2004; Co-author, 2 books; Around 70 academic articles; Approximately 100 articles in popular journals; TV appearances and radio broadcasts. Honours: John Wilkins Prize Lecturer, History of Science, Royal Society of London, 1995; Honorary Doctor, University of Central Lancashire, 2004; Various medals, citations and awards. Memberships: Fellow, Royal Astronomical Society, 1973. Address: Wadham College, Oxford OX1 3PN, England.

**CHAPMAN Barry Lloyd**, b. 6 June 1936, Werris Creek, New South Wales, Australia. Consultant Cardiologist (Retired). 2 sons, 2 daughters. Education: MB, BS, Sydney University, 1960; Member, 1966, Fellow, 1972, Royal Australasian College of Physicians. Appointments: Resident Medical Officer, 1960-62, Medical Registrar, 1963-66, Fellow in Medicine, 1967-70, Foundation Director of Coronary Care, 1968-70, Royal Newcastle Hospital, New South Wales, Australia; Research Fellow, Senior Registrar, West Middlesex Hospital, Isleworth, England, with attachment to Hammersmith Hospital, London, 1971-73; Staff Specialist in Medicine, 1973-91, Consultant

Cardiologist, 1984-87, Senior Consultant Cardiologist, 1988-91, Royal Newcastle Hospital, New South Wales; Senior Consultant Cardiologist, John Hunter Hospital, Newcastle, New South Wales, 1991-2001; Clinical, and later Conjoint, Lecturer in Medicine, Faculty of Medicine and Health Sciences, University of Newcastle, New South Wales, 1979-2001; Retired, 2001. Publications: Numerous original papers on subjects including: Liver cirrhosis, peptic ulcer - particularly risk factors especially aspirin, coeliac disease, dermatitis herpetiformis, polymyalgia rheumatica, acute myocardial infarction - particularly prognostic factors, a new coronary prognostic index, effects of coronary care on myocardial infarction mortality, medical history (coronary artery disease in antiquity and prehistoric times); Papers published in medical journals which include: Medical Journal of Australia; Australasian Annals of Medicine; Gut; Proceedings of the Third Asian Pacific Congress of Gastroenterology; Lancet; Proceedings of the Royal Society of Medicine; British Heart Journal; Papers also read before learned societies. Honours: Efficiency Decoration; Medal, Anniversary of National Service, 1951-72. Memberships include: Retired Fellow: Royal Australasian College of Physicians; Cardiac Society of Australia and New Zealand; Retired Member: Australasian Society of Ultrasound in Medicine; Gastroenterological Society of Australia; Sydney Gut Club; Emeritus Member, American Association for the Advancement of Science; Emeritus Fellow, International College of Angiology; Life Member, New South Wales Society of the History of Medicine; Life Fellow, Royal Society of Medicine. Address: 31 Elbrook Drive, Rankin Park, NSW 2287, Australia.

**CHAPMAN Jean,** b. 30 October 1939, England. Writer. m. Lionel Alan Chapman, 1 son, 2 daughters. Education: BA (Hons), Open University, 1989. Appointments: Creative Writing Tutor for East Midlands Arts and Community Colleges. Publications: The Unreasoning Earth, 1981; Tangled Dynasty, 1984; Forbidden Path, 1986; Savage Legacy, 1987; The Bellmakers, 1990; Fortune's Woman, 1992; A World Apart, 1993; The Red Pavilion, 1995; The Soldier's Girl, 1997; This Time Last Year, 1999; A New Beginning, 2001; And a Golden Pear, 2002; Danced Over The Sea, 2004. Other: Many short stories. Honours: Shortlisted, Romantic Novel of Year, 1982, 1996, and Kathleen Fidler Award, 1990. Memberships: Society of Authors; Chairman, Romantic Novelists Association, 2002-03. Address: 3 Arnesby Lane, Peatling Magna, Leicester LE8 5UN, England.

**CHAPMAN Stanley D(avid),** b. 31 January 1935, Nottingham, England. Professor; Writer. Education: BSc, London School of Economics and Political Science, 1956; MA, University of Nottingham, 1960; PhD, University of London, 1966. Appointments: Lecturer, 1968-73, Pasold Reader in Business History, 1973-, Professor, 1993-97, Emeritus Professor, 1997-University of Nottingham; Editor, Textile History Bi Annual, 1982-2002. Publications: The Early Factory Masters, 1967; The Beginnings of Industrial Britain, 1970; The History of Working Class Housing, 1971; The Cotton Industry in the Industrial Revolution, 1972, new edition, 1987; Jesse Boot of Boots the Chemists, 1974; The Devon Cloth Industry in the 18th Century, 1978; Stanton and Staveley, 1981; The Rise of Merchant Banking, 1984; Merchant Enterprise in Britain from the Industrial Revolution to World War I, 1992; Hosiery and Knitware: Four Centuries of Small-Scale Industry in Britain, 2002. Address: Rochester House, Halam Road, Southwell, Nottinghamshire NG25 0AD, England.

**CHAPPELL Gregory Stephen,** b. 7 August 1948, Adelaide, Australia. Cricketer; Business Executive. m. Judith Elizabeth Donaldson, 1971, 2 sons, 1 daughter. Education: Adelaide College; Prince Alfred College, Adelaide. Appointments: Teams: South Australia, 1966-73, Somerset, 1968-69, Queensland, 1973-84 (Captain 1973-77, 1979-80); Tests for Australia, 1970-84, 48 as Captain, Scoring 7,100 runs (Average 53.8) including 24 Hundreds, and Holding 122 Catches; Scored 108 on Test Debut v England, Perth, 1970; Only Captain to have scored a Century in each innings of 1st Test as Captain (v West Indies, Brisbane 1975); Holds record for most catches in a Test Match (7, v England, Perth 1975); Scored 24,535 1st Class Runs (74 Hundreds); Toured England 1972, 1975, 1977, 1980; Managing Director, AD Sports Technologies, 1993-95, Greg Chappell Sports Marketing, 1995-98; Coach, South Australian Redbacks cricket team, 2002. Publication: Greg Chappell's Health and Fitness Repair Manual, 1998. Honours include: Australian Sportsman of the Year, 1976. Memberships: MCC; South Australian Cricket Association. Address: c/o South Australian Cricket Association, Adelaide Oval, North Adelaide, SA 5006, Australia.

**CHARLIER Roger Henri Liévin Constance Louise,** b. 10 November 1924, Antwerp, Belgium. University Professor. m. Patricia Simonet, 1 son, 1 daughter. Education: Certificate of Political and Adm Sci, Colonial University of Belgium, 1940; MPolSci, Brussels, 1942; MS (Earth and Oceans), Brussels, 1945; PhD, Erlangen, 1947; Postgraduate study, McGill University, 1953; LitD, Paris, 1956; Industrial College of the Armed Forces, 1956; DSc, Paris, 1958; Education Curriculum Diploma, Parsons College, 1962. Appointments include: Major (Intelligence), World War II; Consultant, 20th Century Fox Corporation, 1948; Professor, Poly University, Washington, DC, 1950-54; Professor, Finch College, USA, 1954-56; Special Lecturer, Chairman, Department of Geology and Geography, Hempstead NY, Hofstra University, USA, 1956-59; Visiting Professor, University of Minnesota, USA, 1959-61; Professor of Geology, Parsons College (now University), 1961-62; Professor of Geology, Geography and Oceanography, Northeastern Illinois University, Chicago, 1961-87, Special research Scholar, 1962-64; Professor Extraordinary, 1970-86, Professor Emeritus, 1986-, Vrije Universiteit Brussels, Belgium; Professeur associé, 1970-74, hon, 1986-,Université de Bordeaux I, France; Fulbright Fellow, 1974-76; Kellogg Fellow, 1980-82; Scientific Advisor to CEO HAECON, 1984-88, 1989-2000; Scientific Advisor to CEO SOPEX, 1988-89; Professor Emeritus, Northeastern Illinois University, USA, 1988-; Chair, Task Force Environment and Sustainability, EFCA, 1998-2002; Vice-Chair, same Belgian ORI-OIC Newspaper Correspondent, various US, Belgian, Swiss papers, 1945-60, 1983-99. Publications include: Books: I Was a Male War Bride, 1948; For the Love of Kate, 1958; Pensées, 1962; Economic Oceanography, 1980; Study of Rocks, 1980; Tidal Power, 1982; Ocean Energies, 1993; Coastal Erosion, 1999; Tools for the Black Sea, 2000; Co-editor, Proc 6th Int Congr Hist Oceanog, [UNESCO] Ocean Sciences Bridging the Millennium, 2004, Black Sea Seminar, 2002; Articles include: Small Sources of Methane; The Atmospheric Methane Cycle: Sources, Sinks, Distribution and Role in Global Change; Tourism and the Coastal Zone: The Case of Belgium: Ocean and Coastal Management; I was a Male War Bride. Honours include: Belgian Government Awards, 1939, 1975; Chicago Public Schools Award, 1975, 1987, 1992; Outstanding Achievement Presidential Award, 1980; Paul-Henri Spaak Memorial Lecture Award, 1992. Memberships include: Fellow, Geological Society of America; Charter Member, International Association for the History of Oceanography; Charter Member and Fellow, New Jersey Academy of Science, President, 1954-57, Past President, 1957-58; American Association for the Advancement of Science; Royal Belgian Society for Geographical Studies; Education Committee, Marine Technology Society; Association of American University Professors; Académie Nationale des

Arts, Sciences et Belles-Lettres, France, 1970-; Royal Marine Academy of Belgium, 2005-. Address: 2 Ave du Congo, Box 23, Brussels 1050, Belgium.

**CHARLTON John (Jack),** b. 8 May 1935. Former Football Player; Broadcaster; Football Manager. m. Patricia, 1958, 2 sons, 1 daughter. Appointments: Professional footballer, Leeds Utd FC, 1952-73; Manager, Middlesborough FC, 1973-77, Sheffield Wednesday FC, 1977-83, Newcastle Utd FC, 1984-85, Republic of Ireland Football Team, 1986-95; Played with winning teams in League Championship, 1969, Football Association Cup, 1972, League Cup, 1968, Fairs Cup, 1968, 1971, World Cup (England v Germany), 1966. Publication: Jack Charlton's American World Cup Diary, 1994. Honours: Football Writers Association Footballer of the Year, 1967; OBE. Membership: Sports Council, 1977-82.

**CHARLTON Robert (Bobby) (Sir),** b. 11 October 1937. Former Footballer. m. Norma, 1961, 2 daughters. Career: Footballer with Manchester Utd, 1954-73; Played 751 games scoring 245 goals; FA Cup Winners' Medal, 1963; First Division Championship Medals, 1956-57, 1964-65, 1966-67; World Cup Winners' Medal (England team), 1966; European Cup Winners' Medal, 1968; 106 appearances for England, scoring 49 goals, 1957-73; Manager, Preston North End, 1973-75; Chairman, NW Council for Sport and Recreation, 1982-; Director, Manchester Utd Football Club, 1984-. Publications: My Soccer Life, 1965; Forward for England, 1967; This Game of Soccer, 1967; Book of European Football, Books 1-4, 1969-72. Honours: Honorary Fellow, Manchester Polytechnic, 1979; Honorary MA, Manchester University; Knighthood; CBE. Address: 17 The Square, Hale Barns, Cheshire WA15 8ST, England.

**CHARNEY Lena London,** b. 26 January 1919, Symiatycze, Poland. Retired Teacher; Historian; Poet, Business Woman. m. Roy L Charney, 10 November 1955, 1 son. Education: BA, cum laude, Hunter College, New York City, 1941; MA, Clark University, Worcester, Massachusetts, 1942; PhD. ABD, Columbia University, 1947-53. Contributions to: various anthologies, reviews, magazines, and journals. Appointments: Millinery designer, Sanjour Studio, 1937, 1939-41; Designer, Co-owner, Lenblac Millinery Store, 1938; Co-owner, Co-manager, Golden Dawn bungalow colony, 1939-46; Secretary to New York City Manager, Insurance Field, 1945; Assistant Editor, Insurance Weekly, 1946; Saleslady, Bonwit-Teller, Arnold Constable and Lane Bryant, 1947-49; Director, Teacher, Workmen's Circle Yiddish School, Shrub Oak, New York; Sunday school teacher, Lakeland Jewish Centre and Temple Beth Am; Teacher, Principal, St Basil's Academy, Garisson, 1968-73; Substitute teacher, various districts, 1974-82; Co-manager, London's Studio Apartments, 1950-59; Owner, Manager, London's Studio Apartments, 1959-; Poet, 1984-. Honours: Finalist, Verve Poetry Competition, 1990; Honourable Mention, Nostalgia Poetry Contest, 1991; Finalist, Greenburgh Poetry Competition, 1993; Diamond Homer Award, Famous Poets Society, 1996, 1998 and 1999; Featured poet at, "An Evening of Poetry", Mount Pleasant Public Library, Pleasantville, New York, 2001. Publications: Historical articles in: Wisconsin History, 1948; The Southwestern Historical Quarterly, 1954; Indiana Magazine of History, 1948; Iowa Journal of History, 1950; Military Affairs, 1951; Michigan History, 1952; Poetry in many publications and anthologies. Honours: Featured poet at its first Evening of Poetry, Mount Pleasant Public Library, Pleasantville, New York, 2001. Memberships: Association of American University Women; American Historical Association; Academy of Political Science; National Writers Union; Academy of American Poets; Hudson Valley Writers Centre;

Poetry Society of America; Peregrine Poets. Address: PO Box 145, Mohegan Lake, NY 10547, USA.

**CHATER ROBINSON Geoffrey Michael (Geoffrey Chater),** b. 23 March 1921, Barnet, Hertfordshire, England. Actor. m. Jennifer R F Hill, 2 sons, 1 daughter. Education: Marlborough College, 1933-37; Chillon College, Glion-sur-Montreaux, Switzerland, 1938. Career: Captain WWII Infantry, India and Burma, 1942-45; Assistant Stage manager, Theatre Royal (Repertory), Windsor; Actor Old Vic Shakespeare Season, 1954-55; Subsequently played more than 100 roles on TV, feature films, and on the west End Stage as Geoffrey Chater; Most recently appeared as Brother Robert in Orchis Fatalis in the Midsomer Murder television series, 2005. Membership: MCC. Address: The Elms, Iden, Rye, Sussex, England.

**CHAUDHARY Badri Lal,** b. 10 December 1951, Jeeva Khera, Rajasthan, India. Professor of Botany; Vice-Chancellor. m. Krishna Chaudhary, 1 son, 2 daughters. Education: BSc, 1972, MSc, 1974, PhD, 1980, University of Udaipur. Appointments: Lecturer, MSJ College, 1974-75; Assistant Professor, 1975-90, Associate Professor, 1990-93, Professor, 1993-, Cultural Co-ordinator, 1990-93, Incharge, PG Department of Biotechnology, 1998-2003, Head, Department of Botany, 1995-98, Dean Students Welfare, 1996-2000, Dean, College of Science, 2001-, Chairman, Faculty of Science, 2001-, Vice-Chancellor, 2004-, M L Sukhadia University, Udaipur, Rajasthan, India. Publications: 27 books include in English: Recent Researches in Botanical Sciences (with N C Aery), 1991; Moss Flora of Rajasthan (with G S Deora), 1993; Pharmaceutical Biology Part I, 2004; Pharmaceutical Biology Part II, 2004; Competitive Botany (with Ratnu and Sonie), 2004; Numerous articles in scientific journals. Honours: Honorary Director, State SC/ST Development Corporation, Jaipur, 1990-95; Science Specialist in Rajasthan Hindi Granth Academy, 1994-95; Appreciation from Government of Rajasthan in the field of the environment, 1990-91. Memberships: Life Member, Indian Science Congress; Life Member, Indian Botanical Society; Life Member Indian Bryological Society; New York Academy of Sciences; International Society of Bryologists. Address: Vice-Chancellor M L Sukhadia University, New Campus, Udaipur 313001, Rajasthan, India.

**CHEAL MaryLou,** b. 5 November 1926, Michigan, USA. Research Psychologist. m. James Cheal, 2 sons, 1 daughter. Education: BA, Oakland University, Rochester, Michigan, USA, 1969; PhD, Psychology, University of Michigan, 1973. Appointments include: Assistant to Associate Psychologist, McLean Hospital, Harvard Medical School, 1977-83; Faculty Research Associate, Arizona State University, 1983-87; Visiting Professor, Air Force Systems Command University Resident Research Program Appointment, Williams Air Force Base, Arizona, USA, 1986-88; Research Psychologist, University of Dayton Research Institute at Williams Air Force Base, 1986-94; Adjunct Associate Professor, Professor, Department of Psychology, Arizona State University, USA, 1987-; Senior Research Psychologist, University of Dayton Research Institute at the Air Force Armstrong Laboratory, Mesa, Arizona, USA, 1994-95. Publications: 70 publications including: Timing of facilitatory and inhibitory effects of visual attention, 2002; Inappropriate capture by diversionary dynamic elements, 2002; Efficiency of visual selective attention is related to the type of target, 2002. Honours include: Society of Sigma Xi, 1972; Fellow, American Association for Advancement of Science, 1987; Fellow, American Psychological Association, 1987; Charter Fellow, American Psychological Society, 1988; World Intellectual of 1993; Commemorative Medal of Honor, American Biographical Institute, 1993; Professional Women's

Advisory Board, 1998; The C T Morgan Distinguished Service to Division 6 Award, American Psychological Association, 1999. Memberships include: American Association for Advancement of Science, 1969-87, Fellow, 1987-; Sigma Xi, 1972-; Society for Neuroscience, 1974-; American Psychological Association, member, 1980-86, fellow, 1986-; President, Division 6, 1997-98, Committee. on Division/APA Relation, member, 1997-98, chair, 1999, Representative to Council, 2000-2005, division 6; Member, Committee on Structure and Function of Council, 2004-06; Coalition for Academic Scientific and Applied Research, Member, 2000, Secretary, 2001-2004, President, 2005; The Psychonomic Society, 1988-; American Psychological Society, charter fellow, 1988-; International Brain Research Organization. Address: 127 Loma Vista Drive, Tempe, AZ 85282-3574, USA.

**CHEDID Andrée,** b. 20 March 1920, Cairo, Egypt. Poet; Novelist; Dramatist. m. Louis A Chedid, 23 August 1942, 1 son, 1 daughter. Education: Graduated, American University of Cairo, 1942. Publications: Poetry Collections: Textes pour un poème (1949-1970), 1987; Poèmes pour un texte (1970-91), 1991; Par delà les mots, 1995. Novels: Le Sommeil délivré, 1952, English translation as From Sleep Unbound, 1983; Jonathon, 1955; Le Sixième Jour, 1960, English translation as The Sixth Day, 1988; L'Autre, 1969; La Cité fertile, 1972; Nefertiti et le reve d'Akhnaton, 1974; Les Marches de sable, 1981; La Maison sans racines, 1985, English translation as The Return to Beirut, 1989; L'Enfant multiple, 1989. Plays: Bérénice d'Egypte, Les Nombres, Les Montreur, 1981; Echec à la Reine, 1984; Les saisons de passage, 1996. Other: The Prose and Poetry of Andrée Chedid: Selected Poems, Short Stories, and Essays (Renée Linkhorn, translator), 1990; A la Mort, A la Vie, 1992; La Femme de Job, 1993; les Saisons de passage, 1996; Le Jardin perdue, 1997; Territoires du Souffle, 1999; Le Cœur demeure, 1999; Essays; Children's books. Honours: Prix Louise Labe, 1966; Grand Prix des Lettres Francaise, l'Académie Royale de Belgique, 1975; Prix de l'Académie Mallarmé, 1976; Prix Goncourt de la nouvelle, 1979; Prix de Poèsie, Société des Gens de Lettres, 1991; Prix de PEN Club International, 1992; Prix Albert Camus, 1996; Prix Poésie de la SALEH, 1999; Légion d'honneur, Commandeur des Arts et des Lettres. Membership: PEN Club International. Address: c/o Flammarion, 26 rue Racine, Paris 75006, France.

**CHEFFINS Brian Robert,** b. 21 January 1961, Montreal, Quebec, Canada. Professor of Corporate Law. m. Joanna, 2 daughters. Education: BA, History, University of Victoria, Canada, 1978-81; First Year Law, University of British Columbia, 1981-82; LLB, University of Victoria, 1982-84; LLM, University of Cambridge, England, 1985-86. Appointments: Assistant Professor, 1986-91, Associate Professor, 1991-97, Professor, 1997, Faculty of Law, University of British Columbia; Visiting Scholar, Wolfson College, Oxford, 1992-93; S J Berwin Professor of Corporate Law, Professorial Fellow, Trinity Hall, Faculty of Law, University of Cambridge, 1998-; Visiting Fellow, Duke Global Capital Markets Center/Duke Law School, North Carolina, USA, 2000; Visiting Professor, Harvard Law School, Massachusetts, USA, 2002; Visiting Lecturer/Visiting Fellow, Stanford Law School, California, USA, 2003. Publications: Book, Company Law: Theory, Structure and Operation, 1997; Book, Trajectory of (Corporate Law) Scholarship, 2004; Also contributed book chapters and articles in academic publications. Honours: Co-winner, Society of Public Teachers of Law Prize for Outstanding Legal Scholarship, 1998; John Simon Guggenheim Memorial Fellowship, 2002-03. Address: Faculty of Law, University of Cambridge, 10 West Road, Cambridge CB3 9DZ, England. E-mail: brc21@cam.ac.uk

**CHELLY Faïza Ghariani,** b. 4 September 1942, Zaghouan, Tunisia. Professor of Philosophy; Artist. m. Rached Chelly, 1 son, 2 daughters. Education: BAC; Master's Degree, Philosophy; Certificate, French Literature. Appointments: Research Associate; Professor of Philosophy; Principal Professor of Philosophy; Amateur Artist, 1969-; Professional Artist, 1990-; Solo Exhibitions: "Metaphysique de l'imagination", Galerie Blel, Tunis, 1998; "Réminiscence I", Carthage, 2001; "Réminiscence II", Musée de Sidi Bou Saîd, 2002; "Réminiscence II", Centre Culturel International, Hammamet, 2002; Group Exhibitions include most recently: Ouverture de la saison culturelle, Araina, 2002; Espace des Arts, Bizerte, 2003; Union des Artists Plasticiens Tunisiens, Tunis, 2003, Maison de la culture El Magharibia, Ariana, 2003; Ibn Khaldoun Tunis, Ariana, 2003; Maison de la Culture et de la jeunesse du 7 Novembre, Bizerte, 2004. Publications: Numerous reviews and mentions in newspapers and journals. Honours: Certificate of Congratulations, Libya, 2003; Certificate of Recognition and Congratulations, Bizerte, 2004. Memberships: Philosophical Association of Tunisia, 1995-; Union of Visual Artists of Tunisia. Address: Rue Jemel edine Ressaissi, No 32, El Menzeh IX B, 1004 Tunisia.

**CHELTSOV Vladislav,** b. 24 June 1934, Moscow, Russia. Professor of Physics; Theorist in quantum electrodynamics of emission from microstructures. Divorced, 2 sons. Education: MS Diploma, Moscow Engineering Physical University, 1958; PhD, Kahzan University, 1969; Associate Professor of Physics, Textile Academy, 1972. Appointments: Assistant Professor, 1958-62, Researcher, 1962-69, Department of Theoretical Nuclear Physics of Moscow Engineering Physics University; Senior Instructor, Associate Professor, Higher School, 1969-88; Associate Professor, Department of Physics, Moscow State Mining University, 1988-. Publications: Theory of two proton radioactivity, 1964; Effect of phase mixing of co-operative quantum states in the system of two level atoms and lasing without inversion, 1965, 1969, 1970, 1989; Theory of co-operative resonance fluorescence of two-level atoms, 1981-86; Theory of spontaneous and stimulated emission in semiconductor, Bose-Einstein distribution for photons with non-zero chemical potential, 1969 (thesis), 1971, 1997; New theory (without series expansions and intermediate virtual states but with using the novel algorithm in operating the causal functions) has been elaborated to describe spontaneous emission of resonance photons from atoms trapped in micro-cavities, 1993-95, 2003; Optical Mössbauer effect on the AC Stark-sublevels, 1998-99, 2001; Storage of light by two two-level atoms, 2001; New non-linear optical effects in emission and absorption of resonance photons by two-level atoms, trapped in damped microcavity, 2001; Cavity-controlled spontaneos emission spectral lineshape, 2003. Honour: Nominee for the Peter Kahpitza Grant from the Royal Society, 1991. Memberships: Senior Member, IEEE/LEOS; Individual Member, European Physical Society; CPHYS; Member of the Institute of Physics, UK; Member, Optical Society of America, the SPIE. Address: Post Box 31, 119313 Moscow V313, Russia. E-mail: vcheltsov@mtu-net.ru

**CHEN Bing-Huei,** b. 30 January 1954, Taichung, Taiwan. Professor. m. Wen-Huei Wang, 1 son, 1 daughter. Education: BS, Food Science, Fu Jen University, 1977; MS, Agricultural Chemistry, California State University, Fresno, 1983; PhD, Food Science, Texas A and M University, 1988. Appointments: Associate Professor, 1988-93, Professor and Chair, 1994-2001, Chair Professor in Food Science and Technology, 2004-, Department of Nutrition and Food Science, Fu Jen University, Taipei. Publications: More than 80 research articles have been published in internationally renowned journals. Honours:

Outstanding Research Awards, National Science Council of Taiwan and Chinese Institute of Food Science and Technology. Memberships: Institute of Food Technologists; New York Academy of Science; AOAC International; American Chemical Society. Address: Department of Nutrition and Food Science, Fu Jen University, Taipei, Taiwan 242, ROC. E-mail: nutr100 7@mails.fju.edu.tw

**CHEN Jiann-Chu,** b. 17 February 1946, Kaohsiung, Taiwan. Professor. m. Su-Ching, 1 son, 1 daughter. Education: Doctor of Agriculture, Faculty of Agriculture, Kyushu University, Fukuoka, Japan, 1976. Publications: 169 scientific journal papers. Honours: Outstanding Research Award, 1992-93, 1994-95, 1997-98; Special Appointed Researcher, 1999, 2002; Academic Award, 2001. Membership: World Aquaculture Society. Address: National Taiwan Ocean University, Department Aquaculture, Keelung 202, Taiwan.

**CHEN Pang-Chi,** b. 8 September 1947, Taichung, Taiwan. Physician; Gastroenterologist. m. Ying-Erl Lin, 2 sons. Education: MD, 1973. Appointments: Chief, Division of Gastroenterology and Clinical Professor, Chang Gung Memorial Hospital; Associate Professor, Medical College, Chang Gung University; Editor-in-Chief, Gastroenterological Journal of Taiwan. Publications: Several in professional journals. Honours: Taiwan Medical Association Award, 1979, 1984; 20th Century Achievement Award, 1995; World Lifetime Achievement Award, 1996; Distinguished Taipei Citizen; Dictionary of International Biography; 500 Leaders of Influence; Who's Who in the World; Who's Who in Medicine and Healthcare; 500 Leaders for the New Century; The Barons 500; The Global 500; 500 Founders of the 21st Century. Memberships: ABI; IBC; GEST; DEST; ASGE; IASG; EAGE; AGA. Address: Chang Gung Memorial Hospital, 199 Tun Hwa North Road, Taipei 105, Taiwan.

**CHEN Shilu,** b. 24 September 1920, Dong Yang, Zhejiang, China. Professor. m. Xiaosu Gong, 2 sons, 1 daughter. Education: BSc, Aeronautics, Tsinghua University, China, 1945; PhD, Aeronautics, Moscow Aeronautical Institute, Russia, 1958. Appointments: Honorary Dean, College of Astronautics, Northwestern Polytechnical University, China, 1987-; Foreign Academician, Russian Academy of Astronautics, 1994-; Academician, Chinese Academy of Engineering, 1997-. Publications: Dynamic Stability Coupling and Active Control of Elastic Vehicles with Unsteady Aerodynamic Forces Considered; Longitudinal Stability of Elastic Vehicles; Progress and Development of Space Technology in China, 2000. Honours: Recipient of First Grade Award for Progress in Science and Technology on "Dynamics and Control of Elastic Vehicles", Chinese National Education Committee, 1991; Honoured as "Excellent Postgraduate Supervisor", "Distinguished Specialist", Ministry of Aeronautics and Astronautics, 1992. Memberships: Director, Chinese Society of Aeronautics and Astronautics, 1964-92; Chairman, Session of Aeronautics and Astronautics, China Advisory Committee for Academic Degrees, 1985-91; Honorary President, Shanxi Provincial Society of Astronautics, 1994-; Associate Fellow, AIAA, 1996-. Address: Northwestern Polytechnical University, South Apt 17-1-301, Xian 710072, People's Republic of China. E-mail: s.l.chen@nwpu.edu.cn

**CHEN Xuhui,** b. 25 July 1937, Hunan, China. Scientist. m. Wang Kaidi, 1 son, 2 daughters. Education: BS, Physical Geography, Department of Geography, Lanzhou University, 1959; English Training Center, Department of Science and Technology, Ministry of Agriculture, 1989-90; Tutor to Doctorate, Institute of Geochemistry, Chinese Academy of Science, 1995-98. Appointments: Assistant Professor, Soil and

Fertilizer Institute, Gansu Academy of Agricultural Sciences, 1959-82; Professor, 1983-2005, Director, 1984-97, Soil and Fertilizer Institute, Guizhou Academy of Agricultural Sciences; Specialist Adviser, Guizhou Academy of Agricultural Sciences, 2002-05. Publications: Articles in professional scientific journals. Honours: 2nd Prize, Advancement of Science and Technology, Government of Gansu Province, 1982; 4th Prize, 1990, 3rd Prize, 1991, 3rd Prize, 1999, 3rd Prize, 2000, Advancement of Science and Technology, Government of Guizhou Province; 3rd Prize, Advancement of Science and Technology, Ministry of Agriculture, 1991. Memberships: Vice President, Soil Society of Guizhou Province, 1987-2003; Council Member, Plant Nutrition and Fertilizer Society of China, 1990-2004; Member, International Society of Soil Science, 1994-2002; Council Member, Soil and Water Conservation Society of South China, 1996-2005; Member, Editorial Committee, Plant Nutrition and Fertilizer Science, 1999-2004. Address: Guizhou Academy of Agricultural Sciences, Guiyang, Guizhou 550006, China.

**CHENG Fai Chut,** b. 15 July 1933, Shanghai, China. Researcher in Electrical Engineering. Education: BSc, Electrical Engineering, Tsing Hua University, Beijing, 1957; MPhil, Electrical Engineering, University Hong Kong, 1990. Appointments: Engineer, NE Power Administration, Central Laboratory, Harbin, 1957-73; Technician, Tomoe Electrons Co, Hong Kong, 1973-76; Lecturer, School Science and Technology, Hong Kong, 1976-80; Part-time Demonstrator, University Hong Kong, 1980-88; Temporary Teacher, Haking Wong Technical Institute, Hong Kong, 1987-88; Evening Visiting Lecturer, 1988-89, 1990-93, Research Assistant, 1989-92, Teaching Assistant, 1992-93, Honorary Research Associate, 1993-94, Part-time Research Assistant, 1994-95, Hong Kong Polytechnic, now Hong Kong Polytechnic University; Part-time Research Assistant, 1995-97, Honorary Research Fellow, 1998-99, Honorary Fellow, 2000-02, Hong Kong Polytechnic University; Unemployed Researcher, 2003-. Publications: Insulation Thickness Determination of Polymeric Power Cables, 1994; Discussion on Insulation Thickness Determination of Polymeric Power Cables, in journal IEEE Transactions on Dielectrics and Electrical Insulation, 1995. Honours: Outstanding Achievement Medal, Gold Star Award, Silver Medal, IBC, 1997; Distinguished Leadership Award, 20th Century Achievement Award, Most Admired Man of the Decade, 1997 Man of Year Commemorative Medal, ABI, 1997; 2000 Millennium Medal of Honour, ABI, 1998. Memberships: IEEE, US; Institution of Electronic Engineers, UK. Address: 2-019 Lotus Tower 1, Garden Estate, 297 Ngau Tau Kok Rd, Kowloon, Hong Kong.

**CHENG Huai-Rui,** b. 10 December 1943, Shaanxi, China. Metallurgist. m. Zhu Yong-Zhen, 1 son, 1 daughter. Education: Bachelor of Engineering, Xian Jiao Tong University, 1964-69; Visiting Scholar, TU Graz, Austria, 1980-81; Visiting Scholar, TU, Wien, Austria, 1981-82. Appointments: Manager, Central Laboratory, Xian Aero-Engine Company, 1983-86; Director, Metallurgic Department, Xian Aero-Engine Company, 1986-99; Professor, Senior Engineer; Honorary Professor, North-West Polytechnical University; Deputy General Manager, Xian Airfoil Technology Co Ltd, 1999-2004. Honours: Outstanding Contribution to Scholar Study Abroad, Ministry of Aviation, 1992; Outstanding Contribution to Development of Science and Technology, State Council, China, 1996; Adviser of Superalloy Committee of China for all life. Memberships: China Aviation Society; China Metal Society. Address: Xujiawan, Beijiao, PO Box 13-197 Xian, China. E-mail: cheng@xat.xa.sn.cn

**CHENG Kai,** b. 18 December 1961, Harbin, China. University Professor. m. Lucy Q Lu, 1 son. Education: BEng (Hons)

in Mechanical Engineering, 1983, MSc in Manufacturing Engineering, 1988, Harbin Institute of Technology; PhD in Manufacturing Engineering, Liverpool John Moores University, 1994. Appointments: Postdoctoral Fellow, Liverpool John Moores University, 1994-95; Senior Lecturer, Mechanical Design and Manufacturing, Glasgow Caledonian University, 1995-99; Reader in Manufacturing Engineering, Leeds Metropolitan University, 1999-2001; Chair Professor in Precision Engineering, Leeds Metropolitan University, 2000-. Publications: Over 160 papers in learned international journals and referred conferences; Author and Editor, 4 books; Contributor, 6 book chapters. Honours: Best Paper Award, 16th National Conference on Manufacturing Research, 2000; Research Grant Awards, EU 6th Framework Program, EPSRC (UK), DTI (UK) and other research funding bodies. Memberships: Fellow, Institution of Electrical Engineers; Member, Institution of Mechanical Engineers; Member, European Society of Precision Engineering and Nanotechnology. Address: Advanced Manufacturing Technology Research Group, School of Technology, Leeds Metropolitan University, Leeds LS1 3HE, England. E-mail: k.cheng@leedsmet.ac.uk

**CHENG Taining,** b. 19 December 1935, Nanjing, China. Architect. m. Dongping Xu, 2 sons. Education: Graduate, Architecture Department, Nanjing Institute of Technology (now called Southeast University), 1956. Appointments: Architect China Academy of Building Research, Architect, Shanxi Lingfeng Area Designing Office, 1971-81; Architect, Dean of the Office, The Second Designing Office, Hangzhou Architecture Institute, 1981-84; Director, Architect, Hangzhou Architecture Institute, 1984-92; Honorary Director, Chief Architect, A & U Studio, Hangzhou Architecture Institute, 1992-2003; Chief Architect, China United Engineering Corporation, 2003-; Guest Professor, Zhejiang University and Southeast University; Attended sixteenth, seventeenth and eighteenth representative conferences of UIA; Participant in domestic and overseas academic conferences. Publications: Books: A Guide to Chinese Traditional Architecture, 1980; Contemporary Chinese Architect Cheng Taining Collective Works, 1997; Fraction and Direction (collective papers), 1998; Marketing Economy, Cross-Cultural Development and Architectural Creation (collective papers), 2000; Cheng Taining 1997-2000 Selected Works of Architecture, 2001; Numerous articles in professional architectural journals. Honours include: Architectural projects: 1970's National Design Award of Excellence, Yushan Hotel, Taiyuan, 1977; China Architectural Association Award of Creativity, Yellow Dragon Hotel, Hangzhou, 1992, Ghana, National Opera, Ghana, 1992, Mali Conference Building, Mali, 1991; National Design Award of Excellence, Railway Station, Hanhzhou, 2000; Personal: National Expert with Outstanding Achievement, 1991; Special petition from the Government, 1991; Chinese Architectural Designing Master, 2000; Nominated for Liang Sicheng Architecture Award, 2002. Memberships: Commissioner of Technical Activities Committee, Architectural Society of China; Commisioner of Committee of Experts, International Engineering Consultancy Company. Address: China United Engineering Corporation, Cheng Taining Architectural Research Institute, 11F, No 303, Wenhui Road, Hangzhou, Zhejiang, People's Republic of China. E-mail: ctn@arch.china.com

**CHENG Wenyu,** b. 28 June 1921, Chengdu, China. Professor of Economics. m. Helen Kuomei Huang, 2 sons, 2 daughters. Education: BA, Economics, National Wuhan University, 1943; Graduate Studies, Economics, Harvard University, 1945-46; MA, University of Chicago, 1950; PhD, 1954; University of Cambridge, 1982; UCLA Summer Course Work. Appointments: Professor of Economics, Marietta College, Ohio, 1948-95; Professor, 1960; Senior Distinguished Professor, 1985; Professor of Economics, Muskingum College, Ohio, 1987-91; Honorary Professor of Economics, Wuhan University, 1993-; Adjunct Professor of Economics, Ohio University, 1992-93; Emeritus, 1995. Publications: Survey of Economics; Co-author, Money and Banking; Principles of Economics; Many articles in professional journals. Honours: Scholarship Award, Overseas Dr Sun Yatsen Institute; Honorary Professorship, Wuhan University and Southwestern University of Finance and Economics, China; Omicron Delta Kappa Distinguished Service Key. Memberships: Association for Asian Studies; National Bureau for Asian Research. Address: 928 Glendale Road, Marietta, OH 45750, USA.

**CHENG Yue,** b. 23 August 1958, Wenzhou, Zhejing, China. Molecular Geneticist. m. Yuxing Xiong, 1 daughter. Education: BMed, Anhui Medical College, China, 1982; MMed, Sun Yatsen University of Medical Sciences, China, 1987; PhD, Hong Kong University of Science and Technology, 2002. Appointments: Teaching Assistant, Anhui Medical College, 1982-84; Assistant Professor, Sun Yatsen University of Medical Science, 1989-93; Visiting Assistant Researcher, University of California, Irvine, 1993-95; Visiting Scholar, Hong Kong University of Science and Technology, 1995-2002; Visiting Fellow, Genetics Branch, National Cancer Institute, National Naval Medical Center, USA, 2003-. Publications: Articles in professional scientific journals. Honours: Grant, Sun Yatsen University of Medical Science, 1991; Scholarship, American Chinese Medical Board, 1993; Lifetime Achievement Award, IBC, 2001; Life Fellow, IBA, 2001; Deputy Director General, IBC, 2001; Vice Consul, IBC, 2002; Listed in Who's Who Publications; Fellowship Award, National Institutes of Health, USA, 2003-. Memberships: Chinese Medical Association, 1991-; Hong Kong Professional Teacher's Union, 1998-03; Member, American Association for the Advancement of Science, 2002-; American Association for Cancer Research, 2003-. E-mail: yuecheng@hotmail.com

**CHER (Cherilyn LaPierre Sarkisian),** b. 20 May 1946, El Centro, California, USA. Singer; Actress; Entertainer. m. (1) Sonny Bono, 1964, divorced, deceased, 1 daughter, (2) Gregg Allman, 1975, divorced, 1 son. Career: Worked with Sonny Bono in duo Sonny and Cher, 1964-74; Also solo artiste, 1964-; Performances include: Hollywood Bowl, 1966; Newport Pop Festival, 1968; Television includes: Sonny And Cher Comedy Hour, CBS, 1971; Cher, CBS, 1975-76; Sonny And Cher Show, CBS, 1976-77; Vocalist with rock group Black Rose, including US tour supporting Hall & Oates, 1980; Actress, films: Good Times, 1967; Chastity, 1969; Come Back To The Five And Dime, Jimmy Dean Jimmy Dean, 1982; Silkwood, 1984; Mask, 1985; The Witches Of Eastwick, 1987; Moonstruck, 1987; Suspect, 1987; Mermaids, 1989; Love and Understanding; faithful; If these Walls could Talk; Pret-a-Porter; Tea with Mussolini. Recordings include: Singles: with Sonny And Cher: I Got You Babe (Number 1, UK and US), 1975; Baby Don't Go, 1965; Just You, 1965; But You're Mine, 1965; What Now My Love, 1966; Little Man, 1966; The Beat Goes On, 1967; All I Ever Need Is You, 1971; A Cowboy's Work Is Never Done, 1972; Solo hit singles include: All I Really Want To Do, 1965; Bang Bang, 1966; Gypsies Tramps And Thieves (Number 1, US), 1971; The Way Of Love, 1972; Half Breed (Number 1, US), 1973; Dark Lady (Number 1, US), 1974; Take Me Home, 1979; Dead Ringer For Love, duet with Meatloaf, 1982; I Found Someone, 1987; We All Sleep Alone, 1988; After All, duet with Peter Cetera (for film soundtrack Chances Are), 1989; If I Could Turn Back Time, 1989; Jesse James, 1989; Heart Of Stone, 1990; The Shoop Shoop Song (from film soundtrack Mermaids) (Number 1, UK), 1991; Love And Understanding, 1991; Oh No Not My Baby, 1992; Walking In Memphis, 1995; One By One,

1996; Paradise Is Here, 1996; Believe, 1998; Strong Enough, 1999; Albums: with Sonny and Cher: Look At Us, 1965; All I Really Want To Do, 1965; The Wondrous World Of Sonny And Cher, 1966; Sonny And Cher Live, 1972; Solo albums include: All I Really Want To Do, 1965; The Sonny Side Of Cher, 1966; With Love, 1967; Backstage, 1968; Jackson Highway, 1969; Gypsies Tramps And Thieves, 1972; Foxy Lady, 1972; Greatest Hits, 1974; Stars, 1975; I'd Rather Believe In You, 1976; Take Me Home, 1979; I Paralyze, 1984; Cher, 1988; Heart Of Stone, 1989; Love Hurts, 1991; Cher's Greatest Hits 1965-1992, 1992; It's A Man's World, 1995; Believe, 1999; Black Rose, 1999; Living Proof, 2001. Honours include: Oscar, Best Actress, Moonstruck, 1988; Oscar Nomination, Best Supporting Actress, Silkwood, 1984. Address: Reprise Records, 3000 Warner Boulevard, Burbank, CA 19010, USA.

**CHESNAIS Jean Claude,** b. 27 October 1948, France. Demographer. m. Diane Padureleanu, 2 sons. Education: PhD, Demography, University of Paris, 1975; PhD Economics, Institut d'Etudes Politiques, 1984. Appointments: Senior Research Fellow, Institut National d'Etudes; Professor, Ecole Nationale d'Administration and Ecole Polytechnique; Visiting Professor, School of Advanced International Studies, Johns Hopkins University. Publications: The Demographic Transition. its Stages, Patterns and Economic Implications; Demographic Transition Patterns and their Impact on the Age Structure; Worldwide Historical Trends in Murder and Suicide. Honours: La démographie, Que Sais-Je?, 6th edition, 2005; Academie Francaise Prize, 1996; Prize of the French Speaking Statistician. Memberships: International Statistical Institute; International Union for the Scientific Study of Population; World Humanity Action Trust. Address: INED 133 Boulevard, Davout 75020 Paris, France.

**CHILD Dennis,** b. 10 July 1932, Ulverston, England. Emeritus Professor of Educational Psychology; Author. m. Eveline Barton, 1 son, 1 daughter. Education: teachers' Certificate, St John's College, York, 1957; BSc, London, 1962; M Ed, Leeds, 1968; PhD, Bradford, 1973. Appointments: Teacher of General Science, Easingwold Comprehensive School, near York, 1957-59; Teacher of Physics and Chemistry, Bootham School, York, 1959-62; Lecturer in Physics, 1962-65, Senior Lecturer in Education, 1965-67, City of Leeds College of Education; Lecturer, 1967-73, Senior Lecturer, 1973-76, Psychology of Education, Postgraduate School of Studies of Research on Education, University of Bradford; Visiting Professor, University of Illinois, USA, 1972, 1973; Professor and Head of School of Education, University of Newcastle upon Tyne, 1976-81; Professor of Educational Psychology, School of Education, 1981-92, Head of School, 1984-87, Emeritus Professor of Educational Psychology, School of Education, 1992-, University of Leeds; Author. Publications include: Some technical problems in the use of personality measures in occupational settings illustrated using the "Big Five" (book chapter), 1998; Painters of the Northern Counties of England and Wales, 1994, 2nd edition, 2002; The Yorkshire Union of Artists 1888-1922, 2001; Psychology and the Teacher (7th edition, major revision), 2004; The Yorkshire Union of Artists 1888-1922 in Antique Collecting, 2004; Entry for James Lonsdale (1777-1839) in Dictionary of National Biography, 2004. Honours: OBE, 1997; Directions in Educational Psychology edited by Dianne Shorrocks-Taylor. An appreciation of the works of Dennis Child, 1998; Biography for Dennis Child in European Revue of Applied Psychology, 1999. Memberships: FBPsS; FCST; C Psychol. Address: The Cottage, Main Street, Scholes, Leeds LS15 4DP, England.

**CHILD Mark Sheard,** b. 17 August 1937, Stockton-on-Tees, England. University Professor. m. Daphne Hall, 1 son, 2 daughters. Education: BA (Cantab) Chemistry 1st class, 1959, PhD (Cantab), Theoretical Chemistry, 1962, Clare College, Cambridge. Appointments: Research Fellow, Lawrence Radiation Laboratory, University of California, Berkeley, USA, 1962-63; Lecturer, Theoretical Chemistry, University of Glasgow, 1963-66; Lecturer, Theoretical Chemistry, 1966-89, Aldrachian Praelector in Chemistry, 1989-92, Professor, Chemical Dynamics, 1992-94, Coulson Professor of Theoretical Chemistry, 1994-2004, University of Oxford; Visiting Fellow, University of Wisconsin, Madison, USA, 1963; Visiting Professor, Institute of Advanced Studies, Hebrew University of Jerusalem, 1978-79; Visiting Professor, University of Colorado, USA, 1988-89; Visiting Professor, Université de Paris-Sud, 1989; Visiting Professor, Joseph Fourier University, Grenoble, 1996. Publications: Author and Co-author of over 150 articles in scientific journals; Books: Molecular Collision Theory, 1974, reissued, 1996; Semiclassical mechanisms with molecular applications, 1991. Honour: Fellow of the Royal Society; William Draper Harkins Lecture, University of Chicago, 1985; Tilden Lecture, Royal Society of Chemistry, 1987-87; Condon Lecture, University of Colorado, 1987-88. Memberships: Royal Society; Royal Society of Chemistry.

**CHIN Jacky,** b. 2 April 1960, Ipoh, Perak, Malaysia. Corrosion Scientist. m. Ann Fong, 1 son. Education: Diploma in Technology, Materials Science, Tunku Abdul Rahman College, Malaysia, 1984; Bachelor of Science, Universiti Teknologi Malaysia, 1990; Doctorate, Southern Cross University, Australia, 1996. Appointments: Corrosion Scientist, Corrosion Science Research Centre, 1984-90; Director, Oriental Science Research Centre, 1990-; Visiting Professor, Zhongshan University, Guangzhou, China, 2000-. Publications: Book: Corrosion and Corrosion Protection of Building Materials; Article: Endothermic-based Atmospheres. Honours: The Outstanding Young Malaysian, 2000; Listed in Who's Who publications and biographical dictionaries. Memberships: Institute of Metal Finishing, UK; Institution of Corrosion Science and Technology, UK. Address: 36A Jalan SS15/4B, Subang Jaya, 47500 Selangor Darul Ehsan, Malaysia. E-mail: yschin@mailcity.com

**CHIN Takaaki,** b. 4 October 1960, Kobe, Japan. Medical Doctor. m. K Hayashi, 1 daughter. Education: Bachelor of Medicine, Tokushima University, Tokushima, Japan, 1986; Medical Diplomate, 1986; PhD, Kobe University. Appointments: Resident, University Hospital, Kobe, Japan, 1986-87; Doctor Course, Kobe University, Kobe, Japan, 1987-91; Research Fellow, McGill University, Montreal, Canada, 1990-92; Head Physician, Hyogo Rehabilitation Centre, Kobe, Japan, 1992-. Publications: Articles in medical journals including: Developmental Biology, 1996; Prosthetics and Orthotics International, 1997, 1999, 2002; Journal of Rehabilitation Research and Development, 2001; American Journal of Physical Medicine and rehabilitation, 2002, 2003; Journal of Bone and Joint Surgery (br), 2004. Honour: Iida Prize, Japanese Society of Prosthetics and Orthotics, 2001. Memberships: Japanese Orthopaedic Association; Japanese Association of Rehabilitation Medicine; Councillor, 1998-, Japanese Society of Prosthetics and Orthotics; Vice-President, 2003-, Japan Branch, International Society for Prosthetics and Orthotics; International Society of Orthopaedic Surgery and Traumatology. Address: Hyogo Rehabilitation Centre, 1070 Akebono-Cho, Nishi-Ku, Kobe, 651-2181 Japan. E-mail: t-chin@pure.co.jp

**CHIN Young,** b. 23 October 1950, Seoul, Korea. Lawyer; Member of National Assembly. m. Mi Young Chung, 1 son, 1 daughter. Education: BA, Seoul National University, Seoul,

Korea, 1975; LLM, University of Washington, School of Law, USA, 1984. Appointments: Judge, Seoul Southern District Court, 1980-81; Advisor, 1988 Seoul Olympic Organisation, 1984-88; Director, Korean Taekwondo Association, 1996-97; Professor, Real Estate Studies, Konkuk University, 2001; Chief Secretary to the Chairperson, Grand National Party, 2004-2005. Publications: Book: Comparison of Korea-US Law related to Resale Price Maintenance; Article: Protection of Constitution and Free Enterprise Principle; Many other articles on economy and market system. Membership: Korean Bar Association. Address: # 518 National Assembly Members' Building, Youido-Dong, Yeongdeungpo-Gu, Seoul, Korea. E-mail: ychin21@hanmail.net Website: www.chinyoung.com

**CHIOU Che Wun,** b. 7 February 1960, Taiwan. Professor in Computer Science. m. Whey-Lin Jhung, 1 son, 3 daughters. Education: BS, Electronic Engineering, Chung Yuan University, Taiwan, 1982; MS, 1984, PhD, 1989, Electrical Engineering, National Cheng Kung University, Taiwan. Appointments: Senior Specialist, Chung Shan Institute of Science and Technology, 1990-2000; Professor, Department of Electronic Engineering, Dean, Division of Continuing Education, Ching Yun University, Taiwan. Publications: More than 50 papers. Honours: Listed in international biographical dictionaries. Address: 229, Chien-Hsin Rd, Chung-Li 320, Taiwan. E-mail: cwchiou@cyu.edu.tw

**CHIRAC Jacques René,** b. 29 November 1932, Paris, France. Politician. m. Bernadette Chodron de Courcel, 1956, 2 children. Education: Lycée Carnot; Lycée Louis-le-Grand, Paris; Institute of Political Science, Paris; Harvard University Summer School, USA. Appointments: Military Service, Algeria; Auditor, Cour des Comptes, 1959-62; Special Assistant, Government Secretariat General, 1962 Counsellor, Cour des Comptes, 1965-94; Secretary of State for Employment Problems, 1967-68; Secretary of State for Economy and Finance, 1968-71; Minister for Parliamentary Relations, 1971-72, for Agriculture and Rural Development, 1972-74, of the Interior, 1974; Prime Minister of France, 1974-76, 1986-88; Secretary General, Union des Démocrates pour la République (UDR), 1975, Honorary Secretary General, 1975-76; President, Rassemblement pour la République (formerly UDR), 1976-94, Honorary Secretary General, 1977-80; Mayor of Paris, 1977-95; President of France, 1995-2002; Re-elected President of France, 2002-. Publications: Discours pour la France a l'heure du choix; La lueur de l'espérance: Réflexion du soir pour le matin, 1978; Une Nouvelle France, Reflexion 1, 1994; La France pour tous, 1995. Honours include: Prix Louis Michel, 1986; Grand-Croix de la Légion d'Honneur; Grand Croix de l'Ordre National du Mérite; Chevalier du Mérite. Address: Palais de l'Eysée, 55-57 rue du Faubourg Saint-Honoré, 75008 Paris, France.

**CHISHOLM Alison (Fiona Williams),** b. 25 July 1952, Liverpool, England. Teacher, Writer, Poet. m. Malcolm Chisholm, 10 July 1971, 2 daughters. Education: ATCL, 1969; FLCM, 1971; LLAM, 1973. Appointments: Teacher, Oxford Academy of Speech and Drama, Middlesbrough; Principal, Richmond Academy of Speech, Southport; Poetry and Creative Writing Tutor, Southport College; Poetry Consultant, BBC Radio Merseyside, 1991-1996. Publications: Alone No More (co-author), 1977; Flying Free, 1985; The Need for Unicorns, 1987; Single Return, 1988; Paper Birds, 1990; The Craft of Writing Poetry, 1992; A Practical Poetry Course, 1994; How to Write 5-Minute Features, 1996; Daring the Slipstream, 1997; How to Write About Yourself (co-author), 1999; Writing Competitions: The way to win (co-author), 2001; Mapping the Maze, 2004. Contributions to: Envoi; Outposts; Doors; Orbis; Smoke; Staple; Acumen; Poetry Now; Poetry Nottingham Int;

The Formalist. Others; Various anthologies and children's anthologies; BBC Radio Merseyside and Network Northwest; Articles on poetry in numerous writers' magazines. Honours: Prizes, Mary Wilkins Memorial Competition (twice), Success Open, Grey Friars, Rhyme International, Lace, KQBX, Chester, Banstead, Lake Aske, Envoi, Julia Cairns, Ouse Valley, Sefton, New Prospects, Wells International and Yorkshire Competitions, and US competitions in various categories of World Order of Narrative and Formalist Poets and NFSPS, Ohio Poetry Day Competitions. Memberships: Society of Women Writers and Journalists; Poetry Society; Verse Writers' Guild of Ohio; Association of Christian Writers; Southport Writers' Circle; Society of Authors. Address: 53 Richmond Road, Birkdale, Southport, Merseyside PR8 4SB, England.

**CHITESCU Ion,** b. 19 July 1947, Bucharest, Romania. Professor of Mathematics. m. Rodica Chitescu, 2 daughters. Education: Licencié, Maths, 1970, PhD, Maths, 1975, University of Bucharest. Appointments: Assistant Professor, 1970-80, Lecturer, 1980-91, Associate Professor, 1991-2000, Professor, 2000-, Dean-, Faculty of Mathematics, University of Bucharest. Publications: Main books: Monograph: Function Spaces; Mathematical Analysis Dictionary (in collaboration); Measure Theory (in collaboration); 41 papers (research); Fields of interest: Vector Measures and Integration; Function Spaces; Random Sequences; Probability and Statistics; Optimization; Fractal Theory. Honours: Romanian National Academy Prize, for "Function Spaces", 1985. Memberships: American Mathematical Society; Mathematical Reviews Referee; Mathematical Reports Advisory Board. Address: Str Henri Coanda 44, Sector 1, Bucharest 010668, Romania.

**CHITHAM Edward Harry Gordon,** b. 16 May 1932, Harborne, Birmingham, England. Education Consultant. m. Mary Patricia Tilley, 29 December 1962, 1 son, 2 daughters. Education: BA, MA (Classics), Jesus College, Cambridge, 1952-55; PGCE, University of Birmingham, 1955-56; MA, English, University of Warwick, 1973-77; PhD, University of Sheffield, 1983. Publications: The Black Country, 1972; Ghost in the Water, 1973; The Poems of Anne Brontë, 1979; Brontë Facts and Brontë Problems (with T J Winnifrith), 1983; Selected Brontë Poems (with T J Winnifrith), 1985; The Brontës' Irish Background, 1986; A Life of Emily Brontë, 1987; Charlotte and Emily Brontë (with T J Winnifrith), 1989; A Life of Anne Brontë, 1991; A Bright Start, 1995; The Poems of Emily Brontë (with Derek Roper), 1996; The Birth of Wuthering Heights: Emily Brontë at work, 1998; A Brontë Family Chronology, 2003; Harborne: A History, 2004. Contributions to: Byron Journal; Gaskell Society Journal; ISIS Magazine; Brontë Society Transactions. Memberships: Fellow, Royal Society of Arts, 1997. Joint Association of Classics Teachers; Gaskell Society; Brontë Society. Address: 25 Fugelmere Close, Harborne, Birmingham B17 8SE, England.

**CHIU Dirk M,** b. Malaysia. Engineering Educator. m. Lee H Lim, 1 son, 1 daughter. Education: BSc, Engineering, London, 1969; MSc, Edinburgh, 1976; PhD, Manchester, 1978. Appointments: Telecom Engineer, STC; Electronic Design Engineer, Control Systems Ltd; Electronic Senior Engineer, London University; Electronic Lecturer, Singapore Polytechnic; Microelectronic Lecturer, Paisley University; Course Co-ordinator in Electronics, Victoria University of Technology; Visiting Professor, Nankai University, and Dong Hwa University; Associate Professor, UPM. Publications: Electronic Science and Education (book); Over 100 articles on electronic sciences; Semiconductor Electronics; Power Electronics; Microelectronics; Engineering Education. Honours: Taiwan SRC Research Professorship, 2000. Memberships:

MIEE; CEng; PEng. Address: 71 Long Valley Way, Doncaster East, Victoria 3109, Australia.

**CHIU Wan Cheng,** b. 1 November 1919, Meihsien, Guangdong, China. Professor. m. Margaret C Y Liu, 3 daughters. Education: BS, National Central University, China, 1941; MS, 1947, PhD, Meteorology, 1951, New York University. Appointments: Technician, Fukien Weather Bureau, China, 1941-42; Teacher, Maths, Punshan Model School, Szechwan, China, 1942-43; Graduate Student, Assistant Teacher, Meteorology, National Central University, China, 1943-45; Research Associate, Research Scientist, New York University, 1951-61; Professor, Meteorology, University of Hawaii, 1961-87; Visiting Scientist, 1967-68, Senior Fellow, 1975, National Centre of Atmospheric Research. Publications: The relative importance of different heat-exchange process in the Lower Stratosphere; The spectrums of angular momentum transfer in the atmosphere; The Interpretation of the energy spectrum; The spectral equation of the statistical energy spectrum of atmospheric motion in the frequency domain; A study of the possible statistical relationship between the tropical sea surface temperature and atmospheric circulation. Honours: Fellow, New York University; Listed in numerous Who's Who and biographical publications. Memberships: American Meteorological Society; American Geophysical Union; Royal Meteorological Society of England. Address: 216 Kalalau Street, Honolulu, HI 96825, USA.

**CHO Gilsoo,** b. 24 December 1956, Daejon, Republic of Korea. Professor. m. Changsoon Park, 1 daughter. Education: BS, 1974-78, MS, 1978-80, Seoul National University; PhD, Virginia Tech, USA, 1981-84. Appointments: Professor of Clothing and Textiles, Yonsei University, 1984-; Director of Research Institute of Clothing and Textile Sciences, 2003-. Publications: Book Chapter as co-author: Computational Clothing and Accessories in Fundamentals of Wearable Computers and Augmented Reality (by W Barfield and T Caudell), 2001; Articles as co-author in professional journals: A Fabric Sound Evaluation System for Totally Auditory-Sensible Textiles, 2002; Thermal Properties and Physiological Responses of Vapour-Permeable Water-Repellent Fabrics Treated with Microcapsule Containing PCMs, 2004. Honours: International Scientist of the Year 2004, International Educator of the Year 2004, IBC; Listed in Who's Who publications and biographical dictionaries. Address: Department of Clothing and Textiles, College of Human Ecology, Yonsei University, 134 Shinchon-Dong, Sudaemun-ku, Seoul, Korea 120-749. E-mail: gscho@yansei.ac.kr Website: http://suny.yonsei.ac.kr/~gscho

**CHO Moon-Boo,** b. 13 December 1935, Pukcheju, Republic of Korea. Academic Administrator. m. Hee-Zah Park, 2 sons, 4 daughters. Education: BA, Public Administration, Seoul National University, 1959; PhD, Politics, Seikei University, Japan, 1993. Appointments: Professor, Cheju National University, 1965-97; Visiting Researcher, Law College, Tokyo University, 1980-83; Visiting Scholar, Yale Law School, 1991-92; Dean, College of Social Science, 1985-88; Dean for Academic Affairs, 1998-99; Dean, Graduate School, Public Administration, 1993-95; President, Cheju National University, 1997-2001. Publications: Korean Local Government, 1995; The Structure and Function of Budget Decision Process, 1997. Honours: Presidential Medal, Korea, 1979; Certificate of Meritorious Service, Korean Self-Government, 1995, 1996; Best Decoration in the Decoration of Civil Servants, 2001. Memberships: Cheju Island Education Committee, 1979-80; Vice Chief, Cheju Election Committee, 1984-90; Chief, Regional Consulting Subcommittee, Cheju Provincial Office, 1986-88; Public Welfare Delegate, Cheju Labour Relation Board, 1979-87; Member, Rebuilding Korea, 1998; Member, Director, Korean Association for Public Administration, 1979-; Member, Director, Vice Chief, Korean Association for Public Administrative Law, 1979-; Director, Vice Chief, Korean Association for Local Autonomy, 1989-. Address: 113-7 Il-do-2-dong, Dae-Yoo, Dae-lim Apt 302-501, Cheju-shi, Cheju-do 690-831, Republic of Korea. E-mail: mbc3422@kornet.net

**CHO Myeong-Chan,** b. 19 February, 1958, Kimhae, Republic of Korea. Cardiologist; Professor; Researcher. m. Kwang-Joo Kim, 1 son, 1 daughter. Education: MD, 1983, College of Medicine, PhD, 1992-96, Graduate School, Seoul National University, Seoul, Korea; Postdoctoral Fellow, University of California, San Diego, USA, 1996-97; Postdoctoral Fellow, University of North Carolina, USA, 1997-98. Appointments: Intern, 1983-84, Resident, Department of Internal Medicine, Clinical Fellow, Department of Cardiology, 1990-91, Seoul National University Hospital, Seoul, Korea; Chief in Cardiology, Capital Armed Forces General Hospital Seoul, Korea, 1987-90; Lecturer, 1991-93, Assistant Professor, 1993-98, Associate Professor, 1993-3003, Professor, 2003-, Chief in Cardiology and Director of Cardiovascular/Cath Laboratory, 1998-2004, Director of Department of Planning and Administration, 2003-2004, Chairman, Department of Internal Medicine, 2004-, Chungbuk National University Hospital, Cheongju, Korea; Visiting Professor, Department of Cardiology, Royal Infirmary, Glasgow, Scotland, 1994. Publications: Articles in international medical journals as co-author include most recently: Novel oral formulation of paclitaxel inhibits neointimal hyperplasia in a rat carotid artery injury model, 2004; Local delivery of green tea catchins inhibits neointimal formation in the rat carotid artery injury model, 2004; Implantation of bone marrow mononuclear cells using injectable fibrin matrix enhances neovascularization in infarcted myocardium, 2005. Honours: Cheongnam Scientific Award, Korean Society of Internal Medicine, 2001; Chungbuk Medical Scientific Award, Chungbuk National University, 2002; Best Editor, Korean Society of Circulation, 2003. Memberships include: Korean Medical Association, 1983-; Korean Society of Internal Medicine, 1987-; Associate Member: Korean Society of Hypertension, 1989-, Korean Society of Echocardiography, 1990, Korean Society of Lipidology and Artherosclerosos, 1990-, Korean Society of Tissue Engineering, 1996-, Korean Society of Molecular Biochemistry and Molecular Biology. Address: Department of Cardiology, Chungbuk National University Hospital, 62 Gaeshin-Dong, Heungduk-Gu, Cheongju 361-711, Korea. E-mail: mccho@cbnu.ac.kr

**CHO Sung Won,** b. 10 March 1953. Gastroenterologist. m. 2 sons. Education: Medical Degree, Yonsei University College of Medicine, 1974-78; Master of Medicine, The Graduate School, Yonsei University, 1982-86; Doctor of Philosophy, The Graduate School, Soon Chun Hyang University, 1990-94. Appointments: Intern, Resident, Department of Internal Medicine, 1980-84, Research Fellow, 1984-85, Instructor, 1985-89, Assistant Professor, 1990-93, Associate Professor, 1994-95, Department of Gastroenterology, Soon Chun Hyang University, Seoul; Research Fellow, Liver Section, Academic Department of Medicine, Royal Free Hospital, London, England, 1987-89; Associate Professor, 1995-97, Professor of Medicine, 1998-, Department of Gastroenterology, Ajou University School of Medicine, Suwon. Publications: Reversion form precore/core promoter mutants to wild-type hepatitis B virus during the course of lamivudine therapy, 2000; Effect of virological response on post-treatment durability of lamivudine-induced HbeAg seroconversion, 2002; Blockage of HSP 90 modulates Helicobacter pylori-induced IL-8 productions through the inactivation of transcriptional factors of AP-1 and NF-kappaB, 2004; Amelioration of oxidative stress with ensuing inflammation contributes to chemoprevention of H pylori-associated gastric carcinogenesis, 2004; Restoration of heat shock protein70 suppresses gastric mucosal inducible nitric oxide synthase expression induced by Heliobacter pylori, 2004; Selective induction of apoptosis with proton pump inhibitor in gastric cancer cells, 2004. Honours: Best SCI journal publication, Korean Association of the Study of the Liver, 2001; Best Oral Presentation, Korean Association of the Study of the Liver, 2003; Best Article Publication, Korean Society of Gastroenterology, 2002; Section PI of Genomic Research Centre for Liver and Gastroenterology, Korean Ministry of Health and Welfare, 2001; Section P I of Liver Cirrhosis Research Center, Korean Ministry of Health and Welfare, 2005. Memberships: Korean Society of Internal Medicine; Korean Society of Gastroenterology; Korean Association of the Study of the Liver; Korean Society of Gastrointestinal Endoscopy; Korean Study of Group of Hepacellular Carcinoma; European Association for the Study of the Liver. Address: Department of Gastroenterology, Ajou University Hospital, Suwon 442-721, Korea. E-mail: sung_woncho@hotmail.com

**CHO Zang-Hee,** b. 15 July 1936, Seoul, Korea. Professor of Radiological Sciences (Physics). m. Jung-suk Cho, 3 daughters. Education: MSc, BSc, Seoul University, 1960-62; PhD, Uppsala University, 1966; FilD, Stockholm University, 1972. Appointments: Professor, University of California at Irvine, Columbia University, University of California at Los Angeles, Stockholm University. Publications: 200 scientific peer reviewed publications and books authored. Memberships: US National Academy of Sciences; Institute of Medicine; Korean National Academy of Sciences. Address: 29 Harbour Pointe Drive, Corona Del Mar, CA 92625-1333, USA.

**CHOI Byung-Ok,** b. 2 June 1964, Busan, Republic of Korea. Neurologist. m. Hyun-kyung Song, 1 son. Education: MD, 1983-89, MS, 1994-96, PhD, 1996-2001, Yonsei University, Seoul, Korea; Neurology, Ministry of Health and Welfare, 1998. Appointments: Professor, Pochon CHA University, Sungnam, Korea, 2000-2002; Professor, Ewha Womans University, Seoul, Korea, 2003-; Director, Korean Organisation for Rare Diseases, Seoul, Korea, 2005. Publications: Articles published in journals including: Human Mutation, Neurology, Neurogenetics, British Journal of Pharmacology, Thrombosis Research, European Neurology, Muscle and Nerve, Experimental Molecutlar Medicine etc, Human Mutation. include: Mutational analysis of PMP22, MPZ, Cx32, ERG2 and NEFL in Korean Chacot-Marie-Tooth neuropathy patients; Patents for diagnostic methods and kits for CMT disease and vascular diseases. Honours: Young Investigator's Award, International Society of Haematology, 2002; Presentation Awards: Korean Neurology Association, 2004-2005, Korean Association of Biological Sciences, 2004; Korean EMG Association, 2005, etc. Address: Department of Neurology, College of Medicine, Ewha Womans University, Dongdaemun Hospital, 70 Jongno 6-ga, Jongno-gu, Seoul 110-783, Republic of Korea. E-mail: bochoi@ewha.ac.kr

**CHOI Byung-Tae,** b. 13 August 1961, Kyungnam, Korea. Professor; Anatomist. m. Dae-Jae Ko, 2 sons. Education: BSc, College of Education, 1985, MSc, Graduate School of Education, 1988; PhD, Graduate School, 1993, Pusan National University, Korea. Appointments: Teaching Assistant, 1987-90, Lecturer, 1990-97, Department of Biology Education, Pusan National University; Full-time Lecturer, Assistant Professor, Associate Professor, 1997-, Director, Research Institute of Oriental Medicine, 2002-04, Dong-eui University, Busan, Korea; Visiting Professor, Neuroscience Research Center, Peking University, 2001-2002. Publications: 105 articles about oriental medicine and morphological science. Memberships: Korean Association of Anatomists; Korean Association of Physical Anthropology;

Korean Society for Molecular Biology. Address: Department of Anatomy, College of Oriental Medicine, Dong-eui University, Busan 614-052, Korea. E-mail: choibt@deu.ac.kr

**CHOI Dong Ryong,** b. 15 February 1945, Tokyo, Japan. Consulting Geologist. m. Chong-Ih Kim, 1 son, 1 daughter. Education: Doctor of Science, Hokkaido University, Japan, 1972. Appointments: Chief Engineer, Kokusai Kogyo Co Ltd, Tokyo, Japan, 1973-77; Postdoctoral Fellow, Assistant Professor, University of Miami, 1977-85; Senior Research Scientist, Australian Geological Survey Organization, 1985-89; Consulting Geologist, Mineral Exploration and borehole imaging, 1989-. Publications: Surge Tectonics and Paleolands in the Pacific; Numerous contributions to professional journals. Honours: Research funds from US National Science Foundation; Listed in 500 Leaders of Influence; Co-editor, New Concepts in Global Tectonics Newsletter; Invited Lectures: Japan National Oil Corporation and many others. Memberships: American Association of Petroleum Geology; Geological Society of Australia. Address: 6 Mann Place, Higgins, ACT 2615, Australia.

**CHOI Hyo,** b. 24 August 1949, Namhaegun, Republic of Korea. Professor. m. Mi Sook Lee, 2 sons. Education: BS, Meteorology, 1968-76, MS, Marine Meteorology and Physical Oceanography, 1976-78, Seoul National University, Korea; PhD, Civil Engineering and Coastal Meteorology, University of Texas at Austin, USA, 1980-84; PhD, Atmospheric Chemistry-Pollution Modelling, Peking University, Beijing, China, 1999-2004. Appointments include: Senior Researcher, Korea Ocean Research and Development Institute, KAIST, Seoul, Korea, 1984-88; Investigator, Scientist, Interpreter, 1st Korean Antarctic Expedition Team, King George Island, 1985; Associate Professor, 1988-94, Professor, 1994-, Department of Atmospheric Environmental Sciences, Kangnung National University; General Director, Donghae Coastal Region Research Institute, Kangnung National University, 1989-91;Member, Ocean Reservation Consulting Council, Ministry of Environment, Korean Government, 1992-94; Senior Researcher, National Fishery Research and Development Agency, Korean Government, 1997-99; President, Korean Environmental Sciences Society, 2002-03; Co-President, 3rd International Symposium on Air Quality Management of Urban Regional and Global Scales, Istanbul, Turkey, 2004-; Guest Professor, Peking University, Beijing China, 2005-; Member editorial boards: Advanced in Fracture Mechanics, UK, 1996-98; Damage and Fracture Mechanics, Wessex Institute of Technology, UK, 1999-2001; Geospatial Today, India, 2002-2003. Publications: Articles in scientific journals as author and co-author include: Recycling of suspended particulates by atmospheric boundary depth and coastal circulation, 2004; Effects of atmospheric circulation and boundary layer structure on the dispersion of suspended particulates in the Seoul metropolitan area, 2005; Characteristics of atmospheric circulation in the Sockco coast, 2005; Monthly variation of sea-air temperature difference in the Korean coast, 2005. Honours: National Order, Magnolia, Korean Government, 1986; Meritorious Prize from the Head of Korean Meteorological Administration, 1999; 9th Scientific and Technological Prize for Excellent Paper, Korean Federation of Science and Technology, 1999; Meritorious Prize, Korean Environmental Sciences Society, 2004. Memberships: Korean Meteorological Society; Korean Environmental Sciences Society; La Société Franco-Japonaise D'Oceanographie, Japan; American Meteorological Society; Asia Oceania Geosciences Society; Air and Waste Management Association, USA. Address: Department of Atmospheric Environmental Sciences, Kangnung National University, Kangnung, Kangwondo 210-702, Republic of Korea. E-mail: du8392@hanmail.net

# DICTIONARY OF INTERNATIONAL BIOGRAPHY

**CHOI Hyun-Sik,** b. 29 June 1941, Seoul, Korea. Business Executive. m. Kyung-Ja Kim, 2 sons, 1 daughter. Education: College of Pharmacy, Seoul National University, 1964; Korea University Business School, 1968; Advanced Management Program, Seoul National University, 1995. Appointments: Joined Choong-Wae Pharmaceutical Corporation, 1966, Board Director, 1980-89, Executive Director, Sales and Marketing, 1989-92, Vice-President, 1992-98, President, 1998-2001, Executive Vice-Chairman, 2001-2004; President, 1999-2001, Executive Vice-Chairman, 2001-2004, Choong-Wae Medical Corporation; Executive Vice-Chairman, Daeyoo Pharmaceutical Corporation, 2001-2004; Executive Vice-Chairman, Choong-Wae IT, 2001-2004; General Advisor, GlaxoSmithKline, 2004-; Director, Korea Health Industry Development Institute, 1999-. Honours: CEO Award, Institute for CEOs of Korea, 1999; Sinjisikin (Homo-Knowlegian), Ministry of Commerce, Industry and Energy, 1999; Order of National Service Merit, 2002. Memberships: Chairman, Distribution Committee, -2003, Chairman, Fair Competition Council Operation Committee, -2003, Chairman, Korea Good Manufacturing Practice Committee, -2003, Korea Pharmaceutical Manufacturing Association. Address: D-2702, Michelan Chereville 180, Jeongja-dong, Bundang-gu, Seongnam-si, Kyeonggi-do, 463-858 Korea.

**CHOI Seok Hwa,** b. 11 June 1957; Republic of Korea. Veterinary Surgeon; Professor. m. Hye Jung Kim, 1 son, 1 daughter. Education: DVM, 1985; PhD, Veterinary Surgery, 1990. Appointments: Professor, Chungbuk National University, Korea, 1992-; President, Chungbuk Veterinary Hospital, 1994-96; Secretary in General Affairs, Korean Society of Veterinary Clinics, 2002-2004. Publications: Effect of apitherapy in piglets with preweaning diarrhoea, 2003; Odontoplasty for the treatment of malocclusion of the incisor teeth in a beaver, 2005. Honour: Scientific Award in Medicine and Healthcare, The Korean Federation of Science and Technology Societies. Memberships: Korean Society of Veterinary Medicine; Korean Society of Veterinary Clinics. Address: College of veterinary Medicine, Chungbuk National University, San 48, Gaeshin-dong, Heungduk-gu, Cheongju, Chungbuk, 361-763 Korea. E-mail: shchoi@cbu.ac.kr

**CHOMSKY (Avram) Noam,** b. 7 December 1928, Philadelphia, Pennsylvania, USA. Linguist; Philosopher; Professor; Author. m. Carol Doris Schatz, 24 December 1949, 1 son, 2 daughters. Education: BA, 1949, MA, 1951, PhD, 1955, University of Pennsylvania. Appointments: Assistant Professor, 1955-58, Associate Professor, 1958-61, Professor of Modern Languages, 1961-66, Ferrari P Ward Professor of Modern Languages and Linguistics, 1966-76, Institute Professor, 1976-, Massachusetts Institute of Technology; Visiting Professor, Columbia University, 1957-58; National Science Foundation Fellow, Institute for Advanced Study, Princeton, New Jersey, 1958-59; Resident Fellow, Harvard Cognitive Studies Center, 1964-65; Linguistics Society of America Professor, University of California at Los Angeles, 1966; Beckman Professor, University of California at Berkeley, 1966-67; John Locke Lecturer, Oxford University, 1969; Shearman Lecturer, University College, London, 1969; Bertrand Russell Memorial Lecturer, Cambridge University, 1971; Nehru Memorial Lecturer, University of New Delhi, 1972; Whidden Lecturer, McMaster University, 1975; Huizinga Memorial Lecturer, University of Leiden, 1977; Woodbridge Lecturer, Columbia University, 1978; Kant Lecturer, Stanford University, 1979; Jeanette K Watson Distinguished Visiting Professor, Syracuse University, 1982; Pauling Memorial Lecturer, Oregon State University, 1995. Publications: Syntactic Structures, 1957; Current Issues in Linguistic Theory, 1964; Aspects of the Theory of Syntax, 1965; Cartesian Linguistics, 1966; Topics in the Theory of Generative Grammar, 1966; Language and Mind, 1968; Sound Patterns of English (with Morris Halle), 1968; American Power and the New Mandarins, 1969; At War with Asia, 1970; Problems of Knowledge and Freedom, 1971; Studies on Semantics in Generative Grammar, 1972; For Reasons of State, 1973; The Backroom Boys, 1973; Counterrevolutionary Violence (with Edward Herman), 1973; Peace in the Middle East?, 1974; Bains de Sang (with Edward Herman), 1974; Reflections on Language, 1975; The Logical Structure of Linguistic Theory, 1975; Essays on Form and Interpretation, 1977; Human Rights and American Foreign Policy, 1978; Language and Responsibility, 1979; The Political Economy of Human Rights (with Edward Herman), 2 volumes, 1979; Rules and Representations, 1980; Radical Priorities, 1981; Lectures on Government and Binding, 1981; Towards a New Cold War, 1982; Some Concepts and Consequences of the Theory of Government and Binding, 1982; Fateful Triangle: The United States, Israel and the Palestinians, 1983; Modular Approaches to the Study of the Mind, 1984; Turning the Tide, 1985; Barriers, 1986; Pirates and Emperors, 1986; Knowledge of Language: Its Nature, Origin and Use, 1986; Generative Grammar: Its Basis, Development and Prospects, 1987; On Power and Ideology, 1987; Language in a Psychological Setting, 1987; Language and Problems of Knowledge, 1987; The Chomsky Reader, 1987; The Culture of Terrorism, 1988; Manufacturing Consent (with Edward Herman), 1988; Language and Politics, 1988; Necessary Illusions, 1989; Deterring Democracy, 1991; Chronicles of Dissent, 1992; What Uncle Sam Really Wants, 1992; Year 501: The Conquest Continues, 1993; Rethinking Camelot: JFK, the Vietnam War, and US Political Culture, 1993; Letters from Lexington: Reflections on Propaganda, 1993; The Prosperous Few and the Restless Many, 1993; Language and Thought, 1994; World Orders, Old and New, 1994; The Minimalist Program, 1995; Powers and Prospects, 1996; The Common Good, 1998; Profit over People, 1998; The New Military Humanism, 1999; New Horizons in the Study of Language and Mind, 2000; Rogue States: The Rule of Force in World Affairs, 2000; A New Generation Draws the Line, 2000; Architecture of Language, 2000; 9-11, 2001; Understanding Power, 2002; On Nature and Language, 2002; Contributions to: Scholarly journals. Honours: Distinguished Scientific Contribution Award, American Psychological Association, 1984; George Orwell Awards, National Council of Teachers of English, 1987, 1989; Kyoto Prize in Basic Science, Inamori Foundation, 1988; James Killian Faculty Award, Massachusetts Institute of Technology, 1992; Lannan Literary Award, 1992; Joel Selden Peace Award, Psychologists for Social Responsibility, 1993; Homer Smith Award, New York University School of Medicine, 1994; Loyola Mellon Humanities Award, Loyola University, Chicago, 1994; Helmholtz Medal, Akademie der Wissenschaft, Berlin-Brandenburg, 1996; Benjamin Franklin Medal, Franklin Institute, Philadelphia, 1999; Rabinranath Tagore Centenary Award, Asiatic Society, 2000; Peace Award, Turkish Publishers Association, 2002; Many honorary doctorates. Memberships: American Academy of Arts and Sciences; American Association for the Advancement of Science, fellow; American Philosophical Association; Bertrand Russell Peace Foundation; British Academy, corresponding member; Deutsche Akademie der Naturforscher Leopoldina; Linguistics Society of America; National Academy of Sciences; Royal Anthropological Institute; Utrecht Society of Arts and Sciences. Address: 15 Suzanne Road, Lexington, MA 02420, USA.

**CHONG, Tae Hyong,** b. 5 August 1946, Soonchun City, Korea. Professor. m. Young Sook Song, 2 sons, 1 daughter. Education: Bachelor of Engineering, Department of Mechanical Engineering, Hanyang University, Korea, 1970; Master of

Engineering, 1977, Dr. Eng, 1983, Department of Precision Mechanics, Kyoto University, Japan. Appointments: Lieutenant, Korea Army, 1970-72; Assistant Professor, 1983-87, Associate Professor, 1987-92, Professor, 1992-, Hangyang University, Korea; Foreign Visiting Professor, Kyoto University, Japan, 1986-87; Foreign Visiting Professor, University of Tokyo, Japan, 1996-97. Publications: Simple Stress Formulae for a Thin-Rimmed Spur Gear; Development of a Computer-Aided Concurrent Design System of Mechanical Design; Multiobjective Optimal Design of Cylindrical Gear Pairs for Reduction of Gear Size and Meshing Vibration; A New and Generalised Methology to Design Multi-Stage Gear Drives by Integrating Dimensional and the Configuration Design Process. Honour: Dr. Eng, Kyoto University, Japan, 1983. Memberships: President, KSMTE; Member, KSME; JSME; KSPE; JSPE; AGMA; KGMA. Address: #104-404, Daerim Apt, 501 Daebang-Dong, Dongjak-ku, Seoul, Korea 156-020. E-mail: thchong@hangyang.ac.kr Website: gearlab.hangyang.ac.kr

**CHOPE John Norman,** b. 27 June 1948, Birmingham, England. Dental Surgeon. m. Susan Mary Le Page, 1 daughter. Education: BSc (Hons), Physiology, 1969, BDS (Hons) Bristol University Faculty of Medicine, Department of Physiology and Dental School, 1966-72; LDS RCS Eng, Royal College of Surgeons of England, 1972; MFGDP (UK) RCS Eng, Royal College of Surgeons of England, 1992. Appointments include: Trainee Dental Technician, 1965, Dental Pathology Research Technician, University of Birmingham, 1966; Neurophysiologist, USA, Sudan, 1969, 1973; Senior House Officer, Oral Surgery, United Bristol Hospitals, 1973; Associate Dental Surgeon, Backwell, Somerset, 1973, Stockwood, Bristol and Shepton Mallet, Somerset, 1973-74, Principal Dental Surgeon and Dental Practice Owner, Holsworthy, Devon, 1974-, Hartland, Devon, 1975-, Bude, Cornwall, 1981-90, Okehampton, Devon, 1983-98; Consultant, VDC plc (Veterinary Drug Company), 1996-98; Member, British Dental Association Research Foundation Committee, 1997-2000; National Council Member, 1989-2004, Chairman, 1995-2004, Confederation of Dental Employers; National Council Member, General Dental Practitioners Association, 2004-; Elected Member, General Dental Council, 1996-; Member, Dental Technicians Association Education Committee, 2003-; Editorial Board Member, Dentistry, 2000-; Justice of the Peace, 1993-; Expert Professional Panel Member, Family Health Services Appeal Authority, 2001-. Publications: Recording from taste receptors stimulated by vascular route, 1969; Dental Practice Guide to the Therapeutic Laser, 1995; A Look at Bodies Corporate, 1997; Numerous articles in dental journals, 1974-. Honours: Duke of Edinburgh's Gold Award; Associate Dental Company Scholarships, University of Bristol, 1966-67, 1969-72; Medical Research Council Award, Bristol University, 1967-69 L E Attenborough Medal, 1972, The George Fawn Prize, 1972, Bristol University. Memberships Include: British Dental Association; British Medical and Dental Hypnosis Society; General Dental Practitioners Association; Medical Protection Society; International Dental Federation; Magistrates Association; Country Landowners Association; Fellow, Royal Society of Medicine; Faculty of General Dental Practitioners(UK) Royal College of Surgeons of England. Address: Penroses Dental Practice, Bodmin Street, Holsworthy, Devon EX22 6BB, England.

**CHOU Dean-Yi,** b. 4 December 1954, Taiwan, China. Professor. m. Mei-Jing Shih, 1 son. Education: BS, Physics, National Tsing Hua University, Taiwan, China, 1977; PhD, Astronomy, California Institute of Technology, California, USA, 1986. Appointments: Postdoctoral Research Fellow, Institute for Astronomy, University of Hawaii, Hawaii, USA, 1986-87; Associate professor, 1987-92, Professor, 1992-, Physics

Department, National Tsing Hua University, Taiwan, China. Address: Physics Department, Tsing Hua University, Hsinchu 30043, Taiwan, China. E-mail: chou@phys.nthu.edu.tw

**CHOW YUN-FAT,** b. 1956, Lamma Island, China. Film Actor. m. Jasmine Chow. Appointments: Actor, TV Station, TVB, Hong Kong, 1973, appearing in over 1,000 TV series. Creative Works: Films include: The Story of Woo Viet; A Better Tomorrow, 1986; God of Gamblers, 1989; The Killer; Eighth Happiness; Once a Thief, 1991; Full Contact, 1992; Hard Boiled, 1992; Peace Hotel, 1995; Broken Arrow, 1999; Anna and the King, 1999; Crouching Tiger, Hidden Dragon, 2000; King's Ransom, 2001; Bulletproof Monk, 2001. Address: c/o William Morris Agency, 151 El Camino Drive, Beverly Hills, CA 90212, USA.

**CHRISTENSEN Helena,** b. 25 December 1968, Copenhagen, Denmark. Model. 1 son. Appointments: Former child model; Adult modelling career, 1988-99; Front cover model, major magazine covers; Major contracts with: Versace; Chanel; Lagerfeld; Revlon; Rykiel; Dior; Prada and others; Magazine Photographer, 1999-. Address: c/o Marilyn's Agency, 4 Rue de la Paix, 75003 Paris, France.

**CHRISTIE Julie Frances,** b. 14 April 1940, Assam, India. Actress. Education: Brighton Technical College; Central School of Speech & Drama. Creative Works: Films: Crooks Anonymous, 1962; The Fast Lady, 1962; Billy Liar, 1963; Young Cassidy, 1964; Darling, 1964; Doctor Zhivago, 1965; Fahrenheit 451, 1966; Far From the Madding Crowd, 1966; Petulia, 1967; In Search of Gregory, 1969; The Go-Between, 1971; McCabe & Mrs Miller, 1972; Don't Look Now, 1973; Shampoo, 1974; Demon Seed, Heaven Can Wait, 1978; Memoirs of a Survivor, 1980; Gold, 1980; The Return of the Soldier, 1981; Les Quarantiemes rugissants, 1981; Heat and Dust, 1982; The Gold Diggers, 1984; Miss Mary, 1986; The Tattooed Memory, 1986; Power, 1987; Fathers and Sons, 1988; Dadah is Death (tv), 1988; Fools of Fortune, 1989; McCabe and Mrs Miller, 1990; The Railway Station, 1992; Hamlet, 1995; Afterglow, 1998; The Miracle Maker (voice), 2000; Plays: Old Times, 1995; Suzanna Andler, 1997; Afterglow, 1998. Honours include: Motion Picture Laurel Award, Best Dramatic Actress, 1967; Motion Picture Herald Award, 1967. Address: c/o International Creative Management, 76 Oxford Street, London W1D 1BS, England.

**CHRISTIE Linford,** b. 2 April 1960, St Andrews, Jamaica. Athlete. 1 daughter. Appointments: Cashier, Wandsworth Co-op; Member, Thames Valley Harriers; Winner, UK 100m, 1985, 1987, 200m, 1985 (tie), 1988; Winner, Amateur Athletics Association 100m, 1986, 1988, 200m, 1988; Winner, European 100m Record; Silver Medallist, 100m, Seoul Olympic Games, 1988, Winner 100m Gold Medal, Commonwealth Games, 1990, Olympic Games, 1992; World Athletic Championships, 1993, Weltklasse Grand Prix Games, 1994, European Games, 1994; Winner 100m, Zurich, 1995; Co-Founder (with Colin Jackson), Managing Director, Nuff Respect sports man co, 1992-; Captain, British Athletics Team, 1995-97; Retired, 1997; Successful coach to several prominent UK athletes. Publications: Linford Christie (autobiography), 1989; To Be Honest With You, 1995; A Year in the Life of Linford Christie, 1996. Honours include: Male Athlete of the Year, 1988, 1992; BBC Sports Personality of the Year, 1993. Address: The Coach House, 107 Sherland Road, Twickenham, Middlesex TW9 4HB, England.

**CHRUŚCIEL Tadeusz Lesław,** b. 30 January 1926, Lwów, Poland. Physician. 2 sons, 1 daughter. Education: MD, Faculty of Medicine, Medical Academy, Cracow, 1951; Postgraduate

Fellow, Oxford, England, 1960; Affiliate Member, Royal Society of Medicine, London, 1960; Professorship, State Council, 1986; D hc (doctor honoris causa) Silesian Medical Academy, Katowice, 1998. Appointments: Academy of Medicine, Cracow, 1948-56; Professor, Chairman, Academy of Medicine, Zabrze, 1956-68; Senior Medical Officer, Drug Dependence, WHO, Geneva, 1968-75; Drug Research Institute, Warsaw, 1976-85; Postgraduate Medical School, Warsaw, 1986-97; retired, 1997. Publications: Over 300 research papers and articles contributed to specialist journals. Honours: Polonia Restituta Commander's Cross, 2001; Numerous research awards. Memberships: International Narcotics Control Board, 1979-83; National Physicians' Council, President, 1989-93; WHO expert advisory panel on drug dependence, 1978-99; NPC Member, 2001-; Catholic Association of Polish Physicians, GC Secretary, 2002-; Commission of Social Response to Pharmacotherapy, Polish Academy of Sciences, 2004. Address: 6 Dzika Str, App 284, PL-00-172, Warsaw, Poland.

**CHU Han-Shu,** b. 12 October 1933, Qingtian, Zhejiang, China. Radioastronomer. m. Luo Pei-Fang, 2 daughters. Education: Graduate, Electrical Engineering, National Zhejiang University, 1953; Advanced Study, Institute of Physics, China Academy of Sciences, 1954-56; Advanced Study on Radioastronomy, Academy of Sciences, Russia, 1956-60. Appointments: Research Assistant, 1953, Research Associate, Associate Professor, 1960-, Professor, 1993-, Purple Mountain Observatory, China Academy of Sciences; Worked on Radioastronomy, VLBI Astrophysics: Polarization and high resolution research of Active Galactic nuclei including quasars and BL Lac objects; Design and Construction of advanced sensitive polarization radiotelescopes in cm wave band for studying polarized radiation from sun spots; Pioneered microwave radiometry technology and solar radio astronomy in China; Solution of the problem of the physical nature of spurious polarization in Radioastronomy; Discovery in Active Galactic Nuclei of an unusual 3 jet structure, revealing new unknown non-axial ejection mechanism in AGN; Discovery of CME (Coronal Mass Ejection) and Ejection of Large Scale Magnetic Fields from Active Galactic Nuclei, the CMEs are responsible for Sporadic Ejection of jet components and the drastic variabilities in AGN (including those powerful ejections that produce Ray Burst, and those from BL Lac Objects); Discovery of Helical Magnetic Fields and Intrinsically Asymmetric Jets in AGN, the Helical Magnetic Field is responsible for Collimation of the jet and is crucial for Extraction of Black Hole Rotational Energy; Discovery of dramatic variability in jet direction of BL Lac AO 0235+164, and the successful explanation of the puzzle of exceptional violent variabilities by the CME Model. Publications include: The Physical Nature of Spurious Polarization Transformed from the Background Non-Polarized Radiation of Cosmic Extended Radio Sources, 1988; Unusual Features in QSR 3C147 – A Unified Explanation of the Jets and BLR Clouds, 1993; AO 0235+164 – A Heretic BL Lac, 1994; VLBI Observations of the Puzzling BL Lacertae Object 0235+164, 1996; CME and Ejection of Large Scale Magnetic Fields, Helical Magnetic Fields and Intrinsically Asymmetric Jets - New Findings in AGN (Radio Emission from Galactic and Extragalactic Compact Sources, 1998); Discovery of Helical Magnetic Fields and Intrinsically Asymmetric Jets in AGN; Discovery of CME and Ejection of Large Scale Magnetic Fields from AGN (High Energy Processes and Phenomena in Astrophysics, 2003); Author of numerous papers. Honours: Gold Medal, 7th International Nathiagali Summer College on Physics and Contemporary Needs, 1982; Natural Science Award, China Academy of Sciences, 1995; International Man of the Year, 1997-98, IBC; 20th Century Achievement Award, ABI, 1998; 2000 Millennium Medal of Honour, ABI, 1999; 2000

Commemorative Medal of Honour, ABI, 2000; American Order of Excellence, 2001; Presidential Seal of Honour Medal, ABI, 2001; American Medal of Honour, ABI, 2001; 2000 Outstanding Scientists of the 20th Century (and of the 21st Century) Medal, IBC, 2001, 2002; Congressional Medal of Honor, ABI, 2001; Great Minds of the 21st Century Medal, ABI, 2003; ABI World Laureate Medallion, 2002; Lifetime Achievement Award (Gold), IBC, 2002; International Medal for Scientific Achievement, ABI, 2002; World Lifetime Achievement Award, ABI, 2003; The World-Wide Honours List, IBC, 2003; International Register of Profiles, IBC, 2003; International Scientist of the Year Medal, IBC, 2002, 2003, 2004; International Medal of Honour, IBC, 2003; 21st Century Award for Achievement, IBC, 2003; Eminent Scientists of Today Medal, IBC, 2003; Lifetime of Achievement One Hundred, IBC, 2004; Lifetime of Scientific Achievement Award, IBC, 2004; International Order of Merit, IBS, 2004; IBC Certificate of Distinction, 2004; Order of Distinction, 2000 Outstanding Scientists of the 21st Century, IBC, 2004; Listed in International Book of Honour, ABI, 2000 and several biographical dictionaries including: The First Five Hundred, IBC, 1998; International Book of Honor, ABI, 1999; Leading Intellectuals of the World, ABI, 2000, 2002-03, 2004 (Dedication The Genius Elite Section); 1000 World Leaders of Scientific Influence, ABI, 2002; 500 Founders of the 21st Century, IBC, 2003; 500 Leaders of Science, ABI, 2003; One Thousand Great Scientists, IBC, 2003; American Hall of Fame, ABI, 2003; Dictionary of International Biography, IBC, 2004; Living Legend, Dedication, IBC, 2004; International Register of Profiles, IBC, 2004; Outstanding Scientists of the 21st Century, Dedication, IBC, 2004; Greatest Intellectuals of the 21st Century, 2004; The Cambridge Blue Book, IBC, 2004; Great Minds of the 21st Century Dedication, ABI, 2004; The World Book of Knowledge, ABI, 2005. Memberships: International Astronomical Union; Astronomical Society of China; Electronics Society of China, Senior Member. Address: Purple Mountain Observatory, China Academy of Sciences, Nanjing 210008, China.

**CHU Kent-Man,** b. 12 July 1963, Hong Kong. Doctor; Surgeon. Education: MB, BS, 1987; FRCS (Ed), 1992; FCSHK, 1992; FHKAM (Surgery), 1995; FACS, 1998; MS, 2001. Appointments: Associate Professor, Chief of Division of Upper GI Surgery, Department of Surgery, University of Hong Kong Medical Centre; Director, Surgical Endoscopy Centre; Co-Director, Centre for Education and Training; Honorary Consultant, Department of Surgery, Queen Mary Hospital; Honorary Consultant, Department of Surgery, Tung Wah Hospital. Publications: 1 Master of Surgery thesis; 121 Full Articles; 2 Book Chapters; 105 Abstracts; Invited speaker or faculty, 112 occasions. Honours: International Guest Scholar, The American College of Surgeons, 1999; Akita Award, Japanese Society of Gastroenterological Society, 2001; Faculty Teaching Medal, 2003. Memberships: 12 International or Local Associations and Colleges; Secretary General, Asian Surgical Association, 2005-. Address: Department of Surgery, University of Hong Kong Medical Centre, Queen Mary Hospital, Pokfulam, Hong Kong. Website: www.hku.hk/surgery/

**CHUANG Yii-Der,** b. 1 July 1934, Chekiang, China. Retired Business Executive and Diplomat. m. Chung-Hwa Lee, 2 sons, 1 daughter. Education: BS, Automotive Engineering, Chung-Cheng Institute of Science and Technology, 1957; MS, Metallurgical Engineering, Michigan State University, USA, 1966; PhD, Materials Science, New York University, USA, 1971. Appointments: Director, Hot Laboratory, Nuclear Energy Research Institute, Atomic Energy Council, Taiwan, 1972-82; Senior Scientist, Science and Technology Advisory Group, Executive Yuan, Taipei, Taiwan, 1980-84; Deputy Director,

Preparation Office Materials Research Laboratory, Industrial Technology Research Institute, Taiwan, 1981-82; Deputy Director, Materials Research and Development Centre, Chung Shan Institute of Science and Technology, Taiwan, 1982-84; Director, Science Division, Taipei Economic and Cultural Office, Houston, 1984-86, San Francisco, 1986-92, Washington DC, USA, 1992-2000; President, H & Q Asia Pacific, Taiwan Office, 2000-2002; Senior Advisor, WI Harper Group, 2004-. Publications: 38 articles in scientific journals include: Beta Brass Bicrystal Stress-Strain Relations, 1973; Iodine-Induced Stress Corrosion Cracking of Cu-Barrier Zircaloy-4 Tubes, 1981; A New Processing System and Method for Examination of Irradiated Fuel Elements, 1981. Honours: A Hero Medal, President, Chiang Kai-Shek, Republic of China, 1963; Distinguished Scholar, New York University, 1972; Listed in Who's Who publications and biographical dictionaries. Memberships: Founding Member, Monte Jade Science and Technology Association, West Coast, USA; Alpha Sigma Mu Honor Society; Founding Member, The Chinese Society for Materials Science. Address: 11F-5, No 70, Sec 2, An-He Road, Taipei 10680, Taiwan, Republic of China. E-mail: ydchuang@ms77.hinet.net

**CHUGANI Mahesh Lakhi,** b. 31 October 1964, Bombay, India. Engineer. Education: MS, Electrical Engineering, 1990, PhD, 1996, Rensselaer Polytechnic Institute, USA; BE, Electronics and Telecommunications, College of Engineering, Pune, India, 1987. Appointment: DSP Software Engineer, 1996-2001; Director of Support and Training, 2001-03; Real Estate Consultant, 2003-. Publications: A Mathematical Model of Blood Flow Through Stenotic Arteries, conference presentation, 1994; Labview Signal Processing, 1998; Guide to Practical Signal Filtering, Research and Development, articles, 2000; Digital Signal Processing: A Hands-On Approach, 2005. Honours: Charles M Close Doctoral Research Prize, Rensselaer Polytechnic Institute, 1996; Whitaker Award, 20th Northeast Bioengineering Conference, 1994. Membership: National Association of Realtors. Address: 2017 S Stoneman Ave, Alhambra, CA 91801, USA. E-mail: mchugani@alum.rpi.edu

**CHUKWUJEKWU Ifenna Echezona,** b. 2 February 1953, Onitsha, Nigeria. Estates Surveyor and Valuer. m. Juliet Chukwujekwu, 2 sons. Education: BSc, Estate Management, University of Nigeria, Nsukka, 1977; Masters of Business Administration, University of Benin, Nigeria, 1991. Appointments: Estate Manager, Grade II, 1978-79, Estate Manager, Grade I, 1979-83, Senior Estate Manager, 1983-85, Principal Estate Manager and Head of Project Appraisal and Consultancy Services, 1985-87; Assistant Chief Estates Manager, 1988-92, Chief Estates Manager, 1994-2000, General Manager, Chief Executive, 2000-, Edo Development and Property Authority, Benin City, Nigeria. Publications: Articles and papers presented include: Securitisation of Property Development in Nigeria – A case study of Edo Development and Property Authority Housing Programme, 2001; Property Rating and Other Forms of Land Taxation as sources of revenue to the Local Government Authorities; Management Proposal for a Shopping Centre – case study of Ugbowo Shopping Centre, Benin; Feasibility and Viability Study on Urban Low Cost Housing Estates (Case studies of Iguosa Housing Estate and Ugbiyokho Housing Estate, both in Benin, Edo State). Honours: National Administrative Merit Award; Award of Excellence in Estate Management; Fellow Institute of Administrative Management of Nigeria; Honorary Doctorate Degree, Estate Management, Marlborough University, USA. Memberships: National President and Chairman, Council Association of Housing Corporations of Nigeria; Fellow, Nigerian Institution of Estates Surveyors and Valuers; Fellow, Marborough University

Graduate Association, African Region; Chairman, Edo State Chapter, Nigerian Institution of estates Surveyors and Valuers; External Examiner, Department of Estate Management, Federal Polytechnic, Auchi. Address: Edo Development and Property Authority, Sakpomba Road, PMB 1064, Benin City, Edo State, Nigeria. E-mail: cijek@yahoo.com

**CHUN Jang Ho,** b. 23 November 1948, Koyang, Kyunggido, Korea. Professor; Researcher. m. Kyung Won Hong, 1 son, 1 daughter. Education: Bachelor of Electronic Engineering, Kwangwoon University, Seoul, Korea, 1968-75; Master of Electronic Engineering, Yonsei University, Seoul, Korea, 1976-78; PhD, Electrophysics, Stevens Institute of Technology, New Jersey, USA, 1980-84; Professor and Researcher, Kwangwoon University, 1984-; Technical Advisor, Mission Telecom Company, Seoul, Korea, 2004-; Visiting Scientist, Princeton University, New Jersey, USA, 1988-89; Visiting Scientist, University of Tokyo, Tokyo, Japan, 1994. Publications include: The phase-shift method for determining adsorption isotherms of hydrogen at electrified interfaces; Methods for determining adsorption isotherms in electrochemical systems; Constant conversion factors between adsorption isotherms of hydrogen in electrochemical systems. Honours: Commendation for Excellent Teaching and Research, Korea Government; Fellowships for Visiting Scientists, Korea Science and Engineering Foundation, 1988-1989, 1994; Studying Abroad Scholarship, Korea Government, 1980-84; The Most Excellent Graduation, Kwangwoon University; Listed in Who's who publications and biographical dictionaries. Memberships: The Electrochemical Society; International Association for Hydrogen Energy; The Korean Electrochemical Society. Address: Department of Electronic Engineering, Kwangwoon University, Seoul 139-701, Korea. E-mail: jhchun@daisy.kwangwoon.ac.kr

**CHUN Young Nam,** b. 3 July 1961, Paju, Gyeonggi, Republic of Korea. Professor. m. Eum Mi Kang, 2 daughters. Education: BA, 1983, PhD, 1993, Inha University; Postdoctoral, University of Illinois at Chicago, 1999. Appointments: Visiting Researcher, Institute of IVD, Stuttgart University, Germany, 1990; Research, Development Institute of Korea Gas Corporation, 1990-92; Visiting Researcher, Institute of IVD, Stuttgart University, 1992-93; Visiting Researcher, Russian Academy of Sciences, 1993-94; Visiting Professor, McMaster University, 2004-05; Full Time Lecturer, 1994-96, Assistant Professor, 1996-2000, Associate Professor, 2000-05, Professor, 2005-, Chosun University, Korea. Publications: Air Pollution Engineering, 2000; Incineration and Air Pollution Control, 2002; Environmental Design and CAD, 2004; Environmental and Pollution, 2004. Honours: Best Teacher, Chosun University, 2001; Paper Award, Korea Society of Environmental Engineers; 2003; Listed in Who's Who publications and biographical dictionaries. Memberships: Korean Society of Environmental Engineers; Korean Society of Mechanical Engineers; Korean Society of Combustion. Address: Chosun University, #375 Seosuk-dong, Dong-gu, Gwangju 501-759, Republic of Korea. E-mail: ynchun@chosun.ac.kr

**CHURCH Charlotte Maria,** b. 21 February, 1986, Llandaff, Cardiff, Wales. Singer. Career: Albums include: Voice of an Angel, 1998; Charlotte Church, 1999; Christmas Offering, 2000; Dream a Dream, 2000; Enchantment, 2001; Performances include: Charlotte Church: Voice of an Angel in Concert, 1999; Dream a Dream: Charlotte Church in the Holy Land, 2000; The Royal Variety Performance 2001, 2001; The 43rd Annual Grammy Awards, 2001; Concerts include: Hollywood Bowl; Hyde Park. Preludes include: Pie Jesu; Panis Anjulicus; Dream a Dream; The Prayer (duet with Josh Groban); It's the Heart that Matters; TV Appearances include: Heartbeat, 1999; Touched by an Angel, 1999; Have I Got News For You, 2002; The Kumars at No. 42, 2002; Parkinson, 2002; Friday Night with Jonathon Ross, 2003; Film: I'll Be There, 2003. Publications: Voice of An Angel – My Life (So Far), autobiography, 2001.

**CHURCH Robert,** b. 20 July 1932, London, England. Author. m. Dorothy June Bourton, 15 April 1953, 2 daughters. Education: Beaufoy College, London, 1946-48. Appointments: Army, 1950-52; Metropolitan Police, 1952-78; Probation Service, 1978-88. Publications: Murder in East Anglia, 1987; Accidents of Murder, 1989; More Murder in East Anglia, 1990; Anglian Blood, co-editor, 1995; Well Done Boys, 1996. Contributions to: The Criminologist; Miscellaneous journals. Honour: Winner, Salaman Prize for Non-Fiction, 1997. Address: "Woodside", 7 Crome Walk, Gunton Park, Lowestoft, Suffolk NR32 4NF, England.

**CHURCHILL Caryl,** b. 3 September 1938, London, England. Dramatist. m. David Harter, 1961, 3 sons. Education: BA, Lady Margaret Hall, Oxford, 1960. Publications: Owners, 1973; Light Shining in Buckinghamshire, 1976; Traps, 1977; Vinegar Tom, 1978; Cloud Nine, 1979; Top Girls, 1982; Fen, 1983; Collected Plays, 2 volumes, 1985, 1988; A Mouthful of Birds (with D Lan), 1986; Serious Money, 1987; Ice Cream, 1989; Hot Fudge, 1990; Mad Forest, 1990; Lives of the Great Poisoners (with I Spink and O Gough), 1991; The Skriker, 1994; This is a Chair, 1997; Blue heart, 1997; Faraway, 2000. Other: Various radio and television plays. Address: c/o Casarotto Ramsay Ltd, National House, 60-66 Wardour Street, London W1V 3HP, England.

**CHUTE Janet Elizabeth,** b. 18 November 1952, Halifax, Nova Scotia, Canada. Professor. Education: Art College, London, England; BA, 1st Class Honours, Dalhousie University, Halifax; MA, Memorial University of NHd; MA, University of Toronto, Canada; PhD, McMaster University, Hamilton, Ontario, Canada. Appointments: Postdoctoral Studies, 1989-92; Faculty, Dalhousie University, 1989-; Faculty, Mount Saint Vincent University, 1998-; Writer, 1999-; Consultant for Indian and Northern Affairs, Canada and various Aboriginal organisations across Canada and USA. Publications: The Legacy of Shingwaukonse: A Century of Native Leadership; Numerous articles in journals and books. Honours: Winner, Joseph Brant Award, Multicultural Society of Ontario; Winner, Clio Award, Canadian Historical Association. Memberships: American Anthropological Association; American Ethnohistorical Society. Address: 870 Marlborough Woods, Halifax, Nova Scotia B3H 1H9, Canada.

**CHVOJ Zdenek,** b. 16 March 1948, Prague, Czechoslovakia. Scientist. m. Blanka Svobodova, 1 son, 1 daughter. Education: RNDr, Charles University, Prague, 1976; CSc, Charles University, 1977; DSc, 1990; Doctorate, Technical University, Prague, 1995. Appointments: Lecturer, Technical University Prague, 1969, 1992-; Researcher, Charles University, Prague, 1971-75; Institute of Physics AVCR, 1975-; Editor-in-Chief, Czechoslovak Journal of Physics. Publications: Co-author, Recent Trends in Crystal Growth, 1988; Kinetic Phase Diagrams, 1991; Co-editor, Collective Diffusion on Surfaces, 2001; More than 100 articles and papers contributed to professional journals. Honours: Honorary Appreciation Award, CSAV, 1982; Recipient, Czech Literature Foundation Award, 1986. Memberships: Czech Union of Mathematicians and Physicists. Address: Institute of Physics, AVCR, Cukrovarnicka 10, 16253 Praha 6, Czech Republic.

**CIAMPI Sara,** b. 24 January 1976, Genova, Italy. Writer. Education: Leaving Certificate, Linguistics School; Laurea Honoris Causa, Literature; Laurea Honoris Causa, Philosophy. Career: Literary activity began at 14 years of age stimulated

initially by significant health problems and later by serious illness (tuberculosis and malaria). Publications: Momenti, 1995; Malinconia di Un'anima, 1999; La Maschera Delle Illusioni, 1999; Rassegna di Novelle e Canti, 2000; Giacomo Leopardi, degree thesis, 2000. Honours: Over 100 national and international honours and awards; Included in prestigious Italian and foreign dictionaries; Title of Baroness von Derneck and Dame St Lukas, with Royal Order; Candidate, Nobel Prize in Literature, 2001, 2002. Memberships: Pontzen Academy; Giosuè Carducci Academy; Micenei Academy; Paestum Academy; Costantiniana Academy; Gentium Pro Pace Academy; Marzocco Academy. Address: Via San Fruttuoso 7/4, I 16143 Genova, Italy.

**CIESZYŃSKI Tomasz Maria Tadeusz,** b. 6 November 1920, Poznan, Poland. Professor. m. Maria Elzbieta, 1 son, 1 daughter. Education: Medical Faculty, John Casimir University, Lvov, 1938-44; Diploma, Jagellonian University, Cracow, 1945; Diploma, Faculty of Mathematics, Physics and Chemistry, University of Wroclaw, 1952; MD, 1947; Docent of Surgery, 1968. Appointments: Senior Assistant, Adjunct Chair of Crystallography, University of Wroclaw, 1950-52; Senior Assistant, Orthopaedic Clinic, Medical Academy of Warsaw, 1953; Senior Assistant, Adjunct, Docent, Extraordinary Professor, Second Surgical Clinic, Medical Academy, Wroclaw, 1953-91; Professor of Medical Sciences, 1992-; President and Founder: League of Descendants of Lvov's Professors Murdered by Gestapo in July 1941, 2001-. Publications include: The Natural System of Foods, 1950; Ultrasonic Catheter for Heart Examination, 1956; The idea of quantum thermodynamics and the general function of physical density, 1968; Electrosynthetics, photosynthetics and thermosynthesis of melamin, 1969; About the Need to Protect Biological Increment in Poland, in Polish, 1971; Melting Point of Apatites as Bond Energy Property in Relation to Structure, 1974; Artifical heart propelled by respiratory muscles, 1977; Equalization of Asymmetric Extremities in Children, 1987; Anabolic and Catabolic Processes in Relation to the Polarity of Electric Fields, 1991; Electric Field inside Bone, in Polish, 1991; The Days Strong by Love, poem in Polish, 1999. Honours include: Golden Cross of Merit, 1975; Cross de Chevalier of the Order of Polonia Restituta, 1990; Medal, University of Tokyo, 1982; Medal, Medical Academy, Wroclaw, 1990. Memberships include: Polish Chemical Society; Society of Polish Surgeons; American Society of Bone Mineral Research. Address: Modrzewiowa 20, Oborniki Slaskie 55-120, Poland.

**CINGOSKI Vlatko,** b. 11 June 1962, Ohrid, Macedonia. Assistant Professor; PhD Researcher. m. Vesna Cingoska, 1 daughter. Education: BS, Electrical Engineering, 1986, MS, 1990, University Sts Cyril and Methodious, Macedonia; PhD, Electrical Engineering, Hiroshima University, Graduate School of Engineering, 1996. Appointments: Teaching and Research Assistant, University Sts Cyril and Methodious, 1986-91; Invited Research Assistant, 1991-96, Assistant Professor, 1996-99, Hiroshima University; Assistant General Manager, 1999-2002, Project Manager, 2002-, Electric Power Company of Macedonia. Publications: Over 60 articles in professional journals. Honours: Best Paper Award, Japanese Society for Applied Electromagnetics; Editor, Journal of the Japanese Society for Applied Electromagnetic and Mechanics. Memberships: IEEE; International Compumag Society; Japanese Society of Applied Electromagnetics and Mechanics; New York Academy of Sciences. Address: Electric Power Company of Macedonia, Development and Investments Department, 11 October Str, No 9, 1000 Skopje, Macedonia.

**CIULLI Franco,** b. 19 August 1960, Ancona, Italy. Cardiothoracic Surgeon. Education: St Ignatius College,

Riverview, Sydney, Australia; Medical School, Specialist Cardiovascular Surgery, University of Verona, Italy. Appointments: Transplant Fellow, Career Registrar, Papworth Hospital, Cambridge, England, 1991-93; Senior Registrar, Cardiothoracic Surgery, Glasgow Royal Infirmary, Scotland, 1993-; Senior Transplant Fellow, St Vincent's Hospital, Sydney, Australia, 1994; Consultant Cardiothoracic Surgeon, Transplantation Northern General Hospital, Sheffield, England, 1995-99; Consultant, Cardiothoracic Surgeon, Clinical Director, Bristol Royal Infirmary, England, 1999-. Publications: Essentials Thoracic and Cardiovascular Surgery, 2003. Honours: Speciality Post Graduate Degree, Cardiovascular Surgery, Cum Laude, University of Verona, Italy, 1991. Memberships: European Association Cardiothoracic Surgery; Society of Cardiothoracic Surgeons, Great Britain and Ireland; International Society of Heart and Lung Transplantation. Address: Cardiothoracic Surgery, Camden House, Bristol Royal Infirmary, Bristol BS2 8HW, England. E-mail: franco.ciulli@ubht.swest.nhs.uk

**CLAIRE Regi, (Yvonne Regula Butlin-Staub),** b. 8 June 1962, München/TG, Switzerland. m. Ron Butlin. Fiction Writer. Education: Maturität (Typus E), Frauenfeld, Switzerland, 1981; lic. phil. 1, English and German, Zurich University, Switzerland, 1992. Appointment: Research Assistant, Department of English, Zurich University, 1992-93. Publications: Inside-Outside (short stories), 1998; The Beauty Room (novel), 2002. Honours: Winner of Exchange Scholarship with Aberdeen University, 1983-84; Winner, Semester Prize, Zurich University, 1986; Winner, Edinburgh Review 10th Anniversary Short Story Competition, 1995; Scottish Arts Council Writer's Bursary, 1997; Inside-Outside shortlisted for Saltire First Book Award, 1999; Writer's Bursary from Thurgau Canton, Switzerland, 2002; The Beauty Room longlisted for Allen Lane/MIND Book of the Year Award, 2003; Writer's Bursary from Pro Helvetia (Swiss Arts Council), 2003; UBS Cultural Foundation Award, 2003. Memberships: Scottish PEN; Autorinnen und Autoren der Schweiz. Address: 7 West Newington Place, Edinburgh EH9 1QT, Scotland.

**CLAPTON Eric (Eric Patrick Clapp),** b. 30 March 1945, Ripley, Surrey, England. Musician (guitar); Singer; Songwriter. m. (1) Patti Boyd, 1979, divorced; 1 son, deceased, 1 daughter, (2) Melia McEnery, 2002. Career: Guitarist with groups: The Roosters, 1963; The Yardbirds, 1963-65; John Mayall's Bluebreakers, 1965-66; Cream, 1966-68; Blind Faith, 1969; Derek and the Dominoes, 1970; Delaney And Bonnie, 1970-72; Solo artiste, 1972-; Concerts include: Concert for Bangla Desh, 1971; Last Waltz concert, The Band's farewell concert, 1976; Live Aid, 1985; Record series of 24 concerts, Royal Albert Hall, 1991; Japanese tour with George Harrison, 1991; Film appearance: Tommy, 1974. Compositions include: Presence Of The Lord; Layla; Badge (with George Harrison). Recordings include: Albums: Disraeli Gears, 1967; Wheels Of Fire, 1968; Goodbye Cream, 1969; Layla, 1970; Blind Faith, 1971; Concert For Bangladesh, 1971; Eric Clapton's Rainbow Concert, 1973; 461 Ocean Boulevard, 1974; E C Was Here, 1975; No Reason To Cry, 1976; Slowhand, 1977; Backless, 1978; Just One Night, 1980; Money And Cigarettes, 1983; Behind The Sun, 1985; August, 1986; Journeyman, 1989; 24 Nights, 1992; MTV Unplugged, 1992; From The Cradle, 1994; Rainbow Concert, 1995; Crossroads 2, 1996; Live In Montreux, 1997; Pilgrim, 1998; One More Car One More Rider, 2002; with Jimmy Page and Jeff Beck, 1999; Soundtracks include: Tommy; The Color Of Money; Lethal Weapon; Rush; Hit singles include: I Shot The Sheriff; Layla; Lay Down Sally; Wonderful Tonight; Cocaine; Behind The Mask; Tears In Heaven; Contributed to numerous albums by artists including: Phil Collins; Bob Dylan; Aretha Franklin; Joe Cocker; Roger Daltrey; Dr John; Rick Danko;

Ringo Starr; Roger Waters; Christine McVie; Howlin' Wolf; Sonny Boy Williamson; The Beatles: The White Album (listed as L'Angelo Mysterioso). Honours include: 6 Grammy Awards, 1993; Q Magazine Merit Award, 1995; Grammy Award for best pop instrumental performance, 2002. Address: c/o Michael Eaton, 22 Blades Court, Deodar Road, London, SW15 2NU, England.

**CLARK (Alastair) Trevor,** b. 10 June 1923, Glasgow, Scotland. Retired Overseas Civil Servant; Museums Layman. m. Hilary Agnes Anderson. Education: Glasgow Academy, 1929-35; Edinburgh Academy, 1935-41; BA (Shortened Honours PPE), 1947, MA, 1948, Magdalen College, Oxford; Colonial Administrative Service Course, Oxford and London, 1947-48; Inns of Court, Middle Temple, called to bar, 1963; Advanced Management, Ashridge Management College, 1966; Associateship of Museums Association (AMA), 1998. Appointments include: War Service, Major in Cameron Highlanders & Gambia Regt RWAFF, Nigeria, India and Burma, 1942-46; Assistant District Officer, Azare, Bauchi Province, Nigeria, 1949; ADO I/C Provincial Office, 1949, Assistant District Officer, 1949-53, Divisional Officer, 1953-54, Bauchi, Northern Provinces, Nigeria; Deputy Secretary to Governor and Executive Council, 1954-57, Secretary to Executive Council, 1957-58, Senior District Officer, Igbirra, 1958-59, Northern Region of Nigeria: Assistant Secretary, Colonial Secretariat, 1960-61, Assistant Colonial Secretary and Clerk of Councils, 1961-63, Assistant (and Acting) Director of Social Welfare, 1963-66, Assistant (and Acting) Commissioner for Resettlement, 1966-67, Director of Social Welfare, Member Legislative Council, 1967, Principal Assistant Colonial Secretary, 1967-69, Deputy (and Acting) Director of Urban Services, 1969-72, Hong Kong: Deputy (and Acting) Chief Secretary, Solomon Islands, 1972-74; Chief Secretary, Western Pacific High Commission, Member Executive Council and Legislative Assembly, 1974-75; Deputy (and Acting) Governor, Solomon Islands, 1975-77: Director, Royal Lyceum Theatre, Edinburgh, 1980-88; Councillor, City of Edinburgh District, 1980-88; Member Lothian Health Board, 1981-89; Member, Secretary of State for Scotland's Museums Advisory Board, 1983-85; Trustee, Board of National Museums of Scotland, 1985-87; Conservative Party Advisory Committee on Arts and Heritage, 1988-98; Volunteer Guide, National Museums of Scotland, 1992-2003; Member, Race Relations Panel, Scottish Sheriff Courts, 1983-. Publications: A Right Honourable Gentleman, Abubakar from the Black Rock, 1991; Editor: Was it Only Yesterday?, The Last General of Nigeria's "Turawa", 2002; Good Second Class (But Not Even C3), 2004; Articles and reviews contributed to journals. Honours: LVO, 1974; CBE, 1976; US State Department Country Leader Fellowship, 1972; Leverhulme Trust Grant, 1979-81. Memberships: Fellow Royal Society of Antiquaries of Scotland, 1988; Fellow, Royal Scottish Society of Arts (Science and Technology), 1996. Address: 11 Ramsay Garden, Edinburgh EH1 2NA, Scotland. E-mail: atrevorclark2@tiscali.co.uk

**CLARK (Thomas) Alastair,** b. 27 February 1949, Blackburn, England. Central Banker. m. Shirley Anne Barker, 1 son, 1 daughter (deceased). Education: MA Maths, Emmanuel College, Cambridge; MSc Econ, LSE; Executive Program, Stanford University, 1996. Appointments: PA, Deputy Governor, 1980-81; UK Alternate Director, IMF, 1983-85; UK Alternate Director, EIB, 1986-88; Head, Financial Markets and Institutions Division, 1987-93; Head, European Division, 1993-94; Deputy Director, Financial Structure, 1994-97; Executive Director, Financial Stability, 1997-2003; Adviser to the Governor, 2003-. Membership: Honorary Member, The Association of Corporate Treasurers. Address: Bank of England,

Threadneedle Street, London, EC2R 8AM, England. E-mail: a.clark@bankof england.co.uk

**CLARK Douglas George Duncan,** b. 3 October 1942, Darlington, England. Poet. Education: BSc, Honours, Mathematics, Glasgow University, 1966. Appointments: Actuarial Student, Scottish Widows Fund, Edinburgh, 1966-69; Research Investigator, British Steel, Teesside, 1971-73; Computer Officer, Bath University Computing Services, 1973-93. Publications: The Horseman Trilogy in 4 books: Troubador, 1985; Horsemen, 1988; Coatham, 1989; Disbanded, 1991; Dysholm, 1993; Selected Poems, 1995; Cat Poems, 1997; Wounds, 1997; Lynx: Poetry from Bath (editor), 1997-2000; Kitten Poems, 2002; Finality, 2005. Contributions to: Lines Review; Cencrastus; Avon Literary Intelligencer; Outposts; Acumen; Sand Rivers Journal; Rialto; Completing the Picture: Exiles, Outsiders and Independents; Poet's Voice; Mount Holyoke News; Isibongo; Agnieszka's Dowry; Recursive Angel; Octavo; Perihelion; Autumn Leaves; Fulcrum; Scriberazone. Membership: Bath Writers' Workshop, 1982-1996. Address: 69 Hillcrest Drive, Bath, Avon BA2 1HD, England.

**CLARK Eric,** b. 29 July 1937, Birmingham, England. Author; Journalist. m. Marcelle Bernstein, 12 April 1972, 1 son, 2 daughters. Appointments: Reporter, The Exchange Telegraph news agency, London, 1958-60; Reporter, The Daily Mail, 1960-62; Staff Writer, The Guardian, 1962-64; Home Affairs Correspondent, Investigations Editor, The Observer, London, 1964-72; Author and journalist, 1972-. Publications: Ten Deighton's London Dossier, Part-author, 1967; Everybody's Guide to Survival, 1969; Corps Diplomatique, 1973, US edition as Diplomat, 1973; Black Gambit, 1978; The Sleeper, 1979; Send in the Lions, 1981; Chinese Burn, 1984, US edition as China Run, 1984; The Want Makers (Inside the Hidden World of Advertising), 1988; Hide and Seek, 1994; The Secret Enemy, in progress; Numerous newspaper articles. Honours: Fellow, English Centre, International PEN. Memberships: Society of Authors; Authors Guild; Mystery Writers of America; National Union of Journalist; American Marketing Association. Address: c/o A M Heath Agency, 6 Warwick Court, London WC1R 5DJ, England.

**CLARK Graham Ronald,** b. 10 November 1941, Littleborough, Lancashire, England. Opera Singer. m. Joan, 1 daughter. Education: Loughborough College of education, Leicestershire, 1961-64; Masters degree, Management, Loughborough University, Leicestershire, 1969-70; Singing studies with Bruce Boyce in London. Career: Teacher, Head of Physical Education Departments in 3 schools, 1964-69; Senior Regional Officer, The Sports Council, 1971-75; Operatic début with Scottish Opera, 1975; Principal, English National Opera, 1978-85; Performances with Royal Opera Covent Garden, Opera North and Welsh National Opera in the UK; International performances include: 16 seasons and over 100 performances, Bayreuth Festspiele, 1981-2004; 13 seasons, Metropolitan Opera, New York, 1985-2001; Performances in Aix-en-Provence, Amsterdam, Barcelona, Berlin, Bilbao, Bonn, Brussels, Catania, Chicago, Dallas, Geneva, Madrid, Matsumoto, Milan, Munich, Nice, Paris, Rome, Salzburg, San Francisco, Stockholm, Tokyo, Toronto, Toulouse, Turin, Vancouver, Vienna, Yokohama, Zurich, 1976-2004; Over 300 Wagner performances including over 200 performances of Der Ring des Nibelungen, 1977-2004; International festivals include, Amsterdam, Antwerp, Berlin, Brussels, Chicago, Cologne, Copenhagen, Edinburgh, Lucerne, Milan, Paris, Rome, Tel Aviv, Washington and the London Proms. Recordings with the BBC, BMG, Decca, EMI, Erato, EuroArts, Opera Rara, Philips, Sony, Teldec, The Met, WDR; Videos include: The Makropulos

Case, Canadian Opera, Toronto; The Ghosts of Versailles, The Met, New York; Die Meistersinger, Der fliegende Holländer, Der Ring des Nibelungen, Bayreuther Festspiele; Wozzeck, Deutsche Staatsoper, Berlin and The Met, New York; Ariadne auf Naxos, Opéra National de Paris. Honours: 3 nominations for Outstanding Individual Achievement in Opera, including an American Emmy, 1983, 1986, 1993; Sir Laurence Olivier Award, 1986; Honorary Doctor of Letters, Loughborough University, 1999; Sir Reginald Goodall Prize, 2001. Membership: The Garrick Club. Address: c/o Ingpen & Williams, 7 St George's Court, 131 Putney Bridge Road, London, SW15 2PA, England.

**CLARK Jonathan Charles Douglas,** b. 28 February 1951, London, England. Historian. m. Katherine Redwood Penovich, 1996. Education: BA, 1972, PhD, 1981, Cambridge University. Appointments: Research Fellow, Peterhouse, Cambridge, 1977; Leverhulme Trust, 1983; Fellow, All Souls College, Oxford, 1986; Visiting Professor, Committee on Social Thought, University of Chicago, 1993; Senior Research Fellow, All Souls College, Oxford, 1995; Joyce and Elizabeth Hall Distinguished Professor of British History, University of Kansas, 1995-; Distinguished Visiting Lecturer, University of Manitoba, 1999; Visiting Professor, Forschungszentrum Europäische Aufklärung, Potsdam, 2000; Visiting Professor, University of Northumbria, 2001-03. Publications: The Dynamics of Change, 1982; English Society 1688-1832, 1985, 2nd edition as English Society 1660-1832, 2000; Revolution and Rebellion, 1986; Editor, The Memoirs of James 2nd Earl Waldegrave, 1988; Editor, Ideas and Politics in Modern Britain, 1990; The Language of Liberty, 1993; Samuel Johnson, 1994; Editor, Edmund Burke, Reflections on the Revolution in France, 2001; Joint editor, Samuel Johnson in Historical Context, 2002; Our Shadowed Present, 2003. Contributions to: Scholarly books and journals, and to periodicals.Memberships: Royal Historical Society, fellow; Ecclesiastical History Society; Church of England Record Society; North American Conference on British Studies; British Society for Eighteenth Century Studies. Address: Department of History, University of Kansas, 1445 Jawhawk Boulevard, Lawrence, KS 66045, USA.

**CLARK Patricia Denise (Claire Lorrimer, Patricia Robins, Susan Patrick),** b. 1921, England. Writer; Poet. Publications: As Claire Lorrimer: A Voice in the Dark, 1967; The Shadow Falls, 1974; Relentless Storm, 1975; The Secret of Quarry House, 1976; Mavreen, 1976; Tamarisk, 1978; Chantal, 1980; The Garden (a cameo), 1980; The Chatelaine, 1981; The Wilderling, 1982; Last Year's Nightingale, 1984; Frost in the Sun, 1986; House of Tomorrow (biography), 1987; Ortolans, 1990; The Spinning Wheel, 1991; Variations (short stories), 1991; The Silver Link, 1993; Fool's Curtain, 1994; Beneath the Sun, 1996; Connie's Daughter, 1997; The Reunion, 1997; The Woven Thread, 1998; The Reckoning, 1998; Second Chance, 1998; An Open Door, 1999; Never Say Goodbye, 2000; Search for Love, 2000; For Always, 2001; The Faithful Heart, 2002; Over My Dead Body, 2003; Deception, 2003; Troubled Waters, 2004; Dead Centre, 2005. As Patricia Robins: To the Stars, 1944; See No Evil, 1945; Three Loves, 1949; Awake My Heart, 1950; Beneath the Moon, 1951; Leave My Heart Alone, 1951; The Fair Deal, 1952; Heart's Desire, 1953; So This is Love, 1953; Heaven in Our Hearts, 1954; One Who Cares, 1954; Love Cannot Die, 1955; The Foolish Heart, 1956; Give All to Love, 1956; Where Duty Lies, 1957; He Is Mine, 1957; Love Must Wait, 1958; Lonely Quest, 1959; Lady Chatterley's Daughter, 1961; The Last Chance, 1961; The Long Wait, 1962; The Runaways, 1962; Seven Loves, 1962; With All My Love, 1963; The Constant Heart, 1964; Second Love, 1964; The Night is Thine, 1964; There Is But One, 1965; No More Loving, 1965; Topaz Island, 1965; Love Me Tomorrow, 1966; The Uncertain Joy, 1966; The

Man Behind the Mask, 1967; Forbidden, 1967; Sapphire in the Sand, 1968; Return to Love, 1968; Laugh on Friday, 1969; No Stone Unturned, 1969; Cinnabar House, 1970; Under the Sky, 1970; The Crimson Tapestry, 1972; Play Fair with Love, 1972; None But He, 1973; Fulfilment, 1993; Forsaken, 1993; Forever, 1993; The Legend, 1997; Memberships: Society of Authors; Romantic Novelists Association. Address: Chiswell Barn, Marsh Green, Edenbridge, Kent TN8 5PR, England.

**CLARKE Anthony Peter (Sir),** b. 13 May 1943, Ayr, Scotland. Judge. m. Rosemary, 2 sons, 1 daughter. Education: MA, Economics Part I, Law Part II, King's College, Cambridge. Appointments: Called to Bar, Middle Temple, 1965; QC, 1979; Judge of the High Court QBD, 1993-8; Admiralty Judge, 1993-98; Lord Justice of Appeal, 1998-. Honours: Knight, 1993; PC, 1998. Memberships: Garrick Club; Rye Golf Club. Address: Royal Courts of Justice, Strand, London WC2A 2LL, England.

**CLARKE Arthur C(harles),** b. 16 December 1917, Minehead, Somerset, England. Author. m. Marilyn Mayfield, 1953, divorced 1964. Education: BSc, King's College, London, 1948. Appointments: Assistant Editor, Science Abstracts, 1949-50; Many appearances on UK and US radio and television; Chancellor, Moratuwa University, Sri Lanka, 1979-2002; Vikram Sarabhai Professor, Physical Research Laboratory, Ahmedabad, 1980. Publications: Non-Fiction: Interplanetary Flight, 1950; The Exploration of Space, 1951; The Exploration of the Moon (with R A Smith), 1954; The Challenge of the Spaceship, 1960; The Challenge of the Sea, 1960; Man and Space (with others), 1964; The Coming of the Space Age, 1967; First on the Moon (with the astronauts), 1970; Beyond Jupiter (with Chesley Bonestell), 1973; Arthur C Clarke's Mysterious World (with Simon Welfare and John Fairley), 1980; Arthur C Clarke's World of Strange Powers (with Simon Welfare and John Fairley), 1984; Arthur C Clarke's Chronicles of the Strange and Mysterious (with Simon Welfare and John Fairley), 1987; Astounding Days, 1988; How the World was One, 1992; Arthur C Clarke's A-Z of Mysteries (with Simon Welfare and John Fairley), 1993; The Snows of Olympus, 1994. Fiction: Prelude to Space, 1951; Against the Fall of Night, 1953; Reach for Tomorrow, 1956; The Other Side of the Sky, 1958; Tales of Ten Worlds, 1962; 2001: A Space Odyssey (with Stanley Kubrick), 1968; The Lost World of 2001, 1972; Rendezvous with Rama, 1973; The Fountains of Paradise, 1979; 2010: Space Odyssey II, 1982; The Songs of Distant Earth, 1986; 2061: Odyssey III, 1988; Rama II (with G Lee), 1989; The Garden of Rama (with G Lee), 1991; Beyond the Fall of Night (with Gregory Benford), 1991; The Hammer of God, 1993; Rama Revealed (with G Lee), 1993; 3001: The Final Odyssey, 1997; The Trigger (with Michael Kube-McDowell), 1998; The Light of Other Days (with Stephen Baxter), 2000; Greetings, Carbon-Based Bipeds!, 2000; The Treasure of the Great Reef, 1964; Arthur C Clarke & C S Lewis: A Correspondence; A Time Odyssey ( with Stephen Baxter): Time's Eye; Sunstorm; Wolflings;. Contributions to: Journals and periodicals. Honours: Kalinga Prize, UNESCO, 1961; Stuart Ballantine Medal, Franklin Institute, 1963; Nebula Awards, Science Fiction Writers of America, 1972, 1974, 1979; John Campbell Award, 1974; Hugo Awards, World Science Fiction Convention, 1974, 1980; Vidya Jyothi Medal, 1986; Grand Master, Science Fiction Writers of America, 1986; Charles Lindbergh Award, 1987; Commander of the Order of the British Empire, 1989; Lord Perry Award, 1992; Knighted, 1998; Many honorary doctorates. Memberships: Association for the Advancement of Science; International Science Writers Association, fellow; Royal Astronomical Society, Fellow; Society of Authors. Address: 25 Barnes Place, Colombo 7, Sri Lanka.

**CLARKE Granville Daniel,** b. 26 October 1940, Keighley, Yorkshire, England. Creative Artist. Education: City and Guilds 1st Class Honours, 1957 Full Technological Certificate, 1959, Barnsley College of Art, 1955-60. Career: Professional Artist in pencil and watercolour; Professional musician, writer, performer with Foggy Dew-O, 1965-76; Director, Scarlet Songs Publishing; BBC Radio and TV presenter and performer; Original art expert and commentator, TV Series Watercolour Challenge, Channel 4, 1998; Specialised in watercolour snow scenes for fine art publishers Michael Stewart, Bristol, 1983-86; Member, Community Action in the Rural Environment, 1986-90; Involved in wildflower conservation; Developer of environmental educational initiatives as lecturer and on video resource guides for Kirklees Countryside Department, West Yorkshire, 1992-97; Folk Music Masterclass Lecturer, Bretton College, Wakefield, Yorkshire, 1997; Sponsor of many eye camps in India through Sightsavers International, 1991-2000; Live performances: Visually Vivaldi, Knaresborough Festival, 1999; Classical Manoeuvres in Art, Marlborough College, 2001; Regular lecture tours and tutorials, Marlborough College and Bath University, 1999-2004; Only artist to paint around the world in 90 days, 1990; Exhibitions: Numerous one-man and collective exhibitions, 1977- including House of Commons and Royal Society of British Artists; Works in collections world-wide; Commissions include: English Nature; P&O Cruise Lines; Mercedes Benz; Guardian Newspapers; Artistic commemoration of the first Toll Motorway in the UK, 2003. Publications: Sketches and Impressions, 1991; Works reproduced in limited editions: Silkstone Images of Winter; Wharncliffe Crags in Autumn. Honours include: TV Awards: Firstimers Granada TV, 1967; Queens Documentary Award, YTV, 1977; Presented to Prince Charles at the RIBA/Times Carnegie National Awards; Wildflower Conservation Award, English Nature, 1993; Service to Mankind Award for saving a life, 1997. Memberships: Yorkshire Watercolour Society, 1989; Fellow, Royal Society of Arts, 1997. Address: Huskar Cottage Studio, 8 South Yorkshire Building, Moorend Lane, Silkstone Common, Nr Barnsley, South Yorkshire S75 4 RJ, England. E-mail: g.danny.clarke@virgin.net Website: www.granvilledclarke.com

**CLARKE Hilda Margery,** b. 10 June 1926, Monton, Eccles, Manchester, England. Artist; Gallery Director. Widowed, 2 sons. Education: Studied privately in Manchester with L S Lowry, and in Hamburg; Drawing, Printmaking and Sculpture, Southampton College of Art, part-time, 1960-88; Ruskin School of Art Workshops under Tom Piper, Chris Orr and Norman Ackroyd, 4 weeks, 1975; BA (Honours), Open University, 1975-82. Career: Founder and Director, "The First" Gallery, Southampton, 1984-; Curator, long running national touring exhibitions, 1988-; Exhibitions: Southampton City Art Gallery; FPS Gallery, Buckingham Gate, London; Mall Galleries, London; Chalk Farm Gallery, London; Ditchling, Sussex; Bettles Gallery, Ringwood; New Ashgate Gallery, Farnham; Tib Lane Gallery, Manchester; One man exhibitions: Hamwic Gallery, Southampton, 1970; Westgate Gallery, Winchester, 1973; University of Southampton, 1975; Hiscock Gallery, Southsea, 1977; "The First" Gallery, Southampton, 1989, 1998, 2004; Turner Sims Concert Hall, Southampton (by invitation) for the Inauguration of the Foyer, 1994; Ramsgate Library Gallery, 2001; Works in public collections: Southampton University; Southern Arts Association; St Mary's Hospital, Isle of Wight; Works in private collections: Felder Fine Art, London; Michael Hurd (deceased), Liss; Mr and Mrs B Hunt, Southampton; Dr C Williams, Bristol; Lady Lucas. Publications: Catalogues: Two Memorable Men: Crispin Eurich (1936-76) photographs, LS Lowry (1887-1976) drawings; The Animated Eye; Paintings and Moving Machines by Peter Markey; Showman-Shaman-Showman: Paintings and Prints by Stephen Powell; Architect at Leisure: Watercolours and Drawings by Arthur Mattinson (1853-1932); Passage From India: Paintings and Prints by Jacqueline Mair MA RCA. Membership: FRSA, elected 1996. Address: "The First" Gallery, 1 Burnham Chase, Bitterne, Southampton SO18 5DG, England.

**CLARKE Keith Edward,** b. 1940, United Kingdom. Consultant. m. Barbara, 1 son, 1 daughter. Education: B. Eng, Electrical Engineering, University of Bradford; Diploma, Computing Science, Imperial College of Science and Medicine; M.Phil. Computing Science, University of London; Management, London Business School. Appointments: Adviser, Ministry of Technology, 1969-70; Various management posts, BT Research, 1972-83; Deputy Director of Research, BT, 1985-89; Director, Applications and Services Development, BT Laboratories, Martlesham, Suffolk, 1989-92; Senior Vice-President Engineering, BT North America, San Jose, California, 1992; Director, Group Systems Engineering, BT plc, 1992-95; Director of Engineering Collaboration and Business Planning, BT Global Engineering, 1995-97; Director, Technology External Affairs, BT plc, 1997-2000; Executive Director (part-time), British Approvals Board for Telecommunications, Consultant, 2000-2001; Consultant in ITC with clients in UK and Europe, 2000-; Company Directorships: BT (CBP) Limited, 1989-95; Cellnet Limited, 1989-92; British Approvals Board for telecommunications, 1992-2000; BPS Inc, 2000; BABT Holdings, 2000; Hermont (Holdings, 2000-2002. Publications: Over 60 publications in the field of telecommunications include: How Viewdata Works (editor, R Winsbury), 1981; The Immediate Past and Likely Future of Videotext Display Technology, 1982; On the Road to Worldwide Communication (jointly with J Chidley), 1987; Royal Academy of Engineering Seminar on the Public Perception of Risk-Lessons from the Mobile Phone Industry, 2000. Memberships: Fellow: Institution of Electrical Engineers, British Computer Society, British Institute of Management, Royal Academy of Engineering, RSA; Liveryman of the Worshipful Company of Information Technologists; Freeman of the City of London; Guild of Freeman of the City of London; Naval and Military Club; The City Livery Yacht Club; The Little Ship Club. E-mail: kclarke@totalonline.net

**CLARKE Michael Gilbert,** b. 21 May 1944, Halifax, England. Vice-Principal. m. Angela Mary Cook, 1 son, 2 daughters. Education: BA, Politics and Sociology, 1963-66, MA, Comparative Politics, 1966-67, University of Sussex. Appointments: Lecturer and Director of Studies, Politics, University of Edinburgh, 1969-75; Assistant, 1975-76, Deputy Director, Policy Planning, Lothian Regional Council, 1976-81; Chief Executive, Local Government Training Board, 1981-89; Chief Executive Local Government Management Board, 1989-93; Head School of Public Policy, Professor of Public Policy, 1993-98, Pro-Vice Chancellor, 1998-2002, Vice-Principal, 2002-, University of Birmingham. Publications: Articles and books on UK local governance and constitutional arrangements at sub-national level. Honours: Fellow, Royal Society of Arts, 1988; Honorary Member, Society of Local Authority Chief Executives, 1998; CBE, 2000; DL, 2000; Honorary MA, University College Worcester, 2003; Honorary Member, Chartered Institute of Public Finance and Accounting, 2004. Memberships: West Midlands Regional Assembly; Non-executive Director: Government Office for West Midland, Ikon Gallery, Birmingham, Birmingham Research Park, Malvern Hills Science Park; Chairman: Central Technology Belt, Worcestershire Regional Partnership; Member, General Synod, Church of England; Lay Canon, Worcester Cathedral. Address: Millington House, Lansdowne Crescent, Worcester, WR3 8JE, England. E-mail: m.g.clarke@bham.ac.uk

**CLARKE Robert Henry,** b. 6 March 1919, London, England. Oceanographer. m. Obla Paliza de Clarke, 2 sons, 1 daughter. Education: St Olaves and St Saviours Grammar School, 1932-38; Open Scholar in Natural Science, New College Oxford, 1938-40, 1946-47; Bachelor of Arts and Master of Arts with honours in Zoology, Botany and Chemistry, University of Oxford, 1946; Doctor of Philosophy, University of Oslo, Norway, 1957. Appointments: Lieutenant (Sp), RNVR in British Navy, Admiralty Unexploded Bomb Department with operations in various seas, and Directorate of Admiralty Research and Development(India) with special operations in India, Burma and Ceylon, 1940-46; Biologist in the Discovery Investigations, British Colonial Office, 1947-49; Principal Scientific Officer, British National Institute of Oceanography, conducted oceanographical expeditions in all Oceans and in all Seas except the Caspian Sea and the Dead Sea, 1949-71; Lent to FAO of the United Nations in the grade P5 as a whale biologist in Chile, Ecuador and Peru, 1958-61; Fishing off the coast of Peru, 1971-77; Visiting Professor, Universities of Baja California and Yucatan, Mexico, 1977-82; Currently retired but continuing research. Publications: Author of more than 100 research publications, many of book length and mostly on whales (especially the sperm whale), whale conservation, whaling and on ambergris, squids and deep sea fishes. Honours: Honorary Member, Fundación Ecuatoriana para el Estudio de los Mamíferos Marinos; Honorary Member, Sociedad Geográfica de Lima; Included in the Encyclopaedia of the Azores. Memberships: Scientific Fellow, Zoological Society of London; Institute of Biology of Great Britain; Challenger Society; Marine Biological Association of the United Kingdom; Association of British Zoologists, Member of Council, 1962-65. Address: Apartado 40, Pisco, Peru. E-mail: robertclarke007@hotmail.com

**CLARKE William Malpas,** b. 5 June 1922, Ashton-under-Lyne, England. Author. m. Faith Elizabeth Dawson, 2 daughters. Education: BA Hons, Econ, University of Manchester, England, 1948; Hon DLitt, London Guildhall University, 1992. Appointments: Financial Editor, The Times, 1956-66; Director-General, British Invisible Exports Council, 1967-87; Chairman, ANZ Merchant Bank, 1987-91; Chairman, Central Banking Publications, 1991-. Publications: City's Invisible Earnings, 1958; City in the World Economy, 1965; Private Enterprise in Developing Countries, 1966; The World's Money, 1970; Inside the City, 1979; How the City of London Works, 1986; Secret Life of Wilkie Collins, 1988; Planning for Europe, 1989; Lost Fortune of the Tsars, 1994; Letters of Wilkie Collins, 1999; The Golden Thread, 2000. Contributions to: The Banker; Central Banking; Euromoney; Wilkie Collins Society Journal. Honour: CBE, 1976. Memberships: Thackeray Society; Wilkie Collins Society; Reform Club. Address: 37 Park Vista, Greenwich, London SE10 9LZ, England.

**CLAYTON Peter Arthur,** b. 27 April 1937, London, England. Publishing Consultant; Archaeological Lecturer. m. Janet Frances Manning, 5 September 1964, 2 sons. Education: School of Librarianship; North West Polytechnic, London, 1958; Institute of Archaeology, London University, 1958-62; University College, London, 1968-72. Appointments: Librarian, 1953-63; Archaeological Editor, Thames & Hudson, 1963-73; Humanities Publisher, Longmans, 1973; Managing Editor, British Museum's Publications, 1974-79; Publications Director, BA Seaby, 1980-87; Writer, Lecturer, 1987-; Consulting Editor, Minerva Magazine, 1990-; Expert Advisor (coins and antiquities), Department for Culture Media and Sport (Treasure Committee). Publications: The Rediscovery of Ancient Egypt; Archaeological Sites of Britain; Seven Wonders of the Ancient World; Treasures of Ancient Rome; Companion to Roman Britain; Great Figures of Mythology; Gods and Symbols of Ancient Egypt; Chronicle of the Pharaohs; Family Life in Ancient Egypt; The Valley of the Kings; Egyptian Mythology. Contributions to: Journal of Egyptian Archaeology; Numismatic Chronicle; Coin & Medal Bulletin; Minerva. Honours: Liveryman of the Honourable Company of Farriers of the City of London, 2000; Freeman of the City of London, 2000. Memberships: Chartered Institute of Library and Information Professionals, fellow; Society of Antiquaries of London, fellow; Royal Numismatic Society, fellow. Address: 41 Cardy Road, Boxmoor, Hemel Hempstead, Hertfordshire HP1 1RL, England.

**CLEARE John Silvey,** b. 2 May 1936, London, England. Photographer; Writer. m. (2) Jo Jackson, 12 May 1980, 1 daughter. Education: Wycliffe College, 1945-54; Guildford School of Photography, 1957-60. Appointments: Joint Editor, Mountain Life magazine, 1973-75; Editorial Board, Climber and Rambler magazine, 1975-85. Publications: Rock Climbers in Action in Snowdonia, 1966; Sea-Cliff Climbing in Britain, 1973;Mountains, 1975; World Guide to Mountains, 1979; Mountaineering, 1980; Scrambles Among the Alps, 1986; John Cleare's Best 50 Hill Walks in Britain, 1988; Trekking: Great Walks in the World, 1988; Walking the Great Views, 1991; Discovering the English Lowlands, 1991; On Foot in the Pennines, 1994; On Foot in the Yorkshire Dales, 1996; Mountains of the World, 1997; Distant Mountains, 1999; Britain Then and Now, 2000; On Top of the World, 2000; Pembrokeshire – The Official National Park Guide, 2001; The Tao Te Ching, 2002; Moods of Pembrokeshire & its Coast, 2004; Portrait of Bath, 2004; Books of Songs, 2004; The Tao, 2005. Contributions to: Times; Sunday Times; Independent; Observer; World; Country Living; Boat International; Intercontinental; Alpine Journal; High; Climber; Great Outdoors. Honour: 35mm Prize, Trento Film Festival, for film The Climbers (as Cameraman), 1971. Membership: Outdoor Writers Guild, executive committee. Address: Hill Cottage, Fonthill Gifford, Salisbury, Wiltshire SP3 6QW, England.

**CLEARY Jon (Stephen),** b. 22 November 1917, Sydney, New South Wales, Australia. Author; Screenwriter. Appointments: Journalist, Australian News and Information Bureau, London, 1948-49 and New York City 1949-51. Publications: The Small Glories (short stories), 1945; You Can't See Round Corners, 1947; The Long Shadow, 1949; Just Let Me Be, 1950; The Sundowners, 1952, screenplay 1961; The Climate of Courage, UK edition as Naked in the Night, 1954; Justin Bayard, 1955; The Green Helmet, 1957, screenplay 1960; Back of Sunset, 1959; The Siege of Pinchgut (screenplay with H Watt), 1959; North from Thursday, 1960; The Country of Marriage, 1961; Forest of the Night, 1962; Pillar of Salt (short stories), 1963; A Flight of Chariots, 1964; The Fall of an Eagle, 1965; The Pulse of Danger, 1966; The High Commissioner, 1967; The Long Pursuit, 1968; Season of Doubt, 1969; Remember Jack Hoxie, 1970; Helga's Webb, 1971; The Liberators (UK edition as Mask of the Andes), 1971; The Ninth Marquess (UK edition as Man's Estate), 1972; Ransom, 1973; Peter's Pence, 1974; Sidecar Boys (screenplay), 1974; The Safe House, 1975; A Sound of Lightning, 1976; High Road to China, 1977; Vortex, 1977; The Beaufort Sisters, 1979; A Very Pirate War, 1980; The Golden Sabre, 1981; The Faraway Drums, 1981; Spearfield's Daughter, 1982; The Phoenix Tree, 1984; The City of Fading Light, 1985; Dragons at the Party, 1987; Now and Then, Amen, 1988; Babylon South, 1989; Murder Song, 1990; Pride's Harvest, 1991; Dark Summer, 1992; Bleak Spring, 1993; Autumn Maze, 1994; Winter Chill, 1995; Endpeace, 1996; A Different Turd, 1997; Five Ring Circus, 1998; Dilemma, 1999; Bear Pit, 2000; Yesterday's Shadow, 2001; The Easy Sin, 2002; Degrees if Connection, 2003; Miss Ambar Regrets, 2004; Morning's Gone,

2006. Literary Agent: Vivienne Schuster, Curtis Brown Ltd, Haymarket, London, England. Address: c/o Harper Collins, 77-85 Fulham Palace Road, London W6 8JB, England.

**CLEAVE Brian Elseley,** b. 3 September 1939, Ilford, Essex, England. Barrister. m. Celia Valentine Williams. Education: LLB, Exeter University, 1961, 1958-61; Kansas University, 1961-62; Manchester University, 1962-63. Appointments: Admitted as a solicitor, 1966; Assistant Solicitor, 1978-86, Principal Assistant Solicitor, 1986-90, Solicitor, 1990-99, Inland Revenue; Called to the Bar, Gay's Inn, 1999; Senior Consultant, Tacis Tax Reform Project, Moscow, 2000-2002; Senior Consultant, Europeaid Tax Reform II Project, Moscow, 2003-. Honours: CB, 1995; QC, Honoris Causa, 1999. Membership: FRSA. Address: Gray's Inn Tax Chambers, Third Floor, Gray's Inn Chambers, Gray's Inn, London WC1R 5JA, England. E-mail: bcleave@lawdraft.fsnet.co.uk

**CLEESE John (Marwood),** b. 27 October 1939, Weston-Super-Mare, Somerset, England. Author; Actor. m. (1) Connie Booth, 1968, dissolved 1978, 1 daughter, (2) Barbara Trentham, 1981, dissolved 1990, 1 daughter, (3) Alyce Faye Eichelberger, 1993. Education: MA, Downing College, Cambridge. Career: Began writing and making jokes professionally, 1963; Appeared in and co-wrote TV Series: The Frost Report; At Last the 1948 Show; Monty Python's Flying Circus; Fawlty Towers; The Human Face; Founder and Director, Video Arts Ltd, 1972-89; Films include: Interlude; The Magic Christian; And Now For Something Completely Different; Monty Python and the Holy Grail; Life of Brian; Yellowbeard, 1982; The Meaning of Life, 1983; Silverado, 1985; A Fish Called Wanda, 1988; Mary Shelley's Frankenstein, 1993; The Jungle Book, 1994; Fierce Creatures, 1996; The World Is Not Enough, 1999; The Quantum Project, 2000; Rat Race, 2000; Pluto Nash, 2000; Harry Potter and the Philosopher's Stone, 2001; Die Another Day, 2002; Harry Potter and the Chamber of Secrets, 2002; Charlie's Angels: Full Throttle, 2003; Around the World in 80 Days, 2004. Publications: Families and How to Survive Them, (with Robin Skynner), 1983; The Golden Skits of Wing Commander Muriel Volestrangler FRHS and Bar, 1984; The Complete Fawlty Towers (with Connie Booth), 1989; Life and How to Survive It (with Robin Skynner), 1993. Honour: Honorary LLD, St Andrews. Address: c/o David Wilkinson, 115 Hazlebury Road, London SW6 2LX, England.

**CLEGG Jerry S,** b. 29 September 1933, Haber City, Utah, USA. Professor of Philosophy. m. Karen M, 3 daughters. Education: BA, 1955, MA, 1959, University of Utah, USA; PhD, University of Washington, USA, 1964. Appointment: Philosophy Department, Mills College, Oakland, California USA, 1962-, currently Professor of Philosophy. Publications: Books: The Structure of Plato's Philosophy; On Genius: From Schopenhauer to Wittgenstein; Articles in scientific journals: What Magellan's voyage didn't prove or why the Earth is flat; Symptoms; Self-Predication and Linguistic Reference in Plato's Theory of the Forms; Plato's Vision of Chaos; Wittgenstein on Verification and Private Languages; Faith; Some Artistic Uses of Truths and Lies; Nietzsche and the Ascent of Man in a Cyclical Cosmos; Nietzsche's Gods in the Birth of Tragedy; Freud and the Issue of Pessimism; Logical Mysticism and The Cultural Setting of Wittgenstein's Tractatus; Jung's Quarrel with Freud; Conrad's Reply to Kierkegaard; Mann contra Nietzsche; Freud and the "Homeric" Mind; Life in the Shadow of Christ: Nietzsche on Pistis versus Gnosis ( in Nietzsche and the Gods). Address: 6636 Admiral Way S.W., Seattle, WA 98116, USA.

**CLELAND Helen Isabel,** b. 3 July 1950, Bristol, England. Headteacher. m. J R S Hoult, deceased, 1 son, 1 daughter.

Education: BA, Single Honours, English, University of Exeter, 1968-71; PGCE, Homerton College, Cambridge, 1971-72. Appointments: English Teacher, Dame Alice Owen's School, Islington, London, 1972-76; English Teacher, 1976-79, Head of Sixth Form, Senior Teacher, 1979-86, Haverstock School, Camden, London; Deputy Head, 1986-91, Edmonton School, Enfield; Headteacher, Woodford County High School, 1991-. Address: Woodford County High School, High Road, Woodford Green, Essex IG8 9LA, England. E-mail: head.woodfordcounty high@redbridge.gov.uk

**CLEMENTS Christopher John,** b. 21 January 1946, England. Medical Practitioner. m. Vivienne, 2 sons. Education: MB.BS, London Hospital, University of London, 1969; LRCP, MRCS, 1969; DObst, University of Auckland, 1972; DCH, Royal College of Physicians, London, 1973; MSc, University of Manchester, 1980; MCCM, 1980; MFPHM, 1980; FAFPHM, 1994. Appointments include: Registrar, Waikato Hospital, New Zealand, 1971; Medical Director, Hospital de Valle Apurimac, Peru, 1973-74; Chief Medical Officer, Save the Children Fund, Bangladesh Project, 1977, Afghanistan Project, 1977-78; Assistant Director, National Head of Disease Control, Department of Health, Head Office, Wellington, New Zealand, 1983-85; Medical Officer, Expanded Programme on Immunization, World Health Organisation, Geneva, 1985-2002. Publications: Over 100 articles and chapters contributed to books on public health. Memberships: Royal College of Public Health Physicians. Address: 24 Millbank Drive, Mount Eliza, VIC 3930, Australia. E-mail: john@clem.com.au

**CLEMENTS Teresa Agnes,** b. 18 July 1939, Croydon, Surrey, England. Religious Sister; Theologian. Education: Teachers' Certificate of Education, Coloma College of Education, West Wickham, 1961; Batchelors degree in Sacred Theology, Pontifical University of St Thomas Aquinas (Angelicum), Rome, 1979; Licentiate in Sacred Theology, 1980, Doctorate of Sacred Theology, 1982, Pontifical Gregorian University, Rome. Appointments: Missionary, Kinyamasika Teacher Training College, Fort Portal, Uganda, East Africa, 1962-74; Religious Sister, Cape Coast Diocese, Ghana, West Africa, 1974-76; Lecturer in Theology, Pontifical College, Regina Mundi, 1981-83; Lecturer in Theology, Milltown Institute of Theology and Philosophy, Dublin, Ireland, 1983-89; Member, General Leadership of the Daughters of Mary and Joseph, Rome, 1989-92; Provincial Superior of the Daughters of Mary and Joseph, England, 1992-98; Roman Catholic Representative, Advisory Board for Religious Life to the Bishops of the Church of England, 1993-98; Representative, CoR to Churches Together in Great Britain and Ireland, 1993-96; Member, Executive of the Conference of Religious for England and Wales, 1993-96; President, Conference of Religious for England and Wales, 1996-98; Member, Board of the Catholic Agency for Social Concern, 1999-2003; Member, Board of Caritas: social-action: agency of the Roman Catholic Conference of Bishops for England and Wales, 2003-04; Member, Committee for On-Going Formation of Priests, Roman Catholic Archdiocese of Southwark, 2003-. Publications: Many contributions to Religious Life Review, Milltown Studies and other theological journals. Memberships: Roman Catholic Religious Sister: Daughters of Mary and Joseph, an International Congregation; The Ecumenical Society of the Blessed Virgin Mary; Committee for the Ongoing Formation of Priests, Roman Catholic Southwark Archdiocese; Patient/Carers Advisory Group, The Royal Marsden Hospital, Sutton; Caritas: social action. Address: The Convent, Layhams Road, West Wickham, Kent BR4 9QJ, England. E-mail: tclements@stjosephs45.freeserve.co.uk

**CLEOBURY Stephen John,** b. 31 December 1948, Bromley, Kent, England. Conductor. m. Emma Sian Disley, 3 daughters. Education: MA, Mus. B., St John's College, Cambridge. FRCO; FRCM. Appointments: Director of Music, St Matthew's, Northampton. 1971-74; Sub-organist, Westminster Abbey, 1974-78; Master of Music, Westminster Cathedral, 1979-82; Director of Music, King's College, Cambridge, 1982-; Conductor, Cambridge University Music Society, 1983-; Chief Conductor, BBC Singers, 1995-. Publications: Sundry arrangements and short compositions. Honour: Hon. D. Mus., Anglia Polytechnic University. Memberships: ISM; Vice-President, RCO; Member of Advisory Board, RSCM. Address: King's College, Cambridge CB2 1ST, England. E-mail: sjc1001@cam.ac.uk

**CLIFF Ian Cameron,** b. 11 September 1952, Twickenham, England. Diplomat. m. Caroline Redman, 1 son, 2 daughters. Education: 1st Class Honours, Modern History, Magdalen College, Oxford, 1971-74. Appointments: History Master, Dr Challoner's Grammar School, Amersham, 1975-79; 2nd Secretary, Foreign and Commonwealth Office, 1979-80; Arabic Language Training, Damascus and St Andrews University, 1980-82; 1st Secretary, British Embassy, Khartoum, 1982-85; 1st Secretary, Foreign and Commonwealth Office, 1984-89; 1st Secretary, UK Mission to UN, New York, 1989-93; Director, Exports to the Middle East, Near East and North Africa, Department of Trade and Industry, 1993-96; Deputy Head of Mission, British Embassy, Vienna, 1996-2001; HM Ambassador to Bosnia and Herzegovina, 2001-. Publications: Occasional articles in Railway Magazines. Honour: OBE, 1992. Address: c/o Foreign and Commonwealth Office, London SW1A 2AH, England.

**CLIFFORD Max,** b. April 1943, Kingston-upon-Thames, England. Public Relations Executive. m. Elizabeth, 1 daughter. Appointments: Worker, Department Store; Former Junior Reporter, Merton & Morden News; Former Press Officer, EMI Records (promoted the Beatles); Founder, Max Clifford Associates, clients have included Muhammad Ali, Marlon Brando, David Copperfield, O J Simpson, Frank Sinatra, Simon Cowell. Address: Max Clifford Associates Ltd, 49-50 New Bond Street, London, W1Y 9HA, England.

**CLIFT Roland,** b. 19 November 1942, Epsom, Surrey, England. Professor of Environmental Technology. m. Diana Helen Manning, 2 sons, 1 deceased, 1 daughter. Education: BA, 1963, MA, 1966, Trinity College, Cambridge; PhD, McGill University, Montreal, Canada, 1970. Appointments: Head, Department of Chemical Engineering, 1981-91, Professor of Chemical Engineering, 1981-92, Professor of Environmental Technology and Director of Centre for Environmental Strategy, 1992-, University of Surrey; Editor-in-Chief, Powder Technology, 1987-95; Member, UK Ecolabelling Board, 1992-98; Member, Royal Commission on Environmental Pollution, 1996-; Visiting Professor, University of Göteborg, Sweden, 1999-; Director: ClifMar Associates Ltd, 1996-; Particles Consultants Ltd, 1998-; Merrill Lynch New Energy Technologies Ltd, 1999-; Industrial Ecology Solutions Ltd, 2001-; Member, Research Advisory Committee, Forest Research and Forestry Commission, 2004-. Publications: Bubble, Drops and Particles, 1978; Slurry Transport using Centrifugal Pumps, 1996; Processing of Particulate Solids, 1997; Sustainable Development in Practice: Case Studies for Engineers and Scientists, 2004; Numerous edited books and articles in professional journals. Honours: Henry Marion Howe Medal, American Society for Metals, 1976; Frank Moulton Medal, Institution of Chemical Engineers, 1978; Officer of the Order of the British Empire, 1994; Sir Frank Whittle Medal, Royal Academy of Engineering, 2003. Memberships: Fellow, Royal Academy of Engineering; Fellow,

Institution of Chemical Engineers; Honorary Fellow, Chartered Institute of Waste and Environmental Management; Fellow, Royal Society of Arts. Address: Centre for Environmental Strategy, University of Surrey, Guildford, Surrey GU2 7XH, England. E-mail: r.clift@surrey.ac.uk

**CLINTON Hilary Rodham,** b. 26 October 1947, Chicago, Illinois, USA. Lawyer and Former First Lady of USA. m. Bill Clinton, 1 daughter. Education: Yale University. Career: Rose Law Firm, 1977-, currently Senior Partner; Appointments: Legal Counsel, Nixon Impeachment Staff, 1974; Senator from New York, 2001-; Various teaching positions, committee places, public & private ventures. Publications include: Every Child Needs a Village, 1994; It Takes a Village, 1996; Dear Socks, Dear Buddy, 1998; An Invitation to the White House, 2000; Living History (memoirs), 2003; numerous magazine articles. Honours include: One of Most Influential Lawyers in America, 1988, 1991; AIDS Awareness Award, 1994; Grammy Award, 1997. Address: US Senate, Washington, DC 20510, USA.

**CLINTON William Jefferson (Bill),** b. 19 August 1946, Hope, Arizona, USA. Former President, USA. m. Hillary Rodham, 1975, 1 daughter. Education: BS, International Affairs, Georgetown University, 1964-68; Rhodes Scholar, University College, Oxford, 1968-70; JD, Yale University Law School, 1970-73. Appointments: Professor, University of Arizona Law School, 1974-76; Democrat Nominee, Arizona, 1974; Attorney-General, Arizona, 1977-79; State Governor of Arizona, 1979-81, 1983-92; Member, Wright, Lindsey & Jennings, law firm, 1981-83; Chairman, Southern Growth Policies Board, 1985-86; Chairman, Education Commissioner of the States, 1986-87; Chairman, National Governor's Association, 1986-87; Vice-Chairman, Democrat Governor's Association, 1987-88, Chairman elect, 1988-89, Chairman, 1989-90; Co-Chairman, Task Force on Education, 1990-91; Chairman, Democrat Leadership Council, 1990-91; President, USA, 1993-2001; Impeached by House of Representatives for perjury and obstruction of justice, 1988; Aquitted in the Senate on both counts, 1999; Suspended from practising law in Supreme Court, 2001-06. Honours: National Council of State Human Service Administrators Association Award; Award, Leadership on Welfare Reform; National Energy Efficiency Advocate Award; Honorary Degree, Northeastern University, Boston, 1993; Honorary Fellow, University College, Oxford, 1993; Honorary DCL, Oxford, 1994; Honorary DLitt, Ulster University, 1995. Address: 55 West 125th Street, New York, NY 10027, USA.

**CLOONEY George,** b. 1962, USA. Actor. m. Talia Blasam, divorced. Creative Works: TV Series: ER, 1984-85; The Facts of Life, 1985-86; Roseanne, 1988-89; Sunset Beat, 1990; Baby Talk, 1991; Sisters, 1992-94; ER, 1994-99; Films: Return of the Killer Tomatoes, 1988; Red Surf, 1990; Unbecoming Age, 1993; From Dusk Till Dawn, 1998; Batman and Robin, 1998; The Peacemaker, 1998; Out of Sight, 1998; The Thin Red Line, 1998; Three Kings, 1999; The Perfect Storm, 1999; Where Art Thou? 2000; Spy Kids, 2001; Ocean's Eleven, 2001; Welcome to Collinwood, 2002; Solaris, 2003; Confessions of a Dangerous Mind (director), 2003; Spy Kids 3-D: Game Over, 2003; Intolerable Cruelty, 2003. Address: Creative Artists, 9830 Wilshire Boulevard, Beverly Hills, CA 90212, USA.

**CLOONEY Rosemary,** b. 23 May 1928, Maysville, Kentucky, USA. Singer. Appointments: Early appearances with sister, Betty; Joined saxophonist Tony Pastor's band, 1945; Solo Artiste, 1946-. Creative Works: Films include: The Stars Are Singing, 1953; Here Come The Girls, 1954; Red Garters, 1954; Deep In My Heart, 1954; White Christmas, 1954; Albums include: Deep in My Heart, 1954; Hollywood's Best, 1955; Blue

Rose, 1956; Clooney Times, 1957; Ring A Round Rosie with the Hi-Lo's, 1957; Swing Around Rosie, 1958; Fancy Meeting You Here with Bing Crosby, 1958; The Ferrers At Home, 1958; Hymns From the Heart, 1959; Rosemary Clooney Swings Softly, 1960; A Touch of Tabasco, 1960; Clap Hands, Here Comes Rosie, 1960; Rosie Solves The Swingin' Riddle, 1961; Country Hits From the Past, 1963; Love, 1963; Thanks For Nothing, 1964; That Travelin' Two Beat, 1965; Look My Way, 1976; Nice to be Around, 1977; Here's To My Lady, 1979; Rosemary Clooney Sings Harold Arien, 1983; My Buddy, 1983; Rosemary Clooney Sings The Lyrics of Johnny Mercer, 1987; Show Tunes, 1989; Girl Singer, 1992; Singles include: You're Just In Love; Beautiful Brown Eyes; Come On - My House; Tenderly; Half As Much; Botcha Me; Too Old to Cut the Mustard (with Marlene Dietrich); The Night Before Christmas; Hey There; This Ole House; Mambo Italiano; Mangos. Publication: This For Remembrance. Address: c/o Production Central, 3500 West Olive, Suite 1420, Burbank, CA 91505, USA.

**CLOSE Glenn,** b. 19 March 1947, Greenwich, Connecticut, USA. Actress. m. (1) C Wade, divorced, (2) J Marlas, 1984, divorced, 1 daughter (with J Starke). Education: William and Mary College. Career: Co-owner, The Leaf and Bean Coffee House, 1991-; Films include: The World According to Garp, 1982; The Big Chill, 1983; The Stone Boy, 1984; Jagged Edge, 1985; Fatal Attraction, 1987; Dangerous Liaisons, 1989; Hamlet, 1989; The House of Spirits, 1990; Hamlet, 1990; 101 Dalmatians, 1996; Mars Attacks! 1996; Air Force One, 1997; Paradise Road, 1997; Tarzan, 1999; Cookie's Fortune, 1999; 102 Dalmatians, 2000; The Safety of Objects, 2001; Pinocchio (voice), 2002. Theatre includes: The Rules of the Game; A Streetcar Named Desire; King Lear; The Rose Tattoo; Death and the Maiden; Sunset Boulevard. Address: Creative Artists Agency, 9830 Wilshire Boulevard, Beverly Hills, CA 90212, USA.

**CLOSSICK Peter,** b. 18 May 1948, London. Artist. m. Joyce, 1 daughter. Education: Shoe Design, Leicester College of Art, 1969; BA, Fine Art, Camberwell College of Art, 1978; ATC, Goldsmiths London University, 1979. Appointments: Part-time Art Lecturer: Oxford-Brookes University; Open College of the Arts; Greenwich College; Art Consultant, Blackheath Conservatoire of Music and Art. Publications: Dictionary of Artists in Britain Since 1945, Art Dictionaries Ltd; Who's Who in Art Since 1927, Art Trade Press Ltd; Painting Without A Brush, Studio Vista; The London Group – 90th Anniversary, Tate Britain. Honour: Elected London Group President, 2000. Membership: President, The London Group, 2000-05. Address: 358 Lee High Road, Lee Green, London SE12 8RS, England. E-mail: enquiries@thelondongroup.com Website: www.redstart.net/clossick/index.html

**CLOUDSLEY Anne, ((Jessie) Anne Cloudsley-Thompson),** b. 20 March 1915, Reigate, Surrey, England. Physiotherapist; Artist. m. Professor JL Cloudsley-Thompson, 3 sons. Education: MCSP, ME, LET, University College Hospital, London, England; LCAD, DipBS, Byam Shaw School of Art, University of the Arts, London. Appointments: Established Physiotherapy Department, Hatfield Military Hospital, Hertfordshire, England, 1940-42; Superintendent Physiotherapist, Peripheral Nerve Injuries Centre, Wingfield Orthopaedic Hospital, Oxford, England, 1942-44; Superintendent Physiotherapist, Omdurman General Hospital, Sudan, 1960-71; Founder and Honorary Gallery Curator, Africa Centre, London, 1978-82; Visiting Lecturer, Fine Art, University of Nigeria, Nsukka, 1981; Lecturer, Lithography, Working Men's College, London NW1, 1982-91. Publications: Women of Omdurman: life, love and the cult of virginity, 1983, reprinted 1983, 1984, 1987;

Articles and reviews; Numerous exhibitions: Individual: AFD Gallery, 1977; Mandeer Gallery, 1981; Ecology Centre, 1990; Budapest, 1990; Walk Gallery, 2004; Little Known Aspects of Sudanese Life (throughout Europe 1982-84); Group: The Royal Academy Summer Exhibition, 1992, 1993; Fresh Art, 2001, 2002, 2003; Cork Street, 2003; Discerning Eye, Mall Gallery, 2004; Bankside, 2005. Memberships: Chartered Society of Physiotherapy, 1935-; Print Makers Council, 1996-; Elected to The London Group, 2002-. Address: 10 Battishill Street, London N1 1TE, England.

**CLOUDSLEY-THOMPSON John Leonard,** b. 23 May 1921, Murree, India. Professor of Zoology. m. J Anne Cloudsley, 3 sons. Education: BA, 1947, MA, 1949, PhD, 1950, Pembroke College, Cambridge; DSc, University of London, 1960. Appointments: War Service, 1940-44; Lecturer in Zoology, King's College, University of London, 1950-60; Professor of Zoology, University of Khartoum and Keeper, Sudan Natural History Museum, 1960-71; Professor of Zoology, Birkbeck College, University of London, 1972-86; Professor Emeritus, 1986-. Publications: Over 50 books, including: Ecophysiology of Desert Arthropods and Reptiles, 1991; The Nile Quest, novel, 1994; Biotic Interactions in Arid Lands, 1996; Teach Yourself Ecology, 1998; The Diversity of Amphibians and Reptiles, 1999; Ecology and Behaviour of Mesozoic Reptiles, 2005; Monographs, 11 Children's natural history books: Contributions to Encyclopaedia Britannica, Encyclopedia Americana; Articles in professional journals. Honours: Honorary Captain, 1944; Royal African Society Medal, 1969; Institute of Biology KSS Charter Award, 1981; Honorary DSc, Khartoum and Silver Jubilee Gold Medal, 1981; Biological Council Medal, 1985; J H Grundy Memorial Medal, Royal Army Medical College, 1987; Peter Scott Memorial Award, British Naturalists' Association, 1993; Fellow, Honoris Causa, Linnean Society, 1997; Listed in national and international biographical publications. Memberships: Liveryman, Worshipful Company of Skinners; FI Biol; FWAAS; FRES; FLS; FZS. Address: 10 Battishill Street, Islington, London N1 1TE, England.

**CLOUGH Mark Gerard,** b. 13 May 1953, Kuala Lumpar. Lawyer. m. Joanne Elizabeth Dishington, 2 sons, 1 daughter. Education: Ampleforth; MA, University of St Andrews. Appointments: Called to the Bar, Gray's Inn, 1978; Solicitor, 1995; Partner, Competition and Trade Gp, Ashurst, 1995; Solicitor Advocate, Supreme Court of England and Wales, 1996; Queen's Counsel, 1999. Publications: Shipping and EC Competition Law, 1990; EC Merger Regulation, 1995; Butterworth's European Community Law Service EC Anti-Dumping, Subsidies and Trade Barrier Regulation Sections, 1997; Trade and Telecoms, 2002; A True European Essays for Judge David Edward: Chapter 13 – Collective Dominance – The Contribution of the Community Courts, 2003; Contributed articles to numerous journals. Memberships: Director, Camden People's Theatre; Chairman, Solicitors Association of Higher Court Advocates; Member, Advisory Board, British Institute of International and Comparative Law; Competition Law Forum; Member, IBA Anti-trust and International Trade Law Committee, Associate Member, American Bar Association.

**CLUYSENAAR Anne, (Alice Andrée),** b. 15 March 1936, Brussels, Belgium (Irish citizen). Retired Lecturer; Poet; Songwriter; Librettist; Painter. m. Walter Freeman Jackson, 30 October 1976. Education: BA, Trinity College, Dublin, 1957; University of Edinburgh, 1963; Huddersfield Polytechnic, 1972-73. Appointments: Lecturer, King's College, Aberdeen, 1963-65, University of Lancaster, England, 1965-71, University of Birmingham, England, 1973-76, Sheffield City Polytechnic, England, 1976-89; Part-time Lecturer, University of Wales,

Cardiff, 1989-2002. Publications: A Fan of Shadows, 1967; Nodes, 1971; English Poetry Since 1960 (contributor), 1972; Aspects of Literary Stylistics, 1976; Selected Poems of James Burns Singers (editor), 1977; Poetry Introduction 4, 1978; Double Helix, 1982; Timeslips: New and Selected Poems, 1997; The Life of Metrical and Free Verse by Jon Silkin (contributor), 1997; Poets on Poets, Henry Vaughan, 1997; Henry Vaughan, Selected Poems, 2004; The Hare That Hides Within, 2004. Memberships: Usk Valley Vaughan Association; Second Light; Fellow, Welsh Academy. Address: Little Wentwood Farm, Llantrisant, Usk, Gwent NP15 1ND, Wales. E-mail: anne.cluy senaar@virgin.net

**COBB David Jeffery,** b. 12 March 1926, Harrow, Middlesex, England. Freelance Writer; Poet. 2 sons, 3 daughters. Education: BA, Bristol, 1954; PGCE, 1955. Appointments: German Teacher, Nottinghamshire, 1955-58; Programme Officer, UNESCO Institute of Education, Hamburg, 1958-62; English Teacher, British Council, Bangkok, 1962-68; Assistant Professor, Asian Institute of Technology, Bangkok, 1968-72; Manager, RDU, Longman Group Ltd, 1972-84; Freelance, 1985-. Publications: A Leap in the Light; Mounting Shadows; Jumping From Kiyomizu; Chips off the Old Great Wall; The Shield-Raven of Wittenham; The Spring Journey to the Saxon Shore; The Iron Book of British Haiku; A Bowl of Sloes; The Genius of Haiku, Readings From R H Blyth; Forefathers; Palm; The British Museum Haiku. Contributions to: Rialto; Blithe Spirit; Modern Haiku; Frogpond; HQ; Snapshots. Honours: 1st Prize, Cardiff International Haiku Competition, 1991; 2nd Prize, HSA Merit Book Awards, 1997 and 2002; 1st Prize, Itoen International Contest, Japan, 1993; The Sasakawa Prize for Innovation in the Field of Haikai, 2004. Memberships: British Haiku Society, president, 1997-2002; Haiku Society of America; John Clare Society; Royal Bangkok Sports Club. Address: Sinodun, Shalford, Braintree, Essex CM7 5HN, England.

**COCKCROFT John Anthony Eric,** b. 9 August 1934, England. Freelance Consultant. m. Education: ATI, C Text, Burnley College of Science and Technology, 1954; BA, 1959, MA, 1963, Modern History and Economics, Cambridge University; MLitt, Politics/Strategic Studies, Aberdeen University, 1979; PhD, Strategy & Science & Technology Policy, Manchester University, 1982. Appointments: National Service, Commissioned, Sword of Honour, Army, 1954-56; Management Trainee, UK private industry including Ford Motor Co, 1959-65; Fellow, Ministry of Economic Co-ordination, Athens, Greece, OECD, Paris, 1965-67; Adviser, Inter-ministerial Investment Advisory Committee, Kabul, Afghanistan, FCO/ODA, 1970-71; Expert, Ministry of National Economy, Jordan, UNIDO, Vienna, 1971-72; Managing Director, Anglo-German Textile Manufacturing Co, UK, 1973-78; Fellow, Greece & Turkey, NATO, Brussels, 1979-80; Consultant, Dar Es Salaam, Tanzania, UNIDO, Vienna, 1980; Professor of Economics, University of Makurdi, Nigeria, 1982; Killam Research Fellow, Strategy, Centre for Foreign Policy Studies, Dalhousie University, Canada, 1983-84; Team Leader, Bangladesh, Cotton Industry, World Bank/IFC/PriceWaterhouse, 1985-86; Managing Director, private company spinning, weaving and making-up, UK, 1986-89; Manager, subsidiary of Allied Textiles plc, Bradford, UK, 1990-91; Consultant, Stoddard Sekers plc, Renfrew, Scotland, UK, 1991-94; Team Leader, Cotton Sector Assessment Project, Ethiopia, USAID, Washington, 1994; Team Leader, Agricultural Reform Project, Bangladesh, EU, 1994-97; Consultant, Agricultural Policy, USAID/APRP, Cairo, 1997; Professor and Adviser in International Relations, Queen's University, Dhaka, 1997-98; Senior Management Consultant, Dhaka, Helen Keller, New York, 1998-99; Honorary Visiting Fellow, Centre for Defence Economics, University of York, UK,

2000-03; Consultant, Orissa, India, public sector, DFID/Adam Smith Institute, London, 2000; Consultant, W & E Africa, ITC/UN, Geneva, 2000; Consultant, Kosovo State Enterprise Conversion, EAR/UNMIK, EU, 2000; Product Development Consultant, London, 2001-; Private Consultant, Cairo, Egypt, 2001; Acting Team Leader, EU Enterprise Restructuring Project, Bosnia, 2002; ITC Nominee, IF Mission to Malawi, World Bank, Washington/ITC, Geneva, 2002; Specialist, Kosovo, Support for Economic & Institutional Reform, USAID Washington /SEGIR, 2003; Adviser, Haitian Economic Recovery and Opportunity Act, HERO, USAID Washington, 2003; Adviser, Textiles/Trade, WTO & AGOA, East and Southern Africa, Regional Agricultural Trade Expansion in Support, USAID Washington /RATES, 2003; Adviser, Southern African Global Competitiveness Hub, Regional Activity to promote Integration through Dialogue and Policy Implementation, USAID Washington/RAPID, 2003; Consultant in Mozambique, USAID, Washington/RAPID, 2004; Specialist, Paraguay Exports, USAID, Washington, DC, 2004; Consultant, Africa Caribbean Pacific (ACP) sector study, EU, Brussels, 2004; Expert, Southern Africa Global Competitiveness Hub, USAID, 2004. Publications: Science & Technology in Economic Development: The Pilot Teams, 1968; BMD, NATO, Europe and UK to Y2K, private paper, 2001; An Exercise in Contemporary Strategy: A Study in Military Power, Influence and Science & Technology in Determining Plausibility of a New Soviet Limited War Strategy 1972-81, PhD thesis, 1981; Intra-Alliance Economic Co-operation & Military Assistance, 1980; Over 25 reports for governments and international organisations; 4 letters to the editor on Global Security published in The Times, 2001-02. Honours: Textile Institute, Manchester; Textile Society, Bradford; Marksman, Army; Technical State Scholarship to Cambridge University. Memberships: Cavalry and Guards Club, London; Fellow, Textile Institute. Address: The Old Vicarage, Ledsham LS25 5LT, England. E-mail: cockcroftj@aol.com

**COCKER Jarvis Branson,** b. England. Singer. m. Camille Bidault-Waddington, 1 son. Education: St Martin's College of Art & Design. Appointments: Singer with Pulp (formerly named Arabacus Pulp), 1981-; Made Videos for Pulp, Aphex Twin, Tindersticks; Co-Producer, Do You Remember The First Time? (TV). Creative Works: Singles include: My Legendary Girlfriend, 1991; Razzmatazz, 1992; O U, 1992; Babies, 1992; Common People, 1995; Disco 2000, 1996; Albums include: It; Freaks; Separations; PulpIntro: The Gift Recordings; His 'N' Hers; Different Class, 1995; This is Hardcore, 1998. Address: c/o Savage & Best Ltd, 79 Parkway, London NW1 7PP, England.

**COCKER Joe,** b. 20 May 1944, Sheffield, South Yorkshire, England. Singer; Songwriter. Appointments: Northern Club circuit, with group, The Grease Band, 1965-69; Solo Artist, 1968-; Regular worldwide tours and major concert appearances. Creative Works: Singles: With a Little Help From My Friends, 1968; Delta Lady, 1969; The Letter, 1970; Cry Me a River, 1970; You Are So Beautiful, 1975; Unchain My Heart, 1987; When the Night Comes, 1990; Up Where We Belong. Honours: Grammy, Best Pop Vocal Performance, 1983; Academy Award, Best Film Song, 1983; Grammy Nomination, 1988. Address: c/o Roger Davies Management, 15030 Ventura Blvd #772, Sherman Oaks, CA 91403, USA.

**COCKING Edward Charles Daniel,** b. 26 September 1931, London, England. University Professor. m. Bernadette Keane, 1 son, 1 daughter. Education: Buckhurst Hill County High School, Essex; BSc, PhD, DSc, University of Bristol. Appointments: Head, Department of Botany, 1969-91, Professor of Botany, 1969-97, Emeritus Professor, 1997, Director, Centre for Crop Nitrogen Fixation, 1997-, University of Nottingham; Member,

Board of Trustees, Royal Botanic Gardens, Kew, 1983-93; Council of Royal Society, 1986-88; Member (Chairman, Plants & Environment Research Committee, 1990-94), Council of Agricultural & Food Research Council; Member (Chairman, Board of Directors, 1999-2003), Governing Body Rothamsted Research, 1991-; Research Fellow, 1995-97; Leverhulme Trust Emeritus Research Fellow, 2000-02. Publications: Numerous articles and publications in professional journals. Honours: Fellow, Royal Society, 1983; Member, Academia Europaea, 1993; Honorary Member, Hungarian Academy of Sciences, 1995; Fellow, Indian Academy of Agricultural Sciences, 2000; Fellow, World Innovation Foundation, 2003. Memberships: Fellow, Institute of Biology; Member, Biochemical Society; Member, Royal Microscopic Society; Member, Royal Society of Chemistry. Address: Centre for Crop Nitrogen Fixation, University of Nottingham, Nottingham NG7 2RD, England. E-mail: edward.cocking@nottingham.ac.uk

**COE Sebastian Newbold,** b. 29 September 1956. Member of Parliament. m. Nicola Susan Elliott, 1990, 2 sons, 2 daughters. Education: BSc Hons, Economics, Social History, Loughborough University. Career: Winner, Gold Medal for running 1500m and silver medal for 800m, Moscow Olympics, 1980; Gold medal for 1500m and silver medal for 800m, Los Angeles Olympics, 1984; European 800m Champion, Stuttgart, 1986; World Record Holder at 800m, 1000m and mile, 1981; Research Assistant, Loughborough University, 1981-84; Member, 1983-89, Vice Chairman, 1986-89, Chairman, Olympic Review Group, 1984-85, Sports Council; Member, HEA, 1987-92; Olympic Committee, Medical Commission, 1987-; Conservative MP for Falmouth and Camborne, 1992-; PPS to Deputy PM, 1995-96; Assistant Government Whip, 1996-97; Private Secretary to Leader of the Opposition, The Rt Hon William Hague, MP, 1997-2001; Council Member, International Association of Athletic Federations, 2003-; Chairman, London 2012 Olympic and Paralympic Bid, 2004. Publications: Running Free, with David Miller, 1981; Running for Fitness, with Peter Coe, 1983; The Olympians, 1984, 1996; More Than a Game, 1992; Born to Run (autobiography), 1992. Memberships: Associate Member, Academie des Sports, France; Athletes Commission, IOC; IOC Medical Commission, 1988-94; Member, Sport For All Commission, 1998-; IOC Commission 2000, 1999. Address: House of Lords, London SW1A 0PW, England.

**COEN Ethan,** b. 1958, St Louis Park, Minnesota, USA. Film Producer; Screenwriter. m. Education: Princeton University. Appointments: Screenwriter with Joel Coen, Crime Wave (formerly XYZ Murders); Producer, Screenplay, Editor, Blood Simple, 1984. Creative Works: Films: Raising Arizona, 1987; Miller's Crossing, 1990; Barton Fink, 1991; The Hudsucker Proxy, 1994; Fargo, 1996; The Naked Man; The Big Lebowski, 1998; O Brother, Where Art Thou? 2000; The Man Who Wasn't There, 2001; Fever in the Blood, 2002. Publication: Gates of Eden, 1998. Address: c/o UTA, 9560 Wilshire Boulevard, Beverly Hills, CA 90212, USA.

**COEN Joel,** b. 1955, St Louis Park, Minnesota, USA. Film Director; Screenwriter. Divorced. Education: Simon's Rock College; New York University. Appointments: Assistant Editor, Fear No Evil, Evil Dead; Worked with Rock Video Crews; Screenwriter with Ethan Coen, Crime Wave (formerly XYZ Murders). Creative Works: Films: Blood Simple, 1984; Raising Arizona, 1987; Miller's Crossing, 1990; Barton Fink, 1991; The Hudsucker Proxy, 1994; Fargo, 1996; The Big Lebowski; O Brother, Where Art Thou? 2000; The Man Who Wasn't There, 2001. Honours include: Best Director Award, Cannes International Film Festival, 1996. Address: c/o UTA, 9560 Wilshire Boulevard, Beverly Hills, CA 90212, USA.

**COHEN Leonard,** b. 21 September 1934, Montreal, Canada. Singer; Songwriter. 2 children. Education: McGill University. Creative Works: Recordings include: Songs of Leonard Cohen, 1967; Songs of Love and Hate, 1971; Live Songs, 1972; New Skin for the Old Ceremony, 1973; Best of Leonard Cohen, 1975; Death of a Ladies Man, 1977; Recent Songs, 1979; Songs From A Room, 1969; Various Positions, 1984; I'm Your Man, 1988; The Future, 1992; Cohen Live, 1994; Ten New Songs, 2001; Field Commander Cohen, 2002; The Essential Leonard Cohen, 2003; Dear Heather, 2004. Publications: Let Us Compare Mythologies; The Favorite Game; Beautiful Losers; Energy of Slaves; Death of a Lady's Man; Book of Mercy; Stranger Music. Honours include: McGill Literature Award; Order of Canada. Address: c/o Macklam Feldman Management, 200-1505 W 2nd Ave, Vancouver, BC V6H 3Y4, Canada.

**COHEN Robert,** b. 15 June 1959, London, England. Cellist; Conductor. m. Rachel Smith, 1987, 4 sons. Education: Purcell School; Guildhall School of Music; Cello studies with William Pleeth, Andre Navarra, Jacqueline du Pre and Mstislav Rostropovich. Appointments: Started playing cello, aged 5; Royal Festival Hall debut, aged 12; London recital debut, Wigmore Hall, aged 17; Tanglewood Festival, USA, 1978; Recording debut, Elgar Concerto, 1979; Concerts in USA, Europe and Eastern Europe, 1979-; Concerts worldwide with major orchestras and with conductors including Muti, Abbadao, Dorati, Sinopoli, Otaka, Mazur, Davis, Marriner and Rattle, 1980-; Director, Charleston Manor Festival, East Sussex, 1989-; Regular international radio and TV appearances; Conductor, various chamber orchestras, 1990-, symphony orchestras, 1997-; Visiting Professor, Royal Academy of Music, 1998-; Professor of Advanced Cello Studies, Conservatorio della Svizzera Italiana di Lugano, 2000-. Publications: Recordings include: Walton Concerto, 1995; Britten Cello Suite, 1997; Morton Feldman Concerto, 1997; Britten Cello Symphony, 1998; Sally Beamish Cello Concerto River, 1999; H K Gruber Cello Concerto, 2003. Honours: Winner, Young Concert Artists International Competition, New York, 1978; Piatigorsky Prize, Tanglewood Festival, 1978; Winner, UNESCO International Competition, Czechoslovakia, 1981. Memberships: Fellow, Purcell School for Young Musicians, 1992-. Address: True Music Management, 15 Birchwood Avenue, London N10 3BE, England. E-mail: infor@true-music.com Website: www.robertcohen.info

**COHEN-MUSHLIN Aliza,** b. 8 April 1937, Tel Aviv, Israel. Professor. Education: BSc, Biology and Chemistry, 1965, MA, Art History, 1974, Hebrew University; BMus, Harpsichord and Organ, Rubin Music Academy, 1972; PhD, Art History, Hebrew University and London University, 1981. Appointments: Senior Lecturer, 1989-2000, Director, Centre for Jewish Art, 1990-, Professor, 2000-, Hebrew University; Editor, Jewish Art, 1986-. Publications: 3 books. Honours: Honorary Professor, Braunschweig University, Germany, 2000. Memberships: Committee, Internationale Palaeographie Latine, 1993-; Steering Committee, Religious Heritage, Council of Europe, 1998-; Academy of Science, Braunschweig, Germany, 2000-. Address: Centre for Jewish Art, Hebrew University, Mt Scopus, Jerusalem 91905, Israel. E-mail: cja@vms.huji.ac.il Website: www.hum.huji.ac.il/cja

**COHN Mildred,** b. 12 July 1913, New York, USA. Biochemist. m. Henry Primakoff, 1 son, 2 daughters. Education: BA, Hunter College, 1931; MA, 1932, PhD, 1937, Columbia University. Appointments: Research Associate, Biochemistry, George Washington University, 1937-38; Research Associate, Biochemistry, Cornell Medical College, 1938-46; Research Associate, 1946-58; Associate Professor, 1958-1960, Biochemistry, Washington University, St Louis; Associate

Professor of Biochemistry and Biophysics, 1960-61; Full Professor, 1961-1982, Benjamin Rush Professor, 1978-1982, University of Pennsylvania School of Medicine; Career Investigator, American Heart Association, 1964-1978; Senior Member, Fox Chase Cancer Center, 1982-85. Publications: More than 150 articles and chapters in professional journals and books. Honours include: 9 Honorary Degrees and Garvan Medal, American Chemical Society, 1963; Cresson Medal, Franklin Institute, 1975; Chandler Medal, Columbia University; National Medal of Science; Distinguished Service Award, College of Physicians, Philadelphia; PA Governor's Award for Excellence in Science; Stein-Moore Award, Protein Society and many others. Memberships: Phi Beta Kappa; Sigma Xi; American Chemical Society; American Society of Biochemistry and Molecular Biology; American Academy of Arts and Sciences; National Academy of Sciences; American Philosophical Society. Address: University of Pennsylvania School of Medicine, Department of Biochemistry and Biophysics, 242 Anat/Chem, Philadelphia, PA 19104-6059, USA.

**COHN-SHERBOK Dan,** b. 1 February 1945, Denver Colorado, USA. Professor of Judaism. m. Lavinia Cohn-Sherbok. Education: BA, Williams College, 1962-66; BHL, MAHL, Hebrew Union College, 1966-71; PhD, Cambridge University, 1971-74. Appointments: Lecturer, Theology, University of Kent, Canterbury, 1975-97; Professor of Judaism, University of Wales, Lampeter, 1997-. Publications: The Jewish Heritage; Dictionary of Judaism and Christianity; Atlas of Jewish History; The Jewish Faith; The Hebrew Bible; Fifty Key Jewish Thinkers; Judaism; Judaism: History, Belief and Practice; Understanding the Holocaust; Holocaust Theology; Interfaith Theology; A Concise Encyclopaedia of Judaism; Jewish Mysticism: An Anthology; Judaism and Other Faiths; Jewish Petitionary Prayers; Modern Judaism. Honour: Honorary DD, Hebrew Union College. Memberships: London Society for the Study of Religion; Cymmrodian Society; Athenaeum; Williams Club. Address: Department of Theology and Religious Studies, University of Wales, Lampeter SA48 7ED, Wales.

**COLBORN Nigel,** b. 20 February 1944, Nottingham, England. Journalist; Presenter; Author; Gardener. m. Rosamund F M Hewlett, 10 November 1972, 2 sons, 2 daughters. Education: King's School, Ely, Cambridgeshire, England; BS, Cornell University, USA, 1968. Publications: The Classic Horticulturist, 1987; This Gardening Business (Humour), 1989; Leisurely Gardening, 1989; Family Piles (humour), 1990; The Container Garden, 1990; Short Cuts to Great Gardens, 1993; The Good Old Fashioned Gardener, 1993; Annuals and Bedding Plants, 1994; The Kirkland Acres (novel), 1994; The Congregation (novel), 1996; A Flower for Every Day, 1996; Weather of the Heart (novel), 1998; The Garden Floor, 2000. Contributions to: Newspapers and magazines. Honour: Royal Society of Arts, fellow. Memberships: Society of Authors; Royal Horticultural Society, council; Hardy Plant Society; Alpine Garden Society. Address: Wakefields, Hall Road, Hacconby PE10 0UY, England.

**COLE B J,** b. 17 June 1946, North London, England. Musician (pedal steel guitar); Producer. Career: Musician, Country Music circuit, London, 1964-; Pedal steel guitar player, Cochise; Founder member, producer, Hank Wangford Band; Leading exponent of instrument in UK; Currently prolific session musician and solo artiste; Leader, own group Transparent Music Ensemble; Replacement guitarist for the Verve, 1998-. Recordings: Solo albums: New Hovering Dog, 1972; Transparent Music, 1989; The Heart Of The Moment, 1995; As session musician: Tiny Dancer, Elton John, 1970; Wide Eyed And Legless, Andy Fairweather-Low, 1975; No Regrets, Walker

Brothers, 1976; City To City, Gerry Rafferty, 1978; Everything Must Change, Paul Young, 1984; Silver Moon, David Sylvian, 1986; Diet Of Strange Places, k d lang, 1987; Montagne D'Or, The Orb, 1995; Possibly Maybe, Björk, 1995; with Hank Wangford: Hank Wangford, 1980; Live, 1982; Other recordings with: Johnny Nash; Deacon Blue; Level 42; Danny Thompson; Alan Parsons Project; Shakin' Stevens; Beautiful South; John Cale; Echobelly.

**COLE Barry,** b. 13 November 1936, Woking, Surrey, England. Writer; Poet. m. Rita Linihan, 1959, 3 daughters. Appointments: Northern Arts Fellow in Literature, Universities of Durham and Newcastle-upon-Tyne, England, 1970-72. Publications: Blood Ties, 1967; Ulysses in the Town of Coloured Glass, 1968; A Run Across the Island, 1968; Moonsearch, 1968; Joseph Winter's Patronage, 1969; The Search for Rita, 1970; The Visitors, 1970; The Giver, 1971; Vanessa in the City, 1971; Pathetic Fallacies, 1973; The Rehousing of Scaffardi; Dedications, 1977; The Edge of the Common, 1989; Inside Outside: New and Selected Poems, 1997; Lola and the Train, 1999; Ghosts Are People Too, 2003. Contributions to: New Statesman; Spectator; Listener; Times Educational Supplement; Times Higher Educational Supplement; Critical Survey; Atlantic Monthly; Tribune; London Magazine; Transatlantic Review; Observer; Guardian. Address: 68 Myddelton Square, London EC1R 1XP, England.

**COLE Natalie Maria,** b. 6 February 1950, Los Angeles, California, USA. Singer. m. (1) Marvin J Yancy, 30 July 1976, divorced, (2) Andre Fischer, 17 September 1989, divorced. Education: BA, Child Psychology, University of Massachusetts, 1972. Career: Stage debut, 1962; Solo recording artist, 1975-; Major concerts worldwide include: Tokyo Music Festival, 1979; Nelson Mandela 70th Birthday Concert, Wembley, 1988; Nelson Mandela tribute, Wembley, 1990; John Lennon Tribute Concert, Liverpool, 1990; Homeless benefit concert with Quincy Jones, Pasadena, 1992; Rainforest benefit concert, Carnegie Hall, 1992; Commitment To Life VI, (AIDs benefit concert), Los Angeles, 1992; Television appearances include: Sinatra And Friends, 1977; Host, Big Break, 1990; Motown 30, 1990; Tonight Show, 1991; Entertainers '91, 1991; Recordings: Hit singles: This Will Be, 1975; Sophisticated Lady, 1976; I've Got Love On My Mind, 1977; Our Love (Number 1, US R&B chart), 1977; Gimme Some Time (duet with Peabo Bryson), 1980; What You Won't Do For Love (duet with Peabo Bryson), 1980; Jump Start, 1987; I Live For Your Love, 1988; Pink Cadillac, 1988; Miss You Like Crazy (Number 1, US R&B charts), 1989; Wild Women Do, from film Pretty Woman, 1990; Unforgettable (duet with father Nat "King" Cole), 1991; Smile Like Yours, 1997; Albums: Inseparable, 1975; Natalie, 1976; Unpredictable, 1977; Thankful, 1978; Natalie...Live!, 1978; I Love You So, 1979; Don't Look Back, 1980; Happy Love, 1981; Natalie Cole Collection, 1981; I'm Ready, 1982; Dangerous, 1985; Everlasting, 1987; Good To Be Back, 1989; Unforgettable...With Love (Number 1, US), 1991; The Soul Of Natalie Cole, 1991; Take A Look, 1993; Holly and Ivy, 1994; Stardust, 1996; This Will Be, 1997; Snowfall on the Sahara, 1999; with Peabo Bryson: We're The Best Of Friends, 1980. Honours: Numerous Grammy Awards include: Best New Artist, 1976; Best Female R&B Vocal Performance, 1976, 1977; 5 Grammy Awards for Unforgettable, including Best Song, Best Album, 1992; 5 NAACP Image Awards, 1976, 1988, 1992; American Music Awards: Favourite Female R&B Artist, 1978; Favourite Artist, Favourite Album, 1992; Soul Train Award, Best Single, 1988; Various Gold discs. Memberships: AFTRA; NARAS. Address: c/o Dan Cleary Management Associates, Suite 1101, 1801 Avenue Of The Stars, Los Angeles, CA 90067, USA.

**CÖLFEN Helmut,** b. 24 July 1965, Krefeld, Germany. Scientist; Chemist. m. Stefanie Sender, 2 daughters. Education: Chemistry Studies, Gerhard-Mercator University, Duisburg, 1985-91; PhD, Chemistry, 1993; Postdoctoral Studies, National Centre for Macromolecular Hydrodynamics, Nottingham, England, 1993-95; Habilitation, Max-Planck-Institute for Colloids and Interfaces, 1995-2001. Appointments: Research Assistant, University of Duisburg, 1991-93; Postdoctoral Studies, 1993-95; Scientist, Head of Analytical Services in Colloid Chemistry, Head of Biominetic Mineralisation Group, Max-Planck-Institute for Colloids and Interfaces, 1995-; Private Dozent, Potsdam University, 2004-. Publications: More than 100 papers as co-author and first author in scientific journals. Honours: Graduate Scholarship, University of Duisburg, 1991-93; Hochschulabsolventenpreis, University of Duisburg, 1991; Studienabschlussstipendium, Fonds der chemischen Industrie, 1993; Dr Hermann Schnell Award, German Chemical Society; Travel Award, Macromolecular Chemistry Division, German Chemical Society. Membership: German Chemical Society. Address: Max-Planck-Institute for Colloids and Interfaces, Colloid Chemistry, D-14424 Potsdam, Germany. E-mail: coelfen@mpikg.mpg.de

**COLGAN Michael Anthony,** b. 17 July 1950, Dublin, Ireland. Film and TV Producer; Theatre Producer and Director. m. Susan FitzGerald, 1 son, 2 daughters. Education: BA, Trinity College, Dublin. Appointments: Director, Abbey Theatre, Dublin, 1974-78; Co-Manager, Irish Theatre Company, 1977-78; Manger, 1978-81, Artistic Director, 1981-83, Member Board of Directors, 1983-, Dublin Theatre Festival; Artistic Director, Board Member, Gate Theatre Dublin, 1984-; Executive Director, Little Bird Films, 1986-; Founder, Belacqua Film Company, 1988; Co-Founder, Blue Angel Film Company, 1999 (producers of The Beckett Film Project 2000, commissioned by Channel 4 and RTE to film all 19 of Beckett's plays); Artistic Director Parma Film Festival, 1982; Chairman, St Patrick's Festival, 1996-99; Board Member: Millennium Festivals Ltd, Laura Pels Foundation, New York. Theatre productions include: I'll Go On; Juno and the Paycock; Salomé; Three Sisters; Molly Sweeney; Three Beckett Festivals (all 19 Samuel Beckett stage plays), The Gate, 1991, Lincoln Center, New York, 1996, Barbican, London, 1999; Three Pinter Festivals: The Gate, 1994, 1997, Lincoln Center, New York, 2001. Honours: Sunday Independent Arts Awards, 1985, 1986; Eamonn Andrews Award for Excellence, 1996; People of the Year Award, 1999; Doctor in Laws Honoris Causa, Trinity College, Dublin, 2000; Peabody Award, 2003. Memberships: Irish Arts Council, 1989-94; Governing Authority Dublin City University. Address: The Gate Theatre, 1 Cavendish Road, Dublin 1, Ireland. E-mail: info@gate-theatre.ie

**COLLAZOS Julio,** b. 11 March 1955, Tordehumos, Valladolid, Spain. Medical Doctor. Education: Medical Degree, Complutense University School of Medicine, Madrid, Spain, 1979; Doctor in Medicine, Autonoma University School of Medicine, Madrid, Spain, 1990. Appointments: Residency and Fellowship, Internal Medicine, Jimnez Díaz Foundation, Madrid, Spain, 1980-84; Attending Physician, Hospital Provincial, Alicante, Spain, 1984-87; Associate Professor, Alicante University School of Medicine, Alicante, Spain, 1984-87; Attending Physician, 1987-93, Chief Infectious Diseases Section, 1993-, Hospital de Galdakao, Vizcaya, Spain. Publications: Doctoral Thesis: The Tumor Makers in Benign Liver Disease; Many professional articles and book chapters. Honours: Medical Degree with honours, Complutense University School of Medicine; Doctor in Medicine cum laude, Autonoma University School of Medicine; Nominated for numerous honours and awards from American Biographical Institute and International Biographical Centre, England. Memberships: President, Association of Infectious

Diseases, Vizcaya, Spain; Fellow, American Biographical Institute, Raleigh, North Carolina, USA. Address: Section of Infectious Diseases, Hospital de Galdakao, 48960 Vizcaya, Spain.

**COLLINGBOURNE Stephen,** b. 15 August 1943, Dartington, Devon, England. Artist. 1 son, 1 daughter. Appointments: Lecturer, Dartington College of Art, 1965-70; Worked at Serpentine Gallery, London, 1971; Assistant to Robert Adams, sculptor, 1972; Lived and worked in Malaya, 1972-73; Fellow in Sculpture, University College of Wales, 1974; Lecturer in Sculpture, Edinburgh College of Art, 1976-99; Early retirement, 1999-; One man exhibitions include: Bluecoat Gallery, Liverpool, 1972; British Council, Kuala Lumpur, Malaysia, 1973; Plymouth City Art Gallery, 1977; Southampton City Art Gallery, 1977; Informal Works on Paper, Edinburgh Festival, 1990; High Cross House, Dartington, Devon, 1997; Galleri Viktor, Nykarleby, Finland, 1998; Group exhibitions include: Serpentine Gallery, London, 1972; Kettles Yard, Cambridge, 1973; Built in Scotland Touring Show, Camden Arts Centre, London, 1983; Renlands Konstmuseum, Karleby, Finland, 1998. Honours: Commissions include: Leicester University, 1974; Collections include: Welsh Arts Council; Leicester City Art Centre; Edinburgh City Art Gallery; Awards and prizes from: Arts Council of Great Britain, 1972; John Moore's Liverpool, 1972; The British Council, 1973; Welsh Arts Council, 1975; Arts Council of Great Britain, 1975; Welsh Arts Council, 1976; Royal Scottish Academy, 1977, 1978; Scottish Arts Council, 1985. Address: Tofts, Blyth Bridge, West Linton, EH46 7AJ, Scotland.

**COLLINS Jackie,** b. England. Novelist; Short Story Writer; Actress. m. Oscar Lerman. Creative Works: Screenplays: Yesterday's Hero; The World in Full of Married Men; The Stud. Publications: The World is Full of Married Men, 1968; The Stud, 1969; Sunday Simmons and Charlie Brick, 1971; Sinners, 1981; Lovehead, 1974; The Love Killers, 1977; The World is Full of Divorced Women, 1975; Lovers & Gamblers, 1977; The Bitch, 1979; Chances, 1981; Hollywood Wives, 1983; Lucky, 1985; Hollywood Husbands, 1986; Rock Star, 1988; Lady Boss, 1990; American Star, 1993; The World is Full of Married Men, 1993; Hollywood Kids, 1994; Dangerous Kiss, 1999; Hollywood Wives: The New Generation, 2001; Lethal Seduction, 2001. Address: c/o Simon & Schuster, 1230 Avenue of the Americas, New York, NY 10020, USA.

**COLLINS Joan,** b. 23 May 1933, London, England. Actress. m. (1) Maxwell Reed, 1954, divorced, 1957, (2) Anthony Newley, 1963, divorced, 1970, 1 son, 1 daughter, (3) Ronald Kass, 1972, divorced, 1983, 1 daughter, (4) Peter Holm, 1985, divorced, 1987, (5) Percy Gibson, 2002. Career: Films include: I Believe in You, 1952; Girl in Red Velvet Swing, 1955; Land of the Pharaohs, 1955; The Opposite Sex, 1956; Rally Round Flag Boys, 1957; Sea Wife, 1957; Warning Shot, 1966; The Executioner, 1969; Revenge, 1971; The Big Sleep, Tales of the Unexpected, 1977; Stud, 1979; The Bitch, 1980; Nutcracker, 1982; Decadence, 1994; Hart to Hart, 1995; Annie: A Royal Adventure, 1995; In the Bleak Midwinter, 1995; The Clandestine Marriage, 1998; The Flintstones-Viva Rock Vegas, 1999; Joseph and the Amazing Technicolor Dreamcoat, 1999; These Old Broads, 2000; Ellis in Glamourland, 2004. Numerous TV appearances include: Dynasty, 1981-89; Cartier Affair, 1984; Sins, 1986; Monte Carlo, 1986; Tonight at 8.30, 1991; Pacific Palisades (serial), 1997; Will and Grace (USA), 2000. Publications: J C Beauty Book, 1980; Katy: A Fight for Life, 1981; Past Imperfect, 1984; Prime Time, 1988; Love and Desire and Hate, 1990; My Secrets, 1994; Too Damn Famous, 1995; Second Act, 1996; My Friends' Secrets, 1999; Star Quality,

2002; Joan's Way, 2003; Misfortune's Daughters, 2004. Honours: OBE, 1997. Address: c/o Paul Keylock, 16 Bulbecks Walk, South Woodham Ferrers, Essex, CM3 5ZN, England.

**COLLINS John Vincent,** b. 16 July 1938, London, England. Consultant Physician. m. Helen Eluned, 1 son, 1 daughter. Education: Guy's Hospital Medical and Dental Schools. Appointments: Consultant Physician, Royal Brompton Hospital, 1976-2003; Consultant Physician and Medical Director, Chelsea and Westminster Hospital, 1979-2003; Honorary Physician, Royal Hospital, Chelsea, 1979-2003; Senior Medical Advisor, Benenden Healthcare Society, 1979-; Group Medical Adviser, Smith and Nephew plc, 1987-. Publications: 2 monographs and 20 chapters in books; 150 peer reviewed clinical scientific papers on clinical lung physiology, asthma and heart/lung diseases. Honours: Research grants from: Department of Health, Medical Research Council, Chest, Heart and Stroke Association. Memberships: Fellow, Royal College of Physicians, London; British Thoracic Society; European Respiratory Society, London Society of Apothecaries. Address: Royal Brompton Hospital, Sydney Street, London SW3 6NP, England. E-mail: john.collins@chelwest.nhs.uk

**COLLINS Kenneth Darlington (Sir),** b. 12 August 1939, United Kingdom. Environmentalist. m. Georgina Frances Pollard, 1 son, 1 daughter. Education: BSc (Hons), Glasgow University, 1965; MSc, Strathclyde University, 1973. Appointments: Steelworks Apprentice, 1956-59; Planning Officer, 1965-66; Tutor Organiser, Workers Educational Association, 1966-67; Lecturer: Glasgow College of Building, 1967-69, Paisley College of Technology, 1969-79; Member: East Kilbride Town and District Council, 1973-79, Lanark County Council, 1973-75, East Kilbride Development Corporation, 1976-79; European Parliament: Deputy Leader, Labour Group, 1979-84, Chairman Environment Committee, 1979-84, 1989-99, Vice-Chairman, 1984-87, Socialist Spokesman on Environment, Public Health and Consumer Protection, 1984-89; Chairman, Scottish Environment Protection Agency, 1999-. Publications: Contributed to European Parliament reports; Various articles on European environment policy. Honour: Knights Bachelor, 2003. Honours: Honorary Degree of Doctor, University of Paisley, 2004. Memberships: Fellow, Royal Scottish Geographical Society; Fellow, Royal Geographical Society; Honorary Fellow, Chartered Institution of Water and Environment Management; Honorary Fellow, Chartered Institution of Wastes Management; Fellow, Industry and Parliament Trust; Honorary Senior Research Fellow, Department of Geography, Lancaster University; Board Member; Institute of European Environment Policy, Energy Action, Scotland; Former Board Member, Central Scotland Forest Trust; Board Member of Forward Scotland until 2003; Member, Management Board, European Environment Agency (nominated by the European Parliament); Honorary Vice-President, National Society for Clean Air; Vice-President: Royal Environmental Health Institute of Scotland, International Federation of Environmental Health, Town and Country Planning Association, Trading Standards Institute; Ambassador for Asthma UK; Honorary President, Scottish Association of Geography Teachers. Address: SEPA Erskine Court, The Castle Business Park, Stirling FK9 4TR, Scotland.

**COLLINS Pauline,** b. 3 September 1940, Exmouth, Devon, England. Actress. m. John Alderton, 2 sons, 1 daughter. Education: Central School of Speech & Drama. Creative Works: Stage Appearances: A Gazelle in Park Lane (stage debut, Windsor 1962); Passion Flower Hotel; The Erpingham Camp; The Happy Apple; The Importance of Being Ernest; The Night I Chased the Women with an Eel; Come as You Are; Judies; Engaged; Confusions; Romantic Comedy; Woman in Mind;

Shirley Valentine; Films: Shirley Valentine, 1989; City of Joy, 1992; My Mother's Courage, 1997; Paradise Road, 1997; Mrs Caldicott's Cabbage War, 2002; Man and Boy, 2002; TV appearances: Upstairs Downstairs; Thomas and Sarah; Forever Green; No-Honestly; Tales of the Unexpected; Knockback, 1984; Tropical Moon Over Dorking; The Ambassador, 1998; Man and Boy, 2002; Sparkling Cyanide, 2003. Publication: Letter to Louise, 1992. Honours include: Olivier Award, Best Actress, London; BAFTA Award; Tony, Drama Desk & Outer Critics' Circle Awards, New York; OBE, 2001.

**COLLINS Phil,** b. 30 January 1951, Chiswick, London, England. Pop Singer; Drummer; Composer. m. (1) 1976, 1 son, 1 daughter, (2) Jill Tavelman, 1984, divorced, 1 daughter, (3) Orianne Cevey, 1999, 2 sons. Education: Barbara Speake Stage School. Appointments: Former Actor, Artful Dodger in London Production of Oliver; Joined Rock Group, Genesis as Drummer, 1970, Lead Singer, 1975-96. Creative Works: Albums with Genesis: Selling England by the Pound, 1973; Invisible Touch, 1986; We Can't Dance, 1991; Solo Albums include: Face Value, 1981; Hello I Must Be Going, 1982; No Jacket Required, 1985; 12"Ers, 1987; But Seriously, 1989; Serivous Hits Live, 1990; Dance into the Light, 1996; Hits, 1998; A Hot Night in Paris, 1999; Testify, 2002; The Platinum Collection, 2004; Love Songs: A Compilation … Old and New, 2004; Solo Singles include: In the Air Tonight, 1981; You Can't Hurry Love, 1982; Against All Odds, 1984; One More Night, 1985; Easy Lover, 1985; Separate Lives, 1985; Groovy Kind of Love, 1988; Two Hearts, 1988; Another Day in Paradise, 1989; I Wish It Would Rain Down, 1990; Both Sides of the Story, 1993; Dance Into the Light, 1996; Soundtrack Albums: Against All Odds, 1984; White Nights, 1985; Buster, 1988; Tarzan, 1999; Brother Bear, 2003. Films include: Buster, 1988; Frauds, 1993. Honours include: 7 Grammy's; 6 Ivor Novello Awards; 4 Brits; 2 Awards, Variety Club of Great Britain; 2 Silver Clef's; 2 Elvis Awards; Academy Award for You'll be in my Heart from Tarzan film, 1999; Oscar for Best Original Song, You'll be in my Heart, 2000. Membership: Trustee, Prince of Wales Trust, 1983-97.

**COLLIS Louise Edith,** b. 29 January 1925, Arakan, Burma. Writer. Education: BA, History, Reading University, England, 1945. Publications: Without a Voice, 1951; A Year Passed, 1952; After the Holiday, 1954; The Angel's Name, 1955; Seven in the Tower, 1958; The Apprentice Saint, 1964; Solider in Paradise, 1965; The Great Flood, 1966; A Private View of Stanley Spencer, 1972; Maurice Collis Diaries (editor), 1976; Impetuous Heart: The story of Ethel Smyth, 1984. Contributions to: Books and Bookmen; Connoisseur; Art and Artists; Arts Review; Collectors Guide; Art and Antiques. Memberships: Society of Authors; International Association of Art Critics. Address: 65 Cornwall Gardens, London SW7 4BD, England.

**COLMAN Robert W,** b. 7 June 1935, New York, New York, USA. Physician. m. Roberta, 1 son, 1 daughter. Education: AB, summa cum laude, Harvard College; MD, cum laude, Harvard Medical School. Appointments: Assistant to Associate Professor Medicine, Harvard Medical School; Associate Professor to Professor of Medicine, University of Pennsylvania; Sol Sherry Professor of Medicine and Director, Sol Sherry Thrombosis Research Center, Temple University. Publications: 600 peer reviewed publications. Honours: International Society on Hemostasis and Thrombosis, Distinguished Career Award; Johnson and Johnson Focused Giving Program Award; American Heart Association Senior Investigator Award. Memberships include: American Society Biochemistry and Molecular Biology; American Society Investigative Pathology; American College of Physicians. Address: Sol Sherry Thrombosis Research Center,

Temple University School of Medicine, 3400 N Broad Street, Philadelphia, PA 19140, USA.

**COLOMBINI Fabiano,** b. 21 January 1950, Italy. Professor. m. Clori Giannini, 1 son. Education: Degree, cum laude, Economics, University of Pisa, 1974. Appointments: Assistant Professor, Banking, 1977, Associate Professor, Corporate Finance, 1983, Professor, Economics of Financial Intermediaries, University of Pisa; Research Scholar, London School of Economics and Political Science, 1982-83; Professor, Director, Institute of Economics of Financial Intermediaries, University of Cagliari, 1987-88; Lecturer, Economics of Financial Intermediaries, LUISS "G Carli" University of Rome, 1997-2004. Publications: Several books and articles in professional journals. Honours include: AIDEA Award, 1981. Memberships include: European Finance Association; Accademia Italiana di Economia Aziendale; Società Italiana di Storia della Ragioneria. Address: University of Pisa, Via C Ridolfi 10, 56124 Pisa, Italy.

**COLTART John,** b. 7 October 1943, Poole, Dorset, England. Consultant Cardiologist. 1 son, 3 daughters. Education: MD, MBBS, St Bartholomews Hospital, Medical College, 1962-72; MRCS; MRCP; FRCP, 1982; FACC, 1975; FESC, 1989. Appointments: Consultant, Cardiologist & Clinical Director, Guys & St Thomas Foundation Trust; Consultant Physician, Metropolitan Police; Civilian Consultant in Cardiology, Army & Royal Navy Federation; Consultant Cardiologist, King Edward VII & St Luke's Hospital for the Elderly. Publications: 2 books; Over 250 scientific papers in peer-reviewed journals. Honours: Buckston Browne Prize and Medal, Harveian Society; Paul Philip Reitlinger Prize, University of London. Memberships: FRCP; FACC; FESC; President, Cardiology Section, Royal Society of Medicine; Vice President, NCH Graduate Medical Federation. Address: 47 Weymouth Street, London W16 8NS, England.

**COLTRANE Robbie,** b. 31 March 1950, Glasgow, Scotland. Actor. m. Rhona Irene Gemmel, 2000, 1 son, 1 daughter. Education: Glasgow School. Appointments: Director, Producer, Young Mental Health (documentary), 1973. Creative Works: Stage appearances include: Waiting for God; End Game; The Bug; Mr Joyce is Leaving; The Slab Boys; The Transfiguration of Benno Blimpie; The Loveliest Night of the Year; Snobs and Yobs; Your Obedient Servant (one-man show), 1987; Mistero Buffo; TV: The Comic Strip Presents...; Five Go Mad In Dorset; The Beat Generation; War; Summer School; Five Go Mad in Mescalin; Susie; Gino; Dirty Movie; The Miner's Strike; The Supergrass (feature film); The Ebb-tide; Alice in Wonderland; Guest Roles: The Yong Ones; Kick Up the Eighties; The Tube; Saturday Night Live; Lenny Henry Show; Blackadder; Tutti Frutti; Coltrane in a Cadillac; Cracker; The Plan Man, 2003; Frasier, 2005; TV film: Boswell and Johnson's Tour of the Western Isles; Films include: Mona Lisa; Subway Riders; Britannia Hospital; Defence of the Realm; Caravaggio; Eat The Rich; Absolute Beginners; The Fruit Machine; Slipstream; Nuns on the Run; Huckleberry Finn; Bert Rigby, You're A Fool; Danny Champion of the World; Henry V; Let It Ride; The Adventures of Huckleberry Finn; Goldeneye; Buddy; Montana; Frogs for Snakes; Message in a Bottle; The World is Not Enough, 1999; On the Nose, 2000; From Hell, 2000; Harry Potter and the Philosopher's Stone, 2001; Harry Potter and the Chamber of Secrets, 2002; Van Helsing, 2004; Harry Potter and the Prisoner of Azkaban, 2004; Ocean's 12, 2005; Harry Potter and the Goblet of Fire, 2005. Publications: Coltrane in a Cadillac, 1992; Coltrane's Planes and Automobiles, 1999. Address: c/o CDA, 125 Gloucester Rd, London SW7 4TE, England.

**CONKLIN Patricia Ann,** b. 20 September 1954, New York, USA. Teacher. 1 son. Education: BS, Marymount Manhattan College, 1975. Appointments: Mathematics Teacher, 1981-, Senior Activities Moderator, 2000-, Student Council Moderator, 2003-, Cathedral High School. Honours: Multiple Award Winner; Listed in Who's Who publications and biographical dictionaries. Memberships: National Association of Student Councils; National Catholic Educational Association; NCM. Address: 251-40 &1 Avenue, Bellerose, NY 11426, USA. E-mail: pconlin@cathedralhs.org

**CONLON James,** b. 18 March 1950, New York, USA. Conductor. m. Jennifer Ringo, 2 daughters. Education: Bachelor of Music, Juilliard School of Music, New York, 1972. Appointments: Professional conducting debut, Spoleto Festival, 1971; New York debut, La Boheme, Juilliard School of Music, 1972; Member of orchestral conducting faculty, Juilliard School of Music, 1972-75; Debuts: New York Philharmonic, 1974, Metropolitan Opera, 1976, Covent Garden, 1979, Paris Opera, 1982, Maggio Musicale, Florence, 1985, Lyric Opera of Chicago, 1988, La Scala, Milan, 1993, Kirov Opera, 1994; Music Director, Cincinnati May Festival, 1979-; Music Director, Rotterdam Philharmonic, 1983-91; Chief Conductor, Cologne Opera, 1989-96; General Music Director, City of Cologne, Germany and Principal Conductor, Gurzenich Orchestra-Cologne Philharmonic, 1989-2002; Principal Conductor, Paris Opera, 1996-; Frequent guest conductor at leading music festivals; Conducted virtually all leading orchestras in North America; Numerous television appearances. Honours: Grand Prix du Disque, Cannes Classical Award and ECHO Classical Award; Officier de l'Ordre des Arts et des Lettres, 1996; Zemlinsky Prize, 1999; Legion d'Honneur, 2001. Address: c/o Shuman Associates, 120 West 58th Street, 8D, New York, NY 10019, USA. E-mail: shumanpr@cs.com

**CONNER Angela,** b. 12 July 1938, Great Britain. Sculptor. m. John Bulmer, 1 daughter. Career: Solo exhibitions include: Lincoln Center, New York; Browse and Darby and Hirschl Gallery, Cork Street, London; Friends of the Tate; Group exhibitions include: Gimpel Fils Gallery, New York; Royal Academy Summer Show; Victoria and Albert Museum; Carnegie Museum of Modern Art; Washington Museum; Sculpture by the Sea, Sydney, Australia, etc; Work in Collections include: Arts Council of Great Britain; National Portrait Gallery; Carnegie Museum of Modern Art, Pittsburgh; Jewish Museum, New York; Victoria and Albert Museum; House of Commons; National Trust; 10 Downing Street; French Embassy; and others; Private collections include: HRH Prince of Wales; Paul Mellon; Sir Roy Strong; President Chirac; John Major; Crown Prince of Saudi Arabia; Duke of Devonshire; Lord Sainsbury; Dame Drew Heinz; Gunter Sachs; Evelyn Rothschild; Mrs Henry Ford II; The Most Hon The Marquess of Salisbury; Commissions: Largest mobile sculpture in Europe, Dublin City; Large water mobile for Chatsworth, Derbyshire; Centre pieces for Heinz Hall Plaza, Pittsburgh, USA; Horsham, Surrey; Chesterfield, Derbyshire; Largest indoor mobile sculpture, Lovells, London; Mobile Arch, Longleat; Many bronze portraits and statues: HM The Queen; HM The Queen Mother; Tom Stoppard, Lucien Freud, Sir John Tavener; Dame Janet Baker, John Betjeman, Lord Rothschild, Sir Noel Coward, General de Gaulle, Camilla Parker Bowles, etc. Publications: Numerous in books, newspapers, magazines and TV. Honours: American Architect's Honour Award for Sculpture; British Society of Equestrian Art Annual Award; First Prize, Kinetic Art Organisation. Membership: Fellow, Royal Society of British Sculptors. Address: George and Dragon Hall, Mary Place, London W11 4PL, England. Website: www.angelaconner.co.uk

**CONNERY Sean (Thomas Connery),** b. 25 August 1930. Actor. m. (1) Diane Cilento, 1962, dissolved 1974, 1 son, (2) Micheline Roquebrune, 1975, 2 stepsons, 1 stepdaughter. Creative Works: Appeared in Films: No Road Back, 1956; Action of the Tiger, 1957; Another Time, Another Place, 1957; Hell Drivers, 1958; Tarzan's Greatest Adventure, 1959; Darby O'Gill and the Little People, 1959; On the Fiddle, 1961; The Longest Day, 1962; The Frightened City, 1962; Woman of Straw, 1964; The Hill, 1965; A Fine Madness, 1966; Shalako, 1968; The Molly Maguires, 1968; The Red Tent, 1969; The Anderson Tapes, 1970; The Offence, 1973; Zardoz, 1973; Ransom, 1974; Murder on the Orient Express, 1974; The Wind and the Lion, 1975; The Man Who Would Be King, 1975; Robin and Marian, 1976; The First Great Train robbery, 1978; Cuba, 1978; Meteor, 1979; Outland, 1981; The Man with the Deadly Lens, 1982; Wrong is Right, 1982; Five Days One Summer, 1982; Highlander, 1986; The Name of the Rose, 1987; The Untouchables, 1987; The Presido, 1989; Indiana Jones and the Last Crusade, 1989; Family Business, 1990; the Hunt for Red October, 1990; The Russia House, 1991; Highlander II - The Quickening, 1991; Medicine Man, 1992; Rising Sun, 1993; A Good Man in Africa, 1994; First Knight, 1995; Just Cause, 1995; The Rock, 1996; Dragonheart, 1996; The Avengers, 1998; Entrapment, 1999; Playing By Heart, 1999; Finding Forrester, 2000; The League of Extraordinary Gentlemen, 2003; James Bond in: Dr No, 1963; From Russia with Love, 1964; Goldfinger, 1965; Thunderball, 1965; You Only Live Twice, 1967; Diamonds are Forever, 1971; Never Say Never Again, 1983. Publication: Neither Shaken Nor Stirred, 1994. Honours include: BAFTA Lifetime Achievement Award, 1990; Man of Culture Award, 1990; Rudolph Valentino Award, 1992; Golden Globe Cecil B De Mille Award, 1996 BAFTA Fellowship, 1998. Address: c/o Creative Artists Agency Inc, 9830 Wilshire Boulevard, Beverly Hills, CA 90212, USA.

**CONNICK Harry Jr,** b. 1968, New Orleans, USA. Jazz Musician; Actor; Singer. m. Jill Goodacre, 1994, 3 daughters. Education: New Orleans Centre for the Creative Arts; Hunter College; Manhattan School of Music; Studies with Ellis Marsalis. Creative Works: Albums include: Harry Connick Jr, 1987; 20, 1989; We Are In Love, 1991; Lofty's Roach Soufflé, 1991; Blue Light, Red Light, 1991; Eleven, 1992; 25, 1992; When My Heart Finds Christmas, 1993; She, 1994; Star Turtle, 1996; To See You, 1997; Come By Me, 1999; Contribution to music for film, When Harry Meets Sally; Composed music for Thou Shalt Not (Broadway), 2001; Films as Actor: Memphis Belle; Little Man Tate, 1991; Independence Day; Excess Baggage; Hope Floats; Band Leader Harry Connick's Big Band. Honours include: Grammy Award. Address: Columbia Records, c/o Anita Nanko, 51/12, 550 Madison Avenue, PO Box 4450, New York, NY 10101, USA.

**CONNOLLY Billy,** b. 24 November 1942. Comedian; Actor; Playwright; Presenter. m. (1) Iris Connolly, 1 son, 1 daughter, (2) Pamela Stephenson, 1990, 3 daughters. Appointments: Apprentice Welder; Performed originally with Gerry Rafferty and The Humblebums; 1st Play, The Red Runner, staged at Edinburgh fringe, 1979. Creative Works: Theatre: The Great Northern Welly Boot Show; The Beastly Beatitudes of Balthazar B, 1982; TV include: Androcles and the Lion, 1984; Return to Nose and Beak (Comic Relief); South Bank Show Special (25th Anniversary Commemoration), 1992; Billy; Billy Connolly's World Tour of Scotland (6 part documentary), 1994; The Big Picture, 1995; Billy Connolly's World Tour of Australia, 1996; Erect for 30 Years, 1998; Billy Connolly's World Tour of England, Ireland and Wales, 2002; Gentleman's Relish; World Tour of New Zealand, 2004; Films include: Absolution, 1979; Bullshot, 1984; Water, 1984; The Big Man, 1989; Pocahontas,

1995; Treasure Island (Muppet Movie), 1996; Deacon Brodie (BBC Film), 1996; Mrs Brown, 1997; Ship of Fools, 1997; Still Crazy, 1998; Debt Collector, 1998; Boon Docksaints, 1998; Beautiful Joe, 2000; An Everlasting Piece, 2000; The Man Who Sued God, 2002; White Oleander, 2002; Gabriel and Me, 2002; The Last Samurai, 2003; Numerous video releases of live performances include: Bite Your Bum, 1981; An Audience with Billy Connolly, 1982; Numerous albums include: The Great Northern Welly Boot Show (contains No 1 hit DIVORCE); Pick of Billy Connolly. Publications include: Gullible's Travels, 1982. Honours include: Gold Disc, 1982; CBE, 2003. Address: c/o Tickety-boo Ltd, 94 Charity Street, Victoria, Gozo VCT 105, Malta. E-mail: tickety-boo@tickety-boo.com Website: www.billyconnolly.com

**CONNOR Alexandra,** b. 23 April 1959, England. Writer; Artist; Television Presenter. Education: Harrogate College. Career: One woman exhibitions: Marina Henderson Gallery, Chelsea; Richmond Gallery, London; Exhibited at Old Church Street Gallery, Chelsea; Portraits include: Kenneth Branagh, Brian Blessed, Anthony Sher, Frank Middlemass, Ken Dodd; Portraits commissioned by the Royal Shakespeare Company and exhibited in the RSC Theatre and the RSC Art Gallery; Works commissioned by Aspreys; Paintings collected in Europe, Japan and USA; Television includes: The Time The Place; Crystal Rose Show; Presented series called Past Masters for This Morning; Pebble Mill; Good Afternoon; 40 Minutes; Radio: In The Psychiatrist's Chair; John Dunne Show; Vanessa Felz Show; Dublin Radio; Midweek; Radio 5 Live; Viva Radio; Talk Radio UK. Books: Non-fiction: The Wrong Side of the Canvas, 1989; Rembrandt's Monkey, 1991; Private View, 2002; Fiction: The Witch Mark, 1986; Thomas, 1987; The Hour of the Angel, 1989; The Mask of Fortune, 1990; The Well of Dreams, 1992; The Green Bay Tree, 1993; Winter Women: Midsummer Men, 1994; The Moon is My Witness, 1997; Midnight's Smiling, 1998; Green Baize Road, 1999; An Angel Passing Over, 2000; Hunter's Moon, 2001; The Sixpenny Winner, 2002; A Face in the Locket, 2003; The Turn of the Tide, 2004; The Tailor's Wife, 2005; As Alexandra Hampton: The Experience Buyer, 1994; The Deaf House, 1995; Medical thrillers: Bodily Harm, 1998; Cipher, 1999; Articles in magazines and newspapers. Membership: FRSA. Address: c/o Ed Victor Ltd, 6 Bayley Street, Bedford Square, London WC1B 3HE, England. Website: www.alexandra-connor.co.uk

**CONNORS James Scott (Jimmy),** b. 2 September 1952, Illinois, USA. Tennis Player. m. Patti McGuire, 1978, 1 son, 1 daughter. Education: University of California, Los Angeles. Appointments: Amateur Player, 1970-72; Professional, 1972-; Australian Champion, 1974; Wimbledon Champion, 1974, 1982; USA Champion, 1974, 1976, 1978, 1982, 1983; South Australian Champion, 1973, 1974; WCT Champion, 1977, 1980; Grand Prix Champion, 1978; Commentator, NBC; Played Davis Cup for USA, 1976, 1981. Honour: BBC Overseas Sports Personality, 1982. Address: Tennis Management Inc, 109 Red Fox Road, Belleville, IL 62223, USA.

**CONRAN Jasper Alexander Thirlby,** b. 12 December 1959, London, England. Fashion Designer. Education: Bryanston School, Dorset; Parsons School of Art & Design, New York. Appointments: Fashion Designer, Managing Director, Jasper Conran Ltd, 1978-. Creative Works: Theatre Costumes: Jean Anouilh's The Rehearsal, Almeida Theatre, 1990; My Fair Lady, 1992; Sleeping Beauty, Scottish Ballet, 1994; The Nutcracker Sweeties, Birmingham Royal Ballet, 1996; Edward II, 1997; Arthur, 2000. Honours include: Fil d'Or (International Linen Award), 1982, 1983; British Fashion Council Designer of the Year Award, 1986-87; Fashion Group of America Award,

1987; Laurence Olivier Award for Costume Designer of the Year, 1991; British Collections Award (in British Fashions Awards), 1991. Address: Jasper Conran Ltd, 6 Burnsall Street, London SW3, England.

**CONROY (Donald) Pat(rick),** b. 26 October 1945, Atlanta, Georgia, USA. Writer. m. (1) Barbara Bolling, 1969, divorced 1977, 3 daughters, (2) Lenore Guerewitz, 1981, divorced 1995, 1 son, 5 daughters. Education: BA in English, The Citadel, 1967. Publications: The Boo, 1970; The Water is Wide, 1972; The Great Santini, 1976; The Lords of Discipline, 1980; The Prince of Tides, 1986; Beach Music, 1995. Honours: Ford Foundation Leadership Development Grant, 1971; Anisfield-Wolf Award, Cleveland Foundation, 1972; National Endowment for the Arts Award for Achievement in Education, 1974; Governor's Award for the Arts, Georgia, 1978; Lillian Smith Award for Fiction, Southern Regional Council, 1981; SC Hall of Fame, Academy of Authors, 1988; Golden Plate Award, American Academy of Achievement, 1992; Georgia Commission on the Holocaust Humanitarian Award, 1996; Lotos Medal of Merit for Outstanding Literary Achievement, 1993; Many others. Memberships: Authors Guild of America; PEN; Writers Guild. Address: c/o Houghton Mifflin Co, 222 Berkeley Street, Boston, MA 02116, USA.

**CONTE Amedeo Giovanni,** b. 24 May 1934, Pavia, Italy. Professor. m. Maria-Elisabeth Conte, 1 daughter. Education: Degree in Law, Collegio Ghislieri, University of Pavia, 1957; Research Scholar, Mathematical Logic and Philosophy, Münster, Germany, 1957-58; Research Scholar, Philosophy, Freiburg im Breisgau, Germany, 1959; PhD , University of Turin, 1964. Appointments: Professor, Philosophy of Law, University of Pavia, 1964-; Libero docente (Privatdozent), University of Turin, 1964-. Publications: 261 publications include: Main books: Saggio sulla completezza, 1962; Primi argomenti per una critica del normativismo, 1968; Deontische Logik und Semantik (co-editor), 1977; Filosofia del linguaggio normativo (3 vols), 1989-2001; Filosofia dell'ordinamento, 1997; Nella parola, 2004; Main articles: Minima deontica, 1988; Deontica wittgensteiniana, 1993; Nomotropismo, 2000; Unomia, 2001; Filosofia del baro, 2003; Oggetti falsi, 2003; Filosofia del deontico, 2004; Adelaster, 2004. Honours: Humboldt Scholarship, 1958-59; Member of Accademia Nazionale dei Lincei, Rome, 2000-. Memberships: Accademia Nazionale dei Lincei, Rome, 2000-; Editorial Boards: Doxa; Philosophy of Human Rights; Quaderni della Seconda Università di Napoli; Rivista internazionale di Filosofia del diritto; Sociologia del diritto; Sorites; Text; Theoria. Address: Piazza Castello 35, I-27100 Pavia PV, Italy. E-mail: amedeogiovanni.conte@unipv.it

**CONTI Tom,** b. 22 November 1941, Paisley, Scotland. Actor; Director; Novelist. m. Kara Wilson, 1967, 1 daughter. Education: Royal Scottish Academy of Music. Creative Works: London Theatre include: Savages (Christopher Hampton), 1973; The Devil's Disciple (Shaw), 1976; Whose Life is it Anyway? (Brian Clarke), 1978; They're Playing Our Song (Neil Simon/Marvin Hamlisch), 1980; Romantic Comedy (Bernard Salde); An Italian Straw Hat, 1986; Two Into One; Treats, 1989; Jeffrey Bernard is Unwell, 1990; The Ride Down Mt Morgan, 1991; Present Laughter (also director), 1993; Chapter Two, 1996; Jesus My Boy, 1998; Films include: Dreamer; Saving Grace; Miracles; Heavenly Pursuits; Beyond Therapy; Roman Holiday; Two Brothers Running; White Roses; Shirley Valentine; Chapter Two; Someone Else's America; Crush Depth; Something to Believe In, 1996; Out of Control, 1997; The Enemy, 2000; TV Works include: Madame Bovary; Treats; The Glittering Prizes; The Norman Conquests; The Beate Klarsfeld Story; Fatal Dosage; The Quick and the Dead; Blade on the Feather;

The Wright Verdicts; Deadline; Donovan; Director: Last Licks; Broadway, 1979; Before the Party, 1980; The Housekeeper, 1982; Treats, 1989; Present Laughter, 1993; Last of the Red Hot Lovers, 1999; Author: The Doctor, 2004. Honours: West End Theatre Managers Award; Royal TV Society Award; Variety Club of Great Britain Award, 1978; Tony Award, New York, 1979. Address: Artists Independent Network, 32 Tavistock Street, London, WC2E 7PB, England.

**CONTRERAS C Marcela,** b. 4 January 1942, Chile. Professor in Transfusion Medicine. 1 son, 1 daughter. Education: BSc, Chile, 1963; L Med, Chile, 1967; Medico-Cirujano, Chile, 1968; ECFMG, USA, 1968; MD, Chile, 1972; Specialist in Haematology (Blood Transfusion), JCHMT of the Royal College of Physicians, 1980; MRCPath, 1988; FRCP, Edinburgh, 1992; FRCPath, 1997; FRCP, 1998, Fellow, Academy of Medical Sciences, 2003. Appointments include: Lecturer in Immunology and Immunohaematology, Blood Bank and Centre of Immunohaematology, University of Chile, 1971-72; British Council Scholar, 1972-74; Senior Scientific Officer, 1974-76, Medical Assistant in Blood Transfusion, 1976-78, North London Blood Transfusion Centre, Edgware; Senior Registrar in Haematology, St Mary's Hospital, London and Northwick Park Hospital, Middlesex, 1978-80; Home Office appointed Tester for Paternity Testing, 1980-89; Deputy Director, Consultant, North London Blood Transfusion Centre, Edgware, 1980-84; Honorary Member, MRC Blood Group Unit, 1987-95; Honorary Senior Lecturer, Haematology, St Mary's Hospital Medical School, 1980-98; Chief Executive and Medical Director, North London Blood Transfusion Centre, 1984-95; Executive Director, London and South East Zone, National Blood Service, London, 1995-99; Professor in Transfusion Medicine, Royal Free and University College Hospitals Medical School, 1998-; National Director of Diagnostics, Development and Research, National Blood Service, London, 1999-; Visiting Professor in the Faculty of Applied Sciences, University of the West of England, Bristol, 2004-. Publications: More than 300 including 150 papers in peer-reviewed journals, 36 chapters, 50 letters to the editor, 11 books (some with 3 editions), 123 abstracts. Honours include most recently: Zoutendyk Medal, University of Johannesburg, 1995; President, International Society of Blood Transfusion, 1996-98; President, British Blood Transfusion Society, 2001-2003; H R Nevanlinna Medal, Helsinki, 2002; Fellow, Academy of Medical Sciences, 2003; Transfusion Medicine Award from ACOBASMET & Group CIAMT, Colombia, 2004; ISBT Award for outstanding contribution to blood transfusion and transfusion medicine, 2004. Memberships include: British Society for Haematology; British Medical Association; American Association of Blood Banks; International Society of Blood Transfusion; Chairman of the Committee on Socio-Economic Aspects of Blood Transfusion of ISBT; Board of NATA (Network for Advancement of Transfusion Alternatives); Board of Directors of NetCord (International Network for Cord Blood Banks); Royal Society of Medicine, sections of Pathology and Immunology; Board of the European School of Transfusion Medicine; European Society for Blood and Marrow Transplantation (EBMT); European Society for Haematology; Member of 5 editorial boards of medical journals. Address: c/o National Blood Service, Colindale Avenue, London NW9 5BG, England.

**COOK John Barry,** b. 9 May 1940, Gloucester, England. Educator. m. Vivien Lamb, 2 sons, 1 daughter. Education: BSc, Physics and Mathematics,1961, Associate, Diploma in Theology, 1961 King's College, University of London, 1958-61; PhD, Biophysics, 1965, Guy's Hospital Medical School, University of London, 1961-65. Appointments: Lecturer (part-time), Physics, Royal Veterinary College, 1962-64; Lecturer, Physics, Guy's Hospital Medical School, 1964-65; Physics Teacher, Senior Science Master, Head of Physics Department, Haileybury, Hertford, 1965-72; Headmaster, Christ College, Brecon, 1973-82; Headmaster, Epsom College, 1982-92; Director, Inner Cities Young Peoples Project, 1992-95, Principal, King George VI and Queen Elizabeth Foundation of St Catharine's at Cumberland Lodge, 1995-2000, Educational Consultant, 2000-; OFSTED Inspector of Schools, 1993-; Inspecting, Consultancy and Advisory work for a wide range of schools in UK, Kenya, Egypt, Malaysia, Argentina, Abu Dhabi, France and Austria; Chairman, Academic Policy Committee, Headmasters Conference; Chairman, South Wales Branch, Independent Schools' Information Service; Member, Curriculum Committee of the School's Council, the Council of the Midlands Examining Group, the Oxford and Cambridge Schools' Examination Board and of the Examination Committees of the Universities of Oxford and Cambridge; At various times Governor of 15 schools in Hertfordshire, Wales, Surrey, Staffordshire, Kent, Worcestershire; Chairman of Governors at The Royal School. Publications: Books as joint author: Solid State Biophysics; Multiple Choice Questions in A-level Physics; Multiple Choice Questions in O-level Physics; Papers and articles in: Nature, International Journal of Radiation Biology; Molecular Physics; Journal of Scientific Instruments; School Science Review. Memberships: College of Episcopal Electors and Governing Body of the Church in Wales; Chairman, Children's Hospice Association of the South East. Address: 6 Chantry Road, Bagshot, Surrey GU19 5DB, England.

**COOKE Jonathan Gervaise Fitzpatrick,** b. 26 March 1943, London, England. Sailor; Administrator. m. Henrietta Chamier, 1 son, 2 daughters. Education: Marlborough College, 1956-61; Dartmouth 1961-64; Joint Services Defence College, 1984; Royal College of Defence Studies, 1993. Appointments: Royal Navy, 1961-96; Navigation and Submarine Specialist; Commanded HMS Rorqual, HMS Churchill, HMS Warspite, 1980-84; 3rd Submarine Squadron, 1988-89; Naval Attaché, Paris, 1990-93; Commodore, 1993; Director Intelligence, Ministry of Defence; Chief Executive to Leathersellers Company, 1996-; Director AngloSiberian Oil, 1998-2003. Honours: OBE; Commandeur de L'Ordre Nationale de Merité, France. Memberships: Naval and Military Club; Queen's Club. Address: Downstead House, Morestead, Winchester, Hampshire, SO21 1LF, England. E-mail: jcooke@leathersellers.co.uk

**COOKSON Thomas Richard,** b. 7 July 1942, Bournemouth, England. Schoolmaster. m. Carol, 3 daughters. Education: MA, English Literature, Balliol College, Oxford, 1961-64. Appointments: Hopkins Grammar School, New Haven, Connecticut, USA, 1965-67; English Department and House Tutor, Winchester College, Winchester, 1967-72; Assistant Master, Manchester Grammar School, Manchester, 1972-74; Head of English Department , 1974-83, Housemaster, 1983-90, Winchester College, Winchester; Headmaster, King Edward VI School, Southampton, 1990-96; Headmaster, Sevenoaks School, Sevenoaks, Kent, 1996-2001; Principal, The British School, Colombo, Sri Lanka, 2002; Headmaster, Winchester College, Winchester, 2003-2005. Publications: John Keats, 1972, Bernard Shaw, 1972 (Edward Arnold Portrait Series); Articles on the International Baccalaureate, The London Evening Standard, 1999, The Daily Telegraph, 2001. Honour: MA, Oxford. Memberships: Member of the Committee, 1997-2000, Member of the Sub-committee of Six on the Future Director of the HMC, 1997-98, Chairman and Secretary of the South Eastern Division, 1999-2000, Headmasters Conference; Lecturer at Headmasters Conference Training Conferences, 1996-2001; Governor: Rugby School, 2005-, English School in Prague, 2005-; Rye

Golf Club. Address: Chapel Cottage, Kemsing Road, Wrotham, Kent TN15 7BU, England.

**COOMBE Michael Ambrose Rew,** b. 17 June 1930, Croydon, Surrey, England. Retired Judge. m. Anne Hull, deceased, 3 sons, 1 deceased, 1 daughter. Education: MA, English Language and Literature, New College Oxford, 1951-54; Called to Bar by Middle Temple, 1957. Appointments: Junior Prosecuting Counsel to the Crown, Inner London, 1971-74; Central Criminal Court, 1974-78; Senior Prosecuting Counsel to the Crown, 1978-85; Recorder of the Crown Court, 1976-85; Circuit Judge, 1985; Appointed to Central Criminal Court, 1986-2003. Honours: Middle Temple Harmsworth Scholar; Bencher, 1984; Reader of the Inn, Autumn 2001; Freeman of the City of London. Memberships: Garrick; Liveryman of the Worshipful Company of Stationers; Liveryman of the Worshipful Company of Fruiterers.

**COOMBES Gaz (Gareth).** Singer; Musician (guitar). Career: Member, The Jennifers; Lead singer, guitarist, Supergrass, 1994-; Major concerts include: Support to Blur, Alexandra Palace, 1994; UK tour with Shed Seven, 1994; T In The Park Festival, Glasgow, 1995. Recordings: Albums: I Should Coco (Number 1, UK), 1995; In It for the Money, 1997; Supergrass, 1999; Singles: Caught By The Fuzz, 1994; Mansize Rooster, 1995; Lenny, 1995; Alright, 1995; Going Out, 1996; Sun Hits the Sky, 1997; Pumping On Your Stereo, 1999; Mary, 1999. Honours: Q Award, Best New Act, 1995; BRIT Award Nominations: Best British Newcomer, Best Single, Best Video, 1996. Address: c/o Courtyard Management, 22 The Nursery, Sutton Courtenay, Abingdon, Oxon OX14 4UA, England.

**COONEY Anthony Paul,** b. 3 July 1932, Liverpool, England. Schoolmaster; Poet. m. 12 April 1958, 2 daughters. Education: Gregg Commercial College, Liverpool, 1948-50; Ethel Wormald College of Education, 1968-70; Open University. Appointments: Assistant Master, 1971-91. Publications: Georgian Sequence; The Wheel of Fire; Germinal; Inflections; Mersey Poems; Personations; Land of My Dreams; Bread in the Wilderness; The Story of St George; St George – Knight of Lydda; The Rainbow Has Two Ends; Planet of the Shapes. Contributions to: Various small press magazines. Address: Rose Cottage, 17 Hadassah Grove, Lark Lane, Liverpool L17 8XH, England.

**COONEY Muriel Sharon Taylor,** b. 12 October 1947, Edenton, North Carolina, USA. Nurse. 2 sons. Education: BSN, East Carolina University, Greenville, North Carolina, 1969; MSN, St Louis University, St Louis, Missouri, USA, 1972; Orthopaedic Nurse Certificate. Appointments: Occupational: Staff Nurse, Johns Hopkins Hospital, Baltimore, Maryland, 1969-71; Staff Nurse, Barnes Hospital, St Louis, Missouri, 1971-72; Cardiovascular Clinical Nurse Specialist, Jackson Memorial Hospital, Miami, Florida, 1973-74; Home Healthcare Supervisor, Manager, Co-ordinator Council for Senior Citizens, Durham, North Carolina, 1985; Person County Memorial Hospital, Roxboro, North Carolina, 1989-98; Teaching: Clinical Instructor, Shepherd College, Shepherdstown, West Virginia, 1983; Lecturer, Clinical Instructor, Shepherd College, 1984; Instructor, Piedmont Community College, Roxboro, North Carolina, 1989-90; Instructor, Watts School of Nursing, Durham, North Carolina, 1990-2004; Independent Education Consultant, 2005-. Publications: The Effects of Selected Teaching on the Recognition of Digitalis Toxicity, research thesis. Honours: Life Fellow, IBA; Distinguished Leadership Award for Service to Nursing Profession, 1994. Memberships: American Nurses Association; North Carolina Nurses Association; NCNA Council of Nurse Educators, Chairperson, 1994-97, Vice Chairperson, 1992-93; NCNA Council of Medical Surgical Nursing;

NCNA Cabinet of Education and Resource Development; NCNA Council of Clinical Nurse Specialists National League of Nursing; Academy of Medical Surgery Nursing, Bylaw Commission, 1994; Watts School of Nursing Association of Nursing , Student Advisors, 1993-2004; National Association of Orthopaedic Nurses; Triangle Chapter, Treasurer, 1995, NAON; North Carolina Nurses Association, North Carolina Association of Nursing Students, 2004-. Address: 4812 Bahama Road, Rougement, North Carolina 27572, USA.

**COONEY Thomas,** b. 21 January 1942, Drogheda, Ireland. Catholic Priest; Augustinian. Education: Philosophical Studies, Good Counsel, House of Studies, Ballyboden, Dublin, Ireland, 1960-62; STB, Theological Studies, Gregorian University, Rome Italy, 1963-67; Dip.Catechtics, Corpus Christi College, London, 1968-69; MA, St Louis University, St Louis, Missouri, USA, 1973-75; Dip. Communications, Communication Centre, Hatch End, London, 1989; CPE, Holy Family Hospital and Medical Center, Methuen, Massachusetts, USA, 1990; Dip. Spiritual Direction, Center for Religious Development, Cambridge, Massachusetts, USA, 1990-91; Masters, Clinical Pastoral Counselling, Emmanuel College, Boston, Massachusetts, 1991-93. Appointments: Entered Augustinian Order, Dublin, 1959; Ordained, Rome, 1967; Teaching Chaplain, Vocational School, Dublin, 1967-68; Housemaster and Teacher, St Augustine's College, Dungarvan, 1969-72; Teacher, Good Counsel College, New Ross, 1972-73; Master of Students, Good Counsel, Dublin, 1974-81; Provincial, Irish Province of the Augustinian Order, 1981-89; Executive, CMRS, 1983-89; President, Conference of Major Superiors of Ireland, 1986-89; Prior, St John's Priory, Dublin, 1993-95; Assistant General of the Augustinian Order, North West Europe and Canada, 1995-2001; Director of Pastoral Studies, Milltown Institute of Theology and Philosophy, Dublin, 2001-. Publications: Articles in religious and theological journals. Memberships: Honorary Treasurer and Member of the Executive, National Conference of Priests of Ireland, 1994-95; Theological Faculty, Milltown Institute, 2001-; Member of the Executive and Treasurer, All Ireland Spiritual Guidance Association, 2005; Honorary President, Seapoint, Pitch and Put Golf Club, Termonfeckin, Ireland. Address: The Milltown Institute of Theology and Philosophy, Milltown Park, Dublin 6, Ireland. E-mail: info@milltown-intitute.ie

**COONS Dorothy H,** b. Lewisburg, Ohio, USA. Gerontologist. m. George D Coons. Education: BS, Wittenberg University; Graduate Courses, University of Michigan; European Study Tour of Industrial Therapy Programs for the Elderly; Internship, University of Michigan Mental Health Service. Appointments include: Co-Investigator of Ypsilanti State Hospital Project, 1961-67; Program Director, Milieu Therapy Training Program, 1968-80; Director of Continuing Education, 1975-80; Project Director, Older American Folk Artists, 1979-80; Research Scientist, 1980; Project Director, Project on Alzheimer's Disease, 1981-83; Project Director, Alzheimer's Disease, 1983-87; Associate Research Scientist Emeritus, 1987. Publications include: Co-author, A Better Life, 1986; Co-author, A Manual for Trainers of Direct Service Staff in Special Alzheimer's Units, 1990; Editor, Specialized Dementia Care Units, 1991; Co-author, Quality of Life in Long-Term Care, 1996. Honours: Humanitarian of the Year, ADRDA-Grand Rapids Area Chapter, 1985; Wilbur J Cohen Award, University of Michigan, 1985; Distinguished Service Award, Michigan Non-Profit Homes Association, 1985; Clark Tibbitts Award, Association for Gerontology in Higher Education, 1988; Award for Dedicated Service to the Elderly, Ypsilanti Regional Psychiatric Hospital, 1989. Address: 2031 Winsted Boulevard, Ann Arbor, MI 48103, USA.

**COOPER Alice (Vincent Furnier),** b. 4 February 1948, Detroit, Michigan, USA. Singer. m Sheryl Goddard, 1 sons, 2 daughters. Career: First to stage theatrical rock concert tours; Among first to film conceptual rock promo videos (pre-MTV); Considered among originators and greatest hard rock artists; Known as King of Shock Rock; Many film, television appearances. Recordings: Singles include: I'm Eighteen; Poison; No More Mr Nice Guy; I Never Cry; Only Women Bleed; You And Me; Under My Wheels; Bed Of Nails; Albums include: School's Out, 1972; Billion Dollar Babies, 1973; Welcome To My Nightmare, 1976; From The Inside, 1978; Constrictor, 1986; Raise Your Fist And Yell, 1987; Trash, 1988; Hey Stoopid, 1991; Last Temptation, 1994; He's Back, 1997. Publications: Wrote foreword to short story book: Shock Rock. Honour: Foundations Forum, Lifetime Achievement Award, 1994. Memberships: BMI; NARAS; SAG; AFTRA; AFofM. Address: PO Box 5542, Beverly Hills, CA 90211, USA.

**COOPER Barrington Spencer,** b. 15 January 1923, Cardiff, Wales. Consulting Psychiatrist. m. Jane Eva Livermore Wallace, 1 daughter. Education: BA, Queens' College, Cambridge; MB BS, MRGCP, Bart's Medical School, London. Appointments include: House Physician, Whittington Hospital, 1946; House Physician, Ashford County Hospital, 1947; Medical Registrar, Oster House Hospital, 1947; Captain, Royal Army Medical Corps, Graded Psychiatrist, 1947-49; Chief Assistant, Academic Department of Psychological Medicine, St Bartholomew's Hospital, 1949-51; Clinical Assistant in Psychiatry: St Bartholomew's Hospital, 1951-53, London Jewish Hospital, 1951-53, National Hospital for Nervous Diseases, 1953-55; Elective Visiting Lecturer in Psychosomatic Medicine, University of Athens, University of Rome; Research Fellow, Sloane-Kettering Institute, New York City, 1951; Consulting Psychiatrist, Langham Clinic of Psychotherapy, London, 1970; Consulting Physician, Bowden House Clinic, London, 1974; Attending Physician, Foundation for Manic Depression, Columbia University, New York, 1974; Corresponding Associate, WHO Psychosocial Centre, Stockholm, 1977; Visiting Professor, Boston University Medical School, 1979-82; Consulting Physician, Clinic of Psychotherapy, London; Chairman and Consultant, Allied Medical Diagnostic Care; Currently: Medical Advisor: BACO Entertainment AG, Allied Medical Diagnostic Clinic, World Film Services, New Media Medical University, Fabyan Films Ltd, West One Productions Inc, Glesteams Ltd, Skyy Spirits Ltd, Caplin Cybernetic Ltd; Chairman and Consultant, Allied Medical Corporate Health Care; Private Practice, Devonshire Place, London; Independent Film Producer; The One Eyed Soldiers; The Doctor and the Devils; The Colonel's Children; Winner Takes All; Script Consultant; Director Fabyan Ltd and Fabyan Films Ltd. Publications: Author, Helix (ballet), 1982; Cockpits (novella), 1982; Contributing Editor, Kolokol Press UK, Kolokol Press US and Delos; Professional publications: Travel Medicine, 1982; Travel Sickness, 1982; Thomas Cook Health Passport, 4th edition, 1990; Consumer Guide to Over-the-Counter Medicines, 1996; Your Symptoms Diagnosed, 2nd edition, 1996; Consumer Guide to Prescription Medicines, 2001; Non-Allopathic Medication; Numerous articles in medical journals. Honours include: PhD, Cornell University; PhD, Columbia Pacific University. Memberships include: Member Royal College of General Practitioners, 1964; London Jewish Hospital Society; Life Fellow, Royal Society of Medicine; Fellow, Society of Clinical Psychiatrists; Foundation Member, Medical Section, British Psychological Society; British Association of Counselling; Fellow, American Academy of Arts and Sciences; British Medical Association; World Psychiatric Association; BAFTA; AIP; Founder and Patron, Salerno International Youth Orchestra Festival, Manhattan School of Music.

Address: 10 Devonshire Place, London W1, England. E-mail: drbcooper@btclick.com

**COOPER (Brenda) Clare,** b. 21 January 1935, Falmouth, Cornwall, England. Writer. m. Bill Cooper, 6 April 1953, 2 sons, 1 daughter. Publications: David's Ghost; The Black Horn; Earthchange; Ashar of Qarius; The Skyrifters; Andrews and the Gargoyle; A Wizard Called Jones; Kings of the Mountain; Children of the Camps; The Settlement on Planet B; Miracles and Rubies; Timeloft; Marya's Emmets; Cat of Morfa, 1998; Stonehead, 2000; One Day on Morfa, 2001; Time Ball, 2003. Honour: Runner Up, Tir Na Nog Award. Memberships: PEN; Society of Authors; Welsh Academy. Address: Tyrhibin Newydd, Morfa, Newport, Pembrokeshire SA42 0NT, Wales.

**COOPER Jilly (Sallitt),** b. 21 February 1937, Hornchurch, Essex, England. Writer; Journalist. m. Leo Cooper, 1961, 1 son, 1 daughter. Appointments: Reporter, Middlesex Independent Newspaper, Brentford, 1957-59; Columnist, The Sunday Times, 1969-85, The Mail on Sunday, 1985-. Publications: How to Stay Married, 1969; How to Survive from Nine to Five, 1970; Jolly Super, 1971; Men and Super Men, 1972; Jolly Super Too, 1973; Women and Super Women, 1974; Jolly Superlative, 1975; Emily (romance novel), 1975; Super Men and Super Women (omnibus), 1976; Bella (romance novel), 1976; Harriet (romance novel), 1976; Octavia (romance novel), 1977; Work and Wedlock (omnibus), 1977; Superjilly, 1977; Imogen (romance novel), 1978; Prudence (romance novel), 1978; Class: A View from Middle England, 1979; Supercooper, 1980; Little Mabel series, juvenile, 4 volumes, 1980-85; Violets and Vinegar: An Anthology of Women's Writings and Sayings (editor with Tom Hartman), 1980; The British in Love (editor), 1980; Love and Other Heartaches, 1981; Jolly Marsupial, 1982; Animals in War, 1983; The Common Years, 1984; Leo and Jilly Cooper on Rugby, 1984; Riders, 1985; Hotfoot to Zabriskie Point, 1985; Turn Right at The Spotted Dog, 1987; Rivals, 1988; Angels Rush In, 1990; Polo, 1991; The Man Who Made Husbands Jealous, 1993; Araminta's Wedding, 1993; Appassionata, 1996; How to Survive Christmas, 1996; Score! 1999; Pandora, 2002. Honours: Publishing News Lifetime Achievement Award, 1998; OBE, 2004. Membership: NUJ. Address: c/o Vivienne Schuster, Curtis Brown, 4th Floor, Haymarket House, 28-29 Haymarket, London, SW1Y 4SP, England. E-mail: cb@curtisbrown.co.uk

**COOPER Leon Niels,** b. 28 February 1930, New York, USA. Physicist. m. Kay Anne Allard, 1969, 2 daughters. Education: BA, 1951, MA, 1953, PhD, 1954, Columbia University. Appointments: Institute for Advanced Study, Princeton, 1954-55; Research Associate, University of Illinois, 1955-57; Assistant Professor, Ohio State University, 157-58; Associate Professor, Brown University, Rhode Island, 1958-62; Professor, 1974, Thomas J Watson, Senior Professor of Science , 1974-, Director, Center for Neural Science, 1978-90, Institute for Brain and Neural Systems, 1991-, Brain Science Program, 2000-. Publications: An Introduction to the Meaning and Structure of Physics, 1968; Structure and Meaning, 1992; How We Learn, How We Remember, 1995. Honour: Comstock Prize, NAS, 1968; Joint Winner, Nobel Prize, Physics, 1972; Honorary DSc, Columbia, Sussex, 1973, Illinois, Brown, 1974, Gustavus Adolphus College, 1975, Ohio State University, 1976, Pierre and Marie Curie University, Paris, 1977; Award in Excellence, Columbia University, 1974; Descartes Medal, Academy de Paris, University Rene Descartes, 1977; John Jay Award, Columbia College, 1985. Memberships: National Science Foundation Post-doctoral Fellow, 1954-55; Alfred P Sloan Foundation Research Fellow, 1959-66; John Simon Guggenheim Memorial Foundation Fellow, 1965-66; Fellow, American Physical Society, American Academy of Arts and

Sciences; American Federation of Scientists; Member, NAS, American Philosophical Society. Address: Box 1843, Physics Department, Brown University, Providence, RI 02912, USA.

**COOPER Thomas Joshua,** b. 19 December 1946, San Francisco, California, USA; Artist. m. Catherine Alice, 2 daughters. Education: BA cum laude, Special Studies – Art, Philosophy, Literature, Humboldt State University, California, 1969; MA, Art with Distinction in Photography, University of New Mexico, USA, 1972; California Lifetime Community College Teaching Credential, 1972. Appointments: Founding Head, Department of Photography, 1982-2000, Honorary Professor, 1998-, Elected Chair, School of Fine Art, 2000-2002, Senior Researcher and Professor of Fine Art, 2002-, Glasgow School of Art, Glasgow, Scotland. Publications: Solo publications include: Dialogue with Photography, 1979-2005; Between Dark and Park, 1985; Dreaming the Gokstadt, 1988; Simply Counting Waves, 1995; A Handful of Stones, 1996; Wild, 2001; Some Rivers, Some Trees, Some Rocks, Some Seas, 2003; Point of No Return, 2004 Photographs included in numerous reference books and exhibition catalogues. Honours: John D Phelan Award in Art and Literature (first time ever awarded in photography) San Francisco, California, USA, 1970; Major Photography Bursary (joint award), Arts Council of Great Britain, 1976; Photography Fellow, National Endowment of the Arts, Washington DC, USA, 1978; Major Artists Award, Scottish Arts Council, Edinburgh, Scotland, 1994; Major Artists Award, Lannan Foundation, Santa Fe, New Mexico, USA, 1999-. Memberships: Society for Photographic Education; Founding Member, Scottish Society for the History of Photography; Royal Scottish Geographical Society. Address: The Glasgow School of Art, 167 Renfrew Street, Glasgow G3 6RQ, Scotland. E-mail: t.cooper@gsa.ac.uk

**COPILU Dumitru,** b. 17 February 1931, Şutu, Cluj District, Romania. Professor; Scientific Researcher. 2 sons, 2 daughters. Education: Bachelor Diploma, Faculty of Philology, "M Lomonosov" University of Moscow, 1957; Doctor of Philology, in the interliterary European Relations – a cybernetic approach, Bucharest University, 1988. Appointments: University Assistant, Bucharest University, 1958-66; Principal Philologist, Head of Documentary Department, University Documentary Centre, Expert in the Syntheses Department of the Ministry of Education, Head of Education-Teaching Department, National Centre for Information and Documentation in Education, 1966-73; Principal Philologist and Principal Researcher, Bucharest Institute of Pedagogic and Psychological Research, Department of Pedagogy-Psychology, Babeş-Boliay University, and in the Romanian Academy, Cluj-Napoca; Principal Researcher, Bucharest Institute of Education Sciences, 1974-94, and in the Kishinev Institute of Education Sciences, 1992-2004; Associate Professor at Romanian universities, including Bucharest Public University, "Titu Maiorescu" Independent University, Bucharest Ecological University, Bucharest "Spiru Haret" University, Oradea University and Moldavian University – Kishinev "Ion Creangă" Pedagogic University, Technical University of Moldavia, Tiraspol University of Kishinev, Bălţi "Alecu Russo" Public University. Publications: Over 100 scientific papers presented at national and international conferences; Over 200 studies and articles in 9 languages published in more than 60 periodicals and more than 40 collected volumes; 3 school textbooks; 1 teacher textbook; Contributions in the fields of: Education: Education for International Understanding, 1974; Informative Microsystem regarding the Connection of the Education with Practical Activities, 1977; Formation of Teaching in World Preuniversity Education, 1995; Periodisation of Sciences, 2000; Educational Standards, 2002; Teaching Process Based on Curricular Objectives of Formation, 2002;

Education of Management, 2003; Universal Dimensions of Ignatie Breanceaninov, 2004; Programme of Continuous Formation, School Managers and Professors, 2005; Literary Science: Relationships Between Two National Literatures, 1984; Literary Periodisation, 1995; Romanian Poet Eminescu's University, 2004. Honours: Cultural Merit Medal, Romania, 1970; Man of the Year, 2004, Great Minds of the 21st Century, ABI, 2004; Deputy Director General, IBC, 2005. Memberships: Association of Romanian Scientists; Society of Romanian Journalists; Association of Educational Managers in the Moldavian Republic; "Ateneul Român" as Patron of the Ecological University. Address: Str Aleea Dealul Măcinului nr 1 A, Bloc 452, Sc E, Ap 177, Sector 6, 062043 Bucharest, Romania.

**COPLEY Paul,** b. 25 November 1944, Denby Dale, Yorkshire, England. Actor; Writer. m. Natasha Pyne, 7 July 1972. Education: Teachers Certificate, Northern Counties College of Education. Appointments: Freelance Actor/Writer. Publications: Staged: Pillion, Bush Theatre, London, 1977; Viaduct, Bush Theatre, London, 1979; Tapster, Stephen Joseph Theatre, Scarborough, 1981; Fire-Eaters, Tricycle Theatre, London, 1984; Calling, Stephen Joseph Theatre, Scarborough, 1986; Broadcast: On May-Day, BBC Radio 4 Sunday Play, 1986, repeated World Service, 1987, Radio 4, 1996; Tipperary Smith, BBC Radio 4, 1994; Words Alive, BBC Education Radio, 1996-2003; Publications: Plays for children: Odysseus and the Cyclops, 1998; The Pardoner's Tale, 1999; Loki the Mischief Maker, 2000; Jennifer Jenks and Her Excellent Day Out, 2000. Membership: Writers Guild. Address: Casarotto Ramsay Ltd, 60 Wardour Street, London W1V 4ND, England.

**COPLEY Robert Anthony,** b. 29 January 1960, England. Fine Art Auctioneer. m. Diana Copley, 1 son, 1 daughter. Education: Sherborne School. Appointments: Christie's: Director, 1990, Head of Furniture Department, 1995, Deputy Chairman, Christies International UK, 2000. Membership: Brooks's. Address: Christie's, 8 King Street, St James's, London SW1Y 6QT, England. E-mail: rcopley@christies.com

**COPPOLA Francis Ford,** b. 7 April 1939, Detroit, Michigan, USA. Film writer and director. m. Eleanor Neil, 2 sons (1 deceased), 1 daughter. Education: Hofstra University; University of California. Career: Films include: Dementia 13, 1963; This Property is Condemned, 1965; Is Paris Burning?, 1966; You're A Big Boy Now, 1967; Finian's Rainbow, 1968; The Rain People, 1969; Patton, 1971; The Godfather Part II, 1975; The Great Gatsby, 1974; The Black Stallion (produced), 1977; Apocalypse Now, 1979; One From the Heart, 1982; Hammett (produced), 1982; The Escape Artist, 1982; The Return of the Black Stallion, 1982; Rumble Fish, 1983; The Outsiders, 1983; The Cotton Club, 1984; Peggy Sue Got Married, 1986; Gardens of Stone, 1986; Life Without Zoe, 1988; Tucker: the Man and His Dream, 1988; The Godfather Part III, 1990; Dracula, 1991; My Family/Mia Familia, 1995; Don Huan de Marco, 1995; Jack, 1996; The Rainmaker, 1997; The Florentine, 1999; The Virgin Suicides, 1999; Grapefruit Moon, 2000; Assassination Tango; Supernova; Megalopolis; Executive producer: The Secret Garden, 1993; Mary Shelley's Frankenstein, 1994; Buddy, 1997; The Third Miracle, 1999; Goosed, 1999; Sleepy Hollow, 1999; Monster; Jeepers Creepers; No Such Thing; Pumpkin; Theatre direction includes: Private Lives, The Visit of the Old Lady (San Francisco Opera Co), 1972; Artistic Director, Zoetrope Studios, 1969-; Owner, Niebaum-Coppola Estate, Napa Valley. Honours: Cannes Film Award for The Conversation, 1974; Director's Guild Award for The Godfather; Academy Award for Best Screenplay for Patton, Golden Palm (Cannes), for Apocalypse Now, 1979; Also awarded Best Screenplay, Best Director and

Best Picture Oscars for the Godfather Part II; US Army Civilian Service Award; Commandeur, Ordre des Arts et des Lettres. Address: Zoetrope Studios, 916 Kearny Street, San Francisco, CA 94133, USA.

**CORBET Philip Steven,** b. 21 May 1929, Kuala Lumpur, West Malaysia. University Professor; Consultant Ecologist; Medical Entomologist. 1 daughter. Education: BSc, First Class Honours, Botany, Geology, Zoology, 1949, BSc, First Class Honours, Zoology, 1950, University of Reading; PhD, Entomology, Gonville and Caius College, University of Cambridge, 1953; DSc, Zoology, University of Reading, 1962; ScD, Zoology, Gonville and Caius College, University of Cambridge, 1976; DSc, Zoology, University of Edinburgh, 2003; DSc, University of Dundee, 2005. Appointments: Entomologist, East African Freshwater Fisheries Research Institute, Jinja, Uganda, 1954-57; Entomologist, East African Virus Research Institute, Entebbe, Uganda, 1957-62; Research Scientist (Entomologist), Entomology Research Institute, Canada Department of Agriculture, Ottawa, Ontario, Canada, 1962-67; Director, Research Institute, Canada Department of Agriculture, Belleville, Ontario, Canada, 1967-71; Professor and Chairman, Department of Biology, University of Waterloo, Ontario, Canada, 1971-74; Professor and Director, Centre for Resource Management, University of Canterbury and Lincoln College, Christchurch, New Zealand, 1974-78; Professor of Zoology, Department of Zoology, University of Canterbury, Christchurch, New Zealand, 1978-80; Professor of Zoology, 1980-90, Head of Department, 1983-86, Department of Biological Sciences, Professor Emeritus of Zoology, 1990-, University of Dundee, Scotland; Honorary Professor, University of Edinburgh, Scotland, 1996-. Publications: Author or co-author of over 250 research reports on freshwater biology, medical entomology and conservation biology; 4 books: co-author, Dragonflies, 1960, reprinted 1985; A Biology of Dragonflies, 1962, reprinted 1983; co-author, The Odonata of Canada and Alaska, volume 3, 1975, revised edition, 1978, reprinted 1998; Dragonflies. Behaviour and Ecology of Odonata, 1999, reprinted 2001, 2004. Honours include: President, 1971-72 and Gold Medal for Outstanding Achievement, 1974, Entomological Society of Canada; Commonwealth Visiting Professor, University of Cambridge, 1979-80; President, British Dragonfly Society, 1983-91; President, Worldwide Dragonfly Association, 2001-2003; Neill Prize, Royal Society of Edinburgh, 2002; Elected Fellowships: Institute of Biology, 1967; Entomological Society of Canada, 1977, Royal Society of Tropical Medicine and Hygiene, 1985; Royal Society of Edinburgh, 1987; Royal Society of Arts, 1991; Honorary Memberships: British Dragonfly Society 1991; Société française d'odonatologie, 1997; Dragonfly Society of the Americas, 2000. Memberships: The Arctic Club; Royal Entomological Society; Institute of Ecology and Environmental Management. Address: Crean Mill, Crean, St Buryan, Cornwall TR19 6HA, England. E-mail: pscorbet@creanmill.u-net.com

**CORBETT Peter George,** b. 13 April 1952, Rossett, North Wales. Artist. Education: BA (Honours), Fine Art, Manchester Regional College of Art and Design, 1974. Career: Artist, oil on canvas; Speaker, Workers Educational Association, Liverpool, 1995; Life Drawing Tutor, Bluecoat Chambers, Liverpool, 1996; Originator "Liverpool European Capital of Culture 2008", 1996/1997; Exhibitions include: Centre Gallery Liverpool, 1979; Liverpool Playhouse, 1982; Acorn Gallery Liverpool, 1985; Major Merseyside Artists Exhibition, Port of Liverpool Building, 1988; Merseyside Contemporary Artists Exhibition, Albert Dock, Liverpool; Surreal Objects Exhibition, Tate Gallery, Liverpool, 1989; Unity Theatre, Liverpool, 1990; Royal Liver Building, Liverpool (two person), 1991; Senate House Gallery, Liverpool University (one man), 1993; Academy of Arts, Liverpool (two man), 1994; Grosvenor Museum Exhibition, Chester (open), 1995; Atkinson Gallery, Southport (one man), 1995; Liverpool Academy of Arts, 1998; Hanover Gallery, Liverpool (two man), 1999; Liverpool Biennial of Contemporary Art, 1999; Independent DFN Gallery, New York (mixed), 2000; Influences and Innovations, Agora Gallery, New York (mixed), 2002; Retrospective Painting Exhibition, Senate House Gallery, University of Liverpool, 2004, included in Liverpool Biennial of Contemporary Art (independent); Works included in Liverpool University Art Collection; Atkinson Gallery, Southport; Private Collections in America, Netherlands, Australia, Germany, Britain. Publications: Numerous poems in poetry anthologies including: A Celebration of Poets, 1999; Parnassus of World Poets, 2001; The Best Poems and Poets of 2002; A Shield of Angels, 2002; The Sound of Poetry (Audio-cassette), 2002; Quantum Leap Magazine, 2003; The Pool of Life (Full anthology of own poems), 2003. Honours include: Honorary Professor of Fine Art, Institute of Co-ordinated Research, Victoria, Australia, 1994 Diploma Winner, Scottish International Open Poetry Competition, 1998; International German Art Prize, 1998; Outstanding Achievement Award, Albert Einstein Academy, USA, 1998; Friedrich Holdrein Award and Gold Medal for Poetry, Germany, 2000; International Peace Prize, United Cultural Convention, USA, 2002; World Lifetime Achievement Award, American Biographical Institute, 2002; Minister of Culture, American Biographical Institute, 2003; Poet of the Year, International Society of Poets, USA, 2003; Short listed for the Lexmark European Art Prize, exhibition of finalists in London, 2004. Memberships: Design and Artists Copyright Society, London; Maison International des Intellectuels, Paris, France; International Society of Poets, USA; National Poetry Society, London; Founding Member, American Order of Excellence, American Biographical Institute, 2002. Address: Flat 4, 7 Gambier Terrace, Hope Street, Liverpool L1 7BG, England. Website: www.axisartists.org.uk/all/ref7166.htm

**CORBETT Robin, (Lord Corbett of Castle Vale),** b. 22 December 1933, Fremantle, Australia. Parliamentarian. m. Valerie, 1 son, 2 daughters. Appointments: Trainee, Birmingham Evening Mail; Reporter, Daily Mirror; Deputy Editor, Farmer's Weekly; Editorial Staff Development Executive, IPC Magazines; Labour Relations Executive, IPC; National Executive Committee Member, Honorary Secretary Magazine and Book Branch, National Union of Journalists; Elected Member of Parliament for Hemel Hempstead, 1974-79; Elected Member of Parliament for Birmingham Erdington, 1983-2001; Opposition Front Bench Spokesman on Broadcasting and Media, 1987-94 and Disabled People's Rights, 1994-95; Chairman, House of Commons Home Affairs Select Committee, 1999-2001; Appointed to House of Lords, 2001; Member, Select Committee on the EU (SCF). Memberships: Vice Chairman Indo-British Parliamentary Group; Chairman, Friends of Cyprus; Vice-Chairman, All Party Motor Group, sustainable development, renewable energy; Member, Wilton Park Academic Council; Vice-President, Lotteries Council; Treasurer, ANZAC Group; Member, Friends of Eden Project; Patron, Hope for Children; Director, Rehab UK; Chairman, Castle Vale Neighbourhood Management Board, 2001-04; Chairman, Castle Vale Neighbourhood Partnership, 2004-05; Chairman, Parliamentary Labour Peers' Group, 2005-; Member, Lords PLP Co-ordination Committee, 2004-05. Address: House of Lords, London, SW1A 0PW, England. E-mail: castlevale@corbetts.plus.com

**CORBLUTH Elsa,** b. 2 August 1928, Beckenham, Kent, England. Writer; Photographer. m. David Boadella, divorced 1987, 1 son, 1 daughter, deceased 1980. Education: BA, Combined Creative Arts, 1st Class Honours, Alsager College, 1982; MA, Creative Writing, Lancaster University, 1984.

Publications: St Patrick's Night, poems on daughter's death in charity hostel fire while working there; Various booklets; Wilds, travelling exhibition of poems illustrated by her photographs, accompanied by poetry readings; Group of 7 poems in SW Arts Proof Series of small books, 1998. Contributions to: Poetry Review; Outposts; The Rialto; Times Literary Supplement; Anthologies: Green Book; Arts Council of Great Britain; PEN. Omissions: Publisher of St Patrick's Night – Peterloo poets, and title of another poetry collection published by the same publisher, The Planet Iceland, 2002. Honours: 1st Prizes, South-West Arts Competition, Bridport, 1979-1981; Joint 1st, Cheltenham Festival Competition, 1981; 1st, Sheffield Competition, 1981; 1st, ORBIS Rhyme Revival, 1986, 1993, 1995; 1st Prize Yorkshire Poetry Competition, 1997. Membership: Harbour Poets, Weymouth. Address: Hawthorn Cottage, Rodden, Near Weymouth, Dorset DT3 4JE, England.

**CORBY Peter John Siddons,** b. 8 July 1924, Leamington Spa, England. Businessman. m. (1) Gail Susan Clifford-Marshall, 2 sons, (2) Inés Rosemary Mandow, 1 son. Education: Private Grammar School (Boarding). Appointments: Engineering Apprentice, Coventry Gauge & Tool Co Ltd, 1940-42; Wartime Service: Flight Engineer (Halifax and Lancaster), 78 Squadron, 4 Group, Bomber Command Royal Airforce, 1943-48; Managing Director of family business, Corbys Ltd and John Corby Ltd; Created manufactured and marketed the Corby Electric Trouser Press, also served on the boards of various other manufacturing and service companies, 1949-74; Sold Corby companies to Thomas Jourdan plc, 1974; Various non-executive directorships, including Thomas Jourdan plc, 1974-2004; Company Memberships: Cordeal Limited (family company); SaveTower Ltd (property company); Intercinq (Swiss company). Honours: Freeman of the City of London, 1977; Liveryman (Marketors), 1978. Memberships: Ocean Cruising Club; Island Sailing Club; Honorary Member, Yacht Club de France; Fellow of the Institute of Directors, 1955; Lloyd's of London, 1974. Address: The Sloop, 89 High Street, Cowes, Isle of Wight PO31 7AW, England.

**CORDINGLY David,** b. 5 December 1938, London, England. Writer. m. Shirley, 1 son, 1 daughter. Education: Honours Degree Modern History, MA, Oriel College, Oxford; D Phil, University of Sussex. Appointments: Graphic Designer with various design groups and publishing firms in London; Exhibition Designer, The British Museum; Keeper, Art Gallery and Museum, Brighton; Assistant Director, Museum of London; Keeper of Pictures and the Head of Exhibitions, National Maritime Museum, Greenwich. Publications: Books: Marine Painting in England 1700-1900, 1974; Painters of the Sea, 1979; Nicholas Pocock, Marine Artist, 1986; Life among the Pirates: the romance and the reality, 1995; Pirates: an illustrated history; Ships and Seascapes: an introduction to marine prints, drawings and watercolours, 1997; Heroines and Harlots: women at sea in the great age of sail, 2001; Billy Ruffian: the Bellerophon and the downfall of Napoleon, 2003. Address: 2 Vine Place, Brighton, Sussex BN1 3HE, England.

**CORGIER Monique,** b. 10 October 1947, Lyon, France. Researcher. Education: PhD, National Institute of Applied Sciences, University of Lyon, 1974. Appointments: Researcher, Expert Researcher, CNRS, University of Lyon, INSA, Bayer Crop Science (Environmental Chemistry). Publications: Various articles in scientific periodicals. Membership: Advisory Board, Employee Shareholders. Address: 302 Rue Garibaldi, 69007 Lyon, France.

**CORNFORTH John Warcup,** b. 7 September 1917, Sydney, Australia. Organic Chemist. m. Rita H Harradence, 1 son,

2 daughters. Education: University of Sydney; Doctorate, Oxford University, 1941. Appointments: Worked with Robert Robinson, 1941-46; Scientific Staff, British Medical Research Council, 1946-62; Director, Milstead Laboratory of Chemical Enzymology, Shell Research Ltd, 1962-75; Associate Professor, Warwick University, 1965-71; Visiting Professor, University of Sussex, 1971-75; Royal Society Professor, University of Sussex, 1975-82; Researched stereochemistry of biochemical compounds. Publications: Co-author, The Chemistry of Penicillin, 1949; Numerous papers on chemical and biochemical topics. Honours: Corday-Morgan Medal, Chemical Society, 1953; Flintoff Medal, Chemical Society, 1966; Ciba Medal, Biochemical Society, 1966; Stouffer Prize, 1967; Davy Medal, Royal Society, 1968; Ernest Guenther Award, American Chemical Society, 1969; Prix Roussel, 1972; Honorary DSc, ETH Zurich, 1975, Oxford, Dublin, Liverpool, Warwick universities, 1976, Aberdeen, Hull, Sussex, Sydney universities, 1977; Joint Winner, Nobel Prize for Chemistry, 1975; Royal Medal, Royal Society, 1976; Copley Medal, Royal Society, 1982. Memberships: Corresponding member, Australian Academy of Science, 1977-; Foreign Associate, US National Academy of Sciences, 1978-; Foreign member, Royal Netherlands Academy of Sciences, 1978-; Foreign Honorary member, American Academy, 1973-; Honorary Fellow, 1976-, RSC, 2001, St Catherine's College, Oxford; Honorary Professor, Beijing Medical University, 1986-. Address: Saxon Down, Cuilfail, Lewes, East Sussex, BN7 2BE, England.

**CORNWALL-JONES Mark Ralph,** b. 14 February 1933, Quetta, Pakistan. Investment Manager. m. Priscilla Yeo, 3 sons, 1 daughter. Education: Jesus College, Cambridge. Appointments: National Service, Kings Royal Rifle Corps; Battersea Churches Housing Trust; The Debenture Corporation; John Govett & Co Ltd; Courage Ltd; Halifax Building Society; Govett Oriental Investment Trust; Ecclesiastical Insurance Group; Allchurches Trust. Honours: OBE, 2004. Address: Erin House, 3 Albert Bridge Road, Battersea, London SW11 4PX, England.

**COROIANU Anton Iuliu Demetru,** b. 16 October 1943, Arad, Romania. Engineer. m. Viorica Coroianu. Education: Engineer Diploma, Machine Construction Technology, Polytechnic Institute of Bucharest, 1961-66; Graduate Diploma, Utilisation of Isotopes and Radiation, Faculty of Physics, University of Bucharest, 1967-68; PhD, Non-destructive Control of Nuclear Elements, University of Brasov, 1976-80. Appointments: Engineer, Institute of Atomic Physics, 1967-77, Senior Engineer, Institute for Nuclear Research, Pitesti, 1977-80; Senior Inspector, State Committee for Nuclear Energy (former CNCAN), 1980-90, Chief State Inspector, 1990-97, Director, 1997-, National Commission for Nuclear Activities Control (CNCAN). Publications: 49 articles in the field of non-destructive testing with penetrating radiation and in the field of regulation, authorisation and control of nuclear activities in Romania. Memberships: European Society for Radiation Protection; Founding Member, Romanian Association for Non-destructive Testing; Founding Member, Romanian Society for Radiation Protection; Associate Member, American Society for Non-destructive Testing. Address: National Commission for Nuclear Activities Control, Blvd Libertatii 15, PO Box 42-2, Bucharest 5, Romania 761061. E-mail: anton.corianu@cncan.ro

**CORP Ronald Geoffrey,** b. 4 January 1951, Wells, Somerset, England. Musician; Cleric. Education: MA, Christ Church, Oxford; Dip. Theol., University of Southampton. Appointments: Librarian, Producer and Presenter, BBC Radio 3, 1973-87; Musical Director, Highgate Choral Society, 1984; Musical Director, The London Chorus, 1985; Founder, New London Orchestra, 1988; Founder, New London Children's Choir, 1991;

Non-stipendiary Minister, St Mary's Kilburn with St James' West End Lane, 1998-2002; Non-stipendiary Assistant Curate, Christ Church, Hendon; Compositions include: And All the Trumpets Sounded, 1989; Laudamus, 1994; Four Elizabethan Lyrics, 1994; Cornucopia, 1997; Piano Concerto, 1997; A New Song, 1999; Adonai Echad, 2001; Kaleidoscope, 2002; Missa San Marco, 2002; Dover Beach, 2003; Waters of Time, 2005. Publications: 18 recordings with New London Orchestra; Book: The Choral Singer's Companion, 1987, revised edition, 2000. Memberships: Trustee, 2000-, Chairman, Education Committee, Musician's Benevolent Fund; Vice-President, The Sullivan Society. Address: 76 Brent Street, London NW4 2ES, England. E-mail: ronald.corp@btconnect.com

**CORRY Charles Elmo,** b. 15 May 1938, Salt Lake City, Utah, USA. Geophysicist; Consultant. 2 sons, 1 daughter. Education: BS, Geology, Utah State University, 1970; MS, Geophysics, 1972, University of Utah; PhD, Geophysics, Texas A&M University, 1976. Appointments: Ground Radio Technician, US Marine Corps, 1956-59; Electronic Missile Checkout, GD/Astronautics, San Diego, 1960-64; Research Associate, Scripps Institution of Oceanography, San Diego, 1965-68, Woods Hole Oceanographic Institution, 1968; Manager, Geophysical Research, AMAX, Golden, 1977-82; Vice President, Nonlinear Analysis Incorporated, Bryan, Texas, 1982-84; Visiting and Adjunct Associate Professor, Geophysics, Texas A&M University, 1983-87; Associate Professor, Geophysics, University of Missouri, Rolla, 1984-89; Coordinator, World Ocean Circulation Experiment, Woods Hole Oceanographic Institution, 1990-95; Consultant, Database Administration, Denver and Colorado Springs, 1995-2001; President, Equal Justice Foundation, 2001-. Publications: 3 books; Numerous articles in professional journals. Memberships: American Geophysical Union; IEEE; Society of Exploration Geophysicists; Fellow, Geological Society of America; American Civil Liberties Union, Marine Corps League. Address: 455 Bear Creek Road, Colorado Springs, CO 80906-5820, USA. E-mail: ccorry@ejfi.org

**CORTES Joaquin,** b. 1970, Madrid, Spain. Appointments: Joined Spanish National Ballet, 1985; Principal Dancer, 1987-90; Now appears in own shows, blending gypsy dancing, jazz blues and classical ballet; Films: Pedro Almodóvar's, The Flower Of My Secret; Gitano, 2000.

**CORTI Christopher Winston,** b. 30 July 1940, London, England. Consultant. m. Shirley Anne Mack, 3 sons. Education: Bishopshalt School, Hillingdon, Middlesex, 1951-59; BSc, Metallurgy, Battersea College of Advanced Technology, London, 1959-63; PhD, Metallurgy, University of Surrey, Guildford, 1968-72. Appointments: Student, UK Atomic Energy Authority, Lancashire, 1961-62; Research Officer, Central Electricity Research Laboratories, Leatherhead, Surrey, 1963-68; Scientific Officer, Department of Materials Science & Engineering, University of Surrey, 1968-72; Project Leader, Brown Boveri Research Centre, Baden, Switzerland, 1973-77; Research Manager, Materials Technology, Johnston Matthey Technology Centre, Reading, 1978-88; Technical Director, Colour & Print Division, Johnson Matthey plc, Stoke on Trent, 1988-92; SPT Officer, Department of Trade & Industry, UK Government, 1993-94; Managing Director, International Technology, World Gold Council, London, 1994-2004; Managing Director, COReGOLD Technology Consultancy, 2004-. Publications: Over 70 scientific articles and conference papers in refereed scientific journals. Honours: Chartered Engineer; Chartered Scientist; Fellow, Institute of Materials, Minerals and Mining; Fellow, City & Guilds Institute, London. Memberships: Institute of Materials, Minerals and Mining,

London; City & Guilds Institute, London; Engineering Council, UK; Science Council, UK; Royal Horticultural Society, UK; National Trust, UK. Address: 21 Marchwood Avenue, Emmer Green, Reading, Berkshire RG4 8UH, England. E-mail: chris@corti.force9.co.uk

**COSBY Bill,** b. 12 July 1937, Philadelphia, USA. Actor. m. Camille Hanks, 1964, 5 children (1 son deceased). Education: Temple University; University of Massachusetts. Appointments: Served USNR, 1959-60; President, Rhythm and Blues Hall of Fame, 1968-; TV appearances include: The Bill Cosby Show, 1969, 1972-73, I Spy, The Cosby Show, 1984-92, Cosby Mystery Series, 1994-; Recitals include: Revenge, To Russell, My Brother With Whom I Slept, To Secret, 200 MPH, Why Is There Air, Wonderfulness, It's True, It's True, Bill Cosby is a Very Funny Fellow: Right, I Started Out as a Child, 8:15, 12:15, Hungry, Reunion 1982, Bill Cosby... Himself, 1983, Those of You With or Without Children, You'll Understand; Numerous night club appearances; Executive Producer, A Different Kind of World (TV series), 1987-; Films include: Hickey and Boggs, 1972; Man and Boy, 1972; Uptown Saturday Night, 1974; Let's Do It Again, 1975; Mother, Jugs and Speed, 1976; Aesop's Fables, A Piece of the Action, 1977; California Suite, 1978; Devil and Max Devlin, 1979; Leonard: Part IV, 1987; Ghost Dad, 1990; The Meteor Man, 1993; Jack, 1996; 4 Little Girls. Publications: The Wit and Wisdom of Fat Albert, 1973; Bill Cosby's Personal Guide to Power Tennis, Fatherhood, 1986; Time Flies, 1988; Love and Marriage, 1989; Childhood, 1991; Little Bill Series, 1999; Congratulations! Now What? 1999. Honours: 4 Emmy Awards and 8 Grammy Awards. Address: c/o The Brokaw Co, 9255 Sunset Boulevard, Los Angeles, CA 90069, USA.

**COSH (Ethel Eleanor) Mary,** b. Bristol England. Historian. Education: MA, St Anne's College Oxford, 1946-49. Appointments: Employment Clerk/Officer, Ministry of Labour, 5 years; Member of Design Review, Council of Industrial Design, 1951-52; Free-lance part-time employment includes: Transcriber for Hansard (for Standing Committees) Re-cataloguing Library, Order of St John; Artist's Model at leading London art schools. Publications: The Real World (fiction), 1961; Inveraray and the Dukes of Argyll (with the late Ian G Lindsay), 1973; Edinburgh: The Golden Age, 2002; A History of Islington, 2005; Numerous local publications including: The Squares of Islington (in 2 parts); Contributions to: The Times, Times Educational Supplement, The Spectator, Country Life. Honours: MA; FSA. Memberships: Conservation societies including: National Trust; NACF; Georgian Group; Victorian Society; Architectural Heritage Society of Scotland; Cockburn Association. Address: 10 Albion Mews, Islington, London N1 1JX, England.

**COSTA CABRAL E GIL Luis Manuel,** b. 30 March 1960, Lisbon, Portugal. Researcher; Consultant; Translator. m. Maria Dulce, 1 son. Education: Graduate, Chemical Engineering, 1985; MSc, Technological Organic Chemistry, 1989; Specialisation, Science and Technology Management, 1994. Appointments: Research Engineer, ICTM, 1985-87; Researcher, INETI, 1987-2005; Patent Translator, AGCF, JPC, CM, RCF, 1990-2005; Technical Advisor, ART/Belgium, 1990-94; Researcher, ITIME, 1994-97; Consultant, ZILTCH, 1998-2005; Consultant, AIEC, BETACORK, JPC, 2004-2005. Publications: 66 technical and scientific papers in national and international journals; 84 presentations in international meetings; 6 technical books on cork; 11 patents. Honours: 5 patent awards, 2 national, 3 international. Memberships: Portuguese Engineer Association, 1987; New York Academy of Sciences, 1994; Creativity

Portuguese Association, 1996; Portuguese Materials Society, 1997. E-mail: luis.gil@ineti.pt

**COSTELLO Elvis (Declan McManus),** b. 25 August 1955, London, England. Singer; Songwriter; Musician; Record Producer. m. (1) 1 child, (2) Cait O'Riordan, divorced, (3) Diana Krall, 2004. Career: Lead singer, Elvis Costello And The Attractions, 1977-; Appearances include: UK tour, 1977; US tour, 1978; Grand Ole Opry, 1981; Royal Albert Hall, with Royal Philharmonic, 1982; Cambridge Folk Festival, 1995; Television includes: Appearance in Scully, ITV drama, 1985; Also worked with The Specials; Paul McCartney; Aimee Mann; George Jones; Roy Orbison; Wendy James; Robert Wyatt; Jimmy Cliff; Co-organiser, annual Meltdown festival, South Bank Centre, London. Compositions include: Alison, 1977; Watching The Detectives, 1977; (I Don't Want To Go To) Chelsea, 1979; Crawling To The USA, 1978; Radio Radio, 1978; Stranger In The House, 1978; Girls Talk, 1979; Oliver's Army, 1979; Boy With A Problem, 1982; Every Day I Write The Book, 1983; Music for television series (with Richard Harvey): G.B.H., 1991; Jake's Progress, 1995; Other songs for artists including Johnny Cash; June Tabor. Recordings: Albums include: My Aim Is True, 1977; This Years Model, 1978; Armed Forces, 1979; Get Happy, 1980; Trust, 1980; Almost Blue, 1981; Taking Liberties, 1982; Imperial Bedroom, 1982; Goodbye Cruel World, 1984; Punch The Clock, 1984; The Best Of, 1985; Blood And Chocolate, 1986; King Of America, 1986; Spike, 1989; Mighty Like A Rose, 1991; My Aim Is True, 1991; The Juliet Letters, with the Brodksy Quartet, 1993; Brutal Youth, 1994; The Very Best Of Elvis Costello And The Attractions, 1995; Kojak Variety, 1995; Deep Dead Blue, Live At Meltdown (with Bill Frisell), 1995; All The Useless Beauty, 1996; Terror & Magnificence, 1997; Painted From Memory, 1998; The Sweetest Punch: The Songs of Costello, 1999; Best of Elvis Costello, 1999; For the Stars (with Anne Sofie von Otter), 2001; When I Was Cruel, 2002. Honours include: BAFTA Award, Best Original Television Music, G.B.H., 1992; MTV Video, Best Male Video, 1989; Rolling Stone Award, Best Songwriter, 1990. Address: c/o Jill Taylor, By Eleven Management, 12 Tideway Yard, 125 Mortlake High Street, London SW14 8SN, England.

**COSTELLO R H Brian,** Psychologist; Teacher. Education: Victorian Education Department Certificate, 1964; FCP Thesis, Psychological Special Education, London, 1974; South Australian Psychologists Board Certification, 1975; PhD, International College, Los Angeles, 1982; Victorian Psychologists Board Certification, 1985; Fellow, Royal Chartered College of Teachers (College of Preceptors); ABPS Diplomas in Psychological Disabilities Evaluation and Rehabilitation, 1996; Diplomate, AAIM College of Pain Management, 2003-. Appointments include: Elementary Teacher, 1962; Junior Secondary Teacher, 1963-71; Secondary and Special Education Teacher, 1971-74; Lecturer and Senior Psychology Tutor, Victorian Institute of Social Welfare, SAIT, University of South Australia, Sturt CAE, Elizabeth CAE, Monash University, 1971-86; Research and Private Practice, 1975-; Director Cassel Research Centre (Publishing); Consultant, Management Psychologist, National Drugs Foundations, Government Departments and NGO's 1989-; National Faculty Member, United States Sports Academy, 1986-2002; Visiting Professor of Psychology, University of South Alabama, 1997-; Consultant in Mind-Body Medicine, Swinburne University Hospital, 2001-; PhD and MA Supervisor, Swinburne University of Technology, 2002-. Publications: Author of numerous publications on pain control and mind-body medicine. Honours: US Golden Eagle Award of Excellence, 1997; Award of Distinction for International Forensics Education, South Alabama University, 1997; Outstanding

Service Award, American College of Forensic Examiners, 1999; Honorary Eminent Fellow of Wisdom and Award of Excellence for Education and Research, Wisdom Hall of Fame, Beverley Hills, 2001. Memberships: Australian Chair, Director at Large, International Council of Psychologists, 1978; Fellow and Diplomate, American Board of Medical Psychotherapists, 1986; Fellow American Association of Integrative Medicine, 2002-; Ambassador, International Council of Psychologists. Address: The Ibis Lodge, PO Box 1114, Pearcedale, Australia 3912. E-mail: bcos5371@bigpond.net.au

**COSTNER Kevin,** b. 18 January 1955. Actor. m. Cindy Silva, divorced 1 son, 2 daughter, 1 son by Bridget Rooney. Education: California State University. Appointments: Directing debut in Dances With Wolves, 1990; Films include: Frances, 1982; The Big Chill, 1983; Testament, 1983; Silverado, 1985; The Untouchables, 1987; No Way Out, 1987; Bull Durham, 1988; Field of Dreams, 1989; Revenge, 1989; Robin Hood: Prince of Thieves, 1990; JFK, 1991; The Bodyguard, 1992; A Perfect World, 1993; Wyatt Earp, 1994; Waterworld, 1995; Tin Cup, 1996; Message in a Bottle, 1998; For Love of the Game, 1999; Thirteen Days, 2000; 3000 Miles to Graceland, 2001; Dragonfly, 2002; Open Range, 2003; Co-producer, Rapa Nui; Co-producer, China Moon. Honours include: Academy Award for Best Picture, 1991. Address: TIG Productions, Producers Building 5, 4000 Warner Boulevard, Burbank, CA 91523, USA.

**COTTELL Michael Norman Tizard,** b. 25 July 1931, Southampton, England. Retired Civil Engineer. m. Joan Florence, 2 sons. Education: Southampton University; Birmingham University. Appointments: Assistant County Surveyor, East Suffolk County Council, 1965-73; Deputy County Surveyor, East Sussex County Council, 1973-76; County Surveyor, Northants County Council, 1976-84; County Surveyor, Kent County Council, 1984-91; Executive Consultant, Travers Morgan Consultants, 1991-95; Chairman, Aspen Consultancy Group, 1995-2002. Honour: OBE, 1988.Memberships: F R ENG; FICE; F IHT; MCIM. Address: Salcey Lawn, Harrow Court, Stockbury, Sittingbourne, Kent, ME9 7UQ, England.

**COTTRELL Bryce A M,** b. 16 September 1931, Aldershot, England. Stockbroker. m. Jeane D Monk, 2 sons, 2 daughters. Education: Corpus Christi College, Oxford, 1951-55. Appointments: Partner, 1963-85, Head of Government Bonds, 1970, Senior Partner, 1983-85, Chairman, 1985-88, Phillips & Drew; Fellow, Corpus Christi College, Oxford, 1990-92; Non-Executive Director, Long Term Capital Ltd, 1994-99; Non-Executive Chairman, JWM Partners (UK) Ltd, 1999-; Member, Group Thirty Committee on International Securities Settlement, 1989-90. Memberships: Companion of the Chartered Management Institute; Securities Institute. Address: The Portreeve's House, East Street, Tonbridge, Kent TN9 1HP, England.

**COTTRELL David Milton,** b. 27 March 1969, Fort Dodge, Iowa. Recording Engineer; Writer. Education: Bachelors Degree in Counseling, Almeda University; Consumer Electronics, Dick Grove Music Career Workshop. Appointments: FM Engineer; Songwriter; Recording Engineer/Producer; Music Publisher; Electronics Technician; Counselor; Personal Trainer. Honours: American Medal of Honor; Noble Laureate; Man of the Year, 2004, 2005; International Professional of the Year, 2005; Achievement in Science Award, 2005; Great Minds of the 21st Century; International Order of Merit; Listed in Who's Who publications and biographical dictionaries. Memberships: DeMolay; Natural Resources Defense Council; The Sierra Club. Address: 414 First Street South East, Apartment C, Le Mars, IA 51031, USA. E-mail: davecottrell@frontiernet.net

**COULOURIS Mary Louise,** b. 17 July 1939, New York City, New York, USA. Artist. m. Gordon Wallace, 1 son, 1 daughter. Education: NDD, Chelsea School of Art, 1956-58; Dip AD (Lond), Slade School, London University, 1958-61, Postgraduate, Slade School, 1962; French Government Scholar, 1962-64. Career: Artist; Mosaic Commission, Skyros, Greece, 1999; Tapestry Commission, Yale College, Wrexham, 2002; Work in collections: House of Lords; Sainsburys PLC; Scottish National Heritage; Hambros Bank; Baroness Crawley; Ashmolean, Oxford; Bank of Scotland; Bibliotheque Nationale, Paris, France. Honours: 1st Prize, Scottish Development Agency Design Award, 1988; Artists' Exchange to Athens for Glasgow Year of Culture, 1990; Churchill Fellow, 1992; 1st Prize, Sainsbury Wine Label Design Award, 1996. Membership: Senior Fellow, Royal Society of Painter Etchers. Address: 5 Strawberry Bank, Linlithgow, West Lothian, EH49 6BJ, Scotland. Website: www.artmlc.co.uk

**COULSON-THOMAS Colin Joseph,** b. 26 April 1949, Mullion, Cornwall, England. Professor; Author; Chairman. 1 son, 2 daughters. Education: MSc, London Business School, 1975; DPA, 1977, MSc (Econ), 1980, LSE/London University; PCL, MA, CNAA, 1981, AM, 1982, University of Southern California; UNISA, MPA, 1985, PhD, 1988, University of Aston. Appointments: Consultant, Cooper & Lybrand, 1975-78; Editor, Publisher, Head of Public Relations, ICSA, 1978-81; Publishing Director, Longman Group, 1981-84; Corporate Affairs, Xerox, Rank Xerox, 1984-93; Founder, Chairman of companies including: Adaptation, ASK Europe, Cotoco, Policy Publications, 1987-; Willmot Dixon Professor, Dean of Faculty, Head of Patteridge Bury Campus, University of Luton, 1994-97; Professor, Head, Centre for Competitiveness, 2000-; Professor of Direction and Leadership, University of Lincoln, 2005-; Editor, The Learning Organisation, 2005-. Publications: Author of over 30 books and reports including: The Future of the Organisation, 1997/98; Individuals and Enterprise, 1999; Shaping Things to Come, 2001; Transforming the Company, 2002, 2004; The Knowledge Entrepreneur, 2003; Reports include: Pricing for Profit, 2002; Winning New Business, 2003. Memberships: Chartered Accountant; FCA; FCCA; FCIS; FMS; FCIPR; FCIPD; FRGS; FSCA; Has served on regional and national public sector boards. Address: Mill Reach, Mill Lane, Water Newton, Cambridgeshire PE8 6LY, England. E-mail: colinct@tiscali.co.uk Website: www.ntwkfirm.com/colin.coulson-thomas

**COUPLES Fred,** b. 3 October 1959, Seattle, Washington, USA. Professional Golfer. Education: University of Houston. Appointments: Member, Rider Cup Team, 1989, 1991, 1993; Named All-American, 1979, 1980; Winner, numerous tournaments including Kemper Open, 1983; Tournament Players Championship, 1984, Byron Nelson Golf Classic, 1987, French PGA, 1988, Nissan LA Open, 1990, 1992, Tournai Perrier de Paris, 1991, BC Open, 1991, Federal Express St Jude Classic, 1991, Johnnie Walker World Championship, 1991, 1995, Nestle Invitational, 1992, The Masters, 1992, with Jan Stephenson J C Penney Classic, 1983, with Mike Donald, Sazale Classic, 1990, with Raymond Floyd, RMCC Invitational, 1990, Buick Open, 1994, Dubai Desert Classic, 1995, Players Championship, 1996, Skins Game, 1996, Australian Skins Game, 1997; Member, US Team, Presidents Cup, 1997; Champion, Bob Hope Chrysler Classic, 1998; Champion, Memorial Tournament, 1998; Member, President Cup Team, 1998. Honours: Vardon Trophy, 1991, 1992; Named PGA Player of Year, Golf World magazine, 1991, 1992. Address: c/o PGA Tour, 100 Avenue of the Champions, PO Box 109601, Palm Beach Gardens, FL 33410, USA.

**COURIER Jim (James Spencer),** b. 17 August 1970, Sanford, Florida, USA. Tennis Player. Career: Professional Tennis Player, 1989-; Winner of tournaments including: Orange Bowl, 1986, 1987, Basel, 1989, French Open, 1991, 1992, Indian Wells, 1991, 1993, Key Biscayne, 1991, 1993, Australian Open, 1992-93, Italian Open, 93; Finalist US Open, 1991; Quarterfinalist, Wimbledon, 1991; Runner-up French Open, 1993, Wimbledon, 1993; Semifinalist, Australian Open, 1994, French Open, 1994; Winner of 23 singles titles and six doubles titles and over 16 million dollars in prize money; Retired, 2000. Address: IGM, Suite 300, 1 Erieview Place, Cleveland, OH 44114, USA.

**COURTILLOT Vincent Emmanuel,** b. 6 March 1948, Neuilly, France. Professor of Geophysics. m. Michèle Consolo, 1 son, 1 daughter. Education: Civil Engineer, Paris School of Mines, 1971; MS, Geophysics, Stanford University, 1972; PhD, Geophysics, University of Paris VI, 1974; DSc, Geophysics, University of Paris VII, 1977. Appointments: Assistant, University of Paris VII, 1973-77; Maitre-Assistant, 1977-78; Maitre de Conférences, 1978-83; Professor, 1983-89; Physicien classe exceptionnelle, 1989-94; Director, Ministry of Education, 1989-93; Professor classe exceptionelle, University of Paris VII, 1994-; Director, Graduate School of Earth Sciences, 1995-98; President, European Union of Geosciences, 1995-97; Professor, Institut Universitaire de France, 1996-; Director, Institut de Physique du Globe de Paris, 1996-98, 2004-; Special Adviser to the Minister of Education, Research and Technology, 1997-98; Director, Ministry of Research, 1999-2001; President, Scientific Council of the City of Paris, 2002-; Chief Editor, Earth and Planetary Science Letters, 2003-; President elect, American Geophysical Union, Geomagnetism and Paleomagnetism, 2004-. Publications: Several articles in professional journals, two books. Honours: Prix Gay, French Academy of Sciences, 1981; 1st Franco-British Prize, 1985; Fellow, AGU, 1990; Chevalier, Ordre national du Mérite, 1990, Officier, 1997; Silver Medal, Centre National de la Recherche Scientifique, 1993; Fairchild Distinguished Scholar, 1994; Chevalier, Legion of Honour, 1994; Member, Academia Europea, 1994; Gerald Stanton Ford Lecturer, University of Minnesota, 1996; Associate, Royal Astronomical Society; Commandeur, Ordre National des Palmes Académiques, 1997; Prix Dolomieu, French Academy of Sciences, Moore Distinguished Fellow, CalTech, 2002; Commencement Speaker, University of Lausanne; Member, Paris Academy of Sciences, 2003. Address: IPG, 4 Place Jussieu, 75230 Paris Cedex 5, France.

**COVENEY Peter Vivian,** b. 30 October 1958, London, England. University Professor. m. Samia Coveney-Nehmé, 1 son, 1 daughter. Education: BA, Lincoln College, Oxford, 1981; Jane Eliza Procter Fellow, Princeton University, 1981-82; Senior Scholar, MA, Merton College, Oxford, 1984; Sir Edward Abraham Fellow, DPhil, Keble College, Oxford, 1987. Appointments: Lecturer in Physical Chemistry, University of Wales, Bangor, 1987-90; Leader, Senior Scientist, Schlumberger Cambridge Research Programme, 1991-98; Professor and Head of Physical Chemistry, Director Centre for Computational Science, Queen Mary, University of London, 1999-2002; Professor and Director, Centre for Computational Science, University College, London, 2002-; Chairman, UK Collaborative Computational Projects Steering Panel, 2005-08. Publications: Author of numerous articles in books and scientific journals; 7 patents for technical inventions; Books: The Arrow of Time (with Roger Highfield), 1990; Frontiers of Complexity (with Roger Highfield), 1995; Several edited works include: Scientific Grid Computing, 2005. Honours: Innovative Applications of Artificial Intelligence, 1996; HPC Challenge Award (Supercomputing), 2003; International Supercomputing Conference Award, 2004. Memberships: Fellow, Royal Society of Chemistry; Fellow, Institute of Physics; Scientific Society of the Isaac Newton Institute. Address: Centre for Computational Science, University College London, 20 Gordon Street, London WC1H 0AJ. Website: www.chem.ucl.ac.uk/ccs

**COWDREY Herbert Edward John,** b. 29 November 1926, Basingstoke, Hampshire, England. University Teacher. m. Judith Watson Davis, 14 July 1959, deceased August 2004, 1 son, 2 daughters. Education: BA, 1949, MA, 1951, DD, 2000, Oxford University. Appointments: Chaplain and Tutor, St Stephen's House, Oxford, 1952-56; Fellow, 1956-94, Fellow Emeritus, 1994-, St Edmund Hall, Oxford; Honorary Fellow, St Stephen's House, Oxford, 2005. Publications: The Cluniacs and the Gregorian Reform; The Epistolae Vagantes of Pope Gregory VII; Two Studies in Cluniac History; The Age of Abbot Desiderius; Popes, Monks and Crusaders; Pope Gregory VII, 1073-85; The Crusades and Latin Monasticism, 11th-12th Centuries; Popes and Church Reform in the 11th Century. Contributions to: Many articles. Honour: British Academy, fellow. Memberships: Royal Historical Society; Henry Bradshaw Society. Address: 19 Church Lane, Old Marston, OX3 0NZ, England.

**COWEN Athol Ernest,** b. 18 January 1942, Corbridge, Hexham, Northumberland, England. Writer; Poet; Publisher. Education: Queen Elizabeth Grammar School, Penrith. Career: Artist; Musician, Songwriter; Writer, Poet; Self-employed Publisher. Publications: Word Pictures (Brain Soup), 1989; Huh!, 1991; Work included in various anthologies published in Wales, England, India and the USA. Memberships: Publishers' Association; Poetry Society; Writers' Guild of Great Britain; Musicians' Union; Guild of International Songwriters and Composers; MRI; DG (ABIRA); IOA. Address: 40 Gibson Street, Wrexham, Wrexham County Borough LL13 7TS, Wales.

**COX Charles Brian,** b. 5 September 1928, Grimsby, Lincolnshire, England. Professor Emeritus of English Literature; Writer; Poet; Editor. Education: BA, 1952, MA, 1955, MLitt, 1958, Pembroke College, Cambridge. Appointments: Lecturer, Senior Lecturer, University of Hull, 1954-66; Co-editor, Critical Quarterly, 1959-; Professor of English Literature, 1966-93, Professor Emeritus, 1993-, Pro-Vice Chancellor, 1987-91, University of Manchester; Visiting Professor, King's College, London, 1994; Honorary Fellow, Westminster College, Oxford, 1994; Member, Arts Council 1996-98; Chair, North West Arts Board, 1994-2000. Publications: The Free Spirit, 1963; Modern Poetry (with A E Dyson), 1963; Conrad's Nostromo, 1964; The Practical Criticism of Poetry (with A E Dyson), 1965; Poems of This Century (editor with A E Dyson), 1968; Word in the Desert (editor with A E Dyson), 1968; The Waste Land: A Casebook (editor with A P Hinchliffe), 1968; The Black Papers on Education (editor with A E Dyson), 1971; The Twentieth Century Mind (editor with A E Dyson), 3 volumes, 1972; Conrad: Youth, Heart of Darkness and The End of the Tether (editor), 1974; Joseph Conrad: The Modern Imagination, 1974; Black Paper 1975 (editor with R Boyson), 1975; Black Paper 1977 (editor with R Boyson), 1977; Conrad, 1977; Every Common Sight (verse), 1981; Two Headed Monster (verse), 1985; Cox on Cox: An English Curriculum for the 1990's, 1991; The Great Betrayal: Autobiography, 1992; Collected Poems, 1993; The Battle for the English Curriculum, 1995; African Writers (editor), 1997; Literacy is Not Enough (editor), 1998; Emeritus (verse), 2001. Honours: Commander of the Order of the British Empire, 1990; Fellow, Royal Society of Literature, 1993 DLitt, De Montfort University, 1999. Membership: Chair, North West Arts Board, 1994-2000. Address: 20 Park Gates Drive, Cheadle Hulme, Stockport SK8 7DF, England.

**COX Courteney,** b. 15 June 1964, Birmingham, Alabama, USA. Actress. m. David Arquette, 1999, 1 daughter. Appointments: Modelling career, New York; Appeared Bruce Springsteen music video, Dancing in the Dark, 1984; Films: Down Twisted, 1986; Masters of the Universe, 1987; Cocoon: The Return, 1988; Mr Destiny, 1990; Blue Desert, 1990; Shaking the Tree, 1992; The Opposite Sex, 1993; Ace Ventura, Pet Detective, 1994; Scream, 1996; Commandments, 1996; Scream 2, 1997; The Runner, 1999; Scream 3, 1999; The Shrink Is In, 2000; 3000 Miles to Graceland, 2001; Get Well Soon, 2001; Alien Love Triangle, 2002; November, 2004; TV series: Misfits of Science, 1985-86; Family Ties, 1987-88; The Trouble With Larry, 1993; Friends, 1994-2004; TV films include: Roxanne: The Prize Pulitzer, 1989; Till We Meet Again, 1989; Curiosity Kills, 1990; Morton and Hays, 1991, Tobber, 1992; Sketch Artist II: Hands That See, 1995. Address: c/o Creative Artists Agency, 9830 Wilshire Boulevard, Beverly Hills, CA 90212, USA.

**COX Dennis William,** b. 27 February 1957, Hornchurch, Essex, England. Director. m. Lisette Mermod, 1996, 2 stepdaughters. Education: Hornchurch Grammar School, 1965-75; BSc in Mathematics, Westfield College, London. Appointments: Various positions rising to Senior Manager of Banking and Finance, Arthur Young (now Ernst & Young), 1978-88; Senior Manager of Banking and Finance, BDO Binder Hamlyn, 1988-90; Audit Manager, Midland Bank, rising to Senior Audit Manager (Compliance) HSBC Holdings plc, 1991-97; Director of Risk Management, Prudential Portfolio Managers, 1997-2000; Director of Operational Risk, HSBC Operational Risk Consultancy Division, 2000-01; Chief Executive Officer, Risk Reward Limited, 2002-; CFO, BDKT, 2003-; Chief Executive Officer, Auxetica Ltd, 2004-; Chief Executive Officer, Compliance Edge Ltd, 2004-. Memberships: Institute of Chartered Accountants in England and Wales; Securities and Investments Institute; Financial Authorisation Committee of Institute of Actuaries; Council Member, ICAEW; MIB, 1988; FCA, 1991; ACA, 1981; MSI, 1992. Publications: Banks: Accounts, Audit & Practice, 1993; Author of various articles in professional journals. Address: Risk Reward Limited, Canada House, 9 Walton Gardens, Shenfield, Essex CM13 1EJ, England. E-mail: dwc@riskrewardlimited.com

**COX Richard,** b. 8 March 1931, Winchester, Hampshire, England. Writer. m. 1963, 2 sons, 1 daughter. Honours degree in English, St Catherine's College, Oxford, 1955. Publications: Operation Sealion, 1974; Sam, 1976; Auction, 1978; KGB Directive, 1981; Ground Zero, 1985; An Agent of Influence, 1988; Park Plaza, 1991; Eclipse, 1996; Murder at Wittenham Park, 1998 ( as R W Heber, 1997). Contributions to: Daily Telegraph (Staff Correspondent, 1966-72); Travel & Leisure; Traveller; Orient Express Magazine. Honour: Territorial Decoration, 1966. Membership: Army and Navy Club; Member, CARE International UK, 1989-, (Board Member 1985-1997); Member, States of Alderney, 2001-; Representative States of Guernsey, 2003-. Address: 18 Hauteville, Alderney, Channel Islands GY9 3UA.

**CRAGGS Stewart Roger,** b. 27 July 1943, Ilkley, West Yorkshire, England. Academic Librarian. m. Valerie J Gibson, 28 Sept 1968, 1 son, 1 daughter. Education: ALA, Leeds Polytechnic, 1968; FLA, 1974; MA, University of Strathclyde, Glasgow, 1978; PhD, University of Strathclyde, 1982. Appointments: Teesside Polytechnic, 1968-69; JA Jobling, 1970-72; Sunderland Polytechnic, later University, 1973-95; Consultant to the William Walton Edition, Oxford University Press, 1995-. Publications: William Walton: A Thematic Catalogue, 1977; Arthur Bliss: A Bio-Bibliography, 1988; Richard Rodney Bennett: A Bio-Bibliography, 1990; William

Walton: A Catalogue, 2nd ed, 1990; John McCabe: A Bio-Bibliography, 1991; William Walton: A Source Book, 1993; John Ireland: A Catalogue, Discography and Bibliography, 1993; Alun Hoddinott: A Bio-Bibliography, 1993; Edward Elgar: A Source Book, 1995; William Mathias: A Bio-Bibliography, 1995; Arthur Bliss: A Source Book, 1996; Soundtracks: An International Dictionary of Composers for Films, 1998; Malcolm Arnold: A Bio-Bibliography, 1998; William Walton: Music and Literature, 1999; Lennox Berkeley: A Source Book, 2000; Benjamin Britten: A Bio-Bibliography, 2001; Arthur Bliss: Music and Literature, 2002; Peter Maxwell Davies: A Source Book, 2002. Honour: Professor of Music Bibliography, University of Sunderland, 1993; Library Association McColvin Medal for Best Reference Book, 1990. Address: 106 Mount Road, High Barnes, Sunderland, SR4 7NN, England.

**CRAMPTON Colin Bassett,** b. 31 December 1926, Gillingham, Kent, England. Widower, 2 daughters. Education: Royal Naval Short Course, Economics, University of Edinburgh, 1944-45; BSc, Geology, 1953, PhD, 1956, University of Bristol. Appointments: Soil Surveyor and Researcher, Yorkshire, Principal Scientific Officer in Charge, South Wales region, Rothamsted Experimental Station; Research Scientist, Canadian Forestry Service, 1967-70; Research Scientist, Department of Indian and Northern Affairs, 1970-73; Tenured Full Professor, Department of Geography, Simon Fraser University, 1973-91; Retired, 1991; P Geo membership, 1993; Full time teaching through Distance Education. Publications: Papers published in international journals and conference proceedings. Address: Department of Geography, Simon Fraser University, Burnaby, BC V5A 1S6, Canada.

**CRANE Richard Arthur,** b. 4 December 1944, York, England. Writer. m. Faynia Williams, 5 September 1975, 2 sons, 2 step-daughters. Education: BA (Hons), Classics and English, 1966, MA, 1971, Jesus College, Cambridge. Appointments: Fellow in Theatre, University of Bradford, 1972-74; Resident Dramatist, National Theatre, 1974-75; Fellow in Creative Writing, University of Leicester, 1976; Literary Manager, Royal Court Theatre, 1978-79; Associate Director, Brighton Theatre, 1980-85; Dramaturg, Tron Theatre, Glasgow, 1983-84; Visiting Writers Fellowship, University of East Anglia, 1988; Writer-in-Residence, Birmingham Polytechnic, 1990-91, HM Prison Bedford, 1993; Lecturer in Creative Writing, University of Sussex, 1994-. Publications: Thunder, 1976; Gunslinger, 1979; Crippen, 1993; Under the Stars, 1994. Stage Plays: The Tenant, 1971; Crippen, 1971; Decent Things, 1972; The Blood Stream, 1972; Secrets, 1973; Bleak Midwinter, 1973; The Quest, 1974; Clownmaker, 1975; Humbug, 1975; Venus and Superkid, 1975; Mean Time, 1975; Bloody Neighbours, 1975; Satan's Ball, 1977; Gogol, 1979; Vanity, 1980; Brothers Karamazov, 1981; The Possessed (with Yuri Lyubimov), 1985; Mutiny! (with David Essex), 1985; Soldier Soldier (with Tony Parker) 1986; Envy (with Donald Swann), 1986; Pushkin, 1987; Red Magic, 1988; Rolling the Stone, 1989; Phaedra (with Michael Glenny), 1990; Baggage and Bombshells, 1991; Under the Stars, 1993. Editor: Poems from the Waiting Room, 1993; The Last Minute Book, 1995; Pandora's Books, 1997; TV Plays: Rottingdean, 1980; The Possessed, 1985. Radio Plays: Gogol, 1980; Decent Things, 1984; Optimistic Tragedy, 1986; Anna and Marina, 1991; Understudies, 1992; Vlad the Impaler, 1992; The Sea The Sea (classic serial), 1993; Plutopia (with Donald Swann), 1994; Eugene Onegin, 1999. Contributions to: Edinburgh Fringe; Guardian; Independent; Stage; Index on Censorship, Times Literary Supplement. Honours: Edinburgh Fringe First Awards, 1973, 1974, 1975, 1977, 1980, 1986, 1987, 1988, 1989; Ensemble Award, National Theatre Festival, Hungary, 2004.

Address: c/o Casarotto-Ramsay Ltd, National House, 60-66 Wardour Street, London W1V 3HP, England.

**CRAPON de CAPRONA Noël François Marie, (Comte),** b. 23 May 1928, Chambéry, Savoie, France. Lawyer; UN Senior Official, retired. m. Barbro Sigrid Wenne, 2 sons. Education: Diploma, Institute of Comparative Law, 1951; LLB, University of Paris, 1952; Postgraduate Studies, School of Political Science, 1952-54. Appointments: Assistant Manager, Sta Catalina Estancias, Argentina, 1947-48; Editor, Food and Agriculture Organization of the United Nations, 1954-57; Liaison Officer, UN and Other Organisations, Director General's Office, 1957-65; Chief, Reports and Records, 1966-72; Chief, Conference Operations, 1972-74; Secretary General, Conference and Council, 1974-78; Director, FAO Conference, Council and Protocol Affairs, 1974-83. Publication: The Longobards, a tentative explanation, 1995. Honours: FAO Silver Medal, 25 Years of Service; Medal of Honour, City of Salon de Provence, 1992; Who's Who Medal, 2000; World Medal of Honour, American Biographical Institute, 2003. Memberships: Society in France of the Sons of the American Revolution; Alumni Association College St Martin de France and Ecole des Sciences Politiques. Address: Lojovägen 73-75, S-18147 Lidingö, Sweden; Palais Hadrien, Place dei Tres Mast, 83600 Port-Frejus, France.

**CRAWFORD Alistair,** b. 25 January 1945, Fraserburgh, Aberdeenshire, Scotland. Artist; Writer. m. Joan Martin. Education: Diploma in Art, Glasgow School of Art, 1966; Art Teachers Certificate, Aberdeen College of Education, 1968. Career: Painter; Printmaker; Photographer; Art Historian; Performer; Lecturer, Department of Textile Industries University of Leeds, 1968-71; Senior Lecturer, Graphic Design, Coventry Polytechnic, 1971-73; Lecturer in Graphic Art, 1974-83, Senior Lecturer, 1983, Reader, 1987, Head of Department, 1986-95; Professor of Art, 1990, Head of the new University of Wales, School of Art, Aberystwyth, 1994; Currently Research Professor of Art, University of Wales, Aberystwyth, 1995-; Balsdon Senior Fellow, 1995-96, First Archive Research Fellow, 1997-2001, British School at Rome; Exhibitions: 38 solo exhibitions and 159 selected exhibitions in Britain and Europe and USA; 438 works represented in 59 public and corporate collections and nearly 2000 in private collections world-wide; Recent solo exhibitions include: A Return to Wales, Retrospective 1974-2000; New Paintings, National Library of Wales; Landscape Capriccios, the landscape of the mind, University of Wales, Aberystwyth, 2004-2005; Curator of several major exhibitions of photography in Europe and USA; Performances: An Evening with Eugene Strong, 1996-, Brief Exposure, 2001-; A Little Bit More Brief Exposure, 2004-. Publications: Over 120 publications; Books and catalogues include: John Thomas 1838-1905, Photographer (co-author), 1977; Mario Giacomelli, 1983, 1985; Elio Ciol, Italia Black and White, 1986; Carlo Bevilacqua, 1986; Elio Ciol, Assisi, 1991; George Chapman, 1989; Will Roberts, 1993; Kyffin Williams, 1995; Alistair Crawford Collected Photographs, 1995; The Welsh Lens, 1997; Robert MacPherson 1914-1872, 1999; Made of Wales, 2000; Father P P Mackey (1851-1935) Photographer, 2000; Mario Giacomelli, 2001, 2002, 2004; Erich Lessing Vom Festhalten der Zeit. Reportage – Fotografie 1948-73, 2002, 2003; Column "Brief Exposure", Inscape Magazine, 1999-; Co-editor, Photoresearcher, Vienna, 2004-. Honours include: Arts Council of Wales; British Council; British Academy; Goethe Institute; Winston Churchill Fellow, 1982; Gold Medal in Fine Art, Royal National Eisteddfod of Wales, 1985; Invited Fellow, Royal Photographic Society, 1991; Invited Academician, Royal Cambrian Academy, 1994; Elected Honorary Fellow, Royal Society of Painter-Printmakers, 2000. Memberships: Royal Cambrian Academy; Royal Society of Painter-Printmakers; European Society for the History of Photography. Address: Brynawel, Comins Coch, Aberystwyth SY23 3BD, Wales. E-mail: alc@aber.ac.uk

**CRAWFORD Cindy,** b. 1966, USA. Model. m. (1) Richard Gere, 1991, divorced, (2) Rande Gerber, 1998, 1 son, 1 daughter. Career: Major contracts with Revlon & Pepsi Cola; Presenter on own MTV fashion show; Appearances on numerous magazine covers, model for various designers; Face of Kelloggs Special K, 2000; Film: Fair Game, 1995; Released several exercise videos. Publications: Cindy Crawford's Basic Face, 1996; About Face (for children), 2001. Address: c/o Wolf-Kasteler, 231 South Rodeo Drive, Suite 300, Beverly Hills, CA 90212, USA.

**CRAWFORD Daniel Frank,** b. 11 December 1948, Hackensack, New Jersey, USA. Theatre Director. m. Stephanie, 1 daughter. Appointments: Artistic Director, The King's Head Theatre, 1970-; Adjudicator, Vivian Ellis Prize, 1985-2000; Producer and co-producer, over 20 West End shows; Director, The King's Head, West End, National Tour and abroad; Lighting Designer, over 150 shows. Honours: Olivier Award, Best Performance in a Musical; Most Promising New Playwright, Evening Standard Award; Best Comedy Award, Oliver Award, Evening Standard Award, 1992; Peter Brook Award, 1995; Best Supporting Role in a Musical, 2000; Second Queen's Award for Trainee Directors Programme, 2002. Memberships: The Society of London Theatres. Address: The King's Head Theatre, 115 Upper Street, London N1 1QN, England.

**CRAWFORD Michael,** b. 19 January 1942. Actor; Singer. Appointments: Actor, 1955-; Films for Children's Film Foundation; 100's radio broadcasts; Appeared in original productions of Noyess Fludde and Let's Make an Opera, by Benjamin Britten; Tours, UK, USA, Australia. Stage roles include: Travelling Light, 1965; The Anniversary, 1966; No Sex Please, We're British, 1971; Billy, 1974; Same Time, Next Year, 1976; Flowers for Algernon, 1979; Barnum, 1981-83, 1984-86; Phantom of the Opera, London, 1986-87; Broadway, 1988, Los Angeles, 1989; The Music of Andrew Lloyd Webber (concert tour), USA, Australia, UK, 1992-92; EFX, Las Vegas, 1995-96; Dance of the Vampires, Broadway, 2003; Films include: Soap Box Derby, 1950; Blow Your Own Trumpet, 1954; Two Living One Dead, 1962; The War Lover, 1963; Two Left Feet, 1963; The Knack, 1965; A Funny Thing Happened on the Way to the Forum, 1966; The Jokers, 1966; How I Won the War, 1967; Hello Dolly, 1969; The Games, 1969; Hello Goodbye, 1970; Alice's Adventures in Wonderland, 1972; Condor Man, 1980; TV appearances include: Sir Francis Drake (series), 1962; Some Mothers Do 'Ave 'Em (several series); Chalk and Cheese (series), 1979; Sorry (play), 1979. Publication: Parcel Arrived Safely: Tied with String (autobiography), 2000. Honours: OBE; Tony Award, 1988. Address: c/o ICM Ltd, Oxford House, 76 Oxford Street, London W1D 1BS, England.

**CRAWFORD Robert (Roy) James,** b. 6 April 1949, Lisburn, Northern Ireland. Professor of Engineering Materials. m. Isobel Catherine (Renee) Allen, 2 sons, 1 daughter. Education: BSc, 1st Class Honours, Mechanical Engineering, 1970, PhD, 1973, DSc, 1987, Queen's University, Belfast. Appointments: Engineering Assistant Lecturer, Queen's University Belfast, 1972-73; Technical Service Engineer, ICI, 1973-74; Lecturer, Senior Lecturer and Reader,1974-79, Director, Polymer Processing Research Centre, 1997-99, Director, School of Mechanical and Process Engineering, 1989-97; Professor of Engineering Materials, 1989-99, 2001-05, Pro-Vice-Chancellor, 2001-05, Queen's University Belfast; Professor of Mechanical Engineering, University of Auckland, New Zealand, 1999-2001; Vice-Chancellor, 2005-, University of Waikato, New Zealand, Company Directorships: Hughes & McLeod Ltd, 1991-, Rotosystems, 1991-2005, University Bookshop, 1995-99, QUBIS Ltd, 2001-05; University Challenge Fund, 2001; Investment Belfast Ltd, 2003-05. Publications: 7 books and over 300 papers in learned journals and conferences; Delivered Keynote Addresses at conferences all over the world. Honours: GKN Windsor Prize, 1979; Gaspar Award, 1983, 1990; J S Walker Award, 1983; PMDA Award, 1987; Silver Medal, 1990, 1992; Engineering Employers Federation Trophy, 1992; SMART Award, 1993, 1994; Netlon Medal, 1996; IGDS Quality Award, 1996, ARM Distinguished Service Award, 1998; Best Paper on Rotational Moulding, SPE ANTEC Conferences, 1999, 2000, 2001, 2002. Memberships: F R Eng; Chartered Engineer; Fellow, Institute of Mechanical Engineers; Fellow, Institute of Materials, Minerals and Mining; Fellow Society of Plastics Engineers. Address: Vice-Chancellor's Office, University of Waikato, Private Bag 3105, Hamilton, New Zealand. E-mail: r.crawford@waikato.ac.nz

**CREASEY Richard John,** b. 28 August 1944, Bournemouth, England. Media Executive. m. Vera, 2 sons, 1 daughter. Education: Malvern College. Appointments: Researcher, 1965-73, Producer, 1972-74, Granada TV; Producer, 1974-77, Executive Producer, 1977-78, Head of Documentaries, 1978-92, Director Network Factual Programmes, 1992-94, ATV Network/ Central Television; Expedition Leader, New York to London Overland Challenge, sponsored by Ford, endorsed by United Nations, 1993-94; Founder Director, BUR Media, 1994-; Editor in Chief, The Digital Village, 1995-2001; Executive Producer, BBC, 2001-04; Chairman, Television Trust for the Environment, 2003-. Memberships: Life Member, BAFTA; British Microlight Aircraft Association, 2001-. Address: 11 Regents Park Road, London NW1 7TL, England. E-mail: richard@richardcreasey. net Website: www.richardcreasey.net

**CRESSON Edith,** b. 27 January 1934, Boulogne-sur-Seine, France. Politician. m. J Cresson, 2 daughters. Education: Hautes Etudes Commerciales, Doctorat de Démographie. Appointments: Economist, Conventions des Institutions Republicanes, 1965; Socialist Party National Secretary, 1974; Mayor of Thure, 1977; Member, Eurpean Assembly, 1979; Ministry of Agriculture,1981-83; Mayor of Chatellerault, 1983-97; Adjoint au maire, 1997-; Minister, for Foreign Trade and Tourism, 1983-84, Minister, for Industrial Redeployment and Foreign Trade, 1984-86, Minister for European Affairs, 1988-90; PM, 1990-92; President of Schneider International Services Industries et Environnement, 1990-91, 1992-95; Commissaire européen chargé de la recherche et de l'éducation, 1995-99; Presidente de la Fondation pour les Ecoles de la Deuxième Chance. Publications: Avec le Soleil, 1976; Innover ou subir, 1998; Docteur Honoris Causa de l'Open University, UK and l'Institut Weisman, Israel, 1999; Présidente de la Fondation pour les Écoles de la Deuxième Chance, 2002-. Address: 10 Av. George V, Paris, France.

**CRESTON Bill,** b. 1932, Brooklyn, New York City, USA. Artist; Film Maker. Education: Art Student League; High School of Music and Arts. Appointments: Faculty: Cooper Union, School of Visual Arts, Hunter College; Screenings: Museum of Modern Art, New York City; Exit Art, New York City; Anthology Film Archive, New York City; The Kitchen, New York City. Honours: Fellowship, New York Foundation for the Arts Film Makers Grant, 2004. Address: 463 West Street, A 629, New York, NY 10014-2035, USA. Website: http: //www.emedialoft.org/artistspages/billcreston.htm

**CRICHTON John Michael,** b. 23 October 1942, Chicago, Illinois, USA. Film Director; Author. Education: AB, summa cum laude, 1964, MD, 1969, Harvard University. Appointments: Visiting Lecturer in Anthropology, Cambridge University, 1965; Postdoctoral Fellow, Salk Institute for Biological Sciences, La Jolla, California 1969-70; Visiting Writer, Massachusetts Institute of Technology, 1988; Creator, Co-Executive Producer, ER, NBC, 1994-. Publications: The Andromeda Strain, 1969; Five Patients, 1970; The Terminal Man, 1972; The Great Train Robbery, 1975; Eaters of the Dead, 1976; Jasper Johns, 1977; Congo, 1980; Electronic Life, 1983; Sphere, 1987; Travels, 1988; Jurassic Park, 1990; Rising Sun, 1992; Disclosure, 1994; The Lost World, 1995; The Terminal Man, 1995; Airframe, 1996; Timeline, 1999; Prey, 2002; Non-fiction: Five Patients: The Hospital Explained, 1970; Jasper Johns, 1977, revised edition, 1994; Electronic Life, 1983; Travels, 1988; Screenplays: Westworld, 1975; Twister (with Anne-Marie Martin, 1996; Films include: Westworld, writer, director, 1973; Coma, writer, director, 1978; Jurassic Park, co-writer, 1993; Rising Sun, co-writer, 1993; Disclosure, co-producer, 1994; Twister, co-writer, co-producer, 1996; Sphere, co-producer, 1998; Eaters of the Dead, co-producer, 1998; 13th Warrior, co-producer 1999. Honours include: Edgar Awards, Mystery Writers of America, 1968, 1979; Academy of Motion Pictures Arts and Sciences technical Achievement Award, 1995; Emmy, Best Dramatic Series for "ER", 1996; Ankylosaur named Bienosaurus crichtoni, 2000. Memberships: Authors Guild Council, 1995-; PEN; Phi Beta Kappa; Writers Guild of America; Directors Guild; Academy of Motion Picture Arts and Sciences; Board of Directors, International Design Conference, Aspen, 1985-91; Board of Trustees, West Behavioural Sciences Institute, La Jolla, 1986-91; Board of Overseers, Harvard University, 1990-96. Address: Constant Productions, 2118 Wiltshire Blvd #433, Santa Monica, CA 90403, USA.

**CRICK Francis Harry Compton**, b. 8 June 1916, Northampton, England. Neuroscientist. m. (1) 1 son, (2) Odile Speed, 1949, 2 daughters. Education: Graduated, Physics, University College, London; PhD, Caius College, Cambridge, 1953. Appointments: British Admiralty, work on development of radar and magnetic mines, 1940-47; Medical Research Council Student, Strangeways Research Laboratory, Cambridge University, 1947-49; MRC Laboratory of Molecular Biology, Cambridge, 1949-76; Keickhefer Distinguished Research Professor, 1977-, President, 1994-95, The Salk Institute, La Jolla, California, USA; Adjunct Professor of Psychology, University of California, San Diego; Research to determine the structure of DNA. Publications include: Of Molecules and Men, 1967; Life Itself, 1981; What Mad Pursuit, 1988; The Astonishing Hypothesis, 1994; Numerous papers on molecular and cell biology. Honours: Joint Winner, Nobel Prize for Physiology in Medicine, 1962; Royal Medal, Royal Society, 1972; Copley Medal, Royal Society, 1975; Michelson-Morley Award, Cleveland, USA, 1981; Numerous memorial lectures and other awards. Memberships: Fellow, 1960-61, Honorary Fellow, 1965, Churchill College, Cambridge; Foreign Honorary Member, American Academy of Arts and Sciences, 1962; Fellow, University College, London, 1962; Honorary Member, American Society of Biological Chemistry, 1963; Honorary, MRIA, 1964; Honorary FRSE, 1966; Fellow, AAAS, 1966; Foreign Associate, NAS, 1969; Member, German Academy of Science, 1969; Foreign Member, American Philosophical Society, Philadelphia, 1972; Hellenic Biochemical and Biophysical Society, 1974; Honorary Fellow, Caius College, Cambridge, 1976; Associate, Académie Française, 1978; Fellow, Indian National Science Academy, 1982; Honorary Fellow, Institute of Biology, 1995; Honorary Fellow, Tata Institute of Fundamental Research, Bombay, 1996. Address: The Salk Institute for Biological Studies, PO Box 85800, San Diego, CA 92186-5800, USA.

**CRISP Adrian James**, b. 21 November 1948, Harrow, Middlesex, England. Consultant Rheumatologist. 1 daughter. Education: University College School, London, 1962-66; Magdalene College, Cambridge, 1968-71; University College Hospital, Medical School, London, 1971-74. Appointments: Consultant, Rheumatology and Metabolic Bone Diseases, Addenbrookes Hospital, Cambridge, 1985-; Associate Dean, University of Cambridge Clinical School and Eastern Deanery, 1997-2005; Director of Studies in Clinical Medicine and Fellow, Churchill College, Cambridge, 1991-. Memberships: Member of Council and Executive, and Chairman of Education Committee, British Society for Rheumatology. Address: The Old Forge, 83 High Street, Great Abington, Cambridge CB1 6AE, England.

**CRISTEA Valentin Gabriel**, b. 7 June 1968, Targoviste, Romania. Mathematician. Education: Bachelor Degree, Mathematics, University of Bucharest, Romania, 1987-91; Grant Holder, International Congress of Mathematicians, ICM '98, Technische Universität Berlin, Germany, 1998; Arbeitstagung, Max-Planck-Institut fuer Mathematik, Bonn Germany, 1999. Appointments: Assistant Professor of Mathematics "Valahia" University, Targoviste, Romania, 1995-; Assistant Professor of Mathematics, Politechnic University of Bucharest, 1995-96; Mathematician, Instituto de Fisica Aplicada, CSIC, Madrid, Spain, 1994-95 (6 months); Mathematician, CIMAT, Guanajuato, Mexico, 1998 (1 month); Mathematician Max-Planck-Institut fuer Mathematik, Bonn, Germany, 1999 (7 months). Publications: Considerations sur les paires de superconnexions sur des supervarietes, 1991; Remarks about the Supermanifolds, 1992; Totally geodesic graded Riemannian submanifolds of the (4,4)-dimensional graded Riemannian manifold, 1995; Existence and uniqueness theorem for Frenet frames supercurves, 1999; The reduced bundle of the principal superfibre bundle, 2001; Euler's superequations, 2001; Curvilinear Integral I(C) for problems of variations calculus on supermanifolds, 2002. Honours: Distinguished Leadership Award, American Biographical Institute; Nominated as inaugural member of the Leading Scientists of the World, 2005; Listed in biographical dictionaries. Membership: Romanian Society of Mathematical Sciences. Address: Str G-ral Matei Vladescu, BL 30 Sc A, Ap 6 Targoviste, 0200 Jud Dambovita, Romania. E-mail: valentin_cristea@yahoo.com

**CRONENBERG David**, b. 15 March 1943, Toronto, Canada. Film Director. Education: University of Toronto. Appointments: Directed fillers and short dramas for TV; Films include: Stereo, 1969; Crimes of the Future, 1970; The Parasite Murders/Shivers, 1974; Rabid, 1976; Fast Company, 1979; The Brood, 1979; Scanners, 1980; Videodrome, 1982; The Dead Zone, 1983; The Fly, 1986; Dead Ringers, 1988; The Naked Lunch, 1991; Crash, 1996; Acted in: Nightbreed, 1990; The Naked Lunch (wrote screenplay); Trial by Jury; Henry and Verlin; To Die For, 1995; Extreme Measures, 1996; The Stupids, 1996; Director, writer, producer, actor, Crash, 1996. Publications: Crash 1996; Cronenberg on Cronenberg, 1996. Address: David Cronenberg Productions Ltd, 217 Avenue Road, Toronto, Ontario, M5R 2J3, Canada.

**CRONIN James Watson**, b. 29 September 1931, Chicago, Illinois, USA. Physicist. m. Annette Martin, 1954, 1 son, 2 daughters. Education: BS, Southern Methodist University, 1951; MS, 1953, PhD, Physics, 1955, University of Chicago. Appointments: National Science Foundation Fellow, 1952-55; Assistant Physicist, Brookhaven National Laboratory, 1955-58; Assistant Professor of Physics, 1958-62, Associate Professor, 1962-64, Professor, 1964-71, Princeton University; Professor of Physics, University of Chicago, 1971-; Loeb Lecturer in Physics, Harvard University, 1976. Honours: Research

Corporation Award, 1968; Ernest O Lawrence Award, 1977; John Price Wetherill Medal, Franklin Institute, 1975; Joint Winner, Nobel Prize for Physics, 1980; Honorary DSc, Leeds, 1996; National Medal of Science, 1999. Memberships: NAS; American Academy of Arts and Sciences; American Physical Society. Address: Enrico Fermi Institute, University of Chicago, 5630 South Ellis Avenue, Chicago, IL 60637, USA.

**CROOKS Stanley George,** b. 3 March 1925, London, England. Chartered Engineer. m. Gwendoline Hatch, 1 son, 1 daughter. Education: Bournemouth Municipal College, Bournemouth, 1947-49; Birmingham Central Technical College, Birmingham, 1949-50; University of London Commerce Degree Bureau, London, 1949-50; BSc, Engineering, 1950, BSc, Economics, 1956, University of London; Fellow, Institution of Electrical Engineers, 1965; Companion, Chartered Management Institute, 1960; Chartered Engineer; European Engineer. Appointments: Royal Artillery, 1943-47, Major, 1946, Active service in Burma and French Indo-China; Pirelli General plc, 1941-43, 1950-96: Home Sales Manager, 1959-61, seconded to Pirelli SpA, Italy, 1960, Deputy Manager, Production Division, 1961-63, Manager Production Division, 1963-65, Production Director, 1965-67, Managing Director, 1967-71, Vice-Chairman, 1971-87, Chairman, 1987-94; Vice-Chairman, Pirelli UK plc, 1989-97; Cable Sector, Pirelli Group, 1971-81: Directeur Général Adjoint, 1971-73, Directeur Général, 1973-81, Société Internationale Pirelli, Basle (responsible for subsidiaries in Argentina, Brazil, Canada, Mexico, Peru, Spain and UK, 1971-87 and for expansion into Australia, 1975, USA, 1978, France and Ivory Coast, 1980; CEO, Cable Sector, 1982-87. Publications: Numerous papers presented at national and international conferences include most recently: Succeeding in Europe in the 1990's, 1990; Meeting our Targets Together, 1996; A Skills Passport – The Contribution of Industry, 1996 Books: Twyford – Ringing the Changes, 1999; Twyford – 20th Century Chronicles, 2000, Alfred Waterhouse in Twyford, 2003. Honour: Doctor of Science (Honoris Causa), University of Southampton, 1977. Memberships: Confederation of British Industry, Council member, 1987-97, Chairman, Education Policy Panel, 1995-97; Southampton Institute of Higher Education, Chairman of Governors, 1988-90; University of Southampton, numerous positions include: Trustee, Southampton University Development Trust, 1984-96; Chairman, Management School, 1990-92, Chairman, Southampton Innovations Limited, 1996-99; British Institute of Management, President, Southampton Branch, 1987-92; Itchen College, Southampton, Governor, 1969-71; Southern Science & Technology Forum, Founder Sponsor, 1967, President, 1978-93; Young Enterprise, Member National Executive, 1968-71. Address: Bournewood House, Bourne Lane, Winchester, Hampshire SO21 1NX, England.

**CROSHAW Michael,** b. 12 March 1943, Warwick, England. Poet. m. Theresa Belt, 6 June 1970, div 1976, 2 sons. Appointments: British Telecom, 1973-91; Associate Editor, Orbis Magazine, 1980-87. Publications: Alum Rock, 1992; A Harmony of Lights, 1993. Contributions to: Acumen; Babel; Bogg; Bradford Poetry Quarterly; Bull; Chapman; Completing the Picture; Core; Emotional Geology; Envoi; Envoi Book of Quotes on Poetry; The Interpreter's House; Jennings; Manhattan Poetry Review; Mercia Poets, 1980; The Month; Moorlands Review; New Hope International; Orbis; Ore; Other Poetry; Outposts Poetry Quarterly; Pennine Platform; Poetry Australia; Poetry Business Anthology, 1987-88; Poetry Nottingham; The Poet's Voice; Psychopoetica; Stride; Vigil; Weyfarers. Address: Queen's Road, Nuneaton, Warwickshire CV11 5ND, England.

**CROSLAND Neisha,** b. 11 December 1960, London, England. Textile Designer. m. Stephane Perche, 2 sons. Education: BA,

1st Class Honours, Textile Design, Camberwell School of Arts and Crafts, 1984; MA, Printed Textiles, Royal College of Art, 1986. Career includes: Designed Romagna Collection for Osborne & Little, 1988; Designed Carnival Collection of wall papers and furnishing fabrics for Harlequin Wallcoverings Ltd, 1990-94; Freelance Designer, also contributed to the First Eleven portfolio, 1991; Launch of Neisha Crosland Scarves, 1994; Launched Neisha at Debenhams, 1998; Launched Ginka ready to wear brand, launched first wallpaper collection, 1999; Launched home decorative and stationary collection, opened first retail outlet London, 2000-2001; Started licensed collection for Hankyu, Japan, 2002; unched first collection of furnishing fabrics, 2003.

**CROSSLAND Bernard,** b. 20 October 1923, Sydenham, England. Mechanical Engineer. m. Audrey Elliott Birks, 2 daughters. Education: BSc, 1943, MSc, 1946, Engineering, Nottingham University College; PhD, University of Bristol, 1953; DSc, University of Nottingham, 1960. Appointments: Engineering Apprentice, 1940-44, Technical Assistant, 1943-45, Rolls Royce Ltd, Derby; Lecturer, Luton Regional Technical College, 1945-46; Assistant Lecturer, Lecturer, Senior Lecturer in Mechanical Engineering, University of Bristol, 1946-59; Professor of Mechanical Engineering, Head of Department of Mechanical and Manufacturing Engineering, 1959-84, Dean of the Faculty of Engineering, 1964-67, Senior Pro Vice Chancellor, 1978-82, Queen's University of Belfast; Involved in the investigations of several major disasters including: King's Cross Underground Fire, Bilsthorp Colliery Roof Fall, Southall Train Crash, Ladbroke Grove Rail Crash and numerous others. Publications: Many articles in professional journals and books. Honours: 11 named lectures; 8 prizes; 3 Honorary DEng; 6 Honorary DSc; Honorary Fellowships: FWI, FIEI, Fellow of the University of Luton, FIMechE, FIStructE; CBE, 1980; Kt, 1990. Memberships: Royal Irish Academy; Royal Academy of Engineering; Royal Society; Irish Academy of Engineering. Address: 16 Malone Court, Belfast, BT9 6PA, Northern Ireland.

**CROUCH Colin,** b. 1 March 1944, Isleworth, Middlesex, England. University Professor. m. Joan Ann Freedman, 2 sons. Education: BA, first class, Sociology, London School of Economics, 1969; DPhil, Nuffield College, Oxford, 1975. Appointments: Temporary Lecturer in Sociology, London School of Economics, 1969-70; Research Student, Nuffield College, Oxford, 1970-72; Lecturer in Sociology, University of Bath, 1972-73; Lecturer, 1973-79, Senior Lecturer, 1979-80, Reader, 1980-85, Sociology, London School of Economics and Political Science; Professor of Sociology, Fellow of Trinity College, University of Oxford, 1985-95; Chairman, Department of Social and Political Sciences, Professor of Comparative Social Institutions, European University Institute, Florence, Italy; External Scientific Member, Max-Planck-Institut für Gesellschaftsforschung, Cologne, Germany; Chairman, The Political Quarterly Ltd. Publications: 8 books; Editor, 18 books; 108 other articles and chapters. Honours: Hobhouse Memorial Prize, 1969. Memberships: President of Society for the Advancement of Socio-Economics; Max-Planck-Gesellschaft. Address: Istituto Universitario Europeo, San Domenico Di Fiesole, 50016 FI, Italy. E-mail: colin.crouch@iue.it

**CROUCH Helga Ursula,** b. 18 January 1941, London, England. Botanical Artist. m. Julian Terence Crouch, 1 daughter. Education: Cardiff College of Art, Wales; Central School of Arts and Crafts, London, England. Career: Graphic Designer, 1964-78; Botanical Illustrator specialising in wild flora, fruits and insects on vellum in watercolour; Tutor of Botanical Art. Publications: Books: Contemporary Botanical

Artists; Arte y Botanica; The Art of Botanical Painting; A New Flowering – 1000 Years of Botanical Art; Articles: Country Living Magazine; Kew Magazine; Essex Life. Honours: Certificate of Art and Design (Distinction); Diploma in Art and Design; Certificate of Botanical Merit; Silver Gilt Medal, Royal Horticultural Society. Memberships: Founder Member, Society of Botanical Artists; Fellow, Linnean Society; Cambridge Open Studios; European Boxwood and Topiary Society. Address: The Mill House, Little Sampford, Nr Saffron Walden, Essex CB10 2QT, England. E-mail: botanicalartist@btinternet.com

**CROUCH Sunny Joyce,** b. 11 February 1943, London, England. Director. m. William Crouch. Education: MA, Distinction, University of Lancaster; Diploma, Chartered Institute of Marketing (Distinction); Diploma, Market Research Society. Appointments: Course Director, Honours Degree in Business Studies, University of Portsmouth Business School, 1872-83; Chief Marketing and Tourism Officer, City of Portsmouth, 1983-88; Director of Marketing, London Docklands Development Corporation, 1988-98; Non-Executive Director, Scottish Radio Holdings, 1887-; Managing Director, World Trade Centre, London, 1998-; Non-Executive Director, London First, 2002-; Non-Executive Director, Thurrock Urban Development Corporation, 2004-. Publications: Mass Media and Cultural Relationships, 1975; Marketing Research for Managers, 3rd edition, 2003; Numerous published articles on marketing, tourism, regeneration. Honours: Tourist Authority of the Year, 1987; England for Excellence "Cities" Award, 1988; Freedom of the City of London, 1993; Business Person of the Year, London Docklands, 2000; Civic Award, London Borough of Tower Hamlets. Memberships: Institute of Directors, 1990; First Forum (Top Women's Organisation), 1990; Trustee, Island Health Trust, 1996; Liveryman, Worshipful Company of World Traders, 1998; Trustee, Friends of the Maritime Museum, 1999; Governor, University of East London, 2000. Address: World Trade Centre London, 5 Harbour Exchange Square, London E14 9GE, England. E-mail: sunny.crouch@wtc-london.com

**CROWE Russell,** b. 7 April 1964, New Zealand. Actor. m. Danielle Spencer, 2003, 1 son. Career: Films include: The Crossing, 1993; The Quick and the Dead, 1995; Romper Stomper, 1995; Rough Magic, 1995; Virtuosity, 1995; Under the Gun, 1995; Heaven's Burning, 1997; Breaking Up, 1997; LA Confidential, 1997; Mystery Alaska, 1999; The Insider, 1999; Gladiator, 2000; Proof of Life, 2000; A Beautiful Mind, 2001; Master and Commander: The Far Side of the World, 2003. Honours: Variety Club Award (Australia), 1993; Film Critics Circle Award, 1993; Best Actor, Seattle International Film Festival, 1993; Management Film and TV Awards, Motion Pictures Exhibitors Association, 1993; LA Film Critics Association, 1999; National Board of Review, 1999; National Society of Film Critics, 1999; Academy Award for Best Actor, 2000; Golden Globe, 2001; BAFTA Award, 2001; Screen Actors' Guild Award for Best Actor, 2001. Address: ICM, 8942 Wilshire Blvd, Beverly Hills, CA, 90211, USA.

**CROZIER Brian Rossiter, (John Rossiter),** b. 4 August 1918, Kuridala, Queensland, Australia. Journalist; Writer; Consultant. m. (1) Mary Lillian Samuel, 7 September 1940, deceased 1993, 1 son, 3 daughters (2) Jacqueline Marie Mitchell. Education: Lycée, Montpellier; Peterborough College, Harrow; Trinity College of Music, London. Appointments: Music and Art Critic, London, 1936-39; Reporter, Sub-Editor, Stoke-on-Trent, Stockport, London, 1940-41; Sub-Editor, Reuters, 1943-44; News Chronicle, 1944-48; Sub-Editor and Writer, Sydney Morning Herald, 1948-51; Correspondent, Reuters-AAP, 1951-52; Features Editor, Straits Times, 1952-53; Leader Writer, Correspondent, and Editor, Foreign Report, The Economist,

1954-64; Commentator, BBC English, French, and Spanish Overseas Services, 1954-66; Chairman, Forum World Features, 1965-74; Co-Founder and Director, Institute for the Study of Conflict, 1970-79; Columnist, National Review, New York, 1978-94; Columnist, Now!, 1979-81, The Times, 1982-83, The Free Nation, later Freedom Today, 1982-89; Adjunct Scholar, Heritage Foundation, Washington, DC, 1984-95; Distinguished Visiting Fellow, Hoover Institution, Stanford, California, 1996-2002. Publications: The Rebels, 1960; The Morning After, 1963; Neo-Colonialism, 1964; South-East Asia in Turmoil, 1965, 3rd edition, 1968; The Struggle for the Third World, 1966; Franco, 1967; The Masters of Power, 1969; The Future of Communist Power (US edition as Since Stalin), 1970; De Gaulle, 2 volumes, 1973, 1974; A Theory of Conflict, 1974; The Man Who Lost China (Chiang Kai-shek), 1976; Strategy of Survival, 1978; The Minimum State, 1979; Franco: Crepúsculo de un hombre, 1980; The Price of Peace, 1980, new edition, 1983; Socialism Explained (co-author), 1984; This War Called Peace (co-author), 1984; The Andropov Deception (novel published under the name John Rossiter), 1984 (published in the US under own name), 1986; Socialism: Dream and Reality, 1987; The Grenada Documents (editor), 1987; The Gorbachev Phenomenon, 1990; Communism: Why Prolong its Death-Throes?, 1990; Free Agent, 1993; The KGB Lawsuits, 1995; Le Phénix Rouge (Paris) (co-author), 1995; The Rise and Fall of the Soviet Empire, 1999; Contributions to numerous journals. Memberships: Traveller's Club, 1955-90; Royal Automobile Club, 1990-. Address: 18 Wickliffe Avenue, Finchley, London N3 3EJ, England.

**CRUISE Tom (Thomas Cruise Mapother IV),** b. 3 July 1962, Syracuse, New York, USA. Actor. m. (1) Mimi Rogers, 1987, divorced 1990, (2) Nicole Kidman, 1990, divorced 2001, 1 adopted son, 1 adopted daughter. Career: Actor, films include: Endless Love, 1981; Taps, 1981; All The Right Moves, 1983; Losin' It, 1983; The Outsiders, 1983; Risky Business, 1983; Legend, 1984; Top Gun, 1985; The Color of Money, 1986; Rain Man, 1988; Cocktail, 1989; Born on the Fourth of July, 1989; Daytona, 1990; Rush, 1990; Days of Thunder, 1990; Sure as the Moon, 1991; Far and Away, 1992; A Few Good Men, 1992; The Firm, 1993; Interview with the Vampire, 1994; Jerry Maguire, 1996; Mission Impossible, 1996; Eyes Wide Shut, 1997; Mission Impossible 2, 1999; Magnolia, 1999; Vanilla Sky, 2001; Minority Report, 2002; Space Station 3D, voice, 2002; The Last Samurai, 2003; Collateral, 2004; Producer: Without Limits, 1998. Honours: Golden Globe, 2000. Address: C/W Productions, c/o Paramount Studios, 5555 Melrose Avenue, Hollywood, CA 90038, USA.

**CRUYFF Johan,** b. 25 April 1947, Amsterdam, Netherlands. Footballer. Appointments: Played for Ajax, 1964-73; Top scorer in Dutch league, with 33 goals, 1967; Moved to Barcelona, now Coach of Barcelona; Captained Netherlands, 1974 World Cup Final, 1974; Retired, 1978; Started playing again and signed for Los Angeles Aztecs; Played for Washington Diplomats, 1979-80; Levante, Spain, 1981; Ajax and Feyenoord, 1982; Manager, Ajax, 1987-87, winning European Cup-Winners Cup, 1987; Manager, Barcelona, winning Cup-Winners Cup, 1989; European Cup, 1992, Spanish League, 1991, 1992, 1993, Spanish Super Cup, 1992; Formed Cruyff Foundation for disabled sportspeople and Johan Cruyff University to assist retired sportspeople, 1998. Honour: European Footballer of the Year, 1971, 1973-74.

**CRYSTAL Billy,** b. 14 March 1947, Long Beach, NY, USA. Actor; Comedian. m. Janice Goldfinger, 2 daughters. Education: Marshall University. Appointments: Member of group, 3's Company; Solo appearances as stand-up comedian; TV appearances include: Soap, 1977-81; The Billy Crystal

Hour, 1982; Saturday Night Live, 1984-85; The Love Boat; The Tonight Show; TV films include: Breaking Up is Hard to Do, 1979; Enola Gay; The Men; The Mission; The Atomic Bomb, 1980; Death Flight; Feature films include: The Rabbit Test, 1978; This is Spinal Tap, 1984; Running Scared, 1986; The Princess Bride, 1987; Throw Momma From the Train, 1987; When Harry Met Sally..., 1989; City Slickers, 1991; Mr Saturday Night (Director, Producer, co-screenplay writer), 1993; City Slickers II: The Legend of Curly's Gold, 1994; Forget Paris, 1995; Hamlet; Father's Day; Deconstructing Harry; My Grant, 1998; Analyse This, 1998; The Adventures of Rocky and Bullwinkle, 2000; Monsters Inc (voice), 2001; America's Sweethearts, 2001; Mike's New Car (voice), 2002; Analyze That, 2002. Publication: Absolutley Mahvelous, 1986.

**CSABA György,** b. 31 May 1929, Törökszentmiklos. Physician. m. (1) 1954, (2) Katalin Kallay, 1970, 2 sons, 2 daughters. Education: MD, 1953; PhD, 1957; DSc, 1969. Appointments: Assistant Professor, 1953-59, 1st Assistant, 1959-63, Associate Professor, 1963-70, Professor, 1970-, Director, Department of Biology, Semmelweis University of Medicine, 1971-94; Professor, 1970-99; Professor Emeritus, 2000-. Publications: 24 books, 24 chapters and over 780 scientific publications in peer-reviewed journals. Honours: Huzella Prize, 1983; Pal Bugat Award, Scientific Educational Society, 1989; Hung Higher Education Medal, Ministry of Education, 1994; Golden Signet, Semmelweis University of Medicine, 1994; 5 Prizes for High Level Books; Khwarizmi International Award; Comsats Award. Memberships: President, General and Theoretical Section, Hung Biological Society, 1978-87; Chairman, Book Committee, Scientific Press Council, Budapest, 1980-88; Chairman, Editorial Committee, Semmelweis Publisher, 1989-2001. Address: PO Box 370, H-1445 Budapest, Hungary.

**CSAKY John Bernard,** b. 31 August 1945, Shropshire, England. m. (1) Iryna Zenowia Pasznyk, 1970, divorced 1993, 2 daughters; (2) Tina Jasmine Mohar, 2004, 1 son. Education: Bedales School; Diploma, Art and Design, Portsmouth School of Art, 1967; Master of Art, Royal College of Art, London, 1970. Appointments: Wolff Olins, Design Consultants, 1970-71; Architecture and Planning Team, Milton Keynes Development Corporation, 1971-80; Principal, Special Projects Partnership, 1980-85; Director, Travel and Leisure Division, Fitch & Co, Design Consultants, 1985-92; Managing/Creative Director, John Csaky Associates Ltd, 1994-2005. Major projects include: Lighting and special effects for the 1970 Isle of Wight Music Festival; Loughton Lakes and Milton Keynes Bowl, 1979; Master Plan for Technical Institute, for China Engineering Consultants, Taipei, 1980; Studio building for sculptor, Dame Elisabeth Frink, 1980; The TT Tsui Gallery of Chinese Art and Design, V & A Museum, 1991; The British Pavilion, Expo 88 Brisbane; Kingdom of Saudi Arabia Pavilion, Expo 92; Puerto Rico Pavilion, Expo '92, Seville; FutureVision: This is Tomorrow, interactive exhibition for Granada Studios, 1995; Al Watan, Family Park, Riyadh, Saudi Arabia, 2005; Hail Pavilion, Al Janadriyah Festival Riyadh, 2002; Action Stations! Millennium Exhibition, Portsmouth Historic Dockyard, 2001; Plymouth Mayflower, 2002; Wildwalk@Bristol, Millennium Exhibition, Bristol, 2000; The Deep, Kingston Upon Hull, Millennium Exhibition, 2002; The Twilight Zone, 2005; Amazon to Caribbean exhibition, The Horniman Museum, 2005; Connect Gallery, Royal Museum, Edinburgh, 2005. Publications: Various project articles including: Times, Financial Times, Independent, Building, Building Design, Architects Journal, Designers Journal, RIBA Journal, Design, Garten und Landschaft, Architecture and Urbanism (Japan); Architectural Digest (USA); Landscape, Design Week, Architectural Design, Time Magazine. Honours: MA Silver Medal, Royal College of Art, 1970. Membership: Fellow, Royal Geographical Society; Fellow, Royal Society of Arts; Member, Royal Institution. Address: 12 Prospect Road, London NW2 2JT, England. E-mail: jcsaky@hotmail.com

**CSIKAI Gyula,** b. 31 October 1930, Tiszaladány. Professor in Physics. m. Margit Buczkó, 2 sons. Education: University Diploma in Mathematics and Physics, 1953, Candidate, 1957, DSc, 1966, Corresponding, 1973, and Ordinary Member, 1985, Hungarian Academy of Sciences. Appointments: Head, Neutron Physics Department, ATOMKI, Debrecen, Hungary, 1956-67; Head Institute of Experimental Physics, Debrecen, 1967-95; Deputy Minister of Culture and Education of Hungary, 1987; Professor, 1967, Dean, 1972-75, Rector, 1981-86, Kossuth University, Debrecen, Hungary; Professor Emeritus, 2001-. Publications: More than 240 papers in scientific journals; Handbook of Fast Neutron Generators I-II, 1987; Handbook on Nuclear Data, 1987, 2003; 2 patents. Honours: First Prize of Hungarian Academy of Sciences, 1967; Eötvös Medal, 1980, Golden Medal of Hungary, 1980; State Award, 1983; Named Honorary Freeman of Tiszaladány, 2000-; Honorary Doctor, Kiev National University, 2001. Memberships: Expert UN-IAEA, Vienna, 1976; The New York Academy of Sciences, 1982; Hungarian Academy of Sciences, 1985; Academia Europea, 1991; Secretary, IUPAP Commission, Nuclear Physics, 1993-96. Address: Institute of Experimental Physics, University of Debrecen, H-4010 Debrecen-10, P O Box 105, Hungary.

**CULKIN Macauley,** b. 26 August 1980, NY, USA. Actor. m. Rachel Milner, 1998, separated. Education: George Balanchine's School of Ballet, NY. Appointments: Actor, films: Rocket Gibralter, 1988; Uncle Buck, 1989; See You in the Morning, 1989; Jacob's Ladder, 1990; Home Alone, 1990; My Girl, 1991; Only the Lonely, 1991; Home Alone 2: Lost in New York, 1992; The Nutcracker; The Good Son, 1993; The Pagemaster, 1995; Getting Even with Dad, 1995; Body Piercer, 1998; Party Monster, 2003; Saved! 2004; Play: Madame Melville, Vaudeville Theatre, London, 2001. Address: c/o Brian Gersh, William Morris Agency, 151 S El Camino Drive, Beverley Hills, CA 90212, USA.

**CULL-CANDY Stuart G,** b. 2 November 1946. Professor of Neuroscience. m. Barbara Paterson Fulton, 1 daughter. Education: BSc (Hons), Biology, University of London, 1969; MSc, Physiology, University College London, 1970; PhD, Synaptic Physiology, University of Glasgow, 1974; Postdoctoral Fellow, Institute of Pharmacology, University of Lund, Sweden, 1974-75. Appointments: Beit Memorial Research Fellow and Associate Research Staff, Department of Biophysics, 1975-82, Wellcome Trust Reader in Pharmacology, 1982-90, Professor of Neuroscience, Personal Chair, 1990-, University College London; Medical Research Council Neuroscience Committee, 1987-91; Wellcome Trust International Interest Group Grants Committee, 1991-97; International Research Scholar, Howard Hughes Medical Institute, 1993-98; Royal Society – Wolfson Position, 2003-. Publications: Numerous articles on synaptic transmission and glutamate receptors in the brain and peripheral nervous system in the scientific journals: Nature, Neuron, Journal of Neuroscience, Journal of Physiology; Various book chapters; Editor of scientific journals: Reviewing Editor, Journal of Neuroscience, 2000-; Editor, Neuron, 1994-98; External Editorial Adviser in Neuroscience, Nature, 1993-97; Editor, Journal of Physiology, 1987-95; European Journal of Neuroscience, 1988-. Honours: Appointed International Scholar, Howard Hughes Medical Institute, USA, 1993-98; GL Brown Prize, Physiological Society, 1996; Elected Fellow of the Royal Society, 2002; Wolfson Award, Royal Society, 2003; Elected Fellow of the Academy of Medical Sciences,

2004. Memberships: Royal Society; Academy of Medical Sciences; Society for Neuroscience, USA; Physiological Society, UK; British Neuroscience Association; International Brain Research Organisation; Pharmacological Society, UK. Address: Department of Pharmacology, University College London, Gower Street, London WC1E 6BT, England. E-mail: s.cull-candy@ucl.ac.uk

**CUMMINGS Jasper Lee,** b. 13 September 1936, Snow Hill, North Carolina. College Administrator. m. (1) Barbara, deceased, 2 daughters, (2) Marie Newman, 3 daughters. Education: AA, Business Administration, Strayer College, 1973; BA, Magna Cum Laude, Business Administration, Sojourner-Douglas College, 1990-92. Appointments: US Army, 1956-58; Insurance Agent, North Carolina Mutual Life Company, 1958-59; US Air Force Reserves, 1961-62; Radio Announcer, WFAG, Farmville, North Carolina, 1963-64; Accounting Technician, National Institutes of Health, Bethesda, Maryland, 1964-95; Public Relations Representative, Capital Spotlight newspaper, Washington DC, 1977-87; Currently, Administrator, Sojourner-Douglass College Centre, Prince George's County, Maryland. Publications: Speaking to Excel. Honours: 5000 Personalities of the World; International Directory of Distinguished Leadership; 500 Leaders of Influence; Who's Who Among Students in American Universities; John Edgar Hoover Memorial Gold Medal for Distinguished Public Service; Who's Who in American Law Enforcement, 1989, 1992; Outstanding Service Plaque, Lake Arbor Civic Association; Liberty and Justice Award, American Police Hall of Fame; Able Toastmaster; Membership Service Award, Toastmasters International; Special Achievement Award for Outstanding Performance, NIH; Organizational Award, Division of Financial Management, National Institutes of Health; Award of Merit, 1997; Certificate of Honour, National Association of Chiefs of Police; Certificate of Appreciation, American Federation of Police; World Laureate, ABI; Fellow, ABI; Outstanding Community service Award, Lake Arbor Association, 2001; Certificate of Appreciation of Service, Alpha Nu Omega Fraternity; Master Diploma, Administration, World Academy of Letters; International Peace Prize, United World Cultural Society; Great Minds of the 21st Century, ABI; Lifetime Achievement, IBC; Founder, Bill Clinton Presidential Library; many others. Memberships: Past Member, Toastmasters International; Treasurer, Sojourner-Douglass Alumni Association; President, Newbridge Homeowners Association; Past President, South Greene National Alumni Association; American Federation of Police; American Police Hall of Fame; Education Ministry, First Baptist Church of Glenarden. Address: 11000 Spyglass Hill, Mitchellville, MD, USA.

**CURE Susan Carol,** b. 18 August, Los Angeles, USA. Biologist. m. Michel Y Cure, 1 son, 2 daughters. Education: BA, Biological Science, Stanford University, 1962; PhD, Medical Microbiology, Stanford University, 1967. Appointments: Postdoctoral Fellow, California Department of Health, 1966-1968; Researcher, Centre d'Études de la Biologie Prénatale, 1970-1974; Lecturer, Associate Professor, American University in Paris, 1971-1976, 1987-; Science Co-ordinator, Association Française Contre les Myopathies, 1989-; Researcher, Genethon, Genoscope, French Genome Centres, 1992-. Publications: Many articles in scientific journals: American Journal of Human Genetics; Nature; Journal of Investigative Dermatology. Memberships: AAAS; American Society of Microbiology; Club du Mt St Leger; Sigma Xi. Address: 3 av Robert Schuman, 75007, Paris, France.

**CURIO Eberhard Otto Eugen,** b. 22 October 1932, Berlin, Germany. Professor of Biology. m. Dorothea Curio, 1 son, 1 daughter. Education: Doctor rer. nat., Free University of Berlin, 1957; Professor of Biology, Ruhr University, Bochum, 1970. Appointments: Research Associate, Max-Planck-Institute for Behavioural Physiology, 1957-64; Assistant Professor, 1964-68, Lecturer, 1968-70, Professor, 1970-, Ruhr University Bochum, Germany. Publications: The Ethology of Predation, 1976; Behavior as a Tool for Management Intervention in Birds (book chapter), 1998. Honours: Ornithologists Award, German Ornithologists' Society, 1994; Honorary Member, Ethological Society, 2000; Chair for Biodiversity, ASEAN Regional Center for Biodiversity Conservation, 2001-04. Memberships: Society for Conservation Biology; International Society for Behavioral Ecology; Ethological Society; Association for the Study of Animal Behaviour; German Zoological Society; German Ornithologists' Society; American Society of Naturalists. Address: Conservation Biology Unit, Ruhr University Bochum, 44780 Bochum, Germany. E-mail: eberhard.curio@rub.de Website: www.pescp.org

**CURL James Stevens,** b. 26 March 1937, Belfast, Northern Ireland. Architect; Architectural Historian. m. (1) 2 daughters, (2) Stanisława Dorota Iwaniec, 1993. Education: Queen's University, School of Architecture, Belfast, 1954-58; DiplArch, Oxford School of Architecture, 1961-63; Dip TP, Oxford Department of Land Use Studies, 1963-67; PhD, University College London, 1978-81. Appointment: Retired Professor Emeritus of Architectural History, having held Chairs at two British universities. Publications include: The Londonderry Plantation 1609-1914, 1986; English Architecture: An Illustrated Glossary, 1987; Victorian Architecture, 1990; Encyclopaedia of Architectural Terms, 1993; A Celebration of Death, 1993; Egyptomania, 1994; Victorian Churches, 1995; The Oxford Dictionary of Architecture, 1999, 2000; The Honourable The Irish Society and the Plantation of Ulster 1608-2000: The City of London and the Colonisation of County Londonderry in the Province of Ulster in Ireland – A History and Critique, 2000; The Victorian Celebration of Death, 2000, 2004; The Art and Architecture of Freemasonry, 2002; Georgian Architecture, 2002; Classical Architecture, 2002; Death and Architecture, 2002; The Egyptian Revival, 2005; Victorian Architecture, 2005; The Oxford Dictionary of Architecture and Landscape Architecture, 2005. Honours: British Academy Research Awards, 1982, 1983. 1992, 1994, 1998; Sir Banister Fletcher Award for Best Book of Year (1991) 1992; Building Centre Trust Award, 1992; Interbuild Fund Award, 1992 Royal Institute of British Architects Research Award, 1993; Marc Fitch Fund Award, 2003; Authors Foundation Fund Award, 2004. Memberships: Society of Authors; Royal Institute of British Architects; Royal Institute of the Architects of Ireland; Royal Incorporation of Architects in Scotland ; Society of Antiquaries of Scotland; Society of Antiquaries of London. Address: 15 Torgrange, Holywood, County Down BT18 0NG, Northern Ireland. E-mail: jscurl@btinternet.com

**CURRY Alan Chester,** b. 15 October 1933, Columbus, Ohio, USA. Actuary; Manager. m. Shetalyn Jamison, 3 sons, 1 daughter. Education: Bachelor of Science in Education with honours, Illinois State University, 1957; Management Development Program, State Farm Insurance Company, 1959; Fellow (by examination) The Casualty Actuarial Society, 1965. Appointments: Several actuarial positions at State Farm Insurance Company including Vice-President and Actuary for 25 years; Currently retired and a Member of the Board of Directors, State Farm Insurance Company. Honours: Graduate with honours, Illinois State University; Honour Societies: Pi Gamma Mu; Pi Omega Pi; Kappa Delta Pi. Memberships: Past Member of Board of Directors, Casualty Actuarial Society; Past Board Member, American Academy of Actuaries; Past

President, Midwestern Actuarial Forum. Address: 7 Canterbury Court, Bloomington, IL 61701, USA.

**CURTIS David Roderick,** b. 3 June 1927, Melbourne, Australia. Neuropharmacologist. m. Lauri Sewell, 1 son, 1 daughter. Education: MB BS, University of Melbourne, 1950; PhD, Australian National University, 1957. Appointments: Research Scholar, 1954-56, Research Fellow, 1956-57, Fellow, 1957-59, Senior Fellow, 1959-62, Professorial Fellow, 1962-66, Professor of Pharmacology, 1966-73, Department of Physiology, John Curtin School; Professor and Head, Department of Pharmacology, 1973-88, Chairman, Division of Physiological Sciences, 1988-89, Howard Florey Professor of Medical Research, Director of School, 1989-92, University Fellow, 1993-95, Emeritus Professor, 1993, John Curtin School of Medical Research, Australian National University. Publications: Numerous articles in professional journals; Co-author, The John Curtin School of Medical Research. The First Fifty Years, 1948-1998. Honours: FAA, 1965; FRS, 1974; Burnet Medal, Australian Academy of Science, 1983; President, Australian Academy of Science, 1986-92; FRACP, 1987; AC, 1992; Centenary Medal, 2003. Memberships: Honorary Fellow, The British Pharmacological Society; Honorary Member Emeritus, The Australian Association of Neurologists; Honorary Member: The Neurosurgical Society of Australasia; The Australian Neuroscience Society; The Australian Physiological and Pharmacological Society. Address: 7 Patey Street, Campbell, ACT 2612, Australia.

**CURTIS Jamie Lee,** b. 22 November 1958, Los Angeles, California, USA. m. Christopher Guest, 1 son, 1 daughter. Education: University of the Pacific, California, USA. Career: Films include: Halloween; The Fog; Halloween 2; Prom Night; Trading Places; The Adventures of Buckaroo Banzai: Across the 8th Dimension; 8 Million Ways to Die; A Fish Called Wanda; Blue Steel; My Girl; Forever Young; My Girl 2; True Lies, 1994; House Arrest, 1996; Fierce Creatures, 1996; Halloween H20, 1998; Virus, 1999; The Tailor of Panama (also director), 2000; Daddy and Them; Halloween H2K: Evil Never Dies. TV includes: Dorothy Stratten: Death of a Centrefold; The Love Boat; Columbo Quincy; Charlie's Angels; Mother's Boys; Drowning Mona (director), 2000. Publications: When I Was Little, 1993; Today I Feel Silly and Other Moods That Make My Day, 1999. Address: c/o Rick Kurtsmann, CAA, 9830 Wilshire Boulevard, Beverly Hills, CA 90212, USA.

**CURTIS Sarah,** b. 21 May 1936, Preston, England. Journalist; Writer. m. 3 October 1960, 3 sons. Education: BA, 1958, MA, St Hugh's College, Oxford, England. Appointments: Times Educational Supplement, 1958-59; The Times, 1959-61; Editor, Adoption and Fostering, 1976-87; Editor, RSA Journal and Head of Communications RSA, 1989-95. Publications: Thinkstrip, series, 1976-79; It's Your Life, series, 1983; Juvenile Offending, 1989; Children Who Break the Law, 1999; The Journals of Woodrow Wyatt, editor, Vol 1, 1998, Vol 2, 1999, Vol 3, 2000. Contributions to: Times Literary Supplement, novel reviewer, since 1960s; Contributor, The Sunday Times, New Society, Financial Times, BBC Radio 4. Address: 9 Essex Villas, London W8 7BP, England.

**CURTIS Tony (Bernard Schwarz),** b. 3 June 1925, New York, USA. Film Actor. m. (1) Janet Leigh, divorced, 2 daughters, (2) Christine Kaufmann, divorced, 2 daughters, (3) Leslie Allen, 2 sons, (4) Lisa Deutsch, 1993. Education: New School of Social Research. Appointments: Served in US Navy; Actor, films include: Houdini; Black Shield of Falworth; So This is Paris?; Six Bridges to Cross; Trapeze; Mister Cory; Sweet Smell of Success; Midnight Story; The Vikings; Defiant Ones; Perfect

Furlough; Some Like It Hot, 1959; Spartacus, 1960; The Great Imposter, 1960; Pepe, 1960; The Outsider, 1961; Taras Bulba, 1962; Forty Pounds of Trouble, 1962; The List of Adrian Messenger, 9163; Captain Newman, 1963; Paris When It Sizzles, 1964; Wild and Wonderful, 1964; Sex and the Single Girl, 1964; Goodbye Charlie, 1964; The Great Race, 1965; Boeing, Boeing, 1965; Arriverderci, Baby, 1966; Not With My Wife You Don't, 1966; Don't Make Waves, 1967; Boston Strangler, 1968; Lepke, 1975; Casanova, 1976; The Last Tycoon, 1976; The Manitou, 1978; Sextette, 1978; The Mirror Crack'd, 1980; Venom, 1982; Insignificance, 1985; Club Life, 1986; The Last of Philip Banter, 1988; Balboa, Midnight, Lobster Man from Mars, The High-Flying Mermaid, Prime Target, Center of the Web, Naked in New York, The Reptile Man, The Immortals, 1995; The Celluloid Closet, 1995; Louis and Frank, 1997; Brittle Glory, 1997; TV includes: Third Girl From the Left, 1973; The Persuaders, 1971-72; The Count of Monte Cristo, 1976; Vegas, 1978; Mafia Princess, 1986; Christmas in Connecticut, 1992; A Perry Mason Mystery: The Case of the Grimacing Governor; Elvis Meets Nixon. Publications: Kid Andrew Cody and Julie Sparrow, 1977; The Autobiography, 1993. Honours include: Kt Order of the Republic of Hungary, 1966. Address: c/o William Morris Agency, 151 S El Camino Drive, Beverley Hills, CA 90212, USA.

**CUSACK John,** b. 28 June 1966, Evanston, Illinois, USA. Actor. Appointments: Piven Theatre Workshop, Evanston, from age 9-19; New Criminals Theatrical Company, Chicago; Films include: Class, 1983; Sixteen Candles, 1984; Grandview USA, 1984; The Sure Thing, 1985; One Crazy Summer, 1986; Broadcast News, 1987; Hot Pursuit, 1987; Eight Men Out, 1988; Tapeheads, 1988; Say Anything, 1989; Fatman and Little Boy, 1989; The Thin Red Line, 1989; The Grifters, 1990; True Colors, 1991; Shadows and Fog, 1992; Roadside Prophets, 1992; The Player, 1992; Map of the Human Heart, 1992; Bob Roberts, 1992; Money for Nothing, 1993; Bullets Over Broadway, 1994; The Road to Wellville, 1994; City Hall, 1995; Anastasia, 1997; Con Air, 1997; Hellcab, 1997; Midnight in the Garden of Good and Evil, 1997; This is My Father, 1998; Pushing Tin, 1998; Being John Malkovich, 1999; America's Sweethearts, 2001; Live of the Party, 2000; Serendipity, 2001; Max, 2002; Adaptation, 2002; Identity, 2003; Runaway Jury, 2003; Actor, director, writer: Grosse Pointe Blank, 1997; Arigo (producer, actor), 1998; High Fidelity (actor, writer), 1997; The Cradle Will Rock, 1999. Address: 1325 Avenue of the Americas, New York, NY 10019, USA,

**CUSACK Sinead Mary,** b. 1948. Actress. m. Jeremy Irons, 1977, 2 sons. Appointments: Appearances with RSC include: Lady Amaranth in Wild Oats, Lisa in Children of the Sun, Isabella in Measure for Measure, Celia in As You Like It, Evadne in the Maid's Tragedy, Lady Anne in Richard III, Portia in the Merchant of Venice, Ingrid in Peer Gynt, Kate in the Taming of the Shrew, Beatrice in Much Ado About Nothing, Lady MacBeth in MacBeth, Roxanne in Cyrano de Bergerac; Other stage appearances at Oxford Fest, Gate Theatre (Dublin), Royal Court; Virago in A Lie of the Mind, 2001, Oxford Festival, Gate Theatre, Dublin, Royal Court and others; numerous appearances in TV drama; Films include: Alfred the Great; Tamlyn; Hoffman; David Copperfield; Revenge; The Devil's Widow; Horowitz in Dublin Castle; The Last Remake of Beau Geste; Rocket Gibralter; Venus Peter; Waterland; God on the Rocks; Bad Behaviour; The Cement Garden; The Sparrow; Flemish Board; Stealing Beauty; I Capture the Castle. Address: c/o Curtis Brown Group, 4th Floor, Haymarket House, 28-29 Haymarket, London, SW1Y 4SP, England.

# DICTIONARY OF INTERNATIONAL BIOGRAPHY

**CUSSLER Clive (Eric),** b. 15 July 1931, Aurora, Illinois, USA. Author; Advertising Executive. m. Barbara Knight, 28 August 1955, 3 children. Education: Pasadena City College, 1949-51; Orange Coast College; California State University. Appointments: Advertising Directorships; Author. Owner, Bestgen and Cussler Advertising, Newport Beach, California, 1961-65; Copy Director, Darcy Advertising, Hollywood, California and Instructor in Advertising Communications, Orange Coast College, 1965-67; Advertising Director, Aquatic Marine Corporation, Newport Beach, California, 1967-79; Vice President and Creative Director of Broadcast, Meffon, Wolff and Weir Advertising, Denver, Colorado, 1970-73; Chair, National Underwater and Marine Agency. Publications: The Mediterranean Caper, 1973; Iceberg, 1975; Raise the Titanic, 1976; Vixen O-Three, 1978; Night Probe, 1981; Pacific Vortex, 1982; Deep Six, 1984; Cyclops, 1986; Treasure, 1988; Dragon, 1990; Sahara, 1992; Inca Gold, 1994; Shock Wave, 1996; Flood Tide, 1997; Serpent, 1999; Atlantis Found, 1999; Blue Gold, 2000; Valhalla Rising, 2001; Fire Ice, 2002; Sea Hunters II, 2002. Honours: Numerous advertising awards; Lowell Thomas Award, New York Explorers Club. Memberships: Fellow, New York Explorers Club; Royal Geographical Society.

**CYWIŃSKI Zbigniew,** b. 12 February 1929, Toruń, Poland. University Professor, Emeritus. m. Helena Wilczyńska, 11 April 1956, 1 son, 3 daughters. Education: Inż (BSc Eng), 1953; Mgr inż (MSc Eng), 1955; Dr inz (PhD Eng), 1964; Dr hab inż (DSc Eng), 1968; Professor, 1978. Appointments: Consulting Engineer, University of Baghdad, Iraq, 1965-66; Assistant Professor, University of Mosul, Iraq, 1970-73; UNESCO Expert, Ministry of Education, Mogadishu, Somalia, 1979-80; Professor, University of Tokyo, Japan, 1987-88; Vice Dean, 1975-78, Dean, 1984-87, 1993-99, Head, Structural Division, 1994-98, Faculty of Civil Engineering, Technical University of Gdansk. Publications: 3 textbooks, 2 books on structural mechanics; 2 monographs on bridges and on the TU Gdansk History; 314 published papers; 120 published reviews. Honours: Awards of the Minister of Education, 1964, 1976, 1978; Golden Cross of Merit, 1974; Cavalier Cross, 1980 and Officer's Cross, 1999, Poland's Rebirth Order; Medal, National Commission of Education, 1986; Gdańsk Millennium Medal, 1997. Memberships: Polish Society of Theoretical and Applied Mechanics, Regional Committee Head, 1990-92; International Association of Bridge and Structural Engineering, Alternate Delegate to Permanent Committee, 1994-; Fellow, American Society of Civil Engineers; Polish Society of Bridge Engineers. Address: ul Mściwoja 50/32, 80-357, Gdańsk-Oliwa, Poland.

**CZAPIK Romana Antonina,** b. 26 January 1929, Kraków, Poland. Professor. Education: Magister Philosophy in Botany, 1952, Doctor, 1961, Habilitation in Natural Sciences, 1967, Jagellonian University, Kraków. Appointments: Assistant Teacher of Biology, middle school, 1952; Senior Assistant, 1955; Adjunct, 1964; Docent, 1968; Extraordinary Professor, 1979; Regular Professor, 1976-81; Vice Director of the Botanical Institute; Retired, 1999; Continuing scientific activity. Publications: Papers and reviews in plant cytology, embryology, apomixis, embryology and pollution. Honours: Prize for didactic activity, Ministry of Education, 1966; Prize for habilitation dissertation, 1968; Golden Cross of Merit, 1974; Knight of Polonia Restituta Cross, 1981; Commission of National Education Medal, 1985; S G Navashin Medal, 1990; Dr J L Holub Medal, meritorious for Slovak botany, 1999; dedication of volume 41, Acta Biologica Cracoviensia ser Botanica, 1999. Memberships: 1962 International Association of Plant Taxonomy; 1962 International Organisation of Plant Biosystematists; International Association for Sexual Plant Reproduction Research; Member, 1954-, Honorary

Membership, 2004-, Polish Botanical Society; Member, 1964-, President of the Association, 2001-, Jagellonian Graduates Association. Address: Dept of Plant Cytology and Embryology, Jagellonian University, Grodzka 52, 31-044 Kraków, Poland. E-mail: ubczapik@cyf-kr.edu.pl

**CZECZUGA-SEMENIUK Ewa,** b. 13 April 1957, Mińsk, Belarus. Physician. m. Janusz Włodzimierz Semeniuk, 1 daughter. Education: PhD, Medicine, Medical University, Białystok, Poland, 1986. Appointments: Junior Researcher in Microbiology, 1982-83, Lecturer in Microbiology, 1983-85, Lecturer, 1985-2003, Senior Lecturer, 2003-, in Gynaecological Department, Medical University, Białystok, Poland. Publications: Numerous articles in professional scientific journals. Honours: Award I degree, Medical University, Białystok, Poland, 2000. Memberships: Polish Society of Gynaecology; Polish Society of Endocrinology; Polish Society of Menopause and Andropause. Address: Legionowa 9/54, 15-281, Białystok, Poland.

# D

**D'AGUILAR Paul,** b. 9 September 1924, London, England. Artist. Education: Educated privately in Spain, Italy and France; Trained by Professor Oscar Barblain, Sienna; Royal Academy Schools, 1949-54; Studied Conservation at the Courtauld Institute, London. Career: Artist in oil and watercolour; Critic and Reviewer, 1960-62; Travelled to Italy to restore pictures after the floods in Florence and Venice; Exhibitions: Leeds University, 1953; Daily Express Young Artists, 1953; Redfern and Leicester Galleries; National Society; Young Contemporaries; FPS; NEAC; RBA; Royal Academy; Biennal International de Cherbourg, France; Barcelona and Tarragona, Spain; St Ferme Abbey, Gironde, France, 1991; Retrospective Exhibition, Carlyle Gallery, Chelsea, London, 2003; Work in collections: Lord Rothermere; Wakefield and Bradford Educational Committees. Publication: Drawing Nudes (book), 1965. Honours: Bronze, Gold and Silver Medals, Royal Drawing Society; First Prize for drawing, Royal Academy; Leverhulme Scholarship. Address: 11 Sheen Gate Gardens, London SW14 7PD, England.

**D'ANCONA Matthew Robert Ralph,** b. 27 January 1968, London, England. Journalist. m. Sarah Schaefer, 2 sons. Education: St Dunstan's College; BA, 1st Class Honours, History, 1989, Magdalen College Oxford (Demy; H W C Davis Prize in History, 1987). Appointments: The Times, 1991-95, Assistant Editor, 1994-95; Deputy Editor (Comment), 1996-98, Deputy Editor, 1998-, The Sunday Telegraph. Publications: The Jesus Papyrus (with C P Thiede), 1996; The Ties That Bind Us, 1996; The Quest for the True Cross (with C P Thiede), 2000; Going East (novel), 2003. Honours: Prize Fellow, All Souls College, Oxford, 1989-86; Charles Douglas-Home Memorial Trust Prize, 1995; Political Journalist of the Year, British Press Awards, 2004. Memberships: Member, Board of Directors, Centre for Policy Studies, 1998-; Advisory Council, Demos, 1998-; British Executive, International Press Institute, 1998-; Millennium Commission, 2001-; Policy Advisory Board, Social Market Foundation, 2002-; Member of Hansard Society's Commission on Parliament in the Public Eye, 2004-2005; Fellow, Royal Society of Arts, 2004-. Address: The Sunday Telegraph, 1 Canada Square, Canary Wharf, London E14 5DT, England.

**DAEHNE Siegfried,** b. 13 October 1929, Meissen, Saxony, Germany. Chemist. m. Anneliese Daehne Koelling, 2 sons, 1 daughter. Education: Study of Chemistry, 1949-57, Doctor's Degree, 1961, Habilitation, 1968, Humboldt University, Berlin; Venia Legendi, Technical University, Dresden, 1977. Appointments: Head of Laboratory, Institute of Optics and Spectroscopy, Berlin, 1957-62; Head of Department, 1963-84, Staff Member, 1985-87, Central Institute of Optics and Spectroscopy, Berlin; Head of Department, Analytical Centre, Academy of Sciences of the GDR, Berlin, 1988-91; Head of Laboratory, Federal Institute for Materials Research and Testing, Berlin, 1992-95; Head of Project, DFG Sonderforschungsbereich 337, Free University, Berlin, 1992-98; Consultant, Federal Institute for Materials Research and Testing, Berlin, 1996-2001. Publications: Over 260 research publications in professional journals; 9 patents in field of molecular spectroscopy, colour chemistry and supramolecular chemistry, with basic contributions to the mechanisms of spectral sensitization and desensitization in photography, 1965, 1967, theory of the ideal polymethine state, 1966, history of colour and constitution theories, 1970, 1978, structural principles of conjugated organic compounds (triad theory), 1977, 1985, 1990; spontaneous and enantioselective generation of chiral J-aggregate helices from achiral cyanine dye molecules, 1996, 1997; Artificial light harvesting systems for photo-induced electron transfer reactions, 2003; Initiator, main author, Prognosis of Time-Resolved Spectroscopy, Berlin, 1968; Initiator and organiser, Annual Application Schools of Laser Pulse Spectrometry, Berlin, 1982-86; Fifth Symposium of Photochemistry, Reinhardsbrunn, 1986; NATO Advanced Research Workshop on Syntheses, Optical Properties and Applications of Near-Infrared Dyes in High Technology Fields, Trest, Czech Republic, 1997. Honours: Leibniz Medal of the Academy of Sciences of the GDR, 1976; Lieven Gevaert Medal, Society of Photographic Scientists and Engineers, USA, 1997. Memberships include: Society for German Chemists; European Photochemistry Association; German Bunsen Society of Physical Chemistry. Address: Kastanienallee 6, D-12587, Berlin, Germany.

**DAFOE Willem,** b. 22 July 1955, Appleton, Wisconsin, USA. Actor. Education: Wisconsin University. Appointments: Actor, films include: The Loveless, 1981; New York Nights, 1981; The Hunger, 1982; Communists are Comfortable (and 3 other stories), 1984; Roadhouse 66, 1984; Streets of Fire, 1984; To Live and Die in LA, 1985; Platoon, 1986; The Last Temptation of Christ, 1988; Saigon, 1988; Mississippi Burning, 1989; Triumph of the Spirit, 1989; Born on the Fourth of July, 1990; Flight of the Intruder, 1990; Wild at Heart, 1990; The Light Sleeper, 1991; Body of Evidence, 1992; Far Away, So Close, 1994; Tom and Viv, 1994; The Night and the Moment, 1994; Clear and Present Danger, 1994; The English Patient, 1996; Basquiat, 1996; Speed 2: Cruise Control, 1997; Affliction, 1997; Lulu on the Bridge, 1998; Existenz, 1998; American Psycho, 1999; Shadow of the Vampire, 2000; Bullfighter, 2000; The Animal Factory, 2000; Edges of the Lord, 2001; Spider-Man, 2002; Auto Focus, 2002; Once Upon a Time in Mexico, 2003; The Clearing, 2004; The Reckoning, 2004.

**DAHL Sophie,** b. 1978. Fashion Model. Appointments: Discovered by Isabella Blow; Worked with fashion photographers: Nick Knight, David La Chapelle, Karl Lagerfeld, David Bailey, Enrique Badulescu, Herb Ritts and Ellen Von Unwerth; Appeared in: ID, The Face, Elle, Esquire, Scene magazines; Advertising campaigns for Lainey, Keogh, Bella Freud, Printemps, Nina Ricci, Karl Lagerfeld, Oil of Ulay, Hennes; Music videos for U2, Elton John, Duran Duran; Cameo appearances in films: Mad Cows, Best, 1999; Stage appearance in The Vagina Monologues, Old Vic Theatre, 1999; Judge, Orange Prize for Fiction, 2003. Publication: The Man with the Dancing Eyes, 2003. Address: c/o Storm Model Management, 5 Jubilee Place, London SW3 3TD, England.

**DAICHES David,** b. 2 September 1912, Sunderland, England. Professor Emeritus; Writer. m. (1) Isobel Janet Mackay, 28 July 1937, deceased 1977, 1 son, 2 daughters, (2) Hazel Neville, 1978, deceased 1986. Education: MA, Edinburgh University, 1934; DPhil, Oxford University, 1939. Appointments: Fellow, Balliol College, Oxford, 1936-37; Assistant Professor, University of Chicago, 1939-43; Professor, Cornell University, 1946-51, Sussex University, 1961-77; University Lecturer, 1951-61, Fellow, Jesus College, 1957-62, Cambridge; Director, Institute for Advanced Studies, Edinburgh University, 1980-86. Publications: 45 books including: The Novel and the Modern World, 1939; Robert Burns, 1950; Two Worlds, 1956; A Critical History of English Literature, 1960; The Paradox of Scottish Culture, 1964; God and the Poets, 1984; Edinburgh: A Traveller's Companion, 1986; A Weekly Scotsman and Other Poems, 1994. Honours: Royal Society of Literature, fellow, 1957; Scottish Arts Council Book Award, 1973; Scottish Book of the Year Award, 1984; Commander of the Order of the British Empire, 1991; Various honorary doctorates. Memberships:

Association for Scottish Literary Studies, honorary president; Modern Language Association of America, honorary member; Saltire Society, honorary president. Address: 22 Belgrave Crescent, Edinburgh, EH4 3AL, Scotland.

**DAIMON Hiroshi,** b. 22 July 1953, Japan. Professor. Education: BSc, 1976, MSc, 1978, PhD, 1983, University of Tokyo. Appointments: Educational Staff, 1978, Assistant Professor, 1983, University of Tokyo; Associate Professor, Osaka University, 1990; Visiting Scientist, LBNL, California, USA, 1994-95; Professor, Nara Institute of Science and Technology, 1997-. Publications: About 130 articles. Honours: Award of Young Scholar Lecture Series, The Chemical Society of Japan; Award of Japan Society of Applied Physics; Award of Japan Society of Electron Microscopy; The Ichimura Prize in Technology – Meritorious Achievement Prize; NAIST Prize in Science. Memberships: American Physical Society; Physical Society of Japan; Japanese Society for Synchrotron Radiation Research; Japan Society of Applied Physics; Surface Science Society of Japan; Vacuum Society of Japan. Address: 8916-5 Takayama, Ikoma, Nara 630-0192, Japan. E-mail: daimon@ms.naist.jp

**DAISLEY Miriam Louise,** b. 22 May 1950, Northern Cambria, Pennsylvania, USA. Counsellor. Education: B Ed, Elementary, Clarion University, 1971; M Ed, Guidance, Indiana University of Pennsylvania, 1975; Computer Information and Communications Technology, Cambria, County Community College, 2002. Appointments: Elementary Teacher, Northern Cambria, 1972-74; Elementary Teacher, DDP/Ludwigsburg, Germany, 1974; Teacher of Gifted Children, 1975-91, Counsellor, 1991- Appalachia Indiana School District; Taught English in China, 2002. Publications: Promoted American Association of University Women's book, Women in Cambria County; Author of plays on: Johnstown Artists; No Bullying Programs, for school grades 1-8; Compiled booklets on Women in History; Wrote college courses on Arts and Humanities, Creative Thinking, Critical Thinking, approved by Pennsylvania Department of Education. Honours: Outstanding Woman, American Association of University Women; Taft Scholarship, Cannon University Government Course; National Geographic Alliance Scholarships; Liaison to China. Memberships: Pennsylvania State Counselor's Association; Pennsylvania State Education Association; American Association of University Women. Address: 1148 McKinley Avenue, Johnstown, PA 15905, USA. E-mail: mdaisley@iu08.org

**DAJUN Jin (Aixinjueluo),** b. February 1948, Beijing, China. Chinese Brushwork Painter. Education: Graduate, Beijing Arts and Crafts College, 1968; Studies in traditional Chinese painting with Mr Huang Jun and Mr Yu Zhizhen; Well nurtured in profound Chinese culture. Appointments: Chinese Brushwork Painter. Honours: Prize for Outstanding Art Accomplishment, UNESCO and International Peace Educators' Association, 1999; World Expo Gold Medal for Wonderful Art Works, USA, 2002; Painting, Taizehn and Parrot, collected by China National Arts Museum as a national treasure; Appears in Contemporary Chinese Outstanding Artists Dictionary. Memberships: Member, Beijing Painters Association; Member, China National Outstanding Intellectuals Association; Vice Chairman, Painting Association of Ministry of Health. Address: China Academy of Traditional Chinese Medicine, No 16 South XiaoJie, Dongzhimen, Beijing 100700, China.

**DAKSHINAMURTI Krishnamurti,** b. 20 May 1928, Vellore, India. Professor Emeritus. m. Ganga B, 2 daughters. Education: BSc, University of Madras, 1946; MSc, 1952, PhD, 1957, University of Rajputana. Appointments: Senior Lecturer,

Biochemistry, Christian Medical College, Vellore India, 1952; Research Associate, Nutritional Biochemistry, University of Illinois, USA, 1957; Research Associate, Massachusetts Institute of Technology, 1962; Associate Director of Research, St Joseph Hospital, Lancaster, Pennsylvania, 1963; Associate Professor, Biochemistry, 1965, Professor of Biochemistry and Molecular Biology, 1973-98, Emeritus Professor, Faculty of Medicine, 1998-, Co-Director, Centre for Health Policy Studies, St Boniface Hospital Research Centre, 2004-, University of Manitoba, Canada; Visiting Professor of Cell Biology, Rockefeller University, 1974-75. Publications: Author of over 200 research publications and 4 books. Honours: Fellow of the Royal Society of Chemistry, UK; Borden Award, Nutrition Society of Canada, 1973. Fellow, Canadian College of Neuropsychpharmacology; Fellow, International College of Nutrition; Fellow, American College of Nutrition; President, International College of Nutrition, 1990-92. Memberships: American Society of Biochemistry and Molecular Biology; Society for Neuroscience; American Society of Neurochemistry; American Institute of Nutrition; American Society for Cell Biology; American Diabetes Association; Canadian Biochemical Society; Biochemical Society, UK; Nutrition Society of Canada; International Society of Neurochemistry; International Brain Research Organisation; Charter Member Serotonin Club; American Society of Hypertension; President, India School of Dance, Music and Theatre, Winnipeg; Founder, Manohar Performing Arts of Canada. Address: Faculty of Medicine, University of Manitoba, Winnipeg, Manitoba Canada R3E 0W3. E-mail: dakshin@cc.umanitoba.ca

**DA'LUZ VIEIRA-JONES Lorraine,** b. 30 April 1955, London, England. Physician of Chinese Medicine; Lecturer; Chief Executive Officer. m. Schuyler Jones, 1 son, 1 daughter. Education: Lic. Ac. (Acupuncture, England), 1983; B. Ac., 1986; M. Ac., 1988; M St (Oxford), 1994; M. Phil., distinction (Oxford), 1995; D. Phil. (Oxford), 1999; Dipl. Ac. (USA), 2002; DOM, Chelsea University, London, 2004; M Lett., 2005. Appointments: New Internationalist, 1979-80; World Information Service on Energy, 1980-83; Clinician and Consultant, Acupuncture Physician, 1982-; Lecturer, College of Traditional Acupuncture, England, 1984-99; Anthropology Adjunct Professor, Wichita State University, Kansas, USA, 1999-; Lecturer, Academy of 5 Element Acupuncture, Florida, USA, 2000-; Consultant and Lecturer Workshops, USA, 2000-; Chief Executive Officer, Healing Sanctuaries LLC, 2003-. Publication: The Credence Factor (book explaining placebo effect), forthcoming. Honours: Woman of the Year, 2004; International Peace Prize, 2004; Professional of the Year, 2005; Woman of Achievement, 2005. Memberships: Fellow, American Association of Integrative Medicine, 2002; American Association of Oriental Medicine; British Acupuncture Council; Shakespeare Society, Wichita, USA.. Address: The Prairie House, 1570 N Ridgewood Drive, Wichita, KS 67208, USA. driorijones@cs.com

**DAL MASO Luigino,** b. 13 March 1967, Este, Padua, Italy. Statistican. m. Claudia Braga. Education: Science Doctor, Statistics, Padua University, 1993. Appointments: Researcher, Aviano Cancer Centre, Italy, 1993-2003; Consultant, Pharmacological Institute M Negri, Milan, Italy, 1995-99; Consultant, Pascale Cancer Institute, Naples, Italy, 1996-98; Visiting Scientist, International Agency for Research on Cancer, Lyon, France, 2001-02, 2004. Publications: Articles in professional journals. Honours: Fellow, Italian Association Against Cancer, 1993-95; 2 grants, National Minister of Health, Italy, 2000-03. Memberships: Italian Association of Cancer Registries, 1999-2003; Italian Epidemiological Association, 1994-2002. Address: Aviano Cancer Institute,

via Pedemontana Occidentale 12, I-33081, Aviano (PN), Italy
E-mail: dalmaso@cro.it

**DALAI LAMA The (Tenzin Gyatso),** b. 6 July 1935, Taktser, Amdo Province, North East Tibet. Temporal and Spiritual Head of Tibet 14th Incarnation. Appointments: Enthroned at Lhasa, 1940; Rights exercised by regency, 1934-50; Assumed political power, 1950; Fled to Chumbi in South Tibet, 1950; Agreement with China, 1951; Vice-Chair, Standing Committee, Member, National Committee, CPPCC, 1951-59; Honorary Chairman, Chinese Buddhist Association, 1953-59; Delegate to National People's Congress, 1954-59; Chairman, Preparatory Committee for Autonomous Region of Tibet, 1955-59; Fled to India after suppression of Tibetan national uprising, 1959. Publications: My Land and People, 1962; The Opening of the Wisdom Eye, 1963; The Buddhism of Tibet and the Key to The Middle Way, 1975; Kindness, Charity and Insight, 1984; A Human Approach to World Peace, 1984; Freedom in Exile (autobiography), 1990; The Good Heart, 1996; Ethics for the New Millennium, 1998; Art of Happiness, (co-author), 1999; A Simple Path: basic Buddhist Teachings by His Holiness the Dalai Lama, 2000; Stages of Meditation: training the Mind for Wisdom, 2002; The Spirit of Peace, 2002. Honours: Dr Buddhist Philos (Monasteries of Sera, Drepung and Gaden, Lhasa), 1959; Supreme Head of all Buddhist sections in Tibet; Memory Prize, 1989; Congressional Human Rights Award, 1989; Nobel Prize, 1989; The Freedom Award (USA), 1991. Address: Thekchen Choeling, McLeod Ganj 176219, Dharamsala, Himachal Pradesh, India.

**DALBY John Mark Meredith,** b. 3 January 1938, Southport, Lancashire. Clergyman. Education: MA, Exeter College, Oxford; Ripon Hall, Oxford; PhD, University of Nottingham. Appointments: Ordained Deacon, 1963, Priest, 1964, Oxford; Curate of the Hambledon Valley Group, 1963-68; Vicar of St Peter, Spring Hill, Birmingham, 1968-75; Rural Dean of Birmingham City, 1973-75; Secretary of the Committee for Theological Education, Advisory Council for the Church's Ministry, also Honorary Curate of All Hallows, Tottenham, 1975-80; Vicar, later Team Rector of Worsley, 1980-91; Rural Dean of Eccles, 1987-91; Archdeacon of Rochdale, 1991-2000; Chaplain of the Beauchamp Community, Newland, 2000-. Publications: Open Communion in the Church of England, 1959; The Gospel and the Priest, 1975; Tottenham: Church and Parish, 1979; The Cocker Connection, 1989; Open Baptism, 1989; Anglican Missals and their Canons, 1998; Infant Communion: The New Testament to the Reformation, 2003. Address: The Chaplain's House, The Beauchamp Community, Newland. Malvern, Worcestershire WR13 5AX, England. E-mail: markd alby@dalbyj.fsnet.co.uk

**DALE Peter Grenville Hurst,** b. 14 February 1935, Newcastle upon Tyne, England. Architect. 3 sons. Education: Diploma in Architecture, Durham University, 1961; MA, Architecture, Leeds Metropolitan University, 1994; Certificate in Construction,1958; Certificate in Town Planning, 1970. Appointments: County Architect, Humberside, 1977-85; Senior Lecturer, Leeds Metropolitan University; Professor of Architecture, University of Leeds, 1993-; Honorary Fellow, London College of Management/Information Technology. Publications: 4 Royal Institute of British Architects Training Manuals, 1991 (re-edited 1997); 10 archaeological magazine editorials. Honours: 33 national, regional and local awards; Chairman, Construction Industry Research, Department of the Environment, 1991/1997; Chairman, European Union, Construction Harmonisation Technology, 1997-. Memberships: Chairman, British Brick Association, 2004; Cordwainers Guild; Builders Guild; Freeman of England and Wales. Address: 19 Mile End Park, Pocklington, York YO42 2TH, England.

**DALGLEISH Angus George,** b. 14 May 1950, London, England. m. 1 son. Professor of Oncology. Education: Harrow County Grammar School for Boys; BSc (Hons), Anatomy, University College, London, 1971; MB BS, University of London, University College Hospital, 1974; FRACP, 1984; MRCP, 1984; JCHMT, Certificate in Medial Oncology, 1985; MRCPath, 1992; FRCP, 1993; FRCPath, 1996; F Med Science, 2000. Appointments: House Surgeon, Locum Casualty Officer, St Stephen's Hospital, London, 1975; House Physician, Poole District Hospital, Dorset, 1975; Flying Doctor Service, Queensland, Australia, 1976; Resident Medical Officer, 1977, General Medical Registrar, 1978, 1980, Princess Alexandra Hospital, Brisbane; Cardio-Thoracic Registrar, Prince Charles Hospital, Brisbane, 1980; Registrar in Radiotherapy, Royal Brisbane Hospital, 1981; Senior Registrar in Oncology, 1982, Senior Registrar in Clinical Immunology and Haematology, 1983, Royal Prince Alfred Hospital, Sydney; Clinical Research Fellow, Royal Marsden Hospital, London, 1984; Clinical Scientist MRC, CRC and Honorary Consultant Physician, Immunologist and Oncologist, Northwick Park Hospital, London, 1986; Honorary Senior Lecturer in Oncology and Honorary Consultant Physician, RPMS, Hammersmith, London, 1986; Head, Retrovirus Research Group, MRC, Clinical Research Centre, 1988; Head, Clinical Virology, Senior Lecturer, and Honorary Consultant Physician, The Royal London Hospital Medical College, 1991; Professor, Foundation Chair of Oncology, St George's Hospital Medical School, Honorary Consultant in Medical Oncology, SGH, 1991; Visiting Professor in Oncology, Institute of Cancer Research, 1994; Chairman of Oncology, Gastroenterology and Endocrinology, St George's Hospital Medical School, 1998. Publications: Numerous articles in professional medical journals. Honours: MRC Scholarship for BSc in Anatomy, 1970; Royal Australian College of Radiologists Travelling Fellowship, 1981; New South Wales Clinical Oncology Fellowship, 1984. Memberships: Association of American Immunologists; British Oncology Association; British Society of Immunology; London Cell Molecular Biology Group; UK Molecular Biology of Cancer Network; British Association for Cancer Research; Association of Cancer Physicians; Trustee, London Youth Cancer Holiday Trust; Elected Member, Medical Research Club; Founder Member, European Committee for AIDS Research; European Society Medical Oncology. Address: Department of Oncology, St George's Hospital Medical School, Tooting, London SW17 0RE, England. E-mail: a.dalgleish@sghms.ac.uk Website: www.oncologyresearch.co.uk

**DALGLISH Kenneth (Kenny) Mathieson,** b. 4 March 1951, Glasgow, Scotland. Football Manager. Appointments: Played for Celtic, Scottish League Champions, 1972-74, 1977; Scottish Cup Winners, 1972, 1974, 1975, 1977; Scottish Cup Winners, 1972, 1974, 1975, 1977; Scottish league Cup winners, 1975; Played for Liverpool, European Cup Winners, 1978, 1981, 1984; FA Cup Winners, 1986, 1989; League Cup winners, 1981-84; Manager, 1986-91; Manager Blackburn Rovers, 1991-97; Newcastle United, 1997-98; Director of Football operations, Celtic, 1999-2000; 102 full caps for Scotland scoring 30 goals. Honours: Footballer of the Year, 1979, 1983; MBE; Freeman of Glasgow. Address: c/o Celtic Football Club, Celtic Park, Glasgow, G40 3RE, Scotland.

**DALLAGLIO Lawrence Bruno Nero,** b. 10 August 1976, Sheppards Bush. London, England. Professional Rugby Union Player. Partner, Alice Corbett, 1 son, 2 daughters. Education: Kingston University. Career: Captain Wasps Rugby Union, 1995-; British Lions Tours, 1997, 2001, 2005; Member, World Cup Winning Team, Australia, 2003; Captain of England, 1998-99, 2004. Publications: Diary of a Season, 1997; Know the Modern Game, 1999. Honours: England Captain; Club Captain of Wasps; Freedom of the Borough, City of Rugby; Freedom of the Borough, Richmond, MBE. Address: c/o Sportscast, 11a Laud Street, Croydon CR0 1SU, England. E-mail: ashley@sportscastnet.com

**DALMAS John,** b. 3 September 1926, Chicago, Illinois, USA. Author. m. Gail Hill, 15 September 1954, 1 son, 1 daughter. Education: BSc, Michigan State College, 1954; Master of Forestry, University of Minnesota, 1955; PhD, Colorado State University, 1967. Publications: The Yngling, 1969; The Varkaus Conspiracy, 1983; Touch the Stars: Emergence (with Carl Martin), 1983; Homecoming, 1984; The Scroll of Man, 1985; Fanglith, 1985; The Reality Matrix 1986; The Walkaway Clause, 1986; The Regiment, 1987; The Playmasters (with Rodney Martin), 1987; Return to Fanglith, 1987; The General's President, 1988; The Lantern of God, 1989; The Lizard War, 1989; The White Regiment, 1990; The Kalif's War, 1991; The Yngling and the Circle of Power, 1992; The Orc Wars (collection), 1992; The Regiment's War, 1993; The Yngling in Yamato, 1994; The Lion of Farside, 1995; The Bavarian Gate, 1997; The Three Cornered War, 1999; The Lion Returns, 1999; Soldiers, 2001; The Puppet Master, 2001; Otherwhens, Otherwheres, 2003; The Helverti Invasion, 2003; The Second Coming, 2004; The Regiment: A Trilogy (collection), 2004. Contributions to: Journals, magazines and anthologies. Honours: Xi Sigma Pi Forestry Honorary Society, 1953; Phi Kappa Phi Scholastic Honorary Society, 1954; Sigma Xi Scientific Research Society, 1963. Memberships: Science Fiction Writers of America; Vasa Order of America. Address: 1425 Glass Street, Spokane, WA 99205, USA.

**DALRYMPLE William Benedict,** b. 20 March 1965, Edinburgh, Scotland. Writer. m. Olivia Fraser, 2 sons, 1 daughter. Education: Exhibitioner, 1984, Senior History Scholar, 1986, MA, Honours, 1992, Trinity College, Cambridge. Appointments: Author, 1989-. Publications: In Xanadu, 1989; City of Djinns, 1993; From the Holy Mountain, 1997; The Age of Kali, 1998; White Mughals, 2002. Contributions to: Times Literary Supplement; Spectator; New York Review of Books; Guardian. Honours: Yorkshire Post, Best First Work Award, 1990; Scottish Arts Council, 1990; Thomas Cook, Travel Book Award, 1994; Sunday Times, Young British Writer of the Year, 1994; Scottish Arts Council Autumn Book Award, 1997; Grierson Award for Best Documentary, 2002; Wolfson Prize for History, 2003; Scottish Book of the Year, 2003; Mungo Park Medal (RSGS), 2003; Percy Sykes Medal (RSAA), 2005. Memberships: FRSL, 1993; FRGS, 1993; FRAS, 1998; PEN, 1998. Address: 1 Pages' Yard, Church Street, London W4 2PA, England. E-mail: wdalrymple1@aol.com

**DALTON Ann,** b. 28 October 1933, East Sussex, England. Coloratura Soprano Soloist for classical, folk, cabaret and operatic concerts and recitals; BBC Studio Manager, Programme Producer, Trainer; Accredited Chaperone for children performing on stage (Glyndebourne Opera House and Talisman Film Company). Education: Ursuline Convent, Brentwood, Essex; Guildhall School of Music and Drama Performance Certificate; BBC Programme and Engineering Training Colleges, Evesham & Marylebone Road; Piano & Cello Grade V, Royal Academy of Music; City & Guilds Teaching Certificate. Appointments: Producer and Studio Manager, British Broadcasting Corporation, London, 1955-89; Seconded via BBC International Relations Department to be Head of Training and Operations (later Director, External Affairs) for the International Radio and TV Training Centre at Hatch End, Middlesex, to assist Third World and other communicators, 1972-89; Voluntary vocational assistance as Co-Founder and Manager of this centre (while off-duty from the BBC), 1955-72; Lecturer, Loyola University Summer Communications Courses, USA, 1973-76; Organiser, British Radio & TV UNDA Festivals and competitions; Jury Member, Prix d'Italia UNDA-TV Awards, 1978; Jury Member, Sandford St Martin TV awards, 1987; Selected as Mass Media Commission Representative to present Loyal Address at Buckingham Palace, 1981; Various appearances on radio and television broadcasts; Selected singing candidate in the English National Opera TV series, "Operatunity", 2002; First solo singing broadcast live from BBC Concert Hall, accompanied by Dr George Thalben-Ball. Honours: Pro Ecclesia Cross, 1981; Six Championship Awards from Sussex Singing Contests, 2000-2005; Two Gold Medals for Singing, Eastbourne, 2001, 2005. Memberships: Fellow, Royal Society of Arts; Royal Television Society; Radio Academy; Association of Independent Producers; Associate, Institute of Qualified Private Secretaries; Environmental and Animal Carers. Address: 13 Warrior Square, St Leonards-on-Sea, East Sussex, TN37 6BA, England.

**DALTON Timothy,** b. 21 March 1946. Actor. Education: Royal Academy of Dramatic Art. Career includes: National Youth Theatre; Theatre includes: Toured with Prospect Theatre Company; Guest Artist, RSC; Co-starred with Vivien Merchant in Noel Coward's The Vortex; Anthony and Cleopatra, 1986; The Taming of the Shrew, 1986; A Touch of the Poet, Young Vic, 1988; Lord Asriel in Philip Pullman's His Dark Materials, National Theatre, 2003; Films include: The Lion in Winter, 1968; Cromwell, 1970; Wuthering Heights; Mary, Queen of Scots, 1972; Permission to Kill, 1975; The Man Who Knew Love; Sextette, 1977; Agatha, 1978; Flash Gordon, 1979; James Bond in The Living Daylights, 1987 and Licence to Kill, 1989; The Rocketeer, 1991; The Reef, 1996; The Beautician and the Beast, 1996; Made Men, 1998; Cleopatra, 1998; Possessed, 1999; Timeshare, 2000; American Outlaws, 2001; Looney Tunes – Back in Action, 2002; Hercules, 2004; TV roles include: Mr Rochester in Jane Eyre, BBC TV, 1983; Master of Ballentrae, HTV, 1983; Mistral's Daughter, TV mini-series, 1984; Florence Nightingale, TV mini-series; Sins, TV mini-series, 1985; Philip von Joel in Framed, mini-series, Anglia TV, 1992; Jack in Red Eagle; Rhett Butler in Scarlett, Sky, 1994; Salt Water Moose, comedy, 1995; The Informant, 1996. Membership: Actors' Equity. Address: c/o ICM, Oxford House, 76 Oxford Street, London W1D 1BS, England.

**DALTREY David Joseph,** b. 30 December 1951, London, England. Session Musician (guitar and piano); Guitar Tutor; Composer. Education: Guildhall School of Music and Drama; ALCM, London College of Music, 1969-72; City and Guilds, Adult Teacher Training, 1985-87. Appointments: Recording artist with EMI and DECCA; Worked for BBC, London; Composer; Producer; Session Musician; Tutor; Audio Consultant. Recordings: Tales of Justine-Albert/Monday Morning, UK, 1967; Joseph And The Amazing Technicolour Dreamcoat, UK 1969, USA 1971; Petals from a Sunflower, UK,1998; The Wayfarer, UK, 2004. Honours: Gold Record, Scepter Records, USA, 1971. Memberships: Musicians' Union; Incorporated Society of Musicians; AES; Institute of Acoustics; MIOA; Music Producer's Guild; Radio Academy. Address: Flat 3, Hughesdon House, 122 Northgate Street, Bury St Edmunds, Suffolk, IP33 1HG, England. E-mail: yazzpeachey@aol.com Website: www.byor.com

**DALY John Patrick,** b. 28 April 1966, Carmichael, CA, USA. Golfer. m. 2 children. Education: University of Arkansas. Appointments: Turned professional, 1987; Won Missouri Open, 1987; Ben Hogan Utah Classic, 1990; PGA Championship, Crooked Stick, 1991; BC Open, 1992; Dunhill Cup, 1993, 1998; BellSouth Classic, 1994; British Open, 1995; BMW

International Open, 2001. Recording: My Life (album). Address: c/o PGA America, 100 Avenue of the Champions, Palm Beach Gardens, FL 33418, USA.

**DALYELL Tam,** b. 9 August 1932, Edinburgh, Scotland. Member of Parliament; Writer. m. Kathleen Wheatley, 26 December 1963, 1 son, 1 daughter. Education: Harecroft Hall, Eton; King's College, Cambridge, 1952-56. Appointments: Elected to House of Commons, 1962-2005; Father of the House of Commons, 2001-05. Publications: The Case for Ship Schools, 1958; Ship School Dunera, 1961; One Man's Falklands, 1982; A Science Policy for Britain, 1983; Misrule: How Mrs Thatcher Deceived Parliament, 1987; Dick Crossman: A Portrait, 1988. Contributions to: Weekly Columnist, New Scientist, 1967-; Many Obituaries, Independent Newspaper. Honours: Various Awards of Science; Honorary Doctor of Science, University of Edinburgh, 1994; Honorary Degree, City University, London, 1998; Trustee, History of Parliament, 1999-2005; Chairman, All-Party Latin America Group, 1999-2004; St Andrew's University, 2003; Napier University, Edinburgh, 2004; Northumbria University, 2005. Address: Binns, Linlithgow, EH44 7NA, Scotland.

**DĂNĂILĂ Leon,** b. 1 July 1933, Darabani, Botosani. Neurosurgeon. m. Alexandrina Ionescu. Education: Graduate, Faculty of General Medicine of Jassy, Faculty of Psychology and Philosophy, Bucharest, 1958; Fulbright Scholarship, Neurosurgery Clinic, University Hospital of New York, 1980; PhD, Medicine, 1973; Senior Physician 2nd Degree, 1981. Studies in the Netherlands, Moscow, Budapest, Dusseldorf, Brussels, Glasgow, Edinburgh, Paris. Appointments: General Practitioner, Sanitary District of Comanesti and Darmanesti in Bacau County, 1958-61; Resident Neurosurgeon, Neurosurgery Clinic of Bucharest, 1961-; Head of the Vascular Neurosurgery Department VII, 1981; Professor of Neurosurgery, Bucharest Faculty of Medicine, Head of Neurosurgery Department, 1996-; Professor, Psychoneurology, Titu Maiorescu University of Bucharest, 1992; President, Romanian Neurosurgery, 1997-. Publications: 307 scientific works, 59 in foreign journals; 24 books include: Spinal Neurinoma, 1972; Psychoneurology, 1983; Volumes 2 and 3, Vascular Diseases of the Brain and Spinal Cord, 1985; Romanian Neurosurgery, volumes I and II, 1986, 1987; Cardiovascular Thromboembolism, 1987; Psychiatric Surgery, 1988; Cerebral Atherosclerosis, 1988; The Treatment of Brain Tumors, 1993; Alzheimer Disease, 1996; Sculpture in the Brain, 1998; Apoptosis, 1999, 2002; Dateness and Prospects in Neurosurgery, 2000; Handbook of Neuropsychology, 2000, 2002; Lasers in Neurosurgery, 2001; Arterial and Venous Vascularization of the Brain, 2001; Atlas of Surgical Pathology of the Brain, 2000, 2001; Neurosurgical Synthesis, 2002; Atherosclerosis of the Brain, 2004; Atlas of cerebro-vascular pathology, 2005. Honours: 10 Certificates of Innovator; 18 Certificates of Inventor; Award, Romanian Academy, 1995, 2001, 2002, 2003; RE del Vivo International Award, 1996; Honorary Citizenship of Darabani, 1999 and Dorohoi, 1999; ABI World Laureate, 1999. Memberships include: Titular Member, Romanian Academy; Romanian Medical Academy; Romanian Academy of Scientists; New York Academy of Scientists; L'Union Medical Balakanique; Balkan Society of Angiology and Vascular Surgery; American Association for the Advancement of Science; European Society for Stereotactic and Functional Neurosurgery; Société de Neurochirurgie de Langue Française; Congress of Neurological Surgeons. Address: Traian St, No 2, Bl Fl, Sc III, Et 2, Ap 4, Sector 3, Bucharest, Romania.

**DANCE Charles,** b. 10 October 1946, Rednal, Worcestershire, England. Actor. m. Joanna Haythorn, 1970, 1 son, 1 daughter.

Appointments: Formerly employed in industry; with RSC, 1975-80, 1980-85; TV appearances include: The Fatal Spring; Nancy Astor; Frost in May; Saigon - The Last Day; Thunder Rock (drama); Rainy Day Women; The Jewel in the Crown (nominated for Best Actor BAFTA Award); The Secret Servant; The McGuffin; The Phantom of the Opera, 1989; Rebecca, 1996; In the Presence of Mine Enemies; The Ends of the Earth, 2004; Bleak House, 2004; Fingersmith, 2005; Last Rights, 2005; Films include: For Your Eyes Only; Plenty; The Golden Child; White Mischief; Good Morning Babylon; Hidden City; Pascali's Island, 1988; China Moon, 1990; Alien III, 1991; Limestone, 1991; Kabloonak; Century; Last Action Hero; Exquisite Tenderness, 1993; Short Cut to Paradise, 1993; Undertow; Michael Collins; Space Trucker, 1996; Goldeneye; The Blood Oranges; What Rats Won't Do; Hilary and Jackie, 1998; Don't Go Breaking My Heart, 1999; Jurij, 1999; Dark Blue World, 2000; Gosford Park, 2001; Ali G in da House, 2001; Black and White; Swimming Pool, 2002; Ladies in Lavender (writer/director), 2005; Theatre: Coriolanus (title role), RSC, 1989; Irma La Douce; Turning Over; Henry V; Three Sisters, 1998; Good, 1999; Long Day's Journey Into Night, 2001; The Play What I Wrote, 2002; Radio: The Heart of the Matter, 2001; The Charge of the Light Brigade, 2001. Address: c/o ICM, Oxford House, 76 Oxford Street, London, W1D 1BS, England.

**DANDY Gillian Margaret (Gill),** b. 17 August 1957, Ely, Cambridgeshire, England. Public Relations Consultant. Education: Birmingham College of Food and Domestic Arts, 1976-79. Appointments: Harrison Cowley Public Relations Ltd, Birmingham, 1980-83; Associate Director, Leslie Bishop Company, 1983-90; Director, Shandwick Communications, 1990-96; Director of Development and PR, London Bible College, 1990-2002; Communications Director, Evangelical Alliance, 2002-04; Non-Executive Director, Shared Interest Society Limited, 2004-. Memberships: Chartered Institute of Public Relations; Fellow, Royal Society for the Encouragement of the Arts. Address: 56 Southerton Road, Hammersmith, London, W6 0PH, England. E-mail: gill.dandy@btinternet.com

**DANESI Yusuf Ally,** b. 17 August 1963, Lagos, Nigeria. Advertising Regulator. m. Olufunke Matanmi, 1 son, 2 daughters. Education: BSc, Political Science, University of Ibadan, 1986; MSc, International Relations, University of Lagos, 1988; Diploma, Advertising, 1998. Appointments: Programmes Officer, Radio Nigeria 2, Lagos, 1986-87; Publishing Manager, Friends Foundation Publishers, Lagos, 1989; General Manager, Africa Sings Ltd (Ad Recording Studio) Lagos, 1991; Registration Officer, 1991-94, Assistant Chief Registration Officer/Inspectorate Officer, 1994-99, Chief Registration/Inspectorate Officer, 1999-2004, Acting Director/Head Research, Planning and Statistics, 2004-, Advertising Practitioners Council of Nigeria. Publications: Over 35 articles in professional journals and newspapers include most recently: Tsunamis, Advertising and Our Future, 2005; Advertising Obesity to Children, 2005; Advertising Disrupted! 2005; Discontinuity in Advertising Media, 2005; Research and Statistics as Vital Tools for Nigeria's Advertising Industry; Organic "Tie-Ins": Advertisers' Bouquet of Opportunities, 2005; Valuation of Advertainment: The Marketers' Dilemma, 2005; The Interactive Challenge and Nigeria's Advertising Industry, 2005. Honours: Best Overall Graduating Student (Arts), 1983, Late Sir Samuel Manuwa Prize for the Best A/L Economics Student, 1983, Allison Ayida Prize for the Best A/L Economics Student, 1983, King's College, Lagos; Ten Years of Meritorious Service 1991-2001, Advertising Practitioners Council of Nigeria. Memberships: Registered Practitioner in Advertising; Nigerian Institute of International Affairs; President "The Friends", A Socio-Philanthropic Organisation.

Address: Advertising Practitioners Council of Nigeria, National Theatre Annexe, Iganmu PO Box 50648, Ikoyi, Lagos, Nigeria. E-mail: y_danesi@yahoo.co.uk

**DANIEL Milan,** b. 14 June 1931, Horazdovice, Czech Republic. Scientific Worker in Parasitology. m. Vlasta Pacakova, 1 son, 1 daughter. Education: RNDr, Charles University, Prague, 1956; PhD, 1959; DSc, 1987. Appointments: Assistant Professor, Charles University, Prague, 1954-55; Scientific Worker, Czech Academy of Sciences, Prague, 1956-86, Postgraduate Medical School, Prague, 1987-; Consultant, National Institute of Public Health, Prague, 2000-. Publications: Over 240 articles in scientific journals and 14 books including titles: Biomathematic Study on the Nest Environment of Susliks Citellus citellus, 1983; Small Mammals in Eastern Part of Nepal Himalaya, 1985; Mesostigmatid Mites in Nests of Small Terrestrial Mammals and Features of their Environment, 1988; Medical Entomology and Environment, 1989; Life and Death at the Summits of World; Secret Paths of Disease Vectors. Honours: Award, Czech Academy of Sciences, 1985; Award, Czech Literary Foundation, 1990. Memberships: Czech Society of Parasitology; New York Academy of Sciences. Address: Tomanova 64, CZ-169 00 Prague 6, Czech Republic.

**DANIEL Reginald,** b. 7 December 1939, London, England. Ophthalmic Surgeon. m. Carol Bjorck, 1 son, 1 daughter. Education: University of London, 1959-64; Westminster Hospital Medical School, 1961-64; MB BS, 1964; LRCP, 1964; FRCS, 1970; DO Eng, 1968; AKC, 1960; FRCOphth, 1988. Appointments: Chief Clinical Assistant, Moorfields Eye Hospital; Senior Registrar, Moorfields Eye Hospital; Teacher to University of London; Consultant Ophthalmic Surgeon, Guy's and St Thomas' Hospitals; Consultant Ophthalmic Surgeon, Private Practice, Harley Street, London. Publications: Author of many papers on retinal detachments, cataracts, corneal pathology and squints; Author of ophthalmic chapters in general surgical and medical reference books. Honour: Freeman of the City of London. Memberships: American Academy of Ophthalmology; Ophthalmic Society, UK; European Intraocular Implant Society; Contemporary Society of Ophthalmology in the USA; Moorfields Hospital Surgeons Society; Liveryman, Worshipful Company of Spectacle Makers; City of London Livery Club. Address: 152 Harley Street, London, W1G 7LH, England. E-mail: regandcarol@aol.com

**DANIELS Jeff,** b. 19 February 1955, Athens, Georgia, USA. Actor. Education: Central Michigan University. Appointments: Apprentice Circle Repertory Theatre, New York; Founder, Purple Rose Theatre Company, Chelsea, Michigan; Theatre: The Farm, 1976; Brontosaurus, 1977; My Life, 1977; Feedlot, 1977; Lulu, 1978; Slugger, 1978; The Fifth of July, 1978; Johnny Got His Gun (Obie Award), 1982; The Three Sisters, 1982-83; The Golden Age, 1984; Redwood Curtain, 1993; Short-Changed Review, 1993; Lemon Sky; Films: Ragtime, 1981; Terms of Endearment, 1983; The Purple Rose of Cairo, 1985; Marie, 1985; Heartburn, 1986; Something Wild, 1986; Radio Days, 1987; The House on Carroll Street, 1988; Sweet Hearts Dance, 1988; Grand Tour, 1989; Checking Out, 1989; Arachnophobia, 1990; Welcome Home, Roxy Carmichael, 1990; Love Hurts, 1990; The Butcher's Wife, 1992; Gettysburg, 1993; Speed, 1994; Dumb and Dumber, 1994; Fly Away Home, 1996; Two Days in the Valley, 1996; 101 Dalmatians, 1996; Trial and Error, 1997; Pleasantville, 1998; All the Rage, 1999; My Favourite Martian, 1999; Chasing Sleep, 2000; Escanaba in da Moonlight, 2000; Super Sucker, 2002; Blood Work, 2002; The Hours, 2002; Gods and Generals, 2002; I Witness, 2003; Imaginary Heroes, 2004; The Squid and the Whale, 2005; Because of Winn-Dixie, 2005; TV films: A Rumor of War, 1980; Invasion of Privacy,

1983; The Caine Mutiny Court Martial, 1988; No Place Like Home, 1989; Disaster in Time, 1992; Redwood Curtain, 1995; Teamster Boss: The Jackie Presser Story; (specials) Fifth of July; The Visit (Trying Times). Publications: Author, Plays: Shoeman, 1991; The Tropical Pickle, 1992; The Vast Difference, 1993; Thy Kingdom's Coming, 1994; Escanaba in da Moonlight, 1995; The Goodbye Girl, 2004; The Five People You Meet in Heaven, 2004.

**DANILOV Gennady Stepanovich,** b. 26 March 1935, St Petersburg, Russia. Physicist. m. Kotova Lidya Michajlovna, 1 son, 1 daughter. Education: PhD, 1964, DSc, 1976, Institute of Theoretical and Experimental Physics, Moscow. Appointments: Researcher, 1959-66, Senior Researcher, 1966-71, Physics Technical Institute, St Petersburg; Senior Researcher, 1971-86, Leading Researcher, 1986-, Head of Group, St Petersburg Nuclear Physics Institute. Publications: Several articles for professional journals. Address: St Petersburg Nuclear Physics Institute, 188350 Gatchina, Leningrad district, Russia. E-mail: danilov@thd.pnpi.spb.ru

**DANN Colin Michael,** b. 10 March 1943, Richmond, Surrey, England. Author. m. Janet Elizabeth Stratton, 4 June 1977. Publications: The Animals of Farthing Wood, 1979; In the Grip of Winter, 1981; Fox's Feud, 1982; The Fox Cub Bold, 1983; The Siege of White Deer Park, 1985; The Ram of Sweetriver, 1986; King of the Vagabonds, 1987; The Beach Dogs, 1988; The Flight from Farthing Wood, 1988; Just Nuffin, 1989; In the Path of the Storm, 1989; A Great Escape, 1990; A Legacy of Ghosts, 1991; The City Cats, 1991; Battle for the Park, 1992; The Adventure Begins, 1994; Copycat, 1997; Nobody's Dog, 1999; Journey to Freedom, 1999; Lion Country, 2000; Pride of The Plains 2002. Honour: Arts Council National Award for Children's Literature, 1980. Membership: Society of Authors. Address: Castle Oast, Ewhurst Green, East Sussex, England.

**DANSON Ted,** b. 29 December 1947, San Diego, California, USA. Actor. m. (1) Randell L Gosch, divorced, (2) Cassandra Coates, 1977, divorced, 2 daughters, (3) Mary Steenburgen, 1995. Education: Stanford University; Carnegie-Mellon University. Appointments: Teacher, The Actor's Institute, Los Angeles, 1978; Star, NBC-TV series Cheers, 1982-93; CEO Anasazi Productions (Formerly Danson/Fauci Productions); Off-Broadway plays include: The Real Inspector Hound, 1972; Comedy of Errors; Actor, producer TV films including: When the Bough Breaks, 1986; We Are The Children, 1987; Executive Producer TV films: Walk Me to the Distance, 1989; Down Home, 1989; Mercy Mission: The Rescue of Flight 771, 1993; On Promised Land, 1994; Other appearances in TV drama; Films include: The Onion Field, 1979; Body Heat, 1981; Creepshow, 1983; A Little Treasure, 1985; A Fine Mess, 1986; Just Between Friends, 1986; Three Men and a Little Lady, 1990; Made in America, 1992; Getting Even With Dad, 1993; Pontiac Moon, 1993; Gulliver's Travels (TV), 1995; Loch Ness, 1996; Homegrown, 1998; Thanks of a Grateful Nation, 1998; Saving Private Ryan, 1998; Becker, 1998; Mumford, 1999. Address: c/o Josh Liberman, Creative Artists Agency, 9830 Wilshire Boulevard, Beverly Hills, CA 90212, USA.

**DANTZIG George Bernard,** b. 8 November 1914, Portland, Oregon, USA. Mathematician; Expert in Linear Programming and Operations Research. m. Anne Shmuner, 1936, 2 sons, 1 daughter. Education: BA, University of Maryland, 1936; Horace Rackham Scholar, MA, University of Michigan. Appointments: Statistical Control Headquarters, US Air Force, Chief of Combat Analysis Branch, Mathematical Adviser, 1946-52; Research Mathematician, Rand Corporation, Santa Monica, California, 1952-60; Professor, Chairman of Operations

Research Centre, 1960-66; C A Criley Professor of Operations Research and Computer Science, 1966-97, Emeritus Professor, 1997-, Stanford University, Palo Alto, California; Head of Methodology Project, International Institute for Applied Systems Analysis, 1973-74. Publications: Linear Programming and Extensions, 1963; Compact City, with Thomas L Saaty, 1973; Over 150 technical papers. Honours include: National Medal of Science, 1975; National Academy of Sciences Award in Applied Mathematics and Numerical Analysis, 1977; Harvey Prize, 1985; Silver Medal Operational Research Society, 1986; COORS American Ingenuity Award, 1989; Pender Award, University of Pennsylvania, 1995. Memberships: NAS; National Academy of Engineering; Fellow, American Academy of Arts and Sciences; Honorary member, Institute of Electrical and Electronics Engineers. Address: 821 Tolman Drive, Stanford, CA 94305, USA.

**DANYLAK Joan Kikel**, b. 3 February 1943, Brooklyn, New York, USA. Poet; Author. Education: BA, magna cum laude, English and German, University of Arizona, 1969. Appointments: Secretary, General Electric Corporation, early 1960's; Secretary to the Manager of Public Relations Department, Allied Chemical Corporation; Secretary to the President, World Institute Inc., 1965-66; Bookkeeper, JO-R Pile Lead & Boom Corporation, 1970's; Poet; Publisher; Editor. Publications: Over 15 books include: Honoring Poets and Professional and Creative People; Latin American Culture; Bonjour Dr Sukon Kim; Ya'Sou, A Celebration of Life. Honours: Elected to 3 Honor Societies in College: Psi Chi, Phi Kappa Phi, Delta Phi Alpha; Grant, American Poetry Association; President's Award, National Authors Registry, 1996; Medallion and Trophy, Famous Poets Society; Poet of the Year, 2002; Western Archipelago Review Award; Listed in Great Minds of the 21st Century, ABI. Memberships: New Mirage Academy; Mensa. Address: 111-20, 73 Avenue, #7A Forest Hills, NY 11375, USA.

**DAS Sachi Nandan**, b. 1 August 1944, Cuttack, Orissa, India. Hospital Consultant. m. Subha, 1 son 1 daughter. Education: MBBS (Utkal), Orissa, 1968; DMRT (RCP (Lond), RCS (Eng)), 1971; FRCR (UK), 1977. Appointments: Senior House Officer, Radiotherapy, Plymouth General Hospital, England, 1969-70; Registrar and Senior Registrar, Mersey Regional Centre for Radiotherapy, Liverpool, England, 1970-77; Consultant, Honorary Senior Lecturer, Radiotherapy and Oncology, Ninewells Hospital and Medical School, Dundee, Scotland, 1977-. Publications: Articles in various professional journals. Honours: Long Service Award, NHS Tayside; Listed in national and international biographical dictionaries. Memberships: Fellow, Royal College of Radiologists; Member, British Medical Association; Scottish Radiological Society. Address: Department of Radiotherapy & Oncology, Ninewells Hospital, Dundee DD1 9SY, Scotland.

**DASZEK Jan**, b. 8 June 1956, Tarnow, Poland. Composer; Pianist; Poet. m. Sylvia Daszek, 2 daughters. Education: Attended 8 different schools and college; Self taught composition; Studied with accomplished musicians and composers: Career: Composer from the age of 12; Numerous concerts on piano and other instruments and appearances on radio, televison and at music festivals. Compositions: 100 works include symphonies, passions, music for string quartets, music for solo instruments, music for organs, chamber music, music for choirs, theatre music, jazz and songs including: Preludes for piano; Beati Pauperes Spiritus for mixed accappella choir; Veni Creator Spiritus for choir and orchestra; Gabriel the Archangel of God for choir and three trombones; Missa for mixed choir and oboe; Heavenly Voices for string quartet; Monte Carmelo for orchestra; The Panorama of a Summer Softness for string quartet; Das Debet (Bo Yin Ra) for soprano voice and orchestra; Cantabile for a tenor voice and an orchestra; The Hebrew Songs; Music for Saint Francis from Assisi for accordion; The Symphony of Life for a few instruments; Nativitas Domini, sonata for piano; A Quintet for wind instruments; Compositions for a flute and a string orchestra; De Divinis Nominibus for mixed accappella choir; The Christmas Symphony, instrumental; The Jahve Symphony for chamber band; The Biblical Symphony for piano; Symphony for a symphonic octet; General Score from the "Et Verbum Caro Fatum Est" series; A Short Composition for Alexander for double bass; Aumd for piano; Jazz for the Yamaha PSR 300; Missa for oboe and mixed choir; Ewangeliarz for tenor voice; Psalms for piano; Psalms for organ; Hymns for piano; A Variation for xylophone. Honours: Winner of 5 competitions as a composer; Several Music Awards. Memberships: Polish Composers' Union; ZAIKS; ISCM Polish Section. Address: Ul Nowa 42, 43-460 Wisla-Jawornik, Woj Slaskie, Poland.

**DATTA Dipankar**, b. 30 January 1933, India. Physician. m. Jean Bronwen, 1 son, 1 daughter. Education: MBBS, Calcutta University, 1958; MRCP (UK), 1970; FRCP, Royal College of Physicians and Surgeons of Glasgow, 1980; FRCP, Royal College of Physicians of London, 1996. Appointments: Consultant Physician with special interest in Gastroenterology, 1975-97; Honorary Senior Clinical Lecturer in Medicine, 1984-97, Honorary Clinical Sub-Dean, Faculty of Medicine, 1989-97, Member of the Faculty of Medicine, 1989-95, Member of the Senate, 1991-94, Glasgow University; Member of the Lanarkshire Health Board, 1983-87; President, BMA, Lanarkshire, 1993-95; Chairman, Overseas Doctor's Association, Scotland, 1989-95; Member, General Medical Council, UK, 1994-99; Chairman, South Asia Voluntary Enterprise, 1994-; Director, British Overseas NGO's for Development, 1993. Memberships: Royal College of Physicians and Surgeons of Glasgow; Royal College of Physicians of London. Address: 9 Kirkvale Crescent, Newton Mearns, Glasgow G77 5HB, Scotland.

**DAUDEL Raymond**, b. 2 February 1920, Paris, France. University Professor. m. Salzedo Pascaline, 2 sons. Education: DSc, 1944. Appointments: Assistant of Pr Irene Joliot Curie (Nobel Laureate), 1943; Maitre Assistant of Pr Frederic Joliot (Nobel Laureate), 1956; Associate Professor of Pr Louis de Broglie (Nobel Laureate), 1957; Full Professor, University of Paris, 1962. Publications: 350 articles in international journals; 25 books including: Le Sida (AIDS) (co-author), translated into Italian, Spanish and Portuguese, 1994; La Science et La Métamorphose des Arts (co-author), 1994. Honours: Doctor, honoris causa, universities of Uppsala, Louvain, Barcelona, Iasy. Memberships: 5 national academies and 4 international academies; President, European Academy of Arts, Sciences and Humanities. Address: 60 Rue Monsieur Le Prince, 75006 Paris, France.

**DAUNTON Martin James**, b. 7 February 1949, Cardiff, Wales. University Professor of History. m. Claire Gobbi, 7 January 1984. Education: BA, University of Nottingham, 1970; PhD, University of Kent, 1974; Litt D, Cambridge, 2005. Appointments: Lecturer, University of Durham, 1973-79; Lecturer, 1979-85, Reader, 1985-89, Professor of History, 1989-97, University College London; Convenor, Studies in History series, Royal Historical Society, 1995-2000; Professor Economic History, University of Cambridge, 1997-; Master, Trinity Hall, Cambridge, 2004-; President, Royal Historical Society, 2004-. Publications: Coal Metropolis: Cardiff; House and Home in the Victorian City, 1850-1914; Royal Mail: The Post Office since 1840; A Property Owning Democracy?; Progress and Poverty; Trusting Leviathan; Just Taxes. Contributions to: Economic

History Review; Past & Present; Business History; Historical Research; Charity, Self-Interest and Welfare in the English Past; English Historical Review; Twentieth Century British History; Empire and Others; Politics of Consumption; Organisation of Knowledge. Honour: Fellow of the British Academy, 1997. Membership: Royal Historical Society. Address: Trinity Hall, Cambridge, CB2 1TJ, England.

**DAVE Ramesh Chhabilal,** b. 3 April 1942. Educator. m. Rekha, 18 August 1976, 1 son. Education: Kovid, 1960; STC, 1963; MEd, 1970; MA, 1972. Appointments: Teaching, 1958-; Headmaster, GVSS High School, Kachchh, Gujarat State, 1971-. Publications: Alpana, poems, 1972; Gagan Padechhe Nannun, short stories, 1972; Anant Ane Urmina Parakramo, stories for children, 1994; Educational articles: Dipdiksha 1, 1994; Dipdiksha 2, 1995; 2 prayer cassettes, Vandu Devi Sarswati. Honours: Best Teacher Award, Gujarat State, 1981; Best Teacher National Award, 1987; National Award, National Council for Child Education, 1988; Best Principal, Gujarat Madhyastha Parishad, 1992. Memberships: Member, Educational Committee, Gujarat Secondary Education Board, 1996; Gujarat State Text Book Committee, 1997; Adult Education; All-India Radio Broadcasting; Inspection Panel, Gujarat State. Address: GVSS High School, Gadhaisa 370 445, Gujarat State, India.

**DAVID Joanna Elizabeth,** b. 17 January 1947, Lancaster, England. Actress. m. Edward Fox, 1 son, 1 daughter. Education: Elmhurst Ballet School; Royal Academy of Dance; Webber Douglas Academy of Dramatic Art. Career: Theatre includes: The Family Reunion, The Royal Exchange, 1973; Uncle Vanya, Royal Exchange Manchester, 1977; The Cherry Orchard, 1983 and Breaking the Code, 1986, Theatre Royal Haymarket; Stages, Royal National Theatre, 1992; The Deep Blue Sea, Royal Theatre Northampton, 1997; Ghost Train Tattoo, Royal Exchange Theatre, 2000; Copenhagen, Salisbury Playhouse, 2003; The Importance of Being Earnest, Royal Exchange Theatre, 2004; Television includes: War and Peace; Sense and Sensibility, Last of the Mohicans, Duchess of Duke Street, Rebecca, Carrington and Strachey; Fame is the Spur, First Among Equals; Paying Guests; Unexplained Laughter; Hannay; Children of the North; Secret Friends; Inspector Morse; Maigret; Rumpole of the Bailey; Darling Buds of May; The Good Guys; Sherlock Holmes; The Cardboard Box; Pride and Prejudice; A Touch of Frost; Bramwell; A Dance to the Music of Time; Midsummer Murders; Written in Blood; Dalziel and Pascoe; Blind Date; Heartbeat; The Mill on the Floss; The Dark Room; The Glass; The Way We Live Now; The Forsyte Saga; He Knew He Was Right; Brides in the Bath; Foyles War; Heartbeat; Monarch of the Glen; Falling; Bleak House; Films: In the Name of Pharaoh, 1998; Cotton Mary, 1999; Rogue Trader; The Soul Keeper; Secret Friends; The Tulse Luper Suitcase. Memberships: Trustee, Ralph and Meriel Richardson Foundation; Committee Member, The Theatrical Guild; Council Member, King George V Pension Fund; Board Member, Unicorn Children's Centre. Address: 25 Maida Avenue, London W2 1ST, England.

**DAVID, Baroness of Romsey in the City of Cambridge, Nora Ratcliff David,** b. 23 September 1913, Ashby-de-la-Zouch, Leicestershire. Member of House of Lords. m. Richard William David, 1935, deceased, 2 sons, 2 daughters. Education: MA, Newnham College Cambridge. Appointments: JP, Cambridge City, 1965-; Former Cambridge City Councillor; Cambridge County Councillor, 1974-78; Sits as Labour Peer in the House of Lords, 1978-; Opposition Whip, 1979-83, Deputy Chief Opposition Whip, 1983-87; Opposition Spokesman for Environment and Local Government in Lords, 1986-88; Opposition Spokesman for Education, 1979-83 and 1986-97;

Member of the Board, Peterborough Development Corporation, 1976-78; EC Select Committee, 1991-94; EC Agriculture Committee, 1993-98. Honours: Baroness-in-Waiting to HM The Queen, 1978-79; Honorary Fellow: Newnham College, Cambridge, 1986, Anglia Higher Education College, 1989; Honorary DLitt, Staffordshire University, 1994. Memberships: CPRE; Save The Children; Howard League; All party Children's Group; All party Penal Group; All party Environment Group. Address: The House of Lords, London SW1, England. E-mail: davidn@parliament.uk

**DAVIDSON Donald (Herbert),** b. 6 March 1917, Springfield, Massachusetts, USA. Philosopher; Professor; Writer. m. (1) 1 daughter, (2) Nancy Hirshberg, 4 April 1975, deceased 1979, (3) Marcia Cavell, 3 July 1984. Education: BA, 1939, MA, 1941, PhD, 1949, Harvard University. Appointments: Instructor, Queen's College, New York City, 1947-50; Assistant Professor to Professor, Stanford University, 1951-67; Visiting Professor, University of Tokyo, 1955; Professor, 1967-70, Chairman, Department of Philosophy, 1968-70, Lecturer with rank of Professor, 1970-76, Princeton University; Gavin David Young Lecturer, University of Adelaide, 1968; John Locke Lecturer, Oxford University, 1970; Professor, Rockefeller University, New York City, 1970-76, University of Chicago, 1976-81; Willis S and Marion Slusser Professor University of California at Berkeley, 1981-; John Dewey Lecturer, University of Michigan, 1973; George Eastman Visiting Professor, Balliol College, Oxford, 1984-85; Fulbright Distinguished Lecturer, India, 1985-86; S J Keeling Memorial Lecturer in Greek Philosophy, University College, London, 1986; Thalheimer Lecturer, Johns Hopkins University, 1987; John Dewey Lecturer, Columbia University, 1989; Alfred North Whitehead Lecturer, Harvard University, 1990; Kant Lecturer, University of Munich, 1993; Various other lectureships. Publications: Decision Making: An Experimental Approach (with Patrick Suppes), 1957; Words and Objections (editor with J Hintikka), 1969; Semantics for Natural Language (editor with Gilbert Harman), 1970; The Logic of Grammar (co-editor), 1975; Essays on Actions and Events, 1980; Inquiries into Truth and Interpretation, 1983; Plato's Philebus, 1990; Structure and Content of Truth, 1990; Subjective, Intersubjective, Objective, 2001; numerous essays and articles in philosophical journals. Honours: Teschemacher Fellow in Classics and Philosophy, 1939-41; Rockefeller Fellowship in the Humanities, 1945-46; American Council of Learned Societies Fellowship, 1958-59; National Science Foundation Research Grants, 1964-65, 1968; Fellow, Center for Advanced Study in the Behavioral Sciences, 1969-70; Guggenheim Fellowship, 1973-74; Fellow, All Souls College, Oxford, 1973-74; Honorary Research Fellow, University College, London, 1978; Sherman Fairchild Distinguished Scholar, California Institute of Technology, 1989; Hegel Prize, City Stuttgart, 1991; DDL Honoris causa, Oxford University, 1995; Doctorate of Philosophy, honoris causa, Stockholm University, 1999. Memberships: American Academy of Arts and Sciences; American Association of University Professors; American Philosophical Association; American Philosophical Society; British Academy, corresponding member; Norwegian Academy of Science and Letters, 1987. Address: c/o Department of Philosophy, University of California at Berkeley, Berkeley, CA 94720-2390, USA.

**DAVIE Ronald,** b. 25 November 1929, Birmingham, England. Child Psychologist. m. Kathleen, 1 son, 1 daughter. Education: BA Psychology (Hons), University of Reading, 1954; PGCE, University of Manchester, 1955; Diploma in Educational Psychology, University of Birmingham, 1961; PhD, University of London, 1970. Appointments: Various teaching, psychology and research posts, 1955-67; Co-Director, National Child

Development Study & Deputy Director, National Children's Bureau, 1968-74, Director, NCB, 1982-90; Professor, Educational Psychology, University of Cardiff, 1974-81; Consulting and Forensic Psychologist, 1990-99; Member, SEN Tribunal, 1994-2003; Visiting Professor, University of Gloucestershire, 1997-. Publications include; Living With Handicap, 1970; From Birth to Seven, 1972; Children Appearing Before Juvenile Courts, 1977; The Home and The School, 1979; Street Violence and Schools, 1981; Children and Adversity, 1982; Understanding Behaviour Problems, 1986; Child Sexual Abuse, 1989; Childhood Disability and Parental Appeals, 2001; The Voice of the Child, 1996; Mobile Phone Usage in Pre-Adolescence, 2004. Honours: Hon DEd, CNAA, 1991; Hon Fellow, RCPCH, 1996; Hon DEd, University of West of England, 1998; Hon DLitt, University of Birmingham, 1999. Memberships: Fellow, British Psychological Society; Former President, National Association for SEN; Former Chairman, Association for Child Psychology and Psychiatry; Vice President, Young Minds. Address: Bridge House, Upton, Caldbeck, Wigton, Cumbria, CA7 8EU, England.

**DAVIES (Hilary) Sarah (Ellis),** b. 11 January 1962, Newcastle upon Tyne, England. Corporate Branding Consultant. m. Jeremy Fawcett Bourke, 1 son, 1 daughter. Education: Foundation, Wimbledon School of Art, 1980-81; Kingston Polytechnic, 1981-82. Appointments: Runner, 1982-84, TV Commercials Producer, 1984-85, Director, 1988; Head of Television, 1985-97, Managing Director and Shareholder, 1993-97, Lambie-Nairn Ltd; Commercial Director and Shareholder, The Brand Union Ltd incorporating Lambie-Nairn, Tutssels and The Clinic, 1997-99; The Brand Union sold to WPP Ltd, 1999; Corporate Branding Consultant, clients including: 3i, Pearson Television, Thames Television, 1999-2002; Consultant on Marketing, Sales and Client Services, BBC Broadcast Ltd, 2002-. Publication: Building the Brand – Spectrum Magazine, 1995. Honours: Gold Lion, Cannes Advertising Festival, 1985; D&AD Silver, Most Outstanding Animation, 1985, 1986; Creative Circle Silver – Best Use of Videotape, 1986, 1987, Best Use of Computer Graphics, 1986; D&AD Silver – Most Outstanding Television Graphics, 1987; Lambie-Nairn awarded Queen's Award for Export, 1995. Memberships: Royal Television Society; Chelsea Arts Club; David Lloyd; Trustee, Media Trust, 1994-, Director of the trust's television channel, The Community Channel; Trustee, TimeBank, 2000-. Address: 98 Bennerley Road, London SW11 6DU, England. E-mail: sarah@sarahdavies.demon.co.uk.

**DAVIES Alan Roger,** b. 6 March 1966, Chingford, Essex, England. Actor; Comedian; Writer. Education: BA (Hons), Drama, University of Kent, 1984-88. Career: Television: Jonathan Creek, BBC, 1996-; A Many Splintered Thing, BBC, 1998-2000; Bob and Rose, ITV, 2001; QI, BBC, 2003-; The Brief, ITV, 2004-; Radio: Alan's Big One, Radio 1, 1994-95; The Alan Davies Show, Radio 4, 1998. Publications: Regular contributor to The Times Sports Section; Urban Trauma, DVD/Audio Cassette; Live at the Lyric, DVD/Audio Cassette. Honours: Critics Award for Comedy, Edinburgh Festival, 1994; BAFTA Award for Best Drama for Jonathan Creek, 1997; Best Actor for Bob and Rose, Monte Carlo TV Festival, 2002; DLitt, University of Kent, 2003. Membership: Arsenal Season Ticket Holder. Address: c/o ARG, 4 Great Portland Street, London W1W 8PA, England.

**DAVIES James Atterbury,** b. 25 February 1939, Llandeilo, Dyfed, Wales. Former Senior Lecturer; Writer. m. Jennifer Hicks, 1 January 1966, 1 son, 1 daughter. Education: BA, 1965; PhD, 1969. Appointments: Visiting Professor, Baylor University, Texas, 1981; Senior Lecturer, University College of Swansea, 1990-; Mellon Research Fellow, University of

Texas, 1993; Senior Lecturer, UWS, 1990-98; Part-time Senior Lecturer, UWS, 1998-2001. Publications: John Forster: A Literary Life, 1983; Dylan Thomas's Places, 1987; The Textual Life of Dickens's Characters, 1989; Dannie Abse, The View from Row B: Three Plays (editor), 1990; Leslie Norris, 1991; The Heart of Wales (editor), 1995; A Swansea Anthology (editor), 1996; A Reference Companion to Dylan Thomas, 1998; Dylan Thomas's Swansea, 2000. Honours: Fellow, Welsh Academy, 1999. Address: 93, Rhyd-y-Defaid Drive, Sketty, Swansea SA2 8AW, Wales

**DAVIES Jonathan,** b. 24 October 1962. Rugby Player. m. (1) Karen Marie, 1984, deceased 1997, 2 sons, 1 daughter, (2) Helen Jones, 2002. Appointments: Rugby Union outside-half; Played for following rugby clubs: Trimsaran, Neath, Llanelli; Turned professional, 1989; with Cardiff, 1995-97; Played for Welsh national team (v England), 1985; World cup Squad (6 appearances), 1987; Triple Crown winning team, 1988; Tour New Zealand (2 test appearances), 1988; 29 caps, sometimes Captain; Also played for Barbarians Rugby Football Club; Rugby League career; Played at three-quarters; Widnes (world record transfer fee), 1989; Warrington (free transfer), 1993-95; Reverted to rugby union, 1995; Welsh national team; British national team; Tour New Zealand, 1990; 6 caps, former Captain. Publication: Jonathan, 1989. Address: C/o Cardiff Rugby Football Club, Cardiff Arms Park, Westgate Street, Cardiff, Wales.

**DAVIES Josie Ennis,** b. 8 December 1928, Coventry, Warwickshire, England. Retired School Teacher and College Lecturer; Poet. m. Harold Henry Davies, 26 December 1967. Education: Teaching Diploma, 1952, 1964. Appointments: Tax Officer, Inland Revenue, 1946-50; School Teacher, 1952-62; Lecturer, Coventry Technical College, 1962-72. Publications: Waiting for Hollyhocks; Shadows on the Lawn; The Tuning Tree; Marmalade and Mayhem; Miscellany; Understanding Stone, 1994; A Press of Nails, 1996; Grief Like A Tiger, 1996; Journey to Ride, 1997; Daisies in December, 1999; Alphabet Avenue and Other Tales, 2002; Going Places, 2002; Tunes from the Shopping Trolley, 2003; A Song in My Pocket, 2003; Walking Between Leaves, 2004; Poets on My Mind, 2005. Contributions to: Folio International; Pennine Platform; Iota; Periaktos; Poetry Nottingham; Spokes; Success; The Countryman; Weyfarers; The Writers Voice; The Lady; Vigil; Haiku Quarterly; Period Piece and Paperback; Envoi; Poetry Digest. Membership: National Poetry Foundation. Address: 349 Holyhead Road, Coventry, Warwickshire CV5 8LD, England.

**DAVIES Laura,** b. 5 October 1963, Coventry, England. Golfer. Appointments: Turned professional, 1985; Won Belgian Open, 1985; British Women's Open, 1986; US Women's Open, 1987; AGF Biarritz Open, 1990; Wilkinson Sword English Open, 1995; Irish Open, 1994, 1995; French Masters, 1995; LPGA Championship, 1996; Danish Open, 1997; Chrysler Open, 1998, 1999; WPGA Championship, 1999; Compaq Open, 1999; TSN Ladies World Cup of Golf (Individual), 2000; WPGA International Matchplay, 2001; Norwegian Masters, 2002; Represented, England, World Team Championship, Taiwan, 1992; Europe in Solheim Cup, 1990, 1992, 1994. Publication: Carefree Golf, 1991. Honours: Rookie of the Year, 1985; Order of Merit Winner, 1985, 1986, 1992; Rolex Player of the Year, 1996. Address: c/o Women's Professional Golf European Tour, The Tytherington Club, Dorchester Way, Tytherington, Macclesfield, SK10 2JP, England.

**DAVIES Richard John,** b. 12 August 1949, Swansea, Wales. Government Official. m. Margaret Mary, 1 son, 1 daughter. Education: BA (Hons), 1971, MA, 1976, University of

Liverpool. Appointments: Teaching Assistant, Department of Political Theory and Institutions, University of Liverpool, 1972-73; Entered Civil Service, 1973; Served MOD, FCO, MPO, 1973-84; Assistant Secretary Welsh Office, 1985; Head of Division, Welsh Office: Health Management, Systems and Personnel, 1985-87, Health and Social Services Policy, 1987-89, Housing, 1989-94, School Performance, 1994; Nuffield-Leverhulme Fellow, 1990; Director, Department for Training and Education, National Assembly for Wales, 1997-. Memberships: Fellow Royal Society of Arts; Member Chartered Management Institute. Address: Department for Training and Education, National Assembly for Wales, Cathays Park, Cardiff CF10 3NQ, Wales. E-mail: richard.john.davies@wales.gsi.gov.uk

**DAVIES Ryland,** b. 9 February 1943, Cwym, Ebbw Vale, Wales. Opera and Concert Singer (Tenor). m. (1) Anne Howells (divorced 1981); (2) Deborah Rees, 1983, 1 daughter. Education: FRMCM, Royal Manchester College of Music, 1971. Debut: Almaviva, Barber of Seville, Welsh National Opera, 1964. Career: Glyndebourne Chorus, 1964-66; Soloist and Freelance, Glyndebourne and Sadler's Wells, Royal Opera House, Covent Garden, Welsh National Opera, Scottish Opera, Opera North; Performances in Salzburg, San Francisco, Chicago, New York, Hollywood Bowl, Paris, Geneva, Brussels, Vienna, Lyon, Amsterdam, Mannheim, Rome, Israel, Buenos Aires, Stuttgart, Berlin, Hamburg, Nice, Nancy, Philadelphia; Sang Lysander in A Midsummer Night's Dream at Glyndebourne, 1989, Tichon in Katya Kabanova at the 1990 Festival; Other roles have included Mozart's Ferrando and Don Ottavio, Ernesto, Fenton, Nemorino, Pelléas, (Berlin 1984), Oberon, (Montpellier, 1987); Tamino, Lensky, Belmonte and Enéas in Esclarmonde; Sang Podestà in Mozart's Finta Giardiniera for Welsh National Opera, 1994; Arbace in Idomeneo at Garsington, 1996; Season 1998 with Mozart's Basilio at Chicago; Concert Appearances at home and abroad; Radio and TV Broadcasts; Appeared in films including: Capriccio, Entführung, A Midsummer Night's Dream; Trial by Jury, Don Pasquale. Recordings: include, Die Entführung; Les Troyens; Saul; Così fan tutte; Monteverdi Madrigals, Messiah, Idomeneo, Il Matrimonio Segreto, L'Oracolo (Leoni), Lucia di Lammermoor, Thérèse, Judas Maccabeus, Mozart Requiem, Credo Mass, Mozart Coronation Mass and Vêspres Solenelle. Honours: Boise and Mendelssohn Foundation Scholarship, 1964; Ricordi Prize, 1964; Imperial League of Opera Prize, 1964; John Christie Award, 1965. Address: 71 Fairmile Lane, Cobham, Surrey KT11 2WG, England.

**DAVIS Andrew (Frank) (Sir),** b. 2 February 1944, Ashridge, Hertfordshire, England. Conductor. m. Gianna, 1 son. Education: DMusB (Organ Scholar), King's College, Cambridge; MA (Cantab), 1967; With Franco Ferrara, Rome, 1967-68; DLitt (Hons), York University, Toronto, 1984. Debut: BBC Symphony Orchestra, 1970. Career: Pianist, Harpsichordist, Organist, St Martin-in-the-Fields Academy, London, 1966-70; Assistant Conductor, BBC Scottish Symphony Orchestra, Glasgow, 1970-72; Appearances, major orchestras and festivals internationally including Berlin, Edinburgh, Flanders; Conductor, Glyndebourne Opera Festival, 1973-; Music Director, 1975-88, Conductor Laureate, 1988-; Toronto Symphony; Conductor, China, USA, Japan and Europe tours, 1983, 1986; Principal Guest Conductor, Royal Liverpool Philharmonic Orchestra, 1974-77; Associate Conductor, New Philharmonic Orchestra, London, 1973-77; Conducted: La Scala Milan, Metropolitan Opera, Covent Garden, Paris Opera; Music Director, Glyndebourne, 1988-; Chief Conductor, 1989-2000, Conductor Laureate, 2000-, BBC Symphony Orchestra; Musical Director, Chicago Lyric Opera, 2000-; Conducted La Clemenza di Tito, Chicago, Oct 1989; Szymanowski King Roger, Festival Hall, London, 1990; Katya Kabanova and Tippett's New Year, (1990) Glyndebourne

Festival; Opened 1991 Promenade Concerts, London, with Dream of Gerontius; Glyndebourne, 1992, Gala and The Queen of Spades; Conducted Elektra, at First Night, 1993 London Proms; Berg's Lulu, Festival Hall, 1994, returned 1997, for Stravinsky's Oedipus Rex, Persephone and The Rakes's Progress; Hansel and Gretel, 1996-97, and Capriccio, 1997-98, for the Met; Philadelphia, Chicago and Boston Orchestras, New York Philharmonic, and other leading American and European orchestras; Contracted to become Music Director and Principal Conductor of the Chicago Lyric Opera, 2000; Season 1999 with a new production of Pelléas et Mélisande at Glyndebourne and Tippett's The Mask of Time at the London Prom concerts. Compositions: La Serenissima (Inventions on a Theme by Claudio Monteverdi); Chansons Innocentes. Recordings include: All Dvorák Symphonies, Mendelssohn Symphonies, Borodin Cycle; Enigma Variations, Falstaff, Elgar; Overtures: Coriolan, Leonore No 3, Egmont, Fidelio Beethoven; Symphony No 10, Shostakovich, and violin concertos; Canon and other digital delights, Pachelbel; Cinderella excerpts; The Young Person's Guide to the Orchestra; Concerto No 2, Rachmaninov; The Planets, Gustav Holst; Symphony No 5, Horn Concerto, Piano Concerto No 2, Hoddinott; Brahms piano concertos; Nielsen Symphonies nos 4 and 5; Currently working on The British Line series with the BBC SO including the Elgar Symphonies and Enigma Variations, Vaughan Williams, Delius, Britten and Tippett; Operatic releases including Glyndebourne productions of Katya Kabanova, Jenufa, Queen of Spades, Lulu and Le Comte Ory. Honours: 2 Grand Prix du Disque Awards, Duruflé's Requiem recording with Philharmonic Orchestra; Gramophone of Year Award, 1987, Grand Prix du Disque, 1988, Tippett's Mask of Time; Royal Philharmonic Society/Charles Heidsieck Award, 1991; CBE, 1992; Royal Phiharmonic Society Award, Best musical opera performance of 1994, Eugene Onegin, on behalf of Glyndebourne Festival Opera, 1995; Gramophone Award for Best Video for Lulu; 1998 Award for Best Contemporary recording of Birtwistle's Mask of Orpheus; Critics Choice Award for Elgar/Payne Symphony No 3; Knight Bachelor, New Years Honours List, 1999. Address: c/o Askonas Holt Ltd, Lonsdale Chambers, 27 Chancery Lane, London WC2A 1PF, England.

**DAVIS Bryn Derby,** b. 22 March 1938, Thurnscoe, Yorkshire, England. Professor of Nursing Education. m. Catherine, 3 sons, 1 daughter. Education: RMN, 1961; SRN, 1965; RNT, 1969; BSc (Hons), Psychology, 1973; PhD, Social Psychology, 1983. Appointments: Principal Tutor, Holloway Sanatorium, Virginia Water, Surrey, 1970-73; DHSS, Research Fellow, London School of Economics, 1973-76; Deputy Director, Nursing Research Unit, University of Edinburgh, 1976-84; Principal Lecturer, Head of Nursing Research, Brighton Polytechnic, 1984-89; Professor and Head of School of Nursing, University of Wales College of Medicine, Cardiff, 1989-99; Academic and Professional Nursing Consultant, 1999-; Editor, Journal of Psychiatric and Mental Health Nursing, 1998-2004. Publications: Research into Nursing Education (editor), 1983; Nurse Education: research and developments (editor), 1987; Caring for People in Pain, 2000; Various articles in nursing journals and many chapters in books by others on pain, culture, relationships and mental health. Memberships: Royal College of Nursing; Fellow Royal Astronomical Society. Address: 108 New Road, Brading, Sandown, Isle of Wight, PO36 0AB, England. E-mail: davisbryn3@aol.com

**DAVIS Carl,** b. 1936, New York, USA. Composer; Conductor. m. Jean Boht, 1971, 2 daughters. Education: Studied composition with Hugo Kauder and with Per Norgaard in Copenhagen. Career: Assistant Conductor, New York City Opera, 1958; Associate Conductor, London Philharmonic

Orchestra, 1987-88; Principal Conductor, Bournemouth Pops, 1984-87; Principal Guest Conductor, Munich Symphony Orchestra, 1990-; Artistic Director and Conductor, Royal Liverpool Philharmonic Orchestra, Summer Pops, 1993-; Musical theatre: Diversions, 1958; Twists, 1962; The Projector and Cranford; Pilgrim; The Wind in the Willows, 1985; Alice in Wonderland, 1987; The Vackees, 1987. Incidental music for theatre includes: Prospect Theatre Co; The National Theatre; RSC. Ballet: A Simple Man, 1987; Lipizzaner, 1988; Liaisons Amoureuses, 1988; Madly, Badly, Sadly, Gladly; David and Goliath; Dances of Love and Death; The Picture of Dorian Grey; A Christmas Carol, 1992; The Savoy Suite, 1993; Alice in Wonderland, 1995; Aladdin, 2000. Music for TV includes: The Snow Goose, 1971; The World at War, 1972; The Naked Civil Servant, 1975; Our Mutual Friend, 1978; Hollywood, 1980; Churchill: The Wilderness Years, 1981; Silas Marner, 1985; Hotel du Lac, 1986; The Accountant, 1989; The Secret Life of Ian Fleming, 1989; Separate But Equal, 1991; The Royal Collection, 1991; A Year in Provence, 1992; Fame in the 20th Century: Clive James, 1992; Ghengis Cohn, 1993; Thatcher: The Downing Street Years, 1993; Pride and Prejudice, 1995; Oliver's Travels, 1995; Eurocinema: The Other Hollywood, 1995; Cold War, 1998-99; Goodnight, Mr Tom, 1998; The Great Gatsby, 2000; The Queen's Nose; An Angel for May. Operas for TV: The Arrangement; Who Takes You to the Party?; Orpheus in the Underground; Peace. Film music: The Bofors Gun, 1969; The French Lieutenant's Woman, 1981; Champions, 1984; The Girl on a Swing, 1988; Rainbow, 1988; Scandal, 1988; Frankenstein Unbound, 1989; The Raft of the Medusa, 1991; The Trial, 1992; Voyage, 1993; Widow's Peak, 1994; Topsy Turvy, 2000; series of Thames Silents including Napoleon, 1980, 2000; The Wind; The Big Parade; Greed; The General; Ben Hur; Intolerance; Safety Last; The Four Horsemen of the Apocalypse, 1992; Wings, 1993; Waterloo, 1995; Phantom of the Opera, 1996. Concert works: Music for the Royal Wedding; Variations on a Bus Route; Overture on Australian Themes, Clarinet Concerto, 1984; Lines on London Symphony, 1984; Fantasy for Flute and Harpsichord, 1985; The Searle Suite for Wind Ensemble; Fanfare for Jerusalem, 1987; The Glenlivet Fireworks Music, 1988; Norwegian Brass Music, 1988; Variations for a Polish Beggar's Theme, 1988; Pigeons Progress, 1988; Jazz Age Fanfare, 1989; Everest, 1989; Landscapes, 1990; The Town Fox, 1990; A Duck's Diary, 1990; Paul McCartney's Liverpool Oratorio, 1991. Recordings: Christmas with Kiri, 1986; Beautiful Dreamer, 1986; The Silents, 1987; Ben Hur, 1989; A Simple Man, 1989; The Town Fox and Other Musical Tales, 1990; Leeds Castle Classics, Liverpool Pops at Home, 1995. Honours: Obie Prize Best Review, 1958; Emmy Award, 1972; BAFTA Awards, 1981, 1989; Chevalier des Arts et des Lettres, 1983; Honorary Fellowship, Liverpool University, 1992; Honorary DA, Bard, New York, 1994; Honorary DMus, Liverpool, 2002; Special Achievement Award for Music for Television and Film, 2003. Address: c/o Paul Wing, 16 Highland Road, Amersham, Buckinghamshire, HP7 9AW, England.

**DAVIS Colin (Rex) (Sir),** b. 25 September 1927, Weybridge, Surrey, England. Conductor. m. (1) April Cantelo, 1949, 1 son, 1 daughter, (2) Ashraf Naini, 1964, 3 sons, 2 daughters. Education: Royal College of Music. Career: Conductor Associate, Kalmar Orchestra and Chelsea Opera Group; Assistant Conductor, BBC Scottish Orchestra, 1957-59; Conductor, Sadler's Wells Opera House (ENO), 1959, Principal Conductor, 1960-65, Musical Director, 1961-65; Artistic Director, Bath Festival, 1969; Chief Conductor, BBC Symphony Orchestra, 1967-71, Chief Guest Conductor, 1971-75; Musical Director, Royal Opera House, Covent Garden, 1971-86; Guest Conductor, Metroplitan Opera, New York, 1969 (Peter Grimes), 1970, 1972; Principal Guest Conductor, Boston Symphony Orchestra, 1972-84; Principal

Guest Conductor, London Symphony Orchestra, 1975-95; Bayreuth Festival, first British conductor, 1977 (Tannhäuser); Vienna State Opera, debut, 1986; Music Director and Principal Conductor, Bavarian State Radio Orchestra, 1983-92; Honorary Conductor, Dresden Staatskapelle, 1990-; Principal Conductor, London Symphony Orchestra, 1995; Principal Guest Conductor, New York Philharmonic Orchestra, 1998-; Has worked regularly with many orchestras in Europe and America; Season 1999 with the Choral Symphony at the London Prom concerts and Benvenuto Cellini and Les Troyens at the Barbican Hall, both with the London Symphany Orchestra. Recordings: Extensive recording with Boston Symphony Orchestra, London Symphony Orchestra, Dresden Staatskapelle, Bavarian Radio Symphony Orchestra. Honours: Officier dans L'Ordre National de Legion d'Honneur, 1999; Maximiliansorden, Bavaria, 2000; Best Classical Album and Best Opera Recording (for Les Troyens), Grammy Awards, 2002; Honorary DMus, Keele, 2002, RAM, 2002. Address: c/o Alison Glaister, 39 Huntingdon Street, London N1 1BP, England.

**DAVIS Geena,** b. 21 January 1957, Wareham, Massachusetts, USA. Actress. m. (1) Richard Emmolo, 1981, divorced 1983, (2) Jeff Goldblum, divorced 1990, (3) Renny Harlin, 1993, divorced, (4) Reza Jarrahy, 2001, 1 daughter, 2 sons. Education: Boston University. Appointments: Member, Mt Washington Repertory Theatre Company; Worked as model; TV appearances incude: Buffalo Bill, 1983; Sara, 1985; The Hit List; Family Ties; Remington Steele; Secret Weapons, TV film; The Geena Davis Show, 2000. Films include: Tootsie, 1982; Fletch, 1984; Transylvania 6-5000, 1985; The Fly, 1986; The Accidental Tourist; Earth Girls Are Easy, 1989; Quick Change; The Grifters; Thelma and Louise; A League of Their Own; Hero; Angie; Speechless (also producer); Cutthroat Island; The Long Kiss Goodnight, 1996; Stuart Little, 1999; Stuart Little 2, 2002. Honours: Academy Award, Best Supporting Actress, 1989. Address: C/o ICM, 8942 Wilshire Boulevard, Beverly Hills, CA 90211, USA.

**DAVIS Steve,** b. 22 August 1957, Plumstead, London, England. Snooker Player. m. Judith Lyn Greig, 1990, 2 sons. Appointments: Professional snooker player, 1978; Has won 73 titles; In 99 tournament finals, as at 2002; Major titles include: UK Professional Champion, 1980, 1981, 1984, 1985, 1986, 1987; Masters Champion, 1981, 1982, 1988, 1997; International Champion, 1981, 1983, 1984; World Professional Champion, 1981, 1983, 1984, 1987, 1988, 1989; Winner, Asian Open, 1992, European Open, 1993, Welsh Open, 1994; Member, Board World Professional Billiards and Snooker Association, 1993-. Honours: BBC Sports Personality of Year, 1989; BBC TV Snooker Personality of Year, 1997. Publications: Steve Davis, World Champion, 1981; Frame and Fortune, 1982; Successful, 1982; How to Be Really Interesting, 1988; Steve Davis Plays Chess, 1996. Address: 10 Western Road, Romford, Essex, England.

**DAVISON Geoffrey Joseph,** b. 10 August 1927, Newcastle-upon-Tyne, England. Writer. m. Marlene Margaret Wilson, 15 September 1956, 2 sons. Education: TD; FRICS. Publications: The Spy Who Swapped Shoes, 1967; Nest of Spies, 1968; The Chessboard Spies, 1969; The Fallen Eagles, 1970; The Honorable Assassins, 1971; Spy Puppets, 1973; The Berlin Spy Trap, 1974; No Names on Their Graves, 1978; The Bloody Legionnaires, 1981; The Last Waltz (Vienna May 1945), 2001; The Dead Island, 2001; The Colombian Contract, 2001. Membership: Pen and Palette Club. Address: 95 Cheviot View, Ponteland, Newcastle-upon-Tyne NE20 9BH, England.

**DAWE (Donald) Bruce,** b. 15 February 1930, Fitzroy, Victoria, Australia. Associate Professor; Poet; Writer. m. (1) Gloria Desley Blain, 27 January 1964, deceased 30 December 1997, 2 sons, 2 daughters, (2) Ann Elizabeth Qualtiough, 9 October 1999. Education: BA, 1969, MLitt, 1973, MA, 1975, PhD, 1980, University of Queensland; Hon. DLitt (USQ), 1995; Hon.DLitt (UNSW), 1997. Appointments: Lecturer, 1971-78, Senior Lecturer, 1978-83, DDIAE; Writer-in-Residence, University of Queensland, 1984; Senior Lecturer, 1985-90, Associate Professor, 1990-93, School of Arts, Darling Heights, Toowoomba. Publications: No Fixed Address, 1962; A Need of Similar Name, 1964; Beyond the Subdivisions, 1968; An Eye for a Tooth, 1969; Heat-Wave, 1970; Condolences of the Season: Selected Poems, 1971; Just a Dugong at Twilight, 1974; Sometimes Gladness: Collected Poems, 1978, 5th edition, 1993; Over Here Harv! and Other Stories, 1983; Towards Sunrise, 1986; This Side of Silence, 1990; Bruce Dawe: Essays and Opinions, 1990; Mortal Instruments: Poems 1990-1995, 1995; A Poets' People, 1999; The Chewing-Gum Kid, 2002; No Cat – and That's That!, 2002; Show and Tell, 2003; Luke and Lulu, 2004. Contributions to: Various periodicals. Honours: Myer Poetry Prizes, 1966, 1969; Ampol Arts Award for Creative Literature, 1967; Dame Mary Gilmore Medal, Australian Literary Society, 1973; Braille Book of the Year, 1978; Grace Leven Prize for Poetry, 1978; Patrick White Literary Award, 1980; Christopher Brennan Award, 1984; Philip Hodgins Medal for Literary Excellence, 1997; Order of Australia, 1992; Distinguished Alumni Award, UNE, 1996; Australian Arts Council Emeritus Writers Award, 2000. Memberships: Australian Association for Teaching English, honorary life member; Centre for Australian Studies in Literature; Victorian Association for Teaching of English, honorary life member; Patron, Speech and Drama Teachers' Association of Queensland; Patron, PEN (Sydney). Address: c/o Pearson Education, 95 Coventry St, South Melbourne, Australia, 3205.

**DAWES Hugh Nicholas,** b. 22 February 1935, Blair's Hill, Hanover, Jamaica, West Indies. Economist. m. Yvonne Ionie Dawes, 2 sons. Education: BSc, Economics, Cornell University, 1969; MPA, Public Finance, 1971, MA, Economics, 1976, PhD, Economics, 1979, New York University. Appointments: Instructor, 1971-79, Assistant Professor of Economics,1979-82, Associate Professor of Economics, 1982-89, Professor of Economics, 1989-, BMC College, City University of New York; Associate Professor of Economics, College of New Rochelle, New York, 1988. Publications: Articles in academic journals include: Developed vs Underdeveloped Economics: The Missing Links, 1982; The Consumption Function of Developing Countries, 1987; Books: Public Finance and Economic Development, 1982; Basic Principals of Economics, 2004. Honours: Scholarships: Jamaica, 1968, Cornell University, 1968, New York University, 1970, 1971; Certificate of Achievement Award, BMC College, 1984, 2002; Listed in Who's Who Among American Teachers and other biographical dictionaries. Memberships: American Association of University Professors; Atlantic Economic Society. Address: 1925 McGraw Avenue, Bronx, NY 10462, USA. E-mail: daweseco@earthlink.net

**DAWIDS Richard Greene,** b. 5 January 1941, Copenhagen, Denmark. Business Executive. Education: Davidson College, 1960-61; University of Grenoble, France, 1966-67; University of Copenhagen, 1968. Appointments: W Copenhagen Handelbank, 1968-85; Tokyo, 1985-89; Vice-President, Surongo SA, Brussels, 1987-90, President, 1991-2003; Board of Directors: Cie Bois Sauvage, Brussels; Enterprises et Chemins de Fer en Chine, Brussels; Berenberg Bank, Hamburg, Germany. Address: Groupe Surongo, 17 Rue du Bois Sauvage, 1000 Brussels, Belgium.

**DAWKINS (Clinton) Richard,** b. 26 March 1941, Nairobi, Kenya. Zoologist; Professor of the Public Understanding of Science. m. (1) Marian Stamp, 19 August 1967, divorced 1984, (2) Eve Barham, 1 June 1984, deceased, 1 daughter, (3) Lalla Ward, 15 September 1992. Education: BA, 1962, MA, 1966, DPhil, 1966, Balliol College, Oxford. Appointments: Assistant Professor of Zoology, University of California at Berkeley, 1967-69; Fellow, New College, Oxford, 1970-; Lecturer, 1970-89, Reader in Zoology, 1989-95, Charles Simonyi, Professor of the Public Understanding of Science, 1996-, Oxford University; Editor, Animal Behaviour, 1974-78, Oxford Surveys in Evolutionary Biology, 1983-86; Gifford Lecturer, University of Glasgow, 1988; Sidgwick Memorial Lecturer, Newnham College, Cambridge, 1988; Kovler Visiting Fellow, University of Chicago, 1990; Nelson Lecturer, University of California at Davis, 1990. Publications: The Selfish Gene, 1976, 2nd edition, 1989; The Extended Phenotype, 1982; The Blind Watchmaker, 1986; River Out of Eden, 1995; Climbing Mount Improbable, 1996; Unweaving the Rainbow, 1998; A Devil's Chaplain, 2003; The Ancestor's Tale, 2004. Contributions to: Scholarly journals. Honours: FRS; Royal Society of Literature Prize, 1987; Los Angeles Times Literature Prize, 1987; Honorary Fellow, Regent's College, London, 1988; Silver Medal, Zoological Society, 1989; Michael Faraday Award, Royal Society, 1990; Nakayama Prize, Nakayama Foundation for Human Sciences, 1994; Honorary DLitt, St Andrews University, 1995; Honorary DLitt, Canberra, 1996; International Cosmos Prize, 1997; Honorary DSc, University of Westminster, 1997; Honorary DSc, University of Hull, 2001; Kistler Prize, 2001; Honorary DUniv, Open University, 2003; Honorary DSc, Sussex, 2005; Honorary DSc, Durham, 2005; Honorary DSc, Brussels, 2005; Shakespeare Prize, 2005. Address: c/o Oxford University Museum, Parks Road, Oxford, OX1 3PW, England.

**DAWNAY Charles James Payan,** b. 7 November 1946, Glasgow, Scotland. Investment Trust Company Director. m. Sarah Stogdon, 1 son, 3 daughters. Education: MA (Hons), History, Trinity Hall, University of Cambridge, 1965-68; Investment Management Programme, London Business School, 1976. Appointments: Investment Manager, M & G Group, 1969-78; Export Sales Director, Alginate Industries Ltd, 1978-81; Managing Director, Vannick Products Ltd, 1981-83; SG Warburg & Co Ltd/Mercury Asset Management Group plc, 1983-92: Director SG Warburg & Co Ltd, 1984, Director, Mercury Asset Management Group plc, 1987, Chairman, Mercury Fund Managers Ltd, 1987; Business Development Director, 1992-99, Deputy Chairman, 1999-2000, Martin Currie Ltd; Currently: Chairman, China Heartland Fund Ltd, 1997-; Chairman, Northern Aim VCT plc, 2000-; Chairman, Gurr Johns Ltd, 2000-; Chairman, Investec High Income Trust plc, 2001-; Director, Taiwan Opportunities Trust plc, 2001-; Chairman, Resources Investment Trust plc, 2001-; Chairman, New Opportunities Investment Trust plc, 2002-; CCLA Investment Management Ltd, 2004-. Finance Committee, Investment Panel, The National Trust, 1991-; West Regional Committee, The National Trust for Scotland, 1993-; Chairman, Biggar Museum Trust, 1993-; Governor and Member of Court of Assistants, Corporation of the Sons of Clergy, 1995-; Member, Merchant Company of Edinburgh, 1995-; Chairman, Penicuik House Preservation Trust, 2001-; Member of the Board of Trustees, The National Galleries of Scotland, 2003. Memberships: Brooks; New Club (Edinburgh); Pratts. Address: Symington House, By Biggar, Lanarkshire ML12 6LW, Scotland.

**DAWSON Earl Bliss,** b. 1 February 1930, Perry, Florida, USA. Biochemist. m. Winnie Ruth Isbell, 1 son, 3 daughters. Education: BA, 1955; MA, 1960; PhD, 1964. Appointments: Instructor, University of Texas, Medical Branch (UTMB), 1963-

64; Associate Professor, University of Texas Medical Branch, 1968. Publications: 7 books and manuals; 7 book chapters; 47 articles; 108 abstracts. Honours: Research Fellowships: in Cardiovascular Physiology, Bowman Gray School of Medicine, 1956; Renal Physiology, University of Missouri School of Medicine, 1958-59, Nutrition, Texas A&M University, 1960-61; National Science Foundation Pre-doctoral Scholarship Award (individual award), 1961-62; National Institute of Health Pre-doctoral Research Award (Individual Grant), 1962-63; Moody Foundation Research Award, 1964; Sigma Xi. Memberships: American Institute of Nutrition; American Society of Clinical Nutrition; American Society for Experimental Biology and Medicine; New York Academy of Science; American College of Nutrition; American Society for Reproductive Medicine. Address: 3431 S Peach Hollow CIR No 8, Pearland, TX 77584-8006, USA.

**DAWSON Patricia Vaughan,** b. 23 January 1925, Liverpool, England. Artist; Poet. m. James N Dawson, 25 September 1948, 1 son, 2 daughters. Education: Croydon School of Art, 1941-45; Diploma, Industrial Design. Appointments: Ashfold School, 1947-48; Lecturer, Tate Gallery, London, 1963-66. Creative Works: Etchings in: La Bibliotheque Nationale, Paris, France; British Museum, and many UK museums. Publications: Poems and works represented in: New Education; Pictorial Knowledge; Still, New Knowledge; Observer; Guardian; The Artist Looks At Life; La Lanterne des Morts; The Kiln; The Forge; Reliquaries; Wet Leaves. Address: Flat 1, 3 Albion Villas Rd, London SE26 4DB, England.

**DAY Doris,** b. 3 April 1924, Cincinnati, Ohio, USA. Singer; Actress. m. (1) Al Jorden, March 1941, divorced 1943, 1 son, (2) George Weilder divorced 1949, (3) Marty Melcher, 3 April 1951, deceased 1968. Career: Former dancer, Cincinnati; Singer, shows including: Karlin's Karnival, WCPO-Radio; Bob Hope NBC Radio Show, 1948-50; Doris Day CBS Show, 1952-53; Solo recording artist, 1950-; Actress, numerous films including: Tea For Two, 1950; Lullaby Of Broadway, 1951; April In Paris, 1952; Pajama Game, 1957; Teacher's Pet, 1958; Pillow Talk, 1959; Midnight Lace, 1960; Jumbo, 1962; That Touch Of Mink, 1962; The Thrill Of It All, 1963; Send Me No Flowers, 1964; Do Not Disturb, 1965; The Glass Bottom Boat, 1966; Caprice, 1967; The Ballad Of Josie, 1968; Where Were You When The Lights Went Out, 1968; Own television series, The Doris Day Show, 1970-73; Doris Day And Friends, 1985-86; Doris Day's Best, 1985-86; TV special, The Pet Set, 1972. Honours: Winner (with Jerry Doherty), Best Dance Team, Cincinnati; Laurel Award, Leading New Female Personality In Motion Picture Industry, 1950; Top audience attractor, 1962; American Comedy Lifetime Achievement Award, 1991. Address: c/o Doris Day Animal League, 227 Massachusetts Avenue NE, Washington, DC 20002, USA.

**DAY Elaine,** b. 30 June 1954, Hendon, North London, England. Freelance Writer. m. David John Day, 5 August 1994, 1 daughter. Publications include: Natural Tranquillity, 1997; Crystal Pillars/Fossil Seas Poetry Book, 1997; Poetry Now East Anglia, 1998; A Celebration of Poets, 1997; Acorn Magazine, 1998; The Secret of Twilight, 1998; A Quiet Storm, anthology, 1998; The Star-Laden Sky, anthology, 1997; Light of the World, anthology, 1997; Beyond the Horizon, anthology, 1997; A Celebration of Friendship (anthology), 1999; A Celebration of Poets (anthology), 1999; Prayer for Jesus and other poems, 2000; People Who Counted, 2000; Praying in Poems, 2000; Let's Shout About It, 2000; Praise Poetry Book, 2001; Praise the Lord, 2001; Heaven & Earth, 2003. Contributions to: Old Yorkshire Magazine; Acorn Magazine; One Magazine; Day By Day Magazine; Forward Press; Freehand Magazine; Poetic

Hour Magazine; Citizen Newspaper; Faith in Focus anthology; Gentle Reader Magazine; Animal Crackers Magazine; Linkway Magazine; Science Friction anthology; Monomyth Magazine; Superfluity Magazine; The Snoring Cat Magazine; BBC Children in Need Pamphlet, 2000; Rainstorms & Rainstorms Anthology, 2000; Small Press Poets Anthology, 2000; Roobooth Publications; Poetry Church, 2000; Closer to Heaven, 2005; Christian poetry book, 2005. Honours: 7 Editors Choice Awards for Poetry; British Academy Certificate, 1983. Memberships: Imagine Writing Group; British Academy of Songwriters, Composers and Authors. Address: 141 Turpin Avenue, Collier Row, Romford, Essex RM5 2LU, England.

**DAY Stephen Peter,** b. 19 January 1938, Ilford, Essex. Consultant. m. Angela Waudby, 1 son, 2 daughters. Education: BA, MA, 1957-60, Visiting Fellow, 1987, Corpus Christi College, Cambridge. Appointments: Senior Political Officer in Aden Protectorate, Her Majesty's Overseas Civil Service, 1961-67; Foreign and Commonwealth Office, 1967-93: Ambassador to Qatar; Household of the Prince of Wales; Ambassador to Tunisia; Senior Trade Commissioner, Hong Kong; Currently, Chairman, MBI Foundation and British Tunisian Society. Honours: CMG; Commander of the Republic of Tunisia. Memberships: Oriental Club; Hong Kong Club. Address: 92 West End Lane, Esher, Surrey KT10 8LF, England. E-mail: s.day@claremontassociates.net

**DAY William,** b. 28 August 1946, Hove, England. Music Teacher. m. Education: Bassoon and flute studies, Royal College of Music, London, 1963-66. Appointments: Part time flute and bassoon teacher, Drayton Manor Grammar School, 1964-66; Principal bassoon, D'Oyly Carte Opera Company, 1966-70; Principal bassoon, London Festival Ballet, 1968; Freelance engagements as principal and sub-principal bassoon, New Cantata Chamber Orchestra, 1966-70; Bassoon, BBC Training Orchestra, Bristol, 1970;Flute and bassoon teacher, Wolverhampton Education Authority, 1970-71; Woodwind teacher, Darlington Education Authority, 1971-73; Principal flute, Mid-Sussex Sinfonia, 1973-74; Woodwind coach, Brighton Youth Orchestra, 1973-75; Part time teacher of student teachers, Brighton Teacher Training College, 1973-77; Woodwind teacher, many schools and sixth form colleges, Brighton area, 1973-86; Solo flute, Music Room, Royal Pavilion, Brighton, 1974; Flute teacher, Roedean School, 1976; Various concerts, New Cantata Soloists, 1977-79; Solo flute and bassoon, Cantilena Soloists Ensemble, 1975; Teacher, Oriel School, Ludlow and Grange House School, Leominster, 1987-89; Woodwind tutor, Llandovery College, South Wales, 1999-2001; Education Network, 2001-; Unaccompanied Solo Flautist, 2004. Memberships: Incorporated Society of Musicians. Address: 2 Prospect Place, Newton Street, Craven Arms, Shropshire, SY7 9PH, England.

**DAY-LEWIS Daniel,** b. 20 April, London, England. Actor. m. Rebecca Miller, 1996; 2 sons (1 by Isabelle Adjani). Education: Bristol Old Vic Theatre School. Career: Plays: Class Enemy, Funny Peculiar, Bristol Old Vic; Look Back in Anger, Dracula, Little Theatre, Bristol and Half Moon Theatre, London; Another Country, Queen's Theatre; Futurists, National Theatre; Romeo, Thisbe, Royal Shakespeare Company Hamlet, 1989; TV: A Frost in May; How Many Miles to Babylon?; My Brother Jonathan; Insurance Man; Films: My Beautiful Launderette; A Room with a View; Stars and Bars; The Unbearable Lightness of Being; My Left Foot, 1989; The Last of the Mohicans, 1991; In the Name of the Father, 1993; The Age of Innocence, 1992; The Crucible, 1995; The Boxer, 1997; Gangs of New York, 2002; The Ballad of Jack and Rose, 2004. Honours: Academy Award for Best Actor, BAFTA Award, Best Actor, (for My

Left Foot) 1989; Screen Actors' Guild Award for Best Actor, 2003; BAFTA Award for Best Actor in a Leading Role, 2003. Address: c/o Julian Belfrage Associates, 46 Albemarle Street, London W1S 4DF, England.

**DE ARAUJO Carlos José,** b. 5 October 1967, Rio de Janeiro, Brazil. Professor. m. Gilmara B Da Silva Araujo. Education: Mechanical Engineer, 1991, Master of Science, Mechanical Engineering, 1994, Universidade Federal da Paraíba, Brazil; Doctor in Materials Science and Engineering, INSA of Lyon, France, 1999. Appointment: Associate Professor, Federal University of Campina Grande, Brazil, 1994-. Publications: More than 10 articles published in international journals and more than 30 papers presented in national and international conferences; Papers concerning shape memory alloys (fundamentals and applications). Honours: Listed in Who's Who publications and biographical dictionaries. Memberships: Brazilian Society of Mechanical Sciences. Address: DEM/CCT/UFCG, Caixa Postal: 10069, CEP: 58109-970, Campina Grande – PB, Brazil, Carlos@dem.ufcg.edu.br

**DE BONO Edward (Francis Publius Charles),** b. 19 May 1933, Malta. Author; Physician; Inventor; Lecturer. m. Josephine Hall-White, 1971, 2 sons. Education: St Edward's College, Malta; BSc, 1953, MD, 1955, Royal University of Malta; MA, 1957, DPhil, 1961, Oxford University; PhD, Cambridge University, 1963. Appointments: Research Assistant, 1957-60, Lecturer, 1960-61, Oxford University; Assistant Director of Research, 1963-76, Lecturer in Medicine, 1976-83, Cambridge University; Honorary Director and Founding Member, Cognitive Research Trust, 1971-; Secretary-General, Supranational Independent Thinking Organisation, 1983-; Lecturer. Publications: The Use of Lateral Thinking, 1967; The Five-Day Course in Thinking, 1967; The Mechanism of Mind, 1969; Lateral Thinking: A Textbook of Creativity, 1970; The Dog Exercising Machine, 1970; Lateral Thinking for Management: A Handbook of Creativity, 1971; Practical Thinking: Four Ways to Be Right, Five Ways to Be Wrong, 1971; Children Solve Problems, 1972; PO: A Device for Successful Thinking, 1972; Think Tank, 1973; Eureka: A History of Inventions (editor), 1974; Teaching Thinking, 1976; The Greatest Thinkers, 1976; Wordpower: An Illustrated Dictionary of Vital Words, 1977; Opportunities: A Handbook of Business Opportunity Search, 1978; The Happiness Purpose, 1978; Future Positive, 1979; Atlas of Management Thinking, 1981; De Bono's Thinking Course, 1982; Learn to Think, 1982; Tactics: The Art and Science of Success, 1984; Conflicts: A Better Way to Resolve Them, 1985; Six Thinking Hats: An Essential Approach to Business Management from the Creator of Lateral Thinking, 1985; CoRT Thinking Program: CoRT 1-Breadth, 1987; Letters to Thinkers: Further Thoughts on Lateral Thinking, 1987; Masterthinker II: Six Thinking Hats, 1988; Masterthinker, 1990; Masterthinker's Handbook, 1990; Thinking Skills for Success, 1990; I Am Right, You Are Wrong: From This to the New Renaissance: From Rock Logic to Water Logic, 1990; Handbook for the Positive Revolution, 1991; Six Action Shoes, 1991; Serious Creativity: Using the Power of Lateral Thinking to Create New Ideas, 1992; Surpetition: Creating Value Monopolies When Everyone Else is Merely Competing, 1992; Teach Your Child How to Think, 1993; Water Logic, 1993; Parallel Thinking, 1994; Teach Yourself to Think, 1995; Mind Pack, 1995; Edward do Bono's Textbook of Wisdom, 1996; How to be More Interesting, 1997; Simplicity, 1998; New Thinking for the New Millennium, 1999; Why I Want to be King of Australia, 1999; The Book of Wisdom, 2000; The de Bono Code, 2000; Contributions to: Television series, professional journals, and periodicals. Honour: Rhodes Scholar; Honorary Registrar, St Thomas' Hospital Medical School, Harvard Medical School.

Membership: Medical Research Society. Address: 12 Albany, Piccadilly, London W1V 9RR, England.

**DE BONT Jan,** b. 22 October 1943, Netherlands. Cinematographer and Director. Education: Amsterdam Film Academy. Appointments: Cinematographer: Turkish Delight; Keetje Tippel; Max Heulaar; Soldier of Orange; Private Lessons (American debut), 1981; Roar; I'm Dancing as Fast As I Can; Cujo; All The Right Moves; Bad Manners; The Fourth Man; Mischief; The Jewel of the Nile; Flesh and Blood; The Clan of the Cave Bear; Ruthless People; Who's That Girl; Leonard Part 6; Die Hard, Bert Rigby - You're A Fool; Black Rain; The Hunt for Red October; Flatliners; Shining Through; Basic Instinct; Lethal Weapon 3, 1992; TV Photography: The Ray Mancini Story; Split Personality (episode of Tales From the Crypt); Director, films: Speed (debut), 1994; Twister; Speed 2: Cruise Control (also screenplay and story); The Haunting. Address: C/o David Gersh, The Gersh Agency, 232 North Canon Drive, Beverly Hills, CA 90210, USA.

**DE BURGH Chris (Christopher Davison),** b. 15 October 1948, Argentina. Singer; Songwriter. m. Diane Patricia Morley, 2 sons, 1 daughter. Education: Trinity College, Dublin. Career: Irish tour with Horslips, 1973; Solo artiste, 1974-; Album sales, 40 million to date; Sell-out concerts world-wide; Performances include: Carol Aid, London, 1985; The Simple Truth, benefit concert for Kurdish refugees, Wembley, 1991; Royal Albert Hall, London. Recordings: Singles include: Flying, 1975; Patricia The Stripper, 1976; A Spaceman Came Travelling, 1976; Don't Pay The Ferryman, 1982; High On Emotion, 1984; Lady In Red (Number 1, UK), 1984; Love Is My Decision, theme from film Arthur 2, 1988; Missing You, 1988; Albums: Far Beyond These Castle Walls, 1975; Spanish Train And Other Stories, 1975; At The End Of A Perfect Day, 1977; Crusader, 1979; Eastern Wind, 1980; Best Moves, 1981; The Getaway, 1982; Man On The Line, 1984; The Very Best Of Chris De Burgh, 1985; Into The Light, 1986; Flying Colours, 1988; From A Spark To A Flame - The Very Best Of Chris De Burgh, 1989; High On Emotion - Live From Dublin, 1990; Power Of Ten, 1992; This Way Up, 1994; Beautiful Dreams, 1995; The Love Songs, 1997; Quiet Revolution, 1999; Notes from Planet Earth – The Ultimate Collection, 2001; Timing is Everything, 2002. Honours: ASCAP Award, The Lady In Red, 1985, 1987, 1988, 1990, 1991, 1997; IRMA Awards, Ireland, 1985-90; Beroliner Award, Germany; BAMBI Award, Germany; Midem Trophy, France. Current Management: Kenny Thomson, 754 Fulham Road, London SW6 5SH, England.

**DE BURGH Lydia,** b. 3 July 1923, London, England. Artist. Education: Private education; Studied with Sonya Mervyn, 1948-51; Byam Shaw School of Art, 1952; Edward Wesson. Career: Wrens, 1942; Enigma-Ultra; Red Cross, 1943-45; Professional portrait, landscape and wildlife painter. Exhibitions include: Royal Society of Portrait Painters; Royal Society of British Artists; Royal Glasgow Institute; Royal Birmingham Society; Royal Ulster Academy; Commissions include: H M The Queen, 1955-59; The Late Princess Alice, Duchess of Gloucester; The Late Princess Royal; African Wildlife for Rowland Ward, Kenya and the Sportsmans Gallery, New York; Maze Prison Northern Ireland, 1972; 8 One Person exhibitions including Vose Gallery, Boston, USA; Last exhibition November 2003. Publications: Lydia's Story, 1989; Another Way of Life – Memoirs, 1999; Numerous articles in press and magazines. Honours: Academician Royal Ulster Academy; Diploma Member, Ulster Watercolour Society. Memberships include: NACF; INLP; USPCA; Countryside Alliance; Irish Georgian Society; Ulster Water Colour Society; Royal Ulster

Academy. Address: 4 Church Court, Clough, Downpatrick, Co Down, BT30 8QX, Northern Ireland.

**DE COURCY Anne Grey,** b. London, England. Writer. m. Robert Armitage, deceased 1998, 1 son, 2 daughters. Education: Wroxah Abbey, Leamington, Warwickshire; Millfield, Street, Somerset. Appointments: Woman's Editor, London Evening News, 1973-80; Columnist and Section Editor, Evening Standard, 1980-91; Feature Writer, Daily Mail, 1991-2003. Publications: Kitchens, 1973; Starting from Scratch, 1975; Making Room at the Top, 1979; A Guide to Modern Manners, 1985; 1939, The Last Season, 1989; The Life of Edith, Lady Londonderry, 1992; The Viceroy's Daughters, 2000; Diana Mosley, 2003; Debs at War, 2005. Memberships: Biographers' Club; The Literary Society. Address: c/o Carole Blake, Blake Friedmann, 122 Arlington Road, London NW1 7HP, England. E-mail: anne@de-courcy.freeserve.co.uk

**DE CRESPIGNY (Richard) Rafe (Champion),** b. 16 March 1936, Adelaide, South Australia, Australia. m. Christa Charlotte Boltz, 1 son, 1 daughter. Education: BA, 1957, MA, 1961, Cambridge University; BA, University of Melbourne, 1961; BA, 1962, MA, 1964, PhD, 1968, Australian National University. Appointments: Lecturer, 1965-70, Senior Lecturer, 1970-73, Secretary-General, 28th International Congress of Orientalists, 1971, Reader in Chinese, 1973-1999, Dean of Asian Studies, 1979-1982, Australian National University, Canberra; Master, University House, 1991-2001; Adjunct Professor of Asian Studies, 1999-. Publications: The Biography of Sun Chien, 1966; Official Titles of the Former Han Dynasty (with H H Dubs), 1967; The Last of the Han, 1969; The Records of the Three Kingdoms, 1970; China: The Land and Its People, 1971; China This Century: A History of Modern China, 1975, 2nd edition, 1992; Portents of Protest, 1976; Northern Frontier, 1984; Emperor Huan and Emperor Ling, 1989; Generals of the South, 1990; To Establish Peace, 1996. Membership: Australian Academy of the Humanities, fellow; Chinese Studies, Association of Australia, President, 1999-2001. Address: Faculty of Asian Studies, Australian National University, Canberra 0200, Australia.

**DE DUVE Christian René,** b. 2 October 1917, Thames Ditton, Surrey, England (Belgian Citizen). Biochemist. m. Janine Herman, 1943, 1 son. Education: Graduated in Medicine, University of Louvain, Belgium, 1941. Appointments: Professor of Physiological Chemistry, 1947-85, Emeritus Professor, 1985-, University of Louvain Medical School, Belgium; Professor of Biochemical Cytology, 1962-88, Emeritus Professor, 1988-, Rockefeller University, New York City. Honours: Prix des Alumni, 1949; Prix Pfizer, 1957; Prix Francqui, 1960; Prix Quinquennal Belge des Sciences Médicales, 1967; Gairdner Foundation International Award of Merit, Canada, 1967; Dr H P Heineken Prijs, Netherlands, 1973; Nobel Prize for Medicine, 1974; Honorary DSc, Keele University, 1981; Doctor honoris causa, Rockefeller University, 1997; Numerous other honorary degrees. Memberships: Royal Academy of Medicine, Belgium; Royal Academy of Belgium; American Chemical Society, Biochemical Society; American Society of Biological Chemistry; Pontifical Academy of Sciences; American Society of Cell Biology; Deutsche Akademie der Naturforschung, Leopoldina; Koninklijke Akademie voor Geneeskunde van België; American Academy of Arts and Sciences; Royal Society, London; Royal Society of Canada. Address: c/o Rockefeller University, 1230 York Avenue, New York, NY 10021, USA.

**DE FINIS Lia (Rosalia Carmela),** Head Teacher. Education: Degree in Classic Arts, University of Padua, 1950. Appointments: Full Teacher of Classic Arts in secondary schools, 1960-72;

Head-Mistress, Secondary School "G Prati", Trento, Italy, 1972-98; Director of the Review, Trentino's Studies of Historical Sciences, 1989-. Publications: Editor, 12 volumes concerning Acts of Cultural Conventions; 12 books and articles and some notes about historical-didactic-pedagogical subjects. Honours: Commendatore of the Italian Republic, 1996; Grand' Ufficiale of the Italian Republic, 1998; Decorated with the Trento Town Seal – S Venceslao's Eagle, 1998. Memberships: Chairwoman, Classic Culture Italian Association, Trento's Delegation, 1975-; Agiati's Academy of Sciences, Literature and Arts, 1975-; Chairwoman, Cultural Association A Rosmini, 1989-; Correspondent Member, Veneto's Archives – Deputation of Venetian Land's History; Accesi's Academy, Trento; Co-ordinator, Head Masters of the Superior Secondary Schools, -1988; Government Representative, Trento's University Board, 1985; Representative of the Province of Trento, S Chiara's Cultural Centre Board; Representative of the Province of Trento, Provincial Committee on Equal Opportunities, 1996-99; Chairwoman, Soroptimist International Club, 1989-91. Address: Via G. A. Prato, 24, 1-38100 Trento, Italy.

**DE FRANCIA Peter Laurent,** b. 1921 Beaulieu, Alpes Maritimes, France. Artist; Professor. Education: Academy of Brussels, 1938-40; Slade School, University of London, 1945-48. Appointments: Canadian Government Exhibition Commission, Ottawa, 1949-50; Architects Department, American Museum, New York, USA, 1951; Head of Fine Art Programming, BBC Television, 1952-54; Department of Art History and Complementary Studies, St Martin's School of Art, 1954-61; Department of Art History and Complementary Studies, Royal College of Art, London, 1961-69; Principal, Department of Fine Art, Goldsmiths College, University of London, 1970-72; Professor of Painting (postgraduate), Royal College of Art, 1972-86; Exhibitions: 23 one-man exhibitions include most recently: Centre for Contemporary Art, New Delhi, India, 1991; Gloria Gallery Nicosia, Cyprus, 1995; Austin Desmond Fine Art, London, 1996; The Place London, 1999; Ruskin School of Drawing, Oxford, 1999; British Council, New Delhi, 2002; "The Bombing of Sakiet", Tate Modern, 2003-4; Numerous group exhibitions. Work in collections: Ashmolean Museum, Oxford; British Museum, London; Graves Art Gallery, Sheffield; Imperial War Museum, London; Museum of Modern Art, New York; Museum of Modern Art, Prague, Tate Gallery, London; Victoria and Albert Museum, London; Arts Council of Great Britain; Works in private collections in the UK and overseas. Publications: Leger: The great parade, 1969; The Life and Work of Fernand Leger, 1983; Untitled, 1989; Fables, 1990-2001, 2002. Address: 44 Surrey Square, London SE17 2JX, England.

**DE GIOVANNI-DONNELLY Rosalie Frances,** b. 22 November 1926, Brooklyn, New York, USA. m. Edward F, 2 sons. Education: BA, Brooklyn College, 1947; MA, 1953; PhD, Columbia University, 1961. Appointments: Chief, Microbial Genetics Laboratory, 1962-67; Research Biologist, Food and Drug Administration, 1968-88; Professor, George Washington University Medical School, 1968-. Publications: Articles to Scientific Journals. Honours: Food and Drug Award of Merit, 1970. Memberships: American Association for the Advancement of Science; American Society of Microbiology; Sigma Xi; Sigma Delta; Environmental Mutagen Society. Address: 1712 Strine Dr, McLean, VA 22101, USA.

**DE HAMEL Christopher Francis Rivers,** b. 20 November 1950. Archivist; Librarian. m. (1) 1978, 2 sons, (2) Mette Tang Simpson, 1993. Education: BA, Otago University, New Zealand; DPhil, Oxford University. Appointments: Cataloguer, Medieval Manuscripts, 1975, Assistant Director, 1977, Director, Western and Oriental, later Western Manuscripts, 1982-2000, Sotheby's, London; Visiting Fellow, All Souls College, Oxford, 1999-2000; Donnelley Librarian and Fellow, Corpus Christi College, Cambridge, 2000-. Publications include: Glossed Books of the Bible and the Origins of the Paris Book Trade, 1984; A History of Illuminated Manuscripts, 1986, 2nd edition, 1994; Medieval and Renaissance Manuscripts in New Zealand Collections (with M Manion and V Vines), 1989; Syon Abbey, The Library of the Bridgettine Nuns and their Peregrinations after the Reformation, 1991; Scribes and Illuminators, 1992; The British Library Guide to Manuscript Illumination, 2001; The Book: A History of the Bible, 2001; Various reviews, journal articles and catalogues. Honours: FSA; FRHistS; Hon LittD, St John's Minnesota, 1994; Hon Dlitt, Otago University, 2002 Membership: Chairman, Association for Manuscripts and Archives in Reserve Collections. Address: Corpus Christi College, Trumpington Street, Cambridge CB2 1RH, England.

**DE HAVILLAND Olivia Mary,** b. 1 July 1916, Tokyo, Japan. Actress. m. (1) Marcus Aurelius Goodrich, 1 sons, (2) Pierre Paul Galante, 1955, divorced 1979, 1 daughter. Appointments: Actress, films including: Captain Blood, 1935; Anthony Adverse, 1936; The Adventures of Robin Hood, 1938; Gone With The Wind, 1939; Hold Back the Dawn, 1941; Princess O'Rourke, 1942; To Each His Own (Academy Award), 1946; The Dark Mirror, 1946; The Snake Pit, 1947; The Heiress (Academy Award), 1949; My Cousin Rachel, 1952; Not as a Stranger, 1954; The Proud Rebel, 1957; The Light in the Piazza, 1961; Lady in a Cage, 1963; Hush Hush Sweet Charlotte, 1964; The Adventurers, 1968; Airport '77, 1976; The Swarm, 1978; The Fifth Musketeer; Plays: Romeo and Juliet, 1951; Candida, 1951-52; A Gift of Time, 1962; TV: Noon Wine, 1966; Screaming Women, 1972; Roots, The Next Generations, 1979; Murder is Easy, 1981; Charles and Diana: A Royal Romance, 1982; North and South II, 1986; Anastasia (Golden Globe award), 1986; The Woman He Loved, 1987. Publications: Every Frenchman Has One, 1962; Contributor, Mother and Child, 1975. Honours: Numerous awards include: Academy awards, 1946, 1949; New York Critics Award, 1948, 1949; Look Magazine Award, 1941, 1946, 1949; Venice Film Festival Award, 1948; Filmex Tribute, 1978; American Academy of Achievement Award, 1978; American Exemplar Medal, 1980; Golden Globe, 1988; DRhc, American University of Paris, 1994. Address: BP 156-16, 75764 Paris, Cedex 16 France.

**DE JAGER Cornelis,** b. 29 April 1921, Den Burg, Netherlands. Professor, Space Research and Astrophysics. m. Duotje Rienks, 2 sons, 2 daughters. Education: Doctoral Degree, 1945, Doctor Degree, cum laude, 1952, University of Utrecht. Appointments: Assistant, 1946, Senior Scientist, 1955, Lecturer, 1957, Professor, 1960, University of Utrecht; Professor, University of Brussels, 1961-86. Publications: 33 books, 400 scientific publications, 160 popular publications. Honours: Gold Medal, RAS, London; Hale Medal, AAS; Dr Hon Causa, Paris, Wroclaw. Memberships: Several. Address: Molenstraat 22, 1791 DL Den Burg, Texel, The Netherlands. E-mail: cdej@planet.nl

**DE KLERK Frederik Willem,** b. 18 March 1936, Johannesburg, South Africa. Politician. m. (1) Marike Willemse, 1959, 2 sons, 1 daughter, (2) Elita Georgiadis, 1998. Education: Potchefstrom University. Appointments: In law practice, 1961-72; Member, House of Assembly, 1972; Information Officer, National Party, Transvaal, 1975; Minister, Posts, Telecommunications and Social Welfare and Pensions, 1978; Minister, Posts, Telecommunications and Sport and Recreation, 1978-79; Minister, Mines, Energy and Environmental Planning, 1979-80; Mineral and Energy Affairs, 1980-82; Internal Affairs, 1982-85; National Education and Planning, 1984-89;

Acting State President South Africa, August-September, 1989; State President, South Africa, 1989-94; Executive Deputy President, Government of National Party, 1994-96; Leader of Official Opposition, 1996-97; Former, Chairman, Cabinet and Commander-in-Chief of the Armed Forces; Former, Chairman, Council of Ministers. Publications: The Last Trek: A New Beginning (autobiography), 1999; Various articles and brochures for the National Party Information Service. Honours: Joint winner, Houphouet Boigny Prize (UNESCO), 1991; Asturias Prize, 1992; Liberty Medal (SA), 1993; Shared Nobel Prize for Peace with Nelson Mandela, 1993. Address: 7 Eaton Square, London, SW1, England.

**DE LA BILLIÈRE Peter (Sir),** b. 29 April 1934, Plymouth, Devon, England. Retired Army Officer. m. Bridget Constance Muriel Goode, 1965, 1 son, 2 daughters. Education: Royal College of Defence Studies, Staff College. Appointments: Joined King's Shropshire Light Infantry, 1952; Commissioned Durham Light Infantry; Served Japan, Korea, Malaya, Jordan, Borneo, Egypt, Aden, Gulf States, Sudan, Oman, Falklands; Commanding Officer 22 Special Air Service Regiment (SAS), 1972-74; General Staff Officer 1 (Directing Staff) Staff College, 1974-77; Commander, British Army Training Team, Sudan, 1977-78; Director, SAS, Commander, SAS Group, 1978-83; Commander, British Forces, Falklands and Military Commissioner, 1984-85; General Officer Commanding, Wales, 1985-87; General Officer Commanding South East District and Permanent Peace Time Commander, Joint Forces Operations Staff, 1987-90; Commander, British Forces, Middle East, 1990-91; Adviser to HM Government on Middle East Affairs; Current appointments: Director, Robert Fleming Holdings Ltd, 1977-99; Chairman, FARM Africa; Chairman, Meadowland Meats Ltd, 1994-2002; President, Army Cadet Force, 1992-99. Publications: Storm Command: A Personal Story, 1992; Looking For Trouble (autobiography), 1994. Honours include: Several honorary doctorates; Order of Bahrain, 1st class, 1991; Chief Commander, Legion of Merit, USA, 1992; Meritorious Service Cross, Canada, 1992; Order of Abdul Aziz, 2nd class, Saudi Arabia, 1992; Kuwait Decoration, 1st class, 1992; Qatar Sash of Merit, 1992; KCB; KBE; DSO; MC and Bar; MSC DL. Address: c/o Naval and Military Club, 4 St James's Square, London SW1Y 4JU, England.

**DE LA HOUSSAYE Brette Angelo-Pepe,** b. 20 August 1960, Los Angeles, California, USA. Researcher; Engineer; Educator. Education: BSEET, DeVry Institute, City of Industry, California, 1989. Appointments: Engineer Researcher, private practice, 1990-2003; Calcgate (Software), 2003-; Discovered alternate method for calculating energy using Newton's Second Law of Motion and Work Energy Theorem, applications also include integral calculus. Memberships: IEEE; American Physical Society; Institute of Nanotechnology; National Trust for Historic Preservation; American Museum of Natural History. Address: 7719 Goodland Ave, North Hollywood, CA 91605, USA.

**DE LA MARE Walter Giles Ingpen,** b. 21 October 1934, London, England. Publisher. m. Ursula Steward, 1 son, 1 daughter. Education: MA (Oxon), Trinity College, Oxford, 1955-59. Appointments: National Service, Royal Navy, 1953-55; Midshipman, RNVR, 1954, Sub-lieutenant, 1955; Director, Faber and Faber Ltd, 1969-98; Director, Faber Music Ltd, 1977-87; Director, Geoffrey Faber Holdings Ltd, 1990-; Chairman, Giles de la Mare Publishers Ltd, 1995-; Literary Trustee of Walter de la Mare, 1982-; Founder Walter de la Mare Society, 1997. Publications include: The Complete Poems of Walter de la Mare (editor), 1969; Motley and Other Poems by Walter de la Mare (editor with introduction for Folio Society), 1991; Publishing Now (contributor of general chapter), 1993;

Short Stories 1895-1926 by Walter de la Mare (editor), 1996; Short Stories 1927-1956 by Walter de la Mare (editor), 2001; Richard de la Mare at 75 (editor with Tilly de la Mare), 2004. Memberships: Publishers Association: Chairman, University, College and Professional Publishers Council, 1982-84, Member of PA Council, 1982-85, Chairman of Copyright Committee, 1988, Chairman, Freedom to Publish Committee, 1992-95, 1998-2000; International Publishers Association Freedom to Publish Committee, 1993-96; Stefan Zweig Committee, British Library, 1986-95; Executive Committee, Patrons of British Art, Tate Gallery, 1998-2001; Translation Advisory Group, Arts Council of England, 1995-98; Club: Garrick. Address: PO Box 25351, London NW5 1ZT, England. E-mail: gilesdelamare@dial.pipex.com; www.gilesdelamare.co.uk

**DE LA MAZA Luis M,** b. 12 August 1943, Ribadesella, Spain. Professor. m. Maria, 1 son, 1 daughter. Education: MD, Facultad de Medicina, Madrid, Spain, 1966; PhD, University of Minnesota, USA, 1974. Appointments: Assistant Professor, University of Minnesota, USA, 1974-75; Visiting Associate, National Institutes of Health, USA, 1975-79; Professor, Department of Pathology, University of California, Irvine, USA, 1979-. Publications include: Numerous articles in scientific and medical journals; Books: Medical Virology, Volumes 1-10; Color Atlas of Diagnostic Microbiology. Honours: Excm Diputacion Provincial de Asturias, Spain, 1961; Wasserman Award, Spain, 1964. Memberships: American Society for Microbiology; American Association for the Advancement of Sciences; American Society of Clinical Pathologists. Address: Department of Pathology, Medical Sciences, Room D440, University of California, Irvine, CA 92697, USA.

**DE LA RENTA Oscar,** b. 22 July 1932, Santo Domingo. Fashion Designer. (1) Françoise de Langlade, 1967, deceased 1983, (2) Anne de la Renta, 1989. Education: Santo Domingo University; Academia de San Fernando, Madrid. Appointments: Staff designer, under Cristobel Balenciaga, AISA couture house, Madrid; Assistant to Antonio Castillo, Lanvin-Castillo, Paris, 1961-63; Designer, Elizabeth Arden couture and ready-to-wear collection, New York, 1963-65; Designer and partner, Jane Deby Inc, New York, 1965; After her retirement, firm became Oscar de la Renta Inc, purchased by Richton International, 1969; Chief Executive, Richton's Oscar de la Renta Couture, Oscar de la Renta II, Oscar de la Renta Furs, Oscar de la Renta Jewelry, Member of Board of Directors, Richton Inc, 1969-73; Oscar de la Renta Ltd, 1973; Chief Executive Officer, 1973--; Couturier for Balmain, Paris, Nov, 1992-; Producer, 80 different lines including high-fashion clothing, household linens, accessories and perfumes for shops in USA, Canada, Mexico and Japan; Owner, Oscar de la Renta Shop, Santo Domingo, 1968-. Honours: Recipient, numerous fashion awards; Caballero, Order of San Pablo Duarte, Order of Cristobal Colon. Address: Oscar de la Renta Ltd, 550 7th Avenue, 8th Floor, New York, NY 10018, USA.

**DE LA TOUR Frances,** b. 30 July 1944, Bovingdon, Hertfordshire, England. Actress. m. Tom Kempinski, 1972, divorced 1982, 1 son, 1 daughter. Education: Lycée français de Londres, Drama Centre, London; With the Royal Shakespeare Company, 1965-71. Appointments: Stage appearances include: As You Like It, 1967; The Relapse, 1969; A Midsummer Night's Dream, 1971; The Man of Mode, 1971; Small Craft Warnings, 1973; The Banana Box, 1973; The White Devil, 1976; Hamlet (title role), 1979; Duet for One, 1980; Skirmishes, 1981; Uncle Vanya, 1982; Moon for the Misbegotten , 1983; St Joan, 1984; Dance of Death, 1985; Brighton Beach Memoirs, 1986; Lillian, 1986; Facades, 1988; King Lear, 1989; When She Danced (Olivier Award), 1991; The Pope and the Witch,

1992; Greasepaint, 1993; Les Parents Terrible (Royal National Theatre), 1994; Three Tall Women, 1994-95; Blinded by the Sun (Royal National Theatre), 1996; The Play About the Baby (Almedia Theatre), 1998; The Forest (Royal National Theatre), 1998-99; Antony and Cleopatra (RSC), 1999; Fallen Angels (Apollo), 2000-01; The Good Hope and Sketches by Harold Pinter, (Royal National Theatre), 2001-02; Dance of Death (Lyric), 2003; Films include: Our Miss Fred, 1972; To The Devil a Daughter, 1976; Rising Damp, 1980; The Cherry Orchard, 1998; Love Actually, 2003; TV appearances include: Crimes of Passion, 1973; Rising Damp, 1974, 1976; Cottage to Let, 1976; Flickers, 1980; Skirmishes, 1982; Duet for One, 1985; Partners, 1986; Clem, 1986; A Kind of Living (series), 1987, 1988; Downwardly Mobile (series), 1994; Cold Lazarus, 1996; Tom Jones, 1997. Honours: Best Supporting Actress Plays and Players Award, 1973; 3 Best Actress Awards, 1980; Best Actress Standard Film Award, 1980; Best Actress SWET Award, 1983; Honorary Fellow, Goldsmiths College, University of London, 1999; Best Actress, Royal Variety Club, 2000. Address: c/o Kate Feast Management, 10 Primrose Hill Studios, Fitzroy Road, London, NW1 8TR, England.

**DEL MEL Widanelage Erantha Jayalath Chandrange,** b. 18 November 1959, Colombo, Sri Lanka. Research Scientist. m. Nilwala Gunaratne, 2 sons, 1 daughter. Education: PhD Artificial Intelligence and Robotics, Kensington, 1998; PhD, 2001, DSc, 2004, Applied Psychology, OIUCM. Appointments: Director, Mindtherapy Foundation, Sri Lanka, 2001-; Senior Professor of Psychology, Colombo South Government General University Teaching Hospital, 2004-. Publications: Framework for an Integrated Model of Collaborative Techniques in Counselling and Therapy; Psychology of the Next Generation: Lessons from Modern Consciousness Research; Brain Re-engineering with Assertiveness Training; Brain Re-engineering through Neural Optimisation Technique; Principles & Practice of Neural Optimisation Technique; The Psychology of Consciousness; Mental State – An Analysis of Altered States of Consciousness; The Secret Communication Process of the Mind: A Visual Inquiry into the Mysteries of Consciousness; Trance: From Supernatural to Technology; The Natural Mind: A Revolutionary Approach to Psycho-somatic Disorders; Altered States of Consciousness: An Empirical Analysis for Behavioural Scientists. Honour: William Hughes Award, 1986. Memberships: International Council of Psychologists; Institute of Professional Psychologists. Address: 108/1 De Soysa Road, Rawathwatte, Moratuwa, Sri Lanka. E-mail: erantha@mindtherapy.org

**DE NIRO Robert,** b. 1943, New York, USA. Actor. m. Diahnne Abbott, 1976, 1 son, 1 daughter, 2 children by Toukie Smith. Career: Actor; Producer; Director; Films include: Trois chambres à Manhattan, 1965; Greetings, 1968; The Wedding Party, 1969; Sam's Song, 1969; Bloody Mama, 1970; Jennifer On My Mind, 1971; Born To Win, 1971; The Gang That Couldn't Shoot Straight, 1971; Bang the Drum Slowly, 1973; Mean Streets, 1973; The Godfather Part II, 1974; The Last Tycoon, 1976; Taxi Driver, 1976; 1900, 1976; New York, New York, 1977; The Deer Hunter, 1978; Raging Bull, 1980; True Confessions, 1981; The King of Comedy, 1983; Once Upon a Time in America, 1984; Falling in Love, 1984; Brazil, 1985; The Mission, 1986; Angel Heart, 1987; The Untouchables, 1987; Midnight Run, 1988; We're No Angels, 1989; Jacknife, 1989; Stanley and Iris, 1990; Goodfellas, 1990; Awakenings, 1990; Backdraft, 1991; Cape Fear, 1991; Guilty of Suspicion, 1991; Mistress, 1992; Night and the City, 1992; Mistress, 1992; The Godfather Trilogy: 1901-1980, 1992; Mad Dog and Glory, 1993; This Boy's Life, 1993; A Bronx Tale, 1993; Mary Shelley's Frankenstein, 1994; Heat, 1995; Casino, 1995; Le Cent et une nuits de Simon Cinéma, 1995; The Fan, 1996; Marvin's Room,

1996; Sleepers, 1996; Jackie Brown, 1997; Wag The Dog, 1997; Cop Land, 1997; Great Expectations, 1998; Ronin, 1998; Analyze This, 1999; Flawless, 1999; Men of Honor, 2000; Meet the Parents, 2000; The Adventures of Rocky & Bullwinkle, 2000; 15 Minutes, 2001; The Score, 2001; Showtime, 2002; City by the Sea, 2002; Analyze That, 2002; Godsend, 2004; Shark Tale (voice), 2004; Meet the Fockers, 2004; The Bridge of San Luis Rey, 2004; Hide and Seek, 2005; The Good Shepherd, 2006; Chaos, 2006. Honours include: Commander, Ordre des Arts et des Lettres; Academy Award, Best Supporting Actor, 1974; Academy Award, Best Actor, 1980. Address: CAA, 9830 Wilshire Boulevard, Beverly Hills, CA 90212, USA.

**DE PALMA Brian,** b. 11 September 1940, Newark, New Jersey, USA. Film Director. m. Gale Ann Hurd, 1991, 1 daughter. Education: Sarah Lawrence College, Bronxville; Columbia University. Appointments: Director: (short films) Icarus, 1960; 660124: The Story of an IBM Card, 1961; Wotan's Wake, 1962; (feature length) The Wedding Party, 1964; The Responsive Eye (documentary), 1966; Murder à la Mod, 1967; Greetings, 1968; Dionysus in '69 (co-director), 1969; Hi Mom!, 1970; Get to Know Your Rabbit, 1970; Sisters, 1972; Phantom of the Paradise, 1974; Obsession, 1975; Carrie, 1976; The Fury, 1978; Home Movies, 1979; Dressed to Kill, 1980; Blow Out, 1981; Scarface, 1983; Body Double, 1984; Wise Guys, 1985; The Untouchables, 1987; Casualties of War, 1989; Bonfire of the Vanities, 1990; Raising Cain, 1992; Carlito's Way, 1993; Mission Impossible, 1996; Snake Eyes, 1998; Mission to Mars, 2000; Femme Fatale, 2002. Address: Paramount Pictures, Lubitsch Annex #119, 555 Melrose Avenue #119, W Hollywood, CA 90038, USA.

**DE RANTER Camiel Joseph,** b. 27 August 1937, Hoboken, Antwerp, Belgium. Professor. m. Monique Blaton, 2 sons. Education: Licentiate in Chemistry, 1960, Certificate in High School Teaching, 1960, Certificate in Nuclear Sciences, 1960, DSc, Physical Chemistry, 1964, Catholic University of Leuven. Appointments: Research Scientist, 1960-62, Research Assistant, 1963-67, Senior Research Scientist, 1967-70, Chemistry Department, Faculty of Sciences, Docent in Analytical Chemistry, 1970-74, Professor, 1974-76, Ordinary Professor, 1976-2002, President, 1983-92, Institute of Pharmaceutical Sciences, Vice-Dean, Faculty of Pharmaceutical Sciences, 1992-98, Emeritus Professor, 2002-, Member of the Senate, 2003-, University of Leuven; Visiting Professor, Faculty of Chemistry, Jagiellonian University, Krakow, 1984. Publications: Over 200 scientific articles in professional journals. Memberships: Koninklijke Vlaamse Chemische Vereniging; Koninklijke Nederlandse Chemische Vereniging; American Crystallographic Association; Belgian Pharmaceutical Association; Belgian Association of Biophysics; Netherlands Crystallographic Association, Vice-President, 1999-; The QSAR and Modelling Society. Address: Catholic University Leuven, E Van Evenstraat 4, B 3000 Leuven, Belgium.

**DE SOUSA Alice,** b. 11 January 1966, Portugal. Actress; Producer; Artistic Director. Education: BA, Honours, EEC Law, 1st Class, 1995; MA, Portuguese Studies, 1997. Career: Numerous roles in television, radio and film productions; Lead roles in over 30 productions, including Hermione, The Winter's Tale; Millamant, The Way of the World; Elvira, Blithe Spirit; Producer of more than 60 theatre productions, including: Never Nothing From No One, Hamlet, Company, Pymaglion, Richard III, You're Gonna Love Tomorrow, Hedda Gabler, Peep Show, Cousin Basillio; Shadows on the Sun; The Importance of Being Earnest, Three Sisters, The White Devil, 'Tis Pity She's a Whore, The Ruffian on the Stair and The Erpingham Camp, The Maias, Ines de Castro, King Lear, Absent Friends, A Doll's House, and

The Heiress of the Cane Fields. Address: Greenwich Playhouse, 189 Greenwich High Road, London, SE10 8JA, England.

**DE STACPOOLE Robert George Francis,** b. 30 March 1924, London, England. Historian. m. Susan Mary Angela Trouncer, 1 son, 3 daughters. Education: BA, 1948, MA, 1963, Christ's College, Cambridge. Appointments: Active Academic Historian, 1948-2005; Working Member of Lloyds, 1950-96; Insurer at Lloyds, 1956-93. Publications: Various historical articles relating to Europe, Ireland, USA and the Papacy. Memberships: 1900 Club, 1949-; St James' Club, 1947-75; Brooks Club, 1976-; Catholic Union, 1953-; Kensington Society, 2000-. Address: Flat 2, 57 Gloucester Road, Kensington, London SW7 4QN, England.

**DE VILLIERS François Pierre Rousseau,** b. 10 May 1950, Namibia. Professor of Paediatrics. m. (1) J Gai, deceased 2001, 1 son, 1 daughter (2) Mariana Catharina, 2004. Education: MBChB, 1974; BA, 1983; MMed, 1987; PhD, 1990; FACP, 2000; FCPaed (SA), 2001. Appointments: Professor and Chair, Paediatrics, 1994, Deputy Dean (Research), 1997-2001, Deputy Dean (Academic Matters), 2004-, Medical University of South Africa. Publications: Book: Practical Management of Paediatric Emergencies, 4th Edition, 2004 ; Numerous articles in professional journals. Honour: Research Excellence Award, Medunsa, 1998; Research Excellence Award for Senior Researcher, Medunsa, 2001. Memberships: New York Academy of Sciences; International Society for the Study of Paediatric and Adolescent Diabetes; American College of Physicians. Address: PO Box 480, Medunsa 0204, South Africa.

**DE WET Jacobus Anthony,** b. 27 July 1929, Grahamstown, South Africa. Engineer; Mathematical Physicist. m. P A Van Reenen, 3 sons, 1 daughter. Education: BSc, 1950; MSc, 1952; PhD, 1970. Appointments: Principal Engineer, Department of Water Affairs; Senior Research Officer, Council of Scientific and Industrial Research. Publications: 15 papers on nuclear structure, recently making use of algebraic geometry. Memberships: South African Institute of Physics; South African Natural Scientist; Past Member, New York Academy of Sciences. Address: Box 514, 6600 Plettenberg Bay, South Africa.

**DEAN Christopher,** b. 27 July 1958, Nottingham, England. Ice Skater. m. (1) Isabelle Duchesnay, 1991, divorced, 1993, (2) Jill Ann Trenary, 1994, 2 sons. Appointments: Police Constable, 1974-80; British Ice Dance Champion (with Jayne Torvill), 1978-83, 1993; European Ice Dance Champion (with Jayne Torvill), 1981, 1982, 1984, 1994; World Ice Dance Champion (with Jayne Torvill), 1981-84; World professional Champions, 1984-85, 1990, 1995-96; Choreographed Encounters for English National Ballet, 1996; Stars on Ice, USA, 1998-99, 1999-2000; Ice Dance: World tours with own and international companies of skaters, 1985, 1988, 1994, 1997, tours of Australia and New Zealand, 1984, 1991, UK, 1992, Japan, 1996, USA and Canada, 1997-98. Publications: Torvill and Dean's Face the Music and Dance (with Jayne Torvill), 1993; Torvill and Dean: An Autobiography (with Jayne Torvill), 1994; Facing the Music (with Jayne Torvill), 1996. Honours: BBC Sportsview Personality of the Year (with Jayne Torvill), 1983-84; Honorary MA, 1994. Address: c/o Sue Young, PO Box 32, Heathfield, East Sussex, TN21 0BW, England.

**DEANE Seamus (Francis),** b. 9 February 1940, Derry City, Northern Ireland. Professor of Irish Studies; Writer; Poet. m. Marion Treacy, 19 August 1963, 3 sons, 1 daughter. Education: BA, Honours, 1st Class, 1961, MA, 1st Class, 1963, Queen's University, Belfast; PhD, Cambridge University, 1968. Appointments: Visiting Fulbright and Woodrow Wilson

Scholar, Reed College, Oregon, 1966-67; Visiting Lecturer, 1967-68, Visiting Professor, 1978, University of California at Berkeley; Professor of Modern English and American Literature, University College, Dublin, 1980-93; Walker Ames Professor, University of Washington, Seattle, 1987; Julius Benedict Distinguished Visiting Professor, Carleton College, Minnesota, 1988; Keough Professor of Irish Studies, University of Notre Dame, Indiana, 1993-. Publications: Fiction: Reading in the Dark, 1996. Poetry: Gradual Wars, 1972; Rumours, 1977; History Lessons, 1983; Selected, 1988. Non-Fiction: Celtic Revivals: Essays in Modern Irish Literature, 1880-1980, 1985; A Short History of Irish Literature, 1986, reissued, 1994; The French Revolution and Enlightenment in England, 1789-1832, 1988; Strange Country: Ireland, Modernity and Nationhood, 1790-1970, 1997; Foreign Affections: Essays on Edmund Burke, 2005. Editor: The Adventures of Hugh Trevor by Thomas Holcroft, 1972; The Sale Catalogues of the Libraries of Eminent Persons, Vol IX, 1973; Nationalism, Colonialism and Literature, 1990; The Field Day Anthology of Irish Writing, 3 volumes, 1991; Penguin Twentieth Century Classics: James Joyce, 5 volumes, 1993; Field Day Review 1, 2005. Honours: AE Memorial for Literature, 1973; American-Irish Fund, Literature, 1989; Guardian Fiction Prize, 1997; Irish Times International Fiction Award, 1997; Irish Times Fiction Award, 1997; London Weekend Television South Bank Award for Literature, 1997; Ruffino Antico-Fattore International Literature Award, Florence, 1998; Honorary DLitt, Ulster, 1999. Memberships: Aosdana (Irish Artists' Council); Field Day Theatre and Publishing Company, director; Royal Irish Academy. Address: Institute of Irish Studies, 1145 Flanner Hall, University of Notre Dame, IN 46556, USA.

**DEAR Nick,** b. 11 June 1955, Portsmouth, England. Playwright. m. Penny Downie, 2 sons. Education: BA, Honours, English Literature, University of Essex, 1977. Appointments: Playwright-in-Residence, Essex University, 1985, Royal Exchange Theatre, 1987-88. Publications: Temptation, 1984; The Art of Success, 1986; Food of Love, 1988; A Family Affair (after Ostrovsky), 1988; In the Ruins, 1989; The Last Days of Don Juan (after Tirso), 1990; Le Bourgeois Gentilhomme (after Molière), 1992; Pure Science, 1994; Zenobia, 1995; Summerfolk (after Gorky), 1999; The Villains' Opera, 2000; Power, 2003; Lunch in Venice, 2005; The Turn of the Screw, 2005; The Miracle of Reason, 2005. Opera Libretti: A Family Affair, 1993; Siren Song, 1994; The Palace in the Sky, 2000; Other: Several radio plays. Films: The Monkey Parade, 1983; The Ranter, 1988; Persuasion, 1995; The Gambler, 1997; The Turn of the Screw, 1999; Cinderella, 2000; Byron, 2003; Eroica, 2003; The Hollow, 2004. Honours: John Whiting Award, 1987; Olivier Award nominations, 1987, 1988; BAFTA Award, 1996; Broadcasting Press Guild Award, 1996; South Bank Show Theatre Award, 1999; Prix Italia, 2003. Membership: Writer's Guild of Great Britain. Address: c/o Rosica Colin Ltd, 1 Clareville Grove Mews, London SW7 5AH, England.

**DEARDEN James Shackley,** b. 9 August 1931, Barrow-in-Furness, England. Appointment: Curator, Ruskin Galleries, Bembridge School, Isle of Wight and Brantwood Coniston, 1957-96. Publications: The Professor: Arthur Severn's Memoir of Ruskin, 1967; A Short History of Brantwood, 1967; Iteriad by John Ruskin (editor), 1969; Facets of Ruskin, 1970, Japanese edition, 2001; Ruskin and Coniston (with K G Thorne), 1971; John Ruskin, 1973, 2nd edition, 1981, Japanese edition, 1991, enlarged edition, 2004; Turner's Isle of Wight Sketch Book, 1979; John Ruskin and Les Alpi, 1989; John Ruskin's Camberwell, 1990; A Tour to the Lakes in Cumberland: John Ruskin's Diary for 1830 (editor), 1990; John Ruskin and Victorian Art, 1993; Ruskin, Bembridge and Brantwood, 1994;

Hare Hunting on the Isle of Wight, 1996; John Ruskin, a life in pictures, 1999; King of the Golden River by John Ruskin (editor), 1999. Contributions to: Book Collector; Connoisseur; Apollo; Burlington; Bulletin of John Rylands Library; Country Life; Ruskin Newsletter (editor); Ruskin Research Series (general editor); Journal of Pre-Raphaelite Studies; Ruskin Programme Bulletin; Turner Society News; Whitehouse Edition of Ruskin's Works (joint general editor). Honour: Hon. D. Litt. (Lancaster), 1998. Memberships: Ruskin Society; Ruskin Association, secretary and treasurer; Turner Society; Companion of the Guild of St George, Acting Master and Director for Ruskin Affairs; Old Bembridgians Association, past president; Isle of Wight Foot Beagles, vice president; Friends of Ruskin's Brantwood, vice president. Address: 4 Woodlands, Foreland Road, Bembridge, Isle of Wight, England.

**DEARLOVE Richard Billing (Sir),** b. 23 January 1945, Cornwall, England. Master, Pembroke College, Cambridge. m. Rosalind, 2 sons, 1 daughter. Education: MA, Queens' College Cambridge. Appointments: Entered Foreign Office, 1966; Nairobi, 1968-71; Prague, 1973-76; Foreign and Commonwealth Office, 1976-80; First Secretary Paris, 1980-84; Foreign and Commonwealth Office, 1984-87; Counsellor, UKMIS Geneva, 1987-91; Washington, 1991-93; Director, Personnel and Administration, 1993-94, Director, Operations, 1994-99, Assistant Chief, 1998-99, Chief, 1999-2004, Secret Intelligence Service; Master of Pembroke College, Cambridge, 2004-; Trustee, Kent School, Connecticut, USA, 2001-. Honours: OBE, 1984; KCMG, 2001; Honorary Fellow, Queens' College, Cambridge, 2004. Address: Master's Lodge, Pembroke College, Cambridge, CB2 1RF, England.

**DEBAKEY Lois,** b. Lake Charles, Louisiana, USA. Professor of Scientific Communication; Writer; Editor; Lecturer. Education: BA, Mathematics, Newcomb College, Tulane University; MA, PhD, Literature and Linguistics, Tulane University; Postgraduate Courses in Biostatistics, Medical School, Tulane University. Appointments include: Professor of Scientific Communications, Baylor College of Medicine, 1968-; Consultant, National Library of Medicine, Bethesda, Maryland, 1986-; Member, National Advisory Committee, University of Southern California Development and Demonstration Center in Continuing Education for Health Professionals; Consultant, American Bar Association Legal Writing Committee; Advisory Committee, Society for the Advancement of Good English; Trustee, DeBakey Medical Foundation; Member, Advisory Council, University of Texas at Austin School of Nursing Foundation, 1993-; Member, Usage Panel, American Heritage Dictionary; Team Leader Consultant, Health and Medical Data Base, Encyclopaedia Britannica; Current Editorial Board Member: Journal of the American Medical Association, Core Journals in Cardiology, International Angiology Network, CV Network; Internationally renowned course developer and authority in the field of medical writing; Acclaimed for use of cartoons and humour as teaching aids. Publications: Editor and author of numerous medical and scientific articles, chapters and books; Senior author, The Scientific Journal: Editorial Policies and Practices, 1976; Co-author, Medicine: Preserving the Passion, 1987; Co-author, Medicine: Preserving the Passion in the 21st Century, 2004. Honours include: Phi Beta Kappa; Golden Key National Honor Society; Distinguished Service Award, American Medical Writers Society, 1970; Inaugural John P McGovern Award, Medical Library Association, 1983; Member, Texas Hall of Fame; Life Honorary Member, Medical Library Association, 1989. Memberships include: Founding Board of Directors, Friends of the National Library of Medicine; Fellow, American College of Medical Informatics; Fellow, Royal Society for the Encouragement of Arts, Manufactures and Commerce, UK; Medical Library Association; National Association of Science Writers; Foundation for Advanced Education in the Sciences; Plain English Forum. Address: Baylor College of Medicine, 1 Baylor Plaza, Houston TX 77030 3411, USA.

**DEBAKEY Michael Ellis,** b. 7 September 1908, Lake Charles, Louisiana, USA. Cardiovascular Surgeon. m. Katrin Fehlhaber, 4 sons, 1 daughter. Education: BS, 1930, MD, 1932, MS, 1935, Tulane University. Appointments: Chairman of Surgery, Baylor College of Medicine, 1948-93; Clinical Professor of Surgery, University of Texas Dental Branch, 1952-; President, The DeBakey Medical Foundation, Houston, 1961-; Distinguished Service Professor, Baylor College of Medicine, 1968-; Vice President for Medical Affairs and CEO, Baylor College of Medicine, 1968-69; President Baylor College of Medicine, 1969-79; Distinguished Professor of Surgery, Texas A&M University, 1972-; Chancellor, Baylor College of Medicine, 1978-96; Olga Keith Wiess Professor of Surgery, Baylor College of Medicine, 1981-; Director, The DeBakey Heart Center, Houston, 1985-; Chancellor Emeritus, Baylor College of Medicine, 1996-. Publications: Over 1,600 in books and professional journals. Honours include: More than 50 honorary degrees; US Army Legion of Merit, 1945; American Medical Association Distinguished Service Medal, 1959; Albert Lasker Award for Clinical Research, 1963; Presidential Medal of Freedom with Distinction, presented by Lyndon B Johnson, 1969; Eleanor Roosevelt Humanities Award, 1969; USSR Academy of Sciences 50th Anniversary Jubilee Medal, 1973; National Medal of Science, awarded by President Ronald Reagan, 1987; Academy of Athens induction, 1992; Thomas Jefferson Award, American Institute of Architects, 1993; Children Uniting Nations, Global Peace and Tolerance Lifetime Achievement Award for Science and Technology, 1999; John P McGovern Compleat Physician Award, 1999; Library of Congress Bicentennial Living Legend Award, 2000; Methodist DeBakey Heart Center, 2001; NASA Invention of the Year Award, 2001; Foundation for Biomedical Research Michael E DeBakey Journalism Award, 2002; Lindbergh-Carrell Prize, 2002; Golden Hippocrates International Prize for Excellency in Medicine, Laureate of the Year, 2003; Russian Academy of Sciences, Lomonosov Gold Medal, 2004; American Heart Association National Chapter, Lifetime Achievement Award, 2004; Michael E Debakey Veterans Affairs Medical Center, 2004. Memberships include: World Medical Association; American Medical Association; International Cardiovascular Society; American College of Surgeons; American Surgical Association; Thoracic Surgery Directors Association; Texas Heart Association; Texas Academy of Science; Western Surgical Association. Address: Baylor College of Medicine, One Baylor Plaza, Houston, TX 77030, USA.

**DEBAKEY Selma,** b. Lake Charles, Louisiana, USA. Professor of Scientific Communication. Education: BA, Languages, Newcomb College; Postgraduate studies, French and Philosophy, Tulane University. Appointments: Director, Department of Medical Communications, Ochsner Clinic and Alton Ochsner Medical Foundation, New Orleans, 1942-68; Medical Writer and Editor; Consultant Editor; Internationally renowned course developer. Main professional interests: Internationally recognised authority in the field of medical writing and editing, most especially in the use of humour in the form of cartoons to depict faulty reasoning and language use; Ethics; Literacy; Publishing. Publications: A huge body of work, as writer, editor, consultant, course developer; Co-author, Current Concepts in Breast Cancer, 1967; Numerous articles and papers contributed to specialist peer-reviewed journals; Over 1000 articles as Editor; Judge for several prestigious medical

writing awards, including Modern Medical Monographs Awards, AORN DuPuy Writer's Awards. Honours: Named in Texas Hall of Fame; Listed in numerous international and specialist biographical directories, including: Dictionary of International Biography; Outstanding People of the 21st Century; 2000 Outstanding Intellectuals of the 21st Century; 2000 Outstanding Scientists of the 21st Century; 2000 Outstanding Scholars of the 21st Century; 2000 Outstanding Women of the 20th Century; Who's Who in America; Who's Who in the World; Profiled in numerous newspapers and magazines. Memberships: American Association for the Advancement of Science; American Medical Writers' Association; Association of Teachers of Technical Writing; Council of Biology Editors; Society for Health and Human Values; Society for Technical Communication. Address: Baylor College of Medicine, 1 Baylor Plaza, Houston, TX 77030 3411, USA.

**DEECKE Lüder,** b. 22 June 1938, Lohe, Holstein, Germany. University Professor; Neurologist. m. Gertraud Flinspach, 3 sons. Education: MD, University of Freiburg, Germany, 1965; Examination, Educational Council for Foreign Medical Graduates, Frankfurt, 1966; Research Fellow, Oto-Neurophysiology Laboratory, University of Toronto, Canada, 1970-71; Professorial Thesis (Venia legendi), Neurology and Neurophysiology, University of Ulm, 1973. Appointments: Assistant Professor, 1973, Associate Professor, 1978, University of Ulm Germany; Full Professor, Professor Ordinarius, University of Vienna, Austria, 1985-; Head of Department of Clinical Neurology, University of Vienna (now Medical University of Vienna); Head, Ludwig-Boltzman Institute for Functional Brain Topography. Publications: 550 publications in the fields of neurology and neurophysiology include: Brain potentials prior to voluntary movement, co-discoverer of the readiness potential (co-author, H H Kornhuber, MD thesis), 1965; Voluntary finger movement in man: Cerebral potentials and theory (professorial thesis), 1976. Honours: Stipend of the Studentstiftung des Deutschen Volkes, 1964-65; Scientific Award, The City of Ulm, 1970; Invitation as Faculty Member of the IBRO-UNESCO Workshop on Motor Function at Shiraz, Iran, 1974; Distinguished Visiting Professor, Simon Fraser University, Vancouver, 1982; Dr Herbert Reisner Award, 1989; Citation Classic, Current Contents, Institute for Scientific Information (Kornhuber & Deecke, Pflügers Arch. 284:1-17, 1965), 1990; Distinguished Visiting Professor, University of California, Irvine, 1991; Hoechst Award, 1997; Hans Berger Award of the German Society of Clinical Neurophysiology, 2000; Dr Honoris causa Simon Fraser University, Vancouver, 2003. Memberships: 55 international and national scientific societies. Address: Department of Clinical Neurology, Medical University of Vienna, Währinger Gürtel 18-20, A-1090 Vienna, Austria. E-mail: luederdeecke@meduniwien.ac.at Website: wwww.meduniwien.ac.at/neurologie

**DEEGALLE Mahinda,** b. 31 October 1961, Badulla, Sri Lanka. Academic; University Teacher. Education: BA (Hons) University of Peradeniya, 1985; MTS, Harvard University, 1989; PhD, University of Chicago, 1995. Appointments: Research Collaborator, Kyoto University, 1995-96; Research Fellow, Japan Society for the Promotion of Science, 1997-99; Research Fellow, International College for Advanced Buddhist Studies, 1999; Numata Visiting Professor, McGill University, 1999-2000; Instructor, Cornell University, 2000; Lecturer in the Study of Religions, Bath Spa University College, 2000-. Publications: Pali Buddhism (co-editor), 1996; From Buddhology to Buddhist Theology, 2000; Is Violence Justified? Current Dialogue, 2002; Preacher as a Poet, 2003; Buddhist Prayer, 2003; Austerity as a Virtue, 2003; Sri Lankan Theravada Buddhism in London, 2004; Buddhism, Conflict and Violence in Modern Sri Lanka (editor),

2005. Honours: Honorary Title "Vimalakirti Sri; Fulbright Award, 1987-89; Valedictorian, Harvard University Divinity School, 1989; Bukkyo Dendo Kyokai Fellowship, 1995-96. Memberships: American Academy of Religion; International Association of Buddhist Studies; British Association for the Study of Religion; United Kingdom Association for Buddhist Studies; PTS. Address: Study of Religions, School of Historical and Cultural Studies, Bath Spa University College, Newton Park, Bath BA2 9BN, England. E-mail: m.deegalle@bathspa.ac.uk

**DEEKEN Alfons Theodor,** b. 3 August 1932, Emstek, Niedersachsen, Germany. Philosopher; Educator; Writer. Education: MA, Berchmanskolleg, Munich, Germany, 1958; MA, Sophia University, Tokyo, 1966; PhD, Fordham University, New York, 1973. Appointments: Assistant Professor to Professor, 1973-82, Professor of Philosophy, 1982-2003, Professor Emeritus, 2003-, Sophia University, Tokyo, Japan. Publications: Growing Old and How to Cope With It, 1972; Process and Permanence in Ethics: Max Scheler's Moral Philosophy, 1974; Confronting Death, 1996; Kirisutokyoo to Watakushi (Christianity), 1995; Humor wa Oi to Shi no Myooyaku (Humour), 1995; Death Education, 2001; Hikari no dialogue (Words of the Bible), 2002; Yoku Iki, Yoku Warai, Yoki Shi to Deau (Good living, good humour, good death), 2003. Honours: Best Ethics Book of 1974, Catholic Press Association, America, 1975; Kikuchi Kan Literary Award, Literary Association of Japan, 1991; Cross of the Order of Merit of the German Federal Republic, President of Germany, 1998; Cultural Award, City of Tokyo, 1999. Memberships: Japanese Society of Clinical Thanatology, President, 2001-; Japanese Association of Death Education and Grief Counselling, President 1974-2003; Japanese Association for Clinical Research on Death and Dying; International Work Group on Death, Dying and Bereavement. Sophia University, S J House, Kioicho 7-1, Chiyoda-ku, 102-8571 Tokyo, Japan.

**DEELEY Michael,** b. 6 August 1932, London, England. Film Producer. m. Ruth Spencer, 1 son, 2 daughters. Education: Stowe School, England. Appointments: 2nd Lieutenant, British Army, Malaya, 1951-52; Deputy Chairman, British Screen Advisory Council; Producer of more than 30 films including: Blade Runner; The Deer Hunter; The Italian Job; The Man Who Fell To Earth; Produce of many TV films and series. Honours: Oscar, Best Picture for The Deer Hunter, 1979; Humanitas Award, NAACP. Memberships: Academy of Motion Picture Arts & Sciences; BECTU; Garrick Club, London. Address: 1010 Fairway Road, Santa Barbara, CA 93108, USA.

**DEERING Anne-Lise,** b. Norway. Clay Artist; Medallic Sculptor; Former Potter. Education: Science Degree, Norway, 1954; Oil Painting, Southern Illinois University, Carbondale, Illinois, 1958; Ceramics, Foothill College, Los Altos, California, 1975; BA, Art, Penn State University, University Park, Pennsylvania, 1977; Computer Graphic Design and Medallic Art, Penn State University, 1990-91; Residential Real Estate Appraisal Courses, Marketing Strategy, Sales and Promotion Courses, PA Realtors Institute, 1994-96. Career: Middle Eastern Dance Teacher, 1975-80; Self-employed Clay Artist and Potter, 1977-98; Member, 1977-2000, Juried Member, 1981-2000, Board of Directors, 1984-97, Pennsylvania Guild of Craftsmen (PGC); Participant in PGC Craft Fairs for 10 years; Artist Member, Art Alliance of Central Pennsylvania, 1978-99; Participant in Art Alliance Gallery Shop, 1989-99; Licensed Real Estate Sales Person, 1991-99; Exhibits include: American Medallic Sculpture Association juried exhibit, Newark Museum, New Jersey, 1990; Invitational, Mountain Top Gallery, Cresson, Pennsylvania, 1998; The Pen and Brush Gallery juried exhibit, New York City, 1998, 1999, 2000, 2001; American Numismatic

Association, Colorado Springs, 2001; Penn State University, 2002, Wroclav, Poland, 2002; AMSA juried exhibit, Ornamental Metal Museum, Memphis, Tennessee, 2003; Co-ordinator and chair of AMSA members juried exhibit, Nordic Heritage Museum, Seattle, Washington, 2004; In charge of AMSA medals displays at numerous libraries throughout the greater Seattle area, 2004; Participated in AMSA members exhibit, Forest Lawn Museum, Glendale, California, 2005; Medal in private collections and the permanent collection of the Museum of Medallic Art, Wroclav, Poland. Memberships: Pennsylvania Guild of Craftsmen and Central Pennsylvania Chapter, 1977-2000; Member of American Medallic Sculpture Association (AMSA), 1990-, Newsletter Editor, 2000-, Secretary, 2001-; Charter Member, National Museum of Women in the Arts, 1998-; Board of Directors, Washington Potters Association, 2000-. Address: 24229 92nd Ave W, Edmonds, WA 98020, USA.

**DEGANI Avi,** b. 14 May 1938, Tel-Aviv, Israel. University Professor. m. Rina, 3 sons, 1 daughter. Education: BSc, Hebrew University of Jerusalem, 1961; MA, 1970, PhD, 1971, University of Minnesota, USA. Appointments: Professor, Tel-Aviv University, 1972-; Creator of the term and field of knowledge, Geocartography, 1972; Founder, Chief Executive Officer, Geocartography Knowledge Group, 1987-. Publications: Numerous articles in national and international professional journals. Memberships: Israel national representative, CODATA; ESOMAR; International Association of Financial Crimes Investigators; FIMAT. Address: Geocartography, Bldg. 8 Kehilat Venezia St., Tel Aviv, Israel 69400. E-mail: avidegani@geocartography.com

**DEGARMO Mark B,** b. 2 November 1955, Connecticut, USA. Dancer; Choreographer; Arts Educator. Education: BFA, Dance, Juilliard School for the Performing Arts, 1982; Admittance to the PhD program, School of Interdisciplinary Arts and Science, The Union Institute and University, 2001; PhD Candidate, 2003. Appointments: Founder, Artistic Director, Choreographer, Mark DeGarmo and Dancers, Dynamic Forms Inc, 1982-; Teaching Artist in Aesthetic Education and Dance, Lincoln Center Institute for the Arts in Education, 1986-2000. Publications: Windows on the Work, 6 volumes; 76 dances produced and performed. Honours: Fulbright Senior Scholar Fellowship to Peru, 1998-99; American Cultural Specialist Award to Ecuador, 2000; Honorary Committee of the Martha Hill Award for Leadership in Dance, 2001. Memberships: Founding Board Member, A Room of Her Own Foundation, New Mexico; Member, Fulbright Association, Washington; Advisory Board Member, Clemente Soto Velez Cultural and Educational Center, New York. Address: 107 Suffolk Street, Suite 310, New York City, NY 10002, USA. Email: markdegarmodance@aol.com

**DEGENHARD Andreas,** b. 23 May 1970, Osnabrück, Germany. Physicist. Education: Diploma in Theoretical Physics, 1995; PhD summa cum laude, Mathematical Physics, 1999. Appointments: Postdoctoral, Department of Theoretical Physics, University of Bielefeld, 1999; Postdoctoral Studies, Institute of Cancer Research, in collaboration with King's College, 1999-2002; Lecturer, University of Bielefeld, 2002-. Publications: Articles in professional journals. Honours: Exceptional grade assessment, Institute of Cancer Research, London; Listed in national and international biographical dictionaries. Memberships: German Physical Society; Patents in the research field. Address: Faculty of Physics, University of Bielefeld, Universitätsstrasse 25, D-33615 Bielefeld, Germany. E-mail: adegenha@physik.uni-bielefeld.de Website: www.degenhard.org

**DEGERFELT Kent,** b. 28 March 1946, Gothenburg, Sweden. Ambassador. m. Brunella. Education includes: Interpreter in Russian, Military Interpreters' School, Uppsala, Sweden, 1969-70; BA, History of Economics, Political Sciences, International Development Co-operation, University of Gothenburg, Sweden, 1968-72; Master of Law, University of Lund, Sweden, 1968-73; Studies at Ecole National d'Administration, Paris, 1983-84. Appointments include: Attaché, Ministry for Foreign Affairs, Stockholm, 1973-74; Attaché, Permanent Mission of Sweden to the UN, Geneva, 1975; Second Secretary, Embassy of Sweden, Madrid, 1975-78; Deputy Head of Mission, Embassy of Sweden, Jakarta, Indonesia, 1978-80; First Secretary, Ministry for Foreign Affairs, Stockholm, 1981-82; Deputy Head of Mission, Embassy of Sweden in Guatemala City and Chargé d'Affairs in El Salvador, 1982-83; First Secretary, Embassy of Sweden, Paris, 1984-88; Deputy Head of Division/Head of Section, Ministry for Foreign Affairs, Stockholm, 1988-90; Counsellor, Embassy of Sweden, Nairobi, Kenya, 1991; Deputy Head of Mission, Embassy of Sweden, Rabat, Morocco, 1991-95; Counsellor, 1995-96; Director, 1996, Ministry for Foreign Affairs, Stockholm; Ambassador, Head of Delegation, European Commission, Managua, Nicaragua, 1996-99; Adviser ad personam, Directorate General for External Relations, European Commission, Brussels, 2000-2002; Ambassador, Head of Delegation, European Commission, Khartoum, Sudan, 2002-. Honours: Knight of Isabela la Católica; Knight of Finland's Lion; Officier de L'Ordre du Mérite; Grand Cross of José Marcoleta. Address: Delegation Sudan, Service Valise Diplomatique, European Commission, B-1049 Brussels, Belgium. E-mail: kent.degerfelt@cec.eu.int

**DEHDASHTI Amir R,** b. 21 March 1974, Tehran, Iran. Neurosurgeon. Education: MD, Tehran University of Medical Sciences (Shahid Beheshti); Specialisation in Neurosurgery, Department of Neurosurgery, Geneva University Hospitals; Cerebrovascular Fellowship, Centre Hospitalier Universitaire Vaudois, Lausanne, Switzerland. Appointments: Chef du Clinique, Department of Neurosurgery, Centre Hospitalier Universitaire Vaudois, Lausanne, Switzerland. Publications: Articles in medical journals and conference papers as first author include: Preoperative silk suture embolization of cerebral and dural arteriovenous malformations, 2001; Shunt-dependent hydrocephalus after rupture of intracranial aneurysms: a prospective study of the influence of treatment modality, 2004; The Value of Multislice CT Angiography in Postoperative Control of Clipped Aneurysms, 2005. Honour: Best Score, Top Mark, European Association of Neurological Surgeons Examination. Address: Department of Neurosurgery, 46 Bugnon, Centre Hospitalier Universitaire Vaudois, 1011 Lausanne, Switzerland. E-mail: amir.dehdashti@hospvd.ch

**DEIGHTON Len,** b. 18 February 1929, London, England. Writer. m. Publications: The Ipcress File, 1962; Horse Under Water, 1963; Funeral in Berlin, 1964; Ou Est Le Garlic/Basic French Cooking, 1965, 1979; Action Cook Book, 1965; Cookstrip Cook Book, 1966; Billion Dollar Brain, 1966; An Expensive Place to Die, 1967; Len Leighton's London Dossier, 1967; The Assassination of President Kennedy, co-author, 1967; Only When I Larf, 1968; Bomber, 1970; Declarations of War, 1971; Close-up, 1972; Spy Story, 1974; Eleven Declarations of War, 1975; Yesterday's Spy, 1975; Twinkle, Twinkle, Little Spy, 1976; Catch a Falling Spy, 1976; Fighter, 1977; SS-GB, 1978; Airshipwreck, co-author, 1978; Blitzkreig, 1979; Battle of Britain, co-author, 1980, 1990; XPD, 1981; Goodbye Mickey Mouse, 1982; Berlin Game, 1983; Mexico Set, 1984; London Match, 1985; Game, Set and Match, 13 part TV series; Winter: A Berlin Family 1899-1945, 1987; Spy Hook, 1988; Spy line, 1989; Spy Sinker, 1990; Basic French Cookery Course, 1990;

ABC of French Food, 1989; Mamista, 1991; City of Gold, 1992; Violent Ward, 1993; Blood, Tears and Folly, 1993; Faith, 1994; Hope, 1995; Charity, 1996. Address: c/o Jonathan Clowes Ltd, 10 Iron Bridge House, Bridge House, Bridge Approach, London NW1 8BD, England.

**DEJONCKERE Philippe Henri,** b. 11 July 1949, Ronse, Belgium. Medical Doctor; University Professor. m. Suzanne Thiry, 2 daughters. Education: Final Diploma Conservatory, 1971; MD, 1973; MSc, Occupational Medicine, 1975; Medical Specialist, ENT, 1976; MSc, Statistics, 1978; PhD, 1981; MSc, Legal Medicine, 1987. Appointments: Lecturer, Faculty of Medicine, University of Louvain, Belgium, 1983; Visiting Professor, University of Lille, France, 1985; Professor and Chairman, Institute of Phoniatrics, University of Utrecht, Netherlands, 1991; Visiting Professor, University of Kurume, Japan, 1996; Guest Professor, University of Leuven, Belgium, 2001. Publications: 7 books; About 300 scientific articles. Honours: Paul Guns Prize, phoniatrics, 1975; Van Lawrence Award, British Voice Association, 1997; Officer, Crown Order, Belgium; Knight Order of King Leopold, Belgium. Memberships: President, Collegium Medicorum Theatri, 1999; President, European Laryngological Research Group; Chairman, Committee on Phoniatrics; European Laryngological Society; President, Dutch Society of Voice, Speech and Language Society. Member of Honour, Dutch Society of Lopop. and Phoniatrics, 2002; Member of several societies of ENT and Phoniatrics. Address: Rue Margot 3, B-1435, Corbais, Belgium.

**DEKHTYAR Yuri,** b. 19 June 1947, Riga, Latvia. Head of Institute; Professor. m. Galina, 12 August 1978, 2 daughters. Education: PhD, 1982, DSc, 1992, Riga Technical University. Appointments: Designer, Design Company, Riga, 1971-73; Lecturer, Docent, Professor, Head of Institute, Riga Technical University, 1976-. Publications: About 300 in professional journals. Honour: Latvian State Prize, 1989. Membership: Material Research Society; Latvian Medical Engineering and Physics Society; European Federation of Organisations for Medical Physics; Corresponding Member, Latvian Academy of Sciences. Address: Riga Technical University, 1 Kalku Street, LV-1658 Riga, Latvia.

**DEL GIACCO Sergio G,** b. 2 January 1936, Pavia, Italy. University Professor of Medicine. m. Silvana Grossi, 1 son, 1 daughter. Education: Medical Degree, Milan University, 1959; Assistant Professor, 1965; Associate Professor, 1971; Full Professor of Clinical Immunology, 1980; Full Professor of Internal Medicine, 1983. Appointments: Resident, Milan University, 1959-67; Assistant Professor, Cagliari University, 1967-71; Chief of Medical Division, University Hospital, Cagliari, 1971-98; Head of Medical Department, University Hospital, Cagliari, 1999-; Head of Postgraduate School of Allergology and Clinical Immunology, Cagliari University, 1987-, 2003; Head, Postgraduate School of Internal Medicine, 2003-. Publications: More than 350 articles on autoimmune diseases, allergy, AIDS, in scientific journals of medicine, allergology and clinical immunology; Congress proceedings; Books. Honours: Commendator of Italian Republic; President, Italian Society of Allergology and Clinical Immunology, SIAIC, 1994-98; Past-President, SIAIC, 1998-2001; President of UEMS Section of Allergology and Clinical Immunology, 2001-. Memberships: British Society for Immunology; American Association for Asthma, Allergy and Immunology; European Academy of Allergology and Clinical Immunology; New York Academy of Sciences; American Association for Advanced Sciences; Italian Society for Allergology and Clinical Immunology; Italian Society of Internal Medicine. E-mail: delgiacs@pacs.unica.it

**DELACOTE Jacques,** b. France. Maestro. m. Maria-Lucia Alvares-Machado. Education: Paris Conservatory; Vienna Academy of Music, with Professor Hans Swarowsky. Career: Assistant to Leonard Bernstein and Darius Milhaud; Performed with New York Philharmonic Orchestra, 1972; Guest conductor: Cleveland Orchestra; San Francisco Symphony Orchestra; London Symphony; London Philharmonic and Royal Philharmonic orchestras; English Chamber Orchestra; Montreal and Vienna Symphony orchestras; Orchestre de Paris and Orchestre National de France; Royal Orchestra of Belgium; Danish Royal Orchestra; Scottish National and Scottish Chamber orchestras; Israel Philharmonic Orchestra; Works with various radio orchestras including: BBC London; RIAS Berlin; SDR Stuttgart; SWF Baden-Baden; WDR Köln; BR München; MDR Leipzig; Opera conductor: State Opera houses of Vienna, Munich and Hamburg; Deutsche Oper Berlin; Royal Opera House Covent Garden, London; Welsh National Opera; Scottish Opera; English National Opera; Opéra de Paris; opera houses of Brussels, Zürich, Copenhagen, Chicago, Pittsburgh, Montreal, Toronto, Venice, Colón Buenos Aires, and the Gran Teatre del Liceu in Barceona, among others; Participated in following festivals: Summer Concerts Vienna, Wexford, Inverness, Flandres, Blossom Cleveland, Pablo Casals, Macerata, Mérida, Peralada, Orange, Klangbogen Vienna, Dresden, and Summer Festival at Wiesbaden. Publications: Recordings include: La Traviata; Turandot; Carmen, live from the Royal Opera House, Covent Garden, London; Roméo et Juliet; Hérodiade; Samson et Dalilia, live from the Liceu at Barcelona; Carmen, live from Earls Court, London; Otello, live from the Royal Opera House, Albert Hall, London; José Carreras and Friends, live from the Royal Theatre, Drury Lane, London; French Opera Arias, with José Carreras; Operatic Arias with Samuel Ramey; The Royal Philharmonic Collection (Bizet). Honours: First Prize, Gold Medal, Dimitri-Mitropoulos Competition, New York, 1971. Address: c/o Agency Dr Germinal Hilbert, Maximilianstr 22, 80539, Munich, Germany.

**DELGADO Aldo Rodriguez,** b. 8 July 1955, Havana, Cuba. Guitarist. m. Victoria Diaz de Villegas Rozhkova, 1 son, 2 daughters. Education: National School of Arts, 1968-73; Studies under Professors Issac Nicola and Martha Cuervo, Instituto Superior de Arte de la Habana, 1976-81; Postgraduate studies in counterpoint, harmony, history of music, musical analysis, guitar. Career: Guitar Professor, Basic Music School of Holguin, 1973-76; Guitar Professor, Escuela Nacional de Arte, La Habana, Cuba, 1976-78; Guitar Professor, Escuela de Bellas Artes, Cartagena, Colombia, 1997; Teacher at numerous master classes; Participant in International Music Festivals: Varna, Bulgaria, Morelia, Mexico, Moscow, Russia, Mendoza, Argentina, Rostock, Germany, Ankara, Turkey; International Guitar Festivals: Volos, Greece, Esztergom, Hungary, Havana, Cuba, Tychi, Poland, Istanbul, Turkey, Laredo, Spain, Gotze-Delchev, Bulgaria; Performances with orchestras including: National Symphony Orchestra de Cuba and Matanzas, Cuba; Symphony and Philharmonic Orchestra of Bogota, Colombia; Radio and Television Symphonic Orchestra, Bulgaria; Symphonic Orchestra of Matanzas, Camaguey y Santiago de Cuba; Philharmonic Orchestra of Istanbul, Turkey; Philharmonic Orchestra of Wrocklaw, Poland; Porto Symphony Orchestra, Portugal. Publications: Una Vida a Contramano (book about the life of Maria Luisa Anido); Isaac Nicola: Maestro de Maestros (book about the teacher's life); Metodo de Guitarra (study manual). Compositions include: Cancion y Fuga en Son (2 guitars); La Leyenda del Juglar; Cancion y Danza; Retrato de Mujer; Aire Brasilero. Recordings: Latin American Concert; Album "Rodrigo-Brouwer; Masterly Concert (live); Album "Bach-Vivaldi". Honours include: 1st prize, International Guitar Contest, Esztergom, Hungary, 1979; 3rd Prize, International

Guitar Contest, Alirio Diaz, Caracas, Venezuela, 1979; 1st Prize, Chamber Music Contest, Higher Institute of Arts of Havana, 1981; 3rd Prize, International Guitar Contest of Havana, Cuba, 1982; Laureate, International Guitar Contest, Francisco Tarrega Benicasim, Spain, 1982; 3rd and Special Prize given by La banca de San Paolo di Torino, Italy, Alessandria, 1983; Diploma of Honour, Contest "Maria Canals", Barcelona, Spain, 1985; Egrem Prize for the Most Sold Classical Music Disc, 1987; Egrem Prize for the Greatest Cultural Contribution Disc, 1991. Address: Calle 13, No 108, Apartamento 74 e/ L y M Vedado, La Habana, Cuba. E-mail: aldor@cubarte.cult.cu

**DELILLO Don,** b. 20 November 1936, New York, New York, USA. Author. Education: BA in Communication Arts, Fordham University, 1958. Publications: Americana, 1971; End Zone, 1972; Great Jones Street, 1973; Ratner's Star, 1976; Players, 1977; Running Dog, 1978; Amazons, 1980; The Names, 1982; White Noise, 1985; The Day Room, 1987; Libra, 1988; Mao II, 1991; Underworld, 1997; Valparaiso, 1999; The Body Artist, 2001. Contributions to: Periodicals. Honours: National Book Award, 1985; Irish Times-Aer Lingus International Fiction Prize, 1989; PEN/Faulkner Award, 1992; Jerusalem Prize, 1999; Howells Medal, 2000. Literary Agent: Wallace Literary Agents Inc. Address: c/o Wallace & Sheil, 177 East 70th Street, New York, NY 10021, USA.

**DELLA JUSTINA Masimo,** b. 10 May 1962, Presidente Getulio, Santa Catarina State, Brazil. University Lecturer. Education: BA, Philosophy, Pontifical Catholic University of Parana, 1985; BSc, Economics, 1995, MSc, Economics, 1996, London School of Economics; PhD Production Engineering, Federal University of Santa Catarina, 2004. Appointments: Co-ordinator of development project in Kitwe, Zambia, 1988-91; Lecturer in Macroeconomic Principles, 1997-, Co-ordinator of Social Projects, 2002-, PUCPR. Publications: Do Economists Have a Heart? (article), 1999; Criteria for the Ideal Economic Growth in Brazil (article), 2001. Honours: Listed in Who's Who publications and biographical dictionaries. Membership: LSE's Alumni. Address: Economics Department, PUCPR, 1155 Imaculada Conceicao, Curitiba, PR, Brazil. E-mail: masimo.justina@pucpr.br

**DELPY Julie,** b. 8 November 1969, France. Film Actress. Education: New York University Film School. Appointments: Actress, films include: Detective, 1985; Mauvais Sang, 1986; La Passion Béatrice, 1987; L'Autre Nuit, 1988; La Noche Oscura, 1989; Europa Europa, 1991; Voyager, 1991; Warszawa, 1922; Young and Younger, 1993; The Three Musketeers, 1993; When Pigs Fly, 1993; The Myth of the White Wolf, 1994; Killing Zoe, 1994; Mesmer, 1994; Trois Couleurs Blanc, 1994; Trois Couleurs Rouge, 1994; Before Sunrise, 1995; An American Werewolf in Paris, 1997; The Treat; LA without a Map; Blah, Blah, Blah (director); The Passion of Ayn Rand, 1999; TV: ER. Address: c/o William Morris Agency, 151 El Camino Drive, Beverley Hills, CA 90212, USA.

**DEN Walter,** b. 23 March 1971, Summit, New Jersey, USA. Professor. m. Yi-Hsin Yu, 1 daughter. Education: BS, Mechanical Engineering, University of California, Santa Barbara, 1993; MS, Civil and Environmental Engineering, 1995, PhD, Environmental Engineering, 2000, University of Southern California. Appointments: Research Assistant, University of Southern California, 1996-98; Associate Researcher, National Nano Device Laboratories, 2001-2002; Assistant Professor, Associate Professor, Department of Environmental Science and Engineering, Tunghai University, Taiwan, 2002-. Publications: Over 15 peer-reviewed journal articles; Over 25 conference, workshop and seminar publications. Memberships: American

Chemical Society; Institute of Environmental Science and Technology; Chinese Aerosol Association. Address: Taichung-Kan Road, Section 3, No 181, PO Box 818, Taichung City 407, Taiwan, Republic of China. E-mail: w den@mail.thu.edu.tw

**DENCH Dame Judith (Judi),** b. 9 December 1934, York, Yorkshire, England. Actress. m. Michael Williams, 1971, deceased, 1 daughter. Education: Central School of Speech Training and Dramatic Art. Career: Appeared Old Vic, leading roles, 1957-61; Royal Shakespeare Company, 1961-62; Leading roles include: Anya (The Cherry Tree); Titania (A Midsummer Dream); Isabella (Measure for Measure); West African Tour with Nottingham Playhouse, 1963; Subsequent roles include: Irina (The Three Sisters, Oxford Playhouse, 1964); Title role, St Joan and Barbara (Nottingham Playhouse, 1965); Lika (The Promise, 1967); Sally Bowles (Cabaret, 1968); Numerous appearances in lead roles and tours to Japan, 1970, 1972, and Australia, 1970 as Associate Member Royal Shakespeare Company, 1969-, these include: Viola (Twelfth Night); Beatrice (Much Ado About Nothing); Duchess (Duchess of Malfi); Other Performances include: Miss Trant (The Good Companions, 1974); Nurse (Too Good to Be True, 1975, 1976); Cymbeline, 1979; Lady Bracknell (The Importance of Being Ernest, 1982); Pack of Lies, 1983; Waste, 1985; Antony and Cleopatra, 1987; Hamlet, 1989; The Seagull (Royal National Theatre, 1994); Plays Directed: Much Ado About Nothing, 1988; Look Back in Anger, 1989; The Boys from Syracuse, 1991; Absolute Hell (Royal National Theatre, 1995); A Little Night Music, 1995; Amy's View, 1997; Filumena, 1998. Films include: A Study in Terror, 1965; Four in the Morning, 1966; A Midsummer Night's Dream (RSC, 1968); Dead Cert, Wetherby, 1985; A Room with a View, 1986; 84 Charing Cross Road, 1987; Henry V, 1989; Goldeneye, 1995; Tomorrow Never Dies, 1996; Mrs Brown, 1997, Shakespeare in Love, 1998; Tea with Mussolini, 1998; The World is Not Enough, 1999; Chocolat, 2000; Iris, 2001; The Shipping News, 2001; The Importance of Being Earnest, 2002; Die Another Day, 2002; Ladies in Lavender, 2004; The Chronicles of Riddick, 2004. TV includes: Major Barbara; Talking to a Stranger; The Funambulists; Age of Kings; Jackanory; Neighbours; Marching Song; On Approval; Langrishe Go Down; Love in a Cold Climate; A Fine Romance; Going Gently; Saigon-Year of the Cat, 1982; Ghosts, 1986; Behaving Badly, 1989; Absolute Hell; Can You Hear Me Thinking?; As Time Goes By; Last of the Blonde Bombshells. Publications: Judi Dench: A Great Deal of Laughter (biography); Judi Dench - With a Crack in Her Voice (biography), 1998. Honours include: Numerous Honorary degrees and Honorary Fellowship (Royal Holloway College); Best Actress: Variety London Critic's (Lika, The Promise, 1967); Guild of Directors (Talking to a Stranger, 1967); Society West End Theatre (Lady MacBeth, 1977); New Standard Drama Awards: Juno and the Paycock, 1980; Lady Bracknell (The Importance of Being Ernest, 1983); Deborah (A Kind of Alaska, 1983); Variety Club Award for Best Actress, Filumena, 1998; Academy Award, Best Supporting Actress (Shakespeare in Love), 1999; BAFTA Award for Best Actress (Last of the Blonde Bombshells); BAFTA Award for Best Actress (Iris), 2002; BAFTA Tribute for Lifetime Achievement, 2002; Olivier Award for Lifetime Achievement, Society of London Theatres, 2004; The William Shakespeare Award, The Shakespeare Theatre in Washington, 2004; Honorary Doctorate, Mary Baldwin College, Staunton, Virginia, 2004; Honorary Doctorate, The Juilliard Academy, New York, 2004. Address: c/o Julian Belfrage Associates, 46 Albermarle Street, London, W1X 4PP, England.

**DENECKE Heiko,** b. 5 February 1942, Freiburg, Germany. Surgery. m. Siegrun, 2 sons. Education: Medical Degree, University of Cologne, 1969; Surgical Training, 1973-79,

Habilitation, 1979, Professor of Surgery, 1979, University of Munich; Vascular Surgeon, 1986; Visceral Surgeon, 1996. Appointments: Professor of Surgery, University of Würzburg; Affiliated, Academic Hospital, Schweinfurt, Head of Surgical Department I. Publications: Renovaskulärer Hochdruck - Spätprognose nach Operation, 1980; Kolorektale Anastomosen, 1984, Leberchirurgie, 1996; Spezielle Chirurgische Therapie, 1996; What is New in Stoma-Surgery (German), 2004. Honours: British Council, 1972; Bayer. Chir. Verein., 1974; German Surgical Society, 1982. Memberships: German Surgical Society; German Society for Vascular Surgery; German Thoracic Society. Address: Leopoldina Krankenhaus, Gustav-Adolf-Str 8, 97422 Schweinfurt, Germany. E-mail: chdenecke1@leopoldina.de

**DENEUVE Catherine (Catherine Dorléac),** b. 22 October 1943, Paris, France. Actress. m. David Bailey (divorced), 1 son (by Roger Vadim), 1 daughter (by Marcello Mastroianni). Appointments: Film debut in: Les petitis chats, 1959; President, Director-General, Films de la Citrouille, 1971-79; Films include: Les portes claquent, 1960; L'homme à femmes, 1960; le Vice et la Vertu, 1962; Et Satan conduit le bal, 1962; Vacances portugaises, 1963; Les parapluies de Cherbourg (Palme D'Or, Cannes Festival), 1963; Les plus belles escroqueries du monde, 1963; La chasses à l'homme, 1964; Un monsieur de compagnie, 1964; La Costanza della Ragione, 1964; Repulsion, 1964; Le chant du monde, 1965; La Vie de chateua, 1965; Liebes Karusell, 1965; Les créatures, 1965; Les demoiselles de Rochfort, 1966; Belle de jour (Golden Lion, Venice Festival), 1967; Benjamin, 1967; Manon 70, 1967; Mayerling, 1968; La chamade, 1966; Folies d'avril, 1969; Belles d'un soir, 1969; La sirène du Mississippi, 1969; Tristana, 1970; Peau d'âne, 1971; Ça n'arrive qu'aux autres, 1971; Liza, 1971; Un flic, 1972; Touche pas la femme blanche, 1974; Hustle, 1976; March or Die, 1977; Coup de foudre, 1977; Ecoute voir...1978; L'argent des autres, 1978; A nous deux, 1979; Ils sont grandes ces petits, 1979; Le dernier métro, 1980; Je vous aime, 1980; Hotel des Americaines, 1981; L'africain, 1983; The Hunger, 1983; Le bon plaisir, 1984; Paroles et musiques, 1984; Le lieu du crime, 1986; La reine blanche, 1991; Indochine (César Award), 1992; Ma saison préférée, 1993; La Partie d'Echecs, 1994; The Convent, 1995; Les cent et une nuits, 1995; Les Voleurs, 1995; Genéalogie d'un crime, 1997; Le Vent de la nuit, 1999; Belle-Maman, 1999; Pola x, 1999; Time Regained, 1999; Dancer in the Dark, 2000; Je centre a la maison, 2001; Absolument fabuleux, 2001; 8 Femmes, 2002. Honours: Honorary Golden Bear, Berlin Film Festival, Arts de l'Alliance française de New York Trophy, 1998. Memberships include: Co-Chairman, UNESCO Campaign to protect World's Film Heritage, 1994-. Address: c/o Artmedia, 20 avenue Rapp, 75007 Paris, France.

**DENG Wei,** b. 13 April 1959, Beijing, China. Photographer; Visiting Professor; Researcher. Education: Graduate, Photography Department, Beijing Film Academy, 1982. Appointments: Took portrait photographs of eminent Chinese cultural figures, 1980-85; Took portrait photographs of eminent world figures, 1991-97. Publications: Great Names in Chinese Culture, first portrait photo album of eminent figures in China,, 1986; Deng Wei's Diary, 1999; A Photographic Record of Eminent World Figures, picture album, 2000; Deng Wei, A Look at the World, picture album, 2001; Top-Notch Photographic Works by Deng Wei, picture album, 2003; Selection of Photographic Works by Deng Wei, picture album, 2003; Eight Years, 3 volumes, 2004; Deng Wei & 50 Faces, picture album, 2004. Exhibitions: Photographic Exhibition of Deng Wei, held in China National Museum of Fine Arts and several large cities in China, 2001-2003; United Nations, New York, 2004; The Carter Presidential Center, Atlanta, 2005. Honours: Invited to lecture in Great Britain, 1990; Awarded

FRPS by Royal Photographic Society, 2004; Awarded Golden Statue Prize for China Photography, 2004. Address: Xinjiekou Houmao Hu Tong #5, Beijing 100035, China.

**DEPARDIEU Gerard,** b. 27 December 1948, Chateauroux, France. Actor; Vineyard Owner. m. Elisabeth Guignot, 1970, 1 son, 1 daughter. Education: Cours d'art dramatique de Charles Dullin and Ecole d'art dramatique de Jean Laurent Cochet. Appointments: President, Jury, 45th Cannes International Film Festival, 1992; Appeared in several short films. Creative Works: Feature Films include: Les gaspards, 1973; Les valseuses, 1973; Pas si mechant que ca, 1974; 1900, 1975; La derniere femme, 1975; Sept morts sur ordonnance, 1975; Maîtresse, 1975; Barocco, 1976; René la Canne, 1976; Les plages de l'Atlantique, 1976; Baxter vera Baxter, 1976; Dites-lui que je l'aime, 1977; Le camion, 1977; Reve de singe, 1977; Le sucre, 1978; Buffet froid, 1979; Loulou, 1979; Le dernier metro, 1980 (César award Best Actor, France); Le choix des armes, 1981; La femme d'à côté, 1981; La chèvre, 1981; Le retour de Martin Guerre, 1981 (Best Actor Award, American Society of Film Critics); Danton, 1981; Le grand frère, 1982 La lune dans le carniveau, 1983; Les compères, 1983; Fort Saganne, 1983; Tartuffe (also Director), 1984; Rive Droit, Rive Gauche, 1984; Police, 1984; One Woman or Two, 1985; Jean de Florette, 1985; Tenue de soirée, 1985; Rue de départ, 1986; Les fugitifs, 1986; Cyrano de Bergerac, 1989 (César award Best Actor); Uranus, 1990; Green Card (Golden Globe for Best Comedy Actor), 1991; Mon Pere Ce Heros, 1991; 1492: Conquest of Paradise, 1991; Tous les matins due monde, 1991; Germinal, 1992 A Pure Formality, 1993; Le Colonel Chabert, 1993; La Machine, Elisa, Les Cents et Une Nuits, Les Anges Gardiens, Le Garçu, all 1994; Bogus, 1995; Unhook the Stars, 1995; Secret Agent, 1995; Vatel, 1997; The Man in the Iron Mask, 1997; Les Portes du Ciel, 1999; Astérix et Obélix, 1999; Un pont entre deux rives (also Director), 1999; Vatel, 1999; Les Acteurs, 2000; Chicken Run, 2000; Le Placard, 2001; 102 Dalmatians, 2001; Astérix et Obélix: Mission Cleopatra, 2002; Bon Voyage, 2004. Several plays and television productions. Publication: Lettres volées, 1988. Honours: Numerous national and international awards. Address: Art Media, 10 Avenue George V, 75008 Paris, France.

**DEPP Johnny,** b. 9 June 1963, Owensboro, Kentucky, USA. Actor. m. (1) Lori Anne Allison (divorced), (2) Vanessa Paradis, 1 son, 1 daughter. Appointments: Former rock musician; TV appearances include 21 Jump Street; Films include: A Nightmare on Elm Street; Platoon; Slow Burn; Cry Baby; Edward Scissorhands, 1990; Benny and Joon, 1993; What's Eating Gilbert Grape, 1991; Arizona Dream; Ed Wood; Don Juan de Marco, 1994; Dead Man; Nick of Time; Divine Rapture; The Brave (also writer and director), 1997; Donnie Brasco, 1997; Fear and Loathing in Las Vegas, 1998; The Astronaut's Wife, 1998; The Source, 1999; The Ninth Gate, 1999; The Libertine, 1999; Just to Be Together, 1999; Sleepy Hollow, 1999; Before Night Falls, 2000; The Man Who Cried, 2000; Chocolat, 2000; Blow, 2001; From Hell, 2001; Lost in La Mancha, 2002; Once Upon a Time in Mexico, 2002; Pirates of the Caribbean: The Curse of the Black Pearl, 2003; Secret Window, 2004; Finding Neverland, 2004; The Libertine, 2004; Charlie and the Chocolate Factory, 2005. Address: 500 S Sepulveda Boulevard, Suite 500, Los Angeles, CA 90049, USA.

**DERBYSHIRE Eileen,** b. 6 October 1931, Urmston, Manchester, England. Actress. m. Thomas Wilfrid Holt, 1 son. Education: Northern School of Music. Career: First broadcast, 1948; Appeared in numerous radio productions; First repertory appearance, 1952; Numerous repertory jobs including Manchester Library Theatre, Farnham, Harrogate Festival, Scarborough (Stephen Joseph Theatre in the Round); Touring with the Century Theatre; Played Emily Bishop in Coronation Street, 1961-. Honour: LRAM. Membership: Life Member, British Actors' Equity. Address: c/o Granada Television Ltd, Quay Street, Manchester, M60 9EA, England.

**DERERA Nicholas F,** b. 5 January 1919, Budapest, Hungary. Agricultural Scientist; Plant Breeder. m. Roza E Derera, 1 son. Education: Dip.Agr.Sc, 1942; Dip.PB, 1943; CPAg, 1996. Appointments: Plant Breeder, Hungary, 1943-56; Process Worker, Laboratory Assistant, 1957-58; Research Agronomist, New South Wales Department of Agriculture 1958-61; Plant Breeder, Senior Plant Breeder, Officer-in-Charge, Director, Wheat Breeding, Plant Breeding Institute, North West Wheat Research Institute, Narrabri, 1961-81; Agricultural Science Consultant, 1981-; Adjunct Professor, University of Sydney, 1998-. Publications: Over 96 scientific, semi-popular and major conference papers. Honours: Fellow, Australian Institute of Agricultural Science, 1977; Certificate of Appreciation, RSL, 1979; Farrer Memorial Medal, 1981; Bronze Plaque and Citation, Canada, 1982; Rotary Award for Vocational Excellence, 1983; Member of the Order of Australia, 1994. Address: 5 Lister Street, Winston Hills, NSW 2153, Australia.

**DERN Laura,** b. 10 February 1967, Los Angeles, USA. Actor. 1 son, 1 daughter with Ben Harper. Appointments: Film debut aged 11 in Foxes, 1980; TV appearances include: Happy Endings; Three Wishes of Billy Greer; Afterburn; Down Came a Blackbird; Director, The Gift, 1999; Within These Walls, 2001; Damaged Care, 2002; Films: Teachers; Mask; Smooth Talk; Blue Velvet; Haunted Summer; Wild of Heart; Rambling Rose; Jurassic Park; A Perfect World; Devil Inside; Citizen Ruth, 1996; Bastard Out of Carolina, 1996; Ruby Ridge, 1996; October Sky, 1999; Dr T and the Women, 2000; Daddy and Them, 2001; Focus, 2001; Novocaine, 2001; Jurassic Park III, 2001; I Am Sam, 2001; We Don't Live Here Anymore, 2004; Happy Endings, 2005.

**DERSHOWITZ Alan (Morton),** b. 1 September 1938, New York, New York, USA. Lawyer; Professor of Law; Writer. m. Carolyn Cohen, 2 sons, 1 daughter. Education: BA, Brooklyn College, 1959; LLB, Yale University, 1962. Appointments: Called to the Bar, Washington, DC, 1963, Massachusetts, 1968, US Supreme Court, 1968; Law Clerk to Chief Judge David L Bazelon, US Court of Appeals, 1962-63, to Justice Arthur J Goldberg, US Supreme Court; Faculty, 1964-, Professor of Law, 1967-, Fellow, Center for Advanced Study of Behavioral Sciences, 1971-72, Felix Frankfurter Professor of Law, 1993-, Harvard University. Publications: Psychoanalysis, Psychiatry and the Law (with others), 1967; Criminal Law: Theory and Process, 1974; The Best Defense, 1982; Reversal of Fortune: Inside the von Bulow Case, 1986; Taking Liberties: A Decade of Hard Cases, Bad Laws and Bum Raps, 1988; Chutzpah, 1991; Contrary to Popular Opinion, 1992; The Abuse Excuse, 1994; The Advocate's Devil, 1994; Reasonable Doubt, 1996; The Vanishing American Jew, 1997; Sexual McCarthyism, 1998; Just Revenge, 1999; The Genesis of Justice, 2000; Supreme Injustice, 2001; Letters to a Young Lawyer, 2001; Shouting Fire, 2002. Contributions to: Periodicals. Honours: Guggenheim Fellowship, 1978-79; Honorary doctorates. Memberships: Order of the Coif; Phi Beta Kappa. Address: c/o Harvard University Law School, Cambridge, MA 02138, USA.

**DERVAIRD Lord, John Murray,** b. 8 July 1935, Stranraer, Scotland. Lawyer. m. Bridget Jane, 3 sons. Education: Edinburgh Academy; BA, Lit Hum 1st class, Corpus Christi College, Oxford, 1959; LLB, Edinburgh University, 1962. Appointments: Advocate 1962; QC, 1974; Commissioner, Scottish Law Commission, 1980-88; Judge, Court of Session,

Scotland, 1988-90; Dickson Minto Professor of Company and Commercial Law, 1990-98, Dean Faculty of Law, 1994-96, Professor Emeritus, 1999-, Edinburgh University; Chairman Scottish Committee for Arbitration Law Reform, 1985-96; Chairman, Scottish Council for International Arbitration, 1990-2003. Publications: "Scotland" in Encyclopaedia of International Arbitration; "Agriculture" in Stair Encyclopaedia of Scots Law; Numerous articles in journals on agriculture, arbitration and commercial law. Honour: FCIArb. Memberships: ICC; LCIA; CIArb; IAI (Paris). Address: 4 Moray Place, Edinburgh, EH3 6DS, Scotland.

**DERWENT Richard Austin,** b. 28 September 1953. Chartered Accountant. Education: BA Hons (1st Class), History, London University. Appointments: Chartered Accountant, Deloitte, Haskins and Sells, Southampton, 1972-81; Audit Manager, Brooking Knowles and Lawrence, 1981-82; Audit Manager, Rawlinson and Hunter, 1982-84; Senior Technical Manager, Pannell Kerr Forster, 1984-86; Senior Technical Manager, Clark Whitehill, 1986-91; Self-employed Consultant, 1991-. Publications: Charities: An Industry Accounting and Auditing Guide, 1995, 1997; Contributions to: Financial Reporting: A Survey of UK Published Accounts; The Times; Charity World; Accountancy; Certified Accountant; Corporate Money; True and Fair; The Small Practitioner. Memberships: Secretary and Chairman, London Society Financial Reporting Discussion Group, 1989-91; Financial Reporting Committee, ICAEW, 1990-97. Address: Flat 7, Foxlea, 70 Northlands Road, Southampton SO15 2LH, England.

**DESAI Anita,** b. 24 June 1937, Mussoorie, India. Writer. m. Ashvin Desai, 13 December 1958, 2 sons, 2 daughters. Education: BA, Honours, Miranda House, University of Delhi. Publications: Cry, The Peacock; Voices in the City; Fire on the Mountain; Clear Light of Day; In Custody, (also filmed, 1994); Baumgartner's Bombay; Where Shall We Go This Summer?; Bye Bye Blackbird; The Peacock Garden; Cat on a Houseboat; The Village by the Sea, (also BBC TV Serial, 1992); Games at Twilight; Journey to Ithaca, 1995; Fasting, Feasting, 1999; Diamond Dust and Other Stories, 2000; The Zig Zag Way, 2004. Honours: Winifred Holtby Award, Royal Society of Literature, 1978; Sahitya Akademi Award for English, 1978; Federation of Indian Publishers Award, 1978; Padma Shri Award, India, 1989; Hadassah Magazine Award, 1989; Guardian Prize for Children's Fiction, 1993; Literary Lion, New York Public Library, 1993; Neil Gunn International Writers Fellowship, Scotland, 1994. Memberships: Royal Society of Literature; Sahitya Akademi of India; PEN; Fellow, American Academy of Arts and Letters, 1992; Fellow, Girton College and Clare Hall, Cambridge. Address: c/o Rogers, Coleridge and White Ltd, 20 Powis Mews, London W11 1JN, England.

**DESALVA Christopher Joseph,** b. 16 June 1950. Attorney; Counselor at Law. m. Erika Marie, dissolution pending, 1 daughter. Education: Occupational Education in Real Estate, Associate of Arts in Business Administration and Economics, College of the Desert, California; Bachelor of Art in Political Science, St Vincent College, Pennsylvania; Juris Doctor in Law, American College of Law, California; PhD/MBA in Business Administration, California Coast University, California. Appointments: Tax and Real Property Consultant, 1985-94; Real Estate Broker, 1980-; Life and Disabilities Insurance Agent, 1978-; Founder/President, C J DeSalva & Associates Investment and Marketing Services of La Quinta, 1979-89; CEO/President, The Kings Vault Gallery Inc, 1985; Realtor, 1985-; Certified Law Student, California State Bar Association, 1985-88; Adjunct Faculty Member, Lecturer and Instructor of Property Law, American College of Law, 1989, 1990, 1992, 1993, 1994

and 1995; Attorney and Counselor at Law, 1994-; Admitted to the Supreme Court of the State of California as an Attorney and Counselor at Law, 1994; Admitted to the Federal Jurisdiction of the United States District Courts, Central District of California, 1995, Southern District of California, 1997; Admitted to practice as an Attorney and Counselor at Law before the separate and independent Bar of the United States Tax Court, Washington, DC, 1995; Admitted to practice as an Attorney and Counselor at Law before the separate and independent Bar of the United States Federal Court of Claims, Washington, DC, 1995; Admitted and litigated as defense counsel, PRO HAC VICE Arizona, Colorado and US District Court Wichita, Kansas: Litigated IN PRO SE, New York Supreme Court. Publications: Author, NAFTA, The Hidden Agenda, 1995. Honours: Commemorative Medal of Honor, ABI, 1991; National Republican Congressional Committee's Business Advisory Council, 2003; Businessman of the Year; 2003 National Leadership Award; Medal of Excellence, Legal Professional of the Year, IBC, 2004; Ronald Reagan Republican Gold Medal, Republican House of Representatives, 2004. Memberships: Certified Member, Board of Governors, National Society of Public Accountants, 1984-; California Association of Realtors, 1985-; National Association of Realtors, 1983-; California Bar Association, 1994-; American Bar Association, 1995-; American Association of Trial Lawyers, 1997-; Coachella Valley Bar Association, 2000-. Address: 45-902 Oasis Street, Suite D, Indio, CA 92201, USA.

**DESLIPPE Richard Joseph,** b. 5 September 1962, Windsor, Ontario, Canada. Associate Professor of Ecology. Education: BSc, Biology, Department of Zoology, University of Guelph, 1981-85; MSc, Biology, Department of Biology, University of Windsor, 1987-1989; PhD, Zoology, Department of Zoology, University of Alberta, 1990-94. Appointments: Postdoctoral Fellow, Cornell University, 1994-96; Visiting Assistant Professor, Texas Tech University, 1996-97; Adjunct Professor, The Institute of Environmental and Human Health; Assistant Professor of Ecology, 1997-2003, Associate Professor, 2003-, Texas Tech University. Publications: Numerous papers and articles. Honours: Recipient of various awards. Address: Department of Biological Sciences, Texas Tech University, Lubbock, TX 79409-3131, USA. E-mail: richard.deslippe@ttu.edu

**DETCHEVA Vanya,** b. 28 November 1926, Plovdiv, Bulgaria. Artist; Painter. m. Bernard Allain, 20 December 1977. Education: Academy of Fine Arts, Sofia; National Superior Academy of Fine Arts, Paris. Appointments: Solo Exhibitions include: Galerie du Comité des relations culturelles avec l'Etranger, Sofia, 1962; Galerie Prachna Brana, Prague, 1963; Galerie Deutsche Bücher Stube, Berlin, 1963; Radio Bulgare, Sofia, 1966; Galerie Rakovski 125, Sofia, 1968; Salle d'Exposition de l'Ambassade de Bulgarie, Paris, 1975; Hôtel de Ville, Chateaucoux, 1979; Eglisau H R Galerie, Zürich, 1981; Galerie Voltaire/Lubéron/Vaucluse, Bonnieux, France, 1983; Collective Exhibitions include: Salon d'Automne, Paris, 1976-81; Exposition Grand Prix International de peinture de la Côte d'Azur, Cannes, 1983-94; Exposition Internationale, Rome, I sette colli di Roma, Palazzo Nari, 1985, Museo de la Civilta Romana, 1989; Exposition Panorama de la peinture française contemporaine, London, 1988, Basel, 1988; Geneva, 1989; Salon des Indépendants, Grand Palais, 100th anniversaries of Van Gogh, 1990, Paul Delveaux, 1991, works of Botero, 1992; Galeria d'Art Marabello, Barcelona, Spain, 1998; Commemorative exhibition, Galerie Chipka 6, Sofia, Bulgaria, 1999. Creative works include: Stained glass collects; Tapestries; Lithographies; Public and private collections; Films. Honours include: Silver Medal, 1970, Gold Medal, 1986, art and culture, Bulgaria; Prix René Borel, 1989, 1991, 1992; Official diplomas, medals, from international art competitions including Deauville, 1982-92, Cannes, 1983-95, London, 1988, Basel, 1988, Geneva, 1989, Ypres, 1993, Bruges, 1994, Cambridge, 1998; 2000 Millennium Gold Medal of Honour, for Leading Intellectuals of the World, ABI, USA; Work appears in several critical art volumes and biographical dictionaries including Dictionary of International Biography, IBC, UK. Address: 13 Boulevard des Freres Voisin, 75015 Paris, France.

**DETTORI Lanfranco (Frankie),** b. 15 December 1970, Milan, Italy. Flat Race Jockey. m. Catherine Allen, 1997, 2 sons, 3 daughters. Appointments: Ridden races in England, France, Germany, Italy, USA, Dubai, Australia, Hong Kong and other countries in Far East, 1992-; 1000 rides and 215 wins in UK, 1995; Horses ridden include Lamtarra, Barathea, Vettori, Mark of Distinction, Balanchine, Moonshell, Lochsong, Classic Cliché, Dubai Millennium, Daylami; Sakhee; major race victories include: St Leger (twice), The Oaks (twice); The Breeders Cup Mile; Arc de Triomphe (twice); French 2000 Guineas (twice); English 1000 Guineas; Queen Elizabeth II Stakes; Prix L'Abbaye; The Japan Cup (twice); The Dubai World Cup; Rode winner of all 7 races at Ascot, 28 October 1996. Publication: A Year in the Life of Frankie Dettori, 1996. Honours: Jockey of the Year, 1994, 1995; BBC Sports Personality of the Year, 1996; International Sports Personality of the Year, Variety Club, 2000. Address: c/o Peter Burrell Classic Management, 53 Stewarts Grove, London, SW3 6PH, England. E-mail: pburrell@classicmanagement.com

**DEUCHAR Stephen John,** b. 11 March 1957, United Kingdom. Director, Tate Britain. m. Katie Scott, 1 son, 3 daughters. Education: BA, History 1st Class Honours, University of Southampton; PhD, History of Art, Westfield College, University of London, 1986; Andrew W Mellon Fellow in British Art, Yale University, 1981-82. Appointments: Curator of Paintings, 1985-87, Curator, Armada Exhibition, 1987-88, Corporate Planning Manager, 1988-90; Head of Exhibitions and Displays, 1990-95, Director, Neptune Court Project, 1995-97, National Maritime Museum; Director, Tate Britain, 1998-. Publications: Noble Exercise: the Sporting Ideal in 18th Century British Art, 1982; Paintings, Politics and Porter, Samuel Whitbread and British Art, 1984; Concise Catalogue of Oil Paintings in the National Maritime Museum (jointly), 1988; Sporting Art in 18th Century British Art: A Social and Political History, 1988; Nelson: An Illustrated History (jointly), 1995; Articles on British Art. Memberships: Visual Arts Committee, British Council; Advisory Council, Paul Mellon Centre for Studies in British Art; Council, University of Southampton. Address: Tate Britain, Millbank, London SW1P 4RG, England.

**DEUSSEN Nancy Bloomer,** Composer; Performer; Arts Organiser. m. (1) Charles Webster, 1952, 1 son, 2 daughters, (2) John Hayes Bloomer, 1962, (3) Gary Ronald Deussen, 1982. Education: Manhattan School of Music; The USC School of Music. Appointments: Original works performed throughout US and Canada; Numerous commissions both locally and nationally from performers and ensembles around the world. Publications: CDs include: Amber Waves, piano, 1967; Trio for Violin, clarinet and piano, 1989; San Andreas Suite, 1989; Cascades, a toccata, 1989; Peninsula Suite, string orchestra, 1994; Ascent to Victory, 1998; Trio for Violin, cello and piano, 1998; The Pegasus Suite, 1999; Reflections on the Hudson, 1955; Piano Prelude, 1988. Honours: 2nd Bay Area Composers Symposium Orchestral Award, 1991; 1st Prize, Britten-on-the-Bay, 1996; Winner, Mu Phi Epsilon Original Composition Competitions, 1985, 1999, 2005; Burton Award, Radio Station WOMR-MA, 2000; Winner, Marmor Chamber Music Competition, Stanford University, 2002; Commission for choral work from Foundation for Universal Sacred Music, 2004; Commissions for concert band work for US Continental Army Band, 2005; Commissions for Blackledge Chamber Ensemble, 2005. Address: 3065 Greer Road, Palo Alto, CA 94303, USA. Website: www.nancybloom erdeussen.com

**DEUTSCH Claude,** b. 20 July 1936, Paris, France. Professor of Physics. m. Nimet El Abed, 2 sons. Education: Engineer, ENSCP, Paris, 1959; Master of Theoretical Physics, Orsay, 1961; Doctor of Science, University Paris XI, 1969. Appointments: Director, Paris Sud Informatique, University Paris XI, Orsay, 1985-93; Director GDR-918, CNRS, Ion-plasma Interaction, 1989-96; Director, Physics Laboratory, University Paris XI, 1994-98; Invited Professor, Tokyo Institute of Technology, Japan, 1999-2000; Professor, Physics, Exceptional Class, 1995-. Publications: Numerous articles in professional journals. Honours: Bronze Medal, 1973, Silver Medal, 1980, CNRS; Bronze Medal, Madrid Polytechnic, 1995; Fellow, American Physical Society, 1996. Memberships: Societé Francaise de Physique; American Physical Society. Address: Laboratoire de Physique des Gaz et Plasmas, Bat 210, UPS, 91405-Orsay, France. E-mail: claude.deutsch@lpgp.u-psud.fr

**DEVANARAYANAN Sankaranarayanan,** b. 11 November 1940, Thiruvananthapuram, India. University Professor; Physicist. m. Chitra, 1 son, 1 daughter. Education: BSc, University of Kerala, 1961; MSc, University of Kerala, 1963; PhD, Indian Institute of Science, Bangalore, 1969; Diploma, Uppsala University, Sweden, 1971; DSc, International University, USA, 1999. Appointments: Research Fellow, Indian Institute of Science, 1963-69; Senior Research Assistant, Indian Institute of Science, 1969-70; SIDA Fellow, Institute of Physics, Uppsala, Sweden, 1970-71; Lecturer, 1971-75, Reader, 1975-84, Professor, 1984-2000, Professor and Head, 1993-2000, Physics Department, University of Kerala; Professor, Physics, University of Puerto Rico, Rio Piedras, USA, 1989-91; Principal, KVVS Institute of Technology, Via Adur, 2003-; Computer Software Languages known: FORTRAN; JAVA; JAVASCRIPT; HTML; SERVELETS. Publications: Over 84 research articles in standard scientific journals in science in solid state physics, spectroscopy, crystal growth and atmospheric physics; Thermal Expansion of Crystals, monograph, 1979; Quantum Mechanics, book, 2005. Honours: Merit Scholar, University of Kerala, 1961-63; SIDA Fellowship, Sweden, 1970-71; Visiting Professor, University of Puerto Rico, 1989; Over 18 biographies in national and international publications. Memberships: American Physical Society, 1991-; Indian Physics Association, 1974-; Indian Meteorological Society, 1999-; United Writers' Association, 1998-; Indian Association Physics Teachers, 1974-; Senate, University of Kerala, 1998-2000; Academic Council, University of Kerala, 1991-2001; Chairman, PG Board of Studies in Physics, University of Kerala, 1993-2001; Commission of Enquiry, University of Kerala, 2000; many others. Address: TC 40/239, (G-9) PRS Enclave, Easwara Vilasom Road, Cotton Hill, Thiruvananthapuram – 695014, India. E-mail: sdevanarayanan@yahoo.com

**DEVERALL Brian James.** Education: BSc, Botany, Hons 1, Edinburgh, 1957; DIC, 1960, PhD, 1960, Plant Pathology, London. Appointments include: Harness Fellow, Commonwealth Fund, New York, 1960-62; PostDoctoral Fellow, University of Wisconsin, 1960-61, University of Nebraska, 1961-62; Lecturer, Imperial College, University of London, England, 1962-70; Principal Scientific Officer, Wye College, University of London, England, 1970-72; Professor of Plant Pathology, University of Sydney, Australia, 1973-2001; Emeritus Professor, University of Sydney, 2001-. Publications: 6 Monographs and edited books; Numerous research and review papers in leading international journals; 20 Review Chapters. Memberships: British Mycological Society, 1962-97; British Plant Pathology Society, since foundation in 1982-; Australasian Plant Pathology Society, 1972-, President, 1987-89; American Phytopathological Society, 1993-2002, Fellow, 1999; International Society for Plant Pathology, Vice President, 1993-98. Address: Faculty of Agriculture, Food and Natural Resources, University of Sydney, NSW 2006, Australia.

**DEVERALL Philip Brook,** b. 30 April 1937, London, England. Surgeon. m. Ann, 2 sons, 1 daughter. Education: MB BS (London), 1960; MRCS (Eng), LRCP (London), 1960; FRCS (England), 1964. Appointments: Training in the UK, Leeds and London, USA, Birmingham, Alabama and Leiden, Netherlands; Consultant Heart Surgeon, Leeds, 1970-77; Consultant and Lecturer, 1978-97, Emeritus Consultant, 1998-, Guy's Hospital London; Retired. Publications: Over 200 articles in peer reviewed journals and chapters in specialised books. Honours: State and County Scholarships; MB BS (Honours): Hallett Prize; FRCS. Memberships: All major societies in UK, Europe, USA, Canada and Asia. Address: 3 Northfield Close, Bromley, Kent BR1 2WZ, England. E-mail:phil@pdeverall.freeserve.co.uk

**DEVITO Danny,** b. 1944, New Jersey, USA. Actor; Director. m. Rhea Perlman, 1982, 2 sons, 2 daughters. Education: American Academy of Dramatic Arts; Wilfred Academy of Hair and Beauty Culture. Appointments: Hairdresser for 1 year; Stage appearances include: The Man With a Flower in His Mouth; Down the Morning Line; The Line of Least Existence; The Shrinking Bride; Call Me Charlie; Comedy of Errors; Merry Wives of Windsor; Three by Pirandello; One Flew Over the Cuckoo's Nest; Film appearances include: Lady Liberty; Scalawag; Hurry Up or I'll be 30; One Flew Over the Cuckoo's Nest; Deadly Hero; Car Wash; The Van; World's Greatest Lover; Goin' South; Going Ape; Terms of Endearment; Romancing the Stone; Johnny Dangerously; Head Office; Jewel of the Nile; Wiseguys; Ruthless People; My Little Pony (voice); Tin Men; Throw Momma From the Train (also director); Other People's Money, 1991; Batman Returns, 1992; Hoffa (also producer, director), Other People's Money, 1991; Batman Returns, 1992; Renaissance Man, 1994; Junior, 1994; Matilda (also director, co-producer); Mars Attacks, 1997; The Rainmaker, 1997; LA Confidential, 1997; Man on the Moon, 1999; Drowning Mona, 2000; Screwed, 2000; Heist, 2001; What's the Worst That Could Happen? 2001; Death to Smoochy, 2002; Austin Powers in Goldmember, 2002; Television appearances include: Taxi (also director), Feeling Mary (director only); Valentine; The Rating Game (director); All the Kids Do It, A Very Special Christmas Party; Two Daddies? (voice); The Selling of Vince DeAngelo (director); Amazing Stories (also director); The Simpsons (voice). Address: c/o Fred Specktor, Creative Artists Agency, 9830 Wilshire Boulevard, Beverly Hills, CA 90212, USA.

**DEVLIN Dean,** b. 27 August 1962. Actor; Screenplay Writer; Producer. Creative Works: Film produced: The Patriot, 2000; Films written and produced; Stargate, 1994; Independence Day, 1996; Godzilla, 1998; Film screenplay: Universal Solider, 1992; Actor: My Bodyguard, 1980; The Wild Life, 1984; Real Genius, 1985; City Limits, 1985; Martians Go Home, 1990; Moon 44, 1990; Total Exposure, 1991; TV series: The Visitor (creator, executive producer), 1997; TV appearances in: North Beach, 1985; Rawhide, 1985; Hard Copy, 1987; Generations, 1989; Guest appearances in: LA Law; Happy Days; Misfits of Science. Address: c/o Creative Artists Agency, 9830 Wilshire Boulevard, Beverly Hills, CA 90212, USA.

**DEWHIRST Ian,** b. 17 October 1936, Keighley, Yorkshire, England. Retired Librarian; Writer; Poet. Education: BA

Honours, Victoria University of Manchester, 1958. Appointment: Staff, Keighley Public Library, 1960-91. Publications: The Handloom Weaver and Other Poems, 1965; Scar Top and Other Poems, 1968; Gleanings From Victorian Yorkshire, 1972; A History of Keighley, 1974; Yorkshire Through the Years, 1975; Gleanings from Edwardian Yorkshire, 1975; The Story of a Nobody, 1980; You Don't Remember Bananas, 1985; Keighley in Old Picture Postcards, 1987; In the Reign of the Peacemaker, 1993; Down Memory Lane, 1993; Images of Keighley, 1996; Co-editor, A Century of Yorkshire Dialect, 1997. Contributions to: Yorkshire Ridings Magazine; Lancashire Magazine; Dalesman; Cumbria; Pennine Magazine; Transactions of the Yorkshire Dialect Society; Yorkshire Journal. Honour: Honorary Doctor of Letters, University of Bradford, 1996; MBE, 1999. Memberships: Yorkshire Dialect Society; Edward Thomas Fellowship. Address: 14 Raglan Avenue, Fell Lane, Keighley, West Yorkshire BD22 6BJ, England.

**DEXTER Colin,** b. 29 September 1930, Stamford, Lincolnshire, England. Writer. Education: Christ's College, Cambridge; MA (Cantab): MA (Oxon). Publications: Last Bus to Woodstock, 1975; Last Seen Wearing, 1976; The Silent World of Nicholas Quinn, 1977; Service of All the Dead, 1979; The Dead of Jericho, 1981; The Riddle of the Third Mile, 1983; The Secret of Annexe 3, 1983; The Wench is Dead, 1989; The Jewel That Was Ours, 1991; The Way Through the Woods, 1992; Morse's Greatest Mystery, 1993; The Daughters of Cain, 1994; Death is Now My Neighbour, 1996; The Remorseful Day, 1999. Honours: Silver Dagger, 1979, 1981, Gold Dagger, 1989, 1992, Diamond Dagger, 1997, Crime Writers' Association; Macavity Award, Best Short Story, 1995; Lotos Club Medal of Merit, New York, 1996; Sherlock Holmes Award, 1999; Officer of the Order of the British Empire, 2000; Freedom, City of Oxford, 2001; Fellow, St Cross College, Oxford, 2005. Memberships: Crime Writers' Association; Detection Club. Address: 456 Banbury Road, Oxford OX2 7RG, England.

**DHALL Dharam Pal,** b. 8 December 1937, Kenya. Vascular Surgeon. m. Tehseen, 1 son, 1 daughter. Education: MBChB, 1961; FRCS, 1965; PhD, 1967; MD, 1968; FRACS, 1994, MACE, 2002. Appointments: Senior Registrar, Lecturer, Surgery, Aberdeen University; Professor of Surgery, University of Nairobi; Senior Consultant Surgeon, Canberra Hospital; Visiting Fellow, John Curtin School of Medical Research, Canberra; Director, Institute of Sathya Sai Education, Canberra, Director, Educare Community Services Pty Ltd; Academic Adviser, University of Central Queensland for Master of Learning Management in Human Values, University of Queensland; Adjunct Professor of Bioethics, University of Canberra. Publications: Approximately 200 articles in Scientific Medical Journals; 15 books on the teachings of Sri Sathya Sai Baba including Human Values, The Heart of Dynamic Parenting; Workshops on Dynamic Parenting; Stepping Stones to Peace; Dynamic Dharma; Over one hundred articles in professional journals. Honours include: Hallett Award, 1963; National Heart Foundation; NH and MRC, Australia; Pharmacia Uppsala, Sweden. Memberships: World Education Federation; Associate Member, Australian Counselling Association; Member, Australian College of Educators. Address: PO Box 697, Queanbeyan, NSW 2620, Australia. E-mail: paldhall@aol.com

**DHAR Hirendra Lal,** b. 2 October 1931, Chittagong, Bangladesh. Geriatrician; Medical Centre Director. m. Rikta Dhar, 1 son, 1 daughter. Education: BSc, 1950, MB BS, 1957, PhD, 1963, Calcutta University; DHA, University of Bombay, 1984; MD, Colombo, 1985; FRCP, Colombo, 2001. Appointments: Demonstrator, AIIMS, New Delhi, 1959; Lecturer, Maulana Azad Medical College, New Delhi,

1962; Reader, JIPMER, Pondicherry, 1967; Professor, Seth GS Medical College and Hospital, Mumbai, 1971; Professor and Head, 1972, Dean, 1985, Emeritus Scientist, 1989, LTM Medical College and Hospital, Mumbai; Director, Medical Research Centre, Bombay Hospital Trust, Mumbai, 1991. Publications: Nearly 300 original works in national and international journals. Honours: Honorary, FCAI, 1964; Dr B C Roy National Award, 1991; Honorary DSc, 1992; The Ancient Royal Order of Physicians, Sri Lanka, 1993; Honorary FICG, 1998. Memberships: Member of many national and international research organisations; Fellow, Indian College of Allergy and Immunology, 1963; President, South Asia Chapter, International Association of Asthmology, 1975-90; President, ICAI, 1999. Address: Medical Research Centre, Bombay Hospital Trust, Bombay 400 020, India. E-mail: drdharmrc@hotmail.com

**DIAMA Benjamin,** b. 23 September 1933, Hawaii, USA. Retired Public School Teacher. Education: BFA, School of the Art Institute, Chicago, 1956; State of Hawaii Government Teachers Certificate, 1962. Appointments: Art, Basketball Coach, Waimea High, 1963-67; Music, Art, Campbell High, 1967-68; Maths, Art, Waipahu High, 1968-69; Music, Art, Palisades Elementary, 1969-70; Art, Music, History, Typing, Honokaa High, 1970-73; Music, Kealakehe Elementary-Intermediate, 1973-74; Retired, 1974. Publications include: School One vs School Two on the Same Campus, 1983; The Calendar Clock Theory of the Universe with Faith - Above and Beyond, 1984-88; Inventor, Universal Calendar Clock and Double Washdeck Floating Boat; Benjamin Diama Calendar Clock Theory of the Universe, 1991, 1992, 1993. Honours: Hawaii Government Acquisition Painting Collection Award, 1984; Medal of Honour, ABI, 1998. Memberships include: HEA; HSTA; NEA; ASCAP; New York Academy of Sciences; American Association for the Advancement of Science; American Geophysical Union; Smithsonian Society. Address: PO Box 2997, Kailua-Kona, Hawaii, HI 96745, USA.

**DIAMOND Neil Lesley,** b. 24 January 1941, Brooklyn, New York, USA. Pop Singer; Composer. m. (1) 2 children, (2) Marcia Murphey, 1975, 2 children. Education: New York University. Appointments: Formerly with Bang Records, Uni, MCA Records, Los Angeles; Now recording artist with Columbia Records; Guest Artist, TV network shows. Publications: Songs include: Solitary Man; Cherry, Cherry; Kentucky Woman; I'm A Believer; September Morn; Sweet Caroline; Holly, Holy; A Little Bit Me, A Little Bit You; Longfellow Serenade; Song Sung Blue; America; I am I Said; Recordings: Numerous albums, 1966-; 19 Platinum albums; 28 Gold albums; Composer, film scores; Jonathan Livingston Seagull, 1973; Every Which Way But Loose, 1978; The Jazz Singer (also actor), 1980. Honours include: Grammy Award, Jonathan Livingston Seagull, 1973. Address: c/o Columbia Records, 2100 Colorado Avenue, Santa Monica, CA 90404, USA.

**DIAZ Cameron,** b. 30 August 1972, Long Beach, California, USA. Actress. Appointments: Films include: The Mask, 1994; The Last Supper, 1995; Feeling Minnesota, 1996; She's the One, 1996; A Life Less Ordinary, 1997; There's Something About Mary, 1998; Very Bad Things, 1998; Being John Malkovich, 1999; Invisible Circus, 1999; Any Given Sunday, 1999; Charlie's Angels, 2000; Things You Can Tell Just by Looking at Her, 2000; Shrek (voice), 2001; Vanilla Sky, 2001; The Sweetest Thing, 2002; Gangs of New York, 2002; Minority Report, 2002; Charlie's Angels: Full Throttle, 2003; Shrek 2 (voice), 2004. Address: c/o International Creative Management, 8942 Wilshire Boulevard, Beverly Hills, CA 90211, USA.

**DIAZ Cecilia Isabel,** b. 31 October 1944, Panama, Republic of Panama. Professor of Biochemistry. Education: Licence, Chemistry, Catholic University of Louvain, Belgium; Diploma of Advanced Studies, Doctor, 3rd Cycle, Biochemistry, University of Dijon, France; Diploma, University teaching, University of Panama. Appointments: Technician III, Gorgas Memorial Laboratory, 1969-73; Part-time Professor, University Santa María la Antigua, 1971-74; Chair Assistant, 1973-75, Assistant Professor, 1975-80, Associate Professor of Biochemistry, 1980-84, Full Professor, Biochemistry, 1984-2005, Director Department of Biochemistry and Nutrition, 1994-97, Faculty of Medicine, University of Panama. Publications: 9 manuals and books; 20 articles; 7 short articles. Honours: Apostolic Nunciature Scholar, Catholic University of Louvain; Republic of France Scholar; Educational Commission for Foreign Medical Graduates Fellowship, University of Wisconsin, Madison, Wisconsin, USA; Travel Award, American Society of Biochemistry and Molecular Biology; Honorary Professor, The Albert Schweitzer International University. Memberships: Colegio Panameño de Químicos; American Chemical Society; Asociación Panameña para el Avance de la Ciencia; Asociación Panameña de Bioquímica; Biochemical Society; New York Academy of Sciences; International Association of Medical Science Educators. Address: Faculty of Medicine, Department of Biochemistry, University of Panama, Via Bolivar, Panama, Republic of Panama.

**DICKINS Thomas Edmund,** b. 9 May 1970, Liverpool, England. Principal Lecturer in Psychology. m. Inbal Ringel. Education: BSc, Honours, Psychological Sciences, Polytechnic of East London (CNAA), 1991; MSc, History and Philosophy of Science, University and Imperial College, London, 1992; PhD, Signal to Symbol: The First Stage in Evolution of Language, University of Sheffield, 2000. Appointments: Lecturer in Psychology, University of Greenwich, 1998-99; Lecturer in Psychology, London Guildhall University, 1999-2001; Senior Lecturer in Psychology, Nottingham Trent University, 2001-2003; Senior Lecturer in Psychology, 2003-2004, Principal Lecturer in Psychology, 2004-, University of East London. Publications in scientific journals include: What can evolutionary psychology tell us about cognitive architecture?, 2003; Social Constructionism as Cognitive Science, 2004. Honours: Listed in Who's Who publications and biographical dictionaries. Membership: British Society for the Philosophy of Science. Address: School of Psychology, University of East London, London E15 4LZ, England. E-mail: t.dickins@uel.ac.uk

**DICKINSON Angie (pseudonym of Angeline Brown),** b. 30 September 1931, Kulm, North Dakota, USA. Actress. Education: Glendale College. Appointments: Actress in films: Lucky Me, 1954; Man With the Gun; The Return of Jack Slade; Tennessee's Partner; The Black Whip; Hidden Guns; Tension at Table Rock; Gun the Man Down; Calypso Joe; China Gate; Shoot Out at Medicine Bend; Cry Terror; I Married a Woman; Rio Bravo; The Bramble Bush; Ocean's 11; A Fever in the Blood; The Sins of Rachel Cade; Jessica; Rome Adventure; Captain Newman MD; The Killers; The Art of Love; Cast a Giant Shadow; The Chase; Poppy is Also a Flower; The Last Challenge; Point Blank; Sam Whiskey; Some Kind of Nut; Young Billy Young; Pretty Maids All in A Row; The Resurrection of Zachery Wheeler; The Outside Man; Big Bad Mama; Klondike Fever; Dressed to Kill; Charlie Chan and the Curse of the Dragon Queen; Death Hunt; Big Bad Mama II; Even Cowgirls Get The Blues; The Maddening; Sabrina; The Sun - The Moon and the Stars; Pay it Forward; Sealed with a Kiss, 1999; The Last Producer, 2000; Duets, 2000; Pay It Forward, 2000; Big Bad Love, 2001; Ocean's Eleven, 2001; TV series: Police Woman; Cassie & Co; TV films: The Love War; Thief; See the Man Run; The Norliss Tapes; Pray for the Wildcats; A Sensitive Passionate Man; Overboard; The Suicide's Wife; Dial M for Murder; One Shoe Makes it Murder; Jealousy; A Touch of Scandal; Still Watch; Police Story: The Freeway Killings; Once Upon a Texas Train; Prime Target; Treacherous Crossing; Danielle Steel's Remembrance; Miniseries: Pearl; Hollywood Wives; Wild Palms.

**DIEMER Emma Lou,** b.24 November 1927, Kansas City, Missouri, USA. Composer; Professor; Musician. Education: BM, 1949, MM, 1959, Yale School of Music; PhD, Eastman School of Music, 1960. Appointments: Composer-in-Residence, Arlington Virginia Schools; Professor of Composition, University of Maryland, 1965-70; Professor of Composition, 1971-91, Professor Emeritus, 1991-, University of California. Publications: Over 200 publications, 1957-2005; Orchestra, chamber works, choral works, vocal works and solo instrumental works; Several articles on music. Honours include: Fulbright Scholarship in composition and piano, 1952-53; NEA Fellowship in electronic music, 1980; ASCAP Award annually since 1962; AGO Composer of the Year, 1995; Honorary Doctorate, Central Missouri State University, 1999. Memberships: ASCAP; Mu Phi Epsilon; American Guild of Organists; American Music Center; International Alliance for Women in Music. Address: 2249 Vista del Campo, Santa Barbara, CA 93101, USA. E-mail: eldiemer@cox.net

**DIERINGER Gregg,** b. 18 October 1956, Athens, Ohio, USA. Plant Ecologist. m. Leticia Cabrera, 2 sons. Education: BS cum laude, 1979, MS, 1981, University of Akron; PhD, University of Texas at Austin, 1988. Appointments: Teaching Assistant, University of Akron, 1979-81; Teaching Assistant, 1983, Research Assistant, 1983-84, Teaching Assistant, 1984-88, Instructor, 1990-92, University of Texas at Austin; Instructor, Austin Community College, 1988, 1989-92; Assistant Professor, Southwest Texas State University, 1989; Visiting Professor, Instituto de Ecologia, Veracruz, Mexico, 1992-93; Assistant Professor, 1993-97, Associate Professor, 1997-99, Western Illinois University; Lecturer, University of Texas at Brownsville, 1999-2002; Associate Professor, Chair, Department of Biological Sciences, Northwest Missouri State University, 2003-. Publications: Numerous articles in professional journals; Presentations at scientific meetings; General reports and book reviews. Honours: Eagle Scout, 1973; Phi Sigma Alpha, University of Akron, 1978; Scholarship to attend Rocky Mountain Biological Station, 1983; Several research grants. Memberships: Botanical Society of America; Torrey Botanical Society. Address: Department of Biological Sciences, Northwest Missouri State University, 800 University Dr, Maryville, MO 64468, USA. E-mail: greggd@mail.nwmissouri.edu

**DIETER Peter,** b. 22 February 1952, Neustadt, Germany. Biochemist. m Kathrin Asman, 1 daughter. Education: PhD, 1981; Habilitation, 1991; Full Professor, 1997. Appointments: Canberra, Australia, 1986; NIH, Bethesda, USA, 1989; Freiburg, Germany, 1997; Full Professor, Dresden, Germany, 1997-. Publications: Many articles in journals; Impact factor N 300. Honour: Associate Professor, Thailand, 2004. Memberships: Many societies. Address: Briesnitzer Hoehe 42A, D-01157 Dresden, Germany.

**DIGBY-BELL Christopher,** b. 21 June 1948, Aberdeen, Scotland. m. Claire, 2 sons, 1 daughter. Education: Marlborough College, 1961-65; College of Law. Appointments: Articled at Taylor & Humbert, 1966-71; Taylor Garrett, 1972-89, Managing Partner, Taylor Garrett, 1987-89; Frere Cholmeley Bischoff, 1989-98, International Managing Partner, 1995-97; Chief Executive and Legal Director, Palmer Capital Partners, 1998-. Publications: Regular contributor to Times, Lawyer

and other legal journals. Honours: Special Award, UNICEF Child Rights Lawyer of the Year Awards, 2002; Judges Award, Liberty/Justice Human Rights Lawyer of the Year Awards, 2002. Memberships: Law Society; City of London Law Society; Honorary Legal Advisor, Down's Syndrome Association; City of London Member of Law Society Ruling Council, 2001-03. Address: Palmer Capital Partners, 17 Clifford Street, Mayfair, London W1S 3RQ, England. E-mail: chdb@palmercapital.co.uk

**DILLON Matt,** b. 18 February 1964, New Rochelle, New York, USA. Actor. Appointments: Films include: Over the Edge, 1979; Little Darlings, 1980; My Bodyguard, 1980; Liar's Moon, 1982; Tex, 1982; The Outsiders, 1983; Rumble Fish, 1983; The Flamingo Kid, 1984; Target, 1985; Rebel, 1985; Native Son, 1986; The Big Town (The Arm), 1987; Kansas, 1988; Drugstore Cowboy, 1989; A Kiss Before Dying, 1991; Singles, 1992; The Saint of Fort Washington, 1993; Mr Wonderful, 1993; Golden Gate, 1994; To Die For; Frankie Starlight; Beautiful Girls; Grace of My Heart; Albino Alligator; In and Out, 1997; There's Something About Mary, 1998; One Night at McCool's, 2000; Deuces Wild, 2000; City of Ghosts, 2002; Employee of the Month, 2004; Loverboy, 2005. Address: c/o William Morris Agency, ICM, 151 S El Camino Drive, Beverly Hills, CA 90212, USA.

**DIMBLEBY David,** b. 28 October 1938, London, England. Broadcaster; Newspaper Proprietor. m. (1) Joceline Gaskell, 1967, dissolved, 1 son, 2 daughters, (2) Belinda Giles, 2000, 1 son. Education: Christ Church, Oxford; University of Paris; University of Perugia. Appointments: Presenter and interviewer, BBC Bristol, 1960-61; Broadcasts include: Quest; What's New?; People and Power, 1982-83; General Election Results Programmes, 1979, 1983, 1987; various programmes for the Budget, by-elections, local elections; Presenter, Question Time BBC, 1993-; Documentary films include: Ku-Klux-Klan; The Forgotten Million; Cyprus: The Thin Blue Line, 1964-65; South Africa: The White Tribe, 1979; The Struggle for South Africa, 1990; US-UK Relations: An Ocean Apart, 1988; David Dimbleby's India, 1997; Live commentary on many public occasions including: State Opening of Parliament; Trooping the Colour; Wedding of HRH Prince Andrew and Sarah Ferguson; H M The Queen Mother's 90th Birthday Parade; Funeral of Diana, Princess of Wales, 1997; Memorial Services including Lord Olivier. Publication: An Ocean Apart (with David Reynolds), 1988. Honours: Supreme Documentary Award, Royal TV Society; US Emmy Award, Monte Carlo Golden Nymph; Royal TV Society, Outstanding Documentary Award, 1990, 1997. Address: c/o Coutts & Co, 440 Strand, London WC1R 0QS, England.

**DIMBLEBY Jonathan,** b. 31 July 1944. Broadcaster; Journalist; Author. m. Bel Mooney, 1968, 1 son, 1 daughter. Education: University College, London. Appointments: Reporter, BBC Bristol, 1969-70; BBC Radio, World at One, 1970-71; Reporter, This Week, Thames TV, 1972-78, 1986-88; TV Eye, 1979; Reporter, Yorkshire TV, Jonathan Dimbleby in Evidence: The Police (series); The Bomb, 1980; The Eagle and the Bear, 1981; The Cold War Game, 1982; The American Dream, 1984; Four Years On - The Bomb, 1984; Associate Ed/Presenter, First Tuesday, 1982-86; Presenter/Ed, Jonathan Dimbleby on Sunday, TV AM, 1985-86; On the Record, BBC TV, 1988-93; Charles: The Private Man, The Public Role, Central TV, 1994; Jonathan Dimbleby, London Weekend TV, 1995-; Presenter, Any Questions?, BBC Radio 4, 1987-; Any Answers?, 1989-; Writer/Presenter, The Last Governor, Central TV, 1997; An Ethiopian Journey, LWT, 1998; A Kosovo Journey, LWT, 2000; Michael Heseltine – A Life in the Political

Jungle, LWT, 2000. Publications: Richard Dimbleby, 1975; The Palestinians, 1979; The Prince of Wales: A Biography, 1994; The Last Governor, 1997. Honours: Richard Dimbleby Award, 1974. Memberships: VP, Council for Protection of Rural England, 1997-; Soil Association, 1997-; President, Voluntary Service Overseas, 1999-; Bath Festivals Trust, 2003. Address: c/o David Higham Associates Ltd, 5 Lower John Street, W1R 4HA, England.

**DIMITROV Nikola,** b. 30 September 1972, Skopje, Macedonia. Ambassador. Education: Master of Law Degree, University of Cambridge, England. Appointments: Ambassador Extraordinary and Plenipatentiary of The Republic of Macedonia to the United States of America. Publications: The Framework Convention for the Protection of National Minorities; The Exhumation of Buried Antagonisms, 1998; Historical Background and Theoretical Implications, 1999. Honour: Best Student of Generation Prize. Address: 1101 30th Street, NW Ste 302, Washington DC, WA 20007, USA. E-mail: usoffice@macedonianembassy.org

**DIMOV Maxim Jekov,** b. 1 January 1961. Executive. Education: Attended German Language School, 1975-80; MA, International Economic Relations, University for National and Work Economy, 1986; Appointments: Machinoexport, Sofia, Bulgaria, 1986-89, Berlin, Germany, 1989-91; Chairman of the Board, Homo Ludens Foundation, 1991-; Executive Director, Council Of Ministers, State Fund for Reconstruction and Development, 1993-94; Member of Parliament, Deputy Chairman of Economic Commission, Member of Budget and Finance Commission, 37th National Assembly, 1994-97; Member of the Board, Energoremont Holding, 1994-97; Chairman of the Board, McCup Holding, 1997-; Member of the Board, IF Framlington Bulgaria Fund, London, 1997-2001; Deputy Chairman of the Supervisory Board, DZI Bank, Sofia, Bulgaria, 2001-2002; Regional Director Eurasia, PETMAL Oil Holdings, Malaysia, 2002-. Publications: Financial Engineering of Industrial Company, 1988; Problems of International Co-ordination Against Money Laundering, 1989; Harmonization of the Bulgarian and European Financial Systems, 1993; The role of the National Audit Office in conditions of market economy, 1996; ISO 9000:2000 Quality Management Systems, 2002. Honours: Honorary, Corresponding Member, International Informatization Academy, Moscow; Outstanding Intellectuals of the 21st Century, IBC, Cambridge, England; Man of the Year 2003, ABI, USA; Chairman, Bulgarian Non-Olympic Committee. Memberships: Bulgarian Antarctic Institute; Bulgarian-German Forum; Bulgarian Russian Business Association; National Geographic Society, USA; American Biographical Institute, USA; International Biographical Centre, UK. Address: 42-B Rodopski Izvor, Sofia 1680, Bulgaria.

**DING Tiping,** b. 22 July 1941, Hunan, China. Geologist. m. Xiaoqiu Zou, 2 sons. Education: Department of Geology, Centre-South Institute of Mining and Metallurgy, 1959-64; Postgraduate Study, Chinese Academy of Geological Sciences, 1964-67; Visiting Scholar, Department of Chemistry and Department of Geology, McMaster University, Canada. Appointments: Member, Academic Committee, 1984-, Professor, Chief of the Division of Isotope Geology, 1991-, Institute of Mineral Resources, Chinese Academy of Geological Sciences. Publications: Silicon Isotope Geochemistry; Calibrated sulfur isotope abundance ratios of three IAEA sulfur isotope reference materials and V-CDT with a reassessment of the atomic weight of sulfur; Stable isotope study of the Langshan polymetallic mineral district, Inner Mongolia, China; Silicon isotope compositions of dissolved silicon and suspended matter in the Yangtze River, China. Honours: The Scientist receiving allowance from the Chinese Government, 1991; The Scientist

making prominent contribution to the State, 1996. Memberships: Chairman, Committee of Isotope Abundance and Atomic Weight; Member, International Association of Geochemistry and Cosmochemistry; Member, Geochemical Society; Director, Geological Society of China. Address: Institute of Mineral Resources, Chinese Academy of Geological Sciences, Beijing 100037, P R China.

**DINI Luciana,** b. 19 January 1955, Rome, Italy. Full Professor. Education: MD, Biology, University of Rome "La Sapienza", 1977. Appointments: Researcher, University of Rome "Tor Vergata", Department of Biology, 1982-92; Associate Professor of Comparative Anatomy and Cytology, Department of Biology, 1992-2000, Full Professor of Comparative Anatomy and Cytology, Department of Biological and Environmental Science Technology, 2000-, University of Lecce, Lecce, Italy. Publications: Articles in scientific journals including: Journal of Clinical Investigation, 1994; Blood, 1994; Hepatology, 1995; Microscopy Research Technology, 2002; Cell and Tissue Research, 2003. Honour: Award Winner for best work in the field of cellular biology, Societa Nazionale di Scienza, Lettere ed Arti, 1987. Memberships: European Microscopy Society; European Cell Death Organisation. Address: Department of Biological and Environmental Science Technology, University of Lecce, Via Per Monteroni, Lecce 73100, Italy. E-mail: luciana.dini@unile.it

**DINSDALE Reece,** b. 6 August 1959, Normanton, West Yorkshire, England. Actor. m. Zara Turner, 1 son, 1 daughter. Education: Normanton Grammar, 1970-77; Guildhall School of Music and Drama, 1977-80. Career: Films include: Rabbit on the Moon; Hamlet; Romance and Rejection; ID; A Private Function; Television includes: Conviction; Ahead of the Class; The Trouble with George; Spooks; Murder in Mind; Thief Takers; Young Catherine; Take Me Home; Coppers; Home to Roost; Threads; Winter Flight; Theatre includes: Visiting Mr Green; Love You Too; A Going Concern; Racing Demon; Wild Oats; Observe the Sons of Ulster Marching Towards the Somme. Honours: International Press Award for Best Actor at the Geneva Film Festival for the film ID, 1996; Honorary Vice-President of Huddersfield Town Football Club Patrons Association. Membership: Huddersfield Town Football Club. Address: c/o Jonathan Artaras Associates Ltd, 11 Garrick Street, London WC2E 9AR, England.

**DINWIDDY Bruce Harry,** b. 1 February 1946, Epsom, England. Diplomat. m. Emma Victoria Dinwiddy, 1 son, 1 daughter. Education: MA, Philosophy, Politics and Economics, New College, Oxford, 1964-67. Appointments: British Embassy, Swaziland, 1967-69; Research Officer, ODI, 1970-73; FCO, 1973; First Secretary, UK Delegation (MBFR) Vienna, 1975-77; FCO, 1977-81; Head of Chancery, British Embassy, Cairo, 1981-83; FCO, 1983-86, Cabinet Office, 1986-88; Counsellor, British Embassy, Bonn, 1989-91; Deputy High Commissioner, Ottawa, 1992-95; Head, African Department (Southern), FCO, 1995-98; Commissioner, British Indian Ocean Territory, 1996-98; High Commissioner, Dar Es Salaam, 1998-2001; Seconded to Standard Chartered Bank, 2001-2002; Governor, Cayman Islands, 2002-05. Publication: Promoting African Enterprise, 1974. Honour: CMG, 2003. Memberships: Vincent's Club, Oxford; Aldeburgh Golf Club; Royal Wimbledon Golf Club. Address: c/o FCO (Grand Cayman), King Charles Street, London SW1A 2AH, England.

**DION Celine,** b. 30 March 1968, Charlemagne, Quebec, Canada. Singer. m. Rene Angelil, 17 December 1994, 1 son. Career: Recording Artiste, 1979-; Winner Eurovision Song Contest for Switzerland, 1988; Recorded in French, until, 1990;

35 million albums sold. Creative Works: Albums: Unison, 1990; Dion chante Plamondon, 1991; Sleepless in Seattle, 1993; The Colour of My Love, 1993; D'eux, 1995; Falling Into You, 1996; Let's Talk About Love, 1998; These are Special Times, 1998; All the Way, 1999; A New Day Has Come, 2002. Singles include: Beauty and the Beast, 1992; If You Asked Me To; Nothing Broken But My Heart; Love Can Move Mountains; When I Fall In Love; The Power of Love; Misled; Think Twice; Because You Loved Me; My Heart Will Go On; Immortality, 1998; Treat Her Like a Lady, 1998; That's the Way, It Is, 1999; The First time I Ever Saw your Face, 2000. Publications: All the Way, 2000; My Story, My Dreams, 2001; Honours: Pop Album of Year, 1983; Female Artist of Year, 1983-85, 1988; Discovery of the Year, 1983; Best Quebec Artist Outside Quebec, 1983, 1988; Best Selling Record, 1984, 1985; Best Selling Single, 1985; Pop Song of the Year, 1985, 1988; Journal de Quebec Trophy, 1985; Spectrel Video Award, Best Stage Performance, 1988; Album of the Year, 1991; Female Vocalist of the Year, 1991-93; Academy Award for Best Song written for a motion picture or TV, 1992; Grammy Award, 1993, 1999. Address: Les Productions Feeling, 2540 boulevard Daniel-Johnson, Porte 755, Laval, Quebec H7T 2S3, Canada.

**DIPROSE Noel Blair,** b. 26 December 1931, Camberwell, England. Tutor; Manager. Education: BA (Hons), English, Bournemouth, Dorset; ALAM (Eloc.), Teacher's Diploma, London; Gold Medal LAM (Hons), University of Glasgow; MA, Languages and Philosophy, 1964, University of Paris, course, 1965-66; London Business Management Course; Computer Certificate; Training and work experience in Accountancy. Appointments: Worked for a London law firm, RAF personnel selection section, 1950-52; Business accounts for an American company, London, 1956-59; Assistant, Anglais Lycée D'Etat Mixte Jacques Amyot, Melun Seine-et-Marne, France, 1965-66; Assistant Master, London grammar school; Executive Officer, Academic Department, University of London, 1967; Established Civil Servant; Retail Management; Linguist, French and German Assistant Supervisor, British Telecommunications, 1979-90; Tutor (Manager), English and French to university entrance, Mathematics to common entrance 11+. Publications: Milton and Keats; Questions Philosophiques. Honours: Award for Public Speaking; Listed in Who's Who publications and biographical dictionaries. Memberships: LAMDA Teachers' Association, London; NGP. Address: 10A Sunnyside Road South, London N9 9ST, England.

**DIVINSKY Michael,** b. 26 January 1947 C Romny, Ukraine. Statistician. m. Dinah Divinsky, 1 daughter. Education: MSc, State University, Kiev, Ukraine, 1972; PhD, Research Institute Engineering Survey, Moscow, 1981. Appointments: Senior Engineer, Ukrgiintiz, Kiev, 1972-76; Group Leader, Chief Specialist, Project Research Institute Moscow, 1980-90; Research Scientist Institute Technion, Haifa, Israel, 1992-93; Chief Expert in Statistical Applications, Public Works Department, Tel Aviv, Israel, 1993-. Publications: More than 60 publications including 24 in periodicals and proceedings of international conferences. Honours: Who's Who Historical Society, Certificate of Accomplishment; Listed in several biographical dictionaries. Memberships: Professional Engineers of the State of Israel Design and Research Centre. Address: Public Works Department, Materials and Research Division, 55 Ben Zvi Road, 61940 Tel Aviv, Israel. E-mail: mdivinsky@hotmail.com

**DIXON Alan (Michael),** b. 15 July 1936, Waterloo, Lancashire, England. m. Josephine Stapleton, 13 August 1960. Education: Studied Art, Goldsmiths College, University of London, 1956-63; University of London Diploma in Visual Arts. Appointment:

Teacher of Art, Schools in London and Peterborough, England, 1959-87. Publications: Snails and Reliquaries, 1964; The Upright Position, 1970; The Egotistical Decline, 1978; The Immaculate Magpies, 1982; The Hogweed Lass, 1991; A Far-Off Sound, 1994; Transports, 1996; The Ogling of Lady Luck, 2005. Contributions to: Poetry; Partisan Review; The Observer; The Times Literary Supplement; The Listener; New Statesman; London Review of Books; The Nation; London Magazine; Encounter; The Spectator; Prairie Schooner; The Scotsman. Address: 51 Cherry Garden Road, Eastbourne, BN20 8HG, England.

**DJUPEDAL Øystein,** b. 5 May 1960, Oslo, Norway. Member of Norwegian Parliament. m. Ragnhild Hammer, 2 sons, 1 daughter. Education: Graphics, Upper Secondary School. Appointments: Printer, Wennbergs Printing Works, 1983-93; Member of Norwegian Parliament, 1993-; Member of Committee on Education, Research and Church Affairs, 1993-97; Member of Committee on Financial Affairs, 1997-2005; Member of the extended Committee on Foreign Affairs, 2001-2005. Publications: Fagbevegelsen 2000 – nytt arhyndre, 1997; Kompetansepolitikk 2000, 1997. Memberships: Leader, Rosenborg local Socialist Left Party, 1982-95; Leader, South Trondelag County Socialist Left Party Youth, 1982-85; Member, National Board of Norwegian Socialist Left Party Youth, 1982-85; Board Member, South Trondelag County Socialist Left Party, 1985-86; Vice-Chairperson, 1988-89, Leader, 1989-91, Trodheim Socialist Left Party; Leader, South Trondelag County Socialist Left Party, 1991-93; Member, Norwegian Socialist Left Party National Board, 1991-93; Vice Chairperson, Norwegian Socialist Left Party, 1997-. Address: Stortinget. 0026 Oslo, Norway. E-mail: oystein.djupedal@stortinget.no

**DO Laurent,** b. 8 May 1967, Saint Vallier, France. Neurosurgeon. Education: School of Medicine, Montpellier, France, 1985-91; Residency, Neurosurgery, Marseille, France, 1991-97. Appointments: Neurosurgeon, Centre Hospitalier Universitaire Marseille, France, 1998-2002; Head, Department of Neurosurgery, Centre Hospitalier Universitaire Pointe a Pitre, Guadeloupe, 2002-. Publications: Articles in paediatric neurosurgery, interventional neuroradiology, neurochirurgie; neurosurgery, spine. Memberships: Société Francaise de Neurochirurgie; World Federation of Neurosurgical Societies; European Association of Neurosurgical Societies. Address: Service de Neurochirurgie, Centre Hospitalier Universitaire, BP465, 97159 Pointe a Pitre, Cedex Guadeloupe, France. E-mail: laurent.do@chu-guadeloupe.fr

**DOBBS Michael John,** b. 14 November 1948. Author. m. Amanda L Collingridge, 1981, 2 sons. Education: Christ Church, Oxford; Fletcher School of Law & Diplomacy, USA. Appointments: UK Special Adviser, 1981-87; Chief of Staff, UK Conservative Party, 1986-87; Joint Deputy Chairman, 1994-95; Deputy Chairman, Saatchi & Saatchi, 1983-91; Deputy Chairman, Conservative Party, 1994-95; Chairman, Spirit Advertising, 1998-. Publications: House of Cards, 1989; Wall Ganes, 1990; Last Man to Die, 1991; To Play the King, 1993; The Touch of Innocents, 1994; The Final Cut, 1995; Goodfellowe MP, 1997; The Buddha of Brewer Street, 1998; Whispers of Betrayal, 2000; Winston's War, 2002. Address: 12 Onslow Court, Drayton Gardens, London, SW10 9RL, England. E-mail: michldobbs@aol.com

**DOBER Hans Martin,** 11 March 1959, Neuwied/Rhein, Germany. Clergyman. m. Susanne Dober. 2 sons, 1 daughter. Education: Dr phil, 1990; Privat Dozent, Dr. phil. theol. habil., 2001. Clergyman of the Protestant Church, 1992-; Assistant of Practical Theology, University of Tübingen, Germany, 1994-

2002. Publications: Die Zeit Ernst Nehmen, 1990; Die Moderne Wahrnehmen, 2002; Articles: Flanerie Sammlung Spiel, 2000; Schleiermacher und Levinas, 2002; Ich und mich sind immer zu eifrig im Gespräche, 2002. Address: Eichhoernchenweg 5, 78532 Tuttlingen, Germany.

**DÖBEREINER Jürgen,** b. 1 November 1923, Königsberg Pr, Germany. Veterinarian. m. Johanna Kubelka, deceased 2000, 2 sons, 1 deceased 1996, 1 daughter. Education: DMV, Rio de Janeiro, 1954; MSc, University Wisconsin-Madison, USA, 1963; Dr med vet hc, Justus-Liebig-University Giessen, Germany, 1977. Appointment: Research Worker in Animal Pathology, Ministry Agriculture-Embrapa, Rio de Janeiro, Brazil, 1955-. Publications: More than 170 scientific papers; Co-author, Plantas Tóxicas do Brasil, 2000; Editor-in-Chief, Pesquisa Agropecuaria Brasileira (Brazilian Journal of Agricultural Research), 1965-76; Editor, Pesquisa Veterinária Brasileira (Brazilian Journal of Veterinary Research), 1981-. Membership: President, Brazilian College of Animal Pathology, 1978-2008; President, Brazilian Association of Science Editors, 2000-2004; President, The Johanna Döbereiner Research Society, 2002-2006. Address: Embrapa-CNPAB/Sanidade Animal, Km 47, Seropédica, Rio de Janeiro 23890-000, Brazil.

**DOBRESCU Mircea Virgil,** b. 27 October 1952, Turnu-Magurele, Romania. (German citizen, arrived in Germany, 1983). Veterinary Surgeon; Veterinary Dentist and Periodontist; Consultant; Scientist; Researcher; Writer. Education: DVM, summa cum laude, 1976; PhD Veterinary Medicine, Dentistry Science and Periodontology, 1993, University of Bucharest; Master in Veterinary Dentistry and Periodontology, Munich, Germany, 1992; Studies throughout Europe and Israel. Appointments: Assistant Professor, Pathology, Diagnostics and Clinics, State Veterinary Institute, Beit-Dagan, Ministry of Agriculture of State of Israel, University of Tel Aviv, Weizmann Institute of Sciences, University of Jerusalem, 1978; Specialist in Microbiology, Virology, Pathology and Leukaemia, Central Laboratories for Diagnosis, Ministry of Agriculture, Bucharest, 1978-82; Studies in Germany for Specialist in Veterinary Dentistry and Periodontology, 1983-89; Private practice for Veterinary Dentistry and Peridontology for small animals, Augsburg, Germany, 1989-; Owner and Senior Lecturer, School of Veterinary Dentistry and Periodontology for medical postgraduate training in Europe, 1992-; Presenter, numerous animal and veterinary conferences, seminars and workshops. Publications include: Odonton Therapy: A new human and animal Periodontology therapy; First Periodontal Status and First Dentistry Reference Cards in Veterinary Medicine for Cat and Dog; Use of Periodontal Status in Veterinary Dentistry Science; First Vade-mecum stomatologicum in Veterinary Medicine; Cast crown restorative dentistry of canini in dogs and cats with gold and porcelain, two new methods; Corrective orthodontics of common malocclusions in dogs with acrylic intraorale plates with expansion screw; Corrective Protrusion (corrective orthodontic) of Incisivi in a Rottweiler with chrome-cobalt intraorale plate with expansion screw – a premiere; Books: Da grinst selbst das Pferd (Even the Horse Would Grin); Joyful Stories of a Veterinary Surgeon, edited in Germany, 1996; The Last Secret of the Red Stone, fiction-adventure-novel, forthcoming; 37 articles in professional journals on veterinary dentistry and Periodontology and on animal and human cancer. Honours: International Personality of the Year 2001 in recognition of service to Education; International Scientist of the Year 2001 and of the Year 2003; 2000 Eminent Scientists of Today, 2003; Great Minds of the 21st Century; Man of the Year, 2001; Man of the Year, 2002; Living Legends; American Medal of Honor, 2002; World Medal of Honour, ABI, 2003; Nominated, International Peace Prize, United Cultural

Convention, ABI, USA, 2003; Worldwide Honours List, IBC, 2003; Contemporary Hall of Fame, ABI, 2003; Leading Intellectuals of the World, ABI, 2004; The Contemporary Who's Who of Professionals, ABI, 2005; Listed in several international directories of biography. Memberships: Research Board of Advisors, American Biographical Institute; New York Academy of Sciences; American Association for the Advancement of Science; Federation of European Microbiological Societies; International Union of Microbiological Societies; Romanian Oncological Society. Address: Stettenstr 28, 86150 Augsburg, Bayern, Germany.

**DOHMEN Guenther,** b. 8 April 1926, Heidelberg, Germany. University Professor. m. Karin Dohmen, 2 sons, 2 daughters. Education: PhD, Heidelberg University, 1951; Habilitation, Educational Science, Tuebingen University, 1963. Appointments: Founding Director, German Institute of Distance Studies, 1967-79; Member, Council of Europe's Steering Committee on Educational Technology, 1967-78; Chair, Association of University Teachers of Education, 1979-89; Director, Institute of Education II, University of Tuebingen, 1980-94; Chairman, German Association for Adult Education; Chairman, German Co-operative for Adult Education; Vice-President, European Association for Adult Education; Consultant to Governments, OECD, UNESCO, PHARE, EU; Guest Professor in 33 countries in all continents. Publications: School and Assessment, 1965; Lifelong Learning, 1995; Future of Adult Education in Europe, 1998; Informal Learning, 2001; 200 other publications partly translated to English, French, Spanish, Japanese. Honours: Student Representative in the German Constituant Assembly, 1948-49; UN Prize for International Education, 1954; Honorary Doctor, British Open University, 1981; Man of the Year 2001, American Biographical Institute. Memberships: German Expert Group in the Forum Education; International Adult and Continuing Education Hall Of Fame, USA; Education Council, State Baden-Wuerttemberg. Address: Falkenweg 72, D-72076 Tuebingen, Germany.

**DOIG John,** b. 2 August 1958, Helensburgh, Scotland. Violinist; Conductor. Education: First enrolled pupil, St Mary's Music School, Edinburgh, 1972. Appointments: BBC Symphony Orchestra, 1975-78; Principal Violin, BBC Philharmonic Orchestra, 1979-81; Co-Leader, Orchestra of Scottish Opera, 1981-83; Co-Leader and Guest Leader, Scottish Chamber Orchestra, 1986-90; Leader, Orchestra of Scottish Opera, 1991-98; Founder and Artistic Director, Scottish Bach Consort, 1994-. Honour: Honorary President, Scottish Bach Society. Membership: Society of Musicians. Address: Endrick Mews, Killearn, Stirlingshire G63 9ND, Scotland.

**DOJCINOVIC Uros,** b. 15 May 1959, Belgrade, Yugoslavia. Guitarist; Composer; Pedagogue. m. Vesna Djukic-Dojcinovic, 12 Jan 1984, 1 son. Education: University of Philology, Belgrade, 1979; Music Academy, Zagreb, 1979-83; Graduated in Classical Guitar, 1984; Graduated, Music Pedagogy, Music University of Belgrade, 1985; Postgraduate work in Musicology, University of Belgrade, 1988. Debut: Belgrade Concert Hall, Cultural Centre Stari Grad, 1976. Career: Over 2500 concerts worldwide; Over 500 radio and television appearances; Numerous masterclasses, lecturers and presentations; Professor of Classical Guitar, Chamber Music, various music schools in Belgrade and Zagreb. Compositions: Chamber Music with Guitar, opus 16, 26, 27, 31, 33, 34, 35, 36, 37, 39, 40, 48, includes 10 suites, themes with variations, fantasias, cycle-form compositions, some for different guitar orchestras and chamber groups including classical guitar. Recordings: South American Guitar; Exotic Guitar; Characteristic Guitar; Guitar Recital; Classical and Romantic Music for two guitars; Danza Caracteristica; Chamber Music for Guitar; Exotic Guitar Music. Publications: Magic World of the Guitar, 1984; Yugoslav Guitar History, 1992; The Guitar Triumph, 1994; The First Guitarist Steps, 1995; Anthology of Guitar Music in Serbia, 1996; Anthology of Guitar Music in Montenegro, 1996; Numerous articles in journals. Honours: Over 15 National and International medals, diplomas and prizes; First Republic and Federal Prizes in Guitar Composition, 1975, 1977; First Prize, Cultural Olympiad, Belgrade, 1978. Memberships: Society for Music Artists of Serbia; Society of Composers of Montenegro; Matica Srpska-Novi Sad. Address: Solunska str 12, 11000 Belgrade, Serbia.

**DOKULIL Milos,** b. 23 July 1928, Brno, Czech Republic. University Professor. m. Anna Chudoba, 1 daughter. Education: BA, 1949, MA, 1951, University of Political and Social Sciences, Prague, 1947-51; Charles University, Faculty of Arts, 1948-50; PhD, Czechoslovak Academy of Sciences, 1963; DSc, Charles University, 1993. Appointments: Lecturer, Senior Lecturer, Technical University, 1956-63; Senior Lecturer, Faculty of Pedagogy, 1963-69; For political reasons prevented from academic activity, including publishing of 3 books, 1970-89; Associate Professor, Department Head, 1990; Professor, Masaryk University, 1992-. Publications: A Primer of Logic for Teachers, 1967; Through the Philosophy of History to the History of Philosophy, 1970, enlarged, 1992; The Formation of a Philosopher: Through Toleration Towards the Epistemology of John Locke, 1972; On the Issue over Toleration: Lockean Contemplations, 1995; Ethics, 3 vols (Co-author, co-editor), 1998; Masaryk as a Rear-view Mirror? 2005; Numerous professional articles. Honours: Nominations to Man of Year, International Biographical Centre, American Biographical Institute; Nomination for Ministry of Education Prize (Czech Republic), 1999. Address: Faculty of Informatics, Masaryk University, Botanicka 68a, CZ 602 00 Brno, Czech Republic.

**DOLE Elizabeth Hanford,** b. 29 July 1936, Salisbury, North Carolina, USA. Administrator. m. Robert J Dole, 1975. Education: Duke University; Harvard University; University of Oxford. Appointments: Called to Bar, District of Columbia, 1966; Staff Assistant to Assistant Secretary for Education, Department of Health, Education & Welfare, 1966-67; Practising lawyer, Washington DC, 1967-68; Associate Director Legislative Affairs, then Executive Director Presidents Commission for Consumer Interests, 1968-71; Deputy Assistant, Office of Consumer Affairs, The White House, Washington DC, 1971-73; Commissioner, Federal Trade Commission, 1973-79; Assistant to President for Public Liaison, 1981-83; Secretary of Transport, 1983-87; Candidate for Republican presidential nomination, 1999; Senator from North Carolina, 2003-. Memberships: Trustee, Duke University, 1974-88; Member, Visiting Committee, John F Kennedy School of Government, 1988-; Secretary of Labour, 1989-90; President, American Red Cross, 1991-98; Member, Commission, Harvard School of Public Health, 1992-; Board of Overseers, Harvard University, 1989-95. Address: Office of the Senator from North Carolina, Suite B34, Dirksen Building, US Senate, Washington, DC 20510, USA.

**DOLE Robert J,** b. 22 July 1923, Russell, Kansas, USA. Politician. m. (2) Elizabeth Hanford Dole, 1975, 1 daughter. Education: University of Kansas; Washburn Municipal University. Appointments: Member, Kansas Legislature, 1951-53; Russell County Attorney, 1953-61; Member, House of Representatives, 1960-68; US Senator from Kansas, 1969-96; Senate Majority Leader, 1995-96; Senate Republican Leader, 1987-96; House Majority Leader, 1985-87; Minority Leader, 1987; Chairman, Republic National Committee, 1971-72; Vice-Presidential Candidate, 1976; Presidential Candidate,

1996; Member of Counsel, Verner, Liipfert, Bernhard, McPherson and Hand, Alston and Bird, 2003-. Publications: Great Political Wit (co-ed), 1999; Great Presidential Wits, 2001. Memberships: Chairman, Senate Finance Committee, Dole Foundation, 1981-84; Director, Mainstream Inc; Advisor, US Delegate to FAO Conference, Rome, 1965, 1974, 1977; Member, Congressional delegate to India, 1966, Mid E, 1967; Member, US Helsinki Commission; Delegate to Belgrade Conference, 1977; Trustee, William Allen White Foundation, University of Kansas; Member, National Advisory Committee, The John Wesley Colleges; American Bar Association; National Advisory Committee, on Scouting for the Handicapped, Kansas Association for Retarded Children; Advisory Board of Utd Cerebral Plasy, Kansas; Honorary Member, Advisory Board of Kidney Patients Inc; Presidential Medal of Freedom, 1997; Distinguished Service Award, 1997. Address: Suite 410, 901 15th Street, NW Washington DC 20005, USA.

**DOLEZAL Urszula Marta,** b. 8 September 1933, Krakow, Poland. Microbiologist, Scientific Worker. m. Marian Dolezal. Education: Manager, 1956, Doctor, PhD, 1959, Faculty Biology and Science of Earl Jagiellonian University; Associate Professor, Medical Academy in Cracow, 1965; Professor, sc.title, 1977; Professor ordinary Academy of Physical Education, 1990. Appointments: Head, Department of Mycology Medicine, Medical Academy Institute of Microbiology, 1970, Head of Chair, Department of Hygiene and Health Protection, later Health Promotion of Cracow Academy of Physical Education 1975; Retired, 2003-. Publications: 243 publications of topics: mycological pollution of air, mycology of the human environment and the influence of fungi, mould, yeast on the health of the population, mycoflora of flats and buildings, hygiene and different topics of preventive medicine, new aspect of health promotion, HIV/AIDS. Honours: Zloty Krzyz Zaslugi, 1980; Medal Komisji Edukacji Narodowej, 1983; Krzyz kawalerski Orderu Odrodzenia Polski, 1987. Memberships: Polish Academy of Science Commission of Biology; Commission of Public Health; International Scientific Forum on Home Hygiene, delegate of Poland in ERNA/RECS; Inter. Red Cross and Red Crescent Societies. Address: Daszynskiego 32 app 6, 31534, Poland.

**DOLLFUS Audouin Charles,** b. 12 November 1924, Paris, France. Physicist; Astronomer. m. Catherine Browne, 1959, 4 children. Education: Doctor of Mathematics, Faculty of Sciences, University of Paris. Appointments: Astronomer, Astrophysical Section, Meudon Observatory, Paris, 1946-; Head of Laboratory for Physics of the Solar System; Astronomer, Observatoire de Paris, 1965; Discovered Janus, innermost moon of Saturn, 1966;Emeritus President, Observatoire de Triel, 1994-; Research into polarisation of light. Publications: 350 scientific publications on astrophysics. Honours: Grand Prix of Academie des Sciences; International Award Galabert for Astronautics; Diploma Tissandier, International Federation of Astronautics. Memberships: International Academy of Astronautics; Société Astronomique de France; Aéro-club de France; French Association for the Advancement of Science; Royal Astronomical Society, London; Society of French Explorers; Explorers Club, USA; Société Philomatique de Paris; Honorary member, Royal Astronomical Society of Canada. Address: 77 rue Albert Perdreaux, 92370 Chaville, France.

**DOMEIKA Povilas,** b. 20 November 1938, Radviliskis Region, Lithuania. Economist; Professor. m. Audrone Zilnyte, 2 sons. Education: Economist, Lithuanian Academy of Agriculture (now University), 1963; Dr of Economics, Leningrad Institute of Agriculture (now St Petersburg State University of Agriculture), 1970; Dr Habil of Economics, Lithuanian Institute of Agrarian

Economics, 1991; Professor, Lithuanian Academy of Agriculture (now University), 1993. Appointments: Senior Assistant of Economics and Accounting Department, 1964-67, Dr Senior Assistant, 1970, Dr Associate Professor, 1976, Economical Cybernetics Department, Dr Associate Professor, Vice-Dean of Faculty of Economics, 1971-80; Dr Associate Professor, Head of Department of Economical Cybernetics, 1980-91, Dr Habil Professor, Department of Economical Cybernetics, 1993; Professor Dr Habil, Informatics Department, 1996-, Lithuanian University of Agriculture. Publications: Author of monographs: Mechanization of Accounting in Agricultural Enterprises, 1977, 1978; Co-author of textbooks: Accounting in Agriculture (with Essentials of Computerized Technology), 1974, 1980, 1987; Computerization of Accounting in Agricultural Enterprises, 1984; Author, 90 published scientific articles. Honours include: Academician, International Academy of Informatization of the United Nations, 1999; Order of Merit, Lithuanian University of Agriculture, 2004. Memberships: Member of Senate, Lithuanian University of Agriculture; Council Board: Faculty of Economics and Management; Institute of Information Technologies. Address: Universiteto 10, Akademijos m, LT-53361, Kauno rajonas, Lithuania. E-mail: pdm@eko.lzua.lt

**DOMINGO Placido,** b. 21 January 1941, Madrid, Spain. Singer; Conductor; Administrator. m. Marta Ornelas, 3 sons. Education: Studies in Piano, Conducting and Voice, National Conservatory of Music, Mexico City. Appointments: Operatic debut as Alfredo in La Traviata, Monterrey, Mexico, 1961; 12 roles, 280 performances, Israel National Opera, 2½ years; Title role, Ginastera's Don Rodrigo, New York City Opera, 1966; Debut as Maurizio in Adriana Lecouvreur, Metropolitan Opera, NY, 1968; 41 roles, over 400 performances, Metropolitan Opera, 36 years; Regularly appears at: Milan's La Scala, the Vienna State Opera, London's Covent Garden, Paris' Bastille Opera, the San Francisco Opera, Chicago's Lyric Opera, the Washington National Opera, the Los Angeles Opera, the Lyceo in Barcelona, the Colon in Buenos Aires, the Real in Madrid, and at the Bayreuth and Salzburg Festivals; Conductor of opera performances at the Metropolitan, London's Covent Garden and Vienna State Opera, etc; Conductor of symphonic concerts with the Berlin Philharmonic, London Symphony and Chicago Symphony, etc; Music Director, Seville World's Fair; General Director, Washington National Opera, 1994-; General Director, Los Angeles Opera, 2000-; Over 120 different roles including: Wagner's "Parsifal", "Lohengrin" and Seigmund in "Walkure"; "Meistersinger", "Tannhauser"; "Flying Dutchman"; Richard Strauss's "Die Frau Ohne Schattern"; Weber's "Oberon"; Beethoven's "Fidelio"; Gherman in Tchaikovsky's "Queen of Spades" (in Russian); the Spanish opera "Margarita la Tornera" by Roberto Chapi; Verdi's "La Battaglia di Legnano"; Anton Garcia Abril's "Divinas Palabras"; Rasputin in Deborah Drattell's "Nicholas and Alexandra"; Breton's "La Dolores"; Albeniz's "Merlin";Founder, yearly competition for young singers, "Operalia"; Inaugurated Domingo Cafritz Young Artists Program of the Washington Opera, 2002; Special benefit concerts to help 1985 Mexican earthquake, AIDS charities, Armenian earthquake, mudslides in Acapulco, and others. Publications: Recordings: Over 100 recordings, 97 of which are full-length operas; More than 50 videos; 3 theatrically released films (Zeffirelli's "Traviata" and "Otello", and Rosi's "Carmen"); Recently: double CD of every Verdi aria for the tenor voice; CD of excerpts from Wagner's "Siegfried" and "Gotterdaemmerung". Honours: Total of 11 Grammy Awards; Telecast of "Tosca" seen by audience of more than 1 billion in 117 countries; Sang 18th opening night of a season with "Pagliacci", Metropolitan Opera, 1999-2000; 7 of his CDs appeared on Billboard's top-selling charts of classical and cross-over recordings; 8 records have gone gold; Named Kennedy Center Honoree; Commander of France's Legion of Honor; Recipient, Honorary Knighthood of the British Empire; The United States Medal of Freedom; Honorary Doctorate, Oxford University, England, 2003; President Gorbachev's World Award for Humanitarian Causes. Address: c/o Vincent and Farrell Associates, 165 East 83rd St, #5E, New York, NY 10028, USA.

**DOMINIAN Jack,** b. 25 August 1929, Athens, Greece. Doctor. m. Eddith Mary, 4 daughters. Education: MA; FRCPEd; FRCPsy; DSc (Hons); MBE. Appointments: Qualified as doctor, 1955; Qualified as psychiatrist, 1961; Consultant Psychiatrist, 1964-88; Private Practice, 1988-2003; Retired, 2003-. Publications: 32 books including: Christian Marriage, 1967; Marriage, Faith & Love, 1981; Marital Breakdown, 1968; Authority, 1976; Cycles of Affirmation, 1975; Let's Make Love, 2001; One Like Us, 1998; Living Love, 2004; Over 100 articles in leading Catholic journal, Tablet; Numerous articles in BMJ, Lancet and other scientific journals. Honours: DSc (Hon), Lancaster University, 1976; MBE, 1994. Memberships: Royal College of Psychiatry; Royal College of Physicians, Edinburgh; Fellow, Royal Society of Medicine, London. Address: 19 Clements Road, Chorleywood, Hertfordshire, England.

**DONADIO Mario Dimitrio,** b. 12 March 1969, Yonkers, New York, USA. Clinical Radiologist. Education: Degree in Medicine & Surgery, 1994, Specialisation in Radiology, 1999, II University of Naples, Italy. Appointments: Second Lieutenant Doctor CPL, Italian Army, 231 Rgt Avellino, 1997-98; Consultant Radiologist, Femir-Salus, Naples, 1999-2000; Consultant Radiologist, Sasso Radiological Office, Naples, 1999-2001; Consultant Radiologist, University Hospital, Lewisham, England, 2001-04; Consultant Radiologist, Newham General Hospital, London, England, 2001-04; Consultant Radiologist, S Giuseppe Moscati Hospital, Monteforte, Italy, 2004-. Memberships: Order of Medical Doctors of Avellino, Italy, 1995-; GMC, UK, 1998-; Specialist Register, Clinical Radiologist, GMC, UK, 2000. Address: via S Pionati, 10, 83100 Avellino, Italy. E-mail: dimischek@doctors.org.uk

**DONALD Athene Margaret,** b. 15 May 1953. Professor of Physics. m. 2 children. Education: BA in Natural Sciences (Theoretical Physics), 1971-74, PhD, 1974-77, Cambridge University. Appointments: Postdoctoral Associate, Department of Materials Science and Engineering, Cornell University, 1977-81; SERC Fellowship, Department of Metallurgy and Materials Science, Cambridge University, 1981-83; Royal Society University Research Fellowship, Cavendish Laboratory, Cambridge, 1983-85; Lecturer, Department of Physics, 1985-95, Reader in Experimental Physics, 1995-98, Professor, Department of Physics, 1998-, Deputy Head, 2003-, University of Cambridge. Honours: Charles Vernon Boys Prize of the Institute of Physics, 1989; Samuel Locker Award in Physics, University of Birmingham, 1989; Rosenhain Medal and Prize, Institute of Materials, 1995; Elected Fellow of the Royal Society, 1999; William Hopkins Prize of the Cambridge Philosophical Society, 2003; Mott Prize, Institute of Physics, 2005. Memberships include: BBSRC Strategy Board, 2003-04; Editorial Board, European Physical Journal E; Research Council Panel for Basic Technology; Cambridge Philosophical Society; Dorothy Hodgkin Fellowship Committee; 2nd Target Station Steering Advisory Committee, Rutherford Appleton Laboratory; RAE subpanel E19. Address: Cavendish Laboratory, Madingley Road, Cambridge CB3 0HE, England. E-mail: amd3@cam.ac.uk

**DONALDSON David,** b. 13 February 1936, Birmingham, England. Physician. Education: MB, ChB, University of Birmingham Medical School, 1959; MRCP, London, 1963;

MRCPath, London, 1969; FRCPath, London, 1981; FRCP, London, 1999; FI Biol, London 2002; FRSC, London, 2001. Appointments: House Physician, Selly Oak Hospital, Birmingham, 1959-60; House Surgeon, Children's Hospital, Birmingham, 1960; Senior House Officer, Clinical Pathology, Queen Elizabeth Hospital, Birmingham, 1960-61; Assistant Resident Medical Officer, Registrar in General Medicine, General Infirmary, Leeds, 1961-62; Registrar, General Medicine, Victoria Hospital, Keighley, 1963-64; Lecturer, Honorary Senior Registrar, Chemical Pathology, Institute of Neurology, National Hospitals for Nervous Diseases, London, 1964-70; Consultant, Chemical Pathology, East Surrey Hospital, Redhill, 1970-2001, Crawley Hospital, Crawley, 1970-2001; Gatwick Park Hospital, Horley, 1984-; Vice Chairman, Medical Sub-Committee, Marie Curie Memorial Foundation, 1978-83; Clinical Director, Pathology Department, East Surrey Hospital, 1991-94; Chairman, East Surrey Division, British Medical Association, 1992-93; Chairman, South West Thames Chemical Pathology Advisory Group, South Thames Regional Health Authority, 1995-2000; Deputy Honorary Editor, Editorial Board, Journal of The Royal Society for the Promotion of Health, 1997-. Publications: Over 100 publications in professional journals and chapters in books; Books: Essential Diagnostic Tests in Biochemistry and Haematology (co-author), 1971; Diagnostic Function Tests in Chemical Pathology (co-author), 1989; Psychiatric Disorders with a Biochemical Basis, 1998. Honour: Recipient, Mori Felicitation Award, International College of Nutrition, 2002. Memberships include: Fellow, International College of Nutrition, Royal Society of Medicine, Royal Society for the Promotion of Health, Royal Geographical Society, Medical Society of London, Hunterian Society; Member, American Association for the Advancement of Science, Association of Clinical Biochemists, Association of Clinical Pathologists, European Atherosclerosis Society, British Atherosclerosis Society, British Association for the Advancement of Science, New York Academy of Sciences, Faculty of History and Philosophy of Medicine and Pharmacy (Worshipful Society of Apothecaries of London), Harveian Society of London. Address: 5 Woodfield Way, Redhill, Surrey RH1 2DP, England.

**DONG Yuning,** b. 16 June 1955, Nanjing, China. Professor. Education: B Eng, 1982, M Eng, 1984, Nanjing University of Posts and Telecommunications; PhD, South East University, Nanjing, China, 1988; M Phil, Queen's University, Belfast, Northern Ireland, 1998. Appointments: Lecturer, 1988-92, Associate Professor, 1992-1999, Professor, Information Engineering Department, 1999-, Nanjing University of Posts and Telecommunications; Visiting Scholar, Imperial College, London, England, 1992-93; Postdoctoral Fellow, University of Texas, Galveston, Texas, 1993-95; Research Fellow, Queen's University, Belfast, Northern Ireland and University of Birmingham, England, 1995-98. Publications: 3D reconstruction of irregular shapes, 2001; Fast computation of various templates, 2003; Technical papers in Chinese Journal of Electronics, Chinese Journal of Computers and others, 2000-2003. Honours: Best University Teacher, Jiangsu Province, China, 1992; Best Researcher, Ministry of Posts and Telecommunications, China, 1993. Memberships: Senior Member, China Communications Institute; Senior Member, Chinese Institute of Electronics. Address: Nanjing University of Posts and Telecommunications, PO Box 166, 66 New Mo-fan-ma-lu Road, Nanjing 210003, China. E-mail: dongyn@njupt.edu.cn

**DONIN Valery Il'yich,** b. 11 March 1941, Nerchinsk, Eastern Siberia, Russia. Physicist. m. Tamara Kurtz, 1 daughter. Education: MSc, 1963, Tomsk State University; PhD (CPMSc), 1972; Doctorate in Phys and Math Sc, 1989, Russian Academy

of Sciences. Appointments: Engineer, Research Scientist, Head of Laboratory, quantum electronics, Siberian Branch of Russian Academy of Sciences, 1963-. Publications: Around 100 research papers in field of laser and plasma physics; book, High-Power Gas Ion Lasers, 1991. Honours: First degree diploma, Siberian Branch of Russian Academy of Sciences, 1973; Honorary diplomas, Russian Academy of Sciences, 1974 and 1999; Medal, Exhibition of National Economic Achievements, USSR, 1979; Honorary professor, Albert Schweitzer International University, 2000; American Medal of Honor, ABI, 2001; Inducted into 500 Leaders of World Influence Hall of Fame, ABI, and 500 Founders of 21st Century Honours List, IBC, 2002. Memberships: Rozhdestvensky Optical Society; New York Academy of Sciences. Address: Institute of Automation and Electrometry, Siberian Branch of Russian Academy of Sciences, Acad Koptyuga pr. 1, Novosibirsk 630090, Russia. E-mail: donin@iae.nsk.su

**DONNELLY John David,** b. 23 December 1929, Trichinolpoly, India. Roman Catholic Priest. Education: Beaumont College, Old Windsor; Collegio de Propaganda Fide, Rome; Universita Urbaniana. Appointments: National Service: 2nd Lieutenant, Royal Berkshire Regiment, 1948-50; Secretary to Bishop of Brentwood, 1958-62; Parish Priest, Hainault, 1962-67; Vice-Rector, College of Propaganda Fide, Rome, 1967-69; Parish Priest, Upminster, 1969-81; Vicar General, Diocese of Brentwood, 1981-91; Parish Priest, Frinton and Walton, Essex, 1995-2005. Publication: Stations of the Cross for Brentwood Cathedral. Honours: Licentiate of Philosophy (PhL); Licentiate of Theology (STL); Prelate of Honour to the Pope (Rt Rev Monsignor); Canon of Brentwood Chapter. Membership: Essex Club. Address: 114 Connaught Avenue, Frinton-on-Sea, Essex CO13 9AD, England.

**DONNELLY Martin Eugene,** b. 4 June 1958, Newbury, Berkshire, England. Civil Servant. m. Susan Catchpole, 3 daughters. Education: Philosophy, Politics and Economics, Oxford University, 1976-79; College of Europe, Bruges, 1979-80; Ecole Nationale d'Administration, Paris, 1983-84. Appointments: Joined Treasury, 1980; Private Secretary to the Financial Secretary, 1982; Private Secretary to the Secretary of State for Northern Ireland, 1988-89; Member of Personal Staff of Leon Brittan, European Commission Vice-President, 1989-92; Leader of Treasury Team controlling defence spending, 1993-95; Seconded to French Finance Ministry, 1995-96; Set up Treasury Team dealing with Economic and Monetary Union in Europe, 1996; Deputy Head, European Secretariat, Cabinet Office, 1997-2003; Policy Director, Immigration and Nationality Directorate of the Home Office, 2003-2004; Director General, Economic, Foreign and Commonwealth Office, 2004-. Honour: CMG, 2002. Address: Foreign and Commonwealth Office, King Charles Street, London SW1, England.

**DONNER Richard,** b. 1939, New York, USA. Director; Producer. Appointments: Actor off-Broadway; Collaborated with director Martin Ritt on TV adaption of Somerset Maugham's Of Human Bondage; Moved to California and began commercials, industrial films and documentaries; Films: X 15, 1961; Salt and Pepper, 1968; Twinky, 1969; The Omen, 1976; Superman, 1978; Inside Moves, 1981; The Toy, 1982 Ladyhawke, 1985; The Goonies, 1985; Lethal Weapon, 1987; Scrooged, 1988; Lethal Weapon 2, 1989; Radio Flyer, 1991; The Final Conflict (executive producer), 1991; Lethal Weapon 3, 1992; Free Willy (co-executive producer), 1993; Maverick, 1994; Assassins, 1995; Free Willy 3: The Rescue; Lethal Weapon 4, 1998; Blackheart (producer), 1999; Conspiracy Theory; TV films: Portrait of a Teenage Alcoholic; Senior Year; A Shadow in the Streets; Tales From the Crypt presents Demon

Knight (co-executive producer); Any Given Sunday, 1999; X-Men (executive producer), 2000; Series episodes of: Have Gun Will Travel; Perry Mason; Cannon; Get Smart; The Fugitive; Kojak; Bronk; Twilight Zone; The Banana Splits; Combat; Two Fisted Tales; Conspiracy Theory. Address: The Donners Company, 9465 Wilshire Boulevard, #420, Beverly Hills, CA 90212, USA.

**DONORÀ Luigi,** b. 18 April 1935, Dignano d'Istria (Pola), Italy. Composer. Education: Studies with: Luigi Perracchio, Felice Quaranta, Sandro Fuga, Carlo Pinelli and Franco Donadoni, Conservatoire of Turin; Diploma, Choral Music and Choral Direction, 1963, Composition, 1972, Conservatoir of Milan; Electronic Music Course held by Enore Zaffri, 1968; Conductorship Course held by Mario Rossi, 1967, 1968, 1969; Studies at the Accademia Musicale Chigiana in Siena with Franco Ferrara and Peter Maag, 1968; Specialisation courses in Composition in Siena held by Goffredo Petrassi, 1968 and Boris Porena, 1969; Diploma in High Specialisation in Composition with Franco Donatoni, 1969; Diploma in High Specialisation in Director of Polyphonic Choir with Nino Antonelli, 1969-70; Opera Direction Course with Bruno Rigacci and Gino Bechi, 1970; Workshops with Ligeti, 1973 and Luigi Dallapiccola, 1974. Career: Teacher, Giuseppe Verdi Conservatoire, Turin, 1977-2000; Composer; Piano Accompanist; Patentee of 2 patents for a series of rules to solve musical problems, Ministry of Industry and Commerce. Compositions: Numerous compositions for the theatre, for orchestra, chamber music, vocal music. Publications: Appunti per uno studio sul canto patriarchino, 1977; Antonio Smareglia, 1982; La corale istriana di Torino, 1987. Honours: Awards in national and international composition competitions. Address: Via Tibone 6, 10126 Torino, Italy.

**DONOVAN Marie-Andrée,** b. 1947, Timmins, Ontario, Canada. Writer. 1 daughter. Education: BA, University of Ottawa, Canada. Appointment: Typesetting and Layout, Bibliothèque du Nouveau Monde (Corpus d'Éditions Critiques), University of Ottawa. Publications: Books: Nouvelles volantes (short stories), 1994; L'Envers de toi (novel), 1997, 2000; Mademoiselle Cassie (novel), 1999, 2003; L'Harmonica (novel), 2000; Les Bernaches en voyage (story for children), 2001; Les soleils incendiés (novel), 2004. Honours: Prix littéraire Le Droit 2000 for Mademoiselle Cassie; Prix littéraire de la Fondation franco-ontarienne 2002, for La Couleur des voyages (to be published); Listed in Who's Who publications and biographical dictionaries. Address: Corpus d'Éditions Critiques, University of Ottawa, 60 University, Ottawa, Ontario, Canada K1N 6N5. E-mail: donovan@uottawa.ca

**DONOVAN Paul James Kingsley,** b. 8 April 1949, Sheffield, Yorkshire, England. Writer (Freelance). m. Hazel Case, 27 October 1979, 1 son, 2 daughters. Education: MA, Oriel College, Oxford. Appointments: Staff Journalist, Sunday Mirror, Daily Mail and Today, 1973-88; Radio Columnist, Sunday Times, 1988-. Publications: Roger Moore, 1983; Dudley, 1988; The Radio Companion, 1991; All Our Todays, 1997. Contributions to: Newspapers including The Times, Sunday Times, Observer, Guardian; New Dictionary of National Biography. Memberships: Society of Authors, Broadcasting Committee; Devonshire Association. Address: 11 Stile Hall Gardens, London W4 3BS, England. E-mail: pauldon@scribbler.freeserve.co.uk

**DOOLAN Brian James,** b. 25 August 1943, Birmingham, England. Roman Catholic Priest. Education: City of Birmingham Training College; St Stephen's House, Oxford; St Mary's College, Oscott. Appointments: School Teacher, 1964-66; In Anglican Ministry, 1968-94; Principal, Alan Knight Training Centre, Guyana, South America, 1982-85; Assistant Director,

Maryvale Institute, Birmingham, 1995-96; Parish Priest, St George's, Worcester, 1996-99; Dean of St Chad's Cathedral, Birmingham, 1999-. Publications: St George's, Worcester 1590-1990, 1999; Catholic Bishops of Birmingham, 2003; The Pugins and the Hardmans, 2004; Contributor to: Midland Catholic History; The Basilican; Oxford Dictionary of National Biography. Memberships: Chairman, English Catholic History Association; Chairman, Midland Catholic History Association; Executive Secretary, Archdiocese of Birmingham Historic Churches Committee. Address: Cathedral House, St Chad's Queensway, Birmingham B4 6EU, England.

**DORFF Stephen,** b. 29 July 1973, Atlanta, Georgia, USA. Actor. Appointments: Started acting aged 9; Films: The Gate; The Power of One; An Ambush of Ghosts; Judgement Night; Rescue Me; Backbeat; SFW; Reckless; Innocent Lies; I Shot Andy Warhol; City of Industry, 1997; Blood and Wine, 1997; Blade, 1998; Entropy, 1999; Quantum Project, 2000; Cecil B Demented, 2000; The Last Minute, 2001; Zoolander, 2001; All For Nothin', 2002; Deuces Wild, 2002; Riders, 2002; FearDotCom, 2002; Den of Lions, 2002; Cold Creek Manor, 2003; Alone in the Dark, 2005; Tennis, Anyone?, 2005; TV films: I Know My First Name is Steven, 1989; Always Remember I Love You, 1989; Do You Know the Muffin Man? 1989; A Son's Promise, 1990; Earthly Possessions, 1999; TV series: What a Dummy, 1990. Address: 9350 Wilshire Boulevard, Suite 4, Beverly Hills, CA 90212, USA.

**DORFMAN Ariel,** b. 6 May 1942, Buenos Aires, Argentina (Chilean citizen). Research Professor of Literature and Latin; Author; Dramatist; Poet. Education: Graduated, University of Chile, Santiago, 1967. Appointment: Walter Hines Page Research Professor of Literature and Latin, Centre for International Studies, Duke University, Durham, North Carolina, 1984-. Publications: Fiction: Hard Rain, 1973; My House is On Fire, 1979; Widows, 1983; Dorando la pildora, 1985; Travesia, 1986; The Last Song of Manuel Sendero, 1986; Mascara, 1988; Konfidenz, 1996. Poetry: Last Waltz in Santiago and Other Poems of Exile and Disappearance, 1988. Plays: Widows, 1988; Death and the Maiden, 1991; Reader, 1992; Who's Who (with Rodrigo Dorfman), 1997. Films: Death and the Maiden, 1994; Prisoners in Time, 1995; My House is on Fire, 1997. Non-Fiction: How to Read Donald Duck (with Armand Mattelart), 1971; The Empire's Old Clothes, 1983; Some Write to the Future, 1991; Heading South, Looking North: A Bilingual Journey, 1998. Honours: Olivier Award, London 1991; Time Out Award, 1991; Literary Lion, New York Public Library, 1992; Dora Award, 1994; Charity Randall Citation, International Poetry Forum, 1994; Best Film for Television, Writers Guild of Great Britain, 1996. Address: c/o Centre for International Studies, Duke University, Durham, NC 27708, USA.

**DOUGLAS Brian David,** b.8 July 1948, Scotland. Painter. Education: York School of Art, 1963-67; Maidstone College of Art, 1967-70; Royal Academy Schools, London, 1970-73; Leeds Polytechnic, 1973-74. Career: Teacher, 1974-83; Technician, York University, 1984-89; Painter, 1970-2004. Honours: RAS (Painting and Engraving); NEAC; RBA. Memberships: Royal Society of British Artists; New English Art Club. Address: 26 Whitestone Drive, York YO31 9HZ, England.

**DOUGLAS James Frederick,** b. 22 September 1938, Portadown, Co Armagh, Northern Ireland. Consultant Nephrologist. m. Giselle Sook An Douglas, 3 sons. Education: BA, BCL, 1960, MA, 1964, BM BCh, 1969, Wadham College, Oxford; Middle Temple London, Called to the Bar, 1964; MB BCh, Queen's University, Belfast, 1969; MRCP (UK), 1972; FRCP (UK), 1986. Appointments: Lecturer, College of Law, 1963; Junior Medical Positions: Royal Victoria and City Hospitals, Belfast, Radcliffe Infirmary, Oxford, 1969-72; Tutor in Clinical Pharmacology, 1970-71, Queen's University, Belfast; Specialist in Nephrology, Dialysis and Transplantation, 1972-, Consultant, 1975-, Unit Director, 1988-96; Emeritus Professor, 2003-, Queen's University Belfast; Currently: Consultant Nephrologist, Antrim Area Hospital and Teaching Fellow in Clinical Pharmacology, Queen's University, Belfast. Publications: Over 60 publications on acute and chronic renal failure, transplantation, renal toxicology, law and ethics of renal failure and organ donation. Memberships include: British Transplantation Society; Renal Association; American Society of Nephrology; International Society of Nephrology; Transplantation Society. Address: Ballyrobert House, 5 Coyles Lane, Ballyrobert, Bangor, Co Down, Northern Ireland BT19 1VF. E-mail: jamesfdouglas38@hotmail.com

**DOUGLAS Kirk**, b. 9 December 1916, Amsterdam, New York, USA. Actor. m. (1) Diana Dill, 2 sons, (2) Anne Buydens, 2 sons. Education: St Lawrence University; American Academy of Dramatic Arts. Appointments: President, Bryna Productions, 1955-; Director, Los Angeles Chapt, UN Association. Stage appearances: Spring Again; Three Sisters; Kiss and Tell; The Wind is Ninety; Alice in Arms; Man Bites Dog; The Boys of Autumn; Films include: The Strange Love of Martha Ivers; Letters to Three Wives; Ace in the Hole; The Bad and the Beautiful; 20,000 Leagues under the Sea; Ulysses; Lust for Life; Gunfight at Ok Corral; Paths of Glory; the Vikings; Last Train from Gun Hill; The Devil's Disciple; Spartacus; Strangers When We meet; Seven Days in May; Town Without Pity; The List of Adran Messenger; In Harms Way; Cast a Giant Shadow; The Way West; War Waggon; The Brotherhood; The Arrangement; There Was a Crooked Man; Gunfight, 1971; Light at the Edge of the World; Catch Me a Spy; A Man to Respect, 1972; Cat and Mouse; Scalawag (director), 1973; Once is Not Enough, 1975; Posse (producer, actor), 1975; The Moneychangers (TV), 1976; Holocaust 2000, 1977; The Fury, 1977; Villain, 1978; Saturn 3, 1979; The Final Countdown, 1980; The Man From Snowy River, 1986; Tough Guys, 1986; Queenie (TV mini series), 1987; Oscar, Welcome to Veraz, Greedy, 1994; Diamonds, 1999; Family Jewels, 2002. Publications: The Ragman's Son: an Autobiography, 1988; Novels: Dance With The Devil, 1990; The Secret, 1992; The Gift, 1992; Last Tango in Brooklyn, 1994; Climbing the Mountain: My Search for Meaning, 1997; The Broken Mirror (novel), 1997; My Stroke of Luck, 2002. Honours: Academy awards, critics awards; Commandeur, Ordre des Arts et Lettres, 1979; Légion d'honneur, 1985; Presidential Medal of Freedom, 1981; American Film Industries Lifetime Achievement, 1991; Kennedy Center Honors, 1994; Lifetime Achievement Award, Screen Actors' Guild, 1999; Golden Bear, Berlin Film Festival, 2000; National Medal of Arts, 2002. Address: The Bryna Company, 141 S El Camino Drive, Beverly Hills, CA 90212, USA.

**DOUGLAS Michael Kirk**, b. 25 September 1944, New Brunswick, NJ, USA. m. (1) Diandra Mornell Luker (divorced), 1 son, (2) Catherine Zeta Jones, 2000, 1 son, 1 daughter. Appointments: Actor in films: It's My Turn; Hail Heroll, 1969; Summertime, 1971; Napoleon and Samantha, 1972; Coma, 1978; Running, 1979; Star Chamber, 1983; Romancing the Stone, 1984; A Chorus Line, 1985; Jewel of the Nile, 1985; Fatal Attraction, 1987; Wall Street, 1987; Heidi, 1989; Black Rain, 1989; The War of the Roses, 1990; Shining Through, 1990; Basic Instinct, 1992; Falling Down, 1993; The American President, 1995; The Ghost and the Darkness, 1996; The Game, 1997; A Perfect Murder, 1998; Traffic, 2000; Wonder Boys, 2000; One Night at McCool's, 2000; Don't Say a Word, 2001; A Few Good Years, 2002; It Runs in the Family, 2003; Monkeyface,

2003; Producer, films including: One Flew Over the Cuckoo's Nest, 1975; The China Syndrome; Sarman (executive producer); Romancing the Stone; Jewel of the Nile, Flatliners, 1990; Made in America (co-executive, producer); Disclosure, 1994; A Perfect Murder, 1998; One Night at McCool's, 2000; Godspeed; Lawrence Mann, 2002; Actor in TV series: Streets of San Francisco. Honours include: Academy Award for Best Actor for Wall Street, 1988; Spencer Tracey Award, 1999; UN Messenger of Peace, 2000. Address: C/o Creative Artists Agency Inc, 9830 Wilshire Boulevard, Beverly Hills, CA 90212, USA. Website: www.michaeldouglas.com

**DOWD George Simon**, b. 9 November 1946, Halifax, Yorkshire, England. Consultant Orthopaedic Surgeon. m. Angela Christine, 3 daughters. Education: University of Liverpool. Appointments: House Officer posts, David Lewis Northern Hospital; Registrar and Senior Registrar in several Liverpool Hospitals; Senior Lecturer, University of Liverpool and Consultant Orthopaedic Surgeon; Senior Lecturer University of London Royal National Orthopaedic Hospital, London and Consultant Orthopaedic Surgeon; Consultant Orthopaedic Surgeon, St Bartholomew's Hospital, London; Currently Director, Wellington Knee Surgery Unit, London and Consultant Orthopaedic Surgeon; Consultant Orthopaedic Surgeon, Royal Free Hospital, London. Publications: Publications on trauma, arthritis and disorders of the knee including soft tissue injuries and arthritis of the knee; 2 books on multiple choice questions in orthopaedics and trauma; 11 book chapters on orthopaedics and trauma including knee disorders. Honours: ABC Travelling Fellow; Norman Roberts Prize, President's Medal, British Orthopaedic Research Society; Hunterian Professor Royal College of Surgeons, Munsif Oration, Bombay, India. Memberships: British Orthopaedic Association; British Association of Surgery of the Knee; ISAKOS; Honorary Member, Macedonian Orthopaedic and Sports Association; Arthroscopy Association of North America. Address: Wellington Knee Surgery Unit; Wellington Hospital, Wellington Place, London NW8 9CR, England.

**DOWLING Ann Patricia**, b. 15 July 1952. Professor of Mechanical Engineering. m. Thomas Paul Hynes, 1974. Education: Ursuline Convent School, Westgate, Kent; BA, 1973, MA, 1977, PhD, 1978, Girton College, Cambridge; CEng, FIMechE, 1990; FREng (FEng, 1996); FRAeS, 1997; Fellow, Royal Society, 2003; Fellow, Institute of Acoustics, 1989. Appointments: Research Fellow, 1977-78, Director of Studies in Engineering, 1979-90, Sidney Sussex College, Assistant Lecturer in Engineering, 1979-82, Lecturer, 1982-86, Reader in Acoustics, 1986-93, Deputy Head, Engineering Department, 1990-93, 1996-99, Cambridge University; Jerome C Hunsaker Visiting Professor, MIT, 1999-2000; Moore Distinguished Scholar, CIT, 2001-02. Publications: Sound and Sources of Sound, with J E Ffowes Williams), 1983; Modern Methods in Analytical Acoustics, with D G Crighton et al, 1992; Contributions to scientific and engineering journals. Honours: A B Wood Medal, Institute of Acoustics, 1990. Memberships: AIAA, 1990; Defence and Aerospace Technology Foresight Panel, 1994-97; Defence Scientific Advisory Council, 1998-2001; EPSRC, 2001- (Member, 1998-2002, Chairman, 2003-, Technical Opportunities Panel), Non-executive Director, DRA, 1995-97; Scientific Advisory Board, DERA, 1997-20901; Council, Royal Academy of Engineering, 1998-2002 (Vice President, 1999-2002); Trustee, Ford of Britain Trust, 1993-2002; Cambridge European Trust, 1994-; National Museum of Science and Industry, 1999-; Governor, Felsted School, 1994-99; Foreign Associate, French Academy of Sciences, 2002. Address: Engineering Department, Cambridge University, Trumpington Street, Cambridge CB2 1PZ, England.

**DOWNES Andrew,** b. 20 August 1950, Handsworth, Birmingham, England. Composer; Lecturer. m. Cynthia Cooper, 9 August 1975, 2 daughters. Education: Choral Scholar, 1969-72, BA Hons, 1972, St John's College, Cambridge; MA (Cantab), 1975; Royal College of Music, 1972-74; Singing with Gordon Clinton; Composition with Herbert Howells. Debut: Wigmore Hall, 1969. Career includes: Established Faculty of Composition, 1975, Head of School, 1990, Professor, School of Composition and Creative Studies, 1992-2005, Birmingham Conservatoire, England; Chaired Symposium on Music Criticism, Indian Music Congress, University of Burdwan, 1994; Performances of own works include: Berlin, Kaiser Willhelm Gedächtniskirche, 1980; Israel Philharmonic Guest House, Tel Aviv, 1989, Calcutta School of Music, 1994, Paris, 1995-99, University of New Mexico, 1995, 1997, 1999, Bombay, Delhi, Calcutta, 1996, Barletta, Italy, 1996 New York, 1993, 1996, 2003; Caracas, Venezuela, 1997; Symphony Hall, Birmingham, 1998, 2003, 2004, 2005, Rudolfinum, Prague, 1998, 2001, 2002, 2005 Lichtenstein Palace, Prague, 1999, James Madison University, Virginia, 2000; Boston, Massachusetts, 2000; Phoenix, Arizona, 2001; Washington, DC, 2002; Colorado, Michigan, Las Vegas, 2003; North Carolina, California, Indiana, Columbia and Nashville, Tennessee, 2004. Compositions include: Sonata for 8 Horns Opus 54, University of New Mexico commission, 1994, performed by the horns of the Czech Philharmonic Orchestra, 1998, 2000, 2005; Sonata for 8 Flutes (premiered New York, 1996, subsequent performances worldwide); Songs From Spoon River, performed at Tanglewood Festival and on BBC Radio 3; Towards A New Age, performed by the Royal Philharmonic Orchestra in Birmingham, 1997; New Dawn, oratorio based on American Indian texts, Adrian Boult Hall, Birmingham, 2000, King's College Chapel, Cambridge, 2002; Sonata for 8 Pianists, Birmingham, 2000, Genoa, 2002; Sonata for Horn and Piano for Roland Horvath of Vienna Philharmonic Orchestra; Concerto for 4 Horns and Orchestra for the Czech Philharmonic Orchestra, Prague, 2002, Czech radio, 2003; Songs of Autumn, performed by massed children's choir, Symphony Hall, Birmingham, 2003, Lichfield Cathedral, 2004; Forthcoming: Opera, Far From The Madding Crowd for The Thomas Hardy Society (to be premiered 2006). Recordings include: The Marshes of Glynn, cantata, commission for Royal opening of Adrian Boult Hall, Birmingham, 1986; O Vos Omnes, motet, Cantamus commission (published by Faber Music in anthology, "30 Sacred Masterworks for Upper Voice Choir"); Sonata for 2 Pianos; Fanfare for a Ceremony, commission for Open University; Centenary Firedances, commissioned by City of Birmingham for its centenary celebrations; Shepherd's Carol; 3 Song Cycles on CD entitled "Old Loves Domain", 2000; The Souls of the Righteous, anthem, 1997; Sacred Choral Music on CD entitled "The Lord is My Shepherd", 2001; Sonata for Oboe and Piano, 1998; Sonata for 8 Horns by Horns of Czech Philharmonic Orchestra; Concerto for 2 Guitars and Strings; Flute Choir Music by James Madison University Flute Choir and Massachusetts Flute Choir, 2000. Publications (by Lynwood Music and Faber Music): 88 works including 5 symphonies, 4 large-scale choral works, 2 double concertos, 3 string quartets, 2 brass quintets, flute octet, Sonata for 8 pianists, horn octet, horn sextet and horn quartet, 5 song cycles and many sacred works. Honours include: Prizewinner, Stroud International Composers' Competition, 1980; Trees planted in Israel in name of Andrew Downes in recognition of composition, Sonata for 2 pianos, 1987; Invited by Crane Concert Choir, University of New York, to conduct his choral work A St Luke Passion, 1993; Leather bound presentation copy of Fanfare for a Ceremony given to HRH Prince Edward on his visit to Birmingham Conservatoire, 1995; Bound presentation copy of Fanfare for Madam Speaker given to Rt Hon Betty Boothroyd MP at her installation as Chancellor of Open University, 1995; Awarded Gold Medal by Institution of Mechanical Engineers for composition for their 150th Anniversary, 1997. Memberships include: Representing Birmingham Conservatoire, Indian Music Congress; Leading Patron, Midland Chamber Players' Society; President, Central Composers' Alliance; President, Church Stretton & South Shropshire Arts Festival; Chairman, Birmingham branch, ISM; PRS; MCPS; Fellow, Royal Society of Arts. Address: c/o Lynwood Music, 2 Church Street, West Hagley, West Midlands DY9 0NA, England.

**DOWNES David Anthony,** b. 17 August 1927, Victor, Colorado, USA. Professor of English Emeritus; Writer. m. Audrey Romaine Ernst, 7 September 1949, 1 son, 3 daughters. Education: BA, cum laude, Regis University, 1949; MA, Marquette University, 1950; PhD, University of Washington, 1956. Appointments: Assistant Professor, Professor, Chairman of Department, University of Seattle, 1953-68; Professor of English, Dean of Humanities and Fine Arts, 1968-72, Director of Educational Development Projects, 1972-73, Director of Humanities Programme, 1973-74, Director of Graduate English Studies, 1975-78, Chairman of Department, 1978-84, Professor Emeritus, 1991, California State University, Chico; Consultant Cowles Rare Book Library, Gonzaga University, 1997. Publications: Gerard Manley Hopkins: A Study of His Ignatian Spirit, 1959; Victorian Portraits: Hopkins and Pater, 1965; Pater, Kingsley and Newman, 1972; The Great Sacrifice: Studies in Hopkins, 1983; Ruskin's Landscape of Beatitude, 1984; Hopkins' Sanctifying Imagination, 1985; The Ignatian Personality of Gerard Manley Hopkins, 1990; Hopkins' Achieved Self, 1996; The Belle of Cripple Creek Gold, 2001; Angel in Wax, 2004. Contributions to: Scholarly books and journals. Honours: Exceptional Merit Awards for Scholarship, 1984, 1988, 1990, 1992; Honorary Doctor of laws, Gonzaga University, 1997. Address: 1076 San Ramon Drive, Chico, CA 95973, USA.

**DOWNES Paul Edward,** b. 12 July 1970, Dublin, Ireland. Lecturer in Psychology. Education: LLB, 1992, BA, Psychology, 1995, PhD, 1999, Trinity College, Dublin. Appointments: Lecturer in Psychology and Law, Concordia University, Estonia, 1998-2001; Lecturer in Education and Human Development (Psychology), 2001-05, Director, Educational Disadvantage Centre, 2004-, St Patrick's College, Drumcondra, Dublin (a college of Dublin City University). Publications: Book: Living With Heroin: Identity, Social Exclusion and HIV among the Russian Speaking Minorities in Estonia and Latvia, 2003; Articles in journals: Journal of Analytical Psychology, 2003; Kwartalnik Pedagogiczny (Poland), 2003, 2004; Socialna Pedagogika (Slovenia), 2005; Journal of Cybernetics and Human Knowing, 2005; Froebel Journal of Child Centred Education, Vol 1, 2005; Commissioned Research Reports; Book chapters. Honours: Entrance Exhibition Award, 1988, Butterworth (Ireland) Prize for Law, 1989, Foundation Scholarship Exam for Law, 1990, Graduate Memorial Prize for Psychology, 1994, Postgraduate Award for Psychology, 1995-98, Trinity College, Dublin; Listed in Who's Who publications and biographical dictionaries. Memberships: Board of Directors, Ana Liffey Drug Project, Dublin, 2002-; Designer, Familiscope, Ballyfermot, 2004; Co-ordinator, Member, EdD Programme Board and Interview Board, St Patrick's College, 2004; Board of Directors, Village Project for Young Offenders, Dublin, 2005; Irish National Co-ordinator, 5 year European Union Sixth Framework Project, 2005. Address: 20 The Grove, New Bettyglen, Raheny, Dublin 5, Ireland. E-mail: paul.downes@spd.dcu.ie

**DOWNEY Robert Jr,** b. 4 April 1965, New York, USA. Actor. m. Deborah Falconer, 1 child. Sentenced to probation for possession of cocaine; imprisoned for further drugs offence breaching terms of probation, 1997; released for rehabilitation, 1998; imprisoned again, 1999, freed, 2000, charged with drugs possession, 2000. Appointments: Actor in films including: Pound, 1970; Firstborn; Weird Science; To Live and Die in LA; Back to School; The Pick-Up Artist; Johnny B Good; True Believer; Chances Are; Air America; Soapdish; Chaplin (BAFTA Award); Heart and Souls; Short Cuts; The Last Party; Natural Born Killers; Only You; Restoration; Mussolini; The Untold Story (TV mini-series); Restoration; Danger Zone; Home for the Holidays; Richard III; Bliss Vision, 1997; The Gingerbread Man, 1997; Two Girls and a Guy, 1998; In Dreams, 1999; Friends and Lovers, 1999; Wonder Boys, 2000; Automotives, 2000; Lethargy, 2002; Whatever We Do, 2003; The Singing Detective, 2003; Gothika, 2003; Eros, 2004; Game 6, 2005; Television includes: Ally McBeal, 2000; Black and White, 2000.

**DOWNING Richard,** b. 8 February 1951, Stourbridge, West Midlands, England. Consultant Vascular Surgeon. m. Stella Elizabeth, 2 sons, 2 daughters. Education: BSc (Hons), Physiology, 1972, MB ChB (Distinction in Pharmacology and Therapeutics), 1975, MD, 1983, University of Birmingham; Fellow, Royal College of Surgeons of England, 1980. Appointments: Lecturer in Anatomy, University of Birmingham, 1976-77; Research Associate, Washington University, St Louis, Missouri, USA, 1977-78; Registrar in Surgery, United Birmingham Hospitals, 1979-83; Lecturer in Surgery, 1983-86, Senior Lecturer in Surgery, 1986-90, University of Birmingham; Consultant Vascular Surgeon, Worcestershire Royal Hospital, 1990-. Publications: Publications on pancreatic islet transplantation, peripheral vascular disease. Honours: Examiner, Faculty of Dental Surgery, Royal College of Surgeons of England, 1989-95; Member of the Editorial Board: Journal of the Care of the Injured, 1989-96 and British Journal of Diabetes and Vascular Disease, 2002-. Memberships: Vascular Society of Great Britain and Ireland; European Society of Vascular and Endovascular Surgery; Association of Surgeons of Great Britain and Ireland; International Pancreas and Islet Transplant Society. Address: 46 Lark Hill, Worcester WR5 2EQ, England.

**DOYEL David,** b. 24 August 1946, Lindsay, California, USA. Archaeologist; Anthropologist. m. Sharon S Debowski. Education: BA, 1969, MA, 1972, California State University, Chico, USA; PhD, University of Arizona, Tucson, USA, 1977. Appointments: Director, Navajo Nation Archaeology and Museum Programme, Window Rock, Arizona, 1979-82; Director and Archaeologist, Pueblo Grande Museum, City of Phoenix, 1984-90; Owner, Estrella Cultural Research, Phoenix, Arizona, 1991-2005; Research Director, Archaeological Consulting Service, Tempe, Arizona, 1993-99; Principal Investigator, URS Corporation, 2000-2002; Principal Investigator, LBG Corporation, 2002-2004. Publications: 20 pages personal bibliography, including edited volumes, book reviews, monographs and articles in professional journals. Honour: Outstanding Supervisor, Navajo Nation; Sigma Xi. Membership: Society for American Archaeology. Address: PO Box 60474, Phoenix, AZ 85082-0474, USA.

**DOYLE Roddy,** b. 1958, Dublin Ireland. Writer. m. Bellinda, 2 sons. Publications: The Commitments, 1987, filmed 1991; The Snapper, 1990, filmed, 1992; The Van, 1991; Paddy Clarke Ha Ha Ha, 1993; The Women Who Walked Into Doors, 1996; A Star Called Henry, 1999; The Giggler Treatment, 2000; Rory and Ita, 2002. Honour: Booker Prize for Paddy Clarke Ha Ha Ha, 1993. Address: c/o Patti Kelly, Viking Books, 375 Hudson Street, New York, NY 10014, USA.

**DRABBLE Margaret,** b. 5 June 1939, Sheffield, England. Author. m. (1) Clive Swift, 2 sons, 1 daughter, (2) Michael Holroyd, 1982. Education; Newnham College, Cambridge. Appointments: Editor, The Oxford Companion to England Literature, 1979-84; Chairman, National Book League, 1980-82; Vice-Patron, Child Psychotherapy Trust, 1987-. Publications: A Summer Bird-Cage, 1963; The Garrick Year, 1964; The Millstone, 1965 Jerusalem the Golden, 1967; The Waterfall, 1969; The Needle's Eye, 1972; Arnold Bennett: A Biography, 1974; The Realms of Gold, 1975; The Genius of Thomas Hardy (editor), 1976; The Ice Age, 1977; For Queen and Country: Britain in the Victorian Age, 1978; A Writer's Britain, 1979; The Middle Ground (novel), 1980; The Oxford Companion to English Literature (editor), 1985; The Radiant Way (novel), 1987; A Natural Curiosity, 1989; Safe as Houses, 1990; The Gates of Ivory, 1991; Angus Wilson: A Biography, 1995; The Witch of Exmoor (novel), 1996; The Peppered Moth (novel), 2001; The Seven Sisters (novel), 2002. Honours include: John Llewelyn Rhys Memorial Prize, 1966; E M Forster Award, American Academy of Arts and Letters, 1973; Hon D Litt, Sheffield, 1976, Bradford, 1988, Hull, 1992; Honorary Fellow, Sheffield City Polytechnic, 1989; Honorary member, American Academy of Arts and Letters, 2002. Address: c/o PFD, Drury House, 34-43 Russell Street, London, WC2B 5HA, England.

**DRAGOUN Otokar,** b. 15 March 1937, Sedlec, Czech Republic. Physicist. m. Nadezda Novotná, 5 July 1961, 2 daughters. Education: Diploma in Engineering, Czech Technical University, Prague, 1962; PhD, Physics, 1967, DSc, Physics, 1985, Charles University, Prague. Appointments: Researcher, Nuclear Physics Institute, Czech Academy of Science, 1962-; Head of Research Group, 1971-2005; Postdoctoral Fellow, Max-Planck Institute for Nuclear Physics, Heidelberg, Germany, 1966-69; Visiting Professor, Faculty of Physics Technical University, Munich, Spring 1992, Summer 1994; External Lecturer, Charles University, Prague, 1986-2005; External Lecturer, Czech Technical University, Prague, 1999-; Member of the Karlsruhe Tritium Neutrino Experiment, 2001-. Publications: Contributor of reviews and science papers on nuclear, nuclear atomic and neutrino experimental physics in international journals; Patentee in field. Honours: Medal Science Achievement, Union Czech Mathematicians and Physicists, 1988. Membership: Czech Physical Society. Address: Nuclear Physics Institute of the Academy of Sciences of Czech Republic, CZ-25068, Rez near Prague, Czech Republic.

**DRCHAL Vaclav,** b. 21 May 1945, Prague, Czech Republic. Physicist. m. Jaroslava, 2 sons. Education: Faculty of Mathematics and Physics, 1968, Doctorate, 1974, Charles University; Candidate of Science, 1974. Appointments: Academy of Sciences, Institute of Solid State Physics, 1968-80; Institute of Physics, 1980-. Publications: 178 original scientific articles, 1 monograph. Honours: State Prize, 1982; Prize, Academy of Sciences, 1989, 1998. Membership: Union of Czech Mathematicians and Physicists; American Physical Society. Address: Academy of Sciences, Institute of Physics, Na Slovance 2, CZ-182 21, Prague 8, Czech Republic.

**DREIMANIS Aleksis,** b. 13 August 1914, Valmiera, Latvia. Geologist. m. Anita Kana, 2 daughters. Education: Mag.rer.nat, University of Latvia, 1938; Habilitation, 1941. Appointments: Assistant/Privatdocent, University of Latvia, 1937-44; Military Geologist, Latvian Legion, 1944-45; Associate Professor, Baltic University, 1946-48; Lecturer/Professor Emeritus, University of Western Ontario, 1948-. Publications: Over 200 articles in professional journals. Honours include: Teaching Award, Ontario Confederation of University Faculty Associations, 1978; Fellow, Royal Society of Canada, 1979; Doctor honoris causa,

University of Waterloo, 1969, University of Western Ontario, 1980; Distinguished Career Award, Quaternary Geology and Geomorphology Division of the Geological Society of America, 1987; Foreign Member, Latvian Academy of Sciences, 1990; Doctor geographiae honoris causa Univeritatis Latviensis, 1991; Distinguished Fellow, Geological Association of Canada, 1995; Three Star Order of Latvia, 2003. Address: 287 Neville Drive, London, Ontario, N6G 1C2, Canada.

**DREW David Elliott,** b. 13 April 1952, Gloucestershire, England. Member of Parliament. m. Anne, 2 sons, 2 daughter. Education: BA, University of Nottingham; PGCE, University of Birmingham; MA, Bristol Polytechnic; MEd, University of the West of England. Appointments: Teacher, 1976-86; Lecturer, University of the West of England, 1986-97; Member of Parliament, Labour/Co-operative Party, Stroud, 1997-; Chair, Parliamentary Labour Party Backbench Committee on Agriculture, 1997-2001; Chair, Parliamentary Labour Party Backbench Rural Affairs Group; Member, Select Committee, DEFRA; Town Councillor; Former District and County Councillor. Memberships: Co-operative Party; UNISON. Address: House of Commons, London SW1A 0AA, England. E-mail: drewd@parliament.uk

**DREWS Gerhart,** b. 30 May 1925, Berlin, Germany. Professor of Biology. m. Christiane May. Education: State Examination, 1951, Dr rer nat, 1953, Dr rer nat habil, 1960, University of Halle. Appointments: Scientific Assistant, University of Halle, 1953; Group Leader and Post Doctoral Studies, Institute of Microbiology and Experimental Therapy, Jena, 1954-60; Reader, 1961-63, Full Professor, 1964-93, University of Freiburg. Publications: 330 articles and books on structure, bioenergetics and morphogenesis of photosynthetic bacteria and history of microbiology. Honours: Dr hc, University of Buenos Aires; Werner-Heisenberg Medal, Alexander von Humboldt Foundation; Honorary Member, VAAM. Memberships: ASM; AAAS; SGM; DGHM; VAAM; GBM. Address: Schlossweg 27B, 79249 Merzhausen, Germany. E-mail: gerhart.drews@bio logie.uni-freiburg.de

**DREYFUSS Richard Stephen,** b. 29 October 1947, New York, USA. Actor. m. Jeramie, 1983, 2 sons, 1 daughter. Education: San Fernando Valley State College. Appointments: Alternative military service, Los Angeles County General Hospital, 1969-71; Actor, stage appearances include: Julius Caesar, 1978; The Big Fix (also producer), 1978; Othello, 1979; Death and the Maiden, 1992; The Prison of Second Avenue, 1999; Films include: American Graffiti, 1972; Dillinger, 1973; The Apprenticeship of Duddy Kravitz, 1974; Jaws, 1975; Inserts, 1975; Close Encounters of the Third Kind, 1976; The Goodbye Girl, 1977; The Competition, 1980; Whose Life Is It Anyway?, 1981; Down and Out in Beverly Hills, 1986; Stakeout, 1988; Moon over Parador, 1989; Let It Ride, 1989; Always, 1989; Rosencrantz and Guildenstern are Dead, 1990; Postcards from the Edge, 1990; Once Around, 1990; Randall and Juliet, 1990; Prisoners of Honor, 1991; What About Bob?, 1991; Lost in Yonkers, 1993; Another Stakeout, 1993; The American President, 1995; Mr Holland's Opus, 1995; Mad Dog Time, 1996; James and the Giant Peach, 1996; Night Falls on Manhattan, 1997; The Call of the Wild, 1997; Krippendorf's Tribe, 1998; A Fine and Private Place, 1998; The Crew, 2000; The Old Man Who Read Love Stories, 2000; Who is Cletis Tout? 2001; (TV movie) Oliver Twist, 1997; Director, producer, Nuts, 1987; Hamlet (Birmingham), 1994. Publication: The Two Georges (with Harry Turtledove), 1996. Honours: Golden Globe Award, 1978; Academy Award for Best Actor in the Goodbye Girl, 1978. Memberships: American Civil Liberties Union Screen Actors Guild; Equity Association; American Federation

of TV and Radio Artists; Motion Picture Academy of Arts and Sciences. Address: William Morris Agency, 151 S El Camino Drive, Beverly Hills, CA 90212, USA.

**DRIVER Minnie (Amelia),** b. 21 January 1970. Actress. Appointments: Actress, TV appearances include: God on the Rocks; Mr Wroe's Virgins; The Politician's Wife; Film appearances include: Circle of Friends; Goldeneye; Baggage; Big Night; Sleepers; Grosse Point Blank; Good Will Hunting; The Governess; Hard Rain; An Ideal Husband, 1999; South Park: Bigger, Longer and Uncut, 1999; Slow Burn, 2000; Beautiful, 2000; Return to Me, 2000; The Upgrade, 2000; High Heels and Lowlifes, 2001; D.C. Smalls, 2001; Play: Sexual Perversity in Chicago, Comedy Theatre, London, 2003. Honours: Best Newcomer, 1997, Best Actress, 1988, London Circle of Film Critics. Address: c/o Lou Coulson, 1st Floor, 37 Berwick Street, London, W1V 3LF, England.

**DRIVER Paul William,** b. 14 August 1954, Manchester, England. Music Critic; Writer. Education: MA, Honours, Oxford University, 1979. Appointments: Music Critic, The Boston Globe, 1983-84, Sunday Times, 1985-; Member, Editorial Board, Contemporary Music Review; Patron, Manchester Musical Heritage Trust. Publications: A Diversity of Creatures (editor), 1987; Music and Text (editor), 1989; Manchester Pieces, 1996; Penguin Popular Poetry (editor), 1996. Contributions to: Sunday Times; Financial Times; Tempo; Gramophone; London Review of Books; New York Times; Numerous others; Frequent broadcaster. Membership: Critics Circle. Address: 15 Victoria Road, London NW6 6SX, England.

**DROBENA Thomas John,** b. 23 August 1934, Chicago, Illinois, USA. Educator. m. Wilma S Kucharek, 27 December 1980, 2 sons. Education: BA, Valparaiso University, 1964; ThB, 1961, MDiv, 1974, Concordia Theological Seminary; MA, Hebrew University, Jerusalem, 1968; PhD, California Graduate School, 1975; STM, Lutheran Theological Seminary, 1986. Appointments: Research Scholar, Slavic Heritage Institute, Torrington, Connecticut; Adjunct Professor, State University of New York, Binghamton, 1975-77. Publications: Heritage of the Slavs, 1976; Lutheran Churches in Slovakia (translator), 2005; Numerous articles in professional journals. Honours: DSc, London University; Grantee: US State Department to Israel, 1967-68; Russian and Eastern European Center, University of Illinois at Urbana, 1980-. Memberships: Fellow, Instituto Slovacco, 1973-; Slavic Heritage Institute, Vice-President, Treasurer, 1964-; Chaplain (Major), Civil Air Patrol, USAFA, 1964-; Chair, ELCA Slovak Zion Synod, International Relations Committee, 1995-; Administrative Assistant to the Bishop, 2002-; Editor, The Zion, 1995-; Editor, Slovo, 1998; President, 1990-, Editor, Journal, 1995-, New England Lutheran Historical Society; President, Northwest Connecticut Crime Stoppers, 1988-; Board of Directors, American Red Cross, 1986-99; American Association of Teachers of Slavic and Eastern European Languages; American Association for the Advancement of Slavic Studies; Czechoslovak Society for the Arts and Sciences. Address: c/o Slavic Heritage Institute, PO Box 1003, Torrington, CT 06790-1003, USA.

**DROBNI Sándor,** b. 5 March 1919, Szöd, Hungary. Surgeon. m. Hedda Sárvári, 4 daughters. Education: Graduate, Pázmány Péter Medical University, Budapest, 1944; PhD, Hungarian Academy of Sciences, 1964; Nominal Professor, Semmelweis Medical University, Budapest, 1986. Appointments: Member of Teaching Staff, Lecturer, Medical University, Budapest, 1948-; Specialist in abdominal and cancer surgery; Regular Lecturer, Hungarian Surgical Society; Participant in international congresses all over the world; Introduced his own operational method at Athens, 1961, Rome, 1962, Philadelphia, 1964, Strasbourg, 1968, Nuremberg, 1972, Barcelona, 1982. Publications: Books: Surgery of Rectal Cancer (co-editor), 1969; Recent Progress in the Study of Disorders of the Colon and Rectum (co-editor), 1972; Surgery of the Intestines, 1976, 1982; More than 100 articles in medical journals nationally and internationally include: Factors influencing operability and inoperability of carcinoma of the colon and the rectum, 1974; One state protoolectomy and ileostomy, 1967; Abdominoperineal resection for enormous presacral cysts and tumours, 1975. Honours: Eminent Surgeon, Council of Ministers of Hungary, 1985, 1987; Medal "Pro Hungarian Surgery", Hungarian Surgical Society, 2000; Invited Lecturer, 1st International Conference "European Surgery in the 3rd Millennium", Budapest, 2001; Herczel Mano Award, Association of Coloproctology of Hungary, 2003; Laudatio and Diploma, 11th Biennial Congress of the International Society of University Colon and Rectal Surgeons, 2004. Memberships: Hungarian Surgical Society; Société International de Chirurgie, Brussels; Member of the Founder Committee of the "Hedrologicum Conlegium", Athens; Fellow, Societas Internationalis Universitario Chiurgorum Colonis et Recti, Fundata in Urbe Mexicana; Fellow, American College of Surgeons. Address: Krisztina Krt 79, H-1016 Budapest, Hungary. E-mail: lettner@axelero.hu

**DROZDOV Yuri,** b. 19 March 1936, Habarovsk, Russia. Engineer-Mechanic. m. Tatiana Drozdova, 2 daughters. Education: Graduated, Moscow Bauman State Technical University, 1959; Doctor of Technical Sciences; Professor; Academician of the Russian Space Academy and other academies. Appointment: Deputy Director, Head of the Department of Friction, Wear and Lubrication, Science and Mechanical Engineering Research Institute. Publications: 500 scientific articles, books and patents, mainly in the fields of tribology, reliability and machine resource in extreme conditions. Honours: USSR State Prize Winner; Honoured Worker of Science of Russia; Orders and Medals of Russia and USSR for Space Exploration. Memberships: Editorial Board, Journal of Materials Protection, China; Deputy Chief Editor of the journals Friction and Wear, Problems of Engineering and Reliability of Machines, Russia; Editorial Board Member, Russian Engineering Research. Address: 4-2-248 Zuzinskaya St, Moscow 117418, Russia. E-mail: drozdov@caravan.ru

**DRUCE (Robert) Duncan,** b. 23 May 1939, Nantwich, Cheshire, England. Musician. m. Clare Spalding, 15 September 1964, 2 daughters. Education: Royal College of Music, London, 1956; Kings College, Cambridge, 1957; BA, 1960; MusB, 1961; MA, York University, 1987. Appointments: Lecturer, Leeds University, 1964-65; BBC Radio Music Producer, 1965-68; Freelance Violinist and Composer, 1968-; Member, Fires of London and Academy of Ancient Music; Part-time Appointments at University of East Anglia, University of London Goldsmiths College, Lancaster University; Full time Senior Lecturer, Bretton Hall College, 1978-91, part-time, 1991-2002, Huddersfield University, 1993-. Compositions: Compositions commissioned by BBC, Huddersfield Contemporary Music Festival, Swaledale Festival, Yorkshire Bach Choir. Publications: New Completion, Mozart Requiem (Novello); Several articles in professional music magazines and journals; Regular contributor to Gramophone Magazine, 1996-. Memberships: Musicians Union; British Academy of Composers and Songwriters. Address: Hey Mount, 19a Back Lane, Holmfirth, HD9 1HG, England.

**DUBROVINA Nina Nikolaevna,** b. 10 October 1939, Leningrad, USSR. Aviation Engineer. Widow, 1 daughter. Education: Automatic Control Systems, Moscow High Technical

School, 1963; English Language Courses, Moscow, 1963-66; Training Course, European Commission TACIS Program, 1996. Appointments: Engineer, Automatic Control Systems, 1964-93, Leading Engineer-Constructor, Quality Management Centre, 1993-97, Quality Management Co-ordinator of TACIS Program, 1996, Leading Expert, 1997-2001, AN Tupolev Aviation Scientific – Technical Complex, now Tupolev; Quality Expert on Management of Aviation International Co-operation Programmes, Aviation Euro-Russian Consortium, Moscow, 2001-02; Quality Expert, Norma Scientific Methodical Centre, 2002; Quality Expert, Financial Director Councillor, Aviacor Aviation Plant, Samara, 2003; Quality Director, Polyot Aviation Trading House, Moscow, 2004; Deputy General Director, Moscow Office, Zapolyarye Airline, 2005. Publications: Numerous articles in professional journals. Honours: Veteran of Labour medal; A N Tupolev medal; Several Diplomas of Honour for good work. Memberships: The USSR Interdepartmental Commission on Airworthiness Norms, 1981-91; Expert Council on the Russian Aviation Department, State Duma of Russian Federation, 1998. Address: Studencheskaya street 17, apt 10, Moscow 121151, Russia. E-mail: nnd@zapolyarye.ru

**DUBURS Gunars,** b. 12 June 1934, Riga, Latvia. Chemist. m. Renate, 1 daughter. Education: Chemist, Latvian University, 1957; PhD, 1961; Dr chem habil, 1979; Professor, 1988. Appointments: Research Scientist, 1957-64, Head of Laboratory, 1964-, Scientific Director, 1980-2004, Institute of Organic Synthesis. Publications: 485 science papers, 169 patents. Honours include: D Grindel's Award, 1996; Award of the Latvian Cabinet of Ministers, 1999; Award of the Latvian Academy of Science and Patent Office, 2000; O Schmiedeberg's Medal, 2001; Listed in numerous biographical publications. Memberships: Latvian Academy of Science; International Society of Heterocyclic Chemistry; Albert Schweitzer International University; UNESCO Molecular and Cell Biology Network. Address: 21 Aizkraukles Street, Latvian Institute of Organic Synthesis, Riga, LV 1006, Latvia.

**DUCHOVNY David,** b. 7 August 1960, New York, USA. Actor. m. Tea Leoni, 1997, 1 son, 1 daughter. Education: Yale University; Princeton University. Appointments: Stage appearances include: Off-Broadway plays, The Copulating Machine of Venice, California and Green Cuckatoo; TV series: The X Files; Films include: New Year's Day, 1989; Julia Has Two Lovers, 1990; The Rapture, 1991; Don't Tell Mom The Babysitter's Dead, 1991; Chaplin, 1992; Red Shoe Diaries, 1992; Ruby, 1992; Kalifornia, 1993; Venice, Venice, Apartment Zero; Close Enemy; Loan; Independence Day; Playing God; The X Files, 1998; Return To Me, 2000; Evolution, 2001; Zoolander, 2001; Full Frontal, 2002; XIII, 2003; Connie and Carla, 2004; House of D, 2004; Television includes: Twin Peaks, 1990; The X-Files, 1993-; Life With Bonnie, 2002. Address: 20th Century Fox Film Corporation, PO Box 900, Beverly Hills, CA 90213, USA.

**DUCORNET Erica Lynn, (Rikki Ducornet),** b. 19 April 1943, New York, New York, USA. Writer; Artist; Teacher. 1 son. Education: Bard College, 1964. Appointments: Novelist-in-Residence, University of Denver, 1988-; Visiting Professor, University of Trento, Italy, 1994. Publications: The Stain, 1984; Entering Fire, 1986; The Fountains of Neptune, 1989; Eben Demarst, 1990; The Jade Cabinet, 1993; The Butcher's Tales, 1994; Phosphor in Dreamland, 1995; The Word "Desire", 1997; The Fan-Maker's Inquisition, 1999. Contributions to: Periodicals. Honours: National Book Critics Circle Award Finalist, 1987, 1990, 1993; Critics Choice Award, 1995; Charles Flint Kellogg Award in Arts and Letters, 1998. Membership:

PEN. Address: c/o Department of English, University of Denver, Denver, CO 80208, USA.

**DUDLEY Martin Raymond,** b. 31 May 1953, Birmingham, England. Priest. m. Paula Jones, 2 sons. Education: Royal Military Academy, Sandhurst; BD, MTh, PhD, King's College, London; University College, Cardiff; City University Business School. Appointments: Senior Clerk, Horizon Midlands plc, 1972-74; Assistant Curate of Whitechurch, Cardiff, 1979-83; Vicar of Weston, Hertfordshire, 1983-88; Priest-in-charge, Ardeley, Hertfordshire, 1986-88; Vicar of Owlsmoor, Sandhurst, Berkshire, 1988-95; Rector, The Priory Church of St Bartholomew the Great, West Smithfield, City of London, 1995-; Trustee, Butchers & Drovers Charitable Institution, 1996-2000; Lay Representative, Professional Conduct and Complaints Committee, The Bar Council of England and Wales, 2000-; Governor, The City Literary Institute, 2001-2003; Common Councilman, Ward of Aldersgate, City of London, 2002-; Governor, City of London Academy for Girls, 2002; Governor, City of London Academy, Southwark, 2003-; Trustee, The London Library, 2004. Publications: Books include most recently: A Herald Voice: The Word of God in Advent and Christmas, 2000; Risen, Ascended, Glorified: Daily Meditations from Easter to Trinity, 2002; Crowning the Year: Autumn in the Christian Tradition, 2003; Churchwardens: A Survival Guide (with Virginia Rounding), 2003; The Parish Survival Guide (with Virginia Rounding), 2004. Honours: Freedom, The City of London, 1996; Serving Brother, Order of St John, 1998; Freedom and Livery, 2000, Honorary Freeman, 2000, The Farriers' Company. Memberships: Fellow of the Royal Historical Society; Fellow of the Society of Antiquaries of London. Address: 4 Wallside, Barbican, London EC2Y 8BH, England. E-mail: martin.dudley@btinternet.com

**DUERDEN Brian Ion,** b. 21 June 1948, Nelson, Lancashire, England. Medical Practitioner. m. Marjorie Hudson. Education: BSc, Honours, Medical Science, 1970, MB ChB, 1972, MD, 1979, Edinburgh University Medical School; MRCPath, 1978; FRCPath, 1990; FRCP Edin., 2005. Appointments: House Officer, Thoracic Surgery and Infectious Diseases, Edinburgh City Hospital, 1972-73; Lecturer in Bacteriology, Edinburgh University, 1973-76; Lecturer, 1976-79, Senior Lecturer, 1979-83, Professor, 1983-90, Medical Microbiology, Sheffield University; Honorary Consultant, Microbiology, Sheffield Children's Hospital, 1979-90; Professor of Medical Microbiology, University of Wales College of Medicine/Cardiff University, 1991-; Medical Director, 1995-2002, Director of Service, 2002-2003, Public Health Laboratory Service; Currently, Inspector of Microbiology and Infection Control, Department of Health. Publications: 135 articles in scientific journals; Contributions to text books for undergraduate and postgraduate use; Editor-in-Chief, Journal of Medical Microbiology, 1982-2002; Articles on anaerobic microbiology, antibiotics, healthcare associated infection and public health. Memberships: Society for Anaerobic Microbiology; Fellow, Infectious Diseases Society of America; Society for General Microbiology; Anaerobe Society of the Americas. Address: Department of Health, Skipton House, 80 London Road, London SE1 6LH, England. E-mail: brian.duerden@dh.gsi.gov.uk

**DUFFY Lawrence Kevin,** b. 1 February 1948, Brooklyn, New York, USA. Biochemist; Educator. m. Geraldine, 2 sons, 1 daughter. Education: BS, Chemistry, Fordham University, 1969; MS, Chemistry, University of Alaska, 1972; PhD, Biochemistry, 1977. Laboratory Instructor, University of Alaska, 1969-71; Research Assistant, University of Alaska Fairbanks, 1974-76; Post-doctoral Fellow, Boston University, 1977-78; Post-doctoral Fellow, Roche Institute of Molecular Biology, 1978-80;

James W McLaughlin Fellow, University of Texas, 1980-81; Research Assistant Professor, University of Texas Medical Branch, 1982-83; Instructor, Middlesex Community College, 1983-84; Assistant Biochemist, McLean Hospital, Belmont, 1983-85; Assistant Professor, Biochemistry, Harvard Medical School, 1983-87; Science and Organic Chemistry Instructor, Roxbury Community College, 1984-87; Associate Biochemist, Brigham and Women's Hospital, 1985-87; Research Associate, Duke University Centre, 1986-87; Professor, Chemistry and Biochemistry, University of Alaska Fairbanks, 1987-; Co-ordinator, Program in Biochemistry and Molecular Biology, 1987-90, 1992-93; Adjunct Researcher, Brigham and Women's Hospital, 1987-90; Affiliate Professor, Centre for Alcohol Addiction Studies, 1995-98; Head, Department of Chemistry and Biochemistry, 1994-99; Co-ordinator, RSI Scientist in Residence Programme, 1996-2003; President, UAF Faculty Senate, 2000; Associate Dean for Graduate Studies and Outreach, 2001; Member, Metals Working Groups. Arctic Monitoring and Assessment Program. Publications: 228 scientific papers and abstracts. Honours: Fiest Outstanding Advisor Award; ACS Analytical Chemistry Award; Phi Lambda Upsilon; NIDCD Minority Research Mentoring Award, 1996; University of Alaska Alumni Award for Professional Achievement, 1999; Usibelli Award for Research, 2002. Memberships: American Chemical Society; New York Academy of Sciences; Member of Editorial Board, The Science of the Total Environment, 1999; President Elect, American Institute of Chemists, 2004-2005. Address: 2712 Tall Spruce, Fairbanks, Box 80986, Alaska 99708-0986, USA.

**DUKAKIS Olympia,** b. 20 June 1931. Actress. m. Louis Zorich, 3 sons. Education: Boston University. Appointments: Teacher of Drama, New York University graduate programme for 15 years; Founding member, The Charles Playhouse, Boston, Whole Theatre, Montclair, New Jersey; Appeared in over 100 regional theatre productions; Off-Broadway shows including: Mann Ish Mann; The Marriage of Bette and Boo; Titus Andronicus; Peer Gynt; The Memorandum; The Curse of the Starving Class; Electra; Appearances in Broadway productions of Abraham Cochrane; The Aspern Papers; The Night of the Iguana; Who's Who in Hell; Mike Nichol's Social Security; Numerous TV appearances, TV include: Tales of the City (series); Films include: The Idolmaker; John Loves Mary; Death Wish; Rich Kids; Made for Each Other; Working Girl; Moonstruck; Dad; Look Who's Talking; Steel Magnolias; In the Spirit; Look Who's Talking Too; The Cemetery Club; Digger; Over the Hill; Look Who's Talking Now; Naked Gun 331/3; The Final Insult (Cameo); I Love Trouble; Jeffrey; Mighty Aphrodite; Mr Holland's Opus; Picture Perfect; My Beautiful Son, 2001; Ladies and The Champ, 2001; And Never Let Her Go, 2001; The Intended, 2002. Honours: Academy Award for Best Supporting Actress for Moonstruck, 1988; 2 Obie awards. Membership: Board, National Museum of Women in the Arts, Washington DC. Address: William Morris Agency, 151 S El Camino Drive, Beverly Hills, CA 90212, USA.

**DUKE Chris,** b. 4 October 1938. London. England. Professor; Scholar. m. Elizabeth Sommerlad, 3 sons, 2 daughters. Education: BA, 1st Class Honours, 1960, PGCE, 1961, MA, 1963, Jesus College, Cambridge, England; PhD, King's College, London, England, 1966. Appointments: Woolwich Polytechnic, England, 1961-66; University of Leeds, 1966-69; Director (Founding), Continuing Education, Australian National University, 1969-85; Professor, Continuing Education, 1985-96, Pro-Vice-Chancellor, 1991-95, University of Warwick, England; President, UWS Nepean, Sydney, Australia and Professor of Lifelong Learning, 1996-2000; Director and Professor of Continuing Education, University of Auckland,

New Zealand, 2000-2002; Professor and Director of Community and Regional Partnerships, RMIT University, Melbourne, Australia, 2002-. Publications: Many books, edited volumes, chapters and journal articles in the fields of higher education, adult, continuing and non-formal education and lifelong learning and in policy and management of higher education; Recent books include: The Learning University, 1992, reprinted 1996; The Adult University, 1999; Managing the Learning University, 2002. Honours: Hon. DLitt. Keimyung University, Republic of Korea; Fellow, Australian College of Education. Memberships: Leadership and membership of international and national professional bodies in the fields of adult and continuing education. Address: 26 Nepean Street, Emu Plains, NSW 2750, Australia. E-mail: chris.duke@rmit.edu.au

**DUNAWAY (Dorothy) Faye,** b. 14 January 1941, Bascom, Florida, USA. Actress. m. (1) Peter Wolf, 1974, (2) Terry O'Neill, 1981, 1 son. Education: Florida University; Boston University. Appointments: Lincoln Center Repertory Company, New York, 3 years, appearances in: A Man For All Seasons; After the Fall; Tartuffe; Off-Broadway in Hogan's Goat, 1965; Old Times, Los Angeles; Blanche du Bois in A Streetcar Named Desire, 1973; The Curse of an Aching Heart, 1982; Films include: Hurry Sundown; The Happening; Bonnie and Clyde, 1967; The Thomas Crown Affair, 1968; A Place For Lovers, 1969; The Arrangement, 1969; Little Big Man, 1970, Doc, 1971; The Getaway, 1972; Oklahoma Crude, 1973; The Three Musketeers, 1973; Chinatown, 1974; Damned, 1976; Network, 1976; The Eyes of Laura Mars, 1978; The Camp, 1979; The First Deadly Sin, 1981; Mommie Dearest, 1981; The Wicked Lady, 1982; Supergirl, 1984; Barfly, 1987; Burning Secret, 1988; The Handmaid's Tale, 1989; On A Moonlit Night; Up to Date, 1989; Scorchers; Faithful; Three Weeks in Jerusalem; The Arrowtooth Waltz, 1991; Double Edge; Arizona Dream; The Temp; Dun Juan DeMarco, 1995; Drunks; Dunston Checks In; Albino Alligator; The Chamber; Fanny Hill, 1998; Love Lies Bleeding, 1999; The Yards, 1999; Joan of Arc, 1999; The Thomas Crown Affair, 1999; The Yards, 2000; Stanley's Gig, 2000; Yellow Bird, 2001; Changing Hearts, 2002; Rules of Attraction, 2002; Mid-Century, 2002; The Calling, 2002; TV include: After the Fall, 1974; The Disappearance of Aimee, 1976; Hogan's Goat; Mommie Dearest, 1981; Evita! - First Lady, 1981; 13 at Dinner, 1985; Beverly Hills Madame, 1986; The Country Girl; Casanova; The Raspberry Ripple; Cold Sassy Tree; Silhouette; Rebecca; Gia, 1998; Running Mates, 2000; The Biographer, 2002. Publications: Looking for Gatsby (Autobiography with Betsy Sharkey), 1995. Honours include: Academy Award for Best Actress for Network. Address: c/o Ed Limato, ICM, 8942 Wilshire Boulevard, Beverly Hills, CA 90211, USA.

**DUNBAR Adrian,** b. Enniskillen, Northern Ireland. Actor. m. Anna Nygh, 1 stepson, 1 daughter. Education: Guildhall School of Music and Drama, London, UK. Career: Films include: The Fear; A World Apart; Dealers; My Left Foot; Hear My Song, 1992; The Crying Game, 1993; Widow's Peak, 1994; Richard III, 1995; The Near Room, 1996; The General, 1998; Wild About Harry, 2000; Shooters, 2000; The Wedding Tackle, 2000; How Harry Became a Tree, 2001; Triggerman, 2002; Darkness, 2002; Stage appearances include: Ourselves Alone, Royal Court Theatre, 1985; King Lear, Royal Court; TV appearances include: Reasonable Force; Cracker.

**DUNCAN Doris Gottschalk,** b. 19 November 1944, Seattle, Washington, USA. Professor of Computer Information Systems. Divorced. Education: BA 1967, MBA 1968, University of Washington, Seattle; PhD, Golden Gate University, San Francisco, 1978; Certified Data Processor, 1980; Certified Data Educator, 1984; Certified Systems Professional, 1985; Certified

Computer Professional, 1994, 2003. Appointments: Director of Company Analysis and Monitoring programme, Input, Palo Alto, 1975-76; Lecturer, Associate Professor, Professor, Computer Information Systems, 1976-, Co-ordinator, computer info systems, 1994-97, Co-adviser, grad programmes, computer info systems and electronic business, 1999-, California State University, East Bay, (formerly CSU Hayward); Independent Consultant, Computer Information Systems, part time, 1976-; Director, Information Systems Programme, Golden Gate University, San Francisco, 1982-83; Visiting Professor, Information Systems, University of Washington, Seattle, 1997-98. Publications: Computers and Remote Computing Services, 1983; Author of over 60 journal articles and papers in conference proceedings. Honours include: Computer Educator of the Year, International Association for Computer Information Systems, 1997; Distinguished research award for "Comicstand.com: an E-Commerce Start-Up", Allied Academics, 1999; Service awards from Association of Information Technology Professionals: bronze, silver, gold, emerald, diamond, double diamond, triple diamond, 2000; Meritorious service award as faculty advisor of student chapter, CSUH and grant recipient; Winner of beautiful home awards and decorating, Foster City, 1994, 1995, 1996, 2003. Memberships include: Board member: Institute for Certification of Computer Professionals, Education Foundation Board; AITP Special Interest Group in Education Board; Advisory Board, Ximnet Corp; Editorial Review Board member for 3 journals: Journal of Informatics Education and Research; Journal of Information Technology Education; Journal of Information Systems Education; Associate Editor, Journal of Informatics & Education Research; Member: Association of Information Technology Professionals (Past President, Vice President, Secretary and Committee Chair, San Francisco chapter); Association of Computing Machinery; International Academy of Information Management; International Association of Computer Information Systems; Academy of Business Education; Decision Sciences Institute; Beta Gamma Sigma. Address: California State University, East Bay, Hayward, CA 94542, USA. E-mail: doris_duncan@hotmail.com

**DUNCAN George,** b. 9 November 1933, Edinburgh, Scotland. Director. 1 daughter. Education: BSc Econ, London School of Economics; Wharton School; MBA, University of Pennsylvania. Appointments: Director, City of London Investment Trust, 1977-2000; Director, BET plc, 1981-96; Chairman, ASW Mouldings plc, 1986-2002; Household Mortgage Corporation, 1986-94; Whessoe plc, 1987-97; Calour Group, 1990-97; Chairman, Swan Hill Group, 1993-2003; Director, Alldays plc, 1999-2001; Deputy Chairman, Associated British Ports plc, 1999-2003; Director, Hurlingham Simal Ltd, 2000-. Memberships: Institute of Chartered Accountants; CBI President's Committee, 1980-83; European Advisory Board, Wharton School, 1995-98; Freeman, City of London, 1971; Chairman, CBI Companies Committee, 1980-83. Address: 19 Belgrave Mews West, London, SW1X 8HT, England.

**DUNN Charleta J,** b. 18 January 1927, Clarendon, Texas, USA. Clinical Psychologist. m. Roy E Dunn Jr, 2 sons, 1 daughter. Education: BS, 1951, MEd, 1954, West Texas University at Canyon; EdD, University of Houston, Houston, Texas, 1966; Postdoctorate in Clinical Psychology, University of Texas Medical Branch, Galveston, Texas, 1971. Appointments: Teacher, Amarillo Public Schools, 1951-62; Assistant Professor, University of Houston, 1966-70; Director Pupil Appraisal, Goose Creek, ISD, Baytown, Texas, 1971-73 Full Professor, Texas Women's University, 1974-90. Publications: 6 research-based monographs (Funded Research Grants); 3 books: World of Work, 1971; Sisk: Book of Ages, 1998; Burcham and Allied

Families, 2000. Memberships: National Registrar of Mental Health; American Psycho-Therapy Association.

**DUNN Douglas (Eaglesham)**, b. 23 October 1942, Inchinnan, Scotland. Professor of English; Writer; Poet. m. Lesley Jane Bathgate, 10 August 1985, 1 son, 1 daughter. Education: BA, University of Hull, 1969. Appointments: Writer-in-Residence, University of Hull, 1974-75, Duncan of Jordanstone College of Art, Dundee District Library, 1986-88; Writer-in-Residence, 1981-82, Honorary Visiting Professor, 1987-88, University of Dundee; Fellow in Creative Writing, 1989-91, Professor of English, 1991-, Head, School of English, 1994-99, University of St Andrews; Director, St Andrews Scottish Studies Institute, 1993-. Publications: Terry Street, 1969; The Happier Life, 1972; Love or Nothing, 1974; Barbarians, 1979; St Kilda's Parliament, 1981; Europea's Lover, 1982; Elegies, 1985; Secret Villages, 1985; Selected Poems, 1986; Northlight, 1988; New and Selected Poems, 1989; Poll Tax: The Fiscal Fake, 1990; Andromache, 1990; Scotland: An Anthology (editor), 1991; The Faber Book of 20th Century Scottish Poetry (editor), 1992; Dante's Drum-Kit, 1993; Boyfriends and Girlfriends, 1994; The Oxford Book of Scottish Short Stories (editor), 1995; Norman MacCaig: Selected Poems (editor), 1997; The Donkey's Ears, 2000; 20th Century Scottish Poems (editor), 2000; The Year's Afternoon, 2000. Contributions to: Newspapers, reviews, and journals. Honours: Somerset Maugham Award, 1972; Geoffrey Faber Memorial Prize, 1975; Hawthornden Prize, 1982; Whitbread Poetry Award, 1985; Whitbread Book of the Year Award, 1985; Honorary LLD, University of Dundee, 1987; Cholmondeley Award, 1989; Honorary DLitt, University of Hull, 1995. Membership: Scottish PEN. Address: c/o School of English, University of St Andrews, St Andrews, Fife KY16 9AL, Scotland.

**DUNNETT Alan David Michael**, b. 7 July 1953, London, England. Playwright; Poet; Theatre Director. Education: English Degree, Trinity College, Oxford University, 1971-74. Appointments: Creative Writing Tutor, Aspley Library, Nottingham, 1989-90; Writer-in-Residence, Ashwell Prison, 1991-92. Publications: In the Savage Gap, 1989; Hurt Under Your Arm, 1991. Contributions to: New Poetry 6; Rialto; Other Poems; Smoke; Pennine Platform; Orbis; Staple; Stepping Out; Weyfarers; Poetry Nottingham; Iota; Frogmore Papers; Skoob Occult Review; Envoi; Methuen Book of Theatre Verse; Stand; Outposts; Interpreter's House; Dream Catcher; The Reader; Poetry Salzburg Review. Honour: East Midlands Arts Literature Bursary, 1989. Address: 108 Crofton Road, London SE5 8NA, England.

**DUNNETT Denzil Inglis**, b. 21 October 1917, Sirsa, India. Retired Diplomat; Poet. m. Ruth Rawcliffe, 20 March 1946, 2 sons, 1 daughter. Education: Edinburgh Academy, 1922-35; MA Lit Hum, Corpus Christi College, Oxford, 1939. Appointments: Editorial Staff, The Scotsman, 1946-47; Diplomatic posts: Bulgaria, Paris, Buenos Aires, Congo, Madrid, Mexico, Senegal, 1946-77. Publication: Bird Poems, 1989; The Weight of Shadows, poems descriptive and religious, 2001. Contributions to: Scottish Review; Scottish Bookman; Satire Review; Anthology of the Anarhyme. Address: 11 Victoria Grove, London W8 5RW, England.

**DUNNING John Harry**, b. 26 June 1927. Economist. m. Christine Mary Brown, 1975. Education: BSc, University College London; PhD, University of Southampton. Appointments: Sub Lieutenant, RNVR, 1945-48; Lecturer and Senior Lecturer, Economics, University of Southampton, 1952-64; Foundation Professor of Economics, 1964-75, Esmée Fairburn Professor of International Investment and Business Studies, 1975-88, ICI

Research Professor in International Business, 1988-92, Emeritus Professor of International Business, 1992, University of Reading; Professor of International Business, Rutgers University, 1989-2000; Past Chairman, Economists Advisory Group Ltd; Consultant to Government Departments, OEDC and UNCTAD. Publications: Books include most recently: Multinational Enterprises and the Global Economy, 1993; The Globalization of Business, 1993; Foreign Direct Investment and Governments (with Rajneesh Narula), 1996; Globalization and Developing Countries (with Khalil Hamdani), 1997; Alliance Capitalism and Global Business, 1997; Governments, Globalization and International Business, 1997; Globalization, Trade and Foreign Direct Investment, 1998; Regions, Globalization and the Knowledge Based Economy, 2000; Global Capitalism at Bay? 2001; Theories and Paradigms of International Business Activity, 2002; Global Capitalism, FDI and Competitiveness; Making Globalization Good, 2003; Multinationals and Industrial Competitiveness (with Rajneesh Narula), 2004. Honours: Dr honoris causa, Universidad Autónoma Madrid, Spain, 1990; Honorary PhD: Uppsala University, Sweden, 1975; Antwerpen University, Belgium, 1997; Honorary Professor of International Economics and Business, Beijing, China, 1995. Memberships: Royal Economic Society; Academy of International Business; President, 1987-88, Dean of Fellows, 1994-96, International Trade and Finance Association; President, 1994, Dean of Fellows, 2003-, European Academy of International Business. Address: Holly Dell, Satwell Close, Rotherfield Greys, Henley-on-Thames, Oxon RG9 4QT, England.

**DUNST Kirsten Caroline**, b. 30 April 1982, Point Pleasant, New Jersey, USA. Actor. Career: Over 70 commercials, 1985-; Films include: New York Stories, 1989; Darkness Before Dawn, 1993; Greedy, 1994; Interview with the Vampire: The Vampire Chronicles, 1994; Little Women, 1994; Jumanji, 1995; Small Soldiers, 1998; Dick, 1999; Drop Dead Gorgeous, 1999; The Virgin Suicides, 1999; Deeply, 2000; Bring It On, 2000; Crazy/Beautiful, 2001; The Cat's Meow, 2001; Get Over It, 2001; Spider-Man, 2002; Levity, 2003; Mona Lisa Smile, 2003; Eternal Sunshine of the Spotless Mind, 2004; Spider-Man 2, 2004; TV appearances include: The Tonight Show with Jay Leno, 1992; Rank, 2001; Gun, 1997; Sisters, 1991. Honours include: Academy of Science Fiction, Fantasy & Horror Films, Best Performance by a Young Actor in Interview with the Vampire: The Vampire Chronicles, 1995; Boston Society of Film Critics Award, Supporting Actress, Interview with the Vampire: The Vampire Chronicles,1994; Empire Awards, Best Actress, Spider-Man, 2003; MTV Movie Awards, Best Female Performance, Spider-Man, 2003; MTV Movie Awards, Best Breakthrough Performance, Interview with the Vampire: The Vampire Chronicles, 1995; Young Star Award, Best Performance by a Young Actress in a Drama Film, 1995.

**DUNWOODY Richard**, b. 18 January 1964, Belfast, North Ireland. Jockey. Appointments: Rode winner of: Grand National (West Tip), 1986, (Minnehoma), 1994; Cheltenham Gold Cup (Charter Party), 1988; Champion Hurdle (Kribensis), 1990; Champion National Hunt Jockey, 1992-93, 1993-94, 1994-95; Held record for most wins at retirement in 1999; Group Manager, Partner, Dunwoody Sports Marketing, 2002. Publications: Hell For Leather (with Marcus Armytage); Dual (with Sean Magee); Hands and Heels (with Marcus Armytage); Obsessed. Honours: National Hunt Jockey of the Year 1990, 1992-95; Champion of Champions, 2001. Address: c/o Dunwoody Sports Marketing, The Litten, Newtown Road, Newbury, Berkshire, RG14 7BB, England. E-mail: richard.d@du-mc.co.uk

**DUPONT Olivier**, b. 5 June 1965, Valognes, France. Director Channel Development. m. Flavie Guffroy, 2 daughters.

Education: Graduate, Sales and Marketing, Business School, 1989. Appointments: Sales Representative, 1988-90, Assistant Brand Manager, 1990-91, Area Manager, 1991-93, Kraft; Trade Marketing Director, Kraft Foods International, 1993-96; Key Account Manager, 1996-99, National Field Manager, 1999-2001, Seagram; International Sales Co-ordinator, Yoplait, 2001-2002; Director, Channel Development, Cadbury Schweppes, 2002-. Honours: Listed in Who's Who publications and biographical dictionaries. Address: 6 rue des Abeilles, 78120 Sonchamp, France. E-mail: flavie.olivier.dupont@wanadoo.fr

**DUPUY-ENGELHARDT Hiltraud,** b. 21 December 1940, Mannheim, Germany. Professor. m. Jean-Marie Dupuy. Education: Staatsexamen, 1966, 1968; Dr phil, 1968; Doctorat d'Etat, PhD, 1987. Appointments: Studienrätin zA, 1970; Lectrice d'Allemand, 1971; Assistante Associée, 1971-75; Assistante Non-Agrégée, 1976-81; Maître Assistante, 2nd class, 1981, 1st class, 1987; Maître de Conférences, 1988; University Professor, 2nd class, 1989, 1st class, 2000; Professor Emeritus, 2001. Publications: Numerous articles in national and international journals. Memberships: AGES; ANCA; ASL; GAL; IDS. Address: 17 La Hingrie, F-68660 Rombach-le-Franc, France. E-mail: hiltraud@libertysurf.fr

**DURANT Graham John,** b. 14 March 1934, Newport, Monmouthshire, Wales. Medicinal Chemist. m. Rosemary, 2 sons. Education: BSc, PhD, University of Birmingham, England; Post doctoral studies, University of Iowa, USA. Appointments: Administration, Smith Kline and French Research, 1960-86; Director of Center for Drug Design and Development, Professor of Medicinal Chemistry, University of Toledo, Ohio, USA, 1987-92; Senior Director of Chemistry, Cambridge Neuroscience, USA, 1992-98; Drug Discovery Consultant, 1999-. Publications: Author or co-author of approximately 100 publications in scientific journals; Inventor and co-inventor of approximately 200 US and international patents. Honours: Royal Society of Chemistry Award in Medicinal Chemistry, 1983; Inductee, National Inventors Hall of Fame, USA, 1990. Memberships: Fellow and Life Member, Royal Society of Chemistry; Past Member, American Chemical Society and several other scientific societies. Address: 5 Wingfield, Thurlestone, Kingsbridge, Devon TQ7 3TT, England. E-mail: gradurant@aol.com

**DURDEN-SMITH Neil,** b. 18 August 1933, Richmond, Surrey, England. Co-Director; Broadcaster. m. Judith Chalmers, 1 son, 1 daughter. Education: Aldenham and Royal Naval College. Appointments: Royal Navy, 1952-63; ADC to Governor General of New Zealand, 1957-59; Commanded HMS Rampart, 1960-62; Cricket and Hockey for Royal Navy and Combined Services; Producer, BBC Outside Broadcasts (special responsibility for 1966 World Cup), 1963-66; Radio and television broadcaster, Test Match and County Cricket, Olympic Games (1968 and 1972), International Hockey, Trooping the Colour, Royal Tournament, Money Matters, Sports Special, 1967-74; Director, The Anglo-American Sporting Clubs, 1968-74; Chairman and Managing Director, Durden-Smith Communications, 1974-81; Trustee, The Lord's Taverner's, 1976-2004; Chairman, The Lord's Taverners, 1980-82; Chairman, Sports Sponsorship International, 1982-87; Chairman, The Altro Group, 1982-94; Director, Ruben Sedgwick, 1987-95; Chairman, Woodside Communications, 1992-99; Director, BCM Grandstand, 1993-; President, Middlesex Region, The Lord's Taverners, 1993-; Chairman, Brian Johnston Memorial Trust, 1994-2000; Consultant, AON, 1995-; Trustee, Charlie Walker Memorial Trust, 1997-; Consultant, Tangible Securities, 2003-; Patron, Motor Neurone Disease Association. Publications: Forward for England: Bobby Charlton's Life Story, 1967; World Cup '66,

1967. Honours: OBE, 1997; Freeman of the City of London. Memberships: MCC; The Lord's Taverners; Sparks; I Zingari; Wig & Pen; Cricket Writers; Free Foresters; Lords & Commons Cricket; County Cricketers Golf; Saints & Sinners; Home House; Ritz; 50 St James's; Highgate and Vale Do Lobo Golf Clubs; FAGS; Ladykillers and Surbiton Hockey Clubs. Address: 28 Hillway, Highgate, London N6 6HH, England.

**DUROV Vladimir Alekseevich,** b. 29 January 1950, Arkhangelsk, Russia. Chemist. m. Ol'ga Nikolaevna Durova, 1 daughter. Education: MSc, 1973, PhD, 1978, DSc, 1989, Lomonosov Moscow State University; Professor of Physical Chemistry, Academic Rank, Ministry of Higher Education of Russia, 1993. Appointments: Junior Researcher, 1977-82, Senior Researcher, 1982-90, Leading Researcher, 1991-93, Research Professor, 1994-1995, Professor of Chemistry (Full Professor), 1995-, Department of Physical Chemistry, Lomonosov Moscow State University. Publications: Over 160 articles in refereed journals; 5 monographs; 10 textbooks. Honours: Grantee, Russian Foundation of Basic Research; Grantee, Russian University Foundation; Distinguished Professor of Chemistry Award, International Soros Science Education Program. Memberships include: Bureau of Scientific Council on Chemical Thermodynamics and Thermochemistry, 1987-; Bureau of the Scientific and Methodical Council on Chemistry, 1992-; Joint Task Group of IUPAC and CODATA on Standardisation of Physico-Chemical Properties Electronic Datafile, 1998-; International Advisory Board of the International Conferences on Chemical Thermodynamics, 1999-; International Advisory Committee of the European Molecular Liquids Group, 1999-; Editorial Board of the Journal of Molecular Liquids, 1999-; Academician, International Academy of Creative Endeavours, 2000-; Active member, Academician, International Academy of Sciences. Address: Department of Physical Chemistry, Faculty of Chemistry, Lomonosov Moscow State University, W-234, Moscow 119899, Russia. E-mail: durov@phys.chem.msu.ru

**DURUP Jean,** b. 8 July 1932, Paris, France. Professor Emeritus. m. Nicole Mathez, 1 son, 3 daughters. Baccalaureat, 1947, Licence, 1952, Doctorat, 1959, Paris, France. Appointments: Research Fellow, CNRS, Paris, 1952-61; Research Fellow, CNRS, Orsay, 1961-68; Professor, Université de Paris-Sud, Orsay, 1968-85; Professor, Université Paul Sabatier, Toulouse, 1985-97; Professor Emeritus, 1997-. Publications: Book, Positive ion-molecule reactions in gas phase; Over 100 papers in high-level journals, on physics, biology and chemistry. Honours: Silver Medal of CNRS, 1968; Fellow, American Physical Society, 1980. Address: IRSAMC, Université Paul Sabatier, 118 Route de Narbonne, 31062 Toulouse, France. E-mail: jean.durup@irsamc.ups-tlse.fr

**DUURSMA Egbert Klaas,** b. 27 March 1927, Smallingerland, Netherlands. Professor of Oceanology; Director. m. Caroline Bosch, 3 sons, 1 daughter. Education: Graduated, Organic Chemistry, Free University, Amsterdam; PhD, 1960. Appointments: Research Scientist, dairy industry, Leeuwarden, Netherlands, 1953-56; Senior Scientist, Marine Radioactivity, NIOZ, Den Helder, 1960-65; Chief of Section, Sedimentology, International Laboratory of Marine Radioactivity, IAEA, Monaco, 1965-76; Expert FAO, Jepara, Indonesia, 1975; Director, Delta Institute for Hydrobiological Research, Royal Netherlands Academy of Sciences, Yerseke, Netherlands, 1976-86; Chairman, Dutch Council for Ocean Research and Antarctic Commission, 1985-93; First Scientific, later General, Director, NIOZ, Texel, Netherlands, 1986-89; Professor of Oceanology, University of Groningen, 1986-91; Many Guest Professorships. Publications include: The dissolved organic constituents of sea water, chapter in Chemical Oceanography,

1965; Theoretical, experimental and field studies concerning reactions of radioisotopes with sediments and suspended particles of the sea, 1967; Geochemical aspects and applications of (all) radionuclides in the sea, chapter, 1972; Role of pollution and pesticides in brackish water aquaculture in Indonesia, 1976; Pollution of the North Sea, co-author, 1988; Are tropical estuaries environmental sinks or sources?, 1995; Environmental compartments, equilibria and assessment of processes (of radioactive, metal and organic contaminants), between air, sediments and water, 1996; Stratospheric ozone chemistry: A literature review and synthesis, 1997, 2000; Dumped chemical weapons in the sea, options, Synopsis on the state of the art, emergency actions, first aid and state responsibilities, Editor and co-author, 1999; Global and regional rainfall, river-flow and temperature profile records; consequences for water resources, 2002; Energy and environment; irreversable events, 2005; Numerous book chapters, articles in scientific journals and conference proceedings. Honour: Medal, Royal Netherlands Academy of Art and Sciences, 1986. Memberships: Academia Europaea. Address: 302 Av du Semaphore, 06190 Roquebrune/Cap Martin, France.

**DUVALL Robert,** b. 5 January 1931, San Diego, USA. Actor. m. (1) Gail Youngs, divorced, (2) Sharon Brophy, 1991. Education: Principia College, Illinois, USA; Student, Neighbourhood Playhouse, New York. Appointments: Actor, stage appearances include: A View From the Bridge (Obie Award), 1965; Wait Until Dark, 1966; American Buffalo; Films include: To Kill a Mockingbird, 1963; Captain Newman, MD, 1964; The Chase, 1965; Countdown, 1968; The Detective, 1968; Bullitt, 1968; True Grit, 1969; The Rain People, 1969; M*A*S*H, 1970; The Revolutionary, 1970; The Godfather, 1972; Tomorrow, 1972; The Great Northfield; Minnesota Raid, 1972; Joe Kidd, 1972; Lady Ice, 1973; The Outfit, 1974; The Conversation, 1974; The Godfather Part II, 1974; Breakout, 1975; The Killer Elite, 1975; Network, 1976; The Eagle Has Landed, 1977; The Greatest, 1977; The Betsy, 1978; Apocalypse Now, 1979; The Great Santini, 1980; True Confessions, 1981; Angelo My Love (actor and director), 1983; Tender Mercies, 1983; The Stone Boy, 1984; The Natural, 1984; The Lightship, 1986; Let's Get Harry, 1986; Belizaire the Cajun, 1986; Colors, 1988; Convicts; Roots in Parched Ground; The Handmaid's Tale, 1990; A Show of Force, 1990; Days of Thunder, 1990; Rambling Rose, 1991; Newsies, 1992; The New Boys, 1992; Stalin, 1992; The Plague; Geronimo; Falling Down, 1993; The Paper, 1994; Wrestling Ernest Hemingway, 1994; Something to Talk About: The Stars Fell On Henrietta; The Scarlet Letter; A Family Thing (also co-producer); Phenomenon, 1996; The Apostle, 1997; Gingerbread Man, 1997; A Civil Action, 1999; Gone In Sixty Seconds, 2000; A Shot at Glory (also producer), 2000; The 6th Day, 2000; Apocalypse Now: Redux, 2001; John Q, 2002; Assassination Tango (also producer), 2002; Director, We're Not the Jet Set; Assassination Tango, 2002; Several TV films and appearances. Address: c/o William Morris Agency, 151 S El Camino Drive, Beverly Hills, CA 90212, USA.

**DUVALL Shelley,** b. 7 July 1949, Houston, Texas, USA. Actress; Producer. Appointments: Founder, TV production company, Think Entertainment; Actress in TV films: Brewster McCloud; Mccabe and Mrs Miller; Thieves Like Us; Nashville; Buffalo Bill and the Indians; Three Women (Cannes Festival Prize, 1977); Annie Hall; The Shining; Popeye; Time Bandits; Roxanne; Suburban Commando; The Underneath; Portrait of a Lady; Changing Habits; Alone, 1997; Home Fries, 1998; Space Cadet; Big Monster on Campus; The 4th Floor; Dreams in the Attic; Manna From Heaven, 2001; Television includes: Bernice Bobs Her Hair; Lily; Twilight Zone; Mother Goose Rock'n'Rhyme; Faerie Tale Theatre (Rumpelstiltskin,

Rapunzel); Tall Tales and Legends (Darlin' Clementine); Executive producer: Faerie Tale Theatre; Tall Tales and Legends; Nightmare Classics; Dinner at Eight (film); Mother Goose Rock'n'Rhyme; Stories from Growing Up; Backfield in Motion (film); Bedtime Stories; Mrs Piggle-Wiggle.

**DVORAK Tomas,** b. 26 January 1952, Prague, Czech Republic. Photographer. m. Eva Pikova, 1976, 1 son. Education: High School of Graphic Design, Prague, 1967-71; Magister of Art, Academy of Performing Arts Film and TV School, 1975. Career: Freelance Photographer, 1975-; Founder, DD Studio (with Eva Dvorakova), 1990; Exponent of Digital Imaging, 1996-; Working on building a National Museum of Photography in Czechia, 2000; Teacher, Academy of Performing Arts, Film and TV School, 2005. Civic Activities: Judge at Federation of European Professional Photographers, 1999. Honours: Certificate of QEP for Digital Photography, 2000; Listed in 2000 Outstanding Artists and Designers, Cambridge. Memberships: Asociace Fotografu Praha, 1990; Vice-President, Association of Czech Photographers, 1990; Federation of European Professional Photographers, 1997. Commissions and Creative Works: Advertising campaigns for Coca Cola, 1991, Philip Morris, 1993, Nestlé, 1997. Address: Liliova 7, 11000 Prague 1, Czech Republic.

**DVORAKOVA Eva,** b. 30 December 1954, Prague, Czech Republic. Photographer. m. Tomas Dvorak, 1976, 1 son. Education: Magister of Art, Academy of Performing Arts, Film and TV School, 1978. Appointments: Freelance Photographer, 1978-; Founder, DD Studio (with Tomas Dvorak), 1990; Exponent of Digital Imaging, 1996-; Work on building National Museum of Photography in Czechia, 2000. Honours: Listed in national and international biographical dictionaries. Memberships: Asociace Fotografu, Prague, 1990; Federation of European Professional Photographers, 1997. Commissions and Creative Works: Advertising campaigns for Coca Cola, 1991, Philip Morris, 1993, Nestlé, 1997. Address: Liliova 7, 11000 Prague 1, Czech Republic.

**DVORETZKY Isaac,** b. 24 January 1928, Houston, Texas, USA. Research Chemist; Research Manager (Retired); Consultant. m. Constance Alexandra Schwalbe, 1 son, 2 daughters. Education: BA, Hons, Chemistry, Rice University, 1948; MA, Chemistry, 1950; PhD, Chemistry, 1952. Appointments: Research Chemist, 1952-56, Research Group Leader, 1956-58, 1959-62, Exchange Scientist, Amsterdam, 1958-59, Research Supervisor, 1962-67, 1968-70, Senior Research Liaison, 1967-68, Research Department Manager, 1970-72, Manager, PhD Recruitment and University Relations, 1972-93, Shell Oil Company. Publications: Numerous research papers in journals including Journal of the American Chemical Society, Journal of Organic Chemistry, Analytical Chemistry, Journal of Chromatography; Several papers delivered at conferences and symposia. Honours: Outstanding Volunteer of the Year, National Society of Fund Raising Executives, 1996; Meritorious Service Award, Association of Rice University Alumni, 2003. Memberships include: American Chemical Society; National Consortium for Graduate Degrees for Minorities in Science and Engineering; American Technion Society, President, Greater Houston Chapter; Member, National Board of Directors; International Board of Governors, The Technion-Israel Institute of Technology. Address: 2927 Rimrock Drive, Missouri City, Texas 77459, USA.

**DYBKAER René,** b. 7 February 1926, Copenhagen. Physician. m. Nanna Gjoel, deceased. Education: MD, 1951, Dr Med Sci, 2004, University of Copenhagen; Specialist Clinical Chemistry, 1957. Appointments: Various medical residencies, 1951-55; Reader, Copenhagen University Institute of Medical Microbiology, 1956-70; Head, Department of Medical Microbiology, Royal Dental School of Copenhagen, 1959-70; Head, Department of Clinical Chemistry at De Gamles By, 1970-77, at Frederiksberg Hospital, 1977-96, at Department of Standardization in Laboratory Medicine, H:S Kommunehospitalet, 1997-99, H:S Frederiksberg Hospital, 2000. Publications: Books: Quantities and units in clinical chemistry, 1967; Good practice in decentralised analytical clinical measurement, 1992; Continuous quality improvement in clinical laboratories, 1994; Compendium on terminology and nomenclature in clinical laboratory sciences, 1995; An Ontology on Property for physical, chemical and biological systems, thesis, 2004; numerous articles to professional journals. Honours: Commemorative Lecture Enrique Concustell Bas, 1988; Henry Wishinsky Distinguished International Services Award, 1993; Honorary member of various national clinical laboratory societies; Professor James D Westgard Quality Award, 1998. Memberships: Vice President, 1973-78, President, 1979-84, Past President, 1985-90, International Federation of Clinical Chemistry; President, European Confederation of Laboratory Medicine, 1994-97; Chairman, Danish Society of Clinical Chemistry, 1991-93. Address: H:S Frederiksberg Hospital, Department of Standardization in Laboratory Medicine, Nordre Fasanvej 57, DK-2000 Frederiksberg, Denmark.

**DYER Charles,** b. 17 July 1928, Shrewsbury, England. Playwright. m. Fiona, 20 February 1960, 3 sons. Publications: Turtle in the Soup, 1948; Who On Earth, 1950; Poison in Jest, 1952; Jovial Parasite, 1955; Red Cabbage and Kings, 1958; Rattle of a Simple Man, novel, play, film, 1962; Staircase, novel, play, film, 1966; Mother Adam, 1970; Lovers Dancing, 1982; Those Old Trombones, 2005; Various screenplays. Address: Old Wob, Gerrards Cross, Buckinghamshire SL9 8SF, England.

**DYER James Frederick,** b. 23 February 1934, Luton, England. Archaeological Writer. Education: MA, Leicester University, 1964. Appointment: Editor, Shire Archaeology, 1974-. Publications: Southern England: An Archaeological Guide, 1973; Penguin Guide to Prehistoric England and Wales, 1981; Discovering Archaeology in England and Wales, 1985, 6th enlarged edition, 1997; Ancient Britain, 1990; Discovering Prehistoric England, 1993; The Stopsley Book, 1998; Luton Modern School History, 2004. Contributions to: Bedfordshire Magazine; Illustrated London News; Archaeological Journal. Honours: Honorary Doctor of Arts, University of Luton, 1999. Memberships: Society of Authors; Royal Archaeological Institute; Society of Antiquaries. Address: 6 Rogate Road, Luton, Bedfordshire LU2 8HR, England.

**DYKE Greg,** b. 20 May 1947. Television Executive. 1 son, 1 stepson, 1 daughter, 1 stepdaughter. Education: York University; Harvard Business School. Appointments: Management Trainee, Marks & Spencer; Reporter, local paper; Campaigner for Community Relations Council, Wandsworth; Researcher, The London Programme; London Weekend TV (LWT); Later, Founding Producer, The Six O'Clock Show; Joined TV-AM, 1983; Director of Programmes, LWT, 1987-91; Group Chief Executive, LWT (Holdings) PLC, 1991-94; Chairman, GMTV, 1993-94; Chairman, Chief Executive Officer, Pearson TV, 1995-99; Chairman, Channel 5 Broadcasting, 1997-99; Former TVB Hong Kong; Director, BSkyB, 1995; Phoenix Pictures Inc, New York, Pearson PLC, 1996-99 and others; Director (non-executive) Manchester Utd, 1997-99; Director General, BBC, 2000-04. Memberships: Trustee Science Museum, 1996-; English National Stadium Trust, 1997-99.

**DYKES David Wilmer,** b. 18 December 1933, Swansea, Wales. Retired; Independent Scholar. m. Margaret Anne George, 2 daughters. Education: MA, Corpus Christi College, Oxford, 1952-55; PhD, University of Wales. Appointments: Commissioned Service, RN and RNR, 1955-62; Civil Servant, 1958-59; Administrative Appointments, University of Bristol and University College of Swansea, 1959-63; Deputy Registrar, University College of Swansea, 1963-69; Registrar, University of Warwick, 1969-72; Secretary, 1972-86, Acting Director, 1985-86, Director, 1986-89, National Museum of Wales. Publications: Anglo-Saxon Coins in the National Museum of Wales, 1977; Alan Sorrell: Early Wales Recreated, 1980; Wales in Vanity Fair, 1989; The University College of Swansea, 1992; The Eighteenth Century Token, forthcoming; Articles and reviews in numismatic, historical and other journals. Honours: Parkes-Weber Prize and Medal, Royal Numismatic Society, 1954; K St J, 1993; Honorary Member, President, 1998-2003, British Numismatic Society. Memberships: Liveryman, Worshipful Company of Tin Plate Workers; Freeman City of London; Foundation Member, Welsh Livery Guild, 1993; FSA; FRHistS; FRNS; FRSA; FRSAI. Address: 3 Peverell Avenue East, Poundbury, Dorchester, Dorset, DT1 3RH, England.

**DYKES Richard T B,** b. 7 April 1945. Chairman. Appointments: Ministry of Labour, 1967-74; Assistant Private Secretary to Michael Foot, Secretary of State for Employment, 1974-76; Principal, Economic Policy (Manpower) Division, Department of Employment, 1976; Non-Executive Director, Austin & Pickersgill Ltd, Shipbuilders, Sunderland, 1979-80; Director of Industrial Relations, British Shipbuilders, 1977-80; Principal Private Secretary, Department of Employment, 1980-81; Chief Executive, Unemployment Benefit Service, 1981-85, Head of Inner Cities Central Unit, 1985-86, Department of Employment; Director of Operations, 1986-91, Managing Director, 1992-96, Post Office Counters Ltd; Managing Director, 1996-99, Group Managing Director, 1999-2001, Royal Mail; Chairman, Carrenza Ltd, 2001-. Memberships: Forensic Science Service Advisory Board, 1991-96; Design Council, 1996-2001; Regeneration Committee of Business in the Community, 1996-2003; Chairman, Appeals Committee for Seeability, 1998-2001. Address: 9 Fournier Street, London E1 6QE, England. E-mail: richard@carrenza.com

**DYLAN Bob (Robert Allen Zimmerman),** b. 24 May 1941, Duluth, Minnesota, USA. Singer; Musician (guitar, piano, harmonica, autoharp); Poet; Composer. Musical Education: Self-taught. Career: Solo folk/rock artist, also performed with The Band; The Travelling Wilburys; Grateful Dead; Songs recorded by estimated 3000 artists, including U2, Bruce Springsteen, Rod Stewart, Jimi Hendrix, Eric Clapton, Neil Young; Numerous tours: USA, Europe, Australia, 1961-; Film appearances include: Pat Garrett and Billy The Kid; Concert For Bangladesh; Hearts Of Fire. Compositions include: Blowin' In The Wind; Like A Rolling Stone; Mr Tambourine Man; Lay Lady Lay; Forever Young; Tangled Up In Blue; Gotta Serve Somebody; Don't Think Twice; It's Alright; A Hard Rain's Gonna Fall; The Times They Are A-Changin'; Just Like A Woman; I'll Be Your Baby Tonight; I Shall Be Released; Simple Twist Of Fate; Paths Of Victory; Dignity. Recordings: Over 40 albums include: The Freewheelin' Bob Dylan, 1964; Bringing It All Back Home, 1965; Highway 61 Revisited, 1965; Blonde On Blonde, 1966; John Wesley Harding, 1968; Nashville Skyline, 1969; Self Portrait, 1970; New Morning, 1970; Before The Flood, 1974; Hard Rain, 1976; Desire, 1976; Street Legal, 1978; Slow Train Coming, 1979; Infidels, 1983; Empire Burlesque, 1985; Knocked Out Loaded, 1986; Down In The Groove, 1988; Biograph (5 record set), 1988; Oh Mercy, 1989; Under The Red Sky, 1990; MTV Unplugged, 1995; Time Out of Mind,

1998; Love and Theft, 2001; with The Band: Planet Waves, 1974; Blood On The Tracks, 1975; with Travelling Wilburys: Travelling Wilburys, 1988; Vol 3, 1990; with Grateful Dead, Dylan And The Dead, 1989; Singles include: One Too Many Mornings, 1965; Mr Tambourine Man, 1966; Love Sick, 1997. Publications: Tarantula, 1966; Writings And Drawings, 1973; The Songs Of Bob Dylan 1966-75, 1976; Lyrics 1962-85, 1986; Drawn Blank, 1994; Highway 61 Revisited (interactive CD-ROM). Honours include: Honorary D Mus, Princeton University, 1970; Inducted, Rock and Roll Hall of Fame, 1988; Grammy, 1990. Address: c/o Columbia Records, 550 Madison Avenue, New York, NY 10022, USA.

**DYRBERG Peter,** b. 16 October 1962, Copenhagen, Denmark. Lawyer. 3 sons, 1 daughter. Education: Master of Law, 1985; BA, Political Science, 1996. Appointments: Lawyer with law firm in Copenhagen, 1985-87; European Court of Justice, 1987; Legal Service, European Parliament, 1994-95; Principal Legal Advisor, then Head of the Brussels Antenna, European Ombudsman Office, 1996-1999; Head of the Legal Service, EFTA Surveillance Authority, 1999-2002; Member of Second Board of Appeal, European Union's Trade Mark Office, 2002-2005; Resident Partner in Brussels of the law firm Schjodt, Norway and Director of the European Law Institute, University of Reykjavik, 2005-. Publications: Articles in legal journals including: European Law Review; European Intellectual Property Review; Danish Law Journal "EU-Ret & Menneskeret"; Norwegian Law Journal "Lou og Rett"; Spanish Law Journal "Revista de Derecho Comunitario Europeo". Memberships: University Association for Contemporary European Studies; Danish Association for Community Law; Danish Association for European Studies; German Association "GRUR". Address: Clos du Parnasse 10B, B-1050 Brussels, Belgium. E-mail: peter.dyrberg@schjodt.no Website: www.schjodt.no

**DYSON Freeman J(ohn),** b. 15 December 1923, Crowthorne, England (US citizen, 1957). Professor of Physics Emeritus. m. (1) Verena Haefeli-Huber, 11 August 1950, divorced 1958, 1 son, 1 daughter, (2) Imme Jung, 21 November 1958, 4 daughters. Education: BA, Cambridge University, 1945; Graduate Studies, Cornell University, 1947-48, Institute for Advanced Study, Princeton, New Jersey, 1948-49. Appointments: Research Fellow, Trinity College, Cambridge, 1946-49; Warren Research Fellow, University of Birmingham, England, 1949-51; Professor of Physics, Cornell University, 1951-53; Professor of Physics, 1953-94, Professor Emeritus, 1994-, Institute for Advanced Study. Publications: Symmetry Groups in Nuclear and Particle Physics, 1966; Neutron Stars and Pulsars, 1971; Disturbing the Universe, 1979; Values at War, 1983; Weapons and Hope, 1984; Origins of Life, 1986; Infinite in All Directions, 1988; From Eros to Gaia, 1992; Imagined Worlds, 1997; The Sun The Genome and the Internet, 1999. Honours: Heineman Prize, American Institute of Physics, 1966; Lorentz Medal, Royal Netherlands Academy of Sciences, 1966; Hughes Medal, Royal Society, 1968; Max Planck Medal, German Physical Society, 1969; J Robert Oppenheimer Memorial Prize, Center for Theoretical Studies, 1970; Harvey Prize, Israel Institute of Technology, 1977; Wolf Prize, Wolf Foundation, 1981; National Book Critics Circle Award, 1984; Templeton Prize for Progress in Religion, 2000. Honorary doctorates. Memberships: American Physical Society; National Academy of Sciences; Royal Society, fellow. Address: 105 Battle Road Circle, Princeton, NJ 08540, USA.

**DYSON James,** b. 2 May 1947, Designer. m. Deidre Hindmarsh, 1967, 2 sons, 1 daughter. Education: Royal College of Art. Appointments: Director, Rotork Marine, 1970-74; Managing Director, Kirk Dyson, 1974-79; Developed and designed, Dyson Dual Cyclone vacuum cleaner, 1979-93; Founder, Chairman

Prototypes Ltd, 1979-; Dyson Appliances Ltd, 1992-; Hon DLitt (Staffordshire), 1996; Hon DSc, Oxford Brookes, 1997, Huddersfield, 1997, Bradford, 1998. Publications include: Doing a Dyson, 1996; Against the Odds (autobiography), 1997; History of Great Inventions, 2001. Honours: Numerous design awards and trophies. Address: Dyson Ltd, Tetbury Hill, Malmesbury, Wiltshire SN16 0RP, England.

# E

**EASTHAM Anthony Richard,** b. 21 April 1944, Lingfield, England. Engineer; Professor; University Administrator. m. Judith Anna, 1 son, 1 daughter. Education: BSc, Physics, London, England, 1965; PhD, Applied Physics, Surrey, England, 1969. Appointments: Director of Research Sciences and International Programmes, Professor of Electrical and Computer Engineering, Queen's University, Ontario, Canada, 1985-95; Visiting Professor, University of Tokyo, Japan, 1996; Associate Vice-President for R&D, Professor of Civil Engineering and Electrical Engineering, Hong Kong University of Science and Technology, Hong Kong, 1998-; President, Chief Executive Officer, HKUST RandD Corporation Ltd, 2000-. Publications: 5 chapters and monographs; 65 journal papers; 81 conference proceeding papers; 35 research reports. Honours: Joint Holder, Ross Medal, Engineering Institute of Canada, 1978; Award for Excellence in Teaching, Queen's University, 1980; Queen's University Prize for Excellence in Research, 1982; Commemorative Medal, 125th Anniversary of Confederation of Canada, 1992; Outstanding Service Award, High Speed Rail Association, 1993. Memberships: Professional Engineer, Ontario, Canada; IEEE; Chartered Institute of Logistics and Transport; High Speed Rail Association; Canadian Chamber of Commerce in Hong Kong. Address: 8 Uk Tau Village, Pak Tam Road, Sai Kung Country Park, Sai Kung, NT, Hong Kong. E-mail: rdtony@ust.hk

**EASTWOOD Clint,** b. 31 May 1930, San Francisco, USA. Actor; Film Director. m. (1) Maggie Johnson, 1 son, 1 daughter; 1 daughter by Frances Fisher; m. (2) Dina Ruiz, 1996, 1 daughter. Education: Los Angeles City College. Appointments: Lumberjack, Oregon; Army service; Actor, TV series, Rawhide, 1959-65; Owner, Malposo Productions, 1969-; Mayor, Carmel, 1986-88. Films include: The First Travelling Saleslady; Star in the Dust; Escapade in Japan; Ambush at Cimarron Pass; Lafayette Escadrille; A Fistful of Dollars, 1964; For a Few Dollars More, 1965; The Good, the Bad and the Ugly, 1966; The Witches, 1967; Hang 'Em High, 1968; Coogan's Bluff, 1968; Where Eagles Dare, 1969; Paint Your Wagon, 1968; Kelly's Heroes, 1970; Two Mules for Sister Sara, 1970; Dirty Harry, 1971; Joe Kidd, 1972; High Plains Drifter (also director), 1973; Magnum Force, 1973; Thunderbolt and Lightfoot, 1974; The Eiger Sanction (also director), 1975; The Outlaw Josey Wales (also director), 1976; The Enforcer, 1976; The Gauntlet (also director), 1978; Every Which Way But Loose, 1978; Escape From Alcatraz, 1979; Bronco Billy (also director), 1980; Any Which Way We Can, 1980; Firefox (also director), 1982; Honky Tonk Man (also director), 1982; Sudden Impact (also director), 1983; Tightrope, 1984; City Heat, 1984; Pale Rider (also director), 1985; Heartbreak Ridge (also director); Director, Breezy, 1973; Bird, 1988; The Dead Pool, 1988; Pink Cadillac, 1989; White Hunter, Black Heart (also director), 1989; The Rookie (also director), 1990; Unforgiven (also director), 1992; In the Line of Fire, 1993; A Perfect World (also director), 1993; The Bridges of Madison County (also director, producer), 1995; The Stars Fell on Henrietta (co-producer); Absolute Power (also director), 1997; True Crime, 1998; Director, Midnight in the Garden of Good and Evil, 1997; Space Cowboys (also director), 2000; Blood Work (also director, producer), 2002. Honours: Academy Awards, 1993; Fellow, BFI, 1993; Irving G Thalberg Award, 1995; Legion d'honneur, Commander, Ordre des Arts et Lettres, American Film Institute's Life Achievement Award, 1996; Screen Actors Guild, 2003. Address: c/o Leonard Hirshan, William Morris Agency, 151 S El Camino Drive, Beverly Hills, CA 90212, USA.

**ECCLESTON Christopher,** b. 16 February 1964, Salford, England. Actor. Appointments: Actor, films: Let Him Have It, 1991; Shallow Grave, 1995; Jude, 1996; Elizabeth, 1998; A Price Above Rubies, 1998; Heart, 1999; Old New Borrowed Blue, 1999; Existenz, 1999; Gone in 60 Seconds, 2000; The Invisible Circus, 2001; The Others, 2001; I am Dina, 2002; 28 Days Later, 2002; TV appearances: Cracker, 1993-94; Hearts and Minds, 1995; Our Friends in the North, 1996; Hillsborough, 1996; Strumpet, 2001; Flesh and Blood, 2002; Dr Who, 2005; Theatre includes: Miss June, 2000. Address: Hamilton Asper Management, Ground Floor, 24 Hanway Street, London W1P 9DD, England.

**ECCLESTONE Bernie,** b. October 1930. Business Executive. m. (1) 1 daughter, (2) Slavica, 2 daughters. Education: Woolwich Polytechnic, London. Appointments: Established car and motorcycle dealership, Bexley, Kent; Racing-car driver for short period; Set up Brabham racing team, 1970; Owner, Formula One Holdings, now controls Formula One Constructors Association, representing all top racing-car teams; Vice-President in charge of Promotional Affairs, Federal Institute de l'Automobile (FIA), racing's international governing body. Address: Formula One Administration Limited, 6 Prince's Gate, London SW7 1QJ, England. Website: www.formula1.com

**ECKERSLEY Richard Hilton,** b. 22 February 1941, Warrington, Lancashire, England. Graphic Designer. m. Dika, 1 son, 2 daughters. Education: BA (Hons), English and Italian Literature, 1958-62, Granted an MA, 1990, Trinity College, University of Dublin; BA (Hons) Art and Design, London College of Printing, 1962-66. Appointments: Graphic Designer, London Studio of Percy Lund Humphries, printers and publishers, 1966-68; Freelance Designer in London working for Lund Humphries, University of London, Arts Council of Great Britain, HMSO, Sotheby's, the Wildenstein Gallery, Workers Educational Association, Ward Locke, Heinemann, Anthony Blond, Longman, 1969-74; Senior Graphic Designer, Kilkenny Design Workshops, Ireland, 1974-80; Visiting Associate Professor, Tyler School of Art, Temple University, Philadelphia, USA, 1980-81; Visiting Lecturer: London College of Printing, Maidstone College of Art, Bristol Polytechnic, Limerick College of Art, University of Iowa, Wake Forest University, Washington, University of St Louis, Philadelphia University of the Arts, Rhode Island School of Design; Senior Designer, University of Nebraska Press, 1981-. Publications: Works reproduced in numerous graphic arts magazines and journals and books including: Typography Now: the Next Wave by Rick Poyner, 1991; The Complete Typographer by Christopher Perfect, 1993; Design, Writing, Research by Ellen Lupton, 1996; On Book Design by Richard Hendel, 1999; Becoming a Graphic Designer by Steven Heller, 1999; A Short History of the Printed Word by Warren Chappell, 2000. Honours include: Silver Medal, Leipzig Book Fair, 1989; Carl Herzog Prize for Book Design, 1994; Honorary Associate Professor, University of Nebraska; Royal Designer for Industry, Royal Society of Arts, 1999. Memberships: American Association of Graphic Arts; Association Typographique Internationale. Address:1345 Garfield Street, Lincoln, NE 68502, USA. E-mail: reckersley1@unl.edu

**ECONOMOU Christos,** b. 11 July 1930, Athens, Greece. Civil Engineer. m. Penelope, 1 son, 1 daughter. Education: National Technical University, Athens Greece, 1955; Eidgenössische Technische Hochschule, Zurich, Switzerland, 1955-57; CEBTP, Paris France, 1974. Appointments: Technical Department, National Tourism Organisation; Titan Cement Industry; Lecturer, National Technical University, Athens, Greece; Professor of Reinforced Concrete, Democritus University of Thrace, Greece.

Publications: Prestressed Concrete (in Greek), 1957; Concrete technology (in Greek), 1973; Prestressed Concrete Applications (in Greek), 1993; Many other publications. Memberships: Technical Chamber of Greece; Scientific Society of Concrete Research of Greece. Address: 17A Doxapatrie St, Athens 11471, Greece. E-mail: econet@otenet.gr

**EDBERG Stefan,** b. 19 January 1966, Vastervik, Sweden. Tennis Player. m. Annette, 1 daughter. Appointments: Tennis player, winner of: Junior Grand Slam, 1983; Milan Open, 1984; San Francisco, Basle and Memphis Opens, 1985; Gstaad, Basle and Stockholm Opens, 1986; Australian Open, 1986, 1987; Wimbledon, 1988, 1990, finalist, 1989; US Open, 1991; Masters, 1989; German Open, 1992; US Open, 1992; Winner (with Anders Jarryd) Masters and French Open, 1986, Australian and US Opens, 1987; Member, Swedish Davis Cup Team, 1984, 1987; Semi-finalist, numerous tournaments; Retired in 1996 having won 60 professional titles and more than 20 million dollars in prize money; Founded the Stefan Edberg Foundation to assist young Swedish tennis players. Honour: Adidas Sportsmanship Award (four times). Address: c/o ATP Tour 200, ATP Tour Boulevard, Ponte Vedra Beach, FL 32082, USA.

**EDER Andrew Howard Eric,** b. 21 April 1964, London England. Dental Surgeon. m. Rosina Jayne Saideman, 2 sons, 1 daughter. Education: BDS (Hons), KCHMDS, University of London, 1986; LDS, Royal College of Surgeons of England; MSc, Conservative Dentistry, Eastman Dental Institute, University of London, 1990; Elected to MFGDP, Royal College of Surgeons of England; Membership in Restorative Dentistry, Royal College of Surgeons of England and Glasgow, 1994; Fellowship in Dental Surgery (Ad Eundum), Royal College of Surgeons of Edinburgh, 2003; Elected to ILTM, Institute of Learning and Teaching, 2002. Appointments: House Officer, Paediatric, Orthodontic and Restorative Dentistry, KCHMDS, 1987-88; Clinical Assistant in Restorative Dentistry, King's and Part-time Associate GDP, 1988-89; Registrar in Restorative Dentistry, Eastman, 1990-91; Clinical Lecturer in Restorative Dentistry, Eastman and Associate, GDP, 1991-94; Senior Clinical Lecturer in Restorative Dentistry, Eastman and Associate GDP, 1994-98; Senior Clinical Lecturer in Restorative Dentistry, Eastman and Specialist Practitioner, 1998-2002; Currently: Director of Continuing Professional Development and Visiting Professor and Honorary Consultant in Restorative Dentistry, Eastman Dental Institute (UCL); Honorary Professor, The School of Health and Social Sciences, Middlesex University; Specialist in Restorative Dentistry and Prosthodontics, Private Practice. Publications: 24, single and multi-author papers, edited articles posters and abstracts; Textbook: Tooth Surface Loss (with R Ibbetson), 2000; Editorial Advisory Board: The European Journal of Restorative Dentistry, 1995-; Clinical Adviser, Editorial Advisory Board: Independent Dentistry, 1997-; Board of Advisors, British Dental Journal, 2005-; Clinical Adviser in Restorative Dentistry: smile-on.com, 2002-. Memberships: Council Member, 1986-, President, 1994-95, Chairman of Trustees, 2003-, Alpha Omega; Council Member, 1994-, Fellowship, 1997, President, 2005-2006, British Society for Restorative Dentistry; Council Member, 1998-, British Prosthodontic Conference; Council Member, 1992-2003, President, 2001-2002, Odontological Section, Royal Society of Medicine. Address: Eastman CPD, 123 Gray's Inn Road, London WC1X 8WD, England. E-mail: aeder@eastman.ucl.ac.uk

**EDGE (THE) (David Evans),** b. 8 August 1961, Ireland. Musician. Appointments: Guitarist, Founder Member, U2, 1978-; Toured Australasia, Europe, USA, 1980-84; Live Aid Wembley, 1985; Self Aid Dublin, A Conspiracy of Hope (Amnesty International Tour), 1986; World tour, 100 performances, Europe and USA, 1987; Tour, Australia, 1989; New Year's Eve Concert Point Depot Dublin (Broadcast live to Europe and USSR, 1989; World tour, 1992-93; Dublin Concert, 1993. Recordings: Albums with U2: Boy, 1980; October, 1981; War, 1983; Under A Blood Red Sky, 1983; The Unforgettable Fire, 1984; The Joshua Tree, 1987; Rattle and Hum, 1988; Achtung Baby, 1991; Zooropa, 1993; Pop, 1997; All That You Can't Leave Behind, 2000; How to Dismantle an Atomic Bomb, 2004; Singles with U2 include: With Or Without You; I Still Haven't Found What I'm Looking For; Where the Streets Have No Name, 1988 (all 3 no 1 in US charts); Desire, 1988; Stay, 1993; Discotheque, 1997 (all 3 UK no 1); Sweetest Thing, 1998; Beautiful Day, 2000; Stuck in a Moment You Can's Get Out Of, 2001; Vertigo, 2004. Honours: Gold Disc for War, USA; Platinum Disc for Under a Blood Red Sky, UK; Band of Year (Rolling Stone Writers Poll), 1984; Grammy Awards: Album of Year, Best Rock Performance, Best Video; Best Live Act, BPI Awards, 1993. Address: c/o Regine Moylet Publicity, 9 Ivebury Court, 325 Latimer Road, London, W10 6RA, England.

**EDGECOMBE Jean Marjorie,** b. 28 February 1914, Bathurst, New South Wales, Australia. Author. m. Gordon Henry Edgecombe, 2 February 1945, 2 daughters, 2 sons. Education: BA, Honours, Sydney University, 1935. Publications: Discovering Lord Howe Island, (with Isobel Bennett), 1978; Discovering Norfolk Island, (with Isobel Bennett), 1983; Flinders Island, the Furneaux Group, 1985; Flinders Island and Eastern Bass Strait, 1986, 2nd edition, 1994; Lord Howe Island, World Heritage Area, 1987; Phillip Island and Western Port, 1989; Norfolk Island, South Pacific: Island of History and Many Delights, 1991, revised 2nd edition, 1999; Discovering Flinders Island, 1992, revised 2nd edition, 1999; Discovering King Island, Western Bass Strait, 1993, revised 2nd edition, 2004. Contributions to: Articles and poems to various publications. Honour: Medal of the Order of Australia, 1995. Membership: Australian Society of Authors; Hornsby Shire Historical Society; Australian Conservation Foundation; Furneaux Historical Research Association, life membership; The Australian Museum Society; The National Trust of Australia (New South Wales); State Library of New South Wales Foundation. Address: 7 Oakleigh Avenue, Thornleigh, 2120 New South Wales, Australia.

**EDMONDS Philip Hanbury,** b. 25 April 1940, Sydney, Australia. Real Estate and Business Valuer. m. Janet Gibson, 1 daughter. Education: BEcon (Hons), Sydney University. Appointments: Managing Director, Pacific Securities Pty Ltd, 1972-, Tasman Securities Pty Ltd, 1981-; Edmonds and Associates P/L, 1985. Memberships: Fellow, Australian Property Institute; Fellow, Chartered Institute of Secretaries; Certified Practising Accountant. Address: 44 Harbour Street, Mosman, NSW 2088, Australia.

**EDWARDS Anthony,** b. 19 July 1962, Santa Barbara, California, USA. Education: RADA, London. Appointments: Member, Santa Barbara Youth Theatre in 30 productions, aged 12-17; Commercials aged 16; Stage appearance: Ten Below, New York, 1993. Actor, films: Fast Times at Ridgemont High, 1982; Heart Like a Wheel, 1982; Revenge of the Nerds, 1984; The Sure Thing, 1985; Gotcha!, 1985; Top Gun, 1985; Summer Heat, 1987; Revenge of the Nerds II, 1987; Mr North, 1988; Miracle Mile, 1989; How I Got Into College, 1989; Hawks, 1989; Downtown, 1990; Delta Heat, 1994; The Client, 1994; Us Begins with You, 1998; Don't Go Breaking My Heart, 1999; Jackpot, 2001; TV series: It Takes Two, 1982-83; Northern Exposure, 1992-93; ER, 1994-; Soul Man; TV films: The Killing of Randy Webster, 1981; High School USA, 1983; Going for Gold: The Bill Johnson Story, 1985; El Diablo, 1990;

Hometown Boy Makes Good, 1990; In Cold Blood, 1996; TV specials: Unpublished Letters; Sexual Healing. Address: C/o United Talent Agency, 9560 Wilshire Boulevard, Suite 500, Beverly Hills, CA 90212, USA.

**EDWARDS Blake,** b. 26 July 1922, Tulsa, OK, USA. Film Director; Screen Writer. m. Julie Andrews, 1969. Appointments: US Coast Guard Reserve WWII; Writer for radio shows: Johnny Dollar; Line-Up; Writer, Creator: Richard Diamond; Creator TV shows: Dante's Inferno; Peter Gunn; Mr Lucky; Co-producer and writer: Panhandle, 1947; Stampede, 1948; Writer on films: All Ashore, 1952; Sound Off, 1952; Cruisin' Down the River, 1953; Drive a Crooked Road, 1954; My Sister Eileen (musical version), 1955; Operation Mad Ball, 1957; Notorious Landlady, 1962; Director, writer, films include: Bring Your Smile Along, 1955; He Laughed Last, 1955; Mr Cory, 1956; This Happy Feeling, 1958; Director, films: Operation Petticoat, 1959; High Time, 1960; Breakfast at Tiffany's, 1961; Days of Wine and Roses, 1962; The Carey Treatment, 1972; Producer, co-writer, director: The Soldier in the Rain, 1963; The Pink Panther, 1964; A Shot in the Dark, 1964; What Did You Do in the War, Daddy, 1966; Peter Gunn, 1967; The Party, 1968; Darling Lili, 1969; Wild Rovers, 1971; The Tamarind Seed, 1974; The Return of the Pink Panther, 1975; The Pink Panther Strikes Again, 1976; Revenge of the Pink Panther, 1978; 10, 1979; SOB, 1980; Victor/Victoria, 1981; Trail of the Pink Panther, 1982; Curse of the Pink Panther, 1983; Blind Date, 1986; Sunset, 1988; Skin Deep, 1989; Switch, 1991; Son of the Pink Panther, 1993; Producer, writer: Experiment in Terror, 1962; Co-writer, director: The Great Race, 1964; Writer, director, co-producer: Victor/Victoria (stage musical), Broadway, 1995. Address: c/o Blake Edwards Company, Suite 501, 10520 Wilshire Boulevard, Apt 1002, Los Angeles, CA 90024, USA.

**EDWARDS Elizabeth,** b. 13 October 1915, Holmfirth, Yorkshire, England. Retired Lecturer. m. Harry Lampen Edwards, 28 December 1968. Education: BA, Administration, Teachers Diploma, Manchester University, 1945-49. Appointments: Broadway Secondary Modern School, Cheadle; Leamington Spa Milverton College of Further Education; Buxton College of Further Education; Bournemouth College of Technology. Publications: A History of Bournemouth, 1981; Co-author, Tails of the Famous, 1987, with Margaret Brown; Famous Women in Dorset, 1992; Margaret Brown - Shelley Was Her Life, 1994; Bournemouth Past, 1998. Contributions to: Dorset Life; Hampshire Life; Choice; Yours; Gentlemen's Magazine. Friends Literary Society; Tutor, French Conversation, University of the Third Age. Address: Avon Cliff Residential Home, 50/52 Christchurch Road, Bournemouth, BH1 3PE, England.

**EDWARDS Gareth Owen,** b. 12 July 1947. Rugby Union Player (retired); Businessman. m. Maureen Edwards, 1972, 2 sons. Education: Cardiff College of Education. Appointments: Welsh Secondary Schools Rugby international, 1965-66; English Schools 200 yards Champion (UK under 19 record holder), 1966; Welsh national team: 53 caps, 1967-78; Captain 13 times, youngest captain (aged 20), 1968; Played with clubs: Cardiff, 1966-78; Barbarians, 1967-78; British Lions, 1968, 1971, 1974; Joint Director, Euro-Commercials (South Wales) Ltd, 1982-; Players (UK) Ltd, 1983-889 Chairman, Hamdden Ltd, 1991-; Chairman, Regional Fisheries Advisory Committee, Welsh Water Authority, 1983-89. Publications: Gareth - An Autobiography, 1978; Rugby Skills, 1979; Gareth Edwards on Rugby, 1986; Gareth Edwards' 100 Great Rugby Players, 1987. Address: Hamdden Ltd, Plas y Ffynnon, Cambrian Way, Brecon, Powys, LD3 7HP, Wales.

**EDWARDS Harold (Harry) Raymond,** b. 10 January 1927, Sydney, Australia. Economist. m. Elaine Lance, 18 August 1951, 1 son, 4 daughters. Education: BA, Honours, Sydney, 1948; DPhil, Oxford, 1957; Hon DLitt, Macquarie University, 1992. Appointments: Professor of Economics, University of Sydney, 1962-; Foundation Professor, Economics, Founder, Graduate School of Management, Macquarie University, 1966-72; Member of Parliament, Shadow Minister for Industry, Science, Finance, Leader of Australian Parliament Delegation and Member of International Executive, Inter-Parliamentary Union, Geneva, 1978-82, inaugurated National Prayer Breakfast, 1986, House of Representatives, Canberra, Parliament of Australia, 1972-93; Microfinance Consultant, Development Economics, Adviser 1985- and First Chairman of the Board, Opportunity International Australia Ltd, Overseas Aid Organisation; Emeritus Professor, Macquarie University, 1993-. Publications: Competition and Monopoly in the British Soap Industry, OUP, 1962; Articles in various journals. Honours: Queen Elizabeth Silver Jubilee Medal, 1977; Australia Centenary Medal, 2003; Member of the Order of Australia, AM, 2005. Memberships: Fellow, Academy of the Social Sciences in Australia; Fellow, Australian Institute of Management; Layman, Uniting Church in Australia. Address: 12 John Savage Crescent, West Pennant Hills, NSW 2125, Australia.

**EDWARDS Janet,** b. 18 May 1946, Huddersfield, Yorkshire, England. Singer; Musician (piano). m (1), 2 sons, (2) Thomas Saunders. Education: Associate of the Royal College of Music, 1965; Licentiate of Trinity College London, 1966; Dip Ed, Diploma in Education, 1967; Studied piano, with Dr Michael Kruszynski; Piano soloist and accompanist: Recitals, 1974-; Performed with artists including those from Royal Opera House, ENO soloists; Performances: Italy; France; Germany; UK including South Bank, Wigmore Hall; Devised, performed own shows: Sounds Entertaining; I Say I Play; Munich, London, other UK halls; Solo work, classical, popular, theatre, jazz music, in: Europe; Scandinavia; Middle East; Accompanist, Assistant Musical Director, Royal Gala Performance of works by Stephen Sondheim, Theatre Royal Drury Lane; Work as repertoire voice coach, Royal Academy of Music, early 1980s; Master class group sessions working with professionals and non-professionals, 1989-; Played: Anna in Girls Were Made To Love And Kiss, West End, 1994; Also runs professional seminars in auditioning techniques, workshops and seminars for the general public; Began one-woman show, 'S' Wonderful, 'S' Marvellous, in theatres and venues in the UK, 1997-; London shows including Pizza on the Park, performing own songs and recording, 1999-. Honours: Diploma with distinction, Huddersfield College of Technology; ARCM; LTCL Dip Ed; FRSA, 2003. Memberships: British Academy of Composers and Songwriters; Musicians Union; Equity. Website: www.janetedwards.co.uk

**EDWARDS Jonathan,** b. 10 May 1966, London, England. Athlete. m. Alison Joy Briggs, 2 sons. Career: Athlete, Bronze Medal, World Championships, 1993; Gold Medal, Fifth Athletics World Championships, Gothenburg, twice breaking own record for triple jump, clearing 18.29m, 1995, Edmonton, 2001; Silver Medal, Olympic Games, Atlanta, 1996; World Championships, 1997, 1999; Gold Medal, European Championships, 1998; European Indoor Championships, 1998; Goodwill Games, 1998; Sports Fellowship, University of Durham, 1999; Olympic Games, 2000; World Championships, 2001; Commonwealth Games, 2002; Retired from athletics after 2003 World Championships; Currently working mainly for the BBC as a sports commentator and presenter of programmes including Songs of Praise. Publication: A Time to Jump, 2000. Honours: BBC Sportsman of the Year, 1995; IAAF Athlete of the Year, 1995; BBC Sports Personality of the Year, 1995;

British Male Athlete of the Year, 1995, 2000, 2001; CBE. Address: c/o Jonathan Marks, MTC, 20 York Street, London W1U 6PU, England. E-mail: info@mtc-uk.com Website: www.mtc-uk.com

**EDWARDS Philip Walter,** b. 7 February 1923, Cumbria, England. Retired Professor of English; Writer. m. Sheila Mary Wilkes, 8 May 1952, 3 sons, 1 daughter. Education: BA, 1942, MA, 1946, PhD, 1960, University of Birmingham. Appointments: Lecturer, University of Birmingham, 1946-60; Professor, Trinity College, Dublin, 1960-66, University of Essex, 1966-74, University of Liverpool, 1974-90. Publications: Sir Walter Raleigh, 1953; Kyd, The Spanish Tragedy, 1959; Shakespeare and the Confines of Art, 1968; Massinger: Plays and Poems, 1976; Shakespeare's Pericles, 1976; Threshold of a Nation, 1979; Hamlet, 1985; Shakespeare: A Writers Progress, 1986; Last Voyages, 1988; The Story of the Voyage, 1994; Sea-Mark, 1997; The Journals of Captain Cook, 1999; Pilgrimage and Literary Tradition, 2005. Membership: British Academy, fellow, 1986-. Address: High Gillinggrove, Gillinggate, Kendal, Cumbria LA9 4JB, England.

**EDWARDS Robert,** b. 27 September 1925. Physiologist. m. Ruth E Fowler, 1956, 5 daughters. Education: University of Wales; University of Edinburgh. Appointments: Research Fellow, California Institute of Technology, 1957-58; Scientist, National Institute of Medical Research, Mill Hill, 1958-62; Glasgow University, 1962-63; Department of Physiology, University of Cambridge, 1963-89; Ford Foundation Reader in Physiology, 1969-85; Professor of Human Reproduction, 1985-89, Professor Emeritus, 1989-, University of Cambridge. Publications: A Matter of Life, with P C Steptoe, 1980; Conception in the Human Female, 1980; Mechanisms of Sex Differentiation in Animals and Man, with C R Austin, 1982; Human Conception in Vitro, with J M Purdy, 1982; Implantation of the Human Embryo, with J M Purdy and P C Steptoe, 1985; In Vitro Fertilisation and Embryo Transfer, with M Seppala, 1985; Life Before Birth, 1989; Numerous articles in scientific and medical journals. Honours: Honorary Member, French Society for Infertility; Honorary Citizen of Bordeaux; Hon FRCOG; Hon MRCP; Hon DSc (Hull, York, Free University Brussels); Gold Medal, Spanish Fertility Society, 1985; King Faisal Award, 1989. Memberships: Fellow, Churchill College, Cambridge, now Extraordinary Fellow; Scientific Director, Bourn Hall Clinics, Cambridge and London; Chair, European Society of Human Reproduction and Embryology, 1984-86; Visiting Scientist, Johns Hopkins University, 1965, University of North Carolina, 1966, Free University of Brussels, 1984; Honorary President, British Fertility Society, 1988-; Life Fellow, Australian Fertility Society; Chief Editor, Human Reproduction, 1986-. Address: Duck End Farm, Dry Drayton, Cambridge, CB3 8DB, England.

**EFIMOV Alexander Vasilievich,** b. 12 May 1954, Lugovaya, Orenburg Region, Russia. Chemist. Widower, 1 daughter. Education: Bachelor's Degree, Moscow State University, 1976; Candidate of Science (PhD), 1983; Doctor of Science, Chemistry, 1995. Appointments: Probationer, 1976-79, Junior Researcher, 1979-87; Senior Researcher, 1987-96, Leading Researcher, 1996-1998, Principal Researcher, 1998-, Deputy Director, 2002-, Institute of Protein Research, Russian Academy of Sciences. Publications: Articles in scientific journals including: Journal of Molecular Biology, 1979, 1995; FEBS Letters, 1984, 1987, 1991, 1992, 1993, 1994, 1996, 1997, 1998, 2003; Structure, 1994; Proteins, 1997. Membership: Scientific Secretary, 1989-2000; Deputy Director, 2002-, Institute of Protein Research. Address: Institute of Protein Research,

RAS, 142290 Pushchino, Moscow Region, Russia. E-mail: efimov@protres.ru

**EFROS Victor,** b. 11 June 1942, Ekaterinburg Province of Russia. Physicist. m. N Pushkina, 1 son. Education: MSc, Moscow State University, 1966; PhD, 1974, DSc, 1987, Kurchatov Institute, Moscow. Appointments: Senior Scientist, 1974-89, Head Scientist, 1989-, Russian Research Centre, Kurchatov Institute; Foreign Professor, Department of Physics, University of Trento, Italy, 2000-2002; Research Work: Nills Bohr Institute, University of Surrey, University of Trento, Technical University of Vienna, Chalmers University of Gothenburg, European Centre for Theoretical Nuclear Physics, University of Saskatchewan. Publications: More than 100 articles in professional journals. Honours: Kurchatov Prizes, 1973, 1990, 2001. Address: Russian Research Centre "Kurchatov Institute", 123182 Moscow, Russia.

**EGEE Dale Richardson,** b. 7 February 1934, New York City, New York, USA. Art Consultant (Retired). m. David Egee, 2 sons, 2 daughters. Education: Rosemont College, Rosemont, Pennsylvania, USA, 1953-55; Instituto d'Arte, Florence Italy, 1955-57. Appointments: Tapestry Designer, Lebanon, Italy, Dubai, 1968-78; Art Consultant, Gallery Owner specialising in Middle Eastern and African Art, 1978-2003; Consultant to banks, businesses, governments: Qatar, Kuwait, USA for selection, commission and installation of all art in 8 embassies: Saudi Arabia, Kuwait, Jordan, Yemen, Bangladesh, Egypt, Tanzania and Kenya. Publications: Numerous articles in professional journals including: Arts in the Islamic World; Eastern Art Report; Curator of catalogue of Contemporary Arab Art, Rotterdam Museum, 2001-2002. Memberships: Royal Geographical Society; Chelsea Arts Club. Address: 9 Chelsea Manor Studios, Flood Street, London SW3 5SR, England. E-mail: egee.art@btinternet.com

**EGLETON Clive Frederick William,** b. 25 November 1927. Author; Retired Army Officer; Retired Civil Servant. m. Joan Evelyn Lane, 9 April 1949, deceased 22 February 1996, 2 sons. Education: Staff College, Camberley, 1957. Publications: A Piece of Resistance, 1970; Last Post for a Partisan, 1971; The Judas Mandate, 1973; Seven Days to a Killing, 1973; The October Plot, 1974; Skirmish, 1975; State Visit, 1978; The Mills Bomb, 1978; Backfire, 1979; The Winter Touch, 1982; A Falcon for the Hawks, 1982; The Russian Enigma, 1982; Conflict of Interests, 1984; Troika, 1984; A Different Drummer, 1985; Picture of the Year, 1987; Gone Missing, 1988; Death of a Sahib, 1989; In the Red, 1990; Last Act, 1991; A Double Deception, 1992; Hostile Intent, 1993; A Killing in Moscow, 1994; Death Throes, 1994; A Lethal Involvement, 1995; Warning Shot, 1996; Blood Money, 1997; Dead Reckoning, 1999; The Honey Trap, 2000; One Man Running, 2001; Cry Havoc, 2002; Assassination Day, 2004; The Renegades, 2005. Memberships: Crime Writers Association; Society of Authors. Address: Dolphin House, Beach House Lane, Bembridge, Isle of Wight PO35 5TA, England.

**EGTESADI Shahryar,** b. 6 November 1952, Sanandaj, Iran. Professor of Clinical Nutrition. m. Akhtar Afshari, 3 daughters. Education: BS, Nutrition Science and Food Chemistry, Shahid Beheshti University, 1975, Tehran; MSPH, Nutrition Science, Tehran University, Teheran, 1977; PhD, Nutrition, University of California, Davis, USA, 1986. Appointments: Instructor, Tabriz University, Tabriz, Iran, 1978-86; Assistant Professor, 1986-90, Associate Professor, 1990-95, Professor, 1995-2002, Associate Dean for Education and Research Affairs, School of Public Health, 2002, Tabriz University of Medical Sciences; Chair, Department of Biochemistry and Nutrition, Tabriz, Iran,

1986-93; Visiting Scientist, Human Nutrition Research Center on Aging, Tufts University, USA, 1995; Chair, Department of Biochemistry and Clinical Nutrition, 1996-98; Head of Research Department, School of Public Health and Nutrition, Tabriz, Iran, 1996-2002; Professor, Iran University of Medical Sciences, School of Public Health, Tehran, 2002-. Publications: 98 articles presented or published in Iranian and international journals and congresses mainly on the topics of regulation of metabolism, nutrition assessments of infants and children, growth pattern and nutrition status of adolescents, nutrition behaviour and food choice of adolescents, food insecurity; Copper, iron and antioxidants nutrition and metabolism, and issues of clinical nutrition. Honours: Distinguished Editor of Article presented in the Iranian Research Forum, National Research Centre of Iran, Iranian Ministry of Science, 1999; Distinguished Scientist of Tabriz University of Medical Sciences, School of Public Health and Nutrition, 2000; Listed in Great Minds of 21st Century, ABI, 2001; Distinguished Scientist, Iran University of Medical Sciences, School of Public Health, 2002. Memberships: Iranian Society of Nutrition; Iranian Society of Physiology and Pharmacology; Iranian Board of Nutrition. Address: Iran University of Medical Sciences, School of Public Health, Dept of Nutrition, Argentina Square, Alvand Street, Tehran, Iran. E-mail: egtesadi@iums.ac.ir

**EHRNST Anneka Cecilia,** b. 29 October 1945, Ostersund, Sweden. Physician, Scientist. m. Robert Grundin, 2 sons. Education: MD, 1972, PhD, 1978, Associate Professor 1980, Karolinska Institute; Specialist in Clinical Immunology, 1980; Specialist in Clinical Virology, 1983; Postdoctoral training at Harvard Medical School, 1981-82. Appointments: Laboratory Physician, 1973-82; Deputy Head, Polio Vaccine Development, National Bacterial Laboratory, 1982-83; Clinical Virologist: Stockholm Municipal Laboratory, 1983-93, Huddinge University Hospital, 1993-2003, Karolinska University Hospital, Huddinge, 2004-.; Deputy Head, Clinical Virology, 1992-95; Researcher Microbiology Tumorbiology Centre, Karolinska Institute, Stockholm, 1996-, Adjunct Professor 2004. Publications: Over 100 publications in international medical and scientific journals; approximately 100 presentations at scientific meetings; Scientific Secretary and Editor of Proceedings, V International CMV Conference. Memberships include: New York Academy of Science; European Society Clinical Virology; National Geographic Society; Others. Address: Microbiology and Tumorbiology Centre, Box 280, Karolinska Institute, SE 171 77 Stockholm, Sweden.

**EIDERMAN Boris,** b. 23 February 1934, Kharkov, Ukraine, USSR. Mechanics Researcher. m. Susanna Nuger, 1 son. Education: MSc, engineer-mechanic, Mining Institute, Kharkov, 1957; PhD, 1968, Dr Sci, 1986, Professorship, 1989, Academy, Mining Institute, Moscow. Appointments: Engineer and designer of mining machinery, Machine Build Works, Kharkov, 1957-61; Head, Mechanics Section, Mining Institute, Kharkov, 1961-66; Senior Scientist, Leading Scientist, Professor, Mechanisation Section, Academy Mining Institute, Moscow, 1967-91; Scientist, Researcher, College of Technology, Jerusalem, Israel, 1992-93; Chief Scientist, Sortech Separation Technologies Ltd, Jerusalem, Israel, 1997-2003; Consultant, 2004-. Publications: Mechanisms for Formation of Traffic and Energy Expenditure of Conveyors, 1984; Parameters and Calculation Methods for Conveyors, 1987; Scraper Conveyors, 1993; Triboclassification Technology for Minerals and Fly Ash, 2000; Triboclassification Technology for Bulk Powder, 2001. Honours: Prize Winner, USSR Council of Ministers, 1983; Grantee, Ministry of Industry and Trade of Israel, 1992, 1997. Memberships: New York Academy of Sciences; Forum for Bulk Solids Handling.

Address: Home: Gvirtsman Moshe str 6/4, 97793 Jerusalem, Israel. E-mail: boris@eiderman.com

**EIGEN Manfred,** b. 9 May 1927, Ruhr, Germany. Physical Chemist. m. Elfriede Müller, 1 son, 1 daughter. Education: Doctorate, Göttingen University, 1951. Appointments: Assistant, Professor, Head of Department, 1953-, Director, 1964, Max-Planck Institute of Physical Chemistry, Göttingen; Honorary Professor, Technical University, Göttingen, 1971-; President, Studienstiftung des Deutschen Volkes, 1983-. Honours: Hon Dr, University of Washington, St Louis University, Harvard University, Cambridge University; Numerous other honorary degrees; Foreign Honorary Member, American Academy of Arts and Sciences; Otto Hahn Prize, 1967; Joint Winner, Nobel Prize for Chemistry, 1967. Memberships: Akademie der Wissenschaften, Göttingen; Foreign Associate Member, National Academy of Sciences, USA; Foreign Member, Royal Society, UK; Academie Française, 1978. Address: Georg-Dehio-Weg 14, 37075, Germany.

**EISENREICH Günther,** b. 12 April 1933, Leipzig, Germany Retired Professor of Mathematics. m. Gisela Busse. Education: Studies in Mathematics, Physics and Biology, 1951-56; Degree in Mathematics, 1956; Doctor of Natural Sciences, 1963; Habilitation in Natural sciences, 1968. Appointments: Scientific Worker, Saxon Academy of Sciences, Leipzig, 1957-58; Scientific Assistant, 1959-67; Senior Assistant, 1967-69; University Docent, Mathematical Section, 1969-70, Professor of Theoretical Mathematics, 1970-98, (appointments delayed for political reasons), University of Leipzig. Publications: Books: Vorlesungen über Vektor–und Tensorrechnung; Lineare Algebra und analytische Geometrie; Vorlesung über Funktionentheorie mehrerer Variabler; Lexikon der Algebra; Fachwörterbuch Mathematik Englisch/Deutsch/Französisch/Russisch; Fachwörterbuch Physik Englisch/Deutsch/ Französisch/ Russisch; Articles on mathematics, biology, philosophy, linguistics and biographies which include: Untersuchungen über Ideale in Stellenringen; Eine Dualitätsbeziehung zwischen s-Moduln; Zur Syzygientheorie und Theorie des inversen Systems perfekter Ideale und Vektormoduln in Polynomringen und Stellenringen; Zum Wahrheitsproblem in der Mathematik; Numerous reviews, translations of Scientific books from the English, French, Russian and Hungarian. Honour: General Honouring for Scientific Success, Education of students and Democratizing the University. Memberships: Deutsche Mathematiker-Vereinigung, 1990-98; Mathematische Gesellschaft der DDR; Deutscher Hochschulverband, Speaker of the Saxons; Federation of Trade Unions. Address: Gartenbogen 7, D-04288 Leipzig, Germany.

**EISHINSKII Alexandr Moiseevich,** b. 1 October 1936, Dnepropetrovsk, Ukraine. Mathematician. Divorced. Education: Degrees, 1954, 1965. Appointments: Teacher of Mathematics; Science Research Worker. Publications: Co-author of 9 patents; Author and co-author of 9 books: Etudes of the analytical geotechnology, 1989; Mathematical algorithms of thermochemical geotechnology, 1992; Some questions of destruction of mining rocks, 1995; Mathematical algorithms of chemical cinetics, 1998; Torsion of the anisotrops and nonhomogeneous bodies, 1999; Exact Solutions of some problems of mechanics, 2000; The theory and practice of thermochemical technology of extracting and processing coal, 2000; Exact Solutions of some problems of analytical mechanics, 2003; Exact Solutions of the Einsteins Field Equations, 2005. Honours: Research Board of Advisors, ABI; Order of International Ambassadors, ABI; Silver and Gold Medals, IBC, England. Memberships: New York Academy of Sciences; Member, International Academy of Ecology and Life

# DICTIONARY OF INTERNATIONAL BIOGRAPHY

Protection Sciences, St Petersburg. Address: Ioseftal 24 Apt 9, Kiryat-Ata, 28014 Israel.

**EISNER Michael Dammann**, b. 7 March 1942, Mt Kisco, New York, USA. Entertainment Executive. m. Jane Breckenridge, 1967, 3 sons. Education: Denison University. Appointments: Senior Vice President, prime-time production and development, ABC Entertainment Corporation, 1973-76; President, COO, Paramount Pictures Corporation, 1976-84; Chairman, Chief Executive Officer, The Walt Disney Company, 1984-. Honour: Légion d'honneur. Address: Walt Disney Company, 500 South Buena Vista Street, Burbank, CA 91521, USA.

**EJEH Stephen Pinder**, b. 2 November 1956, Idoma, Benue State, Nigeria. Lecturer; Researcher. m. Eunice Ejeh, 2 sons. Education: B Eng, Civil Engineering, 1979; M Eng, Structural Engineering, 1982; PhD, Structural Engineering, 1990. Appointments: Teacher, Researcher, Supervisor of Undergraduate, Masters and Doctors Degrees in Civil Engineering, University of Ahmadu Bello, Zaria, Nigeria. Publications: 16 journal papers; 7 conference papers; 11 public lectures. Honours: Role Model Award, NUESA; Award of Excellence, NACES, 1998-99; Award for Excellence, NUESA, 2000-2001. Memberships: MNSE; COREN; FICEN; MMSN. Address: Department of Civil Engineering, Ahmadu Bello University, Samaru, Zaria, Nigeria, West Africa. E-mail: spejeh@engineers.com

**EJOBE Evwiere O Olorogun**, b. 28 May 1942, Ajoki, Edo State, Nigeria. Lawyer, Business Consultant. m. Arodovwe, 4 sons, 3 daughters. Education: BSc (Econ) (Hons), University of Ibadan, 1966; MSc, Business Administration, University of Aston, Birmingham, England, 1977; LLB (Hons), Lagos State University, 1990; BL (Hons), Nigerian Law School, Lagos, 1991; Attended and participated in various seminars and business and professional courses within and outside Nigeria including those at: Nigerian Institute of International Affairs, Lagos; International Business School, Lausanne, Switzerland, Oxford and Cambridge Universities, England. Appointments include: Assistant Manager, Electricity Corporation of Nigeria, 1966-67; Trainee, Freeman Lawrence & Partners (Chartered Accountants) Kingsway, London, England, 1967-71; Chief Accountant and Company Secretary, Fox Photos Limited (Photographers to the British Royal Family), London, 1971-73; Adviser (Expatriate) to the Governor, Central Bank of Zambia, London, 1973-76; Principal Assistant Secretary, 1978, Under Secretary, 1979, Nigerian Civil Service, Cabinet Office, Government of the Federal Republic of Nigeria, Lagos, 1978-79; General Manager then Managing Director and Chief Executive Officer, West African Distillers Ltd (Distillers to the Nation), Ikeja, Lagos, 1979-86; Apprenticeship (while at the Lagos Law School), Chief Rotimi Williams Chambers, Lagos, 1991; Chairman, Committee of Finance and Appriation, Chairman, Committee on Assets Sharing Between Delta and Edo States, Member, Committee on Oil and Mineral Resources, Member, Committee on Judicial and Legal Matters, Delta State House of Assembly, 1992-93; Currently Managing Partner, Olorogun Ejobe & Co (Attorneys-at-Law, Barristers, Solicitors and Advocates), Dominion Chambers, Lagos. Publications: Contributed articles to learned journals and presented papers and acted as group leader in various fora as well as submitted essays and dissertations for academic recognition and awards. Honour: Olorogun, The Highest Traditional Chieftancy Title in Oghara Kingdom in Nigeria. Memberships: Fellow of the Society of Company and Commercial Accountants, England; Member of the British Institute of Management, England. Address: Olorogun Ejobe & Co. 4, Aderibigbe Shitta Street, Maryland, Lagos, Nigeria.

**EKELE Bissallah Ahmend**, b. 8 March 1962, Ofante, Nigeria. Obstetrician; Gynaecologist. m. Comfort, 1 son, 1 daughter. Education: MBBS, University of Jos, Nigeria, 1979-85; FWACS, West African Postgraduate College, 1987-94; FICS, International College of Surgeons, 1997. Appointments: Senior House Officer, UMTH, Maidugur, Nigeria, 1987-88; Registrar, Senior Registrar, JUTH, Jos, 1988-94; Lecturer, Consultant, UDUTH, Sokoto, 1994-97; Senior Lecturer, 1997-2000, Reader, 2000-03, UDU, Sokoto, Nigeria. Publications: 49 in peer-reviewed journals including: Lancet, Acta. Obstet. Gynecol. Scand. and International Journal of Obstetrics and Gynaecology; Contributed chapters in 7 books. Honours: Gold Medal, Anatomy and Physiology; Glazo Prize, Anaesthesia; Fredrick Zuspan Award. Memberships: Society of Obstetrics and Gynaecology of Nigeria; International Society for the Study of Hypertension in Pregnancy. Address: Department of Obstetrics and Gynaecology, Usmanu Danfodiyo University Teaching Hospital, Sokoto, Nigeria. E-mail: ekeleba@skannet.com.ng

**EL MIEDANY Yasser**, b. 30 June 1961, Alexandria, Egypt. Clinical Professor of Rheumatology. m. Sally Sayed Youssef, 2 sons, 1 daughter. Education: MB ChB, Ain Shams University, Cairo, Egypt, 1984; Diploma in Internal Medicine, 1987; MSc, Rheumatology and Rehabilitation, 1989; MD, Rheumatology and Rehabilitation, 1994; GMC Registration, 2001. Appointments: House Officer, Ain Shams University Hospitals; Senior House Officer, General Medicine Department, 1986-87, General Medicine, Rheumatology and Rehabilitation Department, 1987-90, Registrar, Rheumatology and Rehabilitation Department, 1990-91, Registrar, Assistant Lecturer, 1992-94, Consultant Lecturer, 1994-95, 1997-2001, Consultant, Associate Professor, 2001-, Ain Shams University Hospitals and Ain Shams University Specialist Hospital, Ain Sham University; Registrar, Glasgow Royal Infirmary, Centre for Rheumatic Diseases, 1991-92; Consultant Rheumatologist, Saudi German Hospital, Jeddah, Saudi Arabia, 1995-97; Consultant Rheumatologist (locum) Broomfield Hospital, Chelmsford, England, 2001-2002; Consultant Rheumatologist (locum), Princess Royal Hospital Haywards Heath, England, 2002; Consultant Rheumatologist (locum), North Hampshire Hospital Basingstoke, England, 2003; Consultant Rheumatologist, Darent Valley Hospital, Dartford, England, 2003-. Publications: Book: Basic Rheumatology for Postgraduates, 1995, 2001; Numerous articles as co-author in medical journals. Honour: Health Professional of the Year 2004. Memberships: Fellow, American College of Rheumatology; British Society for Rheumatology; Royal College of Physicians; Paediatric International Rheumatology Organisation; American Association for Diabetes Mellitus; Egyptian Society for Rheumatology and Rehabilitation. Address: 2 Italian Hospital Street, Abbassia, Cairo, Egypt 11381. E-mail: yasser_elmiedany@yahoo.com Website: www.dryasserelmiedany.egydoc.com

**EL-BAZ Farouk**, b. 1 January 1938, Zagazig, Egypt. Geologist; Educator; Researcher. m. Catherine Patricia O'Leary, 4 daughters. Education: BSc, Ain Shams University, Egypt, 1958; MS, Missouri School of Mines, 1961; PhD, University of Missouri, 1964. Appointments: Assiut University, 1958-69; Heidelberg University, Germany, 1964-66; Belcomm Inc, 1967-72; Smithsonian Institution, 1973-82; Itek Optical Systems, 1982-86; Director and Research Professor, Center for Remote Sensing, Boston University, Boston, Massachusetts, USA, 1986-. Publications: Say It In Arabic, 1968; The Moon as Viewed by Lunar Orbiter, 1970; Apollo Over the Moon, 1978; Astronaut Observations from the Apollo-Soyuz Mission, 1977; Egypt as Seen by Landsat, 1979; Apollo-Soyuz Test Project: Earth Observations and Photography, 1979; The Geology of Egypt: An Annotated Bibliography, 1984; Physics of

Desertification, 1986; The Gulf War and the Environment, 1994; Atlas of Kuwait from Satellite Images, 2000; Wadis of Oman, 2002; Sultanate of Oman: Satellite Image Atlas, 2004. Honours: NASA Apollo Achievement Award; Order of Merit First Class, Egypt; Nevada Medal; Pioneer Award (Arab Thought Foundation); Golden Door Award, International Institute of Boston; Honorary Doctorates: New England College, New Hampshire, 1989; Mansoura University, Egypt, 2003; American University in Cairo, Egypt, 2004; University of Missouri-Rolla, 2004. Memberships: Royal Astronomical Society; US National Academy of Engineering; African Academy of Sciences; Arab Academy of Sciences; Academy of Sciences for the Developing World; Geological Society of America; American Association for the Advancement of Science; Explorers Club. Address: Center for Remote Sensing, 725 Commonwealth Avenue, Boston University, Boston, MA 02215, USA. E-mail: farouk@bu.edu

**EL-SHARKAWY Mabrouk A,** b. 7 April 1937, Shobratana, Gharbia Governate, Egypt. Scientist. m. Stella Navarro, 1 daughter. Education: BSc honours, Agriculture, Alexandria University, Egypt, 1958; Research Assistant, National Research Centre, Dokki, Cairo, 1958-60; Graduate Student, Louisiana State University and University of Arizona, 1960-65; MSc, Agronomy, Louisiana State University, 1962; PhD, Agronomy, University of Arizona, 1965. Appointments: Associate Plant Physiologist, University of California at Davis, 1965-66; Crop Physiologist, Ministry of Agriculture, Cairo, 1966-68; Professor, University of Tripoli, Libya, 1968-78; Head, Agronomy Division, Faculty of Agriculture, 1972-75; Head, Plant Production, Arab Organization of Agricultural Development, 1978-80; Crop Physiologist, Centro Internacional de Agric Tropical, Cali, Colombia, 1980-97; Co-ordinator and Manager of Integrated Cassava Production Project, 1988-96; Discovered C3/C4 Syndrome in plant photosynthesis, farming systems in sandy soil; Discovery of leaf Kranz anatomy and photorespiration reassimilation in C4 photosynthesis species including maize, tropical grasses and amaranthus species; Physiological characteristics of cassava productivity in the tropics; Discovery of mechanisms underlying resistance of cassava to atmospheric and edaphic water-stress; Selection of cassava cultivars resistant to drought and poor soils; Integrated cassava production systems in hillside and marginal lands; Characterisation of cassava germ plasm for leaf photosynthesis in relation to crop productivity in humid, seasonally dry and semi-arid environment; Characterisation of cotton germ plasm for leaf photosynthesis; Genetic inheritance of fibre traits in upland cotton; Selection of wheat and barley cultivars for desert conditions; Research on cropping systems, irrigation and plant-soil relationships in the Libyan Sahara desert; Developed a method to measure plant photorespiration in $CO_2$-free air now in use. Publications: Over 130 in professional journals. Honours: University of Alexandria fellow, 1955-58; University of California fellow, 1965-66; Egyptian Government Scholar, 1959-65; Recipient, Citation Classic Award, Institute of Scientific Information, PA, USA, 1986; Over 600 citations in literature, Citation Index ISI. Memberships: Sigma Xi; New York Academy of Sciences; American Society of Agronomy; Crop Science Society of America; AAAS; American Institute of Biological Sciences, Alpha Zeta. Address: A A 26360 Cali Valle, Colombia, South America. E-mail: elsharkawy@ telesat.com.co

**ELBERN Victor H,** b. 9 June 1918, Düren, Germany. Art Historian. m. Theresia Schager, 2 sons, 1 daughter. Education: University of Bonn; Bacc Phil, Rome Gregorian University; Dr phil, Zurich University; Studies in Philosophy, History, Classical Archaeology, Roman Languages, History of Art.

Appointments: Chief Curator, State Museums of Berlin, Early Christian and Byzantine Department; International Exhibitions: Essen, 1956, Brussels Expo, 1958; Honorary Professor, History of Art, Free University, Berlin, 1970; Chairman, Görres-Gesellschaft, 1982-93; Director, Jerusalem Institute Görres-Gesellschaft, 1987-93; Visiting Professor: Tel-Aviv University, 1979, Zurich University, 1983, Jerusalem Hebrew University, 1983. Publications: Der Goldaltar von Mailand, 1952; Das erste Jahrtausend, 3 volumes, 1962-64; Der eucharistische Kelch in frühen Mittelalter, 1964; St Liudger und die Abtei Werden, 1962; Dom und Domschatz in Hildesheim, 1979; Die Goldschmiedekunst in frühen Mittelalter, 1988; Fructus Operis, Gesammelte Aufsätze, 1998; Fructus Operis II, Beiträge liturgische Kunst, 2003; About 500 articles. Honours: Chevalier Couronne de Belgique, 1958; Cavaliere San Silvestro, 1958; Commendatore S. Gregorio Magno, 1981; Grand Officer, Holy Sepulchre, 1990; Bundesverdienstkreuz Deutschland, 1983. Memberships: Société des Antiquaires, Poitiers, 1961; Deutsches Archäologisches Institut, 1980; Braunschweig Wiss Gesellschaft, 1984; Accademia Nazionale dei Lincei Roma, 1988. Address: Ilsensteinweg 42, D-14129 Berlin, Germany.

**ELDRIDGE Colin Clifford,** b. 16 May 1942, Walthamstow, England. University Reader in History; Writer. m. Ruth Margaret Evans, 3 August 1970, deceased 2003, 1 daughter. Education: BA, 1963, PhD, 1966, Nottingham University. Appointments: Lecturer, 1968-75, Senior Lecturer in History, 1975-92, Reader, 1992-98, Professor, 1998-, University of Wales. Publications: England's Mission: The Imperial Idea in the Age of Gladstone and Disraeli, 1973; Victorian Imperialism, 1978; Essays in Honour of C D Chandaman, 1980; British Imperialism in the 19th Century, 1984; Empire, Politics and Popular Culture, 1989; From Rebellion to Patriation: Canada & Britain in the Nineteenth & Twentieth Centuries, 1989; Disraeli and the Rise of a New Imperialism, 1996; The Imperial Experience: From Carlyle to Forster, 1996; The Zulu War, 1879, 1996; Kith and Kin: Canada, Britain and the United States form the Revolution to the Cold War, 1997. Contributions to: Various learned journals. Honour: Fellow, Royal Historical Society. Memberships: Historical Association; Association of History Teachers in Wales; British Association of Canadian Studies; British Australian Studies Association. Address: Tanerdy, Cilau Aeron, Lampeter, Dyfed SA48 8DL, Wales.

**ELEGANT Robert Sampson,** b. 7 March 1928, New York, New York, USA. Author; Journalist; Novelist. m. (1) Moira Clarissa Brady, 16 April 1956, deceased 20 January 1999, 1 son, 1 daughter, (2) Ursula Rosemary Righer, 10 May 2003. Education: AB, University of Pennsylvania, 1946; Japanese Army Language School, 1947-48; Yale University, 1948; MA, 1950, MS, 1951, Columbia University. Appointments: War, Southeast Asia Correspondent, Various Agencies, 1951-61; Central European Bureau, Newsweek, 1962-64; Others, Los Angeles Times, Washington Post, 1965-70; Foreign Affairs Columnist, 1970-76; Independent Author and Journalist, 1977-. Publications: China's Red Masters, 1951; The Dragon's Seed, 1959; The Centre of the World, 1961; The Seeking, 1969; Mao v Chiang: The Battle for China, 1972; The Great Cities, Hong Kong, 1977; Pacific Destiny, 1990. Novels: A Kind of Treason, 1966; The Seeking, 1969; Dynasty, 1977; Manchu, 1980; Mandarin, 1983; White Sun, Red Star, 1987; Bianca, 1992; The Everlasting Sorrow, 1994; Last Year in Hong Kong, 1997; The Big Brown Bears, 1998; Bianca, 2000. Contributions to: Newspapers and periodicals. Honours: Phi Beta Kappa; Pulitzer Fellow, 1951-52; Ford Foundation Fellowship, 1954-55; Overseas Press Club Awards, 1963, 1966, 1967, 1972; Edgar Allan Poe Award, 1967; Sigma Delta Chi Award, 1967; Fellow, American Institute for Public Policy Research, Washington, DC,

1976-78; Senior Fellow, Institute for Advanced Study, Berlin, 1993-94; Finalist, Pulitzer Prize for International Reporting, twice. Memberships: Authors League of America; Hong Kong Foreign Correspondents Club. Address: 10 Quick Street, London N1 8HL, England.

**ELENAS Anaxagoras,** b. 8 January 1960, Hrisoupolis, Greece. Assistant Professor in Civil Engineering. m. Areti Charissi, 1 son, 1 daughter. Education: Dipl-ing, University of Stuttgart, Germany, 1984; Dr-Ing, Ruhr-University of Bochum, Germany, 1990. Appointments: Researcher, Ruhr-University, Bochum, Germany, 1985-90; Greek Army, 1991; Lecturer, 1992-97, Assistant Professor, 1997-, Democritus University, Thrace, Greece. Publications: Over 60 in refereed international journals and conferences. Memberships: Technical Chamber of Greece; Seismological Society of America; Earthquake Engineering Research Institute. Address: Democritus University of Thrace, Institute of Structural Mechanics and Earthquake Engineering, Vas Sofias 1, GR-67100 Xanthi, Greece.

**ELEY Daniel Douglas,** b. 1 October 1914, Wallasey, Cheshire, England. Physical Chemist. m. Brenda M Eley, deceased 1992, 1 son. Education: BSc (Hons), Chemistry, 1934, MSc, 1935, PhD, 1937, Manchester University; PhD, 1940, ScD, 1956, St John's College and Colloid Science Department, Cambridge University. Appointments: Researcher for Ministry of Supply and Teacher, Natural Science Tripos, Colloid Science Department, Cambridge University, 1940-45; Lecturer in Colloid Chemistry, 1945-51, Reader in Biophysical Chemistry, 1951-54, Bristol University; Professor of Physical Chemistry, 1954-80, Dean, Faculty of Pure Science, 1959-62, Professor Emeritus, 1980-, Nottingham University. Publications: Numerous papers in scientific journals on solutions, surface chemistry and catalysis, organic semiconductors and related topics; Catalysis and the Chemical Bond, Reilly Lectures, University of Notre Dame, Indiana, 1954; Editor, Adhesion, 1961; A Co-editor, Advances in Catalysis, 1956-98. Honours: Woodiwiss Scholar, 1933, Mercer Scholar, 1934, Darbishire Fellow, 1936, Manchester University; Senior Award, Department of Scientific and Industrial Research, 1937; OBE, 1961; FRS, 1964; Corresponding Member, Bavarian Academy of Science, 1971; Leverhulme Emeritus Fellow, 1981. Memberships: Council, 1951-54, 1960-63, Vice-President, 1963-66, Faraday Society; CCHEM, FRSC, Royal Society of Chemistry; Emeritus Member, Biochemical Society; Meetings Secretary, 1961-63, Honorary Secretary, 1963-65, Honorary Member, 1983-, British Biophysical Society. Address: Brooklands, 35 Brookland Drive, Chilwell, Beeston, Nottingham, NG9 4BD, England.

**ELFMAN Danny,** b. 29 May 1954, USA. Composer; Musician (guitar); Vocalist. Career: Lead singer, songwriter, guitarist, band Oingo Boingo; Compositions: Film scores: Pee-Wee's Big Adventure; Beetlejuice; Batman; Batman Returns; Dick Tracy; Darkman; Edward Scissorhands; Sommersby; Other music for films includes: Weird Science; Ghostbusters II; Something Wild; Television series score: The Simpsons. Recordings: Albums: with Oingo Boingo: Only A Lad, 1981; Nothing To Fear, 1982; Good For Your Soul, 1983; Dead Man's Party, 1985; Boingo, 1986; Skeletons In The Closet, 1989; Dark At The End Of The Tunnel, 1990; Article 99, 1992; Batman Returns, 1992; Dolores Claiborne, 1995; Mission Impossible, 1996; The Frighteners, 1996; Mars Attacks! 1996; Men In Black, 1997; Good Will Hunting; Scream 2; My Favorite Martian; Psycho; Sleepy Hollow. Honour: Emmy Nomination, The Simpsons. Current Management: L A Personal Development, 950 N. Kings Road, Suite 266, West Hollywood, CA 90069, USA.

**ELLA Olekwu Benjamin,** b. 6 July 1962, Ogene-Amejo, Nigeria. Civil Engineer. m. Comfort R Ella, 3 sons. Education: BSc, Building, 1986; MSc, Construction Technology, 1992; PhD, Civil Engineering, 2002. Appointments: Acting Head of Department, Department of Civil Engineering, Bayero University, Kano, Nigeria, 1994-95; Rector, Benue State Polytechnic, Ugbokolo, 2003-. Publications: Effects of Rice-Hull Ash (RHA) production method on the strength characteristics of RHA concrete; Geotechnical and engineering properties of some lateritic soils in Kano municipal; Effect of katsi (dye residue) on the performance characteristic of mud renders; Pozzolanic properties of katsi; Strength properties of katsi- cement concrete. Honours: Distinguished Nation Builders Merit Award; Development in Nigeria Merit Award; Rotaract District 9120 Merit Award. Memberships: Nigerian Institute of Building; Associate Member, Nigerian Society of Engineers. Address: Rectory Department, Benue State Polytechnic, PMB 01, Ugbokolo, Nigeria.

**ELLENS Jay Harold,** b. 16 July 1932, McBain, Michigan, USA. Professor. m. Mary Jo, 3 sons, 4 daughters. Education: BA, 1953; BD, 1956; ThM, 1965; PhD, Psychology, 1970; MDiv, 1983; MA, 2000; PhD, Greco Roman Studies, 2005. Appointments: Active Duty US Army, Colonel, 1955-62; Clergy, 1955-2002; Professor, 1965-85; Psychotherapist, 1970-2001; Executive Director, Christian Association for Psychological Studies International, 1974-89; Founder, Editor in Chief, The Journal of Psychology and Christianity, 1974-88. Publications: 111 books; 172 articles in professional journals. Honours: Numerous Military Medals; 4 MSM; 1 Legion of Merit; Numerous Distinguished Lectureships; Knighthood. Memberships: 26 Invited Professional and Military Officers Societies. Address: 26705 Farmington Road, Farmington Hills, MI 48334-4329, USA.

**ELLIOTT John Huxtable (Sir),** b. 23 June 1930, Reading, Berkshire, England. Historian. m. Oonah Sophia Butler. Education: BA, 1952, MA, 1955, PhD, 1955, Cambridge University. Appointments: Lecturer in History and Fellow, Trinity College, Cambridge, 1957-67; Professor of History, King's College, London, 1968-73; Professor, School of Historical Studies, Institute for Advanced Study, Princeton, USA, 1973-90; Regius Professor of Modern History and Fellow of Oriel College, Oxford University, 1990-97. Publications include: The Revolt of the Catalans, 1963; Imperial Spain, 1963; Europe Divided, 1968; The Old World and the New, 1970; A Palace for a King (with Jonathan Brown), 1980; Richelieu and Olivares, 1984; The Count-Duke of Olivares, 1986; Spain and Its World, 1989; Empires of the Atlantic World, 2006. Honours: Grand Cross Order of Alfonso X, 1988; FBA, 1992; Kt, 1994; Prince of Asturias Prize, 1996; Grand Cross Order of Isabel la Católica, 1996; Balzan Prize for History, 1999; Honorary Doctorates: Madrid (Autónoma); Madrid (Complutense); Genoa; Barcelona; Portsmouth; Valencia; Lleida; Warwick; Brown; William and Mary; Honorary Fellow: Trinity College, Cambridge; Oriel College, Oxford. Memberships: American Philosophical Society; American Academy of Arts and Sciences; Accademia dei Lincei. Address: Oriel College, Oxford OX1 4EW, England.

**ELLIS Christopher Matthew,** b. 23 April 1950, Gloucester, England. Lighting Designer; Theatre Producer. m. Georgina Mary Tilley, 2 sons. Education: Dean Close School, Cheltenham, 1958-68. Career: Designed first West End production, Lloyd George Knew My Father, 1972; Planned lighting installation for new Haymarket Theatre with the City Architects, moved there as Head of Lighting, 1973; Designed first production at the New National Theatre, 1977; First production for Royal Shakespeare

Company, 1978; Production Manager, 1980, Associate Director, 1984, Leicester Haymarket Theatre, also continued freelance career; Designed first opera for Royal Opera House; Drama Panel of East Midland Arts, 1998; Appointed Design Consultant to Deutscher Schauspielhause, Hamburg, 1988; Theatre Director, Chief Executive, Leicester Haymarket Theatre, 1990-92; Advisor on church lighting to the Leicester Diocesan Advisory Committee, 1997; Formed Chris Ellis Lighting, 1998; Designed stage and lighting systems for the new Singapore Repertory Theatre, 2001; Designed opening production for Esplanade Theatre, Singapore, 2002; Designed the opening production for Teatro della Luna, Milan, 2003; West End productions include: Singing in the Rain (Sadlers Wells); On Your Toes (Festival Hall); Elaine Stritch at Liberty (Old Vic); Rent, Annie Get Your Gun (Prince of Wales); Taboo (The Venue); La Cava, Mack and Mabel (Piccadilly); Boyband (Gielgud); Ute Lemper, HMS Pinafore, Lloyd George Knew My Father, Lady Harry (Savoy); All You Need is Love, Pirates of Penzance (Queens); Brief Encounter (Lyric); Hotstuff (Cambridge); Hair, Henry IV Part 1 and 2, Henry V, Masterclass, Importance of Being Earnest (Old Vic); Numerous productions for the Royal Shakespeare Company; Opera and ballet productions. Publications: Articles in Lighting and Sound International. Honour: Live 2000 Silver Award for Lighting Designer of the Year. Memberships: Society of British Theatre Lighting Designers, 1972-; Association of British Theatre Technicians, 1974-; Association of Lighting Designers, 1984; Drama Panel, East Midland Arts, 1988-; Board Member, Derby Playhouse Theatre, 1992-. Address:47 Shanklin Drive, Stoneygate, Leicester LE2 3AE, England. E-mail: chrise llis1@compuserve.com

**ELLIS David George,** b. 23 June 1939, Swinton, Lancashire, England. University Teacher. m. 24 September 1966, 2 daughters. Education: MA, 1964, PhD, 1970, University of Cambridge. Appointments: Lecturer, La Trobe University, Melbourne, Victoria, Australia, 1968-72; Lecturer, Senior Lecturer, Professor, University of Kent at Canterbury, England, 1972-. Publications: Stendhal, Memoirs of an Egotist (translation), 1975; Wordsworth, Freud and the Spots of Time: Interpretation in 'The Prelude', 1985; D H Lawrence's Non-Fiction: Art, Thought and Genre (with Howard Mills), 1988; Imitating Art: Essays in Biography (editor), 1993; Dying Game, volume 3, New Cambridge Biography of D H Lawrence, 1998; Literary Lives: Biography and the Search for Understanding, 2000; That Man Shakespeare, 2005. Address: English School, University of Kent at Canterbury, Canterbury CT2 7NX, England.

**ELLIS Harold,** b. 13 January 1926, London, England. Professor of Surgery. m. Wendy Levine, 1 son, 1 daughter. Education: BM BCh, University of Oxford, 1948; FRCS, 1951; MCh, 1956; DM, 1962. Appointments: Resident appointments in: Oxford, Sheffield, Northampton and London, 1948-60; RAMC (Graded Surgical Specialist), 1950-51; Senior Lecturer in Surgery, 1960-62, Professor of Surgery, 1962-89, Westminster Medical School; Professor Emeritus, University of London, 1989; Clinical Anatomist, University of Cambridge, 1989-93; Clinical Anatomist, United Medical and Dental School, Guy's Campus (now School of Biomedical Sciences, King's College, Guy's Campus), 1993-. Publications: 25 books include most recently: Clinical Anatomy for Laparoscopic and Thorascopic Surgery, 1995; Gray's Anatomy (38th edition) Section Editor, 1995; Operations That Made History, 1996; Index to Differential Diagnosis, 1996; Index of Surgical Differential Diagnosis, 1999; Applied Radiological Anatomy, 1999; A History of Surgery, 2000; Numerous book chapters and articles in medical journals. Honours include: CBE, 1987; Honorary, FACS, 1989; Honorary Fellow, Royal Society of Medicine, 1996; Honorary Gold Medal, Royal College of Surgeons of England. Memberships: President, Armed Services Combined Assessment Board in Surgery; Honorary Freeman, Company of Barbers. Address: 16 Bancroft Avenue, London N2 0AS, England.

**ELLIS John Norman,** b. 22 February 1939, Leeds, England. Employment Law Consultant. m. 1 son, 2 stepsons, 1 daughter. Appointments: Civil Servant, 1954-68; Trade Union Full Time Officer, 1968-95; Deputy General Secretary, 1982-86, General Secretary, 1986-92, CPSA: Secretary General Council of Civil Service Unions, 1992-1995; Panel Member, Employment Tribunal, 1992; Associate Consultant, Talking People, an ACS Company. Publications: Published 36 editions of the National Whitley Bulletin, 1992-95: Articles in the Public Policy and Administration Journal. Honours: OBE for services to industrial relations, 1995. Memberships: Labour Party; Civil Service Pensioners' Alliance; Institute of Employment Right. Address: 26 Harestone Valley Road, Caterham, Surrey CR3 6HD, England. E-mail: johnellis60@aol.com

**ELLIS Richard Mackay,** b. 9 July 1941, Chalfont St Peter, England. Consultant Physician. m. Gillian Ann Cole, 1 son, 1 daughter. Education: Wellington College; MB BChir, Clare College, Cambridge, 1965; St Thomas's Hospital Medical School, London; MD, New York, 1982. Appointments: Senior Lecturer in Rheumatology, University of Southampton, 1980; Consultant in Rheumatology and Rehabilitation, Salisbury District Hospital, 1980; Director, Wessex Rehabilitation Unit, Salisbury, 1989. Memberships: Fellow, Royal College of Surgeons, London, 1971; Editor, Journal of Orthopaedic Medicine, 1985; Fellow, Royal College of Physicians, London, 1988; Council Member, British Institute of Musculoskeletal Medicine, 1990; Convenor, Examining Board for Diploma in Musculoskeletal Medicine, Society of Apothecaries of London, 1998; Honorary President, Society of Orthopaedic Medicine, 2000. Address: 161 Bouverie Avenue, Salisbury, Wiltshire SP2 8EB, England.

**ELLSAESSER Hugh Walter,** b. 1 June 1920, USA. Atmospheric Scientist. m. Lois M McCaw, deceased, 1 adopted son, deceased, 1 son, 1 daughter. Education: AA, Bakersfield Junior College, 1941; MA, University of California, Los Angeles, 1947; PhD, University of Chicago, 1964. Appointments: 2nd Lieutenant, USAF, 1943, advanced to Lieutenant Colonel; Weather Officer, Antigua, San Juan, Florida, London, Washington, DC, Omaha; Physicist, Lawrence Livermore National Laboratory, 1963-86; Guest Scientist, 1986-97; Consultant Meteorologist, 1997-. Publications: Numerous articles in professional journals. Honour: Phi Beta Kappa Commendation Medal. Memberships: American Meteorological Society; American Geophysical Union; AAAS. Address: 4293 Stanford Way, Livermore, CA 94550, USA. E-mail: hughel@sbcglobal.net

**ELS Ernie,** b. 17 October 1969, Johannesburg, South Africa. Professional Golfer. m. Leizl Els, 1 son, 1 daughter. Career: Professional, 1989-; Winner, US Open, 1994, 1997; Toyota World Matchplay Championships, 1994, 1995, 1996; South Africa PGA Championship, 1995; Byron Nelson Classic, 1995; Buick Classic, 1996, 1997; Johnny Walker Classic, 1997; Bay Hill Invitational, 1998; Nissan Open, 1999; Int presented by Quest 2000; Standard Life Loch Lomond, 2000; Open Championship, 2002; Genuity Championship, 2002; British Open, 2002; Fourth World Match Play title, 2002; Member, Dunhill Cup Team, 1992-2000; World Cup Team, 1992, 1993, 1996, 1997, 2001; Member, President's Cup, 1996, 1998, 2000; Founder, Ernie Els Foundation to help disadvantaged children,

1999. Honour: South African Sportsman of Year, 1995. Address: 46 Chapman Road, Klippoortjie 1401, South Africa.

**ELSTON Wolfgang E,** b. 13 August 1928, Berlin, Germany. Geologist; Professor. m. Lorraine, deceased, 27 July 2000, 2 sons. Education: BS, cum laude, City College of New York, 1949; MA, Columbia University, 1953; PhD, 1953. Appointments: Assistant Professor, Texas Technological University, 1955-57; Assistant Professor, Professor, University of New Mexico, 1957-92; Senior Research Professor, 1992-, Co-ordinator, University of New Mexico-Los Alamos National Laboratory Volcanology Programme, 1992-2000. Publications: Hundreds of titles on volcanology, planetology, economic geology. Honours: Visiting Research Fellow, Royal Society, UK; Foundation Visitor, University of Auckland, New Zealand; Fellow, Geological Society of America; Exchange Scientist, National Science Foundation, University of Queensland; Honorary Life Member, New Mexico Geological Society. Memberships: American Geophysical Union; Geological Society of America; Society of Economic Geologists; American Association of Petroleum Geologists; Meteoritical Society. Address: Department of Earth and Planetary Sciences, University of New Mexico, Albuquerque, NM 87131-1116, USA.

**ELTIS Walter (Alfred),** b. 23 May 1933, Warnsdorf, Czechoslovakia. Economist. m. Shelagh Mary Owen, 5 September 1959, 1 son, 2 daughters. Education: Emmanuel College, Cambridge; BA, Cambridge University; MA, Nuffield College, 1960; DLitt, Oxford University, 1990. Appointments: Fellow, Tutor, Economics, 1963-88, Emeritus Fellow, 1988-, Exeter College, Oxford; Director General, National Economic Development Office, London, 1988-92; Chief Economic Adviser to the President of the Board of Trade, 1992-95; Visiting Professor, 1992-2004, University of Reading. Publications: Growth and Distribution, 1973; Britain's Economic Problem: Too Few Producers (with Robert Bacon), 1976; The Classical Theory of Economic Growth, 1984 (2nd Edition, Palgrave 2000); Keynes and Economic Policy (with Peter Sinclair), 1988; Classical Economics, Public Expenditure and Growth, 1993; Britain's Economic Problem Revisited, 1996; Condillac, Commerce and Government (editor, with Shelagh M Eltis); Britain, Europe and EMU, 2000. Contributions to: Economic journals and bank reviews. Memberships: Reform Club, chairman, 1994-95; Royal Automobile Club; Political Economy Club; Vice President, European Society for the History of Economic Thought, 2000-04. Address: Danesway, Jarn Way, Boars Hill, Oxford OX1 5JF, England.

**ELTON Ben(jamin Charles),** b. 3 May 1959, England. Writer; Comedian. m. Sophie Gare, 1 son, 1 daughter. Education: BA, Drama, University of Manchester. Appointments: Writer, TV series and for British Comedians; Stand-up Comedian: Tours, 1986, 1987, 1989, 1993, 1996, 1997; Host, Friday Night Live, TV Comedy Showcase, 1986-88; Co-writer, Presenter, South of Watford (documentary TV series), 1982; Writer/Director, Inconceivable, film, 2000. Publications: Bachelor Boys, 1984; Stark, 1989; Gridlock, 1991; This Other Eden, 1993; Popcorn, 1996; Blast from the Past, 1998; Inconceivable, 1999; Dead Famous, 2001; Plays: Gasping, 1990; Silly Cow, 1991; Popcorn, 1996; Blast from the Past, 1998; The Beautiful Game, musical, book and lyrics, 2000; Maybe Baby, writer/director, feature film, 2000; High Society, 2002; We Will Rock You, musical, 2002; Other: Recordings; The Young Ones, 1982; Happy Families, 1985; Blackadder, 1985, 1987, 1989; Filthy Rich and Catflap, 1986; Motormouth, 1987; Motovation (album), 1988; The Man From Auntie, 1990, 1994; The Very Best of Ben Elton Live, 1990; A Farties Guide to the Man From Auntie, 1990; Ben Elton Live, 1993; Stark, 1993; The Thin Blue Line (sitcom);

1995, 1996; Ben Elton Live, 1997; The Ben Elton Show, 1999. Honours: Best Comedy Show Awards, Brit Academy, 1984, 1987; Gold Dagger Award, 1996; TMA Award, 1997; Lawrence Olivier Award, 1998. Address: c/o Phil McIntyre, 2nd Floor, 35 Soho Square, London, W1D 3QX, England.

**EMADI Mohammad Hossein,** b. 22 May 1960, Shiraz, Iran. Agriculturist; System Analyst; Rural Development Strategist. m. Fatima, 2 sons, 1 daughter. Education: Diploma, 1978; BSc, Animal Sciences, Shiraz University, 1986; MSc, Agricultural Education, Tehran University, 1990; PhD, Systems Agricultural and Rural Development, UWS, Australia, 1995. Appointments: Executive Manager, Seed Company, 1988-90; Research Deputy, Rural Research Center, RRC, 1995-; Vice Minister, Ministry of Agriculture, 1997-. Publications: 5 books have been published; 32 articles. Honours: Best Selected PhD Thesis awards and Best Selected Research in Nomadic issues, 2004, Ministry of Culture, Iran. Memberships: IK, Representative of Iran; Member, of ODI; AGRECOL; Resource person for APO; FAO; AAEE; APEAN; Representative of CIRAN in Middle East. Address: P O Box 14155-6371, Tehran, Iran.

**EMANUEL Elizabeth Florence,** b. 5 July 1953, London, England. Fashion Designer. m. David Leslie Emanuel, 1975, separated 1990, 1 son, 1 daughter. Education: Harrow College of Art. Appointments: Opened London salon, 1978; Designer, wedding gown for HRH Princess of Wales, 1981; Costumes for Andrew Lloyd Webber's Song and dance, 1982; Sets and costumes for ballet, Frankenstein, The Modern Prometheus, Roy Opera House, London, La Scala Milan, 1985; Costumes for Stoll Moss production of Cinderella, 1985; Costumes for films: Diamond Skulls, 1990; The Changeling, 1995; Uniforms for Virgin Atlantic Airways, 1990; Britannia Airways, 1995; Launched international fashion label Elizabeth Emanuel, 1991; Launched Bridal Collection for Berkertex Brides UK Ltd, 1994; Launched bridal collection in Japan, 1994; Opened new shop and design studio, 1996; Launched own brand label (with Richard Thompson), 1999. Publications: Style for All Seasons (with David Emanuel), 1982. Address: Ground Floor Studio, 23 Warrington Crescent, London, W9 1ED, England.

**EMBERSON Ian McDonald,** b. 29 July 1936, Hove, Sussex, England. Retired Librarian; Poet and Artist. Publications: Doodles in the Margins of My Life, 1981; Swallows Return, 1986; Pirouette of Earth, a novel in verse, 1995; Natural Light, 1998; The Comet of 1811, 2001; The Snake and The Star, 2003. Contributions to: Pennine Platform; Envoi; Orbis; New Hope International; Bradford Poetry Quarterly; Dalesman; Countryman; Acumen; Poetry Scotland; Brontë Studies; IOTA; Poets Voice; Aireings; Pennine Ink. Honour: William Alwyn International Poetry Society Award, 1981. Memberships: Pennine Poets; Brontë Society; Gaskell Society. Address: Eastroyd, 1 Highcroft Road, Todmorden, Lancashire OL14 5LZ, England. Website: www.ianemberson.co.uk

**EMEL'YANOV Vladimir,** b. 1 June 1943, Moscow, Russia. Physicist. Divorced, 2 daughters. Education: Graduate, Faculty of Physics, 1966, Diploma of Physicist, postgraduate study, Diploma of Candidate of Science (PhD), 1973, Diploma of Doctor of Science, 1988, Moscow State University. Appointments: Research Fellow, 1973-75, Assistant Professor, 1975-89, Full Professor, 1989-, Physics Faculty, Moscow State University. Publications: 300 articles; 3 monographs: Co-operative effects in Optics, 1988; Interaction of strong laser radiation with solids, 1990; Co-operative effects in Optics, Superradiance and Phase Transitions, 1993. Honours: Prize Winner, International Publishing Company "Nauka", 1995; Lomonosov Prize Winner, highest award of Moscow State

University, 1999; Listed in international biographical dictionary. Memberships: SPIE. Address: Physics Faculty, Moscow State University, 119899 Moscow, Russia. E-mail: emel@em.msk.ru

**EMERY Alan E H,** b. 21 August 1928, Manchester, England. Physician. m. Marcia Lynn Maler, 3 sons, 3 daughters. Education: University of Manchester, England; PhD, Johns Hopkins University, USA. Appointments: Reader, Medicine, Manchester University, 1964-68; Foundation Professor, Human Genetics, Edinburgh University, 1968-83; Research Professor and Fellow, Edinburgh University, 1983-90; Research Director, 1990-2000, Chief Scientific Adviser, 2000-, European Neuro-Muscular Centre; Visiting Professor, Peninsula Medical School, Exeter, 2002-. Publications: Around 300 medical science papers; 21 books. Honours: Various visiting professorships and named lectures; Honorary MD, University of Naples and University of Wurzburg; National Foundation USA, International Award; Gaetano Gold Medal; Honorary Membership or Fellowship: Dutch Society of Human Genetics; Association of British Neurologists; Royal Society of South Africa, Hon MD, Naples, Wurzburg; International Award for Genetic Research, USA; Gaetano Conte Prize for Clinical Research, 2000; Pro Finlandiae Gold Medal for contributions to Neuroscience, 2000; Lifetime Achievement Award, WFN, 2002. Memberships: FRCP; FRCPE; FLS; FRSE. Address: Peninsula Medical School, Department of Neurology, Royal Devon and Exeter Hospital, Exeter EX2 5DW, England.

**EMMERICH Roland,** b. 10 November 1955, Stuttgart, Germany. Director; Screenplay Writer; Executive Producer. Education: Film School in Munich. Appointments: Producer (as student) The Noah's Ark Principle, shown at Berlin Film Festival (sold to over 20 countries), 1984; Founder, Centropolis Film Productions; Films: Making Moon 44; Universal Soldier; Stargate; Independence Day; The Thirteenth Floor (producer); The Patriot; TV series: The Visitor (producer), 1997. Address: c/o Creative Artists Agency, 9830 Wilshire Boulevard, Beverly Hills, CA 90212, USA.

**EMMS David Acfield,** b. 16 February 1925, Lowestoft, Suffolk, England. Headmaster. m. Pamela Baker Speed, 3 sons, 1 daughter. Education: MA, Modern Languages, Diploma in Education, Brasenose College, Oxford, 1947-51. Appointments: War Service, Captain, Royal Indian Airborne Artillery, 1943-47; Assistant Master, Head, Modern Languages Department, OC, CCF, 1st XV Rugby Coach, Uppingham School, 1951-50; Headmaster, Cranleigh School, 1960-70; Headmaster, Sherborne School, 1970-74; The Master, Dulwich College, 1975-86; Vice-Chairman, The English Speaking Union, 1984-89; The Director, London House for Overseas Graduates, 1986-95. Publication: HMC Schools and British Industry, 1981. Honours: Rugby Football Blue, Oxford University, 1949, 1950; OBE, 1995. Memberships: FRSA, 1988; Master, Skinners' Company, 1987; Chairman, Headmasters' Conference, 1984; President, Independent Schools Careers Organisation, 2002-; President, Alleyn Club, 1985; Brasenose Society, 1987. Address: The Dove House, Church Lane, Birdham, nr Chichester, West Sussex PO20 7AT, England. Website: dovehouse@emmses.fsnet.co.uk

**ENDERBY Sir John Edwin,** b. 16 January 1931, Grimsby, Lincolnshire, England. Physicist. m. Susan, 1 son, 3 daughters. Education: Westminster College, London; BSc, PhD, Birkbeck College, London. Appointments: Professor of Physics and Head of Department, University of Bristol, 1976-96; Vice President, Royal Society, 1999-2004; Chief Scientific Adviser, Institute of Physics Publishing, 2002-; Chairman, Melys Diagnostics Ltd, 2004-; President, Institute of Physics, 2004-. Publications: Numerous papers and articles in professional journals. Honours:

Westminster College Wright Prize, 1953; College Award, 1956; Guthrie Medal, 1985; Hon DSc, Loughborough University, 1996; CBE, 1997; Honorary Fellowship, Birkbeck College, 2000; Knight Bachelor, 2004. Memberships: Fellow, Institute of Physics; Fellow, Royal Society; Member, Academia Europaea; Atheneum Club. Address: 7 Cotham Lawn Road, Bristol, BS6 6DU, England.

**ENGEL Juergen Kurt,** b. 31 August 1945, Gerbitz, Germany. Chemist; Researcher. m. Rita Busset, 1 son, 1 daughter. Education: Diploma, Engineering, Naturwissenschaft-Technishe Akademie, Isny, Germany, 1969; Diploma, Chemistry, Technische Universität, Braunschweig, Germany, 1972; Diploma, Natural Sciences, 1975; Habilitation, Pharmacy, Universität Regensburg, Regensburg, Germany, 1985. Appointments: Laboratory Leader, Pharmaceutical Division, 1976-1980, Head Research Co-ordination, 1980-87, Head Medicinal Chemistry Synthesis, 1982-87, Degussa AG, Frankfurt, Germany; Head Chemical and Pharmaceutical Research and Development, 1987-93, Head, Research and Development, 1993-2000, ASTA Medica AG, Frankfurt, Germany; Chairman, Managing Director, Zentaris GmbH, Frankfurt, Germany, 2001-; COO Aeterna Zentaris, 2003-; Professor, School of Pharmacy Universität Regensburg, 1990-; Professor, Technical University, Dresden, 1993-. Publications: Memofix Pharmazie, 1995; Pharmaceutical Substances, 2000; Editor: Arzneimittel, 1987; Memofax, 2001; Contributor of numerous articles to professional journals; Chapters to books; Patentee in field. Honours: Recipient Galileo Galilei Silver Medal, 5th International Symposium on Platinum and Other Substances, Padua, Italy; Galenus-von-Pergamon Award, 1995. Memberships: German Chemical Society, Chairman Board of Directors, Medicinal Chemistry Section; German Pharmaceutical Society; International Society for Heterocyclic Chemistry; German Society for Biochemistry and Molecular Biology, Advisory Board. Address: Zentaris GmbH, Weismuellerstrasse 45, 60314 Frankfurt, Germany. E-mail: juergen.engel@zentaris.de

**ENGEL Tala,** b. New York City, USA. Attorney-at-Law. m. James A Colias, deceased 1989. Education: Middlebury College, Middlebury, VT, 1953; BA, Russian and Spanish, University of Miami, 1954; JD, University of Miami, Coral Gables, Florida, 1957. Appointments: Solo Practice, Miami, Florida, 1957-61; Immigration Attorney, Chicago, 1961-87, Washington DC, 1987-90, Chicago, 1990-93, Washington DC, 1993-2002, Miami, Florida, 2002-; Immigration Service, 1961-62, Parole Agent, Illinois Youth Commission, 1963-66, Bar: Florida, 1957, US District Court; Illinois and US District Court, 1962; US Supreme Court, 1965; DC Bar, 1982; Sued Chicago Bar Association for right of women lawyers to participate in activities of the Bar Association in 1970. Publications: 10 MLQ 110 Criminal Law; 10 MLQ 608 Insurance Law. Honours: Miami Law Quarterly, 1955, 1956; Editor, The Lawyer, 1956; Alpha Lambda Delta; Board of Directors, Cordi Marian Settlement, Chicago, 1977-93. Memberships: Chicago Bar Association, Development of Law Committee, 1985-87, Entertainment Committee, 1971-73; Life Member, Chicago Bar Foundation; Life Member, Florida Bar Foundation; ABA, Illinois Bar Association, General Assembly, 1984-87; Federal Bar Association; Florida Bar Association; American Immigration Lawyers. Address: 601 Three Islands Blvd. #215, Hallandale Beach, FL 33009, USA.

**ENGLISH Terence Alexander Hawthorne,** b. 3 October 1932, Pietermaritzburg, South Africa. Cardiac Surgeon (Retired). m. (1) Ann Margaret Dicey, 2 sons, 2 daughters, (2) Judith Francis Milne. Education: BSc, Engineering, Witwatersrand University, South Africa, 1951-54; MB BS, Guy's Hospital Medical School,

1955-62; FRCS (England and Edinburgh), 1967. Appointments: Surgical training at Brompton and National Heart Hospitals, Senior Registrar; Consultant Cardiothoracic Surgeon, Papworth and Addenbrooke's Hospitals, 1972-95; Performed Britain's first successful heart transplant, 1979; President, Royal College of Surgeons of England, 1989-92; Master, St Catharine's College, Cambridge, 1993-2000; President, British Medical Association, 1995-96. Publications: Principles of Cardiac Diagnosis and Treatment, 2nd edition, 1992; 23 contributions to chapters in books; 118 peer-reviewed articles mainly on surgery and cardiac transplantation. Honours: KBE, 1991; Honorary DSc, Universities of Sussex and Hull; Honorary MD, Universities of Nantes and Mahidol, Thailand; Honorary Fellow, Worcester College, Oxford, St Catharine's College and Hughes Hall, Cambridge, King's College, London, American College of Surgeons, Royal College of Physicians and Surgeons of Canada, College of Medicine of South Africa, College of Physicians and Surgeons of Pakistan, Royal College of Anaesthetists, Royal College of Surgeons of Ireland. Memberships: 20 national and international professional societies; Clubs: The Athenaeum; The Hawk's Club, Cambridge, Chairman, 1997-2001. Address: Principal's Lodgings, St Hilda's College, Oxford OX 4 1DY, England. E-mail: tenglish@doctors.org.uk

**ENRIGHT D(ennis) J(oseph),** b. 11 March 1920, Leamington, Warwickshire, England. Writer; Poet; Editor. m. Madeleine Harders, 3 November 1949, 1 daughter. Education: BA, Honours, 1944, MA, 1946, Downing College, Cambridge; DLitt, University of Alexandria, Egypt, 1949. Appointments: Professor of English, Far East, 1947-70; Co-Editor, Encounter, 1970-72; Director, Chatto and Windus Publishers, 1974-82. Publications: The Laughing Hyena and Other Poems, 1953; Academic Year, 1955; Bread Rather Than Blossoms, 1956; Some Men are Brothers, 1960; Selected Poems, 1969; Memoirs of a Mendicant Professor, 1969; Daughters of Earth, 1972; The Terrible Shears: Scenes From a Twenties Childhood, 1974; Sad Ires and Others, 1975; Paradise Illustrated, 1978; A Faust Book, 1979; The Oxford Book of Death (editor), 1983; A Mania for Sentences, 1983; The Alluring Problem, 1986; Collected Poems, 1987; Fields of Vision, 1988; The Faber Book of Fevers and Frets (editor), 1989; Selected Poems, 1990; Under the Circumstances, 1991; The Oxford Book of Friendship (editor with David Rawlinson), 1991; The Way of the Cat, 1992; Old Men and Comets, 1993; The Oxford Book of the Supernatural (editor), 1994; Interplay: A Kind of Commonplace Book, 1995; The Sayings of Goethe (editor), 1996; Collected Poems 1948-1998, 1998; Play Resumed: A Journal, 1999; Signs and Wonders: Selected essays, 2001. Contributions to: Journals, reviews, and magazines. Honours: Cholmondeley Award, 1974; Queen's Gold Medal for Poetry, 1981; Honorary Doctorates, University of Warwick, 1982, University of Surrey, 1985; Officer of the Order of the British Empire, 1991; Companion of Literature, 1998. Membership: Royal Society of Literature, Fellow. Address: 35A Viewfield Road, London SW18 5JD, England.

**ENYA (Eithne Ni Bhraonain),** b. 17 May 1961, Gweedore, County Donegal, Ireland. Singer; Musician (piano, keyboards); Composer. Musical Education: Classical piano; Career: Member, folk group Clannad, 1980-82; Solo artiste, 1988-; 25 million albums sold to date. Compositions: Music for film and television scores: The Frog Prince, 1985; The Celts, BBC, 1987; LA Story, 1990; Green Card, 1990. Recordings: Albums: with Clannad: Crann Ull, 1980; Fuaim, 1982; Solo albums: Watermark, 1988; Shepherd's Moon, 1991; Enya, 1992; The Celts (reissued), 1992; The Book Of Trees, 1996; On My Way Home, 1998; Storms in Africa, 1998; A Day Without Rain, 2000; Singles include: Orinoco Flow (Number 1, UK), 1988; Evening Falls,

1988; Oiche Chiun, 1988; Orinoco Flow, 1988; Storms In Africa (Part II), 1989; Caribbean Blue, 1991; How Can I Keep From Singing, 1991; Book Of Days, 1992; Anywhere Is, 1995; Only If, 1997; May It Be, 2001; Only Time, 2001; Wild Child, 2001. Honours: 3 Grammy Awards; 6 World Music Awards including Best Selling Artist in the World, 2001. Address: 'Manderley', Victoria Road, Killiney, County Dublin, Ireland.

**EÖSZE László,** b. 17 November 1923, Budapest, Hungary. Musicologist. m. (1) 1 son, 1 daughter, (2) Margit Szilléry, 1983. Education: PhD, Aesthetics and Literature. Appointments: Music Teacher and Pianist; Concerts in Hungary and Europe, 1946-51; Editor, 1955-57, Chief Editor, 1957-61, Art Director, 1961-87, Editio Musica, Budapest. Publications: 16 books including: Life and Work of Zoltán Kodály, 1956; Zoltán Kodály's Life in Pictures, 1957; History of Opera, 1960; Giuseppe Verdi, 1961, 2nd edition, 1966, enlarged, 1975; Zoltán Kodály, His Life and Work, in English, 1962, in German, 1965; Zoltán Kodály, 1967; Kodály, His Life in Pictures and Documents, in English and German, 1971; Richard Wagner, 1969; Richard Wagner, Eine Chronik seines Lebens und Schaffens, 1969; Zoltán Kodály, életének krónikája, 1977; 119 római Liszt dokumentum, 1980; Selected studies on Z Kodály, 2000; Essays and articles in various languages; Contributions to numerous professional publications. Honours: Erkel Prize, 1977; Gramma Award, 1978; Medium Cross of the Order of the Hungarian Republic, 1998; Medal for Merit of the President of the Republic, 2003; Grand Prize of the National Society of Creative Artists, 2003. Memberships: Co-president, F Liszt Society; Executive Secretary, 1975-95, International Kodály Society; Hungarian Musicological Society, 1996-. Address: Attila ut 133, 1012 Budapest, Hungary.

**EPHRON Nora,** b. 19 May 1941, New York, USA. Author; Scriptwriter. Education: BA, Wellesley College. m. (1) Dan Greenberg, (2) Carl Bernstein, 2 sons, (3) Nicholas Pileggi. Appointments: Reporter, New York Post, 1963-68; Freelance Writer, 1968-; Contributing Editor, New York Magazine, 1973-74; Film appearances: Crimes and Misdemeanors; Husband and Wives. Publications: Wallflower at the Orgy, 1970; Crazy Salad, 1975; Scribble, Scribble, 1978; Heartburn, 1983; Nora Ephron Collected, 1991; Screenplays: Silkwood (with Alice Arlen), 1983; Heartburn, 1986; When Harry Met Sally..., 1989; Cookie (co-executive producer, co-screenwriter with Delia Ephron); Sleepless in Seattle (also director), 1993; Mixed Nuts (also director); Michael (also director), 1996; You've Got Mail (also director), 1998; Red tails in Love: a Wildlife Drama in Central Park (also producer and director), 2000; Hanging Up (also producer), 2000. Address: c/o Sam Cohm International Creative Management, 40 West 57th Street, New York, NY 10019, USA.

**EPPERT Günter J,** b. 2 August 1933, Friedland, Czechia, Germany. Chemist. m. Christa Traubach, 2 sons, 1 daughter. Education: Diploma, 1958; Dr rer nat, 1961; Dr habil, 1980. Appointments: University Lecturer in Analytical Chemistry, 1982; Collaborator of UNIDO, 1984-89; Founder of the firm SEPSERV Separation Service Berlin, Germany, 1990-. Publications: About 70 publications and patents; Books: Einführung in die Schnelle Flüssigchromatographie; Leitfaden ausgewählter Trennmethoden; HPLC Trouble Shooting; Flüssigchromatographie HPLC - Theorie und Praxis. Membership: Gesellschaft Deutscher Chemiker. Address: Dovestr 1B, 10587 Berlin, Germany. E-mail: sepserv.berlin@t-online.de Website: www.sepserv.com

**EPPSTEIN Ury,** b. 3 February 1925, Saarbrücken, Germany. Israeli Musicologist. m. Kikue Iguchi, 2 sons. Education: MA,

Hebrew University of Jerusalem, 1949; Diploma in Japanese Language, Tokyo University of Foreign Studies, 1959; Diploma in Japanese Music, Tokyo University of Fine Arts and Music, 1963; PhD, Tel Aviv University, 1984. Appointments: Academic Assistant, Music Research Centre, Hebrew University, 1966-1972; Lecturer, Musicology and Theatre Departments, Tel Aviv University, 1972-1977; Lecturer, Departments of Musicology, Theatre, East Asian St, Hebrew University, 1972-; Guest Lecturer, Copenhagen University; East Asian Institute and Musicology Department, Lund University, 1986; Guest Lecturer, Dokkyō University, Japan; Tokyo University of Fine Arts and Music, 1997. Publications: Kanjinchō, translation of Kabuki play from Japanese, 1993; The Beginnings of Western Music in Meiji Era Japan, 1994; Musical Means to Political Ends - Japanese School Songs in Manchuria, 1996; Governmental Policy and Controversy - The Beginnings of Western Music in Japan, 1998; Changing Western Attitudes to Japanese Music in: Collected Articles and Essays in Honour of His Imperial Highness Prince Mikasa on the Occasion of His 88th Birthday, 2004. Honours: Order of the Rising Sun conferred by the Emperor of Japan, 1989; Israel Ministry of Education and Culture Prize for translation of Kabuki drama from Japanese. Memberships: European Association for Japanese Studies, Israel Musicological Society. Address: 80 Tchernihovsky St, Jerusalem, Israel.

**EPSTEIN (Michael) Anthony (Sir),** b. 18 May 1921, London, England. Medical Scientist; University Teacher. 2 sons, 1 daughter. Education: Trinity College, Cambridge; Middlesex Hospital Medical School, London. Appointments: House Surgeon, Middlesex Hospital, London and Addenbrooke's Hospital, Cambridge, 1944; Lieutenant and Captain, Royal Army Medical Corps, 1945-47; Assistant Pathologist, Middlesex Hospital Medical School, 1948-65; Berkeley Travelling Fellow, 1952-53; French Government Scholar, Institut Pasteur, Paris, 1952-53; Visiting Investigator, Rockefeller Institute, New York, 1956; Honorary Consultant Virologist, Middlesex Hospital, 1965-68; Reader in Experimental Pathology, Middlesex Hospital Medical School, 1965-68; Honorary Consultant Pathologist, Bristol Hospitals, 1968-82; Professor of Pathology, 1968-85, Head of Department, 1968-82, University of Bristol; Emeritus Professor of Pathology, University of Bristol and Fellow, Wolfson College, Oxford, 1986-. Publications: Over 240 original contributions to major scientific journals; Joint Founder Editor, International Review of Experimental Pathology, volumes 1-28, 1962-86; Joint Editor, 5 scientific books including The Epstein-Barr Virus 1979; The Epstein-Barr Virus: Recent Advances, 1986; Oncogenic -herpesviruses: An Expanding Family, 2001. Honours include: Paul Ehrlich and Ludwig Darmstaedter Prize and Medal, West Germany, 1973; Fellow, Royal Society, 1979; Honorary Professor, Sun Yat Sen University, China, 1981; Bristol Myers Award for Cancer Research, USA, 1982; Honorary Fellow, Queensland Institute of Medical Research, 1983; CBE, 1985; Prix Grifuel, France, 1986; Honorary Fellow, Royal College of Physicians of London, 1986; Extraordinary Governing Body Fellow, Wolfson College, Oxford, 1986-2001; Honorary MD, University of Edinburgh, 1986; Honorary Professor, Chinese Academy of Preventive Medicine, 1988; Gairdner International Award, Canada, 1988; Honorary Fellow, Royal Medical Society of Edinburgh, 1988; Member, Academia Europea, 1988; Honorary Fellow, Royal Society of Edinburgh, 1991; Knight Bachelor, 1991; Royal Medal, The Royal Society of London, 1992; Fellow, University College London, 1992; Honorary Fellow, Royal College of Pathologists of Australasia, 1995; Honorary DSc, University of Birmingham, 1996; Honorary MD, Charles University of Prague, 1998; Founder Fellow, Academy of Medical Sciences, 1998; Honorary Fellow, Wolfson College Oxford, 2001. Address: Nuffield Department of Clinical Medicine, University of Oxford, John Radcliffe Hospital, Oxford, OX3 9DU, England.

**EPSTEIN Trude Scarlett,** b. 13 July 1922, Vienna, Austria. Development Anthropologist. m. A L Epstein, deceased, 2 daughters. Education: Diploma in Industrial Administration and Economics and Political Science, Oxford; BSc, Economics, PhD, Economics, Manchester. Appointments: Director, PEGS; SESAC & Intervention; Research Professor, Sussex University, England; Senior Fellow, Australian National University, Canberra, Australia; Visiting Professor: Australian National University, University of Minnesota; University of Minneapolis; Adjunct Professor: Maryland University; Bengurion University of the Negev, Israel. Publications: Books: Southern India: Yesterday, Today and Tomorrow; Village Voices - Forty Years of Rural Transformation in South India; Capitalism: Primitive and Modern - A Manual for Culturally Adapted Social Marketing; Articles include: Development, There is Another Way - A Rural-Urban Paradigm. Honours: Sir Murdoch McDonald Award; Rockefeller Research Fellowship; Honorary Fellowship of the Indian Anthropological Association and the British Association of Social Anthropology; The Most Excellent Order of the British Empire (OBE). Memberships: Agricultural Development Council; UK-UNESCO Social Science Advisory Board; Council, Royal Anthropological Institute. Address: 5 Viceroy Lodge, Kingsway, Hove BN3 4RA, England. E-mail: scarlett@epstein.nu Website: www.pegs.org

**ERDEN Aysu Aryel,** b. 16 September 1951, Ankara, Turkey. University Professor. m. Ernur Erden, 1 son. Education: Graduate, Department of English Language and Literature, Faculty of Letters, Hacettepe University, Ankara, Turkey; Fil Dr (PhD), 1979. Appointments: Assistant Professor, 1972-79, Associate Professor, 1989, Professor of Linguistics, 1999, Chair, Department of Linguistics, 2000-2003, Faculty of Arts, Hacettepe University, Ankara, Turkey; Vice-Chair, Department of English Language and Literature, Faculty of Arts and Sciences, Cankaya University, Ankara, Turkey, 2003-. Publications: Book: Linguistic Criticism and Short Stories, 2000; 90 articles on theoretical linguistics, stylistics, literary criticism, translation criticism. Honours: Woman of the Year 2004, ABI, USA; The Outstanding Female Executive Award, ABI, USA. Memberships: Chair of Translation and Linguistic Rights, Turkish PEN Centre; Turkish Authors Association. Address: Cankaya University, Faculty of Arts and Sciences, Department of English Language and Literature. E-mail: aysuerden@cankaya.edu.tr Website: www.aysuerden.org

**EREDIAUWA Eheneden,** b. 20 October 1953, Lagos, Nigeria. Crown Prince of Benin. m. Iroghama, 3 sons, 2 daughters. Education: BSc Econs, University of Wales, Wales, 1973-77; MPA, Rutgers Graduate School, New York, USA, 1979-81; Doctorate Thesis in International Administration (deferred to family commitments), University of London, England, 1985-87. Appointments: Graduate Intern, United Nations Organisation, 1981; Training in Royal Palace Administration, 1982-84, 1986-89; Administrative Officer and Research Assistant, Nigerian Institute of International Affairs, 1984-85; Director, Member of Board of Directors of Integrated Data Services Ltd, Nigerian Petroleum Corporation, 1989-95; Director in private sector with British, Belgian Nigerian and Swiss companies, 1989-97; Advisor, Edo State Government, 1991-93; Ambassador Extraordinary and Plenipotentiary, Ministry of Foreign Affairs, Federal Republic of Nigeria, Abuja, 1997-2004. Publications: Threat Perception in Nigeria Foreign Policy. Memberships: World Association of Former United Nations Interns and Fellows; Nigerian Institute of International Affairs; Petroleum

Institute, London; Edo State Boy Scout Council. Address: The Oba's Palace, P O Box 1, Benin City, Edo State, Nigeria.

**EREMENKO Alexander Ivanovich**, b. 20 April 1942, Russia. Ophthalmologist. m. Tatiana Malisheva, 2 daughters. Education: Graduate, Paediatric Faculty, Tomsk Higher Medical Institute, 1965; Postgraduate, Department of Ophthalmology, Tomsk, 1972; Doctor of Medical Science, 1990; Professor, 1991; Academician, 1994. Appointment: Currently, Professor of Ophthalmology, Kuban State Medical Academy, Krasnodar, Russia. Publications include: 355 articles; 3 monographs; 12 methodic recommentations; Vestnik of Ophthalmology, Moscow; Ophthalmological Journal, Odessa; Ophthalmosurgery, Moscow. Honours: Medal, Russian Federation Honoured Doctor; Kuban and Adygeya Honoured Public Health Worker. Memberships: Presidium of the Board, Society of Ophthalmologists of Russia; Member and Academician, International Implants Academy; Chairman, Krasnodar Society of Ophthalmologists of Russia. Address: Kuban State Medical Academy, Sedin Street 4, Krasnodar 350640, Russia.

**ERGATIS Periklis**, b. 15 March 1969, Athens, Greece. Researcher. Education: BSc Mathematics; PhD, Applied Mathematics. Appointment: Researcher, University of Patras, 1998. Publications: Articles in scientific journals and conference proceedings as author and co-author include: A small axisymmetric obstacle in the presence of an underwater point source field, 1997; A small resistive axisymmetric obstacle in the presence of an underwater point source field, 2001; Sound scattering by hard axisymmetric object in a double layered ocean, 2001; A Computational Method for Railway Track Fault Diagnosis, 2002; Time-Dependent Heat Transfer Coefficient of a Wall, 2003; Sound Scattering by a Resistive and Axially Symmetric Object in a Two-Layer Ocean, 2004. Honours: International Scientist of the Year, 2004; Top 100 Scientists of 2005. Address: 80 P Pavlopoulou Street, Patras 26331, Greece.

**ERITJA Ramon**, b. 9 August 1955, Lleida, Spain. Chemist. m. Elisenda Olivella, 2 sons. Education: BSc, Chemistry, BSc Pharmacy, PhD, Chemistry, 1984, University of Barcelona, Spain. Appointments: Postdoctoral Fellow, Department of Molecular Genetics, Beckman Research Institute of the City of Hope, Duarte, California, USA, 1984-86; Research Associate, Department of Chemistry and Biochemistry, University of Colorado, Boulder, Colorado, USA, 1986-87; Postdoctoral Fellow, Department of Organic Chemistry, University of Barcelona, Spain, 1987-89; Research Associate, Group Leader, Centre for Research and Development, CSIC Barcelona, Spain, 1989-94; Group Leader, European Molecular Biology Laboratory, Heidelberg, Germany, 1994-99; Group Leader, Consejo Superior de Investigaciones Científicas, Barcelona, Spain, 1999-. Publications: 180 publications on synthesis and study of properties of oligonucleotides and peptides in scientific journals. Memberships: American Peptide Society; International Society for Nucleosides, Nucleotides and Nucleic Acids. Address: Viriato 43, 5, 1, E-08014, Barcelona, Spain. E-mail: recgma@cid.csic.es

**ERLICH Victor**, b. 22 November 1914, Petrograd, Russia. University Professor. m. Iza Sznejerson, 2 sons. Education: MA, Free Polish University, Warsaw, 1937; PhD, Columbia University, New York, USA, 1951. Appointments: Assistant Professor, Professor of Slavic Literatures, University of Washington, 1948-62; Bensinger Professor of Russian Literature, Yale University, 1963-85; Professor Emeritus, 1985-. Publications: Russian Formalism: History - Doctrine, 1955; The Double Image, 1964; Gogol, 1969; Modernism and Revolution, 1994. Honours: Guggenheim Fellow, 1958, 1964, 1976-77;

National Endowment for the Humanities Fellow, 1968-69. Memberships: American Association for the Advancement of Slavic Studies, Vice President, 1973-77; Modern Language Association. Address: 25 Glen Parkway, Hamden, CT 06517, USA.

**ERMIS Sitki Samet**, b. 6 May 1969, Istanbul, Turkey. Ophthalmologist. m. Betul Ugur, 3 sons. Education: Medical Doctor, 1993, Ophthalmologist, 1997, University of Istanbul; Fellow, Kyoto Prefectural University of Medicine, Japan, 2003. Appointment: Assistant Professor of Ophthalmology, University of Afyon Kocatepe, Turkey, 2000-. Publications: Articles to professional journals; Chapter in book, Progress in Glaucoma Research. Honour: Japanese Government Scholarship (Mombusho). Memberships: Turkish Ophthalmic Society; American Society of Cataract and Refractive Surgery; European Society of Cataract and Refractive Surgeons; Association for Research in Vision and Ophthalmology. Address: Seyhresmi mah, Yusufziyapasa sk, No:10/3 34240, Fatih, Istanbul, Turkey. E-mail: ssermis@yahoo.com

**ERNST Konstantin**, b. 6 February 1961, Moscow, Russia. Mass Media Company Executive. m. Larisa Sinelshchikova, 1 daughter. Education: Graduate, Faculty of Biology, Leningrad University, 1983; PhD, Biochemistry, 1986. Appointments: Joined "Vzglyad" programme, Channel 1, Central Television, Russia, 1988; Author and Host "Matador" programme, 1990-; General Producer, Obschestvennoe Rossiyskoe Televidenie (ORT), 1995-; General Director of ORT, 1999-; Major productions include: Radio Silence (full-length music film), 1988; Homo Duplex (short film), 1989; Waiting Room (television series), 1998; Impact Force (series), 1999; Memories of Sherlock Holmes, 2000; Co-author and producer, Russian Project-1, 1995; Russian Project-2, 1996; Author and producer, Old Songs about the Eternal - 1, 2,3 (musical series), 1995-97; Co-producer, Checkpoint (feature Film), 1998; Author and producer, Old Songs about the Eternal PS, 2000; Producer, Impact Force-2, Stop by Request, Empire under Strike, Border Taiga. Romance, 2000; Peculiarities of National Hunt in Winter Season (motion picture), 2000; Producer, Impact Force-3, The Fifth Corner, Stop by Request-2, 2001; Producer, Investigated by Znatoki. Case No 23, Azazel, Special Squad, Ice Age, Russians in the City of Angels, Uchstok, Diversionist (all TV series), 72 Meters, Night Watch, The Turkish Gambit (feature films), 2002-2004. Honours: Golden Olive, Bar International Festival, Montenegro, 1995, 2000; Russian Television Academy TEFI Award, 1998, 2000, 2001; Golden Rose, X Open Russian Film Festival Kinotavr, Sochi, 1999; Crystal Globe, XXXIV Karlovy Vary International Film Festival, Czech Republic, 1999; Vesuvius Award, Naples International Film Festival, 1999; Silver Dophin, XV Film Festival in Troy, Greece, 1999; Press Prize, First Open Russian Advertising Competition, 1999; Business-Olympus Award, 2001; Russian State Prizewinner, 2003. Memberships: Russian Television Academy; Board Member, National Association of TV Broadcasters; President, Media Industrial Committee, 2002-. Address: 12 Akademika Koroleva Str, Moscow 127000, Russia. E-mail: first@1tv.ru Website: www.1tv.ru

**ERSKINE Philip Neil**, b. 20 August 1933, United Kingdom. Major (Retired); Artist. m. Alice Fiona Radcliffe, 2 sons, 1 daughter. Education: Sandhurst; Ruth Prowse Art School, Cape Town, South Africa, 1986-88; Slade Summer School, 1990. Appointments: Commissioned in Scots Guards, 1953, 20 years service: Regimental service in Suez Canal Zone, Germany, Persian Gulf; ADC to Lord Cobham, Governor General of New Zealand, 1959-60; Equerry to HRH the Duke of Gloucester, 1962-64; Commanded Royal Guard at Balmoral, 1967; Retired as Major, 1971; Moved with family to South Africa, 1971; Founding Chairman, Cultural Press of South Africa; Joint Editor, Antiques in South Africa, 1976-86; Board Member: South African Military History Museum, Johannesburg, Michaelis Collection, Cape Town, Stellenbosch Museum; Restored (with his wife) the Old cape Homestead of Ida's Valley and 2 other restoration projects; Full-time Artist, 1989-; 15 one-man exhibitions in South Africa; Works in collections: Everard Read Gallery, Johannesburg and Cape Town; Commissions include: Mural at Corndavon for the late Queen Mother. Publications: Articles on South African Antiques, South African history and historical personalities. Honour: Gold Medal for work in the field of restoration, Simon Van der Stel Foundation. Memberships: Founder, Antique Collectors Society of South Africa; Founding Chairman, Historic House Owners Association of South Africa; Chairman, for 5 years, Stellenbosch Action 300 (conservation society); Local Committee Member, for 10 years, Simon Van der Stel Foundation. Address: Ida's Valley Homestead, PO Box 132 Stellenbosch, Cape 7599, South Africa

**ERTLER Klaus-Dieter,** b. 20 November 1954, Feldbach, Austria. Professor. Education: MA, 1982; PhD, 1985; Habilitation, 1999. Appointments: Lecturer, University of Graz, Austria, 1982-2000; Visiting Professor, University of Heidelberg, Germany, 2000-02; Visiting Professor, University of Aachen, Germany, 2002-03; Visiting Professor, University of Kassel, Germany, 2003-04; Professor, University of Graz, 2004-. Publications: Author, 7 books; Editor, 3 books; Articles in professional journals. Memberships: Vice President, Gesellschaft für Kanada-Studien (GKS). Address: Institut fuer Romanistik, Universität Graz, Merangasse 70, A-8010 Graz, Austria.

**ESAKI Leo,** b. 12 March 1925, Osaka, Japan. Physicist. m. (1) Masako Araki, 1959, 1 son, 2 daughters, (2) Masako Kondo, 1986. Education: Graduated, University of Tokyo, 1947, PhD. Appointments: With Sony Corporation, 1956-60; IBM Fellow, 1967-92, IBM T J Watson Research Center, New York, 1960-92, Manager, Device Research, 1962-92, IBM Corporation, USA; Director, IBM Japan, 1976-92, Yamada Science Foundation, 1976-; President, University of Tsukuba, Ibaraki, Japan, 1992-98; Chair, Science and Technology Promotion Foundation of Ibaraki, 1998-; Director General, Tsukuba International Congress Center, 1999-; President, Shibaura Institute of Technology, 2000-. Publications: Numerous articles in professional journals. Honours: Nishina Memorial Award, 1959; Asahi Press Award, 1960; Toyo Rayon Foundation Award, 1961; Morris N Liebmann Memorial Prize, 1961; Stuart Ballantine Medal, Franklin Institute, 1961; Japan Academy Award, 1965; IBM Fellow, 1967; Joint Winner, Nobel Prize for Physics, 1973; Order of Culture, Japanese Government, 1974; Sir John Cass Senior Visiting Research Fellow, London Polytechnic, 1981; US-Asia Institute, Science Achievement Award, 1983; American Physical Society, Institute Prize for New Materials, 1985; IEEE Medal of Honour, 1991; Japan Prize, 1998; Grand Cordon Order of Rising Sun, First Class, 1998. Memberships: Japan Academy; American Philosophical Society; Max-Planck Gesellschaft; Foreign Associate, NAS; American National Academy of Engineering. Address: Shibaura Institute of Technology, 3-9-14 Shibaura, Minato-ku, Tokyo 108, Japan.

**ESSIEN Okon Etim Akpan,** b. 10 January 1942, Ntan Ekere-Ibiono Ibom, Nigeria. University Professor. m. Maria Okon Essien, 2 sons, 3 daughters. Education: BA, University of Nigeria, 1965; MA, University of California, Los Angeles, 1968; PhD, University of Edinburgh, 1974. Appointments: Lecturer, Ahmadu Bello University, Zaria, Nigeria, 1968-76;

Senior Lecturer, Reader, 1976-84, 1985-, University of Calabar, Professor of Linguistics, Head of Department, Languages and Linguistics, 1984-93, Dean, Faculty of Arts, 1991-95, Chairman, Committee of Deans, 1993-95, Member, Governing Council, 1992-96, University of Calabar; Member, Governing Council, Adeyemi College of Education, Ondo, 1992-94; Member, Board of Directors, NERDC, Abuja, 1991-94. Publications: Over 60 articles and papers contributed to specialist peer-reviewed journals; Chapters contributed to books; Textbooks in Nigerian and English Languages, including, A Grammar of the Ibibio Language; The Tense Systems of Nigerian Languages and English. Honours: Final Year Best Student Latin Prize, 1958; Mboho Mkparawa Ibibio Excellence Award, 1992; Federation of Akwa Ibom Women Association, Eminent Persons Award, 1995; Federation of UNESCO Clubs of Nigeria Award, 1998; Fellow, Modern Languages Association of Nigeria, 2001; UNESCO, EXTEA, Spain, Certificate of Appreciation for Collaboration in the World Languages Report, 2000; Title of Mkpisong (Pillar), Akwa Ibom State, 2003; Officer of the Order of the Niger (OON), 2004; Certificate of Excellence, 2004; Language & Culture in Nigeria: A Festschrift for Okon Essien, 2004. Memberships: President, Ibibio Language Writers Association, 1983-; President, Linguistic Association of Nigeria, 1990-95; West African Linguistic Society; Modern Languages Association of Nigeria; Conference of African Linguistics, USA. Address: Department of Linguistics, University of Calabar, Calabar, Cross River State, Nigeria.

**ESSLEMONT Iain,** b. 2 September 1932, Aberdeen, Scotland. General Medical Practitioner (Retired). m. Mary Gibb Mars, 1 son, 2 daughters. Education: MB ChB, 1956; D ObstRCOG, 1960; MRCGP, 1973; Dip Aust COG, 1980; FRACGP, 1981; MCGP (Malaysia), 1982; FAFP (Malaysia), 1997. Appointments: House Surgeon, Ayr County Hospital, Scotland, 1956-57; House Physician, Paediatrician, General Hospital, Dewsbury, England, 1957; RAMC, 1957-50; House Surgeon, Obstetrics, Ayrshire Central Hospital, Scotland, 1960; General Practitioner, Cha'ah, Johore, Malaysia, 1960-62; General Practitioner, Drs Allan and Gunstensen, Penang, Malaysia, 1962-77; MO, Kununurra, Western Australia, 1977-78; Southside After-Hours Medical Service, Perth, Western Australia, 1978-82; General Practitioner, Huntingdale Family Medical Service, Gosnells, Western Australia, 1979-99; General Practitioner, Gosnells Health Care Practice, Gosnells, Western Australia, 1999; Examiner, Royal Australian College of General Practitioners, 1985-2002; President, The Dalton Society, 1994; External Clinical Teacher, Royal Australian College of General Practitioners, 2001-2002. Publications: Articles in the Australian Family Physician: Non surgical treatment for Meibomian Cysts, 1995; Sick doctors – a personal story, 2001; Why use soap? 2001; What is a GP? 2001; The clue was in the ingots, 2001; Birth, death and life, 2001; Where is general practice heading? 2002; Dying, 2002. Honour: Paul Harris Fellowship (Rotary), 1998. Memberships: Royal College of General Practitioners; Royal Australian College of General Practitioners; Academy of Family Physicians Malaysia. Address: 2, Chardonnay Avenue, Margaret River, Western Australia, 6285 Australia. E-mail: esslemont@wn.com.au

**ESTEFAN Gloria (Fajado),** b. 1 September 1957, Havana, Cuba. Singer; Songwriter. m. Emilio Estefan, 1 September 1978. Education: BA, Psychology, University of Miami, 1978. Career: Singer, backed by Miami Sound Machine, 1974-; Billed as Gloria Estefan, 1989-; Appearances include: Tokyo Music Festival, Japan, 1985; World tour, 1991; The Simple Truth, benefit concert for Kurdish refugees, Wembley, 1991; White House State Dinner, for President of Brazil, 1991; South American tour, 1992; Royal Variety Performance, London, before Prince and Princess of Wales, 1992; Co-organiser, benefit concert for victims of Hurricane Andrew, Florida, 1992; 45 million albums sold to date. Compositions include: Anything For You; Don't Wanna Lose You; Oye Mi Canto (co-written with Jorge Casas and Clay Ostwald); Cuts Both Ways; Coming Out Of The Dark (co-written with Emilio Estefan and Jon Secada); Always Tomorrow; Christmas Through Their Eyes (co-written with Dianne Warren). Recordings: Albums: Renacer, 1976; Eyes Of Innocence, 1984; Primitive Love, 1986; Let It Loose, 1988; Anything For You (Number 1, UK), 1989; Cuts Both Ways, 1989; Exitos De Gloria Estefan, 1990; Into The Light, 1991; Greatest Hits, 1992; Mi Tierra, 1993; Christmas Through Your Eyes, 1993; Hold Me, Thrill Me, Kiss Me, 1994; Abriendo Puertas, 1995; Destiny, 1996; Gloria!; Santo Santo, 1999; Alma Caribeño: Caribbean Soul, 2000; Also featured on: Jon Secada, Jon Secada (also co-producer), 1991; Til Their Eyes Shine (The Lullaby Album), 1992; Hit singles include: Dr Beat, 1984; Conga, 1986; Hot Summer Nights, used in film soundtrack Top Gun, 1986; Bad Boy, 1986; Words Get In The Way, 1986; Rhythm Is Gonna Get You, 1987; Can't Stay Away From You, 1988; Anything For You (Number 1, US), 1988; 1-2-3, 1988; Oye Mi Canto (Hear My Voice), 1989; Here We Are, 1989; Don't Wanna Lose You, 1989; Get On Your Feet, 1989; Coming Out of The Dark (Number 1, US), 1991; Remember Me With Love, 1991; Always Tomorrow, 1992; Cuts Both Ways, 1993; Go Away, 1993; Mi Tierra, 1993; Turn the Beat Around, 1994; Abrienda Puertos; Tres Deseos; Mas Alla. Honours: Grand Prize, Tokyo Music Festival, 1985; Numerous Billboard awards, 1986-; American Music Award, Favourite Pop/Rock Duo or Group, 1989; Crystal Globe Award, 21 Club, New York, 1990; Latin Music Award, Crossover Artist Of Year, 1990; Humanitarian Award, B'Nai B'rith, 1992; Desi Entertainment Awards, Performer of Year, Song of Year, 1992; Humanitarian Award, National Music Foundation (for helping victims of Hurricane Andrew), 1993. Address: c/o Estefan Enterprises, 6205 Bird Road, Miami Beach, FL 33155, USA.

**ESTEVEZ Emilio,** b. 12 May 1962, New York, USA. Actor. m. Paula Abdul, 1992, divorced 1994, 1 son, 1 daughter. Appointments: Actor, films include: Tex, 1982; Nightmares, 1983; The Outsiders, 1983; The Breakfast Club, 1984; Repo Man, 1984; St Elmo's Fire, 1984; That Was Then...This is Now, 1985; Maximum Overdrive, 1986; Wisdom (also writer and director), 1986; Stakeout, 1987; Men at Work, 1989; Freejack, 1992; Loaded Weapon, 1993; Another Stakeout, 1993; Champions II, 1993; Judgement Night, 1993; D2: The Mighty Ducks, 1994; The Jerky Boys (co-executive, producer); Mighty Ducks 3; Mission Impossible, 1996; The War at Home, 1996; The Bang Bang Club, 1998; Killer's Head, 1999; Sand, 2000; Rated X, 2000; The LA Riot Spectacular, 2004. Address: c/o UTA, 5th Floor, 9560 Wilshire Boulevard, Beverly Hills, CA 90212, USA.

**ETHERIDGE Melissa Lou,** b. Leavenworth, Kansas, USA. Singer; Songwriter; Musician (guitar). Musical Education: Berklee College of Music, Boston. Career: Musician, Los Angeles bars, 5 years; Recording artiste, 1988-. Recordings: Albums: Melissa Etheridge, 1988; Brave And Crazy, 1989; Never Enough, 1992; Yes I Am, 1993; Your Little Secret, 1995; Breakdown, 1999; Singles: I'm the Only One, 1994; Come to My Window, 1994; If I Wanted To, 1995; Nowhere to Go, 1996; Angels Would Fall, 1999. Honours: Grammy Nomination, Bring Me Some Water, 1988. Current Management: Bill Leopold, W F Leopold Management, 4425 Riverside Drive, Ste 102, Burbank, CA 91505, USA.

**ETIENNE Gilbert,** b. 22 June 1928, Neuchâtel, Switzerland. Emeritus Professor. m. Annette Etienne, 2 sons, 1 daughter.

Education: LLB, University of Neuchâtel, Switzerland, 1951; Diploma, Institute of Oriental Civilisation, Paris, France, 1954; PhD, India's Economy, University of Neuchâtel, Switzerland, 1955. Appointments: Lecturer, Hindu Art, Punjab University, Lahore, India, 1952-53; General Assistant, Favre-Leuba Company (Swiss Watch Company), Bombay, India, 1956-58; Professor of Development Economics, Graduate Institute of International Studies, 1959-96; Professor, Graduate Institute of Development Studies, 1964-96; Professor Emeritus as both institutes, 1996-; Visiting Lecturer, MIT, Cornell and Chicago Universities; Visiting Professor, EDI, World Bank, Collège de France, Paris. Publications: Numerous books include most recently; Chine-Inde, le match du Siècle, 1998, Chinese edition, 2000; Contribution to Le Pakistan (ed C Jaffrelot), 2002; Imprévisible Afghanistan, 2002; Le développement à contre-courant, 2003. Honour: Global Award for outstanding contribution to social and economic development studies, Priyadarshni Academy, Bombay, 2002. Memberships: International Committee of the Red Cross, 1973-85; Founding Member and Vice-chairman of the Board of African Institute (later Institute of Development Studies), 1961-64; Chairman, Geneva Society, 1997-. Address: 10 Chemin de Grange-Bonnet, 1224, Chene-Bougeries Genève, Switzerland.

**ETO Shinkichi,** b. 16 November 1923, Mukden, China. Educationist. m. Kazuko Ono, 1 son, 2 daughters. Education: BL, Law Faculty, University of Tokyo, Japan, 1948. Appointments: Associate Professor of International Relations, 1956, Professor, 1967, Professor Emeritus, 1984, University of Tokyo, Japan; President, Asia University, 1987-95; Chancellor, Tokyo Eiwa Educational Institution, 1998-2002. Publications: My Thirty Three Years Dream: The Autobiography of Miyazaki Toten (translated from the Japanese with M B Jansen), 1982; China's Republican Revolution (editor with H Z Schiffrin), 1994. Honours: Purple Ribbon Medal, Japanese Government, 1991; Second Order of the Sacred Treasure, Emperor of Japan, 2001. Memberships: Director Emeritus, Japan Association of International Law; Director Emeritus, Japan Association of International Relations. Address: 4-46-9 Kugayama, Suginami-ku, Tokyo 168-0082, Japan.

**ETTY Robert,** b. 6 November 1949, Waltham, Lincolnshire, England. Schoolteacher; Poet. m. Anne Levison, 3 April 1975, 1 son, 1 daughter. Education: BA. Publications: Hovendens Violets, 1989; New Pastorals, 1992; Marking Places, 1994; A Selection, 1997; Small Affairs on the Estate, 2000; The Blue Box, 2001. Contributions to: Poetry Review; The North; Spectator; Outposts; Rialto; Staple; Stand; Verse; The Independent. Honours: Lake Aske Award, Nottingham Poetry Society, 1990; 1st Prize, Wykeham Poetry Competition, 1991; 1st Prize, Kent and Sussex Open Poetry Competition, 1992; Other awards, 1989-04 Address: Evenlode, Church Lane, Keddington, Louth, Lincolnshire LN11 7HG, England.

**EUBANK Chris,** b. 8 August 1966, Dulwich, England. Middleweight Boxer. m. 4 children. Career: WBC International Middleweight Boxing Champion, 2 defences, March-November, 1990; WBO Middleweight Boxing Champion, 3 defences, November 1990-August 1991; WBO World Super-Middleweight Boxing Champion, 14 defences, September 1991-March 1995; Lost title to Steve Collins, Cork, Sept 1995; Failed to regain title against Joe Calzaghe, Sheffield, October 1997; Unsuccessful fights for WBO Cruiserweight title against Carl Thompson, Manchester, April 1998, Sheffield, July 1998; Patron Breakthrough; Ambassador, International Fund for Animal Welfare; Spokesperson, National Society for the Prevention of Cruelty to Children. Address: 9 The Upper Drive, Hove, East Sussex, BN3 6GR, England.

**EUN Bang Hee,** b. 25 June 1933, Seoul, Korea. Policy Planner. m. Kuk Kyung Lee, 2 daughters. Education: BA, English Language and Literature, Sookmyung Women's University, 1961. Appointments: Board Member, Yoon-Gook Scholarship Association, 1984-87; Member, Women's Special Committee Auspices under the President, 2000-2001; Member, Judiciary Examining Committee, Ministry of Justice, 2000-2001; Board Member, Korean Foundation for Working Together, 2000-; Chairman, Korea Council for Reconciliation and Co-operation, 2000-; Co-Representative, Citizen's Coalition for Safety, 2000-; Member, Korea Publication Ethics Committee, 2000-2004; Board Member, National Association for Disaster Relief, 2002-; Member, Committee for Refugee Recognition, Ministry of Justice,2002-; Co-ordinator, Korea NGO's Network, 2002-2004; Member, Presidential Committee of Medical System Development, 2002-2003; Member, Tax Reform Committee, MoFE, 2004-; Member, Livelihood Protection Committee, MoHWA, 2004-; Member, Science Korea Committee, Korea Science Foundation, 2004-; Member, Medical Institutions Evaluation Committee, MoHWA, 2004; Member, Committee on 60th Anniversary of Korean Liberation, 2005-; Member, Committee on Women's Policy Review, MoHWA, 2005-2007; President, Korean National Council of Women, 2000-. Publications: Publisher, Korean Women (yearly publication in English), 2000-; Publisher, Women (monthly publication in Korean), 2000-; Crown with Glasses (long novel), 2003. Address: Seudaimoonku, 265-90 Hongeundong, Seoul, Korea. E-mail: kncw@chol.com

**EVANGELISTA Linda,** b. St Catherine, Toronto, Ontario, Canada. Model. m. Gerald Marie (divorced 1993). Career: Face of Yardley Cosmetics; Numerous catwalk appearances. Address: c/o Elite Model Management, 40 Parker Street, London WC2B 5PH, England.

**EVANGELOU Spiros N,** b. 7 July 1954, Kalentzi, Ioannina, Greece. Professor. Education: DPhil, Theoretical Physics, Oxford University, England, 1980. Appointments: Imperial College, 1980-81, University of Oxford, England, 1981-82; Military Service, Greece, 1982-84; Research Centre of Crete, Greece, 1984-86; University of Ioannina, Greece, 1986-. Publications include: 80 Articles in refereed journals and 3 books. Honours: Scholarships; Greek Writers Award. Memberships: IOP; APS. Address: Physics Department, University of Ioannina, Ioannina 45110, Greece. E-mail: sevagel@cc.uoi.gr

**EVANS Chris,** b. 1966, Warrington, England. Broadcaster. m. (1) Carol McGiffin, 1991, divorced, (2) Billie Piper, divorced. Career: Numerous sundry jobs; Joined Piccadilly Radio, Manchester; Producer, GLR Radio, London; Presenter of numerous television programmes including Don't Forget Your Toothbrush, co-presenter, The Big Breakfast; Presenter, Radio 1 Breakfast Show, 1995-97, Virgin Radio Breakfast Show, 1997-; Established Ginger Productions, media production company; Presenter and Executive Producer, TFI Friday, Channel 4. Honours: British Comedy Award Prizes, Best Entertainment Series, Top Channel 4 Entertainment Presenter, 1995. Address: Ginger Productions, 131-151 Great Titchfield Street, London W1P 8DP, England.

**EVANS D John O,** b. 17 November 1953, Morriston, Swansea, South Wales. Broadcaster. Education: BMus, 1975; MA, 1976; PhD, University of Cardiff, Wales. Appointments: First Research Scholar, Britten-Pears Library and Archive, Aldeburgh, England, 1980-84; Music Producer, BBC Radio 3, 1985-89; Senior Producer, BBC Singers, 1989-92; Chief Producer, Series, BBC Radio 3, 1992-93; Head of Music Department, BBC Radio 3, 1993-97; Head of Classical Music,

BBC Radio, 1997-2000; Head of Music Programming, BBC Radio 3, 2000-. Publications: Author with Donald Mitchell, Benjamin Britten: Pictures from a Life 1913-1976, 1978; Editor, Benjamin Britten: His Life and Operas, by Eric Walter White, revised 2nd edition, 1982. Contributions include: A Britten Companion, 1984; A Britten Source Book, 1987; ENO, Royal Opera House and Cambridge Opera Guides on Britten's Peter Grimes, Gloriana, The Turn of the Screw, Death in Venice. Honours: Prix Italia Award and Charles Heidsieck Award, 1989; Royal Philharmonic Society Award, 1994; Sony Radio Award, 1997. Memberships: Director, The Britten Estate; Trustee of Britten-Pears Foundation; Chairman of Concentric Circles Theatre Company; Chair, Opera Jury for RPS Awards; Juror, BBC Singer of the World Competition; Tosti International Singing Competition, BBC Choir of the Year. Address: 44 Brooksby Street, Islington, London, N1 1HA, England. E-mail: john.evans@bbc.co.uk

**EVANS David,** b. 27 August 1942, London, England. Professor of Logic and Metaphysics. Education: BA, MA, PhD, Classics, University of Cambridge. Appointments: Research Fellow, 1964-65, Official Fellow and Lecturer, 1965-78, Sidney Sussex College, Cambridge; Visiting Professor, Philosophy Department, Duke University, USA, 1972-73; Professor of Logic and Metaphysics, 1978, Head of Philosophy Department, 1978-92, Dean of the Faculty of Arts, 1986-89, Director of the School of Philosophical and Anthropological Studies, 1987-95, Chair, Postgraduate Research Committee, 1993-2003, Chair, University Research Ethics Committee, 2004-, Queen's University, Belfast. Publications: Books: Aristotle's Concept of Dialectic, 1977; Aristotle, 1987; Edited books: Moral Philosophy and Contemporary Problems, 1988; Teaching Philosophy on the Eve of the Twenty-First Century (with Ioanna Kuçuradi), 1998. Honours: Craven Student, University of Cambridge, 1963-64; Member of the Royal Irish Academy, 1983. Memberships include: Steering Committee, International Federation of Philosophical Societies; British Philosophical Society; National Committee for Philosophy, Royal Irish Academy; Royal Institute of Philosophy; Aristotelian Society; Association Internationale des Professeurs de Philosophie; Arts Council of Northern Ireland; Governor, Strand Primary School, Belfast. Address: School of Philosophical Studies, Queen's University, Belfast BT7 1NN, Northern Ireland. E-mail: jdg.evans@qub.ac.uk

**EVANS Donald, (Onwy),** b. 12 June 1940, Cardiganshire, Wales. Retired Welsh Teacher m. Pat Thomas, 29 December 1972, 1 son. Education: Honours Degree, Welsh, 1962, Diploma, Education, 1963, University College of Wales Aberystwyth; PhD Thesis in final stages of completion, University of Wales Lampeter, 2004. Appointments: Welsh Master, Ardwyn Grammar School, Aberystwyth, 1963-73; Penglais Comprehensive School, Aberystwyth, 1973-84; Welsh Specialist, Cardigan Junior School, 1984-91; Welsh Supply Teacher in Ceredigion, Primary and Comprehensive Schools, 1991-2002. Publications: Egin (Shoots), 1976; Parsel Persain (Sweet Parcel) (editor), 1976; Haidd (Barley), 1977; Grawn (Seeds), 1979; Blodeugerdd o Gywyddau (Anthology of Alliterative Poems) (editor), 1981; Eden, 1981; Gwenoliaid (Swallows), 1982; Machlud Canrif (Century's Sunset), 1983; Eisiau Byw (Needing to Live), 1984; Cread Crist (Christ's Creation), 1986; O'r Bannau Duon (From the Black Hills), 1987; Iasau (Thrills), 1988; Seren Poets 2 (with others), 1990; The Life and Work of Rhydwen Williams, 1991; Wrth Reddf (By Instinct), 1994; Asgwrn Cefen (Backbone), 1997; Y Cyntefig Cyfoes (The Contemporary Primitive), 2000; Contributions to: Several publications. Honours: National Eisteddfod Crown and Chair, 1977, 1980; Welsh Arts Council Literary Prizes,

1977, 1983, 1989; Welsh Academy Literary Award, 1989. Memberships: Welsh Academy; Welsh Poetry Society; Gorsedd of Bards, National Eisteddfod of Wales. Address: Y Plas, Talgarreg, Llandysul, Ceredigion SA44 4XA, West Wales.

**EVANS Janet M,** b. 16 September 1956, Raleigh, North Carolina, USA. Publisher. 2 sons. Education: Technical and Administrative Training. Appointments: Marketing assistant, Evans and Wade Advertising Ltd, 1977-78; Chief Executive Officer, American Biographical Institute: Chairman, ABI Research Association, 1979-97; Magazine and Newsletter Editor, 1979-; Director, Conference on Culture and Education, 1984; Executive Director, World Institute of Achievement, 1985-; President, American Biographical Institute, 1997-; General-in-Residence, United Cultural Convention, 2001-. Publications: Editor, Publisher, Biographical Reference. Honours: Honorary Life Fellow, International Biographical Association. Memberships: Foundation for International Meetings, Board Member 1992; Publishers' Association of the South; Raleigh Chamber of Commerce; American Society of Professional and Executive Women; National Association of Independent Publishers; Publishers Marketing Association. Address: American Biographical Institute, PO Box 31226, 5126 Bur Oak Circle, Raleigh, NC 27622, USA.

**EVANS Louise,** b. 6 September, San Antonio, Texas, USA. Investor; Clinical Psychologist (retired); Philanthropist. m. Thomas Ross Gambrell. Education: BS, Psychology, Northwestern University, 1949; MS, Clinical Psychology, Purdue University, 1952; Intern, Clinical Psychology, Menninger Foundation, 1953; PhD, Clinical Psychology, Purdue University, 1955; Post-doctoral Fellowship, Clinical Child Psychology, Department of Child Psychology, Menninger Clinic, 1956; Diploma, American Board of Examiners in Professional Psychology, 1966. Appointments: Teaching Assistant, Psychology Department, Purdue University, 1950-51; Intern, Menninger Foundation, 1952-53; Staff Psychologist, Kankakee State Hospital, Illinois, 1954-55; Postdoctoral Fellow, Menninger Clinic, US Public Health Service, 1955-56; Head Staff Psychologist, Child Guidance Clinic, Kings County Hospital, Brooklyn, New York, 1957-58; Clinical Research Consultant, Episcopal Diocese, St Louis, Missouri, 1959-60; Director, Psychology Clinic, Barnes-Renard Hospitals, Instructor, Medical Psychology, Washington University School of Medicine, St Louis, 1959-60; Private Practice, Fullerton, California, 1960-93. Publications: Articles in professional journals. Honours include: Silver Goblet, World's Leading Biographee of 1987, IBC; 25 Year Silver Achievement Award, ABI, 1993; World Lifetime Achievement Award, ABI, 1995; Distinguished Alumni Award, Purdue University, 1993; Old Master Award, Purdue University, 1993; Northwestern University College of Arts and Sciences, Merit Award, 1997; International Woman of the Year, Medal of Honour, 1996-97; 2000 Outstanding Scientists of the 20th Century Medal; Scientific Achievement Award, ABI; American Psychological Association, International Division Award for Lifelong Contributions to the Advancement of Psychology Internationally, 2002; Plaque for Pioneering Leadership in International Psychology, 2003; Certificate as Ambassador in recognition of outstanding leadership and enduring commitment, 2003, International Council of Psychologists. Memberships include: Fellow: Academy of Clinical Psychology, American Psychological Association, Royal Society of Health, UK; Fellow, American Association for the Advancement of Science. Address: PO Box 6067, Beverley Hills, CA 90212-1067, USA.

**EVANS Richard Rowland,** b. 26 May 1936, Tabor, Dolgellau, Wales. Retired Headteacher; Writer; Poet. m. Bronwen Edwards, 21 August 1965, 1 daughter. Education: Teacher's

Certificate, 1958; Diploma in Bilingual Education, 1964; BEd, 1980, University College of Wales; BA, University of Wales, 1998; Mphil, University of Wales, 2003. Appointment: Welsh Editor, The Normalite/Y Normalydd, 1957-58. Publication: Mynd i'r Lleuad, 1973; Marion Eames, 2004. Contributions to: Articles and poetry to Dalen, Godre'r Gader; The Normalite/Y Normalydd; Y Cyfnod; Y Dydd. Honour: Winner, Book Writing Competition, 1970, Bardic Chair, 1988. Memberships: Barddas; Cymdeithas Bob Owen; The Welsh Academy / Yr Academi Gymreig. Address: Brithdir, 93 Ger-y-llen, Penrhyn-coch, Aberystwyth, Ceredigion, West Wales, SY23 3HQ.

**EVANS William John,** b. 23 July 1943, Bridgend, Wales. University Professor. m. Gillian Mary Phillips, 2 sons, 1 daughter. Education: BSc (Hons), PhD, 1969, DSc, 1996, University of Wales Swansea. Appointments: Senior Scientific Officer, 1969-79, Principal Scientific Officer and Head of Mechanical Design Research, 1979-85, (MOD(PE)) National Gas Turbine Establishment, Farnborough; Lecturer, Senior Lecturer, Reader, Interdisciplinary Research Centre and Materials Department, 1985-96, Professor and Director, Interdisciplinary Research Centre, 1997-2002, Director, Welsh Development Agency Centre of Excellence in Materials, 2002-2003, Director, Rolls Royce Technology Centre, 2001-, Head of Materials Research Centre, 2003-, University of Wales Swansea. Publications: Over 200 scientific publications and numerous invitations to lecture at international events; Co-editor, Titanium 95 (3 volumes), 1996; Co-editor, Proceedings of the Component Optimisation Conference at Swansea (COMPASS 1999), 2000; Co-editor, COMPASS 2002, 2003. Honours: Elected Fellow, Royal Academy of Engineering; Visiting Professor, University of New South Wales, Australia. Memberships: Fellow, Institute of Materials, Minerals and Mining (IOM³); Past President, South Wales Metallurgical Association; Chairman, Materials Technology Forum for Wales (Welsh Development Agency sponsored); Editorial Board, Journal of Fatigue of Engineering Materials and Structures. Address: Materials Research Centre, School of Engineering, University of Wales Swansea, Singleton Park, Swansea SA2 8PP, Wales. E-mail: w.j.evans@swansea.ac.uk

**EVDOKIMOV Vyacheslav Borisovich,** b. 25 August 1945, Shadrinsk, Russian Federation. Lawyer. m. Elena Evdokimova, 1 son, 4 daughters. Education: Higher Education Diploma in Law, Sverdlovsk Law Institute, Russia, 1968; Candidate Degree in Law, 1972; Doctorate Degree in Law, 1990; Professor of Law, 1992. Appointments: Sverdlovsk Prosecution Officer, 1968-69; Lawyer, Sverdlovsk Regional Bar, 1969-71; Professor, Sverdlovsk Law Institute (now the Urals State Law Academy) and in the Urals Legal Service Academy, 1971-2000; Chief of Lawmaking Co-ordination Department, Ministry of Justice of Russia, 2000-2001; First Deputy Minister of Justice of Russia, 2001-2004; Chief of Civil and Social Legislature, Ministry of Justice of Russia, 2004-. Publications: About 150 works on state management in law including: Political Parties in Foreign Countries, 1992; Constitutional Legal Proceedings in the USA, 1996; Federalism and Decentralization, 1997; Election Systems in World Countries, 1999; Local Authorities in Foreign Countries, 2001; International Legal Assistance, 2004. Honours: Honoured Lawyer of Russia; Honoured Officer of Justice of Russia; 9 Medals. Address: ul. Vorontsovo Pole 4, 109830 Moscow, Russia

**EVE Trevor,** b. 1 July 1951. Actor. m. Sharon Patricia Maughn, 1980, 2 sons, 1 daughter. Education: Kingston Art College; RADA. Career: Actor, Theatre includes: Children of a Lesser God, 1981; The Genius, 1983; High Society, 1986; Man Beast and Virtue, 1989; The Winter's Tale, 1991; Inadmissible

Evidence, 1993; Uncle Vanya, 1996; TV includes: Shoestring, 1980; Jamaica Inn, 1990; A Sense of Guilt, 1990; Parnell and the Englishwoman, 1991; A Doll's House, 1991; The Politician's Wife, 1995; Black Easter, 1995; Under the Sun, 1997; Evilstreak, 1999; David Copperfield, 1999; Waking The Dead, 2000, 2001, 2002, 2003, 2004, 2005; Films include: Hindle Wakes; Dracula; A Wreath of Roses; The Corsican Brothers; Aspen Extreme; Psychotherapy; The Knight's Tale; The Tribe; Appetite; Possession; Troy; Producer for Projector Productions: Alice Through the Looking Glass, 1998; Cinderella; Twelfth Night, 2002. Honours include: Olivier Award for Best Supporting Actor, 1997. Address: c/o ICM Ltd, Oxford House, 76 Oxford Street, London, W1N 0AX, England.

**EVERETT Rupert,** b. 29 May 1960, Norfolk, England. Actor. Education: Central School for Speech and Drama, London. Appointments: Apprentice, Glasgow Citizen's Theatre, 1979-82; Model, Versace, Milan; Image of Opium perfume for Yves Saint Laurent; Stage appearances include: Another Country, 1982; The Vortex, 1989; Private Lives; The Milk Train Doesn't Stop Here Anymore; The Picture of Dorian Gray; The Importance of Being Earnest; Films include: Another Country, 1984; Dance With a Stranger, 1985; The Right Hand Man, 1985; Duet for One; Chronicle of Death Foretold, 1987; Hearts of Fire, 1987; Haunted Summer, 1988; The Comfort of Strangers, 1989; Inside Monkey Zetterland; Pret à Porter, 1995; The Madness of King George, 1995; Dunstan Checks In; My Best Friend's Wedding, 1997; A Midsummer's Night's Dream, 1998; B Monkey, 1998; An Ideal Husband, 1999; Inspector Gadget, 1999; The Next Best thing, 2000; Unconditional Love, 2002; The Importance of Being Earnest, 2002; TV includes: Arthur the King; The Far Pavilions, 1982; Princess Daisy, 1983. Publications: Hello Darling, Are You Working?, 1992; The Hairdressers of San Tropez, 1995. Address: c/o ICM, 8942 Wilshire Boulevard, Beverly Hills, CA 90211, USA.

**EVERT Chris(tine) Marie,** b. 21 December 1954, Fort Lauderdale, Florida, USA. Former Lawn Tennis Player. m. (1) J Lloyd, 1979, divorced 1987, (2) A Mill, 1988, 3 sons. Education: High School, Ft Lauderdale. Career: Amateur, 1970-72; Professional, 1972-. Winner of: French Championship, 1974, 1975, 1979, 1980, 1982, 1985, 1986; Wimbledon Singles: 1974, 1976, 1981; Italian Championship: 1974, 1975, 1980; South African Championship: 1973; US Open: 1975, 1976, 1977, 1979, 1980, 1982 (record 100 victories); Colgate Series, 1977, 1978; World Championship, 1979; Played Wightman Cup, 1971-73, 1975-82; Federation Cup, 1977-82; Ranked No 1 in the world for seven years; Won 1309 matches in her career; Holds 157 singles titles and 18 Grand Slam titles. Appointments: President, Women's Tennis Association, 1975-76, 1983-91; Director, President's Council on Physical Fitness & Sports, 1991-; NBC TV sports commentator and host for numerous TV shows; Other: Established Chris Evert Charities, 1989; Owner, Evert Enterprises/IMG, 1989-; Chris Evert Pro-celebrity Tennis Classic, 1989-. Publications: Chrissie (autobiography), 1982; Lloyd on Lloyd (with J Lloyd) 1985. Honours include: International Tennis Hall of Fame, 1995; International Tennis Federation Chartrier Award, 1997; Named by ESPN as One of Top 50 Athletes of the 20th Century, 1999. Address: Evert Enterprises, 7200 W Camino Real, Suite 310 Boca Raton, FL 33433, USA.

**EVTIMOVA Zdravka,** b. 24 July 1959, Pernik, Bulgaria. Literary Translator; Author. m. Todor Georgiev, 2 sons, 1 daughter. Education: BA, American Studies, MA, English and American Studies, St Kiril and Methodius University, Bulgaria. Appointments: Translator, Interpreter, National Institute of Scientific Information, Sofia; Chief of Interpreters

Section, Rare Earth Elements Institute, Bulgarian Academy of Sciences; Chief Expert, English and American Sector Translations, Ministry of Defence. Publications: Books published in Bulgaria: Your Shadow Was My Home (novel), 2000; Thursday (novel), 2003; 3 short story collections; Bitter Sky (short story collection) published in the UK, 2003. Honours: Chudomir Short Story National Award; Anna Kamenova National Literary Award, 1995; Gencho Stoev Short Story Award for a Short Story by a Balkan Author; Best Novel of the Year 2003 for the novel, Thursday; Best Short Story Collection by an established author; Award, MAG Press, San Diego, California. Membership: Bulgarian Writers' Union; Bulgarian PEN; International Organisation of Artists without Frontiers. Address: 36/61 Gagarin Street, 2304 Pernik, Bulgaria. E-mail: zevtimova@yahoo.com

**EXLEY Colin Stewart,** b. 13 February 1926, Leeds, England. Retired Lecturer. m. Mary Averil Wilson, 3 sons. Education: RN Course, 1943, MA, 1947-51, D Phil, Burdett-Coutts Scholar in Geology, 1953-55, Hertford College, Oxford. Appointments: RNVR, 1943 47; RNVSR, 1947-57; RNR, 1957-76; Scientific Officer and Senior Scientific Officer, British Ceramic Research Association, 1951-53, 1955-57; Lecturer and Senior Lecturer, University College of North Staffordshire and Keele University, 1957-85, Fellow of Keele University, 1985-. Publications: About 45 including: Magmatic Differentiation and Alteration in the St Austell Granite, 1959; Hercynian Intrusive Rocks (with M Stone) in Igneous Rocks of the British Isles (editor D S Sutherland), 1982; Igneous Rocks of S W England (with P A Floyd and M T Styles), 1993. Honour: RN Reserve Decoration, 1967. Memberships: Senior Fellow, Geological Society of London; Geologists Association; Ussher Society; Royal Geological Society of Cornwall; Mediterranean Landing Craft Association. Address: 50 Pepper Street, Keele, Newcastle, Staffs ST5 5AQ, England.

**EYIME Ronald Nze,** b. 1 January 1956, Kwale, Nigeria. Optometrist. m. Gloria, 2 sons, 1 daughter. Education: BSc in Optometry, 1982; Doctor of Opthometry, 1995; Fellow, Nigerian College of Optometrists (Public Health Optometry), 2003. Appointments: General Manager, Rodway Opticals Ltd, 1982-86; Managing Optometrist, Tripod Ophthalmics Ltd, 1986-92; Registrar and Chief Executive Officer, Optometrists Registration Board of Nigeria, 1992-. Publications: Contributed many articles to professional journals. Honours: International Optometrist of the Year, 2003; Deputy Director General of the IBC, 2003; Nigerian Sectoral Leadership Award, 2004. Memberships: President of the African Council of Optometry, 2000-04; Rotarian; Governing Board Member, World Council of Optometry. Address: 62 Bode Thomas Street, Suru-Lere, Nigeria

**EZIN Jean-Pierre Onvêhoun,** b. 7 December 1944, Guezin, Benin. University Professor. m. Victoire Akele, 3 sons, 1 daughter. Education: Doctorat de 3e cycle, 1972, Doctorat d'Etat, 1981, University of Lille I, France. Appointments: Lecturer, Catholic University of Lille, France, 1972-73; Lecturer, National University of Benin, 1973-77; Associate Professor, University of Lille I, France, 1978-81; Professor, National University of Benin, 1981-. Publications: At least 20 books, papers and articles on mathematics, mathematical physics and Riemannian geometry. Honours: Officier des Palmes Academiques Françaises; Vice-Chancellor of the National University of Benin, 1990-92. Memberships: American Mathematical Society; Societé Mathématique de France; African Mathematical Union; Senior Associate, Abus Salam International Centre for Theoretical Physics; Lions Clubs International. Address: Institut

de Mathématiques et des Sciences Physiques, IMSP, BP 613,
Porto Novo, Benin. E-mail: jp.ezin@imsp-mac.org

# DICTIONARY OF INTERNATIONAL BIOGRAPHY

## F

**FABIANO Nicola,** b. 9 December 1965, Rome, Italy. Physicist. Education: PhD, Theoretical Physics, University of Perugia, Italy, 1995; DSc, Physics, University of Rome, 1991. Appointments: Researcher, Theoretical Physics, Laboratory Nazionali di Frascati Infn, 1992, University of Perugia, Italy, 1995. Publications: Several articles in professional journals. Honours: Research Scholarship, 1992-94; Patrick Blackett Scholarship, 1994. Address: Via Borgorose 15/E, 00189 Rome, Italy.

**FABRE DE LA RIPELLE Michel,** b. 21 December 1924, Paris, France. Director of Research. m. Marie-Pierre de Bon, 1 son, 1 daughter. Education: Physics and Mathematics, La Sorbonne, 1946; Diploma for Higher Studies, Nuclear Physics and Electronics, Probability and Quantum Mechanics, 1947; PhD, Science, Professor Louis de Broglie, 1956. Appointments: Researcher, National Centre for Scientific Research, 1947-; Postdoctoral studies, Kioto University, Japan, 1961-62; Scientific Attaché, French Embassy, Japan, 1964-68; Director of Research, Institute of Nuclear Physics, University Paris-Sud Orsay, France, 1968-. Publications: Over 70 papers in international scientific journals on few and many body problems. Address: Institute of Nuclear Physics, University Paris-Sud, 91406 Orsay, France.

**FAINLIGHT Ruth (Esther),** b. 2 May 1931, New York, New York, USA. Writer; Poet; Translator; Librettist. m. Alan Sillitoe, 19 November 1959, 1 son, 1 daughter. Education: Colleges of Arts and Crafts, Birmingham, Brighton, UK. Appointment: Poet-in-Residence, Vanderbilt University, USA, 1985, 1990. Publications: Poetry: Cages, 1966; To See the Matter Clearly, 1968; The Region's Violence, 1973; Another Full Moon, 1976; Sibyls and Others, 1980; Climates, 1983; Fifteen to Infinity, 1983; Selected Poems, 1987, 2nd edition, revised, 1995; The Knot, 1990; Sibyls, 1991; This Time of Year, 1994; Sugar-Paper Blue, 1997; Burning Wire, 2002; Visitação: Selected Poems in Portuguese translation, 1995; Encore La Pleine Lune, Selected Poems in French translation, 1997; Poemas, translation of selected poems in Spanish, 2000; Bleue Papier-Sucre, 2000; La Verita Sulla Sibilla, selected poems in Italian translation, 2003. Translations: All Citizens Are Soldiers, from Lope de Vega, 1969; Navigations, 1983; Marine Rose: Selected Poems of Sophia de Mello Breyner, 1988. Short Stories: Daylife and Nightlife, 1971; Dr Clock's Last Case, 1994. Libretti: The Dancer Hotoke, 1991; The European Story, 1993; Bedlam Britannica, 1995. Contributions to: Atlantic Monthly; Critical Quarterly; English; Hudson Review; Lettre Internationale; London Magazine; London Review of Books; New Yorker; Poetry Review; Threepenny Review; Times Literary Supplement. Honours: Cholmondeley Award for Poetry, 1994; Hawthornden Award for Poetry, 1994. Memberships: Society of Authors; PEN; Writers in Prison Committee. Address: 14 Ladbroke Terrace, London W11 3PG, England.

**FAIRBRASS Graham John,** b. 14 January 1953, Meopham, Kent, England. Traveller; Writer; Poet; Painter. Education: BA, Arts, Open University, 1991; Coleg Harlech, 1995-96; Diploma, University of Wales, 1996; Norwich School of Art and Design, 1996-99. Publication: Conquistadors Shuffle Moon, 1989. Contributions to: Poetry Now, 1994; Anthology South East; Parnassus of World Poets, 1994, 1995, 1997; Poetry Club Anthology, vol 1, 1995; Birdsuit, 1997-99; Moon on its Bank, 2004; Ashes at the Moon, 2005. Address: 6 Hornfield Cottages, Harvel, Gravesend, Kent DA13 0BU, England.

**FAIRBROTHER Nicola Kim,** b. 14 May 1970, Henley, England. Journalist. Education: Oaklands Infant and Junior Schools; Edgebarrow Comprehensive School. Appointments: Editor, Kokakids Judo Magazine, 2001-; Journalist, Costa Brava News, Alicante, Spain; Sports Writer, Reading Chronicle; BBC Commentator for Judo, Commonwealth Games, 2002, Olympic Games, Athens, 2004. Publications: Numerous sporting articles and some travel reports for variety of newspapers including The Times, Sunday Times, Telegraph and Guardian. Honours: 6th Dan, British Judo; Junior European Silver Medallist, 1986; Junior European Champion, 1987; European Bronze Medallist, 1990; World Bronze Medallist, 1991; European Champion, 1992; Olympic Silver Medallist, 1992; European Champion, 1993; World Champion, 1993; MBE, 1994; European Player of the Year, 1994; European Silver Medallist, 1994; European Champion, 1995; Olympic 5th Place, 1996. Address: 26 Broom Acres, Sandhurst, Berkshire GU47 8PW, England. E-mail: editor@kokakids.co.uk

**FAIRBURN Eleanor M, (Catherine Carfax, Emma Gayle, Elena Lyons),** b. 23 February 1928, Ireland. Author. m. Brian Fairburn, 1 daughter. Appointments: Past Member, Literary Panel for Northern Arts; Tutor, Practical Writing, University of Leeds Adult Education Centre. Publications: The Green Popinjays, 1962; New edition, 1998; The White Seahorse, 1964, 3rd edition, 1996; The Golden Hive, 1966; Crowned Ermine, 1968; The Rose in Spring, 1971; White Rose, Dark Summer, 1972; The Sleeping Salamander, 1973, 3rd edition, 1986; The Rose at Harvest End, 1975; Winter's Rose, 1976. As Catherine Carfax: A Silence with Voices, 1969; The Semper Inheritance, 1972; To Die a Little, 1972; The Sleeping Salamander, 1973. As Emma Gayle: Cousin Caroline, 1980; Frenchman's Harvest, 1980. As Elena Lyons: The Haunting of Abbotsgarth, 1980; A Scent of Lilacs, 1982. Biographies (as Eleanor Fairburn): Edith Cavell, 1985; Mary Hornbeck Glyn, 1987; Grace Darling, 1988. Membership: Middlesbrough Writers Group, president, 1988, 1989, 1990. Address: 27 Minsterley Drive, Acklam, Middlesbrough, Cleveland TS5 8QU, England.

**FAIRFAX John,** b. 9 November 1930, London, England. Writer, Poet. 2 sons. Appointments: Co-Founder and Member of Council of Management, Arvon Foundation; Director, Phoenix Press, Arts Workshop, Newbury; Poetry Editor, Resurgence. Publications: The Fifth Horseman of the Apocalypse, 1969; Double Image, 1971; Adrift on the Star Brow of Taliesin, 1974; Bone Harvest Done, 1980; Wild Children, 1985; The Way to Write, 1981; Creative Writing, 1989; Spindrift Lp, 1981; 100 Poems, 1992; Zuihitsu, 1996; Poem Sent to Satellite E2F3, 1997; Poem on Sculpture, 1998; Poem in Hologram, 1999; Commissioned poems: Boots Herbal Garden, engraved on glass for several institutes, 1999, 2000-05; Poems in Virtual Reality, 2003, 2004. Contributions to: Most major literary magazines. Membership: The Arvon Foundation, co-founder, 1968. Address: The Thatched Cottage, Eling, Hermitage, Newbury, Berkshire RG16 9XR, England.

**FAITHFULL Marianne,** b. 29 December 1947, Hampstead, London, England. Singer. 1 son. Career: Recording artist, 1964-; Tours, appearances include: UK tour with Roy Orbison, 1965; US tour with Gene Pitney, 1965; Uxbridge Blues and Folk Festival, 1965; Montreux, Golden Rose Festival, 1966; Roger Water's The Wall, Berlin, 1990; Chieftains Music Festival, London, 1991; Acting roles include: I'll Never Forget Whatisname, 1967; Three Sisters, Chekkov, London, 1967; Hamlet, 1970; Kurt Weill's Seven Deadly Sins, St Ann's Cathedral, New York, 1990; Film appearance, Girl On A Motorcycle, 1968. Recordings: Singles include: As Tears Go By; Come And Stay With Me; This Little Bird; Summer Nights; Something

Better/Sister Morphine; The Ballad Of Lucy Jordan; Dreaming My Dreams; Electra, 1999; Albums: Come My Way, 1965; Marianne Faithfull, 1965; Go Away From My World, 1966; Faithfull Forever, 1966; Marianne Faithfull's Greatest Hits, 1969; Faithless, with the Grease Band, 1978; Broken English, 1979; Dangerous Acquaintances, 1981; A Child's Adventure, 1983; Strange Weather, 1987; Blazing Away, 1990; A Secret Life, 1995; 20th Century Blues, 1997; The Seven Deadly Sins, 1998; Vagabond Ways, 1999; Contributor, Lost In The Stars - The Music Of Kurt Weill, 1984; The Bells Of Dublin, The Chieftains, 1992. Publications: Faithfull (autobiography), 1994; Marian Faithfull Diaries, 2002. Honours include: Grammy Nomination, Broken English, 1979. Address: c/o The Coalition Group Ltd, 12 Barley Mow Passage, London, W4 4PH, England. Website: pithuit.free.fr/FAITHFULL

**FAKIOLAS Efstathios Tassos**, b. 26 November 1971, Moscow, Russian Federation (Greek Citizen). Strategy Analyst. m. Eirini Tsoucala, 1 son. Education: BA, International Studies, 1989-93, Master of Arts, International Politics and Security, 1993-96, Athens Panteion University; Master of Arts, International Relations and Strategic Studies, Lancaster University, England, 1994-95; Currently PhD Student, Department of War Studies, King's College, London, England. Appointments: Civil Servant, Finance Department, Social Insurance Fund Organisation for the Employees of the Hellenic Broadcasting Corporation and Tourism, September-November 2002; Strategy Analyst, Strategic Planning Department, Group Strategy Division, Agricultural Bank of Greece, 2002-. Publications: 12 peer-reviewed journal articles include most recently: Security, Strategy and Dialectic Realism: Ontological and Epistemological Issues in Constructing a New Approach to International Politics, 1999; Reflecting on the Relationship Between Security and Military Strategy, 2001; Theories of European Integration: A Neglected Dimension, 2002; Co-author, 1 book chapter; Numerous other articles in journals, periodicals and newspapers. Honours include: NATO Science Fellowships, 1994-95, 1996-99; Several scholarships and grants; 4 Distinctions, Athens Panteion University of Political and Social Sciences, 1989-93; Memorial Diploma, Public Benefit Foundation "Alexander S Onasis", 1995; British International Studies Association Research Award, 1998. Memberships include: International Institute for Strategic Studies; Royal United Services Institute for Defence Studies; International Studies Association; International Political Sciences Association; Academy of Political Science, USA; Hellenic Association of International Law and International Relations. Address: 86 Xanthipou Street, Papagou/Holargos, 155 61, Athens, Greece. E-mail: efakiolas@hotmail.com

**FALCK (Adrian) Colin**, b. 14 July 1934, London, England. Poet; Critic; Educator. (1) 1 daughter, (2) 1 son. Education: BA, Philosophy, Politics and Economics, 1957, BA, Philosophy, Psychology and Physiology, 1959, MA, 1986, Magdalen College, Oxford; PhD, Literary Theory, University of London, 1988. Appointments: Military Service: British Army, Royal Artillery, 1952-54, Royal Air Force (Volunteer Reserve), 1954-65; Lecturer in Sociology, London School of Economics and Political Science, 1961-62; Part-time Lecturer in Philosophy and Education, University of Maryland, European Division, London, 1962-64; Lecturer in Modern Literature, Chelsea/King's College, University of London, 1964-84 Adjunct Professor in Literature, Syracuse University, London Program, Antioch University, London Program, 1985-89; Associate Professor in Literature, York College, Pennsylvania, 1989-99; Editorial: Co-Founder, 1962, Associate Editor, 1965-72, The Review; Poetry Editor, The New Review, 1974-78. Publications: The Garden in the Evening: Poems from the Spanish of Antonio Machado, 1964; Promises (poems), 1969; Backwards into

the Smoke (poems), 1973; Poems Since 1900: An Anthology (editor with Ian Hamilton), 1975; In This Dark Light (poems), 1978; Robinson Jeffers: Selected Poems (editor), 1987; Myth, Truth and Literature: Towards a True Post-Modernism, 1989, 2nd edition, 1994; Edna St Vincent Millay: Selected Poems (editor), 1991; Memorabilia (poems), 1992; Post-Modern Love: An Unreliable Narration (poems), 1997; American and British Verse in the Twentieth Century: The Poetry that Matters (critical history), 2003. Address: 20 Thurlow Road, London NW3 5PP, England.

**FALDO Nick**, b. 18 July 1957, Welwyn Garden City, England. Professional Golfer. m. (1) Melanie, divorced, (2) Gill, divorced, 1 son, 2 daughters, (3) Valerie Bercher. Career: Professional, 1976-; Winner numerous tournaments including: Skol Lager Individual, 1977; Colgate PGA Championship, 1978; Sun Alliance PGA Championship, 1980, 1981; Haig Whisky TPC, 1982; Paco Rabanne Open de France, 1983; Martini International, 1983; Car Care Plan International, 1983, 1984; Lawrence Batley International, 1983; Ebel Euro Masters Swiss Open, 1983; Heritage Classic, US, 1984; Peugeot Spanish Open, 1987; 116th Open Gold Championship, 1987; Peugeot Open de France, 1988, 1989; Volvo Masters, 1988; 2nd, US Open Championships, 1988; Masters Tournament, US, 1989; Volvo PGA Championship, 1989; Dunhill British Masters, 1989; Suntory World Match Play, 1989; 119th Open Golf Championship, 1990; Masters Tournament, US, 1991, 1996; Carroll's Irish Open, 1991, 1992, 1993; 121st Open Golf Championship, 1992; Scandinavian Masters, 1992; 2nd, USPGA Championship, 1992; GA European Masters, 1992; Toyota World Match Play, 1992; Volvo Bonus Pool, 1992; Johnnie Walker Classic, 1993; 2nd, 122nd Open Golf Championship, 1993; Alfred Dunhill Open, 1994; Doral-Ryder Open, US, 1995; Nissan Open, US, 1997; World Cup of Golf, 1998; 5th, US Open (including third round record 66), 2002; 8th 132nd Open Golf Championship, 2003; Team Member: Ryder Cup, 1977, 1979, 1981, 1983, 1985 (winners) 1987 (winners) 1989, 1991, 1993, 1995 (winners), 1997 (winners); Alfred Dunhill Cup, 1985, 1986, 1987 (winning team), 1988, 1991, 1993; World Cup of Golf, 1977, 1991, 1998 (winners). Publications: In Search of Perfection, (with Bruce Critchley), 1995; Faldo - A Swing for Life, 1995. E-mail: nfdo@faldodesign.com

**FALK Heinz**, b. 29 April 1939, St Pölten. Professor Organic Chemistry. m. Rotraud, 1 son. Education: Dr Phil, University of Vienna. Appointments: Assistant, University Vienna, 1966; Post-Doctoral ETH, Zurich, 1971; Habilitation, University of Vienna, 1972; Assistant Professor, Physical Organic Chemistry, 1975; University Professor, Organic Chemistry, University Linz, 1979; Guest Professor, University of Barcelona, 1982; Dean, Science Technical Faculty, University of Linz, 1989-91. Publications: 290 papers in refereed journals; Several patents. Honours include: Loschmidt Medal, 1998, and others. Memberships include: Austrian Academy of Science; Austrian Chemical Society; German Chemical Society; European Society of Photochemistry; American Society of Photochemistry Photobiology; New York Academy of Science; European Academy of Sciences. Address: Institute for Organic Chemistry, Johannes Kepler University Linz, Altenbergerstr 14, A 4040 Linz, Austria. E-mail: heinz@falk.net

**FALKOWSKI Bogdan Jaroslaw**, b. 21 January 1955, Warsaw, Poland. Professor; Researcher. m. Beata Olejnicka, 1 son. Education: Master of Electrical Engineering (Hons), Warsaw University of Technology, Warsaw, Poland, 1974-78; PhD, Electrical and Computer Engineering, Portland State University, Portland, USA, 1986-91. Appointments: Research and Development Engineer, Centre of Research in Information

Systems, Blonie, Poland, 1978-80, Centre of Research in Computer Systems, Warsaw, Poland, 1981-86; Research Assistant, Department of Electrical and Computer Engineering, Portland, Oregon, USA, 1986-92; Professor, School of Electrical and Electronic Engineering, Nanyang Technological University, Singapore, 1992-. Publications: Articles in numerous scientific journals including: IEEE Transactions on Computers; IEEE Transactions on CAD of Integrated Circuits and Systems; IEEE Transactions on Circuits and Systems; IEE Proceedings, Circuits, Devices and Systems; IEE Proceedings, Digital Techniques and Computers; IEE Proceedings, Vision, Image and Signal Processing. Honours: IEEE/ACM Design Automation Conference Award, IEE Hartree Best Paper Award, 2002. Memberships: Senior Member, IEEE; Eta Kappa Nu Electrical Engineering Honor Society; Tau Beta Pi Engineering Honor Society. Address: Nanyang Technological University, School of EEE, Nanyang Avenue, 639798, Singapore, Singapore. E-mail: efalkowski@ntu.edu.sg

**FALLOWELL Duncan Richard,** b. 26 September 1948, London, England. Writer. Education: Magdalen College, Oxford. Publications: Drug Tales, 1979; April Ashley's Odyssey, 1982; Satyrday, 1986; The Underbelly, 1987; To Noto, 1989; Twentieth Century Characters, 1994; One Hot Summer in St Petersburg, 1994; Gormenghast, 1998; A History of Facelifting, 2003. Address: 44 Leamington Road Villas, London W11 1HT, England.

**FALQUE Dominique Louis,** b. 14 August 1951, Marseille, France. Business Advisor. m. Florence Dor, 2 sons, 2 daughters. Education: MBA, Ecole Supérieure des Sciences Economiques et Commerciales. Appointments: Financial Analyst, Allia Doulton, Paris, 1976-81; Controller, Schlumberger, Paris, St Etienne Douala, Buenos Aires, 1981-94, Lexmark, Paris, Orleans, 1995-2001; Business Consultant, Financial Advisor, Coach Owners and Entrepreneurs, Geneva, Switzerland, 2001-. Address: Vuache 1, 1201 Geneva, Switzerland. E-mail: dominique@falque.ch Website: www.falque.ch

**FALZEDER Ernst M,** b. 17 February 1955, Linz, Austria. Psychologist. 1 son, 1 daughter. Education: Maturity Certificate, 1973; Graduate university training in Psychology, Psychopathology and Psychiatry, Faculties of Philosophy and Natural Sciences, University of Salzburg, Austria, 1973-85; PhD, University of Salzburg, 1985; Training as Group Therapist, IPG Salzburg, 1974-76; Psychoanalytic training at the Salzburg Study Group for Psychoanalysis, 1985-. Appointments: Assistant, Psychological Institute, University of Salzburg, 1979-85; Lecturer, Universities of Salzburg and Innsbruck, 1985-; Assistant Professor, Psychological Institute, University of Salzburg, 1986-87; Research Fellowships in Switzerland, USA, include: The Foundation Louis Jeantet for the History of Medicine, Geneva, Switzerland, 1992-97; Woodrow Wilson Center, Washington, DC, 1997-98; Department of History of Science, Harvard University, Cambridge, Massachusetts, 1998-99. Publications: More than 100 including main editor of the correspondence of Sigmund Freud and Sándor Ferenczi, 3 vols, 1993-2000; Editor, Freud/Abraham Correspondence, 2002. Honours include: Gustav Hans Graber-Prize of the International Society for Pre and Perinatal Psychology, 1986; Nomination for Gradiva Award, National Association for the Advancement of Psychoanalysis, 1997. Memberships: Founding and Board member, Austrian Society for Sexological Research, 1979; Member, editorial board, journal Psychoanalyse, 1985-86. Address: Spital am Pyhrn Nr 290, A-4582, Austria.

**FAN Charles Chwei-Lin,** b. China. Economic and Statistical Methodologist. Education: BS, National Kwangsi University,

Kwei-Lin, China, 1947; MS, Montana State University, Bozeman, 1961; PhD, University of Hawaii, Honolulu, USA, 1967. Appointments: Assistant Professor, National Kwangsi University, Kwei-Lin, 1947-49; Sugarcane Farm Economist, Taiwan Sugar Company, 1950-58; Editorial Member, Taiwan Sugar Industry Handbook Compilation Committee, 1951; Associate Professor of Statistics and Mathematics, Southern University, Baton Rouge, Louisiana, USA, 1967-69; Statistician, Economist and Methodologist, Ministry of Treasury and Economics, Government of Ontario, 1970-89; Retired, 1990. Publication: The Collected Essays of Cheng Ying, Taipei, 1985 (Cheng Ying is a pen name of Charles C L Fan). Honours: Distinguished Service Award, Ministry of Economic Affairs, Taiwan, 1956; Exchange Visitor, Institute of International Education, New York, 1959-61; Fellow, Council on Economic and Cultural Affairs, New York, 1959-61; Consultant, Chinese/English Dictionary of Agricultural Economics, England, 1973; World Citizen of the Year, ABI, 2002. Memberships: AAUP, 1969-98; Life Member, AAEA; IAAE, 1970-2004; CAES, 1970-2004. Address: Box 38058, Dixie Mall Post Office, 1250 South Service Road, Mississauga, Ontario L5E 3G3, Canada.

**FANE Julian,** b. 25 May 1927, London, England. Writer. m. Gillian Swire, 6 January 1976. Publications: Morning, 1956; A Letter; Memoir in the Middle of the Journey; Gabriel Young; Tug-of-War; Hounds of Spring; Happy Endings; Revolution Island; Gentleman's Gentleman; Memories of My Mother; Rules of Life; Cautionary Tales for Women; Hope Cottage; Best Friends; Small Change; Eleanor; The Duchess of Castile; His Christmas Box; Money Matters; The Social Comedy; Evening; Tales of Love and War; Byron's Diary; The Stepmother; The Sodbury Crucifix; The Collected Works of Julian Fane, Vols I, II, III, IV and V; The Harlequin Edition of Shorter Writings; Awaiting publication: Damnation, 2004; Games of Chance, 2005; The Time Diaries, 2005; According to Robin, 2006; Odd Woman Out, (in preparation). Honour: Fellow, Royal Society of Literature, 1974. Membership: Society of Authors. Address: Rotten Row House, Lewes, East Sussex BN7 1TN, England.

**FANG Jin-Qing,** b. 11 July 1939, Fu-jian, China. Scientific Researcher. m. 1 son, 1 daughter. Education: Graduate, Department of Physics, Qing-Hua University, Beijing, China, 1958-64; Postdoctoral Fellow, Australian National University and University of Texas at Austin, USA, 1987-90. Appointments: Researcher into atomic energy science and technology, non-linear science, nonlinear complex networks and complexity science with applications including chaos control and synchronisation, China Institute of Atomic Energy, 1964; Research Professor (Fellow), 1987-; Head of the Key Program Projects of the National Natural Science Foundation of China, 2005- Visiting Professor in about 20 universities world-wide, 1990-. Publications include: More than 150 articles and more than 50 Science and EI recorded scientific papers; 10 monographs and textbooks from 1976 including most recently: Taming Chaos and Developing High Technology, 2002; Co-author: Chaos Control-Theory and Applications, 2003. Honours: 10 Awards and Prizes, China include: 2nd Prizes of Progress in Science and Technology in National Defence of China, 1998, 2000, 2002 and first prizes in 2005. Memberships: China Institute of Physics; Chinese Institute of System Science. Address: China Institute of Atomic Energy, PO Box 275-81, Beijing 102413, China. E-mail: fangjq@hotmail.com

**FANG Rong Rémi,** b. 10 August 1958, Ping-Jiang, Hunan, China. Physicist. Education: Graduate, Tsinghua University, 1982; Postgraduate, Institute of High Energy Physics, China, 1985; PhD, Louis Pasteur University, France, 1997. Appointments: Lecturer, University of Science and Technology of China, 1958-88; Visiting Associate Professor, Paris University IV, 1989-91; Visiting Scholar, Centre of Research of Nuclear Physics, Strasbourg, France, 1991-92; Engineer, Computer Software, Aerial Nuclear Irradiation Centre, Strasbourg, France, 1993-. Publications: Several articles in professional journals concerning Rule of Charge Accumulation, and Stability Conditions. Honour: Lifetime Achievement Award, ABI. Memberships: AAAS; New York Academy of Sciences; Fellow, ABI. Address: 1 Rue Du Frankenbourg, 67450 Mundolsheim, France. E-mail: r.fang@aerial-crt.com

**FANTHORPE U(rsula) A(skham),** b. 22 July 1929, Kent, England. Writer; Poet. Education: BA, MA, Oxford University. Appointments: Writer in Residence, St Martin's College, Lancaster, 1983-85; Northern Arts Literary Fellow, Universities of Durham and Newcastle, 1987-88. Publications: Side Effects, 1978; Standing To, 1982; Voices Off, 1984; Selected Poems, 1986; A Watching Brief, 1987; Neck Verse, 1992; Safe as Houses, 1995; Penguin Modern Poets 6, 1996; Double Act (audiobook with R V Bailey), 1997; Poetry Quartets 5 (audiobook), 1999; Consequences, 2000; Christmas Poems, 2002; Queueing for the Sun, 2003; Collected Poems, 2005. Contributions to: Times Literary Supplement; Encounter; Outposts; Firebird; Bananas; South West Review; Quarto; Tribune; Country Life; Use of English; Poetry Review; Poetry Book Society Supplement; Writing Women; Spectator; BBC. Honours: The Queen's Gold Medal for Poetry, 2003; Travelling Scholarship, Society of Authors, 1983; Hawthornden Scholarships, 1987, 1997; Arts Council Writers Award, 1994; Chomondeley Award, Society of Authors, 1995; Honorary DLitt, the West of England, 1995; Hon. Ph.D. Cheltenham & Gloucester College, 2000; CBE, 2001; Honorary Fellow, St Anne's College, Oxford, 2003; Honorary Fellow, Sarum College, Salisbury, 2004. Memberships: PEN; Royal Society of Literature, Royal Society of Arts, fellow. Address: Culverhay House, Wotton-under-Edge, Gloucestershire GL12 7LS, England.

**FARAG Radwan Sedkey,** b. 27 November 1941, Cairo, Egypt. Professor of Biochemistry. m. Fatma Mahmoud El-Shishi, 1 son. Education: BSc, 1963, MSc, 1967, Faculty of Agriculture, Cairo University, Egypt; PhD, St Bartholomew's Hospital Medical College, London University, 1974. Appointments: Demonstrator, 1963-67, Associate Lecturer, 1967-74, Lecturer, 1974-79, Director of Central Laboratory, 1975-95, Associate Professor, 1979-84, Professor of Biochemistry, 1984-, Head of Biochemistry Department, 1988-94, Faculty of Agriculture, Cairo University; Over 40 MSC and 45 PhD students obtained their degrees under his direct supervision. Publications: Author; Chromatographic Analysis, 1990; Lipids, 1991; Physical and Chemical Analysis of Fats and Oils, 1995; Principles of Biochemistry, 1999; Modern Methods of Amino Acid Analysis and Assessment of Protein Quality, 2003. Over 120 papers in prominent journals. Honours: Egyptian State Award, Egyptian Academy of Scientific Research and Technology, 1978, 1984; 20th Century Award Achievement, IBC, 1997. Memberships: National Encyclopedia, Egypt; American Oil Chemists Society; International Association for Cereal Science and Technology; New York Academy of Sciences; American Association for the Advancement of Science; National Committee of Biochemistry and Molecular Biology; Advisory Board of J Drug Res. Address: Biochemistry Department, Faculty of Agriculture, Cairo University, PO 12613, El-Gamma St, Giza, Egypt.

**FARHI Musa Moris,** b. 5 July 1935, Ankara, Turkey. Novelist; Poet. m. Nina Ruth Gould, 2 July 1978, 1 stepdaughter. Education: BA, Humanities, Istanbul American College, 1954; Diploma, Royal Academy of Dramatic Art, London, 1956. Publications: The Pleasure of Death, 1972; Voices Within The

Art: The Modern Jewish Poets, 1980; The Last of Days, 1983; Journey Through the Wilderness, 1989; Children of the Rainbow, 1999; Young Turk, 2004. Contributions to: Menard Press; Men Cards; European Judaism; Modern Poetry In Translation; Frank; Jewish Quarterly; Steaua (Romania); Confrontation (USA); North Atlantic Review (USA); Reflections on the Universal Declaration of Human Rights. Honours: MBE. Memberships: Fellow of Royal Society of Literature; Society of Authors; Writers Guild; PEN. Address: 11 North Square, London NW11 7AB, England.

**FARHI Nicole,** b. 25 July 1946. Fashion Designer. m. David Hare, 1992; 1 daughter with Stephen Marks. Education: Cours Berçot Art School, Paris. Appointments: Designer, Pierre d'Albi, 1968; Founder, French Connection with Stephen Marks, 1973; Former designer, Stephen Marks; Founder and designer, Nicole Farhi, 1983-; Nicole Farhi For Men, 1989-; Opened Nicole's Restaurant, 1994. Honours: British Fashion Award for Best Contemporary Design, 1995, 1996, 1997; FHM Awards Menswear Designer of the Year, 2000; Maxim Awards, British Designer of the Year, 2001. Address: 16 Foubert's Place, London W1F 7PJ, England.

**FARINGDON Charles Michael,** b. 3 July 1937, London, England. Stockbroker. m. Sarah Caroline Askew, 3 sons, 1 daughter. Education: BA, Trinity College, Cambridge. Appointments: Treasurer, National Arts Collection Fund; Commissioner, English Heritage; Chairman, Royal Commission on Historic Monuments of England; Chairman, Ludwig Institute, London Branch; Chairman, Royal Marsden Hospital; Partner, Cazenovic & Co; Chairman, Witan Investment Trust plc; Lord-in-Waiting to H M The Queen; Chairman, Institute of Cancer Research. Address: Buscot Park, Faringdon, Oxon SN7 8BU, England. E-mail: farbuscot@aol.com

**FARMAN Allan George,** b. 26 July 1949, Birmingham, England. Professor of Radiology and Imaging Sciences. m. Taeko Takemori. Education: BDS, 1971; LDSRCS, 1972; PhD, 1977; Dip ABOMR, 1982; EdS, 1983; MBA, 1987; DSc, 1996; Dip JBOMR, 1997. Appointments: Professor, Radiology and Imaging Sciences, School of Dentistry, University Louisville; Clinical Professor, Diagnostic Radiology, University Louisville School of Medicine, 1980-. Publications: 300 science articles, numerous texts and contributions to textbooks; Oral and Maxillofacial Diagnostic Imaging; Editor: Panoramic Imaging News, 2001-. Honours: President of Honour, First Latin-American Regional Meeting on Dentomaxillofacial Radiology, 1996. Memberships: International Association of Dentomaxillofacial Radiology, President, 1994-97; American Academy of Oral and Maxillofacial Radiology, Editor, 1988-95 and 2005-; American Dental Association, Representative to International DICOM Committee, 2001-; Founder, Organiser, International Congress Computed Maxillofacial Imaging, 1995-. Address: c/o School of Dentistry, University of Louisville, Louisville, KY 40292, USA.

**FARR Dennis Larry Ashwell,** b. 3 April 1929, Luton, Bedfordshire, England. Art Historian. m. Diana Pullein-Thompson, 1 son, 1 daughter. Education: BA Hons, 1950, MA, 1956, Courtauld Institute of Art, London University. Appointments: Assistant Witt Librarian, Courtauld, 1952-54; Assistant Keeper, Tate Gallery, 1954-64, Curator, Paul Mellon Collection, Washington DC, 1965-66; Deputy Keeper/Senior Lecturer, Glasgow University Art Collection, 1967-69; Director, Birmingham Museums and Art Gallery, 1969-80; Director, Courtauld Institute Galleries, 1980-93. Publications: William Etty, 1958; Tate Gallery Modern British School Catalogue (2 volumes with M Chamot and M Butlin), 1964; English Art 1870-

1940, 1978; Lynn Chadwick, Sculptor (with Eva Chadwick), 1990, second edition, 1998, third edition, 2005; Francis Bacon, A Retrospective Exhibition, Yale Centre for British Art (with M Peppiatt and S Yard), 1999; Lynn Chadwick Retrospective, Tate Britain, 2003; and many exhibition catalogues and publications for the Courtauld Collections; General Editor, Clarendon Studies in History of Art, 1985-2001. Contributions: Burlington Magazine; Museums Journal; TLS; Apollo; DNB, Oxford DNB. Honours: FRSA, 1971; FMA, 1973; Hon DLitt, Birmingham University, 1981; CBE, 1991. Memberships: Athenaeum, 1971; President, Museums Association, 1980; Chairman, Association of Art Historians, 1983-86; Member, Comité Internationale d'Histoire de l'Art, 1983. Address: Orchard Hill, Swan Barn Road, Haslemere, Surrey GU27 2HY, England.

**FARROW Mia Villiers,** b. 9 February 1945, California, USA. Actress. m. (1) Frank Sinatra, 1966, divorced 1968, (2) André Previn, 1970, divorced 1979, 14 children including 1 son with Woody Allen. Career: Stage debut in The Importance of Being Ernest, New York, 1963, other stage appearances include: The Three Sisters, House of Bernard Alba, 1972-73; The Marrying of Ann Leete, Ivanov, RSC, London, 1976; Romantic Comedy, Broadway, 1979; Films include: Guns at Batasi, 1964; Rosemary's Baby, 1968; John and Mary, Secret Ceremony, 1969; The Great Gatsby, 1973; Full Circle, A Wedding, Death on the Nile, 1978; A Midsummer Night's Sex Comedy, 1982; Broadway Danny Rose, 1984; Hannah and Her Sisters, 1986; Radio Days, 1987; Another Woman, 1988; Oedipus Wrecks, 1989; Alice, Crimes and Misdemeanours, 1990; Husband and Wives, Shadows and Fog, 1992; Widow's Peak, 1994; Miami Rhapsody, 1995; Private Parts, 1997; Reckless, 1995; Coming Soon, 2000; TV appearances include: Peyton Place, 1964-66; Peter Pan, 1975. Publication: What Falls Away (autobiography), 1996. Honours: Academy Award; Best Actress, 1969; David Donatello, 1969; Film Festival Award, 1969; San Sebastian Award. Address: International Creative Management, c/o Sam Cohn, 40 West 57th Street, New York, NY 10019, USA. Website: www.mia-farrow.com

**FATEH Pervez,** b. 6 April 1961, Pakistan. Quality Engineer; Metallurgist. m. Ghazala Shaheen, 2 sons, 1 daughter. Education: BSc, Engineering, Metallurgical and Materials Science, University of Engineering and Technology, Lahore, Pakistan, 1983-88; MSc Marketing, University of Huddersfield, 1997-2000; HND, Mechanical Engineering, Swedish Institute, Pakistan; BTEC Management Studies, Bradford Business School; NVQ3 Customer Service, Liverpool University; Diploma in Computer Science, Parklane College, Leeds; Quality Audit and Environmental Audit Statistical Process Control; Six Sigma; Kaizen; Five "S" and Manufacturing Excellence. Appointments: Production Manager, Steel Division, ITTEFAQ Foundries (Pvt)ltd, Lahore, Pakistan, 1988-96; Quality Engineer, Lexicraft Ltd, Liverpool, 1997-98; Quality Manager and Works Metallurgist, Ellison Circlip Group/Transtechnology (GB)Ltd, 1998-2002; Quality Engineer/Metallurgist, Thyssenkrupp Woodhead Ltd, Leeds, 2002-. Publications: Design and Development of Automobile Piston, 1988; Total Quality Management, A Comparative Study, 1998; The Use of Total Quality Management in Relationship Marketing, 2000. Address: 13 Galloway Lane, Pudsey, Leeds LS28 7UG, England. E-mail: pervezf@yahoo.com

**FAULKS Sebastian,** b. 20 April 1953, Newbury, Berkshire, England. Author; Journalist. m. Veronica Youlten, 1989, 2 sons, 1 daughter. Education: Wellington College; Emmanuel College, Cambridge. Appointments: Reporter, Daily Telegraph newspaper, 1979-83; Feature Writer, Sunday Telegraph, 1983-86; Literary Editor, The Independent, 1986-89; Deputy Editor,

The Independent on Sunday, 1989-90, Associate Editor, 1990-91; Columnist, The Guardian, 1992-, Evening Standard, 1997-99; Mail on Sunday, 1999-2000. Television: Churchill's Secret Army, 2000. Publications: The Girl at the Lion d'Or, 1989; A Fool's Alphabet, 1992; Birdsong, 1993; The Fatal Englishman, 1996; Charlotte Gray, 1998; On Green Dolphin Street, 2001. Address: c/o Aitken and Stone, 29 Fernshaw Road, London, SW10 0TG, England.

**FAULL Margaret Lindsay,** b. 4 April 1946, Sydney, Australia (British and Australian citizen). Chief Executive; Company Secretary. Education: BA (II, I), Archaeology, 1966, Diploma in Education, 1967, Sydney University; MA (Hons), England Language, Macquarie University, 1970; PhD, Archaeology, Leeds University, 1979; MA, Leisure Management, Sheffield University, 1990. Appointments: English/History Teacher, New South Wales, Australia, 1970-71; Sub-Warden, Oxley Hall, University of Leeds, 1972-75; Field Archaeologist, West Yorkshire MCC, 1975-83; Deputy County Archaeologist, West Yorkshire MCC, 1983-85; Project Manager, Thwaite Mills Industrial Museum, 1985-86; Director/Company Secretary, Yorkshire Mining Museum/National Coal Mining Museum for England, 1986-. Publications: Over 50 articles in professional and popular journals; Book, Domesday Book, 30: Yorkshire, 1986. Honours: ILAM Manager of the Year, 1996; Doctor of the University, Bradford University, 1997. Memberships: Fellow, Royal Society of Arts, Manufactures and Commerce; Fellow, Institute of Directors; Affiliate, Institute of Mining, Materials and Metals; Fellow, Institute of Leisure and Amenity Management; Fellow, Society of Antiquaries; Member, Institute of Field Archaeologists. Address: National Coal Mining Museum for England, Caphouse Colliery, New Road, Overton, Wakefield WF4 4RH, England. E-mail: margaret.faull@ncm.org.uk

**FAVRET Eduardo Alfredo,** b. 5 May 1962, Moron, Argentina. Physicist. Education: Licentiate, Physical Sciences, University of Buenos Aires, 1992; PhD, Physical Sciences, Faculty of Sciences, University of Buenos Aires, 1998. Appointments: Assistant Professor and Researcher, Institute of Technology, University of San Martin, National Commission on Atomic Energy; Researcher, Fellowships, National Council on Scientific and Technological Research, Argentina; Postdoctoral Fellowship, German Science Foundation, Saarland University, Germany, 2001-02. Publications: Materials Characterization, 1990, 1991, 2003; Practical Metallography, 1996, 1997, 1999, 2003; Optics and Laser Technology, 1997; Microstructural Science, 1999; Kerntechnik, 2000; Journal of Archaeological Science, 2001; Microscopy and Analysis, 2001, 2002; Microscopy Research and Technique, 2001; Microscopy and Microanalysis, 2002, 2003, 2004; Applied Surface Science, 2004; Microscopy Today, 2004. Honours: 2nd Prize, International Metallographic Contest, 1995; Prize, Metallographic Photography, 1988; Honorable Mention Award, International Metallographic Contest, 2001. Memberships: Argentine Society of Microscopy; American Society for Metals; International Metallographic Society; Microscopy Society of America. Address: Lincoln 831, 1712 Castelar, Argentina. E-mail: favret@cnea.gov.ar

**FAWCETT Peter Ernest Sandford,** b. 25 December 1922, Nottingham, England. Solicitor. m. Berit Kier, 1 son, 1 daughter. Education: MA (Oxon), Oriel College, Oxford. Appointments: War Service: Major, The Buffs attached to the King's African Rifles and Free French Forces; Solicitor; President, Founder, Alliance Française (London), 1983-97; Chairman, British Museum Chinese Ivories Exhibition, 1984; Chairman, Sassoon Chinese Ivories Trust, 1991-; Commissioner for Oaths, Quebec; Chairman of Charities. Honours: Officier, Légion d'Honneur, France; Officier, Ordre National du Mérite, France.

Memberships: Travellers Club; FZS; Oriental Ceramic Society. Address: Travellers Club, 106 Pall Mall, London SW1Y 5EP, England.

**FEAST Michael William,** b. 29 December 1926, Deal, Kent, England. Astronomer. m. Constance Elizabeth Maskew, 1 son, 2 daughters. Education: PhD, Physics, Imperial College, London, 1949. Appointments: NRC Postdoctoral Fellow, Ottawa, Canada, 1949-52; Astronomer, Radcliffe Observatory, Pretoria, 1952-74; South African Astronomical Observatory, 1974-92, Director, 1976-92; Royal Society Visiting Fellow, Cambridge University, 1992-93; Honorary Professor, University of Cape Town, 1983-. Publications: About 350 scientific publications. Honours: Vice-President International Astronomical Union, 1979-85; Associate (Honorary Fellow), Royal Astronomical Society, London, 1980; Gill Medal, Astronomical Association of South Africa, 1983; De Beer Gold Medal, South African Institute of Physics, 1992; DSc, honoris causa, University of Cape Town, 1993. Memberships: South African Academy; Fellow, Royal Society of South Africa; Royal Astronomical Society; Astronomical Society of South Africa. Address: Astronomy Department, University of Cape Town, Rondebosch 7701, South Africa. E-mail: mwf@artemisia.ast.uct.ac.za

**FEDERER Roger,** b. 8 August 1981, Basel, Switzerland. Professional Tennis Player. Career: Started playing as junior in 1995, turned professional 1998. Career Titles/Finals: 12/8. Current ATP Rank: 1. Numerous television appearances and interviews. Honours: Winner of the Allianz Suisse Open Singles, Gstaad Singles, Wimbledon Singles, Halle Singles, Hamburg Singles, Australian Open Singles, Dubai Singles, Indian Wells Singles, 2004; Winner of the Marseille Singles, Dubai Singles, Munich Singles, Halle Singles, Wimbledon Singles, Vienna Singles, Tennis Masters Cup Singles, Miami Doubles (Max Mirny), Vienna Doubles (Yves Allegro), 2003. Address: Oberwil, Switzerland.

**FEDOROV Victor,** b. 12 March 1947, Krasnogrosk, Pskov region, Russia. Economist. m. Galina Federova, 1 son, 1 daughter. Education: N A Voznesenskiy Financial and Economic Institute, Leningrad, 1971. Appointments: Deputy, Pskov Regional Soviets, 1968-71; Lecturer, Political Economy, North-Western Polytechnical Institute, 1975-76; Deputy Editor in Chief, Selskaya Molodezh (Rural Youth) journal, 1980-85; Editor in Chief, Director, Molodaya Gvardia publishing house, 1985-97; First Deputy Director, 1997, Director, 1998, Director General, 2001, Russian State Library. Publications: Articles in professional journals; Numerous books. Honours: Medal for Heroic Labour, 1970; Medal for Labour Merit, 1971; Order of the Friendship of the Peoples, 1985; 850th Anniversary of Moscow Medal, 1997; Chinese Medal of Friendship, 2001. Memberships: Member, Council of Workers of Culture, Science and Arts at the Ministry of Foreign Affairs of Russian Federation; Member, Co-ordination Bureau of Library Assembly of Eurasia, 1998; Member, Permanent Committee of International Federation of Library Associations on National Libraries, 1999; Member, Conference of European National Libraries, 1999; Member, Council on Culture and Arts at the President of Russian Federation, 2001; Member, Council Rumyantsev Society of Friends of the Library; Member, editorial board of professional journals, Bibliotekovedenie and Biblioteka; Member, editorial board of Russian Orthodox Church Encyclopaedia. Address: Vozdvizhenka 3/5, Moscow 119019, Russia.

**FEHM Tanja,** b. 23 April 1971, Nuremberg, Germany. Medical Doctor. Education: MD, Medical School, Erlangen, Germany, 1990-97; Postdoctoral Fellow, Adjunct Assistant Professor, University of Texas, Southwestern Medical School, Dallas,

Texas, USA, 1999-2001 Appointments: Clinical Researcher, University of Tuebingen, Germany, 2001-; Adjunct Assistant Professor, Cancer Immunobiology Center, University of Texas, Southwestern Medical School, Dallas, Texas, USA, 2001-. Publications: Original papers in medical journals: Breast Cancer Research and Treatment; Clinical Cancer Research; Oncology; Tumor Biology; Journal of Clinical Oncology. Honours: Poster Prize, German Cancer Society, 2002; Grantee, German Research Society. Memberships: AACR; GMSD. Address: Braunsbacher Str 20, 80765 Fuerth, Germany. E-mail: tanja.fehm@t-online.de

**FEILER Jo Alison,** b. 16 April 1951, Los Angeles, California, USA. Artist-Photographer. Education: University of California, Los Angeles, California; Art Center College of Design, Los Angeles, California. BFA, 1973, MFA, 1975, California Institute of the Arts, Valencia, California. Career: Assistant Director, Frank Perls Gallery, Beverly Hills, California, 1969-70; Photography Editor, Coast Environment Magazine, Los Angeles, California, 1970-72; Art Director, Log/An Inc, Los Angeles, California, 1975-85; Special projects: De Paulo Health Plan, Los Angeles, Annual Report, 1971; Still Photographer, Hawk Films Ltd, Borehamwood, England, 1974; Still Photographer, Warner Brothers Films, London, England, 1974-75; Publicity Photographer, Warner Brothers Records Inc., Burbank, California, 1975; Still Photographer, CRM/McGraw-Hill Productions, Santa Monica California, 1977-79; Commissioned by MCA Inc., to create a photographic portfolio depicting behind the scenes operations at Universal Studios, 1983; Solo exhibitions: Institute of Contemporary Art, London, England, 1975; California Institute of the Arts, Valencia, California, 1975; NUAGE, Los Angeles, California, 1978; Susan Harder Gallery, New York City, 1984; Group exhibitions, 1975-, include: The Museum of Fine Arts, Houston, Texas, 1983; Susan Harder Gallery, New York City, 1984, 1985; Musée de la Photographie, Port Sarrazine Mougins, France, 1993; Santa Barbara Museum of Art, Santa Barbara, California, 1993; Works in permanent collections including: National Portrait Gallery, London; Victoria and Albert Museum, London; The Metropolitan Museum of Art, New York; The Museum of Modern Art, New York City; Los Angeles Count Museum of Art; International Museum of Photography, Rochester, New York; Santa Barbara Museum of Art; Oakland Museum; Museum of Fine Arts, Houston; Smithsonian Institution, Washington, DC; Bioblioteque Nationale, Paris; Musée D'Art Moderne De La Ville de Paris; Fondation Vincent Van Gogh, Arles, France; Works in many private collections. Publications: Works featured in: Books: Portfolio One, Museum Edition Portfolio, 1976; Women on Women, 1978; The Nude 80 (France), 1980; Numerous articles in journals and magazines. Honours: Certificate of Art Excellence, Los Angeles County Museum of Art, 1968; Scholarship Grant (Photography), California Institute of the Arts, 1974; Cash Award, 2nd All California Photography Show, Laguna Beach Museum of Art, 1976. Memberships: Royal Photographic Society of Great Britain; The Friends of Photography, San Francisco, California.

**FEILITZEN Maria Cecilia von,** b. 26 September 1945, Stockholm, Sweden. Scientific Co-ordinator; Senior Researcher; Lecturer. Education: BA, 1969, PhD, 1971, Stockholm University. Appointments: Researcher, Swedish Broadcasting Corporation, 1964-96; Senior Researcher, Department of Journalism, Media and Communication, Stockholm University, 1981-2002; Senior Researcher and Lecturer, 2002-, Head of Department, 2003-, Media and Communication Studies, University College of Södertörn; Scientific Co-Ordinator, The International Clearinghouse on Children, Youth and Media, Nordicom, Göteborg University, 1997-; President,

Member Board of Directors, Association for Swedish Media and Communication Science; Examiner, Board of Films for Children and Young People, Swedish Film Institute, 1983-88; Head of Centre for Mass Communication Research, Stockholm University, 1990-93; Expert Member, The Media Council, The Swedish Ministry of Culture, 1991-; Member, Board of Directors, Swedish National Board of Film Classifications, 2000-; Co-Editor, several international journals on media and communication. Publications: About 175 scientific articles, reports and books in the field of media and communications. Memberships: International Association for Media and Communication Science; Association For Swedish Media And Communication Science; Amnesty International. Address: Media and Communication Studies, University College of Södertörn, 14189 Huddinge, Sweden.

**FEKETE John,** b. 7 August 1946, Budapest, Hungary. Professor of English and Cultural Studies; Writer. Education: BA, Honours, English Literature, 1968, MA, English Literature, 1969, McGill University; PhD, Cambridge University, 1973. Appointments: Visiting Assistant Professor, English, McGill University, Montreal, Quebec, 1973-74; Associate Editor, Telos, 1974-84; Visiting Assistant Professor, Humanities, York University, Toronto, Ontario, 1975-76; Assistant Professor, 1976-78, Associate Professor, 1978-84, Professor, English, Cultural Studies, 1984-, Trent University, Peterborough, Ontario. Publications: The Critical Twilight: Explorations in the Ideology of Anglo-American Literary Theory from Eliot to McLuhan, 1978; The Structural Allegory: Reconstructive Encounters With the New French Thought, 1984; Life After Postmodernism: Essays on Culture and Value, 1987; Moral Panic: Biopolitics Rising, 1994. Contributions to: Canadian Journal of Political and Social Theory; Canadian Journal of Communications; Science-Fiction Studies. Address: 1818 Cherryhill Road, Peterborough, Ontario K9K 1S6, Canada.

**FELBER Ewald,** b. 24 March 1947, Vienna, Austria. Professor, Musician, Composer. m. Elfriede Halmschlager, 1 son. Education: Music Teacher, University of Music, Vienna, 1976; Primary School Teacher, State College, Vienna, 1983; Doctor Phil, Musicology, University of Vienna, 1993; Diploma, Summer Course, University of Santiago de Compostela, Spain, 1980. Appointments: Guitar Teacher, High School, Vienna, 1973-81; Professor, State College of Teacher Education, Vienna, 1981-; Concert Activities, 1970-; Visiting Professor at various foreign universities. Publications: Book: Klangfarben zur Musik von Ewald Felber, 1998; Musical Notes (own compositions), 2004; Records and CDs. Honours: Professor, 1983; Oberstudienrat, 1998; Winner, Composing Competition, 2003. Memberships: Board Member, Vienna International Summer Course for New Music; AKM (Authors, Composers and Music Editors). Address: Rosentalgasse 5-7/2/6, A-1140 Vienna, Austria. E-mail: fee@pabw.at

**FELBER Sonja Veronika,** b. 21 March 1965, St Pölten. Mechanical Engineer. Education: E Grad, University Technology, Vienna, 1992; DSc, 1994. Appointments: Research Scientist, OMV Vienna, Austria, 1991-92; Assistant, 1993-2001, Professor, 2002-, University of Technology, Vienna. Publications: New Findings in Crack-Arrest, Test of Heat Affected Zones, Test Methods, CTOD Tests, Pipeline Steels, Pressure Vessel Steels, TM Steels; Simulation of Heat Affected Zones, Building of Pipelines. Memberships: Austrian Welding Foundation; Austrian Iron and Steel Institute; IIW. Address: TVFA, E 030, Institute for Materials Research and Testing, Vienna University of Technology, A-1040 Vienna, Karlspl 13, Austria.

**FELDMAN Anthony,** b. 27 November 1953, South Africa. Architect and Interior Designer. Education: Architectural Association DIP AA, 1978; RIBA (Part 3), 1981. Appointments: Principal, Anthony Feldman, Architects and Interior Designers, 1983-; Completed projects in UK, USA, Europe and Asia. Publications: Interior Elite; Terence Conran's House Book; House and Garden Magazine; Design Magazine; Casa Vogue. Memberships: RIBA; IIDA; BIDA. Address: 18 Hertford Street, Mayfair, London W1J 7RT, England.

**FELDMAN Keith Stuart,** b. 29 July 1943, London, England. Actuary. m. Teresa Ann Wallace, 1 son, 1 daughter. Education: BSc (Special), 1st Class Honours, Mathematics, Imperial College of Science and Technology, University of London; PhD, Nuclear Physics, 1965. Appointments: Research Officer, Central Electricity Generating Board, 1965-67; Operations Research Officer, International Publishing Corporation, 1967-69; Founder, Inter-Bond Services (Merged with Datastream Plc, 1978), 1969-81; Director, W I Carr (stockbroking subsidiary of Banque Indosuez; formerly Partner: Galloway & Pearson), 1981-93; Research Actuary, Robert Fleming & Co (Investment Bankers), 1993-98; Independent Actuary, Hazell Carr Plc, 1999-. Publications: Articles as sole author and co-author in professional journals. Memberships: Fellow, Institute of Actuaries, 1977; Member of the Stock Exchange, 1984; Fellow, Securities Institute, 1992. Address: Skybreak, The Warren, Radlett, Hertfordshire WD7 7DU, England. E-mail: keith.feldman@hazellcarr.com

**FELDMAN Paula R,** b. 4 July 1948, Washington, District of Columbia, USA. Professor of English; Writer. Education: BA, Bucknell University, 1970; MA, 1971, PhD, 1974, Northwestern University. Appointments: Assistant Professor, English, 1974-79, Associate Professor, English, 1979-89, Professor, English, 1989-, Director, Graduate Studies in English, 1991-93; C Wallace Martin Professor of English, 1999-, Louise Frye Scudder, Professor of Liberal Arts, 2000-, University of South Carolina, Columbia. Publications: The Microcomputer and Business Writing (with David Byrd and Phyllis Fleishel), 1986; The Journals of Mary Shelley (editor with Diana Scott-Kilvert), 2 volumes, 1987; The Wordworthy Computer: Classroom and Research Applications in Language and Literature (with Buford Norman), 1987; Romantic Women Writers: Voices and Countervoices (editor with Theresa Kelley), 1995; British Women Poets of the Romantic Era: An Anthology, 1997; A Century of Sonnets: The Romantic Era Revival 1750-1850 (Editor with Daniel Robinson), 1999; Records of Woman, (Editor), 1999. Contributions to: Papers of the Bibliographical Society of America, 1978; Studies in English Literature, 1980; Approaches to Teaching Shelley's Frankenstein, 1990; Blake: An Illustrated Quarterly, 1993; Keats-Shelley Journal, 1997; New Literary History, 2002. Address: Department of English, University of South Carolina, Columbia, SC 29208, USA.

**FELLGETT Peter Berners,** b. 11 April 1922, Ipswich, Suffolk, England. University Research and Teaching. m. Janet Mary Briggs, 1 son, 2 daughters. Education: The Leys, Cambridge; Cambridge University. Appointments: Senior Assistant Observer, The Observatories, Cambridge University; PSO, Royal Observatory, Edinburgh; Professor of Cybernetics, University of Reading; Emeritus Professor. Publications: Around 100 articles in learned literature. Honours: Fellow, Royal Society. Memberships: FRS; FRSE; Fellow, Royal Astronomy Society; Fellow, IEEE. Address: Little Brightor, St Kew Highway, Bodmin PL30 3DV, England.

**FELLOWES (KITCHENER-FELLOWES) Julian Alexander,** b. 17 August 1949, Cairo, Egypt. Writer; Actor,

Lecturer; Producer. m. Emma Kitchener, 1 son. Education: Magdalene College, Cambridge; Webber Douglas Academy of Dramatic Art; Repertory Theatre, Northampton and Harrogate. Career: Theatre: West End début, A Touch of Spring by Sam Taylor, Comedy Theatre; Futurists by Dusty Hughes, Royal National Theatre; Also played at: the Criterion; the Gielgud, the Vaudeville; TV: Lord Killwillie, The Monarch of the Glen; 2nd Duke of Richmond, Aristocrats; Our Friends in the North; For the Greater Good; Dirty Tricks; Sharpe's Regiment; Films: Shadowlands with Anthony Hopkins; Damage with Jeremy Irons; Place Vendome with Catherine Deneuve; Tomorrow Never Dies with Pierce Brosnan; Numerous lectures from Naples, Florida to Venice, Italy; Director and writer, Separate Lives, starring Emily Watson, Tom Wilkinson and Rupert Everett, 2005; TV Scripts: Little Lord Fauntleroy; The Prince and the Pauper (also producer); Screenplays include: Gosford Park directed by Robert Altman; Vanity Fair starring Reese Witherspoon for Focus Films; Piccadilly Jim by P G Wodehouse starring Sam Rockwell; Book for new stage musical version of Mary Poppins at the Prince Edward Theatre, 2004;. Publications: Script for Gosford Park; Novel: Snobs, 2004; Book of children's stories, forthcoming, 2006. Honours: International EMMY for Little Lord Fauntleroy, 1995; BAFTA nomination for The Prince and the Pauper, 1997; Best Screenplay, New York Critic's Circle and National Film Critics, 2001, Screen Writer of the Year, ShoWest (organisation of American Film Distributors), 2001, Writers Guild Award for Best Original Screenplay, 2001, Academy Award (Oscar), Best Original Screenplay, 2001, all for Gosford Park; Medal of Excellence, The Walpole Group (UK). Address: c/o ICM Oxford House, 76 Oxford Street, London W1D 1BS, England.

**FELLS Ian,** b. 5 September 1932, Sheffield, England. Professor of Energy Conversion. m. Hazel Denton Scott, 4 sons. Education: MA, PhD, Trinity College, Cambridge, 1952-58. Appointments: Lecturer, Chemical Engineering, Sheffield University, 1958-62; Reader, Fuel Science, Durham University, 1962-75; Professor of Energy Conversion, Newcastle University, 1975-88; Chairman, New and Renewable Energy Centre, Blyth, Northumberland, 2002-05; Former Science Adviser, World Energy Council; Special adviser to select committees in House of Lords and House of Commons; Served on several Cabinet and Research Council committees; Former Energy Adviser to the European Union and European Parliament; Made over 500 radio and TV programmes including: The Great Egg Race, Take Nobody's World for It (with Carol Vorderman) and Murphy's Law. Publications include: UK Energy Policy Post Privatisation, 1991; World Energy 1923-1998 and beyond; Turning Point. Independent Review of UK Energy Policy; More than 200 articles. Honours: Royal Society Faraday Medal and Prize, 1993; Melchett Medal, Energy Institute, 1999; Collier Memorial Medal, Institute of Chemical Engineers and Royal Society, 1999; CBE, 2000. Memberships: Fellow, Royal Academy of Engineering; Fellow, Royal Society of Edinburgh; Fellow, Energy Institute; Fellow, Institution of Chemical Engineers. Address: 29 Rectory Terrace, Newcastle upon Tyne, NE3 1YB, England.

**FENG Lida,** b. 23 November 1925, Beijing, China. Medical Doctor; Professor. m. Luo Yuanzheng, 1 son. Education: Chee-Lou University, 1944-46; University of California, Berkeley, 1946-48; College of the Pacific, 1949-55; MD, Leningrad, Russia. Appointments: Professor, Immunology, 1955-58; Medical Doctor, Professor, Chinese Science Academy, 1955-72; Medical Doctor, Professor, Navy General Hospital, 1972-. Publications: Numerous articles in professional medical journals. Address: Xibianmenwai Dajie 10-7-41, Beijing 100045, China.

**FERGUS-THOMPSON Gordon,** b.9 March 1952, Leeds, England. Concert Pianist. Education: Royal Manchester College of Music. Career: Concert pianist; Debut, Wigmore Hall, 1976; Performed as a soloist with orchestras including: The Philharmonia; English Chamber Orchestra; City of Birmingham Symphony Orchestra; Royal Liverpool Philharmonic; Halle Orchestra; Bournemouth Symphony Orchestra; BBC Symphony Orchestra; Over 200 BBC Radio 3 recitals; Toured extensively throughout Europe as recitalist and soloist with the Göteborg Symphony Orchestra and the Residente Orchestra of the Hague, also Australia, Far East, South Africa and USA; Professor of Piano, Royal College of Music, 1996-. Recordings include: The Rachmaninoff Sonatas, 1987; Balakirev and Scriabin Sonatas, 1987; Complete Works of Debussy (5 volumes), 1989; Complete Works of Scriabin (Volume 1 - Sonatas 4, 5, 9 and 10 and Studies Op. 42, 1992; Rachmaninoff's Etudes-Tableaux, 1990; Bach Transcriptions, 1990; Complete Works of Ravel (2 volumes), 1992; Scriabin (Volume 2 - Sonatas 2 and 3 and Studies Op 8), 1994; Scriabin (Volume 3 - Preludes Op 2 - 17), 1994; Headington Piano Concerto, 1997; Scriabin (Volume 4 Complete Mazurkas), 2000; Scriabin (Volume 5 - Preludes Op. 22 - 74, 5 Impromptus), 2001. Honours: Calouste Gulbenkian Fellowship, 1978; Winner, Solo Instrumental Section, Music Retailers' Association Awards, 1991; Winner, Solo Instrumental Section, MRA Awards, 1992. Address: 12, Audley Road, London NW4 3EY, England.

**FERGUSON Alexander Chapman (Sir),** b. 31 December 1941, Glasgow, Scotland. Football Club Manager. m. Catherine Holding, 1966, 3 sons. Appointments: Footballer, Queen's Park, 1958-60, St Johnstone, 1960-64, Dunfermline Athletic, 1964-67, Glasgow Rangers, 1967-69, Falkirk, 1969-73, Ayr Utd, 1973-74; Manager, East Stirling, 1974, St Mirren, 1974-78, Aberdeen, 1978-86, Scottish National Team (assistant manager), 1985-86, Manchester Utd, 1986- (winners FA Cup 1990, 1994, 1996, 1999, 2004; European Cup Winners' Cup, Super Cup, 1991; FA Premier League Championship 1992/93, 1993/94, 1995/ 94, 1996/97, 1998/99, 1999/2000, 2000/01, 2002/03; League and FA Cup double 1994 and 1996 (new record); Champions League European Cup, 1999. Publications: A Light in the North, 1984; Six Years at United, 1992; Just Champion, 1993; A Year in the Life, 1995; A Will to Win, 1997; Managing My Life: My Autobiography, 1999; The Unique Treble, 2000. Honours include: KBE, 1999; CBE; Voted Best Coach in Europe, UEFA Football Gala, 1999; Freeman, Cities of Aberdeen, Glasgow and Manchester. Address: c/o Manchester United Football Club, Old Trafford, Manchester M16 0RA, England.

**FERGUSON James Edward, II,** b. 25 October 1951, Los Angeles, California, USA. Professor. m. Lynn, 3 sons. Education: MD, Bowman Gray School of Medicine, 1973-77; Internship, San Francisco, 1977-78; Residency, Stanford University School of Medicine, 1978-80; Chief Resident, Bowman Gray School of Medicine, 1980-81; Postdoctoral Fellowship, Stanford University School of Medicine, 1982-84. Appointments: Clinical Faculty, Bowman Gray School of Medicine, 1981-82; Assistant Professor, Stanford University School of Medicine, 1984-87; Assistant Professor, University of Virginia School of Medicine, 1987-90; Associate Professor, University of Virginia School of Medicine, 1990-96; Professor, University of Virginia School of Medicine, 1996-2002; The John W Greene, Jr. Professor and Chair, Department of Obstetrics and Gynecology, University of Kentucky, 2002-. Publications: Numerous articles, books, reports. Honours: Elected fellow, American College of Obstetrician and Gynecologists; Listed in several who's who publications; Senior Member, American Institute of Ultrasound Medicine. Memberships include: American Medical Association; Society for Maternal-Fetal Medicine; American Association for the Advancement of Science; American Physiological Society; Society for Gynecological Investigation. Address: Department of Obstetrics and Gynecology, 800 Rose Street, University of Kentucky College of Medicine, Lexington, KY 40536, USA.

**FERGUSON Kenneth Adie,** b. 6 April 1921, Sydney, Australia. m. Helen Viner McVicar, 2 sons, 3 daughters. Education: BVSc, 1942; PhD, 1951. Appointments: Research Scientist, CSIRO, 1947-73; Chairman, Animal Research Laboratories, CSIRO, 1973-78; Director, Institute of Animal and Food Sciences, CSIRO, 1978-86; Consultant, Peptide Technology Ltd, Sydney, Copenhagen, Cambridge, 1986-93. Publications: Articles in professional journals including research on endocrinology and nutrition of wool growth, isolation and characterisation of pituitary hormones, foetal development of immunity to skin grafts, immunological enhancement of growth hormone action, protection of dietary nutrients against microbial degradation in rumen. Honours: Fellowships, Australian College of Veterinary Scientists, 1974, Australian Academy of Technological Sciences and Engineering, 1976. Memberships: Endocrine Society of Australia (President 1972-74); Society for Endocrinology, England; Australian Society of Animal Production; Australian Biochemical Society; Australian Physiological and Pharmacological Society; Australian Veterinary Association. Address: Compton, 595 Captain's Flat Road, Carwoola, NSW 2620, Australia.

**FERGUSON Mark William James,** b. 11 October 1955, United Kingdom. Professor. 3 daughters. Education: BSc, 1st Class Honours, Anatomy, 1976, BDS, 1st Class Honours, Dentistry, 1978, PhD, Anatomy, 1982, Queen's University, Belfast. Appointments include: Lecturer in Anatomy, Queen's University, Belfast, 1979-84; Head of Department of Basic Dental Sciences, 1984-86, Professor, School of Biological Sciences, 1986-, Head of Department of Cell and Structural Biology, 1986-92, Dean School of Biological Sciences, 1994-96, University of Manchester; Founder, Chairman and Chief Executive Officer, Manchester Biotechnology Limited and Manchester Incubator Building Company Limited, 1997-99; Co-Founder, Director and Chief Executive Officer, Renovo Limited, 2000-. Publications: Books: The Structure, Development and Evolution of Reptiles, 1984; Crocodiles & Alligators: an Illustrated Encyclopaedic Survey by International Experts, 1989; Cleft Lip & Palate: Long Term Results & Future Prospects, 1990; Egg Incubation, Its Effects on Embryonic Development in Birds and Reptiles, 1991; Gray's Anatomy (38th edition), The Structure Development and Evolution of Teeth, 2000; Author and co-author of more than 300 papers and book chapters. Honours include: Colyer Prize, Royal Society of Medicine, 1980; Alan J Davies Achievement Award, American Dental Association, 1981; Conway Medal, Royal Academy of Medicine in Ireland, 1985; Darwin Lecturer, British Association for the Advancement of Science; President's Medal British Association of Oral and Maxillofacial Surgeons, 1990; JJ Pindborg International Prize, 1996; Broadhurst Lecture, Harvard Medical School, 1996; CBE, 1999; International Association for Dental Research Craniofacial Biology Award, 2000; Honorary Doctor of Medical Sciences, Queen's University, Belfast, 2002. Memberships: FFDRCSI, 1990; FDSRCSEd, 1992; FMedSci, 1998; Chairman, Health and Life Sciences Panel, UK Government Technology Foresight Programme; Secretary, European Tissue Repair Society; President, Medical Section, British Association for the Advancement of Science; President, Craniofacial Society; Member: Committee on Safety of Medicine Biologicals Sub Group, 1999-; Genome Valley Steering Group, 2000-. Address: Faculty of Life Sciences, University of Manchester, Stopford Building, Manchester M13 9PT, England.

**FERGUSON Robert Thomas,** b. 2 June 1948, Stoke on Trent, England. Writer. m. 3 April 1987. Education: BA, University College, London, 1980. Publications: Enigma: The Life of Knut Hamsun, 1987; Henry Miller: A Life, 1991; Henrik Ibsen: A New Biography, 1996; The Short Sharp Life of T E Hulme, 2002. Contributions to: Best Radio Drama, 1984; Best Radio Drama, 1986. Honours: BBC Methuen Giles Cooper Awards, 1984, 1986; J G Robertson Prize, 1985-87. Address: Bygdoy Allé 63B, 0265 Oslo, Norway.

**FERNANDEZ Mary Joe,** b. 19 August 1971, Dominican Republic. Tennis Player. m. Tony Godsick, 2000. Career: Ranked No 1 USA, 1984; Turned professional, 1986; Reached quarter-finals of French open, 1986, quarter-finals, Geneva, 1987, semi-finals Eastbourne, 1988, semi-finals, French Open, 1989, runner up to Graf in singles and runner up with Fendick in doubles, Australian Open, 1990; Reached semi-finals at Wimbledon and Australian Open, Italian Open, 1991; Runner-up Australian open, 1992; Won Bronze Medal in singles and Gold in doubles with G Fernandez, Olympic Games, 1992; Reached semi-finals US Open, 1992; Reached semi-finals Italian Open, quarter-finals Australian Open, 1993; Won singles title, Strasbourg, 1994; Winner, (with Davenport) French Open Doubles, 1996; Winner doubles, Hilton Head, Carolina, 1997, Madrid, 1997, won singles title German Open, 1997; Member, US Federal Cup Team, Atlantic City, 1991, 1994-99; Spokesperson for Will to Win Scholarship Programme, 1998; Retired, 2000. Publication: Mary Joe Fernandez (with Melanie Cole).

**FERNGREN Gary Burt,** b. 14 April 1942, Bellingham, Washington, USA. Professor of History. m. Agnes, 3 daughters. Education: BA, 1964, MA, 1967, PhD, 1973. Appointments: Assistant Professor of History, 1970-78, Associate Professor, 1978-84, Professor, 1984-, Oregon State University. Publications: General Editor, The History of Science and Religion in the Western Tradition: An Encyclopaedia; Co-Editor, Samuel Kottek et al, From Athens to Jerusalem; Editor, Science and Religion: A Historical Introduction. Honours: Fellowships, National Endowment for the Humanities, Canada Council, College of Physicians of Philadelphia, Ben Gurion University, Israel. Memberships: International Society of the History of Medicine, Associate General Secretary, (formerly Vice President); American Osler Society; American Association for the History of Medicine. Address: 2040 NW 23rd Street, Corvallis, OR 97330, USA.

**FERRARIS Giovanni,** b. 20 March 1937, Prarolo, Italy. Crystallographer. m. Margherita, 2 sons. Education: Laurea in Physics, 1960, Libera Docenza, DSc equivalent, in Crystallography, 1969, University of Turin. Appointments include: Currently Full Professor of Crystallography, Faculty of Sciences, University of Turin; Doctor Honoris Causa, University of Bucharest, Romania and Darmstadt, Germany. Publications: About 200 articles in mineralogical crystallography and crystal chemistry; 1 monograph, 2004. Honours: Plinius Medal, SIMP; Tartufari Prize, Accademia dei Lincei. Membership: Russian Academy of Natural Sciences. Address: Dipartimento di Scienze Mineralogiche e Petrologiche, Università di Torino, Via Valperga Caluso 35, I-10125 Torino, Italy. E-mail: giovanni.fe rraris@unito.it

**FERREIRA Hendrik,** b. 17 July 1954, Germiston, South Africa. Professor. m. Hester Susanna Potgieter. Education: BSc, Electrical Engineering, 1976, MSc, Electronic Engineering, 1978, DSc, Engineering, 1980, University of Pretoria; Professional Engineer Registration, Engineering Council of South Africa, 1982. Appointments: Postdoctoral Study, Linkabit Corporation, San Diego, USA, 1980-81; Consulting Engineer,

GH Marais & Partners, Pretoria, South Africa, 1981-83; Senior Lecturer, 1983-84, Associate Professor, 1985-89, Professor, 1989-, Rand Afrikaans University, South Africa. Publications: Numerous papers and articles in professional journals; Contributions in books; Book reviews. Honours: Presidential Award for Young Investigators, Foundation for Research Development, 1990-93. Memberships: IEEE; SAIEE; AMS; PSA; Fellow, PSSA. Address: Box 984, Melville 2109, South Africa. E-mail: hcf@ing.rau.ac.za

**FERRIGNO Pietro Camillo,** b. 6 February 1962, Bergamo, Italy. Therapist. Education: Black belt of Karate, Milan, 1972; 5th year of Pianoforte, Bergamo, 1979; Classic Maturity Diploma, Treviglio, 1982; Some examinations, Medical Faculty of Milan; Masseur's Certificate (Classical Massage-Shiatsu), Milan, 1995. Appointment: Dott. Commander of Justice of Sovereign Order of St John of Jerusalem (Knights of Malta), Malta, 2003. Honours: Nominations for various awards, American Biographical Institute, 2004-2005; Listed in Who's Who publications and biographical dictionaries. Address: Via Ing Grossi 5, 24047 Treviglio (BG), Italy.

**FERRIS Paul (Frederick),** b. 15 February 1929, Swansea, Wales. Writer. Publications: A Changed Man, 1958; The City, 1960; Then We Fall, 1960; The Church of England, 1962; A Family Affair, 1963; The Doctors, 1965; The Destroyer, 1965; The Nameless: Abortion in Britain Today, 1966; The Dam, 1967; Men and Money: Financial Europe Today, 1968; The House of Northcliffe, 1971; The New Militants, 1972; The Detective, 1976; Talk to Me about England, 1979; Richard Burton, 1981; A Distant Country, 1983; Gentlemen of Fortune, 1984; Children of Dust, 1988; Sex and the British, 1993; Caitlin, 1993; The Divining Heart, 1995; Dr Freud: A Life, 1997; Dylan Thomas: The Biography, 1999; Infidelity, 1999; New Collected Letters of Dylan Thomas, 2000; Cora Crane, 2003; Television Plays: The Revivalist, 1975; Dylan, 1978; Nye, 1982; The Extremist, 1983; The Fasting Girl, 1984. Address: c/o Curtis Brown Ltd, Haymarket House, 28/29 Haymarket, London SW1 4SP, England.

**FERRY Bryan,** b. 26 September 1945, Washington, County Durham, England. Singer; Songwriter; Musician. 4 sons. Education: Fine Art, Newcastle University. Career: Formed Roxy Music, 1971; Solo artiste, 1973-; Worked with: Brian Eno; Phil Manzanera; Andy Mackay; Steve Ferrone; David Williams; Robin Trower; Pino Palladino; Nile Rodgers; Carleen Anderson; Shara Nelson; Jhelisa; Numerous worldwide tours; Major concerts include: Crystal Palace, 1972; Live Aid, Wembley, 1985; Radio City, New York, 1988; Wembley, 1989; Support tours, Alice Cooper, David Bowie; Television appearances include: Subject of Without Walls documentary, 1992; Videos: New Town (live), 1990; Total Recall (documentary), 1990. Recordings: Singles include: Love Is The Drug, 1975; Dance Away, 1979; Angel Eyes, 1979; Over You, 1980; Jealous Guy, 1981; Slave To Love, 1985; The Right Stuff, 1987; I Put A Spell On You, 1993; Albums: Solo: These Foolish Things, 1973; Another Time Another Place, 1974; Let's Stick Together, 1976; In Your Mind, 1977; The Bride Stripped Bare, 1978; Boys And Girls, 1985; Bete Noire, 1987; The Ultimate Collection, 1988; Taxi, 1993; Mamounia, 1994; As Time Goes By, 1999; Frantic, 2002; with Roxy Music: Roxy Music, 1972; For Your Pleasure, 1973; Stranded, 1973; Country Life, 1974; Siren, 1975; Viva Roxy Music, 1976; Manifesto, 1979; Flesh And Blood (Number 1, UK), 1980; Avalon, (Number 1, UK), 1982; The High Road (live mini-album), 1983; The Atlantic Years, 1983; Street Life, 1987; Recent compilations include: The Thrill Of It All, 1995; More Than This - The Best Of Roxy Music and Bryan Ferry, 1995. Honours include: Grand Prix Du Disque, Best Album,

Montreux Golden Rose Festival, 1973. Address: c/o Barry Dickins, ITB, 3rd Floor, 27A Floral Street, London, WC2E 9DQ, England.

**FERZAK Franz Xaver,** b. 27 October 1958, Neuenhinzenhausen, Germany. Publisher; Writer; Engineer. Education: Diploma of Mechanical Engineering, 1982. Appointments: Author, Publisher, 1986-; Translator, MVV Peiting, 1996-97, 2002. Publications: Nikola Tesla, 1986, Karl Freiherr von Reichenbach, 1987; Giordano Bruno, 1996; Wilhelm Reich, 1991; Jesus of Qumran, 1997; Viktor Schauberger, 2001. Honours: Listed in Who's Who publications and biographical dictionaries. Address: Am Bachl 1, 93336 Altmannstein, Germany.

**FETHERSTON Brian,** b. 26 January 1955, Milwaukee, Wisconsin, USA. Artist Sculptor; Painter. m. Marianne, 1 son. Education: Ontario College of Art, Canada. Appointments: Commissions and Creative Works: Solo exhibitions of Fetherston & Fetherston (Brian & Marianne): Galerie Cluny, Geneva, Switzerland, 1986; In permanence, Galerie Cluny, Geneva, 1989-90; Gallery Montserrat, New York, 1996; Six Tech SA, Geneva, Switzerland, 1997; Ballard-Fetherston Gallery, Seattle, Washington, 1998; DWT Gallery, Geneva, 2000-01; Group exhibitions of Fetherston & Fetherston (Brian & Marianne) in Spain, Switzerland, Turkey, France, include: Gallery Ramko, Istanbul, Turkey, 1991; Gallerie du Vieux-Chêne, Geneva, 1991; Museum International Art, Carnac, France, 1996; Finansbank SA, Geneva, 1991; United Nations, Geneva, 1995, 1996; Red Cross, Geneva, 1996; Biennale du Japon Grand Prix de Sapporo, Japan, 1997; Société Générale & Trust, Zurich, 1997; Art EXPO 99, New York, 1999; Barcelona Art Expo, 1999; Mural, Trompe l'Oeil, BPI Investments, Geneva; Mural, Gallay-Jufer, SA; Designer Work Team Gallery, Switzerland, 2000. Mural (Trompe L'Oeil BPI Investments, Geneva; Mural, Gallay-Jufer SA, Geneva. Publications: Gallery Guide Paris, 12th, 13th editions; Business Guide to Switzerland, 1992; Art News Magazine, USA, 1996; Gallery Guide, New York, 1996. Membership: Professor of Fine Arts, Greci Marino, Italy. Address: 8 rue de Fribourg, 1201 Geneva, Switzerland. Website: www.ffetherston.com

**FETHERSTON Marianne,** b. 14 August 1959, Alexandria, Egypt (Swiss citizen). Artist Painter. m. Brian, 1 son. Education: Ontario College of Art, Toronto, Canada. Honour: Gallery Art et Vie, Jury Prize, 1987. Commissions and Creative Works: Solo Exhibitions of Fetherston & Fetherston (Brian & Marianne): Galerie Cluny, Geneva, 1986; (permanent), Circulo Bellas Artes, Salon de Otono, Palma de Mallorca, Spain, 1987; Gallery Bearn, Palma de Mallorca, Spain, 1988; Galerie Cluny, Geneva, 1989-90; Gallery Montserrat, New York, 1996; Six Tech SA, Geneva, 1997; Ballard-Fetherston Gallery, Seattle, Washington, 1998; DWT Gallery, Geneva, 2000-01; Group exhibitions of Fetherston & Fetherston (Brian & Marianne) in Switzerland, Spain, France, Japan, include: Finansbank SA, Geneva, 1991; Museum International Art, Carnac, France, 1996; United Nations, Switzerland, 1995-96; Red Cross, Geneva, 1996; Biennale du Japan Grand Prix de Sapporo, 1997; Société Générale & Trust, Zurich, 1997; Art Expo 99 New York, 1999; Barcelona Art Expo, 1999; Mural (Trompe l'oeil) BPI Investments, Geneva; Mural, Gallay-Jufer, SA. Publication: Gallery Guide, Paris, 12th, 13th edition; Art News Magazine, 1996; Gallery Guide, New York, 1996. Membership: Professor of Fine Arts, Greci Marino, Italy. Address: 8 rue de Fribourg, 1201 Geneva, Switzerland.

**FETTWEIS Günter B L,** b. 17 November 1924, Düsseldorf, Germany. Mining Engineer; University Professor Emeritus.

m. Alice, 1 son, 3 daughters. Education: Diploma in Mining, Technical University of Aachen, 1950; Dr Jng, 1953, Assessor des Bergfachs (a of Mining), 1955. Appointments: Junior Mining Inspector, State of North Rhine-Westfalia, 1953-55; Mining Engineer, 1955-57, Production Manager, Mining Co Neue Hoffnung, Oberhausen, Germany, 1957-59; Professor of Mining, University of Leoben, Austria, 1959-93; Rector, 1968-70, Emeritus, 1993-. Publications: About 250 articles and 15 books about mining and mineral economics. Honours: Dr h C mult Aachen (D), 1980, Miskolc (H), 1987, Petrosani (RO), 1996, Moscow (RG), 1999, Košice (SK), 2003; Several awards, Austria, Germany, Poland and the Vatican. Memberships: Austrian Academy of Sciences; Several other European academies of sciences; Indian National Academy of Engineering; Honorary Member, Austrian Mining Association (BVÖ); German Mining Association (GDMB); International Committee of World Mining Congress; Lions Club, Homburg, Germany; Board of the Austrian Mining Association, 1959-2000; Vice President, International Committee of World Mining Congress, 1976-2001; Explorers Club; Lions Club. Address: Gasteigergasse 5, A 8700 Leoben, Austria.

**FIDLER Peter John Michael,** b. 16 March 1942, Bradford, England. Solicitor. m. Barbara Pinto, 2 sons, 2 daughters. Education: Bradford Grammar School; MA, 1st class honours, St John's College, Oxford. Appointments: Coward Chance Solicitors, 1967-72; Partner, D J Freeman, 1972-84; Partner, Stephenson Harwood, 1984-2002; Consultant, Pinsents, 2002-04; Consultant, CMS Cameron McKenna LLP, 2004-. Memberships: Law Society; City of London Law Society; Association of Business Recovery Professionals (R3). Address: CMS Cameron McKenna LLP, Mitre House, 160 Aldersgate Street, London EC1A 4DD, England. E-mail: peter.fidler@cms-cmck.com

**FIENNES Ranulph (Twisleton-Wykeham),** b. 7 March 1944, Windsor, England. Explorer; Writer. m. (1) Virginia Pepper, deceased 2004, (2) Louise Millington, 2005. Education: Eton College. Appointments: British Army, 1965-70; Special Air Service, 1966; Sultan of Muscat's Armed Forces, 1968-70; Led British Expeditions to White Nile, 1969, Jostedalsbre Glacier, 1970, Headless Valley, British Columbia, 1970; Transglobal expedition, first circumpolar journey round the world, 1979-82, North Pole (5 expeditions), 1985-90, Ubar Expedition (discovered the lost city of Ubar, Oman), 1992, First unsupported crossing of Antarctic continent, 1993; Land Rover 7x7x7 Challenge (7 marathons in 7 days on 7 continents), 2003; Lectures; Television and film documentary appearances. Publications: A Talent for Trouble, 1970; Ice Fall on Norway, 1972; The Headless Valley, 1973; Where Soldiers Fear to Tread, 1975; Hell on Ice, 1979; To the Ends of the Earth: The Transglobe Expedition - The First Pole-to-Pole Circumnavigation of the Globe, 1983; Bothie the Polar Dog (with Virginia Fiennes), 1984; Living Dangerously (autobiography), 1988; The Feather Men, 1991; Atlantis of the Sands, 1992; Mind Over Matter: The Epic Crossing of the Antarctic Continent, 1994; The Sett, 1996; Ranulph Fiennes: Fit For Life, 1998; Beyond the Limits, 2000; The Secret Hunters, 2001; Captain Scott, 2003. Honours: Dhofar Campaign Medal, 1969; Sultan of Muscat Bravery Medal, 1970; Krug Award for Excellence, 1980; Gold Medal and Honorary Life Membership, Explorer's Club of New York, 1983; Livingstone's Gold Medal, Royal Scottish Geographic Society, 1983; Founder's Medal, Royal Geographic Society, 1984; Hon DSc, Loughborough, 1986; Guinness Hall of Fame, 1987; Polar Medal and Bar, 1987, 1994; ITN Award, 1990; Officer of the Order of the British Empire, 1993; Hon DUniv, Birmingham, 1995; British Chapter, The Explorers' Club Millennium Award For Polar Exploration, 2000; Honorary DSc, Portsmouth University, 2000;

Hon DLitt, Glasgow Caledonian, 2002. Membership: Honorary Membership, Royal Institute of Navigation, 1997. Address: Greenlands, Exford, Somerset TA24 7NU, England.

**FIFIELD Christopher (George),** b. 4 September 1945, Croydon, England. Musician; Writer. m. Judith Weyman, 28 Oct 1972, div. Education: Associate, Royal College of Organists, 1967; MusB, 1968; Graduate, Royal Schools of Music, 1969; Associate, Royal Manchester College of Music, 1969. Publications: Max Bruch: His Life and Works, 1988; Wagner in Performance, 1992; True Artist and True Friend: A Biography of Hans Richter, 1993; Letters and Diaries of Kathleen Ferrier, 2003; Ibbs and Tillett, the Rise and Fall of a Musical Empire, 2005. Recordings: Symphony No 1/Cloud and Sunshine, Frederic Cliffe; Symphony Op 60, Xaver Scharwenka. Contributions to: Grove; Grove Opera; DNB; Viking Opera Guide; Oxford Companion to Music; Music on the Web; Music and Letters; BBC Music Magazine. Address: 162 Venner Road, London SE26 5JQ, England.

**FIGES Eva,** b. 15 April 1932, Berlin, Germany. Writer. 1 son, 1 daughter. Education: BA, Honours, English Language and Literature, University of London, 1953. Publications: Winter Journey, 1967; Patriarchal Attitudes, 1970; B, 1972; Nelly's Version, 1977; Little Eden, 1978; Waking, 1981; Sex and Subterfuge, 1982; Light, 1983; The Seven Ages, 1986; Ghosts, 1988; The Tree of Knowledge, 1990; The Tenancy, 1993; The Knot, 1996; Tales of Innocence and Experience, 2003. Honour: Guardian Fiction Prize, 1967. Membership: Society of Authors. Address: c/o Rogers, Coleridge & White Ltd, 20 Powis Mews, London W11 1JN, England.

**FIGGIS Mike,** b. 28 February 1949, Kenya. Film Director; Writer; Musician. Career: Came to England, 1957; Studied music, performing in band, Gas Board; Musician, experimental theatre group, The People Show, early 1970s; Maker of independent films including: Redheugh; Slow Fade; Animals of the City; TV film, The House, Channel 4; Films include: Stormy Monday (also screenplay and music), 1988; Internal Affairs (also music), 1990; Liebestraum (also screenplay and music), 1991; Mr Jones, 1993; The Browning Version, 1994; Leaving Las Vegas (also screenplay and music), 1995; One Night Stand, 1997; Flamenco Women, 1997; Miss Julie, 1999; The Loss of Sexual Innocence, 1999; Time Code, 1999. Honours: IFP Independent Spirit Award, 1996; National Society of Film Critics Award. Address: c/o ICM, 8942 Wilshire Boulevard, Beverly Hills, CA 90211, USA.

**FIGUEROLA PINERA Ramon,** b. 1 November 1955. m. Hilda G, 1981, 1 son, 2 daughters. Education: MS, Operations Research, MS, Statistics, 1983, Stanford University; BS, Actuarial Science, UNAM, 1980; Diploma in TQM, ITAM, 1993; Diploma in Financial Analysis and Information Technology, ITESM, 1996; Credit Analysis Techniques, Euromoney London, 1999; Diploma in Management, IPADE, 2001; Diploma in Corporate Finance, ITAM, 2003. Appointments: Planning and Financial Adviser, Federal Government, 1981-89; Strategic Planning Manager, Mexinox SA de CV, 1989-92; Superintendent of Investment Projects and Information Technology, 1992-96; Submanager of Investment Projects and Budgeting of Exploration and Production, 1996-2000; Pemex Exploration and Production: Administrative and Finance Manager, 2000-. Memberships: Institute of Management Sciences; Colegio Actuarios. Address: Nacajuca 115, Col Prados de Villahermosa, Villahermosa, Tabasco 86030, Mexico. E-mail: rfiguerolap@pep.pemex.com

**FILAR Marian Andrzej,** b. 6 October 1942, Krosno, Poland. Lawyer; Professor of Law. m. Veronika Filar, 1 daughter. Education: Technical studies for miners, Cracow, Poland, 1960-62; MA, Legal Studies, Niclaus Copericus University, Torun, 1962-67; Scholarships: Max Planck's Institute of International Criminal Law and Comparative Law, Freiburg, Germany, 1986; Institute of Criminal Law, University of Rome, 1972; PhD, 1972. Appointments: Assistant, 1967, Lecturer, 1972, Habilitated Doctor of Law, 1977, Vice Dean of the Faculty, 1985-87, Dean of the Faculty, 1987-90, Associate Professor, 1988, Professor, 1991-, Faculty of Law and Administration, Chair of Criminal Law and Criminal Policy, Vice-Rector for Student Affairs, 1990-93, University of Niclaus Copernicus; Vice Chairman of the State Tribunal (Poland), 1997-2001. Publications include: Rape in Polish Criminal Law, 1974; Pornography. Studies in the Field of Criminal policy, 1977; Sexual Offences in Polish criminal Law, 1985; Criminal Justice Policies in the Crossnational Perspective, 1991; Medical Criminal Law, 2000. Honours: Medal, Polish National Education Commission; Knight's Cross "Polonia Restituta". Memberships: International Association of Criminal Law; Former Vice-President, Member of the Board, Scientific Society of Criminal Law; Polish Medicine Academy; Polish Academy of Sexuological Knowledge. Address: Suchatowka 73, 88-140 Gniewkowo, Poland.

**FILIPPOV Igor V,** b. 29 June 1971, Yaroslavl City, Russia. Neurophysiologist; Assistant Professor. Education: MD, 1994; PhD, Physiology, Russian Academy of Sciences, Moscow, Russia, 1997. Appointment: Currently Assistant Professor, Department of Physiology and Biophysics, Yaroslavl State Medical Academy, Yaroslavl City, Russia. Publications: 70 scientific publications, including articles in international peer-reviewed journals and local Russian journals. Honours: Grants from Netherlands Institute for Brain Research; California Institute of Technology and International Brain Research Organisation. Memberships: Pavlov's Russian Physiological Society; International Organisation of Psychophysiology; International Brain Research Organisation. Address: Department of Physiology and Biophysics, Yaroslavl State Medical Academy, Revolutsionnaya Street 5, Yaroslavl City, 150000 Russia. E-mail: filippov@yma.ac.ru Website: http://www.yma.ac.ru

**FINE Anne,** b. 7 December 1947, Leicester, England. Writer. m. Kit Fine, divorced, 2 daughters. Education: BA Honours, Politics and History, University of Warwick, 1965-68. Career, Novelist for both children and adults. Publications include: Novels: The Killjoy, 1986; Taking the Devil's Advice, 1990; In Cold Domain, 1994; Telling Liddy, 1998; All Bones and Lies, 2001; Raking the Ashes, 2005. For Older Children: The Summer House Loon, 1978; The Other Darker Ned, 1979; The Stone Menagerie, 1980; Round Behind the Ice House, 1981; The Granny Project, 1983; Madame Doubtfire, 1987; Goggle Eyes, 1989; The Book of the Banshee, 1991; Flour Babies, 1992; Step by Wicked Step, 1995; The Tulip Touch, 1996; Very Different (short stories), 2001; Up on Cloud Nine, 2002; Numerous books for younger children. Honours include: Guardian Children's Award, 1989; Carnegie Medals, 1989, 1993; Smarties Prize, 1990; Guardian Children's Literature Award, 1990; Publishing News, Children's Author of Year, 1990, 1993; Whitbread Children's Novel Awards, 1993, 1996; Children's Laureate, 2001-2003; Fellow, Royal Society of Literature, 2003; OBE, 2003. Membership: Society of Authors. Address: c/o David Higham Associates, 5-8 Lower John Street, Golden Square, London W1F 9HA, England. Website: www.annefine.co.uk

**FINER Stephen Alan,** b. 27 January 1949, London, England. Artist. Career: Solo Exhibitions: Four Vine Lane, London, 1981, 1982, 1985; Anthony Reynolds Gallery, London, 1986, 1988; Berkeley Square Gallery, London, 1989; Bernard Jacobson Gallery, London, 1992, 1995; Woodlands Art Gallery, 1994; Agnew's, London, 1998; Pallant House Gallery, Chichester, Sussex, 2001, Charleston, Sussex, 2002; Art Space Gallery, London, 2004; Selected Mixed Exhibitions: British Art, 1940-80, from the Arts Council Collection, Hayward Gallery, London, 1980; Collazione Inglese II, Venice Biennale, Italy, 1984; Academicians' Choice, Stephen Finer invited by Kitaj, Mall Galleries, London; The Portrait Now, National Portrait Gallery, London, 1993-94, 1990; The Discerning Eye, Stephen Finer invited by Martin Gayford, Mall Gallery, London, 1996; Men on Women, Touring Exhibition Stephen Finer invited by Peter Edwards, Wales, 1997-98; 50 Contemporary Self-Portraits, Six Chapel Row, Bath, 1998; British Art, 1900-98, Agnew's, London, 1998; About the Figure, Six Chapel Row, Bath, 1999; Painting the Century, 101 Portrait Masterpieces, 1900-2000, National Portrait Gallery, London, 2000-01; The National Portrait Gallery Collects, Bodelwyddan Castle, Wales, 2003; Public Collections: Arts Council; Atkinson Art Gallery, Southport; The British Council; Contemporary Art Society; Los Angeles County Museum of Art; National Portrait Gallery, "David Bowie", London; Pallant House Gallery, "Sir Morris Finer", Chichester, Sussex. Selected publications: Allgemeines Kunstlerlexikon; Dictionary of British Artists Since 1945; Handbook of Modern British Painting and Printmaking, 1900-2000; The Portrait Now, Robin Gibson, National Portrait Gallery, 1993; Painting the Century 101 Portrait Masterpieces, 1900-2000, Robin Gibson, National Portrait Gallery, London, 2000; Stephen Finer: Presence and Identity, Martin Golding, Modern Painters, Spring, 2000; Intimacy and Mortality, Finer's People, Robin Gibson, Charleston Trust, 2002. Address: 20 Kipling Street, London SE1 3RU, England. Websites: www.stephenfiner.com

**FINK Merton, (Matthew Finch, Merton Finch),** b. 17 November 1921, Liverpool, England. Author. m. (1) 15 March 1953, 1 son, 1 daughter, (2) 24 November 1981. Education: School of Military Engineers, 1942; School of Military Intelligence, 1943; LDS, Liverpool University, 1952. Publications: Dentist in the Chair, 1953; Teething Troubles, 1954; The Third Set, 1955; Hang Your Hat on a Pension, 1956; The Empire Builder, 1957; Solo Fiddle, 1959; The Beauty Bazaar, 1960; Matchbreakers, 1961; Five Are the Symbols, 1962; Snakes and Ladders, 1963; Chew this Over, 1965; Eye with Mascara, 1966; Eye Spy, 1967; Jones is a Rainbow, 1968; Simon Bar Cochba, 1971; A Fox Called Flavius, 1973; Open Wide, 1976. Contributions to: Dental Practice, 1956-; Bath Chronicle, 1995. Honour: Richard Edwards Scholar, 1950. Memberships: Civil Service Writers; Deputy Chairman, Bath Literary Society; British Dental Association; Chairman, Service Committee, Bath British Legion. Address: 27 Harbutts, Bathampton, Bath BA2 6TA, England.

**FINKELSTEIN Richard Alan,** b. 5 March 1930, New York City, New York, USA. Microbiologist; Professor Emeritus. m. (1) Helen Rosenberg, 1 son, 2 daughters, (2) Mary Boesman, 1 daughter. Education: BS, University of Oklahoma, 1950; MA, 1952, PhD, 1955, University of Texas, Austin; Postdoctoral work, University of Texas Southwestern Medical School, Dallas, 1955-58. Appointments: Chief, Bioassay Section, Walter Reed Army Institute for Research, Washington DC, 1958-64; Deputy Chief, Chief, Department of Bacteriology and Mycology, US Army Medical Component, SEATO Medical Research Laboratory, Bangkok, Thailand, 1964-67; Associate Professor, Professor, Department of Microbiology, University of Texas Southwestern Medical School, 1967-79; Professor, Chairman, Department of Microbiology, 1979-93, Millsap Distinguished Professor, 1985-2000, Curators' Professor, 1990-2000, School of Medicine, University of Missouri, Columbia; Consultant, editorial boards, National Institutes of Health Study Sections. Publications: Over 230 including articles in scientific journals and texts on cholera, enterotoxins, gonorrhea, role of iron in host-parasite interactions. Honours include: Outstanding Achievement, 1964, Performance, 1965, US Army; Ciba-Geigy Lecturer, 1975; Visiting Scientist, Japanese Science Council, 1976; Robert Koch Prize, Science, Medicine, Bonn, Germany, 1976; Many lectureships, 1980-2000; Chancellor's Award for Outstanding Research, University of Missouri, 1985; Sigma Xi Research Award, 1986; Distinguished Service Award, American Society for Microbiology, 1998. Memberships: American Society for Microbiology, Texas, Missouri and National offices; American Academy of Microbiology, offices; American Association of Immunology; Infectious Diseases Society of America; Society of General Microbiology; Pathology Society of Great Britain and Ireland; Sigma Xi. Address: 3861 S Forest Acres, Columbia, MO 65203, USA.

**FINN Neil**, b. 27 May 1958, Te Awamutu, New Zealand. Singer; Musician (guitar); Songwriter. Career: Member, Split Enz, 1977-85; Founder member, Crowded House, 1985-; Duo with brother Tim, 1995; International concerts include: A Concert For Life, Centennial Park, Sydney, 1992; WOMAD Festival, 1993; Television appearances include: Late Night With David Letterman, NBC; The Tonight Show, NBC; In Concert '91, ABC; Return To The Dome, Ch4; MTV Unplugged; Top Of The Pops, BBC1. Recordings: Albums: with Split Enz: Frenzy, 1978; True Colours, 1979; Beginning Of The Enz, 1980; Waita, 1981; Time And Tide, 1982; Conflicting Emotions, 1984; See Ya Round, 1985; History Never Repeats Itself - The Best Of Split Enz, 1993; Oddz & Endz, 1993; Rear Enz, 1993; with Crowded House: Crowded House, 1986; Temple Of Low Men, 1988; Woodface, 1991; Together Alone, 1993; Seductive & Emotional, 1994; Unplugged in the Byrdhouse, 1995; Recurring Dream, 1996; Originals, 1998; with Tim Finn: Finn, 1995; Solo Albums: Try Whistling This, 1998; Encore!, 1999; Singles: with Split Enz include: I See Red; I Got You; History Never Repeats; Six Months In A Leaky Boat; with Crowded House include: Don't Dream It's Over; Something So Strong; Better Be Home Soon; Chocolate Cake; Fall At Your Feet; Four Seasons In One Day; Distant Sun; Nails In My Feet; Solo Singles: Sinner, 1998; She Will Have Her Way, 1998; Last One Standing, 1999; Can You Hear Us, 1999. Honours: Q Awards: Best Live Act (with Crowded House), 1992; Best Songwriter, 1993; OBE, for services to New Zealand, 1993. Current Management: Grant Thomas Management, 3 Mitchell Road, Rose Bay, NSW 2029, Australia.

**FINNEY Albert**, b. 9 May 1936. Actor. m. (1) Jane Wenham, divorced, 1 son; (2) Anouk Aimée, 1970, divorced, 1978. Education: Royal Academy of Dramatic Art. Appointments: Appointments: Birmingham Repertory Company, 1956-58; Shakespeare Memorial Theatre Company, 1959; National Theatre, 1965, 1975; Formed Memorial Enterprises, 1966; Associate Artistic Director, English Stage Company, 1972-75; Director, United British Artists, 1983-86; Plays include: Julius Caesar; Macbeth; Henry V; The Beaux Strategem; The Alchemist; The Lizard on the Rock; The Party, 1958; King Lear; Othello, 1959; A Midsummer Night's Dream; The Lily-White Boys, 1960; Billy Liar, 1960; Luther, 1961, 1963; Much Ado About About Nothing; Armstrong's Last Goodnight, 1965; Miss Julie, 1965; Black Comedy, 1965; Love for Love, 1965; A Flea in Her Ear, 1966; A Day in the Death of Joe Egg, 1968; Alpha Beta, 1972; Krapp's Last Tape, 1973; Cromwell, 1973; Chez

Nous, 1974; Loot (Director), 1975; Hamlet, 1976; Tamburlaine the Great, 1976; Uncle Vanya, 1977; Present Laughter, 1977; The Country Wife, 1977-78; The Cherry Orchard, 1978; Macbeth, 1978; Has 'Washington' Legs?; The Biko Inquest (director), 1984; Sergeant Musgrave's Dance (director), 1984; Orphans, 1986; J J Farr, 1987; Another Time, 1989; Reflected Glory, 1992; Art, 1996; Films include: The Entertainer; Saturday Night and Sunday Morning, 1960; Tom Jones, 1963; Night Must Fall, 1963; Two For the Road, 1967; Scrooge, 1970; Gumshoe, 1971; Murder on the Orient Express, 1974; Wolfen, 1979; Looker, 1980; Shoot the Moon, 1981; Annie, 1982; Life of John Paul II, 1983; The Dresser, 1983; Under the Volcano, 1983; Miller's Crossing, 1989; The Image, 1989; The Run of the Country, 1995; Washington Square, Breakfast of Champions, 1999; Simpatico, 1999; Delivering Milo, 1999; Erin Brokovich, 2000; TV appearances include: My Uncle Silas, 2001, 2003; The Gathering Storm, 2002. Honours: Hon DLitt (Sussex), 1966; Lawrence Olivier Award, 1986; London Standard Drama Award for Best Actor, 1986; Dilys Powell Award, London Film Critics Circle, 1999; BAFTA Fellowship, 2001; Emmy Award, 2002; BAFTA Award for Best Actor, 2003; Golden Globe, 2003. Address: c/o Michael Simkins, 45/51 Whitfield Street, London W1T 4HB, England.

**FINNEY David John**, b. 3 January 1917, United Kingdom. Consultant Biometrician. m. Mary Elizabeth Connolly, 1 son, 2 daughters. Education: Open Entrance Scholarship, BA Mathematics, Clare College Cambridge, 1934-38; Graduate study, Galton Laboratory, University College, London, 1938-39; MA (Cantab), 1941; MA (Oxon), 1945; ScD (Cantab), 1947. Appointments include: Statistician, Rothamsted Experimental Station, 1939-45; Lecturer in the Design and Analysis of Scientific Experiment, University of Oxford, 1945-54; Consultant, National Foundation for Educational Research, London, 1948-57; Visiting Professor, University of South Carolina, 1949; Seconded as Statistical Expert to UN Food and Agriculture Organisation, Statistics Branch, Indian Council of Agricultural Research, New Delhi India, 1952-53; Reader in Statistics, 1954-63, Professor, 1963-66, University of Aberdeen; Director, Agricultural Research Council's Unit of Statistics, 1954-84; Consultant to Empire Cotton Growing Corporation (later Cotton Research Corporation), 1960-75; Honorary Director, Research Group in Biometric Medicine, University of Aberdeen, 1961-65; Professor of Statistics, University of Edinburgh, 1966-84; Visiting Scientist, International Rice Research Institute, Los Baños, Philippines, 1984-85; Key Consultant, Indian Agricultural Statistics Research Institute, 1984-90; Director, Research Centre, International Statistical Institute, Voorburg, Netherlands, 1987-88; Invited Speaker at Conference of Japanese Toxicological Society, Nagoya, Japan, 1998. Publications: Author and co-author of 9 books; Over 300 scientific papers published in leading statistical, agricultural, biological and medical journals. Honours include: Weldon Memorial Prize, University of Oxford, 1956; Hon Docteur en Sciences Agronomiques, National Faculty of Agriculture, Gembloux, Belgium, 1967; Paul Martini Prize, Deutsche Gesellschaft für Medizinische Dokumentation und Statistik, 1971; Fisher Memorial Lecturer, London, 1972; Honorary DSc: City University London, 1976, Heriot-Watt University, Edinburgh, 1981; CBE, 1978; Honorary Doctor of Mathematics, University of Waterloo, Canada, 1989. Memberships include: Fellow, 1939, President, 1973-74, Royal Statistical Society, 1939; International Statistical Institute, 1951; Honorary Life Fellow, Eugenics Society, 1954; Fellow of the Royal Society, 1955; Fellow of the Royal Society of Edinburgh, 1955; President, 1964-65, Honorary Life Member, 1984, Biometric Society. Address: 13 Oswald Court, South Oswald Road, Edinburgh EH9 2HY, Scotland.

**FIORENTINO Linda,** b. 9 March 1960, Philadelphia, Pennsylvania, USA. Actress. Education: Rosemont College; Circle in the Square Theatre School. Career: Member, Circle in the Square Performing Workshops; Films: Vision Quest, 1985; Gotcha, 1985; After Hours, 1985; The Moderns, 1988; Queens Logic, 1991; Shout, 1991; Wildfire, 1992; Chain of Desire, 1993; The Desperate Trail, 1994; The Last Seduction, 1994; Bodily Harm, 1995; Jade, 1995; Unforgettable, 1997; The Split, 1997; Men in Black, 1997; Kicked in the Head, 1997; Dogma, 1998; Ordinary Decent Criminal, 1999; Where the Money Is, 1999; What Planet Are You From? 2000; Liberty Stands Still, 2002; Films for TV include: The Neon Empire, 1989; The Last Game, 1992; Acting on Impulse, 1993; Beyond the Law, 1994; The Desperate Trail. Address: c/o United Talent Agency, 9560 Wilshire Boulevard, Floor 5, Beverly Hills, CA 90212, USA.

**FIRTH Colin,** b. 10 September 1960. Actor. Education: Drama Center, London. Career: Theatre includes: Another Country, 1983; Doctor's Dilemma, 1984; The Lonely Road, 1985; Desire Under the Elms, 1987; The Caretaker, 1991; Chatsky, 1993; Three Days of Rain, 1999; TV appearances; Dutch Girls, 1984; Lost Empires (series), 1985-86; Robert Lawrence in Tumbledown, 1987; Out of the Blue, 1990; Hostages, 1992; Master of the Moor, 1993; The Deep Blue Sea, 1994; Pride and Prejudice (Mr Darcy), 1994; Nostromo, 1997; The Turn of the Screw, 1999; Donovan Quick, 1999; Radio: Richard II in Two Planks and a Passion, 1986; The One Before the Last (Rupert Brooke), 1987; Films: Another Country, 1983; Camille, 1984; A Month in the Country, 1986; Femme Fatale, 1990; The Hour of the Pig, 1992; Good Girls, 1994; Circle of Friends, 1995; The English Patient, 1996; Fever Pitch, 1996; Shakespeare in Love, 1998; The Secret Laughter of Women, 1999; My Life So Far, 1999; Relative Values, 1999; Londinium, 2000; Bridget Jones's Diary, 2000; The Importance of Being Earnest, 2002; Hope Springs, 2003; Love Actually, 2003. Honours: Radio Times Actor Award for Tumbledown, 1996; Best Actor Award, Broadcasting Press Guild for Pride and Prejudice. Address: c/o ICM Ltd, Oxford House, 76 Oxford Street, London, W1N 0AX, England.

**FISCHER Ernst Otto,** b. 10 November 1918, Munich, Germany. Inorganic Chemist. Education: Diploma in Chemistry, 1949, Doctorate, 1952, Munich Technical University. Appointments: Associate Professor, 1957, Professor, 1959, Professor and Director, Inorganic Chemistry, 1964, Munich Technical University; Research on Organometallic Compounds of Transition Metals. Publications: 500 scientific publications; Fe$(C_5H_5)_2$ Structure, 1952; Cr$(C_6H_6)_2$, 1955; Ubergansmetall-Carben-Komplexe, 1964; Metal-Complexes Vol I, with H Werner, 1966; Ubergansmetall-Carben-Komplexe, 1973. Honour: Gottinger Academy Prize for Chemistry, 1957; Alfred-Stock-Gedachtnis Prize, 1959; Hon Dr rer nat, Munich, 1972, Erlangen, 1977, Veszprem, 1983; Joint Winner, Nobel Prize for Chemistry, 1973; Hon DSc, Strathclyde, 1975; American Chemical Society Centennial Fellow, 1976. Memberships: Bayerische Akademie der Wissenschaften, 1964; Deutsche Akademie der Naturforscher Leopoldina, 1969; Corresponding Member, Austrian Academy of Sciences, 1976; Academy of Sciences, Gottingen, 1977; Foreign Member, Accademi Nazionale dei Lincei, 1976; Foreign Honorary Member, American Academy of Arts and Sciences, 1977. Address: Sohnckestrasse 16, 81479 Munich 71, Germany.

**FISCHER-MÜNSTER Gerhard,** b. 17 November 1952, Münster- Sarmsheim, Germany. Composer, Soloist, Lecturer, Conductor. m. Bettina, 1 son, 1 daughter. Education: Peter Cornelius Konservatorium Mainz, Staatliche Musikhochschule und Johannes-Gutenberg- Universität Mainz, Staatsexamen,

1974; Seminar for conducting, Bingen, Exam. Career: First Compositions in 1965. Concerts as Soloist, Piano and Clarinet; Concerts as Conductor of different orchestras and ensembles. TV records, Radio records/performances in Germany, Italy, Austria, Switzerland, France, Belgium, USA, Japan; Guest Conductor European Symphony Orchestra, Luxembourg 1993; Performances at International Festivals. Guest Lecturer at various Institutes; Founder of Symphonic Wind Orchestra of Conservatory Mainz 1991; Founder of Wind Chamber Ensemble1981; Lecturer Peter-Cornelius Konservatorium, 1975-. Publications: Over 400 compositions (main: 5 Symphonies, Psalm 99, Schizophonie, Sonatas, Haiku-Lieder words by Sigrid Genzken-Dragendorff, Sonett words by Shakespeare, Symphonic Lieder words by Brigitte Pulley-Grein, Piano Concertino, Daliphonie); Harmonie aus dem Einklang (historical/physical work)' Lehrplan Klarinette; Publications in Music Journals; Publications about Fischer-Münster at different Universities; Jury member at numerous music contests; Guest Lecturer, University Mainz. Honours: Award, Adv. Ministry of Culture 1984, 1989, 1992, 2000; Award, Adv. Management of International Music Festival of Switzerland, 1985; Honorary Member, IBC Advisory Council; St. Rochus Cup (Bingen) for cultural achievement; Honorary Member, ABI Research Board of Advisers. Memberships: Deutscher Komponisten-Interessenverband; World Association for Symphonic Bands and Ensemble (WASBE), GEMA, Association for German Lecturers and Artists; Fördergesellschaft Peter-Cornelius-Konservatorium. Address: Auf den Zeilen 11, D-55424 Münster-Sarmsheim, Germany. E-mail: Fischer-Muenster@gmx.de Website: www.fischer-muenster.de

**FISHBURNE Laurence,** b. 30 July 1961, Augusta, Georgia, USA. Actor. m. Hanja Moss, 1985, divorced 1 son, 1 daughter. Career: Stage appearances include: Short Eyes; Two Trains Running; Riff Raff (also writer and director); TV appearances include: One Life to Live (series, debut age 11); Pee-wee's Playhouse; Tribeca; A Rumour of War; I Take These Men; Father Clements Story; Decoration Day; The Tuskagee Airmen; Miss Ever's Boys; Always Outnumbered; Films include: Cornbread Earl and Me, 1975; Fast Break; Apocalypse Now; Willie and Phil; Death Wish II; Rumble Fish; The Cotton Club; The Colour Purple; Quicksilver; Band of the Hand; A Nightmare on Elm Street 3; Dream Warriors; Gardens of Stone; School Daze; Red Heat; King of New York; Cadence; Class Action; Boyz N the Hood; Deep Cover; What's Love Got to Do With It?; Searching for Bobby Fischer; Higher Learning; Bad Company; Just Cause; Othello; Fled; Hoodlums (also exec producer); Event Horizon; Welcome to Hollywood; Once in the Life (also writer); The Matrix, 1999; Michael Jordan to the Max, 2000; Once in the Life, 2000; Osmosis Jones, 2001; The Matrix Reloaded, 2003; The Matrix Revolutions, 2003 Address: c/o Paradigm, 10100 Santa Monica Boulevard, 25th Floor, Los Angeles, CA 90067, USA.

**FISHER Allen,** b. 1 November 1944, Norbury, Surrey, England. Painter; Poet; Art Historian. Education: BA, University of London; MA, University of Essex. Appointment: Head of Art, Professor of Poetry and Art, University of Surrey Roehampton. Publications: Over 100 books including: Place Book One, 1974; Brixton Fractals, 1985; Unpolished Mirrors, 1985; Stepping Out, 1989; Future Exiles, 1991; Fizz, 1994; Civic Crime, 1994; Breadboard, 1994; Now's the Time, 1995; The Topological Shovel (essays), Canada, 1999; Gravity, 2004; Entanglement, 2004, Canada. Contributions to: Various magazines and journals. Honour: Co-Winner, Alice Hunt Bartlett Award, 1975. Address: 14 Hopton Road, Hereford HR1 1BE, England.

# DICTIONARY OF INTERNATIONAL BIOGRAPHY

**FISHER Carrie,** b. USA. Actress and Author. m. Paul Simon, 1983, divorced, 1984. Education: Central School of Speech & Drama, London. Career: First appearances: at a nightclub, with mother, aged 13, Broadway chorus in Irene, aged 15; Stage appearances: Censored Scenes from Hong Kong, Agnes of God, both Broadway; Films include: Star Wars; The Empire Strikes Back; Return of the Jedi; The Blues Brothers; Garbo Talks; The Man With One Red Shoe; When Harry Met Sally; Hannah and Her Sisters; The 'Burbs; Sibling Rivalry; Drop Dead Fred; Soapdish; This is My Life; Austin Powers: International Man of Mystery; Scream 3; Famous; Heartbreakers, 2001; Jay and Silent Bob Strike Back, 2001; A Midsummer Night's Rave, 2002; Several TV appearances. Publications: Postcards from the Edge, also screenplay, 1987; Surrender the Pink, 1990; Delusions of Grandma, 1994; Several short stories. Honours: Photoplay Best Newcomer of the Year, 1974; PEN for first novel (Postcards from the Edge, 1987). Address: Creative Artists Agency, 9830 Wilshire Boulevard, Beverly Hills, CA 90212, USA.

**FISHER Charles Harold,** b. 20 November 1906, Hiawatha, West Virginia, USA. Chemistry Researcher and Teacher. m. Elizabeth Snyder. Education: BS, Roanoke College, 1928; MS, 1929, PhD, 1932, University of Illinois, Urbana. Appointments: Instructor, Chemistry, Harvard University, 1932-35; Research Group Leader, US Bureau of Mines, Pittsburgh, Pennsylvania, 1935-40; Research Group Leader, USDA East Regional Research Center, Philadelphia, 1940-50; Director, USDA Southern Regional Research Center, New Orleans, Louisiana, 1950-72; Consultant, Textile Research, Republic of South Africa, 1967, Food Technology, Pan American Union, 1968; Research Associate, Roanoke College, Salem, Virginia, 1972-; Consultant, Paper Technology, Library of Congress, 1973-76; Established Lawrence D and Mary A Fisher Scholarship, Roanoke College, 1978. Publications: Over 200 including (co-author) book: Eminent American Chemists, 1992; 72 patents include (co-inventor) Acrylic Rubber, 1992. Honours include: Honorary DSc, Tulane University, 1953, Roanoke College, 1963; Southern Chemists Award, 1956; Herty Medal, 1959; Chemical Pioneer Award, 1966; Polymer Science Pioneer, Polymer News, 1981; Distinguished Alumnus, Roanoke College, 1992; Hall of Fame, Salem Educational Foundation, 1996. Memberships include: American Chemical Society, Board, 1969-71; American Institute of Chemists, President, 1962-63, Board Chairman, 1963, 1973-75; Roanoke College Alumni Association, President, 1978-79; Board Member, Salem Educational Foundation, 1990-99; Board Member, Salem Historical Society, 1991-93; American Institute of Chemical Engineers. Address: Roanoke College, 221 College Lane, Salem, VA 24153, USA.

**FISHER John William,** b. 15 February 1931, Ancell, Missouri, USA. Professor Emeritus; Structural Engineer. m. Nelda Rae Adams, 3 sons, 1 daughter. Education: BScE, Washington University, St Louis, Missouri, USA, 1956; MS,1958, PhD, 1964, Lehigh University, Bethlehem, Pennsylvania, USA. Appointments: US Army, 1951-53; Assistant Bridge Research Engineer, National Academy of Sciences, AASHO Road Test, Ottawa, Illinois, 1958-1961; Research Instructor, 1961-1964; Assistant and Associate Professor of Civil Engineering, 1966-1969; Professor of Civil and Environmental Engineering, 1969-2002; Associate Director, Fritz Engineering Laboratory, 1971-1985; Director, ATLSS, 1986-1999; Joseph T Stuart Chair in Civil Engineering, 1988-2002; Co-Director, ATLSS Engineering Research Center (Center for Advanced Technology for Large Structural Systems), 1999-2001; Professor Emeritus, 2002. Publications: Co-author: 269 articles in professional journals; 4 books. Honours: Named Engineer of the Year in Research, Institute of Bridge Integrity and Safety, 1992;

Honorary Member, American Society of Civil Engineers; John A Roebling Medal for Lifetime Achievement in Bridge Engineering, 1995; Transportation Board Distinguished Lecturer, 1997; International Institute of Welding Portevin Lecturer, 1997; Named the Richard J Carrol Memorial Lecture in Civil Engineering, John Hopkins University, 1999; The John Fritz Medal awarded by the five engineering societies of the United Engineering Foundation, 2000; Roy W Crum Distinguished Service in 2000 Award by the Transportation Research Board, 2001; Achievement Educator Award, American Institute of Steel Construction, 2001; Laureate of the International Award of Merit in Structural Engineering, International Association for Bridge and Structural Engineering, 2001; Chairman's Lecture Award American Association of State Highway Officials Subcommittee on Bridges and Structures, 2004. Memberships: National Academy of Engineers; Corresponding Member, Swiss Academy of Engineering Sciences; Transportation Research Board Executive Committee, 1997-2000; Committee A2C02 Steel Bridge Committee; Specification Committee, American Institute of Steel Construction; Honorary Member of American Society of Civil Engineers; Specifications Committee, American Railroad Engineering and Maintenance-of-Way Association; American Welding Society; American Society for Engineering Education. Address: ATLSS Center, Lehigh University, 117 ATLSS Drive, Bethlehem, PA 18015, USA. E-mail: jwf2@lehigh.edu

**FISK Pauline, (Pauline Davies),** b. 27 September 1948, London, England. Writer. m. David Davies, 12 Feb 1972, 2 sons, 3 daughters. Publications: Midnight Blue, 1990; Telling the Sea, 1992; Tyger Pool, 1994; Beast of Whixall Moss, 1997; The Candle House, 1999; Sabrina Fludde, 2001; The Red Judge, 2005; The Mrs Marridge Project, 2005. Contributions to: Homes and Gardens, 1989; Something to Do With Love (anthology), 1996. Honours: Smarties Grand Prix Prize, 1990; Shortlisted, Whitbread Award. Address: c/o Laura Cecil, 17 Alwyne Villas, London N1 2HG, England.

**FISZER-SZAFARZ Berta,** b. Wilnius. Scientist. 1 son, 1 daughter. Education: PhD, University of Buenos Aires, 1956. Appointments: Laboratory Chief, Cancer Institute Villejuif, France, 1961-67; Visiting Scientist, National Cancer Institute of Bethesda, USA; Laboratory Chief, Curie Institute, France. Publications: Articles in scientific journals. Honour: Doctor honoris causa, Shenyang, China. Memberships: European Association Cancer Research; American Association Cancer Research. Address: Institut Curie-Biologie, Bat 110 Centre Universitaire, 91405 Orsay, France.

**FITCH Val Lodgson,** b. 10 March 1923, Nebraska, USA. Physicist. m. (1) Elise Cunningham, 1949, died 1972, 2 sons, 1 deceased, (2) Daisy Harper Sharp, 1976. Education: BEng, McGill University, 1948; PhD, Physics, Columbia University, 1954. Appointments: US Army, 1943-46; Instructor, Columbia University, 1953-54; Instructor, 1954-60, Professor of Physics, 1960-, Chair, Department of Physics, 1976, Cyrus Fogg Bracket Professor of Physics, 1976-84, Princeton University; James S McDonald Distinguished University Professor of Physics, 1984-. Honour: Research Corporation Award, 1968; Ernest Orlando Laurence Award, 1968; John Witherill Medal, Franklin Institute, 1976; Joint Winner, Nobel Prize for Physics, 1980. Membership: Sloan Fellow, 1960-64; Member, NAS, American Academy of Arts and Sciences, President's Science Advisory Committee, 1970-73; American Philosophical Society. Address: PO Box 708, Princeton University, Department of Physics, Princeton, NJ 08544, USA.

**FITZGERALD Tara,** b. 18 September 1969. Actress. Career: Stage debut in Our Song, London; Ophelia in Hamlet, London, 1995; Antigone, 1999; TV appearances include: The Black Candle; The Camomile Lawn; Anglo-Saxon Attitudes; Six Characters in Search of An Author; Fall From Grace; The Tenant of Wildfell Hall; The Student Prince; Women in White; Frenchman's Creek; In the Name of Love; Theatre includes: Our Song (London); Hamlet (New York); Films: Sirens, 1994; The Englishman Who Went up a Hill but Came Down a Mountain, 1995; Brassed Off, 1996; Childhood, 1997; Conquest, 1998; New World Disorder, 1998; The Cherry Orchard, 1999; Rancid Aluminium, 1999; Dark Blue World, 2000. Address: c/o Caroline Dawson Associates, 19 Sydney Mews, London, SW3 6HL, England.

**FITZPATRICK Horace, Earl of Upper Ossory and Castletown,** b. 1934 Louisville, Kentucky, USA (British National). University Research Professor; Musician. Education: BA, 1956, MMus, 1958, Yale University; Diploma (1st Honours); State Academy of Music and Drama, Vienna, 1959; Studied horn with Reginald Morley-Pegge, London, Philip Farkas, Chicago, John Barrows, Yale, Gottfried v. Freiberg, Vienna; Teenage conducting studies with uncle, Glenn Welty, leading free-lance conductor, Chicago Radio; Later with Paul Hindemith (Yale), Hans Swarowsky (Vienna), and Robert Heger (Munich); Doctor of Philosophy, Oxford University, 1965. Career includes: Various orchestral posts as principal horn, 1958-66, including: Metropolitan Opera, Radio Symphony of the Air (New York under Leonard Bernstein), Vienna Philharmonic and State Opera (deputy); Orchestra da Camera di Palazzo Pitti, Florence; Cairo State Opera; Hamburg Kammerorchester; Royal Opera House Covent Garden; London Mozart Players; Deputy Curator, Yale Collection of Musical Instruments, 1956-58; First ever Lecturer in European Music, American University, Cairo, 1959-60; First ever solo recording on 18th century horn, Golden Crest Records, 1959; Solo Debut on Natural Horn, Wigmore Hall, London, 1964; International appearances as Soloist on Natural Horn including, Salzburg, City of London, Flanders (Bruges), Edinburgh and Vienna Festivals, 1964-88; Tutoring in Music History, Wadham College, Oxford University, 1961-64; Stipendiary Lecturer, St Catherine's College, Oxford University, Member of Faculty of Music, History of Instruments, 1963-71; Pioneering research into use of music (mainly Classical period 1740-1830), according to Greek philosophical principles, as a form of healing support, 1996-; Director, International Summer Academy for Historic Performance, Austria, 1971-80; Secured Philip Bate Collection for Oxford University, set up Oxford Foundation for Historic Musical Instruments, 1964-71; Established Atelier for Historic Wind Instruments, Oxford, 1971; Professor of Natural Horn, Guildhall School of Music and Drama, 1972-79; Founded Hanover Band, 1974 and the Florilegium, 1975; Leverhulme Visiting Professor, Johannes Gutenberg-Universität, Mainz, 1981-86; Leverhulme Visiting Research Professor, Music University "Mozarteum", Salzburg, 1985-; Research Unit and Laboratory Orchestra (historic instruments) at Salzburg in dialogue with the Royal Swedish Academy of Music and the Royal Technical Institute, Stockholm, 1985-; Chairman, Aula Classica, a research, education and performance network to study the music of the Mozartean Era through its related disciplines, 1988-; Patronage of the Secretary General of the Council of Europe, 1989; Professorial Research Fellow, Institute of Musicology, University of Vienna, 1994-2000. Publications include: The Horn and Horn-Playing and the Austro-Bohemian Tradition 1680-1830, 1970; Telemann, 1973; 17 articles in The New Grove; Articles in German, French and Spanish music encyclopaedias; Concert and book reviews For The Times, Times Literary Supplement and Oxford Mail. Honours:

Numerous research grants and scholarships; Medaglia d'Oro per la Cultura, Italy, 1959; Order of St Martin, Austria, 1977; Listed in biographical dictionaries. Memberships: Athenaeum, 1981-97; Country Club UK. Address: 16 Sutherland Street, London, SW1V 4LA, England.

**FITZPATRICK Nicholas David,** b. 23 January 1947, Leicester, England. Consulting Actuary. m. Jill Brotherton, 1 son, 1 daughter. Education: Industrial Economics, Nottingham University. Appointments: Investment Analyst, Friends Provident, 1969-72; Portfolio Manager, Abbey Life, 1972-76; Equity Manager and Director of Investments, British Rail Pension Fund, 1976-86; Partner, 1986-92, Head of Investment Consulting, 1992-2001, Bacon & Woodrow; Head of Global Investment Consulting, Hewitt, 2001-. Memberships: CFA; FIA; FRSA. Address: Sommarlek, Woodhurst Park, Oxted, Surrey, RH8 9HA, England. E-mail: nick.fitz@ntlworld.com

**FJERDINGSTAD Erik,** b. 4 October 1940. Physical Chemist. Education: Student, 1959, Filosoficum, 1960, BSc, 1962, Magister Scientiarum, 1966, BEd, 1967, Diploma of Public Health, 1972. Appointments: Instructor, University of Copenhagen, 1962-66; Adjunct Virum Gymnasium, 1966-72; Assistant Professor, University of Copenhagen, 1972-76; Associate Professor, 1976-80; Now retired. Publications: Articles in international journals about the environment, heavy metals; Compendia for university students in biology and hygiene, seminar reports. Honours: Scholarship to Nordic School of Public Health, Affiliation Gothenburg University. Memberships: AAS; NYAS; LFIBA; Dan-Soc Mater Res; Danish Magister Organizations. Address: Bredebovej 23 mf, DK-2800 Kgs Lyngby, Denmark.

**FLAKE Floyd Harold,** b. 30 January 1945, Los Angeles, California. Clergy; Corporate Executive. m. Margarett Elaine McCollins, 2 sons, 2 daughters. Education: BA, Wilberforce University, 1967; DMin, United Theological Seminary, 1994. Appointments: Sales Representative, J Reynolds, 1967-68; Marketing Analyst, Xerox Corporation, 1968-70; Associate Dean of Students, Lincoln University, 1970-73; Dean of Students, Interim Dean of the Chapel, Director of MLK Centre, Boston University, 1973-76; US Congressman, 1986-97; SR Pastor, Chief Executive Officer, The Greater Allen Cathedral AME of New York, 1976-; President, Edison Charter Schools, 1998-2002; President, Wilbeyonce University, 2002-. Publications: Author, The Way of the Bootstrapper; Numerous articles on education and faith-based initiative in various publications; Co-author, Practical Virtues, 2002. Honours: Honorary Doctorates: Boston University, Wilberforce, Cheney and Lincoln; Achievement in Religion, Ebony Magazine. Memberships: Board of Directors, Fannie Mae Foundation; Board of Directors, Edison Schools; Senior Fellow, Manhattan Institute; Brookin Institute for Custom and Metropolitan Policy. Address: 110-31 Merrick Blvd, Jamaica, NY 11433, USA.

**FLEISCHMANN Ernest (Martin),** b. 7 December 1924, Frankfurt, Germany. Music Administrator. Divorced, 1 son, 2 daughters. Education: Bachelor of Commerce, Chartered Accountant, University of the Witwatersrand, South Africa, 1950; Bachelor of Music, University of Cape Town, 1954; Postgraduate work, South African College of Music, 1954-56. Debut: Conductor with Johannesburg Symphony Orchestra, 1942. Career: Conductor of various symphony orchestras and operas, 1942-55; Music Organiser, Van Riebeeck Festival, Cape Town, 1952; Director of Music and Drama, Johannesburg Festival, 1956; General Manager, London Symphony Orchestra, 1959-67; Director for Europe, CBS Records, 1967-69; Managing Director, Los Angeles Philharmonic and General Director,

Hollywood Bowl, 1969-98; Artistic Director, Ojai Festival, 1998-2003; President, Fleischmann Arts, International Arts Management and Consulting Services, (consultant to orchestras, festivals and government bodies in USA and Europe), 1998-. Publications: Commencement address, The Orchestra is Dead, Long Live the Community of Musicians, Cleveland Institute of Music, 1987; The Recession, Cultural Change, and a Glut of Orchestras, paper for Economics of The Arts, Salzburg Seminar, 1993. Honours include: Doctor of Music (honoris causa), Cleveland Institute of Music, 1987; Grand Cross of the Order of Merit, Germany, 1996; First Living Cultural Treasure of the City of Los Angeles, 1998; Officer, Ordre des Arts et Lettres, France, 1998; Knight First Class, Order of the White Rose, Finland, 1999; Gold Baton Award, American Symphony Orchestra League, 1999. Memberships: Board of Councillors, USC Thornton School of Music; Board of Directors, Los Angeles Philharmonic Association. Address: 2225 Maravilla Drive, Los Angeles, CA 90068, USA.

**FLETCHER Philip,** b. 2 May 1946. Director General of OFWAT. m. Margaret Anne Boys, 2 daughters, 1 deceased. Education: MA, Trinity College, Oxford. Appointments: Joined Civil Service, 1968, Director, Central Finance, 1986-89, Director (grade 3), Planning & Development Control, 1990-93, Chief Executive, PSA Services and Property Holdings, 1993-94, Deputy Secretary (grade 2), Cities and Countryside, 1994-95, Department of Environment; Receiver, Metropolitan Police District, 1996-2000; Director General, Water Services, 2000-. Address: OFWAT, Centre City Tower, 7 Hill Street, Birmingham B5 4UA, England. E-mail: philip.fletcher@ofwat.gsi.gov.uk

**FLETCHER Robin,** b. 11 February 1966. Education: NCTJ National Certificate in Journalism, South Glamorgan Institute, Cardiff, 1987; MBA, University of Glamorgan, 1999; MPhil (Journalism), Cardiff University, 2002. Appointments: Trainee Reporter, 1984-87, Senior Reporter, 1987-89, Birmingham Evening Mail/Birmingham Post; Deputy Editor/Acting Editor, Bromsgrove Weekly Mail Series, 1989; News Editor, Focus Newspapers, Birmingham, 1989-90; Senior Editor, Midland Weekly Media & Editor, Solihull News, 1990-92; Editor/Director, Northampton Chronicle & Echo, 1992-94; Editor/Director, Evening Gazette, Blackpool, 1994-95; Editor, Wales on Sunday, Western Mail and Echo, Cardiff, 1996-97; Editor, South Wales Echo, Western Mail and Echo, Cardiff, 1997-2001; Change Development Manager, 2001-02, Communications Director, 2002-03, Trinity Mirror Regionals, London; Founding Director, Reflex Business Services Ltd, Cardiff/London, 2003-. Honours: Highly Commended, Regional Editor of Year Awards, 1994; Honorary Fellow, Royal Society of Arts, 1999; Honorary Fellow, University of Wales Institute, Cardiff, 2002; Joint Winner, Best Consultancy, Communicators in Business South West Awards, 2004. Memberships: Member, Communicators in Business; Affiliate, Institute of Business Advisers; Affiliate, Institute of Management Consultants. Address: Reflex Business Services Ltd, Solstar House, 11 Blackwell Close, Stonehouse, Gloucestershire GL10 2HF, England. E-mail: robinfletcher@reflexservices.com Website: www.reflexservices.com

**FLEXNER Kurt Fisher,** b. 26 September, 1915, Vienna, Austria. Economist. m. Josephine M Moncure, 2 sons. Education: BA, Johns Hopkins University, 1946; PhD, Economics, Columbia University, 1954. Appointments: Professor of Economics, New York University, 1950-1960; Professor Emeritus, The University of Memphis; Chairman, Department of Economics, 1968-87; Chief Economist, Deputy Manager, The American Bankers Association, 1960-67; Chief Financial Institutions Advisor, The Agency of International

Development of the USA, 1967-69. Publications: The European Payments Union, 1955; The Savings and Loan Industry in the State of New York, 1963; The Enlightened Society – The Economy with a Human Face, 1989; The 21st Century – The Best or the Last, awaiting publication; About 100 articles in professional and trade journals. Honours: President, The Economic Club of Memphis, 1984-92; Member, International Advisory Committee to the Austrian Prime Minister, 1990-93; Advisor, Council to the President, Russia, 1992-96. Address: The Fountains at Millbrook, 17 Crestview Road, Millbrook, NY 12545, USA.

**FLID Mark Rafailovich,** b. 8 July 1948, Moscow, USSR. Chemist. 1 daughter. Education: Studies, Moscow Institute of Fine Chemical Technology, 1966-72; PhD, 1978; Doctor of Technical Science, Professor, 2002. Appointments: Research Scientist, 1972-79, Senior Research Scientist, 1979-92, Head of Laboratory, 1992-98, Head of Department, 1998, Vice-Director, JSC Scientific Research Engineering Centre, 2005-, Federal State Scientific Research Institute "Syntez" (former Institute of Chlorine Industry), the leading specialist in the vinyl chloride problem in Russia. Publications: The elaboration and creation of new vinyl chloride production technologies, 1996; The ethane oxidative chlorination process, 1997; The routes of deep oxidation reactions in the ethylene oxychlorination process, 2001. Honours: Listed in Who's Who publications and biographical dictionaries. Memberships: Mendeleev's Russian Chemical Society; United Nations Solvent Options Committee, 2001-. Address: Scientific Research Engineering Centre "Syntez", Vernadsky Prospect 86, 119571, Moscow, Russia. E-mail: mflid@yandex.ru

**FLÖCKINGER Gerda,** b. 8 December 1927, Innsbruck, Austria (naturalised British citizen, 1946). Designer Maker Jewellery; Photographer; Lecturer. Education: Painting, St Martin's School of Art, 1945-50; Etching, Jewellery Design and Enamelling, Central School of Arts and Crafts, 1950-56. Appointments: Creator and Teacher, Modern Jewellery Course, Hornsey College of Art, 1962-68; Invited to be first living woman to have a solo show at the V&A, and numerous group shows throughout the UK and internationally. Honours: CBE, 1991; Freeman of the Goldsmiths' Company, 1998; Entries in biographical dictionaries and in numerous books and magazines. Address: c/o Kathleen Slater, The Crafts Council, 44a Pentonville Road, London N1 1BY, England. Goldsmiths' Company Website: www.whoswhoingoldandsilver.com

**FLOOD Thomas,** b. 21 May 1947, Dublin, Ireland (British Citizen). Chief Executive. Education: BA, English, Metaphysics and Politics, 1967-69, University College, Dublin. Appointments: Market Research Team, A E Herbert Ltd (Machine Tools), Coventry, 1969-70; Secondment to Research Team, W S Atkins Consulting Engineers, Epsom, Surrey, 1970-72; Market Research Department, 1972-73, Marketing Manager, Industrial Product Division, 1973-75, Marketing Manager, Packaging Systems Group, 1975-77, Sales Manager, Strapping Systems Unit, 1977-79, Sales and Marketing Director, Decorative Materials Unit, 1979-82, Group Marketing Manager, Packaging Systems Division, 1982-86, 3M United Kingdom PLC, Bracknell, Berkshire; Marketing Director, Wallingford, 1986-90, Deputy Chief Executive, Wallingford, 1990-92, Charity Chief Executive, Wallingford, 1992-2001, Group Chief Executive, London, 2001-, BTCV (British Trust for Conservation Volunteers). Honours: Fellow, Royal Society of Arts, 1995; Fellow, British Institute of Management, 1995; CBE, 2004. Memberships: Chair of Trustees, 1994-99, Red Admiral Aids Charity; Board Member, 1996-98, Tree Council; Board Member, 1997-99, Age Resource; Trustee, BTCV

Pension Scheme, 1997-; Member, UK Biodiversity Steering Group, 1998-; Member, 1999-2001, New Deal Task Force; Member, Home Office Volunteering Group, 2000-2001; Co-opted to Board, ACEVO, 2002; ODPM, Cleaner, Safer, Greener Communities Fora, 2004-. Address: c/o BTCV, 80 York Way, London N1 9AG, England.

**FLOUD Roderick Castle,** b. 1 April 1942, Barnes, England. University Professor. m. Cynthia Anne, 2 daughters. Education: BA, 1961, MA, D Phil, 1970, Oxford University. Appointments: Lecturer, Economic History, University College London, 1966-69; Lecturer in Economic History and Fellow of Emmanuel College, Cambridge, 1969-75; Professor of Modern History, Birkbeck College, London, 1975-88; Visiting Professor of History and Economics, Stanford University, California, 1980-81; Provost of City of London Polytechnic (later London Guildhall University), 1988-2002; Vice-Chancellor, 2002-2004, President, 2004, London Metropolitan University. Publications include: An Introduction to Quantitative Methods for Historians, 1973-80; The British Machine Tool Industry 1850-1914, 1976; Height, Health and History (with K Wachter and A Gregory), 1990; The Cambridge Economic History of Modern Britain (editor with P Johnson), 2004. Honours: Honorary DLitt, City University; Honorary Fellow, Birkbeck College, Wadham College, Emmanuel College; Fellow British Academy; Fellow of City and Guilds of London Institute. Memberships: Athenaeum; Board, European University Association; Board, Universities UK. Address: London Metropolitan University 31 Jewry, London EC3N 2EY, England. E-mail: rfloud@londonmet.ac.uk

**FLOURNOY Dayl Jean II,** b. 17 December 1944, San Antonio, Texas, USA. Clinical Microbiologist. m. 2 sons, 1 daughter. Education: BS, Southwest Texas State University, San Marcos, Texas, 1965; AS, San Antonio College, Texas, 1966; MT, ASCP, Santa Rosa Medical Center, Texas, 1966; MA, Incarnate Word College, San Antonio, Texas, 1968; PhD, University of Houston, Texas, 1973; Postdoctoral, St Luke's Episcopal Hospital, Houston Texas, 1975; Fellow, Oklahoma Geriatric Education Center, Oklahoma City, 1991. Appointments include: Director of Clinical Microbiology/Serology, Veterans Affairs Medical Center, Oklahoma City, 1975-; Professor of Pathology, OUHSC, 1987-. Publications: Over 200 articles in peer reviewed journals. Honours: Fellowships, awards include: Charlotte S Leebron Memorial Trust Award, Oklahoma State Medical Association, 1993; Advanced Toastmaster Silver Certification, Toastmasters International, 2000; Fellow, American Academy of Microbiology, 1986-; Fellow, Society for Hospital Epidemiology of America, 2004. Memberships include: American Society of Microbiology; Society for Hospital Epidemiology of America; Southwestern Association of Clinical Microbiology; Editorial Board, American Journal of Infection Control, 2000-2003. Address: Dir Micro, VAMC (113) 921 13th Street, Oklahoma City, OK 73104, USA.

**FLOWER David John Colin,** b. 7 June 1956, London, England. Occupational Physician. m. Harriett Ann Sinclair, 1 son, 1 daughter. Education: BSc (Eng), Chemical Engineering, 1977; MB BS, 1982; MD, 1996; Diploma, Royal College of Obstetricians & Gynaecologists, 1986; Member, Royal College of General Practitioners, 1987; Associate, 1993, Member, 1996, Fellow, 2002, Faculty of Occupational Medicine RCP; Diploma in Aviation Medicine, 1999. Appointments: House Surgeon, Professorial Surgical Unit, University College Hospital, London; Principal in General Practice, Wantage, Oxfordshire; Occupational Physician, UK Atomic Energy Authority; Consultant and Senior Consultant, Occupational Physician, British Airways plc; Group Head of Health, Safety and Environment Centrica plc; Part time Consultant, Adviser, UK

Sport. Publications: Scientific and popular articles on alertness, performance and the management of jet lag; Contributing author, British Olympic Association Athlete Publications, Sydney 2000, Athens 2004; Battelle, US Department of Transportation, Handbook on Fatigue in Transportation. Memberships: President, Section of Occupational Medicine; Royal Society of Medicine; Member, Society of Occupational Medicine; American College of Occupational and Environmental Medicine. Address: Centrica plc, Millstream, Maidenhead Road, Windsor, Berkshire SL4 5GD, England.

**FLOWER Roderick John,** b. 29 November 1945, Southampton, England. Pharmacologist. m. Lindsay Joyce Riddell. Education: BSc, University of Sheffield, 1971; PhD, University of London, 1974; DSc, 1985. Appointments: Senior Scientist, Wellcome Foundation, 1973-84; Professor of Pharmacology, University of Bath, 1984-89; Lilly Professor, Biochemical Pharmacology, St Bart's Hospital Medical School, London, 1989-94; Wellcome Trust principal Fellow, Professor of Pharmacology, 1994-; Head of William Harvey Research Institute, 1998-2002; Consultant in field; Co-editor, Glucocorticoids, 2000. Publications: More than 200 peer reviewed papers; More than 200 other publications including reviews, books, book chapters, abstracts, conference proceedings, editorials and published correspondence. Honours: Sandoz Prize,1978, Gaddum Medal, 1986, William Withering Prize, 2003, British Pharmacological Society; Fellow Academy of Medical Sciences; Fellow, Royal Society. Memberships: British Pharmacological Society; Academia Europea, 2002

**FO Dario,** b. 24 March 1926, Leggiuno-Sangiamo, Italy. Dramatist; Actor. m. Franca Rame, 1954, 1 child. Education: Academy of Fine Arts, Milan. Appointments: Dramatist and Actor in agitprog theatre and television; Co-Founder (with Franca Rame), Dramatist, Actor, Nuova Scena acting groupe, 1968, Collettivo Teatrale la Comune, 1970. Publications: Numerous plays, including: Le commedie, I-IX, 1966-91, 1992; Morte accidentale di un anarchico (Accidental Death of an Anarchist), 1974; Non si paga, non si paga! (We Can't Pay? We Won't Pay!), 1974; Tutta casa, letto e chiesa (Adult Orgasm Escapes From the Zoo), 1978; Female Parts (with Franca Rame), 1981; Manuale et minimo dell attore, 1987; Mistero Buffo, 1977; Coming Home; History of Masks; Archangels Don't Play Pinball; Hooters, Trumpets and Raspberries; The Tricks of the Trade, 1991; Il papa e la stega (The Pope and the Witch), 1989; L'Eroina-Grassa e'Bello, 1991; Johan Padan a la Descoverta de le Americhe, 1991; Dario Fo Recita Ruzzante, 1993; Il diavolo con le zinne, 1997. Honour: Hon DLitt, Westminster, 1997; Nobel Prize for Literature, 1997.

**FODOR László,** b. 25 November 1961, Budapest, Hungary. Geologist. m. Judit Fodor, 1 daughter. Education: Master of Geology, Eötvös University, Budapest, Hungary, 1987; PhD, Université P et M Curie, Paris, France, 1991. Appointments: Assistant Lecturer, Department of Applied and Environmental Geology, 1993-98, Assistant Professor, Department of Applied Geology, 1998-2000, Eötvös University; Senior Scientist, Geological Institute of Hungary, 2000-. Publications: Articles in scientific journals as co-author include: Miocene-Pliocene tectonic evolution of the Slovenian Periadriatic line and surrounding area, 1998; Tectonics 17, 690-709. Honours include: Széchenyi Professorial Scholarship, Ministry of Education of Hungary, 1997-2000; Bolyai Janos Scholarship for Research, Hungarian Academy of Sciences, 2001-2004. Memberships: American Geophysical Union; Geological Society of America; International Association of Sedimentologists; Hungarian Geological Society. Address: Geological Institute of Hungary; Stefania ut 14, H-1143 Budapest, Hungary. E-mail: fodor@mafi.hu

# DICTIONARY OF INTERNATIONAL BIOGRAPHY

**FOGEL Steven Anthony**, b. 16 October 1951, United Kingdom. Solicitor. m. Joan Selma Holder, 2 sons, 1 daughter. Education: LLB Honours, 1972, LLM, 1973, King's College, London; ACIArb, 1991. Appointments: Cohen & Meyohas, Paris, 1973-74; Articled, Titmuss Sainer & Webb (now Dechert): Qualified, 1976; Partner since 1980; Head of Property Department, 1990-98; Member of firm's world-wide Finance and Real Estate Executive; Director, Investment Property Forum, 1999-; Blundell Law Lecturer, 1985, 1996; Member of Law Commission Working Party on Landlord and Tenant CWP 95 HMSO, 1985-96; Member of RICS working party on arbitration under the Landlord and Tenant Act 1954, 1993-; Former Governor of Anglo-American Real Property Institute; Member, British Property Federation Customer Focus Working Party, 1996-2000; Former legal advisor to Property Committee of British Retail Consortium and acted for the in the passage through Parliament of the Landlord and Tenant (Covenants) Act 1995; Director of LJCC, 1992-; Trustee "Motivation" wheelchair charity, 1992-. Publications: Encyclopaedia of Forms and Precedents, volume 22, (contributor), 1986, 1997; Landlord and Tenant Factbook (co-author), 1992-; Insurance, Terrorism and Leases (co-author), 1993; Privity of Contract: A Practitioners Guide to the Landlord and Tenant (Covenants) Act (co-author), 1995, 3rd edition, 2001; Handbook of Rent Review (consultant editor). Memberships: Director, Investment Property Forum; Anglo-American Real Property Institute; Associate Member, Chartered Institute of Arbitrators. Address: c/o Dechert LLP, 2 Serjeant's Inn, London EC4Y 1LT, England.

**FONDA Bridget**, b. 27 January 1964, Los Angeles, CA, USA. Actress. Education: NY University theatre programme; Studied acting at Lee Strasburg Institute and with Harold Guskin. Career: Workshop stage performances include Confession and Pastels; Films: Aria (Tristan and Isolde sequence), 1987; You Can't Hurry Love, 1988; Shag, 1988; Scandal, 1989; Strapless, 1989; Frankenstein Unbound, 1990; The Godfather: Part III, 1990; Doc Hollywood, 1991; Out of the Rain, 1991; Single White Female, 1992; Singles, 1992; Bodies Rest and Motion, 1993; Point of No Return, 1993; Little Buddha, 1994; It Could Happen To You, 1994; Camilla, 1994; The Road to Welville, 1994; Rough Magic, 1995; Balto (voice), 1995; Grace of My Heart, 1996; City Hall, 1996; Drop Dead Fred; Light Years (voice); Iron Maze; Army of Darkness; Little Buddha; Touch; Jackie Brown; Finding Graceland; The Break Up; South of Heaven West of Hell; Monkey Bone; Lake Placid; Delivering Milo; TV series: 21 Jump Street; Jacob Have I Loved; WonderWorks (episode), 1989; The Edge (The Professional Man); TV film: Leather Jackets, 1991; In the Gloaming, 1997. Address: c/o IFA, 8730 West Sunset Boulevard, Suite 490, Los Angeles, CA 90069, USA.

**FONDA Jane**, b. 21 December 1937. Actress. m. (1) Roger Vadim, 1967, divorced 1973, deceased 2000, 1 daughter, (2) Tom Hayden, 1973, divorced 1989, 1 son, (3) Ted Turner, 1991, separated. Education: Vassar College. Films include: Tall Story, 1960; A Walk on the Wild Side, 1962; Sunday in New York, 1963; La Ronde, 1964; Barbarella, 1968; They Shoot Horses Don't They? 1969; Steelyard Blues, Tout va Bien, 1972; The Blue Bird, 1975; Fun with Dick and Jane, 1976; Coming Home, California Suite, 1978; The China Syndrome, 1979; Nine to Five, 1980; On Golden Pond, 1981; Agnes of God, 1985; Stanley and Iris, 1990; Lakota Woman, Producer, 1994; Stage Work includes: Invitation to a March; The Fun Couple; Strange Interlude; TV: The Dollmaker, 1984. Publications: Jane Fonda's Workout Book, 1982; Women Coming of Age, 1984; Jane Fonda's Workout and Weightloss Program, 1986; Jane Fonda's New Pregnancy Workout and Total Birth Program, 1989; Jane Fonda Workout Video; Jane Fonda Cooking for Healthy Living, 1996. Honours: Academy Award Best Actress, 1972, 1979; Emmy Award, The Dollmaker, 1984. Address: c/o Kim Hodgert, CAA, 9830 Wilshire Boulevard, Beverly Hills, CA 90212, USA.

**FONDA Peter**, b. 23 February 1940, NY, USA. Film Actor, Director and Producer. m. Susan Brewer, divorced 1974, 2 children. Education: University of Omaha. Career: Tammy and the Doctor, 1963; The Victors, 1963; Lilith, 1964; The Young Lovers, 1964; The Wild Angels, 1966; The Trip, 1967; Easy Rider (also co-screenplay writer, co-producer), 1969; The Last Movie, 1971; The Hired Hand (also director), 1971; Two People (also director), 1973; Dirty Mary, Crazy Harry, 1974; Race With the Devil, 1975; 92 in the Shade, 1975; Killer Force, 1975; Fighting Mad, 1976; Future World, 1976; Outlaw Blues, 1977; High Ballin', 1978; Wanda Nevada (also director), 1979; Open Season; Smokey and the Bandit II, 1980; Split Image, 1982; Certain Fury, 1985; Dead Fall, 1993; Nadja, 1994; Love and a 45, 1994; Painted Hero, 1996; Escape From LA, 1996; Idaho Transfer (also director); Ulee's Gold, 1997; Spasm; Fatal Mission; Reckless; Cannonball Run (cameo); Dance of the Dwarfs; Mercenary Fighters; Jungle Heat; Diajobu My Friend; Peppermint Frieden; The Rose Garden; Family Spirit; South Beach; Bodies Rest and Motion; Deadfall; Molly and Gina; South of Heaven West of Hell; The Limey; Keeping Time; TV films: The Hostage Tower, 1980; Don't Look Back, 1996; A Reason to Live; A Time of Indifference; Sound; Certain Honorable Men; Montana. Address: IFA Talent Agency, 8730 West Sunset Boulevard, Suite 490, Los Angeles, CA 90069, USA.

**FONF Vladimir**, b. 13 August 1949, Michurinsk, Russia. Mathematician. Divorced, 1 daughter. Education: MSc, Mathematics, 1971; PhD, Mathematics, 1979; DSc, Mathematics, 1991. Appointments: Docent, Professor, Kharkov Railroad Institute, Ukraine, 1983-93; Associate Professor, Ben-Gurion University, Israel, 1993-97, Professor, Ben-Gurion University of the Negev, 1997-. Publications: More than 60 articles in mathematical journals in: Bulgaria, Canada, England, Germany, Israel, Poland, Spain, USA, USSR; Co-author, Handbook of Banach Spaces, 2001. Honour: Guastella Fellowship, 1993-96. Membership: Israel Mathematical Union. Address: Department of Mathematics, Ben-Gurion University of the Negev, PO Box 653, Beer-Sheva 84105, Israel. E-mail: fonf@math.bgu.ac.il

**FONG Eileen Peksiew**, b. 1 April 1964, Malaysia. Plastic Surgeon. m. Andreas Kompa. Education: MBBS, Malaya, 1989; FRCS, Edinburgh, 1993; Dipl Plastic Surgery, British Association of Plastic Surgeons, RCS, England, 1997; FAM, Singapore, Plastic Surgery, 2000. Appointments: Residency in General Surgery, UK, 1991; Residency in Plastic Surgery, UK, 1993-97; Registrar in Plastic Surgery, Singapore, 1997-2000; Consultant Plastic Surgeon, University Hospital Kuala Lumpur, Malaysia, 2000-2004; Consultant Plastic Surgeon, Gleneagles Intan Medical Centre, Kuala Lumpur, Malaysia, 2004-, Sunway Medical Centre, Selangor, Malaysia, 2004-. Publications: Articles in medical journals: Immediate Autogenous Breast Reconstruction in Stage 1 to Stage 3 Breast Cancer, 2001; Keloids – The Sebum Hypothesis Revised, 2002. Honour: Excellence in Service Award, University of Malaya, 2003. Memberships: Malaysian Association of Plastic, Aesthetic and Cranomaxillofacial Surgeons; Fellow, Academy of Medicine of Singapore; Fellow of the Royal College of Surgeons of Edinburgh. Address: Suite 1-15, Gleneagles Intan Medical Centre, 282-286 Jalan Ampang, 50450 Kuala Lumpur, West Malaysia. E-mail: dreileenfong@yahoo.com

**FONT-RÉAULX Benoît de,** b. 20 January 1951, Boulogne sur Seine, France. Senior Banker. m. Isabelle de Roussel de Preville, 2 sons, 2 daughters. Education: Bachelor's Degree, Honours, 1968; Ingenieur des Mines de Paris, 1973; Master in Economic Sciences, 1973; Ingenieur au Corps des Mines, 1975. Appointments: Head, Industrial Environment Service, Ministry of Industry, Rouen, 1977-79; Planning Staff Member, Foreign Office, Paris, 1979-80; Private Secretary of the French Foreign Minister, 1980-81; Head of Nuclear Service, Ministry of Industry, Paris, 1981-83; Banker, J P Morgan, 1983-95; Banker, Societe Generale, Paris, 1995-. Address: Societe Generale, 17 Cours Valmy, 92972 Paris La Defense, France. E-mail: benoit.de-font-reaulx@sgcib.com

**FONTANA Edmund Louis,** b. 25 February 1949, Jersey City, New Jersey, USA. Retired Educator. m. Patricia Blizzard. Education: Lea College, Albert Lea, Minnesota, 1967-70; BA, Elementary Education, 1972, MA, Urban Education, 1983, New Jersey City University. Appointments: Teacher, 7th and 8th Slow Learners, Rutherford Junior High, Rutherford, New Jersey, 1972-73; Teacher, 7th Grade Mathematics, Horace Mann Elementary, North Bergen, New Jersey, 1975-86; Teacher, 6th Grade, 1986-87, 5th Grade, 1987-98, Social Studies and Language Art, 1998-2000, JFK School (self contained), North Bergen, New Jersey; Teacher, 5th Grade, Robert Fulton Elementary School, North Bergen, New Jersey, 2000-2004; Minor League Umpire and baseball player; Retired, 2004-. Honours: Pin of Excellence, 1993; "Dare" Teacher of the Year, 1991, 1992; District Teacher of the Year, 1990, 1994; Disney Hand Nominee for Most Innovative Teacher, 2004; Listed in Who's Who publications and biographical dictionaries. Memberships: Coach, Freshman and Junior Varsity Baseball, 1977-81; Elementary School Yearbook Moderator, 1984-86; School Safety Patrol Monitor, 1997-2002; Mentorship for New Faculty, 1997-2004; Family Life Committee, 1986-2004; State Mathematics and Social Study Committees, 1993-96; Member, 1992-96, Chairman, 1994-95, School Based Management; Chairman, School Treasury for Quality Assurance, 1993-97. Address: 3 Sandpiper Court, Carolina Shores, NC 28467, USA. E-mail: fsugarbear@aol.com

**FONTINOY Charles-Marie,** b. 12 March 1920, Stavelot, Belgium. Retired University Professor. Education: Licencié en philosophie et lettres, 1941; Agrégé de l'Enseignement Secondaire Supérieur, 1941; Docteur en langues orientales, 1963. Appointments: Secondary School Teacher, Athénée Royal d'Aywaille, Belgium, 1945-66; Professor, Hebrew Bible and Semitic Languages, State University of Liège, Belgium, 1966-85; Chairman, Department of Oriental Studies, 1980-85. Publications: Articles in professional journals. Honours: Recipient, various grants, 1954-66; Various awards including: Grand Officier de l'ordre de Léopold II, Brussels, 1981. Memberships: Belgian Society of Oriental Studies. Address: La Bovière 3, B-4920 Aywaille, Belgium.

**FORBES Bryan,** b. 22 July 1926, Stratford, London, England. Film Executive; Director; Screenwriter; Author. m. Nanette Newman, 1955, 2 daughters. Education: West Ham Secondary School; Royal Academy of Dramatic Art. Appointments: Writer, Producer, Director of numerous films and TV programmes. Publications: Truth Lies Sleeping, 1951; The Distant Laughter, 1972; Notes for a Life, 1974; The Slipper and the Rose, 1976; Ned's Girl, 1977; International Velvet, 1978; Familiar Strangers, 1979; That Despicable Race, 1980; The Rewrite Man, 1983; The Endless Game, 1986; A Song at Twilight, 1989; A Divided Life, 1992; The Twisted Playground, 1993; Partly Cloudy, 1995; Quicksand, 1996; The Memory of all That, 1999. Honours: Best Screenplay Awards; UN Award; Many Film Festival Prizes;

Honorary DL, London, 1987; Honorary Doctor of Literature, Sussex University, 1999; CBE. Memberships: Ex-President, Writers Guild of Great Britain; Ex-President, Beatrix Potter Society; President, National Youth Theatre of Great Britain. Address: Pinewood Studies, Iver Heath, Buckinghamshire, England.

**FORD Anna,** b. 2 October 1943. Broadcaster. m. (1) Alan Holland Bittles, (2) Charles Mark Edward Boxer, deceased 1988, 2 daughters. Education: Manchester University. Appointments: Work for student interests, Manchester University, 1966-69; Lecturer, Rupert Stanley College of Further Education, Belfast, 1970-72; Staff Tutor, Social sciences, North Ireland Region, Open University, 1972-74; Presenter and Reporter, Granada TV, 1974-76, Man Alive, BBC, 1976-77, Tomorrow's World, BBC, 1977-78; Newscaster, ITN, 1978-80; W TV am, 1980-82; Freelance broadcasting and writing, 1982-86; BBC news and current affairs, 1989-. Publication: Men: A Documentary, 1985. Honour: Hon LLD (Manchester); 1998; Honourable Bencher Middle Temple, 2002. Membership: Trustee, Royal Botanic Gardens, Kew. Address: BBC Television Centre, Wood Lane, London, W12 7RJ, England.

**FORD Harrison,** b. 13 July 1942, Chicago, USA. Actor. m. (1) Mary Ford, 2 sons, (2) Melissa Ford, divorced 2004, 1 son, 1 daughter. Education: Ripon College. Career: Numerous TV appearances; Films include: Dead Heat on a Merry-Go-Round, 1966; Luv, 1967; The Long Ride Home, 1967; Getting Straight, 1970; Zabriskie Point, 1970; The Conversation, 1974; American Graffiti, 1974; Star Wars, 1977; Heroes, 1977; Force 10 from Navarone, 1978; Hanover Street, 1979; Frisco Kid, 1979; The Empire Strikes Back, 1980; Raiders of the Lost Ark, 1981; Blade Runner; Return of the Jedi, 1983; Indiana Jones and the Temple of Doom; Witness; The Mosquito Coast, 1986; Working Girl, 1988; Frantic, 1988; Indiana Jones and the Last Crusade, 1989; Presumed Innocent, 1990; Regarding Henry, 1991; The Fugitive, 1992; Patriot Games, 1992; Clear and Present Danger, 1994; Sabrina, 1995; Air Force One, 1996; Six Days and Seven Nights, 1998; Random Hearts, 1999; What Lies Beneath, 2000; K-19: The Widowmaker (also executive producer), 2002; Hollywood Homicide, 2003. Address: 10279 Century Woods Drive, Los Angeles, CA 90067, USA.

**FORDE Walter Patrick,** b. 17 June 1943, Bunclody, County Wexford, Eire. Education: Maynooth College, Ireland, BA, 1964; BD, 1967; H Dip Ed, 1969; Diploma in Social Science, 1972; Ordained, 1968. Appointments: Teacher, St Peter's College, Wexford, 1969-73; General Secretary, National Youth Federation, 1973-74; Director of Social Services and Press Officer, The Diocese of Ferns, 1974-96; Parish Priest, Castlebridge, Co Wexford. Publications: Books include: Adventuring in Priesthood, 1993; The Christian in the Market Place, 1994; Changing Social Needs, 1995; Changing Christian Concerns, 1999; Joan's People, 2003. Honours: County Wexford Person of the Year, 1988; Honorary Life Member, National Youth Federation; Lifetime Achievement Award, Religious Press Association of Ireland, 1993. Address: The Presbytery, Castlebridge, Co Wexford, Eire.

**FOREMAN Alfred G,** b. 19 March 1960, Sulfur, Louisiana, USA. Theologian; Philosopher. Education: BA, University of Louisiana, Layfayette, Louisiana, 1987; MA, Liberty University, Lynchburg, Virginia, 1991. Appointments: Pastor, Church of God, 1986-2002; Imman Saladin of the Al-Ruh-Al-Amin Mosque (Spirit of Faith and Truth Mosque); Louisiana Philosophical Institute of Humanities; Lecturer, Islamic Center of Lafayette, Louisiana; Founder, South Louisiana Weather Station. Publications: The Ecclesiastic Order: The Apology,

Vol 1, 2002; The Christian and Islamic Thesis in History, 2003; Exposition of Islamic Knowledge: Incoherence of the Secularist, 2004; Book of Islamic Philosophy, Prophetic Wisdom and Directives. Honours: Listed in Who's Who Publications. Membership: International Palm Society; Center for Islam and Science. Address: 130 Palms Road, Crowley, LA 70526, USA.

**FORMAN Milos,** b. 18 February 1932, Caslav. Education: Film Faculty, Academy of Music and Dramatic Art, Prague. Appointments: Director, Film presentations, Czech TV, 1954-56; of Laterna Magika, Prague, 1958-62; Member, artistic committee, Sebor-Bor Film Producing Group; Director, films including: Talent Competition; Peter and Pavla, 1964; The Knave of Spades; A Blonde in Love, 1965; Episode in Zruc; Like a House on Fire (A Fireman's Ball), 1968; Taking Off, 1971; Co-Director, Visions of Eight, 1973; One Flew Over the Cuckoo's Nest, 1975; Hair, 1979; Ragtime, 1980; Amadeus, 1983; Valmont, 1988; The People Vs Larry Flint, 1995; Appeared in New Year's Day, 1989; Keeping the Faith, 2000. Publications. Turnaround: A Memoir (with Jan Novak), 1993. Honours: Czech Film Critics' award for Peter and Pavla, 1963, Grand Prix 17th International Film Festival, Locarno, for Peter and Pavla, 1964; Prize Venice Festival, 1965; Grand Prix, French Film Academy for a Blonde in Love, 1966; Klement Gottwald State Prize, 1967; Academy Award (Best Director) for One Flew Over the Cuckoo's Nest, 1976; Academy Award, César Award, 1985; Golden Globe for Best Director, 1996; Silver Bear for Best Director, Berlin Film Festival, 2000. Address: C/o Robert Lantz, 888 7th Avenue, New York, NY 10106, USA.

**FORSTER Gordon Colin Fawcett,** b. 30 August 1928, Tadcaster, Yorkshire, England. Academic. m. Judith Mary Duffus Passey. Education: BA, University of Leeds, 1949; Institute of Historical Research, University of London, 1950-52. Appointments: Douglas Knoop Research Fellow, University of Sheffield, 1952-55; Assistant Lecturer, Lecturer, Senior Lecturer, School of History, 1955-93; Chairman, School of History, 1982-85, Life Fellow, 1993-, University of Leeds. Publications: Chapters in Victoria County History volumes: York; Hull; Beverley; Chester; The East Riding Justices of the Peace in the Seventeenth Century; Catalogue of the Records of the Borough of Scarborough; Articles in Northern History and county historical journals; Founder-Editor, Northern History, 1966-. Honours: Fellow of the Royal Historical Society; Fellow of the Society of Antiquaries; Silver Medal, Yorkshire Archaeological Society. Memberships: President, Yorkshire Archaeological Society, 1974-79; President, Thoresby Society, 1983-87; President, Conference of Regional and Local Historians; Chairman, Yorkshire Archaeological Society Record Series, 1978-. Address: School of History, University of Leeds, Leeds LS2 9JT, England.

**FORSYTH Frederick,** b. 25 August 1938, Ashford, Kent, England. Writer. m. (1) Carole Cunningham, 1973, 2 sons, (2) Sandy Molloy. Education: University of Granada. Appointments: Reporter, Eastern Daily Press, 1958-61; Reuters News Agency, 1961-65; Reporter, 1965-67, Assistant Diplomatic Correspondent, BBC, 1967-68; Freelance journalist, Nigeria and Biafra, 1968-69; Narrated Soldiers (TV), 1985; Several TV appearances. Publications: Novels: The Day of the Jackal, 1971; The Odessa File, 1972; The Dogs of War, 1974; The Shepherd, 1975; The Devil's Alternative, 1979; The Fourth Protocol, 1984; The Negotiator, 1989; The Deceiver, 1991; Great Flying Stories, 1991; The Fist of God, 1993; Icon, 1996; The Phantom of Manhattan, 1999; Quintet, 2000; The Veteran and Other Stories, 2001; Other: The Biafra Story, 1969, revised edition as The Making of an African Legend: The Biafra Story, 1977; Emeka, 1982; No Comebacks: Collected Short Stories,

1982; The Fourth Protocol (screenplay), 1987. Honour: Edgar Allan Poetry Award, Mystery Writers of America, 1971; CBE. Address: c/o Bantam Books, 62-63 Uxbridge Road, London, W5 5SA, England.

**FORSYTH Peter Joseph Edward,** b. 23 January 1922, Thame, Oxfordshire, England. Research Metallurgist. m. Joan Margaret, 1 son, 1 daughter. Education: HNC, Mechanical Engineering, Oxford School of Technology, 1939-48; Fellow, Institution of Metallurgists, 1973; Doctor of Science, Council for National Academic Awards, 1973; Visiting Professor of Engineering Materials, University of Southampton, 1975-. Appointments: Research Metallurgist, Deputy Chief Scientific Officer (individual merit), Head of Aluminium Alloy Research Section also with responsibility for failures and accident investigations with particular reference to the fatigue of metals, Royal Aircraft Establishment, Farnborough, 1944-82. Publications: The Physical Basis of Metal Fatigue, 1969; Over 100 other publications mainly related to metal fatigue include: Exudation of material from slip bands at the surface of fatigued crystals of aluminium-copper alloy, 1953; A two stage process of fatigue crack growth, 1961; A unified description of micro and macroscopic fatigue crack behaviour, 1983. Honours: Rosenhain Medal for research in physical metallurgy, Institute of Metals, 1967; Prince Phillip Medal for research in aid of industry, City and Guilds of London Institute. Memberships: Fellow, Institution of Materials, Minerals and Mining. Address: 5 Hillary Road, Farnham, Surrey GU9 8QY, England.

**FORTE James Peter,** b. 19 September 1936, Boston, Massachusetts, USA. Composer; Poet; Author. m. Nancy Mosehauer Forte. Education: BA, Music, State University of New York, Albany, 1979; Brandeis University, Lowell State University, Longy School of Music, Boston University. Appointments: Independent poet, 1950-, composer, 1952-, music teacher, 1966-92, concert manager, 1974-, author, 1976-; Music Director, Robbins Library Concert Series, Arlington, Massachusetts, 1973-78; Manager, Northeastern University Symphony Orchestra, 1978-81; Founder, Chairman, Arlington Alive (Arlington Arts Council), 1979-86; Concert series director, Northeastern University Department of Music, 1979-81; Founder, Director, New England Symphony Orchestra (now New Arts Symphony Orchestra), 1981-; Founder, Director, Electric Symphony, 1988-; Director, Electric Symphony Festival, New England, 1990-. Civic Activities include: Member, Arlington Historical Commission, 1972-82; Arlington Citizens' Involvement Committee, 1974-83; Member, Robbins Library Cultural Enrichment Series Committee, 1978-81; Master of Ceremonies, Member, Guidebook Editor, Arlington Town Day Committee, 1978-82; Member, Town Meeting, Town of Arlington, 1980-83; Member, Arlington Cable Access Steering Committee, 1981; Member, Arlington Selectmen's Committee on Service Priorities, 1981. Publications: Books of poetry: Chaconne, 1990; Alone, 1990; Man of Stone, 1992; The Transparent Hero, 1993; The White Eagle, 1995; New Water, 1995; When the Rope is Untied, 1996; White Tiger White Stripes, 2002; Books: Fragments of the Whole, 1990, 1992; The Urban Vegetarian (co-author, cookbook), 1992; Music: Numerous orchestral, choral, chamber works including The Holy Child, 1968; Homeland, 1970; Angel Bells, 1975; Sinfonia for Strings: For Those Who Must Journey Into Eternity, Symphony No. 1, 1971-72; Piano Sonatas, Nos 1-5, 1969, 1971, 1973, 1982, 1983; String Quartets, Nos 3 and 4, 1967, 2002; Electronic music and music for synthesisers, acoustic instruments and voice, including Hidden Mountain, 1990; The Sacred Meadow, 1991; Deep Winter, 1993; CDs: Golden Light, 1997; At the Edge of Dawn, 1998; Rokka's Return, 2000; Through the Mist, 2001; Music of James Forte, 2002; Suite for Strings, 2003; And the Day After I

Die, Choral Music, 2003; Sinfonia for Strings, 2005; 6 cassettes. Honours include: Citizen of the Year, Arlington Chamber of Commerce, 1976; Arlington Town Day Committee Award, 1983; Muse Award, Public Action for the Arts, Boston, 1983; Proclamation, Town of Arlington, 1984; International Man of the Year, IBC, 1998-99; 20th Century Award of Achievement, IBC, 1999; Listed in several international and specialist biographical reference works. Memberships include: Massachusetts Music Teachers Association; Music Teachers National Association; American Federation of Musicians; American Legion; Fellow, International Biographical Association; American Society of Composers, Authors and Publishers. Address: Box 1316, Arlington, MA 02474, USA. E-mail: mail@wildflower publishers.com Website: www.wildflowerpublishers.com

**FOSTER Anthony,** b. 11 April 1926, Gravesend, Kent, England. Composer. m. Barbara Humphries, 26 July 1952, deceased 1991, 1 daughter. Education: LRAM, ARGO; Piano with Anne Collins, Arthur Tracy Robson, Organ with John Cook (Organist, Holy Trinity, Stratford-upon-Avon), John Webster (Organist, Oxford University); Composition and orchestration with Gordon Jacob, Richard Arnell. Career: Schools Music Specialist: Hugh Clopton, Stratford-upon-Avon, 1951; St Barnabas School, Oxford, 1954; Downs School, Brighton, 1957; Organ appointments: All Saints, Perry Street, Northfleet, 1948; All Souls, Brighton, 1957; St Matthias, Brighton, 1960; St Augustine of Canterbury, Brighton, 1969; Composed many works, secular and sacred for solo and choral voices, solo instruments and orchestra; Composed incidental music for BBC productions. Recordings: Jonah and the Whale, Harrow School of Young Musicians, Royal Albert Hall, London, 1983; A Child is Born, 1987, Christ the Lord is Risen Again, 1997, Child of Heaven, 1999, Chichester Cathedral Choir, directed by Alan Thurlow; Jubilate Deo for Organ, Alan Thurlow, Organist, Chichester Cathedral, 1988; Magnificat, Blessed Virgin Mary Service, Carlisle Cathedral Choir, directed by Jeremy Suter 2000. Publication: Jonah and the Whale, 1974. Honour: Honorary Vice-President, Brighton Schools Music and Drama Association, 1977. Memberships: The British Academy of Composers and Songwriters; The Performing Right Society. Address: 1 Cawley Road, Chichester, West Sussex PO 19 1UZ, England.

**FOSTER Brendan,** b. 12 January 1948, Hebburn, County Durham, England. Athlete. m. Susan Margaret Foster, 1972, 1 son, 1 daughter. Education: Sussex University; Carnegie College, Leeds. Career: Competed: Olympic Games, Munich, 5th in 1500 m, 1972; Montreal, bronze medal in 10,000m, 5th in 5000m, 1976; Moscow, 11th in 10, 000m, 1980; Commonwealth Games, Edinburgh, bronze medal at 1500m, 1970; Christchurch, silver medal at 5,000m, 1974; Edmonton, gold medal at 10,000m, bronze medal at 5000m, 1978; European champion at 5000m, 1974 and bronze medallist at 1500m, 1974; World record holder at 3000m and 2 miles; European record holder at 10,000m Olympic record holder at 5000m; Director, Recreation, Gateshead, March, 1982; Managing Director, Nike International, 1982-86; Vice President, Marketing (Worldwide), Vice President (Europe), 1986-87; Chairman and Managing Director, Nova International; BBC TV Commentator, 1980-. Publications: Brendan Foster with Cliff Temple, 1978; Olympic Heroes 1896-1984, 1984. Honours: Hon MEd, Newcastle University; Hon DLitt, Sussex University, 1982; BBC Sports Personality of the Year, 1974. Address: Nova International, Newcastle House, Albany Court, Monarch Road, Newcastle upon Tyne, NE4 7YB, England.

**FOSTER David (Manning),** b. 15 May 1944, Sydney, New South Wales, Australia. Novelist. Education: BSc, Chemistry, University of Sydney, 1967; PhD, Australian National University, Canberra, 1970. Publications: The Pure Land, 1974; The Empathy Experiment, 1977; Moonlite, 1981; Plumbum, 1983; Dog Rock: A Postal Pastoral, 1985; The Adventures of Christian Rosy Cross, 1986; Testostero, 1987; The Pale Blue Crochet Coathanger Cover, 1988; Mates of Mars, 1991; Self Portraits (editor), 1991; A Slab of Fosters, 1994; The Glade Within the Grove, 1996; The Ballad of Erinungarah, 1997; Crossing the Blue Montain (contributor), 1997; In the New Country, 1999; The Land Where Stories End, 2001. Short Stories: North South West: Three Novellas, 1973; Escape to Reality, 1977; Hitting the Wall: Two Novellas, 1989. Honours: The Age Award, 1974; Australian National Book Council Award, 1981; New South Wales Premier's Fellowship, 1986; Keating Fellowship, 1991-94; James Joyce Foundation Award, 1996; Miles Franklin Award, 1997; Courier Mail Award, 1999; Shortlisted, International Dublin IMPAC Award, 1998. Address: PO Box 57, Bundanoon, New South Wales 2578, Australia.

**FOSTER Giles Henry,** b. 30 June 1948, Winchester, England. Film and TV Director. m. Nicole Anne Coates, 2 sons. Education: BA Honours, English, University of York, 1969-72; MA (RCA), Film and TV, Royal College of Art, 1972-75. Career: Film and Television Director and Writer; TV include: Bertie and Elizabeth; The Prince and the Pauper; Coming Home; Oliver's Travels; The Rector's Wife; Adam Bede; Monster Maker; Northanger Abbey; Dutch Girls; The Aerodrome; The Obelisk; 5 Alan Bennett scripts; Hotel du Lac; Silas Marner; A Lady of Letters; Foyle's War; Devices and Desires; Films: Consuming Passions; Tree of Hands (Innocent Victim, USA); The Lilac Bus. Honours: BAFTA Nominations for: Silas Marner, A Lady of Letters, Foyle's War; BAFTA Award for: Hotel du Lac; Grierson Award for Best Short Film for: Devices and Desires. Memberships: British Academy of Film and Television Arts; Groucho Club. Address: c/o Anthony Jones, pfd, Dury House, 34-43, Russell Street, London WC2B 5HA, England. E-mail: ghf@clara.co.uk

**FOSTER Jodie (Alicia Christian),** b. 19 November 1962, Los Angeles, USA. Actress; Film Director and Producer. 2 sons. Education: Yale University. Career: Acting debut in TV programme, Mayberry, 1969; Films include: Napoleon and Samantha, 1972; Kansas City Bomber, 1972; Menace of the Mountain; One Little Indian, 1973; Tom Sawyer, 1973; Alice Doesn't Live Here Any More, 1975; Taxi Driver, 1976; Echoes of a Summer, 1976; Bugsy Malone, 1976; Freaky Friday, 1976; The Girl Who Lives the Lane, 1977; Candleshoe, 1977; Foxes, 1980; Carny, 1980; Hotel New Hampshire, 1984; The Blood of Others, 1984; Siesta, 1986; Five Corners, 1986; The Accused, 1988; Stealing Home, 1988; Catchfire, 1990; The Silence of the Lambs, 1990; Little Man Tate (also director), 1991; Shadows and Fog, 1992; Sommersby, 1993; Maverick, 1994; Nell, 1994; Home for the Holidays (director, co-producer only), 1996; Contact, 1997; The Baby Dance (executive producer only), 1997; Waking the Dead (executive producer only), 1998; Contact, 1998; Anna and the King, 1999; Panic Room, 2002; The Dangerous Lives of Altar Boys (also producer), 2002. Honours: Academy Award for Best Actress, 1989, 1992; Hon DFA, Yale, 1997. Address: E G G Pictures Production Co, 7920 Sunset Boulevard, Suite 200, Los Angeles, CA 90046, USA.

**FOTOPOULOS Takis,** b. 14 October 1940, Greece. Writer; Editor; Senior Lecturer. m. Sia Mamareli, 28 July 1966, 1 son. Education: LLB, 1962, BA, Economics, 1965, University of Athens; MSc, Economics, London School of Economics, 1968. Appointments: Lecturer Grade I, Economics, 1969-70, Lecturer, Grade II, 1970-72, North Western Polytechnic; Senior Lecturer, Economics, University of North London,

1973-89; Editor, Society and Nature, 1992-98, Democracy and Nature, 1999-2003; Editor, International Journal of Inclusive Democracy, 2004-. Publications: Towards An Inclusive Democracy, 1997; Per Una Democrazia Globale, 1999; Vers une democratie generale, 2002; Hacia Una Democracia Inclusiva, 2002; Umfassende Demokratie, 2003; Published in Athens: Dependent Development, 1985; The War in the Gulf, 1991; The Neoliberal Consensus, 1993; The New World Order and Greece, 1997; Inclusive Democracy, 1999; Drugs, liberalisation vs penalisation, 1999; The New Order in the Balkans, 1999; Religion, Autonomy and Democracy, 2000; From Athenian Democracy to Inclusive Democracy, 2000; Globalisation, Left and Inclusive Democracy, 2002; The war against "terrorism", 2003; Chomsky's capitalism, Albert's post-capitalism and inclusive democracy, 2004; The multi-dimensional crisis and Inclusive Democracy, 2004. Contributions to: Education, Culture and Modernization, 1995; Routledge Encyclopedia of International Political Economy, 2001; Defending Public Schools, 2004; Complessita sistemica e svilluppo eco-sostenibil, 2001; Studies on the contemporary Greek Economy, 1978; Environment, Growth and Quality of Life, 1983; Globalisation and Social Economy, 2001; Psyche, Polis, Society – in memory of Castoriadis, 2004. Over 500 articles to English, American, French, German, Dutch, Norwegian and Greek scholarly journals, magazines and newspapers. Memberships: Theomai Editorial Board; Inclusive Democracy (in Greek) Advisory Board. Address: 20 Woodberry Way, London N12 OHG, England. Website: www.inclusivedemocracy.org/fotopoulos/

**FOULKES OF CUMNOCK George (Rt Hon Lord Foulkes of Cumnock),** b. 21 January 1942, Oswestry, England. Director of Voluntary Organisations; Former Member of Parliament. m. Elizabeth Anna Hope, 1970, 2 sons, 1 daughter. Education: BSc, Psychology, Edinburgh University, 1964. Appointments: President, Scottish Union of Students, 1964-66; Director, ELEC, 1966-68; Scottish Organiser, European Movement, 1968-69; Director, Enterprise Youth, 1969-73; Director, Age Concern Scotland, 1973-79; Member of Parliament for Carrick Cumnock & Doon Valley, 1979-2005; Parliamentary Under-Secretary of State, Department of International Development, 1997-2001; Minister of State, Scotland Office, 2001-02. Publications: Editor, 80 Years On (History of Edinburgh University SRC); Chapters in: Scotland – A Claim of Right and Football and the Commons People. Honours: Privy Counsellor, 2000; Justice of the Peace; Wilberforce Medal, 1998. Memberships: Commonweath Parliamentary Association. Address: House of Lords, London SW1A 0WP, England. E-mail: foulkesg@parliament.uk

**FOWLER Harold Gordon,** b. 25 August 1950, Roswell, New Mexico, USA. Entomologist. m. Vilma Elena Martinez, 1 son, 2 daughters. Education: BA, Biology, SUNY Brockport, 1971; MS, Entomology, Rutgers University, 1978; PhD, Entomology, Rutgers University, 1982; LLD, Ecology, UNESP, 1996. Appointments: Consultant Ministry of Education, Peru, 1971-79; Consultant/Researcher, Ministry of Agriculture, Paragum, 1974-74; Graduate Professor, Herman Escobar-Juarez, Mexico, 1979-80; Teaching/Research Assistant, Rutgers University, 1980-82; Research Professor, University of Florida, USA, 1982-86; Professor, Ecology, São Paulo State University, Brazil, 1983-94; Full Professor, State University of São Paulo, 1994-. Publications: 400 scientific publications on biological control, ecology, biodiversity, environmental impact assessment, and others. Honours: Outstanding MS Award, 1978, Outstanding PhD Award, 1980, Entomological Society of America; CC Compton Award. Memberships: AAAS; Ecological Society of America; Association Pualista Environmental Consultants; Argentine Ecological Society; Environmental Defense Society of Rio Claro; American Society of Naturalists; Sigma Xi;

Entomological Society of America. Address: Estrada de Jacutinga, 133, 13500-000 Rio Claro, São Paulo, Brazil. E-mail: hgfowler@rc.unesp.br

**FOWLER Sandra,** b. West Columbia, West Virginia, USA. Poet. Education: Studied poetry with Lilith Lorraine, Founder Director of Avalon; Cultural Doctorate in Literature, World Roundtable, 1981; Honorary Doctorate, Literature, The World Academy of Arts and Culture, 2002. Career: Associate Editor, Ocarina, 1978-89; Guest Editor, Friendship Bridge, India, 1979. Publications: Book of Poetry: In the Shape of the Sun, 1972-73, 1975; The Colors Cry in Rain, 1983; Ever Sunset, 1992; Poetry on Websites: Able Muse, Poetry.Com, Poetry Depth Quarterly, Sandra Fowler Poetry Exhibit, International Poetry Hall of Fame Museum; Works in: The World Anthology of Haiku; Cyber Literature; The Chinese Poetry International Quarterly; Poems recorded on cassette and CD. Honours include: Medal of Honor for Lifetime Achievement, American Biographical Institute, 1980; Inducted into International Poetry Hall of Fame, 1997; Nominated for the Pushcart Prize, 1998; Commemorative Coin for work in human rights, Amnesty International, 1998; Named on Wall of Tolerance, 2001; Honorary Member, Steering Committee, Clinton-Gore Campaign, 1995 and Gore-Lieberman Campaign, 1999. Memberships: Distinguished Member, International Society of Poets; World Academy of Arts and Culture; Founding Member, The United States Holocaust Memorial Museum; Southern Poverty Law Center; World Renaissance for Classical Poetry. Address: Rt 1, Box 50, West Columbia, WV 25287, USA.

**FOX Christopher,** b. 21 July 1949, Yorkshire, England. Police Officer. m. Carol Anne, 1 son, 2 daughters. Education: Loughborough University. Appointments: Police Officer, Nottinghamshire, 1972-90; Assistant and Deputy Chief Constable, Warwickshire Police, 1990-96; Chief Constable Northamptonshire Police, 1996-2003; Chief Constable, President, Association of Chief Police Officers, 2003-. Honours: Police Long Service and Good Conduct, 1995; Queen's Police Medal, 1996. Membership: Trustee, Endeavour (Youth Charity). Address: 25 Victoria Street, London SW1H 0EX. E-mail: chris.fox@ACPO.pnn.police.co.uk

**FOX Edward,** b. 13 April 1937. Actor. m. (1) Tracy Pelissier, 1958, divorced 1961, 1 daughter. 1 daughter by Joanna David. Education: Royal Academy of Dramatic Art. Career: Actor, 1957-; Provincial repertory theatre, 1958; Worked widely in films, stage plays and TV; Stage appearances include: Knuckle, 1973; The Family Reunion, 1979; Anyone for Denis, 1981; Quartermaine's Terms, 1981; Hamlet, 1982; The Dance of Death, 1983; Interpreters, 1986; The Admirable Crichton, 1988; Another Love Story, 1990; The Philanthropist, 1991; My Fair Lady; Father, 1995; A Letter of Resignation, 1997; The Chiltern Hundreds, 1999; The Browning Version, 2000; The Twelve Pound Look, 2000; Films include: The Go-Between, 1971; The Day of the Jackal; A Doll's House, 1973; Galileo, 1976; A Bridge Too far; The Duellists; The Cat and the Canary, 1977; Force Ten from Navarone, 1978; The Mirror Crack'd, 1980; Gandhi, 1982; Never Say Never Again, 1983; Wild Geese; The Bounty, 1984; The Shooting Party; Return from the River Kwai, 1989; Circles of Deceit (TV), 1989; Prince of Thieves, 1990; They Never Slept, 1991; A Month by the Lake, 1996; Prince Valiant, 1997; Television includes: Daniel Deronda, 2002. Honours: Several awards for TV performance as Edward VIII in Edward and Mrs Simpson.

**FOX James,** b. 19 May 1939, London, England. Actor. m. Mary Elizabeth Fox, 1973, 4 sons, 1 daughter. Career: Actor, films include: Mrs Miniver, 1952; The Servant, 1963; King Rat,

1965; Those Magnificent Man in Their Flying Machines, 1965; Thoroughly Modern Millie, 1966; Isadora, 1967; Performance, 1969; Passage to India, 1984; Runners, 1984; Farewell to the King, 1987; Finding Mawbee (video film as the Mighty Quinn), 1988; She's Been Away, 1989; The Russia House, 1990; Afraid of the Dark, 1991; Patriot Games, 1991; As You Like It, 1992; The Remains of the Day, 1993; The Old Curiosity Shop, 1994; Gulliver's Travels, 1995; Elgar's Tenth Muse, 1995; Uncle Vanya, 1995; Anna Karenina, 1997; Mickey Blue Eyes, 1998; Jinnah, 1998; Up at the Villa, 1998; The Golden Bowl, 1999; Sexy Beast, 2000; The Lost World, 2001. Publication: Comeback: An Actor's Direction, 1983. Address: c/o ICM Oxford House, 76 Oxford Street, London, W1D 1BS, England.

**FOX Michael J,** b. 9 June 1961, Edmonton, Alberta, Canada. Actor. m. Tracy Pollan, 1988, 1 son, 2 daughters. Career: TV appearances include: Leo and Me, 1976; Palmerstown USA, 1980; Family Ties, 1982-89; Spin City, 1996-2000; TV films include: Letters from Frank, 1979; Poison Ivy, 1985; High School USA, 1985; Films include: Midnight Madness, 1980; Class of '84, 1981; Back to the Future, 1985; Teen Wolf, 1985; Light of Day, 1986; The Secret of My Success, 1987; Bright Lights, Big City, 1988; Back to the Future II, 1989; Back to the Future III, 1989; The Hard Way, 1991; Doc Hollywood, 1991; The Concierge, 1993; Give Me a Break, 1994; Greedy, 1994; The American President, 1995; Mars Attacks!, 1996; The Frighteners, 1996; Stuart Little (voice), 1999; Atlantis: The Lost Empire (voice), 2001; Interstate 60, 2002; Stuart Little 2 (voice), 2002. Address: c/o Kevin Huvane, CAA, 9830 Wilshire Blvd, Beverly Hills, CA 90212, USA.

**FOXALL Gordon Robert,** b. 16 July 1949, Birmingham, England. Research Professor. m. Jean, 1 daughter. Education: BSc, Honours, Social Studies, 1970, MSc, Management, 1972, University of Salford; PhD, University of Birmingham, 1983; PhD, University of Strathclyde, 1990; D Soc Sc, University of Birmingham, 1995. Appointments: Lecturer, University of Newcastle upon Tyne, 1972-79; Lecturer, Birmingham University, 1980-83; Reader, Cranfield University, 1983-86; Professor, Strathclyde University, 1987-90; Professor, Birmingham University, 1990-97; Distinguished Research Professor, Cardiff University, 1997-. Publications: Books include: Corporate Innovation; Marketing Psychology; Consumer Psychology for Marketing; Understanding Consumer Choice; Context and Cognition; Consumer Behaviour Analysis. Honours: Fellow, British Psychological Society; Fellow, British Academy of Management; Academician of the Academy of Social Science. Address: Cardiff Business School, Cardiff University, Colum Drive, Cardiff CF10 3EU, Wales.

**FRAGOMENI James Mark,** b. 24 September 1962, Columbus Ohio, USA. Engineer; Educator. Education: Bachelor of Science (BS) in Metallurgical Engineering, University of Pittsburgh, Pennsylvania, 1981-85; Master of Science in Engineering (MSE), 1987-89, Doctor of Philosophy (PhD), Mechanical Engineering, 1990-94, Purdue University, College of Engineering, West Lafayette, Indiana. Appointments: Assistant Professor, University of Alabama, 1995-97; NASA Faculty Research Fellow, summers, 1996, 1997; AFOSR/Airforce Faculty Research Fellow, summer, 1998; Assistant Professor, Ohio University, 1997-2000; Assistant Professor, University of Detroit Mercy, 2000-2005; Instructor at Ford Training Center, 2001-2004; Instructor at Focus Hope (part-time), Detroit, Michigan, 2001-2003. Publications: Over 60 technical articles in conference proceedings and scientific journals including: Acta Astronautica, 2002, 2004; Aerospace Science and Technology, 2002; Computer Assisted Mechanics and Engineering Sciences, 2004; Journal of Materials Engineering and Performance, 2005.

Honours: University of Pittsburgh Merit Scholarship, 1981-85; Carpenter Technology Scholarship, 1982; Order of Engineer, 1989; Tau Beta Pi; Phi Eta Sigma; Sigma Xi The Scientific Research Society, 1996-; Listed in Who's Who publications and biographical dictionaries. Memberships: The Materials Society; The American Society for Engineering Education; The American Society for Mechanical Engineers; The American Society for Quality; The American Society for Materials. Address: 25105 Biarritz Circle, #C. Oak Park, MI 48237, USA. E-mail: jamesfrag@yahoo.com Website: www.jamesmatsci.org

**FRAILE Medardo,** b. 21 March 1925, Madrid, Spain. Writer; Emeritus Professor in Spanish. Education: DPh, DLitt, University of Madrid, 1968. Publications: Cuentos con Algun Amor, 1954; A La Luz Cambian las Cosas, 1959; Cuentos de Verdad, 1964; Descubridor de Nada y Otros Cuentos, 1970; Con Los Dias Contados, 1972; Samuel Ros Hacia una Generacion Sin Critica, 1972; La Penultima Inglaterra, 1973; Poesia y Teatro Espanoles Contemporaneos, 1974; Ejemplario, 1979; Autobiografia, 1986; Cuento Espanol de Posguerra, 1986; El gallo puesto en hora, 1987; Entre parentesis, 1988; Santa Engracia, numero dos o tres, 1989; Teatro Espanol en un Acto, 1989; El rey y el pais con granos, 1991; Cuentos Completos, 1991; Claudina y los cacos, 1992; La Familia irreal inglesa, 1993; Los brazos invisibles, 1994; Documento Nacional, 1997; Contrasombras, 1998; Ladrones del Paraiso, 1999; Cuentos de Verdad (anthology), 2000; Descontary Contar, 2000; Escrituray Verdad, 2004. Translation: El Weir de Hermiston by R L Stevenson, 1995. Contributions to: Many publications. Honours: Sesamo Prize, 1956; Literary Grant, Fundacion Juan March, 1960; Critics Book of the Year, 1965; La Estafeta literaria Prize, 1970; Hucha de Oro Prize, 1971; Research Grant, Carnegie Trust for Universities of Scotland, 1975; Colegiado de Honor del Colegio heraldico de España y de las Indias, 1995; Comendador con Placa de la Orden Civil de Alfonso X El Sabio, 1999; Orden venezolana de Primera Clase de Don Balthazar de Leon. Memberships: General Society of Spanish Authors; Working Community of Book Writers, Spain; Association of University Teachers. Address: 24 Etive Crescent, Bishopbriggs, Glasgow G64 1ES, Scotland.

**FRANCE Roger,** b. 7 January 1938, Bedford, England. Consultant Architect; Town Planner. Education: MSc, Linacre College, Oxford; MA, University of York; DIC, Imperial College London; AA Dipl; Dip TP. Appointments: Architectural Assistant, Middlesex County Council, 1961-62, Maguire and Murray, 1962-63; Research Group Town Development Division, GLC, 1963-65; Principal Planning Officer, London Borough of Southwark, 1966-70; Principal, Roger France and Associates, 1968-82; Senior Lecturer in Town Planning, North London Polytechnic, 1970-75; Senior Lecturer in Urban Conservation, Oxford Polytechnic, 1975-92 (Oxford Brookes University, 1992-94); Visiting Lecturer, University of Cambridge, 1991-92; Academic Visitor, 1993-94, 1999-2000; Visiting Lecturer, University of Sheffield, 1996-98; Research Associate, University of Bath, 2000-; Official Lecturer, Civic Trust, 1986-90; Specialist Assessor, Welsh Funding Council, 1995-96; Specialist Adviser, Design and Historic Environmental Panel, RTPI, 1996-; Caseworker: Council for British Archaeology, 1982-86, International Council of Monuments and Sites, 1986-. Publications: Chester: a Study in Conservation (contributor), 1969; Look Before You Change, 1985; Marston: a Case for Conservation, 1988; Methods of Environmental Impact Assessment (contributor), 1995; Numerous reviews and articles for professional journals including: RTPI Journal, The Planner, Context. Honours: Honorary Member: Association of Conservation Officers, 1984, National Trust for Historic Preservation of America, 1985; Freeman, 1993, Worshipful

Company of Chartered Architects, Liveryman, 1994, Master of Students, 1995-, Member, Court of Assistants, 1999; Freeman City of London, 1994. Memberships: Founder Member, Trustee, Association for Small Historic Towns and Villages, 1989-98; Founder, Trustee, Research Council for the Historic Environment, 1990-; Founding Member and Convenor, Conservation Course Director's Forum, 1991; Founding Court Member, Guild of Educators, 2001, Middle Warden, 2004; Member College of Readers, 2000; Licensed Reader, Church of England at University Church of Great St Mary's Cambridge and Sidney Sussex College, Cambridge, 2003-; RIBA, 1964; MRTPI, 1974; FRGS, 1989, IHBC, 1998, ILTM, 2002. Address: 32 Manor Place, Cambridge CB1 1LE, England.

**FRANCHI Giuseppe,** b. 16 November 1924, Siena, Italy. University Professor. m. Rampazzo Rosana, 1 son. Education: Laurea Pharmacy, University of Siena, 1948; Libera Docenza, Pharmaceutical Technology and Legislation, 1958; Libera Docenza, Pharmaceutical Chemistry, 1962. Appointments: Lecturer and Professor, Pharmaceutical Technology and Legislation, 1958-75; Dean Faculty of Pharmacy, University of Siena, Italy, 1976-88; Pharmaceutical Chemistry Department, University of Siena, Director, 1976-81, 1995-97; Retired, 1997. Publications: 92 papers on pharmaceutical chemistry and pharmaceutical techniques, 1951-97; 1 book on analytical chemistry; 2 patents on pharmaceutical technological equipment. Honours: Gold Medal for services to school, culture and art, 1984; Commendatore al merito della Repubblica Italiana, 1997. Memberships: Accademia delle Scienze di Siena, detta dei Fisiocritici, 1954, President, 1990-98; Association of Italian Teachers and Researchers in Pharmaceutical Technology and Legislation, 1971, President, 1981-97; Italian Society of Pharmaceutical Sciences, 1966-2004; Pharmaceutical Society of Latin Mediterranean Countries, 1963; Rotary Club 2070 District, 1980. Address: Via della Sapienza 39, 53100 Siena, Italy.

**FRANCIS Clare,** b. 17 April 1946, Surrey, England. Writer. 1 son. Education: Economics Degree, University College, London. Appointment: Chair, Advisory Committee on Public Lending Right, 2000-2003. Publications: Come Hell or High Water, 1977; Come Wind or Weather, 1978; The Commanding Sea, 1981; Night Sky, 1983; Red Crystal, 1985; Wolf Winter, 1987; Requiem, 1991; Deceit, 1993; Betrayal, 1995; A Dark Devotion, 1997; Keep Me Close, 1999; A Death Divided, 2001; Homeland, 2004. Honours: Member, Order of British Empire; Fellow, University College, London; University of Manchester Institute of Technology, Honorary Fellow. Membership: Society of Authors, Chairman, 1997-99; Royal Society for the Encouragement of Arts, Fellow. Address: c/o Johnson& Alcock, Clerkenwell House, 45-47 Clerkenwell Green, London EC1R 0HT, England.

**FRANCO Jose Eduardo,** b. 17 February 1969, Madeira. Professor; Investigator. m. Fatima Franco, 3 daughters. Education: Master's Degree, History, Faculdade de Letras da Universidade de Lisbon, 1999; PhD, History and Civilisations, Ecole des Hautes Etudes en Science Sociales, Paris, 2004. Appointments: Professor of Literature, Seminario Padre Dehon, Porto, Portugal, 1991-93; Investigator of History, Catholic University of Lisbon, 2000, Centro Faces de Eva-University, Lisbon, 2002-; Professor, Universidade Nova de Lisboa, 2003-. Publications: Brotar Educação, 1999; O Mito de Portugal, 2000; Historia de um Manual Conspiracionista, 2002. Honour: 1st Prize for the book ,Mito de Portugal, Sociedade Historica da Independencia de Portugal, 2004. Memberships: Centro de Estudos Faces de Eva; Centro de Literatura e Cultura Portuguesa e Brasileira; President, Association of Universities, Lisbon, 1999; Member: Instituto, Sao Tomas de Aquino. Address:

Centro Literatura e Cultura Portuguesa-UCP Palma de Cima 1649-023, Lisbon, Portugal.

**FRANIN Dina,** b. 29 March 1959, Zagreb, Croatia. Author; Poet. Education: Graduate, Law Faculty, Zagreb University, 1987. Publications: Poetry: Primal Scream (collection of poems), 1995; Woman's Pride is a Hard Stone (collection of poems), 1996; The Last Juices of Summer (collection of poems), 1999; The Sheltered Moon (collection of haiku), 1999; Blue Nature (collection of poems), 2002; Short stories: Here Beside Me, 1996; The Pair of Scales, 1999; Numerous poems published in anthologies and magazines nationally and internationally. Honours: Honourable Mention, 6th Annual Haiku Competition, Croatian Haiku Association, 1998; 3rd Prize, International Kumamoto Kusamakura Haiku Competition, Japan, 1999; 3rd Honourable Mention, International Competition, Hawaii Education Association, 1999; Editor's Award, International Library of Poetry, Owing Mills, USA, 1999; 1st Prize, 8th Annual Haiku Competition, Croatian Haiku Association, 2000; Commended Haiku, International Yellow Moon Literary Competition, Australia, 2000; Highly Commended Poem, International Yellow Moon Literary Competition, Australia, 2000. Memberships: Matica Hrvatska; The Association of Croatian Haiku Poets; The Association of Artists August Šenoa; The Association of Artists Vjekoslav Majer; The Association of Artists Tin Ujević; Editor's Board of miscellany Naša riječ; Distinguished Member of the International Society of Poets. Address: Republike Austrije 21, 10000 Zagreb, Croatia. E-mail: dinafranin@yahoo.com

**FRANKLAND (Anthony) Noble,** b. 4 July 1922, Ravenstonedale, England. Historian; Biographer. m. (1) Diana Madeline Fovargue Tavernor, 28 February 1944, deceased 1981, 1 son, 1 daughter, (2) Sarah Katharine Davies, 7 May 1982. Education: Open Scholar, MA, 1948, DPhil, 1951, Trinity College, Oxford. Appointments: Served Royal Air Force, 1941-45, Bomber Command, 1943-45; DFC, 1944; Official British Military Historian, 1951-60; Deputy Director of Studies, Royal Institute of International Affairs, 1956-60; Director, Imperial War Museum, 1960-82. Publications: Crown of Tragedy: Nicholas II, 1960; The Strategic Air Offensive Against Germany (co-author), 4 volumes, 1961; The Bombing Offensive Against Germany: Outlines and Perspectives, 1965; Bomber Offensive: The Devastation of Europe, 1970; Prince Henry, Duke of Gloucester, 1980; Witness of a Century: Prince Arthur, Duke of Connaught, 1850-1942, 1993; History at War: The Campaigns of an Historian, 1998; Encyclopaedia of Twentieth Century Warfare (general editor and contributor), 1989; The Politics and Strategy of the Second World War (joint editor), 9 volumes. Contributions to: Encyclopaedia Britannica; Times Literary Supplement; The Times; Daily Telegraph; Observer; Spectator; Military journals. Honours: Companion of the Order of the Bath; Commander of the Order of the British Empire; Holder of the Distinguished Flying Cross. Address: 26/27 River View Terrace, Abingdon, Oxon, OX14 5AE, England.

**FRANKLIN Aretha,** b. 25 March 1942, Memphis, TN, USA. Singer. m. (1) Ted White, divorced, (2) Glynn Turman, 1978. Career: First recordings, father's Baptist church, Detroit; Tours as gospel singer; Moved to New York, signed with Columbia Records, 1960, Atlantic, 1966, Arista, 1980. Publications: Recordings include: Aretha, 1961; The Electrifying Aretha Franklin, 1962; Laughing on the Outside, The Tender, the Moving, the Swinging Aretha Franklin, 1963; Running Out of Fools, The Gospel Sound of Aretha Franklin, 1964; Soul Sister, 1966; I Never Loved a Man the Way I Love You, 1967; Lady Soul, Aretha Now, Aretha in Paris, 1968; Aretha's Gold, 1969; This Girl's in Love With You, Spirit in the Dark, 1970; Live at

Fillmore West, 1971; Young Gifted and Black, Amazing Grace, 1972; Hey Now Hey, The Best of Aretha Franklin, The First Twelve Sides, 1973; Let Me in Your Life, With Everything I Feel in Me, 1974; You, 1975; Sparkle, Ten Years of Gold, 1976; Sweet Passion, 1977; Almighty Fire, 1978; La Diva, 1979; Aretha, 1980; Love All the Hurt Away, 1981; Jump to It, 1982; Get It Right, 1983; One Lord, One Faith, 1988; Through the Storm, 1989; What You Can See is What You Sweat, 1991; Jazz to Soul, 1992; Aretha After Hours, Chain of Fools, 1993; Unforgettable: A Tribute to Dinah Washington, 1995; Love Songs, 1997; The Delta Meets Detroit, 1998; A Rose is Still a Rose, 1998; Amazing Grace, 1999. Publications: Aretha: From these Roots (with David Rib). Honours: Numerous Grammy Awards, 1967-87; American Music Award, 1984; John F Kennedy Centre Award, 1994; Rock and Roll Hall of Fame, 1987. Address: 8450 Linwood Street, Detroit, MI 48206, USA.

**FRANKLIN Raoul Norman,** b. 3 June 1935, New Zealand. Physicist; Engineer. m. (1) Faith Ivens, deceased, 2 sons, (2) Christine Penfold, 2005. Education: BSc, BE, 1st Class Honours, 1955, MSc, 1st Class Honours, 1956, ME, Distinction, 1956, Auckland, New Zealand; D Phil, 1960, DSc, 1978, Oxford University. Appointments: Officer, 1957-63, Reserve, 1963-75, New Zealand Defence Scientific Corps; Civil Service Commission Senior Research Fellow, RMCS Shrivenham, 1961-63; Fellow and Tutor in Engineering, Keble College, Oxford, 1963-78; University Lecturer in Engineering Science, Oxford University, 1967-78; Consultant, Culham Laboratory, 1968-98; Assessor, Fusion Programme, 1984-92, United Kingdom Atomic Energy Authority; Visiting Professor, Open University, Oxford Research Unit, 1998-. Publications: Plasma Phenomena in Gas Discharges, 1976; Physical Kinetics (editor), 1981; Interaction of Intense Electromagnetic Fields with Plasma (editor), 1981; Over 150 papers and articles on plasmas, gas discharges and granular materials. Honours: Honorary Fellow, Keble College, 1980; CBE, 1995; Order of Merit, Poland, 1995; Honorary Doctor of Civil Law, City University, 1999; Foundation Master, Guild of Educators, 1999-2002; Master, 2002-2003, Worshipful Company of Curriers; Distinguished Alumnus Award, University of Auckland, 2004.. Memberships include: Fellow, Institute of Physics; Fellow, Institute of Mathematics and its Applications; Fellow, Institution of Electrical Engineers; Fellow, Royal Academy of Engineering; Fellow, Royal Society of Arts; Member of the Council, University of Buckingham; Trustee, Lloyds Tercentenary Fellowship Fund. Address: 12 Moreton Road, Oxford OX2 7AX, England. E-mail: raoulnfaith@tiscali.co.uk

**FRANKS Michael,** b. 6 May 1928, Kingsclere, Hampshire, England. Strategic Consultant. m. (1) Anne Home, 2 daughters, (2) Nicola Stewart Heath (née Balmain). Education: Epsom College, 1942-46; MA, Classics and Law, Merton College, Oxford, 1946-50; Called to the Bar, Gray's Inn, 1953. Appointments: Sub-Lieutenant, RNVR, National Service, 1951-53; Chancery Bar, 1953-58; Financial and Commercial Management, Royal Dutch/Shell Group, UK, Netherlands, Carribean, Venezuela, 1959-69; Director, Beaverbrook Newspapers, 1969-73; Chairman, Clyde Paper plc, 1971-76; Manager, First National Holdings, 1973-74; Since 1976 involved as Chairman, Director, Consultant or Trouble-Shooter with numerous quoted and private companies; Currently, Strategic Consultant, South & West Investments. Publications: Limitation of Actions, 1959; The Clerk of Basingstoke, A Life of Walter de Merton, 2003. Membership: Royal Thames Yacht Club. Address: South & West Investments, Field House, Mapledurwell, Basingstoke, Hants RG25 2LU, England. E-mail: mf@michaelfranks.freeserve.co.uk

**FRASE Antony Richard Grenville,** b. 8 July 1954, Newcastle upon Tyne, England. Lawyer. m. Sarah Louise Walker, 1 son, 1 daughter. Education: MA (Cantab), Trinity College, Cambridge. Appointments: Solicitor, Allen and Overy, 1980-83; Solicitor, 1983-88, Partner, 1988-92, Denton Hall, seconded to Securities and Futures Authority, 1989-91; Counsel, Mees-Pierson ICS, 1993-94; Head of Litigation, Personal Investment Authority, 1995-98; Of Counsel, Dechert, 1998-; Lecturer and Course Co-ordinator for London and Metropolitan University's Postgraduate Diploma in Financial Services; London Metal Exchange and Securities and Futures Authority Arbitration Panels, 1992-2000. Publications: Contributions to: Law and Regulation of Futures Trading, 1993; Law and Regulation of Hedge Funds, 2001; Practitioners Guide to Designated Investment Business, 2002; Butterworth's Encyclopaedia of Forms and Precedents, Editor, Law and Regulation of Investment Exchanges and Alternative Trading Systems, 2002; Law and Regulation of Investment Management, 2004; Legal Columnist, Risk and Reward Magazine, 2001-2002. Address: c/o Dechert, 2 Serjeants' Inn, London EC4, England. E-mail: richard.frase@dechert.com

**FRASER Lady Antonia, (Lady Antonia Pinter),** b. 27 August 1932, London, England. Author. m. (1) Sir Hugh Fraser, 1956, dissolved 1977, 3 sons, 3 daughters, (2) Harold Pinter, 1980. Education: MA, Lady Margaret Hall, Oxford. Appointment: General Editor, Kings and Queens of England series. Publications: King Arthur and the Knights of the Round Table, 1954; Robin Hood, 1955; Dolls, 1963; A History of Toys, 1966; Mary Queen of Scots, 1969; Cromwell, Our Chief of Men, 1973; King James: VI of Scotland, I of England, 1974; Kings and Queens of England (editor), 1975; Scottish Love Poems: A Personal Anthology (editor), 1975; Love Letters: An Anthology (editor), 1976, revised edition, 1989; Quiet as a Nun, 1977; The Wild Island, 1978; King Charles II, 1979; Heroes and Heroines (editor), 1980; A Splash of Red, 1981; Mary Queen of Scots: Poetry Anthology (editor), 1981; Oxford and Oxfordshire in Verse: An Anthology (editor), 1982; Cool Repentance, 1982; The Weaker Vessel: Woman's Lot in Seventeenth Century England, 1984; Oxford Blood, 1985; Jemima Shore's First Case, 1986; Your Royal Hostage, 1987; Boadicea's Chariot: The Warrior Queens, 1988; The Cavalier Case, 1990; Jemima Shore at the Sunny Grave, 1991; The Six Wives of Henry VIII, 1992; The Pleasure of Reading (editor), 1992; Political Death, 1994; The Gunpowder Plot, 1996; The Lives of the Kings and Queens of England, 1998; Marie Antoinette: the Journey, 2001. Other: Several books adapted for television. Contributions to: Anthologies. Honours: James Tait Black Memorial Prize, 1969; Wolfson History Award, 1984; Prix Caumont-La Force, 1985; Honorary DLitt, Universities of Hull, 1986, Sussex, 1990, Nottingham, 1993 and St Andrews, 1994; St Louis Literary Award, 1996; CWA Non Fiction Gold Dagger, 1996; Shortlisted for NCR Award, 1997; Norten Medlicott Medal, Historical Association, 2000. Memberships: Society of Authors, chairman, 1974-75; Crimewriters' Association, chairman, 1985-86; Writers in Prison Committee, chairman, 1985-88, 1990; English PEN, vice president, 1990-. Address: c/o Curtis Brown Ltd, 162-168 Regent Street, London W1R 5TB, England.

**FRASER Barry John,** b. 8 April 1945, Melbourne, Australia. University Professor. m. Marilyn Denise Fraser, 2 daughters. Education: BSc, University of Melbourne, 1967; DipEd, 1968, BEd, 1971, PhD, 1976, Monash University. Appointments: High School Science Teacher, Victorian Education Department, 1969-71; Senior Tutor in Education, Monash University, 1972-75; Senior Lecturer in Education, Macquarie University, 1976-81; Professor and Director, Science and Mathematics Education Centre, Curtin University of Technology, 1982-. Publications: Classroom Environment, 1986; Windows Into Science

Classrooms, 1990; Educational Environments, 1991; Improving Science Education, 1995; Gender, Science and Mathematics: Shortening the Shadow, 1996; Improving Teaching and Learning in Science and Mathematics, 1996; International Handbook of Science Education, 1998. Honours: Outstanding Science Educator of Year, Association for Education of Teachers of Science (USA), 1991; Distinguished Contributions to Science Education Through Research Award, National Association for Research in Science Teaching (USA), 2003. Outstanding Paper Award, National Association for Research in Science Teaching (USA), 1984, 1986, 1988; Outstanding Paper Award, Special Interest Group on Study of Learning Environments, American Educational Research Association, 1989, 1991, 1994, 1995, 1996, 1998, 1999, 2001, 2004; Fellow, American Association for Advancement of Science; Fellow, International Academy of Education; Fellow, Academy of Social Sciences in Australia; Fellow, Australian College of Education. Memberships include: President, National Association for Research in Science Teaching, 1995-96; Executive Director, International Academy of Education, 1997-; American Educational Research Association. Address: Science and Mathematics Education Centre, Curtin University of Technology, GPO Box U1987, Perth 6845 Western Australia, Australia.

**FRASER George MacDonald,** b. 2 April 1925, Carlisle, England. Author; Journalist. m. Kathleen Margarette Hetherington, 1949, 2 sons, 1 daughter. Education: Glasgow Academy. Appointment: Deputy Editor, Glasgow Herald newspaper, 1964-69. Publications: Flashman, 1969; Royal Flash, 1970, screenplay, 1975; The General Danced at Dawn, 1970; Flash for Freedom, 1971; Steel Bonnets, 1971; Flashman at the Charge, 1973; The Three Musketeers, screenplay, 1973; The Four Musketeers, screenplay, 1974; McAuslan in the Rough, 1974; Flashman in the Great Game, 1975; The Prince and the Pauper, screenplay, 1976; Flashman's Lady, 1977; Mr American, 1980; Flashman and the Redskins, 1982; Octopussy, screenplay, 1983; The Pyrates, 1983; Flashman and the Dragon, 1985; Casanova, television screenplay, 1987; The Hollywood History of the World, 1988; The Sheikh and the Dustbin, 1988; The Return of the Musketeers, screenplay, 1989; Flashman and the Mountain of Light, 1990; Quartered Safe Out Here, 1992; The Candlemass Road, 1993; Flashman and the Angel of the Lord, 1994; Black Ajax, 1997; Flashman and the Tiger, 1999; The Light's on at Signpost, 2002; Flashman on the March, 2005. Honour: OBE, 1999. Address: Baldrine, Isle of Man, Britain.

**FRASER Ian Masson,** b. 15 December 1917, Forres, Moray, Scotland. Ordained Minister. m. Margaret D D Stewart, deceased, 2 sons, 1 daughter. Education: MA, BD (New College for Theology), with distinction in Systematic Theology, 1936-42; PhD, 1955, Edinburgh University, Scotland. Appointments: Manual Working Industrial Chaplain, Fife, Scotland, 1942-44; Interim appointment, Hopemouth Church, Arbroath, Scotland, 1944-45; Scottish Secretary, Student Christian Movement, 1945-48; Parish Minister, Rosyth, Fife, Scotland, 1948-60; Warden of Scottish Churches House, Dunblane, Scotland, 1960-69; Executive Secretary, 1969-73, Consultant and Programme Co-ordinator, 1973-75, World Council of Churches; Dean and Head of the Department of Mission, Selly Oak Colleges, Birmingham, England, 1973-82; Voluntary Research Consultant, Scottish Churches' Council, 1982-90, Action of Churches Together in Scotland, 1990-. Publications: Numerous articles and books including most recently: Strange Fire, a book of life stories and prayers, 1994; A Celebration of Saints, 1997; Signs of Fire (audio cassette), 1998; Salted with Fire, more stories, reflections, prayers, 1999; Caring for Planet Earth, children's stories and prayers, 2002; R B Cunningham Graham – Fighter for Justice, 2002; Action of Churches Together in Scotland, Ecumenical Adventure, beginnings in the 1960's of the work of Scottish Churches House and Council, 2002; Many Cells One Body, 2003. Honours: Cobb Scholarship, Cunningham Fellowship, Gunning Prize, New College, Edinburgh. Address: Ferndale, Gargunnock, by Stirling FK8 3BW, Scotland.

**FRATTI Mario,** b. 5 July 1927, L'Aquila, Italy. (US citizen, 1974). Playwright; Educator. 3 children. Education: PhD, Ca Foscari University, 1951. Appointments: Drama Critic, 1963-, Paese, 1963-, Progresso, 1963-, Ridotto, 1963; Adelphi College, teacher, 1964-65; Faculty, Columbia University, 1965-66; Professor of Literature, New School, Hunter College, 1967-; Faculty, Hofstra University, 1973-74. Publications: Plays: Cage-Suicide, 1964; Academy-Return, 1967; Mafia, 1971; Bridge, 1971; Races, 1972; Eleven Plays in Spanish, 1977; Refrigerators, 1977; Eleonora Duse-Victim, 1981; Nine, 1982; Biography of Fratti, 1982; AIDS, 1987; Porno, 1988, Encounter, musical, 1989; Family, 1990; Friends, 1991; Lovers, 1992; Leningrad Euthanasia, 1993; Holy Father, 1994; Sacrifices, 1995; Jurors, 1996; 8 Plays in Russian, 1997; 4 Plays in Japanese, 7 Mini Dramas in Spanish, 1997; 4 Dramas in Spanish, 1998; Candida and her Friends, 1999; Erotic Adventures in Venice, 2000; Puccini – A Musical, 2000; Terrorist, 2002; Blindness, 2003. Honours: Tony Award, 1982; Other awards for plays and musicals. Memberships: Drama Desk; American Theatre Critics; Outer Critics Circle, Vice-President. Address: 145 West 55th Street, Apt 15D, New York, NY 10019, USA.

**FREASIER Aileen W,** b. 12 November 1924, Edcouch, Texas, USA. Educator. m. Ben C Freasier, deceased, 3 sons, 2 daughters. Education: BS, Home Economics, Texas A&I University, 1944; M Ed, Special Education, 1966, 90 hours above the Master's level, Louisiana Tech University. Appointments: Fourth Grade Teacher, Robstown Elementary School, Robstown, Texas, 1948-49; EMR Class teacher, San Antonio Independent School District, San Antonio, Texas, 1961-62; TMR Day Care Program Teacher, Lincoln Parish Association for Retarded Children, Ruston, Louisiana, 1965-71; Teacher, Lincoln Parish Association for Retarded Children's Summer Program, Ruston, Louisiana, 1969; EMR, TMR Class Teacher, Lincoln Parish Schools, I A Lewis, Lincoln Center, Ruston, Louisiana, 1971-77; EMR Resource Room Teacher, Hico Elementary, Lincoln Parish Schools, Hico Louisiana, 1977-80; Coordinating Teacher, Early Childhood Program, Lincoln Parish Schools, Ruston, Louisiana, 1980-81; IEP Facilitator/Educational Diagnostician, Special Schools District #1, Louisiana Training Institute, Monroe, Louisiana, 1981-95; Retired Senior Program Volunteer PreGED Class Tutor, Lincoln Parish Detention Center, Ruston, Louisiana, 1995-. Publications: 20 publications in professional special education, correctional education, and technology education journals; 11 commercial workbooks/duplicating masters books for special education students; 3 international, 45 national, 24 state presentations to special education, correctional and technology-using educators. Honours include: Mary C Wilson Award, Lincoln Parish Schools, 1978; State Named Bolivar L Hait Research and Projects Endowment Honoree, American Association of University Women, Louisiana Division, 1982; Special Schools District # 1, Teacher of the Year, 1988; Phi Delta Kappa Service Award, 1991; J E Wallace Wallin Education of the Handicapped Children Award, Louisiana Federation of the Council for Exceptional Children, 1994; President's Award for Outstanding Service, Louisiana Council for Exceptional Children, Technology and Media, 1997. Memberships include: American Association of University Women; Council for Exceptional Children, Correctional Education Association; Daughters of the American Revolution; Delta Kappa Gamma; Kappa Kappa Iota; Lincoln Parish Retired Teachers; Louisiana Reading

Association; Phi Delta Kappa; Ruston Mayor's Commission for Women. Address: PO Box 1595, Ruston, LA 71273-1595, USA. E-mail: aileenwf@bayou.com

**FREDERICK Dennis,** b. 23 January 1948, Brooklyn, New York, USA. Maritime Educator. m. Lois, 1 son, 2 daughters. Education: BS, Marine Transportation, 1969, MS, Transportation Management, 1989, State University of New York Maritime College; Certificate, Advanced Chartering Problems, State University of New York Maritime College and Association of Ship Brokers and Agents; STCW 95 Certification (Standards of Training Certification and Watch Keeping); Federal Licences: Chief Mate Oceans; Radar Observer; GMDSS Operator. Appointments: Ships Officer, 1969-72; Marine Superintendent, Global Terminal and Container Services, Jersey City, New Jersey, 1972-73; Ocean Deck Licence Instructor. Merchant Marine School at Seaman's Church Institute, New York, 1973-75; Radar Instructor, US Department of Transportation Maritime Administration Radar School at Seaman's Church Institute, New York, 1975-82; Adjunct Assistant and Assistant Professor, Marine Transportation, 1982-94, Associate Professor of Marine Transportation, 1994-, Chair, Maritime Transportation Department, 1998-2002, State University of New York Maritime College. Publications: Small Passenger Vessel Management in the Northeast Recreational Fishing Industry (thesis); Rapid Radar Plotting, 1975; Celestial Navigation. Honours: Listed in Who's Who publications and biographical dictionaries. Memberships: New York State United Teachers; Captree Boatmen's Association; Captree Boatmen's Joint Venture; Long Island Commercial Passenger Fishing Vessel Association; Freeport Boatmen's Association. Address: 351 Taylor Avenue, Levittown, NY11756, USA. E-mail: dfrederick@sunymaritime

**FREEDMAN David N(oel),** b. 12 May 1922, New York, New York, USA. Professor of Biblical Studies; Writer; Editor. m. Cornelia Anne Pryor, 16 May 1944, 2 sons, 2 daughters. Education: City College of New York, 1935-38; AB, University of California at Los Angeles, 1938-39; ThB, Old Testament, Princeton Theological Seminary, 1944; PhD, Semitic Languages and Literature, Johns Hopkins University, 1948. Appointments: Numerous include: Professor of Biblical Studies, 1971-92, Director, Program on Studies in Religion, 1971-91, Arthur F Thurnau Professor in Old Testament Studies, 1984-92, University of Michigan; Visiting Professor in Old Testament Studies, 1985-86, Professor in Hebrew Biblical Studies, 1987, Endowed Chair in Hebrew Biblical Studies, 1987-, University of California at San Diego; Numerous visiting lectureships and professorships. Publications: More recently: Hosea (Anchor Bible Series; with F I Andersen), 1980; Pottery, Poetry, and Prophecy, 1981; The Paleo-Hebrew Leviticus Scroll (with K A Mathews), 1985; Amos (Anchor Bible Series; with F I Andersen), 1989; The Unity of the Hebrew Bible, 1991; Studies in Hebrew and Aramaic Orthography (with D Forbes and F I Andersen), 1992; The Relationship Between Herodotus' History and Primary History (with Sara Mandell), 1993; Divine Commitment and Human Obligation, 1997; The Leningrad Codex: A Facsimile Edition, 1998; Psalm 119: The Exaltation of Torah, 1999; Micah (Anchor Bible Series; with R I Andersen), 2000; The Nine Commandments, 2000. Other: The Biblical Archaeologist Reader (co-editor), 4 volumes, 1961, 1964, 1970, 1982; Anchor Bible Series (co-editor), 18 volumes, 1964-72; 50 volumes, (general editor), 1972-; Computer Bible Series (co-editor), 18 volumes, 1971-80; Anchor Bible Reference Library (general editor), 16 volumes, 1988-96; Anchor Bible Dictionary (editor-in-chief), 6 volumes, 1992. Honours: Guggenheim Fellowship, 1958-59; AATS Fellowship, 1965; Honorary doctorates. Memberships: American Academy of Religion; American Archaeological Institute; American Oriental Society; American Schools of Oriental Research; Explorers Club; Society of Biblical Literature. Address: c/o Department of History, No 0104, University of California, San Diego, 9500 Gilman Drive, La Jolla, CA 92093-0104, USA.

**FREEMAN Cathy,** b. 16 February 1973, Mackay, Australia. Athlete. m. Alexander Bodecker. Career: Public Relations Adviser; Winner, Australian 200m, 1990-91, 1994, 1996; Australian 100m, 1996; Amateur Athletics Federation 400m, 1992, 200m, 1993; Gold Medallist 4x100m, Commonwealth Games, 1990; Gold Medallist 200m, 400m, Silver Medallist 4x100m, Commonwealth Games, 1994; Silver Medallist 400m, Olympic Games, Atlanta, 1996; Winner, World Championships 400m, Athens (first Aboriginal winner at World Championships), 1997; Set 2 Australian 200m records, 5 Australian 400m records, 1994-96; 1st, World Championships, Seville, 400m, 1999; Gold Medallist, Sydney Olympic Games 400m, 2000; took break from atheletics in 2001; returned to international competition, Gold Medal 4x400m relay, Commonwealth Games, Manchester, 2002; Media and Communications Officer, Australia Post. Honours: Numerous national awards include: Australian of the Year, 1998; OAM, 2001. Address: c/o Melbourne International Track Club, 43 Fletcher Street, Essendon, Vic 3040, Australia.

**FREEMAN David Franklin,** b. 13 April 1925, Raleigh, North Carolina, USA. Adult and Child Psychiatrist and Psychoanalyst. m. Constance Covell Freeman, 1 son, 2 daughters. Education: BS, Wake Forest College, North Carolina, 1948; MD, Bowman Gray School of Medicine, Winston-Salem, 1951; Internship, Philadelphia General Hospital, 1951-52; Resident, Adult and Child Psychiatry, Boston Psychopathic Hospital, Massachusetts, 1952-55; Research Fellow, Psychiatry, Harvard University, 1952-55; 2nd Year Child Psychiatry, Worcester Youth Guidance Center, Massachusetts, 1955-56; Candidate, Adult and Child Psychoanalysis, Boston, Washington, UNC-Duke University Psychoanalytic Institutes, 1955-66. Appointments: Private Practice, Adult and Child Psychiatry, Lincoln, Massachusetts, 1956-61; Director, North Central Mental Health Consultation Service, Fitchburg, Massachusetts, 1956-57; Staff Psychiatrist, Douglas A Thom Clinic for Children, Boston, Massachusetts, 1957-61; Assistant in Child Psychiatry, Boston University School of Medicine, 1960-61; Consultant, several child psychiatry clinics, 1956-66; Clinical Faculty, Assistant Professor to Clinical Professor, University of North Carolina, 1961-95; Adjunct Professor, University of North Carolina at Chapel Hill, 1995-; Training and Supervising Psychoanalyst, UNC-Duke University Psychoanalytic Education Program, 1972-; Psychiatric Consultant, NE Home for Little Wanderers, Boston, Massachusetts, 1959-61; Director, Child Psychiatry Outpatient Clinic, North Carolina Memorial Hospital, Chapel Hill, 1961-63; Private Practice, Adult and Child Psychiatry and Psychoanalysis, Chapel Hill, North Carolina, 1963-. Publications: Several articles in professional medical journals. Honours include: Alpha Omega Alpha, 1950; Herman Lineberger Award, 1997; NC Psychoanalytic Foundation, 2003. Memberships include: Life member: American Psychiatric Association; International Psychoanalytical Association; North Carolina Psychiatric Association; American Academy of Child and Adolescent Psychiatry; North Carolina Medical Society; American Psychoanalytic Association; Association for Child Psychoanalysis; Life Member and Past President: North Carolina Psychoanalytic Society; North Carolina Council of Child Psychiatry; Founder and Chair: North Carolina Psychoanalytic Foundation, 1995-2000. Address: 101 Ashe Place, Chapel Hill, NC 27517, USA.

**FREUD Anthony Peter,** b. 30 October 1957, London, England; Opera Administrator; Barrister. Education: LLB (Hons), King's College, London, 1975-78; Inns of Court School of Law, 1978-79. Appointments: Trained as Barrister; Theatre Manager, Sadler's Wells Theatre, 1980-84; Company Secretary, Director of Opera Planning, Welsh National Opera, 1984-91; Executive Producer Opera, Philips Classics, 1992-94; General Director, Welsh National Opera, 1994-. Honour: Honorary Fellowship of Cardiff University, 2002. Memberships: Member, Honorary Secretary of Gray's Inn, 1979; Chairman of Jury, Cardiff Singer of the World, 1995-; Chairman, Opera Europa, 2002-; Trustee, National Endowment for Science, Technology and the Arts (NESTA), 2004-. Address: Welsh National Opera, Wales Millennium Centre, Bute Place, Cardiff Bay CF10 5AL, Wales. E-mail: anthony.freud@wno.org.uk

**FREUD Bella,** b. 17 April 1961, London, England. Fashion Designer. Education: Accademia di Costuma e di Moda, Rome; Institutto Mariotti, Rome. Appointments: Assistant to Vivienne Westwood on her designer collections, 1986-89; Launched own label presenting autumn/winter collection of tailored knitwear and accessories, 1990; Exhibited, London Designer Show, 1991, London Fashion Week, 1993. Honours: Winner, Innovative Design - the New Generation Category (British Fashion Awards), 1991. Address: 21 St Charles Square, London, W10 6EF, England.

**FREUD Lucian,** b. 8 December 1922. Painter. m. (1) Kathleen Epstein, 1948, divorced 1952, 2 daughters, (2) Lady Caroline Maureen Blackwood, 1953, divorced 1957, deceased 1996. Education: Central School of Art, East Anglian School of Painting and Drawing. Appointments: Teacher, Slade School of Art, London, 1948-58; First one-man exhibition, 1944; Exhibitions, 1946, 1950, 1952, 1958, 1963, 1972, 1978, 1979, 1982, 1983, 1988, 1990-96; Retrospectives: Hayward Gallery, 1974, 1988, 1989; Tate Gallery, Liverpool, 1992; Works included in public collections: Tate Gallery, National Portrait Gallery, Victoria and Albert Museum, Arts Council of Great Britain, British Council, British Museum, Fitzwilliam Museum (Cambridge), National Museum of Wales (Cardiff), Scottish National Gallery of Modern Art (Edinburgh), Walker Art Gallery (Liverpool), Ashmolean Museum of Art, Oxford, in Brisbane, Adelaide, Perth (Australia), Musée National d'Art Moderne (Paris, France), Art Institute of Chicago, Museum of Modern Art (NY), Cleveland Museum of Art (OH), Museum of Art Carnegie Institute (Pittsburgh), Achenbaach Foundation for Graphic Arts and Fine Arts (San Fran), The St Louis Art Museum, Hirshborn Museum and Sculpture Garden, Smithsonian Institute (Wash), Rubenspeis, City of Siegen, 1997. Address: c/o Diana Rawstron, Goodman-Derrick, 90 Fetter Lane, London, EC4A 1EQ, England.

**FREWER Glyn Mervyn Louis, (Mervyn Lewis),** b. 4 September 1931, Oxford, England. Author; Scriptwriter. m. Lorna Townsend, 11 August 1956, 2 sons, 1 daughter. Education: MA, English Language and Literature, St Catherine's College, Oxford, 1952-1955. Appointments: Student Officer, British Council, Oxford, 1955; Copywriter, various agencies, 1955-64; Advertising Agency Associate Director, 1974-85; Retired; Proprietor antiquarian/secondhand bookshop, 1985-2001. Publications: The Hitch-Hikers (BBC Radio Play), 1957; Adventure in Forgotten Valley, 1962; Adventure in the Barren Lands, 1964; The Last of the Wispies, 1965; Death of Gold (as Mervyn Lewis), 1970; The Token of Elkin, 1970; Crossroad, 1970; The Square Peg, 1972; The Raid, 1976; The Trackers, 1976; Tyto: The Odyssey of an Owl, 1978; Bryn of Brockle Hanger, 1980; Fox, 1984; The Call of the Raven, 1987; also scripts for children's television series, industrial films, etc.

Contributions to: Birds; Imagery; The Countryman. Honours: Junior Literary Guild of America Choice, for Adventure in Forgotten Valley, 1964; Freeman of the City of Oxford, 1967. Address: Cottage Farm, Taston, Oxford OX7 3JN, England.

**FREZZOTTI Renato,** b. 19 December 1924, Imperia, Italy. Medical Doctor; Ophthalmologist. m. Angela Tabanelli, 2 sons, 1 daughter. Education: Medical Degree, 1949; Libera Docenza, 1959. Appointments: Past Head, Department of Opthalmological Science, University of Sienna, 1967-2000; Full Professor of Ophthalmology, 1970-2000; Professor Emeritus, 2001-. Publications: Over 400 in professional journals. Memberships: Italian Society of Opthalmology; American Academy of Opthalmology. Address: Viale XXIV Maggio 23, 53100 Siena, Italy.

**FRIEDAN Betty (Naomi),** b. 4 February 1921, Peoria, Illinois, USA. Feminist Activist; Writer. m. Carl Friedan, June 1947, divorced May 1969, 2 sons, 1 daughter. Education: AB, Smith College, 1942. Appointments: Research Fellow, University of California at Berkeley, 1943; Founder-1st President, National Organization for Women, 1966-70; Contributing Editor, McCall's magazine, 1971-74; Senior Research Associate, Columbia University, 1979-81; Research Fellow, Harvard University, 1982-83; Chubb Fellow, Yale University, 1985; Guest Scholar, Woodrow Wilson Center for International Scholars, 1995-96; Many other lectureships. Publications: The Feminine Mystique, 1963; It Changed My Life: Writings on the Women's Movement, 1976; The Second Stage, 1981; The Fountain of Age, 1993; Life So Far: A Memoir, 2000. Contributions to: Periodicals. Honours: Humanist of the Year Award, 1974; Mort Weisinger Award for Outstanding Magazine Journalism, 1979; Author of the Year, 1982, American Society of Journalists and Authors; Eleanor Roosevelt Leadership Award, 1989; Various honorary doctorates. Memberships: American Society of Journalists and Authors; American Sociology Association; Association of Humanistic Psychology; Authors Guild; National Organizatioin for Women; National Press Club; PEN; Phi Beta Kappa. Address: 420 7th Street North West, Apt 1010, Washington, DC 20004, USA.

**FRIEDMAN (Eve) Rosemary, (Robert Tibber, Rosemary Tibber, Rosemary Friedman),** b. 5 February 1929, London, England. Writer. m. Dennis Friedman, 2 February 1949, 4 daughters. Education: Queen's College, Harley Street, London; Law Faculty, University College, London University. Publications: No White Coat, 1957; Love on My List, 1959; We All Fall Down, 1960; Patients of a Saint, 1961; The Fraternity, 1963; The Commonplace Day, 1964; Aristide, 1966; The General Practice, 1967; Practice Makes Perfect, 1969; The Life Situation, 1977; The Long Hot Summer, 1980; Proofs of Affection, 1982; A Loving Mistress, 1983; Rose of Jericho, 1984; A Second Wife, 1986; Aristide in Paris, 1987; An Eligible Man, 1989; Golden Boy, 1994; Vintage, 1996; The Writing Game, 1999; Intensive Care, 2001; Paris Summer, 2004; Others: Home Truths, (stage play), 1997; Change of Heart (stage play), 2004; Commissioned screenplays and television drama; Contributions to and reviewer for: Sunday Times; Times Literary Supplement; Guardian; Jewish Quarterly. Memberships: Royal Society of Literature; Society of Authors; Writers' Guild of Great Britain; British Academy of Film and Television Arts; Fellow, PEN. Address: Apt 5, 3 Cambridge Gate, London NW1 4JX, England. E-mail: rosemaryfriedman@hotmail.com

**FRIEDMAN Isaiah,** b. 28 April, 1921, Luck, Poland. University Professor Emeritus; Historian. m. Barbara Joan Braham, 1 son. Education: BA, 1945, MA, 1945, Jewish History, Hebrew University, Jerusalem; PhD, International History,

London School of Economics and Political Science, University of London, 1964. Appointments: Research Fellow, Hebrew University, 1965-68; Fellow, Deutsche Forschungsgemeinschaft, 1968-71; Associate Professor, Modern Jewish History and Political Science, Dropsie University, Philadelphia, 1971-77; Professor of History, Ben-Gurion University, Beersheba, Israel, 1977-91; Professor Emeritus of History, 1991-. Publications: Books: The Question of Palestine, 1914-1918, British-Jewish-Arab Relations, 1973, 2nd and expanded edition, 1992 (also in Hebrew); Germany, Turkey and Zionism, 1897-1918, 1977, 2nd edition, 1998 (also in Hebrew); The Rise of Israel: A Documentary Record, 12 volumes, 1987; Palestine: A Twice Promised Land? (also in Hebrew), 2000. Honour: Recipient Theodor Körner Foundation Prize, University of Vienna, 1964. Memberships: Fellow, American Philosophical Society, 1971-76; Fellow, American Council Learned Society, 1972; Fellow, The Lucius Littauer Foundation, 1972; Fellow, American Academy for Jewish Research, 1975; Member, World Jewish Studies. Address: 39 Sigalon Street, Omer 84-965, Beersheba, Israel.

**FRIEDMANN Patricia Ann**, b. 29 October 1946, New Orleans, Louisiana, USA. Author. m. (1) Robert Skinner, 17 March 1979, divorced, 1996, 1 son, 1 daughter, (2) Edward Muchmore, 11 November 1999. Education: AB, Smith College, 1968; MEd, Temple University, 1970; ABD on Doctorate, University of Denver, 1975. Appointments: Managing Editor, Diplomat, 1980-82; Editor, Jewish Times, 1976-78; Adjunct Faculty, Loyola University, 1993-; Writer in Residence, Tulane University, 2001. Publications: Reviewer: Publishers Weekly, Times-Picayune, Short Story, Brightleaf, 1993-99; Author: Too Smart to Be Rich, 1988; The Exact Image of Mother (novel), 1991; Eleanor Rushing (novel), 1998; The Accidental Jew, 1994 and Lovely Rita, 2000, as part of Native Tongues stage production; Odds (novel), 2000; Secondhand Smoke (novel), 2002; Short stories in Short Story, Louisiana Literature, Louisiana English Journal, Xavier Review, Anthology, Above Ground; Anthology, Christmas Stories from Louisiana, 2003; Summertime and Litigiousness is Easy in Newsweek; Selections in the New Great American Writers Cookbook, 2003. Honours: Discover Great New Writers, 1999; Original Voices, 1999; Booksense 76, 2002. Memberships: Author's Guild. Address: 8330 Sycamore Place, New Orleans, LA 70118, USA.

**FRIEDRICH Fabian**, b. 2 May 1965, Blumenau, Santa Catarina, Brazil. Biochemist; Molecular Biologist. Education: Graduation, Biochemistry, Universidade Federal de Santa Catarina, Brazil, 1988; Postgraduate Specialisation, Biotechnology, Universidade Federal do Rio Grande do Sul, Brazil, 1988; Master Degree, Parasitology, Molecular Biology, Institute Oswaldo Cruz, Fiocruz, Brazil, 1993; Doctorate (PhD), Cell and Molecular Biology, Instituto Oswaldo Cruz, Fiocruz, Brazil, 1996. Appointments: Working with molecular biology and biotechnology, for past 16 years. Publications: Images of UFOs; UFOs: The Search for Unidentified Flying Objects and Unknown Civilizations Continues ... (exobiology and ufology); Articles in professional biomedical journals and nucleotide sequences published in the gene bank. Honours: Listed in numerous biographical directories. Membership: Brazilian Society of Virology, 1993-2000. Address: Rua Rio de Janeiro, 1756, apto 54 – Centro, Cascavel – Paraná, Cep 85.801-031, Brazil.

**FRIEND Lionel**, b. 13 March 1945, London, England. Orchestral Conductor. m. Jane Hyland, 1 son, 2 daughters. Education: Royal College of Music, 1963-67; London Opera Centre, 1967-68. Appointments: Music Staff and Conductor, Welsh National Opera, 1969-72; Assistant Conductor and Chorus Master, Glyndebourne Opera, 1969-72; Kapellmeister, Kassel, Germany, 1972-75; Staff Conductor, English National Opera, 1976-89; As Guest includes: Philharmonia, BBC Symphony Orchestra, Orchestre National de France, La Monnaie, Brussels, Royal Ballet, Oper Frankfurt, Perth International Arts Festival; Conductor-in-Residence, Birmingham Conservatoire, 2003-. Address: 136 Rosendale Road, London SE21 8LG, England.

**FRIER Brian Murray**. Consultant Physician; Honorary Professor of Diabetes. m. Isobel Wilson, 1 daughter. Education: BSc (Honours Class 1), Physiology, 1969, MB ChB, 1972, MD, 1981, University of Edinburgh. Appointments: Junior medical appointments in Edinburgh and Dundee, 1972-76; Clinical Research Fellow, Cornell University Medical Center, The New York Hospital, New York, USA, 1976-77; Senior Medical Registrar, 1978-82; Consultant Physician, Western Infirmary and Gartnavel General Hospital, Glasgow, 1982-87; Consultant Physician, Royal Infirmary of Edinburgh, 1987-, and Honorary Professor of Diabetes, University of Edinburgh, 2001-. Publications: Books co-edited with B M Fisher: Hypoglycaemia and Diabetes, Clinical and Physiological Aspects, 1993; Hypoglycaemia in Clinical Diabetes, 1999; Original publications in peer reviewed journals, review articles, editorials and book chapters on hypoglycaemia, insulin therapy, complications of diabetes, driving and diabetes etc. Honours: R D Lawrence Lecturer of British Diabetic Association, 1986; Somogyi Award of the Hungarian Diabetes Association for hypoglycaemia research, 2004. Memberships: MRCP (UK) 1974; FRCP (Edin), 1984; FRCP (Glas), 1986; Chairman of Honorary Medical Advisory Committee on Driving and Diabetes to Secretary of State for Transport; Chairman, Chief Scientist's Office Committee on Diabetes Research in Scotland; Council Member 2002-, Royal College of Physicians of Edinburgh. Address: Department of Diabetes, Royal Infirmary, Edinburgh EH16 4SA, Scotland.

**FRISTACKY Norbert**, b. 8 November 1931, Slovakia. Professor of Computer Science and Engineering. m. Hilda Matejcikova, 1 son. Education: Dipl.Ing, Electrical Engineering, 1954, PhD, Technical Cybernetics, 1964, Slovak Technical University. Appointments: Assistant Professor, 1954, Docent, 1970, Head, Computer Science and Engineering Department, 1978-90, Professor, 1985, Rector, 1990-91, Slovak Technical University; Visiting Lecturer, University of Salford, England, 1970-71; External Lecturer, Comenius University, Bratislava, 1974-89; Visiting Professor, Technical University, Dresden, Germany, 1986; External Professor, University of Technology, Vienna. Publications include: Programmable Logic Processors, 1981; Logic Circuits, 1986, 1990. Honours include: Slovak University of Technology Medal, 1997; Czech Technical National Society Prize, 1981; IEEE Computer Society Computer Pioneer Award, 1996; Great Medal of St Gorazd, 2002. Memberships include: Scientific Council for Cybernetics and Electronics, Slovak Academy of Sciences; IEEE; Slovak Society for Cybernetics and Informatics; Slovak Society for Informatics; Slovak Academic Society. Address: Slovak Technical University, Ilkovicova 3, 81219 Bratislava, Slovakia.

**FRITH Christopher Donald**, b. 16 March 1942, Cross-in-Hand, Sussex, England. Professor in Neuropsychology. m. 2 sons. Education: BA, MA, Natural Science Tripos, Christ's College, Cambridge, 1960-63; Diploma in Abnormal Psychology, 1965; PhD, Psychology, 1969, London University. Appointments: Probationer Clinical Psychologist, South West Metropolitan Hospital Board Scheme, 1963-65; Research Worker, 1965-70, Lecturer, 1970-75, Department of Psychology, Institute of Psychiatry; MRC Scientist, 1975-85, Senior Scientist, 1980-89, Special Appointment, 1989-92,

Medical Research Council, Division of Psychiatry, Clinical Research Centre; Special Appointment, Cyclotron Unit, Hammersmith Hospital, Medical Research Council, 1992-94; Currently, Professor in Neuropsychology, Wellcome Department of Imaging Neuroscience and Deputy Director, Leopold Müller Functional Imaging Laboratory, Institute of Neurology, University College, London. Publications: Books: Reminiscence, Motivation and Personality: A Case Study in Experimental Psychology (co-author), 1977; The Cognitive Neuropsychology of Schizophrenia (author), 1992; Human Brain Function (co-author), 1997; Schizophrenia: A Very Short Introduction (co-author), 2003; Numerous articles in peer-reviewed medical journals. Honours include: British Psychological Society Book Award, 1996; Kenneth Craik Award, St John's College, Cambridge, 1999; Elected Fellow, Academy of Medical Sciences; Elected Member Academia Europaea, 1999; Elected Fellow, Royal Society, 2000; Honorary Doctorate, Paris-Lodron University, Salzburg, 2003; IgNobel Prize for Medicine (jointly), 2003. Memberships: Chartered Clinical Psychologist; Experimental Psychology Society; Associate Member, British Psychological Society, British Neuropsychology Society; British Neuropsychiatry Association; Association for the Scientific Study of Consciousness; Society for Neuroscience. Address: Wellcome Department of Imaging Neuroscience, Institute of Neurology, 12 Queen Square, London WC1N 3BG, England. E-mail: cfrith@fil.ion.ucl.ac.uk

**FRITH Uta,** b. 25 May 1941, Rockenhausen, Germany. Professor of Cognitive Development. m. Chris, 2 sons. Education: Vordiplom in Psychology, Universität des Saarlandes, Saarbrücken, Germany, 1964; Diploma in Abnormal Psychology, 1966, PhD in Psychology, 1968, Institute of Psychiatry, University of London. Appointments: MRC Scientist, 1968-; MRC Senior Scientist, 1980; MRC Special Appointment, 1988; MRC External Scientific Staff, 1998; Visiting Professor, 1993, Professor of Cognitive Development, 1996-, Deputy Director, Institute of Cognitive Neuroscience, 1998-, University College, London. Publications: Books: Autism in History: The Case of Hugh Blair of Borgue (with R Houston), 2001; Autism – Explaining the Enigma, 2nd edition, 2003; The Learning Brain – Lessons for Education (with S J Blakemore), 2005; Numerous articles in medical journals. Honours: President's Award, British Psychological Society, 1990; Elected Fellow of the British Academy, 2001; Elected Fellow of the Academy of Medical Sciences, 2001; Elected Fellow of the Royal Society, 2005; Honorary Doctorates: University of Göteborg, Sweden, 1992, University of St Andrews, 2000, University of Palermo, 2004, University of York, 2004. Memberships: British Psychological Society; Experimental Psychology Society; American Psychological Society; Association of Child and Adolescent Mental Health. Address: Institute of Cognitive Neuroscience, University College London, 17 Queen Square, London WC1N 3AR, England. E-mail: u.frith@ucl.ac.uk

**FRITZE Lothar,** b. 5 April 1954, Karl-Marx-Stadt. Researcher; Political analyst. m. Ulrike Fritze Otto, 2 sons. Education: Dipl-Ing oec, Betriebswirtschaft, 1978; Dr phil, Promotion in Philosophie, 1988; Dr phil habil, Habilitation in Politikwissenschaft, 1998. Appointments: Scientific collaborator, Forschungsinstitut fuer Textiltechnologie, Karl-Marx-Stadt, 1978-90; Institut fuer Wirtschafts u Sozialforschung, 1992-93; Hannah-Arendt-Institut fuer Totalitarismusforschung, Dresden, 1993-. Publications: Books: Innenansicht eines Ruins: Gedanken zum Untergang der DDR, 1993; Panoptikum DDR-Wirtschaft: Machtverhaeltnisse, Organisationsstrukturen, Funktionsmechanismen, 1993; Die Gegenwart des Vergangenen: Ueber das Weiterleben der DDR nach ihrem Ende, 1997; Taeter mit gutem Gewissen: Ueber menschliches Versagen im

diktatorischen Sozialismus, 1998; Die Toetung Unschuldiger. Ein Dogma auf dem Pruefstand, 2004; Verfuehrung and Anpassung. Zur Logik der Weltanschauungsdiktatur, 2004; Numerous articles to professional journals. Honours: Privatdozent, Technical University, Chemnitz; Award, Gesellschaft fuer Deutschlandforschung, 1998. Address: Georgistrasse 2, D-09127 Chemnitz, Germany.

**FRIZZELL Edward William,** b. 4 May 1946, Paisley, Scotland. Civil Servant. m. Moira Calderwood, 2 sons, 1 daughter. Education: Paisly Grammar School; MA (Hon), Glasgow University, 1968. Appointments: Marketing Economist, Scottish Milk Marketing Board, 1968-73; Expert Marketing Executive, Scottish Council (Development and Industry), 1973-76; Principal, Department of Agriculture and Fisheries for Scotland, 1976-78; First Secretary, Office of the UK Permanent Representative to the European Communities, Brussels, 1978-82; Head of Division, Scottish Education Department, 1982-86; Head of Division, Scottish Office Finance Group, 1986-89; Director, Industry Department, Scottish Development Agency, 1989-91; Chief Executive, Scottish Prison Service, 1991-99; Head, Scottish Executive, Enterprise, Transport & Lifelong Learning Department, 1999-. Honours: CB, NY, 2000. Memberships: Mortonhall Golf Club, Edinburgh. Address: Scottish Executive, Enterprise, Transport & Lifelong Learning Department, Meridian Court, Glasgow G2 6AT, Scotland, United Kingdom. E-mail: eddie.frizzell@scotla nd.gsi.gov.uk

**FROLOV Sergei Vladimirovich,** b. 14 August 1967, Leningrad, USSR. Mathematician; Physicist; Engineer; Educator. Education: Bachelor's Degree, Physics, 1989, Master's Degree, Mathematical Physics, 1993, St Petersburg State University; Doctor, Processes and Apparatus of Food Technology, St Petersburg State University of Refrigeration and Food Technologies, 1998. Appointments: Scientific Advisor, St Petersburg State University, 1991-95; Associate Professor, 1995-2000, Professor, 2000-, St Petersburg State University of Refrigeration and Food Technologies. Publications: Articles in scientific journals including: Physical Review, Theoretical and Mathematical Physics, Russia; Engineering Physical Journal, Russia; Journal of Applied Chemistry, Russia. Address: Flat 27, Italyanskaya St. 6, 191011, St Petersburg, Russia. E-mail: frol@sf1251.spb.edu

**FROST Christopher Peter,** b. 9 July 1950, Carlisle, England. Journalist; Academic m. Vanessa, 3 daughters. Education: Postgraduate Diploma (Distinction), Higher Education, 1997; MA, Education, 1999. Appointments: Editor and Journalist, Bedfordshire Journal, 1970-80; Journalist, Blackpool Gazette, 1980-90; Senior Lecturer in Journalism, University of Central Lancashire, 1990-2002; Head of Journalism, 2002, Professor of Journalism, 2004-, Liverpool John Moores University. Publications: Media Ethics and Self Regulation, 2000; Reporting for Journalists, 2001; Designing for Newspapers and Magazines, 2003; Various academic papers; Various popular reports. Memberships: National Union of Journalists; Higher Education Academy; Association for Journalism Education. Address: Liverpool John Moores University, Dean Walters Building, St James Road, Liverpool L1 7BR, England. E-mail: c.p.frost@livjm.ac.uk

**FROST David (Paradine) (Sir),** b. 7 April 1939, Tenterden, Kent, England. Television Personality; Author. m. (1) Lynn Frederick, 1981, divorced 1982, (2) Lady Carina Fitzalan-Howard, 1983, 3 sons. Education: MA, Gonville and Caius College, Cambridge. Appointments: Various BBC TV series, 1962-; Many ITV series, 1966-; Chairman and Chief Executive,

David Paradine Ltd, 1966-; Joint Founder and Director, TV-am, 1981-93; Regular appearances on US television. Publications: That Was the Week That Was, 1963; How to Live Under Labour, 1964; Talking with Frost, 1967; To England With Love, 1967; The Presidential Debate 1968, 1968; The Americans, 1970; Whitlam and Frost, 1974; I Gave Them a Sword, 1978; I Could Have Kicked Myself, 1982; Who Wants to be a Millionaire?, 1983; The Mid-Atlantic Companion (jointly), 1986; The Rich Tide (jointly), 1986; The World's Shortest Books, 1987; David Frost: An Autobiography, Part I: From Congregations to Audiences, 1993. Honours: Golden Rose Award, Montreux, 1967; Richard Dimbleby Award, 1967; Silver Medal, Royal Television Society, 1967; Officer of the Order of the British Empire, 1970; Religious Heritage of America Award, 1970; Emmy Awards, 1970, 1971; Albert Einstein Award, 1971; Knighted, 1993. Address: c/o David Paradine Ltd, 5 St Mary Abbots Place, London W8 6LS, England.

**FRY Stephen John,** b. 24 August 1957. Actor; Writer. Education: Queen's College, Cambridge, England. Appointments: Columnist, The Listener, 1988-89; Daily Telegraph, 1990-; Appeared with Cambridge Footlights in revue, The Cellar Tapes, Edinburgh Festival, 1981; Re-wrote script: Me and My Girl, London, Broadway, Sydney, 1984; Plays: Forty Years On, Chichester Festival and London, 1984; The Common Pursuit, London, 1988 (TV, 1992); TV series: Alfresco, 1982-84; The Young Ones, 1983; Happy Families, 1984; Saturday Night Live, 1986-87; A Bit of Fry and Laurie, 1989-95; Blackadder's Christmas Carol, 1988; Blackadder Goes Forth, 1989; Jeeves and Wooster, 1990-92; Stalag Luft, 1993; Laughter and Loathing, 1995; Gormenghast, 2000; Radio: Loose Ends, 1986-87; Whose Line Is It Anyway?, 1987; Saturday Night Fry, 1987; Harry Potter and the Chamber of Secrets (Narrator, CD), 2002; Harry Potter and the Prisoner of Azkaban (Narrator, CD), 2004; Films: The Good Father; A Fish Called Wanda; A Handful of Dust; Peter's Friends, 1992; IQ, 1995; Wind in the Willows, 1997; Wilde, 1997; A Civil Action, 1997; Whatever Happened to Harold Smith? 2000; Relatives Values, 2000; Discovery of Heaven, 2001; Gosford Park, 2001; Thunderpants, 2002; Bright Young Things, 2003; Tooth, 2004; The Life and Death of Peter Sellers, 2004. Publications: Paperweight (collected essays), 1992; The Liar (novel); The Hippopotamus, 1994; Fry and Laurie 4 (with Hugh Laurie), 1994; Paperweight, 1995; Making History, 1996; Moab is My Washpot (autobiography), 1997; The Star's Tennis Balls (novel), 2000. Honour: Hon LLD (Dundee), 1995. Memberships: Patron, Studio 3 (arts for young people); Freeze (nuclear disarmament charity); Amnesty International; Comic Relief. Address: c/o Hamilton Asper Management, Ground Floor, 24 Hanway Street, London, W1P 9DD, England.

**FRYBA Ladislav,** b. 30 May 1929, Studenec. Professor. m. Dagmar Frybova. Education: Ing, 1953, DSc, 1959, Docent, 1966, Professor, 1993, Czech Technical University; Doctor honoris causa, University of Pardubice, 2004. Appointments: Head, Bridge Department, Railway Research Institute, 1972-84; Professor, Institute of Theoretical and Applied Mechanics, Academy of Sciences of the Czech Republic, 1984-. Publications: 6 books, co-author 6 books, 191 papers in 8 world languages; Best known world-wide: Dynamics of Railway Bridges, 2nd edition, 1996; Vibration of Solids and Structures Under Moving Loads, 3rd edition, 1999. Honours: Medals, Czechoslovak Academy of Sciences, Czech Society for Mechanics; 5 medals from Japanese Universities and Society of Japanese Association of Mechanical Engineering; Diploma, European Association for Structural Dynamics; Listed in international biographical dictionaries. Memberships: Chairman, Committees of Experts of the European Rail Research Institute, Utrecht, 1967-2001;

President, Czech Society for Mechanics, 1991-; President, European Association for Structural Dynamics, 1996-99; Member, Engineering Academy of the Czech Republic, 1996-; Research Board of Advisors, American Biographical Institute, 1999; Member, Editorial Board of the Journal of Sound and Vibration, 2001-.

**FUENTES Carlos,** b. 11 November 1928, Panama City, Panama. Professor of Latin American Studies; Writer. m. (1) Rita Macedo, 1957, 1 daughter, (2) Sylvia Lemus, 24 Jan 1973, 1 son, 1 daughter. Education: Law School, National University of Mexico; Institute de Hautes Études Internationales, Geneva. Appointments: Head, Cultural Relations Department, Ministry of Foreign Affairs, Mexico, 1955-58; Mexican Ambassador to France, 1975-77; Professor of English and Romance Languages, University of Pennsylvania, 1978-83; Professor of Comparative Literature, 1984-86, Robert F Kennedy Professor of Latin American Studies, 1987-, Harvard University; Simon Bolivar Professor, Cambridge University, 1986-87; Professor-at-Large, Brown University, 1995-. Publications: La Region Mas Transparente, 1958; Las Buenas Conciencias, 1959; Aura, 1962; La Muerte de Artemio Cruz, 1962; Cantar de Ciegos, 1964; Cambio de Piel, 1967; Zona Sagrada, 1967; Terra Nostra, 1975; Una Familia Lejana, 1980; Agua Quemada, 1983; Gringo Viejo, 1985; Cristóbal Nonato, 1987; Myself with Others (essays), 1987; Orchids in the Moonlight (play), 1987; The Campaign, 1991; The Buried Mirror, 1992; El Naranjo, 1993; Geography of the Novel: Essays, 1993; La frontera de cristal (stories), 1995; Los Años con Laura Diaz (novel), 1999; Los Cincosoles de Mexico (anthology), 2000; Inez, 2000; Ce que je crois, 2002; La Silla de Aguila, 2003. Contributions to: Periodicals. Honours: Biblioteca Breva Prize, Barcelona, 1967; Rómulo Gallegos Prize, Caracas, 1975; National Prize for Literature, Mexico, 1984; Miguel de Cervantes Prize for Literature, Madrid, 1988; Légion d'Honneur, France, 1992; Principe de Asturias Prize, 1992; Latin Civilisation Prize, French and Brazilian Academies, 1999; DLL, Ghent, 2000, Madrid, 2000; Mexican Senate Medal, 2000; Los Angeles Public Library Award, 2001; Commonwealth Award Delaware, 2002. Memberships: American Academy and Institute of Arts and Letters; El Colegio Nacional, Mexico; Mexican National Commission on Human Rights. Literary Agent: Brandt & Brandt. Address: c/o Brandt & Brandt, 1501 Park Avenue, New York, NY 10036, USA.

**FUENTES Martha Ayers,** b. 21 December 1923, Ashland, Alabama, USA. m. Manuel Solomon Fuentes, 11 April 1943. Education: BA, Education University of South Florida, USA, 1969. Appointments: Playwright/Author, at present; Jewellery Sales, Tampa, Florida, 1940; Later served in various business positions; Author, 1953. Publications: Pleasure Button, full length play, 1995-96; Jordan's End, 1998. Honours: Iona Lester Scholarship, Creative Writing, University Southern Florida, George Sergel Drama Award, University of Chicago, Southeastern Writers Conference; Instructor, Playwriting and TV; Feature Writer for national magazines. Memberships: Dramatist Guild; Authors Guild; Florida Theatre Conference; North Carolina Writers' Network; Florida Studio Theatre, Sarasota, Florida; United Daughters of the Confederacy; Southern Heritage Society. Address: 102 Third Street, Belleair Beach, FL 33786-2311, USA.

**FUJIMAKI Norio,** b. 15 February 1953, Niigata, Japan. Researcher. m. 10 July 1988, 2 daughters. Education: BSc, 1975, MSc, 1977, PhD, 1980, Electronic Engineering, University of Tokyo. Appointments: Fujitsu Laboratories Ltd, 1980-99; National Institute of Information and Communication Technology (previous name, Communications Research Laboratories), 1999-. Publications: Neuromagnetism (co-author), 1997; Handbook of Quantum Engineering (co-author), 1999; Several articles in professional journals including: IEEE Transactions; Journal of Applied Physics; Neuroscience Research; Human Brain Mapping; Neuro Image. Memberships: Institute of Electrical and Electronics Engineers; Institute of Electronics, Information and Communications Engineers; Japan Society of Applied Physics; Japan Biomagnetism and Biomagnetics Society; Japan Society of Medical Electronics and Biological Engineering; Society for Neuroscience; Japan Neuroscience Society. Address: Brain Information Group, National Institute of Information and Communications Technology, 588-2, Iwaoka, Iwaoka-cho, Nishi-ku, Kobe 651-2492, Japan. E-mail: fujimaki@po.nict.go.jp

**FUJITA Masayuki,** b. 15 August 1956, Takamatsu, Kagawa, Japan. Biologist; Educator. m. Tomoko, 1 son. Education: BS, Chemistry, Shizuoka University, Faculty of Science, 1975-79; Doctor of Agriculture, Biochemistry, Nagoya University, Graduate School of Bioagricultural Sciences, 1979-83. Appointments: Assistant Professor, 1983-91, Associate Professor, 1991-99, Professor, 1999-, Kagawa University; Serving Concurrently as Professor, Ehime University and The United Graduate School of Agricultural Sciences, 1999-; Researcher, Institute of Biological Chemistry, Washington State University, USA, 1996-97. Publications: Plant Infection, 1982; Handbook of Phytoalexin Metabolism and Action, 1995; Lignin and Lignan Biosynthesis, 1998; Biochemistry and Molecular Biology of Plant Stress, 2001. Honour: Fellow, Co-operative Research Programme: Biological Resource Management for Sustainable Agricultural Systems, Organisation for Economic Co-operation and Development (OECD). Memberships: American Society of Plant Biologists; Phytochemical Society of North America; International Society for Horticultural Science. Address: Kagawa University; 2393 Ikenobe Miki-cho, Kagawa 761-0795, Japan. E-mail: fujita@ag.kagawa-u.ac.jp

**FUKAZAWA Hajime,** b. 1947, Mito-shi, Japan. Oral and Maxillofacial Surgeon. Education: Doctor of Dental Surgery, 1975, Doctorate in Medical Science, 1979, Iwate Medical University, Japan. Appointments: Assistant Professor, Iwate Medical University, 1980-92; Chairman, Assistant Professor, Hachinohe Red Cross Hospital, 1981-82; Clinical Observership in Surgical Oncology, Department of Head and Neck Surgery, M D Anderson Cancer Center, USA, 1988-89; Assistant Professor, Niigata University, 1992-94; Chairman and Assistant Professor, Yuri Nokyo General Hospital, Honjoh-shi, Japan, 1994-2000; Chairman and Assistant Professor, Ookubo Hospital, Mito-shi, Japan, 2000-. Publications: Multidisciplinary Treatment of Head and Neck Cancer, 1994; Many articles and papers in professional journals and conference proceedings. Honours: Citation, Japan Society for Cancer Therapy, 1995; Best Doctor of Head and Neck Cancer, Japan Cancer Hospital, 1999; Indian Medical Culture Award, 2004. Memberships: IPPNW; Corresponding Fellow, American Society for Head and Neck Surgery; Director, Japanese Oral Surgeons; Councillor, Japan Society for Oral Tumors. Address: Department of Oral and Maxillofacial Surgery, Ookubo Hospital, 4-4040-32 Ishikawa, Mito-shi 310-0905, Japan.

**FULLER Cynthia Dorothy,** b. 13 February 1948, Isle of Sheppey, England. Poet; Adult Education Tutor. divorced, 2 sons. Education: BA Honours, English, Sheffield University, 1969; Postgraduate Certificate of Education, Oxford University, 1970; MLitt, Aberdeen University, 1979. Appointments: Teacher of English, Redborne School, 1970-72; Freelance in Adult Education, University Departments at Durham and Newcastle Universities, also Open University and Workers Education Association. Publications: Moving towards Light,

1992; Instructions for the Desert, 1996; Only a Small Boat, 2001. Contributions to: Poems in various magazines including: Other Poetry; Iron; Poetry Durham; Literary Review. Honour: Northern Arts Financial Assistance. Address: 28 South Terrace, Esh Winning, Co Durham DH7 9PR, England.

**FULLER Jean Violet Overton,** b. 7 March 1915, Iver Heath, Bucks, England. Author. Education: Brighton High School, 1927-31; Royal Academy of Dramatic Art, 1931-32; BA, University of London, 1945; University College of London, 1948-50. Publications: The Comte de Saint Germain, 1988; Blavatsky and Her Teachers, 1988; Dericourt: The Chequered Spy, 1989; Sickert and the Ripper Crimes, 1990; Cats and other Immortals, 1992; Krishnamurti and the Wind, 2003; Driven to it (autobiography), 2005. Honour: Writers Manifold Poems of the Decade, 1968. Membership: Society of Authors. Address: Fuller D'Arch Smith Ltd, 37B New Cavendish Street, London, England.

**FULLERTON Alexander Fergus,** b. 20 September 1924, Saxmundham, Suffolk, England. Writer. m. Priscilla Mary Edelston, 10 May 1956, 3 sons. Education: Royal Naval College, Dartmouth, 1938-41; School of Slavonic Studies, Cambridge University, 1947. Appointments: Editorial Director, Peter Davies Ltd, 1961-64; General Manager, Arrow Books, 1964-67. Publications: Surface!, 1953; A Wren Called Smith, 1957; The White Men Sang, 1958; The Everard Series of naval novels: The Blooding of the Guns, 1976; Sixty Minutes for St George, 1977; Patrol to the Golden Horn, 1978; Storm Force to Narvik, 1979; Last Lift from Crete, 1980; All the Drowning Seas, 1981; A Share of Honour, 1982; The Torch Bearers, 1983; The Gatecrashers, 1984. Special Deliverance, 1986; Special Dynamic, 1987; Special Deception, 1988; Bloody Sunset, 1991; Look to the Wolves, 1992; Love for an Enemy, 1993; Not Thinking of Death, 1994; Into the Fire, 1995; Band of Brothers, 1996; Return to the Field, 1997; Final Dive, 1998; In at the Kill, 1999; Wave Cry, 1999; The Floating Madhouse, 2000; Single to Paris, 2001; Flight to Mons, 2003; Westbound, Warbound, 2003; Stark Realities, 2004; Non-Combatants, 2005. Address: c/o Johnson & Alcock Ltd, 45 Clerkenwell Green, London EC1R 0HT, England.

**FUNG Wye-Poh,** b. 9 January 1937, Telok-Anson, Malaysia. Consultant Physician; Gastroenterologist. m. Saw-Lin Fung, 1 son, 1 daughter. Education: MB, BS, University of Malaya, Singapore, 1961; MRACP, Melbourne, 1965; FRACP, 1972; FACG, 1972; MD, University of Singapore, 1972; FAMS, 1978. Appointments: Assistant Lecturer, Clinical Medicine, University of Singapore, 1964-65; Research Fellow, Gastroenterology, A W Morrow, Department of Gastroenterology, Royal Prince Alfred Hospital, Camperdown, Sydney, 1965-66; Lecturer, Clinical Medicine, 1965-70; Senior Lecturer, Medicine, 1970-74, Associate Professor, Medicine, 1975, University of Singapore, Singapore General Hospital; Associate Physician, Department of General Medicine, Royal Perth Hospital, 1975-76; Senior Lecturer, Medicine, University of Western Australia, Royal Perth Hospital, 1976-85; Visiting Associate Professor, Department of Medicine and GI Unit, University of California, San Francisco, 1981-82; Consultant Physician, Gastroenterologist, Private Practice, 1985-; Gastroenterologist, Swan District Hospital, 1985-; St John of God Hospital, Wembly, Australia, 1986-; Osborne Park Hospital, 1986-; Armadale-Kelmscott Hospital, 1987-, Perth, Western Australia. Publications: Numerous articles in professional journals. Memberships: Foundation Secretary, Treasurer, Gastroenterological Society of Singapore, 1967-75; Gastroenterological Society of Australia, 1975-. Address: Suite 2, 11 Colin Grove, West Perth, WA 6005, Australia.

**FURUKUBO-TOKUNAGA Katsuo,** b. 24 September 1954, Nagoya, Japan. Professor. m. Midori Furukubo, 1 daughter. Education: BSc, Kyoto University, 1978; MSc, 1980, Doctorate, Science, 1983, Nagoya University, Japan; Advanced Graduate Course, National Institute of Basic Biology, Okazaki, Japan, 1983. Appointments: Research Fellow, National Institute of Basic Biology, Okazaki, 1983; Senior Researcher, Chiba Cancer Center, Chiba, Japan, 1983-88; Senior Research Associate, 1988-92, Assistant Professor, 1992-95, University of Basle, Switzerland; Associate Professor, University of Tsukuba, Ibaraki, Japan, 1995; Project Leader, Tsukuba Advanced Research Alliance, Ibaraki, Japan, 2000-; Chief research achievement: Discovery of Cross-phylum conservation of genetic programs of brain development between fruitflies and human. Publications: Numerous research papers and articles in specialist peer-reviewed journals such as Cell Press; Proceedings of the National Academy of Sciences, USA; Genes and Development; Development. Honours: Research grant, Roche Research Foundation, 1993-95; Research grant, Swiss National Science Foundation, 1994-97; Research grant, The Yamaha Science Foundation, 1996-97; Research grant, Tsukuba Advanced Research Alliance, 2000-2006. Memberships: Numerous scientific and professional affiliations including, The Genetical Society, UK; The Genetics Society of America; Society for Neuroscience; The Japanese Society of Developmental Biologists; The Molecular Biology Society of Japan; Japan Neuroscience Society. Address: Institute of Biological Sciences, University of Tsukuba, Tennodai 1-1-1-, Tsukuba, Ibaraki, Japan.

**FUTKO Sergey Ivanovich,** b. 11 June 1968, Minsk, Belarus. Research Scientist; Physicist. Education: MSc, Honours, Moscow Physico-Technical Institute, 1991; Internship, University of Illinois at Chicago, USA, 1997; PhD, Honours, Byelorussian Academy of Sciences, 2003. Appointments: Junior Research Scientist, 1994-2001, Research Scientist, 2001-2004, Senior Research Scientist, 2004-, Heat and Mass Transfer Institute, NAS, Minsk, Belarus. Publications: Articles in scientific journals: Models of FCG with Allowance for Flame Turbulence, 2002; Effect of Kinetic Properties of a Mixture on Wave Macrocharacteristics of Filtration Combustion of Gases, 2003; Mechanism of Upper Temperature Limits in a Wave of FCG, 2003; Kinetic Analysis of the Chemical Structure of Waves of FCG in Fuel-Rich Compositions, 2003; Analysis of NOx Formation in FC of methane-air mixtures, 2003; Book: Chemistry of Filtration Combustion of Gases, 2004. Honours: Listed in Who's Who publications and biographical dictionaries; International Scientist of the Year, 2005. Address: Institute of Heat and Mass Transfer, P Brovki 15, Minsk, 220072, Belarus. E-mail: foutko@itmo.by

**FYODOROV Nikolai Vasilyevich,** b. 9 May 1958, Chuvash Republic. Politician. m. Svetlana Yuryevna Fyodorova, 1 son, 1 daughter. Education: Graduate, Law Faculty, Kazan State University, 1980; Cand. Sc. (Law), Moscow Institute of State and Law, 1985; Appointments: Teacher, Chuvash State University, 1980-82, 1986-89; Member, USSR Supreme Soviet, 1989-91; Minister of Justice of Russia, 1990-93; President of Chuvash Republic, 1994-, re-elected, 1997 and 2001; Member, Council of Federation, 1996-2002; Representative of Russia in the Parliamentary Assembly of Council of Europe. Publications: More than 100 books and articles in economy, law and national relations. Honours: State Counsellor of Justice of Russia; The Russian Federation State Prize in the field of science and technology for restoration of the historical part of Cheboxary, 1999; Order, For Merits in Fatherland IV class; The highest All-Russian Femida Prize, 1997; Peter the Great National Prize; Honorary Construction Worker of Russia; Order of the Saint Duke Daniil Moskovskii 1 class and Order of Reverend Sergii Radonezhskii, Russian Orthodox Church. Address: 1 Republic Square, House of Government, 428004 Cheboxary, Chuvash Republic, Russia. E-mail: president@cap.ru

# G

**GABRIEL Peter,** b. 13 February 1950, Cobham, Surrey, England. Singer; Composer. Appointments: Co-Founder, Genesis, 1966; Solo Artiste, 1975-; Appearances worldwide in concerts; Founder, World of Music, Arts and Dance (WOMAD), music from around the world, 1982; Founder, Real World Group, 1985; Real World Studios, 1986; Real World Records, 1989; Real World Multimedia, 1994; Launched Witness Human Rights Programme, 1992. Creative Works: Singles: Solsbury Hill; Games Without Frontiers; Shock The Monkey; Sledgehammer; In Your Eyes; Don't Give Up; Biko; Big Time; Red Rain; Digging in the Dirt; Steam; Blood of Eden; Kiss That Frog; Solo albums: PG I-IV, PG Plays Live, 1983; So, 1986; Shaking the Tree (compilation), 1990; Us, 2992; Ovo, 2000; Up, 2002; Soundtrack albums: Birdy; Passion (Last Temptation of Christ). Honours: Ivor Novello Awards, 1983, 1987; Brit Awards, 1987, 1993; 9 Music Video Awards; Video Vanguard Trophy, 1987; Grammy Awards, 1990, 1993. Address: c/o Real World, Box Mill, Box, Wiltshire, SN14 9PL, England.

**GABRIEL Vincent Albert,** b. 30 August 1942, Singapore. Management Consultant. m. Chua Lim Neo, 2 sons. Education: BSc (Hons) Economics, University of London, England; Certificate in Education, Singapore; Diploma in Marketing, UK; Certificate in Non-Formal Education; Certificate in Urban Education. Appointments: Secondary School Educator, 1961-72; Supervisor in Advanced Training Techniques, 1973-79; Curriculum Advisor, 1979-80; Management Consultant, 1980-. Publications: Management; A Guide to Management of Business; Management of Business; At Your Finger Tips: Physical Geography, Economic Geography, Elective Geography. Honours: Best in the World in English (LCCI); Second Prize, National Banking Essay Competition; Joint First in Asian Productivity Organisation; Joint First, Institute of Administration Management Essay Competition; Prize Winner, Switch Sounds of the Century. Website: home.pacific.net.sg/~ajgabriel

**GADA Manilal Talakshi,** b. 12 January 1947, Gujarat, India. Psychiatrist. m. Manjula, 2 daughters. Education: MBBS, University of Bombay, 1971; DPM, College of Physicians and Surgeons of Bombay, 1975; MD, University of Bombay, 1976. Appointments: Professor of Psychiatry, Padamashree Dr D Y Patil Medical College (deemed University); Head, Department of Psychiatry and Psychiatrist, Rajawadi Municipal General Hospital; (Retired) Specialist (Psychiatrist), Panel Consultant, Air India; Senior Specialist (Psychiatrist), Panel Consultant, Oil and Natural Gas Commission, Bombay Region; Specialist (Psychiatrist), Panel Consultant, Larsen and Toubro Co; Honorary Psychiatrist, Sulabha School for Mentally Retarded Children; Post Graduate Teacher and Examiner for DPM, DNB. Publications include: Defeat Depression: A Guide for Patients and Their Family Members, 1994, 2nd edition, 1998; Mansik Hatasha Hatao (book in local Gujarati language); 1998; Defeat Depression, 4th edition, 2000, reprint, 2001; Stress Management: Holistic Approach, 2001, reprint 2002; Khinnata Nakoj (Defeat Depression, book in local Marathi language), 2003; Co-editor, Essentials of Post-graduate Psychiatry, 2005; 8 book chapters; More than 60 papers in scientific journals. Honours include: Invited by WHO Mental Health Division to participate in a Multicentric Study on Depressive Disease; Tilak Venkoba Rao Oration Award, Indian Psychiatric Society, 1987; President, Lions Club of Bombay Pantnagar, 1994-95; Late Dr R K Menda Oration Award, Indian Medical Association, Nagpur Branch, 1995; Late Dr S M Lulla Oration Award, Bombay Psychiatric Society, 2000; West Zone President's Award, 1984,

1997; District Committee Chairman, Lions District 323A2 of Lions Club International, 1998-; Lions International President's Appreciation Certificate, 2003. Memberships include: Life Fellow, Indian Psychiatric Society; Chair, Biological Psychiatry Section, 1997-99; Chair, Ethics Committee, 2001-03, 2003-05; Chairman, Organising Committee of 58th Annual Conference of Indian Psychiatric Society, 2006; Life Fellow, Indian Psychiatric Society - West Zone, President, 1994-95; Life Fellow, Bombay Psychiatric Society, President, 1989-90; Life Fellow, Indian Association of Private Psychiatry; Founder Life Fellow, Indian Association for Child and Adolescent Mental Health; Life Member, Kutchi Medicos Association , President, 1992-94; Life Member Indian Medical Association. Address: 201 Kumudini, Above Andhra Bank, 7th Road, Rajawadi, Ghatkopar (East), Bombay 400 077, India.

**GADDAFI Colonel Mu'ammar Muhammad al,** b. 1942, Serte, Libya. Libyan Army Officer; Political Leader. m. 1970, 8 children. Education: University of Libya, Benghazi. Appointments: Served, Libyan Army, 1965-; Chair, Revolutionary Command Council, 1969-; Commander-in-Chief of Armed Forces, 1969; Prime Minister, 1970-72; Minister of Defence, 1970-72; Secretary General of General Secretariat of General Peoples Congress, 1977-79; Chair, OAU, 1982-83. Publications: The Green Book, 3 vols; Military Strategy and Mobilization; The Story of the Revolution. Honours: Title, Colonel; Rank of Major-General, 1976. Membership: President, Council, Federation of Arab Republics, 1972. Address: Office of the President, Tripoli, Libya.

**GADSBY Roger,** b. 2 March 1950, Coventry, England. General Practitioner. m. Pamela Joy, 1 son, 1 daughter. Education: BSc (Hons), Medical Biochemical Studies, 1971, MB ChB (Hons), Obstetrics and Gynaecology, 1974, Birmingham University Medical School; Post qualification experience in hospitals in Birmingham and Stoke-on-Trent, GP training in Stoke. Appointments: Full-time General Practitioner, now Senior Partner, Redroofs Practice, Nuneaton Warwickshire, 1979-; Part-time Senior Lecturer in Primary Care, University of Warwick, 1992-; Co-Founder, Warwick Diabetes Care, 2000. Publications: Over 100 papers and articles on diabetes and pregnancy sickness symptoms; 2 textbooks on diabetes; 2 chapters on diabetes issues in primary care in major diabetes textbooks. Honours: DCH, 1978; DRCOG, 1978; MRCGP (by examination), 1978; FRCGP (by election), 1992. Memberships: Fellow, Royal College of General Practitioners; Diabetes (UK); Primary Care Diabetes Society; American Diabetes Association; British Medical Association; Chairman of Trustees, Pregnancy Sickness Support Charity. Address: Rivendell, School Lane, Exhall, Coventry, CV7 6GF, England. E-mail: rgadsby@doctors.org.uk

**GAFITANU Mihai,** b. 16 September 1934, Iasi, Romania. Professor, Engineering. m. Eliza, 2 sons. Education: Mechanical Engineering, Technical University of Iasi, 1957; DSc, Technical University, Polytechnica, Bucharest, Romania, 1968. Appointments: Assistant, 1957-62, Lecturer, 1962-69, Assistant Professor, 1969-72, Professor, 1972-, Vice Dean, 1964-72, Vice Rector, 1972-76, Rector, 1976-84, 1996-2000, Head of Department, 1985-96, Technical University of Iasi. Publications: 9 monographs; 14 texts and handbooks; 275 papers in scientific journals, proceedings; 13 international patents. Honours: Romanian Academy Prize, 1985; Gold Medals, Inventions Expo, Geneva, 1994, Brussels, 1997; Listed in several biographical publications. Memberships: Vice President, Society of Tribology, 1981; Romanian Academy of Technical Sciences, 1998-; National Council, Academy Accred, 1994-; National Council Academic Titles Attest, 1991-98; National Council Scientific Research, 1998-2003; Doctor Honoris Causa

– Technical University of Moldavia, Chisinau, 1999; Northern University of Baia Mare, Romania, 2002. Address: 12B, Al Vlahuta St, Iasi 700487, Romania.

**GAILLARD Mary K,** b. 1 April 1939, New Brunswick, New Jersey, USA. m. Bruno Zumino, 2 sons, 1 daughter. Education: BA, Hollins University, 1960; MA, Columbia University, 1961; Doctorat de Troisième Cycle, 1964, Doctorat d'Etat, 1968, University of Paris, Orsay. Appointments: Attaché de research, 1964-66, Chargé de research, 1968-73, Maître de research, 1973-79 CNRS; Visiting Scientist, Fermilab, 1973-74, 1983; Scientific Associate, Theory Division, CERN, 1964-81; Theory Group Leader, LAPP; Directeur de research, CNRS, 1980-81; Professor of Physics, University of California, Berkeley, Faculty Senior Staff, Lawrence Berkeley Laboratory, 1981-. Publications: 180 articles in scientific journals and conference proceedings; Co-editor: Weak Interactions, 1977; Gauge Theories in High Energy Physics, 1982. Honours: Woodrow Wilson Scholarship, 1960; Prix Thibaud, 1977; Loeb Lecturer in Physics, Harvard University, 1980; Chancellor's Distinguished Lecturer, University of California, Berkeley, 1981; Warner-Lambert Lecturer, University of Michigan, 1984; Fellow, American Physical Society, 1985; Miller Research Professorship, University of California, Berkeley, 1987-88, Fall 1996; E O Lawrence Memorial Award, 1988; Guggenheim Fellow, 1989-90; Fellow, American Academy of Arts and Sciences, 1989; Member, National Academy of Arts and Sciences, 1991; J J Sakurai Prize, 1993; Trustee, Council of Penn Women Lecturers, University of Pennsylvania, 1994; APS Centennial Lecturer, 1998-99; Member, American Philosophical Society, 2000. Memberships: American Physical Society; French Physical Society; European Physical Society; American Association for the Advancement of Science; American Civil Liberties Union; Arms Control Association; Union of Concerned Scientists. Address: Department of Physics, University of California, Berkeley, CA 94720, USA

**GAJDUSEK Daniel Carleton,** b. 9 September 1923, Yonkers, New York, USA. Paediatrician; Virologist. Education: Graduated, Medicine, Harvard University, 1941; Internships and Residencies in several children's hospitals; Physical Chemistry, California Institute of Technology; Research Fellowship, Virology Department, Harvard University. Appointments: Walter Reed Army Medical Center, 1952-53; Institut Pasteur, Tehran, Iran and University of Medicine, 1954-55; Visiting Investigator at Walter and Eliza Hall, Institute, Australia, 1955-57; Laboratory Chief, National Institute of Neurological Disorders and Stroke, NIH, Bethesda, Maryland, USA, 1958-97; Chief of Study of Child Growth and Development and Disease Patterns in Primitive Cultures, and of Laboratory of Slow, Latent and Temperate Virus Infections, 1958-97; Chief of Central Nervous System Studies Laboratory, 1970-97; Professor, Institute of Human Virology, University of Maryland, 1996-. Publications: Hemorrhagic Fevers and Mycotoxicoses, 1959; Slow, Latent and Temperate Virus Infections, 1965; Correspondence on the Discovery of Kuru, 1976; Kuru (with Judith Farquhar), 1980; Research, Travel and Field Expedition Journals (55 vols), 1940-99; Vilinisk Encephalomyelitis, 1996; over 1,000 papers on microbiology, immunology, paediatrics, neurology, cognitive and psychosexual development and genetics. Honours: Several honorary degrees; Meade Johnson Award, American Academy of Pediatrics, 961; Dautrebande Prize, 1976; Shared Nobel Prize for Physiology or Medicine, 1976; Cotzias Prize, 1978; Huxley Medal, Royal Anthropological Institute of Great Britain and Ireland, 1988; Stuart Mudd Prize, 1989; Award of 3rd International Congress on Alzheimer's Disease, 1992; Award of 3rd Pacific Rim Biotechnology Conference, 1992; Gold Medal, Slovak Academy of Science, 1996; Honorary Professor, 10

Chinese universities, 1993-2002; Honorary Adviser, 3 Chinese academies, 1999-2002. Memberships: Society for Paediatric Research; American Pediatric Society; National Academy of Sciences; American Academy of Arts and Sciences; American Philosophica Society; Deutsche Akademie der Naturforscher Leopoldina; Third World Academy of Science; American Academy of Neurology; Russian Academy of Medicine; Sakha (Iakut) Siberian Academy of Science (branch of Russian Academy of Science). Address: Institut Alfred Fessard, CNRS, Avenue de la Terrasse, 91198 Gif-sur-Yvette, Cedex, France.

**GALASKO Charles Samuel Bernard,** b. 29 June 1939, Johannesburg, South Africa. Orthopaedic Surgeon. m. Carol Freyda Lapinsky, 29 October 1967, 1 son, 1 daughter. education: MB, BCh, 1st Class Honours, 1962, ChM, 1970, Witwatersrand; FRCS, Edinburgh, 1966; FRCS, England, 1966; Honorary MSc, Manchester, 1980; FCMSA (Honorary Fellow, College of Medicine of South Africa), 2003; FFSEM, Ireland, 2002; F Med Sci. Appointments include: House positions, Johannesburg and London; Nuffield Scholar, Nuffield Orthopaedic Centre, Oxford, 1969; Registrar, 1970, Senior Orthopaedic Registrar, 1970-73, Radcliffe Infirmary and Nuffield Orthopaedic Centre, Oxford; Director, Orthopaedic Surgery, Assistant Director, Division of Surgery, Royal Postgraduate Medical School, Director, Orthopaedic Surgery, Consultant, Hammersmith Hospital, 1973-76; Member, Unit Management, Royal Manchester Children's Hospital, Clinical Director, Department of Orthopaedic Surgery, Salford General Hospitals, 1989-92; Member, Unit Management Board, 1989-96, Medical Director, 1993-96, Salford Royal Hospitals NHS Trust; Professor, Orthopaedic Surgery, University of Manchester, 1976-2004; Consultant Orthopaedic Surgeon, Hope Hospital and Royal Manchester Children's Hospital, 1976-2004; Director of Education and Training, Salford Royal Hospitals NHS Trust, 2002-. Publications: Numerous articles and papers in the field of orthopaedics; 9 books include: Skeletal Metatases, author, 1986; Competing for the Disabled, co-author, 1989; Editor: Principles of Fracture Management, 1984; Neuromuscular Problems in Orthopaedics, 1987. Honours include: Moynihan Prize, Association of Surgeons of Great Britain and Ireland, 1969; Hunterian Professor, Royal College of Surgeons of England, 1971; AO Fellowship; Australian Commonwealth Fellowship, 1982; Sir Arthur Sims Commonwealth Professor, 1998; Scholarships; Academic prizes; Numerous lectureships, UK and abroad. Memberships include: International Orthopaedic Research Society, Programme Chairman, 1984-87, Membership Committee Chairman, 1987-90, President, 1990-93; International Association Olympic Medical Officers, Treasurer, 1988-2000; British Orthopaedic Association, Council, 1988-91, 1998-2003, Vice President, 1999-2000, President, 2000-2001; Royal College of Surgeons, England, Council, 1991-2003, Vice-President, 1999-2001, Chairman, Training Board, 1995-99; Chairman, Head Injury Working Party, 1997-99; Chairman, Joint Committee on Higher Surgical Training of the United Kingdom and Ireland, 1997-2000; Chairman, Intercollegiate Academic Board for Sport and Exercise Medicine, 2002-. Address: 72 Gatley Road, Gatley, Cheshire, SK8 4AA, England.

**GALE (Gwendoline) Fay,** b. 13 June 1932, Balaklava, South Australia. Social Scientist. 1 son, 1 daughter. Education: BA (Honours), 1954, PhD, 1962, DUniv, 1994, University of Adelaide; Hon DLitt, UWA, 1998. Appointments: Lecturer, 1966-70, Senior Lecturer, 1971-74, Reader, 1975-77, Professor of Geography, 1978-89, University of Adelaide; Pro Vice Chancellor, University of Adelaide, 1988-89; Vice Chancellor, University of Western Australia, 1990-97; President, Australian Vice Chancellors Committee (AVCC), 1996-97; President, Academy of Social Sciences in Australia, 1998-2000; President,

Association of Asian Social Science Research Councils, 2001-03. Publications include: Urban Aborigines, 1970; Race Relations in Australia: The Aboriginal Situation, 1975; Adelaide Aborigines: A Case Study of Urban Life 1966-81, 1982; Tourists and the National Estate: Procedures to Protect Australia's Heritage, 1987; Aboriginal Youth and the Criminal Justice System: The Injustice of Justice, 1990; Juvenile Justice: Debating the Issues, 1993; Tourism and the Protection of Aboriginal Cultural Sites, 1994; Strategies to Redress Gender Imbalance in the Numbers of Senior Academic Women, 1996; Cultural Geographies (editor) 1998. Honours include: Fellow, Academy of Social Sciences, 1978; Emeritus Professor, University of Adelaide, 1989; Officer, Order of Australia, 1989; Honorary Life Member, Institute of Australian Geographers, 1994; Fellow, Australian Institute of Management, 1994; Emeritus Professor, University of Western Australia, 1997; John Lewis Gold Medal, 2000, Honorary Life Fellow, Academy of The Social Sciences, 2001; Griffith Taylor Medal, 2002; Honorary Fellow, Association for Tertiary Education Management, 2003. Address: Academy of the Social Sciences, Box 1956, Canberra, ACT 2600, Australia.

**GALE Raymond Floyd,** b. 12 June 1918, Galesbury, USA. Professor. m. Irma F Gale. Education: BA, Journalism, MSc, 1940, Psychology, 1947, Illinois State University; Counseling Psychology, EdD, North-western University, 1955; Postgraduate work at Illinois, Colorado, University of Southern California, Minnesota and Chicago. Appointments: Teacher, Illinois High School, 1946-50; Teacher, Counselor, Highland Park High School, 1950-55; Dean of Faculty, Wayland Academy, Wisconsin; Professor of Psychology, Ball State University, 1957-83; Guest Professor, Colorado, Millikin, Idaho, New Mexico, Southern California, Wisconsin, Johns Hopkins; Taught graduate Psychology courses to Air Force Officers in England, Germany, Italy and Spain, 1972-75. Publications include: Developmental Behavior: A Humanist Approach, 1969; Discovering Your Unique Self, 1971; Who Are You Really, 1974; Explorations into Humanness, Pilot Study of 30 Cultures, 1977; Toward Human Excellence - Comprehensive Study of 172 Cultures, 1991; Gypsies in the Sky, 2000; Knocking Knees and Noses with the Natives, 2001; Circle the Wagons, 2002; Winter Haven: An Octogenarian's Paradise. Honours: International Scientist of the Year; Outstanding Man of 20th Century; Distinguished Leadership Award; Man of the Year, 2000 and 80 other awards; Hall of Fame, IBC and ABI. Memberships: Phi Delta Kappa; APA; AAHP; AAHP International; American Academy of Sciences. Address: 5801 W Bethel Ave #569-71, Muncie, IN 47304, USA.

**GALL Henderson Alexander (Sandy),** b. 1 October 1927, Penang, Malaysia. Writer; Broadcaster. m. Eleanor Mary Patricia Anne, 1 son, 3 daughters. Education: MA, Aberdeen University, Scotland, 1952. Appointments: National Service, RAF, 1945-48; Foreign Correspondent: Reuters, 1953-63, Independent Television News, 1963-92; Co-presenter, News At Ten, 1970-90; Writer, Presenter, Producer of numerous documentaries including: Cresta Run, 1970, 1985; King Hussein, 1972; Afghanistan, 1982, 1984, 1986; George Adamson, 1989; Richard Leakey, 1995; Empty Quarter, 1996; Imran's Final Test, 1997. Publications: Books: Gold Scoop, 1977; Chasing the Dragon, 1981; Don't Worry about the Money Now, 1983; Behind Russian Lines: An Afghan Journal, 1983; Afghanistan: Agony of a Nation, 1988; Salang, 1989; George Adamson: Lord of the Lions, 1991; News From the Front: The Life of a Television Reporter, 1994; The Bushmen of Southern Africa: Slaughter of the Innocent, 2001. Honours: Rector, 1978-81, Honorary LLD, 1981, Aberdeen University; Sitara-i-Pakistan, 1986; Chairman, Sandy Gall's Afghan Appeal, 1986-; Lawrence of Arabia Memorial Medal; RSAA, 1987; Commander of the Order of the British Empire, 1988. Memberships: Turf; Travellers, Honorary Member; Special Forces; Royal St George's Golf Club; Rye Golf Club; Honorary Member, St Moritz Tobogganing. Address: Doubleton Oast House, Penshurst, Tonbridge, Kent TN11 8JA, England. E-mail: sgaa@btinternet.com Website: www.sandygal lsafghanistanappeal.org

**GALLAGHER Liam,** b. 21 September 1972, Burnage, Manchester. Singer; Musician; Producer. m. Patsy Kensit, 1997, divorced 2000, 1 son; 1 son with partner Nicole Appleton. Career: Singer with Oasis, 1991-; Tours in USA and Britain; Founder and recorded for Big Brother records, 2000-. Publications: Singles include: Supersonic, 1994; Shakermaker; Live Forever; Cigarettes and Alcohol; Some Might Say; Wonderwall; Cast No Shadow; Don't Look Back in Anger; D'You Know What I Mean; All Around the World; Go Let It out; The Hindu Times; Albums: Definitely Maybe, 1994; What's the Story Morning Glory?, 1995; Be Here Be Now, 1997; The Masterplan, 1998; Standing on the Shoulder of Giants, 2000; Familiar to Millions (live), 2001; Heathen Chemistry, 2002. Honours: 4 platinum discs for Definitely Maybe, 8 platinum discs for (What's the Story) Morning Glory, 1996; 3 Brit Awards, 1996. Address: C/o Ignition Management, 54 Linhope Street, London, NW1 6HL, England. Website: www.oasisnet.com

**GALLAGHER Noel,** b. 29 May 1967, Manchester. Songwriter; Musician; Singer. m. Meg Mathews, 1997, divorced, 1 daughter. Career: Formerly worked with Inspiral Carpets; Songwriter, Guitarist and Singer with Oasis, 1991-; Tours in USA and Britain. Publications: Recordings with Oasis, singles include: Supersonic, 1994; Shakermaker; Live Forever; Cigarettes and Alcohol; Some Might Say; Wonderwall; Cast No Shadow; Don't Look Back in Anger; D'You Know What I Mean; All Around the World; Go Let It Out; The Hindu Times; Albums: Definitely Maybe, 1994; (What's the Story) Morning Glory?, 1995; Be Here Now, 1997; The Masterplan, 1998; Standing on the Shoulder of Giants, 2000; Familiar to Millions (live), 2001; Heathen Chemistry, 2002. Honours: 4 platinum discs for Definitely Maybe, 8 platinum discs for (What's the Story) Morning Glory, 1995; Be Here Now, 1997; 3 Brit Awards, 1996; Best song, Grammy Awards (Wonderwall), 1997. Address: c/o Ignition Management, 54 Linhope Street, London, NW1 6HL, England. Website: www.oasisnet.com

**GALLAS John Edward,** b. 11 January 1950, Wellington, New Zealand. Teacher in Student Support Service; Poet. Education: Nelson College, New Zealand, 1961-67; BA, Honours, English, Otago University, Dunedin, New Zealand, 1968-71; MPhil, English Literature, 1100-1400, Merton College, Oxford, 1972-74; PGCE, North Staffs Polytechnic, 1980-81. Publications: Practical Anarchy, 1989; Flying Carpets Over Filbert Street, 1993; Grrrrr, 1997; Resistance is Futile, 1999; The Song Atlas, 2002; Star City, 2004; Robin Hood and the Deer (with Clifford Harper), 1999; The Ballard of Santo Caserio (with Clifford Harper), 1999. Contributions to: PN Review; Landfall; Thames Poetry; Staple; Outposts; Stand; Rialto; Envoi; Poetry London Newsletter, Poetry Ireland. Honours: Rutland Poetry Prize, 1984; Runner-up, National Poetry Prize, 1985; East Midlands Arts Bursary, 1986; Charnwood Poetry Prize, 1987; New Voices Midlands Reading Tour, 1990; Surrey Poetry Centre Prize, 1992; Barnet Poetry Prize, comedy, 1997. Address: 40 London Road, Coalville, Leicestershire LE67 3JA, England.

**GALLETLY Gerard Duncan,** b. 17 March 1928, Bootle, Liverpool, England. Civil Engineer; Emeritus Professor of Applied Mechanics. Education: B Eng, 1947, M Eng, 1950, D Eng, 1977, University of Liverpool; SM, 1950, ScD, 1952, Massachusetts Institute of Technology. Appointments:

Airfield construction service RAF, 1947-49; Flying Officer, Germany; Head, Plates and Shells Section, David Taylor Model Basin, US Navy, Washington DC, 1952-55; Specialist in Structural Mechanics, Shell Development Co, Emeryville, California, 1955-61; Assistant Director, Advanced Materials R&D Laboratory, Pratt & Whitney Aircraft, North Haven, Connecticut, 1961-64; Professor of Applied Mechanics, 1964-95, Alexander Elder Professor, 1987-95, Dean of Engineering, 1980-83, Emeritus Professor, 1995-, Liverpool University. Publications: Over 100 technical papers include: Torispherical Shells – a Caution to Designers; Elastic-Plastic Buckling of Internally-Pressurised Thin Torispherical Shells; Optimun Design of Thin Circular Plates on an Elastic Foundation. Honours: Best Research Paper of the Year, ASME, 1979; Thomas Bernard Hall Prize, 1985, Ernest William Moss Prize, 1986, Donald Julius Groen Prize, 1990, Water Arbitration Prize, 1990, IMechE; Special Medal , International Conference on Shell Buckling, Lyons, 1991; Dr. h.c., Cracow University of Technology, 1995; FICE, 1976; FIMechE, 1977; FREng, 1989. Memberships: FICE; FIMechE, RAF Club. Address: Lantana, 58 Noctorum Lane, Prenton, Wirral, Merseyside, CH43 9UB, England. E-mail: em79@liv.ac.uk

**GALLINER Peter,** b. 19 September 1920, Berlin, Germany. Publisher. m. (1) Edith Marguerite Goldsmidt, 1 daughter, (2) Helga Stenschke. Education: Berlin and London. Appointments: Reuters, London, England, 1944-47; Foreign Manager, Financial Times, London, 1947-60; Chairman of Board, Managing Director, Ullstein Publishing Group, Berlin, Germany, 1961-64; Vice-Chairman, Managing Director, British Printing Corporation, 1965-70; International Publishing Consultant, 1965-67, 1970-75; Chairman, Peter Galliner Associates, 1970-; Director, International Press Institute, 1975-93; Chairman, International Encounters, 1995-. Honours: Order of Merit, 1st Class, Germany, 1965; Ecomienda, Orden de Isabel la Catolica, Spain, 1982; Commander's Cross, Order of Merit, Germany, 1990; Turkish Press Freedom Award, Turkey, 1995; Media and Communication Award, Krakow, Poland, 1998. Address: Bregenzer Str 3, D-10707 Berlin, Germany; Untere Zaeune 9, CH-8001 Zurich, Switzerland.

**GALLOWAY Janice,** b. 2 December 1955, Ayrshire, Scotland. Writer. 1 son. Education: MA, University of Glasgow, 1974-78; Postgraduate Diploma, Secondary Education, Hamilton College of Education, 1979. Appointments: Teacher of English, Garnock Academy, Ayrshire, Scotland, 1980-90; SAC Teacher of Creative Writing HMPs Barlinnie, Cornton Vale and Dungavel, 1994; Times Literary Supplement Research Fellow, The British Library, 1999; Affiliate Tutor, Creative Writing, Glasgow University, 2002-04. Publications: Novels and Short Stories: The Trick is to keep Breathing, 1990; Blood, 1991; Foreign Parts, 1994; Where You Find It, 1996; Clara, 2002; Editor (with Hamish Whyte): The Day I Met the Queen Mother, 1990; Scream if you want to go Faster, 1991; Pig Squealing, 1992; Meantime, 1993; How Would You Feel? An anthology of prisoners' writings, 1995; A wide variety of anthologised work including short stories, novel extracts, poems, prose-poetry and visual arts collaborations. Honours: The Trick is to keep Breathing: Shortlisted, Whitbread First Novel, Scottish First Book, Aer Lingus Awards, Winner, MIND/Allan Lane Prize; Scottish Arts Council Award; Blood: Shortlisted, Guardian Fiction Prize, People's Prize, Satire Award, Winner, Scottish Arts Council Award, Perrier/Cosmopolitan Prize, New York Times Notable Book of the Year 1992; Foreign Parts: Shortlisted, Saltire Award, Winner, McVitie's Prize, Scottish Arts Council Award; American Academy of Arts and Letters, EM Forster Award, 1995; Creative Scotland Award, granted by the Scottish Arts Council, 2001; Clara: Shortlisted, SAC Book

of the Year, nominated for the Dublin IMPAC Award, Winner Saltire Award, 2002. Address: c/o Derek Johns, AP Watt Literary Agency, 20 John Street, London, WC1N 2DR. E-mail: djohns@apwatt.co.uk

**GALLOWAY Peter,** b. 19 July 1954, United Kingdom. Area Dean, Church of England. Education: BA, Goldsmiths College, University of London, 1976; Certificate in Theology, St Stephen's House, Oxford, 1983; PhD, King's College, University of London, 1987. Appointments include: Ordained Deacon, 1984, Ordained Priest, 1984, Church of England; Curate, St John's Wood Church, London, 1986-86; Assistant Master, Arnold House School, 1983-85; Chaplain, Hospital of St John and St Elizabeth, 1983-86; Curate, St Giles-in-the-Fields, London, 1986-90; Chaplain: Moorfields Eye Hospital, 1986-88, St Paul's Hospital and the Shaftesbury Hospital, 1986-90, Cambridge Theatre, 1988-90; Governor, Soho Parish School, 1989-91; Justice of the Peace, City of London, 1989-; Priest-in-Charge, 1990-95, Vicar, 1995-, Emmanuel, West Hampstead, London; Chairman of Governors, Emmanuel School, West Hampstead, 1990-; Joint Chairman, Hampstead Council of Christians and Jews, 1992-99; Member: London Borough of Camden Education Committee, 1997-2001, London Borough of Camden, Schools Organisation Committee, 1999-2004, West End Green Conservation Area Advisory Committee, 1996-2000, Committee of the Friends of Hampstead Cemetery, 2000-; Area Dean of North Camden, 2002-; Member, Edmonton Episcopal Area Bishop's Council, 2002-. Publications: The Order of St Patrick, 1983; Henry Mackay, 1983; Good and faithful servants, 1988; The Cathedrals of Ireland, 1992; The Order of the British Empire, 1996; Royal Service Vol 1 (with others), 1996; The Most Illustrious Order, 1999; A Passionate Humility, Frederick Oakley and the Oxford Movement, 1999; The Cathedrals of Scotland, 2000; The Order of St Michael and St George, 2000; Companions of Honour, 2002; The Order of the Bath, forthcoming 2006. Honours: OBE, 1996; Service Medal of the Order of St John, 1996; KStJ, 1997; Honorary Fellow, Goldsmiths College, 1999; Memberships: Order and Medals Research Society, 1977-, Nikaean Club, 1988-, The Athenaeum, 1990-; Freeman, City of London, 1995-; Fellow, Society of Antiquaries, 2000-; Liveryman, Worshipful Company of Glaziers, 1998-; Sub-Dean, The Order of St John (Priory of England), 1999-; Member, Board of Directors, St John Ambulance, 1999-. Address: The Vicarage, Lyncroft Gardens, London NW6 1JU, England.

**GALPERIN Igor,** b. 11 June 1959, Moscow, Russia. Composer; Pianist; Teacher. m. Alla Epshtein-Galperin. Education: Graduate, Department of Theory and Compositino, Music College, P Tchaikovsky Conservatory, Moscow, 1978; Graduate, 1983, PhD, 1990, Musical-Pedagogical Department, Moscow Pedagogical Institute. Appointments: Teacher, Piano, Moscow Pedagogical College, 1986-91; Teacher, Special Piano and Ensemble, Musical-Pedagogical Department, Moscow Pedagogical Institute, 1987-91; Teacher, Score Reading, Keyboard Harmony and Piano, Department of Musicology, Tel-Aviv University, 1992. Publications: Articles in professional journals; Numerous musical pieces and compositions. Honours: Winner, Israel Prime Minister's Award for Composers, 2004. Memberships: Israel Composers League; Society of Authors, Composers and Music Publishers in Israel. Address: Hirshfeld 29 str, Apt 12, Rishon-le-Tzion, 75244 Israel. E-mail: igorga@post.tau.ac.il

**GALTUNG Johan,** b. 24 October 1930, Oslo, Norway. Director; Professor of Peace Studies. m. Fumiko Nishimura, 3 sons, 1 daughter. Education: PhD, Mathematics, 1956, PhD, Sociology, 1957, University of Oslo. Appointments:

Assistant Professor, Columbia University, 1957-60; Director, Founder, International Peace Research Institute, Oslo, 1959-69; Professor, Peace Research, University of Oslo, 1969-77; Visiting Professor, Peace studies around the world, 1977-99; Director, Founder, TRANSCEND: A Peace and Development Network, 1993-. Publications: Essays in Peace Research, vols I-VI, 1975-88; Essays in Methodology, vols I-IV, 1977-88; Human Rights in Another Key, 1994; Peace by Peaceful Means, 1996; Searching for Peace, 2002. Honours: 8 Dr hon causa degrees, and 4 Honorary Professorships. Memberships: Founder, International Peace Research Association; First President, World Futures Studies Federation. Address: 7 Cret de Neige, F-01210 Versonnex, France.

**GALVIN John Brett,** b. 9 August 1944, Waterbury, Connecticut, USA. Professor of Mathematics. m. Alberta Campoli, 3 daughters. Education: BA, 1966, MA, 1967, Fairfield University. Appointments: Teacher of Mathematics, Watertown High School, 1967-2001; Professor of Mathematics, University of Connecticut, 2001-. Honours: Listed in national and international biographical dictionaries. Memberships: Life Member, Connecticut Education Association; National Educational Association; American Association of University Professors. Address: 113 Newton Terrace, Waterbury, CT 06708, USA.

**GAMACHE Gerald L,** b. 30 December 1942, Des Moines, Iowa, USA. Psychology. Education: AA, Pensacola Junior College, 1974; BA, Psychology, 1975, MA, Psychology, 1976, University of North Florida; PhD, Psychology, Old Dominion University, 1986. Appointments: US Army, 1960-63; US Navy, 1963-82; Director, US Army Safety Studies Program, 1986-89; President, KGA International, 1989-; Associate Professor, Flagler College, 1991-. Publications: 5 books, 25 articles and technical reports. Honours: Civil Service Award, 1987; Honorary DSc, Kiev Polytechnic Institute, 1998; Honorary MD Degree, Cosmopolitan University, Chile. Memberships: American Psychological Association; Human Factors and Ergonomics Society; American Psychological Society; Diplomate, APA; Life Fellow, American College of Forensic Sciences; Diplomate, ABPS. Address: 8 Althea Street, St Augustine, FL 32084, USA. E-Mail: drjerrygamache@bellson74.no7

**GAMBLE Cynthia Joan,** b. 20 December 1941, Much Wenlock, Shropshire, England. University Lecturer. Education: L ès L, Université de Grenoble, Grenoble, France, 1971; BA (Hons), 1971, Diploma in Education, 1974, PhD, 1997, Birkbeck College, University of London; Appointments: Assistante d'Anglais, Lycée de Jeunes Filles, Quimperlé, 1963-64; Assistante d'Anglais, Lycée Stendhal, Grenoble, 1964-65; Head of French Department, Lanfranc School, Croydon, 1965-69; Teacher of French, Ealing Girls' Grammar School, London, 1969-71; Lecturer in French, City of Leeds and Carnegie College of Education, 1971-76; Senior Lecturer in French, Director of International Exchanges, Department of International Relations, 1976-86, Head of European Secretariat, Senior Lecturer in French, Leeds Metropolitan University 1986-89; Head of European Relations, University of East London, 1989-97; Honorary Research Fellow, The Ruskin Programme, Lancaster University, 1997-2001; Honorary Research Fellow, Birkbeck College, London University, 2001-2002; Visiting Fellow, The Ruskin Programme, Lancaster University, 2001-. Publications: Author, Proust as Interpreter of Ruskin: The Seven Lamps of Translation, 2002; Ruskin-Turner: Dessins et Voyages en Picardie romantique (co-author with M Pinette and S Wildman), 2003; Numerous conference papers and invited lectures. Honours: Honorary Secretary and Founder, Ruskin Society, 1997. Memberships: Société des Amis de Marcel

Proust et de Combray; Franco-British Society. Address: Flat 89, 49 Hallam Street, London W1W 6JP, England. E-mail: cgamble@britishlibrary.net

**GAMBON Sir Michael John,** b. 19 October 1940, Dublin, Ireland. Actor. m. Anne Miller, 1962, 1 son. Appointments: Former, Mechanical Engineer; Actor with Edwards/Macliammoir Co, Dublin, 1962, National Theatre, Old Vic, 1963-67, Birmingham Repertory and other provincial theatres, 1967-69; Title roles include: Othello; Macbeth, Coriolanus, King Lear, Anthony and Cleopatra, Old Times; RSC, Aldwych, 1970-71; The Norman Conquests, 1974; Otherwise Engaged, 1976; Just Between Ourselves, 1977; Alice's Boys, 1978; with National Theatre, 1980; with RSC, Stratford and London, 1982-83; TV appearances include: Ghosts; Oscar Wilde; The Holy Experiment; Absurd Person Singular; The Borderers; The Singing Detective; The Heat of the Day; Maigret, 1992; The Entertainer, Truth; Films: The Beast Must Die, 1975; Turtle Diary, 1985; Paris by Night, 1988; The Cook, the thief, his wife and her lover; A Dry White Season, 1989; The Rachel Papers, 1989; State of Grace, 1989; The Heat of the Day, 1989, Mobsters, 1992; Toys, 1992; Clean Slate, 1993; Indian Warrior, 1993; The Browning Version, 1993; Mary Reilly, 1994; Two Deaths, 1994; Midnight in Moscow, 1994; A Man of No Importance, 1995; The Innocent Sleep, 1995; All Our Fault, 1995; Two Deaths, 1996; Nothing Personal, 1996; The Gambler, 1996; Dancing at Lughnasa, 1997; Plunket and McClean, 1997; The Last September, 1998; Sleepy Hollow, 1998; The Insider, End Game, 1999; Charlotte Gray, 2001; Gosford Park, 2001; Ali G Indahouse, 2001; Path to War, 2001; The Actors, 2002; Open Range, 2002; Harry Potter, The Prisoner of Azkaban, 2004. Honours include: London Theatre Critics Award for Best Actor; Olivier Award for Best Comedy Performance; Evening Stand Drama Award. Membership: Trustee, Roy Armouries, 1995-. Address: c/o ICM, Oxford House, 76 Oxford Street, London, W1N 0AX, England.

**GAMMON Philip Greenway,** b. 17 May 1940, Chippenham, Wiltshire, England. Pianist; Conductor. m. Floretta Volovini, 2 sons. Education: Royal Academy of London, London, 1956-61; Badische Müsikhochschule, Karlsruhe, Germany, 1961-64. Appointments: Deputy Piano Teacher, RAM and RASM, 1964; Pianist, Royal Ballet, Covent Garden, 1964-68; Principal Pianist, Ballet for All, 1968-71; Pianist, Royal Ballet, 1971-99; Principal Pianist, Royal Ballet, 1999-2005; Also Conductor with Royal Ballet and as Guest Conductor with the English National Ballet, Hong Kong Ballet and National Ballet of Portugal. Honours: The Recital Diploma, 1960; MacFarren Gold Medal, 1961; Karlsruhe Kultür Preis, 1962; ARCM, 1968; ARAM, 1991; FRAM, 2002. Membership: Musician's Union. Address: 19 Downs Avenue, Pinner, Middlesex HA5 5AQ, England.

**GANELLIN Charon Robin,** b. 25 January 1934, London, England. Medicinal Chemist. m. Tamara Green, deceased, 1 son, 1 daughter. Education: BSc, 1955, PhD, 1958, Queen Mary College, London University; Fellow of the Royal Society of Chemistry, 1968; Chartered Chemist, 1976; DSc, London University, 1986; FRS, 1986. Appointments: Medicinal Chemist, Smith Kline & French, 1958; Research Associate, Massachusetts Institute of Technology, 1960; Medicinal Chemist, 1961-62, Head of Chemistry, 1962-78, Director, 1978-86, Vice-President Research, 1980-84, Vice-President, 1984-86, Smith Kline & French Research Ltd; Smith Kline & French Professor of Medicinal Chemistry, 1986-2002, Emeritus Professor of Medicinal Chemistry, 2002-, University College London. Publications: Books as co-editor: Pharmacology of Histamine Receptors, 1982; Frontiers in Histamine Research (a tribute to Heinz Schild), 1985; Dictionary of Drugs, 1990;

# DICTIONARY OF INTERNATIONAL BIOGRAPHY

Medicinal Chemistry, 1993; Dictionary of Pharmaceutical Agents, 1997; 250 papers and articles as author or co-author in learned scientific journals or books. Honours include: UK Chemical Society Medallion in Medicinal Chemistry, 1977; Prix Charles Mentzer, 1978; Medicinal Chemistry Award, American Chemical Society, 1980; RSC Tilden Medal and Lecture, 1982; SCI Messel Medal and Lecture, 1988; Society for Drug Research Award for Drug Discovery (jointly), 1989; USA National Inventors Hall of Fame, 1990; Fellow, Queen Mary and Westfield College, London, 1992; DSc, Honoris Causa, Aston University, 1995; RSC Adrien Albert Lectureship and Medal, 1999; Nauta Prize for Medicinal Chemistry, European Federation for Medicinal Chemistry, 2004. Memberships: American Chemical Society; British Pharmcological Society; European Histamine Research Society; International Union of Pure and Applied Chemistry; The Royal Society; The Royal Society of Chemistry; Save British Science Society; Society of Chemical Industry; Society for Medicines Research. Address: Department of Chemistry, University College London, 20 Gordon Street, London WC1H 0AJ, England. E-mail: c-r.ganellin@ucl.ac.uk

**GANS-LARTEY Joseph Kojo,** b. 28 August 1951, Accra-Ghana. Barrister. m. Rosmarie Ramrattan, 1 son, 1 daughter. Education: HNC, Business Studies, 1979; LLB, Honours, 1982; Called to the Bar, 1983; LLM, London, 1986. Appointments: Senior Legal Assistant, 1984-86, Crown Prosecutor, 1986-88; Senior Crown Prosecutor, 1988-90; Principal Crown Prosecutor, 1990-92; Prosecution Team Leader, 1992-. Publications: The Challenge Ahead Parts I, II, III. An Analysis of Political and Legal History of Ghana Since Independence. Honour: Times Lawyer of the Week, 2000. Membership: Hon. Society of Lincoln's Inn. Address: Thornhill Road, Croydon, Surrey CRO 2XZ, England. E-mail: ganslartey@aol.com

**GANTI Prasada Rao,** b. 25 August 1942, Seethanagaram (AP), India. Educator. m. Meenakshi Vedula, 1 son, 2 daughters. Education: BE, (Hons), Electrical Engineering, Andhra University, Waltair, India, 1963; M Tech, Control Systems Engineering, 1965, PhD, Electrical Engineering, 1970, Indian Institute of Technology, Kharagpur, India. Appointments: Assistant Professor, Department of Electrical Engineering, PSG College of Technology, Coimbatore, India, 1969-71; Assistant Professor, 1971-78, Professor, 1978-97, Chairman, Curriculum Development Cell, Electrical Engineering, 1978-80, Indian Institute of Technology, Kharagpur, India; Commonwealth Postdoctoral Research Fellow, Control Systems Centre, University of Manchester Institute of Science and Technology, Manchester, England, 1975-76; Alexander von Humboldt Foundation Research Fellow, Ruhr University, Bochum, Germany, 1981-83, 1985, 1991, 2003, 2004; Scientific Advisor, Directorate of Power and Desalination Plants, Water and Electricity Department, Government of Abu Dhabi, 1992-; Visiting Professor, Henri Poincare University, Nancy, France, 2003; Fraunhofer Institut für Rechnerarchitektur und Software Technik (FIRST), Berlin, 2004; Advisor to UNESCO-EOLSS Joint Committee. Publications: Author and Co-author of 4 books and over 150 research papers; Co-editor of 1 book. Honours include: IIT Kharagpur Silver Jubilee Research Award, 1985; The Systems Society of India Award, 1989; International Desalination Association Best Paper award, 1995; Honorary Professor, East China University for Science and Technology. Memberships: Life Fellow, Institution of Engineers, India; Fellow, Institution of Electronic and Telecommunications Engineers, India; Fellow, IEEE, USA; Fellow Indian National Academy of Engineering; Member of numerous editorial boards. Address: PO Box 2623, Abu Dhabi, United Arab Emirates. E-mail: gantirao@emirates.net.ae

**GARAB Győző,** b. 1 January 1948, Szomód, Hungary. Research Scientist. m. Anikó, 27 October 1979, 2 sons, 2 daughters. Education: Physics, University of Szeged, 1971; PhD, Biophysics, 1974; DSc, 1992. Appointments: Research Scientist, Head of Laboratory, 1987-, Deputy Director, 1999-2000, Biology Research Centre, Szeged; Visiting Scientist, University of Illinois, Univ New Mexico, CEA Saclay, Brookhaven National Laboratory. Publications: Photosynthesis: Mechanisms and Effects; More than 100 articles in professional journals. Honours: J Ernst Award, Hungarian Biophysical Society, 1994; Straub Medal, Biology Research Centre, 2001. Memberships: Hungarian Biophysical Society; International Society of Photosynthesis Research. Address: Dózsa György u 7, H-6720 Szeged, Hungary.

**GARDNER Mariana Carmen Zavati,** b. 20 January 1952, Bacau, Romania. Writer. m. John Edward Gardner, 8 August 1980, 1 son, 1 daughter. Education: Baccalauréat with distinction, Vasile Alecsandri Boarding College for Girls, 1971; MSc, Philology, 1st class hons, Alexandru Ioan Cuza University of Iasi, 1975; PGCE, University of Leeds, 1987; Postgraduate Courses: Goethe Institut Rosenheim, Germany, 1991; L'Ecole Normale Supérieure, Auxerre, France, 1991. Appointments: English Teacher, various schools, Part-time Assistant Lecturer, University "Al I Cuza", Iasi, Full-time Assistant Lecturer, University of Bacau, 1975-80; Teacher, Latin, French, German, Spanish and Italian, various schools in England, 1980-2000; Bilingual writer, 2000-. Publications include: Volumes of verse: Whispers; The Journey; Watermarks; Travellers/Calatori; The Spinning Top; Pilgrims/Pelerini; The Remains of the Dream Catcher; Bequests/Mosteniri; Seasons; Poems included in anthologies: Between a Laugh and a Tear; Light of the World; The Sounds of Silence; The Secret of Twilight; A Blossom of Dreams; The Lyre's Song; Honoured Poets of 1988; Last Good-Byes; A Celebration of Poets; The Definitive Version; A Celebration of Poets; Sunrise and Soft Mist; Memories of the Millennium; Nature's Orchard; Lifelines; Antologia Poezia Padurii V; International Notebook of Poetry 2000, 2001, 2002, 2003, 2004, 2005; Journal of the American Romanian Academy of Arts and Sciences; Eastern Voices; Family Ties; Sunkissed; Reflections of Time; Spotlight Poets Anthologies; Science Friction, The Best Poems and Poets of 2002, Pictured Visions, Searching for Paradise, Poetical Reflections, Waters of the Heart; Short Stories: New Fiction Collections; Translations: Cina Cea Fara De Taina/The Lost Mystery of the Last Supper – Poems by Al Florin Tene; Cerul Meu de Hirtie/My Paper Sky – Poems by Al Florin Tene; Journalism: Orizont Bacau; Alma Mater/Dialog Iasi; al cinailea anotimp Oradea; Curierul de Cluj-Napoca; Cetatea Culturala/Cluj-Napoca; Crisana Plus Oredea; Cronica Iasi; Viata Politehnicii Iasi; Ateneu Bacau; Origini-Romanian Roots, USA. Honours: 4 Editor's Choice Awards, UK and USA; Bronze Medal, North American Poetry Competition, USA, 1998; The American Romanian Academy Award, Canada, 2001; The Ionel Jianu Award for Arts, Canada, 2001. Memberships: American Romanian Academy of Arts and Sciences, USA; LiterArt XXI, International Association of Romanian Writers and Artists, USA; National Geographic Society; Associate Member, Poetry Book Society, UK. Address: 14 Andrew Goodall Close, East Dereham, Norfolk NR19 1SR, England.

**GARDNER Nancy Bruff (Nancy Bruff, Nancy Gardner),** b. 15 November 1909, Fairfield County, Connecticut, USA. m. (1) Thurston Clarke, 1 son, 1 daughter, (2) Esmond Gardner, 20 July 1963, deceased. Education: Private School in New York, Connecticut and University of Sorbonne, Paris. Publications: Novels: The Manatee; Cider From Eden; Beloved Woman; The Fig Tree; The Country Club; Mooncussers (in paperback as Mist

# DICTIONARY OF INTERNATIONAL BIOGRAPHY

Maiden); Old is Bold (new book); Poetry: My Talon in Your Heart, 1946; Walk Lightly on the Planet, 1985; Plays (produced off Broadway): The Cast Iron Smile; Mrs Hollister's Trojan Horse; Laughing Liar. Contributions to: Various newspapers; Collection of writings in Boston University Library. Memberships: Authors Guild; Dramatists Guild; Cosmopolitan Club; Mayflowers; Hugeonot; Magna Charta Dames; Pilgrims. Address: 200 East 66th Street, Apt D803, New York, NY 10021, USA.

**GARDNER-THORPE Christopher,** b. 22 August 1941. Consultant Neurologist. Education: St Philip's School, London, 1948-54; Beaumont College, Old Windsor, Berkshire, 1954-59; MB BS, 1964, MD, 1973, University of London, St Thomas' Hospital; FRCP; FACP. Appointments: House Surgeon, Peace Memorial, Watford, 1964; House Physician, Royal South Hants Hospital, Southampton, 1964-65; Senior House Officer in Neurology, 1965-66, Registrar in Neurology, 1967-69, Wessex Neurological Centre, Southampton General Hospital; Medical Registrar, North Staffordshire Infirmary and City General Hospital, Stoke on Trent, 1966-67; Registrar in Neurology, 1969, Neurological Research Registrar, 1969-71, Neurological Registrar, Special Centre for Epilepsy, 1969-71, Bootham Park Hospital, York and General Infirmary, Leeds; Senior Registrar in Neurology, Newcastle General Hospital and Royal Victoria Infirmary, Newcastle-upon-Tyne, 1971-74; Physician in Charge, Newcourt Hospital, Exeter, 1974-88; Consultant Neurologist, South Western Regional Health Authority, 1974-93; Consultant Neurologist, North Devon District Hospital, Barnstable, 1974-95; Consultant Neurologist, Mardon House Neurorehabilitation Centre, 1997-; Consultant Neurologist, Royal Devon and Exeter Hospital, Exeter and Plymouth General Hospital, 1993-, Lead Clinician in Neurology, 1997-, Exeter Healthcare NHS Trust. Publications: Numerous articles in professional and popular journals. Honours: Freeman of the City of London, 1979; Her Majesty's Lieutenant for the City of London, 1981-; Freeman, 1979-80, Liveryman, 1980-, Worshipful Company of Barbers; Esquire, Order of St John, 1980-; Invited Fellow, Royal Society of Arts, 1997. Memberships include: World Federation of Neurology; European Federation of Neurological Societies; Association of British Neurologists; International League Against Epilepsy; British Epilepsy Association; Irish Neurological Association; General Medical Council; Medical Defence Union; British Medical Association; Royal Society of Medicine; Royal College of Physicians; Society of Expert Witnesses. Address: The Coach House, 1a College Road, Exeter, Devon, EX1 1TE, England. E-mail: cgardnerthorpe@ doctors.org.uk

**GAREGNANI Pierangelo,** b. 9 August 1930, Milan, Italy. Professor of Economics. Education: Scholarship student, Degree in Political Sciences, Cum laude, University of Pavia, 1949-53; Foreign Bursar, Trinity College Cambridge, PhD, Economics, Faculty of Economics, Cambridge University, 1953-58; Libera docenza, 1960. Appointments: Assistant, Economics, Faculty of Economics and Commerce, University of Rome "La Sapienza", 1959-61; Researcher, Associazióne per lo Sviluppo del Mezzogiorno, Rome, 1959-61; Rockefeller Fellow, MIT, Cambridge, Massachusetts, USA, 1961-62; Lecturer, Economics, University of Sassari, 1962-63; Full Chair in Economics, University of Sassari, 1963-66, University of Pavia, 1966-69, University of Florence, 1969-74, University of Rome "La Sapienza", 1974-92, University of Rome Three, 1992-; Visiting Professor, Cambridge University, 1973-74, Fellow, Trinity College Cambridge, 1973-74, 1990-91; Director of Research, Research Doctorates, University of Rome; Visiting Professor, Stanford University, USA, 1985-86, New School for Social Research, New York, 1987-91; Participant in numerous

international conferences and seminars. Publications include: Il capitale nelle teorie della distribuzione, 1960, 1972, 1974, 1976, 1982; Notes on Consumption Investment and Effective Demand, 1978, 1979 (reprinted in Keynes's Economics and the Theory of Value and Distribution, editors J Eatwell and M Milgate, 1983); Value and Distribution in the Classical Economists and Marx, 1984; Savings, Investment and the Quantity of Capital in General Intemporal Equilibrium, 2000. Memberships: Academia Europaea, Cambridge, 1988-; Corresponding Member, Accademia Nazionale dei Lincei, 2001-. Address: Viale Gorizia 33, 00198 Rome, Italy.

**GARMANOV Maksim E,** b. 29 May 1961, Moscow, Russia. Chemist; Electrochemist; Researcher; Scientist. Education: Highest Degree with honours, Chemical Faculty, Moscow State University, Russia, 1983; Postgraduate Course, The Karpov's Physico-Chemical Research Institute, Moscow, Russia, 1990. Appointments: Special Researcher, Institute of Physical Chemistry, Academy of Sciences, Moscow, 1983-86; Junior Scientist, 1986-87, Postgraduate Student, 1987-90, The Karpov's Physico-Chemical Research Institute, Moscow; Junior Scientist, 1990-92, Scientist, 1992-, Institute of Physical Chemistry, Academy of Sciences, Moscow; Supernumerary Manager on marketing and production of organic corrosion inhibitors, IPHCAN Ltd, Moscow, 1992-. Publications: Numerous articles in professional scientific journals. Honours: Highest degree with honours, Moscow State University, 1983; Listed in national and international biographical honours and grand editions. Memberships: Trade Union of Scientific Workers; New York Academy of Sciences, 1995-2004. Address: The Institute of Physical Chemistry of RAS, Leninsky Prospect 31, Moscow 119991, Russia. Website: http:// maxsuper.boom.ru/index.html

**GARNER Alan,** b. 17 October 1934, Cheshire, England. Author. m. (1) Ann Cook, 1956, divorced, 1 son, 2 daughters, (2) Griselda Greaves, 1972, 1 son, 1 daughter. Education: Magdalen College, Oxford, 1955-56. Appointment: Member, International Editorial Board, Detskaya Literatura Publishers, Moscow, 1991-. Publications: The Weirdstone of Brisingamen, 1960; The Moon of Gomrath, 1963; Elidor, 1965; Holly from the Bongs, 1966; The Owl Service, 1967; The Book of Goblins, 1969; Red Shift, 1973; The Guizer, 1975; The Stone Book Quartet, 1976-78; Fairy Tales of Gold, 1979; The Lad of the Gad, 1980; British Fairy Tales, 1984; A Bag of Moonshine, 1986; Jack and the Beanstalk, 1992; Once Upon a Time, 1993; Strandloper, 1996; The Voice that Thunders, 1997; The Well of the Wind, 1998. Honours: Carnegie Medal, 1967; Guardian Award, 1968; Lewis Carroll Shelf Award, USA, 1970; Gold Plaque, Chicago International Film Festival, 1981; Children's Literature Association International Phoenix Award, 1996; OBE, 2001. Membership: Portico Library, Manchester. Address: Blackden, Holmes Chapel, Crewe, Cheshire CW4 8BY, England.

**GARNER James (James Baumgardner),** b. 7 April 1928, Norman, Oklahoma, USA. Actor. m. Lois Clarke, 1995, 1 son, 2 daughters. Appointments: Former travelling salesman, oil field worker, carpet layer, bathing suit model; Toured with road companies; Actor, TV appearances include: Cheyenne, Maverick, 1957-62; Nichols, 1971-72; The Rockford Files, 1974-79; Space, 1985; The New Maverick; The Long Summer of George Adams; The Glitter Dome; Heartsounds; Promise (also executive producer); Obsessive Love; My Name is Bill (also executive producer); Decoration Day; Barbarians at the Gate; The Rockford Files; A Blessing in Disguise; Dead Silence; First Monday (series), 2002; Films include: Toward the Unknown; Shoot-Out at Medicine Bend, 1957; Darby's Rangers, 1958; Sayonara; Up Periscope, 1959; The Americanization of Emily, 1964; 36 Hours; The Art Of Love, 1965; A Man Could

Get Killed, 1966; Duel at Diablo, 1966; Master Buddwing, 1966; Grand Prix, 1966; Hour of the Gun, 1967; Marlowe, 1969; Support Your Local Sheriff, 1971; Support Your Local Gunfighter, 1971; Skin Game, 1971; They Only Kill Their Masters, 1972; One Little Indian, 1973; Health, 1979; The Fan, 1980; Victor/Victoria, 1982; Murphy's Romance, 1985; Promise (made for TV), 1986; Sunset, 1987; Decoration Day (TV film), 1990; Fire in the Sky, 1993; Maverick (TV), 1994; My Fellow Americans, 1996; Twilight, 1998; Space Cowboys, 2000; Atlantis: The Lost Empire, 2001; Roughing It (TV), 2002; Divine Secrets of the Ya-Ya Sisterhood, 2002. Honours: Emmy Award; Purple Heart.

**GARNER Richard Clayton,** b. 12 February 1950, London, England. Journalist. m. Anne Wilkinson. Education: Harlow College, 1969-70. Appointments: Islington Journal, 1970-74; Kent Evening Post, 1974-77; Birmingham Evening Mail, 1977-80; Times Educational Supplement, 1980-90; Education Correspondent, Daily Mirror, 1990-2001; Education Editor, Independent, 2001-. Publication: Midsummer Variations: An Anthology of Poetry, 1971. Memberships: King's Head Theatre Club; Middlesex County Cricket Club. Address: 137 The Avenue, Bengeo, Hertford SH14 3DX, England. E-mail: r.garner@independent.co.uk

**GARNETT Richard (Duncan Carey),** b. 8 January 1923, London, England. Writer; Publisher; Translator. Education: BA, King's College, Cambridge, 1948; MA, 1987. Appointments: Production Manager, 1955-59, Director, 1957-66, Rupert Hart-Davis Ltd; Director, Adlard Coles Ltd, 1963-66; Editor, 1966-82, Director, 1972-82, Macmillan London; Director, Macmillan Publishers, 1982-87. Publications: Goldsmith: Selected Works (editor), 1950; Robert Gruss: The Art of the Aqualung (translator), 1955; The Silver Kingdom (in US as The Undersea Treasure), 1956; Bernard Heuvelmans: On the Track of Unknown Animals (translator), 1958; The White Dragon, 1963; Jack of Dover, 1966; Bernard Heuvelmans: In the Wake of the Sea-Serpents (translator), 1968; Joyce (editor with Reggie Grenfell), 1980; Constance Garnett: A Heroic Life, 1991; Sylvia and David, The Townsend Warner/Garnett Letters (editor), 1994; Rupert Hart-Davis Limited: A Brief History, 2004. Address: Hilton Hall, Hilton, Huntingdon, Cambridgeshire PE28 9NE, England.

**GARRETT Godfrey John,** b. 24 July 1937, Beckenham, Kent, England. Former Diplomat; Consultant. m. Elisabeth Margaret Hall, 4 sons, 1 daughter. Education: Degree in Modern Languages, Sidney Sussex College, Cambridge, 1958-61. Appointments: Foreign and Commonwealth Office, 1961-93; Head of International Peace Keeping Missions in Croatia and Ukraine, 1993-95; Consultant to Control Risk Company, 1996-98; Consultant on Eastern Europe, 1998-2005. Honours: OBE, 1982; Swedish Order of the North Star, 1983. Address: White Cottage, Henley, Haslemere, Surrey GU27 3HQ, England.

**GARRETT Lesley,** b. 10 April 1955. Opera Singer. m. 1991, 1 son, 1 daughter. Education: Royal Academy of Music; National Opera Studio. Career: Winner, Kathleen Ferrier Memorial Competition, 1979; Performed with Welsh National Opera; Opera North; At Wexford and Buxton Festivals and at Glyndebourne; Joined ENO (Principal Soprano), 1984; Major roles includes: Susanna, Marriage of Figaro; Despina, Cosi Fan Tutte; Musetta, La Bohème; Jenny, Rise and Fall of the City of Mahaggony; Atalanta, Xerxes; Zerlinda, Don Giovanni; Yum-Yum, The Mikado; Adèle, Die Fledermaus; Oscar, A Masked Ball; Dalinda, Ariodante; Rose, Street Scene; Bella, A Midsummer Marriage; Eurydice, Orpheus and Eurydice; Title roles in the The Cunning Little Vixen and

La Belle Vivette; Numerous concert hall performances in UK and abroad (including Last Night of the Proms); TV and radio appearances. Honours: Hon DArts (Plymouth), 1995; Best selling Classical Artist, Gramophone Award, 1996. Address: The Music Partnership Ltd, 41 Aldebert Terrace, London, SW8 1BH, England.

**GARTON George Alan,** b. 4 June 1922, Scarborough, England. Retired Biochemist. m. Gladys F Davison, 2 daughters. Education: BSc, PhD, DSc, University of Liverpool. Appointments: Service with Ministry of Supply during WWII; Johnston Research and Teaching Fellow, University of Liverpool, 1949-50; Biochemist, 1950-63, Head, Lipid Biochemistry Department, 1963-83, Deputy Director, 1968-83, Honorary Research Associate, 1984-92, Honorary Professorial Fellow, 1992-, Rowett Research Institute; Member, Council, British Nutrition Foundation, 1982-2004; President, International Conferences on Biochemistry of Lipids, 1982-89; Chairman, British National Committee for Nutritional and Food Sciences, 1985-87. Publications: Numerous articles and papers on biochemistry and nutrition. Honours: FRSE, 1966; Visiting Professor of Biochemistry, University of North Carolina, 1967; FRS, 1978; SBStJ, 1986; Honorary Research Fellow, University of Aberdeen, 1987-. Memberships: Farmers Club, London; Fellow, Royal Society, London; Fellow, Royal Society of Edinburgh. Address: 2 St Devenicks Mews, Cults, Aberdeen, AB15 9LH, Scotland.

**GASCOIGNE (Arthur) Bamber,** b. 24 January 1935, London, England. Author; TV Presenter. m. Christina Ditchburn. Education: Eton College; Magdalene College, Cambridge. Appointments: Freelance Author; Chairman, University Challenge TV series, 1962-87; Author and Presenter of numerous TV documentaries including: The Christians, 1977; Man and Music, 1987-89; The Great Moghuls, 1990; Creator and Editor-in-Chief, HistoryWorld, 1994-. Publications: Novels and children's books; History books include: World Theatre, 1968; The Great Moghuls, 1971; Treasures and Dynasties of China, 1975; The Christians, 1977; Encyclopaedia of Britain, 1993. Address: HistoryWorld, 1 St Helena Terrace, Richmond, London TW9 1NR, England. E-mail: bamber@historyworld.net Website: www.historyworld.net

**GASCOIGNE Paul John,** b. 26 May 1967, Gateshead, England. Footballer. m. Sheryl Failes, divorced, 1 son. Career: Played for Newcastle United, 1985-88; Tottenham Hotspur, 1988-92, Lazio, Italy, 1992-95; Glasgow Rangers, 1995-98; Middlesbrough, 1998-2000; Everton, 2000-02; Burnley, 2002; Signed as player/coach, Gansu Tianma (Gansu Sky Horses), Chinese B-League, 2003; Played for England, 13 under 21 caps, 57 full caps, World Cup Italy, 1990. Publication: Paul Gascoigne, autobiography with Paul Simpson, 2001. Honours: BBC Sports Personality of the Year, 1990; FA Cup Winners Medal, 1991. Address: c/o Robertson Craig & Co, Clairmont Gardens, Glasgow, G3 7LW, Scotland.

**GASIC Slobodan,** b. 1 January 1942, Prijedor, Bosnia. Physician; University Professor. m. Anna Chuman, 2 sons, 1 daughter. Education: MD, University of Vienna Medical School, 1968; Qualification in Internal Medicine, 1974, Qualification in Clinical Pharmacology, 1981, Qualification in Cardiology, 1984, Habilitation in Internal Medicine, 1998, Professor of Internal Medicine, University of Vienna. Appointments: Department of Internal Medicine, 1968-72, Department of Cardiology, 1972-75, Department of Internal Medicine, 1977-91, Professor of Internal Medicine, Department of Endocrinology, 1992-, University of Vienna. Publications: Numerous articles in international medical journals; Book contributions. Memberships: European

Society of Cardiology; German Pharmacology Society; Austrian Diabetes Society. Address: University of Vienna Medical School, Waehringer Gurtel 18-20, 1090 Vienna, Austria.

**GASKIN Catherine Marjella,** b. 2 April 1929, County Louth, Dundalk, Ireland. Novelist. m. Sol Cornberg, 1 December 1955, deceased, 1999. Education: Holy Cross College, Sydney, Australia; Conservatorium of Music, Sydney. Publications: This Other Eden, 1946; With Every Year, 1947; Dust in Sunlight, 1950; All Else is Folly, 1951; Daughter of the House, 1952; Sara Dane, 1955; Blake's Reach, 1958; Corporation Wife, 1960; I Know My Love, 1962; The Tilsit Inheritance, 1963; The File on Devlin, 1965; Edge of Glass, 1967; Fiona, 1970; A Falcon for a Queen, 1972; The Property of a Gentleman, 1974; The Lynmara Legacy, 1975; The Summer of the Spanish Woman, 1977; Family Affairs, 1980; Promises, 1982; The Ambassador's Women, 1985; The Charmed Circle, 1988. Memberships: Society of Authors; Author's Guild of America. Address: Villa 139, The Manors, 15 Hale Road, Mosman, NSW 2088, Australia.

**GASPARYAN Vahe Chris,** b. 5 April 1971, Yerevan, Armenia. Cardiac Surgeon. m. Lusine Grigoryan, 2 daughters. Education: MD Degree, Diploma with Excellence, Yerevan State Medical University, Yerevan, Armenia, 1987-93; Residency in Cardiovascular Surgery, 1993-95; Research Scholarship, Assistant Professor Degree, 2000. Appointments: Cardiac Surgeon, Mikaelian Surgical Institute, Yerevan, Armenia, 1995-96; Training in Cardiac Surgery, New York, USA, 1995, Paris, France, 1998; Fellowship in Cardiac Surgery, Singapore, 2002-2003; Chief of Cardiac Surgery Department, Erebouni Medical Centre, Yerevan, 2003-. Publications: Articles in professional medical journals including, Journal of Thoracic and Cardiovascular Surgery, 1999, 2000; Asian Cardiovascular and Thoracic Annals, 2002. Honours: Alexis Carrel Award, Rome, Italy, 1995; Merit Award, Singapore, 2000. Membership: Asian Society for Cardiovascular Surgery, 2001-. Address: 26 Papazian St, Apt 24, 375012, Yerevan, Armenia. E-mail: vahegasparyan@yahoo.com

**GATES William Henry (Bill),** b. 8 October 1955, Seattle, USA. Computer Software Executive. m. Melinda French, 1994, 1 son, 2 daughters. Education: Harvard University. Appointments: Joined MITS, 1975; Programmer, Honeywell, 1975; Founder, Chairman, Board, Microsoft Corporation, 1976-, CEO, 1976-99; Software Architect, 1999-. Publications: The Future, 1994; The Road Ahead, 1996; Business at the Speed of Thought, 1999. Honours: Howard Vollum Award, Reed College, Portland, Oregon, 1984; Named CEO of Year, Chief Executive Magazine. Address: Microsoft Corporation, 1 Microsoft Way, Redmond, WA 98052, USA.

**GATHORNE-HARDY Jonathan,** b. 17 May 1933, Edinburgh, Scotland. Author. m. (1) Sabrina Tennant, 1962, 1 son, 1 daughter, (2) Nicolette Sinclair Loutit, 12 September 1985. Education: BA, Arts, Trinity College, Cambridge, 1957. Publications: One Foot in the Clouds (novel), 1961; Chameleon (novel), 1967; The Office (novel), 1970; The Rise and Fall of the British Nanny, 1972; The Public School Phenomenon, 1977; Love, Sex, Marriage and Divorce, 1981; Doctors, 1983; The Centre of the Universe is 18 Baedeker Strasse (short stories), 1985; The City Beneath the Skin (novel), 1986; The Interior Castle: A Life of Gerald Brenan (biography), 1992; Particle Theory (novel), 1996; Alfred C. Kinsey - Sex The Measure of All Things, A Biography, 1998. Other: 11 novels for children. Contributions to: Numerous magazines and journals. Address: 31 Blacksmith's Yard, Binham, Fakenham, Norfolk NR21 0AL, England.

**GATTING Michael William,** b. 6 June 1957, Kingsbury, Middlesex, England. Cricketer. m. Elaine Mabbott, 1980, 2 sons. Career: Right-hand batsman and right-arm medium bowler, played for Middlesex, 1975-98, Captain, 1983-97; 79 Tests for England, 1977-95, 23 as Captain; Scoring 4,409 runs (average 35.5) including 10 hundreds; Scored 36,549 first-class runs (94 hundreds); Toured Australia (Captain), 1986-87; Captain, rebel cricket tour to South Africa, 1989-90; 92 limited-overs internationals, 37 as Captain; Member, England Selection Committee, 1997-; Director of Coaching, Middlesex Cricket Club, 1999-2000; Director, Ashwell Leisure, 2001-. Publications: Limited Overs, 1986; Triumph in Australia, 1987; Leading From the Front (autobiography), 1988. Honour: OBE; Wisden Cricketer of The Year, 1984. Address: c/o Middlesex County Cricket Club, Lord's Cricket Ground, St John's Wood Road, London, NW8 8QN, England.

**GAUGHAN John Anthony,** b. 19 August 1932, Listowel, Co Kerry, Ireland. Catholic Priest. Education: BA, University College, Dublin, 1953; BD, St Patrick's College, Maymouth, Ireland, 1956; MA, University College, Dublin, 1965; PhD, 1992; DLitt, 1996. Appointments: Chaplain and Vocational School Teacher, Presentation College, Bray, 1957-60; Reader, Most Precious Blood, Cabra West, 1960-62; Curate, Most Sacred Heart: Aughrim-Greenane, 1962-64; Chaplain and University Tutor, University College Dublin, St Mary's Convent, Donnybrook, 1964-65; Curate, St Joseph's, Eastwall, 1965-67, Our Lady of Good Counsel, Drimnagh, 1967-70, St Patrick's, Monkstown, 1970-77, St Thérèse, Mount Merrion, 1977-83, University Church, St Stephen's Green, 1983-88; Parish Priest, Guardian Angels, Blackrock, 1988-. Publications: Contributor of over 95 articles to professional journals; Author of 20 books including most recently: Olivia Mary Taafe (1832-1918): Foundress of St Joseph's Young Priests Society, 1995; Memoirs of Senator Joseph Connolly A Founder of Modern Ireland (editor), 1996; Newmans's University Church: A History and Guide, 1997; Memoirs of Senator James G Douglas: Concerned Citizen (editor), 1998; At the Coal Face: Recollections of a City & Country Priest 1950-2000, 2000; Listowel and Its Vicinity 1973-2003: A Supplement, 2004; Articles and book reviews to various periodicals and newspapers. Memberships: National Library of Ireland Society, Chairman, 2000-; Kerry Archaeological and History Society, Committee Member, 1976-89; Writers Week, Founding Member, 1971, President, 1983-90, Vice-President, 1991-; Irish PEN, Committee Member, 1976-, Chairman, 1981-.

**GAULKE Mary Florence,** b. 24 September 1923, Johnson City, Tennessee, USA. Library Administrator. Divorced. 1 son. Education: BS, Home Economics, Oregon State University, 1963; MS, L S University of Oregon, 1968; PhD, Special Education, 1970. Appointments: Handicapped Learner, Head of Department, Home Economics, Riddle School District, Oregon, 1963-66; Librarian, Douglas County Intermediation Education District, Roseburg, 1966-67; Head Resident, Head Counselor; Prometheus Project, South Oregon College, Ashland, 1966-68; Superintendent Librarian, Medford School District, 1970-73; Instructor, Psychology, South Oregon College, 1970-73; Library Superintendent, Roseburg School District, 1974-91; Resident Psychologist, Black Oaks Boys School, Medford, 1970-75; Member, Oregon Governments Council Library, 1979. Publications: Vo-Ed Course for Junior High; Library Handbook; Instructions for Preparation of Cards for All materials Catalogued for Libraries; Handbook for Training Library Aides. Honours: Delta Kappa Gamma; Phi Delta Kappa. Memberships: Life Member, International Biographical Association; ALA; South Oregon Library Federation; Oregon Library Association;

# DICTIONARY OF INTERNATIONAL BIOGRAPHY

Pacific North West Library Association. Address: 608 Lakeridge Lane, La Vernia, TX 78121, USA.

**GAULTIER Jean-Paul,** b. 24 April 1952, Arcueil, Paris. Fashion Designer. Career: Launched first collection with his Japanese partner, 1978; Since then known on international scale for his men's and women's collections; First junior collection, 1988; Costume designs for film The Cook, The Thief, His Wife and Her Lover, 1989, for ballet le Défilé de Régine Chopinot, 1985; Madonna's World Tour, 1990; Released record, How to Do That (in collaboration with Tony Mansfield), 1989; Launched own perfume, 1993; Designer of costume for Victoria Abril in Pedro Almodóvar's film Koka, 1994; film, La Cité des Enfants Perdus, 1995; The Fifth Element, 1996; Absolutely Fabulous, 2001; Launched perfume brands Jean-Paul Gaultier, 1993, La Mâle, 1995, Fragile, 1999. Honours: Fashion Oscar, 1987; Progetto Leonardo Award for How to Do That, 1989; Chevalier des Arts et des Lettres. Address: Jean-Paul Gaultier SA, 30 rue du Faubourg-Saint-Antoine, 75012 Paris, France.

**GAVAYEVA Nadezhda N,** b. 7 February 1951, Saransk, Russia. Professor of English. Education: Diploma, Mordovian State University, 1973; Candidate of Philological Sciences, 1985; Associate Professor, 1991. Appointments: Postgraduate, Leningrade State University, 1973-77; Assistant, English Language Department, 1978-86, Teacher of English, 1978-86, Senior Teacher, 1986-89, Associate Professor, 1989-, Mordovian State University. Publications: 43 publications on text linguistics, ways of teaching English as a foreign language, cultural aspects of teaching English. Honours: Gold Medal, high school, 1968; Honoured Doctor, Udmurt State University, Russia, 1995. Address: 52-15 Demokraticheskaya Street, Saransk, Mordovia 430000, Russia.

**GEBAUER Phyllis,** b. 17 October 1928, Chicago, Illinois, USA. Novelist; Writer; Teacher. m. Frederick A Gebauer, 2 December 1950, deceased. Education: BS, Northwestern University, 1950; MA, University of Houston, 1966; Postgraduate, several universities. Appointments: Workshop Leader, Santa Barbara Writers' Conference, 1980-; Instructor, University of California at Los Angeles Extension Writers' Program, 1989-; Lecturer, San Diego State University Writers Conference, 1995-. Publications: The Pagan Blessing, 1979; The Cottage, 1985; The Final Murder of Monica Marlowe, 1986; Criticism, The Art of Give and Take, 1987. Honours: 1st Prize for Fiction, Santa Barbara City College, 1972; 1st and 2nd Prizes for Fiction, Santa Barbara City College, 1973. Memberships: PEN Center, USA, West; Dorothy L Sayers Society; Mystery Writers of America. Address: 515 West Scenic Drive, Monrovia, CA 91016-1511, USA.

**GÉBLER Carlo,** b. 21 August 1954, Dublin, Ireland. Writer; Film-Maker. m. Tyga Thomason, 23 August 1990, 3 sons, 2 daughters. Education: BA, English and Related Literature, University of York, 1976; Graduate, National Film and Television School, 1979. Appointments: Part-time Teacher, Creative Writing, HMP Maze, Co Antrim, 1993-95; Appointed Writer-in-Residence, HMP Maghaberry, Co Antrim, 1997. Publications: The Eleventh Summer, 1985; August in July, 1986; Work & Play, 1987; Driving through Cuba, 1988; Malachy and His Family, 1990; The Glass Curtain: Inside an Ulster Community, 1991; Life of a Drum, 1991; The Cure, 1994; W9 and Other Lives, 1998; How to Murder a Man, 1998; Frozen Out, 1998; The Base, 1999; Father & I, 2000; Dance of Death, 2000; Caught on a Train, 2001; 10 Rounds, 2002; August' 44, 2003; The Siege of Derry, A History, 2005; The Bull Raid, 2005. Membership: Elected to Aosdána, Ireland, 1990. Address: c/o Antony Harwood, 103 Walton Street, Oxford, OX2 6EB, England.

**GECKIL Hikmet,** b. 1 March 1963, Elazig, Turkey. Genetic Engineer. m. Berna Geckil, 2 sons. Education: BS, Department of Biology, Firat University, Elazig, Turkey, 1984; MS, Molecular Biology, Inonu University, Malatya, Turkey, 1988; PhD, Molecular Biology-Biotechnology, Illinois Institute of Technology, Chicago, 1995; Postdoctorate, Biochemistry, Department of Life Sciences, Ben-Gurion University of the Negev, Israel, 2000. Appointment: Assistant Professor, Department of Biology, Inonu University, Turkey, 1996-. Publications in scientific journals as co-author: Cell growth and oxygen uptake of Escherichia coli and Pseudomonas aeruginosa are differently affected by the genetically engineered Vitreoscilla hemoglobin gene, 2001; Genetic engineering of Enterobacter aerogenes with Vitreoscilla hemoglobin gene: cell growth survival and antioxidant enzyme status under oxidative stress, 2003. Honours: Scholarship, Scientific and Technical Research Council of Turkey, 1986-87; Honour Member, Scientific and Technical Research Council of Turkey; 1987-88; Scholarship Award, Turkish Ministry of Education, 1988; Post-doctoral Fellow, Council for Higher Education of Israel, 1999-2000. Memberships: European Federation of Biotechnology. Address: Department of Biology, Inonu University, Malatya 44069, Turkey. E-mail: hgeckil@inonu.edu.tr Website: http://web.inonu.edu.tr/~hgeckil

**GEDDES Gary,** b. 9 June 1940, Vancouver, British Columbia, Canada. Professor of English; Writer; Poet. m. (1) Norma Joan Fugler, 1963, divorced 1969, 1 daughter, (2) Jan Macht, 1973, divorced 1999, 2 daughters. Education: BA, University of British Columbia, 1962; Diploma in Education, University of Reading, 1964; MA, 1966, PhD, 1975, University of Toronto. Appointments: Lecturer, Carleton University, Ottawa, Ontario, 1971-72, University of Victoria, British Columbia, 1972-74; Writer-in-Residence, 1976-77, Visiting Associate Professor, 1977-78, University of Alberta, Edmonton; Visiting Associate Professor, 1978-79, Professor of English, 1979-98, Concordia University, Montreal, Quebec; Distinguished Professor of Canadian Culture, Western Washington University, 1999-2001; Adjunct Professor and Writer-in-Residence, University of British Columbia, 2005. Publications: 20th Century Poetry and Poets, 1969, 4th edition, 1996; 15 Canadian Poets (editor with Phyllis Bruce), 1970, 4th edition, 1999; Poems, 1970; Rivers Inlet (verse), 1972; Snakeroot (verse), 1973; Letter of the Master of Horse (verse), 1973; The Acid Test (verse), 1981; The Inner Ear: An Anthology of New Canadian Poets (editor), 1983; The Terracotta Army (verse), 1984; Changes of State (verse), 1986; The Unsettling of the West (stories), 1986; Hong Kong (verse), 1987; Light of Burning Towers (verse), 1990; Letters from Managua: Meditations on Politics or Art (essays), 1990; The Art of Short Fiction: An International Anthology, 1992; Girl By the Water (verse), 1994; The Perfect Cold Warrior (verse), 1995; Active Trading: Selected Poems, 1970-95, 1996; Flying Blind (verse), 1998; Sailing Home: A Journey Through Time, Place and Memory (non-fiction), 2001; Skaldance (verse), 2004; Kingdom of Ten Thousand Things: An Impossible Journey from Kabul to Chiapas (non-fiction), 2005. Honours: E J Pratt Medal; National Poetry Prize, Canadian Authors Association; America's Best Book Award, Commonwealth Poetry Competition, 1985; Writers Choice Award; National Magazine Gold Award; Archibald Lampman Prize; Silver Medal, Milton Acorn Competition; Poetry Book Society Recommendation; Gabriela Mistral Prize, 1996. Memberships: League of Canadian Poets; Writers' Union of Canada; Playwright's Guild of Canada. Address: 2750 Seaside Drive, RR 2, Sooke, British Columbia, V0S 1N0, Canada.

**GEDEONOV Andrei,** b 10 September 1949, Leningrad, USSR. Radiochemist. m. Iulia Basova, 1 daughter. Education:

Chemist, Leningrad State University, Leningrad, USSR, 1966-71, Postgraduate Student, 1971-74; PhD, Postgraduate Study V G Khlopin Radium Institute, Leningrad, 1977; Junior Research Worker, 1974-79, Senior Research Worker, 1979-91, Head of Laboratory, 1991-, V G Khlopin Radium Institute, Saint Petersburg, Russia. Publications: Articles as co-author in scientific journals and conference proceedings including: Journal of Environmental Radioactivity, 2002; Proceedings of the 5th International Conference on Environmental Radioactivity in the Arctic and Antarctic, St Petersburg, Russia, 2002; 3 USSR Patents. Honours: Medal, Exhibition of National Economic Achievement, 1978; Honorary Title, Inventor of the USSR, 1983; Honorary Title Veteran of Atomic Industry, 1998. Membership: Fellow, House of Scientists, Saint Petersburg, Russia. Address: Dzeleznovodskaja St 27-72, 199155 Saint Petersburg, Russia. E-mail: gedeonov @ pop3.rcom.ru

**GEE Arthur,** b. 10 January 1934, Latchford, Warrington, Lancashire. Artist. m. Margaret Ray Robinson, 1 son, 1 daughter. Education: St Helens College of Art and Design, 1983-84. Appointments: Trainee, Wire Industry, 1949-52; RAF, 1952-55; Mechanical Engineering Draughtsman, 1956-83; Full Time Artist, 1983-94; Semi-Retired, 1994-. Creative works: 2 illustrations for Flights of Imagination edited by Mike Mockler; Works in collections: Acrylic titled Mallard in the Sere Wood; Collection at Nature in Art, Twigworth, Gloucester, 2004. Honours: Certificate of Merit, Italian Academy of Art, Salsomaggiore; Drawing Prize, National Exhibition of Wildlife Art, Liverpool; Highly commended acrylic, Welsh Snow, NAPA Show, St Ives, Cornwall, 2003. Memberships: Society of Wildlife Artists, 1969-99; National Acrylic Painters Association, 1992-; Sefton Guild of Artists, 1996-; Warrington Visual Artists Forum, 1998-. Address: 31 Karen Close, Burtonwood, Warrington, Cheshire, WA5 4LL, England.

**GEENEN Vincent,** b. 6 February 1958, Verviers, Belgium. Research Director of Belgian NFSR; Chairman of Liege Centre of Immunology. 2 sons. Education: Saint-Servais College, 1975; MD, Liege University, 1982; PhD, Liege University, 1987; Professor thesis, 1996. Appointments: Research Associate, 1987, Senior Research Associate, 1997, Professor, Liege University, 2001. Publications: Over 100 in professional journals, 6 books, 20 chapters in books, a contribution to Encyclopedia of Neuroscience, 1997, 2002. Honours: Masius Prize, 1985; Semper Prize, 1988; SmithKline Beecham Prize of the Royal Academy of Medicine, 1992; Alumni Prize, University Foundation of Belgium, 1993; Chairman, 3rd Gordon Conference on Neuroendocrine - Immunology, 1997; Patent, Thymus-based tolerogenic theory against Type A diabetes. Memberships: International Society of Neuroendocrinology, 1987; Endocrine Society, 1988; International Society of Neuroimmunomodulation, 1990; International Society of Molecular Evolution, 1993; Molecular Medicine Society, 1995; American Diabetes Association, 1997; European Association for the Study of Diabetes, 1996; Immunology Diabetes Society, 1999. Address: Institute of Pathology, CHU-B23, B-4000 Liege-Sart Tilman, Belgium.

**GEERTZ Clifford (James),** b. 23 August 1926, San Francisco, California, USA. Professor of Social Science; Writer. m. (1) Hildred Storey, 30 October 1948, divorced 1982, 1 son, 1 daughter, (2) Karen Blu, 1987. Education: AB, Antioch College, 1950; PhD, Harvard University, 1956. Appointments: Research Assistant, 1952-56, Research Associate, 1957-58, Massachusetts Institute of Technology; Instructor and Research Associate, Harvard University, 1956-57; Fellow, Center for Advanced Study in the Behavioral Sciences, Stanford, 1958-59; Assistant Professor of Anthropology, University of California at Berkeley,

1958-60; Assistant Professor, 1960-61, Associate Professor, 1962-64, Professor, 1964-68, Divisional Professor, 1968-70, University of Chicago; Senior Research Career Fellow, National Institute for Mental Health, 1964-70; Professor of Social Science, 1970-, Harold F Linder Professor of Social Science, 1982-, Professor Emeritus, 2000-, Institute for Advanced Study, Princeton, New Jersey; Visiting Lecturer with Rank of Professor, Princeton University, 1975-2000; Various guest lectureships. Publications: The Religion of Java, 1960; Old Societies and New States (editor), 1963; Agricultural Involution: The Processes of Ecological Change in Indonesia, 1963; Peddlers and Princes, 1963; The Social History of an Indonesian Town, 1965; Person, Time and Conduct in Bali: An Essay in Cultural Analysis, 1966; Islam Observed: Religious Development in Morocco and Indonesia, 1968; The Interpretation of Cultures: Selected Essays, 1973; Myth, Symbol and Culture (editor), 1974; Kinship in Bali (with Hildred Geertz), 1973; Meaning and Order in Moroccan Society (with Hildred Geertz and Lawrence Rosen), 1979; Negara: The Theatre State in Nineteenth Century Bali, 1980; Local Knowledge: Further Essays in Interpretive Anthropology, 1983; Bali, interprétation d'une culture, 1983; Works and Lives: The Anthropologist as Author, 1988; After the Fact: Two Countries, Four Decades, One Anthropologist, 1995; Available Light: Anthropological Reflections on Philosophical Topics, 2000. Contributions to: Scholarly books and journals. Honours: Talcott Parsons Prize, American Academy of Arts and Sciences, 1974; Sorokin Prize, American Sociological Association, 1974; Distinguished Lecturer, American Anthropological Association, 1983; Huxley Memorial Lecturer and Medallist, Royal Anthropological Institute, 1983; Distinguished Scholar Award, Association for Asian Studies, 1987; National Book Critics Circle Prize in Criticism, 1988; Horace Mann Distinguished Alumnus Award, Antioch College, 1992; Fukuoka Asian Cultural Prize, 1992. Memberships: American Academy of Arts and Sciences, fellow; American Association for the Advancement of Science, fellow; American Philosophical Society, fellow; British Academy, corresponding fellow; Council on Foreign Relations, fellow; National Academy of Sciences, fellow; Royal Anthropological Institute, honorary fellow. Address: c/o School of Social Science, Institute for Advanced Study, Princeton, NJ 08540, USA.

**GEESIN Frances Helene,** b. 21 July 1941, Dulwich, London. Textile Artist; Researcher. m. Ron Geesin, 3 sons. Education: NDD, Painting, West Sussex College of Art, 1963, Design, Woven Textiles, 1966, PhD, 1995, The Royal College of Art. Appointments: Fabric Designer for Wallis Shops, Knitted Fabric Designer for Coram St Margarets, Leicester, Warp Knitted Designer for Frymann & Fletcher, Nottingham, 1966-70; Made costumes for BBC TV, stage, films and dance, 1976-92; Teacher at numerous colleges including: Helsinki University, Finland, The Saga School, Japan, University of Brighton, Nottingham Trent University, John Moores University, Kawashima Textile School, Japan, Royal College of Art, 1966-99; Part-time at Design for Life Department, Brunel University, 1997-99; Consultant, Philips Design and Research Laboratories, 1997-99; Senior Research Fellow, Fashion and Textiles Department, Royal College of Art, 1997-99; Senior Research Fellow, Central St Martins, 1999-2000; Senior Research Fellow, London College of Fashion, 1999-. Publications: Engenious Textile Developments (Textile Forum), 1997; Wearable Computing (internet magazine article), 1998; Encouraging Connections (conference paper), 1997; Revelation. Textile artists addressing issues (catalogue), 1998; Through the Surface. Collaborating artists from Britain and Japan (catalogue), 2004. Honours: Portrait Prize and RSA Bursary, West Sussex College of Art, 1963; Sponsorship by Drapers' Company, 1993; BASF Sponsorship, 1994; Daler-Rowney Prize, 1995; British

Standards Award, 1995; Arts Foundation Fellowship for Textile Design, 2003. Membership: Textile Institute. Address: Head Rest, Street End Lane, Broadoak, Heathfield, East Sussex, TN21 8TU, England.

**GEFFEN David,** b. 21 February 1943, Brooklyn, New York, USA. Film, Recording and Theatre Executive. Appointments: William Morris Talent Agency, 1964; Launched new film studio with Steven Spielberg and Jeffrey Katzenberg; Founder, Music Publishing Company Tunafish Music with Laura Nyro; Joined Ashley Famous Agency; Appointed Vice President, Creative Man (now International Creative Man), 1968; Founder, Asylum Records and Geffen-Roberts Management Company with Elliot Roberts, 1970; Sold Asylum to Warner Communications, but remained President, 1971, merged it with Elektra, signed up Bob Dylan and Joni Mitchell; Vice-Chairman, Warner Bros Pictures, 1975-76; Founder, Geffen Records, President, 1980-, signed up Elton John, John Lennon and Yoko Ono and many others, sold label to Music Corporation of America Inc, 1990; Founder, Geffen Film Company, Producer: Little Shop of Horrors; Beetlejuice, 1988; Men Don't Leave; Defending Your Life; Co-producer, musical, Dreamgirls, 1981-85; Little Shop of Horrors; Cats, 1982; Madame Butterfly, 1986; Social Security; Chess, 1990; Miss Saigon; Founder, DGC record label; Co-founder, Dreamworks, SKG, 1995-. Address: Dreamworks SKG, 100 Universal Plaza, Building 477, Universal City, CA 91608, USA.

**GELMAN Len,** b. 15 April 1949, Ukraine. Professor. 1 daughter. Education: MS (with honours) National Technical University of Ukraine, Kiev, 1972; PhD, 1987, Doctor of Sciences, 1993, Acoustical Institute, Russian Academy of Sciences. Appointments: Visiting Professor, Technion-Israel Institute of Technology, Haifa, Israel, 1999-2000; Visiting Professor, University of South Carolina, Columbia, USA, 2000; Visiting Professor, Milan Polytechnical University-Enitechnologie, Milan, Italy, 2001; Visiting Professor, University of South Carolina, Columbia, USA, 2001; Visiting Professor, Milan Polytechnical University-Enitechnologie, 2002; Professor, Senior Research Officer, Department of Process and Systems Engineering, Cranfield University, UK, 2002-. Publications: More than 150 works; 17 patents. Honours include: USA International Science Foundation Grant, 1995; USA Civilian Research and Development Foundation Grants, 1996, 2000; USA MacArthur Foundation Grant, 1997-98; Acoustical Society of America Scholarship, 1997-98; Lady Davies Grant, Israel, 1999-2000; University of South Carolina Fellowship, 2000, 2001; Landau Network-Centro Volta Fellowship, Italy, 2000; Travel Grant Deemed University, Tamil Nadu, India, 2001; USA National Research Council Grant, 2001-2001; USA National Academy of Sciences Grant, 2002-2003; United Kingdom Royal Society Grant, 2002-2003; United Kingdom DTI Grants, 2004-2005, 2004-2007, 2004-2007, 2005-2007; Keynote Speaker: Workshop on Enhancement of Helicopter Fault Diagnosis Methodologies, Virginia Beach USA, 1998, 6 Topical NDE Conference ASME San Antonio, USA, 1999. National Symposium on Acoustics, India, 2001, Conference of American Institute of Aeronautics and Astronautics, Palm Springs, USA, 2004; Listed in Who's Who publications and biographical dictionaries. Memberships: International Institute of Acoustics and Vibration; London Institute of Electrical Engineering; UK Institution of Diagnostic Engineers; New York Academy of Sciences; Acoustical Society of America; Acoustical Society of Japan; Elesevier Engineering, UK; Fellow, British Institute of NDT. Address: Cranfield University, School of Engineering, AMAC, Cranfield, Bedfordshire MK43 0AL, England. E-mail: l.gelman@cranfield.ac.uk

**GENEL (Guenel) Leonid Samooilovitch,** b. 11 August 1946, Moscow, Russia. Materials Scientist. m. Galkina Valentina Vassilyevna. 2 sons. Education: Moscow Steels and Alloys Institute, 1964-69; Magistre Diploma, 1969; Moscow D I Mendeleev Chemical Processing Institute; Postgraduate Studies, 1976-1979; DrPhil, 1980. Appointments: Engineer, Institute for Sources of Electrical Energy, 1972; Senior Engineer, Research Worker, Institute for Metal Protection from Corrosion, 1982; Chief of Sector, Chief of Department, NPO Polymerbyt, 1991; General Director, Spectroplast Ltd, 1991-. Publications: More than 90 publications in the following fields: Mechanochemistry of gluing, treatment of surface, development of new polymer based materials being produced by mechanochemical technique; Wave approach to the control strength and durability of solids, and also materials based on the approach; Liquid intermediary refrigerants and also concentrates of anti-corrosive, colouring and viscosity controlling additives to them; Formulations for cleaning equipment from depositions; Polymeric compositions with decorative effects; Philosophy and cosmology which origin of great amount of matter and small amount of antimatter in the Universe is explained with the Universe's expansion with acceleration without participation of the original explosion in; Properties, structure of Cosmic Vacuum and its energy as well as any other parameter of something, that may be measured (time, distance, velocity, mass, temperature, power and so on), are considered as a concrete measure of deviation from Ideal Vacuum; Parental Role of the Cosmic Vacuum as a polirizer and water as a matrix in the origin of living from lifeless; The four-lettered alphabet is used in the DNA molecule for writing down a project for activity and development of each living thing on Earth. The project is being realised by means of 20 subordinate letters as a-aminoacids, with whose aid life on Earth is being formed. Such an approach assumes possibility of the existence of a translator from the bio-language to human essential languages, including Hebrew, and vice versa. Such a translator is assumed to make easier understanding between science, religions, philosophies and living nature and also to help in establishing between them the more objective balance of interrelations; Chemical physics of living matter considers an organism and its fragments by analogy with interconnected quantum devices, which emit and absorb bioquanta. The bioquanta in their turn interact with other bioquanta forming a bizone. In the scope of being developed General Theory and Techniques of Knowledge Management an attempt to establish for actual state of a person and society relationship between scientific and technical progress on the one hand and spirituality on the other hand, and also perspectives of change in the relationship is being made for civilisation. Honours: The Outstanding Scholar of the 20th Century Medal, IBC, 2000; The Leading Intellectual of the World Medal, 2004; The World Medal of Freedom, ABI, USA; The Laureate of All-Russian Exhibition Centre Medal; The 10 Year Medal for the Merchants and the Employers Society; Title of Honorary Chemical Industry Worker, Russia. Memberships: Academician of Russian Academy for Sciences and Arts (RooAN); Academician of International Academy of Refrigeration. Address: Spectroplast Ltd, 2nd Vladimirskaya str 11, Moscow 111123, Russia. E-mail: lg@splast.ru

**GENSLER Kinereth Dushkin,** b. 17 September 1922, New York, New York, USA. Poet. Widow, 2 sons, 1 daughter. Education: BA, University of Chicago, 1943; MA, Columbia University, 1946. Appointment: Editor, Alice James Books, 1976-2001. Publications: Threesome Poems, 1976; The Poetry Connection (co-author), 1978; Without Roof, 1981; Journey Fruit, 1997. Contributions to: Anthologies, books, journals, and periodicals. Honours: Members Award, Poetry Society of America, 1969; Power Dalton Award, New England Poetry Club, 1971; Borestone Mountain Award, 1973; Residency,

Ragdale, 1981; Residency, MacDowell Colony, 1982, 1983. Memberships: Academy of American Poets; Alice James Poetry Cooperative Society; Poetry Society of America. Address: 221 Mt Auburn Street, Cambridge, MA 02138, USA.

**GEORGIEV Viden,** b. 1 February 1925, Gintsi, Sofia Region, Bulgaria. Physician. m. Elena Kisselkova, 1 son, 1 daughter. Education: Doctor of Medicine, Medical University, Sofia, Bulgaria, 1954; Doctor of Philosophy, Institute of Experimental Medicine, Saint Petersburg, Russia, 1962. Appointments: Assistant, 1955-58, Senior Assistant, 1959-63, Associate Professor, 1967-75, Professor of Physiology, 1975-, National Sports Academy, Sofia, Bulgaria; Researcher, Sorbonne, Paris, France, 1964-66. Publications: Author: Proprioceptors and Circulation, (monograph), 1965; Vascular Reactions in Sportsmen after Physical Efforts (monograph), 1973; Nervous System and Sport (book), 1975; Peripheral and Brain Circulation at Physical Efforts (monograph), 1991. Memberships: Bulgarian Society of Physiological Sciences; Bulgarian Society of Sports Medicine; New York Academy of Sciences; National movement for development and protections of the science and higher education. Address: 14 Tsar Peter Street, Sofia 1463, Bulgaria.

**GERE Richard,** b. 31 August 1949. Actor. m. Cindy Crawford, 1991, divorced. Education: University of Massachusetts. Career: Formerly played trumpet, piano, guitar and bass and composed music with various groups; Stage performances with Provincetown Playhouse and Off-Broadway; Appeared in London and Broadway productions of The Taming of the Shrew, A Midsummer Night's Dream and Broadway productions of Habeas Corpus and Bent; Founding Chairman and President, Tibet House, New York; Actor, films include: Report to the Commissioner, 1975; Baby Blue Marine, 1976; Looking for Mr Goodbar, 1977; Days of Heaven, 1978; Blood Brothers, 1978; Yanks, 1979; American Gigolo, 1980; An Officer and a Gentleman, 1982; Breathless, 1983; Beyond the Limit, 1983; The Cotton Club, 1984; King David, 1985; Power, 1986; No Mercy, 1986; Miles From Home, 1989; 3000, 1989; Internal Affairs, 1990; Pretty Woman, 1990; Rhapsody in August, 1991; Sommersby (co-executive, producer), 1993; Mr Jones (co-exec producer), 1994; Intersection, 1994; First Knight, 1995; Primal Fear, 1996; Red Corner, 1997; Burn Hollywood Burn, 1998; Runaway Bride, 1999; Dr T and the Women, 2000; Autumn in New York, 2000; The Mothman Prophecies, 2002; Unfaithful, 2002; Chicago, 2002; Shall We Dance, 2004; Bee Season, 2005. Publication: Pilgrim Photo Collection, 1998.

**GERHOLM Tor Ragnar,** b. 21 December 1925, Brooklyn, New York, USA. Retired. m. Maud Birgitta Ellemo, 3 sons, 1 daughter. Education: Matriculation Examination, Norra Latin Stockholm, 1945; Fil Lic, University of Stockholm, 1952; PhD, University of Uppsala, 1956. Appointments: Research Assistant, Royal Institute of Technology, Stockholm, 1951-54; Research Assistant, Uppsala University, Uppsala, 1954-56; Assistant Professor, 1956-62; Professor, Physics, University of Stockholm, 1962-90; Retired. Publications include: Physics and Man; Ide och Samhalle. Honours: Literary Prize, Swedish Authors Association; Cultural Prize, Natur Och Kultur; Cultural Prize, Langmans Cultural Foundation. Memberships: Royal Swedish Academy of Science; The Royal Swedish Academy of Engineering Sciences. Address: Svartmangatan 21, SE 111 29 Stockholm, Sweden.

**GERKE MENDIETA Carlos,** b. 15 April 1942, Sucre, Bolivia. Lawyer. m. Marcela Siles, 1 son, 2 daughters. Education: Licenciado en Derecho, Political and Social Sciences, 1967; Lawyer, 1967. Appointments: Private Practice; University Professor, Commercial Law, Civil Law. President,

La Paz Bar; Member, Andean Judiciary Committee; Member, Advisory Committee of the Bolivian Foreign Office; National President, Bolivian Catholic University. Publications: New Law of Administrative Procedure in Bolivia, 2002; Intellectual Property Law under Bolivian Law; Domicile in the Bolivian Civil Code. Honours: Diploma and Gold Medal, Best Student of Law School; Knight of the Order of Saint Gregorius Magnus, awarded by Pope John Paul II. Memberships: Member of the Honour Council, Andean Judiciary Committee; Order of Saint Gregorius Magnus; Bolivian Genealogy Society; Bolivian Philately Society. Address: PO Box 14606, La Paz, Bolivia.

**GERMANN Richard P(aul),** b. 3 April 1918, Ithaca, New York, USA. Pharmaceutical Research Chemist; Executive; Consultant. m. M(alinda) Jane Plietz, 1 daughter. Education: BA, Chemistry, University of Colorado, 1939; Graduate Scholar 1939-41; Naval Research Fellow, Western Reserve University, 1941-43; Business and Advertising, Brown University, 1954; PhD, Hamilton State University, 1973. Appointments: Chief Analytical Chemist, Taylor Refining Company, 1943-44; Pharmaceutical Research Chemist, American Cyanamid Company, 1944-52; Development Chemist, i/c Pilot Plant, Geigy Chemical Corporation, 1952-55; Chemist, Research Division, W R Grace & Company, 1955-60; Chief Chemist, G H Packwood Manufacturing Company, 1960-61; Co-ordinator, Chemical Product Development, Abbott Laboratories, 1961-71; President, Ramtek International, 1973-2000, Germann International, 1973-82. Publications: Numerous US and Foreign Patents; Decontamination of Plant Wastes: An Overview, 1969; Science's Ultimate Challenge - The Re-evaluation of Ancient Occult Knowledge, 1979; Science and Innovation, 1993. Memberships: American Chemical Society; American Association for the Advancement of Science; Chemical Society, London; Commercial Chemical Development Association; Chemical Market Research Association; Alpha Chi Sigma; Chemists Club, New York and Chicago. Address: Shaker Village, 394 Cleveland Road, Apt 11H, Norwalk, OH 44857-8500, USA

**GERSTER Richard,** b. 29 May 1946, Winterthur, Switzerland. Economist. m. Doris Gerster, 1 son, 2 daughters. Education: PhD Econ, University of St Gall, Switzerland, 1973. Appointments: Programme Co-ordinator, Helvetas, 1972-81; Director, Swiss Coalition of Development Organisations, 1981-98; Director, Gerster Consulting (www.gersterconsulting.ch), for public policy and international development, 1998-. Publications: Switzerland as a Developing Country, 1998; Alternative Approaches to Poverty Reduction Strategies (SDC working paper), 2000; Patents and Development, Third World Network, 2001; Globalisation and Justice, 2nd edition 2005. Honour: Christoph Eckenstein Award for the Relations Switzerland-Third World, 1987; Blue Planet Award, 2002. Memberships: Member of Parliament in the Canton of Zürich, 1987-92; Member, Governing Board of State Bank of Zürich, 1988-2003; Member, Development Advisory Council to the Government of Austria, 2000-. Address: Goeldistr 1, CH-8805 Richterswil, Switzerland.

**GERWIN Thomas,** b. 8 February 1955, Kassel, Germany. Composer; Media Artist. m. Konstanze Thuemmel, 1 son, 2 daughters. Education: Studies in guitar and flute, 1977-79; Magister Artium, Musicology, Linguistics, Philosophy, Tübingen, 1979-83; Musician, Composer, Landes-Theatre, Tübingen; Master Class Diploma, Composition and Electronics, Stuttgart, 1987-91. Appointments: Director, Inter Art Project, Studio for Media Art, Berlin and Karlsruhe; President, Society for Multisensorial Art. Publications: 11 audio CDs; 3 CD-ROMs; 7 experimental film scores; Over 20 large music and video installations. Honours: Karl-Sczuka-Support Award for Radio Art, 1999; Selection Award of American Composers Forum, 1999; Official Sound Composer for European Pavilion at EXPO 2000. Memberships: World Forum for Acoustic Ecology; Canadian Electroacoustic Community; International Computer Music Association; Society for Multisensorial Art; Berliner Gesellschaft fuer Neue Musik. Address: Calvinstr 13, 10557 Berlin, Germany. E-mail: inter.art.project@t-online.de Website: www.inter-art-project.de

**GHAFOOR Abdul,** b. 10 February 1928, Mansehra, Pakistan. m. Tahera, 1 son, 1 daughter, deceased. Education: BA, Honours, Urdu Language and Literature, 1955; PhD, Honours, Engineering, USA, 1995. Appointments: Lt Colonel and Acting Brigadier, Engineer Corps, Pakistan Army, 1952-77; Chief Engineer, Government of Punjab, Provincial Government of Pakistan, 1977-79; Director of Works and Chief Engineer, Private Limited Construction Company, 1979-81; General Manager and Chief Engineer, Saudi Development Company, Jeddah, 1981-82; Chief Resident Engineer, private Consulting Engineers firm, Pakistan, 1982-85; Project Director, Riyadh, Saudi Arabia consultant engineers company, 1985-86; Chief Engineer, consulting engineers firm, Pakistan, 1987; Chief Engineer, construction company, Pakistan, 1988-90; Director of Works in Pakistan, private trading and finance company, 1990; Chairman, Chief Executive, Private Ltd Consulting Engineers, 1990-98; Director General Al-Beruni Group for Education, 1998-. Publications: Anne Frank – Diary of a Young Girl, Urdu Edition; Silver Spoon Guide for Quality English Writing; Numerous articles in professional magazines and newspapers. Honours: Several medals and letters of appreciation. Memberships: Life Fellow, American Society of Civil Engineers, USA; Fellow, Institution of Engineers, Pakistan, Structure Institute of Engineers, USA; PE of Pakistan Engineering Council; Member, Advisory Council, IBC; Deputy Governor, ABIRA, USA. Address: House no 36, Street 5, F-8/3, Islamabad, Pakistan.

**GHANI Abdul Ghani A,** b. 10 April 1956. New Zealand Citizen. Education: BSc, Physics, 1978, MSc, Physics, 1981, Baghdad, Iraq; PhD, Chemical Engineering, Food Engineering, The University of Auckland, New Zealand, 2001. Appointments: Research Associate, Iraqi Atomic Energy Agency, Baghdad, Iraq, 1978-81; Physicist, Private Factory, Iraq, 1981-83; Research Fellow, Solar Energy Research Centre, Iraqi Scientific Research Council, Baghdad, Iraq, 1983-90; Lecturer, Numerical Analysis and Computer Programming, Department of Physics, University of Baghdad, Iraq, 1986-86; Lecturer, Mathematics, Numerical Analysis and Computer Programming, University of Tikrit, Iraq, 1990-91; Technical Manager, Private Factory, Baghdad, Iraq, 1991-95; PhD Student, 1997-2001, Research Fellow, Department of Chemical and Materials Engineering 2001-, The University of Auckland, New Zealand. Publications: Book: Sterilization of Food in Retort Pouches, 2005; Book chapter: Numerical simulation of transient two-dimensional profiles of temperature, concentration and flow of liquid food in a can during sterilization (co-author), 2003; Over 75 articles in professional international journals and presented at conferences as co-author include: A computational and experimental study of heating and cooling cycles during thermal sterilization of liquid foods in pouches using CFD, 2003; Analysis of thermal sterilization of solid-liquid food mixture in cans, 2003. Honours: 2 Scholarships, 1998-2000, Research Fellowship, Department of Chemical and Materials Engineering, University of Auckland, New Zealand; Best Doctoral Thesis in the Faculty of Engineering, 2001; Post Doctoral Fellowship, 2002-2005, New Zealand Foundation of Research Science and Technology; Listed in Who's Who publications and biographical dictionaries.

Memberships include: Food Science and Process Engineering Group, Department of Chemical and Materials Engineering, The University of Auckland; Australian New Zealand Solar Energy Society; International Solar Energy Society; Institute of Professional Engineers of New Zealand; Society of Chemical Engineering New Zealand. Address: Department of Chemical and Materials Engineering, The University of Auckland, Private Bag 92019, Auckland, New Zealand.

**GHEORGHE Calcan,** b. 16 April 1956, Săgeata, Buzău, Romania. Professor. m. Graţiela Georgeta Calcan, 1 son. Education: History-Philosophy Faculty, Al.I.Cuza, University, Iaşi, 1976-80; Doctorate, Al.I.Cuza University, Iaşi, 1990-95. Appointments: Professor of History, Philosophy, History of Art, History of Religions, Practical Technology High School No 6, Ploieşti, 1980-90; National College, Mihai Viteazul, Ploieşti, 1991-2002; Professor, History, Oil and Gas University, Ploieşti. Publications: 4 books; Over 100 studies, articles, reviews about the history of Romanian oil and international recognition of the Alliance achieved by the Romanian people in 1918. Honours: Doctor of Historical Sciences; Headmaster National College, Mihai Viteazul, Ploieşti; Chevalier des Palmes Academiques; Recteur Populaire, University "Dimitrie Gusti", Ploieşti; 1st prize, Session of Scientific Communications, Iaşi, 1979; 1st prize country, Session of pupils scientific communication (co-ordinator), 1987, 1996. Memberships: Vice President, Scientific Foundation (FOSP); Historical Studies Society Prahova; Vice President, Association Cult of the Heroes; Archivist Society; Friends of the Archivists, Prahova. Address: 2C Bulevardul, Bucureşti, Bl 15C, ap 42, Ploieşti 2000, Romania. E-mail: calcan@xnet.ro

**GHISTA Dhanjoo Noshir,** b. 10 January 1940, Bombay, India. Professor. m. Garda Kirsten, 1 son, 2 daughters. Education: PhD, Stanford University, California, 1964. Appointments: Post-Doctoral Research Associate, National Academy of Sciences, National Research Council, Washington DC, 1964-66; Aerospace Engineering and Medical Engineering Scientist, National Academy of Sciences, (NRC) and NASA, Ames Research Centre, 1966-69; Associate Professor, Washington University, St Louis, USA, 1969-71; Professor and Head, Biomedical Engineering Division, Indian Institute of Technology, 1971-75; Senior Scientist, NASA, Ames Research Centre, and Stanford VA Medical Centre, 1975-78; Professor of Biomechanics and Engineering Mechanics, Michigan Technological University, 1979-81; Head, Biomedical Engineering Department, Chedoke-McMasters Hospitals, Ontario, Canada, 1981-84; Professor of Medicine and Engineering Physics, Chairman, Biomedical Engineering, McMaster University, 1981-87; Vice President, Board of Directors, Corporation for Medical Devices and Industry Development, Ontario, 1988-89; Founding Professor and Chairman, Department of Biophysics, Faculty of Medicine and Health Sciences, United Arab Emirates University, Al Ain, United Arab Emirates, 1989-95; Professor and Head, Biomedical Engineering Department, Osmania University, Hyderabad, India, 1995-2000; Professor, Nanyang Technological University, Singapore, 1998-99, 2000-; Vice-chancellor designate, Ananda Marga Gurukula University and Neohumanistic University System, 2000-. Pioneered: Biomedical Engineering, Healthcare Engineering and Management Science, Community-development Engineering of Sustainable Townships (for rural development and urban transformation) and advancement of Third-world countries. Prime Interests: Neo Global Political-Economic Order: Economic democracy, Political (Party-less) Governance based on elected representatives from Soceital/Community sectors, and World Government; Biomedical and Healthcare Sciences and Engineering; Socio-Economic-Political Science and Engineering; Neohumanistic Education System (for liberating the intellect); Consciousness and Cognitive Science; Psychological and Behavioural Science; Sports Science and Medicine; Role of University in Society. Publications: Over 20 books in Biomedical Engineering and Social Sciences: Biomechanics, Engineering-physiology, Cardiovascular physics, Orthopaedic mechanics, Osteo-arthro mechanics, Medical and life physics, Human-body dynamics, Spinal-injury biomedical engineering and African development; Author, Socio-Economic Democracy and the World Government, 2004; Over 300 journal, professional and academic articles; Editor in Chief: Renaissance Universal Journal, 1980-89, Automedica Journal, 1995-. Honours: Rotary Prize, 1959; Bhabha Endowed Professorship, ITT, Madras, 1973-75; Teaching Award, Faculty of Medicine and Health Sciences, UAE University, 1994-95; Kenneth H Clarke Prize, Best Paper, 1994. Memberships: Founding Member, Conference on Mechanics in Medicine and Biology, 1978-; Co-founder and Board Member, Gauss Institute, 1987; Co-Founder, Al Khaleej Institute of Advanced Studies, 1991. Address: School of Chemical and Biomedical Engineering, Nanyang Technological University, 50 Nanyang Avenue, Singapore, 639798. E-mail: mdnghista@ntu.edu.sg

**GHOSAL Kajal,** b. 14 December 1962, India. Chronic Disease and Oncological Homeopathic Consultant. m. Hemanta Ghosal. Education: Bachelor in Homeopathic Medicine and Surgery, Calcutta University; Cardio Pulminary Resuscitation, Basic First Aid, American Red Cross, Duluth; Bachelor of Science, Calcutta University; Bachelor of Education, Madurai Kamraj University. Appointments: Associate researcher and Co-Investigator, Institute of HYDT Research and Education, India and American Institute of HYDT Research and Education, USA; Honorary Consultant to: Dr Pulin Pradhan Swasthya Kendra, Purba Medinipur; Shamayita Jivan Surya, Ranabahal, Amarkanan, Bankura; Nivedita Chikitsalay, Bagbazar, Koltaka; Clinical Observer, Cancer Centre Welfare Home and Research Institute, Thakurpukur, Koltaka; Organiser, 1st International Seminar of HYDT, 1st and 2nd National Seminars on HYDT. Publications include: Research papers as co-author: Homeopathy in the Treatment of Cancer Cervix; Homeopathy in the Treatment of Hyrothyroidism; Homeopathy in the Treatment of Leukaemia; Homeopath in the Treatment of Breast Cancer; HYD Therapy in Cancer of Urinary Bladder; HYD Therapy in Cancer Thyroid; Contributions to: HYDT Times, Medical World. Honour: Bharat Vikash Award, 2003. Address: 49/1 Ramlal Bazar, Koltaka 78, West Bengal, India. E-mail: drghosal_99@rediffmail.com

**GHOSH Chandra,** b. 15 June 1944, Kolkata, India. Consultant Forensic Psychiatrist. m. N A Hindson. Education: MBBS, Calcutta University, India, 1967; Diploma in Psychological Medicine, Conjoint Board of Psychological Medicine, London, 1974; Member, Royal College of Psychiatrists, 1975. Appointments: Senior House Officer, General Psychiatry, 1971-72, Registrar, Group Psychotherapy, 1972-74, Senior Registrar, Subnormality, Forensic Adolescent, Psychogeriatric, 1974-76, East Liverpool Area Health Authority (Teaching); Consultant Psychiatrist, Park Lane Hospital, Maghull, 1977-87; Consultant Forensic Psychiatrist, Clinical Director, Consultant Co-ordinator for Rehabilitation Services, Broadmoor Hospital, 1988-98; Medical Director, Pastoral Homes Limited, 1998-2000; Consultant Forensic Psychiatrist, Blenheim Secure Services, Chadwick Lodge, 2000-2003; Medical Director for Personality Disorder Service and Women's Service, Mayflower Hospitals, Bury. Publications: Letter in Lancet on Popranolol Trial, 1977; Review article in Hospital Doctor, 1981; Book review in Mind Out; Article, Service Needs of Black Women Offender Patients; Chapter in Working with Difference; Several papers presented at conferences on subjects including domestic violence, particularly in relation to South Asian women.

Memberships include: Committee Member, North West MIND, 1980-86;Ethnic Minority Health Group, Community Relations Council, Liverpool, 1979-86; Management Committee, Asian Women's Advisory Centre, Hackney, 1995-2000; Transcultural Psychiatry Interest Group, Royal College of Psychiatrists; Mental Health Unit of NACRO, 1988-2002; Working Party, Southall Black Sisters, 2002-; Secretary, Isambullela (domestic violence umbrella organisation), 2004-. Address: Mayflower Hospitals, Buller Street, Off Bolton Road, Bury, Lancashire BL8 2BS, England.

**GHOSH Narendra Nath,** b. 1 January 1970, Bankura, India. Scientist. m. Swayang Probha Ghosh. Education: BSc (Hons), Chemistry; MSc, Chemistry; PhD, Chemistry. Appointments: Post-Doctoral Fellow, University of Delaware, USA, 1998-2000; Faculty, Chemistry Department, Birla Institute of Technology and Science, Pilani, 2000-2002; Post-Doctoral Fellow, University of Tennessee, 2002-2004; Postdoctoral Research Scientist, University of Kentucky, Lexington, USA, 2004; Faculty, Birla Institute of Technology and Science, Pilani, Goa, India, 2005-. Publications: Papers published in Journal of Nanostructured Materials; British Ceramic Transactions; Journal of Materials Science and Engineering; British Journal of Materials Science and Engineering; Bulletin of Materials Science; Ceramic Transactions; European Journal of Solid State and Inorganic Chemistry; Chemical Communications. Honours: Invited as Chairperson in the Conference, Materials for New Millennium; Eminent Scientist of Today Medal, International Biographical Association. Reviewer of papers for many international journals; Listed in Who's Who publications and biographical dictionaries. Address: Department of Chemistry, Birla Institute of Technology and Science – Pilani (Goa Campus), Zuarinagar, Goa-403726, India. E-mail: naren70@yahoo.com

**GHUBASH Rafia Obaid,** b. 13 November 1956, Dubai. University President. Education: MB, BCh, Cairo University, Cairo, Egypt, 1983; Diploma in Child and Adolescent Psychiatry, 1988, Diploma in Psychiatry, 1988, Board Certification in Psychiatry, 1990, Institute of Psychiatry, University of London, England; Certification in Epidemiology and Medical Statistics, London School of Hygiene and Tropical Medicine, London, England, 1990; PhD, Community and Epidemiological Psychiatry, University of London, England, 1992; Arab Board Certificate in Psychiatry, 1997. Appointments: Clinical Associate, Maudsley and Bethlem Hospitals, Institute of Psychiatry, University of London, 1985-88; Associate Professor of Psychiatry, 1999- Assistant Dean for Female Student Affairs, 1993, Vice Dean 1999, Dean, 2000, Faculty of Medicine and Health Sciences, United Arab Emirates University; President, Arabian Gulf University, Bahrain, 2001-; Member, Advisory Committee, UNDP Arab Human Development Report, 2003; Contributor, UNDP Arab Human Development Report, 2004. Publications: Books: Medicine in the United Arab Emirates, Origin and Development, 1997; Sad Letters, A study of depression among the Arab population, 1998; 35 articles as first author and co-author in scientific medical journals including: Social Psychiatry and Psychiatric Epidemiology; Psychological Medicine; Acta Psychiatria Scandinavica; European Psychiatry; The International Journal of Social Psychiatry and Psychological Reports. Honours include: Rashid Award for Scientific Excellence, 1988, 1992; Al Awis 1st Prize for Research, 1994, 1995; Award of Education, Datamatix, United Arab Emirates, 2002; Shaikh Hamdan Bin Rashid Al-Maktoum Award for Medical Sciences, 2004. Memberships include: Emirates Medical Association, 1983-; Fellow, Royal College of Medicine, 1989-91; General Medical Council, UK, 1997-; Bahrain Centre for Studies and Research Trustees Council; Arab Though

Foundation. Address: Arabian Gulf University, PO Box 26671, Adlya, Kingdom of Bahrain. E-mail: rafia@agu.edu.bh

**GIACCONI Riccardo,** b. 6 October 1931, Genoa, Italy (US Citizen). Astrophysicist. m. Mirella Manaira, 1957, 1 son, 2 daughters. Education: Doctorate, University of Milan, 1954. Appointments: Assistant Professor of Physics, University of Milan, 1954-56; Research Associate, Indiana University, 1956-58; Research Associate, Princeton University, 1958-59; American Science and Engineering Inc, 1958-73; Associate, Harvard College Observatory, 1970-72; Associate Director, Center for Astrophysics, 1973-81; Professor of Astrophysics, Harvard University, 1973-81; Professor of Astrophysics, 1981-99, Research Professor, 1999-, Johns Hopkins University; Director, Space Telescope Science Institute, Baltimore, 1981-92; Professor of Astrophysics, Milan University, Italy, 1991-99; Director General, European Southern Observatory, Garching, Germany, 1993-99; President, Associated Universities Inc, 1999-; Carried out fundamental investigations in the development of x-ray astronomy. Publications X-Ray Astronomy (co-editor), 1974; Physics and Astrophysics of Neutron Stars and Black Holes (co-editor), 1978; A Face of Extremes: The X-ray Universe (co-editor), 1985; Numerous articles in professional journals. Honours: Space Science Award, AIAA, 1976; NASA Medal for Exceptional Scientific Achievement, 1980; Gold Medal, Royal Astronomical Society, 1982; A Cressy Morrison Award in Natural Sciences, New York Academy of Sciences, 1982; Wolf Prize, 1987; Laurea hc in Physics, Rome, 1998; Nobel Prize in Physics, 2002; Numerous other awards. Memberships: American Academy of Arts and Sciences; American Astronomical Society; American Physical Society; Italian Physical Society; International Astronomical Union; Max Planck Society; Foreign member, Accademia Nazionale dei Lincei. Address: Associated Universities Inc, 1400 16th Street, NW, Suite 730, Washington, DC 20036, USA.

**GIANFRANCESCO Fernando,** b. 11 May 1968, Piedimonte Matese (CE), Italy. Scientist. m. Teresa Esposito, 3 sons. Education: Degree in Biology, "Federico II" University of Naples, 1994; PhD, Morphological Human Sciences, University of Bologna, Italy, 2000. Appointments: Biomedical Researcher, Human Genetics, International Institute of Genetics and Biophysics, Italian National Research Council; Visiting Scientist, National Institute of Aging, National Institutes of Health, Baltimore, USA; Scientist Researcher, first Italian genomics research company, 2001-2002; Scientist Researcher, Italian National Research Council, 2002-. Publications: Many articles on human genome evolution and human genetic diseases in professional scientific journals; Patents for diagnostic methods for human genetic diseases. Honours: Speaker at numerous national and international conferences and seminars; Listed in Who's Who publications and biographical dictionaries. Memberships: Italian Society of Human Genetics; American Society of Human Genetics. Address: Via Restaurazione N 46, 81014, Fontegreca, Caserta, Italy. E-mail: fgianfrancesco @isa.cnr.it

**GIBB Barry,** b. 1 September 1947, Isle of Man, emigrated to Australia, 1958, returned to UK, 1967. Singer and Songwriter. m. Linda Gray, 4 children. Career: Formed Bee Gees with brothers Robin and the late Maurice and Andy. Publications: Albums with BeeGees include: Bee Gees 1st; Odessa; Main Course; Children of the World; Saturday Night Fever; Spirits Having Flown; High Civilisation; Size Isn't Everything; Still Waters; One Night Only; This Is Where I Came In; Their Greatest Hits – The Record; Singles include; NY Mining Disaster 1941; Massachusetts; To Love Somebody; Holiday; I've Gotta Get a Message to You; I Started a Joke; Lonely Days; How Can You

Mend a Broken Heart; Jive Talkin'; Staying Alive; Night Fever; How Deep Is Your Love; Too Much Heaven; Tragedy; Love You Inside Out; One; You Win Again; First of May; Writer of songs for other artists including: Elvis Presley (Words); Sarah Vaughn (Run To Me); Al Green, Janis Joplin, Barbara Streisand (Guilty album); Diana Ross (Chain Reaction); Dionne Warwick (Heartbreaker); Dolly Parton and Kenny Rogers (Island in the Stream); Ntrance (staying Alive)Take That (How Deep is Your Love); Boyzone (Words); Yvonne Elliman (If I Can't Have You). Honours: 7 Grammy Awards; elected to Rock and Roll Hall of Fame, 1996; International Achievement, 1997; 5th most successful recording artists ever, have sold over 100 million records worldwide. Address: c/o Middle Ear, Studio, 1801 Bay Road, Miami Beach, FL 33139, USA.

**GIBB Robin,** b. 22 December 1949, Isle of Man, emigrated to Australia, 1958, returned to UK 1967. Singer and Songwriter. m. Divina Murphy, 1 son. Career: Formed Bee Gees with brothers Barry, and the late Maurice and Andy. Publications: Albums with the Bee Gees include: Bee Gees 1st; Odessa; Main Course; Children of the World; Saturday Night Fever; Spirits Having Flown; High Civilisation; Size Isn't Everything; Still Waters; One Night Only; Their Greatest Hits – The Record; Solo album: Magnet, 2003; Singles include: NY Mining Disaster 1941; Massachusetts; To Love Somebody; Holiday; I've Gotta Get a Message to You; I Started a Joke; Lonely Days; How Can You Mend a Broken Heart; Jive Talkin'; Stayin' Alive; Night Fever; How Deep Is Your Love; Too Much Heaven; Tragedy; Love You Inside Out; One; You Win Again; First of May; Writer, songs for other artists including: Elvis Presley (Words); Sarah Vaughn (Run to Me); Al Green, Janis Joplin, Ntrance (Stayin' Alive); Take That (How Deep is Your Love); Boyzone (Words); Yvonne Elliman (If I Can't Have You). Honours: 7 Grammy awards; Elected to Rock and Roll Hall of Fame, 1996; International Achievement Award, American Music Awards, 1997; Brit Award for Outstanding Contribution to Music, 1997; World Music Award for Lifetime Achievement, 1997; 5th most successful recording artists ever, have sold 100 million records worldwide. Address: Middle Ear, 1801 Bay Road, Miami, FL 33139, USA.

**GIBB Thomas R P,** b. 10 February 1916, Belmont, Massachusetts, USA. Retired Professor. m. (1) 1 son, 1 daughter, (2) Reen Meergans. Education: BS, Bowdoin College, 1936; PhD, Chemistry, MIT, 1940. Appointments: Instructor, Assistant Professor, MIT; Professor, Tufts University; Emeritus Professor, 1980. Publications: 2 books; Several papers. Honours: Phi Beta Kappa; Alpha Chi Sigma; Fellow, Sigma Xi and AAAS. Memberships: American Chemical Society; American Association for the Advancement of Science. Address: 55 Main St, Dover, MA 02030, USA.

**GIBSON Mel,** b. 3 January 1956, Peekshill, New York, USA. Actor; Producer. m. Robyn Moore, 5 sons, 1 daughter. Education: National Institute for Dramatic Art, Sydney. Career: Founder, ICONS Productions; Actor, films include: Summer City; Mad Max, 1979; Tim, 1979; Attack Force Z; Gallipoli, 1981; The Road Warrior (Mad Max II), 1982; The Year of Living Dangerously, 1983; The Bounty, 1984; The River, 1984; Mrs Soffel, 1984; Mad Max Beyond the Thunderdome, 1985; Lethal Weapon; Tequila Sunrise; Lethal Weapon II; Bird on a Wire, 1989; Hamlet, 1990; Air America, 1990; Lethal Weapon III, 1991; Man Without a Face (also director), 1992; Maverick, 1994; Braveheart (also director, co-producer), 1995; Ransom, 1996; Conspiracy Theory, 1997; Lethal Weapon 4, 1998; Playback, 1997; The Million Dollar Hotel, 1999; The Patriot, 2000; What Women Want, 2000; We Were Soldiers, 2002; Signs, 2002; The Singing Detective, 2003; Paparazzi,

2004; Plays include: Romeo and Juliet; Waiting for Godot; No Names No Pack Drill; Death of a Salesman. Honours include: Commandeur, Ordre des Arts et des Lettres. Address: c/o ICONS Productions, 4000 Warner Boulevard, Room 17, Burbank, CA 91522, USA.

**GIBSON OF MARKET RASEN, Baroness of Market Rasen in the County of Lincolnshire, Anne Gibson,** b. 10 December 1940, United Kingdom. m. (1) John Donald Gibson, 1 daughter, (2) John Bartell, 1 stepdaughter. Education: BA, University of Essex. Appointments: Full-time Organiser, Labour Party, Saffron Walden, 1965-70; Researcher, House Magazine (journal of Houses of Parliament), 1975-77; Party Candidate, Labour, Bury St Edmunds, 1979; Assistant, Assistant Secretary and Deputy Head of Organisation and Industrial Relations Department, TUC, 1977-87; National Officer Amicus, with special responsibility for voluntary sector and equal rights sections, 1987-96, policy and political work, 1996-2000; Member: General Council, TUC, 1989-2000; Trade Union Sustainable Development Committee; Department of Employment Advisory Group on Older Workers, 1993-96; Board, Bilbao Agency, 1996-2000; Parliamentary and Scientific Committee; Labour Party: NEC Women's Committee, 1990-98, National Constitutional Committee, 1997-2000, Labour Party Policy Reform, 1998-2000; Subcommittees in the House of Lords: Foreign and Commonwealth Affairs Group, Home Affairs Group, Defence Group; Member, BBC Charter Review Group; Equal Opportunities Commissioner, 1991-98, Health and Safety Commissioner, 1996-2000; Member All-Party Parliamentary Groups: Adoption, Brazil, Bullying at Work, Arts and Heritage, Asbestos Sub-Committee, Asthma, BBC, Breast Cancer, Children, Countryside, Fibromualgia, Insurance and Financial Services, Latin America, Rail Freight, Safety and Health, Sex Equality, TU(nion) Group of MP's, Wildlife Protection, World Government. Publications: Numerous TUC and MSF equal opportunities booklets including: Disability and Employer – A Trade Union Guide, 1989; Charter of Equal Opportunities for 1990's, 1990; Lesbian and gay Rights in Employment, 1990; recruitment of Women Workers, 1990; Part-time Workers Rights, 1991; Sexual Harassment at Work, 1993; Caring – A Union Issue, 1993; Women in MSF, 1991. Honours: OBE, 1998; Life Peer, 2000. Memberships: Chair, Andrea Adams Trust, 2002-2004; President, RoSPA; Chair, DTI Dignity at Work Group; Fawcett Society; Fabian Society. Address: House of Lords, London SW1A 0PW, England.

**GIDDENS Anthony,** b. 18 January 1938. University Administrator; Sociologist. m. Jane M Ellwood, 1963. Education; Hull University; London School of Economics; Cambridge University. Appointments: Lecturer, late Reader, Sociology, University of Cambridge, 1969-85; Professor of Sociology, 1985-97; Fellow, King's College, 1969-96; Director, London School of Education, 1997-2003. Publications: Capitalism and Modern Social Theory, 1971; Ed, Sociology of Suicide, 1972; Politics and Sociology in the Thought of Max Weber, 1972; Editor and translator, Emile Durkheim: Selected Writings, 1972; Ed, Positivism and Sociology, 1974; New Rules of Sociological Method, 1976; Studies in Social and Political Theory, 1976; Central Problems in Social Theory, 1979; Class Structure of the Advanced Societies (2nd editor), 1981; Contemporary Critique of Historical Materialism (vol 1), Power, Property and State, 1981, (vol 2), Nation, State and Violence, 1985; Jointly, Classes, Power and Conflict, 1982; Profiles and Critiques in Social Theory, 1983; Joint editor, Social Class and the Division of Labour, 1983; Constitution of Society, 1984; Social Theory and Modern Sociology, 1987; Joint editor, Social Theory Today, 1987; Sociology, 1989; The Consequences of Modernity, 1990; Modernity and Self-Identity, 1991; The Transformation of Intimacy, 1992; Beyond Right and Left, 1994; In Defence of

Sociology, 1996; Third Way, 1998. Honours include: Prince of Asturias Award, Spain, 2002. Address: London School of Economics, Houghton Street, London, WC2A 2AE, England.

**GIELEN Uwe Peter,** b. 15 August 1940, Berlin, Germany. Professor of Psychology. Education: MA, Psychology, Wake Forest University, 1968; PhD, Social Psychology, Harvard University, USA, 1976. Appointments: Assistant Professor of Psychology, City University of New York, 1977-80; Associate Professor, 1980-87, Professor, 1987-, Chairman, 1980-90, Director, Institute for International and Cross-Cultural Psychology, 1998-, St Francis College, New York, USA. Publications: 15 books; 100 other publications; Editor-in-Chief, World Psychology, 1995-97, International Journal of Group Tensions, 1997-2002; Co-editor, Psychology in the Arab Countries; International Perspectives on Human Development; The Family and Family Therapy in International Perspective; Cross-Cultural Topics in Psychology; Migration: Immigration and Emigration in International Perspective; Handbook of Culture, Therapy and Healing; Families in Global Perspective; Childhood and Adolescence. Honours: Kurt Lewin Award, 1993, Wilhelm Wundt Award, 1999, New York State Psychological Association. Memberships: Fellow, American Psychological Association; Fellow, American Psychological Society; President, International Council of Psychologists, 1994-95; President, Society for Cross-Cultural Research, 1998-99. Address: Department of Psychology, St Francis College, Brooklyn, NY 11201, USA. E-mail: ugielen@hotmail.com

**GIESY John Paul,** b. 9 August 1948, Youngstown, Ohio, USA. Professor. m. Susan Elaine Damerell, 1 daughter. Education: BS, Summa Cum Laude, Honours, Biology, Alma College, 1970; MS, Limnology, 1971, PhD, Limnology, 1974, Michigan State University. Appointments include: Adjunct Assistant Professor, Zoology, 1976-80, Graduate Faculty, 1976-80, Ecology Faculty, 1978-80, University of South Carolina, Aitken Campus; Adjunct Assistant Professor of Biology, 1978-81; Adjunct Assistant Professor of Environmental Engineering, 1978-81; Pesticide Research Center, 1981-87; Professor of Fisheries and Wildlife, 1985-97, currently Distinguished Professor of Zoology, Professor of Veterinary Medicine, Michigan State University; Concurrent appointments include: Center for Integrative Toxicology, 1981-, Center for Hazardous Waste Management, 1990-, National Food Safety and Toxicology Center, 1997-; Visiting Scientist: Office of Water, Soil and Air Hygiene, Federal Republic of Germany, Berlin, 1989, Italian Hydrobiological Institute, Italian National Research Council, Pallanza, Italy, 1989-90; Biological Research Station of Helgoland, List/Sylt, Germany, 1993; Visiting Professor, Chair of Ecological Chemistry and Geochemistry, University of Bayreuth, Germany, 1987-88; Chair Professor at Large of Biology and Chemistry, City University of Hong Kong; Professor of Environmental Science, Nanjing University, China. Publications: 5 books include: Microcosms in Ecological Research; Sediments: The Chemistry and Toxicology of In-Place Pollutants; Editor, 6 books; 499 peer reviewed articles in scientific journals as author and co-author; 767 lectures world-wide. Honours include: Chevron Distinguished Lecture, University of California-Davis, 1989; Sigma Xi Meritorious Research Award, 1990; CIBA GEIGY Agricultural Recognition Award, 1990; Willard F. Shepard Award, Michigan Water Pollution Control Association, 1992; Distinguished Professor Award, Michigan State University, 1993; Quintessence Award, 1994; Vollenweider Environmental science Award, 1994; Numerous awards for papers; Founders Award, Society of Environmental Toxicology and Chemistry, 1995; SETAC/Menzie-Curra Environmental Education Award, 2002; 5th most cited author in the field of Ecology/Enviromental Science, 1994-2004; Listed in Who's Who Publications and biographical dictionaries. Memberships include: International Association for Sediment and Water Science; International Association of Great Lakes Research; Sigma Xi; Society of Environmental Toxicology and Chemistry; SETAC Foundation for Environmental Education; American Association for the Advancement of Science; American Chemical Society; American College of Toxicology; American Fisheries Society; American Institute of Biological Sciences; International Water Association. Address: Department of Zoology, Natural Science Building, Michigan State University, East Lancing, MI 48824-122, USA. E-mail: jgiesy@aol.com

**GIFFORD Zerbanoo,** b. 11 May 1950, India. Foundation Director. m. Richard Gifford, 2 sons. Education: Roedean School; Watford College of Technology; London School of Journalism; BA Honours, Open University. Appointments: Director ASHA Foundation; National Endowment of Science, Technology and Arts Fellowship; Adviser to Rt. Hon. Jack Straw on Community Relations at the Home Office; Director Anti-Slavery International. Publications: The Golden Thread – Asian Experiences in Post Raj Britain; Thomas Clarkson and the Campaign Against Slavery; Dadabhai Naoroji – The 1st Asian MP; Celebrating India; Asian Presence in Europe. Honours: Nehru Centenary Award for international work championing the cause of women and children; Freedom of City of Lincoln, Nebraska for work against all forms of slavery and racism. Address: Herga House, London Road, Harrow on the Hill, Middlesex HA1 3JJ, England. E-mail: zerbanoo gifford@hotmail.com

**GIL David Georg,** b. 16 March 1924, Vienna, Austria. Professor of Social Policy; Author. m. Eva Breslauer, 2 August 1947, 2 sons. Education: Certificate in Psychotherapy with Children, Israeli Society for Child Psychiatry, 1952; Diploma in Social Work, School of Social Work, 1953, BA, 1957, Hebrew University, Jerusalem, Israel; MSW, 1958, DSW, 1963, University of Pennsylvania. Appointment: Professor of Social Policy, Brandeis University. Publications: Violence Against Children, 1970; Unravelling Social Policy, 1973, 5th edition, 1992; The Challenge of Social Equality, 1976; Beyond the Jungle, 1979; Child Abuse and Violence (editor), 1979; Toward Social and Economic Justice (editor with Eva Gil), 1985; The Future of Work (editor with Eva Gil), 1987; Confronting Injustice and Oppression, 1998. Contributions to: Over 50 articles to professional journals, book chapters, book reviews. Honours: Leadership in Human Services, Brandeis University, Heller School, 1999; Social Worker of the Year, National Association of Social Workers, Massachusetts, 2000; Mentoring Award, Brandeis University, Heller School, 2005. Memberships: National Association of Social Workers; American Orthopsychiatric Association; Association of Humanist Sociology. Address: Heller School, Brandeis University, Waltham, MA 02454-9110, USA.

**GILBERT Anthony,** b. 26 July 1934, London, England. 2 sons, 1 daughter. Composer. Education: MA, DMus, University of Leeds; Composition with Anthony Milner, Matyas Seiber, Alexander Goehr and Gunther Schuller; Conducting with Lawrence Leonard, Morley College, London. Career: Lecturer in Composition, Goldsmiths College, 1968-73; Composer in Residence, University of Lancaster, 1970-71; Lecturer in Composition, Morley College, 1972-75; Senior Lecturer in Composition, Sydney Conservatorium, Australia, 1978-79; Composer in Residence, City of Bendigo, Victoria, 1981; Senior Tutor in Composition, Royal Northern College of Music, 1973-96; Head of School of Composition and Contemporary Music, Royal Northern College of Music, 1996-99. Compositions: Operas: The Scene-Machine, The Chakravaka-Bird; Orchestra:

Symphony; Sinfonia; Ghost and Dream Dancing; Crow Cry; Towards Asavari; On Beholding a Rainbow; Sheer; Wind orchestra: Dream Carousels; Chamber: 4 string quartets; Saxophone Quartet; Quartet of Beasts; Nine or Ten Osannas; Vasanta With Dancing; Palace of the Winds; Instrumental: Ziggurat; Reflexions, Rose Nord; Moonfaring; Dawnfaring; 3 Piano Sonatas; Spell Respell; The Incredible Flute Music; Treatment of Silence; Osanna for Lady O; Farings; Stars; Rose luisante; Vocal: Certain Lights Reflecting; Love Poems; Inscapes; Long White Moonlight; Beastly Jingles; Vers de Lune; Music Theatre: Upstream River Rewa. Recordings: Moonfaring; Beastly Jingles; Nine or Ten Osannas; Towards Asavari; Dream Carousels; Igorochki; Quartet of Beasts; Six of the Bestiary; Quartet No 3; Farings; Oh Beholding a Rainbow; Certain Lights Reflecting; ... into the Gyre of a Madder Dance; Unrise. Honours: Fellow of Royal Northern College of Music, 1981. Memberships: Society for the Promotion of New Music; Performing Right Society; Mechanical Copyright Protection Society; British Academy of Composers and Songwriters. Address: 4 Oak Brow Cottages, Altrincham Road, Styal, Wilmslow, Cheshire SK9 4JE, England.

**GILBERT Robert Andrew,** b. 6 October 1942, Bristol, England. Antiquarian Bookseller; Editor; Writer. m. Patricia Kathleen Linnell, 20 June 1970, 3 sons, 2 daughters. Education: BA, Honours, Philosophy, Psychology, University of Bristol, 1964. Appointment: Editor, Ars Quatuor Coronatorum, 1994-2000. Publications: The Golden Dawn: Twilight of the Magicians, 1983; A E Waite: A Bibliography, 1983; The Golden Dawn Companion, 1986; A E Waite: Magician of Many Parts, 1987; The Treasure of Montsegur (with W N Birks), 1987; Elements of Mysticism, 1991; World Freemasonry: An Illustrated History, 1992; Freemasonry: A Celebration of the Craft (J M Hamill), 1992; Casting the First Stone, 1993; Editor with M A Cox: The Oxford Book of English Ghost Stories, 1986; Victorian Ghost Stories: An Oxford Anthology, 1991; The Golden Dawn Scrapbook, 1997; Editor, The House of the Hidden Light, 2003. Contributions to: Ars Quatuor Coronatorum; Avallaunius; Christian Parapsychologist; Dictionary of National Biography; Dictionary of 19th Century British Scientists; Dictionary of Gnosis and Western Esotericism; Gnosis; Hermetic Journal; Cauda Pavonis; Yeats Annual. Memberships: Society of Authors; Librarian, Supreme Council for England and Wales (A&A Rite); Prestonian Lecturer, United Grand Lodge of England, 1997. Address: 4 Julius Road, Bishopston, Bristol BS7 8EU, England.

**GILBERT Walter,** b. 21 March 1932, Boston, Massachusetts, USA. Molecular Biologist. m. Celia Stone, 1953, 1 son, 1 daughter. Education: Graduated, Physics, Harvard University, 1954; Doctorate in Mathematics, Cambridge University, 1957. Appointments: National Science Foundation Fellow, 1957-58; Lecturer, Research Fellow, 1958-59, Professor of Biophysics, 1964-68, Professor of Molecular Biology, 1969-72, American Cancer Society Professor of Molecular Biology, 1972, Harvard University; Devised techniques for determining the sequence of bases in DNA. Honours: US Steel Foundation Award in Molecular Biology (NAS), 1968; Joint Winner, Ledlie Prize, Harvard University, 1969; Joint winner, Warren Triennial Prize, Massachusetts General Hospital, 1977; Louis and Bert Freedman Award, New York Academy of Sciences, 1977; Joint winner, Prix Charles-Léopold Mayer, Académie des Sciences, Institute de France, 1977; Harrison Howe Award of the Rochester branch of the American Chemical Society, 1978; Joint winner, Louisa Gross Horowitz Prize, Columbia University, 1979; Gairdner Foundation Annual Award 1979; Joint winner, Albert Lasker Basic Medical Research Award, 1979; Joint winner, Prize for Biochemical Analysis, German Society for Clinical Chemistry,

# DICTIONARY OF INTERNATIONAL BIOGRAPHY

1980; Sober Award, American Society of Biological Chemists, 1980; Joint Winner, Nobel Prize for Chemistry, 1980; New England Entrepreneur of the Year Award, 1991; Ninth National Biotechnology Ventures Award, 1997. Memberships: Foreign member, Royal Society; NAS; American Physical Society; American Society of Biological Chemists; American Academy of Arts and Sciences. Address: Biological Laboratories, 16 Divinity Avenue, Cambridge, MA 02138, USA.

**GILFANOV Marat,** b. 18 July 1962, Kazan, USSR. Astrophysicist. m. Marina Gilfanova, 1 daughter. Education: Diploma Physics, Moscow Physical-Technical Institute, 1985; PhD, Physics, Space Research Institute, Moscow, 1989; Doctor of Physics and Mathematics, Space Research Institute, Moscow, 1996. Appointments: Junior Scientist, Space Research Institute, Moscow, 1985-88; Scientist, 1988-91; Senior Scientist, 1991-96; Leading Scientist, 1996-; Max-Planck-Institut für Astrophysik, Garching, Germany, 1996-. Publications: Over 200 in international scientific journals. Honours: COSPAR, Commission E Zeldovich medal, 1992. Memberships: COSPAR, Commission E; International Astronomical Union, 1994-; Scientific Council of Space Research Institute, 1997-; Wissenschaftlicher Institutsrat, Max-Planck-Institut für Astrophysik. Address: Max-Planck-Institut für Astrophysik, Karl-Schwarzschild-Str 1, 85741 Garching, Germany.

**GILL, Sir Ben,** b. 1 January 1950. Company Director. m. Carolyn Davis, 4 sons. Education: Barnard Castle School, Co Durham, 1960-67; General Agriculture degree, St John's College, Cambridge, 1968-71. Appointments: Worked on family farm, North Yorkshire, 1971; Teacher of science and agriculture, Namasagali College, Uganda, East Africa, 1972-75; Ran 200 sow pig unit, Holderness, East Yorkshire, 1975-77; Family farming business, North Yorkshire, 1978-. Honours: CBE, 1996; Visiting Professorship, Department of Biology, Leeds University, 1996; Fellow, Royal Agriculture Society, 1997; Honorary DSc, Leeds University, 1997; Fellow, Institute of Grocery Distribution, 1998; Honorary DSc, Cranfield University, 2000; Honorary DSc, University of West England, 2002; Honorary D, Civil Law University of East Anglia, 2003. Memberships: Parent Governor, Easingwold County Primary School, 1982-88; Member, Vice Chairman, 1985-86, NFU National Marketing Committee, 1984-87; Member, NFU National Council, 1985-2004; Member, Vice Chairman, 1986-87, Chairman, 1987-2001, National Livestock and Wool Committee, 1985-2001; Vice President, NFU, 1991-92; Deputy President, NFU, 1992-98; President, NFU, 1998-2004; Member, Agriculture and Food Research Council, 1991-94; Member, Chairman of Agricultural Systems Directorate, Biotechnology and Biological Sciences Research Council, 1994-97; Founder and Chairman, Alternative Crops Technology Interaction Network, 1994-2004; OST Technology Foresight, 1994-99; Director of FARM Africa, 1991-98; Executive Member, International Federation of Agricultural Producers, 1998-2004; Member, Council of Food from Britain, 1999-2005; Vice President, Comitee des Organisations Professionelles des Agriculteurs, 1999-2003; President, Confederation of European Agriculture, 2000-04; Member, Governing Council of the John Innes Centre, Norwich, 2002-; Patron: Pentalk, Farmers Overseas Action Group, Plants & Us, Rural Stress Information Network, St John's Ambulance Bricks and Wheels Appeal. Address: Home Farm, Hawkhills, Easingwold, York, North Yorkshire YO61 3EG, England. E-mail: sirbengill@wngill.demon.co.uk

**GILL Christopher J F,** b. 28 October 1936, Wolverhampton, England. m. Patricia M, 1 son, 2 daughters. Education: Birchfield Preparatory School, 1944-50; Shrewsbury School, 1950-54. Appointments: Ordinary Seaman, Royal Naval Reserve, 1952-

55; Joined family meat processing and wholesaling business, F A Gill Ltd, 1959, currently Chairman of the company; Member, Wolverhampton Borough Council, 1965-72; Chairman, Public Works Committee, 1967-69; Chairman, Local Education Authority, 1969-70; Retired as Lieutenant Commander, RNR, 1979; Active member, West Midlands Conservative Associations; Past President, Midlands West European Conservative Council; Elected Member of Parliament for Ludlow, 1987; Former Vice-Chairman, Conservative European Affairs Committee; Vice-Chairman, Conservative Agriculture Committee, 1991-94; Member, Agriculture Select Committee, 1989-94; Member, Welsh Affairs Select Committee, 1995-97; Member, Council of Europe, 1997-99; Past President, Meat Training Council; Past President, British Pig Association. Publications: Whips' Nightmare – Diary of a Maastricht Rebel, 2003. Memberships: Chairman, The Freedom Association. Honours: Reserve Decoration, 1971; Liveryman, Worshipful Company of Butchers; Freeman of the City of London. Address: Billingsley Hall Farm, Bridgnorth, Shropshire, WV16 6PJ, England. E-mail: freedom@christopher-gill.co.uk

**GILLARD David Owen,** b. 8 February 1947, Croydon, Surrey, England. Writer; Critic. m. Valerie Ann. Education: Tavistock School, Croydon, Surrey. Appointments: Scriptwriter and Assistant Director, Associated British Pathé, 1967-70; Film and Theatre Critic, Daily Sketch, 1970-71; Ballet Critic, Daily Mail, 1971-88; Instituted drama preview pages, The Listener, 1982; Founder-Editor, English National Opera Friends Magazine, 1983-92; Radio Correspondent, Radio Times, 1984-91; Classical Music Editor, Radio Times, 2001-2003; Opera Critic, Daily Mail, 1971-. Publications: Play: Oh Brothers! 1971; Beryl Grey: A Biography, 1977. Memberships: National Union of Journalists; Critics Circle; Broadcasting Press Guild. Address: 1 Hambledon Court, 18 Arundel Way, Highcliffe, Christchurch, Dorset, BH23 5DX, England.

**GILLHAM Paul Maurice,** b. 26 November 1931, Carshalton, Surrey, England. Company Director. m. Jane Pickering, 2 sons, 1 daughter. Education: Royal College of Music, 1950-52; Guildhall School of Music, 1954-55; BA,MA, Christ's College, Cambridge. Appointments: Unilever, 1958-70; Chairman, Keith Prowse Group, 1970-80; Chairman, Deyong Golding Ltd, 1984-92; Chairman, Cathedral Capital Plc, 1997-; Director, Wren Underwriting Agencies Ltd, 1993-97; Daisy Chain (Hair and Beauty) Ltd, 1997-. Honours: MA (Cantab); LGSM. Address: Edmonds Farmhouse, Gumshall, Guildford, Surrey GY5 9LQ, England.

**GILLIAM Terry Vance,** b. 22 November 1940, Minnesota, USA. Animator; Film Director; Actor; Illustrator; Writer. m. Margaret Weston, 1 son, 2 daughters. Education: BA, Occidental College. Appointments: Associate Editor, HELP! magazine, 1962-64; Freelance illustrator, 1964-65; Advertising copywriter/art director, 1966-67; with Monty Python's Flying Circus (UK), 1969-76; Animator: And Now For Something Completely Different (film); Co-director, actor, Monty Python and the Holy Grail; Director, Jabberwocky; Designer, actor, animator, Monty Python's Meaning of Life (film), 1983; Co-writer, director, Brazil, 1985; The Adventures of Baron Munchausen, 1988; Director, The Fisher King (film), 1991; Twelve Monkeys, 1996; Presenter, TV series: The Last Machine, 1995; Executive Producer, Monty Python's Complete Waste of Time, 1995; Director and co-writer, Fear and Loathing in Las Vegas, 1998; Executive Producer, Monty Python's Complete Waste of time (CD-Rom), 1995; Appeared in Lost in La Mancha, documentary, 2002; Director and co-writer, The Brothers Grimm (film), 2005; Director and co-writer, Tideland (film), 2005. Publications: Monty Python's Big Red Book; Monty

Python's Paperback, 1977; Monty Python's Scrapbook, 1979; Animations of Mortality, 1979; Monty Python's The Meaning of Life; Monty Python's Flying Circus - Just the Words (co-ed), 1989; DFA (hon), Occidental College, 1987; The Adventures of Baron Munchausen, 1989; Not the Screenplay or Fear and Loathing in Las Vegas, 1998; Gilliam on Gilliam, 1999; Dark Knights and Holy Fools, 1999; The Pythons Autobiography by the Pythons, 2003. Honour: Hon DFA, Occidental College, 1987; Hon DFA, Royal College of Art, London, 1988; Honorary Dr of Arts, Wimbledon School of Art, 2004. Address: c/o Jenne Casarotto, National House, 60-66 Wardour Street, London, W1V 4ND, England.

**GILLIS Richard,** b. 22 April 1950, Dundee, Scotland. Solicitor; Managing Director. m. Ruth J P Garden. Education: Admitted as a Solicitor, 1975; Kenya Advocate, 1978. Appointments: Solicitor, Greater London Council, 1975-77; Solicitor, Archer & Wilcock, Nairobi, Kenya, 1977-80; Shoosmiths, 1980-81; Assistant to the Secretary, TI Group plc, 1981-85; Secretary, ABB Transportation Holdings Ltd (British Rail Engineering Ltd until privatisation), Trustee, Company Pension Scheme, 1985-95; Clerk to the Council and Company Secretary, University of Derby, 1995-2002; Managing Director, family investment companies, 2001-; Secretary, Justice report on perjury; Director then Vice-Chairman, Crewe Development Agency, 1992-95; The Order of St John: Chairman, Property Committee, Derbyshire Council of the Order of St John, 1994-2003; Trustee, Priory of England and the Islands of the Order of St John and Trustee, St John Ambulance, 1999-2003; Chairman, Audit Committee and Priory Regulations Committee, Regional Member of Priory Chapter, 1999-2005; Court of Assistants, Worshipful Company of Basketmakers, 2004-. Honours: OStJ, 1999; Honorary Life Member, Court of the University of Derby, 2003. Memberships: CBI East Midlands Regional Council, 1993-95; Stakeholders' Forum, Derby City Challenge, 1993-98; Guild of Freemen of the City of London; Provincial Grand Lodge of Warwickshire; Bonnetmaker Craft of Dundee; Maccabæans; FRSA; Clubs: Athenæum; City Livery; New (Edinburgh). Address: 2 St Fort Road, Wormit, Newport-on-Tay, Fife, DD6 8LA, Scotland.

**GILLY François-Noel,** b. 1 May 1955, Lyon, France. University Surgeon. 2 daughters. Education: Medical Doctor, 1984; Digestive Surgeon, 1986. Appointments: Surgeon, civil hospitals in Lyon, 1986-; University Professor, 1995; Dean of Medical Faculty, Lyon University, 1999-. Publications: Articles in professional medical journals. Honours: Chevalier des Palmes Academiques; Prix Patey Mathieu; Prix A Ponet. Memberships: Academie Nationale de Chirugie; ICHS; ISIORT; IAGS; AFC. Address: Department of Surgery, Lyon University CHLS, 69495 Pierre Benite Cedex, France. E-mail: francogi@lyon-sud.univ-lyon1.fr

**GILMOUR Pat (McGuire),** b. 19 March 1932, Woodford, Essex, England. Art Historian; Curator. m. Alexander Tate Gilmour, 2 daughters. Education: Sculpture, Glasgow School of Art, 1956-58; Distinction in Art and in Theory of Education, Sidney Webb College, London, 1962-65; Diploma in Design Education, Hornsey College of Art, 1968-70; BA (Hons), History of Art and English Literature, London University, 1971-73. Appointments: Journalist, West Essex Gazette, 1949-55; Assistant to Editor, Percival Marshall Publishers, London, 1959-62; Lecturer II, in charge of Art and Design, Southwark College for Further Education, 1965-74; Founding Curator of Prints, Tate Gallery, London, 1974-77; Senior Lecturer in charge of Contextual Studies, North East London Polytechnic, 1977-79; Head of Art History and Liberal Studies, Central School of Art & Design, London, 1979-81; Senior and Founding Curator in charge of the Department of International Prints & Illustrated

Books, National Gallery of Australia, Canberra, 1981-89; Free-lance Art Historian and Curator, 1990-; Expert Witness on Picasso: Kornfeld v Tunick, 1993; Member of Editorial Board, Print Quarterly, 1996-; Selector and Cataloguer of numerous exhibitions in Great Britain and Australia, 1972-99; Member of many Print Biennale Juries and President of the Ljubljana Jury, 1993. Publications include: Modern Prints, 1970; Henry Moore, Graphics in the Making, 1975; Artists at Curwen, 1977; Artists in Print, BBC TV series, 1981; Ken Tyler: Master Printer, 1986; Lasting Impressions: Lithography as Art, editor and contributor, 1988; The Life and Work of Shikō Munakata, captions and essay, 1991; Innovation in Collaborative Printmaking: Kenneth Tyler 1963-1992, 1993; Numerous entries for the Macmillan Dictionary of Art. Honours: Ken Tyler gift of prints presented to the Tate Gallery in her honour, 2004. Memberships include: Committee, Institute of Contemporary Arts, London, 1979-81; Committee, Print Council of Australia, 1983-89; Guest Editor, The Tamarind Papers, 1990; Contributor and member, Editorial Board, Print Quarterly, 1986-. Address: 3 Christchurch Square, Victoria Park, London E9 7HU, England.

**GINGRICH Newt (Newton Leroy),** b. 17 June 1943, Harrisburg, USA. American Politician. m. (2) Marianne Ginther, 1981, 2 daughters by previous marriage. Education: Emory and Tulane Universities. Appointments: Member, Faculty, West Georgia College, Carrollton, 1970-78, Professor of History, 1978; Member, 96-103rd Congresses from 6th District of Georgia, 1979-92; Chair, GOPAC, now Chair Emeritus; House Republican Whip, 1989; Speaker, House of Representatives, 1994-99; Adjunct Professor, Reinhardt College, Waleska, Georgia, 1994-95; Co-founder, Congressional Military Reform Caucus, Congressional Space Caucus; Chief Executive Officer, The Gingrich Group, Atlanta, 1999-; Board of Directors, Internet Policy Institute; Advisory Board, Museum of the Rockies. Publications: Window of Opportunity, 1945, 1995; To Renew America, 1995. Honour: Distinguished Visiting Scholar, National Defense University, 2001. Membership: AAAS. Address: The Committee for New American Leadership, 1800 K Street #714, Washington, DC 20006, USA.

**GINOLA David,** b. 25 January 1967, Gassin, Var, France. Professional Footballer; Sportsman. m. Coraline Delphin, 1990, 2 daughters. Career: Football clubs: 1st division Toulon clubs, 1986-87; Matraracing, Paris, 1987-88; Racing Paris 1, 1988-89; Brest-Armorique, 1989-90; Paris-Saint-Germain (French national champions, 1993-94, winners Coupe de France, 1993, 1995, winners coupe de la ligue, 1995) 1991-95; Newcastle Utd, England, 1995-97; Tottenham Hotspur, 1997-2000; Aston Villa, 2000-02; 17 international caps; Anti-landmine campaigner for Red Cross, 1998-. Honours: Football Writers' Association, Player of the Year, 1999; Professional Football Association Player of the Year, 1999. Publication: David Ginola: The Autobiography (with Niel Silver), 2000. Website: www.ginola14.com

**GINZBURG Vitaly,** b. 4 October 1916, Moscow, Russia. Physicist. m. Nina Ginzburg, 1946, 1 daughter. Education: Graduated, Physics, Moscow University, 1938, Postgraduate, Physics Institute, Academy of Sciences. Appointments: P N Lebedev Physical Institute, USSR (now Russian) Academy of Sciences, 1940-; Professor, Gorky University, 1945-68; Moscow Institute of Physics, 1968-. Publications: The Physics of a Lifetime, 2001. Honours include: Honorary DSc, Sussex, 1970; Mandelstam Prize, 1947; Lomonosov Prize, 1962; USSR State Prize, 1953; Order of Lenin, 1966; Gold Medal, Royal Astronomical Society; 1991; Bardeen Prize, 1991; Wolf Prize, 1994, 1995; Varilov Gold Medal, Russian Academy of Sciences, 1995; Lomonsov Gold Medal, Russian Academy of Sciences,

1995; UNESCO Nils Bohr Gold Medal, 1998; APS Nicholson Medal, 1998; IUPAP O'Ceallaigh Medal, 2001; Order of Lenin; many others. Memberships: Foreign Member, Royal Danish Academy of Sciences and Letters; Foreign Honorary Member, American Academy of Arts and Science; Honorary Fellow, Indian Academy of Science; Foreign Fellow, Indian National Science Academy; Foreign Associate, NAS, USA; Foreign Member, Royal Society, London; Academia Europaea. Address: P N Lebedev Physical Institute, Russian Academy of Sciences, Leninsky Prospect 53, 117924 GSP, Moscow B-333, Russia.

**GIVENCHY Hubert de,** b. 21 February 1927, Beauvais, France. Fashion Designer. Education: Ecole Nat Supérieure des Beaux-Arts, Paris; Faculté de Droit, Univ de Paris. Appointments: Apprentice, Paris fashion houses of Lucien Lelong, 1945-46, Robert Piguet, 1946-48, Jacques Fath, 1948-49, Elsa Shiaparelli, 1949-51; Established own fashion house in Parc Morceau, Paris, 1952-56, Avenue George V, 1956; President, Director-General Society Givenchy-Couture and Society des Parfums Givenchy, Paris, 1954; Honorary President, Administrative Council Givenchy SA, 1988-; President, Christie's France, 1997-; Work included in Fashion: An Anthology, Victoria & Albert Museum, London, 1971; Costume designer for films: Breakfast at Tiffany's, 1961; Charade, 1963; The VIPs, 1963; Paris When It Sizzles, 1964; How to Steal a Million, 1966. Honour: Chevalier, Légion d'honneur. Address: 3 Avenue George V, 75008 Paris, France.

**GJESSING Ketil,** b. 18 February 1934, Oslo, Norway. Education: Magister Artium and Candidatus Philologae, majoring in Literature, University of Oslo, 1965. Appointments: Teacher, Atlantic College, now United World College of the Atlantic, 1965-66; Dramaturge, Radio Drama Department of Norwegian Broadcasting Corporation, 1965-99, Retired, 2000-. Publications: Collections of poetry: Kransen om et møte, 1962; Frostjern, 1968; Private steiner bl a, 1970; Utgående post, 1975; Snøen som faller i fjor, 1977; Bjelle, malm, 1979; Vinger, røtter, 1982; Slik pila synger i lufta, 1985; Nådefrist, 1988; Dans på roser og glass, 1996; Represented in a Slovak language anthology of Norwegian poetry, German language selection of 60 poems was published in 2000; Short story published in Danish, Japanese and Swedish translation. Honours: Gyldendals legat, 1978; Språklig Samlings Literary Prize, 1995. Memberships: Norwegian Association of Writers; Norwegian Writers' Centre; Norwegian Association of Translators. Address: Dannevigsvn 12, 0463 Oslo, Norway.

**GLADWELL David John,** b. 13 March 1947, Llangynhafal, Sir Ddinbych, Wales. Head of the Civil Appeals Office; Master in the Court of Appeal, Civil Division. m. Ragnhild Kuhbier-Gladwell, 1 stepson. Education: Inns of Court School of Law; Barrister, Gray's Inn, 1972; LLM, European Legal Studies, University of Exeter, 1982; Postgraduate Diploma in Intellectual Property Law, Queen Mary and Westfield College, University of London, 1984; Accredited Mediator, Centre for Dispute Resolution. Appointments: J Henry Schroeder Wagg, Merchant Bankers, 1966-69; Practice at Bar, 1972-74; Office of the Registrar of Criminal Appeals, 1974-81; Private Law Division, 1982-88, International Division, 1988-93, Head of Law Reform Division, 1993-95, Head of Justice Division, 1995-99, Head of Senior Judicial Appointments Division, 1999-2001; Chairman, Review of Crown Immunity from Criminal Prosecution, 2001-2002; Head of Constitutional Policy Division, 2003, Lord Chancellor's Department; Head of Civil Appeals Office and Master in the Court of Appeal, Civil Division, 2003-; Chairman, Working Group on the establishment of the Patents County Court, 1986-87; Vice-Chairman, 1991-92, Chairman, 1992-93 European Committee on Legal Co-operation, Council

of Europe; Chairman, Council of Europe Working Group on Efficiency in Justice, 1998-2000; Member, Civil Justice Council, 1998-2000; Member, Working Group on a Single European Patent Court, 1999-2000; Secretary, Judicial Working Group on Ethics, 2002-2003; Member, EU Assessment Missions to Albania and Croatia; Member, Council of Europe Assessment Missions to Georgia and Montenegro, 2002. Publications: The Exhaustion of Intellectual Property Rights; Patent Litigation; The Patents County Court; Are You Ready for Woolf?; The Civil Justice Reforms in England and Wales; Modern Litigation Culture; Judicial Appointments; Manual of Civil Appeals (jointly); Alternative Dispute Resolution and the Courts. Honours: Fellow of the Society of Advanced Legal Studies. Memberships: Bencher, Gray's Inn; Executive Committee, Anglo-Russian Law Association; Advisory Council, Society for Advanced Legal Studies, Garrick Club. Address: Royal Courts of Justice, Strand, London WC1A 2LL, England. E-mail: david.gladwell@hmcourts-service.gsi.gov.uk

**GLASSMAN George M,** b. 7 September 1935, New York City, USA. Physician; Dermatologist. m. Carol Frankford, 1 son, 1 daughter. Education: BA, Brown University, Providence, Rhode Island, 1957; MD, New York University School of Medicine, New York, 1962; Rotating Internship, Greenwich Hospital, Greenwich, Connecticut, 1962-63; Dermatology Residency, New York University Medical Centre (including Bellevue Hospital, University Hospital, Skin and Cancer Unit and Manhattan VA Hospital), 1963-66. Appointments: Chief of Dermatology, LCDR, MC, US Naval Hospital, St Albans, New York, 1966-68; Private Practice in Dermatology, White Plains, New York, 1968-96; Clinical Assistant Professor, Albert Einstein College of Medicine, 1970-75; Clinical Assistant Professor, New York Medical College, 1975-87; Attending, Westchester County Medical Centre, 1974-87; Attending, White Plains Hospital, 1969-96 (Associate attending, 1969-77) (Honorary, 1996-); Associate Attending, St Agnes Hospital, White Plains, 1978-96 (Assistant attending, 1969-78) (Honorary, 1996-). Publications: 1 article, New York State Journal of Medicine. Honours: Continuing Medical Education Award of American Academy of Dermatology 1980-; Physician's Recognition Award of the American Medical Association, 1980-; Who's Who in Science and Engineering; Who's Who in the World; Who's Who in America; Who's Who in the East. Memberships: American Academy of Dermatology; New York State Society of Dermatology; Westchester County Medical Society; Westchester Academy of Medicine; AMA; Society for Paediatric Dermatology. Address: 268 Stuart Dr, New Rochelle, NY 10804-1423, USA.

**GLATTRE Eystein Junker,** b. 16 April 1934, Kristiansand, Norway. Epidemiologist. m. Ruth Lillian Jordal, 3 daughters. Education: MD, University of Oslo, 1962; Fellowship in Medical Statistics, Medical Statistics Institute, Oslo, 1965-67, Mayo Graduate School of Medicine, Rochester, USA, 1967-68; PhD, History of Ideas (Bio-temporal Structures), University of Aarhus, Denmark, 1980. Appointments: Assistant Professor, Nordic School of Public Health, Sweden, 1968-69; Consultant, Statistics Norway, 1969-70, Amanuensis, Institute of Preventive Medicine, University of Oslo, 1970-79; Senior Epidemiologist, 1980-91, Head of Department, 1992-2002, Cancer Registry of Norway; Leader of Norwegian Thyroid Cancer Project, 1985-; Board Member, Norwegian Canine Cancer Registry, 1990-2000; Professor in Epidemiology, Norwegian Veterinary College, 1992-2002; Main project since 1997 has been the development of fractal epidemiology. Publications: Around 160 papers and books on cancer research, trace element research, disease classification, cartography, vital statistics, theory of science and mathematics including: A Temporal Quantum Model, 1972; (co-author) Atlas of Cancer Incidence in Norway 1970-79, 1985; Prediagnostic s-Selenium in a Case-Control Study of Thyroid Cancer, 1989; Case-control study testing the hypothesis that seafood increases the risk of thyroid cancer, 1993; Human papillomavirus infection as a risk factor for squamous cell carcinoma of the head and neck, 2001; Fractal Analysis of a case-control study, 2002; The Norwegian Thyroid Cancer Project: History, achievements and present view on carcinogenesis, 2003; Fractal meta-analysis and causality embedded in complexity: Advanced understanding of disease aetiology, 2004. Honour: H M King Olav's Award for Young Mathematicians, 1953. Memberships: Norwegian Medical Association; Norwegian Epidemiological Association; European Thyroid Association; Czech Society for Experimental and Clinical Pharmacology and Toxicology; Society for Chaos Theory in Psychology and Life Sciences. Address: Dron Ingeborgs v 14 N-3530 Royse, Norway.

**GLAZEBROOK (Reginald) Mark,** b. 25 June 1936, Burton, Cheshire, England. Painter; Writer; Lecturer; Exhibition Organiser. m. (1) Elisabeth Claridge, 1 daughter, (2) Wanda Osinska, 1 daughter (3) Cherry Long Price. Education: BA Honours, History, Pembroke College, Cambridge University, 1956-59; Slade School of Fine Art, University College, London, 1960-61. Appointments: Exhibitions Officer, Arts Council of Great Britain and Curator of Collection of British Art, 1961-64; Lecturer, Maidstone College of Art, 1965-67; Art Critic, London Magazine, 1967-68; Director, Whitechapel Art Gallery, 1969-71; Head of Modern British Paintings and Drawings, P and P Colraghi and Co Ltd, Gallery Director and Art History Lecturer, San José State University, California, 1977-79; Director, Editions Alecto, 1979-81; Director Albemarle Gallery, 1986-93. Publications: Principal exhibition catalogues written and edited include: John Armstrong, 1957; Artists and Architecture of Bedford Park 1857-1900, 1967; David Hockney Paintings, Prints and Drawings 1960-70, 1970; The Seven and Five Society, 1979; Unitone Spirit of the 30's, 1984; Sean Scully, 1997. Honours: FRSA, 1971; Mark Twain Award, USA, 1977. Memberships: Beefsteak Club; Lansdown Club; Chelsea Arts Club. Address: Flat 1, 29 Draycott Place, London SW3 2SB, England. E-mail: rm.glazebrook@virgin.net

**GLEAVE John Reginald Wallace,** b. 6 April 1925, Coventry, England. Neurosurgeon. m. Margaret Anne Newbolt, 3 sons, 3 daughters. Education: Entrance Scholar, Uppingham, 1938; Student, Magdalen College, Oxford, 1943; Sheppard Prize Exhibition, 1945; BA (Hons School Natural Science - Physiology), 1946; Student, Radcliffe Infirmary, Oxford, 1947; Gask Clinical Prize, 1947; Radcliffe Pathology Prize, 1947; MA, BM, BCh, (Oxon), 1950; FRCS (England), 1957; MA (Cantab), 1974. Appointments: House Officer, Radcliffe Infirmary, Oxford, 1950-52; National Service: Officer in Charge of Neurological Unit, Wheatley Military Hospital, Surgical Specialist: Major, 1952-54; Served in AER as Surgeon in mobile Neurosurgical team until 1968; Registrar, Nuffield Orthopaedic Centre, 1955-56; Registrar, Professorial Surgical Unit, Liverpool, 1956-57; Senior Registrar, Neurosurgical Unit, Radcliffe Infirmary, Oxford, 1958-62; Consultant Neurosurgeon, East Anglian Neurosurgical and Head Injury Service, Addenbrooke's Hospital, Cambridge, 1962-90; College Lecturer, Neuro-Anatomy, Magdalene College, Cambridge, 1962-2000; Lecturer, Neurosurgery, Secretary of M Chir Committee, 1974-82, Examiner in Surgery, 1980-84, University of Cambridge; Examiner in Surgery, University of London, 1985-91; Currently: Consultant Neurosurgeon Emeritus, Addenbrooke's Hospital, Cambridge; Quondam Consultant Neurosurgeon, BUPA Hospital, Cambridge and Norwich; Emeritus Fellow and Praelector, St Edmund's College, Cambridge. Publications: Numerous articles in medical journals, book chapters as author

and co-author on tumours of the brain and spinal cord, head injury, surgical technique include most recently: Litigation and the Cauda Equina. Outcome after head, neck and spinal trauma: A medico-legal Guide (ed. Macfarlane and Hardy), 1997; Occipito-clival intradiploic meningocoele following skull fracture in infancy, 2001; Cauda Equina Syndrome: What is the relationship between timing of surgery and outcome? 2002. Honours: Rowed for Oxford against Cambridge, 1946-48; Olympic Rowing Squad, 1948; Rowed for Leander, 1948-49; Played rugby football for Oxfordshire and RAMC, 1948-54. Memberships: FRCS; FRSM; Society of British Neurological Surgeons; European Society for Stereotactic and Functional Neurosurgery; Worshipful Society and Mystery of Apothecaries of London; Freeman of the City of London; Vincents; Hawks; Leander; Oxford and Cambridge. Address: Riversdale, Great Shelford, Cambridge CB2 5LW, England.

**GLEBOV Dmitri Alexandrovich,** b. 29 July 1967, Kazan, Russia. Chemical Engineer. m. Elena Glebova. Education: MSc, Chemical Engineering, 1990; PhD, Chemical Engineering, 1994. Appointments: Assistant Professor, Kazan State Technology University, 1994-98; Research Engineer, Royal Institute of Technology, Stockholm, Sweden, 1998-2002; Consultant, Fredrik Setterwall Kosult AB, 2002-2004; Development Engineer, Climatewell AB, Stockholm, Sweden, 2004-. Publications: More than 30 papers include: Optimisation of double-jet precipitation process of AgHal microcrystals (PhD Thesis); Low temperature driven absoption chiller, 2001; Marangoni instability analysis in $LiBr/H_2O$-additive system for water vapour absorption, 2002. Honours: Scholarship, Swedish Institute, 1998; Listed in Who's Who publications and biographical dictionaries. Membership: Civilingenjörs Förbundet, Sweden. Address: Trondheimsgatan 7, Tr 7, 16432 Kista, Stockholm, Sweden. E-mail: glebov_euromail@yahoo.com

**GLEITER Herbert,** b. 13 October 1938, Stuttgart, Germany. Professor. m. Erika, 1 son. Education: Diploma, Mechanical Engineering, 1965; PhD, Physics, 1966, University of Stuttgart; DSc, Materials Science, University of Bochum, 1970. Appointments: Assistant Professor, University of Goettingen, 1966-67; Research Fellow, Harvard University, 1967-71; Visiting Professor, MIT, Cambridge, 1971; Professor, University of Bochum, 1972; Chair, Professor, University of Saarbruecken, 1973; Call to University of Hamburg, 1980; Call to Swiss Federal Technical University, Zurich, 1982; Founding Director, Institute of New Materials, Saarbruecken, 1987-90; Vice President, 1994, Director, Institute of Nanotechnology, 1994, Research Center Karlsruhe. Publications: Over 300 publications in international journals on Materials Science and Solid State Physics; 4 Books. Honours: Masing Prize, 1972; Leibniz Prize, 1988; Max Planck Prize, 1993; Gold Medal of FEMS, 1995; Heyn Medal of DGM, 1998; Heisenberg Medal, 2000; Honorary Doctor, University of Darmstadt, 2002; Honorary Professor, University of Lanzhou and Hangzhou, 2003. Memberships: Honorary Member, President, Council, University of Illinois, 1992; Honorary Member, Material Research Society, India, 1994; German Academy of Science, 1999; US National Academy, 2003; American Academy of Arts and Sciences, 2004. Address: Freihamerstrasse 1, 82166 Graefelfing, Germany, E-mail: herbert.gleiter@int.fzk.de

**GLENDINNING Victoria,** b. 23 April 1937, Sheffield, England. Author; Journalist. m. (1) O N V Glendinning, 1958, 4 sons, (2) Terence de Vere White, 1981, (3) K P O'Sullivan, 1996. Education: BA, Honours, Modern Languages, Somerville College, Oxford, 1959; Diploma, Social Administration, 1969. Appointment: Editorial Assistant, Times Literary Supplement,

1970-74. Publications: A Suppressed Cry: Life and Death of a Quaker Daughter, 1969; Elizabeth Bowen: Portrait of a Writer, 1977; Edith Sitwell: A Unicorn Among Lions, 1981; Vita: The Life of Victoria Sackville-West, 1983; Rebecca West: A Life, 1987; The Grown-ups (novel), 1989; Hertfordshire, 1989; Trollope, 1992; Electricity (novel), 1995; Sons and Mothers (co-editor), 1996; Jonathan Swift, 1998; Flight (novel), 2002. Contributions to: Various journals, newspapers and magazines. Honours: Duff Cooper Memorial Award, 1981; James Tait Black Prize, 1981; Whitbread Awards, 1983, 1992; Whitbread Award, Trollope, 1992; Honorary DLitt, Southampton University, 1994, University of Ulster, 1995, Trinity College, Dublin, 1995, University of York, 2000; Commander of the Order of the British Empire, 1998. Memberships: Royal Society of Literature, Vice-President; English PEN, President, 2001-03; Vice-President, English PEN, 2004. Address: David Higham Associates, 5/8 Lower John Street, Golden Square, London W1, England.

**GLENN John Herschel**, b. 18 July 1921, Cambridge, Ohio, USA. US Senator. m. Anna Margaret Castor, 1943, 1 son, 1 daughter. Education: Muskingum College; Naval Aviation Cadet program. Appointments: Marine Corps, 1943; Test Pilot, USN and Marine Corps; 1 of 1st 7 Astronauts in US Space Program, 1959; 1st American to orbit Earth, 1962; Resigned, US Marine Corps, 1965; Director, Roy Crown Cola Company, 1965-74; Consultant, NASA; US Senator, Ohio, 1975-99; Announced return as astronaut, 1997, on board Discovery shuttle, 1998. Publications: We Seven, co-author, 1962; P.S., I Listened to Your Heart Beat. Honours include: DFC 6 times; Air Medal with 18 Clusters; Set environmental speed record for 1st flight to average supersonic speeds from Los Angeles to New York, 1957; Space Congressional Medal of Honour; 1st Senator to win 4 consecutive terms in office. Address: Ohio State University, John Glenn Institute, 100 Bricker Hall, 190 North Oval Mall, Columbus, OH 43210, USA.

**GLENNIE Evelyn**, b. 19 July 1965, Aberdeen, Scotland. Musician. m. Gregorio Malcangi, 1993. Education: Ellon Academy, Aberdeenshire; Royal Academy of Music; Furthered studies in Japan on a Munster Trust Scholarship, 1986. Appointments: Solo debut Wigmore Hall, 1986; Concerts with major orchestras world-wide; Tours UK, Europe, USA, Canada, Australia, New Zealand, Far East, Japan, Middle East, South America, China; Performs many works written for her including Bennett, Bourgeois, Heath, Macmillan, McLeod, Muldowney and Musgrave; First solo percussionist to perform at the Proms, London, 1989, subsequent appearances, 1992, 1994, 1996, 1997. Creative work: Recordings include: Rebounds; Light in Darkness; Dancin'; Rhythm Song; Veni, Veni, Emmanuel; Wind in the Bamboo Grove; Drumming; Sonata for two pianos and percussion – Bela Bartok; Last Night of the Proms – 100th Season; Her Greatest Hits; The Music of Joseph Schwantner; Street Songs, Reflected in Brass; Shadow Behind the Iron Sun. Publications: Good Vibrations (autobiography), 1990; Great Journeys of the World, Beat It! Honours: Honorary Doctorates include: Honorary DMus from the Universities of Aberdeen, 1991, Bristol, 1995, Portsmouth, 1995, Surrey, 1997; Queens University, Belfast, 1998, Exeter, Southampton, 2000; Hon DLitt from Universities of Warwick, 1993, Loughborough, 1995; Numerous prizes include Queen's Commendation Prize (RAM); Gold Medal Shell/LSO Music Scholarship, 1984; Charles Heidsieck Soloist of the Year Award, Royal Philharmonic Society, 1991; OBE, 1993; Personality of the Year, International Classical Music Awards, 1993; Young Deaf Achievers Special Award, 1993; Best studio percussionist, Rhythm Magazine, 1998, 2000; Best Live Percussionist, Rhythm Magazine, 2000; Classic FM Outstanding Contribution to Classical Music, 2002;

Walpole Medal of Excellence, 2002; Musical America, 2003; 2 Grammy Awards.

**GLOAG Julian**, b. 2 July 1930, London, England. Novelist. 1 son, 1 daughter. Education: Exhibitioner, BA, 1953, MA, 1957, Magdalene College, Cambridge. Publications: Our Mother's House, 1963; A Sentence of Life, 1966; Maundy, 1969; A Woman of Character, 1973; Sleeping Dogs Lie, 1980; Lost and Found, 1981; Blood for Blood, 1985; Only Yesterday, 1986; Love as a Foreign Language, 1991; Le passeur de la nuit, 1996; Chambre d'ombre, 1996. Teleplays: Only Yesterday, 1986; The Dark Room, 1988. Memberships: Royal Society of Literature, fellow; Authors Guild. Address: 36 rue Gabrielle, 75018 Paris, France

**GLODOWSKI Shelley Jean**, b. 27 January 1950, Stoughton, Wisconsin, USA. Administrator; Writer. m. Randolph R Glodowski. Education: Bachelor of Arts, Hamline University, 1972. Appointments: Senior Book Reviewer, Midwest Book Review, 1974-; Program Assistant positions, Medical School, Hospital, Sociology Department, School of Music, Physical Sciences Laboratory, 1991-91, Office Manager, Instructional Materials Center, 1987-91, Chair's Secretary, Sociology Department, 1991-94, Administrator, Philosophy Department, 1994-, University of Wisconsin-Madison. Publications: Murder on the Wrong Note, 2002; Murder on a Philosophical Note, in progress; Online reviews for Midwest Book Review monthly under "Internet Watch". Honours: America's Registry, 2003-2004; University of Wisconsin-Madison Exceptional Service Award, 1986, 1995, 1996, 1998, 1999; Discretionary Compensation Award, 2002, 2003, 2004; Listed in Who's Who publications and biographical dictionaries. Membership: Letters and Science Administration Group, University of Wisconsin-Madison. Address: 137 Washington Street, Oregon, WI 53575, USA. E-mail: shelmyst@aol.com

**GLOVER Danny**, b. 22 July 1946, Georgia, USA. Actor. m. Asake Bomani, 1 daughter. Education: San Francisco State University. Appointments: Researcher, Office of Mayor, San Francisco, 1971-75; Member, American Conservatory Theatre's Black Actor Workshop; Broadway debut, Master Harold...and the Boys, 1982; Other stage appearances include: The Blood Knot, 1982; The Island; Sizwe Banzi is Dead; Macbeth; Suicide in B Flat; Nevis Mountain Dew; Jukebox; Appearances in TV films and series; Founder, with wife, Bomani Gallery, San Francisco; Actor films: Escape From Alacatraz, 1979; Chu Chu and the Philly Flash, 1981; Out, 1982; Iceman, 1984; Places in the Heart, 1984; Birdy, 1984; The Color Purple, 1984; Silverado, 1985; Witness, 1985; Lethal Weapon, 1987; Bat 21, 1988; Lethal Weapon II, 1989; To Sleep With Anger, 1990; Predator 2, 1990; Flight of the Intruder, 1991; A Rage in Harlem, 1991; Pure Luck, 1991; Grand Canyon, 1992; Lethal Weapon II, 1992; The Saint of Fort Washington, 1993; Bopha, 1993; Angles in the Outfield, 1994; Operation Dumbo Drop, 1995; America's Dream, 1996; The Rainmaker, 1997; Wings Against the Wind, 1998; Beloved, 1998; Lethal Weapon IV, 1998; Prince of Egypt (voice), 1998; Antz (voice), 1998; The Monster, 1999; Bàttu, 2000; Boseman and Lena, 2000; Wings Against the Wind, 2000; Freedom Song, 2000; 3 A M, 2001; The Royal Tenebaums, 2001; The Real Eve (TV series), 2002; Good Fences (TV), 2003; Saw, 2004; The Cookout, 2004. Address: c/o Cary Productions Inc, PMB 352, 6114 LaSalle Avenue, Oakland, CA 9461, USA.

**GLOVER Judith**, b. 31 March 1943, Wolverhampton, England. Author. 2 daughters. Education: Wolverhampton High School for Girls, 1954-59; Aston Polytechnic, 1960. Publications: Place Names of Sussex (non-fiction), 1975; Place Names of Kent (non-fiction), 1976. Drink Your Own Garden (non-fiction), 1979; The

Sussex Quartet: The Stallion Man, 1982, Sisters and Brothers, 1984, To Everything a Season, 1986; Birds in a Gilded Cage, 1987; The Imagination of the Heart, 1989; Tiger Lilies, 1991; Mirabelle, 1992; Minerva Lane, 1994; Pride of Place, 1995; Sussex Place-Names (non-fiction), 1997. Address: c/o Artellus Ltd, 30 Dorset House, Gloucester Place, London NW1 5AD, England.

**GLUCK Malcolm Richard,** b. 23 January 1942, Hornchurch, Essex, England. Wine Writer, 2 sons, 1 daughter. Education: Watford College of Art. Appointments: Copy Chief, Doyle Dane Bernbach, London, New York, 1966-73; Proprietor, Intellect Games, 1973-75; Director, Abbott Mead Vickers, 1977-80; Director, Collett Dickenson Pearce, 1980-84; Creative Group Head, Ogilvy & Mather, 1984-85; Creative Director, Lintas, 1986-88; Wine Columnist, 1989, Wine Correspondent, 1996-, The Guardian. Publications: Superplonk, 1991, 1992, 1993, 1994, 1995, 1996, 1997, 1998, 1999, 2000, 2001, 2002, 2003; Supernosh (with Anthony Worrall Thompson), 1993; Gluck's Guide to High Street Wine, 1995; Gluck on High, 1996; Gluck, Gluck, Gluck, 1996; Summerplonk, 1997, 1998; Street Plonk, 1998, 1999, 2000; The Sensational Liquid – Gluck's Guide to Wine Tasting, 1999; Wine Matters – Why Water Just Won't Do, 2003; New Media Language (contributor), 2003; Superplonk – The Top One Thousand, 2004; Superplonk, 2005; Supergrub, 2005; The Simple Art of Matching Food and Wine, 2005; Numerous articles in magazines and newspapers; Music: Compiler/Presenter, Vintage Classics, Deutsche Grammophon, 1996; Films/TV: Nosh and Plonk (with Lesley Walters) video, 1993; Presenter, Gluck, Gluck, Gluck, BBC2 TV, 1996; The World of Wine, video, dvd, 2003. Honours: Over 200 advertising awards include: Best Trade Advertising Copy, 1966; Best Colour Advertisement, 1967; Best Black and White Newspaper Advertisement Copy, 1968; Best Newspaper Colour Advertisement, 1972; Best Animated Commercial, 1971; Best Travel Advertising Campaign, 1979; Best use of a Celebrity in a TV Commercial, 1982; Best Cinema Commercial, 1980; Best Outdoor Poster, 1987; Most Original Animated Commercial, 1988. Memberships: Groucho Club; Circle of Wine Writers; Society of Authors.

**GODFREY Sylvia Ann,** b. 3 July 1937, Washington, DC, USA. Real Estate; Mortgage Broker. m. Lynn, deceased, 1 son, 2 daughters. Education: Degree, University of Maryland School of Law, 1960; Business, University of Florida, 1963, 1975; Business, St Leo Jr College, 1973; Environmental Studies, Florida Keys Jr College, 1975; College studies in applied and art history, music and music industry. Appointments: President, Founder, Florida Keys Juvenile Services Inc; President, Founder, God Free Music Ministries Inc; Business Owner, Licensed Real Estate Broker; Business Owner, Licensed Mortgage Broker; President, God Free Music Co; Author; Composer; Publisher; Producer; Administrator, Island Home for Abused and At Risk Youths. Publications: Legislation to provide housing and supportive services for America's homeless; Numerous articles concerning Youth Services, Health Issues, etc; Subject of numerous articles and honours; Numerous songs and recorded works. Honours: Honorary Conch Status for 20 years service to the underprivileged children of Monroe County, Florida; Annual Doing Good Award, 3 years in a row; Good Citizenship Award, 5 times; Honoured by President Bush and Governor Pataki, New York; United Cultural Convention International Peace Prize, 2005. Memberships: South Florida Center for the Arts; American Red Cross; Chamber of Commerce, Key Largo, Florida; Irish American Club. Address: 216 Orange Blossom Road, Tavernier, FL 33070, USA. E-mail: fkjs_island@bellsouth.net Website: www.islandhome.org

**GODINEZ Pedro Oscar,** b. 1948, Havanna, Cuba. Poet; Journalist; Cultural Promoter. Appointments: Director of Havanna's socio-cultural and ecological project "Painting the Prado" (an open air market showing work from over 200 artists); Leader of weekly Dialogue and Meeting and cultural programme; Literary Advisor to the Union of Writers of Cuba; Literary Advisor to the Arab Union of Cuba. Publications (many translated internationally): Atrefedor del Espejo, 1985; La Belle Epoque, 1989; La Rosa Furiosa, 1991; Razones Para Estar Acompandue; El Amor del Poeta, 1992; Confidencia; Homenje Dos Voces. Honours: First Prize, Biennial New Poetry Award; First Prize, Juan Franscisco Manzanao Award; Ruben Martinez Villera Prize of the CTC International; Collection in the book of homages was finalist in the Rafael Alberti Centenary Poetry Prize convened by the Council of Cadiz and the University of Havanna; Book "Estas alas tan Contas" finalist in the Maria Longnar Hispanic-American Poetry Prize; Man of the Year 2003, American Biographical Institute; 2nd Prize National Cuban Poetry Competition, 2004; Shortlisted to top three finalists for Cuba's most prestigious poetry prize, The Nicholas Guillen Poetry Prize, 2005. Membership: Union of Writers and Artists of Cuba. Address: Neptuno #156 (ler.piso), Esq. a Consulado CP 10200, La Habana, Cuba. E-mail: pogodinez@yahoo.com.mx

**GOFF OF CHIEVELEY (Rt Hon Lord Goff of Chieveley) Robert Lionel Archibald,** b. 12 November 1926, Meigle, Perthshire, Scotland. Lawyer. m. Sarah Cousins, 1 son, 2 daughters. Education: MA, 1st class honours Jurisprudence, 1953, DCL, 1972, New College, Oxford. Called to Bar, Inner Temple, 1951. Appointments: Military service, Scots Guards, 1945-48; Fellow and Law Tutor, Lincoln College, Oxford, 1951-55; Practising Barrister, 1956-75, Queen's Counsel, 1967; Judge of the High Court, 1975-82; Judge in charge of the Commercial Court, 1979-81; Lord Justice of Appeal, 1982-86; Chairman of the Council of Legal Education, 1976-82; Chairman of the Court, London University, 1986-91; President, Chartered Institute of Arbitrators, 1986-91; Chairman, British Institute of International and Comparative Law, 1986-2001; Founder, Chairman, 1987-2001, President, 2001-, Pegasus Scholarship Trust; High Steward, Oxford University, 1991-2001; Law Lord, 1986-98; Senior Law Lord, 1996-98. Publications: The Law of Restitution (with Professor Gareth Jones), 1st edition, 1966, now in 6th edition; Numerous published lectures including: Maccabean Lecture, British Academy, 1983; Lionel Cohen Memorial Lecture, Hebrew University of Jerusalem, 1987; Cassel Lecture, Stockholm University, 1993; Presidential Address, Bentham Club, 1986; Presidential Address, Holdsworth Club, 1986; Wilberforce Lecture. Honours: Kt, 1975; Privy Councillor, 1982; Life Peer, 1986; Honorary Fellow: Lincoln College, Oxford, New College, Oxford, Wolfson College, Oxford, American College of Trial Lawyers; Honorary DLitt: City University, London, Reading University; Honorary LLD, Buckingham University, London University, Bristol University; Grand Cross (1st Class) Order of Merit, Federal Republic of Germany; Fellow of the British Academy. Address: House of Lords, Westminster, London SW1 0PW, England.

**GOGO Joseph Oko,** b. 21 July 1946, Takoradi, Ghana. Policy Analyst. m. Frances Gogo, 1 son, 2 daughters. Education: BSc, Geology, University of Ghana, 1972; MSc, Engineering Geology, McGill University, Canada, 1976; MSc, Magna cum Laude, Geotechnical Engineering, 1985, DSc, Summa cum Laude, Geotechnical Engineering, 1990, University of Brussels, Belgium. Appointments: Research Officer, 1977-82, Senior Research Scientist, 1982-95, Principal Research Scientist, 1995-96, Director, Science and Technology Policy Research Institute, 1996-, Council for Scientific and Industrial Research (CSIR), Ghana; Science and Technology Co-ordinator for West Africa,

The New Partnership for Africa's Development (NEPAD), 2004-. Publications: Author of over 40 articles and reports. Honours: Wadell Prize for best student in the Faculty of Science, University of Ghana, 1972; University of Ghana Postgraduate Scholarship, 1974; Max Binz Award for distinguished scholarship, McGill University, Canada 1975; William H Howard Award for outstanding academic performance, McGill University, Canada 1975; UNESCO Fellowship, 1983; Award of Highest Distinction for Doctor of Science thesis, University of Brussels, Belgium. Memberships: Africa Technology Policy Studies Network; New York Academy of Sciences; US Materials Research Society. Address: Council for Scientific and Industrial Research, PO Box M 32, Accra, Ghana. E-mail: jgogo@email.com

**GOLAN Shammai,** b. 5 April 1933, Poland. Emigrated to Israel, 1947. Holocaust Survivor; Hebrew Writer; Diplomat. m. Arna Ben-Dror, 2 sons, 2 daughters. Education: BA, Literature and History, Hebrew University of Jerusalem, 1961. Appointments: Director, Writers' House, Jerusalem, 1971-78; Head, Department of Jewish Education and Culture for the Diaspora, Buenos Aires, Argentina, 1978-81; Chairman, Hebrew Writers' Association, 1981-84, 1989-91; Counsellor, Cultural Affairs, Embassy of Israel, Mexico, 1984-87, Moscow, 1994-99; Director and Secretary, Board of Directors, Society of Authors, Composers and Music Publishers in Israel, 2000-. Publications: Novels and short stories: The Last Watch; Guilt Offerings; The Death of Uri Peled; Escape for Short Distances; Canopy: The Ambush; Holocaust: Anthology; My Travels with Books: Essays; Scenarios; Radio plays; Numerous articles. Honours: Literary Awards: Barash, 1962; Acum, 1965; Ramat-Gan, 1973; The Agnon Jerusalem, 1976; Prime Minister's Prize, 1992. Memberships: Hebrew Writers' Association; PEN Centre; ACUM; Cultural Academy of Mexico; Council, Yad Vashem Museum Memorial. Address: 1 Haamoraim Str, Tel Aviv 69207, Israel.

**GOLD Nicholas Roger,** b. 11 December 1951, Oxford, England. Managing Director. 1 son, 2 daughters. Education: Felsted School, 1965-69; University of Kent, 1970-73; College of Law, 1976-77. Appointments: Touche Ross & Co, 1973-76; Solicitor, Freshfields, 1977-86; Director, Baring Brothers, 1986-95; Managing Director, ING Investment Bank, 1995-; Council of Royal Academy of Dramatic Art, 2003-; Board of Prince of Wales's Foundation for Integrated Health, 2003-. Memberships: Fellow, Institute of Chartered Accountants in England and Wales, 1977; Solicitor of Supreme Court, 1979; Associate, Royal Academy of Dramatic Art; Hurlingham Club. Address: 14 Northumberland Place, London W2 5BS, England. E-mail: nicholasgold@aol.com

**GOLDBERG Abraham (Sir),** b. 7 December 1923, Edinburgh, Scotland. Professor of Medicine. m. Clarice Cussin, 2 sons, 1 daughter. Education: MBChB, University of Edinburgh, 1941-46; MD (Gold Medal), Edinburgh, 1956; FRCP, Glasgow, 1964; FRCP, Edinburgh, 1965; DSc, University of Glasgow, 1966; FRCP, London, 1967; FRSE, 1971; FFPM, 1989. Appointments include: Nuffield Research Fellow, University College Hospital Medical School, 1952-54; Medical Research Council Travelling Fellow in Medicine, University of Utah, USA, 1954-56; Regius Professor of Materia Medica, University of Glasgow, 1970-78; Chairman, Medical Research Council Grants Committee, 1973-77; Regius Professor of the Practice of Medicine, now Emeritus, University of Glasgow, 1978-89; Chairman, Committee on the Safety of Medicines, 1980-86; Honorary Professorial Research Fellow, Department of Modern History, University of Glasgow, 1996-2003. Publications: Diseases of Porphyrin Metabolism (co-author), 1962; Recent Advances in Haematology (co-editor), 1971; Disorders of Porphyrin Metabolism (co-author), 1987; Pharmaceutical Medicine and the Law (co-editor), 1991; Papers on clinical and investigative medicine, 1951-. Honours: Editor, Scottish Medical Journal, 1962-63; Sydney Watson Smith Lecturer, Royal College of Physicians, Edinburgh, 1964; Henry Cohen Lecturer, University of Jerusalem, 1973; Knighted (KB), 1983; Fitzpatrick Lecturer, Royal College of Physicians, London, 1988; Goodall Memorial Lecturer, Royal College of Physicians and Surgeons of Glasgow, 1989; Lord Provost Award for Public Service, City of Glasgow, 1988; Foundation President, Faculty of Pharmaceutical Medicine of the Royal Colleges of Physicians, 1989. Membership: Association of Physicians of Great Britain and Ireland. Address: 16 Birnam Crescent, Bearsden, Glasgow, G61 2AU, Scotland.

**GOLDBERG Whoopi,** b. 13 November 1949, New York, USA. Actress. m. (2) D Claessen, 1986, divorced 1988, 1 daughter, (3) L Trachtenberg, 1994, divorced, 1995. Career: First appearance aged 8, Hudson Guild Theatre, New York; Helen Rubenstein Children's Theatre, San Diego, moved 1974; Co-founder, San Diego Repertory Theatre, appeared in 2 productions, Brecht's Mother Courage and Marsha Norman's Getting Out; Moved to San Francisco, Jointed Blake Street Hawkeyes Theatre, appeared in The Spook Show and Moms, co-wrote, a one-woman show in US Tours, debut, The Lyceum Theatre, Broadway, 1984; Films include: The Color Purple, 1985; Jumpin' Jack Flash, Ghost, 1990; Sister Act; Made in America, 1992; Sister Act II; Corrina Corrina, 1993; Star Trek Generation 5; Moonlight and Valentino; Bogus; Eddie; The Associate, 1996; The Ghost of Mississippi, 1996; How Stella Got Her Groove Back, 1998; Deep End of the Ocean, 1999; Jackie's Back! 1999; Girl Interrupted, 1999; Rat Race, 2001; Call Me Claus, 2001; Kingdom Come, 2001; Monkeybone, 2001; Golden Dreams, 2001; Star Trek: Nemesis, 2002; Blizzard (voice), 2002; TV Appearances in Moonlighting, 1985-86; own TV show, 1992-93. Honours: Several nominations as best actress for The Color Purple including Academy Award, Golden Globe; Emmy Nomination for Moonlighting; Grammy for Best Comedy Album, 1985.

**GOLDBLUM Jeff,** b. 22 October 1952, Pittsburgh, USA. Actor. m. (2) Geena Davis, divorced. Education: Studied at New York Neighbourhood Playhouse. Career: Actor, films include: California Split, 1974; Death Wish, 1974; Nashville, 1975; Next Stop Greenwich Village, 1976; Annie Hall, 1977; Between the Lines, 19777; The Sentinel, 1977; Invasion of the Body Snatchers, 1978; Remember My Name, 1978; Thank God it's Friday, 1978; Escape From Athena, 1979; The Big Chill, 1983; The Right Stuff, 1983; Threshold, 1983; The Adventures of Buckaroo Banzai, 1984; Silverado, 1985; Into the Night, 1985; Transylvania 6-5000, 1985; the Fly, 1986; Beyond Therapy, 1987; The Tall Guy, 1989; Earth Girls Are Easy, 1989; First Born (TV), 1989; The Mad Monkey, 1990; Mister Frost, 1991; Deep Cover, 1992; The Favour, The Watch and the Very Big Fish, 1992; Father and Sons, 1993; Jurassic Park, 1993; Lushlife (TV), 1994; Future Quest (TV), 1994; Hideaway, 1995; Nine Months, 1995; Independence Day, 1996; The Lost World, 1997; Holy Man, 1998; Popcorn, 1999; Chain of Fools, 2000; Angie Rose, 2000; Cats and Dogs, 2001; Producer: Little Surprises, 1995; Holy Man, 1999. Address: c/o Peter Lemie, William Morris Agency, 151 El Camino Drive, Beverly Hills, CA 90212, USA.

**GOLDENBERG Iosif Sukharovich,** b. 1 May 1927, Ukraine. School Teacher. Education: PhD, Philology Department, Kharkov State University, 1949. Publications: Tavolga, English translation as Meadow-sweet; Nad Propast'yu v Tishi, English translation as On the Verge of Abyss in the Silence; Zalozhniki Zaveta, English translation as Hostages of Behest; Izbrannoe,

English translation as Selected Rhymes. Contributions to: Periodicals. Address: Building AB-1, Apt 43, 142292 Pushchino, Moscow Region, Russia.

**GOLDING Allan Peter,** b. 26 March 1960, Jamestown, South Australia. Physician. m. Dymphna, 2 sons, 1 daughter. Education: MBBS, University of Adelaide, Australia, 1984; Diploma in Obstetrics, Gynaecology and Neonatal Care, Royal Australian and New Zealand College of Obstetrics and Gynaecology, 1987; Registered Medical Board of South Australia; Certificate, Civil Aviation Medicine, Australia, 2001. Appointments include: Intern, Royal Adelaide Hospital, Adelaide, 1984; Resident Medical Officer, Lyell McEwin Health Service, Elizabeth Vale, 1985-86; Resident Medical Officer, Modbury Hospital, Modbury, South Australia, 1987; Rural General Practice, Medicine, Surgery and Obstetrics, Port Pirie, South Australia, 1988-; Clinical Lecturer, University of Adelaide, Department of General Practice, 1993-; Designated Aviation Medical Examiner, 2000-; Steering Committee, Mid-North Rural South Australia Division General Practice, 1994-; Chairman, Drug and Therapeutics Committee, Port Pirie Regional Health Service Inc, 1994-2000; Mental Health Advisory Committee, Mid-North Regional Health Service Inc, 1996-2000; Medical Officer, Port Pirie Abattoir, 1991-; Club Surgeon, Port Pirie Racing and Harness Club, 1993-95; Club Doctor, Port Pirie Power Boat Club, 1990-2003. Publications: Articles in medical journals as co-author: South Australian Hypertension Survey. General Practitioner Knowledge and Reported Management Practices – A Cause for Concern? 1992; A Comparison of Outcomes with Angiotensin-Converting Enzyme Inhibitors and Diuretics for Hypertension in the Elderly. Memberships include: Fellow, Royal Australian College of General Practitioners; Fellow, Australian College of Rural and Remote Medicine; Port Pirie Medical Practitioners Society; Australian Medical Association; Sports Medicine Australia; International Federation of Sports Medicine; Arthritis Foundation of Australia; Rural Doctors Association of Australia; Australasian Society of Aerospace Medicine; Port Pirie Asthma Support Group; Life Member, Asthma Foundation; Leader Member, Lord Baden-Powell Society. Address: Central Clinic, 101 Florence Street, Port Pirie, SA 5540, Australia. E-mail: supadocs@westnet.com.au

**GOLDMAN William,** b. 12 August 1931, Chicago, Illinois, USA. Author. m. Ilene Jones, 1961, 2 daughters. Education: Columbia University. Publications: Novels: The Temple of Gold, 1957; Your Turn to Curtsey, My Turn to Bow, 1958; Soldier in the Rain, 1960; Boys and Girls Together, 1964; The Thing of It Is, 1964; No Way to Treat a Lady (as Harry Longbaugh); Father's Day, 1971; Marathon Man, 1974; Wigger, 1974; Magic, 1976; Tinsel, 1979; Control, 1982; The Silent Gondoliers, 1983; The Color of Light, 1984; Play: Blood Sweat and Stanley Poole (with James Goldman), 1961; Musical comedy: A Family Affair (with James Goldman and John Kander), 1962; Non-fiction: Adventures in the Screen Trade, 1983; Hype and Glory, 1990; Four Screenplays, 1995; Five Screenplays, 1997; Screenplays: Harper, 1966; Butch Cassidy and the Sundance Kid, 1969; The Princess Bride, 1973; Marathon Man, 1976; All the President's Men, 1976; A Bridge Too Far, 1977; Magic, 1978; Heat, 1985; Brothers, 1987; Year of the Comet, 1992; Memoirs of an Invisible Man, 1992; Chaplin, 1992; Indecent Proposal, 1993; Maverick, 1994; Ghost and the Darkness, 1996; Absolute Power, 1997; Hearts in Atlantis, 2001. Honours: Academy Awards, 1970, 1977. Address: c/o William Morris, 151 El Camino Drive, Beverly Hills, CA 90212, USA.

**GOLDRING Hon Sir John Bernard,** b. 9 November 1944. High Court Judge. m. Wendy Margaret Lancaster, 2 sons. Education: Exeter University. Appointments: Called to the Bar,

Lincoln's Inn, 1969; Recorder, Midland and Oxford Circuit, 1987; Queen's Counsel, 1987; Deputy Senior Judge, Sovereign Base Areas, Cyprus, 1991; Deputy High Court Judge, 1995; Judge, Courts of Appeal, Jersey and Guernsey, 1998; Judge of the High Court of Justice, 1999-. Honours: Knighthood, 1999; Presiding Judge, Midland Circuit, 2001. Address: Royal Courts of Justice, Strand, London WC2A 2LL, England.

**GOLDSHMIDT Vladimir Y,** b. 26 December 1928, Kirovograd, Ukraine, USSR. Engineer-Geophysicist. m. 1 daughter. Education: MSc, Geophysics, Kazakh Mining-Metallurgical Institute, 1955; PhD, Academy of Sciences of Kazakhstan, 1965; DSc, Moscow State University, 1977; Professor, USSR Supreme Certification Commission, 1989. Appointments: Chief Engineer, Geologic-Geophysical expedition in Kazakhstan, 1955-65; Head of the Department of Interpretation of Geological Data, Institute of Mining Geophysics, Almaty, 1966-1991, Concurrently, Professor-Lecturer, Institute of Qualification Updating of the USSR, Almaty, 1968-91; Professor-Researcher-Geophysicist, 1992-2000, Professor Consultant, 2001-2004, The Geophysical Institute of Israel. Publications: USSR, 1958-92: 20 books, teaching aids, methodical recommendations; 4 author, 7 co-author, 9 participant, Certificates for Inventions; 120 articles, abstracts in Russian; 1 book translated from Russian into Chinese; Israel, USA, Europe, 1992-2005: 60 articles, abstracts and reports; 2002-2003, scientific and other publications in newspapers. Honours: Prospector Award, Ministry of Geology of the USSR, 1978; USSR Inventor, State Committee of Inventions and Discoveries of the USSR, 1984; Honoured Scientist (Meritorious Science Worker) of Kazakhstan, 1989; Medals from USSR and Kazakhstan; Biography and main scientific works published in book: Russian Applied Geophysics of the XXth Century by Biographies, Academy of Sciences, Moscow, 1998; Listed in Encyclopaedia of Kazakhstan. Membership: Israel Geography Society, Jerusalem; Scientists of the South Association. Address: Abarbanel Street 22/11, Beer-Sheva 84759, Israel.

**GOLDSMITH David Julian Alexander,** b. 29 August 1959, Salford, England. Medical Consultant. m. Deborah Mary Gillatt, 1 son, 1 daughter. Education: BA, 1980; MBB Chir, 1983; MA, 1984; MRCP, 1985; FRCP, 1999; Diploma of Teaching, South Thames Deanery, 2001. Appointments include: Surgical House Officer, Warwick Hospital, 1983-84; Medical House Officer, 1984, Senior HP, 1984-85, Renal Registrar, 1987-88, Renal Research Registrar, 1988-91, St Thomas' Hospital; Senior HP, Professorial Renal Unit, Hammersmith Hospital, 1985; Senior HP, Thoracic Medicine, Brompton Hospital, 1985-86; Senior HP, National Hospital for Nervous Diseases, 1986; Registrar, General Medicine, Kingston Hospital, 1986-87; Senior Registrar (Locum), Endocrine Unit, Guy's Hospital, 1991; Senior Registrar, Nephrology, Withington Hospital, 1991-94; Senior Registrar, Nephrology, Manchester Royal Infirmary, 1994-95; Consultant in Nephrology, General Medicine, Brighton, 1995-98; Consultant, Nephrology, Guy's and St Thomas' NHS Trust, 1998-. Publications include: 1 Book and 8 Chapters; 170 Papers; 22 Letters; 130 Abstracts presented at National and International Meetings; Core-reviewer, contributor, Medical Masterclasses; Editor, Journal of Nephrology, 2003-; Educational, 2003-; Editor, Neprology, Dialysis, Transplantation, 2004-. Memberships include: Royal College Committee on Renal Diseases, 1995-2000; South Thames Regional Monospeciality Training Committee, 1998-; Royal College of Physicians, 2000-; UK Renal Association Executive Committee, 2002-; External Grant Review Member, National Kidney Research Fund, 2003-; Honorary Secretary, UK Renal Association, 2004-; Member, Executive Council, European Renal Association, 2004-; Royal Society of Medicine; London Hypertension Society; Medical

Society of London; UK Renal Association; International Society of Nephrology. E-mail: goldsmith@london.com Website: www.dgoldsmith.co.uk

**GOLDSMITH Harvey,** b. 4 March 1946, London, England. Chief Executive; Impresario. m. Diana Gorman, 1971, 1 son. Education: Christ's College; Brighton College of Technology. Appointments: Partner, Big O Posters, 1966-67; Organised first free open-air concert, Parliament Hill Fields, with Michael Alfandary, 1968; Opened Round House, Camden Town, 1968, Crystal Palace Garden Party series concerts, 1969-72; Merged with John Smith Entertainment, 1970; Formed Harvey Goldsmith Entertainment (rock tours promotion co), 1976; Acquired Allied Entertainment Group (rock concert promotions co), 1984; Formed Classical Productions with Mark McCormack, 1986; Promoter and Producer, pop rock, classical musical events including: Concerts: Bruce Springsteen; The Rolling Stones; Elton John; The Who; Pink Floyd; Opera: Aïda, 1988, Carmen, 1989, Tosca, 1991, Earls Court; Pavarotti at Wembley, 1986; Pavarotti in the Park, 1991; The Three Tenors, 1996; Mastercard Masters of Music, 1996; The Eagles, 1996; Music for Monserrat, 1997; The Bee Gees, 1998; Ozzfest, 1998; Paul Weller, 1998. Honour: CBE, 1996. Memberships include: Chairman, Concert Promoters Association, 1986; Chairman, National Music Festival, 1991; Co-Chairman, President's Club, 1994; Vice Chairman, Prince's Trust Action Management Board, 1993; VP, REACT, 1989; VP, Music Users Council, 1994; Trustee, Band Aid, 1985; Trustee, Live Aid Foundation, 1985; Trustee, Royal Opera House, 1995; Trustee, CST, 1995; British Red Cross Coms Panel, 1992; Prague Heritage Fund, 1994; London Tourist Board, 1994. Address: Harvey Goldsmith Entertainment Ltd., Greenland Place, 115-123 Bayham Street, London NW1 0AG, England.

**GOLDSMITH Jerry,** b. 10 February 1929, Los Angeles, USA. Film Music Composer. m. Carol Sheinkopf. Education: Los Angeles City College; Berklee College of Music. Career: Composer, TV scores: Twilight Zone; General Electric Theatre; Doctor Kildare; Gunsmoke; Climax Playhouse 90; Studio One; Star Trek: Voyager; Film scores include: The Stripper, 1962; The Prize, Seven Days in May, 1963; In Harm's Way, The Man From UNCLE, Von Ryan's Express, A Patch of Blue, The Blue Max, Our Man Flint, Seconds, Stagecoach, 1965; The Sand Pebbles, 1966; In Like Flint, 1967; Planet of the Apes, 1968; Tora! Tora! Tora!, Patton, 1970; Wild Rovers, 1971; The Other, The Red Pony, 1972; Papillon, 1973; QB VII, Chinatown, 1974; Logan's Run, 1975; The Omen, Islands in the Stream, 1976; MacArthur, Coma, 1977; The Boys From Brazil, Damien - Omen II, 1978; Alien, 1979; Masada, Star Trek: The Motion Picture, 1979; The Final Conflict, 1981; Outland, Raggedy Man, 1981; Poltergeist, First Blood, Twilight Zone: The Movie, Psycho II, Under Fire, 1983; Gremlins, 1984; Legend, Explorers, Rambo: First Blood II, 1985; Poltergeist II: the Other Side, Hoosiers, 1986; Innerspace, Extreme Prejudice, 1987; Rambo III, 1988; Criminal Law, The `Burbs', Leviathan, Star Trek V: The Final Frontier, Total Recall, Gremlins, The Russia House, 1990; Sleeping With the Enemy, Medicine Man, 1991; Basic Instinct, Forever Young, 1992; The Vanishing, Dennis the Menace, Malice, 1993; City Hall, 1995; Star Trek: First Contact, 1996; LA Confidential, 1997; Air Force One, 1997; The Edge, 1997; Deep Rising, 1997; US Marshals, 1998; Small Soldiers, 1998; Mulan, 1998; Star Trek: Insurrection, 1998; The Mummy, 1999; The 13th Warrior, 1999; The Haunting, 1999; Hollow Man, 2000; Along Came a Spider, 2001; The Last Castle, 2001; The Sum of All Dears, 2002; Star Trek: Nemesis, 2002; Ballet scores include: A patch of Blue, 1970; Othello, 1971; Capricorn One, 1989. Honours: Max Steiner Award, National Film Society, 1982; Richard Kirk Award, BMI, 1987; Golden Score Award, American Society of

Music Arrangers, 1990; Career Achievement Award, Society for Preservation of Film Music, 1993; 1st American Music Legend Award, Variety, 1995. Address: c/o Savitsky & Co, Suite 1450, 1901 Avenue of Stars, Los Angeles, CA 90067, USA.

**GOLDSMITH Zac,** b. 20 January 1975, Westminster, London. Editor. m. Sheherazada Ventura-Bentley, 1 son, 2 daughters. Appointments: Member, International Honours Programme, Global Ecology Course, visiting Eastern Europe, India, Thailand, New Zealand, Mexico, United States, 1993-94; Worked with Redefining Progress, Non-Governmental Organisation, San Francisco, USA, 1994-95; Member, currently Associate Director, International Society for Ecology and Culture based in California, USA, Bristol, UK, Ladakh, India; 1995-97; Ran tourist education programme, Ladakh, India; Editor, The Ecologist Magazine, 1997-; Board Member, JMG Foundation; The Fondation de Sauve; L'Association Goldsmith pour L'Environment, L'Artisanat et le Mond Rural. Founder, FARM, campaigning membership organisation for British farmers; Delivered speeches at venues including: The Schumacher Memorial Lectures; The Oxford Union; Numerous schools colleges and think-tanks in the UK. Publications: Newspaper articles for: The Times, The Sunday Times, The Daily Mail, The Mail on Sunday, The Independent, The Guardian, The Observer, The Standard, The Express, The Telegraph, Tribune, many regional British newspapers; Magazine articles in: The Ecologist Magazine (over 30), Country Life, The Big Issue, The New Statesman, The Week, Global Agenda 2003, Geographical, Tatler, Vanity Fair. Honours: Young Philanthropist of the Year, Beacon Prize, 2003; International Environmental Leadership, Global Green Award, 2004. Memberships: Aspinalls; Travellers; Mark's. Address: Unit 18 Chelsea Wharf, 15 Lots Road, London SW10 0QJ, England. E-mail: zeco@compuserve.com

**GOLDSTEIN Myrna,** b. 5 August 1948, Rochester, New York, USA. Professor; Journalist; Writer; Businesswoman. Education: Master's Degree, Teaching English as a Second/ Foreign Language, St Michael's College, Vermont, USA; BSJ, Journalism, Northwestern University, Illinois, USA; Certification to Teach English Conversation, Perugia Board of Education; Diploma, Italian Language, Certification to Teach Italian, University for Foreigners, Italy; Owner, Euroglobal Communications SNC, Loiri/Porto San Paolo, Sardinia, Italy. Appointments: Journalism: Business Market Editor/Reporter, Fairchild Publications, New York City, 1971-73; Contributing Journalist, Publicist, New York City, 1973-74, Venice Italy, 1981-86; Syndicated Feature Writer and Food Editor promoted to Editorial Board Member, Writer Columnist Opinion Pages; Feature Writer, Gannett Co, Rochester New York and Harrison, Westchester County, New York, 1974-81, 1986-89; Cross-Cultural Journalist, Editor, Copywriter, Publicist, Perugia, Italy, 1990-; Teaching Appointments: Journalism and Mass Communications, State University of New York, 1974; Instructor, Italian Language for Foreigners, Elizabeth Seton College, Yonkers, New York and Manhattan Community College, New York City, 1987-88; Conversation Instructor, Perugia Board of Education, 1995-2004; Professor and Creator "Greatest Hits" Experimental Linguistic Laboratory, Perugia, 1996-98; Professor, Tourism English, 1997-98, Professor, Business Communications and International Marketing, 1997-98, Institute for Commercial Services, Gualdo Tadino; Professor of Journalism, Spoleto and Norcia, 2000; Professor, Italian Army Officers Language Training Centre (SLEE), Perugia, 1998-2003; Lecturer, 2001-2002, Professor, 2002-04, Program for Interpreters and Translators, Faculty of Philosophy and Letters, University of Perugia. Publications: Are You in Your English File? Decoding Listening Comprehension Through Pre-Listening Strategies: A Pilot Case Study, 2002; Sensing Worlds of Worlds – Poem-Songs on Loving and the World, 2004; Stealing Vesuvius, 2004. Honours: Pulitzer Prize Nominee; Reader's Digest Magazine Writing Award. Memberships: European Society for the Study of English (ESSE); International Women's Media Foundation, Washington DC, USA; Italian Association for English Professionals (AIA); SIETAR; TESOL Italy; TESOL, USA. Address: Via dei Narcisi 61/I, 06126 Perugia (Casaglia), Italy. E-mail: myrnagoldstein@libero.it

**GOLDSTEIN Robert Justin,** b. 28 March 1947, Albany, New York, USA. College Professor. Education: BA, University of Illinois, 1969; MA, 1971, PhD, 1976, University of Chicago. Appointments: Research and Administrative Assistant, University of Illinois, 1972-73; Lecturer, San Diego State University, 1974-76; Assistant Professor, Associate Professor, Full Professor, Oakland University, Rochester, Michigan, 1976-. Publications: Political Repression in Modern America, 1978, revised edition, 2001; Political Repression in Nineteenth Century Europe, 1983; Political Censorship of the Press and the Arts in Nineteenth Century Europe, 1989; Censorship of Political Caricature in Nineteenth Century France, 1989; Saving "Old Glory": The History of the American Flag Desecration Controversy, 1995; Burning the Flag: The Great 1989-90 American Flag Desecration Controversy, 1996; Desecrating the American Flag: Key Documents from the Controversy from the Civil War to 1995, 1996; The War for the Public Mind: Political Censorship in Nineteenth Century Europe, 2001; Flag Burning and Free Speech: The Case of Texas V Johnson, 2000; Political Censorship: The New York Times Twentieth Century in Review, 2001. Address: Department of Political Science, Oakland University, Rochester, MI 48309, USA. E-mail: goldstei@oakland.edu

**GOLDSTEIN-JACKSON Kevin Grierson,** b. 2 November 1946, Windsor, Berkshire, England. Writer; Poet. m. Mei Leng Ng, 6 September 1975, 2 daughters. Education: BA, Reading University; MPhil, Southampton University; FRSA. Appointments: Programme Organizer, Southern TV, 1970-73; Assistant Producer, HK-TVB, Hong Kong, 1973; Freelance Writer, TV Producer, 1974-75; Head of Film, Dhofar Region TV Service, Sultanate of Oman, 1975-76; Assistant to Head of Drama, Anglia TV, 1977-81; Founder, Chief Executive and Programme Controller, Television South West, 1981-85; Freelance Writer, 1985-. Contributions to: Sunday Times; Financial Times; Hampshire Poets; Sandwiches; Bogg; Isthmus; Bare Bones; Contemporary Poets; Doors; Envoi; Haiku Quarterly; Iota; Krax; Ellery Queen's Mystery Magazine; Kangaroo; Tidepool; New England Review; Presence; Author of 18 published books. Memberships: Writers' Guild; Society of Authors; Poetry Society. Address: c/o Alcazar, 18 Martello Road, Branksome Park, Poole, Dorset BH13 7DH, England.

**GOLLEDGE Allan David,** b. 30 October 1971, Te Awamutu, New Zealand. 1 daughter. Associate Pastor. Education: Diploma of Ministry, Tabor College, 1996-98. Appointments: Youth Worker, 1991-96; Executive Manager, Pilbara Youth Services Inc; Executive Officer, Pilbara Council of Young People; Youth Leader, Karratha Apostolic Church, 1991-96; Assistant Manager, Cameliers Guest House (a ministry of Fusion WA), 1997-99; Carer Liaison Officer, Baptistcare Mental Health Service, 1999-; Assistant Pastor, Batavia Coast Christian Outreach Centre, 1997-2001; Associate Pastor, New Hope Christian Centre, 2001-. Honours: Commonwealth Nations Youth of the Year Award, 1995; Gold Record of Achievement, American Biographical Institute; Finalist, Citizen of the Year Award, Shire of Roebourne; Listed biographical dictionaries. Address: 7 Koojarra Street, Geraldton, WA 6530, Australia.

**GOMES DE MATOS Francisco Cardoso,** b. 3 September 1933, Crato, Brazil. University Professor. m. Helen Herta Bruning, 1 son, 2 daughters. Education: Bachelor in Law and Languages, Federal University, Pernambuco, 1958; Master's in Linguistics, University of Michigan, 1960; PhD in Applied Linguistics, Catholic University of Sao Paulo, 1973. Appointments: Visiting Professor, Catholic University of Sao Paulo, 1966-79; Fulbright Visiting Professor, University of Georgia, Athens Georgia, USA, 1985-1986; Professor, Federal University of Pernambuco, 1980-; Co-founder, Brazil-America Association. Publications: Plea for Universal Declaration of Linguistic Rights, 1984; Plea for Communicative Peace, 1993. Honours: Benefactor Member, International Society for the Teaching of Portuguese as a Foreign Language; Listed in biographical publications. Memberships: Brazilian Linguistics Association; Brazilian Academy of Philology. Address: Rua Setubal 860-B, Apto 604, 51030-010 Recife, Brazil. E-mail: fcgm@hotlink.com.br

**GOMEZ Rajan Gaetan,** b. 21 November 1938, Kalutara, Sri Lanka. Consultant and Researcher in Parliamentary and Commonwealth Affairs. m. Rosanne Pinto, 2 daughters. Education: BSc (Hons), University of Sri Lanka, 1961; DIC (Diploma of Imperial College), 1973, MSc, Management Studies (with Distinction) Imperial College, 1973. Appointments: Directorates in the Commonwealth Secretariat and the Sri Lanka Administrative Service; Director of Development and Planning, Commonwealth Parliamentary Association, 1992-2003; Senior Research Fellow, University College London. Publications: Several publications in management operations research, human resource development, parliamentary and public administration; Member of Editorial Boards including Journal of Public Administration and Development. Honours: Nominee for Smith-Mundt Fulbright Award, 1961-62; Kluwer-Harrap Award, University of London, 1973. Memberships include: Fellow Royal Society of Chemistry; Fellow Royal Society of Arts. Address: 51 Linkway, London SW20 9AT, England.

**GÖNCZ Árpád,** b. 10 February 1922, Budapest, Hungary. Politician; Writer; Dramatist; Translator. m. Maria Zsuzsanna Göntér, 1947, 2 sons, 2 daughters. Education: DJ, Pázmány Péter University, 1944; University of Agricultural Sciences. Appointments: Active with Independent Smallholders' Party, 1947-48; Imprisoned for political activities, 1957-63; Founding Member, Free Initiative Network, Free Democratic Federation, Historic Justice Committee; Member and Speaker of Parliament, 1990; Acting President, 1990, President, 1990-2000, Republic of Hungary. Publications: Men of God (novel), 1974; Hungarian Medea (play), 1979; Iron Bars (play), 1979; Encounters (short stories), 1980; 6 plays, 1990; Homecoming (short stories), 1991; Shavings (essays), 1991. Honours: Honorary Knight Commander of the Order of St Michael and St George, England, 1991; Dr hc, Butler, 1990, Connecticut, 1991, Oxford, 1995, Sorbonne, 1996, Bologna, 1997; George Washington Prize, 2000; Pro Humanitate Award, 2001; Polish Business Oscar Award, 2002. Membership: Hungarian Writers' Union, President, 1989-90.

**GONZALEZ-MARINA Jacqueline,** b. 19 February 1935, Madrid, Spain. Lecturer; Translator and Official Interpreter in 7 Languages; Poet; Writer; Publisher; Journalist; Editor; Artist. m. (1) 2 sons, 1 daughter, (2) Desmond Savage, 22 December 1982. Education: BA, Modern Philology, 1959, MA, Modern Philology, 1962, University of Barcelona. Appointments: Lecturer, University of Barcelona, 1960-68, St Godrics College, London, 1970-91; Founder, Editor, Dandelion Magazine, 1979-; Editor, Fern Publications, 1979-; Editor, The Student Magazine (International), 2000- Lecturer in Modern Languages, American Intercontinental University, London, 1994-2000; More than 60 art exhibitions, one person and collective in England and Spain. Publications: Dieciocho Segundos, 1953; Tijeras Sin Filo, 1955; Antología de Temas, 1961; Short Stories, 1972; Brian Patten, 1975; A Survival Course, 1975; Once Poemas a Malaga, 1977; Poesía Andaluza, 1977; Adrian Henri, 1980; Historias y Conversaciones, 1995; Mediterranean Poetry, bilingual anthology, 1997; Conversaciones en Español, 1998; Drawing and Painting for Fun, 1998; The Millennium Anthology, poetry and prose, Vol 1, 1999, Vol II, 2000; The International Book of Short Stories, 2002; Cats in the Palm Tree and Other Stories (co-writer), 2002; Dali & I, poems, 2003; Contributions to: Countless anthologies and international magazines; Writer and broadcaster for the BBC, London, 1975-78. Honours: Royal Academician, Royal Academy of St Telmo, Malaga, Spain, 1975; Honorary Member of the Atheneum in Alicante, Spain, 1999. Memberships: Society of Women Writers and Journalists, London, 1980-; The Historical Association Saxoferreo, Cordoba, Spain, 1997-. Address: "Casa Alba", 24 Frosty Hollow, East Hunsbury, Northants NN4 0SY, England.

**GONZALEZ ZUMARRAGA Jose Antonio Eduardo,** b. 18 March 1925, Pujili, Prov Cotopaxi, Ecuador. Priest; Bishop; Cardinal. Education: San Jose Seminary, Quito; Doctorate, Pontificia University of Salamanca, Spain. Appointments: Ordained Priest, 1951; Bishop of Tagarata and Auxiliary of Quito, 1969; Bishop of Machala, 1978; Assistant Archbishop of Quito with right of succession, 1980; Archbishop of Quito, 1985; Cardinal, Presbytery Church Santa Maria in Via, 2001. Publications: Problemas del patronato indiano a traves del 'Gobierno Eclesiastico Pacifico' de Fr Gaspar de Villarroel, 1961; Fray Gaspar de Villarroel, su 'Gobierno Eclesiastico Pacifico' y el patronato indiano, 1990; Mons Antonio Gonzalez Zumarraga, El Episcopado Latinamericano y las Iglesias Locales, 1999; Juan Pablo II "Pastor Supremo de la Iglesia", 2003; Albanzas a la Sma Virgen Maria, 2004. Honours: Gran Cruz de la Orden Nacional al Merito, 1994; Gran Cruz de la Orden de San Lorenzo, 2001. Memberships: Honorary Member, Academica Nacional de Historia; Member, Academica Nacional de Historia Eclesiástica. Address: Apartado 17-01-00106, Quito, Ecuador.

**GONZALEZ-GONZALEZ Jesus Maria,** b. 25 January 1961, Herreros de Suso, Avila, Spain. Stomatologist. m. Maria Teresa Rubio Hortells, separated 2003, 2 children. Education: BMed, University of Salamanca, 1985; Programmer Basic, Pontificia University of Salamanca, 1988; Specialist in Stomatology, University of Murcia, 1992; DMed, University of Alicante, 1992. Appointments: Medical Practitioner, State Health Service, Salamanca and Provence, 1987-88, La Manga, Murcia, 1990; Dentist, State Health Service, Cartagena, Murcia, 1990, 1991, Bejar and Ciudad Rodrigo, Salamanca, 1992; Private Practice in Stomatology, Murcia, 1991, Salamanca, 1991-; Speaker in field, 13 reports in congress. Publications: Several books in Spanish; Articles in professional journals and magazines; 2 patents. Honours: Honorable Mention, Children's Meeting of Painting, Town House of Salamanca, 1974 and Military Service, Lerida, 1986; Listed in numerous Who's Who publications and biographical dictionaries. Memberships: Professional Association of Dentists, Spain; Ski Club of Salamanca; New York Academy of Sciences; Founder President, Asociacion de Padres de Familia Separados de Salamanca y Pro-Derechos de Nuestros Hijos. Address: c/ Avila, No 4, lo A, 37004 Salamanca, Spain.

**GOOCH Graham Alan,** b. 23 July 1953, Leytonstone, England. Cricketer. m. Brenda Daniels, 3 daughters. Career: Right-hand opening batsman, right-arm medium bowler; Played for Essex 1973-97, (captain, 1986-87, 1989-94), West Prov, 1982-83,1983-84; Played in 118 tests for England, 1975 to 1994-95, 34 as captain, scoring 8900 runs (England record, average 42.5) including 20 hundreds (highest score 333 and Test match aggregate of 456 v India, Lord's 1990, becoming only batsman to score triple century and century in a first-class match and holding 103 catches; scored 44,841 runs (128 hundreds) and held 555 catches in first-class cricket; Toured Australia 1978-79, 1979-80, 1990-91 (captain) and 1994-95; 125 limited-overs internationals, including 50 as captain (both England records); Member, England Selection Committee, 1996-; Manager, England Tour to Australia, 1998-99; Head Coach, Essex, 2001-. Publications: Testing Times, 1991; Gooch: My Autobiography, 1995. Honours include: OBE; Wisden Cricketer of the Year, 1980. Address: c/o Essex County Cricket Club, The County Ground, New Writtle Street, Chelmsford, Essex, CM2 0PG, England.

**GOOD-BLACK Edith Elissa,** b. 10 January 1945, Hollywood, California, USA. Writer. m. Michael Lawrence Black, deceased. Education: BA, English, California State University, Northridge, 1974; Student, University of California, Los Angeles and University of California, Berkeley, 1962-92; Explorer, Mayan ruins, Mexico, 1963; Study of Ballet Folklorico, Mexico, 1963. Appointments: Participant, numerous dance, art, music, literature, mathematics and science classes; Dancer, Hajde Dance Troop, Berkeley, California, 1962-66; One-woman shows, Los Angeles, 1962-95; Singer, coffee houses, cafés, nightclubs, half-way houses, libraries, and others, Los Angeles, 1986-; Sole Proprietor, Gull Press. Publications include: (pseudonym, Pearl Williams) The Trickster of Tarzana, 1992; Short Stories, 1995; Mad in Craft, 1995; Missives, 1995; Contributed poetry to CDs, radio broadcasts, internet broadcasts, publications. Honours: Summa Cum Laude, California State University; Writing chosen by a jury of experts for permanent collection in the Library of Congress; Achievement Prize, International Biographical Centre, 2000; Listed in numerous Who's Who and biographical publications. Memberships: MENSA; American Society of Composers, Authors and Publishers; Plummer Park Writers; Westside Writers; Democratic clubs, California and Mexico, 1962-; Supporter, mental health organisations, 1962-; Delegate to local conventions, fundraiser, canvasser, office worker, driver and participant in consciousness raising groups in support of civil rights; CORE, San Francisco, Berkeley, Los Angeles, and Oakland, 1965; Peace in Alliance for Survival, Berkeley, Oakland, Los Angeles, 1964-80; Women's rights, Westside Women's Center, Woman's Building, Los Angeles, 1974-80; Environment in Earth Day, Los Angeles, 1977; Physical and Mental Health; Consultant, tutor and book reviewer, Mental Health Association, Los Angeles, 1962-; Supporter of Residential Collective, 1985-. Address: 1470 South Robertson Blvd, Apt B, Los Angeles, CA 90035-3402, USA.

**GOODBODY Michael Ivan Andrew,** b. 23 January 1942, Wicklow, Ireland. Stockbroker. m. Susannah Elizabeth Pearce, 1 son, 2 daughters. Education: Kingstown School, Dublin, Ireland. Appointments: J & L F Goodbody Ltd, Jute Manufacturers, 1960-62; Member of the Stock Exchange, 1968-87; Member of the Securities Institute, 1987-; Stockbroker, Smith Rice & Hill, 1962-74; Stockbroker, 1974-82, Partner/Director, 1982-89, Divisional Director, 1989-2000, Capel-Cure Myers; Private Client Fund Manager, Carr Sheppards Crosthwaite, 2001-. Publications: The Goodbody Family of Ireland, 1979; A Quaker Wedding at Lisburn; Occasional articles on family history. Memberships: Territorial Army – 289 Parachute Regiment RHA, 1964-75; Society of Genealogists; Treasurer, Colne and Stour Countryside Association; Irish Genealogical Research Society; Quaker Family History Society. Address: The Old Rectory, Wickham St Paul's, Essex CO9 2PJ, England.

**GOODE Barbara Irene,** b. 14 August 1924, Bournemouth, England. Retired. m. (1) Robert George Cowdrey, 2 sons, 1 daughter, (2) Geoffrey George Goode. Appointments: Assistant Matron, Care Home, Bournemouth; Relief Library Assistant, Bournemouth Libraries. Publications: Thoughts of Barbara Goode, 1997; Just Barbara, 1998; The Village Hymnal (words to husband's music); Little Book of Poems; Contributions to: About 500 poetry books and professional publications; Stories for children in hospital magazines; Verse to prison magazines on a voluntary basis. Honours: 5 Certificates for Children's Stories; Runner-up, Robert Burns Contest; 15 small money prizes. Address: 14 The Broadway, Oakington, Cambridge CB4 5BE, England.

**GOODENOUGH Frederick Roger,** b. 21 December 1927, Broadwell, Oxfordshire. Retired Director; Farmer. m. Marguerite June, 1 son, 2 daughters. Education: MA (Cantab), 1955; MA (Oxon), 1975; FCIB; FLS; FRSA. Appointments: RN, 1946-48; Joined Barclays Bank Ltd, 1950; Local Director, Birmingham, 1958-60, Reading, 1960-69, Oxford, 1969-87, Director Barclays, Bank UK, Ltd, 1971-87, Barclays Bank International Ltd, 1977-87, Barclays PLC, 1985-89, Barclays Bank PLC, 1979-89; Advisory Director, Barclays Bank Thames Valley Region, 1988-89; Member, London Committee Barclays Bank DCO, 1966-71, Barclays Bank International Ltd, 1971-80; Senior Partner, Broadwell Manor Farm, 1968-; Curator, Oxford University Chest, 1974-93; President, Oxfordshire Rural Community Council, 1993-98; Trustee: Nuffield Medical Benefaction, 1968-2002 (Chairman, 1987-2002), Nuffield Dominions Trust, 1968-2002 (Chairman, 1987-2002); Nuffield Oxford Hospitals Fund, 1968-2003 (Chairman, 1982-88), Nuffield Orthopaedic Centre Trust, 1978-2003 (Chairman, 1981-2003), Oxford Preservation Trust, 1980-89, Radcliffe Medical Foundation, 1987-98; Governor: Shiplake College, 1963-74 (Chairman, 1966-70),Wellington College, 1968-74, Goodenough College, 1985-; Patron, Anglo Ghanaian Society, 1991-.Publication co-author, Britain's Future in Farming (edited by Sir Frank Engledow and Leonard Amoy, 1980. Honours: High Sheriff, Oxfordshire, 1987-88; Deputy Lieutenant, Oxfordshire, 1989-; Supernumerary Fellow, 1989-95, Honorary Fellow, 1995, Wolfson College, Oxford. Memberships: Fellow, Linnean Society (Member of Council 1968-75, Treasurer, 1970-75, Finance Committee, 1968-); Brooks's, London. Address: Broadwell Manor, Nr Lechlade, Gloucestershire, GL7 3QS, England. E-mail: f.r.goodenough@broadwellmanor.co.uk

**GOODING Cuba Jr,** b. 2 September 1968, Bronx, New York, USA. Actor. m. Sara, 1994, 2 children. Career: TV appearances include: Kill or Be Killed, 1990; Murder with Motive: The Edmund Perry Story, 1992; Daybreak, 1993; The Tuskagee Airmen; Film appearances include: Coming to America, 1988; Sing, 1989; Boyz N the Hood, 1991; Gladiator, 1992; A Few Good Men, 1992; Hitz, 1992; Judgement Night, 1993; Lightning Jack, 1994; Losing Isiah, 1995; Outbreak, 1995; Jerry Maguire, 1996; The Audition, 1996; Old Friends, 1997; As Good As It Gets, 1997; What Dreams May Come, 1998; A Murder of Crows, 1999; Instinct, 1999; Chill Factor, 1999; Men of Honor, 2000; Pearl Harbor, 2001; Rat Race, 2001; In the Shadows, 2001; Snow Dogs, 2002; Boat Trip, 2002; Psychic, 2003; The Fighting Temptations, 2003; Radio, 2003; Honours: 2 NAACP Awards; Academy Award; Best Supporting Actor (for Jerry Maguire), 1997; Chicago Film Critics Award; Screen Actor Guild Award. Address: c/o Rogers and Cowan, 1888 Century Park East, Suite 500, Los Angeles, CA 90067, USA.

**GOODISON Sir Nicholas,** b. 16 May 1934, Radlett, England. Former Chairman, London Stock Exchange. m. Judith Abel Smith, 1960, 1 son, 2 daughters. Education: BA Classics, 1958, MA, PhD, Architecture and History of Art, 1981, King's College, Cambridge. Appointments: H E Goodison & Co (now Morgan Stanley, Quilter & Co Ltd), 1958-86, Chairman, 1975-86; Member of Council, 1968-88, Chairman, 1976-88, Stock Exchange, London; President, International Federation of Stock Exchanges, 1985-86; Member, Panel on Takeovers and Mergers, 1976-88; Member, Council for the Securities Industry, 1978-85; Member, Securities Association, 1986-88; Director, Ottoman Bank, 1986-92; Director, Banque Paribas Capital Markets, 1986-88; Director, General Accident plc, 1987-95; Director, 1989-2002, Deputy Chairman, 1993-99, British Steel plc (from 1999, Corus plc); Chairman, TSB Group plc, 1989-95; Deputy Chairman, Lloyds TSB Group plc, 1995-2000; President, British Bankers' Association, 1991-96; Member, Executive Committee, 1976-2002, Chairman, 1986-2002 National Art Collections Fund; Director, 1975-, Chairman, 2002, Burlington Magazine; Director, 1977-98, Vice-Chairman, 1980-88, English National Opera; Chairman, 1982-2002, Member of Governing Board, 2002-, Courtauld Institute of Art, London University; Trustee, Kathleen Ferrier Memorial Scholarship Fund, 1987-; Trustee, National Heritage Memorial Fund, 1988-97; Member of Council ABSA (now Arts and Business), 1990-99; Chairman, Crafts Council, 1997-; Member of Council, 1965-, President, 1990-, Furniture History Society; Trustee, 2001-, Chairman, 2003-, National Life Story Collection; Governor Marlborough College, 1981-97; Trustee, Harewood House Trust; Chairman of Review Steering Group, National Record of Achievement, (Department for Education and Science) 1996-97; Member, Royal Commission on Long Term Care for the Elderly, 1997-99; Chairman, Goodison Group on Lifelong Learning, 1999-; Member, Further Education Funding Council, 2000-2001; Leader and author, Goodison Review "Securing the Best for our Museums: Private Giving and Government Support" (HM Treasury), 2003. Publications: English Barometers 1680-1860, 1968, 2nd edition, 1977; Ormolu: the Work of Matthew Boulton, 1974, revised as Matthew Boulton: Ormolu, 2003; Hotspur, Eighty Years of Antiques dealing (with Robin Kern), 2004; Articles and lectures on stock exchange, banking, financial regulation, etc; Articles and lectures on arts, history of decorative arts, museums, etc. Honours: KB, 1982; Chevalier, Legion d'Honneur, 1990; Hon DLitt, City University, 1985; Hon LLD, Exeter University, 1989; Hon DSc, Aston University, 1994; Hon DArt, deMontfort University, 1998; Hon DCL, University of Northumbria, 1999; Hon DLitt, University of London, 2003; Honorary Fellow, King's College, Cambridge, 2002; Honorary Fellow, Courtauld Institute of Art, 2003; Honorary Fellow, British Academy, 2004; Honorary Fellow, Royal Academy of Arts; Senior Fellow, Royal College of Art; Honorary Fellow, RIBA. Memberships: Fellow, Society of Antiquaries; Fellow, Royal Society of Arts. Address: PO Box 2512, London W1A 5ZP, England.

**GOODMAN Anthony Eric,** b. 21 July 1936, London, England. Academic. m. Jacqueline, 1 daughter. Education: BLitt, MA (Oxon), Oxford University, 1965. Appointments: Member of Academic Staff, 1961-2001, Professor of Medieval and Renaissance History, 1993-2001; Professor Emeritus, 2001-, History Department, University of Edinburgh. Publications: The Loyal Conspiracy, 1971; A History of England from Edward II to James I, 1977; The Wars of the Roses, 1981; The New Monarchy, 1988; John of Gaunt, 1992; Margery Kempe and her World, 2002; The Wars of the Roses. The Soldiers' Experience, 2005. Honour: Fellow of the Royal Historical Society. Address: 23 Kirkhill Gardens, Edinburgh EH16 5DF, Scotland.

**GOODMAN D Wayne,** b. 14 December 1945, Glen Allen, Mississippi, USA. Professor. m. Sandra Faye Hewitt, 1 son. Education: BS, Mississippi College, 1968; PhD, University of Texas, 1974; NATO Postdoctoral Fellow, Technische Hochschule, Germany, 1975-76. Appointments: National Research Council Research Fellow, 1976-78, Staff Member, 1978-80, National Bureau of Standards; Staff Member, 1980-84, Supervisor, Surface Science Division, 1985-88, Sandia National Laboratories; Adjunct Professor, Department of Chemistry, University of Texas, 1985; Professor of Chemistry, 1988-94, Head, Physical and Nuclear Division, 1991-93, Robert A Welch Professor of Chemistry, 1994-, Robert A Welch Chair of Chemistry, 1998-, Distinguished Professor of Chemistry, 2000-, Texas A&M University. Publications: Over 460 reviewed papers and book chapters, mainly on chemisorption and catalytic reactions on atomically clean and chemically modified metal single crystal surfaces, also fundamental chemistry of processes occurring at the solid-gas/solid-liquid interface relating to coatings and corrosion. Honours: NATO Fellowship, 1975, National Research Council Fellowship, 1976; Distinguished Visiting Lecturer, University of Texas, Austin, 1982; Ipatieff Prize, American Chemical Society, 1983; 1 of 100 Outstanding Young Scientists in America, Science Digest, 1985; Frontiers in Chemistry, Lecturer, Texas A&M University, 1987; Procter and Gamble Lecturer, University of Cincinnati, 1990; Langmuir Lecturer, American Chemical Society, 1991; Ipatieff Lecturer, Northwestern University, 1992; Colloid and Surface Chemistry Award, American Chemical Society, 1993; Yarwood Medal, British Vacuum Society, 1994; Humboldt Research Prize, 1995; Texas A&M University Distinguished Research Award, 1997; Robert Burwell Lecturer, North American Catalysis Society, 1997; Fellow, American Vacuum Society, 1998; Elected Fellow, Institute of Physics, 1999; Giuseppe Parravano Award, 2001; ACS Arthur W Adamson Award for Distinguished Service in the Advancement of Surface Chemistry, 2002; ACS Gabor Somorjai Award, 2005. Memberships: American Chemical Society, Division of Colloid and Surface Chemistry Treasurer, 1979, Division Vice-Chairman, 1984, Division Chairman, 1985, Speaker's Tour, 1984, 1991, Member, Joint Board-Council Committee on Publications, 1998; American Vacuum Society, Executive Committee, Surface Science Division, 1980, 1985; Southwest Catalysis Society, President, 1993. Address: Texas A&M University, Department of Chemistry, PO Box 30012, College Station, TX 77842-3012, USA. E-mail: goodman@mail.chem.tamu.edu

**GOODMAN John,** b. 20 June 1952, St Louis, USA. Film Actor. m. Annabeth Hartzog, 1989, 1 daughter. Education: South West Missouri State University. Career: Broadway appearances in: Loose Ends, 1979; Big River, 1985; TV appearances include: The Mystery of Moro Castle; The Face of Rage; Heart of Steel; Moonlighting, Chiefs (min-series); The Paper Chase; Murder Ordained; The Equalizer; Roseanne (series); Normal, Ohio, 2000; Pigs Next Door, 2000; Films include: The Survivors, 1983; Eddie Macon's Run, 1983; Revenge of the Nerds, 1984; CHUD, 1984; Maria's Lovers, 1985; Sweet Dreams, 1985; True Stories, 1986; The Big Easy, 1987; Burglar, 1987; Raising Arizona, 1987; The Wrong Guys, 1988; Everybody's All-American, 1988; Punchline, 1988; Sea of Love, 1989; Always, 1989; Stella, 1990; Arachnophobia, 1990; King Ralph, 1990; Barton Fink, 1991; The Babe, 1992; Born Yesterday, 1993; The Flintstones, 1994; Kingfish: A Story of Huey P Long, 1995; Pie in the Sky, Mother Night, 1996; Fallen, 1997; Combat!, 1997; The Borrowers, 1997; The Big Lebowski, 1998; Blues Brothers 2000, 1998; Dirty Work, 1998; The Runner, 1999; Coyote Ugly, 2000; One Night at McCool's, 2000; Happy Birthday, 2001; My First Mister, 2001; Storytelling, 2001; Monsters Inc (voice), 2001; Dirty Deeds, 2002. Address: c/o Fred Spektor, CAA 9830 Wilshire Boulevard, Beverly Hills, CA 90212, USA.

**GOODSON-WICKES Charles,** b. 7 November 1945, London, England. Consulting Physician; Company Director; Business Consultant; Charity Executive. m. Judith Hopkinson, 2 sons. Education: MB BS, St Bartholomew's Hospital, 1972; Barrister-at-Law, Inner Temple, 1972. Appointments: House Physician, Cambridge and London, 1971-72; Surgeon Captain The Life Guards, served BAOR, Northern Ireland, Cyprus, 1973-77; Clinical Assistant and Locum Consultant, St Bartholomew's Hospital, London, 1976-80; Consulting Physician, BUPA Medical Centre, 1976-86; Regular Army Reserve of Officers, 1977-2000; Special Liaison and Research, Conservative Central Office, 1979-87; Principal, Private Occupational Health Practices, London, 1980-94; Member of Parliament for Wimbledon, 1987-97; Re-enlisted as Lieutenant Colonel for Gulf Campaign, on active service in advance from Saudi Arabia through Iraq to Kuwait, 1990-91; Parliamentary Private Secretary to: The Department of the Environment, The Treasury, The Department of Transport, 1992-96; Non-Executive Director, Merton Enterprise Agency Ltd, 1988-97; Non-Executive Director, Nestor Healthcare Group plc, 1993-99; Chief Executive, Medarc Ltd, 1982-; Director, Thomas Greg & Sons Ltd, 1992-; Non-Executive Director, Property Reversions I, II, III, 1993-; Non-Executive Director, Gyrus Group plc, 1997-; Chairman, British Field Sports Society, 1994-97; Founder Chairman, The Countryside Alliance, 1997-99; Chairman, The Rural Trust, 1999-; Chief Executive, London Playing Fields Society, 1998-; London Sports Board, 1999-. Publications: The New Corruption, 1984; Another Country (contributor), 1999. Honour: Deputy Lieutenant of Greater London, 1999-. Memberships: Clubs: Boodle's; Pratt's; MCC. Address: Watergate House, Bulford, Wiltshire SP4 9DY, England.

**GOODWIN Timothy Alan,** b. 3 May 1961, New Albany, Mississippi, USA. Information Technologist. Education: Bachelor of Business Administration, Computer Information Systems, Delta State University, 1985; Associate of Applied Science, Information Technology, State Technical Institute, 1999; Mater Diploma, honoris causa, Information Systems, World Academy of Letters, 2005. Appointments: Computer Analyst, Tyler Computers and Office Supplies, 1986-88; Programmer/Analyst, 1988-2002, Web Analyst/Database Administrator, 2002, Commercial Data Corporation. Publications: Co-authored systems: Profitline Solutions accounting, employee management and materials management systems; Commercial Data Corporation's e-Business Solution; Other non-branded systems authored: loans system, ambulatory billing system, retail accounting system, charged-off loans system and financial customer profiling system. Honours: International Medal of Honour; UCC Legion of Honor; World Medal of Freedom; American Medal of Honor; International Peace Prize; ABI World Laureate; World Lifetime Achievement Award, IBC Lifetime Achievement Award; IBC Companion of Honour; IBC Hall of Fame; American Hall of Fame; Leading Intellectuals of the World Hall of Fame; Great Minds of the 21st Century Hall of Fame; Commercial Data Corporation Service Awards; Listed in Who's Who publications and biographical dictionaries. Memberships: International High IQ Society; IBC Deputy Directors General Inner Circle; International Biographical Association; International Order of Merit; International Order of Distinction; Order of International Ambassadors; Order of International Fellowship; World Peace and Diplomacy Forum; Association for Computing Machinery; International Webmaster's Association; HTML Writers Guild; IEEE Computer Society; Phi Theta Kappa; Delta Mu Delta; World Black Belt Bureau. Address: 10307 Riggan Drive, Olive Branch, MS 38654, USA. E-mail: timgoodwin@ieee.org

**GORBACHEV Mikhail Sergeyevich,** b. 2 March 1931, Privolnoye, Krasnogvardeisky, Stavropol, Russia. Politician. m. Raisa Titarenko, 25 September 1953, 1 daughter. Education: Faculty of Law, Moscow State University, 1955; Stavropol Agricultural Institute, 1967. Appointments: Machine Operator, 1946; Joined CPSU, 1952; Deputy Head, Department of Propaganda Stavropol Komsomol Territorial Committee, 1955-56; First Secretary, Stavropol Komsomol City Committee, 1956-58; Second, then First Secretary Komsomol Territorial Committee, 1958-62; Party Organizer, Stavropol Territorial Production Board of Collective and State Farms, 1962; Head Department of Party Bodies of CPSU Territorial Committee, 1963-66; First Secretary, Stavropol City Party Committee, 1966-68; Second Secretary, Stavropol Territorial CPSU Committee, 1968-70, First Secretary, 1970-78; CPSU Central Secretary for Agricultural, 1978-85; General Secretary, CPSU Central Committee, 1985-91; Chairman, Supreme Soviet, 1989-90; President, USSR, 1990-91; Head, International Foundation for Socio-Econ and Political Studies, 1992-; Head, International Green Cross, 1993-; Co-founder, Social Democratic Party of Russia, 2000. Publications: A Time for Peace, 1985; The Coming Century of Peace, 1986; Speeches and Writings, 1986-90; Peace Has No Alternative, 1986; Moratorium, 1986; Perestroika: New Thinking for Our Country and the World, 1987; The August Coup (Its Cause and Results), 1991; December-91, My Stand, 1992; The Years of Hard Decisions, 1993; Life and Reforms, 1995. Honours: Indira Gandhi Award, 1987; Nobel Peace Prize, 1990; Peace Award World Methodist Council, 1990; Albert Schweitzer Leadership Award, Ronald Reagan Freedom Award, 1992; Honorary Citizen, Berlin, 1992; Freeman of Aberdeen, 1993; Urania-Medaille, Berlin, 1996; Honorary Degrees: University of Alaska, 1990; University of Bristol, 1993; University of Durnham, 1995; Order of Lenin, 3 times; Orders of Red Banner of Labour, Badge of Honour and other medals. Address: International Foundation for Socio-Economic and Political Studies, Leningradsky Prosp 49, 125468 Moscow, Russia.

**GORBACHEV Mikhail Yurievich,** b. 14 October 1959, Kishinev, Moldova. Chemist. m. V V Gorbacheva, 3 sons, 1 daughter. Education: MSc, Chemistry, Kishinev State University, 1981; PhD, Chemistry, Rostov-on-Don State University, 1986. Appointments: Post Graduate, 1982-85, Scientific Researcher, 1986-95, Senior Scientific Researcher, 1995-, Institute of Chemistry, Academy of Sciences of Moldova. Publications: 55 scientific publications including articles in the journal Physics and Chemistry of Liquids, 2000, 2001, 2002, 2003, 2004. Honour: Diploma, Russian Mendeleev's Society of Chemistry, Odessa, 1983. Memberships: Russian Mendeleev's Society of Chemistry; International Association of Water Quality; Moldavian Chemical Society. Address: Drumul Viilor Str. 42, Ap 77, Kishinev MD-2021, Republic of Moldova. E-mail: myugorbachev@yahoo.com

**GORDELADZE Maguli,** b. 25 April 1942, Tbilissi, Georgia. Bioenergy-Information-Therapist. Widowed, 2 children. Education: Teaching Diploma, Pushkin Institute for Education, 1965; Studied methods of alternative medicine, State Medical School, Tbilissi, Diploma, 1989. Appointments: Head, Scientific Research Laboratory for Non-traditional Healing Methods, 1990, Head, Department of Alternative Medicine, 1996, First Children's Hospital, Tbilissi; Invited to work as a Scientific Counsellor of Bioenergy-Information-Therapy, German gynaecological practice in Frankfurt am Main, Germany, 1997-; Lectures on the results and discoveries of her empirical work, 1998; Workshops and seminars for doctors and other people working with patients. Publications include: Maguli Gordeladze (by Demiko Loladze), 1996; Heilung durch Bioenergie, 1999;

Bioenergie – Die ärztliche Kunst des 21 Jahrhunderts, 2001; Bioenergowater Therapy, The Medical Art of the 21st century, 2002; Die Flüssigkeitszirkulation in menschlichen Organismus, 2002; Die Schutzenenergie im menschlichen Organismus und die Angst, 2003; Kopfschmerzen, 2003; Bioenergie in der Kinderheilkunde, 2003; Einhundert Jahre – ohne Krankheit, 2004, 2005. Honours: Honorary Diploma, Department of Bioenergy-Information, Georgian Engineering Academy, 2000; Elected Member of the Georgian Women's Council Board, 2000; Decorated for outstanding achievement and contribution to the field of alternative medicine for children as well as for her successful social activity, on the orders of the former President of Georgia, Edward Schewardnadze, Georgian Embassy, Bonn, Germany, 2000. Memberships: Deutsche Gesellschaft für Energetische und Informationsmedizin (DGEIM), Germany; Internationalen BIT-Ärztegesellschaft (Biophysikalische Informationstherapie Deutschland); New York Academy of Sciences; American Association for the Advancement of Science; Honorary Member, Georgian Engineering Academy; Elected Member, Georgian Women's Council Board. Address: Raimundstr. 157, 60320 Frankfurt, Germany.

**GORDON Anthony Grant,** b. 15 October 1942, Carmarthen, Wales. Independent Scientific Researcher. m. (1) Ann Diane Hitchings, divorced, 1 son, 1 daughter, (2) Mavis Anne Frisby, deceased 2002. Education: BSc, Psychology, Birkbeck College, London University, 1966-69; Diploma in Audiology, Southampton University, 1972. Appointments: Research Assistant, Nuffield Speech and Hearing Centre, King's Cross, 1970-71; Senior Audiology Technician, King's College, Hospital, 1973-84; Audiologist, Mayday Hospital, Croydon, 1985-86; Scientific Reader, Oxford English Dictionary, 1989-2003. Publications: Many contributions on a wide range of topics to journals of anaesthesiology, audiology, cardiology, epidemiology, Fortean studies, gastroenterology, infectious diseases, medicine, microbiology, neurology, neurosurgery, ophthalmology, otology, pathology, paediatrics, pharmacology, psychiatry, psychology and science. Membership: Fellow Royal Society of Medicine. Address: 32 Love Walk, London, SE5 8AD, England.

**GORDON Dotsie M,** b. 12 April 1943, Ridge District, St Elizabeth, Jamaica. Human Resource Professional. m. Aston M Gordon, 2 sons. Education: Certified Administrative Manager, 1986; Certificate in Personnel Management, College of Arts Science and Technology, Now University of Technology, 1990; Certified Human Resource Professional, 1996; MA, Law and Employment Relations, University of Leicester, UK, 2002. Appointments: Agricultural Workers' Centre, Department of the Treasury, 1962-64; Building and Loan Trust Company, 1964-66; Citibank, 1966-70; Founder, Managing Director, Dot Personnel Services JA Ltd, 1971-. Honours: Honorary Member, Jamaica Professional Secretaries' Association; CAM Board of Regents; CVSS; Meritorious Award, 1994; Jamaican Employers Federation, Meritorious Award, 1999. Memberships: Institute of Personnel and Development; Human Resource Professionals Association of Ontario; Society for Human Resource Management; Association for the Advancement of Management; Jamaica Association for Training and Development; Jamaica Computer Society; Jamaica Professional Secretaries Association; University of Technology Alumni Association. Address: 1 Oakdale, Kingston 8, Jamaica, West Indies. E-mail: Dotpersonnel@colis.com

**GORDON John William,** b. 19 November 1925, Jarrow-on-Tyne, England. Writer. m. Sylvia Young, 9 January 1954, 1 son, 1 daughter. Publications: The Giant Under the Snow, 1968, sequel, Ride the Wind, 1989; The House on the Brink,

1970; The Ghost on the Hill, 1976; The Waterfall Box, 1978; The Spitfire Grave, 1979; The Edge of the World, 1983; Catch Your Death, 1984; The Quelling Eye, 1986; The Grasshopper, 1987; Secret Corridor, 1990; Blood Brothers, 1991; Ordinary Seaman (autobiography), 1992; The Burning Baby, 1992; Gilray's Ghost, 1995; The Flesh Eater, 1998; The Midwinter Watch, 1998; Skinners, 1999; The Ghosts of Blacklode, 2002. Contributions to: Beginnings (Signal 1989); Ghosts & Scholars 21. Membership: Society of Authors. Address: 99 George Borrow Road, Norwich, NR4 7HU, England.

**GORDON Robert Patterson,** b. 9 November 1945, Belfast, Northern Ireland. University Teacher. m. Helen Ruth, 2 sons, 1 daughter. Education: St Catharine's College, Cambridge, 1964-69: BA, 1968, MA, 1972, PhD, 1973, Litt. D, 2001 (all Cambridge). Appointments: Assistant Lecturer, Hebrew and the Old Testament, 1969-70, Lecturer in Hebrew and Semitic Languages, 1970-79, University of Glasgow; Lecturer in Divinity, 1979-95, Regius Professor of Hebrew, 1995-, University of Cambridge. Publications: 1 and 2 Samuel: Introduction, 1984; 1 and 2 Samuel: A Commentary, 1986; The Targum of the Minor Prophets (jointly), 1989; Studies in the Targum to the Twelve Prophets, 1994; The Old Testament in Syriac: Chronicles, 1998; Hebrews: Commentary, 2000; Holy Land, Holy City, 2004; The Old Testament in its World (jointly), 2005. Honours: Jarrett Scholarship, 1966; Rannoch Hebrew Scholarship, 1966; Senior Scholarship, 1968; Bender Prize, 1968; Tyrwhitt Scholarship, 1969; Mason Prize, 1969. Memberships: Society for Old Testament Studies; British Association of Jewish Studies; National Club. Address: 85 Barrons Way, Comberton, Cambridge CB3 7DR, England.

**GORDON Sheldon Philip,** b. 11 July 1942, New York City, USA. Professor. m. Florence, 27 June 1965, 2 sons. Education: BS, Mathematics, Polytechnic University of New York, 1963; MSc, Mathematics, McGill University, 1965; PhD, Mathematics, McGill University 1969. Appointments: Assistant Professor, Queens College, 1968-74; Professor, Suffolk Community College, 1974-99; Adjunct Professor, SUNY, Stony Brook, 1994-; Professor, Farmingdale State University of New York, 1997-. Honours: Best Project, INPUT; Harvard Calculus Consortium; National Science Foundation Awards. Memberships: Mathematical Association of America; American Mathematics Association of Two Year Colleges. Address: 61 Cedar Road, East Northport, New York 11731, USA.

**GORDON-DUFF-PENNINGTON Patrick Thomas,** b. 12 October 1930, London, England. Landowner; Estate Manager; Farmer. m. Phyllida Pennington, 4 daughters. Education: Modern History, Trinity College Oxford, 1948-51. Appointments: National Service: SUO, Eaton Hall, OCS, 2nd Lieutenant, 1st Battalion, Queen's Own Cameron Highlanders, 1951-53; Student Shepherd, Hill Farms in Perthshire and Inverness-shire, 1953-55; Herded father-in-law's sheep at Muncaster and started work with rhododendrons, farmed small farm in Eskdale on own account, 1955-57; Student Land Agent, Sandringham, 1957-59; Farmed hill and upland farms in Dumfriesshire and Cumbria and managed farms for others, 1959-82; Director, Adverikie Estate, 1970-, Managing Director, 1986-97; Concerned with management of wife's family estate at Muncaster, 1982-; Council, Scottish NFU, 1972-82, Vice-Chairman, Livestock Committee, 1976-80, Convenor, Hill Farming Committee, 1976-82, Honorary President, 1981-83; President, Dumfries and Stewarty NFU, 1976; County Chairman, Cumbria NFU, 1986; Appointed Member, 1987-93, Lake District Special Planning Board, served on Development Control Committee and Chairman, Park Management Committee, 1989-93; Convenor, Scottish Landowners Federation, 1988-91; Chairman, Deer Commission for Scotland, 1993-99; Chairman, Knott End Centre for Complementary Care, 1991-2002; Chairman, Scottish Committee, Association of Electricity Producers, 1991-96; Non-Executive Director, Booker Countryside, 1994-96; European and Parliamentary Fellow, Industry and Parliament Trust, 1995-; Vice-President, Field Studies Council, 1995-; Occasional writer and broadcaster; Poet; Healer. Publications: Patrick of the Hills (Poems), 1998; Those Blue Remembered Hills (autobiography), 2004. Honours: OBE; FRGS; Deputy Lieutenant, Cumbria, 1993. Address: Muncaster Castle, Ravenglass, Cumbria CA18 1RQ, England.

**GORE Albert Jr,** b. 31 March 1948. Politician. m. Mary E Aitcheson, 1970, 1 son, 3 daughters. Education: Harvard University; Vanderbilt University. Appointments: Investigative reporter, editorial writer, The Tennessean, 1971-76; Home-builder and land developer, Tanglewood Home Builders Co, 1971-76; Livestock and tobacco farmer, 1973-; Head, Community Enterprise Board, 1993-; Member, House of Representatives, 1977-79; Senator, from Tennessee, 1985-93; Vice President, USA, 1993-2001; Democrat candidate in Presidential Elections, 2000; Lecturer, Middle Tennessee State, Fisk, Columbia Universities, 2001-; Vice-Chairman, Metropolitan West Financial, 2001-. Publication: Earth in the Balance, 1992. Honours include: Dr hc, Harvard 1994, New York, 1998. Address: Metwest Financial, 11440 San Vicente Boulevard, 3rd Floor, Los Angeles, CA 90049, USA.

**GORE-BOOTH David (Sir),** b. 15 May 1943. Retired Diplomat; Company Director. m. Mary Muirhead, 1 son (from previous marriage), 1 stepson. Education: Christ Church, Oxford; Middle East Centre for Arab Studies, Lebanon. Appointments: HM Diplomatic Service, 1964-98: Third Secretary: Foreign and Commonwealth Office, 1964, Middle East Centre for Arabic Studies, 1964, Baghdad, 1966; Third then Second Secretary, Lusaka, 1967; Second Secretary: Foreign and Commonwealth Office, 1969, Tripoli, 1969; Second then First Secretary, Foreign and Commonwealth Office, 1971; First Secretary, UK permanent representation to European Communities, Brussels, 1974; Assistant Head of Financial Relations Department, Foreign and Commonwealth Office, 1978; Counsellor (Commercial), Jeddah, 1980-83; Counsellor and Head of Chancery, UK Mission to UN, New York, 1983-86; Head of Policy Planning Staff, Foreign and Commonwealth Office, 1987-88; Assistant Under Secretary, Middle East, 1989-92; Ambassador to Saudi Arabia, 1993-96; High Commissioner to India, 1996-98; Special Advisor to the Chairman of HSBC Holdings plc, 1999-; Chairman, Windsor Energy Group, 1999-; Co-Chairman, Dubai/UK Trade and Economic Committee, 2000-, Qatar/Britain Association of Businessmen, 2001-, British Syrian Society, 2003-; Vice-President, Middle East Association, 2002; Director: HSBC Bank Middle East, 1999-, British Arab Commercial Bank, 1999-, HSBC Bank, Egypt, 1999-, Middle East International Magazine, 1999-, Saudi British Bank, 2000-; Group 4 Falck 2000-2004, Group 4 Securicor, 2004-, Arab-British Chamber of Commerce, 2002-, Vedanta Resources plc, 2003-; Trustee, Next Century Foundation, 1997; Member: Advisory Board, Centre for Studies in Security and Diplomacy, University of Birmingham, 1999-, Moroccan-British Business Council, 2002-; Egyptian-British Business Council, 2003-. Honours: Knight Commander of the Order of St Michael and St George, 1997; Knight Commander of the Royal Victorian Order, 1997. Memberships: Clubs: MCC; Travellers'; Garrick. Address: 27 Wetherby Mansions, Earl's Court Square, London SW5 9BH, England.

**GORI Fabio,** b. 5 August 1947, Montale (Pistoia), Italy. Professor. Education: Laurea Degree with Honours, Chemical

Engineering, 1971, Research Scholarship, Engineering, 1971-72, University of Bologna. Appointments: Professor, University of Reggio Calab, 1986-90; Professor, SUNY at Stony Brook, USA, 1988; Professor, Technical University of Milano, 1990-92; Professor, Heat Transfer, University of Rome "Tor Vergata", 1992-. Publications: 2 books on Thermodynamics, in Italian; Chapter on Heat Transfer in the Encyclopedia of Energy; 34 papers in international journals and 62 papers on proceedings of international conferences with referees; 3 patents. Memberships: American Society of Mechanical Engineering; Italian Union of Thermal Fluid-Dynamics. Address: Department of Mechanical Engineering, University of Rome "Tor Vergata", Via Del Politecnico 1, 00 133 Rome, Italy. Website: www.termofluid odinamica.it

**GORMLEY Antony Mark David,** b. 30 August 1950, London, England. Sculptor. m. Vicken Parsons, 2 sons, 1 daughter. Education: BA, History of Art, Trinity College, Cambridge, 1968-71; Central School of Art, London, 1974-75; BA, Fine Art, Goldsmiths School of Art, London, 1975-77; Postgraduate Studies, Slade School of Fine Art, London, 1977-79. Career: Artist and Sculptor; Solo exhibitions include: Whitechapel Art Gallery, London, 1981; Coracle Press, London, 1983; Riverside Studios, 1984; Drawings, 1981-1985, Salvatore Ala Gallery, New York, USA, 1985, 1986; Five Works, Serpentine Gallery, London, England, 1987; The Holbeck Sculpture, Leeds City Art Gallery, 1988; Drawings, Mcquarrie Gallery, Sydney, Australia, 1989; Bearing Light, Burnett Miller Gallery, Los Angeles, USA, 1990; Drawings and Etchings, Frith Street Gallery, London, 1991; American Field (touring), USA, 1992; Antony Gormley (touring), Sweden, England, Ireland, 1993; Field for the British Isles (touring) UK, 1994; Critical Mass, Remise, Vienna, Austria, 1995; Embody, Johnson County Community College, Kansas City, USA, 1996; Total Strangers, Koelnischer Kunstverein, Cologne, Germany, 1997; Angel of the North, The Gallery, Central Library, Gateshead, 1998; Insiders and other Recent Work, Galerie Xavier Hufkens, Brussels, Belgium, 1999; Quantum Cloud (part of North Meadow Sculpture Project), Millennium Dome, London, 2000; New Works, Galerie Nordenhake, Berlin, Germany, 2001; Anthony Gormley Drawing, The British Museum, London, 2003; Asian Field (touring) China, 2003; Domain Field, The Great Hall, Winchester, 2004; Antony Gormley Display, Tate Britain, 2004; Numerous group exhibitions, 1980-; Works in collections including: Arts Council of Great Britain; Tate Gallery; British Council; Southampton Art Gallery; Neue Museum Kassel, Stadt Kassel; Walker Arts Center Minneapolis; Leeds City Art Gallery; Irish Museum of Modern Art; Major commissions include: The Angel of the North, 1998; Quantum Cloud, London, 2000. Honours: Turner Prize, 1994; OBE, 1998; South Bank Art Award, 1999; Honorary Fellow, RIBA, 2001; Honorary Doctorate, Open University, 2001; Honorary Doctorate, Cambridge University; Fellow, Jesus College and Trinity College; RA; Fellow, RSA; Honorary Doctorate, Newcastle University, 2004; Honorary Doctorate, Teeside University, 2004. Address: 15-23 Vale Royal, London N7 9AP, England. E-mail: antony.gormley@ndirect.co.uk

**GOROKHOV Igor M,** b. 6 April 1932, Leningrad, Russia. Professor of Geochemistry. m. Irina A Ostrovskaya, 1 daughter. Education: Certificate of research chemist (honours), Leningrad State University, 1954; PhD, Chemical Sciences, Leningrad Technology Institute, 1965; Senior Research Officer, Geochemistry, Higher Education Board of the USSR, Moscow, 1979; DSc, Geology and Mineralogical Sciences, Institute of Geochemistry, Kiev, Ukraine, 1981. Appointments: Junior Research Fellow, USSR Academy of Science, V G Khlopin Radium Institute, Leningrad, 1954-61; Junior Research Fellow,

USSR Academy of Science, Laboratory of Precambrian Geology, Leningrad, 1961-67; Junior Research Fellow to Head of Laboratory, Russian Academy of Science, Institute of Precambrian Geology and Geochronology, St Petersburg, 1967-. Publications: 2 books; Over 100 articles in scientific journals. Honours: Medal for scientific service, Geological Survey, Prague, 1986; Medal for scientific service, Geological Survey, Bratislava, 1986; State Scientific Grants, 1994, 1997, 2000; Award, INTERPERIODICA Publishing House, 1996, 2004. Memberships: Board of Directors, Council on Isotope Geology and Geochronology, 1973-91, Council on Geochemistry, 1992-93, 1999-; Committee on the Upper Precambrian, Moscow, 1988-; Editorial Board, Chemical Geology, 1987-99; New York Academy of Sciences, 1995. Address: Institute of Precambrian Geology and Geochronology, Russian Academy of Sciences, nab Makarova 2, 199034 St Petersburg, Russia. E-mail: gorokhov@ig1405.spb.edu

**GORRIE Donald Cameron Easterbrook,** b. 2 April 1933, Dehra Dun, India. Member of the Scottish Parliament. m. Astrid Salvesen, 2 sons. Education: MA, Modern History, Corpus Christi College, Oxford, 1953-57. Appointments: School Master: Gordonstoun School, 1957-60, Marlborough College, 1960-66; Director of Research then Administration, Scottish Liberal Party, 1968-75; Liberal Councillor, Edinburgh Town Council, 1971-75, Councillor and Liberal Democrat Group Leader, Lothian Regional Council, 1974-96, City of Edinburgh District Council, 1980-96, City of Edinburgh Council, 1995-97; MP, Liberal Democrat, Edinburgh West, 1997-2001; Member Liberal Democrat Scotland Team, 1997-99; MSP, Liberal Democrat, Central Scotland, 1999-; Spokesman on Local Government, 1999-2000, Finance, 2000-01; Justice, 2001-03; Procedures, 1999-2003; Communities, Culture, Sport, Voluntary Sector, Older People, 2003-. Honours: OBE; DL; Backbencher of the Year, 1999; Free Spirit of the Year, 2001. Publications: Party Manifestos and Political pamphlets. Memberships: Former Chairman, Edinburgh Youth Orchestra; Sometime Board/Committee: Royal Lyceum Theatre; Queen's Hall, Edinburgh; Edinburgh Festival; Scottish Chamber Orchestra; Castle Rock Housing Association; Lothian Association of Youth Clubs; Edinburgh City Youth Café; Diverse Attractions; Edinburgh Zoo. Address: 9 Garscube Terrace, Edinburgh EH12 6BW, Scotland.

**GORYAEVA Elena Mikhailovna,** b. 11 November 1944, Leningrad, Russia. Research Scientist; Physicist. m. Mikhail Alexandrovich Goryaev, 1976, 1 daughter. Education: MS, Opto-Electronics, Leningrad Institute of Optics and Exact Mechanics, 1967. Appointments: Engineer, 1967-72, Junior Research Specialist, 1972-82, Research Specialist, 1982-, Laboratory of Luminescence and Photochemistry, S I Vavilov State Optical Institute, St Petersburg. Publications: Over 40 scientific publications, patents and reports presented. Honours: Labour Veteran Medal, Leningrad City Council of People's Deps, 1988; Listed in national and international biographical dictionaries. Memberships: Member, All Russian Inventors Society. Address: S I Vavilov State Optical Institute, Birzhevaya liniya 12, 199034 St Petersburg, Russia. E-mail: goryaeva@yahoo.com or ogoryaev@og2172.spb.edu

**GOSAVI Mo So,** b. 15 September 1935, Phaltan, Satara, Maharashtra, India. Educator. m. Sunanda Devi, 2 sons, 1 daughter. Education: B. Com, 1st Class Honours, 1954, M. Com., 1st Class Honours, 1956, LLB, 1st Class Honours, PhD, Business Administration, 1st Class Honours, 1968, Pune University, India; Sahityacharya (MA Marathi), 1956. Appointments: Daxina Fellow, Pune University, 1954-56; Lecturer, Assistant Professor, Professor, B M College of

# DICTIONARY OF INTERNATIONAL BIOGRAPHY

Commerce, 1956-58; Professor and Principal, BYK College of Commerce, Pune University, 1958-95 (youngest principal at the age of 22 with longest tenure of 38 years); Founder and Director, MBA Programme at Pune University; Pioneer of management education in India; Founder and Director, JDC Bytco Institute of Management Studies and Research, Nashik, India, 1968-; Elected President, College of Management, Indian Council of Management Executives, Mumbai, 2000-2008; Participant in many national and international conferences and symposia on management education including astrology, futurology and predictive science. Publications: 20 books on management, education and spirituality; Articles in journals of repute in the field of management; Numerous conference presentations. Honours: Rajiv Gandhi Peace Award, 1990; Samaj Bhushan Award, 1993; Shikshan Maharshi Award, 1996; Dnyan Hira Award, 1999; Master Teacher of the Millennium, 2001; Outstanding Management Scientist, India, 2002; Sir, 2004. Memberships: Secretary, Gokhale Education Society, 1973-; Indian Commerce Association; Indian Association for Management Development; Indian Institute of Public Administration (Nashik Chapter); Indian Academy of H.R. Education; National President, National Council of Teacher Educators, 2005-2010. Address: Director, JDC Bytco I.M.S.R., 7 Anubandh Model Colony, Nashik 422005, India. E-mail: gokhale_edu@hotmail.com

**GOSEKI-SONE Masae,** b. 6 May 1956, Tokyo, Japan. Associate Professor. m. Atsushi Goseki, 2 children . Education: Bachelor of Home Economics, 1979, Master of Home Economics, 1981, Japan Women's University; Doctor of Philosophy of Dentistry, Tokyo Medical and Dental University, 1989; Registered Dietician, Ministry of Health and Welfare, 1984; Radiation Protection Supervisor Qualification (First Class), Ministry of Education, Culture, Sports Science and Technology. Appointments: Educational Assistant, Tokyo Medical and Dental University, 1981-97; Lecturer, 1998-2001, Associate Professor, 2002-, Japan Women's University. Publications Articles in scientific journals including: Journal of Dental Research, 1995; Journal of Bone and Mineral Research, 1998, 2001, 2002, 2005; Biochemical and Biophysical Research Communications, 1999, 2002; Patents for: The Prediction Method (Bone Mineral Density and the gene Polymorphism Analysis – Tissue non-specific alkaline phosphatase; Discovery of the registration of the novel gene (Cbfa1, rat partially). Honours: Grant-in-Aid for Scientific Research, Ministry of Education, Culture, Sports and Technology, 1990-93, 1998-99. Memberships: Trustee, International Conference of Alkaline Phosphatase; Trustee, Japan Society of Metabolism and Clinical Nutrition; American Society for Bone and Mineral Research. Address: 2-8-1 Mejirodai, Bunkyo-ku, Tokyo, 112-8681 Japan.

**GOSLING-HARE Paula Louise, (Ainslie Skinner, Holly Baxter),** b. 12 October 1939, Michigan, USA. Author; Crime and Suspense Fiction. m. (1) Christopher Gosling, September 1968, divorced 1978, 2 daughters, (2) John Hare, 1982. Education: BA, Wayne State University. Appointments: Copywriter, Campbell Ewald, USA; Copywriter, Mitchell & Co, London; Copywriter, Pritchard Wood, London: Freelance Copywriter, 1974-. Publications: A Running Duck, 1976; Zero Trap, 1978; The Woman in Red, 1979; Losers Blues, 1980; Minds Eye (as Ainslie Skinner), 1980; Monkey Puzzle, 1982; The Wychford Murders, 1983; Hoodwink, 1985; Backlash, 1987; Death Penalties, 1990; The Body in Blackwater Bay, 1992; A Few Dying Words, 1994; The Dead of Winter, 1995; Death and Shadows, 1999; Underneath Every Stone, 2000; Ricochet, 2002; Tears of the Dragon, 2004. Honours: Gold Dagger, Crime Writers' Association; Arts Achievement Award, Wayne State University. Memberships: Crimewriters' Association, chairman,

1982; Society of Authors. Address: c/o Greene & Heaton Ltd, 37 Goldhawk Road, London W12 8QQ, England.

**GOSNELL Joseph Arthur,** b. 21 June 1936, Arrandale Cannery, British Columbia, Canada. Commercial Fisherman; Politician. m. Audrey Adele Munroe, 5 sons, 2 daughters. Education: St Michael's Indian Residential School, Alert Bay, British Columbia. Appointments: Long-time commercial Fisherman; Former Executive Chairman and President, Nisga'a Tribal Council, 1992; Former Council Member and Chief Councillor, Gitlakdamix Band; Former Member, Pacific Area Regional Council; Former Board Member, Native Brotherhood of British Columbia; Former Commissioner, Pacific Salmon Commission; Chief Negotiator, Nisga'a Negotiating Team; Signed Historic Nisga'a Treaty, 1999; Elected President of new Nisga'a Lisims Government, 2000; Member, First Nations Advisory Council, Simon Fraser University, 2001; Appointed Governor of the Council for Canadian Unity, 2002. Honours: LLD, Royal Roads University, 1997; LLD, Open University, 1999; LLD, University of British Columbia, 2000; LLD, Simon Fraser University, 2000; Order of British Columbia, 1999; Order of Canada, 2001; Award for Contribution to Humanity, Canadian Labour Congress, 1999; Bachelor of Laws, Wilp Wilxo' oskwhl Nisga'a and University of Northern British Columbia; Newsmaker of the Week, CTV, 1998; Newsmaker of the Year, CBC Radio, 1998; Citation from Dialogue Canada for Leadership, 1996; Lifetime Achievement Award, National Aboriginal Achievement Award, 2000; Queen's Golden Jubilee Medal, 2002; Patron, University of Victoria, Education Endowment for Aboriginal Justice, 2000. Address: 4406 Adams Crescent, New Aiyansh, BC V0J1A0, Canada.

**GOSWELL Brian (Sir),** b. 26 November 1935, London, England. Chartered Surveyor. m. Deirdre Gillian Stones, 2 sons. Education: Durham University. Appointments: Military Service: Served with Oxford and Bucks Light Infantry, 1954-56; Healey & Baker (Surveyors and Valuers): Joined 1957, Partner, 1969, Managing Partner, 1977, Deputy Senior Partner, 1988, Deputy Chairman, Board of Management, 1997, Consultant, 2000, Retired, 2002; Director: Guinness Peat Properties Inc, 1982-84; City Merchant Developers Plc, 1984-89; Chairman: Pubmaster, Ltd, 1994-96, The William Hill Group Ltd, 1994-97, The Brent Walker Group Plc, 1993-97, Roux Restaurants Ltd, 1988-96; President: British Council for Offices, 1993-94, American Chamber of Commerce (UK), 1994-98; Director: Avon City Ltd, 1989-98, Carlton Club Political Committee, 1993-98, Sunley Secure II Plc, 1992-99; Currently: Chairman, ISS Group Ltd; Member, Advisory Board of the Fulbright Commission; Member, Duke of Edinburgh's International Fellowship; Member, Board of Management, British Council for Offices; Vice-President, Carlton Club Political Committee; President, The Land Institute. Honour: Knight Bachelor, 1991. Memberships: Fellow Durham University Society; Past President, Incorporated Society of Valuers and Auctioneers; Fellow Royal Institution of Chartered Surveyors; Fellow Land Institute; Fellow Royal Society of Arts; Fellow Institute of Directors; Clubs: Carlton; The Cavalry and Guards; City Livery; Marylebone Cricket Club; Royal Green Jackets London Club; United & Cecil Club; Leander Club. Address: Pipers, Camley Park Drive, Pinkneys Green, Berkshire, SL6 6QF, England.

**GOUGH Douglas Owen,** b. 8 February 1941, Stourport, Worcestershire, England. Astrophysicist. m. Rosanne Penelope, 2 sons, 2 daughters. Education: BA, 1962, MA, PhD, 1966, St John's College, University of Cambridge. Appointments: Research Associate, Joint Institute for Laboratory Astrophysics, and Department of Physics and Astrophysics, University of Colorado, 1966-67; Visiting Member, Courant Institute of Mathematical Sciences, New York University, 1967-69; National Academy of Sciences Senior Postdoctoral Resident/ Research Associate, Goddard Institute for Space Studies, New York, 1967-69; Member, Graduate Staff, Institute of Theoretical Astronomy, 1969-73; Lecturer, Astronomy and Applied Mathematics, 1973-85, Reader in Astrophysics, 1985-93 Institute of Astronomy and Department of Applied Mathematics and Theoretical Physics, Professor of Theoretical Astrophysics, 1993-, Deputy Director, 1993-99, Director, 1999-2004, Institute of Astronomy, University of Cambridge; Associate Professor, University of Toulouse, 1984-85; Fellow Adjoint, Joint Institute for Laboratory Astrophysics, Boulder, Colorado, 1986-; Scientific Co-ordinator, Institute for Theoretical Physics, University of California, Santa Barbara, 1990; Visiting Professor, Department of Physics, Stanford University; Honorary Professor of Astronomy, Queen Mary and Westfield College, University of London, 1996-. Publications: About 300 papers in scientific literature; Books edited include: Problems of Solar and Stellar Oscillations, 1983; Seismology of the Sun and distant stars, 1991; Challenges to theories of the structure of moderate-mass stars, 1991; Equation-of-State and Phase-transition issues in Models of Ordinary Astrophysical Matter, 2004; The Scientific Legacy of Fred Hoyle, 2004. Honours: Gravity Research Foundation Prize (shared with F W W Dilke), 1973; James Arthur Prize, Harvard University, 1982; William Hopkins Prize, Cambridge Philosophical Society, 1984; George Ellery Hale Prize, American Astronomical Society, 1994; Mousquetiere d'Armagnac, 2001; Eddington Medal, Royal Astronomical Society, 2002. Memberships: Fellow, Royal Astronomical Society; American Astronomical Society; International Astronomical Union; Astronomical Society of India; Fellow, Royal Society; Fellow, Institute of Physics; Foreign Member, Royal Danish Academy of Sciences and Letters. Address: Institute of Astronomy, Madingley Road, Cambridge CB3 0HA, England. E-mail: douglas@ast.cam.ac.uk

**GOULD Elliott,** b. 29 August 1938, Brooklyn, New York, USA. Actor. m. (1) Barbra Streisand, 1963, divorced 1971, 1 son, (2) Jenny Bogart, 1 son, 1 daughter. Career: Actor, theatre appearances include: Say Darling, 1958; Irma La Douce, 1960; I Can Get It For You Wholesale, 1962; Drat! The Cat, 1965; Alfred in Little Murders, 1967; Toured in the Fantastiks with Liza Minelli; National tour with Deathtrap; Films include: The Confession, 1966; The Night They Raided Minsky's, 1968; Bob and Carol and Ted and Alice, 1969; Getting Straight, 1970; M*A*S*H, 1970; The Touch, 1971; Little Murders, 1971; The Long Good-Bye, 1972; Nashville, 1974; I Will...I Will...For Now, 1976; Harry and Walter Go to New York, 1976; A Bridge Too Far, 1977; The Silent Partner, 1979; The Lady Vanishes, 1979; Escape to Athens, 1979; The Muppet Movie, 1979; Falling in Love Again, 1980; The Devil and Max Devlin, 1981; Over the Brooklyn Bridge, 1984; The Naked Face, 1984; Act of Betrayal, 1988; Dead Men Don't Die, 1989; Secret Scandal, 1990; Strawanser, The Player, Exchange Lifeguards, Wet and Wild Summer, Naked Gun 331/3, the Final Insult (cameo), White Man's Burden, The Glass Shield, Kicking and Screaming, A Boy Called Hate, Johns, The Big Hit, American History, X, Bugsy, Hoffman's Hunger, Capricorn One; Boys Life 3, 2000; Ocean's Eleven, 2001; Numerous TV appearances including Doggin' Around (BBC TV); Once Upon a Mattress (CBC). Website: www.elliottgould.net

**GOULD Stephen Jay,** b. 10 September 1941, New York, New York, USA. Professor of Geology and Zoology; Curator; Writer. m. Deborah Ann Lee, 3 October 1965, 2 sons. Education: AB, Antioch College, 1963; PhD, Columbia University, 1967. Appointments: Assistant Professor, 1967-71, Associate Professor, 1971-73, Professor of Geology, 1973-,

Alexander Agassiz Professor of Zoology, 1982-, Assistant Curator, 1967-71, Associate Curator, 1971-73, Curator, 1973-, Invertebrate Paleontology, Museum of Comparative Zoology, Harvard University; Lecturer, Cambridge University, 1984, Yale University, 1986, Stanford University, 1989. Publications: Ontogeny and Phylogemy, 1977; Ever Since Darwin, 1977; The Panda's Thumb, 1980; The Mismeasure of Man, 1981; Hen's Teeth and Horse's Toes, 1983; The Flamingo's Smile, 1985; Time's Arrow, Time's Cycle, 1987; An Urchin in the Storm, 1987; Wonderful Life, 1989; Bully for Brontosaurus, 1991; Finders, Keepers (with R W Purcell), 1992; Eight Little Piggies, 1993; Questioning the Millennium: A rationalist's Guide to a Precisely Arbitrary Countdown, 1997; Leonardo's Mountain of Clams and the Diet of Worms, 1998; The Living Stones of Marrakech, 2000. Contributions to: Journals. Honours: American Book Award, 1981; National Book Award, 1981; John D and Catharine T MacArthur Foundation Fellowship, 1981-86; National Book Critics Circle Award, 1982; Outstanding Book Award, American Educational Research Association, 1983; Phi Beta Kappa Book Awards, 1983, 1990; Brandeis University Creative Arts Award, 1986; Medal, City of Edinburgh, 1990; Forkosch Award, 1990; Rhone-Poulenc Prize, 1991; Silver Medal, Linnean Society, 1992; Over 35 honorary doctorates; Numerous other awards, medals, etc. Memberships: American Academy of Arts and Sciences, fellow; American Society of Naturalists, president, 1977-80; History of Science Association; National Academy of Sciences; Paleontological Society, president, 1985-; Sigma Xi; Society for the Study of Evolution, president, 1990; Society for the Systematic Study of Zoology. Address: c/o Museum of Comparative Zoology, Department of Earth Sciences, Harvard University, Cambridge, MA 02138, USA.

**GOURA George Stepanovich,** b. 15 May 1929, Leninacan, Armenia, USSR. Mechanical Engineer. m. Kluyeva Victoriya Alexandrovna, 2 daughters. Education: Higher School: Railway Institute at Rostov at River Don, USSR, 1946-51; Candidate of Technical Science, USSR Academy of Science, Moscow, 1962; Doctor's Degree of Technical Science, Kiev Civil Aviation Institute, USSR, 1974. Appointments: Chief, Service and Supply of Locomotive Maintenance, South-Donetsk and Donetsk Railways Department, USSR Railway Ministry, 1952-; Teacher, Railway Technical Secondary School, Tikhoretsk, Kuban, 1954-55; Teacher, 1955-58, Dean of Mechanical Faculty, 1957-58, Railway Institute, Byelorussia; Post-graduate course, 1958-61, Higher Engineer-Researcher, 1961-62, Institute of Engineering Science, Academy of Sciences USSR, Moscow; Head, Power Transmissions Constructions Department, Lugansk Diesel Locomotive Institute, 1962-65; Senior Lecturer, 1965-76, Professor, 1976, Head of Chair, 1971-99, Dean of General Technical Faculty, 1974-77, Krasnodar Polytechnic Institute, Kuban; Rector, Irkutsk Railway Engineers Institute, 1980-82; Head of Chair, Professor, Sochi State University of Tourism and Resort Business; Involved in the creation of Health Resort of Professional Higher Education, Sochi, 1966-. Publications: Over 160 publications and inventions in professional scientific and engineering journals and bulletins; Author of the modern theory of non-free motion of body with due regard for non-stationary processes and deformations in friction contact zone; Creator of original landing gears of aircrafts; Creator of the testing method of materials on abrasive wearing at high speeds of sliding with applying of a composition elastic-abrasive cloth; Creator of precise processing and assembly technology of fiber connections; Creator of schematic plans of Kursk submarine lift. Honours: Honorary Diploma, International Scientific Congress on Tribology, 1985; Title of Honoured Worker of the Science and Engineering of Russian Federation, President of Russia, 1996; Title of Honorary Worker of Higher Education in Russia,

Minister of Education, 1999; Silver Medal of distinguished contribution to development of Kuban, 1999; Laureate Professor of Zhukovsky Prize, Russian Transport Academy of Science in Aeronautical field of research, 1999; Honourable Citizen of the City of Sochi. Memberships: Society of Researchers, New York Museum of Natural History; Russian Transport Academy of Science; Scientific-Methodical Council on Tribology, Ministry of Education of Russia; Interdepartmental Scientific Council on Tribology of Russia; Russian Association of Tribology Engineers. Address: Abrikosovaya Str 17 A, Room 22, Sochi, Russia 354003. E-mail: goura@mail.ru Website: goura.narod.ru

**GOURLAY Caroline**, b. 10 August 1939, London, England. Poet. m. Simon Gourlay, 17 May 1967, 3 sons. Education: Royal Academy of Music, 1957-60; LRAM, 1962-64. Appointment: Editor, Blithe Spirit, Journal of the British Haiku Society. Publications: Crossing the Field, 1995; Through the Café Door, 1999; Reading All Night, 1999; Lull Before Dark, Brooks Books Press, 2005. Contributions to: Envoi; Poetry Wales; New Welsh Review; Iron; Haiku Quarterly; Outposts; Blithe Spirit, Journal of the British Haiku Society, Planet Tanka Splendor. Honour: James Hackett Award, 1996. Address: Hill House Farm, Knighton, Powys LD7 1NA, Wales.

**GOVAERTS France**, b. Brussels, Belgium. Professor Emeritus of Sociology. m. Pierre-Emeric Mandl, 1 son, 1 daughter. Education: BA, Law, Liège University; LLD, Free University of Brussels; PhD ( Doctorat d'État) Université René Descartes, Paris V/Sorbonne, 1975. Appointments: Research Director, Centre National de Sociologie du Travail, 1962-83; Professor of Sociology of Knowledge, Free University of Brussels, 1971-90; President, International Institute of Sociology, 1974-80; Professor of Methodology in Social Sciences, State University of Mons, 1975-78; NGO Representative to the UN, 1986-2003; Past Consultant or Expert to organisations including: OECD, EC, UN. Publications: Over 200 articles on sociology of knowledge, epistemology, semiotics in advertising, gender, ageing, poverty, social indicators, sociology of leisure, sociology of sports; Author of the seminal book on women's multiple roles: Loisirs des femmes et temps libre, 1999; Works presently on social individuation processes. Honours: Officier de l'ordre de Leopold, 1977; Honorary President, International Institute of Sociology, 1980-; Invited to give keynote addresses and to chair sessions at numerous international meetings and scientific congresses. Memberships: Life Member, Association internationale des sociologues de langue française; Life Member, International Sociological Association; American Association for the Advancement of Science; New York Academy of Sciences; Past memberships in numerous national and international associations, scientific societies and women's organisations. Address: Rue Gabrielle 82, Bte 5, 1180 Brussels, Belgium.

**GOVRIN Nurit**, b. 6 November 1935, Israel. Educationist; Researcher; Writer. m. Shlomo Govrin, 3 sons. Education: BA, Hebrew Literature, Bible Studies; MA, Hebrew Literature; PhD, Hebrew Literature; Tel-Aviv University; Harvard University, USA; University of Oxford, England. Appointments: Administrative positions, Tel-Aviv University; Teaching, University of California at Los Angeles, Columbia University, New York, Hebrew Union College; Assistant, 1965-68, Teacher, 1968-72, Lecturer, 1972-74, Senior Lecturer, 1974-78, Associate Professor 1978-90, Full Professor, 1990-, Tel-Aviv University; Public Council for Culture and Art, Ministry of Education; Judge, Selection Committees for many literary prizes. Publications: 14 books including: G Shoffman: His Life and Work, 2 volumes, 1982; The Brenner Affair - The Fight for Free Speech, 1985; The Literature of Eretz - Israel in the Early Days of the Settlements,

1985; The First Half - The Life and Work of Dvora Baron 1888-1923, 1988; Honey from the Rock, 1989; Brenner - Nonplussed and Mentor, 1991; Burning - Poetry About Brenner, 1995; Literary Geography - Lands and Landmarks on the Map of Hebrew Literature, 1998; Reading the Generations – Contextual Studies in Hebrew Literature, 2 Volumes, 2002; Nurit Govrin: Bibliography: 1950-2004 by Joseph Galrom-Goldshlayer; Nurit Govrin: The Forgotten Traveler: Shlomith F Flaum – Her Life and Work, 2005; Prescriptives on Modern Hebrew Literature – In Honor of Professor Nurit Govrin, edited by Avner Holzman, 2005; Editor of 14 books. Honours: Postgraduate Scholarship, Rothschild Fund, 1973-74; Research Grants: Israel National Academy for Sciences, 1975-78, Jewish Memorial Fund, 1982, Israel Matz Fund, 1982, 1984-86, 1989, American Academy for Jewish Studies, 1984-85, 1989; Haifa Municipality Prize, 1993; Shalom Aleichem Prize, 1996; Creative Woman Prize, Wizo Prize, 1998; Bialik Prize, 1998; Israel Efros Prize, 2001. Memberships: Katz Institute for Research of Hebrew Literature; Literature Committee, Israel National Academy of Sciences and Humanities. Address: 149 Jobotinsky St, Tel-Aviv 62150, Israel.

**GOWANS James**, b. 7 May 1924, Sheffield, England. Medical Scientist. m. Moyra, 1 son, 2 daughters. Education: Kings College, London; Kings College Medical School, London; Lincoln College, Oxford. Appointments: Research Professor, Royal Society, Oxford University, 1962-77; Secretary, UK Medical Research Council, 1977-87; Secretary General, Human Frontier Science Program, Strasbourg, France, 1989-93. Publications: Numerous articles in scientific journals. Honours: FRS; FRCP; Kt; CBE; Royal Medal, Royal Society; Foreign Associate, US National Academy of Sciences; Gairdner Foundation Award, Toronto; Wolf Prize in Medicine, Israel; Honorary Degrees at Yale, Chicago, Rochester, New York, Birmingham, Edinburgh, Glasgow, Southampton. Memberships: Honorary Fellow at Lincoln, Exeter and St Catherine's Colleges, Oxford. Address: 75 Cumnor Hill, Oxford, OX2 9HX.

**GOWER David Ivon**, b. 1 April 1957, Tunbridge Wells, Kent. Cricketer. m. Thorunn Ruth Nash, 1992, 2 daughters. Education: University College, London. Career: Left-hand batsman; Played for Leicestershire, 1975-89, captain, 1984-86, Hampshire, 1990-93; Played in 117 Tests for England, 1978-92, 32 as captain, scoring then England record 8,231 runs (average 44.2) with 18 hundreds; Toured Australia, 1978-79, 1979-80, 1982-83, 1986-87, 1990-91; Scored 26,339 first-class runs with 53 hundreds; 114 limited-overs internationals; Sunday Express Cricket Correspondent, 1993-95; Public Relations Consultant for cricket sponsorship National Westminster Bank, 1993-; Commentator, Sky TV, 1993-; Commentator and presenter, BBC TV, 1994-99; Columnist, Sunday Telegraph, 1995-98; Presenter, Sky TV cricket, 1999-; Columnist, The Sun, 2000-; Television: They Think It's All Over. Publications: A Right Ambition, 1986; On The Rack, 1990; The Autobiography, 1992; Articles in Wisden Cricket Monthly. Address: SFX Sports Group, 35/36 Grosvenor Street, London W1K 4QX, England.

**GRACE Sherrill Elizabeth**, b. Ormstown, Quebec, Canada. University Professor. 2 children. Education: BA, University of Western Ontario, 1962-65; MA, 1968-70, PhD, 1970-74, McGill University. Appointments: Teacher, Netherhall Secondary Girls School, Cambridge, England, 1967-68; Teaching Assistant, 1970-73, Special Lecturer, 1974-75, Assistant Professor, 1975-77, McGill University; Assistant Professor, 1977, Associate Professor, 1981, Professor, 1987-, Departmental Head, 1997-2002, University of British Columbia. Publications include: Violent Duality: A Study of Margaret Atwood, 1980; The Voyage That Never Ends: Malcolm Lowry's Fiction, 1982;

Regression and Apocalypse: Studies in North American Literary Expressionism, 1989; Sursum Corda: The Collected Letters of Malcolm Lowry, 1995, 1996; Staging the North: 12 Canadian Plays, 1999; Canada and the Idea of North, 2002; Performing National Identities: Essays on contemporary Canadian Theatre, 2003; New annotated edition, A Woman's Way Through Unknown Labrador, 2004; Inventing Tom Thomson: From Biographical Fictions to Fictional Autobiographies, 2004. Honours include: University of British Columbia President Killam Research Prize, 1990; FEL Priestley Award, 1993; University of British Columbia Jacob Biely Research Prize, 1998; Fellow, Royal Society of Canada; Richard Plant Prize, 2003; Canada Council Killam Fellowship, 2003-05; Brenda and David McLean Chair in Canadian Studies, 2003-05; UBC Distinguished University Scholar, 2003-. Memberships: International Association of University Professors of English; Modern Language Association; Association of Canadian University Teachers of English. Address: Department of English, University of British Columbia, #397-1873 East Mall, BC V6T 1Z1, Canada.

**GRACIA-BENEYTO Carmen,** b. 29 May 1947, Valencia, Spain. Professor; Art Historian. m. Juan Pecourt, 1 son, 2 daughters. Education: Degree, Filosofia y Letras, 1968; PhD, Geography and History, 1973, University of Valencia, Spain. Appointments: University Teacher, 1975-90, Professor, 1990-, University of Valencia, Spain; Director, Museo de Bellas Artes de Valencia, 1991-93; Director, Instituto de Arte, Institució Valenciana d'Estudios I Investigació, 1992-95. Publications: Books: Las Pensiones de Pintura de la Diputacion de Valencia, 1987; Valencian Painter 1860-1936. From the Collection of the Council of Valencia, 1992; Història de L'Art Valencià, 1995; Arte Valenciano, 1998; La Imagen del Pensamento: El Paisaje en Ignacio Pinazo, 2001. Honours: Honorary Director: Museo de Bellas Artes de Valencia. Memberships: Numerario Institut d'Estudis Catalans. Address: Isabel la Catolica 7, 46113 Moncada (Valencia), Spain. E-mail: carmen.gracia@uv.es

**GRADE Michael Ian,** b. 8 March 1943, London, England. Broadcasting Executive. m. (1) Penelope Jane Levinson, 1967, divorced 1981, 1 son, 1 daughter, (2) Hon Sarah Lawson, 1982, divorced, (3) Francesca Mary Leahy, 1998, 1 son. Education: St Dunstan's College, London, UK. Appointments: Trainee Journalist, Daily Mirror, 1960, Sports Columnist, 1964-66; Theatrical Agent, Grade Organisation, 1966; Joint Managing Director, London Management and Representation, 1969-73; Deputy Controller of Programmes (Entertainment), London Weekend TV, 1973-77; Director of Programmes and Member Board, 1977-81; President, Embassy TV, 1981-84; Controller, BBC 1, 1984-86; Director of Programmes BBC TV, 1986-87; Chief Executie Officer, Channel Four, 1988-87; Chairman, VCI PLC, 1995-98; Director, 1991-2000, non-executive Chairman, 1995-97, Chairman, 1997-98, First Leisure Corp. Honours: CBE, Hon LLD (Nottingham), 1997; Royal TV Society Gold Medal, 1997. Memberships include: Vice President, Children's Film Unit, 1993-; Delfont Macintosh Theatres Ltd, 1994-99; Entertainment Charities Fund, 1994-; Deputy Chairman, Society of Stars, 1995-; RADA, 1996-; Royal Albert Hall, 1997-; Charlton Athletic Football Club, 1997-; Camelot Group, 2000-; Digitaloctopus, 2000-; Chair, Octopus, 2000-; Pinewood Studio Ltd, 2000-; Hemscott.NET, 2000-.

**GRAF Steffi,** b. 14 June 1969, Bruehl, Germany. Tennis Player. m. Andre Agassi, 1 son. Career: Won Orange Bowl 12s, 1981; European 14 and under and European Circuit Masters, 1982, Olympic demonstration event, Los Angeles; Winner, German Open, 1986, French Open, 1987, 1988, 1993, 1995, 1996; Australian open, 1988, 1989, 1990, 1994; Wimbledon, 1988, 1989, 1991, 1992, 1993, 1995, 1996, US Open, 1988, 1989, 1993, 1995, 1996; Ranked No 1, 1987; Official World Champion, 1988; Grand Slam winner, 1988, 1989; Olympic Champion, 1988; German Open, 1989; Youngest player to win 500 Singles victories as professional, 1991; 118 tournament wins, 23 Grand Slam titles, 1996; Won ATP Tour World Championship, 1996; Numerous Women's Doubles Championships with Gabriela Sabatini, Federation Cup, 1992; Retired, 1999. Publication: Wege Zum Erfolg, 1999. Honours: Olympic Order, 1999; German Medal of Honour, 2002. Memberships: Ambassador, World Wildlife Fund, 1984-; Founder and Chair, Children for Tomorrow; Ambassador, EXPO 2000. Address: Stefanie Graf Marketing GmbH, Mallaustrasse 75, 68219 Mannheim, Germany. E-mail: kontakt@stefanie-graf.com Website: stefanie.graf.com

**GRAHAM Bruce Hebenton,** b. 9 November 1941, Dundee, Scotland. Musician (multi-instrumentalist); Composer; Author; Entertainer. m. (1) Phyllis Elizabeth McFarlane, 18 September 1963, 1 (adopted) daughter, (2) Sharon Belinda Maxim, 7 April 1988. Musical Education: Private tuition; Schillinger Course of Composition; Pupil, Henry Nelmes Forbes, ABCA. Career: Session musician; Musical Director, London recording, television and film studios, West End Theatres; Founder, Jingles Records and Jingles Music, 1985; Featured in cabaret, Old Tyme Music Halls, one-man keyboard concerts, 1988; Worked with: Andy Williams; Rock Hudson; Juliet Prowse; Lulu; The Three Degrees; Sacha Distel; Bob Hope; Sir Harry Secombe; Faith Brown; Tommy Steele; Paul Daniels; Cleo Laine and John Dankworth; Matt Monro; Bruce Forsythe; Marti Webb; Richard Chamberlain; Vince Hill; Jimmy Shand; Jeff Wayne; Des O'Connor; Rolf Harris; Val Doonican; Anthony Newley; Helen Reddy; Wayne Sleep; David Hemmings; Michael Crawford; Lionel Blair; Gemma Craven; Tony Basil; Miss World TV Orchestra; Andrew Lloyd Webber; Phil Tate; Ray McVay; Johnny Howard; Ike Isaacs; Geoff Love; Orchestras include: Sydney Thompson's Old Tyme; National Philharmonic; London Concert; BBC Radio; Scottish Radio; Northern Dance; London Palladium; Own small groups. Compositions include: Two Symphonies; A Divertimenti For Strings; Two Suites for Orchestra; Reverie For Brass Band; 10 Suites for Large Jazz Orchestra; One-act Ballet; A Musical; Over 300 songs and shorter pieces. Publications: Magazine articles; Music And The Synthesizer, 1969. Memberships: Musicians' Union; Equity; British Music Writers Council. Address: 25 Milton Road, Wallington, Surrey SM6 9RP, England.

**GRAHAM Henry,** b. 1 December 1930, Liverpool, England. Lecturer; Poet. Education: Liverpool College of Art, 1950-52. Appointment: Poetry Editor, Ambit, London, 1969-. Publications: Good Luck to You Kafka/You'll Need It Boss, 1969; Soup City Zoo, 1969; Passport to Earth, 1971; Poker in Paradise Lost, 1977; Europe After Rain, 1981; Bomb, 1985; The Very Fragrant Death of Paul Gauguin, 1987; Jardin Gobe Avions, 1991; The Eye of the Beholder, 1997; Bar Room Ballads, 1999; Kafka in Liverpool, 2002. Contributions to: Ambit; Transatlantic Review; Prism International Review; Evergreen Review; Numerous anthologies worldwide. Honours: Arts Council Literature Awards, 1969, 1971, 1975. Address: Flat 5, 23 Marmion Road, Liverpool L17 8TT, England.

**GRAHAM James (8th Duke of Montrose),** b. 6 April 1935, Salisbury, Rhodesia. Member of House of Lords. m. Catherine Elizabeth MacDonnell Young, 2 sons, 1 daughter. Appointments: Farmer; Landowner; Lieutenant Queen's Bodyguard for Scotland, Royal Company of Archers, 2003; Member of Council, National Farmers Union of Scotland, 1981-86; Chairman, Buchanan Community Council, 1982-93; Vice-

Chairman, Loch Lomond and Trossachs Working Party, 1991-93; President, The Royal Highland and Agricultural Society of Scotland, 1997-98; Entered House of Lords, 1996; Elected Hereditary Peer, 1999; Opposition Whip, 2001-; Opposition Spokesman for Scottish Affairs, 2001-. Address: House of Lords, Westminster, London SW1A 0PW, England.

**GRAHAM Leona,** b. 18 January 1971, Great Britain. Radio Presenter; Voice Over Artist. Education: BA (QTS) Drama. Appointments: Presenter on Core, Surf 107.2; The Eagle; Power FM; Choice FM, 1994; Currently Virgin Radio Presenter and Virgin Radio Classic Rock Presenter; Voice overs for ITV, BBC, Sky One and many more. Address: 1 Golden Square, London W1F 9DJ, England. Website: www.leonagraham.com

**GRAHAM Tony,** b. 23 November 1951, London, England. Artistic Director. Education: BA Hons, University of Kent, 1971-74; Didsbury College of Education, Manchester University, 1974-75. Appointments: Drama Teacher, Head of Drama and Dance, numerous inner city ILEA secondary schools, 1975-85; ILEA Drama Advisory Team, Inner London Education Authority, 1986-88; Associate Director, 1989-92, Artistic Director, 1992-97, TAG Theatre; Artistic Director, Unicorn Theatre for Children, 1997-. Memberships: Action for Children's Arts; ASSITEU. Address: c/o Unicorn Theatre, St Mark's Studios, Chillingworth Road, London, N7 8QJ. E-mail: tony@unicorntheatre.com

**GRAHAM-DIXON Anthony Philip,** b. 5 November 1929, Woodford, England. Retired Queen's Counsel. m. Suzanne Villar, 1 son, 1 daughter. Education: Westminster School; MA, Christ Church, Oxford, 1948-52; C5 Russian Interpreter Examination, 1955. Appointments: Lieutenant, Special Branch RNVR, 1955; Called to the Bar, Inner Temple, 1956, Bencher, 1982; QC, 1973; Retired from the Bar, 1986; Governor, Bedales School, 1988-96; Deputy Chairman, Public Health Laboratory Service, 1988-95; Chairman of the Trustees, London Jupiter Orchestra, 1999-2003; Chairman of the Trustees, Society for the Promotion of New Music, 1990-95. Publications: Consulting Editor, Competition Law in Western Europe and the USA, 1973. Honours: Scholar, Westminster School and Christ Church Oxford; QC, 1973. Membership: Member of the Livery, Goldsmiths Company. Address: Masketts Manor, Nutley, East Sussex TN22 3HD, England. E-mail: anthony@graham-dixon.com

**GRAHAM-SMITH Francis (Sir),** b. 25 April 1923, Roehampton, Surrey, England. Astronomer. m. Elizabeth Palmer, 3 sons, 1 daughter. Education: Natural Sciences Tripos, Downing College Cambridge, 1941-43, 1946-47; PhD (Cantab), 1952. Appointments: Telecommunications Research Establishment, Malvern, 1943-46; Research into Radio Astronomy Cavendish Laboratory, Cambridge, 1946-64; Jodrell Bank, 1964-74 and 1981-; Director, Royal Greenwich Observatory, 1976-81; Responsible for establishing the Isaac Newton Group of telescopes on La Palma, Canary Islands; Professor of Radio Astronomy, 1964-74, 1981-90, Langworthy Professor of Physics, 1987-90, Pro-Vice-Chancellor, 1988-90, Emeritus Professor, 1990-, University of Manchester; Director, Nuffield Radio Astronomy Laboratories, Jodrell Bank, 1981-88; 13th Astronomer Royal, 1982-90. Publications: Books: Radio Astronomy, 1960; Optics (with J H Thomson), 1971, 2nd edition, 1988; Pulsars, 1977; Pathways to the Universe (with Sir ACB Lovell), 1988; Pulsar Astronomy (with A G Lyne), 1989, 2nd edition, 1998; Optics and Photonics (with T King), 2000; Introduction to Radio Astronomy (with B F Burke), 1997, 2nd edition, 2002. Honours: Fellow, 1953-64, Honorary Fellow, 1970, Downing College, Cambridge; Kt Bachelor, 1986; Royal Medal, Royal Society, 1987; DSc: Queens University Belfast, 1986, Keele University 1987, Birmingham University, 1989, Dublin University, 1990; Nottingham University, 1990, Manchester University, 1993; Salford University, 2003, Liverpool, 2003; Glazebrook Medal, Institute of Physics, 1991. Memberships: Fellow of the Royal Society, Physical Secretary and Vice-President, 1988-94; Fellow of the Royal Astronomical Society, Secretary, 1964-71, President, 1975-77; Foreign Associate, Royal Society of South Africa, 1988; Chairman of the Governors, Manchester Grammar School, 1987-98. Address: Old School House, Henbury, Macclesfield, Cheshire SK11 9PH, England. E-mail: fgsegs@ukonline.co.uk

**GRAMA Elena Viviana,** b. 9 June 1950, Bucharest, Romania. Physicist. 1 son, 1 daughter. Education: License Diploma in Physics (MS), Faculty of Physics, University of Bucharest, 1974. Appointments: Teacher of Physics, High School, Bucharest, 1974-81; Master's Physics Desk, Bucharest, 1981-90; Ambassador Assistant, Romanian Embassy, Japan, 1990-95; Safeguards Expert, 1999-, Section Head, 2000-2004, Director, 2004-, National Commission for Nuclear Activities Control, Bucharest; Participated as an Expert in Physical Protection, IAEA IPPAS Mission, Ukraine, 2003. Publications: Papers presented at conferences and seminars and safety reports include most recently: Romania Nonproliferation Policy, 2001; Transport Packaging and Disposition of Seized Nuclear Material, Regional Pilot Course on Response to Nuclear Terrorism and Incidents Involving the Illicit Trafficking of Radio Active Materials, 2003; Security Design Philosophy, Best Global Practices in Physical Protection, 2004. Membership: Institute for Management of Nuclear Materials. Address: National Commission for Nuclear Activities Control, Blvd Libertatii 14, PO Box 42-2, Bucharest 5, Romania 761061. E-mail: viviana.grama@cncan.ro

**GRANBERG Seth,** b. 22 November 1945, Oulu, Finland. Professor in Gynaecologic Ultrasaound. Education: Medical Doctor, Aarhus, Denmark, 1977; PhD, Associate Professor, University of Gothenburg, Sweden, 1991. Appointments: Physician at various hospitals, 1977-83; Obstetrician/Gynaecologist, 1983-2000, Head of Ultrasound Unit, 1997-2000, Sahlgren Hospital, Gothenburg, Sweden; Professor of Gynaecologic Ultrasound, Centre for Foetal Medicine and Gynaecological Ultrasound, Department of Obstetrics and Gynaecology, Karolinska University Hospital, Sweden, 2001-. Publications: Research articles within the field of gynaecologic ultrasound, oncology, infertility; Several book chapters within the field of gynaecologic ultrasound. Honours: Honorary Citizen of the City of Ixtapa, Mexico, 1996; Academic Affairs Medal, Riyadh, Saudi Arabia, 1996. Memberships: AIUM; American Association of Gynecologic Laparoscopists; SFOG; SGY; Swedish and Finnish Ultrasound Associations. Address: Department of Woman and Child Health, Division of Obstetrics and Gynaecology, Karolinska Hospital, SE-17176, Stockholm, Sweden.

**GRANIK Alex T,** b. 19 August 1939, Tadzhikistan. Physicist. m. Rita Visitei. Education: MS, Engineering, Odessa Institute of Technology, Odessa, USSR, 1956-61; PhD, Theoretical Physics and Mathematical Physics, Physics Department, Odessa University and Institute of Thermal Physics, Academy of Sciences, Novosibirsk, USSR, 1963-66. Appointments: Assistant Professor, Associate Professor, Department of Physics, Odessa Institute of Technology, 1966-76; Application Programmer, PBL Associates, Pt Richmond California, USA, 1978; Associate Professor Physics Department, Kentucky State University, USA, 1979-82; Scientific Consultant, Lawrence Livermore National Laboratory, USA, 1984-88; Associate Professor, Physics Department, University of the Pacific,

California, USA, 1982-2005; Professor Emeritus, 2005-. Publications: More than 50 publications in refereed journals including: Foundations of Physics, Physics of Fluids, Journal of Fluid Mechanics, Astrophysical Journal, Astrophysics and Space Science, Physics Essays; Numerous presentations at national and international conferences. Address: Physics Department, University of the Pacific, Stockton, CA 95211, USA. E-mail: agranik@pacific.edu

**GRANOTT Nira,** b. Petak-Tikva, Israel. Psychology Professor; Researcher. 1 son, 1 daughter. Education: MA, Tel-Aviv University, 1983; Harvard University, EdM, 1988; PhD, Massachusetts Institute of Technology, 1993. Appointments: Multimedia Project Director, Educational TV, Tel Aviv, 1974-80; Senior Analyst, Software Developer, Control Data Corporation, Tel Aviv, 1983-86; Assistant Professor of Psychology, University of Texas at Dallas, 1993-95, 1997-2002; Director, Microdevelopment laboratory, 1993-2002; Visiting Professor, Harvard Graduate School of Education, 1995-96; Co-founder, President, OORIM LLC, 2000-; Visiting Professor, Tufts University, 2002-. Publications: Articles include Unit of analysis, ensemble processes; Developing Learning, chapter contributed to Adult Learning and Development, 1998; Books include Microdevelopment: Transition Processes in Development and Learning, 2001. Honours: Research grant from NSF, 1999, Timberlawn Research Foundation, 1999; Texas Higher Education Coordination Board, 2000; Listed in several international biographical reference works. Memberships: American Psychological Society; American Education Research Association; Jean Piaget Society. E-mail: ngranott@aol.com

**GRANT Hugh John Mungo,** b. 9 September 1960, London, England. Actor. Education: BA, New College, Oxford. Career: Actor in theatre, TV and films, producer for Simian Films; Began career in the in Jockeys of Norfolk (writer with Chris Lang and Andy Taylor); Films include: White Mischief, 1987; Maurice, 1987; Lair of the White Worm, 1988; La Nuit Bengali, 1988; Impromptu, 1989; Bitter Moon, 1992; Remains of the Day, 1993; Four Weddings and a Funeral, 1994; Sirens, 1994; The Englishman who went up a hill but came down a mountain, 1995; Nine Months, 1995; An Awfully Big Adventure, 1995; Sense and Sensibility, 1995; Restoration, 1996; Extreme Measures, 1996; Mickey Blue Eyes, 1998; Notting Hill, 1998; Small Time Crooks, 2000; Bridget Jones' Diary, 2001; About a Boy, 2002; Two Weeks' Notice, 2002; Love Actually, 2003; Bridget Jones: The Edge of Reason, 2004; Travaux, on sait quand ça commence..., 2005. Honours include: Golden Globe Award, BAFTA Award for Best Actor, Four Weddings and a Funeral, 1995; Peter Sellers Award for Comedy; Evening Standard British Film Awards, 2002. Address: c/o Simian Films, 3 Cromwell Place, London SW7 2JE, England.

**GRANT James Russell,** b. 14 December 1924, Bellshill, Scotland. Physician; Poet. m. (1) Olga Zarb, 23 March 1955, divorced, 1 son, (2) Susan Tierney, 22 April 1994. Education: Medal in English, Hamilton Academy, 1941; MB CHb, University of Glasgow, 1951; Institute of Psychiatry, University of London, 1954-55. Appointments: Various medical posts. Publications: Hyphens, 1959; Poems, 1959; The Excitement of Being Sam, 1977; Myths of My Age, 1985; In the 4 Cats, 1997; Jigsaw and the Art of Poetry, 2001; Essays on Anxiety, 2001. Contributions to: Glasgow University Magazine; Botteghe Oscure; Saltire Review; Prism International; Fiddlehead; Chapman; Ambit; BBC; CBC; Agenda; Edinburgh Review; Anthologies: Oxford Book of Travel Verse, 1985; Christian Poetry, 1988; Book of Machars, 1991. Honours: Scottish Open Poetry Competition, 1976; UK National Poetry Competition.

Memberships: British Medical Association. Address: 255 Creighton Avenue, London N2 9BP, England.

**GRANT Richard E,** b. 1957. Actor. m. Joan Washington, 1 daughter. Career: Actor, Theatre appearances include: Man of Mode, 1988; The Importance of Being Earnest, 1993; A Midsummer Night's Dream, 1994; TV appearances include: Honest, Decent, Legal and True, 1986; Here is the News, 1989; Suddenly Last Summer, 1992; Hard Times, 1993; Karaoke, 1996; A Royal Scandal, 1996; The Scarlet Pimpernel, 1998; Hound of the Baskervilles, 2002; Posh Nosh, 2003; Patrick Hamilton: Words, Whisky and Women, 2005; Films: Withnail and I, 1986; How to Get Ahead in Advertising, 1989; Warlock, 1989; Henry and June, 1990; Mountains of the Moon, 1990; LA Story, 1991; Hudson Hawk, 1991; Bram Stoker's Dracula, 1992; The Player, 1993; The Age of Innocence, 1993; Prêt à Porter, 1995; Jack and Sarah, 1995; Portrait of a Lady, 1995; Twelfth Night, 1995; The Serpent's Kiss, 1996; The Match, 1998; A Christmas Carol, 1999; Trial and Retribution, 1999; Little Vampires, 1999; Hildegarde, 2000; Gosford Park, 2001; Monsieur 'N', 2002; Bright Young Things, 2003; Tooth, 2004; The Story of an African Farm, 2005. Publications: With Nails: The Film Diaries of Richard E Grant, 1995; Twelfth Night, 1996; By Design - A Hollywood Novel. Address: c/o ICM, Oxford House, 76 Oxford Street, London W1N 0AX, England. Website: www.richard-e-grant.com

**GRATTON Guy Brian,** b. 16 July 1970, Kirkcaldy, Scotland. Engineer; Writer; Test Pilot. Education: BEng (Hons), Aeronautics and Astronautics, 1992, PhD, Aerospace Engineering, 2005, University of Southampton. Appointments: Flight Test Engineer, 1993-96, Manager, Environmental Test Facilities, 1996-97, Ministry of Defence, Boscombe Down; Chief Technical Officer, British Microlight Aircraft Association, 1997-. Publications: Articles in professional journals including: International Journal of Aerospace Management, 2002; Journal of Aerospace Engineering, 2003. Honours: D G Astridge Prize for Aerospace Safety, 2003; Safety in Mechanical Engineering Award, 2003. Memberships: Institution of Mechanical Engineers; Royal Aeronautical Society; Society of Experimental Test Pilots. Address: c/o British Microlight Aircraft Association, Bullring, Deddington, Banbury, Oxon OX15 0TT, England. E-mail: guy@gratton.org

**GRAY (Edna) Eileen Mary,** b. 25 April 1920, United Kingdom. Cyclist. m. Walter Herbert Gray, deceased 2001, 1 son. Education: St Saviour's; St Olave's Grammar School for Girls, London. Appointments: Inspectorate, Fighting Vehicles, 1940-45; Invited to ride abroad, British Women's Cycling Team, 1946; International Delegation, Paris, 1957; Organiser first international competition for women in UK, 1957; Campaigner for international recognition of women in cycling; Team Manager, inaugural women's world championship, 1958; Member, Executive Committee, British Cycling Federation, 1958-87; Elected to Federation International Amateur de Cyclism, 1977; Vice-President, British Olympic Association, 1992-, Vice-Chairman, 1988-92; Chairman, British Sports Forum, 1991; Member, Manchester Olympic Bid Committee, 1991; Deputy Commandant, British Olympic Team, 1992; International Official, Commonwealth Games, Edmonton and Brisbane; Trustee, London Marathon Trust. Councillor, 1982-98, President, Kingston Sport Council, Mayor, 1990-91, Royal Borough of Kingston upon Thames. Honours: Special Gold Award, Ministry of Education, Taiwan; OBE, 1978; Freeman of the City of London, 1987; Olympic Order, International Olympic Committee, 1993; Grandmaster, Hon Fraternity of Ancient Freemasons (women) and Trustee of its Charity; CBE, 1997. Memberships: Chairman, London Youth Games; Vice-

President: Cyclists Touring Club, 2000; British School Cycling Association, 2001. Address: 129 Grand Avenue, Surbiton, Surrey KT5 9HY, England.

**GRAY Hon Sir Charles Anthony St John,** b. 6 July 1942, London, England. Judge. m. Cindy Elizabeth Gray, 1 son, 1 daughter. Education: Major Scholar, MA, Trinity College, Oxford. Appointments: Barrister, 1966-98; QC, 1984; Recorder, 1990-98; High Court Judge (Queen's Bench), 1998-. Honours: Knighthood, 1998; Honorary Fellow, Trinity College, Oxford, 2004. Membership: Brooks's. Address: Royal Courts of Justice, Strand, London WC2A 2LL, England.

**GRAY Douglas,** b. 17 February 1930, Melbourne, Victoria, Australia. Professor of English; Writer. m. 3 September 1959, 1 son. Education: MA, Victoria University of Wellington, New Zealand, 1952; BA, 1956, MA, 1960, Merton College, Oxford. Appointment: J R R Tolkien Professor of English, Oxford, 1980-97, Emeritus, 1997-. Publications: Themes and Images in the Medieval English Religious Lyric, 1972; Robert Henryson, 1979; The Oxford Book of Late Medieval Verse and Prose (editor), 1985; Selected Poems of Robert Henryson and William Dunbar (editor), 1998; The Oxford Companion to Chaucer (editor), 2003. Contributions to: Scholarly journals. Honours: British Academy, fellow, 1989; Honorary LitD, Victoria University of Wellington, 1995. Memberships: Early English Text Society; Society for the Study of Medieval Languages and Literatures, president, 1982-86. Address: Lady Margaret Hall, Oxford OX2 6QA, England.

**GRAY Dulcie (Winifred Catherine),** b. 20 November 1920, England. Actress; Dramatist; Writer. m. Michael Denison, 29 April 1939. Education: England and Malaysia. Appointments: Numerous stage, film, radio, and television appearances. Publications: Murder on the Stairs, 1957; Baby Face, 1959; For Richer, for Richer, 1970; Ride on a Tiger, 1975; Butterflies on My Mind, 1978; Dark Calypso, 1979; The Glanville Women, 1982; Mirror Image, 1987; Looking Forward, Looking Backward (autobiography), 1991; J B Priestley, biography, 2000. Contributions to: Periodicals. Honours: Queen's Silver Jubilee Medal, 1977; Times Educational Supplement Senior Information Book Prize, 1978; Commander of the Order of the British Empire, 1983. Memberships: British Actors Equity; Linnean Society, fellow; Royal Society of Arts, fellow; Society of Authors. Address: Shardeloes, Amersham, Buckinghamshire HP7 0RL, England.

**GRAY John Clinton,** b. 9 April 1946, Ripon, Yorkshire, England. University Professor. m. Julia Hodgetts, 1 son, 1 daughter. Education: BSc, Biochemistry, 1967, PhD, 1970, University of Birmingham; MA, University of Cambridge, 1977. Appointments: University Research Fellow, University of Birmingham, 1970-73; Research Biochemist, University of California, Los Angeles, 1973-75; Science Research Council Research Fellow, 1975-76, University Demonstrator, 1976-80, University Lecturer, 1980-90, Reader in Plant Molecular Biology, 1990-96, Professor of Plant Molecular Biology, 1996-, Head of Department of Plant Sciences, 2003-, University of Cambridge. Publications: Numerous articles in scientific journals; Ribulose Bisphosphate Carboxylase-Oxygenase (editor with R J Ellis), 1986; Plant Trichomes (editor with D L Hallahan), 2000. Honours: Nuffield Foundation Science Research Fellowship, 1984-85; Royal Society Leverhulme Trust Senior Research Fellowship, 1990-91. Membership: Midlands Association of Mountaineers. Address: 47 Barrons Way, Comberton, Cambridge CB3 7EQ, England. E-mail: jcg2@mole.bio.cam.ac.uk

**GRAY Rose,** b. 28 January 1939. Chef; Restaurateur. m. David Robin MacIlwaine, 2 sons, 2 daughters. Education: BA, Fine Art, Guildford School of Art. Appointments: Teacher of Fine Art, London, 1960-63; Designer and manufacturer of paper lights and furniture, 1963-68; Importer of French cookers, 1969-80; Chef, Nell's Nightclub, New York, 1985-86; Chef, Owner, The River Café, 1987-. Publications: with Ruth Rogers include: The River Café Cook Book, 1995; River Café Cook Book Two, 1997; The Italian Kitchen, accompanying the Channel 4 TV series, 1998; River Café Cook Book Green, 2000; River Café Cook Book Easy, 2003; Rogers and Gray Italian Country Cook Book, USA, 1995; The Café Cook Book, USA, 1997; Italian Easy Recipes from London River Café, USA, 2004. Honours include: Italian Restaurant of the Year, The Times, 1988; Best New Restaurant, Courvoisier Best of the Best Awards, 1989; Eros Awards, Evening Standard, 1994/1995; Michelin Star, 1998; Food Book of the Year, Glenfiddich Awards, 1995; Tatler's Most Consistently Excellent Restaurant Award, 2004; Co-founder, Cooks in Schools charity, 2004. Address: The River Café, Thames Wharf, Rainville Road, London W6 9HA, England. E-mail: info@rivercafe.co.uk

**GRECH Gaetan Anthony,** b. 9 January 1931, Hamrun, Malta. Honorary Consul. m. Filippa, 1 December 1951, 2 daughters. Education: Lyceum, Distinction, Music, Maltese, English, Italian, Mathematics, History, Accountancy, Malta, 1937-49; Qualified Radio Operator, Programme Presenter, 1977. Appointments: Supervisor, Production Control, 1950-74; Actor, Theatre Director, 1956-62; Travel Agent, own business, 1974-91; Honorary Consul, Malta, 1987-; Justice of the Peace. Publications: Author of several poems and plays; Contributor of literature in the book, Connection; Short stories for radio. Memberships: Secretary, Treasurer, Maltese Guild of S Augustine, 1954-56; Journalist, Newspaper & Radio, 1961-; Editor, Newsletter, 1973-88; Secretary, Publicity Officer, Malta United, 1974-76; Secretary, Founder, Maltese Community Radio, 1977; Maltese Community Council, 1978-88; Founder, Maltese Language School, 1981. Honours: 2 certificates, Voluntary Journalism, Maltese Herald, 1961-91; Knight of Grace, Order of St John Knights, Malta, 1976; 2 certificates, Australia Bi-Centennial Celebrations, 1988; Honorary Trustee, Enfield City, SC, 1988-; Shield of Valor, 1992; Order of Australia Medal, 2002. Address: 57 Clifton Street, Camden Park, SA 5038, Australia.

**GRECHISHKIN Vadim Sergeevich,** b. 31 October 1933, St Petersburg, Russia. Physicist; Researcher. m. Rufina Vasiljevna Ershova, 1956, 1 daughter. Education: Candidate of Science, Leningrad University, 1960; Dr of Science, Moscow University, 1968. Appointments: Docent, 1960-63, Head of Chair, 1963-72, Perm University; Vice Rector, 1972-75, Head of Chair, 1975-, Dean of Faculty, 1991-94, Kaliningrad University. Publications: Book: Quadrupole Interaction in Solids, 1973; Introduction to Radiofrequency Spectroscopy, Perm, 1969; Nuclear Spin Resonans, 1990; Theory of Waves, 2001; Contributions to over 585 articles to professional journals; 32 patents in field. Honours: Medal of Peking University, 1990; Honoured Scientist of Russia, 1992; Soros Professor, 1994; Medal of Poznan University, 1997; 4 medals of Russia. Memberships: New York Academy of Sciences; Russian Academy of Science and Art; Vice President of RUAN, 2003; President of Baltic RUAN, 2003. Address: Kaliningrad State University, A Nevsky 14, 236041 Kaliningrad, Russia. E-mail: grechishkin@kern.ru

**GREEN Andrew David (Andy),** b. 15 April 1954, United Kingdom. Professor of Comparative Education. Education: BA (Hons), English Language and Literature, University of Oxford, 1975; MA, Cultural Studies, Centre for Contemporary Cultural

Studies, University of Birmingham, 1979; PGCE, University of London Institute of Education, 1981; PhD, Comparative Education History, University of Birmingham, 1988. Appointments: Consultant for: UNESCO; OECD; European Commission; CEDEFOP; Government of Malta; UK Department of Education and Skills; UK Department for Employment; UK Department for Trade and Industry, 1995-2005; Lecturer in Communications and Sociology, South East London College, 1981-88; Senior Lecturer, Education History and Policy, Thames Polytechnic, 1988-90; Lecturer in Education, 1990, Professor of Education, 1998-2003, Professor of Comparative Education, 2003-, Institute of Education, University of London. Publications: 10 books include most recently: Education, Globalization and the Nation State, 1997, Japanese edition, 1999, Chinese edition, 2003; Convergence and Divergence in European Education and Training Systems (with A Wolf and T Leyney), 1999, Spanish edition, 2001; Where are the Resources for lifelong Learning? (with A Hodgson and G Williams), 2000; Modelling and Measuring the Wider Benefits of Learning (with T Schuller et al), 2001; High Skills: Globalization, Competitiveness and Skills Formation (with P Brown and H Lauder), 2001. Honours: Fulbright Exchange Lecturer, Yuba College, California, 1986; Standing Conference on Education Book Prize , 1991; Consultant to National Skills Task Force, 1999-200; Visiting Professor, Danish University of Education, Copenhagen, 2002, 2004; Member of UK Government's Skills Strategy Steering Group; Various research grants. Memberships: National Association of University Teachers; History of Education Society; Comparative Education Society of Europe. Address: Little Bannisters, Exlade Street, Checkendon, Oxon, RG8 0UA, England. E-mail: andy.green@ioe.ac.uk

**GREEN Bryn(mor) Hugh,** b. 14 January 1941, Mountain Ash, South Wales. Academic. m. Jean Armstrong, 1965, 2 sons. Education: Dartford Grammar School; BSc, Botany, 1962, PhD, Plant Ecology, 1965, The University of Nottingham. Appointments: Lecturer, Department of Botany, University of Manchester, 1965-67; Regional Officer for SE England, Nature Conservancy Council, 1967-74; Lecturer and Senior Lecturer, Wye College, 1974-87; Professor and Head of the Environment Sub-Department, Wye College, University of London, 1987-96; Emeritus Professor of Countryside Management, University of London, 1996-. Publications: Countryside Conservation: landscape ecology, planning and management, 1981, 1985, 1996; Co-author, The Diversion of Land: conservation in a period of farming contraction, 1991; The Changing Role of the Common Agricultural Policy: the future of farming in Europe, 1991; Threatened Landscapes: conserving cultural environments, 2001; Numerous chapters in books and papers in scientific journals. Memberships: Vice President, Kent Wildlife Trust; Vice President, Kent and Sussex Farming and Wildlife Advisory Group; Former Countryside Commissioner; England Committee Member, Nature Conservancy Council; Chairman, Landscape Conservation Working Group of IUCN; Chairman, Kent White Cliffs Heritage Coast Countryside Management Project; Deputy Chairman, The Kent Trust for Nature Conservation; Member, Editorial Advisory Boards of Landscape and Urban Planning; Journal of Environmental Planning and The International Journal of Sustainable Development and World Ecology. Honours: OBE, 1995; Churchill Fellow, 1999. Address: 16 The Granville, Hotel Road, St Margaret's Bay, Dover, Kent CT15 6DX, England.

**GREEN Michael Frederick,** b. 2 January 1927, Leicester, England. Writer. Education: BA, Honours, Open University. Publications: The Art of Coarse Rugby, 1960; The Art of Coarse Sailing, 1962; Even Coarser Rugby, 1963; Don't Print my Name Upside Down, 1963; The Art of Coarse Acting, 1964; The Art of Coarse Golf, 1967; The Art of Coarse Moving, 1969 (TV serial, 1977); The Art of Coarse Drinking, 1973; Squire Haggard's Journal, 1976 (TV serial, 1990 and 1992); Four Plays For Coarse Actors, 1978; The Coarse Acting Show Two, 1980; Tonight Josephine, 1981; The Art of Coarse Sex, 1981; Don't Swing from the Balcony Romeo, 1983; The Art of Coarse Office Life, 1985; The Third Great Coarse Acting Show, 1985; The Boy Who Shot Down an Airship, 1988; Nobody Hurt in Small Earthquake, 1990; Coarse Acting Strikes Back, 2000. Memberships: Society of Authors; Equity; National Union of Journalists. Address: 31 Clive Road, Twickenham, Middlesex, TW1 4SQ, England.

**GREEN Paul John,** b. 27 July 1936, Seattle, Washington, USA. Scholar. Education: BA, Seattle Pacific College, 1957; MA, University of Washington, 1958; MLS, University of California at Berkeley, 1968; PhD, Washington State University, 1981; Further part-time language study, University of Oregon, 2003-05. Appointments: Teaching Assistant, English, University of Washington, 1963-66; Instructor in English, Central Washington University, 1966-67; Research Assistant in Librarianship, University of California, Berkeley, 1967-68; Assistant Serials Librarian, University of Oregon, 1968-69; Teaching Assistant in English, Washington State University, 1974-76; Bibliographic Searching Assistant, Washington State University, 1984-2001. Publications: Contributor of numerous articles, reviews, notes and translations, bibliographies, poems, letters and an abstract; Editor, Student Writing, 1966-67; Novel: The Life of Jack Gray, (privately printed), 1991, new expanded edition, 2002; Previously unpublished literary reviews, 1997-99, 2001; Previously unpublished literary essays, 1992-2000, 2001; From Russia with Love and A Literary Potpourri, 2003; Collected Writings on the Fiction of Franz Kafka, with a Germanics Supplement, 2003; Eighteenth Century Salad with French and Italian Dressing: Swift-Voltaire, Fielding-Manzoni and Reviews Franco-Italian, and Italian, 2003; On Our Mutual Friend and Other Dickensiana, 2003; The Song of Eugene, with expanded introductory materials and nine Heinrich Heine translated poems, 2004. Honours: Freshman Scholarship, Seattle Pacific College, 1954-55; Non-resident Tuition Waiver, University of California, Berkeley, 1967-68; Editorial Board Member, Works and Days, 1984-94; Editorial Board Member, Recovering Literature, 1994-2000; Phi Sigma Iota Consultant, Language Pedagogy, China, 1997; Cavalier, World Order of Science, Education and Culture. Memberships: MLA; American Comparative Literature Association; Order of International Ambassadors; Academy of American Poets; International Comparative Literature Association; LFIBA; DGABIRA; Kafka Society of America; Life Member, London Diplomatic Academy; University of California Alumni Association; Arnold Bennett Hall Society, University of Oregon; Industrial Workers of the World; Sierra Club; People to People International; University of Washington Alumni Association; Oregon Shakespeare Festival; American Civil Liberties Union; Common Cause; Benjamin Ide Wheeler Society, University of California, Berkeley; Henry Suzzallo Society, University of Washington; Jordan Schnitzer Museum of Art, University of Oregon; Bowmer Society, Oregon Shakespeare Festival; American Library Association; Fine Arts Museums, San Francisco. Address: 825 Washington St #20, Eugene, OR 97401-2845, USA.

**GREEN Philip Nevill,** b. 12 May 1953, Walsall, England. Chief Executive. m. Judy Green, 2 daughters. Education: BA (Hons) Economics and Politics, University of Wales; MBA, London Business School. Appointments: Vice-President, Marketing, Crayonne (USA) Inc, 1977-80; Managing Director, Home Furnishing Division, 1980-85, Group Development Director, 1985-89, Group Managing Director, 1989-90,

Coloroll Group plc; Regional Director, Northern Europe and Anglophone Africa, 1990-94, Chief Operating Officer, Europe and Asia, 1994-99, DHL Worldwide Network NV/SA; Chief Executive Officer, Trading Solutions Division, 1999-2001, Chief Operating Officer, Reuters Group, 2001-2003, Reuters Group PLC; Chief Executive Officer, Royal P&O Nedlloyd BV, 2003-. Memberships: Non-executive Director, SKF, Gothenburg, Sweden, Member of Audit Committee, 2000-04; Advisory Board, London Business School, 2000-; Trustee, Philharmonia Orchestra, London, 2002-; International Advisory Council Member, Port of Singapore, 2004-; Board Member, The Chamber of Shipping, London, 2004-. Address: P&O Nedlloyd Limited, Beagle House, Braham Street, London E1 8EP, England. E-mail: philip.n.green@ponl.com

**GREEN Timothy (Seton),** b. 29 May 1936, Beccles, England. Writer. m. Maureen Snowball, October 1959, 1 daughter. Education: BA, Christ's College, Cambridge, 1957; Graduate Diploma in Journalism, University of Western Ontario, 1958. Appointments: London Correspondent, Horizon, and American Heritage, 1959-62, Life, 1962-64; Editor, Illustrated London News, 1964-66. Publications: The World of God, 1968; The Smugglers, 1969; Restless Spirit, UK edition as The Adventurers, 1970; The Universal Eye, 1972; World of Gold Today, 1973; How to Buy Gold, 1975; The Smuggling Business, 1977; The World of Diamonds, 1981; The New World of Gold, 1982, 2nd edition, 1985; The Prospect for Gold, 1987; The World of Gold, 1993; The Good Water Guide, 1994; New Frontiers in Diamonds: The Mining Revolution, 1996; The Gold Companion, 1997; The Millennium in Gold, 1999; The Millennium in Silver, 1999. Address: 8 Ponsonby Place, London, SW1P 4PT, England.

**GREENFIELD Jeanette,** b. Melbourne, Australia. Author; International Lawyer. Education: LLB, University of Melbourne, 1968; LLB, 1973, PhD, International Law, 1976, Cambridge University. Appointments: Called to the Bar, Supreme Court, Victoria, 1969; Teaching Fellow, Law School, Monash University, 1970-71; Consultant and Contributor to Ministerial Review of Australia's Protection of Movable Cultural heritage, 1991; Contributor to House of Commons Parliamentary Report, Cultural Property: Return and Illicit Trade, 2000. Publications: China and the Law of the Sea, Air & Environment, 1979; The Return of Cultural Treasures, 1989, 1996, 2005; China's Practice in the Law of the Sea, 1991; Contributions to: Chambers Biographical Dictionary, 1990, The Law of the Sea in the Asian Pacific Region, 1995, Spoils of War, 1997. Honour: British Academy Award, 1986. Address: GPO Box 4989 WW, Melbourne 3001, Victoria, Australia. E-mail: jeanette0088@yahoo.com.au

**GREENFIELD, Baroness of Ot Moor in the County of Oxfordshire, Susan Adele Greenfield,** b. 1 October 1950, London, England. Professor of Pharmacology. Education: BA (Hons) Oxon, 1973, MA Oxon,1974, DPhil, Oxon, 1974, St Hilda's College, Oxford University. Appointments: Travelling Scholarship to Israel, 1970; MRC Research Scholarship, Department of Pharmacology, 1973-76, Dame Catherine Fulford Senior Scholarship, St Hughes College, 1974, J H Burn Trust Scholarship, Department of Pharmacology, 1977, MRC Training Fellowship, Laboratory of Physiology, 1977-81, Oxford University; Royal Society Study Visit Award, 1978, MRC-INSERM French Exchange Fellow, 1979-80, College de France, Paris; Junior Research Fellow, Green College, 1981-84, Tutorial Fellow in Medicine, Lincoln College, 1985-, University Lecturer in Synaptic Pharmacology, 1985-, Professor of Pharmacology, 1996-, Oxford University; Deputy Director, Squibb Projects, 1988-95; Gresham Chair of Physic, Gresham College, London,

1995-98; Director, Royal Institution of Great Britain, 1998-, Fullerian Professor of Physiology, 1998-; Visiting Fellow in Neurosciences, Institute of La Jolla, USA, 1995; Distinguished Visiting Scholar, Queen's University, Belfast, 1996; Royal Institution Christmas Lecturer (first woman to present series), 1994; Columnist, Independent on Sunday, 1996-98; Brain Story (series BBC 2), 2000; Trustee, Science Museum, 1998-; World Economic Forum Fellow, 2001. Publications: Books: Mindwaves (co-editor with C B Blackmore), 1987; Journey to the Centres of the Brain (with G Ferry), 1994; Journey to the Centres of the Mind, 1995; The Human Mind Explained (editor) 1996, The Human Brain: A Guided Tour, 1997; Brain Power (editor), 2000; The Private Life of the Brain, 2000; Tomorrow's People, 2003; Numerous published research papers and articles to journals. Honours: Michael Faraday Award, Royal Society, 1998; Woman of Distinction of the Year, Jewish Care, 1998; Gave Consultative Seminar at request of Prime Minister, 1999; Woman of the Year, The Observer, 2000; CBE, 2000; Honorary Fellow, University of Cardiff, 2000; Honorary FRCP, 2000; 28 Honorary DScs; Life Peer, 2001; Produced Greefield Report for Department of Trade and Industry, 2002; Ordre National de la Legion d'Honneur, 2003; Golden Plate Award, Academy of Achievement, Washington, 2003; Elected Adelaide's Thinker in Residence, 2004 and 2005; Science and Economy Seminars, 2004-05; Appointed Chancellor of Heriot Watt University, 2005. Address: Department of Pharmacology, Mansfield Road, Oxford OX1 3QT, England. E-mail: susan.greenfield@pharm.ox.ac.uk

**GREENING John David,** b. 20 March 1954, London, England. Teacher of English; Poet. m. Jane Woodland, 29 April 1978, 2 daughters. Education: BA, Honours, English, University College of Swansea, 1975; University of Mannheim, Germany, 1975-76; MA, Drama, University of Exeter, 1977. Appointments: Clerk to Hans Keller, BBC Radio 3; EFL Teacher in Aswan, Upper Egypt and then to Vietnamese Boat People in North-east Scotland; Teacher of English, Kimbolton School, Huntingdon. Publications: Westerners, 1982; Winter Journeys, 1984; Boat People, 1988; The Tutankhamun Variations, 1991; Fotheringhay and Other Poems, 1995; The Coastal Path, 1996; The Bocase Stone, 1996; Nightflights: New and Selected Poems, 1998; Gascoigne's Egg, 1999; OMM SETY, 2001; The Home Key, 2003; The Poets of the First World War, 2004; The Poetry of W B Yeats, 2005. Contributions to: Observer; TLS; Quadrant; Spectator; Encounter; World and I; Stand; Poetry Review; Bananas; Rialto; Poetry Wales; Outposts; Poetry Durham; Oxford Poetry; Cumberland Poetry Review; PBS Anthology; Gregory Anthology. Honours: 1st prize, Alexandria International Poetry Prize, 1981; Scottish Arts Council Writer's Bursary, 1982; Society of Authors Award, 2000. Membership: Poetry Society; Top Prizes, Arvon/Sotheby's International Poetry Competition, 1987, 1989; Bridport Prize, 1998; TLS Centenary Prize. Address: 27 Hatchet Lane, Stonely, St Neots, Cambridgeshire PE19 5EG, England.

**GREENSTOCK Jeremy Quentin (Sir),** b. 27 July 1943, Harrow, Middlesex, England. Diplomat. m. Anne Ashford Hodges, 1 son, 2 daughters. Education: Worcester College, Oxford. Appointments: Assistant Master, Eton College, 1966-69; Diplomatic Postings in Lebanon, Dubai, Washington, Saudi Arabia, Paris, 1969-90; Assistant Under Secretary for Western and Southern Europe, 1990-93; Minister, Washington, 1994-95; Political Director, Foreign and Commonwealth Office, 1996-98; UK Permanent Representative at the United Nations, 1998-2003; UK Special Representative for Iraq, 2003-2004; Director, The Ditchley Foundation, 2004-. Honours: CMG, 1991; KCMG, 1998; GCMG, 2003. Membership: Oxford and Cambridge Club. Address: Ditchley Park, Enstone, Chipping Norton, Oxon OX7 4ER, England. E-mail: director@ditchley.co.uk

**GREENWOOD Duncan Joseph**, b. 16 October 1932, New Barnet, Hertfordshire, England. Research Scientist. Education: Hutton Grammar School; BSc, Liverpool University, 1954; PhD, 1957, DSc, 1972, Aberdeen University. Appointments: Research Fellow, Aberdeen University, 1957-59; Research Leader, National Vegetable Research Station, 1959-66; Head of Soils and Crop Nutrition, Horticultural Research International (formerly National Vegetable Research Station), 1966-92; Emeritus Research Fellow, 1992-2004; Associate Fellow, Warwick University, Warwick HRI, 2004-; Visiting Professor, Leeds University, 1985-93; Honorary Professor, Birmingham University, 1986-93. Publications: 180 scientific publications mostly on soil science, plant nutrition and agronomy. Honours: Sir Gilbert Morgan Medal, Society of Chemical Industry, 1962; Research Medal, Royal Agricultural Society of England, 1979; President's Medal, Institute of Horticulture, 2004; President, International Committee, Plant Nutrition, 1978-82; Elected FRS, 1985; Individual Merit Promotion DCSO (UG5), 1986; President, British Society of Soil Science, 1991-92; CBE, 1993; Inaugural Lifetime Achievement Award, Grower of the Year, 2000; Honorary Life Member, Association of Applied Biologists, 2004; Named Lectures; Blackman, Oxford, 1982; Distinguished Scholars, Belfast, 1982; Hannaford, Adelaide, 1985; Shell, Kent, 1988; Amos, Wye, 1989. Memberships: Elected FRCS, 1977; F.Inst.Hort, 1986; FRS, 1985; British Society of Soil Science; Society of Chemical Industry. Address: 23 Shelley Road, Stratford-upon-Avon CV37 7JR, England.

**GREENWOOD Norman Neill**, b. 19 January 1925, Melbourne, Australia. Emeritus Professor of Chemistry. m. Kirsten Rydland, 3 daughters. Education: BSc, 1st Class, 1946, MSc, 1st Class, 1948, DSc, 1966, University of Melbourne, Australia; PhD, 1951, ScD, 1961, Cambridge University. Appointments: Laboratory Cadet, CSIR(O), Melbourne, 1942-46; Resident Tutor and Lecturer in Chemistry, Trinity College, Melbourne, 1946-48; Senior Harwell Research Fellow, Atomic Energy Research Establishment, Harwell, 1951-53; Lecturer, then Senior Lecturer, Inorganic Chemistry, University of Nottingham, 1953-61; Professor and Head of Department of Inorganic Chemistry, University of Newcastle upon Tyne, 1961-71; Professor and Head of Department of Inorganic and Structural Chemistry, 1971-90, Head of the School of Chemistry, 1971-74, 1983-86, Dean of the Faculty of Science, 1986-88, Emeritus Professor of Chemistry, 1990-, University of Leeds; Numerous visiting professorships, 1966-93. Publications: Some 480 research papers and reviews; 10 books. Honours include: Tilden Lectureship and Medal, Chemical Society, London, 1966; Main Group Element Chemistry Award and Medal, 1974, Liversidge Lectureship and Medal, 1984, Ludwig Mond Lectureship and Medal, 1991, Tertiary Education Award and Medal, 1993, Royal Society of Chemistry; A W von Hofmann, Lectureship, Gesellschaft Deutscher Chemiker, 1983; Foreign Member, l'Académie des Sciences, Institut de France, 1992; Fellow of the Royal Society, 1987; Royal Society Humphry Davy Lectureship, 2000; D de l'university, honoris causa, University de Nancy I, France, 1997; Gold Medal and Honorary Citizenship of the City of Nancy, France, 1977; DSc, honoris causa, Toho University, Tokyo, Japan, 2000. Memberships: FRSC; MRI; FRS. Address: University of Leeds School of Chemistry, Leeds, LS2 9JT, England.

**GREER Germaine** b. 29 January 1939, Melbourne, Victoria, Australia. Writer; Broadcaster. Education: BA, Honours, Melbourne University, 1959; MA, Honours, Sydney University, 1962; PhD, Cambridge University, 1967. Appointments: Senior English Tutor, Sydney University, 1963-64; Assistant Lecturer and Lecturer, English, University of Warwick, 1967-72; Lecturer, American Program Bureau, 1973-78; Visiting Professor, Graduate Faculty of Modern Letters, 1979, Professor of Modern Letters, 1980-83, University of Tulsa; Founder-Director, Tulsa Centre for Studies in Women's Literature, 1981; Proprietor, Stump Cross Books, 1988-; Special Lecturer and Unofficial Fellow, Newnham College, Cambridge, 1989-98. Publications: The Female Eunuch, 1969; The Obstacle Race: The Fortunes of Women Painters and Their Work, 1979; Sex and Destiny: The Politics of Human Fertility, 1984; Shakespeare (editor), 1986; The Madwoman's Underclothes (selected journalism), 1986; Daddy, We Hardly Knew You, 1989; The Change: Women, Ageing and the Menopause, 1991; Slip-Shod Sibyls: Recognition, Rejection and the Woman Poet, 1995; The Whole Woman, 1999. Editor: The Uncollected Verse of Aphra Behn, 1989. Co-Editor: Kissing the Rod: An Anthology of Seventeenth Century Verse, 1988; Surviving Works of Anne Wharton (co-editor), 1997; The Whole Woman, 1999; John Wilmot, Earl of Rochester, 1999; 101 Poems by 191 Women (editor), 2001. Contributions to: Numerous articles in Listener, Spectator, Esquire, Harper's Magazine, Playboy, Private Eye and other journals. Honours: Scholarships, 1952, 1956; Commonwealth Scholarship, 1964; J R Ackerly Prize and Premio Internazionale Mondello, 1989. Address: c/o Aitken and Stone Associates Ltd, 29 Fernshaw Road, London SW10 0TG, England.

**GREGORI Alberto**, b. 1 September 1960. Consultant Orthopaedic Surgeon. Education: St Aloysius College, Glasgow; Glasgow University Medical School, 1977-82. Appointments: Surgeon, MAP, Bourj el Barajneh, Lebanon, 1985; Rotating Registrar, East of Scotland, 1988-92; Registrar and Senior Registrar, Orthopaedics, West of Scotland Training Programme, 1992-97; Leverhulme Fellow, UTH, Lusaka, Zambia, 1996; AO Fellow, Hôpital Sud, Grenoble, France, 1997; Consultant Orthopaedic Surgeon, Hairmyres Hospital, 1997-. Publications: Electronic Textbook CD, Navigation in Total Knee Replacement, 2003; Multiple international and national articles and presentations. Honours: FRCS ORTH; FRCS (Eng); MBChB, Glasgow; DFM, Glasgow. Memberships: Fellow, British Orthopaedic Association; Member, World Orthopaedic Concern; Member, British Medical Association. Address: Department of Orthopaedics, Hairmyres Hospital, East Kilbride, G75 8RG, Scotland.

**GREGORY Jenny (Jennifer Anne)**, b. 11 May 1946, Melbourne, Australia. Historian; Publisher. m. Ross, 1 son, 1 daughter. Education: BA (Hons) History, PhD, University of Western Australia. Appointments: Lecturer, Senior Lecturer, Associate Professor, Department of History, 1991-, Director, Centre for Western Australian History, 1989-, University of Western Australia; Director, University of Western Australia Press, 1998-; President, National Trust of Australia, 1998-; Inaugural President, History Council of Western Australia., 2003-. Publications: Western Australia Between the Wars 1919-1939: Studies in Western Australian History 11, (editor), 1990; On the Homefront: Western Australia and World War II, (editor) 1996; Building a Tradition: a history of Scotch College 1897-1996, 1996; Historical Traces: Studies in Western Australian History, 17 (editor), 1997; Traces of the Past: The National Trust Register of the Built Environment of Western Australia (co-author) CD-ROM, 1997; Claremont: a history (co-author), 1999; City of Light: a History of Perth since the 1950s, 2003. Honours: UWA Excellence in Teaching Award, 1993; WA History Foundation Award for the best first book in the field of Western Australian History, 1997; Centenary Medal, Governor General of Australia, 2001; Champion Award, National Year of the Built Environment, 2004. Memberships: Fellow, Royal Historical Society, London; President, National Trust of Australia; President, History Council of Western Australia;

Professional Member, Professional Historians of WA (Inc); International Committee of Monuments and Sites, Australia; Australian Historical Association; Royal Western Australian Historical Society. Address: UWA Press & Centre for WA History, The University of Western Australia, Crawley, WA 6009, Australia. E-mail: jag@cyllene.uwa.edu.au

**GREGOTTI Vittorio,** b. 10 August 1927, Novara, Italy. Architect. m. Marina Mazza. Education: Graduate, Architecture, Polytechnic of Milan, 1952. Appointments: Collaboration with L Meneghetti and G Stoppino, 1953-68; Founder, President, Gregotti Associati, 1974; Professor of Architectural Composition, Architectural Institute, University of Venice; Visiting Professor, Universities of: Tokyo, Buenos Aires, São Paulo, Lausanne, Harvard, Philadelphia, Princeton, Cambridge (UK), MIT; Director, Edilizia Moderna, 1963-65; Director, Visual Arts and Architectural Section, Biennale di Venezia, 1974-76; Director, Rassegna, 1979-98; Director, Casabella, 1982-96; Works include: University Departments in Palermo and Cosenza, Belem Cultural Centre, Lisbon; Redevelopment of the former industrial area of Bicocca, Milan; Plans for new towns and renewal of urban districts in Shanghai, China. Publications: 17 books and essays on architectural issues; Articles in magazines and newspapers; Books include: New Directions in Italian Architecture, 1968; Inside Architecture, 1996. Honours: Member, Accademia di San Luca, 1976; Accademia di Brora, 1995-; Gold Medal for Science and Culture, President of the Italian Republic, 2000; Degrees of Honoris Causa: Polytechnic of Prague, 1996, Polytechnic of Bucharest, 1999, University of Porto, 2003. Memberships: Bund der deutschen Architekten, 1997-; Honorary Member, American Institute of Architects, 1999-. Address: Via Matteo Bandello 20, 20123 Milan, Italy. E-mail: v.gregotti@gregottiassociati-link.it Website: www.gregottiassociati.it

**GRENVILLE Hugo,** b. 5 August 1958, London, England. Painter. m. Sophia, 2 sons. Education: Life Classes, Chelsea School of Art, 1978; Open Studio, Heatherley's School of Art, 1988-89. Career: H M Armed Forces, Coldstream Guards, served in Northern Ireland, Rhodesia, UK, West Africa, Germany and NATO HQ, 1977-83; J Walter Thompson Advertising Agency, 1983-84; Founder and Director of company dealing in contemporary art, 1984-89; Became full-time painter, 1989; Visiting Tutor to the Gorhambury Art Group as well as teaching one day a week from London Studio, 1990-94; Course Director of Red House Studios, 2001-; Group Exhibitions include: The Chelsea Art Society, 1975, 1993; The Arts Club, London, 1990; Royal Institute of Oil Painters, 1991, 1993, 1996; Royal Institute of Painters in Watercolours, 1992; The Burlington Gallery, London, 1993; Royal Society of British Artists, 1996, 1997, 1998; Fosse Gallery Summer Exhibition, 1998, 1999, 2000; The Tresco Gallery, Tresco, 2002; Summer Exhibition Fraser Fine Art, San Francisco, USA, 2005; Summer Exhibition, Richmond Hill Gallery, 2005; One-Man Shows: New King's Road Gallery, London, 1991; The Newbury Museum, featured artist of the Newbury Festival, 1992; Smith's Gallery, London, 1992; Oliver Swann Galleries, London, 1994; Tryon & Swann Gallery, London, 1995; China Club, Hong Kong, 1995; David Messum Gallery, London, 1997, 1999, 2000, 2001, 2003, 2004, 2005. Works in collections in UK, USA, Canada, France, Hong Kong and Australia include: Edinburgh City Council; The Worshipful Company of Ironmongers; The Ministry of Defence, The China Club, Hong Kong, The Tresco Estate; The Late Duke of Devonshire. Publications: Regular contributor to The Artist and The Literary Review. Membership: The Chelsea Arts Club. Address: The Red House, Mendham, Suffolk IP20 0JD, England. E-mail: hugogrenville@mac.com Website: www.hugogrenville.com

**GRESSER Sy,** b. 9 May 1926, Baltimore, Maryland, USA. Stone Sculptor; Writer; Poet. 4 sons, 1 daughter. Education: BS, 1949, MA, 1972, Zoological Sciences, English and American Literature, University of Maryland; Institute of Contemporary Arts, Washington, DC, 1949-50. Appointments: Publications Consultant for various firms, 1960-; Teacher, 1965-70; Private Students. Publications: Stone Elegies, 1955; Coming of the Atom, 1957; Poems From Mexico, 1964; Voyages, 1969; A Garland for Stephen, 1971; A Departure for Sons, 1973; Fragments and Others, 1982; Hagar and Her Elders, 1989. Contributions to: Poetry Quarterly; Stand; Antioch Review; Western Humanities Review; Johns Hopkins Review; Atavist Magazine; New York Times Book Review. Address: 1015 Ruatan Street, Silver Spring, MD 20903, USA.

**GRETZKY Wayne,** b. 26 January 1961, Brantford, Canada. Ice Hockey Player. m. Janet Jones, 1988, 2 sons, 1 daughter. Career: Former player with Edmonton; Played with Los Angeles Kings, 1988-96, St Louis Blues, 1996, New York Rangers, 1996-99; Retired, 1999; Most prolific scorer in National Hockey League history; Most Valuable Player (9 times). Publication: Gretzky: An Autobiography (with Rick Reilly). Honour: Hockey Hall of Fame, 1999. Address: New York Rangers, Madison Square Garden, 2 Pennsylvania Plaza, New York, NY 10121, USA.

**GRIER Pam,** b. 1949, Winston-Salem, North Carolina, USA. Actress; Writer; Singer. Career: Actress, films: The Big Doll House, 1971; Women in Cages, 1971; Big Bird Cage, 1972; Black Mama, White Mama, 1972; Cool Breeze, 1972; Hit Man, 1972; Twilight People, 1972; Coffy, 1973; Scream, Blacula, Scream!, 1973; The Arena, 1973; Foxy Brown, 1974; Bucktown, 1975; Friday Foster, 1975; Sheba Baby, 1975; Drum, 1976; Greased Lightning, 1977; Fort Apache: The Bronx, 1981; Something Wicked This Way Comes, 1983; Stand Alone, 1985; The Vindicator, 1986; On the Edge, 1986; The Allnighter, 1987; Above the Law, 1988; The Package, 1989; Class of 1999, 1991; Bill and Ted's Bogus Journey, 1991; Tough Enough, Posse, 1993; Serial Killer, 1995; Original Gangstas, 1996; Escape from LA, 1996; Mars Attacks!, 1996; Strip Search, 1997; Fakin' Da Funk, 1997; Jackie Brown, 1997; Holy Smoke, 1999; In Too Deep, 1999; Fortress 2, 1999; Snow Day, 2000; Wilder, 2000; 3 A.M., 2001; Love the Hard Way, 2001; Bones, 2001; John Carpenter's Ghosts of Mars, 2001; Undercover Brother, 2002; The Adventures of Pluto Nash, 2002; Baby of the Family, 2002; TV mini-series: Roots: The Next Generations, 1979; Films: Badge of the Assassin, 1985; A Mother's Right; The Elizabeth Morgan Story, 1992; Stage appearances: Fool for Love; Frankie and Johnnie; In the Claire de Lune. Honour: Best Actress NAACP, 1986.

**GRIEVES John Kerr,** b. 7 November 1935, England. Business Consultant. m. Ann, 1 son, 1 daughter. Education: MA, Keble College, Oxford, 1955-58; Harvard Business School, USA, 1979. Appointments: Joined, 1963, Partner, 1964-74, Departmental Managing Partner, Company Department, 1974-78, Managing Partner, 1979-85, Head of Corporate Finance Group, 1985-89, Senior Partner, 1990-96, Freshfields; Subsequently Non-Executive Director: Northern Electric, Enterprise Oil, Hillsdown Holdings, First Leisure Corporation plc (Chairman), New Look Group plc, (Chairman), Esporta plc (Chairman). Membership: The Athenaeum. Address: 7 Putney Park Avenue, London SW15 5QN, England.

**GRIFFIN James Patrick,** b. 8 July 1933, Wallingford, Connecticut, USA. White's Emeritus Professor of Moral Philosophy. m. Catherine Maulde Von Halban, deceased, 1 son, 1 daughter. Education: BA, Yale University, USA, 1955; D Phil, 1960, MA, 1963 University of Oxford, England. Appointments:

Tutorial Lecturer, Christ Church, Oxford, 1960-66; Lecturer in Philosophy, University of Oxford, 1964-90; Fellow and Tutor in Philosophy, Keble College, University of Oxford, 1966-96; Reader in Philosophy, 1990-96, White's Professor of Moral Philosophy, 1996-2000, University of Oxford; Adjunct Professor, Centre for Applied Philosophy and Public Ethics, Canberra, Australia, 2002-; Distinguished Visiting Professor, Rutgers University, USA, 2002-. Publications: Books: Wittgenstein's Logical Atomism, 1964; Well-Being, 1986; Value Judgement, 1996; Values, Conflict and the Environment (with others), 1996. Honours: Medal, National Education Commission, Poland; Order of Diego de Lusa da Venezuela; Doctor, honoris causa, University of Santiago de Compostela, Spain. Memberships: Brooks's; Oxford and Cambridge Club. Address: 10 Northmoor Road, Oxford OX2 6UP, England.

**GRIFFITH Melanie,** b. 9 August 1957, New York, USA. Actress. m. (1) Don Johnson, 1975, divorced 1976, remarried 1989, divorced 1993, 1 daughter, (2) Steve Bauer, divorced, (3) Antonio Banderas, 1996, 1 daughter. Education: Hollywood Professional School. Career: Films include: Night Moves, 1975; One On One, 1977; Roar, Body Double, 1984; Stormy Monday, 1987; Working Girl, 1988; Bonfire of the Vanities, 1991; Close to Eden, 1993; Nobody's Fool, 1994; Mulholland Falls, 1996; Lolita, 1996; Shadow of Doubt, 1998; Celebrity, 1998; Another Day in Paradise, 1998; Crazy in Alabama, 1999; Cecil B. Demented, 2000; Forever Lulu, 2000; Life with Big Cats, 2000; Tart, 2001; Stuart Little 2 (voice), 2002; The Night We Called It a Day, 2003; Shade, 2003; Tempo, 2003; TV Includes: Once an Eagle (mini-series); Carter Country (series); Steel Cowboy; She's in the Army Now. Address: Creative Artists Agency, 9830 Wilshire Boulevard, Beverly Hills, CA 90212, USA.

**GRIFFITH WILLIAMS, His Honour Judge John,** b. 20 December 1944, Teignmouth, Devon, England. Senior Circuit Judge. m. Mair Tasker Watkins, 2 daughters. Education: BA, Jurisprudence, The Queen's College, Oxford, 1963-66. Appointments: Commissioned 1964, Served 4th Battalion Royal Welch Fusiliers (TA), 1964-68; Lieutenant, Welsh Volunteers (TAVR), 1968-71; Called to the Bar, Gray's Inn, 1968, Bencher, 1994; Recorder of the Crown Court, 1985-2000, Queen's Counsel, 1985; Member, Bar Council, 1990-2000; Deputy High Court Judge, 1993-2000; Assistant Commissioner, Boundary Commission for Wales, 1994-2000; Treasurer, 1993-95, Leader, 1996-98, Wales and Chester Circuit; Deputy Chancellor, 1996-99, Chancellor, 1999, Diocese of Llandaff; Member, Criminal Injuries Compensation Board, 1999-2000; Circuit Judge, 1999; Senior Circuit Judge and Recorder of Cardiff, 2001-. Memberships: Army and Navy Club; Cardiff and County Club; Royal Porthcawl Golf Club. Address: The Crown Court, The Law Courts, Cathays Park, Cardiff CF10 3PG, Wales.

**GRIGGS Ian Macdonald,** b. 17 May 1928, Essex, England. Clergyman. m. Patricia Margaret Vernon-Browne, 3 sons, 1 deceased, 3 daughters. Education: MA, Trinity Hall, Cambridge, 1949-52; Westcott House, Cambridge, 1952-54. Appointments: Curate of St Cuthbert, Portsmouth, 1954-59; Domestic Chaplain to Bishop of Sheffield (half-time), Diocesan Youth Chaplain (half-time), 1959-64; Vicar of St Cuthbert, Fir Vale, Sheffield, 1964-71; Vicar of Kidderminster, Honorary Canon of Worcester, 1971-83; Archdeacon of Ludlow, 1983-87; Bishop of Ludlow, Diocese of Hereford, 1987-94; Honorary Assistant Bishop, Diocese of Carlisle, 1994-. Memberships: Governor, Atlantic College, 1990-2004; Chairman, Churches Council for Health and Healing, 1990-99. Address: Rookings, Patterdale, Cumbria CA11 0NP, England.

**GRIGORYAN Alexander,** b. 2 August 1914, Baku, USSR. Oil Company Executive. 1 daughter. Education: Diploma, Oil-Field Engineer, Azerbaijan Industrial Institute, 1939; Candidate of Technical Sciences, Diploma, Higher Certifying Commission, 1963. Appointments: Driller's Assistant, drilling oil wells, Baku, 1931-34, Senior Engineer, Turbodrilling Enterprise, Baku, 1939-44; Senior Engineer, USSR Ministry of Oil Industry, Moscow, 1944-52; Head of Department, All Union Scientific Research Institute of Drilling Technology, Moscow, 1952-80; President, Grigoryan Branched-Horizontal Wells Company, Los Angeles, California, USA, 1992-. Publications: About 100 publications, scientific works, inventions; Articles including: Multy Bottom Hole Formation Exposing, 1956; Multy Bottom Hold Formation Exposing in Borislav, 1957; The Drilling of Horizontal Wells, 1969; Drilling the Results of the Exploitation of Branched-Horizontal Wells, 1976; Branching-Horizontal Wells are the Nearest Future of the Oil Industry, 1998; Patents: A System for Directional Drilling, 1944; Means of Widening the Bottom Hole Area in Wells in the Pay Zone, 1946, 1949; Means of Lowering the Water Level and Drainage in Carrying Out Boreholes in Mines, 1950; A System for Descending Equipment Tools into Directional Wells, 1953; Turbodrill, 1959; A Means of Increasing the Debit of Wells, 1960; Means of Carrying Out Multy Bottom Hole Wells, 1961; Means of Seeking a Bore Hole for a Blown Out Well, 1965; Means of Drilling Wells, 1969. Honours: Order of the Badge of Honour; Medical for Distinction in Labour; Other Medals and Badges; Diplomas, USSR Ministry of Oil Industry. Membership: Society of Petroleum Engineers. Address: 1637 N Vine Street, # 809, Los Angeles, CA 90028, USA.

**GRIMSBY Bishop of, The Rt Rev David Douglas James Rossdale,** b. 22 May 1953, London, England. Bishop. m. Karen, 2 sons. Education: Westminster College, Oxford; Roehampton Institute. Appointments: Curate of Upminster, 1981-86; Vicar of St Luke's Moulsham, 1986-90; Vicar of Cookham, 1990-2000; Area Dean of Maidenhead, 1994-2000; Honorary Canon, Christ Church, Oxford, 1990-2000; Canon and Prebendary, Lincoln Cathedral, 2000-; Suffragen Bishop of Grimsby, 2000-. Honours: Diploma in Applied Theology, 1990; MA in Applied Theology, 1991; MSc, Management of Ministry, 2001. Memberships: Chairman of the Board of Education for the Diocese of Lincoln; Commissioner on the Churches Regional Commission for Yorkshire and the Humber Region. Address: Bishop's House, Church Lane, Irby, Grimsby, North East Lincolnshire DN37 7JR, England. E-mail: rossdale@btinternet.com

**GRINDE Kjell,** b. 1 August 1929, Bergen, Norway. Civil and Structural Engineer. m. (1) Heidi, divorced, 1 son, 1 daughter, (2) Anneliv, 2 step-daughters. Education: BSc, 1954, MSc, 1956, Technical University of Norway; Diploma, Total Quality Management, Lausanne, Switzerland. Appointments: Scientific Assistant to Professor, Technical University of Norway, 1954-56; Site Engineer, Snowy Mountains Hydro-Electric Authority, Australia, 1956-58; Site Engineer, Norconsult Ethiopia, Koka Power Plant, 1958-60; Site Engineer, Assab Harbour and Water Supply, 1960-62; Chief Engineer and Resident Manager, Norconsult Nigeria, 1962-64; Marketing Director, 1964-68, Managing Director, 1968-81, Norconsult International, Oslo; Projects for World Bank, UN Agencies, Regional Banks, Developing Countries' Governments; Saga Petroleum, Oslo; Corporate Management Technical Director, projects in North Sea, Benin, Caribia, USA, 1981-91; Working Chairman, Senior Expert Group, 1991-. Publications: Professional articles; Conference papers. Honours: Honours Award for Technical Assistance to Developing Countries, Norwegian Natural Sciences Research Council, 1976. Memberships: Director, President, Federation International des Ingenieurs Conseil, 1973-

80; Chairman of the Board, Norwegian Petroleum Consultants, 1975-80; Member, Executive Committee Royal Polytechnical Society, 1979-84; Director, Norwegian Export Council, 1975-80; Chairman, Drammen Technical Society, 1996-. Address: Hanna Winsnesgate 1, 3014 Drammen, Norway. E-mail: annhgr@online.no

**GRISEZ Germain,** b. 30 September 1929, University Heights, Ohio, USA. Professor of Christian Ethics; Writer. m. Jeannette Selby, 9 June 1951, 4 sons. Education: BA, John Carroll University, University Heights, Ohio, 1951; MA and PhL, Dominican College of St Thomas Aquinas, River Forest, Illinois, 1951; PhD, University of Chicago, 1959. Appointments: Assistant Professor to Professor, Georgetown University, 1957-72; Lecturer in Medieval Philosophy, University of Virginia at Charlottesville, 1961-62; Special Assistant to Patrick Cardinal O'Boyle, Archbishop of Washington, DC, 1968-69; Consultant, Archdiocese of Washington, DC, 1969-72; Professor of Philosophy, Campion College, University of Regina, Saskatchewan, Canada, 1972-79; Archbishop Harry J Flynn Professor of Christian Ethics, Mount Saint Mary's College, Emmitsburg, Maryland, 1979-. Publications: Contraception and the Natural Law, 1964; Abortion: The Myths, the Realities, and the Arguments, 1970; Beyond the New Morality: The Responsibilities of Freedom (with Russell Shaw), 1974, 3rd edition, 1988; Beyond the New Theism: A Philosophy of Religion, 1975; Free Choice: A Self-Referential Argument (with Joseph M Boyle Jr and Olaf Tollefsen), 1976; Life and Death with Liberty and Justice: A Contribution to the Euthanasia Debate (with Joseph M Boyle Jr), 1979; The Way of the Lord Jesus, Vol I, Christian Moral Principles (with others), 1983, Vol II, Living a Christian Life (with others), 1993, Vol III, Difficult Moral Questions (with others), 1997; Nuclear Deterrence, Morality and Realism (with John Finnis and Joseph M Boyle Jr), 1987; Fulfilment in Christ: A Summary of Christian Moral Principles (with Russell Shaw), 1991. Contributions to: Many scholarly journals. Honours: Pro ecclesia et pontifice Medal, 1972; Special Award for Scholarly Work, 1981, Cardinal Wright Award for Service to the Church, 1983, Fellowship of Catholic Scholars; Various other fellowships and grants. Memberships: American Catholic Philosophical Association, president, 1983-84; Catholic Theological Society of America. Address: Mount Saint Mary's College, Emmitsburg, MD 21727, USA.

**GRISHAM John,** b. 8 February 1955, Jonesboro, Arkansas, USA. Author; Lawyer. m. Renée Grisham, 1 son, 1 daughter. Education: Mississippi State University; University of Mississippi Law School. Appointment: Ran one-man criminal defence practice in Southaven, Mississippi, 1981-90. Publications: The Pelican Brief; A Time to Kill; Stand in Line at a Super Crown; The Firm; The Client; The Chamber; The Rainmaker; The Runaway Jury; The Partner; The Street Lawyer; The Testament; The Brethren; A Painted House, 2001; Skipping Christmas, 2001; The Summons, 2002; The King of Torts, 2003; Bleachers, 2003; The Last Juror, 2004; The Broker, 2005. Address: Doubleday & Co Inc, 1540 Broadway, New York, NY 10036, USA.

**GROENING Matthew,** b. 15 February 1954, Portland, Oregon, USA. Writer; Cartoonist. m. Deborah Lee Caplan, 2 children. Education: Evergreen State College. Appointments: Cartoonist, Life in Hell syndicated weekly comic strip, Sheridan, Oregon, 1980-; President, Matt Groening Productions Inc, Los Angeles, 1988-, Bongo Entertainment Inc, Los Angeles, 1993-; Creator, The Simpsons interludes, The Tracey Ullman Show, 1987-89; Creator, Executive Producer, The Simpsons TV show, 1989-; Founder and Publisher, Bongo Comics Group; Founder and Publisher, Zongo Comics, including Jimbo, 1995, Fleener, 1996.

Publications: Love is Hell, 1985; Work is Hell, 1986; School is Hell, 1987; Childhood is Hell, 1988; Akbar and Jeff's Guide to Life, 1989; Greetings From Hell, 1989; The Postcards That Ate My Brain, 1990; The Big Book of Hell, 1990; The Simpsons Xmas Book, 1990; Greetings From the Simpsons, 1990; With Love From Hell, 1991; The Simpsons' Rainy Day Fun Book, 1991; The Simpsons' Uncensored Family Album, 1991; The Alphabet Book, 1991; Maggie Simpson's Counting Book, 1991; Maggie Simpson's Book of Colors and Shapes, 1991; Maggie Simpson's Book of Animals, 1991; The Road to Hell, 1992; The Simpson's Fun in Sun Book, 1992; Making Faces with the Simpsons, 1992; Bart Simpson's Guide to Life, 1993; The Simpsons Ultra-Jumbo Rain-Or-Shine Fun Book, 1993; Binky's Guide to Love, 1994; Love is Hell 10th Anniversary Edition, 1994; Simpsons Comics Extravaganza, 1994; Simpsons Comic Spectacular, 1994; Bartman: The Best of the Best, 1994; Simpson Comics Simps-O-Rama, 1995; Simpsons Comics Strike Back, 1995; Simpsons Comics Wing Ding, 1997; The Huge Book of Hell, 1997; Bongo Comics.

**GROS AYMERICH Jose,** Zaragoza, Spain. Physician. Education: Cou, Colegio del Salvador, SI, Zaragoza, 1969; MD, Universidad Autonoma de Madrid, 1976; Specialist in Medical Oncology, 1982; University Specialist in Pharmaceutical Industry Medicine, UCM, 1989. Appointments: Spanish Air Force, 1976-77; Jimenez Diaz Foundation, Madrid, 1978-82; Emergency Service, Social Security, 1979-81, 1983-84; Upjohn, 1984-88; Primary Care Practitioner, Social Security, 1989-; Scientific Advisor, CABYC, 2000-. Publications: Lung Cancer Chemotherapy, 1984, Revista Par. Memberships: SEOM; ASCO; ESMO; NYAS. Address: Jazmin – 76, 3-B, E – 28033 Madrid, Spain. E-mail: jgrosay@telepolis.com

**GROSSMAN Margaret Rosso,** b. 17 October 1947, Illinois, USA. Professor. m. Michael, 2 sons. Education: BMus, highest honours, University of Illinois, 1969; AM, Stanford University, 1970; PhD, Musicology, 1977, JD, summa cum laude, 1979, University of Illinois. Appointments: Bock Chair and Professor, Agricultural Law, Department of Agricultural and Consumer Economics, University of Illinois at Urbana-Champaign; Frequent Visiting Professor, Wageningen University, The Netherlands. Publications: Numerous law review articles, book chapters, books. Honours: Fulbright Research Fellow (3 awards); German Marshall Fund Research Fellow; Silver Medal, European Council for Agricultural Law; Distinguished Service Award, American Agricultural Law Association. Memberships: American Agricultural Law Association; American Veterinary Medical Law Association; European Council for Agricultural Law; Dutch Society for Agrarian Law. Address: 333 Mumford Hall, 1301 W Gregory Dr, Urbana, IL 61801, USA.

**GROVES Paul Raymond,** b. 28 July 1947, Gloucester, England. Teacher; Poet. m. Annette Rushton Kelsall, 1 June 1972, 2 daughters. Education: Teaching Certificate, Caerleon College of Education, 1969. Appointments: Assistant Master in various state schools; evening class lecturer in Creative Writing; visiting poet in schools, Poetry Society. Publications: Poetry Introduction 3, 1975; Green Horse, 1978; Academe, 1988; The Bright Field, 1991; Ménage à Trois, 1995; Eros and Thanatos, 1999; Wowsers, 2002. Honours: Eric Gregory Award, 1976. 1st Prizes: The Times Literary Supplement/Cheltenham Festival, 1986; Green Book, 1986; Yeats Club, 1987; Surrey Poetry Group, 1987, 1988, 1991; Charterhouse International, 1989, 1990; Rainforest Trust, 1991; Orbis International, 1992; Bournemouth Festival, 1994; Cotswold Writers, 1995; Wilkins Memorial, 1997. Address: 4 Cornford Close, Osbaston, Monmouth NP25 3NT, Wales.

**GROVES Philip Denys Baker,** b. 9 January 1928, Watford, Hertfordshire, England. Architect. m. Yvonne Joyce Chapman, 2 sons, 1 daughter. Education: Watford Grammar School, 1939-44; Regent Street Polytechnic School of Architecture, 1948-55. Appointments: RAF, 1945-48: Served in UK, Palestine, Egypt; Architects Co-Partnership: Joined 1955, Partner, 1965, Chairman, 1983-95; Architect for education and health projects, UK, Middle East, Far East and Caribbean; Royal Institute of British Architects; Member of Council, 1962-81, Vice President, 1972-75, 1978-80, Chairman, Board of Education, 1974-75, 1979-80; ARCUK Council, 1962-80; Chairman, 1971-74; Chairman, University of York Centre for Continuing Education, 1978-81; Chairman, CPD in Construction Gp, 1990-96; Construction Industry Council, 1993-96; Comité de Liaison des Architects du Marché Commun, 1986-92; Examiner at Schools of Architecture UK and overseas; Chairman, HCCI, 1985-88; President, 1989, Herts Community Foundation; Chairman, 1988-97, Vice President, 1998-; Chairman, Herts TEC, 1992-97; Business Link Herts, 1993-2003, TEC National Council, 1996-99. Publications: Design for Health Care (jointly); Hospitals and Health Care Facilities (jointly); Various articles in professional journals. Honours: Associate, 1955, Fellow, 1968, Royal Institute of British Architects; FRSA, 1989; Deputy Lieutenant of Hertfordshire, 1988-. Memberships: Fellow, Royal Institute of British Architects; Registered Architect ARB; Fellow Royal Society of Arts. Address: The Dingle, Whisper Wood, Loudwater, Rickmansworth, Hertfordshire WD3 4JU, England.

**GRYNING Sven-Erik,** b. 9 June 1948, Naestved, Denmark. Scientist. m. Susanne, 2 sons. Education: MS, Technical University of Denmark, 1972; PhD, 1982. Appointments: Scientific Staff, Health Physics Department, Riso National Laboratory, 1974-77; Scientific Staff, Physics Department, 1977-84; Scientific Staff, Meteorology and Wind Energy, 1984-; Senior Scientist, 1992-; Adjoint Director, Research, Swedish Defence Research Establishment, 1992-96; Chairman, Convenor, NATO/CCMS International Technical Conference Series on Air Pollution Modelling and its Application, 1992-2000; Project Leader, Oresund Experiment, 1982-90; Chairman, Executive Committee, NOPEX, 1992-; Member, Scientific Panel on Atmospheric Chemistry European Commission, 1995-2000. Publications: Editor, Air Pollution Modeling and Its Application. X, XI, XII, XIII, XIV; Guest Editor, Atmospheric Environment, Theoretical and Applied Climatology, Agricultural and Forest Meteorology; Associate Editor, Quarterly Journal of the Royal Meteorological Society, 2002-. Honours: ITM Scientific Committee Award, 2000; Grantee, Nordic Council of Ministry. Memberships: Danish Meteorological Society; European Association for the Science of Air Pollution. Address: Haraldsborgvej 120, DK-4000 Roskilde, Denmark.

**GU Baoyu,** b. 19 March 1939, Qingdao, China. Artist. m. Jianhua Yang, 2 sons, 1 daughter. Education: Graduate, Shangdong Physical Education Institute, 1962; Graduate, Central Academy of Fine Arts, 1966; Studies with Kuchan Li and Xuetao Wang, 1962-. Career: Art exhibitions in Beijing, Shanghai, Japan, America and more than 30 provinces and countries; President, Shandong Academy of Social Science; President, Qingdao Institute of Traditional Painting Research. Publications: Many books and critical articles include: Traditional Painting Album by Baoyu Gu; Collected Works of Baoyu Gu; Painting Skills of Baoyu Gu (18 volumes). Honours include: First Prize, Art Gallery in China, 1976; Second Place, HongYe Cup, Canada, 1989; Countrywide Champion of Handwriting and Painting, 1996; Worthy Prize of China in the 20th Century, 1999; One of One Hundred most Famous Painters in China. Memberships: Vice-President, China Modern Artists Association; Council Member, China Traditional Painting Artists Association. Address: Room 401, Unit 3 of No 1 Da Yao San Road, Quingdao, China.

**GUESGEN Hans Werner,** b. 24 April 1959, Bonn, Germany. Associate Professor. m. Gaby, 11 August 1984, 3 daughters. Education: Dipl-Inform, University of Bonn, 1983; Dr rer nat, University of Kaiserlautern, 1988; Dr habil, University of Hamburg, 1993. Appointments: Post Doctoral Fellow, ICSI, Berkeley, California, 1989-90; Scientific Researcher, GMD St Augustin, Germany, 1983-92; Associate Professor, Computer Science Department, University of Auckland, 1992-. Publications: 2 monographs; 8 edited books, journals and reports; Over 100 refereed articles in journals, books, conference proceedings and workshop notes; Over 30 technical reports. Memberships: American Association for Artificial Intelligence. Address: Computer Science Department, University of Auckland, Private Bag 92019, Auckland, New Zealand. E-mail: hans@cs.auckland.ac.nz

**GUEST Harry, (Henry Bayly Guest),** b. 6 October 1932, Glamorganshire, Wales. Poet; Writer. m. Lynn Doremus Dunbar, 28 December 1963, 1 son, 1 daughter. Education: BA, Trinity Hall, Cambridge, 1954, DES, Sorbonne, University of Paris, 1955. Appointments: Lecturer, Yokohama National University, 1966-72; Head of Modern Languages, Exeter School, 1972-91; Teacher of Japanese, Exeter University, 1979-96. Publications: Arrangements, 1968; The Cutting-Room, 1970; Post-War Japanese Poetry, (editor and translator), 1972; A House Against the Night, 1976; Days, 1978; The Distance, the Shadows, 1981; Lost and Found, 1983; The Emperor of Outer Space (radio play), 1983; Lost Pictures, 1991; Coming to Terms, 1994; Traveller's Literary Companion to Japan, 1994; So Far, 1998; The Artist on the Artist, 2000; A Puzzling Harvest, Collected Poems, 2002. Contributions to: Reviews, quarterlies, and journals. Honours: Hawthornden Fellow, 1993; Honorary Research Fellow, Exeter University, 1994-; Honorary Doctor of Letters, Plymouth University, 1998. Membership: Poetry Society, General Council, 1972-76. Address: 1 Alexandra Terrace, Exeter, Devon EX4 6SY, England.

**GUEST GORNALL Anthony Richard,** b. 22 July 1936, Grappenhall, Cheshire, England. Literary Agent. m. Judy Redmond, 1 son, 1 daughter. Education: Hertford College, Oxford. Appointments: Cassell & Co Publishers; Hutchinson & Co Publishers; Co-Founder, Intercontinental Literary Agency, 1965-. Memberships: Cheshire Pitt Club; Oxford and Cambridge Club; Sunningdale Golf Club. Address: Ridge Mount Cottage, Sunningdale, Berkshire SL5 9RW, England. E-mail: anthony@ridgeascot.fsworld.co.uk

**GUI Gerald P H,** b. 8 June 1962, Kuala Lumpur, Malaysia. Consultant Surgeon. m. Corina Espinosa, 2 sons. Education: MB BS, University College and Middlesex Hospital Medical School, London, 1981-86; FRCS Edinburgh, 1990; FRCS England, 1991; Master of Surgery, University of London, 1996. Appointments: Previously: Senior Registrar and Lecturer in Surgery, St George's Hospital Medical School; Registrar in Surgery, St Bartholomew's Hospital, London; Currently: Consultant Surgeon, Royal Marsden NHS Trust and Honorary Senior Lecturer, Institute of Cancer Research, London. Publications: Many peer-reviewed original manuscripts in surgery and breast cancer management, tumour biology of breast cancer. Honours: University of London Laurels, 1986; Royal College of Surgeons of England Travelling Fellowship, 1997; Surgeon in Training Medal, Royal College of Surgeons, Edinburgh, 1994. Memberships: British Association of Surgical Oncology; British Breast Group; British Oncological Association; Society of Academic and Research Surgeons;

Fellow, Association of Surgeons of Great Britain and Ireland. Address: Academic Surgery (Breast Unit), Royal Marsden NHS Trust, Fulham Road, London SW3 6JJ, England. E-mail: gerald.gui@rmh.nthames.nhs.uk

**GUILLEBAUD John,** b. 19 January 1941, Burundi, Africa. Physician. m. 3 children. Education: BA, 1961, MB BChir, 1964-65, MA, 1965, St John's College, Cambridge; FRCS (Edin), 1969; RCOG, 1972; FRCOG, 1984; Family Planning Association Certificate, 1972. Appointments include: Various hospital posts, 1964-70; Registrar in Obstetrics and Gynaecology, Stoke Mandeville Hospital, 1970-71; Clinic Surgeon, 1970-, Research Director, Board Member, 1974-, Elliot-Smith Vasectomy Clinic, Churchill Hospital, Oxford; Research Fellow, Nuffield Department of Obstetrics and Gynaecology, John Radcliffe and Churchill Hospitals, Oxford, 1972-76; World Health Organisation Research Fellow, 1976; Lecturer, Senior Registrar, Nuffield Department of Obstetrics and Gynaecology, Oxford, 1976-77; Medical Director, 1978-2002, Trustee, 2003-, Margaret Pyke Centre for Study and Training in Family Planning, 1978-2002; Honorary Consultant, Gynaecology and Reproductive Health, Camden Primary Care Trust, 1978-2002; Honorary Consultant Gynaecologist, University College London Hospitals Trust, 1978-2002; Professor of Family Planning and Reproductive Health, 1993-2002, Professor Emeritus, 2002, University College, London; Honorary Consultant in Family Planning, Oxford Primary Care Trust, 1991-; Self-employed Clinical Practice, Oxford. Publications: More than 300 communications in medical journals; Numerous educational articles and interviews for the lay press and electronic media. Books: The Pill – and other hormonal methods, 1980, sixth edition 2004; Contraception – Your Questions Answered, 1985, 4th edition, 2004; Contraception: Science and Practice (co-editor), 1989; Contraception: Hormonal and Barrier Methods, 1992, 5th edition, 2004. Contraception: A User's Guide (co-author), 1994, 3rd edition, 2000; Oral Contraception Compliance: what you and your patients need to know, 1994; Sexuality and Disability: a guide to everyday practice,, 1999. Honours: Maslen Science Prize, 1956; Open Scholarship, St John's College, Cambridge, 1957; Bentley Prize, St Batholomew's Hospital, 1965; Evian/Birthright Health Award for "his campaign on human numbers, a crucial factor in meeting human needs on a finite planet", 1993. Memberships include: Fellow, Royal College of Surgeons; Fellow, Royal College of Obstetricians and Gynaecologists; Family Planning Association; Founding Member, Faculty of Family Planning and Reproductive Health Care. Address: Whiteleaf Mead, 14 Hid's Copse Road, Cumnor Hill, Oxford OX2 9JJ, England. E-mail: j.guillebaud@lineone.net

**GUILLEMIN Roger Charles Louis,** b. 11 January 1924, Dijon, France (US Citizen). Endocrinologist. m. Lucienne Jeanne Billard, 1951, 1 son, 5 daughters. Education: BA, 1941, BSc, 1942, University of Dijon; Medicine, University of Lyons, medical degree, 1949; PhD, Institute of Experimental Medicine and Surgery, Montreal, 1950. Appointments: Resident Intern, University Hospital, Dijon, 1949-51; Professor, Institute of Experimental Medicine and Surgery, Montreal; Baylor College of Medicine, Houston, Texas, 1953; Associate Director, Department of Experimental Endocrinology, Collège de France, Paris, 1960-63; Resident Fellow and Research Professor, 1970-89, Dean, 1972-73, 1976-77, Distinguished Professor, 1997-, The Salk Institute for Biological Studies, San Diego, California; Distinguished Scientist, 1989-93, Medical and Scientific Director, Director, 1993-94, 1995-97, Whittier Institute for Diabetes and Endocrinology, La Jolla; Adjunct Professor of Medicine, University of California, San Diego, 1995-97. Honours: Bonneau and La Caze Awards in

Physiology, 1957, 1960; Gairdner Award, 1974; Officier, Legion d'honneur, Lasker Foundation Award, 1975; Nobel Prize for Physiology or Medicine, 1977; National Medal of Science, 1977; Barren Gold Medal, 1979; Dale Medallist, UK Society for Endocrinology, 1980. Memberships: NAS; American Academy of Arts and Sciences; American Physiological Society; Society for Experimental Biology and Medicine; International Brain Research Organisation; International Society for Research in Biology and Reproduction; Swedish Society of Medical Sciences; Academie Nacionale de Medecine; Academie des Sciences; Academie Royale de Medecine de Belgique; The Endocrine Society. Address: The Salk Institute, 10010 North Torrey Pines Road, La Jolla, CA 92037, USA.

**GUIMARAES Romeu Cardoso,** b. 29 July 1943, Belo Horizonte MG, Brazil. m. Alexandrina M Guimaraes. Education: MD, 1965; PhD, Pathology, 1970; Full Professor, Genetics, 1987. Appointments: University Federal Minas Gerais, 1966-75; University Estadual Paulista, 1976-93; Currently working on: Origin of Life, Philosophy of Biology. Honour: Illustrious Son of Belo Horizonte. Membership: Sao Paulo Academy of Sciences; Minas Gerais Academy of Medicine. Address: Dpto de Biologia Geral, Institut Ciencias Biologicas, UFMG, 31270-901 Belo Horizonte MG, Brazil. E-mail: romeucg@mono.icb.ufmg.br

**GUINNESS (Cecil) Edward,** b. 1924, Great Britain. Brewery Director. m. Elizabeth Mary Fossett Thompson, 3 daughters, 1 deceased. Education: Stowe School, 1938-42; Army Course, University of Belfast, 1942-43; Ex-Serviceman's Course, School of Brewing, Birmingham, 1946-47. Appointments: WWII: Officer Cadet, Royal Artillery (invalided out due to Battle Course injury), 1942-45; Former Vice-Chairman, Guinness Brewing Worldwide; Joined Guinness as Junior Brewer, 1945; Director: Wolverhampton and Dudley Breweries, 1964-87, Guinness plc, 1971-89; Chairman and Managing Director, Harp Lager Consortium, 1971-87; Chairman: Brewer's Society, 1985-86, Fulmer Parish Council, 1973-81, UK Trustees Duke of Edinburgh's Commonwealth Study Conferences, 1972-86; Licensed Trade Charities Trust, 1981-92, Governing Body, Dame Alice Owen's School, Potters Bar, 1981-92, Scottish Licensed Trade Association, 1972, Wine and Spirit Trade Benevolent Society, 1989-90, Chairman, Executive Committee, Fulmer Sports and Community Association, 2003-2004; President, 2004-, Chairman, Development Trust, 1993-96, Governor and Member of Executive Committee, 1996-, Queen Elizabeth Foundation for Disabled People; President: Performing Arts Centre Campaign, Dame Alice Owen's School, 1997-2002, Fulmer Recreation Ground Campaign, 2000-2003; Former President and Vice-President, 1980 and 1991, Licensed Victuallers National Homes; Member, Governing Body, Lister Institute of Preventive Medicine, 1968-2001, Gerrards Cross with Fulmer Parochial Church Council, 2002-2005. Publication: The Guinness Book of Guinness, 1988. Honours: CVO, 1986; Master, Worshipful Company of Brewers, 1977-78. Membership: Life Member, Industrial Society. Address: Huyton Fold, Fulmer Village, Buckinghamshire SL3 6HD, England.

**GULBENKIAN Boghos Parsegh (Basil Paul),** b. 23 March 1940, London, England. Solicitor; Judge. m. Jacqueline Gulbenkian, 2 daughters. Education: LLB, London School of Economics, London University, 1958-61; Qualified as a Solicitor, 1984. Appointments: Senior Partner, Gulbenkian Andonian Solicitors; Immigration Judge; Honorary Consul, Armenian Embassy. Publications: Editor: Entry and Residence in Europe; Immigration Law and Business in Europe. Honours: Encyclicals from His Holiness Vasken I; St Mesrob Medal; Freeman of the City of London. Memberships: Founder, Solicitors Family

Law Association; Immigration Law Practitioners Association; President, European Immigration Lawyers Group; Council of Immigration Judges. Address: 125 High Holborn, London WC1 6QA, England. E-mail: paulg@gulbenkian.co.uk

**GÜLSOY Tanses Yasemin,** b. Verdun, France. Advertising Executive. Education: BA, Pomona College, Claremont, California, USA, 1985; MA, Journalism and Mass Communication, New York University, New York, New York, 1988. Appointments: Research Assistant, Harry Frank Guggenheim Foundation, New York, New York, 1986-88; Advertising Copywriter, 1989-97, International Advertising Director, 1997-2001, Manajans/Thompson, Istanbul, Turkey; Founder and Owner, Tans Communications Consultancy, Istanbul, Turkey, 2001-2003; General Manager, Gültan Elektrik Tic ve San A S, Istanbul, Turkey, 2003-. Publications: Why the Fight over Peace Studies, 1988; An English-Turkish Dictionary of Advertising with Turkish-English Index, 1999; 38 newspaper articles in American newspapers. Honours: Bogazici University, Business Administration Department Dean's List, 1982; Pomona College Academic Scholarship, 1982-85; Pomona College Honnold Fellowship for Graduate Study, 1985; Harry Frank Guggenheim Foundation Fellowship, 1986-88; Profiled by weekly news magazine Aktüel as one of Turkey's brightest young minds, 2002; Honours Award, Turkey's Association of Advertising Creatives, 2002; Listed in Who's Who 2003, 2004 and 2005 publications and biographical dictionaries. Memberships: American Marketing Association; Turkish Society for Opinion and Marketing Research; Turkish Association of Advertising Creatives; New York University European Alumni Group; Pomona College Alumni Volunteers; Member of Board of Directors, 1994-96, Robert College Alumni Association. Address: Adnan Saygun Cad, Dag Apt 72/10, I.Ulus, 34360 Istanbul, Turkey.

**GUMAA Samia Ahmed,** b. 20 February 1943, Cairo, Egypt. Professor of Microbiology. m. El Tigani El Musharaf, 6 daughters. Education: MBBS, Science and Medicine, University of Khartoum, 1966; Diploma, Bacteriology, University of Manchester, England, 1971; Primary MRC Path, England. Appointments: Rotating house Officer, Khartoum Civil Hospital, 1966-67; Registrar of Immunology, Manchester Royal Infirmary, Manchester Eye Hospital, St Mary's Hospital for Women and Children, Manchester, 1972; Lecturer, Senior Lecturer, 1976, Associate Professor 1977, Associate Professor of Microbiology, 1991, Professor of Microbiology, 1992-94, Head of Department of Microbiology and Parasitology, Faculty of Medicine, University of Khartoum. Publications: Author and co-author of over 30 articles and papers in professional medical journals. Honours: Prize in Medicine, University of Khartoum, 1966; International Woman of the Year, IBC, Cambridge, England, 1998; Twentieth Century Award for Achievement, IBC, Cambridge, England, 1998. Memberships: Member, Senate, University of Khartoum; Society of Dermatologists; Society of Pathologists; Faculty Board of Medicine, University of Khartoum; Post-graduate Medical Board, Academic Board of Academy of Medical Sciences Technology. Address: Faculty of Medicine, Department of Microbiology and Parasitology, PO Box 102, University of Khartoum, Sudan.

**GUMLEY-MASON Frances Jane Miriah Katrina,** b. 28 January 1955, London, England. Headmistress. m. Andrew Samuel Mason, 1 son, 1 daughter. Education: MA, Newnham College, Cambridge. Appointments: Parliamentary Researcher, 1974; Braille Transcriber, 1975; Editorial Assistant, 1975-76, Staff Reporter and Literary Editor, 1976-79, Editor, 1979-81, Catholic Herald; Senior Producer, Religious Broadcasting, BBC, 1981-88; Series Editor, Channel 4, 1988-89; Acting Executive Producer, Religion, BBC World Service, 1989; Guest Producer and Scriptwriter, BBC Radio 4, 1989-95; Headmistress, St Augustine's Priory, Ealing, 1995-. Publications: Books (with Brian Redhead): The Good Book; The Christian Centuries; The Pillars of Islam; Protestors for Paradise; Discovering Turkey (jointly). Honour: MA, Newnham College, Cambridge. Membership: Mistress of the Keys, Catholic Writers' Guild, 1982-87. Address: St Augustine's Priory, Hillcrest Road, Ealing, London W5 2JL, England. E-mail: admin@saintaugust inespriory.org.uk

**GUMPERTZ Werner H,** b. 26 December 1917, Berlin, Germany. Consulting Engineer. Education: BCE Swiss Federal Institute of Technology, 1939; Sanitary Engineering, New York University, 1941; SB in Civil Engineering, MIT, 1948; SM in Building Engineering and Construction, MIT, 1950; Advanced Professional degree of Building Engineer, MIT, 1954; Appointments: Office and Field Engineer, United Engineers and Constructors, 1948-49; Assistant Professor of Building Technology, Massachusetts Institute of Technology, 1949-1957; Senior Principal, Simpson Gumpertz & Heger Inc, 1956-. Publications: Numerous publications, presentations and lectures on field of building and building materials, 1948-. Honours: Sigma Xi; 1st Prize, paper contest, American Society of Civil Engineers, 1948; Citation for Good Citizenship, Freedom Inc, 1957; Award of Merit, Boston Arts Festival, 1958; Commendation for Public Service, member of Engineering Board, City of Newton, Massachusetts, 1961; Honour Award for Design in Urban Transportation, US Department of Housing and Urban Development, 1968; Award of Appreciation, American Society for Testing and Materials, 1980-85; Award of Merit, American Society for Testing and Materials, 1986; ASTM Walter C Voss Award to Engineer for Outstanding Contribution to Advancement of Building Technology, 1987; William C Cullen Award, ASTM, 2005. Memberships: Fellow, ASCE; Fellow, ASTM; ACI; AAA; NFPA; Midwest Roofing Contractors Association. Address: c/o Simpson Gumpertz & Heger Inc, 41 Seyon Street, Waltham, MA 02453, USA.

**GUN-MUNRO Sydney Douglas (Sir),** b. 29 November 1916, Grenada, Windward Islands, West Indies. Medical Practitioner. 2 sons, 1 daughter. Education: MRCP, LRCP, 1942, MBBS Hons, 1943, D.O., 1952; Elected FRCS, 1985, King's College London University and King's College Hospital, London. Appointments: Medical Officer, Lewisham Hospital, 1943-46; District Medical Officer, Grenada, 1946-49; Surgeon, General Hospital St Vincent, 1949-71; District Medical Officer, Bequia, St Vincent, 1972-76; Governor, Associated State, St Vincent, 1977-79; Governor-General, St Vincent and the Grenadines, 1979-85; Retired. Honours: MBE, 1957; Kt.B, 1977; GCMG, 1979. Address: Bequia, St Vincent and the Grenadines, West Indies.

**GUNAWAN Benny,** b. 1 March 1948, Bogor, Indonesia. Senior Lecturer. m. Sri Saptaningsih, 1 son, 2 daughters. Education: BSc, University of Pajajaran, Bandung, 1975; MSc, Department of Animal Husbandry, University of Sydney, Australia, 1980; PhD, School of Fibre Science and Technology, University of New South Wales, Sydney, Australia, 1986; Professor, Postgraduate Studies in Management, University of Satyagama, Jakarta, Indonesia, 1999. Appointments: Director of Research Institute, Department of Agriculture, 1987-90; Director of Postgraduate Studies, University of Satyagama, 1997-; Director of Postgraduate Studies in Business Administration, Stiami, 2001-; Chairman of Foundation for Regional Community Development, 2001-; Dean of Faculty for Political Social Science, University of Pramita, Indonesia, 2005-. Publications: More than 200 articles published in local and international journals since 1976. Honours: Listed in Who's Who publications and biographical dictionaries. Membership: National Geographic Society. Address: Komp MG Cempaka Mas Blok A5, JC Jendsuprapto, Cempaka Putih, Jakarta Pusat 10640, Indonesia. E-mail: bgunawan@cbn.net.id

**GUNN Anthony William,** b. 21 May 1946, Stanmore, England. Master of Wine. m. Amanda Till, 2 daughters. Education: MA, Modern History, Corpus Christi College, Oxford, 1975; Master of Wine, 1974. Appointments: Brand Manager, 1972, Buyer, 1977, Grants of St James's; Wine and Spirits Controller, ASDA, 1981; Director, Dent and Reuss Ltd, 1984; Managing Director, Pol Roger Ltd, 1990-. Publications: Contributor to: Wines of the World, 1981; The Wine Drinker's Handbook, 1982. Honour: Chevalier de L'Ordre de Merite Agricole, 1983. Memberships: Liveryman, Fishmongers Company; Freeman City of London; Member, Oxford and Cambridge Club; Institute of Masters of Wine, Chairman, 1977-78. Address: Pol Roger Ltd, Shelton House, 4 Coningsby Street, Hereford HR1 4QR, England. E-mail: bill.gunn@polroger.co.uk

**GUNNING Christopher,** b. 5 August 1944, Cheltenham, England. Composer. 4 daughters. Education: Hendon County Grammar School; Guildhall School of Music and Drama. Career: Recent scores include: Agatha Christie's Poirot; Piano Concerto; Symphony No 1; Saxophone Concerto; The Lobster; Wild Africa; Karaoke; Cold Lazarus; Rebecca; When the Whales Came; Firelight; Rosemary and Thyme. Publications: The Really Easy Flute Book; First Book of Flute Solos; Second Book of Flute Solos; First Book of Clarinet Solos; Second Book of Clarinet Solos. Honours: 3 BAFTA Awards for Best TV Music (Agatha Christie's Poirot, Porterhouse Blue and Middlemarch); 3 Ivor Novello Awards for Best Film/TV Scores (Firelight, Rebecca, Under Suspicion). Memberships: British Academy of Composers and Songwriters; Director, PRS, 1983-2004. Address: 24 Ranelagh Road, Ealing, London W5 5RJ, England. E-mail: orchmus@dircon.co.uk

**GUNSTON Bill, (William Tudor Gunston),** b. 1 March 1927, London, England. Author. m. Margaret Anne, 10 October 1964, 2 daughters. Education: University College, Durham, 1945-46; City University, London, 1948-51. Appointments: Pilot, Royal Air Force, 1946-48; Editorial Staff, 1951-55, Technical Editor, 1955-64, Flight; Technology Editor, Science Journal, 1964-70; Compiler, Jane's All the World's Aircraft, 1968-; Compiler/Editor, Jane's Aero-Engines, 1996-; Freelance author, 1970-; Director, So Few Ltd. Publications: Over 370 books including: Aircraft of The Soviet Union, 1983; Jane's Aerospace Dictionary, 1980, 4th edition, 1998; Encyclopaedia of World Aero Engines, 1986, 3rd edition, 1995; Encyclopaedia of Aircraft Armament, 1987; Giants of the Sky, 1991; Faster Than Sound, 1992; Jet Bombers, 1993; Piston Aero Engines, 1994, 2nd edition, 1998; Encyclopaedia of Russian Aircraft, 1995; Jet and Turbine Aero Engines, 1995, 2nd edition, 1997; Night Fighters, 2nd edition, 2004; The Cambridge Aerospace Dictionary, 2004; World Encyclopaedia of Aircraft Manufacturers, 2nd edition, 2005; Contributions to: 188 periodicals; 18 partworks; 75 video scripts; Member Association of British Science Writers. Honours: Fellow, Royal Aeronautical Society; Officer of the Order of the British Empire. Address: High Beech, Kingsley Green, Haslemere, Surrey GU27 3LL, England.

**GUPTA Suman,** b. 4 October 1975, Allahabad (UP), India. Research Fellow. Education: BSc, 1996, MSc, 2000, PhD, 2005, University of Allahabad; Certificate, Computer Application course, 2002. Appointments: Research Fellow, Scientist, University Grant's Commission project on Viability and Reproduction of Algae facing periodic Water Stress,

University of Allahabad. Publications: Vegetative Survival and Reproduction under Submerged and Air-Exposed Conditions and Vegetative Survival as Affected by Salts, Pesticides and Metals in Aerial Green Alga 'Trentepohlia aurea'; Zoosporangia Survival, Dehiscence and Zoospore Formation, and Motility in the Green Alga 'Rhizoclonium hieroglyphicum' as Affected by Different Factors; Motility and survival of 'Euglena ignobilis' as affected by different factors, Folia Microbiol, Volume 50, in press. Honours: National Scholarship Holder; Merit Award in Master of Science; Participated, National Symposium on Science and Ethics of Environmental Care and Sustainability, 2002; Presented paper, National Symposium on Biology and Biodiversity of Freshwater Algae, 2004. Memberships: Life Member, Association of Microbiologists of India; IARI, New Delhi. Address: 369-A/140-A, Tula Ram Bagh, P O Daraganj, Allahabad (UP), 211004, India.

**GUPTA Vinod Kumar,** b. 23 March 1954, Jaipur, India. Internist; Researcher; Poet; Ethicist. m. Anjali Dhankani, 10 May 1979, 1 son. Education: MB, BS, 1976, MD, 1980, University of Rajastan, Jaipur, India; MRCP (UK) Part 1, 1988; ECFMG (USA), 1989. Appointments: Junior Resident in Medicine, All India Institute for Medical Sciences, New Delhi, India, 1977-78; Registrar in General Medicine, 1978-79, Senior Registrar in General Medicine, 1979-80, JLN Medical College, Ajmer, India; Consultant Physician, Panacea Medical Clinic, Delhi, 1980-85; General Physician and Medical Doctor, Emirates Diagnostic Clinic, Dubai, United Arab Emirates, 1985-87; Specialist Physician, Al-Rasheed Medical Clinic, Dubai, 1988-89; Physician, Dubai Police, 1989-. Publications: Spirit of Enterprise, 1990; Contributed articles to professor journals. Honours include: Rolex Award, 1990; Certificate of Merit Ministry of Education and Youth Services, Government of India, 1970-71; Lala Ramchander Memorial Award, 1970-71; Merit Scholarship, Board of Secondary Education, 1970-71, University of Rajastan, 1973-75; Prize for Courteous Behavior and Service to Community, Rotary International, 1985; New Century Award, Barons 500, 1999; Leaders for the New Century; Editors Choice Award, 2002; Best Poets of 2002; 3rd place medal, Poetry.com; Nominated for: International Man of the Year 2003; Great Minds of the 21st Century, 2004; American Medal of Honor, 2005; World Medal of Freedom, 2005; Leading Health Professionals of the World, 2005; Man of the Year, 2005; Man of Achievement, 2005; International Peace Prize, 2005. Memberships: American Association for the Advancement of Science; New York Academy of Science; American Headache Society. Address: Dubai Police Medical Services, PO Box 12005, Dubai, United Arab Emirates. E-mail: dr_vkgupta@hotmail.com

**GURDON John Bertrand,** b. 2 October 1933, Dippenhall, Hampshire, England. Molecular Biologist. m. Jean Elizabeth Margaret Curtis, 1964, 1 son, 1 daughter. Education: Graduated, Zoology, Christ Church College, Oxford, 1956; Doctorate, Embryology, Zoology Department, 1960. Appointments: Beit Memorial Fellow, 1958-61; Gosney Research Fellow, California Institute of Technology, 1961-62; Research Fellow, Christ Church, Oxford, 1962-72; Departmental Demonstrator, 1963-64, Lecturer, Department of Zoology, 1966-72; Visiting Research Fellow, Carnegie Institute, Baltimore, 1965; Scientific Staff, 1973-83, Head of Cell Biology Division, 1979-83, John Humphrey Plummer Professor of Cell Biology, 1983-2001, Medical Research Council, Molecular Biology Laboratory, University of Cambridge; Master, Magdalene College, Cambridge, 1995-2002; Fellow, Churchill College, Cambridge, 1973-95; Croonian Lecturer, Royal Society, 1976; Dunham Lecturer, Harvard Medical School, 1974; Carter-Wallace Lecturer, Princeton University, 1978; Fellow, Eton College,

1978-93. Publications: Control of Gene Expression in Animal Development, 1974. Honours: Hon DSc, 1978, 1988, 1998, 2000; Hon Dr, 1982; Albert Brachet Prize, 1968; Scientific Medal of Zoological Society, 1968; Feldberg Foundation Award, 1975; Paul Ehrlich Award, 1977; Nessim Habif Prize, 1979; CIBA Medal, Biochemical Society, 1981; Comfort Crookshank Award for Cancer Research, 1983; William Bate Hardy Triennial Prize, 1983; Charles Leopold Mayer Prize, 1984; Ross Harrison Prize, 1985; Royal Medal, 1985; Emperor Hirohito International Biology Prize, 1987; Wolf Prize for Medicine, jointly, 1989; Distinguished Service Award, Miami, 1992; Knight Bachelor, June 1995; Jean Brachet Memorial Prize, International Society for Differentiation, 2000; Conklin Medal, Society of Developmental Biology, 2001; Copley Medal Royal Society, 2003. Memberships: Honorary Foreign Member, American Academy of Arts and Sciences, 1978; Honorary Student, Christ Church, Oxford, 1985; Fullerian Professor of Physiology and Comparative Anatomy, Royal Institute, 1985-91; President, International Society for Developmental Biology, 1990-94; Foreign Associate, NAS, 1980, Belgian Royal Academy of Science, Letters and Fine Arts, 1984, French Academy of Science, 1990; Foreign Member, American Philosophical Society, 1983; Chair, Wellcome Cancer Campaign Institute, University of Cambridge, 1990-2001; Governor, The Wellcome Trust, 1995-2000; Chair, Company of Biologists, 2001-. Address: Whittlesford Grove, Whittlesford, Cambridge CB2 4NZ, England.

**GUREVICH Alexander,** b. 26 March 1921, Leningrad, USSR. Scientific Worker. m. Selyanina Nina, 1 son, 1 daughter. Education: Leningrad Polytechnic Institute, 1937-41; Diploma of Electrical Engineer, Military Academy of Communication, 1941-44. Appointments: Military Service (Radar Units), 1944-49; Senior Engineer, Senior Scientific Worker, Research and Development Institute, 1959-57; Senior Scientific Worker, Chief of Laboratory, Semiconductor Institute, Academy of Sciences, USSR, 1957-72; Senior Scientific Worker, Chief Scientific Worker, Ioffe Physico-Technical Institute, Russian Academy of Sciences, 1972-. Publications: Monographs: Hollow Resonators and Waveguides (in Russian), 1952; Microwave Ferrites (in Russian, translated into English, Polish, etc), 1960; Magnetic Resonance in Ferrites and Antiferromagnets (in Russian), 1973; Magnetic Oscillations and Waves (with G A Melkov) (in Russian), 1994, (in English), 1996; Solid State Physics (in Russian), 2004; Approximately 160 scientific articles on magnetism and microwaves. Honours: Soros Professor, 1983; USSR Government Premium, 1988; Honoured Scientist of the Russian Federation, 1999. Membership: Council on Condensed Matter Physics, Russian Academy of Sciences. Address: A F Ioffe Physico-Technical Institute, 26 Polytekhnicheskaya Str, St Petersburg, 194021 Russia,

**GURNEY A(lbert) R(amsdell),** b. 1 November 1930, Buffalo, New York, USA. Professor of Literature; Dramatist; Writer. m. Mary Goodyear, 1957, 2 sons, 2 daughters. Education: BA, Williams College, 1952; MFA, Yale University School of Drama, 1958. Appointments: Faculty, 1960-, Professor of Literature, 1970-, Massachusetts Institute of Technology. Publications: Plays: Children, 1974; The Dining Room, 1982; The Perfect Party, 1986; Another Antigone, 1986; Sweet Sue, 1986; The Cocktail Hour, 1988; Love Letters, 1989; The Old Boy, 1991; The Fourth Wall, 1992; Later Life, 1993; A Cheever Evening, 1994; Sylvia, 1995; Overtime, 1995; Labor Day, 1998; The Guest Lecturer, 1999; Far East, 1999; Ancestral Voices, 1999; Human Events, 2000; Buffalo Gal, 2001; O Jerusalem, 2003; Mrs Farnsworth, 2004; Big Bill, 2003; Screen Play, 2005; Novels: The Gospel According to Joe, 1974; The Snow Ball, 1985. Screenplay: The House of Mirth, 1972. Television Play: O

Youth and Beauty (from a story by John Cheever), 1979. Opera libretto: Strawberry Fields. Honours: Drama Desk Award, 1971; Rockefeller Foundation Grant, 1977; National Endowment for the Arts Award, 1982; Theatre Award, American Academy of Arts and Sciences, 1990; Lucille Lortel Award, 1992; William Inge Award, 2000; Theatre Hall of Fame, 2005; Honorary doctorates. Address: 40 Wellers Bridge Road, Roxbury, CT 06783, USA.

**GURR Andrew (John),** b. 23 December 1936, Leicester, England. Professor; Writer. m. Elizabeth Gordon, 1 July 1961, 3 sons. Education: BA, 1957, MA 1958, University of Auckland, New Zealand; PhD, University of Cambridge, 1963. Appointments: Lecturer, Leeds University, 1962; Professor, University of Nairobi, 1969; University of Reading, 1976-2002. Publications: The Shakespeare Stage 1574-1642, 1970, 3rd edition, 1992; Writers in Exile, 1982; Katherine Mansfield, 1982; Playgoing in Shakespeare's London, 1987, 3rd edition, 2004; Studying Shakespeare, 1988; Rebuilding Shakespeare's Globe, 1989; The Shakespearian Playing Companies, 1996; The Shakespeare Company 1594-1642, 2004. Editor: Plays of Shakespeare and Beaumont and Fletcher. Contributions to: Scholarly journals and periodicals. Memberships: International Shakespeare Association; Association of Commonwealth Literature and Language Studies; Society for Theatre Research; Malone Society. Address: c/o Department of English, University of Reading, PO Box 218, Reading, Berkshire RG6 2AA, England.

**GURSES Metin,** b. 2 April 1945, Turkey. Professor of Mathematics. m. Unsal, 1 son, 1 daughter. Education: BS, 1969, MS, 1971, PhD, 1975, Associate Professor, 1981, Physics Department, Middle East Technical University; Professor, Physics Department, Cukurova University, 1988. Appointments: Teaching Assistant, 1969-72, Instructor, 1972-76, Assistant Professor, 1976-81, Associate Professor, 1981-82, Physics Department, Middle East Technical University; Visiting Researcher, Physics Department, Yale University, 1973-75; Visiting Research Fellow, Physics Department, Princeton University, 1979; Visiting Research Fellow, Max-Planck Institute for Astrophysics, Garching, 1979-81; Visiting Scientist, Institute for Theoretical Physics, Koln University, 1987; Senior Research Scientist, Department of Mathematics, TUBITAK Basic Research Institute, 1982-88; Professor, Physics Department, Cukurova University, 1988-91; Professor, Department of Mathematics, Bilkent University, 1991-. Publications: Over 65 papers in refereed international journals. Honours: Fellow, Alexander von Humboldt, 1979-81, 1987; Sedat Simavi Science Prize, 1986; Science and Technical Research Council of Turkey Young Scientist Award, 1984. Memberships: Turkish Physical Society; International Society of General Relativity and Gravitation; Turkish Mathematical Society; Turkish Mechanics Society; American Mathematical Society; American Physical Society; Turkish Academy of Sciences; Abdus Salam Institute of Theoretical Physics. Address: Bilkent University, Matematik Bolumu, 06533 Bilkent, Ankara, Turkey.

**GUSEV Vladimir Aleksandrovitch,** b. 25 April 1945, Kalinin, Russia. Art Administrator. m. Tokareva Marina Evgenievna, 2 daughters. Education: I Repin Leningrad Academy of Painting, Sculpture and Architecture. Appointments: Scholarly Secretary, Leningrad Branch of the Union of Painters, 1974-78; Scientific Researcher, Head of Department, Deputy Director, 1978-88, Director, 1988-, State Russian Museum; Head of Reconstruction of Michailovsky Palace and Marble Palace, St Petersburg; Member, Presidential Committee for State Awards in the field of literature and art; Corresponding Member, Russian Academy of Arts. Publications: Over 60 articles in Russian,

English, German, French, Italian and Spanish. Honours: Medal for Valorous Work, 1971; Honourable Worker of Arts of the Russian Federation, 1996; Active Member, Russian Academy of Arts, 2001; State Award, Russian Federation for Literature and Arts, 2003; Medal in Memory of the 300th Anniversary of St Petersburg, 2003. Memberships: Chairman, Scientific Council, State Russian Museum; Scientific Council, Hermitage; Board of international charitable foundation for St Petersburg Revival; Russian Branch, UNESCO Committee for Culture; St Petersburg Branch, Union of Painters; Board of the Union of Art and Museum Workers, St Petersburg; Board of the Russian Committee, International Museum Council (ICOM); Committee for the State Awards for Literature and Arts, Russian Federation President's Administration. Address: The 34 Suvorovsky prospect, app 35, 193015 St Petersburg, Russia. E-mail: info@rusmuseum.ru Website: www.rusmuseum.ru

**GUSEV Vladimir Georgiyevich,** b. 20 April 1939, Novosibirsk, Russia. Physicist. m. Nikulina N G, 1 daughter. Education: Tomsk State University, 1963. Appointment: Vice-Professor, Tomsk State University. Publications include: Articles in journals: Optics and Spectroscopy, 1989-94; Optics of Atmosphere and Ocean, 1990-93, 1995-97, 1999, 2001-2003; Soviet Journal of Optical Technology, 1990, 1992-93, 1995, 1997-2001; Many articles to other professional journals. Memberships: New York Academy of Sciences. Address: Tomsk State University, Lenina 36, 634050 Tomsk, Russia.

**GUTERSON David,** b. 4 May 1956, Seattle, Washington, USA. Writer. m. Robin Ann Radwick, 1979, 3 sons, 1 daughter. Education: BA, 1978, MA, 1982, University of Washington. Appointment: High School Teacher of English, Bainbridge Island, Washington, 1984-94. Publications: The Country Ahead of Us, The Country Behind, 1989; Family Matters: Why Home Schooling Makes Sense, 1992; Snow Falling on Cedars, 1994; East of the Mountains, 1999. Honour: PEN/Faulkner Award for Fiction, 1995; Barnes and Noble Discovery Award, 1995; Pacific NW Booksellers Award, 1995. Address: c/o Georges Borchardt Inc, 136 East 57th Street, New York, NY 10022, USA.

**GUTHEINZ Joseph Richard,** b. 13 August 1955, Camp Lejune, North Carolina, USA. College Instructor; Author; Attorney. m. Lori Ann Bentley, 6 sons. Education: BA, MA, California State University, Sacramento, California; MS, University of Southern California; JD South Texas College of Law; Teaching Credentials in: Aeronautics, Sociology, Criminal Justice, Military Science, Political Science, Business and Industrial Management, Public Administration, California State. Appointments: Senior Special Agent, National Aeronautics and Space Administration, NASA; Special Agent, US Department of Transportation OIG and the Federal Aviation Administration; Member of Faculty, University of Phoenix and Alvin Community College; Former Member of Faculty, Central Texas College; National Association of Certified Fraud Examiners; Attorney at Law; Retired. Publications: Is it legal to privately own space shuttle tiles?; The Moon Rock Con; Building 265; Cover-up in Space; White Fog, Dark Secrets; Marketing an Asteroid Threat; In Search of the Goodwill Moon Rocks; NASA investigation reports on: Russian Mir Space Station fire and crash; Civilian Astronaut Corps; Honduras Moon Rock. Honours: NASA Exceptional Service Medal; Presidents Council on Integrity and Efficiency Career Achievement Award; Honorary Lieutenant, Governor of Oklahoma. Memberships: Republican National Lawyers Association; Texas Criminal Defense Lawyers Association; National Certified Fraud Examiners Association; Member of the Bar of US Supreme Court. Address: Law Office of Joseph R Gutheinz Jr, 205 Woodcombe, Houston, Texas 77062, USA. E-mail: jgutheinz@sbcglobal.net

**GUTHRIE Robin (Robert Isles Loftus),** b. 27 June 1937, Retired Public Servant. m. Sarah Julia, 2 sons, 1 daughter. Education: MA, Classics, Trinity College, Cambridge, 1958-61; Certificate of Education, Liverpool University, 1961-62; MSc , Economics, London School of Economics, 1966-68. Appointments: Head, Cambridge House, Founder Cambridge House, Literacy Scheme, Teacher at a Brixton Comprehensive School, 1963-69; Social Development Officer, Peterborough Development Corporation, 1969-75; Assistant Director, Social Work Service, DHSS, 1975-79; Director, Joseph Rowntree Memorial Trust (now the Joseph Rowntree Foundation), 1979-88; Chief Charity Commissioner for England and Wales, 1988-92; Director of Economic and Social Affairs, Council of Europe, 1992-98. Publications: Numerous articles and papers in journals including: New Society, The Good European's Dilemma, 2000; New Europe, a graceless trudge – analysis of EU Enlargement; Lectures: First Geraldine Aves Memorial Lecture; First Wynford Vaughan Thomas Memorial Lecture; Fourth Arnold Goodman Charity Lecture; Henri de Koster Memorial Lecture, Strasbourg, 1994. Honour: Honorary DLitt, Bradford University, 1991. Memberships include currently: Chair and Founder, York Museums and Gallery Trust; Chair of Governors, College of York St John; Chair, Jessie's Fund; Chair, Rodolphus Choir; Chair, Holgate and Westfield Branch Labour Party; Trustee, The Thalidomide Trust UK; Governor, Poppleton Road Junior School, York; Governor, Clifton College, Bristol; Member, Parochial Church Council, St Luke's, Clifford; Member of Court, University of York; Member of Council, University of Leeds; Vice-President, Cambridge House. Address: Braeside House, Acomb Road, York, YO24 4EZ, England. E-mail: robin@theguthries.co.uk

**GUTHRIE OF CRAIGIEBANK, Gen. Charles Ronald Llewelyn Guthrie,** b. 17 November 1938, London, England. Company Director. m. Catherine Worrall, 2 sons. Education: Royal Military Academy, Sandhurst. Appointments: Command, Welsh Guards, 1979; Served BAOR and Aden 22 SAS Regiment, 1965-69; Staff College Graduate, 1972; Military Assistant to Chief of General Staff, Ministry of Defence, 1973-74; Brigade Major, Household Division, 1976-77; Commanding Officer, 1 Battalion Welsh Guards, served Berlin and Northern Ireland, 1977-80; Colonel General Staff Military Operations, Ministry of Defence, 1980-82; Command British Forces New Hebrides, 1980, 4 Armed Brigade, 1982-84; Chief of Staff, 1 (British) Corps, 1984-86; General Officer Commanding, North East District Command 2 Infantry Division, 1986-87; Assistant Chief to the General Staff, Ministry of Defence, 1987-89; Command 1 British Corps, 1990-91; Commander in Chief, BAOR, 1992-94; Command, Northern Army Group, 1992-93 (now disbanded); Chief of the General Staff, 1994-97; Chief of the Defence Staff, 1997-2001; Colonel Commandant, Intelligence Corps, 1986-95; Colonel Life Guards (Gold Stick; ADC General to HM The Queen, 1993-2001; Colonel Commandant, SAS Regiment, 2000-; Non-Executive Director: N M Rothschild & Sons; Advanced Interactive Systems Inc; Ashley Gardens Block 2 Limited; BICE Chileconsult; Colt Defence LLC; N M Rothschild & Sons (Brazil) Limitada; N M Rothschild & Sons (Mexico) SA de CV; Rothschilds Continuation Holding AG; Member of Council, Institute of International Strategic Studies. Honours: LVO, 1977, OBE, 1980; KCB, 1990;GCB, 1994; Kt SMO Malta, 1999; Commander, Legion of Merit, USA, 2001; Life Peer, 2001; Freeman City of London, 1988; Liveryman, Painter Stainers Co, 1989. Memberships include: President: Federation of London Youth Clubs, Action Research, Army Benevolent Fund; Chairman of the Advisory Board, King's Centre for Military Health Research; Patron: Canning House Library Appeal, Cardinal Hume Centre, Household Cavalry Museum Appeal, Order of Malta's Care Trust, Second World

War Experience Centre, UK Defence Forum. Address: New Court, St Swithin's Lane, London EC4P 4DU, England. E-mail: lordguthrie@rothschild.co.uk

**GUTIERREZ Julio Roberto,** b. 10 January 1953, Santiago, Chile. Ecologist. m. Angela, 2 sons. Education: Licenciado en Ciencias, Mencion Biologia, Universidad de Chile, Chile, 1977; PhD, Biology, New Mexico State University, USA, 1984. Appointments: Assistant Professor, 1984-85, Associate Professor, 1985-90, Professor, 1990-, Universidad de la Serena, Chile. Publications: 85 publications. Honours: Listed in Who's Who publications and biographical dictionaries. Memberships: Ecological Society of America; Sociedad de Ecologia de Chile. Address: Departamento de Biologia, Universidad de la Serena, La Serena, Casilla 599, Chile. E-mail: jgutierr@userena.cl

**GUTIN Gregory,** b. 17 January 1957, Novozibkov, Russia. University Professor. m. Irina Gutin, 2 sons. Education: MSc, Mathematics, Gomel University, Belarussia, 1979; PhD, Mathematics, Tel Aviv University, Israel, 1993. Appointments: Research Assistant, Lecturer, Odense University, Denmark, 1993-96; Lecturer, Brunel University, UK, 1996-2000; Professor of Computer Science, Royal Holloway, University of London, 2000-. Publications: Digraphs (monograph with J Bang-Jenson), 2000; Traveling Salesman Problem (editor with A Punnen), 2002; More than 80 research papers. Honour: Kirkman Medal, Institute of Combinatorics and Its Applications, 1996. Address: Department of Computer Science, Royal Holloway, University of London. E-mail: gutin@cs.rhul.ac.uk

**GYENGE Csaba,** b. 22 January 1940, Razboieni, Romania. Professor. m. Éva Gyenge, 3 sons. Education: Diploma of Mechanical Engineer, 1961, PhD, 1979, Technical University of Cluj-Napoca, Romania. Appointments: In industry: Manufacturing Engineer, Head of Research Department, Mechanical Enterprise Cugir, Romania, 1961-70; Assistant, Lecturer, Docent, Professor, Head of Department, Department of Manufacturing Engineering, Technical University of Cluj-Napoca, Romania, 1970-2005. Publications: 8 technical and scientific books; 6 university courses; 36 articles in international scientific journals; 18 articles in Romanian scientific journals; 108 papers in proceedings of international scientific conferences; 36 papers in Romanian scientific conferences; 5 patents. Honours: Honorary Professor: University of Transylvania Brasov, Romania, Technical University of Kosice, Slovakia; Signum Aureum of the University of Miskolc, Hungary; Medal, Pro Universitate et Scientia Award, Hungarian Academy. Memberships: Hungarian Academy of Science; Member of International Scientific Committee, Donau Adria Association for Automation and Manufacturing; International Association of Mechanical Transmission Engineers. Nr 18 Str N Cristea, 400184 Cluj-Napoca, Romania. E-mail: gyenge_cs@yahoo.com

# H

**HA Dae Yong,** b. 9 August 1953, Seoul, Korea. University Professor. m. Hyun Sook Kim, 1 son, 1 daughter. Education: BA, Business Administration, Cheongju University, Korea, 1976; MA, Marketing, Yonsei University, Korea, 1980; PhD, Marketing, Hanyang University, Korea, 1986. Appointments: Professor of Marketing, 1983-, Dean of College of Economics and Business Administration, 2000-2001, Dean of Planning and Co-ordination Affairs, 2002-2003, Cheongju University, Korea; Vice-President, Korean Association of Small Business Studies, 2003-; Director, Korean Marketing Association, 2004-. Publications: Contemporary Marketing, 1998; Promotional Strategy, 2001; Marketing, 2004; A Study on the Behavior and the Satisfaction with the User's Motivation for Mobile Internet, 2004; 40 articles. Honours: President's Award, Korean Society of Consumer Studies, 1998; Listed in Who's Who in the World. Memberships: Director, Korean Marketing Association; Director, Korean Marketing Science Association. Address: Division of Business Administration, Cheongju University, 36 Naedock-dong, Cheongju-shi, Korea. E-mail: hdyid@cju.ac.kr

**HABERMAN Mandy Nicola,** b. 19 October 1954, United Kingdom. Inventor; Entrepreneur. m Steven Haberman, 1 son, 2 daughters. Education: BA (Hons), Graphic Design, St Martin's School of Art, London, 1976. Career: Freelance design contract, ILEA adult literacy project, 1976-78; Career change to become inventor and entrepreneur, invented Haberman Feeder, 1982, Founder and Manager, Haberman Feeders Ltd (to establish product in hospitals and mail order), 1984; Invented the Anywayup Cup, 1990, Founder, The Haberman Company, 1995; Principal, Haberman Associates, 1998-; Director, CafeBabe Ltd, 2003-; Founded independent on-line forum: www.makesparksfly.com to promote awareness and debate in intellectual property rights issues, 2002; Member: Intellectual Property Strategic IT Committee, Patent Office, 2001, Chartered Institute of Patents Agents Disciplinary Board, 2001-, Intellectual Property Advisory Committee, 2002-, Advisory Council for Eurpean Commission's Information Society Technologies Programme, 2002, Simfonec Advisory Committee, CASS Business School, 2003; Editorial Board of Patent World, Informa Law; Speaker on innovation, design and intellectual property rights at numerous national and international events. Honours: Anywayup® Cup is a Millennium Product, 2000; 3M Award for Innovation, 2000, Nokia Award for Consumer Product Design, 2000, Design in Business Association; Female Inventor of the Year, 2000; Gold Medal, Geneva Salon des Inventions, 2000; Horners Award for Innovation, British Plastics Federation, 2002; Tommy Award (St Thomas' Hospital) for Most Parent Friendly Innovative Product, 2000 and 2001; Honorary Doctorate in Design and Honorary Fellow, University of Bournemouth, 2002; Special recognition Award, Global Woman Inventors and Innovators Network, 2003; Special Achievement Award, IOD Suffolk, 2003; Recognised as "Pioneer to the Life of the Nation" by HM Queen Elizabeth, 2003; Finalist in Veuve Clicquot Business Woman of the Year Award, 2004. Memberships: Fellow, Royal Society of Arts; Ideas 21. Address: 44 Watford Road, Radlett, Hertfordshire WD7 8LR, England. E-mail: mandy.haberman@virgin.net Website: www.mandyhaberman.com

**HABGOOD Anthony John,** b. 8 November 1946, Woodbastwick, England. Company Director. m. Nancy Atkinson, 2 sons, 1 daughter. Education: BA, Economics, Gonville and Caius College, Cambridge University, 1968; MS, Industrial Administration, Carnegie-Mellon University, Pittsburgh, USA, 1970; MA, Economics, Gonville and Caius College, 1972. Appointments: Director, 1976-86, Member, Management Committee, 1979, Member, Executive Committee, 1981, Boston Consulting Group Inc; Director, 1986-91, Chief Executive Officer, 1991, Tootal Group plc; Non-Executive Director, Geest plc, 1988-93; Chief Executive, 1991-96, Chairman, 1996-, BUNZL plc; Non-Executive Director, Powergen plc, 1993-2001; Non-Executive Director, SVG Capital plc, 1995-; Non-Executive Director, National Westminster Bank plc, 1998-2001; Non-Executive Director, Marks and Spencer plc, 2004-. Address: 110 Park Street, London W1K 6NX, England.

**HABGOOD John Stapylton, Baron of Habgood Calverton,** b. 23 June 1927. Retired Archbishop of York; Author. m. Rosalie Mary Ann Boston, 7 June 1961, 2 sons, 2 daughters. Education: BA, 1948, MA, 1951, PhD, 1952, King's College, Cambridge; Cuddesdon College, Oxford. Appointments: Demonstrator in Pharmacology, Cambridge, 1950-53; Fellow, King's College, Cambridge, 1952-55; Curate, St Mary Abbots, Kensington, 1954-56; Vice Principal, Westcott House, Cambridge, 1956-62; Rector, St John's Church, Jedburgh, 1962-67; Principal, Queen's College, Birmingham, 1967-73; Bishop of Durham, 1973-83; Archbishop of York, 1983-95; Pro Chancellor, University of York, 1985-90; Hulsean Preacher, University of Cambridge, 1987-88; Bampton Lecturer, University of Oxford, 1999; Gifford Lecturer, University of Aberdeen, 2000. Publications: Religion and Science, 1964; A Working Faith: Essays and Addresses on Science, Medicine and Ethics, 1980; Church and Nation in a Secular Age, 1983; Confessions of a Conservative Liberal, 1988; Making Sense, 1993; Faith and Uncertainty, 1997; Being a Person: Where Faith and Science Meet, 1998; Varieties of Unbelief, 2000; The Concept of Nature, 2002. Contributions: Theology and the Sciences, Interdisciplinary Science Reviews, 2000. Honours: Honorary DD, Universities of Durham, 1975, Cambridge, 1984, Aberdeen, 1988, Huron, 1990, Hull, 1991, Oxford, 1996, Manchester, 1996; Honorary DU, York, 1996; Privy Counsellor, 1983; Honorary Fellow, King's College, Cambridge, 1986; Life Peer, 1995. Address: 18 The Mount, Malton, North Yorkshire YO17 7ND, England.

**HACKMAN Gene,** b. 30 January 1930, San Bernardino, California, USA. Actor. m. Fay Maltese 1956, divorced 1985, 1 son, 2 daughters. Education: Studied Acting, Pasadena Playhouse. Appointments: Films including: Lilith, 1964; Hawaii, 1966; Banning, 1967; Lucky Lady, 1975; Night Moves, 1976; Domino Principle, 1977; Superman, 1978; Superman II, 1980; Bat 21, 1987; The Package, 1989; The Von Metz Incident, 1989; Loose Connections, 1989; Full Moon in Blue Water, 1989; Postcards From the Edge, 1989; Cass Action, 1989; Loose Canons, 1990; Narrow Margin, 1990; Necessary Roughness, 1991; The William Munny Killings, 1991; The Unforgiven, 1992; The Firm, 1992; Geronimo, 1994; Wyatt Earp, 1994; Crimson Tide, 1995; The Quick and the Dead, 1995; Get Shorty, 1996; Birds of a Feather, 1996; Extreme Measures, 1996; The Chamber, 1996; Absolute Power, 1996; Twilight, 1998; Enemy of the State, 1998; Under Suspicion, 2000; Heist, 2001; The Royal Tenenbaums, 2001; Numerous TV appearances and stage plays. Publication: Co-author, Wake of the Perdido Star, 2000. Honours: Academy Award, Best Actor; New York Film Critics Award; Golden Globe Award; British Academy Awards; Cannes Film Festival Award; National Review Board Award; Berlin Film Award; Golden Globe for Best Actor in a Musical or Comedy, 2001. Address: c/o Barry Haldeman, 1900 Avenue of the Stars, 2000 Los Angeles, CA 90067, USA.

**HACKNEY Roderick Peter,** b. 3 March 1942, Liverpool, England. Architect. m. Tina, 1 son. Education: John Brights Grammar School; Manchester University. Appointments:

Architectural Practice, 1971-. Publications: The Good, The Bad & The Ugly, 1990. Honours: Prix International d'Architecture, Belgium, 1979; Civic Trust Award, UK, 1980; Gold Medal, Young Architects, Sofia Biennale, Bulgaria, 1983; Award for Good Design, Department of Environment, UK, 1975, 1980; Robert Mathew Prize, International Union of Architects. Memberships: President, International Union of Architects; President, Royal Institute of British Architects; President, Snowdonia National Park Society; Fellow, American Institute of Architects; Fellow, Indian Institute of Architects; Fellow, Royal Architectural Institute of Canada; Fellow, Federation de Colegios de Arquitectos de la Republica Mexicana, Mexico; Fellow, United Architects of the Philippines; Honorary Member, Consejo Superior de Los Colegios de Arquitectos de Espana, Spain. Address: Rod Hackney & Associates Ltd, St Peters House, Windmill Street, Macclesfield, Cheshire SK11 7HS, England. E-mail: rod@stpeter.demon.co.uk

**HADDAD Ghassan,** b. 1926, Lattaqia, Syria. Educationist; Academic. Education, Bachelor, Master, Military Sciences, Military Academy, Damascus, Syria; PhD, Economic Sciences, DSc, International Economic Sciences, University of Humboldt-Berlin, Germany. Appointments: Several important military positions before reaching the rank of Staff Major General, Syria, 1963; Planning Minister, Syria, 1963-66; Researcher then Visiting Professor, Germany, 1866-75; Economic Advisor and Chief of Experts, Ministry of Planning, Baghdad, Iraq, 1975-85; Professor of Postgraduate Studies in Economic Science, Baghdad University, 1975-85; Professor of Postgraduate Studies in Economic Science, Al Mustansyriah, Iraq, 1985-2002; Professor of Postgraduate Studies in Economic Science in several universities in Jordan, 2002-2003; Visiting Professor of Postgraduate Studies in Economic Science, Paris, France, 2003-. Publications: Books of researches in Arabic, French and German. Honours: Many distinguished medals and honours include: Syrian Medal of Merit (Excellent Degree); Syrian Medal of Fidelity; Certificate of Honour, Iraqi Union of Writers; Listed in Who's Who publications and biographical dictionaries. Memberships: Union of Arab Writers; Union of Arab Historians; Union of Arab Economists; Editorial committees of several academic periodicals. Address: 7 Allée du Bosquet, 92310 Sèvres, France. E-mail: ghassanmrhaddad@yahoo.com

**HADFIELD Andrew David,** b. 25 April 1962, Kendal, Cumbria, England. Professor of English. m. Alison Sarah Yarnold, 1 son, 2 daughters. Education: BA, 1st Class Honours, University of Leeds, England, 1984; DPhil, University of Ulster, Northern Ireland, 1988. Appointments: British Academy Postdoctoral Fellow, University of Leeds, 1989-92; Lecturer in English, 1992-96, Senior Lecturer in English, 1996-98, Professor of English, 1998-2003, University of Wales, Aberystwyth; Visiting Professor in English, Columbia University, New York, USA, 2002-2003; Professor of English, University of Sussex, England, 2003-. Publications: Literature, Politics and National Identity, 1994; Spenser's Irish Experience, 1997; Literature Travel and Colonial Writing, 1998; The English Renaissance, 2000; Shakespeare, Spenser and the Matter of Britain, 2003; Shakespeare and Renaissance Politics, 2003; Shakespeare and Republicanism, 2005. Honours: Fellow of the English Association; Leverhulme Major Award, 2001-2004; Chatterton Lecture at the British Academy, 2003. Memberships: English Association; Spenser Society of America. Address: Department of English, University of Sussex, Falmer, Brighton BN1 9QN, England.

**HADID Zaha.** Architect. Education: Diploma Prize, Architectural Association, 1977. Appointments: Partner, Office for Metropolitan Architecture; Teacher, later led own studio,

Architectural Association, -1987; Kenzo Tange Chair, Graduate School of Design, Harvard University, 1987-; Sullivan Chair, University of Illinois, School of Architecture, Chicago; Guest professorships: Hamburg, Ohio and New York; Professor, University of Applied Arts, Vienna, Austria; Eero Saarinen Visiting Professor of Architectural Design (spring semester), Yale University, USA, 2004. Publications: Numerous winning designs in research-based competitions around the world; Work widely published in periodicals and monographs; Paintings and drawings in national and international exhibitions; Work appears in permanent collections of various institutions. Honours include: Tyrolean Architecture Award, Bergisel Ski Jump, Innsbruck, 2002; Commander of the British Empire, 2002; Mies van der Rohe Award, Car Park and Terminus Hoenheim North, Strasbourg, 2003; Blueprint Award, Architect of the Year, 2004; WIRED Rave Award, Rosenthal Centre for Contemporary Art, Cincinnati, 2004; Laureate of the Pritzker Architecture Prize, 2004. Memberships: Honorary Member, American Academy of Arts and Letters; Fellow, American Institute of Architecture; Commander of the British Empire, 2002. Address: Zaha Hadid Architects, Studio 9, 10 Bowling Green Lane, London EC1R 0BQ, England. E-mail: press@zaha-hadid.com Website: www.zaha-hadid.com

**HAEBERLE Rosamond Pauline,** b. 23 October 1914, Clearwater, Kansas, USA. Retired Teacher. Education: Bachelor of Science, Music Education, Kansas State College, 1936; Master of Music, Northwestern University, Evanston Illinois, 1948; Post Graduate Year, Wayne State University, Detroit, Michigan; Professional Registered Parliamentarian. Appointments: Teacher, Plevna, Kansas, 1 year; Esbon, Kansas, 4 years; Frankfurt, Kansas, 2 years, Garden City, Kansas, 1 year; 3 years Music Supervisor, Waterford Township Schools, Waterford, Michigan; 33 years (32 years music and 1 year High School English), Pontiac, Michigan. Honours: Teacher's Day Award, Michigan State Fair; Distinguished Service Award, Michigan Retired School Personnel; Award of Honor and Recognition and Citation, Michigan Federation of Music Clubs; Woman of Achievement and Woman of the Year Award, Pontiac Business and Professional Women; Excellence in Community Service; Daughter of the American Revolution; Listed in 5 Who's Who publications. Memberships: Pontiac Tuesday Musicale; Michigan Federation of Music; Business and Professional Women; American Association of University Women; Daughters of American Revolution; Oakland County Pioneer and Historical Society, Town Hall; Detroit College Women, Junior Pontiac Women, Pontiac Retired School Personnel, Past State President, Michigan Federation of Music Clubs. Address: 125 Post Oak, Wichita, KS 67206, USA.

**HAGA Tatsuya,** b 14 February 1941, Tokyo, Japan. Scientist. m. Kazuko Tsutsumi. Education: Bachelor Degree, Faculty of Science, Tokyo University, 1963; PhD, Department of Biochemistry, Graduate School of Science, Tokyo University, 1970. Appointments: Instructor, Tokyo University, 1969-74; Associate Professor, Hamamatsu University School of Medicine, 1974-88; Professor, Tokyo University, 1988-2001; Director and Professor Gakushuin University, Institute for Biomolecular Science, 2001-. Publications: Solubilization, purification and molecular characterization of receptors: Principles and strategy (Chapter in Receptor Biochemistry, 1990); G Protein-coupled receptors (editor). 1999. Membership: International Society of Neurochemistry. Address: Institute for Biomolecular Science, Gakushuin University, 1-5-1 Mejiro, Toshima-ku, Tokyo 1718588, Japan. E-mail: tatsuya.haga@gakushuin.ac.jp

**HAGANS James A,** b. 9 November 1922, Cincinnati, Ohio, USA. Physician Scientist. Education: AB, Magna cum laude,

Marietta College, 1944; MD, University of Cincinnati College of Medicine, 1946; PhD, University of Oklahoma Graduate School, 1960. Appointments: Professor of Medicine, 1962; Manager, Medical Biostatistics, The Upjohn Company and Merck, Sharpe and Dohme, 1963-72; Chief, VA Co-operative Studies Program, 1972-85. Publications: 22 scientific articles. Honours: Phi Beta Kappa, 1943; Alpha Omega Alpha, 1946; Upjohn Prize, 1969; VA Distinguished Career Award, 1985. Memberships: AMA; ACP Fellow, Biometrics Society; American Society of Clinical Pharmacology and Experimental Therapeutics. Address: 9201 W Broward Blvd, Apt c-115, Ft Lauderdale, FL 33324, USA.

**HAGER Hermann Amadeus,** b. 1 February 1955, Vienna, Austria. Artist; Painter. Education: Bachelor of Medicine, University of Norway, 1980; Doctor of Psychology and Philosophy, University of Italy, 1990. Career: Painter; Musician; Composer; Journalist; Educator; Consultant; Soul-Doctor; Reformer of Psycho-Methods; Inventor of the "Cromo-School" to help people suffering from Crom-anomalies; Advocates the company of cats as a therapy for people suffering from mental illness (and the purring of cats helps also against hypertension, the purring is the fact which enables cats to help patients); Created the painting style "Colourmetry"; Created the music composition style "musimetry"; Created the architectural style "Archimetry" Currently working on the design of his T-Shirt Collection. Publications: Books: How to Communicate Successfully with Austrians; 100 Logical Puzzles; Geometric Colouring Book; 100 Mathematical Puzzles; Train Your Brain; Introduction to Musimetry; Many articles in different magazines. Honours: Numerous honours and awards include: Nominated for man of the Year 2004, American Biographical Institute; Listed in Who's Who publications and biographical dictionaries. Memberships: American Association for the Advancement of Science; New York Academy of Sciences. Address: Piaristengasse 5-7, 1080 Vienna, Austria.

**HAGGER Nicholas Osborne,** b. 22 May 1939, London, England. British Poet; Verse Dramatist; Short Story Writer; Lecturer; Author; Man of Letters; Philosopher; Cultural Historian. m. (1) Caroline Virginia Mary Nixon, 16 September 1961, 1 daughter, (2) Madeline Ann Johnson, 22 February 1974, 2 sons. Education: MA English Literature, Worcester College, Oxford, 1958-61. Appointments: Lecturer in English, University of Baghdad, 1961-62; Professor of English Literature, Tokyo University of Education and Keio University, Tokyo, 1963-67; Tokyo University, 1964-65; Lecturer in English, University of Libya, Tripoli, 1968-70; Freelance Features for Times, 1970-72. Publications: The Fire and the Stones: A Grand Unified Theory of World History and Religion, 1991; Selected Poems: A Metaphysical's Way of Fire, 1991; The Universe and the Light: A New View of the Universe and Reality, 1993; A White Radiance: The Collected Poems 1958-93, 1994; A Mystic Way: A Spiritual Autobiography, 1994; Awakening to the Light: Diaries, Vol 1, 1958-67, 1994; A Spade Fresh with Mud: Collected Stories, Vol 1, 1995; The Warlords: From D-Day to Berlin, A Verse Drama, 1995; A Smell of Leaves and Summer: Collected Stories, Vol 2, 1995; Overlord, The Triumph of Light 1944-1945: An Epic Poem, Books 1 & 2, 1995, Books 3-6, 1996, Books 7-9, 10-12, 1997; The One and the Many, 1999; Wheeling Bats and a Harvest Moon: Collected Stories, Vol 3, 1999; Prince Tudor, A Verse Drama, 1999; The Warm Glow of the Monastery Courtyard: Collected Stories, Vol 4, 1999; The Syndicate: The Story of the Coming World Government, 2004; The Secret History of the West: The Influence of Secret Organisations on Western History from the Renaissance to the 20th Century, 2005; Classical Odes: Poems on England, Europe and a Global Theme, and of Everyday Life in the One, 2005. Membership:

Society of Authors. E-mail: info @nicholashagger.co.uk Website: www.nicholashagger.co.uk

**HAGUE William Jefferson,** b. 26 March 1961, Rotherham, Yorkshire, England. Politician; Management Consultant. m. Ffion Jenkins, December 1997. Education: BA, Honours, Magdalen College, Oxford, England; MBA, Insead Business School, France, 1986. Appointments: Management Consultant, McKinsey & Co, 1983-88; Elected to Parliament, Richmond, Yorkshire, England, 1989; Parlimentary Private Secretary to Chancellor of Exchequer, 1990-93; Parliamentary Under-Secretary of State, Department Social Security, 1993-94; Ministry of State, Department of Social Security, 1994-95; Secretary of State for Wales, 1995-97; Leader, Conservative Party, 1997-2001; Chair, International Democratic Union, 1999-2001; Political Adviser, JCB PLC, 2001-; Non-Executive Director, AES Eng PLC, 2001-; Member, Political Council of Terra Firma Capital Partners, 2001-. Honour: Privy Councillor, 1995. Address: House of Commons, London SW1A 0AA, England.

**HAHN Frank Horace,** b. 26 April 1925, Berlin, Germany. Emeritus Professor of Economics. m. Dorothy Salter. Education: Bournemouth Grammar School; BSc (Econ), 1945, PhD, 1951, London School of Economics; MA, University of Cambridge, 1960. Appointments: Lecturer in Economics, University of Birmingham, 1948-58; Reader in Mathematical Economics, University of Birmingham, 1958-60; Fellow, Churchill College, Cambridge, 1960-; Lecturer in Economics, University of Cambridge, 1960-66; Professor of Economics, London School of Economics, 1967-72; Professor of Economics, 1972-92, Professor Emeritus, 1992-, University of Cambridge; Professor Ordinario, 1989-2000, Emeritus Professor, 2000-, University of Siena. Publications: 135 publications including books written and edited. Honours: D Soc Sci, Birmingham, 1981; Doctor Honoris Causa, Strasbourg, 1984; D Litt, East Anglia, 1984; DSc (Econ), London, 1985; Doctor of the University, York, 1991; Doctor of Letters, Leicester, 1993; Doctor of Philosophy, Athens, 1993; Docteur Honoris Causa de l'Universite Paris X, Nanterre, 1999. Memberships: Fellow, British Academy; Corresponding Fellow, American Academy of Arts and Sciences; Foreign Associate, US National Academy of Sciences; Honorary Member, American Economic Association; Honorary Fellow, London School of Economics; Member, Academia Europaea; Palacky Gold Medal, Czechoslovak Academy of Sciences; Honorary Member, Italian Association for the History of Political Economy; President, Econometric Society, 1968-69; President, Royal Economic Society, 1986-89; President, Section F, British Association for the Advancement of Science, 1990. Address: Churchill College, Cambridge, CB3 0DS, England.

**HAINES John Francis,** b. 30 November 1947, Chelmsford, Essex, England. Government Official; Poet. m. Margaret Rosemary Davies, 19 March 1977. Education: Padgate College of Education, 1966-69; ONC in Public Administration, Millbank College of Commerce, 1972. Appointments: General Assistant; Payments Assistant. Publications: Other Places, Other Times, 1981; Spacewain, 1989; After the Android Wars, 1992; Orders from the Bridge, 1996; Pennine Triangle (with Steve Sneyd & J C Hartley), 2002; A Case Without Gravity (translation), 2005. Contributions to: Dark Horizons; Fantasy Commentator; First Time; Folio; Idomo; Iota; Macabre; New Hope International; Not To Be Named; Overspace; Purple Patch; Sandor; The Scanner; Simply Thrilled Honey; Spokes; Star Line; Stride; Third Half; Yellow Dwarf; A Child's Garden of Olaf; A Northern Chorus; Ammonite; Boggers All; Eldritch Science; Foolscap; Heliocentric Net; Lines of Light; Ore; Pablo Lennis; Pleiade; Premonitions; Mentor; Rampant Guinea Pig; Zone;

Positively Poetry; What Poets Eat; Mexicon 6 - The Party; Terrible Work; Xenophilia; Literae; XUENSê; Dreaming Scryers True Deceivers. Memberships: Science Fiction Poetry Association; British Fantasy Society; The Eight Hand Gang, founder-member. Address: 5 Cross Farm, Station Road, Padgate, Warrington WA2 0QG, England.

**HAINS Gaétan Joseph Daniel Robert,** b. 9 May 1963, Montreal, Canada. Computer Scientist. Education: BSc, honours, Concordia University, 1985; MSc, 1987, DPhil, 1990, Oxford University. Appointments: Researcher, CRIM Montreal, 1989; Assistant Professor, Associate Professor, University of Montreal, 1989-95; Visiting Professor, ENS Lyon, 1994; Visiting Researcher, Fujitsu-ISIS, Japan, 1994-95; Professor, 1995-, Director, 2000-04, 1st Class Professor, 2004-, Laboratoire d'informatique fondamentale d'Orleans, University of Orleans and CNRS. Honours: Commonwealth Scholar, 1986-89; IISF Visiting Scholarship, Japan, 1992. Address: LIFO BP 6759 Batiment IIIA, rue Leonard de Vinci, 45067 Orleans Cedex 2, France. Website: http://hains.org

**HAKIMI Rainer A,** b. 12 March 1960, Stuttgart, Germany. Physician; Medical Consultant. m. Regina Hakimi, 1 son. Education: Medical Faculty, University of Tuebingen, Germany, 1981-87; Robert-Bosch Hospital, Stuttgart, Germany; MBA, 2004. Appointments: Heart Surgery, 1988-90, Internal Medicine, 1990-93, Robert-Bosch Hospital, Stuttgart; Medical Consultant, Hallesche Krankenversicherung, Stuttgart, 1993-; Specialisation: General Medicine, 1993, Naturopathy, 1994, Sports Medicine and Occupational Medicine, 1996, Medical Quality Management, 1998, Psychotherapy, 2000, Emergency Medicine, 2005. Publications: 25 publications in medical journals about insurance medicine and complementary medicine. E-mail: rainerhakimi@aol.com

**HAKKINEN Mika,** b. 28 September 1968, Helsinki, Finland. Racing Driver. m. Erja Honkanen. Appointments: Formerly, go-kart driver, Formula Ford 1600 driver, Finnish, Swedish and Nordic Champion, 1987; Formula 3 driver, British Champion with West Surrey racing, 1990; Formula 1 driver Lotus, 1991-93, McLaren, 1993-2001; Grand Prix wins: European, 1997, Australia, 1998, Brazil, 1998, 1999, Spain, 1998, 1999, 2000, Monaco, 1998, Austria, 1998, 2000, Germany, 1998, Luxembourg, 1998, Japan, 1998, 1999, Malaysia, 1999, Hungary, 1999, 2000, Belgium, 2000; Formula One Driver's Championship Winner, 1998, 1999; Sabbatical, 2001; Retirement from Formula One; FIA European Rally Championship, Finland, 2003. Publication: Mika Hakkinen: Doing What Comes Naturally.

**HALE Marguerite (Grete),** b. 10 May 1929, Ottawa, Ontario, Canada. Business Woman. m. Reginald Britten Hale. Education: Bachelor, Journalism, Carleton University, 1954; Honorary Doctorate, University of Ottawa, 1999. Appointments: President, 1978-89, Chairman, 1989-, Morrison Lamothe Inc. (Independent family controlled Canadian frozen food processor); Directorships and Advisory Board Appointments include: Prior, Military and Hospitaller Order, St Lazarus of Jerusalem; President, Beechwood Cemetery; Executive Committee Member, Director, University of Ottawa; Friends of the National Library of Canada; Salvation Army Advisory Board (Ottawa), Member; Hospice at May Court, Chair; Canhave Children's Centre, Director; Institute of Canadian Studies, Advisory Board; Chair, Leadership, Ottawa. Publication: The Happy Baker of Ottawa, 1990. Honours: Grand Cross, Military Hospitaller Order of St Lazarus of Jerusalem; Ottawa Carleton Philanthropy Award, Outstanding Volunteer of the Year, 1997; Ottawa-Carleton Business Woman of the Year, 1997; Canadian

Woman Entrepreneur of the Year Award, Lifetime Achievement Category, 1998; Ottawa Community Builder of the Year Award, 2001; Honorary Colonel, 78th Fraser Highlanders, Fort Glengarry Garrison. Memberships: Fellow, Royal Canadian Geographic Society; Fellow, Heraldry Society of Canada; Rideau Club of Ottawa; Governor, Royal Canadian Geographical Society; Chair, Community Foundation of Ottawa; Chair, Macdonald Cartier Library; Vice Sénéchale, La Chaine des Rotisseurs. Address: Bayne House, 40 Fuller Street, Ottawa, Ontario K1Y 3R8, Canada. E-mail: ghale@morrisonlamothe.com

**HALIM Youssef,** b. 27 January 1925, Cairo, Egypt. Professor Emeritus. m. Amal, 1 son, 1 daughter. Education: BSc, Zoology and Chemistry, 1948; Diploma, Higher Studies in Oceanography, 1950; Docteurs es Sciences, Paris, 1956. Appointments: Lecturer, 1958-64, Associate Professor, 1964-73, Professor, 1993-, Vice-Dean for Graduate Studies, 1976-82, Department of Oceanography, Faculty of Science, Alexandria, Egypt. Publications include: Human Impacts on Alexandria's Marine Environment; Occurrence and Succession of Potentially Harmful Phytoplankton, 2001; The Nile and the Suez Canal – Effects on Living Resources in Egyptian Waters; The Nile and the Levantine Sea, 2004. Honour: UNEP's Global 500, 1997. Memberships: The Oceanography Society; The Specialised National Councils, Cairo. Address: Department of Oceanography, Faculty of Science, Alexandria 21511, Egypt. E-mail: youssefhalim@hotmail.com

**HALL Christopher Sandford,** b. 9 March 1936, Tunbridge Wells, Kent, England. Solicitor. m. Susanna Bott, 3 sons. Education: MA, Trinity College, Cambridge. Appointments: National Service and Reserve TAVR, 5 Royal Inniskilling Dragoon Guards, 1954-56, 1956-70; Solicitor, 1963, Partner, Senior Partner, 1964-96, Cripps, Harries, Hall, Tunbridge Wells; Consultant, Knights Solicitors, 1999; Currently Director: A Burslem & Son Ltd, Stonemasons; Brighton Race Course Ltd; International League for the Protection of Horses; Racing Welfare. Honours: Territorial Decoration (TD), 1970; Deputy Lieutenant, East Sussex, 1986. Memberships: Tunbridge Wells and Tonbridge District Law Society, President, 1987-; Jockey Club, 1990-, Chairman Disciplinary Committee and Steward, 1996-2000; Member, Jockey Club Appeal Board; Chairman, Jockey Club Arab Horse Racing Committee; South of England Agricultural Society, Chairman, 1984-90; Worshipful Company of Broderers, Master, 1980; Member County Committee for Sussex, Country Landowners Association; Southdown and Eridge Hunt, Chairman, 1978-84; Olympia Show Jumping, Chairman, 2000. Address: Great Danegate, Eridge, Tunbridge Wells TN3 9HU, England. E-mail: cshall.danegate@virgin.net

**HALL Donald (Andrew Jr),** b. 20 September 1928, New Haven, Connecticut, USA. Poet; Writer; Professor of English, retired. m. (1) Kirby Thompson, 1952, divorced 1969, 1 son, 1 daughter, (2) Jane Kenyon, 1972, deceased 1995. Education: BA, Harvard University, 1951; BLitt, Oxford University, 1953; Stanford University, 1953-54. Appointments: Poetry Editor, Paris Review, 1953-62; Assistant Professor, 1957-61, Associate Professor, 1961-66, Professor of English, 1966-75, University of Michigan. Publications: Poetry: Poems, 1952; Exile, 1952; To the Loud Wind and Other Poems, 1955; Exiles and Marriages, 1955; The Dark Houses, 1958; A Roof of Tiger Lilies, 1964; The Alligator Bride: Poems New and Selected, 1969; The Yellow Room: Love Poems, 1971; A Blue Wing Tilts at the Edge of the Sea: Selected Poems 1964-1974, 1975; The Town of Hill, 1975; Kicking the Leaves, 1978; The Toy Bone, 1979; The Twelve Seasons, 1983; Brief Lives, 1983; Great Day at the Cows' House, 1984; The Happy Man, 1986; The One Day: A Poem in Three Parts, 1988; Old and New Poems, 1990; The One

Day and Poems (1947-1990), 1991; The Museum of Clear Ideas, 1993; The Old Life, 1996; Without, 1998. Short Stories: The Ideal Bakery, 1987. Other: Henry Moore: The Life and Work of a Great Sculptor, 1966; Marianne Moore: The Cage and the Animal, 1970; The Gentleman's Alphabet Book, 1972; Writing Well, 1973, 7th edition, revised, 1991; Remembering Poets: Reminiscences and Opinions-Dylan Thomas, Robert Frost, T S Eliot, Ezra Pound, 1978; Goatfoot Milktongue Twinbird: Interviews, Essays and Notes on Poetry 1970-76, 1978; To Read Literature: Fiction, Poetry, Drama, 1981, 3rd edition, revised, 1987; The Weather for Poetry: Essays, Reviews and Notes on Poetry 1977-81, 1982; Poetry and Ambition: Essays 1982-1988, 1988; Anecdotes of Modern Art (with Pat Corrigan Wykes), 1990; Here at Eagle Pond, 1990; Their Ancient Glittering Eyes, 1992; Life Work, 1993; Death to Death of Poetry, 1994; Principal Products of Portugal, 1995. Honours: Edna St Vincent Millay Memorial Prize, 1956; Longview Foundation Award, 1960; Guggenheim Fellowships, 1963, 1972; Sarah Josepha Hale Award, 1983; Poet Laureate of New Hampshire, 1984-89; Lenore Marshall Award, 1987; National Book Critics Circle Award, 1989; Los Angeles Times Book Award, 1989; Robert Frost Silver Medal, Poetry Society of America, 1991; Lifetime Achievement Award, New Hampshire Writers and Publishers Project, 1992; New England Book Award for Non-Fiction, 1993; Ruth Lilly Prize for Poetry, 1994; Honorary doctorates.

**HALL Jerry,** b. 2 July 1956, Texas, USA. Model; Actress. m. Mick Jagger, 1990, divorced 1999, 2 sons, 2 daughters. Education: Trained at the Actors Studio in New York and the National Theatre, London; 2 years Humanities, Open University. Career: Began modelling, Paris, 1970s; Numerous TV appearances including David Letterman Show, USA; Own TV series, Jerry Hall's Gurus, BBC, 2003; Contributing editor, Tatler, 1999-; Stage debut in William Inge's Bus Stop, Lyric Theatre, London, 1990; Films: Batman, Princess Caraboo, 1994; Diana and Me, 1996; RPM, 1996; Plays: The Graduate, Gielgud Theatre, London, 2000; Benchmark, New End Theatre, Hampstead; English tour with Picasso's Women (monologue). Publication: Tell Tales, 1985. Address: c/o Eclipse Management Production, 32 Tavistock Street, London, WC2E 7PB, England.

**HALL J(ohn) C(live),** b. 12 September 1920, London, England. Poet. Education: Oriel College, Oxford. Appointments: Staff, Encounter Magazine, 1955-91; Editor, Literary Executor of Keith Douglas. Publications: Poetry: Selected Poems, 1943; The Summer Dance and Other Poems, 1951; The Burning Hare, 1966; A House of Voices, 1973; Selected and New Poems 1939-84, 1985; Long Shadows: Poems 1938-2002, 2003. Other: Collected Poems of Edwin Muir, 1921-51 (editor), 1952; New Poems (co-editor), 1955; Edwin Muir, 1956. Address: 9 Warwick Road, Mount Sion, Tunbridge Wells, Kent TN1 1YL, England.

**HALL Nigel John,** b. 30 August 1943, Bristol, England. Sculptor. m. Manijeh Yadegar. Education: NDD, West of England College of Art; MA, Royal College of Art; Harkness Fellowship to USA, 1967-69. Career: Tutor, Royal College of Art, 1971-74; Principal Lecturer, Chelsea School of Art, 1974-81; Solo exhibitions include: Robert Elkon Gallery, New York, 1974, 1977, 1979, 1983; Annely Juda Fine Art, London, 1978, 1981, 1985, 1987, 1991, 1996, 2000, 2003; Annely Juda Fine Art, London, 2005; Galerie Maeght, Paris, 1981, 1983; Staatliche Kunsthalle, Baden-Baden, 1982; Nishimura Gallery, Tokyo, 1980, 1984, 1988; Garry Anderson Gallery, Sydney, 1987, 1990; Gallery Hans Mayer, Dusseldorf, 1989, 1999; Park Gallery Seoul, 1997, 2000; Galerie Scheffel, Bad Homburg, 2004; Kunsthalle, Mannheim, 2004; Group Exhibitions include: Documenta Kassel, 1977; Whitechapel Gallery, 1981; Tokyo

Metropolitan Museum, 1982; Le Havre Museum of Fine Art, 1988; MOMA, New York, 1993; Fogg Art Museum, Harvard University, 1994; Schloss Ambras, Innsbruck, 1998; British Council Touring Exhibition, Pakistan, South Africa, Zimbabwe, 1997-99; Bad Homburg, 2001, 2003; Work in public collections include: Tate Gallery; National Museum of Modern Art, Paris; National Gallery, Berlin; MOMA, New York; Australian National Gallery, Canberra; Art Institute of Chicago; Kunsthaus, Zurich; Tokyo Metropolitan Museum; Museum of Modern Art, Brussels; Louisiana Museum, Denmark; National Museum of Art, Osaka; Museum of Contemporary Art, Sydney; Dallas Museum of Fine Art; Tel Aviv Museum; Los Angeles County Museum; National Museum of Contemporary Art, Seoul; Commissions include: Australian National Gallery, Canberra, 1982; IBM London, 1983; Airbus Industries, Toulouse, 1984; Museum of Contemporary Art, Hiroshima, 1985; Olympic Park, Seoul, 1988; Clifford Chance, London, 1992; Glaxo Wellcome Research, Stevenage, 1994; NTT, Tokyo, 1996; Bank of America, London, 2003; Said Business School, University of Oxford, 2005. Honour: Elected, Royal Academy, 2003. Address: 11 Kensington Park Gardens, London, W11 3HD, England.

**HALL Peter (Geoffrey),** b. 19 March 1932, London, England. Professor of Planning; Writer. m. (1) Carla Maria Wartenberg, 1962, divorced 1966, (2) Magdalena Mróz, 1967. Education: MA, PhD, St Catharine's College, Cambridge. Appointments: Assistant Lecturer, 1957-60, Lecturer, 1960-66, Birkbeck College, University of London; Reader in Geography, London School of Economics and Political Science, 1966-68; Professor of Geography, 1968-89, Professor Emeritus, 1989-, University of Reading; Professor of City and Regional Planning, 1980-92, Professor Emeritus, 1992-, University of California at Berkeley; Professor of Planning, 1992-, Director, School of Public Policy, 1995-96, University College, London. Publications: The Industries of London, 1962; London 2000, 1963, revised edition, 1969; Labour's New Frontiers, 1964; Land Values (editor), 1965; The World Cities, 1966, 3rd edition, 1984; Von Thunen's Isolated State (editor), 1966; An Advanced Geography of North West Europe (co-author), 1967; Theory and Practice of Regional Planning, 1970; Containment of Urban England: Urban and Metropolitan Growth Processes or Megapolis Denied (co-author), 1973; Containment of Urban England: The Planning System: Objectives, Operations, Impacts (co-author), 1973; Planning and Urban Growth: An Anglo-American Comparison (with M Clawson), 1973; Urban and Regional Planning: An Introduction, 1974, 2nd edition, 1982; Europe 2000, 1977; Great Planning Disasters, 1980; Growth Centres in the European Urban System, 1980; Transport and Public Policy Planning (editor with D Banister), 1980; The Inner City in Context (editor), 1981; Silicon Landscapes (editor), 1985; Can Rail Save the City? (co-author), 1985; High-Tech America (co-author), 1986; Western Sunrise (co-author), 1987; The Carrier Wave (co-author), 1988; Cities of Tomorrow, 1988; London 2001, 1989; The Rise of the Gunbelt, 1991; Technoples of the World, 1994; Sociable Cities (co-author), 1998; Cities in Civilisation, 1998; Urban Future 21 (co-author), 2000; Working Capital, 2002. Honours: Honorary Fellow, St Catharine's College, Cambridge, 1988; British Academy, fellow, 1983; Member of the Academia Europea, 1989; Knight Bachelor, 1998; Prix Vautrin Lud, 2001; Gold Medal, Royal Town Planning Institute, 2003. Memberships: Fabian Society, chairman, 1971-72; Tawney Society, chairman, 1983-85. Literary Agent: Peters, Fraser, Dunlap. Address: c/o Bartlett School, University College, London, Wates House, 22 Gordon Street, London WC1H 0QB, England.

**HALL Sir Peter (Reginald Frederick),** b. 22 November 1930, Bury St Edmunds, Suffolk, England. Director and Producer for Stage, Film, Television, and Opera; Associate Professor

# DICTIONARY OF INTERNATIONAL BIOGRAPHY

of Drama. m. 1) Leslie Caron, 1956, divorced 1965, 1 son, 1 daughter, (2) Jacqueline Taylor, 1965, divorced 1981, 1 son, 1 daughter, (3) Maria Ewing, 1982, divorced 1990, 1 daughter, (4) Nicola Frei, 1990, 1 daughter. Education: BA, Honours, St Catharine's College, Cambridge. Appointments: Director, Arts Theatre, London, 1955-56, Royal Shakespeare Theatre, 1960, National Theatre, 1973-88; Founder-Director-Producer, International Playwright's Theatre, 1957, Peter Hall Co, 1988; Managing Director, Stratford-on-Avon and Aldwych Theatre, London, 1960-68; Associate Professor of Drama, Warwick University, 1966-; Co-Director, Royal Shakespeare Co, 1968-73; Artistic Director, Glyndebourne Festival, 1984-90; Artistic Director, Old Vic, 1997; Wortham Chair in Performing Arts, Houston University, Texas, 1999; Chancellor, Kingston University, 2000-; Theatre, opera and film productions. Publications: The Wars of the Roses, adaptation after Shakespeare (with John Barton), 1970; John Gabriel Borkman, by Ibsen (translator with Inga-Stina Ewbank), 1975; Peter Hall's Diaries: The Story of a Dramatic Battle (edited by John Goodwin), 1983; Animal Farm, adaptation after Orwell, 1986; The Wild Duck, by Ibsen (translator with Inga-Stina Ewbank), 1990; Making an Exhibition of Myself (autobiography), 1993; An Absolute Turkey, by Feydeau (translator with Nicola Frei), 1994; The Master Builder (with Inga-Stina Ewbank), 1995; Mind Millie For Me (new translation of Feydeau's Occupe-toi d'Amélie, with Nicola Frei), 1999; Cities in Civilization, 1999; The Necessary Theatre, 1999; Exposed by the Mask, 2000. Honours: Commander of the Order of the British Empire, 1963; Honorary Fellow, St Catharine's College, Cambridge, 1964; Chevalier de l'Ordre des Arts et Des Lettres, France, 1965; Tony Award, USA, 1966; Shakespeare Prize, University of Hamburg, 1967; Knighted, 1977; Standard Special Award, 1979; Special Award for Outstanding Achievement in Opera, 1981, and Awards for Best Director, 1981, 1987; Several honorary doctorates. Membership: Theatre Directors' Guild of Great Britain, founder-member, 1983-.

**HALL Roger David,** b. 5 March 1943, Salford, England. University Teacher. m. Joan, 1 son, 1 daughter. Education: Manchester Grammar School; Leeds University; MSc, UMIST; MSc, PhD, Salford University; MEd, Manchester University. Appointments: Management Trainee, Smith & Nephew, 1965-67; Lecturer, Stockport College, 1969-71; Managing Director, Stylo Plastics, 1971-90; Senior Lecturer, Stockport College, 1990-99; Principal Lecturer, Huddersfield University, 1999-. Publications: Many articles and conference papers. Honours: Justice of the Peace; BA (Hons), Leeds. Memberships: Chartered Manager; Fellow, Chartered Management Institute; Chartered Fellow, Chartered Institute of Personnel and Development; Fellow, Royal Society of Arts; Member: British Academy of Management; Association of MBAs; Standing Conference on University Teaching and Research in the Education of Adults; Higher Education Academy. Address: 123 Hill Lane, Manchester, M9 6PW, England. E-mail: rogerdhall@aol.com

**HALLETT Christine Margaret,** b. 4 May 1949, Barnet, Hertfordshire, England. Vice-Chancellor. MA, University of Cambridge; PhD, Loughborough University. Appointments: Civil Servant, 1970-74; Teaching and research posts in Social Policy, Universities of Oxford, Leicester, Western Australia, Keele and Stirling; Principal and Vice-Chancellor, University of Stirling, 2004-. Publications include: Interagency Co-operation in Child Protection, 1995; Women and Social Policy: An Introduction (editor), 1996; Hearing the Voices of Children: Social Policy for a New Century (co-author), 2003. Honour: Fellow of the Royal Society of Edinburgh, 2002. Address: The Principal's Office, University of Stirling, Stirling FK9 4LA, Scotland.

**HALLIGAN Aidan William Francis,** b. 17 September 1957, Dublin, Ireland. Physician. m. Carol Furlong, 3 daughters. Education: Medical School, Trinity College, Dublin, 1978-84; Qualifications: MB BCh, BAO, BA, 1984; MRCOG, 1991; MA, Trinity College Dublin, 1993; MD, Trinity College Dublin, 1993; MRCPI, 1996; FFPHM, 2003; FRCP, 2004; FRCOG, 2004. Appointments: Currently: Director of Clinical Governance for the NHS, 1999-; Deputy Chief Medical Officer for England, 2003-; Honorary Consultant in Obstetrics, Guy's and St Thomas' Hospital NHS Trust, 2003-08; Visiting Professor, Department of Surgical Oncology and Technology of the Division of Surgery, Anaethetics and Intensive Care, Imperial College London, 2005-08; Director General for Clinical Strategy and Development for the National Programme for IT, 2004; Senior Responsible Owner for Benefits Realisation for the National Programme for IT, 2004; Director of the implementation of Modernising Medical Careers, 2003-04. Publications: More than 60 articles as co-author in peer reviewed journals. Honours include: Harold Malkin Prize, Royal College of Obstetricians and Gynaecologists, 1993, 1996; Ethicon Foundation Fund Travel Award, 1994; Katherine Bishop Harman Award, 1994; Paul Millac Award for Evidence Based Care (jointly), 1996; Public Sector Winner of the Inspired Leaders Network, 2005: Naked Leader Award for No Nonsense Authentic and Transparent Leadership, 2005. Memberships include: Fellow, Royal Academy of Medicine in Ireland; Blair Bell Research Society; Royal College of Obstetricians and Gynaecologists; Royal College of Physicians of Ireland; Faculty of Public Health Medicine; Royal College of Physicians; British Medical Association; British Hypertension Society; British Association for Perinatal Medicine. Address: NHS Clinical Governance Support Team, St John's House, East Street, Leicester LE1 6NB, England. E-mail: aidan.halligan@ncgst.nhs.uk

**HALLIWELL Geri Estelle,** b. 7 August 1972, Watford, England. Singer. Career: Member, Spice Girls, -1998; Started as Touch, renamed as Spice Girls; Found manager and obtained major label recording deal; Numerous TV appearances, radio play and press interviews; UK, European and US tours; Nominated United Nations Ambassador, 1998; Solo Career, 1998-; Video and book releases. Recordings: Singles with Spice Girls: Wannabe, 1996; Say You'll Be There, 1996; 2 Become 1, 1996; Mama/Who Do You Think You Are, 1993; Spice Up Your Life, 1997; Too Much, 1997; Stop, 1998; (How Does It Feel to Be) On Top of the World, as part of England United, 1998; Move Over/Generation Next, 1998; Viva Forever, 1998; Albums: Spice, 1996; Spiceworld, 1997; Solo Singles: Look At Me, 1999; Mi Chico Latino, 1999; Lift Me Up, 1999; Bag It Up, 2000; It's Raining Men, 2001; Scream If You Want to Go Faster, 2001; Albums: Schizophonic, 1999; Scream If You Want to Go Faster, 2001. Honours: With Spice Girls, numerous music awards in polls.

**HALLWORTH Grace Norma Leonie Byam,** b. 4 January 1928, Trinidad, West Indies. Ex-Librarian; Author; Storyteller. m. Trevor David Hallworth, 31 October 1964. Education: Exemptions from Matriculation, 1946; Associate of Library Association, 1956; Diploma in Education, London University, 1976; Editorial Board Member, Institute of Education, University of London, 1995. Publications: Listen to this Story, 1977; Mouth Open Story Jump Out, 1984; Web of Stories, 1990; Cric Crac, 1990; Buy a Penny Ginger, 1994; Poor-Me-One, 1995; Rythm and Rhyme, 1995; Down By The River, 1997 Contributions to: Books and journals. Honours: Runner-up for Greenaway Medal. 1997. Membership: Society for Storytelling, patron, 1993-94. Address: Tranquillity, 36 Lighthouse Road, Bacolet Point, Scarborough, Tobago, West Indies.

**HALPERN Daniel,** b. 11 September 1945, Syracuse, New York, USA. Associate Professor; Poet; Writer; Editor. m. Jeanne Catherine Carter, 31 December 1982, 1 daughter. Education: San Francisco State College, 1963-64; BA, California State University at Northridge, 1969; MFA, Columbia University, 1972. Appointments: Founder-Editor, Antaeus literary magazine, 1969-95; Instructor, New School for Social Research, New York City, 1971-76; Editor-in-Chief, Ecco Press, 1971-; Visiting Professor, Princeton University, 1975-76, 1987-88, 1995-96; Associate Professor, Columbia University, 1976-. Publications: Poetry: Traveling on Credit, 1978; Seasonal Rights, 1982; Tango, 1987; Foreign Neon, 1991; Selected Poems, 1994. Other: The Keeper of Height, 1974; Treble Poets, 1975; Our Private Lives: Journals, Notebooks and Diaries, 1990; Not for Bread Alone: Writers on Food, Wine, and the Art of Eating, 1993; The Autobiographical Eye, 1993; Holy Fire: Nine Visionary Poets and the Quest for Enlightenment, 1994; Something Shining, 1998. Editor: Borges on Writing (co-editor), 1973; The American Poetry Anthology, 1975; The Antaeus Anthology, 1986; The Art of the Tale: An International Anthology of Short Stories, 1986; On Nature, 1987; Writers on Artists, 1988; Reading the Fights (with Joyce Carol Oates), 1988; Plays in One Act, 1990; The Sophisticated Cat (with Joyce Carol Oates), 1992; On Music (co-editor), 1994. Contributions to: Various anthologies, reviews, journals, and magazines. Honours: Jesse Rehder Poetry Award, Southern Poetry Review, 1971; YMHA Discovery Award, 1971; Great Lakes Colleges National Book Award, 1973; Borestone Mountain Poetry Award, 1974; Robert Frost Fellowship, Bread Loaf, 1974; National Endowment for the Arts Fellowships, 1974, 1975, 1987; Pushcaft Press Prizes, 1980, 1987, 1988; Carey Thomas Award for Creative Publishing, Publishers Weekly, 1987; Guggenheim Fellowship, 1988; PEN Publisher Citation, 1993. Address: c/o The Ecco Press, 100 West Broad Street, Hopewell, NJ 08525, USA.

**HALSEY Alan,** b. 22 September 1949, Croydon, Surrey, England. Bookseller; Poet. Education: BA, Honours, London. Publications: Yearspace, 1979; Another Loop in Our Days, 1980; Present State, 1981; Perspectives on the Reach, 1981; The Book of Coming Forth in Official Secrecy, 1981; Auto Dada Cafe, 1987; A Book of Changes, 1988; Five Years Out, 1989; Reasonable Distance, 1992; The Text of Shelley's Death, 1995; A Robin Hood Book, 1996; Fit to Print (with Karen McCormack), 1998; Days of '49 , with Gavin Selerie, 1999; Wittgenstein's Devil: Selected Writing 1978-98, 2000; Sonatas and Preliminary Sketches, 2000; Marginalien (Poems, Prose & Graphics 1988-2004), 2005. Contributions to: Critical Quarterly; Conjunctions; North Dakota Quarterly; Writing; Ninth Decade; Poetica; South West Review; Poetry Wales; Poesie Europe; O Ars; Figs; Interstate; Prospice; Reality Studios; Fragmente; Screens and Tasted Parallels; Avec; Purge; Grille; Acumen; Shearsman; Oasis; New American Writing; Agenda; Colorado Review; Talisman; PN Review; Resurgence; West Coast Line; The Gig; Boxkite. Membership: Thomas Lovell Beddoes Society; David Jones Society. Address: 40 Crescent Road, Nether Edge, Sheffield S7 1HN, England.

**HAM Christopher John,** b. 15 May 1951, Cardiff, Wales. University Professor. m. Ioanna Burnell, 2 sons, 1 daughter. Education: BA, 1972, M Phil, 1976, University of Kent, 1972; PhD, University of Bristol, 1983. Appointments: Research Assistant, University of Leeds, 1975-77; Lecturer, University of Bristol, 1977-86; Fellow, King's Fund, 1986-92; Professor, University of Birmingham, 1992-; Seconded to Department of Health as Director of Strategy Unit, 2000-2004. Publications include: Policy Making in the NHS, 1981; Health Policy in Britain, 1982, 5th edition 2004; The Policy Process in the Modern Capitalist State (with M J Hill), 1984, 2nd edition 1993.

Honour: CBE, 2004. Memberships: Fellow, Royal Society of Medicine, 1993; Founder Fellow, The Academy of Medical Sciences, 1998; Honorary Fellow, Royal College of Physicians, 2004. Address: Health Services Management Centre, University of Birmingham, 40 Edgbaston Park Road, Birmingham B15 2RT, England.

**HAMBURGER Michael, (Peter Leopold),** b. 22 March 1924, Berlin, Germany (British Citizen). Poet; Writer; Translator; Editor. m. Anne Ellen File, 1951, 1 son, 2 daughters. Education: MA, Christ Church, Oxford, England. Appointments: Assistant Lecturer in German, University College, London, 1952-55; Lecturer, then Reader in German, University of Reading, 1955-64; Florence Purington Lecturer, Mount Holyoke College, South Hadley, Massachusetts, 1966-67; Visiting Professor, State University of New York at Buffalo, 1969, and at Stony Brook, 1971, University of South Carolina, 1973, Boston University, 1975-77; Visiting Fellow, Wesleyan University, Middletown, Connecticut, 1970; Regent's Lecturer, University of California at San Diego, 1973; Professor (part-time), University of Essex, 1978. Publications: Poetry: Flowering Cactus, 1950; Poems 1950-51, 1952; The Dual Site, 1958; Weather and Season, 1963; Feeding the Chickadees, 1968; Penguin Modern Poets (with A Brownjohn and C Tomlinson), 1969; Travelling, 1969; Travelling I-V, 1973; Ownerless Earth, 1973; Travelling VI, 1975; Real Estate, 1977; Moralities, 1977; Variations, 1981; Collected Poems, 1984; Trees, 1988; Selected Poems, 1988; Roots in the Air, 1991; Collected Poems, 1941-94, 1995, paperback, 1998; Late, 1997; Intersections, 2000; The Take-Over (story), 2000; From a Diary of Non-Events, 2002; Wild and Wounded, 2004. Prose: Reason and Energy, 1957; From Prophecy to Exorcism, 1965; The Truth of Poetry, 1970, new edition, 1996; A Mug's Game (memoirs), 1973, revised edition as String of Beginnings, 1991; Hugo von Hofmannsthal, 1973; Art as a Second Nature, 1975; A Proliferation of Prophets, 1983; After the Second Flood: Essays in Modern German Literature, 1986; Testimonies: Selected Shorter Prose 1950-1987, 1989; Philip Larkin: A Retrospect, 2002; Michael Hamburger in Conversation with Peter Dale, 1998. Translator: Many books, including: Poems of Hölderlin, 1943, revised edition as Hölderlin: Poems, 1952; J C F Hölderlin: Selected Verse, 1961; H von Hofmannsthal: Poems and Verse Plays (with others), 1961; H von Hofmannsthal: Selected Plays and Libretti (with others), 1964; J C F Hölderlin: Poems and Fragments, 1967, new edition, enlarged, 1994, 2004; The Poems of Hans Magnus Enzenberger (with others), 1968; The Poems of Günter Grass (with C Middleton), 1969; Paul Celan: Poems, 1972, new edition, enlarged as Poems of Paul Celan, 1988, 3rd edition, 1995; Selected Poems, 1994; Kiosk, 1997; Günter Grass: Selected Poems and Fragments, 1998; W G Sebald: After Nature, 2002; Unrecounted, 2004. Contributions to: Numerous publications. Honours: Bollingen Foundation Fellow, 1959-61, 1965-66; Translation Prizes, Deutsche Akademie für Sprache und Dichtung, Darmstadt, 1964; Arts Council of Great Britain, 1969; Medal, Institute of Linguistics, 1977; Wilhelm-Heinse Prize, 1978; Schlegel-Tieck Prizes, 1978, 1981; Goethe Medal, 1986; Austrian State Prize for Literary Translation, 1988; Honorary LittD, University of East Anglia, 1988; European Translation Prize, 1990; Hölderlin Prize, Tübingen, 1991; Petrarca Prize, 1992; Officer of the Order of the British Empire, 1992; Honorary DPhil, Technical University, Berlin, 1995; Cholmondeley Award for Poetry, 2000; Horst-Bienek Prize, Munich, 2001. Address: c/o John Johnson Ltd, Clerkenwell House, 45-47 Clerkenwell Green, London EC1 0HT, England.

**HAMBY Gene M Jr,** b. 23 March 1943, Florence, Alabama, USA. Attorney. m. Judy B Hamby, 1 son, 1 daughter. Education, Bachelor of Science with Great Honor, Florence State University (now University of North Alabama), 1965; Juris Doctor, University of Alabama School of Law, 1968. Appointments: Solo Practitioner, focusing on consumers, Sheffield, Alabama; Board Member, Law School Foundation, University of Alabama School of Law; Past District Vice-President, University of Alabama National Alumni Association; Past President, University of North Alabama Alumni Association; Past Member and Chairman of the Board, Sheffield Utilities; Past Chairman of the Board, Sheffield Industrial Development Board; Past President, Colbert County Chamber of Commerce; Past Chairman, Sheffield Education Foundation; Past President, Sheffield Kiwanis Club; President, Colbert County Youth Center; Past Director, Shoals Economic Development Authority. Honours: President Student Government Association; 1963-65; Elected by student body as Mr Florence State University; Bench and Bar Legal Honor Society; Selected Sheffield Citizen of the Year by Sheffield Kiwanis Club, 1991, 2001; Honourable Discharge from US Army as SP5; Listed in Who's Who publications and biographical dictionaries. Memberships: President, Shoals Democrat Club; Board of Directors, Alabama Archaeological Society. Address: PO Box 328, 406 North Nashville Avenue, Sheffield AL 35660, USA.

**HAMDAN Motasem,** b. 1 July 1968, Palestine. Assistant Professor of Health Policy and Management. m. Jale Hamdan, 2 sons. Education: BSc, Health Services Administration,1994, MSc, Health Institutions Administration, 1996, School of Health Services Administration, Hacettepe University, Ankara, Turkey; PhD, Public Health, Catholic University of Leuven, Belgium, 2003. Appointments: Hospital Management Officer, Health Services Management Unit, Technical Assistance Projects, Palestinian Ministry of Health, 1996-98; Faculty and Co-ordinator of the Higher Diploma Programme in Health Management, School of Public Health, Al-Quds University, Jerusalem, 1998-99; Researcher, Centre for Health Services and Nursing Management Research, School of Public Health, Catholic University of Leuven, Belgium, 1999-2003; Head of the Health Policy and Management Unit, Assistant Dean,School of Public Health, Al-Quds University, Jerusalem, 2003-. Publications: Articles in professional journals as author and co-author include most recently: Organising Health Care within Political Turmoil: The Palestinian Case, 2003; Human resources for health in Palestine: A policy analysis. Part I: Current situation and recent developments, 2003; Human resources for health in Palestine: A policy analysis. Part II: The process of policy formulation and implementation, 2003; The dynamics of health policy development during transition and under uncertainty: what can be learned from the Palestinian experience, 2003; 4 papers presented at international conferences in Italy, Sweden, Norway and Spain. Memberships: International Association of Health Policy; International Society on Priorities in Health Care; Member of Board of Associated Editors of international refereed journal Health Policy. Address: The School of Public Health, Al-Quds University, PO Box 5100, Jerusalem. E-mail: mhamdan@med.alquds.edu

**HAMILTON Robert Ross,** b. 28 March 1957, Holmbury St Mary, Dorking, Surrey, England. Academic; Screenwriter; Writer. m. (1) Dolores Batchett, 1977, deceased, 1991, (2) Penelope Monkwell-Harris, 1991, 1 daughter. Education: BA, English and Philosophy, Bristol University, 1978; MSc, Artificial Intelligence Systems, Middlesex College of Technology, 1979; PhD, St Hugh's College, Oxford, 1984. Appointments: Freelance Systems Consultant, various companies; Writer. Publications: Film Scripts: Secret History of Polynesia, 1990; Indigo Blue, 1991, Profit of Doom, 1993; The Solaris Bible, 1995; Numerous articles in literary magazines and contributions to textbooks. Memberships: Classic Car Club; Organisation for improving

East-West understanding; RSPB. Address: 110 Vinery Road, Cambridge, CB2 3DT, England.

**HAMILTON-WEDGWOOD Kenneth Roy,** b. 11 December 1931. Engineer. m. Rita, 1973, dissolved 1979. Appointments: Consultant/Technical Author (electronics), Environmental Instrumentation Satellite Data Collection (Argos) Oceanography; National Service, RAF; Sac airborne wireless communications, early experimental Decca navigator, 1950-52; Resident Engineer, Whessoe Ltd, Darlington, 1960-67; Engineer, Ultra Electronics, London, 1968-69; Engineer, Marine Electronics, 1971-72; Engineer, Partech Electronics Ltd, 1982; Founder, Camba Consultants; Consulting Engineer, Ford of Detroit and Caterpillar Tractor, Illinois, USA and numerous other countries world-wide; Installed complete fuel supply at Heathrow Airport, London. Honour: Opened new ASDA Store, Bodmin, 2002. Membership: Bodmin Probus; Complimentary friend of Eden Project for life. Address: Rosedale, Redmoor, Bodmin, Cornwall, PL30 5AR, England. E-mail: g3xkw@amserve.com

**HAMMETT Louise B, (Biddy Hammett),** b. 18 September 1929, Columbus, Georgia, USA. Community Service Volunteer; Artist; Writer; Playwright; Historian; Publisher. m. Paul Lane Hammett Jr, 2 daughters. Education: BA, Auburn University, Alabama, 1950; Postgraduate Studies, LaGrange College, Georgia, 1962-69; Audited Art Studies; Certified equivalent MA in Art, University of Georgia, 1982. Appointments: School Teacher, LaGrange Public Schools, Georgia, 1950-51; Founder of Art Division, 1970, Volunteer, 1970-71, LaGrange Academy; Co-founder and Art Instructor, Chattahoochee Valley Art Museum Association, LaGrange; Founder and Chair, Chattahoochee Valley Art Association's Sidewalk Art Show; Artist in Residence, Instructor, Chattahoochee Valley Community College; Private Studio Art Instructor, LaGrange, 1963-80; Exhibited Power Crossroads, Coweta Counter, Georgia, 1971; Private Studio Art Instructor, Columbus, 1980-; Oil painting demonstrations; Represented in group shows and in permanent art collections. Publications: Articles in professional and popular journals and magazines; Oil painting, Georgia to Georgia, gifted to Zugdidi, Republic of Georgia; Oil painting, Peach Trees, gifted to Kiryu City, Japan. Honours: Selected for the Vincent Price Contemporary Southern Art Festival, 1964; Selected for Gardens Festival Eight; Award of Excellence, LaGrange Academy Art Program; Award of Appreciation, Ocfuskee Historical Society Inc, 1974; Appreciation Award, Regional Historic Preservation Advisory Council, Chattahoochee Flint Area, 1980; Historic Columbus Foundation Award for Outstanding Contributions in the Field of Historic Preservation in Columbus, Georgia, 1986; 1st place award, Commemorative Events Category, NSDAR; Award for Excellence in Community Service, NSDAR, 1990; Award for Outstanding Supoprt, NSSAR, 1993; Chattahoochee Valley Art Museum, 1994; 6 separate awards under the Seals of two Mayors and Councils of Columbus, Georgia for Meritorious Civic Service. Memberships: Chattahoochee Valley Art Association; Atlanta Art Association; Elms & Roses Garden Club; Highland Country Club Ladies Golf Association. Address: Cherith Creek Designs, P O Box 123, Columbus, GA 31902-0123, USA.

**HAMMOND Jane Dominica,** b. 6 April 1934, London, England. Public Relations Management Training Consultant. m. Rudolph Samuel Brown, deceased, 1 daughter. Education: CAM Diploma in Public Relations (Communication, Advertising and Marketing) with Distinction, 1974; National Vocational Qualification Assessor in Public Relations, Institute of Personnel and Development, 1998. Appointments: Press Office Assistant, Swissair, 1959-61; Assistant Editor, Dairy Industries, 1961-63; Reporter, Public Service Newspaper, NALGO (now UNISON),

1964-65; Health Service Public Relations Officer, 1965-68; Public Relations Officer, St Teresa's Hospital, 1968-70; Senior Information Officer: London Borough of Hammersmith, 1971-73, and Community Relations Commission, 1973-77 and its successor, Commission for Racial Equality, 1977-78; Editor, Hollis Public Relations Weekly, 1978-80; Consultant, Trident Public Relations Ltd, 1980-2002; Trident Training Services, 1986-; Independent; Course Director, London Corporate Training Courses, 1998-; Lecturer, Westminster Kingsway College, 1991-; Lecturer, Birkbeck College, 1999-2002. Publications: Chapter on non-commercial public relations in Public Relations Practice, 1995; Report for DFID on Romanian Government Relations with Public, 1997; Articles in professional journals. Memberships: NUJ, 1962; Associate, 1965, Member, 1968, Fellow, 1981, Chartered Institute of Public Relations; Member, 1974, Fellow, 2000, CAM Foundation: Millennium Founder Member, Guild of Public Relations Practitioners, 1986; Member and past-President, Rotary Club of Putney, 1998. Address: Trident Training Services, Suite 5, 155 Tawc Park Road, London SW15 2EG, England. E-mail: trident @btconnect.com Website: www.tridenttraining.com

**HAMMOND Peter,** b. 13 July 1942. Mining Supervisor. m. Diane Ivy, 12 August 1989. Education: Modules Diploma of Higher Education, 1985. Appointments: Environmental and Mining Supervisor; Public Speaker on Poetry and Literature Black Country in Colleges and Universities, Schools and Art Societies nationwide. Publications: Two in Staffordshire with Graham Metcalf, 1979; Love Poems, 1982. Contributions to: New Age Poetry; Outposts; Charter Poetry; Chase Post; Swansea Festival, 1982. Honour: School Poetry Prize, 1956. Memberships: Rugeley Literary Society; Co-Founder, Cannock Poetry Group; Poetry Society Readings. Address: 6 Gorstey Lea, Burntwood, Staffordshire WS7 9BG, England.

**HAMMONS Thomas James,** b. England. Chartered Engineer; Power Engineer; Consultant, University Teacher. Education: BSc, 1957; PhD, Imperial College, London University, 1961; ACGI, 1957; DIC, 1961. Appointments: Engineer, System Engineering Department, AEI, 1961-62; Fc Engineering, Glasgow University, 1962-2002; Professor, Electrical and Computer Engineering, McMaster University, 1978-79; Visiting Professor, Silesian Polytechnic University, 1978; Visiting Scientist, University Saskatchewan, Canada, 1979; Visiting Academic, Czechoslovak Academic Science, 1982, 1985, 1988; Visiting Professor, Polytechnic University Grenoble, 1984; Consultant, Mawdsleys, 1965-78; NSHEB, 1965-70; GEC, 1975-84. Publications: Over 350 Scientific Papers and Articles. Memberships: Universities Power Engineering Conf; Eur Ing, CEng Institution Mechanical Engineering, CIGRE Institute of Diagnostic Engineers; Institute of Electrical and Electronic Engineers, Energy Development and Power Generation Committee, Synchronous Machinery Subcommittee, Chair, International Practices Subcommittee, Past Chair, Station Control Subcommittee, PES, Standards Voting Committee, Standards committees, Chair, UKRI Power Engineering Chapter, 1994-2004. Honours: Chairman, Institute of Electrical and Electronic Engineers (IEEE) UKRI Section, 2000-2002; Deputy Director General, Life Patron, International Biographic Society; Fellow, Institute of Electrical and Electronic Engineers, 1996; Distinguished Service Award, IEEE/PES, 1996; IEEE PES Outstanding Large Chapter Award, UKRI Chapter, 2003; IEEE Region 8 Chapter of the Year Award, 2001 and 2004; IEEE UKRI Chapter, Outstanding Engineer Award, 2004; State Scholar; Cultural Doctorate, World University. Address: Clairmont, 11c Winton Drive, Kelvinside, Glasgow G12 0PZ, Scotland. E-mail: T.Hammons@ieee.org

**HAMNETT Katherine,** b. 16 August 1948. Designer. 2 sons. Education: St Martin's School of Art. Appointments: Tuttabankem, 1969-74; Designed freelance in New York, Paris, Rome and London, 1974-76; Founder, Katherine Hamnett Ltd, 1979; Launched Choose Life T-shirt collection, 1983; Involved in Fashion Aid, 1985; Opened first Katherine Hamnett shop, London, 1986, 2 more shops, 1988; Production moved to Italy, 1989; Visiting Professor, London Institute, 1997-; International Institute of Cotton Designer of the Year, 1982; British Fashion Industry Designer of the Year, 1984; Bath Costume Museum Menswear Designer of the Year Award, 1984; British Knitting and Clothing Export Council Award for Export, 1988. Publications: Various publications in major fashion magazines and newspapers. Address: Katherine Hamnett Ltd, 202 New North Road, London N1 7BJ, England.

**HAMPSHIRE Stuart (Newton) (Sir),** b. 1 October 1914, Healing, Lincolnshire, England. Retired Professor of Philosophy; Writer. m. (1) Renee Ayer, 1961, deceased 1980, (2) Nancy Cartwright, 1985, 2 daughters. Education: Balliol College, Oxford. Appointments: Fellow and Lecturer in Philosophy, 1936-40, Domestic Bursar and Research Fellow, 1955-60, All Souls College, Oxford; Service in the British Army, 1940-45; Personal Assistant to the Minister of State, British Foreign Office, 1945; Lecturer in Philosophy, University College, London, 1947-50; Fellow, New College, Oxford, 1950-55; Grote Professor of Philosophy of Mind and Logic, University of London, 1960-63; Professor of Philosophy, Princeton University, 1963-70; Warden, Wadham College, Oxford, 1970-84; Professor, Stanford University, 1985-91. Publications: Spinoza, 1951; Thought and Action, 1959; Freedom of the Individual, 1965; Modern Writers and Other Essays, 1969; Freedom of Mind and Other Essays, 1971; The Socialist Idea (co-editor), 1975; Two Theories of Morality, 1977; Public and Private Morality (editor), 1978; Morality and Conflict, 1983; Innocence and Experience, 1989; Justice is Conflict, 1990. Contributions to: Philosophical journals. Honours: Honorary DLitt, University of Glasgow, 1973; Knighted, 1979. Memberships: American Academy of Arts and Sciences, fellow; British Academy, fellow. Address: 7 Beaumont Road, The Quarry, Headington, Oxford, OX3 8JN, England.

**HAMPSHIRE Susan,** b. 12 May 1942, England. Actress. m. (2) Sir Eddie Kulukundis, 1981, 1 son from first marriage. Education: Hampshire School, Knightsbridge. Career: Theatre work includes: Expresso Bongo, 1972; Follow That Girl; Fairy Tales of New York; The Ginger Man; A Doll's House; The Taming of the Shrew; Peter (Peter Pan, 1974); As You Like It; Arms and the Man; Miss Julie; Man and Superman; Elizabeth (The Circle, 1976); Crucifer of Blood; Ruth Carson (Night and Day, 1979); Tribades; Elizabeth (The Revolt, 1980); Stella Drury (House Guest, 1981); Elvira (Blithe Spirit, 1986); Marie Stopes (Married Love, 1989); A Little Night Music; Anna (The King and I, 1990; Countess of Marshwood (Relative Values, 1993); Susanna (Susanna Andler, 1995); Mrs Christie (Black Chiffon, 1996); Sheila Carter (Relatively Speaking), 2000-2001; Felicity Marshwood (Relative Values), 2002; Films include: During One Night, 1961; Three Lives of Thomasina; Night Must Fall and Wonderful Life, 1964; Monte Carlo or Bust, 1969; David Copperfield, Paris in August, Living Free, Malpertius and A Time for Loving, 1972; Bang; TV appearances include: Andromeda; Fleur Forsyte (The Forsyte Saga, 1970); Sarah Churchill; Duchess of Marlborough (The First Churchills, 1971); Becky Sharp (Vanity Fair, 1973); Going to Pot, 1985; Madelaine Neroni (The Barchester Chronicles, 1982); Matha (Leaving, Series I and II, 1984-85); Natasha (Don't Tell Father, 1992); Esme Harkness (The Grand, 1997, series 2, 1998); Molly (Monarch of the Glen, 1999-2003). Publications include: Susan's Story, 1981; Lucy Jane at the Ballet; The Materal Instinct, 1985; Every Letter Counts, 1990; Lucy Jane on Television; Lucy Jane and the Dancing Competition, 1991; Lucy Jane and the Russian Ballet, 1993; Rosie's First Ballet Lesson, 1997. Honours: Best Actress Awards: Emmys for: The Forsyte Saga, 1970; The First Churchills, 1971; Vanity Fair, 1973; E Poe Prizes du Film Fantastique, 1972; Hon DLit City University, London, 1984; Hon DLit, St Andrews University, Scotland; Hon DEd, Kingston University, Surrey, 1994; Hon DArts, Boston, USA, 1994; OBE, 1995. Address: c/o Chatto & Linnit Ltd, 123A King Road, London SW3 4PL, England.

**HAMPSON Norman**, b. 8 April 1922, Leyland, Lancashire, England. Retired University Professor. m. Jacqueline Gardin, 22 April 1948, 2 daughters. Education: University College Oxford, 1940-41, 1945-47. Publications: La Marine de l'An ll, 1959; A Social History of The French Revolution, 1963; The First European Revolution, 1963; The Enlightenment, 1968; The Life and Opinions of Maximilien Robespierre, 1974; A Concise History of the French Revolution, 1975; Danton, 1978; Will and Circumstance: Montesquieu, Rousseau and The French Revolution, 1983; Prelude to Terror, 1988; Saint-Just, 1991; The Perfidy of Albion, 1998; Not Really What You'd Call a War, 2001. Contributions to: Numerous magazines and journals. Honour: D Litt (Edinburgh), 1989. Memberships: Fellow, British Academy; Fellow, Royal Historical Society. Address: 305 Hull Road, York, Y010 3LU, England.

**HAMPTON Christopher (James)**, b. 26 January 1946, Fayal, The Azores. Playwright. m. Laura de Holesch, 1971, 2 daughters. Education: Lancing College, Sussex, 1959-63; BA, Modern Languages, 1968, MA, New College, Oxford. Career: Resident Dramatist, Royal Court Theatre, London, 1968-70; Freelance Writer, 1970-. Publications: Tales from Hollywood, 1983; Tartuffe or The Imposter (adaptation of Moliére's play), 1984; Les Liaisons Dangereuses (adaptation of C de Laclos's novel), 1985; Hedda Gabler and A Doll's House (translations of Ibsen's plays), 1989; Faith, Hope and Charity (translator), 1989; The Ginger Tree (adaptation of Oscar Wynd's novel), 1989; White Chameleon, 1991; The Philanthropist and Other Plays, 1991; Sunset Boulevard, 1993; Alice's Adventures Underground, 1994; Carrington, 1995; Mary Reilly, 1996; The Secret Agent, 1996; Art (translator), 1996; Nostromo, 1997; An Enemy of the People (translator), 1997; The Unexpected Man (translator), 1998; Conversations After a Burial (translator), 2000; Life x Three, 2001; Three Sisters, 2003. Other: Screenplays, radio and television plays. Honours: Evening Standard Award, 1970, 1983, 1986; Plays and Players London Critics' Award, 1970, 1973, 1985; Los Angeles Drama Critics Circle Award, 1974; Laurence Olivier Award, 1986; New York Drama Critics' Award, 1987; Prix Italia, 1988; Writers Guild of America Screenplay Award, 1989; Oscar, 1989; BAFTA, 1990; Special Jury Award, Cannes Film Festival, 1995; 2 Tony Awards, 1995; Scott Moncrieff Prize, 1997; Officier, Ordre des Arts et des Lettres, 1998. Membership: Royal Society of Literature, fellow. Address: National House, 60-66 Wardour Street, London W1V 3HP, England.

**HAN Jin Suk**, b. 11 August 1953, Seoul, Korea. Professor. m. Mi Kyung Choo, 1 son, 2 daughters. Education: MD, Seoul National University College of Medicine, 1978; PhD, Medical Science, Seoul National University, 1988; Boards: Korean Board of Medicine, 1978; Diplomate of Internal Medicine, 1983, Sub-speciality of Nephrology, 1992, Korean Board of Internal Medicine. Appointments: Fulltime Lecturer, Assistant and Associate Professor, 1986-99, Professor, 1999-, Department of Internal Medicine, Seoul National University College of Medicine; Chief, Division of Nephrology, Seoul National

University Hospital, 2001-2004. Articles in medical journals including: Journal of the American Society of Nephrology, 2002, 2004; American Journal of Physiology (Renal Physiology), 2003; Kidney International, 2004. Honours: Visiting Fellow, Laboratory of Kidney Electrolyte Metabolism, NHLBI, Bethesda, Maryland, USA, 1990-92; Presidential Award, Seoul National University, 1978; Award of Excellent Research, The Korean Federation of Science and Technology Societies, 1999, 2003. Memberships: American Physiology Society; American Society of Nephrology; FASEB; ISN; ERA; Korean Society of Nephrology. Address: Department of Internal Medicine, Seoul National University College of Medicine, 28 Yongon-dong, Chongno-gu, Seoul 110-744, Korea. E-mail: jshan@snu.ac.kr

**HAN Moonsik**, b. 15 January 1955, Incheon, South Korea. Professor. m. Sungwon Lee, 1 son. Education: BS, Mechanical Engineering, 1979, MS, Mechanical Engineering, 1981, PhD, Mechanical Engineering, 1986, Inha University, Incheon, Korea. Appointments: Senior Researcher, Structural Fatigue Laboratory, Korea Institute of Machinery and Metal, Daejeon, Korea, 1981-95; Dean of Student Affairs, Dong Yang University, Younju, Korea, 1995-96; Professor, Mechanical and Automotive Engineering Faculty, Keimyung University Daegu, Korea, 1997-; Postdoctoral fellow, Department of Mechanical Engineering, Sheffield University, England, 1989-90; Visiting Researcher, Engine Division, Southwest Research Institute, San Antonio, Texas, USA, 1984. Publications: Articles in scientific journals include most recently: Fracture analysis of thick plate for partial penetration multi-pass weldment using j-integral, 2004; Damage assessment of composites structures subjected to low velocity impact, 2004; Failure analysis of the exhaust valve stem from a Waukersha P9390 GSI gas engine, 2004; Vibration control of a rotating cantilevered beam using piezoactuators: experimental work, 2004; Free nitrogen effect on creep failure and creep crack growth of C-Mn steel, 2004. Honour: Excellent Research Award, Korea Institute of Machinery and Metals, 1988. Memberships: Editor, Transactions of the Korean Hydrogen and new Energy Society, 2000-2001; Editor/Director, Journal of the Korean Society of Precision Engineering, 1998-2003; Steering Committee, Daegu Machinery Institute of Components and Materials Foundation, 2001-; Director, Korean Society of Manufacturing Process Engineers, 2002-; Director, Korean Society of Automotive Engineers, 2000-; Director, Department of Planning, Daegu Technopark, Korea, 2001-2002. Address: Faculty of Mechanical and Automotive Engineering, Keimyung University, 1000 Shindang-Dong, Dalseo-Gu, Daegu 704-701, Republic of Korea. E-mail: sheffhan@kmu.ac.kr

**HAN Sang-Lin**, b. 24 April 1060, Taejon, Korea. Professor. m. Hyoung-Ae Cheon, 2 sons. Education: BBA, Korea University, 1979-82; MBA, State University of New York at Buffalo, 1985-87; PhD, Pennsylvania State University, 1987-91. Appointments: Assistant Professor, University of Michigan-Dearborn; Associate Professor, Chungnam National University, Korea; Professor, School of Business, Hanyang University, Korea; Fulbright Scholar, University of Michigan-Ann Arbor. Publications: Books: Environmental Marketing, 1998; Persona Marketing, 2004; Articles in professional journals: Buyer-Supplier Relationships Today, 1993; Antecedents and Consequences of Service Quality in On-Line Banking, 2004. Honours: Fulbright Scholar, 1999; Listed in Who's Who publications and biographical dictionaries. Memberships: American Marketing Association; American Academy of Marketing Science; Korean Marketing Association. Address: School of Business, Hanyang University, Seoul 133-791, Korea. E-mail: slhan@hanyang.ac.kr

# DICTIONARY OF INTERNATIONAL BIOGRAPHY

**HAN Seung-Kyu,** b. 2 September 1962, Seoul, South Korea. Plastic Surgeon. m. Hee-Yeon Hwang. Education: MD, Korea University College of Medicine, 1981-87; Residency in Plastic Surgery, Korea University Medical Center, 1988-92; PhD, Korea University Graduate School of Medicine, 1988-94. Appointments: Research Scientist, Stanford University Medical Center, USA, 1997-99; Director, Plastic Surgery Research Laboratory, Korea University Medical Center, 1999-; Chairman, Scientific Committee of Korean Research Group for Wound Care, 2002-; Associate Professor, Korea University College of Medicine, 2002-; Fellow, European Academy of Plastic Surgery, 2003-. Publications: 107 articles in professional journals; 5 chapters in 3 plastic surgery textbooks; Editor: Advances in Wound Care, 2002. Memberships: American Society of Plastic Surgeons; European Academy of Cosmetic Surgery. Address: Department of Plastic Surgery, Korea University Guro Hospital, 97 Guro-dong, Guro-ku, Seoul 152-703, South Korea. E-mail: pshan@kumc.or.kr

**HANDLEY Martin Hugh,** b. 8 July 1951, Oxford, England. Conductor; Coach; Broadcaster. 1 son, 1 daughter. Education: MA Honours, Corpus Christi College, Cambridge, 1969-72; Postgraduate Acting Course, Bristol Old Vic Theatre School, 1978-79. Appointments: Repetiteur for Kent Opera, Repetiteur and Conductor, Germany, 1972-81; Chorus Master and Conductor for Australian Opera, 1981-84; Chorus Master and Conductor, English National Opera, 1984-90; Presenter for BBC World Service, 1985-; Conductor for London City Opera, D'Oyly Carte Opera, Travelling Opera etc., 1990-; Head of Music, House Conductor, Royal Opera, Copenhagen, 1996-98; Presenter, BBC Radio 3, 1998-; Conductor for Castleward Opera, 2000-; Guest Coach, Young Artists' Programme, Royal Opera House, Covent Garden, 2002-; Conductor for Grange Park Opera, Carl Rosa Opera, 2004-. Address: c/o BBC Radio 3, Broadcasting House, London W1A 1AA, England.

**HANDLEY Sandra L,** b. 6 June 1938, Healdsburg, California, USA. Appraiser; Author. 1 son, 1 daughter. Education: Pacific Lutheran University, 1956-57; Senoma State University, 1968-71; Graduate Course Work, University of California-Berkeley, 1976-77. Appointments: Licensed Real Estate Appraiser; Vocational Teacher; Teacher and Counsellor, Meditation and Spiritual Life Skills; Consultant, Integrating Integrity into Business; Invited to teach University of Moscow, Russia; Real Estate and Vocational Education; State Chairperson, NRCC; Founder, ROHB; Dean of Secretarial College; Published Author. Publications: Death is Not the End; Lessons in Light; Living in Light. Honours: Woman of the Year, American Biographical Institute of International Research; Gold Medal Recipient, Small Business Council, NRCC; Teacher of the Year, Fort Bragg School District; Humanitarian of the Year, HUSUCon; Listed in Who's Who publications and biographical dictionaries. Memberships: Appraisal Institute; ROHB. Address: 1275 Fourth Street #637, Santa Rosa, CA 95404, USA. E-mail: slhand@msn.com

**HANDOO Surrinder Kumar,** b. 15 January 1950, Srinagar, Kashmir. Scientist. m. Kiran Handoo, 3 daughters. Education: MSc, Physics, 1971; PhD, Physics, 1977. Appointments: Scientist E-1, Cement Research Institute of India, 1977, Scientist E-2, 1981, Scientist E-3, 1983, Programme Leader, Newer Materials and Processes, 1988, Group Manager, Newer Materials and Cements, 1994; General Manager, Marketing, Quality Management, Testing, 2001-, General Manager, Centre for Quality Management, Standards and Calibration Services, 2003, National Council for Cement and Building Materials, Ballabgarh, India. Publications: 53 in national and international journals; 3 patents. Membership: Life Member, Indian Thermal

Analysis Society. Address: National Council for Cement and Building Materials, Ballabgarh-121 004, Haryana, India. E-mail: skhandoo@rediffmail.com

**HANKINSON Michael,** b. Great Britain. Composer; Conductor; Organist. Education: Organ and choral scholar, Hereford Cathedral; Organ studies with John Webster and Conducting studies with Charles Proctor, Trinity College of Music; Organ studies with Stephanus Zondagh; Conducting studies with Francesco Mander, Maurice Handford and Werner Andreas Alberts. Appointments: Resident Composer, RPM Film Studies, South Africa, 1970-; City Organist and City Music Adviser, Durban; Formed Soundwaves contemporary music group, 1980; Revived Durban Philharmonic Orchestra; Resident Conductor and Assistant to Carlo Franci, The State Theatre, Pretoria, 10 years; Conductor, Laureate and Composer in Residence, The Johannesburg Philharmonic Orchestra; Established State Theatre-Tshwane Education Project and The South African Music Education Trust, 1994. Publications: Composed numerous film scores, full length ballet, several choral works and concertos for both organ and for trombone; Orchestral scores and accompaniments for Zulu opera, Princess Magogo; A Mandela Portrait, premiered by The Johannesburg Philharmonic Orchestra with six subsequent performances in the USA. Address: Stone Music Productions, 28 Vincent Ave, Duxberry, Sandton, South Africa.

**HANKS Tom,** b. Oakland, California, USA. Actor. m. (1) Samantha Lewes, 2 children, (2) Rita Wilson, 1988, 2 sons. Career: Began acting with Great Lakes Shakespeare Festival; Appeared in Bosom Buddies, ABC TV, 1980; Films include: Splash; Bachelor Party; The Man with One Red Shoe; Volunteers; The Money Pit; Dragnet; Big; Punch Line; The Burbs; Nothing in Common; Every Time We Say Goodbye; Joe Versus the Volcano, 1990; The Bonfire of the Vanities, 1990; A League of Their Own, 1991; Sleepless in Seattle, 1993; Philadelphia, 1993; Forrest Gump, 1994; Apollo 13, 1995; That Thing You Do (also directed), 1997; Turner & Hooch, 1997; Saving Private Ryan, 1998; You've Got Mail, 1998; Cast Away, 1999; The Green Mile, 1999; Toy Story 2 (voice), 1999; From the Earth to the Moon, 1999; Road to Perdition, 2002; Catch Me If You Can, 2003. Honours: Academy Award, 1994, 1995. Membership: Board of Governors, Academy of Motion Picture Arts and Sciences, 2001-. Address: c/o CAA, 9830 Wilshire Boulevard, Beverly Hills, CA 90212, USA.

**HANNAH Daryl,** b. 1960, Chicago, Illinois, USA. Actress. Education: University of California at Los Angeles; Professional Training: Ballet tuition with Marjorie Tallchief, also studied with Stella Adler. Career: Film appearances include: The Fury; The Final Terror; Hard Country; Blade Runner; Summer Lovers; Splash; The Pope of Greenwich Village; Reckless; Clan of the Cave Bear; Legal Eagles; Roxanne; Wall Street; High Spirits; Steel Magnolias; Crazy People; At Play in the Fields of the Lord; Memoirs of an Invisible Man; Grumpy Old Men; Attack of the 50ft Woman; The Tie That Binds; Grumpier Old Men; Two Much; The Last Days of Frankie the Fly; Wild Flowers, 1999; My Favorite Martian, 1999; Dancing at the Blue Iguana, 2000; Cord, 2000; Speedway Junky, 2001; Jackpot, 2001; A Walk to Remember, 2002; Play: The Seven Year Itch, 2000; Directed: The Last Supper, 1994; A Hundred and One Nights, 1995.

**HANNAH John,** b. 1962, Glasgow, Scotland. Actor. m. Joanna Roth. Education: Royal Scottish Academy of Music and Drama. Career: Formerly electrician, formerly with Worker's Theatre Company; TV appearances include: McCallum; Joan; Faith; Rebus; Film appearances include: Four Weddings and a Funeral, 1994; Sliding Doors, 1998; The James Gang, 1999; The

Mummy, 1999; The Mummy Returns, 2001; Pandaemonium, 2001.

**HANNAH Judith Anna Challenger,** b. 8 October 1948, Baltimore, Maryland, USA. Private Education Tutor. m. (1) Brian Challenger, 1968, divorced, 1994, 1 son, 1 daughter, (2) Rev W P Hannah, 2001. Education: Associate of Arts, Arlington Bible College, 1985; BS, Liberty University, 1991; MEd, Mount St Mary's College, 1996; Maryland State Teacher Certification, 1996-; Diploma, Institute of Children's Literature, Charter Oak College, 1997. Appointments: Assistant Teacher, K-4 Mill Valley School, Owing Mills, Maryland, 1984-85; Teacher, Arlington Baptist School, Baltimore, 1985-86; Nursery Teacher, Mill Valley School, 1986-87; Bookkeeper, Secretary, Challenger Engineering Inc, Finksburg, 1987-92; Assistant Director to Director, Before and After Child Care, ABC Care Inc, 1992-95; Teacher Internship for Master's degree, also long-term Substitute, Frederick County Schools, Maryland, 1995-96; Tutor, Office Manager, Learning Resources, Westminster, Maryland,1996-97; Private Tutor, President, Business Owner, A Lesson Learned Inc, Union Bridge, Maryland, 1997-; Publications: 94,520 People Can't Be Wrong, real estate article, 1981. Honours include: Delegation Member, People to People Ambassador Programme to China, 2001; People to People International, Global Peace, Egypt, 2003; Listed in several biographical dictionaries. Memberships: Volunteer, Crisis Hotline, Baltimore, 1972; Leader-Teacher, Pioneer Girls International, Arlington Baptist Church, 1975-78; Phi Lambda Theta, 1994-; Volunteers in Mission, 1997-; Emmaus, 1999-; International Dyslexia Association; Resident Member, Smithsonian Institution. Address: 48 Bucher John Road, Union Bridge, MD 21791, USA.

**HANNAN Daniel John,** b. 1 September 1971, Lima, Peru. Member of the European Parliament; Journalist. m. Sara Maynard, 2 daughters. Education: Marlborough, 1984-89; MA, Modern History, 1st Class, Oriel College, Oxford, 1990-92. Appointments: Leader Writer, Daily Telegraph, 1996-; Columnist, Sunday Telegraph; Member of the European Parliament for South East England (Conservative), 1999-. Publications: Time for a Fresh Start in Europe, 1993; The Euro – Bad for Business, 1995; A Guide to the Amsterdam Treaty, 1997; The Challenge of the East, 1998; What is Britain Votes No? 2004; Direct Democracy, 2005. Address: 58 Keswick Road, Great Bookham, Surrey KT23 4BH, England.

**HANRAHAN Brian,** b. 22 March 1949, London. Journalist. m. 1 daughter. Education: BA, Essex University. Appointments: Far East Correspondent, Hong Kong, 1983-85; Moscow Correspondent, 1986-88; Foreign Affairs Correspondent, working in Middle East, Balkans and Eastern Europe, 1987-97; Diplomatic Editor, BBC TV News, 1997-. Publications: "I counted them all out and I counted them all back": The Battle for the Falklands (with Robert Fox), 1982; The Day That Shook the World (Essays on 9/11 by BBC journalists), 2002. Honours: Reporter of the Year, Royal Television Society, 1982; Richard Dimbleby Award, British Academy of Film and Television Arts (BAFTA), 1982; Honorary Doctorates, Essex University, Middlesex University. Memberships: Chicken Shed Theatre Trust; Royal Institute of International Affairs; Royal United Services Institute; Frontline Club. Address: c/o BBC TV News, Television Centre, Wood Lane, London W12 7RJ, England.

**HANS-ADAM II (His Serene Highness Prince Hans-Adam II of Liechtenstein),** b. 14 February 1945, Vaduz, Liechtenstein. m. Marie Kinsky von Wchinitz und Tettau, 3 sons, 1 daughter. Education: Advanced Level Diploma and Abitur Certificate, Grammar School, Zuoz, 1960-65; Licentiate Degree,

Management and Economics, University of St Gallen, 1965-69. Appointments: Bank trainee, London, England; Undertook reorganisation of management and administration of assets belonging to the Princely House, 1970; Appointed permanent deputy to Prince Franz Joseph II, 1984; Assumed regency, 1989. Address: Schloss Vaduz, FL-9490 Vaduz, Fürstentum, Liechtenstein.

**HANSON Albert L,** b. 9 July 1952, Gainesville, Florida, USA. Physicist; Engineer. m. Anta LoPiccolo, 2 sons. Education: BS with Honors, Engineering Honors Program, North Carolina State University, 1974; MSE, 1976, PhD, 1979, University of Michigan. Appointments: Research Associate, 1979-81, from Assistant Physicist to Physicist, 1981-, Brookhaven National Laboratory, Upton, New York, USA. Publications: Contributed more than 55 articles to professional journals; 7 Reports for the US Government. Honour: Co-recipient, Research and Development 100 Award, 1988. Memberships: American Nuclear Society; American Association for the Advancement of Science; International Radiation Physics Society. Address: Brookhaven National Laboratory, Department of Energy Sciences and Technology, Building 475, Upton, NY 11973, USA. E-mail: alh@bnl.gov

**HANSON Curtis,** b. 24 March 1945, Los Angeles, USA. Film Director; Screenplay Writer. Career: Editor, Cinema magazine; Began film career as screenplay writer; Director, films: The Arousers, 1970; Sweet Kill (also screenplay), 1972; Little Dragons (also co-producer), 1977; Losin' It, 1983; The Bedroom Window (also screenplay), 1988; Bad Influence, 1990; The Hand That Rocks the Cradle, 1992; The River Wild, 1994; LA Confidential, 19988; The Children of Times Square (TV film); Wonder Boys, 1999; Screenplays: The Dunwich Horror, 1970; The Silent Partner, 1978; White Dog, 1982; Never Cry Wolf, 1983; Television: Hitchcock: Shadow of A Genius, 1999. Address: United Talent Agency, 9560 Wilshire Boulevard, Floor 5, Beverly Hills, CA 90212, USA.

**HANSON John Gilbert (Sir),** b. 16 November 1938, Sheffield, England. Warden of Green College, Oxford. m. Margaret Clark, deceased, 3 sons, 1 deceased. Education: BA Lit. Hum., 1961, MA, 1964, Honorary Fellow, 1977, Wadham College, Oxford; Middle East Centre for Arab Studies, Lebanon, 1966-68; Royal College of Defence Studies, 1983. Appointments: War Office, 1961-63; British Council, 1963-98, service in India, Lebanon, Bahrain and Gulf, London, Iran, Deputy Director General, 1988-93, Director General, 1992-98; Warden, Green College, Oxford, 1998-; Patron GAP, 1989-98; Member: Franco-British Council, 1992-98, UK-Japan 2000 GRP; Council, VSO, 1993-98; Chairman, Bahrain-British Foundation, 1997-2004; President, British Skin Foundation, 1997-2002; Member of Governing Council: Society for Asian Studies, 1989-93, SOAS, 1991-98, University of London, 1996-99. Honours: CBE, 1979; KCMG, 1995; Honorary Fellow, St Edmund's College, Cambridge, 1998; Honorary D. Litt., Oxford Brookes University, 1995; Honorary Doctorate: Humberside University, 1996, Greenwich, 1996. Memberships: Athenaeum; MCC; Royal Overseas League; Gymkhana (Madras). Address: Warden's Lodgings, Green College, Oxford OX2 6HG, England.

**HARARY Keith,** b. 9 February 1953, New York, USA. Research Scientist; Author; Science Journalist; Consultant. m. Darlene Moore. Education: PhD, Psychology, Graduate School of the Union Institute, 1986; BA (distinction), Psychology, Duke University, Durham, North Carolina, 1975; Specialised training in crisis and suicide intervention, individual and family counselling, Mental Health Centre, Durham, North Carolina, 1972-76. Appointments: Crisis Counselor,

Durham Mental Health Centre, 1972-76; Research Associate, Psychical Research Foundation, 1973-76; Research Associate, Maimonides Medical Centre, 1976-79; Director of Counseling, Human Freedom Centre, 1979; Research Consultant, SRI International, Freelance Science Journalist, 1988-98; Editor at Large, Omni Magazine, 1995-98; President and Research Director, Institute for Advanced Psychology, 1986-; Director of Public Relations, Pen's Pals, 2003-; Editorial Director, Stockmat, 2004-. Publications: Author and co-author, numerous books and articles. Memberships: American Psychological Association; Association for Media Psychology. Address: PO Box 56238, Portland, OR 97238, USA.

**HARBINSON-BRYANS Robert, (Robin Bryans)** b. 24 April 1928, Belfast, Northern Ireland. Author. Publications: Gateway to the Khyber, 1959; Madeira, 1959; Summer Saga, 1960; No Surrender, 1960; Song of Erne, 1960; Up Spake the Cabin Boy, 1961; Danish Episode, 1961; Tattoo Lily, 1962; Fanfare for Brazil, 1962; The Protégé, 1963; The Azores, 1963; Ulster, 1964; Lucio, 1964; Malta and Gozo, 1966; The Field of Sighing, 1966; Trinidad and Tobago, 1967; Faber Best True Adventure Stories (editor), 1967; Sons of El Dorado, 1968; Crete, 1969; The Dust Has Never Settled, 1992; Let the Petals Fall, 1993; Checkmate, 1994, Blackmail and Whitewash, 1996. Address: 90 Ferrymead Avenue, Greenford, Middlesex, UB6 9TN, England.

**HARBOUR Malcolm John Charles,** b. 19 February 1947, Woking, Surrey, England. Member of the European Parliament. m. Penny Johnson, 2 daughters. Education: MA, Mechanical Engineering, Trinity College, Cambridge; Diploma in Management Studies, University of Aston in Birmingham. Appointments: Engineering Apprentice, 1967; Designer and Development Engineer, 1969-72, Product Planning Manager, Rover-Triumph, 1972-76; Project Manager, Medium Cars, 1976-80, Director, Business Planning, Austin Rover, 1980-82, Director Marketing, 1982-84, Director, Sales UK and Ireland, 1984-86, Director, Overseas Sales, 1986-89, BMC, Longbridge; Established Harbour Wade Brown, Motor Industry Consultants, 1989-; Jointly founded ICDP (International Car Distribution Programme), 1993; Co-Founder and Project Director, 3 Day Car Programme, 1998-99; Member of the European Parliament for the West Midlands, 1999-, Re-elected 2004-; Committee Member: Legal Affairs and Consumer Protection; Industry, Technology Research and Energy; Co-Chairman, European Forum for the Automobile and Society; Chairman, European Ceramics Industry Forum; Governor, European Internet Foundation; Chairman, Conservative Technology Forum; Leader of European Parliament Delegation to the World Summit on the Information Society, 2003. Publications: Winning Tomorrow's Customers, 1997; Many car industry reports. Memberships: CEng; MIMechE; FIMI; Solihull Conservative Association, 1972-, Former Chairman, Solihull Constituency; International Policy Committee, Royal Society. Address: Manor Cottage, Manor Road, Solihull, West Midlands B91 2BL, England. E-mail: mharbour@europarl.eu.int

**HARCOURT Geoffrey (Colin),** b. 27 June 1931, Melbourne, Australia. Academic; Professor Emeritus; Economist; Writer. m. Joan Margaret Bartrop, 30 July 1955, 2 sons, 2 daughters. Education: BCom, Honours, 1954, MCom, 1956, University of Melbourne; PhD, 1960, LittD, 1988, Cambridge University. Appointments: Professor Emeritus, University of Adelaide, 1988; President, Jesus College, Cambridge, 1988-89, 1990-92; Reader in the History of Economic Theory, Cambridge University, 1990-98; Emeritus Reader, History of Economic Theory, Cambridge, 1998-; Emeritus Fellow, Jesus College, Cambridge, 1998-. Publications: Economic Activity (with P H Karmel and R H Wallace), 1967; Readings in the Concept

and Measurement of Income (editor with R H Parker), 1969; Some Cambridge Controversies in the Theory of Capital, 1972; Theoretical Controversy and Social Significance: An Evaluation of the Cambridge Controversies, 1975; The Microeconomic Foundations of Macroeconomics (editor), 1977; The Social Science Imperialists (selected essays), 1982; Keynes and His Contemporaries: The Sixth and Centennial Keynes Seminar Held in the University of Kent at Canterbury (editor), 1985; Controversies in Political Economy (selected essays), 1986; International Monetary Problems and Supply-Side Economics: Essays in Honour of Lorie Tarshis (editor with Jon S Cohen), 1986; On Political Economists and Modern Political Economy (selected essays), 1992; The Dynamics of the Wealth of Nations. Growth, Distribution and Structural Change. Essays in Honour of Luigi Pasinetti (co-editor with Mauro Baranzini), 1993; Post-Keynesian Essays in Biography: Portraits of Twentieth Century Political Economists, 1993; Income and Employment in Theory and Practice (editor with Alessandro Roncaglia and Robin Rowley), 1994; Capitalism, Socialism and Post-Keynesianism: Selected Essays, 1995; A "Second Edition" of The General Theory (editor, with P A Riach), 2 volumes, 1997; 50 Years a Keynesian and Other Essays, 2001; Selected Essays on Economic Policy, 2001; L'Economie rebelle de Joan Robinson, editor, 2001; Joan Robinson: Critical Assessments of Leading Economists, 5 volumes (editor with Prue Kerr), 2002; Editing Economics: Essays in Honour of Mark Perlman (co-editor), 2002. Contributions to: Many books and scholarly journals. Honours: Fellow, Academy of the Social Sciences in Australia (FASSA), 1971; President, Economic Society of Australia and New Zealand, 1974-77; Officer in the General Division of the Order of Australia (AO), 1994; Economic Society of Australia, Distinguished Fellow, 1996; Honorary DLitt, De Montfort University, 1997; Honorary Fellow, Queen's College, University of Melbourne, 1998; Honorary DComm, Melbourne, 2003; Hon D.h.c.rer.pol., University of Fribourg, Switzerland, 2003; Academician of the Academy of Learned Societies for the Social Sciences (AcSS), 2003; Distinguished Fellow, History of Economics Society, USA, 2004; Honorary Member, European Society for the History of Economic Thought, 2004. Memberships: Royal Economic Society. Address: Jesus College, Cambridge CB5 8BL, England.

**HARDCASTLE Jesse Leslie,** b. 8 December 1926, Croydon, Surrey, England. Retired Film Administrator. m. Vivienne Wendy Richards, 2 sons. Education: St Joseph's College, Croydon. Appointments: British Lion Films; Royal Navy, 1944-47; British Film Institute, 1948-94; Manager Central Booking Agency; General Manager, National Film Theatre; Administrator, London Film Festival, 1957-77; Southbank Controller, British Film Institute; Creator and Curator, Museum of the Moving Image, 1988-94; Retired, 1994; Consultant, Persistence of Vision Company, 1995-. Honours: OBE; Fellow of the British Film Institute; Honorary Fellow, British Kinematograph and Television Society; BAFTA Special Award. Memberships: Trustee, Worthing Dome Regeneration Trust; Executive Committee, National Museum of Cinema Technology, Bletchly Park; Chairman, Uckfield Film Society, Worthing Film Society; Executive Committee, Soho Housing Association; Vice-President, Soho Society. Address: 37C Great Pulteney Street, London W1F 9 NT, England. E-mail: hardcastle@ukonline.co.uk

**HARDCASTLE Michael, (David Clark),** b. 6 February 1933, Huddersfield, England. Author. m. Barbara Ellis Shepherd, 30 August 1979, 4 daughters. Appointment: Literary Editor, Bristol Evening Post, 1960-65. Publications: Author of over 140 children's books, 1966-; One Kick, 1986; James and the TV Star, 1986; Mascot, 1987; Quake, 1988; The Green Machine,

1989; Walking the Goldfish, 1990; Penalty, 1990; Advantage Miss Jackson, 1991; Dog Bites Goalie, 1993; One Good Horse, 1993; Soccer Captain, 1994; Puzzle, 1995; Please Come Home, 1995; Matthew's Goals, 1997; Carole's Camel, 1997; The Price of Football, 1998; Shoot-Out, 1998; Eye for a Goal, 1998; Goal-Getter, 1999; Injury Time, 1999; Rivals United, 1999; Danny's Great Goal, 1999; My Brother's a Keeper, 2000; Mine's a Winner, 2000; Sam's Dream, 2000; The Striker's Revenge, 2000; The Most Dangerous Score, 2001; Archie's Amazing Game, 2002. Contributions to: Numerous articles in magazines and journals. Honour; Member of the Order of the British Empire, 1988. Memberships: Federation of Children's Book Groups, national chair, 1989-90. Address: 17 Molescroft Park, Beverley, East Yorkshire HU17 7EB, England.

**HARDING Anthony Filmer,** b. 20 November 1946, Bromley, Kent, England. Professor of Archaeology. m. Lesley Eleanor, 2 sons. Education: BA, 1968, MA, 1973, PhD, 1973, Cambridge University. Appointments: Lecturer in Archaeology, 1973-87, Senior Lecturer in Archaeology, 1987-90, Professor of Archaeology, 1990-2004, University of Durham; Professor of Archaeology, University of Exeter, 2004-. Publications: The Bronze Age in Europe (with J M Coles), 1979; The Mycenaeans and Europe, 1984; European Societies in the Bronze Age, 2000. Honours: FBA, 2001; President, European Association of Archaeologists, 2003-2006. Address: Department of Archaeology, Laver Building, North Park Road, Exeter EX4 4QE, England. Website: www.ex.ac.uk/sogaer/archaeology/staff-harding.html

**HARDISH Patrick,** b. Perth Amboy, New Jersey, USA. Librarian; Composer. Education: BA, Queens College, CUNY, 1976; MS, Pratt Institute, 1981; Juilliard School, 1969-72; Columbia University, graduate work, 1978-80; Bennington College composition seminar, 1980. Appointments: Library Assistant V, Columbia University, 1978-84; Co-Director and Co-Founder, Composers Concordance and its New Music Now Series, 1983-; Senior Librarian, New York Public Library, 1984-; Editorial Board, New Music Connoisseur, 1994-; Virginia Center for Creative Arts: Fellowships, 1981, 1982, 1986, 1988; Guest Composer Lectures, New York University, 2000. Publications: Reviews in music journal, Notes, 1985, 1994; Music: Sonorities VI (for Vibraphone), 2004; Sonorities VII (for Clarinet), 2004; Duo (for Piano and Percussion), 2005; 2 recordings. Honours: Meet the Composer awards, 1978, 1982 (2x), 1983, 1991, 1997; Margaret Fairbank-Jory Copying Assistance Program from the American Music Center. Memberships: St Ansgar's Scandinavian Catholic League; St George's Society of New York; American Music Center; Music Library Association (and its New York Chapter); Kosciuszko Foundation. Address: PO Box 36-20548, PABT, New York, NY 10129, USA. E-mail: pathardish@hotmail.com

**HARDWICK David Francis,** b. 24 January 1934, Vancouver, Canada. Pathologist; Professor. m. Margaret M, 1 son, 2 daughters. Education: MD, University of British Columbia, 1950-57. Appointments: Research Associate, Paediatrics, University of Southern California, 1960-62; Clinical Instructor, Pathology, 1963-65, Assistant Professor, Pathology, 1965-69, Associate Professor, Pathology, 1969-74, Professor, Pathology, 1974-99, Professor and Head, Pathology, 1976-90, Honorary Associate Professor, Paediatrics, 1972-87, Honorary Professor, Paediatrics, 1974-99, Special Advisor Planning, Medicine, 1997-, Professor Emeritus, Pathology and Paediatrics, 1999-, University of British Columbia. Publications: Author and co-author of numerous refereed journals; books; chapters; abstracts; reports. Honours include: Certificate of Merit, Master Teacher Awards; University of British Columbia Teaching Excellence Award; Canadian Silver Jubilee Medal, 1978; President's Award for service to the University of British Columbia; LLD honoris causa, University of British Columbia, 2001; Senior Member, Canadian Medical Association, 2002; Gold Medal, International Academy of Pathology, 2002; President's Award, US and Canadian Academy of Pathology, 2004; Bartholomew Mosse Memorial Lecturer, Dublin, 2004. Memberships include: BC Association of Pathologists; Canadian Association of Pathologists; Society for Paediatric Pathology; International Academy of Pathology. Address: Dean's Office, Faculty of Medicine, University of British Columbia, #317-2194 Health Sciences Mall, Vancouver, British Columbia, Canada V6T 1Z3. E-mail: david.f.hardwick@ubc.ca

**HARDWICK Elizabeth,** b. 27 July 1916, Lexington, Kentucky, USA. Writer; Critic; Teacher. m. Robert Lowell, 28 July 1949, divorced 1972, 1 daughter. Education: AB, 1938, MA, 1939, University of Kentucky; Columbia University. Appointments: Co-Founder and Advisory Editor, New York Review of Books, 1963-; Adjunct Associate Professor of English, Barnard College. Publications: Fiction: The Ghostly Lover, 1945; The Simple Truth, 1955; Sleepless Nights, 1979. Non-fiction: The Selected Letters of William James (editor), 1960; A View of My Own: Essays on Literature and Society, 1962; Seduction and Betrayal: Women and Literature, 1974; Rediscovered Fiction by American Women: A Personal Selection (editor), 18 volumes, 1977; Bartleby in Manhattan (essays), 1984; The Best American Essays 1986 (editor), 1986; Sight Readings: American Fictions (essays), 1998; Herman Melville, A Life, 2000. Contributions to: Periodicals. Honour: Gold Medal, American Academy and Institute of Arts and Letters, 1993. Address: 15 West 67th Street, New York, NY 10023, USA.

**HARDY Alan William,** b. 10 March 1951, Luton, Bedfordshire, England. Teacher; Poet. m. Sibylle Mory, 24 August 1985, 1 daughter. Education: BA, English and Italian Literature, 1973, MA, Comparative Literature, 1976, Warwick University; Dip TEFL, Christ Church College, Kent University, 1983. Appointments: English Teacher, Sir Joseph Williamson's Mathematical School, Rochester, Kent; English Language Teacher, Whitehill Estate School of English, Flamstead, Hertfordshire. Publication: Wasted Leaves, 1996. Contributions to: Orbis; Envoi; Iota; Poetry Nottingham; The Interpreter's House; South; Poetic Licence; Braquemard; Fire; Borderlines. Honour: 2nd Prize, Hastings National Poetry Competition, 1994. Address: Whitehill Estate School of English, Flamstead, St Albans, Hertfordshire AL3 8EY, England.

**HARDY Robert,** b. 29 October 1925. Actor; Author. m. (1) Elizabeth Fox, 1 son. (2) Sally Pearson, 2 daughters. Career: Theatre appearances include: 4 seasons of Shakespeare, Stratford-on-Avon, 2 at Old Vic; World tours include Henry V and Hamlet, USA; Numerous appearances London and Broadway theatres, 1952-; Winston Churchill in Celui qui a dit Non, Palais des Congres, Paris, 1999-2000; Writer and/or presenter numerous TV programmes including The Picardy Affair, The History of the Longbow, Heritage, Horses in Our Blood, Gordon of Khartoum; Other TV appearances include: Prince Hal and Henry V in Age of Kings; Prince Albert in Edward VII; Malcolm Campbell in Speed King; Winston Churchill in the Wilderness Years; Siegfried Farnon in All Creatures Great and Small; Twiggy Rathbone and Russell Spam in Hot Metal; The Commandant in the Far Pavilions; Sherlock Holmes; Inspector Morse; Middlemarch; Castle Ghosts; Gulliver's Travels; Films include: How I Won the War; Yellow Dog; Dark Places; Young Winston; Ten Rillington Place; Le Silencieux; Gawain and the Green Knight; The Spy Who Came in From the Cold; La Gifle; Robin Hood; The Shooting Party; Paris By Night; War and Remembrance; Mary Shelley's Frankenstein; Sense and Sensibility; Mrs Dalloway; The Tichborne Claimant, 1998; An Ideal Husband, 1999; The Gathering, 2001; Harry Potter and the Chamber of Secrets, 2002; Harry Potter and the Prisoner of Azkaban, 2004; Harry Potter and the Goblet of Fire, 2005. Publications: Longbow, 1976; The Great War Bow, 2005. Honours: Hon DLitt (Reading), 1990; CBE; FSA. Memberships: Consultant, Mary Rose Trust, 1979-, Trustee, WWF, 1991-; Trustee, Royal Armouries, 1984-96; Master of Worshipful Company of Bowyers, 1988-90. Address: c/o Chatto & Linnit, 123A King's Road,, London, SW3 4PL, England.

**HARE David,** b. 5 June 1947, St Leonards, Sussex, England. Dramatist; Director. m. (1) Margaret Matheson, 1970, divorced 1980, 2 sons, 1 daughter, (2) Nicole Farhi, 1992. Education: Lancing College; MA, Honours, Jesus College, Cambridge. Appointments: Founder, Portable Theatre, 1968, Joint Stock Theatre Group, 1975, Greenpoint Films, 1982; Literary Manager and Resident Dramatist, Royal Court, 1969-71; Resident Dramatist, Nottingham Playhouse, 1973; Associate Director, National Theatre, 1984-88, 1989-. Plays: Slag, 1970; The Great Exhibition, 1972; Knuckle, 1974; Brassneck, 1974; Fanshen, 1976; Teeth 'n' Smiles, 1976; Plenty, 1978; Licking Hitler, 1978; Dreams of Leaving, 1980; A Map of the World, 1982; Saigon, 1983; The History Plays, 1984; Pravda, 1985; Wetherby, 1985; The Asian Plays, 1986; The Bay at Nice and Wrecked Eggs, 1986; The Secret Rapture, 1988; Paris by Night, 1989; Straples, 1990; Racing Demon, 1990; Writing Lefthanded, 1991; Heading Home, 1991; The Early Plays, 1991; Murmuring Judges, 1991; The Absence of War, 1993; Asking Around, 1993; Skylight, 1995; Mother Courage, 1995; Skylight, 1995; Ivanov, 1996; Amy's View, 1997; The Judas Kiss, 1998; The Blue Room, 1998; Via Dolorosa, 1998; My Zinc Bed, 2000; Royal Court, 2000; Via Dolorosa, 2000; The Hours, 2001; Lee Miller, 2001. Honours: John Llewellyn Rhys Award, 1974; BAFTA Award, 1978; New York Drama Critics' Circle Award, 1983; London Standard Award, 1985; Plays and Players Awards, 1985, 1990; Drama Award, 1988; Olivier Award, 1990; Critic's Circle Best Play of the Year, 1990; Time Out Award, 1990. Membership: Royal Society of Literature, fellow.

**HARE John Neville,** b. 11 December 1934, Bexhill, England. Explorer; Writer. m. Philippa, 3 daughters. Education: ABU, University of Zaria, Nigeria, 1957; Diploma, Administration/Law. Appointments: District Officer, Colonial Service, Northern Nigeria, 1957-64; Director, Macmillan Publishers, 1965-75; Consultant, Hodder and Stoughton Publishers, 1975-89; United National Environment Programme, 1989-96; Founder, Wild Camel Protection Foundation, 1996-. Publications: The Lost Camels of Tartary, 1998; Shadows Across the Sahara, 2003; 32 books for children on environmental issues; Over 50 articles on the wild Bactrian camel and expeditions in the Gobi and Saharan Deserts. Honours: Ness Award, Royal Geographical Society, 2004; Lawrence of Arabia Memorial Medal, Royal Society of Asian Affairs, 2004. Memberships: Reform Club; Muthaiga Club, Nairobi. Address: School Farm, Benenden, Kent TN17 4EU, England. E-mail: harecamel@aol.com Website: www.wildcamels.com

**HAREWOOD The Earl of (George Henry Hubert Lascelles),** b. 7 February 1923, London, England. Musical Administrator. m. (1) Maria Donata Stein, 1949, divorced 1967, 3 sons, (2) Patricia Tuckwell, 1967, 1 son. Education: King's College, Cambridge University. Career includes: Board Directors, 1951-53, 1969-72, Administrative Executive, 1953-60, Royal Opera House, Covent Garden, London; Chairman, British Council Music Advisory Committee; Director General, 1958-74, Chairman, 1988-90, Leeds Musical Festival; Artistic Director,

Edinburgh International Festival, 1961-65; Arts Council Music Panel, 1966-72; Artistic Advisor, New Philharmonia Orchestra, 1966-76; General Advisory Council, BBC, 1969-77; Managing Director, Sadler's Wells Opera, 1972; Managing Director, 1974-85, Chairman, 1986-95, English National Opera; Governor of BBC, 1985-87; President, British Board of Film Classification, 1985-96; Artistic Director, Adelaide Festival, 1988; Artistic Advisor, Buxton Festival, 1993-98. Publications: Editor, Opera, 1950-53; Editor and compiler, Kobbé's Complete Opera Book, 1954, 1973, 1987, 1989, 1997; Autobiography, The Tongs and The Bones, 1982; Kobbé's Illustrated Opera Book, 1989; Pocket Kobbé, 1994. Honours include: KBE, 1987. Address: Harewood House, Leeds, LS17 9LG, England.

**HARJO Joy,** b. 9 May 1951, Tulsa, Oklahoma, USA. 1 son, 1 daughter. Education: BA, University of New Mexico 1976; MFA, University of Iowa, 1978; Non-degree, Film-making, Anthropology, Film Centre, 1982; Native Screenwriters Workshop, Sundance Institute, 1998; Summer Songwriting Workshop, Berklee School of Music, 1998. Appointments: Assistant Professor, Department of English, University of Colorado, 1985-88; Associate Professor, Department of English, University of Arizona, 1988-90; Professor, Department of English, University of New Mexico, 1991-97; President, Mekko Rabbit Production Inc, 1992-; Visiting Writer, UCLA Department of English, 1998; Professor, UCLA, 2001-. Publications: She Had Some Horses, 1985; Secrets from the Centre of the World, 1989; In Mad Love & War, 1990; The Woman Who Fell From the Sky, 1994; Reinventing the Enemy's Language; A Map To The Next World, poems and tales, 2000; The Good Luck Cat, children's book, 2000; How We Became Human, New and Selected Poems, W W Norton, 2002; CD: Native Joy for Real, Joy Harjo, Mekko Prod; CD: Letter from the End of the 20th Century, music and poetry with her band Joy Harjo and Poetic Justice, 1997. Honours: National Council on the Arts; The London Observer Best Book of 1997 (Reinventing the Enemy's Language); Lila Wallace Reader's Digest Writers Award, 1998-2000; Honorary Doctorate, St Mary-in-the-Woods College, 1998; First American in the Arts, Outstanding Medal of Achievement, 1998; Lifetime Achievement in the Arts, National Writers Circle of America; Western Literature Distinguished Achievement Award, 2000; Oklahoma Book Arts Lifetime Achievement, 2002. Membership: Board of Directors, Russell Moore Foundation; Board of Directors, Arts Research. Address: Mekko Productions Inc, 1140 D Alewa Drive, Honolulu, HI 96817, USA.

**HARNICK Sheldon Mayer,** b. 30 April 1924, Chicago, Illinois, USA. Lyricist. m. (1) Mary Boatner, 1950, (2) Elaine May, 1962, (3) Margery Gray, 1965, 1 son, 1 daughter. Education: Northwestern University. Career: Contributor to revues: New Faces of 1952; Two's Company, 1953; John Murray Anderson's Almanac, 1954; The Shoestring Revue, 1955; The Littlest Revue, 1956; Shoestring 1957, 1957; with composer Jerry Bock: Body Beautiful, 1958; Fiorello, 1959; Tenderloin, 1960; Smiling The Boy Fell Dead (with David Baker), 1961; She Loves Me, 1963; Fiddler On The Roof, 1964; The Apple Tree, 1966; The Rothschilds, 1970; Captain Jinks Of The Horse Marines (opera with Jack Beeson), 1975; Rex (with Richard Rodgers), 1976; Dr Heidegger's Fountain Of Youth (opera with Jack Beeson), 1978; Gold (cantata with Joe Raposo), 1980; Translations: The Merry Widow, 1977; The Umbrellas Of Cherbourg, 1979; Carmen, 1981; A Christmas Carol, 1981; Songs Of The Auvergne (musical; book; lyrics), 1982; The Appeasement of Aeolus, 1990; Cyrano, 1994. Address: Kraft, Haiken & Bell, 551 Fifth Avenue, 9th Floor, New York, NY 10176, USA.

**HARRELSON Woody,** b. 23 July 1961, Midland, Texas, USA. Actor. m. Laura Louie, 1997, 1 child. Education: Hanover College. Career: Theatre includes: The Boys Next Door; 2 on 2 (author, producer, actor); The Zoo Story (author, actor); Brooklyn Laundry; Furthest from the Sun; On An Average Day; TV includes: Cheers; Bay Coven; Killer Instinct; Films include: Wildcats; Cool Blue; LA Story; Doc Hollywood; Ted and Venus; White Men Can't Jump; Indecent Proposal; I'll Do Anything; The Cowboy Way; Natural Born Killers; Money Train; The Sunchaser; The People vs Larry Flint; Kingpin; Wag the Dog, 1997; The Thin Red Line, 1998; EdTV, 1999; Play It to the Bone, 2000; American Saint, 2000. Address: c/o Creative Artists Agency, 9830 Wilshire Boulevard, Beverly Hills, CA 90212, USA.

**HARRIS Alfred,** b. 21 July 1930, London, England. Artist. m. Carmel, 1 son, 2 daughters. Education: Intermediate Arts, Willesden School of Art, 1947-49, 1950-52; ARCA, Royal College of Art, 1952-55. Appointments: Senior Lecturer (retired), University of London, Institute of Education; Chairman, Department of Art and Design; Exhibitions include: New Art Centre London; Beaux Arts Gallery, London; Grosvenor Gallery, London; Ben Uri Gallery, London; Falum Museum, Sweden; Orerro Museum, Sweden; Dalarnas Museum, Sweden; Royal College of Art, London; Tate Gallery, London. Honours: Elected Member, The London Group; Elected Member, Royal West of England Academy; Elected Fellow, Royal Society of Arts. Address: 70 Camden Mews, London NW1 9BX, England.

**HARRIS Angela Felicity (Baroness Harris of Richmond),** b. 4 January 1944, St Annes-on-Sea, Lancashire, England. Member of the House of Lords. m. John Philip Roger Harris, 1 son from previous marriage. Education: Ealing Hotel and Catering College. Appointments: Member, Richmond Town Council, 1978-81, 1991-99, Mayor of Richmond, 1993-94; Member, 1979-89, Chairman, 1987-88, Richmondshire District Council; Member, 1981-2001, First Woman Chair, 1991-92, North Yorkshire County Council; Deputy Chair, Association of Police Authorities, 1997-2001; Chair, North Yorkshire Police Authority, 1994-2001; Appointed to House of Lords, 1999; Member, Refreshment Select Committee, 2000-, Member, EU Select Committee, 2000-04, Chair, EU Select Sub-Committee, 2000-04, House of Lords. Honours: Deputy Lieutenant of North Yorkshire, 1994; Created Liberal Democrat Life Peer, 1999. Memberships: Member, Court of the University of York, 1996-; Former Member: Service Authority, national Crime Squad, 1997-2000, Police Negotiating Board, 1995-2001; Former Justice of the Peace, 1982-98; Former, NHS Trust Non-Executive Director, 1990-97; President, National Association of Chaplains to the Police. Address: House of Lords, London, SW1A 0PW. E-mail: harrisa@parliament.uk

**HARRIS Edward Allen (Ed),** b. 28 November 1950, Englewood, New Jersey, USA. Actor. m. Amy Madigan. Education: Columbia University; University of Oklahoma, Norman; California Institute of Arts. Career: Stage appearances include: A Streetcar Named Desire; Sweetbird of Youth; Julius Caesar; Hamlet; Camelot; Time of Your Life; Grapes of Wrath; Present Laughter; Fool for Love; Prairie Avenue; Scar, 1985; Precious Sons, 1986; Simpatico, 1994; Taking Sides, 1996; Films include: Come, 1978; Borderline, 1978; Knightriders, 1980; Creepshow, 1981; The Right Stuff, 1982; Swing Shift, 1982; Under Fire, 1982; A Flash of Green, 1983; Places in the Heart, 1983; Alamo Bay, 1984; Sweet Dreams, 1985; Code Name: Emerald, 1985; Walker, 1987; To Kill a Priest, 1988; Jacknife, 1989; The Abyss, 1989; State of Grace, 1990; Paris Trout, 1991; Glengarry Glen Ross, 1992; Needful Things, 1993;

The Firm, 1993; China Moon, 1994; Milk Money, 1994; Apollo 13, 1995; Just Cause, 1995; Eye for an Eye, 1995; The Rock, 1996; Riders of the Purple Sage, 1996; Absolute Power, 1997; Stepmom, 1998; The Truman Show, 1998; The Third Miracles, 1999; Enemy at the Gates, 2001; A Beautiful Mind, 2001; The Hours, 2002; TV films include: The Amazing Howard Hughes, 1977; The Seekers, 1979; The Aliens are Coming, 1980; The Last Innocent Man, 1987; Running Mates, 1992; The Stand, 1994. Address: 22031 Carbon Mesa Road, Malibu, CA 90265, USA.

**HARRIS John Eric,** b. 29 April 1932, London, England. Company Director. m. Jacqueline, 1 son, 1 daughter. Education: Plaistow Grammar School, 1943-45; Slough Grammar School, 1945-48. Appointments: Managing Director, Harris Overseas Ltd, 1963-82; Chairman, Harvard International Ltd, 1982-, Chairman, Alba plc, 1982; Chairman, Bush Radio plc, 1988; Chairman, Goodman's Industries Ltd, Director, Roadstar (Swiss), 1997-; Director, Grundig Multi-Media BV, 2004-. Publications: Ovarian Cancer I, II, III, IV, V (as Founder Chairman Helene Harris Memorial Trust). Honours: MBE; Honorary Member, British Gynaecological Cancer Society; CBE, 2005; International Gynaecological Society Special Award, 2004. Memberships: CBI; British Gynaecological Cancer Society; Reform Club; Marks Club. Address: Harvard House, 14 Thames Road, Barking, Essex, IG11 0HX, England. E-mail: harrisje@albaplc.co.uk

**HARRIS Marion Rose, (Rose Glendower, Marion Rose),** b. 12 July 1925, Cardiff, South Wales. Author. m. Kenneth Mackenzie Harris, 18 August 1943, 2 sons, 1 daughter. Appointments: Editor/Owner, Regional Feature Service, 1964-74; Editorial Controller, W Foulsham and Co Ltd, 1974-82. Publications: Captain of Her Heart, 1976, large print edition, 2000; Just a Handsome Stranger, 1983; The Queen's Windsor, 1985; Soldiers' Wives, 1986; Officers' Ladies, 1987; Nesta, 1988, large print edition, 1999; Amelda, 1989, large print edition, 1999; Sighing for the Moon, 1991, large print edition, 1999; To Love and Love Again (as Rose Young), 1993; Writing as Rosie Harris: Turn of the Tide, 2002; Troubled Waters, 2002; Patsy of Paradise Place, 2003; One Step Forward, 2003; Looking for Love, 2003; Pins & Needles, 2004; Winnie of the Waterfront, 2004; At Sixes & Sevens, 2005; The Cobblers Kids, 2005; Sunshine & Showers, 2005; Megan of Merseyside, 2006; The Power of Dreams, 2006. Memberships: Society of Authors; Romantic Novelists Association; Welsh Academy. Address: Walpole Cottage, Long Drive, Burnham, Slough SL1 8AJ, England.

**HARRIS Nigel Henry,** b. 11 July 1924, Grimsby, England. Orthopaedic Surgeon. m. Elizabeth, 2 sons. Education: MA, MB, BChir, FRCS, Trinity College, Cambridge and Middlesex Hospital. Appointments: National Service, RAF, 1949-52; House Surgeon: Orthopaedic Department, Middlesex Hospital, 1947, North Middlesex Hospital, 1952-53, in charge of Casualty and Registrar to Orthopaedic Department, King Edward Memorial Hospital Ealing, 1953-55; Surgical Registrar: Mile End Hospital, 1955-56, Fulham Hospital, 1958-59; Registrar,1959-60, Senior Registrar, 1960, Royal National Orthopaedic Hospital; Consultant Orthopaedic Surgeon: Thames Group of Hospitals, 1963, St Mary's Hospital London and the London Foot Hospital, 1964-90; Assistant Honorary Orthopaedic Surgeon, Hospital for Sick Children, Ormond Street, 1964-87; Honorary Consultant Orthopaedic Surgeon, St Mary's Hospital (after retirement from the NHS, 1990); Currently Private Consultant in Orthopaedic Practice and in Medico-Legal Practice; Expert Witness for clinical negligence and personal injury; Former Orthopaedic Surgeon to The

Football Association and Arsenal Football Club; Medical Examiner for Football League Underwriters. Publications: Postgraduate Textbook of Clinical Orthopaedics (editor), 1984, 2nd edition, 1995; Medical Negligence (joint editor), 1990, 2nd edition, 1994, renamed, Clinical Negligence, 3rd edition, 2000; Numerous articles in medical journals. Honours: European Travelling Scholar, 1962; Geigy Scholar, 1967. Memberships: Fellow, British Orthopaedic Association; Fellow, Royal Society of Medicine; British Orthopaedic Research Society; Hospital Consultants and Specialists Association; Medico-Legal Society; Fellow, Member of Council, British Academy of Experts; Chartered Institute of Arbitrators. Address: 14 Ashworth Road, London W9, England.

**HARRIS Robert Sidney,** b. 30 March 1951, London, England. Engineer. m. Beverely, 1 son, 2 daughters. Education: BSc (Eng) 1st Class Honours, Electrical Engineering, Imperial College, London, 1969-72. Appointments include: Designer, 1972-74, Project Leader on ESTEC Contracts, 1975-79, BAC Bristol, UK; AOCS Group Leader, ESTEC Group Leader, 1980, AOCS Systems Engineer, responsible for design and analysis of L-SAT AOCS work, 1981-82, Design Manager, Hipparcos power subsystem, harness subsysem and AOCS, 1982-87; Proposal preparation for STSP missions, 1987-89, Design Manager for STSP activities (SOHO APCS, CLUSTER AOCS, CLUSTER reaction control subsystem), 1989-94, BAe, Bristol, UK; Design Manager for Integral AOCS, 1997-99, Design Manager of XMM AOCS, 1994-99, Member of SOHO recovery team following the temporary loss of the spacecraft, 1998. Member of SOHO "tiger team", 1998, part of recovery team at NASA leading to a successful transition back to full operations, 1998-99, MMS Bristol, UK; Senior Principal Consultant, working on systems, AOCMS, RCS and operations activities for the Rosetta spacecraft, 1999-2003, working on design and operations for the control system of the GOCE spacecraft, Phase A design for the GAIA spacecraft, supporting launch campaign and post-launch activities for the Rosetta spacecraft at ESOC, 2003-2004, RHEA Systems SA, Louvain-La-Neuve (located at Astrium GmbH, Friedrichshafen, Germany). Publications: Numerous technical reports supporting the design development and operations of the various spacecraft attitude and orbit control systems. Honours: Sylvanus P Thompson Award for achieving the top degree in electrical engineering and electronics, 1972; MBE for contribution to the recovery of the SOHO spacecraft, 2000; Laurels for Team Achievement Award (jointly), International Academy of Astronautics, 2003. Memberships: Associate, City and Guilds Institute; Institute of Electrical Engineers. Address: Hoher Weg 50, 88048 Friedrichshafen, Germany. E-mail: family.harris@t-online.de

**HARRIS Rolf,** b. 30 March 1930, Perth, Australia. Entertainer; Singer; Musician (piano, accordion, digeridoo, wobbleboard); Artist. m. Alwen Myfanwy Wiseman Hughes, 1 March 1958, 1 daughter. Education: West Australian University. Musical Education: Piano Grade 1, AMEB. Career: International television entertainer, artist and host, Cartoon Time; Animal Hospital; Exhibition, Rolf on Art, National Gallery, London, 2002. Recordings: Numerous singles include: Tie Me Kangaroo Down Sport; Jake The Peg; Two Little Boys; Stairway To Heaven; Sun Arise; The Court of King Caractacus. Publications: 12 titles including: How To Write Your Own Pop Song; Can You Tell What It Is Yet?, autobiography. Honours: OBE; AM. Membership: Equity. Address: c/o 174-178 North Gower Street, London NW1 2NB, England.

**HARRIS Rosemary,** b. Ashby, Suffolk, England. Actor. m. John Ehle, 1 daughter. Education: Bancroft Gold Medal, Royal Academy of Dramatic Art, 1952. Career: Bristol Old

Vic; London Old Vic; Chichester Festival Theatre; National Theatre at the Old Vic; West End: Seven Year Itch; Plaza Suite; All My Sons; Heartbreak House; The Petition; Best of Friends; Steel Magnolias; National Theatre: Women of Troy; Broadway: Lion in Winter; A Street Car Named Desire; Hay Fever; An Inspector Calls; A Delicate Balance; Films: Tom & Viv; Sunshine; Spiderman; Spiderman Two. Honours: Evening Standard Award; Golden Globe Award; Emmy Award; Tony Award; Academy Award Nomination. Address: c/o ICM Ltd; 76 Oxford Street, London W1N 0AX, England.

**HARRIS Thomas,** b. 1940, Jackson, Tennessee, USA. Writer. m. divorced, 1 daughter. Education: Baylor University, Texas, USA. Appointments: Worked on newsdesk Waco News-Tribune; Member, Staff, Associated Press, New York. Publications: Black Sunday; Red Dragon (filmed as Manhunter); The Silence of the Lambs (filmed). Address: St Martin's Press, 175 Fifth Avenue, New York, NY 10010, USA.

**HARRISON David,** b. 9 April 1957, Liverpool, England. Journalist. m. Linda Elizabeth Harrison, 2 sons. Education: Open Exhibition, BA, Honours, MA, Modern Languages, Pembroke College, Oxford; Speaks French, Spanish and Mandarin. Appointments: The China Daily, Beijing, 1983-84; Foreign Desk, Sub-Editor Home and Foreign, The Daily Telegraph, 1985-90; News Editor, The European, 1990; Senior Reporter, Home and Foreign, The Observer, 1990; War Correspondent, Iraq, Afghanistan, Kosovo, Environment and Transport Correspondent, 1991-98, Senior Correspondent, 1999-, The Sunday Telegraph. Publications: Numerous articles in a number of national newspapers and magazines. Honours: Oxford Blue, Football; Amnesty International Press Award, 1997. Membership: Frontline Club, London. Address: c/o The Sunday Telegraph, 1 Canada Square, Canary Wharf, London E14 5DT, England. E-mail: david.harrison@telegraph.co.uk

**HARRISON Derek,** b. 5 January 1929, Oswaldtwistle, Lancashire, England. Retired Personal Care Industry Executive; Inventor; Journalist. m. Joyce (Joy) Alice Whitaker, 1 son, 1 daughter. Education: Regional College of Art, 1947-52; Manchester University, 1947-52. Appointments: Assistant Manager, 1955-57, Manager, 1957-71, Principal, 1971-, retired 1986, Consultant, 1986-, Moorside Laundry, Swinton, Manchester; Chairman, 1996-99, Vice-President, 1999-, Manchester Branch, Institute of Management; Member, Trafford Park Quality Forum, 1994; Laundry Wages Council, 1972-88; National Executive Council, Association of British Laundry, Cleaning and Rental Services, 1984-87; Chairman, British Diabetic Association (Salford), 1995-2000; Life Member, Diabetes UK; Member, Executive Council, Manchester Chamber of Trade and Industry, 1996; Governor, Registrar, Bridgewater School, Worsley, 1971, 1972, 1973, 1974; Liveryman, Worshipful Company of Launderers, London, 1980; Senior Lecturer, Hollings College, Manchester, 1962. Publications: Patentee in field. Honours: Drummond Cup, University of Manchester, 1947, 1948; Recipient, Freedom of the City of London, 1979; Ernest Albinson Award for journalism, Guild of Cleaners and Launderers, 1999, 2002. Memberships: Life Member, City Livery Club; Manchester University Motor Club, Vice-President, 1969-70; Guild of Cleaners and Launderers, Honorary Vice-President, 1978, 2000, Deputy Master, College of Fellows, 1989-; Honorary Life Member, Automobile Association. Address: 5 Woodlands Avenue, Swinton, Manchester M27 0DJ, England.

**HARRISON John,** b. 12 November 1944, Stockton-on-Tees, England. Chartered Accountant. m. Patricia Alice Bridget, 1 son, 2 daughters. Education: BA Honours, Economics, Sheffield

University; FCA. Appointments: Articled Clerk, Coopers & Lybrand, 1963-67; Corporate Planner, Tillotson, 1967-70; Partner, DeLoitte & Touche, 1970-2001; Chairman, Portal Ltd, 2001-; Chairman, Spring Grove plc, 2002-. Membership: FRSA. Address: Goodwin Manor, Swaffham Prior, Cambridge CB5 0LG, England. E-mail: john.harrison@swaffham.demon.co.uk

**HARRISON Kenneth Cecil,** b. 29 April 1915, Hyde, Cheshire, England. Librarian; Writer. m. Doris Taylor, 2 sons. Appointments include: Army Service WWII, 1940-46; Rank of Major, 1944-46; Borough Librarian of Hyde and Glossop, 1939-47; Borough Librarian and Curator of Hove, 1947-50; Borough Librarian of Eastbourne, 1950-58; Borough Librarian and Curator of Hendon, 1958-61; City Librarian of Westminster, 1961-80; British Council Cultural Exchange Scholar to Romania, 1972; British Council Visitor to Trinidad & Tobago, 1973; British Council Library Advisor to Sri Lanka, 1974; UNESCO Library Adviser to Seychelles and Mauritius, 1977-78; Consultant to Combridge, Jackson International, 1980-82; Library Consultant to the Government of Bermuda, 1984; Library study tours to 44 countries; Presidencies include: Library Association, 1973, Commonwealth Library Association, 1972-75, Association of Chief Librarians, 1969-70; Lecturer in field. Publications include: First Steps in Librarianship, 1950, 5th edition, 1980; Libraries in Scandinavia, 1961, 2nd edition, 1969; Public Libraries Today, 1963; The Library and the Community, 1963, 3rd edition, 1977; Facts at Your Fingertips, 1964, 2nd edition, 1966; Libraries in Britain, 1968; Public Relations for Librarians, 1973, 2nd edition, 1981; Public Library Buildings, 1975-1983 (editor), 1987; International Librarianship, 1989; Library Buildings, 1984-1989 (editor), 1990; A Librarian's Odyssey: episodes of autobiography, 2000; Contributions to newspapers, journals and encyclopaedias. Honours: Fellow of the Library Association (FLA), 1938; MBE (Mil), 1946; OBE, 1980; Knight, First Class, of the Order of the Lion, Finland, 1976; Gold Badge of Merit, Finnish Library Association, 1980; Honorary Life Member, Malta Library and Information Association, 1986; Honorary Member, Zambia Library Association; Listed in Who's Who publications and biographical dictionaries. Memberships include: Council of the Library Association, 1953, 1957-79; IFLA Public Libraries Committee, 1970-81; National Book League Executive Committee, 1969-75; Governing Body, Paddington Institute, 1973-77; Sussex County Cricket Club Committee, 1953-58; Westminster Abbey Library Committee, 1973-80; MCC Arts and Library Committee, 1974-89; Council of the Association of Past Rotarians, 1996-2004; Trustee, Library Association Benevolent Fund, 1983-97. Address: 5, Tavistock, Devonshire Place, Eastbourne, East Sussex BN21 4AG, England. E-mail: kcharrison88@hotmail.com

**HARRISS-WHITE Barbara,** b. 4 February 1946, Westminster, England. Academic. 2 daughters. Education: BA, MA, Geography, 1968, Diploma, Agricultural Science, 1969, University of Cambridge; PhD, Development Studies, University of East Anglia, 1977. Appointments: Research Officer, Centre of South Asia Studies, Cambridge, 1972-77; Research Associate, Overseas Development Institute, London, 1977-81; Research Fellow, London School of Hygiene and Tropical Medicine, 1981-97; University Lecturer in Agricultural Economics, 1987-96, Reader in Development Studies, 1996, Professor of Development Studies, 1998, Director, Queen Elizabeth House International Development Centre, 2004-, University of Oxford. Publications: 15 authored books, 10 edited books, 11 research reports and 174 papers and chapters; Illfare in India, 1999; Outcast from Social Welfare: Adult Disability in Rural South India, 2002; India Working, 2003; Rural India Facing the 21st Century, 2004. Honours: Cambridge University

Smuts Memorial Commonwealth Lecturer, 1998-99; Asian Development Research Institute Foundation Lecturer, 2002; Radhakamal Mukherjee Lecturer, Indian Society of Labour Economics, 2003; Honorary Research Fellow, Ecole des Hautes Etudes en Sciences Sociales, Paris, 2004. Memberships: Development Studies Association; British Association of South Asian Studies; Alpine Club. Address: Queen Elizabeth House, 21 St Giles, Oxford OX1 3LA, England. E-mail: barbara.harriss @qeh.ox.ac.uk Website: www.qeh.ox.ac.uk/

**HARRY Deborah Ann,** b. 1 July 1945, Miami, Florida, USA. Singer; Songwriter; Actress. Career: Former Playboy bunny waitress; Singer, groups: Wind In The Willows; The Stilettos; Founder, Blondie, 1974-83; Appearances include: New York punk club, CBGBs, 1974; Support to Iggy Pop, US, 1977; Solo recording career, 1981-; Actress, films including: Blank Generation, 1978; The Foreigner, 1978; Union City, 1979; Roadie, 1980; Videodrome; Hairspray; The Killbillies; Tales from the Darkside: The Movie, 1990; Intimate Stranger, 1991; Joe's Day, 1999; 200, 1999; Six Ways to Sunday, 1999; Ghost Light, 2000; Dueces Wild, 2000; Red Lipstick, 2000; TV appearances: Saturday Night Life; The Muppet Show; Tales from the Darkside; Wiseguys; Theatre: Teaneck Tanzi; The Venus Flytrap; Recordings: Hit singles: with Blondie: Denis (Denee), 1978; (I'm Always Touched By Your) Presence Dear, 1978; Picture This, 1978; Hanging On The Telephone, 1978; Heart Of Glass (Number 1, UK), 1979; Sunday Girl (Number 1, UK), 1979; Dreaming, 1979; Union City Blue, 1979; Call Me (Number 1, US and UK), 1980; Atomic, 1980; The Tide Is High (Number 1, UK and US), 1980; Rapture (Number 1, US), 1981; Island Of Lost Souls, 1982; Solo: Backfired, 1981; French Kissin' (In The USA), 1986; I Want That Man, 1989; I Can See Clearly, 1993; Albums with Blondie: Blondie, 1976; Plastic Letters, 1978; Parallel Lines (Number 1, US), 1978; Eat To The Beat (Number 1, UK), 1979; Autoamerican, 1980; The Best Of Blondie, 1981; The Hunter, 1982; Solo albums: Koo Koo, 1981; Rockbird, 1986; Def, Dumb And Blonde, 1989; Debravation, 1993; Compilations: Once More Into The Bleach, 1988; The Complete Picture, 1991; Blonde And Beyond, 1993; Rapture, 1994; Virtuosity, 1995; Rockbird, 1996; Der Einziger Weg, 1999; Contributor, film soundtracks: American Gigolo, 1980; Roadie, 1980; Scarface; Krush Groove, 1984. Publications: Making Tracks - The Rise Of Blondie (co-written with Chris Stein), 1982. Memberships: ASCAP; AFTRA; Equity; Screen Actors Guild. Current Management: Overland Productions, 156 W 56th Street, 5th Floor, New York, NY 10019, USA.

**HARSH Shri,** b. 1 July 1957, Jaunpur, UP, India. Scientist. m. Usha Sharma, 1 son, 1 daughter. Education: BSc (Hons), 1977, MSc, 1979, Chemistry, Aligarh Muslim University; PhD, Chemistry, IIT, Delhi, 1986. Appointments: Deputy Manager, 1986-94, Manager, 1994-2000, Group Manager, 2000, National Council for Cement and Building Materials. Publications: 14 papers in professional journals; 2 patents; 1 book. Honours: Best Scientist Award, National Council for Cement and Building Materials, 2000. Address: D-203, NCB Colony, Sector 7D, Faridabad, PIN-121006, India.

**HART Pamela Walker,** b. Jacksonville, Florida, USA. Artist; Writer; Educator. m. Donald Hart. Education: BA, Fashion Merchandising, Florida State University; BS, Art Education, University of Nebraska at Omaha; MS Education, Elmira College, New York. Appointments: Department Manager, Maas Brothers Department Stores, Florida, 1965-68; Office Manager, Cole of California, Regional Office, Atlanta, Georgia, 1968-70; Human Resources Management Officer, United States Air Force, 1970-74; Visual Arts Educator, K-12 Public Schools, Nebraska, Wisconsin, New York, 1978-89;

Professional Artist, Speaker, Writer, Westernville, New York, 1989-; Commissioner, Commission of the Arts, Rome, New York, 2005. Publications: The Best of Sketching and Drawing, 1999; Cover Art: Fearless Through Fire "Women in Motion", 2004; Artwork and article, Inspiration in snow country "Women in Motion", 2004; The Art of Layering: Making Connections, 2004; Artist and author, Mother Wisdom, 2004; Speaker Presentations: Landscape-based abstractions, 2001; Inner Voice/Artistic Choice, 2001; Represented in: Library of the National Museum of Women in the Arts, Washington DC; Numerous private and public collections, United States and Canada. Honours include: Master's Award, Watercolour, Uttica Art Association, Tri-County Regional, Marcy, New York, 1995; First Prize, Watercolour, State University of New York, Uttica/Rome Campus, New York, 1995; Special Recognition Award, Rome Art Association Regional, Rome, New York, 1997; First Prize, Acrylic, Mowhawk Valley Centre for the Arts, Little Falls, New York, 1997; First Prize, Acrylic, State University of New York, Uttica/Rome Campus, 1999; Merit Award, Watermedia, East Washington Watercolor Society National, Richland, Washington, 1999; Adolph and Clara Obrig Prize for a watercolour by and American artist, National Academy of Design, New York, 2000; Prize for Watermedia, 66th National Exhibition, Art Association Galleries, Cooperstown, New York, 2001. Memberships: Elected Member: National Association of Women Artists, Society of Layerists in Multimedia, Central New York Watercolor Society; National League of American Pen Women; Charter Member: National Museum of Women in the Arts, National Women's History Museum.

**HART Raymond Kenneth,** b. 15 February 1928, Newcastle, New South Wales, Australia. Forensic Metallurgist. m. Betty Joyce Hart, 1 son, 1 daughter. Education: ASTC, Sydney Technical College, 1949; DIC, Imperial College, London, 1952; PhD, Metallurgy, University of Cambridge, 1955; JD, Kennedy Western University, 1991. Appointments: Scientific Officer, Aeronautical Research Laboratories, Melbourne, Victoria, 1955-58; Senior Scientist, Argonne National Laboratory, Illinois, USA, 1958-70; Principal Research Scientist, Georgia Institute of Technology, 1970-74; President, Pasat Research Association Inc, 1974-90; Consultant Metallurgist, Raymond K Hart Ltd, Atlanta, Georgia, 1991. Publications: 22 refereed scientific texts; 5 chapters in technical books; 41 presentations at professional meetings; 400 sworn depositions; 100 trial testimonies. Honours include: NASA Certificate of Recognition, 1976; President's Award, Midwest Society of Electronic Microscopy, 1986; Distinguished Scientist Award, Southeastern Microscopy Society, 1993; Morton D Maser Distinguished Service Award, Microscopy Society of America, 1995; Elected to Guild of Benefactors, Corpus Christi College, Cambridge, 1996; International Order of Merit, IBC, 2000; American Medal of Honor, ABI, 2001; Engineering Sciences Section's Founders Award, American Academy of Forensic Sciences, 2002. Memberships: Fellow, American Academy of Forensic Science; Honorary Life Fellow, Royal Australian Chemistry Institute; American Society of Metals, International Branch; American Physical Society; Microscopy Society of America; Sigma Xi. Address: 145 Grogans Lake Drive, Atlanta, GA 30350-3115, USA. E-mail: r_bhart@comcast.net

**HART William R,** b. 26 October 1940, Flint Michigan, USA; Physician; Pathologist. Education: College of Literature Science and the Arts, University of Michigan, Ann Arbor, 1958-61; MD cum laude, University of Michigan Medical School, 1961-65; Rotating Internship, Highland-Alameda County Hospital, Oakland, California, 1965-66; Residency, Anatomic and Clinical Pathology, The University of Michigan Medical Center and Affiliated Hospitals, 1966-70. Appointments: Military Service, Major MC, United States Army, 1970-72; University Faculty Appointments: Assistant Professor of Pathology and Chief, Section of Gynaecologic Pathology, University of Southern California, 1972-74; Assistant Professor of Pathology, 1974-75, Associate Professor of Pathology (with tenure), 1975-89, Professor of Pathology (with tenure), The University of Michigan Medical School; Professor of Pathology, The Ohio State University College of Medicine, 1997-; Professor and Chairman, Department of Pathology, The Cleveland Clinic, Lerner College of Medicine of Case Western Reserve University, 2003-; Hospital and Administrative Appointments include: Chairman, Department of Anatomic Pathology, 1981-92, Vice-Chairman, 1985-92, Chairman, 1992-, Division of Pathology and Laboratory Medicine, Director of Clinical Laboratories, 1992-, Acting Chair, Department of Regional Pathology Practice, 1997-, The Cleveland Clinic Foundation, Cleveland Ohio, USA. Publications: Over 100 articles in professional medical journals; 6 book chapters and monographs; 50 abstracts; Over 160 scientific presentations. Honours include: The Commissioners' Medal, Commission on Continuing Education, American Society of Clinical Pathologists, 1989; Recognition Award, United States and Canadian Academy of Pathology, 1992; 31st Annual Memorial Lecturer, Los Angeles Society of Pathologists, 1996; The Sixteenth Walter G J Putschar Lecturer, Massachusetts General Hospital, 1999. Memberships include: Alpha Omega Alpha; Fellow, American Society of Clinical Pathologists; Fellow, College of American Pathologists; International Society of Gynaecological Pathologists; United States and Canadian Academy of Pathology. Address: Cleveland Clinic Foundation, Pathology and Laboratory Medicine, l-21 9500 Euclid Avenue, Cleveland, OH 44195, USA.

**HART-DAVIS Duff,** b. 3 June 1936, London, England. Author. Education: BA, Oxford University, 1960. Appointments: Feature Writer, 1972-76, Literary Editor, 1976-77, Assistant Editor, 1977-78, Sunday Telegraph, London; Country Columnist, Independent, 1986-2001. Publications: The Megacull, 1968; The Gold of St Matthew (in USA as The Gold Trackers), 1968; Spider in the Morning, 1972; Ascension: The Story of a South Atlantic Island, 1972; Peter Fleming (biography), 1974; Monarchs of the Glen, 1978; The Heights of Rimring, 1980; Fighter Pilot (with C Strong), 1981; Level Five, 1982; Fire Falcon, 1984; The Man-Eater of Jassapur, 1985; Hitler's Games, 1986; Armada, 1988; The House the Berrys Built, 1990; Horses of War, 1991; Country Matters, 1991; Wildings: The Secret Garden of Eileen Soper, 1992; Further Country Matters, 1993; When the Country Went to Town, 1997; Raoul Millais, 1998; Fauna Britannica, 2003; Audubon's Elephant, 2004. Address: Owlpen Farm, Uley, Dursley, Gloucestershire GL11 5BZ, England.

**HART-DYKE David,** b. 3 October 1938, Havant, Hampshire, England. Retired Naval Officer. m. Diana Luce, 1967, 2 daughters. Education: St Lawrence College, Ramsgate, 1952-57; Britannia Royal Naval College, Dartmouth, 1959-61; Staff Course, Royal Naval College, Greenwich, 1974-75. Appointments: Royal Navy, 1958-90; National Service, Commissioned Midshipman RNVR, 1958-59; Sub-Lieutenant RN, HMS Eastbourne, Far East Fleet, 1961-62; Lieutenant, HM Coastal Forces, 1962; Served in HM Ships Lanton, Palliser and Gurkha; Specialist Navigation Course, HMS Dryad, 1967; Navigating Officer, Promoted to Lieutenant Commander, Frigates HMS Tenby, HMS Scylla, 1968-71; Divisional Officer and Head of Navigation, Britannia Royal Naval College, Dartmouth, 1971-73; Promoted to Commander, 1974, Executive Officer, Guided Missile Destroyer, HMS Hampshire, 1974; Staff, Royal Naval Staff College, Greenwich, 1976; Commander of the Royal Yacht Britannia, 1978; Captain, 1980; Captain, HMS Coventry, 1981-82 when sunk by enemy action in the Falklands

War; Assistant Chief of Staff to the Commander of the Chief Fleet, Northwood, 1982-84; Assistant Naval Attaché and Chief of Staff to the Commander British Naval Staff, Washington DC, 1985-87; Director of Naval Recruiting, Ministry of Defence, 1987; Retired from Royal Navy, 1990; Clerk to the Worshipful Company of Skinners, City of London, 1990-2003. Publications: Articles on experiences in the Falklands War and on Combat Stress published in Naval Review and other related journals. Honours: LVO, 1979; ADC to Her Majesty the Queen, 1988-90; CBE, 1990. Membership: Army and Navy Club. Address: Hambledon House, Hambledon, Hants PO7 4RU, England. E-mail: dhartdyke@tiscali.co.uk

**HARTCUP Adeline,** b. 26 April 1918, Isle of Wight, England. Writer. m. John Hartcup, 11 February 1950, 2 sons. Education: MA, Classics and English Literature, Oxon. Appointments: Editorial Staff, Times Educational Supplement; Honorary Press Officer, Kent Voluntary Service Council. Publications: Angelica, 1954; Morning Faces, 1963; Below Stairs in the Great Country Houses, 1980; Children of the Great Country Houses, 1982, 2000; Love and Marriage in the Great Country Houses, 1984; Spello: Life Today in Ancient Umbria, 1985. Contributions to: Times Educational Supplement; Harper's; Queen; Times Higher Educational Supplement. Address: 8F Compton Road, London N1, England.

**HARTER John J,** b. 31 January 1926, Canyon, Texas, USA. Diplomat; Economic Analyst. m. Irene T Harter, 2 sons, 1 daughter. Education: BA, 1948, MA, 1953, University of Southern California; MA, Economics, Harvard University, 1963. Appointments: Lecturer, History, University of Southern California, 1948-53; Foreign Service Officer, US Department of State with assignments in South Africa, Chile, Thailand, Geneva, Washington, 1954-83; Oral Historian, 1983-; Declassifier, Agency for International Development, 1998-. Publications: Views on Global Economic Development, 1979; The Language of Trade, 1984; Numerous articles in Foreign Service Journal and State Magazine. Memberships: American Foreign Service Association; Diplomatic and Consular Officers Retired. Address: 12109 Kershaw Place, Glen Allen, VA 23059-6978, USA. E-mail: jjitharter@aol.com

**HARTILL Edward Theodore,** b. 23 January 1943, United Kingdom. City Surveyor. m. Gillian Ruth Todd, 2 sons, 2 sons from previous marriage. Education: BSc, Estate Management, College of Estate Management, London University; FRICS. Appointments: Joined Burd and Evans, Land Agents, Shrewsbury, 1963; Estates Department, Legal and General Assurance Company, 1964-73; Property Investment Department, Guardian Royal Exchange Assurance Group, 1973-85, Head Office Manager, 1980-85; City Surveyor, Corporation of London, 1985-; Visiting Lecturer in Law of Town Planning and Compulsory Purchase, Hammersmith and West London College of Advanced Business Studies, 1968-78; Member, General Practice Divisional Council, 1989-97, President, 1992-93, General Council, 1990-2004, Honorary Treasurer, 2000-04, Royal Institution of Chartered Surveyors; Member, 1985-, National Council, 1988-, President, 1996-97, Association of Chief Estates Surveyors and Property Managers in Local Government (formerly Local Authority Valuers' Association); Member, Steering Group, 1992-99, Chairman Property Services Sub-Group, 1992-99, Construction Industry Standing Conference; Founder Member, Chairman, Property Services NTO, 1999-2005; Chair, 2003, Vice Chair, 2004-, Assets Skills (a new sector Skills Council); Member, Governing Council, University of London, 2004-. Publications: Occasional lectures and articles on professional topics. Honours: Honorary Associate, Czech Chamber of Appraisers, 1992; Honorary

Member Investment Property Forum, 1995; OBE, 2004. Memberships: British Schools Exploring Society; FRSA, 1993; Liveryman, 1985-, Court of Assistants, 1991-, Master, 2003-2004, Worshipful Company of Chartered Surveyors. Address: 215 Sheen Lane, East Sheen, London SW14 8LE, England.

**HARTILL Rosemary Jane,** b. 11 August 1949, Oswestry, England. Writer; Broadcaster; Non-executive Board Member. Education: BA Hons, English, University of Bristol, 1970. Appointments: BBC Religious Affairs Correspondent, 1982-88, Presenter of World Service's Meridian Books Programme, 1990-92, 1994, BBC; Board Member: Shared Interest, 1996-2005, National Probation Service, Northumbria, 2001-, Northumbria Courts Board, 2004-, Youth Justice Board for England and Wales, 2005-. Publications: Emily Brontë: Poems (editor), 1973; Wild Animals, 1976; In Perspective, 1988; Writers Revealed, 1989; Were You There?, 1995; Visionary Women: Florence Nightingale, editor, 1996. Contributions to: Times Educational Supplement; Saga magazine; Guardian etc. Honours: Nominated, Sony Award for Radio Reporter of the Year, 1988 and Best Arts Radio Feature, 1990; Sandford St Martin Trust Personal Award, 1994; Honorary DLitt, University of Hull, 1995; Finalist In New York Festivals International Radio Competition, 1996; Honorary DLitt, University of Bristol, 2000. Address: Old Post Office, 24 Eglingham Village, Alnwick, Northumberland NE66 2TX, England.

**HARTLAND Michael,** b. 7 February 1941, Cornwall, England. Writer and Broadcaster. m. 1975, 2 daughters. Education: Christ's College, Cambridge, 1960-63. Appointments: British Diplomatic and Civil Service, 1963-78; United Nations, 1978-83; Full-time Writer, 1983-; Book Reviewer and Feature Writer, The Sunday Times, The Times, Guardian and Daily Telegraph; Resident Thriller Critic, The Times, 1989-90; Daily Telegraph, 1993-2003; Travel Correspondent: The Times, 1993-2003; Television and Radio include: Sonia's Report, ITV documentary, 1990; Masterspy, interviews with KGB defector Oleg Gordievsky, Radio 4, 1991. Publications: Down Among the Dead Men; Seven Steps to Treason (dramatised for BBC Radio 4, 1990); The Third Betrayal; Frontier of Fear; The Year of the Scorpion; As Ruth Carrington: Dead Fish. Honours: Fellow, Royal Society of Arts; Honorary Fellow, University of Exeter; South West Arts Literary Award. Memberships: Executive Committee of PEN, 1997-2001; Detection Club; Mystery Writers of America. Address: Cotte Barton, Branscombe, Devon, EX12 3BH, England.

**HARTMANN Reinhard R K,** b. 8 April 1938. Education: Translator's Diploma, University of Vienna, 1956-60; BSc, Economics, 1956-60, Doctorate, 1960-65, Vienna School of Economics; MA, International Economics, Southern Illinois University, USA, 1961-62. Appointments: Lecturer, Modern Languages, University of Manchester Institute of Science and Technology, 1964-68; Lecturer, Applied Linguistics, University of Nottingham, 1968-74; Director, Language Centre and Head of Linguistics, University of Exeter, 1974-92; Reader, Applied Linguistics, 1991-, Head, Department of Applied Linguistics, 1992-96, in School of English, 1996-2001, University of Exeter; Honorary Professor of Lexicography, Department of English, University of Birmingham, 2000-; Visiting Professor, School of English, University of Exeter, 2001-. Publications: Author/editor of 18 books; Articles in national and international scholarly journals; Papers presented at conferences; Numerous invited contributions. Honours: Fellow, Royal Society of Arts; Fellow, Institute of Linguists (London); Honorary Life Member, European Association for Lexicography; MCB UP/Literati Club award for best specialist reference work, 1998. Memberships include: British Association for Applied Linguistics; Linguistics

Association of Great Britain; Societas Linguistica Europea; Association for Literary and Linguistic Computing; European Association for Lexicography. Address: 40 Velwell Road, Exeter, Devon EX4 4LD, England. E-mail: r.r.k.hartmann@exeter.ac.uk

**HARTNELL St John,** b. 4 August 1939, Bristol, England. Chartered Surveyor; Company Director. m. Sara, 1 son, 1 daughter. Education: King's College, Taunton, Somerset; College of Estate Management, London. Appointments: Senior Partner, Hartnell Taylor Cook, 1979-2003; Chairman, APS Ltd, 1985-2003; Director, Oak Holdings plc, 2000-; Chairman, Coord Ltd, 2003-; Chairman, Cardok Ltd, 2003-; Chairman, Kerwoud Ltd, 2004-; Director of Swanwell Developments and Swanwell Investments, 2003-; Developments include: Privatisation and subsequent management of 2,500 acres for the Bristol Port Company; Planning, development advice and letting of major shopping centres including The Mall, Cribbs Causeway, Bristol, The Galleries, Bristol, The Oracle, Reading, The Drummond Centre, Croydon; Office developments include: Windmill Hill, Swindon, Number One Poultry, City of London. Publications: Numerous articles in newspapers and professional journals. Honours: OBE; Hon DSc, University of the West of England; Former High Sheriff of Bristol, 2000. Memberships: Former Assistant, Society of Merchant Venturers; Fellow, Royal Institution of Chartered Surveyors; Former UK President, FIABCI; Clubs: Garrick; Royal Thames Yacht Club; MCC; Clifton Club. Address: Cameley House, Cameley, Temple Cloud, Nr Bristol BS39 5AJ, England.

**HARVEY Barbara Fitzgerald,** b. 21 January 1928, Teignmouth, Devon, England. University Teacher. Education: BA (Oxon) 1949, MA (Oxon), 1953, B Litt (Oxon), 1953, Somerville College, Oxford. Appointments: Assistant, Department of Scottish History, University of Edinburgh, 1951-52; Assistant Lecturer then Lecturer, Department of History, Queen Mary College, University of London, 1952-55; Tutor in Medieval History, 1955-56, Fellow and Tutor in Medieval History, 1956-93, Emeritus Fellow, 1993-, Somerville College, Oxford. Publications: Books: Westminster Abbey and its Estates in the Middle Ages, 1977; The Westminster Chronicle, 1381-94 (editor with L C Hector), 1982; Living and Dying in England 1100-1540: The monastic experience, 1993; The Twelfth and Thirteenth Centuries, 1066-c.1280 (editor) in Short Oxford History of the British Isles, 2001; Articles in: Transactions of the Royal Historical Society; Bulletin of the Institute of Historical Research; Economic History Review; Journal of Ecclesiastical History and other learned journals and similar works. Honours: FBA, 1982; Ford's Lecturer in English History, University of Oxford, 1989; Joint Winner, Wolfson Foundation Prize for History, 1993; CBE, 1997. Memberships: Fellow, Society of Antiquaries, London, 1964-; President, Henry Bradshaw Society, 1997; Honorary Vice-President, Royal Historical Society, 2003-. Address: 66 Cranham Street, Oxford OX2 6DD, England. E-mail: barbara.harvey@someville.ox.ac.uk

**HARVEY Fiona,** Journalist. Education: Christ's College, Cambridge. Appointments: Editor, PC Week, 1999-2000; Editor, Internet World, 1999; Technology Writer, 200-2004, Environment Correspondent, 2004-, Financial Times. Publications: Contributor to: Encyclopaedia Britannica; Scientific American; Science Columnist, Diva Magazine, 2004-2005. Memberships: British Association of Science Writers; Royal Society of Arts. Address: c/o The Financial Times, 1 Southwork Bridge, London SE1 9HL, England.

**HARVEY John Robert,** b. 25 June 1942, Bishops Stortford, Hertfordshire, England. University Lecturer; Writer. m. Julietta

Chloe Papadopoulou, 1968, 1 daughter. Education: BA, Honours Class 1, English, 1964, MA, 1967, PhD, 1969, University of Cambridge. Appointments: English Faculty, Emmanuel College, Cambridge; Editor, Cambridge Quarterly, 1978-86. Publications: Victorian Novelists and Their Illustrators, 1970. Novels: The Plate Shop, 1979; Coup d'Etat, 1985; The Legend of Captain Space, 1990; Men in Black, 1995. Contributions to: London Review of Books; Sunday Times; Sunday Telegraph; Listener; Encounter; Cambridge Quarterley; Essays in Criticism. Honour: David Higham Prize, 1979. Literary Agent: Curtis Brown. Address: Emmanuel College, Cambridge, England.

**HARVEY Jonathan Dean,** b. 3 May 1939, Sutton Coldfield, England. Composer. m. Rosaleen Marie Harvey, 1 son, 1 daughter. Education: Major Scholar, MA, St John's College Cambridge, 1957-61; PhD, Glasgow University, 1961-63; DMus, Cambridge University, 1970. Appointments: Lecturer, Senior Lecturer, Southampton University, 1964-77; Senior Lecturer, Professor, Sussex University, 1977-92; Full Professor, Stanford University, 1995-2000; Visiting Professor, Imperial College, 1999-2002; About 150 performances per annum. Publications: Books: The Music of Stockhausen, 1975; Music and Inspiration, 1999; In Quest of Spirit, 1999; About 40 articles; About 150 compositions for orchestra, choir, chamber and electronic combinations; 2 operas. Honours: Britten Award, 1993; 2 Koussevitsky Awards; British Academy Composer Award, 2004; Honorary Doctorates: Bristol, Southampton and Sussex Universities; FRCM; Honorary RAM; FRSCM; Honorary Fellow, St John's College, Cambridge. Memberships: British Academy; European Academy. Address: c/o Faber Music, 3 Queen Square, London WC1N 3AU, England.

**HARVEY Pamela Ann,** b. 15 October 1934, Bush Hill Park, Edmonton, London, England. Writer; Poet. Education: 6 GCEs, Edmonton County Grammar; RSA Diploma. Appointments: Secretarial Work, London; Library Work, Southgate Library. Publications: Poetry, 1994; Quiet Lines, 1996; The Wellspring (co-author with Anna Franklin), 2000. Contributions to: The People's Poetry; Romantic Heir; Rubies in the Darkness; Cadmium Blue Literary Journal; Pendragon (stories, articles, poems); Keltria, USA; Celtic Connections; Silver Wheel (articles and poems); Sharkti Laureate; Time Haiku; Azami, Japan; The Lady magazine (short story); Avalon magazine (articles); Poetry Now (new fiction) included: Hold That Thought (story), Timeless Tales (story) and Share Our Worlds Anthology (poem). Memberships: Enfield Writers Group; New Renaissance Poets Society.

**HARVEY Suzanne MacLeod,** b. 2 November 1946, Palmerston, New Zealand. Nursing. Education: Bachelor Health Science (Management), Mitchell CAE, New South Wales; Spinal Injuries Certificate, Stoke Mandeville Hospital, United Kingdom; Registered Nurse, New Zealand; Intensive Care Certificate, Royal Infirmary Edinburgh, Scotland. Appointments include: Staff Nurse, Christchurch Public Hospital, New Zealand, 1968; Registered Nurse, Bourke District Hospital, New South Wales, Australia, 1969; Post-Graduate courses, United Kingdom, 1970-73; Registered Nurse, Shenton Park Rehabilitation Centre, Perth, Western Australia, 1973; Nursing Unit Manager, Intensive Care Unit, Royal Prince Alfred Hospital, Sydney, Australia, 1974-76; Charge Nurse, Intensive Care Unit, Christchurch Hospital, New Zealand, 1977-78; Supervisor, Intensive Care Unit, Westmead Hospital, Sydney, Australia, 1978-81; Assistant Director of Nursing, Accident and Emergency, Westmead Hospital, Sydney, 1981-85; Assistant Director, Nursing Paediatrics, Westmead Hospital, Sydney, New South Wales, 1985-88; Deputy Director of Nursing, Auburn District Hospital, Sydney, 1990; Assistant Director, Nursing Radiology, Nuclear Medicine,

Staff Health, Outpatients, Accident and Emergency, Endoscopy, Geriatric Day Care, Radiation Oncology, Westmead Hospital, Sydney, 1989-90; Deputy Director of Nursing, Royal North Shore Hospital, Sydney, 1990-95; Deputy Director of Nursing and Patient Services, Royal North Shore Hospital, Sydney, 1995; Executive Director of Nursing, Human Resources and Patient Services, Austin and Repatriation Medical Centre, Melbourne, Victoria, 1995-; Executive Director, Nursing and Patient Support Services, 1997-2002; Nurse Adviser, Auckland Hospital, 2000; Nursing Leader, Surgical Services, 2002-, Nurse Leader, 2002-2004, Mananger, Health Information Centre, 2004-, Auckland District Health Board. Honours: Finalist, Victoria Business Woman of the Year, Corporation and Government Section, 1998; Listed in Who's Who publications and biographical dictionaries. Memberships: New South Wales College of Nursing, 1987; Charles Stuart University, Mitchell College Graduates Association, 1989; Australia College of Health Service Executives (Victoria), Associate Fellow, 1990; Australia College of Health Service Executives, Certified Health Executive, 1991; Royal College of Nursing, Australia, 1995; Victorian Nurse Executive Association, Fellow, 1996. Address: 28B Mahara Avenue, Birkenhead, Auckland 1310, New Zealand.

**HARVEY William Graeme,** b. 15 January 1947, Watford, England. Naturalist. m. Pauline, 1 son, 2 daughters. Education: University College, Oxford, 1966-69. Appointments: British Council appointments in London, Tanzania, Indonesia and India, 1969-86; Director, British Council, Bangladesh, 1986-93; General Manager, Technical Co-operation Training, British Council, 1990-93; Regional Director, Eastern and Central Africa, British Council, Nairobi, 1993-98; Director, International Partnerships, British Council, London, 1998-2000; Naturalist, Writer, 2000-. Publications: Articles and papers on birds and conservation in UK, Africa and Asia, 1967-2004; Birds in Bangladesh, 1990; Photographic Guide to the Birds of India, 2002; Tails of Dilli (Animal Stories for Children), 2004. Memberships: British Ornithologists Union; British Ornithologists Club; Life Member: Bombay Natural History Society; East African Wildlife Society; Madras Club, Chennai, India. Address: Pound Farm, Blackham, Tunbridge Wells, TN3 9TY, England. E-mail: bill@poundfarm98.wanadoo.co.uk

**HARVEY WOOD (Elizabeth) Harriet,** b. 1 October 1934, Edinburgh, Scotland. Retired. Education: British Institute, Paris; MA, PhD, University of Edinburgh. Appointments: Manager, Philomusica of London Ltd, 1959-66; Secretary, Faculty of Music, Kings College, London, 1966-68; Joined British Council, 1973; Head of Literature, British Council, 1980-94; Director, The Harvill Press, 1995-2002. Publications: James Watson's Choice Collection of Comic and Serious Scots Poems, volume I, 1977, volume II, 1991; The Percy Letters: The Correspondence of Thomas Percy and John Pinkerton, 1985; Banned Poetry (with Peter Porter), 1997; Selected Poems of William Dunbar, 1999; Sightlines (with P D James), 2001; Sir Walter Scott, 2005. Honour: OBE. Memberships: Wingate Scholarship Committee, 1992-; Biographical Society, 1970-94; Judge, Booker Prize for Fiction, 1992; Booker Management Committee, 2000-2003; English PEN, 1985, Executive Committee, 1994-99; Trustee, Golsoncott Foundation, 1997-; Trustee, Asham Literary Endowment Trust, 1999-; Oxford and Cambridge Club. Address: 158 Coleherne Court, Redcliffe Gardens, London SW5 0DX, England. E-mail: hhw@dircon.co.uk

**HARWOOD Eleanor May Cash,** b. 29 May 1921, Maine, USA. Divorced, 1 son, 1 daughter. Education: BA, American International College, 1943; BSc, S Connecticut State University, 1955. Appointments: Ensign to Lieutenant JG

USSN Waves, 1943-46; Librarian, Rathburn Memorial Library, East Haddam, Connecticut, 1955-56; Assistant Librarian, Kent Boys School, Connecticut, 1956-63; Consultant, Chester Public Library, Connecticut, 1965-71. Publications: The Independent School Library And The Gifted Child; The Age Of Samuel Johnson; Remember When?; Moosely Yours. Honours: WWII 50th Women and 50th Victory Medals; Atlantic Theater; Victory Medal; Gold Star Award for Education 1997; Eleanor Harwood College Library named for her at the Reverend Jacob Memorial Christian College, India, 2003. Memberships include: American and Connecticut Library Associations; Society of the Descendents of The Mayflower; Trustee, Chester Historical Society, 1970-72; Disabled American Veterans; American Legion Aux; Appalachian Mountain Club. Address: 10 Maple Street, Box 255, Chester, CT 06412, USA.

**HASELHURST Alan Gordon Barraclough (Rt Hon Sir),** b. 23 June 1937, South Elmsall, Yorkshire, England. Member of Parliament. m. Angela Margaret Bailey, 2 sons, 1 daughter. Education: Oriel College, Oxford, 1956-60. Appointments: Member of Parliament for Middleton and Prestwich, 1970-74; MP for Saffron Walden, 1977-; Parliamentary Private Secretary to the Home Secretary, 1973-74; Parliamentary Private Secretary to Education Secretary, 1979-81; Chairman of Ways and Means and Deputy Speaker, 1997-; Member of Committee of Essex County Cricket Club, 1996-. Publications: Occasionally Cricket, 1999; Eventually Cricket, 2001; Incidentally Cricket, 2003. Honours: Knight Bachelor, 1995; Privy Counsellor, 1999. Memberships: MCC; Essex County Cricket Club; Yorkshire County Cricket Club. Address: House of Commons, London SW1A 0AA, England. E-mail: haselhursta@parliament.uk Website: www.siralanhaselhurst.net

**HASHIGUCHI Yasuo,** b. 31 July 1924, Sasebo, Japan. Professor of English (retired). m. Eiko Uchida, 1 son, 1 daughter. Education: BA, University of Tokyo, 1948; MEd, Ohio University, USA, 1951. Appointments: Associate Professor, English, Kagoshima University, 1951-64, 1964-68, Professor, 1968-82, Kyushu University; Fukuoka University, 1982-88; President, Fukuoka Jo Gakuin Junior College, 1988-93; Professor, Yasuda Women's University, 1993-96. Publications: Editor, Complete Works of John Steinbeck, 20 vols, 1985. Honours: Dick A Renner Prize, 1977; Special Recognition for Outstanding Publication, 1988; Recognition for Many Years of Outstanding Leadership in American Literature & Steinbeck Studies, 1991; Richard W and Dorothy Burkhardt Award, 1994; John J and Angeline Pruis Award, 1996; John J and Angeline R Pruis Award for the Outstanding Steinbeck Translator in Honour of John Steinbeck's Centennial, 2002. Memberships: President, 1977-89, Advisor, 1989-, Kyushu American Literature Society; President, 1977-91, Honorary President, 1991-, Steinbeck Society of Japan; International Association of University Professors of English, 1999-. Address: 7-29-31-105 Iikura, Sawara-ku, Fukuoka 814-0161 Japan.

**HASHIMOTO Tohru,** b. 3 February 1930, Kumamoto, Japan. Professor. m. Yoshiko Sakamoto, 1 son, deceased, 1 daughter. Education: Tokyo Gakugei University, 1951-53; BSc, Institute of Biology, Tohoku University, Sendai, 1955; MSc, 1957, DSc, 1961, University of Tokyo; Postdoctoral work, University of California at Davis, 1962-63. Appointments: Lecturer of Biology, Musashi University, Tokyo, 1960-63; Assistant, Department of Agricultural Chemistry, University of Tokyo, 1963-70; Senior Research Scientist, Institute of Physical and Chemical Research, Wako, 1970-86; Professor of Plant Physiology, Department of Biology, Kobe University, Kobe, 1986-93; Professor of Biochemistry, 1993-2003, Emeritus Professor, 2003-, Department of Life Sciences,

Kobe Women's University, Kobe; Member, Research Project Evaluation Committee, Ministry of Environment of Japan, 1990-99. Publications: 78 original articles and books on plant photomorphogenesis, including: Harmful and beneficial effects of solar UV light on plant growth, 1993; Phytochrome elicits the cryptic red-light signal which results in amplification of anthocyanin biosynthesis in sorghum, 1999; Photoregulation of seed germination, in Seed Science and Technology, 2004. Honours: University Faculty Exchange Grant, Royal Society, 1992. Memberships: Botanical Society of Japan; Japan Society of Photomedicine and Photobiology; American Society of Plant Biologists. Address: Uozakiminami 5-chome, 9-45-101, Kobe 6580025, Japan. E-mail: hashimt@hotmail.com

**HASKINS Christopher (The Rt Hon The Lord Haskins),** b. 1937, Dublin, Ireland. Businessman; Member of House of Lords. m. Gilda Horsley, 5 children. Education: History (Hons), Trinity College, Dublin. Appointments: De La Rue Trainee, 1959-60; Ford Motors Dagenham Personnel, 1960-62; Manager, Belfast, 1962-68, Pioneered foods in Marks & Spencer, 1968-2002; Director, 1974, Deputy Chair, 1974, Chairman, 1980, Northern Dairies (later Northern Foods); Chairman, Express Dairies (merged with Northern Foods), 1998-2002; Member, MAFF Review of CAP, 1995; Chairman, Better Regulation Task Force, 1997-2002; Member, New Deal Task Force, 1998-2001; Member, Britain in Europe Campaign, 1998-; Non Executive Director, Yorkshire Regional Development Agency, 1998-; Advisor to the Prime Minister on Foot and Mouth "Recovery", 2001; Heading Review of Defra, 2002-2003; Chair, Selby Coalfields Task Force (Managing the impact of closure), 2002-2003; Member, CBI President's Committee, 1995-98; Member, Hampel Committee on Corporate Governance, 1996-98; Member, Irish Economic Policy Review Group, 1998; Member, Commission for Social Justice, 1992-94; Member, UK Round Table on Sustainable Development. 1995-98; Trustee, Runnymede Trust, 1989-98; Chairman, Demos Trustees, 1993-2000; Trustee, Civil Liberties, 1997-99; Trustee, Legal Assistance Trust, 1998-2004; Trustee, Lawes Agricultural Trust, 1999-; Director, Yorkshire TV, 2002-; Trustee, Business Dynamics, 2002; Chair, DEFRA Review Group, 2002-03; Chair, Council, Open University, 2004-; Chair, European Movement, 2004-; Regular speaker and writer about Europe, agriculture, regulation, corporate governance. Honours: Labour Peer, 1998; Honorary Degrees: Dublin, Hull, Essex, Nottingham, Leeds, Metropolitan, Cranfield, Huddersfield. Address: Quarryside Farm, Main Street, Skidby, Nr Cottingham, East Yorkshire HU16 5SG, England.

**HASLAM Michael Trevor,** b. 7 February 1934, Leeds, England. Retired Medical Director. m. Shirley Dunstan, 1 son, 2 daughters. Education: Exhibitioner to St John's College, Cambridge, MA, MD, BChir, 1947-52; LMSSA, FRCP, MRCS, St Bartholomew's Hospital, London, 1955-59; MA, Theology, St John's College, York, 2003; Diploma in Psychological Medicine, 1962; Diploma in Medical Jurisprudence, 1972; FRCPsych, 1980; Certificate in Hypnotherapy, BSMDH, 1982. Appointments: Captain, RAMC, Military Service, 1960-62; Senior Registrar to Sir Martin Roth, Newcastle upon Tyne, 1964-67; Consultant in Psychological Medicine, Doncaster, 1967-70; Consultant in Psychological Medicine, York, 1970-89; Medical Director, Harrogate Clinic, 1989-91; Medical Director, South Durham, NHS Trust, 1994-98; Retired 1999. Publications: Books: Psychiatric Illness in Adolescence, 1975; Sexual Disorders, 1978; Psychosexual Disorders, 1979; Psychiatry Made Simple, 1982; Clifton Hospital an era, 1996; Editor: Transvestism, 1996; Psychiatry in the New Millennium, 2002; Editor of the Celtic Times, 1953-56. Honours: TD (Territorial National Service Decoration); Fellow, Royal College

of Physicians, Glasgow, 1979-; Retired Fellow, Royal College of Psychiatrists, 1980; Freeman of London; Liveryman of the Society of Apothecaries; Retired, Warden of North, Association of Freeman of England and Wales. Memberships: Chairman, Society of Clinical Psychiatrists; Author's Club to 1999; Royal Society of Medicine to 2004; Fellow, Royal College of Psychiatrists, retired 2003; Fellow, Royal College of Physicians and Surgeons in Glasgow. Address: Chapel Garth, Crayke, York, YO61 4TE, England.

**HASSAN IBN TALAL H R H,** b. 20 March 1947, Amman, Jordan. Crown Prince of Jordan. m. Sarrath Khujista Akhter Banu, 1968, 1 son, 3 daughters. Education: Christ Church, Oxford University. Appointments: Regent to the throne of Jordan in absence of King Hussein; Ombudsman for National Development, 1971-; Founder, Royal Science Society of Jordan, 1970; Royal Academy of Islamic Civilization Research (AlAlbait), 1980; Arab Thought Forum, 1981; Forum Humanum (now Arab Youth Forum), 1982; Co-Chairman, Independent Commission on International Council for Science and Technology; Honorary General of Jordan Armed Forces. Publications: A Study on Jerusalem, 1979; Palestinian Self-Determination, 1981; Search for Peace, 1984; Christianity in the Arab World, 1994. Honours: Honorary degrees from universities of Yarmouk, 1980, Bogazici (Turkey), 1982, Jordan, 1987, Durham, 1990, Ulster, 1996; Medal, President, Italian Republic, 1982; Knight of Grand Cross of Order of Self-Merit (Italy), 1983. Address: The Royal Palace, Amman, Jordan.

**HASSAN Syed Tajuddin Bin Syed,** b. 11 October 1948, Perak, Malaysia. Professor. m. Husna Jamaludin, 2 sons, 1 daughter. Education: Royal Military College, Kuala Lumpur, HSC, Cambridge University, 1964-67; BSc, First Class Honours, University of New England, Australia, 1968-71; MSc, 1972-74, PhD, 1976-80, University of Queensland, Australia. Appointments: Tutor, 1974, Lecturer, 1980-, Head of Department of Biology, 1987-88, Associate Professor, 1988-98, Professor, 1998-, Director, Rainforest Academy, 2002-2004, Universiti Putra, Malaysia. Publications: 34 in professional research journals; 85 in proceedings; 4 translated books; 5 original books and booklets; 8 articles in books. Honours: Fulbright Scholar; US Environmental Fellowship; International Editor, Conservation Ecology; London Times Fellowship; UNESCO Travel Award; Colombo Plan Scholar; Excellence Award for Teaching and Research, Universiti Putra, Malaysia; Asia Foundation Advisory Consultant; Australian Government, Ecosystem-Modelling Course Grant; Malaysian Government Research Grant; Putrajaya Environmental Management Consultant. Memberships: System Dynamics Society; Ecological Association of Malaysia; Malaysian Applied Biology; Malaysian Plant Protection Society; Entomological Society of Queensland. Address: 41 Jalan USJ 5/1J, 47610 Subang Jaya, Selangor, Malaysia. E-mail: stsh@streamyx.com Website: www.fsas.upm.edu.my/~stshasan/

**HASTE Catherine Mary (Cate),** b. 6 August 1945, Leeds, England. Writer; Television Documentary Producer/Director. m. Melvyn Bragg (Rt Hon The Lord Bragg), 18 December 1973, 1 son, 1 daughter. Education: BA Honours, English, University of Sussex, 1963-66; Postgraduate Diploma Adult Education, Manchester University, 1967. Appointments: Television: The Secret War (BBC); End of Empire (Granada TV); Writing on the Wall (Channel 4) Munich – The Peace of Paper (Thames); Secret History – Death of a Democrat (Channel 4); The Churchills (ITV); Cold War (Jeremy Isaacs Productions/BBC/CNN); Millennium (Jeremy Isaacs Productions/BBC/CNN); Hitler's Brides (Flashback TV/Channel 4). Publications: Keep the Home Fires Burning: Propaganda to the Home Front in the First World

War, 1977; Rules of Desire: Sex in Britain World War I to the Present, 1992; Nazi Women – Hitler's Seduction of a Nation, 2001; The Goldfish Bowl – Married to the Prime Minister 1955-97, co-authored with Cherie Booth, 2004. Memberships: British PEN; Directors Guild of Great Britain; British Academy of Film and Television Arts. Address: 12 Hampstead Hill Gardens, London NW3 2PL, England. E-mail: cate.haste@virgin.net

**HASTINGS Max Macdonald**, b. 28 December 1945, London, England. Author; Broadcaster; Journalist. m. (1) Patricia Edmondson, 1972, dissolved, 1994, 2 sons, 1 deceased, 1 daughter, (2) Penny Grade, 1999. Education: Exhibitioner, University College, Oxford, 1964-65; Fellow, World Press Institute, St Paul, Minnesota, USA, 1967-68. Appointments: Researcher, BBC TV, 1963-64; Reporter, London Evening Standard, 1965-67, BBC TV Current Affairs, 1970-73; Editor, Evening Standard Londoner's Diary, 1976-77; Editor, Daily Telegraph, 1986-95; Editor, Evening Standard, 1996-2002; Columnist, Daily Express, 1981-83, Sunday Times, 1985-86; Editor-in-Chief and a Director, Daily Telegraph Plc, 1989-96. Publications: The Fire This Time, 1968; Ulster, 1969; The Struggle for Civil Rights in Northern Ireland, 1970; Montrose: The King's Champion, 1977; Yoni: The Hero of Entebbe, 1979; Bomber Command, 1979; The Battle of Britain (with Lee Deighton), 1980; Das Reich, 1981; Battle for the Falklands (with Simon Jenkins), 1983; Overlord: D-Day and the Battle for Normandy, 1984; Oxford Book of Military Anecdotes (editor), 1985; Victory in Europe, 1985; The Korean War, 1987; Outside Days, 1989; Outside Days, 1989; Scattered Shots, 1999; Going to the Wars, 2000; Editor, 2002; Armageddon, 2004; Warriors, 2005; Country Fair, 2005. Honours: Somerset Maugham Prize, 1979; British Press Awards, Journalist of the Year, 1982; Granada TV Reporter of the Year, 1982; Yorkshire Post Book of the Year Awards, 1983, 1984; Editor of the Year, 1988; Honorary DLitt. Leicester University, 1992; Royal Society of Literature, fellow, 1996. Address: c/o PFD, Drury House, 34-43 Russell Street, London WC2B 5HA, England.

**HASTINGS Lady Selina**, b. 5 March 1945, Oxford, England. Writer. Education: St Hugh's College, Oxford, England. Appointments: Daily Telegraph, books page, 1968-82; Harper's & Queen Literary Editor, 1986-94. Publications: Nancy Mitford, biography, 1985; Evelyn Waugh, 1994; Rosamond Lehmann, 2002; various children's books. Contributions to: Daily & Sunday Telegraph; Spectator; TLS; New Yorker; Harper's & Queen. Honour: Marsh Biography Award, 1993-96. Memberships: Royal Society of Literature Committee, 1994-99. Address: c/o Rogers Coleridge & White, 20 Powis Mews, London W11, England.

**HASTINGS Stephen L E (Sir)**, b. 4 May 1921, London, England. Retired. m. (1), 1 son, 1 daughter, (2) Elizabeth Anne Marie Gabrielle Naylor Leyland, deceased. Education: Royal Military College Sandhurst. Appointments: Regular Officer, Scotts Guards, 1939-49; Foreign Service, 1949-60; Member of Parliament for Mid Bedfordshire, 1960-83; Retired, 1983; Currently Owner Manager, Milton Park Thoroughbred Stud Farm. Publications: Feature articles for the Daily Telegraph and other publications; The Murder of TSR2, 1966; The Drums of Memory (autobiography), 1994. Honours: Mention in Despatches, 1942; Military Cross, 1945; Knight Bachelor, 1983; Medalia d'Oro, Italy, 1996. Memberships: Whites; Pratts; Fellow, RGS; Masters of Foxhounds Association; Thoroughbred Breeder Association. Address: Stibbington House, Wansford, Peterborough PE8 6JS, England.

**HATEGAN Cornel**, b. 17 August 1940, Ohaba-Matnic, Romania. Physicist. m. Dora, 9 October 1965, 1 daughter.

Education: University Diploma Physics, University of Bucharest, 1964; Dr, Physics, Institute of Atomic Physics, Bucharest, 1973. Appointments: Assistant Researcher, Researcher, Senior Researcher, Institute of Atomic Physics, 1964-70, 1972-; Humboldt Researcher, University of Erlangen Nuremberg, 1970-71; University of Munich, 2002, 2004. Publications: Scientific papers on Atomic and Nuclear Physics. Honours: Urkunde of Humboldt Foundation; Physics Prize of Romanian Academy; Corresponding Member, Romanian Academy, elected, 1992; Fellow, Institute of Physics, elected, 2000. Memberships: Humboldt Club; Nuclear Physics Division of the Romanian Physical Society; New York Academy of Sciences. Address: Institute of Atomic Physics, CP MG 6, 76900 Bucharest, Magurele, Romania.

**HATTERSLEY Roy, (Sydney George)**, b. 28 December 1932, Sheffield, England. Politician; Writer. m. Molly Loughran, 1956. Education: BSc, Economics, University of Hull. Appointments: Journalist and Health Service Executive, 1956-64; Member, City Council, Sheffield, 1957-65; Member of Parliament, Labour Party, Sparkbrook Division, Birmingham, 1964-97; Parliamentary Private Secretary, Minister of Pensions and National Insurance, 1964-67; Director, Campaign for a European Political Community, 1966-67; Joint Parliamentary Secretary, Ministry of Labour, 1967-69, Minister of Defence for Administration, 1969-70; Visiting Fellow, Harvard University, 1971, 1972, Nuffield College, Oxford, 1984-; Labour Party Spokesman on Defence, 1972, and on Education and Science, 1972-74; Minister of State, Foreign and Commonwealth Office, 1974-76; Secretary of State for Prices and Consumer Protection, 1976-79; Principal Opposition Spokesman on the Environment, 1979-80, Home Affairs, 1980-83, Treasury and Economics Affairs, 1983-87, Home Affairs, 1987-92; Deputy Leader, Labour Party, 1983-92. Publications: Nelson: A Biography, 1974; Goodbye to Yorkshire (essays), 1976; Politics Apart, 1982; Press Gang, 1983; A Yorkshire Boyhood, 1983; Choose Freedom: The Future for Democratic Socialism, 1987; Economic Priorities for a Labour Government, 1987; The Maker's Mark (novel), 1990; In That Quiet Earth (novel), 1991; Skylark Song (novel), 1994; Between Ourselves (novel), 1994; Who Goes Home?, 1995; 50 Years On, 1997; Buster's Diaries: As Told to Roy Hattersley, 1998; Blood and Fire: The Story of William and Catherine Booth and their Salvation Army, 1999; A Brand from the Burning: The Life of John Wesley, 2002. Contributions to: Newspapers and journals. Honours: Privy Counsellor, 1975; Columnist of the Year, Granada, 1982; Honorary doctorates. Address: House of Lords, London SW1A 0PW, England.

**HATTORI Naozo**, b. 13 April 1938, Ashikaga, Tochigi Prefecture, Japan. University Professor. m. Takako Mitsutomi, 2 daughters. Education: Bachelor of Physics, 1963, Master of Physics, 1965, Science University of Tokyo; Doctor of Engineering, University of Tokyo, 1980. Appointments: Researcher, Institute of Space and Aeronautical Science, University of Tokyo, 1965-76; Senior Staff Engineer, Power Reactor and Nuclear Fuel Development Corporation, 1976-88; Professor, Science University of Tokyo, 1988-2005; Guest Researcher, National Institute for Environmental Studies, 1992; Joint Researcher, Research Laboratory for Nuclear Reactors, Tokyo Institute of Technology, 1993-2004; Joint Researcher, Institute of Space and Astronautical Science, 1999-2003. Memberships: Atomic Energy Society of Japan; Heat Transfer Society of Japan; Japan Society of Mechanical Engineers. Address: 104-1-301, 2-1 Kotesashiminami 6-Choume, Tokorozawa, Saitama, 359-1146 Japan. E-mail: n-hatto@qf7.so-net.ne.jp

**HAUGHEY Charles James,** b. 16 September 1925. Member of Parliament, Ireland. m. Maureen Lemass, 1951, 3 sons 1 daughter. Education: Scoil Mhuire, Marino, Dublin; St Joseph's Christian Brothers School, Fairview, Dublin; BCom, University College Dublin. Appointments: Called to Irish Bar, 1949; Member, Dublin Corp, 1953-55; MP, 1957-92; Parliamentary Secretary to Minister for Justice, 1960-61; Minister for Justice, 1961-64, Agriculture, 1964-66, Finance, 1966-70, Health and Social Welfare, 1977-79; Chairman, Irish Parliament Joint Committee on the Secondary Legislation of the European Communities, 1973-77; Taoiseach (Prime Minister), 1979-81, 1982, 1987-92; Minister for the Gaeltacht, 1987-92; Leader of the Opposition, 1981-82, 1982-87. Honours: Hon Fellow, RHA; Honorary Doctorates, Dublin City University, University of Clemont-Ferrand, University of Notre Dame. Publication: The Spirit of the Nation. Address: Abbeville, Kinsealy, Co Dublin, Ireland.

**HÄUSLER Rudolf,** b. 3 February 1944, Berne, Switzerland. Medical Doctor; Ear Nose and Throat and Head and Neck Surgeon. m. Kati. Education: Medical School Training, Berne, 1964-70; Ear Nose and Throat and Head and Neck Surgery Training and Specialisation (FMH), Cantonal University Hospital, Geneva, Switzerland, 1970-76. Appointments: Research Fellowship, Eaton Peabody Laboratory of Auditory Physiology, Harvard Medical School, Boston, USA, 1977-78; Research Associate, Psychophysical Department, Laboratory of Electronics, Massachusetts Institute of Technology, Cambridge, Massachusetts, USA, 1978-79; Head of Neuro-otology Division with full-time staff position and academic appointment, Department of ENT, Head and Neck Surgery, Cantonal University Hospital, Geneva, Switzerland, 1980-90; Director and Chairman, University Department of ENT, Head and Neck Surgery, Inselspital, Berne, 1991-; Research into: Otological microsurgery, otosclerosis and stapes surgery, otoneurology and otoneurological surgery, implantable hearing aids. Publications: 266 scientific or medical articles; 510 international or national conference presentations; Chief Editor of Journal ORL NOVA. Memberships: Editorial Board Member of several scientific journals including: Acta Otolaryngol, Stockholm, Auris Nasus Larynx, ORL and Related Specialities. Address: Department of ENT, Head and Neck Surgery, Inselspital, University of Berne, 3010 Berne, Switzerland. E-mail: rudolf.haeeusler@insel.ch

**HAUSTEIN Knut-Olaf,** b. 20 September 1934, Dresden, Germany. Physician. m. Heidi König, 14 July 1967, 1 son, 1 daughter. Education: MD, 1957; Habilitation, 1967; Professor of Clinical Pharmacology 1978. Appointments: Head, Institute of Clinical Pharmacology, 1985-93; Professor, Clinical Pharmacology, University Jena, 1994-99; Guest Professor, Clinical Pharmacology, University Erlangen, 1995-97; Head, Institute for Nicotine Research and Smoking Cessation, Erfurt, 1999-. Publications: Over 340 articles in professional scientific journals; Four monographs. Listed in: Several Biographical Publications. Memberships include: NY Academy of Science; President, German Society for Nicotine Research since 1998. Address: Fritz–Liekint–7, Institute Nicotine Research & Smoking Cessation, Johannestrasse 85-87, D 99084 Erfurt, Germany.

**HAUSWIRTH Otto Karl,** b. 10 May 1932, Gallspach, Upper Austria. Medical Scientist. Education: MD, University of Vienna, 1958; Habilitation, University of Heidelberg, 1972. Appointments: Assistant, Hospitals Hall, Uni-Clin Vienna (intern), Atlantic City, New Jersey, USA, University Clinic Innsbruck, 1959-64; Research Assistant, Department of Pharmacology, University of Zurich, 1964-71; Grantee, Swiss National Fund and Royal Society (London), staying at University

Laboratory of Physiology, Oxford (Professor D Noble), 1968-69; Associate Professor, 1973, Full Professor, 1980-97, University of Bonn; Active in anti-drug movement. Publications: Multiple contributions to professional science journals and to various books. Memberships: Swiss and German Physiological Society; British Biophysics Society; German Pharmacological Society (DGPT); Co-President, International Hippokratic Society, Zurich, 1999-; President, Austrian Hippokratic Society, Mils, 2000; International Scientific Medical Forum on Drug Abuse (a Division of Drug Free America Foundation), 1999. Address: Schneeburgstrasse 8, A-6068 Mils, Austria.

**HAVE Per Dalsgaard,** b. 30 July 1950, Naestved, Denmark. Veterinary Adviser. m. Varna, 2 sons, 2 daughters. Education: Cand Med Vet, DVM, 1977; PhD, 1980. Appointments: Senior Research Scientist, -1992, Head, Diagnostic Department of Virology, 1992-2002, Adviser 2002-, Danish Veterinary Institute, Lindholm. Publications: Over 30 papers on animal virology. Honours: C O Jensens, Mindefond, 1985; Dyssegaards Legat, 1988. Memberships: EFSA Scientific Panel on Animal Health, 2003-; European Society on Veterinary Virology, FAO EUFMD Research Group, 1994-2004; American Association for the Advancement of Science. Address: Danish Institute for Food and Vererinary Research, Bülowsvej 27, DK-1790 Copenhagen, Denmark. E-mail: ph@dfvf,dk

**HAVERGAL Giles Pollock,** b. 9 June 1938, Edinburgh, Scotland. Education: MA, Oxford University, 1958-61. Appointments: Director, Her Majesty's Theatre, Barrow-in-Furness, 1964; Director, Palace Theatre, Watford, 1964-69; Director, Citizens Theatre, Glasgow, 1969-2003; Freelance Director, Actor, Adapter, Teacher. Honours: OBE, 1987; CBE, 2002; Hon.D.Litt, University of Glasgow, University of Strathclyde; Hon.D.Drama, Royal Scottish Academy of Music and Drama. Address: 45A Prince of Wales Mansions, Prince of Wales Drive, London SW11 4BH, England.

**HAWK Tony,** b. 12 May 1968, San Diego, California, USA. Professional Skateboarder. m. Cindy Dunbar, 1990, 3 sons. Career: Started skateboarding 1978; Turned Professional for Dogtown, 1982; Created own company, Birdhouse skateboards, 1992; Film appearances including: Police Academy 4, 1987; Sight Unseen, Transworld skateboarding, 2001; Tony Hawk's Gigantic Skatepark Tour, 2001; Haggard, 2002; End, 2002; Tony Hawk's Boom Boom Huck Jam, 2004; TV Appearances including: Tony Hawk's Gigantic Skatepark Tour; Various "X-Games" Vert Competitions (televised); Various "Gravity Games" Vert Competitions (televised); Jackass, 2000; Max Steel, 2000; Viva la Bam, 2003. Publications: Tony Hawk, Occupation: Skateboarder, autobiography, 2002; The Tony Hawk Pro Skater series, 1999-2004. Honours include: 16 X Games Medals, all Gold, 1995-2004; Various awards for his games, including best game, 2000; Best sports game, 2003; Transworld, best Vert skater, 2000; Slam City Jam, Best Vert trick, 2003. Address: Carlsbad, California, USA.

**HAWKE Ethan,** b. 6 November 1970, Austin, Texas, USA. Actor. Career: Co-founder, Malaparte Theatre Company; Theatre appearances include: Casanova, 1991; A Joke, The Seagull, 1992; Sophistry; Films include: Explorers, 1985; Dead Poets Society, 1989; Dad, 1989; White Fang, 1991; Mystery Date, 1991; A Midnight Clear, 1992; Waterland, 1992; Alive, 1993; Rich in Love, 1993; Straight to One (director), 1993; Reality Bites, 1994; Quiz Show, 1994; Floundering, 1994; Before Sunrise, 1995; Great Expectations, 1999; Gattaca, 1999; Joe the King, 1999; Hamlet, 2000; Tape, 2001; Waking Life, 2001; Training Day, 2001. Publications: Ash Wednesday, 2002.

Address: Creative Artists Agency, 9830 Wilshire Boulevard, Beverly Hills, CA 90212, USA.

**HAWKESWORTH Pauline Mary,** b. 28 April 1943, Portsmouth, England. Secretary. m. Rex Hawkesworth, 25 October 1961, 2 daughters. Appointments: Secretarial Manager, Administrator, Ladies Athletic Club; Track and Field Judge. Publications: 2 books, 82 poems. Anthologies: Parents Enitharmon, 2000; Spirit of Wilfred Owen, 2001. Contributions to: Envoi; South; Interpreters House; Script; Iota; Poetry Nottingham International; Frogmore Press; Others. Honours: 1st Prize, Short Story, Portsmouth Polytechnic, 1981; 1st Prize, South Wales Miners Eisteddfod, 1990; 1st Prize, Hastings Open Poetry Competition, 1993; Runner-Up, Redbeck Competition, 1996; 1st Prize Tavistock and North Dartmoor, 2000; 1st Prize Newark and Sherwood Millennium Project, 2001; 2nd Prize Richmond Adult CC. Membership: President, Portsmouth Poetry Society. Address: 4 Rampart Gardens, Hilsea, Portsmouth PO3 5LR, England.

**HAWKING Stephen (William),** b. 8 January 1942, Oxford, England. Professor of Mathematics; Writer. m. (1) Jane Wilde, 1965, divorced, 2 sons, 1 daughter, (2) Elaine Mason, 1995. Education: BA, University College, Oxford; PhD, Trinity Hall, Cambridge. Appointments: Research Fellow, 1965-69, Fellow for Distinction in Science, 1969-, Gonville and Caius College, Cambridge; Member, Institute of Theoretical Astronomy, Cambridge, 1968-72; Research Assistant, Institute of Astronomy, Cambridge, 1972-73; Research Assistant, Department of Applied Mathematics and Theoretical Physics, 1973-75, Reader in Gravitational Physics, 1975-77, Professor, 1977-79, Lucasian Professor of Mathematics, 1979-, Cambridge University. Publications: The Large Scale Structure of Space-Time (with G F R Ellis), 1973; General Relativity: An Einstein Centenary Survey (editor with W W Israel), 1979; Is the End in Sight for Theoretical Physics?: An Inaugural Lecture, 1980; Superspace and Supergravity: Proceedings of the Nuffield Workshop (editor with M Rocek), 1981; The Very Early Universe: Proceedings of the Nuffield Workshop (co-editor), 1983; Three Hundred Years of Gravitation (with W W Israel), 1987; A Brief History of Time: From the Big Bang to Black Holes, 1988; Black Holes and Baby Universes and Other Essays, 1993; The Nature of Space and Time (with Roger Penrose), 1996 and other essays; The Universe in a Nutshell, 2001; The Theory of Everything: The Origin and Fate of the Universe, 2002; The Future of Space Time, co-editor, 2001; On the Shoulders of Giants, 2002. Contributions to: Scholarly journals. Honours: Eddington Medal, 1975, Gold Medal, 1985, Royal Academy of Science; Pius XI Gold Medal, Pontifical Academy of Sciences, 1975; William Hopkins Prize, Cambridge Philosophical Society, 1976; Maxwell Medal, Institute of Physics, 1976; Dannie Heinemann Prize for Mathematical Physics, American Physical Society and American Institute of Physics, 1976; Honorary fellow, University College, Oxford, 1977; Trinity Hall, Cambridge, 1984; Commander of the Order of the British Empire, 1982; Paul Dirac Medal and Prize, Institute of Physics, 1987; Wolf Foundation Prize for Physics, 1988; Companion of Honour, 1989; Britannica Award, 1989; Albert Medal, Royal Society of Arts, 1999; Honorary doctorates. Memberships: American Academy of Arts and Sciences; American Philosophical Society; Pontifical Academy of Sciences; Royal Society, fellow. Address: c/o Department of Applied Mathematics and Theoretical Physics, Cambridge University, Silver Street, Cambridge CB3 9EW, England.

**HAWKINS Angus Brian,** b. 12 April 1953, Portsmouth, England. Historian. m. Esther Armstrong, 20 May 1980, 2 daughters. Education: BA Hons, Reading University, 1975; PhD,

London School of Economics, 1980. Publications: Parliament, Party and the Art of Politics in Britain, 1987; Victorian Britain: An Encyclopaedia, 1989; British Party Politics, 1852-1886, 1998; The Political Journals of the First Earl of Kimberley, 1862-1902, 1998. Contributions to: English Historical Review, Parliamentary History, Journal of British Studies, Victorian Studies; Nineteenth Century Prose, Archive. Honours: McCann Award, 1972; Gladstone Memorial Prize, 1978. Memberships: Reform Club; Fellow, Royal Historical Society. Address: Rewley House, University of Oxford, 1 Wellington Square, Oxford, England.

**HAWKINS Peter John,** b. 20 June 1944, Old Welwyn, Hertfordshire, England. Art and Antiques Consultant. Education: MA, Modern Languages, Oxford University. Appointments: Director of Christie's (Auctioneers), 1973-2003; Managing Director of Christie's, Monte Carlo, 1987-89. Publication: The Price Guide to Antique Guns and Pistols, 1973. Honours: Freedom of the City of London; Liveryman of the Worshipful Company of Gunmakers, 1978-; Memberships: Turf Club, 1973-. Address: 20 Ennismore Gardens, London SW7 1AA, England.

**HAWN Goldie,** b. 21 November 1945, Washington, USA. Actress. Divorced, 3 children. Career: debut, Good Morning, World, 1967-68; TV includes: Rowan and Martin's Laugh-In, 1968-70; Pure Goldie, Natural history documentary, 1996; Films include: Cactus Flower; There's a Girl in my Soup; Dollars; The Sugarland Express; The Girl from Petrovka; Shampoo; The Duchess and the Dirtwater Fox; Foul Play; Seems Like Old Times; Private Benjamin; Best Friends; Protocol; Swing Shift; Overboard; Bird on a Wire; Housesitter; Deceived; Death Becomes Her; The First Wives Club, 1996; Everybody Says I Love You, 1996; The Out of Towners, 1999; Town and Country, 2001; The Banger Sisters, 2003; Star and Executive Producer: Goldie Hawn Special, 1978, Private Benjamin, 1980; Executive Producer, Something To Talk About; Co-Executive Producer, My Blue Heaven, 1990. Address: Creative Artists Agency, 9830 Wilshire Boulevard, Beverly Hills, CA 90212, USA.

**HAWORTH John,** b. 13 April 1942, Bury, Lancashire, England. Medical Practitioner. m. W Eleanor Roan, 1 daughter. Education: University of St Andrews (Queen's College, Dundee), 1960-66; MB, ChB, 1966; D Obst RCOG, 1970; MRCGP, 1974; FRCGP, 1991; DFFP, 1993. Appointments: House Physician, Maryfield Hospital, Dundee, 1966-67, House Surgeon, Perth Royal Infirmary, 1976; Senior House Officer: Medicine, Cumberland Infirmary, Carlisle, 1978-68, Obstetrics and Gynaecology, City Maternity Hospital, Carlisle, 1968-69, Accident and Emergency Department, Cumberland Infirmary, Carlisle, 1969; Trainee General Practitioner, 1969-70; Principal in General Practice, Carlisle, 1970-97; Member, Faculty Board, Cumbria Faculty, 1977-, Treasurer, 1980-90, Vice-Chairman, 1992-93, Chairman, 1993-96, Provost Designate, 2004-, Royal College of General Practitioners; Honorary Secretary, East Cumbria Division, 1976-, Member, Representative Body, 1984-, Member, Retired Members Forum, 2004-, British Medical Association; Medical Officer, Carlisle United Association Football Club, 1991-; Medical Officer, Aotearoa Maori Rugby League Team, Rugby League World Cup, 2000; Justice of the Peace, 1997. Publications: Many serious and humorous articles and papers in: The Practitioner, Trainee Supplement to Update, Pulse, Update, The Physician, Prescriber, GP; Chapters in Alimentary, My Dear Doctor and in Nervous Laughter; Author, Deeply Darkly Beautifully Blue, 2005. Memberships include: Royal College of General Practitioners; British Medical Association; Vice-Chairman, Carlisle District Crime Prevention Panel, 2000-; Director, Carlisle Rugby League Football Club,

1983-92; Secretary, 1973-76, President, 1988-89, Carlisle Medical Society; President, Carlisle Branch, Multiple Sclerosis Society, 1989-. Address: 40 Brampton Road, Carlisle, Cumbria CA3 9AT, England.

**HAY Jocelyn,** b. 30 July 1927, Wales, United Kingdom. Writer. m. Andrew Hay, 2 daughters. Education BA (Hons), Open University. Appointments: Freelance Writer and Broadcaster, 1954-83; Work included: Forces Broadcasting Service, Woman's Hour, BBC Radio 2 and 4, World Service; Head, Press and PR Department, Girl Guides Association, Commonwealth Headquarters, 1973-78; Founder and Director, London Media Workshops (training agency), 1978-94; Founder and Honorary Chairman, Voice of the Listener and Viewer( the leading advocate of the citizen and consumer in broadcasting in the UK), 1983-; Honorary Trustee, The Voice of the Listener Trust, 1987-; Honorary Trustee, Presswise, 2003-; President, The European Association of Listeners' and Viewers' Associations, Euralva. Publications: Numerous articles, speeches and broadcasts on broadcasting and cultural issues. Honours: MBE, 1999; Commonwealth Broadcasting Association's Elizabeth R Award for services to public service broadcasting, 1999; CBE, 2005. Memberships: Fellow, Royal Society of Arts; Society of Authors. Address: 101 King's Drive, Gravesend, Kent DA12 5BQ, England.

**HAYMAN, Rt Hon Baroness Helene Valerie,** b. 26 March 1949, Wolverhampton, England. Peer. m. Martin Hayman, 4 sons. Education: BA Law, Newnham College, Cambridge, 1969. Appointments: MP, Labour, Welwyn and Hatfield, 1974-79; Founder Member, Maternity Alliance, Broadcaster, 1979-85; Vice-Chairman, Bloomsbury Health Authority, 1985-92; Chairman, Bloomsbury and Islington District Health Authority, 1992; Chairman, Whittington Hospital National Health Trust, 1992-97; Sits as Labour Peer in The House of Lords, 1995-; Parliamentary Under Secretary for State, Department of Environment, Transport and the Regions, 1997; Parliamentary Under Secretary of State, Department of Health, 1998; Minister of State, Ministry of Agriculture Fisheries and Food, 1999-2001; Chair, Cancer Research UK, 2001-2004; Member, Committee of Privy Counsellors reviewing the Anti-Terrorism, Crime and Security Act, 2001; Trustee, Royal Botanic Gardens, Kew, 2002; Member, Board of Road Safe, 2003; Chair, Specialised Health Care Alliance, Member, Select Committee on the Assisted Dying for the Terminally Ill Bill, 2004; Member, Constitution Committee, 2004; Chair, Human Tissue Authority, 2005. Honours: Life Peerage, 1995; Privy Counsellor, 2000. Address: The House of Lords, Westminster, London SW1A 0PW, England.

**HAYMAN Walter Kurt,** b. 6 January 1926, Cologne, Germany. Mathematician. m. (1) Margaret Riley Crann, 1947, deceased 1994, 3 daughters, (2) Waficka Katifi, 1995, deceased 2001. Education: St John's College, Cambridge, 1943-46; MA ScD Fellow, 1947-50. Appointments: Lecturer, King's College, Newcastle, 1947, Exeter, 1947-53; Reader, 1953-56; Professor of Pure Mathematics, Imperial College, University of London, 1956-85; Dean of RCS, 1978-81; FIC, 1989; Part time Professor, University of York, 1985-93; Professor Emeritus, Universities of London and York, Senior Research Fellow, Imperial College, 1995-. Publications: Multivalent Functions, Cambridge, 1958, 2nd edition, 1994; Meromorphic Functions, Oxford, 1964; Research Problems in Function Theory, 1967; Subharmonic Functions, Vol I 1976, Vol II 1989; Papers in various journals. Honours: 1st Smith's Prize, 1948, shared Adam's Prize, 1949, Cambridge University; Junior Berwick Prize, 1955, Senior Berwick Prize, 1964, de Morgan Medal, 1995, Vice President, 1982-84, London Mathematical Society; Co-founder with

Mrs Hayman, British Mathematical Olympiad. Memberships: London Mathematics Society, 1947-; Visiting Lecturer, Brown University, USA, 1949-50; Fellow, 1956-, Council, 1962-63, Royal Society; Foreign Member, Finnish Academy of Science and Letters; Accademia Nazionale dei Lincei (Rome); Corresponding Member, Bavarian Academy of Science; Hon DSc, Exeter, 1981, Birmingham, 1985, University of Ireland, 1997; Hon Dr rer nat, Giessen, 1992; Hon DPhil, Uppsala, 1992; Visiting Lecturer, American Mathematics Society, 1961. Address: Department of Mathematics, Imperial College London, London SW7 2AZ, England.

**HAYTER Alethea Catharine,** b. 7 November 1911, Cairo, Egypt. Former British Council Representative and Cultural Attaché; Writer. Education: BA, MA, University of Oxford. Publications: Mrs Browning: A Poet's Work and Its Setting, 1962; A Sultry Month: Scenes of London Literary Life in 1846, 1965; Elizabeth Barrett Browning, 1965; Opium and the Romantic Imagination, 1968; Horatio's Version, 1972; A Voyage in Vain, 1973; Fitzgerald to His Friends: Selected Letters of Edward Fitzgerald, 1979; Portrait of a Friendship, Drawn From New Letters of James Russell Lowell to Sybella Lady Lyttelton 1881-1891, 1990; The Backbone: Diaries of a Military Family in the Napoleonic Wars, 1993; Charlotte Yonge, 1996; A Wise Woman: A Memoir of Lavinia Mynors from her Diaries and Letters, 1996; The Wreck of the Abergavenny, 2002. Contributions to: Oxford Companion to English Literature; Sunday Times; Times Literary Supplement; Spectator; New Statesman; History Today; Ariel; London Review of Books; Longman Encyclopaedia. Honours: W.H. Heinemann Prize, Royal Society of Literature, 1963; Rose Mary Crawshay Prize, British Academy, 1968; Officer of the Order of the British Empire. Memberships: Royal Society of Literature, fellow; Society of Authors, committee of management, 1975-79; PEN. Address: 22 Aldebert Terrace, London SW8 1BJ, England.

**HAYTON Philip,** b. 2 November 1947, Yorkshire, England. Journalist; Broadcaster. m. Thelma, 1 son, 1 daughter. Education: Various schools in the UK and USA. Appointments: Reporter, Newscaster, 1968-; BBC Radio Leeds; Look North, Leeds; Roving Correspondent, BBC TV News; Presenter, BBC TV's One, Six and Nine O'Clock News, BBC World, BBC News 24. Address: c/o Arlington Enterprises, 1-3 Charlotte Street, London W1P 1HD, England. E-mail: hayton@talk21.com

**HAYWARD Marie (Pauline).** b. Norwich, England. Opera Singer; Teacher. Widowed, 1 son. Education: Royal Academy of Music; MA, Text and Performance Studies, Royal Academy of Dramatic Art; London Opera Centre; Ricci and Tito Gobbi, Italy; MA; ARAM; LRAM; RAMDipl. Debut: Royal Opera House, Verdi, Wagner and Strauss roles. Career: Numerous world-wide appearances, including Royal Albert Hall, Festival Hall, Musikverein, Vienna, London Coliseum, Kiel Opera House, Germany; Also Ring Cycle at Lubeck, Hamburg and Mannheim under Klaus Tennstedt; Verdi and Wagner roles; Major roles include: Abigail, Northern Ireland Opera, Brunnhilde for English National Opera, Elvira and Fiordiligi at Glyndebourne; Miss Jessel in Turn of the Screw at Geneva and Sadlers Wells, English Opera; Oratorio performances in England and Europe; BBC broadcasts, Melodies for You, Friday Night is Music Night; Workshops and Masterclasses at Milan and Heidelberg Universities; Teacher of Voice and Singing. Recordings: Serenade to Music; Pilgrim's Progress; Adrian Boult, Ave Maria; Robert Stolz; Adorations. Honours: ARAM, 1993; 2nd Prize, s'Hertogenbosch International Competition; Medal of Distinction, Geneva. Membership: ISM; Association of Singers and Speakers; Association of Teachers of Singing.

Address: "Illyria" 27 Cyprus Avenue, Finchley N3 1SS, England. E-mail: marie@angelicvoices.demon.co.uk

**HE Qing-Yu,** b. 12 March 1963, Guangdong, China. Academic Researcher. m. Lihong (Lily) Huang, 1 son. Education: BSc, Chemistry, Jinan University, Guangzhou, China, 1981-85; MSc, Chemistry, Jinan/Sun Yat-Sen University, Guangzhou, China, 1985-88; PhD, Chemistry, University of Sheffield, England, 1992-95. Appointments: Assistant Engineer, RIPP, Beijing, China, 1988-91; Visiting Scholar, University of Oxford, England, 1992; Postdoctoral Fellow and Research Associate, 1996-2001, Assistant Professor(Research), 2001, University of Vermont, USA; Assistant Professor (Research), University of Hong Kong, Hong Kong, 2002-2005; Professor and Director, Institute of Life and Health Engineering, Jinan University, Guangzhou, China, 2005-. Publications: 64 research and review articles in primary international journals with an averaged Impact Factor (SCI)>4. Honours: Scientist Development Grant Award, American Heart Association, 2002; Listed in Who's Who publications and biographical dictionaries. Memberships: Royal Society of Chemistry, UK; American Society for Biochemistry and Molecular Biology. Address: 7N-12 Kadoorie Building, IMB, University of Hong Kong, Pokfulam, Hong Kong. E-mail: qyhe@hku.hk and heqy1@yahoo.com

**HEALD Tim(othy Villiers), (David Lancaster),** b. 28 January 1944, Dorset, England. Journalist; Writer. m. (1) Alison Martina Leslie, 30 March 1968, dissolved, 2 sons, 2 daughters, (2) Penelope Byrne, 1999. Education: MA, Honours, Balliol College, Oxford, 1965. Appointments: Reporter, Sunday Times, 1965-67; Feature Editor, Town magazine, 1967; Feature Writer, Daily Express, 1967-72; Associate Editor, Weekend Magazine, Toronto, 1977-78; Columnist, Observer, 1990; Visiting Fellow, Jane Franklin Hall, University of Tasmania, 1997, 1999; University Tutor, Creative Writing, 1999, 2000; FRSL, 2000; Writer-in-Residence, University of South Australia, 2001. Publications: It's a Dog's Life, 1971; Unbecoming Habits, 1973; Blue Book Will Out, 1974; Deadline, 1975; Let Sleeping Dogs Die, 1976; The Making of Space, 1999, 1976; John Steed: An Authorised Biography, 1977; Just Desserts, 1977; H.R.H: The Man Who Will be King, with M Mohs, 1977; Murder at Moose Jaw, 1981; Caroline R, 1981; Masterstroke, 1982; Networks, 1983; Class Distinctions, 1984; Red Herrings, 1985; The Character of Cricket, 1986; Brought to Book, 1988; Editor, The Newest London Spy, 1988; Business Unusual, 1989; By Appointments: 150 Years of the Royal Warrant, 1989; Editor, A Classic English Crime, 1990; Editor, My Lord's, 1990; The Duke: A Portrait of Prince Philip, 1991; Honourable Estates, 1992; Barbara Cartland: A Life of Love, 1994; Denis: The Authorised Biography of the Incomparable Compton, 1994; Brian Johnston: The Authorised Biography, 1995; Editor, A Classic Christmas Crime, 1995; Beating Retreat: Hong Kong Under the Last Governor, 1997; Stop Press, 1998; A Peerage for Trade, 2001; Village Cricket, 2004; Death and the Visiting Fellow, 2004; Death and the d'Urbervilles, 2005. Contributions: Short stories: EQMM; Strand magazine; Tatler; Mail on Sunday. Memberships: Crime Writers Association, Chairman, 1987-88; PEN; Society of Authors. Address: 66 The Esplanade, Fowey, Cornwall PL23 1JA, England. E-mail: timheald@compuserve.com

**HEALEY Denis (Lord Healey of Riddlesden),** b. 30 August 1917, Keighley, Yorkshire, England. Politician; Writer. m. Edna May Edmunds, 1945, 1 son, 2 daughters. Education: BA, 1940, MA, 1945, Balliol College, Oxford. Appointments include: Served, World War II, 1939-45; Contested, (Labour) Pudsey and Otley Division, 1945; Secretary, International Department, Labour Party, 1945-52; Member of Parliament, South East Leeds, 1952-55, Leeds East, 1955-92; Shadow Cabinet, 1959-64, 1970-74, 1979-87; Secretary of State for Defence, 1964-70; Chancellor of the Exchequer, 1974-79; Opposition Spokesman on Foreign and Commonwealth Affairs, 1980-87; Deputy Leader, Labour Party, 1980-83; Member House of Lords. Publications: The Curtain Falls, 1951; New Fabian Essays, 1952; Neutralism, 1955; Fabian International Essays, 1956; A Neutral Belt in Europe, 1958; NATO and American Security, 1959; The Race Against the H Bomb, 1960; Labour Britain and the World, 1964; Healey's Eye, 1980; Labour and a World Society, 1985; Beyond Nuclear Deterrence, 1986; The Time of My Life (autobiography), 1989; When Shrimps Learn to Whistle (essays), 1990; My Secret Planet, 1992; Denis Healey's Yorkshire Dales, 1995; Healey's World, photographs, 2002. Honours include: Grand Cross of Order of Merit, Germany, 1979; Freeman, City of Leeds, 1992; FRSL, 1993. Membership: President, Birkbeck College, 1992-98. Address: House of Lords, London SW1A 0PQ, England.

**HEALEY Norman J,** b. 2 September 1940, England. Manipulative Physician. m. Maureen Brock, 3 daughters. Education: Guy's Hospital, London, 1959-65; MRCS; DA; DRCOG; FLCOM, 1979; ND, 1994. Appointments: Surgeon Lieutenant, Royal Navy, 1965-71; HMS Albion service in Far East, 1968-69; SHO, Royal Bucks Hospital, Aylesbury, 1972; Tutor, London College of Osteopathic Medicine, 1974; Consultant Medical Osteopath, Manipulative Physician, 1975-; Clinical Assistant, Rheumatology, St Mary's Hospital London, 1975-82; Musculoskeletal Medicine Specialist, Transport Friendly Society, 1982-; Honorary Consultant in Rheumatology, St Luke's Hospital, London, 1987-; PPP and BUPA Recognised Specialist, Musculoskeletal Medicine, 1978-. Publication: Manipulation in Rehabilitation, British Association of Manipulative Medicine Annual Symposium, London, 1979. Honours: Kitchener Scholarship, 1959; Fellowship, London College of Osteopathic Medicine, 1979. Memberships: Fellow, Royal Society of Medicine; British Society for Rheumatology; British Osteopathic Association, Ex Honorary Secretary, 1982; British Naturopathic Association, 1994; Member, Debrett's Society; Royal Western Yacht Club of England. Address: 86 Harley Street, London W1G 7HP, England. E-mail: healeyma@aol.com Website: www.healeyclinic.co.uk

**HEALEY Robin Michael,** b. 16 February 1952, London, England. Historian; Biographer. Education: BA, 1974, MA, 1976, University of Birmingham. Appointments: Documentation Officer, Tamworth Castle and Cambridge Museum of Archaeology and Anthropology, 1977-80; Research Assistant, History of Parliament, 1985-92; Visiting Research Fellow, Manchester University, 1997-, Editor, Lewisletter, 2000-. Publications: Books: Hertfordshire (A Shell County Guide), 1982; Diary of George Mushet (1805-13), 1982; Grigson at Eighty, 1985; A History of Barley School, 1995; My Rebellious and Imperfect Eye: Observing Geoffrey Grigson, 2002; Contributions to: Biographical Dictionary of Modern British Radicals, 1984; Domesday Book, 1985; Secret Britain, 1986; Dictionary of Literary Biography, 1991; Encyclopaedia of Romanticism, 1992; Consumer Magazines of the British Isles, 1993; Postwar Literatures in English, 1998-; I Remember When I Was Young, 2003; Oxford Dictionary of National Biography, 2004. Also: Country Life; Hertfordshire Countryside; Guardian; Literary Review; Private Eye; Book and Magazine Collector; Rare Book Review; Independent; Times Literary Supplement; Art Newspaper; B M Insight; Mensa Magazine; Wyndham Lewis Annual; Charles Lamb Bulletin; Cobbett's New Political Register. Honour: 1st Prize, Birmingham Post Poetry Contest, 1974. Memberships: Executive, Charles Lamb Society, 1987-; Press Officer, Alliance of Literary Societies, 1997-; Wyndham

Lewis Society, 2000-. Address: 80 Hall Lane, Great Chishill, Royston, Herts SG8 8SH, England.

**HEANEY Seamus (Justin),** b. 13 April 1939, County Londonderry, Northern Ireland. Poet; Writer; Professor. m. Marie Devlin, 1965, 2 sons, 1 daughter. Education: St Columb's College, Derry; BA 1st Class, Queen's University, Belfast, 1961. Appointments: Teacher, St Thomas's Secondary School, Belfast, 1962-63; Lecturer, St Joseph's College of Education, Belfast, 1963-66, Queen's University, Belfast, 1966-72, Carysfort College, 1975-81; Senior Visiting Lecturer, 1982-85, Boylston Professor of Rhetoric and Oratory, 1985-97, Harvard University; Professor of Poetry, Oxford University, 1989-94. Publications: Eleven Poems, 1965; Death of a Naturalist, 1966; Door Into the Dark, 1969; Wintering Out, 1972; North, 1975; Field Work, 1979; Selected Poems, 1965-1975, 1980; Sweeney Astray, 1984, revised edition as Sweeney's Flight, 1992; Station Island, 1984; The Haw Lantern, 1987; New Selected Poems, 1966-1987, 1990; Seeing Things, 1991; The Spirit Level, 1996, Opened Ground: Selected Poems, 1966-1996, 1998; Electric Light, 2000. Prose: Preoccupations: Selected Prose, 1968-1978, 1980; The Government of the Tongue, 1988; The Place of Writing, 1989; The Redress of Poetry: Oxford Lectures, 1995; Beowulf: A New Verse Translation and Introduction, 1999; Finders Keepers: Selected Prose, 1971-2001. Honours: Somerset Maugham Award, 1967; Cholmondeley Award, 1968; W H Smith Award, 1975; Duff Cooper Prize, 1975; Whitbread Awards, 1987, 1996; Nobel Prize for Literature, 1995; Whitbread Book of the Year Award, 1997, 1999; Honorary DLitt, Oxford, 1997, Birmingham, 2000. Memberships: Royal Irish Academy; British Academy, American Academy of Arts and Letters. Address: c/o Faber & Faber, 3 Queen Square, London WC1N 3RU, England.

**HEAP Sir Peter William,** b. 13 April 1935, Dunchurch, Warwickshire, England. Former Diplomat; Consultant. m. Ann, 1 son, 1 step son, 2 daughters, 1 step daughter. Appointments: Foreign and Commonwealth Office, 1959-95; Diplomatic assignments to New York, Venezuela, Sri Lanka, Irish Republic, Canada; Head, Energy Science and Space Department, Foreign Office, 1980-83; High Commissioner to the Bahamas, 1983-86; Deputy High Commissioner, Nigeria, 1986-89; Trade Commissioner to Hong Kong and Consul General, Macau, 1989-92; HM Ambassador to Brazil, 1992-95; Adviser to the Board, HSBC Investment Bank Ltd, 1995-98; Chairman, Brazil Chamber of Commerce in Great Britain, 1996-; Chairman, Brazil Britain Business Forum, 1998-2003; Former Non-Executive Director, DS Wolf International Ltd; Former Adviser to the BOC Group plc; Adviser Amerada Hess Ltd, 1996-2005; Deputy Chairman and Director, RCM Group, 2002-; Chairman, Labour Finance & Industry Group, 2003-; Chairman, Regal Petroleum plc, 2005-. Honours: KCMG; CMG. Address: 6 Carlisle Mansions, Carlisle Place, London SW1P 1HX, England. E-mail: pwheap@aol.com

**HEATH Michael John,** b. 13 October 1935, London, England. Cartoonist. m. (1), 2 daughters (2) Martha Swift, 2 daughters. Education: Brighton Art College; Trained as animator, Rank Screen Services. Career: Freelance Cartoonist, 1956-; Contributor, 1958-, Cartoon Editor, 1989-, The Spectator; Supply cartoons to: Punch, 1958-89; London Standard, 1976-86, London Daily News, 1987; Independent, 1986-96, Political Cartoonist, 1991-96; Private Eye, 1964-, strips for Private Eye include: The Gays, The Regulars, Great Bores of Today, Baby; Sunday Times, 1967-; Mail on Sunday, 1985-; Also, Lilliput, Tatler, Melody Maker, John Bull, Man About Town, Men Only, Honey. Publications: Private Eye Cartoon Library, 1973; Punch Cartoons of Michael Heath, 1976; Book of Bores, No1, 1976,

No2, Star Bores, 1979, No 3, Bores Three, 1983; Love All, 1982; Best of Heath, 1984; Welcome to America, 1985; The Complete Heath, 1990, Heath's Nineties. Honours: Glen Grant Cartoonist of the Year, 1978; What the Papers Say Cartoonist of the Year, 1981; Glen Grant Pocket Cartoonist of the Year, 1982; MBE, 2002. Address: c/o The Spectator, 56 Doughty Street, London WC1N 2LL, England.

**HEATH-STUBBS John (Francis Alexander),** b. 9 July 1918, London, England. Poet; Writer; Translator; Editor. Education: Worcester College for the Blind; Queen's College, Oxford. Appointments: English Master, Hall School, Hampstead, 1944-45; Editorial Assistant, Hutchinson's 1945-46; Gregory Fellow in Poetry, University of Leeds, 1952-55; Visiting Professor of English, University of Alexandria, 1955-58, University of Michigan, 1960-61; Lecturer in English Literature, College of St Mark and St John, Chelsea, 1963-73. Publications: Poetry: Wounded Thammuz, 1942; Beauty and the Beast, 1943; The Divided Ways, 1946; The Swarming of the Bees, 1950; A Charm Against the Toothache, 1954; The Triumph of the Muse, 1958; The Blue Fly in His Head, 1962; Selected Poems, 1965; Satires and Epigrams, 1968; Artorius, 1973; A Parliament of Birds, 1975; The Watchman's Flute, 1978; Mouse, the Bird and the Sausage, 1978; Birds Reconvened, 1980; Buzz Buzz, 1981; Naming the Beasts, 1982; The Immolation of Aleph, 1985; Cat's Parnassus, 1987; Time Pieces, 1988; Collected Poems, 1988; A Partridge in a Pear Tree, 1988; A Ninefold of Charms, 1989; Selected Poems, 1990; The Parson's Cat, 1991; Sweetapple Earth, 1993; Chimeras, 1994; Galileo's Salad, 1996; The Torriano Sequences, 1997; The Sound of Light, 2000. Play: Helen in Egypt, 1958. Autobiography: Hindsights, 1993. Criticism: The Darkling Plain, 1950; Charles Williams, 1955; The Pastoral, 1969; The Ode, 1969; The Verse Satire, 1969. Translator: Hafiz of Shiraz (with Peter Avery), 1952; Leopardi: Selected Prose and Poetry (with Iris Origo), 1966; The Poems of Anyte (with Carol A Whiteside), 1974; The Rubaiyat of Omar Khayyam (with Peter Avery), 1979; Sulpicia, 2000. Editor: Several books, including: Faber Book of Twentieth Century Verse (with David Wright), 1953; Poems of Science (with Phillips Salman), 1984. Honours: Queen's Gold Medal for Poetry, 1973; Oscar Williams/Jean Durwood Award, 1977; Officer of the Order of the British Empire, 1989; Commonwealth Poetry Prize, 1989; Cholmondeley Award, 1989; Howard Sargeant Award, 1989; Cross of St Augustine, 1999; Fellow, English Association, 1999. Membership: Royal Society of Literature, Fellow. Address: 22 Artesian Road, London W2 5AR, England.

**HECHT Anthony (Evan),** b. 16 January 1923, New York, New York, USA. Poet; Professor. m. (1) Patricia Harris, 27 February 1954, divorced 1961, 2 sons, (2) Helen D'Alessandro, 12 June 1971, 1 son. Education: BA, Bard College, 1944; MA, Columbia University, 1950. Appointments: Teacher, Kenyon College, 1947-48, State University of Iowa, 1948-49, New York University, 1949-56, Smith College, 1956-59; Associate Professor of English, Bard College, 1961-67; Faculty, 1967-68; John D Deane Professor of English of Rhetoric and Poetry, 1968-85, University of Rochester, New York; Hurst Professor, Washington University, St Louis, 1971; Visiting Professor, Harvard University, 1973, Yale University, 1977; Faculty, Salzburg Seminar in American Studies, 1977; Professor, Georgetown University, 1985-93; Consultant in Poetry, Library of Congress, Washington, DC, 1982-84; Andrew Mellon Lecturer in Fine Arts, National Gallery of Art, Washington, DC, 1992. Publications: A Summoning of Stones, 1954; The Seven Deadly Sins, 1958; A Bestiary, 1960; The Hard Hours, 1968; Millions of Strange Shadows, 1977; The Venetian Vespers, 1977; Obbligati: Essays in Criticism, 1986; The Transparent Man, 1990; Collected Earlier Poems, 1990; The Hidden Law:

The Poetry of W H Auden, 1993; On the Laws of the Poetic Art, 1995; The Presumption of Death, 1995; Flight Among the Tombs, 1996; The Darkness and the Light, 2001. Co-Author and Co-Editor: Jiggery-Pokery: A Compendium of Double Dactyls (with John Hollander), 1967. Editor: The Essential Herbert, 1987. Translator: Seven Against Thebes (with Helen Bacon), 1973. Contributions to: Many anthologies; Hudson Review; New York Review of Books; Quarterly Review of Literature; Transatlantic Review; Voices. Honours: Prix de Rome Fellowship, 1950; Guggenheim Fellowships, 1954, 1959; Hudson Review Fellowship, 1958; Ford Foundation Fellowships, 1960, 1968; Academy of American Poets Fellowship, 1969; Bollingen Prize, 1983; Eugenio Montale Award, 1983; Harriet Monroe Award, 1987; Ruth Lilly Award, 1988; Aiken Taylor Award, Sewanee Review, 1988; National Endowment for the Arts Grant, 1989; Phi Beta Kappa. Memberships: Academy of American Poets, honorary chancellor, 1971-97; American Academy of Arts and Sciences; American Academy of Arts and Letters; Phi Beta Kappa. Address: 4256 Nebraska Avenue North West, Washington, DC 20016, USA.

**HEDGES Patrick Armand**, b. 2 June 1948, Fort Bragg, North Carolina, USA. Computer Science. m. Penelope Ann Huff, divorced, 2 sons, 1 daughter. Education: AA, Human Resource and Management, St Leo College, Florida, 1985; Graduate, Air Command and Staff College, 1990; Air War College, 1993, United States Air Force. Appointments: Tour of duty, 55th Military Intelligence, Headquarters First Field Forces, Nha Trang, Vietnam, 1969-70, Intelligence Center, Headquarters United States Continental Army Command, Fort Bragg, North Carolina, 1970-72, Intelligence Operations, Headquarters United States Europe and Seventh Army, Heidelberg, Germany, 1972-75, Operations Research and System Analysis, United States Army Training and Doctrine Command, Fort Monroe, Virginia, 1975-77; Computer Programmer, Applied Technology Laboratory, Fort Eustis, Virginia, 1978-81; Co-Designer Air Tasking Order Computer System, Deputy Director Intelligence Operations Support, Chief of Systems Programming, Technical Advisor Joint Tactical Systems, 1912 Computer System Group, Langley Air Force Base, 1983-91; Chief of Air Force Computer Security Policy and Doctrine, Air Force Cryptologic Support Center, Texas, 1991-94; Chief of Air Force Computer Security, Chief of Information Protection Technical Support, Chief of Air Force Communications Security Policy, Technical Advisor Theatre Battle Management and Global Command & Control Systems' Security Certification, Air Force Communications Agency, Scott AFB, Illinois, 1994-. Publications: Co-author, US Army Net Assessment of US and Soviet Tank Crew Training; Conceptualised and guided the creation of 32 Air Force Computer Security publications; Authored security articles for the Air Force magazines, The Connection and The Intercom. Honours: Battalion Trophy for Outstanding Army Trainee, 1968; Outstanding Army Leadership Plaque for company, 1968; Non-Commissioned Officer of the Year, 1971; Outstanding Staff Action Officer for Intelligence, 1974; Office of the Secretary of Defense Letter of Appreciation, 1977; various Soldier of the Month and Soldier of the Quarter awards; several Suggestion Award Certificates; United States Presidential Awards: Bronze Star Medal, 1970, Meritorious Service Medal, 1977; Other awards: Army Commendation Medal, 1972 and 1975; 3 Good Conduct Medals; National Defense Medal, 1968; Vietnam Service Medal with three campaign battle stars, 1970; Vietnam Campaign Medal, 1970; Vietnam Cross of Gallantry (unit), 1970; Consistently received Department of the Army and Air Force Superior Performance Awards and Citations throughout government civilian career; Listed in numerous biographical dictionaries. Memberships: Veterans of Foreign Wars.

**HEFNER Hugh Marston**, b. 9 April 1926, Chicago, Illinois, USA. Publisher. m. (1) Mildred Williams, 1 son, 1 daughter, (2) Kimberley Conrad, 1989, 2 daughters. Education: BS, University of Illinois. Appointments: Editor-in-Chief, Playboy magazine, 1953-, Oui magazine, 1972-81; Chairman Emeritus, Playboy Enterprises, 1988-; President, Playboy Club International Inc, 1959-86. Honour: International Press Directory International Publisher Award, 1997. Address: Playboy Enterprises Inc, 9242 Beverly Boulevard, Beverly Hills, CA 90210, USA.

**HEGELER Sten**, b. 28 April 1923, Frederiksberg, Denmark. Psychologist. 1 son, 1 daughter. Education: Candidate for Psychology, University of Copenhagen, 1953. Publications: Peter and Caroline; Men Only; Choosing Toys for Children; What Everybody Should Know About AIDS; On Selenium; An ABZ of Love (with I Hegeler); Ask Inge and Sten; World's Best Slimming Diet; On Being Lonesome; XYZ of Love; Living is Loving. Contributions to: Aktuelt; Info; Editor, Taenk magazine. Honour: Ph-Fund and Honorary member of Danish Psychologists Association. Memberships: Danish Psychological Association; Danish Journalist Association; Danish Authors Association. Address: Frederiksberg Alle 25, DK-1820 Frederiksberg, Denmark.

**HEGGLAND Roar**, b. 25 May 1954, Vikebygd, Norway. Geoscientist. m. Lindis Åslid, 2 daughters. Education: Cand Real (MSc), Physics, University of Bergen, Norway, 1982. Appointment: Geophysicist, Statoil, 1984-. Publications include as author and co-author most recently: Chimneys in the Gulf of Mexico, 2000; Detection of Seismic Chimneys by Neural Networks a New Prospect Evaluation Tool, 2000; Detection of Seismic Objects, the Fastest Way to do Prospect and Geohazard Evaluations, 2001; Identifying gas chimneys and associated features in 3D seismic data by the use of various attributes and special processing, 2001; Mud volcanoes and gas hydrates on the Niger Delta front, 2001; Seismic Evidence of Vertical Fluid Migration Through Faults, Applications of Chimney and Fault Detection, 2002; Method of Seismic Signal Processing including Detection of objects in seismic data like gas chimneys and faults. Address: Statoil ASA, N-4035 Stavanger, Norway. E-mail: rohe@statoil.com

**HEILBRON Hilary Nora Burstein**, b. 2 January 1949, England. Barrister. Education: MA, Jurisprudence, Oxford University. Appointments: Called to the Bar, Gray's Inn, 1971, Bencher of Gray's Inn, 1995; Silk, 1987; Department of Trade and Industry Inspector into Blue Arrow plc, 1989-91; Member of the Bar Council, 1991-99; Chairman, London Common Law and Commercial Bar Association, 1991-93; Chairman, Independent Working Party into Civil Justice set up jointly by General Council of the Bar and the Law Society, 1993; Member, CEDR Advisory Panel, 1996-2002; Member of the Bar of NSW, Australia, 1996; SC NSW, Australia, 1997; Vice-Chairman, Marshall Aid Commemoration Commission, 1998-2002; Member, Civil Justice Council, 1998-2002; Vice-Chairman IBA International Litigation Committee, 2004-05; CEDR Accredited Mediator; Deputy Chairman, City Disputes Panel Limited; Deputy High Court Judge. Memberships: Fellow, RSA; ASA, LCIA. Address: Brick Court Chambers, 7-8 Essex Street, London WC2R 3LD, England. E-mail: hilary.heilbron@brickcourt.co.uk

**HEILBRUN Carolyn (Gold)**, b. 13 January 1926, East Orange, New Jersey, USA. Professor of English Literature Emerita; Writer. m. James Heilbrun, 20 February 1945, 1 son, 2 daughters. Education: BA, Wellesley College, 1947; MA, 1951, PhD, 1959, Columbia University. Appointments: Instructor, Brooklyn College, 1959-60; Instructor, 1960-62, Assistant Professor, 1962-67, Associate Professor, 1967-72, Professor of English Literature, 1972-86, Avalon Foundation Professor of Humanities, 1986-93, Professor Emerita, 1993-, Columbia University; Visiting Professor, University of California at Santa Cruz, 1979, Princeton University, 1981, Yale Law School, 1989. Publications: The Garrett Family, 1961; In the Last Analysis, 1964; Christopher Isherwood, 1970; Toward a Recognition of Androgyny, 1973; Lady Ottoline's Album, 1976; Reinventing Womanhood, 1979; Representation of Women in Fiction (editor), 1983; Writing a Woman's Life, 1988; Hamlet's Mother and Other Women, 1990; The Education of a Woman: The Life of Gloria Steinem, 1995; The Last Gift of Time, 1997; Collected Stories, 1997. Honours: Guggenheim Fellowship, 1966; Rockefeller Foundation Fellowship, 1976; Nero Wolfe Award, 1981; Senior Research Fellow, National Endowment for the Humanities, 1983; Alumnae Achievement Award, Wellesley College, 1984; Award of Excellence, Graduate Faculty of Columbia University Alumni, 1984; Life Achievement Award, Modern Language Association, 1999; Many honorary doctorates. Memberships: Modern Language Association, President, 1984; Mystery Writers of America; Phi Beta Kappa. Address: c/o Department of English, Columbia University, New York, NY 10027, USA.

**HEINE Susanna L,** b. 17 January 1942, Prague, Czechoslovakia. University Professor. m. Peter Pawlowsky. Education: Arbitur, 1960; Mag theol, University of Vienna, 1966; Ordained Pastor, Lutheran Church, 1968; Dr theol, University of Vienna, 1973; Habilitation, University of Vienna, 1979. Appointments: Assistant, New Testament Studies, 1968-79; Dozent (Lecturer) Religious Education, 1979-82; Professor, Religious Education, 1982-90; Professor of Pastoral Theology and Psychology of Religion, University of Zurich, 1990-96; Professor of Pastoral Theology and Psychology of Religion, University of Vienna, 1996-. Publications: Leibhafter Glaube, 1976; Biblische Fachdidaktik, 1976; Women and Early Christianity, 1987, 1990; Christianity and the Goddesses, 1988, 1990; Keines Religiöses Wörterbuch, (editor) 1984; Europa in der Krise der Neuzeit (editor), 1986; Islam Zwischen Selbstbild und Klischee (editor), 1995; Frauenbilder – Menschenrechte, 2000; Gedanken für den Tag, 2001; About 200 articles on education, psychology, feminism, history of ideas, interreligious dialogue. Memberships: European Academic Society of Theology, 1988-, Vice Chairman, 1996-2002; Science Board, Sigmund Freud Society, 1995-; World Conference, Religions and Peace, 1996-; Contact Committee for Questions concerning Islam, 1996-; Abrahamitic Friends, 1996-; Austrian Research Community on Social Ethics, 1997-; Board, International Society of Psychology of Religion, 1998-. Address: Protestant Faculty, University of Vienna, Rooseveltplatz 10, A-1090, Vienna.

**HEJNY Horst,** b. 7 August 1953, Solingen, Germany. Engineer. m. Birgit, 3 daughters. Education: Diploma, Chemical Engineering, University of Dortmund, Germany, 1979; Doctoral studies, Bergbau-Forschung GmbH, Essen, Germany; Doctorate, University of Essen, Germany, 1983. Appointments: Senior Scientist, Mining Engineering and Health and Safety in Mining, 1983-96, Deputy Head of Department, Project and Innovation Manager and Research and Development, 1996-2004, Deutsche Montan Technologie GmbH and the predecessor company, Bergbau-Forschung, GmbH; Independent Consultant in the fields of mining engineering, tunnel safety and innovation and project development and management, 2004-. Publications: Numerous papers in various international professional journals; Book: The Mining Industry Research Handbook (covering the results of the European Thematic Network NESMI). Membership: International Who's Who Historical Society. Address: Dr Horst Hejny Consulting, PO Box 100148, 46521

Dinslaken, Germany. E-mail: info@hejny-consulting.de Website: www.hejny-consulting.de

**HELBIG Klaus,** b. 26 August 1927, Germany. Geophysicist. m. Gerda, 1 son, 2 daughters. Education: MSc, 1952; PhD, 1955; DSc, 1964. Appointments: Seismic Party Chief, 1952, Assistant Professor, University of Munich, 1958, UNESCO Expert, Geophysics, 1959-61; Associate Professor, St Louis University, 1964; Research Director, Texaco, 1965-77; Full Professor, University of Utrecht and University of Amsterdam 1977-92. Publications: 85 articles; 3 books: Editor, Geophysical Prospecting, 1969-88; Co-editor, Handbook of Geophysical Exploration, current. Honours include: University Medal, University of Ghent, 1972; Conrad Schlumberger Award, 1984; Erasmus Award, 2002. Memberships: EAGE (honorary), SEG (honorary), DGG; AGU; EASE. Address: Kiebitzrain 84, D-30657 Hannover, Germany. E-mail: helbig.klaus@t-online.de

**HELLAWELL Keith,** b. 18 May 1942, Yorkshire, England. Anti-Drugs Co-ordinator; Police Officer. m. Brenda Hey, 1963, 1 son, 2 daughters. Education: Dewsbury Technology College; Cranfield Institute of Technology; London University. Appointments: Miner, 5 years; Joined Huddersfield Borough Police, progressed through every rank within West Yorkshire Police to Assistant Chief Constable; Deputy Chief Constable of Humberside, 1985-90; Chief Constable of Cleveland Police, 1990-93; Chief Constable of West Yorkshire Police, 1993-98; First UK Anti Drugs Co-ordinator, 1998-2001; Adviser to Home Secretary on International Drug Issues, 2001-. Publications: The Outsider, autobiography, 2002. Memberships include: Association of Police Officers Spokesman on Drugs; Advisory Council on the Misuse of Drugs; Board, Community Action Trust; Trustee, National Society for the Prevention of Cruelty to Children; Editorial Advisory Board, Journal of Forensic Medicine. Address: Government Offices, George Street, London SW1A 2AL, England.

**HELLWIG Birgitta Öman,** b. 11 June 1932, Borås, Sweden. Mathematician. m. Professor Günter Hellwig, 1 son, 3 daughters. Education: Filosofie Kandidat, Uppsala University, Sweden, 1954. Appointments: Technical Officer, Imperial Chemical Industries Ltd, Birmingham, England, 1957; Assistant, Mathematics Department, Uppsala University, 1958; Teaching Fellow, Harvard University Cambridge, Massachusetts, 1959; Senior Mathematician, Republic Aviation, Farmingdale, New York, 1960; Member, Research Staff, Systems Research Center, Lockheed Electrons Co, Bedminster, New Jersey, 1960-61; Translator Maths Textbooks, Addison-Wesley Publishing Co, Reading, Massachusetts, 1964; Reviewer Mathematics Reviews, Ann Arbor, Michigan, 1968-; Assistant to applicants' lawyers by proceedings European Court Human Rights, Strasbourg, France, 1989-. Publications: Contribution articles on differential operators to scientific journals: Math Zeitschrift 86, 1964; Math Zeitschrift 89, 1965; Journal of Mathematical Analysis and Applications 26, 1969; Wissenschaftliche Zeitschrift der Technischen Hochschule Karl-Marx-Stadt, 1969. Honour: Grantee, University Zürich, Switzerland, 1955-56. Memberships: President, Foreign Students Association, Zürich, 1955-56; Secretary, Swedish Students Association, Zürich, 1955-56; Nordiska Komitten för Mänskliga Rättigheter, 1998-. Listed in: Several Biographical Publications. Address: Pommerotter Weg 37, D-52076 Aachen, Germany.

**HELMER Roger,** b. 25 January 1944, London, England. Politician; Member of the European Parliament. m. Sara Winterbottom, 2 sons, 1 daughter. Education: Churchill College, Cambridge, 1962-65. Appointments: Senior marketing and general management positions with major multinational companies in the UK and East and South East Asia, 1965-98; Member of European Parliament (Conservative), 1999-. Publications: Straight Talking on Europe, 2000; A Declaration of Independence, 2003. Honour: Adam Smith Scholar, American Legislative Exchange Council, 2004. Memberships: European Parliament; Countryside Alliance; Lutyens Trust. Address: 11 Central Park, Lutterworth, Leicestershire LE17 4PN, England. E-mail: rhelmer@europarl.eu.int Website: www.rogerhelmer.com

**HELYAR Jane Penelope Josephine, (Josephine Poole),** b. 12 February 1933, London, England. Writer. m. (1) T R Poole, 1956, (2) V J H Helyar, 1975, 1 son, 5 daughters. Publications: A Dream in the House, 1961; Moon Eyes, 1965; The Lilywhite Boys, 1967; Catch as Catch Can, 1969; Yokeham, 1970; Billy Buck, 1972; Touch and Go, 1976; When Fishes Flew, 1978; The Open Grave, The Forbidden Room (remedial readers), 1979; Hannah Chance, 1980; Diamond Jack, 1983; The Country Diary Companion (to accompany Central TV series), 1983; Three For Luck, 1985; Wildlife Tales, 1986; The Loving Ghosts, 1988; Angel, 1989; This is Me Speaking, 1990; Paul Loves Amy Loves Christo, 1992; Scared to Death, 1994; Deadly Inheritance, 1995; Hero, 1997; Run Rabbit, 1999; Fair Game, 2000; Scorched, 2003. Television scripts: The Harbourer, 1975; The Sabbatical, 1981; The Breakdown, 1981; Miss Constantine, 1981; Ring a Ring a Rosie, 1983; With Love, Belinda, 1983; The Wit to Woo, 1983; Fox, 1984; Buzzard, 1984; Dartmoor Pony, 1984; Snow White (picture book), 1991; Pinocchio (re-written), 1994; Joan of Arc (picture book), 1998; The Water Babies (re-written), 1996; Anne Frank (picture book), 2005. Address: Poundisford Lodge, Poundisford, Taunton, Somerset TA3 7AE, England.

**HEMINGWAY Wayne,** b. 19 January 1961, England. Designer. m. Gerardine, 2 sons, 2 daughters. Education: BSc, Honours, Geography and Town Planning, 1979-82, University College, London; MA, Surrey. Appointments: Joint business, market stall, Camden, London; Creator and Co-founder with Geraldine Hemingway of footwear, clothing and accessory label, Red or Dead, 1992; Collection retailed through 8 Red or Dead shops in England, 3 Red or Dead shops in Japan and wholesaled to international network of retailers; Business sold, 1999; Joint venture with Pentland Group PLC, 1996-; Founder, Hemingway Design, 1999; Designer, new wing for Institute of Directors, Pall Mall, 2001; Current design and consultancy projects include Staiths South Bank, Tyneside (800-unit housing estate), carpet design, wall covering and menswear; projects with local councils including: Lancashire, Copeland Borough Council and the North West development Agency, Newcastle and Gateshead; Chair, Prince's Trust Fashion Initiative; Patron, Morecambe Winter Gardens; Judge, Stirling Prize; Professor, Development and Planning Department, Northumbria University, Newcastle upon Tyne. Publications: The Good, the Bad and the Ugly, with Geraldine Hemingway, 1998; Kitsch Icons, 1999; Just Above the Mantelpiece, 2000. Honours: Second Place, Young Business Person of the Year, 1990; Street Designers of the Year, British Fashion Awards, 1995, 1996, 1997, 1998. Address: Hemingway Design, 15 Wembley Park Drive, Wembley, Middlesex HA9 8HD, England.

**HEMMING John Henry,** b. 5 January 1935, Vancouver, British Columbia, Canada. Author; Publisher. m. Sukie Babington-Smith, 1979, 1 son, 1 daughter. Education: McGill and Oxford Universities; MA; D.Litt. Appointments: Explorations in Peru and Brazil, 1960, 1961, 1971, 1972, 1986-87; Director and Secretary, Royal Geographical Society, 1975-96; Joint Chairman, Hemming Group Ltd, 1976-; Chair, Brintex Ltd., Newman Books Ltd. Publications: The Conquest of the Incas, 1970; Tribes of the Amazon Basin in Brazil (with others), 1973;

Red Gold: The Conquest of the Brazilian Indians, 1978; The Search for El Dorado, 1978; Machu Picchu, 1982; Monuments of the Incas, 1983; Change in the Amazon Basin, (editor), 2 volumes, 1985; Amazon Frontier: The Defeat of the Brazilian Indians, 1987; Maracá, 1988; Roraima: Brazil's Northernmost Frontier, 1990; The Rainforest Edge (editor), 1994; The Golden Age of Discovery, 1998; Die If You Must, Brazilian Indians in the 20th Century, 2003. Honours: CMG; Pitman Literary Prize, 1970; Christopher Award, New York, 1971; Order of Merit (Peru) 1991; Order of the Southern Cross (Brazil), 1998; Honorary doctorates, University of Warwick, University of Stirling; Honorary Fellow, Magdalen College, Oxford; Medals from Royal Geographical Society, Boston Museum of Science, Royal Scottish Geographical Society; Citation of Merit, New York Explorers' Club. Address: Hemming Group Ltd, 32 Vauxhall Bridge Road, London SW1V 2SS, England. E-mail: j.hemming@hgluk.com

**HENDERICKX Willem F M R,** b. 17 March 1962, Lier, Belgium. Composer; Professor. m. Beatrice Steylaerts, 3 sons. Education: First Prizes in Percussion, Harmony, Counterpoint, Fugue, Musical Analysis, Composition, Royal Antwerp Conservatory, 1984-92; Composition Courses in Darmstadt, Germany, 1988; Courses in Electronics, The Hague, The Netherlands, 2001. Appointments: Timpanist, Beethoven Academy, Antwerp, Belgium, 1985-95; Professor of Composition and Musical Analysis: Royal Antwerp Conservatory of Music, 1996-, Lemmensinstitut, Louvain, Belgium, 1989-, Royal Conservatory of Amsterdam, The Netherlands, 2002-; Composer of opera, symphonic works and chamber music; House Composer, Musical Theatre Transparant, Antwerp, 2005-. Publications: Ons Erfdeel: Wim Henderickx by H Heughebaert, 1995; Mens en melodie: The Composer Wim Henderickx by Y Knockaert, 1998. Honours: Prize of Contemporary Music, Quebec, Canada, 1993; Prize of the Province of Antwerp, 1999; Prize of the Royal Flemish Academy, Flanders, Belgium, 2002. Memberships: SABAM (Belgian Copyright); CEBEDEM (Belgian Music Publisher). Address: Florisstraat 8, B-2018 Antwerp, Belgium.

**HENDERSON Douglas James,** b. 28 July 1934, Calgary, Alberta, Canada. Theoretical Physicist. m. Rose-Marie Steen-Nielssen, 3 daughters. Education: BA, 1st Class Honours, 1st place, Mathematics, University of British Columbia, 1956; PhD, Physics, University of Utah, USA, 1961. Appointments include: Assistant Professor, Associate Professor, Professor, Physics, Arizona State University, USA, 1962-69; Associate Professor, Physics, 1964-67, Professor, Applied Mathematics, Physics, 1967-69, Adjunct Professor, Applied Mathematics, 1969-85, University of Waterloo, Canada; Research Scientist, 1969-90, Research Scientist Emeritus, 1992-, IBM Almaden Research Center, San Jose, California; Research Scientist, IBM Corporation, Salt Lake City, Utah, 1990-92; Adjunct Professor, Physics, 1990-93, Adjunct Professor, Chemistry, Mathematics, 1990-95, Research Scientist, Center for High Performance Computing, 1990-95, University of Utah; Manuel Sandoral Vallarta Professor, Physics, 1988; Juan de Oyarzabal Professor, Physics, 1993-95, Juan de Oyarzabal Honorary Professor, 1996-, Universidad Autonoma Metropolitana, Mexico; Honorary Professor of Chemistry, University of Hong Kong, 1993-; Professor, Chemistry, Brigham Young University, 1995-; Many visiting positions. Publications: Over 450 research papers in scientific journals; Co-author, Statistical Mechanics and Dynamics, 1964, 2nd edition, 1982; Co-editor, Physical Chemistry: An Advanced Treatise, 15 volumes, 1966-75; Co-author, Chemical Dynamics, 1971; Co-editor, Advances and Perspectives, 6 volumes, 1973-81; Editor, Fundamentals of Inhomogeneous Fluids, 1992. Honours include: Alfred P Sloan

Foundation Fellowship, 1964, 1966; Ian Potter Foundation Fellowship, 1966; Outstanding Research Contribution Award, 1973, Outstanding Innovation Award, 1987, IBM; Corresponding Member, National Academy of Sciences of Mexico, 1990; Catedra Patrimoniales de Excelencia, Mexico, 1993-95; Premio a las Areas de Investigacion, Universidad Autonoma Metropolitana, 1996; John Simon Guggenheim Memorial Foundation Fellow, 1997; Joel Henry Hildebrand National American Chemical Society Award in Theoretical and Experimental Chemistry of Liquids, 1999; American Chemical Society Utah Award, 2005. Memberships include: Fellow, American Physical Society, 1963-; Fellow, Institute of Physics, UK, 1965-; Fellow, American Institute of Chemists, 1971-; American Chemical Society; Biophysical Society; Canadian Association of Physicists; Mathematical Association of America; New York Academy of Sciences; Phi Kappa Phi; Sigma Xi; Sigma Pi Sigma. Address: Department of Chemistry, Brigham Young University, Provo, UT 84602, USA. E-mail: doug@chem.byu.edu

**HENDERSON George Poland,** b. 24 April 1920, London, England. Company Director. m. Shirley Prudence Ann, 2 sons. Education: University of London. Appointments: Captain, Royal Artillery, 1940-46; Commercial Reference Librarian, Guildhall Library, 1946-63; Director, Kelly's Directories Ltd, 1963-66; Director, now Chairman, CBD Research Ltd, 1966-. Publications: Current British Directories, 6 editions, 1953-71; European Companies: A Guide to Sources of Information, 3 editions, 1961-72; Directory of British Associations, 11 editions, 1965-92. Honours: Freeman, City of London, 1961. Memberships: Association of British Directory Publishers; European Association of Directory Publishers; Royal Institution of Great Britain; Royal Philatelic Society, London; Institute of Directors.

**HENDERSON Michael John Glidden,** b. 19 August 1938, Calcutta, India. Chartered Accountant. m. Stephanie Maria Dyer, 1965, 4 sons. Education: St Benedict's School, Ealing, 1948-56; Qualified as Chartered Accountant (FCA), 1961. Appointments: Williams Dyson Jones (Chartered Accountants), 1956-62; Whinney, Smith & Whinney (Chartered Accountants), 1962-65; Joined, 1965, Director, 1975, Managing Director, 1979, Chief Executive, 1984-90, Chairman, Chief Executive Officer, 1989-90, Goodlass, Wall & Lead Industries, renamed Cookson Group Plc; Chairman, Henderson Crossthwaite Holdings, 1995-2000; Director, Guiness Mahon Holdings, 1988-2000; Director, Quexco Inc (Vice-Chairman), 1999-; Director, Cyril Sweett Ltd, 1998-; Director, Wisley Golf Club Plc, 2002-; Deputy Chairman, 2004-, Governor, 1990-, and Deputy Chairman, 2002-, Chairman, Finance & General Purposes, Committee, 1992-, St George's College, Weybridge; Governor, 1992-, and Deputy Chairman, 1999-, Chairman, Finance and General Purposes Committee, 1992-, Cranmore School, West Horsely; Governor, 2002-, and Chairman, Finance and General Purposes Committee, 2003-, St Teresa's School, Effingham. Memberships: Innovation and Advisory Board, DTI, 1988-93; Trustee, Natural History Museum Development Trust, 1990-2000; FRSA, 1989; Knight of the Holy Sepulchre, 2005; MCC; Queens Club; The Wisley Golf Club. Address: "Langdale" Woodland Drive, East Horsley, Surrey KT24 5AN, England.

**HENDERSON Neil Keir,** b. 7 March 1956, Glasgow, Scotland. Education: MA, English Language, English Literature and Scottish Literature, Glasgow University, 1977. Publications: Maldehyde's Discomfiture, or A Lady Churned, 1997; Fish-Worshipping – As We Know It, 2001; An English Summer In Scotland and other Unlikely Events, 2005. Contributions to: Mystery of the City, poetry anthology, 1997; Loveable Warts: A

Defence of Self-Indulgence, Chapman 87, 1997; Mightier Than the Sword: The Punch-Up of the Poses, Chapman 91, 1998; The Red Candle Treasury, 1998; Labyrinths 6 (written in entirety), 2002. Address: 46 Revoch Drive, Knightswood, Glasgow G13 4SB, Scotland.

**HENDERSON William James Carlaw,** b. 26 September 1948, Galashiels, Selkirkshire, Scotland. Lawyer; Writer to the Signet. Education: George Heriot's School, Edinburgh; Old College, Faculty of Law, University of Edinburgh. Appointments: Trainee Solicitor, Patrick and James WS, 1971-73; Solicitor, Wallace and Guthrie, 1973-74; Solicitor, 1974-76, Partner, 1976-83, Allan McDougall and Co; Partner, Brodies WS, 1983-2003. Publications: 2 seminar papers, Moscow School of Political Studies, 1996, 1997; 1 monograph, 2001. Honours: Bachelor of Laws, LLB, 1971; Notary Public, 1975; Writer to the Signet, 1981. Memberships: Society of HM Writers to the Signet; Fellow, Royal Geographical Society; Royal Scottish Geographical Society; Secretary, 1980-83, Society of Scottish Artists, Honorary Life Member, 2005; Governor, Edinburgh College of Art, 1996 99; Director, Edinburgh Printmakers Workshop, 2001-; Trustee, Mendelssohn on Mull Music Festival, 2003-; Director, Family Mediation, Lothian, 2005-; Member, Royal Highland Yacht Club; Member, Edinburgh Sports Club. Address: 11 Inverleith Place, Edinburgh EH3 5QE, Scotland. E-mail: wjchenderson@suhamet.com

**HENDRY Stephen Gordon,** b. 13 January 1969, Edinburgh, Scotland. Snooker Player. m. Amanda Elizabeth Teresa Tart, 1995, 1 son. Appointments: Professional Player, 1985; Scottish Champion, 1986, 1987, 1988; Winner, Rothmans Grand Prix, 1987; World Doubles Champion, 1987; Australian Masters Champion, 1987; British Open Champion, 1988, 1991, 1999; New Zealand Masters Champion, 1988; Benson and Hedges Master Champion, 1989, 1990, 1991, 1992, 1993, 1996; UK Professional Champion, 1989, 1990, 1994, 1995, 1996; Asian Champion, 1989; Regal Masters Champion, 1989; Dubai Classic Champion, 1989; Embassy World Champion, 1990, 1992, 1993, 1994, 1995, 1996, 1999; Irish Masters, 1992; International Open, 1993. Publication: Snooker Masterclass, 1994. Honours: Dr hc (Stirling), 2000; MacRoberts Trophy, 2001. Address: Stephen Hendry Snooker Ltd, Kerse Road, Stirling FK7 7SG, Scotland.

**HENEIN Fawzi,** b. Balina, Egypt. Pharmacist. m. Erika, 1 daughter. Education: Master's Degree in Pharmacy, University of Vienna, 1968; D Pharm, University of Cairo, Egypt. Appointments: Owner, Chief Executive Officer, Apotheke zum Römer, 1980-2002; Owner and Chief Executive Officer, Beethoven Apotheke, Linz, Austria, 2004-. Publications: About 100 articles in newspapers and magazines; TV presentations, talk shows and interviews, Austrian and German TV. Honours: University of Vienna Master's Degree in Pharmacy, 1968; D Pharm, University of Cairo, awarded by the Ministry of Science and Research in Egypt and presented at the National Library in Vienna. Memberships: Chamber of Pharmacists; Österreicherischer Apothekerverband, Patientinhaber und Erfinderverband (OPEV); Austrian-Egyptian Society. Address: Hauptplatz 1-2, A-2405 Bad Deutsch Altenburg, Austria.

**HENLEY Elizabeth Becker,** b. 8 May 1952, Jackson, Mississippi, USA. Playwright. Education: BFA, Southern Methodist University. Publications: Crimes of the Heart, 1981; The Wake of Jamey Foster, 1982; Am I Blue, 1982; The Miss Firecracker Contest, 1984; The Debutante Ball, 1985, 1991; The Lucky Spot, 1987; Abundance, 1989; Beth Henley: Monologues for Women, 1992; Screenplays: Nobody's Fool, 1986; Crimes of the Heart, 1986; Miss Firecracker, 1989; Signatures, 1990; Control Freaks, 1993; Revelers, 1994. Honours: Pulitzer Prize for Drama, 1981; New York Drama Critics Circle Best Play Award, 1981; George Oppenheimer/Newsday Playwriting Award, 1981. Address: c/o The William Morris Agency, 1350 Avenue of the Americas, New York, NY 10019, USA.

**HENMAN Tim (Timothy Henry)**, b. 6 September 1974, Oxford, England. Professional Tennis Player. m. Lucy, 11 December 1999, 2 daughters. Education: Career: ATP: Winner, Sydney, Tashkent, Finalist, Doha and Antwerp, 1997; Winner, Basel, Tashkent, Finalist, Sydney, Los Angeles, 1998; Finalist, Doha, Rotterdam, Queens, Basel, 1999; Winner, Vienna, Brighton, Finals, Rotterdam, Scottsdale, Cincinnati, 2000; Winner, Copenhagen, Basel, Final, Queens Open, 2001; Winner, Adelaide, Final, Indian Wells TMS, Rotterdam, Queens, 2002; Winner, Washington, Paris TMS, 2003; Doubles Winner, Monte Carlo TMS (w Zimonjic), Final, Indian Wells TMS, 2004; Match Record Won 48 : Lost 24 (67%). Honours: Runner Up, BBC Sports Personality of the Year, 1997; Carlton Sports Personality, 1998. Address: c/o IMG, The Pier House, Strand on the Green, Chiswick, London W4 3NN, England.

**HENNI Amr**, b. 10 January 1957, Cairo, Egypt. Assistant Professor. m. Fatma-Zohra, 1 son, 2 daughters. Education: Diplome d'Ingenieur d'Etat, Gas Engineering, Algerian Institute of Petroleum, 1980; MSc, Mechanical Engineering, Stevens Institute of Technology, Hoboken, New Jersey, USA, 1984; MSc, Chemical Engineering, University of Alberta, Edmonton, Canada; PhD, Industrial Engineering, University of Regina, Canada, 2002. Appointments: Assistant Professor, 1984-89; Associate Professor, Algerian Institute of Petroleum, 1989-91; Assistant Professor, University of Regina, 2002-. Publications: 24 refereed publications; 10 conference papers. Honours: US Scholarship, Algerian Institute of Petroleum, 1981-83; Graduated second in class, High Distinction; Scholarship, King Fahd University, Saudi Arabia, 1989; Scholarship, University of Alberta, Edmonton, 1991-93; D B Robinson Graduate Award, Chemical Engineering, 1991; University of Alberta Bursary, Edmonton, 1994; CIM Graduate Research Award in Petroleum Engineering, 1998 and 2001; Sampson J Goodfellow Scholarship, 2001. Memberships: American Institute of Chemical Engineers; Canadian Society of Chemical Engineering; Canadian Institute of Mining, Metallurgy and Petroleum. Address: Industrial Systems, Engineering Department, Faculty of Engineering, University of Regina, Regina, Saskatchewan, Canada, S4S 0A2. E-mail: amr.henni@uregina.ca

**HENNING Jocelyn Ann Margareta Maria (Countess of Roden)**, b. 5 August 1948, Göteborg, Sweden. Author; Playwright; Translator; Broadcaster. m. Earl of Roden, 13 February 1986, 1 son. Education: BA, Lund University, Sweden, 1975. Publications include: Modern Astrology, 1983, 1985, 1993; The Connemara Whirlwind Trilogy, 1990-94, 2001; Keylines, 2000, 2001, 2005. Plays: Smile. Göteborg, 1972; Baptism of Fire, Galway, 1997, Pernik, 1999; The Alternative, Galway, 1998. Contributions to: Swedish and Irish Radio and Television. Memberships: Irish Writer's Union; Irish Playwrights' and Scriptwriters' Guild. Address: 4 The Boltons, London SW10 9TB, England.

**HENRY Lenny**, b. 29 August 1958, England. m. Dawn French, 1 daughter. Appointments: Numerous tours including Loud!, 1994; Australia, 1995. Creative Works: TV includes: New Faces (debut), Tiswas, Three of a Kind, 1981-83; The Lenny Henry Show, Alive and Kicking, 1991; Bernard and the Genie, 1991; In Dreams, 1992; The Real McCoy, 1992; Chef (title role) (3 series), Lenny Hunts the Funk, New Soul Nation, White Goods, 1994; Funky Black Shorts, 1994; Comic Relief, Lenny Go Home, 1996; Lenny's Big Amazon Adventure, 1997; Lenny

Goes to Town, 1998; The Man, 1998; Hope and Glory, 1999, 2000; Lenny's Big Atlantic Adventure, 2000; Lenny in Pieces, 2000, 2001; Films include: True Identity, 1991; Video: Lenny Henry Live and Unleashed, 1989; Lenny Henry Live and Loud, 1994; Toured Australia with Large! Show, 1998. Publications: The Quest for the Big Woof (autobiography), 1991; Charlie and the Big Chill (childrens book), 1995. Honours include: Monaco Red Cross Award; The Golden Nymph Award; BBC personality of the Year, Radio and TV Industry Club, 1993; Golden Rose of Montreux Award for Lenny in Pieces, 2000. Address: c/o PBJ Management Ltd, 5 Soho Square, London W1V 5DE, England.

**HENSON Ray David**, b. 24 July 1924, Johnston City, Illinois, USA. Lawyer, Professor of Law. Education: BS, 1947, JD, 1949, University of Illinois. Appointments: Counsel, Continental Assurance Co, and Continental Casualty Co, 1952-70; Professor of Law, Wayne State University, 1970-75; Professor of Law, 1975-95, Professor Emeritus, 1995-, University of California, Hastings College of Law. Publications: Landmarks of Law, 1960; Secured Transactions, 1973, 2nd edition, 1977; The Law of Sales, 1985; Documents of Title, 1983, 2nd edition, 1990; Various other books and numerous articles in American law reviews. Honours: Chairman, Business Law Section, American Bar Association, 1969-70; Chairman, Uniform Commercial Code Committee, American Bar Association, Illinois State Bar Association and Chicago Bar Association at various times; Member, Legal Advisory Committee, New York Stock Exchange, 1970-75. Memberships: American Bar Association; Illinois State Bar Association; Chicago Bar Association; American Law Institute; University Club, San Francisco. Address: 1400 Geary Blvd, II 2303, San Francisco, CA 94109-6561, USA.

**HENTSCHEL Erwin Josef**, b. 7 February 1934, Nieder-Mohrau, Sudeten. Professor. m. Eleonore, 1 daughter. Education: Dipl Biol, 1959, Dr rer nat, 1964, Facultas docendi for Animal Physiology, 1970, Dr sc nat, 1980, Dr rer nat habil, 1991, University of Jena. Appointments: Full Professor, University of Greifswald, 1988-89; Councillor, European Comparative Endocrinologists, Salzburg, 1988, Leuven, 1990; Originator, Apidology-Institute, University of Jena, 1989-97; Originator and President, European Society for Promoting the Science of Bees and Beekeeping, 1998; Member, Standing Commission of Bee Biology of APIMONDIA, 33rd International Apicultural Congress in Beijing, China, 1993. Honours: Schiller Medallist, 1986; Bundesverdienstkreuz am Bande, 2000. Memberships: Deutsche Zoologische Gesellschaft. Address: Freiligrathstr 8, D-07743 Jena, Germany.

**HERBERT (Edward) Ivor (Montgomery)**, b. 20 August 1925, Johannesburg, South Africa. Author; Journalist; Scriptwriter. Education: MA, Trinity College, Cambridge, 1949. Appointments: Travel Editor, Racing Editor, The Mail on Sunday, 1982-2002. Publications: Eastern Windows, 1953; Point to Point, 1964; Arkle: The Story of a Champion, 1966, further editions, 1975, 2003; The Great St Trinian's Train Robbery (screenplay), 1966; The Queen Mother's Horses, 1967; The Winter Kings (co- author), 1968, enlarged edition, 1989; The Way to the Top, 1969; Night of the Blue Demands, play (co-author), 1971; Over Our Dead Bodies, 1972; The Diamond Diggers, 1972; Scarlet Fever (co-author), 1972; Winter's Tale, 1974; Red Rum: Story of a Horse of Courage, 1974, further editions, 1974, 1977, 1995, 2005; The Filly (novel), 1977; Six at the Top, 1977; Classic Touch (TV documentary), 1985; Spot the Winner, 1978, updated, 1990; Longacre, 1978; Horse Racing, 1980; Vincent O'Brien's Great Horses, 1984; Revolting Behaviour, 1987; Herbert's Travels, 1987; Reflections on Racing (co-author), 1990; Riding Through My Life (with HRH

The Princess Royal), 1991. Memberships: Society of Authors; Writers' Guild. Address: The Old Rectory, Bradenham, Buckinghamshire HP14 4HD, England.

**HERBERT James (John),** b. 8 April 1943, London, England. Author. Education: Hornsey College of Art, 1959. Publications: The Rats, 1974; The Fog, 1975; The Survivor, 1976; Fluke, 1977; The Spear, 1978; Lair, 1979; The Dark, 1980; The Jonah, 1981; Shrine, 1983; Domain, 1984; Moon, 1985; The Magic Cottage, 1986; Sepulchre, 1987; Haunted, 1988; Creed, 1990; Portent, 1992; James Herbert: By Horror Haunted, 1992; James Herbert's Dark Places, 1993; The City, 1994; The Ghosts of Sleath, 1994; '48, 1996; Others, 1999; Once, 2001; Devil in the Dark, Craig Cabell, 2003; Nobody True, 2003. Films: The Rats, 1982; The Survivor, 1986; Fluke, 1995; Haunted, 1995. Address: c/o Bruce Hunter, David Higham Associates, 5-8 Lower John Street, London W1R 4HA, England.

**HERBIG George Howard,** b. 20 January 1920, Wheeling, West Virginia, USA. Astronomer. m. (1) Delia McMullin, 1943, divorced, 1968, 3 sons, 1 daughter, (2) Hannelore Tillmann, 1968. Education: Graduated, University of California at Los Angeles, 1943. Appointments: Junior Astronomer, 1948-50, Assistant Astronomer, 1950-55, Associate Astronomer, 1955-60, Astronomer, 1960-87, Assistant Director, 1960-63, Acting Director, 1970-71, Lick Observatory, California; Professor of Astronomy, University of California, Santa Cruz, 1967-87; Astronomer, 1987-2001, Astronomer Emeritus, 2001-, Institute for Astronomy, University of Hawaii. Publications: Editor of and contributor to: Non-Stable Stars, 1957; Spectroscopic Astrophysics, 1970; Approximately 220 scientific papers, articles and reviews. Honours: Warner Prize, American Astronomical Society, 1955; Medaille, University de Liege, 1969; Gold Medal, Astronomical Society for Pacific, 1980; Petrie Prize Canadian Astronomical Society, 1995. Memberships: NAS; American Academy of Arts and Sciences; Corresponding member, Societe scientifique Royale de Liege; Foreign Scientific member, Max-Planck-Institute fur Astronomie, Heidelberg; Numerous boards, commissions and consultancies. Address: Institute for Astronomy, University of Hawaii, 2680 Woodlawn Drive, Honolulu, HI 96822, USA.

**HERDMAN John Macmillan,** b. 20 July 1941, Edinburgh, Scotland. Writer. m. (1) Dolina Maclennan, divorced, (2) Mary Ellen Watson, 17 August 2002. Education: BA, 1963, MA, 1967, PhD, 1988, Magdalene College, Cambridge, England. Appointments: Creative Writing Fellow, Edinburgh University, Scotland, 1977-79; William Soutar Fellow, Perth, Scotland, 1990-91. Publications: Descent, 1968; A Truth Lover, 1973; Memoirs of My Aunt Minnie/Clapperton, 1974; Pagan's Pilgrimage, 1978; Stories Short and Tall, 1979; Voice Without Restraint: Bob Dylan's Lyrics, 1982; Three Novellas, 1987; The Double in Nineteenth-Century Fiction, 1990; Imelda and Other Stories, 1993; Ghostwriting, 1996; Cruising (play), 1997; Poets, Pubs, Polls and Pillarboxes, 1999; Four Tales, 2000; The Sinister Cabaret, 2001; Triptych, 2004. Honours: Scottish Arts Council Book Awards, 1978, 1993. Address: Roselea, Bridge of Tilt, Pitlochry, Perthshire PH18 5SX, Scotland.

**HERLEA Alexandre,** b. 11 October 1942, Brasov, Romania (French and Romanian Citizen). Professor. Married, 1 daughter. Education: Mechanical Engineer, Institutul Politechnic, Brasov, Romania, 1965; PhD, History of Science and Technology, Ecole des Hautes Etudes en Sciences Sociales and Conservatoire National des Arts et Métiers (CNAM), 1977; Habilitation, Sciences, Université de Paris Sud – Orsay, Sorbonne, France, 1993. Appointments: Engineer, IRGU Company, Bucharest, Romania, 1966-69; Lecturer, Scoala Technica "23 August",

Bucharest, Romania, 1969-72; University Researcher, History of Technology, CNAM, Paris, 1972-77; Visiting Researcher, Smithsonian Institution and Harvard, Princeton and Pennsylvania Universities, 1978-79; Research Engineer, CNAM, Paris, 1980-88; Associated Professor, Ecole Centrale des Arts et Manufactures, 1980-88; Senior Lecturer, History of Technology, 1988-94, Member of Teaching Staff, PhD Programmes, 1988-2000, CNAM, Paris; Visiting Professor, Michigan Technological University, USA, 1990, Universitatea Bucuresti, Romania, 1994; Professor with tenure, History of Technology, 1995-, Director of Social Science Department, 1995-97, Director of International Relations, 2001-, Université de Technologie, Belfort-Montbeliard, France; Minister for European Integration, Romanian Government, 1996-99; Ambassador, Head of the Romanian Mission to the European Union, 2000-2001. Publications: Author, co-author and editor of 12 books published in France, Italy, United States, United Kingdom including: Histoire générale des techniques. Les techniques de la civilisation industrielle, 1978; Les moteurs, 1985; Over 40 scientific studies and numerous political articles. Honours: Silver Medal, Société d'Encouragement au Progrés, France; The Prize "Soziale Marktwirtschaft, Wirtschaftspolitischer Club, Berlin, Germany; Commandeur de la Légion d'Honneur, France; Mare Ofiter (High Officer) Serviciul Credincios, Romania; Doctor Honoris Causa, University Transilvania Brasov, Romania. Memberships include: Comité das Traveaux Historiques et Scientifiques, France; International Committee for the History of Technology (President); International Academy of the History of Science; Romanian Christian Democrat Party (PNT-CD – Vice-President); Christian Democratic International (Member of the Executive Committee, former Vice-President). Address: 4, rue H. Fragonard, 92130 Issy-les-Moulineaux, France. E-mail: alexandre.herlea@wanadoo.fr

**HERMANN Armin Daniel,** b. 26 November 1937, Neu-Sarata, Moldavia. Nuclear Chemistry Engineer. m. Christine Seidel Hermann, 1970, divorced 1981, 1 son. Education: Diploma in Engineering, 1961, DSc, 1984, Technical University Dresden; PhD, Lomonossow University, Moscow, 1965. Appointments: Scientist, 1965-66, Group Leader, 1966-75, Head of Department, 1975-87, German Academy of Sciences; Project Manager, Paul Scherrer Institute, Switzerland, 1990-; Adviser, Nuclear Fuel Industry Research Group, Palo Alto, 1994-; Member, Co-ordination Council, Council of Mutual Economic Aid, Moscow, 1971-87; Nuclear Chemistry Educator, German Academy of Sciences, Technical High School, Zittau, Technical University, Dresden. Publications: Radiochemical Methods, textbook; 100 articles in scientific publications; Patentee in field of nuclear reactors. Honour: Recipient, Order Banner of Labour, governmental award. Memberships: German Chemical Society; Working Group, Nuclear Chemistry; German Society of Nuclear Technology; Swiss Union Atomic Energy; Christian Parish Control Commission. Address: Sommerhaldenstr 5A, 5200 Brugg, Aargau, Switzerland. E-mail: armin.hermann@ bluewin.ch.

**HERMANN Edward Robert,** b. 9 October 1920, Newport, Kentucky, USA. Professor Emeritus; Consultant. m. Eleanor Hill Hermann, 3 sons, 4 daughters. Education: BSCE, University of Kentucky, 1942; SM, Sanitary Engineering, MIT, 1949; CE, University of Kentucky, 1953; PhD, University of Texas, 1957. Appointments: Director of Industrial Hygiene Graduate Programmes, University of Illinois Medical Centre; Professor of Environmental and Occupational Health Sciences, School of Public Health, University of Illinois at Chicago; Professor, Acting Director, Occupational and Environmental Medicine, University of Illinois School of Public Health; Professor, Environmental Engineering, Department of Civil Engineering,

Mechanics and Metallurgy, University of Illinois at Chicago; Professor, Environmental Health Engineering, Northwestern University; Industrial Health Engineer, Humble Oil and Refining Company, (now Exxon Mobil); Chief Sanitary Engineer and Chief of Public Health, US Atomic Energy Commission, Los Alamos, New Mexico; Consultant to various industries, government agencies, law offices and universities. Publications: Over 100 articles, monographs and book chapters in reviewed scientific, engineering and medical journals. Honours: Harrison Prescott Eddy Medal, 1959; Resources Division Award, American Water Works Association, 1960; Michigan Industrial Hygiene Society Award, 1964; Radebaugh Award, 1976; Award of Merit, Chicago Technical Societies Council, 1978; Borden Foundation Award, 1988; Outstanding Civil Engineering Alumnus Award, University of Kentucky, 1995; Donald Eddy Cummings Memorial Award, 1999; Outstanding Publications Award, American Industrial Hygiene Association, 2000. Memberships include: Fellow, American Association for the Advancement of Science; American Academy of Environmental Engineers; Fellow, American Public Health Association; Fellow, Life Member, American Society of Civil Engineers. Address: 117 Church Road, Winnetka, IL 60093, USA.

**HERRMANN Klaus Peter Bruno,** b. 20 May 1937, Koenigszelt, Silesia. Professor. m. Rosemarie Schauer, 1 son. Education: Diploma in Physics, 1961, PhD, 1964, Habilitation, 1969, MLU Halle-Wittenberg. Appointments: Assistant, Department of Physics, 1961-69, Senior Assistant, 1970-71, MLU; Lecturer, 1973-74, Associate Professor, 1975-77, Institute of Mechanics, University of Karlsruhe; Professor of Mechanics, University of Paderborn, 1977-2002; Visiting Professor, USA, China, Bulgaria, France, 1979-2002. Publications: 290 articles in professional journals; 4 monographs (editor). Honours: Member of Editorial Board, Thermal Stresses, 1994; Member of Advisory Board, Acta Mechanica, 1995; Member of Advisory Board, Prikladnaja Mechanika, 1997; Associate Editor, Applied Mechanics Reviews, 1998; Member of Advisory Board, Archive of Applied Mechanics, 2002. Memberships: Fellow, New York Academy of Science; European Mechanics Society; Association Applied Mathematics and Mechanics; German Association for Materials Testing; Hochschulverband. Address: Department of Mechanical Engineering, Chair of Applied Mechanics, University of Paderborn, Pohlweg 47-49, D-33098 Paderborn, Germany. E-mail: jherr1@ltm.upb.de

**HERTFORD, 9th Marquess of, Henry Jocelyn Seymour,** b. 6 July 1958, Birmingham, England. Landowner. m. Beatriz Karam, 2 sons, 2 daughters. Education: Royal Agricultural College, Cirencester. Appointments: Estate Owner; Farm Manager; Flock Master; Shepherd. Memberships: Country Land and Business Association; National Farmers Union. Address: Ragley Hall, Alcester, Warwickshire B49 5NJ, England. E-mail: info@ragleyhall.com

**HESKETH Ronald David,** b. 16 June 1947, Broughty Ferry, Angus, Scotland. Chaplain. m. Vera, 1 son, 1 daughter. Education: BA Hons, Geography, University of Durham, 1968; Theology, University of Cambridge, 1969; Diploma, Pastoral Studies, St Michael's College, Cardiff, 1971; Diploma, Reformation Studies, Open University, 1977. Appointments: Ordained Deacon, 1971; Priest, 1972; Curate, Holy Trinity Church, Southport, 1971-73; Assistant Chaplain, Mersey Mission to Seamen, 1973-75; RAF Chaplain, 1975-98; Command Chaplain, 1998-2001; Chaplain-in-Chief, 2001. Honours: Honorary Chaplain to HM The Queen, 2001-; Fellow, Royal Geographical Society; Companion of the Most Honourable Order of the Bath; CB; BA; DPS; RAF. Membership: Royal Air Force Club. Address: Ministry

of Defence, RAF Innsworth, Gloucester, GL3 1EZ. E-mail: vera&ron.hesketh@dunelm.org.ok

**HESSLE Sven L,** b. 18 February 1941, Lidköping, Sweden. Professor. m. Marie, 3 sons. Education: Chartered Psychologist, 1968; Group Psychotherapist, 1969; PhD, Stockholm University, 1975. Appointments: Consulting psychology, 1968-; Senior Fulbright, University of California at Berkeley, USA, 1989; Guest professor, Dohto University, Japan, 1992; Distinguished guest professor, Doshisha University, Kyoto, Japan, 1999; Editor-in-Chief, International Journal of Social Welfare, 1992-; International expert on children, families and international social work, Rio de Janeiro, Vietnam, Balkan States, China, 1993-; Professor (Chair) of Social Work, Stockholm University, 1993-. Publications: Numerous books, articles, reports in Swedish and English; Child Welfare and Child Protection on the Eve of the 21st Century, 1997; Co-editor, Social Work with Children in Post War Conditions, 1998; Co-author, Child Welfare in Sweden: an overview, 1999; Co-editor, Valuing the Field: Child Welfare in International Context, 2000; Editor, International Standard Setting of Higher Social Work Education, 2001. Honours: Professor of Honour, Guizhou University for ethnic minorities in China, 1999. Address: Kåkbrinken 11A, Se – 11127 Stockholm, Sweden. E-mail: sven.hessle@socarb.su.se

**HESTON Charlton,** b. 4 October 1924, Evanston, Illinois, USA. Actor. m. Lydia Clark, 1944, 1 son, 1 daughter. Education: Northwestern University, Evanston. Appointments: 1st Broadway appearance in Antony and Cleopatra, 1948; Starred in over 50 films, 1950-. Creative Works: Films include: Julius Caesar, 1950; Dark City, 1950; The Greatest Show on Earth, 1952; The Savage, 1952; Ruby Gentry, 1952; The President's Lady, 1953; Pony Express, 1953; Arrowhead, 1953; Bad for Each Other, 1953; The Naked Jungle, 1953; Secret of the Incas, 1954; The Far Horizons, 1955; Lucy Gallant, 1955; The Private War of Major Benson, 1955; three Violent People, 1956; The Ten Commandments, 1956; Touch of Evil, 1958; The Big Country, 1958; The Buccaneer, 1958; Ben Hur, 1959; The Wreck of the Mary Deare, 1959; El Cid, 1961; The Pigeon that Took Rome, 1962; Diamond Head, 1962; 55 Days at Peking, 1962; Major Dundee, 1964; The Greatest Story Ever Told, 1965; The Agony and the Ecstasy, 1965; The War Lord, 1965; Khartoum, 1966; Counterpoint, 1967; Will Penny, 1967; Planet of the Apes, 1967; Beneath the Planet of the Apes, 1969; The Hawaiians, 1970; Julius Caesar, 1970; The Omega Man, 1971; Antony & Cleopatra, 1972; Skyjacked, 1972; The Call of the Wild, 1972; Soylent Green, 1973; The Three Musketeers, 1973; The Four Musketeers, 1974; Earthquake, 1974; Airport, 1975; Midway, 1975; Two Minute Warning, 1976; The Last hard Men, 1976; The Prince and the Pauper, 1976; Gray Lady Down, 1978; The Awakening, 1980; Mother Lode, 1981; Caine Mutiny Court Martial (also directed), 1988; Treasure Island, 1989; Almost an Angel; Solar Crisis; Wayne's World 2; True Lies, 1994; In the Mouth of Madness; Alaska; Hercules, 1997; Any Given Sunday, 1998; Town and Country, 1998; Toscano, 1999. Publications: The Actor's Life, 1979; In the Arena, 1995; Charlton Heston Presents the Bible, 1997. Honours: Academy Award, 1959; Veterans of Foreign Wars Citizenship Medal, 1982; Golden Medal of the City of Vienna, 1995; Commander Ordre des Arts et des Lettres. Memberships: National Council of Arts; Trustee, American Film Institute; Presidential Task Force on Arts and Humanities; National Rifle Association. Address: c/o Jack Gilardi, ICM, 8942 Wilshire Boulevard, Beverly Hills, CA 90211, USA.

**HETZEL Basil Stuart,** b. 13 June 1922, London, England. Medical Scientist. m. Anne Gilmour Fisher, 3 sons, 2 daughters. Education: MD, 1949; FRACP, 1958; FRCP, 1972;

FFCM, 1980; FTS, 1981. Appointments: Michell Professor of Medicine, Adelaide University, 1964-68; Foundation Professor, Social Preventive Medicine, Monash University, 1968-75; Chief, CSIRO Human Nutrition, 1975-85; Executive Director, International Council for Control of Iodine Deficiency Disorders, 1985-95, Chairman, 1995-; Lieutenant Governor of South Australia, 1992-2000. Publications include: The LS Factor, 1987; The Story of Iodine Deficiency, 1989; SOS for a Billion: The Conquest of Iodine Deficiency Disorders, 1996. Memberships: Public Health Association of Australia; President, Endocrine Society of Australia, 1964-66; Deputy Chairman, International Epidemiological Association, 1977-81; Chancellor, University of South Australia, 1992-98. Address: 139 Kermode Street, North Adelaide, SA 5006, Australia.

**HEWISH Antony,** b. 11 May 1924, Fowey, Cornwall, England. Astronomer; Physicist. m. Marjorie E C Richards, 1950, 1 son and 1 daughter. Education: Graduated, Gonville and Caius College, Cambridge, 1948. Appointments: War Service, 1943-46; Research Fellow, Gonville and Caius College, 1951-54; Supernumerary Fellow, 1956-61; University Assistant Director of Research, 1953-61, Lecturer, 1961-69; Fellow, Churchill College, Cambridge, 1962-; Reader in Radio Astronomy, University of Cambridge, 1969-71, Professor, 1971-89, Professor Emeritus, 1989; Professor, Royal Institute, 1977; Director, Mullard Radio Astronomy Observatory, Cambridge, 1982-88; Vikram Sarabhai Professor, Ahmedabad, 1988. Publications: The First, Second, Third and Fourth Cambridge Catalogues; Seeing Beyond the Invisible, Pulsars and physics laboratories. Honours: Hamilton Prize, 1951; Eddington Medal, Royal Astronomical Society, 1968; Boys Prize, Institute of Physics, 1970; Dellinger Medal, International Union of Radio Science, Hopkins Prize, Cambridge Medal and Prize, Society Francaise de Physique, 1974; Nobel Prize for Physics, 1974; Hughes Medal, Royal Society, 1977; Vainu Bappu Prize, Indian National Science Academy, 1998. Memberships: Foreign Member, American Academy of Arts and Sciences, 1970; Member, Belgian Royal Academy of Arts and Sciences, 1989; Member, Emeritus Academia Europea, 1996; Foreign Fellow, Indian National Science Academy; 6 Honorary ScD. Address: Cavendish Laboratory, Madingley Road, Cambridge, CB3 7NQ, England.

**HIBBERD Alan Ronald,** b. 25 October 1931, Bendigo, Australia. Clinical Ecologist; Toxicologist. m. (1) Doreen Imilda Collier, 2 sons, 2 daughters, (2) Lois Stratton. Education: Ridley College, Melbourne; PhC, Victorian College of Pharmacy; DCC, PhD, Chelsea College, University of London. Appointments: Community Pharmacy Practice, Melbourne, 1953-73; Director: ARH Pharmaceuticals, 1959-74, Pressels Laboratories, 1959-74; Part-time Demonstrator, Practical Pharmaceutics, Victorian College of Pharmacy, 1961-64; Lecturer to Postgraduate Students in Pharmacology and Therapeutics and Consultant in Dental Therapeutics and Prescribing, Victorian Branch, Australian Dental Association, 1966-74; In Charge of Drug Information Department and Ward Pharmacy Services, Hackney Hospital, London, 1975; Research Fellow, Pharmacy Department, Chelsea College, University of London, 1976-79; Lecturer, School of Pharmacy, University of London, 1980-81; Tutor in Clinical Pharmacy, Northwick Park Hospital, Harrow, 1980-81; First Course Organiser and Supervisor MSc Course in Clinical Pharmacy, University of London, 1980-81; Director, Hibbro Research, Hereford, 1981-84; Private Practice in Clinical Ecology, London, 1985-; Consultant, Clinical Pharmacology, Biocare Ltd, 1989-; Consultant in Clinical Biochemistry/ Pharmacology, Society for Promotion of Nutritional Therapy (UK), 1992-97; Scientific Adviser to Register of Nutritional Therapists (UK), 1993-. Publications: Author of numerous

articles and scientific papers on drug metabolism and relating to specialist field; Contributor to numerous learned publications. Memberships: Vice-president, International Academy of Oral Medicine and Toxicology (UK), 1994; Fellow (by examination), Pharmaceutical Society of Victoria, 1961; Royal Society of Victoria, 1968; British Dental Society for Clinical Nutrition, 1985; Nutrition Association, 1987; Environmental Dental Association, USA, 1991; British Society for Allergy, Environmental and Nutritional Medicine, 1993; FRSH, 1971; MRPharmS, 1974; Life Fellow, Pharmaceutical Society of Australia, 1991; Retired Fellow, The Royal Society of Medicine, 2003. Address: Bayswater Clinic, 25B Clanricarde Gardens, London W2 4JL, England.

**HIBBERT Christopher,** b. 5 March 1924, Enderby, Leicestershire, England. Author. m. Susan Piggford, 1948, 2 sons, 1 daughter. Education: MA, Oriel College, Oxford. Appointments: Served in Italy, 1944-45; Captain, London Irish Rifles; Military Cross; Partner, firm of land agents, auctioneers and surveyors, 1948-59. Publications: The Road to Tyburn, 1957; King Mob, 1958; Wolfe at Quebec, 1959, The Destruction of Lord Raglan, 1961; Corunna, 1961; Benito Mussolini, 1962; The Battle of Arnhem, 1962; The Roots of Evil, 1963; The Court at Windsor, 1964; Agincourt, 1964; The Wheatley Diary (editor), 1964; Garibaldi and His Enemies, 1965; The Making of Charles Dickens, 1967; Waterloo: Napoleon's Last Campaign (editor), 1967; An American in Regency England: The Journal of Louis Simond (editor), 1968; Charles I, 1968; The Grand Tour, 1969; London: Biography of a City, 1969; The Search for King Arthur, 1970; Anzio: The Bid for Rome, 1970; The Dragon Wakes: China and the West, 1793-1911, 1970; The Personal History of Samuel Johnson, 1971; George IV, Prince of Wales 1762-1811, 1972; George IV, Regent and King 1812-1830, 1973; The Rise and Fall of the House of Medici, 1974; Edward VII: A Portrait, 1976; The Great Mutiny: India, 1857, 1978; The French Revolution, 1981; Africa Explored: Europeans in the Dark Continent, 1796-1889, 1982; The London Encyclopaedia (editor), 1983; Queen Victoria in Her Letters and Journals, 1984; Rome: The Biography of a City, 1985; Cities and Civilizations, 1985; The English: A Social History, 1987; Venice: Biography of a City, 1988; The Encyclopaedia of Oxford (editor), 1988; Redcoats and Rebels: The War for America 1760-1781, 1990; The Virgin Queen: The Personal History of Elizabeth I, 1990; Captain Gronow: His Reminiscences of Regency and Victorian Life (editor), 1991; Cavaliers and Roundheads: The English at War 1642-1649, 1993; Florence: Biography of a City, 1993; Nelson: A Personal History, 1994; Wellington: A Personal History, 1997; George III: A Personal History, 1998; Queen Victoria: A Personal History, 2000; The Marlboroughs: John and Sarah Churchill, 2001; Napoleon: His Wives and Women, 2002; Disraeli, 2004. Honours: Heinemann Award for Literature, 1962; McColvin Medal, 1989; Honorary DLitt, Leicester University, 1996. Address: Albion Place, 6 West Street, Henley-on-Thames, Oxfordshire RG9 2DT, England.

**HIBBERT Clare Louise,** b. 19 April 1973, London, England. Health Economist. Education: BA, Honours, International Business and Spanish, Sheffield Hallam University, 1995. Appointments: Researcher, Intensive Care Unit, Sheffield Teaching Hospitals NHS Trust, 1995-97; Senior Researcher, 1997-2000, Director of Research, 2000-2001, Medical Economics and Research Centre, Sheffield. MRC Senior Research Fellow, University of Sheffield, 2001-. Publications: Book chapters as co-author: Health Economics of Intensive Care in Yearbook on Intensive Care (editor J L Vincent), 1999; Fungal Infections in the ICU – Disease Management Monograph in Pharmoeconomics of anti-fungal therapy in the ICU; Economic Outcomes in Outcomes in Critical Care (editors:

S Ridley and D Young), 2002; 27 articles in professional journals as author and co-author include most recently: A systematic review of ICU costs, 2002; Funding Critical Care, 2003; Methodological issues in studies reporting the costs of sepsis patients, 2004; A cost survey of 70 adult critical care units: Results from a volunteer sample in England, Scotland and Northern Ireland, 2005; Department of Health reports and papers in conference proceedings. Honour: MRC Fellowship in Health Services Research, 2001. Memberships: Research Associates Network; European Society of Intensive Care Medicine; Health Economists Study Group. Address: Health Economics and Decision Science, School of Health and Related Research, University of Sheffield, Regent Court, 30 Regent Street, Sheffield S1 4DA, England. E-mail: chibbert1@aol.com

**HICK Graeme Ashley,** b. 23 May 1966, Salisbury, Zimbabwe. Cricketer. Appointments: Right-Hand Batsman, Off-Break Bowler, Slip Fielder; Teams: Zimbabwe, 1983-86, Worcestershire, 1984-, Northern Districts, 1987-89, Queensland, 1990-91; Scored 100 aged 6 years; Youngest player to appear in 1983 World Cup and youngest to represent Zimbabwe; 65 tests for England, 1991-97, scoring 3,383 runs (average 31.32), including 6 hundreds; Scored 30,189 1st class runs (average 55.2), with 104 hundreds (including 9 doubles, 1 triple, 1 quadruple (405 not out) to 1 April 1999); Youngest to score 2,000 1st class runs in a season, 1986; Scored 1,019 runs before June 1988, including a record 410 runs in April; Fewest innings for 10,000 runs in county cricket (179); Youngest (24) to score 50 1st class hundreds; Toured Australia, 1994-95; 120 limited-overs ints for 3,846 runs (average 37.33) by December 2002; Scored 315 not out v Durham, June 2002- (highest championship innings of the season). Publication: My Early Life (autobiography), 1992. Honours: Wisden Cricketer of the Year, 1987. Membership: England World Cup Squad, 1996. Address: c/o Worcestershire County Cricket Club, New Road, Worcester WR2 4QQ, England.

**HICKS Philip,** b. 11 October 1928, Leamington Spa, England. Artist; Painter. m. Jill Doreen Tweed, 1 son, 1 daughter. Education: Royal Military Academy, Sandhurst; Chelsea School of Art and Royal Academy Schools, 1949-54. Career: Part-time teacher, various schools of art, London area, 1960-86; Full-time painting, over 40 solo exhibitions, UK and abroad; Work appears in many public and corporate collections, including Tate Britain, Victoria and Albert Museum, Imperial War Museum, Contemporary Art Society, Royal College of Music, Nuffield Foundation; Represented by Messum's Fine Art, Cork Street, London. Publications: Mentioned in numerous journals, magazines and newspapers. Honours: British Council Award, 1977. Memberships: Royal Overseas League, St James's, London; Chelsea Arts Club, London; Past Chairman and Vice President, The Artists General Benevolent Institution. Address: Radcot House, Buckland Road, Bampton, Oxfordshire OX18 2AA, England.

**HIDDLESTON James Andrew,** b. 20 October 1935, Edinburgh, Scotland. Professor of French. Widower, 2 daughters. Education: MA, 1957, PhD, 1961, Edinburgh University. Appointments: Lecturer in French, University of Leeds, 1960-66; Fellow, Exeter College, Oxford, 1966-, Professor of French, University of Oxford, 1996-2003; Retired, 2003. Publications: Books: L'Univers de Jules Supervielle, 1965; Malraux: "La Condition humaine", 1973; Poems: Jules Laforgue, edition with introduction and notes, 1975; Essai sur Laforgue at les derniers vers, suivi de Laforgue et Baudelaire, 1980; Baudelaire and "Le Spleen de Paris", 1987, Japanese translation, 1989; Laforgue aujourd'hui (editor), 1988; Collaboration with Michel Collot in edition of Jules Supervielle, Oeuvres poétiques complètes,

1996; Baudelaire and the Art of Memory, 1999; Victor Hugo, romancier de l'abîme (contributing editor), 2002; A wide variety of articles. Honour: Officier de l'ordre des arts et des lettres. Memberships: Society of French Studies; Nineteenth Century French Studies. Address: 86D Banbury Road, Oxford OX2 6JT, England. E-mail: james.middleton@exeter.ox.ac.uk

**HIEMSTRA Linda Darlene,** b. 10 December 1949, Nanaimo, British Columbia, Canada. Project Manager. m. Gordon Henry Heimstra, 1 son, 1 daughter.. Education: Technical Diploma, Fisheries and Aquaculture, Malaspina University, Canada, 1989; Master's Degree in Project Management, University of Victoria, Canada, 2005; Project Management Professional, Project Management Institute, USA, 2005. Appointments: Laboratory Manager, Research Assistant, Fisheries and Oceans, Canada, 1988-95; Research Projects Co-ordinator, Future Sea Farms Inc, 1996-97; Instructor, 1993-, Manager, Fisheries International Programme, 1995-2000, Manager, Training and Research Laboratory, Fisheries and Aquaculture Department, 1995-2000, Aquaculture Projects Co-ordinator, Fisheries and Aquaculture Extension Programme, 2000-2005, Malaspina University-College, Canada; Owner, Project Management Professional, Mel-More Science, 2005-; Organiser of numerous workshops and conferences. Publications: Articles in scientific journals and book chapters as author and co-author include: Accumulation and depuration of domoic acid by the mussel, Mytilus californians, 1995; Evaluation of particle removal by a microscreen drum filter, 1996; Results of a comparative cost analysis between carboy and bag phytoplankton culture methods, 2001; First Nations Training Strategy at Malaspina University College, Canada, 2004; Papers presented at workshops and conferences. Memberships: Member, 2000-2003, Committee Chair, 2000-2003, National Human Resources Standing Committee for the Aquaculture Industry; Member, 1985-, Director, 1996-2002, President, 2000-2001, Aquaculture Association of Canada; Director, 2000-2002, Canadian Aquaculture Industry Alliance; Member, 1999-, Publication Editor, 2002, National Shellfish Association; World Aquaculture Association, 1994-; International Society of Meeting Planners, 2002-; Project Management Institute, 2003-. Address: Mel-More Science, 6036 Breonna Drive, Nanaimo, BC V9V 1G!, Canada. E-mail: hiemstraas@shaw.ca

**HIGGINBOTHAM Prieur Jay,** b. 16 July 1937, Pascagoula, Mississippi, USA. Author; Archivist. m. Alice Louisa Martin, 27 June 1970, 2 sons, 1 daughter. Education: BA, University Mississippi, 1961; Graduate study, City College of New York; American University, Washington DC. Appointments: Assistant Clerk, MS House of Representatives, 1955-58; Teacher, Mobile City Public Schools, 1962-73; Head, Local History Department, 1973-83; Director, Mobile Municipal Archives, 1983-. Publications include: Old Mobile, 1977; Fast Train Russia, 1983; Autumn in Petrisheva, 1987; Man, Nature and the Infinite, 1998; Mauvila, 2000; Alma, 2002. Honours: Gilbert Chinard Prize, 1978; Alabama Library Literature Award, 1979; Mississippi Historical Society Award, 1979; Louisiana Historical Society Award, 1979; Elizabeth Gould Award, 1980. Alabama Library Association, Humanitarian Award, 1999. Listed in: Several Who's Who Publications. Memberships: Society Mobile-Rostov-on-Don; Society Mobile-La Habana; President, Friends of Freedom; Founder and First President, The Mobile Tricentennial, Inc. Address: 60 North Monterey Street, Mobile, AL 36604, USA.

**HIGGS Peter Ware,** b. 29 May 1929, Newcastle upon Tyne, England. University Teacher (retired). m. JoAnn Williamson, 2 sons. Education: Halesowen Grammar School, 1940-41; Cotham Grammar School, Bristol, 1941-46; City of London School,

1946-47; BSc, 1950, MSc, 1951, PhD, 1954, King's College London. Appointments: Senior Student, Royal Commission for the Exhibition of 1851, King's College London, 1953-54, University of Edinburgh, 1954-55; Senior Research Fellow, University of Edinburgh, 1955-56; ICI Fellow, University of London, 1956-58; Lecturer in Mathematics, University College London, 1959-60; Sabbatical Leave, University of North Carolina, USA, 1965-66; Lecturer in Mathematical Physics, 1960-70, Reader in Mathematical Physics, 1970-80, Professor of Theoretical Physics, 1980-96, University of Edinburgh. Publications: Papers in professional journals. Honours: Hughes Medal, Royal Society, 1981; Rutherford Medal, Institute of Physics, 1984; Scottish Science Award, Saltire Society, 1990; James Scott Prize Lectureship, Royal Society of Edinburgh, 1993; Paul Dirac Medal & Prize, Institute of Physics, 1994; Hon DSc, Bristol, 1997; High Energy & Particle Physics Prize, European Physical Society, 1997; Hon DSc, Edinburgh, 1998; Honorary Fellow, Institute of Physics, 1998; Fellow, King's College London, 1998; Royal Medal, Royal Society of Edinburgh, 2000; Hon DSc, Glasgow, 2002; Wolf Prize in Physics, 2004. Memberships: Fellow, Royal Society of Edinburgh, 1974; Fellow, Royal Society, 1983; Fellow, Institute of Physics. Address: 2 Darnaway Street, Edinburgh EH3 6BG, Scotland.

**HIGSON Philip (Willoughby-),** b. 21 February 1933, Newcastle-under-Lyme, Staffordshire, England. Poet; Translator; Editor; Historian; Art Historian; Playwright. Education: BA, Honours, and Charles Beard Research Studentship in Medieval History, 1956, MA, 1959, Research Fellowship in Modern History, 1963, PhD, 1971, Liverpool University; PGCE, Keele University, 1972. Appointments: Lecturer, Senior Lecturer in History, 1972-89, Visiting Lecturer, 1989-90, the now University of Chester; Chairman, President, Anthology Editor, Chester Poets, 1974-92; President, The Baudelaire Society, Chester and Paris, 1992-. Publications: The Riposte and Other Poems, 1971; A Warning to Europe: The Testimony of Limouse (co-author), 1992; The Complete Poems of Baudelaire with Selected Illustrations by Limouse (editor and principal translator), 1992; Limouse Nudes, 1994; Childhood in Wartime Keele: Poems of Reminiscence, 1995; Poems on the Dee, 1997; Inner City Love-Revolt: Footage from a Fifties Affair, 2000; A Poet's Pilgrimage: The Shaping of a Creative Life, 2000; The Jewelled Nude: A Play about Baudelaire and Queen Pomaré, 2002; Sonnets to My Goddess in This Life and The Next: The Prize-winning Volume Expanded, 2002; Poems of Sauce and Satire: A Humorous Selection, 2002; Maurice Rollinat: A Hundred Poems from Les Névroses (translated and introduced), 2003; Ut Pictura Poesis: Pictorial Poems, 2004; Manichaean Contrasts: a Late Selection of Poetry, 2004; Souvenir of a Triple Launch: play, translations, sonnets, 2004; Contributions: historical articles to Oxford DNB and to journals including: Antiquaries Journal, Genealogists' Magazine, Coat of Arms, Northern History, 2 Lancashire and Cheshire journals; Poems to: Making Love: the Picador Book of Erotic Verse, 1978; Rhyme Revival, 1982; Poets England: Staffordshire, 1987; Red Candle Treasury, 1998 and to journals including: Critical Quarterly, Collegian, Chester Poets Anthologies, Candelabrum, The Eclectic Muse, Mandrake Poetry Review, Cadmium Blue Literary Journal, Lexikon, Rebirth, Solar Flame, Romantic Renaissance, Rubies in the Darkness, Metverse Muse, Poet Tree, A Bard Hair Day, Quantum Leap; Bulletin de la Société "Les Amis de Maurice Rollinat". Honours: 1st Prize for an Established Poet, The Eclectic Muse, Vancouver, 1990; David St John Thomas Poetry Publication Prize, 1996; Prize-winner, Lexikon Poetry Competition, 1996; 1st Prize (Gold Award) Rubies in the Darkness Poetry Competition, 2003. Memberships: FSA; FRHistS; FRSA; Society of Authors.

Address: 1 Westlands Avenue, Newcastle-under-Lyme, Staffordshire, ST5 2PU, England.

**HIHARA Katsuji,** b. 16 February 1949, Hyogo, Japan. University Professor (Accounting Educator). m. Masami Yoshida. 1 son. Education: Bachelor, Commercial Science, Kwansei-gakuin University, 1971; Master Business Administration, 1973, Doctor of Business Administration, 1996, Kobe University. Appointments: Assistant, 1975-76, Assistant Professor, 1976-79, Associate Professor, 1979-88, Professor, 1988-89, Toyama University, Japan; Professor, Kobe University of Commerce, Japan, 1989-2004; University of Hyogo, Japan, 2004-; Head, Graduate School of Business Administration, 1992-93, Head of Department of Business Administration, 1992-93, Kobe University of Commerce. Publications: Inflation Accounting (in Japanese), 1984; Income Concepts of Inflation Accounting (in Japanese), 1995. Memberships: Japan Accounting Association. Address: 2-30-22 Yokoo Suma-ku Kobe Hyogo 654-0131, Japan.

**HILFIGER Tommy,** b. Elmira, New York, USA. Men's Fashion Designer. m. Susie Hilfiger, 4 children. Appointments: Opened 1st store, People's Place, Elmira, 1969; Owned 10 clothes shops, New York State, 1978; Full-time Designer, 1979; Launched own sportswear label, 1984; Acquired fashion business from Mohan Muranji; Founder, Tommy Hilfiger Corporation, 1989. Honours include: Winner, From the Catwalk to the Sidewalk Award, VH-1 Fashion and Music Awards, 1995; Menswear Designer of the Year, Council of Fashion Designers of America, 1995. Memberships: Board, Fresh Air Fund, Race to Erase Multiple Sclerosis.

**HILL (Anthony) Edward,** b. 30 December 1959, Coventry, England. Oceanographer. m. Jacqueline Patricia Caukwell, 2 sons. Education: BSc, 1st Class Special Honours, Applied Mathematics, University of Sheffield, 1978-81; MSc, Physical Oceanography, 1983, PhD, Oceanography, 1987, University of Wales, Bangor (formerly University College of North Wales, Bangor). Appointments: Lecturer, 1986-95, Senior Lecturer, 1995-99, University of Wales, Bangor; Director, Proudman Oceanographic Laboratory, Bidston (relocated to Liverpool, 2004), Visiting Professor of Earth Sciences, University of Liverpool, 1999-2005; Director National Oceanography Centre, Southampton (formerly Southampton Oceanography Centre) (joint centre Natural Environment Research Council and the University of Southampton), Professor of Oceanography, University of Southampton, 2005-. Publications: Numerous articles in learned journals mostly relating to the physical oceanography of continental shelf seas. Memberships: Challenger Society for Marine Science; Oceanography Society. Address: 7 Saracens Road, Scatabout, Chandlers Ford, Hampshire SO53 2NT, England.

**HILL Christina Bernadette Thérèse,** Environmental and Educational Consultant. Education: BA (Hons), University of Wales; MA, PhD, University of Birmingham. Appointments: Field Officer, Midlands Director, Director of Development and Training, Head of Research and Legislation, Tidy Britain Group, 1977-88; National Director, School and Group Travel Association (SAGTA), 1988-94; Director of Public Affairs, Aviation Environment Federation and Trust, 1988-89; Chair, YWCA Steering Group for Major Appeal Committee, Open the Door Appeal Committee and Special Events Committee, 1993-96; General Secretary, UK Environmental Law Association, 1996-; General Commissioner of Income Tax, 1998-; Member, Lord Chancellor's Advisory Committee on JPs, 1998; Non-Executive Director, Berkshire Healthcare NHS Trust, 2001-. Publications: Litter Law —Is It Working? 1988; Editor:

School and Group Travel Association (SAGTA) Conference Papers: Safety During School Travel, 1989; Editor, SAGTA Education Reform Act 1988: Charging for School Activities, 1989; Editor, SAGTA Safety Rules, 1990 and SAGTA Code of Conduct, 1990; Editor, SAGTA Conference Papers, Safety and Good Practice During School and Group Travel, 1991; Editor SAGTA Conference Papers, EC Directive on Package Travel, 1994; Numerous articles in environmental and educational press. Memberships: Fellow, Royal Geographical Society, 1989-; Fellow, Royal Society of Arts, 1989-; Affiliate Member, Institute of Wastes Management, 1994-; Associate Member, Chartered Institution of Environmental Health, 1988-; Fellow Institute of Personnel and Development, 1985-96. Address: Honeycroft House, Pangbourne Road, Upper Basildon, Berkshire RG8 8LP, England.

**HILL Christine L,** b. USA. Educator. Education: BS, Elementary Education, Iowa State University, 1987; MA, Educational Psychology/Gifted Education, University of Connecticut, 1996; PhD, Education Policy, Planning and Leadership, Gifted Education, Administration, The College of William and Mary, Williamsburg, Virginia, 2002. Appointments: Third Grade Teacher, Island Paradise School, Honolulu, Hawaii, 1988-89; Adult Education Instructor, Halawa Correctional Facility, Aiea, Hawaii, 1989; Fourth Grade Teacher, Amboy Elementary School, North Little Rock, Arkansas, 1990-92; Teacher of Gifted, 1992-94, Facilitator of Gifted Programs, 1994, Lawton Public Schools, Lawton, Oklahoma; Computer Laboratory Instructor, DeRidder Junior High School, DeRidder High School, Louisiana, 1994-95; Teacher of Gifted, East Beauregard High School, DeRidder, Louisiana, 1995-97; Graduate Assistant, Center for Gifted Education, The College of William and Mary, Williamsburg, Virginia, 1997-99; Executive Intern, Hampton City Schools, 2000; Educational Consultant, SkyLight Training and Publishing, Inc, Arlington Heights, Illinois, 2001-; Executive Assistant, The Professional Development Center, School of Education, The College of William and Mary, 2000-2002; Assistant professor, University of Louisiana at Lafayette, 2002, 2003-2004; Supervisor, Gifted Services, Newport News Public Schools, Newport News, Virginia, 2004-. Publications: Numerous presentations and articles in professional journals. Honours include: Vergie Bourgeois Award for Scholarship, 1996; Pi Lamba Theta, 1996; Kappa Delta Pi, 1997; School of Education Award for Excellence, 2001, Benjamin Stoddert Ewell Award, 2002, Thatcher Prize for Excellence, 2002, College of William and Mary; Listed in Who's Who publications and biographical dictionaries. Memberships include: National Educational Association; American Association of University Women; National Science Teachers Association; National Association for Gifted Children; Virginia Association for the Gifted; American Educational Research Association; National Staff Development Council. Address: Supervisor Gifted Services, Newport News Public Schools, 12465 Warwick Blvd, Newport News, VA 23606, USA. E-mail: christine.hill@nn.k12.va.us

**HILL Colin Arnold Clifford,** b. 13 February 1929, Cambridge, England. Clerk in Holy Orders. m. (1) Shirley Randall, deceased 1963, (2) Irene Florence Chamberlain, 1 son, 1 stepson. Education: Bristol University, 1955; Ripon Hall Theological College, Oxford, 1957; M Phil, University of Wales, Bangor, 2003; Ordained, Sheffield Cathedral, 1957. Appointments: Curate, Rotherham Parish Church, 1959; Vicar of Brightside, 1961; Rector of Easthampstead, 1964; Vicar of Croydon, 1973-94; Chaplain to The Queen, 1990-99. Publication: Unpublished thesis: Archbishop John Whitgift: Free School and Hospital 1596-1604. Honour: OBE, 1995. Membership: Leander Club.

Address: Silver Birches, Preston Crowmarsh, Wallingford, Oxfordshire OX10 6SL, England.

**HILL Damon Graham Devereux,** b. 17 September 1960, Hamstead, London, England. Motor Racing Driver. m. Georgie Hill, 1988, 2 sons, 2 daughters. Appointments: Began motorcycle racing, 1979; Driver, Canon Williams Team, 1993; Driver, Rothmans Williams Renault Team, 1994-96; Driver, Arrows Yamaha Team, 1997; Benson and Hedges Jordan Team, 1998-99. Honours: First motor racing victory in Formula Ford 1600, Brands Hatch, 1984; First Formula One Grand Prix, Silverstone, 1992; Winner, Hungarian Grand Prix, 1993; Winner, Belgian and Italian Grand Prix, 1993, 1994; 3rd Place, Drivers' World Championship, 1993; Winner, Spanish Grand Prix, Barcelona, 1994; Winner, British Grand Prix , Silverstone, 1994; Winner, Portuguese Grand Prix, 1994; Winner, Japanese Grand Prix, 1994, 1996;French Grand Prix, 1996; Spanish Grand Prix, 1995, 1996; San Marino Grand Prix, 1995, 1996; Hungarian Grand Prix, 1995; Brazilian Grand Prix, 1996; German Grand Prix, 1996; Australian Grand Prix, 1995, 1996; Canadian Grand Prix, 1998; Belgian Grand Prix, 1998; 2nd place, Drivers' World Championship, 1994-95; World Champion, 1996; British Competition Driver of the Year, Autosport Awards, 1995; 84 Grand Prix starts; 22 wins; 20 pole positions; 19 fastest laps; 42 podium finishes; numerous racing and sports personality awards; OBE. Publications: Damon Hill Grand Prix Year, 1994; Damon Hill: My Championship Year, 1996; F1 Through the Eyes of Damon Hill.

**HILL Sonia Geraldine,** b. 26 September 1939, London, England. Artist in Oils. Partner, G H Clarke, deceased 1997. Education: Maidenhead Art College, Berkshire, England, 1955-57; Studied perspective composition with A Hayward, Zambia, 1957-63. Career: Architectural Assistant, contract work, London, 1982-1990; Architectural Assistant, Victoria, London, 1991; Exhibitions: Royal Academy, 1993, 2 oil paintings sold and 2 further works accepted by the selection committee; Royal Academy, 2000, oil painting of Quentin Crisp sold, now hanging in Vancouver; Christies, 2001-2002, 2003, 3 works in oils sold (Art for Life); Exhibitions at Richmond and Paris. Publication: Painting "Jack the Lad" illustrated in Royal Academy Magazine, 1993. Honour: Fine Art, Maidenhead College, 1957; Who's Who Book of Art, 1993-2004. Memberships: Friend: Royal Academy, London, 1993-2004, The Royal Overseas League, London, 2004, The Mall Galleries, London, 2004. Address: 6a Warfield Road, Hampton TW12 2AY, England.

**HILLARY Edmund Percival (Sir),** b. 20 July 1919, Auckland, New Zealand. Explorer; Diplomat; Bee-farmer. m. Louise Mary Rose, 1953, deceased 1975, 1 son, 2 daughters (1 deceased). Education: University of Auckland. Appointments: Director, Field Educational Enterprises of Australia Party Ltd; President, Voluntary Service Abroad, New Zealand, 1963-64; High Commissioner to India, also accredited to Bangladesh, Bhutan and Nepal, 1985-. Career: New Zealand Garhwal Expedition to Himalayas, 1951; British Expedition to Cho Oyu, 1952; First to reach summit of Mount Everest, with Sherpa Tenzing, May 29th 1953, on British expedition, under Sir John Hunt, 1953; Leader, New Zealand Alpine Club expedition to Barun Val, 1954; New Zealand Antarctic Expedition, 1956-58; Reached South Pole, 1957; Leader, Himalayan expeditions, 1961, 1963, 1964; Built hospital for Sherpas in Nepal, 1966; Leader, expedition on Mount Herschel, Antarctica, 1967; River Ganges expedition, 1977; High Commissioner to India (also accredited to India and Nepal), 1984; Consultant to Sear Roebuck & Co, Chicago; UNICEF Special Representative of Children of the Himalayas, 1991-; Also bee-farmer. Publications: Author, High Adventure, 1955; The Crossing of Antarctica (with Sir Vivian Fuchs),

1958; No Latitude for Error, 1961; High in the Thin Cold Air (with Desmond Doig), 1963; Schoolhouse in the Clouds, 1965; Nothing Venture, Nothing Win (autobiography), 1975; From the Ocean to the Sky, 1978; Two Generations (with Peter Hillary), 1983. Honours: KG; KBE; Gurkha Right Hand (1st Class); Star of Nepal (1st Class); Cullum George Medal; Hubbard Medal, 1954; Polar Medal, 1958; Founders Gold Medal, Royal Geographical Society, 1958; James Wattle Book of the Year Award, New Zealand, 1975; Centennial Award, National Geographical Society, 1988; LLD (hon), Victoria University, British Columbia, Canada, University of Victoria, New Zealand. Address: 278A Remuera Road, Auckland 5, New Zealand.

**HILLION Pierre,** b. 31 January 1926, Saint-Brieuc, France. Senior Physicist. m. Jeanne Garde, deceased, 2 sons, 2 daughters. Education: Engineer, Ecole Supérieure d'Electricité, 1952; Licencié ès Sciences, 1955; Docteur ès Sciences, 1957. Appointments: Engineer, Le Materiel Electrique S-W, 1950-55; Mathematical Physicist, Army Technical Section, 1955-64; Head, Mathematical Physics Department, Laboratoire Central de l'Armement, 1964-83; Maître de Conférences, Ecole Nationale Supérieure des Techniques Avancées, 1976-88; Scientific Adviser, Centre d'Analyse de Défense, 1983-91; Senior Physicist, Institut Henri Poincaré, 1991-. Publications: About 200 papers on mathematical physics and electromagnetism in various scientific journals and several books, including: Relativité et Quanta, 1968; Essay on formal aspect of electromagnetism, 1993; Electromagnetic Waves, PIER 18, 1998. Honours: Merit for Research and Invention; Officier, Palmes Académiques; Chevalier, Ordre National du Mérite; Chevalier, Legion d'Honneur. Memberships: Société Mathématique de France; Société Internationale de Physique Mathématique; Member, New York Academy of Sciences; Académie d'Electromagnetisme. Address: 86 bis, Route de Croissy, 78110 Le Vésinet, France.

**HILLIS William Daniel,** b. 12 June 1933, Paris, Arkansas, USA. Professor; Physician. m. Argye Briggs Hillis, 2 sons, 1 daughter. Education: BS, Baylor University, Waco, Texas, USA, 1953; MD, Johns Hopkins, Baltimore, Maryland, USA, 1957. Appointments: Resident Staff, Johns Hopkins Hospital, Baltimore, Maryland, USA, 1957-58; Fellow, Johns Hopkins University, Copenhagen, Denmark, 1958-60; Physician and Epidemiologist, US Air Force, Brooks/Lackland Air Force Base, Texas, 1960-65; Assistant Professor, Associate Professor, Professor, Johns Hopkins University Schools of Public Health and Medicine, and Director Clinical Research Center, Johns Hopkins Hospital, 1965-81; Professor and Chairman, Biology, Baylor University, Waco, Texas, USA, 1981-. Publications: Over 60 articles on virology, epidemiology, hypertension and nephrology in scientific journals, USA and international; Book chapters on virology and epidemiology. Honours: Memberships in: Johns Hopkins Society of Scholars; Phi Beta Kappa; Alpha Omega Alpha; Sigma Xi; Fellow Texas Academy of Sciences; Seaman Prize, Association of Military Surgeons of US. Memberships: American Association of Immunologists; American Society for Microbiology; Society for Experimental Biology and Medicine; New York Academy of Sciences. Address: PO Box 97388, Waco, TX 76798-7388, USA. E-mail: william_hillis@baylor.edu

**HIMMELFARB Gertrude,** b. 8 August 1922, New York, New York, USA. Professor of History Emerita; Writer. m. Irving Kristol, 18 January 1942, 1 son, 1 daughter. Education: Jewish Theological Seminary, 1939-42; BA, Brooklyn College, 1942; MA, 1944, PhD, 1950, University of Chicago; Girton College, Cambridge, 1946-47. Appointments: Professor, 1965-78, Distinguished Professor of History, 1978-88, Professor Emerita, 1988-, Graduate School of the City University of New York. Publications: Lord Acton: A Study in Conscience and Politics, 1952; Darwin and the Darwinian Revolution, 1959, revised edition, 1968; Victorian Minds: Essays on Nineteenth Century Intellectuals, 1968; On Liberty and Liberalism: The Case of John Stuart Mill, 1974; The Idea of Poverty: England in the Industrial Age, 1984; Marriage and Morals Among the Victorians and Other Essays, 1986; The New History and the Old, 1987; Poverty and Compassion: The Moral Imagination of the Late Victorians, 1991; On Looking Into the Abyss: Untimely Thoughts on Culture and Society, 1994; The De-Moralization of Society: From Victorian Virtues to Modern Values, 1995; One Nation, Two Cultures, 1999; The Roads to Modernity: The British, French and American Enlightenments, 2004. Contributions to: Scholarly books and journals. Honours: American Association of University Women Fellowship, 1951-52; American Philosophical Society Fellowship, 1953-54; Guggenheim Fellowships, 1955-56, 1957-58; National Endowment for the Humanities Senior Fellowship, 1968-69; American Council of Learned Societies Fellowship, 1972-73; Phi Beta Kappa Visiting Scholarship, 1972-73; Woodrow Wilson Center Fellowship, 1976-77; Rockefeller Humanities Fellowship, 1980-81; Jefferson Lectureship, National Endowment for the Humanities, 1991; Templeton Foundation Award, 1997; Professional Achievement Citation, University of Chicago Alumni Association, 1998; National Humanities Medal, 2004. Memberships: American Academy of Arts and Sciences; American Historical Association; American Philosophical Society; British Academy, fellow; Royal Historical Society, fellow; Society of American Historians. Address: 2510 Virginia Avenue, NW, Washington, DC 20037, USA.

**HINDIE Elif,** b. 2 August 1959, Aleppo, Syria. Medical Educator; Physician; Researcher. m. Maya Khoury, 1 son, 1 daughter. Education: MD, Faculty of Medicine, Aleppo, 1981; Specialist in Endocrinology, French Board, University of Paris V, 1984; Specialist in Nuclear Medicine, French Board, University of Paris XII, 1987; PhD in Biology and Medical Engineering, University of Paris XII, 1990. Appointments: Assistant Professor, 1989-92, Associate Professor, 1993-99, Faculty of Medicine, Paris XII, Hopital Henri Mondor; Associate Professor, Hopital Saint-Antoine, University of Paris VI; Medical Educator, Board of Nuclear Medicine, Saday, 2002-; Medical Educator, Board of Endocrinology, Paris, 2003-. Publications: Ion Microscopy: A new approach for subcellular localization of labelled molecules, 1988; Pre-operative imaging of the paratlyoid glands, 1999; Non-medical exposure to radioiodines and thyroid cancer, 2002; and others. Honours: PhD Award, VIIth International Conference on Spectrometry SIMS VII, Monterey, USA, 1989; Award from Electricitie de France, 2001. Memberships: Fellow, French Society of Nuclear Medicine; French Society of Endocrinology; French Society of Microscopy; President, MEDALE. Address: Hopital Saint-Antoine, 184 rue du Fanbourg St Antoine, 75571 Paris, France. E-mail: elif.hindie@sat.aphp.fr

**HINE Patrick,** b. 14 July 1932, Chandlers Ford, Hampshire, England. Air Force Officer. m. Jill Adèle Gardner, 1956, 3 sons. Career: Fighter Pilot and Member, RAF Black Arrows and Blue Diamonds Formation Aerobatic Teams, 1957-62; Commander, No 92 Squadron, 1962-64 and 17 Squadron, 1970-71; RAF Germany Harrier Force, 1974-75; Director, RAF Public Relations, 1975-77; Assistant Chief of Air Staff for Policy, 1979-83; Commander in Chief, RAF Germany and Commander, NATO's 2nd Allied Tactical Air Force, 1983-85; Vice Chief of the Defence Staff, 1985-87; Air Member for Supply and Organisation, Air Force Board, 1987-88; Air Officer Commanding in Chief, Strike Command, Commander in Chief,

UK Air Forces, 1988-91; Joint Commander, British Forces in Gulf Conflict, 1990-91; with reserve force, rank of Flying Officer, 1991-; Military Adviser to British Aerospace, 1992-99. Honours: King of Arms, Order of the British Empire, 1997-.

**HINGIS Martina,** b. 30 September 1980, Košice, Czech Republic. Tennis Player. Appointments: 1st Tennis Tournament, 1985; Winner, French Open Junior Championship, 1993, Wimbledon Junior Championship, 1994; Competed in the Italian Open, US Open, Chase Championship (New York) and Wimbledon; Won 1st Professional Tournament, Filderstadt, Germany, 1996; Winner, Australian Open, 1997 (youngest winner of a Grand Slam title in 20th Century), 1998, 1999; Beaten Finalist, Australian Open, 2000, 2001, 2002; Winner, US Open, 1997; Beaten Finalist, US Open, 1998, 1999; Wimbledon Singles Champion, 1997; Winner, Australian Open, 1998; Won US Open, 1997, beaten finalist, 1998, 1999; Wimbledon singles champion, 1997; Swiss Federation Cup Team, 1996-98; Semi-finalist, US Open, 2001; By end of 2002 had won 76 tournament titles including five Grand Slam singles and nine doubles titles; Elected to WTA Tour Players' Council, 2002. Honours: WTA Tour Most Impressive Newcomer, 1995; Most Improved Player, 1996; Player of the Year, 1997. Address: c/o AM Seidenbaum 17, 9377 Truebbach, Switzerland.

**HIRATA Tatsuya,** b. 26 June 1943, Tokyo, Japan. Painter; Ceramic Artist. m. Saeko, 25 February, 2 sons, 1 deceased 29 March 1999. Education: Bachelor, French Language, French Language Department, Sophia University; Professor, Art Department, Accademia del Verbano, Italy. Creative works: Paintings; Ceramic art; Exhibitions include: France: Art Impact, Paris, 1994; Espace Branly Société Nationale des Beaux Arts, Paris 1997; Salon International de Peintures et de sculpture, Nancy, 1997; Salon de la Nationale des Beaux Arts, Paris, 2001, 2002; Triennale de Paris, 2002; Japan: Salon de l'Automne Franco-Japonais, Tokyo, 1994; USA; Galerie Montserrat, New York, 1994; Italy: Accademia Italiana "Gli Etruschi" – L'Aquilla della Liberta, Florence, 2002; Accademia Internazionale d'Arte Moderna, Rome, 2002. Publications: Oil-Water color-Etching, Japan, 1987, France, 1996. Honours: Accademicien del Verbano Italia, 1995; Chevalier de l'Ordre Templier, France, 1997; Academical Official Knight, Arts Department, Greci-Marino, 1998; Honorary Member, Foundation Marabello, Spain; Honorary Professor, Accademia Italiana, Gli Etruschi, 2000; Diploma di Mérite, Chevalier de la Paix, Accademia Internazionale "Il Marzocco, 2002. Memberships: Société Nationale des Beaux Arts; Society of Arts, Sciences, Lettres, Paris; Société des Artistes Français; Le Mérite et Dévoument Français; Accademia del Verbeno; Association Galleria Centro Storico, Italy; Accademia Araldia Internazionale "Il Marzocco", Italy; Accademia Italiana "Gli Etruschi", Italy; Japan International Artists Society; La Société Franco-Japonaise d'Art et d'Archéologie, Japan. Address: 2 Banchi, 2 Bancho, Chiyoda-ku, Tokyo 102-0084, Japan.

**HIRST Damien,** b. 1965, Bristol, England. Artist. 2 sons. Education: Goldsmiths College, London. Creative Works: One-man exhibitions include: Institute of Contemporary Arts (ICA), London, 1991; Emmanuel Perrotin, Paris, 1991; Cohen Gallery, New York, 1992; Regen Projects, Los Angeles, 1993; Galerie Jablonka, Cologne, 1993; Milwaukee Art Museum, 1994; Dallas Museum, 1994; Kukje Gallery, Seoul, 1995; White Cube/Jay Jopling, London, 1995; Prix Eliette von Karajan, 1995; Max Gandolph-Bibliothek, Salzburg, Germany, 1996; Gasogian Gallery, New York, 1996; Bruno Bischofberger, Zurich, 1997; Astrup Fearnley, Oslo, 1997; Southampton City Art Gallery, 1998; Pharmacy, Tate Gallery, London, 1999; Sadler's Wells, London, 2000; Damian Hurst, The Saatchi Gallery, 2003; The Agony and The Ecstacy: Selected Works from 1989-2004, Archaeological Museum, Naples, 2004; MFA, Boston, 2005; Numerous group exhibitions world-wide. Television: Channel 4 documentary about Damien Hirst and exhibition at Gagosian Gallery, directed by Roger Pomphrey, 2000. Publications: I Want to Spend the Rest of My Life Everywhere, One to One, Always, Forever, 1997; Theories, Models, Methods, Approaches, Assumptions, Results and Findings, 2000. Honours: Turner Prize, 1995.

**HIRST Paul Heywood,** b. 10 November 1927, Huddersfield, England. Academic. Education: BA, 1958, MA, Trinity College, Cambridge, 1945-48, 1951-52; Academic Diploma in Education, University of London, 1954; MA, Christ Church Oxford, 1955. Appointments: Lecturer and Tutor, University of Oxford, Department of Education, 1955-59; Lecturer in Philosophy of Education, London University, Institute of Education, 1959-65; Professor of Education, King's College, University of London, 1965-71; Professor of Education and Head, Department of Education, University of Cambridge, Fellow of Wolfson College, Cambridge, 1971-88; Emeritus Professor of Education, University of Cambridge, 1988-; Emeritus Fellow of Wolfson College, Cambridge, 1988-; Visiting Professor, Universities of British Columbia, Malawi, Otago, Melbourne, Puerto Rico, Alberta, Sydney; Visiting Professor, Kingston Polytechnic; Visiting Professor or Visiting Professorial Fellow, University of London, Institute of Education; Member, Swann Committee on Education of Children of Ethnic Minorities, 1981-85; Chair, Universities Council for the Education of Teachers, 1987-88; Chair, Committee for Research, CNAA, 1988-92. Publications: Logic of Education (with R S Peters), 1970; Knowledge and the Curriculum, 1974; Moral Education in a Secular Society, 1974; Educational Theory and Its Foundation Disciplines (editor), 1983; Initial Teacher Training and the Role of the School (with others), 1988; Philosophy of Education: Major Themes in the Analytic Tradition, 4 volumes (co-editor), 1998; 87 papers published in collections and philosophical and educational journals. Honours: Member, Royal Norwegian Society of Sciences and Letters; Honorary DEd, CNAA; Honorary DPhil, Cheltenham and Gloucester College of Higher Education, now University of Gloucestershire; Honorary DLitt, University of Huddersfield. Memberships: Honorary Vice-President, Philosophy of Education Society; Athenaeum Club. Address: Flat 3, 6 Royal Crescent, Brighton BN2 1AL, England.

**HISLOP Ian David,** b. 13 July 1960. Writer; Broadcaster. m. Victoria Hamson, 1988, 1 son, 1 daughter. Education: Ardingly College; BA Honours, English Language and Literature, Magdalen College, Oxford. Appointments: Joined staff, 1981-, Deputy Editor, 1985-86, Editor, 1986-, Private Eye, satirical magazine; Columnist, The Listener magazine, 1985-89; TV Critic, The Spectator magazine, 1994-96; Columnist, Sunday Telegraph, 1996-2003; Radio: Newsquiz, 1985-90; Fourth Column, 1992-96; Lent Talk, 1994; Gush (with Nicholas Newman), 1994; Words on Words, 1999; The Hislop Vote, 2000; A Revolution in 5 Acts, 2001; The Patron Saints, 2002; A Brief History of Tax, 2003; The Choir Invisible, 2003; There'll be Bluebirds Over the White Cliffs of Dover, 2004; Are We Being Offensive Enough? 2004; Television scriptwriting: Spitting Image, 1984-89 (with Nick Newman) The Stone Age, 1989; Briefcase Encounter, 1990; The Case of the Missing, 1991; He Died a Death, 1991; Harry Enfield's Television Programme, 1990-92; Harry Enfield and Chums, 1994-97; Mangez Merveillac, 1994; Dead on Time, 1995; Gobble, 1996; Sermon from St Albion's, 1998; Confessions of a Murderer, BBC2, 1999; My Dad is the Prime Minister, 2003, 2004; Performer: Have I Got News For You, 1990-; Great Railway Journeys, 1999; Documentaries: Canterbury Tales, 1996; School Rules, 1997; Pennies from Bevan, 1998; East to West, 1999;

Who Do You Think You Are? 2004. Publications: various Private Eye collections, 1985-; Contributor to newspapers and magazines on books, current affairs, arts and entertainment. Honours: BAFTA Award for Have I Got News for You, 1991; Editors' Editor, British Society of Magazine Editors, 1991; Magazine of the Year, What the Papers Say, 1991; Editor of the Year, British Society of Magazine Editors, 1998; Award for Political Satire, Channel 4 Political Awards, 2004. Address: c/o Private Eye, 6 Carlisle Street, London W1V 5RG, England.

**HISSEY Jane Elizabeth,** b. 1 September 1952, Norwich, Norfolk, England. Author; Illustrator. m. Ivan James Hissey, 1 August 1979, 2 sons, 1 daughter. Education: Art Foundation Course, Great Yarmouth College of Art and Design, 1970; BA, 1974, Art Teachers Certificate, Brighton Polytechnic, 1975. Publications: Old Bear, 1986; Little Bear's Trousers, 1987; Little Bear Lost, 1989; Jolly Tall, 1990; Jolly Snow, 1991; Old Bear Tales, 1991; Little Bear's Day, Little Bear's Bedtime, 1992; Ruff, 1994; Hoot, 1996; Little Bear's Dragon, 1999; Old Bear's All-together Painting, 2000; Little Bear's Alphabet, 2000; Little Bear's Numbers, 2001; Little Bears Colours, 2002; Little Bear's Shapes, 2003; SPLASH! 2003. TV series: Old Bear Stories, 1993-98. Honours: BAFTA, Best Children's Programme, 1993. Address: c/o Hutchinson Childrens Books, Random House, 61-63 Uxbridge Road, London W5 5SA, England.

**HJERMANN Reidar Kvaal,** b. 17 February 1969, Oslo, Norway. Ombudsman for Children in Norway; Clinical Psychologist. m. Pernilla Slotte Hjermann, 2 daughters. Education: Navy Officers Training School, 1988-89; Vocational studies in Psychology, 1992-96; Specialisation in Clinical Psychology for children and adolescents, 2001-2003. Appointments: Private Practice, 1988-; Reserve Officer, Navy Submarine Service, 1989-90; Psychologist, Department for Children and Adolescents, Safety Deputy, Psychiatric Centre, Vestfold, 1997-2004; Private Practice, expert witness, therapy lecturing, foster home counselling, 1998-2003; Work at Tanum and Fossnes Refugee Centres, 2000-2001; Created www.flyktingbarn.no (website with information on psychosocial rehabilitation of children with war experiences) for Norwegian Directorate of Immigration, 2000-2001; Appointed as the Ombudsman for Children in Norway by the King of Norway, 2004. Memberships: Human Rights Panel, Norwegian Psychologists Union; Reference Group, Save the Children; County Governor of Vestfold's Reference Group for improving the health services offered to refugees and asylum seekers. Address: PO Box 8889, Youngstorget, 0028 Oslo, Norway. E-mail: reidar@barneombudet.no Website: www.barneombudet.no

**HJERTÉN Stellan Vilhelm Einar,** b. 2 April 1928, Forshem, Sweden. Biochemist. m. Laila Elisabet Woxström, 1 daughter. Education: PhD, Uppsala University, Sweden, 1967. Appointments: Assistant Professor, 1967-69, Professor in Biochemistry, 1969-, Uppsala University. Publications: Numerous articles of professional journals and publications including: Journal of Liquid Chromatography; Journal of Chromatography; Journal of Biochemical and Biophysical Methods. Honours: The Björkén Prize, Uppsala University, 1985; Founder's Award, Electrophoresis Society, 1988; Frederick Conference Award, 1993; The Hirai Prize, Japan, 1994; American Chemical Society Award, 1996; The Torbern Bergman Medal, Swedish Chemical Society, 1996; The Pierce Award, International Society for Molecular Recognition, 2001; Honorary Doctor, University Medical School, Pécs, Hungary, 1999 and Vytautas Magnus University, Kaunas, Lithuania, 2001; The only Swede listed in Historica Chromatographica, Today's Chemists at Work, American Chemical Society, 2002; The M J E Golay Award, 2002; The Rudbeck Prize, Uppsala

University, Sweden, 2004; Special issues of Electrophoresis and The Analyst published in his honor Stellen Hjerten for many outstanding acheivements; Featured on the cover of the first issue of the Journal of Capillary Electrophoresis as Founder of capillary electrophoresis. Memberships: Initiator of Scandinavian Electrophoresis Society and Nordic Separation Science Society; Member, Editorial Board of several science journals. Address: Uppsala Biomedical Centre, Institute of Biochemistry, Box 576, SE-751 23, Uppsala, Sweden.

**HOAGLAND Edward,** b. 21 December 1932, New York, New York, USA. Author; Teacher. m. (1) Amy J Ferrara, 1961, divorced 1964, (2) Marion Magid, 28 March 1968, died 1993, 1 daughter. Education: AB, Harvard University, 1954. Appointments: Faculty: New School for Social Research, New York City, 1963-64, Rutgers University, 1966, Sarah Lawrence College, 1967, 1971, City University of New York, 1967, 1968, University of Iowa, 1978, 1982, Columbia University, 1980, 1981, Bennington College, 1987-2001, Brown University, 1988, University of California at Davis, 1990, 1992, Beloit College, Wisconsin, 1995; General Editor, Penguin Nature Library, 1985-. Publications: Cat Man, 1956; The Circle Home, 1960; The Peacock's Tail, 1965; Notes from the Century Before: A Journal from British Columbia, 1969; The Courage of Turtles, 1971; Walking the Dead Diamond River, 1973; The Moose on the Wall: Field Notes from the Vermont Wilderness, 1974; Red Wolves and Black Bears, 1976; African Calliope: A Journey to the Sudan, 1979; The Edward Hoagland Reader, 1979; The Tugman's Passage, 1982; City Tales, 1986; Seven Rivers West, 1986; Heart's Desire, 1988; The Final Fate of the Alligators, 1992; Balancing Acts, 1992; Tigers and Ice, 1999; Compass Points, 2000; Numerous essays and short stories. Honours: Houghton Mifflin Literary Fellowship, 1954; Longview Foundation Award, 1961; Prix de Rome, 1964; Guggenheim Fellowships, 1964, 1975; O Henry Award, 1971; New York State Council on the Arts Award, 1972; National Book Critics Circle Award, 1980; Harold D Vursell Award, 1981; National Endowment for the Arts Award, 1982; Literary Lion Award, New York Public Library, 1988; National Magazine Award, 1989; Lannon Foundation Literary Award, 1993; Literary Lights Award, Boston Public Library, 1995; American Academy of Arts and Letters, 1982. Address: PO Box 51, Barton, VT 05822, USA.

**HOANG Cuong,** b. 27 March 1944, Hue, Vietnam. Composer; Violinist. m. Le Kim Thanh. 1 son, 1 daughter. Education: Intermediate Level, Carl-Maria von Weber Conservatory; Graduate, Tchaikovsky Conservatory, Moscow, Russia; Postgraduate, Chopin Conservatory, Warsaw, Poland; Professor of Music, 1992. Appointments: Violin Teacher, 1965-; Dean of Strings Department, 1984, Vice-Director, 1997, Director, 2000-, HoChiMinh City Conservatory, HoChiMinh City, Vietnam; Member of the Jury, International Violin Competition "SPOHR", Freiburg, Germany, 1997. Compositions: Tranh Tu Binh (Four Pictures), string quartet, 1982; Rang Chieu (Bright Cloud in the Sunset) for violin and piano, 1985; Sonatine in C, string quartet, 1990; Ky Uc Dong Song (Memory of the River), suite for string orchestra, 1996; Trong Trang Thanh (The Drum sounded from the Great Wall's King Palace), ballad sonata for cello, and Piano, 1997; Vu Khuc (Dance Music) for solo piano, 1998; Dem Tran Tro (The Anxious Night), 1999; Ngay Dau Xuan (The First Spring Day), ten variations for string trio, 2000; Millennium Spring, overture, 2000; Quintet for violin, viola, cello, double bass and piano, 2001; Thoa Noi Nho Mong (Meet the Longing Thoughts) for flute, dan bau, cello and piano, 2003; Many other pieces for piano, violin, viola, trumpet, flute and vocal music. Honours: Only student selected by a German teacher to develop musical talent, Dresden, 1959; 2nd prize for

Composition, 1990, 1996, 1997, 2000, 2001, 3rd Prize, 1998, 1999, Vietnamese Composer's Association. Memberships: HoChiMinh City Musicians Association; Vietnamese Composers, Musicologists and Musicians Association. Address: 112 Nguyen Du Street, Dist 1, HoChiMinh City, Vietnam. E-mail: nhacvienhcm@hcm.vnn.vn

**HOANG-NGOC Minh** b. 29 July 1929, Vietnam. Doctor of Medicine. m. Nguyen Thi Long, 2 sons, 2 daughters. Education: MD, 1958, Postgraduate Training Residency, Johns Hopkins, MD, USA, 1958-60. Appointments: Chief, Department Gynaeco-Surgical Tu Du Hospital, Saigon, Vietnam, 1965; Assistant Professor, Saigon Faculty of Medicine, 1968; Associated Professor, CHU Amiens, France, 1971. Publications: 280 publications. Memberships: President, French Society of Gynaecology, 1996-98; General Secretary of French Society of Gynaeco-Pathology; Vice President, European Society of Gynaecology, 2001-2003; Life Member, American Society for Reproductive Medicine, Senior Member: ICGS, ISGYP, New York Academy of Sciences. Address: 4 Rue Eugene Delacroix, 94410 Saint Maurice, France.

**HOBBS Lewis Mankin,** b. 16 May 1937, Upper Darby, Pennsylvania, USA. Astronomer. m. Jo Ann Hagele Hobbs, 2 sons, 1 daughter. Education: BEP, Engineering Physics, Cornell University, Ithaca, New York, 1960; MS, Physics, 1962, PhD, Physics, 1966, University of Wisconsin, Madison, Wisconsin. Appointments: Junior Astronomer, Lick Observatory, University of California, 1965-66; Assistant Professor, 1966-72, Associate Professor, 1972-76, University of Chicago; Director, Yerkes Observatory, University of Chicago, 1974-82; Professor of Astronomy and Astrophysics, University of Chicago, 1976-; Emeritus Professor, 2002. Publications: About 150 articles in professional journals. Honours: Alfred P Sloan Scholar, 1956-60. Memberships: International Astronomical Union; American Astronomical Society; American Physical Society. Address: University of Chicago, Yerkes Observatory, Williams Bay, WI 53191, USA.

**HOBBS Peter Thomas Goddard,** b. 19 March 1938, Gloucester, England. Director. m. Victoria Christabel Matheson, 1 daughter. Education: Waugh Scholar, MA, Exeter College, Oxford; CCIPD, 1988; F Inst D, 1989; FRSA, 1992. Appointments: Manager, ICI Ltd, 1962-79; Director, Wellcome Foundation and Wellcome plc, 1979-92; Founder Chairman, Employers Forum on Disability, 1986-93; HM First Non-Police Inspector of Constabulary, 1993-98; Non-Executive Director, Forensic Science Service, 1996-; Chairman, Learning From Experience Trust, 1992-93, 1998-. Publications: Miscellaneous human resource and organisation matters; Old St Albans Court Archaeologia Cantia, 2005. Honour: Dr hc, IMC, 2000. Memberships: Confederation of British Industry, Education and Training Committee, 1990-94; Institute of Directors, Employment Committee, 1989-93; Chemical Industries Association, Training Committee, Employment Board, Council, 1979-92. Address: Blenheim Crescent, London W11 2EQ, England.

**HOBHOUSE Penelope, (Penelope Malins),** b. 20 November 1929, Castledawson, Northern Ireland. Writer; Designer. m. (1) Paul Hobhouse, 1952, 2 sons, 1 daughter, (2) John Malins, 1 November 1983. Education: Honours, Economics, University of Cambridge, 1951. Publications: The Country Gardener; Colour in Your Garden; Garden Style; Flower Gardens; Guide to the Gardens of Europe; The Smaller Garden; Painted Gardens; Private Gardens of England; Borders; Flower Gardens; Plants in Garden History; Garden Style; The Story of Gardening; The Gardens of Persia. Contributions to: The Garden; Horticulture;

Vogue; Antiques; Plants and Gardens. Honour: Awarded Royal Horticultural Society Victoria Medal of Honour, 1996; Lifetime Achievement Award, Guild of Garden Writers, 1999; MA; Hon DLitt. Address: The Coach House, Bettiscombe, Bridport, Dorset DT6 5NT, England.

**HOBSBAWM Eric John Ernest,** b. 9 June 1917, Alexandria, Egypt (British citizen). Professor of Economic and Social History Emeritus; Writer. m. Marlene Schwarz, 1962, 1 son, 1 daughter. Education: BA, 1939, MA, 1943, PhD, 1951, University of Cambridge. Appointments: Lecturer in History, 1947-59, Reader in History, 1959-70, Professor of Economic and Social History, 1970-82, Professor Emeritus, 1982-, Birkbeck College, University of London; Fellow, King's College, Cambridge, 1949-55 (Honorary Fellow, 1971). Publications: Labour's Turning Point, 1880-1900 (editor), 1948; Primitive Rebels, 1959, US edition as Social Bandits and Primitive Rebels, 1959; The Jazz Scene, 1959, revised edition, 1993; The Age of Revolution, 1789-1848, 1962; Labouring Men, 1964; Industry and Empire: An Economic History of Britain since 1750, 1968, 1999, US edition as Industry and Empire: The Making of Modern English Society, 1968; Captain Swing (with George Rudé), 1969; Bandits, 1969, revised edition, 1981, 2000; Revolutionaries, 1973; The Age of Capital, 1848-1875, 1975; Marxism in Marx's Day (editor), 1982; The Invention of Tradition (editor with Terence Ranger), 1983; Worlds of Labour: Further Studies in the History of Labour, 1984, US edition as Workers: Worlds of Labor, 1984; The Age of Empire, 1875-1914, 1987; Politics for a Rational Left: Political Writing, 1977-1988, 1989; Echoes of the Marseillaise: Two Centuries Look Back on the French Revolution, 1990; Nations and Nationalism since 1780: Programme, Myth, Reality, 1990, 2nd edition, 1992; Age of Extremes: The Short Twentieth Century, 1914-1991, 1994; US edition as The Age of Extremes: A History of the World, 1914-1991, 1994; On History (essays), 1997; Uncommon People: Resistance, Rebellion and Jazz, 1998; On the Edge of the New Century, 2000; Interesting Times, 2002. Contributions to: Scholarly journals and general publications. Honours: Palmes Académiques, France, 1993; Commander, Order of the Southern Cross, Brazil, 1996; Companion of Honour, 1998; Numerous honorary degrees. Memberships: British Academy, fellow; American Academy of Arts and Sciences, honorary foreign member; Hungarian Academy of Sciences, foreign member; Academy of Sciences, Turin; The Japan Academy, honorary foreign member. Address: School of History, Birkbeck College, University of London, Malet Street, London WC1E 7HX, England.

**HOBSON Fred Colby Jr,** b. 23 April 1943, Winston-Salem, North Carolina, USA. Professor of Literature; Writer. m. 17 June 1967, divorced, 1 daughter. Education: AB, English, University of North Carolina, 1965; MA, History, Duke University, 1967; PhD, English, University of North Carolina, 1972. Appointments: Professor of English, University of Alabama, 1972-86; Professor of English and Co-Editor, Southern Review, Louisiana State University, 1986-89; Professor of English; Lineberger Professor in the Humanities and Co-Editor, Southern Literary Journal, University of North Carolina at Chapel Hill, 1989-. Publications: Serpent in Eden: H L Mencken and the South, 1974; Literature at the Barricades: The American Writer in the 1930's (co-editor), 1983; Tell About the South: The Southern Rage to Explain, 1984; South-Watching: Selected Essays of Gerald W Johnson (editor), 1984; The Southern Writer in the Post-Modern World, 1990; Mencken: A Life, 1994; Thirty-Five Years of Newspaper Work by H L Mencken (co-editor), 1994; But Now I See: The Southern White Racial Conversion Narrative, 1999; Faulkner's Absalom, Absalom!: Selected Essays (editor), 2002; South to the Future: An American Region in the Twenty-First Century (editor), 2002. Contributions to: Virginia Quarterly Review; Sewanee Review; Atlantic Monthly; Kenyon Review; New York Times Book Review; American Literature; Times Literary Supplement. Honours: Lillian Smith Award, 1984; Jules F Landry Award, 1994, 1999. Address: Department of English, University of North Carolina at Chapel Hill, NC 27599-3520, USA.

**HOCKNEY David,** b. 9 July 1937, Bradford, England. Artist. Education: Bradford College of Art; Royal College of Art. Appointments: Teacher, Maidstone College of Art, 1962, University of Iowa, 1964, University of Colorado, 1965, University of California, Los Angeles, 1966, University of California, Berkeley, 1967. Creative Works: First one-man exhibition, Kasmin Galley, London, 1963; Subsequent one-man exhibitions include: Nicholas Wilder, Los Angeles, 1976; Galerie Neundorf, Hamburg, 1977; Warehouse Gallery, 1979; Knoedler Gallery, 1979, 1981, 1982, 1983, 1984, 1986; Tate Gallery, 1980, 1986, 1988; Hayward Gallery, 1983, 1985; Los Angeles County Museum, 1988; The Metro Museum of Art, New York, 1988; Knoedler Gallery, London, 1988; A Emmerich Gallery, New York, 1988, 1989; Los Angeles Louvre Gallery, Venice, 1982, 1983, 1985, 1988; Nishimura Gallery, Tokyo, Japan, 1988; Manchester City Art Galleries, 1996; National Museum of American Art, Washington DC, 1997, 1998; Museum Ludwig, Cologne, 1997; Museum of Fine Arts, Boston, 1998; Centre Georges Pompidou, Paris, 1999; Musee Picasso, Paris, 1999; Annely Juda Fine Art, 2003; National Portrait Gallery, 2003. Publications: Hockney by Hockney, 1976; David Hockney, Travel with Pen, Pencil and Ink, 1978; Photographs, 1982; China Diary (with Stephen Spender), 1982; Hockney Paints the Stage, 1983; David Hockney: Cameraworks, 1984; Hockney on Photography: Conversations with Paul Joyce, 1988; David Hockney: A Retrospective, 1988; Hockney's Alphabet, 1991; That's the Way I See It, 1993; Off the Wall: Hockney Posters, 1994; David Hockney's Dog Days, 1998; Hockney on Art: Photography, Painting and Perspective, 1998; Hockney on "Art": Conversation with Paul Joyce, 2000; Secret Knowledge: Rediscovering the Lost Techniques of the Old Masters, 2001. Honours: Numerous. Memberships include: Royal Academy, 1985. Address: c/o 7508 Santa Monica Boulevard, Los Angeles, CA 90046, USA.

**HODDLE Glenn,** b. 27 October 1957, England. Footballer; Football Manager. m. Christine Anne Stirling, divorced, 1 son, 2 daughters. Appointments: Player with Tottenham Hotspur, 1976-86, AS Monaco, France, 1986; (12 under 21 caps, 53 full caps on England National Team 1980-88, played in World Cup 1982, 1986); Player/Manager, Swindon Town, 1991-93 (promoted to FA Premier League 1993); Player/Manager, Chelsea, 1993-96; Coach, English National Team, 1996-99; Manager, Southampton, 2000-01; Manager, Tottenham Hotspur, 2001-. Publication: Spurred to Success (autobiography); Glenn Hoddle: The 1998 World Cup Story, 1998. Honours: FA Cup Winners Medal (Tottenham Hotspur), 1984; French Championship Winners Medal (Monaco), 1988.

**HODGE Ian David,** b. 15 February 1952, Chelmsford, Essex, England. University Reader. m. Bridget Anne, 1 son, 3 daughters. Education: BSc, Agricultural Economics, University of Reading, 1973; PhD, Countryside Planning Unit, Wye College, University of London, 1977. Appointments: Temporary Lecturer and Research Associate in Agricultural Economics, University of Newcastle upon Tyne, 1976-78; Visiting Research Associate, Department of Agricultural Economics, University of Idaho, USA, 1982; Lecturer in Agricultural Economics, University of Queensland, Australia, 1979-83; Gilbey Lecturer in the History and Economics of Agriculture, 1983-2000, Acting

Head, Department of Land Economy, 1998, University Senior Lecturer, 2000-2001, University Reader in Rural Economy, 2001-, Head of Department of Land Economy, 2002-, University of Cambridge; Visiting Professor, Department of Agricultural Economics, University of Wisconsin, 1994; Governor: Macaulay Land Use Research Institute, 1998-2003, Cambridge International Land Institute, 2003-. Publications include: Rural Employment: Trends, Options, Choices (with Martin Whitby), 1981; Environmental Economics: Individual Incentives and Public Choices, 1995; Countryside in Trust, Land management by Conservation, Amenity and recreation Organisations (with Janet Dwyer), 1996; Numerous article in academic journals. Honours: BSc, University of Reading, 1973; PhD, University of London, 1977; Fellow Royal Institution of Chartered Surveyors, 2004. Memberships include: Fellow Hughes Hall Cambridge, 2004; Socio Economic Advisory Group, English Nature, 1994-, Broads Research Advisory Panel, 1999-2003, MAFF/DEFRA Academic Economist Panel, 1999-; MAFF Task Force for the Hills, 2000-2001; Resource Policy Research Consortium, 1989-. Address: Department of Land Economy, University of Cambridge, 19 Silver Street, Cambridge CB3 9EP, England. E-mail: idh3@cam.ac.uk

**HODGE Patricia,** b. Grimsby, England. Actress. m. Peter Owen, 2 sons. Education: London Academy of Music and Dramatic Art. Creative Works: Stage appearances include: No-one Was Saved; All My Sons; Say Who You Are; The Birthday Party; The Anniversary; Popkiss; Two Gentlemen of Verona; Pippin; Maudie; Hair; The Beggar's Opera; Pal Joey; Look Back in Anger; Dick Whittington; Happy Yellow; The Brian Cant Children's Show; Then and Now; The Mitford Girls; As You Like It; Benefactors; Noel and Gertie; Separate Tables; The Prime of Miss Jean Brodie; A Little Night Music; Heartbreak House, 1997; Money, 1999; Noises Off, 2000-01; His Dark Materials, 2004. Film appearances: The Disappearance; Rose Dixon - Night Nurse; The Waterloo Bridge Handicap; The Elephant Man; Heavy Metal; Betrayal; Sunset; Just Ask for Diamond; The Secret Life of Ian Fleming; The Leading Man, 1996; Prague Duet, 1996; Jilting Joe, 1997; TV appearances: Valentine; The Girls of Slender Means; Night of the Father; Great Big Groovy Horse; The Naked Civil Servant; Softly, Softly; Jackanory Playhouse; Act of Rape; Crimewriters; Target; Rumpole of the Bailey; The One and Only Mrs Phyllis Dixey; Edward and Mrs Simpson; Disraeli; The Professionals; Holding the Fort; The Other 'Arf; Jemima Shore Investigates; Hayfever; The Death of the Heart; Robin of Sherwood; OSS; Sherlock Holmes; Time for Murder; Hotel du Lac; The Life and Loves of a She Devil; Rich Tea and Sympathy, 1991; The Cloning of Joanna May, 1991; The Legacy of Reginald Perrin, 1996; The Moonstone, 1996; The Falklands Play, 2002. Award: The Olivier Award, 2000. Address: c/o ICM, Oxford House, 76 Oxford Street, London W1R 1RB, England.

**HODGSON Kenneth Jonah,** b. 2 August 1936, Liverpool, England. Clergyman; Social Worker; Artist. 2 daughters. Education: Ponsbourne Pre-Ordination College, Hertfordshire, 1964-66; Oak Hill College, London, 1966-69; Ordained, 1969; The Open University, 1976-79; North East Wales Institute, Wrexham Cymru, 1987-89. Appointments: Clerical Work, 1952-54; Royal Air Force, 1954-57; Clerical Work, 1957-60; Family Business, 1960-61; School Welfare Officer, 1961-64; Anglican Clergyman, 1969-78; Social Worker, 1978-96; Chaplain, TAVR, 1979-82; Chaplain, Regular Army Reserve, 1982-91; Anglican Clergyman, NSM, 2001; Artist in acrylic, oil and water-colour; Collective exhibitions: Royal Cambrian Arts; Williamson Art Gallery, Wirral; Various Liverpool and Chester galleries; Newcastle, Staffordshire; Ludlow; RBSA Gallery Birmingham; Durham; Flintshire; St Ives, Cornwall,

St David's Hall, Cardiff, Cymru and USA venues; Individual exhibitions on Merseyside and Wirral; Associated with Daylight Group – a joint Tate Liverpool and Metropolitan Borough of Wirral SSD Arts Project, Art Forum, 1993; Paintings in private and public collections in UK and other countries. Memberships: Member, Merseyside Artist's Association; Member, 1983-, Secretary, 1983-87, Committee Member 2005 Wirral Society of Arts; Merseyside Contemporary Artists, Steering Committee Secretary, 1988-89; Director, Founder, National Acrylic Painters' Association, 1985; Honorary Vice-President, International Society of Acrylic Painters, USA, 2005. Address: 134 Rake Lane, Wallasey, Wirral, Merseyside CH45 1JW, England.

**HODGSON Peter Barrie**, b. 12 March 1942, Gosforth, England. Market Research Director. m. Audrone Grudzinskas, 1 son. Education: BA, St Peter's College, Oxford, England. Appointments: Senior Research Executive, Marplan Ltd, 1967-69; Senior Research Planner, Garland Compton Ltd, 1970-72; Director, Opinion Research Centre Ltd, 1973-75; Managing Director, Professional Studies Ltd, 1975-77; Director, Professional Studies Ireland Ltd, 1977-78; Managing Director, Action Research Ltd, 1977-78; Director, City Research Associates, Ltd, 1981-89; Managing Director, Travel and Tourism Research Ltd, 1978-. Publications: Articles published in: Espaces (Paris); Marketing; Journal of the Market Research Society; Journal of the Professional Marketing Research Society of Canada; Tourism Management; Journal of Travel Research; BMRA Bulletin; Synergie. Honours: Fellow, Tourism Society; Fellow, Institute of Travel and Tourism. Memberships: Council Member, Market Research Society, 1978-81; Council Member Tourism Society, 1981-84; Chairman, Association of British Market Research Companies, 1987-89; Chairman, Association of European Market Research Institutes, 1991-93; Deputy Chairman/Honorary Secretary, British Market Research Association, 1998-2004. Address: Travel and Tourism Research Ltd, 4 Cochrane House, Admirals Way, London E14 9UD, England. E-mail: pb.hodgson@virgin.net

**HOE Susanna Leonie**, b. 14 April 1945, Southampton, England. Writer. m. Derek Roebuck, 18 August 1981. Education: London School of Economics, 1980-82; BA, University of Papua New Guinea, 1983-84. Appointments: Campaign Co-ordinator, British Section Amnesty International, 1977-80; TEFL Teacher, Women's Centre, Hong Kong, 1991-97. Publications: Lady in the Chamber, 1971; God Save the Tsar, 1978; The Man Who Gave His Company Away, 1978; The Private Life of Old Hong Kong, 1991; Chinese Footprints, 1996; Stories for Eva: A Reader for Chinese Women Learning English, 1997; The Taking of Hong Kong, with Derek Roebuck, 1999; Women at the Siege, Peking 1900 (history), 2000; At Home in Paradise (Papua New Guinea, travel), 2003; Madeira (history/travel), 2004. Contributions to: Times (Papua New Guinea); Liverpool Post; Women's Feature Service. Honours: Te Rangi Hiroa Pacific History Prize, 1984. Membership: Honorary Research Fellow, Centre of Asian Studies, University of Hong Kong, 1991-. Address: 20A Plantation Road, Oxford OX2 6JD, England.

**HOFER Erwin**, b. 25 June 1949, Windisch, Brugg AG, Switzerland. Swiss Ambassador to Russia. m. Beatrice Gut, 3 daughters. Education: Lic iur, Law, University of Zurich. Appointments: Swiss Diplomatic Service, Federal Department of Foreign Affairs, 1976; Political Secretariat of the Federal Department of Foreign Affairs, 1977-82; Swiss Observer Mission to the UN, New York, USA, 1982-87; Head of Section, United Nations and International Organisations, Department of Foreign Affairs, 1987-91; Deputy Head, Mission in Budapest, 1991-95; Ambassador, Permanent Representative of Switzerland to the Conference on Disarmament and Head of the Multilateral Division of the Swiss Mission to the United Nations and other International Organisations in Geneva, 1996-2000; President, Conference on Disarmament, Geneva, and Co-ordinator on the Expansion of the Conference, 1998; Co-Chair, Standing Committee of Experts of the Ottawa-Convention, 1999; Ambassador and head of the Political Division III, United Nations, International Organisations Culture and Environment, Federal Department of Foreign Affairs, Berne, 2000-03; Ambassador of Switzerland in Moscow for Russia, Kazakstan and Turkmenistran, 2004-. Publications: Numerous articles and contributions to popular and professional journals. Address: Swiss Embassy, per Ogorodnaya Sloboda 2/5, 101000 Moscow, Russia.

**HOFFMAN Dustin Lee**, b. 8 August 1937, Los Angeles, California, USA. Actor. m. (1) Anne Byrne, 1969, divorced, 2 daughters, (2) Lisa Gottsegen, 1980, 2 sons, 2 daughters. Education: Santa Monica City College. Appointments: Attendant, Psychiatric Institute; Demonstrator, Macy's Toy Department. Creative Works: Stage appearances include: Harry, Noon and Night, 1964; Journey of the Fifth Horse, 1966; Star Wagon, 1966; Fragments, 1966; Eh?, 1967; Jimmy Shine, 1968; Death of a Salesman, 1984; The Merchant of Venice, 1989; Films include: The Tiger Makes Out, 1966; Madigan's Millions, 1966; The Graduate, 1967; Midnight Cowboy, 1969; John and Mary, 1969; Little Big Man, 1970; Who is Harry Kellerman..?, 1971; Straw Dogs, 1971; Alfredo Alfredo, Papillon, 1973; Lenny, 1974; All the President's Men, 1975; Marathon Man, 1976; Straight Time, 1978; Agatha, 1979; Kramer vs Kramer, 1979; Tootsie, 1982; Ishtar, 1987; Rain Man, 1988; Family Business, 1989; Dick Tracy, 1990; Hook, 1991; Billy Bathgate, 1991; Hero, 1992; Outbreak, 1995; American Buffalo, 1996; Sleeper, 1996; Wag the Dog, 1997; Mad City, 1997; Sphere, 1997; Joan of Arc, 1999; The Messenger: the Story of Joan of Arc, 1999; Being John Malkovich, 1999. TV appearances in: Death of a Salesman, 1985. Honours include: Obie Award, 1966; Vernon Rice Award, 1967; Academy Award, 1980; New York Film Critics Award, 1980, 1988; Golden Globe Award, 1988; BAFTA Award, 1997. Address: Punch Productions, 1926 Broadway, Suite 305, NY 10023, USA.

**HOGWOOD Christopher (Jarvis Haley)**, b. 10 September 1941, Nottingham, England. Harpischordist; Conductor; Musicologist; Writer; Editor; Broadcaster. Education: BA, Pembroke College, Cambridge, 1964; Charles University, Prague; Academy of Music, Prague. Appointments: Founder-Member, Early Music Consort of London, 1967-76; Founder-Director, The Academy of Ancient Music, 1973-; Faculty, Cambridge University, 1975-; Artistic Director, 1986-2001, Conductor Laureate, 2001-, Handel and Haydn Society, Boston; Honorary Professor of Music, University of Keele, 1986-89; Music Director, 1988-92, Principal Guest Conductor, 1992-98, St Paul Chamber Orchestra, Minnesota; International Professor of Early Music Performance, Royal Academy of Music, London, 1992-; Visiting Professor, King's College, London, 1992-96; Principal Guest Conductor, Kammerorchester Basel, 2000-; Principal Guest Conductor, Orquesta de Granada, 2001-04. Publications: Music at Court, 1977; The Trio Sonata, 1979; Haydn's Visits to England, 1980; Music in Eighteenth-Century England (editor), 1983; Handel, 1984; Holme's Life of Mozart (editor), 1991. Contributions to: The New Grove Dictionary of Music and Musicians, 1980, 2000. Honours: Walter Wilson Cobbett Medal, 1986; Commander of the Order of the British Empire, 1989; Honorary Fellow, Jesus College, Cambridge, 1989, Pembroke College, Cambridge, 1992; Freeman, Worshipful Company of Musicians, 1989; Incorporated Society of Musicians Distinguished Musician Award, 1997; Martinu

Medal, Bohuslav Martinu Foundation, Prague, 1999; Honorary Professor of Music, Cambridge University, 2002-. Membership: Royal Society of Authors, fellow. Address: 10 Brookside, Cambridge CB2 1JE, England.

**HOH Fang Chao,** b. 23 September 1933, Shanghai, China. Physicist. m. Eva Birgitta Kristina Hörlin, 1959, 3 sons. Education: BSEE degree, 1957, MS, Plasma Physics, 1961, DSc, Plasma Physics, 1963, Royal Institute of Technology, Stockholm, Sweden. Research Associate, University of California, San Diego, USA, 1963; Senior Research Scientist, Boeing Company, Seattle, 1964-71; Development Engineer, Cook Electric Company, Chicago; Development Engineer, Zenith Radio Corporation, Chicago; Engineer, Ericsson Corporation, Stockholm, 1983-98. Publications: 18 articles on plasma physics and 16 articles on elementary particle theory published in professional journals; Book, Scalar Strong Interaction Hadron Theory. Honours: Listed in biographical directories. Address: Dragarbrunnsg 55C, 75320 Uppsala, Sweden.

**HOLBROOK David (Kenneth),** b. 9 January 1923, Norwich, England. Author. m. 23 April 1949, 2 sons, 2 daughters. Education: BA, Honours, English, 1946, MA, 1951, Downing College, Cambridge. Appointments: Fellow, King's College, Cambridge, 1961-65; Senior Leverhulme Research Fellow, 1965, Leverhulme Emeritus Research Fellow, 1988-90; Writer-in-Residence, Dartington Hall, 1972-73; Fellow and Director of English Studies, 1981-88, Emeritus Fellow, 1988, Downing College; Publications: English for Maturity, 1961; Imaginings, 1961; Against the Cruel Frost, 1963; English for the Rejected, 1964; The Secret Places, 1964; Flesh Wounds, 1966; Children's Writing, 1967; The Exploring Word, 1967; Object Relations, 1967; Old World New World, 1969; English in Australia Now, 1972; Gustav Mahler and the Courage to Be, 1975; Chance of a Lifetime, 1978; A Play of Passion, 1978, 2004; English for Meaning, 1980; Selected Poems, 1980; Nothing Larger than Life, 1987; The Novel and Authenticity, 1987; A Little Athens, 1990; Edith Wharton and the Unsatisfactory Man, 1991; Jennifer, 1991; The Gold in Father's Heart, 1992; Where D H Lawrence Was Wrong About Women, 1992; Creativity and Popular Culture, 1994; Even If They Fail, 1994; Tolstoy, Women and Death, 1996; Wuthering Heights: a Drama of Being, 1997; Getting it Wrong with Uncle Tom, 1998; Bringing Everything Home (poems), 1999; A Study of George MacDonald and the Image of Woman, 2000; Lewis Carroll: Nonsense Against Sorrow, 2001; Going Off The Rails, 2003. Contributions to: Numerous professional journals. Honour: Festschrift, 1996. Honours: Founding Fellow, English Association, 2000. Membership: Society of Authors. Address: 1 Tennis Court Terrace, Cambridge CB2 1QX, England.

**HOLBROOKE Richard C,** b. 24 April 1941, New York, USA. Diplomat. m. (1) 2 sons, (2) Kati Morton, 1995. Education: Brown University; Woodrow Wilson School; Princeton University. Appointments: Foreign Service Officer, Vietnam and Related Posts, 1962-66; White House Vietnam Staff, 1966-67; Special Assistant to Under-Secretaries of State, Katzenbac and Richardson, Member, US Delegate to Paris Peace Talks on Vietnam, 1967-69; Director, Peace Corporations, Morocco, 1970-72; Managing Director, Foreign Policy (quarterly magazine), 1972-76; Consultant, President's Commission on Organisation of Government for Conduct of Foreign Policy, Contributing Editor, Newsweek, 1974-75; Co-ordinator, National Security Affairs, Carter-Mondale Campaign, 1976; Assistant Secretary of State for East Asian and Pacific Affairs, 1977-81; Vice President of Public Strategies, 1981-85; Managing Director, Lehman Brothers, 1985-93; Ambassador to Germany, 1993-94; Assistant

Secretary of State for European and Canadian Affairs, 1994-96; Vice Chair, Credit Suisse First Boston Corporation, 1996-98; Adviser, Baltic Sea Council, 1996-98; Special Presidential Envoy for Cyprus, 1997-98, to Yugoslavia (on Kosovo crisis); Permanent Representative to UN, 1999-2000; Ambassador to UN, 1999-2001. Publications: Counsel to the President, 1991; To End a War, 1998; Several articles and essays. Honours: 12 honorary degrees; Distinguished Public Service Award, Department of Defense, 1994, 1996; Humanitarian of the Year Award, American Jewish Congress, 1998; Dr Bernard Heller, Prize, Hebrew Union College, 1999. Address: c/o Department of State, 2201 C Street NW, Washington, DC 20520, USA.

**HOLDER Stanley John,** b. 21 September 1928, London, England. Nursing Educator. Education: South East Essex Technical College and School of Art Day School; Battersea College (University of Surrey); Sister Tutor Diploma, Advanced Diploma in Education, Master's Level, Adult Education, London University; Institute of Education; Registered General Nurse, Oldchurch Hospital, Romford, Essex. Appointments include: Charge Nurse, Surgical Unit, 1950-54, Tutor, 1956-60, Oldchurch Hospital; Principal Tutor, Hackney Hospital, London, 1960-65; Assistant Editor, Nursing Times, 1965-67; Principal Tutor, St Mary's Hospital, London, 1967-70; Director of Education, St Mary's Hospital and Parkside Health Authority, 1970-90; Chief Nursing Advisor, BRCS, 1988-93; Consultant: Curriculum Design, Middlesex University, 1991, BBC Nursing Education Series, 1991, Tayside Health Board, Scotland, 1991; Government and Official Appointments: Secretary of State appointments: East London Hospital Management Committee, 1966-74, Tower Hamlets Health Authority, 1980-90; Education Consultant, Rampton Inquiry, 1979; DHSS Working Party, Extended Role of the Nurse, 1974-77; Chairman, King's Fund Working Party overseas recruitment, The Language Barrier, 1973-74; Chairman, Member of Council Royal College of Nursing Representative Body, 1969-74; Chief Assessor, University of London Extra Mural Department, 1965-89; Founding Member, 1978-83, Vice-Chairman, 1981-83, Linacre Centre for Health Care Ethics; Vice-Chairman, Mildmay Mission Hospital (HIV/AIDS), 1983-91; Chairman, Mental Health Managers, Tower Hamlets, 1980-98; Elected Member, Chairman, Adult Nursing Committee, English National Board for Nursing, Midwifery and Health Visiting, 1983-90; Member, UK Council for Nursing and Midwifery, 1983-90. Publications: Founding Editor, Nurse Education Today; UK Editor, Nursing Series, McGraw Hill; Co-author, Programmed Learning text of Physiology of Respiration; Numerous articles on health matters and nursing education. Honours: OBE; Fellow, Royal College of Nursing; Florence Nightingale Scholar, USA and Canada, Florence Nightingale Foundation; Freeman City of London; Badge of Honour for Distinguished Service, BRC Society. Memberships: Freeman of City of London, Freeman's Guild; Rotary International, President, Epping, 2003-2004; University of the Third Age. Address: 155 Theydon Grove, Epping, Essex CM16 4QB, England.

**HOLE Derek Norman,** b. 5 December 1933, Plymouth, Devon. Provost Emeritus of Leicester. Education: Public Central School, Plymouth; Lincoln Theological College, 1957-60. Appointments include: National Service Royal Air Force, 1952-54; Assistant Librarian, Codrington Library, Oxford, 1954-56; Ordained Deacon, 1960, Ordained Priest, 1961, Leicester Cathedral; Assistant Curate, St Mary Magdalene, Knighton, Leicester, 1960-62; Domestic Chaplain to the Archbishop of Cape Town, 1962-64; Assistant Curate, St Nicholas, Kenilworth, Warwickshire, 1964-67; Rector of St Mary the Virgin, Burton Latimer, Kettering, Northants, 1967-73; Independent Member, Burton Latimer Urban District Council, 1971-73; Vicar of St

# DICTIONARY OF INTERNATIONAL BIOGRAPHY

James the Greater, Leicester, 1973-92; Chaplain, Lord Mayor of Leicester, 1976-77, 1994-95, 1996-97; Chaplain, Leicester Branch of the Royal Air Forces Association, 1978-92; Chaplain, Haymarket Theatre, Leicester, 1980-83, 1993-95; Member, Actors' Church Union, 1980-95; Chaplain, High Sheriffs' of Leicestershire, 1980-85, 1987-88, 1999-2000, 2001-02; Honorary Canon, Leicester Cathedral, 1983-92; Rural Dean of Christianity South in the City of Leicester, 1983-92; Chaplain, Leicester High School, 1983-92; Chaplain to the Queen, 1985-92; Chairman, House of Clergy for the Diocese of Leicester, 1986-94; Vice-President, Leicester Diocesan Synod, 1986-94; President, Leicester Rotary Club, 1987-88; Member, Association of English Cathedrals, 1992-99; Provost of Leicester, 1992-99; Governor, Leicester Grammar School, 1992-99; Governor, Leicester High School, 1992-2004; Vice-President, The English Clergy Association, 1993-; Priest Associate, Actors' Church Union, 1995-; Chaplain, Merchant Taylors' Company, 1995-96; Chaplain, Guild of Freemen of the City of Leicester, 1996-99; Commissary to the Bishop of Wellington, New Zealand, 1998-; Senior Fellow, De Montford University, Leicester, 1998-; Trustee, Leicester Grammar School, 1999-; Provost Emeritus of Leicester, 1999-; Chairman of the Leicestershire Branch of the Britain-Australia Society, 2000-05; Chaplain, The Royal Society of St George, 2000-; Chaplain to the Master of the Worshipful Company of Framework Knitters, 2004-06; Chaplain to the Mayor of Oadby & Wigston Borough Council, 2005-06. Publications: Contributions to: The History of St James The Greater, Leicester, edited by Dr Alan C McWhirr; Century to Millennium St James the Greater Leicester 1899-1999. Honours: Honorary D Litt, De Montford University, 1999; Freeman of the City of London, 2003-; Liveryman of the Worshipful Company of Framework Knitters, 2003-; Honorary LLD, Leicester University, 2005. Memberships: Leicestershire Club; The Royal Western Yacht Club of England. Address: 25 Southernhay Close, Leicester LE2 3TW, England. E-mail: dnhole@leicester.anglican.org

**HOLEŇA Martin,** b. 9 March 1958, Brno, Czech Republic. Computer Scientist. m Jiřina Poláková, 1 foster son. Education: MSc, Applied Mathematics, Czech Technical University, Prague, 1982; Dr. rer.nat., Probability and Mathematical Statistics, Charles University, Prague, 1989; CSc (approximately PhD), Computer Science, Czechoslovak Academy of Sciences, Prague, 1990. Appointments: Junior Assistant, Czech Technical University, 1982-85; Centre for Scientific Computing, Czechoslovak Academy of Sciences, 1985-90; Researcher, 1990-2000, Senior Researcher, 2000-, Institute of Computer Science, Czech Academy of Sciences; Lecturer, Czech Technical University, 1993-; Lecturer, Charles University, Prague, 2005-; Visiting Scientist in Germany at University of Paderborn, 1993-95, University of Magdeburg, 1996-98, Brandenburg University of Technology at Cottbus, 1999-2000, Institute of Applied Chemistry, Berlin, 2000-. Publications: Over 80 scientific publications in English, German and Czech, papers in scientific journals including: Theoretical Computer Science; Fuzzy Sets and Systems; International Journal of Medical Informatics; Chapters in scientific monographs and contributions to conference proceedings; 4 student textbooks. Honours: Prize, awarded by the Rector of the Czech Technical University in Prague, 1982; Representative of Junior Scientists in the Scientific Board, Institute of Computer Science, 1991-93; Listed in Who's Who publications and biographical dictionaries. Memberships: Czech Computer Society; Czech Society of Biomedical Engineering. Address: Institute of Computer Science, Czech Academy of Sciences, Pod vodárenskou věží 2, 18200 Prague, Czech Republic. E-mail: martin@cs.cas.cz holena@aca-berlin.de Website: www.cs.cas.cz/~martin

**HOLLAND Jools (Julian),** b. 24 January 1958, London, England. Musician (keyboards); Television Presenter. 1 son, 2 daughters. Career: Founder member, pianist, Squeeze, 1974-81, 1985-90; Solo artiste and bandleader: Jools Holland and his Big Band, 1982-84; Jools Holland and his Rhythm And Blues Orchestra, 1991-; Television presenter, music shows: The Tube, C4, 1981-86; Juke Box Jury, 1989; Sunday Night (with David Sanborn), 1990; The Happening, 1990; Hootenanny, 1992-; Later With Jools Holland, BBC2, 1993-; Various other television specials, including Sunday Night, NBC, 1989; Beat Route, BBC2, 1998-99; Jools Meets the Saint, 1999. Recordings: Albums: with Squeeze: Squeeze, 1978; Cool For Cats, 1979; Argy Bargy, 1980; Cosi Fan Tutti Frutti, 1985; Babylon And On, 1987; Frank, 1989; Solo albums: A World Of His Own, 1990; The Full Complement, 1991; A To Z Of The Piano, 1992; Live Performance, 1994; Solo Piano, 1994; Sex and Jazz and Rock and Roll, 1996; Lift up the Lid, 1997; The Best of Jools Holland, 1998; Sunset Over London, 1999; Hop the Wag, 2000; Small World Big Band – Friends, 2001; Small World Big Band Vol 2 – More Friends; Hit singles include: with Squeeze: Take Me I'm Yours, 1978; Cool For Cats, 1979; Up The Junction, 1979; Slap And Tickle, 1979; Another Nail In My Heart, 1980; Pulling Mussels From A Shell, 1980; Hourglass, 1987; 853 5937, 1988. Memberships: Musicians' Union; Equity; Writer's Guild.

**HOLLINGHURST Alan,** b. 26 May 1954, Stroud, Gloucestershire, England. Novelist. Education: BA, 1975, MLitt, 1979, Magdalen College, Oxford. Appointments: Assistant Editor, 1982-84, Deputy Editor, 1985-90, Poetry Editor, 1991-95, Times Literary Supplement, London. Publications: Novels: The Swimming-Pool Library, 1988; The Folding Star, 1994; The Spell, 1998; The Line of Beauty, 2004. Translator: Bajazet, by Jean Racine, 1991. Honours: Somerset Maugham Award, 1988, E.M. Forster Award of the American Academy of Arts and Letters, 1989; James Tait Black Memorial Prize, 1995; Man Booker Prize, 2004. Memberships: Fellow, The Royal Society of Literature. Address: c/o Antony Harwood, 103 Walton Street, Oxford, OX2 6EB, England.

**HOLLOWAY James,** b. 24 November 1948. Gallery Director. Education: Courtauld Institute of Art, London University, 1969-71. Appointments: Research Assistant, National Gallery of Scotland, 1972-80; Assistant Keeper of Art, National Museum of Wales, 1980-83; Deputy Keeper, Scottish National Portrait Gallery, 1983-97; Director, Scottish National Portrait Gallery, 1997-. Publications: Editor, Scottish Masters booklets for National Gallery of Scotland; Several articles; Frequent lectures on Scottish art and collections. Memberships: Curatorial Committee, National Trust for Scotland; Committee Member, Scottish Sculpture Trust; Committee Member, Scottish-Indian Arts Forum. Address: Scottish National Portrait Gallery, 1 Queen Street, Edinburgh, EH2 1JD, Scotland.

**HOLLOWAY Julian Robert Stanley,** b. 24 June 1944, Watlington, Oxford, England. Actor; Director; Writer; Producer. m. (1) Zena Cecilia Walker, dissolved 1977, 1 daughter, (2) Deborah Jane Wheeler, dissolved 1996. Education: Ludgrove Preparatory School; Harrow School; Royal Academy of Dramatic Art. Career: Actor: Theatre includes: My Fair Lady; Arsenic & Old Lace; The Norman Conquests; Charley's Aunt; Pygmalion; Spitting Image; Films include: Ryan's Daughter; Carry on Up The Khyber; Carry on Loving; Carry on Henry; Carry on Camping; Carry on England; Carry on Doctor; Hostile Witness; Rough Cut; TV includes: The Importance of Being Earnest; An Adventure in Bed; Rebecca; The Scarlet and The Black; Ellis Island; The Endless Game; Michelangelo; Grass Roots; Torch Song; The Vet; Dan Dare; Remember Wenn; My Uncle Silas; Director: Play It Again Sam; When Did You Last

See My Mother; Actor/Producer: Carry on Films; The Spy's Wife; The Chairman's Wife; Loophole. Address: c/o Michelle Braidman Associates, Suite 10, 11 Lower John Street, London W1R 3PE, England.

**HOLLOWAY Laurence,** b. 31 March 1938, Oldham, Lancashire. Musician (Piano); Composer; Musical Director. m. Marion Montgomery, deceased, 2 daughters. Career: Touring Dance Band Pianist, 1950s; Cyril Stapleton Showband; Joe Daniels Hotshots, 1950s; Cunard Line, 1956-57; London Weekend Television, regular pianist, 1967-80; Musical Director, Engelbert Humperdinck, 1970-75; Played at studios in London, 1975-85; Musical Director for many top artistes such as Judy Garland, Cleo Lane, Sacha Distel, Dame Edna Everage, Liza Minelli, Rolf Harris, Frankie Howerd, Mel Torme, Elaine Paige in "Piaf"; Featured pianist on Dame Kiri Te Kanawa's popular music albums; Musical Director for Michael Parkinson on the "Parkinson" series; Musical Director of Strictly Come Dancing, BBC, 2004. Compositions: several saxophone quartets, clarinet quartets, pieces for flute and piano and clarinet and piano; Numerous TV signature tunes including Blind Date, Beadle's About; Walking Fingers selected by Associated Board of the Royal Schools of Music for 2001/2002 Grade 1 Examinations;. Recordings: Solo albums: Blue Skies; Showtime; Cumulus; About Time; Laurie Holloway, Live at Abbey Road, 2000; The Piano Player, 2004; Also recorded with many artists including Kiri Te Kanawa, Marion Montgomery, Robert Farnon, Rolf Harris. Honour: Gold Badge of Merit, BASCA. Membership: Temple Golf Club. Address: Elgin, Fishery Road, Bray, Nr Maidenhead, Berkshire SL6 1UP, England.

**HOLLOWAY Patricia, (Patricia Pogson),** b. 8 March 1944, Rosyth, Scotland. Yoga Teacher; Poet. m. (1) 1 son, 1 daughter, (2) Geoffrey Holloway, 27 August 1977. Education: National Diploma in Design, 1964; Teaching Certificate, 1971; Diploma, British Wheel of Yoga, 1987. Appointments: Draughtswoman Restorer, Ashmolean Museum, Oxford, 1964-66; Part-time Yoga Teacher; Poetry Tutor, Schools and Writing Centres, Libraries. Publications: Before the Road Show, 1983; Snakeskin, Belladonna, 1986; Rattling the Handle, 1991; A Crackle from the Larder, 1991; The Tides in the Basin, 1994; Holding, 2002. Contributions to: Anthologies, journals, reviews and magazines. Honours: 1st Prize, York Open Competition, 1985; 3rd Prize, Manchester Open Competition, 1989; 2nd Prize, National Poetry Competition, 1989; 1st Prize, BBC Kaleidoscope Competition, 1990. Memberships: Brewery Poets, Brewery Arts Centre, Kendal; Keswick Poetry Group. Address: 4 Gowan Crescent, Staveley, nr Kendal, Cumbria LA8 9NF, England.

**HOLM Ian,** b. 12 September 1931, Ilford, England. Actor. m. (1) Lynn Mary Shaw, 1955, 2 daughters, (2) Bee Gilbert, 1 son, 1 daughter, (3) Sophie Baker, 1982, 1 son, (4) Penelope Wilton, 1991, 1 step-daughter. Education: Royal Academy of Dramatic Arts. Creative Works: Roles include: Puck, Ariel, Lorenzo, Henry V, Richard III, the Fool (in King Lear), 1997; Lennie in The Homecoming; Moonlight, 1993; King Lear, 997; Max in The Homecoming, 2001; Films include: Young Winston; Oh!; What a Lovely War; Alien; All Quiet on the Western Front; Chariots of Fire; The Return of the Soldier; Greystoke, 1984; Laughterhouse, 1984; Brazil, 1985; Wetherby, 1985; Dance with a Stranger, 1985; Dreamchild, 1985; Henry V, 1989; Another Woman, 1989; Hamlet, 1990; Kafka, 1991; The Hour of the Pig, 1992; Blue Ice, 1992; The Naked Lunch, 1992; Frankenstein, 1993; The Madness of King George, 1994; Loch Ness, 1994; Big Night, 1995; Night Falls on Manhattan, 1995; The Fifth Element, 1996; A Life Less Ordinary, 1996; The Sweet Hereafter, 1997; Existence, 1998; Simon Magus, 1998; Esther Kahn, 1999; Joe Gould's Secret, 1999; Beautiful Joe, 1999; The

Lord of the Rings, 1999; From Hell, 2000; the Emperor's New Clothes, 2000. TV appearances include: The Lost Boys, 1979; We, the Accused, 1980; The Bell, 1981; Strike, 1981; Inside the Third Reich, 1982; Mr and Mrs Edgehill, 1985; The Browning Version, 1986; Game, Set and Match, 1988; The Endless Game, 1989; The Last Romantics, 1992; The Borrowers, 1993; The Deep Blue Sea, 1994; Landscape, 1995; Little Red Riding Hood, 1996; King Lear, 1997; Alice Through the Looking Glass, 1998. Honour: Laurence Olivier Award, 1998. Address: c/o Julian Belfrage Associates, 46 Albemarle Street, London W1X 4PP, England.

**HOLMES Bryan John, (Charles Langley Hayes, Ethan Wall),** b. 18 May 1939, Birmingham, England. Lecturer (retired); Writer. m. 1962, 2 sons. Education: BA, University of Keele, 1968. Publications: The Avenging Four, 1978; Hazard, 1979; Blood, Sweat and Gold, 1980; Gunfall, 1980; A Noose for Yanqui, 1981; Shard, 1982; Bad Times at Backwheel, 1982; Guns of the Reaper, 1983; On the Spin of a Dollar, 1983; Another Day, Another Dollar, 1984; Dark Rider, 1987; I Rode with Wyatt, 1989; Dollars for the Reaper, 1990; A Legend Called Shatterhand, 1990; Loco, 1991; Shatterhand and the People, 1992; The Last Days of Billy Patch, 1992; Blood on the Reaper, 1992; All Trails Leads to Dodge, 1993; Montana Hit, 1993; A Coffin for the Reaper, 1994; Comes the Reaper, 1995; Utah Hit, 1995; Dakota Hit, 1995; Viva Reaper, 1996; The Shard Brand, 1996; High Plains Death, 1997; Smoking Star, 1997; Crowfeeders, 1999; North of the Bravo, 2000; Pocket Crossword Dictionary, 2001; The Guide to Solving Crosswords, 2002; Jake's Women, 2002; Solving Cryptic Crosswords, 2003; Rio Grande Shoot-Out, 2004; Trail of the Reaper, 2004; Three Graves to Fargo, 2004; The Expediter, 2004; Trouble in Tucson, 2005; Shotgun, 2005. Contributions to: Professional and academic journals. Address: c/o Robert Hale Ltd, Clerkenwell Green, London EC1R 0HT, England.

**HOLMES James Christopher (Jim),** b. 21 November 1948, London, England. Musician; Opera Conductor and Coach. m. Jean Wilkinson, 2 sons. Education: BA (Hons), University of Sheffield; Repetiteurs Diploma, London Opera Centre. Appointments: Principal Coach, Conductor, English National Opera, 1973-96; Numerous productions including: Pacific Overtures, London premiere; Street Scene, also BBC TV; La Belle Vivette, premiere of new version with Michael Frayn; Dr Ox's Experiment, world premiere; Arranger, National Youth Orchestra, BBC Proms; Musical Assistant to Simon Rattle, Glyndebourne Festival Opera, 1986-94; Associate Music Director, Carousel, Royal National Theatre; Conductor, BBC Concert Orchestra, London Sinfonietta, Montreal Symphony Orchestra, City of Birmingham Symphony Orchestra, Sinfonia Viva; Head of Music, Opera North, 1996-; Conductor: Gloriana, Tannhäuser, Sweeney Todd, Of Thee I Sing, Katya Kabanova, Pélléas and Melisande, Genoveva, Paradise Moscow, Cunning Little Vixen, Albert Herring; Arranger: Something Wonderful and If Ever I Would Leave You for Bryn Terfel; Guest Lecturer/Coach: National Opera Studio, Royal Northern College of Music. Publications: Numerous articles for programmes especially relating to American musical theatre; Arrangements of American musical songs for singers including: Bryn Terfel, Sally Burgess, Lesley Garrett; TV Programmes: I'm a Stranger Here Myself, Kurt Weill in America, BBC/HR; Street Scene BBC and WDR. Honours: USA Grammy Nomination for recording of Pacific Overtures; Gramophone Award for recording of Lesley Garrett, Soprano in Red. Memberships: Member, Advisory Board, Kurt Weill Complete Edition; Joint Artistic Advisor, Kurt Weill Festival, Dessau. Address: c/o Opera North, Grand Theatre, New Briggate, Leeds, W Yorkshire LS1 6NU, England.

**HOLMES John Eaton (Sir),** b. 29 April 1951, Preston, England. Diplomat. m. Margaret Penelope Morris, 3 daughters. Education: BA, 1st Class Honours, Literae Humaniores (Greats), 1973, MA, 1975, Balliol College, Oxford. Appointments: Joined Foreign and Commonwealth Office, 1973: Second Secretary, British Embassy, Moscow, 1976-78; Near East and North Africa Department, 1978-82; Assistant Private Secretary to the Foreign Secretary, 1982-84; First Secretary (Economic), British Embassy, Paris, 1984-87; Deputy Head, Soviet Department, Foreign and Commonwealth Office, 1987-89; Seconded to Thomas de la Rue & Co, 1989-91; Economic and Commercial Counsellor, New Delhi, 1991-95; Head of the European Union Department, Foreign and Commonwealth Office, 1995; Private Secretary then Principal Private Secretary to the Prime Minister, 1996-99; British Ambassador to Portugal, 1999-2001; British Ambassador to France, 2001-. Honours: CMG, 1997; CVO, 1998; KBE, 1999; GCVO, 2004. Address: 35 rue du Faubourg St-Honoré, 75383 Paris Cedex 08, France. Website: www.amb-grandebretagne.fr

**HOLMES Jonathan Richard,** b. Stratford-upon-Avon, England. Writer; Comedian. Education: Diploma, Art and Design, NWCTA, Warwickshire; BA, Honours, English, BA, Honours, Radio, Film and Television, University of Kent. Career: Television: Writer: Patrick Kielty Almost Live, BBC1, 2001; V Graham Norton, Channel 4, 2003; Dead Ringers, BBC2, 2003; Sir David Frost's Strategic Humour Initiative, NBC America, 2004; Have I Got News For You, BBC1, 2004; 2004 The Stupid Version, BBC3, 2004; Countdown to the British Comedy Awards, ITV1, 2004; Angus Deayton's New Years Dishonours List, ITV1, 2005; 29 Minutes of Fame, BBC1, 2005; The British Academy Film Awards, BBC1, 2005; Writer/Host: The 11 O'Clock Show (Series 5), Channel 4, 2003; Writer/Presenter: The State We're In, BBC3, 2003-2004; Writer/Performer: Armando Iannucci's Gash, Channel 4, 2003; Writer/Script Editor/Actor: The Impressionable Jon Culshaw, ITV1, 2004; Radio: Writer/Creator/Performer, Grievious Bodily Radio, BBC Radio 4; Writer/Performer: Jon Ronson On...., BBC Radio 4; The Now Show, BBC Radio 4; Writer/Panellist: The 99p Challenge, BBC Radio 4; Writer: The Armando Iannucci Show, BBC Radio 4; Co-creator/Writer/Script Editor: Dead Ringers, BBC Radio 4; Presenter: Jon Holmes on LBC 97.3, LBC 97.3, 2002-2004; Jon Holmes on BBC 6 Music, BBC 6 Music, 2003-2004; Jon Holmes on XFM, XFM, 2001; Jon Holmes on Virgin, Virgin Radio, 2002-2003; Writer Presenter: The Day the Music Died, BBC Radio 2; Other: Writer: The Royal Command Performance, Albert Hall, 2003; Rose d'Or Golden Rose Awards, Montreaux, 2003; Rose d'Or Golden Rose Awards, Lausanne, 2004. Honours: Best New Presenter, Commercial Radio Awards, Gold Best Entertainment Show, Sony Awards, for Jon Holmes on Music Radio, 2000; Bronze Comedy, Sony Awards for the Very World of Milton Jones, 2000; British Comedy Award, Gold Best Comedy, Sony Awards, Broadcasting Guild Award for Dead Ringers, 2003; Bronze Comedy, Sony Awards for The Now Show, 2004; Nominee, Channel 4 Political Awards, 2005; Nominee, Rose d'Or International Television Awards, 2005. Address: c/o Vivienne Clore, The Richard Stone Partnership, 2 Henrietta Street, London WC2E 8PS, England.

**HOLMES Stewart Quentin,** b. 25 December 1929, London, England. Actor; Journalist; Poet. Education: Royal Society of Arts Credits, English-Typewriting, Pitman's Shorthand, 1950; Mandarin Chinese, Hong Kong University, 1971-72. Appointments: BBC Correspondent, Tehran, Iran, 1971; Features Editor, Hong Kong Standard, 1971-72; London Correspondent, International Press Bureau and Union Jack newspaper, USA, 1981. Publications: Odes and Ends, 1985; Once Upon a Rhyme,

1987; Nothing Really Serious, 2002. Contributions to: Outpost; British MENSA Magazine. Honour: Golden Poet, World of Poetry, California, 1990. Memberships: British MENSA; British Actors Equity; Chartered Institute of Journalists; Foreign Press Association, London. Address: 106 Clarence Gate Gardens, Baker Street, London NW1 6AL, England.

**HOLMES-WALKER William Anthony,** b. 26 January 1926, Horwich, Lancashire, England. Scientist. m. Marie-Anne Russ, 2 daughters. Education: BSc (Hons) Chemistry, 1950, PhD, Chemistry, 1953, Queen's University, Belfast, Northern Ireland; DIC, Chemical Engineering, Imperial College, London, 1954. Appointments: Technical Officer, ICI Limited, 1954-59; Head of Plastics R&D, The Metal Box Company, 1959-66; Professor of Polymer Science and Technology, Chairman of School of Materials, Brunel University, 1966-74; Director, The British Plastics Federation, 1974-81; Visiting Professor, The City University, 1981-83; Secretary General, European Brewers' Trade Association, CBMC, Brussels, 1983-87; Director, Industrial Liaison, University of Reading, 1987-90; Director, International Technology and Innovation, 1990-94; Chairman of Working Group, The Executive Committee, 1995-96; Chairman, BioInteractions Ltd, 1991-. Publications: Many articles in scientific journals and business publications; Chapter in Thermoplastics, 1969; Polymer Conversion, 1975; Best Foote Forward, 1995; Life-Enhancing Plastics, forthcoming. Honours: ERD, 1972, TD, 1980; Member, Army Emergency Reserve and TAVR, with rank of Lieutenant Colonel. Memberships: Royal Institution, 1953; FRSC, 1966; FPRI, 1969; FIM, 1972; FSA, 1989; Past Master, Skinners' Company. Address: 7 Alston Road, Boxmoor, Herts HP1 1QT, England. E-mail: anthonyhw@ntl.com.uk

**HOLROYD Michael (de Courcy Fraser),** b. 27 August 1935, London, England. Biographer; Writer. m. Margaret Drabble, 17 September 1982. Appointment: Visiting Fellow, Pennsylvania State University, 1979. Publications: Hugh Kingsmill: A Critical Biography, 1964; Lytton Strachey: A Critical Biography, 2 volumes, 1967, 1968, revised edition, 1994; A Dog's Life (novel), 1969; The Best of Hugh Kingsmill (editor), 1970; Lytton Strachey by Himself: A Self-Portrait (editor), 1971, new edition, 1994; Unreceived Opinions (essays), 1973; Augustus John, 2 volumes, 1974, 1975, revised edition, 1996; The Art of Augustus John (with Malcolm Easton), 1974; The Genius of Shaw (editor), 1979; The Shorter Strachey (editor with Paul Levy), 1980; William Gerhardie's God Fifth Column (editor with Robert Skidelsky), 1981; Essays by Diverse Hands (editor), Vol XLII, 1982; Peterley Harvest: The Private Diary of David Peterley (editor), 1985; Bernard Shaw: Vol I, The Search for Love 1856-1898, 1988, Vol II, The Pursuit of Power 1898-1918, 1989, Vol III, The Lure of Fantasy 1918-1950, 1991, Vol IV, The Last Laugh 1950-1991, 1992, Vol V, The Shaw Companion, 1992, one-volume abridged edition, 1997; Basil Street Blues, 1999; Works on Paper, 2002; Mosaic, 2004. Contributions to: Radio, television, and periodicals. Honours: Saxton Memorial Fellowship, 1964; Bollingen Fellowship, 1966; Winston Churchill Fellowship, 1971; Commander of the Order of the British Empire, 1989; Honorary DLitts, Universities of Ulster, 1992, Sheffield, 1993, Warwick, 1994, and East Anglia, 1994, London School of Economics, 1998. Memberships: Arts Council, chairman, literature panel, 1992-95; National Book League, chairman, 1976-78; PEN, president, British branch, 1985-88; Royal Historical Society, fellow; Royal Society of Literature, chairman, 1998-2001, President, 2003-; Society of Authors, chairman, 1973-74; Royal Society of Arts, fellow; Strachey Trust, chairman, 1990-95; Public Lending Right Advisory Committee, chairman, 1997-2000; Royal Literary

Fund, vice-president, 1997-. Address: c/o A P Watt Ltd, 20 John Street, London WC1N 2DR, England.

**HOLT Derek Francis,** b. 21 March 1949, Wembley, England. Professor of Mathematics. m. Catherine Wattebot, 2 sons. Education: Undergraduate, 1967-70, Postgraduate, 1970-74, University College, Oxford. Appointments: Assistent, University of Tübingen, Germany, 1973-75; Research Fellow, Brasenose College, Oxford, 1975-78; Lecturer, Mathematics, 1978-87, Reader, Mathematics, 1987-2001, Professor of Mathematics, University of Warwick, 2001-. Publications: 80 articles in mathematical journals; Books: Perfect Groups (with W Plesken), 1989; Handbook of Computational Group Theory (with B Eick and E A O'Brien), 2005. Honour: London Mathematical Society Junior Whitehead Prize, 1981. Membership: London Mathematical Society, 1979. Address: Mathematics Institute, University of Warwick, Coventry CV 4 7AL, England. E-mail: dfh@maths.warwick.ac.uk

**HOLT Helen Keil,** b. 23 March 1937, West Palm Beach, Florida, USA. Physicist. m. Lawrence G Holt, 2 daughters. Education: BA, Barnard College, 1958; MS, 1960, PhD, 1965, Yale University. Appointments: Physicist, National Bureau of Standards, 1965-86. Publications: Articles in Physical Review Letters, Physical Review and other journals on the subjects of electron-atom scattering, frequency correlation in spontaneous emission, quantum mechanics, gas lasers and atomic physics. Honours: Fellow, American Physical Society; Sustained Superior Performance, NBS. Memberships: American Physical Society; Sigma Xi. Address: 6740 Melody Lane, Bethesda, MD 20817, USA.

**HOLUB Karel,** b. 9 November 1933, Prague. Seismologist. m. (1) Maria, 1954, divorced 1982, (2) Olga, 1984, 3 sons, 1 daughter. Education: Diploma in Applied Geophysics, 1959, Dr rer nat (MA) 1982, PhD, Mathematics and Physics, 1991, Charles University, Prague; DrSc (DSc), Geology, Czech Academy of Sciences, Prague, 2001. Appointments: Geophysical Institute, AS CR, Prague, 1959-78; Research Mining Institute, Ostrava, 1979-93; Research Worker, Project Leader, Senior Research Worker; Principal Research Worker, Institute of Geonics AS CR, Ostrava, 1994-. Publications: More than 150 papers in different journals, more than 100 research and technical reports. Honour: Award of Czech Academy of Sciences, 1963. Memberships: Czech Association of Applied Geophysicists; Czech Society for Mechanics; New York Academy of Sciences. Address: Horymirova 110, CZ 700 30, Ostrava-Zábřeh, Czech Republic. E-mail: holub@ugn.cas.cz

**HOLUBAR Karl,** b. 3 June 1936, Vienna, Austria. Physician. m. Christine Bodenstein, 2 sons. Education: MD, Vienna, 1960; Residency, Dermatology, University of Vienna; Department of Dermatology, University of Amsterdam, 1968; Department of Microbiology (Immunology), State University of New York at Buffalo, USA, 1972-73; Hebrew University, Jerusalem, Israel, 1982-86. Appointments: Interim Chairman and Professor, Dermatology, University of Vienna, 1980-81; Chairman and Professor of Dermatology, Hebrew University Jerusalem, 1983-86; Professor History of Medicine, 1989-, Professor and Chairman, Institute for the History of Medicine, 1989-2001, University of Vienna. Publications: Over 500 publications, including original articles, book chapters, contributions to handbooks, special issues of journals, congress reports, posters and abstracts; 5 books: Challenge Dermatology, 1993; Sun and Skin, 1994; Med. Terminologie und ärztliche Sprache, 1997; Historical Atlas of Dermatology, 2002; Skin in Watercolours, 2003. Honours: (with co-authors), Hoechst Award, 1969; Max Ritter Award, 1976; AESCA Award, 1979; Unilever Award,

1979; Samuel J Zakon Award (History of Dermatology), 1981; Fellow of the Royal College of Physicians; Honorary Fellow of the College of Physicians of Philadelphia. Memberships include: Royal Society of Medicine; New York Academy of Sciences; Medical Society of London; Société Internationale d'Histoire de la Médicine; Société Française d'Histoire de la Dermatologie, Vice-President; Gesellschaft der Ärzte in Wien; Austrian and German national Dermatological Societies; European Society for the History of Dermatology/Venereology, Honorary President; Numerous honorary memberships. Address: Institute for the History of Medicine, Medical University of Vienna, Wahringer Str 25, A 1090 Vienna, Austria. E-mail: karl.holub ar@meduniwien.ac.at

**HOLYFIELD Evander,** b. 19 October 1962, Atlanta, Georgia, USA. Boxer. Career: Founder, Real Deal Record Label, 1999; Founder, Holyfield Foundation to help inner-city youth; Bronze Medal, Olympic Games, 1984; World Boxing Association Cruiserweight Title, 1986; World Boxing Federation Cruiserweight Title, 1987; World Boxing Council Cruiserweight Title, 1988; World Heavyweight Champion, 1990-92, 1993-94, 1996- (following defeat of Mike Tyson, 1996); Defended title against Mike Tyson 1997 (Tyson disqualified for biting off part of Holyfield's ear); Defended IBF Heavyweight Title against Michael Moorer, 1997; Defended WBA and IBF Titles, and Contested WBC Title, against Lennox Lewis, 1999, bout declared a draw; Lost to Lennox Lewis, November 1999; WBA heavyweight champion, 2000-01. Honours: Epsy Boxer of the Decade, 1990-2000. Address: Main Events, 390 Murray Hill Parkway, East Rutherford, NJ 07073, USA.

**HOMAN Roger Edward,** b. 25 June 1944, Brighton, England. University Professor. m. Caroline Baker. Education: BA, Religious Studies, University of Sussex, 1969; MSc, Government, London School of Economics, 1979; PhD, Sociology, University of Lancaster, 1979. Appointments: School teaching posts, 1966-67, 1969-71; Lecturer, Brighton College of Education, 1971-76; Senior Lecturer in Education, Brighton Polytechnic, 1976-92; Principal Lecturer, 1992-98, Professor of Religious Studies, 1998-, University of Brighton. Publications: 90 articles published in academic and professional journals. Honours: Fellow, Victoria College of Music, 1994. Memberships: Victorian Society; National Vice President, Prayer Book Society; Anglo-Catholic Research Society; Ecclesiological Society. Address: University of Brighton, Falmer, East Sussex, BN1 9PH, England. E-mail: r.homan@bton.ac.uk

**HOME, Earl of, David Alexander Cospatrick Douglas-Home,** b. 20 November 1943, Coldstream, Scotland. Banker. m. Jane Margaret Williams-Wynne, 1 son, 2 daughters. Education: MA, Christ Church, Oxford. Appointments: Director, Morgan Grenfell & Co Ltd, 1974-99; Chairman, Coutts & Co, 1999-; Chairman, Committee for Middle East Trade, 1986-92; Trade Industry and Finance Spokesman, House of Lords, 1997-98. Honours: CVO; CBE; FCIB. Membership: Turf. Address: Coutts & Co, 440 Strand, London WC2R 0QS, England.

**HONEGGER Federico,** b. 11 September 1926, Milan, Italy. Artist; Painter. m. Lucia Carminarti, 3 sons, 1 daughter. Education: Baccalaureat, College of St Michel, Fribourg, 1945; Law Degree, Catholic University, Milan, 1952; Text Prac Vereinigte Seidenwebereien AG, Germany, 1950-51. Appointments: Gaspar Honegger, Milan, 1946-59; Buying Manager, Carminarti Industries, Tessili Sp, Milan, 1960-82; President, Milan Group, Catholic Union of Italian Artists, 1982-92. Publications: Author, numerous art projects; Most recently: The Lord Said Unto My Lord (Psalm 107/108 and 2,7) Birth of Heavens, 2005. Honours: Silver Palette, City of

Milan, 1979; Top 70 winner, Art '95 New York International Competition. Memberships: Symbolicum Art Group. Address: Via Annunciata 23/2, 20121 Milan, Italy. E-mail: federico.honegger@fastwebnet.it

**HONG Jong Wook**, b. 2 October 1963, Seoul, Korea. Ophthalmologist. m. Eun Jin Park, 1 son, 1 daughter. Education: Medical Doctor, Korea University, 1987; Ophthalmologist Special Board, KUMC,1990; Physical Doctor, Korea University, 1996. Appointments: Director, Korea Navy Hospital, 1990-94; Professor, Director of Cornea and Refractive Surgery, Korea University Hospital, 1994-2003; Research Faculty, University of Washington, USA, 2000-2002; Chairman, Korea Eye Centre, Seoul, Korea. Publications: Cornea (in Korean); Cataract Surgery (in Korean); Articles in medical journals include: Bowman's layer structure and function: critical or dispensable to corneal function? A hypothesis, 2000; Differential expression analysis by gene array of cell cycle modulators in human corneal epithelial cells stimulated with epidermal growth factor (EFG), hepatocyte growth factor (HGF), or keratinocyte growth factor (KGF), 2001; The wound healing response after laser in situ keratomileusis and photorefractive keratectomy: elusive control of biological variability and effect on custom laser vision correction, 2001; Keratitis caused by Verticillium species, 2002; Relationship between intraocular pressure and systemic health parameters in a Korean population, 2002. Honour: Outstanding Researcher, KUMC, 2003. Memberships: Korea Ophthalmology Society; KRCRS; ASCRS; ARVO; KEEDO. Address: Shinsa Dong 579-2 (Je Surg Bld) Kang Nam Gu, Seoul, 135-892 Korea. E-mail: ophhong@yahoo.com Website: www.keceye.com

**HONG Kyung Pyo**, b. 17 February 1954, Busan, South Korea. Physician; Educator. m. Hyoun Tae Kim, deceased, 2 sons. Education: MD, Seoul National University College of Medicine, 1978; PhD, Chung-Ang University Medical School, Seoul, Korea, 1990; Fellow, University of Alberta Hospital, Edmonton, Canada, 1988; Fellow, Westminster Hospital, London, England, 1990-91. Appointments: House Officer, Seoul National University Hospital, 1978-83; Professor, Hallym University College of Medicine, 1986-94; Physician, 1994-, Vice Chairman, Cardiac and Vascular Centre, 1999-2001, Chief, Division of Cardiology, 2001-2002, Samsung Medical Centre; Professor, 1997-, Director, Office of Medical Education, 2003-, Associate Dean, 2005-, Sungkyunkwan University School of Medicine; Editor-in-Chief, Korean Circulation Journal, 2000-2002. Publications: Clinical Cardiology (co-author), 1998; Textbook of Cardiovascular Medicine (co-author), 2001; Contributor of articles to professional journals. Honour: President, Korean Society of Cardiovascular Rehabilitation and Prevention, 1997-2000. Memberships: Fellow, American Association of Cardiovascular and Pulmonary Rehabilitation; Fellow, Korean Society of Circulation; Member of Editorial Board, 1998-2001, Korean Association of Internal Medicine; Korean Society of Cardiovascular Rehabilitation and Prevention; Korean Society of Medical Education. Address: Samsung Medical Centre, 50 Irwon-Dong, Gangnam-Gu, 135-710 Seoul, Korea. E-mail: kphong@smc.samsung.co.kr

**HONG Sun Ig**, b. 27 April 1957, Seoul, Korea. Professor. m. Mi-Jung Chang, 1 son, 1 daughter. Education: BS, Korea University, 1975-79; MS, Korea Advanced Institute of Sciences and Technology, 1979-81; PhD, University of Pennsylvania, USA, 1984-89. Appointments: Researcher, Korea Atomic Energy Research Institute, 1981-84; Research Scientist, Los Alamos National Laboratory, USA, 1990-94; Lecturer, Kookmin University, Korea, 1994-95; Professor, Chungnam National University, 1995-; Visiting Professor, University of Michigan, 2003-; Editorial Committee

Member, Journal of Nuclear Materials, 2003-. Publications: 160 scientific papers include: Ultrastructural analysis of nanoscale apatite biomimetically grown on organic template. Honours: Outstanding Professor Awards, 2001, 2003, 2004. Memberships: Korea Materials Research Society; Korea Powder Metallurgy Society; Korea Institute of Metals and Materials. Address: Department of Applied Materials, Chungnam National University, Taedok Science Town, Taejon 305-764, Korea. E-mail: sihong@cnu.ac.kr

**HONG Sung-Yull**, b. 27 December 1953, Kyungbook, Korea. Nuclear Engineer. m. Kyung-Sook Kwon, 2 sons. Education: BS, Seoul National University, 1978; MS, 1982, PhD, 1984, Rensselaer Polytechnic Institute, USA. Appointments: Chief Member of Technical Staff, in charge of Nuclear Power Plant Operation and Maintenance, Research and Development, Nuclear Power Laboratory, Korea Electric Power Research Institute, 1984-. Publications: Papers in scientific journals and conference proceedings including: Third International Topical Meeting on NPPTHOS, 2005; ICAPP Key Engineering Materials, 2004; Nuclear Engineering and Design, 2004; 11th Asia-Pacific Conference on NDT. Honours: Member of LMNPP of OECD/NEA; Expert Group of NPP Life-time Management of IAEA; Award, President of Republic of Korea. Memberships: Korean Nuclear Society; Korean Society of Nondestructive Testing. Address: 305-807 Mog-Ryun Apt, Dusan Seo-gu, Daejeon, 302-120 Republic of Korea. E-mail: syhong@kepri.re.kr

**HONIG Edwin**, b. 3 September 1919, New York, New York, USA. Retired Professor of English and of Comparative Literature; Poet; Writer; Dramatist; Translator. m. (1) Charlotte Gilchrist, 1 April 1940, deceased 1963, (2) Margot Dennes, 15 December 1963, divorced 1978, 2 sons. Education: BA, 1939, MA, 1947, University of Wisconsin at Madison. Appointments: Poetry Editor, New Mexico Quarterly, 1948-52; Instructor, Claremont College, California, 1949; Faculty, 1949-57, Assistant Professor of English, Harvard University; Faculty, 1957-60, Professor of English, 1960-82, Professor of Comparative Literature, 1962-82, Professor Emeritus, 1983-, Brown University; Visiting Professor, University of California at Davis, 1964-65; Mellon Professor, Boston University, 1977. Publications: Poetry: The Moral Circus, 1955; The Gazabos: 41 Poems, 1959; Survivals, 1964; Spring Journal, 1968; Four Springs, 1972; At Sixes, 1974; Shake a Spear with Me, John Berryman, 1974; Selected Poems 1955-1976, 1979; Interrupted Praise, 1983; Gifts of Light, 1983; The Imminence of Love: Poems 1962-1992, 1993; Time and Again: Poems 1940-97, 2000. Stories: Foibles and Fables of an Abstract Man, 1979. Non-Fiction: García Lorca, 1944, revised edition, 1963; Dark Conceit: The Making of Allegory, 1959; Calderón and the Seizures of Honor, 1972; The Poet's Other Voice: Conversations on Literary Translation, 1986. Plays: Ends of the World and Other Plays, 1984. Translations: Over 10 books, 1961-93. Contributions to: books, anthologies, reviews, journals, and periodicals. Honours: Guggenheim Fellowships, 1948, 1962; National Academy of Arts and Letters Grant, 1966; Amy Lowell Traveling Poetry Fellowship, 1968; Rhode Island Governor's Award for Excellence in the Arts, 1970; National Endowment for the Humanities Fellowship, 1975, and Grants, 1977-80; National Endowment for the Arts Fellowship, 1977; Translation Award, Poetry Society of America, 1984; National Award, Columbia University Translation Center, 1985; Decorated by the Portuguese President for translation of Pessoa, 1989; Decorated by the King of Spain for translation of Calderón, 1996. Memberships: Dante Society of America; Poetry Society of America. Address: 229 Medway Street, Apt 305, Providence, RI 02906, USA.

**HONTI László,** b. 27 August 1943, Lengyeltóti, Hungary. Professor. m. Márta Varga, 1 daughter. Education: Diploma, 1969, Hungarian, Russian and Finno-Ugric Linguistics, MA, 1970, University of Budapest; Candidate of Sciences, 1976, Doctor scientiarium, 1989, Hungarian Academy of Sciences, Budapest. Appointments: Junior Research Fellow, Senior Research Fellow, 1969-80, Head, Department of Finno-Ugric Languages, 1980-88, Hungarian Academy of Sciences; Professor, University of Groningen, The Netherlands, 1988-97; Professor, University of Udine, Italy, 1997-. Publications: 7 books. Honours: Zoltain Gombocz Medal, Hungarian Linguistic Society, 1977; Critics Prize, Akademiai Kiado, 1977, 1982; Academic Prize, Hungarian Academy of Sciences, 1993. Memberships: Hungarian Linguistics Society; Societas Uralo-Altaica; Honorary Member, Finno-Ugric Society; Association for Linguistic Typology; External Member, 1998-2004, Corresponding Member, 2004-, Hungarian Academy of Sciences. Address: Dipartimento di Glottologia e Filologia Classica, University of Udine, via Mazzini 3, I-33100 Udine, Italy.

**HOOK Andrew Dunnet,** b. 21 December 1932, Wick, Caithness, Scotland. m. Judith Ann Hibberd, deceased, 1984, 2 sons, 1 daughter, deceased, 1995. Education: MA, University of Edinburgh, Scotland, 1954; PhD, Princeton University, USA, 1960. Appointments: Assistant Lecturer, 1961-63, Lecturer in American Literature, 1963-71, University of Edinburgh; Senior Lecturer in English, University of Aberdeen, 1971-79; Bradley Professor of English Literature, University of Glasgow, 1979-98; Visiting Fellow, English Department, Princeton University, 1999-2000; Gillespie Visiting Professor, The College of Wooster, Wooster, Ohio, 2001-2002; Visiting Professor, Dartmouth College, Hanover, New Hampshire, 2003. Publications: Scott's Waverley (editor), 1972; Charlotte Brontë's Shirley (co-editor), 1974; John Dos Passos, Twentieth Century Views (editor), 1974; Scotland and America 1750-1835, 1975; American Literature in Context 1865-1900, 1983; History of Scottish Literature, Vol II 1660-1800 (editor), 1987; Scott Fitzgerald, 1992; The Glasgow Enlightenment (co-editor), 1995; From Goosecreek to Gandercleugh: Studies in Scottish-American Literary and Cultural History, 1999; Scott's The Fair Maid of Perth (co-editor), 1999; F Scott Fitzgerald: A Literary Life, 2002. Honours: Fellow, Royal Society of Edinburgh, 2000-; Fellow, British Academy, 2002. Memberships: British Association for American Studies; Eighteenth Century Scottish Studies Society; Modern Languages Association; Institute of Contemporary Scotland. Address: 5 Rosslyn Terrace, Glasgow G12 9NB, Scotland.

**HOOKWAY Harry Thurston (Sir),** b. 23 July 1921, London, England. Administrator. m. Barbara Butler, deceased, 1 son, 1 daughter. Education: BSc, PhD, London University. Appointments: Assistant Director, National Chemical Laboratory, 1959; Director, United Kingdom Scientific Mission to North America, Scientific Attaché, British Embassy, Washington, Scientific Advisor, High Commission, Ottawa, 1960-64; Head, Information Division, DSIR, 1964-65; Chief Scientific Officer, Department of Education and Science, 1966-69; Under Secretary, Department of Education and Science, 1969-73; Deputy Chairman and Chief Executive, British Library Board, 1973-84; Pro-Chancellor, Loughborough University, 1987-93. Publications: Papers in learned and professional journals. Honours: Hon LLD; Hon D Litt; HON FLA; Hon F I Inst Sci; Gold Medal, International Federation of Library Associations; Knight Bachelor, 1978; President, Institute of Information Scientists, 1973-76; President Library Association, 1985. Memberships: Royal Commission on Historical Monuments (England), 1981-87; Fellow, Royal Society of Arts.

Address: 3 St James Green, Thirsk, North Yorkshire YO7 1AF, England.

**HOOPER John David,** b. 22 March 1947, United Kingdom. Chartered Director. m. Veronica Jane, 1 son, 1 daughter. Education: BSc, 1972; MSc, 1982; PhD, 1985; Diploma in Business Excellence, 1999; Diploma in Company Direction, 2000; Chartered Director, 2001. Appointments: Chief Executive, Chartered Institute of Building, 1985-88; Director of Pan European Operations, Carlson Marketing Group Inc., 1988-91; Business Strategy Manager, Scottish Hydro Electric plc, 1991-94; Chief Executive, Sports Industries Federation, 1994-97; Chief Executive, Royal Society for the Prevention of Accidents, 1997-2004; Chief Executive, Institute of Clinical Research, 2004-. Publications: Heat Energy Recovery in the Pharmaceutical Industry; Energy Management and Marketing in the Pharmaceutical Industry; Challenges and Trends in Clinical Research. Memberships: Fellow, Institute of Directors; Fellow, Chartered Management Institute; Fellow, Royal Society of Arts; Fellow, Royal Institute of Public Health. Address: 26 Magnolia Close, Abington Vale, Northampton NN3 3XE, England.

**HOOPER Michael Wrenford,** b. 2 May 1941, Gloucester, England. Cleric. m. Rosemary, 2 sons, 2 daughters. Education: St David's College, Lampeter, Dyfed; St Stephen's House, Oxford. Appointments: Curate, Bridgnorth, Shropshire, 1965; Victor of Minsterley, Rural Dean, Pontesbury, 1970; Rector and Rural Dean, Leonminster, 1981; Archdeacon of Hereford, 1997; Suffragan Bishop of Ludlow, Archdeacon of Ludlow, 2002.

**HOPE Christopher David Tully,** b. 26 February 1944, Johannesburg, South Africa. Writer. m. Eleanor Marilyn Margaret Klein, 1967, 2 sons. Education: BA, Natal University, 1969; MA, University of the Witwatersrand, 1972. Publications: Cape Drives, 1974; A Separate Development, 1981; The Country of the Black Pig, 1981; The King, the Cat and the Fiddle, 1983; Kruger's Alp, 1984; The Dragon Wore Pink, 1985; White Boy Running, 1988; My Chocolate Redeemer, 1989; Serenity House, 1992; The Love Songs of Nathan J Swirsky, 1993; Darkest England, 1996; Me, The Moon and Elvis Presley, 1997; Signs of the Heart, 1999; Heaven Forbid, 2001; Brothers Under The Skin (Travels in Tyranny), 2003. Contributions to: Times Literary Supplement; London Magazine; Les Temps Modernes. Honours: Cholmondeley Award, 1974; David Higham Prize, 1981; International PEN Award, 1983; Whitbread Prize, 1985. Memberships: Royal Society of Literature, fellow; Society of Authors. Address: c/o Rogers, Coleridge & White Ltd, 20 Powis Mews, London W11 1JN, England.

**HOPE Ronald (Sidney),** b. 4 April 1921, London, England. Writer. Education: BA, 1941, MA, 1946, DPhil, New College, Oxford. Appointments: Fellow, Brasenose College, Oxford, 1945-47, Director, Seafarers' Education Service, London, 1947-76; Director, The Marine Society, 1976-86. Publications: Spare Time at Sea, 1954; Economic Geography, 1956; Dick Small in the Half Deck, Ships, 1958; The British Shipping Industry, 1959; The Shoregoer's Guide to World Ports, 1963; Seamen and the Sea, 1965; Introduction to the Merchant Navy, 1965; Retirement from the Sea, 1967; In Cabined Ships at Sea, 1969; Twenty Singing Seamen, 1979; The Seamen's World, 1982; A New History of British Shipping, 1990; Poor Jack, 2001. Address: 2 Park Place, Dollar, FK14 7AA, Scotland.

**HOPE Ronald Anthony,** b. 16 March 1951, London, England. Professor of Medical Ethics. m. Sally Hirsh, 2 daughters. Education: MA, New College, Oxford, 1970-73; PhD, National Institute for Medical Research, 1973-76; BM BCh, University of Oxford Clinical School, 1977-80. Appointments:

House Surgeon, Royal United Hospital, Bath, 1980-81; House Physician, John Radcliffe Hospital, Oxford, 1981; Senior House Officer, Registrar rotation in Psychiatry, Oxford Hospital, 1981-85; Wellcome Trust Training Fellow in Psychiatry, 1985-87; Clinical Lecturer in Psychiatry, University of Oxford, 1987-90; Leader, Oxford Practice Skills Project, 1990-95; University Lecturer in Practice Skills, 1995-2000; Reader in Medicine, 1996-2000, Professor of Medical Ethics, 2000-, University of Oxford. Publications: Books: Oxford Handbook of Clinical Medicine, editions, 1, 2, 3, 4 (9 translations), 1985-98; Essential Practice in Patient Centred Care, 1995; Manage Your Mind (4 translations), 1995; Medical Ethics and Law, 2003; A Very Short Introduction to Medical Ethics, 2004; Numerous articles and chapters mainly in fields of medical ethics and behavioural disturbance in Alzheimer's Disease. Honours: Rhodes Travel Scholarship, 1969; Bosanquet Open Scholarship, New College, 1970; Wellcome Trust Training Fellowship, 1985-87; Research Prize and Medal, Royal College of Psychiatrists, 1997; Member, through distinction, Faculty of Public Health, 2003. Memberships: Fellow, St Cross College, Oxford; Fellow, Royal College of Psychiatrists; Member, Faculty of Public Health; Governing Body Member, Institute of Medical Ethics. Address: Departments of Public Health and Primary Care, University of Oxford, Old Road Campus, Oxford OX3 7LF, England. E-mail: admin@ethox.ox.ac.uk

**HOPKIN Julian Meurglyn**, b. 30 August 1948, Ystradgynlais, Wales. Professor of Medicine. m. Janina Hopkin, 2 sons, 1 daughter. Education: MB BCh (Wales), 1972; MRCP (UK), 1974; MSc (Edin), 1978; MD (Wales), 1981; MA (Oxon), 1992. Appointments: Consultant Physician, Oxford Hospitals, 1984-98; Fellow of Brasenose College, Oxford, 1992-98; Professor of Medicine, University of Wales, Swansea, 1999-; Director of Swansea School of Medicine, 2001-. Publications: Over 100 primary medical research publications on subjects of genetics, immunity and infection; Author of Oxford University Press monograph on "Pneumocystis Carinii". Honours: Daiwa-Adrian Prize in Medicine, 2001; Visiting Professor at universities of Kyoto, Rome, Osaka. Memberships: Association of Physicians, UK; Fellow, Royal College of Physicians (London and Edinburgh). Address: Hafod, Llanrhidian, Gwyr SA3 1EH, Wales. E-mail: j.m.hopkin@swan.ac.uk

**HOPKINS Anthony (Philip)**, b. 31 December 1937, Port Talbot, South Wales. Actor. m. (1) Petronella Barker, 1967, divorced 1972, 1 daughter, (2) Jennifer Lynton, 1973, divorced 2002, (3) Stella Arroyave, 2003. Education: Welsh College of Music and Drama. Career: Assistant Stage Manager, Manchester Library Theatre, 1960; Joined Nottingham Repertory Company; Royal Academy of Dramatic Art; Phoenix Theatre, Leicester; Liverpool Playhouse and Hornchurch Repertory Company. Films include: The Lion in Winter, 1967; The Looking Glass War, 1968; Hamlet, 1969; Young Winston, 1971; A Doll's House, 1972; The Girl from Petrovka, 1973; Juggernaut, 1974; Audrey Rose, 1976; A Bridge Too Far, 1976; International Velvet, 1977; Magic, 1978; The Elephant Man, 1979; A Change of Seasons, 1980; The Bounty, 1983; The Good Father, 1985; 84 Charing Cross Road, 1986; The Dawning, 1987; A Chorus of Disapproval, 1988; Desperate Hours, 1989; The Silence of the Lambs, 1990; Free Jack, 1990; One Man's War, 1990; Spotswood, 1990; Howard's End, 1991; Bram Stoker's Dracula, 1991; Chaplin, 1992; The Trial, 1992; The Innocent, 1992; Remains of the Day, 1992; Shadowlands, 1993; Legends of the Fall, 1993; The Road to Wellville, 1993; August, 1994; Nixon, 1995; Surviving Picasso, 1995; The Edge, 1996; The Mask of Zorro, 1997; Amistad, 1997; Meet Joe Black, 1997; Instinct, 1998; Titus, 1999; Hannibal, 2000; Hearts of Atlantis, 2000; Mission Impossible 2, 2001; Hannibal, 2001; The Devil and

Daniel Webster, 2001; Bad Company, 2002; Red Dragon, 2002. Theatre includes: A Flea in Her Ear, 1967; A Woman Killed with Kindness, 1971; Macbeth, 1972; Equus, 1974; The Tempest, USA, 1979; Old Times, USA, 1984; The Lonely Road, 1985; King Lear, 1986. TV includes: A Company of Five, 1968; The Poet Game, 1970; War and Peace, 1971; Lloyd George, 1972; All Creatures Great and Small, 1974; Kean, 1978; The Bunker, 1980; Othello, BBC, 1981; A Married Man, 1982; Blunt, 1985; Across the Lake, 1988; Heartland, 1988; To Be the Best, 1990; A Few Selected Exits, 1993; Big Cats, 1993. Honours include: Variety Club Film and Stage Actor Awards, 1984, 1985, 1993; BAFTA Best Actor Awards, 1973, 1991, 1994, 1995; Emmy Awards, 1976, 1981; Oscar, 1991; Laurence Olivier Awards 1985; CBE, 1987; KB, 1993; Commandeur dans l'Ordre des Arts et des Lettres, France, 1996; Honorary DLit, University of Wales, 1988; Honorary Fellowship, St David's College, Wales, 1992; 2 Los Angeles Film Critics Association, Best Actor Awards, 1993; Donesta, 1998; Numerous other awards. Address: c/o CAA, 9830 Wilshire Blvd, Beverly Hills, CA 90212, USA.

**HOPKINS Antony**, b. 21 March 1921, London, England. Musician; Author. m. Alison Purves, 1947, deceased 1991. Education: Royal College of Music with Cyril Smith and Gordon Jacob. Career: Lecturer, Royal College of Music, 15 years; Director, Intimate Opera Company, 1952-64; Series of radio broadcasts, Talking About Music, 1954-92. Compositions include: Operas: Lady Rohesia; Three's Company; Hands Across the Sky; Dr Musikus; Ten o'Clock Call; The Man from Tuscany; Ballets: Etude; Cafe des Sports; 3 Piano Sonatas; Numerous scores of incidental music including: Oedipus; The Love of Four Colonels; Cast a Dark Shadow; Pickwick Papers; Billy Budd; Decameron Nights. Publications include: Understanding Music, 1979; The Nine Symphonies of Beethoven, 1980; The Concertgoer's Companion, 2 volumes, 1984, 1986. Honours: Gold Medal, Royal College of Music, 1943; Italia Prize for Radio Programme, 1951, 1957; Medal, City of Tokyo for Services to Music, 1973; Commander of the British Empire, 1976. Address: Woodyard, Ashridge, Berkhamsted, Hertfordshire HP4 1PS, England.

**HOPKINS Timothy John**, b. 7 March 1967, Manchester, England. Roman Catholic Priest. Education: MA, Classics, Christ's College, Cambridge, 1985-88; STL, PhB, Venerable English College and Pontifical Gregorian University, Rome, 1988-94. Appointments: Assistant Priest, St Willibrord's, Clayton, 1994-95; Chaplain, St Gregory's RC High School, Openshaw, 1994-99; Diocesan Chaplain to Italian Community, 1994-; Parish Priest, St Brigid's, Beswick and St Vincent's, Openshaw, 1995-2003; Governor, St Brigid's RC Primary Beacon School, 1995-; Secretary, Diocesan Council of Priests, 1997-2003; Chair, East Manchester Education Action Zone, 1999-2004; Vice Chair, University of Manchester Settlement, 1999-; Governor, Corpus Christi with St Anne RC Primary School, 1999-; Chaplain, Lord Mayor of Manchester, 2001-02; Governor, St Bede's College, Manchester, 2001-; Founder and Chair, East Manchester E-Learning Foundation, 2001-; Chaplain, Commonwealth Games, Manchester, 2002; Manchester LEA Join Consultative Committee, 2002-; Manchester City Council Children and Young People Scrutiny Committee, 2002-; Greater Manchester Area Officer, Salford Diocese Boundaries & Sites Board, 2003-; Parish Priest of St Anne, St Brigid, St Michael and St Vincent, East Manchester, 2003-; Education Team, New East Manchester Urban Regeneration Company, 2004-. Publications: The Power of the Holy Spirit in the Sacrament of Reconciliation, 1994; Commonwealth Games Chaplaincy: Going for Gold in Manchester, 2002; Education Action Zone and Microsoft Work Together for a Prosperous Future in East

Manchester, 2003. Address: St Anne's Roman Catholic Church, Carruthers Street, Ancoats, Manchester, M4 7EQ, England. E-mail: tim@vincents.fslife.co.uk

**HOPKINSON Betty Constance,** b. 11 March 1920, Coventry, England. Portrait Painter; Art Teacher. m. George S Hopkinson, deceased, 1 son, 2 daughters. Education: Part-time studies in portrait painting with Bernard Hailstone, Maidstone College of Art, 1952-57 and Goldsmiths College of Art, 1957-63 and life drawing with Sam Rabin; Certificate in Fine and Applied Art (Printmaking), Sir John Cass College, City of London Polytechnic, 1984-86. Career: Professional Portrait Painter, 1964-; Teacher of Art, Portrait Painting, St Alban's College of Further Education, 1967; Teacher of Art, Portrait Painting, Hendon College of Further Education 1984-; Teacher of Art, Harpenden Further Education Centre (renamed Oaklands College, Harpenden Campus); Exhibitions: One Man Shows: North and East Finchley Libraries, 1966; Woodstock Galleries, 1972; Upstairs Gallery, Stamford, 1974; The Crest Gallery, Totteridge, 1978; Camden Arts Centre, 1979; Royal Free Hospital, 1980; Old Bull Gallery, Barnet, 1984; Bow House Gallery, Barnet, 1989; Crypt Gallery, St Martins-in-the-Field, London, 1990; Group Exhibitions: La Société des Artists Française, Paris Salon, 1964, 1967, 1971; Royal Society of Portrait Painters, 1960-; Royal Society of British Artists, 1960-; Royal Society of Oil Painters, 1960-; National Society of Painters, Sculptors and Printmakers; Contemporary Portrait Society; Hampstead Arts Council; Printmakers Council; National Open Print Competition Scarborough; Medici Gallery, London; Royal Festival Hall Printmakers Council Exhibitions; Royal Festival Hall GLC Spirit of London; John Laing Landscape Exhibitions; Works in private collections in USA, Canada, Australia, France, Germany, Belgium, Holland, Zimbabwe and UK. Publication: Birthday Cards, The Medici Society Ltd. Honours: Honourable Mention for "Mr Mears", 1964, Medaille d'Argent for "Homage to Bonnard", 1967; Medaille d'Or for "Someone in the Kitchen", 1971, Société des Artistes Française, Paris Salon. Memberships: Founder and Honorary Member, Harpenden Arts Club; National Society of Painters, Sculptors and Printmakers, 1986; Hampstead Arts Council. Address: 2 Lyndhurst Avenue, Mill Hill, London NW7 2AB, England.

**HOPKIRK Joyce,** b. 2 March 1937, England. Writer; Journalist. 1 son, 1 daughter. Appointments: Reporter, Gateshead Post, 1955; Founder Editor, Majorcan News, 1959; Reporter, Daily Sketch, 1960; Royal Reporter, Daily Express, 1961; Editor, Fashion Magazine, 1967; Woman's Editor, The Sun launch, 1969; Launch Editor, Cosmopolitan, 1971-72; Assistant Editor, Daily Mirror, 1973-78; Women's Editor, Sunday Times, 1982; Editorial Director, Elle launch, 1984; Assistant Editor, Sunday Mirror, 1985; Editor-in-Chief, She Magazine, 1986-89; Director, Editors' Unlimited, 1990-; Founder Editor, Chic Magazine, 1994. Publications: Successful Slimming, 1976; Successful Slimming Cookbook, 1978; Splash! (co-author), 1995; Best of Enemies, 1996; Double Trouble, 1997; Unfinished Business, 1998; Relative Values, 1999; The Affair, 2000. Honours: Editor of the Year, 1972, Women's Magazines Editor of the Year, 1988, British Society of Magazine Editors; Woman of Achievement Award, Women's Advertising Club of London, 1998; Co-Chairman, Periodical Publishers Association Magazine Awards, 1998. Membership: Fellow, Royal Society of Arts; Member, Competition Commission, 1999. Address: Gadespring, 109 Piccotts End, Hemel Hempstead, Hertfordshire HP1 3AT, England.

**HOPPER Dennis,** b. 17 May 1936, Dodge City, USA. Actor; Author; Photographer; Film Director. m. (1) Brooke Hayward, 1 daughter, (2) Doria Halprin, one daughter, (3) Katherine La

Nasa, 1989, 1 son. Creative Works: Film appearances include: Rebel Without a Cause, 1955; I Died a Thousand Times, 1955; Giant, 1956; Story of Mankind, 1957; Gunfight at the O.K. Corral, 1957; Night Tide, 1958; Key Witness, 1958; From Hell to Texas, 1958; Glory Stompers, 1959; The Trip, 1961; The Sons of Katie Elder, 1962; Hang 'Em High, 1966; Cool Hand Luke, 1967; True Grit, 1968; The American Dreamer, 1971; Kid Blue, 1973; The Sky is Falling, 1975; James Dean – The First American Teenager, 1976; Mad Dog Morgan, 1976; Tracks, 1979; American Friend, 1978; Apocalypse Now, 1979; Wild Times, 1980; King of the Mountain, 1981; Human Highway, 1981; Rumble Fish, 1983; The Osterman Weekend, 1984; Black Widow, 1986; Blue Velvet, 1986; River's Edge, 1987; Blood Red, 1989; Flashback, 1989; The American Wars, 1989; Chattahoochie, 1990; Motion and Emotion, 1990; Superstar: The Life and Times of Andy Warhol, 1990; Hot Spot, 1990; True Romance, 1993; Boiling Point, 1993; Super Mario Bros, 1993; Chasers, 1994; Speed, 1994; Waterworld, 1995; Search and Destroy, 1995; Basquiat, 1996; Carried Away, 1996; Star Truckers, 1997; Blackout, 1997; Tycus, 1998; Sources, 1999; Lured Innocence, 1999; Justice, 1999; Straight Shooter, 1999; Actor, Writer, Director: Easy Rider, 1969; The Last Movie, 1971; Paris Trout, 1990; The Indian Runner, 1991; Actor, Director: Out of the Blue, 1980; Director: Colors, 1988; The Hot Spot, 1990; Catchfire, 1991; Nails, 1991; Several public exhibitions of photographs. Publication: Out of the Sixties (photographs), 1988. Honours include: Best New Director, Cannes, 1969; Best Film Award, Venice, 1971, Cannes, 1980. Address: c/o Creative Artists Agency, 9830 Wilshire Boulevard, Beverly Hills, CA 90212, USA.

**HOPPER Hugh,** b. 29 April 1945, Whitstable, Kent, England. Musician; Composer; Author. m. Christine Janet, 2 daughters. Musical Education: Self-taught. Career: Musician with: Wilde Flowers; Soft Machine; Isotope; Carla Bley; Soft Head; Hugh Hopper Band; Bone; Dubious Manner. Compositions: Memories, Robert Wyatt and Whitney Houston; Facelift, Soft Machine; Was A Friend, Shleep, Robert Wyatt. Recordings: Soft Machine 2-6; Hoppertunity Box; 1984; Caveman Hughscore; Delta Flora; Jazzloops; Stolen Hour. Publications: Thirty Kent Churches; Rock Bass Manual; Many articles in music journals. Honours: Melody Maker Readers Poll; Downbeat Poll; Société Pataphysique de France; Comité d'Arts France. Memberships: Musicians' Union; MCPS; PRS Address: 29 Castle Road, Whitstable, Kent CT5 2DZ, England. Website: www.hughhopper.com

**HOPWOOD David Alan (Sir),** b. 19 August 1933, Kinver, Staffordshire, England. Scientist. m. Joyce Lilian Bloom, 2 sons, 1 daughter. Education: BA 1st class honours, Natural Sciences, 1954, PhD, 1958, University of Cambridge; DSc, University of Glasgow, 1974. Appointments: John Stothert Bye-Fellow, Magdalene College, Cambridge, 1956-58; University Demonstrator, Assistant Lecturer in Botany, University of Cambridge, 1957-61; Research Fellow, St John's College, Cambridge, 1958-61; Lecturer in Genetics, University of Glasgow, 1961-68; John Innes Professor of Genetics, University of East Anglia, Norwich and Head of the Genetics Department, John Innes Institute, 1968-98; John Innes Emeritus Fellow, John Innes Centre, Emeritus Professor of Genetics, University of East Anglia, Norwich, 1998-; Visiting Research Fellow, Kosan Biosciences, Inc, 1998-. Publications: Over 270 articles on genetics, microbiology and genetic engineering in scientific publications. Honours: 3 honorary memberships; 4 honorary fellowships; Fellow, Royal Society of London; Foreign Fellowship, Indian National Science Academy; 2 honorary Doctorates of Science; Medal of the Kitasato Institute for Research in New Bioactive Compounds; Hoechst-Roussel

Award for Research in Antimicrobial Chemotherapy; Chiron Biotechnology Award; Knight Bachelor; Mendel Medal of the Czech Academy of Sciences; Gabor Medal of the Royal Society; Stuart Mudd Prize, International Union of Microbiological Societies; Ernst Chain Prize, Imperial College, London; Andre Lwoff Prize, Federation of European Microbiological Societies. Memberships: Genetical Society of Great Britain; Society for General Microbiology; American Society for Microbiology; European Molecular Biology Organisation; Academia Europaea. Address: John Innes Centre, Norwich, Norfolk NR4 7UH, England. E-mail: david.hopwood@bbsrc.ac.uk

**HORDER John Plaistowe**, b. 9 December 1919, Ealing, London, England. Physician; General practitioner. m. Elizabeth June Wilson, 2 sons, 2 daughters. Education: Classical Scholarship, University College Oxford, 1938-40; Army war service; Medical Student, Oxford and London Hospital, 1943-48; Intern Appointments, London Hospital, 1948-51. Appointments: General Practitioner, North West London, 1951-81; Foundation Member, 1952, various offices including President, 1979-82, Royal College of General Practitioners; Vice-President, Royal Society of Medicine, 1987-89; Visiting Professor, Royal Free Hospital Medical School, 1983-92; Founder, 1st President, Centre for the Advancement of Inter Professional Education, 1983-2003. Publications include: Articles in medical journals: Illness in General Practice, 1954; Physicians and Family Doctors, A New Relationship, 1977; Book: The Future General Practitioner. Learning and Teaching, (joint editor and contributor), 1972; Book: General Practice under the National Health Service 1948-1997, (joint editor and contributor), 1998. Honours: OBE, 1971; CBE, 1981; Honorary MD, 1985; Honorary DSc, 2000; FRCGP, 1970; FRCP, 1972; FRCP (Ed), 1981; FRCPsych, 1980; Honorary Fellow, Green College, Oxford, 1985; Honorary Fellow, Queen Mary College University of London, 1997. Memberships: Medical Royal Colleges; Royal Society of Medicine; President, Medical Art Society. Address: 98 Regents Park Road, London NW1 8UG, England.

**HORLOCK John Harold (Sir)**, b. 19 April 1928, Edmonton, England. University Administrator and Engineer. m Sheila J Stutely, 1 son, 2 daughters. Education: MA, Mechanical Sciences, 1953, PhD, Mechanical Engineering, 1955, ScD, Mechanical Engineering, 1975, Cambridge University. Appointments: Design and Development Engineer, Rolls-Royce Ltd, 1948-51, Research Fellow, St John's College Cambridge, 1954-57; Lecturer, Engineering, 1956-58, Professor of Engineering, Cambridge University, 1967-74; Harrison Professor of Mechanical Engineering, University of Liverpool, 1958-67; Vice-Chancellor, University of Salford, 1974-80; Vice-Chancellor, 1981-90, Fellow, 1991-, Open University; Treasurer and Vice-President, Royal Society, 1992-97; Pro-Chancellor UMIST, 1995-2001; President, Association for Science Education, 1999. Publications: Books: Axial Flow Compressors, 1958; Axial Flow Turbines, 1973; Actuator Disc Theory, 1978; The Thermodynamics and Gas Dynamics of Internal Combustion Engines (co-editor), Volume I, 1982, Volume II, 1986; Cogeneration, Combined Heat and Power, 1987; Combined Power Plants, 1992; Energy for the Future (co-editor), 1995; Advanced Gas Turbine Cycles, 2003. Honours include: James Clayton Prize, 1962, Thomas Hawksley Gold Medal, 1969, Arthur Charles Main Prize, 1997, Institution of Mechanical Engineers; Honorary Doctorates: Heriot-Watt University, 1980, University of Salford, 1981, University of East Asia, 1987, University of Liverpool, 1987, Open University, 1991, CNAA, 1991, De Montford University, 1995, Cranfield University, 1997; Honorary Fellowships: St John's College, Cambridge, 1989, UMIST, 1991, Royal Aeronautical Society,

2003; Knighthood, 1996; R Tom Sawyer Award, ASME, 1997; Sir James Ewing Medal, ICE, 2002; ISABE Achievement Award, 2003. Memberships: Fellow, Royal Society; Fellow, Royal Academy of Engineering; Fellow, Institution of Mechanical Engineers; Fellow, American Society of Mechanical Engineers; Foreign Associate, National Academy of Engineering, USA. Address: 2 The Avenue, Ampthill, Bedford MK45 2NR, England. E-mail: john.horlock1@btinternet.com

**HORNE Alistair Allan (Sir)**, b. 9 November 1925, London, England. Author; Journalist; Lecturer. m. (1) Renira Margaret Hawkins, 3 daughters, (2) The Hon Mrs Sheelin Eccles, 1987. Education: MA, Jesus College, Cambridge. Appointments: Served WWII: RAF, 1943-44; Coldstream Guards, 1944-47; Captain attached Intelligence Service MI-5; Director Ropley Trust Ltd, 1948-77; Foreign Correspondent, Daily Telegraph, 1952-55; Founded Alistair Horne Research Fellowship in Modern History, 1969, Honorary Fellow, 1988, St Antony's College, Oxford, 1969; Honorary Fellow, Jesus College Cambridge, 1996-; Fellow Woodrow Wilson Center, Washington DC, 1980-81; Member: Management Committee, Royal Literary Fund, 1969-91; Franco-British Council, 1979-93; Committee of Management, Society of Authors, 1979-82; Trustee, Imperial War Museum, 1975-82. Publications: Back into Power, 1955; The Land is Bright, 1958; Canada and the Canadians, 1961; The Price of Glory: Verdun 1916, 1962; The Fall of Paris 1870-1871, 1965; To Lose a Battle: France 1940, 1969; Death of a Generation, 1970; The Terrible Year: The Paris Commune, 1971, 2005; A Savage War of Peace: Algeria, 1954-62, 1977; Small Earthquake in Chile, 1972; Napoleon, Master of Europe 1805-1807, 1979; The French Army and Politics 1870-1970, 1984; Macmillan, Vol I, 1894-1956, 1985; Vol II, 1957-1986, 1989; A Bundle from Britain, 1993; The Lonely Leader: Monty 1944-45, 1994; How Far From Austerlitz: Napoleon 1805-1815, 1996; Telling Lives (editor), 2000; Seven Ages of Paris, 2002; The Age of Napoleon, 2004; Friend or Foe: An Anglo-Saxon History of France, 2004; Numerous contributions to books and periodicals. Honours: Hawthornden Prize, 1963; Yorkshire Post Book of Year Prize, 1978; Wolfson Literary Award, 1978; Enid Macleod Prize, 1985; Commander of the Order of the British Empire, 1992; Chevalier, Legion d'Honneur, 1993; LittD, Cambridge, 1993; Kt, 2003. Memberships: Society of Authors; Fellow, Royal Society of Literature. Address: The Old Vicarage, Turville, Nr Henley on Thames, Oxon RG9 6QU, England.

**HORNE ROBERTS Jennifer**, b. 15 February 1949, Harrow, London, England. Barrister; Writer. m. Keith M P Roberts, 1 son, 1 daughter. Education: Diploma, Italian, University of Perugia, Italy, 1966; BA, Honours, London University, 1969; Law Diploma CLLE, 1974; Bar Finals, Council of Legal Education, Middle Temple, 1976; Ad eundem Member, Inner Temple. Appointments: In practice at Bar 1976-; Currently, Civil Law, Goldsmith Chambers, Temple, London. Publications: Trade Unionists and Law, 1984; New Frontiers in Family Law (co-author), 1994; Labour's True Way Forward, 1998; Labour's Agenda, 2000; Selected Poems, 2002. Memberships: Executive Committee Member, Chair, Family Law Committee; Society of Labour Lawyers; Founder and First Chair, Association of Women Barristers; Family Law Bar Association; Tate; Royal Academy; Highgate Literary and Scientific Society; Fabian Society. Address: Goldsmith Chambers, Temple, London EC4Y 7BL, England. E-mail: kmpr@btinternet.com

**HORNSBY Bevé**, b. 13 September 1915. Speech Therapist; Psychologist. Widowed, 3 sons, 1 daughter. Education: MSc, 1973, PhD, 1982, University of London; MEd, University College North Wales, 1979. Appointments: Ambulance Driver, First Aid Nursing Yeomanry (FANY) and Mechanical Transport

Corps, 1939-42; Pilot, Civil Air Guard, 1938-39; Head of Speech Therapy Clinic, Kingston, 1969-71; Head, Remedial Teaching, St Thomas's Hospital, 1970-71; Head, Dyslexia Dept, St Bartholomew's Hospital, 1971-80; President, Founder, Trustee, The Hornsby International Dyslexia Centre, 1984-; Private Practice, 1984-; Lecturer on Teacher Training Courses, 1984-; Principal and Founder, Hornsby House School, 1988-. Publications: Alpha to Omega - The A to Z of Teaching Reading, Writing and Spelling, 1974, 5th edition, 1999; Alpha to Omega Flash Cards, 1975, 2nd edition 1989; Overcoming Dyslexia, 1984, 3rd edition, 1997; Before Alpha – Learning Games for the Under Fives, 1989; Alpha to Omega Activity Packs, 1990, 1993; The Alpha to Omega Activity Pack, Stage I Plus, 1998; A Walk Through Guide to Alpha to Omega, 2001; Dyslexics I Have Known. Reaching for the Stars, 2001; Numerous articles in scientific and popular journals. Honours: British Dyslexia Association, 1987; FRSA; MBE, 1997; Professorship, Cheltenham and Gloucester College of Higher Education, 1997; Fellow, College of Preceptors, 1997; Golden Award for Achievement, Help the Aged, 1997. Memberships: Associate Member, British Psychological Society, 1983; Fellow, Royal College of Speech and Language Therapists, 1988; Chartered Psychologist, 1990; Associate, British Dyslexic Association, 1990; Trainer in Instrumental Enrichment, 1991; Honorary Member, PATOSS, for Outstanding Achievement, 1998; Fellow, Royal Society of Medicine, 2001 Address: Glenshee Lodge, 261 Trinity Road, Wandsworth, London SW18 3SN, England. E-mail: beve@dyslexia.com

**HOROVITZ Michael,** b. 4 April 1935, Frankfurt am Main, Germany. Writer; Poet; Editor; Publisher; Songwriter; Singer; Musician; Visual Artist; Impresario. Education: BA, 1959, MA, 1964, Brasenose, College, Oxford. Appointments: Editor and Publisher, New Departures International Review, 1959-; Founder, singer-player, director, Jazz Poetry SuperJam bandwagons, 1969-; Founder, Co-ordinator and Torchbearer, Poetry Olympics Festivals, 1980-. Publications: Europa (translator), 1961; Alan Davie, 1963; Declaration, 1963; Strangers: Poems, 1965; Poetry for the People: An Essay in Bop Prosody, 1966; Bank Holiday: A New Testament for the Love Generation, 1967; Children of Albion (editor), 1969; The Wolverhampton Wanderer: An Epic of Football, Fate and Fun, 1971; Love Poems, 1971; A Contemplation, 1978; Growing Up: Selected Poems and Pictures 1951-1979, 1979; The Egghead Republic (translator), 1983; A Celebration of and for Frances Horovitz, 1984; Midsummer Morning Jog Log, 1986; Bop Paintings, Collages and Drawings, 1989; Grandchildren of Albion (editor), 1992; Wordsounds and Sightlines: New and Selected Poems, 1994; Grandchildren of Albion Live (on cassette and CD) (editor), 1996; The POW! Anthology, 1996; The POP! Anthology, 2000; The POM! Anthology, 2001; Jeff Nuttall's Wake on Paper, 2004; Jeff Nuttall's Wake on CD, 2004; Lost Office Campaign Poem, 2005; A New Waste Land, forthcoming. Honours: Arts Council of Great Britain Writers Award, 1976; Arts Council Translator's Award, 1983; Poetry Book Society Recommendation, 1986; Creative Britons Award, 2000; Officer of the Order of the British Empire, 2002. Address: PO Box 9819, London, W11 2GQ, England.

**HORRIDGE G Adrian,** b. 12 December 1927. Professor. m. Audrey Lightburne, 1 son, 3 daughters. Education: First Class Honours, Natural Sciences Tripos, St John's College, Cambridge, England. Appointments: Scientific Officer, Senior Scientific Officer, Department of Structures, Royal Aircraft Establishment, Farnborough, England, 1953-54; Research Fellowship, St John's College, Cambridge. 1954-56; Lecturer, Reader in Zoology, St Andrews University, Scotland, 1956-59; Visiting Associate Professor, University of California, Los Angeles, USA, 1959-60; Fellow, Center for Advanced Study in the Behavioural Sciences, Stanford, California, USA, 1959-60; Director, Marine Laboratory, St Andrews University, Scotland, 1960-69; Visiting Full Professor, Yale University, USA, 1965; Fellow, Royal Society of London, 1969; Professor of Behavioural Biology, Australian National University, Canberra, Australia, 1969; Fellow, Australian Academy of Science, 1970; Examiner in Biology, University Sains, Penang and University of Malaya, Kuala Lumpar, Malaysia, 1972, 1976, 1980, 1984; Visiting Fellowship, Balliol College, Oxford, England, 1973-74; Chief Scientist, US Research Ship, Alpha Helix, in the Moluccas, East Indonesia, 1975; Visiting Fellow, Churchill College, Cambridge, England, 1976-77; Executive Director, Centre for Visual Sciences, Australian National University, 1987-1990; Royal Society Visiting Professorship, St Andrews, Scotland, 1992; Visiting Fellow, Churchill College, Cambridge, 1993-94; Appointed University Fellow, Australian National University, 1993. Publications: 230 papers on Sciences; 20 titles on Indonesian traditional boats; 10 titles on other topics, including: The Structure and Function of the Nervous Systems of Invertebrates (co-author), 1965, Interneurons, 1968; The Compound Eye of Insects (editor), 1975; The Prahu, Traditional Sailing Boat of Indonesia, 2nd edition, 1985; Sailing Craft of Indonesia, 1986; Outrigger Canoes of Bali and Madura, Indonesia, 1987; Natural and low-level seeing systems (co-editor), 1993. Memberships: Fellow, Royal Society of England; Society for Nautical Research; Fellow, Australian Academy of Science. Address: 76 Mueller Street, Yarralumla, ACT, Australia 2600. E-mail: horridge@rsbs.anu.edu.au

**HORROCKS Jane,** b. 18 January 1964, Lancashire, England. Actress. Partner Nick Vivian, 1 son, 1 daughter. Education: Royal Academy of Dramatic Art. Creative Works: Stage appearances include: The Rise and Fall of Little Voice; TV appearances include: Hunting Venus (film); Red Dwarf (series); Absolutely Fabulous; The Flint Street Nativity, 1999; Film appearances: The Dressmaker, 1989; Life is Sweet, 1991; Little Voice, 1998; Born Romantic, 2001; Chicken Run (voice), 2002. Honour: Best Supporting Actress Los Angeles Critics Award, 1992. Address: ICM, Oxford House, 76 Oxford Street, London W1D 1BS, England.

**HORSBRUGH Oliver Bethune,** b. 13 November 1937, London, England. Freelance Television Director. m. Josephine Elsa Hall, 1 son, 1 daughter. Education: St Paul's School, Hammersmith, London, 1949-54. Appointments: BBC Director, 1968-71; Freelance Director, 1971-; Drama: BBC: Bergerac; Juliet Bravo; Z Cars; 30 Minute Theatres; Granada: Kind of Loving; Cribb; Fallen Hero; Strangers; Coronation Street (over 200 episodes); Crown Court; YTV: Emmerdale (over 250 episodes); Kate; LWT: New Scotland Yard; Channel 4: Scott Inquiry; Birmingham 6 Appeal; Gibraltar Inquest; Other: Corporate productions: Many for Visage, Wardlow Grosvenor, Aspen, CTN, Evolution; Training programmes; Interactive videos; ITN: Numerous News At Ten, Channel 4 and other live news bulletins and outside broadcasts; World This Week (3 series), live political programme for ITN. Honours: GSM (Near East), RN, National Service, 1958; BAFTA for Emmerdale, 2000. Memberships: BAFTA; MCC; Press Officer, Cinema Theatre Association. Address: 21 Harbledown Road, Fulham, London SW6 5TW, England.

**HORWITZ Angela Joan,** b. 14 October 1934, London, England. Sculptress; Painter; Professor. 2 sons, 1 daughter. Education: Lycée Francais de Londres; Studied art, Marylebone Institute, 1978-90; Sir John Cass College, 1983-85; Hampstead Institute, 1990-92. Career: Fashion Designer, owner of own company, 1960-80; Exhibitions: Grand Palais, Paris, 1985, 1986;

RBA, NS, RAS, SWA, Mall Galleries, Civic Centre, Southend, SEFAS, Guildhall, Ridley Society, City of Westminster Arts Council, Alpine Gallery, Smiths Gallery Covent Garden, Wintershall Gallery; The Orangery, Hyde Park Gallery, London (Winchester Cathedral, 1992); Exhibition with City of London Polytechnic, Whitechapel, London, 1985; Salon International du Livre et de la Presse à Geneva, 1997; Miramar Hotel, 1998 and Beaux Arts, Cannes, France, 1999; Raymond Gallery, Beaux Arts, 2000; The Atrium Gallery, London, 2000; Gallery le Carre d'or, Paris, 2000; Le Cannet, St Sauveur, 2005; Work in permanent collections: Sculpture in stone for Winchester Cathedral; Well Woman Centre, The United Elizabeth Garrett Anderson Hospital for Women, London; Private collection: Zurich, Switzerland; National Society Ridley Arts Society. Honours: Academical Knight, Arts, Academia Internazionale Greci-Marino, 1999; Academical Knight, Department of Arts, Ordine Accademico Internatzionale, Italy. Memberships: NS, 1982; RAS, 1983; Beaux Arts, Cannes, France, 1997-2005; Landsdown Club; British Red Cross. Address: 6 Wellington House, Aylmer Drive, Stanmore, Middlesex HA7 3ES, England.

**HOSKING Geoffrey Alan,** b. 28 April 1942, Troon, Scotland. University Teacher. m. Anne Lloyd Hirst, 2 daughters. Education: Kings College, Cambridge, 1960-64; Moscow State University, 1964-65; St Antony's College, Oxford, 1965-66. Appointments: Lecturer in History, University of Essex, 1966-71, 1972-76; Visiting Professor, Department of Political Science, University of Wisconsin-Madison, 1971-72; Gastprofessor, Slavisches Institut, University of Cologne, 1980-81; Senior Lecturer, Reader in Russian History, University of Essex, 1976-80, 1981-84; Professor of Russian History, SSEES, University of London, 1984-99, 2004-; Leverhulme Personal Research Professor in Russian History, SSEES-UCL, 1999-2004. Publications: Author: The Russian Constitutional Experiment, 1973; Beyond Socialist Realism, 1980; The First Socialist Society: A History of the Soviet Union from Within, 1985; The Awakening of the Soviet Union, 1990; The Road to Post-Communism: Independent Political Movements in the Soviet Union 1985-91, 1992; Russia: People and Empire (1552-1917), 1997; Russia and the Russians: A History from Rus to Russian Federation, 2001; Editor: Myths and Nationhood, 1997; Russian Nationalism Past and Present, 1998; Reinterpreting Russia, 1999. Honours: Los Angeles Times History Book Prize, 1986; US Independent Publishers History Book Award, 2002; Fellow, British Academy, 1993; Fellow, Royal Historical Society; Honorary Doctorate, Russian Academy of Sciences, 2000; Member, Council of the Royal Historical Society, 2002-. Memberships: Writers and Scholars Educational Trust; Museum of Contemporary History, Moscow; Moscow School of Political Studies. Address: School of Slavonic and East European Studies, University College London, Senate House, London WC1E 7HU, England. E-mail: g.hosking@ssees.ac.uk

**HOSKINS Bob (Robert William),** b. 26 October 1942. Actor. m. (1) Jane Livesey, 1970, 1 son, 1 daughter: (2) Linda Barnwell, 1984, 1 son, 1 daughter. Career: Several stage roles at the National Theatre; Films include: National Health, 1973; Royal Flash, 1974; Zulu Dawn, 1980; The Long Good Friday, 1980; The Wall, 1982; The Honorary Consul, 1983; Lassiter, 1984; The Cotton Club, 1984; Brazil, 1985; The Woman Who Married Clark Gable, 1985; Sweet Liberty, 1985; Mona Lisa, 1986; A Prayer for the Dying, 1987; The Lonely Passion of Judith Hearne, 1987; Who Framed Roger Rabbit?, 1987; The Raggedy Rawney (director, actor and writer), 1988; Mermaids, 1989; Shattered, 1990; Heart Condition, 1990; The Projectionist, 1990; The Favour, The Watch and the Very Big Fish, 1990; Hook, 1991, The Inner Circle, 1992; Super Mario Brothers,

1992, Nixon, 1995, The Rainbow (also director), 1996; Michael, 1996; Cousin Bette, 1996; Twenty-four-seven, 1998; The Secret Agent, 1998; Felicia's Journey, 1999; Parting Shots, 1999; Enemy at the Gates, 2001; Last Orders, 2001; TV appearances include: Omnibus – It Must be Something in the Water, 1971; Villains, 1972; Thick as Thieves, 1972; Schmoedipus, 1974; Shoulder to Shoulder, 1974; Pennies From Heaven, 1975; Peninsular, 1975; Sheppey, 1980; Flickers, 1980; Othello, 1981; The Beggers' Opera, 1983; Mussolini and I, 1984; The Changeling, 1993; World War Two: Then There Were Giants, 1993; David Copperfield, 1999; The Lost World (film), 2001; Stage: Old Wicked Songs, 1996. Honours: For Mona Lisa, New York Critics Award, Golden Globe Award, Best Actor Award, Cannes Festival, 1986.

**HOSOYA Ken-ichi,** b. 15 October 1966, Odawara, Kanagawa, Japan. Research Scientist. Education: BA, Pure and Applied Science, University of Tokyo, Tokyo, Japan, 1991. Appointments: Research Staff, NEC Corporation, Otsu, Japan, 1991-98; Research Staff, 1998-2000, Assistant Manager, 2000-, NEC Corporation, Tsukuba, Japan. Publications: Articles in scientific journals including: IEEE Transactions on Microwave Theory and Techniques, 1998, 2003 (2). Honour: APMC '99 Microwave Prize, Asia Pacific Microwave Conference, 1999. Memberships: Institute of Electronic, Information and Communications Engineers, Japan, 1996-; Institute of Electrical and Electronic Engineers, 1998-. Address: 2-25-9-501 Matsuhiro, Tsukuba, 305-0035 Japan.

**HOUGH Stephen Andrew Gill,** b. 22 November 1961, Heswall, Wirral, England. Concert Pianist. Education: Royal Northern College of Music; Juilliard School, New York; G Mus; PPRNCM; M Mus. Career: Numerous concert performances with orchestras including all UK orchestras; New York Philharmonic; Chicago Symphony Orchestra; Boston Symphony; Philadelphia Orchestra, Minnesota Orchestra; Los Angeles Philharmonic; Cleveland Orchestra; NHK Symphony; Orchestre National de France; DSO, Berlin; Festivals include: Salzburg; Edinburgh; Proms (4 times); Mostly Mozart; Tanglewood; Hollywood Bowl; Ravinia; Aldeburgh. Recordings: About 40 CD recordings on Hyperion, Chandos, BMG, EMI and Virgin; Several published compositions. Honours: MacArthur Fellowship; Naumberg International Competition; Gramophone Record of the Year; Diapason d'Or; Grammy Nominations. Address: c/o Harrison Paratt Ltd, 12 Penzance Place, London W11 4PA, England. Website: www.stephenhough.com

**HOUGHTON Eric,** b. 4 January 1930, West Yorkshire, England. Teacher; Author. m. Cecile Wolffe, 4 June 1954, 1 son, 1 daughter. Education: Sheffield City College of Education, 1952. Publications: The White Wall, 1961; Summer Silver, 1963; They Marched with Spartacus, 1963; A Giant Can Do Anything, 1975; The Mouse and the Magician, 1976; The Remarkable Feat of King Caboodle, 1978; Steps Out of Time, 1979; Gates of Glass, 1987; Walter's Wand, 1989; The Magic Cheese, 1991; The Backwards Watch, 1991; Vincent the Invisible, 1993; Rosie and the Robbers, 1997; The Crooked Apple Tree, 1999. Honour: American Junior Book Award, 1964. Memberships: Society of Authors; Childrens Writers Group. Address: The Crest, 42 Collier Road, Hastings, East Sussex TN34 3JR, England.

**HOUGHTON Ivan Timothy,** b. 23 February 1942, Royal Leamington Spa, England. Physician. m. Teresa Wan. Education: St John's College, Cambridge, 1960-63; St Thomas's Hospital Medical School, 1963-1966, BA (Cantab), 1963; LMSSA (Lond), 1966; BChir (Cantab), 1966; MB (Cantab), 1966; MA (Cantab), 1967; FFARCS (Eng), 1970; LLB (Lond), 1987; MD, Chinese University of Hong Kong, 1993; DMCC, 1995; Dip

Med Ed (Dundee), 1996; LLM (Wales), 2000. Appointments include: Various positions as House Surgeon, House Officer and Registrar, 1966-72; RAMC, 1972-2002, Brigadier L/RAMC, 1996-2002; Senior Specialist, Anaesthesia, 23 Parachute Field Ambulance, 1973-75; Regimental Medical Officer, 22 Special Air Service Regiment, 1975-76; Second in Command, 19 Airportable Field Ambulance, 1976-77; Consultant Anaesthetist, 6 Field Ambulance, 1977-78; Second in Command, 5 Field Force Ambulance, Münster, 1978-80; Consultant Anaesthetist and Second in Command, Military Wing, Musgrave Park Hospital, Belfast, 1981-82; Consultant Anaesthetist, British Military Hospital, Hong Kong, 1982-85; Senior Consultant, British Military Hospital, Münster, 1985-87; Senior Consultant Anaesthetist, British Military Hospital, Hong Kong, 1987-94; Honorary Lecturer, Anaesthesia, 1982-85, Honorary Lecturer, Anaesthesia and Intensive Care, 1987-94, Chinese University of Hong Kong; Senior Consultant Anaesthetist, 1994-97, Commanding Officer, 1996-97, British Military Hospital, Rinteln; Clinical Director of Clinical Care, Royal Hospital Haslar, 1997-98; Regional Educational Adviser (Armed Forces), Royal College of Anaesthetists, 1998-2001; Consultant Adviser in Anaesthesia and Resuscitation to the Surgeon General, 1998-2001; Queen's Honorary Surgeon, 1999-2002; Currently: Editor, European Journal of Anaesthesiology; Undergraduate, Restoration and Conservation, Sir John Cass Department of Art, Media and Design, London Metropolitan University. Publications: Papers on field anaesthesia, ethnic differences in anaesthesia, history of anaesthesia and conservation. Memberships: Liveryman, Society of Apothecaries; Fellow, Royal Society of Medicine; Army and Navy Club; Hong Kong Jockey Club; British Medical Association; Association of Anaesthetists of Great Britain and Ireland; Medico-Legal Society; United Kingdom Institute for Conservation. Address: Canary Riverside, Canary Wharf, London E14, England. E-mail: ivanhoughton@doctors.org.uk

**HOUNSFIELD Godfrey Newbold (Sir)**, b. 28 August 1919, England. Research Scientist. Education: City and Guilds College, London; Faraday House Electrical Engineering College. Appointments: Served in Royal Air Force during World War II; Medical Systems Section, 1951-, Senior Staff Scientist, 1977-86, Consultant to Laboratories, 1986-, Inventor EMI-scanner computerised transverse axial tomography system for X-ray examinations, Central Research Laboratories of EMI (now THORN EMI); Professorial Fellow, Imaging Sciences, Manchester University, 1978. Honours: Several honorary degrees; MacRobert Award, 1972; Wilhelm-Exner Medal, Austrin Industrial Association, 1974; Wiedses des Plantes Medal, Phsikalisch-Medizinische Gesellschaft, Würzburg, 1974; Prince Philip Medal Award, City and Guilds of London Institute, 1975; ANS Radiation Award, Georgia Institute of Physics, 1975; Lasker Award, 1975; Duddell Bronze Medal, Institute of Physics, 1976; Golden Plate, American Academy of Achievement, 1976; Churchill Gold Medal, 1976; Gairdner Foundation Award, 1976; Shared Nobel Prize for Physiology or Medicine (with Professor A M Cormack), for development of computer-assisted tomography, 1979. Address: Central Research Laboratories, Dawley Road, Hayes, Middx, UB3 1HH, England.

**HOUSE Michael Charles Clutterbuck**, b. 31 May 1927, Weston-super-Mare, Somerset, England. Catholic Priest. Education: Officers Training School, Bangalore, 1946; Kings College, London, 1948-51; Campion College, Osterley, 1952-53; St Mary's College, Oscott, Birmingham, 1954-60. Appointments: 2nd Battalion Queen's Royal Regiment, 1945-48; Ordained Priest, 1960; Assistant Priest: St Joseph's, Bristol, 1960-64, St Gerard Majella, Bristol, 1964-69, St

Patrick's, Bristol, 1968-69; Financial Secretary to the Bishop of Clifton and Diocesan Trustees, 1969-80; Parish Priest: St George's, Warminster, 1980-87, St Mary's, Bath, 1987-91, St Thomas More, Marlborough, 1991-98; Religious Advisor to HTV West, 1966-98; Chairman of Governors, St Augustine's School, Trowbridge, 1985-87 and St Edward's School, Romsey, 1969-98; Catholic Chaplain to Marlborough College, 1991-98; National Conference of Priests, 1992-98. Publications: Articles in local papers and magazines Honours: British Empire War Medal, 1939-45; Associateship of Kings College, London, 1951. Membership: Honorary Member, Portishead Cruising Club, Commodore, 1978-79. Address: c/o Mr P D House, Addington Grange, Addington, Buckingham MK18 2JR, England.

**HOUSTON Whitney**, b. 9 August 1963, Newark, New Jersey, USA. Singer. m. Bobby Brown, 18 July 1992, 1 daughter. Musical Education: Singing lessons with mother, Cissy Houston. Career: New Hope Baptist Junior Choir, age 8; Nightclub performances with mother, 1978; Backing vocalist, Chaka Khan and Lou Rawls, 1978; Model, Glamour and Seventeen magazines; Actress, television shows, USA; Solo artiste, 1985-; First US and European tours, 1986; Montreux Rock Festival, 1987; Nelson Mandela Tribute concert, Wembley, 1988; National anthem, Super Bowl XXV, Miami, 1991; Speaker, HIV/AIDs rally, London, 1991; Television specials include: Welcome Home Heroes (return of Gulf troops), 1991; Whitney Houston - This Is My Life, ABC, 1992; Actress, film The Bodyguard, 1992; 87 million albums sold to date. Recordings: Singles include: You Give Good Love, 1985; Saving All My Love For You (Number 1, UK and US), 1985; How Will I Know, 1986; Greatest Love Of All (Number 1, US), 1986; I Wanna Dance With Somebody (Number 1, US and UK), 1987; Didn't We Almost Have It All (Number 1, US), 1987; So Emotional (Number 1, US), 1987; Where Do Broken Hearts Go (Number 1, US), 1988; Love Will Save The Day, 1988; One Moment In Time (Number 1, UK), 1988; I'm Your Baby Tonight (Number 1, US), 1990; All The Man That I Need (Number 1, US), 1990; Miracle, 1991; My Name Is Not Susan, 1991; I Will Always Love You (Number 1 in 11 countries), 1992; I'm Every Woman, 1993; I Have Nothing, 1993; Run To You, 1993; Queen of the Night, 1994; Why Does It Hurt So Bad, 1996; Step by Step, 1997; When You Believe, 1998; It's Not Right But It's Okay, 1999; I Learned from the Best, 1999; If I Told You That, 2000; Could I Have This Kiss Forever, 2000; Heartbreak Hotel, 2000; Whatchlookinat, 2002; One of Those Days, 2002; Albums: Whitney Houston, 1985; Whitney, 1987; I'm Your Baby Tonight, 1990; My Love Is Your Love, 1998; Whitney: The Greatest Hits, 2000; Love Whitney, 2001; Just Whitney, 2002; Film soundtrack: The Bodyguard (Number 1 in 20 countries), 1992. Also featured on: Life's A Party, Michael Zager Band; Duet with Teddy Pendergrass, Hold Me, 1984; Duet with Aretha Franklin, It Isn't, It Wasn't, It Ain't Ever Gonna Be, 1989. Honours include: 2 Grammy Awards; 7 American Music Awards; Emmy, 1986; Songwriter's Hall Of Fame, 1990; Longest-ever US Number 1 record (14 weeks); highest-ever US 1-week sales total, second best seller in US ever, all for I Will Always Love You, 1992; Numerous Gold and Platinum discs. Current Management: Nippy Inc., 2160 N Central Road, Fort Lee, NJ 07024, USA.

**HOVAGUIMIAN Theodore**, b. 31 January 1949, Geneva, Switzerland. Psychiatrist. m. Annette Haye, 2 sons, 1 daughter. Education: Medical Doctorate, 1973; Specialist Title FMH (Federatio Medicorum Helveticorum) in Psychiatry and Psychotherapy, 1987. Appointments: Chief of Staff, University Hospital in Geneva, 1980-87; Consultant, World Health Organisation, 1980-87; Founding Chairman of the Section on Private Practice of the World Psychiatric Association, 1996-2002; Lecturer, Faculty of Medicine, Geneva, Switzerland,

1999; Chairman of the Foundation Geneva-Prize for Human Rights in Psychiatry, 2000-2003; Private Practice in Psychiatry and Psychotherapy, 1987-. Publications: Author of more than 50 books, chapters in books, articles in scientific and professional journals on various fields in clinical psychiatry. Honours: Recipient of Grants from the Swiss National Funds for Scientific Research, 1983, 1986, 1987; Listed in Who's Who publications and biographical dictionaries. Memberships: Various scientific and disciplinary societies. Address: 12 rue Verdaine, 1204 Geneva, Switzerland.

**HOWARD Anthony Michell,** b. 12 February 1934, London, England. Biographer; Reviewer; Writer. m. Carol Anne Gaynor, 26 May 1965. Education: BA, Christ Church, Oxford, 1955. Appointments: Called to the Bar, Inner Temple, 1956; Political Correspondent, Reynolds News, 1958-59; Editorial Staff, Manchester Guardian, 1959-61; Political Correspondent, 1961-64, Assistant Editor, 1970-72, Editor, 1972-78, New Statesman; Whitehall Correspondent, 1965, Sunday Times; Washington Correspondent, 1966-69, Deputy Editor, 1981-88, Observer; Editor, The Listener, 1979-81; Reporter, BBC TV News and Current Affairs, 1989-92; Obituaries Editor, The Times, 1993-99. Publications: The Making of the Prime Minister (with Richard West), 1965; The Crossman Diaries: Selections from the Diaries of a Cabinet Minister (editor), 1979; Rab: The Life of R A Butler, 1987; Crossman: The Pursuit of Power, 1990; The Times Lives Remembered (editor with David Heaton), 1993; Basil Hume: The Monk Cardinal, 2005. Contributions to: Books, newspapers, and journals. Honours: Harkness Fellowship, USA, 1960; Commander of the Order of the British Empire, 1997; Hon LLD, Nottingham, 2001; Hon DLitt, Leicester, 2003. Address: 11 Campden House Court, 42 Gloucester Walk, London W8 4HU, England.

**HOWARD Catherine Audrey,** b. 5 February 1953, Huddersfield, England. Retired Government Officer. m. Leslie Howard, 3 April 1987. Education: Harold Pitchforth School of Commerce; Ashlar and Spen Valley Further Education Institute; Royal Society of Arts Diplomas. Appointments: Clerk, Treasury Department, 1969-70, Clerk, Housing Department, 1970-74, Elland Urban District Council; Clerk, Telephonist, Housing Department, Calderdale Metropolitan Borough Council, 1974-83; Social Work Assistant; Social Services Department, Calderdale, 1983-88. Publications: Elland in Old Picture Postcards, 1983; Poetry: Down By the Old Mill Stream, 1993; The Flamborough Longsword Dance, 1994; Sacrifice for Christianity, 1994; My Pennine Roots, 1994; The Old and the New, 1994; Having Faith, 1994; The Might of the Meek, 1995; Tough as Old Boots, 1995; Portrait of All Hallows, 1996; Childhood Memories, 1996; Old Ways in Modern Days, 1996; Northern Cornucopia, 1996; A Glimpse of Spring, 1998; Poetry From Yorkshire, 1999. Contributions to: Mercedes-Benz Gazette, 1996; Commemorative Poem presented to Bridlington Public Library on the centenary of Amy Johnson, titled Wonderful Amy, 2003. Honours: National Poet of the Year Commendations, 1996 (3 times); National Open Competition Commendations, 1996, 1997; Robert Bloomfield Memorial Awards Commendation, 1998. Address: 17 Woodlands Close, Bradley Grange, Bradley, Huddersfield, West Yorkshire HD2 1QS, England.

**HOWARD Deborah (Janet),** b. 26 February 1946, London, England. Architectural Historian; Writer. m. Malcolm S Longair, 26 September 1975, 1 son, 1 daughter. Education: BA, Honours, 1968, MA, 1972, Newnham College, Cambridge; MA, 1969, PhD, 1973, University of London. Appointments: Professor of Architectural History, University of Cambridge, 2001-; Fellow, St John's College, Cambridge; Head of Department of History of Art, University of Cambridge. Publications: Jacopo Sansovino: Architecture and Patronage in Renaissance Venice, 1975, 2nd edition, 1987; The Architectural History of Venice, 1980, 3rd edition, 1987, revised and enlarged edition, 2002; Scottish Architecture from the Reformation to the Restoration, 1560-1660, 1995; Venice and the East: The Impact on the Islamic World on Venetian Architecture 1100-1500, 2000. Contributions to: Professional journals. Honour: Honorary Fellow, Royal Incorporation of Architects of Scotland; Fellow, Royal Society of Edinburgh. Memberships: Fellow, Society of Antiquarians of Scotland; Fellow, Society of Antiquaries. Address: St John's College, Cambridge CB2 1TP, England.

**HOWARD Elizabeth Jane,** b. 26 March 1923, London, England. Author. m. (1) Peter Scott, 1941, 1 daughter, (2) James Douglas-Henry, 1959, (3) Kingsley Amis, 1965, divorced 1983. Education: Trained as Actress, London Mask Theatre School, Scott Thorndike Student Repertory. Appointments: BBC TV, modelling, 1939-46; Secretary, Inland Waterways Association, 1947; Honorary Director, Cheltenham Literary Festival, 1962; Co-Director, Salisbury Festival, 1973. Publications: The Beautiful Visit, 1950; The Long View, 1956; The Sea Change, 1959; After Julius, 1965; Odd Girl Out, 1972; Mr Wrong, 1975; Getting It Right, 1982; The Cazalet Chronicles: The Light Years (1st volume), 1990, Marking Time (2nd volume), 1991, Confusion (3rd volume), 1993; Casting Off, volume 4, 1995; Falling, 1999; Slipstream: a Memoir, 2003. Other: The Lovers' Companion (anthology); Green Shades (anthology); 14 television plays; 3 film scripts. Contributions to: The Times; Sunday Times; Telegraph; Encounter; Vogue; Harper's; Queen. Honours: CBE; Yorkshire Post Novel of the Year, 1982. Memberships: Fellow, Royal Society of Literature; Authors Lending and Copyright Society. Address: c/o Jonathan Clowes, Iron Bridge House, Bridge Approach, London NW1 8BD, England.

**HOWARD Grahame Charles William,** b. 15 May 1953, London, England. Consultant Clinical Oncologist. 3 sons. Education: St Thomas Hospital Medical School, London, 1970-76; London University Degrees: BSc, MBBS, MD. Appointments: Registrar, The Royal Free Hospital, London; Senior Registrar and Research Fellow, Addenbrooke's Hospital Cambridge; Honorary Senior Lecturer, University of Edinburgh; Consultant Clinical Oncologist, 1987-, Clinical Director, 1999-, The Edinburgh Cancer Centre. Publications: Author of over 100 publications in scientific journals on various topics related to cancer; Co-author of several evidence based guidelines for various cancers. Professional qualifications: MRCP; FRCP (Ed); FRCR; Assistant Editor, Clinical Oncology; Chair, Scottish Intercollegiate Guideline Network, Cancer Speciality Subgroup; Chair, South East Scotland Urology Oncology Group. Address: 4 Ormelie Terrace, Edinburgh, EH15 2EX, Scotland.

**HOWARD John Winston (The Honourable),** b. 26 July 1939, Earlwood, New South Wales, Australia. Prime Minister of Australia. m. Alison Janette Parker, 4 April 1971, 2 sons, 1 daughter. Education: LLB, University of Sydney, 1961. Appointments: Solicitor, Supreme Court, New South Wales, 1962; Partner, solicitors' firm, 1968-74; MP for Bennelong, New South Wales, Federal Parliament, 1974-; Minister for Business and Consumer Affairs, 1975-77; Minister Assisting Prime Minister, 1977; Minister of State for Special Trade Negotiations, 1977; Federal Treasurer, 1977-83; Minister for Finance, 1979; Deputy Leader of the Opposition, 1983-85; Leader of the Opposition, 1985-89, 1995-96; Leader, Liberal Party, 1985-89; Prime Minister, Government of Australia, 1996-. Memberships: Member State Executive, New South Wales Liberal Party, 1963-74; Vice President, New South Wales Division, Liberal Party,

1972-74. Honours: Named one of the most influential people, TIME magazine, 2005. Address: St MG8 Parliament House, Canberra, ACT 2600, Australia.

**HOWARD Norman,** b. 25 November 1926, London, UK. Medical Practitioner; Consultant Clinical Oncologist. m. Anita, 2 sons. Education: BM BCh, MA, 1952; DM, 1965, Oxford University; FFR, 1958; FRCR, 1975. Appointments: House Physician and Surgeon, 1953-54, Registrar, 1954-56, University College Hospital; Registrar and Senior Registrar, Royal Marsden Hospital, 1956-63; Consultant, Radiotherapy and Oncology, Charing Cross Hospital, 1963-91, Wembley Hospital, 1964-91; Honorary Consultant, Royal Marsden Hospital, 1970-; Consultant in Clinical Oncology, Cromwell Hospital, 1982-2001; Chairman: Royal College of Radiologists Research Appeal, 1993-2003, Gunnar Nilsson Cancer Research Trust Fund, Medical Staff Committee, Charing Cross Hospital, 1974-79. Publications: Mediastinal Obstruction in Lung Cancer, 1967; Numerous chapters and articles concerning cancer, radiotherapy and radioisotopes. Honour: Commendatore Order of Merit Republic of Italy, 1976. Memberships: Royal College of Radiologists; Royal Society of Medicine; British Medical Association. Address: 5A Clarendon Road, London W11 4JA, England. E-mail: norman.anita@btinternet.com

**HOWARD Peter Milner,** b. 27 June 1937, Stockport, Cheshire, England. Journalist; Editor. m. Janet Crownshaw, 1 son, 1 daughter. Education: Further education, Sheffield College of Commerce and Technology. Appointments: National Service, Sergeant in Army Public Relations, GHQ Far East Land Forces, Singapore, 1958-60; Copy-boy, General Reporter, Sports Reporter/Sub-editor, Feature Writer, Sports Editor, The Star, Sheffield, 1952-75; Ministry of Defence: Press Relations for Royal Navy in UK and ships at sea, British Army, Royal Air Force in Germany, All three services in the Falklands, post fighting, Press desk work in MOD main building, Editor, Soldier, 1975-85; Jane's Information Group: Editor, Jane's Defence Weekly, Jane's Missiles and Rockets, Jane's Navy International, 3 years as Managing Editor, Military and Systems Yearbooks, 1985-2000; Freelance journalist, Editor, Jane's Defence Industry, 2001-. Memberships: Military Historical Society; International Military Music Society; Union Jack Club; Petersfield Golf Club. Address: Mildmay Cottage, Hawkley Road, West Liss, Hampshire GU33 6JL, England. E-mail: petermhoward@lineone.net

**HOWARD Ron,** b. 1 March 1954, Duncan, Oklahoma, USA. Film Actor; Director. m. Cheryl Alley, 1975, 2 sons, 2 daughters. Education: University of Southern California; Los Angeles Valley College. Appointments: Director, Co-Author, Star, Grand Theft Auto, 1977; Regular TV series The Andy Griffith Show, 1960-68, The Smith Family, 1971-72, Happy Days, 1974, and many other TV appearances. Creative Works: Films directed include: Night Shift, 1982; Splash, 1984; Cocoon, 1985; Gung Ho, 1986; Return to Mayberry, 1986; Willow, 1988; Parenthood, 1989; Backdraft, 1991; Far and Away (also co-producer), 1992; The Paper, 1994; Apollo 13, 1995; A Beautiful Mind, 2001; Film appearances include: The Journey, 1959; Five Minutes to Live, 1959; Music Man, 1962; The Courtship of Eddie's Father, 1963; Village of the Giants, 1965; Wild Country, 1971; Mother's Day, 1974; American Graffiti, 1974; The Spikes Gang, 1976; Eat My Dust, 1976; The Shootist, 1976; More American Graffiti, 1979; Leo and Loree (TV), 1980; Act of Love, 1980; Skyward, 1981; Through the Magic Pyramid (director, executive producer), 1981; When Your Lover Leaves (co-executive producer), 1983; Return to Mayberry, 1986; Ransom, 1996; Ed TV, 1999. Honours include: Outstanding Directorial Achievement in Motion Picture Award, Directors

Guild of America, 1996; Academy Awards for Best Director and Best Film (producer), 2002; DGA Best Director Award, 2002. Address: c/o Peter Dekom, Bloom Dekom & Hergott, 150 South Rodeo Drive, Beverly Hills, CA 90212, USA.

**HOWARTH Nigel John Graham,** b. 12 December 1936, Manchester, England. Circuit Judge. m. Janice Mary Hooper, 2 sons, 1 daughter. Education: LLB, 1957, LLM, 1959, University of Manchester; Bar Finals, 1st class honours, Inns of Court Law School, 1960; Macaskie Scholar, 1960, Atkin Scholar, 1961, Grays Inn. Appointments: Called to the Bar, Grays Inn, 1960; Private practice, Chancery Bar, Manchester, 1961-92; Assistant Recorder, 1983-89; Acting Deemster, Isle of Man, 1985, 1989; Recorder of Crown Court, 1989-92; Circuit Judge, 1992-. Memberships: Vice President, Disabled Living; Manchester Pedestrian Club; Northern Chancery Bar Association, Chairman, 1990-92. Address: c/o Circuit Administrator, Northern Circuit Office, 15 Quay Street, Manchester, M60 9FD, England. E-mail: nhowarth@lix.compulink.co.uk

**HOWATT William A,** b. Halifax, Nova Scotia, Canada. Teacher; Consultant; Counsellor; Author; Coach. m. Sherrie, 2 sons, 1 daughter. Education: BSc; BA; M Ed; MSc; MBA (C); PhD; Ed D; Postdoctoral, University of California, Los Angeles, School of Medicine. Appointments: Faculty, Nova Scotia Community College; Chief Executive Officer, Howatt Human Resources Consulting Inc. Publications: Addictions Handbook (co-author with John Wiley); Book chapters, Addictions Counseling Review for Comprehensive Certification and Licensing Exam; Addiction Book Series (co-editor with John Wiley); Human Services Counseling Tool Box (author). Honours: Citation for work on ADHD in Antigua, Office of the Mayor of Jersey City; member, Editorial Advisory Board, Counselor Magazine. Memberships: APA; William Glass Institute; ICF. Address: 6585 Highway 221, Kentville NS, Canada B4N 3U7. E-mail: bhowatt@howattcompany.com Website: www.howattcompany.com

**HOWE Elspeth Rosamund Morton (Baroness Howe of Idlicote),** b. 8 February 1932. Member of the House of Lords. m. Lord Howe of Aberavon, 1953, 1 son, 2 daughters. Education: BSc, London School of Economics, 1985. Appointments: Secretary to Principal, A A School of Architecture, 1952-55; Deputy Chairman, Equal Opportunities Commission, Manchester, 1975-79; President, Federation of Recruitment and Employment Services, 1980-94; Non-Executive Director, United Biscuits plc, 1988-94; Non-Executive Director, Kingfisher plc, 1986-2000; Non-Executive Director, Legal and General, 1989-97; Chairman, The BOC Foundation for the Environment, 1990-2003; Chairman, The Broadcasting Standards Commission, 1993-99. Publications: 2 pamphlets; Co-author, Women on the Board, 1990; Articles for newspapers; Lectures, speeches, television and radio broadcasts. Honours: Honorary Doctorates: London University, 1990; The Open University, 1993; Bradford University, 1993; Aberdeen University, 1994; Liverpool University, 1994; Sunderland University, 1995; South Bank University, 1995; Honorary Fellow, London School of Economics, 2001. Memberships: President, the UK Committee of UNICEF, 1993-2002; Vice Chairman, The Open University, 2001-03; Trustee, The Architectural Association; Trustee, The Ann Driver Trust; Institute of Business Ethics; President, The Peckham Settlement; NCVO Advisory Council. Address: House of Lords, London SW1A 0PW, England. E-mail: howee@parliament.uk

**HOWE, 7th Earl, Frederick Richard Curzon,** b. 29 January 1951, London, England. Parliamentarian. m/ Elizabeth Helen, 1 son, 3 daughters. Education: BA, 1973, MA, 1977, Christ

Church College, Oxford. Appointments: Barclays Bank plc, 1973-87; Director, Adam & Co plc, 1987-90; Government Whip, 1991-92; Parliamentary Secretary, Ministry of Agriculture and Fisheries, 1992-95; Parliamentary Under Secretary of State for Defence, 1995-97; Opposition Spokesman for Health and Social Services, 1997-; Chairman, LAPADA, 1999-. Address: House of Lords, London SW1A 0PW, England.

**HOWE Geoffrey (Lord Howe of Aberavon),** b. 20 December 1926. Politician; Lawyer m. Elspeth Rosamund Morton Shand, 1953, 1 son, 2 daughters. Education: MA, LLB, Trinity Hall, Cambridge. Appointments: Lieutenant, Royal Signals, 1945-48; Chairman, Cambridge University Conservative Association, 1951; Chairman, Bow Group, 1955; Contested Aberavon, 1955, 1959; Managing Director, Crossbow, 1957-60; Editor, 1960-62; Called to the Bar, Middle Temple, 1952, QC, 1965, Bencher, 1969, Reader, 1993; Member, General Council of the Bar, 1957-61; Member, Council of Justice, 1963-70; MP, Bebington, 1964-66, Reigate, 1970-74, Surrey East, 1974-92; Secretary, Conservative Parliamentary Health and Social Security Committee, 1964-65; Opposition Front Bench Spokesman on labour and social services, 1965-66; (Latey) Interdepartmental Committee on Age of Majority, 1965-67; Deputy Chairman, Glamorgan Quarter Sessions, 1966-70; (Street) Committee on Racial Discrimination, 1967; (Cripps) Conservative Committee on Discrimination Against Women, 1968-69; Chair, Ely Hospital, Cardiff, Inquiry, 1969; Solicitor-General, 1970-72; Minister for Trade and Consumer Affairs, Department of Trade and Industry, 1972-74; Opposition front bench spokesman on social services, 1974-75, on Treasury and Economic Affairs, 1975-79; Director, Sun Alliance & London Insurance Co Ltd, 1974-79; AGB Research Ltd, 1974-79; EMI Ltd, 1976-79; Chancellor of the Exchequer, 1979-83; Chair, Interim Committee, IMF, 1982-83; Secretary of State, Foreign and Commonwealth Affairs, 1983-89; Lord President of the Council, Leader of House of Commons, Deputy Prime Minister, 1989-90; Visiting Fellow, John F Kennedy School of Government, Harvard University, 1991-92; Glaxo Holdings, 1991-95; Herman Phleger Visiting Professor, Stanford Law School, California, 1993; Glaxo Wellcome plc, 1995-96; BICC plc, 1991-97; Visitor, SOAS, University of London, 1991-2001; Special Adviser, International Affairs, Jones, Day, Reavis & Pogue, 1991-2001; Advisory Council, Bertelsmann Foundation, 1992-97; J P Morgan International Advisory Council, 1992-2001; Chair, Framlington Russian Investment Fund, 1994-2003; Chair, Steering Committee, Tax Law Rewrite Project, Inland Revenue, 1996-; Fuji Wolfensohn International European Advisory Board, 1996-98; Carlyle Group, European Advisory Board, 1997-2001; Fuji Bank International Advisory Council, 1999-. Publications: Conflict of Loyalty (memoirs), 1994; Various political pamphlets. Honours include: Grand Cross, Order of Merit (Portugal), 1987; Hon LLD, Wales, 1988; Honorary Freeman, Port Talbot, 1992; Grand Cross, Order of Merit, Germany, 1992; Life Peer, 1992; Hon DCL, City, 1993; Joseph Bech Prize, FVS Stifting, Hamburg, 1993; Companion of Honour, 1996; Order of Public Service, Ukraine, 2001. Memberships: International Advisory Council; Member, Council of Management, Private Patients' Plan, 1969-70; Honorary Vice President, 1974-92, President, 1992-, Association for Consumer Research; National Union of Conservative and Unionist Associations, 1983-84; Institute of International Studies, Stanford University, California, 1990-; Patron, Enterprise Europe, 1990-2004; Vice President: RUSI, 1991-; Joint President, Wealth of Nations Foundation, 1991-; Member, Advisory Council, Presidium of Supreme Rada of Ukraine, 1991-97; Member, Steering Committee, Project Liberty, 1991-97; Chair, Advisory Board, English Centre for Legal Studies, Warsaw University, 1992-99; Centre for European Policy Studies, 1992-; English College

Foundation in Prague, 1992-; GB China Centre, 1992-; Trustee: Cambridge Commonwealth Trust, 1993-; Cambridge Overseas Trust, 1993-; Paul Harris Fellow, Rotary International, 1995; Thomson Foundation, 1995-, Chair, 2004-; President, Academy of Experts, 1996-; Honorary Fellow: UCW, Swansea, 1996; President: Conservative Political Centre National Advisory Committee, 1997-79; Patron, UK Metric Association, 1999-; UCW, Cardiff, 1999; American Bar Foundation, 2000; Chartered Institute of Taxation, 2000; SOAS, 2003. Address: House of Lords, London SW1A 0PW, England.

**HOWELL David Arthur Russell (Lord Howell of Guildford),** b. 18 January 1936, London, England. Economist; Journalist; Author. m. Davina Wallace, 1 son, 2 daughters. Education: King's College, Foundation Scholar. Appointments: Member of Parliament for Guildford, 1966-97; Parliamentary Secretary, Civil Service Department, 1970-72; Minister of State, Northern Ireland, 1972-74; Secretary of State for Energy, 1979-81; Secretary of State for Transport, 1981-83; Chairman, House of Commons Foreign Affairs Select Committee, 1987-97; Chairman, UK-Japan 21st Century Group, 1989-2001; Visiting Fellow, Nuffield College, Oxford, 1991-99; Director, Monks Investment Trust, 1993-; Advisory Director, UBS Warburg, 1996-2000; Chairman, Lords European Committee, Sub-Committee, 1998-2000; Director, John Laing plc, 1999-2002; Trustee, Shakespeare Globe Theatre, 2000-; Chief Opposition Spokesman on Foreign Affairs, House of Lords, 2000-. Publications: Columnist: The Japan Times; Wall Street Journal; International Herald Tribune; Books: Freedom and Capital, 1979; Blind Victory, 1986; The Edge of Now, 2000; Numerous pamphlets and articles. Honours: Privy Counsellor, 1979; Created Peer of the Realm, 1997; Grand Cordon of the Order of the Sacred Treasure, Japan, 2001. Memberships: Beefsteak Club; County Club, Guildford. Address: House of Lords, London SW1A 0PW, England. E-mail: howelld@parliament.uk

**HOWELL Sister Veronica (formerly known as Sister Mary Aidan),** b. 23 May 1924, Woolwich, London, England. Educator. Education: Mount Pleasant Training College, Liverpool; Corpus Christi Theological College, London; Heythrop Theological College, London University; Licentiate of the Royal College of Music. Appointments: Became a member of the Congregation of the Daughters of Jesus, 1944; Teacher, Our Lady of Lourdes Convent School and Sacred Heart Infants School, Colne, Lancashire, 1946-51; Teacher, St Teresa's, Princes Risborough, Buckinghamshire, 1951-56; Teacher, St Stephen's Primary School, Welling, Kent, 1956-60; Teacher, Sts Thomas More and John Fisher Secondary School, Colne, Lancashire, 1960-63; Head Mistress, St Stephen's Primary School, Welling, Kent, 1963-75; Assistant to National Director and Training Officer of Catholic Information Services of England and Wales also helping to produce audio-visual material for spiritual retreats, 1975-79; Vocation's Director for the English Province of the Daughters of Jesus (Religious Congregation), 1979-84; Communications and Press Officer for female and male religious of England and Wales for the Pope's visit to England and Wales, 1982; Parish Assistant of Our Lady of Grace Parish, Governor of St Augustine's First and Middle School, Sister in Charge of Religious Community, High Wycombe, Buckinghamshire, Co-ordinator of Communications for Diocese of Northampton, Co-Editor of Diocesan newspaper, Member of Steering Committee winning the charter for a Christian radio station, 1986-92; Sister in Charge of Community and Parish Sister, Our Lady Help of Christians Parish, Rickmansworth, Hertfordshire, 1993-99; Parish Sister to Sacred Heart Church, Colne, Lancashire, 2000-; Governor of St Thomas More High School, 2001-. Publication: Founder and Co-editor "The Vine" newspaper, Northampton Diocese. Memberships: Congregation of the Daughters of Jesus;

Founder and Chairperson, Association of Christian Education, Welling, Kent, 1970-75; Co-Founder, Day Centre for Elderly Mentally Infirm, High Wycombe, Buckinghamshire, 1988-92; Caring Church Week Groups, 1979-84; Association of Head Teachers, 1963-75. Address: "Southworth", 6 Netherheys Close, Colne, Lancashire, England. E-mail: vghowell@yahoo.com

**HOWLETT Neville Stanley,** b. 17 April 1927, Prestatyn, Wales. Retired Air Vice-Marshal. m. Sylvia, 1 son, 1 daughter. Education: Liverpool Institute High School and Peterhouse, Cambridge, England. Appointments: Pilot Training, Royal Air Force, 1945-48; 32 and 64 Fighter Squadrons, 1948-56; RAF Staff College, 1957; Squadron Commander, 229 (Fighter) OCU, 1958-59; OC Flying Wing, RAF Coltishall, 1961-63; Directing staff, RAF Staff College, 1967-69; Station Commander, RAF Leuchars, 1970-72; Royal College of Defence Studies, 1973; Director of Operations, Air Defence and Overseas, 1973-74; Air Attaché, Washington DC, USA, 1975-77; Director, Management Support of Intelligence, 1978-80; Director General, Personal Services, 1980-82; Retired, 1982; Member, Lord Chancellors Panel of Independent Inquiry Inspectors, 1982-95; Member, Pensions Appeal Tribunal, 1988-2001. Honour: CB. Memberships: Royal Air Force Club; Royal Air Forces Association, Vice-President, 1984-, Chairman Executive Committee, 1990-97, Chairman Central Council, 1999-2001; Royal Air Force Benevolent Fund; Officers Association; Phyllis Court Club, Henley; Huntercombe Golf Club. Address: Milverton, Bolney Trevor Drive, Lower Shiplake, Oxon RG9 3PG, England.

**HOYLE Trevor,** b. 25 February 1940, Rochdale, England. Writer. m. 15 September 1962, 1 son, 1 daughter. Appointments: Panel Judge, Constable Novel Competition and Portico Literary Prize. Publications: Novels: The Relatively Constant Copywriters, 1972; The Adulterer, 1972; Rule of Night, 1975, 2003; Rock Fix, 1977; Seeking the Mythical Future, science fiction, 1977, 1982; Through the Eye of Time, science fiction, 1977, 1982; The Gods Look Down, science fiction, 1978, 1982; The Man Who Travelled on Motorways, 1979; Earth Cult, science fiction, 1979; The Stigma, 1980; Bullet Train, 1980; The Last Gasp, 1983, 1984, 1990; Vail, 1984, 1989; K.I.D.S., 1988, 1990; Blind Needle, 1994; Mirrorman, 1999. Contributions to: Short stories in: Transatlantic Review; Montrose Review; BBC Morning Story; New Fiction Society Magazine; New Yorkshire Writing; Fireweed; Double Space; Wordworks; Pennine Magazine; Artful Reporter; Ambit. Radio Drama: Conflagration; GIGO; Randle's Scandals; Haunted Hospital. Honours: Winner, Radio Times Drama Award, for Gigo radio play, 1991; Sony Best Actor Award, 1992; Winner, British Short Story, Transatlantic Review; Ray Mort Northern Novel Award. Membership: Society of Authors. Address: c/o Tanja Howarth 19 New Row, London, WC2N 4LA, England.

**HOZAWA Koji,** b. 8 August 1956, Morioka, Japan. Medical Doctor. m. Hiromi Hozawa, 1 son, 2 daughters. Education: MD, Tohoku University School of Medicine, Sendai Japan, 1975-81; Degree of Science, Tohoku University Graduate School of Medicine, Sendai, Japan, 1983-87; Research Fellow, Harvard Medical School, Boston, USA, 1986-88; Visiting Scholar, Washington University, Seattle, USA, 1992. Appointments: Assistant Professor, 1995-2001, Associate Professor, 2001-2002, Department of Otolaryngology, Tohoku University School of Medicine, Sendai, Japan; Chief Director, Department of Otolaryngology, Sendai Shakai Hoken Hospital, Sendai, Japan, 2002-; Visiting Lecturer, Department of Otolaryngology, Chinese Medical School, Shenyang, China, 1997-2000; Lecturer, Japan International Co-operation Agency, Tokyo, Japan, 1997-2000; Authorised Researcher, Ministry of Health and

Welfare of Japan, 1999-2001; Secretary General, International Symposium on Recent Advances in Otitis Media, 1998-2000. Publications: Numerous articles in scientific journals include most recently: Hearing and glycoconjugates, 1993; Sympathetic and CGRP-positive nerve supply to the endolymphatic sac of guinea pig, 1993; Pathogenesis of attic cholesteatoma, 1999; Is Cholesteatoma a Cytokine Disease? – in vitro Model of Cholesteatoma, 2002; Editor, Recent Advances in Otitis Media: Proceedings of Otitis Media 2001, 2001. Honours: Silver Prize, Tohoku University School of Medicine Scholarship, 1988; Listed in Who's Who publications and biographical dictionaries. Memberships: International Otopathology Society; Otolaryngological Society of Japan, Member Public Relations Section, 1997-2002, Journal Reviewer, 2004-; Japanese Bronchoesophageal Society, Councillor, 2004-; Otological Society of Japan, Secretary General, 1997-98; Japan Society of Stomato-Pharyngology, Secretary General, 1998-99; Japan Society for Equilibrium Research, Committee, 2001-2003; Japan Society of Laryngology. Address: Sendai Shakai Hoken Hospital, 3-16-1 Tsutsumi-machi, Aoba-ku, Sendai 981-8501, Japan.

**HOZUMI Motoo,** b. 12 March 1933, Fukushima, Japan. Cancer Research. m. Sakiko Wakabayashi, 1 son, 2 daughters. Education: BSc, 1956, MSc, 1958, DSc, 1961, Tokyo University of Education. Appointments: Research Member, National Cancer Center Research Institute, Tokyo, 1962-64; Chief, Central Laboratory, National Cancer Center Research Institute, Tokyo, 1964-75; Research Member, Roswell Park Memorial Institute, Buffalo, New York, 1965-67; Director, Department of Chemotherapy, Saitama Cancer Center Research Institute, Japan, 1975-93; Visiting Professor, Showa University School of Medicine, Tokyo, 1988-2001; Director, Saitama Cancer Center Research Institute, 1990-93. Publications: Over 300 papers and books on cancer research. Honours: Princess Takamatsu Cancer Research Foundation Prize, Tokyo, 1974. Memberships: Japanese Cancer Association; Japanese Haematological Society; American Cancer Association; American Association for the Advancement of Science. Address: 12-288 Fukasaku, Minuma, Saitama, Saitama 337, Japan.

**HŘIB Jiří Emil,** b. 16 September 1942, Frýdek-Místek, Czech Republic. Plant Physiologist. m. Marie Malá, 16 January 1970, 1 daughter. Education: Engineer, 1966, PhD, 1973, University of Agriculture, Brno (now Mendel University of Agriculture and Forestry, Brno). Appointments: Scientist Aspirant, Scientific Film Laboratory, Institute of Scientific Instruments, 1967-73, Scientist, Institute of Vertebrate Zoology, 1973-74, Scientist, Institute of Botany, 1974-83, Scientist, Institute of Experimental Phytotechnics, 1984-87, Scientist, Institute of Systematic and Ecological Biology, 1987-91, Czechoslovak Academy of Sciences, Brno; Scientist, Institute of Plant Genetics, 1991-97, Principal Scientist, Institute of Plant Genetics and Biotechnology, 1997-98, External Scientific Co-worker, Institute of Plant Genetics and Biotechnology, 1999-, Slovak Academy of Sciences, Nitra. Publications: Over 100 articles in professional scientific journals; The Co-Cultivation of Wood-Rotting Fungi with Tissue Cultures of Forest Tree Species, 1990; Research films: (author) Ontogeny of the Alga Scenedesmus quadricauda, 1973; Co-author, Regeneration of the Cap in the Alga Acetabularia mediterranea, 1980. Honours: Research Board of Advisors, American Biographical Institute, 1999; Consulting Editor, Contemporary Who's Who, 2003. Memberships: Czech Society for Scientific Cinematography, Brno, 1965; Czech Botanical Society, Prague, 1967; International Association for Plant Tissue Culture and Biotechnology, 1990; International Association of Sexual Plant Reproduction Research, 1993; New York Academy of Sciences, 2001; Czechoslovak Biological

Society, Brno, 2001; Czech Algological Society, Prague, 2002. Address: Ukrajinská 17, 625 00 Brno, Czech Republic.

**HRIBERNIK Božidar,** b. 6 November 1934, Maribor, Slovenia. Professor. m. Levina, 2 daughters. Education: Dipl. Ing., University of Ljubljana, 1957-62; MSc, University of Zagreb, 1974; Dr. Sc., University of Ljubljana, 1982. Appointments: Designer, Telephone and Lighting Appliances, 1954-57; Instructor University of Ljubljana, 1959-61; Engineering Analyst, Elektrokovina Corporation, Maribor, 1962-68; Contract Lecturer, Higher School of Engineering, Maribor, 1963-68, 1970-76; Head Development Department, Elektrokovina Corporation, 1968-74; Manager, TSN Corporation, Maribor, 1974-76; Lecturer, 1976-83, Head of Electrical Power Engineering Institute, 1980-99, Head of Research Section, 1982-86, Associate Professor, 1983-88, Vice Dean, 1983-87, Faculty of Technical Sciences, University of Maribor; Full Professor, Faculty of Technical Sciences and Department of Electrical Engineering, Computer Science and Information Technology, University of Maribor 1988-99; Dean, Department of Electrical Engineering, Computer Science and Information Technology, 1997-1999; Professor Emeritus, 2000-. Publications: Numerous articles and papers in scientific journals and conference proceedings; Book chapters and scientific reports. Memberships: member of the Committee for Economy and Technology of the Chamber of Commerce of Slovenia, 1975-80; Electrical Engineering Society of Slovenia, Honorary Member, 2000; Senior Member, IEEE; Member Senate University of Maribor; Member of the Council of Higher Education of the Government of Slovenia; Member of the Committee for Nominations in Higher Education of the Government of Slovenia. Address: University of Maribor, Faculty of Technical Sciences, Department of Electrical Engineering, Computer Science and Information Technology, Smetanova ulica 17, SI-2000 Maribor, Slovenia.

**HRIŞCĂ Traian-Eugen,** b. 4 February 1929, Baia Mare, Romania. Artist. m. (1) Ortansa Coatu, (2) Maria-Rozalia Hutter, 1 son, 1 daughter, (3) Corina-Cătălina Ciornei. Education: Graduate, Nicolae Grigorescu Institute of Arts, Bucharest, 1957; Studies with: Adina Paula Moscu, Ion Marsic, Toni Gheorgiu, Schweitzer-Cumpăna, Sigfried, Camil Ressu, Alexandru Ciucurencu. Career: Professional Artist, 1957-; High School Teacher, Baia Mare, 1961-63; President, Baia Mare branch of the Artist's Union, 1968-70; Member Artist's Union National Committee, 1970-73; Research trip to Holland, 1983; Associate Professor, Painting and Mural Art, University of the North, 2000-. Exhibitions include: State Annual Exhibition, Bucharest, 1956; Prague, 1956; Berlin, 1964; Baia Mare Art Museum (solo exhibition), 1975; Svijndrecht, Holland, 1983; The Hague, Holland (solo exhibition), 1983; Drouot-Richelieu Gallery, Paris, 1993; Retrospective Exhibition, Painter's Colony, Baia Mare, 1997; National Art Museum, Cluj-Napoca (solo exhibition), 1997; National Art Salon, Bucharest, 2001; Baia Mare Centennial, 2003; Satu Mare County Exhibition, 2003. Major works include: Paintings: Toilers in the Harbour, 1956; The Dacians, 1967; Sacrifice, 1968; Fertility, 1968, Permanence, 1968; Ritual, 1970; Sunflower, 1971; Vineyard Harvesting, 1974; Simple Chrysanthemums, Dahlias, Daisies, Apple-Tree Flowers, Apricot Tree Flowers, 1974-75; Maramures Landscape, 1977; Village Street, 1981; Reflection Space, 1982; On the River Iza, 1990; Marine Landscape, 1990; Childhood Village, 1996; The Old Mint, 2001; Across the River Mures, 2003; Others: Marble and travertine decorative panels mounted on some of the interior walls of the Bucharest Hotel Restaurant, Baia Mare, 1970; The Roosters Singing, collage tapestry curtain in the former Youth House of Culture, Baia Mare, 1973; Floor and pavement round the artesian well by the terrace of the Bucharest

Hotel Restaurant, 1973. Honours: Member, Szabolcs-Szatmar-Bereg Section of the Hungarian Academy of Sciences, 1994; Man of the Year, 2003, World Medal of Honor, 2003, American Biographical Institute. Membership: Romanian Artists Union. Address: c/o Uniunea Artistilor Plastici, Filiala Baia Mare, Str Victoriei Nr 21, Baia Mare 4800, Romania.

**HSIEH Ching-Liang,** b. 26 August 1951, Tainan City, Taiwan. Professor; Medical Doctor. m. Li-Chun Tsai, 2 sons. Education: Medical Bachelor, School of Chinese Medicine, China Medical College, Taichung, Taiwan, 1971-78; PhD, Medical Science, Department of Clinical Neurophysiology, Neurological Institute, Faculty of Medicine, Kyushu University, Fukuoka, Japan, 1991-95; Doctor of Philosophy, Acupuncture and Moxibustion Massage Institute, Guangzhou Chinese Medicine University, Guangzhou, China, 2001-2004. Appointments: Associate Professor, 1995-2000, Head, School of Chinese Medicine, 1996-2000, Director, Institute of Chinese Medical Science, 1997-2000, China Medical College, Taichung, Taiwan; Professor, Graduate Institute of Traditional Chinese Medicine, Chang Gung University, Taoyuan, Taiwan, 2000-2001; Professor, Attending Physician, Chang Gung Memory Hospital, Taoyuan, Taiwan, 2000-2001; Attending Physician, 2001-, Vice-President, 2002-, China Medical University Hospital, Taichung, Taiwan; Professor, Institute of Integration Chinese and Western Medicine, China Medical University, Taichung, Taiwan, 2002-. Publications: Articles in medical journals as co-author include: The interaction of somatosensory evoked potentials to simultaneous fingers stimuli in the human central nervous system. A study using direct recordings, 1995; Anticonvulsive and free radical scavenging actions of two herbs, Uncaria Rhynchophylla (MIQ) Jack and Gastrodia Elata BL, in kainic acid-treated rats, 1999; Anticonvulsive and free radical scavenging activities of vanillyl alcohol in ferric chloride-Induced epileptic seizures in Sprague-dawley rats, 2000. Honours: Class A Research Award, National Science Council, 2000; Excellent Doctor, China Medical University Hospital, 2002, 2004; Hong-Yen Hsu Traditional Chinese Medicine Academy Award, 2004; Listed in Who's Who publications and biographical dictionaries. Memberships: Taiwan Neurological Society; Taiwan Society of Internal Medicine; Society for Integration Chinese and Western Medicine, Republic of China. Address: No 2 Yuh Der Road, Taichung, Taiwan, ROC. E-mail: clhsieh@www.cmuh.org.tw

**HTANG Aung,** b. 4 November 1956, Matupi, Chin State, Burma. Dentist; Dental Researcher. m. Martha, 2 sons, 2 daughters. Education: BDS, 1982; PhD, Operative Dentistry, Nagasaki University, Japan, 1996. Appointments: Private Dental Practitioner, 1983-85; Civil Dental Surgeon, State Hospitals, 1985-1991; State Scholar, Japanese Ministry of Education, 1991-96; Lecturer, Institute of Dental Medicine, Yangon, 1996-; Founder, Matupi Baptist Church, Yangon. Publications: Fatigue Resistance of Composite Restorations, 1995; 6 research papers; 4 review articles; 3 case reports. Memberships: International Association for Dental Research; Myanmar Dental Association. Address: 36/801 Mahuya Street, North Dagon New Town, Yangon (Rangoon), Myanmar.

**HTILAR SITTHU (His Excellency U Soe Nyunt),** b. 1932, Shwe Sitthi village, Meikhtila Township, Mandalay Division, Myanmar. Poet. m. Hla Yin Yin Daw, 3 sons, 5 daughters. Appointments: Poet since the age of 14; Army Officer to Lieutenant Colonel, 1950-82; Organiser, National Literary conference, KabaAye Hillock, Yangon, 1964-88; Chairman, Myanmar Literary and Periodicals Association Central Executives, 1989-93; Deputy Minister for Information, 1992; Deputy Minister for Culture, Vice Chairman of the Performing

Arts Competition, central Working Committee, Chairman of the Armed Forces Day Commemorative Poetry and Arts Competitions Working Committee, 1993-. Publications: More than 1,000 poems and 1,500 articles in Myanmar; Work translated into English, Russian, French, German, Chinese and Japanese; Over 40 books, including: 18 books of poetry, 11 novels and 11 works of literary criticism; Recent works include: The Nector of Lotus, 1997; My Beloved Mee from Nickinci of Yugoslavia, novelettes and short stories, 1997; Myanmar Classical Poetry, 1998; The Epic Poems of the Conquering of Hlaing Gyi Island and Pannwa, 1999; I Shall Never Forget Him, novelettes and short stories, 1999; My Precious Pearl, 2002; Keep on Flowing Ayeyarwady, epic novel; Poetry includes: Ayeyarwady and Yansi Sing the Friendship Song, 2000; Anthology of Htilar Sitthu's poems, 2001; Sweet Odour Padauk and Dokchampa, 2002; Several Rivers and Mountains Bringing about Nostalgia, epic poems, 2002; Critiques and research papers on classical and 20th century Myanmar poetry; Review of Myanmar modern history. Honours: Winner of President Marshall Tito's Military Medal Degree, 1954; Sarpay Beikman Literary Prize for Poetry, 1962; Medal for Excellent Performance in Administrative Field, First Class, Myanmar, 1991; National Literacy Award, 1992; The Great Poet Laureate, 1996; Honourable Member, Min-on Concert Association, Japan, 2000; Literary Messenger of Friendship, Writers Association of the People's Republic of China, 2001; Medal for Public Service; Medal for State Peace and Tranquillity; Medal for Law and Order Restoration; Listed in national biographical reference works. Memberships: Patron, Myanmar Music Association; Chairman, ASEAN Leading Committee on Culture and Information (COCI); Executive Member, Myanmar Women's Association. Address: Deputy Minister, Ministry of Culture, 131 Kaba Aye Pagoda Road, Kokkine Junction, Bahan Township, Yangon, Union of Myanmar.

**HU David Chung Kuen,** b. 2 February 1954, Hong Kong. Cardiologist. Education: BSc, summa cum laude, University of Minnesota, USA, 1975; MD, Washington University, USA, 1979. Appointments: Clinical Fellow, Mayo Graduate School of Medicine, Rochester, Minnesota, USA, 1982-85; Clinical Instructor, 1985-86, Clinical Assistant Professor, 1986-, University of British Columbia, Vancouver, British Columbia, Canada; Staff Cardiologist, Vancouver General Hospital, 1986-; Consultant Cardiologist, Health Sciences Centre Hospital, Vancouver, 1986-. Publications: Co-author of over 20 publications in scientific medical journals and conference proceedings including: Atrial Septal Defect in elderly patients, 1984; Effect of alpha and beta adrenergic stimulation on atrial natriuretic peptide release in vitro, 1988; Effects of dietary magnesium on atrial natriuretic peptide (ANP) release, 1990; Modulation of ANF release with dietary magnesium, 1990. Honours: Merck Award, Washington University, 1979; Best Clinical Paper, Vancouver General Hospital, 1986; Several research grants; Listed in several biographical dictionaries and Who's Who publications. Memberships: Fellow, Royal College of Physicians of Canada, Fellow, American College of Cardiology; Member, British Columbia Medical Association; Member, Royal College of Surgeons, England; Member, Canadian Medical Association; Member, British Columbia Cardiac Society; Member, Canadian Cardiovascular Society. Address: Rm 1513, Galleria Building, No 9 Queens Road, Central Hong Kong, China. E-mail: dhu@workmail.com

**HUAN Vu Duong,** b. 24 August 1949, Hai Duong, Vietnam. University Professor; Diplomat. m. Lê Thi Minh, 3 daughters. Education: BA (Hons with distinction), History State University of Voronejo, Former Soviet Union, 1968-73; PhD, International Relations, Institute of International Relations, National Academy of Bulgaria, 1981-85. Appointments: Dean, International Relations Department, University of Diplomacy, Hanoi; 1988-92; Participated in Conflict Resolution course, Uppsala University, Sweden, 1992; Vice-Director General, Institute for International Relations, 1992-95; Ambassador of Vietnam to Poland, 1995-98; Director General , Institute for International Relations, 1998-2002; Editor-in-Chief, International Studies Magazine, 1998-2002; Chairman, CSCAP Vietnam, 1998-2002; Vice-Chairman, Research Council of MOFA Vietnam, 1998-; Chairman of Asian ISIS, 2002; Ambassador of Vietnam to Ukraine and Moldova, 2002-; Elected real member, International Personnel Academy, Kiev, 2002. Publications: Author and co-author of 8 books; Co-author, Vietnamese Encyclopaedia, 4 volumes; Author of 45 articles: Diplomatic Dictionary, 2001; Political System of the USA, 2001; Political System of the Russian Federation, 2001; Diplomacy in Ho Chi Minh's Thought; Relations between USA and Big Powers in Asia-Pacific Region, 2003; History of Vietnam's Diplomacy 1975-2001, 2003; Speciality of Vietnam-Laos Relations, 2003; Diplomacy in Ho Chi Minhs Thought, 2005. Honours: Medal of Achievements in Vietnam Diplomacy; Medal of Achievements in Trade Union of Vietnam. Membership: Labour Union of Vietnam. Address: NGO 1194/12, Duong Lang, Dong Da, Hanoi, Vietnam. E-mail: lehiminh49@hotmail.com

**HUANG Christopher,** b. 28 December 1951, Singapore. Professor of Cell Physiology. Education: BA (Oxford), The Queen's College, Oxford, 1971-74; BM BCh (Oxford), Oxford University Clinical School, 1974-76; Medical Research Council Scholar, Physiological Laboratory and Gonville and Caius College, Cambridge, 1978-79; PhD (Cambridge), 1980; DM (Oxford), 1985; MD (Cambridge), 1986; DSc (Oxford), 1995; ScD (Cambridge), 1995. Appointments: Pre-registration appointments, Nuffield Department of Medicine, University of Oxford, 1977-78; University Demonstrator in Physiology, 1979-84; Fellow and College Lecturer in Physiology, 1979-, Director of Studies in Medical Sciences, 1981-, Professorial Fellow, 2002-, New Hall, Cambridge; University Lecturer in Physiology, 1984-96, University Reader in Cellular Physiology, 1996-2002, University Professor of Cell Physiology, 2002-, Cambridge; Several visiting professorships, 1984-2004. Publications: Monographs and books: Intramembrane charge movements in striated muscle, 1993; Applied Physiology for Surgery and Critical Care (co-editor), 1995; Research in medicine. A guide to writing a thesis in the medical sciences (co-author), 1999; Molecular and cellular biology of bone (co-editor), 1998; 170 scientific papers in medical journals. Honours: Florence Heale Open Scholar, The Queen's College, Oxford, 1971-76; President's Scholar, Republic of Singapore, 1971-76; Benefactor's Prize, The Queen's College, Oxford, 1973; Brian Johnson Prize in Pathology, University of Oxford, 1976; LEPRA Award, British Leprosy Relief Association, 1977; Rolleston Memorial Prize for Physiological Research, University of Oxford, 1980; Gedge Prize in Physiology, University of Cambridge, 1981. Memberships: Physiological Society, UK; Research Defence Society, UK; American Society of General Physiologists, USA; Biophysical Society, USA; Association of Bone and Mineral Research, USA; Ordinary Member of Council, 1994-, Biological Secretary, 2000-, Cambridge Philosophical Society. Address: New Hall, Huntingon Road, Cambridge CB3 0DF, England.

**HUANG Dongzhou,** b. 5 November 1949, Ruijin, China. Scientist; Educator, Civil Engineer. m. Yingying Shu, 1 son. Education: BS, Civil Engineering, 1974; MS, Civil Engineering, 1985; PhD, Structural Engineering, 1989. Appointment: Professor, Civil Engineering, Fuzhou University; Senior Research Scientist, Structural Research Center, FDOT, USA;

Developed finite element methods for analyzing elastic and inelastic lateral buckling of trussed-arch bridges; Developed methods for analyzing dynamic/impact factors of various types of bridges due to moving vehicles; Found basic relationships between static and dynamic responses as well as between impact factor and lateral distribution factor; Developed a practical method for determining lateral load distribution factors of arch and beam bridges, a load capacity rating method of bridges through field test and a shear reinforcement design method for prestressed concrete beam anchorage zones; Developed a design method of end zone reinforcement for precast-prestressed concrete beams and a bridge load rating method through field test. Publications: Over 50 papers in professional journals, 2 books. Honour: 1st Prize, Best Publications. Memberships: ASCE; New York Academy of Sciences; American Association for the Advancement of Science. Address: 5416 Moores Mill Road, Tallahassee, FL 32309, USA

**HUBALEK Zdenek,** b. 22 August 1942, Brno, Czech Republic. Research Microbiologist. m. Dagmar, 2 daughters. Education: MS, Biology, 1964, RNDr, 1970, University of Brno; PhD, 1972, DSc, 1987, Academy of Sciences, Prague. Appointments: Research Assistant, Institute of Fodder Research, 1964-66; Research Assistant, Institute of Parasitology, Academy of Sciences, Prague, 1966-83; Principal Research Worker, Institute of Systematic and Ecological Biology, Institute of Landscape Ecology, Institute of Vetrebrate Biology, Academy of Sciences, Brno, 1984-; Associate Professor, Masaryk University, Brno, 1999-. Publications: 250 scientific articles on the ecology of pathogenic microorganisms which are arthropod-borne; numerical classifications; medical zoology; 1 book: Cryopreservation of Microorganisms, 1996. Honour: J E Purkyne Medal for Achievements in Biology, Czech Academy of Sciences, Prague. Memberships: Czech Scientific Societies of: Biology; Microbiology; Mycology; Zoology; International Society of Vector Ecology. Address: Medical Zoology Laboratory, Institute of Vetrebrate Biology, Academy of Sciences, Klasterni 2, CZ-69142 Valtice, Czech Republic. E-mail: zhubalek@brno.cas.cz

**HUBEL David Hunter,** b. 27 February 1926, Ontario, Canada. Neurophysiologist. m. S Ruth Izzard, 1953, 3 sons. Education: Graduated, Medicine, McGill University, Montreal, Canada. Appointments: Professor of Neurophysiology, Harvard Medical School, 1965-67; George Packer Berry Professor of Physiology and Chairman, Department of Physiology, 1967-68; George Packer Berry Professor of Neurobiology, 1968-92; John Franklin Enders University Professor, 1982-; George Eastman Professor, University of Oxford, 1991-92; First Annual George A Miller Lecture, Cognitive Neuroscience Society, 1995; Worked on the physiology of vision and the way in which the brain processes visual information. Publications: Eye, Brain and Vision, 1987; Articles in scientific journals. Honours: Lewis S Rosenstiel Award for Basic Medical Research, 1972; Friedenwald Award, 1975; Karl Spencer Lashley Prize, 1977; Louisa Gross Horwitz Prize, 1978; Dickson Prize in Medicine, 1979; Society of Scholars, Johns Hopkins University, 1980; Ledlie Prize, 1980; Joint Winner, Nobel Prize for Physiology or Medicine, 1981; New England Ophthalmological Society Award, 1983; Paul Kayser International Award of Merit in Retina Research, 1989; City of Medicine Award, 1990; Gerald Award, 1993; Charles F Prentice Medal, 1993; Helen Keller Prize, 1995. Memberships: NAS; Leopoldina Academy, Board of Syndics, Harvard University Press; Foreign Member, Royal Society, London; Senior Fellow, Harvard Society of Fellows; Fellow, American Academy of Arts and Sciences. Address: Department of Neurobiology, Harvard Medical School, 220 Longwood Avenue, Boston, MA 02115, USA.

**HUCKER Hazel Zoë,** b. 7 August 1937, London, England. Writer. m. Michael Hucker, 7 January 1961, 1 son, 1 daughter. Education: BSc, (Econ), London School of Economics and Political Science, 1960. Appointments: Economics and History Teacher, 1972-78; Justice of the Peace, Winchester City, 1980-90; Justice of the Peace, West London Magistrates, 1992-98; Writer, Novelist, 1992-. Publications: The Aftermath of Oliver, 1993; A Dangerous Happiness, 1994; Cousin Susannah, 1995; Trials of Friendship, 1996; The Real Claudia Charles, 1998; Changing Status, 2000. Address: c/o Kingston Crown Court, 6-8 Penryn Road, Kingston KT1 2BB, England.

**HUCKNALL Mick,** 8 June 1960, Manchester, England. Singer; Songwriter. Career: Formed early band, Frantic Elevators, 1979; Formed Simply Red, essentially a solo career with changing band members; Numerous hit singles, television appearances; Numerous tours and festival dates worldwide; Founder, Blood and Fire label, dedicated to vintage reggae tracks. Recordings: Singles: Money's Too Tight to Mention; Come To My Aid; Holding Back the Years; Jericho; Open Up The Red Box; Ev'ry Time We Say Goodbye; The Right Thing; Infidelity; Maybe Some Day; Ev'ry Time We say Goodbye; I Won't Feel Bad; It's Only Love; If You Don't Know Me By Now; A New Flame; You've Got It; Something Got Me Started; Stars; For Your Babies; Thrill Me; Your Mirror; Fairground; Remembering The First Time; Never Never Love; We're In This Together; Angel; Nightnurse; Say You Love Me; The Air That I Breathe; Ghetto Girl; Ain't That a Lot of Love; Your Eyes; Sunrise; Albums: Picture Book, 1985; Early Years, 1987; Men and Women, 1987; A New Flame, 1989; Stars, 1991; 12"ers, 1995; Life, 1995; Fairground, 1995; Greatest Hits, 1996; Blue, 1998; Love and the Russian Winter, 1999; It's Only Love (greatest hits), 2000; Home, 2003. Address: PO Box 20197, London, W10 6YQ, England.

**HUDÁK Ondrej,** b. 23 April 1953, Michalovce, Slovak Republic. Lecturer; Physicist; Capital Market Consultant. m. Tatianna Hudáková, 1 son, 1 daughter. Education: Theoretical Physics, 1971-76, RNDr, Theoretical Physics, 1981, DrSc, Physics, 1985, Charles University, Prague; Bratislava International Commodity Exchange and The International Financial Services Institute, 1994. Appointments: Scientist, Safarik University, Kosice, 1978-79; Postgraduate, Institute of Physics, Academy of Sciences, Prague, 1979-82; Scientist, Solid State Physics, Institute of Experimental Physics, Kosice, 1982-90; Scientist, Institute of Physics, Czech Academy of Sciences, Prague, 1990-96; Lecturer, Faculty of Finance, Bel's University, 1997-; Scientist, Faculty of Mathematics and Physics, Comenius University, Bratislava, 1998; Scientist, Faculty of Materials and Technologies, Slovak Technical University, Bratislava, 1999-2001; Capital Market Consultant, 1994-. Publications include: Technical Analysis and Our Capital Markets, Brno, 1994; Technical Analysis, Banskà Bystrica, 1999; Portfolio Analysis, Banska Bystrica, 2004; Various scientific papers on physics; Various capital market papers. Honours: Award from Czechoslovak Academy of Science, 1981; Alexander von Humboldt-Stiftung Award, 1992; Who's Who in the World, 1998, 1999, 2000, 2001. Memberships: Slovak Physical Society; European Physical Society; Slovak Statistical and Demographical Society; Slovak Genealogical Heraldic Society; Society of Saint Vojtech; CS TUG Society. Address: Stierova 23, SK-04011 Košice, Slovak Republic. E-mail: hudako@mail.pvt.sk

**HUDIK Martin Francis,** b. 27 March 1949, Chicago, Illinois, USA. Business Manager. m. Eileen Mary Abraham, 1 daughter. Education: Associate of Arts and Science, Morton College, 1969; Bachelor of Science, Mechanical and Aerospace

Engineering, Illinois Institute of Technology, 1971; Bachelor of Public Administration, Jackson State University, 1974; Master of Business Administration, Loyola University of Chicago, 1975. Appointments: Assistant Administrator, Illinois Masonic Medical Center, 1969-94; Facilities Manager, Advocate Bethany Hospital, 1997-98; Business Manager, St Bernardine Parish, 2001-; Auxiliary Captain, Cicero Police Department, 1971-99. Publications: Various. Honours: Awards from the Town of Cicero: Meritorious Service Award, Medal of Merit, Police Achievement Award, Emergency Services Achievement Award; AAL Presidential Sports Award, 1978, 1980, 1981, 2000. Special Service Award, Underwriters Laboratories, 1992; Special Service Award, Cook County Sheriffs, 1993; Excellence in Service Award,1997, Outstanding Effort Award, 1998, Recognition Award, 1999; Outstanding Performance Award, 2001; Outstanding Volunteer Award, 2003. Memberships: Knights of Columbus; Masons. Address: 2116 South 51 Court, Cicero, IL 60804, USA.

**HUDSON Anthony Bruce Edward,** b. 11 October 1938, London, England. Schoolmaster. m. Elizabeth Clare Willis, 1 son, 2 daughters. Education: Grenoble University, 1958-59; MA, Modern History, Lincoln College, Oxford, 1959-62; Dip. Ed., Institute of Education, London University, 1962-63. Appointments: Head of English, La Roseraie, Dieulefit, France, 1963-64; Radley College, 1964-88, Housemaster, 1970-84, Sub-Warden, 1980-88, Acting Warden, 1986; Headmaster, Pangbourne College, 1988-2000. Publication: Just to See His Name, 2002. Honour: MBE. Memberships: Skinners' Company, Master 2004-2005; Vincents; Harlequins Rugby Football Club; MCC; Huntercombe Golf Club. Address: Howgate Boathouse, Cleeve Road, Goring on Thames RG8 9BT, England.

**HUDSON Christopher,** b. 29 September 1946, England. Writer. m. Kirsty McLeod, 10 March 1978, 1 son. Education: Scholar, Jesus College, Cambridge. Appointments: Editor, Faber & Faber, 1968; Literary Editor, The Spectator, 1971, The Standard, 1981; Editorial Page Editor, The Daily Telegraph, 1992. Publications: Overlord, 1975; The Final Act, 1980; Insider Out, 1982; The Killing Fields, 1984; Colombo Heat, 1986; Playing in the Sand, 1989; Spring Street Summer, 1993. Address: Little Dane, Biddenden, Kent TN27 8JT, England.

**HUDSON Harry Robinson,** b. 18 November 1929, Kingston-upon-Hull, England. Emeritus Professor of Chemistry. m. Jacqueline Ruth Feeney, 2 sons, 2 daughters. Education: BSc (Special) Honours, Chemistry, External Student of London University at Hull Municipal Technical College, 1949; ARIC by Examination; PhD, Organic Chemistry, London University, 1960; DSc (London), 1976. Appointments: National Service, Education Branch, Technical Training Command, Royal Air Force, 1949-51; Research and Development Chemist, Distillers Company Ltd, Chemical Division, Hull, 1951-58; Research Assistant, 1958-60, Full-time Member of Academic Staff, 1961-94, Reader in Chemistry, 1969, Professor, 1990-94, Emeritus Professor, 1995-, Northern Polytechnic (subsequently The Polytechnic of North London, University of North London, London Metropolitan University); Consultant: Dermal Laboratories Ltd, 1977-87; KenoGard AB, Stockholm, 1987-91; British Technology Group, 1989-92. Publications: Book: Aminophosphonic and Aminophosphinic Acids: Chemistry and Biological Activity (co-editor), 2000; Author or co-author of 6 book chapters and over 100 research publications and review articles. Honours: Fellow Royal Society of Chemistry, 1964; Honorary Research Fellow, University College, London, 1979-80; Visiting Lecturer, Royal Holloway College, University of London, 1979-82; Medal, Organophosphorous Chemistry, University of Lódz, Poland, 1996. Membership:

Royal Society of Chemistry. Address: Department of Health and Human Sciences, London Metropolitan University, 166-220 Holloway Road, London N7 8DB, England. E-mail: harryrhudson@aol.com

**HUDSON Lucian,** b. 5 July 1960, London, England. Professional Communicator. m. Margaret Prythergch. Education: St Catherine's College, Oxford, 1979-83. Appointments: 16 years in television and radio as Producer, Editor and Senior Executive, BBC and ITV; Director of e-Communications, Cabinet Office, then Deputy Director of Communications, Ministry of Agriculture, Farming and Fisheries, 2000-2001; Director of Communications, Department for Environment, Food and Rural Affairs, 2001-2004; Director of Communications, Department for Constitutional Affairs, 2004-; UK's Official Spokesperson, World Summit on Sustainable Development, Johannesburg and at CAP Reform negotiations, Luxembourg; Chairman, Tavistock Institute; Former Chairman, The Rory Peck Trust. Publications: Talks and presentations on strategic communications, reputation and crisis management, collaboration and negotiation. Honour: MA (Hons). Membership: Chartered Institute of Public Relations. Address: DCA, Selborne House, 54 Victoria Street, London SW1E 6QW, England.

**HUET Denise,** b. 2 February 1931, Nancy, France. Professor Emeritus. Education: Agregation de Mathematiques, 1954; Doctorat d'etat en Mathematiques, Paris, 1959. Appointments: Attachee de Recherche, Centre National de la Recherche Scientifique, Paris, 1955-59; Professor, Faculty of Sciences, Dijon, 1959-66; Visiting Professor, Georgetown University, USA, 1966-67; Visiting Professor, Professor, University of Maryland, USA, 1967-72; Professeur à la l'Université de Nancy I, France, 1972-94; Professor Emeritus, 1994-. Publications: Many publications. Honours: Woman of the Year, American Biographical Institute, 1996; 2000 Millennium Medal of Honor. Memberships: American Mathematical Society; Societe Mathematique de France. Address: 86 Rue Felix Faure, 54000 Nancy, France.

**HUGHES Barry Peter,** b. 29 August 1932, Wolverhampton, England. Professor. m. Pamela Anne Barker, 1 son, 2 daughters. Education: BSc honours, 1953, PhD, 1956, Civil Engineering, University of Birmingham. Appointments: Assistant Civil Engineer, Concrete Engineer, Berkeley Power Station, 1956-59; Civil Engineer, Planning Engineer, John Laing Construction Ltd, 1959-62; Lecturer, 1962-68, Senior Lecturer, 1968-73, Professor of Civil Engineering, 1974-95, Emeritus Professor, 1995-, University of Birmingham; Private Consulting, Concrete and Concrete Structures, 1989-; Visiting Professor, University of Coventry, 1999-. Publications: Numerous research and technical papers on concrete and concrete structures; 2 books. Honours: Reader in Concrete Technology, 1971, DSc, 1972, DEng, 1990, Emeritus Professor, 1995, University of Birmingham. Memberships: Institution of Civil Engineers; Institution of Structural Engineers; Concrete Society. Address: Long Barn, 8 Parkfields, Arden Drive, Dorridge, Solihull, West Midlands, B93 8LL, England. E-mail: bphughes@onetel.net.uk

**HUGHES Christopher Wyndham,** b. 22 November 1941, Ipswich, Suffolk. Solicitor. m. Gail, 3 sons. Education: LL.B. Honours, University College, London, 1960-63; College of Law, London, 1963-64. Appointments: Solicitor then Partner, 1970, Wragge & Co; Managing Partner, Wragge & Co, 1993-95; Head of International Wragge & Co LLP, 2004-; Notary Public; Non-executive roles: Board Member, Severn Trent Water Authority, 1982-84; Chairman, Newman Tonks Group PLC, 1995-97; Member, Board of the Pension Protection Fund, 2004-. Publications: Former Member, Editorial Board, The Guide to

Professional Conduct of Solicitors. Honour: LL.B. (London), 1963. Membership: Warwickshire County Cricket Club. Address: Cuttle Pool Farm, Cuttle Pool Lane, Knowle, Solihull, West Midlands B93 0AP, England. Website: www.wragge.com

**HUGHES Frances Mary Theresa,** b. 15 June 1954, Richmond, Surrey, England. Solicitor. m. Jonathan Buckeridge, 2 sons, 1 daughter. Education: MA (Oxon), St Anne's College, Oxford. Appointments: Articles at Theodore Goddard, 1979-81, Solicitor at Theodore Goddard, 1981-83; Partner and Head of Family Department, Bates, Wells and Braithwaite, 1983-2001; Senior Partner, Hughes Fowler Carruthers Solicitors, 2001-; Regular broadcaster on family law issues. Honours: Governor at Large, International Academy of Matrimonial Lawyers. Memberships: Fellow, Royal Society of Arts; Law Society. Address: Academy Court, 94 Chancery Lane, London WC2A 1DT, England. E-mail: f.hughes@hfclaw.com

**HUGHES John W,** b. 18 February 1950, Detroit, Michigan, USA. Film Producer; Screenplay Writer; Director. m. Nancy Ludwig, 2 sons. Education: University AZ. Appointments: Copywriter, Creative Director, Leo Burnett Co; Editor, National Lampoon Magazine; Founder, President, Hughes Entertainment, 1985-. Creative Works: Films: National Lampoon's Class Reunion, 1982; National Lampoons Vacation, 1983; Mr Mon, 1983; Nate and Hayes, 1983; Sixteen Candles, 1984; National Lampoons European Vacation, 1985; Weird Science, 1985; The Breakfast Club, 1985; Ferris Bueller's Day Off, 1986; Pretty in Pink, 1986; Some Kind of Wonderful, 1987; Planes, Trains and Automobiles, 1987; The Great Outdoors, 1988; She's Having a Baby, 1988; National Lampoons Christmas Vacation, 1989; Uncle Buck, 1989; Home Alone, 1990; Career Opportunities, 1990; Dutch, 1991; Curly Sue, 1991; Only the Lonely, 1991; Beethoven, 1992; Home Alone 2: Lost in New York, 1992; Dennis the Menace, 1993; Baby's Day Out, 1993; Miracle on 34th Street, 1994; 101 Dalmations, 1996; Reach the Rock, 1998; New port South, 1999; 102 Dalmations, 2000; Just Visiting, 2001. Honours include: Commitment to Chicago Award, 1990; NATO/Sho West Producer of the Year, 1990. Address: c/o Jacob Bloom, Bloom & Dekom, 150 South Rodeo Drive, Beverly Hills, CA 90212, USA.

**HUGHES Lee Terence,** b. 16 January 1951, Epsom, Surrey, England. Government Servant. Education: BA (Hons) Business Studies, Middlesex Polytechnic, 1979-82; Postgraduate Certificate, Public Service Management, University of Birmingham, 2000-2001. Appointments: Various posts in Criminal Justice and Police Department, Home Office, 1977-98; Head of Freedom of Information/Data Protection, 1998-2003; Secretary, Hutton Inquiry, 2003-2004; Head Judicial Appointments (Courts), 2004-. Honour: CBE, 2004. Address: Department for Constitutional Affairs, Steel House, 11 Tothill Street, London SW1H 9LJ, England. E-mail: lee.hughes@dca.gsi.gov.uk

**HUGHES Shirley,** b. 16 July 1927, Hoylake, England. Children's Fiction Writer and Illustrator. Education: Liverpool Art School; Ruskin School of Drawing and Fine Arts, Oxford. Appointments: Public Lending Right Registrars Advisory Committee, 1984-88; Library and Information Services Council, 1989-92. Publications: Lucy & Tom Series, 6 volumes, 1960-87; The Trouble with Jack, 1970; Sally's Secret, 1973; It's too Frightening for Me, 1977; Moving Molly, 1978; Up and Up, 1979; Charlie Moon and the Big Bonanza Bust Up, 1982; An Evening at Alfies, 1984; The Nursery Collection, 6 volumes, 1985-86; Another Helping of Chips, 1986; The Big Alfie and Annie Rose Story Book, 1988; Out and About, 1989; The Big Alfie Out of Doors Story Book, 1992; Giving, 1993; Bouncing, 1993; Stories by Firelight, 1993; Chatting Hiding, 1994; Rhymes for Annie Rose, 1995; Enchantment in the Garden, 1996; Alfie and the Birthday Surprise, 1997; The Lion and the Unicorn, 1998; Abel's Moon, 1999; Shirley Hughes Collection, 2000; Alfie Weather, 2001; A Life Drawing (autobiography), 2002; Olly and Me, 2003; Ella's Big Chance, 2003; Alfie Wins a Prize, 2004. Honours: Kate Greenaway Medal for Dogger, 1977; Kate Greenaway Medal for Ella's Big Chance, 2004. Eleanor Farjeon Award, 1984; Honorary Fellow, Library Association, 1997; OBE, 1999; Doctor of Letters, University of East Anglia, 2004; Doctor of Letters, University of Liverpool, 2004; Hon. Fellowship Liverpool John Moores University, 2004. Membership: Society of Authors; Fellow, Royal Society of Literature, 2000. Address: c/o Bodley Head, Random House Children's Books, 61-63 Uxbridge Road, London W5 5SA, England.

**HULMES Edward Dominic Antony,** b. 13 June 1932, Urmston, Manchester, England. Theologian. m. Shirley Dorothy Mary Lester-Taylor, 3 daughters. Education: Oriel College, Oxford; Victoria University of Manchester; MA, BD, DPhil. Appointments: Eaton Hall Officer Cadet School and Commissioned Army Service in the Intelligence Corps, 1956-59; Commercial Administration, West Africa, 1960-66; Various teaching posts, Manchester, 1966-72; Director, Farmington Institute, Oxford, 1972-80; Spalding Professorial Fellow in Comparative Theology, University of Durham, 1981-94; Member of the Center of Theological Inquiry, Princeton, USA, 1986-. Publications: Commitment and Neutrality, 1979; The Religious Dimension of Islam (with Riadh El-Droubie), 1980; Education and Cultural Diversity, 1989; Islam: The Straight Path, 2001; The Ecumenical Imperative, 2001; The Spalding Trust and the Union for the Study of the Great Religions, 2002; Catholic Belief and Inter-Faith Encounter, 2004; Numerous contributions to symposia, articles and book-reviews on comparative theological studies and religious education. Honours: William Belden Noble Lecturer, Harvard University, 1981-82; Lecturer on Missions, Princeton Theological Seminary, USA, 1984; Appointed Knight of the Equestrian Order of the Holy Sepulchre of Jerusalem, 1985, Knight Commander, 2000; Trustee and Archivist of the Spalding Trust for the Study of the Great Religions, 1985-2002. Address: Rock House, Cressbrook, Monsal Dale, Via Buxton, Derbyshire SK17 8SY, England.

**HULTQVIST Bengt K G,** b. 21 August 1927, Hemmesjo, Sweden. Professor; Director. m. Gurli Gustafsson, 2 sons, 1 daughter. Education: Dr Sci Degree, Physics, University of Stockholm, 1956. Appointments: Director, Swedish Institute of Space Physics (and its predecessors). 1957-94; Director, International Space Science Institute, 1995-99; Chairman, Space Science Advisory Committee of ESA, 1998-2000; Secretary General of IAGA, 2001-. Publications: Some 200 articles in scientific journals and books; 3 books; Editor of 6 scientific books. Honours include: Grand Gold Medal, Royal Swedish Academy of Engineering Science, 1988; Cospar Prize for International Co-operation, 1990; King's Medal, 1991; Bartel's Medal, 1998; Hannes Alfvén Medal, 2002. Memberships include: Royal Astronomical Society (UK); International Academy of Astronautics; Academia Europaea; Royal Swedish Academy of Sciences; Royal Swedish Academy of Engineering Science; Academy of Finland; Royal Norwegian Academy of Sciences. Address: Gronstensv 2, S-98140, Kiruna, Sweden. E-mail: hultqv@irf.se

**HUMÁR Anton,** b. 7 April 1946, Brezno, Slovakia. Mechanical Engineer; Teacher; Researcher. m. Marie Brodská, 1 son, 1 daughter. Education: Engineer, 1969, PhD, 1983, Military Academy, Brno, Czech Republic; Docent, BUT, FME,

Production Technology Institute, Brno, Czech Republic, 1988. Appointments: Designer, Carriage Works, Studénka, Brno, Czech Republic, 1970-74; Research Worker, Research Institute of Materials and Technology, Brno, Czech Republic, 1974-85; Docent, Brno University of Technology, Faculty of Mechanical Engineering, Production Technology Institute, Brno, Czech Republic, 1985-. Publications include: Books: Sintered Carbides and Cutting Ceramics for Machining; Tables of Materials and Semi-Products for Mechanical Engineering: Chapter 1.5- Composites, Chapter 2.1 – Tool Materials for Machining; Articles: Built-up Edge and its Formation in the Machining of Feritic Nodular Cast Iron; Machining Fibre Reinforced Plastics; Testing of PVD Coats on HSS Drills; 7 papers in conference proceedings. Membership: Mechanical Engineers Association. Address: Štursova 27, 616 00 Brno, Czech Republic. E-mail: humar@fme.vutbr.cz

**HUME John,** b. 18 January 1937, Londonderry, Northern Ireland. Politician. m. Patricia Hone, 1960, 2 sons, 3 daughters. Education: St Colomb's College, Londonderry; St Patrick's College, Maynooth; National University of Ireland. Appointments: Research Fellow, Trinity College; Associate Fellow, Centre for International Affairs, Harvard; Founder Member, Credit Union, Northern Ireland, President, 1964-68; Non-Violent Civil Rights Leader, 1968-69; Representative, Londonderry, Northern Ireland Parliament, 1969-72, in Northern Ireland Assembly, 1972-73; Minister of Commerce, Powersharing Executive, 1974; Representative, Londonderry in Northern Ireland Convention, 1975-76; Elected to European Parliament, 1979-; Leader, Social Democratic and Labour Party (SDLP), 1979-; Member, Northern Ireland Assembly, 1982-86; MP for Foyle, 1983-; Member for Foyle Northern Ireland Assembly, 1998- (Assembly suspended 2002). Publications: Politics, Peace and Reconciliation in Ireland. Honours include: Nobel Peace Prize (shared), 1998; Martin Luther King Award, 1999; Gandhi Peace Prize, 2002; Numerous honorary doctorates. Address: 5 Bayview Terrace, Derry BT48 7EE, Northern Ireland.

**HUME Robert,** b. 6 January 1928, Glasgow, Scotland. Consultant Physician. m. Kathleen Anne Ogilvie Hume, 2 sons, 1 daughter. Education: Ayr Academy; Bellahouston Academy; University of Glasgow; MB ChB, 1948-53; MD (Commend), 1967; DSc, 1985. Appointments: National Service, Intelligence Corps; Commissioned, Gordon Highlanders, India and Germany, 1946-48; Hutcheson Research Scholar, 1955-56, Hall Fellowship, 1956-59, Honorary Clinical Lecturer, 1965, Honorary Sub-Dean, Faculty of Medicine, 1988, University of Glasgow; Consultant Physician, Southern General Hospital Glasgow, 1965-93; Retired, 1993; Member of the Board of Directors, Healthcare International, 1995-2002. Publications: Author of numerous publications on haematological and vascular disorders. Memberships: BMA, 1954; Scottish Society for Experimental Medicine, 1955; British Society for Haematology, 1960; Member, Research Support Group, Greater Glasgow Health Board, 1978-90; Member, Intercollegiate Standing Committee on Nuclear Medicine, UK, 1980-83; Scottish Council, BMA, 1980-83; Chairman, Sub-Committee on Medicine, Greater Glasgow Health Board, 1955-90; RCPS (Glas), Honorary Registrar for Examinations 1971-83, Chairman, Board of Examiners, 1983-88, Visitor and President Elect, 1988, President, 1990-92; Chairman, Conference of Scottish Royal Colleges and Faculties, 1991-92; Chairman, Joint Committee on Higher Medical Training of Royal Colleges of UK, 1990-93; Member, Scottish Society of Physicians, 1965; FRCPS, 1968; FRCPE, 1969; Honorary Member, Association of Physicians of Great Britain and Ireland, 1971; Honorary FACP, 1991; Honorary RACP, 1991; Member,

Academy of Medicine of Malaysia, 1991; Honorary FCM(SA); Honorary FRCPS (Canada); FRCPath, 1992; FRCSEd, 1992; FRCPI, 1993; Member, Buchanan Castle Golf Club; The Royal Philosophical Society of Glasgow; Glasgow Antiques and Fine Arts Society; National Trust of Scotland. Address: 6 Rubislaw Drive, Bearsden, Glasgow G61 1PR, Scotland.

**HUMPHREY Albert "S",** b. 2 June 1926, Kansas City, Missouri, USA. Specialist in Business Planning and Development. m. Myriam Octaaf de Baere, 3 sons, 3 daughters. Education: BS, Chemical Engineering, University of Illinois, 1946; MS, Chemical Engineering, Massachusetts Institute of Technology, 1948; MBA, Business Administration, Harvard Business School, 1955. Appointments include: Military Service: Ensign USNR, USS Chicago, USSS Springfield, Task Force 77 South Pacific, 1944-46; LTJG USNR, Office of Naval Research, Officer's Training School- Submarine Reserve, 1947-50; LCDR USNR, Korean campaign – LST 306 – LSMR 405 COMPHIBLANT, 1950-52; Retired LCDR, 1968; International Consultant to NASA Office of Advanced Research & Technology; Manager of R&D Planning, P R Mallory & Company Inc; Manager of Value Analysis Programme Small Aircraft Division of GE; Chief of Product Planning, Boeing Airplane Company; Assistant to the President, Penberthy Instrument Company; Chief of Chemical and Protective Group, Office of the Chief Chemical Officer US Army Chemical Corp; Currently Chairman and Chief Executive Officer, Business Planning & Development Inc, London, England; Current Directorships: Parkwood Films, London UK; Tower Lysprodukter a/s, Oslo, Norway; Hidden Valley Ltd, Birmingham, UK; Friborg Instruments plc; Executive Director, European Operations NBCC; Governor, John Kelly's Technology College. Publications: Articles in scientific and professional journals include most recently: How to Cope in a Change Culture, 1999; Balancing Act, 1999; Controlled Expansion Pays Off, 2000; Confused by Business Finance? Understand it with Humph, 2003; Turing Downturn into Major Upturn, 2004. Honours: American Institute of Chemical Engineers; Scientific Research Society of America, Sigma Xi; Tau Beta Phi; Institute of Management Consultants; British Accreditation Bureau. Memberships include: British Institute of Directors; British Institute of Marketing; American Institute of Chemical Engineers; Harvard Alumni Association; MIT Alumni Association; University of Illinois Alumni Association; Phi Delta Theta. Address: 1 Randolph Crescent, Little Venice, London W9 1DP, England. E-mail: humph@bpdev.demon.co.uk Website: www.thisistam.com

**HUMPRHEYS David A,** b. 7 November 1956, Epsom, England. Research Scientist. m. 1 daughter. Education: Sutton Valence School, 1974; BSc (Hons), Electronics, Southampton University, 1978; PhD, Electronic Engineering, London University UCL, 1990. Appointments: Scientific Officer, 1978-83, Higher Scientific Officer, 1983-86, Senior Scientific Officer, 1986-91, Grade 7, Civil Service, 1991-95, Principal Research Scientist, 1995-, National Physical Laboratory, Teddington. Publications: More than 13 journal and 45 conference papers. Honours: IEE Ambrose Fleming Premium, 1987. Memberships: Chartered Engineer, Engineering Council, 1987; Corporate Member, Institution of Electrical Engineers (UK), 1987; Senior Member, Institute of Electrical and Electronic Engineers, USA, 1990; Royal Institution of Great Britain. Address: National Physical Laboratory, Ultrafast & Dielectric Measurements, Hampton Road, Teddington, Middlesex TW11 0LW, England. E-mail: david.a.humphreys@iee.org

**HUMPHREYS Emyr Owen,** b. 15 April 1919, Clwyd, Wales. Author. m. Elinor Myfanwy, 1946, 3 sons, 1 daughter. Education: University College, Aberystwyth; University

College, Bangor. Publications: The Little Kingdom, 1946; The Voice of a Stranger, 1949; A Change of Heart, 1951; Hear and Forgive, 1952; A Man's Estate, 1955; The Italian Wife, 1957; A Toy Epic, 1958; The Gift, 1963; Outside the House of Baal, 1965; Natives, 1968; Ancestor Worship, 1970; National Winner, 1971; Flesh and Blood, 1974; Landscapes, 1976; The Best of Friends, 1978; The Kingdom of Bran, 1979; The Anchor Tree, 1980; Pwyll a Riannon, 1980; Miscellany Two, 1981; The Taliesin Tradition, 1983; Salt of the Earth, 1985; An Absolute Hero, 1986; Open Secrets, 1988; The Triple Net, 1988; Bonds of Attachment, 1990; Outside Time, 1991; Unconditional Surrender, 1996; The Gift of a Daughter, 1998; Collected Poems, 1999; Dal Pen Rheswm, 1999; Ghosts and Strangers, 2000; Conversations and Reflections, 2002; Old People are a Problem, 2003; The Shop, 2005. Honours: Somerset Maugham Award, 1953; Hawthornden Prize, 1959; Society of Authors Travel Award, 1978; Welsh Arts Council Prize, 1983; Honorary DLitt, University of Wales, 1990; Welsh Book of the Year, 1992, 1999; Honorary Professor of English, University College of North Wales, Bangor. Membership: Fellow, The Royal Society of Literature, 1991; Cymmrodorion Medal, 2003. Address: Llinon, Penyberth, Llanfairpwll, Ynys Môn, Gwynedd LL61 5YT, Wales.

**HUMPHRIES (John) Barry,** b. 17 February 1934, Australia. Actor; Writer. m. (1) Rosalind Tong, 1959, 2 daughters, (2) Diane Millstead, 2 sons, (3) Lizzie Spender, 1990. Education: University of Melbourne. Appointments: Various one-man shows; film appearances. Publications: Bizarre I, 1965; Innocent Australian Verse, 1968; Wonderful World of Barry McKenzie, 1968; Bazza Pulls It Off, 1972; Adventures of Barry McKenzie, 1973; Bazza Holds His Own, 1974; Dame Edna's Coffee Table Book, 1976; Bazza Comes Into His Own, 1978; Les Patterson's Australia, 1979; Barry Humphries' Treasury of Australian Kitsch, 1980; Dame Edna's Bedside Companion, 1982; Les Patterson: The Traveller's Tool, 1985; Dame Edna: My Gorgeous Life, 1989; Women in the Background, 1996. Honour: Society of West End Managements Award, 1979. Memberships: President, Frans de Boewer Society, Belgium; Vice President, Betjeman Society, 2001-.

**HUMPHRY Derek John,** b. 29 April 1930, Bath, England. Journalist; Author; Broadcaster. Appointments: Messenger Boy, Yorkshire Post, London, 1945-46; Cub Reporter, Evening World, Bristol, 1946-51; Junior Reporter, Evening News, Manchester, 1951-55; Reporter, Daily Mail, 1955-61; Deputy Editor, The Luton News, 1961-63; Editor, Havering Recorder, 1963-67, Hemlock Quarterly, 1983-92, Euthanasia Review, 1986-88, World Right to Die Newsletter, 1992-04; Home Affairs Correspondent, The Sunday Times, 1966-78; Special Writer, Los Angeles Times, 1978-79. Publications: Because They're Black, 1971; Police Power and Black People, 1972; Passports and Politics, 1974; The Cricket Conspiracy, 1976; False Messiah, 1977; Jean's Way, 1978; Let Me Die Before I Wake, 1982; The Right to Die!: Understanding Euthanasia, 1986; Final Exit, 1991; Dying with Dignity, 1992; Lawful Exit, 1993; Freedom to Die, 1998; The Good Euthanasia Guide, 2004. Contributions to: New Statesman; Independent, London; USA Today. Honours: Martin Luther King Memorial Prize, UK, 1972; The Saba Medal for contribution to the World Right-to-Die Movement, 2000. Memberships: Founder and Chief executive Officer, The Hemlock Society, 1980-92; President, World Federation of Right to Die Societies, 1988-90; Founder and President, The Euthanasia Research and Guidance Organization (ERGO), 1993-. Address: 24829 Norris Lane, Junction City, OR 97448-9559, USA.

**HUMPHRYS John,** b. 17 August 1943. Broadcaster. Divorced, 2 sons, 1 daughter. Appointments: Washington Correspondent, BBC TV, 1971-77, Southern Africa Correspondent, 1977-80, Diplomatic Correspondent, 1981; Presenter, BBC Nine o'Clock News, 1981-87; Presenter, BBC Radio 4 Today Programme, 1987-, On the Record, BBC TV, 1993-, John Humphrys Interview Radio 4, 1995-. Publication: Devil's Advocate, 1999; Great Food Gamble; Lost for Words. Honours: Fellow, Cardiff University, 1998; Honorary DLitt, Dundee, 1996; Honorary MA, University of Wales, 1998; Honorary LLD, St Andrews, 1999. Address: BBC News Centre, Wood Lane, London W12, England.

**HUNT Anthony James,** b. 22 June 1932, London, England. Structural Engineer. m. (1) Patricia Daniels, 1957, dissolved 1972, remarried, 1975, dissolved, 1982, 1 son, 1 daughter, (3) Diana Joyce Collett. Education: CEng, Westminster Technical College, 1961; FIStructE, 1973. Appointments: Articled via Founders' Co to J L Wheeler Consulting Engineer, 1948-51; F J Samuely and Partners, Consulting Engineers, 1951-59; Morton Lupton, Architects, 1960-62; Founded Anthony Hunt Associates, Consulting Engineers, 1962, Stood down as Chairman of Anthony Hunt Associates, became a consultant to them in 2002; Acquired by YRM plc, Building Design Consultants, 1988; Became separate limited company, 1997; Major buildings: Sainsbury Centre for the Visual Arts, Norwich, 1978, 1993; Willis Faber Dumas HQ, Ipswich, 1975; Inmos Micro Electronics Factory, Gwent, 1982; Schlumberger Cambridge Research, 1985; Waterloo International Terminal, 1993; Law Faculty, Cambridge, 1995; National Botanic Garden, Wales, 1998; New Museum of Scotland, Edinburgh, 1998; Lloyd's Register of Shipping, London, 2000; Eden Project, Cornwall, 2001; Willis Visiting Professor of Architecture, Sheffield University, 1994-. Publications: Tony Hunt's Structures Notebook, 1997; Tony Hunt's Sketchbook, 1999. Honours: FRSA, 1989; Honorary FRIBA, 1989; Gold Medallist, IStructE, 1995; Honorary DLitt, Sheffield, 1999; Graham Professor of Architecture, Graduate School of Fine Arts, University of Pennsylvania, 2002; Honorary DEng, Leeds, 2003; Visiting Professor, Chinese University of Hong Kong; Visiting Professor, IST, Lisbon. Address: Stancombe Farm, Bisley with Lippiatt, Stroud, Gloucestershire, GL6 7NF, England. E-mail: tony@huntprojects.co.uk

**HUNT David Roderic Notley,** b. 22 June 1947, Brighton, England. Barrister. m. Alison Connell Jelf, 2 sons. Education: MA Honours, Law, Trinity College, Cambridge, 1968; Inns of Court School of Law, 1968-69. Appointments: Called to the Bar, Gray's Inn, 1969; Queen's Counsel, 1987; Recorder, 1991; Master of the Bench of Gray's Inn, 1995. Publications: Article in the Solicitor's Journal. Address: Blackstone Chambers, Blackstone House, Temple, London EC4Y 9BW, England. E-mail: davidhunt@blackstonechambers.com

**HUNT Georgina,** b. 15 June 1922, Reading, England. Artist. 1 son, 1 daughter. Education: DFA (Lond.), Slade School of Fine Art (William Coldstream); Hunter College, New York. Career: Exhibited widely in the UK and internationally, including: Camden Arts Centre, 1982; Osaka International Triennale '93; The Barbican, 1998; Winchester Cathedral, 1999; Florence International Biennale '97 and '99; The Hunting Prize, 1999-2005; The London Group, 1992-2005; Flowers East/Central, 2001-2005. Publications include: Guy Brett, Solo Exhibition Catalogue, Camden Arts Centre, London, 1982; Judith Collins and Frances Spalding, 20th Century Painters & Sculptors, 1991; Chelsea Arts Club Year Book, 1993; Mike Williams, Modern Painters, Winter 1994; David Buckman, The Dictionary of Artists in Britain since 1945, 1998, 2005; Who's Who in

Art, 2000, 2002, 2004; The London Group, edited by Jane Humphrey, 2003. Honours: Major Award, Greater London Arts Association, 1976; 21st Century Association Prize, Osaka International Triennale, 1993; Lorenzo il Magnifico Prize for Lifetime Achievement, Florence International Biennale, 1999; Work in UK and international collections. Memberships: The London Group; Chelsea Arts Club, UCL Alumni Association. Address: 2 Camden Studios, Camden Street, London NW1 0LG, England. Website: www.thelondongroup.com

**HUNT Helen,** b. 15 June 1963, Los Angeles, USA. Actress. Creative Works: Stage appearances include: Been Taken; Our Town; The Taming of the Shrew; Methusalem; Films include: Rollercoaster; Girls Just Want to Have Fun; Peggy Sue Got Married; Project X; Miles From Hume; Trancers; Stealing Home; Next of Kin; The Waterdance; Only You; Bob Roberts; Mr Saturday Night; Kiss of Death; Twister; As Good As It Gets; Twelfth Night; Pay It Forward, 2000; Dr T and the Women, 2000; Cast Away, 2000; What Women Want, 2000; The Curse of the Jade Scorpion, 2001; TV includes: Swiss Family Robinson; Mad About You. Honours include: Emmy Award, 1996, 1997; Golden Globe Award, 1997; Academy Award, Best Actress, 1998. Address: c/o Connie Tavel, 9171 Wilshire Boulevard, Beverly Hills, CA 90210, USA.

**HUNT Jeffrey H,** b. 18 April 1957, Passaic, New Jersey, USA. Optical Scientist. m. Rebecca Johanna Hunt, 1 daughter. Education: BS, Physics, Massachusetts Institute of Technology, 1979; MA, Physics, 1982, PhD, Physics, 1988, University of California, Berkeley. Appointments: Research Assistant, 1977-79, Teaching Assistant, 1978-79, Massachusetts Institute of Technology; Teaching Assistant, 1979-81, Research Associate, 1980-87, University of California, Berkeley; Engineering Specialist, Rockwell Corporation, 1988-96; Technical Fellow, The Boeing Company, 1997-. Publications include: Laser Beam Diagnostics; Optical Parametric Oscillation. Memberships: American Physical Society. Address: Boeing Company WB54, 6633 Canoga Avenue, Canoga Park, CA 91309-7922, USA.

**HUNT Mary Elizabeth,** b. 1 June 1951, Syracuse, New York, USA. Theologian. Education: Bachelor of Arts, Marquette University, 1972; Master of Theological Studies, Harvard Divinity School, 1974; Master of Divinity, Jesuit School of Theology at Berkeley, 1978; PhD, Philosophical and Systematic Theology, 1980. Appointments: Frontier Internship in Mission, Buenos Aires, 1980-82; Co-founder, Co-director, Women's Alliance for Theology Ethics and Ritual, Silver Spring, 1983-; Visiting Assistant Professor, Religion, Colgate University, New York, 1986-87; Adjunct Assistant Professor, Women's Studies, Georgetown University, Washington, 1995-99; Research Fellow, Center for the Study of Values in Public Life, Harvard Divinity School, 2000-2001. Publications: Fierce Tenderness: A Feminist Theology of Friendship; From Woman-Pain to Woman-Vision (editor); La sfida del femminismo alla teologia (editor); Good Sex: Feminist Perspectives from the World's Religions (co-editor), 2001; A Guide for Woman in Religion – Finding Your Way From A to Z (editor), 2004; Many chapters, articles, book reviews and booklets. Honours: Isaac Hecker Award; Women's Ordination Conference Prophetic Figure Award; Crossroad Women's Studies Prize; Mary Rhodes Award. Memberships: American Academy of Religion; Society for Christian Ethics; Alpha Sigma Nu. Address: 8035 13th Street, Suites 1 and 3, Silver spring, MD 20910, USA.

**HUNT Patrick James (Sir),** b. 26 January 1943, Coalville, Leicestershire, England. High Court Judge. m. Susan Jennifer, 1 son, 3 daughters. Education: MA, Keble College, Oxford; Gray's Inn. Appointments: Barrister, 1968; QC, 1987; Deputy High Court Judge, 1994; High Court Judge, 2000-; Deputy, 1992-95, Leader, 1995-99, Midland and Oxford Circuit. Publications: Numerous in legal journals. Honour: Knighted, 2000. Membership: Royal Automobile Club. Address: Royal Courts of Justice, Strand, London WC2A 2LL, England.

**HUNTER Alan James Herbert,** b. 25 June 1922, Hoveton St John, Norwich, England. Author. m. Adelaide Elizabeth Cecily Cubitt, 6 March 1944, 1 daughter. Education: Royal Air Force, 1940-46. Appointments: Crime Reviewer, Eastern Daily Press, 1955-71. Publications: The Norwich Poems, 1945; Gently Go Man, 1961; Vivienne: Gently Where She Lay, 1972; The Honfleur Decision, 1980; Gabrielles Way, 1981; The Unhung Man, 1984; Traitors End, 1988; Bomber's Moon, 1994; Jackpot!, 1995; The Love of Gods, 1997; Over Here, 1998. Author of 46 crime novels featuring Chief Superintendent George Gently to 1999. Contributions to: Magazines and journals. Memberships: Society of Authors; Crime Writers Association; Authors Licensing and Collecting Society. Address: 3 St Laurence Avenue, Brundall, Norwich NR13 5QH, England.

**HUNTER Alexis,** b. 4 November 1948, Auckland, New Zealand. Artist. m. Baxter Mitchell. Education: Diploma of Fine Arts in Painting, Auckland University, 1970; Teaching Diploma, Auckland Teachers College, 1971; City & Guilds, London, 1972; London Graphics Academy, 2001. Appointments: Curator, UK and overseas, 1973-; Assistant Professor of Painting and Photography, Houston University, Texas, USA; Lecturer, UK and overseas, 1981-98. Publications: Numerous articles and papers. Honours: Major Award, Greater London Arts Association, 1981; Grant, Arts Council of New Zealand, 1981; British Council Travel Award, 1982; Grant, Lake District Residency, Greater London Arts Council, 1983; Travel Grant, British Council, 1986; Grant, Arts Council of New Zealand, 1988; Travel Grant, British Council, 1994. Memberships: Artists Alliance of New Zealand; Foundation of Women's Art; London Institute of Directors; Wellesley Club. Address: 13 Hillier House, 46 Camden Square, London NW1 9XA, England. Website: www.alexishunter.co.uk

**HUNTER David John,** b. 4 November 1949, Maidstone, Kent, England. Retired Nurse. m. Marilyn Carol, 1 son, 1 daughter. Education: RGN, 1971; RMN, 1973; OHNC (pt 1), 1981; Cert Ad Ed, 1987; Cert Ed, 1992; Dip ASE, 1993; BA, 1997; LIC&G, 1998; Cert Man, 2000. Appointments: Student Nurse, 1968-71; Staff Nurse, 1971-72; Student Nurse, 1972-73; Charge Nurse, 1973-75; Nursing Officer, 1975-79; Nursing Officer, 1979-92; Staff Nurse, 1982083; Charge Nurse, 1983-84; Nursing Officer, 1984-90; Nurse Tutor, 1990-2001. Publications: Paramedic UK; 3 articles on suicide. Honours: Knight, Order of St Andrew; Serving Brother, Order of St John; British Fires Services Centenary Medal; Laird of Cranachan. Membership: Royal College of Nursing. Address: 10 Brecon Avenue, Cheadle Hulme, Cheadle, Cheshire SK8 6DA, England.

**HUNTER Holly,** b. 20 March 1958, Atlanta, Georgia, USA. Actress. m. J Kaminski, divorced. Education: Career: Theatre includes: on Broadway: Crimes of the Heart; The Wake of Jamey Foster; The Miss Firecracker Contest; Other Stage Appearances include: The Person I Once Was; Battery (All New York); A Lie of the Mind (Los Angeles); Regional work; Films include: Broadcast News, 187; Raising Arizona, 1987; Once Around, 1990; The Piano and The Firm, 1993; Copycat, 1995; Crash, 1996; Living Out Loud, 1998; Time Code, 2000; O Brother Where Art Thou? 2000; When Billie Beat Bobby, 2001; Festival in Cannes, 2001; Goodbye Hello, 2002; Levity, 2003; Thirteen, 2003. Honours: 2 for TV appearances: Best Actress Emmy for Roe vs Wade, 1989; Best Actress Award, American

TV Awards, 1993; Best Actress Award, Cannes Film Festival Award, 1993; Academy Award, 1994. Memberships: Director, California Abortion Rights Action League. Address: 41 Stutter Street, #1649, San Francisco, CA 94104, USA.

**HUPPERT Herbert E,** b. 26 November 1943, Sydney, Australia. m Felicia Ferster, 2 sons. Education: BSc, Honours, Sydney University, 1964; MSc, Australian National University, 1966; MS, University of California at San Diego, 1967; PhD, California, 1968; MA, Cambridge, 1971; ScD, Cambridge, 1985. Appointments: ICI Research Fellow, 1968-69; Assistant Director of Research in DAMTP, 1970-81; University Lecturer in DAMTP, 1981-88; Reader in Geophysical Dynamics, University of Cambridge, 1988-89, Professor of Theoretical Geophysics and Foundation Director of the Institute of Theoretical Geophysics, 1989-; Professor of Mathematics, University of New South Wales, 1991-96; Member, NERC Council, 1993-99; Visiting Scientist, Australian National University, University of California at San Diego, Canterbury University, Caltech, MIT, University of New South Wales, University of Western Australia, the Weizmann Institute, Woods Hole Oceanographic Institute; Chairman, Royal Society Working Group on Bioterrorism, which published a report, Making the UK Safer, 2004, 2002-. Publications: Author or co-author of approximately 190 papers discussing applied mathematics, crystal growth, fluid mechanics, geology, geophysics, oceanography, meteorology and science in general. Honours: Sydney University Medal and Baker Prize in Mathematics, 1964; Fellow, King's College Cambridge, 1970-; Maurice Hill Research Fellow of the Royal Society, 1977; Royal Society Anglo-Australian Research Fellow, 1991, 1995; Evnin Lecturer, Princeton University, 1995; Midwest Mechanics Lecturer, USA, 1996-97; Henry Charnock Distinguished Lecturer, Southampton Oceanography Centre, 1999; Smith Industries Lecturer, Oxford University, 1999; Elected to National Academy of America's Arthur L Day Prize and Lectureship, 2005. Memberships: Elected Fellow: Royal Society, 1987, American Geophysical Union, 2002, American Physical Society, 2004; Royal Society Dining Club. Address: Institute of Theoretical Geophysics, DAMTP, University of Cambridge, Centre for Mathematical Sciences, Wilberforce Road, Cambridge CB3 0WA, England. E-mail: heh1@esc.cam.ac.uk   Website: www.itg.cam.ac.uk/people/heh/index.html

**HUR Do Haeng,** b. 21 May 1965, Buyeo-gun, ChungCheongNam-do, Korea. Corrosion Scientist. m. Mee Hyang Yeem, 3 sons. Education: BA, 1987, MA, 1989, PhD, 1998, Department of Metallurgical Engineering, Yonsei University, Seoul, Korea. Appointment: Principal Researcher, Korea Atomic Energy Research Institute, 1990-. Publications: About 100 original research papers; 12 patents. Honours: Listed in Who's Who publications and biographical dictionaries. Membership: The Corrosion Science Society of Korea. Address: Korea Atomic Energy Research Institute, 150 Deokjin-dong, Yuseong-gu, Daejeon 305-353, Republic of Korea. E-mail: dhhur@kaeri.re.kr

**HURD Douglas (Richard) (Hurd of Westwell),** b. 8 March 1930, Marlborough, England. Politician; Diplomat; Writer. m. (1) Tatiana Elizabeth Michelle, 1960, divorced, 3 sons, (2) Judy Smart, 1982, 1 son, 1 daughter. Education: Trinity College, Cambridge. Appointments: HM Diplomatic Service, 1952-66; Joined Conservative Research Department, 1966, Head, Foreign Affairs Section, 1968; Private Secretary to the Leader of the Opposition, 1968-70; Political Secretary to the Prime Minister, 1970-74; Member of Parliament, Conservative Party, Mid-Oxon, 1974-83, Witney, 1983-97; Opposition Spokesman on European Affairs, 1976-79; Visiting Fellow, Nuffield College,

1978-86; Minister of State, Foreign and Commonwealth Office, 1979-83, Home Office, 1983-84; Secretary of State for Northern Ireland, 1984-85, Home Secretary, 1985-89, Foreign Secretary, 1989-95; Candidate for Conservative Leadership, 1990; Deputy Chairman, NatWest Markets, 1995-98; Director Natwest Group, 1995-99; Deputy Chairman, Coutts & Co, 1998-; Chairman, Hawkpoint Advisory Committee, 1999-2003; Chairman British Invisibles, 1998-2000; Chairman, Prison Reform Trust, 1997-2001; President, Prison Reform Trust, 2001-; Chairman, The Booker Prize Committee, 1998; Chairman, Council for Effective Dispute Resolution, 2001-04; High Steward, Westminister Abbey, 2000-; Joint President, Royal Institute for Internal Affairs, 2002-. Publications: The Arrow War, 1967; Send Him Victorious (with Andrew Osmond), 1968; The Smile on the Face of the Tiger (with Andrew Osmond), 1969; Scotch on the Rocks (with Andrew Osmond), 1971; Truth Game, 1972; Vote to Kill, 1975; An End to Promises, 1979; War Without Frontiers (with Andrew Osmond), 1982; Palace of Enchantments (with Stephen Lamport), 1985; The Search for Peace (BBC TV Series), 1997; The Shape of Ice, 1998; Ten Minutes to Turn the Devil, 1999; Image in the Water, 2001; Memoirs, 2003. Honours: Commander of the Order of the British Empire, 1974; Privy Councillor, 1982; Spectator Award for Parliamentarian of the Year, 1990; Companion of Honour, 1995; Baron Hurd of Westwell, 1997. Address: House of Lords, London SW1A 0PW, England.

**HURLEY Elizabeth,** b. 10 June 1965, England. Model; Actress; Producer. 1 son. Career: Former model and spokeswoman, Estée Lauder; Head of Development for Simian Films, 1996; Films include: Aria, 1987; The Skipper, 1989; The Orchid House, 1990; Passenger '57, 1992; Mad Dogs and Englishmen, 1994; Dangerous Ground, 1995; Samson and Delilah, 1996; Produced Extreme Measures, 1996; Austin Powers: International Man of Mystery, 1996; Permanent Midnight, 1997; My Favorite Martian, 1999; EdTV, 1999; Austin Powers: The Spy Who Shagged Me, 1999; The Weight of Water, 2000; Bedazzled, 2000; Serving Sara, 2002; Double Whammy, 2002. Address: c/o Simian Films, 3 Cromwell Place, London SW7 2SE, England.

**HURN (John) Bruce,** b. 18 May 1926, Spalding, Lincolnshire, England. Artist; Painter; Designer; Art Educationalist. m. June Barbara Haggard, 1 son, 3 daughters. Education: ATD, Birmingham College of Art, 1942-46 (Royal Navy, provisional medical discharge, summer 1944). Appointments: Visiting Tutor, Bournville, Moseley, Nuneaton Schools of Art, 1946-47; Director of Art and Design, King Edward's School, Birmingham, 1947-73; Concurrently, Headmaster, 1952-68, Co-Head, 1968-72, Adult Education, Moseley Branch School of Art; Her Majesty's Inspector of Schools, Art and Design Specialist, 1973-86; Examiner, variously Welsh and Northern Ireland Examination Boards and Northern Universities Joint Board (pioneered new Appreciation of Design paper) then Chief Examiner, London University Schools Examination O-Level Art, 1958-73; Member, West Midlands Advisory Council for Further Education, 1967-73; Member, Advisory Committee, National Exhibition of Childrens'Art, 1978-88; Painter, commissioned to paint the T C Kemp Memorial Crucifixion, King Edward's School Chapel, 1956; Exhibited in group shows: Birmingham and Coventry City Art Galleries; Hereford; Ludlow; Shrewsbury; Stoke-on-Trent; Summer Exhibition, Royal Academy; Solo Exhibitions: Birmingham, Brunel, Keele, Kent, Leicester and Oxford Universities; Compendium Galleries, London and Moseley; 2 painter exhibitions: Midland Arts Centre; Bakehouse Gallery, Blackheath; Commonwork Centre, Weald; Royal Birmingham Society of Artists; Paintings in private collections, UK and USA and in school, college, university and industrial collections. Publications: Contributions to: Curriculum of the Secondary School, 1952; Co-author with C Dodds, Practical Biology (some 800 drawings), 1964, 1972; Illustrated, Unit Biology, by Wright, 1969; Paper for National Association of Gifted Children, Focus on Art. Honours: Design Prize, Worshipful Company of Goldsmiths, 1947; President, RBSA, 1973-74; Honorary Consultant, National Association for Gifted Children, 1987-; Honorary Art Tutor, Harris Hospice, 1989-; Occasional Inspector, Art and Design, British Accreditation Council, 1994-2000 and Open and Distance Learning Quality Council. Memberships: Life Fellow, Royal Society of Arts, 1965; Elected Member, 1966, Treasurer, President, RBSA; Former Chairman, Midland District of the National Society for Art Education; Governor Bromley College for Adult Education, 1989-; Member Bromley Arts Consultative Forum; Patron, Chislehurst Artists; Chairman, The Chislehurst Society (environmental), 1992-98. Address: Hawk's Wing, Hawkwood Lane, Chislehurst, Kent BR7 5PW, England.

**HURSH Ray**, b. 2 March 1935, Superior, Wisconsin, USA. Retired. m. Helen M Hughes, 3 sons, 1 daughter. Education: Theatre, Arts, Speech and Drama, California College of Theater Arts, Pasadena, California, 1953-55; Communications, University of Minnesota, Duluth, Minnesota, 1957-60; Degree in Marketing and Business Management, Wisconsin Indianhead Technical College, 1972-74; Diploma, Fitness and Nutrition, International Correspondence School, Pennsylvania, 1987; Stress Management, International Business Systems, Las Vegas, Nevada, 1987; Stress Management, University of Wisconsin, 1988. Appointments: Musician and Performer; Psychiatric Technician and E R CNA, Dallas Texas Hospital, 1961-72; CNA, nursing homes and home health care, Minnesota and Wisconsin, 1972-85; Personal Trainer and Fitness Instructor, teaching aerobics, body building and individual sports training, specialised in stress management and psychological training, 1983-94; Fine Dining Waiter, 1994-99; Retired, concentrating on writing, 2000-; Lay Minister, Hospice Volunteer. Publications include: A Prism of Thought, 1997; Best Poets of 1998; Outstanding Poets of 1998; Rustling Leaves, 1998; In the Shadow of Midnight, 2000; America in the Millennium, 2000; Nature's Echoes, 2001; Silk Clouds and Velvet Dreams, 2002; Letters From the Soul, 2003; Theatre of the Mind, 2003; Colours of the Heart, 2004; Desert of Despair, 2004; Many Shades of Pale, 2005; Labours of Love, 2005; Music: Composed full mass for Catholic Church, 2004. Honours include: Outstanding Speaker of the Year, Wisconsin Rotary Club, 1952; Outstanding Achievement in Journalism, University of Minnesota, 1959; Winner Love Poem Contest, Le Courte Oreilles Community College, Hayward, Wisconsin, 1997; Editors Choice Award, 1997, 2002; International Poet of Merit, International Society of Poets; Listed in Who's Who publications and biographical dictionaries. Address: 10654 Reinke Street, Apartment #10, Hayward, WI 54843, USA.

**HURSTHOUSE Miles Wilson**, b. 27 October 1919, Hastings, New Zealand. Medical Practitioner. m. Jillian, 2 sons, 1 daughter. Education: MB, ChB, Auckland University College, Otago University, Sydney University, Australian College of Dermatologists, Sydney, Australia. Appointments: Civil Servant; Army Service WW2, 5 years New Zealand Artillery reaching rank of Captain; Hospital Service as House Surgeon, 2 years; Private Medical Practice, 48 years, including 3 years postgraduate study in Australia; Anaesthetist, Nelson Hospital, 16 years; Lecturer, Obstetrics Nelson Hospital, 10 years; Specialist Dermatologist, Nelson Hospital, 10 years; Retired, still registered medical practitioner for emergencies; Managing Director, Private Property Company. Publications: Autobiography, Vintage Doctor: 50 Years of Tears and Laughter, 2001; 10 scientific papers on subjects including:

Melanoma incidence in the Nelson-Marlborough region of New Zealand, use of topical Retinoic acid in bullous ichthyosiform erythroderma, confusing rashes and exanthemata, basal cell carcinoma in burn scars. Honours: International Silver C Gliding Award; Member of winning car team, Southland Centennial Car Trial (International); New Zealand University Blue, Shooting, 1950; Otago University Blues, Shooting, 1949, 1950; Navigation Cup, Nelson Aero Club, 1964; Numerous cups and trophies for local motor sport; Honorary Life Member, Nelson Car Club and Nelson Gliding Club. Memberships include: President: Nelson Car Club, Nelson Gliding Club, Nelson Division, New Zealand Medical Association, Nelson Branch New Zealand Cancer Society, Nelson Branch, New Zealand Heart Foundation, New Zealand Dermatological Association, New Zealand Faculty Australasian College of Dermatologists, Stoke Tahunanui Probus Club; Member, Nelson Area Health Board. Address: 306 Princes Drive, Nelson, New Zealand.

**HURT John**, b. 22 January 1940, Chesterfield, England. m. (1) Annette Robertson, (2) Donna Peacock, 1984, divorced 1990, (3) Jo Dalton, 1990, divorced 1995, 2 sons. Education: Lincoln Academy of Dramatic Art; Royal Academy of Dramatic Art. Appointments: Painter; Actor. Creative Works: Stage appearances include: Chips With Everything, Vaudeville Theatre, 1962; The Dwarfs, Arts, 1963; Hamp, Edinburgh Festival, 1964; Inadmissible Evidence, Wyndhams, 1965; Little Malcolm and His Struggle Against the Eunuchs, Garrick, 1966; Belcher's Luck, Aldwych, 1966; The Only Street, Dublin Festival and Islington, 1973; Travesties, Aldwych and The Arrest, Bristol Old Vic, 1974; The Shadow of a Gunman, Nottingham Playhouse, 1978; The London Vertigo, Dublin, 1991; A Month in the Country, Albery, 1994; Krapp's Last Tape, New Ambassadors Theatre, 2000, Gate Theatre, Dublin, 2001; Afterplay, Gielgud Theatre, 2002; Films include: The Elephant Man, 1980; King Ralph, 1991; Lapse of Memory, 1991; Dark at Noon, 1992; Monolith, 1994; Even Cowgirls Get the Blues, 1994; Rob Roy, 1994; Wild Bill, 1995; Dead Man, 1996; Contact, 1997; Love and Death on Long Island, 1998; All the Little Animals, 1999; You're Dead, 1999; The Love Letter, 1999; Lost Souls, 2000; Night Train, 2000; Captain Corelli's Mandolin, 2001; Harry Potter and the Philosopher's Stone, 2001; Tabloid, 2001; Bait, 2001; Miranda, 2001; Owning Mahony, 2001; Several TV appearances. Honours: Several. Address: c/o Julian Belfrage & Associates, 46 Albemarle Street, London W1X 4PP, England.

**HURT William**, b. 20 March 1950, Washington, USA. Actor. m. (1) Mary Beth Hurt, (2) Heidi Henderson, 1989, 2 sons. Education: Tufts University; Juilliard School. Creative Works: Stage appearances include: Henry V, 1976; Mary Stuart; My Life; Ulysses in Traction; Lulu; Fifth of July; Childe Byron; The Runner Stumbles; Hamlet; Hurlyburly; Beside Herself, 1989; Ivanov, 1991; Films include: Altered States; Eyewitness; Body Heat; The Big Chill; Corky Park; Kiss of the Spider Woman; Children of a Lesser God; Broadcast News, 1987; A Time of Destiny, 1988; The Accidental Tourist, 1989; The Plastic Nightmare; I Love You to Death, 1990; The House of Spirits, 1990; The Doctor, 1991; Until the End of the World, 1991; Mr Wonderful, 1993; The Plague, 1993; Trial By Jury, 1994; Second Best, 1994; Jane Eyre, 1995; Secrets Shared With a Stranger; Smoke, 1995; Michael; Loved; Lost in Space, 1998; One True Thing, 1998; Dark City, 1998; The Miracle Marker, 2000; AI: Artificial Intelligence, 2001; The Flamingo Rising, 2001. Honours include: Theatre World Award, 1978; Best Actor Award, Cannes Film Festival, 1985; Academy Award, Best Actor, 1985; 1st Spencer Tracy Award, 1988. Address; c/o Hilda Quille, William Morris Agency,151 El Camino Drive, Beverly Hills, CA 90212, USA.

**HUSEYNOV Vugar K,** b. 20 September 1975, Armenia. Forensic Pathologist. m. Gunay R Rustamova. Education: Diploma, Azerbaijan Medical University, 1992-98; Intern Certificate, 1998-99; Postgraduate Course Diploma, 1999-2002. Appointment: Forensic Pathologist, 1998-. Publications: Medico legal age determination by facial wrinkles; Changes in the human face due to ageing in forensic medicine; Face as an object of criminalistics; Wrinkles of facial skin; Caraniofacial research at forensic medical identification of the person. Memberships: International Association of Identification; American Academy of Forensic Sciences. Address: 33, 20 January str, Apt # 58, Baku, AZ 1102, Azerbaijan.

**HUSSAIN Akmal,** b. 5 September 1949, Lahore, Pakistan. Economist. m. Rafia Hussain, 3 sons. Education: BA, Pubjab University, Economics and Philosophy, 1969; BA (Honours), MA, Economics, Cambridge University, England, 1972; D Phil, Economics, Sussex University, England, 1980. Appointments: Lecturer, Assistant Professor, Chairman, Department of Public Administration, University of the Pubjab, 1973-76, 1980-83; Visiting Lecturer, Department of Economics, University of California, Riverside, 1983-84; Managing Director, Sayyed Engineers (Private) Limited, 1984-; Worked as mobilizer in village communities to get basic services for villagers, 1980's; Currently: Adjunct Faculty Member, Lahore University of Management Sciences, 1996-; Member, Economic Advisory Board; Member Prime Ministers Economic Affairs Committee until 1998; Member Board of Directors, Pakistan Poverty Alleviation Fund; Member Advisory Committee, UNDP Project on Poverty Alleviation in South Asia, 1997-; Senior Fellow, Pakistan Institute of Development Economics; Numerous consultancies include: Consultant to World Bank, 1993, 1997; Consultant to ILO, 1992, 1999; Consultant to Dutch Government. Publications: Author, 2 books; Co-author or chapter contributor to 8 books; 29 publications in major journals; Over 100 articles to newspapers on economic and social issues; Distinguished Visiting Professor, Beaconhouse National University; Numerous papers presented at international conferences and seminars. Honours: Honorary Member, Prime Ministers Policy Committee on Economic Affairs, 1997-99; Honorary Chairman Working Group on Poverty Alleviation for the preparation of the Ninth Five-Year Plan, 1998-2003; Vice-Chairman, Honorary Chief Executive Officer, Punjab Rural Support Programme, 1998; Certificate of Honour, European Market Research Centre, Brussels, 1999; International Award of Recognition, American Biographical Institute. Memberships: Pakistan Society for Development Economists; Independent Group for South Asian Co-operation. Address: 11 St John's Park, Lahore Cantt, Pakistan. E-mail: aknalhus@sayyed.com.pk

**HUSSEIN Queen Noor (HM),** b. 23 August 1951. m. King Hussein I of Jordan, deceased 2 February 1999, 4 children. Education: BA, Architecture, Urban Planning, Princeton University, USA 1974. Appointments: Architectural and Urban Planning Projects in Australia, Iran and Jordan; Founded in Jordan, Royal Endowment for Culture and Education, 1979; Annual Arab Children's Congress, 1980; Annual International Jerash Festival for Culture and Arts, 1981; Jubilee School, 1984; Noor Al Hussein Foundation, 1985; National Music Conservatory, 1986; National Task Force for Children; Advisory, Committee for the UN University International Leadership Academy, Amman; Patron of the General Federation of Jordanian Women and the National Federation of Business and Professional Women's Clubs; Patron, Royal Society for the Conservation of Nature; Honorary President, Jordan Red Crescent; The Jordan Society, Washington DC, 1980; Patron, International Union for the Conservation of Nature and Nature Rescue, 1988; Founding Member, International Commission on Peace and Food, 1992; President, United World Colleges, 1995; Honorary President, Birdlife International, 1996; Director, Hunger Project. Honours: Numerous Honorary Doctorates, International Relations, Law, Humane Letters; International Awards and Decorations. Memberships: International Eye Foundation Honorary Board; Trustee, Mentor Foundation; General Assembly of the SOSKinderdorf International; International Council of the Near East Foundation. Address: Bab Al Salam Palace, Amman, Jordan.

**HUSTON Anjelica,** b. 8 July 1951, Los Angeles, California, USA. Actress. m. Robert Graham, 1992. Creative Works: Stage appearances include: Tamara, Los Angeles, 1985; TV appearances include: The Cowboy and the Ballerina, NBC-TV Film, 1984, Faerie Tale Theatre, A Rose for Miss Emily, PBS Film, Lonesome Dove, CBS Mini-Series; Films include: Sinful Davey; A Walk with Love and Death, 1969; The Last Tycoon, 1976; The Postman Always Rings Twice, 1981; Swashbuckler; This is Spinal Tap, 1984; The Ice Pirates, 1984; Prizzi's Honor, 1985; Gardens of Stone; Captain Eo; The Dead; Mr North; A Handful of Dust; The Witches; Enemies; A Love Story; The Grifters; The Addams Family; Addams Family Values; The Player; Manhattan Murder Mystery; The Crossing Guard, 1995; The Perez Family, 1995; Buffalo '66, 1997; Phoenix, 1997; Director, Bastard Out of Carolina, 1995, Phoenix, 1997; Agnes Browne, 1999; The Golden Bowl, 2001; The Royal Tenenbaums, 2002. Honours include: Academy Award, Best Supporting Actress, 1985; NY & Los Angeles Film Critics Awards, 1985. Address: c/o International Creative Management, 8942 Wilshire Boulevard, Beverly Hills, CA 90211, USA.

**HUSZAR Laszlo Istvan,** b. 15 November 1932, Budapest, Hungary. Urban and Regional Development Specialist. m. (1) Esther Pasint Magyar, 21 June 1969, divorced May 1979, 2 sons, 1 daughter. (2) Chularat Jeetniyom, 21 June 1979, 1 son. Education: Dip Ing Arch, Technical University, Budapest, 1956; BSc, Economics, London School of Economics, 1961. Appointments: Research Fellow, Planning, University Science and Technology, Kumasi, Ghana, 1961-65; Seconded to Volta River Authority, to locate and plan sixteen resettlement townships, 1963-65; Senior Lecturer, Regional Planning, Architectural Association School Architecture, London, 1965-70; Lecturer, Regional Planning, Nottingham University, 1967-71; Founding Partner, Huszar Brammah & Associates, London, 1971-; Project Manager, S Thailand Regional Planning Study, Songkhla, 1973-74; Resettlement Studies in Sumatra & Sulawesi, Indonesia, 1975-77; Project Director, Bandung Urban Development Study, Indonesia, 1977-78; Sabah Regional Planning Study, Malaysia, 1979-80; Eastern Seaboard Regional Planning Study, Thailand, 1981-82; National Planning Study, Bandar Seri Begawan, Brunei, 1985-87; Senior Urban Policy Adviser, Indonesian Government & IBRD, Jakarta, 1987-90; Project Director, Medan Urban Development Project, Indonesia, 1994-96. Publications: The Towns of Ghana, 1964; Contribution, The Volta Resettlement Experience, 1970; Author of Reports. Honours: Secretary, Hungarian Revolutionary Studies Committee, Budapest, 1956, London, 1956-61; Part in Round Table Discussions on Current Affairs, BBC Hungarian Programs, London, 1991-93. Memberships: Reform Club, Pall Mall; Member, Highgate Society. Listed in: Several International Publication Dictionaries. Address: 109 Southwood Lane, Highgate, London N6 5TB, England.

**HUTSON Jeremy Mark,** b. 7 May 1957, West Kirby, Cheshire, England. Professor of Chemistry. Education: BA, 1st Class, Chemistry, Wadham College, Oxford University, 1975-79; DPhil, Physical Chemistry, Hertford College, Oxford University, 1979-81. Appointments: NATO/SERC Postdoctoral

Research Fellow, University of Waterloo, Canada, 1981-83; Research Fellow, Pembroke College, Cambridge, and Theoretical Chemistry Department, Cambridge University, 1983-86; Lecturer, 1987-83, Reader, 1993-96, Professor, 1996-, Head of the Department of Chemistry, 1998-2001, University of Durham; Numerous invited lectures at international conferences include most recently: 3rd International Meeting on Photodynamics, Havana, 2004; 27th International Symposium on Free Radicals, Taipei, 2004; 3rd Gordon Conference on Ionic and Molecular Clusters, Aussoix, 2004; ECAMP VIII, Rennes, 2004; 228th ACS National Meeting, Philadelphia, 2004; Indian National Conference on Atomic and Molecular Physics, Ahmedabad, 2004. Publications: Over 4,800 citations up to September 2003; Editor (with Professor Roger E Miller), International Reviews in Physical Chemistry; Specialist Editor, Computer Physics Communications. Honours: Corday-Morgan Medal, Royal Society of Chemistry, 1991; Visiting Fellowship, Joint Institute for Laboratory Astrophysics, Boulder, Colorado, USA, 1991; Nuffield Foundation Science Research Fellowship, 1993-94; Visiting Professorship, University of Colorado, 2001-2002. Memberships. Fellow, Royal Society of Chemistry, UK; Fellow, Institute of Physics, UK. Address: Department of Chemistry, University of Durham, Durham DH1 3LE, England.

**HUTTON Gabriel Bruce,** b. 27 August 1932, Minchinhampton, Gloucestershire, England. Circuit Judge (Retired). m. Deborah Leigh Windus, 1 son, 2 daughters. Education: Trinity College, Cambridge, 1951-54. Appointments: Called to Bar, Inner Temple, 1956; Deputy Chairman, Gloucester Quarter Sessions, 1971; Recorder, Crown Court, 1972-78; Circuit Judge, Western Circuit, 1978-2003; Resident Judge, Gloucester Crown Court, 1987-2003. Address: Chestal House, Dursley, Gloucestershire GL11 5AA, England.

**HUTTON, Baron of Bresagh in the County of Down, (James) Brian Edward Hutton,** b. 29 June 1931, United Kingdom. Retired Law Lord. m. (1) Mary Gillian Murland, deceased, 2000, 2 daughters, (2) Rosalind Anne Nickols, 2 step sons, 1 step daughter. Education: BA, Balliol College, Oxford; Queen's University, Belfast. Appointments: Called to the Bar, Northern Ireland, 1954; Junior Counsel to Attorney General of Northern Ireland, 1969; Queen's Counsel, Northern Ireland, 1970; Senior Crown Counsel, Northern Ireland, 1973-79; Judge of the High Court of Justice, Northern Ireland, 1979-88, Lord Chief Justice of Northern Ireland, 1988-97; a Lord of Appeal in Ordinary, 1997-2004; Chairman, Hutton Inquiry, 2003-2004; Member, Joint Law Enforcement Commission, 1974; Deputy Chairman, Boundary Commission for Northern Ireland, 1985-88. Honours: Kt, 1988; Privy Councillor, 1988; Life Peer, 1997. Memberships: President, Northern Ireland Association for Mental Health, 1983-90; Visitor, University of Ulster, 1999-2004. Address: House of Lords, London SW1A 0PW, England.

**HUTTON Ronald Edmund,** b. 19 December 1953, Ootacamund, India. Historian. m. Lisa Radulovic, 5 August 1988. Education: BA, Cantab, 1976; MA, 1980; DPhil, 1980. Appointments: Professor of British History, Bristol University, 1996-; Professor of History, Bristol University. Publications: The Royalist War Effort, 1981; The Restoration, 1985; Charles II, 1989; The British Republic, 1990; The Pagan Religions of the Ancient British Isles, 1991; The Rise and Fall of Merry England, 1994; The Stations of the Sun, 1996; The Triumph of the Moon: A History of Modern Pagan Witchcraft, 1999; Shamans, 2001; Witches, Druids and King Arthur, 2003; Debates in Stuart History, 2004. Contributions to: Journals. Honour: Benjamin Franklin Prize, 1993. Memberships: Royal Historical Society; Folklore Society; Fellow, Society of Antiquaries. Address: 13 Woodland Road, Bristol BS8 1TB, England.

**HUXLEY Andrew Fielding (Sir),** b. 22 November 1917, London, England. Physiologist. m. Jocelyn Richenda Gammell Pease, 1947, deceased 2003, 1 son, 5 daughters. Education: Graduated, 1938, MA, 1941, Trinity College, Cambridge; Clinical study Addenbrookes Hospital, Cambridge and University College Hospital London, 1939-40 not completed on account of WWII. Appointments: Operational Research in World War II, Antiaircraft Command, 1940-42, Admiralty, 1942-45; Fellow, Trinity College, Cambridge, 1941-60, 1990-; Director of Studies, 1952-60, Honorary Fellow, 1967-90, Master, 1984-90, Trinity College; Demonstrator, Department of Physiology, 1946-50, Assistant Director of Research, 1951-59, Reader in Experimental Biophysics, 1959-60 Cambridge University; Jodrell Professor of Physiology, University College, London, 1960-69; Royal Society Research Professor, 1969-83; Professor Emeritus of Physiology, University of London, 1983-. Publications: Reflections on Muscle, 1977; Papers on nerve conduction and muscle contraction, chiefly in Journal of Physiology. Honours: Joint Winner, Nobel Prize for Physiology or Medicine, 1963; Copley Medal, Royal Society, 1973; Knight Bachelor, 1974; Order of Merit, 1983; Grand Cordon of Sacred Treasure, Japan,1995; Swammerdam Medal, 1997; 27 Honorary Degrees. Memberships include: Fellow, Royal Society, 1955, President, 1980-85; Honorary Fellow, Royal Academy of Engineering, 1986-; Honorary Member, Royal Institution of Great Britain, 1981-; Physiological Society; Foundation for Science and Technology; Academia Europaea. Address: Manor Field, 1 Vicarage Drive, Grantchester, Cambridge CB3 9NG, England.

**HUXLEY Hugh Esmor,** b. 25 February 1924, Birkenhead, England. Physiologist. m. Frances Frigg, 1966, 2 stepsons, 1 daughter, 1 stepdaughter. Education: Graduated, Christ's College, Cambridge, 1943; PhD, 1952. Appointments: Radar Officer, RAF Bomber Command and Telecommunications Research Establishment, Malvern, 1943-47; Research Student, Medical Research Council Unit for Molecular Biology, Cavendish Laboratory, Cambridge, 1948-52; Commonwealth Fund Fellow, Biology Department, MIT, 1952-54; Research Fellow, Christ's College, Cambridge, 1952-56; Member, External Staff, 1962-87, Joint Head, Structural Studies Division, 1976-87, Deputy Director, 1977-87, Medical Research Council Laboratory of Molecular Biology, Cambridge; Professor of Biology, 1987-97, Director, 1988-94, Professor Emeritus, 1997-, Rosenstiel Basic Medical Sciences Research Center, Brandeis University, Boston, Massachusetts; Fellow, King's College, Cambridge, 1961-67; Fellow, Churchill College, Cambridge, 1967-87; Harvey Society Lecturer, New York, 1964-65; Senior Visiting Lecturer, Physiology Course, Woods Hole, Massachusetts, 1966-71; Wilson Lecturer, University of Texas, 1968; Dunham Lecturer, Harvard Medical School, 1969; Croonian Lecturer, Royal Society of London, 1970; Ziskind Visiting Professor of Biology, Brandeis University, 1971; Penn Lecturer, University of Pennsylvania, 1971; Mayer Lecturer, MIT, 1971; Miller Lecturer, State University of New York, 1973; Carter-Wallace Lecturer, Princeton University, 1973; Pauling Lecturer, Stanford University, 1980; Jesse Beams Lecturer, University of Virginia, 1980; Ida Beam Lecturer, University of Iowa, 1981. Publications: Articles in scientific journals. Honours: Feldberg Award for Experimental Medical Research , 1963; William Bate Hardy Prize of the Cambridge Philosophical Society, 1965; Honorary DSc, 1969, 1974, 1976, 1988; Louis Gross Horwitz Prize, 1971; International Feltrinelli Prize for Medicine, 1974; International Award, Gairdner Foundation, 1975; Baly Medal, Royal College of Physicians, 1975; Royal Medal, Royal Society of London, 1977; E B Wilson Medal, American Society for Cell Biology, 1983; Albert Einstein World Award of Science, 1987; Franklin Medal, 1990;

Distinguished Scientist Award, Electron Microscopy Society of America, 1991; Copley Medal, Royal Society of London, 1997. Memberships: Member, Advisory Board, Rosensteil Basic Medical Sciences Center, Brandeis University, 1971-77; Member, Council of Royal Society of London, 1973-75, 1984-86; Member, Scientific Advisory Committee, European Molecular Biology Laboratory, 1975-81; Member, Board of Trustees, Associated Universities Inc, 1987-90; Member, Germany Academy of Science, Leopoldina, 1964; Foreign Associate, NAS, 1978; American Association of Anatomists, 1981; American Physiological Society, 1981; American Society of Zoologists, 1986; Foreign Honorary Member, American Academy of Arts and Sciences, 1965; Danish Academy of Sciences, 1971; American Society of Biological Chemists, 1976; Honorary Fellow, Christ's College, Cambridge, 1981. Address: Rosensteil Basic Medical Sciences Research Center, Brandeis University, Waltham, MA 02254, USA.

**HUXTABLE Ada Louise,** b. New York, New York, USA. Architecture Critic; Writer. m. L Garth Huxtable. Education: AB, magna cum laude, Hunter College, New York City; Postgraduate Studies, Institute of Fine Arts, New York University. Appointments: Assistant Curator of Architecture and Design, Museum of Modern Art, New York, 1946-50; Contributing Editor, Progressive Architecture and Art in America, 1950-63; Architecture Critic, The New York Times, 1963-82, The Wall Street Journal, 1996-; Cook Lecturer in American Institutions, University of Michigan, 1977; Hitchcock Lecturer, University of California at Berkeley, 1982. Publications: Pier Luigi Nervi, 1960; Classic New York, 1964; Will They Ever Finish Bruckner Boulevard?, 1970; Kicked a Building Lately?, 1976; The Tall Building Artistically Reconsidered: The Search for a Skyscraper Style, 1985; Goodbye History, Hello Hamburger, 1986; Architecture Anyone?, 1986; The Unreal America: Architecture and Illusion, 1997. Contributions to: Various publications. Honours: Many honorary doctorates; Fulbright Fellowship, 1950-52; Guggenheim Fellowship, 1958; Architectural Medal for Criticism, American Institute of Architects, 1969; 1st Pulitzer Prize for Distinguished Criticism, 1970; Medal for Literature, National Arts Club, 1971; Diamond Jubilee Medallion, City of New York, 1973; Secretary's Award for Conservation, US Department of the Interior, 1976; Thomas Jefferson Medal, University of Virginia, 1977; John D and Catharine T MacArthur Foundation Fellowship, 1981-86; Henry Allen Moe Prize in the Humanities, American Philosophical Society, 1992. Memberships: American Academy of Arts and Letters; American Philosophical Society; American Academy of Arts and Sciences, fellow; New York Public Library, director's fellow; Society of Architectural Historians. Address: 969 Park Avenue, New York, NY 10028, USA.

**HUY Duc Luu,** b. 11 January 1958, Ha Tay, Vietnam. Chemist; Scientist. Education: BS, Hanoi National University, 1980; PhD, N D Zelinsky Institute of Organic Chemistry, Russian Academy of Sciences, 1992. Appointments: Scientist, Head of Laboratory, Fine Organic Synthesis, 1993-2003; Chemistry of Steroids, 2003-. Publications: New Methods for synthesis of corticoids from Sterols via 17-ketosteroids and 17beta-hydroxy-17alpha-ethynyl steroids. Honours: Vietnam Talent Young Science and Technology Award, 1998; Who's Who in the World, 2000. Memberships: ACS, 1996, 1997, 1998. Address: Institute of Chemistry, Vietnam Academy of Science and Technology, 18-Hoang Quoc Viet-Cau Giay- Ha Noi, Vietnam. E-mail: ldhuy@netnam.vn

**HUYNH My Hang V,** b. 30 May 1962, Saigon, Vietnam. Chemist. m. Michael A Hiskey. Education: BS, Chemistry, BA, Mathematics, State University College of New York at Geneseo,

1987-91; PhD, Co-ordination Chemistry, State University of New York at Buffalo, 1992-98. Appointments: Tutor, Chemistry and Mathematics, 1988-90, Teaching Assistant, 1989, State University College of New York at Geneseo; Teaching Assistant, State University of New York at Buffalo, 1997; Synthetic Organic Chemistry, High Nitrogen Energetic Materials, Dynamic Experimentation Division, Los Alamos National Laboratory, 2001-. Publications: 55 articles in scientific journals and 6 patents. Honours: Foundation Presidential Scholarship Award, State University College of New York at Geneseo, 1989-90; Department of Chemistry Supplemental Awards, 1992-93, Mattern-Tyler Award for Excellence in Teaching, 1995-96, State University of New York at Buffalo; Director-Funded Postdoctoral Fellow, 2001-02, Postdoctoral Distinguished Performance Award, 2002, Los Alamos National Laboratory; Listed in several Who's Who and biographical publications. Address: DX-2: Materials and Dynamic Group, MS C920 Los Alamos National University, North Mexico, USA. E-mail: huynh@lanl.gov

**HWANG Seong Taek,** b. 6 March 1965, Jeongju, Korea. Senior Engineer. m. Kyung-A Kim, 1 son, 1 daughter. Education: Bachelor, 1985-89, Master, 1989-90, Doctor, 1999-2001, Sogang University. Appointments: Researcher, Samsung Advanced Institute of Technology, 1993-95; Senior Engineer, 1996-, Project Leader, 1999-, Samsung Electronics. Publications: Articles in scientific journals including: Electronics Letters; IEEE Photonics Technology Letters; Journal of Lightwave Technology. Honours: Chairman's Prize, Samsung Group, 1995; Who's Who in the World, 2003; Who's Who in Science and Engineering, 2005-2006. Membership: IEEE. Address: 102-303, Daerim Apartment, Dokgok-dong, Pyongtaek, Gyunggi-do, Korea 459-707. Email: shwang@samsung.com

**HYAM Ronald,** b. 16 May 1936, Isleworth, England. Historian. Education: Royal Air Force, 1954-56; St John's College Cambridge, 1956-60; First Class in both parts of the Historical Tripos, 1958-59, BA, 1959, MA, 1963, PhD, 1963. Appointments: Fellow, Magdalene College Cambridge, 1962-; Reader, British Imperial History, University of Cambridge, 1996; Emeritus, 1999-; Sometime Librarian, Archivist, Admissions Tutor and President of Magdalene College, Cambridge. Publications: Books on imperial history including: Empire and Sexuality, 1990, 1991, 1992; Britain's Imperial Century 1915-1914, 3rd edition, 2002; The Lion and the Springbok: Britain and South Africa Since the Boer War (with Peter Henshaw), 2003. Honour: LittD, University of Cambridge, 1993. Membership: Project Committee, British Documents on the End of Empire Project. Address: Magdalene College, Cambridge CB3 0AG, England.

**HYATT Derek James,** b. 21 February 1931, Ilkley, Yorkshire, England. Artist; Teacher; Writer. m. Rosamond Joy Rockey, 1 daughter. Education: NDD Illustration, 1st class honours, Leeds College of Art, 1948-52; Part-time studies, Norwich School of Art, 1953; 1st class honours, Royal College of Art, 1954-58; Part-time courses, Film Studies, 1960, Philosophy, 1962, London University. Career: Solo exhibitions annually, throughout UK, 1958-; Visiting Lecturer, Art History and Foundation Course, Kingston School of Art, Surrey, 1959-64; Senior Lecturer, Visual Studies and Illustration Studies, Leeds Polytechnic, 1964-84; Visiting Professor, Cincinnati University, USA, 1980; Full-time artist and writer, 1984-. Publications: Numerous articles in professional art journals and magazines; Author and Illustrator, The Alphabet Stone, 1992; Co-author, Stone Fires-Liquid Clouds, The Shamanic Art of Derek Hyatt, monograph, 2001. Honours: Phil May Drawing Prize, 1954; Royal Scholar Prize, RCA, 1956; Landscape Painting

Prize, RCA, 1958; Companion of the Guild of St George, Ruskin Society, 1990; Yorkshire Arts Award, Bradford Art Gallery, Retrospective, 2001. Memberships: Artists for Nature Foundation International, Extremadura, Spain, 1998. Address: Rectory Farmhouse, Collingham, Wetherby, Yorkshire LS22 5AS, England.

**HYDON Kenneth John,** b. 3 November 1944, Leicester, England. Accountant. m. Sylvia, 1 son, 1 daughter. Education: FCMA; FCCA; FCT. Appointments: Financial Director: Racal SES Ltd, 1979-81; Racal Defence Radar and Avionics Group Ltd, 1981-85; Vodafone Group plc, 1985-; Non-Executive Director: Verizon Wireless (USA), 2000; Reckitt Benkiser plc, 2003- Tesco plc, 2004. Membership: Leander. Address: c/o Vodafone Group plc, The Connection, Newbury, Berkshire RG14 2FN, England. E-mail: ken.hydon@vodafone.com

**HYLLSETH Bjorn,** b. 30 May 1927, Skoger, Norway. Professor Emeritus. m. Randi, 2 sons, 2 daughters. Education: BVetSci, Sydney, Australia, 1958; PhD, Virology, Royal Veterinary College, Stockholm, Sweden, 1973. Appointments: Veterinarian, Franklin Veterinary Club, New Zealand, 1958-64; Laboratory Veterinarian, National Veterinary Institute, Stockholm, 1965-73; Professor, Virology, The Norwegian School of Veterinary Science, 1973-95. Publications: Several articles in professional journals. Membership: Norwegian Veterinary Association. Address: Leanglia 48, N-1387 Asker, Norway.

**HYMAN Timothy James,** b. 17 April 1946, Hove, Sussex, England. Painter; Writer. m. Judith Ravenscroft. Education: Slade School of Fine Art, 1963-67. Career includes: 7 London solo exhibitions including, Austin/Desmond Fine Art, 1990, 2000, 2003; Has shown widely in mixed exhibitions including: Royal Academy Summer Exhibition; Hayward Annual; Whitechapel Open; National Portrait Gallery; Works in public collections including: Arts Council Collection; British Museum; Government Art Collection; Los Angeles County Museum; Contemporary Art Society; Museum of London; Swindon Art Gallery; Deutsche Bank; Artist-in-Residence, Lincoln Cathedral, 1983-84; Artist-in Residence, Sandown Racecourse, 1992; Curated, Narrative Paintings, ICA, London and tour, 1979-80; Curated, Stanley Spencer, Tate Britain, 2001. Publications include: Bonnard, 1998; Bhupen Khakhar, 1998; Carnivalesque, 2000; Sienese Painting, 2003; Frequent contributions to The Times Literary Supplement, 1990-. Honours: Leverhulme Award, 1992; Wingate Award, 1998; Honorary Research Fellow, University College, London; Beato Angelico Medal, Florence, 2004. Address: 62 Myddelton Square, London EC1R 1XX, England.

**HYNDE Chrissie,** b. 7 September 1951, Akron, Ohio, USA. Singer; Songwriter; Musician. 1 daughter with Ray Davies, m. (1) Jim Kerr, divorced, 1 daughter, (2) Lucho Brieva, 1999. Appointments: Contributor to New Musical Express; Co-Founder, Chrissie Hynde and the Pretenders, 1978, Singer, Songwriter, Guitarist, New Band Formed, 1983; Tours in Britain, Europe & USA. Creative Works: Singles include: Stop Your Sobbing, 1978; Kid; Brass in Pocket; I Go to Sleep, 1982; Back on the Chain Gang, 1982; Middle of the Road, 1984; Thin Line Between Love and Hate; Don't Get Me Wrong; Hymn to Her; Albums include: Pretenders, 1980; Pretenders II, 1981; Extended Play, 1981; Learn to Crawl, 1985; Get Close, 1986; The Singles, 1987. Honours: Platinum and gold discs.

**HYNES H B Noel,** b. 20 December 1917, Devizes, Wiltshire, England. Biologist. m. Mary Hinks, deceased, 1999, 3 sons, 1 daughter. Education: ARCS, BSc Special, Imperial College, University of London, 1938; External Research Student (London), Freshwater Biological Association Laboratory, Ambleside, Westmorland, PhD, 1941, DSc, London, 1958. Appointments: Wireworm Survey, Ministry of Agriculture, Shropshire, England, 1941; Entomologist, Agriculture Branch of the Colonial Office, 1941-46; Training in Tropical Crops, Imperial College of Tropical Agriculture, Trinidad, 1941; Inducted into Locust Control Programme, Colonial Office, served in Ethiopia, Kenya and Somalia; Lecturer then Senior Lecturer, Liverpool University, 1947-64; Invited to make a Department of Biology, University of Waterloo, Canada, 1964; Retired as Distinguished Professor Emeritus, 1983; After retirement taught at new University of Addis Ababa, Ethiopia and University of Louisville, Kentucky, USA; Served on various committees for Canadian Government and World Health Organisation. Publications: Books: The biology of polluted waters, 1960; The ecology of running waters, 1970; Nunc dimittis – a life in the river of time (autobiography), 2001; More than 200 papers in scientific journals. Honours: Canada Centennial Medal; Elected Fellow, Royal Society of Canada; Hilary Jolly Award, Australian Society of Limnology; Honorary DSc, universities of Waterloo and New Brunswick; Naumann/Thieneman Medal, International Association of Limnology, 1998; Man of the Year 2005, American Biographical Institute; Listed in Who's Who publications and biographical dictionaries. Memberships: International Society for Limnology; Freshwater Biological Association; North American Benthological Society. Address: 127 Iroquois Place, Waterloo, Ontario, N2L 2S6, Canada. E-mail: nhynes@sciborg.uwaterloo.ca

**HYODO Haruo,** b. 3 March 1928, Japan. Radiologist. m. Keiko Tomita, 1 son, 2 daughters. Education: Dokkyo University School of Medicine, Japan; Tokushima University, Japan. Appointment: Radiologist. Publications: 2 Japanese patents. Honours: Gold Medal, Honorary Member, Japanese Society of Angiography and Interventional Radiology; Japan Billiary Association; Listed in international biographical publications. Memberships: Several Japanese associations. Address: 1-9-3 Saiwai-cyo, Mibu-machi, Shimotsuga tochigi, 321-0203 Japan. E-mail: hyodo283@green.ocn.ne.jp

# I

**IACONETTA Giorgio,** b. 1 February 1962, Cosenza, Italy. Neurosurgeon. m. Giosetta de Simone, 1 son, 1 daughter. Education: Medical Doctor, Naples University Federico, 1986; Assistant, 1990, Specialist, Nurosurgery, 1991, Assistant Professor of Neurosurgery, 2000, University of Naples "Federico II". Appointments: University of Paris, France, 1987; Department of Neurosurgery, New York University Medical Center, New York, USA, 1989; Research Fellow, Neurosurgery, University Hospital, Basel, Switzerland, 1995-96; Department of Neurosurgery, University of Hannover, Germany, 1997-2000; Department of Neurosurgical Anatomy, University of Vienna, Austria, 2002 and 2004; Currently Professor of Neurosurgery, University of Naples "Federico II". Publications: Book: Anatomical Variants of Cerebral Arteries; 3 book chapters on neurosurgical topics; More than 70 papers in international journals. Honours: Italian Ministry of Health, 1989; Italian National Council of Research, 1988, 1996, 1997, 1998, 1999; University of Naples "Federico II", 1996-97; German Council of Research, 1998. Memberships: Italian Society of Neurosurgery; Italian Skull Base Society; Italian Society of Computer Assisted Surgery; Italian Society of Neuro-onclogy. Address: Via Gravina 2, 80055 Portici (NA), Italy. E-mail: iaconetta@libero.it

**IBBETT Vera,** b. 30 May 1929, Lower Kingswood, Surrey, England. Artist; Calligrapher. m. Raymon Strank. Education: Reigate School of Art, 1943-46; Regent Polytehnic, 1947-48; City & Guilds of London Art School, 1948-53; Diploma, Graphic Reproduction, London College of Printing, 1960-61; Studied under John Nash R.A., 1965, Villu Toots, 1990. Career: Artist, painter and illustrator in oils, watercolour and pastel; Private commissions for animal portraits including North African charity veterinary instruction panels; Award winning seed packet designs; Book jackets, full colour illustrations; National Gallery copying transaction; Tower of London calligraphic display work; Exhibited: RA; RMS; SWA; FBA; Appeared on the TV series "The Craftsmen", 1972; Teacher, Reigate School of Art, 1975-86; Designed manuscript with illustrations and calligraphy, Flowers in Heraldry, 1972-75; Battle of Britain memorial panel for RAF Chapel Biggin Hill, 1982; Life size free standing figures for museum display, 1988; Botanical illustration for educational series, 2000; Sculptured bronze plaque commemorating working donkeys in Covent Garden, 2000; Works in private collections in UK and overseas. Publications include: Flowers in Heraldry, limited edition, The Alcuin Society, Canada, 1977; Work in Alcuin Society's Journal, Amphora, British Columbia, 1996; Works in La Revue Moderne. Honours: Awards for Lettering and Calligraphy, Worshipful Company of Painter Stainers, 1958; Elected Fellow, Society of Scribes and Illustrators, 1969; RHS Grenfell Medal for Botanical Illustration, 1970; Elected Member, RMS, 1990; RMS, Gold Bowl Honourable Mention, 1995; RHS, Silver Gilt Lindley Medal for Botanical Illustrations of Educational and Scientific Merit, 2000; Elected Honorary Member, Royal Society of Miniature Painters, 2003. Address: 89 Chipstead Lane, Lower Kingswood, Surrey KT 20 6RD, England.

**IBITOLA Gilbert Akin,** b. 18 January 1962, Ayere, Nigeria. w. Ruth Anyango Odallo, 1 son, 1 daughter. Education: BSc, University of Sokoto, 1984; MSc, University of Ilorin, 1988; PhD, Devi Ahilya University, Indore, India, 1998; Diploma, CIM, Ambala City, India, 1995. Appointments: NYSC Lecturer, Physics, Electronics, The Polytechnic, Ibadan, Nigeria, 1984-85; Part-time Graduate Assistant, Assistant Lecturer, Physics, University of Ilorin, Ilorin, Nigeria, 1985-88; Lecturer, Physics/Electronics, Kwara State Polytechnic, Ilorin,

Nigeria, 1987-89; Assistant Lecturer, Lecturer I and II, Physics/Electronics, 1989-96; Part-time Lecturer, Electronics, Devi Ahilya University, Indore, India, 1993-96; Part-time Lecturer, Electronics, University of Nairobi, Nairobi, Kenya, 1996-97; Lecturer, Senior Lecturer, Physics with Electronics, Kenyatta University, Nairobi, Kenya, 1997-. Publications: Over 30 papers presented at conferences, workshops and seminars include most recently: Adaptive IIR Filtering of Delta-Sigma Modulated Signals, 2003; Web Caching Policies – A Comparison, 2003; A Multi-Destination Routing Approach to Improve Web Server Response, 2004; Web Server: Browsing of the Web Through E-Mail, 2004. Honours include: Vice-Chancellors Prize to best all-round BSc Student, University of Sokoto, Nigeria, 1984; Commonwealth Scholarship and Fellowship Scheme Award, 1992-96; Great Minds of the 21st Century, ABI, USA, 2004. Memberships: Indian Academy for Instructional Planning; Life Member, Indian National Institute-Industry Forum for Energy; Professional Member, Central Institute of Management of India; Life Member, Kenya Meteorological Society; Life Member, Solar Energy Society of India; New York Academy of Sciences; American Association for the Advancement of Science; Institute of Electrical and Electronics Engineers, USA; Association for Computing Machinery of USA. Address: Department of Physics, Kenyatta University, PO Box 43844, Nairobi, Kenya. E-mail: ibitolaieee1@yahoo.com

**IBRAHIM WUSHISHI Dantani,** b. 5 April 1965, Wushishi, Nigeria. Educator. m. Halima Ibrahim, 2 sons. 1 daughter. Education: BSc Ed, Chemistry, 1998; M Ed, Science Education, 2001; PhD, Science Education, 2005. Appointments: Nigerian Navy (Rating Corp), 1988-2004; Lecturer II, Department of Science and Vocational Education, 2004-, Unit Co-ordinator, Science and Mathematics Education, B Ed Part-time Programme, 2004-, Usmanu Danfodiyo University, Sokoto, Nigeria; President, Muslim Students Society of Nigeria, Niger State Area Unit, 1986. Publications: Books: Islam and Modern Gambling, 1995; Reasons for the Resurgence of Sharia in Nigeria, 2003; Many articles on journals. Honours: Baldaz Prize for Best Student in Physics, 1989; Best Features Writer, National Association of Campus Journalists, Usmanu Danfodiyo University. Membership: Science Teachers Association of Nigeria. Address: Department of Science and Vocational Education, Usmanu Danfodiyo University, Sokoto, Nigeria. E-mail: deewushishi@yahoo.com

**ICE-T (Tracy Marrow),** b. Newark, New Jersey, USA. Rap Singer; Actor. m. Darlene Ortiz, 1 child. Creative Works: Albums: Rhyme Pays, 1987; The Iceberg/Freedom of Speech; Just Watch What You Say, 1989; O G Original Gangster, 1991; Havin' a "T" Party (with King Tee), 1991; Body Count, 1992; Home Invasion, 1993; The Classic Collection, 1993; Born Dead (with Body Count), 1994; 7th Deadly Sin, 1999; Films: Breakin', 1984; New Jack City, 1991; Ricochet, 1991; Trespass, 1992; Surviving the Game, 1994; Tank Girl, 1995; Johnny Mnemonic, 1995; Below Utopia; Final Voyage, 1999; Corrupt, 1999; Leprechaun 5, 2000; Sonic Impact, 2000; The Alternate, 2000; Hip Hop 2000, 2001; Out Kold, 2001. Publication: The Ice Opinion, 1994. Address: Priority Records, 6430 West Sunset Boulevard, Los Angeles, CA 90028, USA. Website: www.mcicet.com

**ICHINOHE Minoru,** b. 5 December 1926, Aomori, Japan. Nematologist. m. Mitsuyo Kuwayama, 2 sons. Education: Graduated, 1950, Doctorate, 1961, Institute of Applied Zoology, Faculty of Agriculture, Hokkaido University, Sapporo, Japan. Appointments: Nematologist, Hokkaido National Agricultural Experiment Station, Sapporo, Japan, 1950-58; Chief of Nematology Laboratory, National Institute of Agricultural

Sciences, Nishigahara, Tokyo, 1958-79; Director, Department of Plant Pathology and Entomology, Hokkaido National Agricultural Experiment Station, Sapporo, 1979-87. Publications: Over 100 articles in peer-reviewed scientific journals and books. Honours: Rockefeller Foundation Fellowship, 1958; Award, Japanese Society of Applied Entomology and Zoology, 1966; Special Honour, Lecture on Nematology to Emperor of Japan, Imperial Palace, 1980; Fellow, Society of Nematologists, 1989. Memberships: Society of Nematologists; Japanese Nematological Society. Address: 2-3-11 Yachiyodai Minami, Yachiyo, Chiba, Japan 276-0033.

**IDONIBOYE Kitchener Okoma Igonikon,** b. 12 September 1941, Buguma, Rivers State, Nigeria. Professor of Engineering. m. Victoria Tariah, 3 sons. Education: Dip Tech, Ryerson Polytechnic University, Toronto, Canada, 1973; BS, New York Institute of Technology, New York, USA, 1974; MSc, Polytechnic University of New York, New York City, USA, 1975-76. Appointments: Studio Manager, Nigerian Broadcasting Corporation, 1959-63; University Lecturer, 1979-85, Senior Lecturer, 1986-91, Professor of Engineering Management, 1992, Professor and Dean of Engineering Faculty, 1995 –99, Rivers State University of Science and Technology. Publications: Over 35 articles in learned professional journals including AMSE, France; British Journal of Energy; Nigerian Journal of Chemical and Industrial Engineers. Honours: Life Patron of all engineering students in Nigeria; Doctorate Fellowship of the Nigerian Institute of Technicians, 1995. Memberships: Board of Fellows of the Nigerian Institute of Technicians; New York Academy of Sciences; University Tender's Board; Committee of University Deans of Nigeria; Past Chairman of a panel of Professors to accredit Nigeria's University of Ibadan; Chairman, Review Panel of Oil and Gas Project, Gbaran/UBIE integrated node, mid-western Nigeria; Chairman, Technical Review Panel of Ogbainbiri Flow Station; Member, Pane Review Meeting on Environmental Impact Assessment in Palm Oil Estates, Edo State, Nigeria; Chairman, National Universities Commission accrediting Engineering facilities of: University of Ibadan, Obafemi Awolowo University, Ife-Ife Benin University, Federal University of Technology in Akwre, University of Ado-Ekiti, University of Ekpoma and Lado Re Akintola University in Ogbomosho; Member, University Curriculum Review Workshops, National University Commission. Address: Faculty of Engineering, Rivers State University of Science and Technology, Port Harcourt, Nigeria.

**IDRUS Zulkifli,** b. 7 April 1965, Singapore. Professor. m. Lily Normala Mahdi, 1 daughter. Education: Doctor of Veterinary Medicine, 1989, MS, 1992, Universiti Pertanian Malaysia; PhD, Virginia Polytechnic Institute and State University, USA, 1994. Appointments: Tutor, 1992-94, Lecturer, 1994-99, Associate Professor, 1999-2004, Professor, 2004-, Universiti Putra Malaysia. Publications: Over 45 articles in scientific journals as first author and co-author include most recently: Fear and stress reactions and the performance of commercial broiler chickens subjected to regular pleasant and unpleasant contacts with human beings, 2004; Growth performance, mortality and immune response of two commercial broiler strains subjected to early age feed restriction and heat conditioning under hot, humid, tropical environment, 2004; Responses of heat stressed broiler chickens to dietary supplementation of virginiamycin and Acid-Pak 4-Way™, and early age feed restriction, 2005; Numerous papers presented at conferences. Honours include: Friskie's Award for the Best Doctor of Veterinary Medicine Graduate in Clinical Conference UPM, 1989; Gamma Sigma Delta, 1994; Sigma Xi, 1994; Excellent Service Certificate, Faculty of Veterinary Medicine and Animal Science 1996; Best Scientific Paper Award, 19th Malaysian Society of Animal Production

Conference, 1998; British Council Award for Animal Welfare Educational Visit to UK, 2001; Joint Gold Medal Winner and Silver Medal Winner, 2002, Joint Winner of 2 Bronze Medals, 2003, Joint Gold Medal Winner, 2005 Universiti Putra Malaysia Research and Development Exhibitions; Listed in Who's Who publications and biographical dictionaries. Memberships: Poultry Science Association; Virginia Polytechnic and State University Alumni; Universiti Putra Malaysia Alumni; Veterinary Association of Malaysia; Malaysian Society of Animal Production; World's Poultry Science Association; Malaysian Zoological Association; Universities Federation of Animal Welfare. Address: Department of Animal Science, Faculty of Agriculture, Universiti Putra Malaysia, 43400 UPM Serdang, Selangor, Malaysia. E-mail: zulkifli@agri.upm.edu.my

**IGIĆ Rajko,** b. 9 November 1937, Despotovo, Vojvodina, Yugoslavia. Physician; Pharmacologist. m. Danica Munitić, 2 sons. Education: MD, University of Belgrade Medical School, 1963; PhD, University of Sarajevo, 1970. Appointments: General Practitioner, Sombor, 1963-65; Assistant Professor, University of Sarajevo, 1966-77; Professor, Head, Department of Pharmacology, University of Tuzla, 1978-92; Director, Department of Scientific, Cultural, Technical and Educational International Exchange for Republic of Bosnia and Herzegovina, Sarajevo, 1990-92; Currently Senior Scientist, Cook County Hospital, Chicago, Illinois, USA. Publications: More than 100 research papers and several books, including contributions to Neuropharmacology, 1970, British Journal of Pharmacology, 1971, Circulation Research, 1972, Journal of Pharmacological and Toxicological Methods, 1996, The Scientist, 1997, American Psychologist, 1999; Eleven Poems and One Story, 2001; The Destiny of Germans in St Ivan and Other Writings, 2002; Current Pharmaceutical Design, 2003. Honours: Fulbright Fellow, 1970-72, 1974; Oklahoma Heart Association Fellowship Award, 1971-72; National Award for Scientific Research, Bosnia and Herzegovina, 1986. Memberships: Yugoslav Society of Biomedical Journals and Bulletins, President, 1992-2000; American Physiological Society. Address: Anesthesiology Research, Room 427DX, 637 S Wood Street, Chicago, IL 60612, USA. E-mail: rigic@hektoen.org

**IIDA Yôichi,** b. 21 August 1940, Kobe, Japan. Chemist; Molecular Biologist. m. Hiroko Yokoyama, 1 son, 1 daughter. Education: BS, University of Tokyo, 1963; MS, University of Tokyo, 1965; DSc, University of Tokyo, 1969. Appointments: Research Associate, 1965-77, Lecturer, 1977-95, Associate Professor, 1995-, Hokkaido University, Japan. Publications: Author, Seminar Book of Basic Physical Chemistry, 1992; Human Genome Project and Bioinformatics, 1995; Handbook of Multivariate Statistical Analysis and Examples, 2002; Contributor of articles to professional journals. Memberships: Physical Society of Japan; Chemical Society of Japan; Biophysical Society of Japan; Molecular Biological Society of Japan. Address: Department of Chemistry, Graduate School of Science, Hokkaido University, 060-0810 Sapporo, Hokkaido, Japan. E-mail: chemjimu@sci.hokudai.ac.jp

**IKE Adebimpe Olurinsola,** b. 29 June 1933, Ijebu Igbo, Ogun State, Nigeria. Librarian; Administrator. m. Chukwuemeka Ike OFR, 1 son. Education: BA (Hons), London, 1960; MA, Ghana, 1974; PG Dip Lib, Ibadan, 1965. Appointments: Sub-Librarian, University of Nigeria, Nsukka, 1962-71; Readers Adviser, Ghana Library Board, Accra, Ghana, 1972-74; Assistant Documentalist, Association of African Universities, Accra, Ghana, 1974-75; Senior Librarian, Principal Librarian, University of Lagos, 1976-81; Pioneer University Librarian, Abubakar Tafawa Balewa University, Bauchi, 1981-93; National Co-Ordinator NADICEST Project, 1988-; Visiting

Lecturer, Department of Library Science and Archives, University of Ghana, Legon, Ghana, 1975-76; Professor of Library Science, Nnamdi Azikiwe University, Awka, 1995-. Publications: 54 contributions in monographs, scholarly journals, conferences and seminars. Honours: Lions Club Merit Award for Professional Excellence; Federal Government Scholarships, Secondary School and University. Memberships include: Life Member, Chartered Institute of Library and Information Professionals, UK; Founding Member, Nigerian Library Association; Nigerian Institute of Management. Address: National Documentation and Information Centre for Science and Technology, Nnamdi Azikiwe University, PO Box 1132, Awka, Anambra State, Nigeria.

**IKEDA Kazuyosi,** b. 15 July 1928, Fukuoka, Japan. Physicist; Poet (trilingual, English/Japanese/Chinese). m. Mieko Akiyama Ikeda, 20 November 1956, 1 son, 1 daughter. Education: Graduate, 1951, post graduate studies, 1951-56; Department of Physics, Kyushu University, DSc, 1957. Appointments: Assistant, 1956-60, Associate Professor, 1960-65, Department of Physics, Kysushu University; Associate Professor, 1965-68, Professor, 1988-92, Professor Emeritus, 1992-, Osaka University, Department of Applied Physics, 1965-89, Department of Mathematical Sciences, 1989-; Professor, 1992-, President, 1995-, International Earth Environment University, Japan; Board Member, Advisory Council, Ansted University, 1999-. Publications include: Mechanics without Use of Mathematical Formulae; From a Moving Stone to Halley's Comet; Statistical Thermodynamics; Invitation to Mechanics With Appendix on a Comet in Ancient Times; Basic Mechanics; Basic Thermodynamics; From Entropy to Osmotic Pressure; Graphical Theory of Relativity, and others; over 100 papers on theoretical physics; Over 30 literary books including: Bansyoo Hyakusi Collection of Poems; The World of God, Creation and Poetry; Poems on the Hearts of Creation; Mountains; North South East West; Hearts of Myriad Things in the Universe; Kazuyosi's Poetry on the Animate and the Inanimate; Poems on Love and Peace; Songs of the Soul; Hearts of Innumerous Things in Heaven and Earth; Kazuyosi's Poems on Myriad Things – For Global Brotherhood and World Peace; The World of Hearts; Peace Offerings; Men and Nature; Spring Rain; Universal Songs; Paeans to Spirit; Journeys of Hearts; Rainbows and Flowers; Dances of Spirit; Serialised Poems of 7-5 syllables Fixed Form; Haiku; Tanka; Chinese classical fixed-form poems; Over 60 Literary Articles, Reviews and Essays on Poetry. Honours include: Yukawa Commemorative Scholarship Award; World Decoration of Excellence Medal; Mandakini Literary Award; Hall of Fame; International Cultural Diploma of Honour; Grand Ambassador of Achievement; International Order of Merit; Cultural Doctorate in Poetical Literature; Honorary Doctor of Literature; Honorary Doctor of Environmental Science; Man of the Year; Personality of the Year; International Man of the Year; One in a Million Award; Sphatica International Poet Award; Global Peace and Friendship Award; International Medal for Scientific Excellence; Chevalier Grand Cross; Golden Academy Award for Lifetime Achievement; International Eminent Poet; International Sash of Academia; Golden Scroll of Excellence; Who's Who of the Year Award; 25 Years Achievement Award; Albert Einstein Academy Award for Outstanding Achievement; Knight of San Ciriaco Order; Prize Libro d'Oro; Silver Shield of Valor; Five-Star Leader Award; Most Admired Man of the Decade, Presidential Seal of Honour; Gold Record Achievement; Ambassador of Great Eminence; Order of Pegasus of Highest Degree; Prize Catania; Prize Pandit; International Artistic-Literary Prize of Primavera Catanese; Diploma of Honour of Institute of International Affairs; Platinum Record of Exceptional Performance; Best World Poet of Year, 1999; Star of Asia Award in Poetry; Award of Homage

to Dante Alighieri for Poetical Work; Top 100 Scientist Medal for Significant Achievements in the Field of Theoretical, Mathematical and Chemical Physics and Environmental Science; World Laureate; Prize Oscar 2000; International Commendation of Success in the Professions of Science and Poetry; Silver Book Prize for Universal Songs; Golden Pen Prize for Poetical Work Landforms; Poet of the Millennium Award; International Scientist of the Year; International Commendation of Success; Genius Elite for Remarkable Achievements in the Field of Poetry and Science; Honour of Greatest Intellectual; Decree of International Letters for Cultural Achievement; Outstanding Man of the 20th Century; Scientific Achievement Award; Outstanding Scientist of the 20th Century; Professional Performance Key Award; Notable Author Award; Biographical Honour Award; Torch of Gold Inspiration; Most Influential Scientist of the Decade; Award of Lifelong Tenure of Einstein Chair of Science; Master Diploma for Special Honours in Science and Poetry; Michael Madhusudan Award; Voice of Kolkata Award; World Lifetime Achievement Award; Knight of Lofsensic Ursinius Order; Knight of the Universal Knights Order; NS Chandra Bose National Award for Excellence in the Field of Poetry and Environmental Science; IBC Lifetime Achievement Award; Torch of Global Inspiration; Oscar 2000 Award; The 20th Century Award for Achievement; Golden Book International Prize; Omaggio a Dennis Kann International Poetry Prize; Award of Poem for the Life; Gold Medal of Outstanding Scientist; Ivory Eagle 2001 Award; The 21st Century Award for Achievement; Vice Consul; Legacy of Honor; American Medal of Honor for Significant Accomplishments in the Field of Poetry and Science; Gran Premio d'Autore; Order of International Ambassadors; Medalla al Merito of International Parliament for Safety and Peace; Companion of Honour; Knight of Templar Order; Knight of Holy Grail Order; Excellence in World Poetry Award; World Citizen of the Year; Knight Commander of Sovereign Order of Ambrosini's; Order of Distinction as Specialist in Theoretical Physics and Poetry; Author of the Year Award; International Peace Prize; Leader in Science Award; Gold Star Award; Poet of the Millennium; International Scientist of the Year 2001; Man of Achievement Award, 2005; Leading Scientist of the Year Award; Region of Honor Award, United Cultural Convention; Great Lives Medal; Cambridge Blue Book Man of the Year; Outstanding Intellectual of the 21st Century Medal; Libro Successo International Prize for Paeans to Spirit; Silver Book Prize for Nosce to Ipsum; Golden Book Prize for Kazuyosi's Poems for Myriad Things; Honour of Greatest Mind; The 21st Century Genius of Distinction Award; Lifetime Achievement Award of the United Cultural Covention; numerous others; Listed in over 50 Who's Who books and over 25 dedication sections. Memberships include: New York Academy of Sciences; Physical Society of Japan; Planetary Society; Cyperwit Net; Director, Kansai Branch, Professors World Peace Academy; Chairman, Osaka Branch and Osaka University Branch, National and Professors-Students Coalition Unification of N E W S; Life Fellow, Life Patron, Board of Governors, IBA; Deputy Director General, Research Board of Advisers, Continental Governor, IBC; Deputy Governor, ABIRA; Honorary Founder and Representative for Japan of Olympoetry Movement; Senator and Minister Plenipotentiary for Japan of International Parliament for Safety and Peace; Senator and Minister Plenipotentiary for Asian States of Council of States for Protection of Life; Senator, Academy MIDI; Director, International Writers and Artists Association; Honorary Director, World Parnasians Guild International; Board Member, Modern Poets Society; Editor, Modern Poetry; Member, Grand Council, Confederation of Chivalry; Academician of Honour, Academy Ferdinandea; Academician of Merit, Academy International Trinacria; Charter Member, Order of International Fellowship; Life Member, WIA;

Life Fellow, WLA; Life Fellow, International Poets Academy; Life Fellow, United Writers' Association; Life Member, World Congress of Poets; Honorary Life Member, Jagruthi Kiran Foundation; Honorary Fellow Member, Academy of Indo-Asian Literature; Patron, Karuna India Society; Executive Member, Commissione Lettura Internazionale; Honorary Adviser, Brain Wave; Founding Charter Member, the Leading Intellectuals of the World; Founder Member, Scientific Faculty of Cambridge; Founding Member, American Order of Excellence; Chief Executive, Michael Madhusudan Academy; Founding Member, London Diplomatic Academy; Corresponding Member and Representative for Japan, Institut des Affaires Internationales; Litterateur Life Chief Patron, Metverse Muse; Founding Member, International Honour Society; Consulting Editor, Contemporary Who's Who; Editor, Rock Pebbles; Editorial Advisor, Titas; Patron-in-Chief, Chetana Literary Group; Patron, Katha Kshetre; Patron, Karuna India Society; Chief Patron, Home of Letters; Patron-in-Chief, Omega Welfare Organisation; Patron-in-Chief, Voice of Kolkata. Address: Nisi-7-7-11 Aomadani, Minoo-si, Osaka 562-0023, Japan.

**IKEUCHI Hiroshi,** b. 5 July 1924, Japan. Orthopaedic Surgeon. m. Setsuko. Education: Graduate, Tohoku University, 1949; PhD, 1960. Appointments: Vice Chairman, 1966, Chairman, 1984, Emeritus Chairman, 1990-94, Department of Orthopaedic Surgery, Tokyo Teishin Hospital, 1949-; Resident Doctor and Fellowship Professor (under instruction of Dr David M Bosworth), Department of Orthopaedic Surgery, St Giles Hospital, Sea View Hospital, St Luke's Hospital and Policlinic Hospital, New York, USA, 1959-62; Visiting Lecturer, Tokyo University, 1974-78; Instructor, UCLA, 1978-85; Visiting Lecturer, Shinshu University, 1982-91; Visiting Professor, Kansas University, 1982. Publications include: Total Meniscectomy of Complete Discoid Lateral Meniscus under Arthroscopic Control; Arthroscopic Peripheral Repair of the Menisci. Honours: Purple Ribbon Medal, Ministry of Science and Technology, 1972; Maejima Hisoka Prize, Tele-Communication Association, 1991; Award, Japanese Orthopaedic Association, 1991; Third Order of Merit with the Sacred Treasure, 1994. Memberships: Japanese Orthopaedic Association; Japanese Rheumatism Association; Arthroscopy Association of North America; German Speaking Association of Arthroscopy; French Arthroscopy Association; Argentina Arthroscopy Association; Ikeuchi Intern Society for Arthroscopy and Musculoskeletal Endoscopy. Address: Ozenji-nishi, 6-chome, 24-14, Asao-ku, Kawasaki-shi, Kanagawa-ken, 215-0017, Japan.

**ILLIS Leon Sebastian,** b. 4 March 1930, London, England. Emeritus Consultant Neurologist; Editor, Neurological Journal. m. Oonagh Mary, 3 sons. Education: BSc; MB BS; MD; FRCP. Appointments: House Physician, Registrar, Senior Registrar, University College Hospital, Guy's Hospital. National Hospital, Queen Square, Hospital for Sick Children, Great Ormond Street; Consultant Neurologist, Southampton University Hospitals; Editor, Spinal Cord. Publications: 16 chapters; More than 70 scientific papers; 6 books. Honours: Gold Medal, Ceylon College of Physicians, 1977, 1987. Memberships: Royal College of Physicians; Royal Society of Medicine; Athenaeum; Royal Lymington Yacht Club. Address: Pond House, Sowley, Nr Lymington, Hampshire SO41 5SQ, England. E-mail: lee@illis.co.uk

**ILLSLEY Eric,** b. 9 April 1955, Barnsley, South Yorkshire, England. Member of Parliament. m. Dawn Illsley, 2 daughters. Education: LLB, Law, University of Leeds. Appointments: Head of Administration, Yorkshire National Union of Mineworkers; Member of Parliament, Barnsley Central, 1987-; Member, Select Committee, on Energy, 1987, 1991, on Televising Proceedings

of the House of Commons, 1988-91, on Procedure, 1991-; on Foreign Affairs, 1997-; Opposition Whip, 1991-94; Opposition spokesperson, on health, 1994-95, on local government, 1995, on Northern Ireland, 1995-97. Memberships: Member, Co-operative Party and MSF; Joint Chair, All Party Parliamentary Glass Committee; Treasurer, Yorkshire Labour Group of Members of Parliament; Member, Chairman's Panel; Vice Chair, Parliamentary and Scientific Committee; Vice Chair, Commonwealth Parliamentary Association UK Branch; Executive Committee Member, Inter Parliamentary Union. Address: House of Commons, London SW1A 0AA, England. E-mail: illsleye@parliament.uk

**ILOZOR Benedict Dozie,** b. 26 September 1964, Agulu, Nigeria. University Professor; Architect. m. Doreen Beng Choo Ilozor, 1 son, 2 daughters. Education: BSc (Hons), Architecture, 1986; MSc, Architecture, 1988; Computer Engineering, 1997; PhD, FM Design, Architecture and Building, University of Technology, Sydney, Australia, 1999. Appointments: Tenured Faculty and Management Discipline Co-ordinator for Architecture and Construction Management, School of Architecture and Building, Deakin University, Australia, 2000-2003; Intercollegiate Professor of Architecture, Department of Architecture, Hampton University, Virginia, USA, 2003-. Publications: Over 100 publications as refereed journals and conference papers, editorial, keynote papers and monographs; Editor (Asia Pacific) ASCE Journal of Performance of Constructed Facilities; Journal of Management and Development; Journal of Engineering, Design and Technology. Honours: UK Prize for Sustainability, Royal Institution of Chartered Surveyors; Listed in Who's Who publications and biographical dictionaries. Memberships: Facility Management Association of Australia; Accredited by the Architects Accrediting Council of Australia for the Royal Australian Institute of Architects. Address: Department of Architecture, Faculty of Engineering and Technology, Hampton University, VA 23668, USA. E-mail: benedict.ilozor@hamptonu.edu

**ILYINA Nataly V,** b. 18 June 1957, Vorkuta, Russia. Geologist. Education: Graduate, Ukhta Industrial Institute (now Technical University), 1974-79; Candidate of Science (PhD), Geology, Mineralogy, 1998. Appointment: Senior Research Associate, Institute of Geology, Komi Science Centre, Ural Division of the Russian Academy of Sciences, 2001-. Publications: Book: Palynostratigraphy of the Middle Triassic in the Timan-Northern Uralian Region. Ekaterinburg: Ural Division of the RAS Press, 2001; 18 articles; 10 abstracts. Honour: The Woman of 1992-93, IBS. Memberships: Palaeontological Society of Russia; Palynological Commission of Russia. Address: Institute of Geology, Komi Science Centre, Ural Division, Russian Academy of Sciences, 54 Pervomayskaya St, 167982 Syktyvkar, Russia. E-mail: institute@geo.komisc.ru

**ILYUMZHINOV Kirsan Nikolayevich,** b. 5 April 1962, Elista, Kalmykia. President of the Republic of Kalmykia. m. 1 son. Education: Graduate, Moscow State University for International Relations, 1989. Appointments: Elected President of the Republic of Kalmykia, 1993, re-elected, 1995, 2002-. Publications: President's Crown of Thorns (a documentary novel), 1995; Kalmykia at the turn of centuries (research work), 1997; Kalmykia. Heading toward democracy (research work), 1998. Honour: Order of Friendship by the Decree of the Russian President, 1997. Address: House of Government, 35800 Elista, Republic of Kalmykia, Russian Federation. E-mail: press_kalm@mail.ru

**ILYUSHIN Michael,** b. 8 June 1945, Chapaevsk Kuibyshev Region, USSR. Professor; Chemistry. m. Shugalei Irina

V, 1 daughter. Education: Engineer Chemist-Technologist Diploma, Leningrad Liensovet Institute of Technology (LTI), 1969; Candidate of Chemical Sciences (PhD), LTI, 1975; Doctor of Chemical Sciences, State Institute of Technology, St Petersburg, 1995. Appointments: Engineer, 1969-72; Aspirant (post-postgraduate), 1972-75; Researcher, 1975-78; Assistant Professor, 1978-93, Associate Professor, 1993-95, Professor, 1995-. Publications: 11 papers, many on explosives, in journals or other professional publications. Honours: Medal, Inventor of the USSR, 1981; Soros Associate Professor, Russia, 1997; Award for Achievement, 1998; 20th Century Award for Achievement, 1999; International Man of the Year, 1997-98, 1999-2000; International Man of the Millennium, 1999. Membership: All-Russian Chemical Society, 1972. Address: St Petersburg State Institute of Technology (Technical University), Moskovsky pr 26, 190013, St Petersburg, Russia.

**IM Ye Hoon,** b. 15 May 1969, Korea. Senior Scientist. m. Mi Young Sung, 2 daughters. Education: BS, Aerospace Engineering, Inha University, 1988-92; MS, Aerospace Engineering, 1992-94, PhD, Aerospace Engineering, 1994-2000, Korea Advanced Institute of Science and Technology. Appointments: Korea Institute of Machinery and Materials, 2000-2001; LG Chem Ltd, 2001-. Publications: 5 journal papers; 24 conference papers; 22 research reports; Unsteady Aerodynamics of a wing ground airfoil moving over a wavy wall, 2000; Application of "Fluent +gPROMS" in R&D and Plants (Application to the industrial acrylic acid reactor), 2005. Memberships: Korean Society for Aeronautical and Space Sciences, 1994; Korean Society for Computational Fluids Engineering, 1995; Korean Institute of Chemical Engineers. 2001. Address: LG Chem Ltd, Research Park, 104-1Moonji-dong, Yuseong-gu, Daejeon 305-380, Korea. E-mail: yehoon@lgchem.com

**IMAMURA Tohru,** b. 29 September 1945, Nagoya, Japan. Physicist. m. Seiko (Kimizuka), 2 daughters. Education: Graduate, Toyama High School, 1964; BSc, Faculty of Science, University of Tokyo, 1969. Appointments: Research Officer, 1969-79, Senior Research Officer, 1979-2001, Office of International Relations, 1985-2001, National Research Laboratory of Metrology; Senior Research Scientist, National Institute of Advanced Industrial Science and Technology, 2001-. Publications: Theoretical and Applied Mechanics, 1973; Scientific papers in professional journals, 1972-. Honours: Letter of thanks for work as Chairman, Parents and Teachers Association of an elementary school; Listed in Who's Who publications and biographical dictionaries. Memberships: Acoustical Society of America; Acoustical Society of Japan; Societe Franco-Japonaise des Techniques Industrielles. Address: 35-10 Midorigaoka, Tsukuba 305-0863, Japan. E-mail: tohru-imamura@aist.go.jp

**IMAN (Iman Abdul Majid),** b. 25 July 1956, Model. m. (1) Spencer Haywood, divorced 1987, 1 child, (2) David Bowie, 1992, 1 daughter. Education: Nairobi University. Appointments: Fashion Model, 1976-90; Has modelled for Claude Montana and Thierry Mugler; Signed Revlon Polish Ambers Contract (1st black model to be signed by an international cosmetics co); 1979; Numerous TV appearances; Appeared in Michael Jackson video. Creative Works: Films include: Star Trek VI: The Undiscovered Country; Houseparty II; Exit to Eden; The Deli, 1997; Omikron: The Nomad Soul, 1999. Address: c/o Elite Model Management, 40-42 Parker Street, London WC2B 5PQ, England.

**IMMELMAN Niel,** b. 13 August 1944, Bloemfontein, South Africa. Pianist. Education: Royal College of Music, 1964-69; Private studies with Ilona Kabos, 1969-70, Maria Curcio, 1970-76; LRAM; ARCM; LGSM; LTCL. Career: Debut with London Philharmonic Orchestra, 1969; Concert appearances, London's Royal Festival Hall, Royal Albert Hall and Amsterdam Concertgebouw; Concert tours of every continent; Compact disc recordings for Etcetera and Meridian labels; Professor of Piano, Royal College of Music, London, 1980-; Masterclasses at Berlin Hochschule, The Chopin Academy, Warsaw and Moscow Conservatoire. Publications: Commercial recordings of Beethoven, Schubert, Schumann, Dale, Suk and Bloch; First pianist in history to record complete piano works of Josef Suk; Articles on pianists Lamar Crowson and Annie Fischer. Honours: Chappell Gold Medal, 1969; Fellow, Royal College of Music, 2000. Memberships: Royal Society of Musicians of Great Britain; EPTA. Address: 41 Ashen Grove, London, SW19 8BL, England. E-mail: immelman@lineone.net

**IMRAN KHAN NIAZI,** b. 25 November 1952, Lahore, Pakistan. Cricketer, Politician. m. Jemima Goldsmith, 1995, divorced 2004, 2 sons. Education: Aitchison College; Cathedral School, Lahore; Keble College, Oxford. Appointments: Right-Arm Fast Bowler, Mid-Order Right-Hand Batsman; Played for Lahore 1969-71, Worcestershire, 1971-76, Oxford University, 1973-75 (Captain 1974), Dawood, 1975-76, PIA, 1975-81, Sussex, 1977-88, NSW, 1984-85; 88 test matches for Pakistan, 1971-92, 48 as Captain, scoring 3,807 runs (average 37.6) and taking 362 wickets (average 22.8); Toured England, 1971, 1974, 1975, 1979, 1982, 1983, 1987; Scored 17,771 first class runs and took 1,287 first class wickets; 175 limited-overs ints, 139 as Captain (including World Cup victory); 2nd player to score a century and take 10 wickets in a Test, 1983; Only 3rd player to score over 3,000 test runs and take 300 wickets; Special representative for Sports, UNICEF, 1989; Editor-in-Chief, Cricket life, 1989-90; Founder, Imran Khan Cancer Hospital Appeal, 1991-; Founder, Movement for Justice. Publications: Imran, 1983; All-Round View (autobiography), 1988; Indus Journey, 1990; Warrior Race, 1993; Writer, Syndicated newspaper column. Honours include: Fellow, Keble College, Oxford, 1988; Hilal-e-Imtiaz, 1993. Address: c/o Shankat Khanum Memorial Trust, 29 Shah Jamal, Lahore 546000, Pakistan.

**IMYANITOV Naum Solomonovich,** b. 31 December 1935, Novocherkassk, Russia. Scientist. m. Kira Rozinova, 1 son. Education: MS, 1958; PhD, 1964; DSc, 1980; Diplomas: Fine Chemical Engineering, 1958; Research Chemist, 1962; Senior Research Chemist, 1967. Appointments: Research Scientist, 1958-65; Senior Scientist, 1965-76; Department Leader, 1976-86; Chief Scientist, 1986-, VNII Neftekhim, Leningrad, St. Petersburg; Project Leader, SciVision, St Petersburg, Academic Press, 1998-2000; Project Leader, MDL Information Systems, Inc, St Petersburg, 2000-. Publications: Author, 230 articles and patents; Editor, 2 monographs. Honours: Badge, Inventor of Chechoslovakia, 1979; Badge, Inventor of USSR, 1986; Medal, Veteran of Labour, 1988. Memberships: Mendeleev Chemical Society, 1959; World Wide Club Chemical Community, 1999. Address: ul Bryantseva 18, kv 155, 195269 St Petersburg, Russia. E-mail: naum@itcwin.com

**INALCIK Halil,** b. 26 May 1916, Istanbul, Turkey. University Professor. m. Sevkiye, deceased 1989, 1 daughter. Education: PhD, Ankara University, 1940. Appointments: Professor of History, University of Ankara, 1942-72; University Professor, University of Chicago, 1972-86; Bilkent University, Ankara, Founder of the History Department, 1993-. Publications: The Ottoman Empire: The Classical Age, 1973; Studies in Ottoman Social and Economic History, 1985-; An Economic and Social History of the Ottoman Empire, 1994; Essays in Ottoman History, 1998. Honours: Honorary member: Middle East Studies of USA and Canada; American Historical Association. Memberships: Corresponding Member, The Royal Historical

Society, 1974; Honorary, Royal Asiatic Society, 1978; Corresponding Fellow, British Academy; American Academy of Arts and Sciences, 1983; Turkish Academy of Sciences, 1995. Address: Bilkent University, History Department, 06800 Bilkent, Ankara, Turkey.

**INCZE Ferenc József,** b. 28 December 1928, Budapest, Hungary. Anaesthesiologist; Pathologist; Surgeon. m. Maria Ágnes, 2 sons, 1 daughter. Education: MD, Medical University, Budapest, 1947-53; Board Certification in Pathology, 1957, Surgery, 1960, Anaethesiology and Intensive Care, 1963; Fellow, American College of Anaesthesiologists, 1973; PhD, Hungarian Academy of Sciences, 1977; Fellow, Medical College of Wisconsin, USA, 1981. Appointments: Intern and Resident, 2nd Department of Pathology, Medical University, Budapest, 1952-55; Resident, 1955-60, Assistant Professor, 1960-65, 1st & 2nd Department of Surgery, Medical University, 1955-65; Specialist in Surgery, Polyclinic of XXth District of Budapest, 1965-70; Head Anaesthesist, Metropolitan Istvan/Stephan/Hospital, Budapest, 1970-79; Resident, Medical College of Wisconsin, USA, 1971-73; Head, Department of Anaesthesiology Intensive Care, Saint Roche Hospital, Pest County, Budapest, 1979-95. Publications: Author of 89 scientific publications including : Book, Surgery of Rectal Cancer, 1969; Numerous articles. Honours: 2 awards for Prominent Work, Ministry of Health, 1978, 1986; Ignatius Semmelweis Prize, Pest County, 1996; Award for Scientific and Educational Work, Chamber of Physicians, 1996; Lajos Markusovszky Award, Springer Medical Publishing, 1999; Pro Anaesthesia and Therapia Intensiva honorary diploma and bronze plaque, Hungarian Society of Anaesthesia and Intensive Care, 2003. Memberships: Fellow, American College of Anaesthesiologists; Hungarian Chamber of Physicians; Redactor, Orvosi Hetilap; Hungarian Society of Anaesthesiology and Intensive Care; Public Body of Hungarian Academy of Sciences. Address: H-1077, Budapest, Dohany u 30/B Hungary

**ING Bruce,** b. 1 September 1937, London, England. Mycologist. m. Eleanor Scouller, 1 son, 1 daughter. Education: BA, 1960, MA, 1964, Cambridge University; MSc, St Andrews University, 1967; PhD, Liverpool University, 1979. Appointments: Assistant Organiser, Conservation Corps, 1960-64; Director, Kindrogan Field Study Centre, 1964-67; Conservation Officer, Hertfordshire and Middlesex Trust, 1967-71; Lecturer, Senior Lecturer in Biology, Chester College, 1971-94; Professor of Environmental Biology, University College, Chester, 1999-. Publications: Over 200 papers on myxomycetes, fungi, ecology and conservation, 1959-; Publications in over 10 countries; The Phytosociology of Myxomycetes, 1994; The Myxomycetes of Britain and Ireland, 1999. Honours: Benefactors Medal, British Mycological Society, 1995. Memberships: Institute of Biology; Linmean Society; British Mycological Society; many other botanical, mycological and natural history societies worldwide. Address: 24 Avon Court, Mold, Flintshire, CH7 1JP, England. E-mail: bruce.ing@which.net

**INGEL Lev,** b. 15 May 1946, Nizhny Tagil, USSR. Geophysicist. m. Irina Sklobovskaya, 1 daughter. Education: Graduate, Gorky State University, 1968; PhD, Institute of Experimental Meteorology, Obninsk, 1979; Dr in Physics and Mathematics, Hydrometeo Centre, Moscow, 1998. Appointments: Engineer, Institute 'Salute', Gorky, 1969-73; Engineer, Institute of Experimental Meteorology, Obninsk, 1973-75; Scientist, Senior Scientist, Institute of Experimental Meteorology, Obninsk, 1975-. Publications: More than 140 articles in scientific journals in meteorology, geophysics, hydrodynamics, astrophysics, quantum electronics. Honours: Grantee, International Science Foundation; Russian Foundation of Basic Research, 1997,

1998, 2001, 2004. Membership: Academic Board, Institute of Experimental Meteorology; Izvestia Newspaper Club, Moscow Address: Mira St 4, Flat 45, 249038 Obninsk, Kaluga Reg, Russia. E-mail: lingel@obninsk.com

**INGLE Stephen James,** b. 6 November 1940, Ripon, Yorkshire, England. University Professor. m. Margaret Anne Farmer, 5 August 1964, 2 sons, 1 daughter. Education: BA, 1962, DipEd, 1963, MA, 1965, University of Sheffield; PhD, Victoria University, New Zealand, 1967. Appointment: Professor, University of Stirling. Publications: Socialist Thought in Imaginative Literature, 1979; Parliament and Health Policy, 1981; British Party System, 1989; George Orwell: A Political Life, 1993; British Party System (3), 2000; Narratives & British Socialism, 2002. Many contributions to fields of Politics and Literature. Honours: Commonwealth Scholar, 1964-67; Erasmus Scholar, 1989; Visiting Research Fellow, Victoria University, New Zealand, 1993. Memberships: Political Studies Association. Address: Department of Politics, University of Stirling, Stirling FK9 4LA, Scotland.

**INGLIS-JONES Nigel John,** b. 7 May 1935, London, England. Queen's Counsel. m. (1) Lenette Bromley-Davenport, deceased 1986, 2 sons, 2 daughters, (2) Ursula Jane Drury Culverwell, 1 son. Education: Trinity College, Oxford, 1955-58. Appointments: Subaltern, Grenadier Guards, National Service, 1953-55; Called to the Bar, 1959; Recorder of the Crown Court, 1978-93; Took Silk, 1982; Deputy Social Security Commissioner, 1993-2002; Bencher of the Inner Temple, 1981-. Publication: The Law of Occupational Pension Schemes, 1989. Honour: Queen's Counsel. Membership: MCC. Address: Outer Temple Chambers, 222 The Strand, London WC2R 1BA, England.

**INGRAM David Stanley,** b. 10 October 1941, Birmingham, England. Scientist; Horticulturalist; Conservationist. m. Alison, 2 sons. Education: Yardley Grammar School, Birmingham; BSc, PhD, University of Hull; MA, ScD Cantab. Appointments: Research Fellow, University of Glasgow; Senior Scientific Officer, Agricultural Research Council Unit of Developmental Botany; Lecturer, then Reader in Plant Pathology, University of Cambridge; Regius Keeper, Royal Botanic Garden, Edinburgh; Master, St Catharine's College, Cambridge. Publications: 9 books; Newspaper and magazine articles; Research papers, reviews and articles in peer-reviewed scientific and specialist journals. Honours: OBE; FIBiol, 1986; FRSE, 1993; FIHort, 1995; FRCPEd, 1998; Hon FRSGS, 1998; Hon D University, Open University, 2000; Victoria Medal of Honour, Royal Horticultural Society, 2004. Memberships: Senior Visiting Fellow, Department of Plant Sciences, University of Cambridge; Honorary Professor and Special Adviser to University of Edinburgh on the Public Understanding of Science, Engineering and Technology; Visiting Professor, Glasgow University and Napier University; Honorary Fellow and Visiting Professor, Myerscough College, Lancashire; Honorary Fellow, Royal Botanic Garden, Edinburgh; Downing College, Cambridge; Worcester College, Oxford; Chairman, Darwin Initiative for the Survival of Species; Independent Member, Joint Nature Conservation Committee and Acting Chair; Member, Forestry Commissioner" Advisory Panel. Address: St Catharine's College, Cambridge CB2 1RL, England. E-mail: master@caths.cam.ac.uk

**INMAN Edward Oliver,** b. 12 August 1948, Oslo, Norway. Chief Executive. 1 son, 2 daughters, 2 stepdaughters. Education: MA, Gonville and Caius College, 1969; School of Slavonic Studies, London, 1970. Appointments: Research Assistant, then Directing Staff, Imperial War Museum, London, 1972-78;

Keeper, 1978-82, Director, 1982-2004, Imperial War Museum, Duxford, Cambridge; Chief Executive, South Bank Employers' Group, 2004-. Honours: Order of the British Empire, 1998; Fellow, Royal Aeronautical Society, 1999. Address: South Bank Employers' Group, 103 Waterloo Road, London SE1 8UL, England. E-mail: einman@iwm.org.uk

**INMAN Melbourne Donald,** b. 1 April 1957, Sutton Coldfield, England. Barrister. m. Catherine Inman. Education: MA, Regent's Park College, Oxford; Inn's of Court, School of Law. Appointments: Called to Bar, Inner Temple, 1979; Recorder, 1996; Silk, 1998; Head of Advocacy Training and Development for the Midland Circuit, 1998; Head, 1 Fountain Court, Birmingham, 2001-. Honours: Queen's Counsel.

**INNES Brian,** b. 4 May 1928, Croydon, Surrey, England. Writer; Publisher. m. (1) Felicity McNair Wilson, 5 October 1956, (2) Eunice Lynch, 2 April 1971, 3 sons. Education: BSc, King's College, London, 1946-49. Appointments: Assistant Editor, Chemical Age, 1953-55; Associate Editor, The British Printer, 1955-60; Art Director, Hamlyn Group, 1960-62; Director, Temperance Seven Ltd, 1961-; Proprietor, Brian Innes Agency, 1964-66; Immediate Books, 1966-70, FOT Library, 1970-; Creative Director, Deputy Chairman, Orbis Publishing Ltd, 1970-86; Editorial Director, Mirror Publishing, 1986-88. Publications: Book of Pirates, 1966; Book of Spies, 1967; Book of Revolutions, 1967; Book of Outlaws, 1968; Flight, 1970; Saga of the Railways, 1972; Horoscopes, 1976; The Tarot, 1977; Book of Change, 1979; The Red Baron Lives, 1981; Red Red Baron, 1983; The Havana Cigar, 1983; Crooks and Conmen, 1993; Catalogue of Ghost Sightings, 1996; The History of Torture, 1998; Death and The Afterlife, 1999; Dreams, 1999; Bodies of Evidence, 2000; Profile of a Criminal Mind, 2003; The Body in Question, 2005; Fakes and Forgeries, 2005. Contributions to: Encyclopaedia Britannica; Grove Dictionary of Jazz; Man, Myth & Magic; Take Off; Real Life Crimes; Fire Power; The Story of Scotland; Discover Scotland; Marshall Cavendish Encyclopaedia of Science; Numerous recordings, films, radio and television broadcasts; Many photographs published. Honour: Royal Variety Command Performance, 1961. Memberships: Chartered Society of Designers; Royal Society of Literature; Royal Society of Chemistry; Royal Society of Arts; Institute of Printing; Crime Writers Association; British Actors' Equity. Address: Les Forges de Montgaillard, 11330 Mouthoumet, France.

**INOMATA Nobumichi,** b. 14 November 1936, Ashio Tochigi, Japan. Professor. m. Nobuko Kuraoka, 13 June 1971, 1 son, 1 daughter. Education: BAgri, 1961; MAgri, 1963; DAgri, 1973. Appointments: Assistant, Osaka Prefectural University, 1970; Associate Professor, Okayama University 1977, Professor, Okayama University, 1982, Emeritus Professor, 1999, Okayama University; Professor, Koman Women's University, 1999. Publications: Experimental Manipulation of Ovule Tissues, 1985; Biotechnology in Agriculture and Forestry, 1990; Breeding Oilseed Brasica, 1993; Recent Advances in Oilseed Brassicas, 1997. Memberships: Genetic Society of Japan; Plant Breeding Society of Japan; Japan Society for Plant Molecular Biology; New York Academy of Sciences; American Society of Plant Biologists. Address: Konan Women's University, 6-2-23 Morikita, Higashinada, Kobe 658-0001, Japan. E-mail: inomata@konan-wu.ac.jp

**INOUE Shintaro,** b. 14 July 1952, Osaka, Japan. Biomedical Engineer; Researcher. m. Takako Hashimoto, 1 son, 1 daughter. Education: BA, 1975, MS, 1977, Osaka University, Japan; Registered Professional Engineer, Bio-Technology, Japan, 1995. Appointments: Researcher, Kyoto University, 1979-

83; Researcher, University of Tokyo, 1986-87; Registered Professional Engineer, Japan, 1995-; Guest Researcher, Toyama Institute of Health, Toyama Prefecture, Japan, 2001; Deputy Director, Basic Research Laboratory, Kanebo Ltd, 2000-04; Deputy Director, Kannpo Healthcare Research Laboratory, Kanebo Ltd, 2001-04; Director, Basic Research Laboratory, Kanebo Cosmetics Inc, 2004-. Publications: Numerous original articles and reviews in international dermatological, biochemical and cosmetic journals; Reviews in books for dermatology, biotechnology and cosmetics; Patent invention of medical and cosmetic ingredients. Memberships: Institution of Professional Engineers, Japan; Society for Investigative Dermatology; Biochemistry Society, Japan; Pharmacology Society, Japan; Japanese Society of Inflammation and Regeneration; American Diabetes Association Professional Section. Address: Basic Research Laboratory, Kanebo Cosmetics Inc, 5-3-28 Kotobuki Cho, Odawara, Kanagawa, 250-0002, Japan. E-mail: inoshin@kanebocos.co.jp

**INOUE Takashi,** b. 20 November 1944, Dairen, Manchuria, China. President; Chief Executive Officer. m. Yasuko, 3 sons. Education: Graduate, Marketing and Administration, Waseda University. Appointments: Marketing, Yamaha Corporation, 1968-70; Founded Inoue Public Relations, 1970, currently President and Chief executive Officer; Member, Japan Public Relations Institute, 2004. Publications: An Introduction to Public Relations (editor); The Global Public Relations Handbook: Theory and Practice (co-author). Honours: The Golden World Award for Excellence in Public Relations, International Public Relations Association (Top Award); PRIDE Award for the Global Public Relations Handbook, National Communication Association, USA, 2003. Memberships: Fellow, International Public Relations Association; Public Relations Society of Japan; Council Member, Japan Society for Corporate Communication Studies; Chairman, Industrial Committee, Japan Information-Culturology Society; Board Member, UNDPDEVNET Japan Association; Foreign Correspondents Club of Japan. Address: Shinjuku-gyoenmae Annex 6F, 4-34 Yotsuya, Shinjuku-ku, Tokyo 160-0004, Japan. E-mail: inouetak@inoue-pr.com

**INSALL Donald William,** b. 7 February 1926, Clifton, Bristol, England. Architect. m. Amy Elizabeth (Libby) Moss, 2 sons, 1 daughter. Education: RWA School of Architecture, Bristol University, Bristol; Royal Academy School of Architecture, London; School of Planning and Research for Regional Development; Lethaby Scholar, The SPAB. Appointments: Founder Director, Donald Insall Associates, Architects and Historic Building Consultants, London, Bath, Canterbury, Cambridge, Chester, Shrewsbury, 1957-; Member, Historic Buildings Council for England, 1971-84; Founder-Commissioner, English Heritage, 1984-89. Publications: The Care of Old Buildings Today; Historic Buildings: Action to Maintain the Expertise for their Care and Repair, Council of Europe; Chester: A Study in Conservation; Contributor: Encyclopaedia Britannica and numerous technical journals; Arts Council Film: Buildings: Who Cares? Honours: Queen's Silver Jubilee Medal, 1977; OBE, 1981; CBE, 1995; Honorary LLD, 2004; Honorary Freeman of the City of Chester; Europa Nostra Medal of Honour. Memberships include: Fellow, RIBA; Fellow, RTPI; Fellow, Society of Antiquaries of London; Academician, Royal West of England Academy; Liveryman, Worshipful Company of Goldsmiths; Council Member, SPAB; Member, Europa Nostra; Member of Committees, European Union; Council Member, ICOMOS, UK; UK Committee, World Monument Fund; Past and present Member of Fabric Committees, Westminster Abbey, Canterbury and Southwark Cathedrals; Vice-president, City of Winchester Trust; Honorary Life Member, Bath Preservation Trust; Patron; Kew Society,

Environmental Trust for Richmond upon Thames, Bedford Park Society; Fellow, Royal Society of Arts; Rolls Royce Enthusiasts' Club. Address: Donald Insall Associates, 19 West Eaton Place, London SW1X 8LT, England. E-mail: donald.insall@insall-lon.co.uk

**INSAROV Gregory E,** b. 14 November 1948, Moscow, USSR. Ecologist. m. Irina D, 1 daughter. Education: MS, Mathematics, Moscow State University, USSR, 1970; PhD, Biology, Moscow State Forestry University, Moscow, USSR, 1975; Junior Research Scientist, 1976-77, Senior Research Scientist, 1978-79, Institute of Applied Geophysics, Moscow, USSR; Senior Research Scientist, Natural Environment and Climate Monitoring Laboratory, Moscow, USSR/Russia, 1979-91; Leading Research Scientist, Institute of Global Climate and Ecology, Moscow, Russia, 1991-. Publications: Over 100 publications as author or co-author; Books: Mathematical methods in forest protection, 1980; Effects of S0$_2$ on plants, 1984; Quantitative characteristics of the state of epiphytic lichenflora of biosphere reserves. The Zakatal reserve, 1987; Numerous book chapters, articles in scientific journals and conference proceedings include most recently: Assessment of lichen sensitivity to climate change, 1996; Computer-aided multi-access key IDENT for identification of the Negev lichens, 1997; A system to monitor climate change with epilithic lichens, 1999; Long term monitoring of lichen communities response to climate change and diversity of lichens in the Central Negev Highlands, Israel, 2001; Lichen Monitoring and Global Change, 2002; Towards an Early Warning System for Global Change, 2004. Honours: Expedition leader, former USSR and Sweden, co-ordinated and guided expeditions to remote protected areas with emphasis on lichen monitoring, 1978-92; Visiting Professor, University of Arkansas at Monticello, USA, 1990; Research Associate, Swedish Environmental Protection Agency, Sweden, 1991-92; Research Associate, Ben-Gurion University of the Negev, Israel 1993-97; Marie Curie Experienced Fellow, University of Evora, Portugal, 1997; Research Fellow, Acid Deposition and Oxidant Research Center, Japan, 2004; Editorial Board, Series Problems of Ecological Monitoring and Ecosystem Modelling, 1987-; Director, NATO Advanced Research Workshop on Lichen Monitoring, Wales UK, 2000; Expert, Intergovernmental Panel on Climate Change, 2001-. Memberships: Moscow Society of Naturalists, 1972-; British Lichen Society, 1993-; American Association for the Advancement of Science, 1997-98; American Bryological and Lichenological Society, 1998-; Russian National Committee on Human Dimensions on Global Environmental Change, 2004. Address: Institute of Global Climate and Ecology, Glebovskaya 20B, Moscow 107258, Russia. E-mail: insarov@lichenfield.com

**INTUWONGSE Chai-Sit,** b. Nakornpranom, Thailand. Doctor of Medicine. m. Siriporn Intuwongse, 1 son, 2 daughters. Education: Doctor of Medicine, Siriraj Hospital, Mahidol University, Thonburi, Thailand, 1959; Thai Orthopaedics Board, Thailand, 1975; Thai Board of Family Medicine, Thailand, 2004. Appointments: Lieutenant, Royal Thai Navy, 1959; Head, Orthopaedic Department, Lerd-Sin General Hospital, Bangkok, Thailand, 1966-96; Medical Consultant, Tanksin General Hospital, Chareonkrung General Hospital, Bangkok Metropolitan Administration; Medical Consultant, Sports Authority of Thailand; Medical Consultant, Department of Medical Services, Ministry of Public Health, Thailand; Member, Sub-committee of Medical Board, Department of Labour, Thailand. Publications: Articles in medical publications including: Clinical Orthopaedics and Related Research, 1996; The Journal of Hand Surgery, 1998. Honours: Listed in Who's Who publications and biographical dictionaries. Memberships: Brain Bank, National Economic and Social Development

Board; Royal College of Orthopaedic Surgeons of Thailand; International College of Surgeons. Address: 2 Soi 1 Saeree 1 Rankamhaeng 24, Haumark, Bangkapi, Bangkok, 10250 Thailand.

**IOFFE Boris Lazarevich,** b. 6 July 1926, Moscow, Russia. Physicist. m. Libova Nina, 1 son. Education: MS, Moscow University, 1949; PhD I, Candidate of Science, 1954, PhD II, Dr of Science, 1961, ITEP, Moscow. Appointments: Junior Scientist, 1950-55, Senior Scientist, 1955-77, Head of Laboratory, 1977-, Chairman of ITEP Scientific Council, 1990-97, Institute of Theoretical and Experimental Physics, ITEP, Moscow. Publications: Hard Processes, 1984; Osobo sekretnoe zadanie (essay), 1999; The Top Secret Assignment in: Handbook of QCD, 2001; Without Retouching, 2004; 270 scientific papers. Honours: Badge of Honour of USSR, 1954, 1974; Award of Discovery of USSR, 1986, 1990; Humboldt Award, Germany, 1994; Medal 850 Years of Moscow, 1997; The Novy Mir Magazine Prize, 1999; Listed in Who's Who publications and biographical dictionaries. Memberships: Russian Academy of Science; Fellow of American Physical Society; Executive Committee, United Physical Society of Russia. Address: Bolotnikovskaya 40-4-16, 113209 Moscow, Russia.

**IOKU Koji,** b. 22 December 1960, Okayama, Japan. Professor. m. Akiko, 1 son, 1 daughter. Education: BSc, Engineering, 1984, MSc, Engineering, 1986, Sophia University, Tokyo, Japan; DSc, Engineering, Tokyo Institute of Technology, Tokyo, Japan, 1989. Appointments: Research Associate, Kochi University, Japan, 1989-94; Professor, Yamaguchi University, Japan, 1994-2004; Professor, Tohoku University, Japan, 2003; Government Researcher, University of Tokyo, Japan, 1990-91; Guest Researcher, Juntendo University, 2000-2001. Publications: Over 200 articles in professional journals. Honours: Award for Encouragement of Research in Materials Science, MRS Institute Meeting on Advanced Materials, 1988; Young Scientist Award, Japanese Association for Inorganic Phosphorus Chemistry, 1998; Award for Young Scientist in Memory of Professor Nagai; Listed in Who's Who publications and biographical dictionaries. Address: Aoba 6-6-20, Aramaki, Aoba-ku, Sendai, Miyagi 980-8579, Japan. E-mail: ioku@mail.kankyo.tohoku.ac.jp

**IOSEBASHVILI Alexander,** b. 26 January 1965, City of Tbilisi, Georgia, USSR. Scientist. Education: Doctor of Science, 1991; Scientific Diploma, 1993; Professor, 1993. Appointments: Scientist; Researcher; Philosopher; Psychologist; Applied Mathematician; Lawyer; Medical Reformer; Medical Student; Fraud and Corruption Investigator. Publications include: Physico-cosmological works on Psychology, Politics and Ethics; An Alternative of the Criticism of the Science admitting Pychoanalisis; Albert Einstein and Mendelev and his Periodical Table of Chemical Element for Myth? Honours: Noble Prize, 2002; American Medal of Honor, 2002, 2003, 2004; International Peace Prize, 2002; The World Order of Science-Education-Culture, 2002, 2005. Memberships: Smithsonian; American Association for the Advancement of Science; New York Academy of Sciences; Academy of Political Science; American Psychological Society; National Geographic Society; American Institute of Chemical Engineers; American Museum of Natural History; The Mathematical Association of America; American Chemical Society; American Bar Association; London Diplomatic Academy. Address: 99-05, 63rd Dr Apt 9-V, Rego-Park, NY 11374, USA.

**IOSIF Serafim Constantin,** b. 5 May 1940, Bucharest, Romania. Doctor. m. Elena, 2 sons. Education: MD, Medical Faculty, Bucharest, 1965; Speciality Obstetrics and Gynaecology, Sweden, 1976; Thesis, University of Lund, Sweden, 1981;

Associate Professor, Obstetric Gynaecology, University of Lund, 1983-. Appointments: Employed by Department of Obstetrics and Gynaecology, University Hospital, Lund, Sweden; Fields of interest: Urinary incontinence, menopause, sex steroid hormones, gynaecological oncology. Publications: 120 scientific publications. Honour: Participant in many international medical congresses in Europe, Japan, Australia, America, Canada. Memberships: Swedish Gynaecological Obstetrics Society; International Continence Society; Menopause Society. Address: Nations Gatan 22, Lund 22363, Sweden.

**IP David,** b. 21 August 1960, Hong Kong. Orthopaedic Surgeon. m. Fu Nga Yue. Education: Graduate, Hong Kong University Medical School, 1985; Fellow Royal College of Surgeons of Edinburgh, 1999; Fellow, Hong Kong College of Orthopaedic Surgeons. Publications: Numerous articles in scientific journals as chief author include: Comparison of two total knee prostheses on the incidence of patella clunk syndrome; Management of forearm deformities in multiple exostoses; Early results of nexgen total knee anthroplasty; Premature fixation failure of distal fixation screws of IC nail; Rare complications of segmental medullary tube breakage of intramedullary nailing; Orthopaedic Principles – A Resident's Guide, 2005; Orthopaedic Traumatology – A Resident's Guide, forthcoming. Honours: Lifetime Achievement Award, IBC; Deputy Director General, IBC; Scientific Advisor, IBC; Member, Order of International Fellowship; International Healthcare Professional of the Year Award, 2004; IBC Award of Biographical Recognition; Order of Distinction, IBC; Member, Order of Ambassadors, ABI; Winner of the Universal Award for Achievement for the Year 2004, ABI; Universal Award of Accomplishment, ABI; Outstanding Professional Award, ABI; IBC Award of Biographical Recognition; Key Award, Leader in Science, ABI; International Peace Prize, United Cultural Convention, USA; Scientific Advisor, ABI; Deputy Governor, ABI Research Association; American Medal of Honor, IBA; Elected Fellow of American Biographical Institute Listed in Who's Who publications and biographical dictionaries including: Who's Who in the World; Great Minds of the 21st Century; 2000 Intellectuals of the 21st Century; Leading Intellectuals of the 21st Century; The Cambridge Blue Book; Who's Who in Science and Engineering. Memberships: Royal College of Surgeons of Edinburgh; Life Fellow, IBC; World Peace and Diplomacy Forum; Hong Kong College of Orthopaedic Surgeons; Overseas Member, American Association of Orthopaedic Surgeons; Fellow, American Biographical Institute. Address: 3B Highland Mansion, Cleveland Street, Causeway Bay, Hong Kong. E-mail: ipd8686@pacific.net.hk

**IPATOV Sergei Ivanovich,** b. 10 November 1952, Moscow, Russia. Applied Mathematician in Astronomy. m. Valentina Ipatova (Artiouhova), 1 son. Education: Moscow State University, Department of Mechanics and Mathematics, 1970-75; PhD (Kandidat of Physical and Mathematical Sciences), 1982; Doctor of Physical and Mathematical Sciences, 1997. Appointments: From Probationer Investigator to Leading Scientist, Keldysh Institute of Applied Mathematics of Russian Academy of Sciences, Moscow, 1975-2003; Lecturer, Moscow State University, 1998; Visiting USA via NASA grant, July 2001- April 2002; NRC Senior Research Associate in NASA Goddard Space Flight Centre, May 2002-April 2003; Visiting Senior Research Associate, George Mason University, May 2003-April 2004; Research Associate, Catholic University of America, 2004; Research Associate, University of Maryland, 2005-. Publications: Published 200 scientific works including papers in international, Soviet and Russian journals, and the book: Migration of Celestial Bodies in the Solar System, (in Russian), 2000. Honours: Medals: Outstanding People of the

20th Century, 2000 Outstanding Scientists of the 20th Century, 2000 Outstanding Intellectuals of the 21st Century, 2000 Outstanding Scientists of the 21st Century, One Thousand Great Intellectuals, International Scientist of the Year, International Biographical Centre, Cambridge, England, 1998, 2002 and 2003; Medal of Honor, 1999, Leading Intellectuals of the World, 2002, American Medal of Honor, 2003, American Biographical Institute; Various grants. Memberships: European Astronomical Society, 1995-; Euro-Asian Astronomical Society, 1995-; New York Academy of Sciences, 1995-96, 2004-; Associate, Committee on Space Research, 1996-; Russian Academy of Natural Sciences, 2000-; Russian Academy of Sciences and Arts, 2000-; American Astronomical Society, 2002-; International Astronomical Union, 2003-; Member, Editorial Board of the Journal, Solar System Research, 2003-. Address: Department of Astronomy, University of Maryland, College Park, MD 20742-2421, USA. E-mail: siipatov@hotmail.com

**IRONS Jeremy,** b. 19 September 1948, Isle of Wight, England. Actor. m. (2) Sinead Cusack, 1978, 2 sons. Creative Works: TV appearances include: Notorious Woman; Love for Lydia; Langrishe Go Down; Voysey Inheritance; Brideshead Revisited; The Captain's Doll; Tales From Hollywood, 1991; Longtitude 2000; Films: Nijinsky, 1980; The French Lieutenant's Woman, 1980; Moonlighting, 1981; Betrayal, 1982; The Wild Duck, 1983; Swann in Love, 1983; The Mission, 1986; A Chorus of Disapproval, 1988; Dead Ringers, 1988; Australia, 1989; Danny, The Champion of the World, 1989; Reversal of Fortune, 1990; Kafka, 1991; Damage, 1991; Waterland, 1992; M. Butterfly, 1994; House of the Spirits, 1994; Die Hard with a Vengeance, 1995; Stealing Beauty, 1996; Lolita, 1996; The Man in the Iron Mask, 1997; Chinese Box, 1998; Dungeons and Dragons, 2000; The Time Machine, 2001; Stage appearances: The Real Thing, Broadway, 1984; Rover, 1986; The Winter's Tale, 1986; Richard II, Stratford, 1986. Honours include: NY Critics Best Actor Award, 1988; Academy Award, 1991; Tony Award; European Film Academy Special Achievement Award, 1998.

**IRONSIDE 2nd Baron, Edmund Oslac Ironside,** b. 21 September 1924, Camberley, Surrey, England. Businessman. m. Audrey Marigold Morgan-Grenville, 1 son, 1 daughter. Education: Tonbridge School. Appointments: Lieutenant Royal Navy, 1943-52; Marconi Co, 1952-59; English Electric Leo Computers, 1959-64; International research and Development Co Ltd, 1968-84; NEI plc, 1984-89; Defence Consultant, Rolls Royce IPG, 1989-95. Publication: Book: Highroad to Command, 1972. Honours: Honorary FCGI, 1986; Member of Court of Assistants, Worshipful Company of Skinners, Master, 1981-82; Honorary Fellow, City and Guilds Institute (Hon FCGI). Memberships: Organising Committee, British Library, 1972-74, Select Committee European Communities, 1974-90; Chairman, Science Reference Library Advisory Committee, 1975-85; President: Electric Vehicle Association of Great Britain, 1975-83, European Electric Road Vehicle Association, 1980-82, Sea Cadet Corps, Chelmsford, 1959-88; Vice-President: Institute of Patentees and Inventors, 1976-90, Parliamentary and Scientific Committee, 1977-80, 1983-86; Treasurer, All Party Energy Studies Group, 1979-92; Honorary Secretary, 1992-94, Chairman 1994-2000, All-Party Defence Study Group; Privy Council Member of Court, City University, 1971-96 and Council, 1987-89; Court, University of Essex, 1982; Club: Royal Ocean Racing. Address: Priory House, Old House Lane, Boxted, Colchester, Essex CO4 5RB, England.

**IRVIN Albert,** b. 21 August 1922, London, England. Artist. m. Beatrice Nicolson, 2 daughters. Education: Northampton School of Art, 1940-41; Navigator, Royal Air Force, 1944-46; Goldsmiths College, University of London, 1946-50. Career:

Teacher, Goldsmiths College, 1962-83; Solo exhibitions include: New Art Centre, London, regularly during 1960's and 70's; Gimpel Fils Gallery, London, regularly since 1982; Aberdeen Art Gallery, 1976, 1983; Third Eye Centre, Glasgow, 1983; Ikon Gallery, Birmingham, 1983; Talbot Rice Gallery, Edinburgh, 1989; Spacex Gallery, Exeter, 1990; Serpentine Gallery, London, 1990; Welsh Arts Council, Cardiff, 1990; Royal Hibernian Academy, Dublin, 1995; Centre d'Art Contemporain, Meymac, France, 1998; Royal West of England Academy, 1999; Storey Gallery, Lancaster and Scott Gallery, Lancaster University, 2003; Galleries and museums in USA, Australia, Austria, Germany, France, Belgium, Spain; Works in public collections including Tate Gallery, Royal Academy, Victoria and Albert Museum, Arts Council, British Council and in public collections internationally; Commissions include: Painting for Homerton Hospital, Hackney, 1987; Design for Diversions Dance Company, 1994; Painting for Chelsea and Westminster Hospital, 1996. Publications: Albert Irvin: Life to Painting by Paul Moorhouse, 1998; Television: A Feeling for Paint, BBC2, 1983; Off the Wall: The Byker Show, BBC2 1994; Albert Irvin: Artist At Work, Artsworld, 2000; Albert Irvin: Portrait, Injam, Paris, 2001; Radio: Interview with Joan Bakewell, BBC Radio 3, 1990. Honours: Arts Council Awards, 1968, 1975, 1980; Prize Winner, John Moores Liverpool Exhibition, 1982; Gulbenkian Award for Printmaking, 1983; Giles Bequest Award, Victoria and Albert and British Museum, 1986; Korn/Ferry Award, Royal Academy, 1989; Honorary Fellow, Goldsmiths College, 2002. Memberships: London Group, 1965; Royal Academician, 1998, Honorary Member, Royal West of England Academy, 2000. Address: 19 Gorst Road, London SW11 6JB, England.

**IRVINE Robin Francis,** b. 10 February 1950, Wales. Professor of Molecular Pharmacology. m. Sandra Jane, 2 sons. Education: MA, BA (Hons), Biochemistry, St Catherine's College, Oxford, 1972; PhD, Agricultural Research Council Unit of Developmental Botany, Cambridge, 1976. Appointments: Beit Memorial Fellow, 1975-78, Higher Scientific Officer, 1978, Senior Scientific Officer, 1980, Principal Scientific Officer, 1983, Senior Principal Scientific Officer (UG6), 1987, Deputy Chief Scientific Officer (UG5) and Head of Development and Signalling, 1993-95, AFRC Institute of Animal Physiology, Babraham, Cambridge; Royal Society Research Professor of Molecular Pharmacology, Department of Pharmacology, University of Cambridge. Publications: Over 150 papers as author, co-author and first author published in refereed journals include: Back in the water: the return of the insitol phosphates, 2001; Inositol lipids are regulated during cell cycle progression in the nuclei of murine erythroleukaemia cells, 2001; Inositol 1,4,5-triphosphate 3-kinase A associates with F-actin and dendritic spines via its N terminus, 2001; Type Ii phosphatidylinositol phosphate kinase associates with the plasma membrane via interaction with type I isoforms, 2002. Honours: Pfizer Academic Award, 1988; Transoceanic Lecturer, The Endocrine Society, USA, 1989; FEBS Lecturer, 1993; FRS, 1993; Morton Lecturer, Biochemical Society, 1993; FIBiol, 1998; FMedSci (Founding Fellow), 1998. Memberships: Editorial Boards: Cellular Signalling, 1989-, Current Biology, 1994, Cell, 1996, Molecular Pharmacology, 2000-; Chairman, Molecular and Cellular Pharmacology Group 1999-, Council Member, 1999-, Biochemical Society; Royal Society Council, 1999-2001; Royal Society Research Fellowships Committee, 2000-. Address: Department of Pharmacology, University of Cambridge, Tennis Court Road, Cambridge CB2 1PD, England. E-mail: rfi20@cam.ac.uk

**IRWIN Flavia,** b. 15 December 1916, London, England. m. Roger de Grey, 2 sons, 1 daughter. Artist; Tutor. Education: Chelsea School of Art, with Graham Sutherland, Henry Moore

and Robert Medley. Career: Artist on acrylic on canvas, mixed media on paper; Tutor, Medway College of Art and Design; Head of Decorative Arts Department, City & Guilds of London Art School; Solo Exhibitions include: Zwemmers; London Group; Royal Academy; Gallery 10; Phoenix Gallery; Curwen Gallery; Peoples Theatre, Newcastle; Arts Council Gallery, Bury St Edmunds; Public Collections: Carlisle Art Gallery; Chelsea & Westminster Hospital; Royal Academy. Honours: Senior Academician, 1996. Address: Camer Street, Meopham, Kent DA13 0XR, England.

**ISAACS Jeremy Israel,** b. 28 September 1932. Arts Administrator. m. (1) Tamara Weinreich, 1958, 1 son, 1 daughter, (2) Gillian Widdicombe, 1988. Education: Glasgow Academy; Merton College, Oxford. Appointments: TV Producer, Granada TV, 1958, Associated Rediffusion, 1963, BBC TV, 1965; Controller of Features, Associated Rediffusion, 1967; Thames TV, 1968-78; Producer, The World at War, 1974, Cold War, 1998; Director of Programmes, 1974-78; Special Independent Consultant, TV Series, Hollywood ITV, A Sense of Freedom, ITV Ireland, TV Documentary, BBC, Battle for Crete, NZ TV, Cold War, Turner Broadcasting; CEO, Channel 4 TV Co, 1981-88; General Director, Royal Opera House, 1988-96 (director 1985-97); Chief Executive, Jeremy Isaacs Productions, 1998-. Publications: Storm Over Four: A Personal Account, 1989; Cold War, 1999; Never Mind the Moon, 1999. Honours include: Desmond Davis Award, Outstanding Creative Contribution to TV, 1972; George Polk Memorial Award, 1973; Cyril Bennett Award, 1982; Lord Willis Award, Distinguished Service to TV, 1985. Memberships include: British Film Institute; Fellow, Royal TV Society, 1978.

**ISAYEV Avraam,** b. 17 October 1942, Privolnoe, Azerbaijan. Engineer; Educator. m. Lubov M Dadasheva, 1 daughter. Education: MSChemE Azerbaijan Institute of Oil and Chemistry, Baku, 1964; PhD, Polymer Engineering, Russian Academy of Sciences, Moscow, 1970; MS, Applied Mathematics, Institute of Electronic Machine Building, Moscow, 1975. Appointments: Research Associate, State Research Institute of Nitrogen Industries, Severodonetsk, Russia, 1965-66; Predoctoral, Institute of Petrochemical Synthesis, Russian Academy of Sciences, Moscow, 1967-69, Research Associate, 1970-76; Senior Research Fellow, Israel Institute of Technology, Haifa, 1977-78; Senior Research Associate, Cornell University, Ithaca, New York, 1979-83; Associate Professor, Institute of Polymer Engineering, 1983-87, Professor, 1987-2000, Director, Moulding Technology, 1987-, Distinguished Professor, 2001-, University of Akron, Ohio; Visiting Professor, several universities and institutions. Publications: Numerous articles in professional journals; Books and encyclopaedias; Edited 4 books. Honours include: Distinguished Corporation Inventor, American Society of Patent Holders, 1995; Silver Medal, Institute of Materials, London, 1997; Melvin Mooney Distinguished Technology Award, Rubber Division, American Chemical Society, 1999; OMNOVA Solutions University Signature Award, 2000 and 2002; Vinogradov Prize, GV Vinogradov Society of Rheology, Moscow, 2000. Memberships: American Chemical Society; New York Academy of Sciences; Society of Plastic Engineers; Polymer Processing Society; Society of Rheology. Address: University of Akron, Institute of Polymer Engineering, 250 South Forge Street, Akron, OH 44325-0301, USA.

**ISEKHURE Nosakhare,** b. 19 December 1950, Nigeria. Political Scientist; Journalist. m. Ekinadose Isekhure, 6 sons, 2 daughters. Education: Diploma, Journalism and Creative Writing, 1979; Bachelors degree, Political Science and Journalism, 1981-; Masters Degree, Public Administration, 1982. Appointments: Member, World Youth Parliament,

Canada, 1980; Appointed Member of Board, Member, Benin Traditional Council, 1983, Bendel Radio and Television, 1984; Appointed Member of Board, BDPA; Appointed Member of the Constituent Assembly, 1988. Publications: 220 articles in newspapers; 4 books on Nigerian Politics; Book on September 11th Tragedy; Book on Nigeria's 2003 elections, forthcoming. Honours: Book Publishing Award, 1992; 22 cultural and University bodies awards; Tradomedical Award; Honorary Rotarian; Justice of the Peace; Honorary Citizen, State of Massachusetts, USA. Memberships: The Rosicrucian Order; Honorary Member IBC; Honorary Rotarian; Member, BTC, Edo State, Nigeria. Address: No 7, 9, 11, Sokponba Road, Benin City, Edo State, Nigeria. E-mail: isekhurenosa@yahoo.com

**ISHIGURO Kazuo,** b. 8 November 1954, Nagasaki, Japan. Writer. Education: BA, University of Kent, 1978; MA, University of East Anglia. Publications: A Pale View of Hills, 1982; A Profile of Arthur J Mason (TV play), 1985; An Artist of the Floating World, 1986; The Gourmet (TV play), 1987; The Remains of the Day, 1989; The Unconsoled, 1995; When We Were Orphans, 2000; Never Let Me Go, 2005. Honours: Winifred Holtby Prize, 1983; Whitbread Book of Year Award, 1986; Booker Prize, 1989; Fellow, Royal Society of Literature, 1989; Honorary Doctor of Letters, 1990, 1995, 2003; Officer of the Order of the British Empire, 1995; Cheltenham Prize, 1995; Chevalier de l'Ordre des Arts at des Lettres, 1998. Membership: Royal Society of Arts, fellow, 1990. Address: c/o Faber & Faber Ltd, 3 Queen Square, London WC1N 3AU, England.

**ISHIMURA Misako,** b. 8 October 1951, Osaka, Japan. Fly Fishing Instructor; Federation Fly Fishers Certified Casting Instructor. Education: Graduate, Special Casting Instructors' Course, Joan Wulff School, 1998. Appointments: Director, Juliana Anglers, 1997-98; Director, 1998-2001, Chair, Club Liaison Committee, 1998-2001, Goodwill Ambassador, 2004-, International Women Fly Fishers; Director, Theodore Gordon Fly Fishers, 1998-2003; President, World Fly Fishing of Japan, 2000-; Fly Fishing Instructor, M & M Fly Fishing School, 2000-; Team Japan Captain for FIPS Mouche World Fly Fishing Championship and Conservation Symposium, 2000-. Publications: Article, Willowemoe Creek, in A Woman's No Nonsense Guide to Fly Fishing Favorite Waters; Poem in Voices from the Soul; Pen drawings in International Woman Fly Fishers Newsletters; Water colour drawings presented at Wild Wood Gallery, 2002. Honours: Appreciation Awards, Japan Fly Fishers, 2003; Awarded The First Woman Fly Fisher at FIPS Mouche World Fly Fishing Championship, 2004. Memberships: CIPS-FIPS Mouche; Catskill Fly Tyers Guild; Theodore Gordon Fly Fishers; Federation Fly Fishers. Address: 94 Yorktown Road, Roscoe, NY 12776, USA. E-mail: misakoflyfish@hotmail.com Website: www.wffj.org

**ISHIZAKI Teruhiko,** b. 9 January 1928, Tokyo, Japan. Professor Emeritus. m. Tazuko, 2 sons, 1 daughter. Education: Graduate School of Economics, 1958, DEcon, 1963, Tokyo University. Appointments: Professor, Kanagawa University, 1968-98; Chairman, Society for Industrial Studies, Japan, 1998-2000; Director, Institute of Economics and Trade, Kanagawa University, 1992-98. Publications include: The Evolution of Finance Capitalism in the United States, 1962; The New Economic Nationalism, 1979; The Japanese Economic Challenge to US Economy, 1990. Membership: Society of Industrial Studies, Japan. Address: 5-1-47 Shoodo Sakaeku, Yokohama 247, Japan.

**ISNARDI PARENTE Margherita,** b. 4 October 1928, Catanzaro, Italy. University Professor. m. Fausto Parente. Education: University of Pisa, 1947-51; Study Course, Paris,

1955; Study Course, Göttingen and Hamburg, Germany, 1956-57; Libera Docenza, 1963. Appointments: Professor of the History of Ancient Philosophy, University of Cagliari. Currently, Professor of the History of Philosophy and the History of Ancient Philosophy, Faculty of Letters and Philosophy, University of Rome. Publications: Essays: Tecne. Momenti del pensiero greco da Platone ad Epicuro, 1966; Filosofia e politica nelle lettere di Platone, 1970; Aggiornamento di Zeller-Mondolfo, II, 3, 1975; Studi sull'Accademia platonica antica, 1979; L'eredità di Platone nell'Accademia antica, 1989; Filosofia e scienza nel pensiero dell'Ellenismo, 1991; Platone (I pensatori politici), 1996; Introduzione alla filosofia di Plotino, 1984 ( many new editions); Introduzione allo stoicismo ellenistico, 1993; I mici maestri, 2003. Editions (with introductions and notes): Speusippo, Frammenti, 1980; Senocrate-Ermodoro, Frammenti, 1982; Plotino, Enneadi VI, 1-3, Sui generi dell'essere, 1994; Platone, Lettere, 2002. Translations (with introductions and notes): Bodin, I sei libri dello Stato, 1964-90; Erasmo da Rotterdam, L'educazione del principe cristiano, 1977; Epicuro, Opere, 1975, 1984; Stoici antichi, 1989. Honours: Socia Corrispondente: Accademia Nazionale Lincei, Rome, Accademia Lombarda Scienze e Lettere, Milan; Emerita, Faculty of Letters and Philosophy, University of Rome; Grande Ufficiale Republica d'Italia. Address: via Nizza 45, 00198 Rome, Italy.

**ISOYAMA Shogen,** b. 16 July 1947, Ibaraki prefecture, Japan. Professor; Medical Doctor. m. Yoko Nakamura, 3 sons. Education: BS, Tohoku University, Sendai, 1968; MD, Tohoku University School of Medicine, 1972; PhD, Tohoku University, 1980. Appointments: Resident, Tohoku University Hospital, 1973-74; Research Fellow, Harvard Medical School and Beth Israel Hospital, Boston, USA, 1984-87; Associate Professor, Tohoku University School of Medicine, 1990-99; Visiting Professor, China Medical School, Sjenyan, China, 1990; Visiting Professor, University of California, San Francisco, USA, 1998; Professor of Medicine, Faculty of Medical Science and Welfare, Tohoku Bunka Gakuen University, Sendai, Japan, 1999-. Publications: Original articles for professional medical journals. Honours: Cardiovascular Research Award, American Heart Association, 1985-86. Memberships: American Heart Association; Japanese Circulation Society; Japanese Society of Internal Medicine; Japanese Society of Geriatrics; Japanese Heart Failure Society. Address: 2-24 Akaishidai 4-chome, Tomiya-machi, Kurokawa-gun, Miyagi 981-3332, Japan. E-mail: shogen@rehab.tbgu.ac.jp

**ISSING Otmar,** b. 27 March 1936, Würzburg, Germany. Banking Executive; Economist. m. Sieglinde Böhm. Education: Diploma, University of Würzburg, 1960; Dr rer. pol., 1961; Habilitation, 1965. Appointments: Research Assistant, Institute of Economic and Social Sciences, 1960-66, Lecturer, 1965-66, Professor, 1973-90, University of Würzburg; Professor, University of Erlangen-Nuremburg, 1967-73; Member of the Board, Deutsche Bundesbank, 1990-98; Member of Executive Board, European Central Bank, 1998-; Council of Economic Experts, Federal Republic of Germany, 1988-90. Publications: Books: Introduction to Monetary Policy, 6th edition, 1996; Introduction to Monetary Theory, 13th edition, 2003. Memberships: American Economic Association; Academy of Sciences and Literature; List Gesellschaft; Verein für Socialpolitik. Address: European Central Bank, Kaiserstr 29, 60311 Frankfurt am Main, Germany. E-mail: info@ecb.int

**ITO Atsuko,** b. 7 July 1933, Tokyo, Japan. Professor Emeritus. Education: BSc, Ochanomizu University, 1956; MSc, 1959, DSc, 1962, University of Tokyo, Japan. Appointments: Assistant, University of Tokyo, 1963-68; Assistant Professor,

1968-77, Professor, 1977-99, Retired, 1999, Ochanomizu University; Research Adviser, RIKEN. Publications: 170 papers published in scientific journals. Memberships: Physical Society of Japan, 1958-; Council for University Chartering and School Juridical Person, 1993-2000; University Council Subcommittee on organisation and management, 1993-99; Educational Personnel Training Council, 1993-95; Geodesy Council, 1994-2000; Textbook Authorisation Council, 2001-02; University Administrative Council, Yamanashi University, 2000-04; Research Advisor, RIKEN, 1999-; IIAS Fellow, International Institute for Advanced Studies, 2003-. Address: Advanced Meson Science Laboratory, RIKEN, Hirosawa 2-1, Wako-Shi, Saitama 351-0198, Japan.

**ITOH Chiaki,** b. 4 February 1939, Akita, Japan. Professor. m. Katsuko, 1 son, 1 daughter. Education: PhD, Tokyo University of Education, 1966. Appointments: Lecturer, Meiji Gakuin University, Tokyo, 1968-71; Assistant Professor, 1971-78; Professor, 1978-. Publications: Unified Gauge Theory of Weak Electromagnetic and Strong Interactions, 1973. Honours: International Man of the Year, IBC, 1994-95; Most Admired Man of the Decade, ABI, 1995; The International Order of Merit, IBC, 1996. Memberships: Physical Society of Japan; The American Physical Society. Address: Department of Physics, Meiji Gakuin University, 1518 Kamikuratacho, Totsuka, Yokohama 244-8539, Japan. Website: http://www.meijigakuin.ac.jp/~citoh/eng.htm/

**IVANISEVIC Goran,** b. 13 September 1971, Split, Croatia. Tennis Player. Appointments: Winner, US Open Junior Doubles with Nargiso, 1987; Turned Professional, 1988; Joined Yugoslav Davis Cup Squad, 1988; Runner-up, Wimbledon Championship, 1992, 1994, 1998; Semi-Finalist, ATP World Championship, 1992; Winner, numerous ATP tournaments, include Kremlin Cup, Moscow, 1996; Winner, Wimbledon Championship, 2001; Winner, 22 tours singles and 9 doubles titles to date. Honours include: Bronze Medal, Men's Doubles, Barcelona Olympic Games, 1992; BBC Overseas Sports Personality of the Year Award, 2001. Membership: President, Children in Need Foundation, 1995. Website: www.goranivanisevic.com

**IVANOV Victor Petrovich,** b. 12 May 1950, Novgorod, Russia. Deputy Head of Administration of the President of the Russian Federation. m. 1 son, 1 daughter. Education: Graduate, Leningrad Professor M. Bonch-Bruyevich Electrical Engineering Institute of Communications, 1974; Served in Soviet Army, 1974-75; Engineer, Leningrad Scientific-Production Association "Vector", 1975-77; Served in State Security Bodies, Specialisation - fight against organised crime, 1977-; Head, Directorate of Administrative Bodies, St Petersburg Mayor's Office, 1994-96; Director General, Teleplus Television Company, 1996-98; Head of Directorate, Federal Security Service of the Russian Federation, 1998-99; Deputy Director, Head of Department of Economic Security, Federal Security Service of the Russian Federation, 1999-2000; Deputy Head of Administration of the President of the Russian Federation, 2000-. Honours: Order "For Merits to the Motherland" 4th class; Order of Honour; Medal "For Merits in Combat". Address: Administration of President of Russian Federation, Staraya pl 4, 103132 Moscow, Russia.

**IVASCHENKO Fiodar I,** b. 20 February 1920, Filevo-Soroehin, Ukraine. Psychologist. m. Galina Dyachenko, deceased, 2 daughters. Education: Kabardino-Balkarski Pedagogical Institute, Nalehik, Russia, 1943; Institute of Psychology, Moscow, Russia, 1952; Doctor's Degree in Psychology, 1976. Appointments: War Service, Great Patriotic War (WWII), 1943-45; Schoolmaster, Secondary School,

Ordzhonikidze, North Osetia, Russia, 1946-49; Postgraduate Student, Institute of Psychology, Moscow, Russia, 1948-52; Teacher, Docent, Pedagogical Institute, Stavropol, Russia, 1952-74; Manager of Chair of Psychology, 1974-87, Professor, 1987-, Pedagogical University, Minsk, Belarus. Publications: Pupilary industrial teams, 1961; Peculiarities of self assessment of senior pupils during, professional teaching, 1978; Work and formation of personal attitude of schoolchildren, 1999; The psychological education for schoolchildren, 1999; Establishing psychological contact with pupils, 1999; Use of pupil's previous success in forming an experiment, 2000; Experiencing on methodology psychological research, 2003. Honours: Order "Patriotic War II Degree"; Medal for Fighting Merit; 13 Jubilee Medals; Honorary Title of KD Ushinsky Presidium Academy of Russian Federation, Moscow, for monograph: Pupilary industrial teams, 1961. Address: Str Mavea 5, Ap 10, Minsk 220092, Belarus. E-mail: ivaschenko@jbaw.iba.by

**IVES Kenneth James,** b. 29 November 1926, St Pancras, London, England. Civil Engineer. m. Brenda Grace Tilley, 1 son, 1 daughter. Education: BSc, Engineering, 1948, PhD, 1955, DSc, Engineering, 1967, University College London. Appointments: Junior Engineer, Metropolitan Water Board, London, 1948-55; Lecturer, Reader, Professor of Civil Engineering, 1955-92, Emeritus Professor, 1992-, University College London; Postdoctoral Fellow, Harvard University, USA, 1958-59; Visiting Professor, University of North Carolina, USA, 1964; Adviser on Environmental Health, World Health Organisation, 1967-86; Visiting Professor, Delft University, Netherlands, 1977. Publications: About 120 scientific papers and articles; 3 books: The Scientific Basis of Filtration, 1975; The Scientific Basis of Flocculation, 1978; The Scientific Basis of Flotation, 1984. Honours: Gans Medal of the Society for Water Treatment and Examination, 1966; Gold Medal, Filtration Society, 1983; Jenkins Memorial Medal, International Association for Water Pollution Research and Control, 1990; Freeze Award and Lecture, American Society of Civil Engineers, 1994; Commander of the Order of the British Empire, CBE, 1996. Memberships: Fellow, Royal Academy of Engineering; Life Fellow, Institution of Civil Engineers; Foreign Associate, National Academy of Engineering, USA; Life Member, American Society of Civil Engineers; Life Member, American Water Works Association; Life Member, Water Environment Federation, USA. Address: Department of Civil and Environmental Engineering, University College London, Gower St, London WC1E 6BT, England.

**IVES William George Herbert,** b. 30 September 1922, Woodlea Municipality, Manitoba, Canada. Forest Entomology. m. Marion Florence Taylor, deceased, 3 daughters. Education: BSc, Agriculture, The University of Manitoba, 1951; MSc, The Iowa State College, 1953. Appointments: Lead Aircraftsman, Royal Canadian Air Force, 1942-46; Student Assistant, 1949-50, Technical Officer and Research Officer, Grades 1 through 4, 1951-67, Forest Insect Laboratory, Winnipeg, Manitoba; Research Scientist 2, Forest Biology Laboratory, Winnipeg, 1967-70; Research Scientist 3, 1970-89, Research Scientist 4 (part time), 1989-92, Canadian Forestry Service, Edmonton, Alberta. Publications: Numerous books, articles and papers in professional scientific journals include: Environmental factors affecting 21 forest insect defoliators in Manitoba and Saskatchewan, 1945-69, 1981; Dispersal of Olesicampe benefactor and Mesochorus dimidiatus in western Canada, 1984; Tree and Shrub Insects of the Prairie Provinces (co-author), 1988; Factors affecting the survival of immature lodgepole pine in foothills of west-central Alberta (co-author), 1993; Forest Insect Pests in Canada (co-editor), 1995. Honours: Founders Award, Executive of the Western Forest Insect

Work Conference, 1999; Great Mind of the 21st Century, ABI, 2004; Top 100 Scientists, IBC, 2005. Memberships: New York Academy of Sciences; American Association for the Advancement of Science. Address: 11459 – 42 Avenue, Edmonton, Alberta T6J 0W2, Canada.

**IWAMA Hiroshi,** b. 27 February 1939, Tokyo, Japan. University Professor. m. Yoko, 1 son, 1 daughter. Education: BA in Education, 1963, MA in Education, Graduate School of Waseda University, 1965, Candidate of PhD in Education, 1968, Waseda University, Japan; PhD in Educational Theory and Policy, Graduate School of Pennsylvania State University, 1990. Appointments: Associate Professor, Shibaura Junior College of Technology, Japan, 1969-76; Associate Professor of Shibaura Institute of Technology, 1977-83; Principal, Central Pennsylvania Japanese Language Supplemental School, USA, 1985-87; Professor of Kokushikan University, Tokyo, Japan, 1990-; Professor of Graduate School of Kokushikan University, 1998-. Publications: Articles in professional journals: South Africa and the New Education Fellowship, 2001; The Creation of UNESCO and the NEF, 1999; Books: Japanese Schooling, 1989; Education for Sharing, 1996; The Rise of the New Education Fellowships in India: The Educational Ideas and Projects of R Tagore, 2004. Honours: Listed in national and international biographical dictionaries. Memberships: Director, General Secretary, World Education Fellowship, Japan Section; Member, Holistic Education Society in Japan. Address: 1-26-9 Zenpakuji, Suginami-ku, Tokyo 167-0041, Japan. E-mail: hiwama@m78.com

# J

**JACK Ronald Dyce Sadler,** b. 3 April 1941, Ayr, Scotland. University Professor. m. Kirsty Nicolson, 8 July 1967, 2 daughters. Education: MA, Glasgow, 1964; PhD, Edinburgh, 1968; DLitt, Glasgow. Appointments: Lecturer, Department of English Literature, Edinburgh University, 1965; Reader, 1978; Professor, 1987; Visiting Professor, University of Virginia, 1973-74; Director, Universities Central Council on Admissions, 1988-94; Visiting Professor, University of Strathclyde, 1993; Distinguished Visiting Professor, University of Connecticut, 1998. Publications: Scottish Prose 1550-1700, 1972; The Italian Influence on Scottish Literature, 1972; A Choice of Scottish Verse 1560-1660, 1978; The Art of Robert Burns (co-author), 1982; Sir Thomas Urquhart (co-author), 1984; Alexander Montgomerie, 1985; Scottish Literature's Debt to Italy, 1986; The History of Scottish Literature, Vol I, 1988; Patterns of Divine Comedy, 1989; The Road to the Never Land, 1991; Of Lion and Unicorn, 1993; The Poems of William Dunbar, 1997; Mercat Anthology of Early Scottish Literature, 1997, 2nd revised edition, 2000; New Oxford Dictionary of National Biography (associate editor), 2004. Contributions to: Review of English Studies; Modern Language Review; Comparative Literature; Studies in Scottish Literature. Memberships: Medieval Academy of America; Scottish Text Society. Address: David Hume Tower, George Square, Edinburgh EH8 9JX, Scotland.

**JACKEVICIUS Algirdas,** b. 3 August 1926, Panevezis reg, Lithuania. Surgeon. m. Marija Jackeviciene, 1 daughter. Education: MD, Vilnius University, 1948; Presentation of thesis of doctor of medicine, 1953; Surgeon, Vilnius First Hospital, 1951-1957; Habil Doctor of Medicine, Vilnius, 1969. Appointments: Senior Research Worker, Lithuanian Institute of Oncology, 1957-79; Chief of the Department of Thoracic Surgery, Lithuanian Institute of Oncology, 1979-90; Professor, 1994; Professor of the Clinic of Surgery, Lithuanian Oncology Center, 1990-2002; Professor of the Clinic of Oncology, Vilnius University, 2004- Publications: 262, 1952-2004; 6 books include: Lung Cancer, 1975; Textbook: Oncology (editor), 1992; Lung and Mediastinum Tumors, 2002. Honours: Medal: Veteran of Works, 1986; Sign of Advanced Worker of Health Service. Memberships: International Association for the Study of Lung Cancer; European Association for Cardio-Thoracic Surgery; Lithuanian Society of Thoracic and Cardio Surgeons; Lithuanian Society Against Cancer; Society of Surgeons, Vilnius. Address: Department of Thoracic Surgery, Institute of Oncology, Vilnius University, Santariskiu 1, Vilnius 08660, Lithuania. E-mail: algirdasj@is.lt

**JACKLIN Tony,** b. 7 July 1944, Scunthorpe, England. Golfer. m. Vivien Jacklin, 1966, deceased 1988, 2 sons, 1 daughter, (2) Astrid May Waagen, 1988, 1 son, 1 step-son, 1 step-daughter. Appointments: Lincolnshire Open Champion, 1961; Professional, 1962-85, 1988-; Won, British Assistant Professional's Title, 1965; Won, Dunlop Masters, 1967, 1973; First British player to win British Open since 1951, 1969; US Open Champion, 1970; First British player to win US Open since 1920 and first since 1900 to hold US and British Open titles simultaneously; Greater Greensboro Open Champion, USA, 1968, 1972; Won, Italian Open, 1973, German Open, 1979, Venezuelan Open, 1979, Jersey Open, 1981, British PGA Champion, 1982 and 15 major tournaments in various parts of the world; Played in 8 Ryder Cup matches and 4 times for England in World Cup; Captain of 1983 GB and European Ryder Cup Team; Captain of European Ryder Cup Team, 1985 (1st win for Europe since 1957), 1987; BBC TV Golf Commentator; Director of Golf, San Roque Club, 1988-; Golf course designer.

Publications: Golf With Tony Jacklin, 1969; The Price of Success, 1979; Jacklin's Golfing Secrets, with Peter Dobereiner; The First Forty Years, with Renton Laidlaw, 1985; Your Game and Mine, with Bill Robertson, 1999. Honours include: Honorary Fellow, Birmingham Polytechnic, 1989. Memberships include: British Professional Golfers Association. Address: Tony Jacklin Golf Academy, Plaza del Rio Office Centre, 101 Riverfront Boulevard, Suite 610, Bradenton, FL 34205, USA.

**JACKMAN Brian,** b. 25 April 1935, Epsom, Surrey, England. Freelance Journalist; Writer. m. (1) 14 February 1964, divorced December 1992, 1 daughter, (2) January 1993. Education: Grammar School. Appointment: Staff, Sunday Times, 1970-90. Publications: We Learned to Ski, 1974; Dorset Coast Path, 1977; The Marsh Lions, 1982; The Countryside in Winter, 1986; My Serengeti Years, editor, 1987; Roaring at the Dawn, 1996; The Big Cat Diary, 1996; Touching the Wild, 2003. Contributions to: Sunday Times; The Times; Daily Telegraph; Daily Mail; Country Living; Condé Nast Traveller; BBC Wildlife. Honours: TTG Travel Writer of Year, 1982; Wildscreen Award, 1982. Memberships: Royal Geographical Society; Fauna and Flora Preservation Society. Address: Spick Hatch, West Milton, Nr Bridport, Dorset DT6 3SH, England.

**JACKMAN Sydney Wayne,** b. 25 March 1925, USA. Professor. Education: PhD, Harvard University, 1953. Appointments: Professor of History, 1960-90; Fellow Commoner St Edmund's College, 1991-. Publications: Romanov Relations; Man of Mercury; Deviating Voices; A Stranger in the Hague. Honours: Honorary D Litt, University of Lethbridge, Alberta, Canada; Honorary D Litt, University of Victoria, British Columbia, Canada. Memberships: FSA; FRHistSoc; FRHist (Scot); FRHistSoc (Ireland). Address: #1-159 Cook Street, Victoria, BC, Canada V8V 2N9.

**JACKSON Andrew John,** b. 27 October 1962, Winchester, Hampshire, England. Poet. Education: BA, Honours, History/English, College of Ripon and York St John, 1985-89. Appointments: Civil Service, 1982; Archaeological Assistant, Southampton and Winchester, 1984-85, 1990-91; Administrative Assistant, Benefits Agency, Winchester, 1992-94, currently on permanent contract as Students Grant Assistant, Hampshire County Council. Contributions to: Poetry Now Anthology: Love Lines, 1995; Poetry Now Anthology: Book of Traditional Verse, 1995; Poetry Now: Indelible Ink (anthology), 1995; Poetry Now magazine; Rivet magazine. Address: 100 Priors Dean Road, Harestock, Winchester, Hampshire SO22 6LA, England.

**JACKSON Betty,** b. 24 June 1949, Lancashire, England. Couturier. m. David Cohen, 1985, 1 son, 1 daughter. Education: Birmingham College of Art and Design. Appointments: Chief Designer, Quorum, 1975-81; Founder, Betty Jackson Ltd, 1981, Director, 1981-; Opened, Betty Jackson Retail Shop, 1991; Part-time Tutor, 1982-. Memberships: Fellow, Birmingham Polytechnic, 1989; University of Central Lancashire, 1993. Honours: Designer of the Year, 1985; Royal Designer for Industry, Royal Society of Arts, 1988, 1989; Fil d'Or, International Linen, 1989; Honorary Fellow, 1989, part time tutor, 1982-, visiting professor, 1999, RCA; Contemporary Designer of the Year, 1999. Address: Betty Jackson Ltd, 1 Netherwood Place, Netherwood Road, London W14 0BW, England.

**JACKSON Christopher Murray,** b. 24 May 1935, Norwich, Norfolk, England. Politician; Businessman. m. Carlie Elizabeth Keeling, 1 son, 1 daughter. Education: BA Hons (Physics), Magdalen College, Oxford; ; Studies in German and Economics, Frankfurt University; Postgraduate studies in Economics and

Accounting, London School of Economics. Appointments: Commissioned Pilot, Royal Air Force, 1954-56; Member, Unilever Management Development Scheme, Marketing Manager, Lever Bros, 1966, Senior Manager, 1967, Unilever plc, 1959-69; General Marketing Manager, Director of S&P Services, Save & Prosper Group, 1969-71; Contested UK General Election, East Ham South, 1970; Head of Corporate Planning, Donald Macpherson Group plc, 1971-74; Contested UK General Election, Northampton North, 1974; Director of Corporate Development, Spillers Group, 1974-80; Member, European Parliament for Kent East, 1974-94; Non-executive Director, Westminster Communications Ltd, 1988-95; Non-executive Director, Politics International Ltd, 1995-98; National Chairman, Agriculture & Countryside Forum, 1995-98; Chairman, Natural Resources International Ltd, Chatham, 1997-2003; Director and Former Chairman, CJA Consultants Ltd, 1995-; Chairman, Board of Governors, Bethany School, 1999-. Publications: Numerous articles in popular press and professional journals. Honours: Honorary Member of European Parliament. Memberships: Member, Conservative Party, -1999; Royal Institute of International Affairs; Executive Committee, Society for Long Range Planning, 1969-79; Voluntary Social Worker, Royal Parish Church of St Martin-in-the-Fields, 1963-67; PCC, 1965-69, Treasurer, 1968-69, St Martin-in-the-Fields. Address: 8 Wellmeade Drive, Sevenoaks, Kent TN13 1QA, England. E-mail: c.jackson@btconnect.com

**JACKSON Colin Ray,** b. 18 February 1967. Athlete. Career: Honours for 110m hurdles include: Silver Medal, European Junior Championships, 1985; Gold Medal, World Junior Championships, 1986; Silver Medal, Commonwealth Games, 1986; Silver Medal, European Cup, 1987; Bronze Medal, World Championships, 1987; Silver Medal, Olympic Games, 1988; Silver Medal, World Cup, 1989; Gold Medal, European Cup, 1989, 1993; Gold Medal, Commonwealth Games, 1990; Gold Medal, World Cup, 1992; Gold Medal (new world record), Silver Medal (relay), World Championships, 1993; Honours for 60 hurdles include: Silver Medal World Indoor Championships, 1989, 1993; Silver Medal, 1987, Gold Medal 1989, 1994, European Indoor Championships; Gold Medal, European and Commonwealth Championships, 1994; Gold Medal, European Championships, 1998, 2002; Gold Medal, World Championships, 1999; Numerous Welsh, UK, European and Commonwealth records; Most capped British athlete ever (70 vests), 2003; Total of 25 medals; Announced retirement in 2003. Honours: Hon BA, Aberystwyth, 1994; Hon BSc, University of Wales, 1999; Athlete of the Decade, French Sporting Council; Hurdler of the Century, German Athletic Association; Athlete of the Year, 1993-94; British Athletics Writers Sportsman of the Year, 1994; Sports Writers Association. Memberships: Brecon Athletics Club UK International, 1985-. Address: 4 Jackson Close, Rhoose, Vale of Glamorgan, CF62 3DQ, Wales. Website: www.mtc-uk.com

**JACKSON Glenda,** b. 9 May 1936, Birkenhead, Cheshire, England. Member of Parliament; Actress. m. Roy Hodges, 1958, divorced 1976, 1 son. Education: Royal Academy of Dramatic Art. Appointments: Actress, Royal Shakespeare Company; Other Theatre includes: The Investigation, Hamlet, US, 1965; Three Sisters, 1967; The Maids, 1974; Hedda Gabler, 1975; The White Devil, 1976; Antony and Cleopatra, 1978; The House of Bernada Alba, 1986; Scenes from an Execution, 1990; Mermaid, 1990; Mother Courage, 1990; Mourning Becomes Electra, 1991; Films include: Women in Love, 1969; Sunday, Bloody Sunday, Mary, Queen of Scots and The Boyfriend, 1971; A Touch of Class, 1973; The Abbess of Crewe, 1976; House Calls, 1978; Salome's Last Dance, 1988; The Rainbow, 1989; The Secret Life of Sir Arnold Bax, 1992; TV includes: Elizabeth

R, 1971; The Morecambe and Wise Show; Elected Labour MP Hampstead and Highgate, 1992-; Parliamentary Under Secretary of State, Department for the Environment and Transport, 1997-99; Adviser on Homelessness, GLA, 2000-. Honours: CBE, Honorary DLitt, Liverpool, 1978; Honorary LLM, Nottingham, 1992; Honorary Fellow, Liverpool Polytechnic, 1987; 2 Academy Awards, 1971, 1974. Memberships: President, Play Matters, 1976-; Director, United British Artists, 1986-. Address: c/o House of Commons, London SW1A 0AA, England.

**JACKSON Jesse Louis,** b. 8 October 1941, Greenville, North Carolina, USA. Clergyman; Civic Leader. m. Jacqueline Lavinia Brown, 1964, 3 sons, 2 daughters. Education: University of Illinois; Illinois Agricultural and Technical College; Chicago Theological Seminary. Appointments: Ordained to Ministry Baptist Church, 1968; Active, Black Coalition for United Community Action, 1969; Co-Founder, Operation Breadbasket, Southern Christian Leadership Conference; Coordinating Council, Community Organsations, Chicago, 1966, National Director, 1966-77; Founder, Executive Director, Operation PUSH (People United to Save Humanity), Chicago, 1971-; TV Host, Voices of America, 1990-. Honours include: President's Award, National Medical Association, 1969; Humanitarian Father of the Year Award, National Father's Day Committee, 1971. Address: c/o Rainbow PUSH Coalition, 930 East 50th Street, Chicago, IL 60615, USA.

**JACKSON Michael David, (Gen Sir Mike)** b. 21 March 1944, Sheffield, England. Soldier. m. Sarah Coombe, 4 May 1985, 2 sons, 1 daughter. Education: BSoc Sc, Birmingham University, 1967. Appointments: Chief of Staff Berlin Infantry Brigade, 1977-78; Co-Commander, 2nd Battalion, The Parachute Regiment, 1979-80; Directing Staff, Staff College, 1981-83; Commanding Officer, 1st Battalion, The Parachute Regiment, 1984-86; Directing Staff, Joint Services Defence College, 1987-88; Service Fellow, Wolfson College Cambridge 89; Commander, 39 Infantry Brigade, 1990-91; Director Personal Services, 1992-93; Commander 3 (UK) Division, 1994-96; Commander Multinational Division South West, Bosnia, 1996; Director, Development and Doctrine, MOD, 1996-97; Commander, Allied Command Europe Rapid Reaction Corps, 1997-1999; Commander, Kosovo Force, 1999; Commander in Chief, UK Land Force, 2000-03; Chief of the General Staff, 2003-. Honours: MBE, 1979; Freeman, City of London, 1988; CBE, 1992; CB, 1996; KCB, 1998; DS0, 1999. Membership: RUSI. Address: Office of the Chief of the General Staff, Ministry of Defence, Main Building, Whitehall, London, SW1A 2HB, England. E-mail: webmaster@dgics.mod.uk Website: www.mod.uki

**JACKSON Michael Joseph,** b. 29 August 1958, Gary, Indiana, USA. m. (1) Lisa Marie Presley, divorced, (2) Debbie Rowe, divorced, 2 sons, 1 daughter. Career: Lead singer, family singing group Jackson Five (later the Jacksons), 1969-75; Solo artist, 1971-; Lengthy world tours, including Bad Tour 1987; Dangerous World Tour, 1992; Film appearances: The Wiz, 1978; Captain Eo, 1986; Moonwalker, 1988; Founder, Heal The World Foundation (children's charity); Owner, ATV Music Company (including rights for John Lennon and Paul McCartney songs); Owner, MJJ record label. Compositions include: Co-writer with Lionel Richie, We Are The World, USA For Africa famine relief single, 1985. Recordings: Albums: with Jackson Five/Jacksons include: Diana Ross Presents The Jackson Five, 1969; ABC, 1970; Third Album, 1970; Goin' Back To Indiana, 1971; Maybe Tomorrow, 1971; Looking Through The Windows, 1972; Farewell My Summer, 1973; Get It Together, 1973; Skywriter, 1973; Dancing Machine, 1974; Moving Violation, 1975; Joyfull Jukebox, Music, 1976; The Jacksons, 1976; Goin' Places, 1977;

Destiny, 1978; Triumph, 1980; Boogie, 1980; Live, 1981; Victory, 1984; Solo albums: Got To Be There, 1971; Ben, 1972; Music And Me, 1973; Forever Michael, 1975; The Best Of, 1975; The Wiz (film soundtrack), 1978; Off The Wall, 1979; ET - The Extra Terrestrial (film soundtrack), 1982; Thriller (Number 1 in every Western country), 1982; Bad (Number 1, UK and US), 1987; Dangerous (Number 1, US and UK), 1991; HIStory - Past, Present And Future Book I, 1995; Scream, 1995; Childhood, 1995; Invincible, 2001; Numerous solo hit singles include: Got To Be There, 1971; Rockin' Robin, 1972; Ain't No Sunshine, 1972; Ben (Number 1, US), 1972; Don't Stop Till You Get Enough (Number 1, US), 1979; Off The Wall, 1979; Rock With You (Number 1, US), 1980; One Day In Your Life (Number 1, UK), 1981; She's Out Of My Life, 1980; The Girl Is Mine, duet with Paul McCartney (Number 1, UK), 1982; Billie Jean (Number 1, US and UK), 1983; Beat It (Number 1, US), 1983; Wanna Be Startin' Somethin', 1983; Human Nature, 1983; Say Say Say, duet with Paul McCartney, 1983; Thriller, 1983; I Can't Stop Loving You (Number 1, UK and US), 1987; Bad (Number 1, US), 1987; The Way You Make Me Feel (Number 1, US), 1988; Dirty Diana (Number 1, US), 1988; Leave Me Alone, 1989; Black And White (Number 1, UK and US), 1991; Remember The Time, 1992; Heal The World, 1992; Give In To Me, 1992; Scream (with Janet Jackson), 1995; You Are Not Alone, 1995; Earth Song, 1995; They Don't Care About Us, 1996; Ghosts, 1997; Stranger in Moscow, 1997; Blood on the Dance Floor, 1997; You Rock My World, 2001; Cry, 2001; Contributor, recordings by Minnie Ripperton; Carol Bayer Sager; Donna Summer; Paul McCartney. Publications: Moonwalk (autobiography), 1988; Dancing The Dream (poems and reflections), 1992. Honours include: Numerous Grammy Awards, 1980- (including 7 awards, 1984; Song Of The Year, 1986; Legend Award, 1993) Numerous American Music Awards, 1980- (including 11 awards, 1984; Special Award of Achievement, 1989); BRIT Awards: Best International Artist, 1984, 1988, 1989; Artist Of A Generation, 1996; Soul Train Awards, 1988-; MTV Video Vanguard Award, 1988; 2 NAACP Image Awards, 1988; Entertainer of the Decade, American Cinema Awards Foundation, 1990; First recipient, BMI Michael Jackson Award, 1990; 3 World Music Awards, 1993; Most successful album ever, Thriller (50 million copies sold worldwide); Star on Hollywood Walk Of Fame, 1984; Numerous magazine poll wins and awards; Gold and Platinum records; Honorary Director, Exeter City Football Club, 2002-.

**JACKSON Peter,** b. 31 October 1961, Pukerua Bay, North Island, New Zealand. Film Director. m. Frances Walsh, 1 son, 1 daughter. Films: Bad Taste, 1987; Meet the Feebles, 1989; Valley of the Stereos, 1992; Ship to Shore, 1993; Heavenly Creatures, 1994; Jack Brown Genius, 1994; Forgotten Silver, 1995; The Frighteners, 1996; The Lord of the Rings: The Fellowship of the Ring, 2001; The Lord of the Rings: The Two Towers, 2002; The Long and Short of It, 2003; The Lord of the Rings: The Return of the King, 2003. Honours: Honorary Graduation, Massey University, 2001; BAFTA Award for Best Director, 2001; Voted Man of the Year 2002, Australian Empire Magazine, 2003; Best Director Oscar for Lord of the Rings: The Return of the King, 2004. Member: New Zealand Order of Merit, 2002. Address: c/o ICM, 8942 Wilshire Boulevard, Beverly Hills, CA 90211, USA.

**JACKSON Samuel L,** b. 1949, Washington, USA. Actor. m. LaTanya Richardson, 1 daughter. Education: Morehouse College. Appointments: Co-Founder, Member, Just Us Theatre Company, Atlanta. Creative Works: Stage appearances: Home; A Soldier's Story; Sally/Prince; Colored People's Time; Mother Courage; Spell No 7; The Mighty Gents; The Piano Lesson; Two Trains Running; Fences; TV appearances: Movin' On,

1972; Ghostwriter, 1992; The Trial of the Moke, 1978; Uncle Tom's Cabin, 1987; Common Ground, 1990; Dead and Alive: The Race for Gus Farace, 1991; Simple Justice, 1993; Assault at West Point, 1994; Against the Wall, 1994; Films include: Together for Days, 1972; Ragtime, 1981; Eddie Murphy Raw, 1987; Coming to America, 1988; School Daze, 1988; Do The Right Thing, 1989; Sea of Love, 1989; A Shock to the System, 1990; Def by Temptation, 1990; Betsy's Wedding, 1990; Mo' Better Blues, 1990; The Exorcist III, 1990; GoodFellas, 1990; Return of the Superfly, 1990; Jungle Fever, 1991; Strictly Business, 1991; Jumpin' at the Boneyard, 1992; Patriot Games, 1992; Johnny Suede, 1992; Jurassic Park, 1993; True Romance, 1993; Hail Caesar, 1994; Fresh, 1994; The New Age, 1994; Pulp Fiction, 1994; Losing Isaiah, 1995; Kiss of Death, 1995; Die Hard With a Vengeance, 1995; The Great White Hype, 1996; A Time to Kill, 1996; The Long Kiss Goodnight; Jackie Brown; Trees Lounge; Hard Eight; Out of Sight; The Negotiator; Deep Blue Sea; Sphere; Eve's Bayou; Star Wars Episode I: The Phantom Menace, 1999; Rules of Engagement, 1999; Shaft, 2000; Unbreakable, 2000; The Caveman's Valentine, 2001; The 51st State, 2001; Changing Lanes, 2002; Star Wars Episode II: Attack of the Clones, 2002; The House on Turk Street, 2002; XXX, 2002; Basic, 2003; S.W.A.T, 2003; Country of My Skull, 2004; Twisted, 2004; Kill Bill: Vol 2, 2004. Honours include: Best Actor Award, Cannes International Film Festival; New York Film Critics Award. Address: c/o ICM, 8942 Wilshire Boulevard, Beverly Hills, CA 90211, USA.

**JACKSON Siti Mariah Mansor,** b. 29 May 1953, Kedah, Malaysia. Artist. m. Billy Morrow Jackson. Education: Diploma in Art and Design (Textile Design) and Art Teacher's Diploma, Mara Institute of Technology, Malaysia, 1978-79; MA, Art Education, University of Illinois, 1988. Appointments: Art Teacher, Lecturer, Malaysian Schools and Teachers Colleges, 1979-85; Ceramic Sculptor, 1988-; Vice President, Jackson Studios, Illinois. Civic Activities: Invitational and Juried Local and National Group Art Exhibitions and Show Cases. Honours: First Award, Fabric Design on Paper for Stewardess Uniform, Malaysian Airline System, 1978; Federal Teaching Art Scholarship, Ministry of Education, Malaysia, 1985; Elected Member, Kappa Delta Pi, 1987; Award of Excellence, Manhattan Arts International Cover Art Competition, New York, 1995; 2nd Place, Watercolour, 10th International Juried Exhibition, Laredo Center for the Arts, 2002. Memberships: Smithsonian Institution, Washington, DC; National Museum of Women in the Arts, Washington, DC; International Women Artists Council, USA-Malaysia; Krannert Art Museum, University of Illinois, Champaign; Art Exhibition Advisory Committee, Springer Cultural Center, Champaign. Address: 706 West White Street, Champaign, IL 61820, USA. Web site: http://www.soltec.net/jacksonstudios/

**JACKSON Victoria (Vicky),** b. 6 August 1934, London, England. m. Antoine Jackson, 1 son, 1 daughter. Education: Colchester College of Further Education; Dartington College of Arts. Appointments: Professional Singer, 1969-78; Singing Teacher, 1980-83; BBC Recording Artist; Accounts Controller, Executive Director, Chief Executive Officer, 1987-. Honour: Life Fellow, International Biographical Association. Memberships: Membership Secretary, World Foundation of Successful Women; Royal Horticultural Society. Address: Withycot, Ely Road, Prickwillow, Cambridgeshire CB7 4UJ, England.

**JACKSON William David,** b. 15 July 1947, Liverpool, England. Freelance Journalist; Translator; Poet. m. Christa Antonie Range, 3 June 1972, 1 son, 1 daughter. Education: BA, Honours, English Language and Literature, St Catherine's College, Oxford, 1968. Publication: Then and Now, book,

2002. Contributions to: Acumen; Babel; Blithe Spirit; The Dark Horse; Haiku Quarterly; Iron; Leviathan Quarterly; Metre; Modern Poetry in Translation; Oasis; Orbis; Outposts; Oxford Poetry; Pennine Platform; Poetry Nottingham; Poetry Review; Poetry Wales; The Rialto; The Shop; Stand; Staple. Address: Clemensstrasse 66, 80796 Munich, Germany.

**JACKSON (William) Keith,** b. 5 September 1928, Colchester, Essex, England. Emeritus Professor. m. (1) 3 children, (2) Jennifer Mary Louch, 21 December 1990. Education: London University Teaching Certificate, 1947; BA, Honours, University of Nottingham, 1953; PhD, University of Otago, New Zealand, 1967. Publications: New Zealand Politics in Action (with A V Mitchell and R M Chapman), 1962; New Zealand (with J Harré), 1969; Editor, Fight for Life, New Zealand, Britain and the EEC, 1971; New Zealand Legislative Council, 1972; Politics of Change, 1972; The Dilemma of Parliament, 1987; Historical Dictionary of New Zealand (with A D McRobie), 1996; New Zealand Adopts Proportional Representation: Accident? Design? Evolution? (with Alan McRobie), 1998. Contributions to: Numerous professional journals. Honours: Mobil Award for Best Spoken Current Affairs Programme, Radio New Zealand, 1979; Henry Chapman Fellow, Institute of Commonwealth Studies, London, 1963; Canterbury Fellowship, 1987; Asia 2000 Fellowship, 1996. Address: 92A, Hinau Street, Christchurch 4, New Zealand.

**JACOBI Derek George,** b. 22 October 1938, London, England. Actor. Education: St Johns College, Cambridge. Appointments: Birmingham Repertory Theatre, 1960-63; National Theatre, 1963-71; Prospect Theatre Company, 1972, 1974, 1976-78; Artistic Association, 1976-; Old Vic Company, 1978-79; Joined Royal Shakespeare Company, 1982; Vice-President, National Youth Theatre, 1982-; Artistic Director, Chichester Festival, 1995-. Creative Works: TV appearances include: She Stoops to Conquer; Man of Straw; The Pallisers; I Claudius; Philby; Burgess and Maclean; Tales of the Unexpected; A Stranger in Town; Mr Pye; Brother Cadfael TV series, 1994-; Films: Odessa File; Day of the Jackal; The Medusa Touch; Othello; Three Sisters; Interlude; The Human Factor; Charlotte, 1981; The Man Who Went up in Smoke, 1981; The Hunchback of Notre Dame, 1981; Inside the Third Reich, 1982; Little Dorrit, 1986; The Tenth Man, 1988; Henry V, The Fool, 1990; Dead Again, 1996; Hamlet, 1996; Love is the Devil, 1997; Gladiator, 2000; Gosford Park, 2002; Plays: The Lunatic; Lover and the Poet), 1980; The Suicide, 1980; Much Ado About Nothing; Peer Gynt; The Tempest, 1982; Cyrano de Bergerac, 1983; Breaking the Code, 1986; Richard II, 1988; Richard III, 1989; Kean, 1990; Becket, 1991; Mad, Bad and Dangerous to Know; Ambassadors, 1992; Macbeth, 1993; Hadrian VII, 1995; Playing the Wife, 1995; Uncle Vanya, 1996; God Only Knows, 2000; Director: Hamlet, 1988, 2000. Honours: Honorary Fellow, St Johns College, Cambridge; Variety Club Award, 1976; British Academy Award, 1976; Press Guild Award, 1976; Royal TV Society Award, 1976; Evening Standard Award Best Actor, 1998. Address: Chichester Festival Theatre, Oaklands Park, Chichester, West Sussex PO19 4AP, England.

**JACOBS David Lewis,** b. 19 May 1926, London, England. Broadcaster. m. (1) Patricia Bradlaw, 16 September 1949, div 1972, 1 son deceased, 3 daughters; (2) Caroline Munro, 1975, deceased 1975; (3) Lindsay Stuart Hutcheson, 1 August 1979, 1 stepson. Education: Belmont College, London. Career: Royal Navy; Impressionist, Navy Mixture, 1944; Chief Announcer, Radio SEAC, Ceylon; BBC announcer and newsreader; Freelance broadcaster; Radio includes: Housewives Choice; BBC Jazz Club; Pick Of The Pops; Saturday Show Band Show; Any Questions?; Any Answers?; Melodies For You; Founder

member, Capital Radio; Own programme, BBC Radio 2, 6 years; Television includes: Juke Box Jury; Top Of The Pops; David Jacobs' Words And Music; Sunday Night With David Jacobs; Where Are They Now?; What's My Line?; Eurovision Song Contest; A Song For Europe; Miss World; Little Women; Come Dancing; Presents musical concerts and one-man show, An Evening with David Jacobs; Currently presenting The David Jacobs Collection, BBC Radio 2 and touring the country with the shows: David Jacobs Goes Name Dropping; David Jacobs Presents a Night in Old Vienna with English Serenata; David Jacobs Presents Ain't She Sweet the music of the Roaring 20's and 30's with Charleston Chasers; David Jacobs Presents the Wonderful West End, An Evening of Gershwin and Marti Webb; The Legend of Sinatra with Gary Williams. Publications: Jacobs Ladder; Caroline; Any Questions? (with Michael Bowen). Honours: 6 Royal Command Performances; Top British DJ, BBC and Radio Luxembourg, 6 years; TV Personality of Year, Variety Club of Great Britain, 1960; BBC Radio Personality of Year, 1975; Sony Gold Award, 1984; Sony Hall of Fame; Richard Martin Award (animal welfare); Honorary Doctorate, Kingston University, 1994; CBE, 1996; Deputy Lieutenant of and for Greater London, 1983-2001; Representative Deputy Lieutenant for the Royal Borough of Kingston-upon-Thames; Honorary Freeman of the Royal Borough of Kingston-upon-Thames, 1997; High Steward of the Royal Borough of Kingston Upon Thames, 2001; Chairman, Thames Radio; Radio Academy Hall of Fame, 2004. Memberships include: Vice-President, Society of Stars; Vice-President, Royal Star & Garter Home, Richmond; Vice-President, Kingston Arts Festival; Director, Chairman, Kingston Theatre Trust. Address: 203 Pavilion Road, London SW1X 0BJ, England.

**JACOBS Juergen Carl,** b. 17 May 1936, Aachen, Germany. University Professor. Education: Studies in Law, Literature, Philosophy and Sociology at Göttingen, Munich, Bonn, Cologne, 1956-64; Wiss.Ass., Cologne, 1964-71; Dr Jur. Utr, 1962; Dr Phil, 1964; Habilitation, 1971. Appointments: Professor of German Literature, Bonn, 1972-83; Professor of German Literature, Wuppertal, 1983-. Publications: Wielands Romane, 1969; Wilhelm Meister und seine Brüder, 1971; Prosader Aufklärung, 1976; Der Deutsche Schelmenroman, 1983; Lessing, 1986; Don Quixote in der Aufklärung, 1992; Aporien der Aufklärung, 2001; Zwischenbilanzendes Lebens, 2005; Many articles in learned journals on German and European literature. Honour: Member, Nordrhein-Westfälische Akademie der Wissenschaften. Address: Lindenburger Allee 26, 50831 Cologne, Germany.

**JACOBS Paul Martin,** b. 11 December 1951, Plymouth, England. Consultant Ophthalmic Surgeon. m. Marie Colette McMahon, 1 son. Education: The Queen's College, Oxford; University of Liverpool. Appointments: Resident Surgical Officer, Fellow in Vitreo-Retinal Surgery, Moorfields Eye Hospital, 1982-88; Consultant Ophthalmic Surgeon, University Hospital, Nottingham, 1988-92; Consultant Ophthalmic Surgeon, Borders General Hospital, Melrose, 1992-95; Consultant Ophthalmic Surgeon, York Hospital, 1995-. Publications: Papers and book chapters on vitreo-retinal surgery and cataract surgery. Memberships: Fellow, Royal College of Surgeons of Glasgow; Fellow, Royal College of Ophthalmologists; Fellow, Royal College of Surgeons of Edinburgh; Fellow, Royal Society of Medicine. Address: York Hospital, Wigginton Road, York YO31 8HE, England. E-mail: paul.jacobs@yeork.nhs.uk

**JACOBSON Dan,** b. 7 March 1929, Johannesburg, South Africa. Professor Emeritus; Writer. m. Margaret Pye, 3 sons, 1 daughter. Education: BA, University of the Witwatersrand; Honorary Ph.D., University of Witwatersrand. Appointments:

Visiting Fellow, Stanford University, California, 1956-57; Professor, Syracuse University, New York, 1965-66; Fellow, 1981, Australian National University; Lecturer, 1975-80, Reader, 1980-87, Professor, 1988-94, Professor Emeritus, 1994-, University College, London. Publications: The Trap, 1955; A Dance in the Sun, 1956; The Price of Diamonds, 1957; The Evidence of Love, 1960; The Beginners, 1965; The Rape of Tamar, 1970; The Confessions of Josef Baisz, 1979; The Story of the Stories, 1982; Time and Time Again, 1985; Adult Pleasures, 1988; Hidden in the Heart, 1991; The God Fearer, 1992; The Electronic Elephant, 1994; Heshel's Kingdom, 1998; A Mouthful of Glass, translation, 2000; Ian Hamilton in Conversation with Dan Jacobson, interview, 2002; All for Love, 2005. Contributions to: Periodicals and newspapers. Honours: John Llewelyn Rhys Memorial Award, 1958; W Somerset Maugham Award, 1964; H H Wingate Award, 1979; J R Ackerley Award, 1986; Honorary DLitt, University of the Witwatersrand, 1987; Mary Elinore Smith Prize, 1992; Honorary Fellow, University College, London, 2005. Address: c/o A M Heath & Co Ltd, 79 St Martins Lane, London WC2, England.

**JACOBSON Howard,** b. 25 August 1942, Manchester, England. Novelist. m. Rosalin Sadler, 1978, divorced 2004, 1 son. Education: BA, Downing College, Cambridge. Appointments: Lecturer, University of Sydney, 1965-68; Supervisor, Selwyn College, Cambridge, 1969-72; Senior Lecturer, Wolverhampton Polytechnic, 1974-80; Television Critic, The Sunday Correspondent, 1989-90; Into the Land of Oz, (Channel 4), 1991; Writer/Presenter, Yo, Mrs Askew! (BBC2), 1991, Roots Schmoots (Channel 4 TV), 1993, Sorry, Judas (Channel 4 TV), 1993, Seriously Funny: An Argument for Comedy (Channel 4 TV), 1997; Columnist, The Independent, 1998-; Howard Jackson Takes on the Turner (Channel 4 TV), 2000; Why The Novel Matters: A South Bank Show Special (ITV), 2002. Publications: Shakespeare's Magnanimity: Four Tragic Heroes, Their Friends and Families, 1978; Coming From Behind, 1983; Peeping Tom, 1984; Redback, 1986; In the Land of Oz, 1987; The Very Model of a Man, 1992; Roots Schmoots, 1993; Seeing With the Eye: The Peter Fuller Memorial Lecture, 1993; Seriously Funny, 1997; No More Mister Nice Guy, 1998; The Mighty Walzer, 1999; Who's Sorry Now?, 2002; The Making of Henry, 2004. Honours: Winner Jewish Quarterly and Wingate Prize, 2000; Winner of the first Bollinger Everyman Wodehouse Prize, 2000. Membership: Modern Painters, editorial board. Address: Curtis Brown, Haymarket House, 28-29 Haymarket, London SW1Y 4SP, England.

**JADHAV Meenal,** b. 9 May 1953, Ahmednagar, Maharashtra State, India. Professor of Pathology. m. Vittal Jadhav, 1 daughter. Education: MBBS, MD, Pathology. Appointments: Lecturer, 1980-88, Associate professor, 1988-2004, professor of pathology, 2004-, BJ Medical College, Pune, India; Teaching Experience: Undergraduates, 25 years; Postgraduates, 22 years; University recognised postgraduate guide, 15 years; Undergraduate and postgraduate examiner, 15 years. Publications: 20 in national and international journals of which 11 are Pubmed indexed. Memberships: Indian Association of Pathologists; Indian Association of Cytologists. Address: 8 Mulay Classic, Bhosalenagar, Pune, Maharashtra State, India 411007. E-mail: drvhjadhav@hotmail.com

**JAEGGI Eva Maria,** b. 12 February 1934, Vienna, Austria. Professor. Divorced, 1 daughter. Education: PhD, Psychology; Habilitation, Clinical Psychology, Psychoanalysis. Appointments: Assistant, Sozialforschungsstelle, Dortmund, 1957-60; Head, Student Counselling, Bochum, 1966-72; Assistant Professor, Freie University, Berlin, 1972-78;

Professor, Techn University, Berlin, 1978-99. Publications: 12 books on psychotherapy and/or lifestyle; Many articles. Honours: Silbernes Ehrenzeichen der Stadt, Wien, 1995; Auzeichnung fuer die beste Lehre, 1997; Wissenschaftsbuch des Jahres, 2002. Memberships: Neue Gesellschaft fuer Psychologie; DGPT. Address: Forststr 25, D-14163, Berlin, Germany. E-mail: eva.jaeggi@tu-berlin.de

**JAFFE Edward E,** b. 22 September 1928, Vilna, Poland. Chemist. m. Ann Swirski, 1 son, 2 daughters. Education: BS, City College, City of New York, 1952; MS, 1954, PhD, 1957, New York University. Appointments: Research Chemist, 1957-63, Senior Research Chemist, 1963-65, Research Associate, 1965-73, Research Supervisor, 1973-75, Technical Superintendent, 1975-78, Research Manager, 1978-80, Research Fellow, 1980-84, DuPont Company; Distinguished Research Fellow, 1984-87, Director of Research, 1987-88, Vice President of R&D, 1988-95, CIBA-GEIGY Corporation; Retired, 1995-; Exclusive Consultant to CIBA Speciality Chemical Corp, 1995-2003; Independent consultant, 2003-. Publications: 67 US patents; Over 300 international patents; Many articles in professional journals and chapters in scientific books. Honours: Founders Day Award, New York University; Armin J Bruning Award, Outstanding Contribution to the Science of Colour; Recipient of the American Chemical Society Delaware Section Award, for Conspicuous Scientific Achievement in the Area of Chemistry, 2000. Memberships: American Chemical Society; Delaware Chemical Society Chapter; Organic Section of ACS; Sigma Xi Society. Address: 6 Penny Lane Court, Wilmington, Delaware 19803, USA. E-mail: eejaffe@comcast.net

**JAGGER Mick,** b. 26 July 1943, Dartford, Kent, England. Singer; Songwriter. m. (1) Bianca Pérez Morena de Macias, 1971, divorced, 1979, 1 daughter, (2) Jerry Hall, 2 sons, 2 daughters; 1 daughter by Marsha Hunt. Education: London School of Economics. Career: Member, Rolling Stones, 1962-; Numerous tours, concerts include: National Jazz & Blues Festival, Richmond, 1963; Debut UK tour, 1963; Debut US tour, 1964; Free concert, Hyde Park, 1969; Free concert, Altamont Speedway, 1969; Knebworth Festival, 1976; Live Aid, Philadelphia, 1985; Solo tour including Japan, 1988; Steel Wheels North American tour, 1989; National Music Day Celebration Of The Blues, with Gary Moore, 1992; Voodoo Lounge World Tour, 1994-95; Bridges to Babylon Tour, 1997-98; Films include: Ned Kelly, 1970; Performance, 1970; Freejack, 1992; Bent, 1996. Compositions: Co-writer for the Rolling Stones, with Keith Richards (under the pseudonym The Glimmer Twins). Recordings: Albums include: The Rolling Stones, 1964; The Rolling Stones No 2, 1965; Out Of Our Heads, 1965; Aftermath, 1966; Between The Buttons, 1967; Their Satanic Majesties Request, 1967; Beggar's Banquet, 1968; Let It Bleed, 1969; Get Yer Ya-Ya's Out, 1969; Sticky Fingers, 1971; Exile On Main Street, 1972; Goat's Head Soup, 1973; It's Only Rock And Roll, 1974; Black And Blue, 1976; Some Girls, 1978; Emotional Rescue, 1980; Still Life, 1982; Steel Wheels, 1989; Flashpoint, 1991; Stripped, 1995; Bridges to Babylon, 1997; Solo albums: She's The Boss, 1985; Primitive Cool, 1987; Wandering Spirit, 1993; Goddess in the Doorway, 2001; Singles include: It's All Over Now; Little Red Rooster; (I Can't Get No) Satisfaction; Get Off Of My Cloud; Jumping Jack Flash; Let's Spend The Night Together; Brown Sugar; 19th Nervous Breakdown; Harlem Shuffle; Ruby Tuesday; Paint It Black; It's Only Rock'n'Roll; Start Me Up; Undercover Of The Night; Dancing In The Street (with David Bowie). Honours: with Rolling Stones include: Grammy Lifetime Achievement Award, 1986; Inducted into Rock And Roll Hall Of Fame, 1989; Q Award, Best Live Act, 1990; Ivor Novello Award, Outstanding

Contribution To British Music, 1991. Address: c/o Rupert Loewenstein, 2 King Street, London SW1Y 6QL, England.

**JAHN Ilse Margarete (Trommer),** b. 2 February 1922, Chemnitz (Sachsen). Biologist. m. Wilhelm Jahn, deceased 12 April 1945, 1 daughter. Education: Studied Biology, 1941-42, 1952-56, Diploma in Biology, 1956, Dr rer nat, 1963; University of Jena; DrScNat (habil), Humboldt University, 1979; Docent, Berlin, 1980. Appointments: Assistant Ernst-Haeckel-Haus Jena, 1956-62; Research Fellow (Editor), A-Von-Humboldt Commission, Academy of Science, Berlin, 1962-67; Curator of exposition in Museum für Naturkunde, Humboldt University, 1967-80; Docent of Museology, Humboldt University, Berlin, 1980-82. Publications: Dem Leben auf der Spur, 1969; Die Jugendbriefe Alexander von Humboldts (co-editor), 1973; Charles Darwin, 1982; Geschichte der Biologie (co-editor), 1982, 1985, 1998; Grundzüge der Biologieschichte, 1990; Darwin and Co (co-editor), 2001; 220 scientific articles and biographies. Honours: Vice-Director, Museum für Naturkunde, 1971-74; President, section/biological museums, (council of museums GDR) 1971-82; Title, Obermuseumsrat (Ministry of Culture), 1984; German Society of History and Theory of Biology; President, 1991-93. Memberships: Deutsche Akademie der Naturforscher Leopoldina, 1986-; Corresponding Member, Senckenberg Naturf Ges (SNG), 1992-; New York Academy of Sciences, 1995-; Dr h c, University of Jena, 2002. Address: Eyke-von-Repkow-Pl.2, 10555 Berlin, Germany.

**JAHRREISS Heribert,** b. 15 January 1924, Leipzig, Germany. University Professor of Physics. m. Ingeborg Kunkel, 1 son, 1 daughter. Education: Diploma, Physics, 1951; DPhil, 1952; Habilitation, 1959. Appointments: Scientific Assistant, 1952, Assistant, Lecturer, 1959, Assistant Professor, 1966, Associate Professor, 1970, Professor, 1980. Publications include: Introduction to Physics, 1977, 5th edition, 1993. Honours: Cross of Honour, President of the Federal Republic of Germany; Medal of Honour, University of Köln. Memberships include: Secretary General, 1974-83, Vice President, 1983-86, 1989-92, President, 1986-89, International Union for Vacuum Science, Technique and Application. Address: Nassestr 36, D-50939 Cologne, Germany.

**JAKOBSSON Thor Edward,** b. 5 October 1936, Wynyard, Sask, Canada. Research Scientist. m. Johanna Johannesdottir, 1 son, 1 daughter. Education: Cand Mag, University of Oslo and Bergen, Norway, 1964; Cand Real, Meteorology, University of Bergen, Norway, 1966; PhD, Meteorology, McGill University, Montreal, Canada, 1973. Appointments: Research Assistant, University of Bergen, Norway, 1966-68; Research Scientist, Atmospheric Environment Service, Toronto, Canada, 1973-79; Research Scientist and Project Manager, Icelandic Meteorological Office, Reykjavik, Iceland, 1979-; Adjunct Professor, University of Iceland, 1980-2002. Publications: Popular and scientific articles, reports and book chapters; numerous articles on various subjects in newspapers and journals. Memberships: American Meteorological Society; Canadian Meteorological and Oceanographic Society; International Biometeorological Society. Address: Espigerdi 2 (2E), IS-108 Reykjavik, Iceland, Europe.

**JAMES Alan Morien,** b. 20 January 1933, Newport, Monmouthshire, Wales. Retired University Teacher. m. (1) Valerie Hancox, 4 sons, 2 daughters, (2) Lorna Lloyd. Education: BSc Economics, first class honours, London School of Economics and Political Science, 1954. Appointments: Civil service, 1955-57; Assistant Lecturer, Lecturer, Senior Lecturer, Reader in International Relations, London School of Economics, 1957-73; Professor of International Relations, Keele University,

1974-98. Publications: 8 books. Honours: Rockefeller Research Fellow, Columbia University, 1968; Visiting Professor, University of Ife, 1981; Visiting Professor, Jawaharlal Nehru University, 1983; Guest Professor, National Institute for Defense Studies, Japan, 1993. Memberships: Committees of Social Science Research Council; Council for National Academic Awards; University Grants Committee. Address: 23 Park Lane, Congleton, Cheshire CW12 3DG, England.

**JAMES Anthony, (A R James),** b. 17 March 1931, London, England. Literary Researcher; Author. m. (1) Jacqueline, 19 April 1952, deceased, (2) Anne, 27 September 1997, 1 son, 2 daughters. Appointments: General Manager, Wimbledon Stadium, 1956-91; Secretary, NGRC Racecourse Promoters, 1989-. Publications: W W Jacobs Companion, 1990; Wimbledon Stadium - The First Sixty Years, 1993, new enlarged edition, 2000; Informing the People, 1996; W W Jacobs (biography), 1999; WW Jacobs Book: Hunter's Field Guide, 2001. Contributions to: Book and Magazine Collector; Antiquarian Book Monthly; W W Jacobs Appreciation Society Newsletter; WWII HMSO Paperbacks Society Newsletter. Memberships: Secretary and Editor, W W Jacobs Appreciation Society, WWII HMSO Paperbacks Society. Address: 3 Roman Road, Southwick, W Sussex BN42 4TP, England.

**JAMES Clive Vivian Leopold,** b. 7 October 1939. Writer; Broadcaster; Journalist. Education: Sydney University; Pembroke College, Cambridge. Appointments: President, Footlights, Cambridge; TV Critic, 1972-82, Feature Writer, 1972-, The Observer; Director, Watchmaker Productions, 1994-; Lyricist for Pete Atkin; TV series including: Cinema; Up Sunday; So It Goes; A Question of Sex; Saturday Night People; Clive James on Television; The Late Clive James; The Late Show with Clive James; Saturday Night Clive; Fame in the 20th Century; Sunday Night Clive; The Clive James Show; Numerous TV documentaries including: Clive James meets Katherine Hepburn, 1986; Clive James meets Jane Fonda; Clive James meets Mel Gibson, 1998; Clive James meets the Supermodels, 1998; Postcard series, 1989-; Publications: Non-Fiction: The Metropolitan Critic, 1974; The Fate of Felicity Fark in the Land of the Media, 1975; Peregrine Prykke's Pilgrimage Through the London Literary World, 1976; Britannia Bright's Bewilderment in the Wilderness of Westminster, 1976; Visions Before Midnight, 1977; At the Pillars of Hercules, 1979; First Reactions, 1980; The Crystal Bucket, 1981; Charles Charming's Challenges on the Pathway to the Throne, 1981; From the Land of Shadows, 1982; Glued to the Box, 1982; Flying Visits, 1984; Snakecharmers in Texas, 1988; The Dreaming Swimmer, 1992; Fame, 1993; The Speaker in Ground Zero, 1999; Novels: Brilliant Creatures, 1983; The Remake, 1987; Unreliable Memoirs (autobiography), 1980; Falling Towards England: Unreliable Memoirs Vol II, 1985; Unreliable Memoirs Vol III, 1990; May Week Was in June, 1990; Brrm! Brrm! or The Man From Japan or Perfume at Anchorage, 1991; Fame in the 20th Century, 1993; The Metropolitan Critic, 1993; Criticism: Clive James on Television, 1993; The Silver Castle, 1996; 3 volumes of poetry. Address: c/o Watchmaker Productions, The Chrysalis Building, Bramley Road, London W10 6SP, England.

**JAMES David Geraint,** b. 2 January 1922, Treherbert, Wales. Doctor of Medicine. m. Sheila Sherlock, deceased, 2 daughters. Education: MA, MD, Jesus College, Cambridge; MRCS, LRCP, MRCP, Middlesex Hospital, University of London. Appointments: Surgeon-Lieutenant RNVR, 1946-48; Consultant Physician, Royal Navy, 1972-85; Dean of Studies, 1968-88, Consultant Physician, 1959-, Royal Northern Hospital, London; Professor of Medicine, University of London and Miami; Consultant Ophthalmic Physician, St Thomas'

Hospital, London. Publications: Textbook of Infections, 1957; Colour Atlas of Respiratory Diseases, 1981; Sarcoidosis, 1985. Honours: Worshipful Society of Apothecaries, 1960-; Freeman, City of London; Honorary LLD University of Wales, 1982; FRCP, 1964; Honorary FACP, 1990. Memberships: President: Harvey Society, London; Osler Club, London; Medical Society, London; Member: London Medical Ophthalmology Society; World Congress History of Medicine; RCP; Hunterian Society; World Association of Sarcoidosis; International Journal of Sarcoidosis; Postgraduate Medical Federation; Thoracic Society of France, Italy and Portugal; French National Academy of Medicine; London Glamorganshire Society; White Robed Member, Bardic Circle of Wales. Address: 41 York Terrace East, London NW1 4PT, England.

**JAMES Geraldine,** b. 6 July 1950, Maidenhead, Berkshire, England. Actress. m. Joseph Blatchley, 1 daughter. Education: The Drama Centre, London. Career: Theatre includes: The Cherry Orchard for Oxford Stage Company; Home, Oxford Stage Company; UN Inspector, Royal National Theatre; Faith Healer, Almeida Kings Cross and Give Me your Answer Do, Hampstead Theatre, both by Brian Friel; Death and the Maiden, West End; Hedda Gabler, Manchester Royal Exchange; Lysistrata, West End; The Merchant of Venice, West End and Broadway; Cymbeline, Royal National Theatre; The White Devil, Oxford Playhouse; 4 years repertory including 18 months with the Northcott Theatre, Exeter; TV includes: White Teeth; The Sins; Kavanagh QC; Band of Gold; Blott on the Landscape; The Jewel in the Crown; The History Man; Dummy, Hearts of Gold; He Knew He Was Right; Jane Hall's Big Bad Bus Ride; Hex; Little Britain; Films: Gandhi; The Tall Guy; Wolves of Willoughby Chase; She's Been Away; The Luzhin Defense; An Angel for May; Calendar Girls for Buena Vista; Radio includes most recently: Turtle Diaries; King Lear; The Master and Marguerita; Alexander the Great; The Deptford Wives; The Hours. Honours: TV Critics Award, Best Actress, 1978; Venice Film Festival Best Actress, 1989; Drama Desk Award, New York, 1990; OBE, 2003. Address: c/o Julian Belfrage Associates, 46 Albermarle St, London W1, England.

**JAMES Glen William,** b. 22 August 1952, London, England. Solicitor. m. Amanda Claire Dorrell, 3 daughters. Education: New College, Oxford. Appointments: Articled Clerk, 1974-76, Assistant Solicitor, 1976-83, Partner, 1983-, Slaughter and May. Publications: Various professional articles contributed to books and other publications associated with corporate and commercial law. Memberships: Law Society; City of London Solicitors' Company; Securities Institute; Royal Automobile Club. Address: c/o 1 Bunhill Row, London EC1Y 8YY, England.

**JAMES Michael Leonard,** b. 7 February 1941, Cornwall, England. Government Official; Writer and Broadcaster. m. Jill Tarján, 2 daughters. Education: MA, Christ's College, Cambridge; FRSA. Appointments: Entered Government Service, GCHQ, 1963; Private Secretary to Rt Hon Jennie Lee, Minister for the Arts, 1966-68; DES, 1968-71; Planning Unit of Rt Hon Margaret Thatcher, Secretary of State for Education and Science, 1971-73; Assistant Secretary, 1973; Deputy Chief Scientific Officer, 1974; Adviser, OECD, Paris and UK Governor, International Institute for Management of Technology, Milan, 1973-75; International Negotiations on Non-Proliferation of Nuclear Weapons, 1975-78; Director, IAEA Vienna, 1978-83; Adviser, International Relations, 1983-85, Consultant, 1985-2001, Commission of the European Union, Brussels; Chair, Civil Service Selection Boards, 1983-93; Chair, The Hartland Press Ltd, 1985-2001, Wade Hartland Films Ltd, 1991-2000; Feature Writer and Book Reviewer for The Times, (Resident Thriller Critic, 1990-91); Sunday Times, Guardian and Daily Telegraph, (Resident Thriller Critic, 1993-). Publications: Co-author, Internationalization to Prevent the Spread of Nuclear Weapons, 1980; Novels, as Michael Hartland: Down Among the Dead Men, 1983; Seven Steps to Treason, 1985 (South West Arts Literary Award, dramatised for BBC Radio 4, 1990); The Third Betrayal, 1986; Frontier of Fear, 1989; The Year of the Scorpion, 1991; As Ruth Carrington: Dead Fish, 1998; TV and radio include: Sonja's Report, ITV, 1990; Masterspy (interviews with KGB defector Oleg Gordievsky), BBC Radio 4, 1991. Honours: Honorary Fellow, University of Exeter, 1985-. Memberships: Governor, East Devon College of Further Education, Tiverton, 1985-91, Colyton Grammar School, 1985-90, Sidmouth Community College, 1988-; (Chair, Board of Governors, 1998-2002); Chair, Board of Governors, Axe Vale Further Education College, Seaton, 1987-91; Member, Immigration Appeal Tribunal, 1987-; Devon and Cornwall Rent Assessment Panel, 1990-; Chairman, General Medical Council, Professional Conduct Committee, 2000-. Address: Cotte Barton, Branscombe, Devon, EX12 3BH, England.

**JAMES P(hyllis) D(orothy) (Baroness James of Holland Park).** b. 3 August 1920, Oxford, England. Author. m. Ernest Connor Bantry White, 9 August 1941, deceased 1964, 2 daughters. Appointments: Member, BBC General Advisory Council, 1987-88, Arts Council, 1988-92, British Council, 1988-93; Chairman, Booker Prize Panel of Judges, 1987; Governor, BBC, 1988-93; President, Society of Authors, 1997-. Publications: Cover Her Face, 1962; A Mind to Murder, 1963; Unnatural Causes, 1967; Shroud for a Nightingale, 1971; The Maul and the Pear Tree (with T A Critchley), 1971; An Unsuitable Job for a Woman, 1972; Innocent Blood, 1980; The Skull Beneath the Skin, 1982; A Taste for Death, 1986; Devices and Desires, 1989; The Children of Men, 1992; Original Sin, 1994; A Certain Justice, 1997; Time to be in Earnest, 1999; Death in Holy Orders, 2001; The Murder Room, 2003; The Lighthouse, 2005. Honours: Order of the British Empire; Honorary Fellow, St Hilda's College, Oxford, 1996, Downing College, Cambridge, 2000, Girton College, Cambridge, 2000; Honorary DLitt, University of Buckingham, 1992, University of Hertfordshire, 1994, University of Glasgow, 1995, University of Durham, 1988, University of Portsmouth, 1999; Honorary LittD, University of London, 1993; Dr hc, University of Essex, 1996; Grand Master Award, Mystery Writers of America, 1999. Memberships: Fellow, Royal Society of Literature; Fellow, Royal Society of Arts. Address: c/o Greene & Heaton Ltd, 37 Goldhawk Road, London W12 8QQ, England.

**JAN Tony,** b. 2 February 1971, Seoul, South Korea. Professor. m. Lisa Noh Jan. Education: Bachelor in Engineering with honours, 1998; Doctor of Philosophy in Engineering, 2002. Appointments: Senior Research Engineer, Australian Defence Science Technology Organisation; Assistant Professor (Lecturer A), Associate Professor (Lecturer C), University of Technology, Sydney, Australia. Publications: More than 50 articles on computational intelligence in refereed international journals and conference proceedings. Honours: Chancellor's Prize for PhD thesis; Australian Computing Society Early Career Prize; Invited Chair of IEEE Conferences; Best Paper Prize, IVCNZ; Research Contribution Award, University of Technology, Sydney. Membership: Institute of Electrical and Electronic Engineering. Address: PO Box 123, Broadway, New South Wales 2007, Australia.

**JANES Dominic Timothy Shane,** b. 27 December 1970. Academic. Education: MA, Ancient and Modern History, Oxford, 1992; PhD, Cambridge, 1995. Appointments: Temporary lecturer, History, Lancaster University, 1995-96; Research Fellow, Cambridge University, 1996-99; Research

Fellow, Kings College, London, 1999-2001; Academic Director, Foundation for International Education, 2001-; Part-time Lecturer, Birkbeck College, London. Publications: God and Gold in Late Antiquity, 1998; Romans and Christians, 2002. Memberships: National Liberal Club; Fellow, Royal Historical Society. Address: Foundation for International Education, 114 Cromwell Road, London SW7 4ES, England. E-mail; djanes@fie.org.uk Website: www.fie.org.uk

**JANES J(oseph) Robert,** b. 23 May 1935, Toronto, Ontario, Canada. Writer. m. Gracia Joyce Lind, 16 May 1958, 2 sons, 2 daughters. Education: BSc, Mining Engineering, 1958, MEng, Geology, 1967, University of Toronto. Publications: Children's books: The Tree-Fort War, 1977; Theft of Gold, 1980; Danger on the River, 1982; Spies for Dinner, 1984; Murder in the Market, 1985. Adult books: The Toy Shop, 1981; The Watcher, 1982; The Third Story, 1983; The Hiding Place, 1984; The Alice Factor, 1991; Mayhem, 1992; Carousel, 1992; Kaleidoscope, 1993; Salamander, 1994; Mannequin, 1994; Dollmaker, 1995; Stonekiller, 1995; Sandman, 1996; Gypsy, 1997; Madrigal, 1999; Beekeeper, 2001; Flykiller, 2002. Non-Fiction: The Great Canadian Outback, 1978. Textbooks: Holt Geophoto Resource Kits, 1972; Rocks, Minerals and Fossils, 1973; Earth Science, 1974; Geology and the New Global Tectonics, 1976; Searching for Structure (co-author), 1977. Teacher's Guide: Searching for Structure (co-author), 1977; Airphoto Interpretation and the Canadian Landscape (with J D Mollard), 1984. Contributions to: Toronto Star; Toronto Globe and Mail; The Canadian; Winnipeg Free Press; Canadian Children's Annual. Honours: Grants: Canada Council; Ontario Arts Council; J P Bickell Foundation; Thesis Award, Canadian Institute of Mining and Metallurgy; Works-in-progress Grant, Ontario Arts Council, 1991; Hammett Award Nominee, International Association of Crime Writers (North American Branch). Memberships: Crime Writers Association (UK); Historical Novel Society (UK); International Association of Crime Writers (North American Branch). Address: PO Box 1590, Niagara-on-the-Lake, Ontario L0S 1J0, Canada.

**JANG Joonkyung,** b. 6 September 1967, Busan, South Korea. Professor. m. Sui Rhane Chung, 1 daughter. Education: BS, 1990, MS, Chemistry, 1992, Seoul National University; PhD, Chemistry, Brown University, USA, 2000. Appointments: Postdoctoral Fellow, Northwestern University, 2000-2003, Assistant Professor, School of Nano Science and Technology, Pusan National University, 2003-. Publications: Articles as co-author in scientific journals including: Physical Review Letters, 2003 (2), 2004; Journal of Chemical Physics, 2004. Honours: Potter Prize in Chemistry for a doctoral thesis of outstanding merit, Brown University, 2000; Sigma Xi Award for excellence in research, Brown University, 2000. Memberships: American Chemical Society; Korean Chemical Society. Address: School of Nano Science and Technology, Pusan National University, Busan, South Korea 609-735. E-mail: jkjang@pusan.ac.kr Website: http://home.pusan.ac.kr/~joonjang

**JANG Sung Ho,** b. 18 August 1964, Jin-Chon, South Korea. Professor; Medical Doctor. m. Sook Ja Back, 2 sons. Education: Bachelor's Degree in Medicine, College of Medicine, Yonsei University, Seoul, Korea, 1983-90; Graduate School of Medicine, Kyungpook National University, Taegu, Korea, 2000-2002. Appointments: Lecturer, 1999-2001, Assistant Professor, 2001-2005, Associate Professor, 2005-, Department of Rehabilitation Medicine, Yeungnam University College of Medicine. Publications: Over 30 articles in scientific medical journals include most recently as co-author: Radiation therapy for heterotopic ossification in a patient with traumatic brain injury, 2000; Cortical reoraniszation induced by task-

oriented training in chronic hemiplegic stroke patients, 2004; The Effect of Selective Tibial Neurotomy and Rehabilitation in a Quadriplegic Patient with Ankle Spasticity Following Traumatic Brain Injury: A Case Report, 2004; Ipsilateral Motor Pathway Confirmed by Diffusion Tensor Tractography in a patient with Schizencephaly, 2004; Virtual Reality-Induced Cortical Reorganization and Associated Locomotor Recovery in Chronic Stroke: An Experimenter-Blind Randomized Study, in press, 2005; Restoration of Corticospinal Tract Compressed by Hematoma: a Diffusion Tensor Tractography Study, in press, 2005. Honours: Listed in Who's Who publications and biographical dictionaries. Memberships: Korean Academy of Physical Medicine and Rehabilitation; Korean Brain Mapping and Plasticity Research Group; Human Brain Mapping; Director, Association of Korean Human Brain Mapping. Address: Department of Rehabilitation Medicine, Yeungnam University College of Medicine, 3117-1 Daemyung-Dong, Nam-Gu, Taegu 705-717 South Korea. E-mail: belado@med.yu.ac.kr

**JANG Young-Chul,** b. 13 March 1954, Seoul, Korea. Medical Doctor; Professor. m. Jay R Shim, 1 daughter. Education: MD, 1980, School of Medicine, MS, 1988, Graduate School, PhD, 1992, Graduate School, Kyung Hee University. Appointments: Fellow, Chief of Department of Plastic Surgery, 1989-90, Full-time Instructor, Assistant Professor, Chief of Department of Plastic and Reconstructive Surgery, Dongsan Sacred Heart Hospital, 1996-2003, Associate Professor, 1996-2003, Chief of Department of Plastic and Reconstructive Surgery, 1999-, Professor, 2003-, Head of Professor, Department of Plastic and Reconstructive Surgery, 2003-, Hangang Sacred Heart Hospital, School of Medicine, Hallym University, Seoul, Korea. Visiting Scientist, University of Washington, Seattle, Washington, USA, 1996-98; Consulting Medical Staff, University of Washington Medical Centre, Seattle, Washington, USA, 1997-98; Consulting Surgeon, Smith and Nephew Korea, 2003-; Numerous official positions in scientific and academic associations and societies. Publications: 12 articles in international journals as co-author include most recently: Paediatric electrical burn: outlet injury caused by steel chopstick misuse, 2004; A retrospective analysis of 19,157 burns patients: 18 year experience from Hallym Burn Center in Seoul, Korea. 2005; Paediatric hand injury induced by treadmill, 2005; 45 articles in Korean journals. Honours: Scientific Prize of the Year, Korean Society of Plastic and Reconstructive Surgeons, 1989, 1993; Exemplary Duty Award, Hangang Sacred Heart Hospital, Ilsong Foundation, 2002; Scientific Prize of the Year, Korean Burn Society, 2003; Presidential Citation, Korea Institute for Family Health and Welfare, 2004; Encouragement Award in Hospital Management Education. Hallym Medical Center Chairman, 2004. Memberships: Korean Society of Plastic and Reconstructive Surgeons, 1989-; Korean Society of Hand Surgery, 1991; Korean Society of Aesthetic Surgery, 1992-; International Confederation for Plastic, Reconstructive and Aesthetic Surgery, 1993; International Society for Burns Injuries, 1996-; American Burn Association, 1996-; Korean Burn Association, 1998-; Korean Society of Medical Biochemistry and Molecular Biology, 1999-; Korean Association of Tissue Bank, 2000; Korea Cleft Palate and Craniofacial Association, 2002. Address: Department of Plastic and Reconstructive Surgery, Hangang Sacred Heart Hospital, College of Medicine, Hallym University, 94-200, Youngdungpo-Dong 2 ga, Youngdungpo-Gu, Seoul, Republic of Korea. E-mail: ycjang54@paran.com

**JANNER Greville Ewan, Baron Janner of Braunstone,** b. 11 July 1928, Cardiff, South Wales. Working Peer; Barrister; Queen's Counsel; Author; Jewish Leader. m. Myra Louise Sheink, deceased, 1 son, 2 daughters. Education: MA, Trinity Hall, Cambridge, 1946-49; Harvard Law School, 1950-51; Hon

PhD, Haifa, 1984; Hon LLD, De Montfort University, Leicester, 1998. Appointments: Member of Parliament, Leicester North West, 1970-74; Member of Parliament, Leicester West, 1974-97; Chairman, Select Committee on Employment, 1992-96; Vice Chairman, British Israel and British India Parliamentary Groups; Vice President, World Jewish Congress; Founder President, Commonwealth Jewish Council; Chairman, Holocaust Educational Trust; President, Maimonides Foundation; Former President, Board of Deputies of British Jews, 1978-84; Founder, President, JSB Ltd; Former Director, Labroke plc. Publications: Author, 65 books mainly on employment and industrial relations law, presentational skills and public speaking; One Hand Alone Cannot Clap. Memberships: Magic Circle; International Brotherhood of Magicians. Address: House of Lords, London SW1A 0PW, England.

**JANSEN N Elly,** b. 5 October 1929, Wisch, Holland. Retired Charity Director. m. (1) Alan Brian Stewart, 3 daughters, (2) George Whitehouse. Education: Paedologisch Institute, Free University, Amsterdam, Boerhave Kliniek (SRN), University of London. Appointments: Founder and CEO, Richmond Fellowship for Community Mental Health, 1959-91; Founder, Richmond Fellowship College, 1967; Founder and CEO, Richmond Fellowship International, 1981-2000; Founder and Executive Trustee, Fellowship Charitable Foundation (now Community Housing and Therapy), 1983-93; Founder, Richmond Fellowship Workshops, 1986; Founded: Richmond Fellowship of America (1968), Australia (1973), New Zealand (1977), Austria (1978), and subsequently of Barbados, Bangladesh, Bolivia, Canada, Costa Rica, France, Ghana, Grenada, Hong Kong, India, Israel, Jamaica, Malta, Mexico, Nigeria, Peru, Philippines, Trinidad & Tobago, Uruguay and Zimbabwe; Organised international conferences on therapeutic communities and courses on mental illness and drug rehabilitation; Acted as adviser to many governments on issues of community care. Publications: The Therapeutic Community Outside the Hospital, 1980; Mental Health and the Community, 1983; Towards a Whole Society, 1985; R D Laing, Creative Destroyer, 1997; Contributions to American Journal of Psychiatry, L'Information Psychiatrique and other journals. Honours: Fellowship, German Marshall Memorial Fund, 1977-78; OBE, 1980; Templeton Award, 1985. Address: Clyde House, 109 Strawberry Vale, Twickenham, TW1 4SJ, England.

**JANTUAH Kwame Sanaa-Poku (formerly John Ernest Jantuah),** b. 21 December 1922, Kumasi, Ashanti, Ghana. Educationist; Lawyer; Diplomat; Politician. m. (1) 2 sons, 5 daughters, (2) Agnes Owusua, 1 son, 1 daughter. Education: Cambridge (UK) Senior Secondary School Certificate, 1941; Teacher's Certificate A Grade 1, St Augustine's Teacher Training College, 1943-44; Politics & Economics Diploma course, Catholic Workers College (now Plater College), Oxford, 1946-48; BL and LLB (Hons Lond), Gibson & Weldon School of Law, London, England, 1964-66; Called to the English Bar, Lincoln's Inn, 1966 and to the Ghana Bar, 1967. Appointments: Teacher, Roman Catholic Senior School, Ejisu, 1945-46; Headmaster, Asante Youth Association Day Secondary School, Kumasi, 1953; Deputy General Secretary, Asante-man Council, Kumasi, 1948-50; Elected CPP Member, Kumasi Town Council, 1950; Editor, The Asante Sentinel, Kumasi, 1950-51; Elected Member, Gold Coast Legislative Assembly, 1951 and appointed Ministerial Secretary to Minister of Justice & Attorney General; Minister of Agriculture & Fisheries, 1954-56; Deputy High Commissioner of Ghana to London, 1957-59 (Acting High Commissioner for latter part of 1959); Ambassador of Ghana to France, 1959-62, to Brazil, 1962-64, to Berlin (GDR), 1985-90; Legal Practice, City Chambers, Accra, 1967-79; Minister of Local Government, Rural Development & Co-operatives,

1979-81; Minister of Interior, October to December, 1981 (interrupted by coup d'etat of December 1981). Publications: Ne Nos Inducas in Tentationem (dissenting comment on the Lord's Prayer), 1989; Christianity, Culture and Change, 1997. Honours: Grand Officier de l'Ordre du Mèrite (Republic of Senegal), 1981. Memberships: Royal Oyoko Abohyen Clan of Ashanti; President, Asante Youth Association (AYA), 1952-53; Platernian Association, Oxford; Guild of Catholic Lawyers, Ghana; Ghana Bar Association; Oxford and Cambridge Association of Ghana, Accra; United Gold Coast Convention; Convention People's Party; People's National Party. Address: PO Box AN6467, Accra-North, Accra, Ghana.

**JARQUE Carlos Manuel,** b. 18 October 1954, Mexico City, Mexico. Minister for Social Development, Mexican Government. m. Coral Lira Coria, 2 sons, 2 daughters. Education: Bachelor, Actuarial Science, (Honorary Mention) Anahuac University, Mexico City; Postgraduate Diploma, Statistics, MSc, Statistics and Econometrics, London School Economics & Political Science; Postgraduate Diploma in Planning and Economic Policy, University of Oslo, Norway; PhD, Economics, Australian National University, Canberra; Postdoctorate, Economics, Harvard University. Appointments: General Director, Mexican Central Bureau of Statistics, 1983-86, Director, Department Economic Studies at TELMEX, 1982-83; Secretary, Mexican National Development Plan, 1995-2000; President, INEGI, 1988-99; President, UN Statistical Commission, 1996-98; Secretary, Sedesol, 1999-2000; Manager, Inter American Development Bank, 2000-04. Publications: Over 100 in econometrics, statistics, economics, demography, technology in journals and books. Honours: BANAMEX National Award of Science & Technology, 1979; National Award in Actuarial Science, 1982; Medal President Benito Juarez; Adolphe Quetelet Medal. Memberships: American Statistical Association; Actuaries College of Mexico; Royal Statistical Society; Econometric Society; American Economic Association; Institute of Actuaries. Address: Benjamin Franklin 197, Condesa, Mexico, D F Mexico, CP 06140.

**JARRATT Alexander Anthony,** b. 19 January 1924, London, England. Retired Civil Servant; Company Executive. m. Mary Philomena Keogh, 1 son, 2 daughters. Education: BCom, 1st Class Honours, Birmingham University, 1946-49. Appointments: Petty Officer Fleet Air Arm; Civil Servant Ministry of Power, 1949-64; Seconded to the Treasury, 1953-54; Cabinet Office, 1964-65; Secretary, Prices and Incomes Board, 1964-68; Deputy Under Secretary, Department of Employment and Productivity, 1968-70; Deputy Secretary Ministry of Agriculture, 1970; Chief Executive IPC and IPC Newspapers, 1970-74; Chairman and Chief Executive, Reed International, 1974-85, Director, 1970-85; Chairman, Smiths Industries plc, 1985-91, Director, 1984-96; Director, Thyssen-Bornemisza Supervisory Board, 1972-89; Deputy Chairman: Midland Bank plc, 1980-91, Prudential Corporation, 1987-91 and 1992-94; Non-Executive Director, ICI plc, 1975-91; President Advertising Association, 1979-83; Former Member, NEDC; Former Chairman, CBI Economic Policy Committee; CBI Employment Policy Committee; Former Member, Presidents Committee, CBI; Chairman, Industrial Society, 1975-79; Henley Administrative Staff College, 1976-89; Centre for Dispute Resolution, 1990-2000, president, 2001-; Chancellor, University of Birmingham, 1983-2002. Honours: Companion of the Bath, 1968; Knight Bachelor, 1979; Honorary LLD, University of Birmingham; Honorary DSc, Cranfield; Honorary D Univ, Brunel and Essex; Honorary, CGIA; FRSA; Honorary FCGI. Address: Barn Mead, Fryerning, Essex CM4 0NP, England.

**JARRE Jean-Michel,** b. 24 August 1948, Lyons, France. Musician (synthesizers, keyboards); Composer; Record Producer. m. Charlotte Rampling, 1977. Musical Education: Piano and guitar from age 5; Conservatoire de Paris, with Jeanine Reuff. Career: Solo debut, Paris Opera, 1971; Youngest composer to appear, Palais Garnier, 1971; Major concerts, often including lasers and fireworks, filmed for video releases include: Beijing, China, 1981; Bastille Day, Place De La Concorde, 1979; Houston, Texas (1.3 million audience), 1986; London Docklands, 1988; La Defense, Paris (2.5 million audience), 1990; Sun City, Johannesburg, South Africa, 1993; Member of jury, First International Visual Music Awards, Midem, France, 1992. Compositions include: Oxygène Part IV, used for several television themes; Ballet and film scores include: Des Garçons Et Des Filles, 1968; Deserted Palace, 1972; Les Granges Brûlées, 1973; La Maladie De Hambourg, 1978; Gallipoli, 1979. Recordings: Albums (all self-composed and produced): Deserted Palace, 1971; Oxygène, 1977; Magnetic Fields, 1981; The Concerts In China, 1982; The Essential Jean-Michel Jarre, 1983; Zoolook, 1984; Rendez-Vous, 1986; In Concert Lyons/Houston, 1987; Revelations (Number 2, UK), 1988; Jarre Live, 1989; Waiting For Cousteau, 1990; Images - The Best Of Jean-Michel Jarre, 1991; Chronologie, 1993; Jarre Hong Kong, 1994; Cities in Concert, 1997; Oxygène 7-13, 1997; China Concert, 1999. Honours: First Western artist to play in China, 1981; Grand Prix, Academie Du Disque, Zoolook, 1985; Best Instrumental Album, Victoire de la Musique, 1986; Numerous Platinum and Gold discs worldwide. Address: c/o Dreyfus Records, 26 Avenue Kléber, 75116 Paris, France.

**JARRE Maurice Alexis,** b. 13 September 1924, Lyons, France. Composer. m. (1) France Pejot, 1946, 1 son, (2) Dany Saval, 1965, 1 daughter, (3) Laura Devon, 1967, (4) Khong Fui Fong, 1984. Musical Education: Conservatoire National Supéreur de Musique. Career: Musician, Radiodiffusion Française, 1946-50; Director of Music, Théatre National Populaire (TNP), 1950-63. Compositions: Symphonic music; Music for theatre and ballet include: Roland Petit's Notre-Dame de Paris (Paris Opera), 1966; Numerous film scores include: Lawrence Of Arabia, 1963; Dr Zhivago, 1965; Ryan's Daughter, 1970; Shogun, 1980; Doctors In Love, 1982; A Passage To India, 1985; The Mosquito Coast, 1987; Tai-Pan, 1987; Gaby, 1988; Gorillas In The Mist, 1989; Ghost; Dead Poets Society, 1990; Fatal Attraction; Les Vendanges de feu, 1994; Sunchaser, 1996. Honours: Officer, Légion d'Honneur, Commander des Arts et Lettres; Prix Italia, 1955, 1962; Grand Prix du Disque, Academy Charles Cross, 1962; Hollywood Golden Globe, 1965, 1984; People's Choice Award, 1988. Address: c/o Paul Kohner Inc, 9169 Sunset Boulevard, Los Angeles, CA 90069, USA.

**JASON David,** b. 2 February 1940, England. Actor. Creative Works: Theatre includes: Under Milk Wood, 1971; The Rivals, 1972; No Sex Please...We're British!, 1972; Darling Mr London (tour), 1975; Charley's Aunt (tour), 1975; The Norman Conquests, 1976; The Relapse, 1978; Cinderella, 1979; The Unvarnished Truth (Middle/Far East tour), 1983; Look No Hands! (tour and West End), 1985; Films: Under Milk Wood, 1970; Royal Flash, 1974; The Odd Job, 1978; Only Fools and Horses, 1983; Wind in the Willows, 1983; TV includes: Do Not Adjust Your Set, 1967; The Top Secret Life of Edgar Briggs, 1973-74; Mr Stabbs, 1974; Ronnie Barker Shows, 1975; Open All Hours, 1975; Porridge, 1975; Lucky Feller, 1975; A Sharp Intake of Breath, 1978; Del Trotter in Only Fools and Horses, 1981-91; Porterhouse Blue, 1986; Jackanory, 1988; A Bit of A Do, 1988-89; Single Voices: The Chemist, 1989; Amongst Barbarians, 1989; Pa Larkin in The Darling Buds of May, 1990-92; A Touch of Frost, 1992, 2001; The Bullion Boys, 1993; Micawber, 2001; Voice work: Dangermouse; Count Duckula;

The Wind in the Willows. Honours include: Best Actor Award, BAFTA, 1988; BAFTA Fellowship, 2003.

**JASPER David,** b. 1 August 1951, Stockton on Tees, England. University Teacher; Clergyman. m. Alison Elizabeth Collins, 29 October 1976, 3 daughters. Education: Dulwich College, 1959-69; Jesus College, Cambridge, 1969-72; BA, MA, 1976, BD, 1980, Keble College, Oxford; PhD, Hatfield College, Durham, 1983; DD, Keble College, Oxford, 2002. Appointments: Director, Centre for the Study of Literature and Theology, Durham University, 1986-91, Glasgow University, 1991-; Editor, Literature and Theology; Professor of Literature and Theology, University of Glasgow, 1998-. Publications: Coleridge as Poet and Religious Thinker, 1985; The New Testament and the Literary Imagination, 1987; The Study of Literature and Religion, 1989; Rhetoric Power and Community, 1992; Reading in the Canon of Scripture, 1995; The Sacred and Secular Canon in Romanticism, 1999; The Sacred Desert, 2004; General Editor, Macmillan Series, Studies in Religion and Culture. Honours: Dana Fellow, Emory University, Atlanta, 1991; Honorary Fellow, Research Foundation, Durham University, 1991; Ida Cordelia Bean Distinguished Visiting Professor, University of Iowa, 2003. Memberships: International Society for Religion, Literature and Culture secretary; American Academy of Religion; Fellow and Director, Society for Arts, Religion and Culture, 2000. Address: Netherwood, 124 Old Manse Road, Wishaw, Lanarkshire ML2 0EP, Scotland.

**JAWIEN Jacek,** b. 28 November 1965, Krakow, Poland. Pharmacologist. Education: MD with honours, Medicine, 1990; PhD with honours, 1994, Jagiellonian University School of Medicine, Krakow, Poland. Appointments: Assistant, Department of Internal Medicine, 1990-97, Assistant Professor, Department of Pharmacology 1997-, Jagiellonian University School of Medicine, Krakow, Poland. Guest Researcher, Karolinska Institute, Stockholm, Sweden, 2001-2003. Publications: Articles in scientific journals including: Annals of the New York Academy of Sciences, 1995; Clin. Exp. Allergy, 1996; Allergy, 1997; Cardiovascular Research, 2003; Am J Pathol, 2004; Arterioscler Thomb Vasc Bio, 2005. Honours: Prize, Polish Foundation of Sciences, 1995; Research Award, Prime Minister of Poland, 1995; Councillor, 1998-2000, Vice-President, 2000-2001, European Society for Clinical Investigation. Memberships: European Society for Clinical Investigation, 1993-; New York Academy of Sciences, 1996-. Address: Kolberga str. 14, Krakow 31-160, Poland.

**JAY Peter,** b. 7 February 1937. Writer; Broadcaster. m. (1) Margaret Ann Callaghan, 1961, dissolved 1986, 1 son, 2 daughters, (2) Emma Thornton, 1986, 3 sons. Education: MA, 1st class honours, Politics, Philosophy and Economics, Christ Church Oxford, 1960. Appointments: Midshipman and Sub-Lieutenant, RNVR, 1956-57; Assistant Principal, 1961-64, Private Secretary to Joint Permanent Secretary, 1964, Principal, 1964-67, HM Treasury; Economics Editor, The Time, 1967-77; Associate Editor, Times Business News, 1969-77; Presenter, Weekend World, ITV series, 1972-77; The Jay Interview, ITV series, 1975-76; Ambassador to USA, 1977-79; Director, Economist Intelligence University, 1979-83; Consultant, Economist Group, 1979-81; Chairman and Chief Executive, TV-AM Ltd, 1980-83, and TV-AM News, 1982-83; President, TV-AM, 1983-; Presenter, A Week in Politics, Channel 4, 1983-86; COS to Robert Maxwell, Chairman of Mirror Group Newspapers Ltd, 1986-89; Visiting Scholar, Brookings Institution, Washington, 1979-80; Wincott Memorial Lecturer, 1975; Copland Memorial Lecturer, Australia, 1980; Shell Lecturer, Glasgow, 1985; Governor, Ditchley Foundation, 1982-; Author and Presenter, Road to Riches, BBC TV series,

2000. Publications: The Budget, 1972; Contributor, America and the World, 1979, 1980; The Crisis for Western Political Economy and other Essays, 1984; Apocalypse 2000, with Michael Stewart, 1987; Contributor, Foreign Affairs journal, Road to Riches, or The Wealth of Man, 2000. Honours: Political Broadcaster of the Year, 1973; Harold Wincott Financial and Economic Journalist of the Year, 1973; RTS Male Personality of the Year, Pye Award, 1974; SFTA Shell International TV Award, 1974; RTS Home News Award, 1992; Honorary DH, Ohio State University, 1978; Honorary DLitt, Wake Forest University, 1979; Berkeley Citation, University of California, 1979. Address: Hensington Farmhouse, Woodstock, Oxfordshire OX20 1LH, England.

**JAYACHANDRAN Divakaran,** b. 10 November 1957, Kokkottukonam, Trivandrum, India. Medical Social Worker. m. S Lissa, 1 son, 1 daughter. Education: BSc, 1979, MA, Sociology, 1981, MA, Psychology, 1995; PhD in Behavioural Science in progress. Appointments: Research Scientist, Loyola College of Social Sciences, 1981-82; Psychiatric Social Worker, Medical College, Kozhikode, 1982-85; Medical Social Worker Comprehensive Epilepsy Program, SCT Institute of Medical Sciences, Trivandrum, 1985-. Publications: Numerous articles in medical journals. Honours: Best Scientific Paper award. Memberships: Governing Council IEA, Governing Body, State Resource Centre, Kerala; Patron, Epilepsy Self Group, Advisory Committee Newsletters; ISHA; ARDSI; ISSA; IAUP. Address: Comprehensive Epilepsy Program, SCTIMST, Trivandrum 695011, India.

**JAYAWARDENA Amithirigala Widhanelage,** b. 21 November 1940, Imbulana, Sri Lanka. Engineering Educator. m. Hatsuyo Fujii, 1 son, 1 daughter. Education: BSc(Eng), University of Ceylon, 1963; M Eng, University of Tokyo, Japan; MS, University of California at Berkeley, USA; PhD, University of London, England. Appointments: Engineer, Irrigation Department, Government of Sri Lanka; Senior Engineer, Howard Humphreys & Sons Consulting Engineers, UK; Lecturer and Senior Lecturer, The University of Hong Kong. Publications: Over 100 articles in international journals and conference proceedings in the area of hydrology. Honour: International Visiting Fellowship, American Society of Civil Engineers 2002. Memberships: Fellow, Institution of Civil Engineers; Fellow, Hong Kong Institution of Engineers. Address: Department of Civil Engineering, The University of Hong Kong, Hong Kong. E-mail: hrecjaw@hkucc.hku.hk Website: http://web.hku.hk/~hrecjaw

**JAYAWARDENE Kirikankanange Albert Thistlethwayte Wilhelm Perera,** b. 9 November 1928, Moratuwa, Sri Lanka. Consultant Anaesthetist. m. Amara, 1 son, 2 daughters. Education: MBBS, Ceylon, 1956; DA, London, 1962; FRCA, England, 1963; FACC, USA, 1985. Appointments: Retired Consultant Anaesthetist, Cardiothoracic Unit and Surgical Intensive Care Unit, National Hospital, Sri Lanka. Publications: Several articles in professional medical journals. Honours: Most Outstanding Citizen Award for Medicine, 1995; 20th Century Achievement Award; Vishva Prasadhini Award for Distinguished Service to the Nation, 1996; Listed in national and international biographical dictionaries. Memberships: President, College of Anaesthesiologists of Sri Lanka, 1984, 1985, 1986; President, Sri Lanka Medical Association, 1991; Vice President, Sri Lanka Heart Association, 1994-; Vice President, Organisation of Professional Associations of Sri Lanka, 2001; Patron, Sri Lankan Critical Care and Emergency Medicine Society, 2002-; Director and Vice President, Critical Care, Ceylon Hospitals Ltd; Director, Durdans Heart Surgical Centre. Address: 14 Albert Place, Dehiwela, Sri Lanka.

**JEAL Tim,** b. 27 January 1945, London, England. Author. m. Joyce Timewell, 11 October 1969, 3 daughters. Education: MA, Christ Church, Oxford. Publications: For Love of Money, 1967; Somewhere Beyond Reproach, 1969; Livingstone, 1973; Cushing's Crusade, 1974; Until the Colours Fade, 1976; A Marriage of Convenience, 1979; Baden-Powell, 1989; The Missionary's Wife, 1997; Deep Water, 2000; Swimming with my Father, 2004. Honours: Joint Winner, Llewellyn Rhys Memorial Prize, 1974; Writers Guild Laurel Award. Membership: Society of Authors. Address: 29 Willow Road, London NW3 1TL, England.

**JEFFCOAT Rupert Edward Elessing,** b. 23 June 1970, Edinburgh, Scotland. Musician. m. Catherine, 1 daughter. Education: Chorister under Dr Dennis Townhill, St Mary's Cathedral, Edinburgh, 1978-83; Music Scholar, Glenalmond College, Perthshire, 1983-88; Organ Scholar and Scholar (Music Tripos), St Catherine's College, Cambridge, 1989-92; Musical studies with Alexander Goehr, Robin Holloway, Peter Hurford, Peter le Huray; West Midlands Ministerial Training Course, Birmingham, 2002-2005; Ordained Deacon in the Church of England, 2005. Appointments: Composer, arranger, organist, pianist, director, adjudicator, writer; Acting Assistant Organist, Guildford Cathedral, 1989; Music Teacher and Tutor, Ampleforth College, 1993-95; Assistant Director of Music, St Philip's Cathedral, Birmingham, 1995-97; Musical Director, Bournemouth Sinfonietta Choir, 1996-99; Director of Music, Coventry Cathedral: Choirs sing in 15 languages from 10 centuries of music, 1997-; Freelance Musician, 1976-; Church Appointments in Pickering, Egham, Northampton; Involved with Mendelssohn on Mull Festival from its inception; Musical Assistant, Edinburgh International Festival; Staff Member, Birmingham Conservatoire; Music Teacher, Blue Coat School, Birmingham; Accompanist to Birmingham Bach Choir; Continuo player for Armonico Baroque, performing nationwide; Directed music for National Service with HM the Queen, the Prime Minister and the Archbishop of Canterbury in attendance, March 2000; Organ recitalist, UK and Europe; Directed 10 foreign tours including: Russia, Japan, South Africa and Germany; Many recordings, broadcasts and major musical events including several premiers, hundreds of concerts as organist, pianist, continuo player and director. Compositions: Over 150 compositions mostly choral and liturgical; Works performed throughout Great Britain and the USA include: The Prophet, 2000; The Third Service, 2000 and Psalm settings. Publications: Numerous programme notes. Honours: Prizewinner, Associateship Examination, 1989, Fellowship Examination, 1991, Royal College of Organists; Royal Television Society Award, 2003. Memberships include: Royal College of Organists; Cathedral Organists Association; Incorporated Society of Musicians; Friends of Cathedral Music; Royal Philharmonic Society; Scottish Arts Club. Address: 10a, Priory Row, Coventry, West Midlands CV1 5EX, England. E-mail: rupert@fabjeff.co.uk

**JEFFCOTT Leo B,** b. England. Professor of Veterinary Science. m. Tisza Jacqueline Hubbard, 14 June 1969, 2 daughters. Education: Bachelor of Veterinary Medicine, Royal Veterinary College, University of London, 1961-66; PhD, 1972; FRCVS, 1978; DVr Pt 1, 1973; DVSc, 1989; Specialist in Equine Medicine, 1990; MA, 1994; VetMedDr hc (Uppsala), 2000. Appointments: Assistant Pathologist, 1967-71, Radiologist, 1972-77, Head of Clinical Department, 1977-82, Equine Research Station, Animal Health Trust, Newmarket, England; Professor of Clinical Radiology, 1981-82, Visiting Professor, 1990-91, Swedish University of Agricultural Sciences, Uppsala, Sweden; Professor of Veterinary Clinical Sciences, 1982-91, Deputy Dean, Faculty of Veterinary Science,

1985, Head of Department, Veterinary Clinical Sciences, 1985-89, Director, Department of Veterinary Clinic & Hospital, 1986-91, University of Melbourne, Australia; Professor of Veterinary Clinical Studies, Department of Clinical Veterinary Medicine, 1991-2004, Dean, Veterinary School, 1991-2004, Professorial Fellow, Pembroke College, 1993-2004, University of Cambridge, England; Dean, Faculty of Veterinary Science, University of Sydney, 2004-. Honours include: Share Jones Lectureship in Veterinary Anatomy, 1993; Animal Health Trust Outstanding Scientific Achievement Award, 1994; Sefton Award 1997 for services to Equestrian Safety, 1997; Dalrymple Champneys Prize and Cup, 2001; J D Stewart Address, 2004; R R Pascoe Peroration, 2005. Memberships: British Veterinary Association; British Equine Veterinary Association; Federation Equestre Internationale; Royal College of Veterinary Surgeons; World Society for the Protection of Animals; International Committee on Equine Exercise Physiology. Address: Faculty of Veterinary Science, University of Sydney, J D Stewart Building B01, NSW 2006, Australia. E-mail: leoj@vetsci.usyd.edu.au

**JEFFS Julian,** b. 5 April 1931, Wolverhampton, England. Author; Editor. m. Deborah Bevan, 3 sons. Education: Downing College, Cambridge. Appointments: Sherry Shipper's Assistant, Spain, 1956; Barrister, Gray's Inn, 1958; QC, 1975; Recorder, 1975-96; Bencher of Hon Society of Gray's Inn, 1981; Deputy High Court Judge (Chancery Division), 1981-96; Retired from practice, 1991. Publications: Sherry, 1961, 5th edition, 2004; Clerk & Lindsell on Torts, 13th edition, 1969 to 16th edition, 1989 (an editor); The Wines of Europe, 1971; Little Dictionary of Drink, 1973; Encyclopaedia of UK and European Patent Law, 1977, co-editor; The Wines of Spain, 1999. Honours: Office International de la Vigne et du Vin, 1962, 2001; Gran Orden de Caballeros del Vino; Glenfiddich Wine Writers Award, 1974 and 1978. Memberships: Member of Committee, Wine and Food Society, 1965-67, 1971-82; Chairman, Patent Bar Association, 1980-89; President, Circle of Wine Writers, 1992-96. Address: Church Farm House, East Ilsley, Newbury, Berkshire RG20 7LP, England.

**JENKINS David,** 1 March 1926, Birmingham, England. Ecologist. m. Margaret Wellwood Johnston, 1 son, 1 daughter. Education: MRCVS, Royal Veterinary College, 1948; Degree in Zoology, MA,1952, Emmanuel College, Cambridge; D Phil, 1956, Bureau of Animal Population, Zoology Department, Oxford University; DSc (Oxon); FRSE, 1986. Appointments: Team Leader, Nature Conservancy/Aberdeen University Unit of Grouse and Moorland Ecology, 1956-66; Assistant Director, Research (Scotland), Nature Conservancy, 1966-72; Head of Banchory Research Station, Institute of Terrestrial Ecology, 1972-86; Honorary Research Fellow, 1956-86, Honorary Professor of Zoology, 1986-, Aberdeen University; Chairman, Scientific Advisory Committee, World Pheasant Association, 1975-94; Member, North-east Regional Board, Nature Conservancy Council for Scotland/Scottish Natural Heritage, 1992-98. Publications: Population studies in partridges, 1961 et seq; Population studies on red grouse in north-east Scotland (with A Watson and G R Miller), 1963 et seq.; Structure and regulation of a shelduck population (with M G Murray and P Hall), 1975 et seq.; Ecology of otters in north-east Scotland (alone and with others), 1976 et seq.; Of Partridges and Peacocks – And Of Other Things About Which I Knew Nothing, 2003. Address: Whitewalls, 1 Barclay Park, Aboyne, Aberdeenshire AB34 5JF, Scotland.

**JENKINS Ivor,** b. 25 July 1913, Gorseinon, South Wales. Metallurgist. m. Caroline Wijnanda James. 2 sons. Education: Folland Scholar in Metallurgy, BSc, MSc, DSc, University College of Wales, 1931-34; Industrial Bursar, GEC Research Laboratories, Wembley, England, 1934-36. Appointments: Scientific Staff, GEC Research Laboratories, Wembley, 1936-44; Deputy Chief Metallurgist, Whitehead Iron and Steel Co, Newport, Monmouthshire, Wales, 1944-46; Head of Metallurgy Department, 1946-52, Chief Metallurgist, 1952-61, GEC, Wembley; Director and Director of Research, Manganese Bronze Holdings, Ltd, 1961-69; Director of Research, Delta Metal Co and Director, Delta Metal (BW) Ltd, 1969-73; Deputy Chairman, Delta Materials Research Ltd, 1977-78; Group Director of Research, Delta Metal Co Ltd and Managing Director, Delta Materials Research Ltd, 1973-78; Consultant, 1978-95; Retired, 1995. Publications: Controlled Atmospheres for the Heat Treatment of Metals, 1946; Joint Editor, Powder Metallurgy Series, Institute of Metals, 1993-; More than 100 contributions to learned societies at home and abroad on metallurgical and related topics. Honours: Williams Prize, Iron and Steel Institute, 1946; CBE, 1970; Fellow, American Society of Metals, 1974; Platinum Medallist, Institute of Metals, 1978; Fellow, University College, Swansea, 1985. Memberships: Fellow, Royal Academy of Engineering; Institute of Metals 1932-, President, 1969-70; Iron and Steel Institute, 1937-; Fellow, Institution of Metallurgists, 1948, President, 1965-66; Fellow, Royal Society of the Arts; Honorary Member, European Powder Metallurgy Association, 1992; American Society of Metals. Address: 31 Trotyn Croft, Aldwick Fields, Bognor Regis, West Sussex PO21 3TX, England.

**JENKINS Margaret Anne,** b. 20 April 1944. Biochemist. m. Ian McPherson Jenkins, 28 January 1966, 1 son, 1 daughter. Education: BS, Monash University, 1964; MAACB (Member, Australian Association of Clinical Biochemists), 1982; Diploma, Financial Planning, Deakin University, 1992. Appointments: Biochemist, Queen Victoria Hospital, Melbourne, Australia, 1965; Sole Technology, 1965-68, Relieving Technology, 1968-72, Sole Biochemist, West Gippsland Hospital, Warragul, Australia, 1972-76; Biochemist, Preston and Northcote Community Hospital, Preston, 1976-83; Biochemist, Repatriation Campus, 1983-95, Biochemist, Austin Campus, Austin Health, Heidelberg, Australia, 1995-. Publications: 19 papers, 4 reviews and 4 chapters in professional journals including: Laboratory Investigation of Paraproteins by Capillary Electrophoresis, 1996; Automated Capillary Electrophoresis, 1998; Introduction Chapter: Clinical Applications of Capillary Electrophoresis, 1999. Honours: Travelling Scholarship, Australian Association of Clinical Biochemists Annual Science Meeting, 1991; Nancy Dale Scholarship, Australian Association of Clinical Biochemists, 1993; Roche Poster Prize, Australian Association of Clinical Biochemists, 1999; Listed in Who's Who publications and biographical dictionaries. Memberships: Australasian Association of Clinical Biochemists, 1981-, Committee Member, Victorian Branch; Branch Education Representative, Victorian Branch, 1987-91; Australian Electrophoresis Society, 1994-, Committee Member, 1996-98. Address: Austin Campus, Austin Health, Studley Road, Heidelberg, Vic 3084, Australia.

**JENKINS Michael Nicholas Howard (Sir),** b. 13 October 1932, Sevenoaks, Kent, England. Company Chairman. m. Jacqueline Frances, 3 sons. Education: Merton College, Oxford, 1953-56. Appointments: IBM, 1962-67; Management Consultant, Robson Morrow & Co, 1967-71; Technical Director, London Stock Exchange, 1971-77; Managing Director, European Options Exchange, 1977-80; Chief Executive, London International Futures and Options Exchange, 1981-92; Chairman, Futures and Options Association, 1992-2000; Chairman, London Commodity Exchange, 1992-96; London Clearing House, 1991- Chairman, 1996-; Deputy Chairman, Easyscreen plc, 1999-; Chairman, E. Crossnet Ltd, 1999-. Honours: OBE, 1991; Knighthood, 1997.

# DICTIONARY OF INTERNATIONAL BIOGRAPHY

Address: London Clearing House, Aldgate House, 33 Aldgate High Street, London EC3N 1EA, England.

**JENKINS Michael R (Sir)**, b. 9 January 1936. President, Boeing UK. m. Maxine Louise Hodson, 1 son, 1 daughter. Education: BA Honours, King's College, Cambridge. Appointments: Entered HM Diplomatic Service, 1959; Foreign and Commonwealth Office and British Embassies, Paris and Moscow, 1959-68; Seconded, General Electric Company, London, 1968-70; British Embassy, Bonn, 1970-73; European Commission, Brussels, 1973-83; Assistant Under-Secretary of State, Foreign and Commonwealth Office, 1983-85; Minister and Deputy Head of Mission, British Embassy, Washington DC, 1985-87; British Ambassador, The Netherlands, 1988-93; Executive Director and Member of Group Board, Kleinwort Benson Group, 1993-96; Vice-Chairman, Dresdner Kleinwort Wasserstein, 1996-2003; President, Boeing UK, 2003-; President's Advisory Council, Atlantic Council, 1994; Non-Executive Director, Aegon NV, 1995; Chairman of Directors, Action Centre for Europe, 1995; Chairman, British Group, Member of the European Executive Committee, Trilateral Commission, 1996-98; Adviser, Sage International, 1997; Chairman, Dataroam Ltd, 1999-2002; Non-Executive Director, EO, 2000; Chairman, MCC, 2000-02, Trustee, 2002-; Council of Britain in Europe, 2000-; The Pilgrims, 2001-; Advisory Council Prince's Trust, 2002-. Publications: Arakcheev, Grand Vizier of the Russian Empire, 1969; A House in Flanders, 1992. Honour: KCMG, 1989. Address: The Boeing Company, 16 St James's Street, St James's, London SW1A 1ER, England.

**JENKINS Simon David**, b. 10 June 1943, Birmingham, England. Journalist; Editor. m. Gayle Hunnicutt, 1978. Education: BA, St John's College, Oxford. Appointments: Staff, Country Life Magazine, 1965; News Editor, Times Educational Supplement, 1966-68; Leader Writer, Columnist, Features Editor, 1968-74, Editor, 1977-78, Evening Standard; Insight Editor, Sunday Times, 1974-76; Political Editor, The Economist, 1979-86; Editor, 1990-92, Columnist, 1992-, The Times; Columnist, Evening Standard, 1993-; Director, Faber and Faber (Publishers) Ltd., 1981-90. Publications: A City at Risk, 1971; Landlords to London, 1974; Newspapers: The Power and the Money, 1979; The Companion Guide to Outer London, 1981; Images of Hampstead, 1982; The Battle for the Falklands, 1983; With Respect, Ambassador, 1985; Market for Glory, 1986; The Selling of Mary Davies, 1993; England's Thousand Best Churches, 1999; England's 1000 Best Houses, 2002. Address: 174 Regents Park Road, London NW1, England.

**JENKYNS Richard Henry Austen**, b. 18 March 1949, Steyning, Sussex, England. University Professor. Education: Balliol College, Oxford, 1966-71; Corpus Christi College, Oxford, 1971-72, BA, 1971, M Litt, 1975. Appointments: Fellow of All Souls College, Oxford, 1972-81; Lecturer in Classics, University of Bristol, 1978-81; Fellow in Classics, Lady Margaret Hall, Oxford, 1981-; Reader in Classical Languages and Literature, University of Oxford, 1996-99; Professor of the Classical Tradition, University of Oxford, 1999-. Publications: The Victorians and Ancient Greece, 1980; Three Classical Poets, 1982; Dignity and Decadence, 1991; Classical Epic, 1992; The Legacy of Rome (editor), 1992; Virgil's Experience, 1998; Westminster Abbey, 2004; A Fine Brush on Ivory, 2004. Honours: Arts Council Book Award for creative Non-Fiction, 1980; Yorkshire Post "Best First Work 1980" Prize. Address: Lady Margaret Hall, Oxford OX2 6QA, England. E-mail: richard.jenkyns@lmh.ox.ac.uk

**JENNINGS Alex Michael**, b. 10 May 1957, Upminster, Essex. Actor. Partner: Lesley Moors, 1 son, 1 daughter. Education: BA

honours, Warwick University, 1978; Bristol Old Vic Theatre School, 1978-80. Career: Theatre includes: Richard II, 1990-91; The Importance of Being Ernest, 1993; Hamlet, 1997-98; Speer, 2000; The Winter's Tale, 2001; The Relapse, 2001; My Fair Lady, 2002 Films include: War Requiem, 1988; A Midsummer Night's Dream, 1996; The Wings of the Dove, 1997; The Hunley, 1998; Four Feathers, 2002; TV includes: Smiley's People; Inspector Morse; Ashenden, 1991; Inspector Alleyn Mysteries; Hard Times; Bad Blood, 1999. Honours: Best Actor for Too Clever By Half, London Theatre Critics Awards; Olivier Award, Best Comedy Performance for Too Clever By Half; Oliver Award, Best Actor for Peer Gynt; Helen Hayes Award, Best Actor for Hamlet, 1998; Hon D Litt, Warwick University, 2000; Best Actor, Evening Standard Drama Award, 2001. Address: c/o ICM, Oxford House, 76 Oxford Street, London W1N 0AX, England.

**JENNINGS Elizabeth (Joan)**, b. 18 July 1926, Boston, Lincolnshire, England. Education: MA, St Anne's College, Oxford. Appointments: Assistant, Oxford City Library, 1950-58; Reader, Chatto & Windus Ltd, 1958-60. Publications: Poetry: Poems, 1953; A Way of Looking, 1955; A Sense of the World, 1958; Song for a Birth or a Death, 1961; Recoveries, 1964; The Mind has Mountains, 1966; The Secret Brother, 1966; Collected Poems, 1967; The Animals' Arrival, 1969; Lucidities, 1970; Relationships, 1972; Growing Points, 1975; Consequently I Rejoice, 1977; After the Ark, 1978; Selected Poems, 1980; Moments of Grace, 1980; Celebrations and Elegies, 1982; Extending the Territory, 1985; Collected Poems, 1953-86, 1986; Tributes, 1989; Times and Seasons, 1992; Familiar Spirits, 1994; A Spell of Words, 1997. Editor: The Batsford Book of Children's Verse, 1958; A Choice of Christina Rossetti's Verse, 1970; The Batsford Book of Religious Verse, 1981. Other: Let's Have Some Poetry, 1960; Every Changing Shape, 1961; Robert Frost, 1964; Christianity and Poetry, 1965; Seven Men of Vision, 1976. Contributions to: Newspapers, journals, and magazines. Honours: Arts Council Prize, 1953, and Bursary, 1969; Somerset Maugham Award, 1956; Richard Hillary Prize, 1966; W H Smith Award, 1987; Commander of the Order of the British Empire, 1992; Paul Hamlyn Award, 1997. Memberships: Society of Authors. Address: c/o David Higham Associates Ltd, 5-8 Lower John Street, London W1R 4HA, England.

**JENNINGS John Michael**, b. 27 August 1944, Christchurch, New Zealand. Academic Auditor. m. Cynthia Margaret Bensemann, 1 son, 1 daughter. Education: BMus with honours, University of Canterbury, New Zealand, 1966; MMus, University of Sydney, Australia, 1969; Licentiate of the Royal Schools of Music, London, 1963; Licentiate of the Trinity College of Music, London, 1965. Appointments: Assistant Lecturer, 1967-69, Lecturer, 1969-77, Senior Lecturer, 1978-2003, Dean of Arts, 1986-92, Deputy Chair, Chair, Academic Administration Committee, 1995-98, Quality Assurance Facilitator, 1998-2001, University of Canterbury; Director, New Zealand Universities Academic Audit Unit, 2002-. Publications: Articles in professional journals. Honours: University Prize Award, Commonwealth Scholarship and Fellowship Plan, 1966-67; Fellow, Institute of Registered Music Teachers in New Zealand, 1989. Memberships: Institute of Registered Music Teachers in New Zealand, 1972-; New Zealand Organisation for Quality, 1999-. Address: New Zealand Universities Academic Audit Unit, 178 Willis Street, Wellington, New Zealand. E-mail: director@aau.ac.nz Website: www.aau.ac.nz

**JENNINGS Marie Patricia**, b. 25 December 1930, Quetta, India. Author; Consumer Affairs Consultant. m. Brian Locke, 1 son, 1 stepson, 3 stepdaughters. Education: Presentation Convent College, Strinagar, Kashmir. Appointments: Managing

Director, The Roy Bernand Co Ltd, 1960-65; Special Adviser, Stanley Tools, 1961-89, The Unit Trust Association, 1976-90, The Midland Bank, now HSBC, 1978-2004; Director, Lexington Ltd, 1971-75, The PR Consultants Association, 1979-84, Cadogan Management Ltd, 1984-90; Patron and Former President, National Association of Womens Clubs, 1998-; Member, Council and Deputy Chairman, Insurance Ombudsman Bureau, 1986-2001; Member, Council of Financial International Managers and Borkers Regulatory Association, 1986-98; Executive Committee Member, Wider Share Ownership Council, 1987-91; Consumer Panel, Personal Investment Authority, PIA, Chairman, National Federation of Consumer Groups, 1998-2000; Chairman, President and Founder, Consumer Policy Institute, 2000-; Consultant Editor, Finance, Good Housekeeping Magazine, 1992-2000; Founder and President, The Money Management Council, 1984-; Member, FSA Consumer Education Forum, 1998-2004. Publications: Many books including: Women and Money; Ten Steps to the Top; Guide to Good Corporate Citizenship; Perfect Insurance; National TV series: Money Spinner, C4; Money Go Round, LWT; Translations; Articles for newspapers. Honours: MBE. Memberships: Institute of Directors; Honorary Member, Public Relations Consultants Association; Institute of Public Relations; National Union of Journalists. Address: Cadogan Grange, Bisley, Stroud, Gloucestershire, GL6 7AT, England. Email: mlocke1162@aol.com

**JENNINGS Robert Yewdall (Sir),** b. 19 October 1913, Idle, Bradford. Professor; Barrister; International Tribunals Judge. m. Christine Dorothy Bennett, 1 son, 2 daughters. Education: BA, 1935, LLB, 1936, Downing College, Cambridge; Choate Fellow, Harvard University Law School, 1936-37. Appointments: Assistant Lecturer, Law, London School of Economics, 1937-39; Fellow, Jesus College, Cambridge, 1939-; HM British Army, retired with rank of Major, 1940-46; University Lecturer in Law, Cambridge University, 1946-55; Senior Tutor, Jesus College, 1949-55; Whewell Professor of International Law, Cambridge University, 1955-81; Queen's Counsel, 1969; Honorary Bencher of Lincoln's Inn, 1970; Judge, 1982-96, President, 1991-94, International Court of Justice; Appointing Authority of the Iran/US Claims Tribunal, The Hague, 1991-; Ad Hoc Judge Libya v. UK case. Publications: Editor, British Yearbook of International Law, 1959-81; The Acquisition of Territory in International Law, 1961; General Course on the Principles of International Law, 1967 Editor with Sir Arthur Watts QC, Oppenheim on International Law, 2 volumes, 1992; Collected Writings of Sir Robert Jennings, 2 volumes, 1998. Honours: Knighthood, 1982; Honorary Fellow, Jesus College, Cambridge, 1982; Honorary Fellow, Downing College, Cambridge, 1984; Honorary Fellow, London School of Economics, 1996; Honorary LLD, Cantab 1994; Honorary DCL, Oxford, 1996; Honorary DL, University of Hull, The Saarland, Leicester, Rome. Membership: Institut de droit international 1951-, President, 1983.

**JENSEN Arthur S,** b. 24 December 1917, Trenton, New Jersey, USA. Engineering Physicist. m. Lillian Elizabeth Reed, 2 sons, 1 daughter. Education: BS, Physics, 1938, MS, Physics, 1939, PhD, Physics, 1941, University of Pennsylvania; Diploma of Advanced Engineering, 1972, Computer Science, 1977, Westinghouse School of Applied Science, Baltimore. Appointments: Teacher of Physics and Physics of Aviation, Department of Electrical Engineering, US Naval Academy, 1941-46; Research Physicist, RCA Laboratories, Princeton, NJ, 1946-57; Consulting Physicist, Westinghouse Defence and Space Centre, 1957-94. Publications: 25 patents; 60 articles in physics and engineering journals and conferences. Honours: Captain, US Navy, retired; Westinghouse Special Corporate Patent Award; American Defence Service Medal; American Campaign Medal;

World War II Victory Medal; Naval Reserve Medal; Armed Forces Reserve Medal; Biographical listing in several Who's Who books; Maryland Governor's Citation; Engineers' Council of Maryland's Outstanding Service Award. Memberships: American Association for Advancement of Science; Fellow, Institute of Electrical and Electronic Engineers; American Physical Society; SPIE; Fellow, Washington Academy of Science; Maryland Academy of Science; New York Academy of Science; Life Member, Retired Officers' Association; National Eagle Scout Association; Sigma Xi; American Association of Physics Teachers. Address: Chapel Gate 1104, Oak Crest Village, 8820 Walther Boulevard, Parkville, MD 21234-9022, USA.

**JENSH Ronald P,** b. 14 June 1938. Professor of Pathology, Anatomy and Cellular Biology. m. Ruth-Eleanor Dobson, 1962, 2 daughters. Education: BA, 1960, MA, 1962, Bucknell University; PhD, Jefferson Medical College, 1966. Appointments include: Faculty Member, Jefferson Medical College, 1966-; Faculty Member, Graduate School, Thomas Jefferson University, 1970-; Assistant Professor, Radiology and Anatomy, 1974-82, Associate Professor, Anatomy, 1974-82, Associate Professor, Radiology, 1974-91, Professor of Anatomy, 1982-94, Vice Chairman, Department of Anatomy, 1984-94, Section Chief, Microscopic Anatomy, 1988-, Associate Professor, Pediatrics, 1991-, Professor, Department of Pathology, Anatomy and Cellular Biology, 1994-, Jefferson Medical College. Publications: (author or co-author) 68 papers and books; 69 abstracts; 32 computer programs; 2 Sound and Light Programs - produced; 2 8mm movies produced, 1975; 11 photographic art exhibits including One-Man Shows, Haddonfield, New Jersey, 1987, 1988, Thomas Jefferson University, 1996; 10 photographs published, 1979-. Honours include: Phi Sigma, 1961; Psi Chi, 1961; Sigma Xi, 1967-; Phi Beta Kappa, Mu Chapter, 1986; Hon Life Member, Jefferson Medical College Alumni Association, 1994; Alumni Award, Bucknell University, Lewisburg, Pennsylvania, 1997; Borough of Haddonfield (New Jersey) "Dr Ronald Jensh Recognition Day", 31 May 1997. Memberships include: Neurobehavioral Teratology Society, President, 1985-86; American Association of Anatomists; American Association of University Professors; Teratology Society; International Association of Human Biologists; Radiation Research Society; Society for Experimental Biology and Medicine. Address: 230 East Park Ave, Haddonfield, NJ 08033-1835, USA.

**JEON Jae-Ho,** b. 22 March 1961, Busan, Korea. Research Scientist. m. Sun-Mi Jin, 4 daughters. Education: BS, Busan National University, Korea, 1984; PhD, Korea Advanced Institute of Science and Technology (KAIST), 1994. Appointments: Research Assistant, 1988-93, Researcher, 1994-95, Korea Advanced Institute of Science and Technology; Research Fellow, IRC, Birmingham University, England, 1996-98; Principal Research Scientist, Korea Institute of Machinery and Materials (KIMM), 1995-. Publications: Over 20 articles in international journals as co-author include most recently: Synthesis of Nanostructured $MoSi_2$-TiC Composite Powders by Mechanical Alloying, 2003; Effect of $SrTiO_3$ concentration and sintering temperature on microstructure and dielectric property of $Ba_{1-x}Sr_xTiO_3$, 2004; Effect of Initial Porosity on mechanical properties of C/SiC Composites Fabricated by Silicon Melt Infiltration Process, 2004; Development of Functionally Graded Anti-oxidation Coatings for Carbon/Carbon Composites, 2004; Densification and Dielectric Property of $B_2O_3$-doped $Ba_{1-x}Sr_xTiO_3$ Graded Ceramics, 2004; Constitutional Design and Dielectric Properties of BST Graded Ceramics, 2004; 5 articles in domestic journals; 28 papers in conference proceedings; 3 patents. Honour: Best Researcher in 2003, Korea Institute of Machinery and Materials. Memberships: Korean Ceramic

Society; Korean Institute of Metals and Materials; Korea Powder Metallurgy Institute; Materials Research Society of Korea; International Association of Layered and Graded Materials; Korean Go Association. Address: 106-401 Seongwon 1st Apt, Namyang-Dong, Changwon, 641-751, Korea. E-mail: jjh@kmail.kimm.re.kr

**JEON Wan-Ho,** b. 1 November 1970, Taejon, Korea. Research Engineer. m. Eun-Kyung Cho, 2 daughters. Education: Bachelor, Inha University, Korea, 1992; Master, 1994, PhD, 1999, Korea Advanced Institute of Science and Technology. Appointments: Postdoctoral Course, Korea Advanced Institute of Science and Technology, 1999; Chief Research Engineer, LG Electronics, 200-2004; Research Engineer, Fiber Noise Research Laboratory, ECIM Ltd, 2004-. Publications: Articles in scientific journals as author and co-author: An analysis of the flow and aerodynamic acoustic sources of a centrifugal impeller, 1999; A numerical study on the effects of the design parameters upon fan performance and noise of centrifugal fan, 2003; A numerical study on the flow and sound fields of a centrifugal impeller located near a wedge, 2003; Analysis of the aeroacoustic characteristics of the centrifugal fan in a vacuum cleaner, 2003; Aeroacoustic characteristics and noise reduction of a centrifugal fan for a vacuum cleaner, 2004; An application of the acoustic similarity law to the centrifugal fan noise by numerical calculation, 2004; Numerical analysis on the unsteady flow field and flow noise of a fan system. Honours: Listed in Who's Who publications and biographical dictionaries. Memberships: International Noise Control Engineering; International Institute of Acoustics and Vibration. Address: 115-2302 YongNam, Topsville Apt, Majeon-Dong, Seo-gu, Incheon, Korea. E-mail: whjeon@chol.com

**JEON Yun-Churl,** b. 15 June 1939, Mokpo, Jeollanam-do, Korea. Chairman of the Board of Audit and Inspection of Korea. m. Jung Ja Kim, 1 son, 1 daughter. Education: LLB, College of Law, Seoul National University, Korea, 1965. Appointments: Assistant Director, Ministry of Legislation, 1967-71; Assistant Director, 1971-76, Director, 1976-83, Principal Deputy Director General, Budget Office, 1983-90, Director General, Price Policy Bureau, Assistant Minister for Planning and Management, 1994, Economic Planning Board; Standing Commissioner, Fair Trade Commission, 1991-94; Administrator, National Fisheries Administration, 1995-96; Chairman, Fair Trade Commission, 1997-2000; Minister of Planning and Budget, 2000-2002; Chief of Staff, Office of the President, Republic of Korea, 2002; Deputy Prime Minister and Minister of Finance and Economy, 2002-2003; Chair Professor, College of Law and Political Science, Jeju National University, Jeju, Korea, 2003; Chairman of the Board of Audit and Inspection, 2003-; Chairman of the Governing Board, 2003-2004, Member of the Governing Board and the Finance and Administration Committee, 2004-, International Organisation of Supreme Audit Institutions. Publications: In Korean: Market Economy Where Competition Blossoms, 1999; The Past, the Present and the Future of Market Economy, 2000. Honours: Order of Service Merit, Red Stripes, 1983, Order of Service Merit, Yellow Stripes, 1996, Government of the Republic of Korea; Honorary Doctorate of Law, Kwangwoon University, Seoul, Korea, 1998; Honorary Doctorate of Business Administration, Soonchunhyang University, Seoul, Korea, 1999; Honorary Doctorate of Economics, Mokpo National University, Mokpo, Korea, 1999. Address: 7-802 Sindonga Apt, Bangbaedong, Sheochogu, Seoul, Korea.

**JEONG Yoonchan,** b. 9 March 1971, Daegu, Korea. Senior Research Fellow. m. Hyejeong Han, 1 daughter. Education: BSc, 1994, MSc, 1996, PhD, 1999, Electrical Engineering, Seoul National University. Appointments: Research Associate, School of Electrical Engineering, 1999, Research Staff, Inter-University Semiconductor Research Center, 1999-2001, Post-Doctoral Researcher, 2000-01, School of Electrical Engineering, Seoul National University; Research Fellow, 2001-03, Senior Research Fellow, 2003-, Optoelectronics Research Centre, University of Southampton. Publications: Over 100 articles in professional journals and conference proceedings. Honours: Postdoctoral Fellowship, Korea Science & Engineering Foundation, 2001; Distinguished Alumni Award, Optical Engineering and Quantum Electronics Laboratory, School of Electrical Engineering, Seoul National University, 2003. Memberships: Institute of Electrical and Electronics Engineers; Optical Society of America; Optical Society of America. Address: 42 Castle Street, Inner Avenue, Southampton SO14 6HF, England. E-mail: cherisho@ieee.org

**JEREMIC John,** b. 21 March 1938, Nis, Yugoslavia. Self Employed General Manager. m. Shirley, 1 son, 3 daughters. Education: Qualified Fitter and Turner; Bachelor of Arts, Honours, Theology; Doctor of Divinity; PhD (Africa), 2003. Appointments: Preacher and Evangelist; Running Evangelist Crusades around the world; Most recently, evangelistic crusade in Papua New Guinea with 30,000-35,000 people in attendance; Helped to build "Jeremic Library", Avondale College, New South Wales, Australia; School in Africa named Jeremic Adventist Academy; Has built with associates, 25 churches the largest of which is in Kiberra, Africa; Barton-Jeremic Medical Center, Africa, opened in 2004. Publications: Many religious sermons and church programmes. Honours: Doctor of Divinity; PhD (Africa), 2003. Membership: Senior Elder, Seventh Day Adventist Church. Address: Hospital and Medical Care Pty, PO Box 1200, Box Hill, Vic 3128, Australia. E-mail: hmc-amaz.discoveries@bigpond.com

**JERVIS Simon Swynfen,** b. 9 January 1943, Yoxford, Suffolk, England. Art Historian. m. Fionnuala MacMahon, 1 son, 1 daughter. Education: Corpus Christi College, Cambridge, 1961-64. Appointments: Student Assistant, Assistant Keeper of Art, Leicester Museum and Art Gallery, 1964-66; Assistant Keeper, 1966-75, Deputy Keeper, 1975-89, Acting Keeper, 1989, Curator, 1989-90, Department of Furniture, Victoria and Albert Museum; Director and Marlay Curator, Fitzwilliam Museum, Cambridge, 1990-95; Director of Historic Buildings, The National Trust, 1995-2002. Publications: 7 books on furniture and design; Many articles in learned journals. Memberships: Member, 1964-, Arts Panel, 1982-95, Chairman, 1987-95, Properties Committee, 1987-95, National Trust; Member, 1966-, Council, 1977-79, 1981-83, 1986-87, Editor, 1988-92, Chairman, 1999-, Furniture History Society; Member, 1968-, Stafford Terrace Committee, 1980-90, Victorian Society; Member, Southwark Diocesan Advisory Committee, 1978-87; Member, 1982-, Council, 1987-1991, Royal Archaeological Institute; Elected Fellow, 1983, Council, 1986-88, Executive Committee, 1987-92, House Working party, 1988-, President, 1995-2001, Kelmscott Committee, 2001-, Society of Antiquaries of London; Director, 1993-, Trustee, 1996-, The Burlington Magazine; Member, 1988-, Council, Walpole Society, 1990-95; Guest Scholar, The J Paul Getty Museum, 1988-89, 2003; Member, Museums and Galleries Commission, Acceptance in Lieu Panel, 1992-2000; Trustee, The Royal Collection Trust, 1993-2001; Trustee, 1998-2002, Life Trustee, 2002-, Sir John Soane's Museum; Member, Advisory Council, National Art Collections Fund, 2002-. Address: 45 Bedford Gardens, London W8 7EF, England.

**JESS Digby Charles,** b. 14 November 1953, Plymouth, England. Barrister; Chartered Arbitrator. m. Bridie, 1 son, 1 daughter. Education: BSc Honours, Aston University, 1976;

Called to the Bar, 1978; LLM, 1986, PhD, 1999, University of Manchester; FCIArb, 1992; Chartered Arbitrator, 1999. Appointments: Barrister, Private Practice specialising in insurance claims and building disputes, 1978-; Treasury Counsel (Northern Region), 1990-2003; Legal Assessor, General Medical Council, Council Fitness to Practice Committees, 2002-; Member, Association of Chartered Accountants' Disciplinary and Licensing Committees, 2002-; Chairman CIArb North West Branch, 1992-93; Chairman, BIIBA Liability Society (NW), 1995-99; Sometime Part-time Lecturer in Law, University of Manchester. Publications: The Insurance of Commercial Risks: Law and Practice, 1986, 3rd edition 2001; The Insurance of Professional Negligence Risks: Law and Practice, 1982, 2nd edition, 1989. Memberships: FRSA; Northern Circuit Commercial Bar Association; Technology and Construction Court Bar Association. Address: Exchange Chambers, 7 Ralli Courts, West Riverside, Manchester M3 5FT, England. E-mail: jess@exchangechambers.co.uk

**JESTY Ronald Cyril Benjamin,** b. 7 May 1926, Weymouth, Dorset, England. Graphic Designer; Artist. m. Margaret Ellen Johnson. Appointments: Apprentice Draughtsman, Vickers Armstrong, 1941-45; Freelance Graphic Designer, 1947-78; Artist (watercolours), 1978-; Part-time Art Teacher, 1978-2002. Publications: Learn To Paint Seascapes, 1996; Various articles in Leisure Painter Magazine and International Artist Magazine; Contributor to several books on art and painting. Membership: Royal Society of British Artists, 1982-92. Address: 11 Pegasus Court, South Street, Yeovil, Somerset, BA20 1ND, England.

**JIMBOW Kowichi,** b. 4 June 1941, Nagoya, Japan. Physician; Dermatologist; Professor. m. Mihoko Jimbow, 1 son, 4 daughters. Education: MD, Sapporo Medical College, Sapporo, Japan, 1966; PhD, Sapporo Medical College Graduate School, Sapporo, Japan, 1974. Appointments: Professor and Chair, Department of Dermatology, Sapporo Medical University, School of Medicine, 1995-; Chief, Division of Dermatology, Division of Plastic Surgery (Adjunct), Sapporo Medical University Hospital, 1995-; Adjunct Professor, Department of Medicine, Dermatology and Cutaneous Sciences, University of Alberta, Edmonton, Canada, 1996-; Dean, Sapporo Medical University, Graduate School of Medicine, 2000-; Dean, Sapporo Medical University School of Medicine, 2000-. Honours include: Alfred Marchionini Prize, International Association of Dermatology, 1982; Seiji Memorial Award, Japanese Society of Dermatology, 1984; Alberta Heritage Medical Scientist Award, Canada, 1988, 1993; Henry Stanley Raper Award, European Society of Pigment Cell; Hokkaido Physician Award, Japan, 2001; Hokkaido Science and Technology Award, Japan, 2002. Memberships: Alberta Medical Association; American Academy of Dermatology; American Association for Cancer Research; American Society for Cell Biology; American Society of Photobiology; Canadian Dermatological Association; Canadian Society for Clinical Investigation; Canadian Society for Investigative Dermatology; International Society of Pigment Cell Research; Society for Investigative Dermatology; Japanese Dermatological Association; Japanese Burn Association; WHO Councillor for Evaluation and Methods of Diagnosis and Treatment of Melanoma. Address: Sapporo Medical University, Department of Dermatology, School of Medicine, South 1 West 16, Chuo-ku, Sapporo, Hokkaido, Japan, 005-0832. E-mail: jimbow@sapmed.ac.jp

**JIN Byung-Rae,** b. 13 October 1963, Kyungnam, Korea. Professor. m. Hyung-Joo Yoon, 1 son. Education: BSc, Dong-A University, Korea 1985; MSc, 1987, PhD, 1994, Seoul National University, Korea. Appointments: Doctoral Researcher, University of California, Davis, USA, 1996-97; Professor,

Department of Biotechnology, 1998-, Department Head of Biotechnology, 2002-2003, Vice Dean, College of Natural Resources and Life Science, 2005-; Dong-A University, Korea; Editor-in-Chief, International Journal of Industrial Entomology, 2002-2004; Editor, Journal of Asia-Pacific Entomology, 2002-. Publications: About 200 articles; 1 US Patent; 10 Korean Patents. Honour: Excellent Research Award, KOFST, 1991. Memberships: Korean Society of Molecular and Cellular Biology; Korean Society of Applied Entomology. Address: Department of Biotechnology, College of Natural Resources and Life Science, Dong-A University, Busan 604-714, Korea. E-mail: brjin@dau.ac.kr

**JIN Moon-Seog,** b. 17 April 1960, Naju, Chonnam, Korea. Professor. m. Sun-Young Park, 1 son, 1 daughter. Education: PhD, Chonnam National University, Korea, 1994. Appointment: Researcher, R&D Center, Kumho Company. Publications: 71 articles in scientific journals include: Spin-Orbit Coupling Effect of $Co^{2+}$ Ion in $CuAlSe_2$ Single Crystals. Address: Department of Physics, Dongshin University, Dae-Ho Dong 252, Naju, Chonnam 520-714, Republic of Korea. E-mail: msjin@dsu.ac.kr

**JIN Sung-Ho,** b. 27 March 1964, Busan, Korea. Professor. m. Yeon-Sook Seo, 2 daughters. Education: BS, Department of Chemistry, Pusan National University, 1984-88; MS, 1988-90, PhD, 1990-93, Korea Advanced Institute of Science and Technology. Appointments: Research and Teaching Assistant, Department of Chemistry, Korea Advanced Institute of Science and Technology, 1990-99; Principal Scientist, Samsung Advanced Institute of Technology, 1999-2003; Assistant Professor, Pusan National University, 2003; Associate Professor, Pusan National University, 2003-; Director, Center for Plastic Information System, 2003-. Publications: Over 150 communications, papers and review articles include: Poly (1, 6-heptadiyne)-Based Materials by Metathesis Polymerization, 2000; 30 patents. Memberships: Society for Information Display; Korean Chemical Society; Polymer Society of Korea. Address: Department of Chemistry, Pusan National University, Changjeon-dong, Kumjeong-ku, Busan 609-735, Korea. E-mail: shjin@pusan.ac.kr

**JIN Wei Min,** b. 6 February 1963, China. Physicist. 1 son. Education: BS, University of Science and Technology of China, 1985; PhD, State University of New York at Buffalo, USA, 1999. Appointment: Estimator, a private company, 1998-. Publications: Articles in scientific journals: From Time Inversion to Nonlinear QED, 2000; Quantization of Dirac fields in static spacetime, 2000. Honours: Outstanding Professional Award, ABI; Listed in biographical dictionaries. Address: 2209 Carrington Court, Lexington, KY 40513, USA. E-mail: weiminjin@netscape.net Website: http://www.weiminjin.com/

**JING Weixing,** b. 10 December 1955, China. Comprehensive Financial Planner. m. Ying Fu, 1 daughter. Education: B Eng, 1978, M Eng, 1986, Zhengzhou University of Technology, China; M Ph, Queen's University, Belfast, UK, 1996. Appointments: Certified Financial Planner; Chartered Life Underwriter and Chartered Financial Consultant, Great West/London Life, Canada, 1977-. Honours: Million Dollar Round Table, 2000, 2001, 2003; Listed in Who's Who publications and biographical dictionaries. Memberships: Financial Planner Standard Council, Canada; CLU Institute; Advocis, Canada. Address: 3200 Dufferin Street, Suite 210, Toronto, Ontario, M6A 3B2 Canada. E-mail: weixing.jing@freedom55 financial.com

**JINGA,** b. 15 February 1950, Beceni, Buzau, Romania. Orthodox Priest. m. Gabriela, 1 son, 2 daughters. Education: Graduate, Theological Faculty, University of Bucharest, Romania, 1973. Appointments: Priest in several rural and urban parishes; Secretary of the Arch-Priest of Drobeta Turnu Severin, 1987-; Priest, Iconom-Stauroforus. Publications: Poetry: Vision of a White Stubble Field, 1984; The Struggle in Dawn, 1988; Vertige, 1995; Imbroglio, 1997; Glory to the Waste Ground Dog, 2000; Prose: A Dream of Guardians, 1996; Chief Editor of Terra Griphonis and Apollodor. Honours: The Writers' Union Award for Poetry for Glory to the Waste Ground Dog, 2000; Honorary Citizen of Orşova, 2005. Membership: Writers' Union of Romania, 1997-. Address: Bld 1Dec 1918, Nr 7, Ap 6, Orşova 225200, MH, Romania.

**JOEL Billy (William Martin Joel),** b. 9 May 1949, Bronx, New York, USA. Musician; Singer; Songwriter. m. Christie Brinkley, 23 March 1989, divorced 1994, 1 daughter. Education: LHD (honorary), Fairfield University, 1991; HMD (honorary), Berklee College of Music, 1993. Appointment: Solo Recording Artist, 1972-. Creative Works: Turnstiles; Streetlife Serenade; The Stranger, 1978; 52nd Street, 1978; Glass Houses, 1980; Songs In the Attic, 1981; Nylon Curtain, 1982; An Innocent Man, 1983; Cold Spring Harbour, 1984; Piano Man, 1984; Greatest Hits, Vols I & II, 1985; The Bridge, 1986; KOHUEPT-Live in Leningrad, 1987; Storm Front, 1989; River of Dreams, 1994; 2000 Years: Millennium Concert, 2000. Honours: 6 Grammy Awards; 10 Grammy Nominations; Grammy Legend Award, 1990; Songwriters Hall of Fame, 1992.

**JOFFE Joel Goodman (Lord Joffe),** b. 12 May 1932. Human Rights Lawyer; Businessman; Chairman and Trustee of Charities; National Health Services Chairman. m. Vanetta Joffe, 3 daughters. Education: B Com LLB, Witwatersrand University, Johannesburg. Appointments: Solicitor, then Barrister, Johannesburg, 1952-65; Secretary and Administrative Director, Abbey Life Assurance, London, 1965-70; Founder Director, Joint Managing Director, Deputy Chairman, Allied Dunbar Assurance, 1971-91; Founding Trustee, Chairman, Allied Dunbar Charitable Trust, 1974-93; Chairman, Thamesdown Voluntary Services Council, 1974-1980; Trustee, Honorary Secretary, Chairman of the Executive Committee, Chair, Oxfam, 1979-2001; Chairman, Swindon Private Hospital plc, 1982-87; Council Member, IMPACT, 1984-; Chairman, Swindon Health Authority, 1988-93; Campaigner to protect consumers from the excesses of the Financial Services Industry, 1992-97; Chairman, Swindon and Marlborough National Health Trust, 1993-95; Special Adviser to South African Minister of Transport, 1997-98; Chair of The Giving Campaign, 2000-04; Trustee, J G and V L Joffe Charitable Trust. Memberships: Member, Royal Commission for the Care of the Elderly, 1997-99; Member, Home Officer Working Group on the Active Community, 1998-99. Address: Liddington Manor, Liddington, Swindon, Wiltshire SN4 0HD, England.

**JOGLEKAR Satish Dinkar,** b. 25 February 1949, Junnar, Pune District, India. Physicist. Education: Indian Institute of Technology, Bombay; Doctorate SUNY, Stony Brook, 1975. Appointments: Post-doctoral work: Fermi National Accelerator Laboratory, 1975; Institute of Advanced Study, Princeton, 1975-77; University of California, Berkeley, 1977-79; Professor, Indian Institute of Technology, Kanpur; Taught at postgraduate/undergraduate level for 20 years. Publications: 70 published original works in the field of High Energy Physics. Honours: Fellow, Maharashtra Academy of Sciences India; Fellow, National Academy of Sciences, India; Founder Member, American Order of Excellence; Lifetime Achievement Award, IBC, 2002; World Lifetime Achievement Award, ABI,

2002; Top 100 Scientists, 2005; Top 100 Scientists Pinnacle of Achievement Award; Order of International Ambassadors, ABI; Listed in numerous biographical dictionaries. Membership: American Physical Society. Address: Department of Physics, Indian Institute of Technology, Kanpur 208016, India.

**JOHANSEN Roberto M,** b. 19 September 1944, Chihuahua, Mexico. Entomologist. Education: BSc Biology, Faculty of Sciences, 1972; Colegio de Postgraduados, Escuela Nacional de Agricultura, Chapingo, Mexico, 1972-73; MSc, Biology, 1974, National Autonomous University of Mexico; DSc, Biology, Faculty of Sciences, National Autonomous University of Mexico, 1977; Diplomat, 1997, Diplomat, 1999, Colegio de Postgraduados en Ciencias Agricolas, Mexico. Appointments: Associate Researcher, Institute of Biology, 1975-88; Senior Researcher, 1989-; Professor, Insect Morphology, Division of Higher Studies, Faculty of Sciences, UNAM, 1982-84; Head of Department, 1985-87; Coordinator, Editorial and Publishing Unit of the Instituto de Biología, UNAM, 1987-91. Guest lecturer, Agricultural Thysanopterology, Instituto de Fitosanidad; Colegio de Postgraduados en Ciencias Agricolas, Montecillo, Texcoco, México, 1995-. Publications: Author of some 120 publications; Articles; Reports; Monographs; Book Chapters about Insecta Thysanoptera. Honours: Medals, Diplomas, UNAM, 1986, 1990, 1995, 2000, 2001; The International Cultural Diploma of Honor (1998), by The American Biographical Institute, USA, Title, National Researcher, (1984-1993); Board Certified Entomologist, 1996-, Entomological Society of America; President, Sociedad Mexicana de Entomología, (1999-2001); UNAM Award for University Merit for 25 years of Academic work, 2001; National Researcher, 2002-2005; Cavalier of the World Order of Science, Education and Culture, Académie Européenne d' Informatisation, Brussels, Belgium, 2002; Grand Doctor of Philosophy, Doctor of Philosophy and Full Professor, The World Information Distributed University and the Académie Européenne d'Informatisation, 2003; Listed in biographical dictionaries. Memberships: Sociedad Mexicana de Historia Natural; Sociedad Mexicana de Entomologia; Sociedade Entomologica do Brasil; Academia Mexicana de Ciencias; Asociación Etnobiológica Mexicana; Entomological Society of America; Real Sociedad Española de Historia Natural; Sociedad Mexicana para el Progreso de la Ciencia y Tecnología, Founder Diplomatic Counsellor, 2000; London Diplomatic Academy, England; Lifetime Deputy Governor, 1998, Board of Governors, American Biographical Institute, Research Association, Sociedad Mexicana de Control Biológico; Ingenieros Agrónomos Parasitólogos. Address: Instituto De Biología UNAM, Departamento de Zoología; AP 70-153 México 04510, DF, México.

**JOHANNSON Scarlett,** b. 22 November 1984, New York, USA. Film Actress. Career: North, 1994; Just Cause, 1995; If Lucy Fell, 1996; Manny & Lo, 1996; Fall, 1997; Home Alone 3, 1997; The Horse Whisperer, 1998; My Brother the Pig, 1999; Ghost World, 2000; An American Rhapsody, 2001; The Man Who Wasn't There, 2001; Eight Legged Freaks, 2002; The Girl with a Pearl Earring, 2003; Lost in Translation, 2003; The Perfect Score, 2004. Honours: BAFTA Award for Best Actress, Lost in Translation, 2004.

**JOHN Elton (Sir) (Reginald Kenneth Dwight),** b. 25 March 1947, Pinner, Middlesex, England. Singer; Songwriter; Musician (piano). m. Renate Blauer, 14 February 1984, divorced 1988. Musical Education: Piano lessons aged 4; Royal Academy of Music, 1958. Career: Member, Bluesology, 1961-67; Worked at Mills Music Publishers; Solo artiste, 1968-; Long-term writing partnership with Bernie Taupin, 1967-; Partnership wrote for Dick James Music; Founder, Rocket Records, 1973; Own publishing company, Big Pig Music, 1974; Performances include: Wembley Stadium, 1975; First Western star to perform in Israel and USSR, 1979; Live Aid, Wembley, 1985; Wham's farewell concert, Wembley, 1985; Prince's Trust concerts, London, 1986, 1988; Farm Aid IV, 1990; AIDS Project Los Angeles - Commitment To Life VI, 1992; Chair, The Old Vic Theatre Trust, 2002-; Film appearance, Tommy, 1975. Recordings: Hit singles include: Your Song, 1971; Rocket Man, 1972; Crocodile Rock (Number 1, US), 1973; Daniel, 1973; Saturday Night's Alright For Fighting, 1973; Goodbye Yellow Brick Road, 1973; Candle In The Wind, 1974; Don't Let The Sun Go Down On Me, 1974 (live version with George Michael, Number 1, UK and US, 1991); Philadelphia Freedom, 1975; Lucy In The Sky With Diamonds (Number 1, US), 1975; Island Girl (Number 1, US), 1975; Pinball Wizard, from film Tommy, 1976; Don't Go Breaking My Heart, duet with Kiki Dee (Number 1, UK and US), 1976; Sorry Seems To Be The Hardest Word, 1976; Song For Guy, 1979; Blue Eyes, 1982; I Guess That's Why They Call It The Blues, 1983; I'm Still Standing, 1983; Kiss The Bride, 1983; Sad Songs (Say So Much), 1984; Nikita, 1986; Sacrifice (Number 1, UK), 1989; True Love (with Kiki Dee), 1993; Made In England, 1995; Blessed, 1995; Believe, 1995; You Can Make History, 1996; If The River Can Bend, 1998; Written in the Stars, 1999; Contributor, That's What Friends Are For, Dionne Warwick And Friends (charity record), 1986; Albums include: Elton John, 1970; Tumbleweed Connection, 1971; Friends, 1971; 17-11-70, 1971; Madman Across The Water, 1972; Honky Chateau, 1972; Don't Shoot Me, I'm Only The Piano Player, 1973; Goodbye Yellow Brick Road, 1973; Caribou, 1974; Captain Fantastic And The Brown Dirt Cowboy, 1975; Rock Of The Westies, 1975; Here And There, 1976; Blue Moves, 1976; A Single Man, 1978; Lady Samantha, 1980; 21 At 33, 1980; Jump Up!, 1982; Too Low For Zero, 1983; Breaking Hearts, 1984; Ice On Fire, 1985; Leather Jackets, 1986; Live In Australia, 1987; Reg Strikes Back, 1988; Sleeping With The Past, 1989; The One, 1992; Made In England, 1995; Big Picture, 1997; Love Songs, 1995; Aida, 1999; El Dorado, 2000; Songs From the West Coast, 2001; Elton John – Greatest Hits, 1970-2002, 2002; Achievements: Wrote music for The Lion King, 1994, stage musical The Lion King plays at six theatre worldwide, 2001. Honours include: First album to go straight to Number 1 in US charts, Captain Fantastic..., 1975; Numerous Ivor Novello Awards for: Daniel, 1974; Don't Go Breaking My Heart, 1977; Song For Guy, 1979; Nikita, 1986; Sacrifice, 1991; Outstanding Contribution To British Music, 1986; Star on Hollywood Walk Of Fame, 1975; Madison Square Gardens Honours: Hall Of Fame, 1977; Walk Of Fame (first non-athlete), 1992; American Music Awards: Favourite Male Artist, Favourite Single, 1977; Silver Clef Award, Nordoff-Robbins Music Therapy, 1979; BRIT Awards: Outstanding Contribution To British Music, 1986; Best British Male Artist, 1991; Grammy, Best Vocal Performance By A Group, 1987; MTV Special Recognition Trophy, 1987; Hitmaker Award, National Academy of Popular Music, 1989; Honorary Life President, Watford Football Club, 1989; Inducted into Songwriters Hall Of Fame (with Bernie Taupin), 1992; Q Magazine Merit Award, 1993; Officer of Arts And Letters, Paris, 1993; KBE, 1998; Dr hc Royal Academy of Music, 2002; Grammy Lifetime, Achievement Award, 2000. Address: c/o Simon Prytherch, Elton Management, 7 King Street Cloisters, Clifton Walk, London, W6 0GY, England.

**JOHN Ricky,** b. 2 May 1957, Trinidad, West Indies. Education: BSc, Electrical Engineering, New Jersey Institute of Technology (NJIT), 1981; MSc, Management, NJIT, 1992; PhD, Engineering Management, Kennedy-Western University, 2000. Appointments: Flight Test Engineer for experimental test flights of US Space Shuttle Columbia, member, NASA Space Shuttle Launch Team, Kennedy Space Center, 1981-82; Systems Engineer, Airway Facilities Modernization Program, US Federal Aviation Administration (FAA), 1983-85, Selected to test one of world's first Weather Radar Display Systems, 1983; Program Administrator, New Jersey Department of Energy, 1985; Conceptual designer and installer: first multi-campus integrated computerized energy management system, New Jersey University of Medicine and Dentistry; Largest geothermal energy system of its kind, Stockton State College, New Jersey; Visiting Lecturer, John Donaldson Technical Institute in Port-of-Spain, Trinidad, 1982; Member, New Jersey Martin Luther King Commission Education Committee, 1987-90; Technical Advisor, New Jersey Board of Public Utilities, 1996-; Judge and presenter, NASA Awards for annual North New Jersey Regional Science Fair for secondary students, 1993-. Memberships: New Jersey Institute of Technology Alumni Association, Board of Trustees, 1991-, Vice President for Public Relations, 1996-98; Institute of Electrical and Electronic Engineers; New Jersey Aviation Hall of Fame; Notary Public, State of New Jersey, 1988-. Address: 350 Davis Avenue, Kearny, NJ 07032, USA.

**JOHNS David John,** b. 29 April 1931, Bristol, England. Chartered Engineer. Education: BSc (Eng), Aero Engineering, 1950-53, MSc (Eng), 1959, University of Bristol; PhD, 1967, DSc, 1985, Loughborough University. Appointments: Apprentice up to Section Leader, Bristol Aeroplane Co Ltd, 1949-57; Technical Officer, Sir W G Armstrong Whitworth Aircraft Ltd, 1957-58; Lecturer, Cranfield College of Aeronautics, 1958-64; Reader, Professor, 1964-83, Head of Department of Transport Technology, 1972-82; Senior Pro-Vice-Chancellor, 1982-83, Loughborough University; Foundation Director, City Polytechnic of Hong Kong, 1983-89; Vice-Chancellor and Principal, University of Bradford, 1989-98; Chairman, Prescription Pricing Authority, 1998-2001; Chairman, North and East Yorkshire and Northern Lincolnshire Strategic Health Authority; Chairman, Genetics and Insurance Committee. Publications: Monograph, Thermal Stress Analyses; 126 Technical articles; 40 papers on education, training et al. Honours: British Association for the Advancement of Science Brunel Lectureship in Engineering; Commander of the Order of the British Empire (CBE). Memberships: Chartered Engineer, Engineering Council, 1964; Fellow, Royal Aeronautical Society, 1969; Fellow, Institute of Acoustics, 1977-85; Fellow, Chartered Institute of Transport, 1977-85; Fellow, Hong Kong Institution of Engineers, 1984; Life Fellow, Aeronautical Society of India, 1986; Fellow, Royal Academy of Engineering, 1990. Address: 8 Swan Court, York Road, Harrogate, N. Yorks HG1 2QH, England. E-mail: david@johnshg1.fsnet.co.uk

**JOHNSON Alan Michael Borthwick,** b. 7 June 1944, Liverpool, England. Barrister. Education: Liverpool College, 1951-63; Corpus Christi College, Oxford, 1963-67. Appointments: Barrister at 1, Gray's Inn Square; Called to the Bar 1971; Member of the Middle Temple and Gray's Inn. Honours: MA; Harmsworth Scholarship, Middle Temple. Memberships: Oxford Society; South Eastern Circuit; Criminal Bar Association. Address: 1, Gray's Inn Square, Gray's Inn, London WC1R 5AA, England.

**JOHNSON Benjamin Sinclair Jr,** b. 30 December 1961, Falmouth, Jamaica. Professional Athlete; Coach. Honours: Phil Edwards Memorial Outstanding Track Athlete, 1984, 1985, 1986, 1987; Inducted into the Canadian Amateur Hall of Fame, 1985; Olympic Champion Award, 1985; Morton Crowe Award for Male Athlete of the Year, 1985, 1986, 1987; CTFA Track Jack W Davies Outstanding Athlete of the Year, 1985, 1986, 1987; Athlete of the Month, October 1985, January 1986, August 1987, January 1988, Sports Federation of Canada; Sports Excellence Award, 1986; IAAF/Mobil Grand Prix Standings

(Indoor), 1986; Lionel Connacher Award for Male Athlete of the Year, 1986, 1987; Jesse Owens International Trophy for Athletic Excellence, 1987; World Champion Award, 1987; The Tribute to Champions; Outstanding Athlete of the Year, 1986, 1987; Order of Canada, 1987. E-mail: benjohnson979@mail.com

**JOHNSON Betsey Lee,** b. 10 August 1942, Hartford, Connecticut, USA. Fashion Designer. m. (1) John Cale, 1966, 1 daughter, (2) Jeffrey Olivier, 1981. Education: Pratt Institute, New York; Syracuse University. Appointments: Editorial Assistant, Mademoiselle Magazine, 1964-65; Partner, Co-Owner, Betsey, Bunky & Nini, New York, 1969-; Shops in New York, Los Angeles, San Francisco, Coconut Grove, Florida, Venice, California, Boston, Chicago, Seattle; Principal Designer for Paraphernalia, 1965-69; Designer, Alvin Duskin Co, San Francisco, 1970; Head Designer, Alley Cat by Betsey Johnson (division of LeDamor Inc), 1970-74; Freelance Designer for Junior Women's Division, Butterick Pattern Co, 1971, Betsey Johnson for Jeanette Maternities Inc, 1974-75; Designer for Gant Shirtmakers Inc (women's clothing), 1974-75; Tric-Trac by Betsey Johnson (women's knitwear), 1974-76, Butterick's Home Sewing Catalog (children's wear), 1975-; Head Designer, Junior Sportswear Co; Designed for Star Ferry by Betsey Johnson & Michael Miles (children's wear), 1975-77; Owner, Head Designer, B J Inc, Designer, Wholesale Co, New York, 1978; President, Treasurer, B J Vines, New York; Opened Betsey Johnson Store, New York, 1979. Honours include: Merit Award, Mademoiselle Magazine, 1970; Coty Award, 1971; 2 Tommy Print Awards. Memberships: Council of Fashion Designers; American Women's Forum. Address: 110 East 9th Street, Suite A889, Los Angeles, CA 90079, USA.

**JOHNSON (Alexander) Boris de Pfeffel,** b. 19 June 1964, New York, USA. Member of Parliament. m. Marina Wheeler, 2 sons, 2 daughters. Education: Brakenbury Scholar, BA, Balliol College, Oxford. Appointments: Reporter, LEK Management Consultants, 1987, Trainee Reporter, The Times, 1987; Reporter, Wolverhampton Express and Star, 1988; Leader Writer, 1988, European Community Correspondent, Brussels, 1989-94, Assistant Editor, 1994, The Daily Telegraph; Editor, The Spectator, 1999-; Member of Parliament, Conservative, Henley-on-Thames, 2001-; Shadow Minister for the Arts, April-November 2004; Appearances on Radio and TV. Publications: Books: Friends, Voters and Country Men; Lend Me your Ears; Weekly column for the Daily Telegraph. Honours: Political Commentator of the Year, What the Papers Say, 1997; National Journalist of the Year, Pagan Federation of Great Britain, 1998; Editors' Editor of the Year, 2003; Columnist of the Year, British Press Awards, 2004; Channel 4 News Award for the person who made the biggest impression on the politics of 2004, 2005. Address: House of Commons, London SW1A 0AA, England.

**JOHNSON Charles (Richard),** b. 23 April 1948, Evanston, Illinois, USA. Professor of English; Writer. m. Joan New, June 1970, 1 son, 1 daughter. Education: BA, 1971, MA, 1973, Southern Illinois University; Postgraduate Studies, State University of New York at Stony Brook, 1973-76. Appointments: Assistant Professor, 1976-79, Associate Professor, 1979-82, Professor of English, 1982-, University of Washington, Seattle. Publications: Faith and the Good Thing, 1974; Oxherding Tale, 1982; The Sorcerer's Apprentice: Tales and Conjurations, 1986; Being and Race: Black Writing Since 1970, 1988; Middle Passage, 1990; All This and Moonlight, 1990; In Search of a Voice (with Ron Chernow), 1991; Dreamer, 1998. Honours: Governor's Award for Literature, State of Washington, 1983; National Book Award, 1990. Address: c/o Department of English, University of Washington, Seattle, WA 98105, USA.

**JOHNSON Christopher Louis McIntosh,** b. 12 June 1931, Thornton Heath, England. Economic Adviser. m. Anne Robbins, 1958, 1 son, 3 daughters. Education: MA 1st class honours, Philosophy, Politics and Economics, Magdalen College, Oxford. Appointments: Journalist, 1954-76, Paris Correspondent, 1959-63, The Times and Financial Times; Diplomatic Correspondent, Foreign Editor, Managing Editor, Director, Financial Times, 1963-76; Chief Economic Adviser, 1977-91, General Manager, 1985-91, Lloyds Bank; Visiting Professor of Economics, Surrey University, 1986-90; Visiting Scholar, IMF, 1993; Specialist Adviser to the Treasury Select Committee, House of Commons, 1981-97; Chairman, British Section of the Franco-British Council, 1993-97; UK Adviser, Association for the Monetary Union of Europe, 1991-2002. Publications: Editor, Lloyds Bank Review and Lloyds Bank Economic Bulletin, 1985-91; 4 books; Newspaper articles; Lectures on the euro and other economic and financial topics. Honours: Chevalier de la Legion d'Honneur, 1996. Memberships: Member, National Commission on Education, 1991-92; Member, Council of the Britain in Europe Campaign for the Euro; Member, Council of the Institute for Fiscal Studies; Chairman, New London Orchestra, 2001-04. Address: 39 Wood Lane, London N6 5UD, England. E-mail: johnson.c@blueyonder.co.uk

**JOHNSON Daniel Benedict,** b. 26 August 1957, London, England. Journalist; Writer. m. Sarah Johnson, 2 sons, 2 daughters. Education: BA 1st class, Modern History, Magdalen College, Oxford, 1978; Research Student, Cambridge, 1978-81; Shakespeare Scholar, Berlin, 1979-80. Appointments: Teaching Assistant, German History, Queen Mary College, London, 1982-84; Director of Publications, Centre for Policy Studies, 1983-84; The Daily Telegraph: Leader Writer, 1986-87; Bonn Correspondent, 1987-89; Eastern Europe Correspondent, 1989-90; The Times: Leader Writer, 1990-91; Literary Editor, 1992-96; Assistant Editor, Comment, 1996-98; The Daily Telegraph, Associate Editor, Culture, 1998-. Publications: Contributions to: The New Yorker; New York Times; Wall Street Journal; Washington Post; Commentary; The National Interest; Civilisation; The Spectator; Times Literary Supplement; Literary Review; Prospect; Encounter; many other journals; Books: Co-editor, German Neo-Liberals and the Social Market Economy, 1989; Introduction, Thomas Mann: Death in Venice and Other Stories; Introduction, Collected Stories, 2001. Address: c/o The Daily Telegraph, 1 Canada Square, Canary Wharf, London, E14 5DT, England. E-mail: daniel.johnson@telegraph.co.uk

**JOHNSON David,** b. 26 August 1927, Meir, Staffordshire, England. Historian. Education: Repton; Sandhurst. Publications: Sabre General, 1959; Promenade in Champagne, 1960; Lanterns in Gascony, 1965; A Candle in Aragon, 1970; Regency Revolution, 1974; Napoleon's Cavalry and its Leaders, 1978; The French Cavalry 1792-1815, 1989; Bonaparte's Sabres, 2003. Contributions to: The Armourer (1914: The Riddle of the Marne); Skirmish Magazine. Address: 64B John Street, Porthcawl, Mid-Glam CF36 3BD, Wales.

**JOHNSON Earvin (Magic Johnson),** b. 14 August 1959, Lansing, Michigan, USA. Basketball Player. m. Cookie Kelly, 1 son. Education: Michigan University. Appointments: Professional Basketball Player, Los Angeles Lakers National Basketball Association (NBA), 1979-91, (retired), Returned to professional sport, 1992, later announced abandonment of plans to resume sporting career; Chairman, Johnson Development Corporation, 1993-, Magic Johnson Entertainment, 1997-; Vice-President, Co-Owner, Los Angeles Lakers, 1994-, Head Coach, 1994; Presenter, TV Show, The Magic Hour, 1998-. Publications: Magic, 1983; What You Can Do to Avoid AIDS, 1992; My Life (autobiography), 1992. Honours include: Named,

Most Valuable Player, NBA Playoffs, 1980, 1982, 1987, NBA, 1987, 1989, 1990. Memberships include: NCAA Championship Team, 1979; National Basketball All-Star Team, 1980, 1982-89; National Basketball Association Championship Team, 1980, 1982, 1985, 1987, 1988; National AIDS Association. Address: Magic Johnson Foundation, Suite 1080, 1600 Corporate Pointe, Culver City, CA 90230, USA.

**JOHNSON Graham Lee,** b. 2 January 1953, Brighton, Sussex. Prison Governor. m. Aline, 1 son, 1 daughter. Education: Radio and Television Technician, Brighton Technical College; NVQ, Level 5, Operational Management; NVQ Level 5 Strategic Management; Professional Diploma in Management Studies. Appointments: Officer, HMP Lewes, 1977-88; Senior Officer, HMP Aldington, 1988-92; Principal Officer, Residential Governor, HMP High Down, 1992-96; Deputy Governor, HMHC Haslar, 1996-97; Deputy Governor, Governor, HMP Guys Marsh, 1997-2000; Project and Development Officer, South West Area Office, 2000-2001; Governor, HMP Dartmoor, 2001-2003; Performance Improvement Manager, Efficiency and Consultancy Group, Prison Service Headquarters, London, 2003-. Honour: Honours Award, Institute of Supervisory Management. Memberships: Fellow, Institute of Management; Fellow, Institute of Supervisory Management; Member, The Debrett's Society. Address: HM Prison Service Headquarters, Room 610, Abell House, John Islip Street, London SW1P 4LH, England. E-mail: graham.johnsonDA@hmps.gsi.gov.uk

**JOHNSON Hugh Eric Allan,** b. 10 March 1939, London, England. Author; Editor. m. Judith Eve Grinling, 1965, 1 son, 2 daughters. Education: BA, MA, King's College, Cambridge. Appointments: Feature Writer, Condé Nast Magazines, 1960-63; Editor, Wine and Food Magazine, 1962-63; Wine Correspondent, Sunday Times, 1963-67; Travel Editor, 1967; Editor, Queen Magazine, 1968-70; Wine Editor, Cuisine Magazine, New York, 1983-84; Editorial Director, 1975-90, Editorial Consultant, 1990-2005, The Garden; Chairman, Winestar Productions Ltd, The Movie Business, The Hugh Johnson Collection Ltd. Publications: Wine, 1966; The World Atlas of Wine, 1971, 4th edition, 1994, 5th edition with Jancis Robinson, 2001; The International Book of Trees, 1973, 2nd edition, 1994; The California Wine Book, with Bob Thompson, 1975; Hugh Johnson's Pocket Wine Book, annually, 1977-; The Principles of Gardening, 1979, revised edition, 1996; Hugh Johnson's Wine Companion, 1983, 5th edition, 2003; Hugh Johnson's Cellar Book, 1986; The Atlas of German Wines, 1986; Understanding Wine, A Sainsbury Guide, 1986; Atlas of the Wines of France, with Hubrecht Duijker, 1987; The Story of Wine, 1989, reissued, 1998; The Art and Science of Wine, with James Halliday, 1992; Hugh Johnson on Gardening, 1993; Tuscany and its Wines, 2000; Wine: A Life Uncorked, 2005; many articles on gastronomy, gardening and travel. Other: How to Handle a Wine, video, 1984; A History of Wine, Channel 4 TV series, 1989; Return Voyage, Star TV Hong Kong, 1992. Honours: Honorary Doctorate, University of Essex, 1998; Honorary Trustee, The American Institute for Wine, Food and the Arts, 2000; Fellow Commoner, King's, Cambridge, 2001; Chevalier De L'Ordre National Du Mérite, 2003; Hon. President, The International Wine & Food Society. Membership: President, Sunday Times Wine Club, 1973-; Founder Member, Tree Council, 1974; Circle of Wine Writers, President 1997-. Address: 73 St James's St, London, SW1A 1PH, England.

**JOHNSON Jenny, (Jennifer Hilary Harrower),** b. 2 November 1945, Bristol, England. Writer. m. Noel David Harrower, 28 April 1990, 1 son. Publications: Poetry: The Wisdom Tree, 1993; Neptune's Daughters, 1999; Recent contributions to: Poetry Salzburg Review. Honours: 4 Literary

Awards, Southwest Arts, 1978-92. Address: Ground Floor Flat, 6 Lyndhurst Road, Exmouth, Devon EX8 3DT, England. E-mail: jennyharrower@btinternet.com

**JOHNSON Michael,** b. 13 September 1967, Dallas, USA. Athlete. Education: Baylor University. Appointments: World Champion 200m, 1991, 400m & 4 x 400m, 1993, 200m, 400m & 4 x 400m (world record), 1995, 400m, 1997; Olympic Champion 4 x 400m (world record), 1992, 200m, 400m, 1996, World Record Holder 400m (indoors) 44.63 seconds, 1995, 4 x 400m (outdoors) 2.55.74, 1992, 2.54.29, 1993; Undefeated at 400m, 1989-97; First man to be ranked World No 1 at 200m and 400m simultaneously, 1990, 1991, 1994, 1995; World Record Holder for 400m Relay, 42.93 seconds; Olympic Champion, 200m (world record), 400m, Atlanta, 1996; Olympic Champion, 400m, Sydney 2000. Awards: Jesse Owens Award, 1994; Track and Field US Athlete of the Year (four times). Address: USA Track & Field, PO Box 120, Indianapolis, IN 46206, USA.

**JOHNSON Peter Alec Barwell,** b. 26 July 1936, England. m. Gay Marilyn Lindsay, 2 daughters. Education: Uppingham. Appointments: Founder, The British Sporting Art Trust; East Anglian Committee and Member, Executive Council, Historic Houses Association; Chairman and Managing Director, Arthur Ackermann & Peter Johnson Ltd; Council Member, British Antique Dealers' Association, 1970-80; Chairman, Hans Town Ward Conservatives, 1969-72; Chairman, Cleaner Royal Borough, 1989-91; British Delegate, Conseil Internationale de la Chasse; Governor, Kimbolton School, 1993-2000; Member, Cromwell Museum Management Committee; Founder Trustee, Colvin Fire Prevention Trust, 2000-; Guide, Chelsea Physic Garden; Inventor (with John Barwell) of a weed-gathering hoe (Jo-Hoe), 1994. Publication: Book, The Nasmyth Family (with E Money, 1977). Memberships: Buck's; Hurlingham. Address: 86 Onslow Gardens, London SW7 3BS, England.

**JOHNSON Rex Sutherland,** b. 24 August 1928, Essex, England. Chartered Architect; Arbitrator; Expert Witness. m. Betty E Johnson, deceased, 2 sons. Education: Diploma of Architecture, London University. Appointments: Assistant Architect, Senior Architect, T P Bennett and Son; Junior Partner, Oliver Law and Partners, 1961-63; T P Bennett and Son, 1963-65; Associate Partner, 1965-69, Senior Partner, 1969-90, Ronald Ward and Partners; Retired, 1990; Consultant, Design 5, London. Memberships: Fellow, Royal Institute of British Architects; Fellow, Chartered Institute of Arbitrators; Founder Member, Society of Expert Witnesses; Trustee, Royal Wanstead Childrens Foundation. Address: Whitepines, Longmill Lane, Crouch, Nr Sevenoaks, Kent TN15 8QB, England. Email: beejons@aol.com

**JOHNSON Robin Stanley,** b. 23 January 1944, High Wycombe, Buckinghamshire, England. University Lecturer; Academic Mathematician. m. Rosalind Ann, 2 sons. Education: BSc (Eng), Aeronautics, MSc, Theoretical Aerodynamics, 1962-66, PhD, 1967-69, Imperial College, London. Appointments: Lecturer, Applied Mathematics, 1969-81, Senior Lecturer, Applied Mathematics, 1981-94, Reader, Applied Mathematics, 1994-, University of Newcastle upon Tyne. Publications: Books: Solitons: an Introduction (with P G Drazin), 1989, reprinted with corrections, 1993; An introduction to the mathematical theory of water waves, 1997; Singular perturbation theory, in press 2004; Articles in scientific journals include most recently: The classical problem of water waves: a reservoir of integrable and nearly integrable equations, 2003; The Camassa-Holm equation for water waves moving over a shear flow, 2003; On solutions of the Camassa-Holm equation, 2003; Some contributions to the theory of edge waves, to appear. Memberships: Fellow, Institute of Mathematics and its Applications; Chartered Mathematician. Address: School of Mathematics and Statistics, University of Newcastle upon Tyne, Newcastle upon Tyne NE1 7RU. E-mail: r.s.johnson@ncl.ac.uk

**JOHNSON Sallie Jean,** b. 25 September 1954, San Marcos, Texas, USA. Dean of Distance Learning. m. Charles M Johnson, 4 sons. Education: AS, Liberal Arts, Education and Music 1989, BS, Liberal Arts, Psychology and Education, 1990, University of The State of New York; MA, Human Resources Development, Webster University, St Louis, Missouri, 1991; PhD, Computing Technology in Education, Nova Southeastern University, Fort Lauderdale, Florida, 2001; Distance Education Certificate, State University of West Georgia, 2001. Appointments: Assistant Center Director, Embry-Riddle Aeronautical University, 1985-89; Adjunct Faculty Member, Asian Division, University of Maryland, Okinawa, Japan, 1990-93, Multimedia Learning/Distance Learning Center Director, Asian Division, 1991-93 University of Maryland; Human Resources Training Co-ordinator, Humana Health Care Plans, Corpus Christi, Texas, 1994-95; Administrator, NAS Corpus Christi and NS Ingleside, 1995-96, Centre Director, Corpus Christi and Honolulu, Hawaii, 1996-99, Embry-Riddle Aeronautical University; Associate Director of Distance Learning, 1999-2001, Dean of Distance Learning, 2001-, Troy University, Troy Alabama. Publications: Articles in professional journals and conference proceedings include most recently: Computer Concepts and Application, 2001; Using Student Feedback to Improve and Revise Your Course, 2004; Using Color to Enhance Student Learning, 2004; Meeting Students 24/7 Needs Through Selective Outsourcing, 2004; Dynamic Training for Distance Inductors: The Key to Enhancing Online Learning, 2005. Honours include: Award for Best Symposium Presentation, 2nd Alabama Distance Learning Symposium, 2001; Presenter, World-Wide Department of Defense Conference, 2003; Guest speaker and Keynote speaker at numerous conferences and symposia; Excellence in Distance Learning Administrative Award, 2005; Empire Who's Who Among Executives and Professionals Award, 2005; Woman of the Year 2005, American Biographical Institute; Listed in Who's Who publications and biographical dictionaries. Memberships: Association for Computing Machinery; Western Co-operative of Educational Telecommunications; United States Distance Learning Association; The Learning Resources Network. Address: 304 Wallace Hall, Troy University, Troy, AL 36082, USA. E-mail: s.johnson@troy.edu

**JOHNSON Stanley P,** b. 18 August 1940. Consultant. m. (1) Charlotte Fawcett, 1963, dissolved 1979, 3 sons, 1 daughter, (2) Jennifer Arnell, 1981, 1 son, 1 daughter. Education: BA, MA, Exeter College, Oxford, 1959-63; Harkness or Commonwealth Fund Fellowship, State University of Iowa and Columbia University, New York, 1964; MSc, Agricultural Economics, Oxford, 1964-65. Appointments: United Kingdom Foreign Office, 1964-65; World Bank, Washington DC, 1966-69; United Nations Association of the United States, UNA-USA, 1968-69; Ford Foundation Fellow, London School of Economics, 1969-70; Conservative Research Department, 1969-70; International Planned Parenthood Federation, 1970-73; Head of EC's Prevention of Pollution and Nuisances Division, Adviser to EC Director-General for Environment, European Commission, Brussels, 1973-79; MEP for East Hampshire and the Isle of Wight, Vice Chairman of Committee on the Environment, Public Health and Consumer Protection, European Parliament, 1979-84; Adviser to Director-General Environment, Director of Energy Policy (DG XVII), European Commission, Brussels, 1984-90; Food and Agriculture Organisation of the United Nations, 1990-92; Director, International and Policy Services, Environmental Resources Management, 1992-94; Special

Adviser on the Environment to Coopers and Lybrand, 1994-96; Senior Adviser, International Fund for Animal Welfare, 1996-2003. Publications: Author, 20 books (11 non-fiction and 9 fiction); Articles in professor and popular journals; Speeches at national and international conferences. Honours: Newdigate Prize for English Verse, Oxford University, 1962; Greenpeace Prize for Outstanding Services to the Environment, 1984; Royal Society for the Prevention of Cruelty to Animals, Richard Martin Award for Outstanding Services to Animal Welfare, 1984; Cited by London Times as "environmentalist of the year" for world on EU habitats directive, 1989. Memberships: Consultant, UNDP/UNFPA, 1969-97;Consultant, World Bank Operations Evaluation Unit, 1970; Member, UK Countryside Commission, 1971-73; Fellow, Overseas Development Institute, London; Fellow, Institute for the Study of International Organisations, Sussex University, 1970-73; General Editor, Kluwer Law International series of books on Environmental Law and Policy, 1987-97; Consultant (at Coopers and Lybrand) to UNEP, 1992-92; Consultant FAO for follow-up to Rio Forest Principles, 1994; Trustee, Earthwatch Institute Europe, 1995-2001; Trustee, Plantlife International, 2002-; Trustee, Dian Fossey Gorilla Fund, 2004-. Address: 60 Regents Park Road, London NW1 7SX, England.

**JOHNSON William,** b. 20 April 1922, Manchester, England. University Professor. m. Heather M Thornber, 1946, 3 sons, 2 daughters. Education: BSc.Tech., UMIST, 1943; REME Commd. 1943-47; BSc Mathematics, London, 1948; DSc, Manchester University, 1960; FRS, 1982 FREng, 1983. Appointments: Professor of Mechanical Engineering, UMIST, 1960-75; Professor of Mechanics, Engineering Department, University of Cambridge, 1975-82; Visiting Professor, Industrial Engineering Department, 1984-85, United Technologies Distinguished Professor of Engineering, 1987-89, Purdue University, Indiana, USA; Visiting Professor of Mechanical Engineering and History of Science, UMIST, 1992-94. Publications (with co-author): Plasticity for Mechanical Engineers, 1962; Mechanics of Metal Extrusion, 1962; Bibliography of Slip Line Fields, 1968; Impact Strength of Materials, 1972; Engineering Plasticity, 1973; Engineering Plasticity: Metal Forming Processes, 1978; Crashworthiness of Vehicles, 1978; Bibliography of Slip Line Fields, 1982; Collected papers on Benjamin Robins, 2001-03; Record and Services Satisfactory, 2003. Honours include: Safety in Mechanical Engineering Prize, 1980, 1990; James Clayton Prize, Institution of Mechanical Engineers, 1987; Bernard Hall Prize, 1965, 1967; Silver Medal, Institute of Sheet Metal, 1987; AMPT Gold Medal, Dublin, 1995; ASME Engineer-Historian Award, 2001; Honorary DSc, Bradford University, 1976, Sheffield University, 1986, UMIST, 1995. Memberships: Foreign Fellow, Academy of Athens, 1982; Foreign Member, Russian Academy of Science, Ural Branch, 1993; Indian National Academy of Engineering, 1999; Fellow of University College, London, 1981. Address: 62 Beach Road, Carlyon Bay, St Austell, Cornwall PL25 3PJ, England.

**JOHNSTON Barrie Colin,** b. 7 August 1925, London, England. Retired Merchant Banker. m. Cynthia Anne, 1 son, 1 daughter. Appointments: Junior Clerk, Helbert Wagg & Co Ltd, 1941-43; War Service, Royal Marines, Commissioned, 1945, Qualified as Intelligence Officer, Served in 34th Amphibious Regiment RM in SEAC, 1943-46; Rejoined Helbert Wagg, 1946, amalgamated in 1960 to J Henry Schroder Wagg & Co Ltd; Promoted later to Assistant Director of the Bank; Created Schroder Life Assurance, on the Board for 2 years; Member of team that formed first Property Unit Trust for Pension Funds in 1966, began lecturing on Pension and Property matters, 1946-72; Director, Charterhouse Japhet, 1972-84; Chairman, Charterhouse Bank, Jersey for 5 years; Retired, 1984; Non-executive Director,

Charterhouse Investment Management, 1984-86; Additional Business Interests: The Pension Fund Property Unit Trust, 1966-89; The Charities Property Unit Trust, 1967-88; The Pension Fund Agricultural Property Trust, 1976-89; Non-executive Director, T H White Ltd, 1980-87; Director, Mornington Building Society, 1988-91; Director, ML-MIM European Equity Revival Fund NV, 1990-98; Chairman, Honorary Treasurer, or Trustee of 20 charities, 1984-2003. Publications: Articles in professional magazines and newspapers; lectures to professional bodies; Book, Life's a Lottery – or is it?, 2001. Honour OBE, 1994. Memberships: Fellow, Pensions Management Institute; Associate UK Society of Investment Professionals; Honorary Fellow, Royal College of Radiologists; Honorary Member, Royal Electrical and Mechanical Engineers Institution; Fellow, Royal Society of the Arts. Address: Yew Cottage, 8 The Green, Ewell, Surrey KT17 3JN, England.

**JOLLEY (Monica) Elizabeth,** b. 4 June 1923, Birmingham, England. Writer; Tutor. m. Leonard Jolley, 1 son, 2 daughters. Education: Nursing Training, 1940-46. Appointment: Writer-in-Residence, Western Australia Institute of Technology, later Curtin University of Technology, Perth, 1980-. Publications: Five Acre Virgin and Other Stories, 1976; The Travelling Entertainer, 1979; Palomino, 1980; The Newspaper of Claremont Street, 1981; Mr Scobie's Riddle, 1983; Woman in a Lampshade, 1983; Miss Peabody's Inheritance, 1983; Milk and Honey, 1984; The Well, 1986; The Sugar Mother, 1988; My Father's Moon, 1989; Cabin Fever, 1990; Central Mischief, 1992; The Georges' Wife, 1993; Diary of a Weekend Farmer (poems), 1993; The Orchard Thieves, 1995; Lovesong, 1997; An Accommodating Spouse, 1998. Honours: Honorary Doctorate, Western Australia Institute of Technology, 1986; Officer of the Order of Australia, 1988; Honorary Doctor of Literature, Macquarie University, Sydney, 1995, University of New South Wales, 2000; Honorary Doctorate, University of Queensland, 1997. Address: 28 Agett Road, Claremont, Western Australia 6010, Australia.

**JONAS Hilda (Klestadt),** b. 21 January 1913, Düsseldorf, Germany. Concert Harpsichordist and Pianist; Teacher of Harpsichord and Piano. m. Gerald Jonas, 30 January 1938, 2 daughters. Education: Hochschule für Musik, Cologne, 1932-33; Honour Diploma, Gumpert Conservatory, 1934; Studies with Professor Michael Wittels, Cologne, Rudolf Serkin, Switzerland and Wanda Landowska, Paris, France. Career: Concert soloist and recitalist worldwide with recitals in France, Germany, Spain, Italy, Austria, Belgium, Australia, New Zealand, Hawaii, USA; Colleges, Universities, museums and art centres, Harvard, Carnegie-Mellon, Cincinnati Taft Museum, Haifa Music Museum, Milano Centro Culturale San Fedele, Empire Saal of Schloss Esterházy, Eisenstadt, Brussel's Musée Instrumental, Castello Buonconsiglio, Trento, Palais Wittgenstein, Düsseldorf, Stanford University, California, Palace of the Legion of Honour San Francisco, San Francisco State University, Goethe Institute, California West Coast from Olympia Evergreen State College to Santa Barbara, Westmont, Ventura, Monterey Peninsula Colleges, Sacramento Crocker Art Museum, Ojai Valley Art Center and other cultural centres in Marin County and San Francisco; Soloist with major symphony orchestras including: Cleveland, Cincinnati; Regular series and May festivals under Max Rudolf and Josef Krips, Honolulu, Oxford, Jerusalem, Strasbourg and elsewhere; Owner of private piano studio, Honolulu, 1938-42 and Cincinnati, 1942-75; Founder, 1965, Director, 1965-75, Harpsichord Festival Put-in-Bay, Ohio. Recordings include: Listen Rebecca, The Harpsichord Sounds, for children of all ages; Johann Kuhnau: Six Biblical Sonatas, with text based on authentic edition; Hilda Plays Bach: Italian Concerto, Chromatic Fantasia and Fugue, Partita 1, Capriccio on the departure of his beloved brother, and others; Johann Sebastian Bach: Goldberg Variations. Contributions to: Various music magazines. Memberships: Life Member, Hadassah; Life Member, Brandeis University. Address: 50 Chumasero Drive 1-L, San Francisco, CA 94132, USA.

**JONAS Peter (Sir),** b. 14 October 1946, London, England. General and Artistic Director, Bavarian State Opera. m. Lucy Hull, 1989, divorced 2001. Education: BA honours, University of Sussex; LRAM, FRNCM, 2000, Royal Northern College of Music; CAMS, Fellow, FRCM 1989, Royal College of Music; Eastman School of Music, University of Rochester, USA. Appointments: Assistant to Music Director, 1974-76, Artistic Administrator, 1976-85, Chicago Symphony Orchestra; Director of Artistic Administration, Orchestral Association of Chicago, Chicago Symphony Orchestra, Chicago Civic Orchestra, Chicago Symphony Chorus, Allied Arts Association, Orchestra Hall, 1977-85; General Director, ENO, 1985-93; General and Artistic Director, Bavarian State Opera, 1993-; Chairman, Deutsche Opernkonferenz (Congress of German and European Opera House Directors), 1999-2005. Publications: with Mark Elder and David Pountney, Power House, 1992; Co-author, Eliten und Demokratie, 1999-2005; Lecturer, University of St Gallen (CH), 2001-; Lecturer, University of Zürich, 2003-. Honours: FRSA, 1989; CBE, 1993; Honorary DrMus, Sussex, 1994; Knighted 2000; Bayerische Verdienstorden (Distinguished Service Cross), 2001; Bavarian Constitutional Medal, 2001; Member, Bavarian Academy of Fine Arts, 2005-; Queen's Lecture, Berlin, 2001. Memberships: Advisory Board, Hypo-Vereinsbank, 1994-2004; Board of Governors, Bayerische Rundfunk, 1999-2006; Board of Management, National Opera Studio, 1985-93; Council, RCM, 1988-95; Council, London Lighthouse, 1990-94. Address: Bayerische Staätsoper, Nationaltheater, Max-Joseph-Platz 2, 80539 München, Germany.

**JONES Catherine Zeta,** b. England. Actress. m. Michael Douglas, 1 son, 1 daughter. Creative Works: Stage appearances include: The Pyjama Game; Annie; Bugsy Malone; 42nd Street; Street Scene; TV appearances include: Darling Buds of May; Out of the Blue; Cinder Path, 1994; Return of the Native, 1995; Titanic, 1996; Film appearances include: Scheherazade; Coup de Foudre; Splitting Heirs, 1993; Blue Juice, 1995; The Phantom, 1996; The Mask of Zorro, 1997; Entrapment, 1998; The Haunting, 1999; Traffic, 2000; America's Sweethearts, 2001; Chicago, 2002; Monkeyface, 2003. Honours: Best Supporting Actress, BAFTA Awards, 2003; Screen Actors Guild Awards, 2003; Academy Awards, 2003. Address: c/o ICM Ltd, Oxford House, 76 Oxford Street, London W1N 0AX, England.

**JONES Della,** b. Neath, South Wales, United Kingdom. Opera/Concert Singer. m. Paul Vigars, 1 son. Education; Neath Girls' Grammar School; GRSM, Royal College of Music; LRAM (Singing), ARCM (Piano), Kathleen Ferrier Scholarship. Appointments: Member, with leading roles, ENO, 1977-82; Guest Artist, ENO, also ROH; Currently sings with all major opera companies, overseas concert and operatic appearances in all major European countries, also Russia, Japan, and USA; Prolific recordings on radio and television with all major recording companies. Honours: Honorary FWCMD, 1995; Honorary Fellow, University of Wales, Swansea, 1999. Address: c/o Music International, 13 Ardilaun Road, Highbury, N5 2QR, London, England.

**JONES Douglas Gordon,** b. 1 January 1929, Bancroft, Ontario, Canada. Retired Professor; Poet. Education: MA, Queen's University, Kingston, Ontario, 1954. Appointment: Professor, University of Sherbrooke, Quebec, 1963-94. Publications: Poetry: Frost on the Sun, 1957; The Sun Is Axeman, 1961;

Phrases from Orpheus, 1967; Under the Thunder the Flowers Light Up the Earth, 1977; A Throw of Particles: Selected and New Poems, 1983; Balthazar and Other Poems, 1988; The Floating Garden, 1995; Wild Asterisks in Cloud, 1997; Grounding Sight (poetry), 1999. Other: Butterfly on Rock: A Study of Themes and Images in Canadian Literature, 1970. Honours: President's Medal, University of Western Ontario, 1976; Governor General's Award for Poetry, 1977, and for Translation, 1993; Honorary DLitt, Guelph University, 1982. Address: 120 Hougton Street, North Hatley, Quebec JOB 2CO, Canada.

**JONES George Glenn,** b. 12 September 1931, Saratoga, Texas, USA. Country Singer; Musician (guitar). m. Tammy Wynette, 1969-75; Nancy Sepulveda, 1983. Career: Recording artist, 1953-; Worked under names of Johnny Williams, Hank Davis, Glen Patterson; Worked with The Big Bopper; Johnny Preston; Johnny Paycheck; Recorded duets with Gene Pitney; Melba Montgomery; Tammy Wynette; Elvis Costello; James Taylor; Willie Nelson. Compositions include: The Window Up Above, Mickey Gilley; Seasons Of My Heart, Johnny Cash, Jerry Lee Lewis. Recordings: 150 Country hits include: Why Baby Why; White Lightning; Tender Years; She Still Thinks I Care; You Comb Her Hair; Who Shot Sam?; The Grand Tour; He Stopped Loving Her Today; Recorded over 450 albums; Recent albums include: First Time Live, 1985; Who's Gonna Fill Their Shoes, 1985; Wine Coloured Roses, 1986; Super Hits, 1987; Too Wild Too Long, 1987; One Woman Man, 1989; Hallelujah Weekend, 1990; You Oughta Be Here With Me, 1990; And Along Came Jones, 1991; Friends In High Places, 1991; Salutes Bob Wills and Hank Williams, 1992; Live At Dancetown USA, 1992; Walls Can Fall, 1992; One, 1995; I Lived to Tell It All, 1996; In a Gospel Way, 1997; It Don't Get Any Better Than This, 1998; The Cold Hard Truth, 1999; Live with the Possum, 1999; with Tammy Wynette: We Can Go Together, 1971; Me And The First Lady, 1972; Golden Ring, 1976; Together Again, 1980. Address: Razor & Tie, 214 Sullivan Street, Suite 4A, New York, NY 10012, USA.

**JONES George William,** b. 4 February 1938, Wolverhampton, England. Retired University Professor. m. Diana Mary, 1 son, 1 daughter. Education: Jesus College, Oxford, 1957-60; Nuffield College, Oxford, 1960-63. Appointments: Assistant Lecturer in Government, 1963-65, Lecturer in Government, 1965-66, Leeds University; Lecturer in Political Science, 1966-71, Senior Lecturer in Political Science, 1971-74, Reader in Political Science, 1974-76, Professor of Government, 1976-2003, Professor Emeritus, 2003-, London School of Economics. Publications: Borough Politics, 1969; Herbert Morrison, 1973, 2nd edition 2001; Case for Local Government, 2nd edition 1985; West European Prime Ministers, 1991; At the Centre of Whitehall, 1998; Regulation Inside Government, 1999. Honours: BA, 1960; MA, 1965; D Phil, 1965; FRHisS, 1980; OBE, 1999. Memberships: Honorary Fellow, University of Wolverhampton, 1986; Layfield Committee on Local Government Finance, 1974-76; Joint Working Party on Internal Management of Local Authorities, 1992-93; Beacon Council's Advisory Panel, 1999-2002; National Consumer Council, 1991-99. Address: Department of Government, LSE, Houghton Street, London WC2A 2AE, England. E-mail: g.w.jones@lse.ac.uk

**JONES Grace,** b. 19 May 1952, Spanishtown, Jamaica. Singer; Model; Actress. m. Atila Altaunbay, 1996. Education: Syracuse University. Appointments: Fashion Model, New York, Paris; Made 1st Album, Portfolio, for Island Records, 1977; Debut as Disco Singer, New York, 1977; Founder, La Vie en Rose Restaurant, New York, 1987. Creative Works: Films include: Conan the Destroyer; A View to a Kill, 1985; Vamp; Straight to

Hell; Siesta; Boomerang, 1991; Albums include: Fame; Muse; Island Life; Slave to the Rhythm.

**JONES Hazel Emma (Main),** b. 6 April 1919. Retired Librarian. m. Clifford Henry Jones, deceased, 2 sons, 3 daughters. Education: BA, University of Melbourne, 1943; Certificate of Costume Designer, School of Art, Queensland University of Technology, 1966-68; ALAA, 1974; Certificate of Graduation, Sheffield School of Interior Design, 1995. Appointments: Cataloguer, Medical Librarian, University of Melbourne, 1935-45; Catalogued at Church Grammar School, 1969; Graduate Clerk, Library, Department of Works, Australia, 1970-71; Temporary Librarian, Greenslopes Repatriation Hospital, 1971-72; Deputy Librarian to Acting Librarian, State Department of Health, 1973-84; Since retirement, Cataloguer, Trinity Theological College; Cataloguer, Morningside College of Art, Griffith University Campus. Publications: Financial statements and annual reports. Honours: Member, Australian Institute of Librarians, 1940; Fellow, International Biographical Centre, Cambridge; Joined American Biographical Institute. Memberships: Friends of Queensland Art Gallery; Friends of the Conservatorium , 1976-; Life Member, AILIA; ARLIS/ANZ; Research Officer, IBC; ABI Genealogical Society, 1997. Address: 35 Greer Street, Bardon 4065, Brisbane, Queensland, Australia.

**JONES Huw,** b. 5 May 1948, Manchester, England. Broadcasting Executive. m. Siân Marylka Miarczynska, 1979, 1 son, 1 daughter. Education: BA, Modern Languages (French), MA, Oxon. Appointments: Pop Singer, Recording Artist, Television Presenter, 1968-76; Director, General Manager, Sain Recording Company, 1969-81; Chairman, Barcud Cyf (TV Facilities), 1981-93; Managing Director, Producer, Teledu'r Tir Glas Cyf (independent production company), 1982-93; First Chairman, Teledwyr Annibynnol Cymru (Welsh Independent Producers), 1984-86; Chief Executive, S4C (Welsh Fourth Channel), 1994-2005. Honours: Honorary Fellow, University of Wales, Aberystwyth; Member, Gorsedd of Bards National Eisteddfod of Wales; Fellow, Royal Television Society. Memberships: Chairman, Celtic Film and Television Co Ltd, 2001-2004; Director, Sgrin Cyf; Director, Skillset Ltd; Chairman, Skillset Cymru; Member, British Screen Advisory Council. Address: S4C, Parc Ty Glas, Llanishen, Cardiff, C14 5DU, Wales. E-mail: huw.jones@s4c.co.uk

**JONES James Earl,** b. 17 January 1931, Mississippi, USA. Actor. m. Cecilia Hurt, 1982. Education: University of Michigan. Creative Works: Numerous stage appearances on Broadway and elsewhere including, Master Harold...And the Boys, Othello, King Lear, Hamlet, Paul Robeson, A Lesson From Aloes, Of Mice & Men, The Iceman Cometh, A Hand is on the Gate, The Cherry Orchard, Danton's Death, Fences; Frequent TV appearances; Voice of Darth Vader in films Star Wars, The Empire Strikes Back, The Return of the Jedi; Films include: Matewan; Gardens of Stone; Soul Man; My Little Girl; The Man; The End of the Road; Dr Strangelove; Conan the Barbarian; The Red Tide; A Piece of the Action; The Last Remake of Beau Geste; The Greatest; The Heretic; The River Niger; Deadly Hero; Claudine; The Great White Hope; The Comedians; Coming to America; Three Fugitives; Field of Dreams; Patriot Games; Sommersby; The Lion King (voice); Clear and Present Danger; Cry the Beloved Country; Lone Star; A Family Thing; Gang Related; Rebound; Summer's End; Undercover Angel, 1999; Quest for Atlantis, 1999; On the Q.T., 1999; Finder's Fee, 2001; Recess Christmas: A Miracle on Third Street (voice), 2001. Honours include: Tony Award; Golden Globe Award; Honorary DFA, Princeton, Yale, Michigan.

**JONES Lucy,** b. 1955, London, England. Artist. Education: Byam Shaw School of Drawing and Painting, 1974-76; BA, 1st Class Honours, Camberwell School of Art, 1976-79; Master of Arts, Royal College of Art, 1979-82; The Rome Scholarship in Painting, The British School at Rome, 1982-84. Career: One Person Exhibitions: Artist of the Day, Angela Flowers Gallery, London, 1986; Paintings and Drawings, Spitalfields Health Centre (in association with the Whitechapel Art Gallery, London), 1987; Angela Flowers Gallery, 1987, 1989; Lucy Jones on Lucy Jones, Drumcroon Art Education Centre, Wigan, 1989; Flowers East, London, 1991, 1993, 1995, 1997, 1999, 2000, 2001; Riverside Studios, London, 1996; Flowers Graphics, London, 1998, 1999, 2001, 2003; Flowers West, Santa Monica, California, 1999; Flowers Central, 2002; Numerous group exhibitions 1981-; Works in many public collections. Publications: Works featured in catalogues, newspapers and magazines, nationally and internationally. Honours and Commissions: Cubitt Award for Painting, 1980; Anstruther Award for Painting, 1982; Rome Scholarship for Painting, 1982-84; Oppenheim-John Downes Memorial Trust, 1986; RA Summer Exhibition, Daler-Rowney Award for the best work in oil, 1989; Prize Winner, John Moore's Exhibition, Walker Art Gallery, Liverpool, 1995; The Cabinet Office, Admiralty Arch, London, 2002; Graham Young Print Prize, Royal Academy Summer Exhibition, 2002; Hunting Art Prize, 2004. Address: c/o Flowers East, 82 Kingsland Road, London E2 8DP, England.

**JONES Marjorie Pope,** b. 15 August 1947, Bronx, New York, USA. Elementary Teacher. m. Maurice Jones Jr, 2 sons, 1 daughter. Education: Clark University; Teacher's College, Colombia University. Appointments: Operating Room Technician; Actress, appeared in The Edge of the Night and The Doctors (Soaps), 1965-66; Teacher, Uniondale Public Schools. Honours: Principals Award for 18 Years of Perfect Attendance; Leading Educator of the World, International Biographical Centre, 2005; Listed in Who's Who publications and biographical dictionaries. Memberships: New York State United Teachers; Uniondale Teachers Association; NACCP; African American Genealogical Society. Address: 383 Washington Avenue, Roosevelt, NY 11575, USA. E-mail: milavelt@yahoo.com

**JONES Martyn David,** b. 1 March 1947, Crewe, Cheshire, England. Member of Parliament. Divorced, 1 son, 1 daughter. Education: Liverpool College of Commerce; CIBiol, Liverpool Polytechnic; MIBiol, Trent Polytechnic. Appointments: Microbiologist, Wrexham Lager Beer Company, 1969-87; Councillor, Clwyd County Council, 1981-89; MP for Clwyd South (formerly Clwyd South West), 1987-; Opposition Spokesperson on Food, Agriculture and Rural Affairs, 1994-95; Labour Whip; 1988-92; Speaker's Panel of Chairmen, 1993-94; Chairman, Welsh Affairs Select Committee, 1997. Memberships: Council Member, Royal College of Veterinary Surgeons; SERA, Fabian Society; Christian Socialist Movement; Federation of Economic Development Authorities; Institute of Biology. Address: House of Commons, London, SW1A 0AA, England. E-mail: jonesst@parliament.uk

**JONES Mike,** b. 7 March 1951, Cheshire, England. Post Office Employee; Poet. Publication: Scars and Glory, 1980. Contributions to: Countryman; Outposts; Orbis; New Poetry; Envoi; Candelabrum; Artful reporter; Ipsel; Weyfarers; Chester Poets, Vols 6-12; Meridian; Allusions. Memberships: Mid Cheshire Writers Group, founder; Crewe and District Writers Group; Chester Poets. Address: Glyndwr Cottage, Birch Heath, Tarporley, Cheshire CW6 9UR, England.

**JONES Peter Howard,** b. 18 December 1935, London, England. Emeritus Professor of Philosophy. 2 daughters. Education: Queens' College, Cambridge. Appointments: Lecturer then Reader in Philosophy, 1964-84, Professor of Philosophy, 1984-98, now Emeritus, Director, Institute for Advanced Studies in the Humanities, 1986-2000, University of Edinburgh; Director and Trustee, Foundation for Advanced Studies in the Humanities, 1997-2002; Visiting Professor of Philosophy, University of Rochester, New York, 1969-70; Visiting Professor of Philosophy, Carleton College, Minnesota, 1974; Visiting Professor of Philosophy, Oklahoma University, 1978; Visiting Professor of Philosophy, Baylor University, 1978; Visiting Professor of Philosophy, Dartmouth College, New Hampshire, 1973, 1983; Visiting Fellow, Calgary Institute for Humanities, 1992; Visiting Professor of Philosophy, University of Malta, 1993; Visiting Professor of Philosophy, Belarussian State University, 1997; Visiting Fellow, Humanities Research Centre, ANU, 1984, 2002; Member Spoliation Advisory Panel, 2000-; Visiting Professor of Philosophy, Jagiellonian University, Krakow, 2001-. Publications: Over 100 articles and reviews on philosophy and cultural topics; Books: Philosophy and the Novel, 1975; Hume's Sentiments, 1982; A Hotbed of Genius (editor), 1986; Philosophy and Science in the Scottish Enlightenment (editor), 1988; Philosophy and Science in the Scottish Enlightenment (editor), 1989; Adam Smith Reviewed (editor), 1992; Investigation of the Principles of Knowledge, by James Hutton (editor), 1999; The Enlightenment World (editor), 2004; Elements of Criticism, by Lord Kames (editor), 2005; The Reception of David Hume in Europe (editor), 2005. Honours: FRSE, 1989; FRSA, 1990; FSAScot, 1993; Lothian Lecturer, City of Edinburgh, 1993; Gifford Lecturer, University of Aberdeen, 1994-95; Loemker Lecturer, Emory University, Georgia, USA, 1995-96. Memberships: UNESCO Forum on Tolerance, Tbilisi, 1995; UNESCO Dialogue on Europe and Islam, 1997-; Trustee, National Museums of Scotland, 1987-99; Member Court, University of Edinburgh, 1987-90; Member, Council, Royal Society of Edinburgh, 1992-95; Trustee, Fettes College, 1995-; Trustee, Scots at War, 1999-; Trustee Policy Institute, 1999-. Address: 6 Greenhill Terrace, Edinburgh EH10 4BS, Scotland.

**JONES Peter Ivan,** b. 14 December 1942, Cosham, Hampshire, England. Chairman of the Tote. m. Elizabeth Gent, 2 sons, 2 daughters. Education: BSc Economics, London School of Economics, 1964; MIPA, 1967. Appointments: Chief Executive, Boase Massimi Pollitt, 1988-89; Chief Executive, 1989-93, Director, 1989-97, Omnicom UK plc; President, Racehorse Owners Association, 1990-93; Member, Horserace Betting Levy Board, 1993-95; Director, British Horseracing Board, 1993-97; President, Diversified Agency Services, 1993-97; Chairman, Dorset Police Authority, 1997-2003; Director, 1995-97, Chairman, 1997-, Horserace Totalisator Board. Publications: Trainers Record, annually, 1973-87; Editor, Ed Byrne's Racing Year, annually, 1980-83. Memberships: Bridport and West Dorset Golf Club. Address: Melplash Farmhouse, Melplash, Bridport, Dorset DT6 3UH, England. E-mail: pjones@tote.co.uk

**JONES Quincy,** b. 14 March 1933, Chicago, Illinois, USA. Record Producer; Composer; Arranger; Musician; Conductor. m. (1) 3 children, (2) Peggy Lipton, 2 daughters. Education: Seattle University; Berklee College of Music; Boston Conservatory. Appointments: Trumpeter, Arranger, Lionel Hampton Orchestra, 1950-53; Arranger, various singers; Leader, own orchestra, concerts, TV appearances, 1960-; Music Director, Mercury Records, 1961, Vice-President, 1964. Creative Works: Solo Albums: You've Got It Bad Girl, 1973; Walking In Space, 1974; Body Heat, 1974; Mellow Madness, 1975; I Heard That!,

1976; Quintessence, 1977; Sounds And Stuff Like That, 1978; The Dude, 1981; Bossa Nova, 1983; The Q, 1984; Back On The Block, 1989. Honours: Golden Note, ASCAP, 1982; Honorary Degree, Berklee College, 1983; Over 20 Grammy Awards; Lifetime Achievement, National Academy of Songwriters, 1989; Jean Hersholt Humanitarian Award, 1995; Scopus Award; Producers' Guild of America Award, 1995; Crystal Award, World Economic Forum, 2000; Marian Anderson Award, 2001; Ted Arison Prize, National Foundation for Advancement in the Arts, 2001; Kennedy Center Honor, 2001. Address: Rogers and Cowan, 3800 Barham Boulevard, Suite 503, Los Angeles, CA 90068, USA.

**JONES Russell Alan,** b. 26 May 1960. Director. Education: BA Honours, British Government and Politics and History (also studied with conductor and musicologist, Harry Newstone), University of Kent at Canterbury, 1978-81. Appointments: Orchestra Manager, Royal Liverpool Philharmonic, 1981-86; Concerts Manager, Scottish Chamber Orchestra, 1986; Chief Executive, National Federation of Music Societies, 1987-97; Chairman, National Music Council, 1995-2000; Numerous appointments (Director of Operations and Director of Policy & Public Affairs), ABSA/Arts and Business, 1997-2002; Co-creator, Arts & Business New Partners programme; Director, Association of British Orchestras, 2002-; Former Chairman, Young Musicians Symphony Orchestra; Former Vice Chairman, Academy of Live & Recorded Arts, -2005. Memberships: President, International Alliance of Orchestral Associations; Freeman, City of London; Liveryman, Worshipful Company of Musicians; Past Master, Billingsgate Ward Club; Fellow, Royal Society of Arts; Lords Taverner; Chevalier, Order of Champagne. Address: 12 Eastern Road, Bounds Green, London N22 4DD, England.

**JONES Tom (Thomas Jones Woodward),** b. 7 June 1940, Pontypridd, Wales. Entertainer. m. Melinda Trenchard, 1956, 1 son. Career: Former bricklayer, factory worker, construction worker; Singing debut, aged 3, later sang in clubs, dance halls, with self-formed group The Playboys; Became Tom Jones, 1963; First hit record It's Not Unusual, 1964; Appeared on radio, television; Toured US, 1965; Television show, This Is Tom Jones, 1969-71; Many international hits, albums in Top 10 charts, Europe, USA; Over 30 million discs sold by 1970; Toured continuously, television appearances, 1970s-; Score, musical play Matador; Hit single: A Boy From Nowhere, 1987; Frequent Amnesty International; Simple Truth, 1991; Rainforest Foundation, 1993; Shelter, 1993; Television series: The Right Time, 1992; Glastonbury Festival of Contemporary Performing Arts, 1992; Live stage appearance, Under Milk Wood, Prince's Trust, 1992; Performed in Amnesty International 40th Anniversary Special, 2001. Recordings: Hits include: It's Not Unusual, 1964; What's New Pussycat, 1965; Thunderball, 1966; Green Green Grass Of Home, 1966; Delilah, 1968; Love Me Tonight, 1969; Can't Stop Loving You; She's A Lady; Letter To Lucille, 1973; Say You Stay Until Tomorrow, 1976; A Boy From Nowhere, 1987; It's Not Unusual (reissue), 1987; If I Only Knew, 1994; Burning Down the House, 1999; Baby It's Cold Outside, 1999; Mama Told Me Not To Come, 2000; Sex Bomb, 2000; You Need Love Like I Do, 2000; Tom Jones International, 2002. Albums include: Green Green Grass Of Home, 1967; Delilah, 1968; This Is Tom Jones, 1969; Tom, 1970; I Who Have Nothing, 1970; Close Up, 1972; The Body and Soul Of TJ, 1973; I'm Coming Home, 1978; At This Moment, 1989; After Dark, 1989; The Lead And How To Swing It, 1994; Reload, 1999; Mr Jones, 2002; Reload 2, 2002. Honours: BRIT Award for Best British Male Solo Artist, 2000; Nodnoff Robbins Music Therapy Silver Clef Award, 2001; Q Magazine Merit Prize, 2002; BRIT Award for Outstanding Contribution

to Music, 2003. Memberships: SAG; AFTRA: AGVA. Address: Tom Jones Enterprises, 10100 Santa Monica Blvd, Ste 205, Los Angeles, CA 90067, USA.

**JONES Tommy Lee,** b. 15 September 1946, San Saba, Texas, USA. Actor. m. (1) Kimberlea Cloughley, 1981, (2) Dawn Laurel, 2001. Education: Harvard University. Creative Works: Broadway appearances include: A Patriot for Me; Four in a Garden; Ulysses in Night Town; Fortune and Men's Eyes; TV appearances include: The Amazing Howard Hughes; Lonesome Dove; The Rainmaker; Cat on a Hot Tin Roof; Yuri Nosenko; KGB; April Morning; Films include: Love Story, 1970; Eliza's Horoscope; Jackson County Jail; Rolling Thunder; The Betsy; Eyes of Laura Mars; Coal Miner's Daughter; Back Roads; Nate and Hayes; River Rat; Black Moon Rising; The Big Town; Stormy Monday; The Package; Firebirds; JFK; Under Siege; House of Cards; The Fugitive; Blue Sky; Heaven and Earth; Natural Born Killers; The Client; Blue Sky; Cobb; Batman Forever; Men in Black, 1997; Volcano, 1997; Marshals, 1997; Small Soldiers (voice), 1998; Rules of Engagement, 1999; Double Jeopardy, 1999; Space Cowboys, 2000; Men in Black II, 2002; The Hunted, 2003; The Missing, 2003. Honours include: Emmy Award.

**JONES Trevor Mervyn,** b. 19 August 1942, Wolverhampton, England. Director. m. Verity Ann Bates, 1 son, 1 daughter. Education: BPharm, Honours, PhD, Kings College, London. Appointments: Lecturer, University of Nottingham; Head of Development, The Boots Co Ltd; Director, Research and Development, Wellcome Foundation; Chairman, Reneuron Holdings plc; Director of Merlin Fund, Merlin Biosciences; Director General, Association of the British Pharmaceutical Industry; Director, Allergan Inc; Director, NextPharm Ltd. Publications: Numerous scientific papers in learned journals; Books: Drug Delivery to the Respiratory Tract; Advances in Pharmaceutical Science. Honours: Honorary degrees: PhD, University of Athens; DSc, University of Nottingham; DSc, University of Strathclyde; DSc, University of Bath; Honorary Fellowships: Royal College of Physicians, Faculty of Pharmaceutical Medicine; British Pharmacological Society; The School of Pharmacy; Charter Gold Medal, Pharmaceutical Society; Gold Medal, Comenius University. Memberships: Fellow, Kings College London; Fellow, Royal Society of Chemists; Fellow, Royal Pharmaceutical Society; Member, College of Pharmacy Practice; Member, WHO Commission on Intellectual Property Rights Innovation and Public Health; Liveryman, Worshipful Society of Apothecaries; Atheneum Club; Surrey County Cricket Club. Address: 18 Friths Drive, Reigate, Surrey, RH2 0DS, England. E-mail: trevor.m.jones@ btinternet.com

**JONES Tudor Bowden,** b. 8 November 1934, Ystradgynlais, Wales. University Professor. m. Patricia, 2 sons. Education: BSc (Hons), 1956, PhD, 1959, DSc, 1979, University of Wales, Swansea. Appointments: Research Fellow, Department of Physics, University of Wales, Aberystwyth, 1959-60; Lecturer, Senior Lecturer, Reader, 1960-80, Professor of Ionosphere Physics, 1980, Head of Department, 1998-2001; Emeritus Professor, 1998-, Department of Physics and Astronomy, University of Leicester; National Co-ordinator for Ground Based Solar Terrestrial Physics, Particle Physics and Astronomy Research Council, 1998-2001; Visiting Professor, Department of Communications Systems, University of Lancaster, 1998-. Publications: Over 200 papers in international journals in the fields of radio/radar propagation and ionospheric physics; Book: Propagation of Radio Waves near the Luf, 1964. Honours: Appleton Prize, Royal Society and International Union of Radio Science, 1993; Charles Chree Medal and Prize, Institute of Physics, 1995; IEE Appleton Lecture, 1997; Leverhulme Emeritus Fellow, 2001-2002. Memberships: Fellow Institute of Electrical Engineers; Fellow, Institute of Physics; Fellow, Royal Astronomical Society. Address: Department of Physics and Astronomy, University Road, University of Leicester, Leicester LE1 7RH, England. E-mail: tbj@ion.le.ac.uk

**JONES Zebedee,** b. 12 March 1970, London, England, Artist. Education: Foundation, Camberwell School of Art, 1988-89; BA (Hons), Fine Art, Norwich School of Art, 1989-92; MA (Hons), Chelsea School of Art, 1992-93. Career: Artist living and working in London; Solo Exhibitions: Karsten Schubert, London, 1995; Waddington Galleries, London, 1997; Patrick De Brock Gallery, Knokke, 1997; Green on Red Gallery, Dublin, 1998; Waddington Galleries, London, 1998; Danese, New York, 1999; Slewe, Amsterdam, 2001; Danese, New York, USA, 2002; New Art Centre Sculpture Park & Gallery, 2003-2004; Group exhibitions include most recently: Elegant Austerity, Waddington Galleries, London, 1998; Passion, Gasworks, London, 1999; Visione Britannica III, Valentina Moncada, Rome, 1999; I Melancholy: Emotional States in British Art, Southampton City Art Gallery, 2001; At Sea, Tate, Liverpool, 2001; British Abstract Painting 2001, Flowers East, London, 2001; Trailer, London, 2001; Zebedee Jones and Mark Sheinkman, Houldsworth, London, 2002; Black/White, Danese Gallery, New York, 2003; Focus London, Galerie Lelong, Zurich, 2003-2004. Publications: Works featured in numerous publications including most recently: Zebedee Jones: New Paintings (Catalogue) Waddington Galleries, New Statesman, The Irish Times, The Tribune Magazine, The Guardian Guide, Elegant Austerity (Catalogue), Waddington Galleries, 1998; The New York Times, Contemporary Visual Arts, Artforum International, 1999; The Observer, The Independent on Sunday, The Sunday Times Culture Magazine, 2001. Honours: BA; MA. Address: 77B Peckham Road, London SE5 8UH, England. E-mail: zebedeejones@btinternet.com

**JONES-LEE Michael Whittaker,** b. 3 April 1944, Stirling, Scotland. Professor of Economics. m. Hazel, 2 sons, 1 daughter. Education: B Eng (1st class Hons), Mechanical Engineering, University of Sheffield, 1965; D Phil, Economics, York, 1971. Appointments: Joel Dean Associates (USA) and EAG (Economic Consultants), 1965-66; Teaching Fellow, 1966-67, Esmee Fairbairn Lecturer in Finance, 1967-71, Department of Economics, University of York; Senior Lecturer, Department of Political Economy, University of St Andrews, 1971-72; Senior Lecturer, 1972-75, Reader, 1976-77, University of York; Professor, 1977-, Head of the Department of Economics, 1984-95, Co-Director, Centre for the Analysis of Safety Policy and Attitudes to Risk, 1996- Department of Economics, Dean Faculty of Social Sciences, 1984-88, University of Newcastle upon Tyne. Publications: Books and monographs: The Value of Life: An Economic Analysis, 1976; The Value of Life and Safety: Proceedings of a Conference Held by the Geneva Association (editor), 1982; The Economics of Safety and Physical Risk, 1989; Economic Valuation with Stated-Preference Techniques (co-author), 2002; Numerous articles as author and co-author published in academic journals and conference proceedings. Honours: John Brown Prize for Mechanical Engineering (shared), Sheffield, 1965; Associate Editor, The Journal of Risk and Uncertainty. Membership: Association of University Teachers. Address: Business School-Economics, Ridley Building, University of Newcastle upon Tyne, Newcastle upon Tyne NE1 7RU, England. E-mail: michael.jones-lee@ncl.ac.uk

**JONG Erica (Mann),** b. 26 March 1942, New York, New York, USA. Author; Poet. m. (4) Kenneth David Burrows, 5 August 1989, 1 daughter. Education: BA, Barnard College,

1963; MA, Columbia University, 1965. Appointments: Lecturer in English, City College of the City University of New York, 1964-66, 1969-70; University of Maryland Overseas Division, 1967-69; Faculty, Bread Loaf Writers Conference, Middlebury, Vermont, 1982, Salzburg Seminar, Austria, 1993. Publications: Fear of Flying, 1973; How to Save Your Own Life, 1977; Fanny, Being the True History of the Adventures of Fanny Hackabout-Jones, 1980; Parachutes and Kisses, 1984; Serenissima: A Novel of Venice, (reissued as Shylock), 1987; Any Woman's Blues, 1990; Fear of Fifty: A Midlife Memoir, 1994. Poetry: Fruits and Vegetables, 1971, 2nd edition, 1997; Half-Lives, 1973; Loveroot, 1975; The Poetry of Erica Jong, 1976; At the Edge of the Body, 1979; Ordinary Miracles, 1983; Becoming Light: Poems, New and Selected, 1992; Inventing Memory, 1997. Other: Four Visions of America (with others), 1977; Witches, 1981; Megan's Book of Divorce: A Kid's Book for Adults, (reissued Megan's Two Houses), 1984; Erica Jong on Henry Miller: The Devil at Large, memoir, 1994; Lyrics: Zipless: Songs of Abandon, from the Erotic Poetry of Erica Jong, 1995. Contributions to: Various publications. Honours: Academy of American Poets Award, 1963; Bess Hokin Prize, 1971; New York State Council on the Arts Grant, 1971; Alice Faye di Castagnola Award, 1972; National Endowment for the Arts Grant, 1973; Woodrow Wilson fellow; Mother of the Year, 1982; Memberships: PEN; Authors Guild USA, Council, 1975-, President, 1991-93; Phi Beta Kappa; Poetry Society of America; Poets and Writers; Writers Guild of America (West). Address: C/o Burrows, 451 Park Avenue South, New York, NY 10016, USA.

**JONSON Guy,** b. 5 November 1913, London, England. Concert Pianist. m. Patricia Burrell, deceased, 2 daughters. Education: Royal Academy of Music, London, 1930-35. Appointments: Professor of Pianoforte, Tobias Matthay Pianoforte School, London, 1936-39; Professor, Tutor, Royal Academy of Music, 1939-85; Examiner, Royal Schools of Music, 1947-89; Solo Recitalist, Soloist with major orchestras world-wide. Honours: FRAM; Hon FTCL; FRSA. Memberships: Incorporated Society of Musicians; Royal Philharmonic Society; RAM Club; Royal Society of Arts. Address: 18 Bracknell Gardens, Hampstead, NW3 7EB, London, England. E-mail: guyjonson@blueyonder.co.uk

**JONUŠIENĖ Laimutė,** b. 30 January 1939, Lithuania. Journalist. m. Antanas Jonušas, 1 son. Education: Philology, Vilnius University, 1961; Private studies of art, music and history in Lithuania and abroad. Appointments: Editor, Culture Life Department at the Lithuania National Radio, 1964-2002; Culture Life Observer for the press, 2002-; Broadcasts for International Radio University (URTI), 1994-98. Publications: Reports on the most prestigious summer festivals for Lithuanian National Radio and the Magazine "Muzikos Barai" (traditions, innovations and personalities); Reports on world-wide places of culture for "Muzikos Barai" and "Kelionių magija". Honours: Grants for cultural initiatives: URTI, Paris, 1994-98, Kultur Kontakt, Vienna, 1996, 1998, Open Society Fund, 1996, Lucerne Summer Festival, 2002, Salzburger Festspiele, 1998-2001, Bayreuther Festspiele, 2000-2001. Memberships: Lithuanian Journalists Union; International Federation of Journalists. Address: Basanavičiaus 17-21, LT-03108 Vilnius, Lithuania. E-mail: laima.jonusiene@takas.lt

**JORDAN Bill (Lord),** b. 1936, Birmingham, England. m. Jean, 3 daughters. Appointments: Machine Tool Fitter, 1951; Joined engineering union, served as Shop Steward, Convenor at GKN and District President; Elected Divisional Organiser, West Midlands Division, 1977; Elected National President, Amalgamated Engineering Union, 1986; General Secretary,

# DICTIONARY OF INTERNATIONAL BIOGRAPHY

International Confederation of Free Trade Unions, 1994-2002. Honours: CBE; Honorary Doctorate, University of Central England, 1993; Honorary Doctorate, University of Cranfield, 1995. Memberships: General Council of the British TUC; National Economic Development Council; European Metalworkers' Federation; International Metalworkers' Federation; European Trade Union Confederation; Victim Support Advisory Committee; English Partnership; Winston Churchill Trust; Governor, London School of Economics; Governor, Ashridge Management College; RSA; Member, UN High Level Panel on Youth Employment; Member, UN Global Compact Advisory Council; Chairman, English Partnerships Pension Scheme, 2003-.

**JORDAN Michael Jeffrey**, b. 17 February 1963, Brooklyn, New York, USA. Basketball and Baseball Player. m. Juanita Vanoy, 1989, 2 sons, 1 daughter. Education: University of North Carolina. Appointments: Player, Chicago Bulls National Basketball Association (NBA), 1984-93, 1995-98, (NBA Champions, 1991, 1992, 1993, 1996, 1997, 1998), Birmingham Barons Baseball Team, 1993; Member, NCAA Championship Team, 1982, US Olympic Team, 1984, NBA All-Star Team, 1985-91; with Nashville Sounds, 1994-95; Holds record for most points in NBA Playoff Game with 63; Retired, 1998-; Came out of retirement to play for Washington Wizards, 2001-. Publications: Rare Air: Michael on Michael (autobiography), 1993; I Can't Accept Not Trying: Michael Jordan on the Pursuit of Excellence. Honours include: Seagram's NBA Player of the Year, 1987; Most Valuable Player, NBA All-Star Game, 1988; NBA Most Valuable Player, 1988, 1991, 1992, 1996, 1998; Named, World's Highest Paid Athlete, Forbes Magazine, 1992. Memberships: President, Basketball Operations, Washington Wizards, 1999-. Address: Washington Wizards, 718 7th Street NW, Washington, DC 20004, USA.

**JORDAN Neil Patrick**, b. 25 February 1950, Sligo, Ireland. Author; Director. 3 sons, 2 daughters. Education: BA, 1st Class Honours, History/English Literature, University College, Dublin, 1972. Appointment: Co-Founder, Irish Writers Cooperative, Dublin, 1974. Publications: Night in Tunisia, 1976; The Past, 1979; The Dream of a Beast, 1983; Sunrise with Sea Monster, 1994; Nightlines, 1995. Films as a Director: Angel, 1982; The Company of Wolves, 1984; Mona Lisa, 1986; High Spirits, 1988; We're No Angels, 1989; The Miracle, 1990; The Crying Game, 1992; Interview With the Vampire, 1994; Michael Collins, 1996; The Butcher Boy, 1997; In Dreams, 1999; The End of the Affair, 1999; Double Dawn, 2001. Honours: Guardian Fiction Prize, 1979; The London Evening Standard's Most Promising Newcomer Award, 1982; London Film Critics Circle Awards, 1984; Oscar, 1992; Los Angeles Film Critics Award, 1992; New York Film Critics Circle Award, 1992; Writers Guild of America Award, 1992; BAFTA Award, 1992; Golden Lion, Venice Film Festival, 1996; Silver Bear, Berlin Film Festival, 1997; BAFTA Award, 2000. Address: c/o Jenne Casarotto Co Ltd, National House, 60-66 Wardour Street, London W1V 3HP, England.

**JORTNER Joshua**, b. 14 March 1933, Poland. Professor of Chemistry. m. Ruth Thea Sanger, 1 son, 1 daughter. Education: MSc, Physical Chemistry, The Hebrew University of Jerusalem, Israel, 1951-56; PhD, Physical Chemistry, 1960. Appointments: Lecturer, 1961-63, Senior Lecturer, 1963-65, Department of Physical Chemistry, Hebrew University; Associate Professor, Physical Chemistry, 1965-66, Professor, Chemistry, 1966-, Head, Institute of Chemistry, 1966-72, Tel Aviv University; Deputy Rector, 1966-69, Acting Rector, 1969, Vice President, 1970-72, Heinemann Professor, Chemistry, 1973-2003, Vice President, 1980-86, President, 1986-95, Israel National

Academy of Sciences; Vice-President, 1995-97, President, 1998-99, Past President, 2000-01, International Union of Pure and Applied Chemistry. Publications: Author and Co-author of over 700 articles in scientific journals; Co-author and editor of 23 books. Honours: International Academy of Quantum Science Award; Rothschild Prize; Israel Prize in Exact Sciences; The Wolf Prize in Chemistry; August Wilhelm von Hofmann Medal; The Joseph O Hirschfelder Prize in Theoretical Chemistry; Maria Skoldowksa-Curie Medal of the Polish Chemical Society; Many others. Memberships: Member of learned societies including: Israel National Academy of Sciences and Humanities; International Academy of Quantum Molecular Science; Royal Danish Academy of Sciences and Letters; Polish Academy of Sciences; Russian Academy of Sciences; National Academy of Sciences of the United States of America; Others. Address: School of Chemistry, Tel Aviv University, Ramat Aviv, 69978 Tel Aviv, Israel.

**JOSÉ Alan Spencer MacIntosh**, b. 19 October 1953. Registrar. m. Gwendoline Elizabeth Emmerson, 1 daughter. Education: Harrow High School, Harrow College of Education. Appointments: A carer spanning some 30 years, mostly with local government, specialising in crematoria and cemetery management. Publications: Articles in Journal of ICCM and Motoring Club magazines. Honours: Freeman of the City of London, 1991. Memberships: Institute of Cemetery and Crematorium Management (AInstICCM), 1989-; St Cuthbert's Church Parish Council, 1992-; Secretary, ICCM Northern Branch Forum, 1995-; Chair, St Cuthbert's Church, Building Committee, 1997-; Chair, Community Service Committee, Rotary Club of Durham, 2003-; Catenian Association Provincial Councillor for Durham Circle. Address: Links View, South Road, Durham, DH1 3TQ, England and Le Pont, 53600 Voutré, France.

**JOSEPH Jane Elizabeth**, b. 7 June 1942, Dorking, Surrey. Painter; Printmaker. Education: Camberwell School of Arts & Crafts, 1961-65. Career: Solo shows, 1973-, include: Morley Gallery, London, 1973; The Minories, Colchester, 1982; Angela Flowers Gallery, London, 1987; Flowers East, London, 1989; Flowers East, London, 1992; Edinburgh Printmakers, 1994; Chelsea and Westminster Hospital, London, 1995; Morely Gallery, London, 1997; Scarborough Art Gallery, 1999; "Twenty Etchings for Primo Levi", Morley Gallery, London, Hebrew Union College, New York, Italian Cultural Institute, London, 2000; The Stanley Picker Gallery, Kingston University, 2000; Worcester City Art Gallery, 2001; "Etchings 1985-2001", Victoria Art Gallery, Bath, 2002; Group shows, 1971- include: Royal Academy Summer Exhibition, London, 1971-97/01; Flowers East, 1990, 1994, 1999; Rocket Gallery, London, 1996; Inaugural exhibition, Artsway, Lymington, 1997; The Hunting Art Prizes, London, 1997, 2003; Cheltenham Open Drawing Exhibition and tour (prizewinner) 1998; Portrait of the Artist, touring exhibition, UK, 1999; Printworks, Eagle Gallery, London, 2002; The Art of Aging, Hebrew Union College, New York, 2003; Work in collections: Birmingham City Museum and Art Gallery; School of Art Gallery, Aberystwyth; Arts Council of Wales; Government Art Collection; Castle Museum, Norwich; The British Museum; Unilever House; Imperial College; Chelsea and Westminster Hospital; Ben Uri Society; New Hall College, Cambridge; Fitzwilliam Museum, Cambridge; Hebrew Union College, New York; The City Art Gallery, Worcester; Lindley Library, London; The National Art Library; Victoria and Albert Museum; Yale Center for British Art, New Haven, Connecticut, USA; Ashmolean, Oxford. Commission: Chelsea and Westminster Hospital, 1994; Folio Society, etchings for "If This is a Man" by Primo Levi, 1999, and "The Truce" by Primo Levi, 2002. Publications: Illustrations for "A Little Flora of Common

Plants" with text by Mel Gooding, 2002. Honours: Leverhulme Travelling Award, 1965-66; Invited Artist, Pécs Workshop for Graphic Art, Hungary, 1989, Abbey Award in Painting, British School at Rome, 1991, 1995; Elephant Trust Award, 1997; Wimbledon School of Art Research and Development Grant, 2000. Address: 6A Eynham Road, London W12 0HA, England. E-mail: jane_joseph2003@yahoo.co.uk

**JOSEPHSON Brian David,** b. 4 January 1940, Cardiff, Wales. Physicist. Education: Cambridge University. Appointments: Fellow, Trinity College, Cambridge, 1962-; Research Assistant Professor, University of Illinois, 1965-66; Professor of Physics, Cambridge University, 1974-; Faculty Member, Maharishi European Research University, 1975; Helped discover the tunnelling effect in superconductivity, called the Josephson effect. Publications: Co-editor, Consciousness and the Physical World, 1980; The Paranormal and the Platonic Worlds, in Japanese, 1997; Research papers on superconductivity, critical phenomena, theory of intelligence, science and mysticism. Honours: Honorary Member, Institute of Electrical and Electronic Engineers; Foreign Honorary Member, American Academy of Arts and Sciences; New Scientist Award, 1969; Research Corporation Award, 1969; Fritz London Award, 1970; Hughes Medal, Royal Society, 1972; Joint Winner, Nobel Prize for Physics, 1973. Address: Cavendish Laboratory, Madingley Road, Cambridge, CB3 0HE, England. E-mail: bdj10@cam.ac.uk

**JOSHI Rangnath Nathrao,** b. 29 July 1940, Aite Tq Bhoom district Osmanabad, Maharashtra, India. Retired Superintendent in Law and Judiciary Department; Poet; Writer; Actor; Sweet Poetry Singer; Music Director. Education: HMDs; BTMD; DLit, Colombo; DLit, Nanded; PhD, Calcutta; 17 other literary degrees. Appointments: Composer of poems and lyrics in Marathi, Hindi, English and Sanskrit, Proze and Poetry; Singer of own compositions, 2551 performances in various states and cities in India; Singer, Actor, Director, Literary researcher, artist of radio and television; Many Performances; Approved Poet of AIR; Prominent personality in various posts in several sansthas and state institutions. Publications: 7,000 poems (gits); Publications include: Sangram Tutari; Dhaktya Tuljapurchi Tuljabhavani; Bhavdhara; Shri Tuljabhavani Mahima; Gitbhavani; Dundubhi; Sachitra Gitashree; Lokmata Ahilya deviholkar; Shri Manik Prabhu Gitayan; Bhaktikaustubha; Ahilyadevi Holkar Gitayan; Shrikashi Jagadguru Charitra Gitganga; Dharmatma; Shri Mahadev Maharaj Lilamrut; Shri Sadguru Ramrang Darshan Kavya; Chan Chan bad bad gite. Honours: Six First prizes, 1953, 1974, 1976, 1980, 1999, 2001; Special Merit Certificate Pune, 1976; Numerous medals, awards, cups, certificates for literary, musical, dramatic, poetic work; International Man of the Year 2001; Presided at several literary conferences; Life member, Maharashtra Shahir Parishad Pune; Invited Chief Poet for Kavi Sammelen, arranged by Station Director of All India Radio Aurangabad, 1981, etc; Chief guest, invitee, president, inauguarator, examiner, many literary, musical, dramatic and social institutions; Chief and Judge in numerous competitions. Memberships include: All India Rajendra Samajik Kalyan Parishad Patna 1974-; Gita Ramayan Prachar Sangha Swargashram, 1975, etc; Chief Consultant, Editor, Dharma Prbha magazine, 1984-, and others; Master in Palmistry; ShakatiPat [Kundlini] diksha Sadguru; Jyotish Maharshi; Pandit Samrat. Address: 335 Kaviraj, Near Papnash Tirtha, At PO Tq, Tuljapur District, Osmanabad 413601, Maharashtra State, India.

**JOSIPOVICI Gabriel David,** b. 8 October 1940, Nice, France. Professor of English; Writer; Dramatist. Education: BA, Honours, 1st Class, St Edmund Hall, Oxford, 1961.

Appointments: Lecturer in English, 1963-76, Reader in English, 1976-84, Professor of English, 1984-99, Research Professor, Graduate School of Humanities, 1999-, University of Sussex. Publications: Novels: The Inventory, 1968; Words, 1971; Mobius the Stripper: Stories and Short Plays, 1974; The Present, 1975; Migrations, 1977; The Echo Chamber, 1979; The Air We Breath, 1981; Conversations in Another Room, 1984; Contre-Jour, 1986; In the Fertile Land, Shorter Fiction, 1987; The Big Glass, 1990; In a Hotel Garden, 1993; Moo Pak, 1994; Now, 1998; Goldberg: Variations, 2002; Everything Passes, 2006. Non-Fiction: The World and the Book, 1971; The Lessons of Modernism, 1977; Writing and the Body, 1982 The Book of God: A Response to the Bible, 1988; Text and Voice, 1992; Touch, 1996; On Trust, 1999; A Life, 2001; The Singer on the Shore, 2006. Contributions to: Encounter; New York Review of Books; London Review of Books; Times Literary Supplement. Honours: Sunday Times Playwriting Award, 1969; BBC nominations for Italia Prize, 1977, 1989; South East Arts Literature Prize, 1978; Lord Northcliffe Lecturer, University of London, 1981; Lord Weidenfeld Visiting Professor of Comparative Literature, University of Oxford, 1996-97; Fellow of the Royal Society of Literature, 1997; Fellow of the British Academy, 2001. Address: c/o John Johnson, Clerkenwell House, 45-47 Clerkenwell Green, London EC1R 0HT, England.

**JOSS Timothy Hans,** b. 27 June 1955, London, England. Artistic Director. m. Elizabeth Morag Wallace, 1 daughter. Education: The Queen's College, Oxford, England, 1973-76; University of Grenoble, 1976; Royal Academy of Music, England, 1976-79. Appointments: Mathematics lecturer, Davies's College, London WC1; Community worker, Pitt Street Settlement, London SE15; Commissioned composer and record producer for 1980 World Energy Conference; Researcher for Richard Baker, 1979-81; Assistant Administrator, Live Music Now!, 1981-82; Music and Dance Officer, North West Arts, 1982-89; Concerts Director, Bournemouth Sinfonietta rising to Senior Manager, Bournemouth Orchestras, 1989-93; Director (Artistic Director and Chief Executive), Bath Festivals Trust, 1993-. Publications: Editor: UK Directory of Black, Asian and Chinese Musics, 1989; UK Directory of Community Music, 1992. Honours: Fellow, Royal Society of Arts; Honorary Associate, Royal Academy of Music. Memberships: Chairman, British Arts Festivals Association. Address: The Old Barn, West Yatton, Chippenham, Wiltshire SN14 7EW. E-mail: timjoss@aol.com

**JOYNER-KERSEE Jaqueline,** b. 3 March 1962, East St Louis, Illinois, USA. Athlete. m. Bobby Kersee, 1986. Education: University of California, Los Angeles; Training: Husband as coach. Career: Athlete in the Heptathlon; Assistant Basketball Coach, UCLA; World Record Heptathlon Scores: 7,158 points, Houston, 1986; 7,215 points, US Olympic Trial, Indianapolis, 1988; 7,291 points, Seoul, 1988; 7,044 points, Olympic Games, Barcelona 1992; Honours: 3 Olympic Gold Medals; 4 World Championships; Record erased by IAAF, 1999; With Richmond Rage in American Basketball League; Winner, IAAF Mobil Grand Prix, 1994; Chair, St Louis Sports Commission, 1996-; Jim Thorpe Award, 1993; Jackie Robinson Robie Award, 1994; Jesse Owens Humanitarian Award, 1999; Hon DHL, Spellman College, 1998, Howard University, 1999, George Washington University, 1999. Publications: A Kind of Grace, autobiography, 1997. Address: Elite International Sports Marketing Inc, 1034 South Brentwood Boulevard, Suite 1530, St Louis, MO 63117, USA.

**JOZUKA Hajime,** b. 9 November 1946, Takaoka City, Japan. Medical Doctor. m. Emiko, 1 son, 1 daughter. Education: Medical Department, University of Kanazawa; Trainee,

Department of Psychiatry, University of Nagoya-City; Private education in Psychopathology with Bin Kimura and Jungian Psychology with Dora Kalf. Appointments: Head Doctor, Department of Psychiatry, Mikatabara Hospital, 1975; Head Doctor, Department of Psychoneurology, Toyohashi National Hospital, 1979; Invited Lecturer, Aichi Prefectural College of Kindergarten Teachers, 1979; Head Doctor, Department of Psychoneurology, Nagoya Health Administration Centre of National Telephone and Telegram, 1983; Assistant President, Yahagigawa Psychosomatic Centre, 1991; Invited Lecturer, University of California Irvine, 1993; President of Jozuka Mental Clinic and President of JMC Stress Medical Institute, 1994. Publications: Books in English: Psychoneuroimmuno-pathology, 2000; Introduction to Psychoneuroimmuno-pathology and Clinical Practice, 2004; 6 books in Japanese include: Personality Disorder, 2004; Sexology, 2005; More than 30 articles in medical journals include: Immunological changes and other psychosomatic variations in obese patient, 1989; Immunological study of anxiety and depression, 1990; Immune responses in relaxation therapy for psychosomatic diseases, 1992. Honours include: Representative of Association of Psychosomatic Medicine; National Authorised Psychiatric Tester; Japanese Representative of IOCD. Memberships: Japanese Medical Association; International College of Psychosomatic Medicine; International Organisation of Sexology; International Organisation of Obsessive-Compulsive Disorder; Psychosomatic Association in Japan; Association of Psychiatry and Neurology in Japan; International Association of Allergology; International Association of Immunology; Japanese Association of Immunology; Japanese Association of Allergology; Japanese Psychoanalytic Association. Address: 4-38 Takahatacho, Nishio, Aichi 445-0064, Japan. E-mail: hjozuka@athena.ocn.ne.jp

**JUAN CARLOS I (King of Spain),** b. 5 January 1938, Rome. Education: Private, Fribourg, Switzerland, Madrid, San Sebastian; Institute of San Isidro, Madrid; Colegio del Carmen; General Military Academy, Zaragoza; University Madrid. Appointments: Inaugurated as King of Spain, 1975; Named as Captain-General of the Armed Forces, 1975. Honours include: Charlemagne Prize, 1982; Bolivar Prize, UNESCO, 1983; Gold Medal Order, 1985; Candenhove Kalergi Prize, Switzerland, 1986; Nansen Medal, 1987; Humanitarian Award, Elie Wiesel, USA, 1991; Houphouet Boigny Peace Prize, UNESCO, 1995; Franklin D Roosevelt Four Freedoms Award, 1995. Memberships include: Foreign Member, Académie des sciences morales et politiques. Address: Palacio de la Zarzuela, 28071 Madrid, Spain.

**JUANBARÓ Dr Josep,** b. 9 August 1959, Manresa, Spain. Technologist. Education: Bachelor of Chemistry, 1981, Master of Chemistry, 1982, Doctor of Chemistry, 1990, University of Barcelona, Spain. Appointments: Professor of Chemistry at a private school, 1982-83; Secretary of White Book of Research, 1982-88; Technologist with an industrial company, 1986-. Publications: Articles in scientific journals: Bioengineering and Biotechnology; Quimica e Industria, Barcelona; Publication of the Institut d'Estudis Catalans. Honour: Master of Chemistry awarded by the Institut d'Estudis Catalans (Academic Entity). Address: Nicaragua 139A, 3R, 1A, 08029 Barcelona, Spain. E-mail: josepjip@menta.net

**JUDD Denis (O'Nan),** b. 28 October 1938, Byfield, Northamptonshire, England. Historian; Writer. m. Dorothy Woolf, 10 July 1964, 3 sons, 1 daughter. Education: BA, Honours, Modern History, Oxford University, 1961; PGCEd, 1962, PhD, 1967, London University. Appointments: Trustee of Alison Uttley's Literary Estate; Advisor to BBC History

Magazine. Publications: Balfour and the British Empire, 1968; The Boer War, 1977; Radical Joe: Joseph Chamberlain, 1977; Prince Philip, 1981; Lord Reading, 1982; Alison Uttley, 1986; Jawaharlal Nehru, 1993; Empire: The British Imperial Experience, 1996; The Boer War, 2002; The Lion and the Tiger; The Rise and Fall of the British Raj, 2004; 2 novels/books and stories for children; Other history books and biographies. Contributions to: History Today; History; Journal of Imperial and Commonwealth History; Literary Review; Daily Telegraph; New Statesman; International Herald Tribune; Guardian; Independent; BBC History Magazine; Mail on Sunday. Honours: Fellow, Royal Historical Society, 1977; Awarded Professorship, 1990. Address: 20 Mount Pleasant Road, London NW10 3EL, England.

**JUDD Frank Ashcroft, Lord Judd,** b. 28 March 1935, Sutton, Surrey, England. Specialist in International Affairs. m. Christine Willington, 2 daughters. Education: City of London School, BScEcon, London School of Economics and Political Science, 1953-56. Appointments: F/O RAF, 1957-59; Secretary General, International Voluntary Service, 1960-66; Member of Parliament, Labour, Portsmouth West, 1966-74, Portsmouth North, 1974-79; Parliamentary Private Secretary to Leader of the Opposition, 1970-72; Member of the Parliamentary Delegation to the Council of Europe and Western European Union, 1970-73; Shadow Navy Minister, 1972-74; Parliamentary Under Secretary of State for Defence (Navy), 1974-76; Minister of State for Overseas Development, 1976-77; Minister of State, Foreign and Commonwealth Office, 1977-79; Associate Director, International Defence and Aid Fund for Southern Africa, 1979-80; Director, Voluntary Service Overseas, 1980-85; Director, Oxfam, 1985-91; Created Life Peer, 1991; Member, Sub-committee, (Environment, Agriculture, Public Health and Consumer Protection) of the European Community Committee in the House of Lords, 1997-2001; Member, Procedure Committee, 2001-04, and Ecclesiastical Committee in the House of Lords, 2001-; Joint Committee (Commons & Lords) on Human Rights, 2003-; Member, Parliamentary Assembly of the Council of Europe & Western European Union, 1997-2005; Joint Chair, Joint Working Group on Chechnya, Council of Europe, 2000-03; A Non-Executive Director, Portsmouth Harbour Renaissance Ltd; Trustee of Saferworld and of the Ruskin Foundation; Consultant Advisor to De Montfort University. Publications: Radical Future (jointly), 1967; Fabian International Essays (jointly), 1970; Purpose in Socialism (jointly), 1973; Imagining Tomorrow (jointly), 2000. Honours: Honorary DLitt, University of Bradford, University of Portsmouth; Honorary LLD, University of Greenwich; Honorary Fellow, University of Portsmouth and Selly Oak Colleges; Freeman of the City of Portsmouth; Member of Court, London School of Economics; Member of Court, University of Lancaster and University of Newcastle. Memberships include: Royal Institute of International Affairs; The Royal Society of Arts; The British Council; The Oxfam Association; The Labour Party; The Fabian Society; President, YMCA (England), 1996-2005; Vice-President Council for National Parks and United Nations Association; Convenor, Social Responsibility Forum of Churches Together in Cumbria, 1999-2005. Address: House of Lords, London SW1A 0PW, England.

**JUERGENS Uwe,** b. 29 January 1942, Frankfurt am Main, Germany. Zoologist. m. Christl, 1 daughter. Education: Abitur, Luitpold Gymnasium, Munich, 1961; Doctor Degree, 1969, Habilitation, 1976, University of Munich, Germany. Appointments: Research Associate, Max Planck Institute of Psychiatry, Munich, 1969-91; Professor, Zoological Institute, Head, Neurobiology Department, German Primate Centre, Goettingen, 1991-. Publications: Over 140 articles in international journals; Co-Editor, Nonverbal Vocal Communication, 1992; Co-Editor, Current Topics in Primate Vocal Communication, 1995; Associate Editor, Journal of Medical Primatology, 1996-2004. Honour: Corresponding Member, German Society of Phoniatrics and Paedaudiology. Memberships: International Primatological Society; International Behavioural Neuroscience Society; European Brain and Behaviour Society; Language Origins Society. Address: German Primate Centre, Kellnerweg 4, 37077 Goettingen, Germany. E-mail: ujuerge@gwdg.de

**JUHAS Pavol,** b. 4 July 1941, Teplicany, District Kosice, Slovak Republic. Civil Engineer; Professor. m. Emilia. 2 sons. Education: Ing, Civil Engineering Faculty, Technical University, 1965; PhD, Scientific Study, 1973; Doctor of Sciences, 1988; Associate Professor, 1992; University Professor, 1993. Appointments: Designer, Eastern Slovak Steel Works, 1965-68; Scientific Worker, Institute of Construction and Architecture, 1968-93; Scientific Secretary, 1980-85; Vice Director, 1985-90; Professor, Civil Engineering Faculty, 1993-; Dean, 1994-2000. Publications: Theory and design of civil engineering steel structures; Elasto plastic analyses; Global and local stability; Postcritical behaviour and load carrying capacity; Fatigue strength and lifetime of structures. Honours: Award, Slovak Academy of Sciences; Medals, Technical University; Member, Scientific Committee and Boards. Memberships: Slovak Association for Steel Structures; International Association for Bridge and Structural Engineering; Structural Stability Research Council. Address: Civil Engineering Faculty, Technical University Kosice, Vysokoskolska 4, 042 00 Kosice, Slovak Republic.

**JULIUSON Adetominiyi D Akinsanya,** Diplomat; Parliamentarian; Businessman. Education: BFC, Certified Business Finance Consultant, GB, 1997; Doctoral, Institute of Professional Financial Managers, GB, 2004; BA (Hons); CMBA, Business Management Association, UK, 2004; Honorary Doctor of Business Administration, IIU, Europe, 2004; Executive MBA, Cambridge University Business School, 2004. Appointments: Managing Director, Fandell Property Investment and International Finance, 1996-98; Managing Executive, FCG Commerce Group, 1998-2000; Founder and Chief Executive Officer, Delberg Professional Books, UK, Australia and Philippines, 2000-; Currently, Consultant and Representative, (Humanitarian Issues, Diplomatic Affairs and Political Strategy). Honours include: Fellow, The Rosae Croix; Honorary Fellow, Australian-Asian Institute of Civil Leadership; Freedom of the City of London, 1999; Freedom of the City of Coventry, 1999; First African Liveryman of the City of London, 2000; Noble Order Global Award of Excellence for Charity and Community Service, Philippines, 2003; International Order of Merit; Certificate of Distinction; Knight Grand Commander of the Most Noble Order of Rizal, 2003; Stevie Award for Best Executive, USA, 2003; Honoured by the National Society for the Prevention of Cruelty to Children, 2003; Listed in Who's Who publications and biographical dictionaries. Memberships include: Chairman and Founder, The Diplomatic Affairs Congress; Member of the Court of the Order of Honour for Diplomatic Excellence; Member (Middle East Association), High Level British Trade Mission to Libya and Algeria, Iran, Saudi Arabia, Gulf States (Kuwait, Bahrain, Qatar, Dubai, Abu Dhabi and Oman); Fellow, Atlantic Council of the UK (NATO and ATA General Assembly); Member, Dubai Society; Japan Society; Companion of The Nautical Institute; Member, Royal Television Society; Society of Young Freemen of the City; Vice Chairman, Bachelors Hall Club, London; Member, Royal Institute of International Affairs; Assembly Member, International Diplomatic Academy; Diplomatic Member, London Diplomatic Academy; Guild of Freemen of the City of London; Member of Defence and Security Forum; Member, United Wards Club; Founding Member, City of London Branch of the Agency for Bank of England's Business Panel; Parliamentarian/Member, European Atlantic Council; Member of the 1912 Club (Palace of Westminster), Fellow, Royal Institution of Great Britain; Cities of London and Westminster Conservatives; Political Studies Association; Royal Society of St George of England and Wales; Institute of Directors; Member, Guild of Freemen of the City of York; City Livery Yacht Club, UK; Cripplegate, Lime Street, Broad Street and Bridge Wards of the City of London. Address: PO Box 50561, London E16 3WY, England. E-mail djuliuson@usa.com

**JUNG Yeon-Joo,** b. 15 March, 1950, Daegu, Republic of Korea. Company President; Chief Executive Officer. m. Jong-Im Kim, 2 daughters. Education: Bachelor of Business Administration, Dong-kuk University, 1973; Master of Tax Accounting, Hong-ik University, 1998; Completed Chief Executive Officer e-Business Courses, Seoul National University, 2003. Appointments: Associate, Accounting Division, Samsung Fire Insurance Co Ltd, Seoul, Korea, 1976-78; Manger of Accounting Division, 1982-87; General Manager, Finance and Accounting Team, 1987-93; Assistant Director, Finance and Accounting Team, 1994-95; Director, Finance and Accounting Division, 1996-97, Samsung Corporation, Seoul, Korea (corporate name changed to Samsung Corporation from Samsung Engineering and Construction as a result of a merger, 1995); Executive Managing Director, Finance and Accounting Division, 1998-2000, Executive Vice President and Chief Executive Officer, 2001-2003, Samsung SDI, Seoul, Korea; Elected as Chairman of Board of Directors, President and Chief Executive Officer, Samsung Engineering Co Ltd, 2003-. Honours: Outstanding Achievement Award, 50th Anniversary of the Samsung Group, 1988 Distinguished Service Memorial Award, 5th Anniversary of Second Generation Samsung Group, 1993; Corporate awards: Best Corporate Award for Respect for Shareholders, Ministry of Finance and Economy, 2001; Knowledge Management Award, Maekyung-Booz Allen, 2001; Presidential Award of Korea e-Business, Ministry of Commerce, Industry and Energy, 2001; Best Corporate Management Award (among large-sized companies), Daeshin Economic Research Institute, 2002; Transparent Accounting Award, Korea Accounting Association, 2002; Digital Knowledge Management Award, Ministry of Information and Communication, 2002. Memberships: Director, Greenfund; Executive Director, International Contractors Association of Korea; Director General, Korea Engineering and Consulting Association; Vice-Chairman, Korea Plant Industry Association; Federation of Korean Industries; Korean Management Association. Address: Samsung Engineering Co Ltd, Samsung Sei Tower, 467-14, Dogok-2Dong, Gangnam-Gu, Seoul, Korea. E-mail: yj0315@samsung.com Website: www.samsungengineering.com

**JURKOVIĆ Milan,** b. 3 October 1936, Cetinje, Montenegro. Engineer; Scientific Researcher. m. Zdravka Bukovac, 2 sons. Education: BSc, Mechanical Engineer, University of Mostar, 1966; MSc, Mechanical Engineer, University of Zagreb, Croatia, 1974; Habilitation hc, University of Sarajevo, Bosnia and Herzegovina, 1975; Dr Sc, Mechanical Engineer, University of Banja Luka, 1982; Professional and scientific specialisation: England, 1969, Germany, 1971, 1979, 1988, 1990, Czech Republic, 1974, Poland, 1977, Sweden, 1979, Russia, 1989, etc. Appointments: Head and Educator, mechanical and technical design in industry, 1957-62; Technical educator, 1966-67; Head of project team, Belgrade, Yugoslavia, 1968-69; Head, Department of Production Engineering, Main Engineer, Director of Development and Technical Director, 1969-75; Assistant Professor, University of Sarajevo and University of Banja Luka, Bosnia and Herzegovina, 1975-81; Technical Consultant, Business and Productions Company, 1975-; Dean, 1977-80, 1983-85, Head of Laboratory for Technology of Plastic and Machining Systems, Head of Chair of Manufacturing Engineering, 1985-92, Faculty of Mechanical Engineering, Banja Luka; Associate Professor, 1982-87, Full Professor, 1987-90, 1990-92, Vice Rector, 1981-83, 1988-92, University of Banja Luka; National Expert Team, Ministry of Science, Sarajevo and Belgrad, Yugoslavia, 1986-90; Full Professor, University of Rijeka, 1995- and University of Bihać, 2003-2005; Head, Department of Production Engineering, 1998-2003, Head, Chair of Manufacturing Technologies, 2001-04, Faculty of Engineering, University of Rijeka, Croatia; Visiting Professor: University of Tuzla, 1988-91, 1996-2005, University of Bihać, Bosnia and Herzegovina, 1996-2003 and University of Rijeka, Croatia, 1993-95. Publications: 8 university books; 5 scientific books; 10 monographs; Numerous scientific articles published in professional journals abd conferene proceedings; Scientific books in 21 countries. Honours: Many diplomas and awards including: Medal of Works, Yugoslavia, 1970; Order of Works, Yugoslavia, 1983; Diploma and Medal, Croatian Association of Production Engineers, 2000; Diploma and Certificate, International Symposium on Revitalization and Modernization of Production, 2001; Diploma and Certificate, International Scientific Conference on Development and Modernization of Production, 2001, 2003. Memberships: Croatian Association of Production Engineering; Croatian Society for Communications, Computing, Electronics, Measurement and Control; Croatian Metallurgical Society; Society for Robotics of Bosnia and Herzegovina; President, International Scientific Board: International Scientific Conference on Production Engineering, 1997-2001, International Conference on Development and Moderisation, 2002-2005; Member of Scientific Committee: International DAAAM Symposium, Austria, 2002-2005; International ATDC, Croatia, 2002-2004, International Research Expert, TMT, Bosnia and Herzegovina, 1995-2002, Spain, 2002-2003, Turkey, 2004-2005; International ICIT, Slovenia, 1997-2005, International CIM, Croatia, 1997-2005. Address: Kucina 10, HR-51000 Rijeka, Croatia. E-mail: milanj@riteh.hr Website: www.riteh.hr

**JURUKOVA Zanka Borissova,** b. 18 March 1932, Plovidiv, Bulgaria. m. Peter Georgiev, 1 son, 1 daughter. Education: MD, High Medical School, Sofia, 1957; Bd Cert, Pathologist, 1964; PhD, 1968, DSc, 1978, Professor of Pathology, 1986, Medical Academy, Sofia; Fellow Humboldt Foundation, Medical Faculty, Hamburg, 1965-67; Ultrastructural Pathology, Medical Faculty Salpetriere, Paris, 1973-74. Appointments: Research Fellow, Cardiovascular Pathology, Bulgarian Academy of Sciences, 1964-73; Associate Professor of Pathology, 1974-85, Professor of Pathology, 1986-, Medical Faculty, Medical University, Sofia, Bulgaria. Publications: Over 180 articles in domestic and international journals; Over 110 reports at Bulgarian and International congresses and symposium; Contribution to 4 textbooks of Pathology, 1982, 1990, 1992, 1998. Awards: Best Monography Award, Medical Academy of Sofia, 1980. Memberships: Bulgarian Society of Pathologists; German Society of Pathologists; European Society of Pathologists; French Society of Ultrastructural Pathologists; European Society of Atherosclerosis; International Society of Atherosclerosis; New York Academy of Sciences; Bulgarian Academy of Medicine. Address: Boulevard "Vitosha" 28, Sofia 1000, Bulgaria.

**JUSTICE James Walcott,** b, 16 December 1932, New York City, New York, USA. Physician. m. M A Harras, 3 sons, 1 daughter. Education: BA, Chemistry, Bucknell University, 1954; MD, Medicine, New York Medical College, 1958; Master

of Public Health, Johns Hopkins School of Hygiene and Public Health, 1962. Appointments: Commissioned, 1959-85, retired, 1985, United States Department of Health, Education and Welfare; Served in Indian Health Service, Alaska, Oklahoma, Arizona; On loan to United States Department of State, Peace Corps, Korea; Community Medicine, Health Science Centre, University of Arizona, 1987-. Publications: Twenty Years of Diabetes on the Warm Springs Indian Reservation, 1989; Cancer Profiles of Two American Indian Tribes, 1992; Diabetes in the Desert People, 1993. Honours: Public Health Service Meritorious Service Award; Foreign Service Award; Hazardous Duty Award. Memberships: American Public Health Association; Physicians for Social Responsibility; Clinical Society of US Public Health Service. Address: Native American Research and Training Centre, Arizona Health Science Centre, 1642 E Helen Street, Tucson, AZ 85719, USA.

# DICTIONARY OF INTERNATIONAL BIOGRAPHY

# K

**KABANOV Modest,** b. 19 March 1926, St Petersburg, Russia. Psychiatrist. m. Lydia Kabanova. Education: St Petersburg Medical University, 1948. Appointments: Head Physician, District Psychoneurological Dispensary, St Petersburg, 1958-60; Head Physician, IVth City Mental Hospital, 1960-64; Director, V M Bekhterev Psychoneurological Research Institute, 1964-2002; International Programmes Director, V M Bekhterev Psychoneurological Research Institute, 2002-. Publications: Over 260 in Russian and foreign languages including 9 Monographs. Honours: Honoured Scientist of the Russian Federation. Memberships: President World Association for Dynamic Psychiatry; World Association for Psychosocial Rehabilitation; World Association for Social Psychiatry. Address: V M Bekhterev Psychoneurological Research Institute 3, Bekhterev Street, St Petersburg 192019, Russia.

**KABASAWA Uki,** b. 21 January 1965, Namerikawa, Japan. Physicist. Education: Bachelor Degree, 1988, Master Degree, 1990, Osaka University. Appointments: Researcher, Central Research Laboratory, 1990-96, Engineer, Electronic Device Manufacturing Equipment and Engineering Division, 1996-99, Engineer, Instruments, Beam Technology Centre, 1999-2001, Hitachi Ltd; Engineer, Hitachi High-Technologies Corporation, Beam Technologies Center, 2001-. Publications include: Studies of High Temperature Superconductors, volume 1, 1989, volume 6, 1990; Advances in Superconductivity VI, vol 2, 1994; Quantum Theory of Many-Body Systems, 1999; Elements of Advanced Quantum Theory, 2000; Introduction to Mesoscopic Physics (translator), 2000; The Physics of Quantum Fields (translator), 2002; The Case of the Missing Neutrinos (translator), 2002; The Physics of Low-Dimensional Semiconductor, translator, 2004. Memberships: American Association for the Advancement of Science; New York Academy of Sciences; Physical Society of Japan; Japan Society of Applied Physics. Address: Hitachi High-Technologies Corporation, Beam Technology Centre, 882 Ichige, Hitachinaka-shi, Ibaraki-ken 312-8504, Japan. E-mail: kabasawa-uki@naka.hitachi-hitec.com

**KABIR Shahjahan,** b. 24 January 1943, Jessore, Bangladesh. Biomedical Researcher. m. Ingrid Birgitta Sterner, 12 August 1971. Education: BSc, Rajshahi College, Bangladesh, 1961; MSc, Rajshahi University, 1963; MSc, 1970, PhD, 1971, University of British Columbia, Canada. Appointments: Research Associate, NIH, Beth, Maryland, USA, 1974-756; Scientist, Johns Hopkins University, Baltimore, USA, 1977-78; Scientist, International Centre for Diarrhoeal Disease Research, Bangladesh, 1979-82; National Institute of Public Health and University of Groningen, Bilthoven, The Netherlands, 1983-85; Scientist, Karolinska Institute, Stockholm, 1986-90; Consultant, Sultan Qaboos, University College of Medicine, Oman, 1990-95; Consultant, University of Science and Technology, Chittagong, Bangladesh, 1996-97; Chief Executive Officer, Academic Research and Information Management, Stockholm, Sweden, 1998-. Publications: Author, Contributor, several original scientific articles in journals. Honours: Scientific invention related to cholera bacteria, selected on the journal cover of Society for General Microbiology Quarterly, 1987. Memberships: President, Bangladesh Association, British Columbia, Canada, 1971-72; Governing Committee, Bangladesh Association, Washington, DC, 1974-75; New York Academy of Sciences, 1991-. Address: Murargatan 16A. 754 37 Uppsala, Sweden. E-mail: skabir43@yahoo.com

**KAČALA Ján,** b. 8 April 1937, Dobšiná, Slovakia. Professor. m. Anna Kačalová, 1 son. Education: Pedagogical University in Bratislava, 1954-58; Candidatus Scientiarum (CSc), 1968; PhDr, 1969; DrSc, 1983. Appointments: Editor-in-Chief, Kultura slova, 1971-91; Director, Ludovit Stur Linguistics Institute of the Slovak Academy of Sciences, 1981-91; Chairman, Accrediting Committee, 1995-99, Advisory Board of the Slovak Government, Head of the Slovak Language Department, Pedagogical Faculty of Comenius University, 1992-2004. Publications: The Second Predicate in Slovak, 1971; The Verb and Semantic Structure of the Sentence, 1989; The Syntactic System of Language, 1998. Honours: Honorable Plaque of J Dobrovsky, Czecho-Slovak Academy of Sciences, 1987; Golden Honorable Plaque of L Stur, Slovak Academy of Sciences, 1997. Memberships: Corresponding Member, Slovak Academy of Sciences, 1987-; Societas Linguistica Europaea; Slovak Linguistic Society. Address: Bagarova 4, 841 01 Bratislava, Slovak Republic.

**KAČERGIENÈ Nella (Vernickaitè),** b. 19 October 1935, Minsk. Physician; Paediatrician. Education: Doctor's Assistant, Obstetrician, Kaunas Paramedical and Obstetrical School, 1954; Physician, Kaunas Medical Institute, 1962; Clinical Physician diploma, 1970, Postgraduate, 1973, Diploma, Candidate of Medical Science, Institute of Paediatrics, USSR, Academy of Medical Sciences, Moscow, 1973; Senior Research Diploma, USSR, 1984; Diploma, Med Sci Doctor's degree, USSR Academy of Medical Sciences, 1987; Senior scientific researcher, Vilnius, 1984; Paediatrician of highest category, Vilnius, 1991; Diploma, Dr Sci habilitas, 1993. Appointments: Nurse, Surgery Department, Kaunas Town Hospital No 2, 1952-54; Doctor's Assistant-Obstetrician, Jieznas Hospital, 1954-56; Paediatrician, Prienai District Hospital, 1962-67, Republican Vilnius Children's Hospital, 1967-68; Clinical Physician of the Institute of Paediatrics, USSR, Academy of Medical Sciences, Moscow, 1968-73; Junior Research Worker, 1973-79, Senior Research Worker, 1979-85, Department of Paediatrics of the Lithuanian Scientific Research Institute of Experimental and Clinical Medicine; Senior Research Worker, Lithuanian Scientific Research Institute of Mother and Child Care, 1985-91; Chief Scientific Researcher, Centre of Paediatrics of Vilnius University Children's Hospital, 1991-97, Centre of Paediatrics of Vilnius University, 1998-2001. Publications: (monograph) SOS to the Life on Earth: The Effect of Environmental Factors and Atmospheric Chemical Pollutants on the Human Organism at Certain Periods of Its Ontogenesis, 1999; 210 scientific works and 2 inventions. Honours include: Gold Record of Achievement in Honour of Career Excellence and Outstanding Contributions to International Society, ABI, USA; 20th Century Award for Achievement, IBC, MCM, 1900-2000, England, Silver Medal, 1998; Gold Medal, Leading Intellectuals of the World, ABI, 1998; Gold and Silver Medal, 2000 Outstanding Scientists of the 20th Century, IBC, England, 1999; Gold Medal, International Scientist of the Year, IBC, England, 2001; The IBC Millennium Time Capsule, IBC, England, 1999; Torch of Global Inspiration, ABI, USA, 2000; Presidential Seal of Honour, for Exemplary Achievements in the Fields of Pediatry and Ecology, USA, 2000; Scientific Excellence – Gold Medal, USA, 2001; Secretary General of the United Cultural Convention, USA, 2001; Great Minds of the 21st Century Gold Medal, USA, 2002; International Peace Prize, United Cultural Convention, USA, 2003; The World Order of Science-Education-Culture, European Academy of Informatisation, Brussels, 2002; Albert Schweitzer Gold Medal for Science and Peace, Albert Schweitzer International University, Spain, 2004; American Medal of Honor, ABI, USA, 2004; Da Vinci Diamond, IBC, 2004; Proclamation: The Genius Elite (Documented in Leading Intellectuals of the World, ABI, 2004); Numerous diplomas including: Greatest and Great Minds of the 21st Century Diploma, USA, 2002; Ambassador of Grand Eminence, Diploma, USA, 2002; Researcher of the Year, 2001,

Diploma, USA, 2002-; The World Order of Science – Education – Culture, European Academy of Informatisation, Brussels, 2002; Da Vinci Diamond, IBC, 2004. Memberships include: Lithuanian Paediatric Academic Council, 1973-; Russian Academy of Medical Science Committee of Chronobiology and Chronomedicine, 1985; National Geographic Society, USA, 1991; International Society of Biometeorology, USA, 1991; International Committee for Research and Study of Environmental Factors, Brussels, Belgium, 1992; Founder Diplomatic Counsellor, London Diplomatic Academy, 2000; Member of the Assembly of the International Diplomatic Academy, Geneva, 2002. Address: Viršuliškių 89-22, LT-05117 Vilnius, Lithuania.

**KACZMAREK Bozydar Leon Jan,** b. 11 August 1946, Jarocin, Poland. Psychologist; Neuropsychologist; Psychologist of Communications. m. Renata Kusmierzak, 1 son. Education: MA, 1969; Diplomat, 1972; PhD, 1979; DSc, 1985; Professor, 1992. Appointments: Assistant, 1974-79, Assistant Professor, 1979-86, Associate Professor, 1986-91, Head, Developmental Psychology and Neurolinguistics Department, 1986-, Director, Psychology Institute, 1991-2002, Professor, 1991-, University Maria Curie Sklodowska. Publications include: Brain Organisation of Language, 1985-93; Brain Language Behaviour, 1994, 3rd edition, 1998. Honours: Golden Cross of Merit, 1994. Membership: Polish Neurolinguistic Society. Address: 20-633 Lublin, ul Skrzatow 2 m. 10, Poland.

**KADRI S Manzoor,** b. India. Physician. Education: MBBS, Government Medical College, Srinagar, Kashmir, India, University of Kashmir, Srinagar, Kashmir, India; Postgraduate Training: Certified Course in HIV/AIDS & STD Management, 2002, Certified Course in Geriatric Medicine, 2004, Indian Medical Association. Appointments: Currently, Faculty Member, Regional Institute of Health and Family Welfare, Directorate of Health Services, Kashmir, India; Associated with undergraduate theoretical and practical teaching programme for MBBS, BDS students and laboratory technologists; Associated with laboratory work, serology, bacteriology, screening of tuberculosis and voluntary counselling and testing centre for HIV/AIDS at the SMHS Hospital, Srinagar; Involved in training of medical doctors and para-medics in newer concepts of disease like revised national tuberculosis control programme, awareness regarding HIV/AIDS, reproductive and child health, disease surveillance and working as a Nodal Officer for disease surveillance for the districts of Kupwara and Leh under the National Surveillance Programme for Communicable Diseases. Publications: Book chapters in: Psychology, 2004; Agricultural Development and Vector Borne Disease, 2004; A Guide to Common Diseases, 2004; Epidemiology for Health Professionals, 2004; Health Care Waste Management (An Introduction) for the Health Care Worker, 2004; Food, Waste and Family Health – A Manual for Health Educators, 2004; More than 30 articles in medical journals: Scientific Reviewer for Chest, Journal of the American College of Chest Physicians; Scientific Reviewer for Thorax (BMJ Group of Publications); Editorial Board, Indian Journal for the Practising Doctor. Memberships: Medical Advisor, Gerson Lehrman Group's Council of Healthcare Advisors, New York, USA. New York Academy of Sciences; All India Advisory Board, Journal of the Indian Medical Association; Indian Medical Association; Indian Society of Health Administrators; Indian Association of Medical Informatics; Computer Society of India; Brand Ambassador, Bioinformatics Institute of India. Address: Post Pox 1143, GPO, Srinagar 190001, Kashmir, India. E-mail: kadrism@sancharnet.in Website: http://rihfwk.indmedica.com

**KAFELNIKOV Yevgeny Aleksandrovich,** b. 18 February 1974, Sochi, Russia. Tennis Player. m. 2 daughters. Education: Krasnodar Pedagogical Institute. Appointments: Started playing tennis in Sochi Children Sports School, 1982; Later with coach Anatoly Lepeshin; ATP Professional, 1992-; Won 17 ATP tournaments including Milan, St Petersburg, Gstaad, Long Island; Won French Open (singles and doubles), 1996; Won, Moscow Kremlin Cup, 1997; Won, Australian Open, 1999; Member, Russian Federation Davis Cup Championship Team, 1993; Runner-up, World Championship, Hanover, 1997; Highest ATP Rating 1st, 1999; Olympic singles champion, Sydney, 2000; Winner of 51 pro titles by 2002. Address: All-Russian Tennis Association, Luzhnetskaya nab 8, 119871 Moscow, Russia.

**KAJI Akira,** b. 13 January 1930, Tokyo, Japan (US citizen). Professor. m. Hideko Kaji, 2 sons, 2 daughters. Education: BS, University of Tokyo, 1953; PhD, Johns Hopkins University, 1958. Appointments: Research Fellow, Johns Hopkins Hospital, 1958-59; Guest Investigator, Rockefeller Institute, 1959; Research Associate, Department of Microbiology, Nashville, 1959-62; Visiting Scientist, Oak Ridge National Laboratory, Tennessee, 1962-63; Associate, 1963-64, Assistant Professor, 1964-67, Associate Professor, 1967-72, Department of Microbiology, University of Pennsylvania; Professor, Hygienic Chemistry, University of Tokyo, 1972-73; Professor, Department of Microbiology, University of Pennsylvania, 1972-; John Simon Guggenheim Scholar, Imperial Cancer Research Fund Laboratories, London, 1972-73; Visiting Professor, Fogarty International Senior Fellow, Kyoto University, Japan, 1985. Publications: 110 articles. Honours include: Special Fellowship, Japanese Government; Dazian Predoctoral Fellowship; Japan Society Fellowship. Memberships: Sigma Xi; American Society for Microbiology; British Society of Biological Chemists; American Society of Biological Chemists; Japanese Society of Biological Chemists; American Society of Chemistry; American Society of Cell Biology. Address: Department of Microbiology, University of Pennsylvania School of Medicine, 225 Johnson Pavilion, 3610 Hamilton Walk, Philadelphia, PA 19104-6076, USA. E-mail: kaji@mail.med.upenn.edu

**KALABUKHOVA Tatyana Nikolaevna,** b. 19 April 1939, Moscow, USSR. Biophysicist; Lecturer; Poet; Writer. Education: Diploma with distinction, Moscow State University, Moscow, 1962; Postgraduate, Institute of Biophysics, USSR Academy of Sciences, Moscow, 1965-68; Diploma of Candidate of Science, Moscow, 1971. Appointments: Stager, Researcher, 1962-64, Junior Scientist, Collaborator, 1964-65, Institute of Biophysics, USSR Academy of Sciences, Moscow; Scientist, Collaborator, Institute of Biophysics, USSR Academy of Sciences, Pushchino, 1968-90; Scientist, Collaborator, Institute of Cell Biophysics, USSR Academy of Sciences, Pushchino, 1991; Senior Scientist, Collaborator, Institute of Cell Biophysics, Russian Academy of Sciences, Pushchino, 1992-; Lecturer, Pushchino Ecology Museum, 2003-. Publications: Numerous articles published in professional scientific journals. Honours: Medal of Veteran of Labour of Presidium of Supreme Soviet of USSR, 1988; Medal of President of Russian Federation, 1997; Grantee, Russian Fund for Basic Researches, 1996-98. Memberships: Chairman, Pushchino Branch of Ultraviolet Radiation Section of Science Council on Biophysics Problems, USSR Academy of Sciences, 1976-1980. Address: Microregion (G)-25-116, Pushchino-on-Oka, Moscow Region, 142290, Russia.

**KALININ George,** b. 24 September 1947, Kazakhstan, Petropavlovsk. Materials Science. m. Nikitina Svetlana, 1 son, 1 daughter. Education: BS, Physics of Metals, 1971; PhD, Materials Science, 1980; Scientific Management, Management

Certificate, 1985, 1989. Appointments: Engineer, 1971, Senior Engineer, 1974, Senior Scientist, 1981, Head, Materials Laboratory, 1983, Head of Department, 1987, Research and Development Institute of Power Engineering; International Joint Central Team, ITER, 1994; Engineering Center of Nuclear Equipment Strength, Reliability and Lifetime of Fission Reactors (ENES), 2002. Publications: Over 80 contributions to professional journals, 4 patents. Honours: Bronze Medal, All-Union Exhibition, Moscow, 1980; Honour Certificate, Minister of Atomic Energy, Minatom RF, 1989. Membership: Nuclear Society; RF; Scientific and Technical Society of Materials Scientists. Address: Engineering Center of Nuclear Equipment Strength, Reliability and Lifetime (ENES), PO Box 788, Moscow, 101 000, Russia.

**KALMBACH Gudrun,** b. 27 May 1937, Grosserlach, Germany. Professor. Education: Dr rer. nat. University of Göttingen, Germany. Appointments: Assistant, University of Göttingen, Germany, 1963-66; Lecturer, University of Illinois, Urbana, USA, 1967-69; Assistant Professor, University of Massachusetts, Amherst, USA, 1970-71; Assistant Professor, Pennsylvania State University, University Park, USA, 1969-75; Professor, University of Ulm, Germany, 1975-2002; Director, MINT, 2003-. Publications: 12 books; Articles in professional journals on algebra, topology, quantum structures, education; Chief Editor, Journal MINT. Honours: 4 medals; 2 titles; 2 books in honour of 60th Birthday. Memberships: AMS; AWM; ECHA; Emmy-Noether-Verein (Chair); FDP; LDA; OIA. Address: PF 1533, D-86818 Bad Woerishofen, Germany. E-mail: mint-01@web.de

**KALPAKIOTIS Athanasios,** b. 2 May 1947, Brakpan, South Africa. Composer; Industrial Stylist. Education: Matric, Advanced Academic Grade; NTC5, Mechanotecnics (Machine Tools and Machine Design); Various certificates and diplomas. Appointments: Many contract jobs; Currently pursuing interest in composing and making music and clipart; Web presence, 2000-. Publications: Composer and copyright holder of many songs. Honours: Sons of England Essay Competition, Vryheid, South Africa, 1958; Various art prizes; Finalist in various poetry competitions, 2000-. Memberships: Science of the Soul. Address: PO Box 28559, Kensington 2101, South Africa. E-mail: zeusmachine@netscape.net

**KALRA G L,** b. 1 July 1941, Londkhor, Pakistan. Teacher; Researcher. m. Raj Kalra, 2 daughters. Education: MSc, 1962, PhD, 1967, University of Delhi. Appointments: Senior Research Fellow, University of Delhi, 1966-69; Fellow, Flinders University of South Australia, 1969-70; RA, University of Delhi, 1969-70; Lecturer, 1974-84; Reader, 1984-86; Associate Professor, Al Fateh University, Tripoli, 1986-87; Reader, University of Delhi, 1984-94; Professor in Physics, University of Delhi, 1994-. Publications: 48 research papers mostly in international scientific journals. Honours: Dr Vikram Sarabhai Award, 1986; Australia VC's Committee Visiting Fellowship, 1990; Offered New York Academy of Sciences Membership. Memberships: Founder Member, Astronomical Society of India; Plasma Science Society of India; Listed in Who's Who and biographical publications. Address: Department of Physics and Astrophysics, University of Delhi, Delhi 110 007, India.

**KALTENBACH Anneliese Elisabeth,** b. Karlsruhe-Durlach, Germany. Retired Senior Civil Servant. Education: Diplomas, Commercial French and English Studies, Russian Language and Literature, Karlsruhe, Germanic, General Linguistics, and History Studies; Paris Lic-ès-Lettres, 1957; PhD, Paris, 1962; Appointments: Employee, German Embassy Paris and Ministry for Foreign Affairs, Bonn, 1951-60; Deputy Chief for West European Affairs, Press and Information Office, Federal Government of Bonn, 1961-82. Publications include: Ludwig Haeusser, Historien et patriote (1818-1867), 1965. Honours include: Gold Medal, Robert Schuman, Silver Gilt Medal, Municipality of Paris, Bronze Medal Académie Française, 1966; Commander Order of Oranje-Nassau, 1972; Order of Leopold II, 1972; Commandeur de l'Ordre du Mérite du Grand-Duché de Luxembourg, 1973; Silver Medal, French-German Youth Office, 1982; Commandeur de l'Ordre National du Mérite de la République Française, 1980; Merit Cross First Class, Federal Republic of Germany, 1982; Officer dans l'ordre des Palmes Académiques, 1995. Address: Duerenstrasse 29, D 53173 Bonn, Germany.

**KALVARSKAYA Valeria Pavlovna,** b. 26 January 1930, Krasnodar, USSR. Geologist; Geophysicist. m. Yevgeny Lvovich Kalvarsky, 1 son. Education: Graduate, St Petersburg State University, 1954; PhD, Technical Sciences, 1963; Professor of Geology and Mineralogy, 1990; Corresponding Member, Russian Academy of Natural Sciences, 2001. Appointments: Laboratory Head of Magnetic Logging and Department Head of Logging and Mining Geophysics, 25 years until 1990, Principal Researcher, 1990-, VIRG-Rudgeofizika (FGUNPP "Geologorazvedka" since 2004); Scientific Curator for Geophysical Well Logging of Ore Deposits, 1978-90; Chairman of the Scientific and Methodic Council on Geological-Geophysical Technologies of Exploration for Hard Minerals, 1989-, Ministry of Geology of the USSR (now Ministry of Natural Resources of the Russian Federation); Chairman, St Petersburg Branch, EurAsian Geophysical Society, 1994-. Publications: Author of over 200 scientific papers (industry instructions, guides, articles, methodical recommendations) of which more than 120 have been published. Honours: Honoured Geologist of Russia; Medal of the Second Class Order of Merit to the Motherland; Medal of Merit in Revival of Russian Sciences, International Academy of Nature and Society Sciences; Honorary Subsurface Explorer; Medal for Labour Valour in commemoration of V I Lenin 100th anniversary, 1970; Excellent Subsurface Explorer, 1982; Medal of Merit in Subsurface Exploration, 1982; Medals for Achievement in the USSR National Economy, 1964, 1980, 1983; Honorary Diplomas from Mintopenergo, 2001 and EAGO, 2000, 2005. Memberships: EurAsian Geophysical Society; Society of Naturalists; Scientific Councils of FGUNPP "Geologorazvedka" and NPP "Sevmorgeo". Address: Basseynaya Str 75, Apr 44, 196211 St Petersburg, Russia. E-mail: eago@newmail.ru

**KALYANE Venkatrao Lakshmanrao,** b. 1 June 1955, Talwada (Maratha), Bhalki, India. Publication Officer. m. Sangeeta, 2 daughters. Education: BSc, B Lib Sc, MSc, DIIT, BEd, Postgraduate Diploma in Journalism and Mass Communications, MEd, Postgraduate Diploma in Higher Education, MLIS. Appointments: Senior Research Fellow, 1977-81; Research Associate, 1981-83; Technical Assistant T-II-3, 1983-88; T-4, 1989-90; Junior Scientific Officer T-6, 1990-93; Scientific Officer SD, 1993-95; Scientific Officer D, 1996-2000; Scientific Officer E, 2000-. Publications: 100 research articles; Scientometric studies on individual scientists as scholarly communication stars: Nobel laureates (C V Raman, P G de Gennes, S Chandrasekhar, Barbara McClintock, D C Hodgkin, A H Zewail, Harold W Kroto, Wolfgang Ketterle, Leland H Hartwell), Citation studies (R Chidambaram, Vikram Sarabhai, H J Bhabha); Greatest contributor to Bio-Bibliometrics; Advisory Editorial Board Member, Indian Journal of Information, Library and Society; E-LIS Editor for India at eprints.rclis.org. Memberships: United Writers' Association; Bombay Science Librarians' Association; Indian Science Writers' Association; Indian Library Association; Society for

Information Science. Address: Scientific Information Resource Division, Knowledge Management Group, BARC, Trombay, Mumbai-400 085, India. E-mail: vlkalyane@rediffmail.com

**KAMANDA Kama Sywor,** b. 11 November 1952, Luebo, Congo-Kinshasa. Writer; Poet; Novelist; Playwright; Essayist; Lecturer; Storyteller. Education: State Diploma in Literary Humanities, 1968; Degree in Journalism, Journalism School, Kinshasa, Congo, 1969; Degree in Political Sciences, University of Kinshasa, 1973; HD, University of Liège, 1981. Appointments: Lecturer, various universities, schools and cultural centres; Literary Critic, various newspapers. Publications: Les Contes du griot, Volume 3 (Les Contes des veillées africaines), 1967, 1985, 1998; Les Résignations, 1986, 1997; Éclipse d'étoiles, 1987, 1997; Les Contes du griot, Volume 1, 1988, 1997; La Somme du néant, 1989, 1999; Les Contes du griot, Volume 2 (La Nuit des griots), 1991, 1996; L'Exil des songes, 1992; Les Myriades des temps vécus, 1992, 1999; Les Vents de l'épreuve, 1993, 1997; Quand dans l'âme les mers s'agitent, 1994, 1998; Lointaines sont les rives du destin, 1994, 2000; L'Étreinte des mots, 1995; Chants de brumes, 1997, 2002; Œuvre poétique, 1999; Les Contes du crépuscule, 2000; Le Sang des solitudes, 2002; Contes, 2003, 2004. Honours: Paul Verlaine Award, French Academy, 1987; Louise Labé Award Jury, 1990; Literature Award, Black African Association of French-Speaking Writers, 1991; Special Poetry Award, Academy Institute in Paris, 1992; Silver Jasmin for Poetical Originality, 1992; Special Prize, French-Speaking Countries General Council Agency, 1992; Théophile Gautier Award, French Academy, 1993; Subject of: Kama Kamanda au Pays du Conte (M C De Connick), 1993; Kama Kamanda, Poète de l'Exil (Pierrette Sartin), 1994; Kama Sywor Kamanda, chantre de la mémoire égyptienne (Isabella Cata and Frank Nyalendo), 2003. Memberships: Society of French Poets; French Society of Men of Letters; Association of African Writers; PEN Club; Association of French-Speaking Writers; International Council of French-Speaking Studies; SABAM. Address: 18 Am Moul, L-7418 Buschdorf, Luxembourg. E-mail: kamanda@pt.lu

**KAMEDA Hisao,** b. 15 April 1942, Gifu-City, Gifu, Japan. University Professor. m. Mieko Kameda, 3 sons. Education: Bachelor of Science, 1965, Master of Science, 1967, Doctor of Science, 1970, University of Tokyo, Tokyo, Japan. Appointments: Research Assistant, University of Tokyo, 1970-71; Assistant Professor, University of Electro-Communications, 1971-73; Visiting Scientist, IBM T J Watson Research Center, 1973-74; Visiting Researcher, University of Toronto, 1974-75; Associate Professor, 1973-85, Professor, 1985-92, University of Electro-Communications; Professor, University of Tsukuba, 1992-. Publications: Articles in professional journals including: JACM, 1982, 2002, ACM Transactions Computer Systems, 1984, 1986; IEEE Transactions Software Engineering, 1986; IEEE Transactions Computers, 1998. Honours: Fellow, IEICE; Fellow, IPSJ; Best Paper Award, IEEE NACON '97. Address: Department CS, Graduate School of SIE, University of Tsukuba, 1-1-1 Tennodai, Tsukuba Science City, Ibaraki 305-8573 Japan. Website: www.osdp.cs.tsukuba.ac.jp/~kameda

**KAMENAR Boris,** b. 20 February 1929, Susak-Rijeka. University Professor. m. Maja Perusko, Vedrana. Education: Diploma in Chemical Technology, University of Zagreb, 1953; PhD, Chemistry, University of Zagreb, 1960; Postdoctoral Fellowship, University of Oxford, England, 1964. Appointments: Head, Testing Laboratory, Metal Factory, Rijeka, 1953-56; Research Scientist, Rudjer Boskovic Institute, Zagreb, 1956-62; Assistant and Associate Professor, University of Zagreb, 1962-72; Professor of Chemistry, University of Zagreb, 1972-99; Professor Emeritus, 1999-; Visiting Fellow, All Souls College,

Oxford, 1971-72; Visiting Professor, University of Auckland, New Zealand, 1980; Visiting Professor, Massey University, Palmerston North, New Zealand, 1989-90, 1995. Publications: About 160 articles in scientific journals. Honours: Scientific Award, Republic of Croatia, 1970; Scientific Award, City of Zagreb, 1980; Scientific Award for Life Achievement, Republic of Croatia, 1999. Memberships: President, Croatian Chemical Society, 1976-80; President, European Crystallographic Committee, 1978-81; Croatian Academy of Sciences and Arts, 1988-, Foreign Secretary, 2000-2004; Fellow of the World Academy of Art and Science, 2005-; President, Croatian Crystallographic Association, 1992-. Address: Laboratory of General and Inorganic Chemistry, Faculty of Science, University of Zagreb, Ulica Kralja Zvonimira 8, 10000 Zagreb, Croatia.

**KAMERER Jocelyne Maria,** b. 6 September 1950, Port-a-Moussons, France. Poet. Education: Upsala College, East Orange, New Jersey. Publications: Reflections, 1990; Life Within. Contributions to: Periodicals and many additional small journals. Honours: Gold Quill Award, 1990; Silver Quill Award, 1991; 1st Place, Plowman, 1991; 4 Blue Ribbon Awards, Southern Poetry Association, 1991; 3rd Place, Khepera, 1994; More than 12 1st Place, Robert Bennett's Viewpoint. Memberships: National Association. Address: 6256 Village Lane, Colorado Springs, CO 80918, USA.

**KAMEYAMA Michitaka,** b. 12 May 1950, Utsunomiya, Japan. Professor. m. Kimiko Owashi, 1 son, 2 daughters. Education: Bachelor Degree, Electronic Engineering, 1973, Master Degree, Electronic Engineering, 1975, Doctor Degree, Electronic Engineering, 1978, Tohoku University. Appointments: Research Associate, 1978-81, Associate Professor, 1981-91, Professor, 1991-, Tohoku University. Publications include: A Multiplier Chip with Multiple-Valved Bidirectional Current-Mode Logic Circuits, 1988. Membership: IEEE. Address: 6-10-8 Minami-Yoshinari, Aoba-ku, Sendai, Japan.

**KAMINEK Miroslav,** b. 11 November 1933, Prague, Czech Republic. Plant Physiologist. m. Jana Kaminkova, 2 sons. Education: Dipl Ing, Horticulture, Mendels Agricultural University, Brno, 1959; PhD, Plant Physiology, Czechoslovak Academy of Sciences, 1965. Appointments: Lecturer, Plant Physiology, University of Baghdad, Iraq, 1965-67; Scientist, Institute of Experimental Botany, Academy of Sciences if the Czech Republic, 1967-; Research Fellow, Department of Botany, University of Wisconsin, USA, 1969-70; Visiting Scientist, ARCO Plant Cell Research Institute, Dublin, California, USA, 1986-87; Visiting Professor, Oregon State University, Department of Botany and Plant Pathology, 1987; Visiting Professor, Department of Biochemistry, Universities of Missouri, Columbia and Michigan, 1992-93. Publications: Author of 150 scientific papers. Honours: Award, Czech Academy of Sciences, 1989; Medal for achievements in biological sciences, Czech Academy of Sciences, 2003. Memberships: American Society of Plant Biologists; European Federation of Plant Physiology Societies. Address: Vratislovova 30, Prague 2, Czech Republic. E-mail: kaminek@ueb.cas.cz

**KAMINSKI Wlodzimierz,** b. 16 April 1924, Skierniewice, Poland. Scientist; Economist. m. Krystyna Tyszkowska, 1 son. Education: MS, 1947, LLD, 1948, University of Cracow; DAgricEcon, 1961, Professor, Economic Sciences, 1973-92, doctor honoris causa, 2000, Agricultural University, Warsaw. Appointments: Researcher, Economist, 1959-92, Extraordinary Professor, 1973-80, Ordinary Professor, 1980-92, Faculty of Food Technology, Agricultural University, Warsaw; Ordinary Professor, 1997-, Prorector, 1998-2004, Warsaw College of Economics, Warsaw; Visiting Professor, various universities and institutions; Head, Division for Spatial Research, 1983-92, Director, 1990, Institute of Agricultural and Food Economics. Publications: 24 books, over 300 publications in 8 languages. Honours: Knight, Officer and Commander Cross of Polonia Restituta, 1964, 1979, 1987; Cross of National Army, Polish Government, 1994; Croix d'Officier du Merite Agricole, French Government, 1995; Man of the Year, 2004. Memberships: Polish Scientific Society of Food Industry; Polish Academy of Sciences; 2 committees, Association of Agricultural Economists; Hungarian Scientific Society of Food Industry; French Academy of Agriculture; International Institute of Refrigeration, Paris; New York Academy of Sciences. Address: Smolna 15, Room 11, 00375 Warsaw, Poland.

**KAMLI Ali Ahmad,** b. 11 November 1963, Saudi Arabia. Professor. m. Intesar, 2 sons, 2 daughters. Education: Diploma, Essex University, England, 1988; MS, 1989, PhD, 1991, Southampton University, England. Appointments: Associate Professor, 2000-, Head of Physics Department, 2002-2003, Dean of College of Engineering and Computer Science, 2003-05, King Khalid University, Saudi Arabia. Publications: Articles as co-author in scientific journals including: Physical Review; Journal of Physics; Journal of Modern Optics; Canadian Journal of Physics; Journal of Optics B; Physica E. Honours: British Summer Award; Scholarship from King Khalid University as Visiting Professor at University of Rochester, USA. Memberships: Optical Society of America; Saudi Physical Society; Founder, Saudi Physical Society. Address: Department of Physics, King Khalid University, Abha, PO Box 9003, Saudi Arabia. E-mail: aakamli@kku.edu.sa

**KAMU Okko,** b. 7 March 1946, Helsinki, Finland. Conductor. Education: Violin studies with Väinö Arjava from 1949 and with Professor Onni Suhonen at the Sibelius Academy, Helsinki, 1952-67. Career: Leader of the Suhonen Quartet, 1964; Leader of the Finnish National Opera Orchestra, 1966-69; Conducted Britten's The Turn of the Screw in Helsinki, 1968; Guest Conductor, Swedish Royal Opera, 1969; Chief Conductor, Finnish Radio Symphony Orchestra, 1971-77; Music Director, Oslo Philharmonic, 1975-79; Music Director, Helsinki Philharmonic,1981-88; Principal Conductor, Dutch Radio Symphony, 1983-86; Principal Guest Conductor, City of Birmingham Symphony Orchestra, 1985-88; Principal Conductor, Sjaelland Symphony Orchestra (Copenhagen Philharmonic), 1988-89; Guest engagements with the Berlin Philharmonic, Suisse Romande Orchestra, Vienna Symphony Orchestra and orchestras in the USA, Far East, Australia, South America and Europe; Conducted the premieres of Sallinen's operas The Red Line and The King Goes Forth to France; Metropolitan Opera, 1983, US premiere of The Red Line; Covent Garden, 1987, in the British premiere of The King Goes Forth to France; Principal Conductor of the Helsingborg Symphony Orchestra, 1991-2000; Music Director of the Finnish National Opera, 1996-2000; Principal Guest Conductor, Singapore Symphony Orchestra, 1995-2001 and principal Guest Conductor of Lausanne Chamber Orchestra, 1999-2002. Recordings: About 70 recordings for various labels; Sallinen's Shadows, Cello Concerto and 5th Symphony. Honours: Winner, 1st Herbert von Karajan Conductors' Competition, Berlin, 1969; Member of the Royal Swedish Academy of Music. Address: Villa Arcadia, C/Mozart 7, Rancho Domingo, 29639 Benalmadena Pueblo, Spain.

**KANAZAWA Takafumi,** b. 5 December 1926, Tokyo, Japan. Chemist; Educator. m. Taiko Suzuki, 1 son. Education: Bachelor of Engineering, 1948, Doctor of Engineering, 1961, University of Tokyo. Appointments: Research Associate, 1952, Lecturer, 1957, Associate Professor, 1962, Professor, 1966-90, Professor

Emeritus, 1990, Tokyo Metropolitan University; Professor, Chiba Institute of Technology, 1992- 2004. Publications: Books: Industrial Mineral Chemistry; Inorganic Phosphorous Chemistry; Inorganic Phosphate Materials; Inorganic Industrial Chemistry; Phosphorous; My Essay Technology. Honours: Science Award, The Ceramic Society of Japan; Treatise Award, The Society of Gypsum and Lime; Science Award, Japanese Association of Inorganic Phosphorous Chemistry. Memberships: The Chemical Society of Japan; The Ceramic Society of Japan; The Society of Inorganic Materials, Japan; Japanese Association of Inorganic Phosphorous Chemistry. Address: Sakura 1-62-12, Setagaya-ku, Tokyo 156-0053, Japan.

**KANDA Seiichi,** b. 22 May 1927, Kobe, Japan. Professor of Chemistry. m. Atsuko Takagi, 1 son. Education: BSc, Osaka University, 1953; DSc, 1962. Appointments: Assistant, Osaka City University, 1953; Assistant, Osaka University, 1962; Associate Professor, 1965, Professor, 1968, Tokushima University; Professor, Kobe Womens Junior College, 1993, Retired, 1998. Publications include: Organic Semiconducting Polymers, 1968. Membership: Chemical Society of Japan. Address: 498 Kamihachiman Nishiyama, Tokushima 770-8041, Japan.

**KANDADE Raghunath R,** b. 23 June 1932, Mysore, India. Engineer; Consultant. m. Sundara, 3 daughters. Education: BSc, Nagpur, 1951; BE, Jabalpur, 1954; SMIEEE, IEEE, New York, 1956; FIE, IEI, Calcutta, 1957; FIETE, IETE, New Delhi, 1970. Appointments: British Orgn – Power Generation, Transmission, Distribution. Speciality-Energy Conservation, Temperature Measurement and Control, 1954-1960; Various capacities in Cement and Sugar Section, 1960-68; General Manager of Indo-French Special Steel Project, 1968-74; Head of Manufacturing and Consulting Company, Fykays Engineering , 1974-. Publications: More than 60 papers published including Institute of Foundrymen; Indian Institute of Metals, Arm International others. Honours: National Award for Best Entrepreneur; President's Gold Medal for Energy Conservation. Memberships: ASM International; Institute of Foundrymen, past chapter Chairman; Institute of Metals Indo-German; Indo-Australian Business Councils. Address: Fykays Engineering Pvt Ltd. 10/11 Subhash Road, Jogeshwari East, Mumbai 400 060, India. E-mail: fykays@vsnl.com

**KANEKO Noboru,** b. 15 June 1942, Suttsu, Hokkaido, Japan. Astronomer. m. Hisako Fukushima, 3 sons. Education: Bachelor of Science, 1966, Master of Science, 1968, Doctor of Science, 1971, Hokkaido University, Japan. Appointments: Assistant, 1971-77, Lecturer, 1977-89, Associate Professor, 1989, Hokkaido University, Japan. Publication: Sayfert Galaxies (in Japanese), 1983. Memberships: Astronomical Society of Japan; International Astronomical Union. Address: Izumimachi 3-1-10, Makomanai, Sapporo 005-0015, Japan.

**KANTARIS Sylvia,** b. 9 January 1936, Grindleford, Derbyshire, England. Poet; Writer; Teacher. m. Emmanuel Kantaris, 11 January 1958, 1 son, 1 daughter. Education: Diplôme d'Études Civilisation Française, Sorbonne, University of Paris, 1955; BA, Honours, 1957, Cert.Ed, 1958, Bristol University; MA, 1967, PhD, 1972, University of Queensland, Australia. Appointments: Tutor, University of Queensland, Australia, 1963-66, Open University, England, 1974-84; Extra-Mural Lecturer, Exeter University, 1974-. Publications: Time and Motion, 1975; Stocking Up, 1981; The Tenth Muse, 1983; News From the Front (with D M Thomas), 1983; The Sea at the Door, 1985; The Air Mines of Mistila (with Philip Gross), 1988; Dirty Washing: New and Selected Poems, 1989; Lad's Love, 1993. Contributions to: Many anthologies, newspapers, and magazines. Honours:

National Poetry Competition Award, 1982; Honorary Doctor of Letters, Exeter University, 1989; Major Arts Council Literature Award, 1991; Society of Authors Award, 1992. Memberships: Poetry Society of Great Britain; South West Arts, literature panel, 1983-87, literary consultant, 1990-. Address: 14 Osborne Parc, Helston, Cornwall TR13 8PB, England.

**KAPGATE Dashrath Kisanji,** b. 6 November 1954. Paleobotanist. Education: MSc; PhD; DSc (Paleobotany); LLM, International Law; MA, Public Administration, History, Political Science. Appointments: University teacher, 18 years; Research experience, 25 years; Currently, Head, PG Botany Department, J M Patel College, Bhandara, India; Research Supervisor, 4 awarded PhD students, 2 students registered for PhD; Visited, Australia, Europe and America for research purposes. Publications: 12 books on botany; 75 research papers in various journals and conferences. Honours: Several awards and medals. Memberships: Life Member various national and international social and scientific organisations and societies. Address: PG Department of Botany, J M Patel College, Bhandara (MS), 441904 India.

**KARAN Donna,** b. 2 October 1948, Forest Hills, New York, USA. Fashion Designer. m. (1) Mark Karan, 1 daughter, (2) Stephen Weiss, 1983, deceased 2001. Education: Parsons School of Design, New York. Appointments: Designer, Anne Klein & Co, Addenda Co, 1968; Returned to Anne Klein, 1968, Associate Designer, 1971, Director of Design, 1974-84; Owner, Designer, Donna Karan Co, New York, 1984-96; Designer, Donna Karan International, 1996-2001; Chief Designer, LVMH, 2001-. Honours: Coty Awards, 1977, 1981; Fashion Designers of America Women's Wear Award, 1996. Membership: Fashion Designers of American. Address: Donna Karan International, 15th Floor, 5550 Seventh Avenue, New York, NY 10018, USA.

**KARANDE Sunil,** b. 29 July 1961, Bombay, India. Paediatrician; Researcher. Education: MBBS, 1984; DCH, 1988; MD, 1989; Diploma in Information Technology, Advanced Computing Training School, Pune, 2000. Appointments: Medical Officer, Government of India, 1990-91; Surgeon Lieutenant, Indian Navy, 1991-92; Lecturer, Paediatrics, Seth GS Medical College and KEM Hospital, Bombay, 1992-98; Associate Professor, Paediatrics, Lokmanya Tilak Municipal Medical College and Lokmanya Tilak Municipal General Hospital, Bombay, 1998-; Committee Member and Resource Person for AIDS Awareness in Junior Colleges in Mumbai, UNICEF and Mumbai Districts AIDS Control Society, 2000-. Publications: 56 indexed articles in peer reviewed journals; Written chapters in 2 books. Honours: Expert, Essential Drug List, Indian Pharmacological Society of Clinicians and Pharmacologists, 1994; First Prize, Free Paper, VII Maharashtra State Indian Academy of Paediatrics Conference, 1996; Reviewer for Indian Pediatrics, Indian Journal of Pediatrics, Journal of Postgraduate Medicine and Neurology India, indexed journals. Memberships: Member of Technical Committee: WHO/Adverse Drug Reaction Monitoring Programme, 1997-99; Life Member, Indian Academy of Paediatrics; Life Member, Indian Medical Association; Member, New York Academy of Sciences, 1996. Address: Flat 24, Joothica, 5th Floor, 22A Naushir Bharucha Road, Mumbai 400007, India. E-mail: karandesunil@yahoo.com

**KARASIN Grigory B,** b. 1949, Moscow, Russia. Diplomat; Ambassador Extraordinary and Plenipotentiary. m. Olga V Karasina, 2 daughters. Education: Graduate, College of Oriental Languages, Moscow State University, 1971. Appointments: Embassy in Senegal, 1972-76; Embassy in Australia, 1979-85; Embassy in the United Kingdom, 1988-92; Director, Department

of Africa, MFA, 1992-93; Director, Department of Information and Press, MFA, 1993-96; Deputy Minister of Foreign Affairs of the Russian Federation, 1996-2000; Ambassador to the Court of St James's, 2000-. Address: The Russian Embassy, 13 Kensington Palace Gardens, London W8 4QX, England.

**KARAVANIĆ Ivor,** b. 27 June 1965, Zagreb, Croatia. Archaeologist. m. Snježana. Education: BA, Archaeology, 1990, MA, Archaeology, 1993, University of Zagreb; PhD, Archaeology, 1999, University of Zagreb. Appointments: Research Assistant, 1991-2001; Assistant, 1993-99, Senior Assistant, 1999-2001, Assistant Professor, 2001-05, Associate Professor, 2005-, Department of Archaeology, Faculty of Philosophy, University of Zagreb, 1991-. Publications include: Néandertaliens et Paléolithique supérieur dans la grotte de Vindija, co-author, 1998; Gornjopaleolitičke kamene i koštane rukotvorine iz špilje Vindije, 1994; Upper Paleolithic occupation levels and late-occurring Neanderthal at Vindija Cave (Croatia) in the Context of Central Europe and the Balkans, 1995; The Middle/Upper Paleolithic Interface and the Relationship of Neanderthals and Early Modern Humans in the Hrvatsko Zagorje, co-author, 1998; The Early Upper Paleolithic of Croatia, 1998; Neanderthal Diet at Vindija and Neanderthal Predation: The Evidence from Stable Isotopes, co-author, 2000; Stones that Speak, Šandalja in the Light of Lithic Technology, co-author, 2000; Olschewian and Appearance of Bone Technology in Croatia and Slovenia, 2000; ESR and AMS-based $^{14}$C dating of Mousterian Levels at Mujina Pećina, Dalmatia, Croatia, co-author, 2002; Osvit tehnologije, co-author, 2003; Zivot neandertalaca, 2004. Honours: Fellowship, French Government, 1995, 2001; Constantin-Jireček Fellowship, 1995; Fulbright Fellowship, 1996-97; International Scientist of the Year, IBC, 2001; Listed in several Who's Who and biographical publications. Memberships: National Geographic Society; Croatian Archaeological Society; Society for American Archaeology; European Association of Archaeologists; INQUA National Committee, Croatia; Serra International, Zagreb; Croatian Fulbright Alumni Association; L'Association croate des boursiers du governement Français. Address: Department of Archaeology, Faculty of Philosophy, University of Zagreb, Ivana Lučića 3, 10000 Zagreb, Croatia. E-mail: ikaravan@ffzg.hr

**KAREV George Bentchev,** b. 23 August 1943, Shoumen, Bulgaria. Medical Leader. m. Pavlina, 23 November 1969, 1 daughter. Education: MD, Medical Faculty, Varna, 1969; PhD, Medical Academy, Sofia, 1984. Appointments: Assistant Professor, Department of Medical Biology, Medical Faculty of Varna, 1969-74; Senior Assistant Professor, 1974-77; Head Assistant Professor, 1977-93; Senior Researcher, Bulgarian Academy of Sciences, 1993; Chairman, Committee on Health Care, 36th National Assembly, 1991-94; Vice Chairman, 37th National Assembly, 1994-97; Ambassador, Republic of Bulgaria, Rabat, Morocco, 1998. Publications: Parliamentary Slips by Freud; Articles to various professional journals: American Journal of Physical Anthropology, American Journal of Human Biology, Anthropologischer Anzeiger, Cortex. Honours: 11 diplomas for work with prominent students; Abroad Special Prize of Slavic Academy of Sciences. Memberships: Intl Dermatologystic Association; American Deimatoglyphic Association; European Anthropology Association; New York Academy of Sciences. Address: Institute of Experimental Morphology and Anthropology, Bulgarian Academy of Sciences, Academy G Bontchev Str, Bl 25, Sofia 1113, Bulgaria.

**KARIN Sidney,** b. 7 August 1943, Baltimore, Maryland, USA. Professor of Computer Science and Engineering. Education: BE, Mechanical Engineering, City College of New York, 1966; MSE, Nuclear Engineering, University of Michigan, 1967;

PhD, Nuclear Engineering, University of Michigan, 1973. Appointments include: Director, San Diego Supercomputer Centre, 1985-95, 1997-2001; Director, National Partnership for Advanced Computational Infrastructure, 1997-2001; Professor, Computer Science and Engineering, University of California, San Diego, 1986-. Publications include: Numerous articles in scientific journals; author and co-author of selected publications; books and chapters of books; numerous invited lectures. Honours: Outstanding Alumnus, University of Michigan Nuclear Engineering Department, 1989; IEEE Eighth Annual Symposium on High Performance Distributed Computing Recognition Award, 1999; Strathmore's Who's Who in America, Science and Engineering; Fellow, American Association for the Advancement of Science; Fellow, Association for Computing Machinery. Memberships: Several committees including: Member, IEEE Computer Society; AAAS; Association for Computing Machinery. Address: 748 Avocado Ct, Del Mar, CA 92014-3911, USA.

**KARIVAN Klara-Branka,** b. 4 December 1942, Zagreb, Croatia. Chief Executive Officer. m. Bojan, 1 son. Education: BSc, Faculty of Economics, Zagreb; Postgraduate study of marketing. Appointments: Chief, Business Centre Večer, 1979; General Manager, Marketing Agency, Večer, 1990; Owner, Company Večer, 1992; Chief Executive Officer, EAN Croatia, Croatian Article Numbering Association, 1996. Publications: Vjesnik; Večernji List. Honours: President of MB EAN Croatia/ CRO EAN; Regional Co-ordinator of CEE Region (EAN International). Memberships: EAN International, Regional Co-ordinator, Advisory Board, CEE Region. Address: Novi Goljak 23, 10000 Zagreb, Croatia. E-mail: karivan@ean-croatia.hr

**KARLOV Nikolai Vasilyevich,** b. 15 October 1939, Leningrad, USSR. Physicist. m. Elena, 1 son, 1 daughter. Education: Master of Physics, Moscow State University, 1947-52; PhD, Physics, P N Lebedev Physical Institute, 1956. Appointments: Worker, Aviation Plant, Moscow, 1943-47; Senior Researcher then Head of Sector, Lebedev Physical Institute, USSR Academy of Sciences, 1955-83; Head of Sector then Head of Division, Institute of General Physics, 1983-87; Rector, Moscow Institute of Physics and Technology, 1987-97; USSR People's Deputy, 1989-91; Chair, Higher Attestation Committee, 1992-98; Adviser to the Russian Academy of Sciences, 1999-. Publications: 15 scientific books including: Intense Resonant Interactions in Quantum Electronics (with V M Akulin), 1992; Lectures on Quantum Electronics, 1993; Oscillations, Waves, Structures, 2001; Initial Chapters on Quantum Mechanics, 2004. Honours: USSR State Prize, 1976; Order of Friendship, 1995. Memberships: Corresponding Member, Russian Academy of Sciences; American Physical Society. Address: Moscow Institute of Physics and Technology, Institutsky per, 9, 141700 Dolgoprudny, Moscow, Russia. E-mail: nkarlov@mfti.ru

**KARRAZ Mazen,** b. 7 July 1964, Sednaya, Syria. Physician; Anaesthesiologist. Education: MD, University of Damascus, Syria, 1987; Certificate, Anaesthesia Specialist: Damascus University, Syria, 1993; University of Paris V, 1995; Acupuncture Specialist diploma, University of Paris XIII, 1999; Pain Management Diploma, University of Paris, XII, France, 2000. Appointments: Anaesthesiologist: Bicetre University Hospital, Paris, 1994-95; Beauvais Hospital, 1996-2001; Evry Hospital, 2001-02, Verdun Hospital, 2003-; Expert: Columnist Sociedad Iberoamnericana de Information Cientifica, 2003-; Consultant, Council of Healthcare Advisors, 2003-. Publications: Numerous articles in professional medical journals. Honours: Nominated finalist, loco-regional Anaesthesia Prize, French Association of Anaesthesiologists, 2002, 2003. Memberships: French Pain Management Association; French Anaesthesia Association; Euroanaesthesia Association; World Anaesthesia Association. Address: 57 Planchat St, 75020 Paris, France. E-mail: mazenkarraz@hotmail.com

**KARWOWSKI Jacek Andrzej,** b. 23 March 1940, Vilna, Lithuania. Physicist. m. Anna Maria Karwowska, 2 sons, 1 daughter. Education: MSc, 1962; Doctorate, 1968; Dr hab, 1974; Professor, 1988. Appointments: Assistant, 1962-69, Adjunct, 1969-75, Docent, 1975-88, Professor, 1988-, N Copernicus University, Torun, Poland; Postdoctoral Fellow, Department of Chemistry, University of Alberta, Edmonton, Canada, 1972-73; Visiting Scientist, Max Planck Institute für Astrophysik, Garching bei München, Germany, 1-3 months yearly, 1984-2000; Visiting Professor, Consejo Superior de Investigaciones Cientificas, Madrid, Spain, 1987-88. Publications: 175 scientific papers in international journals; Co-author, 2 books. Honour: Cavalier Cross, Order of Polonia Restituta, 1994. Memberships: Polish Physical Society; European Physical Society; International Society for Theoretical Chemical Physics; Polish Chemical Society; Polish Alpine Society. Address: Instytut Fizyki, Uniwersytet Mikolaja Kopernika, ul Grudziadzka 5, PL-87100 Torun, Poland. E-mail: jka@phys.uni.torun.pl

**KASEJE Dan C Owino,** b. 29 April 1946, Bondo District, Kenya. Medical Doctor. m. Margaret Kaseje, 2 sons, 2 daughters. Education: MB ChB, Nairobi University, Kenya, 1975; MPH, Harvard University, USA, 1978; PhD, Liverpool University, England, 1989. Appointments: Lecturer, Nairobi University, 1976-87; Director, Christian Medical Commission, 1988-92; International Federation of the Red Cross, 1992-96; Director, Christian Health Association, Kenya, 1992-2000; Director, Tropical Institute of Community Health, Kenya, 2000-. Publication: Journal article: Health Poverty and Dignified Living (with C Oyaya), 2001. Membership: Royal Society of Tropical Medicine. Address: Tropical Institute of Community Health, PO Box 2224, Kisumu, Kenya.

**KASER Michael Charles,** b. 2 May 1926, London, England. Economist. m. Elizabeth Piggford, 4 sons, 1 daughter. Education: BA, 1946, MA, 1950, Economics, King's College, Cambridge; MA, 1960, DLitt, 1993, Oxford University. Career: Chief Scientific Advisor's Department, Ministry of Works, 1946-47; HM Foreign Service, including HM Embassy, Moscow as Second Secretary, Commercial Secretariat, 1947-51; United Nations Economic Commission for Europe, Geneva, 1951-63; Lecturer, 1963-93, Reader, 1972-93, Emeritus Fellowship, 1993-, St Antony's College; Honorary Chair, Institute for German Studies, University of Birmingham, 1993-. Publications: Author, Editor, 23 books and 350 articles in journals on the East European, Russian and Central Asian economies; Books include: Soviet Economics, 1970; Health Care in the Soviet Union and Eastern Europe, 1976; Privatisation in the CIS, 1995; The Economics of Kazakstan and Uzbekistan, 1997. Memberships: General Editor, International Economic Association, 1986-; Chairman, Councillor, 1980-92, Central Asia and Caucasus Advisory Board, Royal Institute of International Affairs; Trustee, Council of the Keston Institute and Academic Advisory Committee of Cumberland Lodge, Windsor; Former President, British Association of Former UN Civil Servants; Former President, Albania Society of Britain; Member, Advisory Group on Former Soviet and East European Studies of the Higher Education Funding Council for England, 1995-2000 Reform Club. Honours: Papal Knighthood, Order of St Gregory; Knight's Cross of the Order of Merit, Poland; Order of Naim Frasheri, Albania; Hon DSocSc, Birmingham. Address: 7 Chadlington Road, Oxford, OX2 6SY, England.

**KASHYAP Ajit Singh,** b. 6 June 1959, Palwal, Haryana, India. Endocrinologist. m. Surekha Kashyap, 1 son. Education: MBBS, 1980, MD, 1986, Pune University; DM, Endocrinology, Post Graduate Institute of Medical Education and Research, Chandigarh, India, 1998. Appointments: Clinical Tutor, Medicine, 1986-88, Physician, Armed Forces, 1988-96, Senior Resident, Endocrinology, 1996-98, Associate Professor, Medicine, Endocrinology, 1998-, Armed Forces Medical College, Pune, India. Publications: Author or Co-author of 72 articles published in international medical journals; Papers presented at international conferences in: Birmingham, Harrogate and Brighton, England; Sydney, Australia; Belfast, Northern Ireland; Glasgow, Scotland; Lisbon, Portugal. Honours: Chief of Army Staff Commendation Medal; Listed in Who's Who publications. Address: Department of Medicine, Armed Forces Medical College, Pune 411040, India. E-mail: kashyapajits@hotmail.com

**KASIPATHI Chinta,** b. 17 October 1955, Rajahmundry, India. Professor of Geology. m. Hemalatha, 2 sons. Education: BSc, 1973, M Sc (Tech), 1976, PhD, 1981, Andhra University. Appointments: Research Assistant, 1976-80; Research Associate, 1980-84, Officer Pool, 1984; Lecturer, Assistant Professor, 1984-86; Reader, Associate Professor, 1986-94; Professor, 1994-; Supervised doctoral and masters theses; organised two national seminars; Consultant, several mining organisations; Adviser, national and international bodies. Publications: 98 research papers in field of Indian ore mineral studies; Editorial Board, 5 journals. Honour: Young Scientist Award, 1984; Recognised Qualified Person, Government of India. Memberships: New York Academy of Sciences; AGID; Secretary, IGC; GSI; GMMSI; IMSA; IEA; IGC, India; IMA; IGI; IAGS; SGAT; MMR; JDW; FGW; INS; AEG; ISAG; Secretary, Andhra University Geology Alumni Association; FISCA; FAPA Sc; F GARC. Address: Department of Geology, Andhra University, Visakhapatnam 530003, Andhra Pradesh, India.

**KASPAREK Karel,** b. 14 June 1923, Olesnice, Czech Republic. Journalist. m. Johanna Paula Koidl. Education: Medical Studies, 1945-48, Masaryk University, Brno, Czech Republic; Economic Studies, Franz Joseph University, Innsbruck, Austria, 1949-52. Appointments: Correspondent, Radio Free Europe, Austria, 1953-58; Chairman, Radio Free Europe/Radio Liberty Works Council, 1979-87; Acting Director, RFE Czechoslovak Broadcasting Service, 1989. Publications: Political commentaries in Czech and Western media; Author, Operations of the KGB and Communist State Securities Services against Radio Free Europe and Radio Liberty, 1951-89, in progress. Honours: Letter of Appreciation from Mr William Buckley, President of Radio Free Europe/Radio Liberty, 1985; Honorary Diploma, Masaryk University, Brno Czech Republic, 1990; Honorary Diploma: In gratitude and recognition from the citizens of Olesnice for your contribution towards regaining the freedom of the nation, Town of Olesnice, 1991. Memberships: Chairman, Academic Club, Czechoslovak Christian Democratic Party (People's Party), 1946-48; American Newspaper Guild. Address: Goerresstrasse 28, 80798 Munich, Germany.

**KASPAROV Garri Kimovich,** b. 13 April 1963, Baku. Chess Player. m. (1) Masha Kasparova, 1 daughter, (2) Yulia Kasparova, 1 son. Education: Azerbaijan Pedagogical Institute of Foreign Languages. Appointments: Azerbaijan Champion, 1975; USSR Junior Champion, 1975; International Master, 1979, International Grandmaster, 1980; World Junior Champion, 1980; Won USSR Championship, 1981, subsequently replacing Anatoliy Karpov at top of world ranking list; Won match against Viktor Korchnoi, challenged Karpov for World Title in Moscow, 1985, the match being adjourned due to the illness of both players; Won rescheduled match to become the youngest ever World Champion; Successfully defended his title against Karpov, 1986, 1987, 1990; Series of promotional matches in London, 1987; Won Times World Championship against Nigel Short, 1993; Stripped of title by World Chess Federation, 1993. Publication: Child of Change (with Donald Trelford), 1987; London-Leningrad Championship Games, 1987; Unlimited Challenge, 1990. Honours include: Oscar Chess Prize, 1982-83, 1985-89; World Chess Cup, 1989. Membership: Professional Chess Association. Address: Mezhdunarodnaya-2, Suite 1108, Krasnopresnenskaya nab 12, 123610 Moscow, Russia. E-mail: maiavia@dol.ru Website: www.kasparovchess.com

**KASSAM Amirali Hassanali,** b. 30 June 1943, Zanzibar. Agricultural Scientist. m. Parin Suleman Kassam, 1 son, 3 daughters. Education: BSc (Hons) Agricultural Science, University of Reading, 1966; MS, Irrigation Science, University of California, Davis, USA, 1966; PhD, Agricultural Botany, University of Reading, 1971. Appointments: Research Fellow, Institute for Agricultural Research, Ahmadu Bello University, Samaru, Northern Nigeria, 1971-74; International Scientist, International Crops Research Institute for the Semi-Arid Tropics, Hyderabad, India, 1974-76; Director, ECHEMESS Ltd, Management and Development Consultants, London, 1977-89; Senior Agricultural Officer, CGIAR Technical Advisory Committee, FAO-UN, Rome, 1990-98, 2001-2003; Deputy Director General, West African Rice Development Association, Bouake, Ivory Coast, 1998-2000; Executive Secretary, CGIAR Science Council, FAO-UN, Rome Italy, 2003-. Publications: Articles as author or co-author include most recently: Research Towards Integrated Natural Resources Management, 2003; A Framework for Enhancing and Guarding the Relevance and Quality of Science, 2004; Natural Resource Management Research in the CGIAR: The Role of the Technical Advisory Committee, 2004; Researching the Culture in AgriCulture: Social Research for International Agriculture Development, 2004. Honours: King George VI Memorial Fellow, 1966; Fellow Institute of Biology, London, 1991-; Visiting Principal Research Fellow, School of Agriculture, Policy and Development, University of Reading, 1995-; Ismaili Award for Excellence in Science and Technology, Aga Khan National Council for the United Kingdom, 2002. Memberships: Chairman, Aga Khan Foundation (UK) National Committee, London, 1985-89; Advisory Committee, Overseas Development Institute, London, 1988-91; Chairman, FOCUS Humanitarian Assistance Europe Foundation, 1995-98; Convenor, World Faith Development Dialogue Engagement Group on Hunger and Food Security, 1998-2001; Co-editor, Irrigation Science Journal, 1976-; Editorial Board, Journal of Experimental Agriculture, 1998-. Address: 88 Gunnersbury Avenue, Ealing, London W5 4HA, England. E-mail: Kassamamir@aol.com

**KASUYA Koichi,** b. 1 February 1943, Osaka, Japan. University Professor. m. Keiko Nakamura, 2 sons. Education: BSME, 1965, MSME, 1967, PhD, Engineering, 1970, Osaka University, Japan. Appointments: Research Associate, Osaka University, 1970-78; Humbolt Fellow, University of Karsruhe, Germany, 1976-77; Associate Professor, Tokyo Institute of Technology, 1978-; Member, Advisory Committee, International Symposium on Gas Flow and Chemical Lasers and High Power Laser Conference, 1982-; Research Collaborator, Nagoya University, 1978-91, Osaka University, 1992-. Publications: Several books and many research reports on plasma engineering, laser developments, plasma and laser applications, nuclear fusion (science and technology). Honours: Prize of Kudo Foundation in Japan; Travels Grants, 1967-; Grants-in-Aid for Research Work, Ministry of Education and Hattori Foundation.

Memberships: Institute of Electrical Engineering of Japan; Institute of Electric and Electronic Engineers, USA; American Physical Society; Japan Society of Aeronautics; Japan Society of Plasma Science and Nuclear Fusion; Laser Society of Japan. Address: Department of Energy Sciences, Interdisciplinary Graduate School of Science and Engineering, Tokyo Institute of Technology, G3-35, 4259 Nagatuta, Midori-ku, Yokohama, Kanagawa 226-8502, Japan G3-35.

**KATILIUS Ramunas,** b. 15 October 1935, Kaunas, Lithuania. Physicist; Scientific Researcher. m. Elmira Sabirova, 2 sons. Education: Diploma (cum laude), Faculty of Physics and Mathematics, Vilnius University, 1959; Postgraduate Studies, Institute of Physics and Mathematics, Lithuanian Academy of Sciences, Vilnius, 1959-62; Candidate of Physics and Mathematics (PhD), Institute for Semiconductors of the Academy of Sciences of the USSR, Leningrad, 1969; Doctor of Science (Physics and Mathematics), Ioffe Physical-Technical Institute of the Academy of Sciences of the USSR, Leningrad, 1986; Senior Research Fellow, Academy of Sciences of the USSR, 1989; Doctor Habilitatus (Nat Sci), Republic of Lithuania, 1993; Professor (Nat Sci), Vytautas Magnus University, 1993. Appointments: Junior Research Fellow, Institute of Physics and Mathematics of the Lithuanian Academy of Sciences, Vilnius, 1962-66; Junior Research Fellow, Institute for Semiconductors of the Academy of Sciences of the USSR, Leningrad, 1966-72; Junior Research Fellow, Senior Research Fellow, Ioffe Physical-Technical Institute of the Academy of Sciences of the USSR, Leningrad, 1972-88; Extraordinary Professor, Faculty of Physics and Mathematics, 1992-93, Professor of Physics, Environment Research Faculty, 1993-2000, Vytautas Magnus University, Kaunas; Principal Research Fellow, Semiconductor Physics Institute, Vilnius, 1988-. Publications: Over 130 papers in professional journals; 7 review articles and book chapters; 3 books. Honours: Lithuanian National Science Award, 1995; ISI Citation Index: 500+. Memberships: Lithuanian Physical Society; Associate Member, Institute of Physics, UK; Board Member, Lithuanian Association of Non-Linear Analysis; Editorial Board Member, Nonlinear Analysis – Modelling and Control; Board Member, Open Society Fund, Lithuania, 1990-2000. Address: Semiconductor Physics Institute, Gostauto 11, Vilnius, LT-01108, Lithuania. E-mail: ramunas@osf.lt

**KATSOURIS Andreas G,** b. 1940, Meniko, Cyprus. Professor. m. Despoina, 2 daughters. Education: BA, MA, University of Athens, Greece, 1963; PhD, Greek Drama, University of Leeds, England, 1972. Appointments: Lecturer in Classics, 1973, Associate Professor, 1982, Full Professor, 1997-, University of Ioannina. Publications: 10 books; Many articles. Honours: Stipendiat, Alexander von Humboldt-Stiftung; Fellow, Center for Hellenic Studies. Address: Department of Classics, University of Ioannina, 45332 Ioannina, Greece.

**KATSURA Fumiko,** b. 21 February 1944, Kyoto, Japan. Professor. Education: BA, 1966, MA, 1968, Kyoto University; Visiting Scholar, UCLA, 1977-78; Visiting Scholar, St Edmunds College, 1989-90; Visiting Scholar, Cambridge, 1997; Research Fellow, Kyoto University, 2001-02. Appointments: Assistant, Kyoto University, 1970-72; Instructor, 1972-76, Associate Professor, 1976-91, Professor, 1991-, Ryukoku University. Publications: A History of English Poetry; Men and Literature; For Those Who Read English Poetry; George Meredith's The Ordeal of Richard Feveral; B T Gates' Victorian Suicide; E B Browning's Aurora Leigh; English Sonnets from Southey to Swinburne. Memberships: The Browning Institute; The Renaissance Institute; The English Literary Society of Japan; The Victorian Studies Society of Japan. The owner and manager of "Kameoka Katsura Hall", (a private hall for classical music

and cultural activities). Address: 51 Hatago-Cho, Kameoka, Kyoto, Japan 621-0866.

**KATSURA Isao,** b. 20 August 1945, Kamakura, Kanagawa, Japan. Professor. m. Masae Takahara. Education: BSc, 1968, DSc, 1973, University of Tokyo. Appointments: Postdoctoral Fellow, 1973, University of Basel; Assistant Professor, 1976, Associate Professor, 1988, University of Tokyo; Professor, National Institute of Genetics, 1991. Publications: Author and co-author of numerous articles in scientific journals. Memberships: The Molecular Biology Society of Japan; The Biophysical Society of Japan; The Genetics Society of Japan; The Genetics Society of America. Address: National Institute of Genetics, 1111 Yata, Mishima, Shizuoka 411-8540, Japan.

**KATTI Muralidhar,** b. 15 April 1959, Gulbarga, Karnataka State, India. Educator; Researcher in Medical Sciences. m. Ashwini, 2 daughters. Education: BSc, Natural Sciences, 1978; MSc, Microbiology, 1981; PhD, Microbiology and Immunology, 1991; FISCD (Fellow of Indian Society of Malaria and Communicable Diseases), 1998. Appointments: Assistant Professor, SDU Medical College, Kolar, India, 1993-1995; Assistant Professor, 1995-2002, Associate Professor, 2002-, SCTIMST, Trivandrum, India; Visiting Faculty, Rajiv Gandhi Centre for Biotechnology, Trivandrum, India, 1995-96; Visiting Faculty, Bangalore University, Bangalore India, 1994-95; Visiting Scientist, University of Texas Medical School at Houston, USA, 2002-2003. Publications: 23 publications: 12 original articles, 1 review, 10 brief communications/ correspondence. Honours: FISCD, Indian Society of Communicable Diseases, 1998; Overseas Associateship Award, Government of India, New Delhi, 2001-2002; Listed in Who's Who publications and biographical dictionaries. Memberships: Life Member, Indian Immunologists Society; Life Member, Association of Microbiologists of India; Life Member, Indian Association of Biomedical Scientists; International Society of Infectious Diseases. Address: # 31, 4th Cross, 5th Main, Srinidhi Layout, Bangalore 560062, India. E-mail: mkk@sctimst.ker.nic.in

**KATZ Bernhard,** b. 26 March 1911, Leipzig, Germany (British Citizen). Physiologist. m. Marguerite Penly, 1945, 2 sons. Education: Graduated, Medicine, University of Leipzig, 1934; PhD, 1938, Doctor of Science, 1943, University College, London. Appointments: Beit Memorial Research Fellow, Sydney Hospital, 1939-42; Royal Australian Air Force, 1942-45; Assistant Director of Research, Biophysics Research Unit, Henry Head Research Fellow, 1946-50, Reader in Physiology, 1950-51, Professor and Head of Biophysics, 1952-78, University College, London; Noted for research into the physiology of the nervous system. Publications: Electric Excitation of Nerve, 1939; Nerve, Muscle and Synapse, 1966; The Release of Neural Transmitter Substances, 1969. Honours: Knighted, 1969; Joint Winner, Nobel Prize for Physiology or Medicine, 1970. Address: Department of Physiology, University College, Gower Street, London, WC1E 6BT, England.

**KATZENBERG Jeffrey,** b. 1950, USA. Film Executive. m. Marilyn Siegal, 1 son, 1 daughter. Appointments: Assistant to Chair, CEO, Paramount Pictures, NY, 1975-77; Executive Director, Marketing, Paramount TV, California, 1977, Vice President, Programming, 1977-78; Vice President, Feature Production, Paramount Pictures, 1978-80, Senior Vice President, Production, Motion Picture Division, 1980-82, President, Production, Motion Pictures & TV, 1982-94; Chairman, Walt Disney Studios, Burbank, California, 1994-; Co-Founder, Dreamworks SKG, 1995-. Address: Dreamworks SKG, 100 Flower Street, Glendale, CA 91201, USA.

**KAUFFMAN Teresa Jo,** b. 24 August 1951, San Francisco, California, USA. Professor; Creative Artist; Therapist; TV Writer; Producer; Director; Journalist. Education: BA, summa cum laude, Journalism, University of California, Berkeley, 1974; masters degree, summa cum laude, Communication, University of Texas, Austin, 1980; PhD, Psychology, Communication and Creative Expression Therapy, The Union Institute, 1996, with distinction. Appointments: Writer, film and TV producer and director, artist, poet, composer of lyrics and melody, vocalist, expressive arts and communication therapist; Worked in television, radio and video for over 25 years; TV news anchor and reporter, ABC affiliate, 1974, Texas; Researcher, Writer, Alberta Educational Television, Canada, 1976; Senior writer-producer-director, Ampex Corporation, California, 1981; Lecturer, Department of Communication, North Carolina State University, 1985-2000; Early frame by frame computer art animation in the world; Adjunct faculty in Arts and Studies at NCSU, Adjunct Professor, Meredith College in Raleigh, former Adjunct Faculty, Department of Radio, Television and Motion Pictures, University of North Carolina in Chapel Hill; Teacher of a variety of arts and communication courses; Founder and Director of Creative Spaces. Publications include: Poetry; Textbook: The Script as Blueprint: Content and Form Working Together - Writing for Radio, television, Video and Film, 1997. Honours: 1 Emmy nomination; more than 15 first-place national television and video awards; national Broadcasting Society Outstanding Professional member of the Year, 1994; Outstanding Lecturer of the Year, College of Humanities and Social Sciences at North Carolina State University, 1996; Finalist Outstanding Teacher, North Carolina State University; Phi Kappa Phi. Memberships include: American Psychological Association; Berkeley Honor Society; California Scholastic Federation; National Association of Television Arts and Sciences; Also Community Service work in professional field. Address: 407 Furches St, Raleigh, NC 27607, USA.

**KAUFMANN Myron S,** b. 27 August 1921, Boston, Massachusetts, USA. Novelist. m. Paula Goldberg, 6 February 1960, divorced 1980, 1 son, 2 daughters. Education: AB, Harvard University, 1943. Publications: Novels: Remember Me To God, 1957; Thy Daughter's Nakedness, 1968; The Love of Elspeth Baker, 1982. Address: 59 Pond Street, apt 104, Sharon, MA 02067, USA.

**KAUL Hari Krishen,** b. 21 December 1941, Srinagar, Kashmir, India. Library Networking. m. Kamal, 1 daughter. Education: M Lib Sc, Bombay University; PhD, University of Pune. Appointments: Chief Librarian, India International Centre, New Delhi, 1973-; Founder-Director, DELNET, 1992-. Publications: Library Networks: An Indian Experience; Library and Information Networking; Library Resource Sharing and Networks; Sri Aurobindo: A Descriptive Bibliography; Periodicals in Humanities; Early Writings on India; Export of Indian Books: Promotion and Marketing; A New Journey; Handbook for Indian Writers; Poetry of the Raj; On the Waves; The Deep Seas; Poetry India; Poetry of the Young; Many other publications. Honours: Professor D N Marshall Felicitation Prize; Senior Fellowship, Department of Culture, Government of India; Punjab Librarian Award; Best Librarian Award. Memberships: Indian Library Association; Authors Guild of India; Indian Association of Special Libraries and Information Centre; The Poetry Society, India; others. Address: DELNET, India International Centre, 40 Lodi Estate, New Delhi 110003, India. E-mail: hkkaul@delnet.ren.nic.in

**KAUSHAL Radhey Shyam,** b. 30 June 1944, Aligarh, India. Researcher; Teacher. m. Shashi Kaushal, 1 son, 3 daughters. Education: BSc, Agra University, 1963; MSc, Aligarh University, 1965; PhD, Physics, IIT Kanpur, 1970; PhD, Philosophy, Delhi University, 2000. Appointments: Lecturer, 1971-83, Lecturer (Reader) 1983-86, Reader, 1986-88, Ramjas College, UGC Research Scientist, Department of Physics, Delhi University, 1988-2003; Senior Reader, Ramjas College, 2003-. Publications: Over 90 research papers, 4 books. Honours: Alexander von Humboldt Fellow, 1978-80, 1984, 1991, 1993, 1995, 2000. Memberships: IAMP; Indian Physical Society; Indian Physics Association; Academy of Sciences, India; Life Member, Society for Scientific Values; Indian Chapter, ICTP, Trieste; Senior Associate, IUCCA. Address: Department of Physics, Ramjas College, University Enclave, University of Delhi, Delhi 110007, India.

**KAVATKAR Anita,** b. 9 August 1969, Wai, Satara, India. Medical Doctor; Pathologist. m. Neelkanth C Kavatkar. Education: MBBS, 1990; MD, 1994. Appointments: Lecturer, 1995-2004, Associate Professor, 2004-, Department of Pathology, B J (Byranjee Jeejeebhoy) Medical College, Pune, Maharashtra, India. Publications: Articles in medical journals as co-author: Cytological study of neck masses with special emphasis on tuberculosis, 1996; Sclerosing mediastinitis with oesophageal involvement in military tuberculosis – A case report, 2000; Infantile Hepatic Hemangiendothelioma – A Case Report, 2003; Fatal Outcome of Colloid Cyst of Third Ventricle – A report of three cases, 2003; Fine needle aspiration cytology in lymphadenopathy of HIV positive patients, 2003; Autopsy study of maternal deaths, 2003; Benign linitis plastica – a case report, 2004. Honours: Smt Kuntidevi Mehrotra Award for research publication; Listed in Who's Who publications and biographical dictionaries. Memberships: Life Member: Indian Association of Pathologists and Microbiologists, Research Society, BJ Medical College, Indian Academy of Cytologists. Address: BJ Medical College, Department of Pathology, Sassoon Road, Pune 411001, Maharashtra, India. E-mail: kavatkaranita@rediffmail.com

**KAWAHATA Masahiro,** b. 8 September 1936, Tokyo, Japan. Professor; Executive. m. Keiko Kohra, 1 son. Education: BE, Mechanical Engineering, 1960; ME, Control Engineering, 1963; PhD, Systems Engineering, 1966, University of Tokyo. Appointments: Consulting Professor, Electrical Engineering, Stanford University; Provost's Distinguished Visiting Professor, University of Southern California; Full Professor, Management Engineering, Tokai University; Visiting Professor, Industrial Engineering, University of Washington; Chairman/CEO of eCharge Co Ltd; Member of the Board of Directors, Terabeam Corporation; Senior Vice President, eCharge$^2$ Corp, Chief Advisor, Visualant Inc, CEO Nextelligent Inc. Publications: 130 books and articles for professional journals. Honours: Awarded by Minister of International Trade and Industry for outstanding contribution to the development of Information Society of Japan, 1986; University of Washington Pioneer Award, 1995; Honoured by MITI for outstanding contribution for Public Understanding of High Technologies, 1996; University of Southern California Provost's Distinguished Visiting Professor, 1997. Memberships: Numerous memberships including: Board of Trustees, Japan Systems Engineering Society; Board of Trustees, Japan CAI Society; Board of Trustees, Seijo University and Affiliated Schools; Secretary IEEE Tokyo Branch. Address: 3-18-2 Denenchofu Ota-ku, Tokyo 145-0071, Japan.

**KAWATSU Shoji,** b. 24 July 1956, Nagoya City, Japan. Radiologist. m. Midori. Education: Bachelor's degree, Mathematics, University of Tokyo; MSc, Mathematics, Graduate School of Kyoto University; Medical Doctor, Nagoya University; PhD, Graduate School, Nagoya University. Appointments: Visiting Lecturer, Osaka Institute of Technology; Radiologist, Toyota Municipal Hospital, Japan; Guest

Researcher, Nagoya University, School of Medicine, Department of Radiology; Guest Scientist, National Center for Geriatrics and Gerantology; Visiting Lecturer, China City School of Nursing; Chairman, Department of Radiology, Kyoritsu General Hospital. Publications: Couchy problem for abstract evolution equations of parabolic type, 1990; New insight into the analysis of 6-[Hf] fluro-L-POPA PET dynamic data in brain tissue without an irreversible compartment, 2003. Honours: Licentiate, Japan Society for Radiologists; Licentiate, Japan Society for Nuclear Medicine. Memberships: Japan Society for Mathematics; Japan Society for Radiologists; Japan Society for Nuclear Medicine, IEEE. Address: 3-14-9 Taiho, Atsuta-ku, Nagoya city, Aichi Prefecture, Japan. E-mail: b6rgw@fantasy.plala.or.jp

**KAY Steven Walton,** b. 4 August 1954, Amman, Jordan. Lawyer; Barrister. m. Valerie, 1 son, 1 daughter. Education: LLB (Hons), Leeds University; Inns of Court School of Law, 1976-77. Appointments: Called to the Bar, Inner Temple, 1977; Bar Rights of Audience in the Crown Court, 1995; Bar Council Committee, Efficiency in the Criminal Justice System, 1994; Prime Minister's Special Committee on Victims in the Criminal Justice System, 1995; Secretary Criminal Bar Association, 1993-96; Queens Counsel, 1997; Treasurer, European Criminal Bar Association, 1998-2000; Formed an association to deal with international work with Michail Wladimiroff of Wladimiroff and Partners Law Firm, The Hague, The Netherlands; Defence Counsel, Dusko Tadic, UN International Criminal Tribunal for the Former Yugoslavia , 1996; Defence Counsel, Alfred Musema, UN Criminal Tribunal for Rwanda, 1997-; Amicus Curiae, Trial of Slobodan Milosevic, UN International Tribunal for the Former Yugoslavia, 2001-04; Assigned Counsel, Slobodan Milosevic, 2004-; Other notable trials include: R-v-Winzar (an allegation of murder by insulin injection); R-v-Lomas (a European agricultural regulations fraud); R-v-Hannon (an international time share fraud); R-v-Clemente (an international money laundering case). Publication: Role of Defence in International Criminal Court, Commentary on ICC (editors: Casese, Jones, Gaeta), 2003. Honour: QC, 1997. Memberships: Criminal Bar Association; Forensic Science Society; International Bar Association; International Criminal Law Network; Justice. Address: 25 Bedford Row, London WC1R 4HD, England. E-mail: goodnightvienna@btopenworld.com

**KAZANTZIS Judith,** b. 14 August 1940, Oxford, England. Poet; Fiction Writer. 1 son, 1 daughter. Education: Honours Degree, Modern History, Oxford, 1961. Appointments: General Council, Poetry Society, member, 1991-94; Royal Literary Fund fellow, University of Sussex, 2005-2006. Publications: Poetry Collections: Minefield, 1977; The Wicked Queen, 1980; Touch Papers (co-author), 1982; Let's Pretend, 1984; Flame Tree, 1988; A Poem for Guatemala, pamphlet, 1988; The Rabbit Magician Plate, 1992; Selected Poems 1977-92, 1995; Swimming Through the Grand Hotel, 1997; The Odysseus Papers: Fictions on the Odyssey of Homer, 1999; In Cyclops' Cave, Homeric translation, 2002; Just After Midnight, 2004; Fiction: Of Love And Terror, 2002. Contributions to: Stand; Agenda; London Magazine; Poetry London; Poetry Wales; New Statesman; Red Pepper; Poetry Review; Ambit; Verse; Honest Ulsterman; Bete Noire; Key West Reader; Faber Book of Blue Verse; Virago Book of Love Poetry; Comparative Criticism; Mind Readings; Red Sky at Night. Honours: Judge, Sheffield Hallam Poetry Competition, 1995-96; Judge, Stand International Poetry Competition, 1998; Royal Literary Fund Fellow, University of Sussex, 2005-06. Memberships: Poetry Society; English PEN; CND; Palestine Solidarity Campaign. Address: 32 St Annes Crescent, Lewes, East Sussex, England.

**KEANE Fergal Patrick,** b. 6 January 1961, Ireland. Journalist; Broadcaster. m. Anne Frances Flaherty, 1986, 1 son. Education: Terenure College, Dublin; Presentation College, Cork. Appointments: Trainee Reporter, Limerick Leader, 1979-82; Reporter, Irish Press Group, Dublin, 1982-84, Radio Telefis, Eireann, Belfast, 1986-89 (Dublin 1984-86); Northern Ireland Correspondent, BBC Radio, 1989-91, South Africa Correspondent, 1991-94, Asia Correspondent, 1994-97, Special Correspondent, 1997-; Presenter, Fergal Keane's Forgotten Britain, BBC, 2000. Publications: Irish Politics Now, 1987; The Bondage of Fear, 1994; Season of Blood: A Rwandan Journey, 1995; Letter to Daniel, 1996; Letters Home, 1999; A Stranger's Eye, 2000. Honours: Reporter of the Year Sony Silver Award, 1992, Sony Gold Award, 1993; International Reporter of the Year, 1993; Amnesty International Press Awards; RTS Journalist of the Year, 1994; BAFTA Award, 1997; Hon DLitt, Strathclyde, 2001. Address: c/o BBC Television, Wood Lane, London W12 7RJ, England.

**KEATING Henry Reymond Fitzwalter,** b. 31 October 1926, St Leonards-on-Sea, Sussex, England. Author. m. Sheila Mary Mitchell, 1953, 3 sons, 1 daughter. Education: BA, Trinity College, Dublin. Publications: The Perfect Murder, 1964; Inspector Ghote Trusts the Heart, 1972; The Lucky Alphonse, 1982; Under a Monsoon Cloud, 1986; Dead on Time, 1989; The Iciest Sin, 1990; The Man Who (editor), 1992; The Rich Detective, 1993; Doing Wrong, 1994; The Good Detective, 1995; The Bad Detective, 1996; Asking Questions, 1996; The Soft Detective, 1997; Bribery, Corruption Also, 1999; Jack the Lady Killer, 1999; The Hard Detective, 2000; Breaking and Entering, 2000; The Dreaming Detective, 2002; A Detective at Death's Door, 2003. Contributions to: Crime books reviews, The Times, 1967-83. Honours: Gold Dagger Awards, 1964, 1980, Diamond Dagger Award, 1996, Crime Writers Association. Memberships: Crime Writers Association, chairman, 1970-71; Detection Club, president, 1986-2001; Royal Society of Literature, fellow; Society of Authors, chairman, 1982-83. Address: 35 Northumberland Place, London W2 5AS, England.

**KEATING Paul John,** b. 18 January 1944. Australian Politician. m. Anna Johanna Maria Van Iersel, 1975, 1 son, 3 daughters. Education: De La Salle College, Bankstown, New South Wales. Appointments: Research Officer, Federal Municipal & Shire Council Employees Union of Australia, 1967; MP for Blaxland, 1969-96; Minister for Northern Australia, 1975; Shadow Minister for Agriculture, 1976, for Minerals & Energy, 1976-80, for Resources & Energy, 1980-83; Shadow Treasurer, 1983; Federal Treasurer of Australia, 1983-91; Deputy Prime Minister, 1990-91; Prime Minister of Australia, 1991-96. Publication: Engagement: Australia Faces the Asia Pacific, 2000. Memberships: Chairman, Australian Institute of Music, 1999-; Board of Architects of New South Wales, 2000-.

**KEATON Diane,** b. 5 January 1946, CA, USA. Education: Student at Neighbourhood Playhouse, New York. Career: Theatre in New York includes: Hair, 1968; The Primary English Class, 1976; Films include: Lovers and Other Strangers, 1970; The Godfather, 1972; Sleeper, 1973; Annie Hall, 1977; Manhattan, 1979; Shoot the Moon, 1982; Crimes of the Heart, 1986; Baby Boom, 1988; The Godfather III, 1991; Manhattan Murder Mystery, 1993; Father of Bride II, 1995; Marvins's Room, 1996; The First Wives Club, 1996; The Only Thrill, 1997; Hanging Up (also director), 1999; The Other Sister, 1999; Town and Country, 1999; Sister Mary Explains It All, 2001; Director: Heaven, 1987; Wildflower, 1991; Unsung Heroes, 1995. Publications: Reservations, Still Life, editor. Address:

c/o John Burnham, William Morris Agency, 151 El Camino, Beverly Hills, CA 90212, USA.

**KEATON Michael,** b. 9 September 1951, Pittsburgh, USA. Actor. m. Caroline MacWilliams, divorced, 1 son. Education: Kent State University. Appointments: With Comedy Group, Second City, Los Angeles; TV appearances include: All in the Family; Maude; Mary Tyler Moore Show; Working Stiffs; Report to Murphy; Roosevelt and Truman (TV film); Body Shots (producer), 1999. Creative Works: Films: Night Shift, 1982; Mr Mom, 1983; Johnny Dangerously, 1984; Touch and Go, 1987; Gung Ho, 1987; Beetlejuice, 1988; Clean and Sober, 1988; The Dream Team, 1989; Batman, 1989; Much Ado About Nothing, 1992; My Life, The Paper, 1994; Speechless, 1994; Multiplicity, Jackie Brown, 1997; Desperate Measures, 1998; Jack Frost, 1998; A Shot at Glory, 2000; Quicksand, 2001; First Daughter, 2004. Address: c/o ICM Management, 8942 Wilshire Boulevard, Beverly Hills, CA 90211, USA.

**KEATS Reynold Gilbert,** b. 15 February 1918, Pt Pirie, South Australia, Australia. Emeritus Professor of Mathematics. m. Verna Joy, 2 daughters. Education: Diploma in Accountancy, 1939; BSc, 1948, PhD, 1966, University of Adelaide. Appointments: Clerk, Savings Bank of South Australia, 1934-40; Private to Lieutenant, 2/48th Battalion, Australian Imperial Forces, 1940-45; Visiting Research Scientist, Royal Aircraft Establishment, Farnborough, England, 1948-51; Scientific Officer, Australian Government Department of Supply, Melbourne, Victoria, 1951, 1952; Senior Scientific Officer, 1952-57, Principal Scientific Officer, 1957-61, Australian Government Department of Supply, Weapons Research Establishment, Salisbury, South Australia; Senior Lecturer, University of Adelaide, South Australia, 1961-67; Professor of Mathematics, 1968-83, Dean, Faculty of Mathematics, 1971-76, 1980-83, Member of Council, 1977, 1978, Deputy Chairman of Senate, 1977, 1978, Emeritus Professor, 1983-, Honorary Professor, 1984-88, University of Newcastle, New South Wales. Honours: Fellow, Australian Society of Certified Practising Accountants, 1952; Fellow, Institute of Mathematics and its Applications, 1973; Honorary DMath, University of Waterloo, Ontario, Canada, 1979; Chartered Mathematician, Institute of Mathematics and its Applications, 1993; Fellow, Australian Mathematical Society, 1995; Fellow, Australian Computer Society, 1997. Membership: The Legacy Club of Newcastle. Address: 39 Woodward St, Merewether, NSW 2291, Australia.

**KEATS-ROHAN Katharine S B,** b. 3 June 1957. Historian. m. John Lyttleton Lloyd, deceased 2004, 1 son. Education: BA, History, 1984, MA, Medieval Studies, 1985, PhD, Classics, 1987, London. Appointments: Junior Research Fellow, Linacre College, Oxford, 1987-89; Research Assistant, Department of History, University of Sheffield, 1988-89; Adjunct (Research) Fellow, Linacre College, Oxford, 1992-97; Founder and Director, Unit for Prosopographical Research, 1993-; Fellow, European Humanities Research Centre, Oxford, 1997-. Publications include: Ioannis Saresberiensis Metalogicon (co-editor), 1991; Ioannis Saresberiensis Policraticus Libri I-IV (V-VII to follow), 1993; Domesday Names: An Index of personal and Place Names in Domesday Book, 1997; Domesday People: A Prosopography of Persons Occurring in English Documents 1066-1166, Volume I, Domesday Book, 1999; Continental Origins of English Landholders 1966-1166 Database, 2002; Domesday Descendants: A Prosopography of Persons Occurring in English Documents 1066-1166 Volume II Pipe Rolls to Cartae Baronum, 2002; Numerous articles in academic journals and conference proceedings. Honours: W F Masom Scholarship in Classics, University of London, 1986-88; Clay Scholarship, Bedford College, London, 1985-86; British Council research Visitor

to the University of Prague, 1985; Leverhulme Trust Grant, 1992-96; Prix Brant IV de Koskull 1998 for Domesday People, Confédération Internationale de Généalogie et d'Héraldique. Memberships: Société d'Histoire et d'Archéologie de Bretagne, 1991-; Haskins Society, 1991-; Fellow, Royal Historical Society, 2002. Address: European Humanities Research Centre, 41 Wellington Square, Oxford OX1 2JF, England. E-mail: katharine.keats-rohan@history.ox.ac.uk

**KEAY John (Stanley Melville),** b. 18 September 1941, Devon, England. Author. Education: BA, Magdalen College, Oxford, 1963. Publications: Into India, 1973; When Men and Mountains Meet, 1977; The Gilgit Game, 1979; India Discovered, 1981; Eccentric Travellers, 1982; Highland Drove, 1984; Explorers Extraordinary, 1985; The Royal Geographical Society's History of World Exploration, 1991; The Honourable Company, 1991; Collins Encyclopaedia of Scotland, 1994; Indonesia: From Sabang to Meranke, 1995; The Explorers of the Western Himalayas, 1996; Last Post, 1997; India: A History, 2000; The Great Arc, 2000; Sowing the Wind, 2003; Mad About the Mekong, 2005; The Spice Route, 2005. Address: Succoth, Dalmally, Argyll, Scotland.

**KEEFFE Barrie (Colin),** b. 31 October 1945, London, England. Playwright. m. (1) Dee Truman, 1969, divorced 1979, (2) Verity Bargate, 1981, deceased 1981, 2 stepsons, (3) Julia Lindsay, 1983, divorced 1993. Appointments: Writer; Actor; Director; Journalist; Dramatist-in-Residence, Shaw Theatre, London, 1977, Royal Shakespeare Company, 1978; Associate Writer, Theatre Royal Stratford East, London, 1986-91; Board of Directors, Soho Poly Theatre, 1976-81; Associate Director, Soho Poly Theatre, 1989-; Board of Directors, Theatre Royal, Stratford East, 1981-89; Ambassador, United Nations, 50th anniversary year, 1995; Tutor, City University, London, 2002-; Judith E Wilson Fellow, Christ's College Cambridge, 2003-4. Publications: Plays: A Mad World, My Masters, 1977, revised version, 1984; Methuen, 1977; Gimme Shelter, 1977; Barbarians, 1977; Frozen Assets, 1978, revised version, 1987; Sus, 1979; Heaven Scent, 1979; Bastard Angel, 1980; Black Lear, 1980; She's So Modern, 1980; Chorus Girls, 1981; A Gentle Spirit (with Jules Croiset), 1981; The Long Good Friday (screenplay), 1984; Better Times, 1985; King of England, 1986; My Girl, 1989; Not Fade Away, 1990; Wild Justice, 1990; I Only Want to Be With You, 1997; Barrie Keeffe Plays, Volume 1, 2001; Shadows on the Sun, 2001; Novels: Gadabout, 1969; No Excuses, 1983; Journalism: Numerous articles contributed to national newspapers, including Sunday Times; The Independent; The Guardian; Evening Standard. As Director: A Certain Vincent, 1974; A Gentle Spirit, 1980; The Gary Oldman Fan Club, 1998. Radio Plays: Good Old Uncle Jack, 1975; Pigeon Skyline, 1975; Self-Portrait, 1977; Paradise, 1990; On the Eve of the Millennium, 1999; Tales, 2000; Feng Shui and Me, 2000; The Five of Us, 2002. Television Plays: Gotcha, 1977; Champions, 1978; Hanging Around, 1978; Nipper, 1978; Waterloo Sunset, 1979; No Excuses Series, 1983; King, 1984; Honours: French Critics Prix Revelation, 1978; Giles Cooper Award, Best Radio Plays, 1978; Edgar Allan Poe Award, Mystery Writers of America, 1982; Ambassador for United Nations 50th Anniversary, 1995. Membership: Société des Auteurs et Compositeurs Dramatiques. Address: 110 Annandale Road, London SE10 0JZ, England.

**KEEFFE Emmet Britton,** b. 12 April 1942, San Francisco, California, USA. Physician. m. Melenie Marie Laskey, 2 sons, 1 daughter. Education: BS, 1964, Teaching Credential, 1965, University of San Francisco, California, USA; MD, Creighton University, 1969; Intern and Resident, Gastrointestinal Fellow, Oregon Health Science University, 1974; Liver Fellow,

University of California, San Francisco, 1979. Appointments: Professor of Medicine, Oregon Health Science University, 1979-92, Clinical Professor of Medicine, UCSF, 1992-95; Medical Director, Liver Transplant Program and Chief, Division of Gastroenteology, California Pacific Medical Center, 1992-95; Professor of Medicine, Chief of Hepatology, Medical Director of Liver Transplant Program, Stanford University Medical Center, 1995-. Publication: Flexible Sigmoidoscopy, 1985; Handbook of Liver Disease, 1998, 2004; Atlas of Gastrointestinal Endoscopy, 1998. Honours: Best Doctors in America, Cited, 1992, 1994; America's Top Doctors, 2000-04. Memberships: President, 1995, American Society for Gastrointestinal Ensocopy; Board of Directors, 1991-95, American Liver Foundation; President, 1991, Western Gut Club; President, 2004, American Gastroenterological Association; American Association for the Study of Liver Diseases; Fellow, American College of Physicians; Fellow, American College of Gastroenterology; American Medical Association. Address: Stanford University Medical Center, 750 Welch Road, Suite 210, Palo Alto CA 94304-1509, USA

**KEEGAN John (Desmond Patrick) (Sir),** b. 15 May 1934, London, England. Editor; Writer; Defence Correspondent. m. Susanne Everett, 1960, 2 sons, 2 daughters. Education: BA, 1957, MA, 1962, Balliol College, Oxford. Appointments: Senior Lecturer in Military History, Royal Military Academy, Sandhurst, 1960-86; Fellow, Princeton University, 1984; Defence Editor, Daily Telegraph, 1986-; Delmas Distinguished Professor of History, Vassar College, 1997. Publications: The Face of Battle, 1976; Who's Who in Miltary History (co-author), 1976; World Armies (editor), 1979, new edition, 1982; Six Armies in Normandy, 1982; Zones of Conflict (co-author), 1986; The Mask of Command, 1987; The Price of Admiralty, 1988, reissued as Battle at Sea, 1993; The Times Atlas of the Second World War, 1989; Churchill's Generals (editor), 1991; A History of Warfare, 1993; Warpaths: Travels of a Military Historian in North America, 1995; War and Our World: The Reith Lectures, 1998; The Penguin Book of War: great miltary writings (editor), 1999. Honours: Officer of the Order of the British Empire, 1991; Duff Cooper Prize, 1994; Honorary Doctor of Law, University of New Brunswick, 1997; Honorary Doctor of Literature, Queen's University, Belfast, 2000; Knighted, 2000; Honorary Doctor of Letters, University of Bath, 2001. Address: The Manor House, Kilmington, near Warminster, Wilts BA12 6RD, England.

**KEEN Richard,** b. 29 March 1954, Rustington, Sussex, England. Queen's Counsel. m. Jane Carolyn Anderson, 1 son, 1 daughter. Education: Beckman Scholar, University of Edinburgh. Appointments: Admitted to Faculty of Advocates (Scottish Bar), 1980; Counsel to DTI in Scotland, 1986-93; Queen's Counsel, 1993-; Chairman, Appeal Committee, Institute of Chartered Accountants Scotland (ICAS), 1996-. Address: The Castle, Elie, Fife KY9 1DN, Scotland. E-mail: rskeenqc@compuserve.com

**KEENE Raymond Dennis,** b. 29 January 1948, London, England. Author; Publisher. m. Annette Sara Goodman Keene, 1 son. Education: MA, Trinity College, Cambridge, 1967-72. Career: Chess Correspondent, The Spectator, 1977-; The Times, 1985-; The Sunday Times, 1996-; International Herald Tribune, 2001- Organiser, World Chess Championships, London, 1986, 1993, 2000; Director, Hardinge Simpole Publishing. Publications: 120 books written and published on chess; Daily chess article in The Times; Weekly chess column in The Spectator and the Sunday Times; Weekly IQ column in The Times. Honours: International Chess Grandmaster, 1976; OBE, 1985. Memberships: The Athenaeum; St Stephens. Address: 86

Clapham Common, North Side, London SW4 9SE, UK. E-mail: rdkobe@aol.com

**KEEY Roger Brian,** b. 11 March 1934, Birmingham, England. Chemical Engineer. m. Daphne Pearl Griffiths, 18 March 1959, 1 son, 3 daughters. Education: BSc, 1954; PhD, University of Birmingham, 1957; DSc (Hon), Technical University of Lódź, 2002. Appointments: Chemical Engineer, DCL Ltd, Saltend, 1957-62; Lecturer, Senior Lecturer, Reader, University of Canterbury, New Zealand, 1962-78; Professor, Chemical Engineering, 1978-97; Director, Wood Technology Research Centre, 1997-2001; Forest Guardian, Hurunui District Council, 1999-; Hanmer Springs Community Board, 2001-. Publications: Drying Principles and Practice; Introduction to Industrial Drying Operations; Reliability in the Process Industries; Drying of Loose and Particulate Materials; Wainui Incident; Kiln-Drying of Lumber; Management of Engineering Risk. Honours: Cadman Medal; NZIE Angus Award; NZIE Skellerup Award; IPENZ Rabone Award; IPENZ Skellerup Award; Proctor and Gamble Award, Excellence in Drying Research; Award for outstanding achievement and excellence in Drying R and D, 1st Nordic Drying Conference. Listed in several Who's Who publications. Memberships: former Council Member IPENZ; former Council Member, Christchurch Polytechnic; former Council Member, New Zealand Dairy Research Institute; FRSNZ; FIChemE; FIPENZ; FNZIC; CEng. Address: PO Box 31080, Ilam, Christchurch, New Zealand 8030.

**KEIGHTLEY Richard Charles,** b. 2 July 1933, Aldershot, England. Army Major General. m. Caroline Rosemary Butler, 3 daughters. Education: Royal Military Academy Sandhurst, 1951-53; Army Staff College, 1963; National Defence College, 1971-72; Royal College of Defence Studies, 1980. Appointments: Various Regimental and Staff appointments, 1953-70; Commander, 5th Royal Inniskilling Dragoon Guards, 1972-75; Colonel GS, 1st Division, 1977; Commander 33 Armoured Brigade, 1978-79; Brigadier General Staff, UK Land Forces, 1981; GOC Western District, 1982-83; Commandant, Royal Military Academy Sandhurst, 1983-87; Chairman, Dorset Healthcare NHS Trust, 1995-97; Chairman, Dorset Health Authority, 1988-95, 1998-2001; Chairman, Southampton University Hospitals NHS Trust, 2002-. Honour: CB, 1987. Memberships: President, Dorset County Royal British Legion; President, Dorset Relate; Member, St John Council for Dorset. Address: Kennels Farmhouse, Tarrant Gunville, Dorset DT 11 8JQ, England.

**KEILLOR Garrison, (born Gary Edward Keillor),** b. 7 August 1942, Anoka, Minnesota, USA. Writer; Radio Host. Education: BA, University of Minnesota, 1966. Appointments: Creator-Host, national public radio programmes, A Prairie Home Companion and American Radio Company. Publications: Happy to Be Here, 1982; Lake Wobegon Days, 1985; Leaving Home, 1987; We Are Still Married: Stories and Letters, 1989; WLT: A Radio Romance, 1991; The Book of Guys, 1993; Wobegon Boy, 1997; Lake Wobegon Summer 1956, 2001. Children's Books: Cat, You Better Come Home, 1995; The Old Man Who Loved Cheese, 1996; Sandy Bottom Orchestra, 1997; ME by Jimmy (Big Boy) Valente as Told to Garrison Keillor, 1999. Contributions to: Newspapers and magazines. Honours: George Foster Peabody Award, 1980; Grammy Award, 1987; Ace Award, 1988; Best Music and Entertainment Host Awards, 1988, 1989; American Academy and Institute of Arts and Letters Medal, 1990; Music Broadcast Communications Radio Hall of Fame, 1994; National Humanities Medal, 1999. Address: c/o Minnesota Public Radio, 45 East 7th Street, St Paul, MN 55101, USA.

**KEINÄNEN Matti Tapio,** b. 1 January 1953, Kuopio, Finland. Docent. m. Kristina, 2 sons, 1 daughter. Education: Licentiate of Medicine, 1977; Doctor of Medicine and Surgery, 1981; Specialist in Psychiatry, 1985; Psychoanalytic Psychotherapy Training, 1986; Specialist-level Psychotherapy Training, 1992; Advanced Specialist-level Individual Psychotherapy Training, 1997; Docent in Psychiatry, Turku University, 2002; Family Therapy Training, Finnish Mental Health Society, 1987; Licentiate Psychotherapist, 1995; Licentiate Advanced Specialist-level Individual Psychotherapist, 1998, National Authority for Medicolegal Affairs; Supervising Member, Finnish Balint-Group Organisation, 1999; Docent in Clinical Psychology, Jyväskylä University, 2000. Appointments: Psychiatrist, Finnish Student Health Service, Turku; Docent in Psychiatry, Turku University; Docent in Clinical Psychology, Jyväskylä University. Publications: Articles on biological basic study of psychiatry, family research and symbolic function research in individual psychoanalytic psychotherapy. Honours: International Peace Prize, 2005. Memberships: Finnish Medical Association; Finnish Psychiatric Association; International Semiotic Association; Finnish Psychodynamic Psychotherapy Association; Finnish Adolescent Psychiatry Association; Finnish Balint-Group Association. Address: Finnish Student Health Service, Kirkkotie 13, FIN-20540 Turku, Finland.

**KEIR James Dewar,** b. 30 November 1921, Edinburgh, Scotland. Retired Barrister. m. Jean Mary Orr, 2 sons, 2 daughters. Education: MA, Christ Church, Oxford, 1948; Inner Temple, 1949-50; Yarborough-Anderson Scholar, Inner Temple, 1950. Appointments: Legal Adviser, 1954-66, Secretary, 1966-73, United Africa Co Ltd; Deputy Head, Legal Services, Unilever Ltd, 1973-76; Joint Secretary, Unilever plc and Unilever NV, 1976-84; Chairman, 1969-72, President, 1980-82, Bar Association Commerce, Finance and Industry; Member, Monopolies and Mergers Commission, 1987-92; Director, Open University Educational Enterprises, 1983-88; Chairman, Pharmacists Review Panel, 1986-97; Chairman, Professional Committee, Royal College of Speech and Language Therapists, 1993-2000. Honour: Queen's Counsel, 1980. Membership: Caledonian Club. Address: 15 Clay's Close, East Grinstead, West Sussex RH 19 4DJ, England. E-mail: jamesdewarkeir@aol.com

**KEITA Mobidu,** b. 13 January 1953, Bamako, Republic of Mali. Professor of Social Sciences. m. Anne Keita, 2 sons, 1 daughter. Education: Studies in Education, Psychology, Sociology, Universities of Heidelberg and Mannheim, Germany, 1974-75; Master's Degree in Education, 1975-78, PhD in Social Sciences, 1979-83, University of Tübingen, Germany. Appointments: Professor for Education and Psychology, Ecole Normale Supérieure of Bamako, 1984-87; Set up CEK-Kala Saba (Cabinet d'Etudes Keita-Kala Saba for consulting and research in development issues, 1996; Co-ordinator for West African Region of Urban Waste Expertise Program (research program funded by the Dutch Government), 1997-2003; Co-ordinator of the Malian network "Making Decentralisation Work", IIED Program, 2000-. Publications: Notions fondementales de la Pédagogie de développement, 1986; Partenariat entre la municipalité et la société civile: exemple de la gestion des déchets solides urbains à Bamako, 2001; Improving the stakeholder involvement in solid waste collection in Bamako, 2003; NRP (Nature, Richesse et Pouvoir): Gestion Durable des ressources naturelle, 2004. Memberships: Association "Sigiyoro Damun", Bamako; Coalition contre la Pauvreté en Milieu Urbain, Bamako; Fédération Nationale des Consultants de Mali, Bamako; SURCO (Global consortium for promoting healthy urban environment) based in Gouda, The Netherlands. Address: BP 9014, Bamako, Republic of Mali. E-mail: cek@afribone.net.ml

**KEITEL Harvey,** b. 13 May 1939, USA. Actor. m. Lorraine Bracco, divorced, 1 daughter. Education: Actors Studio. Appointments: US Marines. Creative Works: Stage appearances: Death of a Salesman, Hurlyburly; Films: Mean Streets; Alice Doesn't Live Here Anymore; That's the Way of the World; Taxi Driver; Mother Jugs and Speed Buffalo Bill and the Indians; Welcome to LA; The Duelists; Fingers; Blue Collar; Eagle's Wing; Deathwatch; Saturn 3; Bad Timing; The Border; Exposed; La Nuit de Varennes; Corrupt; Falling in Love; Knight of the Dragon Camorra; Off Beat; Wise Guys; The Men's Club; The Investigation; The Pick-up Artist; The January Man; The Last Temptation of Christ; The Two Jakes; Two Evil Eyes (The Black Cat); Thelma & Louise; Tipperary; Bugsy; Reservoir Dogs; Bad Lieutenant; Mean Streets; The Assassin; The Young Americans; The Piano; Snake Eyes; Rising Sun; Monkey Trouble; Clockers; Dangerous Game; Pulp Fiction; Smoke; Imaginary Crimes; Ulyssees' Gaze, 1995; Blue in the Face, 1995; City of Industry; Cop Land, 1996; Head Above Water; Somebody to Love, 1996; Simpatico, 1999; Little Nicky, 2000; U-571, 2000; Holy Smoke, 2000. Address: c/o William Morris Agency, 151 South El Camino Drive, Beverly Hills, CA 90212, USA.

**KEITH Penelope Anne Constance,** b. 2 April 1940, Sutton, Surrey, England. Actress. m. Rodney Timson, 1978. Education: Webber Douglas School, London. Creative Works: Stage appearances include: Suddenly at Home, 1971; The Norman Conquests, 1974; Donkey's Years, 1976; The Apple Cart, 1977; The Millionairess, 1978; Moving, 1980; Hobson's Choice, 1982; Captain Brassbound's Conversation, 1982; Hay Fever, 1983; The Dragon's Tail, 1985; Miranda, 1987; The Deep Blue Sea, 1988; Dear Charles, 1990; The Merry Wives of Windsor, 1990; The Importance of Being Ernest, 1991; On Approval, 1992; Relatively Speaking, 1992; Glyn and It, 1994; Monsieur Amilcar, 1995; Mrs Warren's Profession, 1997; Good Grief, 1998; Star Quality, 2001; Film appearances include: Rentadick; Take a Girl Like You; Every Home Should Have One; Sherlock Holmes; The Priest of Love; TV appearances include: The Good Life (Good Neighbors in USA), 1974-77; Private Lives, 1976; The Norman Conquests, 1977; To the Manor Born, 1979-81; On Approval, 1980; Spider's Web; Sweet Sixteen; Waters of the Moon; Hay Fever; Moving; Executive Stress; What's My Line?, 1988; Growing Places; No Job for a Lady, 1990; Law and Disorder, 1994; Next of Kin; Coming Home, 1999. Honours include: Best Light Entertainment Performance, British Academy of Film & TV Arts, 1976; Best Actress, 1977; Show Business Personality, Variety Club of Great Britain, 1976; BBC TV Personality, 1979; Comedy Performance of the Year, Society of West End Theatre, 1976; Female TV Personality; TV Times Awards, 1976-78; BBC TV Personality of the Year, 1978-79; TV Female Personality, Daily Express, 1979-82. Address: London Management, 2-4 Noel Street, London W1V 3RB, England.

**KELLEHER Graeme George,** b. 2 May 1933, Sydney, Australia. Civil Engineer; National Resource Manager. m. Fleur Meachen, 1 son, 2 daughters. Education: BE (Civil), 1955. Appointments: Engineer Project Manager, 1955-75; Commissioner, Ranger Uranium Inquiry, 1976-77; Deputy Chair, Non-proliferation Task Force, 1977-78; Chair, CEO, Great Barrier Reef Marine Park Authority, 1979-94; Professor, Systems Engineering, James Cook University, 1991-94; Vice Chair, World Commission on Protected Areas, 1986-98; Senior Advisor and Leader on High Seas Marine Protected Areas Task Force, World Commission on Protected Areas, 1999-; Chair, CSIRO Marine Advisory Committee, 1995-99; Co Chair, Life

Sciences, Co-operative Research Centres Program, 1995-2002; Director, Graeme Kelleher and Associates, 1995-; Member, Religious and Scientific Committee, Religion, Science and the Environment, 1996-; Member, Independent Community Engagement Panel, Murray-Darling Ministerial Council, 2002-2004. Publications: Ranger Uranium Environmental Inquiry; Guidelines for Marine Protected Areas; A Global Representative System of Marine Protected Areas; Many papers and articles. Honours: Churchill Fellowship, 1972; Monash Medal, 1986; Member, Order of Australia, 1988; Officer of the Order of Australia, 1996; Packard International Parks Merit Award, 1998; Centenary Medal, 2003; Institution of Engineers, Canberra Hall of Fame, 2005 Memberships: Institution of Engineers (Fellow); Australian Academy of Technological Sciences and Engineering (Fellow); Environmental Institute of Australia and New Zealand (Fellow). Address: 12 Marulda Street, Aranda, Canberra ACT 2614, Australia.

**KELLER Evelyn Fox,** b. 20 March 1936, New York, New York, USA. Professor of History and Philosophy of Science; Writer. 1 son, 1 daughter. Education: BA, Brandeis University, 1957; MA, Radcliffe College, 1959; PhD, Harvard University, 1963. Appointments: Professor of Mathematics and Humanities, Northeastern University, 1982-88; Senior Fellow, Cornell University, 1987; Member, Institute for Advanced Study, Princeton, New Jersey, 1987-88; Professor, University of California at Berkeley, 1988-92; Professor of History and Philosophy of Science, Massachusetts Institute of Technology, 1992-. Publications: A Feeling for the Organism: The Life and Work of Barbara McClintock, 1983, 2nd edition, 1992; Reflections on Gender and Science, 1985, new edition, 1995; Women, Science and the Body (editor with Mary Jacobus and Sally Shuttleworth), 1989; Conflicts in Feminism (editor with Marianne Hirsch), 1990; Keywords in Evolutionary Biology (editor with Elisabeth Lloyd), 1992; Secrets of Life, Secrets of Death: Essays on Language, Gender, and Science, 1992; Refiguring Life: Metaphors of Twentieth Century Biology, 1995; Feminism and Science (editor with Helen Longino), 1996; The Century of the Gene, 2000; Making Sense of Life, 2002. Contributions to: Scholarly journals. Honours: Distinguished Publication Award, Association for Women in Psychology, 1986; Alumni Achievement Award, Brandeis University, 1991; Honorary Doctorates, Holyoke College, 1991, University of Amsterdam, 1995, Simmons College, 1995, Rensselaer Polytechnic Institute, 1995, Technical University of Lulea, Sweden, 1996; John D and Catharine T MacArthur Foundation Fellowship, 1992-97; Numerous honorary degrees. Address: c/o Program in Science, Technology and Society, Massachusetts Institute of Technology, 77 Massachusetts Avenue, Cambridge, MA 02139, USA.

**KELLEY Patricia Marie Hagelin,** b. 8 December 1953, Cleveland, Ohio, USA. Geology Educator. m. Jonathan Robert Kelley, 1 son, 1 daughter. Education: BA, Geology, College of Wooster, 1975; AM, Geology, 1977; PhD, Geology, Harvard University, 1979. Appointments: Instructor, New England College, 1979; Assistant Professor, 1979-85, Associate Professor, 1985-89, Acting Associate Vice-Chancellor for Academic Affairs, 1988, Professor of Geology and Geological Engineering, 1989-90, University of Mississippi; Programme Director for Geology and Paleontology and Geological Record of Global Change Programmes, National Science Foundation, 1990-92; Professor and Chair of the Department of Geology and Geological Engineering, University of North Dakota, 1992-97; Professor and Chair, Department of Earth Sciences, 1997-2003, Professor of Geology, 2003-, University of North Carolina at Wilmington. Publications: Over 60 books, articles in scientific journals and book chapters as author and co-author include most

recently: The fossil record of drilling predation on bivalves and gastropods, in Predator-Prey Interactions in the Fossil Record, 2003; Moonsnail Project: a scientific collaboration with middle school teachers and students, 2003; Predators, Prey and Their Fossil record: The PS Short Course, 2003; Paleoecological patterns in molluscan extinctions and recoveries: Comparison of Cretaceous-Tertiary and Eocene-Oligocene extinctions in North America, 2004. Honours include: Sigma Xi, 1975; National Science Foundation Graduate Fellowship, 1976-79; An Outstanding Young Woman of America, 1983; Outstanding Faculty Member, School of Engineering, University of Mississippi, 1989-90; Award Paper, 13th Annual Conference on College Teaching and Learning, 2002; Association for Women Geoscientists Outstanding Educator Award, 2003. Memberships include: Fellow, Geological Society of America; Fellow, American Association for the Advancement of Science; President, Paleontological Society, 2000-2002; President, Board of Trustees, Paleontological Research Institution, 2004-2006; National Center for Science Education; Society for Sedimentary Geology; Association for Women Geoscientists. Address: Department of Earth Sciences, University of North Carolina at Wilmington, 601 South College Road, Wilmington, NC 28403-5944, USA. E-mail: kelleyp@uncw.edu

**KELLY Anthony,** b. 25 January 1929, Hillingdon, Middlesex, England. Consultant. Education: BSc, 1st class, Physics, University of Reading, 1949; PhD, Trinity College, Cambridge, 1953; ScD, University of Cambridge, 1968. Appointments: Research Associate, University of Illinois, 1953-55; ICI Fellow, University of Birmingham, 1955; Assistant Professor, Associate Professor, The Technological Institute, Northwestern University, Chicago, 1956-59; University Lecturer, University of Cambridge, 1959-67; Superintendent, 1967-69, Deputy Director, 1969-75, National Physical Laboratory, Middlesex; Seconded to ICI plc, 1973-75; Consultant to many international companies, 1973-; Vice Chancellor and Chief Executive, University of Surrey, 1975-94; Founder, Surrey Research Park, 1979; Director, Johnson Wax UK Ltd, 1981-96; Director, QUO-TEC Ltd, 1984-2000; Director, NPL Management Ltd, 1994-2001; Distinguished Research Fellow, Department of Materials Science and Metallurgy, University of Cambridge, 1994-. Publications: 200 papers in scientific and technical journals; Numerous books; Many lectures. Honours include: CBE, 1988; Gold Medal, American Society of Materials, 1991; Platinum Medal, Institute of Materials, 1992; Knight of St Gregory, 1992; Deputy Lieutenant for the County of Surrey, 1993; DUniv, University of Surrey, 1994; Honorary Fellow, Institution of Structural Engineers, 1996; Hon DSc, University of Birmingham, 1997; Honorary Fellow, Institution of Civil Engineers, 1997; Acta Metallurgica Gold Medal, 2000; Honorary DEng, Hanyang University, Korea, 2001; Honorary Doctor of Science, University of Reading, 2002. Memberships: Institute of Metals; British Non-Ferrous Metals Research Association; Engineering Materials Requirements Board, Department of Trade and Industry; European Association of Composite Materials; Royal National Institute for the Deaf; Institute of Materials. Address: Churchill College, Cambridge, CB3 0DS, England. E-mail: ak209@cam.ac.uk

**KELMAN James,** b. 9 June 1946, Glasgow, Scotland. Author; Dramatist; Essayist. m. Marie Connors, 2 daughters. Publications: The Busconductor Hines, 1984; A Chancer, 1985; A Disaffection, 1989; How Late it Was, How Late, 1994; Translated Accounts, 2001; You Have to be Careful in the Land of the Free, 2004. Short Stories: An Old Pub Near the Angel, 1973; Short Tales from the Nightshift, 1978; Not Not While the Giro and Other Stories, 1983; Lean Tales, 1985; Greyhound for Breakfast, 1987; The Burn, 1991; Busted Scotch,

1997; The Good Times, 1998. Plays: The Busker, 1985; In the Night, 1988; Hardie and Baird, The Last, 1990; One, Two – Hey, 1994; The Art of the Big Bass Drum, Radio 3, 1998; Essays, Some Recent Attacks, 1991; And The Judges Said…, 2002; CD, Seven Stories, 1997. Screenplay: The Return, 1990. Honours: Cheltenham Prize, 1987; James Tait Black Memorial Prize, 1989; Writers Guild Award; Booker Prize, 1994. Address: c/o Rodgers, Coleridge and White Ltd, 20 Powis Mews, London W11 1JN, England.

**KELSALL Malcolm Miles,** b. 27 February 1938, London, England. Professor of English. m. Mary Emily Ives, 5 August 1961. Education: BA, Oxon, 1961; BLitt, Oxon, 1964; MA, Oxon, 1965. Appointments: Staff Reporter, The Guardian newspaper, 1961; Assistant Lecturer, Exeter University, 1963-64; Lecturer, Reading University, 1964-75; Professor, University of Wales, Cardiff, 1975-. Publications: Editor, Sarah Fielding, David Simple, 1969; Editor, Thomas Otway, Venice Preserved, 1969; Christopher Marlowe, 1981; Congreve: The Way of the World, 1981; Byron's Politics, 1985; Byron's Politics, 1987; Editor, Encyclopedia of Literature and Criticism, 1990; The Great Good Place: The Country House and English Literature, 1992; Editor, J M Synge, The Playboy of the Western World, 1997; Editor, William Congreve, Love For Love, 1999; Jefferson and the Iconography of Romanticism, 1999; Literary Representations of the Irish Country House, 2003. Contributions to: Byron Journal; Essays in Criticism; Irish University Review; Theatre Research International; Review of English Studies; Studies in Romanticism. Honours: Elma Dangerfield Prize, 1991; British Academy Warton Lecturer, 1992. Address: School of English, Cardiff University, PO Box 94, Cardiff CF10 3XB, Wales.

**KEMP Terence James,** b. 26 June 1938, Watford, Hertfordshire, England. Professor. m. Sheila Therese, 1 son, 2 daughters. Education: BA, 1961, MA, DPhil, 1963, Jesus College, Oxford. Appointments: DSIR Research Fellow, Cookridge Laboratory, University of Leeds, 1962; Assistant Lecturer, 1966-66, Lecturer, 1966-70, Senior Lecturer in Chemistry, 1970-74, Reader in Chemistry, 1974-80, Professor of Chemistry, 1980-, Pro-Vice Chancellor, 1983-89, University of Warwick. Publications: Introductory Photochemistry, 1971; Dictionary of Physical Chemistry, 1992; 240 original scientific articles. Honours: Meldola Medal, Royal Institute of Chemistry, 1967; Order of Merit, Polish People's Republic, 1978; Nagroda, 2nd prize, Marie Curie-Slodowska Society for Radiation Research, 1992. Address: Department of Chemistry, University of Warwick, Coventry CV4 7AL, England. E-mail: t.j.kemp@warwick.ac.uk

**KEMPA Edward Stanislaw,** b. 27 September 1927, Ruda Śląska, Poland. Professor of Environmental Engineering. m. Lidia Mudry, 2 daughters. Education: MSc, Sanitary Engineering, Wroclaw Technical University, 1956; Dr. rer.techn., Water and Environmental Engineering, Warsaw Technical University, 1963; Dr Sc. (Habilitatus), Environmental Engineering, Wroclaw Technical University, 1976. Appointments: Process Design Engineer, Design Office of Municipal Management, Wroclaw, 1955-62; Director, Wroclaw Technical University Publishing House, 1972-75; Deputy Director, Institute of Environmental Protection Engineering, 1976-79; Professor, Sanitary Engineering Department 1979, Dean, 1981-84, Wroclaw Technical University; Chief Scientific Adviser, ECOSYSTEM Consultants Ltd, Zielona Gora, 1988-; Emeritus Professor, Chair of Water and Waste Technology, Zielona Gora University of Technology, 1986-97; UNIDO split mission expert in India, 1985-88; Adviser, World Health Organisation, 1972, 1980, 1981, 1983; UNEP Adviser, 1981, 1991, 1992; IMO Adviser,

1993; Some 340 technical expertises and opinions, 1954-2004; General Designer of some 30 wastewater treatment plants. Publications: 15 books include: Wastewater treatment, 1972, 1983; Systematics of Wastewater Sludge, 1976; Fundamentals of Environment Protection, 1976, 1985; Systems of Wastewater Treatment, 1981; Municipal Solid Waste Management, 1983; Environmental Impact of Hazardous Waste (editor), 1991; Some 310 papers in journals and conference proceedings; Editor-in-Chief, Acta Politechnicae Wratislaviensis, 1972-85; Editorial Board, Environmental Protection, 1976-; Editorial Board, Waste Magazin, Vienna, 1991-. Honours: Golden Cross of Merit, 1974; Knight's Cross, 1980, Commanders Cross, 1997, of Polonia Restituta; Scientific Award, City of Zielona Gora, 1995; Professor Zygmunt Rudolf Medal, 2000, Honorary Member, 2004-, Polish Association of Sanitary Engineers; Doctor honoris causa, Czestochowa University of Technology, 2004. Memberships: Polish Association of Sanitary Engineers and Technicians; Polish Academy of Sciences; Deutsche Vereinigung für Wasserwirtschaft, Abwasser und Abfall; Wroclaw Scientific Society; International Water Association; Polish Association of United Nations Experts; New York Academy of Sciences. Address: Okrzei 6/2, PO Box 34, 51-673 Wroclaw 9, Poland. E-mail: eskem@neosrada.pl

**KENDALL Bridget,** b. 27 April 1956, Oxford, England. Journalist. Education: Lady Margaret Hall, Oxford, 1974-78; Harvard, USA, 1978-80; St Antony's College, Oxford, 1980-83; Voronegh State University, 1976-77; Moscow State University, 1981-82. Appointments: Trainee, BBC World Service, 1983; Presenter and Producer, Newsnight, BBC2, 1983-84; Producer, Reporter, Editor, BBC World Service Radio, 1984-89; BBC Moscow Correspondent, 1989-93; BBC Washington Correspondent, 1994-98; BBC Diplomatic Correspondent, 1998-. Publications: Co-author, David the Invincible, annotated translation (classical Armenian philosophy), 1980; Kosovo and After: The future of spin in the digital age (Jubilee Lecture for St Antony's College, Oxford), 2000; Co-author, The Day that Shook the World (BBC correspondents on September 11th 2001), 2001. Honours: British Council Scholar to USSR, 1976-77, 1981-82; Harkness Fellow, USA, 1978-80; Sony Award, Reporter of the Year (Bronze Award), 1992; James Cameron Award for distinguished journalism, 1992; Voice of the Listener and Viewer Award, 1993; MBE, 1994; Honorary Doctorate, University of Central England, Birmingham, 1999; Honorary Doctorate in Law, St Andrew's University, 2001; Honorary Doctorate in Law, Exeter University, 2002; Honorary Fellow, St Anthony's College, Oxford. Memberships: Advisory Board, Russian and Eurasian Programme at Chatham House, Royal Institute of International Affairs, 2000-; Member of Council, Royal United Services Institute, 2001-05; Member of Advisory Council, European Research Institute, University of Birmingham. Address: BBC Television Centre, Wood Lane, London W12, England.

**KENNEDY Alexander,** b. 20 April 1933, Manchester, England. Retired Consultant Histopathologist. Education: MB ChB, Liverpool, 1956; MD, Liverpool, 1964; MRCPath, 1967; FRCPath, 1985. Appointments: House Office, Stanley and Royal Liverpool Children's Hospitals, 1956-58; Short Service Commission, Royal Air Force Medical Branch, 1958-61; Pathologist, RAF Hospital, Wroughton, 1958-61; Lecturer, University of Liverpool, 1961-67; Visiting Assistant Professor, University of Chicago, 1968; Senior Lecturer, University of Sheffield, 1969-77; Consultant Histopatholgist, 1977-97, Retired, 1997-, Northern General Hospital, Sheffield. Publications: 4 books; Over 50 articles in professional journals; Abstracts, letters and other publications. Memberships: Pathological Society of Great Britain and Ireland; British Thoracic Society;

British Division of the International Academy of Pathology; Trent Regional Thoracic Society; Sheffield Medico-Chirurgical Society. Address: 16 Brincliffe Gardens, Sheffield, S11 9BG, England. E-mail: sandy.kennedy@care4free.net

**KENNEDY (George) Michael (Sinclair),** b. 19 February 1926, Manchester, England. Music Critic; Author. m. (1) Eslyn Durdle, 16 May 1947, deceased 2 January 1999, (2) Joyce Bourne, 10 October 1999. Education: Berkhamsted School. Appointments: Staff, 1941-, Northern Music Critic, 1950-, Northern Editor, 1960-86, Joint Chief Music Critic, 1986-89, The Daily Telegraph; Music Critic, The Sunday Telegraph, 1989-. Publications: The Hallé Tradition: A Century of Music, 1960; The Works of Ralph Vaughan Williams, 1964, revised edition, 1980; Portrait of Elgar, 1968, 3rd edition, 1987; Elgar: Orchestral Music, 1969; Portrait of Manchester, 1970; A History of the Royal Manchester College of Music, 1971; Barbirolli: Conductor Laureate, 1971; Mahler, 1974, revised edition, 1990; The Autobiography of Charles Hallé, with Correspondence and Diaries (editor), 1976; Richard Strauss, 1976, revised edition, 1995; The Concise Oxford Dictionary of Music (editor), 1980, revised edition, 1995; Britten, 1981, revised edition, 1993; The Hallé 1858-1983, 1983; Strauss: Tone Poems, 1984; The Oxford Dictionary of Music (editor), 1985, 2nd edition, revised, 1994; Adrian Boult, 1987; Portrait of Walton, 1989; Music Enriches All: The First 21 Years of the Royal Northern College of Music, Manchester, 1994; Richard Strauss, Man, Musician, Enigma, 1999; The Life of Elgar, 2004. Contributions to: Newspapers and magazines. Honours: Fellow, Institute of Journalists, 1967; Honorary MA, Manchester, 1975; Officer of the Order of the British Empire, 1981; Fellow, Royal Northern College of Music, 1981; Commander of the Order of the British Empire, 1997; Companion, Royal Northern College of Music, 1999; Hon DMus, Manchester, 2003. Address: The Bungalow, 62 Edilom Road, Manchester M8 4HZ, England.

**KENNEDY Iain Manning,** b. 15 September 1942, Northampton, England. Company Director. m. Ingrid Annette, 2 daughters. Education: Pembroke College, Cambridge, 1961-64. Appointments: Joined staff, 1969, Production Director, 1976, Chief Executive, 1998, Chairman, 2001, Church and Co plc; Chairman, SATRA, 1989; Governor, University College, Northampton, 1998; Retired, 2001. Honours: OBE, 2002. Address: 3 Townsend Close, Hanging Houghton, Northampton, NN6 9HP, England. E-mail: iain@hanghoughton.fsnet.co.uk

**KENNEDY Jane Hope,** b. 28 February 1953, Loughborough, England. Architect. m. John Maddison, 2 sons. Education: Dip Arch, Manchester Polytechnic; Registered Architect, RIBA. Appointments: British Waterways Board, 1978-80; Assistant, David Jeffcoate Architect, 1980-81; Self-employed, 1981-86; Norwich City Council Planning Department, 1986-88; Architect, 1988-, Partner, 1992-, Purcell Miller Tritton; Surveyor to the fabric of Ely Cathedral, 1994-. Memberships: Institute of Historic Building Conservation; Fellow, Royal Society of Arts; Architect Accredited in Building Conservation. Address: Purcell Miller Tritton, 46 St Mary's Street, Ely, Cambridgeshire CB7 4EY, England. E-mail: janekennedy@pmt.co.uk

**KENNEDY John Maxwell,** b. 9 July 1934, Cardiff, Wales. Solicitor. m. Margaret, 4 sons. Education: LLB, University College, London University, 1954. Appointments: Allen & Overy: Joined, 1954, qualified as a Solicitor, 1957, Partner, 1962, Senior Partner, 1986; Involved in advising major international corporations, banks, governments on a wide variety of commercial, financial and oil-related work; International capital markets, involving debt and equity financings by governments and international corporations Acted

for the national oil company in Saudi Arabia and the central bank and the Ministry of Defence; Retired, 1994; Chairman, Law Debenture Corporation plc (Investment Trust), 1994-2000; Board Member, Financial Services Authority, 1994-1999; Chairman, 1996-98, Director and Chairman, Remuneration Committee and Member of the Audit Committee, 1993-2004, Amlin plc (formerly Angerstein Underwriting Trust plc); Chairman, Lloyd's Corporate Capital Association, 1995-98; Trustee, Director (appointed by the Secretary of State)of the Nuclear Trust (fund set up to provide for the decommissioning costs of British Energy's nuclear power stations), 1996-; Carried out Senior Management Review on behalf of the Cabinet Office on the Treasury Solicitor's Department, 1996. Memberships: City of London Club; City Law Club; Hurlingham Club; Royal Wimbledon Golf Club. Address: 16 Kensington Park Road, London W11 3BU, England.

**KENNEDY Nigel,** b. 28 December 1956, England. Violinist. Partner, Eve Westmore, 1 son. Education: Yehudi Menuhin School; Juilliard School of Performing Arts. Creative Works: Chosen by the BBC as the subject of a 5 year documentary on the development of a soloist following his debut with the Philharmonic Orchestra, 1977; Appeared with all the major British orchestras; Appearances at all the leading UK Festivals and in Europe at Stresa, Lucerne, Gstaad, Berlin & Lockenhaus; Debut at the Tanglewood Festival with the Boston Symphony under André Previn, 1985, at MN with Sir Neville Marriner, at Montreal with Charles Dutoit; Given concerts in the field of jazz with Stephane Grappelli at Carnegie Hall and Edinburgh, runs his own jazz group; Recordings include: Elgar Sonata with Peter Pettinger; Tchaikovsky; Sibelius; Vivaldi; Mendelssohn; Bruch; Walton Viola & Violin Concertos; Elgar Concerto with London Philharmonic Orchestra. Publication: Always Playing, 1991. Honours include: Best Classical Disc of the Year Award, London, 1985; Hon DLitt, Bath, 1991. Memberships include: Senior Vice President, Aston Villa FC, 1990-. Address: c/o Russells Solicitors, Regency House, 1-4 Warwick Street, London W1R 5WB, England.

**KENNEDY, Rt Hon Lord Justice, Rt Hon Sir Paul Joseph Morrow Kennedy,** b.12 June 1935, Sheffield, England. m. Virginia Devlin, 2 sons, 2 daughters. Education: MA, LLM, Gonville and Caius College, Cambridge, 1955-59; Called to Bar at Gray's Inn, 1960, Bencher, 1982, Vice-Treasurer, 2001, Treasurer, 2002. Appointments: Recorder, 1972-83; Queen's Counsel, 1973; Presiding Judge, North East Circuit, 1985-89; High Court Judge, Queen's Bench Division, 1983-92; Lord Justice of Appeal, 1992-; Member Judicial Studies Board and Chairman of Criminal Committee, 1993-96; Vice-President, Queen's Bench Division, 1997-2002; Member Sentencing Guidelines Council, 2004-. Honours: Kt, 1983; PC, 1992; Honorary Fellow, Gonville and Caius College, Cambridge, 1998; Honorary LLD, University of Sheffield, 2000. Address: Royal Courts of Justice, Strand, London WC2A 2LL, England.

**KENNEDY Peter Graham Edward,** b. 28 March 1951, London, England. Professor of Neurology. m. Catherine Ann Kennedy, 1 son, 1 daughter. Education: University College London and University College Hospital Medical School, 1969-74; MB BS, 1974; PhD, 1980; MD, 1983; FRCP (London), 1988; FRCP (Glasgow), 1989; DSc, 1991; FRSE, 1992; MPhil, 1993; MLitt, 1995; FRCPath, 1996; FMedSci, 1998. Appointments: Honorary Research Assistant, MRC Neuroimmunology Project, University College, London, 1978-80; Registrar, then Senior Registrar, National Hospital for Nervous Diseases, London, 1982-84; Visiting Assistant Professor of Neurology, Johns Hopkins University Hospital, USA, 1985; Senior Lecturer, Neurology and Virology, University of Glasgow, 1986-87; Burton Professor of

Neurology, University of Glasgow and Consultant Neurologist, Institute of Neurological Sciences, Southern General Hospital, Glasgow, Scotland, 1987-. Publications: Numerous articles in learned journals on Neurology and Neurovirology; Books: Infections of the Nervous System (with R T Johnson), 1987; Infectious Diseases of the Nervous System (with L E Davis), 2000. Honours: BUPA Medical Foundation Doctor of the Year Research Award, 1990; Linacre Medal and Lectureship, Royal College of Physicians, London, 1991; TS Srinivasan Gold Medal and Endowment Lecturer, Madras, 1993; Fogarty International Scholar-in-Residence, National Institutes of Health, Bethesda, USA, 1993-94; James W Stephens Honored Visiting Professor, Department of Neurology, University of Colorado Health Sciences Center, Denver, USA, 1994; Livingstone Lecture, Royal College of Physicians and Surgeons of Glasgow, 2004. Memberships: Association of Physicians of Great Britain and Ireland; Corresponding Member, American Neurological Association; Association of British Neurologists; Fellow of the Royal Society of Edinburgh; Founder Fellow, Academy of Medical Sciences; Secretary, 2000-03, President, 2004-, International Society for Neurovirology; Chairman, EFNS Scientist Panel on Infections including AIDS; Member Editorial Boards several medical journals. Address: Glasgow University Department of Neurology, Institute of Neurological Sciences, Southern General Hospital, Glasgow G51 4TF, Scotland. E-mail: p.g.kennedy@clinmed.gla.ac.uk

**KENNEFICK Christine Marie,** b. 4 July 1962, Washington DC, USA. Materials Scientist. Education: BSc, 1984, MSc, 1986, Stanford University; PhD, Cornell University, 1991. Appointments: National Research Council Associate, NASA Lewis Research Center, Cleveland, Ohio, 1991-93; Guest Scientist, Max-Planck Institute, Stuttgart, Germany, 1994-96; ASEE Postdoctoral Fellow, US Army Research Laboratory, Aberdeen, Maryland, 1997-98; Senior Research Associate, Air Force Research Laboratory, Dayton, Ohio, 1998-2000; Visiting Assistant Professor, Shippensburg University, Pennsylvania, 2001-02. Honours: BSc with Distinction and in Departmental Honors Program; International Woman of Year, IBC, 1998-2001; Outstanding Woman of the Twentieth Century, ABI, 1999; Listed in biographical publications. Memberships: Life Fellow, International Biographical Association; Fellow, Deputy Governor, American Biographical Institute; New York Academy of Sciences; American Physical Society; International Order of Merit; Order of International Ambassadors. Address: 2029 Turtle Pond Drive, Reston, VA 20191, USA.

**KENNET 2nd Baron, (Wayland Hilton Young),** b. 2 August 1923, England. Politician; Writer; Journalist. m. Elizabeth Ann Adams, 24 January 1948, 1 son, 5 daughters. Education: Trinity College, Cambridge. Appointments: Royal Navy, 1942-45; Staff, Foreign Office, 1946-47, 1949-51; Delegate, Parliamentary Assemblies, Western European Union and Council of Europe, 1962-65; Editor, Disarmament and Arms Control, 1962-65; Parliamentary Secretary, Ministry of Housing and Local Government, 1966-70; Opposition Spokesman on Foreign Affairs and Science Policy, 1971-74; Member, European Parliament, 1978-79; Chief Whip, 1981-83; Spokesman on Foreign Affairs and Defence, 1981-90, Social Democratic Party, House of Lords; Vice President, Parliamentary and Scientific Committee, 1989-. Publications: As Wayland Young: The Italian Left, 1949; The Deadweight, 1952; Now or Never, 1953; Old London Churches (with Elizabeth Young), 1956; The Montesi Scandal, 1957; Still Alive Tomorrow, 1958; Strategy for Survival, 1959; The Profumo Affair, 1963; Eros Denied, 1965; Thirty-Four Articles (editor), 1965; Existing Mechanisms of Arms Control, 1965. As Wayland Kennet: Preservation, 1972; The Futures of Europe, 1976; The Rebirth of Britain, 1982;

London's Churches (with Elizabeth Young), 1986; Northern Lazio; An Unknown Italy (with Elizabeth Young), 1990; Parliaments and Screening, 1995. Address: 100 Bayswater Road, London, W2 3HJ, England.

**KENSIT Patsy (Jude),** b. 4 March 1968, London, England. Film Actress. m. (1) Dan Donovan, (2) Jim Kerr, divorced, 1 son, (3) Liam Gallagher, divorced, 1 son. Creative Works: Films include: The Great Gatsby; The Bluebird; Absolute Beginners; Chorus of Disapproval; The Skipper; Chicago Joe and The Showgirl; Lethal Weapon II; Twenty-One; Prince of Shadows; Does This Mean We're Married; Blame It On the Bellboy; The Turn of the Screw; Beltenebros; Bitter Harvest; Angels and Insects; Grace of My Heart; Human Bomb; Janice Beard; Pavillions, 1999; Best; Things Behind the Sun, 2000; Bad Karma; Who's Your Daddy, 2001; The One and Only, 2001; TV appearances: Great Expectations; Silas Marner; Tycoon: The Story of a Woman; Adam Bede; The Corsican Brothers (US TV); Aladdin; Emmerdale.

**KENT Paul Welberry,** b. 19 April 1923, Doncaster, England. Chemist. m. Rosemary Shepherd, 3 sons, 1 daughter. Education: BSc, PhD, Birmingham University; MA, DPhil, DSc, Jesus College, Oxford University. Appointments: Assistant Lecturer then ICI Fellow, Birmingham University; Visiting Fellow, Princeton University, New Jersey, 1948-49; Demonstrator in Biochemistry, Oxford University, 1950-72; Tutor and Dr Lees Reader, 1955-72, Emeritus Fellow (Student), 1973-Christ Church, Oxford; Master, Van Mildert College, Durham University, 1972-82. Publications: Biochemistry of Amino Sugars, 1955; Membrane-Mediated Information, 1973; Some Scientists in the Life of Christ Church, Oxford, 2001; Robert Hooke and the English Renaissance, 2005. Honours: JP; Honorary DSc, CNAA; Honorary LittD, Drury University, USA; Order of Merit, Germany. Memberships: Royal Society of Chemistry; Biochemical Society; Athenaeum. Address: 18 Arnolds Way, Cumnor Hill, Oxford OX2 9JB, England.

**KENTFIELD Graham Edward Alfred,** b. 3 September 1940, Buckhurst Hill, Essex, England. Retired Bank of England Official. m. Ann Hewetson, 2 daughters. Education: BA (Lit Hum, 1st Class), St Edmund Hall, Oxford, 1963. Appointments: Head of Monetary Policy Forecasting, 1974-76, Governor's Speechwriter, 1976-77, Editor, Quarterly Bulletin, 1977-80, Senior Manager, Banking and Money Supply Statistics, 1980-84, Adviser, Banking Department, 1984-85; Deputy Chief Cashier, 1985-91, Chief Cashier and Chief of Banking Department, 1991-94, Chief Cashier and Deputy Director, 1994-98, Bank of England. Honour: Fellow of Chartered Institute of Bankers, 1991; Memberships: Bank of England Director BACS Ltd, 1988-95; Bank of England Director, Financial Law Panel, 1994-98; Bank of England Representative, Council of Chartered Institute of Bankers, 1991-98; Bank of England Representative, APACS Council, 1991-98; Member, Building Societies Investor Protection Board, 1991-2001; Member, Deposit Protection Board (Banks), 1991-98; Chairman, Insolvency Practices Council, 2000-04; Honorary Treasurer, Society for the Promotion of Roman Studies, 1991-; Trustee, 1994- Chairman, 2000-, Chartered Institute for Bankers Pension Fund; Trustee, 1999-, Chairman, 2005-, Overseas Bishoprics Fund; Member, Council of London University, 2000-. Address: 27 Elgood Avenue, Northwood, Middlesex, HA6 3QL, England.

**KENTON Jeremy Martin,** b. 11 December 1955, Glasgow, Scotland. Osteopath; Expert Witness; Writer; Broadcaster. m. Sharon Anna Calder, 2 daughters. Education: Chigwell, 1966-75; ND DO, British College of Osteopathic Medicine, 1975-79. Appointments: Advisor, All Party Parliamentary

Group on Alternative Medicine, 1957-92; Member, Council GCRO, 1987-93; Council Member, 1980-90, President, 1988-91, British Naturopathic and Osteopathic Association; Founder Member, CCAM, 1985; Senior Clinician, BCOM, 1980-92; Regular broadcaster and writer on health topics; Private Osteopathic Practitioner, London and Essex; Expert Medical Witness. Publications: Numerous articles in national press, 1980-; Co-author, Competence in Osteopathic Practice, 1990; Regular broadcaster on national and local radio and television. Memberships: General Osteopathic Council. Address: 148 Harley Street, London W1G 7LG, England. E-mail: jmkost1@aol.com

**KENWRIGHT Bill,** b. 4 September 1945, England. Theatre Producer. Education: Liverpool Institute. Appointments: Actor, 1964-70; Theatre Producer, 1970-; Director, Everton Football Club. Creative Works: Plays directed include: Joseph and The Amazing Technicolor Dreamcoat, 1979; The Business of Murder, 1981; A Streetcare Named Desire, 1984; Stepping Out, 1984; Blood Brothers, 1988; Shirley Valentine, 1989; Travels With My Aunt, 1993; Piaf, 1994; Lysistrata, 1993; Medea, 1993; Pygmalion, 1997; A Doll's House; An Ideal Husband; The Chairs, 2000; Blood Brothers; Ghosts; The Female Odd Couple. Address: Bill Kenwright Ltd, 106 Harrow Road, London, W2 1RR, England.

**KENYON Ronald James,** b. 24 May 1951, Penrith, England. Chartered Accountant. m. Ann Christine Kenyon, 1 son, 1 daughter. Education: Trent Polytechnic, Nottingham; Foundation Course, Institute of Chartered Accountants. Appointments: Pricewaterhouse, Leeds, 1968-69; Chartered Accountant, 1974-, Partner, 1980-, F T Kenyon and Son, Kyle and Kenyon, Kyle Saint and Co, Saint and Co; Chairman, Cumberland Society of Chartered Accountants, 1991. Publications: Rock Climbing in the North of England, 1978; Rock Climbing Guide to Borrowdale, 1986, 1990. Honours: Fellow, Institute of Chartered Accountants; Vice President, Fell and Rock Climbing Club. Memberships: Fell and Rock Climbing Club; Eden Valley Mountaineering Club; Penrith Agriculture Society; Eden Sports Council; Penrith Partnership; Penrith Mountain Rescue Team, 1967-92; Penrith Lions Club, 1979-2004.

**KERC Janez,** b. 22 May 1962, Podrecje. Pharmacist. Education: BSc, 1987, MSc, 1990, PhD, 1995. Appointments: Researcher, 1988-94, Senior Researcher, 1994-2002, Head of NDS Department, 2002-, Lek Pharmaceuticals d.d. Ljubljana; Assistant Professor, Faculty of Pharmacy, University of Ljubljana. Publications: Patents in pharmaceutical field; Articles in professional journals. Honours: KRKA Award, 1985; Minarik Award, 1999. Memberships: Slovenian Pharmaceutical Society; Controlled Release Society. Address: Ulica Bratov Ucakar 86, 1000 Ljubljana, Slovenia.

**KERNICK Robert Charles,** b. 11 May 1927, Istanbul, Turkey. Wine Merchant. m. (1) Gillian Burne, 1 son, 1 daughter, (2) Adelaide Anne Elizabeth White. Education: Blundells and Sidney Sussex, Cambridge. Appointments: Director, Grandmetropolitan Ltd, 1972-75; Managing Director, International Distillers and Vintners, 1972-75; Clerk of the Royal Cellars, 1979-92; Chairman, Corney and Barrow Ltd, 1981-88; Clerk of the Prince of Wales's Cellar, 1992-99. Honours: Commander of the Royal Victorian Order; Chevalier de l'Ordre du Merite Agricole. Memberships: Merchant Taylors' Company; Leathersellers' Company; Cavalry and Guards Club; MCC; Swinley Forest Golf Club. Address: 79 Canfield Gardens, London NW6 3EA, England.

**KERR (Anne) Judith,** b. 14 June 1923, Berlin, Germany. Children's Fiction Writer. Appointments: Secretary, Red Cross, London, England, 1941-45; Teacher and Textile Designer, 1948-53; Script Editor, Script Writer, BBC-TV, London, 1953-58. Publications: The Tiger Who Came to Tea, 1968; Mog the Forgetful Cat, 1970; When Hitler Stole Pink Rabbit, 1971; When Willy Went to the Wedding, 1972; The Other Way Round, 1975; Mog's Christmas, 1976; A Small Person Far Away, 1978; Mog and the Baby, 1980; Mog in the Dark, 1983; Mog and Me, 1984; Mog's Family of Cats, 1985; Mog's Amazing Birthday Caper, 1986; Mog and Bunny, 1988; Mog and Barnaby, 1990; How Mrs Monkey Missed the Ark, 1992; The Adventures of Mog, 1993; Mog on Fox Night, 1993; Mog in the Garden, 1994; Mog's Kittens, 1994; Mog and the Vee Ee Tee, 1996; The Big Mog Book, 1997; Birdie Halleluyah, 1998; Mog's Bad Thing, 2002; The Other Goose, 2001; Goodbye Mog, 2002; Mog Time, 2004. Address: c/o Harper Collins Publishers, 77-85 Fulham Palace Road, London W6 8JB, England.

**KERR Deborah Jane,** b. 30 September 1921, Dumbarton, Scotland. Actress. m. (1) Anthony Bartley, divorced, 2 daughters, (2) Peter Viertel, 1960, 1 step-daughter. Education: Northumberland House, Bristol. Career: Open Air Theatre, Regent's Park, London, 1939; Films include: Contraband, Jenny (Major Barbara, 1940); Love on the Dole, 1940; The Day Will Dawn, 1941; Black Narcissus, 1945; The Huckster, 1946; If Winter Comes, 1947; The Prisoner of Zenda, 1948; King Solomon's Mines, 1950; Dream Wife, 1952; From Here to Eternity, 1953; The King and I, 1956; An Affair to Remember, 1957; Beloved Infidel, 1960; the Innocents, 1961; The Night of the Iguana, 1963; Marriage on the Rocks, 1965; Gypsy Moths, 1968; Reunion at Fairborough, 1984; Theatre includes: Heartbreak House, 1943; Tea and Sympathy, 1953, US 1954-55; Souvenir, 1975; Overheard, 1981; The Corn is Green, 1985; TV includes: A Song at Twilight, 1981; Ann & Debbie and A Woman of Substance, 1984; Hold the Dream, 1986. Honours: NY Drama Critic's Award, 2 in 1947, 1957, 1960; Hollywood For Press Association Award, 1956; The King and I, 1958; Variety Club of Great Britain Award, 1961; BAFTA Special Award, 1991; 6 nominations for Academy Awards. Address: Klosters, 7250 Grisons, Switzerland.

**KESBY John Douglas,** b. 14 April 1938, London, England. Anthropologist; Educator. m. Sheila Anne Gregory. Education: BA, 1960, Diploma in Anthropology, 1961, BLitt, 1963, MA, 1967, DPhil, 1971, Oxford University, England. Appointments: Lecturer, Pitt Rivers Museum, Oxford, 1967-68; College Lecturer, King's and Newnham Colleges, Cambridge, 1968-71; Lecturer, University of Kent, Canterbury, 1971-98. Publications include: The Cultural Regions of East Africa, 1977; The Rangi of Tanzania, 1981; Progress and the Past among the Rangi of Tanzania, 1982; Rangi Natural History, 1986; Entry in Encyclopaedia Britannica: Eastern Africa: the Peoples: East Africa. Memberships include: Association of Social Anthropologists; Association of University Teachers; Royal Society for the Protection of Birds; Kent Trust. Address: 32 St Michael's Place, Canterbury, Kent CT2 7HQ, England.

**KESZEI János,** b. 1 June 1936. Timpanist; Percussionist. 2 sons, 1 daughter. Education: Music High School, Budapest, Hungary; Béla Bartók Conservatorium and Franz Liszt Academy of Music, Budapest, Hungary. Debut: Principal Percussionist, RESO, Dublin, 1957; Principal Timpanist, RESO, Dublin, 1964. Career: Principal Timpanist, Ulster Orchestra, 1966; Principal Timpanist, City of Birmingham Symphony Orchestra, 1969; Principal Timpanist, P Boulez BBC Symphony Orchestra, 1972-78; Freelance, 1978- with: ECO; RPO; LMP; CLS; English Symphonia; OAE; GTO; Solo Timpanist, Rotterdam

Philharmonic, 1984-87; Toured and recorded ROH; Contributed to more than 320 films, records CD's, lectures, master classes in UK and abroad; Involved in early and baroque, Hanover Band, King's Consort and OAE in Glyndebourne summer seasons, Salzburg, New York, Paris, Vienna, Berlin; Professor of Timpani, Royal College of Music, 1973-. Honour: Honorary RCM, 1982. Membership: Royal Society of Musicians of Great Britain. Address: 17 Grove Gardens, Tring, Hertfordshire HP23 5PX, England. E-mail: family@keszeil.fsnet.co.uk

**KETTLEY John Graham,** b. 11 July 1952, Halifax, West Yorkshire, England. Presenter; Weather Consultant. m. Lynn, 2 sons. Education: BSc honours, Applied Physics, Coventry University. Appointments: Meteorological Office, 1970-2000; National BBC TV broadcast meteorologist, Domestic TV manager and lead presenter, 1985-2000; Appearances on numerous TV series; Ambassador for Cricket World Cup, 1999; Presenter and host, Triangular NatWest One-day International cricket, 2001; Freelance presenter and weather consultant, John Kettley Enterprises; Contract weather presenter and sporting features for BBC Radio 5Live, 2001-. Publications: Several articles for cricket journals, travel and leisure brochures; Foreword, Rain Stops Play, book by Andrew Hignell, 2002. Memberships: Lord's Taverner, 1990-; Institute of Broadcast Meteorology, 1995-; Fellow, Royal Meteorological Society, 2001-. Address: c/o PVA Management, Hallow Park, Hallow, Worcester WR2 6PG, England. E-mail: johnkettley@bbc.co.uk

**KEUNING Steven,** b. 7 September 1955, The Hague, The Netherlands. Director General. m. Jacomien Van Dam, 1 son, 1 daughter. Education: MA, Econometrics, Groningen University, 1980; PhD, Economics, Erasmus University, Rotterdam, 1995. Appointments: Head, National Accounts, 1994-2000, Director, Macroeconomic Statistics & Dissemination, 2000-02, Statistics, The Netherlands; Director General, Statistics, European Central Bank, 2002-. Publications: Accounting for Economic Development and Social Change, 1996; Numerous articles in The Review of Income and Wealth, Economic Systems Review and International Statistical Review. Memberships: International Statistical Institute; International Association for Research on Income and Wealth. Address: Director General Statistics, Kaiserstrasse 29, 60311 Frankfurt am Main, Germany. E-mail: steven.keuning@ecb.int

**KEVELAITIS Egidijus,** b. 27 July 1961, Kaunas, Lithuania. Medical Doctor. m. Sigita, 2 sons. Education: MD, 1985; PhD, 1988; DSc, 1993; Docent diploma, 1994. Appointments: Assistant Professor, Department of Physiology and Pathophysiology, Kaunas Medical Institute, 1985-88; Senior Lecturer, Department of Physiology and Pathophysiology, Kaunas Medical Academy, 1988-92; Associate Professor, Department of Physiology, 1992-2001, Professor, Department of Physiology, 2001-, Chairman, Department of Physiology, 2002-, Kaunas Medical University. Publications: Articles to medical journals; Editor, textbook: Human Physiology, 1999, 2002; Journal, Medicina, 2001-. Honours: Award, Lithuanian Academy of Sciences, 1984; Research Fellowship, European Society of Cardiology, 1997. Memberships: Lithuanian Physiological Society, Vice-President, 1992-; European Society of Cardiology; New York Academy of Sciences; Danish Society of Pharmacology. Address: Department of Physiology, 9 Mickeviciaus, Kaunas Medical University, 3000 Kaunas, Lithuania.

**KHAIT Boris Grigoryevich,** b. 7 December 1951, Grodno, Byelorussia. Company President. m. Vasiliyeva Lilya Georgiyevna. 1 son. Education: Diploma of Power Engineering Specialist, Energy Department, Moscow Institute of Rail Transport Engineers, 1974; Darden Business School, Virginia University, USA, 1991. Appointments: Leading processing Engineer, Ministry of railways of USSR, 1974-79; Vice-President of Maintenance Department, Moscow Scientific Research Institute of X-Ray and Radiology, 1979-90; General Director, President, ZAO Insurance Group "Spasskiye Vorota", 1999-. Honours: Order of Friendship, 1997; Medal "In Memory of the 850th Anniversary of Moscow", 1997. Membership Chairman of Public Relations Committee, 1998-, Vice-President, 1998-, All-Russian Insurance Union. Address: Noviy Arbat 36/9, 121205 Moscow, Russia. E-mail: bkhait@svi.ru Website: www.svi.ru

**KHAJA Naseeruddin,** b. 1 April 1954, Gulbarga, India. Medical Teacher. m. Syeda Mahmooda Banu, 2 sons. Education: MBBS, Karnatak University, Dharwad, 1975; DLO, Mysore University, 1978; MS (ENT), Bangalore University, 1981. Appointments: Lecturer in ENT, GMC Bellary, 1982-88; Assistant Professor in ENT, MMC, Mysore, 1988-93; Professor of ENT, KMC, Hubli, 1993-95; Professor & HOD of ENT, KIMS, Hubli, 1995-. Publications: Papers and articles in professional journals. Honours: First PhD Guid at Department of ENT, KIMS, Hubli; Fellowship of Indian Academy of Otolaryngology; President, AOI Karnatak Branch, 2004-05. Memberships: IMA & IMA-AMS; AOI; ISO; APOI; NES; FHNO; Academy of Allergy; Life Associate, MAAS; Life Member, Telemedicine Society of India. Address: Department of ENT, Karnatak Institute of Medical Sciences, Hubli 580022, Karnatak, India. E-mail: drknaseeruddin@rediffmail.com

**KHALATBAREE Farideh,** b. Iran. Author; Publisher. Education includes: Business studies, Institute of Taxation, admitted as an Associate Member, 1972; Fellow, Iranian Association of Accountants, 1974; Fellow, Society of Commercial and Company Accountants, 1978; Member, British Institute of Management, 1978; Fellow, Association of Certified Accountants, 1980; Fellow, Iranian Association of Certified Public Accountants, 2001. Appointments include: Personal Assistant to Partner and in charge of Tax Department, Percy Phillips and Co (London), 1970-73; Senior Accountant, Whinney Murray & Co (Tehran), 1974; Senior Accountant, Coopers & Lyebrand (Tehran), 1974; Deputy Managing Director, Franklin Book Programs Inc, 1974-76; Deputy Managing Director, Iranian Bankers Investment Co (Tehran), 1976-79, Board Member, Pooshesh Industry of Iran, Pooshesh Spinning and Weaving, Pooshesh Velvet, Pooshesh Towel and Blue Jeans, 1977-79, Board Member, Danesh Noo Printing and Publishing, 1977-79, Board Member, Bicycle & Motor Cycle Manufacturing of Iran, 1979-80, Board Member, Aliaf, 1979-80; Board Member, Filver, 1979-81, Board Member, Jahan Oil Company, 1980-82; Chairman, S & H Company, management and finance consultancy firm, 1982-84; Managing Director, Ketab Sara Company, publisher and book-seller, 1982-84; Currently since 1984-, Chairman and Managing Director, Shabaviz Publishing Company, specialising in children's and young adults' books; Member, Parliament's Research Centre, 1998-. Publications: Numerous books include: Financial Dictionary, English/Farsi and Farsi/English; The Cat on the Picture; The Woodpecker who became a Woodpecker; Sweeter than Honey; Red Ball; Happiness; The Fountain of Youth; The Ghoul of Darkness; Coloured Poems; Parinaz or Nazpari; Yusef and Zoleikha; Wings to Fly; A House to Let; The Cricket Who Could Not Sing; The Myths of Yausht; The Old Lyrist; What A Mistake; The Doctor; Isthmus; Kianouri and His Claims; More than 100 articles. Honours include: With Shabaviz Publishing Company: Best Iranian Publisher of the Year, 2001-02, 2003-04, 2004-05; Best Publisher of the 5th Tehran Biennial of Illustrations, 2002; Appraised Publisher of the 42nd Belgrade

Biennial of Illustrations, 2003; Winner, New Horizons Award, Bologna Children's Book Fair, 2004. Address: 2 Nouri Alley, Jomhouri Eslami Avenue, between Golshan St and Bastan St, Tehran 13186-45163, Iran. E-mail: shabaviz@shabaviz.com Website: www.shabaviz.com

**KHALIFA Mohamed Abd-El Hamid**, b. 17 May 1943, Sharkia, Egypt. President, National Gene Bank. m. Appointments: Researcher, 1965, 1976, Director, Gemmeiza, 1976, Senior Researcher, 1981, Chief Researcher, 1986, Maize Research Section; Director, Gemmeiza Research & Extension Center, 1980; Director, Middle Delta Regional Stations for Production & Research, 1983; Under-Secretary, Agricultural Sector, Behera Governate, 1987; Under-Secretary for Pest Control, Ministry of Agriculture, MALR, 1989; Deputy Director, 1991, 2001, President, 2002, Agricultural Research Center; Agricultural Counselor, Representative of Egypt to the United Nations Organisation, Rome, 1997; President, The National Gene Bank, MALR, 2003. Publications: Numerous articles in professional scientific journals. Honours. Membership in international conferences, councils and committees; Country speeches at ministerial and international meetings; Many scientific visits around the world. Memberships include: Executive Council of Behera Governate, 1988; Cotton Council, 1990; Agricultural Research Center, 1991; National Council for Agricultural Research, 1997; Bio-Safety National Committee, 2002. Address: National Gene Bank, MALR, 9 Gamaa St, Giza, Egypt. E-mail: info@ngb.gov.eg

**KHAN Mohammad Mohabbat**, b. 16 January 1949, Dhaka, Bangladesh. Teacher. m. Rokeya Khan, 2 sons. Education: BA (Hons), 1968, MA, 1970, University of Dhaka, Bangladesh; MPA, Syracuse University, USA, 1974; MPA, 1976, PhD, 1976, University of Southern California, USA. Appointments: Associate Professor, University of Benin, Nigeria, 1981-82; Professor, Department of Public Administration, University of Dhaka, Bangladesh, 1983-; Professor, Yarmouk University, Jordan, 1991-92; Member, Bangladesh Public Service Commission, 1999-2004. Publications: 12 books; 6 monographs; 150 chapters and articles in edited books and national and international professional journals. Honours: Awarded in many categories by IBC and ABI. Memberships: American Society for Public Administration; Commonwealth Association for Public Administration and Management; International Political Science Association; International Institute of Administration Science. Address: Department of Public Administration, University of Dhaka, Dhaka-1000, Bangladesh. E-mail: mmkhan@bangla.net

**KHANG Gilson**, b. 5 July 1961, Chungnam, Korea. Professor. m. Seong Hee Koh Khang, 2 sons. Education: BS, 1981, MS, 1985, Department of Polymer Science and Engineering, Inha University, Korea; PhD, Department of Biomedical Engineering, University of Iowa, USA, 1995. Appointments: Instructor, Inha University, 1985-87; Senior Research Scientist, Korea Research Institute of Chemical Technology, 1987-98; Currently Professor, Department of Polymer Science and Technology, Chonbuk National University, Korea. Publications: 53 books, book chapters and reviews; 123 papers; 340 presentations; 29 patents; 54 technical reports. Honours: Best Professor at Chonbuk National University, 2002; Triangle Research Award for Biomaterials and DDS, 2002; Listed in Who's Who publications and biographical dictionaries. Memberships: Society for Biomaterials; Controlled Release Society; American Association of Pharmaceutical Science; Tissue Engineering Society International; Polymer Society of Korea; Korea Society of Biomaterials; Korea Tissue Engineering Society. Address: Department of Polymer Science and Technology, Chonbuk

National University, 664-14 Dukjim, Jeonju, 561-756 South Korea.

**KHARE Mukesh**, b. 1 January 1956, Varanasi, India. Civil Engineer. Education: BEng in Civil Engineering, 1977; MEng in Civil Engineering, Environmental Engineering, 1979, University of Roorkee; PhD, Faculty of Engineering, University of Newcastle upon Tyne, 1989. Appointments: Assistant Design Engineer, Uttar Pradesh State Irrigation Department, 1979-81; Assistant Environmental Engineer, Pollution Control Board, Agra, 1981-84; Research Scholar, Demonstrator, University of Newcastle upon Tyne, England, 1984-89; Fellow to Council of Scientific and Industrial Research, National Environmental Engineering Research Institute, India, 1989-90; Lecturer, Assistant Professor, 1990-96, Assistant Professor, 1997-2000, Associate Professor, February 2000-2005, Professor, 2005- Department of Civil Engineering, Indian Institute of Technology, Delhi; Lecturer II, University of Technology, Lae, Papua New Guinea, 1996-97; Invited Lecturer, Urban Vehicular Pollution, Department of Environmental and Applied Sciences, Harvard University, USA, 2002 and EMN, Nantes, France, 2002; Founder, Co-Ordinator, Indo-French unit on Water and Waste Technologies, joint venture between, Institute of Technology, Delhi and Ministry of Education, France; Co-ordinator, IITD-ENPC, France MOU on Transport and Environment, and Remote Sensing; Reviewer: Research Management Group, Philip Morris Inc, USA, National Research Foundation, Pretoria, S Africa, Foundation for Research Development, Pretoria, S Africa. Publications: More than 50 in international and national refereed journals, proceedings, symposia, 1990-, in field of industrial and water pollution, indoor and outdoor air pollution; Author, Institute Water Quality Monitoring Programme; Book: Modelling Urban Vehicle Emissions, 2002; WIT Press UK; Contributed chapter, Fuel Options, to Handbook of Transport and Environment Vol 4, 2003; Sectoral Analysis of Air Pollution Control in Delhi, 2004; Reviews: Expert reviewer, Foundation for Research Development and National Research Council, South Africa; Research Management Group, USA; Additional Director (India), International Sustainable Technology Alliance (ISTA): Sustainable Development programme, Arizona State University, USA; Member, Expert, Examination Committee, All India Council for Technical Education, India; University Grant Commission, India; Union Public Service Commission, India, Consultant to Associate in Rural Development (ARD), USA and Central Pollution Control Board, India. Honours: National Merit Scholar, 1969-77; Best Outgoing Student, Civil Engineering Department, University of Roorkee, 1977; Best Solo Singer, University of Roorkee Cultural Society, 1977; Fellowship, University Grant Commission, 1977-79; National Scholarship for Study Abroad, 1984-89; Overseas Research Student Award, Committee of Vice-Chancellors and Principals, UK, 1987-89. Memberships include: Fellow, Wessex Institute of Great Britain; Fellow, Indian Water Works Association; Life Member: Indian Society for Wind Engineers; Indian Association for Environmental Management; Indian Society for Environmental Management; Indian Association for Air Pollution Control; Newcastle University and Roorkee University Alumni Associations. Address: Indian Institute of Technology, Hauz Khas, New Delhi 110016, India. E-mail: mukeshk@civil.iitd.ernet.in

**KHARISSOV Boris Ildusovich**, b. 19 January 1964, Uglegorsk, Russia (Mexican citizenship, 2003). Researcher; Chemist. m. Oxana V Kharissova, 2 daughters. Education: Department of Chemistry, 1986, PhD, 1993, Moscow State University, Russia. Appointments: Engineer, Moscow Institute of Chemical Technology, Russia, 1986-89; Researcher, Moscow State University, 1989-94; Researcher and Professor,

Autonomous University Nuevo León, Monterrey, Mexico, 1994-; Participated in recovery work at Chernobyl, 1987; Worked on projects for Mexican National Agency for Science and Technology, 1996, 1998, 2003-; Expert on scientific projects for the Foundation for Research and Technology of Argentina, 2001; Guest Editor, 3 special issues of the international journals, Polyhedron and Journal of Co-ordination Chemistry dedicated to inorganic and co-ordination chemistry in Latin America, 2000, 2001, 2003. Publications: More than 50 published and accepted articles; 3 monographs: Direct Synthesis of Co-ordination Compounds, co-author, 1997; Direct Synthesis of Co-ordination and Organometallic Compounds, co-author and co-editor, 1999; Synthetic Co-ordination and Organometallic Chemistry, co-author and co-editor, 2003; 2 patents; Attended many international scientific congresses. Honours: National Researcher of Mexico, 1999; Best Research Work in the UANL, 2002; Listed in biographical dictionaries. Membership: Mexican Academy of Inorganic Chemistry; Regular Member, Mexican Academy of Sciences, 2002-. Address: A P 18-F, CP 66450 Ciudad Universitaria UANL, San Nicolás de los Garza, NL, Mexico. E-mail: bkhariss@hotmail.com

**KHATIB Hisham,** b. 5 January 1936, Palestine. International Consultant. m. Maha, 21 August 1968, 2 sons, 1 daughter. Education: BSc, Engineering, 1959, University of Cairo; BSc, Economics, 1967, PhD, Engineering, 1974, University of London. Appointments: Energy Expert, Arab Fund, 1976-80; Director General, Jordan Electricity Authority, 1980-84; Minister of Energy, 1984-90, Minister of Planning, 1993-95, Government of Jordan. Publications: 1 history book: Palestine and Egypt under the Ottomans; 3 books on engineering and economics. Honours: Achievement Medal, Institute of Electrical Engineers, UK, 1998; Decorated in Italy, Indonesia, Austria, Jordan, Vatican. Memberships: Fellow, IEE (UK); Fellow, IEEE (USA). Address: PO Box 410, Amman 11831, Jordan.

**KHINTIBIDZE Elguja,** b. 7 June 1937, Georgia. Philologist. m. Mzia Menabde, 2 sons. Education: Student of Tbilisi State University, 1955-60; Postgrad Student, 1960-63; Cand Philol, 1963; DrPhilol, 1971; Professor, 1973; Corresponding Member, Georgian Academy Sciences, 1997. Appointments: Assistant Professor, 1966, Professor, 1973, Deputy Dean Philology Department, 1965-66, The Dean of Philology Department, 1976-85, Vice Rector, Tbilisi State University, 1985-93; Director, Centre of Georgian Studies, 1992-; Head, Laboratory of Georgian-Foreign Literature Contacts, 1993-; Head, Chair of Old Georgian Literature, 2000-. Publications: 180 scholarly works including 14 monographs; Georgian-Byzantine Literary Contacts, 1996; The Designation of Georgians and Their Etymology, 1998; Georgian Literature in European Scholarship, 2001. Honours: Ivane Javakhishvili Prize, 1983; International Order of Merit, 1994. Memberships: Membre Titulaire de Société Internationale pour l'Etude de la Philosophie Médiévale (Belgique Louvan La Neuve). Address: Side Street Ateni 18A Apt 13, Tbilisi 380079, Georgia.

**KHORANA Har Gobind,** b. 9 January 1922, Raipur, Punjab Region, India (US Citizen). Chemist. m Esther Elizabeth Sibler, 1952, 1 son, 2 daughters. Education: Bachelor's Degree, 1943, Master's Degree, 1945, Chemistry, Punjab University; Doctorate, Liverpool University; Postdoctoral work in Zurich, Switzerland. Appointments: Organic Chemist, working with Sir Alexander Todd, Cambridge, 1950-52; Organic Chemist, National Research Institute, Canada, 1952-60; Professor and Co-Director, Institute of Enzyme Chemistry, University of Wisconsin, 1960-64; Conrad A Elvehjem Professor in Life Sciences, 1964-70; Andrew D White Professor at Large, Cornell University, Ithaca, 1974-80; Alfred P Sloan Professor,

1970-97, Professor Emeritus and Senior Lecturer, 1997-, Massachusetts Institute of Technology. Publications: Some Recent Developments in the Chemistry of Phosphate Esters of Biological Interest, 1961; Articles on Biochemistry in various journals. Honours: Joint Winner, Nobel Prize for Physiology or Medicine, 1968; Louisa Gross Horwitz for Biochemistry, 1968; American Chemical Society Award for creative work in Synthetic Chemistry, 1968; Lasker Foundation Award, 1968; American Academy of Achievement Award, 1971; Willard Gibbs Medal, 1974; Gairdner Foundation Annual Award, 1980; National Medal of Science, 1987; Paul Kayser International Award of Merit, 1987; Numerous honorary degrees and international awards. Memberships: NAS; Foreign Academician, USSR Academy of Sciences; Foreign Member, Royal Society, London; Pontifical Academy of Sciences. Address: Departments of Biology and Chemistry, Massachusetts Institute of Technology, 77 Massachusetts Avenue, Room 68-680, Cambridge, MA 02139, USA.

**KHOROSHAYA Emma,** b. 30 August 1936, Moscow, Russia. Mechanical Engineer. m. Georgi Shimelmits, 1 son. Education: MSc, 1959, PhD, 1971, Moscow Technological Institute of Food Industry. Appointments: Senior Researcher, 1963-85, Leading Researcher, 1985-93, Head of Research Laboratory, 1993-96, All Union (Russia) Research Institute of Food Machinery Construction. Publications: More than 70 articles and publications in various Russian scientific journals. Honours: 3 times Silver Award winner, Exhibition of National Economic Achievements; Winner, Russian Council of Ministers' Prize, 1989. Address: Ha-Gat 16/16, Rishon-Le-Zion, Israel. E-mail: shoroh36@mail.ru

**KHOROSHY Eduard,** b. 30 June 1931, Moscow, Russia. Painter. m. Ella Zilz, 1 daughter. Education: Studies at Leningrad School of Art, 1948-53; Graduated from the Painting Faculty of the Painting, Sculpture and Architecture Academy of Arts, Leningrad, 1953-59. Career: Principal Exhibitions: All Union Exhibition of Graduation Works of Art Students, USSR Art Academy, 1959; "Leningrad", Academy of Fine Art's Museum, Leningrad, 1960; "Soviet Russia", Moscow Exhibition Hall, Moscow, 1961; All Union Exhibition of Pieces by Young Artists, USSR Academy, Moscow, 1961; "Leningrad", State Museum of Russian Art, Leningrad, 1964; Moscow's Artists for the 50th Anniversary of the October Revolution, Moscow, 1967; "Historical Moscow", Moscow, 1972; "Self Portrait" Exhibition, Moscow, 1985; Solo Exhibition, Ryback Museum, Israel, 1994; "Art Focus", Tel-Aviv, Israel, 1995; Solo Exhibition, Artist Union's House, Tel-Aviv, Israel, 1996; "International Art Salon", Moscow, Russia, 1998; Exhibition in the Fickler Gallery, Blonckenheim, Germany, 1999; Friendship's House, Belgium-Russia, Brussels, Belgium, 1999; La-Botegha Gallery Auction, Lugano, Switzerland, 1999; Solo Exhibition, Museum of Russian Art, Israel, 2000; Solo Exhibition, Wilfrid Israel Museum of Oriental Art, Israel, 2001. Publications: Numerous articles in magazines and newspapers; Exhibition catalogues. Book: Artists Association of Painters and Sculptors in Israel, 2003. Honour: Diploma of the Exhibition "Moscow's Artists for the 50th Anniversary of the October Revolution" for the painting " My Father Goes to the Front", 1967. Memberships: Union of Painters, USSR, 1963; Israel Council of Painters and Sculptors, 1993; Israel Professional Artists Association, 2004. Address: Ort-Israel 7, Apt 811, 59590 Bat-Yam, Israel.

**KHUDAYBERDIYEV Ruzikul,** b. 1931, Gizhduvan City, Bukhara Region, Uzbekistan. Botanist; Palaeobotanist; Palaeoxilologist. m. 4 daughters. Education: Graduate, Middle Asia State University, Tashkent City; Postgraduate, Botanical Institute Academy of Sciences of Uzbekistan attached to the V. L.

Komorov Botanical Institute Academy of Sciences of the USSR, Leningrad, 1955-58; Candidate of Biology Degree, 1958; Doctor of Biological Sciences, 1985. Appointments: Junior Researcher, 1958, Senior Researcher, Head of Palaeobotanical Laboratory, Botanical Institute, Academy of Sciences of Uzbekistan, Tashkent (since 2001, Botanika Scientific Production Center, Academy of Sciences, Republic of Uzbekistan). Publications: 2 monographs, more than 115 scientific articles as author and co-author include: Palaeobotany of Uzbekistan, 1-3 volumes, 1968, 1971, 1981; The Lower Cretaceous Stratigraphy of the Central Kyzylkum, 1985; The Cretaceous representatives of the genus Taxodioxylon in the Kyzylkum, 1990; The fossil wood of Chamaecyparixylon from the Upper Cretaceous of Kyzylkum, 1997 ; Book chapter: About the history of development of some plant genera in West Tein-Shan in Biodiverse of West of Tien-Shan: protection and efficient use, 2002. Address: ¼ Flat 23, I. Muminov Street, Tashkent, 700041, 700000 Uzbekistan. E-mail: ruzikul@hotmail.com

**KHURAIJAM Gourashyam Singh,** b. 1 March 1941, Imphal Manipur, India. Medical Doctor. m. Mema Devi Nongthombam, 2 daughters. Education: BSc (Hons in Chemistry), 1961; MB BS, 1966, MD, General Medicine, 1973, Delhi University; MRCP (UK), 1981; FRCP (Glasgow), 1992; FRCP (Edinburgh); FRCP (London). Appointments: Assistant Professor, Medicine, North Eastern Regional Institute of Medical Science, Imphal Mainipur, India, 1974-77; Consultant Physician in General Medicine, Respiratory Medicine and Geriatric Medicine, Noble's Isle of Man Hospital, Isle of Man, UK, 1984-. Publications: Books as author: General Science and Hygiene (in Manipuri), 1969; Yaipha-Yumbal (Family Planning in Manipuri), 1969; Articles in scientific journals: An unusual case of Mixed Bacterial Meningitis in an Immunocompetant Adult (co-author), 1999; Acute Confusion and Blindness from Quinine Toxicity, 2003; Acquired Haemophilia in the Elderly, 2004; Primary Thyroid Lymphoma in Elderly, 2004. Honour: Merit Award "C" in Medicine. Memberships: President, Isle of Medical Society, 2000-01; President, The Manx Stroke Foundation; President Burma Star Association, Isle of Man; Chief Patron, Smoke Buster, Isle of Man; Member of Disability Appeal Tribunal, Isle of Man. Address: 12 Cronk Drean, Douglas, Isle of Man, IM2 6AY, United Kingdom.

**KIDD Jodie,** b. 1979, Surrey, England. Fashion Model. Education: St Michael's School, W Sussex. Appointments: Modelled for numerous fashion magazines, also top international catwalk model for designers include: Gucci, Prada, Karl Lagerfeld, Yves Saint Laurent, Chanel, John Galliano, Calvin Klein, Yohji Yamamoto; Make-up Model for Chanel, 1999 season. Honours: Former National Junior Athletics Champion; Holder, Under 15s High Jump Record for Sussex; Many awards as junior show jumper. Address: c/o IMG Models, Bentinck House, 3-8 Bolsover Street, London, W1P 7HG, England.

**KIDMAN Fiona (Judith) (Dame),** b. 26 March 1940, Hawera, New Zealand. Writer; Poet. m. Ernest Ian Kidman, 20 August 1960, 1 son, 1 daughter. Appointments: Founding Secretary/ Organiser, New Zealand Book Council, 1972-75; Secretary, 1972-76, President, 1981-83, New Zealand Centre, PEN; President, 1992-95, President of Honour, 1997-, New Zealand Book Council. Publications: Novels: A Breed of Women, 1979; Mandarin Summer, 1981; Paddy's Puzzle, 1983, US edition as In the Clear Light, 1985; The Book of Secrets, 1987; True Stars, 1990; Ricochet Baby, 1996; The House Within, 1997; Songs from the Violet Café, 2003; Short stories: Unsuitable Friends, 1988; The Foreign Woman, 1994; The Best of Fiona Kidman's Short Stories, 1998; A Needle in the Heart, 2002; Poetry: Honey and Bitters, 1975; On the Tightrope, 1978;

Going to the Chathams, Poems: 1977-1984, 1985; Wakeful Nights: Poems Selected and New, 1991; Other: Search for Sister Blue (radio play), 1975; Gone North (with Jane Ussher), 1984; Wellington (with Grant Sheehan), 1989; Palm Prints (autobiographical essays), 1995; New Zealand Love Stories: An Oxford Anthology (editor), Best New Zealand Fiction, 1999. Contributions to: Periodicals. Honours: Scholarships in Letters, 1981, 1985, 1991, 1995; Mobil Short Story Award, 1987; Queen Elizabeth II Arts Council Award for Achievement, 1988; Officer of the Order of the British Empire, 1988; Victoria University Writing Fellowship, 1988; President of Honour, New Zealand Book Council, 1997; Dame Companion of the New Zealand Order of Merit, for services to literature, 1998. Memberships: International PEN; Media Women; New Zealand Book Council, president, 1992-95; Patron, Cambodia Trust Aotearoa. Address: 28 Rakau Road, Hataitai, Wellington 3, New Zealand.

**KIDMAN Nicole,** b. 20 June 1967, Hawaii, USA, Australian nationality. Actress. m. Tom Cruise, 1990, divorced 2001, 1 adopted son, 1 adopted daughter. Education: St Martin's Youth Theatre, Melbourne; Australian Theatre for Young People, Sydney. Appointments: Goodwill Ambassador, UNICEF. Acting début in Australian film aged 14; Actress, TV mini-series, Vietnam, 1987; Bangkok Hilton, 1989. Creative Works: Films: The Emerald City; The Year My Voice Broke; Flirting; Dead Calm, 1990; Days of Thunder, 1990; Billy Bathgate, 1991; Far and Away, 1992; Malice, 1993; My Life, 1993; Batman Forever, 1995; To Die For, 1995; Portrait of a Lady, 1996; The Peacemaker, Eyes Wide Shut, 1998; Practical Magic, 1999; Moulin Rouge, 1999; The Others, 2000; Moulin Rouge, 2001; Birthday Girl, 2001; The Hours, 2001; Dogville, 2003; Cold Mountain, 2003; The Human Stain, 2003; Birth, 2003; The Interpreter, 2004; Alexander the Great, 2004. Play: The Blue Room, 1998-99. Honours: Best Actress Award, Australian Film Institute; Actress of the Year, Australia; Seattle International Film Festival Award, 1995; London Film Critics Award, 1996; Best Actress, Golden Globe Award, 1996; BAFTA Nominee, 1996; Best Actress in a Musical, Golden Globe Award, 2001; Best Dramatic Actress, Golden Globe Award, 2003; BAFTA Award for Best Actress in a Leading Role, 2003; Academy Award for Best Actress, 2003. Address: c/o Ann Churchill-Brown, Shanahan Management, PO Box 478, Kings Cross, NSW 2011, Australia.

**KIEHL Reinhold,** b. 8 October 1947, Worms, Germany. Chemist; Biochemist; Human Biologist. m. Ilse Gertraud Schoyerer, divorced, 2 daughters. Education: BEng, Engineering School, Mannheim, 1971; MS, Chemistry, University of Heidelberg, 1974; DSc, 1977; MEng, Fachhochschule, Mannheim, 1982. Appointments: Registered Eco-Audit Specialist, Research Fellow Max Planck Institute, Heidelburg, 1977; Postdoctoral Fellow Scripps Clinic, La Jolla, 1977-79; Assistant Professor, Ruhr University, Bochum, 1979-85; Associate Professor, Bielefeld University, 1985-87; Head of Laboratory And Research, Clinic Neukirchen, 1987-94; Professor, Director; Freelance Workshop And Course Instructor, 1995-. Publications: Over 50 articles to professional journals. Memberships: American Heart Association; Max Planck Society; Royal Society of Chemistry; AAAS; British Society of Allergy and Clinical Immunology; International Union of Pure and Applied Chemistry; New York Academy of Science. Address: RKI Institut(e) (Lab Research Molecular Med/Biol), Saliterweg 1, 93437 Furth Im Wald, Germany. Website: www.rki-i.com

**KIHARA Noriyasu (Yosetsu Kashii),** b. 22 October 1934, Fukayama City, Hiroshima-Ken, Japan. Author; Professor. m. Hiroko, 4 children. Education: Lecturer, Kyushu Sangyo

University, 1963-67; BA, Literature, Kita Kyushu University, 1958; MA, Literature, Kyushu University, 1960; PhD, Social Science, Iond University, 2001. Appointments: Lecturer, Assistant Professor, Fukuoka Women's Junior College, 1967-70; Lecturer, Assistant Professor, Full Professor, Kinki University's Kyushu School of Engineering, 1971-2003; Part-time Professor, Kyushu-Sangyo University, 2003- . Publications: Atomic Dome; An Angel in White; Parent's Headache Street; The Key Word and Key Sentence, Volume 2; Editor, Man Language Culture, Volume 4 academic journal, Japan Anthropological Linguistic Association. Honours: Literature Award, Association of the Study of Japanese Spiritual Culture; Deputy Director General, Life Fellow, International Biographical Centre. Memberships: Japanese Centre of International PEN; The Japan Writers' Association; Vice President, Japan Anthropological Linguistic Association; Vice-President, Association of the Study of Japanese Spiritual Culture; Secretary-General, United Cultural Convention. Address: 53-17 Igisu, Iizuka City, Fukuoka-Ken, 820-0053, Japan.

**KIHARA Yasuki,** b. 8 February 1955, Hiroshima, Japan. Cardiologist. m. Miho Yukitoshi, 1 son, 2 daughters. Education: BSc, 1973-75, MD (School of Medicine), 1975-79, PhD, Graduate School of Medicine, 1982-86, Kyoto University, Japan; Speciality Board, Internal Medicine, Japan Society of Internal Medicine, 1985; Speciality Board of Cardiology, Japanese Circulation Society, 1992. Appointments: Residencies, Tenri Hospital, Nara, 1979-82; Clinical Fellow, Kyoto University, 1986; Research Fellow in Medicine, 1986-87, Instructor, 1987-89, Harvard Medical School; Assistant Professor, Toyama Medical and Pharmaceutical University, 1989-93, Kyoto University Graduate School of Medicine, 1993-2002; Visiting Professor, Case Western Reserve University, 1999-; Visiting Professor, Boston university, 1999-; Visiting Scholar, Stanford University, 2001-; Director, Outpatient Clinic, Department of Cardiovascular Medicine, Kyoto University Hospital, 1998-; Associate Professor, Kyoto University Graduate School of Medicine, 2002-. Publications: Articles in medical journals. Honours: Research Awards: Yamanouchi Foundation, Tokyo, 1986, (Fellowship) American Heart Association, Massachusetts Affiliate, 1987-88, Japan Heart Foundation, 1992, Yokohama Foundation, Nagoya, 1992; R I Bing Award, International Society for Heart Research, 1989; Sagawa Young Investigator Award, Cardiovascular System Dynamics Society, Kobe, 1992; Pfizer Health Research Award, 1999; Sigma Xi. Memberships: Fellow, American College of Cardiology; Councilor, Japan Society of Ultrasonics in Medicine; Japan Society of Internal Medicine; Japan Circulation Society; American Association for the Advancement of Science; International Society for Heart Research. Address: Department of Cardiovascular Medicine, Kyoto University Graduate School of Medicine, 54 Shogoin, Sakyo, Kyoto 606-8507, Japan.

**KILMER Val,** b. 31 December 1959, Los Angeles, USA. Actor. m. Joanne Whalley, divorced, 1 son, 1 daughter. Education: Hollywood's Professional's School; Juilliard. Creative Works: Stage appearances include: Electra and Orestes, Henry IV Part One, 1981; As You Like It, 1982; Slab Boys, 1983; Hamlet, 1988; Tis Pity She's A Whore, 1992; TV Films: Top Secret, 1984; Real Genius, 1985; Top Gun, 1986; Willow, 1988; Kill Me Again, 1989; The Doors, 1991; Thunderheart, 1991; True Romance, 1993; The Real McCoy, 1993; Tombstone, 1993; Wings of Courage, 1995; Batman Forever, 1995; Heat, 1995; The Saint, 1996; The Island of Dr Moreau, 1996; The Ghost and the Darkness, 1996; Dead Girl, 1996; Joe the King, 1999; Pollock, 2000; Red Planet, 2000; The Salton Sea, 2002; Run for the Money, 2002; Masked and Anonymous, 2003; Wonderland, 2003; The Missing, 2003; Spartan, 2004; Mind Hunters, 2004.

Address: c/o CAA, 9830 Wilshire Boulevard, Beverly Hills, CA 90212, USA.

**KIM Chan-Ki,** b. 17 December 1968, Chug-Ju, Korea. Senior Researcher; Project Leader. m. 2 sons, 1 daughter. Education: Bachelor's Degree, Electrical Engineering, Seoul National University of Technology, 1987-91; Master's Degree, 1991-93; Doctor's Degree, 1993-96, Electrical Engineering, Chung-Ang University Graduate School. Appointments: Senior Researcher, Project Leader, Korea Electric Power Research Institute, 1996-. Publications: Effect of an Excitation System on Turbine Generator Torsional Stress in an HVDC, 2004; High Pulse Conversion Techniques for HVDC Transmission System; Dynamic Performance of HVDC system according to Exciter of Synch Comp in a Weak AC system; Text book: Electric Control and Applications for High School. Honours: Korea Electric Power Research Institute's Chief Prize, 2002; KIEE Best Paper Award, 2002; Korea Energy Technology Award, 2004. Memberships: KIEE; KIPE; IEE; IEEE. Address: 109-102 Samsung Pureun apts, Jeonmin Dong, Yuseong Gu, Deajeon 305-390, Korea. E-mail: ckkim@kepri.re.kr

**KIM Deok Won,** b. 5 September 1952, Seoul, Korea. Professor. m. Lim Misula, 1 son, 1 daughter. Education: BE, Seoul National University, Korea, 1976; MS, Northwestern University, USA, 1980; PhD, University of Texas at Austin, USA, 1986. Appointments: Assistant Professor, Yonsei University, 1987-96; Associate Professor, 1996-2001; Professor, 2001-; Editorial Board, Yonsei Medical Journal, 1996-2004; Editor in Chief, Journal of Korean Society of Medical and Biological Engineering (KOSOMBE), 1996-97; Academic Director, KOSOMBE, 1998-99; Chairman, Department of Medical Engineering, 1999-2005. Publications: Development of a frequency dependent type apex locator with automatic compensation, 1998; Measurement of leg arterial compliance of normal and diabetics using impedance plethysmography, 1999; A nominvasive estimation of hypernasality using a linear predictive model, 2001; Objective evaluation of treatment effects on port-wine stains using Lab color coordinates, 2001; Root canal length measurement in teeth with electrolyte compensation, 2002; Optimum electrode configuration for detection of arm movement using bio-impedance, 2003; Development and evaluation of an automated stainer for acid-fast bacilli, 2003; An improved approach for measurement of stroke volume during treadmill exercise, 2003. Honours: Recipient, Medison Biomedical Engineering Award, 1996; IEEK Distinguished Service Award, 2003. Memberships: New York Academy of Sciences; IEEE; The Biomedical Engineering Society. Address: Dept of Medical Engineering, Yonsei University College of Medicine, CPO Box 8044, Seoul, Korea. E-mail: kdw@yumc.yonsei.ac.kr

**KIM Dong Yun,** b. 18 February 1969, Busan, South Korea. Medical Doctor. m. Jae Hee Kwon, 1 son, 1 daughter. Education: MD, 1987-93, MS, 1997-98, Seoul National University College of Medicine; Neurosurgical Resident, Seoul National University Hospital, 1994-98. Appointments: Faculty, Cheju Medical Centre, 1998-2001; Spine Fellowship, Seoul National University Hospital, 2001-2002; Faculty, Wooridul Spine Hospital, 2002-. Publications: Over 15 articles in medical journals as co-author include most recently: Intravertebral vacuum phenomenon in osteoporotic compression fracture: report of 67 cases with quantitative evaluation on intravertebral instability, 2004; Effect of PDN® (Prosthetic Disc Nucleus) on the Mobility and Height of the Invertebral Disc: Preliminary Report, 2004; percutaneous ventral decompression for L4-L5 degenerative spondylolisthesis in medically compromised elderly patients: technical case report, 2004' Avascular necrosis of spine: a rare appearance, 2004; Comparison of Multifidus Muscle Atrophy and Trunk

Extension Muscle Strength: Percutaneous Versus Open Pedicle Screw Fixation, 2005; Validation of the Korean Version of the Oswestry Disability Index, 2005. Honour: Sanofi Award for Young Investigator, 2004; Memberships: Korean Neurosurgical; Korean Society of Spine Surgery. Address: Wooridul Spine Hospital, 49-4 Chungdam-Dong, Kongnam-Gu, Seoul Korea 135-100. E-mail: dongyunk@gmail.com

**KIM Hee-Je,** b. 16 May 1965, Seoul, Korea. Physician; Scientist. m. Kyung Kim, 2 sons. Education: MD, 1983-89, PhD, 1997-99, Catholic University of Korea College of Medicine, Seoul, Korea; Postdoctoral Fellowship, Division of Immunology and Hematopoiesis, Comprehensive Oncology Center, Johns Hopkins University School of Medicine, Baltimore, USA, 1999-2001. Appointments: Instructor of Internal Medicine, St Mary's Hospital, Hemopoietic Stem Cell Transplantation Centre, Catholic University of Korea College of Medicine, 1998-2001; Assistant Professor, 2002-2005, Associate Professor, 2005-, Internal Medicine, Catholic University of Korea School of Medicine. Publications: Articles in medical journals as co-author include most recently: Autologous stem cell transplantation using modified TAM or combination of triple-alkylating agents conditioning regimens as one of the post-remission treatments in patients with adult acute myeloid leukemia in first complete remission, 2004; Infectious complications and outcomes after allogenetic hematopoietic stem cell transplantation in Korea, 2004; Early prediction of molecular remission by monitoring BCR-ABL transcript levels in patients achieving a complete cytogenetic response after imatinib therapy for posttransplantation chronic myelogenous leukemia relapse, 2004; Risk-adapted preemptive therapy for cytomegalovirus disease after allogeneic stem cell transplantation: A single-centre experience in Korea, 2005. Honours: Several research and travel grant awards; Best Article of the Year 2003, Korean Journal of Medicine; Best Presentation of the Year 2004, Korean Society of Hematopoietic Stem Cell Transplantation. Memberships: Korean Society of Hematology; Korean Society of Hematopoietic Stem Cell Transplantation; Korean Society of Immunology; Korean Society of Internal Medicine; Korean Association of Medicine; Korean Cancer Association; Asian-Pacific BMT Group, Division of International Society of Hematology; American Society of Hematology; European Hematology Association; International Society for Experimental Hematology. Address: St Mary's Hospital, Catholic Hemopoietic Stem Cell Transplantation Centre, Catholic University of Korea College of Medicine, 62, Youido-dong, Youngdungpo-ku, Seoul 150-713, Korea.

**KIM Hyung-Dong,** b. 22 November 1948, Pusan, Korea. Professor. m. Soon-Ok Jung, 2 sons, 1 daughter. Education: MS, School of Medicine, 1973, MS, Graduate School, 1984, Pusan National University; PhD, Graduate School, Korea University, 1987. Appointments: Internship, 1973-74; Residency, Neurosurgery, 1974-78, National Medical Centre; Navy Military Doctor (Major), 1978-81; Instructor, Assistant Professor, Associate Professor, Inje University, College of Medicine, 1981-89; Research Fellow, Osaka City University, College of Medicine, Japan, 1982-83; Professor and Chairman, Dong-A University College of Medicine, 1989-; Visiting Professor, Baylor College of Medicine, Houston, Texas, USA, 1990; President, Pusan and Kyung-nam Neurosurgical Society, 1996-97; President, Korean Brain Tumor Society, 1999-2000; Congress President, Korean Neurosurgical Society, 2003-2004; President, Young-Honam and Kyushu Neurosurgical Joint Meeting, 2003-. Publications: Numerous articles in medical journals include most recently: Therapeutic Tactics for Giant Pituitary Adenoma, 2003; Clinical Therapeutic Trial of Recurred Craniopharyngiomas, 2004; Intracerebral Hemorrhage Secondary to Ruptured Middle Cerebral Artery Aneury:

Therapeutic Consideration and Prognostic Factors Related to the Site of hemorrhage, 2004; Cerebellar Ectopia Associated with Unilateral Agenesis of Posterior Arch of Atlas, 2004; Preliminary surgical results open sella method with intentionally stages transsphenoidal approach for patients with giant pituitary adenomas, 2005. Memberships: Korean Neurosurgical Society; International Member, Japan Neurosurgical Society; International Member, American Association of Neurological Surgeons; World Federation of Neurological Societies. Address: Department of Neurosurgery, College of Medicine, Dong-A University, 3 Ga-1 Dongdaesin-dong, Seo-gu, Busan 602-715, Korea.

**KIM In-Ju,** b. 17 October 1961, Seoul, Korea. Researcher; Lecturer. m. Eun-Sun Oh, 1 daughter. Education: MSc, Applied Biomechanics, 1996, PhD, 2001, University of Sydney. Appointments: Research Assistant, 1997-2001, Teaching Staff and Honorary Research Fellow, 2002, School of Exercise and Sport Science, Faculty of Health Sciences, University of Sydney; Research Fellow and Lecturer, School of Sport and Health Sciences, University of Exeter, England, 2003. Publications: Numerous articles in professional journals. Honours: Research Award for Generating Innovative Research Ideas to Prevent Fatalities and Injuries in the Workplace, American Society of Safety Engineers Foundation, 2002; Best Paper Award, Journal of Korean Association of Science and Technology, Australia, 2003; Research Grant (Category 1), ACT Health and Medical Research Council's Research Support Program, Australia, 2004; Listed in national and international biographical dictionaries. Memberships: British Association of Sport and Exercise Sciences; The Ergonomics Society; International Society of Biomechanics; International Researcher, Contact Group for Slips, Trips and Falls; International Ergonomics Association; Ergonomics Society of Australia; and many others. Address: 9 Derry Street, Monash, ACT 2904, Australia. E-mail: i.kim@exeter.ac.uk

**KIM In S,** b. Korea. Professor of Environmental Science and Engineering. m. 2 daughters. Education: BS, 1982, MS, 1984, Environmental Engineering, National Fisheries University of Busan, Korea; PhD, Civil and Environmental Engineering, University of Arkansas, Fayetteville, Arkansas, USA, 1991. Appointments: Research and Teaching Assistant, Department of Environmental Engineering, Pusan National University, Busan, Korea, 1984-87; Post-doctoral Research Associate, Department of Chemical Engineering, University of Cincinnati/Risk Reduction Engineering Laboratory of US EPA Research Center, Cincinnati, Ohio, USA, 1991-94; Assistant Professor, 1994-96, Associate Professor, 1996-2001, Professor, 2001-, Department of Environmental Science and Engineering, Director, Water Reuse Technology Centre, Gwangju Institute of Science and Technology, Gwangju, Korea; Visiting Professor, Imperial College of Science, Technology and Medicine, University of London, England, 2000. Publications: Over 80 international refereed journal papers (SCI); Over 90 international conference proceeding papers; Over 160 national refereed journal and conference proceeding papers; 6 book chapters; 7 patents. Honours: Outstanding Performance Award, 1995, 2004, Gwangju Institute of Science and Technology; Chevening Fellowship, British Council, 2000; Best Paper Award, Korean Federation of Science and Technology, 2001; Best Paper Award, Korean Society on Water Quality, 2004, 2005; Best Paper Award, Korean Society of Environmental Engineers, 2005. Memberships: Editorial Board Member: Journal of Korea Solid Waste Engineering Society, 1998-2002; Journal of Korean Society of Environmental Engineers, 1997-2003; Journal of the Korean Hydrogen and New Energy Society, 2003-; Journal of Water and Health, IWA, 2003-; Associate Editor,

Journal of Environmental Engineering and Science, NRC, Canada, 2004; AD Specialist Group, 2001-; Strategic Council Member, 2001-2004; Vice-Chairman, Water Reuse Specialist Group, 2002-; Scientific Programme Committee, 2003-06, IWA, London; Chairman, the 5th International Conference on Wastewater Reclamation & Reuse for Sustainability, Jeju, Korea, 2005. Address: Department of Environmental Science and Engineering, Gwangju Institute of Science and Technology, 1 Oryong-dong, Buk-gu, Gwangju 500-712, Korea. E-mail: iskim@gist.ac.kr

**KIM Jeong-Kyun**, b. 29 August 1960, Kwang-Ju, South Korea. Senior Scientist. m. Eun-Young Jang, 2 sons, 1 daughter. Education: BS, Materials and Metallurgical Engineering, Chunnam National University, Korea, 1987; MS, Materials and Metallurgical Engineering, Korea Advanced Institute of Science and Technology, Korea, 1990; PhD, Materials Engineering, University of Wisconsin-Milwaukee, 1997. Appointments: Researcher, Korea Atomic Energy Research Institute, 1990-92; Research Assistant, 1992-97, Post Doctoral Research, 1997-98, Research Assistant, 1998-2000, University of Wisconsin-Milwaukee; Senior Scientist, MER Corporation, Tucson, Arizona, 2000-. Publications: 17 papers in journals; 13 papers in proceedings. Honours: Listed in national and international biographical dictionaries; M Schiel Award for Honourable Mention in Metallography, 1997; M Schiel Award for Excellence in Metallography, 2000. Address: 4781 N Hollywood Ave, Milwaukee, WI 53211, USA. E-mail: jkkim40@hotmail.com

**KIM Jin-Sun**, b. 10 November 1946, Gangwon-do, South Korea. Provincial Governor. m. Boon-hee Lee, 1 son, 2 daughters. Education: BA, Public Administration, Dongguk University. Appointments: Mayor of Yeongwol-gun, Gangwon-do, 1983-85; Legal Affairs Officer, Ministry of Home Affairs, Officer of Planning and Budget, Senior Financial Officer and Tax Director, 1985-91; Mayor of Gangneung City, 1991-92; Planning and Management Officer, Gangwon-do, 1992-93; Mayor of Bucheon City, Gyonggi-do, 1994-95; Deputy Governor of Administration, Gangwon-do, 1995-98; 32nd Governor of Gangwon-do, 1998-2002, 33rd Governor of Gangwon-do, 2002-; Associate Professor, Dongguk University and Hanyang University, 1999-. Publication: Book: The choices for Gangwon-do Province in the 21st Century. Honours: Hwang-jo-geun-jeong Medal; Honour of Contribution, Korean Veteran's Association; Honour of Contribution, Korean Youth Association; Mugunghwa Gold Decoration, Korean Boy Scouts; Silver Medal for Contribution, Korean Red Cross; Environment Protector Award for the Year 2000, Korea Federation of Environmental Movements. Memberships: Korea Photographers' Association; Honorary Chairman, Association of War Veterans of International Conflicts; Honorary Member, Association of Marine Veterans; Honorary Member, Association of Artists; Yeomaek Volunteer Group, Korean Red Cross; Director, Yulgok Academic Association; Korean Hiking Society; Korean Gardening Society. Address: Governor's Office, Gangwon Provincial Government, 2nd Floor, 15 Bongui-dong, Chuncheon-si, Gangwon-do, 200-700 South Korea.

**KIM Jong Il**, b. 16 February 1942, Mount Paekdu, Korea. Leader of the Democratic People's Republic of Korea; General Secretary of the Workers' Party of Korea; Chairman of the National Defence Commission of the Democratic People's Republic of Korea. Education: Graduated, Kim Il Sung University, Pyongyang. Career: Officer, Section Chief, Deputy Director, Director, Department of the Central Committee of the Worker's Party of Korea, 1964-73; Member, Central Committee of the Workers' Party of Korea, 1972; Secretary,

Central Committee of the Workers' Party of Korea, 1973; Member, Political Committee Central Committee of the Workers' Party of Korea, 1974; Member, Presidium of Political Bureau, Central Committee of the Workers' Party of Korea and Member, Military Commission of the Central Committee of the Workers' Party of Korea, 1980; Deputy, Supreme People's Assembly of the Democratic People's Republic of Korea, 1982-; First Vice-Chairman, National Defence Commission, Democratic People's Republic of Korea, 1990-93; Chairman, National Defence Commission, Democratic People's Republic of Korea, 1993-; Supreme Commander, Korean People's Army, 1991-; Marshal, Democratic People's Republic of Korea, 1992-; General Secretary, Worker's Party of Korea, 1997. Publications: Kim Jong Il Selected Works, 14 volumes; For the Completion of the Juche Revolutionary Cause, 10 volumes; Many other works. Honours: 3 times, The Hero of the Democratic People's Republic of Korea; 3 times, The Kim Il Sung Order; The Kim Il Sung Prize; Many other domestic and foreign orders and medals, honorary titles and titles of doctorate. Address: The Central Committee of the Workers' Party of Korea, Pyongyang, Democratic People's Republic of Korea.

**KIM Jung-sook**, b. 21 August 1946, Seoul, Korea. Politician; Professor. m. Kwang-Yul Cho, 1 son. Education: BA, Education, Korea University, Seoul, Korea, 1969; MA, Education, Ewha Women's University, Seoul, Korea, Ed D, Higher Education, George Washington University, Washington DC, USA, 1988. Appointments include: CITI Bank, Seoul Branch, Korea, 1969-74; Managing Executive Director, Hansung Hospital, Anyang, Korea, 1974-84; District Chairperson for Anyang City Constituency, Democratic Justice Party (forerunner of GNP), ROK, 1988-90; Founder, Chair, Korean Institute for Women & Politics, 1989; Visiting Professor, Cheonbuk National University, Cheonju, Korea, 1994-95; Visiting Associate, Harvard University, USA, 1996-97; GO/NGO Delegate to 38th-49th UN Commission on the Status of Women (CSW), New York, USA, 1994-2005; Vice-Minister of the Ministry for Political Affairs (responsible for the advancement of women), ROK, 1993; Chairperson, Special Committee on Women's Affairs, National Assembly, ROK, 1998-2000; Member, Central Executive Council GNP, ROK, 1998-2003; Chairperson, Women's Affairs Committee, 1998-2004; Member Education Committee, Women's Committee, Budget and Account Committee, National Assembly, ROK, 1998-2004; Vice-Chair, Korean Association of Public Policy Studies, Korea, 1995-; Chair, Korea Tourism Forum, 1995-; Chair, Korean Women & Politics Association, 2000-; President, Center for Asia-Pacific Women in Politics, Manila, The Philippines, 2003-; Member, Supreme Council (Co-Chair), Grand National Party, 2002-2003; Member, 14th National Assembly, 1995-96, 15th and 16th National Assemblies Republic of Korea, 1998-2004; Visiting Professor, Graduate School of Education, Korea University, 2004-. Publications: Numerous articles on women and politics, education and policy studies in professional journals. Honours: Presidential Medal for Exemplary Government Service, Government of the Republic of Korea, 1994; Distinguished Alumni Award, George Washington University, 2004. Memberships: Zonta International; World Association of Girl Guides and Girl Scouts; Korean Association of University Women; Girl Scouts of Korea, Vice-President, 2002-. Address: 3-305 Jinheung Apt, Samsung-dong, Kangnam-gu, Seoul 135-090, Korea. E-mail: kiwp89@hanmail.net Website: www.kiwp.or.kr

**KIM Ki Hang**, b. 5 August 1936, Pyong-Nam, Korea. Distinguished Professor of Mathematics. m. Myong-Ja Hwang, 1 son, 1 daughter. Education: BSc, 1960, MSc, 1961, Mathematics, University of Southern Mississippi; MPhil, 1970, PhD (Dissertation guided by Gian-Carlo Rota of MIT), 1971,

Mathematics, George Washington University. Appointments: Instructor of Mathematics, University of Hartford, 1961-66; Lecturer of Mathematics, George Washington University, 1966-68; Associate Professor of Maths and Chairman, St Mary's College of Maryland, 1968-70; Associate Professor of Mathematics, University of North Carolina at Pembroke, 1970-74; Distinguished Professor of Mathematics, Alabama State University, 1974-. Publications: 7 books and over 150 articles in Mathematics; Mathematical Social Sciences, Editor-in-Chief, 1981-94. Honours: 6 National Science Foundation research grant awards. Memberships: Korean Academy of Science and Technology. Address: 416 Arrowhead Drive, Montgomery, AL 36117, USA.

**KIM Kuk-Nyon,** b. 17 March 1940, Uiseong-Gun, Gyeongsang Buk-Do Province, Korea. Chief Executive Officer. m. Jung-Ja Hwang, 2 sons. Education: Bachelor of Law, College of Law, Korea University, Korea, 1964; Honorary Doctor in Business Administration, Kyungnam National University, Korea, 2004. Appointments: Executive Vice President, 1988, Standing Auditor, 1992, Director & Deputy Chief Executive Officer, 1996, Chairman of the Board and Chief Executive Officer, 2000, Daegu Bank. Honours: Best Chief Executive Officer, Towers Perrin & The Hankyung Business Weekly, 2001; Order of Industrial Service Merit (Bronze Tower) for the support of small and medium enterprises, 2002; Grand Prize in Leadership, Korea Management Innovation Association, 2003. Memberships: Executive Vice President, Korea Federation of Banks, 2000; Deputy Chairman, Dae Gyeong Research Institute, 2000; Executive Vice President, Daegu Chamber of Commerce & Industry, 2003. Address: 103-502 Woobang Mijin Heights Apt, 670, Beommul-dong, Suseong-gu, Daegu, Korea.

**KIM Kyeong Uk,** b. 20 August 1951, Jeomchon, Korea. Professor. m. Jung Sook Kang, 2 daughters. Education: BS, 1975, MS, 1978, Seoul National University, Korea; PhD, University of Illinois, USA, 1981. Appointments: Research Scholar, International Rice Research Institute, 1976-77; Professor, Seoul National University, Korea, 1981-; Visiting Scholar, Cornell University, USA, 1986-87; Visiting Scholar, Technical University of Munich, 1990-91; Visiting Scholar, University of Nebraska-Lincoln, USA, 2003-04. Publications Articles in professional scientific journals include: Analysis of transmission load of agricultural tractors, 2000; Analysis of tractor transmission and driving axle loads, 2001; Development of a seedling pick-up device for vegetable transplanters, 2002. Honours: Academic Award, Korean Society for Agricultural Machinery, 1996; Agricultural Science and Technical Award, Ministry of Agriculture, 1998. Memberships: Korean Society for Agricultural Machinery; American Society of Agricultural Engineers. Address: Department of Biosystems & Biomaterials Sciences and Engineering, College of Agriculture and Life Science, Seoul National University, Shillin-dong san 56-1, Kwanak-ku, 151-742 Seoul, Korea. E-mail: kukim@plaza.snu.ac.kr

**KIM Kyoung Soo,** b. 15 March 1964, Seoul, Korea. Chief Executive Officer. m. Chun Kyun Park, 2 daughters. Education: BS, Chemistry, Kyung Hee University, Korea, 1986; MS, Chemistry, 1988, PhD, Chemistry, 1990, Korea Advanced Institute of Science and Technology (KAIST); Appointments: Senior Researcher, Korea Research Institute of Chemical Technology, 1990-95; Research Manager, Hanmi Pharmaceutical Co. Ltd., 1995-98; Research Director, ChemTech Research Incorporation, 1998-2002; Chief Executive Officer, Chirogenix Co. Ltd., 2002-. Publications: Articles in scientific journals including: Chemistry Letters, 1988; Tetrahedron Letters, 1989 (2), 1991; Journal of Physical

Organic Chemistry, 1990; Chemical Industry (London), 1992; Synthetic Communications, 1992; Pure and Applied Chemistry, 1993; Reviews on Heteroatomic Chemistry, 1990; WO, 1997 (2), 1998, 2002 (2), 2004; 35 patents. Honour: Award in Great Achievement, Korea Research Institute of Chemical Technology, 1993; 2000 Outstanding Scientists of the 21st Century Honours List, IBC, England, 2005. Memberships: Life Fellow, Korean Chemical Society; Life Fellow, International Biographical Association, England, 2005. Address: Chirogenix Ltd, 801, Kowoon Institute of Technology Innovation; Suwon University, Whasung-City, Kyunggi-do, Korea 445-743. E-mail: kskimpc@chirogenix.com

**KIM Nam-Kyoung,** b. 19 May 1956, Kangnung, Korea. Professor. m. Hyunjoo Cho, 2 sons. Education: BS, MS, Engineering, Department of Ceramic Engineering, Seoul National University; PhD, University of Illinois, Urbana-Champaign. Appointments: Research Associate, 1987-89, Visiting Research Associate, 1992-93, University of Illinois, Urbana-Champaign; Lecturer-Associate Professor, 1989-2000, Department Chairman, 1995-96, 2001-02, Planning Committee, College of Engineering, 1998-2002, Full Professor, 2000-, Kyungpook National University. Publications: Over 70 papers mostly in international professional journals. Honours: Best Paper Award, Journal of the American Ceramic Society, 1996; Presentation Award, Korean Ceramic Society, 2002. Membership: Life member, Korean Ceramic Society. Address: Department of Inorganic Materials Engineering, Kyungpook National University, 1370 Sankyuk-Dong, Buk-Gu, Daegu 702-701, Korea. E-mail: nkkim@knu.ac.kr

**KIM Pankoo,** b. 6 April 1964, Gwangju, Korea. Professor. m. Soosan Choi, 3 sons. Education: BS, Chosun University, Korea, 1988; MSc, 1988-90, PhD, 1990-94, Seoul National University, Seoul, Korea. Appointments: Research Institute of Computer Technology, Seoul National University, 1994-95; Lecturer, 1995-97, Assistant Professor, 1997-2001, Associate Professor, 2001-, Chosun University; Visiting Professor, Arizona State University, USA, 2000-2001; Editor, IEEE Multimedia, 2001-; Paper Editor of KIPS, 2002-; Paper Editor of KISS, 2003-. Publications: Articles in scientific journals: A Logical Framework for Visual Information Modeling and Management, 2001; Concept Based Image Retrieval Using the New Semantic Similarity Measurement, 2003; Representing the Spatial Relations in the Semantic Web Ontologies, 2003; Semantic Image Analysis Based on the Representation of the Spatial Relations Between Objects in Images, 2004. Memberships: IEEE; ACM; KISS; KIPS. Address: Chosun University #375 Susuk-Dong, Dong-Gu, Gwangju 501-759, Republic of Korea. E-mail: pkkim@chosun.ac.kr Website: http: //vector.chosun.ac.kr/~pkkim

**KIM Sanghoon,** b. 28 December 1968, Seoul, South Korea. Engineer; Scientist; Consultant (Engineering/ Technology Management); Analyst (Business/Technology); Researcher; Professor. Education: BS, Metallurgical Engineering, 1991, MS, Metallurgical Engineering, 1993, Yonsei University, South Korea; D Phil, Materials Science, University of Oxford, England, 1999. Appointments: Research Engineer, South Korea Institute of Industrial Technology, Ministry of Commerce, Industry and Resources, Incheon, South Korea, 1992-93; Staff Researcher, Korea Electric Power Research Institute, Ministry of Commerce Industry and Resources, Taejon, South Korea, 1994-98; SPIRT Research Fellow/Lecturer, School of Physics and Materials Engineering, Monash University, Clayton, Victoria, Australia, 1999-2001; Deputy Director, Technology Appraisal Specialist, Korea Technology Credit Guarantee Fund, Seoul, South Korea, 2001-; Lecturer, Department of Metallurgical

System Engineering, Yonsei University, Seoul, South Korea, 2004-; Adjunct Professor, Department of Materials Engineering, Daelim College, Anyang, South Korea, 2005-. Publications: More than 20 papers in international journals include: Alloying Elements Partitioning in TiAl-Ru Intermetallic Alloys, 1999; Site Preference of Ru and Pd additions to g Based TiAl Intermetallics, 2000; Microstructure and Microchemistry Variation during Thermal Exposure of Low Alloy Steels, 2002; Improved Technology Scoring Model for Credit Guarantee Fund, in press, 2005; More than 10 internationally invited talks and more than 20 domestic and international conferences in the field of materials science. Honour: Award of Merit, for most distinguished achievement in technology financing, Korea Technology Credit Guarantee Fund, Ministry of Finance and Economy. Memberships: Institute of Materials, Minerals and Mining, UK; American Society for Metals, USA; Minerals Metals and Materials, USA; Materials Research Society, USA; Korea Management and Technology Consulting Association, South Korea. Address: 103dong 1302ho Ssangyong sweet-dot-home Apt, Keun-ma-eul, 130 Tanhyeon-dong, Ilsan-gu, Goyang-city, Kyeonggi-do, 411-840 South Korea. E-mail: sanghoon.kim@kibo.co.kr; sk1228@shinbiro.com

**KIM Se-Kwon,** b. 18 April 1948, Seoul, Korea. Professor. m. Noh Young Run, 2 daughters. Education: BS, 1976, MS, 1978, PhD, 1982, Department of Food Science and Technology, National Fisheries University of Busan; Postdoctoral, Bioprocesses Center, University of Illinois, Urbana-Champaign, 1988. Appointments: Professor, 1989-, Dean of the College of Natural Sciences and Basic Science Research Institute, 2002-2004, Pukyong National University, Korea; Editor-in-Chief, Korean Journal of Life Sciences, 1995-99; Visiting Professor, Memorial University of Newfoundland, Canada, 1999-2000; International Advisory Board, Worldnutra Conference, 2003-; Vice-President, Korean Society of Biotechnology and Bioengineering, 2004; Director, National Marine Bio Research Center, 2004-; Chairman, 7th Asia-Pacific Chitin and Chitosan Symposium, 2006. Publications: More than 200 scientific research articles in journals include: Continuous production of COS using a dual reactor system; Purification and characterization of a lectin from the hard roe of tuna; 18 books; Patents for the development and optimum utilization of marine processing byproducts. Honours: The Best Paper in Chemical Nutrition awarded by the American Oil Chemist's Society, 2002; Grand Prize for the relationship between industry and education, Korea Sanhak Foundation. Memberships: President, Korean Society for Chitin and Chitosan, 1999-2000; Director, Korean Society of Biochemistry and Molecular Biology, 2001-2002. Address: Pukyong National University, Department of Chemistry, 599-1 Daeyeon-Dong, Nam-Gu, Busan 608-739, Korea. E-mail: sknkim@pknu.ac.kr

**KIM Seok Hyeon,** b. 15 May 1949, Kwang San Gun Samdo, Chullanamdo, Korea. High School Teacher; Poet. m. Yeun Gyung Kim, 1 son, 1 daughter. Education: Seoul National Teacher's Educational, 1967-69; Bachelor of Art, Korean and Literature, Meong Ji University, 1970-72; Master of Education, Department of Educational Administration, Graduate School of Public Administration, Dongguk University, 1978-80; Completion, Department of English Language Education, Hankuk University of Foreign Studies, 1985-2002; Doctor of Arts, Department of Literary Creative Writing, Graduate school, Dankook University, 2002-2005. Appointments: Teacher, Tapdong Elementary School, Seoul, Korea, 1973-88; Teacher, Dailim Middle School, Sillim Middle School, Chonho, Middle School, Banpo Middle School, Jangchung Girls' Middle School, 1969-73; Teacher, Gaipo High School, Inhun High School, Jamsin High School, Dunchon High School, Seoul, Korea,

1988-2005. Publications: The Barrier of Communication in the Teacher's Organisation (MA thesis); A Study of Archetype of Korean Modern Poetry – Self Consciousness and Poetic Transformation Through the Archetype (doctoral thesis); Poetry: My Thought for the Spring Day (Korean and English translation); Looking at the Han River (Korean); Thought of Spring Day (Korean). Honours: Award of the Union of Korean National Education, 2001; Poet's Award for Publication, 2003; New Face Award of Poetry and Poet, 2003; Li Yeok Sa Literary Great Award, 2003. Memberships: Korean Poets' Association; Member, Korean Literature Association; Korean PEN; Korean Poet Association. Address: Kang Dong-gu, Dunchon-Dong, Nobabil Apt, 202-1204, 134-060 Seoul, Korea. E-mail: purondol@freechal.com

**KIM Su Gwan,** b. 23 August 1964, Haenam, Korea. Professor; Oral and Maxillofacial Surgeon; Educator. Education: DDS, 1989, MSD, 1992, PhD, 1998, Chosun University, Gwangju, Korea. Appointments: Associate Professor, Vice-Dean, Chosun University, Gwangju, Korea; Chairman, Department of Oral and Maxillofacial Surgery, Chosun University Dental Hospital, Gwangju, Korea, 1999; Director, Korean Academy of Laser Dentistry, 2001; Director, Korean Association of Maxillofacial Plastic and Reconstructive Surgeons, 1990; Director, Korean Association of Oral and Maxillofacial Surgeons, 1990. Publications: Over 370 publications in scientific journals and books include: Grafting of large defects of the jaws with a particulate dentin-plaster of Paris combination, 1999; Combined implantation of particulate dentin, plaster of Paris and a bone xenograft (Bio-Oss) for bone regeneration in rats, 2001; The use of particulate dentin-plaster of Paris combination with/without platelet-rich plasma in the treatment of bone defects around implants, 2002; The Effect of High Local Concentrations of Antibiotics on Demineralized Bone Induction in Rats, 2004. Honours include: Presidential Award, 5 times, 1999-2003; Scientific Research Award, 37 times. Memberships: Affiliate Member, American Association of Oral and Maxillofacial Surgeons; Fellow, International Association of Oral and Maxillofacial Surgeons, 1998; Academy of Laser Dentistry, 2001; Academy of Osseointegration, 2002; International Association of Dental Research; American College of Oral and Maxillofacial Surgeons, 2003; Official Journal of the Asian Association of Oral and Maxillofacial Surgeons; International Congress of Oral Implantologists; European Association of Osseointegration, 2005. Address: 421, Seosuk-dong, Dong-gu, Gwangju-City, Korea, 501-825. E-mail: sgckim@mail.chosun.ac.kr

**KIM Sun-Hoon,** b. 26 September 1960, Seoul, Republic of Korea. Professor. m. Jung-Joo Park, 1 son, 1 daughter. Education: BS, Department of Civil Engineering, Yonsei University, 1983; MS, 1985, PhD, 1988, Department of Civil Engineering, Korea Advanced Institute of Science and Technology. Appointments: Research Assistant, Korea Advanced Institute of Science and Technology, 1985-88; Senior Researcher, Korea Atomic Energy Research Institute, 1988-96; Postdoctoral, University of Wisconsin, Madison, 1993-94; Senior Researcher, Korea Electric Power Research Institute, 1996-97; Associate Professor, Department of Civil Engineering, Youngdong University, 1997-. Publications: 11 international journal papers, 30 international conference papers, 16 domestic journal papers and 25 domestic conference papers include: Three dimensional dynamic response of underground openings in saturated rock masses, 2001; Hysteretic Behaviour of RC Shear Walls, 2004; An adaptive nodal generation with halftoning algorithm for meshfree analysis, 2004. Honours: Distinguished Service Award, The Wind Engineering Institute of Korea, 2002; Best Paper Award, The Computational Structural Engineering

Institute of Korea, 2004. Memberships: General Council, Asian-Pacific Association for Computational Mechanics; Director, International Association for Structural Engineering and Mechanics; Director, Wind Engineering Institute of Korea; Korean Society of Civil Engineers; Computational Structural Engineering Institute of Korea; Korean Society of Steel Engineers; Korean Society of Ocean Engineers; Korean Nuclear Society. Address: Department of Civil Engineering, Youngdong University, San 12-1, Seolgye-ri, Youngdong-eup, Youngdong-kun, Chungbuk 370-701, Republic of Korea. E-mail: kimsh@youngdong.ac.kr Website: http://shkim.vv.st

**KIM Sung Soo,** b. 12 April 1945, Sungsong, Korea. Vocational Education Educator. m. Young Hee Kim, 1 son, 2 daughters. Education: BS, Seoul National University, 1967; MEd summa cum laude, 1971; PhD, University of Minnesota, 1978. Appointments: 1st Lieutenant, Korean Artillery, 1967-69; Assistant, Seoul National University, 1971-75; Consultant, Ministry of Education, Seoul, 1972-75; Assistant University of Minnesota, St Paul, USA, 1976-80; Senior Researcher, Korea Educational Development Institute, 1980-81; Assistant Professor to Professor, Seoul National University, 1981-; Consultant, Ministry of Education, Seoul, 1983-84; Extension Specialist, Rural Development Administration, Suwon, 1990-; Head Professor, Agricultural Management Course, 1993-. Publications: Rural Community Development, 1984; Methodology for Adult Education, 1988; Integrated Rural Development, 1989; Agricultural Extension, 1992; Editor, Journal Korean Agricultural Education, 1982-. Honours: Ever Green Cultural Award, College of Agriculture, Seoul National University, 1966; Chief of Staff Award, Korean Army, 1967; Student Leadership Award, President, University of Minnesota, 1978; Honorary State FFA Degree, Minnesota FFA, 1980; Honorary American FFA Degree, 1999. Memberships: Life Member, Society of Korean Agricultural Education; Life Member, Korean Society of Study Education; Life Member, Korean Association for Adult Education; Executive Secretary and Vice-President, 1982-, President, 1995-, Korean Vocational Association; Secretary, 1994-96, President, 1997-, Korean Association for Agricultural Extension; Phi Delta Kappa; Secretary general 1982-, Korean Association for Rural Youth Education. Address: College of Agriculture & Life Sciences, Seoul National University, Seoul 151-921 Korea. E-mail: agkss@snu.ac.kr

**KIM Sunhyo,** b. 16 August 1958, Kongju, Korea. Nutritionist; Educator. m. Byungchul Ryu, 1 son, 1 daughter. Education: BS, Department of Home Economics Education, Kongju National Teacher's College, 1981; MS, Department of Food and Nutrition, Ewha Womans University, 1983; PhD, Food and Nutrition major, Chungang University, 1990. Appointments: Professor, Department of Home Economics Education, 1990-2002, Counseling Director, 1993-95, 2004-, Chair, Department of Home Economics Education, 1999-2001, Professor, 2003-, Chair, 2005-, Department of Food Service Management and Nutrition, Kongju National University; Visiting Scholar, Department of Human Nutrition, University of Otago, New Zealand, 1994; Visiting Scholar, 1996-97, Postgraduate Researcher, 2002-04, Department of Nutrition, University of California at Davis, USA; Editor, Korean Nutrition Society, 2002-; Editor, Korean Society of Community Nutrition, 2003-; Reviewer, Korean Dietary Reference Intakes, 2005. Publications: Articles in professional scientific journals including: Comparison of dietary patterns and nutrient intakes of elementary schoolchildren living in remote rural and urban areas in Korea: their potential impact on school performance, Nutrition Research, 2005. Honours: Listed in Who's Who in Medicine and Healthcare, 2004-05. Memberships: Korean Nutrition Society;

Korean Society of Community Nutrition; Korean Society of Food Culture; Asian Regional Association for Home Economics. Address: Department of Food Service Management & Nutrition, Kongju National University, 182 Shinwkan-dong, Kongju 314-70, South Korea. E-mail: shkim@kongju.ac.kr

**KIM Tae-Heung,** b. 17 March 1959, Taegu, Korea. Doctor of Medicine. m. Eun-Mee Gil, 1 son, 1 daughter. Education: BS, MD, College of Medicine, 1978-84, MSc, 1989-91, PhD, College of Medicine, 1992-95, Seoul National University. Appointments: Intern, Resident in Dermatology, Seoul National University Hospital, 1986-91; Professor and Chairman, Department of Dermatology, College of Medicine, Gyeongsang National University, Jinju, Kyungnam, Korea, 1991-2003; Postdoctoral Fellowship on Photoimmunology, Department of Immunology, University of Texas MD Anderson Cancer Center, USA, 1996-98; President, White-Line Skin Clinic Group, Kyungnam, Korea, 2003-. Publications: 99 articles including: Treatment of solitary mastomcytoma with intralesional injections of steroid, 2002; Hailey-Hailey disease on the sun-exposed areas, 2002; Artificial reproduction of lesions of atypical hydroa vacciniforme induced by latent EBV infection, 2003; Advantages of the SKH/Hr-1 hairless mouse model to test sunscreen efficacy against photoimmune suppression, 2003; Treatment of acquired syndactyly with epidermal graft after radiosurgery, 2003; Viability of the antigen determines whether DNA or urocanic acid act as initiator molecules for UV-induced suppression of the delayed type hypersensitivity, 2003. Memberships: Korean Dermatological Association; American Society for Photobiologist; European Society for Photobiologist; Photomedicine Society; International Society of Dermatologic Surgery; American Academy of Dermatology. Address: White-Line Skin Clinic & Aesthetics, Fl-5 Handok Bldg, 15-2 Sangnam-Dong, Changwon, Kyungnam 641-832, Korea. E-mail: derkim@hanmail.net Website: www.kimsskin.com

**KIM Taek-Har,** b. 1 January 1933, Republic of Korea. Chairman of World Peace and Missions Corps; Chairman, Korea Unification and Diplomacy Institute. m. Jeong-Jah Lim, 2 sons, 3 daughters. Education: Major in Law, National Jeon Buk University, 1953; BA, Law, Won-Gwang University, 1958; Graduate School Major, MA, International Politics, 1965, PhD course, International Politics, 1975, Joon-Ang University. Appointments: President Korea Lumber Industrial Co Ltd, 1958; Chairman, Kim-Jeh Gun Prosperity Committee, 1964; Chairman, 5 Districts Combined Promotion Committee to Construct West Coast Railway, 1965; Member, National Assembly, Republic of Korea and Vice-Chairman Foreign Affairs Committee, 1973; Chairman, Korea Unification and Diplomacy Institute, 1973; Established International Goodwill Associations between Korea, Brazil, Senegal and Spain, 1977; Normalised Diplomatic Relations between Korea and Nigeria, 1980; Chairman of Korea United Foods Co Ltd, 1980; Chairman Korea Corporation, 1983; Chairman, Korea General Trading Corporation, 1991; Chairman, World Peace and Missions Corps, 1999. Publications: Politics and Elections in Korea; Modernisation on Fishing and Agricultural Fields in Korea; Study for Nationalism of Malaysia; The World Strategy of Korea; Sunshine policy better than sunbeam policy for North Korea; The Vision for Non-Partisan Representative; Wisdom of Switzerland, translation. Honour: Good Conduct Citation, Minister of Home Affairs, 1962. Memberships: Vice President, Korea Saw Mill Association, 1966; Chairman, Korea Handball Association, 1971; Member of Standing, Korea Olympic Committee, 1971; Adviser, Korea International Politics Institute, 1975; Adviser, World International Law Association, 1975; Lions Club; Founding Cabinet, World Peace and Diplomacy Forum, England. Address: #805-1105 Korea National Housing

Apt, 636 Sang-Ha Ri, Gang-nam Maeul, Gu-Seoung Eup, Yong-in Shi, Gyung-gi Do, 449-914 Republic of Korea. E-mail: wpmc21@hanafos.com

**KIM Yong-In (Luke)**, b. 15 July 1957, Chunnam, South Korea. Professor; Doctor. m. Mi-Kyung Agnes Choi, 2 sons, 1 daughter. Education: MD, Kyung Hee University, Seoul, Korea, 1982; ECFMG Certificate, USA, 1984; Board Certificate of Cardiothoracic Surgery, Belgium, 1992; Board Certificate of Cardiothoracic Surgery, Korea, 1997; Physician's License, Pennsylvania, USA, 1998; PhD, Katholieke Universiteit, Leuven, Belgium, 2000. Appointments: Military Physician, military duty, Korea, 1982-85; Residency training, General and Cardiothoracic Surgery, Leuven, Belgium, 1986-92; Research and Clinical Fellow, Cardiac Surgery, Catholic University of Leuven, 1992-95; Department Head, Cardiothoracic Surgery, Pundang CHA Hospital, Korea, 1995-98; Assistant Professor, Kyung Hee University, Seoul, Korea, 1995-97; Associate Staff, Cardiothoracic Surgery, St Francis Medical Center, Pittsburgh, PA, USA, 1998-2001; Department Head of Cardiothoracic Surgery, Inje University, Seoul Paik Hospital, Seoul, Korea, 2002-. Publications: Many articles published in medical journals; 1 textbook; 3 poems in English. Honours: Great Minds of the 21st Century, ABI; Award of Excellent Article, Kyung Hee University Medical School Alumni, 1995; Editor's Choice Award, International Society of Poets, 2001. Memberships: European Association for Cardiothoracic Surgery; The International Society for Minimally Invasive Cardiac Surgery; Korean Society of Cardiothoracic Surgery; Korean Medical Association; Belgian Society of Cardiothoracic Surgery. Address: 1403 HO, 935 Dong, Lotte Apt, Mirinal-maeul, Joong-dong, Wonmi-gu, Pucheon-city, Kyonggi-province, 420-710, South Korea. E-mail: yongin@hotmailcom

**KIM Yong Kyu**, b. 7 July 1943, Gim-Po, Korea. m. Kyu Seong, 2 children. Senior Research Scientist. Education: BS, Biology, Kyung Hee University, 1961; MS, Animal Physiology, Kyung Hee University Graduate School, 1969; PhD, Clinical Pharmacology, Toyama Medical Pharmaceutical University, Japan, 1981. Appointments: Teacher, Academic Affair and Vice Principal, Yumkwang Girls Commercial High School, Seoul, 1965-77; Research Student and PhD Course, Graduate School of Toyama Medical and Pharmaceutical University, Toyama, Japan, 1977-81; Postdoctoral Fellow, Medical College of Georgia, Augusta, USA, 1981-83; Postdoctoral Associate, Yale University, New Haven, USA, 1983-85; Research Associate, University of Southern California, Los Angeles, USA, 1985-91; Assistant Professor, Albany Medical College, USA, 1991-94; Senior Research Scientist, Korea Food and Drug Administration, Seoul, 1995-. Publications: Numerous papers and articles in scientific journals. Honours: Research Fellow, Japan Ministry of Education and Science, 1977-81; Excellent Paper in the Poster Section, Korea Society for Cell and Molecular Biology, 1998; Excellent Paper, Korea Food and Drug Administration, 1998, 1999. Memberships: Associate Member, American Association for the Advancement of Science; Associate Member, Cell Press; Associate Member, Nature; Associate Member, Journal of Biochemistry and Molecular Biology, Korea. Address: 199-26 Jangwi-1-dong, Sungbukgu, Seoul 136-833, Korea.

**KIM Young Gon**, b. 27 September 1947, Iksan, Korea. Professor. m. Seongja Song, 1 son. Education: BS, Biology, Chosun University, 1975; MS, Biology, Chosun University Graduate School, 1977; PhD, Biology (Cellular and Molecular Biology), New Mexico University Graduate school, USA, 1990. Appointments: Research Assistant, 1984-90, Assistant Professor, Associate Professor, 1990-99, Professor, Life Science Institute Director, 1999-Biology, Chasun University

Natural Science; Visiting Scholar, North Carolina State University, USA, 1995-96. Publications: Articles in scientific journals include: The effects of pyonogenol on DNA damage in vitro and expression of superoxide dismutase and HPI in Escherichia coli SOD and catalase deficient mutant cells, 2004; Phytotherapy research. Honours: Award, Superintendent of Chunbuk Educational Affairs, 1964; Scholarship for all school year of Chosun University, 1969-75; New Literature, Literature World, 1998; Best Columnist, Issue Today, 2001. Memberships: International Free Radical Society; American Association for the Advancement of Science. Address: 101-608 Samik Apt, Bongsundong, Namku, Kwangju 503-060, Korea. E-mail: ygnkim@mail.chosun.ac.kr

**KIM Yun-Hee**, b. 25 December 1957, Iksan, Korea. Professor. 2 sons. Education: MD, College of Medicine, 1982, PhD, Graduate School, Department of Neuroanatomy, 1996, Yonsei University; Internships, 1982-83, Residency, Physical Medicine and Rehabilitation, 1983-86, Presbyterian Medical Centre, Chonjou, Korea; Visiting Residency, Frazier Rehabilitation Centre, Louisville, Kentucky, USA, 1985. Appointments: Attending Staff and Chief, Department of Rehabilitation Medicine, Presbyterian Medical Centre, Chonju, Korea, 1986-92; Supervisor, North-Wanju Community Based Rehabilitation Project, Korea, 1988-92; Assistant Professor, 1992-98, Associate Professor, 1998-2002, Chief, Department of Rehabilitation Medicine, 1992-2002, Chonbuk National University Medical School, Chonju, Korea; Visiting Scholar, Cognitive Neurology and Alzheimer's Disease Center, Department of Neurology, Northwestern University Medical School, Chicago, Illinois, USA, 1998-2002; Associate Professor and Chief, Department of Rehabilitation Medicine, College of Medicine, Ponchon CHA University, Budang CHA General Hospital, Sungnam, Korea, 2002-2003; Professor, Department of Rehabilitation Medicine, School of Medicine, Sungkyunkwang University, Samsung Medical Centre, 2003-. Publications: Numerous articles as co-author in medical journals include: Quantitative assessment of static and dynamic postural sway using COBETS in patients with balance problem, 1997; Brain language network and lateralization using spoken and written Korean words in normal adults: A functional MRI study, 2000; Effect of methylphenidate on cognitive impairment following head injury: A double-blind placebo controlled study, 2000; Effect of Computer-Assisted Cognitive Rehabilitation Program in Patients with Brain Injury, 2002. Honours: Clinical Research Awards, Korean Academy of Rehabilitation Medicine, 1997, 2000, 2002; President's Citation Award, American Academy of Physical Medicine and Rehabilitation, 2000. Memberships include: Korean Academy of Rehabilitation Medicine; Korean Society for Neuroscience; Korean Society for Human Brain Mapping; Korean Association of Speech Science; Society for Neuroscience; American Association of Physical Medicine and Rehabilitation; American Society of Neurorehabilitation; American Academy of Electrodiagnostic Medicine. Address: Department of Rehabilitation Medicine, School of Medicine, Samsung Medical Center, Sungkyunkwan University, 50 Ilwon-dong, Kangnam-ku, Seoul 135-710, Republic of Korea. E-mail: yunkim@smc.samsung.co.kr

**KIM Yung-Chul**, b. 27 April 1947, Masan, Korea. Chief Executive Officer and President. m. Sung-Hee Suh, 1 son, 3 daughters. Education: BA, Agricultural Chemistry, 1969, Graduate School of Public Administration, 1972-75, Seoul National University, Seoul, Korea; Department of Economics, University of Missouri-Columbia, Missouri, USA, 1991. Appointments: Secretary to the President, Office of Chief of Staff to the President, Office of the President, 1995-96; Assistant Minister, Secretary to the President for Political Affairs, Office of the President, 1996-98; Deputy Commissioner, Korea Intellectual Property Office, 1998-99; President, Korea District Heating Corporation, 1999-2002; President, Korea Midland Power Corporation, 2002-. Honours: Ministers Award for Excellent Job Performance, 1973; Yellow Stripes Order of Service Merit, 1997. Address: #108-101 Mokryon Town Apt, 716 Ilwon-dong, Gongnam-Gu, Seoul 135-991, Korea.

**KIMŌTŌ Kyoji,** b. 20 June 1942, Osaka, Japan. Professor of Mechanical Engineering. m. Kyoko Komatsu, 1 son, 3 daughters. Education: BSc, Kobe University, 1965; Dr of Engineering, Kyoto University, 1978. Appointments: Professor of Engineering, Department of Mechanical Engineering, Osaka Prefectural College of Technology. Publications: Article: Education for Engineers to the Students in Colleges of Technology, 1998. Editor: Textbook Series of Mechanical Engineering; Author: Engineering Heat Transfer, 1992; Engineering Thermodynamics, 2001; Engineering of Thermal Energy and Environment Conservation, 2002; Introduction to Mechanical Engineering, 2002. Memberships: Japanese Society for Engineering Education; Heat Transfer Society of Japan; Japan Society of Energy and Resources; The Japan Society of Waste Management Experts; Japan Society of Mechanical Engineers. Address: 19-2 Scifu-Cho, Otsu, Shiga Prefecture, 520-0225 Japan. E-mail: kimoto@ipc.osaka-pct.ac.jp

**KIMURA Masashi,** b. 26 January 1966, Japan. Research Scientist. Education: Biological Sciences, 1986-93,PhD, Department of Biological Sciences, 1999, University of Tsukuba; Appointment: Research Scientist, Department of Molecular Pathobiochemistry, Division of Disease Control, Gifu University School of Medicine, 1993-. Publications: Articles in scientific journals including: Journal of Biological Chemistry, 1997, 1999; Cancer Research, 1999; Molecular Cell Biology, 2002; Book: Function of Aurora Kinases in Mitosis and Cancer, 2005. Honours: International Scientist of the Year, IBC, 2004; Greatest Living Legends, IBC, 2004; Outstanding Professional Award, ABI, 2004; Universal Award of Accomplishment, ABI, 2004; Lifetime Achievement Award, IBC, 2005; Top 100 Scientist, IBC, 2005; Leading Scientists of the World, IBC, 2005; Hall of Fame, IBC; Universal Award of Accomplishment, ABI, 2004; Outstanding Professional Award, ABI, 2004; Man of the Year 2005; World Lifetime Achievement Award, ABI, 2005; Listed in Who's Who publications and biographical dictionaries. Memberships: Molecular Biology Society of Japan; Japanese Biochemical Society; Japan Society for Cell Biology; American Society for Cell Biology. Address: Department of Molecular Pathobiochemistry, Division of Disease Control, Gifu University Graduate School of Medicine, Yanagido 1-1, Gifu 50-1194, Japan. E-mail: yo@cc.gifu-u.ac.jp

**KINDERSLEY Tania,** b. 30 January 1967, London, England. Writer. Education: MA, Christ Church, Oxford. Publications: Goodbye, Johnny Thunders, 1997; Don't Ask Me Why, 1998; Elvis Has Left the Building, 2001; Nothing to Lose, 2002. Address: Home Farm, Aboyne, Aberdeenshire AB34 5JP, Scotland. E-mail: pulch66@totalscne.co.uk

**KING B B,** b. 16 September 1925, Itta Bena, Michigan, USA. Singer; Musician. Education: Selftaught Guitar. Appointments: Member, Elkhorn Singers; Played with Sonny Boy Williamson, 1946; Regular broadcast slot, The Sepia Swing Show, Radio WDIA; 300 Performances a Year, 1950s-70s; Numerous worldwide tours. Creative Works: Singles: Three O'Clock Blues; You Didn't Want Me; Please Love Me; You Upset Me Baby; Sweet Sixteen; Rock Me Baby; The B B Jones; The Thrill is Gone. Honours: Grammy Awards, 1971, 1982; Best Traditional Blues Recording, 1984, 1986, 1991, 1992; Rock'n'Roll Hall of

Fame, 1987; NARAS, 1988; Songwriters Hall of Fame, 1990; Gibson Guitars, 1991; Star in Hollywood Walk of Fame, 1990; MTV Video Award, with U2, 1989; Q Inspiration Award, 1992. Membership: Co-Chairman, Foundation for the Advancement of Inmate Rehabilitation & Recreation. Address: 1414 6th Avenue, New York, NY 10019, USA.

**KING Billie Jean,** b. 22 November 1943, California, USA. Tennis Player. m. Larry King, 1965, divorced. Education: Los Angeles State University. Career: Amateur status, 1958-67; Professional, 1967-; Championship Titles: Australia, 1968; South Africa, 1966, 1967, 1969; Wimbledon 20 Titles, 10 doubles, 4 mixed and 6 singles, 1966, 1967, 1968, 1972, 1973, 1975, Italy, 1970; Federal Republic of Germany, 1971; France, 1972; Winner, 1/046 singles tournaments, 1984; Other: Sports Commentator ABC-TV, 1975-78; Founded Women's Tennis Association, 1973; Publisher of Women's Sports, 1974-; US Tennis Team Commissioner, 1981-; CEO World Team Tennis, 1985-; US Federation Cup Team Captain, 1995-; Women's Olympic Tennis Coach, 1996, 2000; Virginia Simms Championship Series Consultant. Publications: Tennis to Win, 1970; Billie Jean, w K Chapin, 1974; We Have Come a Long Way: The Story of Women's Tennis, 1988. Honour: Top Woman Athlete of the Year, 1973. Address: c/o World Team Tennis, 445 North Wells, Suite 404, Chicago, IL 60610, USA.

**KING David John,** b. 25 November 1940, Liverpool, England. Professor of Clinical Psychopharmacology (Retired). m. Anne Logan, 2 sons. Education: Queen's University, Belfast, 1958-64. Appointments: PRHO, Belfast City Hospital, 1964-65; SHO and Registrar in Psychiatry, Belfast and University of Sheffield, 1965-69; Andy Darlington Memorial Fellow, Mental Health Research Fund, 1969-72; Assistant Professor of Psychiatry, Dalhousie University, Nova Scotia, Canada, 1973-75; Senior Lecturer, 1975-86, Reader, 1986-95, Department of Therapeutics and Pharmacology, Queen's University, Belfast; Medical Director, Homefirst Community HSS Trust, 1996-99; Professor of Clinical Psychopharmacology, 1995-2003, Assistant Head of School of Medicine (Research), 1998-2003, Queen's University, Belfast; Consultant Psychiatrist, Holywell Hospital, Antrim, 1972-73, 1975-2003; Retired, 2003. Publications: Editor, Seminars in Clinical Psychopharmacology, First Edition, 1995, Second Edition, 2004; Over 90 scientific publications on the pharmacology of antipsychotic drugs and biological aspects of psychosis. Honour: Royal Irish Academy Award of Merit and Silver Medal in Pharmacology and Toxicology. Memberships: British Association for Psychopharmacology, Council, 1992-96; British Pharmacological Society; Collegium Internationale Neuro-psychopharmacologicum; European College of Neuropsychopharmacology; Ulster Neuropsychiatric Society, President, 1996-98; Ulster Medical Society. Address: The School House, 2 Ladyhill Road, Antrim BT41 2RF, Northern Ireland. E-mail: david.king86@btinternet.com

**KING Francis Henry, (Frank Cauldwell),** b. 4 March 1923, Adelboden, Switzerland. Author; Drama and Literary Critic. Education: BA, 1949, MA, 1951, Balliol College, Oxford. Appointment: Drama Critic, Sunday Telegraph, 1978-88. Publications: Novels: To the Dark Tower, 1946; Never Again, 1947; An Air That Kills, 1948; The Dividing Stream, 1951; The Dark Glasses, 1954; The Firewalkers, 1956; The Widow, 1957; The Man on the Rock, 1957; The Custom House, 1961; The Last of the Pleasure Gardens, 1965; The Waves Behind the Boat, 1967; A Domestic Animal, 1970; Flights, 1973; A Game of Patience, 1974; The Needle, 1975; Danny Hill, 1977; The Action, 1978; Act of Darkness, 1983; Voices in an Empty Room, 1984; Frozen Music, 1987; The Woman Who Was God, 1988; Punishments, 1989; Visiting Cards, 1990; The Ant

Colony, 1991; Secret Lives (with Tom Wakefield and Patrick Gale), 1991; The One and Only, 1994; Ash on an Old Man's Sleeve, 1996; Dead Letters, 1997; Prodigies, 2001; The Nick of Time, 2003. Short Stories: So Hurt and Humiliated, 1959; The Japanese Umbrella, 1964; The Brighton Belle, 1968; Hard Feelings, 1976; Indirect Method, 1980; One is a Wanderer, 1985; A Hand at the Shutter, 1996; The Sunlight on the Garden, 2005. Other: E M Forster and His World, 1978; A Literary Companion to Florence, 1991; Autobiography: Yesterday Came Suddenly, 1993. Honours: Somerset Maugham Award, 1952; Katherine Mansfield Short Story Prize, 1965; Officer, 1979, Commander, 1985, of the Order of the British Empire. Memberships: English PEN, president, 1976-86; International PEN, president, 1986-89, vice-president, 1989-; Royal Society of Literature, fellow. Address: 19 Gordon Place, London W8 4JE, England. E-mail: fhk@dircon.co.uk

**KING Larry,** b. 19 November 1933, Brooklyn, USA. Broadcaster. m. (1) Alene Akins, 1 daughter, (2) Sharon Lepore, 1976, (3) Julia Alexander, 1989, 1 son, (4) Shawn Southwick, 1997. Appointments: Disc Jockey, various radio stations, Miami, Florida, 1957-71; Freelance Writer, Broadcaster, 1972-75; Radio Personality, Station WIOD, Miami, 1975-78; Writer, Entertainment Sections, Miami Herald, 7 years; Host, The Larry King Show, 1978-, 1990 Goodwill Games, WLA-TV Let's Talk, Washington DC; Columnist, USA Today, Sporting News; Appeared in films, Ghostbusters, 1984, Lost in America, 1985. Publications: Mr King, You're Having a Heart Attack (with B D Colen), 1989; Larry King: Tell Me More, When You're From Brooklyn, Everything Else is Tokyo, 1992; On the Line (jointly), 1993; Daddy Day, Daughter Day (jointly), 1997. Honours: Several broadcasting and journalism awards. Address: c/o CNN Larry King Live, 820 1st Street NE, Washington, DC 20002, USA.

**KING Mervyn Allister,** b. 30 March 1948, Chesham Bois, England. Economist; Central Banker. Education: BA honours, King's College, Cambridge. Appointments: Junior Research Officer, 1969-73; Kennedy Scholarship, Harvard University, 1971-72; Research Officer, 1972-76; Lecturer, Faculty of Economics, Cambridge, 1976-77; Fellow, St John's College, Cambridge, 1972-77; Esmee Fairbairn Professor of Investment, University of Birmingham, 1977-84; Visiting Professor of Economics, Harvard University, 1982-83, Massachusetts Institute of Technology, 1983-84; Visiting Professor of Economics, Harvard University, and Senior Olin Fellow, National Bureau of Economic Research, 1990; Professor of Economics, London School of Economics, 1984-95; Chief Economist and Executive Director, Bank of England, 1991-98; Visiting Professor of Economics, London School of Economics, 1996-; Deputy Governor, Bank of England, 1998-2003; Governor, Bank of England, 2003-. Publications: Indexing for Inflation, 1975; Public Policy and the Corporation, 1977; The British Tax System, 1978, 5th edition, 1990; The Taxation of Income from Capital, 1984; Numerous articles in various journals. Honours include: Stevenson Prize, Cambridge University, 1970; Medal of the University of Helsinki, 1982; Honorary Fellow, St John's College, Cambridge, 1997; Honorary degrees from Birmingham and London Guildhall and City (London) and Wolverhampton Universities and London School of Economics; Honorary Fellow, King's College, Cambridge, 2004; Other activities: Advisory Council, London Symphony Orchestra, 2001-; Chairman of OEDC's Working Party 3 Committee, 2001-03; Member, Group of Thirty, 1997-; President of Institute for Fiscal Studies, 1999-2003; Visiting Fellow, Nuffield College, Oxford, 2002-; Patron, Worcestershire County Cricket Club; Trustee, National Gallery; Member, All

England Lawn Tennis and Croquet Club. Address: Bank of England, Threadneedle Street, London EC2R 8AH, England.

**KING Stephen Edwin, (Richard Bachman),** b. 21 September 1947, Portland, Maine, USA. Author. m. Tabitha J Spruce, 1971, 2 sons, 1 daughter. Education: University Maine. Appointments: Teacher, English, Hampden Academy, Maine, 1971-73; Writer-in-Residence, University of Maine, Orono, 1978-79. Publications: Carrie, 1974; Salem's Lot, 1975; The Shining, 1977; The Stand, 1978; The Dead Zone, 1979; Firestarter, 1980; Danse Macabre, 1981; Cujo, 1981; Christine, 1983; Pet Sematary, 1983; The Talisman (w Peter Straub), 1984; Cycle of the Werewolf, 1985; It, 1986; The Eyes of the Dragon, 1987; Misery, 1987; The Tommyknockers, 1987; The Dark Half, 1989; Four Past Midnight, 1990; Needful Things, 1991; Gerald's Game, 1992; The Girl Who Loved Tom Jordan, 1999; Hearts in Atlantis, 1999; Storm of the Century (adapted to mini-series), 1999; Riding the Bullet, 2000; On Writing, 2000; Dreamcatcher, 2001; Everything's Eventual, 2002; The Dark Tower Stories: Volume 1: The Gunslinger, 1982, Volume 2: The Drawing of the Three, 1984. Short Story Collections: Night Shift, 1978; Different Seasons, 1982; Skeleton Crew, 1985; Gerald's Game, 1992; Dolores Claiborne, 1993; Nightmares & Dreamscapes, 1993; Insomnia, 1994; As Richard Bachman: Thinner, 1984; The Bachman Books: Rage, The Long Walk, Roadwork, The Running Man, 1985; Numerous other short stories. Memberships: Authors Guild of America; Screen Artists Guild; Screen Writers of America; Writers Guild. Address: 49 Florida Avenue, Bangor, ME 04401, USA. Website: www.stephenking.com

**KINGSLEY Ben,** b. 31 December 1943, England. Actor. m. 3 sons, 1 daughter. Appointments: RSC, 1970-80, National Theatre, 1977-78; Associate Artist, RSC. Creative Works: Stage appearances include: A Midsummer Night's Dream; Occupations; The Tempest; Hamlet (title role); The Merry Wives of Windsor; Baal; Nicholas Nickleby; Volpone; The Cherry Orchard; The Country Wife; Judgement; Statements After An Arrest; Othello (title role); Caracol in Melons; Waiting for God; TV appearances include: The Love School, 1974; Kean; Silas Marner; The Train, 1987; Murderous Amongst Us, 1988; Anne Frank; Several plays; Films: Gandhi, 1982; Betrayal, 1982; Harem, 1985; Turtle Diary, 1985; Without A Clue, 1988; Testimony, 1988; Pascali's Island, 1988; Bugsy, 1991; Sneakers, 1992; Innocent Moves, 1992; Dave, 1992; Schindler's List, 1993; Death and the Maiden, 1994; Species, 1995; Twelfth Night, 1996; Photographing Fairies, 1997; The Assignment, 1998; Weapons of Mass Destruction, 1998; Sweeney Todd, 1998; The Confession, 1999; Sexy Beast, 1999; Rules of Engagement, 1999; What planet Are You From? 1999; Spooky House, 1999; A.I., 2000; Triumph of Love, 2000; Anne Frank, 2000; Tuck Everlasting, 2001; Sound of Thunder, 2002; Suspect Zero, 2002; House of Sand and Fog, 2002. Honours include: 2 Hollywood Golden Globe Awards, 1982; NY Film Critics Award; 2 BAFTA Awards; Los Angeles Film Critics Award, 1983; Best Actor, British Industry Film Awards, 2001; Screen Actors' Guild Award for Best Actor, 2002. Address: c/o ICM, 76 Oxford Street, London W1N 0AX, England.

**KINGSLEY David John,** b. 10 July 1929, London, England. Marketing and Communications Consultant. m. Gisela, 2 sons, 2 daughters. Education: BSc (Econ), London School of Economics. Appointments: Served RAF Command 1948; President LSE Students Union, 1952; Vice-President, National Union of Students, 1953; Prospective Parliamentary Candidate, East Grinstead, 1952-54; Founded, Kingsley, Manton, Palmer Advertising Group, 1964; Publicity Advisor to Labour Party and Government, General Elections, 1964, 1966, 1970; Advisor to President of Zambia, 1974-82; Advisor to Prime Minister and Government of Mauritius, 1976-81; Publicity Advisor to SDP, 1981-87; Member, CNAA Boards, 1970-82; Chairman, Worldaware, 1992-96; Chairman, Children 2000, 1994-; Chair, Children's Discovery Centre, 2003-; Director, Fun Radio, 2005-; Vice-Chair, Royal Philharmonic Orchestra, 1972-77; Honorary President, LSE Environmental Network, 1998-; Director, Mediawise, 2003-; Chair, Cartoon Arts Trust, 1994-2001, Chair, Creative Summit, 1999; Advisor, Institute of Global Ethics, 2003-; Adviser, Learning for Life, 2005-. Publications: Albion in China, 1979; How World War II Was Won in the Playing Fields of LSE, 2003; Various articles. Honours: Honorary Fellow, London School of Economics; Honorary Member, Royal College of Music; Honorary Doctorate, Soka University, Tokyo, Japan; FIPA; FRSA; MCSD. Memberships: Reform Club; Governor of LSE, 1965-. Address: 81 Mortimer Street, London N1 5AR, England. E-mail: kingsley@dircon.co.uk

**KINGSOLVER Barbara**, b. 8 April 1955, Annapolis, Maryland, USA. Author, Poet. m. (1) Joseph Hoffmann, 1985, divorced 1993, 1 daughter, (2) Steven Hopp, 1995, 1 daughter. Education: BA, DePauw University, 1977; MS, University of Arizona, 1981. Appointments: Research Assistant, Department of Physiology, 1977-79, Technical Writer, Office of Arid Land Studies, 1981-85, University of Arizona, Tucson; Journalist, 1985-87; Author, 1987-; Founder, Bellwether Prize to recognize a first novel of social significance, 1997. Publications: The Bean Trees (novel), 1988; Homeland and Other Stories, 1989; Holding the Line: Women in the Great Arizona Mine Strike of 1983 (non-fiction), 1989; Animal Dreams (novel), 1990; Pigs in Heaven (novel), 1993; Another America (poems), 1994, new edition, 1998; High Tide in Tucson: Essays from Now or Never, 1995; The Poisonwood Bible (novel), 1998; Prodigal Summer (stories), 2000; Small Wonder, 2002; Last Stand, 2002. Contributions to: Many anthologies and periodicals. Honours: Feature-Writing Award, Arizona Press Club, 1986; American Library Association Awards, 1988, 1990; PEN Fiction Prize, 1991; Edward Abbey Ecofiction Award, 1991; Los Angeles Times Book Award for Fiction, 1993; PEN Faulkner, 1999; American Booksellers Book of the Year, 2000; National Humanities Medal, 2000; Governor's National Award in the Arts, Kentucky, 2002; John P McGovern Award for the Family, 2002; Physicians for Social Responsibility National Award, 2002; Academy of Achievement Golden Plate Award, 2003. Address: PO Box 31870, Tucson, AZ 85751, USA.

**KINNOCK Glenys**, b. 7 July 1944, Roade, Northamptonshire, England. Member of European Parliament, Wales. m. Neil Kinnock, 1 son, 1 daughter. Education: BA, Dip Ed, University College, Cardiff, 1962-66. Appointments: Primary and Secondary School Teacher, 1966-93; European Parliamentary Labour Party Spokesperson on Development, Co-President of the African, Caribbean and Pacific States ACP-EU Joint Parliamentary Assembly; Member of European Parliament, South Wales East, 1994-99; Member of European Parliament, Wales, 1999-. Publications: Books: Voices for One World, 1987; Eritrea – Images of War and Peace, 1989; Nambia - Birth of a Nation, 1991; Could Do Better – Where is British Education in the European League Tables?; By Faith and Daring, 1993; Zimbabwe: On the brink, 2003. Honours: Honorary Fellow, University of Wales College, Newport and University of Wales, Bangor; Honorary Doctorates from: Thames Valley, Brunel and Kingston Universities; Fellow, Royal Society of Arts. Memberships: NUT; GMB; President, One World Action; Patron, Saferworld; Council Member, Voluntary Service Overseas; Patron, Drop the Debt Campaign; Vice President, Parliamentarians for Global Action; Board Member, World Parliamentarian Magazine; President, Coleg Harlech; Patron,

Welsh Woman of the Year; Vice President, Wales Council for Voluntary Action, South East Wales Racial Equality Council; Vice President, St David's Foundation; Special Needs Advisory Project, Cymru; UK National Breast Cancer Coalition Wales; Community Enterprise Wales and Charter Housing; Patron, Burma Campaign UK; Crusaid; Elizabeth Hardie Ferguson Trust; Medical Foundation for Victims of Torture; National Deaf Children's Society; Council Member, Britain in Europe.

**KINNOCK Neil Gordon (Lord Kinnock of Bedwellty)**, b. 28 March 1942, Wales, United Kingdom. Politician. m. Glenys Elizabeth Parry, 1967, 1 son, 1 daughter. Education: Lewis School, Pengam; University College, Cardiff. Appointments: Elected President, University College Cardiff Students Union, 1965-66; Tutor, Organizer, Industrial & Trade Union Studies, Workers' Educational Association, 1966-70; Labour MP for Bedwellty, 1970-83, for Islwyn, 1983-95; Member, Welsh Hospital Board, 1969-71; Parliamentary Private Secretary to Secretary of State for Employment, 1974-75; Member, National Executive Committee, Labour Party, 1978-94; Leader of Labour Pty, 1983-92; Leader of the Opposition, 1983-92; EC Commissioner with Responsibility for Transport, 1995-99; President, Cardiff University, 1998-; Vice-President, European Commission, 1999-2004; Chairman, British Council, 2004-; Life Peer, 2005. Publications: Wales and the Common Market, 1971; Making Our Way, 1986; Thorns and Roses, 1992; Numerous contributions in periodicals, newspapers and books including The Future of Social Democracy, 1999. Honours: Several honorary doctorates; Alex de Tocqueville Prize, 2003. Address: British Council, 10 Spring Gardens, London SW1A 2BN, England.

**KINNUNEN Aarne Einari**, b. 4 February 1930, Lieksa, Finland. Emeritus Professor. m. Aino-Maija Tikkanen, 1 son, 2 daughters. Education: MA, 1952, PhD, 1967, Helsinki University, Finland. Appointments: Assistant Teacher, 1963-67, Assistant Professor, 1968-85, Extraordinary Professor, Aesthetics, 1986-94, Helsinki University. Publications (in Finnish): Drama of A Kivi, 1967; Seven Brothers of A Kivi, 1973, 2002; World of Drama, 1985, Theory of Narrative, 1989; Humour and Comedy, 1994; Aesthetics, 2000. Honours: Elias Lönnroth, 1977; Wsoy, 1983; Yrjö Hirn, 1995; Lauri Jäntti, 2001. Membership: Academia Scientiarum Fennica. Address: Vironkatu 9A 14, 00170 Helsinki, Finland.

**KINSKI Natassja**, b. 24 January 1961, West Berlin, Germany. Actress. m. I Moussa, 1984, 1 son, 1 daughter; 1 daughter with Quincy Jones. Career: Debut in Falsche Bewegung, 1975; Films include: Stay as You Are, 1978; Cat People, 1982; Moon in the Gutter, 1983; Unfaithfully Yours; Paris; Texas and the Hotel New Hampshire, 1984; Magdalene, 1989; Terminal Velocity, 1994; One Night Stand, 1997; Sunshine, 1998; Town and Country, 1999; The Claim, 2000; The Day the World Ended, 2001; An American Rhapsody, 2001. Address: c/o Peter Levine, William Morris Agency, 151 South El Camino Drive, Beverly Hills, CA 90212, USA.

**KIRBY Gordon William**, b. 20 June 1934, Wallasey, Cheshire, England. Chemist; Emeritus Professor. m. Audrey Jean Rusbridge, div 1983, 2 sons. Education: Liverpool Technical College, 1950-52; Exhibitioner, 1953-54, Minor Scholar, 1954-55, Dunlop Research Student, 1955-58, BA, 1955, MA, 1959, PhD, 1958, ScD, 1971, Gonville and Caius College, Cambridge. Appointments: 1851 Exhibition Senior Studentship, 1958-60, Assistant Lecturer, 1960-61, Lecturer, 1961-67, Imperial College, London; Professor of Organic Chemistry, Loughborough University of Technology, 1967-72; Regius Professor of Chemistry, 1972-96, Professor of Chemistry,

1997, currently Emeritus Professor of Chemistry, University of Glasgow. Publications: Research papers mainly in the Journals of the Royal Society of Chemistry; Co-editor, Progress in the Chemistry of Organic Natural Products, 1971-. Honours: Schuldam Plate, Gonville and Caius College, Cambridge, 1956; Corday-Morgan Medal and Prize, Royal Society of Chemistry, 1969; Tilden Lecturership and Medal, Royal Society of Chemistry, 1974-75. Memberships: FRSC and C.Chem, 1970; FRSE, 1975; Member, American Chemical Society; Member, Royal Philosophical Society of Glasgow.

**KIRCHNER Celina,** b. 22 April 1970, Krzyżowce, Poland. Graphic Artist. m. Adam Kirchner, 1 daughter. Education: Graduate, Fine Arts Academy, Cracow, Graphic Faculty, Katowice, 1990-95. Career: Printmaker; Draftsman; 6 solo exhibitions; Group exhibitions include: Gielniak Graphic Art Competition, Jelenia Góra, Poland, 1997, 2000, 2003; Polish Print Triennial, Katowice, Poland, 1997, 2003; AGART World Print Festival, Ljubljana, Slovenia, 1998; International Tallinn Print Triennial, 1998, 2001-; International Biennial of Graphic Art, Ljubljana, Slovenia, 1999; International Exhibition of Graphic Art, Frechen, Germany, 1999, 2002; International Print Biennial, Varna, Bulgaria, 1999, 2001; Small Graphic Forms, Łódź, Poland, 1999, 2002, 2005; International Print Triennial, Bitola, Macedonia, 2000, 2003; International Prize of Engraving, Ferrol, Spain, 2000, 2002, 2002, 2004, 2005; International Miniature Print Exhibition, Bristol, England, 2000, Dumfries, Scotland, 2003; International Drawing Competition, Wrocław, Poland, 2000; International Biennial of Miniature Art, Ville Marie, Canada, 2000, 2002; International Exhibition of Miniature Print, Tetovo, Macedonia, 2001, 2003; The Society of Wood Engravers Annual Exhibition, UK, 2001, 2002, 2003;; International Exhibition of Print and Drawing, Vaasa, Finland, 2002; International Small Engraving Salon, Baia Mare, Romania, 2003, 2004, 2005; International Biennial of Engraving, Liege, Belgium, 2003; International Contemporary Print Biennial, Trois Rivieres, Canada, 2003; Linocut Today IV, Bietigheim-Bissingen, Germany, 2004; International Biennial of Graphic Art, Ourense, Spain, 2004; International Mini Print de Sarajevo, Bosnia and Hercegovina, 2004; International Small Print Biennial, Ostrów Wielkopolski, Poland, 2001, 2003, 2005; International Engraving Biennial of Douro, Alijo, Portugal, 2005. Honours include: Grand Prize, Work of the Year 1995, Katowice, Poland, 1996; 1st Prize, International Graphic Art Competition, Jelenia Góra, Poland, 1997; Grant, Polish Ministry of Culture, 2000; 3rd prize, International Prize for Engraving, Ferrol, Spain, 2000; Joint Prize, International Exhibition of Miniature Print, Tetovo, Macedonia, 2001; 2nd Prize, International Miniature Print Biennial, Boguszów Gorce, Poland, 2002; Grant from Marshall of Silesian Voividship, 2003; 3rd Prize, International Miniature Print Biennial, Boguszów Gorce, Poland, 2004; Distinction, International Biennial of Small Graphic Forms, Gniezno, Poland, 2005. Address: ul. Szeroka 23/1a, 40-231 Katowice, Poland. E-mail: ckirchner@poczta.onet.pl

**KIRIYAMA Hiromitsu,** b. 1 October 1970, Osaka, Japan. Researcher. m. Chise Hata, 2 sons. Education: BS, Electrical Engineering, Kansai University, Osaka, Japan, 1993; MS, 1995, PhD, 1998, Electrical Engineering, Osaka University, Osaka, Japan. Appointment: Researcher, Advanced Photon Research Center, Kansai Research Establishment, Japan Atomic Energy Research Institute, Kyoto, Japan, 1998-. Publications: First-author of over 10 research articles which include most recently: High efficiency second-harmonic generation in four-pass quadrature frequency conversion scheme, 2000; Quadrature frequency conversion scheme using CsLiB6O10 crystals for the efficient second-harmonic generation of high power Nd:YAG

laser, 2000; Highly efficient second-harmonic generation in novel four-pass quadrature frequency conversion, 2000; High efficiency frequency doubling of Nd:YAG laser in a two-pass quadrature frequency conversion scheme using $CsLiB_6O_{10}$ crystals, 2002; High energy second-harmonic generation of Nd:glass laser radiation with large aperture $CsLIB_6O_{10}$ crystals, 2002; 25 J green-beam generation using large aperture $CsLIB_6O_{10}$ frequency doubler, 2003; 360-W average power operation with a single stage diode-pumped Nd:YAG amplifier at a 1-kHz repetition rate, 2003; High power pulsed green lasers, 2003 Memberships: Japan Society of Applied Physics; Laser Society of Japan. Address: Japan Atomic Energy Research Institute, Umemidai 8-1, Kizu-cho, Kyoto 619-0215, Japan. E-mail: kiriyama@apr.jaeri.go.jp

**KIRK Nicholas Kenneth,** b. 27 December 1945, Bradford, West Yorkshire, England. Musician (New Orleans Jazz Banjo); Electronics Engineer. Education: BSc, Honours, University of Wales; Postgraduate Diploma in Communications, Southampton University; Postgraduate Diploma in R F and Microwave, Bradford University. Career: Appearances on radio and television Wales with Clive Evans' River City Stompers, 1966-67; Appeared at the Keswick Jazz Festival, Bude Jazz Festival, Marsden Jazz Festival, and at jazz clubs and pubs in Yorkshire, Wales and South of England, with the Dennis Browne Creole Band; Appeared at the 100 Club in London with the New Era Jazzband; Currently proprietor, P&P Electronics and P&P Electrical Publications: Author of British Patent for apparatus for Recording and Replaying Music (The Musical Arranger and Sequencer), subsequent sale of patent rights to Waddingtons House of Games. Composition: Clouds. Recording: Float Me Down The River, with the Dennis Browne Creole Band, cassette; City Of A Million Dreams, cassette. Memberships: Fellow, Royal Microscopical Society. Address: 36 Kilpin Hill Lane, Staincliffe, Near Dewsbury, West Yorkshire WF13 4BH, England.

**KIRK Raymond Maurice,** b. 31 October 1923, Beeston, Nottinghamshire, England. Surgeon, retired. m. Margaret Schafran, 1 son, 2 daughters. Education: King's College, London; Charing Cross Hospital, London; University of London. Appointments: Ordinary Seaman to Lieutenant RNVR, 1942-46; House Surgeon and Casualty Officer, Charing Cross Hospital, 1952; Lecturer in Anatomy, King's College, London, 1952-53; House Surgeon and Resident Surgical Officer, Royal Postgraduate Medical School, Hammersmith Hospital, London, 1953-56; Registrar and Senior Registrar, Charing Cross Hospital, 1956-60; Senior Surgical Registrar, Royal Free Hospital, 1961; Consultant Surgeon, Willesden General Hospital, 1962-72; Consultant Surgeon and Honorary Senior Lecturer, Royal Free Hospital, 1964; Part-time Lecturer in Anatomy and Developmental Biology, University College, London; Honorary Professor of Surgery, Honorary Consulting Surgeon, Royal Free Hospital and Royal Free and University College, London School of Medicine, 1989-. Publications: Author and co-author, 8 books; Numerous articles and chapters in professional medical journals. Memberships: Royal College of Surgeons of England; Court of Examiners; Royal Society of Medicine; Hunterian Society; Medical Society of London; Association of Surgeons of Poland; Association of Surgeons of Sri Lanka. Address: 10 Southwood Lane, Highgate Village, London N6 5EE, England. E-mail: r.kirk@medsch.ucl.ac.uk

**KIRK-GREENE Anthony (Hamilton Millard),** b. 16 May 1925, Tunbridge Wells, England. m. Helen Sellar, 1967. University Lecturer; Fellow; Writer; Editor. Education: BA, 1949, MA, 1954, Clare College, Cambridge; MA, Oxford University, 1967. Appointments: Senior Lecturer in Government,

Institute of Administration, Zaria, Nigeria, 1957-62; Professor of Government, Ahmadu Bello University, Nigeria, 1962-65; University Lecturer and Fellow, St Antony's College, Oxford, 1967-92, Emeritus Fellow, 1992-, Director, Foreign Service Programme, Oxford University, 1986-90; Associate Professor, Stanford University (Oxford Campus), 1992-99; Associate Editor, New Dictionary of National Biography, 1996-2005. Publications: Barth's Travels in Nigeria, 1962; Crisis and Conflict in Nigeria, 1971; A Biographical Dictionary of the British Colonial Service, 1939-66, 1991; On Crown Service, 1999; Britain's Imperial Administrators, 2000; The British Intellectual Engagement with Africa in the 20th Century (co-editor), 2000; Glimpses of Empire, 2001; . Contributions to: Numerous reference books and scholarly journals. Honours: Member of the Order of the British Empire, 1963; Hans Wolff Memorial Lecturer, 1973; Fellow, Royal Historical Society, 1985; Festschrift, 1993; Leverhulme Emeritus Fellowship, 1993; Companion of the Order of St Michael and St George, 2001. Memberships: Royal African Society; International African Institute; Britain – Nigeria Association, Council Member, 1985-; African Studies Association of UK, President, 1988-90; Vice President, Royal African Society, 1992-. Address: c/o St Antony's College, Oxford OX2 6JF, England.

**KIRKHOPE Timothy John Robert,** b. 29 April 1945, Newcastle upon Tyne, England. Solicitor. m. Caroline Maling, 4 sons. Education: Law Society College of Law, Guildford, Surrey. Appointments: Qualified as Solicitor, 1973; Partner, Wilkinson Maughan, now Eversheds, Newcastle upon Tyne, 1977-87; Conservative, Member of Parliament, Leeds North East, 1987-97; Government Whip, 1990-95; Vice Chamberlain to HM the Queen, 1995; Under Secretary of State, Home Office, 1995-97; Business Consultant, 1997-; Member of European Parliament, Yorkshire and the Humber, 1999-; Spokesman on Citizens Rights, Justice and Home Affairs, 1999-; Chief Whip, Conservative Delegation, 1999-2001; Member, Future of Europe Convention, 2002-. Memberships: Fountain Society; Northern Counties Club; Dunstanburgh Castle Golf Club; Newcastle Aero Club, private pilot. Address: c/o ASP 14E, 246 European Parliament, Rue Wiertz, B-1047 Brussels, Belgium. E-mail: tkirkhope@europarl.eu.int

**KIRSZENSTEIN-SZEWINSKA Irena,** b. 24 May 1946, Leningrad, Russia. Athlete. m. 2 sons. Education: Warsaw University. Appointments: Athlete, 1961-80 (100m, 200m, long jump, 4 x 100m relay, 4 x 400m relay); Took part in Olympic Games, Tokyo, 1964, Munich, 1972; 10 times world record holder for 100m, 200m, 400m; President, Polish Women's Sport Association, 1994-, Polish Athletic Association, 1997-; Vice President, Polish Olympic Committee, 1988, Polish Olympians Association, 1993, World Olympians Association, 1995-; Member, Council European Athletic Association, 1995-, Women's Committee, International Association of Athletics' Federation, International Olympic Committee, 1998-, President, Irena Szewinska Foundation-Vita-Aktiva, 1998, IOC Coordination Committee, Athens, 2004-. Honours include: Gold Cross of Merit, 1964; Officer Cross, Order of Polonia Restituta, 1968; Commander's Cross, Order of Polonia Restituta, 1972, with Star, 1999; Order of Banner of Labour, 2nd class, 1976. Address: Polish Athletic Association, ul Ceglowska 68/70, 01-809 Warsaw, Poland.

**KISA Jack Jacob,** b. 12 June 1937, Maragoli, Kenya. Economist. m. Priscilla Wesa, 3 daughters. Education: BSc (Hons), Economics, University of London, England, 1964; Diploma, International Development, York University, Toronto, Canada, 1969; MPA, Economic Development, Harvard University, USA, 1971. Appointments: Senior Economist, Principal Economist,

Ministry of Finance and Planning, Kenya Government; Director, World Employment Programme in Africa, UN; Economist, Senior Economist, The World Bank. Publications: Numerous publications in professional journals. Honours: Shell BP Prize for Best Economics Student; Who's Who in the World, 1998, 2000-01, 2002. Memberships: American Economic Association; Karen Country Club. Address: 15 Ngong View Rise, Karen, PO Box 24204, Nairobi 00502, Kenya.

**KISLIK Vladimir,** b. 1 February 1935, Kislovodsk, USSR. Chemist; Researcher; Consultant. m. Bella Gulko, 1 son. Education: MSc, Institute of Rare Metals, Moscow, 1958; PhD, Institute of Radioactive Metals, Moscow, 1965; Professor, The Hebrew University of Jerusalem, Israel, 1998. Appointments: Engineer, Researcher, Nuclear Industry, Ural, USSR, 1958-66; Lecturer, Physical Engineering Institute, Ural, 1961-64; Consultant, Plutonium Production Plant, Ural, 1962-64; Head, R&D Department, Isotope Institute, Kiev, USSR, 1966-68; Head, R&D Group, Institute of Nuclear Energy, Academy of Science, Kiev, USSR, 1968-73; Consultant, Missiles Enterprises, Moscow, 1970-73; Activist Underground Jewish Movement, Kiev, 1974-81, Moscow, 1984-89; Prisoner of Zion, Gulag Prison Camp, Ukraine, 1981-84; Researcher, R&D Company, Jerusalem, Israel, 1989-91; Senior Researcher, Associate Professor, The Hebrew University of Jerusalem, Israel, 1991-2001. Publications: Author: Plutonium Chemistry and Production Technology (prizewinning book), 1962; Contributor of more than 70 articles to professional journals. Honours: Prizes for New Technology, Ministry of Nuclear Energy, Moscow, 1964, 1966; Ministry of the Chemical Industry, Kiev, 1968; Missile Industry, Moscow, 1971. Memberships: AAAS; New York Academy of Science; Israel Chemical Society; European Membrane Society. Address: The Hebrew University of Jerusalem, Campus Givat Ram, 91904 Jerusalem, Israel. E-mail: vkislik@vms.huji.ac.il

**KISNISCI Reha S,** b. 11 March 1961, Ankara, Turkey. Oral/Maxillofacial Surgeon. m. Sibel, 1 daughter. Education: DDS, 1984, PhD, 1987, Ankara University, Turkey; Fellowship, Southwestern Medical Center, Texas, USA, 1985. Appointments: Resident, Oral/Maxillofacial Surgery, Ankara University, 1984-88; Registrar, Department of Oral/Maxillofacial Surgery, Edinburgh University, Scotland, 1988-89; Chief Resident, 1989-90, Professor in Oral/Maxillofacial Surgery, 1990-, Ankara University; Visiting Professorships: Royal London Hospital, Walton-Aintree Hospital, Manchester Royal Infirmary. Publications: Over 60 scientific articles; Over 80 scientific presentations; Over 30 invited speeches and keynote lectures. Honours: Several international and national prizes; Merit Award, International Foundation of Cleft Lip and Palate. Memberships: Turkish Association of Oral/Maxillofacial Surgery; American Association of Oral/Maxillofacial Surgery; American College of Oral/Maxillofacial Surgery; International Association of Oral/Maxillofacial Surgery; International College of Maxillofacial Surgery; International Cleft Palate. Address: Department of Oral/Maxillofacial Surgery, Faculty of Dentistry, Ankara University; Konya Yolu Ozeri, 06500, Ankara, Turkey. E-mail: kisnisci@tr.net

**KISSANE Sharon Florence,** b. 2 July 1940, Chicago, Illinois, USA. Writer; Educator. m. James Q Kissane, dec, 2 July 1966, 2 daughters. Education: BA, English and Speech, DePaul University, 1962; MA, Communications, Northwestern University, Evanston, Illinois, 1963; PhD, English Education, Loyola University's School of Education, Chicago, 1970. Appointments: Technical Writer, Editor, Commerce Clearing House, Chicago, 1962-63; Night Editor, Daily Herald newspapers, Des Plaines and Park Ridge Editions, 1964-66;

President, Kissane Communications Ltd, 1979-; Columnist, Daily Herald, Barrington and Palatine Editions, 1982-; Business and Financial Correspondent, Chicago Tribune, 1983-85; Fiction Instructor, Harper College, Palatine, Illinois, 1985-88. Publications: Career Success for People with Physical Disabilities, 1966; Polish Biographical Dictionary (co-author), 1993; What is Child Abuse?, 1994; Gang Awareness, 1995; Autobiography of Paul "Mousie" Garner: A Broadway Stooge, 1999. Contributions to: Journals and magazines. Memberships: Founding Member, Barrington Area Arts Council; Founder, Creative Writing Sub-Group; Member, Writer's Guild of America; Member, Northwestern University's Entertainment Alliance; Council on Exceptional Children; Kappa Gamma Pi; Phi Kappa Delta. Address: 15 Turning Shores, South Barrington, IL 60010, USA.

**KITANO Hirohisa**, b. 28 January 1931, Toyama, Japan. Tax Law Educator. m. Hachie Aoyama, 3 sons. Education: LLB, Ritsumeikan University, Kyoto, Japan, 1955; LLM, Waseda University, Tokyo, 1962; LLD, Ritsumeikan University, 1974. Appointments: Staff, Bureau of Tax, Ministry of Finance, Tokyo, 1955-60; Lecturer, University of Toyama, 1962-89; Lecturer University of Tokyo, 1963-64, 1977-79; Assistant Professor, 1964-66, Associate Professor, 1966-71, Professor, 1971-2001, Professor Emeritus, 2001-, Nihon University, Tokyo; Chief, Nihon University Comparative Law Institute, 1996-98, President, Nihon University Law Library, 1998-99; Visiting Scholar, University of California, Berkeley, 1975-76. Publications: Structures of Modern Tax Law, 1972; Rights of Taxpayers, 1981; Japanese Constitution and Public Finance 1983; Taxpayers Fundamental Rights, 1991; Theory of Business Tax Law, 1994; Japanese General Consumption Tax, 1996; Study of Tax Professional, 1997; Fundamental Theory of Science of Tax Law, 2003. Honours: Onoazusa Prize, Waseda University, 1962; Nihon University Award, 1977, 1995; Prize, Japan Association of Tax Consultants, 1973, 1977; Honorary Professor, Southwest University of Political Science and Law, China, 2000. Memberships: President, Japan Taxpayers Association, 1977-; Director, Japan Civil Liberties Union, 1978-2002; Tokyo Bar Association, 1981-; President, Japan Association of Public Financial Law, 1991-2000; President, Japan Democratic Lawyers Association, 1993-; President, Japan Association of Science of Taxation, 1995-; Science Council of Japan, 1994-2003; Vice-president, Japan Lawyers International Solidarity Association, 1995-. Address: 5-9-25 Kitamachi, Kokubunji, Tokyo 1850001, Japan.

**KITE Thomas O Jr**, b. 9 December 1949, Austin, Texas, USA. Golfer. m. Christy Kite, 2 sons, 1 daughter. Appointments: Won Walker Cup, 1971; Turned Professional, 1972; Won Ryder Cup, 1979, 1981, 1983, 1985, 1987, 1989, 1993, European Open, 1980, US Open, Pebble Beach, CA, 1992; LA Open, 1993; 10 US PGA Wins; Appointed Captain, US Team for 1997 Ryder Cup, Valderrama, Spain; Joined Sr PGA Tour 2000; Numerous wins including The Countryside Tradition, 2000; MasterCard Championship, 2002; Spokesman for Chrysler Jr Golf Scholarship Programme. Address: c/o PGA Tour, 112 Tpc Boulevard, Ponte Vedra Beach, FL 32082, USA.

**KITIS Eliza**, b. 27 February 1946, Thessaloniki. Professor; Linguistics. m. George Kitis, 2 sons. Education: MA, Theoretical Linguistics, University of Essex, England, 1975; PhD, Philosophy of Language, University of Warwick, England, 1982. Appointments: Lecturing at Department of English, Aristotle University, Thessaloniki, Greece, 1981-. Publications: Names of periodicals, Journal of Pragmatics, 1987, 1997, 1999; Word and Image, 1997; Pragmatics and Cognition, 2000, many others. Honours: Various studentships, Department of Education

and Science, England; Major 3 year studentship, 1976. Memberships: LAGB, IASS, AIMAV, ESSE, HASE, ICLA; IPrA. Address: Department of English, Aristotle University, Thessaloniki 54124, Greece. E-mail: ekitis@enl.auth.gr

**KITT Eartha Mae**, b. 26 January 1928, South Carolina, USA. Actress; Singer. m. William MacDonald, 1960, divorced, 1 daughter. Career: Soloist, Katherine Graham Dance Group, 1948; Night Club Singer, 1949-; Theatre Work includes: Dr Faustus, Paris, 1951; New Faces, 1952; Timbuktu, 1978; Blues in the Night, 1985; The Wizard of Oz, 1998; The Wild Party, 2000; Films include: New Faces, 1953; Accused, 1957; Anna Lucasta, 1958; Synanon, 1965; Up the Chastity Belt, 1971; Boomerang, 1991; Fatal Instinct, 1993; Numerous TV appearances. Publications: Thursday's Child, 1956; A Tart is Not a Sweet, Alone with Me, 1976; I'm Still Here, 1990; Confessions of a Sex Kitten, 1991. Publications: Thursday's Child, 1956; A Tart is Not a Sweet, Alone with Me, 1976; I'm Still Here, 1990; Confessions of a Sex Kitten, 1991; Down to Earth (jointly), 2000; How to Rejuvenate: It's Not Too Late (jointly), 2000. Honour: National Association of Negro Musicians Woman of the Year, 1968. Address: c/o Eartha Kitt Productions, Flat 37, 888 7th Avenue, New York, NY 10106, USA.

**KITTLEMAN Martha Adrienne**, b. 31 December 1936, Houston, Texas, USA. Caterer; Decorator; Florist. m. Edmund Taylor Kittleman, 3 sons, 2 daughters. Education: BA, University of Mississippi; 2 years, University of Tulsa; UNC; Silver Jubilee, Oxford University, England, 1977; Correspondence degrees, Floristry, Interior Decorating, Antiques. Appointments: Owner, Chef, Adrienne's Tea Room, Bartlesville, Oklahoma, 1979; Head Cook, Bluestem Girl Scout Council, Bartlesville, 1993; Head Cook, Washington/Nowata Counties Community Action Fund Inc (WNCCAF), Dewey, Oklahoma, 1993; Supervisor, Aftercare Program, St John School, Bartlesville, 1994-95; Gourmet Cook, International Mozart Festival, Bartlesville, 1998; Sampler, Auntie Anne's Pretzels, Bartlesville, 1998; Director Associate of RBC; Abundant Health Associates, Independent Member of RBC. Honours: Advisory Council, IBC; Nominee, Woman of the Year, IBC; Member, Society of Descendants of Knights of the Most Noble Order of the Garter; Listed in biographical dictionaries. Memberships: Bartlesville Choral Society; Eucharistic Minister; Magna Carta Dames; Plantagenet Society; Delta Delta Delta Sorority. Address: 110 Fleetwood Place, Bartlesville, OK 74006, USA. E-mail: aewkm7p8@aol.com

**KIVELÄ Sirkka-Liisa**, b. 14 January 1947, Temmes, Finland. Professor. m. Mauri Akkanen. Education: Medical Doctor, 1971; Doctor of Philosophy, 1983; Associate professor in Family Medicine, 1984; Specialist in Family Medicine, 1976; Specialist in Geriatrics, 1985. Appointments: Chief Physician, Posio Health Centre, 1971-80; Senior Lecturer in Geriatrics, Tampere University, 1980-88; Professor in Public Health, Oulu University, 1988-90; Professor in Family Medicine, Oulu University, 1990-2000; Professor in Family Medicine, Turku University, 2000-. Publications: Over 300 scientific articles in national and international journals on depression, falls, abuse, coronary heart disease, chronic pulmonary diseases in old age; 40 publications for medical education; 2 books. Honours: Eeva Jalavisto Prize, 1996; Sv Aa og Magda Friederichens Prize, 1999. Membership: International Association of Psychogeriatrics. Address: University of Turku, Department of Family Medicine, Lemminkaisenkatu 1, 20014 University of Turku, Finland. Website: www.med.utu.fi/yleislaak/kivela.html

**KIWERSKI Jerzy Edward**, b. 24 June 1937, Warsaw, Poland. Physician. m. Szymczak Dorota, 1 son, 3 daughters.

Education: Physician, 1963; Doctor of Medical Sciences, 1971; Habilitation, 1975; Professor of Medicine, 1984. Appointments: Head and Chairman, Rehabilitation Clinic, Warsaw Medical University, 1982-; Regional Consultant in Rehabilitation, 1981-2002; National Consultant in Rehabilitation, 2002-; Vice President, 1990, President, 1999-, Committee of Rehabilitation, Polish Academy of Sciences; Director, Metropolitan Rehabilitation Center, 1991-98; President, Polish Society of Rehabilitation, 1992-99; Honorary Member, Polish Society of Rehabilitation, 2002-; New York Academy of Sciences, 1993; Vice-President, Polish Society of Biomechanics, 1994-2000. Publications: 17 handbooks; Over 530 articles in national and international periodicals; Over 340 lecture and congress papers. Honours: Ministry of Health Awards; President of Warsaw Award, National Orders; Outstanding Man of 21st Century, ABI; 2000 Outstanding Intellectuals of the 20th Century, IBC; Man of the Year 2001, 2004 ABI; One of the Genius Elite, ABI, 2004; Listed in several biographical publications. Memberships: International Medical Society of Paraplegia; European Spine Society; International Rehabilitation Medical Association; European Board of Physical Medicine and Rehabilitation; The World Federation for Neurorehabilitation. Address: Chyliczki, Orchidei 4, 05-500 Piaseczno, Poland.

**KIZAWA Makoto,** b. 18 April 1925, Kiryu, Japan. Former University Professor. m. Yukiko Nishi, 21 January 1951, 2 sons, Education: BA, Dept of EE, University of Tokyo, 1948; DEng, University of Tokyo, 1969. Appointments: Electrotechnical Laboratory, 1948-70; Professor, Osaka University, 1970-80; Professor, Vice-President, 1983-87, University of Library and Information Science. Publications: Digital Magnetic Recording, 1979; A Treatise of Data in Science and Technology, in Japanese, 1983; Co-Editor, Dictionary of Terms in Computer Technology, in Japanese, 1973. Honours: Niwa Prize, Japan Information Centre of Science and Technology, 1969; Standardisation Award, Ministry of International Trade and Industry, Japan, 1989; Decorated with the Third Order of the Sacred Treasure, 2002. Memberships: ICSU/CODATA Task Group on Computer Use, 1967-76; Secretary, ICSU/CODATA Task Group on Accessibility and Dissemination of Data, 1972-80; Member, CODATA Nomination Committee, 1986-98. Address: 3-13-6 Hachimanyama, Setagaya-ku, Tokyo, 156-0056, Japan.

**KLEES Pierre,** b. 20 June 1933, Brussels, Belgium. Company Director. m. Marianne Delange, 2 sons, 1 daughter. Education: Degree of Mechanical and Electrical Civil Engineer, Brussels University, 1956; Advanced Management, Westinghouse Learning Corporation, USA, 1960. Appointments: General Manager, 1986-87, Director General Manager, 1987-89, ACEC; Director General Manager and Vice-Chairman of the Management Committee, Union Minière, 1989-92; Managing Director, 1993-2003, Executive Chairman, 2003-2004, BIAC; Currently: Director of Concours Musical International Reine Elisabeth; Director, European Confederation of Directors Associations; Chairman, Belgian Association of Directors; Director, Airport Council International Fund; Director of Proviron; Director of MCM (Metaal Constructies/Constructions Métalliques; Director of Alstrom ACEC ENERGIE; Director of Trasys S.A.; Vice-Chairman, Commission Energie 2003; Chairman of the Belgian Post; Chairman of the Vinçotte Group; Academic appointments: Chairman: Comité de l'Académie pour les Applications de la Science, Royal Belgian Academy Council for Applied Sciences, Impact Cooremans; Visiting Professor, Université de Mons-Hainaut; Member: Conseil Stratégique de l'Université Libre de Bruxelles (ULB), Schumpeter Group (Group gathering of entrepreneurs), ULB, Conseil Scientifique de la Chaire de l'Ethique des Affaires, ULB. Publications: Author of over 120 reports on subjects including: Technical

and economic aspects of nuclear power stations and gas turbine power stations, on the potential development of alternative energy sources, on the sustainable development of transports, on the management, security and environmental protection of airports. Honours: Honorary Chairman and Managing Director, Brussels International Airport Company; Honorary Chairman, Alcatel-Etca; Honorary Professor, Université Libre de Brussels; Honorary Chairman, Société Royale Belge des Ingénieurs et des Industriels; Expert for the European Commission DG-IV Airport Competition, 1995; Man of the Year 1995, Aviation Press Club; Nominated Manager of the Year 1998, Trends Tendences; Commandeur de l'Ordre de Leopold; Commandeur de l'Ordre de Leopold II. Memberships: ASME; New York Academy of Science, Fondation Tolson D'Or; American Nuclear Society. Address: 120 rue Dodonée, 1180 Brussels, Belgium. E-mail: pklees@aib-vincotte.be

**KLEIN Calvin Richard,** b. 19 November 1942, New York, USA. Fashion Designer. m. (1) Jayne Centre, 1964, 1 daughter, (2) Kelly Rector, 1986. Education: Fashion Institute of Technology, New York. Appointments: Own Fashion Business, 1968; President, Designer, Calvin Klein Ltd, 1969-; Consultant, Fashion Institute of Technology, 1975-. Honours: Coty Award, 1973, 1974, 1975; Coty Hall of Fame; FIT President's Award, Outstanding Design Council of Fashion Designers of America. Memberships: Council of Fashion Designers. Address: Calvin Klein Industries Inc, 205 West 39th Street, NY 10018, USA.

**KLEMBARA Jozef,** b. 5 October 1953, Martin, Slovakia. Vertebrate Paleontologist. Education: Department of Paleontology, 1977, PhD, 1987, Faculty of National Science, Charles University, Prague. Appointments: Head of Division of Morphology of Vertebrates, 1991-93, Head of Division of Ecology and Evol Morphology of Vertebrates, 1994-96, Department of Ecology, Faculty of National Science, Comenius University; Research Worker, 1995-. Publications: Numerous scientific articles for professional journals. Memberships: Society of Vertebrate Paleontology; International Society of Vertebrate Morphology; Slovak Zoological Society. Address: Comenius University in Bratislava, Faculty of Natural Sciences, Department of Ecology, Mlynská dolina, 842 15 Bratislava, Slovak Republic. E-mail: klembara@fns.uniba.sk

**KLEMP Harold,** b. USA. Ministry Writer; Lecturer. Education: Colleges in Milwaukee, Fort Wayne, Indiana. Appointments: US Air Force; Radio Intercept Operator, Goodfellow AFB, Texas. Publications: The Wind of Change; Soul Travelers of the Far Country; Child in the Wilderness; The Living Word, Books 1 and 2; The Book of ECK Parables, vols 1-4; The Spiritual Exercises of ECK; Ask the Master, Books 1 and 2; The Dream Master; We Come as Eagles; The Drumbeat of Time; The Slow Burning Love of God; The Secret of Love; Our Spiritual Wake-Up Calls; A Modern Prophet Answers Your Questions About Life; The Art of Spiritual Dreaming, 1999; Autobiography of a Modern Prophet, 2000; How to Survive Spiritually in Our Times, 2001; The Spiritual Laws of Life, 2002; Past Lives, Dreams and Soul Travel, 2003; The Language of Soul, 2003; Your Road Map to the ECK Teachings: ECKANKAR Study Guide, 2 vols, 2003. Address: c/o Eckankar, PO Box 27300, Minneapolis, MN 55427, USA.

**KLETZ Trevor Asher,** b. 23 October 1922, Darlington, England. Chemical Engineer. m. Denise, deceased, 2 sons. Education: BSc, Chemistry, Liverpool University, 1941-44; DSc, Chemical Engineering, Loughborough University, 1986. Appointments: Various Research, Production and Safety appointments, ICI Ltd, 1944-82; Professor, Department of Chemical Engineering, 1978-86, Senior Visiting Research

Fellow, 1986-2000, Visiting Professor, 2000-, Loughborough University; Adjunct Professor, Texas A&M University, 2003-. Address: 64 Twining Brook Road, Cheadle Hulme, Cheadle, Cheshire SK8 5RJ, England. E-mail: t.kletz@lboro.ac.uk

**KLEVER Paul, b.** Germany. Entrepreneur; Scientist; Educator. Education: Master of Science in Mechanical Engineering (MEng), University of Applied Sciences, Cologne, Germany; Master of Science in Chemical Engineering (MSc), Technical University of Berlin, Germany; Doctor of Science in Chemistry (DSc), University of North London, England; Doctor of Science in Chemistry (Dr), Vasile Goldis Western University, Arad, Romania; Master of Business Administration in Economics (MBA), Trinity College & University, Texas, USA; Doctor of Business Administration (DBA), Universidad Empresarial de Costa Rica, San Jose, Costa Rica; Doctor in Economics (Dr), Moscow State University, Moscow, Russia; Numerous training and business courses. Appointments: Managing Director,, K + K Publishing Group, Bonn, Germany; Sales Manager Computer Systems, Control Data GmbH, Frankfurt and Hamburg, Germany; Sales Manager Computer Systems, Computervision GmbH, Hamburg and Munich, Germany; Director Marketing and Key Account Sales Manager, McDonnel Douglas Information Systems Group, Frankfurt and London; Managing Director, Data Business Partner GmbH, Dusseldorf and Frankfurt, Germany; Researcher and Lecturer, University of Essen, and Technical University of Dortmund, Germany; Director & CEO, Lexington Asset Trust & Holdings Corp, Palm Beach and New York, USA and London, UK; Visiting Professor, Vasile Goldis Western University, Arad, Romania; Vice-Rector and Honorary Professor, Albert Schweitzer International University, Geneva, Madrid and New York; Official Representative and Counsellor to the United Nations Geneva, International Commission on Distance Education (CODE), Geneva, Switzerland and Madrid, Spain; Senior Professor and Dean, Universidad Empresarial de San Jose, Costa Rica; Counsellor and Advisory in Trans American European Businesses over 15 years. Publications: Numerous articles, research papers and technical journals; Presented numerous papers in his areas of expertise. Honours: Honorary PhD in Business Economics, University at Jefferson City, Mississippi, USA; Honorary PhD in Business Economics, Harvard University, Massachusetts, USA; Honorary PhD in Business Economics, Harvard University. Massachusetts, USA; Honorary PhD, St Thomas-a-Becket University, Canterbury, England; Netaji Subhash Chandra Bose National Award for Excellence, UNESCO, Nagpur, India; Kentucky Colonel, awarded by the Governor of the State of Kentucky, Frankfort, Kentucky, USA; Meritorious Service Medal awarded by the United States Army (USAVR), Los Angeles, California, USA. Memberships include: Chamber of Commerce, Boca Raton, Florida, USA; Knight Grand Cross, Sovereign Order of the Knights of Justice, Malta and UK; Knight Commander, Order of Saint Constantine the Great, USA; Royal Yachting Association and Coastal Skipper, England; Grand Commander, World Order of Science, Education and Culture, Belgium and England; Counsel Project Manager, Turbon Tunzini Klimatechnik, Berlin and Cologne, Germany; Researcher and Lecturer, University of Essen, and Technical University of Dortmund, Germany; Counsellor, London Diplomatic Academy, London, England; Honorary Life Member, Albert Schweitzer International Society, Geneva, Madrid, New York; Honorary Life Member, Jagruthi Kiran Foundation, Nagpur, India; Fellow, The Augustan Society, California, USA; Membre, Chambre Européenne Experts (CEE) Commission Parlement Européenne, Brussels - Paris - Rome. Address: London, England. E-mail: euroclass@gmx.net

**KLINE Kevin Delaney, b.** 24 October 1947, St Louis, USA. Actor. m. Phoebe Cates, 1989, 1 son, 1 daughter. Education:

Indiana University; Julliard School of Drama. Appointments: Founding Member, The Acting Co, NY, 1972-76. Creative Works: Films include: Sophie's Choice; Pirates of Penzance; The Big Chill, 1983; Silverado, 1985; Violets Are Blue, 1985; Cry Freedom, 1987; A Fish Called Wanda, 1988; January Man, 1989; I Love You to Death, 1989; Soapdish, 1991; Grand Canyon, 1991; Consenting Adults, 1992; Chaplin, 1992; Dave, 1993; Princess Caraboo, 1994; Paris Match, 1995; French Kiss, 1995; Fierce Creatures, 1996; The Ice Storm, 1997; In and Out, 1997; A Midsummer Night's Dream, 1999; Wild Wild West, 1999; The Anniversary Party, 2001; Life as a House, 2001; Orange County, 2002; The Emperor's Club, 2002; The Hunchback of Notre Dame II (voice), 2002; De-Lovely, 2004; Theatre includes: Numerous Broadway appearances in On the Twentieth Century, 1978; Pirates of Penzance, 1980; Arms and the Man, 1985; Several off-Broadway appearances including Richard III, 1983; Henry V, 1984; Hamlet (also director), 1986, 1990; Much Ado About Nothing, 1988; Measure for Measure, 1995; The Seagull, 2001. Honours include: Tony Award, 1978, 1980; Academy Award, Best Supporting Actor, 1989. Address: c/o William Morris Agency, 1325 Avenue of the Americas, New York, NY 10019, USA.

**KLINGER Thomas Scott, b.** 4 May 1955, Kalamazoo, Michigan, USA. Professor. 1 son, 1 daughter. Education: AA, Bradford College, 1974; BA, Macalester College, 1975; MA, 1979, PhD, 1984, University of South Florida. Appointments: Adjunct Assistant Professor, Saint Leo College, 1984-85; Assistant Professor, 1985-90, Associate Professor, 1990-96, Professor, 1996-, Bloomsburg University. Publications include: Numerous articles in scientific journals. Honours: Fellowship, University of South Florida, 1978-80; Honorable mention, Florida Academy of Sciences, 1980; Science Departmental Award, Bradford College; Midwest Newspapers Scholarship Prize; Mary C Scholarship Prize; Mary C Community Service Award; Antarctic Service Medal, 1999; Listed in numerous Who's Who and biographical publications. Memberships: Society for Integrative and Comparative Biology; American Microscopial Society; Sigma Xi; American Association for the Advancement of Science. Address: Department of Biology, Bloomsburg University, 900 East Second Street, Bloomsburg, PA 17815, USA. E-mail: tklinger@bloomu.edu

**KLINSMANN Jurgen, b.** 30 June 1964, Germany. Footballer. m. Debbie, 1995, 1 son. Appointments: Started career with Stuttgarter Kickers, before moving to Stuttgart, 1984-89; Member, Winning Team, World Cup, 1990, UEFA Cup with Inter Milan, 1991 and Bayern Munich, 1996; With Inter Milan, 1989-92; AS Monaco, 1992-94; Tottenham Hotspur, 1994-95, 1997-98, played for Bayern Munich, 1995-97, Sampdoria, 1997; International Ambassador for SOS Children's Villages in partnership with FIFA; Founder, children's care charity AGAPEDIA; Vice President, Soccer Solutions. Honour: Footballer of the Year, 1988, 1994; English Footballer of the Year, 1995. Address: Soccer Solutions LLC, 744 SW Regency Place, Portland, OR 97225, USA. Website: www.soccersolutions.com

**KLUGMANN Eugeniusz, b.** 22 November 1933, Starogard, Poland. Physicist; Assistant Professor; Researcher. m. Teresa Galaska, 1 son, 1 daughter. Education: MS, Physics, 1955; PhD, Physics, 1966. Appointments: Assistant, Department of Physics, Gdansk University, 1957-66; Senior Technologist, Technical University, Gdansk, 1966-69; Assistant Professor, 1969-; Visiting Reader, University of Nigeria, Nsukka, 1977-79; Visiting Professor, University of Sheffield, 1982, 1983, 1985. Publications: 54 papers in professional journals include: as co-author: Semiconducting diamond, 1998; Diamond semiconducting devices, 1999; Magnetic relaxation in CoPt alloy caused by short range ordering, 1999; Effect of the Martensitic Phase Transition on the Magnetic Properties of Pure Cobalt, 2000; Influence of Temperature on Conversion Efficiency of a Solar Module Working in PV/T Integrated System, 2000; Relationship between Structure and Internal Friction in CoPt and FePd Alloys, 2001; As author: Influence of ion implantation on permeability disaccommodation and magnetic losses in cobalt, 1994; Effects of radiation damage on core loss of conducting ferromagnetics, 1999; Internal friction in pure Co and Co Pt alloy during ordering, 2003. Honours: Gold Medal of Merit, 1980; Bachelors Medal, 1990; Medal, National Education Committee, 1998. Memberships: Fellow, Polish Physical Society; Member, New York Academy of Sciences, 1995-. Address: Gryglewskiego 21, 80-301 Gdansk, Poland.

**KLUTZOW Friedrich Wilhelm,** b. 6 August 1923, Bandoeng, Dutch East Indies. Neuropathologist. 1 son, 1 daughter. Education: MD, University of Utrecht, Netherlands, 1951. Appointments: Residency, Lawrence Memorial Hospital, 1954-56; Private Practice, Madison, Maine, 1956-59, Gillett, Wisconsin, 1959-68; Residency, Anatomic Pathology, DVA Medical Center, Madison, 1968-69, University of Wisconsin Medical School, 1969-71; Fellowship, Neuropathology, Armed Forces Institute of Pathology, Washington, DC, 1971-72; Staff, Neuropathologist, DVA Medical Center, Minneapolis, 1972-75; Chief, Pathology and Laboratory Medicine Service, DVA Medical Center, Brockton, Massachusetts, 1975-83, Wichita, Kansas, 1983-87; Chief of Staff, All Clinical Services, DVA Medical Center, Bath, New York, 1987-90; Consultant, Teacher, Neuropathology, DVA Medical Center, Bay Pines, Florida, 1991-; Consultant in Neuropathology, Minnesota Board of Medical Practice, 1999-; Retired Full Colonel US Army Reserve, 1979-85. Publications include: Incontinence Associated with Bilateral Putamen Lesions, 1989; The Autopsy: Its Role in the Evaluation of Patient Care, 1989; Neuropathology Manual: The Practical Approach, 1996. Honour: Outstanding Career Award, Department of Veterans Affairs, Washington DC, 1990. Memberships include: New York Academy of Sciences; College of American Pathologists; American Association of Neuropathologists; Medical Education Council, University of Rochester; International Society of Neuropathologists. Address: PO Box 3387, West Columbia, SC 29171-3387, USA.

**KLYUSOV Anatoly,** b. 2 July 1940, Jenisejsk, Russia. Chemistry Researcher. m. Lubov, 2 sons. Education: Degree, Engineering, Technical Institute, St Petersburg, 1963; PhD, Mendeleev Chemical and Technical Institute, Moscow, 1973; DSc, Mendeleev Chemical and Technical University, 1993; Professorial Degree, 1995. Appointments: Master Cement Plant, St Petersburg, 1963-64; Head of Laboratory, Industrial Institute, Tyumen, 1964-68; Oil and Gas Geological Institute, Tyumen, 1968-75; Scientific Research Institute Gas Industry, Tyumen, 1975-94; Head of Chair, Professor, Academy of Architecture and Civil Engineering, Tyumen, 1994-95; Head of Laboratory, All Russian Scientific Research Institute for Gas Technology, Moscow, 1995-. Publications: 1 monograph, 10 scientific reviews, 198 scientific articles and 43 patents in the field of Arctic oil and gas cements. Honours: Honoured Inventor of Russia, Presidium of the Supreme Soviet of RSFSR,1987; Russian State Prize Winner, 1989; Four State Awards; 10 silver medals of the Exhibition of National Economic Achievement. Memberships: Academician, President of the Regional Office, International Informatization Academy, 1994; New York Academy of Sciences, 1995; Fellow Cchem FRSC, 1998. Address: Brateevskaya st 16, Korp 6, KV 343, Moscow 115408, Russia.

**KNAPMAN Roger Maurice,** b. 20 February 1944, Crediton, Devon, England. Chartered Surveyor. m. Carolyn Eastman, 1 son, 1 daughter. Education: Royal Agricultural College, Cirencester, England. Appointments: Conservative Member of Parliament for Stroud, 1987-97; Parliamentary Private Secretary to the Minister of State for the Armed Forces, 1991-93; Junior Government Whip, 1995-96; Senior Government Whip and Lord Commissioner of the Treasury, 1996-97; UKIP Political Advisor, 2000-01, Leader, 2001-, UK Independence Party; UKIP MEP for South West of England, 2004-. Address: Coryton House, Coryton, Okehampton, Devon, EX20 4PA, England.

**KNECHT Robert Jean,** b. 20 September 1926, London, England. Professor of French History Emeritus. m. (1) Sonia Hodge, deceased 1984 (2) Maureen White, 28 August 1986. Education: BA, 1948, MA, 1953, King's College, London; D.Litt, Birmingham, 1984. Appointments: Assistant Lecturer, Modern History, 1956-59, Lecturer, Modern History, 1959-68, Senior Lecturer, Modern History, 1968-78, Reader in French History, 1978-85, Professor of French History, 1985-94, Emeritus Professor of French History and Honorary fellow of Institute for Advanced Research in the Humanities, 1998-, University of Birmingham. Publications: The Voyage of Sir Nicholas Carewe, 1959; Francis I and Absolute Monarchy, 1969; The Fronde, 1975; Francis I, 1982; French Renaissance Monarchy, 1984; The French Wars of Religion, 1989; Richelieu, 1991; Renaissance Warrior and Patron, 1994; The Rise and Fall of Renaissance France, 1996; Catherine de'Medici, 1998; Un Prince de la Renaissance: François Ier et son royaume, 1998; The French Civil Wars, 2000; The Valois, 2004. Honour: Chevalier dans l'Ordre des Palmes académiques, 2001. Memberships: Fellow, Royal Historical Society; Society of Renaissance Studies, chairman, 1989-92; Société de l'Histoire de France. Address: 79 Reddings Road, Moseley, Birmingham B13 8LP, England.

**KNIGHT Alanna,** b. South Shields, Tyne and Wear, England. Novelist; Biographer. m. Alexander Harrow Knight, 2 sons. Appointments: Founder, Chairman, Aberdeen Writers Workshop, 1967; Lecturer, Creative Writing, Workers Educational Association, and Andrews' University Summer School, 1971-75; Tutor, Arvon Foundation, 1982, 2005; Secretary, Society of Authors in Scotland, 1991-98. Publications: Legend of the Loch, 1969; October Witch, 1971; Castle Clodha, 1972; Lament for Lost Lovers, 1972; White Rose, 1974; A Stranger Came By, 1974; Passionate Kindness, 1974; A Drink for the Bridge, 1976; Black Duchess, 1980; Castle of Foxes, 1981; Colla's Children, 1982; Robert Louis Stevenson Treasury, 1985; The Clan, 1985; Robert Louis Stevenson in the South Seas, 1986; Estella, 1986; Enter Second Murderer, 1998; Deadly Beloved, 1989; Killing Cousins, 1990; A Quiet Death, 1991; To Kill a Queen, 1992; The Evil that Men Do, 1993; The Missing Duchess, 1994; Sweet Cheat Gone, 1993; Bright Ring of Words (with E S Warfel), 1994; This is Outward Angel, 1994; Inspector Faro and the Edinburgh Mysteries, 1994; The Bull Slayers, 1995; Inspector Faro's Casebook, 1996; Murder by Appointment, 1996, 2000; Angel Eyes, 1998; Coffin Lane Murders, 1998; The Royal Park Murder, 1999; Monster in the Loch, 1999; Dead Beckoning, 1999; The Inspector's Daughter, 2000; The Dagger in the Crown, 2001; Dangerous Pursuits, 2001; Close and Deadly, 2002; An Orkney Murder, 2003; The Gowrie Conspiracy, 2003; Ghost Walk, 2004; Faro and the Royals, 2005. Contributions to: Various publications. Honour: 1st Novel Award, Romantic Novelists Association, 1969; Honorary President Edinburgh Writers Club, 1996-. Memberships: Secretary, Society of Authors, Scotland, 1991-98; Scottish PEN; Committee of Crime Writers Association, 1992-95; Mystery Women; Romantic Novelists Association; Fellow, Royal Society of Antiquaries,

Scotland. Address: 24 March Hall Crescent, Edinburgh EH16 5HL, Scotland.

**KNIGHT Edith Joan,** b. 18 May 1932, Great Houghton, Barnsley, England. Retired Teacher; Singer; Poet. m. John Wyndham Knight, deceased. Education: Certificate in Education, Leeds University; RSA Diplomas in Shorthand, Typewriting Teaching, 1969; Qualifications in Music and Singing. Appointments: Secretarial Posts including Confidential Secretary, Barnsley British Co-operative Society, 1949-56; Head of Commercial Studies, 1969-87, Deputy Head of Middle School, 1973-76, Assistant to Head of Upper School, 1976-87, Wombwell High School; Solo singer for 63 years; Formerly, Oratorio Contralto Soloist, Joan Parkin; Currently singing in the Barnsley Circuit of the Methodist Church. Publications: Anthologies: Voices on the Wind, 1996; A Lasting Calm, 1997; The Secret of Twilight, 1998; Millennium Memories, 2000; Books including: Way Back Then, 1999; A Word of Peace, 2000; The Triplet Times, 2001; Sweet Memories, 2002; Rondeau Challenge, 2003; Love Hurts, 2004; Poetry in magazines including: Poems of the World; Retford Writers; Triumph Herald (hymn). Honour: Bronze Medallion, International Society of Poets' Washington Convention, 1997. Membership: Retford Writers; Fellow of the Faculty of Teachers of Commerce. Address: Great Houghton, Barnsley, South Yorkshire, England.

**KNIGHT Gregory,** b. 4 April 1949, Blaby, Leicestershire, England. Member of Parliament; Solicitor. Education: College of Law, London. Appointments: Member of Parliament for Derby North, 1983-97; Assistant Government Whip, 1989-90; Lord Commissioner of the Treasury, 1990-93; Government Deputy Chief Whip, 1993-96; Minister of State for Industry, Department of Trade and Industry, 1996-97; MP for East Yorkshire, 2001-; Shadow Deputy Leader, House of Commons, 2001-03; Shadow Minister for Culture, 2003; Shadow Minister for Railways and Aviation, 2003-05; Shadow Minister for Roads, 2005-. Publications: Westminster Words, 1988; Honourable Insults, 1990; Parliamentary Sauce, 1993; Right Honourable Insults, 1998. Honour: Privy Councillor, 1995. Memberships: Member of Conservative Party, 1966-; Member of Law Society, 1973; Member, Bridlington Conservative Club, 2001-. Address: House of Commons, Westminster, London SW1A 0AA, England. E-mail: secretary@gregknight.com

**KNIGHT Michael James,** b. 29 August 1939, London, England. Surgeon. m. Phyllis Mary, 1 son, 1 daughter. Education: MB BS (London), 1963; LRCP MRCS (Conjoint Board), 1963; FRCS (Royal College of Surgeons), 1967; MS, London, 1975. Appointments: Consultant Surgeon, St Georges Hospital, London, St James Hospital, London, Royal Masonic Hospital, London. Publications: Chapters and articles on gastroenterology, pancreatic and biliary diseases. Honours: Hunterian Professor, 1975; Member, Court of Examiners of the Royal College of Surgeons. Membership: President, Pancreatic Society of Great Britain and Ireland. Address: 1 St Aubyn's Avenue, Wimbledon, London SW19 7BL, England.

**KNIGHT (Sir) Peter,** b. 12 August 1947, Bedford, England. Professor. m. Christine Knight, 2 sons, 1 daughter. Education: BSc, 1968, DPhil, 1972, University of Sussex. Appointments: Research Associate, University of Rochester, USA, 1972-74; SRC Research Fellow, Sussex University, 1974-76; Jubilee Research Fellow, Royal Holloway College, 1976-78; SERC Advanced Fellow, 1978-83, Lecturer, 1983-87, Reader, 1987-88, Professor, 1988-, Head of Quantum Optics and Laser Science Group, 1992-2001, Head of Physics Department, 2001-, Acting Principal of the Faculty of Physical Sciences, 2004-05, Imperial

College, London. Publications: Over 400 scientific papers in international journals; 2 textbooks, Concepts of Quantum Optics, 1983; Introductory Quantum Optics, 2005. Honours: Fellow, Royal Society; Fellow, Institute of Physics; Fellow, Optical Society of America; Thomas Young Medal, Institute of Physics; Einstein Medal and Prize, Eastman Kodak Co; Parsons Medal, Royal Society and Institute of Physics; Elected Vice President, 2002, President Elect, 2003, President, 2004, Optical Society of America; Knight Bachelor, 2005. Memberships: Royal Society; Optical Society of America; Institute of Physics. E-mail: p.knight@imperial.ac.uk

**KNIGHT Peter Leonard,** b. 12 August 1947, Bedford, England. Educator. m. Christine, 2 sons, 1 daughter. Education: BSc, 1968, DPhil, 1972, University of Sussex. Appointments: Research Associate, University of Rochester, New York, USA, 1972-74; SRC Research Fellow, Sussex University, 1974-76; Jubilee Research Fellow, 1976-78, SERC Advanced Fellow, 1978, Royal Holloway College London; SERC Advanced Fellow, 1978-83, Lecturer, 1983-87, Reader, 1987-88, Professor, 1988-, Head of Physics Department, 2002-, Imperial College London; Chief Scientific Advisor, National Physical Laboratory, 2002-. Publications: Principles of Quantum Optics, 1983; Introductory Quantum Optics, 2004; Author of over 400 articles in scientific literature. Honours: Honorary Doctorates: INAOE Mexico, Slovak Academy of Sciences; Alexander von Humboldt Research Award, 1993; Einstein Medal and Prize for Laser Science, Society of Optical and Quantum Electronics, 1996; Parsons Medal Institute of Physics and Royal Society, 1997; European Physical Society Lecturer, 1998-99; Thomas Young Medal and Prize, Institute of Physics, 1999; President, Optical Society of America, 2004. Memberships: Fellow, Institute of Physics; Fellow, Optical Society of America; European Physical Society; The Royal Society; Mexican Academy of Sciences; Academia Europaea. Address: Blackett Laboratory, Imperial College London, London SW7 2BW, England.

**KNOBLER Robert,** b. 6 December 1945, Bolivia. Professor of Dermatology. Education: BA, 1967, BS, 1969, Columbia University; MD, University of Vienna, 1977. Appointments: Lecturer, Department of Dermatology, Columbia University, 1983-; Professor, Dermatology, University of Vienna Medical School, 1996-; Head, Photoimmunotherapy Center, Dermatology, Vienna; Chairman, EORTC Cutaneous Lymphoma Project Group, 2000-. Publications: Over 100 in professional medical journals. Honours: Unilever Award, 1981; Gold Medal, American Academy of Dermatology, 1992; Research Award, AESCA & Company, 1993. Memberships: New York Academy of Sciences; AAD; ILDS; SID; ESDR; EORTC; SIDLA. Address: Medical University of Vienna General Hospital, Department of Dermatology, Wahringerguertel 18-20, A-1090 Vienna, Austria.

**KNOPFLER Mark,** b. 12 August 1949, England. Guitarist; Songwriter. m. Lourdes Salomone, 1983. Education: Leeds University. Appointments: Former Journalist, Yorkshire Evening Post; Founder, Dire Straits, 1977, Guitarist; 1st Concert, 1977; Group has toured worldwide. Creative Works: Albums include: Making Movies; Brothers in Arms; On Every Street; Songs include: Romeo and Juliet; Money For Nothing; Calling Elvis; Toured with Eric Clapton and recorded with Chet Atkins; Founder, Notting Hillbillies. Honours include: Ivor Novello Award; Grammy Award. Address: c/o Damage Management, 16 Lambton Place, London W11 2SH, England.

**KNOWLES Colin George,** b. 11 April 1939, Southport, England. Retired. m. Rosalie Marion Lander, 3 daughters. Education: CEDEP, Fontainebleau France; MA, PhD, Trinity

College, Delaware, USA. Appointments: Company Secretary and Head of Public Affairs, Imperial Tobacco Ltd, 1960-80; Chairman, Griffin Associates, Ltd, UK, 1980-83; Director, TWS Public Relations (Pty) Ltd, Johannesburg, 1984; Chairman, Concept Communications (Pty) Ltd, Johannesburg, 1983-84; Director of Development and Public Affairs, University of Bophuthatswana, 1985-95; Chairman, Bophuthatswana Region Public Relations Institute of South Africa, 1988-91; Chairman, St John Ambulance Foundation, Bophutharswana, 1989-94; Member Chapter (Governing Body) Priory of St John for South Africa, 1992-99; Director, The Consumer Council of Bobhuthatswana, 1991-94; Director, Association for Business Sponsorship of the Arts, 1975-84, Chairman, 1975-80; Director, The Bristol Hippodrome Trust Ltd, 1977-81; Director, The Bath Archaeological Trust Ltd, 1978-81; Director, The Palladian Trust Ltd, 1978-81; Memberships: Chancellor of the Duchy of Lancaster's Committee of Honour on Business and the Arts, 1980-81; Freeman City of London, 1974; Liveryman, Worshipful Company of Tobacco Pipe Makers and Tobacco Blenders, London, 1973; MInstM; MIPR; FIMgt; FRSA; FPRI (SA); APR; Associate Member, Association of Arbitrators of South Africa (AAArb); OStJ, 1977, CStJ, 1991; KStJ, 1995; Carlton Club; MCC. Address: 15 Standen Park House, Lancaster LA1 3FF, England. E-mail: cgk@waitrose.com

**KNOWLES Evelyn,** b. 14 April 1931, London, England. City Councillor. 1 son, 2 daughters. Education: BA Honours, Psychology, Ealing College of Higher Education. Appointments: President, Cambridge MS Society; Chair, Cambridge Citizens Advice Bureau; Cambridge City Councillor, 1986-2002; Director, St Lukes Community Centre, 1989-98; Mayor of Cambridge, 2000-01; Non-executive Director, Cambridge Primary Care Trust, 1998-2005. Memberships: Fellow, Royal Society of Arts; Member, Liberal Democrat Party; Chair, Liberal Democrat Council Group; Member, Fawcett Society; Friends of the Earth. Address: Carisbrooke, 1b Madeira Road, Ventnor, PO38 1QP, England.

**KNOWLING Michael John,** b. 26 April 1953, Edinburgh, Scotland. Journalist; Writer. Education: Master of Arts (honours), History and Geography, University of Glasgow, 1971-75; Master of Letters in History, University of New England, Armidale, New South Wales, Australia, 1987. Appointments: Journalist and Editor, Northern Newspapers Pty Ltd, Armidale, New South Wales, 1980-88; Media Relations Co-ordinator, The University of New England, 1989; Editor, The University of New England Gazette, 1990-92; Principal, Drummond College, The University of New England, 1990-96; Editor, The Ipswich Advertiser, Ipswich, Queensland, 1996-99; Sub-Editor, Gold Coast Bulletin, Gold Coast, Queensland, 1999-2000; Sub-Editor, Capricornia Newspapers Pty Ltd, Rockhampton, Queensland, 2000-2004; Sub-Editor, The Cairns Post, Cairns, Queensland, 2005-. Publications: Collins Concise Encyclopaedia (assistant editor), 1977; Race Relations in Australia: A History (with A T Yarwood), 1982; The University of New England Gazette (editor), 1990-92. Honours: Association of Rhodes Scholars in Australia Scholarship, 1977; Editor Most Improved Newspaper (Free), 1997, Editor Best Newspaper (Free) and Award for Individual Journalistic Excellence, 1998, Award for Feature Writing, 1999, Queensland Country Press Association; Finalist (Best Headlines), Queensland Media Awards, 2004. Memberships: Association of Rhodes Scholars in Australia; Media, Entertainment and Arts Alliance; Australian and New Zealand Communication Association. Address: PO Box 994, Yeppoon, Queensland 4703, Australia. E-mail: mike@cqinsight.com.au

**KNOX (Alexander John) Keith,** b. 27 November 1933, Belper, Derbyshire, England. Electronic Engineer (retired); Record Producer. m. Ingrid Zakrisson Knox, 1 son. Education: BSc, Physics and Maths, Southampton University, London; Brighton College of Advanced Technology; Course with Richard Goodman, Decision Mathematics for Management. Appointments: Electronic Engineer, with EMI, 1957-59, Brush Clevite Company, Hythe, Hampshire, UK, 1959-62; Redifon Ltd, Crawley, Sussex, UK, 1962-64; Amplivox Ltd, Wembley, Middlesex, UK, 1964-65, Transitron Electronic SA, Switzerland, 1965-67; Transitron Electronic Sweden AB, 1967-72; Freelance sound record producer, Caprice Records/Sonet Records/ WEA-Metronome Records (Stockholm), Storyville Records (Copenhagen), 1971-85; Manager for music group, "Sevda", 1971-74; Manager for music group "Music for Xaba", 1972-73; Marketing and liaison engineer, Sonab AB, Solna, Sweden, 1972-74; Support Engineer, Royal Institute of Technology (KTH), Stockholm, Sweden, 1975-98; English language copywriter for advertising agency, Andersson and Lembke AB, Sundbyberg, Sweden, 1974-75; Executive Producer, Silkheart Records, Stockholm, Sweden, 1986-. Publications: (biography) Jazz Amour Affair, 1986; Numerous articles for jazz publications and underground press. Address: Silkheart Records, Dalagatan 33, SE 11323 Stockholm, Sweden.

**KNOX David Laidlaw (Sir),** b. 30 May 1933, Lockerbie, Dumfriesshire, Scotland. Member of Parliament, retired. m. Margaret Eva Mackenzie, 2 stepsons, 1 deceased. Education: BSc Honours, Economics, London University. Appointments: Production Manager, printing industry, 1956-62; Internal Company Management Consultant, 1962-70; Parliamentary Adviser, Chartered Institute of Management Accountants, 1980-97; Member of European Legislation Select Committee, 1976-97; Member of Speakers Panel of Chairmen, 1983-97; Member of Parliament for Leek, 1970-83; Vice Chairman, Conservative Party, 1974-75; Member of Parliament for Staffordshire Moorlands, 1983-97; Chairman, London Union of Youth Clubs, 1998-99; Deputy Chairman, London Youth, 1999-. Publications: 4 pamphlets. Honours: Knighted, 1993. Memberships: Past member, Federation of Economic Development Authorities; Past member, Industry and Parliament Trust; Past Honorary Fellowship, Staffordshire University; Member, Conservative Party; Member, Conservative Group for Europe; Member, Tory Reform Group; Member, One World Trust. Address: The Mount, Alstonefield, Ashbourne, Derbyshire, DE6 2FS, England.

**KNOX-JOHNSTON, Sir Robin,** b. 17 March 1939, Putney, London, England. Master Mariner; Author. m. 6 January 1962, deceased 2003, 1 daughter. Education: Berkhamsted School; Master's Certificate, 1965. Career: First person to sail single-handed and non-stop around the world, 1968-69. Publications: A World of My Own, 1969; Sailing, 1974; Twilight of Sail, 1978; Last But Not Least, 1978; Seamanship, 1986; The BOC Challenge 1986-87, 1987; The Cape of Good Hope, 1989; The History of Yachting, 1990; The Columbus Venture, 1991; Sea Ice Rock (with Chris Bonington), 1992; Cape Horn, 1994; Beyond Jules Verne, 1995. Contributions to: Yachting World; Cruising World; Guardian. Honours: Knight Bachelor, 1995; Commander of the Order of the British Empire 1969; Honorary DSc, Maine Maritime Academy; Honorary Doctor of Technology, Nottingham Trent University, 1993. Memberships: Younger Brother, Trinity House; Honourable Company of Master Mariners; Royal Institute of Navigation; Council, RNLI. Address: St Francis Cottage, Torbryan, Newton Abbot, Devon TQ12 5UR, England.

**KNUDSEN Dagfinn Andreas,** b. 11 April 1942, Drevja, Norway. Metallurgist. m. Karin Nilssen, 1 daughter. Education:

Engineering Degree, Metallurgical Techniques, Trondheim Tekniske Skole, 1967. Appointments: Assistant Engineer, Årdal Verk, ÅSV, 1967-72; Project Engineer, Sunndal Verk, ÅSV, 1972-86; Process Engineer, Franzefoss Bruk, 1986; Service Engineer, Østlandsmeieriet, 1989; Service Engineer, Autodisplay AS, 1991. Publications: Articles in technical journals; Essay on sensational journalism, 1991; about industrial culture, employees management, company and loyalty; Essay on Norway's fishing industry. Address: Rådhusgata 29, N 8657 Mosjøen, Norway.

**KNUTSSON Henry Hoffding,** b. 4 August 1930, Copenhagen, Denmark. Structural Engineer. 1 son, 1 daughter. Education: Structural Engineer, 1954. Appointments: Chairman or Secretary, Code of Practise for Lightweight Concrete, 1965-84; Masonry, 1978-97; Safety of Structures and Load for Design, 1974-99. Secretary for CEN/TC 124, Timber Structures, 1989-96. Publications: 10 directions (in Danish) and several papers in professional journals. Address: Askevaenget 39, 2830 Virum, Denmark.

**KNYAZEV Sergey P,** b. 18 February 1956, Moscow, Russia. Biologist. 1 daughter. Education: Biologist, Department of Biology and Soil, Voronezh State University, Voronezh, 1978; Postgraduate Student, 1978-82, Candidate of Biological Science, PhD equivalent, 1983, USSR Academy of Sciences, Novosibirsk. Appointments: Scientific Researcher, Institute of Cytology and Genetics, USSR Academy of Sciences, Novosibirsk, 1982-87; Associate Professor, Department of Animal Genetics, Novosibirsk State Agrarian University, 1987-2001; Professor, 2001-; Visiting Scientist, Humboldt University, Berlin, Germany, 1995-96. Publications: More than 100 in journals in the field of animal genetics and evolution, genetic polymorphism and stress resistance, including: Russian Journal of Genetics, 1995,31,3, 1996,32,10, 1998,34,10, 1998,34,12, 1999,35,4, 1999,35,5, 2001,37,4, 2001,32,20, 2003,39,6; Books including: Morphology and Genetics of Hybrid Pigs, 1992; Genetics of Dog, 1999; Co-author, Animal Health and Production Compendium, 2001, 2003, 2004. Honours: Award, International Science Foundation and Russian Academy of Natural Sciences, 1993; Soros Associate Professor International Soros Scientific and Educational Programme Award, 1995, 1997, 1998, 1999, 2000, 2001; Man of the Year, ABI, 2000. Memberships: Active Member, New York Academy of Sciences; International Society on Animal Genetics; Russian Academy of Natural Sciences. Address: Leningradskaya 37, Novosibirsk 630008, Russia. E-mail: knyazev@nsau.edu.ru

**KOBASKO Nikolai Mykola Ivanovich,** b. 6 December 1934, Chornivka, Ukraine. Thermal Science Scientist. m. Olga Letiy, 3 sons. Education: Physicist, Chernovtsy State University, 1959; PhD, National Academy of Sciences, Ukraine, Kiev, 1969. Appointments: Physics Teacher, High School Letychev, 1959-60; Engineer, Machine Construction Plant, Kiev, 1960-62; Researcher, Head of Laboratory, Head of Research Group, Thermophysics Engineering Institute, NAS of Ukraine, 1962-99; Co-founder IQ Technologies Inc, USA, 1999-; Co-founder and President, Intensive Technologies Ltd, Kiev, Ukraine, 2000-. Publications: 6 books; Monograph, Steel Quenching in Liquid Media Under Pressure, 1980; Over 200 articles include: Practical Application of Intensive Quenching Technology for Steel Parts, 2000; Over 30 patents and inventor's Certificates include: Quenching Apparatus and method of hardening Steel Parts, 2000. Honours: Best Inventor's Certificate, Academy of Sciences of Ukraine; Certificates of Appreciation, ASM International, USA. Memberships: ASM International, USA; International Federation of Heat Treatment and Surface

Engineering. Address: 4938 Lindsey Lane, Cleveland, OH 44143-2930, USA.

**KOBAYASHI Nagao,** b. 21 January 1950, Nagano, Japan. Professor of Chemistry. m. Yayoi Enomoto, 2 daughters. Education: MTech, 1975; DSc, 1978; DPharm, 1986. Appointments: Technician, Pharmacy Institute, Tohoku University, 1978-83; Assistant Professor, Chemical Research Institute, Tohoku University, 1983-85; Assistant Professor, Pharmacy Institute, Tohoku University, 1986-95; Professor, Department of Chemistry, Graduate School of Science, Tohoku University, 1995-. Publications: Several articles in professional journals. Memberships: Chemical Society of Japan; Polymer Society of Japan; Japan Society of Co-ordination Chemistry, Society of Porphyrins and Phthalocyanines. Address: Department of Chemistry, Graduate School of Science, Tohoku University, Sendai 980-8578, Japan.

**KOCH-BRANDT Claudia,** b. 21 January 1952, Halle, Germany. Professor of Biochemistry. m. Hans Peter Brandt, 1 son, 1 daughter. Education: Graduate, Pharmaceutical Sciences, 1976, PhD, Biochemistry, 1980, Venia Legendi, 1985, University of Frankfurt. Appointments: Guest Investigator, G Blobel, Rockefeller University, New York, USA, 1977, 1978; DFG Fellow, EMBL Heidelberg, 1980-84; Staff Member, EMBL Heidelberg, 1984-85; Assistant Professor, University of Frankfurt, 1985-91; Professor, University of Mainz, 1991-. Publications: Over 40 articles in professional journals. Honours: Heinz Maier-Leibnitz Award, Minister for Science and Education, 1984; Research Grants, DFG, Ministry of Research and Technology, Fonds Chemistry Industry, 1985-. Memberships: German Society of Biological Chemistry; German Society of Cell Biology; German Society of Pharmacological Toxicology; German Pharmaceutical Sciences; American Association for the Advancement of Sciences; American Association of Cell Biology. Address: Institute of Biochemistry, Becherweg 30, 55099 Mainz, Germany.

**KOCHEVSKY Alexey Nikolayevich,** b. 18 December 1974, Sumy, Ukraine. Research Scientist. Education: MSc, Hydraulic Machines, Hydraulic Drive and Hydraulic and Pneumatic Automatics, 1996, PhD, Hydraulic and Pneumatic Machines, 2002, Sumy State University, Ukraine. Appointments: Junior Scientist, 1999-2001, Research Scientist, 2001-, Department of Applied Fluid Mechanics, Sumy State University, Ukraine. Publications: Numerical Investigation of Swirling Flow in Annular Diffusers with a Rotating Hub Installed at the Exit of Hydraulic Machines, 2001; Investigation of Swirling Flow in Diffusers Installed at the Exit of an Axial-Flow Pump, 2001. Honours: Listed in Who's Who publications and biographical dictionaries. Address: Sumy State University, Rimsky-Korsakov Str 2, Sumy, 40007, Ukraine.

**KOENIGSBERGER Helmut Georg,** b. 24 October 1918, Berlin, Germany. Historian. m. Dorothy Romano, 2 daughters. Education: BA, 1940, MA, 1944, PhD, 1949, Gonville and Caius College, Cambridge. Appointments: Royal Navy, 1944-45; Lecturer, Economic History, Queen's University, Belfast, 1948-51; Senior Lecturer, Economic History, Manchester University, 1951-60; Professor of Modern History, Nottingham University, 1960-66; Professor of History, Cornell University, USA, 1966-73; Professor of History, King's College, London, 1973-84. Publications: The Practice of Empire, 1951, 1969; Europe in the 16th Century (with G L Mosse), 1968, 1989; Estates and Revolutions, 1971; The Habsburgs and Europe, 1971; Politicians and Virtuosi, 1986; Medieval Europe 400-1500, 1987; Early Modern Europe 1500-1789, 1987; Republiken und Republikanismus (editor), 1988; Monarchies, States Generals and Parliaments, 2001. Honours: Guggenheim Fellow, 1970-71; Fellow, Historical College, Munich, 1984-85; Encomienda Order of Isobel the Catholic, 1997; Fellow of King's College London, 1999. Membership: Royal Historical Society, Vice-President, 1982-85; Fellow, British Academy, 1989-. Address: 116 Waterfall Road, Southgate, London N14 7JN, England.

**KOEPPEN Stefanka,** b. 8 November 1937, Bourgas, Bulgaria. Music Educator. m. Helmut, 1 son. Education: Student, Academy of Arts and Music, Sofia, Bulgaria, 1958-63. Appointments: Violinist, Symphonic Orchestra of Bourgas, 1956-58; Teacher of Violin and Viola, College of Music, Bourgas, 1963-67; Symphonic Orchestra of Berlin, 1967-70; Private Instructor of Violin and Viola, Berlin, 1970-; Assistant Professor of Viola, Academy of Arts and Music, Berlin, 1984-. Address: Leo-Baeck-Str 46, 14167 Berlin, Germany.

**KOGAN Norman,** b. 15 June 1919, Chicago, Illinois, USA. Professor Emeritus of Political Science. m. Meryl Reich, 18 May 1946, 2 sons. Education: BA, 1940, PhD, 1949, University of Chicago. Appointments: Faculty, University of Connecticut, 1949-88; Visiting Professor, University of Rome, 1973, 1979, 1987. Publications: Italy and the Allies, 1956; The Government of Italy, 1962; The Politics of Italian Foreign Policy, 1963; A Political History of Postwar Italy, 1966; Storia Politica dell' Italia Repubblicana, 1982, 2nd edition, revised and expanded, 1990; A Political History of Italy: The Postwar Years, 1983. Contributions to: Yale Law Journal; Il Ponte; Western Political Quarterly; Journal of Politics; Comparative Politics; Indiana Law Journal. Honour: Lifetime of Achievement Award, 2003. Address: 13 Westwood Road, Storrs, CT 06268, USA.

**KOGAN Shimshon Boris,** b. 2 September 1937, Leningrad, USSR. Catalysis Chemist. m. Ester Brenner, 2 sons. Education: MSc, Medical Chemistry, Chemical and Pharmaceutical Institute, Leningrad, USSR, 1959; PhD, Hydrocarbon Processing, All Union Petrochemical Processing Research Institute, Leningrad, USSR 1968; DSc, Catalysis, Zelinsky Institute of Organic Chemistry, Moscow, USSR, 1987. Appointments: Researcher, 1960-72, Senior Researcher, 1972-86, Associate Researcher, 1986-90, Head Researcher, 1990-91, All Union Petrochemical Processing Research Institute, Leningrad, USSR; Senior Researcher, Ben Gurion University, Blechner Center for Industrial Catalysis and Process Development, Beer Sheva, Israel, 1991-. Publications: More than 120 papers in scientific journals and presented at conferences as co-author include most recently: Development of novel heterogeneous catalysts for oxidative reactions: preparation and performance of Co-N catalysts in partial oxidation of n-butane and toluene, 2002; Dehydrogenation of neohexane on platinum polymetallic catalysts, 2002; Catalytic process for production of 3-methyl-2-butene-1-al, 2003; Low temperature oxidative cracking of butane and propane into ethylene and propylene, 2003; More than 50 patents. Honours: Prizes of the All Union Chemical Mendeleev's Society (Leningrad Branch), 1966, 1976, 1986, 1988. Memberships: All Union Chemical Mendeleev's Society, 1966-91; Israel Institute of Chemical Engineers, 2001-. Address: 43/5 h-Zvi Str, 84732 Beer Sheva, Israel. E-mail: kogans@bgumail.bgu.ac.il

**KÖHLER Johann Michael,** b. 19 January 1956, Halle, Saale, Germany. Chemist. m. Gabriele Neubert, 14 October 1978, 3 sons, 1 daughter. Education: Diploma Chemistry, 1981; Dr rer nat, Academy of Science, Berlin, 1986; Dr rer nat habil, University of Jena, 1992. Appointments: Aspirant University, Jena, 1981-82; Scientific Co-worker Physical Technology Institute, Jena, 1982-86; Project Leader, 1986-; Research Grant, Max-Planck Society, Dortmund, 1991; Head, Microfabrication Department, Institute of Physics High Technology, 1992-94; Head, Microsystem Department, 1994-99; Head Biotechnical Microsystems Department, 1999-2001; Professor, Physical Chemistry and Micro Reaction Technology, Technical University, Ilmenau, 2001-. Publications include: Nonlinear analysis of heart rate and respiratory dynamics, 1997; Chip Reactor for Microfluid Calorimetry, 1998; Microstructured Polymer Tips for Scanning Near-Field Optical Microscopy, 1998; Chipstrategien Für Diagnostik und Wirkstoffentwicklung, 1998; Characterization of Biomolecule Immobilization by Scanning Force Microscopy Using Wet-Masking Technique, 1998; In-Situ-Formation of Ag-Containing Nanoparticles in Thin Polymer Films, 1998; Making Electrical Contacts to Single Molecules, 1998; Etching in Microsystem Technology, 1999; Microsystem Technology: a Powerful Tool for Biomolecular Studies (co-editor), 1999; Umweltdiagnostik mit Mikrosystemen (co-editor), 1999; Selective labeling of oligouncleotide monolayers by metallic nanobeads for fast optical readont of DNA chips, 2000; Nanotechnologie; Nanoparticle Reactions on Chip, 2004; Generation of metal nanoparticles in a microchannel reactor, 2004; Digital reaction technology by micro segmented flow – components, concepts and applicatinos, 2004; Characterisation of lithographically patterned organosilane monolayers by preferential adsorption of dye molecules, 2004; Segmented flow generation by chip reactors for highly parallelized cell cultivation, 2004; Papers in professional journals. Honour: Science Award, Technical University Cottbus, 1997. Memberships: Gesellschaft Deutscher Chemiker, 1984-; Electrochemical Society, 1994. Address: Technical University Ilmenau, PO Box 100565, D-98684 Ilmenau, Germany.

**KOIDE Samuel S,** b. 6 October 1923, Honolulu, Hawaii, USA. Physician. m. Sumi M Mitsudo, 2 sons. Education: BS, University of Hawaii, 1945; MD, 1953, MS, 1954, PhD, 1960, Northwestern University. Appointments: Associate, Sloan Kettering Institute for Cancer Research, New York, USA, 1960-65; Senior Scientist, Population Council, New York, USA, 1965-2002. Publications: Over 300 paper in Biomedical Journals. Honours: Career Development Award, NIH, PHS, USA, 1963-65. Memberships: American Society of Molecular Biology and Biochemistry; The Biochemical Society; American Society of Cell Biology; Marine Biological Laboratory; USA Society for Experimental Biology and Medicine. Address: Koide Desk, 134 Lefurgy Ave, Dobbs Ferry, NY 10522, USA. E-mail: koide@optonline.net

**KOJIĆ-PRODIĆ Biserka,** b. 29 August 1938, Čakovec, Croatia. Scientist. m. Dragutin Kojić, 1 daughter. Education: BSc, 1961, MSc, 1963, PhD, Chemistry, 1968, Faculty of Science, University of Zagreb, Croatia. Appointments: Head of Laboratory for Chemical and Biological Crystallography, Project Leader, Rudjer Bošković Institute, Zagreb, Croatia; Senior Scientist, Visiting Scientist: University of Uppsala, University of Utrecht, Medical Foundation of Buffalo, Texas Christian University, Fort Worth, USA. Publications: 232 scientific articles in international journals; Chapter in Encyclopaedia of Agrochemicals, 2002. Honours: National Science Award, 1971; National Academy of Science and Art Award, 1997; DAAD Visiting Science Award, 1995, 2000. Memberships: Croatian Crystallographic Association; Croatian Biochemical Society; International Union of Crystallography; European Academy of Science. Address: Rudjer Bošković Institute, POB 180, HR-10002 Zagreb, Croatia. E-mail: kojic@irb.hr

**KOKOSALAKI Sophia,** b. 3 November 1972, Athens, Greece. Fashion Designer. Education: BA, Greek and English Literature, University of Athens, 1991-95; MA, Womenswear, Central

St Martins, 1996-98. Appointments: Catwalk show, London Fashion Week, 1999; Contracted Designer, Ruffo Research, 2000; Chief Designer, Olympic Games, Athens, 2004; Debut catwalk presentation of 12th collection for Spring/Summer 2005, Paris Fashion Week, 2004; Second catwalk presentation of 13th collection for Autumn/Winter 2005-06, Paris Fashion Week, 2005; Designer, costumes for Antigone of Sophocles, performed at ancient theatre of Syracuse, 2005. Honours: Winner, Elle Style Awards, Best New Designer, 2001; Winner, Art Foundation Award for Fashion, 2002; Winner, Best New Generation Designer, Lycra British Style Award, 2003; Voted one of Britain's Cool Brand Leaders, 2004. Address: Unit 7, 47-49 Tudor Road, London E9 7SN, England. E-mail: sophia@sophiakokosalaki.com

**KOKOT Franciszek,** b. 24 November 1929, Olesno Slaskie, Poland. Physician. m. Malgorzata Skrzypczyk, 4 sons. Education: Medical Studies, 1948-53; MD, 1957; PhD, 1962; Associate Professor, 1962-69; Extraordinary Professor, 1969-82; Ordinary Professor, 1982-. Appointments: Technician, Department of Chemistry, 1949-50, Department of Pharmacology, 1950-57, Assistant Senior Assistant, Department of Internal Medicine, Assistant Professor, Associate Professor, 1957-74, Professor, Head of Department of Nephrology, 1974-2000, Rector, 1982-84, Silesian School of Medicine. Publications: Over 650 scientific publications; Several chapters in 30 textbooks. Honours: Honorary Member, 7 foreign societies of Nephrology, L Pasteur Medal (Strasbourg), 1985; Dr hc of the Medical School of: Wroclaw, 1990, Katowice, 1993, Szczecin, 1995, Kosice, 1997, Lublin, 1997; Warsaw, 1999; Jagiellonian University, Cracow, 1999, Medical Academy of Bialestok, 2001, Lodz, 2004; F Volhard Golden Medal, 1991; International Distinguished Medal, 1991. Memberships: International Society of Nephrology; European Society of Nephrology; President, Polish Society Nephrology, 1989-98. Address: Al Korfantego 8/162, 40-004 Katowice, Poland.

**KOLACHEV Boris,** b. 4 April, Kimri Tver Region, Russia. Educator. m. Sinizina Galina, 2 daughters. Education: Engineer, 1952; Candidate of Science, 1955; Doctor of Science, 1967; Professor, 1968. Appointments: Assistant, 1955-58, Senior Lecturer, 1959-68, Full Professor, 1968-90, Honoured Professor, 1990-, Moscow Institute of Aircraft and Technology; Expert of High Certification Committee, USSR Government, 1975-92. Publications: 28 books. Honours: Honoured Man of Science and Technology; State Prize Winner; Honoured Professor. Memberships: New York Academy of Science; Permanent Working International Committee on Hydrogen Treatment of Materials. Address: Andropov Avenue 41/8 - 106, 142800 Stoopino, Moscow Region, Russia.

**KOLTOVER Vitaliy Kiva,** b. 15 May 1944, Orekhovo-Zuyevo, Russia. Biophysicist. 1 son. Education: MS, Physics, Kiev State University, 1966; PhD, Physics and Mathematics, Institute of Chemical Physics, Moscow, 1971; DSc, Biophysics, Moscow, 1988. Appointments: Plant Physiology Institute, Kiev, Ukraine, 1966-68; Predoctoral Fellow, Junior Scientist, Senior Scientist, Head Bioreliability Group Institute of Problems of Chemical Physics, 1968-. Publications: Books and articles in professional journals on reliability, aging, radiation ecology, metallofullerenes. Honours: Outstanding Achievement Diploma of President of Russian Academy of Sciences. Memberships: International Union of Radioecology; American Academy of Anti-Aging Medicine, Expert Consultant, Russian Foundation for Basic Research. Address: Institute of Problems of Chemical Physics, Russian Academy of Sciences, Chernogolovka 142432, Moscow, Russia.

**KOMISSAROV Yuriy Alexeyevitch,** b. 11 February 1938, Astrakhan, Russia. Chemical Engineer. m. L S Komissarova, 1 daughter. Education: Engineer, Astrakhan State Institute, 1965; Candidate Degree, Moscow Chemical Technology Institute, 1974; Doctor Degree, D I Mendeleev University of Chemical Technology of Russia, 1991. Appointments: Engineer, All-Union Institute of Light Alloys, Moscow, 1965-71; Postgraduate, 1971-74; Reader, Professor, Head of Department, D I Mendeleev University of Chemical Technology of Russia, 1975-2004. Publications: 190 articles, 15 books, 15 patents. Honours: Medal, Veteran of Labour, 1987; Medal, 850th Anniversary of Moscow, 1998; Medal, Zhukov 100th Anniversary, 1998; Honoured Science Worker of Russia, 2005. Membership: Russian Academy of Systems Research; International Academy of System Studies. Address: Babakins Street 1-6, Apt 249, Hymki City, Moscow 141407, Russia.

**KONG Lihong,** b. 12 January 1965, China. Senior Engineer. 1 daughter. Education: BSc, 1986; Master of Engineering, 1989; PhD, Biomedical Engineering, 1999-2004. Appointments: Senior Engineer and Researcher, Aviation Medicine, Electrical Engineering, 1989-99; Biomedical Engineering, 1999-. Publications: 10 articles in international conferences; 5 articles in international journals; 1 article in Proceedings of World Congress on Medical Physics and Biomedical Engineering; 22 articles in Chinese journals. Honours: Third Award of Science-Technology Progress, 1990; Second Award of Science-Technology Progress, 1992; Third Award of News Report, 1995; Second Award of Science-Technology Progress, 1995; Second Award of Science-Technology Progress, 1995; Finalist, Space Medicine Branch Young Investigator Award Competition, 1996; One presentation was judged to represent one of the top 10% of the performances from a field of some 88 contestants in the year's competition. Address: Graduate School of Biomedical Engineering, University of New South Wales, Sydney 2052, Australia. E-mail: rheakong@yahoo.com

**KONURALP Cüneyt,** b. 21 February 1967, Ankara, Turkey. Physician; Cardiovascular Surgeon. m. Zeynep, 1 son. Education: BS, Bahçelievler Deneme Lisesi, Ankara, 1984; MD, Ankara University School of Medicine, Ankara, 1990; Cardiovascular Surgery Specialist, Siyami Ersek Thoracic and Cardiovascular Surgery Center, Istanbul, 1996. Appointments: Resident, 1990-96, Staff Surgeon, 1996, Cardiovascular Surgery Department, Siyami Ersek Thoracic and Cardiovascular Surgery Center, Istanbul, Turkey; Clinical Fellow, Cardiothoracic Surgery Department, 1996-98, 1999-2000, Cardiothoracic Transplantation Department, 1998-99; Texas Heart Institute, St Luke's Episcopal Hospital, Houston, Texas; Staff Surgeon, Cardiovascular Surgery Department, Siyami Ersek Thoracic and Cardiovascular Surgery Center, Istanbul Turkey, 2000-. Publications: 35 congress presentations; 49 published scientific articles; 2 invited reviews; 19 abstracts; 3 book chapters; 2 invited talks; 1 patent pending. Honours include: Superior Performance on Track and Field, Turkish Ministry of Youth and Sport, 1986; Grant, Turkish Society of Cardiology, 2001; Winner, Edip Kürklü Award, Turkish Heart Foundation, 2001; Runner-up, C Walton Lillehei Young Investigator's Award, European Association for Cardio-Thoracic Surgery, 2001; Best Paper Prize, World Society of Cardio-Thoracic Surgeons, 2002; International Health Professional of the Year Award, IBC, 2003; Award of Biographical Recognition, IBC, 2004; Lifetime Achievement Award, IBC, 2004; Universal Award of Accomplishment, ABI, 2004; Deputy Governor, ABI Research Association; Outstanding Professional Award, ABI, 2004; International Scientist of the Year, IBC, 2004; Member, Research Board of Advisors, ABI; Scientific Advisor, IBC; The Da Vinci Diamond, IBC, 2004; The Key Award, ABI,

2004. Memberships include: Fellow, International College of Surgeons; Fellow, American College of Chest Physicians; Fellow, American Heart Association; Fellow, European Society of Cardiology; Fellow, American College of Cardiology; Life Fellow, International Biographical Association; Life Fellow, American Biographical Association; Turkish Medical Association; Cardiovascular Surgery Network; Denton A Cooley Cardiovascular Surgery Society; International Society for Heart and Lung Transplantation; Society of Thoracic Surgeons; Turkish Society of Cardiology; World Heart Federation; Heart Failure Society of America; Turkish Society of Perfusionists; Turkish Society of Thoracic and Cardiovascular Anaesthesia and Intensive Care; European Society for Artificial Organs; American Stroke Association; European Association for Cardio-Thoracic Surgery; Turkish Society of Cardiovascular Surgery; New York Academy of Sciences; Galatasaray Sports Club. Address: Ayşe Çavuş Sokak, No 7/6, Huri Apt Suadiye, Istanbul 34740, Turkey. E-mail: ckonuralp@usa.net

**KOOK Abraham Izhak,** b. 29 August 1937, Haifa, Israel. Professor; Researcher. 1 son, 2 daughters. Education: MSc, Hebrew University, Jerusalem, Tel-Aviv University, 1964; Cornell University, New York, USA, 1964-65; PhD, with distinction, Biochemistry, McGill University, Montreal, Canada, 1970. Appointments: Teaching Assistant, Department of Chemistry, Cornell University, 1964-66; Research Fellow, 1966-99, Canadian Heart Foundation Research and Teaching Assistant, 1969-70 Department of Biochemistry, McGill University, Canada; Lecturer, Tel Aviv University Medical School, Department of Chemical Pathology, Tel Hashomer Hospital, Tel Aviv, 1970-71; Lecturer, The Hebrew University, Department of Biochemistry, Lipid Research Laboratory, Hadassah Medical Centre, Jerusalem, 1971-72; Scientist,, 1972-75, Senior Scientist, 1975-80, Department of Cell Biology, The Weizmann Institute of Science, Israel; Associate Professor, Faculty of Medicine, Department of Immunology, Technion-Israel Institute of Technology, Haifa, Israel, 1980-81; Director, Laboratories and Research Division, Wolfson Hospital, Holon, Israel, 1981-84; Associate Professor of Research, Tulane University Medical, New Orleans, USA, 1984-87; Visiting Professor, NIH-NIMH, Brain Biochemistry, Bethesda, Maryland, USA, 1987-89; Professor, New York Academy of Sciences, Director, Research Department, Rebecca Sieff Government Medical Centre, Safed, Israel, 1989-2003. Publications: Over 100 in the fields of biochemistry, immunology and psychoneuro-immunology. Honours: Paulina Erlich Award, Israel, 1963; Canadian Heart Foundation Fellow, 1970; Listed in Who's Who publications and biographical dictionaries. Memberships: Canadian Heart Foundation; Canadian Biochemical Society; Israel Biochemical Society; Israel Immunological Society; New York Academy of Science; American Association for the Advancement of Science. Address: 11 Hazaitim Street, Rosh Pinna, Upper Galilee, 12000 Israel. E-mail: kookai@zahov.net.il

**KOONTZ Dean R(ay), (David Axton, Brian Coffey, Deanna Dwyer, K R Dwyer, John Hill, Leigh Nichols, Anthony North, Richard Paige, Owen West),** b. 9 July 1945, Everett, Pennsylvania, USA. Writer. m. Gerda Ann Cerra, 15 October 1966. Education: BS, Shippensburg University, 1966. Publications: Star Quest, 1968; The Fall of the Dream Machine, 1969; Fear That Man, 1969; Anti-Man, 1970; Beastchild, 1970; Dark of the Woods, 1970; The Dark Symphony, 1970; Hell's Gate, 1970; The Crimson Witch, 1971; A Darkness in My Soul, 1972; The Flesh in the Furnace, 1972; Starblood, 1972; Time Thieves, 1972; Warlock, 1972; A Werewolf Among Us, 1973; Hanging On, 1973; The Haunted Earth, 1973; Demon Seed, 1973; Strike Deep, 1974; After the Last Race, 1974; Nightmare Journey, 1975; The Long Sleep, 1975; Night Chills, 1976;

Prison of Ice, 1976, revised edition as Icebound, 1995; The Vision, 1977; Whispers, 1980; Phantoms, 1983; Darkfall, 1984; Twilight Eyes, 1985; The Door to December, 1985; Strangers, 1986; Watchers, 1987; Lightning, 1988; Midnight, 1989; The Bad Place, 1990; Cold Fire, 1991; Hideaway, 1992; Dragon Tears, 1992; Mr Murder, 1993; Winter Moon, 1993; Dark Rivers of the Heart, 1994; Strange Hideways, 1995; Intensity, 1995; Tick-Tock, 1996; Fear Nothing, 1998; False Memory, 1999; From the Corner of the Eye, 2000. Contributions to: Books, journals, and magazines. Honours: Daedalus Award, 1988; Honorary DLitt, Shippensburg University, 1989. Address: William Morris Agency, 1325 Avenue of the Americas, New York, NY 10019, USA.

**KOÓS Attila,** b. 5 May 1968, Györ, Hungary. Engineer. m. Gyöng-Yi, 2 daughters. Education: BME, Faculty of Electrical Engineering, Technical University of Budapest, 1986-92; Ongoing technical training and study visits, 1992-2000. Appointments: EWSD Specialist, Technical Support Centre, 1992-96, Leader, National Switching Centre, 1996-2000, MATÁV Ltd; Technical Advisor for CTO, Croatian Telecom (HT), 2001-2002; Leader, National Switching Centre, 2003-2004, Director, PKI Telecommunications Development Institute, 2004-, MATÁV Ltd; Projects include: Acceptance tests of several EWSD switches; Work in introduction of No 7 signalling in MATÁV network; Participation in MATÁV – DeTeCon research in Bulgaria at gas company; Work in reorganisation project; Work in introduction of SNOMS switching management systems; Participation in Due Diligence at Croatian Telecom (HT); Elaboration of HT's network management strategy and work in realisation; Elaboration of HT's new O&M organisation; Leading MATÁV – Siemens and MATÁV – Ericsson expert steerings. Address: Arany J, Ut 66, Györujbarat, Hungary 9081. E-mail: koos.attila@ln.matav.hu

**KOPECKÝ Miloslav,** b. 4 May 1928, Prague, Czechoslovakia. Astrophysicist. m. Františka née Matysová, 1927-94, 2 sons. Education: Charles University, Prague, 1947-51; RNDr (rerum naturalium doktor), 1953; DrSc (doctor of physical mathematical science), 1969; Corresponding Member, Czechoslovak Academy of Sciences, 1977. Appointments: Worker of the Astronomical Institute, Ondrejov, 1949-93; Head of the Solar Department, 1971-75; Vice-Director of the Institute, 1975-90; Pensioner, Emeritus Worker of the Institute, 1993-. Publications: Over 200 scientific papers; 4 scientific monographs. Honours: State Prize, 1961; State Distinction, 1988; Various medals from different academies of sciences, universities. Membership: International Astronomical Union; Astronomische Gesellschaft. Address: 25165 Ondrejov 234, Czech Republic.

**KORALEK Paul George,** b. 7 April 1933, Vienna, Austria. Architect. m. Jennifer Koralek, 1 son, 2 daughters. Education: AA School of Architecture. Appointments include: Architect with Powell and Moya, London, 1956-57; Various work in France and Canada, 1957-59; Architect with Marcel Breuer, New York, USA, 1959-60; Founding Partner and Director, Ahrends Burton and Koralek, 1961-; Member of Development Advisory Panel, Cardiff Bay Development Corporation, 1990-2000; Chair Works Committee, 1996, Member of Management Committee, 1997, Member of Architecture Committee, 2002-, Royal Academy of Arts; Chair, South East Regional Design Panel, 2002-; Assessor and Advisor for numerous design awards and competitions; External Examiner, Luton University School of Architecture, 1999-; Principal projects include most recently: North Tipperary County Council Offices, Nenagh, 2000; Trinity College Arts Faculty Building Extension, Dublin, 2000; Trinity College Dublin Innovation Centre, 2001; Trinity College Dublin Pearce Street Competition, 2002; Trinity College Dublin

Enterprise Centre Bio Tech Units, 2003; Stockport Town Centre Design Competition, 2003; Collen House Extension, 2004. Publications: Ahrends Burton and Koralek (monograph), 1991; Collaborations: The Architecture of ABK, August/Birkhäuser; Numerous papers and lectures presented at national and international conferences and seminars. Honours: CBE, 1984; Associate, 1986, Member, 1993, Royal Academy of Arts. Memberships: RIBA; FRIAI. Address: Ahrends Burton and Koralek, 7 Chalcot Road, London NW1 8LH, England. E-mail: abk@abklondon.com Website: www.abk.co.uk

**KORDA Petr,** b. 23 January 1968, Prague, Czech Republic. Tennis Player. m. Regina Rajchrtova, 1992, 1 son, 2 daughters. Appointments: Coached by his father until 18 years old; Coached by Tomas Petera, 1991-; Winner, Wimbledon Junior Doubles, 1986; Turned Professional, 1987; Winner, Stuttgart Open, 1997, Australian Open, 1998, Qatar Open, 1998; Member, Czechoslovak Davis Cup Team, 1988, 1996; Retired, 1999, after winning 20 professional titles including 10 singles titles; Currently plays in Seniors Tour; Winner, Honda Challenge, 2002; Chairman, Board of Supervisors, Karlštejn golf resort.

**KORNBERG Arthur,** b. 3 March 1918, Brooklyn, New York, USA. Biochemist. m. (1) Sylvy R Levy, deceased 1986, 3 sons, (2) Charlene W Levering, 1988, deceased 1995. Education: Pre-Medical Course, College of the City of New York, BS, 1937; Medical Degree, University of Rochester School of Medicine, 1941. Appointments: Commissioned Officer, US PUBLIC Health Service, 1941-42; National Institutes of Health, Bethesda, Maryland, 1942-52; Professor and Chairman, Department of Microbiology, Washington University School of Medicine, 1953-59; Executive Head, 1959-69, Professor, 1959-88, Professor Emeritus, 1988-, Department of Biochemistry, Stanford University School of Medicine, Palo Alto; Made the first synthetic molecules of DNA; Synthesized a biologically active artificial viral DNA. Publications: For the love of Enzymes: the odyssey and a biochemist (autobiography), 1989; Numerous original research papers and reviews on subjects in biochemistry, particularly enzymatic mechanisms of biosynthetic reactions. Honour: Joint Winner, Nobel Prize in Medicine and Physiology, 1959; Several honorary degrees; numerous other awards. Memberships: NAS; American Philosophical Society; American Academy of Arts and Sciences, Foreign member, Royal Society, 1970. Address: Department of Biochemistry, Stanford, University Medical Center, Stanford, CA 94305, USA.

**KORNBERG Hans Leo,** b. 14 January 1928, Herford, Germany (British Citizen). Professor of Biochemistry. Education: BSc, 1949, PhD, 1953, Sheffield University. Appointments: John Stokes Research Fellow, University of Sheffield, 1952-53; Member, Medical Research Council Cell Metabolism Research Unit, University of Oxford, 1955-61; Lecturer in Biochemistry, Worcester College, Oxford, 1958-61; Professor of Biochemistry, University of Leicester, 1961-75; Sir William Dunn Professor of Biochemistry, University of Cambridge, 1975-95; University Professor and Professor of Biology, Boston University, Massachusetts, USA, 1995-; Fellow, 1975-, Master, 1982-95, Christ's College, Cambridge. Publications: Numerous articles in scientific journals. Honours: Commonwealth Fund Fellow, Yale University and Public Health Research Institute, New York, 1953-55; Colworth Medal, Biochemical Society, 1963; Warburg Medal, Gesellschaft für biologische Chemie der Bundersrepublik, 1973; Honorary member of: Society of Biological Chemistry (USA), 1972; Japanese Biochemical Society, 1981; American Academy of Arts and Sciences, 1987; Honorary FRCP, 1989; Numerous honorary fellowships and degrees. Memberships: German Academy of Sciences,

Leopoldina, 1982; Foreign associate, NAS, 1986; Academie Europaea, 1988; Fellow, American Academy of Microbiology, 1992; Foreign member, American Philosophical Society, 1993; Foreign member, Accademia Nazionale dei Lincei, Italy, 1997. Address: The University Professors, Boston University, 745 Commonwealth Avenue, Boston, MA 02215, USA.

**KORNFELD Robert Jonathan,** b. 3 March 1919, Newtonville, Massachusetts, USA. Dramatist; Writer; Poet. m. Celia Seiferth, 23 August 1945, 1 son. Education: AB, Harvard University, 1941; Attended, Columbia University, Tulane University, New York University, New School for Social Research, Circle-in-the-Square School of Theatre, and Playwrights Horizons Theatre School and Laboratory. Appointment: Playwright-in-Residence, University of Wisconsin, 1998. Publications: Plays: Great Southern Mansions, 1977; A Dream Within a Dream, 1987; Landmarks of the Bronx, 1990; Music For Saint Nicholas, 1992; Hot Wind From the South, 1995; The Hanged Man, 1996. Plays produced: Father New Orleans, 1997; The Queen of Carnival, 1997; The Celestials, 1998; Passage in Purgatory, Shanghai, China, 2000; The Gates of Hell, New York, 2002; Starry Night, New York, 2003; The Celestials, New York, 2005. Other: Fiction and poetry. Contributions to: Various publications; Six play readings (theatres, universities and clubs), 2005. Honours: Numerous awards and prizes; Visiting Artist, Fellow, American Academy, Rome, 1996. Memberships: Authors League; Dramatists Guild; National Arts Club; New York Drama League; PEN Freedom to Write Committee. Address: The Withers Cottage, 5286 Sycamore Avenue, Riverdale, NY 10471, USA.

**KORNOWSKI Robert R,** b. 1 June 1943, Green Bay, Wisconsin, USA. Principal Staff Engineer; Inventor; Educator. 1 son, 2 daughters. Education: Bachelor Degree, Electronics Engineering Technology. Appointments: Engineering Positions, Motorola, 1965-; Educator Positions, William Rainey Harper College, 1972-. Publications: Numerous patents, presentations and publications relating to electronic component technology development. Honours: Best Paper of Session Award, IMAPS, ISPS'97. Membership: International Microelectronics and Packaging Society. Address: Motorola GEMS, Room 3025, 1301 East Algonquin Road, Schaumburg, IL 60196-4041, USA.

**KOROLEV Mikhail Antonovich,** b. 12 September 1931, Alma-Ata. Statistician. m. E Letalina-Koroleva, 1957, 1 daughter. Education: Moscow Plekhanov Institute of National Economy. Appointments: Assistant, Moscow Plekhanov Institute of National Economy, 1954-56; Assistant Dean, Department Head, 1956-66, Rector, 1966-72, Professor, 1967-, Moscow Institute of Economics and Statistics; Deputy, First Deputy Director, 1972-85, Director, 1985-87, Central Statistics Board of USSR; Vice-Chair, 1976-79, 1989-91, Chair, Statistical Commission of UN, 1979-81; President, USSR State Committee on Statistics, 1987-89; Advisor to Prime Minister of USSR, 1991; President, Interstate Statistical Committee, CIS, 1992-. Publications: 20 books, numerous articles. Honour: PhD on Economics; Professor, Honorary Scientist, member, International Informatics Academy. Membership: International Statistical Institute. Address: Interstate Statistical Committee of the Commonwealth of Independent States, Build 1, 39 Myasnitskaya Street, 107450 Moscow, Russian Federation.

**KORZENIK Diana,** b. 15 March 1941, New York, New York, USA. Professor Emerita; Painter; Writer. Education: Oberlin College; BA, Vassar College; Master's Programme, Columbia University; EdD, Graduate School of Education, Harvard University. Appointments: Professor Emerita, Massachusetts College of Art, Boston. Publications: Chapter in Art and Cognition (editors, Leondar and Perkins), 1977; Drawn to Art, 1986; Art Making and Education (with Maurice Brown), 1993; The Cultivation of American Artists (co-editor with Sloat and Barnhill), 1997; The Objects of Art Education, 2004. Contributions to: Professional journals and to magazines. Honours: American Library Association Leab Award 2005; Boston Globe L L Winship Literary Award, 1986; National Art Education Association Lowenfeld Award, 1998. Memberships: Friends of Longfellow House, founder, board member; American Antiquarian Society; Massachusetts Historical Society. Address: 7 Norman Road, Newton Highlands, MA 02461, USA.

**KOS Serdjo,** b. 24 January 1957, Rijeka, Croatia. University Professor. m. Gordana Topić. 2 daughters. Education: BSc, Nautical Science, 1986; MSc, Technical Science, 1992, Faculty of Maritime Studies at Rijeka; PhD, Technical Sciences, University of Rijeka, 1994. Appointments: 2nd, 3rd and Chief Officer, Croatia Line (ex Jugolinija), 1980-89; Lecturer, 1992, Assistant Professor, 1998, Associate Professor, 2001, Professor, 2004, Faculty of Maritime Studies of University of Rijeka; Editor-in-Chief, Journal of Maritime Studies, 2003-. Publications: Articles: Differential equation of loxodrome on a sphere; Calculation of distance off by two horizontal angles; Calculation of the rhumb line intersection with the equator; Calculation of navigational parameters in meridian equator and parallel sailing by means of relative co-ordinates. Honours: Listed in Who's Who publications and biographical dictionaries. Memberships: Collaboration Member, Croatian Academy of Engineering; Member of the Council for Maritime Affairs, Croatian Academy of Sciences and Arts. Address: Faculty of Maritime Studies, University of Rijeka, Studentska 2, 51000 Rijeka, Croatia. E-mail: skos@pfri.hr

**KOSINSKY Anatoly Vasilievich,** b. 12 February 1930, Krasnodar, Russia. Researcher; Educator. m. Troshkina Valentina Aphanasievna. Education: Degree, Engineer in Electromechanics, Moscow Energy Institute, 1952; PhD, Radio Institute, Moscow, 1960; DSc, Moscow Institute of Electronics and Mathematics, 1985. Appointments: Engineer, M V Lomonosov State University, 1952-54; Engineer, Radio Institute, Moscow, 1955-57; Head of Research Group, 1958-61; Head, Laboratory of Control, 1961-63; Associate Professor, 1863-86, Professor, 1986, Moscow Institute of Electronics and Mathematics. Publications: Details and Equipment of Automation (with M A Babikov), 1975; Analogous-digital Converters of Moves (with V R Matveevsky and A A Kholomonov), 1991; Over 200 articles and 40 patents in field. Honours: Splendid Worker Medal, USSR 1970; Prize, USSR Economy Exhibition, 1983; Veteran of Work Medal, USSR, 1986; 850 Years of Moscow Medal, 1997. Memberships: New York Academy of Sciences; Sciensec-Technical Society "Aparatus"; Academic Council of Graduation of PhD and DSc. Address: Lomonosovsky Prospekt, D 14, kv 116, 119296 Moscow, Russia.

**KOSTOW Kathryn Eileen,** b. 30 May 1956, Pocatello, Idaho, USA. Conservation Biologist. Education: BSc honours, Biology, College of Idaho, 1978; MSc, Ecology, University of Minnesota, 1981. Appointments: Employed by several agencies in the Columbia River Basin: US Forest Service, US Army Corps of Engineers, National Marine Fisheries Service, and private utility industry; Currently Policy Analyst, Oregon Department of Fish and Wildlife, State of Oregon, 1990-. Publications: Articles and major presentations in popular and professional journals. Honours: Henry Lawrence Gipson Honours, College of Idaho, 1974-78; Webster Fellowship, 1979, Research Fellowship, 1980-81, Delta Waterfowl Research Station, Manitoba, Canada; Achievement Award, National Marine Fisheries Service, 1997.

Memberships: Society of Conservation Biology; American Society of Ichthyologists and Herpetologists; American Fisheries Society; Gilbert Ichthyological Society; Nature Conservancy; World Wildlife Fund. Address: Oregon Department of Fish and Wildlife Fish Division, 17330 SE Evelyn St, Clackamas, OR 97015, USA. E-mail: kathryn.e.kostow@state.or.us Website: www.dfw.state.or.us

**KOSZTOLNYIK Zoltan J,** b. 15 December 1930, Heves, Hungary. Professor Emeritus of History. m. Penelope South Kosztolnyik, 2 daughters. Education: BA, St Bonaventure University, 1959; MA, Fordham University, 1961; PhD, New York University, 1968. Appointments: Instructor in History, 1967-68, Assistant Professor, 1968-72, Associate Professor, 1972-81, Professor of History, 1981-2003; Professor Emeritus, 2003-; Texas A and M University; Guest Professor of Medieval History, Janus Pannonius University, Hungary. Publications: Five Eleventh Century Hungarian Kings, 1981; From Coloman the Learned to Bela III (1095-1196): Hungarian domestic policy and its impact upon foreign affairs, 1987; Hungary in the 13th Century, 1996; Hungary under the early Arpads, 890's to 1063, 2002; Over 50 articles, and over 50 book reviews published in scholarly journals. Honours: New York University Founders Day Award, 1969; Phi Kappa Phi, 1979-; TAMU/College of Liberal Arts Distinguished Teaching Award, 1995. Memberships: Medieval Academy of America; American Historical Association; American Catholic Historical Association. Address: Department of History, Texas A&M University, College Station, TX 77843-4236, USA.

**KOUBA Vaclav,** b. 16 January 1929, Vrabi, Czech Republic. Epizootiologist. m. Anna Holcapkova, 1 son, 1 daughter. Education: Diploma, Veterinary Medicine, 1953, PhD, 1961, Habil Docent 1966, DrSc, 1978, Professor, Epizootiology, 1988, University of Veterinary Medicine, Brno, Czech Republic. Appointments: Lecturer, 1952-56, University of Veterinary Medicine, Brno, Czech Republic; National Chief Epizootiologist, Prague, 1956-78; Visiting Professor, University of Havana, 1967-71; Animal Health Officer (Research/ Education), Senior Animal Health Officer, FAO-UN, Rome, Italy, 1978-85; Professor, Founder of faculty and Institute of Tropical Veterinary Medicine, Brno, 1985-88; Chief, Animal Health Service, Food and Agriculture Organisation of the United Nations, Rome, 1988-91; Visiting Professor, Mexico City, 1993; Visiting Professor, University of Kosice, 1993-98; Visiting Professor, University of Prague, 1999-; Founder of modern epizootiology; Achievements as leading specialist: Eradication of bovine brucellosis, 1964, bovine tuberculosis, 1968, Teschen disease, 1973 and foot and mouth disease, 1975 in Czechoslovakia; Foot and mouth disease in Mongolia, 1964; African swine fever in Cuba, 1971; Myiasis Cochliomyia hominivorax in Northern Africa, 1991 regaining free status of the whole Eastern hemisphere; First isolation of Aujeszky disease virus in Czechoslovakia, 1954. Publications include: General Epizootiology textbooks; FAO-WHO-OIE World Animal Health Yearbook, editor; Over 700 articles on epizootiology; Software: Epizoo, Epizmeth, Epiztext, electronic textbook. Honours: Polar Star Order, Mongolian Government; Outstanding Work Order, Czechoslovak Government; Veterinary Public Health Expert, World Health Organization, Geneva; Informatics Expert, International Office of Epizootics, Paris; Honourable President, Cuban Veterinary Scientific Society. Memberships: World Veterinary Association, Education Committee; International Society of Veterinary Epidemiology and Economics; World Association for the History of Veterinary Medicine. Address: PB 516, 17000 Praha 7, Czech Republic. Website: www.cbox.cz/ vaclavkouba

**KOUMAKIS George,** b. 13 April 1937, Heraclion, Crete. Associate Professor. m. Efstathia, 26 December 1971, 1 son, 3 daughters. Education: Diploma of Philosophy and Philology, University of Athens, 1960; Master of Arts, Philosophy, University of Bonn, Germany, 1967; PhD, 1970. Appointment: Associate Professor, Greek, English, German and French Language, University of Ioannina. Publications: Numerous books and articles in professional journals. Honours: Prize of Municipality, Haraclion, Crete, for book, Nikos Kazantzakis; Scholarship, DAAD; United Cultural Convention's International Peace Prize, 2003; Participated in many Greek, international and world congresses. Memberships: Greek Philosophical Association; American Philosophical Association. Address: Keramikou str 6, 15125 Maroussi, Athens, Greece.

**KOUNO Akihisa,** b. 10 November 1961, Osaka, Japan. Medical Doctor. m. Mika Akamatsu, 1 daughter. Education: MD, School of Medicine, Fujita-Gakuen Health University, 1987; PhD, Graduate School of Osaka University Medical School, 2000; Supervisor, Medico-Legal Society of Japan, 2001; Registered Anaesthesiologist, Japanese Society of Anaesthesiologists. Appointments: Medical Examiner, Osaka Medical Examiners Office, 1989; Executive Director, Kouno Clinic, Sakai, Japan, 1995-; Medical Adviser on Child Abuse, Osaka and Hyogo Prefectures; Assistant Professor, Shiga University of Medical Science, 2004-. Publications: Development of haemoglobin subtypes and extramedullary haematopoiesis in young rats, 2000; Child Suffering in the World (book chapter), 2000; Child Abuse, a global view (book chapter), 2001. Memberships include: International Society for Prevention of Child Abuse and Neglect; Medico-Legal Society, Japan. Address: 2-2-6 Wakamatsu-dai, Sakai-Osaka, 590-0116 Japan. E-mail: kouno 333@skyblue.ocn.ne.jp

**KOVACHEV Ljubomir,** b. 26 November 1942, Dimitrovgrad, Bulgaria. Surgeon. m. Anelia Panteleeva, 1 son. Education: MD, Higher Medical Institute, Sofia, 1972; MD, Surgery, Medical Academy, Sofia, 1978; PhD, Highest Certifying Commission, Sofia, 1985. Appointments: Registrar in Surgery, in hospitals of Dulovo and Pernik, 1972-75; Assistant Professor, 1976-85, Associate Professor, 1986-2002, Head of Department, 1987-2002, Dean of Foreign Students, 1987-93, Higher Medical Institute, Pleven. Publications: Professional journals. Honours: Man of the Year, ABI, 1998; Listed in biographical publications. Membership: Eurosurgery. Address: George Kochev Street 39, Entr D, Ap 2, 5800 Pleven, Bulgaria.

**KOVACS George,** b. 30 October 1943, Budapest. Professor. m. Noemi Farago, 2 sons, 1 daughter. Education: Electrical Engineer, 1966; Dr Techn, 1976, PhD, 1978, Technical University of Budapest; Dr, Hungarian Academy, Hungarian Academy of Sciences, 1996. Appointments: Visiting Researcher in USA, 1972-73, Russia, 1977-79, Germany, 1983; Visiting Professor in Mexico, 1986, Italy, 1994; Computer and Automation Institute, Head of CIM Research Laboratory, 1990-; Professor at the Technical University, Budapest, 1995-; Professor at the University of Pecs, 2003. Publications: Over 300 mostly in English on automation, manufacturing, artificial intelligence. Honours: Excellent Innovator, 1991; IFIP Silver Core, 2004; O. Benedikt Prize, 2003; Best Researcher, 4 times. Memberships: IEEE; IFAC; IFIP. Address: 1025 Budapest, Verecke ut 116, Hungary.

**KOVALEV Alexei Gennadievich,** b. 1 July 1966, Moscow, Russia. Mathematician. Education: Honours Diploma in Mathematics, Moscow State University, 1988; D Phil in Mathematics, Worcester College, Oxford, 1995. Appointments: Research Fellow, University of Edinburgh, 1995-2001;

University Lecturer, Cambridge University and Fellow, Fitzwilliam College, Cambridge, 2001-. Publications: Papers in professional journals. Membership: London Mathematical Society, 1999. Address: Fitzwilliam College, Cambridge CB3 0DG, England. E-mail: a.g.kovalev@dpmms.cam.ac.uk

**KOVENSKY Barbara Jane,** b. 24 October 1945, Cambridge, USA. Chemist. m. Sheldon, 2 daughters. Education: BA, Chemistry, Wheaton College, 1967; MSc, Food Chemistry, University of Toronto, 1972. Appointments: Head, Instrumentation Methodology and Analytical Research Laboratories, RP Scherer Corporation, Detroit, 1968-70; Technical Consultant, Smith, Miller and Patch (Canada) Ltd and Sterile Pharmaceutical Ltd, Toronto, 1971-72; Director, Quality Control, Sterile Pharmaceutical Ltd, Toronto, 1972-75; Director, Envirolab Division, Surveyor, Nenniger and Chenevert (SNC), Montreal, 1975-76; Manager, Organic Analysis Division, Technitrol Canada Ltd, 1967-83; Vice President, Technitrol Expertise Incorporated, Downsview, Ontario, 1983-98; President, Experchem Laboratories Incorporated, Downsview, 1998-. Publications: Several articles in professional journals. Honours: Listed in several biographical dictionaries including: Who's Who of Canadian Women; Who's Who in Canadian Business. Memberships: Order of Professional Chemists; Association of the Chemical Profession of Ontario; Canadian Institute of Food Science and Technology; Canadian Cosmetic, Toiletry and Fragrance Association; Association of Official Analytical Chemists; Fellow, IBA. Address: Experchem Laboratories Incorporated, 1111 Flint Road Units 40-41, Downsview, Ontario M3J 3C7, Canada.

**KOWALSKA Maria T,** b. 8 June 1932, Wielun, Poland. Research Scientist. m. W Kowalski, 1 son, 1 daughter. Education: BA, Lyceum of General Education, Lodz, Poland, 1950; MS in Pharmacy, 1954, PhD in Pharmacy, 1964, Dr Hab in Phytochemistry, 1978, Medical Academy, Poznan. Appointments: Assistant Professor, Pharmacy, Medical Academy, Poznan, 1955-67; Postdoctoral Fellowship, Department of Pharmacy, University of Paris, France, 1969-70; Associate Professor of Agriculture, Department of Technology of Wood, Poznan, 1970-80; Professor of Pharmacognosy, National University of Kinshasa, Zaire, 1980-82; Research Associate, Research Center, Fairchild Tropical Garden, Miami, Florida, USA, 1985-90; Adjunct Assistant Professor, Department of Biochemistry and Molecular Biology, University of Miami, School of Medicine, 1990-2001. Publications: 53 scientific publications in the field of phytochemistry and pharmacognosy in international scientific periodicals. Honours: Dean's Award, Medical Academy in Poznan, 1962-64; PI grants, International Palm Society, 1986-87; PI grants, World Wildlife Fund, 1988. Memberships: Polish Pharmaceutical Society, 1960-72; American Society of Phytochemistry, 1990-92. Address: 6421 SW 106 Street, Miami, FL 33156, USA. E-mail: kellin242@aol.com

**KOZÁK János,** b. 20 December 1945, Kenderes, Hungary. Professor. m. Erzsébet Barna, 3 sons, 2 daughters. Education: Agricultural Engineer, 1968, Professional Agricultural Engineer, 1975, Agricultural Doctor of the University, 1979, University of Agricultural Sciences, Gödöllő, Hungary; Candidate of Economy (PhD), The Hungarian Committee of Scientific Qualifications, Budapest, Hungary, 1988; Habilitation, Szent István University, Gödöllő, Hungary 1998. Appointments: Assistant, Co-operative Farm, Aranykalász, Törökszentmiklós; Manager, Farm Machinery Institute, Gödöllő, 1970; Chief Animal Breeder, Co-operative Farm, Lenin, Kunság Népe, Kunhegyes, 1970-78; Assistant Professor, Professor, University of Agricultural Sciences, Gödöllő, 1978-99; Professor, Szent István University,

Gödöllő, 2000-. Publications: Books: Vertical relations and possibilities for the improvement of interest in goose production; Miscellaneous poultry breeding; Examination of environmental conditions in the light of European Union requirements; Poultry Industry in Hungary; Works on technologies, market regulation and animal welfare. Honour: Outstanding Worker of Agriculture Award, Ministry of Agriculture and Food Industry. Memberships: World's Poultry Science Association Working Group No 8 Waterfowl, Hungarian Branch; Technical Commission of International Down and Feather Bureau; Chairman, Hungarian Standard National Technical Committee MSZT/MB 626, Feather and Down; Poultry Breeding Department, Association of Hungarian Foodstuffs Industry Science; World Rabbit Science Association, Hungarian Branch; Hungarian Association of Agricultural Economists; World Council of Hungarian University Professors; Association of Hungarian Specialists; Public Body of the Hungarian Academy of Sciences. Address: Szent István University; Department of Pig and Poultry Breeding; Páter Károly u 1, H-2103 Gödöllő, Hungary. E-mail: kozak.janos@mkk.szie.hu

**KOZLOVA Ariadna**, b. 28 May 1957, Russia. Senior Researcher. Education: Physics Educator, Orekhovo-Zuevo Pedagogical Institute, 1974-78; Mathematics Educator, Orekhovo-Zuevo, 1981-83; PhD, High Temp Institute, Academy of Sciences, Moscow, 1991; Postdoctoral, Moscow, 1993-96. Appointments: Teacher, Physics, Adelino, Ryazan Region, Russia, 1978-79; Senior Technician, EORRIB Electrogorsk, Moscow, 1979-80; Teacher, Physics and Mathematics, School, Electrogorsk, Russia, 1980-81; Tutor, Dept of Physics, Orekhovo-Zuevo Pedagogical Institute, 1981-83; Engineer, Department of Physics, 1983-84, Corresponding Postgraduate, 1984-88, Research Worker, Department of Physics, 1987-93, Postdoctoral Student, 1993-96, Research Worker, Department of Physics, 1996-, Moscow Aviation Institute. Publications include: High Power Laser-Science and Engineering, 1996; Solar Ultraviolet Radiation, (Modelling, Measurements, Effects), 1997; Surface Diffusion: Atomistic and Collective Processes, 1997. Memberships: New York Academy of Sciences; National Geographic Society; Russian Pushkin Society. Address: Moscow Aviation Institute, Volokolamskoye shosse 4, 125 871 Moscow, Russia.

**KOZLOWSKI Jerzy Marek**, b. 25 January 1931, Krakow, Poland. Educator; Planner; Architect. m. Zofia, 1 son. Education: B Arch, M Arch, Polytechnic, Krakow, 1953-55; Diplome Urbanisme, Ministere de la Construction, Paris, 1963; PhD, University of Edinburgh, 1971; Dr Habil, Polytechnic, Krakow, 1981; Professor (life nomination), Poland, 1991. Appointments: Town Planner, Team Leader, Urban Planning Office, Krakow, Poland, 1955-65; Town Planner, Research Fellow, Planning Research Unit, University of Edinburgh, 1965-71; Director, Research Institute on Environmental Development, Krakow, Poland, 1972-82; Professor, 1982-96, Head of Department of Regional and Town Planning, 1984-87, Director, Planning Programme, 1988-92, Emeritus Professor, 1996-, University of Queensland, Australia. Publications: 19 books; 2 textbooks; 20 research projects; 12 long-term town plans (team leader or member); 3 sub-regional plans (team member); Plan for Tatry National Park (team leader); 3 handbooks; 80 articles, papers at conferences (9 in UK, 20 in Poland, 12 in Italy, 19 in Australia, 3 in Sri Lanka, 2 in New Zealand, 1 in Ireland, Mexico, Turkey, Canada, China, Germany, Indonesia and Saudi Arabia). Honours: State Prizes for: Town plans of Tarnow, 1959, Zakopane and sub-region, 1961, development of threshold analysis, 1977; Scientific Award, Polish Academy of Sciences, 1980. Memberships: Association of Polish Architects; Association of Polish Urban Planners; Commission on Environmental Planning; International Union for Conservation; Planning Institute of Australia; World Society for Ekistics. Address: 118 Mildura Dr, Helensvale, Queensland 4212, Australia. E-mail: j.kozlowski@uq.edu.au

**KOZLOWSKI Wlodzimierz**, b. 12 August 1955, Warsaw, Poland. Physicist. Education: MSc, 1979, PhD, 1983, Moscow Power Engineering Institute – Technical University. Appointments: Expert, Institute of Nuclear Research, Poland, 1980-84; Assistant Professor, Institute of Fundamental Technological Research, Polish Academy of Sciences, Warsaw, 1984-91; Assist Professor, Institute of Nuclear Chemistry and Technology, Warsaw, 1992-94; Assistant professor, Institute of Biocybernetics and Biomedical Engineering, Polish Academy of Sciences, Warsaw, 1994-2002. Publications include most recently: Method of Discrete Displacements..., 1996; A Note on Varying Lattice Isotropy, 2002; Opportunity for Regulating the Collective Effect of Random Expansion with Manifestations of Finite Size Effects in a Moderate Number of Finite Systems, 2003 (http://arxiv.org/cond-mat/0307215). Honours: Listed in Who's Who publications and biographical dictionaries. Address: Bialostocka 9, Apt 25, Warsaw 03-741, Poland. E-mail: wlodekak@ibb.waw.pl

**KPANJA Edward**, b. 1953, Angwa-Madaki, Wamba, Nigeria. Lecturer. m. Edith H Kpanja, 1 son, 4 daughters. Education: B Ed, University of Ilorin, 1990; M. Ed, University of Zaria, 2000; Cert Ed/NCE, Ahmadu Bello University, Zaria, 2000. Appointments: Headmaster, Ministry of Education, Plateau State, Kango, Nigeria, 1976-79; Vice-Principal, Ministry of Education, Government College, Keffi, Nigeria, 1980-89; Principal, Ministry of Education, Nasarawa, Nigeria, 1996-98; Director, Ministry of Education, Nasarawa State, Lafia, Nigeria, 1999-2000; Lecturer, Head of Department, Ministry of Education, College of Education, Akwanga, Nasarawa State, Nigeria, 2001-. Publications: 29 articles in professional journals. Honours: 5 National Awards. Memberships: Member of associations and societies at a national level. Address: Department of Curriculum Studies, College of Education, Akwanga, Nasarawa State, Nigeria.

**KRAJICEK Richard**, b. 6 December 1972, Rotterdam, Netherlands. Tennis Player. m. Daphne Dekkers, 1999, 1 son, 1 daughter. Appointments: Started playing tennis, 3 years; Reached semi-finals, Australian Open, 1992; Wimbledon Men's Singles Champion, 1996; Won 20 titles to date Address: ATP Tour, 201 ATP Tour Boulevard, Ponte Vedra Beach, FL 32082, USA.

**KRALJEVIĆ Miro**, b. 16 February 1949, Ljubljana, Slovenia. Ichthyologist; Scientific Researcher. m. Živana Crvelin, 1 son. Education: BSc, Faculty of Natural Science and Mathematics, 1974, MSc, 1977, PhD, 1995, University of Zagreb, Croatia; Qualified as Assistant Professor, Faculty of Marine Fishery, University of Split, 1998. Appointments: Research Assistant, 1977-95, Senior Research Assistant, 1995-98, Assistant Professor, 1998-2002, Professor, 2002-, Institute of Oceanography and Fisheries, University of Split, Croatia. Publications: Numerous articles as co-author in scientific journals including most recently: Occurrence of bluefish, Pomatomus saltator (Linnaeus, 1766) and butterfish, Stromateus fiatola (Linnaeus, 1758), juveniles in the eastern central Adriatic, 2000; The occurrence of the lesser weever, Echiichthys vipera, in the eastern Adriatic, 2001; Fishing of Norway lobster, Nephrops norvegicus (L), with lobster pot in the Velebit Channel (eastern Adriatic), 2001; Effects of three diets on growth and body composition of gilthead sea bream, Sparus aurata (L), 2004. Honours: Listed in numerous biographical publications.

Memberships: Croatian Biology Association; Croatian Ecological Association; CIESM Association. Address: Institute of Oceanography and Fisheries, Šetalište Ivana Meštrovića 63, 21000 Split, Dalmatia, Croatia. E-mail: kraljević@izor.hr

**KRAMER Stephen Ernest,** b. 12 September 1947, Hampton Court, England. Circuit Judge. m. Miriam Leopold, 1 son, 1 daughter. Education: BA, 1969, MA, 1987, Keble College, Oxford; Université de Nancy, France. Appointments: Called to the Bar (Gray's Inn), 1970; Assistant Recorder, 1987-91, Recorder of the Crown Court, 1991-; Standing Counsel (Crime) to HM Customs and Excise South Eastern Circuit, 1989-95; Member, Bar Council, 1993-95, Committee, South Eastern Circuit, 1997-2000; Chairman Liaison Committee, Bar Council/ Institute of Barristers' Clerks, 1996-99; Committee Member, 1993-98, Acting Vice Chairman, 1998-99, Vice Chairman, 1999-2000, Chairman, 2000-2001, Criminal Bar Association; Queen's Counsel, 1995; Bencher Gray's Inn, 2001-; Head of Chambers, 2 Hare Court Temple, London, 1996-2003; Circuit Judge, 2003-05, Senior Circuit Judge sitting at Central Criminal Court, Old Bailey, 2005-.

**KRASILNIKOV Nikolay,** b. 22 January 1927, Irkutsk, USSR. Communications Educator; Researcher. m. Olga Krasilnikova, 1 son. Education: Graduate, Leningrad Politechnical Institute, 1950; PhD, Leningrad Institute of Aviation Instrument Making, 1952; DSc, Academy of Communication, Leningrad, 1964; Diploma of Professor, 1965. Appointments: Engineer, Institute of Television, Leningrad, 1950-54; Assistant Professor, 1954-57, Head of Department of Transmitting and TV Devices, Leningrad Institute of Aviation Instrument Making, 1957-1994; Professor, State University of Aerospace Instrumentation, Saint Petersburg, 1994-. Publications: 181 including 5 monographs, 1961, 1976, 1986, 1999, 2001; Articles in professional journals. Honours: Medal for Leningrad Defence, 1944; Honoured Scientific and Technical Worker of Russia, 1992; Honoured Professor of State University of Aerospace Instrumentation, St Petersburg, 1997. Memberships: Fellow, Science and Technology Society of Radio Engineering, Electronics and Communications, 1951; New York Academy of Sciences, 1995. Address: State University of Aerospace Instrumentation, 67 Bolshaia Morskaia, 190000 Saint Petersburg, Russia.

**KRATZ Karl-Ludwig,** b. 23 April 1941, Jena, Germany. Professor, Nuclear Chemistry. Education: Diploma, Chemistry, 1967; PhD, summa cum laude, 1972; Habilitation, 1979. Appointments: Professor of Nuclear Chemistry, University of Mainz, 1991-; Adjunct Professor, Nuclear Physics, University of Notre Dame, 2002-; Director, VISTARS. Publications: Numerous scientific papers and articles for professional journals. Honours: ACS Award for Nuclear Chemistry, 1999; GSI GENCO Award, 2004; Listed in several Who's Who and biographical publications. Memberships: Deutsche Physikal Ges; Ges Deutscher Chemiker; Astonom Ges; American Chemistry Society. Address: Johannes Gutenberg-Universität, Instut für Kernchemie, Fritz-Strassmann-Weg 2, D-55128, Mainz, Germany. E-mail: klkratz@uni-mainz.de

**KRAU Edgar,** b. 9 April 1929, Stanislau, Poland. University Professor; Scientist; Educator. m. Mary Epure, 1 daughter. Education: MA, Psychology, Education, 1951, PhD, Psychology, 1964, University of Cluj, Romania. Appointments include: High School Teacher, Gherla, Romania, 1952-61; Chief Research Fellow, Institute of Pedagogical Sciences, Cluj, 1961-63; Consecutive positions, University of Cluj, 1963-77; Head, Psychological Department, Academy of the Romanian Republic, Cluj Branch, 1968-77; Professor, University of Haifa, Israel, 1977-81; Professor, Tel-Aviv University, 1981-97. Publications:

Books: Coauthor, Treatise of Industrial Psychology, 1967; Author, editor, Self-realization, Success and Adjustment, 1989; Author, The Contradictory Immigrant Problem, 1991; Co-author: Project professionnel - projet de vie, 1992; Organizations and Management: Towards the Future, 1993; Author: The Realization of Life Aspirations through Vocational Careers, 1997; Social and Economic Management in the Competitive Society, 1998; A Meta-Psychological Perspective on the Individual Course of Life, 2003; Over 70 papers in leading scientific journals. Honours include: Vasile Conta Prize, Romanian Academy, 1972; Award, High Centre for Logic and Comparative Sciences, Bologna, Italy, 1972; Honorary Mention, Journal of Vocational Behavior, 1986; Homagial Biography, Bibliography, Revue Européenne de Psychologie Appliquée, 1993; Dedication, Outstanding People of the 20th Century, IBC; 20th Century Achievement Award, ABI, 1999; Honours List, International Biographical Centre, 2000; Cavalier, World Order of Science, Education and Culture, 2002; American Order of Excellence, 2003; Legion of Honor, United Cultural Convention, 2005; Listed in numerous international biographical publications. Memberships: International Association of Applied Psychology, 1970-, Executive Committee, Division of Psychology and National Development, 1982-86; Member-Instructor, Israeli Psychological Association, 1978-; Affiliate, American Psychological Association, 1993-; Active Member, New York Academy of Sciences, 1998-; Member of Academic Council, London Diplomatic Academy, 2002; Einsteinian Chair of Sciences, World Academy of Letters, 2004-. Address: 2 Hess Str, 33398 Haifa, Israel.

**KRAVCHENKO Lev Nikolaevich,** b. 24 September 1941, Ulianovsk, Russia. Radio Electronics Engineer; Professor. m. Liudmila Maslova, 2 sons. Education: Higher Education, Ulianovsk Polytechnical Institute, 1966; Candidate of Technical Sciences, Moscow Institute of Electronic Engineering and Technology, 1971; PhD, 1990. Appointments: Teacher, Chair of Radio Electronics, Ulianovsk Polytechnical Institute, 1966-68; Chief Specialist, JSC Research Institute of Molecular Electronics and Plant "Mikron" 1971-; Chief Designer of High Speed Circuits, Ministry of Electronics of the USSR, 1980-91. Publications: More than 100 scientific articles; 76 inventions and patents. Honours; Government Prize Winner in the field of engineering; Medal for Labour Valour, 2001. Memberships: Academician, Academy of Engineering Sciences of the Russian Federation; Corresponding Member, International Academy of Informatics at the UN. E-mail: lev@mikron.ru

**KRAVCHENKO Peter,** b. 21 June 1921, Kyiv, Ukraine. Designer of Special Effects. m. Valentyna Ponomarenko, 1 son, 1 daughter. Education: Diploma, Kyiv State Taras Shevchenko Art School; Diploma, Institute of Commercial Art, Australia; Diploma, School of Television Skill, Australia. Appointments: Visual Artist, Designer of Special Effects, Wardrobe Department, TV Studio, ABN 2, 20 years; Director, Board of Directors of Ukrainian Studies Foundation in Australia; Participated in art exhibitions in Australia and Ukraine. Publications: Many articles published as Approbated Correspondent, Ukrainian Weekly, The Free Thought; Book: Costumes of Ukraine, 1999. Honours: Honourable Diplomas from: President of Ukraine; Mayor of Kyiv, Ukraine; Minister of Culture and Art in Ukraine; Council Ukrainian Organisation in Australia; International Charity Funds: Spiritual Legacy, Ukrainian Khata, Cambridge University; International Peace Award, Cultural Assembly of USA. Memberships: Honorary Member, National Society of Artists in Ukraine; International Charity Fund, Spiritual Heritage, Kyiv; Co-founder, Member and Secretary, Ukrainian Artists Society in Australia. Address: 57 Georges Avenue, Lidcombe, New South Wales, Australia 2141.

**KRICHMAR Sava I Krichmar,** b. 11 December 1928, Odessa, Ukraine. Chemist. 1 daughter. Education: Physical Chemist, Dnepropetrovsk University, 1950; Doctor of Chemical Science, 1969; Professor, 1979. Appointments: Engineer, Nitrogenfertilizer works, Dneprodzerginsk, 1950; Manager, Laboratory, Institute of Nitrogen, 1959; Chief, Department of Chemistry, Industrial Institute, 1972; Professor, Main Scientist, Technical University, Kherson, 1994. Publications: More than 290 publications; Polarization Mechanism of the Smoothing by Electrochemical Burnishing of the Metals; Coulometric Detector for Gas Chromatography; Polarographic Analysis with Polymicroelectrode; Passage of Gas Convectional Barrier; Preparation of Calibrational Limiting Diluting of Gas Mixtures; Association within the Classical Theory of Fetus Formation of New Phase; Sanitary Gas Sensors. Honours: Medal, Inventor of USSR; Medal, Veteran of Work; IBC Outstanding People of the 21st Century Medal; Soros Grant. Memberships: New York Academy of Sciences; American National Geographic Society. Address: Bereslavskoe Street 24, Technical University, Kherson 73008, Ukraine.

**KRIKLER Dennis,** b. 10 December 1928. Cardiologist. m. Education: MB, ChB, with honours, 1951, MD, 1973, University of Cape Town. Appointments: House Physician and House Surgeon, 1952, Medical Registrar, 1954-55, Senior Medical Registrar, 1957-58, Groote Schuur Hospital, Cape Town; Registrar in Parthology and Tutor, University of Cape Town, 1953; Fellow in Medicine, Lahey Clinic, Boston, USA, 1956-57; Consultant Physician, Salisbury Area Hospital, Rhodesia, 1958-66; Clinical Assistant, Westminster Hospital, 1966-68; Clinical Tutor, North London Postgraduate Medical Centre, 1969-73; Consultant Physician, Prince of Wales's General Hospital and St Ann's General Hospital, London, 1967-73; Consultant Cardiologist, King Edward Memorial Hospital and Ealing Hospital, 1973-89; Consultant Cardiologist and Reader in Cardiovascular Diseases, Hammersmith Hospital and Royal Postgraduate Medical School, 1973-94; Emeritus Editor, British Heart Journal. Publications: Numerous articles in professional medical journals. Honours include: Freeman of the City of London, 1990; Medal of Honour, European Society of Cardiology, 1990; Silver Medal, British Cardiac Society, 1992; Chevalier dans l'Ordre National de la Legion d'Honneur, France, 1999. Memberships: Fellow, American College of Cardiology; Honorary Member, Societa' di cultura Medica Vercellese; Honorary Member, Societa di Medical de Levante, Valencia; Former Committee Member, British Cardiac Society and Ex-Officio Councillor; Corresponding Member, Societe Francaise de Cardiologie; Honorary Fellow, Council on Clinical Cardiology; Fellow, American Heart Association. Address: 2 Garden Court, Grove End Road, London NW8 9PP, England.

**KRŇANSKY Jan,** b. 17 October 1956, Prague, Czech Republic. University Teacher. m. Eva Krňanská, 1 daughter. Education: Dipl. Eng., Faculty of Civil Engineering,, 1981, PhD, 1987, Associate Professor, 1989, Technical University, Prague, 1981. Appointments: Assistant Professor, Civil Engineering, 1981-88, Associate Professor, 1989-93, Technical University, Prague; Technical Consultant for building industry, 1994-2002; Head of Department of Civil Engineering, Technical University of Liberec, Scholarly Consultant for building industry, 2003-. Publications: About 20 scientific articles published in professional journals; Author and co-author of 6 publications for Technical University Prague Press; Author of scripts in preparation for Technical University of Liberec Press. Honours: Honourable Recognition of the Rector, Technical University, Prague, 1987. Address: U Starého Mlyna 311, 10400 Prague-10, Czech Republic. E-mail: jan.krnansky@worldonline.cz

**KROCKOVER Gerald Howard,** b. 12 November 1942, Sioux City, Iowa, USA. Professor. m. Sharon Diane Shulkin, 2 sons. Education: BA, Chemistry, Secondary Education, 1964; MA, Science Education, Geology, 1966, PhD, Science Education, Geology, 1970, University of Iowa. Appointments: Science Teacher, Bettendorf and Iowa City, 1964-70; Assistant Professor, Associate Professor, Purdue University, West Lafayette, Indiana, 1970-80; Professor of Earth and Atmospheric Science Education, Purdue University, 1980-. Publications: 13 textbooks; 2 elementary science series; 2 video tape series. Honours include: Outstanding Science Educator, Association for the Education of Teachers of Science, 1973; Distinguished Teacher Educator Award, National Association of Teacher Educators, 1990. Memberships include: American Association for the Advancement of Science; International Organisation for Science and Technology Education. Address: Purdue University, 550 Stadium Drive, West Lafayette, IN 47907-2051, USA.

**KROGH Geo Von,** b. 25 January 1943, Bergen, Norway. Medical Doctor. Education: Graduate, University of Bergen, Norway, 1967; Training in Sweden, 1970-; Specialist in Dermatovenereology, 1978. Appointments: Associate Professor, Karolinska University Hospital Solna, Stockholm, Sweden; Currently working at Karolinska Department for Dermatovenereology. Publications: 119 publication of which 51 are original research contributions; 80 articles and 2 textbooks relating to the management of condylomas; Articles in medical journals as co-author include: Adolescent girls investigated for sexual abuse: history, physical findings and legal outcome, 1999; European course on HPV associated pathology: guidelines for primary care physicians for the diagnosis and management of anogenital warts, 2000; European guideline for the management of anogenital warts, 2001; Condyloma eradication: self-therapy with 0.15%-0.5% podophyllotoxin versus 20-25% podophyllin – an integrated safety assessment, 2001; Potential human papillomavirus reactivation following topical corticosteroid therapy of genital lichen sclerosus and erosive lichen planus, 2002; Screening and genotyping of genital Chlamydia trachomatis in urine specimens from male and female clients of youth-health centres in Stockholm County, 2002; The cost-effectiveness of patient-applied treatments for anogenital warts, 2003; Numerous surveys. Memberships include: Swedish Academy of Dermatology; Scandinavian Society of Genito-urinary Medicine; International Society for the Study of Vulvar Disease; Swedish Physicians Against AIDS; European Academy of Dermatology and Venereology; International AIDS Society; European Academy of Dermatology and Venereology; International Society for STD Research; Medical Society for the Study of Venereal Diseases; American Venereal Disease Association; Swedish Society for Dermatologic Surgery; American Academy of Dermatology; International Union against Sexually Transmitted Infections, European Branch, Honorary Treasurer, 2002-2003. Address: Department of Dermatovenereology, Karolinska University Hospital Solna, 171 76, Stockholm, Sweden. E-mail: geo.von.krogh@ood.ki.se

**KRONDAHL Hans,** Professor Emeritus; Fibre Artist; Fabric Designer. Education: Graduate, University College of Arts Crafts and Design, Stockholm, Sweden; Further studies in Europe and the Far East. Appointments: Teacher, Fibre Art and Textile Design in art schools, 1960-; Working in own studio for Tapestry Weaving and Fabric Design, 1963-; Senior Lecturer, Head of Textile Department, University College of Arts Crafts and Design, Stockholm, Sweden, 1977-78; Head of Textile Design Department, National College of Art and Design, Oslo, Norway, 1978-79; Head of Textile Design Department, HDK College, 1981-88, Professor of Textile Art, 1988-94 Gothenburg University, Sweden, 1981-88; Worked as UNIDO Expert in

Textile Design, Indonesia, 1979-80; Exhibits in Sweden and abroad most recently works included in "Katja of Sweden", Kulturen Museum, Lund, 2002-2003; Permanent representation in museum collections in Europe and USA; Tapestries, front curtains, rugs, carpets, ecclesiastical textiles and vestments commissioned for the public environment. Publications: Works included in: The Lunning Prize Exhibition Catalogue, 1986; Svenska Textilier 1890-1990, by Jan Brunius, etc, 1994; Contemporary Textile Art by Charles S Talley, 1982; Fiberarts Magazine, 1996. Address: Smedjegatan 8, S 21421 Malmö, Sweden.

**KROPACHEV Nikolay,** b. 8 February 1959, Leningrad, Russia. Lawyer; Judge. m. Natalia Alexandrovna Sidorova, 1 son. Education: Graduate, Law Faculty, 1981, PhD Student, 1981-84, PhD (Candidate of Law), Law Faculty, 1985, Doctor of Law Degree, 2000, St Petersburg State University. Appointments: Assistant (Junior) Lecturer, 1985-92, Senior Lecturer, 1992-2000, Professor, 2000-, Dean of the Special Law Faculty, 1992-98, Dean of the Law Faculty, St Petersburg State University, 1998-; Chairman, St Petersburg Charter Court, 2000-. Publications: Mechanism of Criminal Law Regulation, 1989; Penal Law (textbook), 1989; Criminology (textbook), 1992, 2003; Criminal Law on a Contemporary Stage, 1992; Russian Criminal Legislation (Comparative Analysis), 1996; Criminal Law Regulation: Mechanism and System, 1999; Criminal Law Regulation: the criminal liability, 2000. Honours: A F Koni Medal, Ministry of Justice, 1999; Russian President's Prize, 2002; Order of Honour, 2004. Memberships: Vice-President, Interregional Association of Law Schools, 1996; President, St Petersburg and Lenningrad Region Association of Lawyers. Address: Faculty of Law, St Petersburg State University, 22 aya liniya 7, R-199026 VO St Petersburg, Russia. E-mail: office@jurfak.spb.ru

**KROSNICK Mary Lou Wesley,** b. 11 June 1934, Bayonne, New Jersey, USA. Musician; Pianist; Teacher. m. Aaron B Krosnick, 1 son. Education: BS, Juilliard School of Music, 1957; MA, University of Wisconsin, 1958; MM, Yale University School of Music, 1961. Appointments: Head of Piano Department, Sewanee Summer Music Center, 1976-85; Assistant Professor of Music, 1978, Associate Professor of Music, 1985, Professor of Music, 1992, Distinguished Performer-in-Residence, 2000, Professor Emeritus, 2004-, Jacksonville University, Florida; Performances: Soloist with The Boston Pops Orchestra under Arthur Fiedler, 1961; Soloist with The Jacksonville Symphony Orchestra, Kennedy Center and Carnegie Hall under Willis Page, 1972; Soloist with The Jacksonville Symphony Orchestra under Morton Gould, 1981; Performances as a soloist and composer on Radio Stations: WAXR, WNYC, WOR-TV, Radio Free Europe, 1950-51; Composition: The Rain Comes (performed under Leopold Stokowsky in a version orchestrated by him by the New York Philharmonic-Symphony Orchestra, 1949). Publication: Book chapter in Isabella Vengerova: Beloved Tyranna by Joseph Rezits, 1995. Honours: 1st Place, New York Philharmonic Symphony's Young Composers' Contest, 1949; 1st Place, National Guild of Piano Teachers' International Recording Competition, Collegiate Division, 1957, Teachers' Division, 1972; 1st Place, University of Redlands, California, National American Music Competition, 1961. Memberships include: Florida State Music Teachers; Music Teachers National Association; National Federation of Music Clubs; Address: 12734 Bermuda Cay Court, Jacksonville, FL 32225, USA. E-mail: abkmlk@hotmail.com

**KRUG Arno,** b. 16 February 1935, Schneidemuhl, Germany. Surgeon. m. Christine, 3 sons, 1 daughter. Education: MD, Berlin-Marburg, 1959; PhD, Surgery, 1972, Professor, 1978,

Kiel. Appointments: Chief Surgeon, City Hospital, Hof/Saale, Germany, 1978-98; Retired, 1998-. Publications: Blood supply of the myocardium after temporary coronary occlusion; Alteration in myocardial hydrogen concentration: a sign of irreversible cell damage; The extent of ischemic damage in the myocardium of the cat after permanent and temporary coronary occlusion. Memberships: German Society of Surgery. Address: Theodor-Fontane-Str 20, D-95032 Hof/Saale, Germany. E-mail: arnokrug@yahoo.de

**KRUG Edward Charles,** b. 24 August 1947, New Brunswick, New Jersey, USA. Biogeochemist. m. Nancy Wegner. Education: BSc, Environmental Science, 1975, MSc, Soil Chemistry, 1978, PhD, Soil Science, 1981, Rutgers University. Appointments: Assistant Soil Scientist, Connecticut Agricultural Experiment Station, Connecticut, 1981-85; Associate Professional Scientist, Illinois State Water Survey, 1985-90; Independent Consultant, Minnesota, 1991-2000; Biogeochemist, Office of the Chief, Illinois State Water Survey, 2000-. Publications: Numerous articles in professional journals; 10 book chapters. Honours: Frank G Helyar Award, Rutgers University, 1973; Excellence in Review Award, Journal of Environmental Quality, 1991; Listed in several biographical publications. Memberships: American Geophysical Union; Soil Science Society of America; International Society of Soil Science; Certified Professional Soil Scientist; American Society of Agronomy. Address: Illinois State Water Survey, 2204 Griffith Dr, Champaign, IL 61820, USA. E-mail: ekrug@uiuc.edu

**KRUKOWSKI Zygmunt Henderson,** b. 11 December 1948, Crimond, Aberdeenshire, Scotland. Surgeon. m. Margaret Anne, 1 son, 2 daughters. Education: MB ChB, 1966-72, PhD, 1978, University of Aberdeen; FRCS (Edinburgh), 1976; FRCP (Edinburgh), 2001. Appointments: Basic and higher surgical training in Aberdeen, Inverness and London, Ontario; Lecturer in Surgery, 1977-86, Senior Lecturer, 1988-96, Reader, 1996-99, Professor of Clinical Surgery, 1999-, University of Aberdeen; Consultant Surgeon, 1986-; Surgeon to the Queen, 2004-. Publications: Publications on surgical audit, surgical infections, surgical technique, laparoscopic surgery, endocrine surgery and health services research. Honour: Honorary FRCS (Glasgow), 2000. Memberships: National Committees on Audit and Quality; President, British Association of Endocrine Surgeons, 2005-. Address: Aberdeen Royal Infirmary, Foresterhill, Aberdeen AB25 2ZN, Scotland.

**KRUPATKIN Alexander Ilych,** b. 17 February 1961, Moscow, Russia. Medical Doctor. Education: MD, Medical Institute, Tver, 1983; Dr.Neurologist, 1984; Consultant, Psychotherapy, 1987; PhD, 1989; Doctor of Medical Sciences, 1999. Appointments: Physician, Regional Hospital, Tver, 1983-84; Junior Researcher, Senior Researcher, Central Institute of Traumatology and Orthopaedics, Moscow, 1984-; Leading Researcher, 1999-. Publications: Several articles in professional journals; 2 books: Polarographic Method in Traumatology and Orthopaedics, Moscow, 1986; Clinical Neuroangiophysiology of the Limbs (perivascular innervation and nervous trophics), Moscow, 2003. Memberships: New York Academy of Sciences; Russian Association of Functional Diagnosis; Russian Association of Microcirculation, 1994-. Address: Voljsky bulvar kvartal 95, Korpus 3, Kvartira 4, 109125 Moscow, Russia.

**KRUSE-GRAUMANN Lenelis,** b. 16 February 1942, Berlin, Germany. University Professor. m. Carl F Graumann. Education: Diploma, Psychology, 1966; Dr Phil, 1972; Habilitation, 1976. Appointments: Heisenberg Scholarship, German Science Foundation, 1978-84; Professor of Psychology, Fern Universitaet in Hagen, Germany, 1985-; Honorary Professor,

University of Heidelberg, 1988-. Publications: Räumliche Umwelt, 1974; Privatheit als Problem und Gegenstand der Psychologie, 1980; More than 100 articles on environmental psychology, social psychology and psychology of language. Honour: Award for Best Dissertation, University of Heidelberg, 1973. Memberships: German Psychological Society; Associate Member, APA; Environmental Design Research Association. Address: Fern Universitaet in Hagen, Institute for Psychology, PO Box 940, D-58084 Hagen, Germany

**KRUSZEWSKI Eugeniusz Stanislaw**, b. 13 November 1929, Zbaszyn, Poland. University Professor; Historian. m. Marta Bialecka, 2 daughters. Education: MAEc, Poland, 1962; Postgraduate studies, Denmark, 1971-74; PhD, 1975, Dr. hab., 1980, Polish University, London. Appointments: Drafted into Polish Army, 1950-57, 1962-64, Financial Officer, Warsaw, Gdynia; Teacher, Secondary School, Gdańsk, 1965-69; Civil Servant, Governmental Centre of Documentation and Information, Copenhagen, Denmark, 1976-97; Reader, 1980-85, Professor of the History of International Relations, 1985-, Polish University, London; Director, Polish-Scandinavian Research Institute, Copenhagen, Denmark, 1985-. Publications: 6 books on Polish-Scandinavian history, immigration and emigrations history; Over 150 scientific articles, reviews, biographical articles. Honours: Army Medal, 1948; Home Army Cross, London, 1973; Knight Cross of the White Cross International, Sydney, Australia, 1990; Gold Medal of the Polish Cultural Congress, 1985, 1995; The Writers Award, Polish Combatants Association, London, 1992; Award of the Polish Union of Polish Writers Abroad, London, UK, 2000. Memberships: Danish Catholic Historians Society; Polish Historical Society in Great Britain; Polish Society of Arts and Sciences Abroad, London, UK; Union of Polish Writers Abroad, London; Albert Schweitzer Society, Cracow, Poland. Address: POB 2584, DK-2100 Copenhagen Ø – Denmark.

**KRUTILIN Zoya Paprikova**, b. 6 August 1951, Sofia, Bulgaria. Art Editor. m. Feodor Krutilin, deceased, 1 son, 1 daughter. Education: MA, History of Art Department, National Art Academy, Sofia, Bulgaria, 1975. Appointments: Art Historian, National Art Gallery, 1976-79; Art Editor with the Bulgarian Academy of Sciences, 1979-; Founder and Manager of a club for retired people of the arts and sciences, 2000-. Publications: Encyclopaedia A-Z; Bulgarian Encyclopaedia, 7 volumes; CD-ROM Encyclopaedia; Encyclopaedia "Nobel Award Winners"; Encyclopaedia "Bulgarian Traditions Calendar" (co-author). Memberships: Union of Bulgarian Scientists; Union of Bulgarian Journalists. Address: 6 Murgash Str, Sofia 1504, Bulgaria.

**KSHIRSAGAR Vitthal Sadashiv (K'Sagar)**, b. 27 October 1954, Pune, Maharashtra, India. Author. m. 1 son, 2 daughters. Education: BCom, 2nd Class with honours, 1976, LLB, 1st Class with Special Merit, 1979, Pune University. Appointments: Qualified and or selected for the posts: Government Labour Officer, Block Development Officer, Tahasildar, Revenue Officer, Deputy Collector, etc; Worked as: Government Labour Officer, Labour Welfare Officer, Investigating Officer, Industrial Court and In-Charge Assistant Labour Commissioner, State Services, Government of Maharashtra; Voluntary retirement, 1998; Author, educational literature, 1985-. Publications: Author of 42 books including: Adhunik Bharatacha Itihas; Adhunik Jagacha Itihas; Maharashtratil Samajsudharak; Assa Ha Bharat; Co-author of 18 books including: Bharatachi Rajyaghatana….; Rajyashastra Siddhanta Aani Vichar; Editor of 22 books including: India's Struggle for Independence (Marathi Version); India After Independence (Marathi Version); Human geography (Marathi Version). Address: K'Sagar Publications,

"Suvarna-Shilpa", 444/1 Shaniwar Peth, Pune-411030, India. E-mail: k_sagar_v@vsnl.net

**KUAN Shu-chuang**, b. 8 September 1919, Liaoning Province, China. Economist. m. Sheng-shu Ting, 1 daughter. Education: Tsinghua University, China, 1936-37; BA, Economics, Yenching University, China, 1940; AM, Economics, 1945; PhD, Economics, 1948; Radcliffe College, Harvard University, USA. Appointments: Economic Affairs Officer, UN Secretariat, New York City, USA, 1948-56; Research Associate, State Statistical Bureau, China, 1957-58; Research Associate, 1958-79; Senior Research Fellow, Institute of Economics, Chinese Academy of Social Sciences, Beijing, China, 1979-. Publications: Reconsidering the conditions of perfect competition; Simple dynamics in income, investment and consumption; A simple device for approximating solution of dynamic systems occurring in economics; An econometric article forecasting the American economy with reduced military expenditures. Honours: Phi Tau Phi; Phi Beta Kappa; Teaching Excellence Award. Address: 6-1-201 Tuanjichu Bcili, Beijing 100026, China.

**KUBIK Gerhard**, b. 10 December 1934, Vienna, Austria. Cultural Anthropologist; Ethnomusicologist; Psychoanalyst. m. Lidiya Malamusi. Education: PhD, University Vienna, 1971; Habilitation with the work Theory of African Music, 1980. Appointments: Field work since 1959 in 16 countries of sub-Saharan Africa, since 1974 also in Venezuela and Brazil, leading to the world's most comprehensive collection of documented recordings of African music and oral literature; Present status, University Professor. Publications: 260 works, including several books. Honours: Twice a recipient of a Körner Foundation Prize in Vienna; Life affiliateship to the Centre for Social Research, University of Malawi; Elected to Honorary Fellowship of the Royal Anthropological Institute of Great Britain and Ireland, London, 1995. Memberships: Sigmund Freud Museum, Vienna; Centre for Black Music Research, Chicago; Royal Anthropological Institute of Great Britain and Ireland, London; Oral Literature Research Programme, Blantyre, Malawi. Address: Burghardtgasse 6/9, A 1200 Vienna, Austria.

**KUBILIUS Jonas**, b. 27 July 1921, District Jurbarkas, Lithuania. Mathematician. m. Valerija Pilypaité, 1 son, 1 daughter. Education: Diploma with Honours, Vilnius University, 1945; Candidate of Science, Leningrad University, 1951; DSc, Steklov Institute, Moscow, 1957. Appointments: Laboratory Assistant, Assistant Professor, 1945-48, Associate Professor, Professor, 1951-, Rector, 1958-92, Vilnius University; Member, Praesidium, Academy of Sciences of Lithuania, 1962-92; People's Deputy of USSR, 1989-91; Member of Parliament of Lithuania, 1992-96. Publications: Probability methods in the Number Theory (7 editions), 1959; Real Analysis, 1970; Probability and Statistics (2 editions), 1980; Limit Theorems, 1988; Book of Essays, 1996; Antanas Baranauskas and Mathematics, 2001; Several hundred papers. Honours: State Prize in Sciences, 1958, 1980; Dr hc, Greifswald, Prague, Latvian, Salzburg universities, several orders. Memberships: Founder and President, Lithuanian Mathematical Society, 1962-; President, Lithuanian-USA Association, 1991-; President, Club, Experience, 1999-. Address: Faculty of Mathematics and Informatics, Vilnius University, Naugarduko 24, Vilnius LT-2006, Lithuania.

**KUDRYAVTSEVA Natalia**, b. 1 June 1946, Vyksa, Russia. Researcher. 1 son. Education: MD, Novosibirsk State University, 1969; PhD, 1977, Dr Sci, 1992, I P Pavlov Institute of Physiology. Appointments: Research Assistant, Laboratory of Central Regulation of Endocrine Functions, Institute of Physiology, Novosibirsk, 1970-71; Junior Researcher, Senior

Researcher, Leading Researcher, Laboratory of Behavioural Phenogenetics, Institute of Cytology and Genetics, Siberian Department of Russian Academy of Sciences, Novosibirsk, 1971-96; Lecturer, Department of Physiology, Novosibirsk State University, 1988-2001; Head, Neurogenetics of Social Behaviour Sector, Institute of Cytology and Genetics SD RAD, Novosibirsk, 1997-. Publications: 114 articles in scientific journals include most recently as author and co-author: Use of the "partition" test in behavioral and pharmacological experiments, 2003; Changes in the expression of monoaminergic genes under the influence of repeated experience of agonistic interactions: From behavior to genes, 2004; Lorenz was right! Or does aggressive energy accumulate?, 2004; Sociobiology of aggression: mice and people, in Russian, 2004; Dynamic changes of serotonergic and dopaminerge activities during development of anxious depression: Experimental study, in Russian, 2004; Modulation of anxiety-related behaviours by μ- and -opioid receptor agonists depends on the social status of mice, 2004. Honours: 8 research grants; Stipend for Leading Scientist of Russia, 1994-96, 2000-2002. Memberships: International Brain Research Organisation; International Society for Research on Aggression. Address: Institute of Cytology and Genetics, Siberian Department of the Russian Academy of Sciences, pr Ak. Lavrentjeva 10, Novosibirsk 630090, Russia.

**KUEHN Arthur H,** b. 31 October 1936, Cincinnati, Ohio, USA. Minister. m. Gladys M George. Education: BA, Wilmington College, Ohio, 1958; MDiv, Colgate Rochester Divinity School, 1961; Ordination, American Baptist Churches, USA, 1961. Appointments: Associate Minister, 1st Baptist Church, Columbus, Ohio, 1961-63; Pastor, 1st Baptist Church, Hudson, Wisconsin, 1963-67; Director of Visitation and Counselling, Central Baptist Church, Hartford, Connecticut, 1967-77; Senior Minister, United Baptist Church, Lewiston, ME, 1977-88; Executive Director, Opportunity Farm for Boys, New Gloucester, ME, 1988-90; Senior Minister, The Inter-Faith Chapel, Silver Springs, MD, 1990-99; Retired, 1999; Protestant Chaplain, Holland America Line, 2003-present. Publications: Editor, The Wilmingtonian, 1958; Contributor to: The Secret Place; The Baptist Leader; The Word in Season. Memberships: The Ministers and Missionaries Benefit Board; Board of Trustees, Vice President, The Central Presbyterian Church of Chambersburg, PA; Board of Directors, Lutheran Home Care Services, Inc, Chambersburg, PA; Torch Club of Chambersburg, PA; Vice President, Penn National Home Owners Association, Fayetteville, PA; Bronze Medallist, Summer National Senior Games (Softball), The Senior Olympics, 2005. Address: 6887 St Annes Drive, Fayetteville, PA 17222-9442, USA.

**KUHN Alfred Karl,** b. 19 January 1933, Basel, Switzerland. Chemical Engineer. m. Elizabeth A Bierwert, 1 son. Education: Diploma, (MS), 1956. Appointments: Research and Development Engineer, Brown Boveri, 1957-62; Lummus Process Engineer, 1975; ANG Process Engineer, Manager, Director, 1975-84; Process Development Manager, ANG and DGC, 1985-97; Retired, 1997; Part-time Consultant, 1998-. Honours: Distinguished Service Award, 1996. Membership: GEP. Address: 7425 South Houstoun Waring Circle, Littleton, CO 80120, USA.

**KÜHNE Andreas,** b. 28 September 1952, Halle, Saale, Germany. Historian of Science. 1 daughter. Education: Dipl Ing, 1975, Dr Ing, 1982, TU Ilmenau; Dr rer nat habil, Ludwig-Maximilians University, München, 2000; Priv Doz, University of München, 2000. Appointments: Archivist, Deutsche Akademie fur Naturforscher, Halle/Saale, 1982-86; Professor, Co-editor, Nicolaus-Copernicus-Edition, Ludwig-Maximilians University, 1991-; Professor, Academy of Fine Arts, München,

1994-. Publications: Numerous articles in professional scientific journals. Memberships: Society for the History of Science. Address: Wendl-Dietrich-Str 18, 80634 München, Germany. Email: a.kuehne@lrz.uni-muenchen.de

**KUHRT Gordon Wilfred,** b. 15 February 1941, Madras, South India. Clergyman. m. Olive, 3 sons. Education: BD, Honours, London University, 1960-63; Oakhill Theological College, 1965-67; Doctor in Professional Studies, Middlesex University, 2001. Appointments: Religious Education Teacher, 1963-65; Curate, St Illogan, Truro, England, 1967-70; Curate, Holy Trinity, Wallington, England, 1970-73; Vicar of Shenstone, Lichfield, England, 1973-79; Vicar of Emmanuel, South Croydon, England, 1979-89; Rural Dean, Croydon Central, 1981-86; Honorary Canon of Southwark Cathedral, 1987-89; Archdeacon of Lewisham, 1989-96; Chief Secretary of the Advisory Board for Ministry, 1996-98; Director of Ministry, Ministry Division, Archbishop's Council, 1999-. Publications: Handbook for Council and Committee Members, 1985; Believing in Baptism, 1987; Doctrine Matters (editor), 1993; To Proclaim Afresh (editor), 1995; Issues in Theological Education and Training, 1998; Clergy Security, 1999; An Introduction to Christian Ministry, 2000; Ministry Issues for the Church of England – Mapping the Trends, 2001; Bridging the Gap: Reader Ministry Today, 2002. Membership: Fellow of the College of Preachers. Address: Ministry Division, Archbishops' Council, Church House, Great Smith Street, London SW1P 3NZ, England. E-mail: gordon.kuhrt@mindiv.c-of-e.org.uk

**KUIJKEN Barthold,** b. 1949, Belgium. Musician. Education: Modern Flute, Bruges Conservatory and the Royal Conservatories of Brussels and The Hague. Career: Researcher on authentic instruments in museums and private collections; Specialist on the performance of early music from the 17th and 18th centuries on original instruments; Member of Brussels-based ensemble Musiques Nouvelles focusing on avant garde music; Performances with his brothers Wieland (viola da gamba, baroque cello) and Sigiswald (baroque violin, viola da gamba); Performances with Rene Jacobs (counter tenor), Paul Dombrecht (baroque oboe), Lucy van Dael (baroque violin) and with harpsichordists, Robert Kohnen, Gustav Leonhardt, Ewald Demeyere and Bob van Asperen; Baroque Flutist in the Orchestra, Collegium Aureum and in La petite Bande; Chamber music concerts world-wide; Professor of Baroque Flute, Royal Conservatories of Brussels and The Hague; Guest Professor and Member of International Juries. Publications: Numerous scholarly works include: Annotated Urtext edition of J S Bach's Flute Music. Recordings: Numerous recordings on various record labels. Honours: Le Choc de l'Année 2001, France; Diapason d'Or de l'Année 2002, France. Address: Zwartschaapstraat 38, B-1755 Gooik, Belgium.

**KUKLA Cynthia Mary,** b. 23 June 1952, Chicago, Illinois, USA. Artist; Art Professor. 2 sons. Education: BFA, School of the Art Institute of Chicago, Chicago, Illinois, 1973; MFA, University of Wisconsin-Madison, Madison, Wisconsin, 1983. Appointments: Assistant Professor of Art, 1983-1989, Associate Professor of Art, 1989-93, Northern Kentucky University, Highland Heights, Kentucky; Associate Professor of Art, 1993-2003, Professor of Art, 2004-, Illinois State University, Normal, Illinois. Exhibitions: Over 50 solo exhibitions include: Headley Whitney Museum, Lexington, Kentucky, 1985; Armory Art Gallery, Blacksburg, Virginia, 1985; Chautauqua Art Center, New York, 1995; University of Illinois, 2000; Contemporary Art Center, Peoria, Illinois, 2005; Over 200 group exhibitions include: Laguna Beach Art Museum, Laguna Beach, California, 1983; American Embassy, Quito, Ecuador, 1989; Grand European National Centre, Arts e Lettres, Nice, France, 1990;

Canton Art Institute, Canton, Ohio, 1992; Kharkov Art Museum, Ukraine, 1992; Arrowmount Center, Gatlinburg, Tennessee, 1993, 1993, 2005; Rockford Art Museum, Rockford, Illinois, 1995; Ft. Sztuki Association, Krakow, Poland, 1998; Palace of Art, Budapest, Hungary, 1999; Lakeview Art Museum, Peoria, Illinois, 2002; Vivarosi Gallery, Budapest, Hungary, 2004. Honours: University grants for sculpture, 1994, 1997, 2003; University technology grants to develop "Lost Art" website: www.cfa.ilstu.edu/cmkukla, 1997, 1998, 1999; Fellowships, Hungarian Multicultural Council, Balatonfured, Hungary and Vermont Studio Center, Johnson, Vermont, 2003; Keynote Speaker, Cincinnati Art Museum,2004; Fellowship, Virginia Center for Creative Arts, Amhurst, 2005; Travel grant for panel participation in Impact.kontakt Art Conference, Berlin and Poznan, 2005; Commission: 5 paintings for inauguration of Spurlock Museum of World Culture, University of Illinois, Champaign-Urbana, 2001. Memberships: American Institute of University Women; Art Institute of Chicago; College Art Association; Contemporary Art Center, Cincinnati; McLean County Art Center, Bloomington; National Museum of Women Artist, Washington, DC; Rotary International. Address: 1001 Broadmoor Drive, Bloomington, IL 61704-6109. E-mail: cmkukla@ilstu.edu

**KULICHENKO Anatoly,** b. 18 March 1948, St Petersburg, Russia. Textile and Clothing Scientist. Divorced, 2 daughters. Education: Engineer, Leningrad Institute of Textile and Light Industry (LITLI), 1972; Candidate of Technical Sciences (PhD), LITLI, 1978; Docent, LITLI, 1985; Professor, St Petersburg University of Technology and Design, SUTD (former LITLI), 1995; Visiting Professor, De Montfort University, Leicester, UK, 1998; Doctor of Technical Sciences, 2005. Appointments: Engineer, Technologist, Designer, Clothing Manufacturing Companies, Leningrad, 1972-75; Research Course, Department of Textile Science, LITLI, 1975-78; Lecturer, Senior Lecturer (Docent), Professor, Department of Textile Science, LITLI-SUTD, 1978-. Dean of Faculty, Clothing Design and Technology, SUTD, 1994-2002; Head, Department of Textile Science, 2000-, Pro-Rector for University Development, 2002, SUTD-; Doctor of Technical Sciences Degree, 2005, Moscow-. Publications: About 100 publications in the area of textile and clothing science and higher education in Russia, UK, USA, Canada, Hong Kong, Ukraine, France, Finland and others. Honours: Distinguished Leadership Diploma; Man of the Year, 2000, ABI; Meritus Worker of Higher Professional Education Medal, Russian Federation, 2000; Honorary Degree of Doctor of Technology, De Montfort University, UK, 2003. Memberships: European Textile Network; The Textile Institute, UK; The Fibre Society, USA. Address: State University of Technology and Design, 18 Bolshaja Morskaja Str, St Petersburg, Russia 191186.

**KUMAR Perikala Vijayananda,** b. 1 June 1949, Neppalli, India. Doctor; Pathologist. m. Sandhya Kumar, 2 daughters. Education: MBBS, Kurnool Medical College, India, 1973; MD, Shiraz Medical School, Iran, 1980. Appointment: Professor of Pathology, Shiraz Medical School, Shiraz University of Medical Sciences, Iran. Publications: 100 papers published in national and international journals. Membership: International Academy of Cytology. Address: Department of Pathology, Shiraz Medical School, Shiraz University of Medical Sciences, Shiraz, Iran. E-mail: kumar@sums.ac.ir

**KUMM Dietmar Alfred,** b. 20 January 1959, Munich, Germany; Orthopaedic Surgeon. m. Patricia Anne Schneider, 1 son, 2 daughters. Education: Medical Student, Frierich-Wilhelms University, Bonn Germany, 1978-84; MD, University of Bonn, 1984; PhD, 1985. Appointments: Intern, Basle

University, Switzerland, 1984; Assistant Surgeon, EV Hospital, Badgodesberg, 1984-89; Assistant, University of Cologne, Cologne, Germany, 1989-94; Assistant Professor, University of Cologne, Cologne, Germany, 1984-86; Senior Doctor, University of Witten-Herdecke, Witten, 1996-2003; Chief Doctor, Department Director, Head of Department, Bethesda, Hospital, Duisburg, Germany, 2003. Publications: Consultant in field; Contributor of articles to professional journals; Numerous patents: Achievements include: Invention of Periprothet Halterungs Systeme; Gewindestift fuer Femurepiphyse. Memberships: New York Academy of Sciences; German Association for Orthopaedics and Traumatology; BVO; American Association for the Advancement of Science; German Association for Sports Medicine. Address: Orthopädische Klinik, Bethesda KRHS, Heerstr 219, D-47053 Duisburg, Germany.

**KUMPINSKY Enio,** b. Porto Alegre, Brazil. Chemical Engineer. m. Marsha Gail Brum, 4 children. Education: BSChemE, Federal University of Rio Grande do Sul, 1976; MSChemE, Federal University of Rio de Janeiro, 1978; PhD, Chemical Engineering, University of Houston, 1983. Appointments: Research Engineer, DuPont, Wilmington, Delaware, 1984-89; Division Engineer, DuPont, Louisville, 1989-91; Senior Staff Research Engineer, 1991-98, Principal Engineer, 1998-2004, Research Fellow, 2004-, Ashland Speciality Chemical Company, Columbus; Calorimetry and Heat Transfer Consultant, Ashland Speciality Chemical Company Worldwide, 1995-2002; Lean Six Sigma and Design for Six Sigma Initiatives, 2003-; Six Sigma Master Black Belt. Publications: Several articles in professional journals. Address: Ashland Speciality Chemical Company, PO Box 2219, Columbus, OH 43216, USA.

**KUNDT Wolfgang Helmut,** b. 3 June 1931, Hamburg, Germany. Astrophysics Professor. m. Ulrike Schümann, 1 son, 1 daughter. Education: Dipl Phys, 1956, Promotion, 1959, Habilitation, 1965, Hamburg University, under Pascual Jordan. Career: Professor, Hamburg, Bielefeld, Bonn; Visiting Scientist: Pittsburgh, Pennsylvania; Edmonton; Cern; Kyoto; Boston; Bangalore; Linz; Maribor. Publications: Over 250 articles on astrophysics, geophysics and biophysics; 6 books including: Astrophysics: a New Approach, 2004. Honours: NASA Group Achievement Award, 1975. Memberships: AG; EPS. Address: Institut für Astrophysik der Universität, Auf Dem Hügel 71, D-53121, Bonn, Germany. E-mail: wkundt@astro.uni-bonn.de

**KUNDU Anjan,** b. 24 January 1953, Calcutta, India. Scientist. m. Liudmila Kundu, 1 daughter. Education: Diploma in Journalism, 1975, Diploma in Teaching, Interpreter's Diploma, 1977, MSc, Physics, 1977, PhD, Physics, Mathematics, Science, 1981, P.L. University, Moscow. Appointments include: Research Associate, JINR, Dubna, USSR, 1981-83; Lecturer in Physics, BITS, Pilani, 1983-85; Professor, SINP, Calcutta, 1985-; Visiting Scientist: P L University, Moscow, USSR, 1987; University Rome 'La Sapienza', Italy, 1986, 1991, 1992, 1994, 2004; University GH Kassel, Germany, 1993; University Genova, Italy, 1994; Prague Technical University, Czech, 1994; University Bonn, Germany, 1994, 1996; University North Carolina, USA, 1997; University Hannover, Germany, 1999; LAPTH, Annecy, France, 2000; University Rome III, Italy, 2000, 2004; University Dortmund, Frei University, Germany, 2001; University of Wuppertal, Germany, 2004; University of Connecticut, University of Rochester, Ohio State University, USA, 2005. Publications: More than 75 original Scientific Research Contributions in National and International Journals; Book publications, editor and contributor, IOP (UK), 2003; Other publications features, short stories in journals and newspapers; Amateur movie making. Honours include: TPSC Lecturership Award (Senior),

# DICTIONARY OF INTERNATIONAL BIOGRAPHY

1990, 1992, 1995, 1996, 2000-2; AvH Foundation, Germany Fellowship, 1993-4, 1996, 1999, 2001. Listed in: Biographical Publications. Memberships: American Mathematical Society; Indian Physical Society; Advisory Committee of DST project; Member, Planning Committee, SERC School of Non-Linear Dynamics. Address: Theory Group, Saha Institute of Nuclear Physics, 1/AF Bidhan Nagar, Calcutta 700 064, India. E-mail: anjan@tnp.saha.ernet.in

**KUNERT Günter**, b. 6 March 1929, Berlin, Germany. Poet; Author; Dramatist. m. Marianne Todten. Education: Hochschule für angewandte Kunst, Berlin-Weissensee. Publications: Poetry: Wegschilder und Mauerinschriften, 1950; Erinnerung an einen Planeten: Gedichte aus Fünfzehn Jahren, 1963; Der ungebetene Gast, 1965; Verkündigung des Wetters, 1966; Warnung vor Spiegeln, 1970; Im weiteren Fortgang, 1974; Unterwegs nach Utopia, 1977; Abtötungsverfahren, 1980; Stilleben, 1983; Berlin beizeiten, 1987; Fremd daheim, 1990; Mein Golem, 1996; Erwachsenenspiele, autobiography, 1997; Nachtvorstellung, poems, 1999. Novel: Im Namen der Hüte, 1967. Other: Der ewige Detektiv und andere Geschichten, 1954; Kramen in Fächen: Geschichten, Parabeln, Merkmale, 1968; Die Beerdigung findet in aller Stille statt, 1968; Tagträume in Berlin und andernorts, 1972; Gast aus England, 1973; Der andere Planet: Ansichten von Amerika, 1974; Warum schreiben?: Notizen ins Paradies, 1978; Ziellose Umtriebe: Nachrichten von Reisen und Daheimsein, 1979; Verspätete Monologe, 1981; Leben und Schreiben, 1983; Vor der Sintflut: Das Gedicht als Arche Noah, 1985; Die letzten Indianer Europas, 1991. Honours: Heinrich Mann Prize, 1962; Heinrich Heine Prize, Düsseldorf, 1985; Hölderlin Prize, 1991; Georg-Trakl Prize, Austria, 1997. Memberships: Deutsche Akademie für Sprache und Dichtung e.v., Darmstadt. Address: Schulstrasse 7, D-25560 Kaisborstel, Germany.

**KÜNG Hans**, b. 19 March 1928, Lucerne, Switzerland. Professor of Ecumenical Theology Emeritus; Author. Education: Gregorian University, Rome; Institut Catholique, Paris; Sorbonne, University of Paris. Appointments: Ordained Roman Catholic Priest, 1954; Practical Ministry, Lucerne Cathedral, 1957-59; Scientific Assistant for Dogmatic Catholic Theology, University of Münster/Westfalen, 1959-60; Professor of Fundamental Theology, 1960-63, Professor of Dogmatic and Ecumenical Theology, 1963-80, Director, Institute of Ecumenical Research, 1963-96, Professor of Ecumenical Theology, 1980-96, Professor Emeritus, 1996-, University of Tübingen; President, Foundation Global Ethic, Germany, 1995, Switzerland, 1997; Various guest professorships and lectureships throughout the world. Publications: The Council: Reform and Reunion, 1961; That the World May Believe, 1963; The Council in Action, 1963; Justification: The Doctrine of Karl Barth and a Catholic Reflection, 1964, new edition, 1981; Structures of the Church, 1964, new edition, 1982; Freedom Today, 1966; The Church, 1967; Truthfulness, 1968; Infallible?: An Inquiry, 1971; Why Priests?, 1972; On Being a Christian, 1976; Signposts for the Future, 1978; The Christian Challenge, 1979; Freud and the Problem of God, 1979; Does God Exist?, 1980; The Church: Maintained in Truth, 1980; Eternal Life?, 1984; Christianity and the World Religions: Paths to Dialogue with Islam, Hinduism and Buddhism (with others), 1986; The Incarnation of God, 1986; Church and Change: The Irish Experience, 1986; Why I Am Still A Christian, 1987; Theology for a Third Millennium: An Ecumenical View, 1988; Christianity and Chinese Religions (with Julia Ching), 1989; Paradigm Change in Theology: A Symposium for the Future, 1989; Reforming the Church Today, 1990; Global Responsibility: In Search of a New World Ethic, 1991; Judaism, 1992; Mozart: Traces of Transcendence, 1992; Credo: The Apostles' Creed Explained for Today, 1993; Great Christian Thinkers, 1994; Christianity, Its Essence and History,

1995; Islam, in preparation; A Dignified Dying; A plea for personal responsibility (with Walter Jens) 1995; A Global Ethic for Global Politics and Economics, 1997; The Catholic Church, A Short History, 2001; Tracing the Way, Spiritual Dimensions of the World Religions, 2002; My Struggle for Freedom, Memoirs I, 2003. Honours: Oskar Pfister Award, American Psychiatric Association, 1986; Göttingen Peace Award, 2002; 22nd Niwano Peace Prize, Tokyo, 2005; Many honorary doctorates. Address: Waldhäuserstrasse 23, 72076 Tübingen, Germany.

**KUNJAPPU Joy**, b. 18 January 1951, Trichur, India. Research Chemist. m. Mercy Joseph, 1 son, 1 daughter. Education: MSc, 1972; PhD, 1985; DSc, 1996. Appointments: Lecturer, Chemistry, Star Tutorial College, Trichur, 1972-74; Scientific Officer, Bhabha Atomic Research Centre, India, 1974-87, 1989-94; Associate Research Scientist, Postdoctoral, Columbia University, New York, 1987-89, 1994-96; Research Chemist, Polytex Environmentalinks, New York, 1997-98; Consultant, Chemical Sciences, 1999-; Consultant and Adjunct Faculty, Yeshiva University, New York, 2001-; Visiting Professor of Chemistry, Barnard College of Columbia University, New York, 2000-; Adjunct Research Scientist, Chemistry Department, Columbia University, New York, 2004-; Adjunct Professor, Brooklyn College of CUNY, New York, 2004-. Publications: 80 including research articles; Book: Essays in Ink Chemistry, 2002; Poems in Malayalam. Honours: Deputy Director General, International Biographical Association; Advisor to the American biographical Institute; Netaji Subash Chandra Bose Award for Excellence in Surface Science, 2004. Memberships: Association for Surface Scientists; New York Academy of Sciences; American Chemical Society, USA; Association for the Advancement of Medical Instrumentation, USA. Address: 11 Fort George Hill, # 20B, New York, NY10040, USA

**KURODA Haruhiko**, b. 25 October 1944, Japan. Banker. Education: BA, Law, University of Tokyo, Japan, 1967; M Phil, Economics, University of Oxford, England, 1971. Appointments: Joined Japan's Ministry of Finance, 1967. Secondment to International Monetary Fund, Washington DC, USA, 1975-78; Director, International Organisations Division, International Finance Bureau, 1987-88; Secretary to the Minister of Finance, 1988-89; Director of several divisions including International Tax Affairs Division, Tax Bureau, 1989-92; Deputy Vice Minister of Finance for International Affairs, 1992-93; Commissioner, Osaka Regional Taxation Bureau, 1993-94; Deputy Director-General, International Finance Bureau, 1994-96; President, Institute of Fiscal and Monetary Policy, 1996-97; Director-General International Finance Bureau, 1997-99; Vice Minister of Finance for International Affairs, 1999-2003; Special Adviser to the Cabinet, 2003-2005; Professor, Hitotsubashi University, Graduate School of Economics, 2003-2005; President, Asian Development Bank, 2005-. Publications: Several books on monetary policy, exchange rate, international finance policy co-ordination, international taxation and international negotiations. Address: Asian Development Bank, 6 ADB Avenue, Mandaluyong City, 1550 Metro Manila, Philippines. E-mail: e-mail@adb.org

**KUROKAWA Kisho**, b. 8 April 1934, Aichi, Japan. m. Ayako Wakao, 7 December 1984. Education: BArch, Kyoto University, 1957; MArch, 1959, Doctor's course of Architecture, 1964, University of Tokyo. Appointments: President, Kisho Kurokawa Architect and Associates, 1962-; Academician, Japan Art Academy, 1998-; President, The Japan Society of Landscape Design; Professor, Qinghua University, Beijing, China; Advisor, Prime Minister of the Republic of Kazakhstan, 2000-; Senior Advisor, Institute of Urban Planning Board of Capital, Province of Henan, China, 2001-; Advisor, People's Government of

Kunming, China, 2004-; Major works include: Japan: The National Ethnological Museum; Hiroshima City Museum of Contemporary Art; Nagoya City Art Museum, National Art Center; Osaka International Convention Centre; Melbourne Central, Australia; Republic Plaza, Singapore; Kuala Lumpur International Airport, Malaysia; New Wing of the Van Gogh Museum, Amsterdam. Publications: Urban Design, 1965; Homo Movens, 1969; Thesis on Architecture I, 1982; The Philosophy of Symbiosis, 1987, revised version, 1996, English version, 1997, German version, 2005; The Era of Nomad, 1989; Thesis on Architecture II, 1990; Hanasuki, 1991; Poems of Architecture, 1993; Kisho Kurakawa Note, 1994; Kuala Lumpur International Airport, 1998; Millennium Kisho Kurakawa, 2000; Kisho Kurakawa Architect & Associates, 2001; Kisho Kurakawa: The London Texts, 2002. Honours include: First Order, Madara, Bulgarian Government, 1979; Commandeur de l'Ordre du Lion de Finlande, 1985; Gold Medal, Academy of Architecture, France, 1986; Richard Neutra Award for Architecture, California State Polytechnic University, USA, 1988; Honorary Citizen of Sofia, Bulgaria; Officier de l'Ordre des Arts et des Lettres, Le Ministere de la Culture, France, 2003. Memberships: Honorary Fellow, American Institute of Architects; Honorary Fellow, Royal Institute of British Architects; Honorary Member, Union of Architects, Bulgaria; Member, Ordre des Architectes, France; Honorary Member, Bund Deutscher Architeken; Life Patron, IBA. Address: Kisho Kurokawa Architect & Associates, 11F Aoyama Building, 1-2-3 Kita-Aoyama, Minato-ku, Tokyo 107-0061, Japan.

**KURUVILLA Bill (Kollanparampil),** b. 20 July 1943, Kodukulanji, Kerala, India. Engineer. m. Santha, 1 son, 3 daughters. Education: BSc, Electrical Engineering, Kerala, India, 1965; MBA, Business Administration, USA; Student in Theology, USA; PhD programme in Philosophy and Apologetics; PhD, Business Administration, USA, 1997; Diploma in Children's Writing, CT, USA, 2000. Appointments: Lecturer, MA College of Engineering, Kerala, India, 1965-66; Executive Engineer, Kerala State Electricity Board, India, 1966-88; Electrical Engineer, Zesco, Lusaka, Zambia, 1972-75; Chief of Power Station, Sher, Ministry of Power, Mozambique, 1979-81; Design Engineer, Septa, Philadelphia, PA, USA, 1989-. Publications: Numerous articles; 3 books; 1 US patent. Honours: Lifetime Royal Patronage and Citizen of the Year, 1994, 1996; Listed in Who's Who in America and Who's Who in the World; Honored Member, America's Registry of Outstanding Professionals for the Year, 2000-01, 2001-02, 2002-03, 2003-04. Memberships: World Affairs Council of Philadelphia; Institute of Engineers (India); Associate, Library of Congress, USA; Handiham Club of USA. Address: 133A Dawn Drive, Lansdale, PA 19446, USA.

**KUSHKUMBAYEV Sanat,** b. 2 December 1972, Russia. Scholar; Political Scientist. Education: Diploma with honours, Kazakh State National University, 1996; Postgraduate Degree, PhD, 1999. Appointments: Teacher of Political Science and Theory of International Relations, Humanities Institute "D A Kunaev", 1996-97; Research Fellow, Institute of Development of Kazakhstan, 1997-99; Deputy Director, Head of Analysis and Prognosis Department, 1999-2004, Head of the Department of International Studies, 2004-, Institute of Oriental Studies; Regular participant in forums on implementation of initiative of the Conference on Interaction and Confidence Building Measures in Asia, 1998-; Participant in more than 40 international conferences and organiser of 12 international conferences. Publications: Book: Central Asia on the way to integration: geopolitics, ethnicity and security, 2002; More than 60 papers in national and foreign journals; Author of articles, analytical materials and books on the problems of international and regional security in the area of Central Asia and the Caspian. Honour: Winner, M Auezov Award (Diploma and Medal) for young scholars in the field of science in the Republic of Kazakhstan, 2000. Memberships: European Association of Central Asian Studies; National Association of Political Science of Kazakhstan. Address: Institute of Oriental Studies, Kurmangazy Str 29, Almaty, Kazakhstan. E-mail: kushkumbayev@yahoo.com

**KUTCHER Ashton (Christopher),** b. 7 February 1978, Ceder Rapids, Iowa, USA. Actor. Education: Biochemical Engineering Student, University of Iowa. Career: Sweeper, General Mills plant; Modeling. Film Appearances include: Coming Soon, 1999; Down To You, 2000; Reindeer Games, 2000; Dude Where's My Car?, 2000; Texas Ranger, 2001; Just Married, 2003; My Boss's Daughter, 2003; Cheaper by the Dozen, 2003; The Butterfly Effect, 2004. TV Appearances include: Just Shoot Me, 1997; That 70's Show, 1998; Grounded for Life, 2002; The Tonight Show with Jay Leno, 2003; RI:SE, 2003; Entertainment Tonight, 1981; Celebrities Uncensored, 2003; The Bernie Mac Show, 2004, T4, 2004. Honours: Young Artist Award, 1999; Sierra Award, 2000; MTV Movie Award, 2001; Razzie Award, 2004.

**KUTILEK Miroslav,** b. 8 October 1927, Trutnov, Czech Republic. Professor of Soil Science and Soil Physics. m. Xena Radova, 1 son, 1 daughter. Education: Ing, CTU, Prague, 1946-51; CSc, 1952-55; DrSc, 1966. Appointments: Associate Professor, CTU Prague, 1968-73; Reader, University of Khartoum, Sudan, 1965-68; Professor, CTU, Prague, 1973-90, 1992-93; Deputy Dean, 1974-85; Visiting Professor, Institute de Mechanique, Grenoble, France, 1979-80, 1985, 1991; Visiting Professor, University of California, 1981-82; Visiting Professor, Technische Universitat, Braunschweig, 1989; Professor, Bayreuth University, Fachbereich Geookologie, Germany, 1990-92. Publications: Research papers in journals; Scientific Books in Czech; Four books on Soil Science, Soil Hydrology, Porous Materials; Scientific books and monograph chapters in English; Others; Seven fiction books in Czech. Honours: Felber's Award, Technical Sciences; Mendel's Award, Biological Sciences; Honorary Member, IUSS. Memberships: International Soil Science Society; New York Academy of Sciences; International Commission on Irrigation and Drainage; International Council of Scientific Unions; European Cultural Club; Others. Address: Nad Patankou 34, 160 00 Prague 6, Czech Republic.

**KUZNETSOV Vladimir,** b. 14 June 1949, Frunze, USSR. Mathematical and Computational Biologist. m. Ann Ivshina, 1 son. Education: MS, Physics, Kyrgyz State University, 1966-71; PhD Student, Biophysics, Institute of Molecular Biology of the Russian Academy of Science, 1978-80; PhD, Biophysics, Moscow University, 1984; Dr Sci, Mathematics and Physics, Scientific and Technical Union, Russian Academy of Sciences, 1992. Appointments: Junior Researcher, Research Institute of Oncology and Radiology, Frunze, Kyrgyzstan, USSR, 1972-81; Lecturer, Mathematical Department, Kyrgyz State University, 1977-81; Scientist, Head of Laboratory, Institute of Chemical Physics, Russian Academy of Science, Moscow Russia, 1982-98; Research Scholar, Center for Biological Evaluation and Research, USA, 1995-97; Exchange Scientist, National Cancer Institute, NIH, Maryland, USA, 1997-98; Chief Scientist, Civilized Software Inc, Maryland, USA, 1998-99; Senior Research Fellow, National Institute of Child Health and Human Development, NIH, 1999-2004; Senior Member of Professional Staff, Systems Research and Applications International Inc, Fairfax, Virginia, USA, 2004; Senior Group Leader, Department of Information and Mathematical Science, Genome Institute of Singapore, 2004-. Publications: Articles in scientific journals as co-author including: Bulletin of Mathematical Biology, 1994; Mathematical and Computer Modeling, 1994; Journal of Theoretical Biology, 1996; Journal of Urology, 1998; Immunology Today, 1998; AIDS, 1998; Biophysical Journal, 1999; Nature Medicine, 2001; Genetics, 2002; Signal Processing, 2003; Fluctuation and Noise Letters, 2003; Journal of Applied Microbiology, 2004; Journal of Clinical Virology, 2004; Mathematical, Medical and Biological Journal of IMA, 2004; PNAS USA, 2003, 2004; PLOS Genetics, 2005. Honours: Silver Medal, Russian Academy of Natural Sciences, 1994; American Cancer Society Grantee, 1995-96; National Cancer Institute/NIH Grantee, 1996-98. Memberships: Corresponding Member, Russian Academy of Natural Sciences; American Association for Cancer Research; London Mathematical Society; American Statistical Association; American Mathematical Society; International Society for Computational Biology. Address: Genome Institute of Singapore, 80 Biopolis Str # 02-01, Singapore 138672. E-mail: kuznetsov@gis.a-star.edu.sg

**KVAMME Elsa**, b. 12 January 1954, New York, USA. Writer; Director; Actress. m. Per Johan Isdahl, 1 daughter. Education: Examen philosophicum, Språkvitenskap og linguistikk, University of Oslo, Norway; Acting Student, Odin Teatret, 1973-75; Studies at International School of Theatre Anthropology, 1980-81; Film Direction, Tisch School of Arts, New York, 1991-92; Russian Studies, University of Oslo, 1993-94, St Petersburg, 1994. Career: Founder with Yves Liébert, Klovnegruppen Max & Mini, one of Norway's first fringe groups (later Saltkompagniet), 1976; Worked as Actress, Writer and Director of 8 plays with Saltkompagniet, 1977-83; Plays performed in Bilbao, international festivals of Santarcangelo, Italy, Copenhagen International Theatre Festival; First solo performance: The man who gave birth to a woman, performed at international theatre festivals of Sitges, Philadelphia, USA, Manizales, Colombia, 1982; Lady out of work performed at the Festival de Blois, France, 1984; Translated Jacques Brel into Norwegians ithicolarts cabarets, Frederik, 1985 and When I was a horse, 1987; Played in theatre project Medea and wrote and directed the play The girl with the blue eye in co-operation with Det Norske Teater and Riksteatret, 1992-93; Wrote feature film Maya Stoneface, 1995; Directed war documentaries Students at War, 1997 and A Lady with a Hat, 1999; Wrote and directed feature film Fia!, 2003. Publications: Books: Ting som små piker liker, 1991; Maja Steinansikt, 1995, 1997; Tingenes magi, 1997; Dame med hatt, 2001; Kjaere Jens, Kjaere Eugenio - om Jens Bjørneboe, Eugenio Barba og opprørernes teater, 2004; Articles, CDs, DVD and VHS. Honours: The Lysistrata Prize, Sitges Festival, 1983; Guaranteed minimum salary as an artist by the Cultural Ministry of Norway, 1984-; Cultural Scholarship, City of Oslo, 1994; Et Håndtrykk, Norwegian Playwright Society, 1999; Numerous prizes for the feature film Fia! include: best Nordic children and youth film, Nordische Filmtage, Lübeck, 2003; Special Prize of the Kinder Jury, Kinder Festival of Tokyo, 2004; The Moscow Teddy Bear for best film, 21st Festival for Children's and Youth Films, Moscow, 2004; Amanda (Norwegian 'Oscar') for Best Script, 2004. Memberships: Norsk skuespillerforbund; Norske sceneinstruktørers forening; Norsk Dramatisk forbund; Norske filmregissører; NOPA; NFFF. Address: Elisenbergvn 3, 0265 Oslo, Norway. E-mail: elkvamme@online.no

**KWOK Hong Kin.** Assistant Professor; Researcher. Education: BSSc, Sociology, 1978, MPhil, Sociology, 1980, PhD, Sociology, 2000, The Chinese University of Hong Kong, Hong Kong. Appointments: Lecturer, Department of Social Sciences, Lingnan College, Hong Kong, 1980-96; Assistant Professor, Department of Politics and Sociology, Lingnan University, Hong Kong, 1996-; Researcher, Global Development Network (GDN), World Bank Institute of the World Bank; External Examiner, Springboard Programme, Lingnan Institute of Further Education, Lingnan University, 2001-; Assessor, Research grant proposal of research Grants Council of Hong Kong, University Grants Committee, 2002. Publications: Analysing Hong Kong Society, 1989; Chinese Family in Transition, 1997; Theory and Practice of Mother-tongue Education, 1998; Quality Education in the 21st Century: The Development of Mainland China, Hong Kong, Macau and Taiwan, 2000; 70 Years of Education in Hong Kong, 2004; Numerous journal articles. Honours: 1st Class Award, Best Chinese Thesis, Committee for the Scientific Studies in Chinese Management, 2002; Listed in numerous Who's Who and biographical publications: Memberships: Hong Kong Professional Teachers' Union, 1988-; Canadian Sociology and Anthropology Association, 1994-; Hong Kong Sociological Association, 1998-; Hong Kong Teachers' Association, 1998-; Board Member, International Sociological Association, Research Committee on Sociology of Ageing, 2002-06. Address: Department of Politics and Sociology, Lingnan University, 8 Castle Peak Road, Tuen Mun, New Territories, Hong Kong. E-mail: kwokhk@in.edu.hk

**KWOK Lai Yin Percy**, b. 16 August 1967, Hong Kong. Professor and Principal. Education: BA, Philosophy, Mathematics, 1991, P C Ed, Mathematics Education, 1997, PhD, Comparative Education, 2001, University of Hong Kong. Appointments: Teacher, primary, secondary and special schools in Hong Kong, 1991-97; Teacher Consultant, Curriculum Developer, 1997-2001, Tutor, Department of Education, 1999-2001, Full-time Research Assistant, Centre for Information Technology in School and Teacher Education, 2001, The University of Hong Kong; Part-time Lecturer, Hong Kong Institute of Educational Research, Chinese University of Hong Kong, 2001-2004; Full-time Project Manager, 2001-2002, Full-time Tutor, 2001-2002, Part-time Lecturer, 2002-2003, Centre for Information Technology in School and Teacher Education, University of Hong Kong; Part-time Project/Dissertation Supervisor, Hong Kong Institute of Educational Research, Chinese University of Hong Kong, Centre for Information Technology in School and Teacher Education, University of Hong Kong, Faculty of Education, University of Macao, 2002-2004; Full-time Course Co-ordinator and Research Project Manager, School of Education and Languages, Open University of Hong Kong, 2002-2004; Full-time lecturer and Full-time Practicum Tutor, Department of Educational Policy and Administration, Hong Kong Institute of Education, 2002-2003, 2003-2004; Full-time Principal, Pui Ching Education Centre, 2004-. Publications: Numerous articles and conference papers as author and co-author in the field of mathematics education, IT education, special education, comparative education include most recently: Postmodern mappings of archaeology and genealogy of comparative education in China: discourse formation and cultural synthesis for Asian education in the 21st century, 2001; Tensions between localisation and globalisation of distance e-learning for workplace education in mainland China, 2003; Sustaining links between school improvement and educational leadership, 2004. Honours: Listed in Who's Who publications and biographical dictionaries. Memberships: Co-opted Committee Member, Comparative Education Society of Hong Kong; Comparative Education Society in Europe; Hong Kong Association for Mathematics Education; Sub-committee Member, Hong Kong Association for Science and Mathematics Education. Address: Flat F, 19/F, Ko Nga Court, 9 High Street, Hong Kong, China. E-mail: drpercykwok@yahoo.com

**KWON Soon-Kyoung**, b. 14 October 1940, Anjoo, Korea. Professor. m. Sin-Kang Park, 1 son, 1 daughter. Education: BS, Seoul, 1962; MS, Seoul, 1964; PhD, Munster, Germany,

1975. Appointments: Assistant Professor, 1978-82, Associate Professor, 1982-87, Professor, 1987-, Vice President, 1992-93, Dean, College Pharmacy, 1998-2000; President, 2001, Duk-Sung Women's University. Publications: Medicinal Chemistry, 1985, 1996, 1999, 2005; The World of Drugs, 1988; The Advices of Drugs and Health, 2000. Honours: Prize for Distinguished Scientist, 1980; Golden Tower Prize for Distinguished Pharmacist, 1992; Prize for Commentator on Pharmaceutical Affairs, 1997; Dong-Am prize in pharmacy, Korean Pharmaceutical Industry News, 2001. Memberships: American Chemical Society; Pharmaceutical Society of Korea; Korean Chemical Society; Korean Society of Applied Pharmacology. Address: Sooyoo-dong 572-25, Kangbook-Ku, Seoul 142-880, Korea.

**KYLBERG Jan Peter Henrik,** b. 29 November 1938, Stockholm, Sweden. Film Director. m. Margaret Wickham, divorced, 2 sons, 2 daughters. Education: Institution of Physical Chemistry, Stockholm Royal Institute of Technology. Appointments: Film Director; Composer; Artist. Publications: Films: Kadens, 1960; En Kortfilm av Peter Kylberg, 1963; Paris D-Moll, 1964; Jag, 1966; Konsert för Piano, Två Ansikten Och En Fortsättning, 1968; Opus 25, 1978; Du, 1985; F42, 1990; I Ställes För Ett Äventyr, 1996. Honours: Four film awards; Many diplomas. Address: Angsklockevagen 50B, 181 57 Lidingo, Sweden.

**KYRIAKOPOULOS Grigorios,** b. 11 September 1972, Athens, Greece. Research Scientist. Education: Degree, Chemical Engineering, National Technical University of Athens, 1996; MS, Hellenic Open University, Patra, Greece, 2004; PhD, School of Chemical Engineering, National Technical University of Athens, Greece, 2004. Appointments: Research Fellow, Organic Chemical Technology, Laboratory of National Technical University of Athens, 1996-; Participant in the postgraduate programme "Protection of Monuments" organised by the Schools of Architectural Engineering, Chemical Engineering, Civil Engineering and Agronomist-Topographer Engineering, National Technical University of Athens with the experimental study: Removal of pesticides from aqueous solution by adsorption on polymeric resins, 1998-99 and 1999-2000. Publications: Articles in scientific journals and papers in conference proceedings as co-author include: Adsorption of pesticides on resins, 2003; Removal of pesticides from aqueous solutions by adsorption, 2004; Effect of ionic strength and pH on the adsorption of selected herbicides on amberlite, 2005. Honours: Scholarships: National Technical University of Athens, 1998-2001; Hellenic Open University, 2001-2002, 2002-2003, 2003-2004; Prix Afas, 2000, Société d'Encouragement au Progrès (French Institution) in the Municipality of Athens, 2000; Thomaidio Award, National Technical University of Athens, 2003 and 2004; Reviewer in the following journals: Chemical Engineering Science, Journal of Hazardous Materials and Chemosphere. Memberships: Technical Chamber of Greece; Panhellenic Society of Chemical Engineers. Address: School of Chemical Engineering, Section IV, National Technical University of Athens, Zografou Campus, 9 Heroon Polytechniou Street, Athens GR 15780, Greece. E-mail: gregkyr@chemeng.ntua.gr

**KYTE Peter Eric,** b. 8 May 1945, Rawalpindi, Pakistan. Barrister. m. Virginia Cameron, 1 son, 1 daughter. Education: MA, Trinity Hall, Cambridge, 1968. Appointments: Teacher of Classics and French, 1964-65; Manager, Charter Consolidated Ltd, London, Mauritania and Congo, 1968-73; Account Executive, Merrill Lynch, London and New York, 1973-74; Joined Chambers of Daniel Hollis QC, now Hollis Whiteman Chambers, 1974-; Recorder, 1988; Queen's Counsel, 1996; Legal Assessor for the General Medical Council and General Dental Council. Honours: Recommended as Leading Silk in the field of Criminal Fraud in Chambers Guide to the Legal Profession, 2000-. Memberships: New York Stock Exchange; Chicago Board of Trade; Gray's Inn; Criminal Bar Association; Aula Club. Address: Forge House, Lower Heyford, Oxfordshire, OX25 5NS, England. E-mail: peter@kyte.u-net.com

# L

**LA PLANTE Lynda,** b. England. Television Dramatist. m. Richard La Plante. Education: Royal College of Dramatic Art. Appointments: Former Actress. Creative Works: Appeared in The Gentle Touch, Out, Minder; TV dramas include: Prime Suspect, 1991; Civvies; Framed; Seekers; Widows, series; Comics, 2 part drama, 1993; Cold Shoulder 2, 1996; Cold Blood; Bella Mafia, 1997; Trial and Retribution, 1997-; Killer Net, 1998; Mind Games, 2000. Publications include: Entwined; Cold Shoulder; The Governor; She's Out; Cold Heart, 1998; Sleeping Cruelty, 2000. Address: La Plante Productions Ltd, Paramount House, 162-170 Wardour Street, London, W1V 3AT, England.

**LAAR Mart,** b. 22 April 1960, Tallinn, Estonia. Prime Minister. m. Katrin Laar, 1981, 1 son, 1 daughter. Education: MA, Philosophy, BA, History, Tartu University. Appointments: Member, Supreme Council, 1990-92; Member, Constitutional Assembly, 1992; Prime Minister of Estonia, 1992-94, 1999-2002; National Coalition Fatherland Party Chairman, 1992 95; Member of Parliament, Riikogu, VII Session, 1992-95; Member of Parliament, Riigikogu, VIII Session, 1995-98; Chairman, Pro Patria, 1998-; Prime Minister, Republic of Estonia, 1999. Publications: Variety of Estonian and English language books and publications on history. Honours: The Year's Best Young Politician in the World Award, 1993; European Tax Payer Association Year Prize, 2001; European Bull, Davastoeconomic Forum, Global Link Award, 2001; Adam Smith Award, 2002. Memberships: Chairman, Jaan Tonisson Institute; Estonian Christian Democratic Union; Pen Club; Estonian University Students Society. Address: State Chancellery, Lossi Plats 1a, Tallinn 15161, Estonia.

**LACEY Aaron Michael,** b. 26 May 1969, Washington, USA. Motion Picture Actor; Director; Writer. Education: Advanced Certificate, National Conservatory of Drama Arts, 1993. Career: Chief Executive Officer AML Productions, Washington, 1987-; 7 year contract for CBS, starred in In Our Lives, television series; Films include: Twelve Monkeys; West Wing; The Wire; America's Most Wanted; Lincoln; One Way Out; The Accidental Tourist; Running Out of Time; Fatal Mix; Road House; How I Got Into College; In Country; Cumulus 9; Born Yesterday; Dave; In the Line of Fire; Forrest Gump; Clear and Present Danger; Edge; Xscape; Georgetown; Red Dragon; Master Spy: The Robert Hanssen Story; The Recruit; Homicide: Life on the Street; Plays include: Gustave in Jean Anouilh's "Carnival", 1993; Jerome Brace, Gus, Young Man and Man in Edward Albee's "Malcolm"; The Gunman in Clifford Odett's "Waiting for Lefty, 1993; Tye McCool in Tennessee Williams' "Vieux Carre", 1993; Nels in "I Remember Mama". Honours: 2 time Emmy Award winning actor, National Academy of Television Arts and Sciences Capital Region; Phi Theta Kappa; Elected Official Representative, Virginia's Collegiate Honors Council Executive Committee; 1st Degree Black Belt Tae Kwon Do. Memberships: Screen Actors Guild; American Television and Radio Artists; Actors Equity Association; Society of American Flight Directors; International Alliance of Theatrical Stage Employees; Motion Picture Machine Operators; Amateur Athletic Union; Presidential Fitness Marksman. Address: 21034 Thoureau Court, Sterling, VA 20164, USA. E-mail: amlfilms@aol.com

**LACEY Nicholas Stephen,** b. 20 December 1943, London, England. Architect. m. (1) Nicola, (2) Juliet, 2 sons, 3 daughters. Education: MA, Emmanuel College Cambridge; AADipl, Architectural Association, London. Appointments: Partner, Nicholas Lacey and Associates, 1971-83; Partner, Nicholas

Lacey and Partners, 1983-. Honours: Winner, Wallingford Competition; Winner, Crown Reach (Millbank) Competition; Joint Winner, Arunbridge Competition; Prize Winner, Paris Opera House Competition; RIBA Regional Awards; Civic Trust Awards. Memberships: Royal Institute of British Architects (RIBA); Architecture Club; Athenaeum; Royal Dorset Yacht Club. Address: Reeds Wharf, 33 Mill Street, London SE1 2AX, England. E-mail: nicholaslacey@lineone.net

**LACHELIN Gillian Claire Liborel,** b. 5 February 1940, Reigate, Surrey, England. Emeritus Consultant in Obstetrics and Gynaecology. Education: MA, MB, BChir, 1964, MRCOG, 1969, MD (London), 1981, FRCOG, 1982, Cambridge University and St Thomas' Hospital Medical School. Appointments: Reader and Consultant in Obstetrics and Gynaecology, 1977-2000, Emeritus Reader and Consultant in Obstetrics and Gynaecology, 2000-, University College London and University College Hospitals Trust. Publications: Numerous articles on reproductive endocrinology; Books: Miscarriage: The Facts; Introduction to Clinical Reproductive Endocrinology. Memberships: Committee on Safety of Medicines, 1993-96; Society for Gynecologic Investigation (USA), 1982-. Address: Department of Obstetrics and Gynaecology, Royal Free and University College Medical School, 88-96 Chenies Mews, London WC1E 6HX, England.

**LACHINOV Mikhail,** b. 31 March 1957, Gorkovskaya Region, Russia. Engineer; Economist. 1 son, 1 daughter. Education: M Eng, Moscow Civil Engineering University, 1979; PhD, 1987; Master of Economics, State Financial Academy of the Russian Federation Government, 1991; Postgraduate Courses, London School of Business, Holborn College, London, England, 1994. Appointments: Professor of Economics, Moscow State Civil Engineering University, 1995-2002; Head, Director, Institution of Civil Engineers representation in Russia, 1996-2003; Deputy Director, Economics, "Mospromstroi" Construction Corporation, 2002-. Publications: Textbook: Foreign Economic Relations in Construction, 2001; More than 30 scientific articles. Honours: Medal, Krasnoyarsk Region Development Award; Medal, For International Links Development. Memberships: Fellow, Institution of Civil Engineers (UK); Fellow, Russian Society of Civil Engineering; Chartered Engineer. Address: Flat 19, Building 10, Pokrovskyi Blvd 4/17, 101000 Moscow, Russia. E-mail: lachinov@rambler.ru

**LACHOWICZ Tadeusz Zygmunt,** b. 11 December 1919, Drohobycz. Physician; Microbiologist; Chemist. m. Wanda Jadwiga Schmager, deceased. Education: MD, 1948, Master's degree in Chemistry, 1951, Jagiellonian University; Candidate of Medical Sciences, 1958; Lecturer, 1960; Extraordinary Professor, 1968; Ordinary Professor, 1974. Appointments: Assistant, Adjunct, State Institute of Hygiene, 1946-50; Lecturer in Epidemiology in Military Service, 1951-52, Chief of Laboratory; Chief of the Microbiological Department in District Laboratory, 1954-63; Chief of Microbiology Department, Military Institute of Hygiene and Epidemiology, 1963-65; Chief of the Centre, 1965-1980, Retired, 1980. Publications: 135 experimental works, 2 manuals, 2 patents, over 100 interviews to radio, press and television; Investigations on Staphylococcins, 1962; Purification and properties of Staphylococcin A, 1968; The use of Immunofluorescence Adsorption Test for Titrating Tetanus Anatoxins, 1968. Honours: Awards of Ministry of Military Affairs, I, II, II, Grade, 1971, 1977, 1980; Awards of City of Krakow, 1973, 1978; Knight Cross, 1963; Man of the Year, ABI, 1991, 1992, 1993, 1995, 1999, 2000 with Commemorative Medal, 2004; Man of the Year, IBC, 1991-92, 1995-96, IBC; International Order of Merit, 1994; ABI Laureate of Poland, 1999; Key of Success Medical Excellence from ABI,

2000; 2000 Outstanding Scientists of the 20th Century, IBC, 2000; 2000 Outstanding Scholars of the 20th Century, IBC, 2000; Companion of Honour, IBC, 2002; Adviser to the Director General, IBC, 2003; Scroll of Legend, Medal, Living Legends, IBC, 2003; Honorary Member, IBC, 2003; International Register of Profiles, 12th Edition, 2003; International Peace Prize, United Cultural Convention United States of America; The First Five Hundred, IBC, 2003; International Medal of Honour, IBC, 2003; Ambassador of Grand Eminence, ABI, 2003; Greatest Lives, IBC, 2004; Personality of the Year, 2004; Great Minds of the 21st Century, 2004; Noble Laureate, 2004; American Hall of Fame and Medal, ABI, 2004; The Genius Elite, ABI, 2004; Certificate of Authenticity in the Book of Knowledge, ABI, 2005; IBC Hall of Fame, 2005; Top 100 Scientists, IBC, 2005. Memberships: International Society of Pathology of Infectious Diseases; Polish Physician Society; International Biographical Association; American Biographical Institute's Research Association. Address: Krowoderskich Zuchow 23m44, 31-271 Krakow, Poland.

**LACKEY Kayle Diann Ogborn,** b. 22 October 1937, Alexander County, Illinois, USA. Elementary and Special Teacher. m. Joseph Donald Lackey, 1 daughter. Education: BA, History, Asbury College, Wilmore, Kentucky, 1958; MA with honours, Webster University, 1975; Certified, Reading Specialist, 1977; Certificate, Gifted and Talented Educator, South Illinois University, Edwardsville, 1990; Ltd Certified Elementary Education, Illinois; Certified Public School Teacher (life), Missouri; Certified Reading Specialist, Missouri; Registered Professional Real Estate Salesperson, Missouri. Appointments: Teacher, Kindergarten District # 196, 1959-63, Reading Specialist, 1973-79, Teacher, 2nd Grade, 1979-84, Teacher, 4th Grade, 1984-93, Teacher, Gifted and Talented, 1990-92, Dupo, Illinois; Teacher, 1st Grade Mehlville R-9 District, St Louis, Substitute Teacher, 1965-72, 1993-; Clinical Co-operative Teacher, South Illinois University, Edwardsville, 1989; Salesperson, Coldwell Banker Real Estate, St Louis, 1985-2000; Representative for Teachers, 1975-77, Negotiation Committee, 1981, American Federation of Teachers, Dupo, Illinois; Teacher, US Division, Laubach Literacy International, St Louis, 1987-89; Author, Teacher, Gifted and Talented Enrichment Summer Program, 1991; Participant, Asbury College Seminary on Near-Eastern studies, 1985; Representative, Ecumenical Committee, 1986-89, Trustee, 2000-2002, Community Resource Services; Chairman, Board of Education Preschool, 1987-88, Administrative Board, Religion and Race and Church and Society, 1989-93, Financial Secretary, 1999, Board of Directors, 2000, Zion United Methodists, St Louis. Honours: Appreciation for Teaching Excellence Award, Board of Education, Dupo, 1993; Award of Excellence, Illinois Mathematical and Science Academy, 1999. Memberships: Illinois Teachers Retirement System, 1993-; Methodist Congregations United of St Louis, 2001-2004; Gerhardt for Congress, St Louis, 1993-95; Volunteer, American Cancer Society, 2000, 2004; St Louis Art Museum; Missouri Botanical Society; St Louis Zoological Society. Address: 6511 Towne Woods Drive, St Louis, MO 63129, USA.

**LACROIX Christian Marie Marc,** b. 16 May 1951, Arles, France. Fashion Designer. m. Francoise Roesenstiehl, 1989. Education: Université Paul Valéry, Montpellier; Université Paris, Sorbonne; Ecole du Louvre. Appointments: Assistant, Hermès, 1978-79, Guy Paulin, 1980-81; Artistic Director, Jean Patou, 1981-87, Christian Lacroix, 1987-, Emilio Pucci, 2002-; Design for Carmen, Nîmes, France, 1988, for L'as-tu revue?, 1991, for Les Caprices de Marianne, 1994, for Phèdre a la Comèdie Francaise, 1995; Created costumes for Yoyaux, Opera Garnier, 2000; Decorated the TGV Mediterranee, 2001.

Publications: Pieces of a Pattern, 1992; Illustrations for albums, Styles d'aujourd'hui, 1995; Journal d'une collection, 1996. Honours include: Des d'or, 1986, 1988; Prix Balzac, 1989; Goldene Spinnrad Award, Germany, 1990; Chevalier, Arts es Lettres, 1991; Prix Moliere, for costumes in Phèdre, 1996. Membership: Council, Fashion Designers of America. Address: 73 rue de Faubourg Saint Honoré, 75008 Paris, France.

**LADIANA Beatriz B,** b. 5 November 1928, Moncada, Tarlac, Philippines. Concert Artist. m. Vincent James Ladiana, deceased. Education: Music Education Certificate; Music Specialisation Certificate; BSc, Elementary Education; BSc, Education; MSc, Education. Appointments: School Teacher; Educational Director, Day Care Center; Concert Singer; Song Writer; Recording Artist. Publications: Articles in various popular newspapers; Credits in Concert Singer, Julliard School of Music, New York City. Honours: Music (Voice) Scholar, Philippines; First Place, Voice Competition, Philippines. Memberships: Moncadenians of North America Inc, Clifton, New Jersey; Eurasia Millennium Foundation Inc, New York. Address: 479 Jewett Ave, Staten Island, NY 10302, USA.

**LADYMAN Stephen John,** b. 6 November 1952, Ormskirk, Lancashire, England. Member of Parliament. m. Janet Ladyman, 2 stepsons, 1 daughter, 1 stepdaughter. Education: BSc, Applied Biology, Liverpool Polytechnic; PhD, Strathclyde University. Appointments: Research Scientist, MRC Radiobiology Unit, 1979-85; Head of Computing, Kennedy Institute, 1985-91; Head, Computer Support, Pfizer Central Research, 1991-97; Member of Parliament, South Thanet, 1997-; Treasurer, All Party British Fruit Industry Group, 2000-; Chair, All Party Parliamentary Group on Autism, 2000-; Liaison MP for The Netherlands, 2001-; Chair, All Party British-Dutch Group, 2001-; Parliamentary Private Secretary to the Minister for the Armed Forces, 2001-. Address: House of Commons, London SW1A 0AA, England. E-mail: ladymans@parliament.uk

**LAGERFELD Karl-Otto,** b. 1938, Hamburg, Germany. Fashion Designer. Education: Art School, Hamburg. Appointments: Fashion Apprentice, Balmain and Patou, 1959; Freelance Designer, associated with Fendi, Rome, 1963-, Chloe, Paris, 1964-83, Chanel, Paris, 1982-, Isetan, Japan; Designer, Karl Lagerfeld's Women's Wear, Karl Lagerfeld France Inc, 1983-; First collection under own name, 1984; Honorary Teacher, Vienna, 1983; Costume Designer for film, Comédie d'Amour, 1989. Publications: Lagerfeld's Sketchbook, 1990; Karl Lagerfeld Off the Record, 1995. Honours include: Golden Thimble, 1986. Address: Karl Lagerfeld France Inc, 75008 Paris, France.

**LAGOS Ricardo,** b. 2 March 1938, Santiago, Chile. Politician. m. Luisa Durán, 5 children. Education: University of Chile; Duke University, North Carolina, USA; PhD. Appointments: Professor, 1963-72, former Head, School of Political and Administrative Sciences, former Director, Institute of Economics, General Secretary, 1971, University of Chile; Chairman, Alianza Democrática, 1983-84; Chairman, Partido por la Democracia, 1987-90; Minister of Education, 1990-92; Minister of Public Works, 1994; President of Chile, 2000-. Publications: Numerous books and articles on economics and politics. Address: Office of the President, Palacio de la Moneda, Santiago, Chile.

**LAGRAVENESE Richard,** b. 30 October 1959, Brooklyn, New York, USA. Film Screenplay Writer, Director and Producer. m. Ann Weiss, 1986, 1 daughter. Education: Emerson College; BFA, New York University. Appointments: Producer, The Ref, film, 1994; Director, Living Out Loud, film, 1998.

Creative Works: Screenplays: Rude Awakening, 1991; The Fisher King, 1991; The Ref, 1994; A Little Princess, 1995; The Bridges of Madison County, 1995; The Horse Whisperer, 1998; Living Out Loud (also Director), 1998; Unstrung Heroes; Defective Detective, 2002. Honours: Independent Film Project Writer of the Year. Address: c/o Kirsten Bonelli, 8383 Wilshire Boulevard, Suite 340, Beverly Hills, CA 90211, USA.

**LAGUEUX Maurice,** b. 19 December 1940, Montreal, Canada. Professor. m. Gisèle Houle, 1 son, 1 daughter. Education: License Philosophy, University of Montreal, 1961-63; PhD, Philosophy, University of Paris, Nanterre, 1963-65; MA Economics, McGill University, 1968-70. Appointments: Invited Professor, University of Ottawa, 1976-77; Professor, 1965-, Full Professor, 1982-, Department of Philosophy, University of Montreal. Publications: 2 books; More than 20 book chapters; 40 articles in various journals. Honours: General Governor's prize, Le marxisme des années soixante. Memberships: Canadian Philosophical Association; European Society for History of Economic Thought; History of Economic Society; Canadian Society of Aesthetics; Société de Philosophie du Québec. Address: Department of Philosophy, University of Montreal, CP 6128, Succ. Centre-ville, Montreal H3C 3J7, Canada. E-mail: maurice.lagueux@umontreal.ca

**LAHOUD Emile (General),** b. 1936, Baabdate, Lebanon. Politician; Naval Officer. m. Andrée Amadouni, 2 sons, 1 daughter. Education: Brumana High School; Cadet Officer, Military Academy, 1956; Naval Academy courses, UK, USA, 1958-80. Appointments: Ensign, 1959, Sub-Lieutenant, 1962, Lieutenant, 1968, Lieutenant-Commander, 1974, Commander, 1976, Captain, 1980, Rear-Admiral, 1985, General, 1989; Commander of Second Fleet, 1966-68, First Fleet, 1968-70; Staff of Army Fourth Bureau, 1970-72; Chief of Personal Staff of General and Commander of Armed Forces, 1973-79; Director of Personnel, Army Headquarters, 1980-83; President of Military Office, Ministry of Defence, 1983-89; General and Commander of Armed Forces, 1989-; President of Lebanon, 1998-. Publications: Procedure and Modus Operandi, 1998. Honours: Medal of Merit and Honour, Haiti, 1974; Lebanese Medal of Merit, General Officer, 1989; War Medals, 1991, 1992; Dawn of the South Medal, 1993; National Unity Medal, 1993; Medal of Esteem, 1994; Grand Cordon, Order of the Cedar, Lebanon, 1993; Commandeur, Légion d' Honneur, France, 1993; Order of Merit, Senior Officer Level, Italy, 1997; Grand Cross of Argentina, 1998; Order of Hussein ibn Ali, Jordan, 1999; Necklace of Independence, Qatar, 1999. Address: Presidential Palace, Baabda, Lebanon. E-mail: opendoor@presidency.gov.lb

**LAI Shih-Kung,** b. 15 November 1957, Taiwan. Professor. m. Chiung-Ku Lee, 15 October 1993. Education: BSE, Urban Planning, National Cheng Kung University, 1979; MCRP, City and Regional Planning, Ohio State University, 1985; PhD, Regional Planning, University of Illinois at Urbana-Champaign, 1990. Appointment: Director, Centre for Land and Environmental Planning, Associate Professor, Professor, Department of Real Estate and Built Environment, National Taipei University. Publication: Meanings and Measurements of Multiattribute Preferences, 1996; Omega, Environment and Planning B, Decision Sciences. Honour: Research awards of National Science Council, Republic of China, 1993-2005. Memberships: American Planning Association; INFORMS; Chinese Planning Association. Address: 67, Section 3, Min Sheng East Road, Taipei, Taiwan, Republic of China. E-mail: lai@mail.ntpu.edu.tw

**LAIDLAW (Henry) Renton,** b. 6 July 1939, Edinburgh, Scotland. Journalist. Education: James Gillespie's School, Edinburgh, Scotland; Daniel Stewart's College, Edinburgh, Scotland. Appointments: Sports Reporter, Edinburgh Evening News, 1957-68; Newsreader, Interviewer, Grampian Television, 1968-70; Golf Reporter, Evening Standard, London, 1973-98; BBC radio, ITV, TWI, Eurosport, Screensport, Sport on 2, BBC Radio Scotland, PGA European Tour Productions, 1985-2002; Golf Channel, USA, 1995-. Publications: Golfers Handbook (editor); Tony Jacklin – the First 40 Years; Play Better Golf; Play Golf (with Peter Alliss); Golfing Heroes; Ryder Cup 1985; Ryder Cup, 1987; Ryder Cup, 1989; Captain at Kiawah (with Bernard Gallacher); Wentworth – 70 Years; Sunningdale Centenary. Honours: Lifetime Achievement Award in Journalism, PGA of America, 2003; Memorial Journalism Award, USA, 2001. Memberships: R and A; Sunningdale; Royal Burgess; Ballybunion; Caledonian Club. Address: c/o Kay Clarkson, 10 Buckingham Place, London SW1E 6HX. E-mail: rlaidlaw@compuserve.com

**LAIDLAW Christopher Charles Fraser (Sir),** b. 9 August 1922. Business Executive. m. Nina Mary Prichard, 1952, 1 son, 3 daughters. Education: St John's College, Cambridge. Appointments: War Service, Europe, Far East, Major on General Staff, 1939-45; With British Petroleum Co Ltd, 1948-83: Representative, Hamburg, 1959-61, General Manager, Marketing Department, 1963-67, Director, BP Trading, 1967, President, BP Belgium, 1967-71, Director of Operations, 1971-72, Chairman, BP Germany, 1972-83, Managing Director, BP Co Ltd, 1972-81, Deputy Chairman, BP Co Ltd, 1980-81, Chairman, BP Oil Ltd, 1977-81, Chairman, BP Oil International 1981; Director, Commercial Union Assurance Co, 1978-83, Barclays Bank International Ltd, 1980-87, Barclays Bank, 1981-88; Chairman, ICL, 1981-84; President, ICL France, 1983; Director, Amerada Hess Corporation, 1983-94; Director, Barclays Merchant Bank, 1984-87; Chairman, Boving and Co, 1984-85; Chairman, UK Advisory Board, 1984-91, Director, 1987-94, INSEAD; Director, Amerada Ltd, 1985-98; Chairman, Bridon PLC, 1985-90; Director, Daimler-Benz UK Ltd, 1994-99. Honours: Honorary Fellow, St John's College, Cambridge. Memberships: President, German Chamber of Industry and Commerce, 1983-86; Master, Tallow Chandlers Company, 1988-89; Vice-President, British-German Society, 1996-. Address: 49 Chelsea Square, London SW3 6LH, England.

**LAINE Cleo (Clementina Dinah Dankworth),** b. 28 October 1927, Southall, Middlesex, England. Singer. m. (1) George Langridge, 1947, 1 son, (2) John Philip William Dankworth, 1958, 1 son, 1 daughter. Appointments: Joined, Dankworth Orchestra, 1953; Lead, Seven Deadly Sins, Edinburgh Festival and Sadler's Wells, 1961; Acting roles in Edinburgh Festival, 1966, 1967; Founder, Wavendon Stables Performing Arts Centre, 1970; Many appearances with symphony orchestras; Frequent tours and TV appearances and productions including Last of the Blonde Bombshells, 2000. Publications: Cleo: An Autobiography, 1994; You Can Sing If You Want To, 1997. Honours include: Woman of the Year, 9th Annual Golden Feather Awards, 1973; Edison Award, 1974; Variety Club of GB Show Business Personality Award, 1977; TV Times Viewers' Award for Most Exciting Female Singer on TV, 1978; Grammy Award, Best Jazz Vocalist, Female, 1985; Best Actress in a Musical, 1986; Theatre World Award, 1986; Lifetime Achievement Award, 1990; Vocalist of the Year, British Jazz Awards, 1990; Lifetime Achievement Award, USA, 1991; ISPA Distinguished Artists Award, 1999. Memberships include: National Association of Recording Merchandisers. Address: The Old Rectory, Wavendon, Milton Keynes MK17 8LT, England.

**LAINSON Ralph,** b. 21 February 1927, Upper Beeding, Sussex, England. Parasitologist. m. Zéa Constante Lins-Lainson, 1 son, 2 daughters. Education: BSc, 1947-51, London University; PhD, 1952-55, DSc, 1964, University of London, London School of Hygiene and Tropical Medicine. Appointments: Lecturer, Department of Medical Protozoology, London School of Hygiene and Tropical Medicine, 1955-59; Director, Leishmaniasis Unit, Baking Pot, Cayo, Belize, Central America, 1959-62; Research Worker, London School of Hygiene and Tropical Medicine, 1962-65; Director, Wellcome Parasitology Unit, Instituto Evandro Chagas, Belém, Pará, Brazil, 1965-92. Publications: 350 articles in scientific journals and textbooks of parasitic diseases, particularly Leishmaniasis, Malaria and Toxoplasmosis. Honours: Chalmer's Medal, Royal Society of Tropical Medicine and Hygiene, 1971; Manson Medal, Royal Society of Tropical Medicine and Hygiene, 1984; Fellow, Royal Society of London, 1982; Associate Fellow, Third World Academy of Sciences, 1989; OBE, 1996; American Medal of Honour, 2004; Listed in National and international biographical dictionaries. Memberships: Honorary Member, London School of Tropical Medicine and Hygiene; Honorary Member, British Society of Parasitology; Honorary Member, Royal Society of Tropical Medicine and Hygiene; Honorary Member, Society of Protozoologists. Address: Avenida Visconde de Souza Franco 1237, Apto 902, 66053-000, Belém, Pará, Brazil. E-mail: ralphlainson@iec.pa.gov.br

**LAIRD Elizabeth Mary Risk,** b. 21 October 1943, Wellington, New Zealand. Writer. m. David Buchanan McDowall, 19 April 1975, 2 sons. Education: BA, Bristol University, 1966; MLitt, Edinburgh University, 1972. Publications: Red Sky in the Morning, 1988; Arcadia, 1990; Kiss the Dust, 1991; Hiding Out, 1993; Secret Friends, 1996; Jay, 1997; Forbidden Ground, 1997; Jake's Tower, 2001; The Garbage King, 2003; A Little Piece of Ground, 2003; Secrets of the Fearless, 2005. Honours: Children's Book Award, 1992; Smarties Young Judges Award, 1994. Membership: Society of Authors. Address: c/o Rosemary Sandberg, 6 Bailey Street, London WC1B 3HB, England

**LAIRD Gavin Harry (Sir),** b. 14 March 1933, Clydebank, Scotland. Trade Union Official. m. Catherine Gillies Campbell, 1956. Appointments: Shop Stewards Convener, Singer, Clydebank, 7 years; Regional Officer, 1972-75, Executive Councillor for Scotland and North-West England, 1975-82, General Secretary, Union Section, 1992-95, Amalgamated Engineering Union, formerly Amalgamated Union of Engineering Workers; Scottish Trades Union Congress General Council, 1973-75; Part-time Director, Highlands and Islands Development Board, 1974-75; Part-time Director, British National Oil Corporation, 1976-86; Trades Union Congress General Council, 1979-82; Industrial Development Advisory Board, 1979-86; Chairman, The Foundries Economic Development Committee, 1982-85; Arts Council, 1983-86; Director, Bank of England, 1986-94; Non-Executive Director, Scottish TV Media Group PLC, 1986-99; Non-Executive Director, Britannia Life, 1988-; Non-Executive Director, GEC Scotland, 1991-99; Non-Executive Director, Edinburgh Investment Trust, 1994-; Chairman, Greater Manchester Buses North, 1994-96; Armed Forces Pay Review Body, 1995-98; Employment Appeal Tribunal, 1996-; Non-Executive Director, Britannia Investment Managers Ltd and Britannia Fund Managers Ltd, now Britannia Asset Managers Ltd, 1996-; Chairman, Murray Johnstone Venture Capital Trust 4, 1999-; Murray Johnstone Private Acquisition Partnership Advisory Committee, 1999-. Honours: Commander, Order of the British Empire. Memberships: Trustee, John Smith Memorial Trust; Advisory Board, Know-How Fund for Poland, 1990-95; Trustee, Anglo-German Foundation, 1994-; President, Kent Active Retirement Association, 1999-; Vice-President, Pre-Retirement Association of Great Britain and Northern Ireland, 1999-; Editorial Board, European Business Journal. Address: 9 Cleavedon House, Holmbury Park, Bromley BR1 2WG, England.

**LAKATANI Sani,** Politician. Appointments: Leader, Niue People's Party; Prime Minister of Niue, 1999-2001; Minister for External Affairs, Finance, Customs and Revenue, Economic and Planning Development and Statistics, Business and Private Sector Development, Civil Aviation, Tourism, International Business Company and Offshore Banking, Niue Development Bank, 1999-2001; Chancellor, University of the South Pacific, Fiji, 2000-03; Deputy Premier and Minister for Planning, Economic Development and Statistics, the Niue Development Bank, Post, Telecommunication and Information Computer Technology Development, Philatelic Bureau and Numismatics, Shipping, Investment and Trade, Civil Aviation and Police, Immigration and Disaster Management, 2002-. Address: c/o Office of the Prime Minister, Alofi, Niue, South Pacific.

**LAKE (Charles) Michael,** b. 17 May 1944, United Kingdom. Director General. m Christine Warner, 3 daughters. Education: Royal Military Academy, Sandhurst; Army Staff College. Appointments: Commissioned, RTC, 1965; Various regimental appointments in Germany, Hong Kong, Northern Ireland and Oman, 1965-77; Attached Commandant General RM, 1977-78; Directing Staff, Staff College, 1982-83; Command, 1st Division Transport Regiment, 1983-86; Commander, Transport HQ British Forces Riyadh, Gulf War, 1990-91; Regimental Colonel, Logistic Corps, 1992-96; Retired, 1997; Director General, Help the Aged, 1996-; Director, Chelsea Arts Club, 1997. Honours: CBE, 1995; Freeman City of London, 1995; Liveryman Worshipful Company of Carmen, 1995; British Gerontology Society Medal, 1999. Memberships: Board, Help Aged International, 1996-2004; Chairman, Management Board, Chelsea Arts Club, 1997; Benevolent and Strategy Committee, Royal British Legion, 1997-2005; Council, Occupational Pensions Advisory Service, 1997-2005; Trustee, Disasters Emergency Committee, 1999; Board, Network Housing Association, 1999-2001; Trustee, Pensions Policy Institute, 2001; Council, Oxford Institute of Ageing, 2000; Lay Member, Lord Chancellor's Advisory Committee on Conscientious Objectors, 2002; Vice Chair, Air Ambulance Foundation, 2003-04; Chairman, British Gas Energy Trust, 2004; Penguin International Rugby Club; West Cornwall GC; North Hants GC; MCC. Address: Help the Aged, 207-221 Pentonville Road, London N1 9UZ, England. E-mail: mlake@helptheaged.org.uk

**LAKER Frederick Alfred (Sir),** b. 6 August 1922. Business Executive. m. (4) Jacqueline Harvey. Appointments: Short Bros, Rochester, 1938-40; General Aircraft, 1940-41; Served with Air Transport Auxiliary, 1941-46; Aviation Traders, 1946-60; British United Airways, 1960-65; Chairman, Managing Director, Laker Airways Ltd, 1966-82; Director, Skytrain Holidays, 1982-83; Director, Sir Freddie Laker Ltd, 1982-; Director, Northeastern International Airlines Inc, USA, 1984-; Chairman, Managing Director, Laker Airways Bahamas Ltd, 1992-. Honours: Honorary Fellow, University of Manchester Institute of Technology, 1978; Honorary DSc, City University, 1979; Honorary DSc, Cranfield Institute of Technology, 1980; Honorary LLD, Victoria University of Manchester, 1981. Memberships: Jockey Club, 1979-; Chairman, Guild of Air Pilots and Navigators Benevolent Fund. Address: Princess Tower, West Sunrise, Box F-4207, Freeport, Grand Bahama, Bahamas.

**LAKHAN V Chris,** Professor of Earth Sciences. Education: Graduate, Geography, University of Guyana; Postgraduate Studies, MA, University of Windsor; PhD, University of Toronto. Appointments: Ministry of Education, Guyana, 1967-74; Lecturer, University of Guyana, 1973-74; Graduate Teaching Assistant, University of Windsor and University of Toronto; Full Professor, Earth Sciences Department, University of Windsor, Canada. Publications: Books on Geographical Information Systems; Editor 3 books on coastal modelling; Author and co-author of over 50 articles in books and national and international scientific journals on systems and coastal modelling; Editor-in-Chief, Journal of Indo-Caribbean Research. Honours: Canadian Government Commonwealth Scholarship; University of Windsor Scholarship; University of Toronto Open Fellowships for 4 years; Certified Environmental Inspector; Certified Environmental Specialist, and Systems Scientist, International Computing Labs Inc.; Several Teaching Merit Awards, University of Windsor; Faculty of Social Science Teaching Award, University of Windsor. Memberships: Fellow, Royal Geographical Society; International Society for Computer Simulation; Environmental Assessment Association; Urban and Regional Information Systems Association; International Geographical Union; Coastal Education and Research Foundation. Address: Earth Sciences, School of Physical Sciences, University of Windsor, Windsor, Ontario, Canada N9B 3P4. E-mail: lakan@uwindsor.ca

**LALLAAICHA (HRH Princess),** Diplomatist. Appointments: Moroccan Ambassador to UK, 1965-69; Moroccan Ambassador to Italy and accredited to Greece, 1969-73. Honours: Grand Cordon, Order of the Throne of Morocco. Membership: President, Moroccan Red Crescent. Address: c/o Ministry of Foreign Affairs, ave Franklin Roosevelt, Rabat, Morocco.

**LAM Fai Lun Alan,** b. 14 December 1966, Hong Kong. Educator. Education: Diploma of Business, Royal Brisbane International College, Australia; Master of Education, Doctor of Education and Doctor of Philosophy (Business Administration), Empresarial University, Costa Rica. Appointments: Visiting Professor, Empresarial University, Costa Rica; Visiting Professor, China Programme, Southern Queensland University, Australia; Managing Director, Children and Youth Gifted Education Courses Management Committee, China Service Center for Youth Development; Executive Director (voluntary), Pillar Education Foundation Ltd (charitable body); Managing Director, Hong Kong Kee Ling Consultant Co Ltd. Honours: Knight of Justice (KOJ); The Sovereign Order of the Knights of Justice, Malta. Memberships: Charter Member, The 3rd Vice President, International Lions Clubs, The Jiabin Lions Club of 380 District Shenzen, China; Deputy Secretary General, Chinese National and Cultural Foundation; Deputy Secretary General, Hong Kong Buddhist Culture Foundation. Address: No 2 Pai Tau Village, Shatin, Hong Kong. E-mail: alan@pillaredf.com.hk

**LAMAZE Jean-Hugues de,** b. 11 April 1965, Paris, France. Equity Research Executive. m. Aude de Chassey. Education: INSEAD Executive Programme, Fontainbleau, France; Institut Superieur de Gestion, Paris; LLB, Business Law, Paris II ASSAS; Centre de Formation a l'Analyse Financière. Appointments: Platoon Commander, French Cavalry, 1988-89; Enskilda Securities, London, 1989-96; Director, Equity Research, Credit Suisse First Boston, London, 1996-2002; Executive Director, Global Investment Research, Goldman Sachs International, London, 2002-. Honours: French National Defence Medal, 1989. Memberships: INSEAD Alumni Association; Cercle du Bois de Boulogne; Cercle du Jockey Club. Address: Goldman Sachs International, Peterborough Court, 133 Fleet Street, London EC4A 2BB, England. E-mail: jean-hugues.delamaze@gs.com

**LAMB Allan Joseph,** b. 20 June 1954, Langebaanweg, Cape Province, South Africa. Cricketer. m. Lindsay Lamb, 1979, 1 son, 1 daughter. Education: Abbotts College. Appointments: Mid-Order Right-Hand Batsman; Teams: Western Province, 1972-82, 1992-93, OFS, 1987-88, Northamptonshire, 1978-95, Captain 1989-95; Qualified for England 19 82 and played in 79 Tests, 1982-92, 3 as Captain, scoring 4,656 runs, average 36.0, including 14 hundreds; Toured Australia, 1982-83, 1986-87, 1990-91; Scored 32,502 1st Class Runs, 89 hundreds; 1,000 15 times; 122 limited-overs internationals; Director, Lamb Associates Event Management Company, Grenada Sports Ltd; Contributor, Sky Sports Cricket. Publication: Silence of the Lamb, autobiography, 1995. Address: Lamb Associates, First Floor, 4 St Giles Street, Northampton NN1 1JB, England.

**LAMB Andrew (Martin),** b. 23 September 1942, Oldham, Lancashire, England. Writer on Music. m. Wendy Ann Davies, 1 April 1970, 1 son, 2 daughters. Education: Corpus Christi College, Oxford, 1960-63; MA, Honours, Oxford University. Publications: Jerome Kern in Edwardian London, 1985; Ganzl's Book of the Musical Theatre (with Kurt Ganzl), 1988; Skaters' Waltz: The Story of the Waldteufels, 1995; An Offenbach Family Album, 1997; Shirley House to Trinity School, 1999; 150 Years of Popular Musical Theatre, 2000; Leslie Stuart: Composer of Florodora, 2002; Fragson: The Triumphs and the Tragedy (with Julian Myerscough), 2004. Editor: The Moulin Rouge, 1990; Light Music from Austria, 1992; Leslie Stuart: My Bohemian Life, 2003. Contributions to: The New Grove Dictionary of Music and Musicians; The New Grove Dictionary of American Music; The New Grove Dictionary of Opera; Gramophone; Musical Times; Classic CD; BBC Music Magazine; American Music; Music and Letters; Wisden Cricket Monthly; Cricketer; Listener; Notes. Memberships: Fellow, Institute of Actuaries; Lancashire County Cricket Club. Address: 12 Fullers Wood, Croydon CR0 8HZ, England.

**LAMB Willis Eugene Jr,** b. 12 July 1913, Los Angeles, California, USA. Physicist. m. (1) Ursula Schaefer, 1939, deceased 1996, (2) Bruria Kaufman, 1996. Education: University of California; PhD. Appointments: Instructor, 1938, Professor of Physics, 1948-52, Columbia University, New York City; Loeb Lecturer, Harvard University, 1953-54; Professor of Physics, Stanford University, Stanford, California, 1951-56; Wykeham Professor of Physics and Fellow, New College, University of Oxford, England, 1956-62; Henry Ford II Professor of Physics, 1962-72, J Willard Gibbs Professor of Physics, 1972-74, Yale University, USA; Professor of Physics and Optical Sciences, 1974-, Regents Professor, 1990-, University of Arizona, Tucson; Senior Alexander von Humboldt Fellow, 1992-94. Honours: Rumford Premium, American Academy of Arts and Sciences, 1953; Honorary ScD, University of Pennsylvania, 1953; Co-recipient, Nobel Prize in Physics, 1955; Research Corporation Award, 1955; Guggenheim Fellow, 1960; Honorary LHD, Yeshiva University, 1964; Honorary ScD, Gustavus Adolphus College, 1975; Honorary ScD, Columbia University, 1990; Humboldt Fellowship, 1992; Honorary Fellow, Royal Society of Edinburgh. Memberships: National Academy of Sciences. Address: Optical Sciences Center, University of Arizona, Tucson, AZ 85721, USA.

**LAMBERT Nigel Robert Woolf,** b. 5 August 1949, London, England. Barrister; Queens Counsel. m. Roamie Elisabeth Sado, 1 son, 1 daughter. Education: College of Law, London. Appointments: Called to the Bar, Gray's Inn, 1974; Ad eundem Member of Inner Temple, 1986; Chairman, South Eastern

Circuit, Institute of Barristers Clerks Committee; Assistant Recorder, 1992-96; Recorder, 1996-; Queens Counsel, 1999; Chairman, North London Bar Mess, 2001-; Bencher, Gray's Inn, 2003. Memberships: Life Vice President, Cokethorpe Old Boys Association; North London Bar Mess Committee, 1991-; Criminal Bar Association, Committee, 1993-2000; Member, Bar Council, 1993-2000; Member, South Eastern Circuit, Executive Committee, 2001-; Inner Temple Bar Liaison Committee, 2002-04. Address: 2-4 Tudor Street, London EC4Y 0AA, England. E-mail: nigellambertqc@hotmail.com

**LAMBERT Richard Peter,** b. 23 September 1944. Journalist. m. Harriet Murray-Browne, 1973, 1 son, 1 daughter. Education: Balliol College, Oxford; BA Oxon. Appointments: Staff, 1966-2001, Lex Column, 1972, Financial Editor, 1978, New York Correspondent, 1982, Deputy Editor, 1983, Editor, 1991-2001, Financial Times; Lecturer and Contributor to The Times, 2001-; External Member, Bank of England Monetary Policy Committee, 2003-. Honours: Hon DLitt, City University, London, 2000; Princess of Wales Ambassador Award, 2001; World Leadership Forum Business Journalist Decade of Excellence Award, 2001. Memberships: Director, London International Financial Futures Exchange; AXA Investment Mans, International Rescue Committee, UK; Chair, Visiting Arts; Governor, Royal Shakespeare Co; UK Chair, Franco-British Colloque; Member, UK-India Round Table; Member, International Advisory Board, British-American Business Inc. Address: Bank of England, Threadneedle Street, London EC2R 8AH, England.

**LAMINE LOUM Mamadou,** b. Senegal. Politician. Appointments: Formerly Minister of Economics, Finance and Planning, Senegal; Prime Minister of Senegal, 1998-99. Memberships: Parti Socialiste. Address: Office of the Prime Minister, ave Leopold Sedar Senghor, Dakar, Senegal.

**LAMONT Norman Stewart Hughson (Baron Lamont of Lerwick in the Shetland Islands),** b. 8 May 1942, Lerwick, Shetland, Scotland. Politician; Writer; Businessman. m. Alice Rosemary White, 1971. Education: BA Economics, Fitzwilliam College, Cambridge. Appointments: Personal Assistant to Duncan Sandys MP, 1965; Staff, Conservative Research Department, 1966-68; Merchant Banker, N M Rothschild and Sons, 1968-79; Director, Rothschild Asset Management; Conservative Member of Parliament for Kingston-upon-Thames, 1972-97; Parliamentary Private Secretary to Norman St John Stevas, 1974, Opposition Spokesman on Prices and Consumer Affairs, 1975-76, Opposition Spokesman on Industry, 1976-79, Parliamentary Under-Secretary of State, Department of Energy, 1979-81, Minister of State, Department of Trade and Industry, 1981-85, Minister of State, Department of Defence Procurement, 1985-86, Financial Secretary to Treasury, 1986-89, Chief Secretary to Treasury, 1989-90, Chancellor of the Exchequer, 1990-93; Non-Executive Director, N M Rothschild and Sons Ltd, 1993-95; Chairman, Archipelago Fund, Food Fund and Indonesia Investment Trust, 1995-; Chairman, Conservatives Against a Federal Europe, 1998; Vice-Chairman, International Nuclear Safety Commission; Vice-President, Bruges Group; House of Lords Select Committee on European Union; Director, Balli Group PLC. Publications: Sovereign Britain, 1995; In Office, 1999. Honour: Life Peeerage, 1998; Privy Councillor. Memberships: Chairman, Cambridge University Conservative Association, 1963; President, Cambridge Union, 1966. Address: c/o Balli Group plc, 5 Stanhope Gate, London, W1Y 5LA, England.

**LAMPI Rauno Andrew,** b. 12 August 1929, Gardner, Massachusetts, USA. Food Scientist; Engineer. m. Betty, 3 sons, 1 daughter. Education: BS, 1951, MS, 1955, PhD, 1957, Food Technology, University of Massachusetts. Appointments: Technical Director, New England Apple Products; Manager, Food Technology Section, Central Engineering, FMC Corporation; Research Physical Scientist, US Army Natick R and D Centre; Physical Science Administrator, N Labs; Independent Food Scientist/Engineer. Publications: Over 80, including 5 book chapters: 3 patents. Honours: US Army Exceptional Civilian Service Medal; Institute of Food Technology's Industrial Achievement Award; Institute of Food Technology Riester-Davis Award. Memberships: Institute of Food Technology. Address: 20 Wheeler Road, Westborough, MA 01581, USA.

**LANCHBERY John Arthur,** b. 15 May 1923, London, England. Conductor; Composer. m. Elaine Fifield, 1951, divorced 1960, 1 daughter. Education: ARAM, FRAM, Royal Academy of Music. Appointments: Served, Royal Armoured Corps, 1943-45; Musical Director, Metropolitan Ballet, 1948-50; Sadler's Wells Theatre Ballet, 1951-57; Conductor, 1957-59, Principal Conductor, 1959-72, Royal Ballet; Musical Director, Australian Ballet, 1972-77; Musical Director, American Ballet Theatre, 1978-80; Composer and Arranger, ballet music, Pleasuredrome, 1949, Eve of St Agnes, 1950, House of Birds, 1955, La Fille Mal Gardée, 1960, The Dream, 1964, Don Quixote, 1966, Giselle, 1968, La Sylphide, 1970, Hoffman, 1972, Merry Widow, 1975, Month in the Country, 1976, Mayerling, 1978, Rosalinda, 1979, Papillon, 1979, La Bayadère, 1980, Peer Gynt, 1981, The Sentimental Bloke, 1985, Le Chat Botté, 1985, A Midsummer Night's Dream, 1985, Hunchback of Notre Dame, 1988, Figaro, 1992, Robinson Crusoe, opéra comique, 1986, Madame Butterfly, 1995, Dracula, 1997, Snow Maiden, 1998, Cleopatra, 2000, Mr Toad, 2000; For films, Tales of Beatrix Potter, 1971, Don Quixote, 1972, The Turning Point, 1977, Nijinsky, 1980, Evil Under the Sun, 1982, Birth of a Nation, 1992, The Iron Horse, 1994. Honours: Bolshoi Theatre Medal, 1961; Carina Ari Medal, Stockholm, 1984; Queen Elizabeth II Coronation Award, Royal Academy of Dancing, 1989. Address: 71 Park Street, St Kilda West, VIC 3182, Australia.

**LANDAU David,** b. 22 April 1950, Tel Aviv, Israel. Company Chairman. m. Marie-Rose Kahane, 1 son, 1 daughter. Education: MD, University of Pavia, Italy, 1978; MA, Worcester College, Oxford, 1979. Appointments: Supernumary Fellow, Worcester College, Oxford, 1980-; Print Curator, The Genius of Venice, Royal Academy, 1983; Founder and Editor, Print Quarterly, 1984-; Founder and Joint Managing Director, Loot, 1985-95; Founder, 1986, Chairman, 1990-91, Free-Ad Papers International Association; Chairman, Steering Committee, Andrea Mantegna Exhibition, Royal Academy and Metropolitan Museum of Art, New York, 1992; Chairman, Loot Group of Companies, 1994-2000; Director, 1995-2003, Chairman, 1998-2003, National Gallery Company (formerly National Gallery Publications); Director, Getty Images, 2003-; Chairman, Saffron Hill Ventures, 2000-. Publications: Georg Pencz, 1978; Federica Galli, 1982; The Renaissance Print (with Prof. P Parshall), 1994; Articles in Print Quarterly; Master Drawings, The Burlington Magazine, etc. Memberships: Trustee: British Friends of Art Museums of Israel, 1995-; National Gallery Trust, 1996-; National Art Collections Fund, 1996-; National Gallery, 1996-2003; Venice in Peril Fund, 1996-, Treasurer, 1997-; Courtauld Institute, 2002-. Address: 51 Kelso Place, London W8 5QQ, England. E-mail: dlandau@saffronhill.com

**LANDSBERGIENE Grazina,** b. 28 January 1930, Anyksciai, Lithuania. m.Vytautas Landsbergis, 1 son, 1 daughter. Education: Panevezys Gymnasium for Girls, 1948; Lithuanian Academy of Music, 1959. Appointments: Accompanist, National Theatre of Opera and Ballet, 1958-85; Associate Professor, Professor,

# DICTIONARY OF INTERNATIONAL BIOGRAPHY

Lithuanian Academy of Music, 1990-; Numerous concerts and records with various singers. Honours: Vilnius Glory Award, 1998; Order of Grand Duke Gediminas, 1999; Barbora Radvilaite Award, Vilnius, 2005. Memberships: Lithuanian Society of Political Prisoners and Deportees; Chairperson, Vytautas Landsbergis Foundation. Address: Traidenio 34-15, LT 2004 Vilnius, Lithuania.

**LANDSBERGIS Vytautas,** b. 18 October 1932, Kaunas, Lithuania. Musicologist; Politician. m. Grazina Rucyte, 1 son, 2 daughters. Education: J Gruodis Music School, 1949, Ausra gymnasium, Kaunas, 1950; Lithuanian Music Academy, Vilnius, 1955. Appointments include: Chairman, 1988-90, Honorary Chairman, 1991-, Lithuanian Reform Movement, Sajudis; President of the Supreme Council of the Republic of Lithuania (Head of State), 1990-92; Member of Seimas (Parliament), Republic of Lithuania and Leader of Opposition, 1992-96, member, Lithuanian Delegation to Parliamentary Assembly of Council of Europe, 1992-96, 2002-02, and to the Baltic Assembly, 1992-96, 2000-04; Chairman, Lithuanian Conservative Party, 1993-2003; President, Seimas (Parliament) Republic of Lithuania, 1996-2000; Candidate, Presidential elections, 1997; Member of the Seimas (Parliament) of the Republic of Lithuania, 2000-04; Observer to the European Parliament, 2003-04, and MEP, 2004-. Publications: Books: (in Lithuanian) The Hope Regained, 1990, 1991; The Case of Freedom, 1992; The Cross-roads, 1995; Autobiography, Years of Decision (in German and Lithuanian), 1997, Lithuania Independent Again (in English), 2000; Numerous others include: Monographs on the artist and composer M K Ciurlionis, 1965, 1971 and 1975 (in Russian), 1976, 1986, 1992 (in English); Intermezzo (poems), 1991, 2004; Who are We? (poems), 2004; Waves Give Me the Road (memories of the kid), 2004; Editions of Documents: Together. The Council of the Baltic States 1990-92 (in English), 1996; The Act of 11 March. Facsimiles, 2000; The Heavy Freedom (in Lithuanian) volumes I-III, 2000; The Cousin Mathew. The Book on Stasys Lozoraitis from His Letters and Messages (in Lithuanian), 2002, 2003; Koenigsberg and Lithuania, 2003; Unknown Documents on January 13 (in Lithuanian), 2003, 2004; Lithuania's Road to NATO (in Lithuanian), 2005. Honours include: Norwegian People's Peace Prize, 1991; Fondation de Future (France), 1991; Hermann-Ehlers-Preis, Germany, 1992; 9th International Ramon Llull Prize of the Catalonian Culture Congress Foundation (Spain), 1994; Legion of Honour Order 2nd Class, France, 1997; Order of Grand Duke Vytautas, 1st Class, Lithuania, 1998; Vibo Valentia Testimony Prize, Italy, 1998; Royal Norwegian Order of Merit (Grand Cross), 1998; Grand Cross Order of the Republic of Poland, 1999; UNESCO Medal, 1999; Order of Merit (Grand Cross) of the Order of Malta, 1999; Grand Croix de l'Ordre de l'Honneur of Greece, 1999; Truman-Reagan Freedom Award (USA), 1999; Pleiade Ordre de la Frankophonie (France), 2000; Three Stars Order, 2nd Class, Latvia, 2001; Order of the Cross of St Mary's Land, 1st Class, Estonia, 2002; Order of Grand Duke Vytautas with Golden Collar, 2003; Nine Honorary doctorates, including University of Sorbonne. Memberships: Lithuanian Composers Union; European St Sebastian's Order of Knights; Honorary Doctor of St Lucas Academy, The Netherlands, 2004; Chairman: M K Ciurlionis Society; M K Ciurlionis International Competition. Address: Traidenio 34-15, LT 2004 Vilnius, Lithuania.

**LANDYSHEV Yury Sergeevich,** b. 28 December 1928, Stavropol, Russia. Physician; Researcher. m. Iraida Vasilyevna Nefedyeva-Landysheva, 1 son. Education: Higher Medical Education, Stavropol Medical Institute, 1949-55; Postgraduate Education, Department of the Faculty Therapy, Stavropol Medical Institute, 1955-57; Postgraduate Scientific Course, 1968-61, PhD, 1962, Siberian Medical University, Tomsk; Doctor of Medicine, Moscow, 1978. Appointments: Assistant Professor, 1961-63, Associate Professor, 1973-68, Blagoveshchnsk State Medical Institute; Head of the Department of Hospital Therapy, Amur State Medical Academy, 1968-. Publications: 496 published scientific works include: The role of the adrenals in the pathogenesis of asthma, 1991; The basis of the clinic and pathogenesis in allergic diseases, prevention and treatment, 1992; Clinical and functional morphology of the endocrine glands and bronchi in patients with asthma with different methods of treatment, 1997; Guidance of Pulmonology, 2003; 5 patent; 15 books; 12 textbooks, Director of 11 MD and 52 PhD students. Honours: Medal for Services to the Healthcare of the Fatherland; Medal for Services to the Fatherland II Degree; Order of the Red Banner of Labour; Head of specialised delegation meeting; Member, Russian Academy of Natural Sciences, 1997; Honoured Scientific Member of the Russian Federation, 2001. Memberships: President, Association of Medical Workers of the Amur Region/Blagoveshchenk; Head, Regional Scientific and Practical Society of Therapists, Blagoveshchenk, Head, Regional Rehabilitation Asthma Centre. Address: Pionersky Street 5, app 19, Blagoveshchenk, Amur Region, Russia 675000.

**LANEVE Cosimo Raffaele,** b. 14 January 1940, Taranto, Italy. Professor. m. Emilia Salvatore, 1 son, 1 daughter. Education: Degree in Pedagogy, University of Bari, Italy, 1964. Appointment: Professor of Education, Universita degli Studi di Bari, Italy. Publications: Books: Rhetoric and Education. 1981; Language and Person, 1987; Elements of Didactic, 1998; Cultural Drifts and Pedagogic Criticism, 2001; Didactic Between Theory and Practice, 2003. Honours: Recipient, Peschara, 1997; Abroed, 1996. Membership: Italian Society of Pedagogy. Address: Universita degli Studi di Bari, Piazza Umberto I –1, 70120 Bari, Italy.

**LANFREDI Silvania,** b. 28 January 1967, Monte-Alto, SP, Brazil. Researcher. m. Marcos Augusto De Lima Nobre. Education: Chemist, 1990, Master, Inorganic Chemistry, 1990-93, Doctoral, Physical Chemistry, 1994-98, Federal University of São Carlos, Brazil; Doctoral, Physical Chemistry, Institut Nationale Polytechnique de Grenoble-INPG, Saint Martin d'Hères, France, 1995-97. Appointments: Postdoctoral, Science and Engineering of Materials, Institute of Physics, São Paulo-USP-Brazil, 1998-2001; Researcher, Faculty of Science and Technology, University Estadual Paulista-UNESP-Presidente Prudente-SP-Brazil. Publications: Articles as co-author in scientific journals including: Applied Physics Letters, 2003; Catalysis Today, 2003; Journal of Physical Chemistry of Solids, 2003; Journal of the American Ceramic Society, 2003; Journal of Applied Physics, 2003. Honours: Listed in Who's Who publications and biographical dictionaries. Memberships: Sociedade Brasiliera de Quimica; Associação Brasiliera de Ceramica; Sociedade Brasiliera de Pesquisa em Materiais. Address: Rua Roberto Simonsen 305, FCT-UNESP/DFQB, PO Box 467, CEP: 19060-900, Presidente Prudente-SP-Brazil. E-mail: silvania@prudente.unesp.br

**LANG Helmut,** b. 10 March 1956, Vienna, Austria. Fashion Designer. Career: Established own studio, Vienna, 1977; Opened made-to-measure shop, Vienna, 1979; Developed ready-to-wear collections, 1984-86; Presented Helmut Lang's Women's Wear, 1986, Helmut Lang's Menswear, 1987-, Paris Fashion Week; Started licensed business, 1988; Professor, Masterclass of Fashion, University of Applied Arts, Vienna, 1993-; Helmut Lang Underwear, 1994; Helmut Lang Protective Eyewear, 1995. Honours: Council of American Fashion Designers of the Year

Award, 1996. Address: c/o Michele Montagne, 184 rue St Maur, 75010 Paris, france.

**LANG Johannes-Karl,** b. 28 January 1967, Einbeck, Germany. Consultant; Neurosurgeon. Education: Medical Trainee: University of Goettingen, Germany, 1988-94, University of Aberdeen, Scotland, 1992, Hospital of Bressannone, Italy, 1993-94; MD, 1995-2003; Egyptian Medicine, University of Hamburg, 1998-2000; Diploma of Specialisation, 2003-04. Appointments: Assistant Researcher, Therapist, University of Goettingen, 1995-2002; Consultant Researcher, Therapist, LKH Klagenfurt, Austria, 2004-; Research in ancient Etruscan and Egyptian Medicine. Publications: Surgical Neurology: Cerebral bloodflow and role of coloid osmotic pressure on cerebral spinal fluid formations, 1999; Invention of description of evolution of fundamental medical terms in ancient Egypt. Honours: Member of Honour, Italian Etruscan Medicine, 2004. Memberships: Germany Neurolosurgical Society; Arbeitsgemeinschaft Osteosynthese; Swiss Italian Society of Ancient Etruscan Medicine. Address: Department of Neurosurgery, LKH, St Veiter Str, 9010 Klagenfurt, Austria. E-mail: jk_lang@chello.at

**LANG k d (Kathryn Dawn Lang),** b. 2 November 1961, Consort, Alberta, Canada. Singer; Composer; Actress. Career: Played North American clubs with own band, 1982-87; Performed at closing ceremony, Winter Olympics, Calgary, 1988; Headlining US tour, 1992; Royal Albert Hall, 1992; Earth Day benefit concert, Hollywood Bowl, 1993; Sang with Andy Bell, BRIT Awards, 1993; Television includes: Late Night with David Letterman; Wogan; The Arsenio Hall Show; The Tonight Show; Top of the Pops; Subject, South Bank Show documentary, ITV, 1995; Film appearance, Salmonberries, 1991. Recordings: Albums: A Truly Western Experience, 1984; Angel with a Lariat, 1986; Shadowland, 1988; Absolute Torch and Twang, 1990; Ingénue, 1992; Even Cowgirls Get the Blues (soundtrack), 1993; All You Can Eat, 1995; Drag, 1997; Australian Tour, 1997; Invincible Summer, 2000; Live By Request, 2001; Features on soundtrack to Dick Tracy; Hit singles include: Crying (duet with Roy Orbison); Constant Craving; Mind of Love; Miss Chatelaine; Just Keep Me Moving; If I Were You. Honours: Canadian CMA Awards: Entertainer of Year, 1989; Album of Year, 1990; Grammy Awards: Best Female Country Vocal Performance, 1990; Best Pop Vocal, 1993; Album of the Year, Ingénue, 1993; American Music Award: Favourite New Artist, 1993; Songwriter of The Year, with Ben Mink, 1993; BRIT Award, Best International Female, 1995.

**LANG Marie-Claude Elizabeth,** b. 30 September 1948, Neuilly/Seine, France. Research Scientist. m. Izak Rejzman. Education: Masters Degree, Physical Chemistry, 1970, 3rd Cycle Doctorate, Physical Chemistry, 1974, University of Paris 6; Doctorate es-Science, Biophysics, University of Strasbourg, 1983. Appointments: Research Fellow, French National League Against Cancer, 1976-78; Research Scientist, National Institute of Health and Medical Research, 1979-2005, including several positions as Researcher, Pasteur Institute, Paris, 1987-93; Principal Investigator, HIV Virology, Centre National de la Recheche Scientifique, CNRS, Paris, 1994-2000; Principal Investigator, Genodics in collaboration with Joël Sternheimer, Laboratory of Structural and Macromolecular Physical Chemistry, Paris, 2001-2004. Publications include: Do retroviruses preferentially integrate within highly plastic regions of the human genome (co-author), 2004. Honour: Award, French National League Against Cancer, 1984. Memberships: American Association for the Advancement of Science; New York Academy of Sciences. Address: 121 Avenue Général Leclerc, 75014 Paris, France. E-mail: langmcb@aol.com

**LANG Wharton Dietrich Faust,** b. 13 June 1925, Oberammergau, Germany. Sculptor; Carver in Wood. m. Ingrid, 1 son. Education: Leonard Fuller School of Painting, 1946; Sculpture with his father, Faust Lang, 1947-50. Career: Full-time Sculptor in Wood, 1950-; Participating as Council Member and in Selection Committee, SWL and RSMA art exhibitions and St Ives Society of Artists; Work in collections: Ulster Museum, Belfast, RSMA, Diploma Collection, National Maritime Museum, Greenwich, Carving in Relief "Castle of Mey" presented to HM The Queen Mother, 1967. Publications: Various articles in magazines and newspapers since 1950; Featured in book, Creating a Splash (as a member of The St Ives Society of Artists) by Philip Tovey. Honour: Fellow of the Royal Society of Arts, 1983-. Memberships: St Ives Society of Artists; Wildlife Art Society; Former Member, Society of Wildlife Artists; Honorary Member, Royal Society of Marine Artists. Address: Fauna Studio, Mount Zion, St Ives, Cornwall, England.

**LANGE Jessica,** b. 20 April 1949, Cloquet, Minnesota, USA. Actress. m. Paco Grande, 1970, divorced, 1 daughter with Mikhail Baryshnikov; 1 son, 1 daughter with Sam Shepard. Education: University of Minnesota; Mime, Etienne DeCroux, Paris. Appointments: Dancer, Opera Comique, Paris; Model, Wilhelmina Agency, New York. Creative Works: Films include: King Kong, 1976; All That Jazz, 1979; How to Beat the High Cost of Living, 1980; The Postman Always Rings Twice, 1981; Frances, 1982; Tootsie, 1982; Country, 1984; Sweet Dreams, 1985; Crimes of the Heart, 1986; Everybody's All American, 1989; Far North, 1991; Night and the City, 1993; Losing Isaiah, 1994; Rob Roy, 1994; Blue Sky, 1994; A Thousand Acres, 1997; Hush, 1998; Cousin Bette, 1998; Titus, 1999; Play: Long Day's Journey Into Night, 2000; Star Showtime TV Production, Cat On A Hot Tin Roof, 1984. Honours include: Theatre World Award, Golden Globe, 1996. Address: c/o CAA, Ron Meyer, 9830 Wilshire Boulevard, Beverly Hills, CA 90212, USA.

**LANGHAM John Michael,** b. 12 January 1924, Stroxton, UK. Chartered Engineer. m. Irene Elizabeth Morley, 2 sons, 1 daughter. Education: MA (Cantab), Mechanical Sciences Tripos, Queen's College, Cambridge, England; Administrative Staff College. Appointments: Engineer Officer, Royal Navy, 1944-46; Various Appointments, 1947-67, Executive Director, 1967-80, Stone-Platt Industries, plc; Director, BPB Industries plc, 1976-92; Chairman: Vacu-Lug Traction Tyres Ltd, 1973-95; Chairman, Langham Industries, Ltd, 1980-; External Appointments: Member, CBI Council, 1967-79; Chairman, CBI Production Committee, 1970-79; Member, Executive Board, British Standards Institute, 1969-76; Deputy Chairman, Quality Assurance Council, 1971-79; Member, General Council, 1974-82, Member, Management Board, 1979-82, Vice-President, Executive Committee, 1978-82, E.E.F. Publications: Presented British Exchange Paper to 21st International Foundry Congress, Italy; Article: The Manufacture of Marine Propellers with Particular Reference to the Foundry. Honours: Commander of the Order of the British Empire (CBE); Diploma, Institute of British Foundrymen, 1954, 1963; British Foundry Medal and Prize, 1955; Award of American Foundrymen's Society, Detroit Congress, 1962, Dorset Business Man of the Year, 1996. Memberships: Fellow, Institution of Mechanical Engineers; Fellow, Institute of Marine Engineers; Fellow, Institute of British Foundrymen, Companion of the Institute of Management. Address: Bingham's Melcombe, Dorchester, Dorset DT2 7PZ, England.

**LANKA Vaclav,** b. 25 October 1941, Hredle, near Rakovník, Czech Republic. Teacher. 1 son. Education: Diploma, Faculty of Natural Science, Charles University, Prague, 1974; Diploma

Biologist. Appointments: Teacher, to 1994; Vice-Mayor, Town of Rakovník, 1994-98; Currently Teacher. Publications: Co-author, books: Amphibians and Reptiles, 11 editions, 6 languages, 1985; Wolfgang Böhme, 1999; Handbuch der Reptilien und Amphibien Europas, Vol 3/IIA; Monographs: Dice Snake, Natrix tessellata, 1975; Variabilität und Biologie der Würfelnatter, Natrix tessellata LAURENTI, 1976; Several hundred popular articles on nature and ecology; Several hundred specialist and popular lectures. Membership: Entomological Society of the Czech Republic, 1956-; Species Survival Commission, International Union for the Conservation of Nature and Natural Resources. Address: Jilská ul. 1061, 269 01 Rakovník, Czech Republic.

**LANSBURY Angela Brigid**, b. 16 October 1925, United Kingdom. Actress. m. (2) P Shaw, 1949, 1 son, 1 step-son, 1 daughter. Education: School of Singing and Dramatic Art, London; School of Drama and Radio, New York. Career: with MGM, 1943-50; Freelance, 1951-; Films include: Gas Light, National Velvet, 1944; The Picture of Dorian Gray, 1945; If Winter Comes, The Three Musketeers, 1948; Kind Lady, 1951; Please Murder Me, 1956; The Reluctant Debutante, 1958; Blue Hawaii, 1961; The Greatest Story Ever Told, The Amorous Adventures of Moll Flanders, 1965; Bedknobs and Broomsticks, 1971; Death on the Nile, 1978; The Mirror Crack'd, The Lady Vanishes, 1980; The Pirates of Penzance, 1982; The Company of Wolves, 1983; Voice of Mrs Potts in Beauty and the Beast, 1991; Theatre includes: Broadway debut in Hotel Paradiso, 1957; Mame, New York Winter Garden, 1966-68; Gypsy, 1974; Anna, The King and I, 1978; Sweeny Todd, 1979; TV includes: Madeira! Madeira!, The Ming Llama, Lace, Murder She Wrote, 1984-96; The Shell Seekers, 1989; Miss Arris Goes to Paris, 1992; Mrs Santa Claus, 1996; South by Southwest, 1997; A Story to Die For, 2000. Publication: Positive Moves, co-author and video. Honours include: Academy Award Nomination, Best Supporting Actress, 1944; Nomination, Academy Award, The Manchurian Candidate; Pudding Theatre Woman of the Year, 1968; Antoinette Perry Awards for Mame, 1968; Dear World, 1969; Gypsy, 1975; Sweeney Todd, 1982; Sarah Siddons Awards, 1974, 1980; BAFTA Lifetime Achievement Award, 1992; CBE; National Medal of Arts, 1997; Nomination, 16 Emmy Awards; Winner, 6 Golden Globe Awards, nominated 8 Golden Globe Awards. Address: c/o MCA Universal, 100 Universal City Plaza, Universal City, CA 91608, USA.

**LANSING Sherry**, b. 31 July 1944, Chicago, Illinois, USA. Business Executive. m. (2) William Friedkin, 1991. Education: BS, Northwestern University, Evanston, Illinois. Appointments: Mathematics Teacher, Public High Schools, Los Angeles, California, 1966-69; Model, TV commercials, Max Factor Co and Alberto-Culver, 1969-70; Appeared in films Loving and Rio Lobo, 1970; Executive Story Editor, Wagner International, 1970-93; Vice-President for Production, Heyday Productions, 1973-75; Executive Story Editor, then Vice-President for Creative Affairs, MGM Studios, 1975-77; Vice-President, then Senior Vice-President for Production, Columbia Pictures, 1977-80; President, 20th Century Fox Productions, 1980-83; Founder, Jaffe-Lansing Productions, Los Angeles, 1982-; Produced films including Racing with the Moon, 1984, Firstborn, 1984; Fatal Attraction, 1987; The Accused, 1989; Black Rain, 1990; School Ties, 1992; Indecent Proposal, 1993; Chairperson, Paramount Pictures, 1992-. Address: Paramount Pictures Corporation, 555 Melrose Avenue, Los Angeles, CA 90038, USA.

**LANZINGER Klaus**, b. 16 February 1928, Wörgl, Tyrol, Austria. University Professor. m. Aida Schüssl, 1 son, 1 daughter. Education: BA, Bowdoin College, Brunswick, Maine, USA, 1951; PhD, University of Innsbruck, Austria, 1952.

Appointments: Research Assistant, University of Innsbruck, 1957-67; Associate Professor, 1967-77, Professor of Modern Languages, 1977-97, Professor Emeritus, 1997-, University of Notre Dame, Indiana; Chairman, Department of German and Russian, 1989-96. Publications: Epik im amerikanischen Roman, 1965; Editor, Americana-Austriaca, 5 vols, 1966-83; Jason's Voyage: The Search for the Old World in American Literature, 1989; Amerika-Europa: Ein transatlantisches Tagebuch 1961-1989 (online 2003); Articles include: The Foreign Response to the Declaration of Independence, 1978; Thomas Wolfe's Modern Hero: Goethe's Faust, 1983; Jason's Voyage: The International Theme of Thomas Wolfe, 1992. Honours: Fulbright Research Grant, 1961; Zelda Gitlin Literary Prize, Thomas Wolfe Society, 1993. Memberships: Modern Language Association of America (MLA); Deutsche Gesellschaft für Amerkastudien; European Association for American Studies; Thomas Wolfe Society. Address: 52703 Helvie Drive, South Bend, IN 46635, USA.

**LAPHAM Lewis H**, b. 8 January 1935, San Francisco, California, USA. Writer. m. 3 children. Education: BA, Yale University, 1956; Cambridge University. Appointments: Reporter, San Francisco Examiner, 1957-59, New York Herald Tribune, 1960-62; Editor, Harper's Magazine, 1976-81, 1983-; Syndicated newspaper columnist, 1981-87; Lecturer in universities including Yale, Stanford, Michigan, Virginia and Oregon; Host, Author, six-part documentary series, America's Century, 1989; Host, Executive Editor, Book Mark, 1989-1991; Appearances on American and British television, National Public Radio and Canadian Public Radio. Publications: Fortune's Child (essays), 1980; Money and Class in America, 1988; Imperial Masquerade, 1990; The Wish for Kings, 1993; Hotel America: Scenes in the Lobby of the Fin-de-Siècle, 1995; Waiting for the Barbarians, 1997; The Agony of Mammon, 1999; Theater of War, 2002; 30 Satires, 2003; Gag Rule, 2004. Contributions to: Monthly essay for Harper's magazine as "Notebook"; Commentary; National Review; Yale Literary Magazine; Elle; Fortune; Forbes; American Spectator; Vanity Fair; Parade; Channels; Maclean's; London Observer; New York Times; Wall Street Journal. Honour: National Magazine Award for Essays, 1995. Address: c/o Harper's Magazine, 666 Broadway, New York, NY 10012, USA.

**LAPTEV Vladimir**, b. 28 April 1924, Moscow, Russia. Professor of Law. m. Maya Lapteva, 2 sons. Education: Graduate, Law Department, Moscow Institute for Foreign Trade, 1949. Appointments: Chief of Section of Economic Law, Institute of State and Law of Russian Academy of Sciences, Moscow, 1959; Chief, Centre of Entrepreneurial and Economic Law, 1992; Chief scientific researcher of the Institute, 1997; Head of Chair of Entrepreneurial Law of Academic Law University, Moscow, 1997. Publications: More than 350 scientific books and articles in fields of economic and entrepreneurial law. Honour: Professor, Doctor of Law, Honoured Scientist of Russian Federation. Membership: Russian Academy of Sciences. Address: Institute of State and Law, Znamenka 10, Moscow, Russia.

**LAPTYONOK Sergei**, b. 1 May 1935, Vasilievka, Minsk Region, Belarus. Research Worker. m. Anna Laptyonok, 1 son, 1 daughter. Education: Philologist Diploma, 1953-58, Doctor of Philosophy, 1964, Doctor of Philosophical Sciences, 1984, Certificate of Professor, 1986, Belarussian State University. Appointments: Lecturer, 1958-99, Head of Chair for History of Philosophy, Director of Sociological Centre, Belarussian State University; Chief Research Worker, Institute of Social and Political Studies ( under the administration of the President of the Republic of Belarus), 1999-2005. Publications: More than 260 research works including 50 monographs, books, brochures and textbooks: Morals and Family (monograph),

1967; Family and Intellectual Development of Personality (monograph), 1967; Ethics for Youth (book), 1975; Ethics and Etiquette (textbook), 1998 and 2002; Intellectual-Moral World of Students (textbook), 2001. Honours: Certificate of Honour of the Supreme Soviet of BSSR; Medals for Valiant Work; Medal of Labour Veteran. Memberships: Member of the Committee on the Theory of Sociology, World Sociological Association, 1974; Belarussian Academy of Education, 1999; International Academy of Technical Education, 2002, International Academy of Organisation and Management Science, 2004. Address: Institute of Social and Political Studies, Pobeditelei Avenue 7, Office 720, Minsk 220004, Belarus. E-mail: ispi@ispigov.by

**LARA Brian Charles,** b. 2 May 1969, Santa Cruz. Cricketer. Appointments: Started playing cricket aged 6; Played football for Trinidad Under 14; Played cricket for West Indies Under-19; Captain, West Indies Youth XI against India, scoring 186; Left-Hand Batsman; Teams: Trinidad and Tobago, 1987-, Captain 1993-; Warwickshire, 1994, Captain 1988; Making world record 1st class score of 501 not out, including most runs in a day, 390, and most boundaries in an innings, 72, v Durham, Edgbaston, 1994; 90 Tests for West Indies 1990-2002, 18 as Captain, scoring 7,572 runs, average 50.49, including 18 hundreds, highest score 375, world record v England, St John's, Antigua, 1994; Has scored 16,737 1st class runs, 45 hundreds, to 2002, including 2,066 off 2,262 balls for Warwickshire, 1994, with 6 hundreds in his first 7 innings; Toured England, 1991, 1995; 203 One Day Internationals, -2002 for 7,549 runs (average 42.65). Honours: Federation of International Cricketers' Associations International Cricketer of the Year, 1999. Publication: Beating the Field, autobiography, 1995. Address: c/o West Indies Cricket Board, PO Box 616, St John's, Antigua.

**LARGE Andrew McLeod Brooks (Sir),** b. 7 August 1942, Goudhurst, Kent, England. Banker and Regulatory Official. m. Susan Melville, 1967, 2 sons, 1 daughter. Education: University of Cambridge; Euorpean Institute of Business Administration, Fontainebleau; MA, Economics; MBA. Appointments: British Petroleum, 1964-71; Orion Bank Ltd, 1971-79; With Swiss Bank Corporation, 1980-89, as Managing Director, 1980-83, Chief Executive, Deputy Chairman, 1983-87, Group Chief Executive, 1987-88, SBCI London; Board, Swiss Bank Corporation, 1988-90; Non-Executive Director, English China Clays, 1991-96; Chairman, Large, Smith and Walter, 1990-92; Chairman, Securities and Investments Board, 1992-97; Member, Board on Banking Supervision, 1996-97, Deputy Governor, 2002-, Bank of England; Deputy Chairman, 1997-2002, Director, 1998-2002, Barclays Bank; Chairman, Euroclear, 1998-2000. Address: Bank of England, Threadneedle Street, London EC2R 8AH, England. Website: www.bankofengland.co.uk

**LARSEN Donald,** b. 18 April 1951, Oceanside, New York, USA. Teacher; Musician. m. Susan. Education: Bachelor of Science in Music Education, Hofstra University, Hempstead, New York, 1974; Master of Science in Music Education, Queens College, Queens, New York, 1977. Appointments: High School Band, 1974-89, Elementary School Band, 1980-89, Middle School Band, 1989, Hicksville Public Schools, Hicksville, New York; New York State School Music Association Adjudicator, 1977-; Freelance Musician. Honours: Guest Conductor, Rockville Centre All-Diocesan Band, 1994; Guest Conductor, Suffolk County Music Educators Division 2 Band, 1995; Hicksville Public Schools Founders' Day Honoree, 2000; Listed in Who's Who publications and biographical dictionaries. Memberships: Music Educators National Conference; New York State School Music Association; Local 802, American Federation of Music Teachers; New York State United Teachers; Hicksville Congress of Teachers; Percussive Arts Society.

Address: 77 Wyoming Drive, Huntington Sta., NY 11746-2656, USA. E-mail: djlarsen18@juno.com

**LASHKARIPOUR Gholam Reza,** b. 10 October 1954, Nehbandan, Iran. Professor. m. Najmeh Rezanezhad-Joulaei, 2 sons, 1 daughter. Education: BSc, Geology, University of Ferdowsi, Iran; MSc, Engineering Geology, Tarbiat Modaress, Iran; PhD, Civil Engineering, University of Newcastle upon Tyne, England. Appointments: Head of Geology Department, Professor of Geology, University of Sistan and Baluchestan, Iran. Publications: 92 papers. Honours: First Position in Research among all Academic Members, University of Sistan and Baluchestan, 2000, 2001, 2002, 2003. Memberships: International Association of Engineering Geology; International Society of Rock Mechanics. Address: Department of Geology, University of Sistan and Baluchestan, Zahedan, 98135-655 Iran. E-mail: lashkarg@hamoon.usb.ac.ir

**LASKIER Michael M,** b. 5 May 1949, Givataim, Israel. Historian. m. Anat, 1 son, 1 daughter. Education: BA (magna cum laude), 1971, MA, 1973, PhD, 1979, University of California at Los Angeles. Appointments: Associate Director, New York Office, Alliance Israelite Universelle, 1979-80; Lecturer, Jewish and Middle East History Departments, Tel-Aviv University, 1980-89; Louis Susman Associate Professor of History, Spertus College of Judaica, Chicago, USA, 1990-91; Executive Director, The Sephardic Educational Center, Los Angeles, USA, 1992-94; Adjunct Associate Professor of History, 1993-94; Associate Professor of History and Political Science, Chair, Political Science Department, Ashqelon Academic College, 1995-2003; Associate Professor, Department of Middle East History, Bar-Ilan University, 2002-. Publications: Author/editor, numerous books; Over 40 refereed chapters in books; 86 refereed articles in journals; 27 book reviews. Honours: US National Jewish Book Award, 1994. Memberships: Association for Jewish Studies, USA; Israel Oriental Society. Address: Shimon Ben-Tzvi 40, Apt #63, Givataim 53633, Israel. E-mail: michael1949@barak-online.net

**LASOK Karol Paul Edward,** b. 16 July 1953, London, England. Barrister. m. Karen Bridget Morgan Griffith, 2 daughters. Education: MA, Law, Jesus College, Cambridge, 1972-75; LLM, European Legal Studies, 1975-77, PhD (external student), 1982-86, University of Exeter. Appointments: Called to the Bar of England and Wales, Middle Temple, 1977; Queen's Counsel, 1994; Called to the Bar of Northern Ireland, 2002; Trainee, Legal Service of the Commission of the European Communities, 1979; Legal Secretary (Law Clerk), Court of Justice of the European Communities in the Chambers of Advocate General J-P Warner and Advocate General Sir Gordon Slynn, 1980-84 (and March-May 1985 locum tenens); Private Practice in Brussels, specialising in European Community Law, 1985-87; Private Practice in London specialising in European Community Law, 1988-; Recorder (part-time criminal court judge), 1999- Publications: Books: The European Court of Justice: Practice and Procedure, 2nd edition, 1994, 3rd edition in the course of preparation; Law and Institutions of the European Union, 2001; Contributions to 10 books; Numerous articles in legal journals. Honour: Bencher, Honourable Society of the Middle Temple. Address: Monckton Chambers, 4 Raymond Buildings, Gray's Inn, London WC1R 5BP, England.

**LATHAM Anthony John Heaton,** b. 30 October 1940, Wigan, England. University Lecturer; Musician; Writer. m. Dawn Catherine Farleigh, 10 November 1990, 1 son. Education: Merton College, Oxford, 1959-60; BA (Hons) Medieval and Modern History, Birmingham, 1964; PhD, African Studies, Birmingham, 1970. Appointments: Lecturer and Senior

Lecturer, University of Wales, Swansea, 1967-2003; Visiting Professor, University of Illinois, 1979, 1988. Publications: CD, John Latham's Jazz Timers, Sandy & Co, 1998; CD, Oxford Jazz Through the Years 1926-1963, 2002; CD, John Latham's Jazz Timers, with Bill Nicholes, 2004; Discographies: Sandy Brown, 1995; Al Fairweather, 1994; Stan Greig, 1995; Articles in Jazz Journal, Journal of International Association of Jazz Record Collectors, Jazz Rag, Just Jazz; British Jazz Times; New Orleans Music; Oxford Today; New Oxford Dictionary of National Biography, 2004. Honours: Postmastership, Merton College, Oxford, 1959. Membership: Musicians' Union; Secretary, Sandy Brown Society. Address: 2 Church Meadow, Reynoldston, Swansea SA3 1AF, Wales.

**LATIMER Mark David,** b. 3 January 1970, London, England. Orthopaedic Surgeon. m. Mandy Gibbs. Education: BA (Hons), Engineering and Economics, 1989-92, M Eng, 1992-93, First MB Exemption, Medicine, 1993-95, St Hughes College, Oxford; MB BChir, Clare College, Cambridge, 1995-97. Appointments: Clinical Supervisor in Medicine, Newnham College, Cambridge, 2000-2001, King's College, Cambridge, 2002-2004, St John's College, Cambridge, 2004-; Specialist Registrar in Trauma and Orthopaedics, Luton and Dunstable Hospital, 2002-2003, Bedford Hospital, 2003-2004, West Suffolk Hospital, 2004-2005. Publications: Articles in medical journals as co-author: Enoximone potentiates the inotropic effects of $_1$ and $_2$ stimulation in atrial myocardium, 1990; Inotropic effects of Milrinone and Proximone: a comparison, 1995; A comparison of the inotropic effects of Milrinone and Proximone, 2001; measurement of outcome in patients with cervical spondylotic myelopathy treated surgically, 2002; Stopping warfarin therapy is unnecessary for hand surgery, 2004. Honours: ICI and Monsanto Engineering Students Awards; Geissler Prize in Immunology; Neurology and Neurosurgery Awards; BMA Elective Award. Memberships: Royal College of Surgeons of England; Royal College of Surgeons of Edinburgh; Christian Medical Fellowship. Address: 103 Norwich Street, Cambridge, CB2 1ND, England. E-mail: mdlatimer@hotmail.com

**LATYSHEV Pyotr Mikhailovich,** b. 30 August 1948, Khmelnitsky, Ukraine. Politician; Security Officer. m. 2 sons. Education: Omsk Higher School of Ministry of Internal Affairs, Academy of Ministry of Internal Affairs. Appointments: Inspector, the Head, Perm Division for the Fight against Economic Crime, 1970-86; Head, Department of Internal Affairs, Perm oblast, 1986-91; People's Deputy of the Russian Federation, 1990-93; Member of the Committee of Supreme Soviet on Law and the Fight against Crime, 1993; Head, Department of Internal Affairs Krasnador Territory, 1991-94; Deputy Minister of Internal Affairs Russian Federation, 1994-2000; Plenipotentiary Representative of the President of the Russian Federation in the Urals Federal District, 2000-. Honours: State Orders. Address: Office of the Plenipotentiary Representative of the President of the Russian Federation in the Urals Federal District, Oktyabrskaya pl 3, 620031 Yekaterinburg, Russia. Website: www.uralfo.ru

**LAU Mo Kiu,** b. 28 December 1955, Toishan, Canton, China. Radiologist. m. Mei Chen Li, 1 son. Education: MD, China Medical College, Taiwan, 1986; Resident, Cathay General Hospital, Taipei, 1986-90; Resident, National Taiwan University Hospital, 1990; Diplomate, Diagnostic Radiology. Appointments: Attendant Radiologist, Cathay General Hospital, Taipei, 1990-98; Director of Medical Imaging, Yee Zen General Hospital, Taiwan, 1998-. Publications: A custom-made remote injection device for HSG and others; Production of High Quality Black and White Slides with Colour Film and Standard Viewboxes; Is it infallible to identify opaque stone on a single KUB before an IVP study; The value of after contrast opaque stone in IVU; Alagille syndrome a case report; MRI of normal aortomesenteric angle related data; MRI of Ebstein's anomaly; MRI in Asplenia with congenital cardiovascular disease; MRI of acoustic schwannoma; The policy of reduced CT dose in children in Taiwan. Honours: Listed in Who's Who publications and biographical dictionaries. Memberships: American Roentgen Ray Society; European Society of Paediatric Radiology. Address: No 2 Chang Ping Street, Lane 82, 4th Floor, Hsin Chuang 242, Taipei, Taiwan, Republic of China.

**LAUDA Andreas-Nikolaus,** b. 22 February 1949, Vienna. Racing Driver. m. Marlene Knaus, 1976, 2 sons. Appointments: Competed in hill climbs, 1968, later in Formula 3, Formula 2, Sports Car Racing; Winner, 1972 John Player Brit Formula 2 Championship; Started Formula 1 racing in 1971; World Champion, 1975, 1977, 1984, runner-up, 1976; Founder, Owner, Own Airline, Austria. Creative Works: Grand Prix Wins: 1974 Spanish, Ferrari, 1974 Dutch, Ferrari, 1975 Monaco, Ferrari, 1975 Belgian, Ferrari, 1975 Swedish, Ferrari, 1975 French, Ferrari, 1975 US, Ferrari, 1976 Brazillian, Ferrari, 1976 South African, Ferrari, 1976 Belgian, Ferrari, 1976 British, Ferrari, 1977 South African, Ferrari, 1977 German, Ferrari, 1977 Dutch, Ferrari, 1978 Swedish, Brabham-Alfa Romeo, 1978 Italian, Brabham-Alfa Romeo; Retired, 1979; Returned to racing, 1981; Won US Formula 1 Grand Prix, British Grand Prix, 1982, Dutch Grand Prix, 1985; Retired, 1985; Chair, Lauda Air, -2000; CEO Ford's Premier Performance Division, 2001-02; Head, Jaguar Racing Team, 2001-02. Honours include: Victoria Sporting Club International Award for Valour, 1977. Address: Sta Eulalia, Ibiza, Spain.

**LAUDER Leonard Alan,** b. 19 March 1933, New York City, New York, USA. Business Executive. m. Evelyn Hausner, 1959, 2 sons. Education: Wharton School, University of Pennsylvania. Appointments: Joined, 1958, Executive Vice-President, 1962-72, President, 1972-, Chief Executive Officer, 1982-, now also Chairman, Estee Lauder Inc, cosmetics and fragrance company, New York; Trustee, University of Pennsylvania, 1977-; President, Whitney Museum of American Art, 1977-; Trustee, Aspen Institute for Humanistic Studies, 1978-; Governor, Joseph H Lauder Institute of Management and International Studies, 1983-. Address: Estee Lauder Inc, 767 Fifth Avenue, New York, NY 10153, USA.

**LAUGHTON Anthony Seymour (Sir),** b. 29 April 1927. Oceanographic Scientist. m. (1) Juliet A Chapman, 1957, dissolved 1962, 1 son, (2) Barbara C Bosanquet, 1973, 2 daughters. Education: King's College, Cambridge; John Murray Student, Columbia University, New York, 1954-55; PhD. Appointments: Served Royal Naval Volunteer Reserve, 1945-48; Oceanographer, 1955-88, later Director, National Institute of Oceanography, later Institute of Oceanographic Sciences; Member, 1974-, Chairman, 1986-, Joint IOC-IHO Guiding Committee, GEBCO, ocean charts; Member, 1981-, Chairman, 1995-, Governing Body, Charterhouse School; Council, University College, London, 1983-93; Co-ordinating Committee for Marine Science and Technology, 1987-91; Trustee, Natural History Museum, 1990-95. Publications: Papers on marine geophysics. Honours: Silver Medal, Royal Society of Arts, 1958; Prince Albert the 1st of Monaco Gold Medal, 1980; Founders Medal, Royal Geographical Society, 1987; Murchison, Geological Society, 1989. Memberships: Fellow, Royal Society; President, Challenger Society for Marine Science, 1988-80; President, Society for Underwater Technology, 1995-97; President, Hydrographic Society, 1997-99. Address: Okelands, Pickhurst Road, Chiddingfold, Surrey GU8 4TS, England.

**LAURELL Göran Frans Emanuel,** b. 19 January 1954, Stockholm, Sweden. Medical Doctor; Otolaryngologist. m. Birgitta, 1 son, 1 daughter. Education: MD, 1983, PhD, 1991, Karolinska Institute. Appointments: Associate Professor, Karolinska Institute, 1996; Consultant, Department of Otolaryngology, Karolinska Hospital, 1997. Memberships: Swedish Medical Association; Association of Research in Otolaryngology, USA. Address: Department of Otolaryngology and Head and Neck Surgery, Karolinska University Hospital, SE-17176 Stockholm, Sweden. E-mail: goran.laurell@ks.se

**LAUREN Ralph,** b. 14 October 1939, Bronx, New York, USA. Couturier. m. Ricky L Beer, 1964, 3 sons. Appointments: Salesman, Bloomingdale's, New York, Brooks Brothers, New York; Assistant Buyer, Allied Stores, New York; Representative, Rivetz Necktie Manufacturers, New York; Neckwear Designer, Polo Division, Beau Brummel, New York, 1967-69; Founder, Polo Menswear Company, New York, 1968-, Ralph Lauren's Women's Wear, New York, 1971-, Polo Leathergoods, 1978-, Polo Ralph Lauren Luggage, 1982-, Ralph Lauren Home Collection, 1983-; Chair, Polo Ralph Lauren Corporation, 66 stores in USA, over 140 worldwide. Honours: Several fashion awards, including: American Fashion Award, 1975; Council of Fashion Designers of America Award, 1981. Address: Polo Ralph Lauren Corporation, 650 Madison Avenue, New York, NY 10022, USA.

**LAURENTS Arthur,** b. 14 July 1917, New York, New York, USA. Dramatist; Writer; Director. Education: BA, Cornell University, 1937. Publications: Plays: Home of the Brave, 1946; The Bird Cage, 1950; The Time of the Cuckoo, 1952; A Clearing in the Woods, 1956; Invitation to a March, 1960; The Enclave, 1973; Scream, Houston, 1978; The Hunting Season, 1995; The Radical Mystique, 1995; Jolson Sings Again, 1995; My Good Name, 1997; Big Potato, 2000; Venecia, 2001; Claude Lazlo, 2001. Musical Plays: West Side Story, 1957; Gypsy, 1959; Anyone Can Whistle, 1964; Do I Hear a Waltz?, 1964; Hallelujah Baby, 1967; Nick and Nora, 1991; Memoir, Original Story By, 2000. Screenplays: The Snake Pit, 1948; Rope, 1948; Caught, 1948; Anna Lucasta, 1949; Anastasia, 1956; Bonjour Tristesse, 1958; The Way We Were, 1973; The Turning Point, 1977. Novels: The Way We Were, 1972; The Turning Point, 1977. Honours: Tony Awards, 1967, 1984; Drama Desk Awards, 1974, 1978; Golden Glove Award, 1977; Writers Guild of America, 1977; Best Director Award, 1985. Memberships: Academy of Motion Picture Arts and Sciences; Authors League; Dramatists Guild; PEN; Screenwriters Guild; Theatre Hall of Fame. Address: c/o William Morris Agency, 1325 Avenue of the Americas, New York, NY 10019, USA.

**LAURIE Hugh,** b. 11 June 1959, Oxford, England. Actor; Comedian. m. Jo, 2 sons, 1 daughter. Education: Cambridge University. Appointments: President, Footlights, Cambridge University; TV Appearances include: with Stephen Fry, A bit of Fry and Laurie, 1989-91; Jeeves and Wooster, 1990-92; Film Appearances include: Peter's Friends; Cousin Bette, 1998; Maybe Baby, 2000; Stuart Little, 2000. Publications: Fry and Laurie 4, (with Stephen Fry), 1994; The Gun Seller, 1996. Address: Hamilton Asper Ltd, Ground Floor, 24 Hanway Street, London W1P 9DD, England.

**LAURIE Richard Thomas,** b. 4 October 1935, Bagshot, Surrey, England. Writer; Musician; Gardener. m. Susan Dring, 2 sons; 1 daughter. Education: Bradfield College 1949-1954. Appointments: National Service, 2 Lieutenant, RASC; Creative Director, Brockie Haslam, 1970-81; Ted Bates, 1982-84; Band Leader, Dick Laurie's Elastic Band, 1983-; Breen Bryan Laurie and Dempsey, 1985-89; Creative Director, The Medicine Men

1993-; Producer, Zephyr Records, 1995-2000; Director, The Jobbing Gardener, 2002. Publications: Editor: Soho Clarion, 1977-99, Docklands Business News, 1994-96, Journal for European Private Hospitals, 1995-96; Founder/Publisher/Editor, Allegedly Hot News International, 1987-; Numerous articles, reviews and interviews. Memberships: Soho Society Executive Committee, 1976-2000. Address: 27 Clarendon Drive, Putney, London SW15 1AW. E-mail: alasdick@elastic.fsnet.co.uk

**LAURITSEN Nanette Diann,** b. 10 September 1949, Des Moines, Iowa, USA. Caregiver; Student. Divorced, 1 son. Education: Secretarial Graduate, Des Moines Community College, Iowa, 1982. Appointments: Customer services career, 12 years; Bookseller and Head Cashier, Barnes and Noble, Independence, Missouri, 2001-04; Caregiver for ailing mother; Student, American Writers and Artists Institute. Publications: Currently writing inspirational poetry. Honours: Listed in national biographical dictionaries. Memberships: Audubon Society; Norman Vincent Peale Center; KCPT Television; NAFE. Address: 1309 NW Delwood Drive, Blue Springs, Missouri 64015, USA. Website: www.nannet@netzero.com

**LAVENDER Justin,** b. 4 June 1951, Bedford, England. Opera Singer. m. Louise Crane, 1 son, 1 daughter. Education: Queen Mary College, University of London; Guildhall School of Music and Drama. Career: Operatic Tenor; Leading roles with most of the world's major opera houses, 1980-; Title role, Faust (Gounod) Royal Opera, Covent Garden, 2004; Concert engagements with major orchestras and conductors worldwide; Numerous recordings, most recently Schnittka's Faust Cantata. Publications: Regular contributions to The Irish Examiner, original articles and book reviews, 1996-; Contributions to various professional journals. Membership: Newlands Rowing Club. Address: c/o Athole Still International Management Ltd, 25-27 Westow Street, London SE19 3RY, England.

**LAVER Rod(ney) George,** b. 9 August 1938, Rockhampton, Queensland, Australia. Tennis Player. m. Mary Benson, 1966, 1 son. Education: Rockhampton High School. Career: Played Davis Cup for Australia, 1958, 1959, 1960, 1961, 1962, and first open Davis Cup, 1973; Australian Champion, 1960, 1962, 1969; Wimbledon Champion, 1961, 1962, 1968, 1969; USA Champion, 1962, 1969; French Champion, 1962, 1969; First player to win double Grand Slam, 1962, 1969; Professional from 1963; First Player to win over 1,000,000 US $ in prize money. Publications: How to Play Winning Tennis, 1964; Education of a Tennis Player, 1971. Honours: Member, Order of the British Empire; Melbourne Park centre court renamed Rod Laver Arena in his honour, 2000. Address: c/o Tennis Australia, Private Bag 6060, Richmond South, VIC 3121, Australia.

**LAVIELLE Lisette,** b. 14 April 1941, Mulhouse, France. Retired Researcher. m. Jean-Pierre Lavielle, 2 daughters. Education: Graduate, Chemical Engineering, École Nationale Supérieure de Chimie, Mulhouse, 1964; Doctor of Engineering, University of Strasbourg, France, 1968; DSc, University of Haute-Alsace, Mulhouse, 1971. Appointments: Research Associate, Thin Films Laboratory, CNRS, École Nationale Supérieure de Chimie, Mulhouse, 1964-70; Research Associate, Mineral Chemistry Laboratory, CNRS, Mulhouse, 1971-76; Engineer, European Society of Propulsion, Vernon, 1978-79; Research Associate, Macromolecular Chemistry Laboratory, CNRS, Rouen, 1980-81; Research Associate, Centre for Physical Chemistry Solid Surfaces, CNRS, Mulhouse, 1981-94; Research Associate, General Photochemistry Department, CNRS, 1995-2001. Publications: Polymer Surface Dynamics, chapter, 1987; Polymer Characterisation by Inverse Gas Chromotography, chapter, 1989; UV Phototreatment of Polymer Film Surface:

Self-Organization and Thermodynamics of Irreversible Processes, chapter, 1999. Honour: Recipient, Emilio Noelting Prize, École Nationale Supérieure de Chimie de Mulhouse, 1964. Memberships: French Society of Chemistry. Address: 6 rue la Fayette, 68100 Mulhouse, France.

**LAW Chun-Kong,** b. 24 June 1959, Hong Kong. Professor. m. Shuk-kwan Susan Leung, 2 sons. Education: BSc, MPhil, The Chinese University of Hong Kong, Hong Kong; PhD, University of Pittsburgh, USA. Appointments: Associate Professor, 1992-98, Professor, 1998-, Chairman, 2000-2003, Department of Applied Mathematics, National Sun Yat-sen University. Publications: Articles in professional journals as co-author include: Archive for Rational Mechanics and Analysis, 1998; Inverse Problems, 1998, 1999, 2001; Transactions AMS, 2002. Honours: Andrew Mellon Predoctoral Fellowship, University of Pittsburgh, 1990-92; Research Grant Award for Young Investigators, National Science Council, Taiwan, 1997-98; Research Award, National Science Council, Taiwan, 1994-2000. Memberships: Mathematics Society, Taiwan; American Mathematics Society. Address: Department of Applied Mathematics, National Sun Yat-sen University, Kaohsiung, Taiwan 804, ROC.

**LAW Jude,** b. 29 December 1972, London, England. Actor. m. Sadie Frost, 1997, divorced 2003, 2 sons, 1 daughter. Appointments: National Youth Music Theatre; Co-founder Natural Nylon (production Company); Stage appearances include: Joseph and the Amazing Technicolour Dreamcoat; Les Parents Terribles; Film appearances include: Shopping; Wilde; Gattaca; Midnight in the Garden of Good and Evil; Bent; Music From Another Room; The Wisdom of Crocodiles; eXistenZ; The Talented Mr Ripley; Final Cut; Enemy at the Gates; Artificial Intelligence: AI; Road to Perdition; Cold Mountain. Address: c/o Julian Belfrage Associates, 46 Albemarle Street, London, W1S 4DF, England.

**LAWRENCE Margaret Elizabeth,** b. Richmond, Victoria, Australia. Retired Writer; Television and Radio Producer. Widow. Education: Intermediate Certificate, Swinburne Technical College. Appointments: Manager, TV and Radio Producer for an advertising agency, 20 years; Founder and Editor of 2 Yachting Magazines; Victorian Correspondent for Modern Boating; Sculptor; Painter; News Reporter and Broadcaster for regional ABC Radio/TV; Volunteer Broadcaster, Community Radio; Founding Chairman, Noosa Federation of the Arts Incorporated, 1989; President, Friends of the Queensland Conservatorium of Music, 4 years; First Australian female reporter into Japan after the Second World War to film and record documentaries and interviews for Australian radio and television, working with Japanese film and recording crews; Crewmember on "Gretel", skippered by Jock Sturrock when she broke the Melbourne-Devonport race record by 2hrs 58mins. Publications: Articles in Advertising Age, Short History of Strauss, plus many editorials on the arts. Honours: Silver Medal, New York TV and Film Industry Award; Bronze Medal, Chicago TV and Film Industry Award; Grand Prix, Australian Film and TV Awards; Cultural Award, Noosa Shire; 2003 Citizen of the Year Award, Noosa Shire; Order of Australia Medal, 2004. Memberships: Order of Australia Association; Noosa Federation of the Arts Inc; Executive Member, Noosa Sister Cities and Friendship Links Association; Sunshine Beach Surf Life Saving Club; Life Member, Noosa Yacht and Rowing Club; Noosa Heads Bowls Club; Community Radio 101.5, Caboolture. Address: 3/3 Pilchers Gap, Sunshine Beach, Qld 4567, Australia. E-mail: meglawrence@westnet.com.au

**LAWRENCE Roderick John,** b. 30 August 1949, Adelaide, Australia. m. Clarisse Christine Gonet, 3 sons. Education: BArch, University of Adelaide, 1972; MLitt, University of Cambridge, England, 1978; DSc, Ecole Polytechnique Fédérale de Lausanne, Switzerland, 1983. Appointments: Design-Research Architect, South Australian Housing Trust, Adelaide, 1974; Architect, Percy Thomas Partnership, Cardiff, Wales, 1978; Tutor, Department of Architecture, Ecole Polytechnique Fédérale de Lausanne, 1978-84; Consultant, Committee on Housing Building and Planning, Economic Commission for Europe, 1984-85; Visiting Lecturer, Faculty of Architecture and Town Planning, University of Adelaide, Visiting Research Fellow, School of Social Sciences, Flinders University, 1985; Master of Teaching and Research, Centre for Human Ecology and Environmental Sciences, University of Geneva, 1986; Professor, Faculty of Social and Economic Sciences, 1999-. Publications include: An Ecological Blueprint for Healthy Housing, 1993; Mythical and Ritual Constituents of the City, 1994; Type as Analytical Tool: Reinterpretation and Application, 1994; Sustaining Human Settlement: A Challenge for the New Millennium, 2000. Over 120 articles in scientific journals and 50 book reviews. Honours: Wormald Prize in Architecture, University of Adelaide, 1971; Milne Travelling Scholarship, 1974; Lawson Postgraduate Research Fellowship, 1974; Travel and Study Scholarship, National Science Foundation of Switzerland, 1984; Listed in national and international biographical dictionaries. Memberships: Associate Member, Royal British Institute of Architects, 1973-98; People and Physical Environment Research, Sydney; International Association for People – Environment Studies, Guildford, England; Co-ordinator, European Network for Housing Research, Working Group on Housing and Health; Member, Scientific Advisory Board of the World Health Organisation's European Centre for Environment and Health, 1994-98; Member, The New York Academy of Sciences, 1997-; Chairperson, Evaluation Advisory Committee of World Health Organisation's Healthy Cities Project, 1998-; Member, World Health Organization's European Taskforce on Housing and Health, 2001-. Address: Centre for Human Ecology and Environmental Sciences, University of Geneva, 40 Boulevard du Pont D'Arve, 1211 Geneva 4, Switzerland. E-mail: roderick. lawrence@cueh.unige.ch

**LAWRENCE Ruth (Anderson),** b. 15 August 1924, New York, New York, USA. Physician; Paediatrician. m. Robert M Lawrence, 5 sons, 4 daughters. Education: MD, University of Rochester, 1949, Paediatric Residency, Yale New Haven Hospital, 1949-51. Appointments: Research Paediatrician, Monroe Company Health Department, 1953-58; Professor of Paediatrics and Obstetrics and Gynaecology, Faculty Department Paediatrics University of Rochester, 1958-. Publications: Breastfeeding and Guide for the Medical Profession, 6th edition, 2005. Honours: Recognition from MCHB for breastfeeding work; Edward Mott Moore Award, Monroe Company Medical Society, 2001. Memberships: American Academy Paediatrics; American Paediatric Society; American Academic Clinical Toxicology; Co-Founder, Academy of Breastfeeding Medicine. Address: University of Rochester School Medicine, 601 Elmwood Avenue Box 777, Rochester, NY 14642, USA.

**LAWSON Charles Nicholas,** b. 4 May 1940, Crawley, Sussex, England. Publisher. m. Marion Victoria Lawrence, 1 son, 1 daughter. Education: Wellington College, Berkshire, England, 1967-71; Surrey County Technical College, 1971-73, Cambridge College of Arts and Technology, 1973-74. Appointments: Production Director, Hawthorne Press Ltd, 1982-88; Chief Executive, Snipe Publishing, 1988-; Director, Eddison Press Ltd, 1986-; Director, Academy of Children's Writers Ltd, 1986-.

Memberships: International Platform Association; Cambridge Business and Professional Club; University of Cambridge Club; National Trust. Address: The Poplars, 90 Aldreth Road, Haddenham, Ely, Cambridgeshire CB6 3PN, England.

**LAWSON Dominic Ralph Campbell (Hon),** b. 17 December 1956, London, England. Journalist; Editor. m. (1) Jane Fiona Wastell Whytenead, 1982, divorced 1991, (2) Hon Rosamond Monckton, 1991, 2 daughters. Education: Christchurch, Oxford; BA Oxon. Appointments: World Tonight and The Financial World Tonight, BBC, 1979-81; Staff, Energy Correspondent, Lex Columnist, 1987-90, Columnist, 1991-94 The Financial Times; Deputy Editor, 1987-90, Editor, 1990-95, The Spectator; Editor, The Spectator Cartoon Book; Columnist, Sunday Correspondent, 1990; Columnist, Daily Telegraph, 1994-95; Editor, The Sunday Telegraph, 1995-. Publications: Korchnoi, Kasparov, 1983; Britain in the Eighties, co-author, 1989; The Spectator Annual, editor, 1992, 1993, 1994; The Inner Game, editor, 1993. Honours: Editor of the Year, Society of Magazine Editors, 1990. Memberships: Fellow, Royal Society of Arts. Address: The Sunday Telegraph, 1 Canada Square, Canary Wharf, London E14 5AR, England.

**LAWSON Lesley (Twiggy),** b. 19 September 1949, London. England. Model; Singer; Actress. m. (1) Michael Whitney Armstrong, 1977, deceased, 1983, 1 daughter, (2) Leigh Lawson, 1988. Career: Model, 1966-70; Manager, Director, Twiggy Enterprises Ltd, 1966-; Own musical series, British TV, 1975-76; Founder, Twiggy and Co, 1998-; Made several LP records; Appearances in numerous TV dramas, UK and USA; Appeared in films including The Boy Friend, 1971, There Goes the Bride, 1979, Blues Brothers, 1981, The Doctor and the Devils, 1986, Club Paradise, 1986, Harem Hotel, Istanbul, 1988, Young Charlie Chaplin, TV film, 1989, Madame Sousatzka, 1989, Woundings, 1998; Appeared in plays: Cinderella, 1976; Captain Beaky, 1982; My One and Only, 1983-84; Blithe Spirit, Chichester, 1997; Noel and Gertie, USA, 1998; If Love Were All, New York, 1999; Blithe Spirit, New York, 2002; Play What I Wrote, 2002; Mrs Warren's Profession, 2003. Publications: Twiggy: An Autobiography, 1975; An Open Look,1985; Twiggy in Black and White, co-author, 1997. Honours: 2 Golden Globe Awards, 1970. Address: c/o Peters Fraser and Dunlop, Drury House, 34-43 Russell Street, London WC2B 5HA, England. E-mail: postmaster@pfd.co.uk

**LAWSON of BLABY, Baron of Newnham in the County of Northamptonshire, Nigel Lawson,** b. 11 March 1932, London, England. Politician. m. (1) Vanessa Salmon, divorced. 1980, deceased. 1985, (2) Thérèse Mary Maclear, 1980, 2 sons, 4 daughters, 1 deceased. Education: Christ Church, Oxford; MA Oxon. Appointments: Sub-Lieutenant, Royal Naval Volunteer Reserve, 1954-56; Editorial Staff, Financial Times, 2956-60; City Editor, Sunday Telegraph, 1961-63; Special Assistant to Prime Minister, 1963-64; Columnist, Financial Times and Broadcaster, BBC, 1965; Editor, The Spectator, 1966-70; Regular Contributor to Sunday Times and Evening Standard, 1970-71, The Times, 1971-72; Fellow, Nuffield College, Oxford, 1972-73; Special Political Adviser, Conservative Party Headquarters, 1973-74; Member of Parliament for Blaby, Leicestershire, 1974-92; Opposition Whip, 1976-77; Opposition Spokesman on Treasury and Economic Affairs, 1977-79; Financial Secretary to the Treasury, 1979-81; Secretary of State for Energy, 1981-83; Chancellor of the Exchequer, 1983-89; Non-Executive Director, Barclays Bank, 1990-98; Chairman, Central European Trust, 1990-; Adviser, BZW, 1990-91; Non-Executive Director, Consultant, Guinness Peat Aviation, 1990-93; Director, Institute for International Economics, Washington DC, 1991-; International Advisory Board,

Creditanstalt Bankverein, 1991-; International Advisory Board, Total SA, 1994-; Advisory Council, Prince's Youth Business Trust, 1994-; President, British Institute of Energy Economics, 1995-; Chairman, CAIB Emerging Russia Fund, 1997-; Privy Councillor. Publications: The Power Game, co-author, 1976; The View from No 11: Memoirs from a Tory Radical, 1992; The Nigel Lawson Diet Book, co-author, 1996; Various pamphlets. Memberships: President, British Institute of Energy Economics, 1995-; Governing Body, Westminster School, 1999-. Honours: Finance Minister of the Year, Euromoney Magazine, 1988; Honorary Student, Christ Church, Oxford, 1996. Address: House of Lords, London SW1A 0PW, England.

**LAYARD, Baron of Highgate in the London Borough of Haringey, Peter Richard Grenville,** b. 15 March 1934, Welwyn Garden City. Economist. m. Molly Meacher, 1991. Education: BA, Cambridge University; MSc, London School of Economics. Appointments: Schoolteacher, London County Council, 1959-61; Senior Research Officer, Robbins Committee on Higher Education, 1961-64; Deputy Director, Higher Education Research Unit, 1964-74, Lecturer, 1968-75, Head, Centre for Labour Economics, 1974-90, Reader, 1975-80, Professor of Economics, 1980-99, Director, Centre for Economic Performance, 1990-, London School of Economics; Consultant, Centre for European Policy Studies, Brussels, 1982-86; University Grants Committee, 1985-89; Chairman, Employment Institute, 1987-92; Ch-Chairman, World Economy Group, World Institute for Development Economics Research, 1989-; Economic Adviser to Russian Government, 1991-97. Publications: Cost Benefit Analysis, 1973; Causes of Poverty, co-author, 1978; Microeconomic Theory, co-author, 1978; More Jobs, Less Inflation, 1982; The Causes of Unemployment, co-editor, 1984; The Rise in Unemployment, co-editor, 1986; How to Beat Unemployment, 1986; Handbook of Labour Economics, co-editor, 1987; The Performance of the British Economy, co-author, 1988; Unemployment: Macroeconomic Performance and the Labour Market, co-author, 1991; East-West Migration: the alternatives, co-author, 1992; Post-Communist Reform: pain and progress, co-author, 1993; Macroeconomics: a text for Russia, 1994; The Coming Russian Boom, co-author, 1996; What Labour Can Do, 1997; Tackling Unemployment, 1999; Tackling Inequality, 1999. Honours: Created Life Peer, 2000. Memberships: Fellow, Econometric Society. Address: 45 Cholmeley Park, London N6 5EL, England.

**LE Tuan Hung,** b. 15 October 1960, Vietnam. Composer; Performer; Musicologist. Education: Graduate Diploma, Information Services, Royal Melbourne Institute of Technology, 1992; Bachelor of Music, University of Melbourne, 1986; Doctor of Philosophy, Musicology, Monash University, 1991. Career: Freelance Composer, Performer and Musicologist, 1987-; Program Director, Music, Australia Asia Foundation, 1994-. Compositions: Reflections, 1990; Spring, 1991; Prayer for Land, 1991; Longing for Wind, 1996; Calm Water, 1996; Water Ways, 1997; Scent of Memories, 1998; Three Musical Poems, 2002; On the Wings of a Butterfly, 2004. Recordings: Quivering String, 1992; Musical Transfigurations, 1993; Landscapes of Time, 1996; Echoes of Ancestral Voices, 1997; Scent of Time, 2002. Publications: Dan Tranh Music of Vietnam: Traditions and Innovations, 1998; Numerous articles in magazines, reviews and journals. Honour: Overseas Fellowship, Australian Academy of Humanities, 1993. Memberships: Australasian Performing Rights Association. Address: PO Box 387, Springvale, Vic 3171, Australia.

**LE BLANC Matthew,** b. 25 July 1967, Newton, Massachusetts, USA. Actor. m. Melissa McKnight, 2003, 1 daughter, 2004. Education: Newton High School; Trained as Carpenter.

Television Includes: TV 101, 1988; Top of the Heap, 1991; Vinnie and Bobby, 1992; Red Shoes Diaries, 1993; Friends, 1994; Reform School Girl, 1994; Red Shoes Diaries 7,1997; Joey, 2004; Commercials, Levi's 501 jeans, Coca Cola, Doritos, Heinz Ketchup. Films include: Lookin' Italian, 1994; Ed, 1996; Lost in Space, 1998; Charlie's Angels, 2000; All the Queens Men, 2001; Charlie's Angels: Full Throttle, 2003. TV Guest Appearances include: Just the Ten of us, 1989; Monsters, 1990; Married... with Children, 1991; The Rosie O'Donald Show, 1996; The Tonight Show with Jay Leno, 1996; Entertainment Tonight, 2003; Opera Winfrey Show, 2003; Celebrities Uncensored, 2003; Tonight with Jay Leno, 2004. Honours: TV Guide Award, 2000; Teen Choice Award, 2002. Address: c/o United Talent Agency, 9560 Wilshire Boulevard, Suite 500, Beverly Hills, CA 90212, USA.

**LE BRAS Michel,** b. 16 January 1947, Meaux, France, Research Engineer. m. Michèle Guilbert, 2 sons, 1 daughter. Education: Philosophical Dissertation in Structural Engineering, 1977; Doctorate in Physical Sciences, 1997. Appointments: Ingénieur de Recherche Hors Classe, École Nationale Supérieure de Chimie de Lille, 1979-; Senior Lecturer, Chemistry (CNAM Lille). Publications: Editor, 3 books, 3 journals (special issue); 2 extended abstracts; 118 papers in international journals; 44 chapters in books; 23 other papers; 175 communications in conferences; 3 French patents, 1 international patent. Membership: International Editorial Board, Polym Polym Composites (RAPRA p46); Journal of Fire Science. Address: ENSCL, BP59 108, 59652 Villeneuve d'Ascq Cedex, France.

**LE BRUN Christopher Mark,** b. 20 December 1951, Portsmouth, England. Artist. m. Charlotte Verity, 2 sons, 1 daughter. Education: DFA, Slade School of Fine Art, 1970-74; MA, Chelsea School of Art, 1974-75. Career: Visiting Lecturer: Brighton Polytechnic, 1975-82, Slade School of Fine Art, 1978-83, Wimbledon School of Art, 1981-83; Professor of Drawing RA, 2000-02, Chair, Education Committee RA, 2000-, Royal Academy; Trustee, Prince of Wales's Drawing School, 2004-; Trustee: Tate Gallery, 1990-95, National Gallery, 1996-2003, Dulwich Picture Gallery, 2000-05; Numerous one-man and group exhibitions internationally since 1979; Public Collections include: Tate Gallery, British Museum, Victoria and Albert, MOMA, New York; British Council; National Portrait Gallery; Scottish National Gallery of Modern Art; Walker Art Gallery. Publications: Works feature in: 50 Etchings, 1991; Christopher Le Brun, 2001. Honours: John Moores Liverpool Prizewinner, 1978, 1980; Gulbenkian Printmakers Commission, 1983; DAAD Fellowship, Berlin, 1987-88; Turner Watercolour Medal, 2005. Membership: Royal Academician (RA), 1996. Address: Royal Academy of Arts, Piccadilly, London W1J 0BD, England.

**LE MARCHANT Francis Arthur (Sir),** b. 6 October 1939, Hungerton, UK. Artist; Farmer. Education: Byam Shaw School of Drawing and Painting; Certificate, RAS, Royal Academy Schools. Career: One man exhibitions include: Museum of Art and Science, Evansville, USA; Agnews; Roy Miles Fine Art; Group exhibitions include: Royal Academy Summer Exhibitions; Leicester Galleries, Spink; Bilan de l'Art Contemporain, Paris; Spink; Collections include: Government Art Collections, 2 paintings; Financial Times; The Museum of Evansville, USA; University of Evansville, USA; Collection of the late Mrs Anne Kessler. Honour: Silver Medal, Bilan de l'Art Contemporain, Paris. Memberships: Savile Club; Reynolds Club (Alumni Association of Royal Academy Schools). Address: c/o HSBC, 88 Westgate, Grantham, Lincolnshire NG31 6LF, England.

**LEACH Henry (Conyers) (Admiral of the Fleet Sir),** b. 18 November 1923. Naval Officer. m. Mary Jean McCall, 1958, deceased 1991, 2 daughters. Education: Royal Naval College, Dartmouth. Appointments: Served cruiser Mauritius, South Atlantic and Indian Ocean, 1941-42, battleship Duke of York, 1943-45, destroyers, Mediterranean, 1945-46; gunnery, 1947; Gunnery appointments, 1948-51; Gunnery Officer, cruiser Newcastle, Far East, 1953-55; Staff appointments, 1955-59; Commanded destroyer Dunkirk, 1959-61; Captain, 27th Squadron and Mediterranean, frigate Galatea, 1965-67; Director of Naval Plans, 1968-70; Commanded Commando Ship Albion, 1970; Assistant Chief of Naval Staff, Policy, 1971-73; Flag Officer, First Flotilla, 1974-75; Vice-Chief of Defence Staff, 1976-77; Commander-in-Chief and Allied Commander-in-Chief, Channel and Eastern Atlantic, 1977-79; Chief of Naval Staff, First Sea Lord, 1979-82; First and Principal ADC to the Queen, 1979-82; Deputy Lieutenant; Chairman, 1987-98, Honorary Vice-President, 1991-, Council, King Edward VII Hospital; Governor, Cranleigh School, 1983-93; Chairman, 1983-98, Honorary Vice-President, 1999-, St Dunstan's; Governor, St Catherine's, 1987-93. Publications: Endure No Makeshifts, autobiography. Honours: Knight Grand Cross, Order of the Bath; Honorary Freeman, Merchant Taylors, Shipwrights, City of London. Memberships: Royal Bath and West of England Society, President, 1993, Vice-President, 1994-; Royal Naval Benevolent Society, President, 1984-93; Sea Cadet Association, President, 1984-93; Patron, Meridian Trust Association, 1994-; Patron, Hampshire Royal British Legion, 1994-. Address: Wonston Lea, Wonston, Winchester, Hants SO21 3LS, England.

**LEAHY John H G (Sir),** b. 7 February 1928, Worthing, Sussex, England. Retired Diplomatist. m. Elizabeth Anne Pitchford, 1954, 2 sons, 2 daughters. Education: Clare College, Cambridge; Yale University; MA. Appointments: Joined Diplomatic Service, 1951; Third Secretary, Singapore, 1955-57; Second Secretary, then First Secretary, Paris, 1958-62; First Secretary, Tehran, 1965-68; Counsellor, Paris, 1973-75; Attached to Northern Ireland Office, Belfast, 1975-76; Ambassador to South Africa, 1979-82; Deputy Under-Secretary for Africa and Middle East, Foreign and Commonwealth Office, 1982-84; High Commissioner to Australia, 1984-88; Director, The Observer, 1989-92; Pro-Chancellor, City University, 1991-97; Non-Executive Director, 1993-98, Chairman, 1994-97, Lonrho PLC; Chairman, Governors Committee, Tonbridge School, 1994-99. Honours: Knight Commander, Order of St Michael and St George; Honorary DCL, City University, 1997; Officier, Légion d'Honneur, France. Memberships: Franco-British Council, Chairman, 1989-93; Master, Skinners Company, 1993-94; Chairman, Britain-Australia Society, 1994-97. Address: Manor Stables, Bishopstone, Near Seaford, East Sussex BN25 2UD, England.

**LEAL José H,** Museum Director. Education: BS, Marine Biology, 1974-1977, MS Zoology, 1980-84, Federal University of Rio de Janeiro, Brazil; PhD, Marine Biology and Fisheries, University of Miami, Florida, USA, 1985-90. Appointments: Research Assistant, Division of Mollusks, National Museum, Rio de Janeiro, Brazil, 1981-84; Visiting Professor, Laboratoire de Biologie des Invertébrés Marins et Malacologie, Muséum National d'Histoire Naturelle, Paris, France, 1988; Research Associate, 1991-92, Postdoctoral Associate, 1994-95, Electron Microscopy Laboratory, Adjunct Professor of Marine Biology and Fisheries, 1994-, Division of Marine Geology and Geophysics, University of Miami's Rosenstiel School of Marine and Atmospheric Science; Post Doctoral Fellow, Department of Invertebrate Zoology, National Museum of Natural History, Smithsonian Institution, Washington DC, 1992-94; Scientific

Director, 1996, Director, 1996-, The Bailey-Matthews Shell Museum, Sanibel Island, Florida, USA; Editor-in-Chief, The Nautilus, 1998- Temporary Member, Graduate Faculty, University of Alabama, Tuscaloosa, 1999-; Courtesy Faculty Member, College of Arts and Sciences, Florida Gulf Coast University, Fort Myers, 1999-. Publications: Book, Marine Prosobranch Gastropods from Oceanic Islands off Brazil: Species Composition and Biogeography, 1991; 36 articles in peer-reviewed journals; Numerous papers presented at conferences and workshops; several popular articles and contributions to educational websites. Honours: Numerous research grants and fellowships, 1978-. Memberships include: Biological Society of Washington; California Malacozoological Society; Unitas Malacologica; American Malacological Society, President, 2003-04; Malacological Society of London, Conchologists of America, Society of Systematic Biology; American Association of Museums; Natural Science Collections Alliance. Address: The Bailey-Matthews Shell Museum, PO Box 1580, Sanibel Island, FL 33957, USA. E-mail: jleal@shellmuseum.org

**LEAPER David John,** b. 23 July 1947, York, England. Professor of Surgery. m. Francesca Ann, 1 son, 1 daughter. Education: Leeds Modern Grammar School, 1957-65; MBChB with honours, University of Leeds Medical School, 1970; MD, 1979, ChM, 1982. Appointments: House Officer, Leeds General Infirmary, 1970-71; MRC Fellow, 1971-73; Registrar, Leeds General Infirmary and Scarborough, 1973-76; Senior Registrar in Surgery, CRC Fellow, Westminster and Kings College Hospitals, London, 1976-87; Professor of Surgery, University of Hong Kong, 1988-90; Senior Lecturer in Surgery, University of Bristol, 1981-95; Professor of Surgery, 1995-2004, Emeritus Professor, 2004-, University of Newcastle; Visiting Professor, Cardiff University, 2004-. Publications: Books: International Surgical Practice; Oxford Handbook of Clinical Surgery; Oxford Handbook of Operative Surgery; Handbook of Postoperative Complications: Series: Your Operation; Member, Editorial Board of Medical, Educational and Surgical Journals; Papers on wound healing, surgical infections, colorectal and breast cancer. Honours: Fellow, Royal College of Surgeons of England, 1975, of Edinburgh, 1974, of Glasgow, 1998; Hunterian Professor, 1981-82; Zachary Cope Lecturer, 1998; Fellow, American College of Surgeons, 1998; Past Member, Court of Examiners, Royal College of Surgeons of England; Intercollegiate Fellowship Examiner, 2000-04. Memberships: Founder Member, Past Recorder and Past President, European Wound Management Association; Surgical Infection Society of Europe; Past Vice President, Section of Surgery, Royal Society of Medicine; Past Committee Member, Surgical Research Society; Programme Director, Higher Surgical Training, Northern Deanery, 2000-04; Member, Specialist Advisory Committee, Higher Surgical Training, UK, 2000-05; Chair, Subcommittee Surgical Site Infection, Steering Group on Healthcare Associated Infection; Day Case Champion, Modernisation Agency, 2002-04. Address: 33 Peverell Avenue East, Poundbury, Dorchester, Dorset DT1 3RH, England. E-mail: profdavidjohnleaper@doctors.org.uk

**LEAPMAN Michael Henry,** b. 24 April 1938, London, England. Writer; Journalist. m. Olga Mason, 15 July 1965, 1 son. Appointment: Journalist, The Times, 1969-81. Publications: One Man and His Plot, 1976; Yankee Doodles, 1982; Companion Guide to New York, 1983; Barefaced Cheek, 1983; Treachery, 1984; The Last Days of the Beeb, 1986; Kinnock, 1987; The Book of London (editor), 1989; London's River, 1991; Treacherous Estate, 1992; Eyewitness Guide to London, 1993; Master Race (with Catrine Clay), 1995; Witnesses to War, 1998; The Ingenious Mr Fairchild, 2000; The World for a Shilling 2001; Inigo, 2003. Contributions to: Numerous magazines and journals. Honours: Campaigning Journalist of the Year, British Press Award, 1968; Thomas Cook Travel Book Award, Best Guide Book of 1983; Garden Writers Guild Award, 1995; Times Education Supplement Senior Book Award, 1999. Memberships: Society of Authors; Royal Society of Arts, National Union of Journalists; Garden Writers' Guild. Address: 13 Aldebert Terrace, London SW8 1BH, England.

**LEAVER Christopher (Sir),** b. 3 November 1937, London, England. Business Executive. m. Helen Mireille Molyneux Benton, 1975, 1 son, 2 daughters. Appointments: Commissioned, Royal Army Ordnance Corps, 1956-58; Member, Retail Food Trades Wages Council, 1963-64; Justice of the Peace, Inner London, 1970-83; Council, Royal Borough of Kensington and Chelsea, 1970-73; Court of Common Council, Ward of Dowgate, 1973, Sheriff, 1979-80, Lord Mayor, 1981-82, City of London; Justice of the Peace, City, 1974-93; Board, Brixton Prison, 1975-78; Governor, Christ's Hospital School, 1975; Governor, City of London Girls School, 1975-78; Board of Governors, 1978-, Chancellor, 1981-82, City University; Chairman, Young Musicians Symphony Orchestra Trust, 1979-81; Trustee, Chichester Festival Theatre, 1982-97; Church Commissioner, 1982-83, 1996-; Chairman, London Tourist Board Ltd, 1983-89, Trustee, London Symphony Orchestra, 1983-91; Deputy Chairman, 1989-93, Chairman, 1993-94, Vice-Chairman, 1994-2000, Thames Water PLC; Adviser to Secretary of State on Royal Parks, 1993-96; Non-Executive Director, Unionamerica Holdings, 1994-97; Chairman, Eastbourne College. Honours: Knight Grand Cross, Order of the British Empire; Knight, Order of St John of Jerusalem; Honorary Colonel, 151 Regiment, Royal Corps of Transport (Volunteers), 1983-89; Honorary Colonel, Royal Corps of Transport, 1988-91; Honorary Liveryman, Farmers Company; Fellow, Chartered Institute of Transport; Honorary Freeman, Company of Water Conservators; Freeman, Company of Watermen and Lightermen; Order of Oman. Memberships: Vice-President, Playing Fields Association. Address: c/o Thames Water PLC, 14 Cavendish Place, London W1M 0NU, England.

**LEAVER Peter Lawrence Oppenheim,** b. 28 November 1944. Lawyer; Football Executive. m. Jane Rachel Pearl, 1969, 3 sons, 1 daughter. Education: Trinity College, Dublin; Called to Bar, Lincoln's Inn, 1967. Appointments: Member, Committee on Future of the Legal Profession, 1986-88, Council of Legal Education, 1986-91, General Council of the Bar, 1987-90; Chairman, Bar Committee, 1989, International Practice Committee, 1990; Director, Investment Management Regulatory Organisation, 1994-2000; Recorder, 1994-; Bencher, 1995; Queen's Counsel; Chief Executive, Football Association Premier League, 1997-99; Deputy High Court Judge. Memberships: Chartered Institute of Arbitrators; Member, Dispute Resolution Panel for Winter Olympics, Salt Lake City, 2002. Address: 5 Hamilton Terrace, London NW8 9RE, England.

**LEBED Aleksander Ivanovich (Lieutenant General),** b. 20 April 1950, Novocherkassk, Russia. Army Officer. m. 2 sons, 1 daughter. Education: Ryazan Higher School of Airborne Troops; M Frunze Military Academy. Appointments: Platoon then Company Commander, Ryazan Higher Airborne Troops Commanding School, 1973-81; Battalion Commander, Afghanistan, 1981-82; Regimental Commander, 1985-86; Deputy Commander, Airborne Troops Formation, 1986-88; Commander, Tula Airborne Troops Division, 1989-92; Stood guard with paratrooper battalion at Supreme Soviet building during attempted coup, August, 1991; Deputy Commander, Airborne Troops and Military Education Institute, 1991; Commander, 14th Russian Army, Pridniestr Republic, 1992-94; Deputy Chairman, National Council, Congress of Russian Communities, 1995-96; Member, State Duma, 1995-96;

Candidate, Presidential Election, 1996; Secretary, Security Council of Russia, 1996; Started negotiations with Chechen separatists; Founder, Russian People's Republican Party; Governor, Krasnoyarsk Territory; Member, Council of Russian Federation, 1998-. Publications: It is a Pity for the Power, 1995; My Life and My Country, 1997; Ideology of Common Sense, 1997. Honours: Several military orders. Address: House of Administration, Mira prospect 110, 660009 Mrasnoyarsk, Russia.

**LEBED Aleksey Ivanovich,** b. 14 April 1955, Novocherkassk, Rostov Region, Russia. m. Yelizaveta Vladimirovna, 1 son, 1 daughter. Education: Ryazan Higher School of Airborne Troops; Military Academy; Saint Petersburg State University. Appointments: Served in the Soviet Army, 1979-88; Served in Afghanistan, 1982, Pskov, 1991; Military operations, various parts of USSR, 1980-92; Regimental Commander, 300th Paratroop Regiment, 1995-96; State Duma Deputy, 1996-; Head of Government, Republic of Khakassia, 1996-2001; Member, Council of Russian Federation, 1996-; Member, Congress of Russian Communities. Honours: Order of the Red Star; Medal for Courage; Honoris Causa Degree, Khakassia Kalanov State University; Peter the Great Prize, 2001. Address: House of Government, Prospect Lenina 67, R-665019 Abakan, Russia. E-mail: pressa@khakasnet.ru

**LEBLANC Bruce,** b. 4 June 1957, Gardner, Massachusetts, USA. Professor; Bishop. Education: Bachelor of Science, Psychology, Magna Cum Laude, Towson State University, 1981; MPA, Public Administration, Consortium of the California State University, 1987; Certificate, Paralegal Studies, Southern Career Institute, 1989; Certificate, Sexological Instructor/Advisor of AIDS/STD Prevention, Institute for Advanced Study of Human Sexuality, 1989; MA, Sociology, Idaho State University, 1990; EdD, Curriculum and Instruction, University of Sarasota, 1996; Diploma, Certified Massage Therapist, Academy of Massage Therapy, 1997; Certificate, Moderator Trainer, Environmental Issues Forum, 1997; MA, Transpersonal Studies, Atlantic University, 2001-; MS, Psychology, California Coast University, 2004-; Advanced doctoral studies in Political Science, Idaho State University; Board Certified Sexologist, The American College of Sexologists. Appointments: Teaching Assistant, Department of Psychology, Towson State University, Maryland, 1978-80; Director, Trinity Day Camp, Maryland, 1977-80; Supervisor/Group Worker, Rancho San Antonio, California, 1981-85; Deputy Probation Officer, County of Ventura Corrections Services Agency, California, 1986-90; Teaching Assistant, Instructor, Department of Sociology, Idaho State University, Idaho, 1989-91; Pocatello AIDS ETC Program Director, Mountain States Health Corporation, Idaho, 1991; Educational Co-ordinator and Adjunct Professor, Academy of Massage Therapy, Illinois, 1992-98; Professor, Department of Social, Behavioral & Educational Studies, 1991-, ALS Program Advisor/Faculty Co-ordinator of Alternative Educational Assessments, 1997-, Black Hawk College, Illinois. Publications: Co-author, 1 book; Author, 2 study guides and 1 instruction manual; Several articles published in professional journals. Honours: Listed in national and international biographical directories. Memberships: National Social Science Association; Illinois Sociological Association. Address: Black Hawk College, Department of Social and Behavioral Studies, 6600 34th Avenue, Moline, IL 61265, USA. E-mail: leblancb@bhc.edu Website: http://rtrevdrleblanc.faithweb.com

**LECHEVALIER Hubert Arthur,** b. 12 May 1926, Tours, France. Microbiologist. m. Mary Jean Pfeil, 2 sons. Education: Licence ès Sciences, 1947, MS, 1948, Laval University, Quebec, Canada; PhD, Rutgers University, New Brunswick, New Jersey,

1951. Appointments: Assistant Professor, Microbiology, College of Agriculture then Waksman Institute, Rutgers University, 1951-56; Associate Professor, Microbiology, 1956-66, Professor, Microbiology, 1966-91, Associate Director, 1980-88, Waksman Institute of Microbiology, Rutgers University; Professor Emeritus, Rutgers, The State University of New Jersey, 1991-. Publications: Author or co-author of over 140 scientific papers, co-author or co-editor of 10 books including: A Guide to the Actinomycetes and Their Antibiotics, 1953; Antibiotics of Actinomycetes, 1962; Three Centuries of Microbiology, 1965, reprint 1974; The Microbes, 1971; 4 US patents. Honours include: Honorary Member, the Société Française de Microbiologie 1972-; Charles Thom Award (jointly with Mary P Lechevalier), 1982; DSc, Laval University, 1983; Bergey Trust Award for contributions to bacterial taxonomy, 1989; New Jersey Inventors Hall of Fame, 1990; Honorary member of the Society for Actinomycetes, Japan, 1997. Address: 131 Goddard-Nisbet Rd, Morrisville, VT 05661-8041, USA. E-mail: hubartlech@msn.com

**LEE (Edward) Adam (Michael),** b. 29 June 1942, Londonderry, Northern Ireland. Barrister; Company Director. m. Carola Jean Anderson, 2 sons. Education: 1 Jurisprudence, Christ Church, Oxford. Appointments: Barrister-at-Law, called to the Bar, Middle Temple, 1964; Cadet Director, Glyn, Mills & Co, 1964-70; Williams & Glyn's Bank, 1970-85: Senior Planner for Merger (leading to formation of Williams & Glyn's Bank), Deputy Director City Division, 1974-76; Local Director Child & Co, 1977-87, Holts, 1978-87, Drummonds, 1985-87; Assistant General Manager, Royal Bank of Scotland, 1985-87; Group Development Director, Adam & Company Group, 1988-90; Director: Duncan Lawrie Trust Corporation, 1990-92, Unison International, 1992-94, Trustee Resources, 1993-96, Minmet, 1993-96, Crediton Minerals, 1996-98; Investment Advisor, RAF Central Fund, 1983-2000; Consultant; Family farm and associated enterprises. Publications: Articles in: Three Banks Review; Royal Bank of Scotland Review; Humberts Commentary. Memberships: Secretary: Inverforth Charitable Trust, Matthews Wrightson Charitable Trust; Fellow, Chartered Institute of Bankers; Prime Warden, The Dyer's Company, 2003-04; Chairman of Trustees: Explosion! The Museum of Naval Firepower, Gosport, 2000-2002; Former Chairman, House Committee, Trinity Hospice; Trustee, Chelsea Opera Group; Advisory Council Member, Grange Park Opera; Former Vice-Chairman, Kent Opera; Former Director, Rehearsal Orchestra. Address: The Farm, Northington, Alresford, Hampshire SO24 9TH, England. E-mail: adam.lee@northingtonso24.fsnet.co.uk

**LEE Byeong-Kyu,** b. 3 July 1963, Jinju, Korea. Professor. m. 1 son, 1 daughter. Education: MS, 1995, PhD, 1996, University of Massachusetts, USA. Appointments: Director, Environmental Engineering Program, Ulsan University, Korea; Visiting Scientist, Harvard School of Public Health, USA; Visiting Scientist, Bio-Rad Digilab, USA. Publications: Atmospheric Environment; Chemosphere; Journal of Aerosol Science; Waste Management; Environmental Management; Water, Air Soil Pollution. Honours: Honoured Citizen: City of Tulsa and State of Oklahoma, USA; Listed in Who's Who publications and biographical dictionaries. Memberships: AWMA; KOSAE. Address: Department of Civil and Environmental Engineering, University of Ulsan, Ulsan 680-749, Korea. E-mail; bklee@ulsan.ac.kr

**LEE Chan-Yun,** b. 19 July 1952, Hwa-Liang, Taiwan. Technical Staff Member Associate Professor of Physics. m. Chia-Li Grace Yang, 1 son, 2 daughters. Education: BS, Physics, Soochow University, 1974; MS, Physics, University of Southern California, 1980; PhD, Physics, University of

Notre Dame, 1994. Appointments: Assistant Professor, Physics, TIT, 1982-86; Associate Professor, Physics, TIT, 1986-88; Chairman, Physics Section, TIT, 1986-88; Consultant, TSD, 1983-88; Director, TNSM, 1986-88; Senior Engineer, LRC, 1994-99; Professor, Physics, SJCC, 1998-2000; Key Account for South Asia Area, LRC, 1997-99; Technical Staff, 1999-, West Coast Process Co-ordinator, 2000, TEA. Publications: Over 20 articles published in professional journals. Honours: 27th Science and Technology Personnel Research Award, 1988; Excellent Researchers Prize, 1986, 1987; Outstanding Academic Publication Prize, 1987, 1988. Memberships: Chinese Physics Association; American Vacuum Association. Address: 471 Via Vera Cruz, Fremont, CA 94539-5325, USA.

**LEE Christopher Frank Carandini,** b. 27 May 1922, London, England. Actor; Author; Singer. m. Birgit Kroenke, 1961, 1 daughter. Education: Wellington College. Appointments: Served RAF, 1941-46; Mentioned in Despatches, 1944; Film industry, 1947-; Appeared in over 200 motion pictures; Films include: Moulin Rouge, 1953; The Curse of Frankenstein, 1956; Tale of Two Cities, 1957; Dracula, 1958; The Hound of the Baskervilles, 1959; The Mummy, 1959; Rasputin the Mad Monk, 1965; The Wicker Man, 1973; The Three Musketeers, 1973; The Private Life of Sherlock Holmes, 1973; The Four Musketeers, 1975; The Man with the Golden Gun, 1975; To the Devil a Daughter, 1976; Airport 77, 1977; Return from Witch Mountain, 1977; How the West Was Won, 1977; Caravans, 1977; The Silent Flute, 1977; The Passage, 1978; 1941, 1978I Bear Island, 1978; The Serial, 1979; The Salamander, 1980; An Eye for an Eye; Goliath Awaits; Charles and Diana; The Return of Captain Invincible; The Howling Z; Behind the Mask; Roadstrip; Shaka Zulu; Mio my Mio; The Girl. Un Metier du Seigneur; Casanova; The Disputation (TV); Murder Story; Round the World in 80 Days (TV); Return of the Musketeers; Outlaws; Gremlins II, 1989; Sherlock Holmes; Rainbow Thief; L'Avaro; Wahre Wunder, 1990; Young Indy, 1991; Cybereden, 1991; Death Train, 1992; The Funny Man, 1993; Police Academy, Mission in Moscow, 1993; A Feast at Midnight, 1994; The Stupids, 1995; Moses, 1995; Jinnah, 1997; Sleepy Hollow, 1999; The Lord of the Rings, 2000, 2001, 2003; Star Wars Episode II, 2002 and Episode III, 2005; Charlie and the Chocolate Factory, 2005; The Corpse Bride, 2005; Greyfriars Bobby, 2005. Publications: Christopher Lee's Treasury of Terror, Christopher Lee's Archive of Evil, 1975; Christopher Lee's The Great Villains, 1977; Tall Dark and Gruesome, 1977, 2002; Christopher Lee: Lord of Misrule, 2004. Honours: Officier, Ordre des Arts et des Lettres, 1973; Commander, St John of Jerusalem, 1997; Commander of the Order of the British Empire, 2001. Address: c/o Diamond Management, 31 Percy Street, London, W1T 2DD, England.

**LEE Eun Hwa,** b. 3 September 1971, South Korea. Lawyer. m. Olivier Ravel. Education: Bachelor of Arts, International Relations, with honours and distinction, 1992, Master of Arts, Sociology, 1992, Stanford University, USA; Juris Doctor, Georgetown, USA, 1996. Appointments: Jean Monnet Fellow, SOLLAC SA, Paris, 1992-93; Dean Acheson Legal Stagiaire, Court of Justice of the European Communities, Luxembourg, 1996; Associate, Rosenman & Colin LLP, New York, USA, 1997-98; Associate, Weil Gotshal & Manges LLP, London, 1998-2000; Associate, Debevoise & Plimpton LLP, New York and Paris, 2001-. Publications: Co-author: Update, Going Private, 1998; Author, pamphlet, A Practical Guide to the Dean Acheson Legal Stage program, 1996; Individual Development Accounts and Illinois Women's Business Development Center in State Support for Women-Owned Businesses, 1996; Korean Women's Development Institute (Honours Thesis), 1992. Honours: Awards at Stanford University; Staff Award and Scholarship, World Affairs Council, 1992; Academic

Dean's List, Georgetown, 1994-96. Memberships: New York Bar; International Bar Association; World Association of International Studies; Cap and Gown Women's Honors Society. Address: Debevoise & Plimpton LLP, 21 ave George V, 75008 Paris, France. E-mail: ehlee@debevoise.com

**LEE Eung Sun,** b. 3 May 1934, Seoul, Korea. Executive. m. Sook Hee Lee, 1 son, 1 daughter. Education: BA, College of Engineering, Department of Architecture, Seoul National University, 1953-57; Department of Architecture, Graduate School, University of Illinois, USA, 1959-60; Graduate School of Public Administration, Seoul National University, 1962-63. Appointments: Director, Survey Division, Economic Planning Board, 1962-67; Director General, International Co-operation Bureau, Ministry of Science and Technology, 1967-79; Vice-Minister, Ministry of Science and Technology and Vice-Chairman, Atomic Energy Committee, 1979-82; President, Korea Vocational Training and Management Agency, 1982-88; Member, 13th National Assembly, 1988-92: Commerce and Industry Committee, 1988-90, Vice Chairman, Culture and Information Committee, National Assembly, 1990-92; Vice-Chairman, Central Standing Committee, Democratic Liberal Party, 1993-97; Member 15th National Assembly, 1996-2000: Telecommunication, Science and Technology Committee, 1996, Finance and Economic Committee on Budget and Account, 1996-2000; Chairman, Central Ethics Committee, New Korean Party, 1997; Chairman, Central Ethics Committee, Central Executive Council Committee, 1997-98, Chairman, Kangwon Province Secretariat,1998-2000, Grand National Party; Chairman and Chief Executive Officer: Korea Steel and Petrochemical Company, 2000-2001, Korea Steel Chemical Company, 2000-2001, Samkwang Glass Company, 2000-2005; Advisor of DC Chemical Co, Ltd, 2005-. Publication: Memoires of Jae Hak Lee, 2004. Honours: Red Stripe Order of Service Merit, 1973; Commandeur l'Ordre du Lion, Senegal, 1979; Yellow Stripe Order of Service Merit, 1982; Silver Tower Order of Industrial Service Merit, 1983; Gold Tower Order of Industrial Service Merit, 1988. Memberships: Chairman, 1979-82, Asia Science Co-operation Association; Honorary Member, International Organization for the Promotion of Vocational Training and International Youth Skill Olympics, 1989-; Vice-Chairman, 1996-2000, Korea-Russia Inter-parliamentary Co-operation Association. Address: 108-1603 LG Hangang Xi Apartment, Dongbuichon-Dong, Yongsan-Ku, Seoul, Korea. E-mail: eslee@dcchem.co.kr

**LEE Gregory Price,** b. 3 July 1952, Orange, New Jersey, USA. Professor of Neurology (Clinical and Experimental Neuropsychology). m. Susan L Haverstock, 1 son. Education: BA, Psychology, University of Northern Colorado, Greeley, 1975; MA, Clinical Psychology, Lone Mountain College, San Francisco, 1975; PhD, Clinical Psychology, Florida Institute of Technology, Melbourne, Florida, 1980; Fellowship in Neuropsychology, University of Houston and Baylor College of Medicine, Houston, Texas, 1984; Fellowship in Neuropsychology, University of Wisconsin Medical School, Milwaukee, 1986. Appointments: Research Associate, Texas Research Institute of Mental Science, Texas Medical Centre, Houston, 1983-84; Assistant Professor, Department of Surgery, Medical College of Georgia, Augusta, 1986-90; Director, Neuropsychology Services, Department of Surgery, 1986-2001; Clinical Psychology Internship Faculty, Department of Psychiatry, 1987-2001; Associate Professor, Department of Surgery, 1990-95, Professor, Departments of Surgery and Psychiatry and Health Behaviour, 1995-2001; Professor, Department of Neurology, 2001-; Consulting Neuropsychologist, Veteran's Administration Medical Center, Augusta, 1998-2001. Publications: Over 200 scientific publications in professional journals, book chapters and books on human cerebral hemispheric specialization for memory functions, language and emotional expression. Memberships: Fellow, American Psychological Association, 1996; Fellow, National Academy of Neuropsychology; American Academy of Neurology; American Epilepsy Society; International Neuropsychological Society; Sigma Xi; American Academy of Clinical Neuropsychology. Address: Department of Neurology (BA-3278), Medical College of Georgia, 1120 15th Street, Augusta, GA 30912, USA. E-mail: glee@mail.mcg.edu

**LEE Hae-Wan,** b. 19 October 1957, Seoul, Korea. Medical Doctor. m. Mi Young Kim, 1 son, 1 daughter. Education: MD, Seoul National University, 1977-83; MS, 1991-94, PhD, 1993-98, Seoul National University Graduate School; Korean Board of Surgery, 1991-. Appointments: Served in Korean Army, 1983-86; Internship, 1986-87, Residency in Surgery, 1987-91, Fellow in Surgery, 1991-92, Seoul National University Hospital, Seoul, Korea; Postdoctoral Research Fellow, Gastrointestinal Research Laboratory, Veterans Affairs Medical Center, Department of Medicine, University of California, San Francisco, USA, 1998-99; Associate Professor, 1998-2004, Professor, 2004-, Hallym University College of Medicine, Korea. Publications: Articles in medical journals include: Phorbol 12-myristate 13-acetate up-regulates the transcription of MUV2 intestinal mucin via Ras, ERK and NF-kappa, 2002; Immunoreactivity of CD99 in stomach cancer, 2002; Multiple symmetric lipomatosis: Korean experience, 2003. Memberships: Korean Surgical Society, 1983-; Korean Cancer Association, 1991-; Korean Gastric Cancer Association, 1995-. Address: Hallym University Sacred Heart Hospital, 896 Pyungchon-Dong, Dongan-Gu, Anyang-Si, Kyungki-Do, 431-070, Korea. E-mail: leehw@hallym.or.kr

**LEE Hong Sik,** b. 20 June 1954, Seoul, Korea. University Professor. m. Hyung Sun Kim, 2 sons. Education: BA, Engineering, Yonsei University, Seoul, Korea, 1981; MA, Engineering, 1983, PhD, 1986, Nihon University, Tokyo, Japan. Appointments: Technical Review Committee, Ministry of Maritime Affairs and Fisheries, 2002; Dean, College of Construction Engineering, Chung-Ang University, 2003-2005; Technical Review Committee, Incheon Metropolitan City, 2004-. Publications: Articles in scientific journals including: Boundary element modeling of multidirectional random waves in a harbor with partially reflecting boundaries, Ocean Engineering, 2002; Diffraction of multidirectional random waves by multiple rectangular pits, 2003, Ocean Engineering; ASME Journal of Offshore Mechanics and Arctic Engineering, 2004; Engineering Analysis with Boundary Elements, 2004. Honour: KSCE Award, Korean Society of Civil Engineers. Memberships: Korean Society of Civil Engineers; Korean Society of Coastal and Ocean Engineers. Address: Department of Civil Engineering, College of Construction Engineering, Chung-Ang University, Anseong, Gyeonggi-Do 456-756, Korea. E-mail: hongsik@cau.ac.kr Website: http://cau.ac.kr/~hongsik/

**LEE Hong-Koo,** b. 9 May 1934, Seoul, Korea. Politician; Political Scientist. m., 1 son, 2 daughters. Education: Seoul National University; Emory University; Yale University; PhD. Appointments: Assistant Professor, Emory University, USA, 1963-64; Assistant Professor, Case Western Reserve University, 1964-67; Assistant Professor, Associate Professor, Professor of Political Science,1968-88, Director, Institute of Social Sciences, 1979-82, Seoul National University, Korea; Fellow, Woodrow Wilson International Center for Scholars, Smithsonian Institution, Washington DC, 1973-74; Fellow, Harvard Law School, 1974-75; Minister of National Unification, Korea, 1988-90; Special Assistant to President, 1990-91; Ambassador

to UK, 1991-93; Commission on Global Governance, 1991-95; Senior Vice-Chairman, Advisory Council for Unification, Chairman, Seoul 21st Century Committee, The World Cup 2002 Bidding Committee, 1993-94; Deputy Prime Minister, Minister of National Unification, 1994; Prime Minister, 1994-95; Chairman, New Korea Party, 1996; Ambassador to USA, 1998-. Publications: An Introduction to Political Science; One Hundred Years of Marxism; Modernization. Address: Embassy of the Republic of South Korea, 2450 Massachusetts Avenue NW, Washington, DC 20008, USA. E-mail:korinfo@koreaemb.org

**LEE Hulbert Austin,** b. 17 June 1923, Chelsea, Quebec, Canada. Geologist. m. Katherine A Lee, 2 sons, 3 daughters. Education: BSc, Geology and Mineralogy, Queens University, 1945-49; PhD, Geology, University of Chicago, 1949-53. Appointments: Technician, Physics, National Research Council, Canada, 1941-42; Flight Lieutenant, RCAF, 1942-45; Research Scientist, Geological Survey of Canada, 1950-69; Lecturer, University of New Brunswick, 1966-67; Scientist, Geological Survey of Canada, 1952-1969, President, Lee Geo-Indicators Ltd, 1970-2002. Publications: Correlation of Quaternary Events Around Hudson Bay, the Tyrrell Sea and Keewatin Ice Divide; Quaternary Studies in New Brunswick; Esker and Till Methods of Mineral Exploration; Kimberlite Petrology; Engineering Terrain Analysis of Ontario; Diamond and Gold Studies in Russia, Sierra Leone, Ghana. Honours: Susan Near Award, Proficiency Geology; Pioneer in Helicopter Mapping. Memberships: Fellow, Geological Society of America; Canadian Institute of Mining, Metallurgy and Petroleum; Prospectors and Developers Association; Aircrew Association. Address: 10 Andrew Alexander Street, Box 68, Stittsville, Ontario K2S 1A2, Canada.

**LEE Hung,** b. 21 November 1954, Taiwan. Professor. m. Colleen McCann, 1 son, 1 daughter. Education: BSc, honours, Biochemistry, University of British Columbia, 1977; PhD, Biochemistry, McGill University, 1982. Appointments: Research Associate, Division of Biological Sciences, National Research Council, Canada, 1983-86; Assistant Professor, Department of Environmental Biology, 1986-91, Adjunct Professor, School of Engineering, 1992-, Associate Professor, Department of Environmental Biology, 1991-99, University of Guelph; Visiting Professor, Biotechnology Laboratory, University of British Columbia, 1992-93; Affiliated Network Investigator, Protein Engineering Network Center of Excellence, 1998-; Professor, Department of Environmental Biology, University of Guelph, 1999-; Regional Associate Editor for the journal, Environmental Toxicology, 2000-; Network Investigator, Canadian Water Network Centre of Excellence, 2001-. Publications: 134 original research papers, 25 original review papers, 14 book chapters, 1 patent, 170 conference abstracts, 12 non-refereed technical reports, 4 disclosures. Honours include: Canadian MRC Studentship, McGill University, 1978-82; Research Excellence Citation, Imperial Oil Limited, 1990; Presidential Distinguished Professor Award, University of Guelph, 2002-04. Memberships: American Society for Microbiology; Society for Industrial Microbiology. Address: Department of Environmental Biology, University of Guelph, Guelph, Ontario N1G 2W1, Canada.

**LEE Inkyu,** b. 26 June 1957, Taegu, Korea. Professor. m. Eun-Mee Park, 1 son. Education: Premedical Course, College of Liberal Arts and Sciences, 1976-78, MD, School of Medicine, 1978-82, MS, School of Medicine, 1983-85, PhD, School of Medicine, 1985-88, Kyungpook National University, Taegu, Korea. Appointments: Rotating Internship, 1982-83; Residency in Internal Medicine, 1983-86, Dong-san Medical Centre, Taegu, Korea; Clinical Fellow, 1987-88, Research Fellow, 1994-95, Joslin Diabetes Center, Harvard Medical

School, Boston, USA; Professor, Department of Internal Medicine, Keimyung University Medical School, Taegu, Staff in Medicine, Endocrine Section, Dong-san Medical Centre, Taegu, 1998-; Professor, Department of Internal Medicine, Kyungpook National University Medical School, Taegu, Staff in Medicine, Endocrine Section, Kyungpook National University Hospital, Taegu, 2005-. Publications: 14 articles as co-author in medical journals include most recently: Differential regulation of human and mouse orphan nuclear receptor SHP promoter by sterol regulatory element binding protein-1 (SREBP-1), 2004; SREBP-1c mediates the insulin dependent hepatic glukokinase expression, 2004; Tumor necrosis factor-alpha induces fractalkine expression preferentially in arterial endothelial cells and mithramycin A suppresses TNF-alpha-induced fractalkine expression, 2004. Honour: Award of Best Scientist, Society of Korean Internal Medicine. Memberships: Korean Internal Medicine; Korean Diabetic Association; Korean Endocrine Society; Korean Society of Biochemical and Molecular Biology; American Diabetic Association. Address: Section of Endocrinology, Department of Internal Medicine, Kyungpook University Medical School, 50 Samduk 2Ga, Jung-Gu, Taegu, 700-721, Korea. E-mail: leei@knu.ac.kr

**LEE John B.** Author; Poet; Teacher. Education: BA, Honours, English, University of Western Ontario, Canada, 1974; Bachelor of Education, Althouse College, Ontario, 1975; Master of Arts in Teaching English, University of Western Ontario, 1985. Appointments: Author of poetry, children's poetry, fiction, non-fiction, spoken word texts, 1969-; Editor, 1973-; Teacher, Secondary School English and Dramatic Arts, 1975-83, Teacher, Secondary School English, Creative Writing and Dramatic Arts, 1984-89, Waterford District High School; Publisher, 1980-; Teaching Assistant, English Department, University of Western Ontario, 1983-84. Publications: Over 20 poetry books; 10 chapbooks and flyers; 5 books of non-fiction. Honours include: American Poetry Association's Annual Poetry Award, 1985; Roundhouse Poetry Award, 1989, 1990; The Nova Scotia Poetry Award, 1989; Matrix Magazine Travel Writing Award, 1994; The Tilden Award, 1995; People's Poetry Award, 1996; Petro-Canada Poet Laureate, 1996; People's Political Poem Award, 1997; Amethyst Magazine Harbour Writing Award, 1997; Cranberry Tree Press Poetry Award, 2000; Lexikon Poetry Award, 2000; Editor's Prize Open Window II; Certificate of Excellence for Outstanding Achievement in Literature, Ridgetown District High School Hall of Fame, 2002; Eric Hill Award of Literary Excellence in Poetry, Qwerty Magazine and University of New Brunswick, 2003; Poet Laureate of Brantford, 2005; Eric Hill Award of Excellence in Poetry, 2005; Honorary Life Member, Canadian Poetry Association, 2005. Memberships: Life Member, Ontario Poetry Society. Address: 176 St George Street, Brantford, Ontario N3R 1W2, Canada. E-mail: johnb.lee@rogers.com

**LEE Joon Hyun,** b. 15 May 1956, Seoul, South Korea. Professor. m. Hyun Sun Kim, 2 sons. Education: BSc, Pusan National University, 1983; MSc, 1986, PhD, 1989, Tohoku University. Appointments: Research Scientist, Center for Quality Engineering and Failure Prevention, Northwestern University; Director, Center for Failure Analysis and Reliability, Professor School of Mechanical Engineering, Pusan National University. Publications: Application of Laser Based Ultrasound for Quantitiative Evaluation and Imaging of Surface-Breaking Crack; Application of Shearography in Nondestructive Evaluation of Internal Defects for Composite Materials. Honours: Best Research Paper Award, Korean Society for Nondestructive Testing; Best Research Award, Korean Society for Mechanical Engineers. Memberships: ASNT; ASME; JCNDI; KSME; KSNT. Address: School of Mechanical

Engineering, Pusan National University, Busan 609-735, Korea. E-mail: jhlee@pusan.ac.kr Website: www.ndekorea.net

**LEE Jung Eun,** b. 4 January 1972, Seoul, Korea. Doctoral Candidate. Education: BS, Chemistry, 1994, MS, Physical Chemistry, 1997, Sookmyung Women's University; Diploma, Computer Aided Molecular Design Centre Soong Sil University; Currently, PhD Candidate, School of Environmental Science and Engineering Pohang University of Science and Technology; Invited Researcher, University of California Davis, 2003. Publications: Articles as co-author in scientific journals including: Bulletin of the Korean Chemical Society, 1999, 2003; Journal of Molecular Spectroscopy, 2000; Journal of the American Chemical Society, 2002; Journal of Physical Chemistry A, 2003, 2004. Memberships: American Chemical Society; Korean Chemical Society; Global Association of Culture and Peace; Christian Gospel Missionary. Address: School of Environmental Science and Engineering, Pohang University of Science and Technology, Pohang 790-784, Korea. E-mail: lje4523@postech.ac.kr Website: www.postech.ac.kr/lab/see/art

**LEE Kenneth K C,** b. 30 September 1953, Hong Kong. Professor. m. Cindia Y H Ng, 1 son, 2 daughters. Education: BSc (Pharm), University of Washington, 1978; MPhil, 1991, PhD, 1999, The Chinese University of Hong Kong. Appointments: Professor, School of Pharmacy, The Chinese University of Hong Kong; Honorary Senior Lecturer, School of Pharmacy, University of London, England. Publications: Over 30 articles as co-author in peer-reviewed journals include most recently: Economic analysis of celecoxib versus diclofenac plus omeprazole for the treatment of arthritis in patients at risk from ulcer disease, 2003; Evaluation of the Tradition Chinese Medicine knowledge of current undergraduate pharmacy students, 2004; A cost comparison of management of chronic hepatitis B and its associated complications in Hong Kong and Singapore, 2004; Clopidogrel versus aspirin and esomeprazole to prevent ulcer bleeding, 2005; Cost of acute myocardial infarction in Hong Kong, 2005; 42 abstracts presented at national and international meetings; 1 book chapter. Honours: Best Podium Presentation Award, 2nd Annual European Conference, Edinburgh, 1999, Best Contributed Paper Award, 6th Annual International Meeting, Arlington, Virginia, USA, 2001, International Society for Pharmaeconomics and Outcomes Research; Justice of the Peace, HKSAR. Memberships: International Society for Pharmoeconomics and Outcomes Research; Society of Hospital Pharmacists of Hong Kong; Hong Kong Pharmacology Society. Address: School of Pharmacy, The Chinese University of Hong Kong, 6/F BMSB, Shatin, N.T., Hong Kong. E-mail: kclee@cuhk.edu.hk

**LEE Ki-Young,** b. 1 January 1958, Seoul, Korea. Research Scientist. m. Eun-Ae Jang, 2 sons. Education: BS, Metallurgy, Seoul National University, 1981; MS, Materials Science, KAIST, 1983; PhD, Mechanical Engineering, University of Newcastle, Australia, 1994. Appointments: Section Manager, Daewoo Heavy Industry, 1983-89; Visiting Scientist, KFA-IFF, Jülich, Germany, 1992; Postdoctoral Research, University of Vermont, USA, 1993; Research Scientist, KAIST, Korea, 1994-95; Principal Research Scientist, Battery Research Institute, 1996-2003, Vice President, Director of Battery R&D, 2004-, Vice President, Research Fellow, Battery R&D, 2005-, LG Chemical Research Park. Publications: 30 papers in international journals; 10 international conference papers; 2 US patents. Honours: LG Research and Development Award, 1999; Chang Young Shil Award, 1999; Candidate Member, The National Academy of Engineering of Korea, 2002-. Address: Battery Research and Development, LG Chemical Research

Park, 104-1 Moonji-dong, Yusong, Taejon 305-380, Korea. E-mail: kyleeb@lgchem.com

**LEE Kok Loong**, b. 23 June 1976, Kuala Lumpur, Malaysia. Materials Technologist. Education: BEng, Mechanical Engineering, 1998, PhD, Materials Science, 2004, Leicester University, England. Appointments: Researcher, Chungnam National University, Korea, 2003; Currently, Materials Technologist, Corus UK. Publications: Structure Property Relations in Non Ferrous Metals (materials science textbook); Articles in scientific journals: Metallurgical and Materials Transaction A; Scripta Materialia; Materials Science and Engineering A; Journal of Materials Science; Composites Part A: Applied Science and Manufacturing. Honours: PhD Scholarship; Winner of the Lincolnshire Iron and Steel Institute Ironmaster's Young Members Paper; Listed in Who's Who publications and biographical dictionaries. Membership: Institute of Materials. Address: 1 Donnington Gardens, Scunthorpe DN15 7RJ, England. E-mail: kokloong1@yahoo.co.uk

**LEE Kyoo-Yong**, b. 23 December 1955, Seoul, Republic of Korea. Government Official. m. Kyoo-Ok Kim, 2 sons. Education: Bachelor of Arts in Law, 1974-78, Completed course work for Master of Arts, Graduate School of Public Administration, 1979-85, Seoul National University, Seoul, Korea; Master of Engineering, College of Urban Sciences, University of Seoul, Korea, 2002; Guest Researcher, Centre for Energy and Environmental Policy, University of Delaware, USA, 2002-2003. Appointments: Deputy Director, Ministry of Legislation, 1978-86; Director, Ministry of Environment, Office of the President, Ministry of Legislation, 1986-97; Director, Public Information Office, Ministry of Environment, 1997-98; Director General, Environmental Policy, Water Quality Management, Air Quality Management, Ministry of Environment, 1998-2003; Deputy Minister for Planning and Management, Ministry of Environment, 2003-. Publications: Books: Introduction of Tax Law on Real Estate, 1984; Theory of Administrative Appeals, 1995; Comparative Study for Emission Estimation Methodologies of Air Pollutants Using TMS Data and Emission Factors in Emission Sources, 2002; Articles: Study on Fostering Environmental Technologies for Sustainable Development, 1002; Direction of Environmental Policies in Korea, 2004. Honours: Service Merit Medal, 1985; Order of Service Merit, 2000. Memberships: Vice-President, 2004-, Korea Society of Environmental Law Association; Vice-President, 2002-2004, Korean Society of Environmental Engineers; Executive Director, 2000-2002, Korean Society of Atmospheric Environment. Address: 502-802 Samick Park Apt, Gil-dong, Gangdong-gu, Seoul 134-765, Republic of Korea.

**LEE Kyung-Yil**, b. 19 April 1954, Seoul, Republic of Korea. Paediatrician; Educator. m. Moon-Sun Lee, 2 sons. Education: Graduate, Catholic University of Korea College of Medicine, 1979; Master's Degree, 1989, Doctor of Philosophy, 1992, Catholic University Graduate School. Appointments: Military Service, Korean Air Force, 1979-82; Internship and Residency, Catholic Medical Centre, University of Korea, 1982-86; Instructor, 1986-88, Assistant Professor, 1989-96, Associate Professor, 1997-2001, Professor of Paediatrics, 2001-, The Catholic University of Korea College of Medicine; Postdoctoral Visiting Researcher, Institute of Bioregulation, Kushu University, Japan, 1994-95. Publications: Articles as co-author in international medical journals including: Pediatrics, 2004; Pediatric Infectious Disease Journal, 2003, 2004; Acta Pediatrica, 2002; European Journal of Pediatrics, 2004; Journal of Tropical Pediatrics, 2005; 7 other scientific articles; 72 domestic articles in Korean. Honours: Educator of the Year, 2000, 2002, 2004, Catholic University of Korea, The

Catholic Medical Centre; Listed in Who's Who publications and biographical dictionaries. Memberships: Korean Medical Association; Korean Society of Pediatrics. Address: Department of Pediatrics, Catholic University of Korea; Daejeon St Mary's Hospital, 520-2 Daeheung-dong, Jung-gu, Daejeon 301-723, Republic of Korea. E-mail: leekyungyil@catholic.ac.kr

**LEE Lung-Sheng**, b. 15 May 1954, Nantou, Taiwan. Professor. m. Chun-Chin Lai, 1 son, 1 daughter. Education: Bachelor in Industrial Education, National Taiwan Normal University, 1978; Master in Industrial Education, National Taiwan Normal University, 1980; PhD, Technology Education, Ohio State University, 1991. Appointments: Instructor, National Taipei Institute of Technology, 1982-84; Instructor, National Taiwan Normal University, 1984-86; Associate Professor, National Taiwan Normal University, 1986-93; Professor, National Taiwan Normal University, 1993-; Dept Chair, National Taiwan Normal University, 1995-2001; College Dean, National Taiwan Normal University, 2001-2004; Adviser, Ministry of Education, Taiwan, Republic of China, 1997-2000; President, National United University, 2005-. Publications: Over 100 articles; Issues in Technology Education and Vocational Education. Honours: Leader to Watch, International Technology Education Association, 1996; Alumni Award of Excellence, Technology Education, Ohio State University, 1999; Prakken Professional Co-operation Award, ITEA, 2002. Memberships: ITEA; Industrial Technology Education Association, Taiwan. Address: National United University, 1 Lien Da, Kung Ching Li, Miaoli 360, Taiwan. E-mail: lslee@nuu.edu.tw Website: www.nuu.edu.tw/~president/

**LEE Martin Chu Ming**, b. 8 June 1938, Hong Kong. Politician; Barrister. m. Amelia Lee, 1969, 1 son. Education: BA, University of Hong Kong. Appointments: Queen's Counsel; Justice of the Peace; Hong Kong Legislative Council, 1985-; Basic Law Drafting Committee, 1985-90; Hong Kong Law Reform Commission, 1985-91; Chairman, Hong Kong Consumer Council, 1988-91; Founder, 1989, Leader, 1990-, United Democrats of Hong Kong; Chairman, Democratic Party, 1994-; Goodman Fellow, University of Toronto, 2000. Publications: The Basic Law: some basic flaws, co-author, 1988. Honours: International Human Rights Award, American Bar Association, 1995; Prize for Freedom, Liberal International, 1996; Democracy Award, National Endowment for Democracy, USA, 1997; Honorary LLD, Holy Cross College, 1997; Honorary LLD, Amherst College, USA, 1997; Statesmanship Award, Claremont Institute, USA, 1998; Schuman Medal, European Parliament, 2000. Memberships: Chairman, Hong Kong Bar Association, 1980-83. Address: Democratic Party of Hong Kong, 4th Floor, Hanley House, 776-778 Nathan Road, Kowloon, Hong Kong Special Administrative Region, China. E-mail: oml@martinlee.org.hk Website: www.martinlee.org.hk

**LEE Myung Bak**, b. 19 December 1941, Korea. Mayor of Seoul. m. Yoon Ok Kim, 1 son, 3 daughters. Education: BA, Business Administration, Korea University, Seoul, Korea, 1965; Advanced Programme of Business Administration for CEO, Seoul National University, Seoul, 1985; Executive Programme, Graduate School of Mass Communication, Korea University, Seoul, 1995, Yonsei University, Seoul, 1996; Honorary Doctor of Physical Science, Korea National University of Physical Education, Seoul, 1998; Fellow Scholarship, George Washington University, Washington DC, USA, 1999. Appointments include: Chief Executive Officer of 8 Affiliates of Hyundai Group, 1977-92; Assemblyman of the 14th National Assembly, 1992-96; Assemblyman of the 15th National Assembly, 1996-98; Commissioner, Subcommittee on Future Competitiveness, National Reform Committee, Grand

National Party, 2001; Mayor of Seoul, 2002-; Vice-President, Korea Management Association, 1983; Vice-Chairman, World Federation of Korean Association of Commerce, 1993; Professor Emeritus: Undergraduate School of Business Administration, Korea University, Seoul, 1993-; Professor Emeritus, Graduate School of Political Science, Kookmin University, Seoul, 1995-; Emeritus Professor, Graduate School of Business Administration, Korea University, Seoul, 1997; Founder and Chairman East Asia Foundation, 1994-; Adviser to Overseas Korean Traders Association, 2001-; Advisor to Hun Sen, Prime Minister of the Kingdom of Cambodia, 2000-. Publications: History of the June 3rd Student Movement, 1994; There is No Such Thing as a Myth (autobiographical essay), 1995; I See Hope When Everyone Else Talks Despair (essay), 2002. Honours include: Baekma National Medal, Order of Sport Merit, 1982; Excellent Enterprise Award, Business Management Research Centre, Korea University, 1983; Order of Industrial Service Merit, 1985; Selected as one of the 50 Leaders Contributing to National Development, Daily Chosun, 1998; Honorary Ambassador, Arkansas State USA, 1992-. Memberships: Chairman: Korea Atomic Industry Inc, 1980, International Contractors Association of Korea, 1980, North East Asia Economics Association, 1991; Deputy Chairman: Korea Chamber of Commerce, 1982, Korea-USSR Economic Association, 1989. Address: Office of the Mayor, Seoul Metropolitan Government, 31 Taepyeongno 1-ga, Jung-gu, Seoul 100-744, Korea.

**LEE Sang-Keun**, b. 25 November 1929, Korea. Obstetrician; Gynaecologist. m. Soo-Nam Yoon, 1 son, 4 daughters. Education: Graduate, Chonnam National University Medical School, 1950-56; Master's Degree, Medical Science, Graduate School, Chonnam National University, 1956-62; Master's Degree, Public Health, Johns Hopkins University School of Public Health, USA, 1963-64; Doctor's Degree, Medical Science, Graduate School, Chonnam National University, 1964-67. Appointments: Internship, 1956-57, Residency, Specialisation in Obstetrics and Gynaecology, 1960-63, Chonnam University Hospital; Army Surgeon, Captain, Republic of Korea Army, 1957-60; Assistant, 1956-63, Instructor, 1964-68, Assistant Professor, 1968-72, Associate Professor, 1972-74, Chonnam University Medical School; Fellowship, Miami University Hospital, USA, 1972; Medical Director, Dr Lee's Clinic of Obstetrics and Gynaecology, 1974-95; Vice-President, 1983-84, President, 1995-95, Korean Society of Obstetrics and Gynaecology; District Governor, District 3710, Rotary International, 1994-95; President, Alumni Association of Chonnam National University Medical School, 1996-98. Publications: Some Amines and Their Blocking Agents on Response of Myoepithelium of Rabbit Mammary Duct to Oxytoxin; Diagnostic Significance of subphrenic pneumoperitoneum; Comparative Study of Gravindox Slide Test with other Tests for Pregnancy; Clinico-radiographic study on the changes of Lippes loop by use; Clinical appraisal on the accidental pregnancy with Lippes loop; Antepartal education and postpartal family planning performance. Honours: MD; MPH; PhD; Specialist Qualification of Obstetrics and Gynaecology; License of Physician; Plaque of Citation for Meritorious Service, Plaque of Distinguished Service Award, The Rotary Foundation International; Plaque of Appreciation for Community Service, City of Gwangju. Memberships: The Rotary Club of Gwangju-South; Planned Parenthood Federation of Korea; American Association of Gynaecologic Laparoscopists; International Microsurgical Society; Royal Asiatic Society, Korea Branch; American Fertility Society; Korean-British Society; Green Club of Gwangju; Korean Society of Maternal and Child Health; United Nations Association of Republic of Korea; Attending Doctor, Doctor Lee's Obstetrics and Gynaecology Clinic,

Gwangju. Address: 38 Daein-dong, Dong-gu, Gwangju City 501030, Republic of Korea. E-mail: sklee1929@yahoo.com

**LEE Spike (Shelton Jackson Lee)**, b. 20 March 1957, Atlanta, Georgia, USA. Film Maker; Actor. m. Tonya Lewis, 1993, 1 daughter. Education: Morehouse College; Atlanta University; New York University; Institute of Film and TV. Appointments: Wrote Scripts for Black College; The Talented Tenth; Last Hustle in Brooklyn; Produced, Wrote, Directed, Joe's Bed-Stuy Barbershop; We Cut Heads; Has directed music videos; TV Commercials; Films include: She's Gotta Have It, 1985; School Daze, 1988; Do the Right Thing, 1989; Love Supreme, 1990; Mo' Better Blues, 1990; Jungle Fever, 1991; Malcolm X, 1992; Crooklyn; Girl 6; Clockers, 1995; Girl 6; Get on the Bus; 4 Little Girls; He Got Game, 1998; Summer of Sam, 1999; Tales from the Hood, 1995; Bamboozled, 2000; The Original Kings of Comedy, 2000; Lisa Picard is Famous, 2001; A Huey P Newton Story, 2001; The 25th Hour, 2003. Publications: Spike Lee's Gotta Have It: Inside Guerilla Filmmaking, 1987; Uplift the Race, 1988; The Trials and Tribulations of the Making of Malcolm X, 1992; Girl 6; Get on the Bus, 1996. Honours: Cannes Film Festival Prize for Best New Film; Dr h c, New York University, 1998. Address: Forty Acres and a Mule Filmworks, 124 De Kalb Avenue, Brooklyn, New York, NY 11217, USA.

**LEE Ven-Gen**, b. 28 February 1965, Taichung, Taiwan. University Faculty Member. m. Chang-Hung Kuo. Education: BS, Civil Engineering, National Taiwan University, Taiwan, 1988; PhD, Theoretical and Applied Mechanics, Northwestern University, USA, 1993. Appointments: Research Assistant, National Taiwan University, 1988-89; Research Assistant, Northwestern University, 1989-93; Research Associate, University of Illinois at Chicago, USA, 1993-96; Associate Professor, National Chi Nan University, Taiwan, 1997. Publications: Articles in scientific journals including: Journal of Applied Mechanics, 1992, 1993, 1994; Quarterly Journal of Mechanics and Applied Mathematics, 1997; International Journal of Engineering Science, 2002; The Chinese Journal of Mechanics, Series A, 2003; Mechanics Research Communications, 2003. Honours: Research Award, National Science Council, Taiwan, 1997; Listed in Who's Who publications and biographical dictionaries. Memberships: American Society of Mechanical Engineers; American Institute of Aeronautics and Astronautics. Address: Department of Civil Engineering, National Chi Nan University, 1 University Road, Puli, Nantou, Taiwan 545. E-mail: vglee@ncnu.edu.tw

**LEE William Johnson**, b. 13 January 1924, Oneida, Tennessee, USA. Attorney. m. Marjorie Young, 20 August 1949, 2 sons. Education: Akron University; Denison University; Harvard University Graduate School; Ohio State University Law School; Admitted, Ohio Bar, Florida Bar, Federal US District Court Northern and Southern Districts, Ohio and the Southern District of Florida. Appointments: Research Assistant, Ohio State University Law School, 1948-49; Served in the USAF; Attorney Examiner, Assistant State Permit Chief, State Permit Chief, Assistant State Liquor Control Director, Liquor Purchases Chief, Ohio Department of Liquor Control, 1951-57; Assistant Counsel, Hupp Corporation,1957-58; Lawyer in general practice, Acting Municipal Judge, Ohio, 1959-62; Part-time Instructor, College Business Administration, Kent State University, 1961-62; Papy & Carruthers law firm, Florida, 1962-63; Special Counsel, City Attorney's Office, Fort Lauderdale, Florida, 1963-65; Private practice in law, Fort Lauderdale, 1965-66; Assistant Attorney General, Office of the Attorney General, State of Ohio, 1966-70; Administrator, State Medical Board, Ohio, 1970-85; Member, Editorial Board, Ohio State Law Journal; Member, Federated State Board's National

Commission for Evaluation of Foreign Medical Schools, 1981-83; Member, Flex 1/Flex 2 Transitional Taskforce, 1983-84. Publications: Several articles. Honours: Outstanding People of the 20th Century; Wall of Tolerance, Montgomery, Alabama. Memberships: Broward County Bar Association; Akron Bar Association; Columbus Bar Association; Franklin County Trial Lawyers Association; Association of Trial Lawyers of America; American Legion; Phi Kappa Tau; Pi Kappa Delta; Delta Theta Phi; Experimental Aviation Association of South West Florida. Address: 704 Country Club Drive, Apple Valley, Howard, OH 43028, USA.

**LEE Won Je,** b. 1 March 1966, Suwon, Korea. Professor. m. Nam Joo Park, 1 son, 2 daughters. Education: BSc, 1989, MsD, 1993, Department of Oceanography, Inha University, Korea; PhD, School of Biological Sciences, University of Sydney, Australia, 2001. Appointments: First Lieutenant, Korean Army, 1989-91; Research Assistant, Department of Oceanography, Inha University, 1994-95; Visiting Scholar, University of Sydney, 2001-2003; Researcher, Korea Ocean Research and Development Institute, 2003-2004; Assistant Professor, Kyungnam University, 2004-. Publications: Numerous articles, book sections and conference papers include most recently as co-author: Preliminary results of planktonic copepod, Acartia omorii as biomarker for environmental toxicology, 2004; Free-living heterotrophic flagellates from Tasmania (Australia), a field survey, 2005; Summer patterns of phytoplankton distribution at a station in Jangmok Bay, 2005 (in press). Honours: University Postgraduate Awards; University of Sydney Jabez King Heydon Memorial Prize in Biological Sciences for Best PhD Thesis, 2001; Leading Scientists of the World, IBC, 2005. Memberships: Society of Protozoology; International Association of Meiobentologists; Korean Society of Oceanography; Korean Society of Phycology; The Royal Zoological Society of New South Wales. Address: Department of Environmental Engineering, Kyungnam University, 449 Wolyong-dong, Masan 631-701, Korea. E-mail: wonje@kyungnam.ac.kr

**LEE Young Ki,** b. 25 July 1946, Korea. Economist. m. Soo-Jung Kang, 2 sons. Education: BA, Engineering, 1969, MBA, Management, 1972, Seoul National University; MBA, Financial Management, Boston University, 1976; DBA, Finance/Economics, Boston University, 1983. Appointments: Senior Research Fellow, 1984-, Director of Research Planning, 1992-94, Vice President, 1996-98, Director of International Development Exchange Program, 2001; Professor of KDI School, 2001-, Korea Development Institute (KDI); Counselor to the Minister of Finance, Korea, 1987-89; Member, Board of Directors, Korea Stock Exchange, 1990-99; Visiting Professor, University of California, San Diego, 1995; Member, Committee on Corporate Governance in Korea, 1999-2000; Chairman, Advisory Committee of the Bankruptcy Court in Korea, 1998-99; Outside Directors of Public Companies, 1998-; Director, Vice President, Korea Finance Association. Publications: Author, Development of the Korean Corporate Ownership and Governance Structure in the Era of Global Competition, 1996; Editor, An Agenda for Economic Reform in Korea, 2000. Honours: Summa cum Laude, Graduate School of Management, Seoul National University, 1972. Address: Korea Development Institute, PO Box 113, Cheong Kyang, Dong Dae Moon, Seoul, Korea 130-012. Email: yklee@hdiux.hdi.re.kr

**LEE Young-Ho,** b. 12 February 1960, Busan, Korea. Professor. m. Ki-Roung Kim, 1 son, 1 daughters. Education: MD, College of Medicine, 1984, MA,, 1988, PhD, 1992, Department of Anatomy, Graduate School, Hanyang University, Seoul, Korea; Korean Board in Paediatrics, Department of Paediatrics, Inje University, Busan Paik Hospital, Busan, Korea, 1988.

Appointments: Intern, 1984-85, Resident, 1984-85, Inje University Busan Paik Hospital, Busan, Korea. 1985-88; Instructor, 1989-92, Assistant Professor, 1992-96, Associate Professor, 1996-2001, Professor, Chairman, 2001-2005, Department of Paediatrics, Director, Department of Education and Research, University Medical Centre, 2003-2004, Vice-Dean, 2004, Dong-A University College of Medicine, Busan, Korea; Professor, Department of paediatrics, Hanyang University College of Medicine, Seoul, Korea, 2005-; Postgraduate Researcher, Department of Paediatric Hematology-Oncology, University of California, Los Angeles, School of Medicine, 1991-92, Visiting Professor, Baylor College of Medicine, Houston, Texas, 1996. Publications: Articles in medical journals as first author and co-author include most recently: Mutational Analysis of the WASP Gene in 2 Korean families with Wiskott-Aldrich Syndrome, 2003; Autologous stem cell transplantation for the treatment of neuroblastoma in Korea, 2003; Homing-Associated Cell Adhesion Molecules and Cell Cycle Status on the Nucleated Cells in the Bone Marrow, Mobilized Peripheral Blood and Cord Blood, 2004; Establishment and characterization of an ST1571-resistant human myelogenous leukemia cell line, SR-1, 2004; Stem Cell Expressing Homing Receptors could be expanded from Cyropreserved and Unselected Cord Blood, 2004. Honours: Awards, Korean Society of Hematopoietic Stem Cell Transplantation, 2003; Grants, Korean Ministry of Health and Welfare, 2003, 2005. Memberships: American Society of Hematology; International Society of Hematology; International Society of Hematotherapy and Graft Engineering; International Cord Blood Society; Korean Medical Association; Korean Cancer Association; Korean Marrow Donor Program; Korean Societies of: Pedatrics, Pediatric Hemato-Oncology, Hematopoietic Stem Cell Transplantation; Hematology, Biological Response Modifier, Hemostasis and Thrombosis, Blood Transfusion. Address: #102-1601, Shin-Gudeok Woo-sung Apt, Hakjang-Dong, Sasang-Ku, 617-020 Busan, Korea. E-mail: yhlee1@dau.ac.kr

**LEE Youngrahn,** b. 8 November 1948, Seoul, Korea. Professor. m. Youngtai Kim, 2 sons, 1 daughter. Education: Bachelor of Laws, Seoul National University, 1967-71; Master of Laws, 1971-73, Doctor of Law, 1982-87, Seoul National University Graduate School; Studies at University of Paris, France, 1977-79. Appointments: Professor, Korea National Police Academy, 1980-85; Professor, Sookmyung Women's University, 1985-, Exchange Professor, Harvard Law School, USA, 1991-92; Exchange Professor, Illinois Law School, USA, 1997-98; Member: Regulatory Reform Committee, 1991-94, Parole Examination Committee, 1998-2000, Ministry of Justice; Member, Competition Policy Committee, Fair Trade Commission, 1999-2001; Chairperson, Korean Trade Commission, Ministry of Commerce, Industry and Energy, 2002-2005. Publications: Books: Korean Criminal Sentencing: An Empirical Study, 1996; For the innumerable silent people, 2000; Korean Criminal Law: General Principles, 2003; Korean Criminal Law: Particulars, 2003; 5 translations into Korean; 12 articles. Honours: Hongjo Keunjeong Medal, Republic of Korea; Korea Prize of Publication and Culture. Memberships: Korea Criminal Law Association; Korea Association of Comparative Criminal Law; Korean Association of Criminology. Address: College of Law, Sookmyung Women's University, 53-12 Cheonpa-dong 2ga, Yongsan-gu, Seoul, Korea. E-mail: yrlee@sookmyung.ac.kr

**LEE Yuan Tseh,** b. 29 November 1936, Hsinchu, Taiwan. Professor of Chemistry. m. Bernice W Lee, 1963, 2 sons, 1 daughter. Education: National Taiwan University; National Tsinghua University, Taiwan; University of California, Berkeley; PhD. Appointments: Assistant Professor, 1968-71,

Associate Professor, 1971-72, Professor of Chemistry, 1973-74, James Franck Institute and Department of Chemistry, University of Chicago, Illinois, USA; Professor of Chemistry, 1974-94, Professor Emeritus, 1994-, University of California, Berkeley; Head, Academia Sinica, 1994. Publications: Articles in professional journals. Honours: Sloan Fellow, 1969; Guggenheim Fellow, 1976; Miller Professorship, 1981; E O Lawrence Award, US Department of Environment, 1981; Co-recipient, Nobel Prize for Chemistry, 1986; Many other awards and prizes. Memberships: American Academy of Arts and Sciences. Address: Department of Chemistry, University of California, Berkeley, CA 94720, USA.

**LEECH Geoffrey Neil,** b. 16 January 1936, Gloucester, England. Emeritus Professor of English Linguistics; Writer. m. Frances Anne Berman, 29 July 1961, 1 son, 1 daughter. Education: BA, English Language and Literature, 1959, MA, 1963, PhD, 1968, University College London. Appointments: Assistant Lecturer, 1962-64, Lecturer, 1965-69, University College, London; Reader, 1969-74, Professor of Linguistics and Modern English, 1974-2001, Emeritus professor of English Linguistics, 2002-, University of Lancaster; Visiting Professor, Brown University, 1972, Kobe University, 1984, Kyoto University, 1991, Meikai University, Japan, 1999. Publications: English in Advertising, 1966; A Linguistic Guide to English Poetry, 1969; Towards a Semantic Description of English, 1969; Meaning and the English Verb, 1971, 2nd edition, 1987, 3rd edition 2004; A Grammar of Contemporary English (with R Quirk, S Greenbaum, and J Svartvik), 1972; Semantics, 1974, 2nd edition, 1981; A Communicative Grammar of English (with J Svartvik), 1975, 2nd edition, 1994, 3rd edition, 2002; Explorations in Semantics and Pragmatics, 1980; Style in Fiction (with Michael H Short), 1981; English Grammar for Today (with R Hoogenraad and M Deuchar), 1982; Principles of Pragmatics, 1983; A Comprehensive Grammar of the English Language (with R Quirk, S Greenbaum, and J Svartvik), 1985; Computers in English Language Teaching and Research (editor with C N Candlin), 1986; The Computational Analysis of English (editor with R Garside and G Sampson), 1987; An A-Z of English Grammar and Usage, 1989, 2nd edition (with B Cruickshank and R Ivanič), 2001; Introducing English Grammar, 1992; Statistically-driven Computer Grammars in English (editor with E Black and R Garside), 1993; Spoken English on Computer (editor with G Myers and J Thomas), 1995; Corpus Annotation (editor with R. Garside and T. McEnery), 1997; Longman Grammar of Spoken and Written English (with D Biber, S Johansson, S Conrad and E Finegan), 1999; Longman Student Grammar of Spoken and Written English (with D Biber and S Conrad), 2002. Contributions to: A Review of English Literature; Lingua; New Society; Linguistics; Dutch Quarterly Review of Anglo-American Letters; Times Literary Supplement; Prose Studies; The Rising Generation; Transactions of the Philological Society; Language Learning; International Journal of Corpus Linguistics; English Language and Linguistics. Honours: FilDr, University of Lund, 1987; British Academy, fellow, 1987. Membership: Academia Europea. Address: Department of Linguistics and Modern English Language, Lancaster University, Lancaster, LA1 4YT, England.

**LEES Andrew John,** b. 27 September 1947, Liverpool, England. Professor of Neurology. m. Juana Luisa Pulin Perez Lopez, 1 son, 1 daughter. Education: Royal London Hospital Medical College, University of London; Post Graduate Training, L'Hopital Salpetriere, Paris, University College London Hospitals, National Hospital for Neurology and Neurosurgery. Appointments: Consultant Neurologist, National Hospital for Neurology and Neurosurgery; Professor of Neurology,

Institute of Neurology; Director, Reta Lila Weston Institute of Neurological Science; Appeal Steward to the British Boxing Board of Control. Publications: Ray of Hope, authorised biography of Ray Kennedy; Tic and Related Disorders; 820 articles in peer reviewed medical journals. Honours: Charles Smith Lecturer, Jerusalem, 1999; Cotzias Lecturer 2000, Spanish Neurological Association. Memberships: Member, Royal Society of Medicine; Fellow, Royal College of Physicians; President, of the Movement Disorders Society; Former Editor-in-Chief, Movement Disorders. Address: The Reta Lila Weston Institute for Neurological Studies, The Windeyer Building, 46 Cleveland Street, London, W1T 3AA, England. E-mail: a.lees@ion.ucl.ac.uk

**LEES David (Bryan) (Sir),** b. 23 November 1936, Aberdeen, Scotland. Business Executive. m. Edith Bernard, 1961, 2 sons, 1 daughter. Education: Chartered Accountant. Appointments: Articled Clerk, 1957-62, Senior Audit Clerk, 1962-63, Binder Hamlyn and Co, Chartered Accountants; Chief Accountant, Handley Page Ltd, 19640-68; Financial Director, Handley Page Aircraft Ltd, 1969; Chief Accountant, 1970-72, Deputy Controller, 1972-73, Director, Secretary, Controller, 1973-76, GKN Sankey Ltd; Group Finance Executive, 1976-77, General Manager Finance, 1977-82, GKN Ltd; Finance Director, 1982-87, Group Managing Director, 1987-88, Chairman, 1988-, Chief Executive Officer, 1988-97, GKN PLC; Commissioner, Audit Commission, 1983-90; Council Member, 1988-, Chairman, Economic Affairs Committee, 1988-94, Member, President's Committee, currently, Confederation of British Industry; Governor, Shrewsbury School, 1986-; Listed Companies Advisory Committee, 1990-97; Director, 1991-, Chairman, Courtaulds, 1996-98; Director, Bank of England, 1991-99; National Defence Council, 1995-; European Round Table, 1995-2002; Panel on Takeovers and Mergers, 2001-; Governor, Sutton's Hospital in Charterhouse, 1995-; Director, Royal Opera House, 1998-; Currently Chairman, Tate and Lyle PLC. Honours: Officer's Cross, Order of Merit, Germany, 1996; Founding Societies Centenary Award for Chartered Accountants, 1999. Memberships: Companion, British Institute of Management; Fellow, Institute of Chartered Accountants; Fellow, Royal Society of Arts; President, Engineering Employers Federation, 1990-92; President, Society of Business Economists, 1994-99. Address: Tate and Lyle PLC, Sugar Quay, Lower Thames Street, London EC3R 6DQ, England.

**LEGGE-BOURKE Victoria Lindsay,** b. 12 February 1950, Witchford, Cambridgeshire, England. Business Executive. Education: Benenden and St Hilda's College, Oxford. Appointments: Social Attaché, British Embassy, Washington, USA, 1971-73; Director, Junior Tourism LTD, 1974-81; Lady-in-Waiting, HRH The Princess Royal, 1974-86; Extra Lady-in-Waiting, HRH The Princess Royal, 1986-; Special Assistant, 1983-89, Head of Protocol, 1991-94, American Embassy, London; Council of the American Museum in Britain, 1995-; Executive Director, 1995-98, Executive Director of Cultural and Social Affairs, 1999-, Goldman Sachs International; Governor of the English Speaking Union, 1996-99; Director, Lehman Brothers, 1998-99. Honours: LVO, 1986; Meritorious Honor Award, US State Department, 1994. Membership: The Pilgrims. Address: 72 Albany Mansions, Albert Bridge Road, London SW11 4PQ, England. E-mail: victoria.legge-bourke@gs.com

**LEGH Davis Piers Carlis (The Hon),** b. 21 November 1951, Compton, England. Chartered Surveyor. m. Jane Wynter Bee, 2 sons, 2 daughters. Education: Eton, Royal Agricultural College, Cirencester. Appointments: Senior Partner, John German, 1994-99; Senior Partner, Germans, 1999-2000; Chairman, Fisher, German Chartered Surveyors, 2000-. Honour: FRICS.

Memberships: Chairman, Taxation Committee, CLA. 1993-97; Chairman, East Midlands Region Country Land and Business Association (CLA), 2002-. Address: Cubley Lodge, Ashbourne, Derbyshire DE6 2FB, England.

**LEGRIS Manuel Christopher,** b. 19 October 1964, Paris, France. Ballet Dancer. Education: Paris Opera School of Dancing. Career: Member, Corps de Ballet, 1980, Danseur Etoile, 1986-, Paris Opéra; Major roles, Paris Opéra, include Arepo, Béjart, 1986, In the Middle Somewhat Elevated, Forsythe, 1987, Magnificat, Neumeier, 1987, Rules of the Game, Twyla Tharp, 1989, La Belle au Bois Dormant, Nureyev, 1989, Manon, MacMillan, 1990, Dances at the Gathering, Robbins, 1992; In Hamburg created Cinderella Story and Spring and Fall, Neumeier; Appearances, Bolshoi Ballet, Moscow, La Scala, Milan, Royal Ballet, London, New York City Ballet, Tokyo Ballet, Stuttgart Ballet, elsewhere. Honours: Gold Medal, Osaka Competition, 1984; Prix du Cercle Corpeaux, 1986; Nijinsky Prize, 1988; Benois de la Danse Prize, 1998; Chevalier des Arts et des Lettres, 1998; Nijinsky Award, 2000. Address: Théâtre National de l'Opéra de Paris, 8 rue Scribe, 75009 Paris, France.

**LEHOTKA Gabor,** b. 20 July 1938, Vác, Hungary. Organist; Composer; Educator. Education: Degree of Organist-Educator, 1963, Degree of Composer-Music Theory Teacher, 1965, Ferenc Liszt Academy of Music. Career: Soloist, National Philharmonic Society, 1963-80; Organ Teacher, Béla Bartók Conservatoire, 1969-85; Organ Teacher, Ferenc Liszt Academy of Music, 1975-; Organ Construction: Vác (organ built by Jehmlich Company of Dresden), 1976; Training organ for in-practice organists, Vigadó, Budapest (Aqunincum Organ Factory), 1978; Franciscan Church, Vác (Aquincum Organ Factory), 1979; Bartók Hall, Szombathely (Jehmlich Co), 1980; Kodály Grammar School, Kecskemét (Jehmlich Co), 1983; The House of Arts, Szekszárd (Jehmlich Co), 1989; Music Academy of Budapest (Jehmlich Co), 1995; Dohány Street Synagogue, Budapest (Jehmlich Co), 1996; Jury Member of several organ competitions, 1978-99. Compositions: Numerous compositions from 1959 onwards include: Works published in print: Published in USA: Noël pour Orgue, 1981; Suite Française pour Orgue, 1984; Organ Symphony No 4 for Organ Solo, 1983; Veni, Creator Spiritus for SATB Chorus and Organ, 1993; Sabbato ad vesperas Hymn for SATB Soli, SATB Chorus and Organ, 1994; Published in Germany: Präludium, Choral und Fuge für eine Silbermannorgel, 1988; Barock-Sonate für Trompete und Orgel, 1988; Published in France: Quintette pour instruments à vent, 1991; Major works: Sermon on the Mount – Oratorio for mixed choir, soloists and full orchestra, 2002; Eszter (Esther) – Opera in three acts, 2005; The Jáki Mass for mixed choir and full orchestra (re-orchestrated in 1999); Hommage à Händel – Organ Concerto (re-orchestrated in 1999; 2nd Organ Concerto for organ and full orchestra, 2003; Violin Concerto for full orchestra, 1984; Amor Sanctus, fifteen choral works with organ accompaniment on Medieval poems, 1990-92; Latin Mass for mixed choir, 1993. Recordings: Almost 50 recordings including solo albums, collaborations, accompaniments and continuo, 1965-. Publications: Books: My Instrument, the Organ, 1993; The 20th Anniversary of the Vác Organ, 1996; The Methodology of Teaching to Play the Organ, 2000; Articles in music journals. Honours include: Ferenc Liszt Prize, 1974; Artist of Merit of the People's Republic of Hungary, 1978; Chevalier de l'Ordre des Arts et des Lettres, 1986. Memberships: Founding Member, Ferenc Liszt Society; Founding Member, Zoltán Kodály Society. Address: Vam Utca 6, 2600 Vác, Hungary

**LEIBOWITZ Annie,** b. 2 October 1949, Connecticut, USA. Photographer. Education: San Francisco Art Institute. Career: Photographed rock'n'roll stars and other celebrities for Rolling Stone magazine, 1970s; Chief Photographer, Vanity Fair, 1983-; Proprietor, Annie Leibovitz Studio, New York; Celebrity portraits include studies of John Lennon, Mick Jagger, Bette Midler, Louis Armstrong, Ella Fitzgerald, Jessye Norman, Mikhail Baryshnikov, Arnold Schwarzenegger, Tom Wolfe; Retrospective exhibition, Smithsonian National Portrait Gallery, Washington DC, 1991. Publications: Photographs 1970-90, 1992; Women, with Susan Sontag, 2000. Honours: Innovation in Photography Award, American Society of Magazine Photographers, 1987. Address: Annie Leibowitz Studio, 55 Vandam Street, New York, NY 10013, USA.

**LEIGH Elisabeth Sarah,** b. 14 July 1939, London, England. Writer; Lecturer. Education: BA, French and Italian, Somerville College, Oxford; Piccolo Teatro School of Mime, Milan; Central School of Speech and Drama, London. Appointments: Researcher, Producer, Director, BBC Television, 1963-68; Producer, Director, Yorkshire Television, 1969; Independent documentary film producer/director, films for BBCTV, Thames TV and Yorkshire TV, 1969-82; Contributor, food and magazine features, Sunday Times, 1984-91; Novelist, 1989-; Lecturer in Creative Writing, City of Westminister College, London, 1999-. Publications: 5 novels; Sunday Times Guide to Enlightened Eating; Articles for Sunday Times, Elle and Evening Standard. Honours: British Association for the Advancement of Science: Experiment in Time, 1969; BISFA Award, Call for Help, 1971; Argos Award for Consumer Journalism, 1987. Memberships: Society of Authors. Address: c/o David Higham Associates, 5-8 Lower John Street, London W1R 4HA, England.

**LEIGH Jennifer Jason,** b. 5 February 1962, Los Angeles, California, USA. Actress. Career: Appeared in Walt Disney TV movie The Young Runaways, age 15; Other TV films include The Killing of Randy Webster, 1981, The Best Little Girl in the World, 1981; Film appearances including Eyes of a Stranger, 1981, Fast Times at Ridgemont High, 1982, Grandview, USA, 1984, Flesh and Blood, 1985, The Hitcher, 1986, The Men's Club, 1986, Heart of Midnight, 1989, The Big Picture, 1989, Miami Blues, 1990, Last Exit to Brooklyn, 1990, Crooked Hearts, 1991, Backdraft, 1991, Rush, 1992, Single White Female, 1992, Short Cuts, 1993, The Hudsucker Proxy, 1994, Mrs Parker and the Vicious Circle, 1994, Georgia, 1995, Kansas City, 1996, Washington Square, 1997, eXistenZ, 1999; The King is Alive, 2000; The Anniversary Party, 2001; Crossed Over, 2002; Road to Perdition, 2002; In The Cut, 2003; Stage appearances including Sunshine, Off-Broadway, 1989. Address: c/o Elaine Rich, 2400 Whitman Place, Los Angeles, CA 90211, USA.

**LEIGH Mike,** b. 20 February 1943, Salford, Lancashire, England. Dramatist; Film and Theatre Director. m. Alison Steadman, 1973, divorced 2001, 2 sons. Education: Royal Academy of Dramatic Arts; Camberwell School of Arts and Crafts; Central School of Art and Design; London Film School. Publications: Plays: The Box Play, 1965; My Parents Have Gone to Carlisle, The Last Crusade of the Five Little Nuns, 1966; Nenaa, 1967; Individual Fruit Pies, Down Here and Up There, Big Basil, 1968; Epilogue, Glum Victoria and the Lad with Specs, 1969; Bleak Moments, 1970; A Rancid Pong, 1971; Wholesome Glory, The Jaws of Death, Dick Whittington and His Cat, 1973; Babies Grow Old, The Silent Majority, 1974; Abigail's Party, 1977, also TV play; Ecstasy, 1979; Goose-Pimples, 1981; Smelling a Rat, 1988; Greek Tragedy, 1989; It's a Great Big Shame!, 1993. TV films: A Mug's Game, Hard Labour, 1973; The Permissive Society, The Bath of the 2001 F A Cup, Final Goalie, Old Chums, Probation, A Light Snack, Afternoon, 1975; Nuts in May, Knock for Knock, 1976; The Kiss of Death, 1977; Who's Who, 1978; Grown Ups, 1980;

Home Sweet Home, 1981; Meantime, 1983; Four Days in July, 1984; Feature films: Bleak Moments, 1971; The Short and Curlies, 1987; High Hopes, 1988; Life is Sweet, 1990; Naked, 1993; Secrets and Lies, 1996; Career Girls, 1997; Topsy Turvy, 1999; All or Nothing, 2002. Radio Play: Too Much of a Good Thing, 1979. Honours: Golden Leopard, Locarno Film Festival, 1972; Golden Hugo, Chicago Film Festival, 1972; George Devine Award, 1973; Evening Standard Award, 1981; Drama Critics Choice, London, 1981; Critics Prize, Venice Film Festival, 1988; Honorary MA, Salford University, 1991, Northampton, 2000; OBE, 1993; Best Director Award, Cannes Film Festival, 1993; Palme D'Or, Cannes Film Festival, 1996; Honorary DLitt, Stafford, 2000, Essex, 2002. Address: The Peters, Fraser and Dunlop Group Ltd, 503/4 The Chambers, Chelsea Harbour, London SW10 0XF, England.

**LEITH Jake Quintin,** b. 18 November 1958, Bushey, Hertfordshire, England. Chartered Designer. Education: BA, Honours, Textiles (Printed and Woven), Loughborough College of Art and Design, 1981; MA, Textiles and Fashion, Birmingham Institute of Art and Design, 1982. Appointments: Export Designer, Everest Fabrics, Ghaziabad, India, 1983-84; Design Consultant, Europa Shop Equipment Ltd, 1984-85; Interior Designer, Fantasy Finishes, London, 1985-86; Senior Partner, The Jake Leith Partnership (an interior design consultancy), 1986-. Publications: Article: Realising Entrepreneurial Ambition, CSD Magazine, 2001; The Designer Magazine, 2002. Memberships: Fellow, Chartered Society of Designers, 1995-, Vice President, 2004-; FRSA, 1996. Address: Holly Cottage, 16 Chapel Cottages, Hemel Hempstead, Hertfordshire HP2 5DJ, England. E-mail: jake@jlp.uk.com Website: jlp.uk.com

**LEITH Prudence Margaret,** b. 18 February 1940, Cape Town, South Africa. Caterer; Author. m. Rayne Kruger, 1 son, 1 daughter. Education: Haywards Heath, Sussex; St Mary's, Johannesburg; Cape Town University; Sorbonne, Paris; Cordon Bleu School, London. Appointments: Founder and Managing Director: Leith's Ltd (formerly Leith's Good Food Ltd), 1960-65; Leith's Restaurant, 1969-95; Leith's School of Food and Wine, 1975-95; Board Member: Whitbread plc, 1995-2005; Triven VCT, 1999-2003; Halifax plc, 1995-99; Safeway plc (formerly Argyll Group plc), 1989-96; Leeds Permanent Building Society, 1992-95; British Railways Board, 1980-85; British Transport Hotels, 1977-83; Cookery Correspondent: Daily Mail, 1969-73; Sunday Express, 1976-80; The Guardian, 1980-85; The Mirror, 1995-98; Non-Executive Director: Woolworths, 2001-; Omega International plc, 2004-; Consultant, Compass Group plc, 2001-. Publications include: 12 cookbooks including Leith's Cookery Bible with Caroline Waldegrave; 3 novels in print; TV series include: Best of British, BBC2; Take 6 Cooks, Channel 4; Tricks of the Trade, BBC1. Honours: Corning Award Food Journalist of the Year, 1979; Glenfiddich Trade Journalist of the Year, 1983; Honorary Fellow, Hotel, Catering and Institutional Management Association, 1986; Order of the British Empire; Veuve Clicquot Business Woman of the Year, 1990; Honorary Fellow, Salford University, 1992; Honorary Fellow, The City and Guilds of London Institute, 1992-97; Visiting Professor, University of North London, 1993; Freedom of the City of London, 1994; Honorary DSc, The University of Manchester, 1996; Honorary Doctor of Business Administration, Greenwich University, 1996; Honorary Doctor of Letters, Queen Margaret College, Edinburgh, 1997; Honorary Doctorate, The Open University, 1997; Master of the University of North London, 1997; Deputy Lieutenant of Greater London, 1998-; Doctor of the University, Oxford Brookes, 2000; Honorary Doctorate, City University, 2005. Memberships: Trustee/Director, Training for Life, 1999; Commissioner, Lord Griffiths Debt Commission, 2004-05; Chairman: The British Food Trust, 1997-; 3E's Enterprises

Ltd, 1998; Kings College for Technology and the Arts, 2000-; Ashridge Management College, 2002-; 3C's Limited, 2002-. Address: Castleton Glebe, Moreton in Marsh, Gloucester, GL56 0SZ, England.

**LEMPER Ute,** b. 4 July 1963, Munster, Germany. Singer; Dancer; Actress. Education: Max Reinhardt-Seminar, Vienna. Appointments: Leading Role, Viennese Production of Cats, 1983; Appeared in Peter Pan, Berlin, Cabaret, Düsseldorf and Paris; Chicago, 1997-99; Life's A Swindle tour, 1999; Punishing Kiss tour, 2000; Albums include: Ute Lemper Sings Kurt Weill, 1988; Vol 2, 1993; Threepenny Opera, 1988; Mahoganny Songspiel, 1989; Illusions, 1992; Espace Indécent, 1993; City of Strangers, 1995; Berlin Cabaret Songs, 1996; All that Jazz/ The Best of Ute Lemper, 1998; Punishing Kiss, 2000; Film appearances include: L'Autrichienne, 1989; Moscou Parade, 1992; Coupable d'Innocence, 1993; Prêt à Porter, 1995; Bogus, 1996; Combat de Fauves; A River Made to Drown In; Appetite. Honours: Moliere Award, 1987; Laurence Oliver Award; French Culture Prize, 1993. Address: c/o Oliver Gluzman, 40 rue de la Folie Regnault, 75011 Paris, France.

**LENDL Ivan,** b. 7 March 1960, Czechoslovakia, US citizen, 1992. Retired Professional Tennis Player. m. Samantha Frankel, 1989, 5 daughters. Appointments: Winner, Italian Junior Singles, 1978; French Junior Singles, 1978; Wimbledon Junior Singles, 1978; Spanish Open Singles, 1980, 1981; South American Open Singles, 1981; Canadian Open Singles, 1980, 1981; WCT Tournament of Champion Singles, 1982; WCT Masters Singles, 1982; WCT Finals Singles, 1982; Masters Champion, 1985. 1986; French Open Champion, 1984, 1986, 1987; US Open Champion, 1985, 1986, 1987; US Clay Court Champion, 1985; Italian Open Champion, 1986; Australian Open Champion, 1989, 1990; Finalist Wimbledon, 1986; Held, World No 1 Ranking for a Record 270 weeks; Named World Champion, 1985, 1986, 1990; Retired, 1994. Publication: Ivan Lendl's Power Tennis. Honours: Granted American Citizenship, 1992; ATP Player of the Year, 1985, 1986, 1987; Inducted, International Tennis Hall of Fame, 2001. Memberships: Laureus World Sports Academy. Address: c/o Laureus World Sports Academy, 15 Hill Street, London W1 5QT, England.

**LENGYEL Alfonz,** b. 21 October 1921, Gödöllő, Hungary. Professor. m. Hongying Liu. Education: Law Degree, Miskolc Law Academy, 1948; BA, Art History, San Jose State College, 1958; MA, Art History, 1959; Doctorate, Institute of Art and Archaeology, University of Paris, 1964; Internship, Ecole du Louvre, Paris, 1964-65. Appointments: Assistant Professor, Art History, San Jose State College, 1961-63; Lecturer, University of Maryland, 1963-68; Professor, Wayne State University, 1968-72; Professor, Northern Kentucky University, 1972-77; Founder, Dean, Institute of Mediterranean Art and Archaeology, Cincinnati, Ohio, 1977-82; Co-ordinator, Rosemont College, 1982-85; Professor, Eastern College, St Davids, 1985-87; Member, Advisory Board, US Department of Interior, 1987-91; American Director of Sino-American Field School of Archaeology, Xi'an, China; Advisory Professor, Fudan University, Shanghai, 1987-; Consulting Professor, 1988-, American Director, Sino-American Field School of Archaeology, 1990, Xi'an Jiaotong University, China; Board of Directors, Museum of Asian Art, Sarasota, Florida, 2000-. Publications: Public Relations for Museums; Archaeology for Museologists; Chinese Chronological History. Honours: Honorary Doctorate in Law; Gold Medal, Brazil Academy of Humanities; Certificate in Merit, Classical Archaeology; Director's Award, UPAO; Hungarian Officer's Cross of Merit. Memberships: New York Academy of Sciences; International Academy of Sciences and Letters; Michigan Academy of Sciences, Letters and Arts;

Hungarian Academy of Sciences; Institute of Social Murumbi; American Associations of Museums; Others. Address: 4206-73rd Terrace East, Sarasota, FL 34243, USA.

**LENGYEL Gyorgy,** b. 20 March 1951, Budapest, Hungary. Sociologist. Education: LMA in Economics, Karl Marx University of Economics, Budapest, Hungary, 1975; UD in Economics, 1977; MA, History and Sociology, 1981; PhD, Sociology, 1991; Habil doc, Sociology, 1998. Appointments: Research Fellow, City Archives, Budapest, Hungary, 1975-78; Karl Marx University of Economics, Budapest, Hungary, 1978-91; Chairman, Department of Sociology, Budapest University of Economic Sciences, Hungary, 1991-2003, Professor, Department of Sociology, Corvinus University of Budapest, 2003-. Publications: Author: Entrepreneurs, Bankers, Merchants (in Hungarian), 1989; Co-ed, Spread of Entrepreneurship in Eastern Europe, 1996; Co-author: The Transformation of East-European Economic Elites, 1996; Author: The Transformation of the Hungarian Economic Elite (in Hungarian), 1997; Co-editor, Entrepreneurship in Eastern Europe, 1997-98, in International Journal of Sociology; Co-editor, Elites After State Socialism, 2000; Co-editor, The Small Transformation, 2001. Memberships: International Sociological Association, Research Committee on Economy and Society; European Sociological Association, Organiser Research Network on Economic Sociology; Hungarian Academy of Sciences, Committee of Human Resources, 1994-1998, Committee of Sociology; European Sociological Association, Executive Committee Member, 1999-2001. Address: Corvinus University of Budapest, Department of Sociology, Fovam ter 8, H-1093 Budapest, Hungary.

**LENHARO Neide Polos Plaza,** b. 27 June 1950, São Paulo, Brazil. Business Owner. m. Ariel Lenharo, 1 son, 1 daughter. Education: Decoration Designer, Escola Panamerican de Arte, São Paulo, Brazil. Appointments: General Manager, Sales and Marketing, 3i Implants Innovations Inc, Biomet Do Brazil, -2002; Executive Director, Sin Sistema de Implante, 2003-. Address: Avenida Paes de Barros, 485 São Paulo, Cose 03115-020, Brazil. Website: www.implantsin.com

**LENNARTSSON Olof Walter,** b. 27 October 1943, Sweden. Physicist. m. Nancy Karllee, 1 son. Education: MEng, 1969, PhD, Plasma Physics, 1974, Royal Institute of Technology, Stockholm, Sweden. Appointments: NAS/NRC Research Associate, 1974-76; Docent, Royal Institute of Technology, Sweden, 1976-78; Staff Scientist, Lockheed Martin Missiles and Space, 1979-. Publications: Numerous articles in scientific journals and books. Memberships: American Geophysical Union; American Institute of Physics. Address: Lockheed Martin Space Systems Co, Advanced Technology Center, ADCS, B255, 3251 Hanover Street, Palo Alto, CA 94304, USA.

**LEONARD Elmore (John, Jr),** b. 11 October 1925, New Orleans, Louisiana, USA. Novelist. m. (1) Beverly Cline, 30 August 1949, 3 sons, 2 daughters, divorced 7 October 1977, (2) Joan Shepard, 15 September 1979, deceased, 13 January 1993, (3) Christine Kent, 15 August 1993. Education: BA, University of Detroit, 1950. Publications: 33 novels including: Hombre, 1961; City Primeval, 1980; Split Images, 1981; Cat Chaser, 1982; Stick, 1983; Labrava, 1983; Glitz, 1985; Bandits, 1986; Touch, 1987; Freaky Deaky, 1988; Killshot, 1989; Get Shorty, 1990; Maximum Bob, 1991; Rum Punch, 1992; Pronto, 1993; Riding the Rap, 1995; Out of Sight, 1996; Pagan Babies, 2000. Other: The Tonto Woman and Other Western Stories, 1998; Screenplays: Cuba Libre, 1998; Be Cool, 1999. Honours: Edgar Allan Poe Award, 1984, and Grand Master Award, 1992, Mystery Writers of America; Michigan Foundation for the

Arts Award for Literature, 1985; Honorary degrees in Letters from Florida Atlantic University, 1995, University of Detroit Mercy, 1997. Memberships: Writers Guild of America; PEN; Authors Guild; Western Writers of America; Mystery Writers of America. Address: c/o Michael Siegel, Brillstein-Grey Entertainment, 9150 Wilshire Boulevard, Beverly Hills, CA 90212, USA.

**LEONARD Hugh, (John Keyes Byrne),** b. 9 November 1926, Dublin, Ireland. Playwright. m. Paule Jacquet, 1955, 1 daughter. Publications: Plays: The Big Birthday, 1957; A Leap in the Dark, 1957; Madigan's Lock, 1958; A Walk on the Water, 1960; The Passion of Peter Ginty, 1961; Stephen D, 1962; The Poker Session, 1963; Dublin 1, 1963; The Saints Go Cycling In, 1965; Mick and Mick, 1966; The Quick and the Dead, 1967; The Au Pair Man, 1968; The Barracks, 1969; The Patrick Pearse Motel, 1971; Da, 1973; Thieves, 1973; Summer, 1974; Times of Wolves and Tigers, 1974; Irishmen, 1975; Time Was, 1976; A Life, 1977; Moving Days, 1981; The Mask of Moriarty, 1984. Television: Silent Song, 1967; Nicholas Nickleby, 1977; London Belongs to Me, 1977; The Last Campaign, 1978; The Ring and the Rose, 1978; Strumpet City, 1979; The Little World of Don Camillo, 1980; Kill, 1982; Good Behaviour, 1982; O'Neill, 1983; Beyond the Pale, 1984; The Irish RM, 1985; A Life, 1986; Troubles, 1987; Parnell and the Englishwoman, 1988; A Wild People, 2001. Films: Herself Surprised, 1977; Da, 1984; Widows' Peak, 1984; Troubles, 1984; Books: Home Before Night, autobiography, 1979; Out After Dark, autobiography, 1988; Parnell and the Englishwoman, 1989; I, Orla! 1990; Rover and other Cats, a memoir, 1992; The Off-Shore Island, novel, 1993; The Mogs, for children, 1995; Magic, 1997; Fillums, 2003. Honours: Honorary DHL (RI); Writers Guild Award, 1966; Tony Award; Critics Circle Award; Drama Desk Award; Outer Critics Award, 1978; Doctor of Literature, Trinity College, Dublin, 1988. Address: 6 Rossaun Pilot View, Dalkey, County Dublin, Ireland.

**LEONARD Ray Charles (Sugar Ray),** b. 17 May 1956, Wilmington, North Carolina, USA. Boxer. m. Juanita Wilkinson, 1980, divorced 1990, 2 sons. Appointments: Amateur Boxer, 1970-77; won 140 of 145 amateur fights; World amateur champion, 1974; US amateur athletic union champion, 1974; Pan-American Games Gold Medallist, 1975; Olympic Gold Medallist, 1976; Guaranteed Record Purse of $25,000 for first professional fight, 1977; Won, North American Welterweight title from Pete Ranzany, 1979; Won World Boxing Council Version of World Welterweight title from Wilfred Benitez, 1979; Retained title against Dave Green, 1980; Lost it to Roberto Duran, Montreal, 1980; Regained title from Duran, New Orleans, 1980; World Junior Middleweight title, World Boxing Association, 1981; Won, WBA World Welterweight title from Tommy Hearns to become undisputed World Champion, 1981; Drew rematch, 1989; 36 professional fights, 33 wins, lost 2, 1 draw; Retired from boxing, 1982; returned to ring, 1987; Won World Middleweight title; Lost to Terry Norris, 1991; retired, 1991, 1997; returned to ring, 1997; Lost International Boxing Council Middleweight title fight to Hector Camacho, 1992; Commentator, Home Box Office TV Co; Motivational speaker. Address: Suite 303, 4401 East West Highway, Bethesda, MD 20814, USA.

**LEONARD Todd Jay,** b. 16 November 1961, Shelbyville, Indiana, USA. University Professor. Education: BA with Honors and Distinction, Humanities, 1985, MA, History, 1987, Purdue University, Indiana, USA; Diploma, Teaching English as a Foreign Language, English Language Centre, London, England, 1993; PhD, Social Science, Empresarial University of Costa Rica, 2004. Appointments include: Visiting Professor,

La Universidad de las Americas, Costa Rica, 1987; Visiting Lecturer, 1988, Course Coordinator, 1988-89, Department of Foreign Languages and Literatures, Purdue University, Indiana, USA; Assistant English Teacher, Japan Exchange and Teaching Programme, 1989-92; Associate Professor of English, Hirosaki Gakuin University, Japan, 1992-; Part-time Lecturer, Faculty of Education, 1993-, Part-time Lecturer, Faculty of Liberal Arts, 1993-, Hirosaki University, Japan; English Language Committee Member, National Entrance Examination, Daigaku Nyushi Center, Tokyo, 1998-2002; Ordained Minister, Universal Spiritualist Association, Muncie, Indiana, 2003. Publications: Academic books include: East Meets West: Understanding Misunderstandings between ALTs and JTEs, 1999; Orbit English Reading, 2004; ESL related textbooks include: Team-Teaching Together: A Bilingual Resource Handbook for JTES and AETS; East Meets West: An American in Japan, 1998; Trendy Traditions! A Cross-Cultural Skills-Based Reader of Essays on the United States, 2001; Business as Usual: An Integrated Approach to Learning English, 2004; Numerous academic articles and book reviews. Honours include: Dean's List, Purdue University; Outstanding and Distinguished Graduate Instructor, Purdue University, 1987; Rotary Scholar, La Universidad de Costa Rica, 1987; Governor Appointed Trustee for the Committee on Foreigners Living in Aomori, Aomori Foundation for International Relations, 1991-92; Pi Sigma Alpha; Sigma Delta Pi; Phi Alpha Theta; Phi Kappa Phi. Memberships include: Japan Association for Language Teachers; Modern Language Journal Association; Japan Association of Comparative Culture; Life Member Purdue Alumni Association. Address: Jyonan 4-3-19, Hirosaki-shi, Aomori-ken 036-8232 Japan. E-mail: tleonard@infoaomori.ne.jp Website: www.toddjayleonard.com

**LEONARD Tom, (Thomas Anthony Leonard),** b. 22 August 1944, Glasgow, Scotland. Writer. m. Sonya Maria O'Brien, 24 December 1971, 2 sons. Education: MA, Glasgow University, 1976. Appointments: Writer-in-Residence, Renfrew District Libraries, 1986-89, Glasgow University/Strathclyde University, 1991-92, Bell College of Technology, 1993-94; Professor of Creative Writing, Glasgow University, 2001-. Publications: Intimate Voices (writing), 1965-83, 1984; Situations Theoretical and Contemporary, 1986; Radical Renfrew (editor), 1990; Nora's Place, 1990; Places of the Mind: The Life and Work of James Thomson 'BV' Cafe, 1993; Reports From the Present: Selected Works 1982-94, 1995; inside looking in, 2004; access to the silence (poems and Posters 1984-2004), 2004. Contributions to: Edinburgh Review. Honour: Joint Winner, Saltire Scottish Book of the Year Award, 1984. Address: 56 Eldon Street, Glasgow G3 6NJ, Scotland.

**LEONHARDT Joyce LaVon,** b. 17 December 1927, Aurora, Nebraska, USA. Poet. Education: BS, Union College, Lincoln, 1952. Appointments: High School Teacher, 1952-76; Junior College Instructor, 1981-90. Contributions to: Several books of poems. Honours: Honourable Mention Certificates; Golden Poet; Silver Poet. Membership: World of Poetry. Address: 1824 Atwood Street, Longmont, CO 80501, USA.

**LEONI Tea,** b. 25 February 1966, New York, USA. Actress. m. David Duchovny, 1997, 1 son, 1 daughter. Career: Film appearances in Switch, 1991, A League of Their Own, 1992, Wyatt Earp, 1994, Bad Boys, 1995, Flirting with Disaster, 1996, Deep Impact, 1998, There's No Fish Food in Heaven, 1999; The Family Man, 2000; Jurassic Park III, 2001; Hollywood Ending, 2002; People I Know, 2002; House of D, 2004; Appeared in TV sitcoms Naked Truth, 1995, Flying Blind, 1995. Address: c/o ICM, 8942 Wilshire Boulevard, Beverly Hills, CA 90211, USA.

**LEONIDOPOULOS Georgios,** b. 19 April 1958, Kalamata, Messinia, Greece. Electrical, Computer and Electronics Engineer; Researcher; Educator. Education: Diploma, Electrical and Computer Engineering, Patra University, Greece, 1981; Postgraduate, Iowa State University, USA, 1982, Wayne State University, USA, 1983; MSc, 1984; PhD, Electronic and Electrical Engineering, Strathclyde University, Glasgow, Scotland, 1988. Appointments: Trainee Electrical Engineer, Public Electricity Co, Kalamata, Greece, 1979; Teaching Assistant, Strathclyde University, Scotland, 1984-87; Engineering Educator, Secondary School, Kalamata, Greece, 1991-94; Professor, Engineering, Institute of Technology, Kalamata, Greece, 1994-97; Professor, Engineering, Electrical Engineering Department, Institute of Technology, Lamia, Greece, 1997-. Publications include: A method for locating polymeric insulation failure of underground cables, 1998; On the convergence of three series, 1998; Root investigation of third degree algebraic equation, 1998; A mathematical method for solving a particular type of linear differential equations using complex symbolism, 2000; Trigonometric form of the quadratic algebraic equation solution, 2000; Greenhouse dimensions estimation and short time forecast of greenhouse temperature based on net heat losses through the polymeric cover, 2000; Greenhouse daily sun-radiation intensity variation, daily temperature variation and heat profits through the polymeric cover, 2000; Test methods of the four basic mathematical operations, 2001. Honours: Referee of research articles; Patentee in field; Examiner for Greek postgraduate scholarships; Selectee, Euratom research position, Joint European Torus, Culham, Oxford, England, 1990; Head of Electrical Engineering Department, 2000-03; Listee, expert evaluator of European Commission's scientific research and development programmes; European programme Socrates, Greece, 2000-; Grant, Schilizzi Foundation, 1987; Grant, Empeirikeion Foundation, 1994. Memberships: New York Academy of Sciences; IEEE; National Geographic Society; AMSE. Address: Kilkis 11, Kalamata 24100, Messinia, Greece. E-mail: georgiosleonidopoulos@yahoo.gr

**LEONOV Aleksey Arkhipovich (Major-General),** b. 30 May 1934, Listianka, Kamerovo Region, Russia. Cosmonaut. m. Svetlana Leonova, 2 daughters. Education: Chuguevsky Air Force School for Pilots; Zhukovsky Air Force Engineering Academy; Cosmonaut Training, 1960. Appointments: Pilot, 1956-59; Member, CPSU, 1957-91; Participant, space-ship Voskhod 2 flight, becoming first man to walk in space, 1965; Pilot Cosmonaut of USSR; Chairman, Council of Founders, Novosti Press Agency, 1969-90; Deputy Commander, Gagarin Cosmonauts Training Centre, 1971; Participant, Soyuz 19-Apollo joint flight, 1975; Major-General, 1975; Deputy Head, Centre of Cosmonaut Training, 1975-92; Director, Cheteck-Cosmos Co, 1992-; Vice-President, Investment Fund Alfa-Capital, 1997-; Vice President, Alpha Bank, 2000. Honours: Honorary DrScEng; Hero of the Soviet Union, 1965, 1975; Hero of Bulgaria; Hero of Vietnam; Order of Lenin, twice; USSR State Prize, 1981. Memberships: Co-Chairman, Board, International Association of Cosmonauts. Address: Alfa-Capital, Academician Sakharov Prospect 12, 107078 Moscow, Russia.

**LÉOTARD François Gérard Marie,** b. 26 March 1942, Cannes, France. Politician. m. (1) France Reynier, 1976, (2) Isabelle Duret, 1992, 1 son, 1 daughter. Education: Faculté de Droit, Paris; Institut d'Etudes Politiques, Paris; Ecole Nationale d'Administration. Appointments: Secretary of Chancellery, Ministry of Foreign Affairs, 1968-71; Administration, Town Planning, 1973-76; Sous-Préfet, 1974-77; Mayor of Fréjus, 1977-92, 1993-97; Deputy to National Assembly, for Var, 1978-86, 1988-92, 1995-97, 1997-2002; Conseiller-Général,

Var, 1980-88; Secretary, 1982-88, President, 1988-90, 1995-97, Honorary President, 1990-95, Général Parti Républican; Vice-President, 1983-84, President, 1996-, Union pour la Démocratie Française; Minister of Culture and Communications, 1986-88; Member, Municipal Council, Fréjus, 1992; Minister of National Defence, 1993-95; With EU Special Envoy to Macedonia, 2001-; Inspector General de Finances pour l'extérieur, 2001-. Publications: A Mots Découverts, 1987; Culture: Les Chemins de Printemps, 1988; La Ville aimée: mes chemins de Fréjus, 1989; Pendant la Crise, le spectacle continue, 1989; Adresse au Président des Républiques françaises, 1991; Place de la République, 1992; Ma Liberté, 1995; Pour l'honneur, 1997; Je vous hais tous avec douceur, 2000; Paroles d'immortels, 2001. Honours: Chevalier, Order Nationale du Mérite. Address: Nouvelle UDF, 133 bis rue de l'Université, 75007 Paris, France.

**LEOW Melvin Khee-Shing**, b. 13 May 1966, Singapore. Endocrinologist; Physician. m. Jane Sim-Joo Tan, 2 daughters. Education: MB BS, 1990; MMed (Int. Med), 1998; FAMS (Endocrinology), 2003; FACE (USA), 2004; FACP (USA), 2005. Appointments: Medical Officer, 1991-98; Medical Officer, Specialist, Haematology, 1998; Registrar, Endocrinology, 1999-2001; Clinical cum Research Fellow, Harvard Medical School, 2001-02; Associate Consultant, Endocrinology, 2003-2004; Clinical Lecturer, Faculty of Medicine, National University of Singapore, 2004-; Consultant Endocrinologist and Physician, Department of Endocrinology, Tan Tock Seng Hospital, Division of Medicine, 2005-. Publications: Articles in scientific journals including: Annals of the Academy of Medicine (Singapore), 1998, 2003, 2003; Journal of Neurology, 2002; Journal of the American College of Surgeons, 2002; Journal of Clinical Endocrinology and Metabolism, 2003; Critical Care and Shock, 2003; The Singapore Family Physician, 2003; European Respiratory Journal, 2004; Hormone and Metabolic Research, 2005; Postgraduate Medical Journal, 2005; Clinical Endocrinology (Oxford), 2005; Chest, 2005; Singapore Medical Journal, 2005; Endocrine Practice, 2005; Journal of Peripheral Nervous System, 2005. Honours: Excellence Award for Quality Service, 1993; Health Manpower Development Program Scholarship Award, 2001; 10-Year Long Service Award, National Healthcare Group, 2002; Courage Award for the treatment of SARS patients, 2003; Young Investigator, National Health Care Group Doctor Award, 2004; Listed in Who's Who publications and biographical dictionaries. Memberships: Endocrine Society, USA, 2001-; Massachusetts Medical Society, 2001-; American Association of Clinical Endicrinologists, 2001-; Fellow, Academy of Medicine (Singapore); Fellow, International Society for Philosophical Enquiry; Fellow, American College of Endocrinology; Fellow, American College of Physicians. Address: Department of Endocrinology, Division of Medicine, Tan Tock Seng Hospital, 11 Jalan Tan Tock Seng, Singapore 308433. E-mail: mleowsj@massmed.org

**LEROY Miss Joy**, b. 8 September 1927, Riverdale, Illinois, USA. Miss LeRoy - Model; Narrator; Designer; Author. Education: Texas Technological College, Lubbock, 1946; BS (Honours), Purdue University, West Lafayette, Indiana, 1949. Further studies include sewing, theatre, computer programming, fine arts, music, photography. Appointments: Model, sales representative for Jacques and sales representative for the book department at Loebs, Lafayette; Window trimmer, Marshall Fields and Co, 1952-53, and sales and display representative, Emerald House, 1954-55, Evanston, Illinois; Turned professional in field of design, modelling and narrating; Model and narrator for companies including: American Motors Corp (Auto and Kelvinator); Speedway Petroleum Co; Ford Motor Company (Auto and Tractor); The Sykes Co; Coca Cola Co; Hoover Vacuum Co; General Motors Co (Chevrolet and Oldsmobile), J L Hudson; Jam Handy Organization; Boston, 1962-70 as a model for "Copley 7" and a tour guide, model, free lance writer for The Christian Science Monitor and The Christian Science Publishing Society; later, Special Events Co-ordinator for Opening of the Sheraton Hotel and Prudential Insurance Co; From 1976 to 2005 she has travelled around the seven continents and has earned awards from Maupintours, INTRAV and the Crystal Society. Publications: Articles in field of fashion writing, creative ideas for Youth, and educational Puzz-its, copyright from 1986-. Honours: Numerous include: Congressional Certificate of Appreciation, 1991; Republican National Hall of Honour, 1992; Republican Presidential Legion of Honour, Republican Presidential Task Force, Wall of Honour, 1993; Republican Senatorial Medal of Freedom, Order of Liberty National Republican Committee, Republican Presidential Legion of Merit and National Republican Senatorial Order of Merit, 1993; Republican Campaign Council, 1994; Ronald Wilson Reagan Eternal Flame of Freedom, 1995; Grand Club, Republican Party of Florida, 1996; International Women of the Year, 1996-98; Woman of the Year, 1998-99, 2001, 2002, 2004; Presidential Task Force Medal of Merit, Republican Party, 1997; Distinguished 20th Century Republican Leader, 1998; Republican Senatorial Millennium Medal of Freedom, World Laureate of England, Deputy Director General in1999; Presidential Roundtable Representative from Florida, 2000 to 2005, Ronald Wilson Reagan Founder's Wall, 2002; ABI: 2000 Notable American Women; Deputy Governor and Continental Governor; Millennium Medal of Honour and Presidential Medal of Honour; a Noble Member of the Order of International Ambassadors; International Order of Merit, 2000; Presidential Seal of Honor, 2000; American Order of Excellence, 2000; Secretary-General and Noble Prize, and International Peace Prize, United Cultural Convention, 500 Leaders of Influence, Hall of Fame, 2001; Leading Intellectuals of the World; IBC: 2000 Outstanding Intellectuals of the 20th and 21st Century; 500 Founders of the 21st Century; Honours List and American Medal of Honor, 2002; International Medal of Honour, IBC, 2003; Outstanding People of the 21st Century and Who's Who in the 21st Century Medals, 2003; Intellectual of the Year; Charter Member, International Honour Society, 2002; One Thousand Great Americans, 2003; International Register of Profiles, 2003-2005; Vice Consul, 2002; Lifetime Achievement Award, IBC, 2002; Congressional Medal of Excellence, ABI, 2002; World Lifetime Achievement Award, ABI, 2003; Republican Senatorial Medal of Freedom and Star "The highest honor the Republican members of the US Senate can bestow", 2003; International Visual Artist of the Year, International Hall of Fame, World Academy of Letters, with honours, Living Legends, Da Vinci Diamond and Statesman's Award as Ambassador of Grand Eminence, 2004;World Peace and Diplomacy Presidential Dedication, International Register of Profiles and Living Legends, 13th edition, World Medal of Freedom, Noble Laureate and Top 100 Artists, 2005. Address: Apt 2104, 2100 S Ocean Lane, Fort Lauderdale, FL 33316-3827, USA.

**LESLIE John**, b. 11 July 1923, Philadelphia, USA. Artist; Designer; Sculptor; Fine Art; Photographer. m. (1) Kathryn Elizabeth Frame, (2) Mary Frances Huggins, 3 children. Education: Graduate, Commercial Art with Harry Brodsky, Murrell Dobbins Tech, Philadelphia, 1941; Postgraduate, Fleisher Art Memorial, Philadelphia, 1939-42, Philadelphia Museum School of Industrial Art, 1944, Philadelphia Musical Academy, 1965-67, Pennsylvania State University, 1982-. Appointments include: Staff Artist, Philadelphia Daily News, 1942; Founder, Creative Director, Graphic-Ad Displays Inc, Philadelphia, 1944; Collaborative Designer, Thanksgiving Day

Parade and Fashion Show Stage Set Designer, Gimbel Brothers, Philadelphia, 1945; Artist, Muralist, Bonwit Teller, Philadelphia Eagles Football Team, PSFS Bank; Stage Set Designer, Bessie V Hicks School of Dramatic Arts, Philadelphia, 1944-46; Art Director, Dupiex Display and Manufacturing Company Inc, Philadelphia, 1947-54; Designer, Leslie Creations Inc, Lafayette Hill, 1954-65; Founder, Mail Order Methods Inc, Lafayette Hill, Pennsylvania, 1954-57; Artist-Designer, World Treasures, Seven Seas House Inc, Lafayette Hill, Pennsylvania, 1960-65; President, Lions, Lafayette Hill, 1960-71; Founder, Creative Director & Designer of 150 Kopy Kat Inc, franchised Instant Printing Centers in 31 States, Ft Washington, PA, 1968-77; Art Director, Designer, Jesse Jones Industries Inc, Philadelphia, 1978-79; Co-Founder, Art Director, Galerie Marjole Inc, Sanatoga, PA, 1987-89; Lecturer, Limited Edition Fine Arts Prints, 1987-; Fine Art Spokesman, Radio and Television, 1989-; Author, Lasting Impressions, a weekly column on fine art photography, Englewood Herald, Florida, 2000-. Honours: Walter Emerson Baum Award for American Impressionist Painting; Sellers Museum Award for Impressionism in Fine Art Photography; King of Prussia Pastel Painting Award; AMVETS Award for Outstanding Artistic Designs; Playboy Magazine Award for Artistic Merit; Japanese Graphic Arts Industry Award; Works in 23 US museums, US Embassy, Paris, France, and numerous private collections. Memberships: Woodmere Art Museum, Philadelphia; Arts and Humanities Council, Port Charlotte, Florida; Boca Grande, Florida, Art Alliance; New York Oil Pastel Association; US Army's 8th Armored Division Association; National AMVETS; Military Heritage & Aviation Museum, Punta Gorda, FL; Les Amis de Veterans Français. Commissions and Creative Works: Designer, Mannequettes, 3-D miniature human figures with cylindrical wooden heads and paper sculptured clothing; Plasti-Coil: An expandable-retractable coil of multicoloured plastic tubing wound over a soft wire core; 3-D's (3 dimensional collages of paper sculpture, painted artwork & layered composition board), all used in major specialty shop and department store windows and interiors across the USA; The Crystal Mall: a climate controlled glass atrium enclosing entire existing downtown shopping districts; Proposed US Veterans of WWII Memorial Hall of Honor; Proposed museum building & interior design for Military Heritage & Aviation Museum, Punta Gorda, Florida; Designer, First avant-garde A-Frame Home on US Atlantic Coast; Collaborative designer of 11 Coarctare Homes, Englewood, Florida, 1997-99; Creator, Inventor: Functional Metal Sculpture – a collection of welded-chromed steel occasional furniture pieces; The Slab Chair: of interlocking leather-covered foam rubber panels; Numerous exhibitions and works in public and private collections. Address: Blueberry Hill Studios, 6318 Zeno Circle, Port Charlotte, FL 33981, USA.

**LESLIE Peter Evelyn (Sir)**, b. 24 March 1931, Oxford, England. Banker. m. Charlotte Chapman-Andrews, 1975, 2 stepsons, 2 stepdaughters. Education: New College, Oxford; MA Oxon. Appointments: Joined Barclays Bank DCO, 1955, serving in Sudan, Algeria, Zaire, Kenya and Bahamas; General Manager, 1973-76, Director, 1979-91, Barclays Bank Ltd; Chairman, British Bankers Association Executive Committee, 1978-79; Member, 1978-81, Chairman, 1987-92, Export Guarantees Advisory Council; Senior General Manager, Barclays Bank International, 1980-83; Chief General Manager, 1985-87, Managing Director, 1987-88, Deputy Chairman, 1987-91, Barclays Bank PLC; Governor, 1983-2001, Chairman, 1994-2001, Stowe School; Chairman, Committee, London and Scottish Clearing Bankers, 1986-88; Council for Industry and Higher Education, 1987-91; Chairman, Overseas Development Institute, 1988-95; Board of Banking Supervision, Bank of England, 1989-94; Chairman, Commonwealth Development

Corporation, 1989-95; Chairman, Queen's College, London, 1989-94; Curator, University Chest, Oxford, 1990-95; Deputy Chairman, Midland Group, 1991-92; Council, Ranfurly Library Service, 1991-94; Council, Royal Institute of International Affairs, Chatham House, 1991-97; Oxford University Audit Committee, 1992-2001; Board, International Institute for Environment and Development, 1992-95; Chairman, NCM UK, 1995-98; Supervisory Board, NCM Holding NV, Amsterdam, 1995-2000. Memberships: Fellow, Institute of Bankers; Fellow, Linnean Society. Address: 153 Sutherland Avenue, London W9 1ES, England.

**LESSING Doris May,** b. 22 October 1919, Kermanshah, Persia. Writer. m. (1) Frank Charles Wisdom, 1939, divorced 1943, 1 son, 1 daughter, (2) Gottfried Anton Nicholas Lessing, 1945, divorced 1949, 1 son. Publications: Novels: The Grass Is Singing 1950; Children of Violence, 1952; A Proper Marriage, 1954; A Ripple from the Storm, 1965; The Four-Gated City, 1969; Retreat to Innocence, 1956; The Golden Notebook, 1962; Briefing for a Descent into Hell, 1971; The Summer Before the Dark, 1973; The Memoirs of a Survivor, 1974; Canopus in Argos: Archives, 1979-1983; The Diary of a Good Neighbour, 1983; If the Old Could, 1984; The Diaries of Jane Somers, 1984; The Good Terrorist, 1985; The Fifth Child, 1988; Love, Again, 1996; Mara and Dann, 1999; Ben, in the World, 2000; The Old Age of El Magnifico, 2000; The Sweetest Dream, 2001; The Story of General Dann and Mara's Daughter, Griot and the Snow Dog, 2005; Short stories: Collected African Stories, 2 volumes, 1951, 1973; Five, 1953; The Habit of Loving, 1957; A Man and Two Women, 1963; African Stories, 1964; Winter in July, 1966; The Black Madonna, 1966; The Story of a Non-Marrying Man and Other Stories, 1972; A Sunrise on the Veld, 1975; A Mild Attack of Locusts, 1977; Collected Stories, 2 volumes, 1978; London Observed: Stories and Sketches, 1992; The Grandmothers, 2004; Non-fiction includes: Going Home, 1957, 1968; Particularly Cats, 1967; Particularly Cats and More Cats, 1989; African Laughter: Four Visits to Zimbabwe, 1992; Under My Skin, 1994; Walking in the Shade, 1997. Plays: Each to His Own Wilderness, 1958; Play with a Tiger, 1962; The Singing Door, 1973; Other publications include: Fourteen Poems, 1959; A Small Personal Voice, 1974; Doris Lessing Reader, 1990; Timebites, 2005. Honours: 5 Somerset Maugham Awards, Society of Authors, 1954-; Prix Médicis for French translation, Carnet d'or, 1976; Austrian State Prize for European Literature, 1981; Shakespeare Prize, Hamburg, 1982; W H Smith Literary Award, 1986; Palermo Prize and Premio Internazionale Mondello, 1987; Grinzane Cavour Award, Italy, 1989; Woman of the Year, Norway, 1995; Los Angeles Times Book Prize, 1995; James Tait Memorial Prize, 1995; Premi Internacional Catalunya, Spain, 1999; David Cohen Literary Prize, 2001; Principe de Asturias, Spain, 2001; PEN Award, 2002. Memberships: Associate Member, American Academy of Arts and Letters, 1974; National Institute of Arts and Letters, USA, 1974; Member, Institute for Cultural Research, 1974; President, Book Trust, 1996-. Address: c/o Jonathon Clowes Ltd, Iron Bridge House, Bridge Approach, London NW1 8BD, England.

**LESSING Kolja,** b. 15 October 1961, Karlsruhe, Germany. Violinist; Pianist; Musicologist. Musical Education: Basic training both in violin and piano with his mother; Studies at the Musikhochschule Basel with soloist-diplomas in violin and piano; private conducting lessons with Berthold Goldschmidt, London. Debut: Violinist, 1981; Pianist, 1982; Conducting, 1995. Appointments: Performing as violinist and pianist both in recital and as soloist with major orchestras, many first performances of violin compositions, many radio appearances; Professor, violin/chamber music, at Musikhochschule, Stuttgart.

Publications include: Major compositions: Gleitende Figuren, flute and viola, others; CD recordings include: Goldschmidt, complete Piano music, LARGO; Jarnach, Composer's Portrait, DIVOX; Telemann, Violin Fantasies, CAPRICCIO; Ignace Strasfogel, Piano Music, DECCA; Werthoff: Complete Solo Violin Suitor Capriccio; Contributions to Dissonanz, Zürich/Lausanne. Honours: Preis der deutschen Schallplattenkritik, 3/1992; Stamitz-Sonderpreis, 1999. Address: Steinbachtal 52, D 97082 Würzburg, Germany.

**LESTER Adrian Anthony,** b. 14 August 1968, Birmingham, England. Actor. Education: Royal Academy of Dramatic Art, London. Career: Theatre appearances including Cory in Fences, Garrick, 1990, Paul Poitier in Six Degrees of Separation, Royal Court and Comedy Theatre, 1992, Anthony Hope in Sweeney Todd, Royal National Theatre, 1994, Rosalind in As You Like It, Albery and Bouffes du Nord, 1995, Company, Albery and Donmar, 1996; Hamlet, Bouffes du Nord and Young Vic, 2001; TV appearances: For the Greater Good; In the Dark; The Tragedy of Hamlet, Hustle; Film appearances include Ray in The Affair, 1995, Up on the Roof, Primary Colors, 1997, Storm Damage, Love's Labour's Lost, 1999; Dust, 2001; Final Curtain, 2001; Tomorrow, 2002. Honours: Time Out Award, 1992, 1995; Olivier Award, 1996. Memberships: Amnesty International; Greenpeace. Address: c/o Artists Rights Group (ARG), 4 Great Portland Street, London W1W 8PA, England.

**LESTER Alexander Norman Charles Phillips,** b. 11 May 1956, Walsall, England. Broadcaster. Education: Diploma, Communication Studies, Birmingham Polytechnic, 1978. Appointments: BBC Local and Independent Radio, 1977-86; BBC Radio 2, 1987-; Alex Lester Show, Radio 2, 1991-; Presenter, The Boat Show, BBC2 TV, Appearances on: Call My Bluff, BBC TV; Waterworld, Carlton TV; Lunchtime Live, Meridian TV; Announcer/Voice Over on numerous satellite and terrestrial TV and radio channels. Honours: Patron St Michael's Hospice, St Leonards-on-Sea; Ambassador, Hospital Radio Association. Memberships: Hastings Winkle Club; Equity. Address: c/o MPC Management, MPC House, 15-16 Maple Mews, Maida Vale, London NW6 6UZ, England. E-mail: alex.lester@bbc.co.uk

**LESTER Richard,** b. 19 January 1932, Philadelphia, USA. American Film Director. m. Deirdre V Smith, 1956, 1 son, 1 daughter. Education: William Penn Carter School; University of Pennsylvania. Appointments: TV Director, CBS, 1952-54; ITV, 1955-59; Composer, 1954-57; Film Director, 1959-; Films directed: The Running, Jumping and Standing Still Film, 1959; It's Trad ad, 1962; The Mouse on the Moon, 1963; A Hard Day's Night, 1963; The Knack, 1965; Help!, 1965; A Funny Thing Happened on the Way to the Forum, 1966; How I Won the War, 1967; Petulia, 1969; The Bed Sitting Room, 1969; The Three Musketeers, 1973; Juggernaut, 1974; The Four Musketeers, 1974; Royal Flash, 1975; Robin and Marian, 1976; The Ritz, 1976; Butch and Sundance: The Early Days, 1979; Cuba, 1979; Superman II, 1980; Superman III, 1983; Finders Keepers, 1984; The Return of the Musketeers, 1989; Get Back, 1990. Honours: Academy Award Nomination, 1960; Grand Prix, Cannes Film Festival, 1965; Best Director, Rio de Janeiro Festival, 1966; Gandhi Peace Prize, Berlin Festival, 1969; Best Director, Tehran Festival, 1974. Address: c/o Creative Artists Agency, 9830 Wilshire Boulevard, Beverley Hills, CA 90212, USA.

**LESTER OF HERNE HILL, Baron of Herne Hill in the London Borough of Southwark, Anthony Paul Lester,** b. 3 July 1936, London, England. Lawyer. m. Catherine Elizabeth Debora Wassey, 1971, 1 son, 1 daughter. Education: Trinity College, Cambridge; BA, Cantab; LLM, Harvard Law School; Called to Bar, Lincoln's Inn, 1963, Bencher, 1985. Appointments: Special Adviser to Home Secretary, 1974-76, to Northern Ireland Standing Advisory Commission on Human Rights, 1975-77; Appointed Queen's Counsel, 1975; Member, Board of Overseers, University of Pennsylvania Law School, Council of Justice, 1977-90; Member, Court of Governors, London School of Economics, 1980-94; Honorary Visiting Professor, University College London, 1983-; Board of Directors, Salzburg Seminar; President, Interights, 1996-2000; Recorder, South-Eastern Circuit, 1987-93; Co-Chair, Board, European Roma Rights Center; Governor, British Institute of Human Rights; Chair, Board of Governors, James Allen's Girls' School, 1987-93; Chair, Runnymede Trust, 1990-93; Governor, Westminster School, 1998-; Member, Advisory Committee, Centre for Public Law, University of Cambridge, 1999-; International Advisory Board, Open Society Institute, 2000-; Parliamentary Joint Human Rights Commission, 2001-; Foreign Honorary Member, American Academy of Arts and Sciences, 2002. Publications: Justice in the American South, 1964; Race and Law, co-author, 1972; Butterworth's Human Rights Cases, editor-in-chief; Halsbury's Laws of England Title Constitutional Law and Human Rights, 4th edition, consultant editor, contributor, 1996; Human Rights Law and Practice, co-editor, 1999; Articles on race relations, public affairs and international law. Honours: Honorary degrees and fellowships, Open University, University College, London University, Ulster University, South Bank University; Liberty Human Rights Lawyer of the Year, 1997. Address: Blackstone Chambers, Blackstone House, Temple, London EC4Y 9BW, England.

**LETSIE III, King of Lesotho,** b. 17 July 1963, Morija, Lesotho. Monarch. Education: National University of Lesotho; Universities of Bristol, Cambridge and London. Appointments: Principal Chief of Matsieng, 1989; Installed as King of Lesotho, 1990, abdicated, 1995, reinstated after father's death, 1996-; Patron, Prince Mohato Award. Address: Royal Palace, Masero, Lesotho.

**LETTE Kathy,** b. 11 November 1958, Sydney. Australian Author. m. Geoffrey Robertson, 1990, 1 son, 1 daughter. Education: Sylvania High School, Sydney. Publications: Puberty Blues, 1980; HIT and MS, 1984; Girl's Night Out, 1988; The Llama Parlour, 1991; Foetal Attraction, 1993; Mad Cows, 1996; Altar Ego, 1998; Nip 'n Tuck, 2001; Dead Sexy, 2003; Plays: Wet Dreams, 1985; Perfect Mismatch, 1985; Grommitts, 1988; I'm So Sorry For You, I Really Am, 1994; Radio: I'm So Happy For You, I Really Am; Essays: She Done Him Wrong, 1995; The Constant Sinner in Introduction to Mae West, 1995. Address: c/o Ed Victor, 6 Bayley Street, London, WC1B 3HB, England.

**LETTERMAN David,** b. 12 April 1947, Indianapolis. American Broadcaster. m. Michelle Cook, 1969, divorced 1977. Education: Ball State University. Appointments: Radio and TV Announcer, Indianapolis; Performer, The Comedy Store, Los Angeles, 1975-; TV Appearances include: Rock Concert, Gong Show; Frequent guest host, The Twilight Show; Host, David Letterman Show, 1980; Late Night with David Letterman, 1982; The Late Show with David Letterman, CBS, 1993-; TV Scriptwriting includes, Bob Hope Special; Good Times; Paul Lynde Comedy Hour; John Denver Special. Publications: David Letterman's Book of Top Ten Lists, 1996. Honours: Recipient, Six Emmy Awards. Address: Late Show with David Letterman, Ed Sullivan Theater, 1697 Broadway, New York, NY 10019, USA.

**LETTS Quentin Richard Stephen,** b. 6 February 1963, Cirencester, Gloucestershire, England. Journalist. m. Lois Rathbone, 1 son, 1 daughter. Education: Trinity College,

Dublin; Jesus College, Cambridge. Appointments: Daily Telegraph, 1988-95, 1997-2000; New York Bureau Chief, The Times, 1995-97; Parliamentary Sketchwriter, Daily Mail, 2000-. Membership: The Savile Club. Address: Scrubs' Bottom, Bisley, Gloucestershire GL6 7BU, England.

**LETTS-CIARRAPICO Rosa Maria,** b. 30 May 1937, Rome, Italy. Art Historian. m. Anthony A Letts, 1 son, 1 daughter. Education: Maturitá Classica, 1955; Degree in Law, University of Rome, 1955-59; MA Course, Brandeis University, Massachusetts, USA (Fulbright Scholarship), 1959-60; BA (Hons), European History of Art, Courtauld Institute, University of London, 1966-69; MPhil (Hons), Combined Historical Studies on the Renaissance, Warburg Institute, University of London. Appointments: Lecturer, History of Art and Architecture, University of London Extra Mural Department, 1966-80; Lecturer on Italian European Art (Renaissance and Baroque), Exhibitions Consultant, Victoria and Albert Museum, 1975-82; Lecturer in Renaissance and Baroque Art, Italian Modern Art, Design and Architecture, Sotheby's Art Courses, 1978-85; Phillips Courses on Contemporary Design, Architecture and Fashion, 1985-86; Founding Director, Accademia Italiana delle Arti delle Arti Applicate, London, 1988-2002; Cultural Counsellor, Italian Embassy, London, 1992-96; Juror, European Design Award, Royal Society of Arts, 1992-93; Accademia Club, London, 2002-; Art Consultant, Italian Consul, Manchester, 2004-; Curator of numerous exhibitions, 1981-2002. Publications: Books: La Pittura Fiorentina, 1970; Art Treasures of London (in the series English Art Guides), 1981; Renaissance, Cambridge Introduction to the History of Art, 1981, 3rd edition, 1991; Catalogues include: Italia Ao Luar, 1989; Italy by Moonlight 1550-1850, 1990, 2nd edition, 1991; Catalogues essays and articles. Honours: Cavaliere Ufficiale della Repubblica Italiana; Fiorino D'Oro della Cittá di Milano offerta dal Sindaco di Milano. Address: Accademia Club Ltd, 59 Knightsbridge, London SW1X 7RA, England. E-mail: rmletts@accademia-club.com

**LEU Paul,** b. 26 June 1927, Carja-Murgeni, Romania. Educator and Researcher. m. Magdalena, 2 sons, 1 daughter. Education: Philology Graduate (Head of Promotion), Al I Cuza University, Iasi, Romania, 1954; Diploma in Teaching Language, Literature and Literature Theory. Appointments: Teacher, 1949-96; Associate Professor, 1965; Lecturer, 1968; Extensive researches into subjects including: literary history, ethnography, history of music, teaching and history of teaching, history of Bucovina during Austria's domination, also researches into the unpublished works of S Fl Marian, Ciprian Porumbescu, Iraclie Porumbescu, Bishop Grigore Leu, Archbishop Victor Leu and others. Publications: 32 books include: Ciprian Porumbescu – documente si marturii, 1971; Ciprian Porumbescu, monograph, 1972, 1978; Basme din Tara de Sus, 1975; Legende istorice din Bucovina, 1981; Marthir of the Heart, monograph, 1995; Nuvele si amintiri, 1996; Simion Florea Marian, monograph, 1996; Romanian Folk Stories II, III and IV, 1997-98; The S Fl Marian Academician - Monograph, 1998; S Fl Marian, Facerea lumii, 1998; S Fl Marian, Legende botanice, 1999; Founder of the Romanian Ethnography – Monograph I and II, 1998-99; S Fl Marian, Plantele noastre, 2000; Colegiul National Stefan cel Mare Suceava – Monograph I, Etapia austriacă, 2000; Iraclie Prumbescu - Monograph, 2000; Quo vadis romane!, 2001; Gr-or KK Obergymnasium din Suceava, in intampinarea unirii Bucovinei cu Romania, 2003; S Fl Marian, Cosmogeneza, 2004; Basme populare romanesti, I and II, 1986-2004; Martiri ai credintei in Hristos, 2005; Episcopi romani rapiti si asasinati de KGB, 2005; 547 articles, documents and book reviews; Script for the short TV Movie, Remember Ciprian Porumbescu, 1996. Honours: Front Ranking Teacher Award, Romanian Ministry of Education, 1964; Second Degree Teacher Diploma, 1965; First Degree teaching Diploma, 1976; A Pen on Two Continents, summary of Paul Leu's works by Octavian Nestor; Listed in: The Romanian Ethnology Dictionary, I and II, 1998; Bibliographie zur Kultur und Landeskunde der Bukowina, 1965-1990; Muzica in Bucovina, 1981; Scriitori bucovineni Mic dictionar, 1992; Dictionar de literature – Bucovina, 1993; The International Directory of Distinguished Leadership, 11th edition, 2003; The Contemporary Who's Who, 2nd edition, 2005; 2000 Outstanding Intellectuals of the 21st Century, 2004; Enciclopedia Bucovinei, I and II, 2005; Books stored in the most important national, academical and university libraries in the world. Membership: Member and President, Society of Romanian Language and Literature. Address: 7217 175th Street, Unit #113, NE, Kenmore, WA 98028, USA. E-mail: paulleu@hotmail.com

**LEUNG Kam Tim,** b. 21 June 1931, China. Educator. Education: Sun Yat-sen University, 1953. Appointments: Teacher, secondary schools, college and universities, mainland China, 1953-95; Tutor, Open University of Hong Kong, 1997-99; Part-time Tutor, Hong Kong University, 2001. Publications: 30 articles in top journals. Honours: Senior Lecturer Certificate, Educational Department of Guangdong Province, China, 1987; Listed in national and international biographical publications. Memberships: Regular Member, International Association of Chinese Linguistics, 1994-. Address: PO Box 91360, Tsim Sha Tsui Post Office, Kowloon, Hong Kong.

**LEUNG Nigel Chun Ming,** b. 19 July 1977, Hong Kong. Airline Pilot. Education: MEng (First Class Honours), Aeronautical Engineering, Imperial College, London, 2001. Appointments: Principal Engineer, BMT Reliability Consultants Ltd, Hampshire, 2001-02; Cadet Pilot Programme, HK Dragon Airlines Ltd, Adelaide, Australia, 2002-03; Australian Private Pilot Licence (Multi Engine), HK Commercial Pilot Licence and Command Instrument Rating, Junior First Officer, Airbus A330-300, HK Dragon Airlines Ltd, 2004-. Honours: Numerous academic and sports awards and titles during academic life. Memberships: Associate Member, Royal Aeronautical Society. E-mail: aerofoil2415@hotmail.com

**LEUNG Thomas Kim-Ping,** b. 28 July 1955, Hong Kong. Associate Professor. m. May Mei-Lin Leung, 1 son. BA, University of Saskatchewan, Canada; MComm, University of New South Wales, Australia; PhD, University of Western Sydney, Australia. Appointments: Various executive positions in multi-national companies, 1980-91; Lecturer, Assistant Professor, Associate Professor, Hong Kong Polytechnic University, 1991-. Publications: Over 70 articles in international referred journals, book chapters and referred conferences; Book: Guanxi: Relationship in a Chinese Context (co-author), The Haworth Press. Address: Department of Management and Marketing, The Hong Kong Polytechnic University, Hung Hom, Hong Kong. E-mail: msthomas@polyu.edu.hk

**LEVASSEUR Lee,** b. 8 April 1950, Hartford, USA. Fine Artist. 1 son. Education: BS, Art Education: Southern Connecticut State University, 1973. Appointments: Owner, Organic Surrealism, 1989-; Joint Director, Exhibitor, Touring of Quintcentennial Fine Art Exhibition "America 500"; Board of Governors, American Biographical Institute. Honours: Soho International Art Competition, Ariel Gallery, New York City, 1989; Artitudes International Art Competition, New York. Memberships: New Haven Art Council; Branford Chamber of Commerce; Shoreline Alliance of Artists. Address: 525 East Main Street #40, Branford, CT 06405, USA.

**LEVENE OF PORTSOKEN, Baron of Portsoken in the City of London, Peter Keith Levene,** b. 8 December 1941, Pinner, Middlesex, England. Business Executive; Justice of the Peace. m. Wendy Ann Levene, 1966, 2 sons, 1 daughter. Education: BA, University of Manchester. Appointments: Joined, 1963, Managing Director, 1968, Chair, 1982, United Scientific Holdings; Member, South-East Asia Trade Advisory Group, 1979-83; Personal Adviser to Secretary of State for Defence, 1984; Alderman, 1984, Sheriff, 1995-96, Lord Mayor, 1998-99, City of London; Chair, European NATO National Armaments Directors, 1990-91; Special Adviser to Secretary of State for the Environment, 1991-92; Chair, Docklands Light Railway Ltd, 1991-94; Chair, Public Competition and Purchasing Unit, H M Treasury, 1991-92; Deputy Chair, Wasserstein Perella and Co Ltd, 1991-94; Adviser to Prime Minister on Efficiency, 1992-97; Special Adviser to President of Board of Trade, 1992-95; Chair, Chief Executive Officer, Canary Wharf Ltd, 1993-96; Senior Adviser, Morgan Stanley and Co Ltd, 1996-98; Chair, Bankers Trust International, 1998-99; Chair, Investment Banking Europe, Deutsche Bank AG, 1999-2001; Vice Chair, Deutsche Bank, UK, 2001-02; Chair, Lloyds of London, 2002-. Honours: Honorary Colonel Commandant, Royal Corps of Transport, 1991-93; Master, Worshipful Company of Carmen, 1992-93; Honorary Colonel Commandant, Royal Logistics Corps, 1993-; Fellow, Queen Mary and Westfield College, London University, 1995; Knight Commander, Order of St John of Jerusalem; Commander, Ordre National du Mérite, 1996; Honorary DSc, City University, 1998; Knight Commandants Order of Merit, Germany, 1998; Middle Cross Order of Merit, Hungary, 1999; Knight Commander, Order of the British Empire. Memberships: Fellow, Chartered Institute of Transport; Companion, Institute of Management; Defence Manufacturers Association, Council, 1982-85, Vice-Chair, 1983-84, Chair, 1984-85. Address: 1 Great Winchester Street, London EC2N 2DB, England. E-mail: peter.k.levene@db.com

**LEVENSON David,** b. 8 October 1965, Bronx, New York, USA. Physician. m. Marissa, 4 sons. Education: BA cum laude, 1985, BS cum laude, 1985, University of Miami; MD, Honours in Physiology and Biophysics, New York University School of Medicine, 1989. Appointments: Residency Training Programme, Long Island Jewish Medical Centre, 1989-92; Endocrinology Fellowship, Cornell University Programme, 1992-94; Geriatric Fellowship, University of Miami, Florida, 1994-95; Private Practice, 1995-. Publications: Electrophysiologic Changes Accompanying Wallerian Degeneration in Frog Sciatic Nerve Brain Research; Candida Zeylenoides: Another opportunistic yeast; Peripheral facial nerve palsy after high dose radio iodine therapy in patients with papillary thyroid cancer; A review of calcium preparations; A multi-centre trail of Gallium Nitrate in patients with advanced Pagets disease of bone. Honour: AMA Physicians' Recognition Award. Memberships: Fellow, American College of Endocrinology; Fellow, American College of Physicians; American Association of Clinical Endocrinology; Endocrine Society. Address: 7301 West Palmetto Park Road, Suite 108B, Boca Raton, FL 33433, USA.

**LEVER, His Honour Judge Bernard Lewis,** b. 1 February 1951, Manchester, UK. Judge. m. Anne Helen Ballingall, 2 daughters. Education: MA, The Queen's College, Oxford. Appointments: Called to the Bar, Middle Temple, 1975; Barrister, Northern Circuit, 1975-2001; Recorder, 1995-2001; Standing Counsel to the Inland Revenue, 1997-2001; Circuit Judge, 2001. Honour: Neale Exhibitioner, Oxford University. Membership: Vincent's Club. Address: Manchester Crown Court, Minshull Street, Manchester M1 3FS, England.

**LEVER Tresham Christopher Arthur Lindsay (Sir) (3rd Baronet),** b. 9 January 1932, London, England. Naturalist; Writer. m. Linda Weightman McDowell Goulden, 6 November 1975. Education: Eton College, 1945-49; BA, 1954, MA, 1957, Trinity College, Cambridge. Publications: Goldsmiths and Silversmiths of England, 1975; The Naturalized Animals of the British Isles, 1977; Naturalized Mammals of the World, 1985; Naturalized Birds of the World, 1987; The Mandarin Duck, 1990; They Dined on Eland: The Story of the Acclimatisation Societies, 1992; Naturalized Animals: The Ecology of Successfully Introduced Species, 1994; Naturalized Fishes of the World, 1996; The Cane Toad: The History and Ecology of a Successful Colonist, 2001; Naturalized Reptiles and Amphibians of the World, 2003; Naturalised Birds of the World, 2005. Contributions to: Books, Art, Scientific and general publications. Memberships: Fellow, Linnean Society of London; Fellow, Royal Geographical Society; World Conservation Union Species' Survival Commission; Council of Ambassadors, WWF (UK); Honorary Life Member, Brontë Society, 1988. Address: Newell House, Winkfield, Berkshire SL4 4SE, England.

**LEVERKUS (Carl) Erich,** b. 15 March 1926, Duisburg, Germany. Retired Banker. m. Ingrid Nottebohm, 4 sons, 1 daughter. Education: Studied Chemistry and Economics, Diplom-Volkswirt, 1955, Dr. rer. pol., 1957, University of Tuebingen. Appointments: Chairman, Vereinigte Ultramarinfabriken AG, Bensheim, Germany, 1957-72; Managing Partner, William Ree Jr, Hamburg, Germany, 1961-86; General Partner, Leverkus and Co, Hamburg, Germany, 1987-. Publications: Nordelbische Pastorenfamilien und ihre Nachkommen, 1973; Beautiful Lakes of the Canadian Rockies, 1979; Alberta's Forestry Trunk Road, 1979; Freier Tausch und Fauler Zauber – vom Gelt und seiner Geschichte, 1990; Wie der Neandertaler zu seinem Namen kam, 1999; Evolution und Geist, 1999; Childhood under Hitler's Rule, 2000; Geld, Währung, Währungsdeckung, 2001; Carl Leverkus, 2004. Honours: Chairman, Versammlung Eines Ehrbahren Kaufmanns zu Hamburg, 1982-90; Knight of Honour, 1951, Knight of Justice, 1966, Johanniterorden. Memberships: Rotary Club of Hamburg; Uebersee Club, Hamburg. Address: Schauenburger Strasse 55-57, D-20095 Hamburg, Germany.

**LEVEY Michael (Vincent) (Sir),** b. 8 June 1927, London, England. Writer. m. Brigid Brophy, deceased 1995, 1 daughter. Education: Exeter College, Oxford. Appointments: Assistant Keeper, 1951-66, Deputy Keeper, 1966-68, Keeper, 1968-73, Deputy Director, 1970-73, Director, 1973-87, National Gallery, London; Slade Professor of Fine Art, Cambridge, 1963-64, Oxford, 1994-95. Publications: Six Great Painters, 1956; National Gallery Catalogues: 18th Century Italian Schools, 1956; The German School, 1959; Painting in 18th Century Venice, 1959, 3rd edition, 1994; From Giotto to Cézanne, 1962; Dürer, 1964; The Later Italian Paintings in the Collection of HM The Queen, 1964, revised edition, 1991; Canaletto Paintings in the Royal Collection, 1964; Tiepolo's Banquet of Cleopatra, 1966; Rococo to Revolution, 1966; Bronzino, 1967; Early Renaissance, 1967; Fifty Works of English Literature We Could Do Without (co-author), 1967; Holbein's Christina of Denmark, Duchess of Milan, 1968; A History of Western Art, 1968; Painting at Court, 1971; The Life and Death of Mozart, 1971, 2nd edition, 1988; The Nude: Themes and Painters in the National Gallery, 1972; Art and Architecture in 18th Century France (co-author), 1972; The Venetian Scene, 1973; Botticelli, 1974; High Renaissance, 1975; The World of the Ottoman Art, 1976; Jacob van Ruisdael, 1977; The Case of Walter Pater, 1978; The Painter Depicted, 1981; Tempting Fate, 1982; An Affair on the Appian Way, 1984; Pater's Marius the Epicurean (editor), 1985; Giambattista Tiepolo, 1986; The National Gallery Collection: A Selection, 1987; Men at Work, 1989; The Soul of the Eye: Anthology of Painters and Painting (editor), 1990; Painting and Sculpture in France 1700-1789, 1992; Florence: A Portrait, 1996; The Chapel is on Fire (memoir), 2000; The Burlington Magazine, anthology, 2003; Sir Thomas Lawrence, 2005. Contributions to: Periodicals. Honours: Hawthornden Prize, 1968; Knighted, 1981; Honorary Fellow, Royal Academy, 1986; Banister Fletcher Prize, 1987; Lieutenant, Royal Victoria Order, 1965. Memberships: Ateneo Veneto, foreign member; British Academy, fellow; Royal Society of Literature, fellow. Address: 36 Little Lane, Louth, Lincolnshire LN11 9DU, England.

**LEVI-MONTALCINI Rita, b.** 22 April 1909, Turin, Italy. Neuroscientist. Education: Graduated, Medicine, University of Turin, 1936. Appointments: Neurological research in Turin and Brussels, 1936-41, in Piemonte, 1941-43; In hiding in Florence during German occupation, 1943-44; Medical Doctor working among war refugees, Florence, 1944-45; Resumed academic positions at University of Turin, 1945; Worked with Professor Viktor Hamburger, 1947, Associate Professor, 1956, Professor, 1958-77, St Louis, USA; Director, 1969-78, Guest Professor, 1979-89, Guest Professor, Institute of Neurobiology, 1989-, Institute of Cell Biology of Italian National Council of Research, Rome. Publications: In Praise of Imperfection: My Life and Work, 1988. Honour: Joint Winner, Nobel Prize for Medicine, 1986. Address: Institute of Neurobiology, CNR Viale Marx 15, 00137, Rome, Italy.

**LÉVI-STRAUSS Claude, b.** 28 November 1908, Brussels, Belgium. Anthropologist; University Professor; Writer. m. (1) Dina Dreyfus, 1932, (2) Rose Marie Ullmo, 1946, 1 son, (3) Monique Roman, 1954, 1 son. Education: University of Paris-Sorbonne. Appointments: Professor, University of São Paulo, Brazil, 1935-39; Visiting Professor, New School of Social Research, New York, USA, 1942-45; Cultural Counsellor, French Embassy, USA, 1946-47; Associate Director, Musée de l'Homme, Paris, France, 1949-50; Director of Studies, Ecole Pratique des Hautes Etudes, Paris, 1950-74; Professor, 1959-82, Honorary Professor, 1983-, Collège de France. Publications: La vie familiale et sociale des indiens Nambikwara, 1948; Les structures élémentaires de la parenté, 1949; Tristes tropiques,, 1955; Anthropologie structurale, 1958; Le totémisme aujourd'hui, 1962; La pensée sauvage, 1962; Le cru et le cuit, 1964; Du miel aux centres, 1967; L'origine des manières de table, 1968; L'homme nu, 1971; Anthropologie structurale deux, 1973; La voie des masques, 1975, 1979; Le regard éloigné, 1983; Paroles données, 1984; La potière jalouse, 1985; De près et de loin, co-author, 1988; Histoire de Lynx, 1991; Regarder, écouter, lire, 1983; Saudades do Brasil, 1994. Honours: Dr hc, Brussels, Harvard, Yale, Chicago, Columbia, Oxford, Stirling, Zaire, Mexico, Uppsala, Johns Hopkins, Montreal, Québec and Visva-Bharati University, India; Prix Paul Pelliot, 1949; Huxley Memorial Medal, 1965; Viking Fund Gold Medal, 1966; Gold Medal, Centre National de la Recherche Scientifique, 1967; Erasmus Prize, 1973; Aby M Warburg Prize, 1996; Grand Croix, Légion d'Honneur; Commandeur, Ordre National du Mérite, des Palmes Académiques, des Arts et des Lettres. Memberships: Académie Française; Foreign Member, Royal Academy of the Netherlands, Norwegian Academy of Sciences and Letters, American Academy of Arts and Sciences, American Academy and Institute of Arts and Letters, British Academy; Foreign Associate, National Academy of Sciences, USA; Honorary Member, Royal Anthropological Institute, American Philosophical Society, London School of Oriental and African Studies. Address: 2 rue des Marronniers, 75016 Paris, France.

**LEVICK William Russell, b.** 5 December 1931, Sydney, Australia. Neuroscience Researcher. m. Patricia Lathwell, 1

son, 1 son deceased, 1 daughter. Education: BSc, honours, 1953, MSc, 1954, MBBS, honours, 1957, University of Sydney. Appointments: C J Martin Travelling Fellow, Cambridge University, University of California, Berkeley, 1963-64; Professorial Fellow, 1967-83, Professor, 1983-96, Australian National University, Canberra. Honours: Fellowship, Australian Academy of Sciences, 1973, Optical Society of America, 1977, Royal Society of London, 1982. Memberships: Society for Neuroscience; Australian Neuroscience Society; Australian Physiological and Pharmacological Society. Address: 33 Quiros Street, Red Hill, ACT 2603, Australia.

**LEVIN Ira, b.** 27 August 1929, New York, New York, USA. Novelist; Dramatist. m. (1) Gabrielle Aronsohn, 20 August 1960, divorced January 1968, 3 sons, (2) Phyllis Finkel, 1979, divorced 1981. Education: Drake University, 1946-48; AB, New York University, 1950. Appointments: US Army, 1953-55. Publications: Novels: A Kiss Before Dying, 1953; Rosemary's Baby, 1967; This Perfect Day, 1970; The Stepford Wives, 1972; The Boys From Brazil, 1976; Silver, 1991; Son of Rosemary, 1997. Plays: No Time for Sergeants, 1956; Interlock, 1958; Critic's Choice, 1961; General Seeger, 1962; Drat! The Cat! 1965; Dr Cook's Garden, 1968; Veronica's Room, 1974; Deathtrap, 1979; Break a Leg, 1981; Cantorial, 1990. Contributions to: Television and films. Honours: Edgar Allan Poe Awards, Mystery Writers of America, 1953, 1980. Memberships: American Society of Composers, Authors and Publishers; Authors Guild; Authors League of America; Dramatists Guild. Address: c/o Harold Ober Associates, 425 Madison Avenue, New York, NY 10017, USA.

**LEVIN Nikolay Ivanovich, b.** 19 December 1958, Kirov Region, USSR. Politician. m. Tatyana Ivanovna Levina, 2 sons. Education: Trade Union Movement Higher School, Moscow, 1990; North Western Academy of State Service, St Petersburg, 1999. Appointments: Sailor, 1978-83; Production Engineer, sea port of Belomorsk, 1983; Chairman, Trade Union Committee, sea port of Belomorsk, 1984; Deputy Head of Organisation Department of Belomorsk Area CPSU Committee, 1988-90; Chairman, Belomorsk City Soviet of People's Deputies, 1990-91; Deputy Manager, Agroprom Bank, 1991-95; Head of Local Self Government, Belomorsk Area, 1995-2000; Chairman of the Chamber of Representatives, Legislative Assembly, Republic of Karelia, 2000-2002; Chairman of the Legislative Assembly, Republic of Karelia, 2002-. Honours: Honour Diploma, Government of Karelia, 1998; Honoured Worker of National Economy of the Republic of Karelia, 2003; Candidate of Economic Sciences. Memberships: United Russia Party. Address: Kuibysheva St 5, Petrozavodsk, 185610 Republic of Karelia. E-mail: inbox@zsrk.onego.ru

**LEVINSON Barry, b.** 6 April 1942, Baltimore, Maryland, USA. American Screenwriter; Director. m. Diana. Education: American University. Appointments: Wrote and acted on TV Comedy Show, Los Angeles; Later worked on Network TV; Wrote and appeared, The Carol Burnett Show; Worked on film scripts for Silent Movie and High Anxiety; TV work includes: Writer, Tim Conway Comedy Hour; The Marty Feldman Comedy Machine; The Carol Burnett Show; Executive Producer, Harry 30 Minutes of Investigative Ticking; Diner; Homicide; Life on the Street; Films directed: Diner; The Natural; Young Sherlock Holmes; Tin Men; Good Morning Vietnam; Rain Man; Disclosure, 1995; Director, Producer, Avalon; Bugsy; Toys; Jimmy Hollywood, 1994; Sleepers, 1996; Wag the Dog, 1997; Sphere, 1998; Liberty Heights, 2000; An Everlasting Piece, 2001; Bandits, 2001; Writer: Diner; Tin Men; Avalon; Co-wrote screenplays with Valerie Curtin for: And Justice for All; Inside Movies; Best Friends; Unfaithfully Yours; Toys; Liberty

Heights; Actor: Quiz Show, 1994. Honours: Emy Awards, 1974, 1975; Academy Award, 1988. Address: c/o Baltimore/Spring Creek Pictures, Building 133-208, 4000 Warner Boulevard, Burbank, CA 91522, USA.

**LEVITAS Valery,** b. 3 April 1956, Kiev, Ukraine. Researcher; Educator. m. Natasha Levitas, 20 January 1993, 2 sons. Education: MS honours, Mechanical Engineering, Kiev Polytechnic Institute, 1978; PhD, Materials Science, Institute of Superhard Materials, Kiev, 1981; DSc, Continuum Mechanics, Institute of Electronic Machine Building, Moscow, 1988; DEng habil, Continuum Mechanics, University of Hannover, Germany, 1995; Registered Professional Engineer, Texas, 2001. Appointments: Leader, Research Group, 1982-95, Associate Research Professor, 1984-88, Research Professor, 1989-95, Consultant, 1995-, Institute for Superhard Materials, Ukrainian Academy of Sciences, Kiev; Humboldt Research Fellow, 1993-95, Visiting and Research Professor, 1995-99, University of Hannover, Germany; Associate Professor, 1999-2002, Professor, 2002-, Director, Center for Mechanochemistry and Synthesis of New Materials, 2002-, Texas Tech University, Lubbock; President, Firm "Material Modeling", Lubbock, 2002-; Consultant, Los Alamos National Laboratory, 2001-. Publications include: Large Elastoplastic Deformations of Materials at High Pressure, 1987; Thermomechanics of Phase Transformations and Inelastic Deformations in Microinhomogeneous Materials, 1992; Large Deformation of Materials with Complex Rheological Properties at Normal and High Pressure, 1996; Continuum Mechanical Fundamentals of Mechanochemistry, 2004. Honours: Medal, Ukrainian Academy of Sciences, 1984; Alexander von Humboldt Foundation Fellowship, Germany, 1993-95; International Journal of Engineering Sciences Distinguished Paper Award, 1995; Richard von Mises Award, Society of Applied Mathematics and Mechanics, 1998; Best Professor Award, Pi Tau Sigma, Mechanical Engineering Department, Texas Tech University, 2001; American Medal of Honor, ABI, 2004; Barnie E Rushing Jr Faculty Distinguished Research Award, Texas Tech University, 2005. Memberships: International Association for the Advancement of High Pressure Science and Technology; American Society of Mechanical Engineers; American Physical Society; Society of Engineering Science; Society of Applied Mathematics and Mechanics. Address: Texas Tech University, Department of Mechanical Engineering, Lubbock, TX 79409-1021, USA.

**LEVITT Arthur, Jr,** b. 3 February 1931, Brooklyn, New York, USA. Business Executive. m. Marylin Blauner, 1955, 1 son, 1 daughter. Education: Williams College. Appointments: Assistant Promotion Director, Time Inc, New York, 1954-59; Executive Vice-President, Director, Oppenheimer Industries Inc, Kansas City, 1959-62; Joined, 1962, President, 1969-78, Shearson Hayden Stone Inc, now Shearson Lehmann Bros Inc, New York; Chair, Chief Executive Officer, Director, American Stock Exchange, New York, 1978-89; Chair, Levitt Media Co, New York, 1989-93; Chair, New York City Economic Development Corporation, 1990-93; Chair, Securities and Exchange Commission, 1993-2001; Various directorships and other business and public appointments. Honours: Honorary LLD, Williams College, 1980, Pace, 1980, Hamilton College, 1981, Long Island, 1984, Hofstra, 1985. Address: Securities and Exchange Commission, 450 Fifth Street NW, Washington, DC 20001, USA.

**LEVITT Stephen Hillyer,** b. 9 February 1943, Brooklyn, New York, USA. Indologist. Education: Diploma, High School of Music and Art, New York City, 1956-60; BA, Columbia College, Anthropology, 1960-64; PhD, University of Pennsylvania,

Department of Oriental Studies, 1964-73. Appointments: Cataloguer, Indic MSS, University of Pennsylvania Library for Institute for Advanced Studies of World Religions, Stony Brook, New York, 1971-72; Research Assistant, to Emeritus Professor, Dr W Norman Brown, University of Pennsylvania, 1972-74; Visiting Assistant Professor, Anthropology Department and Humanities Program, University of Denver, 1974-76; Tutor, English Department and Student/Faculty Co-ordinator, Humanities Program, Queensborough Community College, New York City, 1977-78; Private tutor, consulting work for University of Pennsylvania Library, Center for Judaic Studies, University of Pennsylvania (formerly Annenberg Research Institute), Burke Library, Union Theological Seminary, 1978-. Publications: Articles in professional journals. Honours: National Defense Foreign Language Fellowship (Tamil), 1964-67; American Council of Learned Societies Fellowship for Summer Study in Linguistics, 1967; American Institute of Indian Studies Travel-Study Award, 1974; University of Denver Faculty Research Grant, 1975. Memberships: American Oriental Society; Friends of the Library of the University of Pennsylvania; Societas Linguistica Euro Paea; Bhandarkar Oriental Research Institute, Dravidian Linguistics Association. Address: 144-30 78th Road, Apt 1H, Flushing, New York 11367-3572, USA.

**LEVY Alain M,** b. 19 December 1946, France. Record Company Executive. Education: Ecole des Mines, France; MBA, University of Pennsylvania. Appointments: With CBS, Assistant to the President, CBS International, New York, 1972, Vice-President, Marketing for Europe, Paris, 1973, Vice-President, Creative Operations for Europe and Manager, CBS Italy, 1978; Managing Director, CBS Disques, France, 1979; Chief Executive Officer, PolyGram, 1984; Executive Vice-President, PolyGram Group, France and Federal Republic of Germany, 1988; Manager, US Operations PolyGram Group, 1990-; President, Chief Executive Officer, Member, Board of Management, PolyGram USA, 1991-; Member, Group Management Committee, Philips Electronics, 1991-; Majority Shareholder, PolyGram USA, 1991-98; Chair, Board EMI Group plc, 2001-; Chair and Chief Executive Officer, EMI Recorded Music, 2001-. Address: EMI Group plc, 4 Tenterden Street, Hanover Square, London W1A 2AY, England.

**LEVY, His Honour Judge Dennis Martyn,** b. 20 February 1936, Liverpool, England. Queen's Counsel. m. Rachel Jonah, 1 son, 1 daughter. Education: BA, 1960, MA, 1963, Gonville and Caius College, Cambridge. Appointments: Called to the Bar, Gray's Inn, 1960, Hong Kong, 1985, Turks and Caicos Islands, 1987; Granada Group, 1960-63; Time Products Ltd, 1963-67; In practice at the Bar, 1967-91; Queen's Counsel, 1982; Recorder, 1989-91; Circuit Judge, 1991-; Member: Employment Appeals Tribunal, 1994-, Lands Tribunal, 1998; Trustee of Fair Trials Abroad. Address: c/o Gonville and Caius College, Cambridge, CB2 1TA, England.

**LEVY John Court (Jack),** b. 16 February 1926, London, England. Engineer; Consultant; Managing Director. m. Sheila F Krisman, 2 sons, 1 daughter. Education: BSc, Engineering, Imperial College of Science and Technology, London, England, 1943-46; MS, University of Illinois, USA, 1953-54; PhD, University of London, 1961. Appointments: Stress Analyst, Boulton Paul Aircraft, 1946-48; Assistant to Chief Engineer, Fullers Ltd, 1948-52; Lecturer, Senior Lecturer, Reader, 1952-66, Head (Professor) of Mechanical and Manufacturing Engineering, 1966-83, City University, London; Director, Engineering Profession at Engineering Council, 1983-90; Consulting Engineer, 1990-97; Consultant to Engineering Council, 1997-; Managing Director, Levytator Ltd, 2000-. Publications: Most recent publications include: UK

Manufacturing – Facing International Challenge, 1994; Co-author, Sustaining Recovery, 1995; The University Education and Industrial Training of Manufacturing Engineers for the Global Market, 1996; UK Developments in Engineering Education, Including the Matching Section, 1998; Keynote address at international conference, The Impact of Globalization on Engineering Education and Practice, Balaton, Hungary, 1999. Honours: OBE, 1984; Member, Board of Governors, Middlesex University, 1990-2003; Freeman of City of London, 1991; Honorary Doctorates, City University, London, University of Portsmouth, Leeds Metropolitan University. Memberships: Fellow, Royal Academy of Engineering; Fellow, Institution of Mechanical Engineers; Fellow, Royal Aeronautical Society; Fellow, City and Guilds of London Institute; Fellow, Royal Society of Arts; Fellow, Institution of Engineers of Ireland. Address: 18 Woodberry Way, Finchley, London N12 0HG, England. E-mail: jack.levy1@btopenworld.com

**LEVY, Baron of Mill Hill, Michael Abraham Levy,** b. 11 July 1944, London, England. Consultant. m. Gilda Altbach, 1 son, 1 daughter. Education: Hackney Downs Grammar School (formerly the Grocers Company School); Qualified as Chartered Accountant. Appointments: Accountancy practice, 1966-73; Built up MAGNET, worldwide record and music publishing group of companies (sold to Warner Brothers) (now part of Time Warner), 1973-88; Built up and sold a second successful company in the music and entertainment business, 1992-97; Consultant to various international companies, 1998-. Honours: B'nai B'rith First Lodge Award, 1994; Elevated to the Peerage as Baron Levy of Mill Hill, 1997; Friends of the Hebrew University of Jerusalem Scopus Award, 1998; Honorary Doctorate, Middlesex University, 1999; Israel Policy Forum (USA) Special Recognition Award, 2003. Memberships: Vice Chairman, Central Council for Jewish Social Services, 1994-; Chairman, Chief Rabbinate Awards for Excellence, 1992-; Chairman, Foundation for Education, 1993-; Patron, British Music Industry Awards, 1995-; Member, World Commission on Israel-Diaspora Relations, 1995-; Chairman, Jewish Care Community Foundation, 1995-; Member, Advisory Council to the Foreign Policy Centre, 1997-; Patron, Prostate Cancer Charitable Trust, 1997-; Member, International Board of Governors, Peres Center for Peace, 1997-; Member, NCVO Advisory Committee, 1998-; Patron, Friends of Israel Educational Trust, 1998-; President, Community Service Volunteers, 1998-; Trustee, Holocaust Educational Trust, 1998-; President, Jewish Care, 1998-; Member, Community Legal Service Champions Panel, 1999-; Chairman, Board of Trustees, New Policy Network Foundation, 2000-; Patron, Save A Child's Heart Foundation, 2000-; Member, Honorary Committee of the Israel Britain and the Commonwealth Association, 2000-; Honorary President, UJIA, 2000-; President, JFS School, 2001-; Patron, Simon Marks Jewish Primary School Trust, 2002-; Honorary Patron, Cambridge University Jewish Society, 2002-; Former positions: Founder, Former Chairman, British Music Industry Awards Committee; Vice-Chairman, British Phonograph Industry Ltd, 1984-87; Vice-Chairman, Phonographic Performance Ltd, 1979-84; Honorary Vice-president, UJIA, 1994-2000; Chairman, Jewish Care, 1992-97; National Campaign Chairman, JIA, 1982-85; Member, Keren Hayesod World Board of Governors, 1991-95; Member, World Board of Governors of the Jewish Agency, representing Great Britain, 1990-95; World Chairman, Youth Aliyah Committee, Jewish Agency Board of Governors, 1991-95; Governor, JFS School, 1990-95; Executive Committee Member, Chai-Lifeline, 2001-2002. Address: House of Lords, Westminster, London SW1, England.

**LEVY Suzy Hug,** b. 2 June 1944, Istanbul, Turkey. Plastic Arts; Sculptor; Installation, Performance, Video Artist. m.

Henry Levy, 1 son, 1 daughter. Education: BA, Robert College, American College for Girls. Career: Artist and Sculptor; Numerous national and international exhibitions include most recently: Solo exhibitions: Newspapers, APEL Gallery, Istanbul and Emlak Bank Gallery, Ankara, Turkey, 1999; A Celebration, installation, video, performance, Milli Reasurans Art Gallery, Istanbul, Turkey, 2000; Fragile Images, installation, photography, performance, video, Iş Sanat Gallery, Istanbul, 2001; Arcadia, installation, performance, video, Milli Reasurans Art Gallery, Istanbul, 2001; INAX Gallery, Tokyo, Japan, 2001; To be a woman, G-art Gallery, Istanbul, 2005; Selected international group exhibitions: Designed Landscape Forum, San Francisco Museum of Modern Art, USA, 1996; Global Fine Arts Gallery, JCCNV, Pilgrims Gallery, DFI Gallery, Washington DC, USA; Documenta, Detroit Museum of Modern Art, USA, 2001; As You See Me But I Am Not, Frauen Museum, Bonn and Communale Gallerie, Berlin, Germany, 2001; Tunis Biennial, Tunis, 2002; Between Two Quays, MAAS Gallery, Rotterdam, Holland, 2002; Nazim Hikmet Commemoration Day, Nakano, Japan, 2002; Comparisons, Tokyo and Kyoto University, Japan, 2003; Gunther Verheugen's Choice, Contemporary Painting and Sculpture from Turkey, European Union Building, Brussels, Belgium, 2003; Dialogues Plastiques, Hotel de Ville Gallery, Brussels, Belgium, 2004; Contemporary Painting and Sculpture from Turkey, Lyngby Cultural Centre, Denmark and Melina Mercouri Cultural Centre, Athens, Greece, 2004; Finalists Show, London Jewish Museum of Art, Ben Uri Gallery and Tram Studios, London, England, 2004; Installed the Flying Carpets exhibit at Dolmabahçe Cultural Centre, Istanbul, 2000; Curator, Auschwitz exhibit, 2001, Anne Frank: A History for Today exhibit, 2002, Terezin Children's drawings exhibit, 2004, Schneidertempel Cultural Centre, Istanbul; Designed the Holocaust Menorah, 2002; Installed the Kuzgun Acar Retrospective exhibit, Kibele Art Gallery, Istanbul, 2004. Honours: Contemporary Artist of the Year Award, Painting and Sculpture Museum Association, Istanbul, 1991; Il Sharjah Biennial Award, United Arab Emirates, 1997; Artist of the Year on Sculpture, Ankara Arts Council, 1998, 1999, 2000; Tunis Biennial Award, 2002; International Jewish Artist of the Year Award in Sculpture, London Jewish Museum of Art, Ben Uri Gallery, 2004. Memberships: Founder, Istanbul Modern Art Museum Foundation; Founder, Schneidertempel Cultural Centre; Istanbul Philharmonic Orchestra Association; PCD-UNESCO Plastic Arts Association; SANART Art and Cultural Organisation. Address: Karakütük Cad. 52, Sariyer, Istanbul, Turkey. E-mail: suzy@levi.com.tr

**LEW Julian D M,** b. 3 February 1948, South Africa. Lawyer; Queen's Counsel. m. Margot Gillian Perk, 2 daughters. Education: LLB honours, University of London, 1969; Doctorat special en droit international, Catholic University of Louvain, Belgium, 1977; Fellow, Chartered Institute of Arbitrators. Appointments: Called to Bar in England, 1970; Admitted Solicitor, 1981; New York State Bar, 1985; Barrister, Arbitrator, 20 Essex Street, London; Visiting Professor, Head of School of International Arbitration, Centre for Commercial Law Studies, Queen Mary, University of London; Partner, Herbert Smith, 1995-2005. Publications: Numerous books and articles on international commercial arbitration and international trade including: Applicable Law in International Commercial Arbitration, Oceana, 1978; Comparative International Commercial Arbitration, co-author, Kluwer, 2003. Memberships: General Council of the Bar of England and Wales; International Bar Association; American Bar Association; Swiss Arbitration Association; American Arbitration Association; French Committee for Arbitration; British Institute of International and Comparative Law; Chairman, Committee on arbitration practice guidelines of Chartered Institute of Arbitrators, 1996-

2001; Chairman, Committee on Intellectual Property Disputes and Arbitration, International Chamber of Commerce, 1995-99; Member, Council of the ICC Institute of World Business Law; Director and Member of Court, London Court of International Arbitration. Address: 20 Essex Street, London WC2R 3AL, England. E-mail: jlew@20essexst.com

**LEWCOCK Ronald Bentley,** b. 27 September 1929, Brisbane, Australia. Architect; Professor. m. Barbara Sansoni. Education: Student, University of Queensland, 1947-49; BArch, Cape Town University, South Africa, 1951; PhD, University of Cape Town, South Africa, 1961; MA, Cambridge University, England,1970. Appointments include: Lecturer, 1952-57, Senior Lecturer, 1958-69, University of Natal, South Africa; Whitehead Research Fellow, Clare Hall, University of Cambridge, 1970-72, Official Fellow, 1976-84; Research Officer, Middle East Centre, Cambridge University, 1973-80; Lecturer, Architectural Associates School, London, 1971-82; Aga Khan Professor of Architecture for Islamic Culture, Director of Program in Architecture for Islamic Societies, MIT, Cambridge, Massachusetts, 1984-91; Chairman, Aga Khan Program for Islamic Architecture, MIT and Harvard University, 1985-97; Professor of Architecture, Georgia Institute of Technology, Atlanta, 1991-; Consultant to: UNESCO, 1978-98, Habitat, World Bank, British Council, 1978-83. Publications: Author: Early 19th Century Architecture in South Africa, 1963; Traditional Architecture in Kuwait and the Northern Gulf, 1978, 2nd edition, 1981; Wadi Hadramaut and the Walled City of Shibam, 1986, internet edition, 2994; The Old World City of San'a, 1986, internet edition, 2004; Architecture of an Island – Sri Lanka, 1998, 2001; San'a an Arabian Islamic City (editor with R B Serjeant), 1983; Contributor of articles to professional journals; Architecture in the Islamic World, 1976; New Grove Dictionary of Music and Musicians, 1980, 1997. Honours: University of Cape Town Festival Prize, 1951; Eliza Howard Visiting Fellowship to Columbia University, 1963; Honorary Doctorate in Architecture, University of Natal, 1999; Keynote speaker at many international conferences, 1958-2005. Memberships: Royal Institute of British Architects; Council, Institute of History and Archaeology of East Africa, 1976-86; Middle East Centre, Cambridge, 1981-88; British School of Archaeology in Jerusalem, London, 1981-98; Technical Co-ordinator, International Campaign for the Conservation of Sana'a, Shibam and Wadi Hadramaut, Yemen, 19878-93; UNRSCO/UNDP Campaign for Conservation of Monuments and Cities in Uzbekistan, 1994-97; Steering Committee Member, Aga Khan Award, 1990-93, Aga Khan Trust for Culture, Geneva, 1993-98. Address: Clare Hall, Cambridge CB3 9AL, England. E-mail: ron.lewcock@arch.gatech.edu

**LEWIN Christopher George,** b. 15 December 1940, Poole, Dorset. Actuary. m. Robin Lynn, 2 sons. Education: Cooper's Company School, London, 1951-55; Actuaries Tuition Course, Institute of Actuaries 1956-62. Appointments: Actuarial Assistant, Equity & Law Life, 1956-63; Actuarial Assistant, London Transport, 1963-67; Actuarial Assistant, 1967-70, Controller, Corporate Pensions, 1970-80, Co-ordinator, Private Capital, 1980-89, British Rail; Pensions Director, Associated Newspapers, 1989-92; Head of Group Pensions, Guinness PLC, 1992-98; Head of UK Pensions, Unilever PLC, 1998-2003; Pensions Manager, EDF Energy plc, 2005; Part-time appointments: Member of Investment Committee, The Pensions Trust, 2004-; Chairman of Training Standards Initiative, National Association of Pension Funds, 2004-; Chairman of Trustees, Marconi Pension Fund, 2004-05. Publications: Book: Pensions and Insurance Before 1800 - A Social History, 2003; Article: The Philosophers' Game (Games and Puzzles Magazine), 1973; Various papers in technical journals on investment appraisal, manpower planning, funding of pension schemes and capital projects. Honours: Sir Joseph Burn Prize, Institute of Actuaries, 1962; Finlaison Medal, Institute of Actuaries, 1999; Pensions Manager of the Year, Professional Pensions Magazine, 2003. Memberships: Fellow Institute of Actuaries, 1962; Fellow, Pensions Management Institute, 1976; Governor, Pensions Policy Institute; Governor, National Institute for Economic and Social Research; Chairman of joint working party with the Actuarial Profession and the Institution of Civil Engineers to develop a successful risk methodology for projects known as RAMP, 1992-; Member of Steering Group for the Stratrisk Initiative, 2002-. Address: Thirlestane House, Broughton, Biggar ML12 6HQ, Scotland.

**LEWIN Michael Zinn,** b. 21 July 1942, Cambridge, Massachusetts, USA. Writer; Dramatist. 1 son, 1 daughter. Education: AB, Harvard University, 1964; Churchill College, Cambridge, England. Appointment: Co-Editor, Crime Writers Association Annual Anthology, 1992-94. Publications: Author of 18 novels including: Called by a Panther, 1991; Underdog, 1993; Family Business, 1995; Rover's Tales, 1998; Cutting Loose, 1999; Family Planning, 1999; Eye opener, 2004. Other: Various radio plays, stage plays and short stories Contributions to: Indianapolis for New York Times Sophisticated Traveller. Honours: Maltese Falcon Society Best Novel, 1987; Raymond Chandler Society of Germany Best Novel, 1992; Mystery Masters Award, 1994. Memberships: Detection Club; Crime Writers Association; Private Eye Writers Association; Authors Guild. Address: Garden Flat, 15 Bladud Buildings, Bath BA1 5LS, England.

**LEWIN Russell Mark Ellerker,** b. 21 March 1958, Woolwich, England. Solicitor. 2 sons. Education: BA, Jurisprudence, 1980, MA, Jurisprudence, 1990, St John's College, Oxford. Appointments: Articled Clerk, 1981-83, Solicitor, 1983-, Partner, 1990, Recruitment Partner, 1994-98, European Regional Council, 1997-, Policy Committee, 1998-, Managing Partner, 1998, Baker & McKenzie, London. Publications: Various articles on topics of Intellectual Property and EU Competition Law. Memberships: City of London Solicitors' Guild; Academy for Chief Executives; Liberal Democrats. Address: c/o Baker & McKenzie, 100 New Bridge Street, London EC4V 6JA, England. E-mail: russell.lewin@bakernet.com

**LEWIS Adrian Mark,** b. 25 June 1951, Swansea, Wales. University Lecturer. m. Valerie Josephine Barber. Publication: BA, Modern History, Oxford University, 1973; MA, History of Art, University of London, 1975; PhD, History of Art, University of Manchester, 1996. Appointments: Lecturer, Bristol Polytechnic, 1975-76; Education Officer, Walker Art Gallery, Liverpool, 1970-79; Lecturer, 1979, MA Course Leader, 2000-2003, History of Art, De Montfort University Leicester; Visiting Associate Professor, Creighton University, Omaha, USA, 1999; External Assessor, Bristol Polytechnic, 1988-92. Publications: Books: The Last Days of Hilton, 1996; Roger Hilton, 2003; Exhibition catalogue: Roger Hilton: The Early Years, 1984; 76 reviews and articles in Art History; Art Monthly; Art Book; Artscribe; Burlington Magazine; Connoisseur; Sculpture Journal. Address: History of Art and Material Culture, De Montfort University, The Gateway, Leicester LE1 9BH, England. E-mail: alewis@dmu.ac.uk

**LEWIS Bernard Walter,** b. 24 July 1917, Lincoln, England. Flour Miller. m. Joyce Ilston Storey, 1943, 1 son, 1 daughter. Education: University of Manchester. Appointments: Joined King's Own Regiment, served in Middle East, 1940-46; RASC, 1941; Captain, 1942; Major, 1943; Chairman and Managing Director, Green's Flour Mills Ltd, 1955-90; General Tax

Commissioner, 1957-93; Chairman, Dengie and Maldon Essex Bench, 1970-88; Chairman, Maldon Harbour Commissioners, 1978-2001; Chairman, Flour Advisory Bureau, 1979-88; President, National Association of British and Irish Millers, 1985-86; Chairman, Edward Baker Holdings Ltd, 1983-89; Retired, 1989. Honour: CBE, 1973. Memberships: Financial Board, Conservative Party, 1966-75; Chairman, Board of Governors, Plume School, 1968-83; Liveryman, Worshipful Company of Bakers, 1973. Address: Roughlees, 68 Highlands Drive, Maldon, Essex CM9 6HY, England.

**LEWIS Carl,** b. 1 July 1961, Birmingham, Alabama, USA. American Athlete. Education: University of Houston. Appointments: Bronze Medal, Long Jump, Pan-American Games, 1979; Won World Cup Competition, 1981; First World Championships (with 8.55 metres); Achieved World Record 8.79 metre jump, 1983; Gold Medals, Olympic Games, 100 metres, 200 metres, Long Jump, 4x100m, 1984; 65 Consecutive wins in Long Jump, 1985; Silver Medal, 200 metres; Gold Medal, 100 metres, Olympic Games, 1988; Jumped 8.64 metres, New York, 1991; World Record, 100 metres 9.86 seconds, 1991; Gold Medal, Long Jump, Olympic Games, 1992; Gold Medal for long jump (27ft. 10.75 in), Olympic Games, 1996; Retired, 1997; Attached to Trialtir, 1997. Honours: Track and Field News Athlete of the Decade, 1980-89; Athlete of the Century, IAAF, 1999. Address: c/o Carl Lewis International Fan Club, P O Box 57-1990, Houston, TX 77257-1990, USA.

**LEWIS Conrad Strafford,** b. 15 July 1922, Woodford, Essex, England. Sculptor; Printmaker. m. Marjory Rae, 2 sons, 3 daughters. Education: Ealing School of Art; Hornsey School of Art. Career: WWII Service, Royal Corps of Signals, India, Burma, 1941-46; Lecturer, Modelling, Woodcarving, Chester School of Art; Lecturer in Charge, Art History and Drawing, West Cheshire College; Early retirement to continue own work, 1982-; Various commissions; Freelance Lecturer, St Albans and Chester; Work in several exhibitions including: Liverpool; North Wales, Cardiff, Chester, St Albans, Amsterdam, New York, Manchester. Publications: Works mentioned in several publications. Honours: Epsom College: Rugby 1st XV, Cricket 1st XI; National Diploma Design, 1948; Art Teachers Diploma, 1950; Elected Associate of Royal Cambrian Academy, 1960. Memberships: RCA; National Society for Art Education. Address: Appletrees, Fish Street, Redbourn, Herts AL3 7LP, England.

**LEWIS David K(ellogg),** b. 28 September 1941, Oberlin, Ohio, USA. Professor of Philosophy; Writer. m. Stephanie Robinson, 5 September 1965. Education: BA, Swarthmore College, 1962; MA, 1964, PhD, 1967, Harvard University. Appointments: Assistant Professor of Philosophy, University of California, Los Angeles, 1966-70; Faculty, 1970-73, Professor of Philosophy, 1973-, Princeton University; Fulbright Lecturer, Australia, 1971; John Locke Lecturer, Oxford University, 1984; Kant Lecturer, Stanford University, 1988. Publications: Convention: A Philosophical Study, 1969; Counterfactuals, 1973; Philosophical Papers, 2 volumes, 1983, 1986; On the Plurality of Worlds, 1986; Parts of Classes, 1991; Papers in Philosophical Logic, 1998; Papers in Metaphysics and Epistemology, 1999; Papers in Ethics and Social Philosophy, 2000. Honours: Matchette Prize for Philosophical Writing, 1972; Fulbright Research Fellow, New Zealand, 1976; Santayana Fellow, Harvard University, 1988; Doctor of Letters, University of Melbourne, 1995; Doctor of the University, University of York, 1999. Memberships: American Association of University Professors; Australian Academy of the Humanities; British Academy; National Association of Scholars; American Academy of Arts and Sciences. Address: c/o Department of Philosophy, Princeton University, Princeton, NJ 08544, USA.

**LEWIS Denise,** b. 27 August 1972, West Bromwich, England. Athlete. Career: Specialises in heptathlon; Commonwealth Heptathlon Record Holder (6,736 points), 1977; Fifth European Junior Championships, 1991; Gold Medal, Commonwealth Games, 1994; Gold Medal, European Cup, 1995; Bronze Medal, Olympic Games, 1996; Silver Medal, World Championships, 1997; Gold Medal, European Championships, 1998; Gold Medal, Commonwealth Championships, 1998; Silver Medal World Championship, 1999; New Commonwealth Record (6,831 points), 2000; Gold Medal, Olympic Games, 2000. Publications: Denise Lewis: Faster, Higher, Stronger, autobiography, 2001. Honours: British Athletics Writers Female Athlete of the Year, 1998, 2000; Sports Writers Association Sportswoman of the Year, 2000. Address: c/o MTC (UK) Ltd, 20 York Street, London, W1U 6PU, England. E-mail: info.mtc-uk.com

**LEWIS Edward B,** b. 20 May 1918, Wilkes-Barre, USA. Professor of Biology. m. Pamela Harrah, 1946, 3 sons, 1 deceased. Education: Minnesota University; California Institute of Technology; PhD. Appointments: Instructor, 1946-48, Assistant Professor, 1948-49, Associate Professor, 1949-56, Professor, 1956-88, Thomas Hunt Morgan Professor of Biology Emeritus, 1988-; Rockefeller Foundation Fellow, Cambridge University, England, 1947-48; Guest Professor, Institute of Genetics, Copenhagen University, Denmark, 1975-76. Honours: Honorary PhD, Umeå University, Sweden, 1981; Thomas Hunt Morgan Medal, Gairdner Foundation International Award, 1987; Co-recipient, Wolf Prize for Medicine, 1989; Rosentiel Medical Research Award, 1990; National Medal of Science, USA, 1990; Co-recipient, Albert Lasker Basic Medical Research Award, 1991; Louisa Gross Horwitz Prize, 1992; Honorary DSc, Minnesota University, 1993; Co-recipient, Nobel Prize for Medicine, 1995. Memberships: Genetics Society of America, Secretary, 1962-64, Vice-President, 1966-67, President, 1967; National Academy of Sciences; American Academy of Arts and Sciences; American Philosophical Society; Foreign Member, Royal Society, 1989; Honorary Member, Genetical Society of Great Britain, 1990. Address: 805 Winthrop Road, San Marino, CA 91108, USA.

**LEWIS Esyr ap Gwilym,** b. 11 January 1926, Clydach Vale, Glamorgan, Wales. Retired Judge. m. Elizabeth Hoffmann, 4 daughters. Education: Exhibitioner and Foundation Scholar, Trinity Hall, Cambridge, 1947-50. Appointments: Army Intelligence Corps, 1944-47; Called to Bar at Gray's Inn, 1951; Law Superviser, Trinity Hall, Cambridge, 1951-57; Queens Counsel, 1971; Recorder, Crown Court, 1972-84; Deputy High Court Judge, 1978-84; Official Referee, London Official Referees Courts, 1984-98, Senior Official Referee, 1994-98; Leader, Welsh Circuit, 1978-82; Member, Criminal Injuries Compensation Board, 1977-84. Publications: Articles in legal publications. Honour: Queen's Counsel. Memberships: Fellow, Chartered Institute of Arbitrators; Vice-President, Academy of Experts; Honorary Fellow, Society of Advanced Legal Studies; Bencher of Gray's Inn, 1978-, Treasurer, 1997. Address: 2 South Square, Gray's Inn, London WC1R 5HT, England.

**LEWIS Geoffrey David,** b. 13 April 1933, Brighton, East Sussex, England. Museum Consultant. m. Frances May Wilderspin, 3 daughters. Education: MA, University of Liverpool; Diploma of the Museums Association. Appointments include: Museum Assistant, 1950-58, Assistant Curator, 1958-60, Worthing Museum and Art Gallery; Deputy Director and Keeper of Antiquities, Sheffield City Museum, 1960-65; Honorary Lecturer in British Prehistory, University of Sheffield,

1965-72; Director, Sheffield City Museums, 1966-72; Director, Liverpool City Museums, 1974-77; Director, Merseyside County Museums, 1974-77; Director of Museum Studies, University of Leicester, 1977-89; Museum Consultant, 1989-; President, 1983-89, Chair, Ethics Committee, 1996-, International Council of Museums; Chair of Governors, Wolvey School, 1998-2003; President, Museums Association, 1980-81. Publications: The South Yorkshire Glass Industry, 1964; Prehistoric and Roman Times in the Sheffield Area (co-author), 1968; For instruction and recreation: a centenary history of the Museums Association, 1989; Manual of Curatorship: A guide to museum practice (co-editor), 1984, 2nd edition, 1992; Contributor to Encyclopaedia Britannica, 1984, 1998, Britannica On-line, 2004; Contributor to many books and articles relating to archaeology, ethics and museums. Honours: Honorary Fellow, Museums Association, 1989; Honorary Member, International Council of Museums, 2004. Memberships: Diploma and Associate, 1958, Fellow, 1966, Museums Association; Fellow, Society of Antiquaries of London, 1969. Address: 4 Orchard Close, Wolvey, Hinckley LE 10 3LR, England. E-mail: geoffrey_lewis@btinternet.com

**LEWIS, Baron of Newnham in the County of Cambridgeshire, Jack Lewis** b. 13 February 1928, Barrow, England. Professor of Chemistry. m. Elfreida M Lamb, 1951, 1 son, 1 daughter. Education: Universities of London and Nottingham; PhD. Appointments: Lecturer, University of Sheffield, 1954-56; Lecturer, Imperial College, London, 1956-57; Lecturer-Reader, 1957-61, Professor of Chemistry, 1967-70, University College, London; Professor of Chemistry, University of Manchester, 1961-67; Professor of Chemistry, University of Cambridge, 1970-95; Fellow, Sidney Sussex College, Cambridge, 1970-77; Warden, Robinson College, Cambridge, 1975-. Publications: Papers in scientific journals. Honours include: Honorary Fellow, Sidney Sussex College, Cambridge; Honorary Fellow, Royal Society of Chemistry; 21 honorary degrees; Davy Medal, Royal Society, 1985; Chevalier, Ordre des Palmes Académiques; Commander Cross of the Order of Merit, Poland. Memberships: Fellow, Royal Society; Foreign Associate, National Academy of Sciences, USA; Foreign Member, American Philosophical Society, 1994; Foreign Member, Accademia Nazionale dei Lincei, 1995; Numerous committees. Address: Robinson College, Grange Road, Cambridge CB3 9AN, England.

**LEWIS Jeremy Morley,** b. 15 March 1942, Salisbury, Wiltshire, England. Writer. m. Petra Lewis, 28 July 1968, 2 daughters. Education: BA, Trinity College, Dublin, 1965; MA, Sussex University, 1967. Appointments: Editor, Andre Deutsch Ltd, 1969-70, Oxford University Press, 1977-79; Literary Agent, A P Watt Ltd, 1970-76; Director, Chatto and Windus, 1979-89; Deputy Editor, London Magazine, 1991-94; Editorial Consultant, Peters, Fraser and Dunlop Group Ltd; Commissioning Editor, The Oldie, 1997-. Publications: Playing for Time, 1987; Chatto Book of Office Life, 1992; Kindred Spirits, 1995; Cyril Connolly: A Life, 1997; Tobias Smollett, 2003. Memberships: Royal Society of Literature Fellow; R S Surtees Society, Secretary. Address: c/o Gillon Aitken, Aitken and Stone Ltd, London, England. E-mail: jeremy.lewis5@btinternet.com

**LEWIS Jerry (Joseph Levitch),** b. 16 March 1926, Newark, New Jersey, USA. Comedian; Writer; Director; Producer; Actor. m. (1) Patti Palmer, 1944, divorced, 5 sons, (2) SanDee Pitnick, 1983, 1 daughter. Career: Comedian, night-clubs, then with Dean Martin, 500 Club, Atlantic City, New Jersey, 1946; Professor of Cinema, University of Southern California; Film debut with Dean Martin in My Friend Irma, 1949; Other films, many also as producer and director, include My Friend Irma Goes West, 1950, That's My Boy, 1951, The Caddy, 1952,

Sailor Beware, 1952, Jumping Jacks, 1953,; The Stooge, 1953, Scared Stiff, 1953, Living It Up, 1954, Three Ring Circus, 1954, You're Never Too Young, 1955, Partners, 1956, Hollywood or Bust, 1956, The Delicate Delinquent, 1957, The Sad Sack, 1958, Rock a Bye Baby, 1958, The Geisha Boy, 1958, Visit to a Small Planet, 1959, The Bellboy, 1960, Cinderfella, 1960, It's Only Money, 1961, The Errand Boy, 1962, The Patsy, 1964, The Disorderly Orderly, 1964, The Family Jewels, 1965, Boeing-Boeing, 1965, Three On a Couch, 1965, Way Way Out, 1966, The Big Mouth, 1967, Don't Raise the Bridge, Lower the River, 1968, One More Time, 1969, Hook, Line and Sinker, 1969, Which way to the Front?, 1970, The Day the Clown Cried, 1972, Hardly Working, 1979, King of Comedy, 1981, Slapstick of Another Kind, 1982, Smörgåsbord, 1983, How Did You Get In?, 1985, Mr Saturday Night, 1992, Funny Bones, 1995; Appeared in play, Damn Yankees, 1995, on tour, 1995-97; Television appearances including Startime, The Ed Sullivan Show and the Jazz Singer. Publications: The Total Film-Maker, 1971; Jerry Lewis in Person, 1982. Address: Jerry Lewis Films Inc, 3160 W Sahara Avenue, C-16, Las Vegas, NV 89102, USA. Website: www.jerrylewiscomedy.com

**LEWIS Jerry Lee,** b. 29 September 1935, Ferriday, Louisiana, USA. Singer; Musician (piano); Entertainer. m. 6 times. Career: Appeared on Louisiana Hayride, 1954; Film appearances: Jamboree, 1957; High School Confidential, 1958; Be My Guest, 1965; Concerts include: National Jazz & Blues Festival, 1968; Rock'n'Revival Concert, Toronto, 1969; First appearance, Grand Ole Opry, 1973; Rock'n'Roll Festival, Wembley, 1974; Numerous appearances with own Greatest Show On Earth; Subject of biographical film, Great Balls Of Fire, 1989. Recordings: Hit singles include: Whole Lotta Shakin' Goin' On', 1957; Great Balls Of Fire, 1958; Breathless, 1958; High School Confidential, 1958; What I'd Say, 1961; Good Golly Miss Molly, 1963; To Make Love Sweeter For You, 1969; There Must Be More To Love Than This, 1970; Would You Take Another Chance On Me?, 1971; Me And Bobby Gee, 1972; Chantilly Lace, 1972. Albums include: Jerry Lee Lewis, 1957; Jerry Lee's Greatest, 1961; Live At The Star Club, 1965; The Greatest Live Show On Earth, 1965; The Return Of Rock, 1965; Whole Lotta Shakin' Goin' On, 1965; Country Songs For City Folks, 1965; By Request - More Greatest Live Show On Earth, 1967; Breathless, 1967; Together, with Linda Gail Lewis, 1970; Rockin' Rhythm And Blues, 1971; Sunday Down South, with Johnny Cash, 1972; The Session, with Peter Frampton, Rory Gallagher, 1973; Jerry Lee Lewis, 1979; When Two Worlds Collide, 1980; My Fingers Do The Talking, 1983; I Am What I Am, 1984; Keep Your Hands Off It, 1987; Don't Drop It, 1988; Great Balls Of Fire! (film soundtrack), 1989; Rocket, 1990; Young Blood, 1995; Many compilations; Contributor, film soundtracks: Roadie, 1980; Dick Tracy, 1990. Honours include: Inducted into Rock'n'Roll Hall Of Fame, 1986; Star on Hollywood Walk Of Fame, 1989. Address: Warner Bros Records, 75 Rockefeller Plaza, New York, NY 10019, USA.

**LEWIS Juliette,** b. 21 June 1973, Fernando Valley, California. Film Actress. Appointments: TV Appearances include: Homefires (mini-series); I Married Dora, 1988; Too Young to Die (movie), 1989; A Family for Joe, 1990; Films include: My Stepmother is an Alien, 1988; Meet the Hollowheads, 1989; National Lampoons Christmas Vacation, 1989; Cape Fear, 1991; Crooked Hearts, 1991; Husbands and Wives, 1992; Kalifornia, 1993; One Hot Summer, That Night, 1993; What's Eating Gilbert Grape, 1993; Romeo is Bleeding, 1994; Natural Born Killers, 1994; Mixed Nuts, 1994; The Basketball Diaries, 1995; Strange Days, 1995; From Dusk Till Dawn, 1996; The Evening Star, 1996; The Audition, Full Tilt Boogie, 1997; The Other Sister, 1999; The 4th Floor, 1999; Way of the Gun, 2000; My

Louisiana Sky, 2001. Address: c/o Willia, Morris Agency, 151 El Camino Boulevard, Beverley Hills, CA 80212, USA.

**LEWIS Lennox,** b. 2 September 1965, Heavyweight Boxer. Career: Defeated Jean Chanet to win European Heavyweight Title, Crystal Palace, 1990; Defeated Gary Mason to win British Heavyweight Title, Wembley, 1991; Commonwealth Heavyweight; WBC Heavyweight, 1992; WBC World Champion, 1993-94, 1997-; Defended WBC Title, and challenged for World Boxing Association (WBA) and International Boxing Federation (IBF) Titles against Evander Holyfield, 1999, Bout declared a draw; Undisputed World Heavyweight Champion, 1999-2001 (lost WBC and IBF titles when defeated by Hasim Rahman, 2001); Defeated Frank Bruno, 1993; Founder, Lennox Lewis College, Hackney, London, 1994; regained title of world heavyweight champion from Hashim Rahman, November 2001; retained title of undisputed world heavyweight champion after beating Mike Tyson, June 2002-; 40 professional wins (20 losses, 1 draw, 31 knock-outs); Film appearance in Ocean's Eleven, 2002. Publications: Lennox Lewis, autobiography, 1993; Lennox, 2002. Honour: Honorary Doctorate, University of London, 1999. Address: Office of Lennox Lewis, Suite 206, Gainsborough House, 81 Oxford Street, London, W1D 2EU, England. E-mail: rose@lennoxlewis.com

**LEWIS Peter Tyndale,** b. 1929, London, England. Retail Businessman. m. Deborah Anne Collins, 1 son, 1 daughter. Education: Christ Church, Oxford, 1949-52. Appointments: 2nd Lieutenant, Coldstream Guards, 1948-49; Pilot Officer, RAFVR, 1951-52; Barrister, Middle Temple, 1955-59; Joined John Lewis Partnership, 1959; Director, John Lewis Department Stores, 1967-71; Chairman, John Lewis Partnership plc and John Lewis plc, 1972-93. Honours: Companion, Institute of Management; Fellow, Royal Society of Arts. Memberships: Executive Committee, Industrial Society, 1968-79; Executive Committee, Design Council, 1971-74; Chairman, Retail Distributors Association, 1971-72; Governor, Windlesham House School, 1979-95; Governor, NIESR, 1983-2000; Trustee, Bell Educational Trust, 1987-97; Governor, Queen's College, Harley Street, 1994-2000; Trustee, Southampton University Development Trust, 1994-2004. Address: 34 Victoria Road, London W8 5RG, England.

**LEWIS-FRANCIS Mark,** b. 4 September 1982, Birmingham, England. Athlete. 1 son. Career includes: World Youth 100m Champion, 1999; UK Under 20, 100m Champion, 1999; 100m Silver Medallist, European Junior Championships, 1999; UK Under 20, 100m Champion, 2000; 1st, 100m B Race, IAAF Grand Prix, London, 2000; 1st, 100m Loughborough, 2000; European Junior Record, World Junior 4 x 100m Champion, 2000; Championship Record, World Junior 100m Champion, 2000; Bronze Medallist, World Junior Record, 60m, World Indoor Championships, Lisbon, 2001; 2nd 60m, Glasgow Indoor Match, 2001; 1st, 100m, Tallahassee, 2001; 1st, DVL Junior Gala, Mannheim, 2001; 1st, 100m, European Cup Super League, 2001; 2nd, 100m, UK Championships, 2001; European Junior 100m Champion, European Junior 4 x 100m Champion, 2001; Semi-Finalist, 100m, IAAF World Championships, 2001; European Indoor 60m Silver Medallist, 2002; 1st 200m, 2nd, 100m, Tallahassee, 2002; 1st, 100m, Loughborough, 2002; 2nd, 100m, Commonwealth Games Trials; UK 100m Champion, 2002; 5th, 100m, IAAF Golden League, Brussels, 2002; 3rd, IAAF Grand Prix II, Reiti, 2002; UK 60m Indoor Champion, 2003; 4th, 60m, World Indoor Championships, Birmingham, 2003; 1st, 100m, IAAF Super Grand Prix, Ostrava, 2003; 1st, 100m, European Cup, 2003; 1st, 100m, IAAF Golden League, Oslo, 2003; 4th IAAF, Golden League, Paris, 2003; 2nd 100m, IAAF Super Grand Prix, Gateshead, 2003; 1st, 100m, Bedford,

2004; 3rd, 100m, IAAF Super Grand Prix, Gateshead, 2004; Olympic Games 4 x 100 m Champion, Athens, 2004; European Indoor Silver Medallist, 2005. Address: c/o PACE Sports Management, 6 The Causeway, Teddington, Middlesex TW11 0HE, England. E-mail: r.simms@pacesportsmanagement.com

**LEWIS-SMITH Anne Elizabeth,** b. 14 April 1925, London, England. Poet; Writer; Editor; Publisher. m. Peter Lewis-Smith, 17 May 1944, 1 son, 2 daughters. Appointments: Assistant Editor, 1967-83, Editor, Envoi Poetry Magazine, 1984-90; Editor, Aerostat, 1972-77; Editor, WWNT Bulletin, 1981-83; British Association of Friends of Museums Yearbook, 1984-91; Publisher, Traeth Publications, 1990-; Publisher, Envoi Poets Publications, 1990-; Balloonist, 1969-. Publications: The Beginning, 1964; Seventh Bridge, 1965; Flesh and Flowers (three impressions), 1967; Dandelion Flavour, 1971; Dinas Head, 1980; Places and Passions, 1986; In the Dawn, 1986; Circling Sound, 1996; Feathers Fancies and Feelings, 1999; Poetry in over 40 different poetry magazines world-wide and 16 anthologies translated into various languages, including Hebrew and Spanish; Regular Contributor to Newspapers and magazines. Honours: Swedish Ballooniana-Prizet for Services to Aviation; Tissandier Award for Services to Aviation, 1983; Debby Warley Award for Services to International Aviation; Dorothy Tutin Award for Services to Poetry. Memberships: PEN; Society of Women Writers and Journalists; Honorary member, Balloon Federation of America; Balloon Club of South Africa. Address: Pen Ffordd, Newport, Pembrokeshire, SA42 0QT, Wales.

**LEYCEGUI Beatriz,** b. 10 November 1964, Veracruz, Mexico. Lawyer. 2 sons, 1 daughter. Education: Master of International Affairs, Columbia University, New York City, USA, 1988-90; JD, Escuela Libre de Derccho, Mexico City, 1982-87. Appointments: Legal Assistant, Ministry of the Interior, Mexico City, 1984-88; Research Assistant, Columbia University, New York City; Legal Counsel, Ministry of Foreign Affairs, Mexico City, 1990; Director, Legal Analysis, Office in Charge of NAFTA negotiations, Ministry of Trade and Industrial Development, Mexico City, 1990-92; Professor and Researcher, ITAM, Mexico City, 1993-99; Partner, SAI Consultores, SC, 1999-. Publications: Books: Some Thoughts Regarding the Prevention, Administration and Resolution of Disputes under NAFTA Chapters 18 & 20, 1993; Trading Punches: Trade Remedy Law Disputes under NAFTA, US, 1995, Mexico, 1997; Natural Partners?: Five Years of the North American Free Trade Agreement (NAFTA), 2000; Articles: Prevention of Disputes under the Free Trade Agreement: Chapter XVIII Analysis, 1994; A Legal Analysis of Mexico's Antidumping and Countervailing Regulatory Framework, 1995; Eliminating Unfairness within North America Region: A Look at Antidumping, 1997; Agreement to disagree: Dispute Resolution under NAFTA, 2000; Trading Remedies to Remedy Trade: the NAFTA Experience, 2003-04; The Ten Major Problems with the Anti-dumping Instrument in Mexico, 2005. Honours: 1st Class Award, Escuela Libre de Derccho; Honorary Mention, Professional Exam, Ford Foundation, Columbia University and Bank of Mexico Scholarships. Memberships: Mexican Bar Law College, Mexican Council for Foreign Affairs; Institute of Latin American Studies; Advisory Board, Columbia University; Legal Studies Department, CIDE; Member, Advisory Board, International Business Law Masters Degree, Iberoamerican University. Address: Prolongación Reforma 600-103, Santa Fe Pena Blanca, Mexico DF 01210, Mexico City, Mexico. E-mail: blg@sai.com.mx Website: www.sai.com.mx

**LI Ching-Chung,** b. 30 March 1932, Changshu, China. Professor of Electrical Engineering and Computer Science. m. Hanna Wu Li, 2 sons. Education: BSEE, National Taiwan

University, 1954; MSEE, 1956, PhD, 1961, Northwestern University. Appointments: Professor, Electrical Engineering, University of Pittsburgh, 1967-; Professor, Computer Science, University of Pittsburgh, 1977-. Publications: Over 200 papers. Memberships: Fellow, IEEE; Biomedical Engineering Society; Pattern Recognition Society. Address: 2130 Garrick Drive, Pittsburgh, PA 15235-5033, USA.

**LI Hua,** b. 25 August 1960, Wuhan, People's Republic of China. Research Scientist; Division Manager. m. Dong-Ping Yuan, 1 daughter. Education: BSc, 1982, MSc, 1987, Wuhan University of Technology; PhD, National University of Singapore, 1999. Appointments: Managing Director, Wuhan University of Technology Press, 1990-94; Research Scholar, Senior Research Engineer, Institute of High performance Computing, National University of Singapore, 1994-2000; Postdoctoral Associate, University of Illinois Urbana-Champaign, USA, 2000-2001; Research Scientist, Division Manager, Institute of High Performance Computing, Singapore, 2001-. Publication: Rotating Shell Dynamics, 2005. Honour: NUS Research Scholarship for PhD Programme. Memberships: China Society for Vibration Engineering; China Society of Mechanics. Address: Blk 612 #09-302, Clementi West St 1, Singapore 120612. E-mail: lihua@ihpc.a-star.edu.sg

**LI Huaizhong,** b. 13 September 1965, China. Research Fellow. m. Aiying Cheng. 1 daughter. Education: B Eng, Tsinghua University, China, 1983-88; M Eng, Xi'an Jiaotong University, 1988-91; PhD, National University of Singapore, 1998-2002. Appointments: Engineer, Project Manager, Xi'an Hi Tech Industrial Development Zone, 1993-98; Software Engineer, GTech Far East Pte Ltd, 2001; Research Fellow, Senior Research Engineer. Singapore Institute of Manufacturing Technology, 2001-. Publications: Over 10 journal papers published in prestigious international journals; 1 book chapter; 15 conference papers/technical reports. Honours: Research Scholarship, National University of Singapore, 1998-2001. Membership: ASME. Address: SIMTech, 71 Nanyang Drive, Singapore 638075. E-mail: hzli@simtech.a-star.edu.sg

**LI Lingwei,** b. 1964. Badminton Player. Career: Participant in international championships; Won Women's Singles Title, 3rd World Badminton Championships, Copenhagen, 1982; Won Women's Singles and Women's Doubles, 5th ALBA World Cup, Jakarta, 1985; Won Women's Singles, World Badminton Grand Prix finals, Tokyo, 1985; Won Women's Singles at Dunhill China Open Badminton Championship, Nanjing, and Malaysian Badminton Open, Kuala Lumpur, 1987; Won Women's Singles at World Grand Prix, Hong Kong, China Badminton Open, and Danish Badminton Open, Odense, 1988; Won Women's Singles, All-England Badminton Championships, 1989; Winner, Women's Singles, 6th World Badminton Championships, Jakarta. Honours: Elected 7th in list of 10 Best Chinese Athletes. Address: China Sports Federation, Beijing, People's Republic of China.

**LI QianLong,** b. 19 August 1945, TaiXing, JiangSu, China. Senior Engineer. m. Mizhenzhong, 1 son, 1 daughter. Education: Engineer, Peijing Chemical Engineering University, 1968; MS, Degree, ZhengZhou University, 1979-82. Appointments: Lanzhou Chemical Corporation, 1968-70; Henan PingDing Shan Power Plant, 1970-78; Senior Engineer, Henan Electric Power Research Institute, 1982-2000; Retired, 2000; Manageress, ZhengZhou Tenglong Environmental Protection Research Institute for Electric Power Industry, 2000-. Publications: The technology of cleaning the scaling of the calcium carbonate from ash pipe line with flue gas and water, 1988; Recovery technology for overflowing ash-slurry of concentration pond,

1998; Recovery technique of industrial waste water in power plant, 1998; Recovery technology for overflowing ash-sluice of the concentration pond in power plants, 2000; Research and practice of the recovery technique to the waste water of power plants, 2002; 5 patents. Honours: 7 Science and Technology Progress Prizes; March 8 Standard Bearers in Henan Power, 1987; The Female Leaders in Science and Technology in Henan Province, 1999; March 8 Standard Bearers in Henan Province, 1999; Patents given 2nd Prize of Scientific and Technical Achievements in Henan Province, 1999; Listed in Who's Who publications and biographical dictionaries. Address: No 3 XingHua North Road, Zhengzhou City 450052, China. E-mail: LQL819@yahoo.com.cn

**LI Tzu-yin,** b. 3 March 1931, Gulangyu District, Xiamen Municipality, Fujian Province, China. Professor; Research Scientist. m. Qing-Liang Huang, 3 daughters. Education: BS, Department of Biology, Beijing Normal University, China, 1954; MS, 1987; PhD, 1990; Postdoctor, 1990-93, Department of Entomology, Texas A and M University, USA. Appointments: Biology Teacher, Beijing 15th Middle School, 1954-56; Lecturer, Professor, Department of Biology, Beijing Normal University, 1956-85; Visiting Scientist, Department of Zoology, J W Gothe University, Frankfurt, Germany, 1981-82; Research Assistant, Postdoctoral Research Scientist, Department of Entomology, Texas A and M University, USA, 1983-2001. Publications: 6 books (4 co-author); Numerous articles for scientific journals. Honours: Certified Outstanding Teacher in Beijing, 1956; Certificate of Honour for lifelong scientist, Department of Zoology, J W Gothe University, 1982; Board Certified Entomologist, 1993, Emeritus Membership, 1996, Entomology Society of America; Certified as one of 2000 Outstanding Scientists of the 20th Century by IBC, Cambridge England, 2000; Award for Scientific Achievement as one of 500 World Leaders of Influence, ABI, USA, 2001; Honourable Professor, Beijing Normal University, China, 2002; included in several most reputed international biographical dictionaries. Memberships: Entomological Society of America; Sigma Xi, Scientific Research Society; Honour Society of Agriculture, Gamma Sigma Delta. Address: 35-30 73rd Street, Apt 3H, Jackson Heights, NY 11372, USA. E-mail: tzuyinli@yahoo.com

**LI Xiuqing,** b. 24 September 1962, Jilin, People's Republic of China. Engineer. m. Zidong Liu, 1 daughter. Education: BSc, Physics, 1984; MSc, Physics, 1987; PhD, Materials Science, 1997. Appointments: Lecturer, Central China Normal University, 1987-93; Research Fellow, University of Leeds, 1997-99; Senior Materials Scientist, ThermoTech Ltd, 1999-2003; Develement Engineer, Heatric, 2003-. Publications: The Coarsening Kinetics of  Particles in Ni-based Alloys, 2002; Modelling of Materials Properties in Duplex Stainless Steels, 2002. Address: 46 Holton Road, Holton Heath, Poole, Dorset BH16 6LT, England. E-mail: xiuqing.li@heatric.com

**LI-LAN,** b. 28 January 1943, New York, New York, USA. Artist. Appointments: Regional Council, Parrish Art Museum, Southampton, New York, 1984-87; Artists Advisory Board, East Hampton Center for Contemporary Art, East Hampton, New York, 1989-90. Publications: Canvas With an Unpainted Part: An Autobiography, Tokyo, Japan, 1976; Texts in exhibition catalogues and books, numerous articles. Commissions and Creative Works: Collections in numerous museums including: Virginia Museum of Fine Arts, Richmond, Virginia; The Parrish Art Museum, Southampton, New York; William Benton Museum of Art, Storrs, Connecticut; Arkansas Arts Center, Little Rock; The Sezon Museum of Modern Art, Karuizawa, Japan; Ohara Museum of Art, Kurashiki,

Japan; Other collections include: Estee Lauder Inc, Mobil Oil Corporation, Lifetime TV, Chermayeff and Geismer Associates, New York; Gap Inc, Flagship Store, Oahu, Hawaii; Art For Peace Collection, Fischer Pharmaceuticals Ltd, Tel Aviv, Israel; Seattle First National Bank, Washington; Security Pacific National Bank, Los Angeles, California; Weatherspoon Art Gallery, Greensboro, North Carolina; Werner Kramarsky Collection, New York; Solo exhibitions in USA, Japan, Taiwan include: Robert Miller Gallery, New York, 1978; OK Harris Gallery, New York, 1983, 1985, 1987; The William Benton Museum of Art, Storrs, Connecticut, 1990; Lin & Keng Gallery, Taipei, Taiwan, 1995, 1997, 2001; Art Projects International, New York, New York, 1994, 1996; DoubleVision Gallery, Los Angeles, California, 2003; Nabi Gallery, New York, 2004; Numerous group exhibitions in USA, Japan and Taiwan. Honours: Artists Grant, Artists Space, New York, 1988, 1990; Certificate of Merit: Chinese American Cultural Pioneer, New York City Council, 1993.

**LIANG Xue-Zhang,** b. 1 December 1939, Pingdu, Shandong, China. University Professor. m. Feng-Jie, 2 sons, 1 daughter. Education: Diploma, 1962; Postgraduate thesis and diploma, 1965. Appointments: Assistant, 1965; Lecturer, 1978; Associate Professor, 1983; Professor, 1990; PhD Supervisor, 1993. Publications: Articles in journals: Lagrange representation of multivariate interpolation, 1989; On the convergence of Hakopian interpolation and cubature, 1997; On the integral convergence of Kergin interpolation on the disk, 1998; Solving second kind integral equation by Galerkin methods with continous orthogonal wavelets, 2001; The application of Cayley-Bacharach theotem to bivariate Lagrange interpolation, 2004. Honours: Natural Science Award, China, 1982; Scientific and Technical Progress Award, Education Committee of China, 1988. Membership: Jilin Province Expert Association of China. Address: Institute of Mathematics, Jilin University, Changchun, Jilin 130012, China.

**LIAO Shutsung,** b. 1 January 1931, Taiwan. m. Shuching, 4 daughters. Education: BS, Agricultural Chemistry, 1953, MS, Biochem, 1956, National Taiwan University; PhD, Biochemistry, University of Chicago, 1961. Appointments: Research Associate, 1960-63; Assistant Professor, 1964-69, Associate Professor, 1969-71, Professor, 1972, Department of Biochemistry and Molecular Biology Ben May Institute for Cancer Research, University of Chicago, 1972; Director, Tang Center for Herbal Medicine Research, 2000-2002; Consultant to various national and international conferences, agencies, foundations and workshops. Publications: Member, Editorial Board: Journal Steroid Biochemistry and Molecular Biology, The Prostate and Receptors and Signal Transduction; Associate Editor, Cancer Research, 1982-89; Over 250 articles to professional journals. Honours: NIH Grantee, 1962-; Pfizer Lecture Fellow Award, Clinical Research Institute, Montreal, 1972; Science-Technology Achievement Prize, Taiwanese-American Foundation, 1983; Gregory Pincus Medal and Award, Worcester Federation for Experimental Biology, 1992; Tzongming Tu Award, Formosan Medical Association, 1993; C H Li Memorial Lecture Award, 1994; Achievements include: Discovery of androgen activation mechanism and androgen receptors; Cloning and structural determination of androgen receptors, and other nuclear receptors, receptor gene mutation, molecular basis of cancer growth and progression, molecular approaches to chemoprevention and therapeutic treatment of hormone sensitive and insensitive cancers as well as cardiovascular and Alzheimer diseases; Memberships: American Society of Biochemistry and Molecular Biology; American Association of Cancer Research; Endocrine Society; North American Taiwanese Professors Association, President,

1980-81, Executive Director, 1981-; Member, National Academy, Taiwan, 1994; Fellow, American Academy of Arts and Sciences, 1997. Address: University of Chicago, Ben May Institute for Cancer Research, 5841 S Maryland Avenue, Chicago, IL 60637-1463, USA.

**LICARY Cheryl,** b. 15 March 1951, Beloit, Wisconsin, USA. Education. 1 son, 1 daughter. Education: BA, Music Education, Luther College, Decorah, Iowa, USA, 1972; Master of Science in Teaching, Kodály Emphasis, University of Wisconsin, 1976; 30 post graduate credits, various universities. Appointments: Vocal Music and Department Chairperson, School District of Beloit, Wisconsin, USA, 31 years; Organist and Choir Director, Our Saviour's Lutheran Church; Choral Adjudicator and Clinician. Publication: Beyond Ratings: Enriching the Solo and Ensemble Experience, Wisconsin School Music Association, 2003. Honours: Rotary Educator Recognition, 2001; Wisconsin Award for Excellence in Music Teaching, 2003; Choirs have appeared twice in Carnegie Hall on public radio – Garrison Kiellor; Listed in Who's Who publications and biographical dictionaries. Memberships: American Choral Directors Association; Wisconsin School Music Association; Wisconsin Choral Directors Association; Music Educators National Conference; American Guild of Organists. Address: 1305 11th Street, Beloit, WI 53511, USA. E-mail: clicary@sdb.k12.wi.us

**LICHFIELD 5th Earl of, Thomas Patrick John Anson,** b. 25 April 1939. British Photographer. m. Lady Leonora Grosvenor, 1975, divorced 1986, 1 son, 2 daughters. Education: Harrow; Sandhurst RMA. Appointments: Army Service, Grenadier Guards, 1957-62; Photographer. Publications: The Most Beautiful Women, 1981; Lichfield on Photography, 1981; A Royal Album, 1982; Patrick Lichfield's Unipart Calendar book, 1982; Patrick Lichfield Creating the Unipart Calendar, 1983; Hot Foot to Zabriske Point, 1985; Lichfield on Travel Photography, 1986; Not the Whole Truth, 1986; Lichfield in Retrospect, 1988; Queen Mother: The Lichfield Selection, 1990; Elizabeth R: a Photographic Celebration of 40 Years, 1991. Honours: Hon DL, Stafford, 1996. Memberships: Fellow, British Institute of Professional Photographers; Fellow, Royal Photographic Society. Address: Shugborough, Stafford ST17 0XB, England. E-mail: lichfield@lichfieldstudios.co.uk

**LIDDELL-GRAINGER David Ian,** b. 26 January 1930. Landowner. m. (1) Anne Mary Sibylla, 14 December 1957, dissolved 1982, 4 sons, 1 daughter, (2) Christine, Lady de la Rue, 2 sons, 1 deceased. Education: Eton; St Peters College, Adelaide, South Australia; College of Estate Management, London. Appointments: Scots Guards, 1948-50; Farmer; County Councillor, 1958-73; Council Member: Scottish Gas Council; RNLI; Scottish Scout Association; National Trust for Scotland; Royal Agricultural Society of England; Scottish Landowners Federation; Deputy Chairman, Timber Growers UK, 1985-88; Area Commissioner, Scouts Scottish Borders; Trustee, Shackleton Preservation Trust; President, Berwick-on-Tweed Wildlife Trust. Memberships: Member, Queen's Body Guard for Scotland, Royal Company of Archers, 1955-83; DL, 1962-85; Grand Master Mason of Scotland, 1969-74; Knight of St John, 1974; Hospitaller Order of St John, Scotland, 1977-82; FSA, Scotland; Member, Regional Advisory Committee Forestry Commission. Address: Ayton Castle, Berwickshire, TD14 5RD, Scotland.

**LIDDLE Peter (Hammond),** b. 26 December 1934, Sunderland, England. Senior Lecturer in History; Writer. Education: BA, University of Sheffield, 1956; Teacher's Certificate, University of Nottingham, 1957; Diploma in Physical Education, Loughborough University of Technology,

1958. Appointments: History Teacher, Havelock School, Sunderland, 1957; Head, History Department, Gateacre Comprehensive School, Liverpool, 1958-67; Lecturer, Notre Dame College of Education, 1967; Lecturer, 1967-70, Senior Lecturer in History, 1970-, Sunderland Polytechnic; Keeper of the Liddle Collection, University of Leeds, 1988-99; Director, The Second World War Experience Centre, Leeds, 1999-; Founder and Editor, The Poppy and the Owl, 1990; Founder and Editor, Everyone's War, 1999. Publications: Men of Gallipoli, 1976; World War One: Personal Experience Material for Use in Schools, 1977; Testimony of War 1914-18, 1979; The Sailor's War 1914-18, 1985; Gallipoli: Pens, Pencils and Cameras at War, 1985; 1916: Aspects of Conflict, 1985; Home Fires and Foreign Fields (editor and contributor), 1985; The Airman's War 1914-18, 1987; The Soldier's War 1914-18, 1988; Voices of War, 1988; The Battle of the Somme, 1992; The Worst Ordeal: Britons at Home and Abroad 1914-18, 1994; Facing Armageddon: The First World War Experienced (co-editor and contributor), 1996; Passchendaele in Perspective: The Third Battle of Ypres (editor and contributor), 1997; At the Eleventh Hour (co-editor and contributor), 1998; For Five Shillings a Day (co-author), 2000; The Great World War, 1914-45, volume I, 2000, volume II, 2001, (co-editor and contributor); D-Day: By Those Who Were There, 2004. Contributions to: Journals and other books. Honours: MLitt, University of Newcastle, 1975; PhD, University of Leeds, 1997. Memberships: British Audio Visual Trust; Fellow, Royal Historical Society. Address: Prospect House, 39 Leeds Road, Rawdon, Leeds LS19 6NW, England.

**LIEBERMAN Josefa Nina,** b. 16 May 1921, Jaroslaw, Poland. Developmental Psychologist. m. Meyer F Lieberman. Education: BS, Psychology, 1957, MA, Developmental Psychology, 1959, PhD, Educational Psychology, 1964, Columbia University; Certification as psychologist in New York State, 1966. Appointments: Assistant Regional Secretary, Refugee Children's Movement, Cambridge, England, 1940-46; Professor Emerita of Education, Brooklyn College, City University of New York; Lecturer to Full Professor, Brooklyn College Brooklyn, New York, 1961-83. Publications: Playfulness and Non-Playfulness in High-School Students, NIMH Report, 1967; Playfulness: Its Relationships to Imagination and Creativity, 1977, Japanese translation, 1981; Articles in professional journals; (biography) He Came to Cambridge: Rabbi David Samuel Margules, 1982; (memoir) The Salzburg Connection: An Adolescence Remembered, 2004. Honours: Phi Beta Kappa; Sigma Xi; General Studies Scholar; Columbia NIMH Doctoral Research Fellow; NIMH Grants, 1966-68; Listed in numerous Who's Who and biographical publications. Memberships: American Psychological Association. Address: 648 Zena Road, Woodstock, NY 12498-2413, USA. E-mail: jnina@aol.com

**LIEBERMAN Louis Stuart,** b. 23 May 1938, Swan Hill, Victoria, Australia. Barrister; Solicitor; Director. m. Marjorie Cox, 2 sons, 1 daughter. Education: New South Wales Barristers and Solicitors Admission Board; Studied and worked as Articled Law Clerk; Qualified as a Solicitor, New South Wales and High Court and Barrister and Solicitor, Victoria; Diploma in Law (SAB). Appointments include: Senior Partner, Harris Lieberman & Co Barristers and Solicitors, 1974-76; Chair, House of Representatives Standing Committee on Aboriginal and Torres Strait Islander Affairs; Parliamentary Secretary to Leader of Opposition, Commonwealth Parliament; Shadow Minister for Health, Further Education, Water Resources, Property and Services; Minister for Planning, Assistant Health, Minerals and Energy, Mines; Member for Benambra, Legislative Assembly, Parliament of Victoria, 1976-92, retired; Member for Indi, House of Representatives, Commonwealth of Australia, 1993-2001,

retired; Director, Hume Building Society Ltd. Memberships: Fellow, Australian Institute of Company Directors; Law Society of New South Wales; Law Institute, Victoria; Australian War Memorial Foundation; Patron Bandiana Military Museum; La Trobe University Council; Wodonga Technical College Council; Rotary. Address: PO Box 151, Wodonga, Victoria, Australia 3689.

**LIEBERSON Stanley,** b. 20 April 1933, Montreal, Canada. Professor of Sociology. Education: MA, Sociology, 1958, PhD, Sociology, 1960, University of Chicago, USA. Appointments: Instructor to Assistant Professor of Sociology, 1959-61, University of Iowa, USA; Assistant Professor to Professor of Sociology, University of Wisconsin, 1961-67; Professor of Sociology, University of Washington, 1967-71; Professor of Sociology, University of Chicago, 1971-74; Professor of Sociology, University of Arizona, 1974-83; Professor of Sociology, University of California, Berkeley, 1983-88, Professor of Sociology, 1988-, Abbott Lawrence Lowell Professor, 1991-, Harvard University. Publications include most recently: Book: A Matter of Taste: How Names, Fashions, and Culture Change, 2000; Articles in academic journals: The Instability of Androgynous Names: The Symbolic Maintenance of Gender Boundaries, 2000; Barking Up the Wrong Branch: Scientific Alternatives to the Current Model of Sociological Science (co-author), 2002; Book chapters: Index of Isolation in the Encyclopedia of Housing, 1998; Examples, Submerged Statements and the Neglected Application of Philosophy to Social Theory in What is Social Theory?: The Philosophical Debates, 1998; Jewish Names and the Names of Jews in These Are the Names: Studies in Jewish Onomastics, 2003. Honours include: Guggenheim Fellowship, 1972-73; Distinguished Contribution to Scholarship Award, American Sociological Association, 1982; Honorary MA, Harvard University, 1988; Honorary Degree of Doctor of Humane Letters, University of Arizona, 1993; Christensen Visiting Fellow, St Catherine's College, University of Oxford, 2001; Co-recipient, Best Book in the Sociology of Culture, Culture Section, American Sociological Association, 2001; Mirra Komarovsky Book Award, Eastern Sociological Association, 2002. Memberships include: Population Association of America; American Sociological Association; Sociological Research Association; American Academy of Arts and Sciences; National Academy of Sciences. Address: Department of Sociology, Harvard University, William James Hall, Room 436, 33 Kirkland Street, Cambridge, MA 02138, USA.

**LIEBESCHUETZ John Hugo Wolfgang Gideon,** b. 22 June 1927, Hamburg, Germany. Retired Professor of Classical and Archaeological Studies; Writer. m. Margaret Rosa Taylor, 9 April 1955, 1 son, 3 daughters. Education: BA, 1951, PhD, 1957, University of London. Appointments: Professor and Head of Department of Classical and Archaeological Studies, University of Nottingham, 1979-92. Publications: Antioch, 1972; Continuity and Change in Roman Religion, 1979; Barbarians and Bishops, 1992; From Diocletian to the Arab Conquest, 1992; The Decline and Fall of the Roman City, 2001. Honours: Fellow, British Academy, 1992; Corresponding Fellow, German Archaeological Institute, 1994; Fellow, University College, London, 1997; Fellow, Society of Antiquaries. Address: 1 Clare Valley, The Park, Nottingham NG7 1BU, England.

**LIGAA Urtnasangiin,** b. 10 March 1932, Galt sum, Khovsgol aimag, Mongolia. Botanist; Economic Botanist. m. Norjingiina Ninjil, 1 son, 4 daughters. Education: BS, Biological Sciences, Mongolian State University, Ulaanbaatar, Mongolia. 1951-56; Chemistry and Pharmacology of Medicinal Plants, Veterinary Institute and Institute of Medicinal Plants, Budapest, Hungary,

1965-66; Postgraduate Botany, Economic Botany, (PhD), V L Komarov Botanical Institute, Academy of Sciences of Leningrad (St Petersburg), Russia, 1969-72. Appointments: Veterinary, State Farm "Erentsav", 1956-63; Scientific Researcher, Agricultural Institute of Mongolian Academy of Sciences, 1964-68; Scientific Researcher, Chief Scientist, Leading Scientist, Chief Advisor for Economic Botany Sector, Member, Academic Council, Institute of Botany, Mongolian Academy of Science, 1973-92; Teacher, Traditional Medicine Institute "Mamba Datsan", 1993-94; Leading Scientist, National Institute of Mongolian Traditional Medicine, 1995-97; Teacher of Medicinal and Useful Plants, 1998-2000, Senior Leading Scientist, Project Executor, 2001-, Mongolian State University of Agriculture. Publications: 21 books and numerous papers to specialist journals, conferences and seminars. Address: Ulaanbaatar 46, POB 743, Mongolia.

**LILLEY, Right Honourable Peter Bruce,** b. 23 August 1943, Kent, England. Politician. m. Gail Ansell, 1979. Education: Clare College, Cambridge; MA, Cantab. Appointments: Chairman, Bow Group, 1973; Member of Parliament for St Albans, 1983-97, for Hitchin and Harpenden, 1997-; Economic Secretary, 1987-89, Financial Secretary, 1989-90, to Treasury; Secretary of State for Trade and Industry, 1990-92, for Social Security, 1992-97; Opposition Front Bench Spokesman for Treasury, 1997-98; Deputy Leader of the Opposition, 1998-99; Former Director, Greenwell Montague, Oil Analyst. Publications: The Delusion of Incomes Policy, co-author, 1977; The End of the Keynesian Era, 1980; Thatcherism: The Next Generation, 1990; Winning the Welfare Debate, 1996; Patient Power, 2000; Common Sense on Cannabis, 2001; Taking Liberties, 2002. Honour: Privy Councillor. Address: House of Commons, London SW1A 0AA, England.

**LILLIE Betty Jane,** b. 11 April 1926, Cincinnati, Ohio, USA. Professor of Biblical Studies. Education: BSEd, 1955, BA, 1961, College of Mt St Joseph; MA, 1967, MA, 1975, Providence College, Rhode Island; PhD, Hebrew Union College, Cincinnati, Ohio, 1982. Appointments: Teaching at graduate and undergraduate levels, Faculty, Athenaeum of Ohio, Cincinnati, Ohio, 1982-2005; Athenaeum Summer Program: Progoff Intensive Journal I, 1986, Progoff Intensive Journal II, 1987, Women in the Biblical Tradition, 1988; Athenaeum Israel Study Program in Israel, Summer 1989; Athenaeum Summer Lecture Series: Women in the Biblical Tradition, 1990; Participant in faculty development workshops, 1992, 1993, 1996, 1997, 1999, 2002, 2003, 2004 and 2005; Faculty, Evening College of the University of Cincinnati, 1984-2003; Academic committees; Involvement in Church ministry and life. Publications: Book: A History of the Scholarship on the Wisdom of Solomon from the Nineteenth Century to our Time; Biblical Exegesis for Weekday Homily Helps; Weekly column on Sunday Scripture readings every third month, 1988-; Numerous articles and papers on religious topics. Honours include: Named Woman of the Year, 1993, 1994, 1995, 1996, 1997, 1999, 2000; International Woman of the Year, 1992-93, 1996-97, 1998-99, 1999-2000, 2001-02; Named for: Decree of International Letters for Cultural Achievement, 1996, 1997; Lifetime Achievement Award, ABI, 1997; International Cultural Diploma of Honour, 1997, 1999; Presidential Seal of Honor, 1997; Order of International Fellowship, 1997; Millennium Hall of Fame, 1998. Memberships: Catholic Biblical Association; Society for Biblical Literature; Biblical Archaeology Society; Eastern Great Lakes Biblical Society, Vice President, 1992; President, 1993; Council of Societies for the Study of Religion; Women's Center for Theological Studies; Ohio Humanities Council. Address: 2704 Cypress Way=3, Cincinnati, OH 45212-1773, USA.

**LIM Chee Wah,** b. 27 January 1965, Batu Pahat, Johor, Malaysia. Professor. m. Moi Peng Choo, 1 son, 1 daughter. Education: BEng (honours), Mechanical Engineering (Aeronautics), University of Technology, Malaysia, 1989; MEng, Mechanical Engineering, National University of Singapore, 1992; PhD, Mechanical Engineering, Nanyang Technological University, Singapore, 1995. Appointments: Research Assistant, National University of Singapore, 1989-91; Research Assistant, Teaching Assistant, Nanyang Technological University, Singapore, 1992-94; Research Assistant, 1994-95, Postdoctoral Research Fellow, 1995-97, University of Queensland, Australia; Research Fellow, University of Hong Kong, 1998-2000; Assistant Professor, 2000-03, Associate Professor, 2003-, City University of Hong Kong; Professional Consultant, Green Technology Consultants Limited, Hong Kong, 2000-; Associate Editor (Asia-Pacific Region), Advances in Vibration Engineering, 2002-; Technical Reviewer for John Wiley & Sons, Kluwer Academic Publishers and more than 10 international journals. Publications: Contributed more than 95 technical papers to professional journals; 1 book chapter; More than 35 international conference papers; miscellaneous research reports; Associate Editor (Asia-Pacific region), Advances in Vibration Engineering. Honours: Public Service Commission Scholarship, Malaysia, 1985-89; Best Academic Performance, Mechanical Engineering, (Aeronautics), 1989; University of Queensland Postdoctoral Research Fellowship, 1995-97; University of Hong Kong Research Fellowship, 1998-2000; Listed in several biographical dictionaries; Fellowship, International Biographical Association. Memberships: American Society of Mechanical Engineers; American Society of Civil Engineers; Acoustical Society of America; Structural Engineering Institute of ASCE. Address: Department of Building and Construction, City University of Hong Kong, Tat Chee Avenue, Kowloon, Hong Kong. E-mail: bccwlim@cityu.edu.hk

**LIM Chwen Jeng,** b. 1964, Malaysia. Architect. Education: AA Dipl, Architectural Association, School of Architecture, London, England, 1982-87. Appointments: Director, Studio 8 Architects, 1994-; Director, Bartlett Architecture Research Laboratory, University College, London, 1999-; Visiting Professor, Glasgow School of Art, 2001-; Exhibitions include: RMIT, Melbourne, Australia, 1996; Stadelschule, Frankfurt, 1997; ARCHILAB Fonds Regional d'Art Contemporain du Centre, France, 1999; Mackintosh Museum, Glasgow, 2004; Venice Architecture Biennale 04, British Pavilion, 2004; Other group exhibitions include: Dulwich Picture Gallery, 1990; National Gallery Alexandros Soutzos Museum, Athens, 1990; Museo Nazionale Di Castel St Angelo, Rome, 1994; Nara World Architecture Triennale, Japan, 1996; Defence Corp Building, Jyvaskyla, Finland, 1997; CUBE Gallery, Manchester, 2000; Academie de France, Rome, 2000; RIBA, London, 2000; Architecture Foundation, London, 2001; Gallery 312, Chicago, USA, 2001; Rubelle + Norman Schafler Gallery, New York, 2001; Storefront Gallery, New York, 2001; Thread Waxing Gallery, New York, 2001; Chicago Architecture Foundation, USA, 2001; Mediatheque d'Orleans, France, 2002; Drawings in permanent collections include: The Victoria and Albert Museum, London; Fonds Regional d'Art Contemporain du Centre, France; RIBA British Architectural Library, London. Publications: Articles in international periodicals and newspapers; Monographs include: Sins and Other Spatial Relatives, 2001; How Green is Your Garden, 2003; Neo Architecture, 2005; 5 edited books. Honours: Award winning research-based architectural competitions include: Housing: A Demonstration Project, UK, 1987; Bridge of the Future, Japan, 1987; UCL Museum, UK, 1996; Ideal Home Concept House, UK, 1999; GlassHouse, Japan, 2001. RIBA Award for Academic Contribution in Architectural Education, 1997, 1998, 1999; Selected to represent the UK in the Venice Architecture Biennale 04, 2004; Chosen as one of the New British Talent in Architecture by the Guardian and Independent Newspapers, 2004. Address: Studio 8 Architects, 95 Greencroft Gardens, London NW6 3PG, England. E-mail: mail@cjlim-studio8.com Website: www.cjlim-studio8.com

**LIM Won Kyun,** b. 4 July 1953, Incheon, South Korea. Professor. m. Chung-Hyo Lee, 2 sons. Education: BS, Mechanical Engineering, 1972-76, MS, Mechanical Engineering, 1979-81, PhD, Mechanical Engineering, 1981-88, Inha University, Incheon, South Korea. Appointments: Professor, 1981-, Mechanical Department Chairman, MyongJi University, Kyonggido, South Korea, 1986-88; Visiting Professor, University of Florida, Gainesville, Florida, USA, 1999-2000; Standard Development Committee Member, Korea Automotive Technology Institute, Cheonan, South Korea, 2001-. Publications: Articles in scientific journals including: Engineering Fracture Mechanics, 1998, 2001; Journal of Composite Materials, 2002; International Journal of Fatigue, 2003. Honours: Full Scholarship, Inha University, 1972-76; Grants, Korea Research Foundation, 1995-97 Memberships: Korean Society of Mechanical Engineers; Editor, Journal of Korean Society of Precision Engineering. Address: Department of Mechanical Engineering, MyongJi University, 38-2 Namdong, Yongin, Kyonggido 449-728, South Korea. E-mail: limwk@mju.ac.kr

**LIM Young Bae,** b. 25 July 1955, Seoul, Korea. Businessman. m. 1 son, 1 daughter. Education: BA, Physics, Dong Kuk University, Korea, 1981; Marketing, Company training with Roche, 2001, 2004; Leadership, London Business School, 2004. Appointments: Pfizer, Korea, 1982-85; Marketing Manager, Sanofi, Korea, 1986-89; Marketing Manager, Novartis, Korea, 1991-98; Senior Director, Head of Diabetes Care Business Area, Roche Diagnostic, Korea, 1998-. Address: Roche Diagnostics Korea Co, Ltd, 15F, Samhwa Building, 144-17, Samsung-dong, Kangnam-ku, Seoul 135-745, Korea. E-mail: young_bae.lim@roche.com

**LIMERICK, Sylvia Countess of; Sylvia Rosalind Pery,** b. 7 December 1935, Cairo, Egypt. m. 6th Earl of Limerick, deceased 2003, 2 sons, 1 daughter. Education: MA, Lady Margaret Hall, Oxford. Appointments include: Research Assistant, Foreign and Commonwealth Office, 1959-62; Volunteer, British Red Cross, 1962-66; President and Chairman, Kensington and Chelsea Division, British Red Cross, 1966-72; Member of Board of Governors, St Bartholomew's Hospital, 1970-74; Vice Chairman, Foundation for the Study of Infant Deaths, 1971-; President, 1972-79, Vice President, 1979-99, UK Committee for UNICEF; Vice-Chairman, Community Health Council, 1974-77; Member, Committee of Management, Institute of Child Health, London, 1976-96; Member Area Health Authority, Kensington, Chelsea and Westminster, 1977-82; Council Member, King Edward's Hospital Fund for London, 1977-; Vice President, 1978-84, President, 1984-2002, Community Practitioners and Health Visitors' Association; Trustee, Child Accident Prevention Trust, 1979-87; President, 1973-84, Vice President, 1985-90, National Association for Maternal and Child Welfare; Reviewed National Association of Citizens' Advice Bureau for H M Government, 1983; Vice-Chairman, 1984-85, Chairman of Council, 1985-95, Chairman Emeritus, 1995-97, British Red Cross Society; Advisory Board, Civil Service Occupational Health Service, 1989-92; Board Member, Eastman Dental Hospital Special Health Authority, 1990-96; Trustee, Voluntary Hospital of St Bartholomew, 1991-2004; Vice President, International Federation of Red Cross and Red Crescent Societies, 1993-97; Vice Chairman, Institute of Neurology/Hospital for Neurology and Neurosurgery Joint Research Ethics Committee, 1993-

2004; Non-Executive Director, University College London Hospitals NHS Trust, 1996-97; Chairman, CMO's Expert Group to Investigate Cot Death Theories, 1994-98; Trustee, Child Health Research Appeal Trust, 1995-; Chairman, Committee of Management, Eastman Dental Institute, 1996-99; Chairman, Eastman Dental Research Foundation, 1996-2002; Chairman, CPHVA Charitable Trust, 1997-2002; Patron, Child Advocacy International, 1998-; Honorary Vice President, British Red Cross Society, 1999-; Patron, CRUSE. Publications: Co-author, Sudden Infant Death: patterns, puzzles and problems, 1985; Over 65 articles in medical journals; Articles on International Red Cross and Red Crescent Movement. Honours: CBE, 1991; Hugh Greenwood Lecturer, Exeter University, 1987; Hon D Litt, Council for National Academic Awards, 1990; Samuel Gee Lecturer, RCP, 1994; European Women of Achievement Humanitarian Award, 1995; Hon LLD, University of Bristol, 1998. Memberships: Fellow, Royal Society of Medicine, 1977-; Hon MRCP, 1990, Hon FRCP, 1994, Royal College of Physicians; Freeman Honoris Causa, Worshipful Company of Salters, 1992; Honorary Fellow, Institute of Child Health, London, 1996; Honorary Member, 1986-, Honorary Fellow, 1996, Royal College of Paediatrics and Child Health; Freeman, Worshipful Company of World Traders, 2003; Order of the Croatian Star, 2003. Address: Chiddinglye, West Hoathly, West Sussex, RH19 4QT. E-mail: srlimerick@aol.com

**LIN Hai,** b. 23 February 1979, Hangzhou, China. Physicist. Education: BS, Physics, Peking University, 2001; MA, Physics, Princeton University, 2003. Appointments: Assistant in Instruction, Princeton University, 2002-. Publications: Numerous articles in professional journals. Honours: Fellowship in Science and Engineering, Princeton University, 2001; Outstanding Professional Award, ABI, 2004; Award of Achievement, National Scholars Honor Society, 2004; Medal, Great Minds of the 21st Century, ABI, 2004. Memberships: American Physical Society; American Mathematical Society; Biophysical Society; American Chemical Society; SIAM; IMS; New York Academy of Sciences. Address: Jadwin Hall, Department of Physics, Princeton University, Princeton, NJ 08544, USA. E-mail: hailin@princeton.edu

**LIN Jonqlan,** b. 21 September 1961, Taiwan. Professor. m. Ruey-Hwa Yeh, 2 sons, 1 daughter. Education: BS, National Taiwan University, 1984; ME, 1990, PhD, 1994, University of Texas at Arlington. Publications: Fuzzy controller for flexible link robot arm by reduced order techniques, 2002; Application of fuzzy set theory to the change intervals at a signalized intersection. Honours: Listed in national and international biographical dictionaries. Address: Ching Yun University, 229 Chien Hsin Road, Chung Li, Taiwan 320, Republic of China. E-mail: jlin@eyu.edu.tw

**LIN Mao-Tsun,** b. 1 July 1942, Taipei, Taiwan. Medical Researcher. m. Hai-chuan Chow, 3 sons. Education: DDS, 1968; PhD, 1977. Appointments: Professor, Chairman, Department of Physiology, National Cheng-Kung University Medical College, Tainan, Taiwan, 1986-96; Professor, Chairman, Department of Physiology, National Yang-Ming University Medical College, Taipei, Taiwan, 1996-2000; Professor, Department of Medical Research, Chi-Mei Medical Center, Yung Kang, Tainan, Taiwan, 2000-. Publications: Numerous papers and articles for professional journals. Honours: Dr Ming-Lian Wang Foundation Outstanding Medical Research Award, 1997; Mr Chin-Ling Yuan Foundation Outstanding Basic Medical Research Award, 1998; National Outstanding Research Award of Republic of China, 2002. Memberships: International Brain Research Organization, 1990-; New York Academy of Sciences, 1995-; International Association of Cerebral Blood Flow and

Metabolism, 1996-. Address: Department of Medical Research, Chi-Mei Medical Center, 901 Chung-Hwa Road, Yung Kang City, Tainan Hsien, Taiwan. E-mail: mtlin@ym.edu.tw

**LIN Yuh-Ling,** b. 8 March 1960, Taiwan. Professor. m. Wei-Wu Wang, 2 sons, 1 daughter. Education: BS, Department of Biology, Tung-Hi University, Taichung, Taiwan; MS, Department of Botany, Chung-Hsin University, Taichung, Taiwan; PhD, Institute of Life Science, National Tsing-Hua University, Hsin-Chu, Taiwan. Appointments: Investigator, Ever-Life Pharmaceutical Factory, Tai-Pei, 1993094; Postdoctoral Researcher, Chang-Guan University, Tao-Yuan, Taiwan, 1994-97; Assistant Professor, 1997-2001, Associate Professor, 2001-2002, Taipei Medical University; Associate Professor, Fu-Jen Catholic University, 2003-; Consultant, Microbio Biotechnology Company, Taipei, Taiwan, 2000-. Address: 510 Chung-Cheng Road, Hsin-Chuang, Taipei-Hsien, Taiwan, ROC. E-mail: med0018@mails.fju.edu.tw

**LIN Zhisheng,** b. 10 December 1944, Puning, Guangdong, People's Republic of China. Professor. m. Xiaodong Lian, 1 son, 1 daughter. Education: University Diploma in Physics, Department of Physics, Sun Yat-Sen (Zhongshan) University, Guangzhou, Guangdong, People's Republic of China, 1964-69. Appointments: Assistant Lecturer, Department of Physics, 1969-79, Assistant Lecturer, 1979-83, Lecturer, 1983-93, Associate Professor, 1992-98, Department of Radio Electronics, Associate professor, 1998-2001, Professor, 2001-, Department of Electronics and Communications Engineering, Sun Yat-Sen (Zhongshan) University, Guangzhou, Guangdong, People's Republic of China. Publications: Books: Principal and Service of Black and White Television Sets, 1994; Electronic Circuits and AM Radio Sets, 1995; Signals and Systems (Chinese Translation of the book Signals and Systems by Simon Haykin et al), 2004; Over 30 journal papers. Honours: Prizes for 2 research projects and 4 science and technology articles. Listed in Who's Who publications and biographical dictionaries. Membership: Senior Member, Chinese Institute of Electronics. Address: Department of Electronics and Communication Engineering, Zhonshan University, Guangzhou, People's Republic of China. E-mail: isslzs@zsu.edu.cn

**LIN Zone-Ching,** b. 22 January 1951, Taiwan. Professor. m. S J Lin, 1 son, 1 daughter. Education: PhD, School of Industrial Engineering, Purdue University, USA, 1980-84. Appointments: Professor Department of Mechanical Engineering, 1989-, Dean of College of Engineering, 1997-2003, Chairman of Mechanical Engineering, 1993-1997, National Taiwan University of Science and Technology; General Secretary, Chinese Society of Mechanical Engineers, 1999-; Chapter Chair, Society of Manufacturing Engineers, USA, Taipei Chapter, 2001-2003; President, Association of Technological and Vocational Education Development, 2003-; Director of Mechanical Solid Division and Automation Division of National Science Council in Taiwan, 2001-2003. Publications: Over 130 international journal papers in the field of: Metal cutting, metal forming, die and measurement, micro/nano fabrication and mechanics. Honours: Distinguished Research Award, National Science Council in Taiwan, 1997, 2000, 2003; Distinguished Engineering Professor, Chinese Engineers Association, 1997; Journal Paper Award, Chinese Society of Mechanical Engineers, 2003; Outstanding Industrial Engineering Award, Purdue University, USA, 2004. Memberships: Committee Member, Appeal Committee of the Ministry of Economic Affairs, Taiwan; Supervisor, Society of Railway Engineering; Editorial Committee Member, International Journal of Manufacturing Technology and Management; Associate Editor of the Chinese Mechanical Engineering Journal. Address: Department of

Mechanical Engineering, National Taiwan University of Science and Technology, No 43, Sec 4 Keejung Road, Taipei 106, Taiwan, Republic of China. E-mail: zclin@mail.ntust.edu.tw

**LINDEN Eddie (Sean),** b. 5 May 1935, Northern Ireland. Poet; Writer; Editor. Education: Holy Family, Mossend; St Patrick's, New Stevenson; Catholic Workers College, Oxford. Appointment: Founder-Editor, Aquarius literary magazine, 1969-. Publications: Who is Eddie Linden? (with Sebastian Barker) (autobiographical account of a Catholic childhood in a Lanarkshire mining-village), 1979; City of Razors (poems), 1980; Who is Eddie Linden (adapted for stage by William Tanner) first produced at the Old Red Lion Theatre, Islington, London, 1997; Represented in anthologies: The Poolbeg Book of Irish Poetry (editor Shaun Traynor), 1979; The Best of Scottish Poetry (editor Robin Bell), 1989; Life Doesn't Frighten Me at All (editor John Agard), 1989; Readings: BBC1 television; BBC Radio 3; BBC Radio Scotland; Radio Clyde; LBC Radio; Live readings throughout Scotland, Ireland, England, Wales, Canada (Toronto, Calgary, Edmonton), New York, Boston, Cambridge, Massachusetts, Paris, 1983, British Council, Paris, 2004. Membership: Poetry Society. Address: Flat 4, Room B, 116 Sutherland Avenue, London W9, England.

**LINDSAY (John) Maurice,** b. 21 July 1918, Glasgow, Scotland. Poet; Writer; Editor. m. Aileen Joyce Gordon, 3 August 1946, 1 son, 3 daughters. Education: Glasgow Academy, 1928-36; Scottish National Academy of Music, 1936-39. Appointments: Programme Controller, 1961-63, Production Controller, 1963-66, Chief Interviewer, 1966-67, Border Television; Director, The Scottish Civic Trust, 1967-83; Consultant, 1983-2002, Honorary Trustee, 2000-, The Scottish Civic Trust; Editor, Scottish Review, 1975-85; Honorary Secretary General, Europa Nostra, 1983-90; President, Association for Scottish Literary Studies, 1982-83. Publications: The Advancing Day, 1940; Predicament, 1942; No Crown for Laughter, 1943; The Enemies of Love: Poems, 1941-45, 1946; Selected Poems, 1947; At the Wood's Edge, 1950; Ode for St Andrew's Night and Other Poems, 1951; The Exiled Heart: Poems, 1941-56, 1957; Snow Warning and Other Poems, 1962; One Later Day and Other Poems, 1964; This Business of Living, 1971; Comings and Goings, 1971; Selected Poems, 1942-72, 1973; The Run from Life: More Poems, 1942-72, 1975; Walking Without an Overcoat: Poems, 1972-76, 1977; Collected Poems, 2 volumes, 1979, 1993; A Net to Catch the Wind and Other Poems, 1981; The French Mosquito's Woman and Other Diversions, 1985; Requiem for a Sexual Athlete and Other Poems and Diversions, 1988; The Scottish Dog, with Joyce Lindsay, 1989; The Theatre and Opera Lover's Quotation Book, with Joyce Lindsay, 1993; News of the World: Last Poems, 1995; Speaking Likenesses, 1997; Worlds Apart, poems, 2000; Glasgow: Fabric of a City, 2000; The Edinburgh Book of 20th Century Scottish Poetry, with Lesley Duncan, 2005. Other: Editions of poetry, plays, etc. Honours: Territorial Decoration; Commander of the Order of the British Empire, 1979; DLitt, University of Glasgow, 1982. Memberships: Association of Scottish Literary Studies; Honorary Fellow, Royal Incorporation of Architects in Scotland. Address: Park House, 104 Dumbarton Road, Bowling, G60 5BB, Scotland.

**LINDSAY Kathryn Elizabeth,** b. 15 February 1953, Renfrew, Ontario, Canada. Research Ecologist. m. Timothy Holden Freemark, 1 son, 2 daughters. Education: BSc, honours, Queens University, Kingston, Ontario, 1977; PhD, Biology, Carleton University, Ottawa, 1984; Loeb Fellowship, Harvard University, Cambridge, 1998-99. Appointments: Research Associate, University of Illinois, Champaign, 1980-83; Strategic Grants Officer, Natural Sciences and Engineering Research, Council of Canada, Ottawa, 1984-86; Pesticides Evaluation

Officer, 1986-88, Research Scientist, 1988-, National Wildlife Research Center, Canadian Wildlife Service. Publications: Many articles in professional journals. Honours: Research Grant, Natural Sciences and Engineering Research Council of Canada, 1998-2002. Memberships: Ecological Society of America; Society of Conservation Biology; International Association of Landscape Ecology; Society of Canadian Ornithologists. Address: National Wildlife Research Centre, Canadian Wildlife Service, Environment Canada, Ottawa, ON K1A 0H3, Canada.

**LINDSAY Oliver John Martin,** b. 30 August 1938, Lincolnshire, England. Author; Editor; Historian. m. Lady Clare Giffard, 1 son, 2 daughters. Education: Royal Military Academy, Sandhurst, UK; Staff College, Camberley, UK; National Defence College, Latimer, UK. Appointments: Commissioned in the Grenadier Guards and on the Staff serving in many parts of the world including: Cameroons, Germany, Cyprus, Rhodesia, Hong Kong and Canada, 1957-93; Retired in rank of Colonel; Trust Director and Fund Raiser, Treloar Trust for 300 disabled children, 1993-99; Editor, Guards Magazine, 1993-. Publications: Books: The Lasting Honour: the Fall of Hong Kong 1941, 1978; At the Going Down of the Sun: Hong Kong and South East Asia 1941-45, 1981; A Guards General: the Memoirs of Sir Allan Adair (editor), 1986; Once a Grenadier: the History of the Grenadier Guards 1945-1995, 1996; Articles published in three continents. Honours: CBE; FRHist S; Member of the Queen's Body Guard for Scotland, Royal Company of Archers. Membership: Boodles Club. Address: Church Farm, Beer Hackett, Sherborne, Dorset DT9 6QT, England.

**LINDSAY Robert,** b. 1951, Ilkeston, Derbyshire, England. Actor. m. Cheryl Hall, divorced; 1 daughter with Diana Weston; 2 sons with Rosemarie Ford. Education: Royal Academy of Dramatic Art. Career: Stage career commenced at Manchester Royal Exchange; Appeared in Me and My Girl, London, Broadway and Los Angeles, 1985-87; Appeared as Henry II in Anouilh's Beckett, London, 1991, Cyrano de Bergerac, London, 1992; Film appearances in Bert Rigby, You're a Fool, Loser Takes All, Strike It Rich, Fierce Creatures, 1996; Television appearances including Edmund in King Lear, Granada, Wolfie in comedy series Citizen Smith, Michael Murray in serial GBH, Channel 4, 1991; My Family, BBC, 2000-; Space Race (narrator), BBC2, 2005; Tony Blair in A Very Social Secretary, More4, 2005; Jericho, ITV1, 2005; Other performances in Genghis Cohn, Jake's Progress, Goodbye My Love, 1996, Oliver, 1998, Richard III, 1998, Fagin in Oliver Twist, 1999. Honours: Olivier, Tony and Fred Astaire Awards for performance in Me and My Girl; Olivier Award for Best Actor in a Musical, 1998. Address: Hamilton Asper Management, Ground Floor, 24 Hanway Street, London W1P 9DD, England.

**LINEKER Gary Winston,** b. 30 November 1960, Leicester, England. Former Footballer; Television Host. m. Michelle Denise Cockayne, 1986, 4 sons. Career: Debut as professional footballer, Leicester City, 1978; Everton, 1985; Represented England, 1986 World Cup, Mexico, 1990 World Cup, Italy; Captain, England, 1991-92; FC Barcelona, Spain, 1986-89; Transferred to Tottenham Hotspur, 1989-92; 80 international caps; Scored 48 goals, June 1992; Grampus Eight Team, Japan, 1994; Presenter, Match of the Day, BBC TV, 1995-. Honour: MA, Leicester, 1992, Loughborough, 1992; OBE, 1992. Address: c/o SFX Sports Group, 35/36 Grosvenor Street, London W1K 4QX, England.

**LING Sergey Stepanovich,** b. 7 May 1937. Politician and Agronomist. m. 3 children. Education: Belarus Agricultural Academy; Higher CPSU School, CPSU Central Committee. Appointments: Agronomist Sovkhoz, Lesnoye Kopylsk District;

Chief Agronomist Sovkhoz, Chief Agronomist, Krynitsa Kopylsk District; Deputy Director, Lyuban Production Co; Chief, Soligorsk Production Agricultural Administration; Deputy Chairman, then Chairman, Slutsk District Executive Committee, Secretary, Smolevichi District CPSU Committee, 1960-72; Chief, Agricultural Division, Secretary, Minsk Regional Belarus Communist Party Committee, 1972-82; First Deputy Chairman, then Chairman, Executive Committee, Minsk Regional Soviet, 1982-86; Chairman, Belarus State Committee on Prices, Deputy Chairman, State Planning Committee, 1986-90; Head, Agricultural Division, Secretary, Central Committee, Belarus Communist Party, 1990-91; Deputy Chairman, Belarus Council of Ministers; Chairman, State Committee on Economics and Planning, 1991-; Deputy Prime Minister, 1994-96, Acting Prime Minister, 1996-97, Prime Minister, 1997-2000, Belarus. Address: c/o Council of Ministers, pl Nezavisimosti, 220010 Minsk, Belarus.

**LINGARD Brian Hallwood,** b. 2 November 1926, Melbourne, Australia. Architect. m. Dorothy, 2 sons, 1 daughter. Education: DA, Manchester College of Art, School of Architecture. Appointments: Royal Navy, 1944-46; Associate, Royal Institute of British Architects (ARIBA), 1949; Commenced private architectural practice, 1950; Fellow, Royal Institute of British Architects (FRIBA), 1957; Formed architectural partnership, Brian Lingard and Partners, 1972; Formed landscape architecture partnership, Ecoscape (now Lingard Styles Landscape), 1975; Formed architectural historians partnership, Gallery Lingard, 1982; Chairman, Architects Benevolent Society, 1988-92. Publications: The Opportunities for the Conservation and Enhancement of Our Historic Resorts; Special Houses for Special People. Honours: RIBA Regional Award (Wales); DOE/RIBA Housing Medals/Commendations (7 awards); Civic Trust Awards/Commendations (21 awards); TIMES/RICS Conservation Awards (2 awards); Prince of Wales Conservation Awards (3 awards); Life Vice-President, Architects Benevolent Society, 2002. Memberships: Carlton Club; Royal Automobile Club; Sloane Club. Address: Le Bouillon House, St George's Esplanade, St Peter Port, Guernsey.

**LINIECKI Julian,** b. 13 March 1930, Lodz, Poland. Physician. m. Janina, 1 son, 1 daughter. Education: Graduated as MD, Medical University of Lodz, 1953; PhD, 1959; Dr habil (Dr Sc), 1967. Appointments: Assistant, Adjunct and Associate Professor, Chief of the Department of Radiological Protection, Professor, Deputy Director (1968-72), Institute of Occupational Medicine, Lodz, 1953-72; Professor, 1974, Chief, Department of Nuclear Medicine, 1974-2000, Vice-Dean, 1974-80, Pro-Rector, 1980-82, Pro-Rector for Research, 1990-96, University of Lodz; Scientific Expert, UNSCEAR, 1964-66 and 1979-86; AEA and WHO expert on radiation; Editor-in-Chief, Nuclear Medicine Review, CEE,1998-. Publications: Over 100 articles and papers contributed to specialist scientific and medical journals, mainly in the fields of nuclear medicine, radiobiology and radiological protection; Worked on 4 scientific annexes for UNSCEAR, 1964, 1966, 1986; Several book chapters; Co-author of numerous ICPRP reports. Honours: Honorary Member, Polish Society of Nuclear Medicine; Polish Health Department Award for Nuclear Medicine Studies in Oncology, 1986; Commander, Polonia Restituta Order. Memberships: Numerous professional and learned societies, including, Member, 1969-, Main Commissioner, 1972-96, Chairman, 1980-92; Vice-Chairman, 1996, of the Committee on Protection in Medicine; International Commission on of Radiological Protection (ICRP); EANM; ESRB, IRPA. Address: Dept of Nuclear Medicine, Medical University of Lodz, Czecholowacka 8-10, PL 92216 Lodz, Poland. E-mail: linieck@csk.am.lodz.pl

**LINKLATER Richard,** b. 30 July 1960, Houston, Texas, USA. Film Director. Appointments: Founder, Director, own film company, Detour Films, Austin, Texas; Founder, Artistic Director, Austin Film Society; Director, films, Slacker, 1991, Dazed and Confused, 1993, Before Sunrise, 1995, Suburbia, 1997, The Newton Boys, 1998; Waking Life, 2001; Tape, 2001; Live From Shiva's Dance Floor, 2003; The School of Rock, 2003; Before Sunset, 2004; $5.15/Hr, 2004. Honours: Silver Bear, Berlin Film Festival, 1995.

**LINSCOTT Gillian,** b. 27 September 1944, Windsor, England. Journalist; Writer. m. Tony Geraghty, 18 June 1988. Education: Honours Degree, English Language and Literature, Somerville College, Oxford University, 1966. Appointments: Journalist, Liverpool Post, 1967-70; Northern Ireland Correspondent, Birmingham Post, 1970-72; Reporter, The Guardian,1972-79; Sub Editor, BBC Radio News, Local Radio Parliamentary Reporter, 1979-90; Freelance Writer, 1990-. Publications: A Healthy Body, 1984; Murder Makes Tracks, 1985; Knightfall, 1986; A Whiff of Sulphur, 1987; Unknown Hand, 1988; Murder, I Presume, 1990; Sister Beneath the Sheet, 1991; Hanging on the Wire, 1992; Stage Fright, 1993; Widow's Peak, 1994; Crown Witness, 1995; Dead Man's Music, 1996; Dance on Blood, 1998; Absent Friends, 1999; The Perfect Daughter, 2000; Dead Man Riding, 2002; The Garden, 2002; Blood on the Wood, 2003. Honours: Herodotus Award, The Historical Mystery Appreciation Society, 1999; Ellis Peters Historical Dagger, Crime Writers Association, 2000. Memberships: Society of Authors; Crime Writers Association. Address: Wood View, Hope Under Dinmore, Leominster, Herefordshire HR6 0PP, England.

**LIOTTA Ray,** b. 18 December 1955, Newark, New Jersey, USA. Actor. m Michelle Grace, 1997, 1 daughter. Education: BFA, University of Miami. Career: Various television appearances including Another World, NBC, 1978-80, Hardhat & Legs, CBS movie, 1980, Crazy Times, ABC pilot, 1981, Casablanca, NBC, 1983, Our Family Honour, NBC, 1985-86, Women Men – In Love there Are No Rules, 1991; The Rat Pack, 1998; Point of Origin, 2002; Film appearances in The Lonely Lady, 1983, Something Wild, 1986, Arena Brains, 1987, Dominick and Eugene, 1988, Field of Dreams, 1989, Goodfellas, 1990, Article 99, 1992, Unlawful Entry, 1992, No Escape, 1994, Corrina, Corrina, 1994, Operation Dumbo Drop, 1995, Unforgettable, 1996, Turbulence, 1997, Phoenix, 1997, Copland, 1997, The Rat Pack, 1998, Forever Mine, 1999, Muppets From Space, 1999; Blow, 2001; Heartbreakers, 2001; Hannibal, 2001; John Q, 2002; A Rumor of Angels, 2002; Narc, 2002. Address: c/o Endeavour Talent Agency, 9701 Wilshire Boulevard, 10th Floor, Beverly Hills, CA 90212, USA.

**LIPMAN Maureen,** b. 10 May 1946, Hull, England. Actor. m. Jack Rosenthal, deceased, 1 son, 1 daughter. Education: Newland High School for Girls, Hull; London Academy of Music and Dramatic Art. Appointments: TV: Cold Enough for Snow, 1997; Hampstead on the Couch, 2002; Coronation Street, 2002; George Eliot: A Scandalous Life, 2002; Jonathan Creek, 2002; Winter Solstice, 2003; Art Deco Designs, 2004; Stage: The Rivals, 1996; Okahoma! 1998, 1999, 2002; Peggy For You, 1999; Sitting Pretty, 2001; The Vagina Monologues, 2001; The Play What I Wrote, 2001; Thoroughly Modern Milly, 2004; Film: Captain Jack, 1997; Solomon & Gaenor, 1998; The Discovery of Heaven, 2001; The Pianist, 2001; Lighthouse Hill, 2002; Supertex, 2002; Radio: The Lipman Test, 1996-97; Choice Grenfell, 1998; Home Truths, 2002. Publications: How Was It For You? 1985; Something to Fall Back On, 1987; You Got an 'Ology?, with Richard Phillips, 1989; Thank You For Having Me, 1990; When's It Coming Out? 1992; You Can Read Me Like a Book, 1995; Lip Reading, 1999. Honours: CBE; Hon D Litt, Hull and Sheffield; Hon MA, Salford. Memberships: BAFTA; Equity. Address: c/o Conway van Gelder Ltd, 18-21 Jerryn Street, London SW1Y 6HP, England.

**LIPPITT John Andrew,** b. 17 January 1967, Wolverhampton, England. Academic. Education: BSc, Honours, Maths and Philosophy, University of Manchester, 1988; M Litt, Philosophy, University of Durham, 1992; PhD, Philosophy, University of Essex, 2000. Appointments: Lecturer in Philosophy, 1992-94, Senior Lecturer in Philosophy, 1994-2001, Reader in Ethics and Philosophy of Religion, 2001-, University of Hertfordshire. Publications: Books: Nietzsche's Futures (edited), 1999; Nietzsche and the Divine (co-edited with Jim Urpeth), 2000; Humour and Irony in Kierkegaard's Thought, 2000; Kierkegaard and Fear and Trembling, 2003; Numerous articles in refereed journals and book collections. Honours: AHRB Research Leave Scheme Award, 1999; Kierkegaard House Foundation Visiting Research Fellow, St Olaf College, Minnesota, 2004-2005. Memberships: American Philosophical Association; British Philosophical Association; Søren Kierkegaard Society of the UK, Secretary 1998-2001. Address: Philosophy Group, University of Hertfordshire, De Havilland Campus, Hatfield, Herts AL10 9AB, England.

**LIPWORTH Maurice Sydney (Sir),** b. 13 May 1931, Johannesburg, South Africa. Barrister; Businessman. m. Rosa Liwarek, 1957, 2 sons. Education: BCom, LLB, University of Witwatersrand. Appointments: Practising Barrister, Johannesburg, 1956-64; Non-Executive Director, Liberty Life Association of Africa Ltd, 1956-64; Executive, Private Trading Companies, 1964-67; Executive Director, Abbey Life Assurance PLC, 1968-70; Vice-President, Director, Abbey International Corporation Inc, 1968-70; Co-Founder, Director, 1970-88, Deputy Managing Director, 1977-79, Joint Managing Director, 1979-84, Deputy Chairman, 1984-88, Allied Dunbar Assurance PLC; Director, J Rothschild Holdings PLC, 1984-87; Director, BAT Industries PLC, 1985-88; Deputy Chairman of Trustees, 1986-93, Chairman, 1993-, Philharmonia Orchestra; Chairman, Monopolies and Mergers Commission, 1988-92; Non-Executive Director, Carlton Communications PLC, 1993-; Deputy Chairman, Non-Executive Director, National Westminster Bank, 1993-2000; Chairman, Financial Reporting Council, 1993-2001; Non-Executive Director, 1994-99, Chairman, 1995-99, Zeneca Group PLC; Member, Senior Salaries Review Body, 1994-; Trustee, South Bank Ltd, 1996-. Honours: Honorary Queen's Council, 1993. Memberships: Chairman, Bar Association for Commerce, Finance and Industry, 1991-91; European Policy Forum. Address: 41 Lothbury, London EC2P 2BP, England.

**LISBERG Harvey Brian,** b. 2 March 1940, Manchester, England. Impressario; Artist Manager. m. Carole Gottlieb, 5 November 1969, 2 sons. Education: Manchester University. Musical Education: Self-taught piano, guitar. Career: First in discovering: Graham Gouldman; Andrew Lloyd Webber; Tim Rice; Herman's Hermits; Tony Christie; Sad Cafe; Godley and Creme; 10cc; Currently representing: 10cc; Graham Gouldman; Eric Stewart; George Stiles; Anthony Drewe; Cleopatra. Address: Kennedy House, 31 Stamford Street, Altrincham, Cheshire WA14 1ES, England.

**LISICYNAS Vladimiras,** b. 10 August 1946, Latvia. Martial Arts Specialist. Education: Purveying College, Moscow, Russia, 1961-64; Moscow Polygraphic Institute Courses in Riga, 1964-65; Radio Electronics Military School, Vilnius, 1966-69; Military Academy, Kcharkov, Ukraine, 1972-76; Studies, Economics Department, 1982-84, Philosophy Department, 1985-87, Vilnius University; Ministry of Communication Courses,

1987-89; Coaches Requalification Courses, Vilnius Pedagogical University, 2001-2003. Appointments include: Military Service, Soviet Army, 1965-80; Senior Engineer, Enterprise "Vilma", 1980-93; Photographer Artist, Children's Photographic Studio, 1981-90; Started to teach Aikido and self defence systems, 1988-; Supervisor, Lithuanian Independence Restoration Headquarters, 1989-92; Senior Self Defence Instructor, Lithuanian Police Supporters Union, 1990-95; President, Traditional Aikido Club, Vilnius, 1993-97; President, Traditional Aikido Centre, Vilnius, 1997-; Signatory, World Martial Arts Federation, 1997-; Professor of Martial Arts Self-Defence, 1998; Member, Representative for Lithuania, World Martial Arts Coalition, 2000-; Signatory, President, Lithuanian Traditional Aikido Federation, 2001-; Vice-President, Signatory, World Korosu Federation, 2003-; Member, Country Representative for Lithuania, International Bodyguards and Security Services Association, 2004-; Founder, Creator "KoKoro Su Ryu" Martial Arts Systems, 2004-; Founder, Creator, "Lithuanian Savigyna" Martial Arts Systems, 2004-; Master Level: Rated one of the 100 World Masters, 1997; Presented with 8 level black belt in Moroko Self Defence, 1998; Member of the World Martial Arts Union Martial Arts Festival in South Korea, 2000-2004; Presented with Aikido and Akijutsu of Korosu 7th Degree 1 Black Belts, 2001; Recognition as Grand Master, 10th Degree Black Belt of "KoKoro Su Ryu", 2004; Recognition as Founder, Creator, Patriarch and Grand Master of "Lithuanian Savigyna", 2004. Honours include: Rewards of the USSR and Soviet Army, 1967-80; Medal, Lithuanian Sports Department, 2003; Medal, For Service to Lithuanian Paraolympic Sport, 2003; Medal and Certificate, for services to 21st century, IBC; Medal and Honourable Diploma, Ukrainian Ministry of Physical Culture and Sport, 2004. Address: Naugarduko Str 7, Vilnius, Lithuania. E-mail:ltaf@centras.lt Website: www.aiki.lt

**LIST Anneliese,** b. 6 January 1922, Heroldsberg, Germany. Author. m. Huldreich List, deceased. Education: Opera House, Nürnberg; Degree in Dance, German Chamber of Theatres, Munich, 1939. Appointments: Dancer, Municipal Theatre Guben, 1939, 40; Dance Soubrette, Municipal Theatre, Landsberg/Warthe, 1941, 1942; Dance Soubrette, Municipal Theatre of Thorn, 1943, 1944, Operetten-Soubrette, Municipal Theatre of Elbing, 1944, 1945; Clerk, Secretary, Nuremberg Field Office, American Consulate General, US Embassy's Escapee Program, 1954-60; Clerk-in-Charge, Foreigners Office, City of Nuremberg, 1960-82, Retired, 1982. Publications: Many stories and poems include: What I'll Never be Able to Forget in All my Life, 1975; My Long Way from the War until Today, 1975; How I Earned My First Money, 1977; The First Dance, 1977; The Luck Behind the Mountains (booklet with 4 stories), 1978; Dedicated to My Little Cat, 1990; Jubilate, 1991; The Rainbow, 1992; The Window, 1992; Her Most Beautiful Christmas, 1992; The Open Chimney, 1992; The Heroine, 1993; The Forest-Sea, 1995; Unbelievable Stories, 1995; Just a Poor Devil, 1994; The Revenge is Mine, 1994; The Ways of God are Miraculous, 1997; Dedicated to My Guardian Angels, 1998; Patience, 1999; Book: Ein Künstlerleben in schwerer Zeit (memoirs), 2002; Present Editions: Schoenbuch-Verlag and Friedmann-Verlag. Honours include: 2nd Prize for the Best Story, What I'll Never be Able to Forget in All My Life; Gold Medal of the City of Nürnberg, 1982; World Literary Academy, International Biographical Centre, 1986; International Cultural Diploma of Honour, ABI, 1988; Cultural Doctorate in Literature, World University Roundtable, 1988; Commemorative Medal of Honour, 1988; World Decoration of Excellence Medallion, 1989; Biographical Roll of Honor, Historical Preservations of America, 1989; World Lifetime Achievement Award, 1992; Diplome d'Honneur, Institute des Affaires Internationales, France, 1995; Named to Order of International Ambassadors, IBC, 1997; Twentieth Century Achievement Award, 1997; Millennium Hall of Fame, Medal and Award, 1997; 2000 Millennium Medal of Honor, 2000; Included in the IBC Millennium Time-Capsule, 2001. Membership: World Literary Academy, IBC, England. Address: Ritter-von-Schuh Platz 15, 90459 Nürnberg, Germany.

**LISTE Hartmut Manfred Heinz,** b. 20 August 1947, Berlin, Germany. Language Professor. Education: Russian, Czech, Slovac and French Languages, Humboldt University, Berlin, 1966-1971; Diplom-Philologe, Humboldt University, Berlin, 1971-1973; Dr Phil, 1975. Appointments: Scientific Assistant, Humboldt University, Berlin, 1971-1973; Researcher, Professor of Languages, Humboldt University, Berlin, 1973-. Publications: Pocket Education Manual of the Czech Language, 1980, 2nd edition, 1983, 3rd edition, 1985, 4th edition, 1987, 5th edition, 1990; Pocket Dictionary Czech-German, 1986, 2nd edition, 1987, 3rd edition, 1990. Memberships: Trade Union Education Sciences; Evangelical German Church. Address: Schivelbeiner Str. 26, D-10439, Berlin, Germany. E-mail: hartmut.liste@rz.hu-berlin.de

**LISTER Richard Percival,** b. 23 November 1914, Nottingham, England. Author; Poet; Painter. m. Ione Mary Wynniatt-Husey, 24 June 1985. Education: BSc, Manchester University. Publications: Novels: The Way Backwards, 1950; The Oyster and the Torpedo, 1951; Rebecca Redfern, 1953; The Rhyme and the Reason, 1963; The Questing Beast, 1965; One Short Summer, 1974. Poetry: The Idle Demon, 1958; The Albatross, 1986. Travel: A Journey in Lapland, 1965; Turkey Observed, 1967; Glimpses of a Planet, 1997. Biography: The Secret History of Genghis Khan, 1969; Marco Polo's Travels, 1976; The Travels of Herodotus, 1979. Short Stories: Nine Legends, 1991; Two Northern Stories, 1996. Contributions to: Punch; New Yorker; Atlantic Monthly. Honour: Royal Society of Literature, fellow, 1970. Address: Flat 11, 42 St James's Gardens, London W11 4RQ, England.

**LITHERLAND Sheila Jacqueline,** b. 18 September 1936, Birmingham, England. Poet; Creative Writing/Literature Tutor. Divorced, 1 son, 1 daughter. Education: Regent Street Polytechnic, 1955; Ruskin College, Oxford, 1986; BA, University College, London, 1989. Publications: The Long Interval; Fourpack; Half Light; Modern Poets of Northern England; New Women Poets; The Poetry of Perestroika; Flowers of Fever; The Apple Exchange. Contributions to: Iron Magazine; Writing Women Magazine; Oxford Magazine; Green Book. Honour: Annaghmakerrig Residence, 1994; Nothern Writers Award, 2000. Memberships: Colpitts Poetry; Poetry Society. Address: 6 Waddington Street, Durham City DH1 4BG, England.

**LITTEN Nancy Magaret,** b. 30 September 1951, Dartford, Kent, England. Musician. m. Clinton Davis, 2 sons, 1 daughter. Education: LRAM Violin (Teacher's), 1970, LRAM Piano (Teacher's), 1971, Royal Academy of Music; Cert Ed, Exeter, 1972; ATCL Voice (Performer's), 2001. Appointments: Teacher of Piano, Singing, Violin and Keyboard, Kent Music School, 1997-; ABRSM Examiner, 1998-; Founder, Director, Kent Keyboard Orchestra, 1999-, and Kent Music's Singing Days for Instrumentalists; Freelance Accompanist and Adjudicator. Publications: Contributor to the Federation of Music Services, A Common Approach, 2002, keyboard section; Consultant to ABRSM for Electronic Keyboard Music Medals, 2004-. Honours: Elizabeth Stokes Open Piano Scholarship, 1968; Janet Duff Greet Prize for most deserving British scholar, 1970, 1971. Membership: Incorporated Society of Musicians. Address: Springfield, 39 Ashford Road, Maidstone, Kent ME14 5DP, England.

**LITTLE RICHARD (Richard Penniman),** b. 5 December 1935, Macon, Georgia, USA. Singer; Musician (piano). Education: Theological college, 1957. Career: R&B singer, various bands; Tours and film work with own band, The Upsetters; Gospel singer, 1960-62; World-wide tours and concerts include: Star Club, Hamburg, Germany, with Beatles, 1962; European tour, with Beatles, Rolling Stones, 1963; UK tour with Everly Brothers, 1963; Rock'n'Revival Concert, Toronto, with Chuck Berry, Fats Domino, Jerry Lee Lewis, Gene Vincent, Bo Diddley, 1969; Toronto Pop Festival, 1970; Randall Island Rock Festival, with Jimi Hendrix, Jethro Tull, 1970; Rock'n'Roll Spectaculars, Madison Square Garden, 1972-; Muhammad Ali's 50th Birthday; Benefit For Lupus Foundation, Universal City, 1992; Westbury Music Fair, 1992; Giants Of Rock'n'Roll, Wembley Arena, 1992; Film appearances: Don't Knock The Rock, 1956; Mr Rock'n'Roll, 1957; The Girl Can't Help It, 1957; Keep On Rockin', 1970; Down And Out In Beverly Hills, 1986; Mother Goose Rock'n'Rhyme, Disney Channel, 1989. Recordings: Albums: Here's Little Richard, 1957; Little Richard Is Back, 1965; Greatest Hits, 1965; Freedom Blues, 1970; The King Of Rock'n'Roll, 1971; God's Beautiful City, 1979; Lifetime Friend, 1987; Featured on: Folkways - A Vision Shared (Woody Guthrie tribute), 1988; For Our Children, 1991; Shake It All About, 1992; Little Richard and Jimi Hendrix, 1993; Shag on Down by the Union Hall,1996; Hit singles include: Tutti Frutti, 1956; Long Tall Sally, 1956; The Girl Can't Help It, 1957; Lucille, 1957; She's Got It, 1957; Jenny Jenny, 1957; Keep A Knockin', 1957; Good Golly Miss Molly, 1958, Baby Face, 1959; Bama Lama Bama Loo, 1964. Honours include: Inducted, Rock'n'Roll Hall of Fame, 1986; Star, Hollywood Walk Of Fame, 1990; Little Richard Day, Los Angeles, 1990; Penniman Boulevard, Macon, named in his honour; Platinum Star, Lupus Foundation Of America, 1992; Grammy Lifetime Achievement Award, 1993.

**LITTLEFIELD Larry James,** b. 7 February 1938, Ft Smith, Arkansas, USA. Plant Pathologist. m. Julianne Hooper Littlefield, 1 son, 2 daughters. Education: BS, Cornell University, 1960; MS, 1962, PhD, 1964, University of Minnesota. Appointments: Assistant Professor, Associate Professor, Full Professor, North Dakota State University, Fargo, North Dakota, 1965-85; International Programmes Specialist, US Department of Agriculture, Washington, DC, 1980-82; Professor and Head, Department of Plant Pathology, 1985-96, Professor Department of Entomology and Plant Pathology, 1996-2004, Professor Emeritus, 2004-, Oklahoma State University. Publications: 43 research papers in scientific journals and 2 books on anatomy of host parasite relations on plants and fungal pathogens, and developmental anatomy of plant parasite fungi; Numerous abstracts, primary emphasis on rust diseases and rust fungi. Honour: National Science Foundation Postdoctoral Fellow, Uppsala University, Sweden, 1964-65. Memberships: American Phytopathological Society; Mycological Society of America. Address: Department of Entomology and Plant Pathology, Oklahoma State University, Stillwater, OK 74078, USA. E-mail: ljlplpa@okstate.edu

**LITTLEJOHN Joan Anne,** b. 20 April 1937, London, England. Creative Artist. Education: Royal College of Music, 1955-59; Postgraduate Study, Howells and Others; LRAM, 1957; GRSM, 1958. Appointments: Freelance Composer, Musicologist, Photographer, 1959-; Administrative Staff, Royal College of Music, 1960-83; Piano Teacher, Harrow School, 1972-73. Publications: Poems and Music. Honours: RVW Trust and Patrons Fund Awards in the 1970's; Recipient Howells' Composing Piano, 1984; Award of Merit, Golden Poet Award, 1985 and Silver Poet Award, 1986; Millennium Medal of Honour, 1998; Archives destined for The Nation, to be housed

at The Devon Record Office. Memberships: PRS; ABIRA. Address: Shepherds Delight, 49 Hamilton Lane, Exmouth, Devon EX8 2LW, England.

**LITTLEMORE Christopher Paul,** b. 8 March 1959, Warwickshire, England. Architect. m. Jane Evelyn Chalk, 1 son, 1 daughter. Education: BA (Hons), B.Arch, Manchester University, 1977-83; MSc, Conservation of Historic Buildings, Bath University, 1998-99. Appointments: Associate, 1986, Director, 1989, Managing Director, 2002, The Charter Partnership, Architects. Membership: Royal Institute of British Architects. Address: Meadow House, Broad Chalke, Nr Salisbury, Wilts, England. E-mail: cplittlemore@charter. eu.com

**LITTON Andrew,** b. 16 May 1959, New York City, New York, USA. Orchestral Conductor; Pianist. Education: Mozarteum, Salzburg; Juilliard School of Music; MM. Appointments: Assistant Conductor, La Scala, Milan, 1980-81; Exxon-Arts Endowment Assistant Conductor, then Associate Conductor, National Symphony Orchestra, Washington DC, 1982-86; Principal Guest Conductor, 1986-88, Principal Conductor, Artistic Adviser, 1988-94, Conductor Laureate, 1994-, Bournemouth Symphony Orchestra; Music Director, Dallas Symphony Orchestra, 1994-; Guest Conductor, many leading orchestras world-wide including Chicago Symphony, Philadelphia, Los Angeles Philharmonic, Pittsburgh Symphony, Toronto Symphony, Montreal Symphony, Vancouver Symphony, London Philharmonic, Royal Philharmonic, London Symphony, English Chamber, Leipzig Gewandhaus, Moscow State Symphony, Stockholm Philharmonic, RSO Berlin, RAI Milan, Orchestre National de France, Suisse Romande, Tokyo Philharmonic, Melbourne Symphony and Sydney Symphony orchestras; Opera debut with Eugene Onegin, Metropolitan Opera, New York, 1989; Conducted Leoncavallo, La Bohème and Falstaff, St Louis Opera, Hansel and Gretel, Los Angeles Opera, 1992, Porgy and Bess, Royal Opera House, Covent Garden, 1992, Salome, English National Opera, 1996; Music Consultant to film The Chosen. Publications: Recordings including Mahler Symphony No 1 and Songs of a Wayfarer, Elgar Enigma Variations, complete Tchaikovsky symphony cycle, complete Rachmaninov symphony cycle, Shostakovich Symphony No 10, Gershwin Rhapsody in Blue, Concerto in F, Bernstein Symphony No 2, Brahms Symphony No 1; As piano soloist and conductor, Ravel Concerto in G. Honours: Winner, William Kapell Memorial US National Piano Competition, 1978; Winner, Bruno Walter Conducting Fellowship, 1981; Winner, BBC-Rupert Foundation International Conductors Competition, 1982; Honorary DMus, Bournemouth, 1992. Address: c/o IMG Artists Europe, Media House, 3 Burlington Lane, London W4 2TH, England.

**LITVINENKO Ivan T,** b. 25 February 1932, Novosibirsk Region, Russia. Agricultural Engineer. m. Tamara Bazilevitch, 1 daughter. Education: Diploma, Siberian Construction University, Novosibirsk, 1955; Candidate of Architecture, Novosibirsk, 1964; Doctor of Agricultural Sciences, Tashkent, Uzbekistan, 1985; Degree of Professor, Novosibirsk, 1990. Appointments: Worked on virgin soils, Kazakhstan, 1955-57; Postgraduate Research Student, Research Institute of Rural Structures, Moscow, 1958-64; Researcher, Head of Laboratory, Dairy Complexes, Ministry of Agriculture of USSR, Novosibirsk, 1962-69; Department Head, Deputy Director, Siberian Institute of Animal Husbandry, SO RASKHN, Novosibirsk, 1970-88; Scientific Secretary-in-Chief, Head of International Co-operation Department, Presidium of Siberian Branch of the Russian Academy of Agricultural Sciences (SO RASKHN), Novosibirsk, 1989-. Publications: 228 publications in scientific editions including 5 monographs, 14 brochures, 7 album-reference books among them: Industrial Milk Production in Siberia, 1978; Beef Production on Industrial Scale in Siberia, 1982; Reference Book of Siberian Cattle Breeder, 2000. Honours: Order of Honour; Honoured Worker of Agriculture; Medal "Veteran of Labour"; Laureate of State Prize, USSR; Medal "The Best People of Russia"; Bearer of the Golden Badge "Property of Siberia". Memberships: Russian Ecological Academy; Presidium of the Siberian Branch of the Russian Academy of Agricultural Sciences; Novosibirsk Regional Committee of the Agricultural Workers Trade Union. Address: PO Box 463, Presidium SO RASKHN, 630501 Krasnoobsk, Novosibirsk Region, Russia. E-mail: vik@online.bu1at.ru

**LIU Huizhen,** b. 12 July 1942, Shanghai Municipality, China. Therapist; Historian of the Development of Traditional Chinese Medicine. m. Zhang Jian, deceased, 2 sons. Education: BA, Beijing University of Traditional Chinese Medicine; MA, China Research Institute of Traditional Chinese Medicine. Appointment: Researcher on Medical Literature, China Institute for the History of Chinese Traditional Medicine. Publications: The New Meaning of Chinese Medical History (co-editor); Medical History, 2004; Over 20 articles including: The Researches on Prevention and Cure of Infectious Diseases by Modern Doctors of Traditional Chinese Medicine. Honours: Gold Medal for National Excellent Work on Chinese Medical History; First Prize, China Society of Chinese Traditional Medicine, 2004. Membership: Jiusan Society. Address: Rm 241, Unit 4, Bldg 6, No 1 Caochang Road, Haidian District, Beijing, China. E-mail: zhangjin@bbn.cn

**LIU Kai,** b. 1 December 1964, Yunnan, China. Mathematician; Lecturer. Education: BSc, Mathematics, Department of Mathematics, Beijing Normal University, People's Republic of China, 1983-97; MSc, Probability and Statistics, Research Department, Central South University, People's Republic of China, 1987-90; PhD, Probability and Statistics, Department of Statistics and Modelling Science, University of Strathclyde, Scotland, 1995-98. Appointments: Assistant Professor, Department of Mathematics, Changsha Railway University, People's Republic of China, 1990-93; Research Fellow, 1993-94, Reader, 1994-95, Department of Mathematics, Huazhong University of Science and Technology; Postdoctoral Senior Research Fellow, 1998-99, Lecturer (fixed term),1999-2000, Department of Mathematics, University of Wales, Swansea, Wales; Lecturer (fixed term), Department of Probability and Statistics, University of Sheffield, England, 2000-2002; Lecturer, Department of Mathematical Sciences, Division of Statistics and OR, University of Liverpool, England, 2002-. Publications: Book: Stability of Stochastic Differential Equations in Infinite Dimensions, in preparation; Articles in scientific journals include most recently as co-author: Piecewise Birth-Death processes with an instantaneous reflection barrier, 2003; Birth-Death processes with disaster and instantaneous resurrection, 2004; Robustness of pathwise stability of semilinear perturbed stochastic evolution equations, 2004. Honours include: Research Fellowship, Daikô Foundation, 1993-94; National Science Funding for Young Scientists, 1994-95; Overseas Research Scholarship, 1995-98; Standard Studentship, Strathclyde University, 1995-98; EPSRC Grants, 2002-2004; Research Development Fund, 2003-2004; LMS Collaborative Small Grant, 2004-2004; 4 invited lectures. Address: Division of Statistics & OR, Department of Mathematical Sciences, University of Liverpool, Liverpool L68 7ZL, England. E-mail: k.liu@liv.ac.uk

**LIU Zhaorong,** b. 1 June 1937, Zuoquan County, Shanxi Province, China. Educator. m. Shaohua Zhao, 1 son, 3 daughters. Education: Mathematical Department, Harbin Teachers' College.

Appointment: Teacher, Yuci Railway Middle School, 1962-95. Publications: The Proof of Goldbach's Conjecture; Numerous other mathematical research papers. Honours: Listed in Who's Who publications and biographical dictionaries. Membership: American Mathematical Society. Address: #168 Anning Street, Yuci District, Jinzhong City, Shanxi Province 030600, People's Republic of China. E-mail: qingqingcao830@yahoo.com

**LIU Zong-Lin,** b. 1 June 1930, Jiang-Yin City, Jiang-Su Province, China. Power Plant and Supply Engineer. m. Jian-Hua Xie, 2 sons. Education: Graduate, National Shanghai Chiao Tung University, 1953. Appointments: Chief Engineer, North China Electric Power Testing and Research Institute, 1983-91; Professorial Senior Engineer, NCEPRI's Association Society of Science and Technique, 1991-2000. Publications: Electric Instrument, 1959; More than 20 articles include: The improvement of the waveform of the ferrous-magnetic saturated stabilizator; The rapid method for calculation of the synthetic measurement errors of PT & CT in the 3-phase, 3-wire electric circuit. The technical supervision experience for the electrical measurement instruments (article popularised to apply to all power plants and substations by Electric Power Ministry of China in 1963). Honours: Advanced Worker of Science and Technique of Beijing, 1977; Advanced Worker of Science and Technique of the Electric Power Ministry of China, 1979. Memberships: Communist of CPC; Senior Member, Society of Electrical Engineering of China. Address: No 1 Dizang-an Nanxiang, Fuxingmen wai, Beijing 100045, China

**LIVELY Penelope Margaret,** b. 17 March 1933, Cairo, Egypt. Writer. m. Jack Lively, 27 June 1957, 1 son, 1 daughter. Education: Honours Degree, Modern History, Oxford University, England. Publications: Fiction: The Road to Lichfield, 1977; Nothing Missing But the Samovar, and Other Stories, 1978; Treasures of Time, 1979; Judgement Day, 1980; Next to Nature, Art, 1982; Perfect Happiness, 1983; Corruption and Other Stories, 1984; According to Mark, 1984; Moon Tiger, 1986; Pack of Cards: Stories 1978-86, 1987; Passing On, 1989; City of the Mind, 1991; Cleopatra's Sister, 1993; Heat Wave, 1996; Beyond the Blue Mountains: Stories, 1997; Spider Web, 1998; The Photograph, 2003; Making It Up, 2005. Non-Fiction: The Presence of the Past: An Introduction to Landscape History, 1976; Oleander, Jacaranda, 1992; A House Unlocked, 2001. Children's Books: Astercote, 1970; The Whispering Knights, 1971; The Driftway, 1972; Going Back, 1973; The Ghost of Thomas Kempe, 1974; Boy Without a Name, 1975; Fanny's Sister, 1976; The Stained Glass Window, 1976; A Stitch in Time, 1976; Fanny and the Monsters, 1978; The Voyage of QV66, 1978; Fanny and the Battle of Potter's Piece, 1980; The Revenge of Samuel Stokes, 1981; Uninvited Ghosts and Other Stories, 1984; Dragon Trouble, Debbie and the Little Devil, 1984; A House Inside Out, 1987; In Search of A Homeland: The Story of the Aeneid, 2001. Contributions to: Numerous journals and magazines. Honours: Officer of the Order of the British Empire, 1989; Commander of the British Empire, 2002; Several honorary degrees and literary awards. Address: c/o David Higham Associates, 5-8 Lower John Street, Golden Square, London W1R 4HA, England.

**LIVERPOOL, Bishop of, Rt Rev James Stuart Jones,** b. 1948, Glasgow, Scotland. Anglican Bishop. m. Sarah Jones, 3 daughters. Education: BA honours, Theology, Exeter University, 1970; PGCE, Drama and Religious Education, 1971; Theological Training, Wycliffe Hall, Oxford. Appointments: Teacher of Religious Education and Latin; Producer at Scripture Union; Reader, 1976; Deacon, 1982; Priest, 1983; Bishop, 1994; Curate and then Associate Vicar, Christ Church with Emmanuel, Clifton, Bristol; Visiting Lecturer, Media Studies, Trinity

College, Bristol; Vicar of Emmanuel Church, South Croydon, 1990; Bishop of Southwark's Examining Chaplain; Bishop's Selector; Bishop of Hull, 1994; Bishop of Liverpool, 1998-. Publications: Author of books on Christian spirituality; Various articles for newspapers. Honours: Honorary Doctor of Divinity, University of Hull, 1999; Honorary Doctor of Letters, University of Lincolnshire and Humberside, 2001. Memberships: Chair, North West Constitutional Convention; Chair, Governing Body Kensington City Academy; Vice Chair, Board of Mission and Public Affairs for Church of England; Chair, Wycliffe Hall, Oxford; President Church Pastoral Aid Society; Co-president, Liverpool Hope College; Member, Governing Council of Liverpool University; Fellow, University of Gloucestershire; Foundation Governor, Blue Coat School, Liverpool; Visitor, Liverpool College, Liverpool; Member, Urban Bishops Panel of the Church of England; Vice President, Tear Fund. Address: Bishop's Lodge, Woolton Park, Liverpool L25 6DT, England.

**LIVESLEY Brian,** b. 31 August 1936, Southport, Lancashire, England. Medical Practitioner. m. Valerie Anne Nuttall, 1 son, 2 daughters. Education: MB, ChB, Leeds University Medical School, 1960. Appointments: Clinical Training and Teaching posts, University and District Hospitals, Leeds, Manchester and Liverpool, 1961-69; Harvey Research Fellow, King's College Hospital Medical School, London, 1969-72; Consultant Physician, Geriatric Medicine, Southwark, London, 1973-88; University of London's Foundation Professor in the Care of the Elderly, Honorary Consultant Physician in General and Geriatric Medicine, Chelsea and Westminster Hospital NHS Trust, London, 1988-2001; North West Thames Regional Adviser, Postgraduate Education, British Postgraduate Medical Federation, 1990-96; Invited Expert on the care of elderly persons for several Police Constabularies and HM Coroner's offices, 1999-; The University of London's Emeritus Professor in the Care of the Elderly, 2003-. Publications: Over 150 professional publications. Honours: Officer Brother, 1992, Knight, 1994, Most Venerable Order of St John of Jerusalem. Memberships: Master, 2005-, Worshipful Society of Apothecaries of London; Royal Society of Medicine; Royal College of Physicians of London; British Medical Association; British Academy of Forensic Sciences; Association of Forensic Physicians. Address: PO Box 295, Oxford OX2 9GD, England. E-mail: brian.livesley@btinternet.com

**LIVINGSTON Dorothy Kirby,** b. 6 January 1948, Gosforth, Northumberland. Solicitor. 2 daughters. Education: MA, Jurisprudence, Hugh's College, Oxford, 1966-69. Appointments: Trainee, 1970, Assistant Solicitor, 1972, Partner, 1980, Herbert Smith; Member, Advisory Board, Centre for European Law, King's College, London, 1996; Member, City of London Law Society Competition Law Committee, 1998; Chairman, City of London Law Society Financial Law Committee, 1999; Member, Bank of England Financial Markets Law Committee, 2002. Publications: Competition Law and Practice, 1995; The Competition Act 1998: A Practitioner's Guide, 2001; Competition Law chapters in Leasing and Asset Finance, 3rd edition 1997, 4th edition 2003. Address: Herbert Smith, Exchange House, Primrose Street, London EC2A 2HS, England. E-mail: dorothy.livingston@herbertsmith.com

**LIVINGSTONE Kenneth Robert,** b. 17 June 1945, London, England. Politician. m. Christine Pamela Chapman, 1973, divorced 1982. Education: Phillipa Fawcett College of Education. Appointments: Technician, Cancer Research Unit, Royal Marsden Hospital, 1962-70; Joined, 1969, Member, Regional Executive, 1974-86, National Executive Council, 1987-89, 1997-, Northern Ireland Select Committee, 1997-99, Labour Party; Councillor, Borough of Lambeth, 1971-78;

Councillor, Borough of Camden, 1978-82; Councillor, 1973-86, Leader, 1981-86, Greater London Council; Member of Parliament for Brent East, 1987-; Elected Mayor of London, 2000-2004, Re-elected 2004-. Publications: If Voting Changed Anything They'd Abolish It, 1987; Livingstone's Labour, 1989. Memberships: Zoological Society of London, Council, 1994-, Vice-President, 1996-98. Address: Greater London Authority, Romney House, Marsham Street, London, SW1P 3PY. E-mail: mayor@london.gov.uk

**LIYANAGE Sunil,** b. 27 September 1941, Colombo, Sri Lanka. Consultant Rheumatologist. m. Isabella Nallamanickam, 2 sons. Education: MBBS (Ceylon), 1965; FRCP (UK); DCH (Eng); DipMedAc. Appointments: Consultant Rheumatologist in East Berkshire, 1975-; Medical Director, Heatherwood and Wexham Park NHS Trust, 1991-95. Publications: Chapters in: Recent Advances in Rheumatology; Textbook of Rheumatology; Handbook of Drug Interactions. Memberships: British Society for Rheumatology; American Society for Bone and Mineral Research; British Medical Acupuncture Society, former Chairman. Address: The Princess Margaret Hospital, Windsor, SL4 3SJ, England. E-mail: rheumatology@lineone.net Website: www.medicalacupuncture.co.uk

**LJUBENOV Todor Todorov,** b. 31 March 1942, Sofia, Bulgaria. Physician; Radiotherapist; Oncologist. m. Dimitra Furnadjieva Ljubenova, 1 daughter. Education: Graduate, Medical University, Sofia, Bulgaria, 1969; Postgraduate School, Berlin-Buch, Germany, 1970-71; MD, Berlin, 1970; Specialisation, Medical University, Geneva, Switzerland, 1984. Appointments: Lecturer, School of Radiology, 1976-80, Chief Assistant Professor, Department of Nuclear Medicine and Radiotherapy, Faculty of Medicine, Medical University, Sofia, 1973-2003; Collaborator in Cyclophasotron, Joint Institute for Nuclear Research, Dubna, Russia, 2002. Honours: Listed in Who's Who publications and biographical dictionaries. Publications: Chapters in books and articles in scientific journals including: Handbook of Rentgenology and Radiology, 1985; The British Journal of Radiology, 1992; Oral Oncology vol II, 1991; Radiobiology, Radiotherapy, 1988; Diabolisme in Medical Mundi parts I, II, III, 1999-2003. Memberships: Member Elect, American Diabetes Society, 2001. Address: 8 Nikolai Pavlovich Street, 1142 Sofia, Bulgaria.

**LLEWELLIN (John) Richard (Allan),** b. 30 September 1938, Haverfordwest, South Wales. Bishop. m. Jennifer Sally House, 1 son, 2 daughters. Education: Clifton College, Bristol; Theological studies, Westcott House and Fitzwilliam College, Cambridge, 1961-64. Appointments: Articled to Messrs Farrer and Co of Lincoln's Inn Fields; Solicitor, Messrs Field Roscoe and Co, London; Assistant Curate, Radlett, Hertfordshire, 1964-68; Assistant Priest, Johannesburg Cathedral, South Africa, 1968-71; Vicar of Waltham Cross, 1971-79; Rector of Harpenden, 1979; Bishop of St Germans, 1985; Bishop of Dover and Bishop in Canterbury, 1992; Bishop at Lambeth and Head of Staff to the Archbishop of Canterbury, 1999-. Address: Lambeth Palace, London, SE1 7JU, England. Email: richard.llewellin@1 ampal.c-of-e.org.uk

**LLEWELLYN SMITH Christopher Hubert (Sir),** b. 19 November 1942, Giggleswick, England. Physicist. m. Virginia Grey, 1 son, 1 daughter. Education: BA, Physics with First Class Honours, 1964, DPhil, Theoretical Physics, 1967, Oxford University. Appointments: Royal Society Exchange Fellow, Physical Institute, Academy of Sciences, Moscow, USSR, 1967-68; Fellow in the Theoretical Studies Division, European Laboratory for Particle Physics (CERN), Geneva, Switzerland, 1968-70; Research Associate, Stanford Linear Accelerator

Center, Stanford, California, USA, 1970-72; Staff Member, Theoretical Studies Division, CERN, Geneva, 1972-74; Fellow, St John's College, Oxford, 1974-98; Lecturer, 1974-80, Reader, 1980-87, Professor of Theoretical Physics, 1987-98, Chairman of Physics, 1987-92; Science Research Council Senior Fellow, 1978-81; Director General of CERN (on secondment from Oxford), 1994-98; Provost and President, University College, London, 1999-2002; Senior Research Fellow, Department of Physics, University of Oxford, 2002-2003; Director, UKAEA Culham Division and Head of the Euratom/UKAEA Fusion Association, 2003-; Chairman, Consultative Committee for Euratom on Fusion, 2004-. Publications: Numerous articles on high energy physics, fusion energy, science policy and international collaboration in science. Honours: Maxwell Prize and Medal, Institute of Physics, Fellow of the Royal Society, 1984; Academia Europaea, 1989; Fellow, American Physical Society, 1994; Honorary DSc, Bristol, UK, 1997; Honorary D.Cien., Granada, Spain, 1997; Honorary DSc, Shandong China, 1997; Medal, Japanese Association of Medical Sciences, 1997; Gold Medal, Slovak Academy of Science, 1997; Foreign Fellow, Indian National Science Academy; Honorary Fellow, University of Wales, Cardiff, 1998; Distinguished Associate Award, US Department of Energy, 1998; Distinguished Service Award, US National Science Foundation, 1998; Glazebrook Medal, Institute of Physics, 1999; Honorary Fellow, St John's College, Oxford, 2000; Knight Bachelor, 2001; Honorary Fellow, New College, Oxford, 2002; Honorary Fellow, Institute of Mathematics and its Applications, 2003. Address: Culham Science Centre, Abingdon, Oxon OX14 3DB, England. E-mail: chris.llewellyn-smith@akaea.org.uk

**LLOYD Christopher,** b. 22 October 1938, Stamford, Connecticut, USA. Actor. m. Carol. Education: Neighbourhood Playhouse, New York. Appointments: Film Debut, One Flew Over the Cuckoo's Nest, 1975; Films include: Butch and Sundance: The Early Days; The Onion Field; The Black Marble; The Legend of the Lone Ranger; Mr Mom; To Be or Not to Be; Star Trek III: The Search for Spock; Adventures of Buckaroo Banzai; Back to the Future; Clue; Who Framed Roger Rabbit?; Track 29; Walk Like a Man; Eight Men Out; The Dream Team; Why Me?; Back to the Future, Part II; Back to the Future, Part III; The Addams Family; Twenty Bucks; Dennis the Menace; Addams Family Values; The Pagemaster; Camp Nowhere; The Radioland Murders; Things To Do in Denver When You're Dead; Cadillac Ranch; Changing Habits; Dinner at Fred's; Baby Geniuses; My Favorite Martian; Man on the Moon; Chasing Destiny, 2000; When Good Ghouls Go Bad, 2001; Wit, 2001; Wish You Were Dead, 2003; Interstate 60, 2003; TV includes: Taxi; Best of the West; The Dictator; Tales from Hollywood Hills; Pat Hobby - Teamed with Genius; September Gun; Avonlea; Alice in Wonderland. Honours: Winner, Drama Desk and Obie Awards, Kaspar, 1973. Address: The Gersh Agency, 252 North Canon Drive, Beverly Hills, CA 90210, USA.

**LLOYD Clive Hubert,** b. 31 August 1944, British Guiana, now Guyana. Cricketer. m. Waveney Benjamin, 1 son, 2 daughters. Career: Left-Hard Batsman, Right-Arm Medium-Paced Bowler; Played for British Guiana and Guyana, 1963-83; Played, 1968-86, Captain, 1981-83, 1986, for Lancashire; 110 Tests for West Indies, 1966-85, with record 74 as Captain, scoring 7,515 runs, averaging 46.6, including 19 centuries; Toured England, 1969, 1973, 1975 in World Cup, 1976, 1979 in World Cup, 1980, 1983 in World Cup, 1984; Scored 31,232 first-class runs including 79 centuries; Director, Red Rose Radio PLC, 1981; Executive Promotions Officer, Project Fullemploy, 1987-; West Indies Team Man, 1988-89, 1996-; International Cricket Council Referee, 1992-95. Publications: Living for Cricket, co-author, 1980; Winning Captaincy, co-author, 1995.

Honours: Commander, Order of the British Empire. Address: c/o Harefield, Harefield Drive, Wilmslow, Cheshire SK9 1NJ, England.

**LLOYD (David) Huw (Owen),** b. 14 April 1950, London, England. Family Doctor. m. Mary Eileen, 1 son, 3 daughters. Education: Gonville and Caius College, Cambridge, 1968-71; Guy's Hospital, London, 1971-74; Somerset Vocational Training Scheme, 1976-79. Appointments: Principal, Cadwgan Surgery, Old Colwyn; Clinical Governance Lead, Conwy Local Health Group. Memberships: Fellow, Royal College of General Practitioners; Chairman, Mental Health Task Group, RCGP; Deputy Chairman, North Wales Local Medical Committee; Member, Welsh Council, RCGP; General Practitioners Committee, Wales. Address: Maes yr Onnen, Abergele Road, Llanddulas; Abergele LL22 8EN, Wales. E-mail: huwlloyd@welshnet.co.uk

**LLOYD Elisabeth Anne,** b. 3 September 1956, Morristown, New Jersey, USA. Professor. Education: BA Science and Political Theory, University of Colorado, Boulder, 1980; PhD, Princeton University, 1984. Appointments: Assistant Professor, Department of Philosophy, University of California, San Diego, 1985-88; Assistant Professor, Department of Philosophy, 1988-90, Associate Professor, 1990-97, University of California, Berkeley; Affiliated Faculty, History and Philosophy of Science Programme, University of California, Davis, 1990-98; Professor, Department of Philosophy, University of California, Berkeley, 1997-99; Professor, Department History and Philosophy of Science, 1998-, Chair, Department of History and Philosophy of Science, 2000-04; Tanis Chair of History and Philosophy of Science, 2001-, Indiana University, Bloomington. Publications: 3 books; 38 articles in professional journals; 4 book reviews; numerous presentations and invited lectures; Articles and books in progress. Honours: University of California: Resident Fellow and Fellow, UC Humanities Research Institute; National Science Foundation Scholar's Award; Humanities Graduate Research Assistance Fellowship; Several grants; Regents Summer Faculty Fellowship; Princeton University: National Science Foundation Graduate Fellow; Garden State Graduate Award; University of Colorado: Phi Beta Kappa; Van Ek Award. Memberships include: American Philosophical Association; Philosophy of Science Association; International Society for the History, Philosophy and Social Studies of Biology. Address: History and Philosophy of Science Department, Goodbody Hall 130, Indiana University, Bloomington, IN 47405-2401, USA. E-mail: ealloyd@indiana.edu

**LLOYD Geoffrey (Ernest Richard) (Sir),** b. 25 January 1933, London, England. Emeritus Professor of Ancient Philosophy and Science; Writer. m. Janet Elizabeth Lloyd, 1956, 3 sons. Education: BA, 1954, MA, 1958, PhD, 1958, King's College, Cambridge. Appointments: Fellow, 1957, Senior Tutor, 1969-73, King's College, Cambridge; Assistant Lecturer in Classics, 1965-67, Lecturer in Classics, 1967-74, Reader in Ancient Philosophy and Science, 1974-83, Professor of Ancient Philosophy and Science, 1983-2000, Cambridge University; Bonsall Professor, Stanford University, 1981; Sather Professor, University of California at Berkeley, 1984; Visiting Professor, Beijing University and Academy of Sciences, 1987; Master, Darwin College, 1989-2000; Professor at Large, Cornell University, 1990-96; Zhu Kezhen Visiting Professor, Institute for the History of Natural Science, Beijing, 2002. Publications: Polarity and Analogy, 1966; Early Greek Science: Thales to Aristotle, 1970; Greek Science After Aristotle, 1973; Magic, Reason and Experience, 1979; Science, Folklore and Ideology, 1983; Science and Morality in Greco-Roman Antiquity, 1985; The Revolution of Wisdom, 1987; Demystifying Mentalities,

1990; Methods and Problems in Greek Science, 1991; Adversaries and Authorities, 1996; Aristotelian Explorations, 1996; The Way and the Word (with N Jivin), 2002; In the Grip of Disease, Studies in the Greek Imagination, 2003; Ancient Worlds, Modern Reflections, 2004; The Delusions of Invulnerability, 2005; Editor: Hippocratic Writings, 1978; Aristotle on Mind and Senses (with G E L Owen), 1978; Le Savoir Grec (with Jacques Brunschwig), 1996, English edition, 2000. Contributions to: Books and journals. Honours: Sarton Medal, 1987; Honorary Fellow, King's College, Cambridge, 1990; Honorary Foreign Member, American Academy of Arts and Sciences, 1995; Knighted, 1997. Memberships: British Academy, fellow; East Asian History of Science Trust, chairman, 1992-; International Academy of the History of Science, 1997; Hon Litt D, University of Athens, 2003. Address: 2 Prospect Row, Cambridge CB1 1DU, England.

**LLOYD John Nicol Fortune,** b. 15 April 1946. Journalist. m. (1) Judith Ferguson, 1974, divorced 1979, (2) Marcia Levy, 1983, divorced 1997, 1 son. Education: MA, University of Edinburgh. Appointments: Editor, Time Out, 1972-73; Reporter, London Programme, 1974-76; Producer, Weekend World, 1976-77; Industrial Reporter, Labour Correspondent, Industrial and Labour Editor, Financial Times; 1977-86; Editor, 1986-87, Associate Editor, 1996-, New Statesman; Other Financial Times assignments, 1987-, including Moscow Correspondent, 1991-95; Freelance journalist, 1996-. Publications: The Politics of Industrial Change, co-author, 1982; The Miners' Strike: Loss Without Limit, co-author, 1986; In Search of Work, co-author, 1987; Counterblasts, contributor, 1989; Rebirth of a Nation: an Anatomy of Russia, 1998; Re-engaging Russia, 2000; The Protest Ethic, 2001. Honours: Journalist of the Year, Granada Awards, 1984; Specialist Writer of the Year, IPC Awards, 1985; Rio Tinto David Watt Memorial Prize, 1997. Address: New Statesman, Victoria Station House, 7th Floor, 191 Victoria Street, London SW1E 5NE, England. E-mail: info@newstatesman.co.uk

**LLOYD Kathleen Annie, (Kathleen Conlon, Kate North),** b. 4 January 1943, Southport, England. Writer. m. Frank Lloyd, 3 August 1962, divorced, 1 son. Education: BA, Honours, King's College, Durham University. Publications: Apollo's Summer Look, 1968; Tomorrow's Fortune, 1971; My Father's House, 1972; A Twisted Skein, 1975; A Move in the Game, 1979; A Forgotten Season, 1980; Consequences, 1981; The Best of Friends, 1984; Face Values, 1985; Distant Relations, 1989; Unfinished Business, 1990; As Kate North: Land of My Dreams, 1997; Gollancz, 1997. Contributions to: Atlantic Review; Cosmopolitan; Woman's Journal; Woman; Woman's Own. Membership: Society of Authors. Address: 26A Brighton Road, Birkdale, Southport PR8 4DD, England.

**LLOYD Robert Andrew,** b. 2 March 1940, Southend-on-Sea, England. Broadcaster; Opera Singer; Teacher; Writer. m. Lynda Anne Powell, 1 son, 3 daughters. Education: MA, Modern History, Keble College, Oxford, 1962; London Opera Centre Certificate, 1969. Appointments: Teacher, various secondary schools, 1962; Lieutenant, Royal Navy, 1962-65; Civilian Tutor, Bramshill Police College, 1966-68; Student, London Opera Centre, 1968-69; Principal Bass, Sadlers Wells Opera, 1969-72; Principal Resident Bass, Royal Opera, Covent Garden, 1972-83; Freelance Broadcaster, Opera Singer, Teacher and Writer, 1983-; Senior Artist, Royal Opera Covent Garden, 2004; Master Teacher, San Francisco Merola Program, 2004. Publications: Over 80 recordings; Radio and TV performances. Honours: Charles Santley Award; Chaliapin Commemoration Medal, St Petersburg; Best Foreign Singer Award, Buenos Aires; Commander of the British Empire, 1990; Honorary

Fellow, Keble College; Honorary Member, Royal Academy of Music, Fellow of Royal Welsh College of Music and Drama. Memberships: President, British Youth Opera; Member, Executive Committee, Musicians Benevolent Fund; President, Abertillery Orpheus Male Voice Choir; President, Southend Choral Society; President 2005-6, Incorporated Society of Musicians; Sponsor, Brecon Cathedral Endowment Appeal; Tooley Committee, HEFCE, Advisory Committee of Friends of Covent Garden. Address: 57 Cholmeley Crescent, London N6 5EX, England. E-mail: robtlloyd@blueyonder.co.uk

**LLOYD Ursula E,** b. 10 July 1943, London, England. Consultant Obstetrician and Gynaecologist. m. William Lloyd, 2 daughters. Education: MB BS, MRCS, LRCP, 1967; FRCOG, 1987. Appointments: Training posts in Obstetrics and Gynaecology, 1967-81; Consultant, St George's Hospital, 1981-92; Private Medical Practice, Portland Hospital, London, 1992-. Memberships: Royal Society of Medicine; British Medical Association; Apothecaries Livery Co. Address: 8 Southwick Place, London W2 2TN, England.

**LLOYD WEBBER Andrew, (Baron Lloyd Webber of Sydmonton)** b. 22 March 1948, London, England. Composer. m. (1) Sarah Jane Hugill, 1971, divorced 1983, 1 son, 1 daughter, (2) Sarah Brightman, 1984, divorced 1990, (3) Madeleine Gurdon, 1991, 2 sons, 1 daughter. Education: Magdalen College, Oxford; Royal College of Music, FRCM, 1988. Career: Composer and producer, musicals; Composer, film scores; Deviser, board game, And They're Off; Owner, Really Useful Group. Compositions: Musicals: Joseph And The Amazing Technicolour Dreamcoat (lyrics by Tim Rice), 1968; Jesus Christ Superstar (lyrics by Tim Rice), 1970; Jeeves (lyrics by Alan Ayckbourn), 1975; Evita (lyrics by Tim Rice), 1976; Tell Me On A Sunday (lyrics by Don Black), 1980; Cats (based on poems by T S Eliot), 1981; Song And Dance, 1982; Starlight Express (lyrics by Richard Stilgoe), 1984; The Phantom Of The Opera (lyrics by Richard Stilgoe and Charles Hart), 1986; Aspects Of Love (lyrics by Don Black and Charles Hart), 1989; Sunset Boulevard (lyrics by Don Black and Christopher Hampton), 1993; By Jeeves (lyrics by Alan Ayckbourn), 1996; Whistle Down The Wind (lyrics by Jim Steinman), 1996; The Beautiful Game (book and lyrics by Ben Elton), 2000; The Woman in White (book by Charlotte Jones, lyrics by David Zippel), 2004; Film Scores: Gumshoe, 1971; The Odessa File, 1974; Jesus Christ Superstar, 1974; Others: Requiem, 1985; Variations On A Theme Of Paganini For Orchestra, 1986; Amigos Para Siempre (official theme for 1992 Olympic Games), 1992; When Children Rule The World (official theme for the opening ceremony 1998 Winter Olympics). Publications: Evita (with Tim Rice), 1978; Cats: The Book of the Musical, 1981; Joseph And The Amazing Technicolour Dreamcoat (with Tim Rice), 1982; The Complete Phantom of the Opera, 1987; The Complete Aspects of Love, 1989; Sunset Boulevard: From Movie to Musical, 1993; Restaurant Columnist, the Daily Telegraph, 1996-99. Honours include: 5 Laurence Olivier Awards; 6 Tony Awards; 4 Drama Desk Awards; 3 Grammy Awards; Triple Play Award, ASCAP, 1988; Knighthood, 1992; Praemium Imperiale Award, 1995; Richard Rogers Award, 1996; Oscar, Best Song, (with Tim Rice), 1997; Honorary Life Peer, 1997; Critics Circle Award Best Musical, 2000. Address: 22 Tower Street, London WC2H 9NS, England.

**LLOYD WEBBER Julian,** b. 14 April 1951, London, England. Cellist. m. (1) Celia M Ballantyne, 1974, divorced 1989, (2) Zohra Mahmoud Ghazi, 1989, divorced, 1999, son, (3) Kheira Bourahla, 2001. Education: Royal College of Music. Appointments: Debut, Queen Elizabeth Hall, 1972; Debut, Berlin Philharmonic Orchestra, 1984; Appears in major international concert halls; Undertaken concert tours throughout Europe, North and South America, Australasia, Singapore, Japan, Hong Kong and Korea; Numerous TV appearances and broadcasts in UK, Netherlands, Africa, Germany, Scandinavia, France, Belgium, Spain, Australasia, USA; Recordings include: World Premieres of Britten's 3rd Suite for Solo Cello; Bridge's Oration; Rodrigo's Cello Concerto; Holst's Invocation; Gavin Bryar's Cello Concerto; Philip Glass Cello Concerto; Tchaikovsky Rococo Variations; Sullivan's Cello Concerto; Vaughan Williams' Fantasia on Sussex Folk Tunes; Andrew Lloyd Webber's Variations; Elgar's Cello Concerto; Dvorak Concerto; Saint Saens Concerto; Lalo Concerto; Walton Concerto; Britten Cello Symphony; Philip Glass Cello Concerto, Phantasia. Publications: Frank Bridge, Six Pieces, 1982; Young Cellist's Repertoire, 1984; Travels with my Cello, 1984; Song of the Birds, 1985; Recital Repertoire for Cellists, 1986; Short Sharp Shocks, 1990; The Great Cello Solos, 1992; The Essential Cello, 1997; Cello Moods, 1999; Classical Journeys, 2004; Elgar Cello Concerto, 2005. Honours: British Phonographic Industry Award for Best Classical Recording, 1986; Crystal Award World Economic Forum, 1998; FRCM. Address: c/o IMG Artists Europe, Lovell House, 616 Chiswick High Road, London, W4 5RX, England. Website: www.julianlloydwebber.com

**LLOYD-JONES Sir (Peter) Hugh (Jefferd),** b. 21 September 1922, St Peter Port, Jersey, Channel Islands. Classical Scholar. m. (1) Frances Hedley, 1953, divorced 1981, 2 sons, 1 daughter, (2) Mary R Lefkowitz, 1982. Education: Christ Church, Oxford; MA (Oxon), 1947. Appointments: Fellow, Jesus College, Cambridge, 1948-54; Fellow, Corpus Christi College, Oxford, 1954-60; Regius Professor of Greek and Student of Christ Church, Oxford, 1960-89. Publications: The Justice of Zeus, 1971, 2nd edition, 1983; Blood for the Ghosts, 1982; Supplementum Hellenisticum (with P J Parsons), 1983; Sophoclis Fabulae (with N G Wilson), 1990; Sophoclea (with N G Wilson), 1990; Academic Papers, 2 volumes, 1990; Greek in a Cold Climate, 1991; Sophocles (editor and translator), 3 volumes, 1994-96; Sophocles: Second Thoughts (with N G Wilson), 1997. Contributions to: Numerous periodicals. Honours: Honorary DHL, University of Chicago, 1970; Honorary PhD, University of Tel Aviv, 1984; Knighted, 1989; Honorary DPhil, University of Thessalonica, 1999, Göttingen, 2002. Memberships: British Academy, fellow; Academy of Athens, fellow; Corresponding Member; American Academy of Arts and Sciences; American Philosophical Society; Rheinisch-Westfälische Akademie; Bayerische Akademie der Wissenschaften; Accademia di Lettere, Archeologia e Belle Arti, Naples. Address: 15 West Riding, Wellesley, MA 02482, USA.

**LO Kam Wah,** b. 4 October 1961, Hong Kong. Senior Research Scientist. m. Kit Ping Li. Education: BSc, Applied Mathematics, 1983; BEng, Electrical Engineering, 1985; PhD, Electrical Engineering, 1989. Appointments: Research Associate, School of Electrical Engineering, University of New South Wales, Sydney, Australia, 1988-89; Lecturer, Department of Electronic Engineering, Hong Kong Polytechnic University, 1989-92; Research Scientist, Microwave Radar Division, DSTO, Adelaide, Australia, 1992-93; Microwave Engineer, Division of Radiophysics, Commonwealth Scientific and Industrial Research Organisation, Sydney, 1993-95; Research Scientist, 1995-99, Senior Research Scientist, 1999-, Maritime Operations Division, DSTO, Sydney. Publications: Over 62 in international scientific and engineering journals and conference proceedings, including IEEE Transactions on Aerospace and Electronic Systems, IEEE Journal of Oceanic Engineering, IEE Proceedings, Journal of the Acoustical Society of America, Microwave and Optical Technology Letters, IEE Electronic Letters. Honour: Postgraduate Research Scholarship, University

of New South Wales, 1985-88. Memberships: Senior Member, Institute of Electrical and Electronic Engineers; Life Member, University of New South Wales Union. Address: DSTO Maritime Operations Division, PO Box 44, Pyrmont, New South Wales 2009, Australia. E-mail: kam.lo@dsto.defence.gov.au

**LO Wen-Lin,** b. 1 January 1958, Kaohsiung, Taiwan. Dermatologist. m. Yung-Jung Ho, 1 son, 1 daughter. Education: MD, National Yang-Ming Medical College, Taipei, 1982. Appointments: Resident, Dermatology, 1984-89, Attending Physician, 1989-91, Veterans General Hospital, Taipei; Lecturer, National Yang-Ming Medical College, 1989-91; Attending Physician, 1991-93, Section Chief, 1993-94, Chutong (Taiwan) Veterans Hospital; Private Practice, 1994-. Publications: Contributor of articles in professional journals. Memberships: Fellow, American Academy of Dermatology; Asian Dermatological Association; International Society of Dermatology; Chinese Dermatological Society; Laser Medicine Society. Address: 2/F #2 Lane 14, Chung Shan North Sec 7, Taipei 111, Taiwan.

**LOACH Kenneth,** b. 17 June 1936, Nuneaton, England. Film Director. m. Lesley Ashton, 1962, 3 sons (one deceased), 2 daughters. Education: St Peter's Hall, Oxford. Appointments: BBC Trainee, Drama Department, 1963; Freelance Film Director, 1963-; Films include: Poor Cow, 1967; Kes, 1969; In Black and White, 1970; Family Life, 1971; Black Jack, 1979; Looks and Smiles, 1981; Fatherland, 1986; Hidden Agenda, 1990; Riff Raff, 1991; Raining Stones, 1993; Ladybird Ladybird, 1994; Land and Freedom, 1995; Carla's Song, 1996; My Name is Joe, 1998; Bread and Roses, 2001; The Navigators, 2001; Sweet Sixteen, 2002; 11.09.01 UK Segment, 2002; TV includes: Diary of a Young Man, 1964; Three Clear Sundays, 1965; The End of Arthur's Marriage, 1965; Up the Junction, 1965; Coming Out Party, 1965; Cathy Come Home, 1966; In Two Minds, 1966; The Golden Vision, 1969; The Big Flame, 1970; After a Lifetime, 1971; The Rank of File, 1972; Auditions, 1980; A Question of Leadership, 1980; The Red and the Blue, 1983; Questions of Leadership, 1983; Which Side are You On?, 1984; The View from the Woodpile, 1988; Time to Go, 1989; Dispatches: Arthur Scargill, 1991; The Flickering Flame, 1996; Another City, 1998. Honours: Hon DLitt, St Andrews; Staffordshire University, Bristol; Dr hc, Royal College of Art, 1988; Honorary Fellow, St Peter's College, Oxford. Address: c/o Parallax Pictures, 7 Denmark Street, London, WC2H 8LS, England.

**LOADER Clive Robert.** Air Marshal. Education: Judd School, Tonbridge; University of Southampton. Appointments: University Cadet, RAF, 1972; Officer Training, 1973-74; Flying Training (Jet Provost, Gnat, Hunter), 1974-76; Joined Harrier Force, 1976; Served tours on all front-line Harrier squadrons including: Cmd 3 (Fighter) Squadron, 1993-95, OC RAF Laarbruch, Germany, 1996-99; Flown on ops in Belize, Falkland Islands, Iraq, Bosnia; Personal Staff Officer to Commander-in-Chief Strike Command, 1991-93, head major review of administration support in RAF, 1999-2000, Air Commodore Harrier RAF High Wycombe, 2000-01, ACOS J3 UK Permanent Joint HQ, 2001-02, ACDS (Ops) MOD, UK, 2002-04, Deputy Commander-in-Chief, Strike Command, 2004-. Honour: OBE, 1996. Memberships: FRAeS; President, RAF Microlight Flying Association; President, RAF Cricket. Address: Deputy Commander-in-Chief Strike Command, Headquarters Strike Command, RAF High Wycombe, Buckinghamshire HP14 4UE, England.

**LOADES David Michael,** b. 19 January 1934, Cambridge, England. Retired Professor of History; Writer. m. Judith

Anne Atkins, 18 April 1987. Education: Emmanuel College, Cambridge, 1955-61, BA, 1958, MA, PhD, 1961, LittD, 1981. Appointments: Lecturer in Political Science, University of St Andrews, 1961-63; Lecturer in History, University of Durham, 1963-70; Senior Lecturer, 1970-77, Reader, 1977-80, Professor of History, 1980-96, University College of North Wales, Bangor; Director, British Academy John Foxe Project, 1993; Honorary Research professor, University of Sheffield, 1996-. Publications: 22 books and collections include: Two Tudor Conspiracies, 1965; The Oxford Martyrs, 1970; The Reign of Mary Tudor, 1979; The Tudor Court, 1986; Mary Tudor: A Life, 1989; The Tudor Navy, 1992; John Dudley: Duke of Northumberland, 1996; Tudor Government, 1997; England's Maritime Empire, 2000; The Chronicles of the Tudor Queens, 2002; Elizabeth I, 2003; Intrigue and Treason: the Tudor Court 1547-1558, 2004. Editor: The Papers of George Wyatt, 1968; The End of Strife, 1984; Faith and Identity, 1990; John Foxe and the English Reformation, 1997; John Foxe: an historical perspective, 1999; with C S Knighton, The Anthony Roll of Henry VIII, 2000; Letters from the Mary Rose, 2002; John Foxe: At Home and Abroad, 2004; Contributions to academic journals. Memberships: Royal Historical Society, Fellow; Society of Antiquaries of London, Fellow; Ecclesiastical History Society; Navy Records Society. Address: The Cottage, Priory Lane, Burford, Oxon OX18 4SG, England.

**LOBOCKI Mieczyslaw Henryk,** b. 18 August 1929, Starogard, Poland. Research Worker. Education: Doctor Philosophy, 1968; Docent, 1977; Associate Professor, 1986; Professor, 1992. Appointments: Head of Education Theory Department, 1972-99, Vice-Director, Pedagogy Institute, 1978-81, Vice-Dean, Pedagogy and Psychology Faculty, 1982-87, Maria Curie-Sklodowska University. Publications include: 25 books together with 8 scripts for students; Over 300 articles; Over 150 reviews of scientific books and journals. Honours: State distinctions 1973, 1977, 1979, 1987, 2003; Awards of Ministry of Education 1971, 1976, 1983, 1986, 1995. Memberships: Scientific Society of the Lublin Catholic University; Lublin Scientific Society; Polish Psychological Society; Polish Pedagogical Society. Address: ul Skrzetuskiego 6/26, 20-628 Lublin, Poland.

**LOBODA-CACKOVIC Jasna,** b. Homec, Slovenia, resident in Berlin, Germany, 1970-. Scientist; Physicist; Artist; Sculptor; Painter; Photographer (art). m. Hinko Cackovic. Education: Art education: Sculpturing and painting in the artist's studio of the Father, Peter Loboda, Artist, Sculptor, Professor at the Academy Ljubljana, Slovenia; Self Education from 1952; Education in Music, Literature, Theatre from Mother, Jelena Loboda Zrinski, Artist, Writer; Science Education: Diploma in Science, Physics, 1960, MSc, Solid State Physics, 1964, University of Zagreb, Croatia; PhD, 1970, Fritz-Haber-Institut der Max-Planck-Gesellschaft, Berlin-Dahlem, Germany and University of Zagreb. Appointments: Scientist, Atom Institute Ruder Boskovic, Zagreb, 1960-71; Hon Assistant, University of Zagreb, 1961-65; Postdoctoral, 1970-71, Scientist, 1965-67, 1970-97, Fritz-Haber-Institut der Max-Planck-Gesellschaft, Berlin-Dahlem; Freelance in multidisciplinary fields, concerning universal art and new fields in science and technology, different aspects of human living and activity, 1997-; Scientific achievements include: Physics of Polymers, synthetic and biological molecules; Reactions at the surface of single crystal and alloys; Self-ordering of the matter; Memory of Solid and Fluid Matter; Order/disorder phenomena in the atomic, molecular and colloidal dimensions; Mutual dependence of order between atomic and colloidal entities; Theoretical and Experimental development of small and wide angle X-rays scattering analysis and of broad line nuclear magnetic resonance analysis. Creative Art Works include new principals of creation in art, "Fracture as a Principle of Forming", developed in the 80th, as complex scopes of expression: Rebuilding a new volume and aesthetic relations from fragments of an already finished sculpture or painting; In spite of fracturing this is a live affirming process; The presence of time is the fourth dimension in the sculptures; Arrangement of several identical or different sculptures, or paintings, to multiple-artworks: Composition of sculptures and paintings into volume-collages; Creative activity in sculpturing/painting/photography and science (physics, mathematics, chemistry) influenced by literature, music, theatre, astrophysics and cosmology; Developing of Universal Art including mentioned multidisciplinary fields; Intention to contribute: to synthesis of science, art and harmony, to the ethic and aesthetic part of human living and activity, to freedom in all it's facet's through culture in the widest sense; Over 380 sculptures and reliefs, over 1000 paintings presented at exhibitions in Germany, Austria, France, Monaco, Switzerland, Croatia, Luxembourg, 1968-, and Internet galleries, 1998-; Innovative Works, Two-Artist Group Jashin, with Hinko Cackovic from 1997; Permanent collections in Gallery for Sculpture (Bildhauergalerie Plinthe), Berlin, 1987-95, Paintings in Gallery Kleiner Prinz, Baden-Baden, Germany, 1987-; In Internet, 1999-: Cyber Museum wwwARTchannel (www.art-channel.net), Gallery of Forschungs-Institut Bildender Künste, and now Gallery "artgala" by Forschungs-Institut Bildender Kunste and Jean-Gebser-Akademie eV, Germany (www.artgala.de); Permanent representation of art and science biography by Brigitte Schellmann Who's Who in German® (www.whoswho-german.de). Publications: About 70 articles to professional scientific journals and in books; Featured in art journals, books and numerous catalogues. Honours: Grants: Atom Institute Ruder Boskovic, Zagreb, Croatia, 1965-66; Deutsche Forschungsgemeinschaft Germany, 1966; Deutscher Akademischer Austauschdient, Germany, 1966-67; Alexander von Humboldt Stiftung, Bad Godesberg, Germany, 1970-71; 20th Century Achievement Award, 1999; New Century Award, Europe 500, 2000; Presidential Award, 500 Great Minds, 2001; 21st Century Achievement Award, 2003; Award for Art, Science and their Creative Interaction: The Da Vinci Diamond, 2004; Art awards include: Euro gold medal, Art and Culture, Exhibition Zürich, Switzerland, 1989; Euro Art Plaquette, Exhibition Paris, France, 1989; 3 Euro honorary prizes, Exhibitions, Berlin, Dresden and Baden-Baden, Germany, 1993, 1994, 1995; Sculpture Prize, 5th Open Art Prize, Bad Nauheim, Germany, 1995; International Virtual Internet Art Competitions of the Forschungs-Instituts Bildender Kunste, Germany, 1998, 2000, 2001; magna cum laude for the oeuvre at the Virtual Internet Art Competitions of the Jean-Gebser-Akademie, Germany, 2002/2003. Memberships: New York Academy of Science, 1996; Deutsche Physikalishe Gesellschaft, 1972-95; Fellow, International Biographical Association, 1998-2001; Member of the Virtual Gallery "artgala.de" by Forschungs-Institut Bildende Künste (FIBK) and Jean-Gebser-Akademie eV, Germany, 1999-; Founding Member of the BWW (Bibliotheque World Wide) Society, 2001; Europäischer Kulturkreis Baden-Baden, 2002-; Archaeology, Astronautics and Seti Research Association, 2002-. Address: Im Dol 60, 14195 Berlin, Germany.

**LOCKLEY John,** b. 10 February 1948, Sale, Cheshire, England. General Practitioner. m. Mavis June Watt, 5 Aug 1972, 2 sons, 1 daughter. Education: Gonville and Caius College, Cambridge, England, 1966-69; MA, 1975; MB BChir (Cantab), 1973. Appointments: House Surgeon, Royal London Hospital, 1972; Vocational Training Course for General Practice, Colchester, 1973; General Practitioner, Ampthill, Bedfordshire, England, 1976-; Editor, Torus, 2000. Publications: The Complete BBC Computer User Handbook, 1988; Acorn to PC: Changing from DFS and ADFS to DOS, 1990; A Practical Workbook for the Depressed Christian, 1991; Headaches - A Comprehensive

Guide to Relieving Headaches and Migraine, 1993; After the Fire, 1994; After the Fire II - A Still Small Voice, 1996; After the Fire III - Chronicles, 1998. Contributions to: Many articles to General Practitioner, Daily Telegraph, Daily Mail and Guardian; Doctor Magazine. Honour: Medeconomics GP Writer of Year, 1989. Membership: Society of Authors. Address: 107 Flitwick Road, Ampthill, Bedfordshire MK45 2NT, England.

**LODER Robert Reginald (Robin),** b. 12 November 1943, Titchfield, Hampshire, England. Landowner. m. Jane Royden, 2 sons, 2 daughters. Education: MA, Trinity College, Cambridge. Appointments: Owner, Leonardslee Gardens; High Sheriff of West Sussex, 2000-01. Address: Leonardslee Gardens, Lower Beeding, Horsham, West Sussex RH13 6PP, England. E-mail: gardens@leonardslee.com

**LODGE David John,** b. 28 January 1935. Honorary Professor of Modern English Literature. m. Mary Frances Jacob, 1959, 2 sons, 1 daughter. Education: BA, honours, MA (London); PhD, Birmingham; National Service, RAC, 1955-57. Appointments: British Council, London, 1959-60; Assistant Lecturer, 1960-62, Lecturer, 1963-71, Senior Lecturer, 1971-73, Reader of English, 1973-76, Professor of Modern English Literature, 1976-87, Honorary Professor, 1987-2000, Emeritus Professor, 2001-, University of Birmingham; Harkness Commonwealth Fellow, 1964-65; Visiting Associate Professor, University of California, Berkeley, 1969; Henfield Writing Fellow, University of East Anglia, 1977. Publications: Novels: The Picturegoers, 1960; Ginger, You're Barmy, 1962; The British Museum is Falling Down, 1965; Out of the Shelter, 1970, revised edition, 1985; Changing Places, 1975; How Far Can You Go?, 1980; Small World, 1984; Nice Work, 1988; Paradise News, 1991; Therapy, 1995; Home Truths, 1999; Thinks...., 2001; Author, Author, 2004. Criticism: Language of Fiction, 1966; The Novelist at the Crossroads, 1971; The Modes of Modern Writing, 1977; Working with Structuralism, 1981; Write On, 1986; After Bakhtin (essays), 1990; The Art of Fiction, 1992; The Practice of Writing, 1996; Consciousness and the Novel, 2002. Honours: Yorkshire Post Fiction Prize, 1975; Hawthornden Prize, 1976; Whitbread Book of the Year Award, 1980; Sunday Express Book of the Year Award, 1988; Chevalier de L'Ordre des Arts et des Lettres, 1997; CBE, 1998. Address: Department of English, University of Birmingham, Birmingham B15 2TT, England.

**LODGE Oliver Raymond William Wynlayne,** b, 2 September 1922, Painswick, Goucestershire, England. Retired Barrister. m. Charlotte Young, deceased, 1990, 1 son, 2 daughters. Education: Officer Cadet, Royal Fusiliers, 1942; BA, 1943, MA, 1947, King's College, Cambridge. Appointments: Called to the Bar by Inner Temple, 1945; Practiced at Chancery Bar, 1945-74; Admitted ad eundam to Lincoln's Inn, 1949; Member of Bar Council, 1952-56, 1967-71; Member of Supreme Court Rules Committee, 1968-71; Bencher of Lincoln's Inn, 1973; Permanent Chairman of Industrial Tribunals, 1975-92, Part-time Chairman, 1992-94; Regional Chairman of London South Region of Industrial Tribunals, 1980-92; General Commissioner of Income Tax for Lincoln's Inn District, 1983-91; Treasurer of Lincoln's Inn, 1995. Publications: Editor, 3rd edition, Rivington's Epitome of Snedl's Equity, 1948; Editor, article on Fraudulent and Voidable Conveyances in 3rd edition of Halsbury's Laws of England, 1956. Memberships: Garrick Club; Bar Yacht Club. Address: Southridge House, Hindon, Salisbury, Wiltshire SP3 6ER, England.

**LOFTHOUSE Geoffrey (Lord Lofthouse of Pontefract),** b. 18 December 1925, Featherstone, England. Deputy Speaker, House of Lords. m. Sarah, deceased, 1 daughter. Education: Leeds University, 1954-57. Appointments: Member, Pontefract Borough Council, 1962; Mayor of Pontefract, 1967-68; Leader, Pontefract Borough Council, 1969-73; First Chairman, Wakefield MDC, 1973; Chairman, Housing Committee, 1973-79; Elected Member of Parliament for Pontefract and Castleford, 1978; Elected Deputy Speaker of the House of Commons, 1992-97; Elected Deputy Speaker of the House of Lords, 1997-; Chairman of Wakefield Health Authority, 1998. Publications: A Very Miner MP (autobiography), 1985; Coal Sack to Woolsack (autobiography), 1999. Honours: Knighthood, 1995; Peerage, 1997. Memberships: Member of the Imperial Society of Knights Bachelor; Appointed Magistrate, 1970; President, British Amateur Rugby League Association. Address: 67 Carleton Crest, Pontefract, West Yorkshire WF8 2QR, England.

**LOGUE Christopher (John),** b. 23 November 1926, Portsmouth, Hampshire, England. Poet; Writer; Dramatist. m. Rosemary Hill, 1985. Education: Prior College, Bath. Publications: Poetry: Wand and Quadrant, 1953; Devil, Maggot and Son, 1954; The Weakdream Sonnets, 1955; The Man Who Told His Love: 20 Poems Based on P Neruda's "Los Cantos d'amores", 1958, 2nd edition, 1959; Songs, 1960; Songs from "The Lily-White Boys", 1960; The Establishment Songs, 1966; The Girls, 1969; New Numbers, 1970; Abecedary, 1977; Ode to the Dodo, 1981; War Music: An Account of Books 16 to 19 of Homer's Iliad, 1981; Fluff, 1984; Kings: An Account of Books 1 and 2 of Homer's Iliad, 1991, revised edition, 1992; The Husbands: An Account of Books 3 and 4 of Homer's Iliad, 1994; Selected Poems (edited by Christopher Reid), 1996; All Day Permanent Red, 2003. Plays: The Lily-White Boys (with Harry Cookson), 1959; The Trial of Cob and Leach, 1959; Antigone, 1961; War Music, 1978; Kings, 1993. Screenplays: Savage Messiah, 1972; The End of Arthur's Marriage, 1965; Crusoe (with Walter Green), 1986. Other: Lust, by Count Plamiro Vicarion, 1955; The Arrival of the Poet in the City: A Treatment for a Film, 1964; True Stories, 1966; The Bumper Book of True Stories, 1980. Editor: Count Palmiro Vicarion's Book of Limericks, 1959; The Children's Book of Comic Verse, 1979; London in Verse, 1982; Sweet & Sour: An Anthology of Comic Verse, 1983; The Children's Book of Children's Rhymes, 1986. Honour: 1st Wilfred Owen Award, 1998. Address: 41 Camberwell Grove, London SE5 8JA, England.

**LOH I-To,** b. 28 September 1936, Tamsui, Taiwan. Church Musician; Ethnomusicologist. m. Hui-chin Su, 2 sons, 1 daughter. Education: M Div, Tainan Theological College and Seminary, 1963; SMM, Union Theological Seminary, School of Sacred Music, New York, USA, 1966; PhD, University of California at Los Angeles, 1982. Appointments: Asian Institute for Liturgy and Music, Manila, Philippines, 1982-94; Professor of Worship, Church Music and Ethnomusicology, 1967-74, 1994-2002, President and Head of Department of Church Music, 1995-2002, Tainan Theological College and Seminary, Taiwan. Publications: Over 20 books and collections of songs including most recently: Sound the Bamboo: CCA Hymnal, 2000; Taiwan Church Press for the Christian Council of Asia, 2000; Teach us to Praise (Chinese) revised edition, 2002. Honour: Fellow of the Hymn Society of America and Canada. Memberships: Hymn Society of America and Canada; Charter Member, World Association for Chinese Church Music. Address: 23 Dong-Rong St #4F, Tainan, Taiwan 70144. E-mail: intoeglobalchurchmusic.org

**LOHMANN Jan,** b. 29031944, Copenhagen, Denmark. Goldsmith. m. Bodil Lohmann, 1 son, 1 daughter. Education: Qualified as Goldsmith with Silver Medal, 1964; Worked in Switzerland, 1966-68; Workshop, Refractory Metals, Dublin, 1983. Career: Co-owner, Galerie Metal, Copenhagen, 1978-98; Studio Kunstnerhuset in Frederiksværk, 1990-; Guest Teacher,

Danish College of Jewellery and Silversmithing, 1986-96; Work in Collections: The Danish State Art Foundation, Denmark; The City Museum, Flensborg, Denmark; Museum of Decorative Art, Copenhagen, Denmark; National Museum of Fine Art, Stockholm, Sweden; The Röhss Museum of Art and Crafts, Göterborg, Sweden; Museum of Applied Art, Trondheim, Norway; Schleswig-Holsteinische Landesmuseum, Schloss Gottorp, Schleswig, Germany; Schmuckmuseum, Pforzheim, Germany; Koldinhus, Kolding, Denmark. Publications: Works featured in: Scandinavian Modern Design 1880-1980, 1980; IIIème Triennale du Bijou, Museé des Arts Décoratifs, 1992; Nordic Images, 1994; Nordic Jewellery (co-editor), 1995; The Art of Danish Jewellery 1960-2000, 2001; Flashes of Danish Jewellery in the 20th Century, 2002; Scandinavian Style Classic and Modern. Scandinavian Design and Its Influence on the World, 2003; Kraks Blä Bog, 2004/2005. Honours: Prize and Silver Medal, 1966; Prizes, Scandinavian Design Competition, Copenhagen, 1972, 1976; Danish Craftsman Prize, 1989. Membership: Billedkunstnernes Forbund, Copenhagen. Address: Kunstnerhuset, Gjethusparken 4, DK-3300 Frederiksværk, Denmark. E-mail: jan@janlohmann.dk Website: www.janlohman.dk

**LOHSE Andrea,** b. 28 April 1964, Kellinghusen, Schleswig-Holstein, Germany. University Lecturer. Education: First State Examination, Christian-Albrechts University, Kiel, 1988; Dr iur, LLD, Christian-Albrechts University, Kiel, 1991; Second State Examination, after 3 years practical training in judicial or other legal work, Schleswig-Holstein, 1993. Appointments: Research Assistant, Christian-Albrechts University, 1984-89; Stagaire, trainee, Commission, European Community, Direction General IV, Brussels, 1989-90; Administrative Assistant, ERASMUS, student exchange, program, 1990-93, Academic Assistant, civil law, 1993-94, Christian-Albrechts University; Lecturer, Academy of the Savings Banks, Kiel, 1991-94; Academic Assistant, civil, business and competition law, Free University Berlin, 1994-2001; Lawyer, Hengeler Mueller, 2003-04; University Lecturer, Johann Wolfgang Goethe University, 2004-05. Publications: Indonesian law concerning prohibition of monopolistic practices and unfair business competition, 2000, 2001; Law in Cases: Antitrust Law and Unfair Business Competition Law, 2001; The Prohibition of Cartels and the EEC Umbrella Regulation, 2001; Corporate Governance – the duties of the members of the management and supervisory board, 2005. Honours: Scholarships: Schleswig-Holstein, 1989-90, University Association Schleswig-Holstein, 1992; Faculty Award, Law, Christian-Albrechts University, 1992; Kieler Doctores Juris Association, 1993; Furtherance Honor, Hermann-Ehlers-Foundation, 1992; Scholarship, German Research Foundation, 2002-03. Membership: Protestant Church, 1964-. Address: Uhlenweg 30A, 25548 Kellinghusen, Germany. E-mail: lohse.andrea@web.de

**LOJDA Ladislav,** b. 18 January 1926, Litohor, Czech Republic. Senior Research Worker. m. Jirina Simova, 8 September 1951, 2 sons. Education: Diploma, Veterinary Medicine, 1950; DVM, 1950; Candidate of Science, 1968. Appointments: Veterinary General Practitioner, 1950-56; Special, Reproduction of Domestic Animals, 1956-58; Regional Veterinary Special, 1958-62; Introduced the health progeny testing (Animal hereditary health control) and matched it with breeding selection, Czechoslovakia, 1958-62; Senior Research Worker, 1962-92. Publications include: Heredopathology of Reproduction in Domestic Animals, 1971; Methods of Chromosomal Study, 1977; Cytogenetics of Animals, 1989; History and Perspectives of Genetic Prevention in Veterinary Medicine, 1996. Honours: Listed in numerous national and international biographical dictionaries; Many others. Memberships: Genetic Society,

Academy of Sciences, Brno; Cytogenetic Society, Academy of Sciences, Praha; Czech Biology Society, Academy of Sciences, Brno. Address: Listi 7, 61400 Brno, Czech Republic.

**LÖKER Altan,** b. 6 November 1927, Kütahya, Turkey. Electrical Engineer, retired. Education: MS in Electrical Engineering, Technical University of Istanbul, 1951; MS in Physics, Stevens Institute of Technology, USA, 1957. Appointments: Electrical Engineer in Turkey, USA, Canada, and Saudi Arabia; Project Manager, Subcontractor, Contractor in Turkey; Graduate Assistant at the Technical University of Istanbul and Physics Department of Stevens Institute of Technology. Publications: Film and Suspense, 1976, 2nd edition, 2005; Dreams and Psychosynthesis, 1987; Cognitive-Cybernetic Theory and Therapy, 1993; Dreams, Migraine, Neuralgia, 1993; Theory in Psychology: The Journal of Mind and Behaviour, 1999; Cognitive Behavioural Cybernetics of Symptoms, Dreams, Lateralization, 2001, 2nd edition, 2002; Migraines and Dreams, 2003. Memberships: Turkish Chamber of Electrical Engineers, retired. Address: Lalasam 23/5, Ferikoy, Istanbul 80260, Turkey. E-mail: alloker@superonline.com

**LOLLOBRIGIDA Gina,** b. 4 July 1927, Sibiaco. Italian Actress. m. Milko Skofic, 1949, 1 son. Education: Liceo Artistico, Rome. Appointments: First Screen Role, Pagliacci, 1947; Appeared in numerous films including: Campane a Martello, 1948; Cuori Senza Frontiere, 1949; Achtung, bandit!, 1951; Enrico Caruso, 1951; Fanfan la Tulipe, 1951; Altri Tempi, 1952; The Wayward Wife, 1952; Les belles de la nuit, 1952; Pane, amour e fantasia, 1953; La Provinciale, 1953; Pane, amour e gelosia, La Romana, 1954; Il Grande Gioco, 1954; La Donna piu Bella del Mondo, 1955; Trapeze, 1956; Notre Dame de Paris, 1956; Solomon and Sheba, 1959; Never So Few, 1960; Go Naked in the World, 1961; She Got What She Asked For, 1963; Woman of Straw, 1964; Le Bambole, 1965; Hotel Paradiso, 1966; Buona Sera Mrs Campbell, 1968; King, Queen, Knave, 1972; The Bocce Showdown, 1990; Plucked, Bad Man's River; The Lonely Woman; Bambole. Publications: Italia Mia, 1974; The Philippines. Address: Via Appia Antica 223, 00178 Rome, Italy.

**LOMAS Herbert,** b. 7 February 1924, Yorkshire, England. Poet; Critic; Translator. m. Mary Marshall Phelps, 29 June 1968, 1 son, 1 daughter. Education: BA, 1949, MA, 1952, University of Liverpool. Appointments: Teacher, Spetsai, Greece, 1950-51; Lecturer, Senior Lecturer, University of Helsinki, 1952-65; Senior Lecturer, 1966-72, Principal Lecturer, 1972-82, Borough Road College. Publications: Chimpanzees are Blameless Creatures, 1969; Who Needs Money?, 1972; Private and Confidential, 1974; Public Footpath, 1981; Fire in the Garden, 1984; Letters in the Dark, 1986; Trouble, 1992; Selected Poems, 1995; A Useless Passion, 1998; The Vale of Todmorden, 2003. Translations: Territorial Song, 1991; Contemporary Finnish Poetry, 1991; Fugue, 1992; Wings of Hope and Daring, 1992; The Eyes of the Fingertips are Opening, 1993; Black and Red, 1993; Narcissus in Winter, 1994; The Year of the Hare, 1994; Two Sequences for Kuhmo, 1994; In Wandering Hall, 1995; Selected Poems, Eeva-Lisa Manner, 1997; Three Finnish Poets, 1999; A Tenant Here, 1999; Not Before Sundown, 2003. Contributions to: London Magazine and other reviews, journals, and magazines. Honours: Prize, Guinness Poetry Competition; Runner Up, Arvon Foundation Poetry Competition; Cholmondeley Award; Poetry Book Society Biennial Translation Award; Knight First Class, Order of the White Rose of Finland, 1991: Finnish State Prize for Translation, 1991. Memberships: Society of Authors; Finnish Academy; Finnish Literary Society; President, Suffolk Poetry

Society, 1999-. Address: North Gable, 30 Crag Path, Aldeburgh, Suffolk IP15 5BS, England.

**LOMAX Alan,** b. 31 January 1915, Austin, Texas, USA. Ethnomusicologist; Writer. m. E Harold, 1937, 1 daughter. Education: Harvard University, 1932-33; BA, University of Texas at Austin, 1936; Graduate Studies in Anthropology, Columbia University, 1939. Appointments: Folk Song Collector, US and Europe; Director, Bureau of Applied Social Research, 1963, Cantometrics Project, Columbia University, 1963. Publications: American Folk Song and Folk Lore: A Regional Bibliography (with S Cowell), 1942; Mr Jelly Roll, 1950, 2nd edition, 1973; Harriett and Her Harmonium, 1955; The Rainbow Sign, 1959; Cantometrics: A Handbook and Training Method, 1976; Index of World Song, 1977; The Land Where the Blues Began, 1993. Editor: American Ballads and Folksongs (with John Lomax), 1934; Negro Folk Songs as Sung by Leadbelly (with John Lomax), 1936; Our Singing Country (with John Lomax), 1941; Folk Song: USA (with John Lomax), 1947, 4th edition, 1954; Leadbelly: A Collection of World Famous Songs (with John Lomax), 1959, 2nd edition, 1965; The Folk Songs of North America in the English Language, 1960; The Penguin Book of American Folk Songs, 1966; Hard-Hitting Songs for Hard-Hit People, 1967; Folk Song Style and Culture, 1968. Honours: National Medal of Arts, 1986; National Book Critics Circle Award, 1993. Memberships: American Association for the Advancement of Science; American Folklore Society, fellow; American Anthropological Association. Address: c/o Association for Cultural Equity, 450 West 41st Street, 6th Floor, New York, NY 10036, USA.

**LOMU Jonah,** b. 12 May 1975, Auckland, New Zealand. Rugby Football Player; Athlete. m. (1) Tanya Rutter, divorced, (2) Fiona Taylor, 2003. Appointments: Bank Officer, ASB Bank of New Zealand; Youngest Ever Capped All Black; Wing; International Debut, New Zealand versus France, 1994; Semi Finalist at World Cup, South Africa, 1995; Affiliiated to Rugby Union; Ran 100m in 10.7 Seconds; With All Blacks, 1999; Signed for Cardiff Blues, 2005. Website: www.jonahlomu.com

**LONG Derek Albert,** b. 11 August 1925, Gloucester, England. Scientist; Author; Antiquarian. m. Moira Hastings (Gilmore), 3 sons. Education: MA, D Phil, Jesus College, Oxford. Appointments: Fellow, University of Minnesota, USA, 1949-50; Research Fellow, Spectroscopy, University of Oxford, 1950-55; Lecturer, Senior Lecturer, Reader in Chemistry, University College, Swansea, 1956-66; Professor of Structural Chemistry, 1966-92, Professor Emeritus, 1992-, Chairman of the Board of Physical Sciences, 1976-79, Director, Molecular Spectroscopy Unit, 1982-88, University of Bradford; OECD Travelling Fellow, Canada and USA, 1964; Leverhulme Research Fellow, 1970-71; Visiting Professor: Reims, Lille, Bordeaux, Paris, Bologna, Florence, Keele; Chairman, Second International Conference on Raman Spectroscopy, Oxford, 1970; Co-Director, NATO Advanced Studies Institute, Bad Winsheim, 1982; Member, Italian-UK Mixed Commission for Implementation of Cultural Convention, 1985; Vice Chairman, Euro Laboratory for Non-Linear Spectroscopy, Florence, 1986-92; Founder, Editor, Editor-in-Chief, Emeritus Editor, 2000-, Journal of Raman Spectroscopy. Publications: Books (sole author): Raman Spectroscopy, 1977; The Raman Effect, 2002; Books (joint editor): Essays in Structural Chemistry, 1971; Specialist Periodical Reports in Molecular Spectroscopy (vols 1-6), 1973-79; Non-Linear Raman Spectroscopy and Its Chemical Applications, 1988; Proceedings Eleventh International Conference on Raman Spectroscopy, 1988; About 200 papers in scientific journals relating to Raman Spectroscopy; Other papers: Sevres Service des Arts Industriels, 1997; The

Goodmanham Plane, 2002. Honours: Fellow, Royal Society of Chemistry, Chartered Chemist; Foreign Member, Lincei Academy, Rome, Italy; Honorary, Docteur es Sciences, Reims, France. Membership: Oxford and Cambridge Club. Address: 19 Hollingwood Rise, Ilkley, W Yorks, LS29 9PW, England. E-mail: profdalong@debrett.net

**LONGFORD Countess of, (Elizabeth Pakenham),** b. 30 August 1906, London, England. Author. m. F A Pakenham, 1931, deceased 2001, 4 sons, 3 daughters. Education: MA, Lady Margaret Hall, Oxford. Publications: Points for Parents, 1956; Catholic Approaches (editor), 1959; Jameson's Raid, 1960, new edition, 1982; Victoria RI, 1964; Wellington: Years of the Sword, 1969; Wellington: Pillar of State, 1972; The Royal House of Windsor, 1974; Churchill, 1974; Byron's Greece, 1975; Life of Byron, 1976; A Pilgrimage of Passion: The Life of Wilfrid Scawen Blunt, 1979; Louisa: Lady in Waiting (editor), 1979; Images of Chelsea, 1980; The Queen Mother: A Biography, 1981; Eminent Victorian Women, 1981; Elizabeth R, 1983; The Pebbled Shore (autobiography), 1986, The Oxford Book of Royal Anecdotes (editor), 1989; Darling Loosy: Letters to Princess Louise 1856-1939 (editor), 1991; Poet's Corner: An Anthology (editor), 1992; Royal Throne: The Future of the Monarchy, 1993. Honours: James Tait Black Memorial Prize for Non-Fiction, 1964; Yorkshire Post Prize, 1969; Honorary DLitt, Sussex University, 1970; Commander of the Order of the British Empire, 1974. Membership: Women Writers and Journalists, honorary life president, 1979-.

**LONGMORE, Rt Hon Lord Justice, Rt Hon Sir Andrew Centlivres,** b. 25 August 1944, Liverpool, England. Judge. m. Margaret McNair, 1 son. Education: Lincoln College, Oxford. Appointments: Called to Bar, 1966; Queen's Counsel, 1983; Recorder of Crown Court, 1992; High Court Judge, 1993; Lord Justice of Appeal, 2001. Publications: Co-editor, 6th, 7th, 8th and 9th edition of MacGillirray's Law of Insurance. Honours: Knight, 1993; Privy Councillor, 2001. Memberships: Middle Temple, 1962-. Address: Royal Courts of Justice, London WC2A 2LL, England.

**LONGO Daniel Robert,** b. 20 February 1952, Jersey City, New Jersey, USA. Health Services Researcher; Medical Educator. m. Karen Ann Ludy, 1 son, 1 daughter. Education: BS, cum laude, Villanova University, 1974; Master of Hospital Administration, George Washington University, 1976; ScD, Health Policy Management, Johns Hopkins University, 1982. Appointments: Consultant, American Hospital Association, Chicago, 1980-82; Director of Research, Director, Multihospital Systems Project, Joint Commission on Accreditation of Healthcare Organizations, Chicago, 1982-86; Assistant Executive Director for Quality Management, Chicago Affiliated Healthcare Group, Ancilla Systems Inc, Chicago, 1986-87; Vice-President, Quality Assurance, Hospital Association of New York State, Albany, 1987-89; President, The Hospital Research and Education Trust, Chicago, 1989-92; Associate Professor of Family and Community Medicine, 1992-99, Director of Graduate Studies, 2000-2004, Professor, Department of Family and Community Medicine, 2000-, School of Medicine, University of Missouri-Columbia; Bohan Visiting Professor of Family Medicine, University of Kansas Medical Center, 2003. Publications: Numerous publications in professional journals and books include: How to Reform the Health Care System Given the Experience of Past Failures, 2002; Tobacco Induced Diseases: A World-Wide Concern, 2003; The Relationship of Spirituality and Health in the Modern Age: Spiritual Food in the Desert of Modern Life, 2003; Health Care Consumer Reports: An Evaluation of Employer Perspectives, 2004; Youth Smoking: Toward a Better Understanding and Realistic Solutions, 2004.

Honours: Best Research Paper Award, 1997, Best Research Paper Honorable Mention Award, 1999, Society of Teachers of Family Medicine; President's Recognition Award, North American Primary Care Research Group, 2002; Best Contributor Award, Journal of the American Medical Directors Association, 2003. Memberships include: American Academy of Family Physicians; International Society for the Prevention of Tobacco Induced Diseases; Society of Teachers of Family Medicine; International Society for Quality Assurance in Health Care. Address: 2991 W Ridley Wood, Columbia, MO 65203, USA. E-mail: Londod@health.missouri.edu

**LONGO Jeannie Michèle Alice,** b. 31 October 1958, Annecy, France. Cyclist. m. Patrice Ciprelli, 1985. Education: Institut d'Etudes Commerciales, Grenoble; University of Limoges. Career: French Cycling Champion, 1979-86; Winner, 13 world titles including World Champion, Road, 1985, 1987, World Champion, 1988, 1989, World Champion, Against the Clock, Spain, 1997; Winner, Tour of Colorado, 1987, 1987, Tour of Colombia, 1987, 1988, Tour of Norway, 1987, Tour de France, 1987; Silver Medal, World Track Race, 1987; Holder, several world records including World Record for 3 km, Covered Track, Grenoble, 1992; Winner, French Cycle Racing Championship, 1992; Silver Medallist, Olympic Games, Barcelona, 1992; Gold Medallist, Olympic Games, Atlanta, 1996; Consultant, France Télévision, 1999-. Honours: Médaille d'Or, La Jeunesse et des Sports; Medaille d'Or, Académie des Sports. Address: Fédération Française de Cyclisme, 5 rue de Rome, 93561 Rosny-sous-Bois, France.

**LONGUET-HIGGINS Hugh Christopher,** b. 11 April 1923, Lenham, Kent, England. Theoretical Chemist. Education: Doctorate, Balliol College, Oxford, 1947. Appointments: Research Fellow, Balliol College, 1947-48; Research Associate, University of Chicago, 1948-49; Lecturer, Reader, Theoretical Chemistry, Victoria University of Manchester, 1949-52; Professor of Theoretical Physics, King's College, London University, 1952-54; Fellow, Corpus Christi College and Professor of Theoretical Chemistry, Cambridge University, 1954-67; Royal Society Research Professor, 1968-74, Sussex University, 1974-89, Professor Emeritus, 1989-, Edinburgh University. Developed the application of precise mathematical analyses to chemical problems. Publications: The Nature of Mind, 1972; Mental Processes, 1987; About 200 papers in scientific journals. Honours: Honorary Fellow, Balliol College, Oxford; Honorary Fellow, Wolfson College, Cambridge; Dr hc York, 1973, Essex, 1981, Bristol, 1983, Sussex, 1989, Sheffield, 1995. Memberships: Foreign Member, American Academy of Arts and Sciences; Foreign Associate, NAS; Life Fellow, Corpus Christi College, Cambridge. Address: Centre for Research on Perception and Cognition, Laboratory of Experimental Psychology, University of Sussex, Falmer, Brighton, BN1 9QG, England.

**LONIGAN Paul R,** b. 27 May 1935, New York City, USA. Professor of Romance Languages. m. Cynthia Hartley Lonigan, 2 daughters. Education: BA, Romance Languages and Classics, Queens College, New York, 1960; PhD, Romance Languages, Johns Hopkins University, 1967. Appointments: Instructor, Russell Sage College, Troy, New York, 1963-65; Associate Professor, State University College, Oswego, New York, 1965-67; Queens College, CUNY, 1967-, Professor, 1983; Professor, CUNY Graduate Center, 1968-. Publications on subjects: Medieval epic, romance, hagiography, Early Irish church, the Druids, Chrétien de Troyes, Villon, Rabelais, Montaigne, Ruben Darío, women in the Middle Ages, Shamanism in the Old Irish Tradition, The Romance Languages and the Celtic Monks, The Three Kings of the Nativity, Napoleon's Irish

Legion; Editor, poetry of María Victoria Carreño Montás, Respuestas Del Corazón, 1999. Honours: National Defence Fellow; Phi Beta Kappa; Delta Phi Alpha; Magna cum laude; Chevalier dans l'Ordre des Palmes Académiques; International Order of Merit, 1999; Commemorative Medal of Honour, 2001; Listed in national and international biographical dictionaries. Memberships: Círculo de Cultura Panamericano; Irish Texts Society; Contributing Editor of Oidhreacht, Newsletter of Celtic Heritage Books; Association of Literary Scholars and Critics; Archaeological Institute of America; American Society of the French Academic Palms. Address: PO Box 243, Montgomery, NY 12549, USA.

**LOOS Katja,** b. 11 February 1971, Frankfurt am Main, Germany. Chemist. Education: Vordiplom, Chemistry, 1990-92, Diploma, Organic Chemistry, 1993-96, Johannes Gutenberg Universität, Mainz, Germany; Dr rer nat, Polymer Science, Universität Bayreuth, Germany. Publications: Several articles in scientific journals. Honours: DAAD Fellowship, University of Massachusetts, Amherst, USA, 1997; DAAD Fellowship, Universidade Rio Grande do Sul, Brazil, 1999; Feodor-Lynen Research Fellowship Polytechnic University, Brooklyn, USA, 2001-03; State University, Groningen, The Netherlands, 2003-; Poster Award Makromolekulares Kolloquium, Freiburg, Germany, 1999, and others. Address: Hattersheimer Str 14, 65779 Kelkheim, Germany. E-mail: katjaloos@web.de

**LOPASIC Alexander,** b. 13 November 1928, Belgrade, Yugoslavia. University Lecturer. Education: Studies in Folklore, Ethnology and World History, 1948-51, Degree in History, 1951, University of Zagreb; Dr Phil, Anthropology and African Linguistics, University of Vienna, 1955. Appointments: Research Fellow, University of London, 1957-59; Curator, Nigerian Museum, Lagos, Nigeria, 1960-61; Assistant Lecturer in Anthropology, University of Cologne, Germany, 1962-65; Lecturer in Social and Cultural Anthropology, University of Reading, England, 1965-94; Visiting Lecturer in Anthropology, University State International University of San Diego, USA, 1971-72; Visiting Professor of Social Anthropology, University of Ljubljana, Slovenia, 1995-. Publications: Commissaire-général D Lerman (1863-1918): a Contribution to the History of Central Africa, 1971; Editor, Mediterranean Societies: Tradition and Change, University of Zagreb, 1994; 42 articles or parts of books on anthropology, Islamic studies, Islam in the Mediterranean and traditional Africa, art, politics and social organisation in Africa, South of Sahara; Fieldwork: Mediterranean Islands, 1962-2003; Coast of Montenegro, 1956, 2002-03; Africa: Western Nigeria, 1960-61, 1997; Lamu, Kenya, 1970; Zanzibar, 2002. Honours: Wenner-Gren Foundation Research Fellowship, University of London, 1957-59; Social Science Research Council Grant, 1972-73; University of Reading Grant, 1974; British Council Grant, 1993. Memberships: Association of Social Anthropologists; Royal Anthropological Institute; British Society for Middle Eastern Studies; Deutsche, Österreichische, Schweizerische Gesellschaft für Völkerkunde; Anglo-Turkish Society; Royal Institute of International Affairs, London. Address: 20 Allison Court, 136 Oxford Road, Reading, Berkshire RG1 7ND, England.

**LOPEZ Jennifer,** b. 24 July 1970, Bronx, New York. Actress; Dancer; Singer. m. (1) Ojani Noa, 1997, (2) Cris Judd, 2001, (3) Marc Anthony, 2004. Appointments: Album: On the 6; J Lo, 2001; Film appearances include: My Little Girl, 1996; My Family – Mia Familia, 1995; Money Train, 1995; Jack, 1996; Blood and Wine, 1996; Anaconda, 1997; Selena, 1997; U-Turn, 1997; Out of Sight, 1998; Thieves, 1999; Pluto Nash, 1999; The Cell, 2000; The Wedding Planner, 2000; Angel Eyes, 2001; Enough, 2002; Maid in Manhattan, 2002; Gigli, 2003; TV appearances include: Second Chances; Hotel Malibu; Nurses on the Line; The Crash of Flight 7. Honours: Golden Globe, 1998; MTV Movie Award, 1999. Address: United Talent Agency, 9560 Wilshire Boulevard, 5th Floor, Beverley Hills, CA 90212, USA.

**LOPEZ DEL CID Rafael,** b. 13 April 1921, Madrid, Spain. Musician. m. Dolores Lucas Castillo, 2 daughters. Education: Studies flute with father Rafael Lopez Cerquera; Student of Manuel Garijo; Course in flute under René de Leroy (of Paris Conservatory of Music, Athenaeum, Madrid; Professional Training, Oscar Esplá Higher Conservatory of Music, Alicante. Career: Flautist and Piccolo Player Arbós Symphonic Orchestra, Madrid, 1939; Professor, Municipal Band, Madrid and Founder National Orchestra of Spain, 1940; Flute Soloist, National Orchestra of Spain, 1940-65; Debut of "Concierto para flauta y orquesta" by Federico de Freitas Vlanco, Lisbon, Portugal, 1961; Founder and Flute Soloist, RTVE Orchestra and Wind Quintet, 1965; Pioneer concert performer in Musical Youth; Flute Instructor, Oscar Esplá Higher Conservatory of Music, Alicante; Flute Soloist, Chamber Orchestra, Toulouse, France, 1966; Soloist, Circle of Spanish Performers, 1972; Flute and Chamber Music Instructor, in international university music courses, Santiago de Compostela/Corunna, 1973; Flute Instructor, German Embassy, Madrid, 1974-77; Jury Member international flute and piccolo competitions; Professor, Royal Higher Conservatory of Music, Madrid, 1981-83, 1988, 1996; Master Classes in honour of Theobald Böhn, Conservatory of Music, Murcia, 1994; Numerous concerts in Spain and abroad. Publications: Books: La flauta y sus recursos: La respiración continua; Método de Manuel Garijo. Recordings include: Octavario for solo flute by Tomás Marco; Homenaje a Manuel de Falla for flute and piano by Jesús Arámbarri; Aria antigua for flute and piano by Moreno Torroba; Suite in B Minor for flute and orchestra by JS Bach. Honours: National Prize for Chamber Music for Wind Instruments; Gold Insignia, Musical Youth; Gold Medal for Fine Arts, City of Madrid. Membership: Honorary President, Association of Spanish Flautists. Address: C/Porto Cristo 13, 28934 Alcorcón (Madrid), Spain.

**LOPEZ GARCIA Angel,** b. Madrid, Spain. Telecommunication Engineer. m. Maria Del Mar, 2 daughters. Education: Telecommunication Engineer, ETSIT, Madrid, Spain, 1980-1986. Appointments: Systems Analyst, Siemens S A, 1986-1989; Project Leader, Sener S A, 1989-1991; Project Leader, Indra Sistemas S A, 1991-2005; Senior Consultant, IT Deusto SA, 2005-. Honours: Graduate with honours, Telecommunication Engineering. Address: Caleruega, 73, 28033, Madrid, Spain. E-mail: alopezg@itdeusto.com

**LÓPEZ-COBOS Jesús,** b. 25 February 1940, Toro, Spain. Orchestral Conductor. Education: DPhil, Madrid University; Composition, Madrid Conservatory; Conducting, Vienna Academy. Appointments: Worked with major orchestras including London Symphony, Royal Philharmonic, Philharmonia, Concertgebouw, Vienna Philharmonic, Vienna Symphony, Berlin Philharmonic, Hamburg NDR, Munich Philharmonic, Cleveland, Chicago Symphony, New York Philharmonic, Philadelphia, Pittsburgh; Conducted new opera productions at La Scala, Milan, Covent Garden, London, Metropolitan Opera, New York; General Musikdirektor, Deutsche Oper, Berlin, 1981-90; Principal Guest Conductor, London Philharmonic Orchestra, 1981-86; Principal Guest Conductor, Artistic Director, Spanish National Orchestra, 1984-89; Music Director, Cincinnati Symphony Orchestra, 1986-; Music Director, Lausanne Chamber Orchestra, 1990-2000; Orchestre Français des Jeunes, 1998-2001. Publications: Recordings including: Bruckner symphonies; Haydn

symphonies; Donizetti's Lucia di Lammermoor; Rossini's Otello; Recital discs with José Carreras. Honours: 1st Prize, Besançon International Conductors Competition, 1969; Prince of Asturias Award, Spanish Government, 1981; Founders Award, American Society of Composers, Authors and Publishers, 1988; Cross of Merit, 1st Class, Federal Republic of Germany, 1989. Address: c/o Terry Harrison Artists, The Orchard, Market Street, Charlbury, Oxon OX7 3PJ, England.

**LOPUSZANSKI Jan (Tadeusz),** b. 21 October 1923, Lwów (Leopol), Poland. Theoretical Physicist. m. (1) Halina Pidek, (2) Barbara Zaslonka, 1 son. Education: MA, University Wroclaw, Poland, 1950; PhD, Jagellonian University, Cracow, Poland, 1955. Appointments: Assistant to Associate Professor, University of Wroclaw, 1947-68, Full Professor, 1968-95 Retired, 1995; Vice Dean, Mathematics, Physics and Chemistry Faculty, University of Wroclaw, 1957-58, Dean, 1962-64; Visiting Professor, University of Utrecht, 1958, NYU, 1960-61; Institute for Advanced Study, Princeton, 1964-65, SUNY, Stony Brook, 1970 71, University of Göttingen, 1984, 1991-92; Director, Institute of Theoretical Physics, University of Wroclaw, 1970-84. Publications: Books: Fizyka Statystyczna, 1969 (Coll A Pawlikowski) An Introduction to the Conventional Quantum Field Theory, 1976; Rachunek Spinorow, 1985; An Introduction to Symmetry and Supersymmetry in Quantum Field Theory, 1991; The Inverse Variational Problem in Classical Mechanics, 1999; Over 100 articles in professional journals. Honours: Member, Editorial Board, Reports on Mathematical Physics and Fortschritte der Physik; Recipient: Chevalry Cross Order Polonia Restituta, 1965; Officer Cross OPR, 1991; Member, Polish Academy of Sciences, correspondent, 1976-86, permanent, 1986-; Polish Academy of Arts and Sciences, Cracow, correspondent, 1996-. Memberships: Polish Physics Society; Association of Members of the Institute for Advanced Study in Princeton; International Association of Mathematical Physics; International Union of Pure and Applied Physics. Address: Institute of Theoretical Physics, University of Wroclaw Pl Max Born 9, 50204 Wroclaw, Poland. E-mail: lopus@ift.uni.wroc.pl

**LOREN Sophia,** b. 20 September 1934, Rome, Italy. Actress. m. Carlo Ponti, 1957 (marriage annulled 1962) m. 1966, 2 sons. Education: Scuole Magistrali Superiori. Appointments: First Screen Appearance, as an extra in Quo Vadis; Appeared in many Italian and other Films including: E Arrivato l'Accordatore, 1951; Africa sotto i Mari (first leading role); La Tratta delle Bianche, La Favorita, 1952; Aida, 1953; Il Paesedei Campanelli, Miseria e Nobilta, Il Segno di Venere, 1953; Tempi Nostri, 1953; Carosello Napoletano, 1953; L'Oro di Napoli, 1954; Attila, 1954; Peccatoche sia una canaglia, la Bella Mugnaia, La Donna del Fiume, 1955; Boccaccio, 1970; Matromonio All; Italiana; American Films include: The Pride and the Passion, 1955; Boy on a Dolphin, Legend of the Lost, 1956; Desire Under the Elms, 1957; That Kind of Woman, 1958; Houseboat, 1958; The Key, 1958; The Black Orchid, 1959; The Millionairess, 1961; Two Women, 1961; El Cid, 1961; Yesterday, Today and Tomorrow, 1963; The Fall of the Roman Empire, 1964; Lady L, 1965; Judith, 1965; A Countess from Hong Kong, 1965; Arabesque, 1966; More than a Miracle, 1967; The Priest's Wife, 1970; Sunflower, 1970; Man of La Mancha, 1972; Brief Encounter, (TV), 1974; The Verdict, 1974; The Cassandra Crossing, 1977; A Special Day, 1977; Firepower, 1978; Brass Target, 1979; Blood Feud, 1981; Mother Courage, 1986; Two Women, 1989; Pret a Porter, 1995; Grumpier Old men; Chair, National Alliance for Prevention and Treatment of Child Abuse and Maltreatment. Publications: Eat with Me, 1972; Sophia Loren on Women and Beauty, 1984. Honours: Venice Festival Award for the Black Orchid, 1958; Cannes Film Festival Award for Best Actress,

1961; Honorary Academy Award, 1991; Chevalier Legion d'Honneur; Goodwill Ambassador for Refugees, 1992. Address: Chalet Daniel, Burgenstock, Luzern, Switzerland.

**LORENZINI Enrico,** b. 24 September 1940, Bologna, Italy. Professor. Education: Degree, Electronic Engineering, 1965; Master in Industrial Safety, 1966. Appointments: Teaching Professor, Parma, University, Italy, 1970-73; Member, CNR National Research Team, 1977-94; Vice-President, CNR Engineering Committee, 1987-94; Dean, Faculty of Engineering, Bologna University, Italy, 1989-95; Member, University Administration Committee. Publications: Author of more than 170 scientific papers; Editor-in-Chief, Scientific Review: International Journal of Heat and Technology. Honours: Member, New York Academy; Member, International Centre for heat and Mass Transfer. Memberships: ASME; ANS; UIT; ATI. Address: Faculty of Engineering, University of Bologna, Viale Risorgimento 2, 40136 Bologna, Italy. E-mail: enrico.lorenzini@unibo.it

**LÖTHMAN Per Arvid,** b. 13 November 1965, Enköping, Sweden. Researcher; Scientist. Education: New York State College of Ceramics, Alfred University, Alfred, USA, 1994; Friedrich-Alexander-Universität, Erlangen-Nürnberg, 1997; MSc. Appointments: Engineer, Scaba AB, Stockholm, Sweden; Application and Sales Engineer, Corning International, Wiesbaden, Germany; Researcher in the Cellular Metals Group, Fraunhofer Institute for Manufacturing and Materials Research, Powder Metallurgy & Composite Materials, Dresden, Germany; Researcher in BioNanotechnology, Bacterial S-layer, Max Bergman Center for Biomaterials Dresden and Dresden University of Technology Institute for Materials Science and Nanotechnology, BioNanotechnology and Structureformation Group (BNS), Dresden, Germany; Project Manager and Researcher, Dresden University of Technology, Biology Department, Institute of Botany, BioNanotechnology group, Dresden, Germany; Referee, Journal of Bioanalytical and Analytical Chemistry. Publications include: Metallic Hollow Spheres – Materials for the Future, 2000; Cell Wall Mechanics of IFAM-Dresden Hollow Sphere Structures, 2000; Metallic Hollow Spheres – a new PM product, 2000; New Lightweight Structures Based on low-cost Metallic Hollow Sphere Structures, 2000; Steel Hollow Spheres made from Iron Oxides, 2000; Powder Metallurgy of Ultralight Materials, 2000; Modelling and Simulation of the Meso- and Macromechanical Properties of Hollow Sphere Structures, 2001; Manufacture and properties of Hollow Sphere Structures in Sound Absorption Applications, 2001; Metallic Hollow Spheres and Hollow Sphere Structures for Automotive Applications, 2001; Investigation and Image Processing of Cellular Metals with Highly Resolving 3D-micro-tomography (μCT), 2002; Metallic Hollow Sphere Structure – a possible Biomaterial with Adjustable Mechanical Properties, 2003; Catalysis of carbon monoxide oxidation by biotemplated platinum clusters, 2005; Nanostructuring of Tetraetherlipid surfaces, 2005; Small angle X-ray transmission characterisation of nano-metersized Pt-clusters in a ceramic thin film on metal substrate, 2005; Lotus Effekt & Wölbstrukturen (invited lecture), 2005. Honours: Listed in biographical publications. Memberships: German Engineering Society; German Society for Biomaterials; Junior Chamber of Commerce International; German Society for Biomechanics; German Society for Materials Science; German Biologist Society; German Society for Biochemistry and Molecular Biology. Address: Niederwaldstrasse 7, 01309 Dresden, Germany. E-mail: per-loethman@web.de Website: http://www.per-loethman.de

**LOTOREV Alexander Nikolaevich,** b. 10 September 1948, Alexandrovka Village, Zolotukhinsky District, Kursk Region,

USSR. Public Servant. m. Liubov Lotoreva, 2 sons, 1 daughter. Education: Postgraduate Diplomas, Kursk State Pedagogical Institute and Russian Academy of Public Service; Valid State Adviser of the Russian Federation 1st class. Appointments: Served in the Red Army, 1967-69; Toolmaker and Secretary of the Comsomol Committee, State Steel Bearing Factory, Kursk, 1970-76; Assistant to the Commander of a Company and Commander of a Company, Armed Forces, 1976-78; Director, Technical Training College No 22, Kursk, 1978-82; Deputy Director, Technical Training College, Surgut, Director of the Technical Training College, Nefteyugansk, Autonomous Region of Khanty, 1982-90; Elected Chairman, Executive Committee of the City of Nefteyugansk, 1990-92, Vice-Head, Administration of Nefteyugansk, 1992-; Elected Deputy of the State Duma of Khanty-Mansyisk. 1995, re-elected. 1999; Vice-President of the Deputy Group "Regions of Russia"; State Duma Committee on Power Transport and Communication; State Duma Mandate Committee; Co-ordinator of the deputy group on relations with Turkmenia; Active participant in the Co-ordinations Council of the Centrist Deputy Association "Unity", "Fatherland-All Russia" "People's Deputy", "Regions of Russia"; Secretary General (Head of Staff), State Duma of the Federal Assembly, Russian Federation, 2002-. Honours: Honorary PhD, Economics; Medals: 60 Years of the USSR Armed Forces, 1978, In Memory of 850 Years of Moscow, 1997, 300 Years of Saint Petersburg, 2003; Honoured Certificate of the State Duma of the Federal Assembly of the Russian Federation, 2002; Order of Honour, 2003. Address: State Duma of the Federal Assembly of the Russian Federation, Okhotny ryad 1, 103265 Moscow, Russian Federation. E-mail: lotorev@duma.gov.ru

**LOUISY Calliopa Pearlette,** b. 8 June 1946, St Lucia, West Indies. Governor General. Education: BA, University of the West Indies, 1969; MA, Laval University, 1975; PhD, University of Bristol, 1994. Appointments: Principal, St Lucia A Level College, 1981-86; Dean, 1986-94, Vice Principal, 1994-95, Principal, 1996-97, Sir Arthur Lewis Community College; Governor General, 1997. Publications: The Changing Role of the Small State in Higher Education; Globalisation and Comparative Education: A Caribbean Perspective; Nation Languages and National Development in the Caribbean: Reclaiming Our Own Voices. Honours: Student of the Year, 1968; Grand Cross of the Order of St Lucia, 1997; International Woman of the Year, 1998, 2001; Grand Cross of the Order of St Michael and St George, 1999; Honorary Degree of Doctor of Law (LL.D) University of Bristol, 1999 and University of Sheffield, 2003; Dame of Grace of the Most Venerable Order of the Hospital of St John of Jerusalem, 2001; Listed in International Biographical Dictionaries. Membership: Fellow, Royal Society of Arts, 2000. Address: Government House, Morne Fortune, Castries, St Lucia, West Indies.

**LOUKIANOV Nikolai,** b. 7 December 1944, Moscow, Russia. Businessman. m. Nina, 2 sons, 1 daughter. Education: Institute of International Affairs, 1971; Academy of Foreign Trade, 1987. Appointments: Commercial Director, Felchimex SA, Belgium, 1974-80; Director, V/O Soyuzpromexport, Moscow, 1980-87; Vice-President, Aspec Pte, Bangkok, 1987-92; Managing Director, Chairman, Agrosia Pte Ltd, Singapore, 1992-; Managing Director, International Potash Company Ltd (UK), 2000-. Honours: Several Medals. Membership: Who's Who membership. Address: Links, Links Drive, Totteridge, London N20 8QU, England.

**LOVE Courtney,** b. 1965. Singer; Musician (guitar); Actress. m. Kurt Cobain, 24 February 1992, deceased, 1 daughter. Career: Member, Faith No More, 1 year; Founder, singer/guitarist, Hole, 1991-; Tours include: Support tour to Nine Inch Nails; Reading

Festival, 1994, 1995; Film appearances: Straight To Hell; Sid And Nancy; Feeling Minnesota; The People vs Larry Flynt; Man on the Moon; Beat, 2000; Julie Johnson, 2001; Trapped, 2002. Recordings: Albums: Pretty On The Inside, 1991; Live Through This, 1994; Celebrity Skin, 1998. Singles: Doll Parts, 1994; Ask for It, 1995; Celebrity Skin, 1998; Malibu, 1998; Awful, 1999. Address: c/o Q-Prime Inc, 729 7th Avenue, 14th Floor, New York, NY 10019, USA.

**LOVELL (Alfred Charles) Bernard (Sir),** b. 31 August 1913, Oldland Common, Gloucestershire, England. Professor of Radio Astronomy Emeritus; Writer. m. Mary Joyce Chesterman, 1937, deceased 1993, 2 sons, 3 daughters. Education: University of Bristol. Appointments: Professor of Radio Astronomy, 1951-80, Professor Emeritus, 1980-, University of Manchester; Director, Jodrell Bank Experimental Station, later Nuffield Radio Astronomy Laboratories, 1951-81; Various visiting lectureships. Publications: Science and Civilisation, 1939; World Power Resources and Social Development, 1945; Radio Astronomy, 1951; Meteor Astronomy, 1954; The Exploration of Space by Radio, 1957; The Individual and the Universe, 1958; The Exploration of Outer Space, 1961; Discovering the Universe, 1963; Our Present Knowledge of the Universe, 1967; The Explosion of Science: The Physical Universe (editor with T Margerison), 1967; The Story of Jodrell Bank, 1968; The Origins and International Economics of Space Exploration, 1973; Out of the Zenith, 1973; Man's Relation to the Universe, 1975; P M S Blackett: A Biographical Memoir, 1976; In the Centre of Immensities, 1978; Emerging Cosmology, 1981; The Jodrell Bank Telescopes, 1985; Voice of the Universe, 1987; Pathways to the Universe (with Sir Francis Graham Smith), 1988; Astronomer By Chance (autobiography), 1990; Echoes of War, 1991. Contributions to: Professional journals. Honours: Officer of the Order of the British Empire, 1946; Duddell Medal, 1954; Royal Medal, 1960; Knighted, 1961; Ordre du Mérite pour la Recherche et l'Invention, 1962; Churchill Gold Medal, 1964; Gold Medal, Royal Astronomical Society, 1981; Many honorary doctorates. Memberships: American Academy of Arts and Sciences, honorary foreign member; American Philosophical Society; International Astronomical Union, vice-president, 1970-76; New York Academy; Royal Astronomical Society, president, 1969-71; Royal Society, fellow; Royal Swedish Academy, honorary member. Address: The Quinta, Swettenham, Cheshire CW12 2LD, England.

**LOVELL Mary Sybilla,** b. 23 October 1941, Prestatyn, North Wales. Writer. m. (2) Geoffrey A H Watts, 11 July 1991, 1 son, 2 stepsons, 2 stepdaughters. Publications: Hunting Pageant, 1980; Cats as Pets, 1982; Boys Book of Boats, 1983; Straight on till Morning, 1987; The Splendid Outcast, 1988; The Sound of Wings, 1989; Cast No Shadow, 1991; A Scandalous Life, 1995; The Rebel Heart, 1996; A Rage to Live, 1998; The Mitford Sisters, 2001; Bess of Hardwick, 2005. Contributions to: Many technical articles on the subjects of accounting and software. Memberships: Society of Authors; R S Surtees Society, vice president, 1980-; Fellow, Royal Geographical Society. Literary Agent: Louise Ducas. Address: Stroat House, Stroat, Gloucestershire NP6 7LR, England.

**LOVESEY Peter, (Peter Lear),** b. 10 September 1936, Whitton, Middlesex, England. Writer. m. Jacqueline Ruth Lewis, 30 May 1959, 1 son, 1 daughter. Education: BA, Honours, English, University of Reading, 1958. Publications: The Kings of Distance, 1968; Wobble to Death, 1970; The Detective Wore Silk Drawers, 1971; Abracadaver, 1972; Mad Hatters Holiday, 1973; Invitation to a Dynamite Party, 1974; A Case of Spirits, 1975; Swing, Swing Together, 1976; Goldengirl, 1977; Waxwork, 1978; Official Centenary History of the Amateur Athletic Association, 1979; Spider Girl, 1980; The False Inspector Dew, 1982; Keystone, 1983; Butchers (short stories), 1985; The Secret of Spandau, 1986; Rough Cider, 1986; Bertie and the Tinman, 1987; On the Edge, 1989; Bertie and the Seven Bodies, 1990; The Last Detective, 1991; Diamond Solitaire, 1992; Bertie and the Crime of Passion, 1993; The Crime of Miss Oyster Brown (short stories), 1994; The Summons, 1995; Bloodhounds, 1996; Upon a Dark Night, 1997; Do Not Exceed the Stated Dose (short stories), 1998; The Vault, 1999; The Reaper, 2000; Diamond Dust, 2002; The Sedgemoor Strangler (short stories), 2002; The House Sitter, 2003; The Circle, 2005. Honours: Macmillan/Panther 1st Crime Novel Award, 1970; Crime Writers Association Silver Dagger, 1978, 1995, 1996 and Gold Dagger, 1982 and Cartier Diamond Dagger, 2000; Grand Prix de Littérature Policière, 1985; Prix du Roman D'Aventures, 1987; Anthony Award, 1992; Macavity Award 1997, 2004. Memberships: Crime Writers Association, chairman, 1991-92; Detection Club; Society of Authors. Address: 59 Crescent Road, Leigh-on-Sea, Essex SS9 2PF, England.

**LOWE Gordon,** b. 31 May 1933, Halifax, England. University Professor. m. Gwynneth Hunter, 2 sons. Education: BSc, ARCS, 1954, PhD, DIC, 1957, Royal College of Science, Imperial College, London University; MA, Oxford University, 1960. Appointments: University Demonstrator, 1959-65, Weir Junior Research Fellow, University College, 1959-61, Official Fellow, Tutor in Organic Chemistry, Lincoln College, 1962-99, University Lecturer, 1965-88, Sub-Rector, Lincoln College, 1986-89, Aldrichian Praelector in Chemistry, 1988-89, Professor of Biological Chemistry, 1989-2000, Emeritus Professor of Biological Chemistry, Supernumerary Fellow, 2000-, Oxford University; Director, Founder, Scientific Consultant, Pharminox Ltd, 2002-. Publications: Around 240 articles in learned journals. Honours: CChem, FRSC, 1981; Charmian Medal for Enzyme Chemistry, Royal Society of Chemistry, 1983; FRS, 1984; DSc, Oxon, 1985; Royal Society of Chemistry Award for Stereochemistry, 1992. Memberships: Fellow, Royal Society, London; Fellow, Royal Society of Chemistry, London. Address: 17 Norman Avenue, Abingdon, Oxfordshire, OX14 2HQ, England. E-mail: gordon.lowe@chem.ox.ac.uk

**LOWE Stephen,** b. 1 December 1947, Nottingham, England. Playwright. m. (1) Tina Barclay, (2) Tany Myers, 1 son, 1 daughter. Education: BA, Honours, English and Drama, 1969; Postgraduate Research, 1969-70. Appointments: Senior Tutor in Writing for Performance, Dartington College of Arts Performance, 1978-82; Resident Playwright, Riverside Studios, London, 1982-84; Senior Tutor, Birmingham University, 1987-88; Nottingham Trent University Advisory Board to Theatre Design Degree, 1987-. Publications: Touched, 1981; Cards, 1983; Moving Pictures and Other Plays, 1985; Body and Soul in Peace Plays, 2 volumes, 1985, 1990; Divine Gossip/Tibetan Inroads, 1988; Ragged Trousered Philanthropists, 1991; Revelations, 2004; The Spirit of the Man, 2005. Contributions to: Books and journals. Honour: George Devine Award for Playwriting, 1977. Memberships: Theatre Writers Union; Writers Guild; PEN. Address: c/o Sara Stroud, Judy Daish Associates, 2 St Charles Place, London W10 6EG, England.

**LOWRY John Christopher,** b. 6 June 1942, Timperley, Cheshire, England. Consultant Surgeon. m. Valerie Joyce Smethurst, 1 son, 1 daughter. Education: BDS, 1963; MB ChB, 1970, University of Manchester; FDSRCS (Eng), 1968; FRCS (Ed), 1984; MHSM (OU), 1994; FDSRCS (Ed), Ad Ho, 1999; FRCS (Eng) by election, 2002; FFGDP (UK) Ad Eund, 2005. Appointments: House Officer, Senior House Officer, University of Manchester, Manchester Royal Infirmary, 1963-65; Registrar, Plastic and Maxillofacial Unit, Bradford,

1965-67; House Officer, Professorial Surgical and Medical Units, University Hospital South Manchester, Senior House Officer in Surgery, University Hospital South Manchester, 1970-72; Senior Registrar, North West Region, 1972-76; Consultant Maxillofacial and Oral Surgeon, Royal Bolton Hospital, 1976-; Part-time Lecturer in Biological Sciences, University of Manchester, 1976-2000; Visiting Professor of Surgery, University of Central Lancashire, 2004-. Publications: Maxillofacial Trauma; Economics of Healthcare Delivery; Salivary Disease; Telemedicine. Honours: Honorary Member, Hungarian Association for Maxillofacial Surgery; Honorary Fellow, American Association for Oral and Maxillofacial Surgery; Honorary Member, Croatian Society for Maxillofacial, Plastic and Reconstructive Head and Neck Surgery; Down Surgical Prize, British Association for Oral and Maxillofacial Surgery; Tomes Medal, British Dental Association; CBE, 2003. Memberships: European Association for Cranio-Maxillo-Facial Surgery, Secretary General, 1998-; British Association of Oral and Maxillofacial Surgeons, Honorary Secretary, 1989-92, President, 2001; Manchester Medical Society, President, 2004-2005; Royal College of Surgeons (Eng), Dean of Faculty, 2001-2004, Member of Council, 2001-, Examiner Surgical Royal Colleges of UK and Ireland, 1996-2001. Address: The Valley House, 50 Ravens Wood, Heaton, Bolton BL1 5TL, England. E-mail: johnlowry1@btinternet.com

**LOYD Francis Alfred (Sir),** b. 5 September 1916, Berkhamsted, England. Colonial Service Officer. m. (1) Katharine Layzell, deceased 1981, 2 daughters, (2) Monica Murray Brown. Education: Trinity College, Oxford, England. Appointments: Appointed to Colonial Service, 1938; District Officer, Kenya, 1939; Military Service, East Africa, 1940-42; Private Secretary to Governor of Kenya, 1942-45; District and Provincial Commissioner, 1945-62; Commonwealth Fund Fellowship to USA, 1953-54; Permanent Secretary, Governor's Office, 1962-63; H.M. Commissioner for Swaziland, 1964-68; Director, London House for Overseas Graduates, 1969-79; Chairman, Oxfam Africa Committee, 1979-85. Honours: MBE, 1951; OBE, 1954; CMG, 1961; KCMG, 1965. Memberships: Vincent's Club (Oxford). Address: 53 Park Road, Aldeburgh, Suffolk IP15 5EN, England.

**LUCAS George,** b. 14 May 1944, Modesto, California, USA. Film Director. Education: University of South California. Appointments: Warner Brothers Studio; Assistant to Francis Ford Cappola, The Rain People; Director, Documentary on making The Rain People; Formed, Lucasfilm Ltd; Director, Co-Author, Screenplay Films THX-1138, 1970; American Graffiti, 1973; Director, Author, Star Wars, 1977; Director, Author, To Prequel The Phantom Menace, 1999; Executive Producer, More American Graffiti, 1979; The Empire Strikes Back, 1980; Raiders of the Lost Ark, 1981; Return of the Jedi, 1982; Indiana Jones and the Temple of Doom, 1984; Howard the Duck, 1986; Labyrinth, 1988; Willow, 1988; Tucker: The Man and His Dream, 1988; Co-Executive Producer, Mishima, 1985; Indiana Jones and the Last Crusade, 1989; Star Wars Episode I: The Phantom Menace, 1999; Star Wars Episode II: Attack of the Clones, 2002; Star Wars Episode III: Revenge of the Sith, 2005; Executive Producer, The Young Indiana Jones Chronicles (TV series), 1992-93; Radioland Murders, 1994. Honours: Dr hc, University of South California, 1994; Irving Thalberg Award, 1992. Address: Lucasfilm Ltd, P O Box 2009, San Rafael, CA 94912, USA.

**LUCAS John (Randolph),** b. 18 June 1929, England. Philosopher; Writer. m. Morar Portal, 1961, 2 sons, 2 daughters. Education: St Mary's College, Winchester; MA, Balliol College, Oxford, 1952. Appointments: Junior Research Fellow, 1953-56,

Fellow and Tutor, 1960-96, Merton College, Oxford; Fellow and Assistant Tutor, Corpus Christi College, Cambridge, 1956-59; Jane Eliza Procter Visiting Fellow, Princeton University, 1957-58; Leverhulme Research Fellow, Leeds University, 1959-60; Gifford Lecturer, University of Edinburgh, 1971-73; Margaret Harris Lecturer, University of Dundee, 1981; Harry Jelema Lecturer, Calvin College, Grand Rapids, 1987; Reader in Philosophy, Oxford University, 1990-96. Publications: Principles of Politics, 1966, 2nd edition, 1985; The Concept of Probability, 1970; The Freedom of the Will, 1970; The Nature of Mind, 1972; The Development of Mind, 1973; A Treatise on Time and Space, 1973; Essays on Freedom and Grace, 1976; Democracy and Participation, 1976; On Justice, 1980; Space, Time and Causality, 1985; The Future, 1989; Spacetime and Electromagnetism, 1990; Responsibility, 1993; Ethical Economics, 1996; The Conceptual Roots of Mathematics, 1999; An Engagement with Plato's Republic; Contributions to scholarly journals. Memberships: British Academy, Fellow; British Society for the Philosophy of Science, president, 1991-93. Address: Lambrook House, East Lambrook, Somerset TA13 5HW, England. Website: http://users.ox.ac.uk/~jrlucas

**LUGTON Charles Michael Arber,** b. 5 April 1951, Johannesburg, South Africa. Government Civil Servant. m. Elizabeth Joyce Graham, 2 sons. Education: St John's College, Johannesburg; The Edinburgh Academy; University of Edinburgh. Appointments: Private Secretary to Permanent Under Secretary of State, Scottish Office, 1976-78; Head of Branch, Police Division, 1978-83; Head of Town and Country Planning Policy Branch, 1983-87; Head of Public Health Division, 1988-90; Head of Criminal Justice and Licensing Division, Scottish Home and Health Department, 1990-95; Principal Private Secretary to the Secretary of State for Scotland, 1995-97; Director of Corporate Development, 1998-99; Head of Constitution and Parliamentary Secretariat, Scottish Executive, 1999-2004; Head of Constitution and Legal Services Group, 2004-. Memberships: Governor, Merchiston Castle School, Edinburgh; Board Member, Civil Service Healthcare Society Limited. Address: Scottish Executive, Victoria Quay, Edinburgh EH6 6QQ, Scotland. E-mail: michael.lugton@scotland.gsi.gov.uk

**LUKASZCZYK Maciej,** b. 11 March 1934, Warsaw, Poland. Concert Pianist. Education: Diploma with Honours, High School of Music, Warsaw, 1956. Career: Performed in concerts as a piano-duo with his brother Jacek Lukaszczyk all over the world; Founder and President of the Chopin Society in Germany. Honours: Order of Merit of the Federal Republic of Germany, First Class, 1991; Order of Merit of the Republic of Poland, 1999; Prizes for concert performances. Address: Kasinostr 3, Kennedy-Haus, Darmstadt, 64293, Germany.

**LUKE William Ross,** b. 8 October 1943, Glasgow, Scotland. Chartered Accountant. m. Deborah Jacqueline Gordon Luke, 3 daughters, 1 deceased. Appointment: Senior Partner, Luke, Gordon & Co, Chartered Accountants, 1983-. Honours: Metropolitan Police Commendation, 1983; Life Vice-President, London Scottish Rugby Football Club, 1995-. Memberships: Fellow, Institute of Chartered Accountants in England and Wales; Member, London Scottish Rugby Football Club; Member, Caledonian Society of London; Qualified Sub-Aqua Advanced Open Water Diver (PADI). Address: 105 Palewell Park, London SW14 8JJ, England.

**LUKOSEVICIUS Leonardas,** b. 28 March 1937, Kaunas, Lithuania. Professor. m. Natalia, 2 sons. Education: Medical Faculty, Kaunas Medical Institute, 1955-61; PhD Student, Biochemistry, Kaunas Medical Institute, 1965-68. Appointments:

Physician, 1961-63; Assistant, Microbiology Department, 1963-64; Assistant, Physiology Department, Kaunas Medical Institute, 1964-65; PhD, Student, 1965-68; Assistant, Biochemistry Department, 1968-71; Associate Professor, 1971-91; Professor, Kaunas Medical University, 1991-; Dean of the Faculty of Healthy Living, University of the Third Millennium (Branch of the Kaunas District), 1999-2002. Publications: Co-author, Lipids and their metabolism; Protein metabolism; Biochemistry; Tissue Biochemistry; Blood Biochemistry; Clinical Biochemistry; Healthy Living since Childhood, 1999; Hormones, 2002; Biochemistry of Tissue and Organ Systems, 2003; Basics in Family Medicine, 2003; Biochemistry, 2003; Co-author of 70 scientific articles. Honours: Lithuanian State Award Laureate, 1978, 1987; Lithuanian Republic President Cup Copy, 1997. Memberships: Chief Editor, Biological Medicine. Address: Taikos av 44-30, LT-50234 Kaunas, Lithuania.

**LUKOSEVICIUS Viktoras**, b. 9 August 1939, Kaunas, Lithuania. University Teacher. m. Emilija Lukoseviciene, 2 sons. Education. Diploma Engineer of Geodesy, Kaunas Polytechnical Institute, Lithuania, 1962; PhD, Engineering, Institute of Surveying, Aerial Photography and Cartography, Moscow, 1966; Associate Professor, Kaunas Polytechnical Institute, 1970. Appointments: Head of Basic Science Department, 1967-70, Head of Civil Engineering Department, 1970-81, KPI; Vice Dean and Associate Professor, Panevezys Faculty, Kaunas University of Technology, 1981-87, Head of Civil Engineering Department, Associate Professor and Faculty Council Chair of Panevezys Campus, Kaunas University of Technology, 1988-2001; Head of Civil Engineering Department, Associate Professor of Panevezys Institute, KTU, 2002-. Publications: Over 60 scientific articles; Participant in conferences in USA, Brazil, Sweden, Norway, Russia. Honours: Certificate, Governor of State of Ohio, USA for outstanding contribution of the continued success of the Columbus National Program, 1995; Fellowship Winner, NATO and Italy National Science Competition, 1996. Memberships: Senate Member, Kaunas University of Technology, 1992-2001; Council Member, KTU, Panevezys Institute, Faculty of Technology; International Association for Continuing Engineering Education; Association for the Advancement of Baltic Studies; Council Member, Lithuanian Liberal Society, 1992-2004; Candidate, Lithuanian Republic Parliament, 1992,1996; Board Member, Panevezys Department, Lithuanian Scientists Union; President, Panevezys Lithuanian and Swedes Society. Address: Statybininku 56-66, Lt 37348 Panevezys, Lithuania.

**LUMB William V**, b. 26 November 1921, Sioux City, Iowa. University Professor. m. Lilly I Carlson, 25 June 1949, 1 son. Education: DVM, Kansas State University, 1943; MSc, Texas A&M University, 1953 Graduate Studies, 1952-54, PhD, 1957, University of Minnesota; Doctor of Science (Honorary), The Ohio State University, 1999. Appointments: Us Army Veterinary Corps, 1943-46; Intern, Resident, Angell Memorial Animal Hospital, Boston, 1946-48; Assistant and Associate Professor, Texas A&M University, 1949-52; Associate Professor, Department of Clinics and Surgery, 1954-58, Colorado State University; Associate Professor, Department of Surgery and Medicine, Michigan State University, 1958-60; Associate Professor, Department of Medicine, 1960-63, Professor and Director of Surgical Laboratory, Department of Clinical Sciences, College of Veterinary Medicine and Biomedical Sciences, 1963-82, Colorado State University; Professor Emeritus, Colorado State University, 1982; Professor, Ross University, St Kitts, West Indies, 1986; President and Chief Executive Officer, The Lubra Company, 1972-99. Publications: Numerous articles in professional journals; Books: Small Animal Anesthesia, 1963; Veterinary Anesthesia (co-author), 1979, 2nd edition, 1984; Book chapters, papers, films; 2 patents. Honours include: The Gaines Medal, 1965; Ralston Purina Award, 1980; Colorado Veterinarian of the Year, 1981; Distinguished Service Award, Veterinary Medicine, Kansas State University, 1982; American College of Veterinary Anesthesiologists, Service Award, 1982; Jacob Markowitz Award, Academy of Surgical Research, 1987; Phi Zeta; Gamma Sigma Delta; Sigma Xi; Glover Distinguished Faculty Award, 2004, Colorado State University. Memberships include: President and Chairman of the Board, American College of Veterinary Surgeons, 1974-75; Founding Diplomate, American College of Veterinary Anesthesiologists; American Veterinary Medical Association; American Animal Hospital Association; Fellow, American Association for the Advancement of Science. Address: 1905 Mohawk Street, Fort Collins, CO 80525-1501, USA.

**LUMLEY Joanna**, b. 1 May 1946, Kashmir, India. Actress. m. (1) Jeremy Lloyd, divorced, (2) Stephen Barlow, 1 son. Career: TV includes: Release; Comedy Playhouse; Satanic Rites of Dracula, 1973, Coronation Street, General Hospital, 1974-75, The New Avengers, 1976-77; Steptoe & Son; Are You Being Served?; Sapphire & Steel, 1978; Absolutely Fabulous, 1992-94, 1996, 2001; Class Act, 1994; Joanna Lumley in the Kingdom of the Thunder Dragon, 1997; Coming Home, 1998; A Rather English Marriage, 1998; Nancherrow; Dr Willoughby MD; Mirrorball, 1999; Giraffes on the Move, 2001; Up In Town, 2002; Films include: Some Girls Do; Tam Lin; The Breaking of Bumbo; Games That Lovers Play; Don't Just Lie There, Say Something; On Her Majesty's Secret Service; Trail of the Pink Panther; Curse of the Pink Panther; That Was Tory; Mistral's Daughter; A Ghost in Monte Carlo; Shirley Valentine; Forces Sweetheart; Innocent Lies; James and the Giant Peach; Cold Comfort Farm; Prince Valiant; Parting Shots; Mad Cows; Maybe Baby; The Cat's Meow; Ella Enchanted; Theatre includes: Blithe Spirit, 1986; Vanilla, 1990; The Letter, 1995; all in London. Publications: Stare Back and Smile, memoirs, 1989; Girl Friday, 1994; Joanna Lumley in the Kingdom of the Thunder Dragon, 1997. Honours: OBE; Hon DLitt, Kent, 1994; D University, Oxford Brookes, 2000; BAFTA Award, 1992, 1994; Special BAFTA, 2000. Address: c/o Caroline Renton, 23 Crescent Lane, London SW4, England.

**LUMSDEN David (James) (Sir)**, b. 19 March 1928, Newcastle upon Tyne, England. Musician. m. Sheila Gladys Daniels, 28 July 1951, 2 sons, 2 daughters. Education: Selwyn College, Cambridge; MA, 1955; DPhil, 1957. Career: Fellow, Organist at New College Oxford; Rector, chori, Southwell Minster; Founder and Conductor of Nottingham Bach Society; Director of Music, Keele University; Visiting Professor at Yale University; Principal: Royal Scottish Academy of Music and Drama and Royal Academy of Music, London; Hugh Porter Lecturer at Union Theological Seminary, New York, 1967; Director, European Union Baroque Orchestra, 1985-. Publications: An Anthology of English Lute Music, 1954; Thomas Robinson's Schoole Musike 1603, 1971. Contributions to: The Listener; The Score; Music and Letters; Galpin Society Journal; La Luth et sa Musique; La musique de la Renaissance. Honours: Knight, 1985; Honorary Fellow, Selwyn College, Cambridge, 1986; Honorary DLitt, Reading, 1990; Honorary Fellow of Kings College, London, 1991; Honorary Fellow, New College, Oxford, 1996. Memberships: Incorporated Society of Musicians, President, 1984-85; Royal College of Organists, President, 1986-88; Incorporated Association of Organists, President, 1966-68; Honorary Editor, Church Music Society, 1970-73; Chairman, National Youth Orchestra of Great Britain, 1985-94; Chairman, Early Music Society, 1985-89; Board, Scottish Opera, 1977-83; Board, ENO, 1983-88. Address: Melton House, Soham, Cambridgeshire CB7 5DB, England.

**LUNAN (Charles) Burnett,** b. 28 September 1941, London, England. Medical Practitioner. m. Helen Russell Ferrie, 2 sons, 1 daughter. Education: MB ChB, 1965, MD, 1977, University of Glasgow. Appointments: Research Fellow, MRC Unit, Strathclyde University, UK, 1971-72; Lecturer, University of Aberdeen, UK, 1973-75; Senior Lecturer, University of Nairobi, Kenya, 1975-77; Consultant Obstetrician, Gynaecologist, North Glasgow University NHS Trust, 1977-; Consultant to WHO, Bangladesh, 1984-85; Short term Consultant to WHO, ODA, Bangladesh, 1988-94. Publications: Various chapters and articles on female sterilisation, infection in pregnancy, diabetes in pregnancy, Caesarean section, health care in the developing world. Honours: MRCOG, 1970, FRCOG, 1983, Royal College of Obstetricians and Gynaecologists, London; FRCS, 1985, Royal College of Physicians and Surgeons of Glasgow. Memberships: Secretary, 1978-82, Vice President, 1998-2002, President, 2002-, Glasgow Obstetrical and Gynaecological Society; Treasurer, 1982-90, Vice President, 1990-91, President, 1991-92, Royal Medico-Chirurgical Society of Glasgow. Address: Princess Royal Maternity, 16 Alexandra Parade, Glasgow G31 2ER, Scotland.

**LUNKIM Tongkhojang,** b. 1 January 1937, Kamu village, Manipur, India. Doctor of Theology; Minister. m. Chongnu, 2 sons, 4 daughters. Education: D Div, M Div, Serampore College (University); M Theol, Fuller Theological Seminary, USA. Appointments: Administrative Secretary, Kuki Christian Church, 1979-; Kuki Bible Translator, 1964-72; President, Kuki Baptist Convention, 1958-59, General Secretary, 1959-68; Chairman, Kuki Movement for Human Rights, 1996-; Co-worker, Disaster Emergency Service Incorporation, and Senior Minister of Imphal Christian Church, 1982-. Address: K C C Office, PO Imphal 795001, Manipur, India.

**LUO Zhi-Shan,** b. 20 August 1936, Da-pu, Guangdong, China. Teacher; Researcher of Mechanics. m. Wang Xiu-Yin, 2 sons. Education: Graduate, Tianjin University, China, 1958. Address: Assistant, 1958-79, Lecturer, 1979-85, Associate Professor, 1986-93, Director, Laboratory of Mechanics, 1984-85; Director, Teaching and Research Section, 1985-86, Professor of Mechanics, 1993-, Tianjin University; Visiting Professor, Mechanical Engineering, University of Hong Kong, 1992; Technical Consultant, Shanton Jingyi Machinery Co, Shanton, China, 1992-94, Hong Kong Press Publications, 1996-97; Chief Engineer, Director of Research, Tianjin Xingu Intelligent Optical Measuring Technique Company, 2000-. Publications: The Principle and Application of Sticking Film Moire Interferometry; Ultra-high Sensitivity Moiré Interferometry for Subdynamic Tests in Normal Light Environment; Research of Instrumentation and Intellectualization for Moiré Interferometry; Ultra-High Sensitivity Moiré Interferometry by the Aid of Electronic-liquid Phase Shifter and Computer; Moiré Interferometer of Intelligent Mode and Its Application; New Computer Adjusted-and-Processing Moiré Interferometer's Applied Research to Mechanical Property Measure of Concrete; Application of Moiré Interferometry in study for Destructive Mechanism of Concrete. Honours: Medal of Gold, 2nd Invention Exhibition of China, 1986; Advanced Award of Science and Technology, China Education, 1986, 1997; Medal of Gilding, 15th International Exhibition of Invention and New Technique, Geneva, 1987; National Award of Invention, China, 1987. Memberships: China Mechanics Society; China Invention Society; Society for Experimental Mechanics, Inc. Address: Four Season Village, 29-5-401, Tianjin University, Tianjin 300072, China. E-mail: lzstju@public.tpt.tj.cn

**LUPESCU Grigore,** b. 30 August 1931, Târgu-Jiu, România. Doctor of Medicine; Specialist in Cardiology. m. Iuliana, 1 son, 1 daughter. Education: PhD, Medical Sciences, Faculty of General Medicine, Bucharest, 1983. Appointments: Doctor of Medicine, Specialist in Cardiology, Târgu-Jiu Hospital. Publications: Over 70 papers and abstracts in diverse journals. Honours: Citizen of Honour, Târgu-Jiu; Honorary Member, IBC Advisory Council; Member, ABI Research Board of Advisors. Memberships: New York Academy of Sciences; Academy of Medical Sciences of Romania; Mediterranean Society of Cardiology; Balkan Medical Union; Society of Writers and Journalist Doctors of Romania. Address: Str Traian No 3, 1400, Târgu-Jiu, Gorj, Romania.

**LURIE Alison,** b. 3 September 1926, Chicago, Illinois, USA. Professor of English; Author. 3 sons. Education: AB, magna cum laude, Radcliffe College, 1947. Appointments: Lecturer, 1969-73, Adjunct Associate Professor, 1973-76, Associate Professor, 1976-79, Professor of English, 1979-, Cornell University. Publications: Love and Friendship, 1962; The Nowhere City, 1965; Imaginary Friends, 1967; Real People, 1969; The War Between the Tates, 1974; V R Lang: Poems and Plays, With a memoir by Alison Lurie, 1975; Only Children, 1979; Clever Gretchen and Other Forgotten Folktales (juvenile), 1980; The Heavenly Zoo (juvenile), 1980; The Language of Clothes (non-fiction), 1981; Fabulous Beasts (juvenile), 1981; Foreign Affairs, 1984; The Truth About Lorin Jones, 1988; Don't Tell the Grownups: Subversive Children's Literature, 1990; Women and Ghosts, 1994; The Last Resort, 1998; Familiar Spirits, 2001. Contributions to: Many publications. Honours: Guggenheim Fellowship, 1966-67; Rockefeller Foundation Grant, 1968-69; New York State Cultural Council Foundation Grant, 1972-73; American Academy of Arts and Letters Award, 1984; Pulitzer Prize in Fiction, 1985; Radcliffe College Alumnae Recognition Award, 1987; Prix Femina Etranger, 1989; Parents' Choice Foundation Award, 1996. Address: c/o Department of English, Cornell University, Ithaca, NY 14853, USA.

**LUSCOMBE Lawrence Edward,** b. 10 November 1924, Torquay, England. Anglican Bishop. m. Doris Luscombe, deceased, 1 daughter. Education: Kings College, London, 1963-64; LLD, 1987, MPhil, 1991, PhD, 1993, University of Dundee. Appointments: Indian Army, 1942-47; Chartered Accountant, Partner, Galbraith, Dunlop and Co, later Watson and Galbraith, 1952-63; Rector, St Barnabas, Paisley, 1966-71; Provost of St Paul's Cathedral, Dundee, 1971-75; Bishop of Brechin, 1975-90; Primus of the Scottish Episcopal Church, 1985-90. Publications: The Scottish Episcopal Church in the Twentieth Century; A Seminary of Learning; Matthew Luscombe, Missionary Bishop; The Representative Man. Honours: Chaplain, Order of St John; Honorary Research Fellow, University of Dundee; Honorary Canon, Trinity Cathedral, Davenport, Iowa, USA. Memberships: Institute of Chartered Accountants of Scotland; Society of Antiquaries of Scotland; Royal Society of Arts. Address: Woodville, Kirkton of Tealing, By Dundee, DD4 0RD, Scotland.

**LUTTWAK Edward N(icholae),** b. 4 November 1942, Arad, Romania (US citizen, 1981). Political Scientist; Author. m. Dalya Iaari, 14 December 1970, 1 son, 1 daughter. Education: Carmel College, England; BSc, London School of Economics and Political Science, 1964; PhD, Johns Hopkins University, 1975. Appointments: Associate Director, Washington Center of Foreign Policy Research, District of Columbia, 1972-75; Visiting Professor of Political Science, Johns Hopkins University, 1973-78; Senior Fellow, 1976-87, Research Professor in International Security Affairs, 1978-82, Arleigh Burke Chair in Strategy, 1987-, Director, Geo-Economics, 1991-, Center for Strategic and International Studies, Washington, DC; Nimitz Lecturer, University of California, Berkeley, 1987; Tanner Lecturer, Yale University, 1989. Publications: A Dictionary of Modern War,

# DICTIONARY OF INTERNATIONAL BIOGRAPHY

1971, new edition with Stuart Koehl, 1991; The Grand Strategy of the Roman Empire: From the First Century A.D. to the Third, 1976; The Economic and Military Balance Between East and West 1951-1978 (editor with Herbert Block), 1978; Sea Power in the Mediterranean (with R G Weinland), 1979; Strategy and Politics: Collected Essays, 1980; The Grand Strategy of the Soviet Union, 1983; The Pentagon and the Art of War: The Question of Military Reform, 1985; Strategy and History, 1985; On the Meaning of Victory: Essays on Strategy, 1986; Global Security: A Review of Strategic and Economic Issues (editor with Barry M Blechman), 1987; Strategy: The Logic of War and Peace, 1987; The Endangered American Dream: How to Stop the United States from Becoming a Third World Country and How to Win the Geo-Economic Struggle for Industrial Supremacy, 1993; Turbo-Capitalism: Winners and Losers in the Global Economy, 1999; La renaissance de la puissance aerienne stategique, 1999; Che cos'é davvero la democrazia (with Susanna Creperio Verratti); Il Libro delle Liberta, 2000; Strategy Now (editor), 2000; Strategy: The Logic of War and Peace, 2002. Contributions to Numerous books and periodicals. Address: c/o Center for Strategic and International Studies, Georgetown University, 1800 K Street North West, Washington, DC 20006, USA.

**LUX Jonathan Sidney,** b. 30 October 1951, London, England. Solicitor. m. Simone, 1 son, 2 daughters. LLB Honours, Nottingham University, 1973; Diplom d'Etudes Superieures, University of Aix-Marseilles, 1974; Solicitor: England and Wales, 1977, Hong Kong, 1986. Appointments: Trainee Solicitor, 1975-77, Solicitor, 1977-83, Partner, London Office, 1983-2001 and 2004-, Managing Partner, Hamburg, Germany, 2001-2003, Ince & Co (international law firm). Publications: Co-author: The Law of Tug, Tow and Pilotage, 1994; The Law and Practice of Marine Insurance and Average, 1996; Alternative Dispute Resolution, 2002; Bunkers, 2004; Corporate Social Responsibility, expected 2005; Editor: Classification Societies, 1993; Maritime Law Handbook, ongoing. Contributor of articles to professional journals. Honours: University Exhibition, 1972; French Government Scholarship, 1973; Freeman of City of London; Fellow, Chartered Institute of Arbitrators. Memberships: Law Society; Fellow, Chartered Institute of Arbitrators; Accredited Mediator (CEDR, The Academy of Experts, ADR Net); London Maritime Arbitrators Association; German Maritime Arbitrators Association; China Maritime Arbitration Commission; Association of Average Adjusters; Steering Committee, London Shipping Law Centre; Former Chair and current Chair of various Committees, International Bar Association; Athenaeum Club; Royal Overseas League. Address: c/o Ince & Co, Knollys House, 11 Byward Street, London EC3R 5EN, England. E-mail: jonathan.lux@incelaw.com

**LYKLEMA Johannes,** b. 23 November 1930, Apeldoorn, The Netherlands. Professor. m. 2 children. Education: Studies in Chemistry and Physics, State University of Utrecht, 1948-55; PhD, Utrecht, 1956; Honorary Doctorate, Universite Catholic, Louvain-la-Neuve, Belgium, 1988, Royal Institute of Technology, Stockholm, Sweden, 1997. Appointments: Military Service, 1956-58; Science Co-Worker, University of Utrecht, 1958-61; Visiting Associate Professor, University of South California, Los Angeles, USA, 1961-62; Professor, Physical and Colloid Chemistry, Wageningen Agricultural University, 1962-; Visiting Professor, University of Bristol, England, 1971; Australian National University, Canberra, 1976, University of Tokyo, Japan, 1988; Visiting Professor, University of Florida, Gainesville, USA, 1997-. Publications: Over 300 articles in professional journals. Honours: Nightingale Award for Medical Electronics, 1963; Gold Medal, Centre for Marine Research, Ruder Boskovic, Zagreb, 1986; Knight in the Order of the Dutch

Lion, 1991; Koninklijke Shell Prize, 1995; Thomas Graham Prize, 1995. Memberships: 90 national and local committees; 95 international. Address: Wageningen University, Department of Physical Chemistry and Colloid Science, De Dreijen 6, 6703 HB Wageningen, The Netherlands.

**LYNCH David,** b. 20 January 1946, Missoula, Montana, USA. Film Director. m. (1) Peggy Reavey, 1967, divorced, 1 daughter, (2) Mary Fisk, 1977, divorced, 1 son. Education: Hammond High School, Alexandria; Corcoran School of Art, Washington, DC; School of Museum of Fine Arts, Boston; Pennsylvania Academy of Fine Arts, Philadelphia. Appointments: Films include: The Grandmother, 1970; Eraserhead, 1977; The Elephant Man, 1980; Dune, 1984; Blue Velvet, 1986; Wild at Heart, 1990; Storyville, 1991; Twin Peaks; Fire Walk With Me, 1992; Lost Highway, 1997; Crumb, 1999; The Straight Story, 1999. TV includes: Twin Peaks, 1990; Mulholland Drive, 2000. Honours: Fellow, Centre for Advanced Film Study, American Film Institute, Los Angeles, 1970; Dr hc, Royal College of Art; Golden Palm, Cannes. Address: c/o CAA, 9830 Wilshire Boulevard, Beverly Hills, CA 90212, USA.

**LYNCH John,** b. 11 January 1927, Boldon, England. Professor Emeritus; Historian. Education: MA, University of Edinburgh, 1952; PhD, University of London, 1955. Appointments: Lecturer in History, University of Liverpool, 1954-61; Lecturer, Reader and Professor of Latin American History, University College, London, 1961-74; Professor of Latin American History and Director of Institute of Latin American Studies, University of London, 1974-87. Publications: Spanish Colonial Administration 1782-1810: The Intendant System in the Viceroyalty of the Río de la Plata, 1958; Spain Under the Habsburgs, 2 volumes, 1964, 1967, 2nd edition, revised, 1981; The Origins of the Latin American Revolutions 1808-1826 (with R A Humphreys), 1965; The Spanish American Revolutions 1808-1826, 1973, 2nd edition, revised, 1986; Argentine Dictator: Juan Manuel de Rosas 1829-1852, 1981; The Cambridge History of Latin America (with others), Vol 3, 1985, Vol 4, 1986; Bourbon Spain 1700-1808, 1989; Caudillos in Spanish America 1800-1850, 1992; Latin American Revolutions 1808-1826: Old and New World Origins, 1994; Massacre in the Pampas, 1872: Britain and Argentina in the Age of Migration, 1998; Latin America between Colony and Nation, 2001. Honours: Encomienda Isabel La Católica, Spain, 1988; Doctor, Honoris Causa, University of Seville, 1990; Order of Andres Bello, 1st Class, Venezuela, 1995. Membership: Royal Historical Society, fellow. Address: 8 Templars Crescent, London N3 3QS, England.

**LYNCH John Edward Jr,** b. 3 May 1952, Lansing, Michigan, USA. Lawyer. m. Brenda Jayne Clark, 4 sons, 1 daughter. Education: AB, Hamilton College, 1974; JD, Case Western Reserve University, 1977; Appointments: Bar: Connecticut, 1978, Ohio, 1980; US District Court (no. dist), Ohio, 1980, US Court of Appeals (6th Circuit), 1980, Texas, 2000; Associate, Thompson, Weir & Barclay, 1977-78; Law Clerk, US District Judge, Cleveland, 1978-80; Associate, 1980-86, Partner, 1986-96, Squire, Sanders and Dempsey, Cleveland; Vice President, General Counsel, Secretary, Caliber System Inc, Akron, Ohio, 1996-98; Senior Vice-President, General Counsel, BP America Inc, 1998-99; Associate General Counsel, Upstream Western Hemisphere BP, 1999-2002; Associate General Counsel, E&P, GP&R; Global BP plc, London, 2003-. Memberships: Master Bencher, American Inns of Court Foundation, 1987-98; Member, Civil Justice Reform Act Advisory Group, US District Court (no.dist.) Ohio; Delegate, Hamilton College Alumni Council, 1992-97; Regional Chair, Alumni Admissions, 1993-97; Trustee, The Catholic Charities Corporation, 1995-97; Member, Cuyahoga County Republican Executive Committee,

Cleveland, 1984-98; Member, Seton Society St Vincent Hospital Fund. Address: BP Plc, Building 200, 1st Floor, Chertsey Road, Sunbury-on-Thames TW16 7LN, England. E-mail: lynchj@bp.com

**LYNDEN-BELL Donald,** b. 5 April 1935. Astronomer. m. Ruth Marion Truscott, 1 son, 1 daughter. Education: Marlborough College, Wiltshire, 1948-53; PhD, Theoretical Astrophysics, Clare College, University of Cambridge, 1960. Appointments: Harkness Fellow of the Commonwealth Fund New York, California Institute of Technology & Mt Wilson & Palomar Observatories, 1960-62; Research Fellow, Clare College, 1960-62; Assistant Lecturer in Mathematics, University of Cambridge, 1962-65; Director of Studies in Mathematics, Clare College, 1962-65; Official Fellow of Clare College, 1962-65; Principal Scientific Officer, later Senior Principal Scientific Officer, Royal Greenwich Observatory, Herstmonceux Castle, Sussex, 1965-72; Professor of Astrophysics, University of Cambridge, 1972-2001; Visiting Appointments: Oort Professor, Leiden University; Visiting Professor, University of Sussex, 1969-72; South African Astronomical Observatory, 1973-90; Fairchild Scholar, CALTECH, 1979; Mt Stromlo Observatory, Australia, 1987; Einstein Fellow, Israeli Academy, Jerusalem, 1990; Carnegie Observatories, Pasadena, California, 2002; Queen's University, Belfast, 1996-2003, David Bates Lecturer, 2003. Publications: Numerous papers in scientific journals; Monthly Notices of Royal Astronomical Society. Honours: Murgoci Prize for Physics, Clare College, 1956; Honorary Scholar of Clare College, 1957; Schwarzschild Lecturer and Medallist of the Astronomische Gesellschaft, 1983; Eddington Medal, 1984, Gold Medal, 1993, Royal Astronomical Society; Medal, Science Faculty, Charles University, Prague; Honorary DSc, Sussex, 1987; Brouwer Award in Dynamical Astronomy of the AAS, 1990; Bruce Medal of the Astronomical Society of the Pacific, 1998; J J Carty Award, NAS, 1999; Russell Lecturer, American Astronomical Society, 2000; CBE, 2000. Membership: Fellow, Clare College; Fellow, Royal Society; Fellow, Royal Astronomical Society; Fellow, Cambridge Philosophical Society; Honorary Fellow, Inter-University Centre for Astronomy and Astrophysics, Pune, India; Foreign Associate, US National Academy of Sciences; Honorary Foreign Member, American Academy of Arts and Sciences; Foreign Associate, Royal Society of South Africa; Honorary Member, American Astronomical Society. Address: 9 Storey's Way, Cambridge CB3 0DP, England. E-mail: dlb@ast.cam.ac.uk

**LYNDON SKEGGS Barbara Noel,** b. 29 December 1924, London, England. Retired. m. Michael Lyndon Skeggs, 2 sons, 2 daughters. Appointments include: Served 6 months in Aircraft Factory and 2½ years in the WRNS during World War II; Joined Conservative Party, holding various constituency positions over the years, 1945-; Manager of Ford Primary School, 1963-88; Appointed Justice of the Peace, 1966-94; Conservative County Councillor for Crookham, 1968-81; Appointed Tax Commissioner, 1984-94; Appointed Deputy Lieutenant for Northumberland, 1988-; Appointed High Sheriff of Northumberland, 1994-95. Honours: Freeman of the City of London, 1973; Badge of Honour for Distinguished Service, BRCS, 1987; MBE, 1990. Memberships: Berwick Infirmary Management Committee, 1966-74; Area Health Authority, 1974-90; Northumberland Family Practitioner Committee, 1980-90; Northumberland Magistrates Committee, 1980-94; Ford and Etal PCC, 1961-96; Board of Northern Opera, 1971-81. Address: Dalgheal, Evanton, Ross-shire IV16 9XH, Scotland.

**LYNN Vera (Margaret Lewis) (Dame),** b. 20 March 1917. Singer. m. Harry Lewis, 1941, 1 daughter. Career: Debut performance, 1924; Appeared with Joe Loss, Charlie Kunz,

1935; Ambrose, 1937-40; Applesauce, Palladium, London, 1941; Became known as the Forces Sweetheart, 1939-45; Radio show Sincerely Yours, 1941-47; Tour of Burma, entertaining troops, 1944; 7 Command performances; Appearances, Europe; Australia; Canada; New Zealand; Performed at 50th Anniversary of VE Day Celebrations, London, 1995; Own television shows: ITV, 1955; BBC1, 1956; BBC2, 1970; First British artist to top Hit Parade. Numerous recordings include: Auf Wiederseh'n (over 12 million copies sold). Publication: Vocal Refrain (autobiography), 1975. Honours: Order of St John; LLD; MMus. Address: c/o Anglo-American Enterprises, 806 Keyes House, Dolphin Square, London SW1V 3NB, England.

**LYON Martin,** b. 10 February 1954, Romford, Essex, England. Librarian; Poet. Education: BA, 1976. Appointments: Principal Library Assistant, University of London. Contributions to: Acumen; Agenda; Orbis; Outposts Poetry Quarterly; Pen International; Spokes. Honour: Lake Aske Memorial Award. Address: 63 Malford Court, The Drive, South Woodford, London E18 2HS, England.

**LYONS Roger Alan,** b. 14 September 1942, London, England. Consultant. m. Kitty Horvath, 2 sons, 2 daughters. Education: BSc (Econ) Hons, University College London, 1966. Appointments: General Secretary, MSF Union, 1992-2002; Member, Merger and Monopolies Commission, 1996-2002; Member, Design Council, 1998-2004; Member, Central Arbitration Committee, 1998-2005; Judge, Employment Appeals Tribunal, 1999-2005; Joint General Secretary, Amicus Union, 2002-04; President, TUC, 2003-04; Adviser to Business Services Association, 2005-. Publications: Contributions to: Handbook on Industrial Relations; Handbook on Management Development; Free and Fair, 2004. Memberships: Fellow, University College London; Fellow, Royal Society of Arts. Address: 22 Park Crescent, London N3 2NJ, England. E-mail: rogerlyons22@hotmail.com

**LYU Min-Young,** b. 9 October 1964, Jeongjoo, Jeonbok, South Korea. Professor. m. Youlee Pae, 1 daughter. Education: BS, Hanyang University, South Korea, 1987; MS, Korea Advanced Institute of Science and Technology, 1989; PhD, University of Akron, USA, 1997. Appointments: Associate Engineer, LG Production Research Centre, 1989-92; Principal Compounding Engineer, Institute of Polymer Engineering, 1996-97; Principal Researcher, Group Leader, Samyang Corporation, 1997-2001; Professor, Department of Die and Mould Design, Seoul National University of Technology, 2001-. Publications: More than 30 articles in scientific journals include: Development of Modern Buss Kneader and the Study of its Flow and Mixing Mechanisms, 1998; Bottom Design of Carbonated Soft Drink PET Bottle to Prevent Solvent Cracking, 2003. Honours: Outstanding Research paper, LG Production Research Centre, 1990; Outstanding Student Achievement, Hoechst-Celanese Corporation Award, The University of Akron, 1996. Memberships: Polymer Processing Society; Silver Member, Society of Plastics Engineers. Address: Department of Die and Mould Design, Seoul National University of Technology, 172 Gongneung 2-dong, Nowon-gu, Seoul 139-743, South Korea. E-mail: mylyu@snut.ac.kr

# M

**MacCARTHY Fiona,** b. 23 January 1940, London, England. Biographer; Cultural Historian. m. David Mellor, 1966, 1 son, 1 daughter. Education: MA, English Language and Literature, Oxford University, 1961. Appointments: Reviewer, The Times, 1981-91, The Observer, 1991-98. Publications: The Simple Life: C R Ashbee in the Cotswolds, 1981; The Omega Workshops: Decorative Arts of Bloomsbury, 1984; Eric Gill, 1989; William Morris: A Life for our Time, 1994; Stanley Spencer, 1997; Byron Life and Legend, 2002. Contributions to: Times Literary Supplement; New York Review of Books. Honours: Royal Society of Arts Bicentenary Medal, 1987; Honorary Fellowship, Royal College of Art, 1989; Wolfson History Prize, 1995; Honorary D Litt, University of Sheffield, 1996; Senior Fellowship, Royal College of Art, 1997; Fellow, Royal Society of Literature, 1997; Honorary Doctorate, Sheffield Hallam University, 2001. Memberships: PEN Club; Royal Society of Literature. Address: The Round Building, Hathersage, Sheffield S32 1BA, England.

**MacCORMAC Richard Cornelius (Sir),** b. 3 September 1938, United Kingdom. Architect; Businessman. m. Susan Karen Landen, separated, 2 sons, 1 deceased. Education: BA, Trinity College, Cambridge, 1962; MA, University College, London, 1965; RIBA, 1967. Appointments: Served Royal Navy, 1957-59; Project Architect, London Borough of Merton, 1967-69; Established private practice, 1969; Major works include: Cable and Wireless College, Coventry, 1994; Garden Quadrangle, St John's College, Oxford, 1994; Bowra Building, Wadham College, Oxford; Burrell's Fields, Trinity College, Cambridge, 1997; Ruskin Library, Lancaster University, 1996; Southwark Station, Jubilee Line Extension, 2000; Wellcome Wing, Science Museum, 2001; Phoenix Initiative, Coventry, 2004; Chairman, MacCormac Jamieson Pritchard Ltd (incorporated in 2002), formerly a partnership since, 1972; Taught in Department of Architecture, Cambridge University, 1969-75 and 1979-81; University Lecturer, 1976-77, Studio Tutor, LSE, 1998; Visiting Professor, Department of Architecture, University of Edinburgh, 1982-85, Hull University, 1998-99; Director, Spitalfields Workspace, 1981-; Chairman, Good Design in Housing Awards, RIBA, London Region, 1977. Publications: Articles in Architectural Review and Architects Journal. Honours include: Kt, 2001; CBE, 1994; RA, 1993; Royal Fine Art Commission/Sunday Times Building of the Year, 1994; Independent on Sunday Building of the Year Award, 1994, 1996; RIBA Regional Award, 1997; Civic Trust Award, 1997; RFAC/BSkyB Building of the Year, Universities Winner, 1998; Millennium Building of the Year Award, RFCA Trust/BSkyB, 2000; Celebrating Construction Achievement, Regional Award for Greater London, 2000. Memberships: President, Royal Institute of British Architects, 1991-93; Member, Royal Fine Art Commission, 1983-93; Commissioner, English Heritage, 1995-98; Royal Academy: Chairman: Architecture Committee, 1997-, Exhibitions Committee, 1998-, Council, 1998; Advisor, British Council, 1993; Urban Task Force, 1998-; President, London Forum of Amenity and Civic Societies, 1997-; Trustee, Greenwich Foundation for RNC, 1998-2002; FRSA, 1982. Address: 9 Heneage Street, Spitalfields, London E1 5LJ. Website: www.mjarchitects.co.uk

**MacCORMACK Geoffrey Dennis,** b. 15 April 1937, Canterbury, Kent, England. Retired Professor of Law. 1 daughter. Education: University of Sydney, Australia, 1954-60; University of Oxford, England, 1960-65. Appointment: Professor of Jurisprudence, University of Aberdeen, 1971-96. Publications: Traditional Chinese Law, 1990; The Spirit of Traditional Chinese Law, 1996. Address: School of Law, King's College, University of Aberdeen, Old Aberdeen AB24 3UB, Scotland. E-mail: g.maccormack@abdn.ac.uk

**MacCRACKEN Michael,** b. 20 May 1942, USA. Atmospheric Scientist. m. Sandra Svets, 2 sons. Education: BS, Engineering, Princeton University, 1964; PhD, University of California, Davis, 1968. Appointments: Physicist, Atmospheric Scientist, University of California, Lawrence Livermore National Laboratory, 1968-2002; Executive Director, National Assessment Co-ordination Office, 1997-2001; Senior Scientist, Office US Global Change Research Program, 2001-2002; Chief Scientist for Climate Change Programs, Climate Institute, Washington, DC, 2003-. Publications: Co-editor 5 books; Several dozen articles in professional journals. Memberships: Fellow, American Association for the Advancement of Science; American Geophysical Union; American Meteorological Society; International Association of Meteorology and Atmospheric Sciences, President 2003-2007; The Oceanography Society. Address: 6308 Berkshire Drive, Bethesda, MD 20814, USA.

**MacDONALD Angus D,** b. 9 October 1950, Edinburgh, Scotland. Headmaster. m. Isabelle M Ross, 2 daughters. Education: MA (Hons), Cambridge University, 1969-71; Dip Ed, Edinburgh University, 1971-72. Appointments: Assistant Teacher, Alloa Academy, 1972-73; Assistant Teacher, King's School, Paramatta, 1978-79; Assistant Teacher, Edinburgh Academy, 1973-82; Head of Geography, 1982, Deputy Principal, 1982-86, George Watson's College; Headmaster, Lomond School, 1986-. Honour: Exhibition to Cambridge University. Membership: Chairman, Clan Donald Lands Trust. Address: 8 Millig Street, Helensburgh, Argyll & Bute, Scotland.

**MacDONALD Betty Ann Kipniss,** b. August 1936, Brooklyn, New York, USA. m. Gordon J F MacDonald, 4 children. Education: Art School, Museum of Modern Art, Manhattan; Art Students League; Sumie Drawing, Chinese Institute night school. Appointments: Teacher of Art, elementary school and junior high school, 5 years; Editorial Assistant of children's books; Teacher of Art, Montshire Museum; Board Member, New Hampshire Art Association; Teacher, Lebanon College; Printmaking; Teacher, Smithsonian Institution, 10 years; Artist, Central Intelligence Agency. Publications: Poetry published in the Potomac Quarterly; Commissions for music book covers; Commissions for murals for a shelter for the homeless. Honours: Purchase Award Prize, Delta National Small Prints Exhibition; Museum Award for Graphics, Washington County Museum of Fine Arts; Best in Show in "Small Prints, Big Impressions", Maryland Federation of Arts; Washington Women's Investment Club Funded Murals; Artwork held in a dozen galleries across the USA and in many museums and permanent collections around the world. Memberships: President, Washington Printmakers Gallery. Address: 7222 Vistas Lane, McLean, VA 22101, USA.

**MacDONALD Ian,** b. 22 December 1921, London, England. Emeritus Professor of Applied Physiology. m. (1), 2 sons, 1 daughter, (2) Rose Philomena. Education: MB BS, PhD, MD, DSc, University of London and Guy's Hospital. Appointments: RAMC, 1946-48; Professor of Applied Physiology, 1967-89, Head, Department of Physiology, 1977-89, Professor Emeritus, 1989-, Guy's Hospital, London; Member, UK Food Additives and Contaminants Committee, 1977-83; President, UK Nutrition Society, 1980-83; Chairman, Joint WHO/FAO Expert Committee of Dietary Carbohydrates, 1980; Chairman, 1983-85, Vice-President, 1990-2005, British Nutrition Foundation; Member, UK Food Advisory Committee, 1983-86;

Chairman, Nutrition Consultative Panel, UK Dairy Industry, 1984-88. Publications: Books: Effects of Carbohydrates on Lipid Metabolism (editor), 1973; Metabolic Effects of Dietary Carbohydrates (editor), 1986; Sucrose (editor), 1988; Published research on gastric physiology and on foetal growth, main research interest: dietary carbohydrate in man. Honours: Freeman of the City of London, 1967; Freeman, Worshipful Society of Apothecaries, 1967; International Award for Modern Nutrition, 1973. Memberships: American Society of Clinical Nutrition; FIBiol. E-mail: rosian@onetel.com

**MacDONALD Lewis,** b. 1 January 1957, Stornoway, Isle of Lewis, Scotland. Member of the Scottish Parliament. m. Sandra, 2 daughters. Education: MA, 1978, PhD, 1984, University of Aberdeen. Appointments: Scottish Executive: MSP for Aberdeen Central, 1999-; Deputy Minister for Transport and Planning, 2001; Deputy Minister for Enterprise, Transport and Lifelong Learning, 2001-2003; Deputy Minister for Enterprise and Lifelong Learning, 2003-. Memberships: Patron, Aberdeen Football Club Supporters Trust; Trustee, Aberdeen Safer Communities Trust. E-mail: lewis.macdonald.msp@scottish.parliament.uk

**MacDONALD Simon Gavin George,** b. 5 September 1923, Beauly, Inverness-shire, Scotland. University Professor of Physics, retired. m. Eva Leonie Austerlitz, 1 son, 1 daughter. Education: First Class Honours, Mathematics and Natural Philosophy, Edinburgh University, 1941-43, 1946-48; PhD, St Andrews University, 1953. Appointments: Junior Scientific Officer, Royal Aircraft Establishment, Farnborough, 1943-46; Lecturer in Physics, 1948-57, Senior Lecturer in Physics, 1962-67, University of St Andrews; Senior Lecturer in Physics, University College of the West Indies, Jamaica, 1957-62; Senior Lecturer in Physics, 1967-72, Dean, Faculty of Science, 1970-73, Professor of Physics, 1973-88, Vice-principal, 1974-79, University of Dundee. Publications: 3 books; Numerous articles in scientific journals on x-ray crystallography. Honours: Fellow, Institute of Physics, 1958; Fellow, Royal Society of Edinburgh 1972; Chairman, Dundee Repertory Theatre; Chairman, Federation of Scottish Theatres. Address: 7a Windmill Road, St Andrews, Fife KY16 9JJ, Scotland.

**MacDOWELL Andie,** b. 21 April 1958, South Carolina, USA. Film Actress. m. (1) Paul Qualley, divorced, 1 son, 2 daughters, (2) Rhett DeCamp Hartzog, 2001. Appointments: TV appearances include: Women and Men 2, In Love There are No Rules, 1991; Sahara's Secret; Films include: Greystoke, 1984; St Elmo's Fire, 1985; Sex, Lies and Videotape, 1989; Green Card, 1990; Hudson Hawk, 1991; The Object of Beauty, 1991; The Player, 1992; Ruby, 1992; Groundhog Day, 1993; Short Cuts, 1993; Bad Girls, 1994; Four Weddings and a Funeral, 1994; Unstrung Heros, 1995; My Life and Me, 1996; Multiplicity, 1996; The End of Violence, 1997; Town and Country, 1998; Shadrack, 1998; The Scalper, 1998; Just the Ticket, 1998; Muppets From Space, 1999; The Music, 2000; Harrison's Flowers, 2000; Town and Country, 2001; Crush, 2001; Ginostra, 2002. Address: c/o ICM 8942 Wilshire Boulevard, Beverly Hills, CA 90211, USA.

**MacDOWELL Douglas Maurice,** b. 8 March 1931, London, England. Professor of Greek; Writer. Education: BA, 1954, MA, 1958, DLitt, 1992, Balliol College, Oxford. Appointments: Assistant Lecturer, Lecturer, Senior Lecturer, Reader in Greek and Latin, University of Manchester, 1958-71; Professor of Greek, 1971-2001, Professor Emeritus, Honorary Research Fellow, 2001-, University of Glasgow. Publications: Andokides: On the Mysteries (editor), 1962; Athenian Homicide Law, 1963; Aristophanes: Wasps (editor), 1971; The Law in Classical

Athens, 1978; Spartan Law, 1986; Demosthenes: Against Meidias (editor), 1990; Aristophanes and Athens, 1995; Antiphon and Andocides (with M Gagarin), 1998; Demosthenes: On the False Embassy (editor), 2000; Demosthenes: Speeches 27-38 (translator), 2004. Honours: Fellow, Royal Society of Edinburgh, 1991; Fellow, British Academy, 1993. Address: Department of Classics, University of Glasgow, Glasgow G12 8QQ, Scotland.

**MacFARLANE Sheila Margaret,** b. 2 May 1943, Aberdeen, Scotland. Artist. 1 daughter. Education: DA, Edinburgh College of Art, 1960-64, Dip Ed, Morray House College of Education, 1964-65; Atelier 17, Paris, 1967-68. Appointments: Lecturer in Charge of Printmaking, Duncan of Jordanstone College, Dundee, 1970-76; Founder, Director, Kirktower House Print Studio, Montrose, 1976-88; Art-Drama Specialist to children with special needs in Angus, Occasional Visiting Lecturer to Ruskin School, Oxford University, 1984-2004; Selector, Researcher for SAC Exhibition "Relief Printing", 1984-85. Publications: The Finella Prints, Printmaking Today, 1997; The Finella Prints, The Leopard Magazine, 2002. Membership: Dundee Contemporary Arts Print Studio. Address: 1 Tangleha, St Cyrus, Montrose, Angus, DD10 0DQ, Scotland.

**MacGREGOR John Roddick Russell (Lord MacGregor of Pulham Market),** b. 14 February 1937, Glasgow, Scotland. Politician; Businessman. m. Jean Mary Elizabeth Dungey, 1 son, 2 daughters. Education: MA, First Class Honours, St Andrew's University; LLB, King's College, London. Appointments: University Administrator, 1961-62; Editorial Staff, New Society, 1962-63; Hill Samuel & Co, 1968-79; Director, Hill Samuel and Co, 1973-79; Deputy Chairman, Hill Samuel Bank Ltd, 1994-96; Non-Executive Director: Slough Estates plc, 1995-, Associated British Foods plc, 1994, Unigate plc (now Uniq), 1996-, Friends Provident plc, 1998-; European Supervisory Board, DAFS Netherlands NV; Political Career: Special Assistant to Prime Minister, 1963-64; Head, Leader of Opposition's Office, 1965-68; Member of Parliament for South Norfolk, 1974-2001; Lord Commissioner of the Treasury, 1979-81; Parliamentary Under Secretary of State for Industry with particular responsibility for small businesses, 1981-83; Minister of State for Agriculture, Fisheries and Food, 1983-85; Chief Secretary to the Treasury, 1985-87; Minister for Agriculture, Fisheries and Food, 1987-89; Secretary of State for Education, 1989-90; Lord President of the Council and Leader of the Commons, 1990-92; Secretary of State for Transport, 1992-94; Member of the House of Lords, 1991-. Honours: OBE, 1971; PC, 1985; Honorary Fellow, King's College, London, 1990; Honorary LLD, University of Westminster, 1995. Address: House of Lords, London SW1A 0PW, England.

**MACHIDA Curtis A,** b. 1 April 1954, San Francisco, USA. Molecular Neurobiologist. Education: AB, University of California, Berkeley, 1976; PhD, Oregon Health Sciences University, 1982. Appointments: Postdoctoral Fellow, Biochemistry, Oregon Health Sciences University, 1982-85; Postdoctoral Fellow, Vollum Institute, 1985-88; Assistant Scientist, 1988-95, Assistant Professor, 1989-95; Associate Scientist, Associate Professor, 1995-2002 Neuroscience, Oregon National Primate Research Center, Oregon Health Sciences University; Research Associate Professor, Integrative Biosciences, Oregon Health Sciences University, 2002-; Adjunct Faculty, Biochemistry and Biophysics, Oregon State University, 1997-2001. Publications: Over 100 articles and abstracts in professional journals; Patent holder; Editor, Adrenergic Receptor Protocols; Editor, Viral Vectors for Gene Therapy: Methods and Protocols; Member, Editorial Boards, Molecular Biotechnology and Frontiers in Bioscience. Honours include: NIH First Award;

AHA Established Investigator Award; NIH Grant Recipient. Memberships: AAAS; ASM; ASBMB; ASGT; AHA Scientific Council. Address: Department of Integrative Biosciences, School of Dentistry, Oregon Health Sciences University, 611 SW Campus Drive, Portland, OR 97239, USA.

**MacINTYRE Iain**, b. 30 August 1924, Glasgow, Scotland. Research Director. m. Mabel Wilson Jamieson, 1 daughter. Education: MBChB, Glasgow, 1947; PhD, London, 1960; MRCPath, 1963, (Founder Member); MRCP, 1969; FRCPath, 1971; FRCP, 1977; DSc, London, 1970; MD Honoris Causa, Turin, 1985; FRS, 1996; FMedSci, 1998, (Founder Fellow); MD Honoris Causa, Sheffield, 2002. Appointments: Honorary Demonstrator, Biochemistry, University of Sheffield, 1948-52; Registrar, Chemical Pathology, Royal Postgraduate Medical School, 1952-54; Sir Jack Drummond Research Fellow, 1954-56; Assistant Lecturer, Lecturer, Reader, Chemical Pathology, Royal Postgraduate School, 1956-67; Director, Endocrine Unit, Wellcome Unit of Endocrinology, later Royal Postgraduate Medical School Endocrine Unit, 1967-90; Professor of Endocrine Chemistry and Chemical Pathology, 1967-90; Chairman of Academic Board, Royal Postgraduate Medical School, 1986-90. Publications: Numerous articles in endocrinology to professional journals. Honours: Gairdner International Award (jointly with DH Copp) for the discovery of the existence and origin of calcitonin, 1967; Elsevier International Award, 1992; Paget Foundation John B Johnson Award, 1995; Elected Fellow, The Royal Society, 1996; Elected Honorary Fellow, Association of American Physicians, 1998; Founder Fellow, Academy of Medical Sciences, 1998; Honorary MD, University of Sheffield, 2002. Memberships: Society for Endocrinology; Physiological Society; Biochemical Society; European Society for Clinical Investigation; Thyroid Club; Association of Clinical Biochemists; American Endocrine Society; American Society for Bone and Mineral Research; European Calcified Tissue Society. Address: The William Harvey Research Institute, St Bartholomew's and the Royal London School of Medicine and Dentistry, Charterhouse Square, London EC1M 6BQ, England. E-mail: i.macintyre@qmul.ac.uk

**MACKAY, His Honour Judge David Ian**, b. 11 November 1945, Birkenhead, England. Circuit Judge. m. Mary Elizabeth Smith, 1974, 1 son, 2 daughters. Education: Birkenhead School; Brasenose College Oxford (Open Scholar); MA. Appointments: Barrister, Inner Temple, 1969; Circuit Judge, 1992; Official Referee, 1993; Provincial Judge of the Technology and Construction Court, 1998; Chairman of the Governors, Birkenhead School, 1991-2001; Chairman, Birkenhead School Foundation Trust, 1998-2004. Membership: Athenaeum, Liverpool. Address: Queen Elizabeth II Law Courts, Derby Square, Liverpool L2 1XA, England.

**MacKENZIE Kenneth John**, b. 1 May 1943, Glasgow, Scotland. Civil Servant. m. Irene Mary Hogarth, 1 son, 1 daughter. Education: Open Exhibitioner, BA, Modern History, 1964, MA, 1970, Pembroke College, University of Oxford; Dorothy Chandos Smyllie Scholarship in Department of History, Stanford University, California, 1964-65; Fulbright Travel Scholarship, 1964; Graduate AM in History, Stanford, 1965. Appointments: Principal Private Secretary to Secretaries of State for Scotland, 1977-79; 2 Assistant Secretary Posts in Scottish Office, 1979-85; 3 Under Secretary Posts in Scottish Office including Principal Finance Officer, 1985-92; Member, Biotechnology and Biological Sciences Research Council, 1992-95; Head of Scottish Office Agriculture and Fisheries Department, 1992-95; Head of Economic and Domestic Secretariat, 1995-97; Head of Constitution Secretariat, 1997-98, Cabinet Office; Head of Scottish Executive Development Department, 1998-2001;

Quinquennial Reviewer, Lord Chancellor's Department, 2001-2002; Chairman, Historic Scotland Foundation, 2001-; Member, British Waterways Scotland Group, 2002-; Honorary Professor, Department of Politics, University of Aberdeen, 2001-04; Lead Consultant with Public Administration International advising the Government of Kosovo on structure and organisation of a Prime Minister's Office, 2004-; Board Member, Christian Aid, 2005-. Publications: Articles: Planner Shortage in Strathclyde, 1976; Tears Before Bedtime: A Look Back at the Constitutional Reform Programme since 1997, 2005. Honour: Companion of the Bath (CB), 1996. Address: 30 Regent Terrace, Edinburgh EH7 5BS, Scotland. E-mail: kjmackenzie@freeuk.com

**MACKERRAS Sir (Alan) Charles**, b. 17 November 1925, Schenectady, New York, USA. Orchestral Conductor. m. Helena Judith Wilkins, 22 August 1947, 2 daughters. Education: Sydney Grammar School, Sydney Conservatorium of Music, Studies with Vaclav Talich, Prague Academy of Music, 1947-48. Appointments: Principal Oboist, Sydney Symphony Orchestra, 1943-46; Oboist, Sadler's Wells Opera Orchestra, 1947; Staff Conductor, Sadler's Wells Opera, 1948-54; Freelance Conductor, orchestras in Britain, European Continent, USA, Australia, 1957-66; First Conductor, Hamburg State Opera, 1966-69; Musical Director, Sadler's Wells Opera, later English National Opera, 1970-77; Chief Guest, Conductor, BBC Symphony Orchestra, 1976-79; Chief Conductor, Sydney Symphony Orchestra, Australian Broadcasting Company, 1982-85; Principal Guest Conductor, Royal Liverpool Philharmonic, 1986-88; Scottish Chamber Orchestra, 1992-95; Conductor Laureate, 1995-; Musical Director, Welsh National Opera, 1987-92; Conductor Emeritus, 1992-; Principal Guest Conductor, San Francisco Opera, 1993-96; Conductor Emeritus, 1996-; Royal Philharmonic Orchestra, 1993-96; Czech Philharmonic Orchestra, 1997-2003; Music Director, Orchestra of St Luke's, 1998-2001, Music Director Emeritus, 2001-; Principal Guest Conductor, Philharmonia Orchestra, 2002-; President, Trinity College of Music, 2000-. Publications: Ballet arrangement of Pineapple Poll, 1951 (Sullivan) and The Lady and the Fool, 1954 (Verdi); Reconstruction of Arthur Sullivan's lost cello concerto, 1986; Contributed 4 appendices to Charles Mackerras: a musicians' musician, by Nancy Phelan, 1987; Numerous articles in musical journals and magazines. Honours: CBE, 1974; Knighthood, 1979; AC (Companion of Order of Australia), 1997; Medal of Merit, Czech Republic, 1996; CH, 2003; Hon RAM, 1969; Hon FRCM, 1987; Honorary Fellow, Royal Northern College of Music, Manchester, 1999; Honorary Fellow, Trinity College of Music, London, 1999; Honorary Fellow, Saint Peter's College, Oxford, 1999; Cardiff University, 2003; Honorary DMus: University of Hull, 1990, Nottingham, 1991, Brno (Czech Republic), York and Griffith (Brisbane), 1994, Oxford, 1997; Prague Academy of Music, 1999; Napier University, 2000; Melbourne and Sydney, 2003; Janacek Academy of Music, Brno, 2004; University of London, 2005; First Recipient, Queen's Medal for Music, 2005; Royal Philharmonic Society Gold Medal, 2005; BBC Radio 3 Listeners' Award for Artist of the Year, 2005. Address: c/o Askonas Hold Limited, Lonsdale Chambers, 28 Chancery Lane, London WC2A 1PF, England.

**MACKESY Piers Gerald**, b. 15 September 1924, Cults, Aberdeenshire, Scotland. Historian; Writer. Education: BA, Christ Church, Oxford, 1950; DPhil, Oriel College, Oxford, 1953; DLitt, Oxford, 1978. Appointments: War Service: Lieutenant, The Royal Scots Greys, N.W. Europe, 1943-7; Harkness Fellow, Harvard University, 1953-54; Fellow, 1954-87, Emeritus, 1988-, Pembroke College, Oxford; Visiting Fellow, Institute for Advanced Study, Princeton, New Jersey, 1961-62; Visiting Professor, California Institute of Technology,

1966. Publications: The War in the Mediterranean 1803-1810, 1957; The War for America 1775-1783, 1964, 1993; Statesmen at War: The Strategy of Overthrow 1798-1799, 1974; The Coward of Minden: The Affair of Lord George Sackville, 1979; War without Victory: The Downfall of Pitt 1799-1802, 1984; British Victory in Egypt, 1801: The End of Napoleon's Conquest (Templer Medal), 1995. Memberships: National Army Museum, council member, 1983-92; Society for Army Historical Research, council member, 1985-94, currently Vice President; British Academy, fellow, 1988. Address: Westerton Farmhouse, Dess, by Aboyne, Aberdeenshire AB34 5AY, Scotland.

**MacKIERNAN Francis Joseph,** b. 3 February 1926, Co Leitrim, Ireland. Catholic Bishop. Education: BA (Honours), 1947, BD, (Honours), 1950, Higher Diploma in Education, 1953, St Patrick's College, Maynooth and University College, Dublin. Appointments: Teacher of Classics, St Malachy's College, Belfast, 1951-52; Teacher of Classics and Irish, St Patrick's College, Cavan, 1952-62; President, St Felim's College, Ballinamore, Co Leitrim, 1962-72; Bishop of Kilmore, 1972-88; Retired, 1988. Publications: Bishops and Priests of the Diocese of Kilmore 1136-1988, 1988; St Mary's Abbey, Cavan, 2000; Many historical articles in Breifne, Journal of the Breifne Historical Society, 1958-. Membership: Editor of Breifne Journal, Secretary, Breifne Historical Society. Address: 5 Brookside, Cavan, Ireland.

**MACKINTOSH Cameron Anthony (Sir),** b. 17 October 1946, Enfield, England. Theatre Producer. Education: Prior Park College, Bath. Appointments: Stage Hand, Theatre Royal, Drury Lane; Assistant Stage Manager; Worked with Emile Littler, 1966; Robin Alexander, 1967; Producer, 1969-; Chair, Cameron Mackintosh, 1981-; Director, Delfont Mackintosh, 1991-; Productions: Little Women, 1967; Anything Goes, 1969; Trelawney, 1972; The Card, 1973; Winnie the Pooh, 1974; Owl and the Pussycat Went to Sea, 1975; Godspell, 1975; Side by Side by Sondheim, 1976; Oliver!, 1977; Diary of a Madam, 1977; After Shave, 1977; Gingerbread Man, 1978; Out on a Limb, 1978; My Fair Lady, 1979; Oklahoma!, 1990; Tomfoolery, 1980; Jeeves Takes Charge, 1981; Cats, 1981; Song and Dance, 1982; Blondel, 1983; Little Shop of Horrors, 1983; Abbacadabra, 1983; The Boyfriend, 1984; Les Miserables, 1985; Cafe Puccini, 1985; Phantom of the Opera, 1986; Follies, 1987; Miss Saigon, 1989; Just So, 1990; Five Guys Named Moe, 1990; Moby Dick, 1992; Putting it Together, 1992; The Card, 1992; Carousel, 1993; Oliver!, 1994; Martin Guerre, 1996; The Fix, 1997; Oklahoma!, 1999; The Witches of Eastwick, 2000; My Fair Lady, 2001. Honours: Observer Award for Outstanding Achievement; Laurence Oliver Award, 1991; Knighted. Address: Cameron Mackintosh Ltd, 1 Bedford Square, London, WC1B 3RA, England.

**MACKLIN Elizabeth,** b. 28 October 1952, Poughkeepsie, New York, USA. Poet. Education: BA in Spanish, State University of New York at Potsdam, 1973; Graduate School of Arts and Sciences, New York University, 1975-78. Appointment: Editorial Staff, 1974-99, Query Editor, 1981-99, The New Yorker Magazine; Poetry Editor, Wigwag Magazine, 1989-91; Freelance Editor and Writer, 2000-. Publication: A Woman Kneeling in the Big City, 1992; You've Just Been Told, poems, 2000. Contributions to: Nation; New Republic; New York Times; New Yorker; Paris Review; Threepenny Review. Honours: Ingram Merrill Foundation Award in Poetry, 1990; Guggenheim Fellowship, 1994; Amy Lowell Poetry Travelling Scholarship, 1998-99; PEN Translation Fund grant, 2005. Memberships: Authors Guild; PEN American Center, executive board, 1995-96. Address: 207 West 14th Street, 5F, New York, NY 10011, USA.

**MACKMIN Michael,** b. 20 April 1941, London, England. Psychotherapist; Poet; Editor. Divorced, 2 daughters. Education: BA, 1963; MA, 1965. Appointment: Editor, The Rialto. Publications: The Play of Rainbow; Connemara Shore. Address: PO Box 309, Aylsham, Norwich NR11 6LN, England.

**MACKSEY K(enneth) J(ohn),** b. 1 July 1923, Epsom, Surrey, England. Army Officer (retired); Historian. m. Joan, 1 son, 1 daughter. Education: Royal Military College, Sandhurst, 1943-44; British Army Staff College,1956. Appointments: Officer, Royal Tank Regiment, British Army, 1941-68, until retirement with rank of Major, 1968; Deputy Editor, History of the Second World War, History of the First World War, 1968-70. Publications: The Shadow of Vimy Ridge, 1965; To the Green Fields Beyond, 1965; Armoured Crusader: General Sir Percy Hobart, 1967, 2004; Africa Korps, Panzer Division, 1968; Crucible of Power: The Fight for Tunisia, 1969; Tank Force, 1970; Tank: A History of AFVs, 1970; Tank Warfare, Beda Fomm, 1971; The Guinness History of Land (Sea, Air) Warfare, 3 volumes, 1973-76; Battle (in US as Anatomy of a Battle), 1974; The Partisans of Europe in the Second World War, 1975; The Guinness Guide to Feminine Achievements, 1975; Guderian: Panzer General, 1975; The Guinness Book 1952 (1953, 1954), 3 volumes, 1977-79; Kesselring, 1978; Rommel's Campaigns and Battles, 1979; The Tanks, Vol III of the History of the Royal Tank Regiment, 1979; Invasion: The German Invasion of England, July 1940, 1980; The Tank Pioneers, 1981; History of the Royal Armoured Corps 1914-1975, 1983; Commando Strike, 1985; First Clash, 1985; Technology in War, 1986; Godwin's Saga, 1987; Military Errors of World War II, 1987; Tank Versus Tank, 1988; For Want of a Nail, 1989; The Penguin Encyclopaedia of Modern Warfare, 1991; Penguin Encyclopaedia and Technology, 1993; The Hitler Options, 1994; From Triumph to Disaster, 1996; Turning Points (memoirs), 1997; Without Enigma, 2000; They Never Looked Back, 2002; The Searchers, 2003. Membership: Beaminster Town Council, 1972-83. Honour: Military Cross, 1944. Address: Whatley Mill, Beaminster, Dorset DT8 3EN, England.

**MacLAINE Shirley,** b. 24 April 1934, Richmond, Virginia, USA. Film Actress; Writer; Film Director. m. Steve Parker, 1954, 1 daughter. Education: Grammar School; Lee High School, Washington. Appointments: Chorus Girl and Dancer; Films include: The Trouble with Harry Artists and Models; Around the World in 80 Days; Hot Spell; The Matchmaker; Can-Can; Career; The Apartment; Two for the Seesaw; The Children's Hour; Irma La Douce; What a Way to go; The Yellow Rolls-Royce; Gambit; Woman Times Seven; The Bliss of Mrs Blossom; Sweet Charity; Two Mules for Sister Sara; Desperate Characters; The Possessions of Joel Delaney; The Turning Point, 1977; Being There, 1979; Loving Couples, 1980; The Change of Seasons, 1981; Slapstick, 1981; Terms of Endearment, 1984; Out on a Limb, 1987; Madame Sousatzka, 1989; Steel Magnolias, 1989; Waiting for the Light, 1990; Postcards from the Edge, 1990; Used People, 1993; Wrestling Ernest Hemingway, 1994; Guarding Tess, 1994; Mrs Westbourne, 1995; The Evening Star, 1995; Mrs Winterbourne, 1996; Revues: If My Friends Could See Me Now, 1974; To London with Love, 1976; London, 1982; Out There Tonight, 1990; TV Film: The West Side Waltz, 1994; Video: Shirley MacLaines's Inner Workout, 1989; Producer and Co-director, The Other Half of the Sky - A China Memoir, 1973. Publications: Don't Fall From Here, 1975; Out on a Limb, 1983; Dancing in the Light, 1985; It's all in the playing, 1987; Going Within, 1989; Dance While You Can, 1991; My Lucky Stars, 1995; The Camino, 2000. Honours: Star of the Year Award, Theatre Owners of America, 1967; Best Actress Award, Desperate Characters, Berlin Film Festival, 1971; Academy Award, Best Actress, 1984; Golden Globe Award, Best Actress,

1989; Lifetime Achievement Award, Berlin Film Festival, 1999. Address: MacLaine Enterprises Inc, 25200 Malibu Road, Suit 101, Santa Monica, CA 90265, USA.

**MACLAVERTY Bernard,** b. 14 September 1942, Belfast, Northern Ireland. Novelist; Dramatist. m. Madeline McGuckin, 1967, 1 son, 3 daughters. Education: BA, Honours, Queen's University, Belfast, 1974. Publications: Bibliography: Secrets and Other Stories, 1977; Lamb (novel), 1980; A Time to Dance and Other Stories, 1982; Cal (novel), 1983; The Great Profundo and Other Stories, 1987; Walking the Dog and Other Stories, 1994; Grace Notes (novel), 1997; The Anatomy School (novel), 2001. For Young Children: A Man in Search of a Pet, 1978; Andrew McAndrew, 1988, US edition, 1993. Radio Plays: My Dear Palestrina, 1980; Secrets, 1981; No Joke, 1983; The Break, 1988; Some Surrender, 1988; Lamb, 1992. Television Plays: My Dear Palestrina, 1980; Phonefun Limited, 1982; The Daily Woman, 1986; Sometime in August, 1989. Screenplays: Cal, 1984; Lamb, 1985; Bye-Child, 2003. Drama Documentary: Hostages, 1992, US edition, 1993; Television Adaptation: The Real Charlotte by Somerville and Ross, 1989. Honours: Northern Ireland and Scottish Arts Councils Awards; Irish Sunday Independent Award, 1983; London Evening Standard Award for Screenplay, 1984; Joint Winner, Scottish Writer of the Year, 1988; Society of Authors Travelling Scholarship, 1994; Shortlisted, Saltire Society Scottish Book of the Year, 1994, 2001; Grace Notes awarded The Saltire Scottish Book of the Year Award, 1997; A Scottish Arts Council Book Award; Shortlisted for: The Booker Prize; the Writers Guild Best Fiction Book; The Stakis Scottish Writer of the Year; The Whitbread Novel of the Year; Creative Scotland Award, the Scottish Arts Council, 2003; Nominated, BAFTA Best Short Film for Bye-Child, 2004; BAFTA Scotland, Best First Director for Bye-Child, 2004.

**MACLEAY John (Iain) Henry James,** b. 7 December 1931, Inverness Scotland. Retired Clergyman. m. Jane Speirs Cuthbert, 1 son, 1 daughter. Education: BA, 1954, MA, 1960, St Edmund Hall, Oxford; College of the Resurrection, Mirfield, Yorkshire. Appointments: Deacon, 1957; Priest, 1958; Curate, St John's, East Dulwich, England, 1957-60; Curate, 1960-62, Rector, 1962-70, St Michael's, Inverness, Scotland; Priest-in-Charge, St Columba's, Grantown-on-Spey with St John the Baptist, Rothiemurchus, Scotland, 1970-78; Canon, St Andrew's Cathedral, Inverness, 1977-78; Rector of St Andrew's, Fort William, 1978-99; Synod Clerk of Argyll and the Isles, Canon of St John's Cathedral, Oban, 1980-87; Dean of Argyll and the Isles, 1987-99; Honorary Canon of Oban, 2001. Address: 47 Riverside Park, Lochyside, Fort William PH33 7RB, Scotland.

**MACLEOD Alison,** b, 12 April 1920, Hendon, Middlesex, England. Writer. Publications: The Heretics (in US as The Heretic), 1965; The Hireling (in UK as The Trusted Servant), 1968; City of Light (in UK as No Need of the Sun), 1969; The Muscovite, 1971; The Jesuit (in US as Prisoner of the Queen), 1972; The Portingale, 1976; The Death of Uncle Joe, 1997. Address: Room 27, 1 View Road, London N6 4DJ, England.

**MacMAHON Eithne Mary Edana,** b. 27 April 1957. Consultant; Honorary Senior Lecturer. Education: MB BCh BAO, University College Dublin, National University of Ireland, 1982. Appointments: Intern, 1982-83, Senior House Officer Rotation in Medicine, 1983-85, Mater Misericordiae Hospital, Dublin; Senior House Officer in Paediatrics, Our Lady's Hospital, Crumlin, 1985; Senior House Officer in Medical Microbiology, St James' Hospital, Dublin, 1986-87; Fellowship in Infectious Diseases, Johns Hopkins University School of Medicine, Maryland, USA, 1987-92; Junior Faculty

Appointment, Instructor, Division of Infection Diseases, University of Minnesota Medical School, Minnesota, USA, 1992-93; Clinical Lecturer, Honorary Senior Registrar, Royal Free Hospital School of Medicine, London, England, 1993-96; Consultant, Department of Infection, Guy's and St Thomas' NHS Foundation Trust, 1996-; Honorary Senior Lecturer, Department of Infectious Diseases, Guy's, King's & St Thomas' School of Medicine, King's College London, 1996-; Recognised Teacher, University of London, 1996-. Publications: Numerous articles, research papers and letters in professional medical journals; Books and book chapters. Memberships include: Member, 1985, Fellow, 2003, Royal College of Physicians of Ireland; British Medical Association, 1996; Member, Royal College of Pathologists, 1998; British Transplantation Society, 2005; American Society of Transplantation, 2005. Address: Department of Infection, St Thomas' Hospital, Lambeth Palace Road, London SE1 7EH, England.

**MacMAHON James Ardle,** b. 25 November 1924, Curragh, Co Kildare, Ireland. Catholic Priest. Education: St Macartan's College, Monaghan; Holy Cross College, Clonliffe, Dublin; University College, Dublin; Gregorian University, Rome. Appointments: Ordained Priest, 1949; Doctorate in Canon Law, 1954; Secretary to the Archbishop of Dublin, 1954-72; Parish Priest, 1975-2000; Commission for Charitable Donations and Bequests for Ireland, 1975-2000; Director of Religious Education in Vocational Schools, 1976-79; Vicar Forane, 1977-80; Episcopal Vicar for Religious, 1980-86; Prelate of Honour of His Holiness, 1985; Chancellor, Dublin Metropolitan Chapter of Canons, 2003. Honour: Silver Medal in Licentiate in Canon Law, 1954. Membership, Foxrock Golf Club, Dublin. Address: Queen of Peace Centre, 6 Garville Avenue, Rathgar, Dublin 6, Ireland.

**MACPHERSON Elle,** b. 29 March 1963, Killara, Australia. Model; Actress; Business Executive. m. G Bensimon, divorced 1990, 1 son with Arpad Busson. Career: Founder, Elle Macpherson Intimates, and Macpherson Men lingerie and underwear companies; Released fitness video, Stretch and Strengthen, The Body Workout, 1995; Chief Executive, Elle Macpherson Inc; Co-owner, Fashion Café, New York; Films: Sirens; Jane Eyre; If Lucy Fell; The Mirror Has Two Faces; Batman and Robin; The Edge; Beautopia; With Friends Like These. Address: c/o Artistmanagement Associates Inc, 414 East 52nd Street, Penthouse B, New York, NY 10022, USA.

**MacQUEEN Hector Lewis,** b. 13 June 1956, Ely, Cambridgeshire, England. Professor of Law. m. Frances Mary, 2 sons, 1 daughter. Education: LLB Honours, 1974-78, PhD, 1985, University of Edinburgh. Appointments: Lecturer, Senior Lecturer, Reader, 1979-94, Professor of Private Law, 1994-, Faculty of Law, Dean of the Faculty of Law, 1999-, University of Edinburgh; Visiting Professor, Cornell University, USA, 1991, Utrecht University, Netherlands, 1997; Director, The David Hume Institute, 1991-99. Publications: Copyright, Competition and Industrial Design, 1989, 2nd edition, 1995; Common Law and Feudal Society in Medieval Scotland, 1993; Studying Scots Law, 1993, 2nd edition, 1999; Contract Law in Scotland (with J M Thomson), 2000; Numerous articles in learned and professional journals and collections. Honour: Fellow of the Royal Society of Edinburgh. Memberships: Chair, Scottish Records Advisory Council, 2001-; Literary Director, Stair Society, 1999-; Heriots FP Cricket Club. Address: Faculty of Law, University of Edinburgh, Edinburgh EH8 9YL, Scotland. E-mail: hector.macqueen@ed.ac.uk

**MacRAE (Alastair) Christopher (Donald) (Summerhayes) (Sir),** b. 3 May 1937, Burleigh, Gloucestershire, England. Retired

Diplomat. m. Mette Willert, 2 daughters. Education: BA Hons, Lincoln College, Oxford; Henry Fellow, Harvard University, USA. Appointments: Royal Navy, 1956-58; Second Secretary, Dar es Salaam, Tanzania, 1963-65; Middle East Centre for Arab Studies, 1965-67; Second Secretary, Beirut, Lebanon, 1967-68; Principal, Near East Department, Foreign and Commonwealth Office, 1968-70; 1st Secretary and Head of Chancery, Baghdad, Iraq, 1970-71; 1st Secretary and Head of Chancery, Brussels, Belgium, 1972-76; On loan to European Commission, 1976-78; Ambassador to Gabon, 1978-80, concurrently to Sao Tome and Principe; Head of West Africa Department, Foreign and Commonwealth Office, and Non-resident Ambassador to Chad, 1980-83; Political Counsellor, Paris, France, 1983-87; Head of Mission, Tehran, Iran, 1987; Assistant Under Secretary, Cabinet Office, 1988-91; British High Commissioner to Nigeria, 1991-94 and concurrently Ambassador to Benin; British High Commissioner to Pakistan, 1994-97; Secretary General Order of St John, 1997-2000. Honours: CMG, 1987; KCMG, 1993; KStJ, 1997. Memberships: Royal Commonwealth Society; Board Member, Aga Khan Foundation (UK); Chairman, Pakistan Society; President St John Ambulance, Ashford District. Address: 4 Church Street, Wye, Kent TN25 5BJ, England. E-mail: christophermacrae@btinternet.com

**MACRORY Richard Brabazon,** b. 30 March 1950, Headley, Surrey, England. Lawyer. m. Sarah Briant, 2 sons. Education: MA, Jurisprudence, Oxford University; Barrister, Gray's Inn, 1974. Appointments: Legal Adviser, Friends of the Earth, 1975-78; Standing Counsel, Council for the Protection of Rural England, 1981-92; Legal Correspondent, Ends Report, 1987-; Member, Royal Commission on Environmental Pollution, 1991-2003; Chairman, Merchant Ivory Film Productions, 1992-2004; Director Environmental Change Unit, Oxford University, 1995-96; Professor, Imperial College London, 1991-94, 1996-99; Board Member, Environment Agency, England and Wales, 1999-2004; Professor of Environmental Law, Faculty of Laws, University College London, 1999-. Publications: Water Law – Principles and Practice, 1988; Bibliography of European Environmental Law (with S Hollins), 1995; Principles of European Environmental Law, 2004; Numerous articles in journals; Editor-in-Chief, Journal of Environmental Law. Honours: CBE, 2000; Honorary Fellow, Chartered Institute of Water Management, 2004; Memberships: UK Environmental Law Association, First Chairman, 1986-88; Honorary President, National Society of Clean Air and Environmental Protection, 2004-. Address: Crossing Farmhouse, Nethercote Road, Tackley, Oxon OX5 3AT, England. E-mail: r.macrory@ucl.ac.uk

**MACY William H,** b. 13 March 1950, Miami, Florida, USA. Actor. Education: Goddard College, Vermont. Appointments: Co-founder, St Nicholas Theatre Company; Atlantic Theatre Company; Stage appearances include: The Man in 605, 1980; Twelfth Night; Beaurecrat; A Call from the East; The Dining Room; Speakeasy; Wild Life; Flirtations; Baby With the Bathwater; The Nice and the Nasty; Bodies Rest and Motion; Oh Hell!; Prairie du Chien; The Shawl; An Evening With Dorothy Parker; The Dining Room; A Call From the Sea; The Beaver Coat; Life During Wartime; Mr Gogol and Mr Preen; Oleanna; Our Town; Play director: Boy's Life; Film appearances include: Without a Trace; The Last Dragon; Radio Days; Somewhere in Time; Hello Again; House of Games; Things Change; Homicide; Shadows and Fog; Benny and Joon; Searching for Bobby Fischer; The Client; Oleanna; The Silence of the Lambs; Murder in the First; Mr Holland's Opus; Down Periscope; Fargo; Ghosts of Mississippi; Air Force One; Wag the Dog; Pleasantville; A Civil Action; Psycho; Magnolia; State and Maine; Panic; Focus; Jurassic Park III; Welcome to Collinwood; The Cooler; Stealing Sinatra; Out of Order; Film

director: Lip Service; TV appearances include: Chicago Hope; The Murder of Mary Phagan; Texan; A Murderous Affair; The Water Engine; Heart of Justice; A Private Matter; The Con; A Slight Case of Murder.

**MADDEN John,** b. 8 April 1949, Portsmouth, England. Film Director. Appointments: TV includes: Inspector Morse; Prime Suspect IV; Ethan Frome; Films: Mrs Brown, 1997; Shakespeare in Love, 1998; Captain Corelli's Mandolin, 2001. Honours: Academy Award for Best Film; BAFTA Award for Best Film, 1998.

**MADDOCKS Morris Henry St John,** b. 28 April 1928, Elland, West Yorkshire, England. Bishop. m. Anne. Education: MA (Cantab), Trinity College, Cambridge, 1956; Chichester Theological College. Appointments: Curate, St Peter's Ealing, London, 1954-55; Curate, St Andrew's, Uxbridge, 1955-58; Vicar, Weaverthorpe, Helperthorpe and Luttons Ambo, 1958-61; Vicar, St Martin's-on-the-Hill, Scarborough, 1961-71; Bishop of Selby, 1972-83; Co-founder, with Anne Maddocks, The Acorn Christian Healing Trust, 1983; Adviser to the Archbishops of Canterbury and York for the ministry of health and healing, 1983-95; Assistant Bishop, Diocese of Chichester, 1987-; Canon of Chichester Cathedral, 1992. Publications: Books: The Christian Healing Ministry, 1981; The Christian Adventure, 1983; Journey to Wholeness, 1986; A Healing House of Prayer, 1987; Twenty Questions About Healing, 1988; The Vision of Dorothy Kerin, 1991. Honour: Cross of St Augustine, 1995. Membership: Founding Life President (with Anne Maddocks), The Acorn Christian Foundation. Address: 3 The Chantry, Cathedral Close, Chichester, West Sussex PO 19 1PZ, England.

**MADDY Penelope Jo,** b. 7 April 1950, Tulsa, Oklahoma, USA. Professor. Education: BA, Mathematics, University of California, Berkeley, 1972; PhD, Philosophy, Princeton University, 1979. Appointments: Assistant Professor, University of Notre Dame, 1978-83; Associate Professor, University of Illinois, Chicago, 1983-87; Associate Professor, 1987-89, Full Professor, 1989-, University of California, Irvine. Publications: Believing the Axioms, 1988; Realism in Mathematics, 1990; Nationalism in Mathematics, 1997. Honours: Westing House Scholarship, 1968; Marshall Scholarship, 1972; American Academy of Arts & Science, 1998; Lakatos Prize, 2002. Memberships: Association for Symbolic Logic; American Philosophical Association; Philosophical Science Association. Address: Department of Logic & Philosophy of Science, University of California Irvine, Irvine, CA 92697-5100, USA.

**MADONNA (Madonna Louise Veronica Ciccone),** b. 16 August 1958, Bay City, Michigan, USA. Singer; Songwriter; Actress. m. (1) Sean Penn, 1985, divorced 1989; 1 daughter with Carlos Leon, (2) Guy Ritchie, 2000, 1 son. Education: University Of Michigan, 1976-78. Career: Dancer, New York, 1979; Actress, 1980-; Solo singer, 1983-; Film appearances include: Vision Quest, 1985; Desperately Seeking Susan, 1985; Shanghai Surprise, 1986; Who's That Girl, 1987; Bloodhounds On Broadway, 1990; Dick Tracy, 1990; A League Of Their Own, 1992; Evita, 1996; The Next Best Thing, 2000; Swept Away, 2002; Die Another Day, 2002; Numerous worldwide concerts, 1983-; Major appearances include: Live Aid, Philadelphia, 1985; Don't Bungle The Jungle, ecological awareness benefit, 1989; Television includes: In Bed With Madonna, documentary, 1991; Stage performance, Speed The Plow, Broadway, 1988; Up For Grabs, Wyndhams Theatre, 2002; Owner, Maverick record label. Compositions include: Co-writer, own hits: Live To Tell; Open Your Heart; Justify My Love; Co-writer, Each Time You Break My Heart, Nick Kamen, 1986. Recordings: Hit singles include: Holiday, 1983; Lucky Star, 1984; Borderline, 1984; Like A Virgin, 1984; Material Girl, 1985; Crazy For You, 1985; Angel, 1985; Into The Groove, 1985; Dress You Up, 1985; Gambler, 1985; Live To Tell, 1986; Papa Don't Preach, 1986; True Blue, 1986; Open Your Heart, 1986; La Isla Bonita, 1987; Who's That Girl, 1987; Causin' A Commotion, 1987; The Look Of Love, 1987; Like A Prayer, 1989; Express Yourself, 1989; Cherish, 1989; Dear Jessie, 1989; Oh Father, 1990; Keep It Together, 1991; Vogue, 1991; I'm Breathless, 1991; Hanky Panky, 1991; Justify My Love, 1991; Rescue Me, 1991; This Used To Be My Playground, 1992; Erotica, 1992; Deeper And Deeper, 1992; Bad Girl, 1993; Fever, 1993; Rain, 1993; Frozen, 1998; Ray of Light, 1998; Power of Goodbye, 1998; Nothing Really Matters, 1999; Beautiful Stranger: theme song from Austin Powers: The Spy Who Shagged Me, 1999; American Pie, 2000; Music, 2000; Don't Tell Me, 2000; What It Feels Like For A Girl, 2001; Die Another Day, 2002; American Life, 2003. Albums: Madonna, 1983; Like A Virgin, 1985; True Blue, 1986; Who's That Girl?, film soundtrack, 1987; You Can Dance, 1988; Like A Prayer, 1989; I'm Breathless, 1990; The Immaculate Collection, 1990; Dick Tracy, film soundtrack, 1990; Erotica, 1992; Bedtime Stories, 1994; Something To Remember, 1995; Evita, film soundtrack, 1996; Ray of Light, 1997; Music, 2000; American Life, 2003. Publications: Sex, 1992; The English Roses, 2003; Mr Peabody's Apples, 2003. Honours include: Numerous MTV Video Awards, including Vanguard Award, 1986; American Music Awards: Favourite Female Video Artist, 1987; Favourite Dance Single, 1991; Oscar, Best Song, 1991; Juno Award, International Song Of The Year, 1991; Grammy Award, Best Longform Music Video, 1992; Numerous awards from Billboard, Vogue and Rolling Stone magazines. Address: c/o Norman West Management, 9348 Civic Centre Drive, Beverly Hills, CA 90210, USA.

**MADSEN Michael,** b. 25 September 1958, Chicago, USA. Actor. m. Jeannine Bisignano, 1 son. Appointments: Began acting career, Steppenwolf Theatre, Chicago; Appeared in plays including: Of Mice and Men; A Streetcar Named Desire; Appeared in Broadway Production of A Streetcar Named Desire, 1992; Films: Wargames, debut, 1983; The Natural; Racing with the Moon, 1984; The Killing Time, 1987; Shadows in the Storm; Iguana, 1988; Blood Red, 1989; Kill Me Again, 1990; The Doors, 1991; The End of Innocence, 1991; Thelma and Louise, 1991; Fatal Instinct, 1992; Inside Edge, 1992; Reservoir Dogs, 1992; Straight Talk, 1992; Almost Blue, 1992; Free Willy, 1993; A House in the Hills, 1993; Money for Nothing, 1993; Trouble Bound, 1993; Wyatt Earp, 1993; The Getaway, 1994; Dead Connection, 1994; Species; Free Willy II: The Adventure Home, 1995; The Winner, 1996; Red Line, 1996; Mulholland Falls, 1996; Man with a Gun, 1996; The Last Days of Frankie the Fly, 1996; Rough Draft, 1997; The Marker, 1997; Donnie Brasco, 1997; Catherine's Grove, 1997; Papertrail, 1997; The Girl Gets Moe, 1997; Executive Target, 1997; The Thief and the Stripper, 1998; Supreme Sanction, 1998; The Florentine, 1998; Species II, 1998; Detour, 1999; Code of the Dragon, 2000; The Ghost, 2000; High Noon, 2000; LAPD Conspiracy, 2001; LAPD To Protect and Serve, 2001; TV: Our Family House, 1985-86; Special Bulletin, 1983; War and Remembrance, 1988; Montana, 1990; Baby Snatcher, 1992; Beyond the Law, 1994. Address: Grant and Tane, 9100 Wilshire Boulevard, Beverley Hills, CA 90212, USA.

**MADUAKOR Obiajuru,** b. 5 July 1938, Isulo, Anambra State, Nigeria. University Professor of English Language and Literature and of African Literature. m. Chijioke Obiageli, 3 sons. Education: BA, Honours English, University of Ibadan, Nigeria, 1962-65; MA, English Literature, University of Leeds, UK, 1971-72; PhD, English Literature, University of Ottawa,

Canada, 1972-77. Appointments: Lecturer, English Literature, University of Ife, Nigeria, 1978-81; Senior Lecturer, 1981-84, Associate Professor, 1984-87, Professor, English Literature, 1987-, University of Nigeria, Nsukka, Nigeria. Publications: Book: Wole Soyinka: An Introduction to His Writing, 1986; 50 articles. Honours: DAAD Scholar, University of Mainz, 1993; Visiting Fellow, University of Hull, 1992; Visiting Fellow, University of Leeds, 1993; Visiting Professor, University of Guelph, 1997-99; Adjunct Professor, Tyndale University College, Toronto, 2004-. Memberships: African Literature Association; Modern Language Association; Literary Society of Nigeria; American Studies Association of Nigeria. Address: Department of English, University of Nigeria, Nsukka, Nigeria. E-mail: obimaduakor@hotmail.com

**MAEHLER Herwig Gustav Theodor,** b. 29 April 1935, Berlin, Germany. Emeritus Professor of Papyrology. m. Margaret, 2 daughters. Education: Classics and Classical Archaeology, Universities of Hamburg, Tübingen and Basel, 1955-61; PhD, University of Hamburg, 1961; Postdoctoral British Council Fellowship, Oxford University, England, 1961-62; Habilitation, Freie Universität, Berlin, 1975. Appointments: Research Assistant, University of Hamburg, 1962-63; Research Assistant, Hamburg University Library, 1963-64; Keeper of Greek Papyri, Egyptian Museum, West Berlin, 1964-79; Reader in Papyrology, 1979-81, Professor of Papyrology, 1981-2000, Professor Emeritus, 2000-, University College, London. Publications: Die Auffassung des Dichterberufs im frühen Griechentum bis zur Zeit Pindars, 1963; Die Handschriften der S Jacobi-Kirche in Hamburg, 1967; Urkunden römischer Zeit, 1968; Papyri aus Hermupolis, 1974; Die Lieder des Bakchylides Part I, 1982, Part II, 1997; Greek Bookhands of the Early Byzantine Period (with G Cavallo), 1987; Editions of Bacchylides, 1970 and Pindar, 1971, 1975, 1989; About 120 articles in learned journals. Honours: Fellow, British Academy, 1986; Fellow, Accademia Nazionale dei Lincei, Rome 2001; Honorary Fellow, University College London, 2001; Honorary PhDs: University of Helsinki, 2000, University of Budapest, 2001, Rome II Tor Vergata, 2003. Membership: Corresponding Member, German Archaeological Institute, 1979. Address: Department of Greek and Latin, University College London, Gower Street, London, WC1E 6BT, England. E-mail: hgt.maehler@virgin.net

**MAES Michael H J,** b. 10 March 1954, Ghent. Professor; Psychiatrist. m. Michaleva Olga, 2 daughters. Education: MD, 1979; Psychiatrist, 1986; PhD, 1991. Appointments: Assistant Professor of Psychiatry, University of Antwerp, Belgium, 1986-91; Assistant Professor of Psychiatry, CWRU, Cleveland, Ohio, USA, 1991-96; Director, Clinical Research, Centre of Mental Health, Antwerp, 1995-; Adjunct Professor, Vanderbilt University, Nashville, Tennessee, USA, 1997-; Professor of Psychiatry, Department of Psychiatry, University of Maastricht, The Netherlands, 1999-. Publications: Over 400 articles in international journals. Honours: ECNP Award, 1991; The Klerman Award for Outstanding Research, NARSAD, 1998; Prize, Rimauz-Bartier, FWO, 1999; Listed in several biographical publications. Memberships: World Psychiatric Association; Society of Biological Psychiatry. Address: M-CARE4U Outpatient Clinics, Grote Markt 1, 2500 Lier, Belgium. E-mail: crc.mh@telenet.be

**MAGEE Bryan,** b. 12 April 1930, London, England. Writer. m. Ingrid Söderlund, 1 daughter. Education: MA, Keble College, Oxford University, 1956; Yale University, 1955-56. Appointments: Theatre Critic, The Listener, 1966-67; Lecturer in Philosophy, Balliol College, Oxford, 1970-71; Visiting Fellow, All Souls College, Oxford, 1973-74; Regular Columnist, The Times, 1974-76; Member of Parliament for Leyton, 1974-

83; President, Critics Circle of Great Britain, 1983-84; Honorary Senior Research Fellow, 1984-94, Visiting Professor, 1994-2000, King's College, London; Honorary Fellow, Queen Mary College, London, 1988-; Fellow, Queen Mary and Westfield College, London, 1989-; Visiting Fellow: Wolfson College, Oxford, 1991-94, New College, Oxford, 1995, Merton College, Oxford, 1998, St Catherine's College, Oxford, 2000, Peterhouse College, Cambridge, 2001. Publications: Go West Young Man, 1958; To Live in Danger, 1960; The New Radicalism, 1962; The Democratic Revolution, 1964; Towards 2000, 1965; One in Twenty, 1966; The Television Interviewer, 1966; Aspects of Wagner, 1968; Modern British Philosophy, 1971; Popper, 1973; Facing Death, 1977; Men of Ideas, 1978, reissued as Talking Philosophy, 2001; The Philosophy of Schopenhauer, 1983; The Great Philosophers, 1987; On Blindness, 1995, reissued as Sight Unseen, 1998; Confessions of a Philosopher, 1997; The Story of Philosophy, 1998; Wagner and Philosophy, 2000; Clouds of Glory, 2003. Contributions to: Numerous journals. Honours: Silver Medal, Royal Television Society, 1978; J R Ackerley Prize for Autobiography, 2004. Memberships: Critics Circle; Society of Authors; Arts Council of Great Britain and Chair, Music Panel, 1993-94; Honorary Fellow, Keble College, Oxford, 1994-; Silver Medal, Royal TV Society; Life Member, Clare Hall, Cambridge, 2004. Address: Wolfson College, Oxford OX 2 6UD, England.

**MAGER Peter Paul,** b. 18 June 1946, Klostergeringswalde, Saxony, Germany. m. Christine, 2 daughters. Education: Approbation in Medicine, Leipzig, 1973; MD, 1974; Mathematics in Chemistry, 1975, Degree in Pharmacology and Toxicology, 1978, Halle; DSc, 1982; Degree in Educational and Didactic Methodology in University Teaching, 1983; Facultas docendi, 1990; Dr med habil, 1991. Appointments: Assistant, Pharmacology and Toxicology, University of Greifswald, 1973-75; Assistant in Internal Medicine, Doesen/Saxony, 1975-76; Senior Researcher, Institute of Pharmacy, University of Halle, 1976-80; Head of Research Group of Pharmacochemistry, University of Leipzig, 1980-; Co-ordinator, Research Programme, FMC Co, Princeton, New Jersey, USA, 1984-90; Consultant, Clinical Pharmacology, Leipzig, 1985-90; Consultant, Biostructure SA, France, 1991-94; Managing Director, Institute of Pharmacology and Toxicology, University of Leipzig, 1993-95; Professor, 1996. Publications: Co-editor and Referee of scientific periodicals; Around 200 papers in scientific periodicals and handbooks; 3 monographs. Honour: Leibniz Award. Memberships include: New York Academy of Sciences; American Association for the Advancement of Science; Affiliate, International Union of Pure and Applied Chemistry; German Society of Pharmacology and Toxicology; Medicinal Chemistry Division, Computer Chemistry Division, German Chemical Society; Deutsche Hochschulverband. Address: Institute of Pharmacology and Toxicology, Haertelstr 16-18, Leipzig D-04107, Germany. E-mail: magp@server3.medizin.uni-leipzig.de

**MAGNUSSON Magnus,** b. 12 October 1929, Reykjavík, Iceland. Writer; Broadcaster. m. Mamie Baird, 1954, 1 son, 3 daughters. Education: Edinburgh Academy; Jesus College, Oxford. Appointments: Assistant Editor, Scottish Daily Express; The Scotsman; Presenter, various TV and radio programmes including: Chronicle; Mastermind; Pebble Mill and One; BC, The Archaeology of the Bible Lands; Tonight; Cause for Concern; All Things Considered; Living Legends; Vikings!; Birds for All Seasons; Editor, The Bodley Head Archaeologies; Popular Archaeology, 1979-80; Chair, Ancient Monuments Board for Scotland, 1981-89; Cairngorms Working Party, 1991-93; NCC for Scotland, 1991-92; Scottish National Heritage, 1992-99; Rector, Edinburgh University, 1975-78; Member,

UK Committee for European Year of the Environment, 1987; Board of Trustees, National Museum of Scotland, 1985-89; President, RSPB, 1985-90; Honorary Vice President, Age Concern Scotland; RSSPCC; FSA, Scotland, 1974. Publications: Introducing Archaeology, 1972; The Clacken and the Slate, 1974; Hammer of the North, 1976; BC, The Archaeology of the Bible Lands, 1977; Landlords or Tenant?; A View of Irish History, 1978; Iceland, 1979; Vikings! Magnus on the Move, 1980; Treasures of Scotland, 1981; Lindisfarne: The Cradle Island, 1984; Iceland Saga, 1987; I've Started So I'll Finish, 1997; Rum: Nature's Island, 1997; Magnus Magnusson's Quiz Book, 2000; Scotland: The Story of a Nation, 2000; Contributions to various historical and novelty books; Introductions to numerous books on historical, geographical and cultural themes; Editor: Echoes in Stone, 1983; Readers Digest Book of Facts, 1985; Chambers Biographical Dictionary, 1990; Others. Honours: Honorary Fellow, Oxford, 1990; Honorary FRIAS, 1987; FRSGS, 1991; Dr hc, Edinburgh, 1978; Hon D Univ, York, 1981; Paisley, 1993; Hon D Litt, Strathclyde, 1993, Naiper, 1984, Glasgow, 2001, Glasgow Caledonian, 2001; Iceland Media Award, 1985; Silver Jubilee Medal, 1977; Medlicott Medal, 1989; Knight of Order of the Falcon, Iceland, 1975; Commander, 1986; Honorary KBE. Address: Blairhaith House, Balmore-Tottance, Glasgow, G64 4AX, Scotland.

**MAGNUSSON Tomas Herbert,** b. 1 April 1949, Linköping. Dentist. m. Annica Birgitta Hedmo, 3 daughters. Education: L D S, 1974; Odont Dr, PhD, 1981; Docent, Reader, 1986; Certified Specialist in Stomatognathic Physiology, 1993. Appointments: General Practitioner, Jokkmokk, Sweden, 1974-1979; Assistant Professor, University of Göteberg, Sweden, 1979-1980; Head, Senior Consultant, Lulea, Sweden, 1980-1988; Senior Consultant, 1988-2000, Head, Senior Consultant, 2000-, Jonkoping, Sweden. Publications: Published more than 60 scientific papers in peer review national and international journals mainly in the field of temporomandibular disorders; One out of two authors of four textbooks and author of four separate book chapters, all in the field of temporomandibular disorders. Honours: The Forsberg Dental Foundation Award for extraordinary clinical achievements, 1990; The Henry Beyron Award for unique research, 2000; Corresponding member, Finnish Dental Society, 2002. Memberships: Swedish Dental Society; Swedish Dental Society; Swedish Academy of Temporo Mandibular Disorders; Board member and past president of the Society of Oral Physiology. Address: The Institute for Postgraduate Dental Education, Box 1030, SE-55111 Jonkoping, Sweden. E-mail: tomas.magnusson@ltjkpg.se

**MAGUIRE Adrian Edward,** b. 29 April 1971, Ireland. Jockey. m. Sabrina, 1995, 1 daughter. Education: Kilmessan National School; Trim Vocational School. Appointments: Champion Pony Race Rider, 1986; Champion Point to Point Rider, 1990-91; Champion Conditional Jockey, 1991-92; Winner of the Following Races: Cheltenham Gold Cup; Irish Grand National; Galway Plate; Imperial Cup; Greenalls Gold Cup; Queen Mother Champion Chase; King George VI Chase; Triumph Hurdle and Cathcort Chase; Holds record for most Point to Point winners in a season; Most winners in a season for a conditional jockey (71), 1991-92; Retired due to neck injury having won over 1,000 races, 2002. Address: The Jockey Club (Jockey Section), 42 Portman Square, London, W1H 0EM, England.

**MAGUIRE Robert Alfred,** b. 6 June 1931, London, England. Retired Architect; Sculptor. m. Alison Margaret, 4 daughters. Education: Leverhulme Scholar, AA Diploma with Honours, Architectural Association School of Architecture, London, 1948-53. Appointments: Buildings Editor, Architect's Journal, 1954-59; Partner, Robert Maguire & Keith Murray, 1959-

89; Chairman, Maguire & Co, 1988-2003, Maguire & Co International, 1989-2002; Consultant, Maguire & Co, 2003-2004; Surveyor of the Fabric to The Queen's Free Chapel of St George at Windsor Castle, 1975-87; Head, Oxford School of Architecture, 1976-85; Trustee, Stowe House Preservation Trust, 1998-. Publications: Book: Modern Churches of the World (co-author with Keith Murray); Numerous articles on architectural theory, architectural critiques and conservation; Major paper: Continuity and Modernity in the Holy Place (Annual Lecture to the Society of Architectural Historians of Great Britain), 1995. Honours: OBE, 1983; 4 buildings of his own design listed as Buildings of Historic Interest: St Paul's Church, Bow Common, London; St Matthew's Church, Perry Beeches, Birmingham; St Mary's Abbey Church, West Malling; Residences at St Mary's Abbey, West Malling. Memberships: Royal Society of Arts; Oxford University Club. Address: Hopewater House, Ettrickbridge, Selkirk TD7 5JN, Scotland.

**MAGUIRE Tobey Vincent,** b. 27 June 1975, Santa Monica, California, USA. Actor. Career: Various Commercials as child; Films include: Pleasantville, 1998; Ride with the Devil, 1999; Tales from the Whoop: Hot Rod Brown Class Clown, 1990; Empire Records, 1995; Fear and Loathing in Las Vegas, 1998; The Cider House Rules, 1999; Wonder Boys, 2000; Cats and Dogs, voice, 2001; Dons Plum, 2001; Spider-Man, 2002; Seabiscuit, 2003; Spider-Man 2, 2004; TV appearances include: Celebrities Uncensored, 2003; The Tonight show with Jay Leno, 1992; Rove Live, 2000; Tracey Takes On…, 1996; Roseanne, 1988; The Wild and Crazy Kids, 1990; Great Scott!, 1992. Honours include: Academy of Science Fiction, Fantasy & Horror Films, USA, Best Performance by a Young Actor, Pleasantville, 1999.

**MAHADIK Kakasaheb,** b. 1 June 1958, Nevri, Sangli District, India. Pharmacist. m. Shobha, 1 son, 1 daughter. Education: B Pharm; M Pharm; PhD. Appointments: Lecturer, Assistant Professor and Vice Principal, Professor and Vice Principal, Bharati Vidypeeth Deemed University, Poona College of Pharmacy, Pune. Publications: 22 and 39 international presentations; 55 and 40 national presentations. Honours: Best Teacher Award, Government of Maharastra, 2004; Chartered Chemist, Institution of Chemists, India. Memberships: ACS; IPA; IPS; ISTE; ISCPT; ISAS; IDMA; IIPA; APA; and others. Address: Ashoka, G Bharatinagar, Paud Road, Kothsud, Pune 411029 (MS), India. E-mail: krmahadik@rediffmail.com

**MAHAJAN Harpreet,** b. November 1953, Simla, India. Computer Consultant; Teacher. Education: BSc, University of Delhi, India, 1973; MA, Political Science, 1975, MPhil, International Affairs, 1976, PhD, International Affairs, 1980, Jawaharlal Nehru University, India; MPhil, Political Science, Columbia University, 1983. Appointments: Executive Director of Information Technology, School of International and Public Affairs, Columbia University, 1995-; Adjunct Associate Professor, School of International Public Affairs, Columbia University, 1993-; Director of Information Technology, Institute for Social and Economic Research and Policy, Columbia, 1998-2002; Consultant, Institute for Social and Economic Research and Policy, 2002-03. Publications: Arms Transfers to India, Pakistan and the Third World, 1982; Peace and Disputed Sovereignty, 1985; Computers: Personal Computers, 2003. Honours: President's Fellow, Political Science, Columbia University, 1980-81; Fellow, Political Science, Columbia, 1978-80; Research Fellow, Delhi University, 1975-79; Listed in national and international biographical dictionaries. Address: 420 W 118th Street, #1514 IAB, Columbia University, New York, NY 10027, USA. Website: www.sipa.columbia.edu

**MAHBOOB Soltanali,** b. 14 April 1944, Meshkinshahr, Iran. Professor. m. Lakestani-Amineh, 1 son, 1 daughter. Education: BS, MSc Degrees, Iran, 1965; CES, DEA, Doctorate Degree, France, 1969; Sabbatical Leave, USA, 1974-75. Appointments: Dean of Pharmacy School, 1974-75; Head of Biochemistry and Nutrition Department, 1976-80; Associate Visiting Professor, USA, 1984-85; Dean of Health and Nutrition School, Tabriz University of Medical Sciences, Tabriz, Iran, 1990-2002; Director of Food and Nutrition Security Program in Tabriz, 2002-. Publications: 40 articles in national and international journals; 90 articles presented at international and national congresses. Honours: Outstanding Professor of Tabriz University of Medical Science, 1985, 1996, 1998; Outstanding Professor of Iran, 1997; Outstanding Researcher of Tabriz University of Medical Science, 1998, 1999, 2003; Outstanding Researcher of Iran, 1998; Outstanding Manager of Tabriz University of Medical Science, 2000. Memberships: Iranian Society of Nutrition; Iranian Society of Physiology and Pharmacology; FASEB; Sigma Xi Scientific Research Society; Nutrition Today. Address: Department of Biochemistry and Clinical Nutrition, Faculty of Public Health and Nutrition; Tabriz University of Medical Science, Tabriz, Iran. E-mail: mahbooba@tbzmed.ac.ir

**MAHECHA GÓMEZ Jorge Eduardo,** b. 8 August 1948, La Palma, Cundinamarca, Colombia. Physicist. m. Clara Inés Botero, 2 sons. Education: BSc, Physics, University of Antioquia, Medellin, Colombia, 1973; MSc Physics, 1979, PhD Physics, 1995, University of Belgrade, Yugoslavia. Appointment: Professor of Physics, Institute of Physics, University of Antioquia, Medellin, Colombia. Publications: Books: Advanced Classical Mechanics; Computational Packages in Science and Engineering; Course on Atomic Doubly Excited States, editor; Articles include: On Riemann Zeta Function; Confined one-electron atom; One-electron atom near metal surfaces; Confined electron hole-systems; Coulomb 3-body systems. Honours: Associate Fellowship, The Abdus Salam, International Centre for Theoretical Physics, Trieste, Italy, 1987-93, 1995-2001. Memberships: Sociedad Mexicana de Fisica; Sociedad Colombiana de Fisica; American Physical Society. Address: Institute of Physics, University of Antioquia, Calle 67 No 53-108, AA 1226, Medellin, Colombia. E-mail: mahecha@fisica.udea.edu.co

**MAHFOUZ Soheir Mahmoud,** b. 12 April 1950, Cairo, Egypt. Professor. m. Khalid Aly Sorour, 1 son, 1 daughter. Education: MBBCh, 1974, MSc, Pathology, 1980; PhD, Pathology, 1984, Faculty of Medicine, Cairo University. Appointments: Pathology Instructor, 1976-78; Assistant Lecturer, 1980-84; Assistant Professor of Pathology, 1989-94; Head of Cytology, 1989-, Professor of Pathology, 1994-, Pathology Department, Kasr Al Ainy Hospital, Cairo University. Publications: Articles in scientific journals: Distribution of the major connective matrix components of the stromal reaction of breast carcinoma, 1987; Synovial Sarcoma, 1990. Honour: Graduated Excellent with Honours, Faculty of Medicine, Cairo University. Memberships: Egyptian Society of Pathologists; Arab Division of the International Academy of Pathology. Address: Pathology Department, Kasr Al Ainy Hospital, Cairo University, Manial, Cairo, Egypt. E-mail: smahfouz@access.com.eg

**MAHJOUB Bechir Mohamed,** b. 18 June 1935, Mahdia, Tunisia. Professor. m. Aicha Zouari, 2 sons, 1 daughter. Education: Licence de Mathématiques, Institut des Hautes Études de Tunis, 1960; Diplôme D'Études Supérieures, University of Tunis, 1963; Doctorat d'État es Sciences Mathématiques, Paris Sorbonne, 1970. Appointments: Professor of Mathematics, University of Tunis, 1974-; Director General, Higher Education of Tunisia, 1977-88; Delegate of Tunisia at

UNESCO, 1988-92; Professor, University of Qatar, 1992-2000. Publications: Book: Cours D'Analyse, 1983; Numerous articles on mathematics published in the proceedings of the Academy of Sciences of Paris and in the annals of the Institute Henri Poincaré. Honours: Officier de l'Ordre de la Republique, Tunisia, 1978; Officier de la Légion d'Honneur, France, 1983; Officier de l'Ordre National du Merite, France, 1984. Memberships: Société Mathématique de Tunisie; Association Tunisienne des Sciences Mathématiques. Address: 9 rue des Narcisses, 1004 Elmenzah 5, Tunisia. E-mail: b.mahjoub@planet.tn

**MAILER Norman (Kingsley),** b. 31 January 1923, Long Beach, California, USA. Writer. m. (1) Beatrice Silverman, 1944, divorced 1951, 1 daughter, (2) Adele Morales, 1954, divorced 1962, 2 daughters, (3) Lady Jeanne Campbell, 1962, divorced 1963, 1 daughter, (4) Beverly Rentz Bentley, 1963, divorced 1980, 2 sons, 1 daughter, (5) Carol Stevens, divorced, 1 daughter, (6) Norris Church, 1980, 1 son. Education: BS, Harvard University. Publications: The Naked and the Dead, 1948; Barbary Shore, 1951; The Deer Park, 1955 (dramatised 1967); Advertisements for Myself, 1959; Deaths for the Ladies (poems), 1962; The Presidential Papers, 1963; An American Dream, 1964; Cannibals and Christians, 1966; Why are We in Vietnam?, 1967; The Armies of the Night, 1968; Miami and the Siege of Chicago, 1968; Moonshot, 1969; A Fire on the Moon, 1970; The Prisoner of Sex, 1971; Existential Errands, 1972; St George and the Godfather, 1972; Marilyn, 1973; The Faith of Graffiti, 1974; The Fight, 1975; Some Honourable Men, 1976; Genius and Lust: A Journey Through the Writings of Henry Miller, 1976; A Transit to Narcissus, 1978; The Executioner's Song, 1979; Of Women and Their Elegance, 1980; The Essential Mailer, 1982; Pieces and Pontifications, 1982; Ancient Evenings, 1983; Tough Guys Don't Dance, 1983; Harlot's Ghost, 1991; How the Wimp Won the War, 1991; Oswald's Tale, 1995; Portrait of Picasso as a Young Man, 1995; The Gospel According to the Son, 1997; The Time of Our Time, 1998; The Spooky Art: Thoughts on Writing, 2003; Why Are We At War? 2003. Contributions to: Numerous journals and magazines. Honours: National Book Award for Arts and Letters, 1969; Pulitzer Prize for Non-Fiction, 1969; Award for Outstanding Service to the Arts, McDowell Colony, 1973. Memberships: PEN, president, 1984-86; American Academy of Arts and Letters. Address: c/o Rembar, 19th West 44th Street, New York, NY 10036, USA.

**MAINI Ravinder Nath (Sir),** b. 17 November 1937, India. Emeritus Professor of Rheumatology. m. Geraldine Room, 3 sons, 1 daughter. Education: BA, Sidney Sussex College, University of Cambridge, 1959; MB BChir, Guy's Hospital Medical College, London, 1962. Appointments: Junior hospital posts at Guy's Hospital, Brompton Hospital, Charing Cross Hospital, London, 1962-70; Consultant Physician, Charing Cross Hospital, West London Hospital, St Stephen's Hospital, London, 1970-79; Honorary Consultant Physician, Charing Cross Hospital, London, 1970-2002; Professor and Head of Department of Immunology of Rheumatic Diseases, Charing Cross and Westminster Medical School, 1979-89, Professor of Rheumatology, 1989; Head of the Division of Clinical Immunology, Kennedy Institute of Rheumatology, 1979-2002; Professor of Rheumatology, 1989-2002, Professor Emeritus, 2002-, University of London at Imperial College; Head of the Department of Rheumatology, 1989-2002, Honorary Consultant Physician, 2002-, Charing Cross Hospital, Hammersmith Hospitals Trust, London; Director, Kennedy Institute of Rheumatology, London, 1990-2000; Head, Kennedy Institute of Rheumatology Division, Faculty of Medicine, Imperial College of Science, Technology and Medicine, 2000-02. Publications: Over 470 include as co-author: Treatment of rheumatoid arthritis

with chimeric monoclonal antibodies to tumour necrosis factor α, 1993; Randomised double-blind comparison of chimeric monoclonal antibody to tumour necrosis factor α (cA2) versus placebo in rheumatoid arthritis, 1994; Repeated therapy with a monoclonal antibody to tumour necrosis factor α in patients with rheumatoid arthritis, 1994; TNF defined as a therapeutic target for rheumatoid arthritis and other autoimmune diseases, 2003. Honours: Gold Medal in Clinical Medicine, First Prize in Surgery, First Prize in Cardiology, Guy's Hospital Medical School, 1962; Doctor honoris causa, University René Descartes, Paris, 1994; Carol Nachman Prize for Rheumatology, Germany, 1999; American College of Rheumatology Distinguished Investigator Award, 1999; Courtin-Clarins Prize, 2000; Crafoord Prize (jointly with Professor Feldmann), Royal Swedish Academy of Sciences, 2000; Kt, 2003; Albert Lasker Clinical Medical Research Award (with Professor Feldmann), 2003; Honorary Doctorate of Science, University of Glasgow, 2004; Outstanding Achievement in Clinical Research Award, The Institute of Clinical Research, UK, 2004; Fothergillian medal, The Medical Society of London, 2004; Honorary Fellowship, Sidney Sussex College, University of Cambridge, 2004; Honorary Fellowship, The Royal Society of Medicine, 2004; Master, The American College of Rheumatology, 2004; Cameron Prize, University of Edinburgh, 2004. Memberships include: American College of Rheumatology; Fellow, British Society for Rheumatology; Fellow, Royal College of Physicians, London; Fellow, Royal College of Physicians, Edinburgh; Fellow, Academy of Medical Sciences (FMedSci); British Society for Immunology; Association of Physicians of Great Britain and Northern Ireland; Antibody Club; Royal Society of Medicine. Address: The Kennedy Institute of Rheumatology Division; Imperial College London, 1 Aspenlea Road, London W6 8LH, England.

**MAINWARING Scott Patterson,** b. 18 July 1954, Pittsburgh, Pennsylvania, USA. Political Scientist; Educator. m. Susan M Elfin, 1 son, 1 daughter. Education: BA, Political Science, 1972-76, MA, Political Science, 1975-76, Yale University; PhD, Political Science, Stanford University, 1978-83. Appointments: Assistant Professor, Government, 1983-88, Associate Professor, Government, 1988-93, Professor of Government, 1993-96, Chair, Government Department 1996-97, Eugene Conley Professor of Political Science, 1996-, Director, Kellogg Institute for International Studies, 1997-2002, 2003-06 University of Notre Dame, Indiana, USA. Publications: Author, The Catholic Church and Politics in Brazil 1916-1985, 1986; Author, Rethinking Party Systems in the Third Wave of Democratization: The Case of Brazil, 1999; Edited books: The progressive Church in Latin America, 1989; Issues in Democratic Consolidation, 1992; Building Democratic Institutions: Party Systems in Latin America, 1995; Presidentialism and Democracy in Latin America, 1997; Christian Democracy in Latin America, 2003; The Third Wave of Democratization in Latin America, 2005; Democratic Accountability in Latin America, 2003. Honours: Phi Beta Kappa, Yale University; Magna Cum Laude, Yale University, 1976; Washburn Clark Prize, Yale University, 1976; Hubert Herring Prize for the best dissertation on a Latin American subject, 1983-84; 7 Research Grants and Fellowships include: Fulbright Hays, 1980-81; Social Science Research Council, 1980-81; Fulbright-Hays, 1987-88; Hoover Institute, Stanford, 1990-91; Woodrow Wilson Centre, 1995-96; Guggenheim Fellow, 2000. Memberships: Council on Foreign Relations, 1986-91; Research Council, International Forum for Democratic Studies, National Endowment for Democracy, Washington DC, 1994-; Consultant, The Ford Foundation, New York; Inter-American Dialogue, Washington DC; MacArthur Foundation, Chicago. Address: Kellogg Institute for International Studies, 231 Hesburgh Center, Notre Dame, IN 46556, USA. E-mail: mainwaring.1@nd.edu

**MAJOR Clarence,** b. 31 December 1936, Atlanta, Georgia, USA. Poet; Writer; Artist; Professor. m. (1) Joyce Sparrow, 1958, divorced 1964, (2) Pamela Ritter. Education: BS, State University of New York at Albany, 1976; PhD, Union Graduate School, 1978. Appointments: Editor, Coercion Review, 1958-66, Writer-in-Residence, Center for Urban Education, New York, 1967-68, Teachers and Writers Collaborative-Teachers College, Columbia University, 1967-71, Aurora College, Illinois, 1974, Albany State College, Georgia, 1984, Clayton College, Denver, 1986, 1987; Associate Editor, Caw, 1967-70, Journal of Black Poetry, 1967-70; Lecturer, Brooklyn College of the City University of New York, 1968-69, 1973, 1974-75, Cazenovia Collge, New York, 1969, Wisconsin State University, 1969, Queens College of the City University of New York, 1972, 1973, 1975, Sarah Lawrence College, 1972-75, School of Continuing Education, New York University, 1975; Columnist, 1973-76, Contributing Editor, 1976-86, American Poetry Review; Assistant Professor, Howard University, 1974-76, University of Washington, 1976-77; Visiting Assistant Professor, University of Maryland at College Park, 1976, State University of New York at Buffalo, 1976; Associate Professor, 1977-81, Professor, 1981-89, University of Colorado at Boulder; Editor, 1977-78, Associate Editor, 1978-, American Book Review; Professor, 1989-, Director, Creative Writing, 1991-, University of California at Davis. Publications: Poetry: The Fires That Burn in Heaven, 1954; Love Poems of a Black Man, 1965; Human Juices, 1965; Swallow the Lake, 1970; Symptoms and Madness, 1971; Private Line, 1971; The Cotton Club: New Poems, 1972; The Syncopated Cakewalk, 1974; Inside Diameter: The France Poems, 1985; Surfaces and Masks, 1988; Some Observations of a Stranger at Zuni in the Latter Part of the Century, 1989; Parking Lots, 1992; Configurations: New and Selected Poems 1958-1998, 1998; Waiting for Sweet Baby, 2002. Fiction: All-Night Visitors, 1969; new version, 1998; NO, 1973; Reflex and Bone Structure, 1975; Emergency Exit, 1979; My Amputations, 1986; Such Was the Season, 1987; Painted Turtle: Woman with Guitar, 1988; Fun and Games, 1990; Dirty Bird Blues, 1996. Other: Dictionary of Afro-American Slang, 1970; The Dark and Feeling: Black American Writers and Their Work, 1974; Juba to Jive: A Dictionary of African-American Slang, 1994; Necessary Distance: Essays and Criticism, 2001; Come by Here: My Mother's Life, 2002. Editor: Writers Workshop Anthology, 1967; Man is Like a Child: An Anthology of Creative Writing by Students, 1968; The New Black Poetry, 1969; Calling the Wind: Twentieth Century African-American Short Stories, 1993; The Garden Thrives: Twentieth Century African-American Poetry, 1995. Honours: Fulbright-Hays Exchange Award, 1981-83; Western States Book Award, 1986; Pushcart Prize, 1989; National Book Award Bronze Medal Finalist, 1998. Address: c/o Department of English, 1 Shields Avenue, University of California at Davis, Davis, CA 95616, USA.

**MAJOR John,** b. 29 March 1943. Politician; Former Member of Parliament. m. Norma Major, 1970, 1 son, 1 daughter. Education: Associate, Institute of Bankers. Appointments: Various executive positions, Stand Chartered Bank, UK and overseas, 1965-80; Served, Lambeth Borough Council, 1968-71, including Housing and Finance Committees, also Chairman, Accounts Committee and Housing Committee, 1969; Contested Camden, St Pancras North, February and October 1974; Member, Board, Warden Housing Association, 1975-93; Member of Parliament for Huntingdonshire, 1979-83, for Huntingdon, 1983-2001; Parliamentary Private Secretary to Ministers of State, Home Office, 1981-83; Assistant Government Whip, 1983-84; Lord Commissioner of Treasury,

Senior Government Whip, 1984-85; Parliamentary Under-Secretary of State, Department of Health and Social Security, 1985-86; Minister of State, Social Security and the Disabled, 1986-87; Chief Secretary to the Treasury, 1987-89; Secretary of State for Foreign and Commonwealth Affairs, 1989; Chancellor of the Exchequer, 1989-90; Elected Leader, Conservative Party, 1990; Prime Minister, 1st Lord of the Treasury, Minister for the Civil Service, 1990-97. Memberships: Parlimentary Consultant to Guild of Glass Engravers, 1979-83; President, Eastern Area Young Conservatives, 1983-85; National Asthma Campaign, 1998-; Chair, Carlyle Group, 2001-; Non-Executive Director, Mayflower Corporation, 2000-; Member, Main Committee, MCC, 2001-; Honorary Master of the Bench of the Middle Temple, 1992. Publications: The Autobiography, 1999. Address: House of Commons, London, SW1A 0AA, England.

**MAJOR Malvina (Lorraine) (Dame),** b. 28 January 1943, Hamilton, New Zealand. Opera Singer (Soprano). m. Winston William Richard Fleming, 16 January 1965, deceased 1990, 1 son, 2 daughters. Education: Grade VIII, Piano, Singing, Theory, Convent at Ngaruawahia, Waikato; Singing continued under Dame Sister Mary Leo, St Mary's Music School, Auckland, 1960-65 and Ruth Packer, Royal College of Music, London, London Opera Centre, UK, 1965-67. Debut: Camden Town Festival, 1968 in Rossini's La Donna del Lago. Career includes: Performances as: Belle, Belle of New York, New Zealand, 1963; Pamina, Magic Flute, London Opera Centre, 1967; 1st non Mormon Soloist to sing with Mormon Tabernacle Choir, 1987; Matilda in Elisabetta Regina d'Inghilterra, Camden Town, 1968; Rosina, Barber of Seville, Salzburg (conductor, Claudio Abbado), 1968-69; Gala Concert, King and Queen of Belgium, Centenary Antwerp Zoological Society, 1969; Marguerite, Gounod's Faust, Neath and London, 1969; Bruckner's Te Deum, conductor Daniel Barenboim, 1968; Cio Cio San, Madam Butterfly; Widow, The Merry Widow; Gilda in Rigoletto; Tosca; Constanze in Die Entführung; Arminda in La Finta Giardiniera, Brussels, 1986; Donna Elvira, Don Giovanni, Brighton Festival, 1987; Donna Anna in Don Giovanni at Sydney, Australia, 1987; Operas include recent productions of Rosalinda (Die Fledermaus) and Lucia di Lammermoor, Mimi in La Bohème and Constanze in New York and Australia; Sang Arminda at Lausanne, 1989, Constanze with the Lyric Opera of Queensland; Season 1992-93 with Lucia at Adelaide, Arminda at Salzburg, Violetta and Gilda at Wellington; Sang in Eugene Onegin and Don Giovanni with Wellington City Opera, 1997. Recordings: To The Glory of God, 1964; L'amico Fritz, opera (Caterina), 1969; Songs for All Seasons, Mahler Symphony No 4, 1970; Scottish Soldiers Abroad, 1975; Alleluia, 1974; Operatic Arias, conductor John Matheson, 1987; La Finta Giardiniera, Brussels. Contributions to: London Sunday Times (article by Desmond Shawe-Taylor). Honours: New Zealand Mobil Song Quest, 1963; Melbourne Sun Aria, Australia, 1964; Kathleen Ferrier Scholarship, London, 1966; OBE, 1985; DBE, 1991; Honorary D Litt, 1993; Honorary D Waik, 1993. Address: P O Box 4184, New Plymouth, New Zealand.

**MAK Ka-Fung Henry,** b. 26 May 1960, Hong Kong. Medical Doctor; Radiologist. Education: BSc (cum laude), Public Health, University of the Philippines, 1984; MBChB, Chinese University of Hong Kong, 1989; Fellow, Royal College of Radiologists, 1995. Appointments: Medical Officer, Queen Mary Hospital, HKSAR, 1992-96; Senior Medical Officer, Yan Chai/Princess Margaret Hospital, HKSAR, 1997-. Publications: Articles in professional medical journals. Honours: Phi Sigma Society, University of Philippines, 1984; Fellow, Hong Kong Stroke Society; Listed in international biographical dictionaries. Memberships: International Society for MRI in Medicine; American Heart Association; Radiological Society of North America. Address: 7-11 Yan Chai Street, Yan Chai Hospital, Tsuen Wan, NT, Hong Kong SAR, China. E-mail: kfmakhk@netvigator.com

**MAKARCHIAN Masoud,** b. 23 July 1959, Hamadan, Iran. Education: MSc, Engineering, Faculty of Engineering, University of Tehran, Iran, 1987; PhD, Geotechnical Engineering, School of Civil and Mining Engineering, The University of Sydney, Australia, 1995. Appointments: Employed as Lecturer, Bu-Ali Sina University, Iran and transferred to the Ministry of Culture and Higher Education; Design, Control and supervision of bridges (over 15 designed), Civil Engineering Committee, Ministry of Jehad-e-Sazandegi, Iran, 1986-88; Manager, Academic Staff Employment Section, Office of Supervision and Evaluation of Education, Ministry of Culture and Higher Education, Iran, 1988-90; Some casual jobs in teaching and civil engineering design, 1995-; Assistant Professor, Bu-Ali Sina University, Hamadan, Iran, 1995-. Publications: 18 papers published in English include most recently: Review of Rock Slop Stability, 1998; An Experimental Study of Foundation Underpinning by Piles, 2002; $K_0$ Triaxial Tests on C1C Kaolin Clay, 2003; Primary and Secondary Consolidation of Kaolin Clay, 2003 (under review). Memberships: British Geotechnical Association; Iranian Society of Civil Engineers; International Society of Soil Mechanics and Geotechnical Engineering; Indian Geotechnical Society; Iranian Geotechnical Society; Iranian Association of Rail Transport Engineering. Address: Faculty of Engineering, Bu-Ali Sina University, PO Box 65178-4161, Hamadan, Iran. E-mail: makarchian@basu.ac.ir

**MAKEPEACE John,** b. 6 July 1939, Solihull, Warwickshire, England. Designer; Furniture Maker. Education: Denstone College, Staffordshire, 1952-57; Pupil to Keith Cooper, Furniture Maker, 1957-59; City and Guilds Teaching Certificate (Crafts), 1957-59; Study tours in: Scandinavia, 1957; USA, 1961, 1974; Italy, 1968; West Africa, 1972. Appointments: Teacher, City of Birmingham, 1959-61; Established own furniture-making business Director, John Makepeace Furniture Ltd, 1963-; Founder Member, Crafts Council, 1972-77; Furniture commissioned by corporate and private clients in UK, Europe and USA; Consultancy Tours: India, 1974, 1977; Australia, 1980; Japan, 1978, 1994; Korea, 2001; Trustee, Victoria and Albert Museum, 1987-91; Founder and Director, The Parnham Trust, 1976-2001. Publications: Book about his work: Makepeace: A Spirit of Adventure in Craft and Design by Professor Jeremy Myerson; Numerous articles in professional and popular journals. Honours: Observer Design Award, 1972; OBE for services to furniture design, 1988; Master's Award, Worshipful Company of Furniture Makers, 1999; Award of Distinction, The Furniture Society, USA, 2002. Memberships: Fellow: Institute of Management; Chartered Society of Designers; Royal Society for the Arts; Member, Contemporary Art Society; Member, Contemporary Applied Arts. Address: Farrs, Whitcombe Road, Beaminster, Dorset DT8 3NB, England.

**MAKINDE Amos Morakinyo,** b. 3 November 1954, Ado-Ekiti, Nigeria. University Senior Lecturer. m. Foluke, 2 sons, 1 daughter. Education: BSc (Hons), Biology, 1980, MSc, Botany, 1984, Unife; PhD, Botany, Obafemi Awolowo University (Unife), 1991. Appointments: Lecturer, Adeyemi College, Ondo, 1985-94; Botany Lecturer, Obafemi Awolowo University, Ile Ife, 1994-. Publications: Articles in scientific journals including: New Botanist, 1993; Nigerian Journal of Botany, 1993; Experientia, 1994; Journal of Agriculture, Science and Technology, 1994; NJB, 1999; African Journal of Science, 1999. Honour: Reviewer of journal papers for: Nigerian Journal of Botany, Journal of Agriculture Science and

Technology, Environtropica. Memberships: Botanical Society of Nigeria; Nigerian Field Society; Board of Studies, Institute of Agriculture Research and Training, Obafemi Awolowo University, Ibadan. Address: Department of Botany, Obafemi Awolowo University, Ile Ife, Nigeria.

**MAKOWER Peter,** b. 12 September 1932, Greenwich, London, England. Architect; Town Planner. m. Katharine Chadburn, 2 sons, 1 daughter. Education: The Royal Engineers, 1951-52; Territorial Army, 1952-56; Master of Arts, Trinity College, University of Cambridge, 1959; Diploma in Architecture, The Polytechnic, London, 1959; Diploma in Town Planning, University of London, 1969. Appointments: Architect, 1959-62, Associate, 1962-82, Frederick Gibberd Partners, London; Executive Architect, Chapman Taylor Partners, 1982-85; Solo Principal, Peter Makower Architects and Planners, 1985-99. Publications: The World is Not Enough – an account of the filming of part of the river chase in the Bond film of that name; The Boater, The Quarterly Magazine of the Thames Vintage Boat Club, 2000. Honours: Conservation and Design Award, London Borough of Richmond upon Thames and the Mortlake with East Sheen Society; Lay Reader, Church of England. Memberships: Associate, 1961-70, Fellow, 1970-, Royal Institute of British Architects; Royal Town Planning Institute, 1972-. Address: 89 Hartington Road, Chiswick, London W4 3TU, England.

**MAKSIMOVIĆ Čedo,** b. 28 February 1947, Glamočani, Srbac, Yugoslavia. University Professor. m. Kovinka Maksimović, 2 daughters. Education: Dipl Ing, Civil (Water) Engineering, 1971; MSc, Hydraulics, 1974; DSc (PhD), Fluid Mechanics, 1982. Appointment: Professor of Civil and Environmental Engineering, Imperial College, London, 1996-. Publications include: Frontiers in Urban Water Management, 2001; Advances in Water Supply Management, 2003; Life in Wetland, 2004. Honour: IAHR Lecturer of the Year 2003. Memberships: FICE; Chairman, European Division IAHR. Address: 44 Hanover Steps, London W2 2YG, England. E-mail: c.maksimovic@imperial.ac.uk

**MAKTOUM H H Sheikh Maktoum bin Rashid al,** b. 1941. Ruler of Dubai. m. 1971. Appointments: Succeeded his father Sheikh Rashid bin Said al Maktoum, as 5th Sheikh, 1990; Prime Minister, United Arab Emirates, 1971-79, 1991-; Deputy Prime Minister, 1979-90; Vice-President, 1990-. Address: Ruler's Palace, Dubai, United Arab Emirates.

**MAKTOUM Sheikh Mohammed bin Rashid al,** b. 1948. Crown Prince of Dubai; Race Horse Owner. Appointments: Trained in British Army and RAF; Minister of Defence, Dubai; with Brothers Sheikh Maktoum al Maktoum, Sheikh Hamden al-Maktoum and Sheikh Ahmed al-Maktoum has had Racing interests in UK, 1976-; first winner, Hatta, Goodwood, 1977; with Brothers now owns studs, stables, country house and sporting estates in Newmarket and elsewhere in UK; Worldwide racing interests based at Delham Hall Stud, Newmarket; Horses trained in England, Ireland and France; Director, Godolphin Racing, Dubai; f Racing Post (daily), 1986; Owner, Balanchine, winner, Irish Derby, 1994; Winner, numerous classic races, Leading Owner, 1985-1989, 1991-93. Address: Ministry of Defence, PO Box 2838, Dubai, UAE.

**MALFITANO Catherine,** b. 18 April 1948, New York City, New York, USA. Singer (Soprano). Education: High School of Music and Art; Manhattan School of Music; With violinist father and dancer/actress mother; Voice with Henry Lewis. Debut: Nannetta in Falstaff, Central City Opera, 1972. Career: With Minnesota Opera, 1973, New York City Opera, 1973-79, debut as Mimi/La BohÈme; Netherlands Opera:

Susanna in Figaro, 1974, Eurydice, 1975, Mimi, 1977; Tosca 1998; Salzburg Festival: Servilia in Tito, 1976, 1977, 1979, 3 Hoffmann roles, 1981, 1982, Salome, 1992, 1993, Elvira in Giovanni, 1994, 1995, 1996; Jenny in Mahagonny, 1998; Met debut as Gretel, 1979, returning for many other roles; Vienna Staatsoper: Violetta, 1982, Manon, 1984, Grete in Schreker's Der Ferne Klang, 1991, Salome and Butterfly, 1993; Wozzeck, 1997; Maggio Musicale Florence: Suor Angelica, 1983, Jenny in Weill's Mahagonny, 1990, Salome, 1994; Teatro Comunale, Florence: Antonia in Hoffmann, 1980-81, Mimi, 1983, Faust, 1985, Butterfly, 1988, Poppea, 1992; Munich: Berg's Lulu, 1985, Mimi, 1986, Daphne, 1988; Covent Garden: Susanna, Zerlina, 1976, Butterfly, 1988, Lina (Stiffelio), Tosca, Tatyana, 1993, Salome, 1995, 1997; Berlin Deutsche Oper: Butterfly, 1987, Amelia in Boccanegra, Mimi, Susanna, 1989, Salome, 1990; Berlin Staatsoper, Marie (Wozzeck), 1994, Leonore (Fidelio), 1995; Geneva: Fiorilla (Turco), 1985, Poppea, Manon, 1989, Leonore, 1994; La Scala: Daphne, 1988, Butterfly, 1990; Wozzeck, 1997; Lyric Opera, Chicago: Susanna, 1975, Violetta, 1985, Lulu, 1987, Barber's Cleopatra, 1991, Butterfly, 1991-92, Liu, 1992; McTeague/Bolcom, 1992; Makropulos Case, 1995-96; 3 Roles/Il Trittico, 1996; Salome, 1996; Butterfly 1997, 1998; Mahagonny, 1998; View from Bridge/Bolcom, 1999; Macbeth, 1999; World premiere roles created: Conrad Susa's Transformations, 1973, Bilby's Doll (Carlisle Floyd), 1976, Thomas Pasatieri's Washington Square, 1976, William Bolcom's McTeague, 1992. Recordings: Rossini Stabat Mater, conductor Muti; Gounod Roméo et Juliette, conductor Plasson; Strauss's Salome, conductor Dohnányi; Music for Voice and Violin with Joseph Malfitano; Tosca - Zubin Mehta; Others; Videos include Tosca with Domingo; Stiffelio with Carreras and Salome. Honours: Emmy, Best Performance in Tosca film; Honorary Doctorate De Paul University, Chicago.

**MALICK Terrence**, b. 30 November 1943, Ottawa, Illinois, USA. Film Director. Education: Center for Advanced Film Study; American Film Institute. Appointments: Films: Bedlands; Days of Heaven, 1978; The Thin Red Line, 1998; The Moviegoer. Honours: NewYork Film Critics Award, National Society of Film Critics Award, 1978; Cannes Film Festival Award, 1978; Golden Berlin Bear Award, 1999; Chicago Film Critics Association Award, 1999; Golden Satellite Award, 1999. Address: c/o DGA, 7920 Sunset Boulevard, Los Angeles, CA 90046, USA.

**MALIK Zubeida.** Journalist. Appointments: Correspondent, Today programme, Radio 4, Reporter, Newsnight, BBC2; Interviewed key figures including: Kofi Anan, President Musharraf, Tony Blair, Prince Saud Al Faisal, Archbishop Tutu, Hamas Sheikh Yassin. Honours: BT Press Award for Radio News Broadcaster of the Year, 1997; Young Journalist of the Year, Foreign Press Association, 2000; Best Radio News Journalist, EMMA, 2001, 2002; Media Personality of the Year, Asian Women of Achievement Awards, 2002; Winner, Carlton TV Multicultural Achievement Award for Television and Radio, 2003; Voted as one of the Good Housekeeping Role Models, 2004. Publications: Contributions to September 11 2001, Feminist Perceptives. Address: Today Programme, BBC Radio 4, Room G630, Stage 6, Television Centre, Wood Lane, London W12 7RJ, England.

**MALIŃSKI Mirosław**, b. 17 May 1955, Koszalin, Poland. Physicist. m. Teresa Glоćkо, 1 son, 1 daughter. Education: Master of Science, 1979, PhD, 1988, N C University, Toruń, Poland. Appointments: Reliability Specialist, Semicond Research and Product Centre, 1979-93; Tutor, Technical University of Koszalin, 1993-2003; Press Agent of Technical University of Koszalin, 1999-2003. Publications: 66 pieces

in professional scientific journals. Honours: Science Awards of the Rector, Technical University of Koszalin, 1998, 2003; Outstanding Paper Award, IEEE, USA, 1998; West-Pomeranian Nobel Prize Winner, 2003. Address: 30/10 Krzyzanowskiego St, 75-328 Koszalin, Poland. E-mail: mmalin@tu.koszalin.pl

**MALKOVICH John**, b. 9 December 1953, Christopher. m. Glenne Headley, 1982, divorced, 1 daughter, 1 son by Nicoletta Peyran. Education: Eastern Illinois and Illinois State University. Appointments: Co-Founder, Steppenwolf Theatre, Chicago, 1976; Theatre appearances include: True West, 1982; Death of a Salesman, 1984; Burn This, 1987; Director, Balm in Gilead, 1984-85; Arms and the Man, 1985; Coyote Ugly, 1985; The Caretaker, 1986; Burn This, 1990; A Slip of the Tongue, 1992; Libra, 1994; Steppenwolfe, 1994; Film appearances include: Places in the Heart, 1984; The Killing Fields, 1984; Eleni, 1985; Making Mr Right, 1987; The Glass Menagerie, 1987; Empire of the Sun, 1987; Miles from Home, 1988; Dangerous Liaisons, 1989; Jane, La Putaine du roi, 1989; Queen's Logic, 1989; The Sheltering Sky, 1989; The Object of Beauty, 1991; Shadows and Fog, 1992; Of Mice and Men, 1992; Jennifer Eight; Alive; In the Line of Fire; Mary Reilly, 1994; The Ogre, 1995; Mulholland Falls, 1996; Portrait of a Lady, 1996; Con Air; The Man in the Iron Mask, 1997; Rounders, 1998; Tune Regained, 1998; Being John Malkovich, 1999; The Libertine, 1999; Ladies Room, 1999; Joan of Arc, 1999; Shadow of the Vampire, 2000; Je Rentre à la Maison, 2001; Hotel, 2001; Knockaround Guys, 2001; The Dancer Upstairs, director and producer, 2002; Ripley's Game, 2003; Johnny English, 2003; Executive Producer, The Accidental Tourist. Address: c/o Artists Independent Network, 32 Tavistock Street, London, WC2E 7PB, England.

**MALLARD John Rowland**, b. 14 January 1927, Northampton, England. Professor of Medical Physics and Medical Engineering. m. Fiona Lawrance, 1 son, 1 daughter. Education: BSc honours, Physics, University College, Nottingham, 1947; PhD, Magnetism, 1952, DSc, Medical Physics, 1972, University of Nottingham. Appointments: Assistant Physicist, Radium Institute, Liverpool, 1951-53; Senior then Principal Physicist 1953-56, Head, Department of Physics, 1956-62, Hammersmith Hospital, London; Reader, Medical Physics, Postgraduate Medical School, University of London, 1962-64; Reader, Biophysics, St Thomas's Hospital Medical School, London, 1964-65; Professor of Medical Physics, Head of Department of Bio-Medical Physics and Bio-Engineering, University of Aberdeen and Grampian Health Board, 1965-92. Publications: Over 240 papers, review articles and lectures in medical and scientific journals. Honours include: OBE, 1992; Royal Society Wellcome Gold Medal, 1984; Royal Society Mullard Gold Medal, 1990; Honorary DSc, University of Hull, 1994; Norman Veall Prize Medal, British Nuclear Medicine Society, 1995; Honorary DSc, University of Nottingham, 1996; Keith of Dunottar Silver Medal, Royal Scottish Society of Arts, 1996; Honorary DSc, University of Aberdeen, 1997; Royal Gold Medal, Royal Society of Edinburgh, 2002; Gold Medal, Royal College of Radiologists, 2004; Medal of European Federation of Organisations of Medical Physics, 2004; Freedom of the City of Aberdeen as a Pioneer of Medical Imaging, 2004. Memberships include: Fellow: Royal Society of Edinburgh; Royal Academy of Engineering; Institution of Electrical Engineers; Institute of Physics; Royal College of Pathologists; Honorary Fellow: Institute of Physics and Engineering in Medicine; British Institute of Radiology; British Nuclear Medicine Society; Founder Fellow, International Society of Magnetic Resonance and Medicine; Founder President, International Union of Physics and Engineering in Medicine. Address: 121 Anderson Drive, Aberdeen, AB15 6BG, Scotland. E-mail: h.parry@biom ed.abdn.ac.uk

**MALLET Philip Louis Victor,** b. 3 February 1926, London, England. Member of HM Diplomatic Service (Retired). m. Mary Moyle Grenfell Borlase, 3 sons. Education: Balliol College, Oxford, England. Appointments: Army, 1944-47; HM Foreign Diplomatic Service, 1949-82; Served in Iraq, Cyprus, Aden, Germany, Tunisia, Sudan and Sweden; British High Commissioner in Guyana and non-resident Ambassador to Suriname, 1978-82. Honour: CMG. Address: Wittersham House, Wittersham, Kent TN30 7ED, England.

**MALLICK Netar Prakash,** b. 3 August 1935. Emeritus Professor; Deputy Lieutenant of Greater Manchester. m. Mary Wilcockson, 1960, 3 daughters. Education: Queen Elizabeth's Grammar School, Blackburn; BSc (Hons), 1956, MB ChB, 1969, Manchester University. Appointments: Surgical Resident, Fellow, Harvard University, 1960; Department of Medicine, Welsh National School of Medicine, 1963-67; Lecturer, 1967-72, Senior Lecturer, 1972-92, Honorary Professor in Renal Medicine, 1992-94, Professor in Renal Medicine, 1994-2000, Emeritus Professor in Renal Medicine, 2000-, Manchester University; Physician in Charge, Department of Renal Medicine, Manchester Royal Infirmary, 1973-92; Vice Chairman, Blackburn, Hyndburn and Ribble Valley Health Authority, 1985-90; Medical Director, Central Manchester Hospitals Healthcare Trust, 1997-2000; Adviser on renal disease to Chief Medical Officer, Department of Health, 1991-97; Deputy Lieutenant of Greater Manchester, 1999-; Medical Director, Advisory Committee on Distinction Awards, 1999-2003; High Sheriff of Greater Manchester, 2002-03; Medical Director, Advisory Committee on Clinical Excellence Awards, 2003-. Publications: Papers on renal disease and health provision in learned journals. Honours: Knight Bachelor,1998; Maitre Commanderie de Bordeaux a Manchester, 2001-; Lifetime Achievement Award, Lloyds TSB Asian Jewel Awards, 2002. Memberships: FRCP, 1976; President, Manchester Literary and Philosophical Society, 1986-88; President, Renal Association of Great Britain and Ireland, 1988-91; Chairman, European Dialysis and Transplantation Association Registry, 1991-94; FRCPE, 1992; President, Union Europeene des Medecins Specialites, 1993-97; FRCPI (Hon), 2000; FRCS (Ed) hon, 2005; Inaugural Fellow, British Renal Society, 2002. Address: Department of Renal Medicine, Central Manchester and Manchester Children's Healthcare NHS Trust, Manchester Royal Infirmary, Manchester M13 9WL, England.

**MALLYA Ramesh,** b. 15 May 1943, Mangalore, India. Consultant Physician and Rheumatologist. m. Sheila Mallya. Education: MBBS, 1970; MCRP (UK), 1976; FRCP Lond., 1992; FRCP Edin., 1996; FACR (USA), 1998. Appointments: House Officer, 1969-70, Senior House Officer, Medicine, 1971-73, Registrar, Medicine, 1974-79, Essex County Hospital, Colchester, Royal Victoria Infirmary, Bournemouth, Westminster Hospital, London; Senior Registrar Rheumatology, 1980-83; King's Hospital, London, Senior Registrar in General Medicine and Rheumatology, 1983-85; Guy's Hospital, London; Currently Consultant Physician and Rheumatologist, Halton General Hospital, Runcorn, Cheshire, BUPA North Cheshire Hospital Stretton, Cheshire, Grosvenor Nuffield Hospital, Chester, Cheshire. Publications: Index of disease activity in Rheumatoid Arthritis (RA); Anti-keratin antibodies in RA; Immune complexes in RA and Acute phase proteins in Rheumatic disorders; Several hundreds of citations on these articles from all over the world. Honours: Registrar to Sir Richard Bayliss KCVO and Professor Malcolm Milne FRS; Examiner, 1995-, Senior Examiner, 1999-, for Royal College of Physicians, London and Edinburgh; Examiner for MB ChB, University of Liverpool, 1999-; Cleveland Foundation sponsorship to visit medical schools and universities in China, 2001; Sponsorship by University of Colombo to act as external examiner on behalf of Royal College of Physicians (UK) and produce a report on the conduct and standard of MD clinical examination, 2004; Member of Peer Review Group, North West Rheumatology; Representative of Royal College of Physicians, Consultant Appointment Committee. Memberships: British Medical Association, Royal College of Physicians, London and Edinburgh; Royal Society of Medicine; British Society for Rheumatology; American College of Rheumatology. Address: North Cheshire Hospitals NHS Trust, Halton General Hospital, Hospital Way, Runcorn, Cheshire WA7 2DA, England. E-mail: ramesh.mallya@nch.nhs.uk

**MALONE Vincent,** b. 11 September 1931, Liverpool, England. Bishop. Education: BSc, Liverpool University, 1959; Cert Ed, 1960, Dip Ed, 1962, Cambridge University. Appointments: Chaplain to Notre Dame Training College, Liverpool, 1955-59; Assistant Priest, St Anne's, Liverpool, 1960-61; Assistant Master, Cardinal Allen Grammar School, Liverpool, 1961-71; Chaplain to Liverpool University, 1971-79; Administrator (Dean), Liverpool Metropolitan Cathedral, 1979-89; Auxiliary Bishop of Liverpool, 1989-. Membership: Fellow, College of Preceptors. Address: 17 West Oakhill Park, Liverpool L13 4BN, England. E-mail: vmalone@onetel.com

**MALOUF (George Joseph) David,** b. 20 March 1934, Brisbane, Queensland, Australia. Poet; Novelist. Education: BA, University of Queensland, 1954. Appointments: Assistant Lecturer in English, University of Queensland, 1955-57; Supply Teacher, London, 1959-61; Teacher of Latin and English, Holland Park Comprehensive, 1962; Teacher, St Anselm's Grammar School, 1962-68; Senior Tutor and Lecturer in English, University of Sydney, 1968-77. Publications: Poetry: Bicycle and Other Poems, 1970; Neighbours in a Thicket: Poems, 1974; Poems, 1975-1976, 1976; Wild Lemons, 1980; First Things Last, 1981; Selected Poems, 1981; Selected Poems, 1959-1989, 1994. Fiction: Johnno (novel), 1975; An Imaginary Life (novel), 1978; Child's Play (novella), 1981; The Bread of Time to Come (novella), 1981, republished as Fly Away Peter, 1982; Eustace (short story), 1982; The Prowler (short story), 1982; Harland's Half Acre (novel), 1984; Antipodes (short stories), 1985; The Great World (novel), 1990; Remembering Babylon (novel), 1993; The Conversations at Curlow Creek (novel), 1996; Dream Stuff (stories), 2000. Play: Blood Relations, 1988. Opera Libretti: Voss, 1986; Mer de Glace; Baa Baa Black Sheep, 1993. Memoir: Twelve Edmondstone Street, 1985. Editor: We Took Their Orders and Are Dead: An Anti-War Anthology, 1971; Gesture of a Hand (anthology), 1975. Contributions to: Four Poets: David Malouf, Don Maynard, Judith Green, Rodney Hall, 1962; Australian; New York Review of Books; Poetry Australia; Southerly; Sydney Morning Herald. Honours: Grace Leven Prize for Poetry, 1974; Gold Medals, Australian Literature Society, 1975, 1982; Australian Council Fellowship, 1978; New South Wales Premier's Award for Fiction, 1979; Victorian Premier's Award for Fiction, 1985; New South Wales Premier's Award for Drama, 1987; Commonwealth Writer's Prize, 1991; Miles Franklin Award, 1991; Prix Femina Etranger, 1991; Inaugural International IMPAC Dublin Literary Award, 1996; Neustadt Laureat, 2000. Address: 53 Myrtle Street, Chippendale, New South Wales 2008, Australia.

**MALPAS James Spencer,** b. 15 September 1931, Wolverhampton, England. Medical Practitioner. m. Joyce May Cathcart, 2 sons. Education: St Bartholomew's Hospital Medical College, University of London, England 1949-55; Postgraduate, Royal Postgraduate Medical School, Hammersmith Hospital, London, 1960, Nuffield Department of Medicine, Oxford, England, 1962-65. Appointments: Medical Specialist, Royal

Airforce, 1957-60; House Physician, Hammersmith Hospital Royal Postgraduate Medical School, 1960-61; Lecturer in Medicine, Oxford University, 1962-65; Dean of the Medical College, 1969-72, Director, ICRF Department of Medical Oncology, 1976-85, Clinical Director, ICRF, 1985-90, Professor of Medical Oncology, 1979-95, Vice President, Medical College, 1987-95, St Bartholomew's Hospital; Professor Emeritus, London University, 1995-; Elected Master of the London Charterhouse, 1996-2001; Currently Trustee, St Bartholomew's London Charitable Foundation. Publications: Over 200 peer-reviewed articles on adult and paediatric cancer and haematology; Co-editor, Myeloma Biology and Management, 3rd edition 2003; Editor, Cancer in Children, 1996. Honours include: Lockyer Lecture, Royal College of Physicians, 1978; Skinner Medal, Royal College of Radiologists, 1986; Freeman of the City of London, 1988; Subhod-Mitra Gold Medal, Delhi, India, 1991; Medicus Hippocraticus Prize, Greece, 1996, Memberships: Member of many medical societies; Fellow, Royal College of Physicians; Fellow, Royal College of Radiology; Fellow, Royal College of Paediatricians and Child Health; Fellow, Royal Institution of Great Britain and Northern Ireland. Address: 253 Lauderdale Tower, Barbican, London EC2Y 8BY, England. E-mail: jmalpas@aol.com

**MALPAS John Peter Ramsden,** b. 14 December 1927, Colombo, Ceylon. Stockbroker. m. Rosamond Margaret Burn, 3 sons. Education: MA (Oxon), P.P.E., New College Oxford. Appointments: Imperial Chemical Industries, 1951-56; Chase, Henderson and Tennant, 1956-58; Deputy Chairman, Quilter Goodison, 1959-87; London Stock Exchange, 1961-88; Non Executive Director, Penny & Giles International, 1988-92; Management Board, 1988-2002, Honorary Treasurer, 1988-98, Royal Hospital for Neuro Disability; Non Executive Director, West Wittering Estate, 1998. Honour: MA (Oxon). Memberships: Itchenor Sailing Club; Ski Club Great Britain. Address: 48 Berwyn Road, Richmond, Surrey TW10 5BS, England. E-mail: peter.malpas@ukgateway.net

**MAMET David Alan,** b. 30 November 1947, Chicago, USA. Playwright; Director. m. (1) Lindsay Crouse, 1977, divorced, (2) Rebecca Pidgeon, 1991. Education: Goddard College, Plainfield, Vermont. Appointments: Artist in Residence, Goddard College, 1971-73; Artistic Director, St Nicholas Theatre Company, Chicago, 1973-75; Guest Lecturer, University of Chicago, 1975, 1979; New York University, 1981; Associate Artistic Director, Goodman Theatre, Chicago, 1978; Associate Professor of Film, Columbia University, 1988; Director, House of Games, 1986; Things Change, 1987; Homicide, 1991; Play, A Life in the Theatre, 1989. Publications: The Duck Variations, 1971; Sexual Perversity in Chicago, 1973; The Reunion, 1973; Squirrels, 1974; American Buffalo, 1976; A Life in the Theatre, 1976; The Water Engine, 1976; The Woods, 1977; Lone Canoe, 1978; Prairie du Chien, 1978; Lakeboat, 1980; Donny March, 1981; Edmond, 1982; The Disappearance of the Jews, 1983; The Shawl, 1985; Glengarry Glen Ross, 1984; Speed-the-Plow, 1987; Bobby, Guild in Hell, 1989; The Old Neighborhood, 1991; Oleanna, 1992; Ricky Jay and his 52 Assistants, 1994; Death Defying Acts, 1996; Boston Marriage, 1999; Screenplays: The Postman Always Rings Twice, 1979; The Verdict, 1980; The Untouchables, 1986; House of Games, 1986; Things Change, 1987; We're No Angels, 1987; Oh Hell!, 1991; Homicide, 1991; Hoffa, 1991; Glengarry Glen Ross, 1992; The Rising Sun, 1992; Oleanna, 1994; The Edge, 1996; The Spanish Prisoner, 1996; Wag the Dog, 1997; Boston Marriage, 2001; Childrens' books: Mr Warm and Cold, 1985; The Owl, 1987; The Winslow Bay, 1999; Essays: Writing in Restaurants, 1986; Some Freaks, 1989; On Directing Film, 1990; The Hero Pony, 1990; The Cabin, 1992; A Whore's Profession, 1993; The Cryptogram, 1994; The

Village (novel), 1994; Passover, 1995; Make-Believe Town: Essays and Remembrances, 1996; Plays, 1996; Plays 2, 1996; The Duck and the Goat, 1996; The Old Religion, 1996; True and False, 1996; The Old Neighbourhood, 1998; Jafsie and John Henry, 2000; State and Maine, (writer, director), 2000. Honours: Outer Critics Circle Award, for contributions to American Theatre, 1978; Honorary DLitt (Dartmouth College), 1996; Pulitzer Prize for Drama, New York Drama Critics Award. Address: c/o Howard Rosenstone, Rosenstone/Wender Agency, 38 East 29th Street, 10th Floor, New York, NY 10016, USA.

**MAN Shiu Wai Sebastian,** b. 11 June 1957, Hong Kong. Businessman. m. Chan Miu Lan Christina, 2 sons. Education: BS, 1979, MS, 1980, Massachusetts Institute of Technology, USA; MBA, Harvard Business School, USA, 1985. Appointments: Assistant Director, Chemical Asia Limited, 1987-89; Director, Hoare Govertt Asia Limited, 1987-89; Chief Executive, Chung Mei International Holding Limited, 1990-. Memberships: Board Member, Massachusetts Institute of Technology HK Alumni Association, 1980-; Board Member, Harvard University Alumni Association, 1985-; Director, Tung Wah Group of Hospitals, 1994-98; Charter Member, 1995-, President, 1996-97, Lions Club of Metropolitan Hong Kong; Member, 1995-, Forum Chairman, 1997-99, Young Presidents Organisation; Honorary President, Man Clansmen Association, 1997-; Executive Committee Member, International Chamber of Commerce, Hong Kong, China Business Council, 1998-; Hong Kong Racehorse Owners Association, 1999-; Committee Member, Hong Kong and China Committee United National Volunteers, 1999-; The Chinese People's Political Consultative Conference, Shenzhen-Baoan Committee, 1999-; Supporter Member, Pacific Basin Economic Council, Hong Kong, China Member Committee, 1999-; Committee Member, Hong Kong Committee for Pacific Economic Co-operation, 2002-; Director, Chinese Entrepreneurs Organisation, 2002-; Vice-Secretary, The Return of Chinese Fellowship Association, Shenzhen-Baoan, 2000-; HKSAR Costs Committee (Legal Society), 2004-2007. Address: Chung Mei Industries Ltd, Blk B, 11/F, Chung Mei Centre, 15B Hing Yip Street, Kwun Tong, KLN, Hong Kong. E-mail: chungmei@chungmei.com

**MANA Samira Al,** b. 25 December 1935, Basra, Iraq. Writer. m. Salah Niazi, July 1959, 2 daughters. Education: BA, Honours, University of Baghdad, 1958; Postgraduate Diploma in Librarianship, Ealing Technical College, 1976; Chartered Librarian, British Library Association, 1980. Appointments: Arabic Language and Literature Teacher, Secondary School, Baghdad, 1958-65; Chief Librarian, Iraqi Cultural Centre, London, 1976-81; Assistant Editor, Alightrab Al-Adabi (Literature of the Exiled), 1985-2002. Publications: The Forerunners and the Newcomers (novel), 1972; The Song (short stories), 1976; A London Sequel (novel), 1979; Only a Half (play in two acts), 1979; The Umbilical Cord (novel), 1990; The Oppressers (novel), 1997; The Soul and Other Stories, 1999; Just Look at Me (novel), 2002. Contributions to: Alightrab Al-Adabi; Many short stories in Arabic magazines; Translations in Dutch and English periodicals. Address: 46 Tudor Drive, Kingston-Upon-Thames, Surrey KT2 5PZ, England.

**MANABE Syukuro,** b. 21 September 1931, Japan. Research Scientist. m. Nobuko Nakamura, 26 February 1962, 2 daughters. Education: BA, 1953, MA, 1956, DSc, 1958, University of Tokyo; Honorary Doctor of Science, McGill University, 2004. Appointments: Research Meteorologist, General Circulation Research Section, US Weather Bureau, Washington, DC, 1958-63; Senior Research Meteorologist, Geophysical Fluid Dymanics Laboratory, Environmental Science Services Administration, Washington, DC, 1963-68; Senior Research Meteorologist,

Geophysical Fluid Dynamics Laboratory, National Oceanic and Atmospheric Administration, Princeton, New Jersey, 1968-97; Director, Global Warming Research Program, Frontier Research System for Global Change, Tokyo, Japan, 1997-2001; Visiting Research Collaborator, Program in Atmospheric and Organic Sciences, Princeton University, USA, 2002-. Publications: Over 140 papers in professional journals. Honours: Rossby Research Medal, American Meterological Society; Revelle Medal, American Geophysical Union; Milankovich Medal, European Geophysical Society; Blue Planet Prize, Asahi Glass Foundation; Asah Prize, Asahi Newspaper Publishing Co; Volvo Prize, Volvo Prize Foundation. Memberships: US National Academy of Sciences; Academia Europaea; Royal Society of Canada; Honorary Member, American Meteorological Society; Honorary Member, Japan Meterological Society; Fellow, American Geophysical Union; Fellow, AAAS. Address: 6 Governors Lane, Princeton, NJ 08540, USA.

**MANDAI Shigemi,** b. 24 February 1947, Kobe City, Hyogo Prefecture, Japan. Mechanical Engineer; Researcher. m. Mikiko Yoshinaka, 1 son, 2 daughters. Education: BS, Doshisha University, Kyoto, Japan, 1969; PhD, Osaka University, Suita, Japan, 1996. Appointments: Researcher, 1969-, Chief Engineer, 2001-, R & D Center, Mitsubishi Heavy Industries, Ltd; Executive Advisory Engineer, Koryo Engineering, Ltd, 2003; Lecturer, Doshisha University, 1996-2000; Chairman, Combustion Technology and the Relating Issues, Japan Society of Mechanical Engineers, 1993-95; Vice-President, 1997-98, Director, 1995-2000, Combustion Society of Japan. Publications: High Temperature Gasification of Coal and its Utilization, 1994; Combustion Engineering Handbook, 1995; New Energy Engineering Book, 1996; Catalysis series volume 12 1996; Practical Combustor Design and its Control, 2001. Honours: J P Davis Best Application Paper Award, ASME, 1986; Engineering Award, JSME, 1994; Best Paper Award, Japan Institute of Energy, 1999; Invention Bounty Award of Kinki district, 2003; Invention Award of Hyogo Prefecture, 2004. Memberships: Japan Society of Mechanical Engineers; Combustion Society Japan; Japan Institute of Energy; Japanese Gas Turbine Society. Address: Koryo Engineering Ltd, 2-1-1 Shinhama Arai-cho, Takasago, Hyogo 676-8686, Japan. E-mail: sigemi_mandai@mhi.co.jp

**MANDAL Anil Kumar,** b. 2 January 1958, West Bengal, India. Doctor. m. Vijaya Kumari Gothwal. Education: MBBS, NRS Medical College, Calcutta, India, 1983. MD, All India Institute of Medical Sciences, New Delhi, 1987; Diplomate, National Board for Practice of Ophthalmology, 1987. Appointments: Junior Ophthalmologist, 1990, Assistant Ophthalmologist, 1991-94, Associate Ophthalmologist, 1994-97, Head, Children's Eye Care Center, 1997-, Professor of Ophthalmology, 1998-, L V Prasad Eye Institute, Hyderabad. Publications: In professional journals. Honours: Best Resident, Ophthalmologic Research Association, AIIMS, New Delhi, 1990; Best Thematic Film, All India Ophthalmological Society, India, 1997; Professor P Siva Reddy Gold Medal, All India Ophthalmological Society, 1997; Shanti Swarup Bhatnager Prize, CSIR, 2003. Memberships: Life Member, All India Ophthalmological Society; Elected International Member, American Academy of Ophthalmology; International Member, Association for Research and Vision in Ophthalmology. Address: LV Prasad Eye Institute, L V Prasad Marq, Banjara Hills, Hyderabad 500 034 AP, India.

**MANDEL H(arold) George,** b. 6 June 1924, Berlin. Pharmacologist. m. Marianne Klein, 2 daughters. Education: BS, 1944, Yale University; PhD, 1949. Appointments: Laboratory Instructor in Chemistry, Yale University, 1942-44; 1947-49; Research Associate, Department of Pharmacology,

George Washington University, 1949-50, Assistant Research Professor, 1950-52, Associate Professor Pharmacology, 1952-58, Professor, 1958-, Chairman, Department of Pharmacology, 1960-96. Publications: Numerous publications on cancer chemotherapy, mechanism of growth inhibition, antimetabolites, drug disposition, chemical carcinogenesis. Honours: Advanced Commonwealth Fund Fellow, Molteno Institute, Cambridge (England) University, 1956; Commonwealth Fund Fellow, University Auckland, New Zealand, and University Medical Sciences, Bangkok, Thailand, 1964; American Cancer Society Eleanor Roosevelt International Fellow, Chester Beatty Research Institute, London, 1970-71; several other scholarships and research grants; Recipient, John J Abel Award in Pharmacology, Eli Lilly & Co, 1958; Distinguished Achievement Award, Washington Academy of Sciences, 1958; Golden Apple Teaching Award, AMA, 1969, 1985, 1997; George Washington Award, 1998. Memberships: Fellow, Medical Research Council Toxicology Unit, Carshalton, England, 1986; Cancer Chemotherapy Com International Union Against Cancer, 1966-73; Board of Advisors, Roswell Park Cancer Institute, Buffalo, New York, 1972-74; Fellow, Lyon, France, 1989; Honorary Fellow, University College, London, 1993-; Consultant, Bureau of Drugs, FDA, 1975-79, EPA, 1978-82; Member various NRC-NAS committees, 1965-86; AAAS; American Chemical Society; American Society Biochemistry and Molecular Biology; President, 1973-74, American Society Pharmacology and Experimental Therapeutics; Chairman, National Caucus of Basic Biomedical Science Chairs, 1991-; American Association for Cancer Research; President, 1976-78, Association for Medical School Pharmacology. Address: 4956 Sentinel Drive, Bethesda, MD 20816 3562, USA.

**MANDELA Nelson Rolihlahla,** b. 1918, Umtata, Transkei. President (retired); Lawyer. m. (1) Evelyn Mandela, divorced 1957, 4 children, 2 deceased, (2) Winnie Mandela, 1958, divorced 1996, 2 daughters, (3) Graca Machel, 1998. Education: University College, Fort Hare; University of Witwatersrand. Appointments: Legal Practice, Johannesburg, 1952; On trial for treason, 1956-61 (acquitted); Sentenced to 5 years imprisonment, 1962; Tried for further charges, 1963-64; sentenced to life imprisonment; Released, 1990; President, African National Congress, 1991-97; President of South Africa, 1994-99; Chancellor, University of the North, 1992-; Joint President, United World Colleges, 1995-. Publications: No Easy Walk to Freedom, 1965; How Far We Slaves Have Come: South Africa and Cuba in Today's World, co-author, 1991; Nelson Mandela Speaks: Forging a non-racial democratic South Africa, 1993; Long Walk to Freedom, 1994. Honours: Jawaharlal Nehru Award, India, 1979; Simon Bolivar Prize, UNESCO, 1983; Sakharov Prize, 1988; Liberty Medal, USA, 1993; Nobel Peace Prize (Joint Winner), 1993; Mandela-Fulbright Prize, 1993; Honorary Bencher, Lincoln's Inn, 1994; Tun Abdul Razak Award, 1994; Anne Frank Medal, 1994; International Freedom Award, 2000; Honorary QC, 2000; Honorary Freeman of London; Numerous honorary doctorates. Address: c/o ANC, 51 Plein Street, Johannesburg 2001, South Africa.

**MANDELBROT Benoit B,** b. 20 November 1924, Warsaw, Poland (French Citizen). Mathematician. Education: Graduated, Ecole Polytechnique, Paris, 1947; MS, California Institute of Technology, 1948; PhD, Sorbonne, Paris, 1952. Appointments: Staff Member, Centre National de la Recherche Scientifique, Paris, 1949-57; Institute of Advance Study, New Jersey, 1953-54; Assistant Professor of Mathematics, University of Geneva, 1955-57; Junior Professor of Applied Mathematics, Lille University; Professor of Mathematical Analysis, Ecole Polytechnique, Paris; Research Staff Member, IBM Thomas J Watson Research Centre, New York, 1958; IBM Fellow, 1974;

Abraham Robinson Professor of Mathematical Science, 1987-99, Sterling Professor, 1999-, Yale University, New Haven, Connecticut; Visiting Professor, Harvard University, 1962-64, 1979-80, 1984-87; Devised the term Fractal to describe a curve or surface. Publications: Logique, Langage et Théorie de l'Information, co-author, 1957; Fractals: Form, Chance and Dimension, 1977; Fractal Geometry of Nature, 1982; Fractals and Scaling in Finance: Discontinuity, Concentration, Risk, 1997; Fractales, hasard et finance, 1997; Multifractals and Low-Frequency Noise: Wild Self-Affinity in Physics, 1998; Gaussian Self-Similarity and Fractals, 2000; Nel mondo dei frattali, 2001; Globality, The Earth, Low-frequency Noise and R/S, 2002; Fractals, Graphics and Mathematical Education, with M L Frame, 2002; Fractals in Chaos and Statistical Physics, 2003; Numerous scientific papers; Editorial Boards, several journals. Honours: Several honorary degrees; Numerous awards and medals including Chevalier, L'Ordre de la Légion d'Honneur, 1989; L F Richardson Medal for Geophysics, 2000; Procter Prize of Sigma Xi, 2002; Japan Prize for Science and Tech, 2002. Address: Mathematics Department, Yale University, New Haven, CT 06520, USA.

**MANDELL Gordon Keith, S,** b. 6 March 1947, New York City, New York, USA. Aerospace Engineer. Education: BS, Aeronautics, Astronautics, 1969, MS, Aeronautics, Astronautics, 1970, Massachusetts Institute of Technology. Appointments: Staff Member, Fluid Dynamics Research Laboratory, Massachusetts Institute of Technology, 1970-72; Consulting Aerospace Engineer, 1973-76; Federal Aviation Administration Designated Engineering Representative, 1976-82; Federal Aviation Administration Aerospace Engineer, determining compliance of aircraft designs with safety standards, 1982-. Publications: Missile Recovery by Extensible Flexwing, 1966; Numerous articles in Model Rocketry magazine, 1968-72; Co-author, Lenticular Re-entry Vehicle, 1970; Co-author, editor, book, Topics in Advanced Model Rocketry, 1973. Honours: Louis de Florez Award; James Means Memorial Prize; Grumman Scholar, Massachusetts Institute of Technology, 1965-69; National Science Foundation Fellow, Massachusetts Institute of Technology, 1969-70; Admitted to: Tau Beta Pi; Sigma Gamma Tau; Sigma Xi. Memberships: National Association of Rocketry; National Space Society; Planetary Society; Team Seti. Address: Post Office Box 671388, Chugiak, AK 99567-1388, USA.

**MANDELSON Peter Benjamin,** b. 21 October 1953, England. Politician. Education: St Catherine's College, Oxford. Appointments: Joined TUC, with Economic Department, 1977-78; Chair, British Youth Council, 1978-80; Producer, London Weekend TV, 1982-85; Director of Campaigns and Communications, Labour Party, 1985-90; MP for Hartlepool, 1992-2004; Opposition Whip, 1994-97, Shadow Frontbench Spokesman on Civil Service, 1995-96, on Election Planning, 1996-97; Chair, General Election Planning Group, 1995-97; Minister without Portfolio, 1997-98; Secretary of State for Trade and Industry, 1998; for Northern Ireland, 1999-2001 (resigned); EU Commissioner for Trade, 2004-; Vice-Chair, British Council, 1999-. Publications: Youth Unemployment: Causes and Cures, 1977; Broadcasting and Youth, 1980; The Blair Revolution: Can New Labour Deliver? 1996. Memberships include: Council, London Borough of Lambeth, 1979-82; International Advisory Committee, Centre for European Policy Studies, 1993-; Trustee, Whitechapel Art Gallery, 1994-; Panel 2000, 1998-.

**MANFREDI Roberto,** b. 22 June 1964, Bologna, Italy. Researcher. Education: MD, 1988; Infectious Disease Specialist, University of Bologna, 1992. Appointments: Researcher, Grantee, 1986-91, Medical Assistant, Infectious Diseases, 1991-93, Associate, 1993-, Contract Professor of Infectious Diseases, Postgraduate School of Infectious Diseases, 1996-, University of Bologna; Board of Associate Professors of Infectious Diseases, 2003. Publications: Over 1500 scientific publications in textbooks, congress proceedings and professional journals; 12 monographs. Honours: L Concato Award, University of Bologna, 1988; F Schiassi Award, 1989; G Salvioli Award, University of Bologna, 1991; FESCI Young Investigator Award, 2000. Memberships: International Society of Infectious Diseases; Italian Society for Infectious and Parasite Diseases; European AIDS Clinical Society; Editorial Board and Reviewer of many scientific journals. Address: Via di Corticella 45, I-40128, Bologna, Italy.

**MANILOW Barry (Pinkus),** b. 17 June 1946, Brooklyn, New York, USA. Singer; Musician (piano); Songwriter. Education: Advertising, New York City College; Musical Education: NY College Of Music; Juilliard School Of Music. Career: Film Editor, CBS-TV; Writer, numerous radio and television commercials; Member, cabaret duo Jeanne and Barry, 1970-72; MD, arranger, producer for Bette Midler; Solo entertainer, 1974-; Numerous world-wide tours; Major concerts include: Gala charity concert for Prince and Princess of Wales, Royal Albert Hall, 1983; Arista Records 15th Anniversary concert, Radio City Music Hall, 1990; Royal Variety performance, London, 1992; Television film Copacabana, 1985; Numerous television specials and television appearances; Broadway show, Barry Manilow At The Gershwin, 1989; West End musical, Copacabana, 1994. Recordings: Albums include: Barry Manilow, 1973; Barry Manilow II, 1975; Tryin' To Get The Feelin', 1976; This One's For You, 1977; Barry Manilow Live (Number 1, US), 1977; Even Now, 1978; Manilow Magic, 1979; Greatest Hits, 1979; One Voice, 1979; Barry, 1981; If I Should Love Again, 1981; Barry Live In Britain, 1982; I Wanna Do It With You, 1982; Here Comes The Night, 1983; A Touch More Magic, 1983; Greatest Hits Volume II, 1984; 2.00 AM Paradise Café, 1984; Barry Manilow, Grandes Exitos En Espanol, 1986; Swing Street, 1988; Songs To Make The Whole World Sing, 1989; Live On Broadway, 1990; The Songs 1975-1990, 1990; Because It's Christmas, 1990; Showstoppers, 1991; The Complete Collection And Then Some, 1992; Hidden Treasures, 1993; The Platinum Collection, 1993; Singin' with the Big Bands, 1994; Another Life, 1995; Summer of '78, 1996; Manilow Sings Sinatra, 1998; Hit singles include: Mandy (Number 1, US), 1975; Could It Be Magic, 1975; I Write The Songs (Number 1, US), 1976; Tryin' To Get The Feelin', 1976; Weekend In New England, 1977; Looks Like We Made It (Number 1, US), 1977; Can't Smile Without You, 1978; Copacabana (At The Copa), from film Foul Play, 1978; Somewhere In The Night, 1979; Ships, 1979; I Made It Through The Rain, 1981; Let's Hang On, 1981; Bermuda Triangle, 1981; I Wanna Do It With You, 1982. Honours: Grammy Awards: Song Of The Year, I Write The Songs, 1977; Best Male Pop Vocal Performance, Copacabana (At The Copa), 1979; Emmy Award, The Barry Manilow Special, 1977; American Music Awards, Favourite Male Artist, 1978-80; Star on Hollywood Walk Of Fame, 1980; Tony Award, Barry Manilow On Broadway show, 1976; Academy Award Nomination, Ready To Take A Chance Again, 1978; Hitmaker Award, Songwriters Hall Of Fame, 1991; Named, Humanitarian of the Year, Starlight Foundation, 1991; Platinum and Gold records. Address: Arista Records, 6 W 57th Street, NY 10019, USA.

**MANJORO Bartholomew,** b. 25 December 1945, Rusapi, Zimbabwe. Bishop. m. Apphia, 2 sons, 1 daughter. Education: Diploma, Administration, ICS London, 1976; Associate of Practical Theology Degree, Christ for the Nations, Dallas, Texas, USA, 1984; Doctor of Divinity, Brownwell University,

1986. Appointments: Founder and President of: Faith World Ministries, Faith World Bible College, Faith Heights Business Fellowship. Publications: Gifts and Ministry of the Holy Spirit; Destined to Rule; Church Administration; Dynamics of Faith; The Five Fold Ministry. Honour: Nominated Man of the Year 2003. Memberships: CFN Association of Bible Colleges; CFN Alumni Ministers Fellowship; Full Gospel Businessmen's Fellowship; International Charismatic Bible Ministries; Representative C. Embassy Jerusalem. Address: PO Box 3772, Harare, Zimbabwe. E-mail: fwm@ecoweb.co.zw Website www.fwm.co.zw

**MANKUTA Harry,** b. 15 February 1924, Ciechanowiec, Poland. Aeronautical Engineer. m. Sara Akerman, 2 sons, 2 daughters. Education: BS, Mechanical Engineering, City College of New York, 1944; ESMDT, Fluid Mechanics, Vector Analysis, NACA, Cleveland, Ohio, 1946; MS, Aeronautical Engineering, Case Institute of Technology, 1948. Appointments: Guest Lecturer in Heat Power Engineering, Israel Institute of Technology, 1954-55; Development testing of axial-flow compressors for Fairchild J-83 engine, Gas Turbine Laboratory, Fairchild Engine Division, Deerpark; Preliminary design, propulsion analysis for VTOL aircraft, proposals on various ground effect machine concepts, preliminary design, US Navy Hydroskimmers, Bell Aerosystems Co, Buffalo, New York, 1958-63. Publications: Performance Comparisons of Propulsion Systems for a Peripheral Jet Ground Effect Machine, Institute of Aero Science, Washington DC, 1962; Preliminary Design of the ARAVA STOL Airplane, 9th Conference on Aviation & Astro Ad Hoc Committee on Ducted Propellers, 1962. Honour: Po Tau Sigma, Mechanical Engineering Honor Society. Address: 29A Alexandroni St, Raanana 43337, Israel.

**MANN (Colin) Nicholas Jocelyn,** b. 24 October 1942, Salisbury, Wiltshire, England. Dean. m. (1) Joëlle Bourcart, 1 son, 1 daughter, divorced, (2) Helen Stevenson, 2 daughters. Education: BA 1st class, Modern and Medieval Languages, 1964, MA, PhD, 1968, King's College, Cambridge. Appointments: Research Fellow, Clare College, Cambridge, 1965-67; Lecturer in French, University of Warwick, 1967-72; Visiting Fellow, All Souls College, Oxford, 1972; Fellow and Tutor in Modern Languages, 1973-90, Emeritus Fellow, 1991-, Pembroke College, Oxford; Director of the Warburg Institute and Professor of the History of the Classical Tradition, University of London, 1990-2001, Senior Research Fellow of the Warburg Institute, 2002-; Dean of the School of Advanced Study and Professor of Renaissance Studies, 2002-, Pro-Vice Chancellor, 2003-, University of London. Publications: Books and articles on Petrarch and other topics in professional journals. Honours: CBE, 1999; Member of many advisory and editorial boards. Memberships: Fellow, 1992, Vice-President and Foreign Secretary, 1999-, British Academy; Council of Contemporary Applied Arts; Council of the Museum of Modern Art, 1984-92. Address: School of Advanced Study, University of London, Senate House, Malet Street, London WC1E 7HU, England. E-mail: deans.office@sas.ac.uk

**MANN Jessica,** b. England. Writer. Publications: A Charitable End, 1971; Mrs Knox's Profession, 1972; The Only Security, 1973; The Sticking Place, 1974; Captive Audience, 1975; The Eighth Deadly Sin, 1976; The Sting of Death, 1978; Funeral Sites, 1981; Deadlier Than the Male, 1981; No Man's Island, 1983; Grave Goods, 1984; A Kind of Healthy Grave, 1986; Death Beyond the Nile, 1988; Faith, Hope and Homicide, 1991; Telling Only Lies, 1992; A Private Inquiry, 1996; Hanging Fire, 1997; The Survivor's Revenge, 1998; Under a Dark Sun, 2000; The Voice From the Grave, 2002; Out of Harm's Way (non-fiction), 2005. Contributions to: Daily Telegraph; Sunday Telegraph;

Various magazines and journals. Memberships: Detection Club; Society of Authors: PEN; Crime Writers Association. Address: Lambessow, St Clement, Cornwall, England.

**MANN Michael K,** b. Chicago, USA. Producer; Director; Writer. Education: University of Wisconsin; London Film School. Appointments: Executive Producer, (TV) Miami Vice, Crime Story, Drug Wars: Camarena Story, Drug Wars: Cocaine Cartel, Police Story, Starsky & Hutch. Creative Works: Films directed include: The Jericho Mile, 1981; The Keep, 1981; Manhunter, 1986; Last of the Mohicans, 1992; Heat, 1995; The Insider, 1999. Honours include: 2 Emmy Awards. Memberships: Writers Guild; Directors Guild. Address: c/o Creative Artists Agency, 9830 Wilshire Boulevard, Beverly Hills, CA 90212, USA.

**MANNERS Crispin Luke,** b. 2 August 1957, Bristol, England. Consultant. 2 sons. Education: Bedford College, London. Appointments: Territory Sales Representative, CPC (UK)Ltd, 1978-80; Executive Assistant to the Chairman, 1980-82, Director, 1982-86, Finance Director, 1986-89, Managing Director, 1989-90, Chief Executive, 1990-, The Argyll Consultancies PLC (including Kaizo). Publication: When two worlds collide.... when sales met marketing. Honours: Salesman of the Year, CPC (UK) Ltd, 1980; Chief Executive of Kaizo, CBI's Innovative Company of the Year, 2003. Memberships: Chairman, Public Relations Consultants Association; Fellow, Institute of Public Relations; Fellow, Institute of Directors. Address: Kaizo, 66-68 Margaret Street, London W1W 8SR, England. E-mail: crispin.manners@kaizo.net

**MANNERS Gerald,** b. 7 August 1932, Ferryhill, County Durham, England. Economic Geographer. m. Joy Edith Roberta Turner, 2 sons, 2 daughters. Education: BA, 1954, MA, 1958, Undergraduate and Scholar, First Class Geographical Tripos, St Catharine's College Cambridge. Appointments: Commissioned Officer, Royal Air Force, 1955-57; Lecturer, Geography, University College, Swansea, 1957-67; Visiting Scholar, Resources for the Future Inc., Washington DC, USA, 1964-65; Reader in Geography, University College London, 1968-80; Visiting Associate, Joint Center for Urban Studies, Harvard University and Massachusetts Institute of Technology, 1972-73; Visiting Fellow, Centre for Resource and Environmental Studies, Australian National University, 1991; Professor of Geography, 1980-97, Emeritus Professor, 1997-, University College London. Publications include: The Geography of Energy, 1964; South Wales in the Sixties, 1964; Spatial Policy Problems of the British Economy, 1971; The Changing World Market for Iron Ore 1950-1980, 1971; Regional Development in Britain, 1972; Minerals and Men, 1974; Coal in Britain: an Uncertain Future, 1981; Office Policy in Britain, 1986. Honours include: Governor, 1978-95, Chairman, 1986-95, Vice-President, 1995-99, Sadler's Wells Foundation; Trustee, 1993-, Eaga Partnership Charitable Trust; Specialist Adviser to the House of Lords Select Committee on Sustainable Development, 1994-95; Trustee, 1977-, Chairman, 1996-2004, City Parochial Foundation and the Trust for London; Specialist Adviser, House of Commons Environmental Audit Committee, 1999-2001; Chairman, Association of Charitable Foundations, 2003-; OBE, 2005. Memberships: Fellow, Royal Geographical Society (with the Institute of British Geographers); British Institute of Energy Economics; Regional Studies Association, Address: 338 Liverpool Road, London N7 8PZ, England. E-mail: g.manners@ucl.ac.uk

**MANNING Jane Marian,** b. 20 September 1938, Norwich, Norfolk, England. Singer (Soprano); Lecturer. m. Anthony Payne. Education: Royal Academy of Music, London; Scuola di Canto, Cureglia, Switzerland. Career: Freelance solo singer specialising in contemporary music; More than 350 world premiers including operas; Regular appearances in London, Europe, USA, Australia, with leading orchestras, conductors, ensembles and at major festivals; Lectures and master classes at major universities in USA including Harvard, Princeton, Cornell, Stanford; UK universities and leading conservatories in Europe and Australia; Visiting Professor, Mills College, Oakland, USA, 1981, 1984, 1986; Artistic Director, Jane's Minstrels, 1988-; Artist-in-Residence, universities in USA, Canada, Australia and New Zealand; Currently AHRC Creative Arts Research Fellow, Kingston University, UK, 2004-07; Visiting Professor, Royal College of Music, London; Honorary Professor, Keele University, 1996-2002; Many CDs, radio broadcasts worldwide. Publications: Books, New Vocal Repertory – An Introduction; New Vocal Repertory 2; Chapter on the vocal cycles in A Messiaen Companion; Numerous articles and reviews in newspapers and professional journals. Honours: Special Award, Composers Guild of Great Britain; FRAM, 1980; Honorary Doctorate, University of York, 1988, OBE, 1990; FRCM, 1998; Hon Doctorate, University of Keele, 2004. Memberships: Vice-President, Society for the Promotion of New Music; Chairman, Nettlefold Trust (Colourscape Festival); Executive Committee, Musicians Benevolent Fund; Royal Philharmonic Society; Incorporated Society of Musicians. Address: 2 Wilton Square, London N1 3DL, England. E-mail: janetone@gmail.com

**MANOCHA Anshu,** b. 10 October 1971, India. Pharmacologist. Education: B Pharm, 1993, M Pharm, 1995, Faculty of Pharmacy, Jamia Hamdard (Hamdard University), India; PhD, Pharmacology, University College of Medical Sciences and Guru Teg Bahadur Hospital, Delhi University, India, 2000. Appointments: Junior Research Fellow, Department of Pharmacology, Faculty of Pharmacy, Jamia Hamdard, India, 1993-95; Senior Research Fellow, Department of Pharmacology, University College of Medical Sciences and Guru Teg Bahadur Hospital, Shahdara, India, 1996-2000; Lecturer, Department of Pharmacology, Faculty of Pharmacy, Jamia Hamdard, New Delhi, India, 2000-. Publications: 11 published articles in national and international journals; 7 published abstracts. Honours include: University Gold Medal for B Pharm and M Pharm, Jamia Hamdard; National Merit Scholarship, 1987; Hakim Abdul Majeed Scholarship, 1992-93; Junior Research Fellowship, Indian Institute of Technology, 1993-95; Senior Research Fellowship, Council of Scientific and Industrial Research 1996-2000; Servier Young Investigators' Award, Institutet de Recherches Internationales Servier, France, 1999. Memberships: Life Member, Indian Pharmaceutical Association; Life Member, Indian Pharmacological Society. Address: Department of Pharmacology, Faculty of Pharmacy, Jamia Hamdard, New Delhi 110062, India. E-mail: anshumanocha@hotmail.com

**MANSELL Nigel,** b. 8 August 1953, Upton-on-Severn, England. Racing Driver. m. Rosanne Perry, 2 sons, 1 daughter. Appointments: Began in Kart-racing, then Formula Ford, Formula 2, 1978-79, first Grand Prix, Austria, 1980; Winner, South African Grand Prix, 1992; Member, Lotus Grand Prix Team, 1980-84, Williams Team, 1985-88, 1991-92, Ferrari Team, 1989-90, Newman-Haas IndyCar Team, 1992-95, McLaren Team, 1995; Winner of 31 Grand Prix; Surpassed Jackie Stewart's British Record of 27 wins; World Champion, 1992; PPG IndyCar World Series Champion, 1993; Editor-in-Chief, Formula One Magazine, 2001. Publications: Mansell and Williams (with Derick Allsop), 1992; Nigel Mansell's IndyCar Racing (with Jeremy Shaw), 1993; My Autobiography (with James Allen), 1995. Honours include: Honorary DEng, Birmingham, 1993; OBE, 1990; BBC Sports Personality of

the Year, 1986, 1992; Special Constable for 12 years; Awarded Honorary Fellowship of Centre for Management of Industrial Reliability, Cost and Effectiveness (MIRCE), 1997; Awarded Grand Fellowship of the MIRCE Akademy, 2000; Appointed President, UK Youth Charity, 2002. Address: c/o Nicki Dance, Woodbury Park Golf & Country Club, Woodbury Castle, Woodbury, Exeter, Devon EX5 1JJ, England.

**MANSER Martin Hugh,** b. 11 January 1952, Bromley, England. Reference Book Editor. m. Yusandra Tun, 1979, 1 son, 1 daughter. Education: BA, Honours, University of York, 1974; MPhil, C.N.A.A., 1977. Publications: Concise Book of Bible Quotations, 1982; A Dictionary of Everyday Idioms, 1983, 2nd edition, 1997; Listening to God, 1984; Pocket Thesaurus of English Words, 1984; Children's Dictionary, 1984; Macmillan Student's Dictionary, 1985, 2nd edition, 1996; Penguin Wordmaster Dictionary, 1987; Guinness Book of Words, 1988; Dictionary of Eponyms, 1988; Visual Dictionary, Bloomsbury Good Word Guide, 1988; Printing and Publishing Terms, 1988; Marketing Terms, 1988, Guinness Book of Words, 1988, 2nd edition, 1991; Bible Promises: Outlines for Christian Living, 1989; Oxford Learner's Pocket Dictionary, 2nd edition, 1991; Get To the Roots: A Dictionary of Words and Phrase Origins, 1992; The Lion Book of Bible Quotations, 1992; Oxford Learner's Pocket Dictionary with Illustrations, 1992; Guide to Better English, 1994; Chambers Compact Thesaurus, 1994; Bloomsbury Key to English Usage, 1994; Collins Gem Daily Guidance, 1995; NIV Thematic Study Bible, 1996; Chambers English Thesaurus, 1997; Dictionary of Bible Themes, 1997; NIV Shorter Concordance, 1997; Guide to English Grammar, 1998; Crash Course in Christian Teaching, 1998; Dictionary of the Bible, 1998; Christian Prayer (large print), 1998; Bible Stories, 1999; Editor: Millennium Quiz Book, 1999; I Never Knew That Was in the Bible, 1999; Pub Quiz Book, 1999; Trivia Quiz Book, 1999; Children's Dictionary, 1999; Compiler, Lion Bible Quotation Collection, 1999; Common Worship Lectionary, 1999; The Eagle Handbook of Bible Promises, 2000; The Westminster Collection of Christian Quotation, 2001; Wordsworth Crossword Companion, 2001; Biblical Quotations: A Reference Guide, 2001; NIV Comprehensive Concordance, 2001; 365 Inspirational Quotations, 2001; Writer's Manual, 2001; The Facts On File Dictionary of Proverbs, 2001; Dictionary of Foreign Words and Phrases, 2002; Getting to Grips with Grammar, 2003; A Treasury of Psalms, 2003; Dictionary of Classical and Biblical Allusions, 2003; The Joy of Christmas, 2003; Editor, Synonyms and Antonyms, 2004; Editor, The Chambers Thesaurus, 2004; Compiler, Best Loved Hymns, Poems and Readings, 2004; Editor, The Really Useful Concise English Dictionary, 2004; Editor, Dictionary of Saints, 2004; Editor, World's Best Mother, A Treasury of Quotations, 2005. Address: 102 Northern Road, Aylesbury, Bucks HP19 9QY, England.

**MANSFIELD Eric Arthur,** b. 14 April 1932, Southend, Essex, England. RAF Officer; Consulting Engineer. m. Marion Byrne, 1 son, 1 daughter. Education: RAF Apprenticeship, 1949-52; MA, St John's College, Cambridge, England, 1953-56; RAF Flying and Training to Wings Standard, 1957-58; MSc, Southampton University, 1962-63; RAF Staff College, 1968-69. Appointments: Tours with RAF Chief Scientist, Exchange with USAF, 1963-68; Nimrod Aircraft Engineering Authority and OC Engineering Wing, RAF Cottesmore, 1969-74; Chief Electrical Engineer, HQ RAF Germany, 1974-78; Staff, HQ 18 Group, 1978-82; Staff, Ministry of Defence, 1983-86; Staff, NATO HQ AFSOUTH, 1986-88; Staff, RAF Support Command, 1986-89; Association of Consulting Engineers, 1989-94; Independent Consultant, 1994-95; Retired, 1995. Memberships: Royal Aeronautical Society; Chartered Engineer. Address: 33

Chalgrove End, Stoke Mandeville, Bucks HP22 5UH. E-mail: ericandmarion@eamansfield.freeserve.co.uk

**MANSFIELD Michael,** b. 12 October 1941, London, England. Barrister. m. (1) Melian Mansfield, 1967, divorced 1992, 3 sons, 2 daughters, (2) Yvette Mansfield, 1992, 1 son. Education: Keele University. Appointments: Began Practising, 1967; Founder, Tooks Court Chambers, 1984; Speciality, Civil Liberties Work; Professor of Law, Westminster University, 1996. Creative Works: Films for BBC TV: Inside Story, 1991; Presumed Guilty. Publication: Presumed Guilty. Honours: Honorary Fellow, Kent University; Several Honorary Degrees. Membership: Patron Acre Lane Neighbourhood Chambers, Brixton, 1997-. Address: Tooks Court Chambers, 14 Tooks Court, Cursitor Street, London EC4Y 1JY, England.

**MANTHIRAM Arumugam,** b. 15 March 1951, Amarapuram, India. Teacher; Researcher. m. Rajeswari, 1 son, 1 daughter. Education: BS, 1974; MS, 1976; PhD, 1980. Appointments: Lecturer, Madurai Kamaraj University, 1981-85; Postdoctoral Fellow, University of Oxford, 1985-86; Postdoctoral Researcher, University of Texas, Austin, 1986-91, Assistant Professor, 1991-96, Associate Professor, 1996-2000, Professor, 2000-. Publications: 250 research papers. Honours: Faculty Excellence Award, 1994; Faculty Leadership Award, 1996; Charlotte Maer Patton Centennial Fellowship in Engineering, 1998; Ashley H Priddy Centennial Professorship in Engineering, 2002; Fellow, American Ceramic Society, 2004. Memberships: American Ceramic Society; American Chemical Society; Materials Research Society; Electrochemical Society; National Institute of Ceramic Engineers. Address: Department of Mechanical Engineering, 1 University Station C2200, University of Texas, Austin, TX 78712, USA.

**MANTOVANI John F,** b. 17 January 1949, St Louis, Missouri, USA. Paediatric Neurologist. m. Janice, 1 son, 1 daughter. Education: BA, cum laude, Chemistry, University of Evansville, Indiana, 1971; MD, with honours, University of Missouri, 1974; Residencies in Paediatrics, Neurology and Child Neurology, Washington University School of Medicine, 1974-79. Appointments include: Assistant Professor, Clinical Neurology, University of Wisconsin, 1980-84; Instructor, Clinical Paediatrics and Neurology, 1985-94, Assistant Professor, 1994-99, Associate Professor, Clinical Paediatrics and Neurology, 1999-, Washington University School of Medicine; Currently, Director of Child Neurology, Medical Director, Mercy Child Development Center; Vice-Chairman, Department of Paediatrics, St John's Mercy Medical Center. Publications: 15 articles as first author and co-author in peer-reviewed professional journals; 6 abstracts, letters and book chapters; Over 70 scientific presentations and invited lectures. Honours: Board Certifications: Paediatrics, 1980, Neurology and Child Neurology, 1981; Neurodevelopmental Disabilities, 2001; Outstanding Resident Teacher in Neurology, Washington University School of Medicine, 1977; Professional Leadership Award in the Field of Developmental Disabilities, University of Missouri, 1989; Listed in Who's Who publications and biographical dictionaries. Memberships: American Academy for Cerebral Palsy and Developmental Medicine; American Academy of Pediatrics; American Board of Psychiatry and Neurology. Address: 621 South New Ballas Road, Suite 5009, St Louis, MO 63141, USA.

**MANVILLE Stewart Roebling,** b. 15 January 1927, White Plains, New York, USA. Archivist; Curator. m. Ella Viola Brandelius-Ström Grainger, 17 January 1972. Education: Hunter College Opera Workshop, 1950-52; Akademie für Musik und Darstellende Kunst, Vienna, 1952-53; BS, Columbia University,

1962. Appointments: Assistant Stage Director, European Opera Houses, 1952-57; Editor, 1959-63; Archivist of Percy Grainger's music, curator of the Percy Grainger House in White Plains New York, 1963-. Publications: Manville-Manvel Genealogy, 1948-; Seeing Opera in Italy, 1955; Seeing Opera in Central Europe, 1956. Memberships include: Soc des Antiquaires de Picardie; National Trust for Historic Preservation; Westchester County Historical Society; St Nicholas Society of New York. Address: 46 Ogden Ave, White Plains, NY 10605-2323, USA.

**MAO Zai-Sha,** b. 3 July 1943, Chengdu, China. Research Chemical Engineer. m. Junxian Zhou, 2 daughters. Education: BEng, Department of Chemical Engineering, Tsinghua University, Beijing, China, 1966; MS, Institute of Chemical Metallurgy, Chinese Academy of Sciences, Beijing, China, 1981; PhD, Department of Chemical Engineering, University of Houston, Texas, USA, 1988. Appointments: Research Professor, Institute of Process Engineering, Chinese Academy of Sciences; Professor, Graduate School, Chinese Academy of Sciences; Associate Editor in Chief, Chinese Journal of Chemical Engineering, Beijing; Associate Editor in Chief, Chinese Journal of Process Engineering, Beijing. Publications: 80 papers in peer-reviewed journals; 60 conference presentations; 5 patents on multiphase chemical reactor design. Honours: Best Fundamental Paper, South Texas Section, AIChE, USA, 1992; Excellent Postgraduate Adviser, Graduate School, Chinese Academy of Sciences, Beijing, 2001. Memberships: Member, Chemical Industry and Engineering Society of China. Address: Institute of Process Engineering, CAS, PO Box 353, Beijing 100080, China.

**MAR AND KELLIE, Earl of, James Thomas Erskine (Jamie),** b. 10 March 1949, Edinburgh, Scotland. Peer. m. Mary. Education: Diploma in Social Work, Moray House College of Education, 1968-71; Certificate in Building, Inverness College, 1987-88. Career: Social Work, 20 years; Building Work, 4 years; Hereditary Peer, 1994-99; Life Peer, 2000-; Liberal Democrt Assistant Whip; Liberal Democrat Assistant Transport Spokesman. Honours: Life Peerage: Lord Erskine of Alloa Tower, 2000. Memberships: Chairman, Clackmannanshire Heritage Trust; Non-Executive Director, Clackmannanshire Enterprise; Select Committee on the Constitution, 2001-04. Address: Hilton Farm, Alloa FK10 3PS, Scotland.

**MARABLE Darwin William,** b. 15 January 1937, Los Angeles, California, USA. Lecturer; Critic; Curator. m. Joan Ynez Frazell. 1 daughter. Education: BA, University of California at Berkeley, 1960; MA, San Francisco State University, 1972; PhD, History of Photography, University of New Mexico, 1980. Appointments: Lecturer, San Francisco State University, 1977-78, 1982, California College of Arts and Crafts, Oakland, 1977-79, St Mary's College, Moraga, 1990-91, 1995; Instructor, University of California at Berkeley Extension, 1995-; San Francisco Art Institute and Academy of Art College, 2001; Mentor, University of California at Berkeley Student-Alumni Mentor Program; Volunteer, University of New Mexico Outreach; Board Member, Diablo Symphony Orchestra, Walnut Creek, 1979-81, Lafayette Arts and Science Foundation, 1980-81, Contra Costa Alliance for the Arts, 1981-82; Docent, Friends of Photography, San Francisco, 1995-2001; Arts Commissioner, Contra Costa County Arts Commission, 2003-. Memberships: History of Photography Group; Friends of Photography; San Francisco Museum of Modern Art; Society for Photographic Education; Photo Alliance, San Francisco. Commissions and Creative Works: Guest Curator: Hearst Art Gallery, St Mary's College, Moraga, The Crucifixion in Modern Art, 1992; California College of Arts and Crafts, Oakland, Vilem Kriz Memorial Exhibition, 1996; JJ Brookings Gallery,

# DICTIONARY OF INTERNATIONAL BIOGRAPHY

San Francisco, Visual Dialogue Foundation, Revisited, 2000. Address: 3337 South Lucille Lane, Lafayette, CA 94549, USA.

**MARABLE Simeon-David**, b. 10 May 1948, Philadelphia, USA. Artist. m. Pamela Joyce Sorenson, 4 sons (1 deceased), 1 daughter. Education: BA, Art and English, Lea College, Minnesota, 1970; Postgraduate, Tyler School of Art, Philadelphia. Appointments: Art-Teacher, 7-8th Grade, Pennsbury, School System, Pennsylvania, 1970-88; Art Teacher, 9-10th Grade, Charles H Boehm High School, Pennsbury, 1988-, Medill Bair High School, Pennsbury, 1990-; Art Teacher, 9-12th Grade, Pennsbury High School West, 2002-; Teacher, Neshaminy Adult Education, 1972-82; Resident Artist, Three Arches Corporation, 1975, Middletown Historical Association, 1976; Manager, Boys Soccer League, Boys Little League, Middletown Township; Senior Babe Ruth Coach, Manager, Langhorn Athletic Association, 1988-89; Senior Coach, Babe Ruth League, 1989; JV Basketball Coach, 1989; Founder Creator, Rivulet Art, 2000; Creator, Olde Philadelphia Educational Programme and Pennsylvania Statehood Programme, National Republican Convention, Philadelphia, 2000; President, Levittown Internationally Known Communities Inc, 2004; Curator, Levittown Exhibit Center North. Creative works include: Portraits of Mike Schmidt, Lee Elia; Creator, Philadelphia City of Champs Logo; 50th Anniversary Logo, 1951-2001 Celebration, Fairless Hills, Pennsylvania; Artwork represented in Middletown Township Calendar and Falls Township Calendar, 1992; Creator, Scale Model Homes Exhibition, Pennsylvania Historic Museum, 2002; Author, Creator, Levittown Pennsylvania, 1952-2002 A Garden Community, 2002; Sketch presented to Governor of Pennsylvania, 2002; Works in permanent collections include: Albert Lea Library, Minnesota, Chapel, Fort Dix, New Jersey; James A Michener Museum. Honour: Artist of the Year, Albert Lea Lions Club, 1970. Memberships: Presidential Task Force; National Trust for Historic Preservation; Buck County Art Educators, President, 1974-74; Levittown Artists Association; National Society of Arts and Literature; International Platform Association. Address: 18 Spindletree Road, Levittown, PA19056-2215, USA. E-mail: amx_12345@hotmail.com

**MARADONA Diego Armando**, b. 1960, Lanus, Argentina. Footballer. m. Claudia Villafane, 2 daughters. Appointments: Boca Juniors, Argentina, 1982; Barcelona Football Club; Naples Football Club, 1984-91, Sevilla (Spain), 1992, Boca Juniors, 1997, Badajoz, 1998-; Founder, Maradona Producciones; Former Ambassador for UNICEF; Banned from football for 15 months after drugs test; Convicted by Naples Court on charges of possession of cocaine, 14 month suspended sentence and fine of 4 million lira, 1991; Federal Court in Buenos Aires ruled he had complied with the treatment; Suspended for 15 months for taking performance-enhancing drugs in World Cup Finals, 1994; Indicted for shooting an air rifle at journalists, 1994; Resigned as coach of Deporto Mandiyu, 1994; Captain of Argentina, 1993. Honour: Footballer of the Century Award, Féderation Internationale de Football Association (France), 2000. Membership: President, International Association of Professional Footballers, 1995-.

**MARBER Patrick**, b. 19 September 1964, London, England. Playwright; Director. 1 son. Education: BA, English Language and Literature, Wadham College, Oxford University, 1983-86. Publications: Plays: Dealer's Choice, 1995; After Miss Julie, 1996; Closer, 1997; Howard Katz, 2001. Honours: Writer's Guild Award for Best West End Play, 1995; Evening Standard Award for Best Comedy, 1995; Evening Standard Award for Best Comedy, 1997; Critic's Circle Award for Best Play, 1997; Olivier Award for Best Play, 1997; New York Critics' Award

for Best Foreign Play, 1999. Address: c/o Judy Daish Associates, Ltd, 2 St Charles Place, London W10 6EG, England.

**MARC'HADOUR Germain**, b. 16 April 1921, Langonnet, Brittany. Priest; Professor. Education: Licence ès Lettres, 1945; Doctorat ès Lettres, 1969; Honorary Doctorate of Theology, 1999. Appointments: High School Teacher, 1945-52; Assistant Professor, 1952, Professor, 1969, Catholic University; Founding Secretary, Amici Thomae Mori, 1963. Publications: 6-volume work on Thomas More and the Bible; 200 articles in professional journals; 10 books. Honours: 4 medals; Dedicatee of a Festschrift, 1989. Memberships: Renaissance Society of America; Modern Language Association; Third Order of St Francis. Address: 126, rue Chèvre, 49044 Angers.

**MARCEAU Marcel**, b. 22 March 1923, Strasbourg, France. Mime Artist. m. (1) Huguette Mallet, divorced, 2 sons, (2) Ella Jaroszewicz, 1966, divorced, (3) Anne Sicco, 1975, divorced, 2 daughters. Education: Lille and Strasbourg Lycees. Appointments: Director, Compagnie de Mime Marcel Marceau, 1948-64; Annual world tours and numerous TV appearances world-wide; Created Don Juan (mime drama), 1964, Candide (ballet), Hamburg, 1971; Creator of the character "Bip"; Director, Ecole de Mimodrame Marcel Marceau, 1978-. Creative Works: Mimes include: Le manteau, Exercices des style (both filmed); Mort avant l'aube; Le joueur de flute; Moriana et Galvau; Pierrot de Montmartre; Les trois perruques. Publications: Les sept péchés capitaux; Les reveries de Bip; Alphabet Book; Counting Book; L'histoire de Bip; The Third Eye; Pimporello, 1987. Honours: Académie des Beaux Arts, 1991; Officier, Légion d'honneur; Commander, Ordre nationale du Mérite; Commander, des Arts et des Lettres; Honorary Degrees from Princeton and Oregon Universities, 1987; Grand Officier du Merite, 1998. Address: c/o Compagnie de Mime Marcel Marceau, 32 rue de Londres, 75009 Paris, France.

**MARCEAU Sophie (Sophie Danièle, Sylvie Maupu)**, b. 17 November 1966, Paris, France. Actress. 1 son, 1 daughter. Creative Works: Stage appearances include: Eurydice, 1991; Pygmalion, 1993; Films: La Boum, 1981; La Boum 2, 1982; Fort Saganne, 1984; Joyeuses Pâques, 1985; L'Amour Braque, 1985; Police, 1985; Descente aux Enfers, 1986; Chouans!, 1987; L'Etudiante, 1988; Mes Nuits Sont Plus Belles Que Vos Jours, 1989; Pacific Palisades, 1989; Pour Sacha, 1991; La Note Bleue, 1991; Fanfan, 1993; La Fille de D'Artagnan, 1994; Braveheart, 1995; Beyond the Clouds, 1995; Firelight, 1988; Anna Karenina, 1996; Marquise, 1997; The World is Not Enough, 1998; La Fidelité, 1999; Belphégor, 2001; Alex and Emma, 2003; Je reste! 2003; Les Clefs de bagnole, 2003; Nelly, 2004; Anthony Zommer, 2005. Publication: Menteuse, 1996. Address: c/o Artmedia, 10 avenue George V, 75008 Paris, France.

**MARCHI Lorraine**, b. 5 June 1923, San Francisco, California, USA. Health Care Executive. m. (1) Robert L Fastie, deceased, (2) Gene Marchi Snr, divorced, 2 sons, 2 daughters. Education: Stanford University, California; University of California, Berkeley; Honorary doctorate, State University of New York, 2002. Appointment: Founder and CEO, National Association for Visually Handicapped. Publications: Several articles in professional journals. Honours: L HD, State University of New York, 2002; Listed in numerous biographical publications. Address: 22 West 21st Street, New York, NY 10010, USA. E-mail: staff@navh.org

**MARCINIAK Jan Jozef**, b. 10 March 1943, Tarnowskie Gory, Poland. Mechanical Engineer. m. Marianna Joanna Melcer, 3 daughters. Education: MA, Silesian Technical University, Gliwice, Poland, 1968; PhD, 1972; DSc, 1982; Professor, 1990.

Appointments: Master of Metal Physics Team, Institute of Metal Science, Silesian Technical University, 1975-80; Director of Science, 1982-85; Head, Metal Science Department, 1984-88; Director of Institute, 1985-93; Head, Special Materials and Techniques, 1991; President, Association of Faculty Mechanics, Gliwice, 1983-88; Chairman of Board, Silesian Technical University, 1985; Director of Centre of Bioengineering since 1999. Publications: Biomaterials in Surgery, 1992; Biomaterials, 2002; Menace of Electromagnetic Environment, 1995, 2000; Co-author: Metal Science and Head Treatment of Tool Materials, 1990; Patents in field. Honours: Award in Gold, Chief Technical Organization, Katowice, 1980; Order of Merits for Development, Voivode of Katowice 1986; Order of Merits, Leszno, 1988; Gold Medal, INPEX XIII, Pittsburgh, 1997; Golden Key Award, London International Inventions Fair, 1997. Memberships: Association of Polish Mechanical Engineers, Chairman, Metal Science Section, 1971-98; Polish Society of Biomechanics; Polish Society of Applied Electromagnetics, Science Section; Polish Society of Biomaterials; Polish Academy of Sciences; Polish Club of Ecology. Address: Silesian Technical University, Institute of Engineering and Biomedical Materials, Konarskiego 18a, 44-100 Gliwice, Poland.

**MARCUS DeLAMBERT Jordan,** b. 2 March 1929, Barbados. Managing Director. m. Grace Enid, 1 son, 1 daughter. Education: Life Insurance Diploma, Canada, Harrison College, 1941-48; Inter BA, University of London, 1949. Appointments: Sub Editor, Barbados Advocate; School Teacher, Combermere High School; Life Underwriter, Branch Manager, Manufacturers Life Insurance Co; Senator, Government of Barbados; Honorary Consul of Cyprus to Barbados; Managing Director, Wildey Shopping Plaza Ltd; Lamberts Ltd; Bank of Nova Scotia International; Scotia Insurance; President of the Senate, Government of Barbados. Membership: Chairman, Barbados Tourism Authority; Founding member of Kiwanis Club, Barbados, Member, Commonwealth Parliamentary Association, Royal Commonwealth Society. Address: Lambert's, Dover Terrace, Christ Church, Barbados. Website: wildeyplaza@sun beach.net

**MARDANI Masoud,** b. 22 November 1956, Masjed, Soleiman, Iran. Medical Doctor. m. Simin Keyan, 2 daughters. Education: MD, Ahvaz University, Iran, 1982; Speciality in Infectious Diseases, University of Shaheed Beheshti, Iran, 1985; MPH, Tehran University, Iran, 1986; Postdoctoral Fellowship in Infectious Diseases in Cancer Patients, University of Texas, USA, 1999. Appointments: Assistant Professor of Medicine, Associate Professor of Medicine, Full Professor of Medicine, Head of Infectious Diseases Department, Dean of Medical Faculty, Shaheed Beheshti University of Medical Sciences and Health Services, Tehran, Iran. Publications: Articles in professional journals include: Candida Krusei fungemia in cancer, 2000; The epidemiology of Candia Glabrata, 2002; Environmental sources of fusarium in patients with cancer, 2002; Infection control and hospital epidemiology, 2002; Rift Valley Fever, 2003; The efficacy of oral Ribavarin in the treatment of Crimean-Congo haemorrhagic fever in Iran, 2003; Management of central venous catheters in patients with cancer and candidemia, 2004. Honours: Honorary Fellowship offered by Japanese International Co-operation Agency, 1994; Documentation of the first confirmed case of Crimean-Congo Hemorrhagic Fever in Iran, 1999. Memberships: European Society of Clinical Microbiology and Infectious Diseases; American Society of HIV; International Society of Hepatitis; Iranian Society of Infectious Diseases and Tropical Medicine; Infectious Diseases Society of America. Address: Office of Dean, Faculty of Medicine, Shaheed Beheshti University of Medical Sciences, Evin, Tehran 19395-4139, Iran. E-mail: mmardani@sbmu.ac.ir

**MARDI Shalva,** b. 10 May 1933, Georgia, Former USSR. Medical Doctor; Professor. m Rosa-Maria Mardi, 1 son, 1 daughter. Education includes: BC, College of the City of Kutaisi, USSR, 1953; Medical Doctor, National Russian Academy of Medicine, Moscow, 1959; Professor of Oncology, Cand med sci, Academy of Medical Sciences, St Petersburg, Russia, 1963; Doctor of Science in Medicine, Academy of Medical Sciences, Kiev, Ukraine, USSR, 1968; PhD, Moscow, 1968. Appointments include: Clinical Professor of Oncology, Tbilisi, Georgia, USSR, 1970; Numerous Visiting and Guest Professorships including: Tel-Aviv; Munich; Vienna; Milan; Houston, Texas; Buffalo, New York; Tokyo; Basel; Zurich; Rio de Janeiro, Brazil; Moscow; Paris; London; Kiev; St Petersburg; University Hospitals and Clinics; Director of Medical Institute of Skin Treatment, Kiron, Israel; President of Scientific, Medical, Pharmaceutical and Cosmetic Laboratory, Binningen, Switzerland; Head of Department and Professor of Dermatological Division, SOLCO-Basel AG, Switzerland; Chief Scientist and Consultant, Rishardson-Meryll Company, USA, Basotherm AG, Germany; ABIC and TEVA Pharmaceuticals, Israel. Publications: More than 250 Scientific publications, books, monographs; 12 international new patents in medicine and for the invention of Mardi's Shark Caviar as an alternative for natural Beluga Caviar and as a food supplement for preventing cancer diseases as well as for the development of new lines in cosmeto-dermatology: Marditalia and Mardisrael.Global projects for United Nations and World Health Organisation: Stop and Solve Skin Cancer Epidemics, 2003. Honours: Numerous United Nations, international and national prizes, honour awards, medals and diplomas in scientific medicine. Memberships include: UNO, American, including: USA, European and Asian Scientific Academies and Societies of Onco-Dermatology; Active Member, International Informatization Academy of the United Nations, 2003-. Address: 3 Bleicherweg, Binningen, CH-4102 Switzerland. E-mail: shavla33@bluewin.ch

**MARETINA Irina Alexandrovna,** b. 11 October 1932, Leningrad, Russia. Chemistry Educator; Researcher. m. Mironov V E, 1 son, 1 daughter. Education: Engineer-Technologist-Chemist Diploma, 1955; Cand Chem Sci Diploma, Moscow, 1962; Doctor Chem Sci Diploma, Moscow, 1976; Professor Diploma, Moscow, 1981. Appointments: Engineer, Lensoviet Leningrad Technological Institute, Leningrad, Russia, 1955-62; Assistant, 1962-65; Assistant Professor, 1965-79; Professor, 1979-98, Lecturer, 1998-2004; Scientific Research, A E Favorsky Irkutsk Institute of Chemistry, Russian Academy of Sciences, 1998-2001, 2004-. Publications: Author of 274 Scientific Publications and Patents including: Utilization of Diacetylene in Basic Industrial Organic Synthesis, 1996; Recovery and Utilization of Diacetylene in Production of Acetylene by Oxidative Pyrolysis of Methane, 2000; Diacetylene: a candidate for industrially important reaction, co-author, 2000; Dialetylene and its Derivatives in Heterocyclization Reaction, co-author, 2002; Peculiarity of the Alkenynamines Synthesys, 2003; Industrial Synthese of 1, 1-Diethoxybutan-3-on from diacetylene, 2003; 1,1-Dialkoxybutan-3-ones, 2005. Honours: Medal, Citizen of the Blockade Leningrad, 1991; Order Znak Pocheta, Moscow, 1981; Medal, The SU Inventor, Moscow, 1981. Memberships: Mendeleev Russian Chemical Society, St Petersburg, 1955-2003; Chairman, St Petersburg State of Technological Institute branch of Mendeleev Russian Chemical Society, 1986-2001. Address: A E Favorsky Irkutsk Institute of Chemistry, Russian Academy of Sciences, Favorsky St 1, 66433 Irkutsk, Russia. E-mail: tba@irioch.irk.ru

**MARGOLYES Miriam,** b. 18 May 1941, Oxford, England. Actor. Education: BA (Hons) English Literature, Cambridge University. Career: Films: Stand Up Virgin Soldiers; The Awakening; The Apple; Reds; Coming Out Of The Ice; Scrubbers; Yentl; Electric Dreams; Handel - Honour, Profit And Pleasure; The Good Father; Little Shop Of Horrors; Little Dorrit; Wiesenthal - The Murderers Among Us; I Love You To Death; Pacific Heights; The Fool; Dead Again; The Butcher's Wife; As You Like It; The Age Of Innocence; Ed And His Dead Mother; The White Horse; Immortal Beloved; Babe (Voice); James And The Giant Peach; Crossing The Border; Romeo and Juliet; Sunshine; End Of Days; Alone; Harry Potter and the Chamber of Secrets; Cold Comfort Farm; Different For Girls; Dreaming Of Josephe Lees; Cats & Dogs; The First Snow Of Winter; The Life And Death Of Peter Sellers; Modigliani; Being Julia; Ladies In Lavender; Television: Fall Of Eagles; Girls Of Slender Means; Kizzy; The Widowing Of Mrs Holroyd; Glittering Prizes; Stanley Baxter Christmas Show; Tales Of The Unexpected: Fat Chance; The History Man; The Lost Tribe; Take A Letter Mr Jones; A Kick Up The 80s (Various); Scotch And Wry; The First Schlemiel; Freud; Strange But True: Flight Of Fancy; A Rough State: The Mexican Rebels; The Young Ones; Alternative Society; Oliver Twist; Blackadder; Blackadder II; Blackadder III; Life And Loves Of A She Devil; The Little Princess; Poor Little Rich Girl; Body Contact; Mr Majeika; The Finding; Doss; City Lights; Old Flames; Orpheus Decending; Hands Across The Sea; Ways And Means; The Comic Strip - Secret Ingredient; Frannie's Turn; Just William; Phoenix And The Carpet; Fall Of The House Of Windsor; The Lost Tribe; Tuscany To Go; Miss Marple; Wallis And Edward; Theatre: The Cherry Orchard; The Killing Of Sister George; She Stoops To Conquer; Dickens' Women; Orpheus Descending; Man Equals Man; Gertrude Stein And A Companion; 84 Charing Cross Rd; Flaming Bodies; Cloud Nine; The White Devil; Threepenny Opera; Kennedy's Children; Canterbury Tales; Fiddler On The Roof; Romeo And Juliet; The Vagina Monologues; The Way Of The World; Blithe Spirit. Honours: Joint winner (with Genevieve Bujold), Best Supporting Actress, LA Critics Circle, 1989; Talkies Performer of the Year, 1991; BAFTA Best Supporting Actor, 1993; Sony Radio Best Actress on Radio, 1993; Best Children's Entertainment, The Royal Television Society, 1999; Best Animation for Children, BAFTA, 1999; Best Independent Production, The Prix Danube, 1999; 2nd Prize, Children's Jury for Best Animation, Chicago International Children's Film Festival, 1999; Grand Prize, Best Short Film, Kinderfilmfest, Tokyo, 1999; Best Film Audience Award Jury Award, Washington DC International Film Festival, 1999 Prix Jeunesse, Best Children's Programme (0-6 fiction), 2000; OBE, 2001. Memberships: BAFTA: Equity; AFTRA; Academy of Motion Pictures. Address: c/o PFD, Drury House, 34-43 Russell Street, London WC2B 5HA, England. Website: www.miriammargolyes.com

**MARGRETHE II H.M. (Queen of Denmark),** b. 16 April 1940, Denmark. m. Count Henri de Laborde de Monpezat (now Prince Henrik of Denmark), 1967, 2 sons. Education: University of Copenhagen; University of Aarhus; University of Cambridge; University of Sorbonne, Paris; London School of Economics. Appointments: Illustrator, The Lord of the Rings, 1977, Norse Legends as Told by Jorgen Stegelmann, 1979, Bjarkemaal, 1982; Poul Oerum's Comedy in Florens, 1990; Cantabile poems by HRH the Prince Consort, 2000. Publications: (trans) All Men are Mortal (with Prince Henrik), 1981; The Valley, 1988; The Fields, 1989; The Forest (trans), 1989. Honours include: Honorary LLD, Cambridge, 1975, London, 1980; Honorary Bencher, Middle Temple, 1992; Honorary Fellow, Girton College, Cambridge, 1992; Medal of the Headmastership,

University of Paris, 1987; Hon KG, 1979. Address: Amalienborg Palace, 1257 Copenhagen K, Denmark.

**MARGULIS Lynn,** b. 5 March 1938, Chicago, Illinois, USA. Scientist; Professor. 3 sons, 1 daughter. Education: AB, Liberal Arts, University of Chicago, 1957; MS, University of Wisconsin, 1960; PhD, University of California, Berkeley, 1965. Appointments: Research Associate, Brandeis University, 1963-65; Elementary Science Study Consultant, 1963-67; US Peace Corps-Colombia Instructor, 1965-66; Adjunct Assistant Professor, 1966-67, Assistant Professor, 1967-71, Associate Professor, 1971-77, Professor, 1977-88, University Professor, 1986-88, Boston University; Visiting Professor, University of California, San Diego, 1980; Co-administrator, NASA, Planetary Biology Internship Program, 1981-; NASA, Planetary Biology Microbial Ecology, 1980, 1982, 1984; Visiting Professor, Universidad Autónoma de Barcelona, 1985, 1986; Visiting Scholar, Marine Science Research Center, SUNY, Stony Brook, 1986; Distinguished University Professor, Department of Botany, 1988-93, Distinguished University Professor, Department of Biology, 1993-97, University of Massachusetts, Amherst; Visiting Professor, Boston University Marine Program, 1994-99; Visiting Professor, George Mason University, 1995; Distinguished University Professor, Department of Geosciences, University of Massachusetts, Amherst, 1997-. Publications: Many publications and articles to professional journals; Author: Symbiosis in Cell Evolution, 2nd edition; Co-author: Five Kingdom, 3rd edition; Acquiring Genomes: A Theory of the Origins of Species and more than 14 other books. Honours: US National Medal of Science, 1999; Collegium Helveticum Fellow, Zurich, 2001; Alexander von Humboldt Prize, German Government, 2002; Hanse Wissenschaft-Kolleg Fellow, 2002. Memberships: National Academy of Sciences; Russian Academy of Natural Science; American Academy of Arts and Science; World Academy of Arts and Sciences. Address: Department of Geosciences, University of Massachusetts, 611 North Pleasant Street, Amherst, MA 01003-9297, USA. Website: www.sciencewriters.org

**MARINELLI Carlo,** b. 13 December 1926, Rome, Italy. Musicologist; Discologist; Discographer. 1 son, 1 daughter. Education: Degree in Letters, La Sapienza University of Rome, 1948. Career: Founder and Editor, Microsolco magazine, 1952-59; Professor, History of Music, 1970-98, Associate, 1985-98, Associate, History of Modern and Contemporary Music, 1992-98, Department of Comparative Cultures, Faculty of Letters, University of L'Aquila; Professor, Discography and Musical Videography, 1998-2002, DAMS, Faculty of Letters, University of Bologna; President, Institute for Research on Musical Theatre, Rome. Publications: Discographies of Mozart, Rossini, Monteverdi, Donizetti, Bellini, Verdi, Puccini; Editor, catalogues of Italian audiovisual and sound sources of Mozart and Rossini; Editor: Notizie Videoarchivio Opera e Balletto, Notizie Archivio Sonoro Musica Contemporanea, IRTEM "Quaderni"; Le cantate profane di J S Bach, 1966; La musica strumentale da camera di Goffredo Petrassi, 1967; Lettura di Messiaen, 1972; Cronache di musica contemporanea, 1974; L'opera ceca, l'opera russa, l'opera in Polonia e Ungheria, 1977; Opere in disco. Da Monteverdi a Berg, 1982; Di Goffredo Petrassi, un'antologia, 1983; Prolegomeni ad una nuova disciplina scientifica: Discografia e videografia musicale, 1998; Prolegomena to a new scientific discipline: musical discography and videography, 2000; I documenti musicali sonori e visivi quali fonti di conoscenza, informazione e trasmissione, 2002; Sound and Visual Musical Documents as Sources of Knowledge, Information and Transmission, 2002; Rilettura digitale come alterazione di documenti sonori originali, 2004; Discological Critical Edition: Giovanni Paisiello, Il re Teodoro in Venezia,

1994. Discographies: Faust e Mefistofele nelle opere sinfonico-vocali, 1986; Le opere di Mozart su libretti di Da Ponte, 1988; Mozart Singspiele, 1993; Mozart, Opere serie italiane, 1995; Monteverdi, Balli e Madrigali in genere rappresentativo, 1996; De Falla, Atalantida, 1996; Rossini, Il barbiere di Siviglia, 1998; Verdi, Rigoletto, Il trovatore, La traviata, 1999; Monteverdi, Opere teatrali, 2000; Rossini, Opere teatrali 1820-1829, 2001; Verdi, Don Carlo, Otello, Falstaff, 2002; Verdi, Oberto, Giorno di regno, Nabucco, Lombardi, Ernani, Due Fascari, 2003; Verdi, Don Carlos, La forza del destino, 2003, Verdi, Aida, 2004; Operatic Discography Encyclopaedia, 2004. Honours: Honorary Member, International Association of Sound and Audiovisual Archives; Academician, Accademia Sante Cecilia, Rome: Memberships: President, Associazione Italiana Archivi Sonori Audiovisivi; Board Member, Internationales Musik Zentrum, 1993-95; Chairman, Discography Committee, IASA, 1996-99; International, American, Australian, French, Spanish and Italian Musicological Societies; International Association of Music Libraries; Association of Recorded Sound Collectors; Australasian Sound Recording Association; Association Française Archives Sonores; Associazione Italiana Studi Nord Americani; Associazione Docenti Universitari Italiani Musica. Address: Via Francesco Tamagno 65-67, I-00168 Rome, Italy. E-mail: carlomarinelli@mclink.it Website: www.carlomarinelli.it

**MARINO Marialuisa,** b. 4 January 1945, Milan, Italy. Artist; Poet; Writer. 3 sons. Education: Ballet Diploma, La Scala Opera House, Italy, 1962; Teachers Diploma, Advanced Diploma, Chechetti, Italy, 1963; Principal Soloist, Performing Arts Council of Transvaal, South Africa; Studies in art, Witwatersrand Technical College of Art, South Africa. Appointments: 6 appointments for voluntary community and honorary officer, 1976-85; First solo art exhibition, 1990; Joined family business founded by father in 1967, became Managing Director, 1978, Marmernova and Building Products Pty Ltd; Only woman member, Master Mason Association and the Building Industries Federation; Trustee and Director of Events, City Ballet of London. Publications: Beyond Fantasy, painting and poetry book, 2000; Merry Mischief – A Childhood Celebration of Queen Elizabeth, The Queen Mother, 2001. Honours: La Scala Opera House, 1962; 10 gold medals, South Africa Premiere Exhibition, Witwatersrand Easter Show, 1976-85; Paul Harris Fellow, Rotary Foundation; Citta di Firenze: Professore HC, for painting "Diana, Princess of Wales", 2000; Cavaliere dell'Etruria: Grosetto, Italy, 2000; Coppa Libertas, for Symphony No 9, 2001; New Art Promotion "Sirena del Mare", Cervia, Italy, 2001; Statua della Liberta, Accademia del Fiorano, New York, USA, 2001; Award for "Merry Mischief", Accademia Italiana Etruschi, Cita di Milano, 2001; Cavaliere della Pace, Firenze, Italy, for painting of President Nelson Mandela, 2001; N D MarialuisaMarino, Accademica Gentilizia (Classe) Belle Arti, 2001; Associazione Culturale: Amici del Quadro Gold Medal, Milan, 2003; Accademia il Marzocco, Gran Premio Internazionale, Genova la Superba citta della Cultura, 2004; Promotore della Pace, for Celebration: A Portrait of Julian Lloyd Webber, 2004; Accademia Internazionale Città Di Roma Award for Venus Through a Mirror of Time, 2004. Memberships: Life Member, British/Italian Society; International Society of Poets, 2000; Accademia Il Marzocco ND for Belle Arte, 2001; Rotary International Rotary Club of Kensington; The Fine Art Trade Guild, 2000; Academical Commander Ordine Accademico del Verbano, 2004. Address: West Eaton Place, London SW1X 8LU, England.

**MARKESINIS Basil,** b. 10 July 1944, Athens, Greece. Barrister; Professor of Law. m. Eugenie Trypanis, 1 son, 1 daughter. Education: LLB "starred first", 1965, Doctor Iuris,

Summa Cum Laude, 1968, Athens; MA, PhD, 1970, LLD, 1988, Cambridge; DCL, Oxford, 1996. Appointments: Advocate, Supreme Court, Athens, 1976-86; Acting Director, 1987-88, Deputy Director, Centre for Commercial Law Studies, 1986-93, Director International Affairs for the Faculty of Laws, 1989-93, Professor of Comparative Law, 1986-95, Queen Mary College, London; Founder-Director, Institute of Anglo-American Law, Leiden, The Netherlands, 1987-99; Professor of European Law, 1995-98, Professor of Comparative Law, 1998-2000, University of Oxford; Founder-Director, Oxford Institute of European and Comparative Law, 1997-2001; Founder-Director, Institute of Transnational Law, University of Texas at Austin, USA, 1999; Clifford Chance Special Adviser for European Affairs, 1998-2001; Professor of Common and Civil Law, 2000-, Founder and first Chairman, Institute of Global Law, 2001-, University College London; Conseiller Scientifique du Premier Président de la Cour de Cassation, France, 2002-. Publications: 25 books include most recently: Always on the Same Path: Essays on Foreign Law and Comparative Methodology vol 2, 2001; The German Law of Tort: A Comparative Treatise (co-author), 2002; Comparative Law in the Courtroom and Classroom, 2003; Compensation for Personal Injury in England, Germany and Italy, 2004; Rechtsvergleichung in Theorie und Praxis, 2004; Over 100 articles in national and international legal journals. Honours include: Honorary degrees from: University of Gent, Paris I, University of Munich; Officier des Palmes Academiques, France, 1991; Queens Counsel, honoris causa, 1998; Commander of the Order of Honour, Greece, 2000; Knight Grand Cross of the Order of Merit, Italy, 2002; Knight Commander of the Order of Merit, Germany, 2003; Commander of the Order of the Légion d'Honneur, France, 2004. Memberships: American Law Institute; Fellow, Royal Belgian Academy; Corresponding Fellow, Academy of Athens; Foreign Fellow, Royal Dutch Academy; Fellow, British Academy; Fellow, Greek Archaeological Society; Corresponding Fellow, French Academy. Address: Middleton Stoney House, Middleton Stoney, Bicester, Oxon OX25 4TE, England.

**MARKHAM Jehane,** b. 12 February 1949, Sussex, England. Poet; Playwright. 3 sons. Education: Central School of Art, 1969-71. Publications: The Captain's Death; Ten Poems, 1993; Virago New Poets, 1993; Twenty Poems, 1999; Between Sessions and Beyond the Couch, 2002; In The Company of Poets, 2003; Thirty Poems, 2004. Radio Plays: More Cherry Cake, 1980; Thanksgiving, 1984; The Bell Jar; Frost in May. Television Play: Nina, 1978. Theatre Plays: One White Day, 1976; The Birth of Pleasure, 1997. Contributions to: Women's Press; Longmans Study; Sunday Times; BBC 2 Epilogue; Bananas Literary Magazine; Camden Voices; Independent; Observer; Acorn; Ambit; New Statesman; Cork Literary Review. Memberships: Poetry Society; Highgate Literary and Scientific Society; NFT; Poetry Book Society.

**MARKHAM Richard,** b. 23 June 1952, Grimsby, England. Concert Pianist. Education: Piano privately with Shirley Kemp and Max Pirani; National Youth Orchestra of Great Britain; Royal Academy of Music, London, 1969-73. Career: Concert Pianist; Tours in over 40 countries as David Nettle/Richard Markham Piano Duo, 1977-; Examiner for Associated Board of the Royal Schools of Music, 1984-. Recordings include: Nettle and Markham in America; Nettle and Markham in England; Nettle and Markham in France; Complete Two-Piano Works of Brahms. Honours: ARCM, 1967; LRAM, 1968; Nora Naismith Scholarship, 1969; Bronze Medal, Geneva International Competition, 1972; Countess of Munster Musical Trust Awards, 1973, 1974; Frederick Shinn Fellowship, 1975; Gulbenkian Foundation Fellowship, 1976-78; ARAM 1983; MRA Award for Excellence, 1985. Memberships: Incorporated Society of

Musicians; RAM Club; Gymnos; Friend of Stonewall. Address: The Old Power House, Atherton Street, London SW11 2JE, England. E-mail: richardpiano@aol.com

**MARKS Isaac,** b. 16 February 1935, Cape Town, South Africa. Doctor. m. Shula, 1 son, 1 daughter. Education: MB ChB, 1956, MD, 1963, Cape Town University; DPM, London University, 1963; FRCPsych, 1970. Appointments: Professor, Consultant Psychiatrist, Institute of Psychiatry, Bethlem-Maudsley Hospital, Kings College London, 1978-2000; Professor Emeritus, 2000-. Publications: 430 scientific articles; 13 books. Honours: Salmon Medallist, New York Academy of Medicine, 1978; Fellow, Centre for Advanced Study in Behavioural Science, Stanford, USA. Membership: Fellow, Royal College of Psychiatrists. Address: 43 Dulwich Common, London, SE21 7EU, England.

**MARKS Peter,** b. 7 April 1945, Buckinghamshire, England. Medical Doctor; Barrister. Education: MD ChB, 1971; MRCP, 1973; MSc, 1976; LLB, 1986; Entry into Inns of Court School of Law, 1986; LLM, 1994; Appointment of Pupil Master, Inns of Court School of Law, 1999; DCH, 2003; PhD, 2004. Appointments: Registration as Doctor, 1971; House Officer to Dr Gavey, 1971, House Officer to Mr Drew, 1971, Senior House Officer, Coronary Care Unit, 1972-73, Westminster Hospital; Senior House Officer, Professor Fraser, Royal Postgraduate Medical School, 1974; Senior Research Registrar, Coronary Care Unit and Thoracic Unit, Westminster Hospital, 1974-78; Lecturer in Medicine, Kings College Hospital, 1978-81; Visiting Professor of Medicine, 1984-95, Assistant Professor of Medicine, 1995-98, Visiting Professor of Medicine, 1998-, Slovakia; Called to the Bar, 1987, Pupillage at Chambers of Peter Rowland; Tenant at Chambers of Peter Rowland, later called Chambers of Ellis Meyer, 1991. Publications: Numerous publications in medical and legal journals and presented at conferences include: Drug dependence caused by Dihydrocodeine, 1978; The Use of Highly Specific Antibodies in the Investigation of Treatment in Hypertension, 1986; The Effects of Weight Reduction in the Treatment of Obese Hypertensive Patients, 1994; Drink Driving Legislation: Medicine and the Law. Lung Function Tests and Failure to Supply a Specimen, 1995; Blood Alcohol Level: The Law and Medicine, 1996; Aetology and outcome of 53 cases of Native Valve Staphylococcal Endocarditis, 1999; Doctrine of Informed Consent – A Trend of the Future, 1999; Hepatitis B vaccination programme at the workplace and the National Policy; 2000; Bakerialna Endokarditida U Onkologickuch Pacientov, 2000; Enigma of Consent, 2001. Honour: Gold Medal of the University for ten years work in infectious diseases, 1999. Membership: Royal College of Physicians. Address: 1 Maxted Road, London SE15 4LL, England.

**MARLAND Michael,** b. 28 December 1934, London, England. Retired Headteacher; Educational Author. m. (1) Eileen, deceased 1968, 4 sons, 1 daughter, (2) Linda, 1 son. Education: BA, Sidney Sussex College, Cambridge, 1954-57. Appointments: English Teacher: Dear Halepaghen Oberschule, Buxtehude, Germany; Simon Langton Grammar School, Canterbury; Head of English: Abbey Wood Comprehensive School, London; Crown Woods Comprehensive School, London then Director of Studies at that school; Headteacher: Woodberry Down School, London; Founder Headteacher, North Westminster Community School, London; General Editor: Blackie: Student Drama Series, Longman: Imprint Books, Heinemann: School Management Series. Publications: Numerous books include: School Management Tasks, 1985; Multilingual Britain, 1987; The Tutor and Tutor Group, 1989; Headship Matters (with Peter Ribbins), 1994; The Art of the Tutor (with Rick Rogers), 1997; Managing Arts in the Curriculum (with Rick Rogers), 2002; The Craft of the Classroom (revised version), 2002; A Vision

for Today (with Gillian Klein), 2003; How to be a Successful Form Tutor (with Rick Rogers), 2004; The Complete Teacher, 2006; Compiled and edited 30 literary anthologies for classroom study, 1969-84; Over 100 articles in journals, booklets, newspapers and symposia on educational matters. Honours: CBE; Fellow, College of Preceptors; Hon. Dr. Education, Kingston; Kidscape Children's Champion; Hon. Dr. University, Surrey Roehampton; Honorary Fellow, Institute of Education, London; Fellow, British Educational Leadership, Management and Administration Society. Memberships: National Council, BELMAS; Vice-President, City of Westminster Arts Council; Education Committee, English Speaking Union; Master of Teaching Steering Committee, Institute of Education; Editorial Board, NAPCE; Patron, Tagore Centre, UK; Chair, Upper Street Association, Islington, London; Board Member, Young Person's Concert Foundation. Address: 22 Compton Terrace, London N1 2UN, England.

**MAROVIC Pavao,** b. 26 January 1954, Split, Croatia. University Professor; Civil Engineer. m. Vladica Herak, 1 son. Education: Faculty of Civil Engineering, University of Zagreb, 1972-77; Graduate, Civil Engineer, 1977; PhD, Faculty of Civil Engineering, University of Zagreb, 1987. Appointments: Teaching Assistant, 1978-88, Assistant Professor, 1988-92, Head of Department, Testing and Technology of Materials, 1988-91, Vice Dean of the Faculty, 1991-94, President, University Assembly, 1991-93, Associated Professor, 1992-96, Vice Rector, 1994-98, Professor, 1996-, Head of the Chair for Strength of Materials, Testing of Structures, 1998-, Dean of the Faculty, 2000-, University of Split; Associated Member, Croatian Academy of Technical Sciences, 2000. Publications: International Conference on Nonlinear Engineering Computations, 1991; Nonlinear Calculations of R/C Structures, 1993; International Congress of Croatian Society of Mechanics, 1997, 2000; Symposium on The Use of Computers in Civil Engineering; Co-editor of 25 Croatian Conference proceedings; Approximately 160 scientific and professional papers in journals and conference proceedings; Many others. Honours: Rector's Student Award; Plaque of the CAD/CAM Congress; Decorated by the President of the Republic of Croatia; County Splitsko-dalmatinska Yearly Award for Science; 2000 Outstanding Scientists of the 20th Century Silver Medal, International Biographical Centre; World Lifetime Achievement Award, American Biographical Institute. Memberships: International Association for Computer Methods in Geomechanics; International Association for Bridge and Structural Engineering; Central European Association for Computational Mechanics; European Scientific Association of Material Forming; National Geographic Society; Croatian Society of Mechanics; Croatian Society of Structural Engineers; Many others. Address: Faculty of Civil Engineering and Architecture, University of Split, Matice hrvatske 15, HR-21000 Split, Croatia.

**MARSDEN Simon Neville Llewelyn (Sir),** b. 1 December 1948, Lincoln, Lincolnshire, England. Photographer; Author. m. Caroline Stanton, 1 son, 1 daughter. Education: Ampleforth College, Yorkshire, England; Sorbonne, Paris, France. Career: Professional photographer and author; Photographs in the following collections: J Paul Getty Museum, California, USA; Victoria and Albert Museum, London; Bibliothéque Nationale, Paris, France; The Cleveland Museum of Art, USA; The Maryland Historical Society, Baltimore, USA; The University of Arizona, USA; Flanders Field Museum, Ypres, Belgium. Publications: In Ruins: The Once Great Houses of Ireland, 1980; The Haunted Realm – Ghosts, Witches and Other Strange Tales, 1986; Visions of Poe- A Personal Selection of E A Poe's Stories and Poems, 1988; Phantoms of the Isles – Further Tales from the Haunted Realm, 1990; The Journal of a Ghosthunter – In search of the Undead from Ireland to Transylvania, 1994; Beyond the Wall – The Lost World of East Germany, 1999; Venice - City of Haunting Dreams, 2002; The Twilight Hour – Celtic Visions from the Past, 2003; This Spectred Isle – A Journey Through Haunted England, 2005. Memberships: Chelsea Arts Club; The Arthur Machen Society. Address: The Presbytery, Hainton, Market Rasen, Lincolnshire LN8 6LR, England. E-mail: info@marsdenarchive.com Website: www.simonmarsden.co.uk

**MARSDEN-SMEDLEY Christopher,** b. 9 February 1931, London, England. Retired Architect. m. Susan Penelope King, 2 sons 1 daughter. Education: BA, (Arch), University College, London, 1956. Appointments: Partner, 1961-96, Senior Partner, 1990-96, Nealon Tanner Partnership; High Sheriff, Avon, 1994-95; Deputy Lieutenant, Somerset, 2000. Publications: Burrington, Church and Village; Articles in various architectural papers. Honours: ARIBA, 1959; FRIBA, 1969. Memberships: Honorary Secretary, Bristol Civic Society, 1966-71; Governor, 1969-75, Chairman, 1972-75, Fairfield School; Committee Member, 1974-97, Chairman, 1988-97, Vice President, 1997-, Bristol Age Care; President, Bristol Commercial Rooms, 1988; Trustee, Wells Cathedral, 1997-; Committee Member, 1997-, President 2000-2001, Canynges Society. Address: Church Farm, Burrington, Near Bristol BS40 7AD, England.

**MARSH Eric M,** b. 25 July 1943, Preston, England. Hotelier. m. Elizabeth Margaret, 2 sons, 2 daughters. Education: National Diploma in Hotelkeeping and Catering, Courtfield Catering College, Blackpool, Lancashire, England, 1960-63. Appointments: Dorchester Hotel, London, 1963-68; Rank Hotels, London, 1968-73; Director and General Manager, Newling Ward Hotels, St Albans, Hertfordshire, England, 1973-1975; Tenant of Cavendish Hotel from Chatsworth Estate, 1975-; Managing Director, Paludis Ltd (Trading as Cavendish Hotel), 1975-; Managing Director of Eudaemonic Leisure Ltd (Trading as George Hotel), 1996-; Managing Director, Cavendish Aviation Ltd (Operating at Gamston Airfield), 1975-. Publications: Several articles in Caterer and Hotelkeeper magazine and Pilot magazine. Memberships: Institute of Marketing; Institute of Advanced Motorists; Director, Committee Member, British Aerobatic Association. Address: Cavendish Hotel, Baslow, Derbyshire DE45 1SP, England. E-mail: info@cavendish-hotel.net

**MARSH Francis Patrick,** b. 15 April 1936, Birmingham, England. Consultant Physician. m. Pamela Anne Campbell, 1 son, 2 daughters. Education: BA, Natural Science Tripos, Gonville and Caius College, 1957; London Hospital Medical College, 1957-60; MB BChir, Cambridge, 1960; MA, Cambridge, 1961; MRCP, London, 1963; FRCP, London, 1976. Appointments: House Physician, 1960-61, House Surgeon, 1961, The London Hospital; Senior House Officer in Medicine, Kent and Canterbury Hospital, 1961-62; Registrar in Medicine, Royal Free Hospital, 1962-63; Registrar in Medicine, The London Hospital, 1963-65; Research Fellow, 1965-67, Lecturer, Senior Registrar, 1967-70, The London Hospital and London Hospital Medical College; Honorary Consultant Physician, Bethnal Green Hospital, 1970-71; Senior Lecturer in Medicine, The London Hospital Medical College, now St Bartholomew's and the Royal London School of Medicine and Dentistry, 1970-2001; Consultant Nephrologist, Barts and the London NHS Trust, 1971-2001; Dean of Medical Studies and Governor, The London Hospital Medical College, 1990-95; Board of Directors, American University of the Caribbean, 2000-; Honorary Senior Lecturer in Medicine, Bartholomew's and the Royal London School of Medicine and Dentistry, 2001-; Emeritus Consultant Nephrologist, Barts and the London NHS Trust, 2001-. Publications: Around 80 original research papers;

Author, 26 book chapters; Editor, Postgraduate Nephrology; Refereed many medical journals and for regional and national prizes. Memberships include: Joint Formulary Committee, British National Formulary; Renal Association; Specialist Advisory Committee on Renal Disease; North East Thames Regional Medical Advisory Committee; North East Thames Regional Committee for Hospital Medical Services; Council of the Section of Medicine, Experimental Medicine and Therapeutics (Royal Society of Medicine); Central Committee for Hospital Medical Services. Address: Butchers End, 20 Butchers Lane, East Dean, West Sussex, PO18 0JF, England. E-mail: frank.marsh@virgin.net

**MARSH Laurie Peter.** Consultant; Property Restoration. Education: National Service RASC and Intelligence Corps, 1950-51, commissioned; Reserve Captain, 1954. Appointments: Chairman, Chief Executive Officer, Raincheque Ltd sold to Blacketts Stores plc, Director of plc, 1956; Chairman, Chief Executive Officer, Wadey Davison and L P Marsh (Properties) Ltd, Director, Greenaways (Builders), London, 1958; Chairman, Booty Jewellery, London, 1962; Director, Tigon Film Group, 1969; Acquired Classic Cinemas, 1971; Chairman, Town and District Properties plc and Laurie Marsh Group plc, 1971; Aquired Essoldo Cinema Group and part Rank cinemas, expanded multiple cinemas; LMG expanded into Europe, name changed to Intereuropean Prop Holdings plc, 1974; Chairman and Director, theatre group with Brian Rix and Ray Cooney, acquired 6 London theatres and 1 on Broadway, New York, 1976; Elected Vice President, 1978, President, 1979, Cinematograph Exhibitors Association; Sold IPH plc to ACC Leisure Group, Lord Grade, 1980; Chairman, Cosgrove Hall Properties Inc, New York, 1980; Chairman, Theatre Royal Bath; Restored theatres in London and New York, 1981; Chairman, F and GP LAMDA, UK National Charity, 1991; Founder, Libertas Charity Group, Chairman, Soundalive Tours Group (now International Heritage Group), 1986-98; Non-Executive Chairman, Cole Kitchen Theatre Group, 1994; Non-Executive Chairman, London Crystal Cleaners and Capital Property Services, 1999; Consultant to major property groups; Property restoration, theatre, financial consultancy. Address: 30 Grove End Road, St John's Wood, London NW8 9LJ, England. E-mail: lauriemarsh@onetel.com

**MARSHALL Albert Selwyn,** b. 26 September 1934, Tatsfield, Surrey, England. Retired Diplomat. m. Joan Margaret Lashwood, deceased, 1985, 1 son, 1 daughter. Education: Kent Horticultural College, Kent, England. Appointments: Royal Corps of Signals, Korea, Suez Canal, Cyprus, 1952-57; Foreign Office, 1957-61; Communications Officer, UK Mission to UN, New York, 1961-64; Archivist, British Embassy, Prague, 1954-65; ECO, British High Commission, Kingston, Jamaica, 1965-68; Foreign and Commonwealth Office, London, England, 1968-72; Management Officer, British Embassy, Addis Ababa, Ethiopia, 1972-75; British Vice-Consul, Belgrade, Yugoslavia, 1975-77; HM Vice-Consul, Tokyo, Japan, 1977-81; Foreign and Commonwealth Office, London, England, 1981-86; Management Officer, British Embassy, Washington DC, USA, 1986-90; HM Consul, Tel Aviv, Israel, 1990-94; Retired, 1994. Honour: MBE, 1968. Memberships: Treasurer, Merrow Horticultural Society; Volunteer, National Trust, Polesden Lacey. Address: 4 Tansy Close, Guildford, Surrrey GU4 7XN, England. E-mail: albert@asmarshall.freeserve.co.uk

**MARSHALL Enid Ann,** b. 10 July 1932, Boyndie, Scotland. University Academic. Education: 1st Class Honours, Classics, 1950-55, LLB, with distinction, 1955-58, PhD (part-time), Scots Company Law, 1960-66, University of St Andrews, Fife, Scotland. Appointments: Apprentice Solicitor, Cupar, Fife,

1956-59; Lecturer in Law, Dundee College of Technology, Dundee, Scotland, 1959-72; Lecturer in Business Law, 1972-74, Senior Lecturer in Business Law, 1974-77, Reader in Business Law, 1977-94, Head of Scots Law Research Unit, 1994-99, University of Stirling, Scotland. Publications: General Principles of Scots Law, 1971, 7th edition, 1999; Scots Mercantile Law, 1983, 3d edition, 1997; Scottish Cases on Contract, 1978, 2nd edition, 1993; Scottish Cases on Agency, 1980; Scottish Cases on Partnerships and Companies, 1980; Oliver and Marshall's Company Law, 10th edition, 1987, 11th edition, 1991, 12th edition, 1994; Gill: The Law of Arbitration, 3rd edition, 1983, 4th edition, 2001; Editor, Arbitration Section, Journal of Business Law, 1976-; Editor, Scottish Law Gazette, 1983-2001. Honours: Honorary Associate, RICS; Solicitor. Memberships: ACI arb; FRSA; Law Society of Scotland. Address: 3 Ballater Drive, Stirling FK9 5JH, Scotland.

**MARSHALL Hugh Phillips,** b. 13 July 1934, London, England. Anglican Priest (Retired). m. Diana Elizabeth Gosling, 1 son, 3 daughters. Education: BA, MA, Sidney Sussex College, Cambridge; Bishops Hostel, Lincoln. Appointments: Royal Navy, 1952-54; Ordained Deacon, 1959, Priest, 1960, Diocese of London; Curate, St Stephen and St John, Westminster, 1959-65; Vicar of St Paul, Tupsey, Hereford, 1965-74; Vicar and Team Rector of Wimbledon, 1974-87; Rural Dean of Merton, 1979-85; Vicar of Mitcham, Surrey, 1987-90; Chief Secretary, ABM, 1990-96; Vicar of Wendover, 1996-2001. Honours: Honorary Canon, Southwark Cathedral, 1989; Honorary Canon Emeritus, 1990; Canon St John's Cathedral Bulawayo, 1996; Commissary to Bishop of Matabeleland, 1989-. Memberships: Chairman, Betty Rhodes Fund, 1966, Member, 1989-; South East Regional Committee, National Lottery Charities Board, 1998-2002; Honorary Secretary, Oxford Diocesan Board of Patronage, 2001-; Foundation Governor, Deddington Voluntary Aided School, 2002. Address: 7 The Daedings, Deddington, Oxon OX15 0RT, England

**MARSHALL Valerie Ann,** b. 23 September 1939, Middlesex, England. Senior Supervisor. m. Derek, 29 April 1970, 2 sons, 1 daughter. Appointments: Private Secretary, The War Office; Senior School Supervisor, 31 years. Publication: Starlight Dreams, 1998; A Week of Special Happenings, Childrens Stories and Poems and Fully Illustrated By Myself, 2000. Contributions to: Anthologies, reviews, quarterlies, journals, magazines, periodicals and newspapers. Honours: Editor's Choice Awards, 1997, 1998; Special Commendation, 1997; Showcase Award, 1998. Address: 147 Warwick Road, Scunthorpe, North Lincs DN16 1HH, England.

**MARSHALL-ANDREWS Robert,** b. 10 April 1944, London, England. Member of Parliament; Queen's Counsel; Writer. m. Gillian Diana, 1 son, 1 daughter. Education: University of Bristol; Gray's Inn. Appointments: Member of Bar, 1967; Recorder, Crown Court, 1982; Queen's Counsel, 1987; Deputy High Court Judge, 1996; Bencher, Gray's Inn, 1996; Member of Parliament, 1997-. Publications: Numerous political articles in national (UK) newspapers and publications: Novels: Palace of Wisdom, 1989; A Man Without Guilt, 2002. Honours: Winner Observer Mace, 1967; Spectator Parliamentary Award, 1997. Address: House of Commons, London SW1A 0AA, England.

**MARSLAND David,** b. 3 February 1939, Leavesden, Hertfordshire, England. University Professor. m. Athena Marsland, 3 daughters. Education: Open Classics Scholarship, Christ's College, Cambridge University, 1957-61, MA, Classics, Cambridge University; State Studentship, Post Graduate Study, London School of Economics, 1961-64; PhD, Brunel University, 1984. Appointments: Lecturer, Senior Lecturer, Professor in Sociology, Department of Sociology, Brunel University, 1964-83; Assistant Director, Social Affairs Unit, Senior Researcher, MVA Consultancy, 1983-89; Professor of Social Science, West London Institute, 1989-97; Director of Research, Department of Health and Social Care, Brunel University, 1997-. Publications: Seeds of Bankruptcy: Sociological Bias against Business and Freedom, 1988; Understanding Youth, 1993; Welfare of Welfare State? 1996. Honours: Morris Ginsberg Fellow, London School of Economics, 1974; Thatcher Award for Services to Freedom, 1991. Memberships: Fellow, Royal Society for Health; Arts Club. Address: CER, Brunel University, Borough Road, Isleworth, Middlesex TN7 5DU, England. E-mail: david. marsland@brunel.ac.uk

**MARSTON Jeffery Adrian Priestley,** b. 15 December 1927, London, England. Surgeon. m. Sylvie Colin, 2 sons, 1 daughter. Education: MA (Oxon), 1952, DM MCh, 1963, Magdalen College, Oxford; St Thomas' Hospital Medical School; Harvard University; FRCS (Eng), 1958. Appointments: Training Posts at St Thomas' Hospital, St Mark's Hospital, 1959-65; Consultant Surgeon, The Middlesex Hospital, The Royal Northern Hospital, 1970-85, University College Hospital, 1985-92; Consultant Vascular Surgeon, The Manor House Hospital, 1974-93, The National Heart Hospital, 1985-91, The Royal National Orthopaedic Hospital, 1985-91; Emeritus Consultant Surgeon, University College London Hospitals, 1993-; Dean, Royal Society of Medicine. Publications: Books: Intestinal Ischaemia, 1977, Contemporary Operative Surgery, 1979; Vascular Disease of the Gut, 1980; Visceral Artery Reconstruction, 1984; Splanchnic Ischaemia and Multiple Organ failure, 1989; Hamilton Bailey: A Surgeons Life, 1999; Over 130 papers on vascular surgery and gastro-enterology. Honours: MD (honoris causa), Université de Nice, 1983; Gimbernat Prize, University of Barcelona, 1986; Honorary Fellow, Collegio Brasileiro de Cirugões; Honorary Fellow, College of Physicians and Surgeons of Pakistan; Chevalier d'Honneur, Ordre National du Mérite de la République Française. Memberships include: Vice-President, Royal College of Surgeons of England; President, Association of Surgeons of Great Britain and Ireland; President Vascular Surgery Society; British Medical Association; Royal Society of Medicine; Association of Surgeons; Medical Society of London; Membre d'Honneur, Association Française de Chirurgie; Socio de Honor, Asociación Española de Cirugía. Address: 4 Hereford Square, London SW7 4TT, England. E-mail: adrimar@btinternet.com

**MARTIN Archer John Porter,** b. 1 March 1910, London, England. Biochemist. m. Judith Bagenal, 1943, 2 sons, 3 daughters. Education: Graduated, 1932, PhD, 1935, Peterhouse, Cambridge University. Appointments: Dunn Nutritional Laboratories, 1936-38; Wool Industries Research Association, Leeds, 1938; Head, Biochemistry Division, Research Department, Boots Pure Drug Company, Nottingham, 1946-48; Staff, Medical Research Council; Lister Institute of Preventive Medicine, Head, Division of Physical Chemistry, National Institute for Medical Research, 1952-56, Chemical Consultant, 1956-59; Director, Abbotsbury Laboratory, 1959-70; Extraordinary Professor, Eindhoven Technological University, Holland, 1964-74; Consultant, Wellcome Research Laboratories, University of Sussex, 1970-73; Invited Professor of Chemistry, Ecole Polytechnique, Lausanne, Switzerland, 1980; Developed paper chromatography. Honours: Berzelius Gold Medal of Swedish Medical Society, 1951; Joint Winner, Nobel Prize for Chemistry, 1952; John Scott Award, 1958; Leverhulme Medal, 1963; Kolthoff Medal, 1969; Callendar Medal, 1971; Randolf Major Medal, Connecticut University, 1979; Fritz Pregl Medal, Austria, 1985; Order of the Rising Sun, 2nd Class, Japan; Several honorary degrees.

**MARTIN Bill,** b. 9 November 1938, Govan, Glasgow, Scotland. Songwriter; Music Publisher. m. Jan, 1 son, 3 daughters. Education: Govan High School; Royal Scottish Academy of Music Certificate. Career: Songwriter; First song, Kiss Me Now, released 1963; Writing partnership with Tommy Scott, 1964-65; Writing partnership with Phil Coulter, 1965-83; Martin-Coulter publishing company, 1970-; Producer of musical, Jukebox, 1983; Producer, publisher and writer, Angus Publications; Acquisitions and Back Catalogue Consultant, SONY/ATV Music, 2000-. Honours: 20 Gold albums; 4 Platinum albums; 3 Ivor Novello Awards; 3 ASCAP Awards; First British Winner, Eurovision Song Contest with Puppet on a String, 1967; Rio de Janeiro Award of Excellence, 1967, 1969; Antibes Song Festival Award for the Best Song, 1971; Japanese Yamaha Best Song Award, 1978; Variety Club Silver Heart, 1979; Scotland's Songwriter of the Decade, 1980; Four No 1s in the UK and three in USA. Memberships: BASCA; PRS; Society of Distinguished Songwriters; Freeman of the City of London; Freeman of the City of Glasgow; Member, Worshipful Company of Distillers; Member, MCC; Past Golf Captain, Royal Automobile Club; Member, St George's Hill Golf Club. Address: 14 Graham Terrace, Belgravia, London SW1W 8JH, England. E-mail: bill.puppetmartin@virgin.net Website: www.billmartinsngwriter.com

**MARTIN David (Alfred),** b. 30 June 1929, London, England. Professor of Sociology Emeritus; Priest; International Fellow; Writer. m. (1) Daphne Sylvia Treherne, 1953, 1 son, (2) Bernice Thompson, 30 June 1962, 2 sons, 1 daughter. Education: DipEd, Westminster College, 1952; External BSc, 1st Class Honours, 1959, PhD, 1964, University of London; Postgraduate Scholar, London School of Economics and Political Science, 1959-61. Appointments: Assistant Lecturer, Sheffield University, 1961-62; Lecturer, 1962-67, Reader, 1967-71, Professor of Sociology, 1971-89, Professor Emeritus, 1989-, London School of Economics and Political Science; Ordained Deacon, 1983, Priest, 1984; Scurlock Professor of Human Values, Southern Methodist University, Dallas, 1986-90; International Fellow, Institute for the Study of Economic Culture, Boston University, 1990-; Various visiting lectureships. Publications: Pacifism, 1965; A Sociology of English Religion, 1967; The Religious and the Secular, 1969; Tracts Against the Times, 1973; A General Theory of Secularisation, 1978; Dilemmas of Contemporary Religion, 1978; Crisis for Cranmer and King James (editor), 1978; The Breaking of the Image, 1980; Theology and Sociology (co-editor), 1980; No Alternative (co-editor), 1981; Unholy Warfare (co-editor), 1983; Divinity in a Grain of Bread, 1989; Tongues of Fire, 1990; The Forbidden Revolution, 1996; Reflections on Sociology and Theology, 1997; Does Christianity Cause War?, 1997; Pentecostalism: The World Their Parish, 2000; Christian Language and the Secular City, 2002; Christian Language and its Mutations; On Secularization, 2005. Honours: Honorary Assistant Priest, Guildford Cathedral, 1983-; Honorary Professor, Lancaster University, 1993-2002; Sarum Lecturer, Oxford University, 1994-95; Honorary Doctor of Theology, Helsinki, 2000. Membership: International Conference of the Sociology of Religion, president, 1975-83. Address: Cripplegate Cottage, 174 St John's Road, Woking, Surrey GU21 7PQ, England.

**MARTIN David McLeod,** b. 30 December 1922, Glasgow, Scotland. Artist; Teacher. m. Isobel A F Smith, deceased, 2000, 4 sons. Education: Glasgow School of Art, 1940-42; RAF War Service, 1942-46; Completed training at Glasgow School of Art, 1948; Diploma in Art, 1948; Jordanhill Teachers' Training College, 1948-49. Career: Commenced a teaching career in Glasgow schools in 1949 ending as a Principal Teacher of Art, Hamilton Grammar School; Retired early in 1983 to paint full-time. Publications: Works appear in books including: Paintings from the Clydesdale Bank Collection by Patrick Bourne; Scottish Watercolour Painting by Jack Firth; Articles in the Artist Magazine. Honours: Elected professional Member: Society of Scottish Artists, 1949, Royal Society of Painters in Watercolour, 1961, Royal Glasgow Institute of the Fine Arts, 1982; Listed in biographical dictionaries. Address: The Old Schoolhouse, 53 Gilmour St, Eaglesham, Glasgow G76 0LG, Scotland.

**MARTIN George (Henry),** b. 3 January 1926, England. Music Industry Executive; Producer; Composer. m. (1) Sheena Rose Chisholm, 1948, 1 son, 1 daughter, (2) Judy Lockhart Smith, 1966, 1 son, 1 daughter. Education: Guildhall School of Music and Drama. Appointments: Sub-Lieutenant, RNVR, 1944-47; Worker, BBC, 1950, EMI Records Ltd, 1950-65, Chair, 1965-; Built AIR Studios, 1969; Built AIR Studios, Montserrat, 1979; Completed new AIR Studios, Lyndhurst Hall, Hampstead, 1992; Co-merged with Chrysalis Group, 1974, Director, 1978-; Chair, Heart of London Radio, 1994-; Scored the music of 15 films. Publications: All You Need is Ears, 1979; Making Music, 1983; Summer of Love, 1994. Honours include: Ivor Novello Awards, 1963, 1979; Grammy Awards, 1964, 1967 (two), 1973, 1993, 1996. Address: c/o AIR Studios, Lyndhurst Hall, Hampstead, London, NW3 5NG, England.

**MARTIN Kevin Joseph,** b. 15 June 1947, Coventry, England. Solicitor. m. Maureen, 2 sons. Education: Cotton College, North Staffordshire; College of Law. Appointments: Partner, Mackintosh & Co, Birmingham, 1972-79; Partner, K J Martin & Co, Balsall Common, 1979-2001; Consultant, Ladders Solicitors, Stratford-upon-Avon, 2001-; Member of Council for Coventry and Warwickshire, 1996-, Deputy Vice-President, 2003, Vice-President, 2004-, President, 2005, The Law Society. Memberships: The Law Society; The Warwickshire Law Society; The Birmingham Law Society; Ladbrook Park Golf Club; The Catenian Association. Address: The Law Society, 113 Chancery Lane, London WC2A 1PL, England. E-mail: kevin.martin@lawsociety.org.uk

**MARTIN Michael John,** b. 3 July 1945. Politician. m. Mary McLay, 1 son, 1 daughter. Education: St Patrick's Boys' School, Glasgow, Scotland. Appointments: Glasgow City Councillor, 1973-79; Member of Parliament, Glasgow, Springburn (now Glasgow North East), 1979-; Deputy Speaker and Deputy Chairman of Ways and Means, 1997-2000; Speaker of the House of Commons, 2000-. Address: Speaker's House, House of Commons, London SW1A 0AA, England.

**MARTIN Rhona (Madeline),** b. 3 June 1922, London, England. Writer; Artist. m. (1) Peter Wilfrid Alcock, 9 May 1941, divorced, 2 daughters, (2) Thomas Edward Neighbour. Appointment: Part-time Tutor, Creative Writing, University of Sussex, 1986-91. Publications: Gallows Wedding, 1978; Mango Walk, 1981; The Unicorn Summer, 1984; Goodbye Sally, 1987; Writing Historical Fiction, 1988. Contributions to: London Evening News; South East Arts Review; Cosmopolitan; Prima. Honour: Georgette Heyer Historical Novel Award, 1978. Memberships: Romantic Novelists Association; Society of Authors; Friends of the Arvon Foundation; Society of Limners. Address: 25 Henwood Crescent, Pembury, Kent TN2 4LJ, England.

**MARTIN Ricky, (Enrique Martin Morales),** b. 24 December 1971, Puerto Rico. Singer; Actor. Career: Joined group Menudo, aged 13; Numerous tours and recordings; Left Menudo, 1989; Acted in Mexican soap opera Alcanzur una Estrella II; Began releasing Spanish language albums; Role as bartender in General Hospital; Won the role of Marius in Broadway production of

Les Miserables; Dubbed voice in Spanish version of Disney film Hercules; Released first English Language album including a duet with Madonna; Numerous television appearances and tour dates. Recordings: Singles: Maria, 1996; 1 2 3 Maria, 1997; Cup of Life, 1998; La Bomba, 1999; Livin' La Vida Loca, 1999; She's All I Have Had, 1999; Shake Your Bon-Bon; Story, with Christine Aguilera; Albums: Ricky Martin, 1991; Me Amarás, 1993; A Medio Vivir, 1995; Vuelve, 1998; Ricky Martin, 1999; Sound Loaded, 2000; La Historia, 2001. Honour: Grammy Award, Best Latin Pop Album, 1999. Address: c/o Sony Music Latin, 550 Madison Avenue, New York, NY 10022, USA.

**MARTIN Stephen Alexander,** b. 13 April 1959, Bangor, Co. Down, Northern Ireland. Deputy Chief Executive. m. Dorothy Armstrong, 1 son, 1 daughter. Education: Sports Science Degree, University of Ulster, Northern Ireland. Appointments: Former hockey player; Coaching Director, Ulster Hockey; High performance Manager, Sports Council, Northern Ireland; Currently: Deputy Chief Executive Officer, British Olympic Association. Honours. Olympic Bronze Medal, 1984; Olympic Gold Medal, 1988; 6th Place, 1992 Olympic Games, Great Britain Hockey; 229 International Caps; MBE for services to hockey, 1993; Honorary DUniv, University of Ulster, 2000. Membership: Olympians Club. Address: 5 The Coaches, Holywood, Co Down BT18 0LE, Northern Ireland.

**MARTIN Steve,** b. 1945, Waco, Texas, USA. Actor; Comedian. m. Victoria Tennant, 1986, divorced. Education: Long Beach State College; University of California, Los Angeles. Appointments: TV Writer, several shows; Nightclub Comedian; TV Special, Steve Martin: A Wild and Crazy Guy, 1978. Creative Works: Recordings: Let's Get Small, 1977; A Wild and Crazy Guy, 1978; Comedy is Not Pretty, 1979; The Steve Martin Bros; Film appearances include: The Absent Minded Waiter; Sgt Pepper's Lonely Hearts Club Band, 1978; The Muppet Movie, 1979; The Jerk, 1979; Pennies From Heaven, 1981; Dead Men Don't Wear Plaid, 1982; The Man With Two Brains, 1983; The Lonely Guy, 1984; All of Me, 1984; Three Amigos, 1986; Little Shop of Horrors, 1986; Roxanne, 1987; Planes, Trains and Automobiles, 1987; Parenthood, 1989; My Blue Heaven; L.A. Story; Grand Canyon; Father of the Bride; Housesitter, 1992; Leap of Faith, 1992; Twist of Fate, 1994; Mixed Nuts, 1994; Father of the Bride 2; Sgt Bilko, 1995; The Spanish Prisoner; The Out of Towners; Bowfinger, 1999; Joe Gould's Secret, 2000; Novocaine, 2002; Bring Down the House, 2003; Cheaper By The Dozen, 2003. Honours: Grammy Award, 1977, 1978; National Society of Film Critics Actor's Award. Address: ICM, 8942 Wilshire Boulevard, Beverly Hills, CA 90211, USA.

**MARTIN Todd,** b. 8 July 1970, Hinsdale, Illinois, USA. Tennis Player. Education: Northwestern College. Appointments: Winner, New Haven Challenger, 1989; Turned professional, 1990; Semi-Finalist, Stella Artois Grass Court Championships, London, 1993, Champion, 1994, Champion (doubles with Pete Sampras), 1995; Finalist, Australian Open, 1994, Grand Slam Cup, Munich, 1995; Semi-Finalist, US Open, 1994, Wimbledon, 1994, 1996, Paris Open, 1998; Champion, Scania Stockholm Open, 1998; Winner of 13 pro titles by end of 2002. Honours include: Adidas/ATP Tour Sportsmanship Award, 1993, 1994; ATP Tour Most Improved Player, 1993. Memberships: US Davis Cup Team, 1994-99; President, ATP Players' Council, 1996-97. Address: c/o Advantage International, 1751 Pinnacle Drive, Suite 1500, McLean, VA 22102, USA.

**MARTIN Victoria Carolyn,** b. 22 May 1945, Windsor, Berkshire, England. Writer. m. Tom Storey, 28 July 1969, 4 daughters. Education: Winkfield Place, Berks, 1961-62; Byam Shaw School of Art, 1963-66. Publications: September Song,

1970; Windmill Years, 1975; Seeds of the Sun, 1980; Opposite House, 1984; Tigers of the Night, 1985; Obey the Moon, 1987. Contributions to: Woman; Woman's Own; Woman's Realm; Woman's Journal; Good Housekeeping; Woman's Weekly; Redbook; Honey, 1967-87. Address: Newells Farm House, Lower Beeding, Horsham, Sussex RH13 6LN, England.

**MARTIN Vivian,** b. Detroit, Michigan. Opera and Concert Singer. m. Education: Conservatoire de Fountainebleau, France; Detroit Conservatory of Music; France; New York; Munich; Berlin; Detroit. Debut: Operatic debut, Leonardo, Verdi's La Forza Del Destino, 1971. Career: Major opera roles including Leonora, Verdi's Il Trovatore; Rezia, Weber's Oberon; Selika, Meyerbeer's L'Africane; Bess, Gershwin's Porgy and Bess, more than 500 times; Major opera houses and concert halls in Europe, Asia, USA, South America; TV and radio appearances; Toured and soloist with numerous orchestras; Symphonies in Sweden, Berlin, Munich, Nurenberg; Philharmonic orchestras in Germany, Slovenska Philharmonia, Detroit Symphony Orchestra; Sang in Tivoli Garden, Copenhagen, Denmark; Grosser Konzert Saal, Vienna, Austria; Théâtre des Champs Elysees, Paris, France, Kongress Saal, Munich, Germany; Participated in World of Gershwin; Festival with concerts with St Petersburg National Symphony Orchestra in Shostakovich Philharmonic Hall, St Petersburg; Moscow Symphony Orchestra in Tschaikovsky, Moscow, Russia; Concerts and performances in USA and abroad during 1994-2004. Honours: First prize and Jean Paul award, Conservatoire de Fountainbleau, 1953; Eighteen singing scholarships and awards. Memberships: AFTRA; American Guild of Music Artists; Actors Equity Association; Wayne State University Alumni Association; Alpha Kappa Alpha. Address: c/o Dr Gösta Schwark International APS, Opera-Concert-Theatre, 18 Groennegade, 1 Floor, DK-1107 Copenhagen, Denmark.

**MARTIN-QUIRK Howard Richard Newell,** b. 8 August 1937, Sanderstead, Surrey, England. Architectural Historian. m. Mitzi Quirk. 1 son. Education: BA (Cantab), 1959, MA, 1961, Christs College, Cambridge University; BSc, Bartlett School of Architecture, London University, 1967; MSc, University College, London, 1985. Appointments: Architectural Assistant, Greater London Council, 1966-67; Senior Research Assistant, Kingston College of Art, 1967-70; Director of Undergraduate Studies, School of Architecture, Kingston Polytechnic, 1970-94; Principal Lecturer and Director of History, School of Architecture, Kingston University, 1994-; Chief Oenologist, Chiddingstone Vineyards, 1971-83; Partner, Martin Quirk Associates Architects, 1980-90; Freelance Writer and Journalist. Publications: Meaning and Metaphor in Architecture, 1983; The Crime of the Century (with Kinglsey Amis), 1989; Fame in Architecture, 2001; Articles and reviews in many architectural publications. Honours: Silver Medal, International Wine and Spirit Society, 1991. Memberships: Society of Architectural Historians; Victorian Society; Wagner Society; Architectural Association; NATFHE; Ecclesiological Society. Address: The Old Coach Road, Chiddingstone, Kent TN8 7BH, England. E-mail: howardmartinquirk@hotmail.com

**MARTINEZ Conchita,** b. 16 April 1972, Monzon, Spain. Tennis Player. Appointments: Turned Professional, 1988; Reached last 16, French Open, 1988, quarter-finals, French Open, 1989, 1990, 1991, 1992, 1993, semi-finals, Italian Open, 1991, French Open, 1994, Australian and US Opens and Wimbledon, 1995, French and US Opens, 1996, quarter-finals, Olympic Games, 1992; With Arantxa Sanchez-Vicario, won Olympic Doubles Silver Medal, 1992; Won, Italian Open, 1993, Hilton Head (SC), Italian Open, Stratton (Vt), 1994; Wimbledon Singles Champion, 1994; by end of 2002 had won 42 WTA tour titles. Honours: WTA Tour Most Impressive Newcomer, 1989; Most Improved Player, Tennis Magazine, 1994; ITF Award of Excellence, 2001; International Tennis Hall of Fame, 2001.

**MARTINEZ Richard Isaac,** b. 16 August 1944, Havana, Cuba. Science Administrator. 1 son, 1 daughter. Education: BSc, Chemistry, McGill University, Montreal, Canada, 1964; PhD, Physical Chemistry, University of California, Los Angeles, 1976. Appointments: Teaching Assistant, McGill University, Montreal, Canada, 1964-65; Teaching and Research Assistant, San Diego State University, San Diego, California, 1965-67; Chemist, Shell Chemical Company, Torrance, California, 1967-70; Postgraduate Research Chemist, University of California, Los Angeles, 1971-76; Research Chemist, National Institute of Standards and Technology, Gaithersburg, Maryland, 1976-92; National Institute of General Medical Sciences, Bethesda, Maryland, 1992-. Publications: 45 refereed journal articles and invited book chapters in well-respected internationally acclaimed science journals and book series on physical, analytical and organic chemistry; Chemical physics; Reaction mechanisms; Mass spectrometry; 2 US patents. Honours: Doctoral Fellowship, University of California, Los Angeles, 1970-73; NRC Postdoctoral Research Associate, National Academy of Sciences, 1976-78; Bronze medal, US Department of Commerce, 1981; I-R 100 Award for patented Flue-Gas Desulfurization Process, 1983; President and Chairman of Board of Directors, Bethesda-Chevy Chase Jewish Community Group, 1991-93; Fellow, 1995-96, Senior Fellow, 1996-, Council for Excellence in Government; Listed in Who's Who in the World, 18th Edition, and numerous Who's Who publications. Memberships: American Chemical Society; Society for the Advancement of Chicanos and Native Americans in Science. Address: National Institute of General Medical Sciences, 45 Center Dr, Bethesda, MD 20892-6200, USA. E-mail: rm63f@nih.gov

**MARTINEZ Seledon C,** b. 19 December 1921, Chimayo, New Mexico, USA. Retired Educational Administrator; Real Estate and Land Developer. m. Josephine V Martinez, 1 son, 3 daughters. Education: Kansas State Teachers College, 1940-42; BA, Inter-American Affairs, Education, University of New Mexico, Albuquerque, 1945; Advanced Graduate Work, University of California at Los Angeles, 1952-53; MA, Public School Administration, Counselling and Guidance, Physical Education, Highlands University, Las Vegas, New Mexico, 1953; Colorado State University, 1965. Appointments: Military Service, US Marine Corps, South Pacific Theatre Operations, 1943-44; Coach, Director, Athletics, Social Science Teacher, Santa Cruz High School, New Mexico, 1945-56; Superintendent, Rio Arriba County Schools, Tierra Amarilla, New Mexico, 1957-58; Principal, Dulce Independent Schools, New Mexico, 1959-62; Assistant to President, Director, Curriculum, Planing, Counselling, Northern New Mexico Technical Vocational School, El Rito, 1962-69; Assistant to President, Campus Director, Northern New Mexico Technical Vocational School, Espanola Campus, 1969-72; Director, Federal Programs, Title I and Migrant Education, Espanola Municipal Schools, 1972-81; Board Regents, Northern New Mexico Community College, El Rito and Espanola, 1989-94; Currently: Real Estate and Land Developer; Owner, Rancho Los Barrancos, Lower Chimayo, New Mexico; Consultant, American Bureau International Education, Caracas, Venezuela. Publications: Policies, Practices and Procedures for Espanola Board of Education, 1973; Career Education Guide (K-12), Espanola Municipal Schools, 1978; Affirmative Action Plan, Espanola Municipal Schools, 1979. Honours include: Full Track Scholarship to Kansas State Teachers College, 1940; Ford Foundation Scholarship, 1952-53; Technical-Vocational Fellowship, 1965; Menaul High

School Athletic Hall of Fame, 1990; Northern Rio Grande Conference Hall of Fame, 1993; Living Legends, Tesoro Vivo de Rio Arriba, 1997; ZIA Award, University of New Mexico Alumni Association, 1997; Listed in Who's Who publications and biographical dictionaries. Memberships: Disabled Veterans of America; American Legion, Chimayo, New Mexico; VFW; American Association Vocational Educators; Foreign Policy Issues Association. Address: PO Box 182, Chimayo, NM 87522, USA.

**MARTYNOV Arthur,** b. 2 July 1973, Kharkov, Ukraine. Pharmacist; Virology Researcher. Education: Magister of Pharmacy, 1995, PhD, Pharmacy, 1997, Ukrainian Pharmaceutical Academy, Kharkov; Postgraduate Diploma in Microbiology, 1999, Postgraduate Diploma in Immunology, 2001, Kharkov Medical Postgraduate Academy; Diploma of Scientific Doctor in Pharmacy, Kiev Medical Postgraduate Academy, 2005. Appointments: Scientific Employee in Allergology and Immunology, 1997-99, Senior Scientific Employee, 1999, Academic Secretary, 2001-, Mechnicov Institute of Microbiology and Immunology, Ukrainian Medical Sciences Academy, Kharkov, Ukraine; Academic Secretary of the scientific journal "Annals of Mechnicov's Institute", 2001-. Publications: 53 scientific articles; 7 patents. Membership: International Association of Microbiologists. Address: Mechnicov Institute of Microbiology and Immunology, 14 Pushkinskaya Str, Kharkov 61057, Ukraine. E-mail: imiamn@mail.ru

**MARWICK Gavin,** b. 29 August 1969, Edinburgh, Scotland. Musician (fiddle). Career: Youngest of family of traditional/ folk musicians; Involved in resurgence of Scottish music and dance, 1980s; Numerous television and radio broadcasts; Festivals and extensive tours mainly with Iron Horse, Europe, and (occasionally) US, Africa, 1988-; Composer, television soundtracks; Recording artist and teacher; Recording sessions include: Wolfstone; Talitha MacKenzie; Old Blind Dogs; The Electrics; The Humff Family; Other projects: Twin fiddle-led trio (with members of Old Blind Dogs) Burach; Theatre music. Recordings: with The Iron Horse: The Iron Horse, 1991; Thro Water Earth And Stone, 1993; Five Hands High, 1994; The Gamekeeper, 1995; Demons And Lovers, 1997; with Jonny Hardie and Davy Cattanach: Up In The Air, 1995; with Burach: The Weird Set, 1995; with the Marwicks: Ceilidh Sets, 1998; with Jonny Hardie: The Blue Lamp, 1999. Honour: Belhaven Best New Folk Band, Burach, 1995. Memberships: Musicians' Union; PRS; PAMRA. Current Management: Peter Stott. Address: 11 Harling Drive, Troon, Ayrshire KA10 6NF, Scotland.

**MASADA Hiromitsu,** b. 3 February 1938, Nishinomiya, Hyogo, Japan. Chemistry Researcher. m. Yoko Danno, 1 daughter. Education: Bachelor of Engineering, Osaka University, 1962; Master of Engineering, 1964, Doctor of Engineering, 1967, Kyoto University. Appointments: Assistant Professor, 1967-72, Associate Professor, 1972-96, Professor, 1996-2003, Kanazawa University. Honour: Seikyo Newspaper Culture Award, Tokyo, 1986; Who's Who in the World, 1998; Nominator, Nobel Prize in Chemistry, 2001. Address: 7-6 Hongo 3 Chome, Kashiwara City, Osaka Prefecture 582-0001, Japan.

**MASAKI Daisaku,** b. 15 February 1964, Kobe, Japan. Aerospace Engineer. Education: Bachelor of Science, 1987, Master of Science, 1989, PhD, 1995, Aeronautical and Astronautical Engineering, University of Tokyo, Japan. Appointments: Technical Staff, 1990-91, 1996-98, Assistant Manager, 1999-2003, Kawasaki Heavy Industries Ltd, Akashi, Japan; Company Sponsored Scholarship, University of

Tokyo, 1992-95; Senior Research Scientist, Institute of Space Technology and Aeronautics/Japan Aerospace Exploration Agency, Tokyo, Japan, 2004-. Publications: Articles in scientific journals and presented at conferences include: Three-dimensional Navier-Stokes Calculations of Transonic Compressor Flowfields with Tip Clearance, 1996; Numerical Investigation of Transonic Compressor Flowfields near Stall, Part I and II, 1997; A Study on the Convergence of Roe's Approximate Riemann Solver, 1997; Numerical Analysis of Transonic Compressor Rotor Flow near Stall Points, 1997; Discussion on A Study on the Convergence of Roe's Approximate Riemann Solver, 1999; Design Study of a Pre-Cooled Turbojet Engine for Flight Experiments, co-author, 2005. Honours: Listed in numerous Who's Who publications and biographical dictionaries. Memberships: Japan Society for Aeronautical and Space Sciences, 1996; Gas Turbine Society of Japan, 1996; American Society of Mechanical Engineers, 1999; Senior Member, American Institute of Aeronautics and Astronautics, 1999. Address: 7-44-1 Jindaiji-Higashimachi, Chofu, Tokyo 182-8522, Japan. E-mail: daimasa@mall.interq.or.jp, also masakid@chofu.jaxa.jp

**MASAMURA Masao,** b. 9 December 1958, Kyoto, Japan. Computational Chemist. Education: Bachelor of dentistry, Kagoshima University Dental School, 1985; DDS, 1985; PhD, University of Tsukuba, 2000. Appointments: Assistant Professor, Okayama University Dental School, 1985-; Assistant Professor, Okayama Graduate School of Medicine and Dentistry, 2001-. Publications: Articles in scientific journals including: Theoretical Chemistry Accounts, 2001; Journal of Chemical Physics, 2002, 2003; Journal of Physical Chemistry A, 2002; Journal of Computational Chemistry, 2004. Honour: Fundamental Information Technology Engineer, Trade and Industry Ministry, 2001. Membership: American Chemical Society. Address: Tushimafukui 1-6-16, Okayama, 700-0088, Japan. E-mail: tokin@mx3.tiki.ne.jp

**MASHHOON Bahram,** b. 9 September 1947, Tehran, Iran. Physicist. 1 daughter. Education: AB Physics, University of California at Berkeley, 1969; PhD, Physics, Princeton University, 1972. Appointments: Assistant Professor, Arya-Mehr University, Tehran, Iran, 1972-73; Research Associate, Princeton University, 1973-74; Postdoctoral Fellow, Center for Theoretical Physics, University of Maryland, 1974-76; Research Associate and Instructor, University of Utah, 1976-78; Lecturer and Research Fellow, California Institute of Technology, 1978-80; Research Fellow, University of Cologne, Germany, 1980-85; Associate Professor of Physics, 1985-95, Professor of Physics, 1995-, Department of Physics and Astronomy, University of Missouri-Columbia. Publications More than 140 scientific publications as author and co-author which include most recently: Ultrarelativistic Motion: Inertial and Tidal Effects in Fermi Coordinates, 2005; Spinning Particles in the Vacuum C Metric, 2005; Non-locality of Accelerated Systems, 2005. Honours: University of California Medal, 1969; Princeton National Fellow, 1969-70; Honourable Mention: Gravity Research Foundation, 1981; Alexander von Humboldt Fellow, 1981-82, 1997; Award Winning Essay, 1983, Honourable Mention, 1984, Gravity Research Foundation; Summer Fellowship, University of Missouri-Columbia, 1986. Address: Department of Physics and Astronomy, University of Missouri-Columbia, Columbia, MO 65211, USA. E-mail: mashhoonb@missouri.edu

**MASHKOVTSEV Mikhail Borisovich,** b. 1 January 1947, Minsk, Byelorussia, USSR. Electronics Engineer; Regional Governor. m. Tatiana Borisovna Mashkovtseva, 2 daughters. Education: Electronics Engineering, Leningrad Institute of Aviation Apparatus. Appointments: Elected Governor, Kamchatka Region, Russia, 2000-; Promoted by the Communist Party of the Russian Federation; Policy Maker; Social Relations Expert. Publications: Articles in local and national newspapers. Honours: Numerous Awards for Achievements in the Social Economic Sector. Membership: Communist Party of the Russian Federation. Address: Kamchatka Regional Administration, 1 Lenin Square, Petropavlovsk-Kamchatski, Kamchatka Region, Russia 683040. E-mail: press@ako.kamchatka.ru

**MASLIYAH Jacob Heskel,** b. 9 August 1942, Baghdad, Iraq. Professor. m. Odette Ishayek, 1 son, 2 daughters. Education: BSc Chemical Engineering, University College, London, 1964; MSc Chemical Engineering, University of New Brunswick, Canada, 1966; PhD, Chemical Engineering, University of British Columbia, Canada, 1970. Appointments: Assistant Professor, 1972-75, Associate Professor, 1975-77, University of Saskatchewan; Visiting Consultant, Alberta Research Council, Edmonton, 1976; Associate Professor, 1977-80, Professor of Chemical Engineering, 1980-, University Professor, 2000-, University of Alberta; NSERC Industrial Research Chair in Oil Sands, Syncrude Canada Ltd, 1996-2001; NSERC Industrial Research Chair in Oil Sands, Albian, Suncor, Canadian Natural Resources Ltd, Champion Technologies and Syncrude, 2001-06. Publications: 263 refereed publications; 1 book, Electronkinetic Transport Phenomena, 1994. Honours: Century of Achievement Award; University Cup; Canada Research Chair; JS Jane Memorial Award. Memberships: Chemical Institute of Canada; Royal Society of Canada; Canadian Academy of Engineering. Address: University of Alberta, 536 Chemical Materials Building, Edmonton, Alberta, T2G 2G6, Canada. E-mail: jacob.masliyah@alberta.ca Website: www.ualberta.ca/masliyah/

**MASON OF BARNSLEY, Baron of Barnsley in the County of South Yorkshire, Roy Mason,** b. 18 April 1924, England. Member of the House of Lords. m. Marjorie Sowden, 2 daughters. Education: TUC Scholarship, London School of Economics; D University, Hallam University, Sheffield. Appointments: Coal Miner, 1938-53; Labour Candidate for Bridlington, 1951-53; Member of Parliament for Barnsley, 1953-83, Barnsley Central, 1983-87; Opposition Spokesman on Defence and Post Office Affairs, 1960-64; Minister of State for Shipping, Board of Trade, 1964-67; Minister of Defence Equipment, 1967-68; Postmaster General, 1968; Minister of Power, 1968-69; President, Board of Trade, 1969-70; Principal Spokesman on Board of Trade Affairs, 1970-74; Member, Council of Europe and Western European Union, 1973; Secretary of State for Defence, 1974-76; Secretary of State for Northern Ireland, 1976-79; Principal Opposition Spokesman on Agriculture, Fisheries and Food, 1979-81. Publication: Paying the Price, autobiography. Honours: PC, 1968; Peerage, 1987. Memberships: Yorkshire Miners' Council, 1949-53; Council of Europe, 1970-71; Yorkshire Group of Labour MPs, 1970-74, 1981-84; Miners' Group of MPs, 1973-74, 1980-81; Railway and Steel Union MPs, 1979-80; National Rivers Authority, 1989-92. Address: 12 Victoria Avenue, Barnsley, South Yorkshire, S70 2BH, England.

**MASSEY Alan Randolph Charles,** b. 6 June 1932, Berkshire, England. Librarian; Poet. m. Gillian Elizabeth Petty, 30 September 1974. Publications: Trajectories in the Air; The Fire Garden. Contributions to: Agenda; Poetry Review; Workshop; Expression. Membership: Poetry Society. Address: 41 Albany Road, Windsor, Berkshire SL4 1HL, England.

**MASSEY Roy Cyril,** b. 9 May 1934, Birmingham, England. Cathedral Organist. m. Ruth Carol Craddock. Education: University of Birmingham, 1953-56; Private tuition under Sir David Willcocks, Worcester Cathedral. Appointments: Accompanist, City of Birmingham Choir, 1953-60; Church and School appointments, 1956-65; Warden, Royal School of Church Music, 1965-68; Organist and Master of the Choristers, Birmingham Cathedral, 1968-74; Organist and Master of the Choristers, Hereford Cathedral, 1974-2001. Publication: The Organs of Hereford Cathedral (in Hereford Cathedral, a history), 2000. Honours: Honorary Fellowship, Royal School of Church Music, 1971; Lambeth Degree, Doctor of Music, 1991; MBE for Services to Music, 1997; Honorary Fellowship, Guild of Church Musicians, 2000; President, Royal College of Organists, 2003-05. Address: 2 King John's Court, Tewkesbury, Gloucestershire GL20 6EG, England. E-mail: drroymassey@ukonline.co.uk

**MASTERSON Kleber Sanlin, Jr,** b. 26 September 1932, San Diego, California, USA. Physicist; Military Operations Researcher. m. Sara Cooper Masterson, 2 sons. Education: BS (Engineering), US Naval Academy, 1954; MS (Physics), US Naval Postgraduate School, 1961; PhD (Physics), University of California at San Diego, 1963; Graduate, Advanced Management Programme, Harvard Business School, 1980. Appointments: Commanding Officer, USS Preble; Antiship Missile Defence Project Manager; Assistant Deputy Commander, Naval Sea Systems Command for Anti-Air and Surface Warfare Systems; Chief, Studies Analysis and Gaming Agency; Office of the Joint Chiefs of Staff; Retired as Rear Admiral, US Navy, 1950-82; Principal, 1982-87, Vice President, Partner, 1987-92 Booz, Allen and Hamilton; Senior Vice President, Science Applications International Corporation, 1992-96; President, The Riverside Group Ltd, 1994-; President, Military Operations Research Society, 1988-89; President, Massachusetts Society of the Cincinnati, 2001-04; Assistant Secretary-General, The Society of the Cincinnati, 2001-04; Treasurer General, The Society of the Cincinnati, 2004-. Publications: Numerous articles and invited presentations; Created NELIAC ALGOL compiler, 1958-59. Honours: Defence Superior Service Medal; Legion of Merit with 2 gold stars for subsequent awards; Navy Commendation Medal with Combat 'V' and 2 gold stars. Memberships: American Physical Society; Society of Sigma Xi; Society of the Cincinnati. E-mail: skidmasterson@compu serve.com

**MATA-SEGREDA Julio F R,** b. 3 August 1948, San José, Costa Rica. Professor. m. Luisa Díaz-Sánchez, 2 sons, 3 daughters. Education: BSc, Chemistry, 1970, Licentiate, Chemistry, 1971, University of Costa Rica; PhD, Chemistry, University of Kansas, USA. Appointments: Instructor, 1975, Professor, 1984, University of Costa Rica; Invited Researcher, Ritsumeikan University, Kyoto, Japan, 1982; Invited Researcher, University of Kansas, USA, 1986-87; Invited Professor, University of the Andes, Merida, Venezuela, 1991. Publications: 65 scientific papers in professional journals; Some book chapters. Honours: National Science Award, 1981; Fullbright Fellowship, 1986; Matsumae Fellowship and Medal, Tokyo, Japan, 1982; Fellow, National Academy of Science, 1994. Memberships: Physical Chemistry Section of the American Chemical Society; Costa Rican Association of Philosophy and History of Science; National Academy of Science, Costa Rica. Address: School of Chemistry, University of Costa Rica, 2060 Costa Rica. E-mail: jmata@cariari.ucr.ac.cr

**MATASOVIC Ranko,** b. 14 May 1968, Zagreb, Croatia. Linguist. m. Maja Rupnik, 2 sons. Education: BA, Linguistics and Philosophy, 1990, MA, Linguistics, 1992, PhD, Comparative Linguistics, 1995, University of Zagreb. Appointments: Assistant Professor of Comparative Linguistics, 1996, Full Professor of Linguistics, 2004, University of Zagreb; Fulbright Visiting Scholar, University of Wisconsin, Madison, USA, 1997-98; Humbold Fellow, Bonn University, 2002-03. Publications: A Theory of Textual Reconstruction in Indo-European Linguistics,

1996; Kratka Poredbenopovijesna Gramatika Latinsuoga Jezika, 1997; Uvod Uporedbenu Lingvistiku, 2001. Honours: Award of the Croatian Academy of Sciences and Arts for a lasting contribution to science, 2002. Memberships: Indogermanische Gesellschaft, Wiesbaden. Address: I Bukovacki Ogranak II, 10 000 Zagreb, Croatia. E-mail: rmatasov@ffzg.hr Website: http: //deenas.ffzg.hr/~rmatasov

**MATHESON Michael,** b. 8 September 1970, Glasgow, Scotland. Member of the Scottish Parliament. Education: BSc, Occupational Therapy, Queen Margaret College, Edinburgh, 1988-92; BA, Diploma in Applied Social Sciences, Open University, 1992-96. Appointments: Community Occupational Therapist, Stirling Council, Central Regional Council and Highland Regional Council, 1992-99; Member of the Scottish Parliament, 1999-; Shadow Minister for Culture and Sport. Memberships: State Registered Occupational Therapist, Health Professions Council; Member, Ochils Mountain Rescue Team; Former Member, Scottish Parliament Justice Committee; Member, Enterprise and Culture Committee. Address: The Scottish Parliament, Edinburgh, EH99 1SP, Scotland. E-mail: michael.matheson.msp@scottish.parliament.uk

**MATHIAS Peter,** b. 10 January 1928. Historian. m. Elizabeth Ann Blackmore, 2 sons, 1 daughter. Education: BA, 1951, MA, 1954, Jesus College, Cambridge; LittD (Oxon), 1985; DLitt (Cantab), 1987. Appointments include: Research Fellow, Jesus College, Cambridge, 1952-55; Assistant Lecturer, Lecturer, Faculty of History, University of Cambridge, 1955-68; Director of Studies in History, Fellow, Queens' College, Cambridge, 1955-68; Tutor, 1957-68, Senior Proctor, 1965-66, University of Cambridge; Chichele Professor of Economic History, University of Oxford, Fellow All Souls College, 1969-87; Curator Bodleian Library, 1972-87; Master, Downing College, Cambridge, 1987-95; Visiting Professor: Toronto University, 1961; Delhi University, 1967; California University, Berkeley, 1967; Pennsylvania University, 1972; Virginia Gildersleeve Professor, Columbia University, 1972; Johns Hopkins University, 1979; Natal University, 1980; Australian National University, 1981; Geneva University, 1986; Leuven University, 1990; San Marino University, 1990; Waseda University, 1996; Osaka Gakuin University, 1998; Bolzano Free University, 1999; Chairman, International Advisory Committee, University of Buckingham, 1979-84; National Advisory Council, British Library, 1994-2000; Great Britain Sasakawa Foundation, 1997-; Member Syndicate Fitzwilliam Museum, Cambridge, 1987-98; Chairman, Fitzwilliam Museum Enterprises, 1990-99; Member, Board of Patrons, European Association for Banking History; Honorary Treasurer, British Academy, 1980-89. Publications: The Brewing Industry in England 1700-1830, 1959, reprinted 1993; English Trade Tokens, 1962; Retailing Revolution, 1967; The First Industrial Nation, 1969, revised edition, 1983; The Transformation of England, 1979; Editor and contributor, Science and Society, 1972; Co-editor and contributor, The First Industrial Revolutions, 1989; Co-editor and contributor, Innovation and technology in Europe, 1991; L'Economia Britannica dal 1815-1914, 1994; Cinque lezioni de teoria e storia, Naples, 2003; General editor, Cambridge Economic History of Europe, 1968-93. Honours: CBE, 1984; Honorary Fellow, Jesus College, 1987, Queens' College, 1987, Downing College, 1995; Honorary LittD, University of Buckingham, 1985, University of Hull, 1992, University of Warwick, 1995, De Montfort University, 1995; Honorary DLitt, University of Birmingham, 1988, UEA, 1999; Honorary Doctorate, Russian Academy of sciences, 2002; Grand Cordon, Order of the Rising Sun, 2003; Fellow, Royal History Society, 1972; Fellow, British Academy, 1977. Memberships include: President, 1974-78, Honorary President, 1978- International Economic History

Society; Vice-President, 1975-80, Honorary Vice-president, 2001-, Royal Historical Society; President, 1989-92, Economic History Society; Academia Europaea; Foreign Member: Royal Danish Academy, Royal Belgian Academy. Address: 33 Church Street, Chesterton, Cambridge, CB4 1DT, England.

**MATOUŠEK Jiří,** b. 4 April 1930, Příbram, Czech Republic. Chemical Engineer. m. Dagmar Matoušková, 1 son, 1 daughter. Education: Dipl Eng (Chem), Czech Technical University, Prague and Military Technical Academy, Brno, 1954; PhD (CSc), Military Technical Academy, Brno, 1958; DSc, Military Academy of Chemical Protection, Moscow, 1967; Associate Professor, Special Technology, Military Academy, Brno, 1966; Professor, Organic Chemistry, Palacký University, Olomouc, 1983. Appointments: Assistant Professor, Military Technical Academy, Brno, 1954-59, Head of Department, 1959-63; Director, NBC Defence R & D Establishment, Brno, 1963-71; Deputy Head, Department of Toxicology, Purkyne Medical Research Institute, Hradec Králové, 1971-81; Director for Research, NBC Defence R & D Establishment, Brno, 1981-89; Senior Research Fellow, Academy of Science, Prague, 1989-90; Professor of Toxicology, Masaryk University, Brno, 1990-; Visiting Professor International Institute for Peace, Vienna, 1990-; Director Institute of Environmental Chemistry and Technology, Brno University of Technology, 1992-2000. Publications: Over 500 articles in professional and scientific journals; About 130 research reports, 90 patents and improvement suggestions, mostly realised in production and use; More than 420 conference papers, mostly international; 21 books and 36 chapters in monographs dealing with chemistry and analysis of toxic agents, chemical and biological disarmament, verification, conversion, ecological, environmental and other global problems, mostly in English but also in German, French, Russian, Czech and Slovak. Honours: 7 state and military orders and medals; Memorial Medal of Masaryk University, 1991; Memorial Medal of Brno University of Technology, 1999; American Medal of Honor, 2002. Memberships: International Network of Engineers and Scientists; World Federation of Scientific Workers; Pugwash Conferences; Accredited Representative of World Federation of Scientific Workers at UNO and conference of NGOs; Chairman, Scientific Advisory Board, Organisation for the Prohibition of Chemical Weapons; Many other professional organisations. Address: Krásného 26, CZ-636 00 Brno, Czech Republic. E-mail: matousek@recetox.muni.cz

**MATSUDA Masafumi,** b. 15 January 1956, Yamaguchi-ken, Japan. Medical Doctor. m. Yoshiko Matsuda, 1 daughter. Education: MD, Faculty of Medicine, University of Tokyo, 1982; PhD, Yamaguchi University, 1989; Boards: Medical Examination of the National Board, Japan, 1982; Standard ECFMG Certificate, USA, 1991. Appointments: Resident, University of Tokyo Hospital, 1982; Resident, 1983, Staff Physician, 1984-87, Assistant, 1987-88, Staff Physician, 1988-90, Yamaguchi University Hospital; Visiting Scientist, 1990-93, Clinical Instructor, 1993-96, Assistant Professor, 1996-98, University of Texas Health Science Center at San Antonio; Co-Director, 1996-97, Medical Research Director, 1998, Clinical Research Center, Texas Diabetes Institute; Lecturer, Kawasaki Medical School, 1999-. Publications:58 original scientific papers; 52 review articles. Honours: Man of the Year 2004, Great Minds of the 21st Century, ABI, USA. Memberships: Councillor, Japan Diabetes Association; Councillor, Japan Society of Clinical Nutrition. Address: Diabetes and Endocrine Division, Department of Medicine, Kawasaki Medical School, 577 Matsushima, Kurashiki-shi, Oyakama-ken, 701-0192, Japan. E-mail: matsudam-ind@umin.ac.jp

**MATSUDA Wakoto,** b. 6 April 1968, Onomichi, Hiroshima, Japan. Neurosurgeon; Researcher. m. Kiyoe Nakazawa, 1 son, 1 daughter. Education: MD, Faculty of Medicine, University of Tsukuba, Ibaraki, Japan, 1990-96; Diplomate in Neurosurgery, Japan Neurosurgical Society, 2002. Appointments: Residency, Department of Neurosurgery, University of Tsukuba Hospital, Tsukuba, Ibaraki Japan, 1996-2002; Clinical Fellow, Department of Neurosurgery, Tsukuba Medical Centre Hospital, Tsukuba, Ibaraki, Japan, 2002-2003; Postgraduate, Department of Morphological Brain Science, 2003-, Research Assistant, 2004-, Graduate School of Medicine, Kyoto University, Kyoto, Japan. Publications: Articles in: Journal of Neurology, Neurosurgery and Psychiatry, 2003, 2004; Neuropsychological Rehabilitation, 2005. Honours: The Best Resident Award of the Year, Department of Neurosurgery, Institute of Clinical Medicine, University of Tsukuba, 2002; Iwadare Scholarship, Iwadare Scholarship Foundation, 2003. Memberships: Japan Neurosurgical Society, Tokyo, Japan; Japanese Congress of Neurological Surgery, Tokyo, Japan. Address: Department of Morphological Brain Science, Graduate School of Medicine, Kyoto University, Building C, 1st & 2nd Floors, Konoe-cho, Yoshida, Sakyo-ku, Kyoto 606-8501, Japan. E-mail: wako@mua.biglobe.ne.jp

**MATSUHASHI Nobuyuki,** b. 7 November 1956, Tokyo. Physician. 3 daughters. Education: BM, 1982, MD, 1991, University of Tokyo. Appointments: Resident, University of Tokyo, 1982-84; Assistant Professor, Tokyo Women's Medical College, 1984-85; Resident, Jichi Medical School, 1985-86; Research Fellow, National Institute of Radiological Sciences, 1988-89; Assistant Professor, University of Tokyo, 1989-2003; Chairman, Department of Endoscopy, Kanto Medical Center, NTT East, 2004-. Publications: Articles in professional medical journals including: Journal of Immunology, Gut, Lancet, Gastroenterology, Gastrointestinal Endoscopy, Journal of Experimental Medicine, Cancer Research. Honours: Academic Prize of the Japanese Gastroenterological Endoscopy Society, 1999. Memberships: Japanese Society for Gastroenterology; Japanese Society for Gastroenterological Endoscopy; Japanese Society for Immunology; Japanese Society for Internal Medicine; American Gastroenterological Association; Society for Mucosal Immunology; American Society for Gastrointestinal Endoscopy. Address: Department of Endoscopy, Kanto Medical Center, NTT East, 5-9-22 Higashi-gotanda, Shinagawa-ku, Tokyo 141-8625 Japan. E-mail: nmatuha-tky@umin.ac.jp

**MATSUMOTO Seiichi,** b. 8 November 1916, Kamakura, Japan. President, Japan Family Planning Association. m. Sadako Ohkochi, 8 November 1948, 1 son, 1 daughter. Education: Graduate, Tokyo University School of Medicine, 1941; Dr Med Sci, Tokyo University, 1947. Appointments: Assistant Professor, Showa Medical College, 1945-60; Chief, Department of Maternal Health, Aiiku Institute, 1950-54; Chief, Department of Obstetrics and Gynaecology, Kanto Teishin Hospital, 1954-58; Professor, Obstetrics and Gynaecology, Gunma University School of Medicine, 1958-72; Professor, Obstetrics and Gynaecology, 1972-92, Director, 1974-85, Professor Emeritus, 1992-; Jichi Medical School Hospital; President, Jichi Medical School, School of Nursing, 1987-91; Professor Emeritus, Gunma University, 1988-. Publications: Menstruation and its Disorders, 1956; Maternal Care, 1968; Introduction to Maternal and Child Health, 1973; Recent Contraceptive Methods, 1975; Maternal Health Care, 1977; Adolescent Health, 1982; Studies on Women's Senses and Behaviours about Menstruation, 1990; Adolescent Clinic, 1995; Studies on PMS, 1995; Menstruation of Japanese Women, 1999. Honours: Award, Minister of Health and Welfare, 1977; Public Health Award, 1989; Order of Sacred Treasure, Gold and Silver Star, 1991; Award, FIGO, 1994; Gold

Medal, World Association for Sexology, 1995. Memberships: Honorary President, Japan Federation of Sexology; Honorary Chairman, Japan Society of Adolescentology; Japan Society of Maternal Health; Executive Board Member, Japan Association of Sex Education. Address: 1-11-17 Yuigahama, 248-0014, Japan.

**MATTESSICH Richard,** b. 9 August 1922, Trieste, Italy. Professor Emeritus. m. Hermine. Education: Mech Engineer Diploma, 1940; Dipl Kaufmann, 1944; Dr rer pol, 1945; Dr honoris causa, 1998. Appointments: Research Fellow, Austrian Institute of Economic Research, 1945-47; Lecturer, Rosenberg College, Switzerland, 1947-52; Department Head, Mount Allison University, Canada, 1953-58; Associate Professor, University of California, Berkeley, 1959-67; Professor, Ruhr University, Bochum, 1965-66; Professor, University of British Columbia, 1967-88; Professor, University of Technology, Vienna, 1976-78; Professor Emeritus, University of British Columbia, 1988-. Publications: Books: Accounting and Analytic Methods, 1964; Simulation of the Firm, 1964; Instrumental Reasoning and Systems Methods, 1978; Modern Accounting Research, 1984; Accounting Research in the 1980's, 1991; Critique of Accounting, 1995; Foundational Research in Accounting, 1995; The Beginnings of Accounting, 2000. Honours: Ford Founding Fellow, USA, 1961, 62; Erskine Fellow, New Zealand, 1970; Killam Senior Fellow, Canada, 1971; Literary Awards, AICPA, 1972, CAAA, 1991. Memberships: Accademia Italiana di Econ Aziendale, 1980-; Austrian Academy of Science, 1984-; Life member, American Accounting Association; Life member, Academy of Accounting Historians; Officially Nominated for the Nobel Prize in Economics, 2002; Dr.h.c. (Univ. of Madrid, 1998; Univ. of Málaga, 2005). Address: c/o Faculty of Commerce and Business Administrator, University of British Columbia, Vancouver, British Columbia, Canada V6T 1Z2. E-mail: richard.mattessich@sauder.ubc.ca

**MATTHEW Christopher Charles Forrest,** b. 8 May 1939, London, England. Novelist; Journalist; Broadcaster. m. Wendy Mary Matthew, 19 October 1979, 2 sons, 1 daughter. Education: BA, Honours, MA, Honours, St Peter's College, Oxford. Appointments: Editor, Times Travel Guide, 1972-73. Publications: A Different World; Stories of Great Hotels, 1976; Diary of a Somebody, 1978; Loosely Engaged, 1980; The Long-Haired Boy, 1980; The Crisp Report, 1981; Three Men in a Boat, annotated edition, with Benny Green, 1982; The Junket Man, 1983; How to Survive Middle Age, 1983; Family Matters, 1987; The Amber Room, 1995; A Nightingale Sang in Fernhurst Road, 1998; Now We Are Sixty, 1999; Knocking On, 2000; Now We Are Sixty (And a Bit), 2003. Contributions to: Many leading newspapers; Columnist for Punch, 1983-88; Restaurant Critic for English Vogue, 1983-86; Book and TV reviewer for Daily Mail. Membership: Society of Authors. Address: 35 Drayton Gardens, London SW10 9RY, England.

**MATTHIESEN Patrick David Albert Francis Jonathan,** b. 1 March 1943, London, England. Art Dealer. m. Hiromi Kaminishi, 2 daughters. Education: Briscoe Owen Scholar, MA, Oriel College, Oxford; Courtauld Institute of Art, London. Appointments: Supervisor of restoration sculpture project in Florence after floods, 1966-67; Supervisor in founding Conservation Institute in Venice in liaison with the Victoria and Albert Museum, 1968-69; Independent Art Dealer, 1970; Associate, Queensbury Investments Ltd property developers, 1970-71; Associate Independent Consultant, 1972, In Charge of the Research Department, 1973-73, General Manager, 1973-75, Director, Old Master Paintings Department, 1976-77, P & D Colnaghi Ltd; Founder, Chairman and Managing Director, Matthiesen Fine Art Ltd, 1978-; Exhibitions mounted by Matthiesen Fine Art include: Important Italian Painting 1600-1700, 1981; Early Italian Paintings and Works of Art 1300-1400, 1983; From Borso to Cesare d'Este: School of Ferrara 1450-1628, 1984; Around 1610: The Onset of Baroque, 1985, Varlin, 1985, Baroque III, 1986; Paintings from Emila 1500-1700, 1987; The Settecento: Italian Rococo and Early Neoclassical Paintings 1700-1800, 1987; A Selection of French Paintings 1700-1840, 1989; Louis Léopold Boilly's L'Entrée du Jardin Turc, 1991; Fifty Paintings 1535-1925, 1993; Paintings 1600-1912, 1996; Gold Backs 1250-1480, 1996; An Eye on Nature, 1997; Collectanea: 1700-1800, 1998; A Del Sarto Rediscovered, 2002; Il Porto di Ripetta, 2002; Chardin's Têtes d'Études au Pastel, 2003. Publications include most recently: Virtuous Virgins: Classical Heroines, Romantic Passion and the Art of Suicide, 2004; Bertin's Ideal Landscapes, 2004; Polidoro Da Caravaggio: La Lignamine's Lamentation. Memberships: RAC; Chairman and Founder, The Matthiesen Foundation. Address: Matthiesen Gallery, 7-8 Mason's Yard, Duke Street, London SW1, England. E-mail: gallery@matthiesengallery.com

**MATULIONIS Arvydas,** b. 1 April 1940, Kupiskis, Lithuania. Professor of Physics. m. Ilona, 3 sons, 1 daughter. Education: Diploma in Physics, Vilnius University, Lithuania, 1961; Candidate of Science, Physics and Mathematics, 1967, DSc, Physics and Mathematics, 1981, Vilnius University, Lithuania; Doctor Habilitus, Nature Science, Lithuania, 1993. Appointments: Research Associate, Institute of Optics, University of Rochester, USA, 1969-70; Senior Research Associate, 1972-74, Head of Laboratory, 1974-91, Associate Professor (part-time), 1983-85, Professor of Physics and Principal Research Associate, 1991-95, Professor of Physics and Head of Fluctuation Research Laboratory, 1995-, Semiconductor Physics Institute, Vilnius; Professor of Physic (part-time), Vytautas Magnus University, Kaunas, Lithuania, 1991-95. Publications: Over 160 in professional journals; Monograph: H L Hartnagel, R Katilius, A Matulionis, Microwave Noise in Semiconductor Devices, John Wiley and Sons, New York, 2001. Honours: Lithuanian National Award in Science, 1983, 1995. Memberships: Lithuanian Physical Society; International Advisory Committee, International Conference on Noise and Fluctuations; International Advisory Committee, European Workshop on Compound Semiconductor Devices and Integrated Circuits (WOCSDICE). Address: Fluctuation Research Laboratory, Semiconductor Physics Institute Vilnius, 11 A Gostauto, Vilnius 01108, Lithuania.

**MATUSSEK Thomas,** b. 18 September 1947, Lauda, Germany. Ambassador. m. Ursula Matussek, 1 son, 2 daughters. Education: Studied Law and History at the Universities of Paris (Sorbonne) and Bonn, 1979-72; First State Examination in Law, 1973. Appointments: Judge's Assistant/Assistant Lecturer, University of Bonn, 1973-76; German Foreign Office, Bonn, 1975-77; German Embassy, London, 1977-80; Federal Chancellery, European Affairs, 1980-83; German Embassy, New Delhi, 1983-86; German Embassy, Lisbon, 1986-88; German Foreign Office, Bonn, 1988-92; Head of the Minister's Office, 1992-93, Chief of the Cabinet of the Minister, 1993-94, Foreign Office, Bonn; Deputy Chief of Mission, German Embassy, Washington, 1994-99; Director-General, Political Department, Foreign Office, Berlin, 1999; Ambassador of the Federal Republic of Germany to the Court of St James's, 2002-. Memberships: Athenaeum; Royal Automobile; Naval and Military Club; Travellers Club; Beefsteak Club; Capital Club. Address: German Embassy, 23 Belgrave Square, London SW1X 8PZ, England. E-mail: ambofffice@german-embassy.org.uk

**MATVEEV Victor,** b. 23 October 1962, Archangel, Russia. Shipping Manager. m. Elena Matveeva, 2 daughters. Education:

Admiral Makarov State Maritime Academy, St Petersburg, Russia. Appointments: 3rd Mate, Merchant Vessels, 1987-88; Cargo Officer, Merchant Ships, 1988-90; Deputy Manager, Claims and Insurance Department, Northern Shipping Co, Archangel, Russia, 1990-93; Managing Director, Boreal Shipping, Archangel, 1993-96; Managing Director, Chairman, OY Solchart Ltd, Helsinki, Finland, 1996-. Honour: Listed in Who's Who publications and biographical dictionaries. Address: Silkinku tojankuja 7B, 00950 Helsinki, Finland. E-mail: victor@solchart.fi

**MATZON Akos**, b. 19 April 1945, Budapest, Hungary. Painter; Artist; Architect. m. Gertrud Gergo, 1 son, 2 daughters. Education: Architect, 1963; Studies in drawing school, 1965-70; University of Technical Sciences, Pecs, Budapest, 1980-86; Technical Professor; Free School of Art, 1986; Art study trip to Germany, France and Switzerland, 1993. Appointments: j X Museum, Györ, 1990; German Embassy, Budapest, 1995; Kunstlergilde Esslingen, Germany, 1998; Wüstenrot; Haus Ungarn, Berlin, 2000; Kiscelli Museum, Budapest, 2002; German Haus, Budapest, 2003; Kassak Museum, Budapest, 2003; Culture Institute, Stuttgart, 2004; Embassy Hungary, Berlin, 2004; Collegium Hungarycum Wien, 2004; TPK Karlsruhe, Germany, 2005; I Kalman Museum Siofok, Hungary, 2005. Publications: Numerous articles in professional journals. Honours: Winner, Pollock-Krasner Foundation Prize, New York, 1998. Memberships: Association of Hungarian Creative Artists; International Madi; Vudak, Germany; Kunstlergilde Esslingen, Germany; International Kepes Society. Address: 52 Rozsika Street, Solymar 2083, Hungary. E-mail: akos@matzon.com Website: www.matzon.com

**MAUPIN Armistead**, b. 13 May 1944, Washington, District of Columbia, USA. Writer. Education: BA, University of North Carolina at Chapel Hill, 1966. Appointments: Reporter, News and Courier, Charleston, 1970-71, Associated Press, 1971-72; Columnist, Pacific Sun, San Francisco, 1974, San Francisco Chronicle, 1976-77. Publications: Tales of the City, 1978; More Tales of the City, 1980; Further Tales of the City, 1982; Babycakes, 1984; Significant Others, 1987; Sure of You, 1989; 28 Barbary Lane, 1990; Back to Barbary Lane, 1991; Maybe the Moon, 1992; The Night Listener, 2000. Other: Libretto for the musical Heart's Desire, 1990. Television Programme: Armistead Maupin's Tales of the City, 1993. Contributions to: Periodicals. Honours: Best Dramatic Serial Award, Royal TV Society, 1994; George Foster Peabody Award, 1994. Address: 584 Castro Street, # 528, San Francisco, CA 94114, USA.

**MAURICE-WILLIAMS Robert Stephen**, b. 14 June 1942, Southampton, England. Consultant Neurosurgeon. m. Elizabeth Anne Meadows, 1 son, 3 daughters. Education: Pembroke College, Cambridge, St Thomas' Hospital Medical School, London; MA, MB, BChir, Cambridge; FRSC (England); FRCP( London). Appointments: Chief Assistant in Neurosurgery, St Bartholomew's Hospital, 1973-77; Consultant Neurosurgeon, Brook Hospital, 1977-80; Consultant Neurosurgeon, 1980-; Senior Neurosurgeon, 1982-, The Royal Free Hospital; Editor, British Journal of Neurosurgery, 1992-99; Member, Court of Examiners, Royal College of Surgeons, 1992-98. Publications: Books: Spinal Degenerative Disease, 1981; Subarachnoid Haemorrhage, 1988; Over 80 papers in peer-reviewed scientific journals and 8 chapters in medical textbooks. Honours: Open Scholarship in Natural Sciences, Pembroke College, Cambridge, 1960; First Class Honours, Natural Sciences Tripos, Cambridge, 1964; Cheselden Medal, St Thomas' Hospital, 1967; Hallett Prize, Royal College of Surgeons, 1971. Memberships: Athenaeum Club, London; Pitt Club, Cambridge; Society of British Neurological Surgeons, Officer, 1996-, Member of

the Council, 1992-. Address: Neurosurgical Unit, Wellington Hospital, London NW8 9LE, England.

**MAUROUARD Elvire**, b. 5 January 1971, Jérémie, Haiti. Writer; Teacher. m. Oliver Maurouard. Education: Licence, French Language and Literature, 1995-99; Master of French Language and Literature, 1998-99; DEA, French Language and Literature, 1999; Doctoral Scholarship of Excellence, 1999-2000; Doctor, French Caribbean Literature, University of Paris, 2004. Appointments: Teacher, Port au Prince, Haiti, 1989-94; Tutor in French, CFA- Châlons en Champagne, 1999-2000; Tutor in French as a Foreign Language, Association pour L'Epanouissement et la Formation des Travailleurs Immigrés, Paris, 2000-2001; Professor of French Language and Literature, 1ére STI-TMA-2GT Lycée Monge, Savigny-sur-Orge, 2004-; In 2005 as a writer and published scholar participated in several intellectual activities in Europe, the USA and Canada: Gave a talk at California State University, Long Beach, delivered a lecture at the Senate, at the anthropological school in Paris and at the Overseas Academy of Sciences, France; Gave a paper, a presentation and a poetry reading at the International Congress of the Council on International Francophone Studies, Ottawa-Gatineau, Canada, 2005. Publications: The black woman and the Haitian novel, 2001; Tales and poems from savoury islands, 2004; The black beauties of Baudelaire, 2005; The alchemy of dreams (poetry), 2005. Honours: Gold Medal, Lutece Academy; Prize, Presence of the Arts, 2005. Memberships: Association of French Speaking Writers; Society of Men and Women of Letters of France. Address: 4 square Anatole-France, 94600 Choisy-le-Roi, France. E-mail: elvirejj@noos.fr

**MAVOR Elizabeth (Osborne)**, b. 17 December 1927, Glasgow, Scotland. Author. Education: St Andrews, 1940-45; St Leonard's and St Anne's College, Oxford, England, 1947-50. Publications: Summer in the Greenhouse, 1959; The Temple of Flora, 1961; The Virgin Mistress: A Biography of the Duchess of Kingston (US edition as The Virgin Mistress: A Study in Survival: The Life of the Duchess of Kingston), 1964; The Redoubt, 1967; The Ladies of Llangollen: A Study in Romantic Friendship, 1971; A Green Equinox, 1973; Life with the Ladies of Llangollen, 1984; The Grand Tour of William Beckford, 1986; The White Solitaire, 1988; The American Journals of Fanny Kemble, 1990; The Grand Tours of Katherine Wilmot, France 1801-3 and Russia 1805-7, 1992; The Captain's Wife, The South American Journals of Maria Graham 1821-23, 1993. Address: Curtis Brown Ltd, 28-29 Haymarket, London SW1Y 4SP, England.

**MAVRIDOU-TSOCHA Elisabeth Apostolos**, b. 28 February 1933, Salonica, Greece. Emeritus Professor of Medicine. m. Constantin Athanasios Tsochas, 1 daughter. Education: Medical Diploma, 1961, Postgraduate Degree, Specialist in Biopathology, 1964, Aristotelian University of Salonica; PhD, Medical School, National and Kapodestrian University of Athens, 1992. Appointments: Assistant, Medical School, Aristotelian University of Salonica, 1961-67; Biopathologist, Private Laboratory, Salonica, 1964-70, Athens, 1971-2000; Professor, Higher Nurses School of Salonica, 1966-70; Professor, School of Health and Caring Professions, 1984-2001, Director, Department of Medical Laboratories, 1990, Advisor on professional education for students, 1989-2001, Consultant on professional education for students, Department of Medical Laboratories, European Community Program, 1998-2001, Honorary Professor Emeritus, Faculty of Health and Caring Professions, 2001-, Technological Educational Institution of Athens. Publications: Books: General Microbiology, 2001; General Microbiology – Laboratory Methods, 2001; Lessons of General Microbiology for Students of Technological Educational

Institution (Yearly Edition, 1984-2000); Lessons of Laboratory Methods for Students of Technological Educational Institution of Athens (Yearly Edition 1994-2000). Honours: Member, Advisory Council for Drugs, Greek Ministry of Health, 1995-98; Honour Diploma, Hellenic Club of Writers, 1997; Honour Diploma, Panhellenic Society of Civilisation, of Learning and of the Fine Arts, 1998. Memberships: New York Academy of Sciences; RSH, England; Medical Association of Athens; Hellenic Society of Microbiology; Hellenic Club of Writers; Panhellenic Society of Civilisation, of Learning and of the Fine Arts. Address: 12 Laskaratou Str, Athens 111 41, Greece.

**MAXWELL DAVIES Peter (Sir),** b. 8 September 1934, Manchester, England. Composer. Education: Royal Manchester College of Music; Mus B (Hons), Manchester University, 1956. Musical Education: Studies with Goffredo Petrassi in Rome, 1957; Harkness Fellowship, Graduate School, Princeton University, studied with Roger Sessions, Milton Babbitt, Earl Kim. Career: Director of Music, Cirencester Grammar School, 1959-62; Founder and co-director (with Harrison Birtwistle) of the Pierrot Players, 1967-71; Founder, Artistic Director, Fires of London, 1971-87; Founder, Artistic Director, St. Magnus Festival, Orkney Islands, Scotland, 1977-86; Artistic Director, Dartington Summer School of Music, 1979-84; President, Schools Music Association, 1983-; President, North of England Education Conference, 1985; Visiting Fromm Professor of Composition, Harvard University, 1985; Associate Composer/Conductor, Scottish Chamber Orchestra, 1985-94; President, Composer's Guild of Great Britain, 1986-; President, St Magnus Festival, Orkney Islands, 1986-; President, National Federation of Music Societies, 1989-; Major retrospective festival as South Bank Centre, London, 1990; Conductor/Composer, BBC Philharmonic, 1992-; Associate Conductor/Composer, Royal Philharmonic Orchestra, 1992-; President, Cheltenham Arts Festival, 1994-; Composer Laureate of Scottish Chamber Orchestra, 1994-; President, Society for the Promotion of New Music, 1995-. Compositions: Stage: Operas Taverner 1962-70; The Martydom of St Magnus 1976-77; The Two Fiddlers 1978; The Lighthouse, 1979; Theatre Pieces: Notre Dame des Fleurs 1966; Vesalii Icones 1969; Eight Songs for a Mad King 1969; Nocturnal Dances, ballet 1969; Blind Man's Buff 1972; Miss Donnithorne's Maggot 1974; Salome, ballet 1978; Le Jongleur de Notre Dame 1978; Cinderella 1980; The Medium 1981; The No 11 Bus 1983-84; Caroline Mathilde, ballet, 1990; Operas: Resurrection 1987 and The Doctor of Myddfai 1996. Orchestra and Ensemble: Alma Redemptoris Mater for 6 wind instruments 1957; St Michael, sonata for 17 wind instruments 1957; Prolation 1958; Ricercar and Doubles for 8 instruments 1959; 5 Klee Pictures 1959, rev 1976; Sinfonia 1962; 2 Fantasias on an In Nomine of John Taverner 1962-64; 7 In Nomine 1963-65; Shakespeare Music 1965; Antechrist 1967; Stedman Caters 1968; St Thomas Wake 1969; Worldes Blis 1969; Renaissance Scottish Dances 1973; Ave Maris Stela 1975; 4 Symphonies 1973-76, 1980, 1984, 1988; Runes from a Holy Island 1977; A mirror of Whitening Light 1977; Dances from Salome, 1979; The Bairns of Brugh 1981; Image Reflection, Shadow 1982; Sinfonia Concertante 1982; Sinfonietta Accademica 1983; Unbroken Circle 1984; An Orkney Wedding, with Sunrise 1985; Jimmack the Postie, overture 1986; 10 Strathclyde Concertos for Violin 1985, Trumpet 1987, Oboe 1988, Clarinet 1990, Violin and Viola, 1991, Flute 1991, Doublebass 1992, Bassoon, 1993, Chamber Ensemble 1994, Orchestra 1995; Vocal: 5 Motets 1959; O Magnum Mysterium 1960; Te Lucis ante Terminum 1961; Frammenti di Leopardi, cantata 1962; Veni Sancte Spiritus 1963; Revelation and Fall; The Shepherds' Calendar 1965; Missa super L'Homme Arme 1968, rev 1971; From Stone to Thorn 1971; Hymn to St Magnus 1972; Tenebrae super Gesualdo 1972; Stone Litany 1973; Fiddlers at the Wedding

1974; Anakreontika 1976; Kirkwall Shopping Songs 1979; Black Pentecost 1979; Solstice of Light 1979; The Yellow Cake Review, 6 cabaret songs 1980; Songs of Hoy 1981; Into The Labyrinth for tenor and orchestra 1983; First Ferry to Hoy 1985; The Peat Cutters 1985; House of Winter 1986; Excuse Me 1986; Sea Runes, vocal sextet 1986; Hymn to the Word of God, for tenor and chorus, 1990; The Turn of the Tide for orchestra and children's choir, 1992; Chamber music includes: String Quartet 1961; The Kestrel Paced Round the Sun 1975; Sonatina 1981; The Pole Star 1982; Sea Eagle 1982; Sonata for violin and cimbalon 1984; Piano Sonata 1981; Organ Sonata, 1982; Latest works: Sails in St Magnus I-III, 1997-98; Job, oratorio for chorus, orchestra and soloists, 1998; A Reel of Seven Fishermen for orchestra, 1998; Sea Elegy, for chorus, orchestra and soloists, 1998; Roma Amor Labyrinths, 1998; Maxwell's Reel with Northern Lights, 1998; Swinton Jig, 1998; Temenos with Mermaids and Angels, for flute and orchestra, 1998; Spinning Jenny, 1999; Sails in Orkney Saga III: An Orkney Wintering, for alto saxophone and orchestra, 1999; Trumpet Quintet, for string quartet and trumpet, 1999; Mr Emmet Takes a Walk, 1999; Horn Concerto, 1999; Orkney Saga IV: Westerly Gale in Biscay, Salt in the Bread Broken, 2000, Symphony No 7, 2000; Antarctic Symphony, Symphony No 8, 2000; Canticum Canticorum, 2001; De Assumtione Beatae Mariae Virginis, 2001; Crossing Kings Reach, 2001; Mass, 2002; Naxos Quartet No 1, 2002; Piano Trip, 2002; Naxos Quartet No 2, 2003. Honours: Many honours including: Fellow, Royal Northern College of Music, 1978; Honorary Member, Royal Academy of Music, 1979; Honorary Member, Guildhall School of Music and Drama, 1981; CBE, 1981; Knight Bachelor, for services to music, 1987; L'officier dans L'Ordre des Arts et des Lettres, France, 1988; First Award, Association of British Orchestras, outstanding contribution and promotion of orchestral life in UK; Gulliver Award for Performing Arts in Scotland, 1991; Fellowship, Royal Scottish Academy of Music and Drama, 1994; Charles Grove Award, outstanding contribution to British Music, 1995; Member of the Bayerische Akademie der Schönen Künste, 1998. Address: c/o 50 Hogarth Road, London SW5 0PU, England.

**MAY Brian James,** b. 7 January 1945. Retired Teacher; Poet. m. 29 July 1967, 1 son, 2 daughters. Education: BA, 1967; MA, 1971; PGCE, 1973; MA, Education, 1991. Appointments: Assistant Warden, Adult Education, Dartington, 1968-70; Head of Drama, Arthur Terry School, Birmingham, 1970-81; Tutor, Open University, 1973-; Head of English, Swanshurst School, Birmingham, 1981-83; Head of Arts Faculty, Chamberlain College, 1983-88; Vice Principal, Josiah Mason College, 1988-93. Contributions to: Orbis; Illuminations; Christ's College Magazine; Times Educational Supplement; Poetry Now. Membership: Fellow, College of Teachers. Address: 3 Holte Drive, Sutton Coldfield, Birmingham B75 6PR, England.

**MAY Derwent James,** b. 29 April 1930, Eastbourne, Sussex, England. Author; Journalist. m. Yolanta Izabella Sypniewska, 1 son, 1 daughter. Education: MA, Lincoln College, Oxford, 1952. Appointments: Theatre and Film Critic, Continental Daily Mail, Paris, 1952-53; Lecturer in English, University of Indonesia, 1955-58; Senior Lecturer in English, Universities of Lodz and Warsaw, 1959-63; Chief Leader Writer, Times Literary Supplement, 1963-65; Literary Editor, The Listener, 1965-86; Literary and Arts Editor, Sunday Telegraph, 1986-90, The European, 1990-91; European Arts Editor, The Times, 1992-. Publications: Novels: The Professionals, 1964; Dear Parson, 1969; The Laughter in Djakarta, 1973; A Revenger's Comedy, 1979. Non-Fiction: Proust, 1983; The Times Nature Diary, 1983; Hannah Arendt, 1986; The New Times Nature Diary, 1993; Feather Reports, 1996; Critical Times: The History of the Times Literary Supplement, 2001; The Times: A Year in Nature

Notes, 2004. Contributions to: Encounter; Hudson Review. Honours: Member, Booker Prize Jury, 1978; Hawthornden Prize Committee, 1987-; FRSL. Membership: Beefsteak Club; Garrick Club. Address: 201 Albany Street, London NW1 4AB, England.

**MAY Geoffrey John,** b. 7 May 1948, London, England. Chartered Engineer. m. Sarah, 2 sons. Education: MA, Double First Class Honours, Natural Sciences Tripos, Materials Science, Fitzwilliam College, University of Cambridge; PhD, Department of Metallurgy and Materials Science; Fellow of the Institute of Metals; Chartered Engineer. Appointments: Research Officer, Central Electricity Generating Board, 1973-74; Technical Manager, Chloride Silent Power Ltd, 1974-78; Design and Development Manager, Chloride Technical Ltd, 1978-82; Technical Director, 1982-86, Operations Director, 1986-88, Tungstone Batteries Ltd; General Manager, Brush Fusegear Ltd, 1988-90; Managing Director, Barton Abrasives Ltd, 1990-91; Group Director of Technology, Hawker Batteries, 1991-97; Group Director of Technology, BTR Power Systems, 1997-2000; Chief Technology Officer, Fiamm SpA, 2000-03; Principal, The Focus Partnership, 2003-. Publications: Numerous publications in technical and trade journals and conference proceedings. Address: Troutbeck House, Main Street, Swithland, Loughborough, Leicestershire LE12 8TJ, England. E-mail: geoffrey.may@tiscali.co.uk

**MAY John F,** b. 10 March 1950, Elisabethville, Belgian Congo. Demographer. m. Anne Legrand, 1 son, 1 daughter. Education: BA, Modern History, 1973; MA, Demography, 1985, University of Louvain, Leuven; PhD, Demography, University of Paris, Sorbonne, 1996. Appointments: Associate Expert in Demography, United Nations, Haiti, 1976-79; Expert in Demography, United Nations South Pacific Commission, 1980-83; Training Co-ordinator, International Union for the Scientific Study of Population, 1985-86; Senior Scientist, The Futures Group International, 1987-97; Senior Population Specialist, Africa Region, World Bank, 1997-. Publications: Numerous papers in peer-reviewed journals. Honours: Andrew W Mellon Foundation Visiting Scholarship at the Population Reference Bureau. Memberships: International Union for the Scientific Study of Population; Population Association of America. Address: The World Bank, 1818 H Street NW, Washington, DC 20433, USA. E-mail: jmay@worldbank.org

**MAY Naomi Young,** b. 27 March 1934, Glasgow, Scotland. Novelist; Journalist; Painter. m. Nigel May, 3 October 1964, 2 sons, 1 daughter. Education: Slade School of Fine Art, London, 1953-56; Diploma, Fine Art, University of London. Publications: At Home, 1969, radio adaptation, 1987; The Adventurer, 1970; Troubles, 1976. Contributions to: Anthologies, newspapers, and magazines. Honour: History of Art Prize, Slade School of Fine Art. Membership: PEN. Address: 6 Lion Gate Gardens, Richmond, Surrey TW9 2DF, England.

**MAY OF OXFORD, Baron of Oxford in the County of Oxfordshire, Sir Robert McCredie May,** b. 1 August 1936, Professor. Education: BSc, PhD, Theoretical Physics, Sydney University. Appointments: Gordon MacKay Lecturer, Applied Mathematics, Harvard University; Senior Lecturer in Theoretical Physics, Personal Chair in Physics, Sydney University; Class of 1877 Professor of Zoology, 1973, Chairman of the Research Board, 1977-88, Princeton University, USA; Royal Society Research Professor, 1988; Chief Scientific Adviser, UK Government, 1995-2000; Head, UK Officer of Science and Technology, 1995-2000; Joint Professorship, Department of Zoology, Oxford University and Imperial College, London; Fellow, Merton College, Oxford University; President, The

Royal Society, 2000-05. Publications: Numerous books; Several hundred papers in major scientific journals; Broader contributions to scientific journalism in newspapers, radio and TV. Honours: Knighthood, 1996; Companion of the Order of Australia, 1998; Craoford Prize, Royal Swedish Academy; Swiss-Italian Balzan Prize; Japanese Blue Planet Prize; Order of Merit (OM), 2002. Memberships: Foreign Member, US National Academy of Sciences; Overseas Fellow, Australian Academy of Sciences. Address: Department of Zoology, University of Oxford, South Parks Road, Oxford, OX1 3PS, England. E-mail: robert.may@zoo.ox.ac.uk

**MAYALL Richard Michael (Rik),** b. 7 March 1958, England. Comedian; Actor; Writer. m. Barbara Robin, 1 son, 2 daughters. Education: University of Manchester. Creative Works: Theatre includes: The Common Pursuit, 1988; Waiting for God, 1991-92; The Government Inspector, 1995; Cell Mates, 1995; TV includes: The Young Ones (also creator and co-writer), 1982, 1984; The Comic Strip Presents, 1983-84, 1992; George's Marvellous Medicine, 1985; The New Statesman, 1987-88, 1990, 1994; Bottom, 1990, 1992, 1994; Rik Mayall Presents, 1992-94; Wham Bham Strawberry Jam!, 1995; The Alan B'Stard Interview with Brian Walden, 1995; In the Red, 1998; The Bill, 1999; Jonathan Creek, 1999; The Knock, 2000; Murder Rooms, 2000; Tales of Uplift and Moral Improvement, 2000; All About George, 2005; Films include: Whoops Apocalypse, 1982; Drop Dead Fred, 1990; Horse Opera, 1992; Remember Me, 1996; Bring Me the Head of Mavis Davis, 1996; Guest House Paradiso, 1999; Merlin – The Return, 1999; Kevin of the North, 2000; Jesus Christ, Super Star, 2000; Several voices for animations; Live Stand Up includes: Comic Strip, 1982; Kevin Turvey and Bastard Squad, 1983; Rik Mayall, Ben Elton, Andy De La Tour, UK tour and Edinburgh Fringe 1983; Rik Mayall and Ben Elton, 1984-85, Australian tour 1986, 1992; Rik Mayall and Andy De La Tour, 1989-90; Rik Mayall and Adrian Edmondson, UK tours, 1993, 1995, 1997, 2001. Honours include: BAFTA, Best New Comedy, 1990; British Comedy Awards, Best New Comedy, 1992, Best Comedy Actor, 1993. Address: c/o The Brunskill Management Ltd, Suite 8A, 169 Queen's Gate, London SW7 5HE, England.

**MAYER Sydney L,** b. 2 August 1937, Chicago, USA. Publisher. m. Charlotte W M Bouter. Education: BA, MA, University of Michigan; MPhil, Yale University. Appointments: Lecturer, University of Maryland, USA, 1966-77; Visiting Assistant Professor, University of Southern California, 1969-74; UK Director, University of Maryland, 1972-73; Managing Director, Bison Books Ltd, 1973-95; President, CEO, Brompton Books Corporation, 1982-98; President, Twin Books Corporation, 1985-98; Chairman, Twin Films Ltd, 1997-. Publications: 22 books including: The World of Southeast Asia (with Harry J Benda), 1971; The Two World Wars (with William J Koenig), 1976; Signal, 1975; World War Two, 1981; hundreds of articles. Honours: Angell Society, University of Michigan, 1989; Honorary Fellow, Oriel College, Oxford, 1993; Fulbright Advisory Board, London, 1993-. Address: 2 Shrewsbury House, 42 Cheyne Walk, London, SW3 5LN, England.

**MAYNE Michael Clement Otway,** b. 10 September 1929, Harlestone, Northamptonshire, England. Anglican Priest. m. Alison, 1 son, 1 daughter. Education: King's School, Canterbury; Corpus Christi College, Cambridge, 1951-55; Cuddesdon College, Oxford, 1955-57. Appointments: Curate, St John the Baptist, Harpenden, 1957-59; Chaplain to Bishop of Southwark, 1959-65; Vicar of Norton, Letchworth, 1965-72; Head of Religious Programmes, BBC Radio, 1972-79; Vicar of Great St Mary's (University Church), Cambridge, 1979-86; Dean of Westminster, 1986-96; Dean Emeritus of Westminster,

1996-. Publications: Prayers for Pastoral Occasions, 1982; Editor, Encounters, 1985; A Year Lost and Found, 1987; This Sunrise of Wonder, 1994; Pray, Love, Remember, 1998; Learning to Dance, 2001; Various articles. Honours: MA (Cantab), 1956; KCVO, 1996. Memberships: Dean of the Order of the Bath, 1986-92; Chairman of Governors, Westminster School, 1986-92; Member of Council, St Christopher's Hospice, 1988-2004; Vice President, St Christopher's Hospice, 2005-; Trustee, Cumberland Lodge, Windsor, 1992-; Chairman, London Ecumenical Aids Forum, 1992-96; Chairman, Sandford St Martin Trust, 1993-2000; Select Preacher, University of Cambridge, 1988; Select Preacher, University of Oxford, 1989, 1993. Address: 37 St Mark's Road, Salisbury, SP1 3AY, England. E-mail: maynem@tiscali.co.uk

**MAYNE Richard (John)**, b. 2 April 1926, London, England. Writer; Broadcaster. m. Jocelyn Mudie Ferguson, 2 daughters. Education: MA, PhD, Trinity College, Cambridge, 1947-53. Appointments: Rome Correspondent, New Statesman, 1953-54; Assistant, Tutor, Cambridge Institute of Education, 1954-56; Official of the European Community, Luxembourg and Brussels, 1956-63; Personal Assistant to Jean Monnet, Paris, 1963-66; Paris Correspondent, 1963-73, Co-Editor, 1990-94; Encounter; Visiting Professor, University of Chicago, 1970; Director, Federal Trust, London, 1971-73; Head, UK Offices of the European Commission, London, 1973-79; Film Critic, Sunday Telegraph, London, 1987-89; The European, 1990-98. Publications: The Community of Europe, 1962; The Institutions of the European Community, 1968; The Recovery of Europe, 1970; The Europeans, 1972; Europe Tomorrow (editor), 1972; The New Atlantic Challenge (editor), 1975; The Memoirs of Jean Monnet (translator), 1978; Postwar: The Dawn of Today's Europe, 1983; Western Europe: A Handbook (editor), 1987; Federal Union: The Pioneers (with John Pinder), 1990; Europe: A History of its Peoples (translator), 1990; History of Europe (translator), 1993; A History of Civilizations (translator), 1994; The Language of Sailing, 2000; In Victory, Magnanimity, in Peace, Goodwill: a History of Wilton Park, 2003; Cross Channel Currents: 100 Years of the Entente Cordiale, co-editor, 2004. Contributions to: Newspapers and magazines. Honour: Scott-Moncrieff Prize for Translation from French, 1978; Officier de L'Ordre des Arts et des Lettres, 2003. Memberships: Society of Authors; Royal Institute of International Affairs; Federal Trust for Education and Research. Address: Albany Cottage, 24 Park Village East, Regent's Park, London NW1 7PZ, England.

**MAYO Edward John**, b. 24 May 1931, Lyme Regis, England. Army Officer. m. (1) Jacqueline Margaret Anne Armstrong, deceased, 1 son, (2) Pamela Joyce Shimwell. Education: King's College, Taunton, 1943-49. Appointments: Commissioned, Royal Artillery, 1951; ADC to Governor of Malta, 1953-54, 2 RHA, 1955-57; ADC to Commander in Chief, BAOR, 1958-60; Adjutant 20 FD Regiment, Malaya, 1961-63; Instructor, RMAS, 1964-66; Instructor, Staff College, 1970-72; Commanded 17 Training Regiment, 1972-75; Colonel General Staff, 1979-93; Director General, Help the Aged, 1983-97; Trustee, Helpage, India, 1984-2001; Trustee, Helpage, Sri Lanka, 1986-; Trustee, Helpage, Kenya, 1984-; Trustee, Ex-Services Mental Welfare, 1996-2005; Trustee, Global Cancer, 1996-2004; Patron, The Homeless Fund, 1998-2000; Patron, Employers Retirement Association, 2004; Chairman of Commissioners, Jurby, Isle of Man, 2002-2004; Director, Executive Communication Consultants, 1999-. Publications: Miscellaneous articles on military matters; Articles on ageing. Honour: OBE, 1976. Memberships: Army and Navy Club; Special Forces Club; MCC; Royal Society of Arts, 1985-97; Woodroffes. Address: Ballamoar Castle, Sandygate, Jurby, Isle of Man, IM7 3AJ, United Kingdom. E-mail: mayo@manx.net

**MAYS Sally**, b. Melbourne, Australia. Pianist; Composer; Teacher. m. John Elsom, 2 sons. Education: AMusA, aged 13 years; LRSM, aged 15 years; ARCM, aged 19 years; Studied at University Conservatorium; Clarke Scholarship, Royal College of Music, London; Further studies with Marcel Ciampi in Paris and Irene Kohler in London. Appointments: Recital pianist in Australia, aged 12 years; First UK recital, Wigmore Hall, 1956; Numerous tours of Australia, New Zealand and South Africa; Appearances in Europe, San Diego, Singapore and Abu Dhabi; Piano tuition and music appreciation, Goldsmiths College, University of London, the City Literary Institute, Marylebone Institute and Roehampton Institute in London; Examiner for the Associated Board of the Royal Schools of Music, in UK and all over the world, 1984-2005; Played with Alexandra Ensemble and leading orchestras around the world; Featured solo performer with London Ballet Orchestra on Margot Fonteyn's Farewell Tour; Premiered: Ann Carr-Boyd's Piano Concerto in Hobart, 1991; Eric Gross's Piano Concerto in Melbourne and Perth, 1983-84; and Edwin Carr's Second Piano Concerto in Wellington and Perth, 1987 and 1992; Broadcasts for Australian Broadcasting Corporation and other broadcasting stations annually; Currently, member of Trio LaVolta and Sounds Positive. Publications: Compiler and editor, four volume series of contemporary Australian Piano Music; Composed for Sounds Positive and for the stage. Honours: Sounds Australia Award for services to music; Chappell Gold Medal, Royal College of Music. Memberships: Founder Member, The Mouth of Hermes, 1968-72; Member, Sounds Positive, 1988-; Fellow, Trinity College, London. Address: 14 Homersham Road, Norbiton, Kingston-upon-Thames, Surrey KT1 3PN, England.

**MAZID Muhammad Abdul**, b. 31 December 1952, Mymensingh, Bangladesh. Public Servant. m. 25 April 1976, 2 sons, 1 daughter. Education: BSc, Bangladesh Agricultural University, 1972; MSc, 1978, Postdoctoral studies, 1983, Kagoshima University, Japan; PhD, Tokyo University of Agriculture, 1980. Appointments: Lecturer, 1976-79, Assistant Professor, 1979-85, Bangladesh Agricultural University; Chief Scientific Officer, Bangladesh Fisheries Research Institute, 1985-89; Additional Director, 1989-92, Director, 1992-97, Director General, 1997, Ministry of Fisheries and Livestock. Publications: Over 100 in professional national and international journals. Honours: 20th Century Achievement Award, ABI; Award for Fisheries Research and Technology Development by Prime Minister, Government of the People's Republic of Bangladesh, 1997; Award for Scientific Printing and Publication, Prime Minister, Government of the People's Republic of Bangladesh, 1999 and 2004. Memberships: WorldFish Nutrition Society, USA; Asian Fisheries Society, Manila; International Network of Genetics in Aquaculture, WorldFish Center, Penang, Malaysia; Fellow of Zoological Society of Bangladesh, Dhaka University; Members, Bangladesh Academy of Agriculture, Dhaka, Bangladesh; Bangla Academy, Dhaka. Address: Bangladesh Fisheries Research Institute, PO Kewotkhali, Mymensingh 2201, Bangladesh.

**MAZZOLENI Donatella**, b. 14 May 1943, Florence, Italy. Architect; Professor. 1 son, 1 daughter. Education: Maturità classica, Classical Lyceum Umberto 1°, Naples, Italy, 1961; Laurea in architettura, Università degli Studi di Napoli "Federico II", Italy, 1967. Appointments: Visiting Professor, University of North Carolina at Charlotte, USA, 1986; Lecturer, universities of Shanghai, Beijing and Tianjin, Peoples Republic of China, 1994; Lecturer, Queensland University of Brisbane, Australia, 1995; Professor, Department of Progettazione Urbana, University of Napoli "Federico II". Publications: Author and co-author, 12 articles in professional journals. Honours: 3rd, IV Concorso Nazionale IN/ARCH Domosic "Per un idea architettonica", Rome, 1968; Nombre d'or, Grand Prix International d'Urbanisme et d'Architecture, 1970; Recherche pour une ville nouvelle, Cannes-Paris, 1969-70; 1st, National Competition for the conservation and systemisation of Rione Terra di Pozzuoli, 1975; 1st, National Competition for the Cityhall, Comunita Montana Hall and Civic Piazza in the city of Montella, 1989; Special Mention for symbolical conception at International Competition "Jardin europèen", APRIAS, Paris, Dunkerque, 1989. Memberships: Ordine degli Architetti di Napoli, 1968-; Fellow, Accademia Pontaniana, Classe Storia, Archeologia e Filologia, 1982-; Special List of Architects who are full-time university teachers, 1984. Address: via Egiziaca a Pizzofalcone 43, 80132 Naples, Italy. E-mail: donatella.mazzol eni@unina.it

**MBOYIYA-HLAM Thandiwe L,** b. 9 January 1958, Adelaide, South Africa. Teacher-Educator. m. Richard Hlam, 2 children. Education: Primary Teachers Course, Lovedale Training College, 1979; Junior Primary Diploma, Rhodes University, 1991; Instruction Course for Teaching and Learning of Mathematics, Leeds University, England, 1993; Diploma in Mathematics Education, Cambridge/Rhodes Universities, 1994; Certificate in Research Methods, Miami University, USA, 1998; Further Diploma in Mathematics Education, Rhodes University, 1999; Bachelor Degree in Education (B.Ed.),Rhodes University, 2000; Currently enrolled for Masters Degree in Mathematics Education, Rhodes University. Appointments: Teacher, Vulindela Public School, Adelaide, South Africa, 1981-94; Junior Lecturer, Junior Field Officer, 1994-96; lecturer, Farm School Co-ordinator, 1996-99, Lecturer, Cluster Project Co-ordinator, 2000-2004, Rhodes University Mathematics Education Project; Regional Project Manager, Co-operative Organisation for Upgrading of Numeracy Training (COUNT Eastern Cape Region), 2004-. Publications: Implications of adopting problem solving approach in the classroom; Farm School Mathematics Education "A project in action"; Pupil Assessment Tasks in RUMEP Farm Schools; Measuring impact in the classroom; Benchmark Assessment grade 4 & 5. Honours: B.Ed. Honours, Rhodes University; Presidential Premier Award for RUMEP Farm School Project, 1995, 1999. Memberships: Association for Mathematics Education in South Africa; Uniting Presbyterian Church in Southern Africa Women Fellowship; Rhodes University Women Association. Address: PO Box 1388, Main Street, Port Elizabeth 6000, South Africa. E-mail: mwcount@iafrica.com

**McALEESE Mary Patricia,** b. 27 June 1951, Belfast, Northern Ireland. President of Ireland. m. Martin, 1976, 1 son, 2 daughters. Education: LLB, The Queen's University, Belfast, 1969-73; BL, Inn of Court of Northern Ireland, 1973-74; MA, Trinity College, Dublin, 1986; Diploma in Spanish, Institute of Linguistics, 1991-94. Appointments: Reid Professor, Criminal Law, Criminology and Penology, Trinity College, Dublin, 1975-79, 1981-87; Current Affairs Journalist, Presenter, Irish National TV, 1979-81; Part-time Presenter, -1975; Director, Institute of Professional Legal Study, Queen's University of Belfast, 1987-97; Pro-Vice Chancellor, 1994-97; President, Ireland, 1997-. Publications: The Irish Martyrs, 1995; Reconciled Beings, 1997. Honours: Several honorary degrees; Silver Jubilee Commemoration Medal, Charles University, Prague. Memberships: European Bar Association; International Bar Association; Inns of Court, North Ireland; King's Inn, Dublin; Former Member: Institute of Advanced Study; Irish Association of Law Teachers; Society of Public Teachers of Law; British and Irish Legal Technology Association. Address: Áras an Uachtaráin, Phoenix Park, Dublin 8, Ireland. E-mail: webmaster@aras.irigov.ie

**McARTHUR Christine Louise,** b. 14 March 1953, Lennox Town, Scotland. Artist. m. (1) Alistair Lyon, divorced, 2 daughters, (2) Roger Billcliffe. Education: Glasgow School of Art, 1971-76. Career: Artist full-time , 1980-; Part-time Lecturer, Glasgow School of Art and Glasgow University Extra Mural Department, 1980-96. Exhibitions: Peter Potter Gallery, Haddington, 1984; Sue Rankin Gallery, London, 1986, 1990; Fine Art Society Glasgow, 1990; Portland Gallery, London, 1992; Roger Billcliffe Fine Art, Glasgow, 1992, 1994, 1996, 1998, 2000, 2002 (2); Ancrum Gallery, Roxburgh, 1993; Open Eye Gallery, Edinburgh, 1993, 1996; Thackeray Gallery, London, 1995; John Martin of London, Summer Show, 1996, 1998; Courtyard Gallery, Crail, 1997; John Martin of London, 1999, 2001, 2003; Gertsev Gallery, Moscow, 2004; Gertsev Gallery, Atlanta, USA, 2004; Lemon Street Gallery, Truro, 2005; Works in collections: Lord Irvine of Lairg; Scottish Arts Council; Arthur Anderson; Scottish Nuclear PLC; University of Strathclyde; Amerada Hess Corporation; Craig Capital Organisation; Lillie Art Gallery, Milngavie; Argyll Group PLC; Clydesdale Bank PLC; MacFarlane Group (Clansman) PLC; Royal Bank of Scotland; Export and Import Bank of Japan, John Lewis Partnership (Glasgow, Nottingham, Edinburgh and Peter Jones, London); Gertsev Gallery, Moscow. Honours: Arts Council Award, Glasgow Society of Women Artist's Trust Fund Award, Lauder Award; N S McFarlane Award, RGI; Alexander Graham Munro Prize, RSW; Scottish Arts Council Travel Bursary; Commissions: 4 large murals for the John Lewis Glasgow Store, 1999; Murals for extension to John Lewis Peter Jones Store, Sloane Square, London, 2002. Memberships: Honorary Secretary, 2000-02, Royal Glasgow Institute of Fine Arts; Royal Scottish Society of Painters in Watercolour. Address: Glen Rowan, Shore Road, Cove, Argyll & Bute, G84 0NU, Scotland. E-mail: clm@rbfa.demon.co.uk

**McCALL Davina,** b. 16 October 1967, London, England. TV Presenter. m. Mathew Robinson, 2 daughters. Education: St Catherine's, Bramley; Godolphin & Latymer, London. Appointments: God's Gift, MTV; Don't Try This At Home, 4 series; The Brits, 2000, 2003; Big Brother, 6 series, 2000-05; Sam's Game, 2001; Popstars – The Rivals, 2002; Reborn in the USA, 2003; Love on a Saturday Night, 2004; Comic Relief, 2004; The BAFTA Television Awards, 2004. Address: c/o John Noel Management, 2nd Floor, 10A Belmont Street, London NW1 8HH, England.

**McCANNY John Vincent,** b. 25 June 1952, Ballymoney, Co. Antrim, Northern Ireland. m. Mary (Maureen) Bernadette Mellon, 1 son, 1 daughter. Education: BSc, Physics, Manchester, 1973, Chartered Engineer and Physicist; PhD, Physics, Ulster, 1978; DSc, Electronic Engineering, Queen's University Belfast, 1998. Appointments: Lecturer in Physics, University of Ulster, Coleraine, 1977-79; Higher Scientific Officer, 1979-81, Senior Scientific Officer, 1981-83, Principal Scientific Officer, 1983-84, RSRE (now Qinetiq), Malvern; EPSRC IT Research Lecturer, 1984-87; Director, Institute of Advanced Microelectronics in Ireland (involving Queen's University Belfast, Trinity College Dublin, National Microelectronics Research Centre at University College Cork, 1989-92; Reader, 1984-87, Professor of Microelectronics Engineering, 1988-, Director, Institute of Electronics, Communications and Information Technology, 2000-, Queen's University Belfast. Publications: 300 research papers in learned journals and major international conferences; 5 research books; 25 patents; Associate Editor, Journal of VLSI Signal Processing, 1988-; Associate Editor, IEEE Transactions. Circuits, Systems and Devices; Analog and Digital Signal Processing, 2000-05. Honours: Northern Ireland Information Technology Award, 1987; UK Royal Academy of Engineering Silver Medal, 1996; IEEE (USA) Millennium Medal, 2000;

CBE, 2002; Royal Dublin Society/Irish Times Boyle Medal, 2003; British Computer Society (Belfast Branch) IT Professional of the Year, 2004. Memberships: Fellow: Institution of Electrical Engineers, Institute of Physics, Royal Academy of Engineering, Institute of Electrical and Electronic Engineers, USA, Royal Society of London; Member, Royal Irish Academy; European Academy of Sciences. Address: Institute of Electronics, Communications and Information Technology, Queen's University Belfast, Northern Ireland Science Park, Queen's Road, Queen's Island, Belfast BT3 9DT, Northern Ireland.

**McCARTER Keith Ian,** b. 15 March 1936, Scotland. Sculptor. m. Brenda, 1 son, 1 daughter. Education: The Royal High School of Edinburgh, 1948-54; Edinburgh College of Art, 1956-60. Appointments: Designer, Steuben Glass, New York, USA, 1961-63; Self-employed Sculptor, 1964-. Publications: Many articles published relative to work. Honours: Otto Beit Medal, Royal Society of British Sculptors; Fellow, Royal Society of Arts; DA (Edin). Memberships: The Farmers Club; Melrose RFC. Address: 10 Coopersknowe Crescent, Galashiels, TD1 2DS, Scotland.

**McCARTHY Cormac, (Charles McCarthy Jr),** b. 20 July 1933, Providence, Rhode Island, USA. Author; Dramatist. m. Lee Holleman, 1961, divorced 1 child, (2) Anne deLisle, 1967, divorced. Publications: Novels: The Orchard Keeper, 1965; Outer Dark, 1968; Child of God, 1974; Suttree, 1979; Blood Meridian, or The Evening Redness in the West, 1985; All the Pretty Horses, 1992; The Crossing, 1994; Cities of the Plain, 1998. Plays: The Gardner's Son, 1977; The Stonemason, 1994. Honours: Ingram Merrill Foundation Grant, 1960; William Faulkner Foundation Award, 1965; American Academy of Arts and Letters Travelling Fellowship, 1965-66; Rockefeller Foundation Grant, 1966; Guggenheim Fellowship, 1976; John D and Catharine T MacArthur Foundation Fellowship, 1981; National Book Award, 1992; National Book Critics Circle Award, 1993. Address: 1011 N Mesa Street, El Paso, TX 79902, USA.

**McCARTNEY (James) Paul (Sir),** b. 18 June 1942, Liverpool, England. Singer; Songwriter; Musician. m. (1) Linda Eastman, 12 March 1969, deceased 1998, 1 son, 2 daughters, 1 stepdaughter, (2) Heather Mills, 2002, 1 daughter. Education: Self-taught in music. Appointments: Member, The Quarrymen, 1957-59, The Beatles, 1960-70; Founder, Apple Corporation Ltd; Founder, MPL Group of Companies; Founder, Wings, 1970-81; Solo Artiste, 1970-; International tours, concerts, TV, radio, films; Founder, Liverpool Institute of Performing Arts, 1995. Creative Works: Numerous albums with The Beatles. Solo Albums: McCartney, 1970; Ram, 1971; McCartney II, 1980; Tug of War, 1982; Pipes of Peace, 1983; Give My Regards to Broad Street, 1984; Press to Play, 1986; All the Best, 1987; Flowers in the Dirt, 1989; Tripping the Light Fantastic, 1990; Unplugged, 1991; Choba b CCCP, 1991; Paul McCartney's Liverpool Oratorio, 1991; Off the Ground, 1993; Paul is Live, 1993; Flaming Pie, 1997; Standing Stone, symphonic work, 1997; A Garland for Linda, composition with 8 other composers for a capella choir, 2000; Paul McCartney: The Music and Animation Collection, DVD, 2004. Publications: Paintings, 2000; The Beatles Anthology (with George Harrison and Ringo Starr), 2000; Sun Prints (with Linda McCartney), 2001; Many Years From Now, autobiography, 2001; Blackbird Singing: Poems and Lyrics 1965-1999, 2001. Honours: MBE, 1965; Numerous Grammy Awards; 3 Ivor Novello Awards; Freeman, City of Liverpool, 1984; Doctorate, University of Sussex, 1988; Guinness Book of Records Award, 1979; Q Merit Award, 1990; Knighted, 1997; Fellowship, British Academy of Composers

and Songwriters, 2000. Address: c/o MPL Communications, 1 Soho Square, London W1V 6BQ, England.

**McCARTNEY Stella,** b. 1972. Fashion Designer. Education: Central St Martins College of Art and Design. Appointments: Work with Christian Lacroix at age 15 and later with Betty Jackson; Work experience in Fashion Department, Vogue magazine; After graduation, set up own design company in London; Chief Designer for Chloe, Paris; Designed collection for Gucci, 2001; VH/1Vogue Fashion and Music Designer of the Year, 2000. Address: Gucci Group, via Don Lorenzo Perosi, 6 Casellina di Scandici, 50018 Florence, Italy. Website: www.stellamccartney.com

**McCLURE Gillian Mary,** b. 29 October 1948, Bradford, England. Author; Illustrator. 3 sons. Education: BA, Combined Honours in French, English and History of Art, Bristol University; Teaching Diploma, Moray House. Publications: 18 children's books, 1974-06. Honours: Shortlisted for Smarties Award and Highly Commended in Kate Greenaway Award, 1985; US Parents Guide to Children's Media Award for Outstanding Achievement in Children's Books. Membership: CWIG Society of Authors, committee member, 1989-; PLR Advisory Committee, 1992. Address: 9 Trafalgar Street, Cambridge CB4 1ET, England.

**McCOLGAN Elizabeth,** b. 24 May 1964, Dundee, Scotland. Athlete. m. Peter McColgan, 1 daughter. Education: Coached by Grete Waitz. Appointments: Gold Medal Commonwealth Games 10,000 m, 1986, 1990; Silver Medal, Olympic Games 10,000m, 1988; Silver Medal, World Indoor Championships 3,000m, 1989; Bronze Medal, Commonwealth Games, 3,000m, 1990; Gold Medal, World Championships 10,000m, 1991; Gold Medal, World Half Marathon Championships, 1992; First in New York City Marathon, 1991; First in Tokyo Marathon, 1992; Third in London Marathon, 1993; Fifth in 1995; First in 1996; Second in 1997, 1998; Retired, 2001; Runs own fitness centre and coaches young athletes in Dundee. Address: c/o Marquee UK, 6 George Street, Nottingham NG1 3BE, England.

**McCONAUGHEY Matthew,** b. 4 November 1969, Ulvade, Texas, USA. Actor. Education: University of Texas, Austin. Appointments: Film appearances include: Dazed and Confused; The Return of the Texas Chainsaw Massacre; Boys on the Side; My Boyfriend's Back, 1993; Angels in the Outfield, 1994; Scorpion Spring; Submission, 1995; Glory Daze; Lone Star; A Time to Kill, 1996; Larger Than Life, 1997; Amistad; Contact; Making Sandwiches; Last Flight of the Raven; Newton Boys; South Beach; EdTV, 1999; U-571, 2000; The Wedding Planner, 2001; Reign of Fire, 2001; Frailty, 2001; 13 Conversations About One Thing, 2001; Tiptoes, 2003; How to Lose a Guy in Ten Days, 2003. Address: c/o Warner Brothers Incorporated, 4000 Warner Boulevard, Suite 1101, Burbank, CA 91522, USA.

**McCONNELL Charles Stephen,** b. 20 June 1951, Yorkshire, England. Chief Executive. m. Natasha Valentinovna, 1 son, 1 daughter. Education: BA honours, Politics, MPhil, Community Development. Appointments: Youth and Community Worker, Dobroyd Community School, Yorkshire, 1974-75; Action Research Worker in Community Education, Scottish Local Government Research Unit, Strathclyde, 1975-77; Lecturer, Community Education, Dundee College of Education, 1977-84; Senior Policy Development Officer, National Consumer Council, London, 1984-87; Deputy Director, Action Resource Centre, London, 1987-88; Assistant Director, Community Development Foundation, London, 1988-89; European and Public Affairs Director, London, 1989-93; Chief Executive,

Scottish Community Education Council, 1993-99; Director, Secretary General, International Association for Community Development, 1998-2002; Chief Executive, Community Learning Scotland, 1999-2002; Chairman, UK National Training Organisation for Community Learning and Development, 2000-2002. Publications: Author, editor, co-editor, over 15 books; Many other articles, research and conference papers. Membership: Fellow, Royal Society of Arts. Address: Corrieway House, Easter Balgedie, Kinross, Perthshire, KY13 9HQ, Scotland. E-mail: charlie.mcconnell@virgin.net

**McCORMICK John Owen,** b. 20 September 1918, Thief River Falls, Minnesota, USA. Professor of Comparative Literature Emeritus; Writer. m. Mairi MacInnes, 4 February 1954, 3 sons, 1 daughter. Education: BA, 1941, MA, 1947, University of Minnesota; PhD, Harvard University, 1951. Appointments: Senior Tutor and Teaching Assistant, Harvard University, 1946-51; Lecturer, Salzburg Seminar in American Studies, Austria, 1951-52; Professor of American Studies, Free University of Berlin, 1952-53, 1954-59; Professor of Comparative Literature, 1959-, now Emeritus, Rutgers University, New Brunswick, New Jersey. Publications: Catastrophe and Imagination, 1957, 1998; Versions of Censorship (with Mairi MacInnes), 1962; The Complete Aficionado, 1967, 2nd edition, 1998; The Middle Distance: A Comparative History of American Imaginative Literature, 1919-1932, 1971; Fiction as Knowledge: The Modern Post-Romantic Novel, 1975, 1998; George Santayana: A Biography, 1987; Sallies of the Mind: Essays of Francis Fergusson (editor with G Core), 1997; Seagoing: Memoir, 2000. Contributions to: Numerous magazines, journals and reviews. Honours: Longview Award for Non-Fiction, 1960; Guggenheim Fellowships, 1964-65, 1980-81; National Endowments for the Humanities Senior Fellow, 1983-84; American Academy and Institute of Arts and Letters Prize, 1988. Address: 31 Huntington Road, York YO31 8RL, England.

**McCOY Anthony Peter,** b. 5 May 1974, Ballymena, Northern Ireland. National Hunt Jockey. Education: St Ollans School, Randalstown, Northern Ireland. Career: 10 times record breaking Champion National Hunt Jockey. Publications: Autobiography: McCoy, 2002; DVD Documentary "The Real McCoy", 2002. Honours: Honorary Doctorate for services to sport, Queens University, Belfast, 2002; MBE, 2003; Winner, Variety Club of Great Britain Award, 2004. Address: Hilltop House, Kingston Lisle, Wantage, Oxfordshire OX12 9HQ, England. E-mail: ap.mccoy@talk21.com

**McCREA Anna Maria,** b. 1 February 1959, Lodz, Poland. Civil Engineer. m. Peter Whitehouse. Education: MEng, Civil Engineering, Lodz Institute of Technology, Poland, 1977-82; MSc, Structures, 1985-87, PhD, Robotics and Automation in Construction, 1993-99, City University, London; Programme of IT Courses, Learning Tree International, London, 1998-99; Diploma in Management Studies, South Bank University, 1998-99. Appointments: Assistant Civil Engineer, Construction and Repair Department of District Administration of Penitentiaries, Lodz, Poland, 1983-84; Assistant Civil and Structural Engineer, Alan Baxter and Associates, London, 1987-89; Structural Engineer, Aukett Europe, 1989-92; Senior Lecturer, South Bank University, 1992-98; Co-ordinator of EU-funded Construction Project Futurehome for Communication, Dissemination and Commercial Exploitation, City University, 1998-2000; Product Development Manager, Minglo.com, 2000; Online Product and Content Developer, Construction Plus – Emap Construction Network, 2000-2002; Contract-based Expert for Assessment of Technical Projects submitted for EU funding, European Commission, 2000-; Visiting Lecturer in IT and Structural Form and Function, University College London, 2000; Research and

Management Senior Consultant, Davis Langdon Management Consulting, 2002-. Publication: 3 publications in refereed journals and 9 at refereed conferences. Honours: MEng; MSc; PhD. Memberships: MASCE; MICE. Address: 340 King's Road, London SW3 5UR, England. E-mail: anna.mccrea@da vislangdon.com

**McCRYSTAL Cahal, (Cal McCrystal),** b. 20 December 1935, Belfast, Northern Ireland. Journalist; Broadcaster; Author. m. Stella Doyle, 15 October 1958, 3 sons. Education: St Mary's College, Dundalk; St Malachy's College, Belfast. Appointments: Reporter, Northern Herald; Labour Correspondent, Belfast Telegraph; Crime Reporter, Chief Reporter, Foreign Correspondent, New York Bureau Chief, News Editor, Foreign Features Editor, Sunday Times, London; Senior Writer, Independent-on-Sunday; Senior Writer, The Observer. Publications: Watergate: The Full Inside Story (co-author), 1973; Reflections on A Quiet Rebel, 1997. Contributions to: Vanity Fair, British Magazines, and British Journalism Review; Independent-on-Sunday and Financial Times (book reviews); Poetry, Ireland Review. Honours: Various journalism awards; Belfast Arts Council Literary Award, 1998; Broadcasts for BBC, Radio Eireann, ABC TV and CBC. Membership: Editorial Board, British Journalism Review. Address: c/o 37 Goldhawk Road, London W12 8QQ, England.

**McCULLOCH Nigel Simeon (The Right Reverend Bishop of Wakefield),** b. 17 January 1942, Anglican Bishop. m. Celia Hume, 2 daughters. Education: Selwyn College, Cambridge; Cuddesdon College, Oxford. Appointments: Assistant Curate, Ellesmere Port, 1966-70; Chaplain and Director of Studies in Theology, Christ's College, Cambridge, 1970-73; Diocesan Missioner, Norwich, 1973-78; Rector of St Thomas's, Salisbury, 1978-86; Archdeacon of Sarum, 1979-86; Bishop of Taunton, 1986-92; Bishop of Wakefield, 1992-; Member of the House of Lords, 1997-; Lord High Almoner to H.M. The Queen, 1997-. Publications: A Gospel to Proclaim; Barriers to Belief; Credo Columnist for the Times, 1996-2000. Honour: MA. Memberships: Chairman, Sandford St Martin Religious Broadcasters Awards; National Chaplain, The Royal British Legion; National Chaplain, The Royal School of Church Music. Address: Bishop's Lodge, Wakefield WF2 6JL, England. E-mail: bishop@wakefield.anglican.org

**McCULLOUGH Colleen,** b. 1 June 1937, Wellington, New South Wales, Australia. Writer. m. Ric Robinson, 1984. Education: Holy Cross College, Woollahra, Sydney University; Institute of Child Health, London University. Appointments: Neurophysiologist, Sydney, London and Yale University Medical School, New Haven, Connecticut, USA, 1967-77; Relocated to Norfolk Island, South Pacific, 1980. Publications: Tim, 1974; The Thorn Birds, 1977; An Indecent Obsession, 1981; Cooking with Colleen McCullough and Jean Easthope, 1982; A Creed for the Third Millennium, 1985; The Ladies of Missalonghi, 1987; The First Man in Rome, 1990; The Grass Crown, 1991; Fortune's Favorites, 1993; Caesar's Women, 1996; Caesar, 1997; The Song of Troy, 1998; Roden Cutler, V.C. (biography), 1998; Morgan's Run, 2000; The October Horse, 2002; The Touch, 2003; Angel Puss, 2004. Honour: Doctor of Letters (honoris causa), Macquarie University, Sydney, 1993. Address: "Out Yenna", Norfolk Island, Oceania (via Australia).

**McDAID Perry, (Phoenix Martin, Pam Louis, Blythe Stitt, Naomi de Plume),** b. 10 October 1959, Derry City, Ireland. Writer; Poet. Education: BTEC, Business Studies, 1984; BA (Hons), Social Sciences. Appointments: Branch Secretary, NICSA, 1980; Civil Servant; Regional Administrative Officer,

Industrial Development Board; Manager, Foyle Chess Club; Accounting Officer, Author Operations Manual for Civil Service Pensions; Quizmaster; Retired due to ill health; Managing Editor, Narwhal Publishing. Publications: Over 500 different poems in 600 listings worldwide; Operations Manual for Civil Service Pensions; Short stories; Banksnotes, Australia. Honours: Honorary Appointment, The Research Board of Advisors, ABI, 2005; Numerous editor's choice awards; Distinguished Member, International Society of Poets. Memberships: Academi Cardiff; Lifetime member, Metverse, ISP; PCOF. Address: 6 Rathmore Road, Rathmore Estate, Derry, BT48 9BS, Northern Ireland.

**McDERMOTT Patrick Anthony,** b. 8 September 1941, Ripley, Surrey, England. Her Majesty's Diplomatic Service, Retired. m. (1) 2 sons, (2) Christa Herminghaus, 2 sons. Education: Clapham College, London. Appointments: Foreign and Commonwealth Office, London, 1961-63; Mexico City, 1963-66; New York, 1966-71; Belgrade, 1971-73; Foreign and Commonwealth Office, London, 1973; Bonn, 1973-76; Paris, 1976-79; Foreign and Commonwealth Office, London, 1979-83; HM Consul-General and Economic and Financial Adviser to the British Military Government, West Berlin, 1984-88; Foreign and Commonwealth Office, London, 1988-89; Counsellor, Paris, 1990-95; Foreign and Commonwealth Office, London, 1996-97; HM Consul General, Moscow and to the Republic of Moldovia, 1998-2001; Retired, 2001-; Management Consultant, Diplomatic Consulting, 2001-02; Deputy Burser, Ampleforth College, 2002-; Board of Trustees, Helmsley Walled Garden, 2005-. Honours: Member, Royal Victorian Order, 1972; Freeman of the City of London, 1986. Address: Linkfoot House, 10 Acres Close, Helmsley, York YO62 5DS, England.

**McDONALD Catherine Donna,** b. 20 December 1942, Vancouver, British Columbia, Canada. Writer; Arts Administrator. m. Robert Francis McDonald, 28 August 1965. Education: BA, 1964. Publications: Illustrated News: Juliana Horatia Ewing's Canadian Pictures 1867-1869; The Odyssey of the Philip Jones Brass Ensemble; Lord Strathcona; A Biography of Donald Alexander Smith; Milkmaids and Maharajas: A History of 1 Palace Street. Contributions to: Periodicals and journals. Address: 10 Chelwood Gardens, Richmond, Surrey TW9 4JQ, England.

**McDONALD Forrest,** b. 7 January 1927, Orange, Texas, USA. Distinguished University Research Professor; Historian; Writer. m. (1) 3 sons, 2 daughters, (2) Ellen Shapiro, 1 August 1963. Education: BA, MA, 1949, PhD, 1955, University of Texas. Appointments: Executive Secretary, American History Research Centre, Madison, Wisconsin, 1953-58; Associate Professor, 1959-63, Professor of History, 1963-67, Brown University; Professor, Wayne State University, 1967-76; Professor, 1976-87, Distinguished University Research Professor, 1987-, University of Alabama, Tuscaloosa; Presidential Appointee, Board of Foreign Scholarships, Washington, DC, 1985-87; Advisor, Centre of Judicial Studies, Cumberland, Virginia, 1985-92; James Pinckney Harrison Professor, College of William and Mary, 1986-87; Jefferson Lecturer, National Endowment for the Humanities, 1987. Publications: We the People: The Economic Origins of the Constitution, 1958; Insull, 1962; E Pluribus Unum: The Formation of the American Republic, 1965; The Presidency of George Washington, 1974; The Phaeton Ride, 1974; The Presidency of Thomas Jefferson, 1976; Alexander Hamilton: A Biography, 1979; Novus Ordo Seclorum, 1985; Requiem, 1988; The American Presidency: An Intellectual History, 1994; States' Rights and the Union 1776-1876, 2000. Contributions to: Professional journals. Honours: Guggenheim Fellowship, 1962-63; George Washington Medal, Freedom's Foundation, 1980; Frances Tavern Book Award,

1980; Best Book Award, American Revolution Round Table, 1986; Richard M Weaver Award, Ingersoll Foundation, 1990; First Salvatori Award, Intercollegiate Studies Institute, 1992; Salvatori Book Award, Intercollegiate Studies Institute, 1994; Mount Vernon Society Choice, One of the Ten Great Books on George Washington, 1998. Memberships: American Antiquarian Society; Philadelphia Society; The Historical Society. Address: PO Box 155, Coker, AL 35452, USA.

**McDONALD Paul Ian,** b. 20 December 1946, Stockport, England. Managing Director. Education: BA (Hons), Geography, University College London, 1965-68; PhD, Civil Engineering, University of Leeds, 1968-71; Cert Ed, New College Oxford, 1971-72. Appointments: Research Fellow, University of Aston, 1975-78; Head of Information Services, National Oil Company of Saudi Arabia, 1978-83; Senior Oil Analyst, Shearson Lehman Brothers, 1983-86; Managing Director, Pearl Oil Ltd, Hong Kong, 1986-2003; Managing Director, Pearl Oil, Great Britain. Publications: Various articles in Nature; New Scientist; Times Literary Supplement; Economist Foreign Report; Books on Middle East and North Africa; Oil Trading in Asia; Deregulation in Japan; Chinese Oil Industry; Oil and Gas in Iraq; The Oil Industry in the USSR; Agriculture in Thailand. Honour: University research exhibited at the Science Museum, London. Memberships: Institute of Petroleum; Oxford Union; Sri Lanka Club, Hong Kong. Address: Springfields, Hawker's Lane, Hambridge, Langport, Somerset TA10 0AU, England.

**McDONALD Trevor,** b. 16 August 1939, Trinidad. Broadcasting Journalist. m. 2 sons, 1 daughter. Appointments: Worked on newspapers, radio and TV, Trinidad, 1960-69; Producer, BBC Caribbean Service and World Service, London, 1969-73; Reporter, Independent TV News, 1973-78; Sports Correspondent, 1978-80; Diplomatic Correspondent, 1980-87; Newscaster, 1982-87; Diplomatic Editor, Channel 4 News, 1987-89; Newscaster, News at 5.40, 1989-90; News at Ten, 1990-99; ITV Evening News, 1999-2000; ITV News at Ten, 2001-; Chairman, Better English Campaign, 1995-97; Nuffield Language Inquiry, 1998-2000; Governor, English-Speaking Union of the Commonwealth, 2000; President, European Year of Languages, 2000. Publications: Clive Lloyd: a biography, 1985; Vivian Richard's biography, 1987; Queen and Commonwealth, 1989; Fortunate Circumstances, 1993; Favourite Poems, 1997; World of Poems, 1999. Honours: Hon DLitt, Nottingham, 1997; Dr hc, Open University, 1997; Honorary Fellow, Liverpool John Moores University, 1998; Newscaster of the Year, TV and Radio Industries Club, 1993, 1997, 1999; Gold Medal, Royal Television Society, 1998; Richard Dimbleby Award for Outstanding Contribution to Television, BAFTA, 1999; Knighted; OBE. Address: c/o ITN, 200 Gray's Inn Road, London, WC1 8XZ, England.

**McDONALD SMITH Paul,** b. 26 November 1956, Melbourne, Australia. Artist. Education: HSC, Scotch College Melbourne, 1975; Fine Art (Painting), RMIT, 1976-78; Private Study, 1973-1979; Numerous European Study Tours; Camberwell Travel Scholarship, 1986; Studies and painted in England, Italy, France, Holland, Belgium, Denmark, Austria and Greece. Appointments: Artist, Painter, Tutor, Judge, Curator; Tutorial Appointments, 1977-; Many guest lecture appointments in Victoria and interstate; Self Employed Artist, 1978-; Various Community Arts Appointments, 1981-; Established and tutored a wide range of painting classes in Eastern, Western and Northern suburbs of Melbourne, oil, water colour, media in plein-air and studio landscape painting, portrait, still-life and life subjects; Numerous Judging Appointments, 1982-; Convenor, Cato Gallery Committee, 1992-97; Editor, VAS Publications, 1997-; President, Victorian Artists Society, 1998-2003; Chairman,

Camberwell Judging Panel, 2002; Exhibitions include: Major solo exhibitions in Melbourne: Mansourah Galleries, 1980; Ash Tree Galleries, 1980, 1983; Gallery 21, Cato Gallery, 1990, 1993; Numerous commissions: Portrait, Landscape, Flowers; Works in Private, corporate, municipal and public collections in Australia and private collections in UK, USA, Japan, the Philippines, New Guinea. Publications: Oils, The Medium of The Masters, 1989; Biographical Catalogues include: Alan Moore, 1994; Ludmilla Meilerts, 1994; Euguene Fromentin, 1996; VAS President's Message, 1998-; Numerous editorial contributions to VAS Newsletter, magazines and professional journals. Honours: Numerous including, VAS Signatory Award, 1991; Norwich Landscape Award, 1992; Heidelberg Prize, 1994; RSPCA National Australia Bank Award, 1995; Outstanding Achievement Award, 1998; Camberwell Club Award, 1998; Norman Kaye Memorial Medallion, 1998 and 1999; Bright '99; Mt Waverley, 1999; Mildura, 1999; Major Award Royal Overseas League, Australia, 2000; Cardinia Shire Award, 2001, VAS Artist of the Year, 2001; Alexandra Award, 2002; Finalist, Victorian Artist of the Year Exhibition, 1990-94, 1996-2003 (no exhibition, 1995). Memberships: FVAS; FRSA; Bottle Brush Club; Twenty Melbourne Painters' Society; RAS, NSW; MOIF; FIBA; LFABI; DDG. Address: 3 Perry Court, Kew, Victoria 3101, Australia. E-mail: paulmcds@cosmos.net.au

**McDORMAND Frances,** b. 23 June 1957, Illinois, USA. Actress. m. Joel Coen, 1 son. Education: Yale University, School of Drama. Appointments: Stage Appearances include: Awake and Sing, 1984; Painting Churches, 1984; The Three Sisters, 1985; All My Sons, 1986; A Streetcar Named Desire, 1988; Moon for the Misbegotten, 1992; Sisters Rosenweig, 1993; The Swan, 1993; Films include: Blood Simple, 1984; Raising Arizona, 1987; Mississippi Burning, 1988; Chattaboochee, 1990; Darkman, 1990; Miller's Crossing, 1990; Hidden Agenda, 1990; The Butcher's Wife, 1991; Passed Away, 1992; Short Cuts, 1993; Beyond Rangoon, 1995; Fargo, 1996; Paradise Road, 1997; Johnny Skidmarks, 1997; Madeline, 1998; Talk of Angels, 1998; Wonder Boys, 1999; Almost Famous, 2000; The Man Who Wasn't There, 2001; Upheaval, 2001; Laurel Canyon, 2002; City By the Sea, 2003; Something's Gotta Give, 2003; Catwoman, 2004; Has appeared in several TV series. Honours: Screen Actors' Guild Award, 1996; London Film Critics' Circle Award, 1996; Independent Spirit Award, 1996; American Comedy Award, 1997; LA Film Critics Award, 2000. Address: c/o William Morris Agency, 1325 Avenue of the Americas, New York, NY 10019, USA.

**McDOUGALL Bonnie Suzanne,** b. 12 March 1941, Sydney, Australia. Professor of Chinese. m. H Anders Hansson, 1 son. Education: BA honours, 1965, MA honours, University Medal, 1967, PhD, 1970, University of Sydney. Appointments: Lecturer in Oriental Studies, University of Sydney, 1972-76; Research Fellow, East Asian Research Center, Harvard University, 1976-79; Associate in East Asian Studies, John King Fairbank Center, Harvard University, 1979-80; Visiting Lecturer on Chinese, Harvard University, 1977-78; Editor and Translator, Foreign Languages Press, Peking, 1980-83; Teacher of English, College of Foreign Affairs, Peking, 1984-86; Senior Lecturer in Chinese, University of Oslo, 1986-87; Professor of Modern Chinese, University of Oslo, 1987-90; Professor of Chinese, University of Edinburgh, 1990-. Publications: Numerous books and articles on Chinese Literature. Memberships: Association for Asian Studies; European Association of Chinese Studies; British Association of Chinese Studies; Universities' China Committee in London; Scots Australian Council. Address: Scottish Centre for Chinese Studies, School of Asian Studies, University of Edinburgh, 8 Buccleuch Place, Edinburgh EH8 9LW, Scotland.

**McDOWALL David Buchanan,** b. 14 April 1945, London, England. Writer. m. Elizabeth Mary Risk Laird, 19 April 1975, 2 sons. Education: MA, 1966-69, M.Litt, 1970-72, St John's College, Oxford. Appointments: Subaltern, Royal Artillery, UK and Hong Kong, 1963-70; British Council, Bombay, Baghdad and London Headquarters, 1972-77; Contributions Officer, United Nations Relief and Works Agency for Palestine Refugees in the Near East, 1977-79; Consultant to voluntary agencies re development in Middle East, 1979-84; Full-time Writer, 1984-. Publications: Lebanon: A Conflict of Minorities, 1984 Palestine and Israel: The Uprising and Beyond, 1989; An Illustrated History of Britain, 1989; Europe and the Arabs: Discord or Symbiosis?, 1992; Britain in Close Up, 1993, 1998; The Palestinians: The Road to Nationhood, 1994; A Modern History of the Kurds, 1996; Richmond Park: The Walker's Historical Guide, 1996; Hampstead Heath: The Walker's Guide (co-author Deborah Wolton), 1998; The Kurds of Syria, 1998; The Thames from Hampton to Richmond Bridge: The Walkers Guide, 2002; The Thames From Richmond to Putney Bridge: The Walker's Guide, 2005. Contributions to: World Directory of Minorities, Middle East section, 1997. Honour: The Other Award. Address: 31 Cambrian Road, Richmond, Surrey TW10 6JQ, England.

**McDOWELL Malcolm,** b. 13 June 1943, Leeds, England. Actor. m. (1) Mary Steenburgen, 1980, 1 son, 1 daughter, (2) Kelley Kuhr, 1992. Appointments: Began career with Royal Shakespeare Company, Stratford, 1965-66; Early TV appearances in such series as Dixon of Dock Green; Z Cars; Stage Appearances: RSC, Stratford, 1965-66; Entertaining Mr Sloane, Royal Court, 1975; Look Back in Anger, New York, 1980; In Celebration, New York, 1984; Holiday Old Vic, 1987; Another Time, Old Vic, 1993; Films Include: If..., 1969; Figures in a Landscape, 1970; The Raging Moon, 1971; A Clockwork Orange, 1971; O Lucky Man, 1973; Royal Flash, 1975; Aces High, 1976; Voyage of the Damned, 1977; Caligula, 1977; The Passage, 1978; Time After Time, 1979; Cat People, 1981; Blue Thunder, 1983; Get Crazy, 1983; Britannia Hospital, 1984; Gulag, 1985; The Caller, 1987; Sunset, 1987; Sunrise, 1988; Class of 1999, Il Maestro, 1989; Moon 44; Double Game; Class of 1999; Snake Eyes, Schweitzer; Assassin of the Tsar, 1991; The Player; Chain of Desire; East Wind; Night Train to Venice; Star Trek: Generations, 1995; Tank Girl, 1995; Kids of the Round Table; Where Truth Lies; Mr Magoo, 1998; Gangster No 1, 2000; TV includes: Our Friends in the North. Address: c/o Markham and Froggatt, 4 Windmill Street, London, W1P 1HF, England.

**McELLISTREM Marcus T,** b. 19 April 1926, St Paul, Minnesota, USA. Emeritus Professor of Physics. m. Eleanor, 1 son, 5 daughters. Education: BA, St Thomas College, St Paul; MS, 1952, PhD, 1956, University of Wisconsin, Madison. Appointments: Research Associate, Indiana University, 1955-57; Assistant Professor, 1957-60, Associate Professor, 1960-65, Professor, 1965-, University of Kentucky; Director, Accelerator Laboratory, University of Kentucky, 1974-. Publications: 95 articles in professional journals. Honours: Distinguished Professor, Arts and Sciences, 1981-82; Kentucky Distinguished Scientist Award, 1992; President, Kentucky Academy of Sciences, 1997. Memberships: Fellow, American Physical Society; Kentucky Academy of Sciences. Address: Department of Physics and Astronomy, University of Kentucky, Lexington, KY 40506-0055, USA.

**McENROE John Patrick,** b. 16 February 1959, Wiesbaden, Federal Republic of Germany. Lawn Tennis Player. m. (1) Tatum O'Neil, 1986, 2 sons, 1 daughter, (2) Patty Smyth, 2 daughters, 1 step-daughter. Education: Trinity High School, New Jersey; Stanford University, California. Appointments: Amateur Player,

1976-78; Professional, 1978-93; USA Singles Champion, 1979, 1980, 1981, 1984; USA Doubles Champion, 1979, 1981, 1989; Wimbledon Champion (doubles), 1979, 1981, 1983, 1984, 1992 (singles) 1981, 1983, 1984; WCT Champion, 1979, 1981, 1983, 1984, 1989; Grand Prix Champion, 1979, 1983, 1984; Played Davis Cup for USA, 1978, 1979, 1980, 1982, 1983, 1984, 1985; Only Player to have reached Wimbledon semi-finals (1977) as pre-tournament qualifier; Semi Finalist, 1989; Tennis Sportscaster, USA Network, 1993; Member, Men's Senior's Tours Circuits, 1994; Winner, Quality Challenge, Worldwide Senior Tennis Circuit, 1999; Owner, John McEnroe Gallery. Publication: You Cannot Be Serious, autobiography, 2002. Honour: International Tennis Hall of Fame, 1999. Address: c/o John P McEnroe Sr, Paul Weiss Rifkind Wharton and Garrison, 1285 Avenue of the Americas, New York, NY 10019, USA.

**McEWAN Ian,** b. 21 June 1948, Aldershot, Hampshire, England. Author. m. (1) Penny Allen, 1982, divorced, 1995, 2 sons, 2 step daughters, (2) Annalena McAfee, 1997. Education: Woolverstone Hall; University of Sussex; University of East Anglia; Hon D Phil, Sussex, 1989; East Anglia, 1993. Publications: First Love, Last Rites, 1975; In Between the Sheets, 1978; The Cement Gardens, 1978; The Imitation Game, 1980; The Comfort of Strangers, 1981; Or Shall we Die?, 1983; The Ploughman's Lunch, 1983; The Child in Time, 1987; Soursweet (screenplay), 1987; A Move Abroad, 1989; The Innocent, 1990; Black Dogs, 1992; The Daydreamer, 1994; The Short Stories, 1995; Enduring Love, 1997; Amsterdam (novel), 1998; Atonement, 2001; Saturday, 2005. Honours: Somerset Maugham Prize, 1975; Primo Letterario, Prato, 1982; Whitbread Fiction Prize, 1987; Prix Femina, 1993; Booker Prize, 1998; Shakespeare Prize, 1999; National Book Critics Circle Award, 2003. Address: c/o Jonathan Cape, Random Century House, 20 Vauxhall Bridge Road, London SW1V 2SA, England. Website: www.ianmcewan.com

**McFALL John,** b. 1944, Member of Parliament. m. Joan McFall, 3 sons, 1 daughter. Education: BSc honours, Chemistry; BA honours, Education; MBA. Appointments: School Teacher, Assistant Head Teacher, -1987; Member of Parliament for Dumbarton, 1987-; Opposition Whip with responsibility for Foreign Affairs, Defence and Trade and Industry, 1990; Deputy Shadow Secretary of State for Scotland with responsibility for Industry and Economic Affairs; Employment and Training; Home Affairs, Transport and Roads; Highland and Islands, 1992-97; Lord Commissioner, 1997-98; Parliamentary Under Secretary of State, Northern Ireland Office, 1998-99; Chairman of the Treasury Select Committee, 2001-05. Memberships: British/Hong Kong Group; British/Italian Group; British/Peru Group; Retail Industry Group; Roads Study Group; Scotch Whisky Group; Parliamentary and Scientific Committee; Select Committee on Defence; Select Committee on Sittings of the House; Executive Committee Parliamentary Group for Energy Studies; Information Committee; Executive Committee Parliamentary Group for Energy Studies. Address: House of Commons, London SW1A 0AA, England. E-mail: mcfallj@parliament.uk

**McFARLANE John,** b. 14 June 1947, Dumfries, Scotland. Bank Chief Executive. 3 daughters. Education: MA, University of Edinburgh, 1969; MBA, Cranfield School of Management, 1975. Appointments: Ford Motor Co, UK, 1969-74; Citibank, 1975-93, ultimately Head, Citibank United Kingdom Region; Group Executive Director, Standard Chartered Plc, (London and Hong Kong), 1993-97; Chief Executive Officer, Australia and New Zealand Banking Group, Melbourne, Australia, 1997-; Former Directorships in the UK: London Stock Exchange, Capital Radio Plc, Securities Association, Auditing Practices Board, Financial Law Panel, Cranfield School of Management; Former Australian Directorships: Business Council of Australia, Australian Graduate School of Management, Axiss Australia; Chairman of the Committee: The Future Development of Auditing in the United Kingdom and Ireland, 1992; Currently: Chairman, Australian Bankers Association; President, International Monetary Conference; Director, Australian Business Arts Foundation; Director, Financial Markets Foundation for Children; Instituted the McFarlane Prizes for Leadership at Cranfield and the University of Edinburgh. Honours: OBE, 1995; Australian Centenary Medal, 2003; Inaugural Distinguished Alumnus Award, Cranfield School of Management, 2003. Memberships: Fellow, Royal Society for the Arts; Hong Kong Institute of Bankers; Australian Institute of Banking and Finance. Address: 100 Queen Street, Melbourne, Victoria 2000, Australia.

**McFAYDEN Jock,** b. 18 September 1950, Paisley, Scotland. Artist. m. (1) Carol Hambleton, divorced, 1 son, (2) Susie Honeyman, 1 daughter, 1 son. Education: BA, MA, Chelsea School of Art, London, 1973-77. Career: Over 40 solo exhibitions including: National Gallery, 1982; Artist-in-Residence, Camden Arts Centre, 1988; Imperial War Museum, 1991; Talbot Rice Gallery, Edinburgh, 1998; Pier Arts Centre, Orkney, 1999; Agnew's Gallery, London, 2001; Works in over 30 public collections, including the Tate Gallery, the National Gallery, the Victoria and Albert Museum, the British Museum; Works in many private and corporate collections in Britain, Europe and America. Publication: Jock McFayden – A Book About a Painter, by David Cohen, 2001. Honours: Arts Council Major Award, 1979; Prizewinner John Moores Liverpool, 1991; Designed sets and costumes for Sir Kenneth MacMillan's ballet, The Judas Tree, Royal Opera House, 1992. Membership: Vintage Japanese Motorcycle Club. Address: 15 Victoria Park Square, Bethnal Green, London E2 9PB, England.

**McGEACHIE Daniel,** b. 10 June 1935, Barrhead, Glasgow, Scotland. Journalist; Company Director. m. Sylvia Andrew, 1 daughter. Appointments: Journalist, Scotland and Fleet Street, 1955-60; Foreign Correspondent, Daily Express, 1960-65; Parliamentary Correspondent, Diplomatic and Political Correspondent, Daily Express, 1965-75; Political Advisor, Conoco UK Ltd, 1975-77; Director, General Manager, Government and Public Affairs, Conoco UK Ltd, 1977-2000. Honours: OBE for services to Industry and Government relations, 1992. Memberships: Member, Royal Institute of International Affairs; Member, Reform Club. Address: 27 Hitherwood Drive, London SE19 1XA, England. E-mail: danmcgeachie@ukgateway.net

**McGEOCH Ian Lachlan Mackay,** b. 26 March 1914, Helensburgh, Scotland. Naval Officer. m. Eleanor Somers Farrie, 2 sons, 2 daughters. Education: Nautical College, Pangbourne, England. Appointments: Cadet, Royal Navy, 1931; Commanded HMS submarine Splendid, 1942-43; Commanded HMS Fernie, 1946-47; Commanded 4th Submarine Flotilla, 1949-51; Naval Liaison Officer, RAF Coastal and Bomber Commands, 1955-57; Commanded HMS Adamant and third submarine flotilla, 1957-58; Director, Undersurface Warfare Division Naval Staff, 1959-60; Imperial Defence College, 1961; Commanded HMS Lion, 1962-64; Flag Officer, Submarines and NATO Commander Submarines, Eastern Atlantic, 1965-67; Vice Admiral, Flag Officer Scotland and Northern Ireland, and NATO Commander Northern Sub-Area, Eastern Atlantic and Commander Nore Sub-Area, Channel, 1968-70; Director, Midar Systems Ltd, 1986-. Publications: Editor, The Naval Review, 1972-80; Co-author: The Third World War: a future history, 1978; The Third World War: the untold story, 1982; Author:

An Affair of Chances, 1991; The Princely Sailor: Mountbatten of Burma, 1996. Honours: Companion of Distinguished Service Order, 1943; Mentioned in Despatches, 1944; Distinguished Service Cross, 1944; Companion of the Most Honourable Order of the Bath, 1966; Knight Commander of the Most Honourable Order of the Bath, 1969; MPhil, Edinburgh University, 1975. Memberships: Member, Honourable Company of Master Mariners; Fellow, Royal Institute of Navigation; Fellow, Nautical Institute; Naval Member, Royal Yacht Squadron; Life Vice Commodore, Royal Naval Sailing Association; Member, Pin Mill Sailing Club. Address: c/o Coutts, 440 Strand, London WC2R 0QS, England.

**McGEOUGH Joseph Anthony,** b. 29 May 1940, Kilwinning, Ayrshire, Scotland. University Professor. m. Brenda Nicholson, 2 sons, 1 daughter. Education: BSc, 1963, PhD, 1967, Glasgow University; DSc, Aberdeen University, 1982. Appointments: Senior Research Fellow, Queensland University, 1967; Research Metallurgist, International Research and Development Co Ltd, Newcastle, 1968-69; Senior Research Fellow, Strathclyde University, 1969-72; Lecturer, 1972-77, Senior Lecturer, 1977-80, Reader, 1980-83, University of Aberdeen; Regius Professor of Engineering, University of Edinburgh, 1983-2005. Publications: Books include: Principles of Electrochemical Machining, 1974; Advanced Methods of Machining, 1988; Micromachining of Engineering Materials (editor), 2001. Honour: FRSE, 1990. Memberships: FIMechE; FIEE; MIMMM. Address: 39 Dreghorn Loan, Edinburgh EH13 0DF, Scotland. E-mail: j.a.mcgeough@ed.ac.uk

**McGILL Bryant Harrison,** 7 November 1969, Mobile, Alabama, USA. Poet; Author; Computer Scientist. m. Rachel Roberts McGill, 2 daughters. Education: Computer Science Graduate, US Navy 1988; Student of M Newman, protégé of W H Auden, Connecticut, 1993-94; George Plimpton, 1994-2003; Dr Alan W Eckert, Ohio, 1997-2002; Doctorate Humane Letters (Hon), Adam Smith University, Boissy-St-Leger, France, 1998. Appointments: Chief Software Architect, Lionheart International, Salt Lake City, Utah, 1994-98; Vice-President of Technology, Mark Steel, Spring City, Utah, 1997-98; Engineer, Borland International, Scotts Valley, California, 1998-99; Chief Research Scientist, Computational Scientific Laboratories, 1999-2001; Chief Technology Officer, Webiness Inc/Artesian Direct, Spokane, Washington, 2001-2005. Publications: McGill English Dictionary of Rhyme; Existence, 2004; Poet's Muse; Associative Reference for Writer's Block, 2005; McGill English Thesaurus for Poets; Drawing the Human Body: A Computational Study for the Artist; Living Language: Proximal Frequency Research Reference. Honours: Humanitarian of the Year, Uranium Publishers, SLC, 1995; Contemporary Poets Hall of Fame Inductee, University of North Carolina at Chapel Hill, 2004. Memberships: Fellow Researcher at Xammon, the Society of Inquiry and Innovation; International Society for Computers and their Applications. Address: 243 Fifth Avenue, Suite 220, New York, NY10016, USA. Website: www.bryantmcgill.com

**McGOUGH Roger,** b. 9 November 1937, Liverpool, England. Poet. m. Hilary Clough, 1986, 3 sons, 1 daughter. Education: St Mary's College, Crosby; BA and Graduate Certificate of Education, Hull University. Appointments: Fellow of Poetry, University of Loughborough, 1973-75; Writer-in-Residence, West Australian College of Advanced Education, Perth, 1986. Publications: The Mersey Sound (with Brian Patten and Adrian Henri), 1967; Strictly Private (editor), 1982; An Imaginary Menagerie, 1989; Blazing Fruit (selected poems 1967-87), 1990; Pillow Talk, 1990; The Lighthouse That Ran Away, 1991; You at the Back (selected poems 1967-87, Vol 2), 1991; My Dad's a Fire Eater, 1992; Defying Gravity, 1992; The Elements, 1993;

Lucky, 1993; Stinkers Ahoy!, 1994; The Magic Fountain, 1995; The Kite and Caitlin, 1996; Sporting Relations, 1996; Bad, Bad Cats, 1997; Until I Met Dudley, 1997; The Spotted Unicorn, 1998; The Ring of Words (editor), 1998; The Way Things Are, 1999; Everyday Eclipses, 2002; Good Enough to Eat, 2002; Moonthief, 2002; Wicked Poems (editor), 2002; Collected Poems of Roger McGough, 2003; What on Earth Can It Be? 2003. Honours: Honorary Professor, Thames Valley University, 1993; Officer of the Order of the British Empire, 1997; Honorary MA, 1998; Cholmondeley Award, 1998; Fellow, John Moores University, Liverpool, 1999. Address: c/o The Peters, Fraser and Dunlop Group Ltd, Drury House, 34 – 43 Russell Street, London WC2B 5HA, England.

**McGREGOR Ewan,** b. 31 March 1971, Perth, Scotland. Actor. m. Eve Mavrakis, 1995, 2 daughters. Education: Guildhall School of Music and Drama. Appointments: Formerly with Perth Repertory Theatre; Theatre includes: What the Butler Saw; Little Malcolm and his Struggle against the Eunuchs, Hampstead Theatre Club, 1989; TV includes: Lipstick on Your Collar; Scarlet and Black; Kavanagh QC, Doggin Around; Tales from the Crypt; ER; Films include: Being Human; Family Style; Shallow Grave; Blue Juice; The Pillow Book; Trainspotting; Emma; Brassed Off; Nightwatch; The Serpent's Kiss; A Life Less Ordinary; Velvet Goldmine; Star Wars Episode I: The Phantom Menace; Little Voice; Rogue Trader; Eye of the Beholder; Nora; Moulin Rouge, 2001; Black Hawk Down, 2002; Stars Wars Episode II: Attack of the Clones, 2002; Down with Love, 2003; Young Adam, 2003; Faster, 2003; Big Fish, 2003; Robots (voice), 2005; Stay, 2005; Valiant (voice), 2005; Star Wars Episode III: Revenge of the Sith, 2005; The Island, 2005; Flora Plum, 2005; Documentary and book: The Long Way Round, motorcycle trip around the world for UNICEF with Charley Boorman, 2004. Honours: Best Actor Dinard Film Festival, 1994; Best Actor, Berlin Film Festival; Empire Award; Variety Club Awards; Film Critics' Awards.

**McGREGOR Harvey,** b. 25 February 1926, Aberdeen, Scotland. Barrister. Education: The Queen's College, Oxford University; Harvard University. Appointments: Flying Officer, Royal Air Force, 1946-48; Barrister in Private Practice, 1955-58, 1965-; Executive, J Walter Thompson, 1959-62; Visiting Professor, New York University, USA, 1963-64; Visiting Professor, Rutgers University, USA, 1964-65; Consultant to Law Commission, 1965-73; Fellow, 1972-85, Warden, 1985-96, New College, Oxford; Visiting Professor, University of Edinburgh, 1998-. Publications: International Encyclopaedia of Comparative Law (contributor), 1972; Contract Code, 1993; McGregor on Damages, 17th edition, 2003; European Contract Code (translation from French), 2004. Honours: MA (Oxon); Doctor of Civil Law (DCL), Oxford; Doctor of Juridical Science (SJD), Harvard; Queen's Counsel; Bencher, Inner Temple; Honorary Fellow, New College, Oxford. Memberships: Past President, Harvard Law School Association of UK, 1981-2001; Member of Editorial Board, Modern Law Review, 1986-; Chairman, London Theatre Council and Theatre Council, 1992-; President, Oxford Stage Co, 1992-; Member, Academy of European Private Lawyers, 1994-; Past Chairman, Trustees of Oxford Union, 1994-2004; Trustee, Migraine Trust, 1999-; Privilegiate, St Hilda's College, Oxford, 2001; Associate Member of Writers to the Signet, 2002-. Address: 29 Howard Place, Edinburgh EH3 5JY, Scotland. E-mail: harvey.mcgregor @hailshamchambers.com

**McGUIGAN Finbar Patrick (Barry),** b. 28 February 1961, Monaghan, Ireland. Sports Commentator; Journalist. m. Sandra Mealiff, 3 sons, 1 daughter. Education: St Louis Convent, Clones, Ireland; Largy School, Clones, Ireland; St Patrick's High

School, Clones Ireland. Career: Irish Juvenile Title and Best Boxer, 1977; Irish Under 19 and Irish Senior Bantam Weight Title, 1978; Commonwealth Gold Medal at Bantam Weight, Edmonton, Canada, 1978; European Bronze at Featherweight, 1980; Turned professional, 1981; British Featherweight Champion, 1983; European Featherweight Champion, 1983; WBA World Featherweight Champion, 1985. Publications: Leave the Fighting to McGuigan, 1985; McGuigan the Untold Story, 1990. Honours: Voted British Boxing Board of Control's Young Boxer of the Year, 1983; World Boxing Association Fight of the Year (v. E Pedroza), 1985; British Boxing Board of Control Fighter of the Year, 1985; MBE, 1994; Voted into the International Boxing Hall of Fame, 2005. Memberships: President and Founder, British Boxers Association (formerly the Professional Boxers Association). Address: c/o Phil Hughes, 3548 North End Road, Fulham, London, SW6 1NY, England.

**McGUINNESS Martin,** b. Derry, Northern Ireland. Politican. m. 4 children. Appointments: Took part in secret London Talks between Secretary of State for Northern Ireland and Irish Republicans Army (IRA), 1972; Imprisoned for six months during 1973, Irish Republic, after conviction for IRA membership; Elected to North Ireland Association, Refused Seat; Stood against John Hume in General Elections of 1982, 1987, 1992; MP for Mid-Ulster, House of Commons, 1997-; Member, Ulster-Mid, Northern Ireland Association, 1998-2000, Association suspended 11 February 2000; Minister of Education, 1999-2000; Spokesperson for Sinn Féin; Member of National Executive; Involved in Peace Negotiations with British Government.

**McGURN Barrett,** b. 6 August 1914, New York, New York, USA. Author. m. Janice Ann McLaughlin, 5 sons, 1 daughter. Education: AB, Fordham University, 1935. Appointments: Reporter, New York Herald Tribune, 1935-66, Bureau Chief, Rome, Paris, Moscow, 1946-62; US Foreign Service, Rome, Saigon; Foreign Service Officer, State Department, Washington, 1966-72; Communications Director, US Supreme Court, 1973-82; Communications Director, Archdiocese of Washington, 1983-89. Publications: Decade in Europe, 1958; A Reporter Looks at the Vatican, 1962; A Reporter Looks at American Catholicism, 1967; America's Court, The Supreme Court and the People, 1997; The Pilgrim's Guide to Rome for the Millennium, 1999; Yank, Reporting the Greatest Generation, 2004. Honours: Best US Foreign Correspondent, Long Island University Award, New York, 1956; Best US Foreign Correspondent, Overseas Press Club, 1957; Honorary Doctorate of Letters, Fordham University, New York, 1958; Grand Knight, Italian National Order of Merit, 1962; Pulitzer Prize Nomination, 1966; US State Department Meritorious Honour Award, 1972. Memberships: Overseas Press Club of America, President, 1963-65; Association of Foreign Correspondents in Italy, President, 1961, 1962; National Press Club, Washington DC; Cosmos Club, Washington DC. Address: 5229 Duvall Drive, Bethesda, MD 20816, USA. E-mail: jmcgurn@erols.com

**McINERNEY Jay,** b. USA. Writer. m. (1) Linda Rossiter, (2) Merry Raymond, (3) Helen Bransford, 1991, 1 son, 1 daughter. Education: Williams University. Publications: Bright Lights, Big City, 1984; Ransom, 1986; Story of My Life, 1988; Brightness Falls, 1992; The Last of the Savages, 1996; Model Behaviour, 1998; How It Ended, 2000.

**McINTYRE Ian (James),** b. 9 December 1931, Banchory, Kincardineshire, Scotland. Writer; Broadcaster. m. Leik Sommerfelt Vogt, 1954, 2 sons, 2 daughters. Education: BA, 1953, MA, 1960, St John's College, Cambridge; College of Europe, Bruges, Belgium, 1953-54. Appointments include:

National Service, Commissioned in the Intelligence Corps, 1955-57; BBC Current Affairs Talks Producer, 1957; Editor, At Home and Abroad, 1959; Programme Services Officer, Independent Television Authority, 1961-62; Director of Information and Research, Scottish Conservative Central Office, 1962-70; Writer, Broadcaster, 1970-76, Controller, Radio 4, 1976-78, Controller, Radio 3, 1978-87, British Broadcasting Corporation; Associate Editor, The Times, London, 1989-90. Publications: The Proud Doers: Israel After Twenty Years, 1968; Words: Reflections on the Uses of Language, editor, contributor, 1975; Dogfight: The Transatlantic Battle over Airbus, 1992; The Expense of Glory: A Life of John Reith, 1993; Dirt and Deity: A Life of Robert Burns, 1996; Garrick, 1999; Joshua Reynolds: The Life and Times of the First President of the Royal Academy, 2003. Honour: Winner, Theatre Book Prize, 1999. Memberships; Union Society, Cambridge; Beefsteak Club. Address: Spylaw House, Newlands Avenue, Radlett, Hertfordshire WD7 8EL, England.

**McINTYRE James Archibald,** b. 2 September 1926, Stranraer, Scotland. Retired Farmer. m. Hilma Wilson Brown, 1 son, 2 daughters. Education: Oxford University, 1944, 6 months short army course. Commissioned 12 H Royal Lancers, 1945-47; West of Scotland Horticultural College, 1948-49. Appointments: Council Member, 1962-72, President, 1969, National Farmers Union, Scotland; Member, 1973-, Chairman, 1985-95, Dumfries and Galloway Health Board; Board Member, NFU Mutual Insurance, 1983-93. Honours: JP, 1989; OBE, 1989; CBE, 1995; O St J, 1979; C St J, 2000. Memberships: National Farmers Union, Scotland, 1950-; Member, Order of St John, 1972-. Address: Glenorchy, Broadstone Road, Stranraer, Scotland.

**McINTYRE Michael Edgeworth,** b. 28 July 1941, Sydney, Australia. Scientist. m. Ruth Hecht, 2 step-sons, 1 step-daughter. Education: BSc Hons (1st class), Mathematics, University of Otago, New Zealand, 1963; PhD, Geophysical Fluid Dynamics, University of Cambridge, England, 1967. Appointments: Assistant Lecturer, Mathematics, University of Otago New Zealand, 1963; Postdoctoral Research Associate, Department of Meteorology, Massachusetts Institute of Technology, USA, 1967-69; Assistant Director of Research in Dynamical Meteorology, 1969-72, University Lecturer, 1972-87, Reader, Atmospheric Dynamics, 1987-93, Professor, Atmospheric Dynamics, 1993-, Department of Applied Mathematics and Theoretical Physics, University of Cambridge; Co-Director, Cambridge Centre for Atmospheric Science, 1992-2003; Principal Investigator, UK Universities' Global Atmospheric Modelling Programme, Natural Environmental Research Council, 1990-; Senior Consultant, Jet Propulsion Laboratory, Pasadena, California, USA, 1991-2002; Scientific Steering Committee, STRATEOLE experiment (quasi-Lagrangian tracers in the Antarctic stratospheric vortex), 1992-2002. Publications: Author and co-author of over 100 articles in learned scientific journals and conference proceedings, including most recently: Lucidity and Science, Parts I-III, 1997-98; On shear-generated gravity waves that reach the mesosphere, 1999; Potential-vorticity inversion on a hemisphere, 2000; Balance and the slow quasimanifold: some explicit results, 2000; Balance, potential-vorticity inversion, Lighthill radiation and the slow quasimanifold, 2001; Some fundamental aspects of atmospheric dynamics with a solar spin-off, 2002; Wind-generated water waves: two overlooked mechanisms?, 2004; Solar tachocline dynamics: eddy viscosity, anti-friction, or something in between?, 2003; Remote recoil: a new wave-mean interaction effect, 2003; Wave capture and wave-vortex duality, 2005. Honours include: Research Fellowship, St John's College, Cambridge, 1968-71; Adams Prize, University of Cambridge, 1981; Carl-Gustaf Rossby Research Medal,

# DICTIONARY OF INTERNATIONAL BIOGRAPHY

American Meteorological Society, 1987; Distinguished Sackler Lecturer, University of Tel Aviv, Israel, 1995; Julius Bartels Medal, European Geophysical Society, 1999. Memberships include: Academia Europaea, 1989-; Fellow of the Royal Society, 1990-; Fellow, American Meteorological Society, 1990-; Fellow, American Association for the Advancement of Science, 1999. Address: Department of Applied Mathematics and Theoretical Physics, Centre for Mathematical Sciences, Wilberforce Road, Cambridge, CB3 0WA, England. Website: www.atm.damtp.cam.ac.uk/people/mem

**McINTYRE Richard Harold,** b. 20 August 1947, Sydney, Australia. Musician. m. Megan Anne Taylor, 4 sons, 1 daughter. Education: Bachelor of Music, Sydney University, 1968. Appointments: Associate Principal Bassoon, Sydney Symphony Orchestra, 1968-78; Lecturer then Senior Lecturer in Bassoon, Canberra School of Music, Australian National University, 1978-; Founding Member, The Canberra Wind Soloists, 1980-; Principal Bassoon, Canberra Symphony Orchestra, 1978-; Chief Conductor and Music Director, Canberra Youth Orchestra, 1980-90; Conductor and Music Director, The Llewellyn Choir, 1992-, Oriana Chorale, 2000-2002; Freelance Conductor; Guest Principal Bassoon, most leading Australian orchestras, 1973-. Recordings: 1 Vinyl recording and 3 compact discs as member of the Canberra Wind Soloists; Wind quintet arrangements of Ravel "Mother Goose", Mussorgsky "Pictures at an Exhibition", Stravinsky "Petrushka"(with piano), "Pulcinella". Honours: Canberran of the Year 1986; Advance Australia Award, 1991; Sounds Australian Award, 1991; Medal of the Order of Australia, 1992. Memberships: International Double Reed Society; Australian Double Reed Society; Media, Entertainment and Arts Alliance; National Tertiary Education Union. Address: 48 Green Street, Narrabundah, ACT 2604, Australia. E-mail: rmac@apex.net.au

**McISAAC Ian,** b. 13 July 1945. Chartered Accountant. m. (1) Joanna Copland, dissolved, 1 son, 1 daughter, (2) Debrah Ball, 1 son, 1 daughter. Education: Charterhouse scholar. Appointments: Partner, Touche Ross (UK), 1979-88; Touche Ross (Canada), 1983-85; Chief Executive, Richard Ellis Finanacial Services, 1988-91; Partner, Deloitte and Touche (formerly Touche Ross), 1991-; Global Head, Reorganisation Service, 1999-, UK Chairman, Emerging Markets, 2000-; Chairman, Society of Turaround Professionals, Director, Care International (UK). Honours: Freeman of the City of London; Member of the Worshipful Company of Chartered Accountants; ACA, 1969; FCA, 1979. Memberships: City of London Club; Hurlingham Club; Royal Mid-Surrey Golf Club; High Post Golf Club; OCYC. Address: 28 Hereford Square, London SW7. E-mail: imcisaac@deloitte.co.uk

**McIVOR Terence Anthony Joseph,** b. 2 September 1970, Londonderry, Northern Ireland. Lecturer. Partner: Michelle, 1 son, 3 daughters. Education: BSc (Hons) Applied Biochemical Sciences with Diploma in Industrial Studies, 1996; Postgraduate Certificate in Further and Higher Education, 1998; Postgraduate Certificate in Educational Technology, 2001, University of Ulster; Doctor of Chemistry, (Chemical Education), University of Canterbury, 2003; Master of Arts in Education, Almeda University, 2005. Appointments: Textile Chemist, Lintrend Textiles, 1994-95; Assistant Engineer, Seagate, 1998; Lecturer, North West Institute of Further Education, 1996-2005; Associate Dean, Faculty of Science, Pepplehills University (responsible for heading and developing BSc Honours or MSc Honours and PhD programme). Publications: Analysis of Thiols as Anticancer Agents Using Cyclic Voltammetry, 1996; Development of ICT within Technology, 2002; Theoretical Chemical Techniques, 2003; Curriculum Development in Science Education, 2005.

Honour: Award for innovative excellence, Lintrend Textiles. Memberships: American Chemical Society; Scientific Chemical Industry; British Computer Society; British Society of Educational Studies; American Institute of Chemists; Institute of Biochemistry; Federation of American Scientists. Address: North West Institute of Further and Higher Education, Strand Road, Londonderry, Northern Ireland. E-mail: terence.mcivor @nwi.ac.uk

**McKEEVER Paul Edward,** b. 3 December 1946, Pasadena, California. Professor. m. Mary Olivia, 1 son, 2 daughters. Education: BS Biology, Brown University, Providence Rhode Island, 1964-68; MD, University of California, 1972; PhD, Medical University of South Carolina, 1976. Appointments: Anatomic Pathology Intern and Cardiopulmonary Trainee, University of California, 1972-73; Neuropathology Fellow and Anatomic Pathology Resident, Medical University of South Carolina, 1973-6; Research Associate, 1976-79, Consultant in Neuropathology, 1976-83, Clinical Associate Professor, 1978-83, Neuropathologist, 1979-83, Pathology Consultant, 1980-83, Bethesda, Maryland; Chief, Department of Pathology, 1983-, Staff Physician, 1983-, Associate Professor, 1983-99, Director, Nerve and Muscle Biopsy Service, 1985-89, Director, Neurohistology Laboratory, 1996, Professor, University of Michigan, 1999-. Publications: Numerous books and articles. Honours include: Mosby Book Award, 1972; Who's Who in the East, 1978; American Men and Women of Science, 1980. Memberships: Editorial Board, American Association of Neuropathologists; Society for Neuroscience; American Association of Pathologists; Children's Oncology Group; Histochemical Society, Publications Committee, Future Directions Committee. Address: Pathology Department, University of Michigan, Box 0602, 1301 Catherine St, Rm M4207, Ann Arbor, MI 48109-0602, USA.

**McKELLEN Ian Murray (Sir),** b. 25 May 1939, Burnley, Lancashire, England. Actor. Education: Bolton School; St Catherines College, Cambridge. Appointments: First stage appearance, Roper (A Man for All Seasons), Belgrade Theatre, Coventry, 1961; Numerous other parts including: Royal National Theatre: Bent, Max; King Lear, Kent; Richard III, world tour then US tour, 1990-92; Napoli Milionaria, 1991; Uncle Vanya, 1992; An Enemy of the People, 1997; Peter Pan, 1997; The Seagull, Present Laughter, The Tempest, West Yorkshire Playhouse, 1998-99; Dance of Death, Broadhurst Theatre, New York, 2001; Films include: Alfred the Great, 1969; The Promise, 1969; A Touch of Love, 1969; Priest of Love, 1981; The Keep, 1982; Plenty, Zina, 1985; Scandal, 1988; The Ballad of Little Jo, 1992; I'll do Anything, 1992; Last Action Hero, 1993; Six Degrees of Seperation, 1993; The Shadow, 1994; Jack and Sarah, 1994; Restoration, 1994; Richard III, 1995; Bent, 1996; Swept From Sea, 1996; Apt Pupil, 1997; Gods and Monsters, 1998; X-Men, 1999; Lord of the Rings: The Fellowship of the Ring, 2001; Lord of the Rings: The Two Towers, 2002; X-Men 2, 2003; Emile, 2003; Lord of the Rings: The Return of the King, 2003; TV appearances include: David Copperfield, 1965; Ross, 1969; Richard II; Edward II; Hamlet, 1970; Hedda Gabler, 1974; Macbeth; Every Good Boy Deserves Favour, Dying Day, 1979; Acting Shakespeare, 1981; Walter; The Scarlet Pimpernel, 1982; Walter and June, 1983; Countdown to War, 1989; Othello, 1990; Tales of the City, 1993; Cold Comfort Farm, 1995; Cameron Mackintosh Professor of Contemporary Theatre Oxford University, 1991. Publications: William Shakespeare's Richard III, 1996. Honours: Clarence Derwent Award, 1964; Hon D Litt, 1989; Variety and Plays and Players Awards, 1966; Actor of the Year, Plays and Players, 1976; Society of West End Theatres Award for Best Actor in a Revival, 1977, for Best Comedy Performance, 1978, for Best Actor in a New Play, 1979; Tony

Award, 1981; Drama Desk, 1981; Outer Critics Circle Award, 1981; Royal TV Society Performer of the Year, 1983; Laurence Olivier Award, 1984, 1991; Evening Standard Best Actor Award, 1984, 1989; Screen Actor's Guild Award for besting supporting Actor, 2000. Address: c/o ICM 76 Oxford Street, London, W1N 0AX, England.

**McKENDRICK Melveena Christine,** b. 23 March 1941, Crynant, Neath, Wales. Hispanist. m. Neil McKendrick, 2 daughters. Education: BA 1st class honours, Spanish, King's College, London; PhD, Girton College, Cambridge, 1967. Appointments: Jex-Blake Research Fellow, 1967-70, Tutor, 1970-83, Senior Tutor, 1974-81, Director of Studies in Modern Languages, 1984-95, Girton College, Cambridge; Lecturer in Spanish, 1980-92, Reader in Spanish Literature and Society, 1992-99, Professor of Spanish, Golden-Age Literature, Culture and Society, 1999-, University of Cambridge; British Academy Reader, 1992-94, Visiting Professor, University of Victoria, 1997; Fellow of the British Academy, 1999-; Pro-Vice-Chancellor (Education), University of Cambridge, 2004-. Publications: Author and co-author, numerous books; Articles on Early Modern Spanish theatre in many journals. Memberships: General Board, Cambridge University, 1993-97; Humanities Research Board, British Academy, 1996-98; Arts and Humanities Research Board, 1998-99; Consultant Hispanic Editor, Everyman, 1993-99; Editorial board, Donaire, 1994-; Revista Canadiense de Estudios Hispanicos, 1995-; Bulletin of Hispanic Studies, Glasgow, 1998-. Address: Department of Spanish & Portuguese, Faculty of Modern and Medieval Languages, University of Cambridge, Sidgwick Avenue, Cambridge, CB3 9DA, England.

**McKENDRICK Neil,** b. 28 July 1935, Formby, Lancashire, England. Historian. m. Melveena Jones, 2 daughters. Education: BA 1st class honours with Distinction, History, 1956, MA, 1960, Christ's College, Cambridge; FRHistS, 1971. Appointments: Research Fellow, 1958, Christ's College Cambridge; Assistant Lecturer in History, 1961-64, Lecturer, 1964-95, Secretary to Faculty Board of History, 1975-77, Chairman, History Faculty, 1985-87, Cambridge University; Fellow, 1958-96, Lecturer in History, 1958-96, Reader in Social and Economic History, 1995-2002, Director of Studies in History, 1959-96, Tutor, 1961-69, Master, 1996-2005, Gonville and Caius College; Lectures: Earl, University of Keele, 1963; Inaugural, Wallace Gallery, Colonial Williamsburg, 1985; Chettyar Memorial, University of Madras, 1990. Publications: Author and Editor of numerous publications; Author of articles in learned journals. Memberships: Tancred's Charities, 1996; Sir John Plumb Charitable Trust, 1999-; Properties Committee, National Trust, 1999-; Vice President, Caius Foundation in America, 1998-; Glenfield Trust, 2001-. Address: The Master's Lodge, Gonville and Caius College, Cambridge, CB2 1TA, England.

**McKENNA Virginia Anne,** b. 7 June 1931, London, England. Actress; Conservationist. m. Bill Travers, deceased 1994, 3 sons, 1 daughter. Education: Central School of Speech and Drama, London. Career: TV includes: The Whistle Blower; Pucini; The Camomile Lawn; The Deep Blue Sea; A Passage to India; Waters of the Moon; September; Films include: Born Free; Ring of Bright Water; Carve Her Name with Pride; The Cruel Sea; The Smallest Show on Earth; Waterloo; The Barretts of Wimpole Street; Staggered; An Elephant Called Slowly; Theatre includes: Season, Old Vic; The Devils; A Winters Tale; Penny for a Song; The River Line; A Little Night Music; The Beggars Opera; Winnie; I Capture the Castle; Hamlet; The King and I. Publications: Books: On Playing with Lions (with Bill Travers); Some of My Friends Have Tails; Into the Blue; Back to the Blue; Journey to Freedom; Co-editor and contributor to: Beyond the

Bars; Contributor to: Women at Work. Honours: Best Actress Award for Born Free, Variety Club; Belgian Prix Femina for Carve Her Name with Pride; SWET Award for The King and I (theatre); Best Actress Award, Romeo and Juliet (TV); Best Actress Award for A Town Like Alice, BAFTA; OBE, 2004. Memberships: Special Forces Club; Patron of: Plan International UK, Children of the Andes, Elizabeth Fitzroy Support; Wildlife Aid, Swallows and Amazons; Founder, Trustee, The Born Free Foundation. Address: The Born Free Foundation, 3 Grove House, Foundry Lane, Horsham, West Sussex RH13 5PL, England. E-mail: wildlife@bornfree.org.uk

**McKENZIE Dan Peter,** b. 21 February 1942, Cheltenham, England. Earth Scientist. m. Indira Margaret, 1 son. Education: BA, MA, PhD, King's College, University of Cambridge. Appointments: Senior Assistant in Research, 1969-75, Assistant Director of Research, 1975-79, Reader in Tectonics, 1979-84, Royal Society Professor of Earth Sciences, Department of Earth Sciences, University of Cambridge. Publications: Author of various papers in learned journals. Honours: Honorary MA, University of Cambridge, 1966; Fellow, Royal Society, 1976; Foreign Associate, US National Academy of Sciences, 1989; Balzan Prize (with F J Vine and D H Matthews), International Balzan Foundation, 1981; Japan Prize (with W J Morgan and X Le Pichon), Technological Foundation of Japan, 1990; Royal Medal of the Royal Society, 1991; Crafoord Prize, 2002. Address: Bullard Laboratories, Madingley Road, Cambridge CB3 0EZ, England.

**McKENZIE Kathleen Julianna,** b. 20 January 1957, South Bend, Indiana. m. Myron Roy McKenzie, 1 son, 1 daughter. Education: Studied under the following painting mentors: Richard Borden, 1979-82; Arthur Getz, 1987-90; Curt Hanson, 1992-. Publications: Listed in Encyclopedia of Living Artists in America, 7th, 9th and 11th Editions; New England Artists' Directory, 2001; International Encyclopaedic Dictionary of Modern and Contemporary Art, Italy, 2003-2004. Honours: 3rd Place, Mystic Outdoor Art Festival; Connecticut Women Artists Inc; Woman of the Year 2003, American Biographical Institute; Listed in several international biographies of artists and Who's Who publications. Memberships: International Peace and Diplomacy Forum; American Biographical Institute Research Association Deputy Governors. Address: 1655 Mountain Road, Torrington, CT 06790, USA.

**McKITTERICK Rosamond Deborah,** b. 31 May 1949, Chesterfield, Derbyshire, England. Professor of Medieval History. m. David John McKitterick, 1 daughter. Education: BA, 1st Class Honours, University of Western Australia, 1967-70; Research for PhD, University of Cambridge, Clare Hall, 1971-74; Seminar für Lateinische Philologie des Mittelalters (Grad 1), University of Munich, 1974-75; PhD, 1976, MA, 1977, LittD, 1991, University of Cambridge. Appointments: Temporary Tutor, Department of History, University of Western Australia, 1971; University Assistant Lecturer, 1979-84, University lecturer, 1984-91, University Reader in Early Medieval European History, 1991-97, University Professor in Early Medieval European History (Personal Chair), 1997-99; Professor of Medieval History, 1999-, University of Cambridge; Fellow, 1974-, Research Fellow, 1974-77, Vice-Principal, 1996-98, Professorial Fellow, 1997-, Newnham College, Cambridge; Hugh Balsdon Fellow, British School at Rome, 2002; Council Henry Bradshaw Society, 1998-; Membre, CNRS ERA 247 Études Méridionales, Toulouse, 1990-; British Co-ordinator, Repertorium Fontium Historiae Medii Aevi (based in Rome), 1992-; British National Committee of the International Congress of Historical Sciences, 1998-2003. Publications: 8 books include: The Frankish Church and the Carolingian Reforms

789-895, 1977; The Frankish Kingdoms under the Carolingians 751-987, 1983; The Caroligians and the Written Word, 1989; Books, scribes and learning in the Frankish Kingdoms, sixth to ninth centuries, 1994; Frankish kings and culture in the early middle ages, 1995; History and Memory in the Carolingian World, 2004; 8 edited books; 66 commissioned book chapters; 30 articles in several languages in scholarly journals; Over 40 conference papers and seminars and numerous guest lectures in Britain, Continental Europe, North America and Australia. Honours: Commonwealth University Scholarship, 1967-70; Amy Jane Best Prize in English Literature, 1968; Hackett Overseas Studentship, 1971-74; Fellow, Royal Historical Society, 1980; Fellow, European Medieval Academy, 1993; Korrespondierendes Mitglied der Monumenta Germaniae Historica, 1999; Fellow, Royal Society of Arts, Manufacturing and Commerce, 2001. Address: Newnham College, Cambridge CB3 9DF, England.

**McLAIN John (Anthony Lain),** b. 5 June 1933, Chingford, London, England. Composer, Songwriter; Retired Statistician. Education: BSc Mathematics, London University, 1955. Appointments: National Service, REME, 1955-57; CAV Ltd, 1957-59; Statistical Officer, Royal Society for the Prevention of Accidents, 1959-70; Manpower Planner, ICI Plastics, 1970-85; British Aerospace, 1985-87; Television work: Our Father, Who Art in Heaven, performed by the Gibside Singers, Tyne Tees TV. Recordings: Now You Have Gone, by Tony Jacobs with Jim Barry (piano); Why Don't They Write the Songs?, by Tony Jacobs with Jim Barry Sextet; Adlestrop (poem by Edward Thomas); I Came to Oxford (Gerald Gould); The Old Railway Line (Anne Allinson); The Demise of Harpenden Junction Box (Sue Woodward), by Gordon Pullin (tenor) with John Gough (piano); Other published compositions: Psalm (The Lord is my Shepherd); Mamble (poem by John Drinkwater); Dream Awhile; The Poop Scoop Song. Memberships: Performing Right Society Ltd; BACS; Light Music Society; Robert Farnon Society; South Herts Golf Club; Mensa. Address: 42 Osidge Lane, Southgate, London N14 5JG, England.

**McLANE Wilhelmina,** b. 30 September 1912, Franklin, Ohio, USA. Music Educator. m. E S Vinnell. Education: BM, MMus, Cincinnati Conservatory of Music; Studied with Nadia Boulanger, Conservatory of the Palais de Fontainbleu, Paris, France; Piano Pedagogy with Louise Robyn and Ethel Lyon, American Conservatory, Chicago, Illinois. Career: Adjudicator, National Guild of Piano Teachers, American Scholarship Association; Currently, Organist, United Methodist Church, Springboro, Ohio, USA; Private Piano and Organ Teacher. Honours: George Ward Nicholas Scholarship; Springer Postgraduate Award of Merit. Membership: Special Active Member, Dayton Ohio Music Club. Address: 1618 Gage Drive, Middletown, OH 45042, USA.

**McLEAN Don,** b. 2 October 1945, New Rochelle, New York, USA. Singer; Instrumentalist; Composer. m. Patrisha Shnier, 1987, 1 son, 1 daughter. Education: Villanova University; Iona College. Appointments: President, Benny Bird Corporation Inc; Member, Hudson River Slope Singers, 1969; Solo concert tours throughout USA, Canada, Australia, Europe, Far East; Numerous TV appearances; Composer of film scores for Fraternity Row; Flight of Dragons; Composer of over 200 songs including Prime Time; American Pie; Tapestry; Vincent; And I Love You So; Castles in the Air; Recordings include: Tapestry, 1970; American Pie, 1971; Don McLean, 1972; Playin' Favourites, 1973; Homeless Brother, 1974; Solo, 1976; PrimeTime, 1977; Chain Lightning, 1979; Believers, 1982; For the Memories, Vol I, Vol II, 1986; Love Tracks, 1988; Headroom, 1991; Don McLean Christmas, 1992; Favourites and

Rarities, 1993; The River of Love, 1995; Numerous compilation packages. Publications: Songs of Don McLean, 1972; The Songs of Don McLean, Vol II, 1974. Honours: Recipient of many gold discs in USA, Australia, UK and Ireland; Israel Cultural Award, 1981. Address: Benny Bird Co, 1838 Black Rock Turnpike, Fairfield, Connecticut 06432, USA.

**McLEAN Donald Millis,** b. 26 July 1926, Melbourne, Australia. Professor Emeritus of Pathology. m. Joyce. Education: MBBS, 1950; MD, University of Melbourne, 1954; MRCPath, 1963; FRCPC, 1967; FRCPath, 1970. Appointments: Harrison Watson Research Fellow, Clare College, Cambridge, 1955-56; Virologist, The Hospital for Sick Children, Toronto, 1958-67; Professor, Medical Microbiology, University of British Columbia, 1967-91; Professor Emeritus, Pathology, 1991-. Publications: 6 books, 120 original scientific papers. Memberships include: British Medical Association; American Society of Virology. Address: 6-5885 Yew Street, Vancouver, British Columbia V6M 3Y5, Canada.

**MCLELLAN David Thorburn,** b. 10 February 1940, Hertford, England. Professor of Political Theory; Writer. m. Annie Brassart, 1 July 1967, 2 daughters. Education: MA, 1962, DPhil, 1968, St John's College, Oxford. Appointment: Professor of Political Theory, Goldsmiths College, University of London. Publications: The Young Hegelians and Karl Marx, 1969; Karl Marx: His Life and Thought, 1974; Engels, 1977; Marxism After Marx, 1980; Ideology, 1986; Marxism and Religion, 1987; Simone Weil: Utopian Pessimist, 1989; Unto Caesar: The Political Importance of Christianity, 1993; Political Christianity, 1997. Contributions to: Professional journals. Address: 13 Ivy Lane, Canterbury, Kent, CT1 1TU, England. E-mail: david@mclellankent.com

**McLEOD James Graham,** b. 18 January 1932, Sydney, Australia. Neurologist. m. Robyn Edith Rule, 13 January 1962, 2 sons, 2 daughters. Education: BSc, 1953, MB BS, 1959, DSc, 1997, University of Sydney; DPhil, Oxon, 1956; Institute of Neurology, London University, 1963-65; Harvard University, Department of Neurology, 1965-66. Appointments: Pro-Dean, Faculty of Medicine, University of Sydney, 1974-94; Chairman, Department of Neurology, Royal Prince Alfred Hospital, 1978-95; Bosch Professor of Medicine, 1972-97, Bushell Professor of Neurology, 1978-97, Professor Emeritus, 1997-, University of Sydney; Consultant Neurologist, Royal Prince Alfred Hospital, Sydney, 1997-. Publications: A Physiological Approach to Clinical Neurology (co-author), 1981; Introductory Neurology (co-author), 1995; Peripheral Neuropathy in Childhood (co-author), 1991, 1999; More than 200 principal scientific publications. Honours: Rhodes Scholarship, 1953; Nuffield Travelling Fellowship, 1964-65; Sir Arthur Sims Commonwealth Travelling Professorship, 1983; AO, 1986; Commonwealth Medical Senior Fellowship; Honorary Doctorate, University of Aix-Marseille. Memberships: Fellow, Royal Australian College of Physicians, 1971; Fellow, Royal College of Physicians, 1977; Fellow, Australian Academy of Science, 1981; Fellow, Australian Academy of Technological Sciences and Engineering, 1987; Australian Science and Technology Council, 1987-93. Address: 2 James Street, Woollahra, NSW 2025, Australia. E-mail: jmcl7953@mail.usyd.edu.au

**McMAHAN Michael Lee,** b. 17 May 1946, Memphis, Tennessee, USA. Professor of Biology. m. Brenda Perry McMahan, 2 sons. Education: BS, 1968, MS, 1971, University of Mississippi; PhD, Louisiana State University, 1976. Appointments: Assistant Professor, Associate Professor, Department of Biology, Campbellsville University, 1975-80; Assistant Professor, Associate Professor, Professor, University

Professor, Department of Biology, Union University, Jackson, Tennessee, USA, 1980-. Publications: Articles in scientific journals as co-author: A Re-evaluation of Pristina longiseta (Oligochaeta:Naididae) in North America, 1975; Solenopsis invicta Buren: Influence on Louisiana pasture soil chemistry, 1976; As author: Protozoan parasites of some terrestrial oligochaetes, 1975; Preliminary notes on a new megadrile species, genus and family from the southeastern United States, 1976; Anatomical notes on Lutodrilus multivesiculatus (Annelida: Oligochaeta), 1979; Ecology of the limicolous megadrile Lutodrilus multivesiculatus, 1998. Memberships: American Microscopical Society; Biological Society of Washington; Association of Southeastern Biologists. Address: Department of Biology, Union University, 1050 Union University Drive, Jackson, TN38305, USA.

**McMANUS Jonathan Richard,** b. 15 September 1958, Heywood, England. Barrister. Education: First Class Honours in Law, Downing College, Cambridge, 1978-81; Called to the Bar, 1982; Appointments: Commenced practice at the bar, 1983; Government A panel of Counsel, 1992-1999; QC, 1999. Publication: Education and the Courts, 1998. Honour: Maxwell Law Prize, Cambridge, 1981. Memberships: Administrative Law, Bar Association; National Trust; English Heritage; Friend of the Royal Opera House. Address: 4 and 5, Gray's Inn Square, Gray's Inn. London WC1R 5AH, England.

**McMICKLE Robert Hawley,** b. 30 July 1924, Paterson, New Jersey, USA. Physicist. m. Gwendolyn Gill, 3 sons, 2 daughters. Education: BA, Physics, Oberlin College, 1947; MS, Physics, University of Illinois, 1948; PhD, Physics, Pennsylvania State University, 1952. Appointments: Research Physicist, BF Goodrich Company, Brecksville, Ohio, 1952-59; Professor, Physics, Robert College, Istanbul, Turkey, 1959-71; University of the Bosphorus, Istanbul, Turkey, 1971-79; Schreiner College, Kerrville, Texas, 1979-80; Luther College, Decorah, Iowa, 1980-81; Adjunct Professor, Physics, Memphis State University, Tennessee, 1981-83; Accreditation Co-ordinator, Northeast Utilities, Seabrook, New Hampshire, 1983-94, Retired, 1994. Publications include: Diffusion Controlled Stress Relaxation, 1955; The Compressions of Several High Molecular Weight Hydrocarbons, 1958; Introduction to Modern Physics, 1979. Honours include: Fellowship, American Petroleum Institute, 1950-52; Research grant, Optics, Innovative Systems Research Inc, Pennsauken, New Jersey, 1976; Distinguished Service Award, University of the Bosphorus, Istanbul, Turkey, 1989. Memberships: American Association of Physics Teachers; Physical Society of Turkey; Sigma Xi. Address: 3032 Fernor Street, Allentown, PA 18103, USA.

**McMILLAN James (Coriolanus),** b. 30 October 1925. Journalist. m. Doreen Smith, 7 April 1953, 3 sons, 1 daughter. Education: MA, Economics, University of Glasgow. Publications: The Glass Lie, 1964; American Take-Over, 1967; Anatomy of Scotland, 1969; The Honours Game, 1970; Roots of Corruption, 1971; British Genius (with Peter Grosvenor), 1972; The Way We Were 1900-1950 (trilogy), 1977-80; Five Men at Nuremberg, 1984; The Dunlop Story, 1989; From Finchley to the World - Margaret Thatcher, 1990. Address: Thurleston, Fairmile Park Road, Cobham, Surrey KT11 2PL, England.

**McQUEEN Alexander,** b. London. Education: St Martin's School of Art, London; Appointments: London Tailors, Anderson and Shepherd, Gieves and Hawkes; Theatrical Costumiers, Berman and Nathans; Des Koji Tatsuno; Romeo Gigli, Rome; Final Collection, St Martin's, 1992 established his reputation; Subsequent shows include: The Birds; Highland Rape; The Hunger; Dante; La Poupee; It's a Jungle Out There;

Untitled; Aquired Italian manufacturing company Onward Kashiyama; Chief Designer, Givenchy, Paris, 1996-2000, of Gucci, 2000-. Honours: Designer of the Year, London Fashion Awards, 1996, 2000; Joint Winner, with John Galliano, 1997; Special Achievement Award, London Fashion Awards, 1998. Address: c/o Gucci Group NV Rembrandt Tower, 1 Amstelplein, 1096 MA Amsterdam, The Netherlands. Website: www.gucci.com

**McVIE J Gordon,** b. 13 January 1945, Glasgow, Scotland. Director Cancer Intelligence; Professor. Education: BSc (Hons), Pathology, 1967, MB, ChB, 1969, University of Edinburgh, Scotland; ECFMG, USA, 1971; Accreditation in Internal Medicine and Medical oncology, Joint Committee on Higher Medical Training, 1977; MD, Edinburgh, 1978; FRCPE, Edinburgh, 1981; FRCPS, Glasgow, 1987; DSc (Hon), University of Abertay, Dundee, Scotland, 1996; DSc (Hon), University of Nottingham, England, 1997; FRCP, 1997; FMedSci, 1998; DSc (Hon), University of Portsmouth, England; FRCSE, Edinburgh, 2001. Appointments: House Officer, Royal Infirmary, Edinburgh and Royal Hospital for Sick Children, Edinburgh, 1969-1970; Medical Research Council Research Fellow, Department of Pathology and Therapeutics, Edinburgh University; 1970-1971; Temporary Lecturer in Therapeutics, 1971-73, Lecturer in Therapeutics, 1973-76, Edinburgh University; Honorary Registrar, 1971-73, Honorary Senior Registrar, 1973-76, Lothian Health Board, Scotland; Senior Lecturer, The Cancer Research Campaign Department of Clinical Oncology, University of Glasgow, 1976-1980; Honorary Consultant in Medical Oncology, Greater Glasgow Health Board, 1976-1980; Head, Clinical Research Unit, Consultant Physician, and Chairman, Division of Experimental Therapy, The National Cancer Institute, Amsterdam, The Netherlands, 1980-84; Clinical Research Director, The National Cancer Institute of the Netherlands, 1984-1989; Scientific Director, 1989-1996, Director General, 1996-2002, The Cancer Research Campaign; Director General, Cancer Research UK, 2002-; Director, Cancer Intelligence, 2003-. Publications: Extensive within this field; Membership of numerous medical editorial boards. Honours: Gunning Victoria Jubilee Prize in Pathology, 1967; Honeyman Gillespie Lecturer in Oncology 1977; Visiting Fellow, Department of Medical Oncology, University of Paris, 1978; Visiting Fellow, Netherlands Cancer Institute, Amsterdam; Consultant, Carcinogenesis of Cytostatic Drugs, International Agency, Research in Cancer, WHO, Lyon, 1980; Visiting Professor, University of Sydney, NSW, Australia; Visiting Professor, British Postgraduate Medical Federation, London University; 1990-96; Chairman, UICC Fellowships Program, 1990-98; President, European Organisation for Research and Treatment of Cancer, 1994-97; First European Editor of Journal of the National Cancer Institute, 1994-; Visiting Professor, University of Glasgow, 1996-; Semmelweis Medal for Excellence in Science. Memberships: European Organisation for Research on Treatment of Cancer (EORTC), 1979-; Numerous advisory committees and examination boards including: Member, Steering Committee, Alliance of World Cancer Research Organisations, 1999; Cancer Research Funders Forum, 1999-2001; Member, AACR Membership Committee, 2000-01; Member, AACR Clinical Cancer Research Committee, 2001-. Address: Cancer Intelligence, 4 Stanley Rd, Cotham, Bristol BS6 6NW, England. E-mail: gordonmcvie@doctors. org.uk

**MEACHER Michael Hugh (Rt Hon),** b. 4 November 1939, Hemel Hempstead, Hertfordshire, England. Member of Parliament. m. Lucianne Sawyer, 2 sons, 2 daughters. Education: Greats, Class 1, New College, Oxford; Diploma in Social Administration, London School of Economics. Appointments:

Lecturer, Social Administration, York and London School of Economics, 1966-70; Member of Parliament for Oldham West, 1970-; Minister for Industry, 1974-75; Minister for the Department of Health and Social Security, 1975-76; Minister for Trade, 1976-79; Member of the Shadow Cabinet, 1983-97; Minister for the Environment, 1997-2003. Publications: Taken for a Ride (about the care of the elderly), 1972; Socialism with a Human Face, 1982; Diffusing Power, 1992. Memberships: Labour Party; Fabian Society; Child Poverty Action Group. Address: House of Commons, Westminster, London, SW1A 0AA, England.

**MEDRANO HERNÁNDEZ Hugo Adrián,** b. 13 February 1958, Tequila, Jalisco, Mexico. Teacher. m. Patricia Gascón González, 1 daughter. Education: Doctor of Latin American Letters, University of Guadalajara, College of Mexico, 2000. Appointments include: Co-director, Literary Magazine, Pulses, 1982-84; Professor of Philosophy, Writing, Spanish Literature and Latin American Literature, Regional Preparatory School of Colotlán, Jalisco, 1984-87; Professor of Spanish, Secondary School, Anáhuac Garibaldi, Guadalajara 1987-90; Professor of the Chair of General Writing and Journalism, Technical College of Monterrery, Guadalajara Campus, 1994-99; Professor of Written Communication and Invited Lecturer, Institute of Technology and Higher Education of the West, Guadalajara 1998-2001; Professor of Writing, Methodology and Research, National Pedagogical University, 1992-99; Professor of Academic Text Writing for the Doctorate of Education, University of La Salle, Guadalajara Campus, 1997-2001; Professor of Advanced Writing for the Doctorate of Science, University Centre, University of Guadalajara, 2000-2005; Visiting Professor, Antelope Valley College, California, USA, 1995; Invited Lecturer, California State University, 1995; Participant in numerous conferences and national and international poetry festivals. Publications: Numerous poems, stories and essays in national and international newspapers and magazines; Anthology of Mexican Literature; Anthology of Latin American Literature; Guide to the Study of the Spanish Language; Novel: Las paredes del cielo, 2003. Honours: Honour, University of Guadalajara, 2002; Honour, Consejo Mexicano de Posgrado (COMPEO), Culiacán, Sinaloa, Mexico, 2004; Honour, Lexicographic Association, University of Coruna, Spain, 2004; Honour: UNESCO-OEI, Havana, Cuba, 2004. Memberships: International Pragmatics Association, Antwerp, Belgium; Asociación de Lexicografía, La Coruña, Spain; Editorial Board: La Tarea, La Girafa. Address: Isla Timor 3459-101, Jardines de San José, Guadalajara, Jalisco, Mexico 44950. E-mail: hmedrano2@hormail.com

**MEDVEDEVA Irina,** b. 17 August 1939, Moscow, Russia. Musicologist; Historian. 1 son. Education: Moscow Conservatory, 1961-66; Postgraduate, 1966-69; Master of Arts, Thesis: Francis Poulenc and his opera creativity. Appointments: Assistant, Faculty of the History of Foreign Music, Main Bibliographic Chief of the Department of Rare Books, Moscow Conservatory, 1969-73; Head of the Group "Music", Information and Culture Centre, 1973-83; Scientific Editor of the magazine "Sovietskaya Musica", 1983-86; Deputy of the General Director and Chief of the Museum's Scientific Work, 1986-, Glinka State Central Museum of Musical Culture; Curator of the Glinka Museum's part in a collective exhibition with the Bolshoi Theatre Museum and New York Public Library: Prokofiev and his contemporaries: The Impact of Soviet Culture, Vincent Astor Gallery, New York, 2003-2004. Publications: Books: Francis Poulenc; Alexander Dargomijsky; More than 150 articles in musical encyclopaedias, magazines and newspapers; Member of the Editorial Board of the Critical Edition of the Complete Works of Sergei Rachmaninov. Memberships: International

Council of Museums; International Association of Museum Libraries, Archives and Documentation Centres; Union of Russian Composers. Address: Glinka State Central Museum of Musical Culture, Fadeyev Str, 125047 Moscow, Russia.

**MEERS Jeffrey,** b. 10 February 1953, London, England. Company Director. m. Louise Michelle, 2 sons. Education: BSc (Hons), Psychology, Nottingham University, 1972-76. Appointments: Senior Psychologist, Ministry of Defence, Royal Navy; Strategic Planner, BMP/DDB Advertising; Director, WCRS Advertising; Vice-President, Bozell Advertising; Global President, IDG; Chief Executive Officer, Officeshopper.com Sparza; Chief Executive Officer, Brightstation E-commerce Division; Non-executive Directorships; Consultant. Publication: Advertising Effectiveness. Membership: Marketing Society. Address: Oakley House, Old Avenue, Weybridge, Surrey KT13 0PS, England. E-mail: jeffmeers@brightstation.com

**MEFED Anatoly Egorovich,** b. 7 December 1938, Gorodische, Dryansk, Russia. Physicist; Researcher of NMR in solids; Consultant. m. Lyudmila Ivanovna Putilova, 1 daughter. Education: Graduate, Moscow University, 1962; PhD, Russian Academy of Sciences, 1972. Appointments: Professor, Physics and Maths, Institute Radioengineering and Electronics Russian Academy of Sciences, Fryazino, 1989; Professor, Kazan State University, 1989. Publications: Author and co-author: Discovery, A New Physical Law in Spin Thermodynamics in Solids, 1968; Contribution to more than 80 research papers to professional journals. Honours: Recipient USSR diploma for discovery of a new physics law in spin thermodynamics in solids, 1987; USSR inventor medal Russian Academy of Sciences; Listed in biographical publications. Membership: New York Academy of Sciences, Russian Academy of Natural Sciences. Address: Russian Academy of Sciences Institute of Radioengineering & Electronics, Vvedenskogo Sq, 141190 Fryazino, Moscow, Russia. E-mail: aem228@ire216.msk.su

**MEHANDJIEV Marin Roussev,** b. 8 March 1927, Sofia, Bulgaria. Chemical Engineer; Ecologist. m. Krassimira Kercheva-Mehandjieva, 1 son, 1 daughter. Education: MSc, Diploma Engineer, Chemistry, Polytechnic of Sofia, 1949; Associate Professor Degree, Non-Ferrous Metallurgy, Polytechnic of Sofia, 1970; PhD, High Chemical Institute in Bourgas, 1971; Associate Professor Degree in Non-Equilibrium Thermodynamics of Accumulation Processes, Institute of Physical Chemistry of Bulgarian Academy of Sciences, 1989; PhD, International Relations, Alabama University, 1999; Professor, Human Rights and Environment, International Association of Lecturers. Appointments: Consultant: UNESCO, UNICEF, ECOSOC/UNO, 1999; Academician World Peace Academy, USA, 1999. Publications: More than 400 scientific publications, including 18 monographs. Honours: Doctor of Philosophy Honoris Causa, Political Science, International Academy of Culture and Political Science, USA, 1999; Honorary Member, Spanish Association of Professionals in Occupational Health and Environment, Spain, 1998; Honorary Member, Ansted University Board of Advisory Council, Malaysia, 1999; Man of the Year, 1998-99, International Biographical Centre, Cambridge, England, 1998; Honorary-Citizen of the Museum-town Koprivhtitsa, Bulgaria, 2001; Nominee, Nobel Prize Award for Chemistry, 2004, by Ansted University, England for his contribution to non-equilibrium thermodynamics of accumulation processes and its applications, particularly the carcinogenic theory based on the proper protective mechanism of cellular tissues. Memberships include: Founding Member, Balkan Union of Oncology, 1995-; Corresponding Member, Ukrainian Ecological Academy of Sciences, 1995-; Active Member, New York Academy of Sciences, 1996-; Lecturer in

Ecological Modelling in South-Western University, N Rilski, Blagoevgrad, 1995-; High Council of Environmental Experts in the Ministry of Environment and Water of Bulgaria, 1997-; President, Foundation, Science and Environmental Analyses, 1998-; Member, International Administration, World University Roundtable, Benson, Arizona, USA, 1999; Academician, Central European Academy of Science and Art, 2000-; Academician, Romanian Ecological Academy, 2000-; Founding Member, Scientific Vice-President and Academician, Balkan Academy of Sciences, New Culture and Sustainable Development, D Jersov, 2001-; Corresponding Member, Royal Academy of Pharmacy, Spain, 2002-; Honourable Academician, Academia Mundial de Ciencias, Technologia, Education y Humanidades, Valencia, Spain, 2003-. Address: Ent A Ste 26, Compl Nadejda Bl 533, 1229 Sofia, Bulgaria.

**MEHIĆ-BASARA Nermana,** b. 10 March 1957, Sarajevo, Bosnia and Herzegovina. Medical Doctor; Psychiatrist. m. Bakir Mehić, 2 daughters. Education: MD, Medical Faculty, University of Sarajevo, 1975-81; Psychiatry, Institute for Alcoholism and Substance Abuse, Sarajevo, 1989; Post Graduate Study, Experimental Medicine, 1995-97. Appointments: Primary Health Care Centre, Fojnica, 1981-82; Staff Member, Psychiatrist, 1982-, Team Member, Project War Victims Rehabilitation, 1992, Chief of Department for Alcoholism, 1992-2000, Director of Institute, 2000-, Institute for Alcoholism and Substance Abuse, Sarajevo; National Co-ordinator for Alcoholism for WHO, 1992-; Leader, Methadone Maintenance and Detox Program, Canton Sarajevo. Publications: 30 papers as author published in various publications including: Medical Archive, Community Mental Health Magazine, Elsevier, book abstracts from different congresses. Honours: Honorable title, Chief Physician "Primarijus", Ministry of Health, Federation of B&H, 2003; Woman of the Year 2003, American Biographical Institute; Nyswander-Dole "Marie" Award, American Association for the Treatment of Opioid Dependence, 2004; Listed in Who's Who publications and biographical dictionaries. Memberships: South Eastern European Addictions Network; Editorial Boards, Mental Health Communications and Addictions; American Biographical Institute's Professional Women's Advisory Board. Address: Institute for Alcoholism and Substance Abuse of Canton Sarajevo, Bolnicka 25, 7100 Sarajevo, Bosnia and Herzegovina. E-mail: zalcnarc@bih.net.ba

**MEINARDUS Otto Friedrich August,** b. 29 September 1925, Hamburg, Germany. Coptologist; Professor. m. Eva Zimmermann, 1 son, 1 daughter. Education: Studies at Hamburg University, London University, Richmond College; BD, Concordia Seminary, St Louis, Missouri, 1949; STM, 1950, PhD, 1955, Boston University; Postdoctoral Studies, Harvard University; FICS, Institute of Coptic Studies, Cairo, 1960. Appointments: Methodist Minister: Christchurch, New Zealand, 1950-51, Adelaide, South Australia, 1951, Peabody, Massachusetts, 1952-56, Maadi Church, Cairo, 1956-68, St Andrew's Church, Athens, Greece, 1968-75; Professor, American University, Cairo, 1956-68; Professor, Athens College, Athens, Greece, 1968-72; Minister, Evangelical Church, Rheinland, 1975-84. Publications: Christian Egypt, Ancient and Modern, 1965, 1977; Monks and Monasteries of the Egyptian Deserts, 1961, 1989, 1992; 2000 Years of Coptic Christianity, 1999; Coptic Saints and Pilgrimages, 2002; Christian Egypt and Life, 1990; St Paul in Greece, 1972; St John of Palmos, 1974; many others. Honours: BD; STM; PhD; FICS. Memberships: German Archaeological Society. Address: Stettiner Str 11, D-25479 Ellerau, Germany.

**MEIR Ephraim,** b. 23 January 1949, Belgium. Professor. m. Shoshana, 2 sons, 3 daughters. Education: BA, MA, Sciences of Religion, Louvain University, 1967-72; BA, MA, Biblical Philology, 1972-75; BA, MA, Theology, 1972-75; PhD, Theology, 1979; Professor, Department of Philosophy, Bar Ilan University, Ramat Gan. Appointments: Head, Department of Philosophy, 1996-98. Publications: Many books published; Tens of articles published. Honours: Various Scholarships from Belgium, Israel and Germany. Address: Sderot ha-Meiri 12, 96107 Jerusalem.

**MELENDRES Carlos A,** b. 4 November 1939, Manila, Philippines. Physical Electrochemist. m. Priscilla Melendres, 1 son, 2 daughters. Education: BS, Chemical Engineering, Mapua Institute of Engineering, Manila, 1961; MS, Chemical Engineering, 1966, PhD, Physical Chemistry, 1968, University of California, Berkeley, USA; Postdoctoral Research, University of Karlsruhe, Germany, 1971. Appointments: Senior Development Engineer, Olin Research Centre, New Haven, Connecticut, 1972-74; Scientific Staff, Argonne National Laboratory, Argonne, Illinois, 1974-; Director of Research, CNRS UMR 6503, 2000-, Invited Professor, University of Poitiers, France, 2000-. Publications: Over 100 publications in peer-reviewed journals; Editor, 3 books; Author, 8 book articles; 3 patents. Honours: Co-director, NATO Advanced Study Institute, Tenerife, 1988, Viana do Castelo, 1989; Director, NATO Advance Research Workshop, Madeira, 1992. Memberships: International Society of Electrochemistry; Electrochemical Society; Society for Electroanalytical Chemistry; Neutron Scattering Society of America; International XAFS Society. Address: 1 rue du Grand Foc, Saint Benoit, France. Email: camelendres@hotmail.com

**MELEZINEK Adolf,** b. 3 October 1932, Vienna, Austria. Emeritus University Professor. m. Vera Melezinek, 1 son, 1 daughter. Education: Dipl Ing, Electronics, 1957; Dr phil, Pedagogy, 1969. Appointments: Chief Engineer; Assistant Professor; University Professor, Chair of Engineering Pedagogy. Publications: More than 200 publications including 20 specialist books such as: Ingenieurpädagogik, in German, Czech, Hungarian, Slovenian, Ukrainian, Polish and Russian editions. Honours: Gold Ring, International Society for Engineering Education; Golden Felber Medal, Czech Technical University, Prague; Honorary Senator, Technical University, Budapest; Grand Gold Medal, Carinthia; Austrian Honorary Cross 1st Class for Science and Art; Dr honoris causa, 1997, 2000, 2001; Listed in several Who's Who and biographical publications. Membership: Founder and Honorary Life President, International Society for Engineering Education (IGIP). Address: Akazienhofstrasse 79, A-9020 Klagenfurt, Austria. E-mail: adolf.melezinek@uni-klu.ac.at

**MELKIKH Alexey V,** b. 17 August 1966, Sverdlovsk, Russia. Reader of Physics. m. Elena Tretjakova, 1 daughter. Education: Engineer-Physicist, Ural State Technical University, Sverdlovsk, 1983-89; Postgraduate School, Ural State Technical University, Yekaterinburg, 1989-92; Candidate of Science, Physics and Mathematics, 1995. Appointments: Assistant, 1992-95, Assistant Professor, 1995-, Ural State Technical University, Yekaterinburg. Publications: Internal structure of elementary particle and possible deterministic mechanism of biological evolution, 2004; Models of active transport of ions in biomembranes of various types of cells (with V D Seleznev), 2005. Memberships: IEEE; Supporter, WWF. Address: Ural State Technical University, Mira Street 19, 620002 Yekaterinburg, Russia. E-mail: mav@dpt.ustu.ru

**MELLERS Wilfrid (Howard),** b. 26 April 1914, Leamington, Warwickshire, England. Professor of Music (retired); Composer; Author. m. (1) Vera M Hobbs, (2) Pauline P Lewis, 3 daughters, (3) Robin S Hildyard. Education: Leamington College, 1933;

BA, 1936, MA, 1938, Cambridge University; DMus, University of Birmingham, 1960. Appointments: Staff Tutor in Music, University of Birmingham, 1948-60; Andrew Mellon Professor of Music, University of Pittsburgh, 1960-63; Professor of Music, University of York, 1964-81; Visiting Professor, City University, 1984-. Publications: Music and Society: England and the European Tradition, 1946; Studies in Contemporary Music, 1947; François Couperin and the French Classical Tradition, 1950, 2nd edition, revised, 1987; Music in the Making, 1952; Romanticism and the 20th Century, 1957, 2nd edition, revised, 1988; The Sonata Principle, 1957, 2nd edition, revised, 1988; Music in a New Found Land: Themes and Developments in History of American Music, 1964, 2nd edition, revised, 1987; Harmonious Meeting: A Study of the Relationship between English Music, Poetry, and Theatre, c.1600-1900, 1965; Caliban Reborn: Renewal in Twentieth-Century Music, 1967; Twilight of the Gods: The Music of the Beatles, 1973; Bach and the Dance of God, 1980; Beethoven and the Voice of God, 1983; A Darker Shade of Pale: A Backdrop to Bob Dylan, 1984; Angels of the Night: Popular Female Singers of Our Time, 1986; The Masks of Orpheus: Seven Stages in the Story of European Music, 1987; Le Jardin Retrouvé: Homage to Federico Mompou, 1989; Vaughan Williams and the Vision of Albion, 1989, new enlarged edition, 1997; The Music of Percy Grainger, 1992; Francis Poulenc, 1994; Between Old Worlds and New: Occasional Writings on Music by Wilfrid Mellers, 1998; Singing in the Wilderness, 2001; Celestial Music, 2002. Contributions to: Reference works and journals. Honours: Honorary DPhil, City University, 1981; Officer of the Order of the British Empire, 1982. Membership: Sonneck Society, honorary member. Address: Oliver Sheldon House, 17 Aldwark, York, YO1 7BX, England.

**MELLING John Kennedy,** b. 11 January 1927, Westcliff-on-Sea, Essex, England. Drama Critic; Editor; Writer; Lecturer; Broadcaster; Chartered Accountant. Appointments: Drama Critic, The Stage, 1957-90; Drama Critic, Fur Weekly News, 1968-73; Editor, The Liveryman Magazine, 1970-75, Chivers Black Dagger Series of Crime Classics, 1986-91; Radio Crime Book Critic, BBC London, 1984-85, BBC Essex, 1987. Publications: Discovering Lost Theatres, 1969; Southend Playhouses from 1793, 1969; Discovering London's Guilds and Liveries, 6 editions, 1973-03; Discovering Theatre Ephemera, 1974; The Poulters of London Booklet, 1977; She Shall Have Murder, 1987; Murder in the Library, 1987; Crime Writers' Handbook of Practical Information (editor), 1989; Gwendoline Butler: Inventor of the Women's Police Procedural, 1993; Alchemy of Murder, 1993; Murder Done to Death, 1996; Scaling the High C's (with John L Brecknock), 1996; A Little Manual of Etiquette for Gentlemen, 2004; The Constructors: Genesis and Growth, 2004; Plays include: George....From Caroline, 1971; Diarists' Pleasures, 1982; Murder at St Dunstan's, 1983; The Toast Is ... (series); Regular columnist, Crime Time magazine, 1996-2002. Honours: Knight Grand Cross; Order of St Michael; Master of the Worshipful Company of Poulters, 1980-81; Police Medal of Honour, USA, 1984; Knight, Order of St Basil, 1984; Crime Writers Association Award for Outstanding Services, 1989; Listed in national and international biographical dictionaries. Memberships: British Academy of Film and Television Arts; Institute of Taxation, fellow; Faculty of Building, Royal Society of Arts, fellow; Crime Writers' Association, committee member, 1985-88; Governor of the Corporation of the Sons of the Clergy, 1981-; Member, Drugs Task Force, National Association of Chiefs of Police, USA; Honorary International Life Vice-President, American Federation of Police; Founder-President, First Honorary Life Member, Westcliff Film and Video Club; Member, Cookery and Food Association; Member, City Livery Club; Liveryman, Worshipful Companies of Bakers, Farriers, and Constructors; Marylebone Rifle and Pistol Club; Edinburgh Press Club. Addresses: 44 A Tranquil Vale, Blackheath, London SE3 0BD, England; 85 Chalkwell Avenue, Westcliff-on-Sea, Essex, SS0 8NL, England.

**MELLOR D(avid) H(ugh),** b. 10 July 1938, England. Professor of Philosophy; Writer. Education: BA, Natural Sciences and Chemical Engineering, 1960, PhD, 1968, ScD, 1990, M in English, 1992, Pembroke College, Cambridge; MSc, Chemical Engineering, University of Minnesota, 1962. Appointments: Research Student in Philosophy, Pembroke College, 1963-68, Fellow, Pembroke College, 1965-70, University Assistant Lecturer in Philosophy, 1965-70, University Lecturer in Philosophy, 1970-83, Fellow, 1971-, and Vice-Master, 1983-87, Darwin College, University Reader in Metaphysics, 1983-85, Professor of Philosophy, 1986-99, Professor Emeritus, 1999-, Pro-Vice-Chancellor, 2000-01, Cambridge University; Visiting Fellow in Philosophy, Australian National University, Canberra, 1975; Honorary Professor of Philosophy, University of Keele, 1989-92. Publications: The Matter of Chance, 1971; Real Time, 1981; Cambridge Studies in Philosophy, (editor) 1978-82; Matters of Metaphysics, 1991; The Facts of Causation, 1995; Real Time II, 1998; numerous articles on philosophy of science, metaphysics and philosophy of mind. Contributions to: Scholarly journals. Memberships: Aristotelian Society, president, 1992-93; British Academy, fellow; British Society for the Philosophy of Science, president, 1985-87. Address: 25 Orchard Street, Cambridge CB1 1JS, England.

**MELLY (Alan) George (Heywood),** b. 17 August 1926, Liverpool, England. Jazz Singer; Critic. m. (1) Victoria Vaughn, 1955, divorced 1962, (2) Diana, 1963, 1 son, 1 stepdaughter. Career: Assistant, London Gallery, 1948-50; Singer, Mick Mulligan's Jazz Band, 1949-61; Cartoon strip writer with Trog, 1956-71; As critic for The Observer: Pop Music, 1965-67; Television, 1967-71; Films, 1971-73; Film scriptwriter, Smashing Time, 1968; Take A Girl Like You, 1970; Singer, John Chilton's Feetwarmers, 1974-; Concerts include: Royal Festival Hall; Royal Albert Hall; Edinburgh Festival; Television includes: Subject, This Is Your Life. Recordings: 30 albums; George Melly and John Chilton's Feetwarmers: Best of Live; Anything Goes; Frankie & Johnny; Puttin' On The Ritz. Publications: I Flook, 1962; Owning Up, 1965; Revolt Into Style, 1970; Flook By Trog, 1970; Rum Bum And Concertina, 1977; The Media Mob (with Barry Fantoni), 1980; Tribe Of One, 1981; Great Lovers, (with Walter Dorin), 1981; Mellymobile, 1982; Scouse Mouse, 1984; It's All Writ Out For You, 1986; Paris And The Surrealists (with Michael Woods), 1991; Don't Tell Sybil: An Intimate Memoir of E L T Mesens, 1997. Honours: Critic Of The Year, IPC National Press Awards, 1970; Fellow, John Moores University; Doctor, Middlesex and Glamorgan University; President, British Humanist Society, 1972-74; BT British Jazz Awards, 1998; Award for Lifetime Acheivement For Jazz. Address: 82 Frithville Gardens, Shepherds Bush, London W12 7JQ, England.

**MELROSE Margaret Elstob,** b. 2 May 1928, Birmingham, England. Retired Politician; Deputy Lieutenant for Cheshire. m. Kenneth R Watson (marriage dissolved), 1 daughter. Education: Howell's School, Denbigh; Drapers' Company Scholarship, Honours Geography Tripos Part 1, Girton College, Cambridge, 1947; Secretarial and Computer Qualifications. Appointments: Vice-Consul for Lebanon for Northern England, Scotland and Northern Ireland, 1963-; Elected Member, Cheshire County Council, 1967-2001; Chairman (1st Woman), 1984-85, 1986-87; "Father" of the Council, 1997-2001; Member Cheshire Police Authority, 1985-97; Chairman of Governors of Crewe and Alsager College of Higher Education, 1978-92; Governor, Manchester Metropolitan University, 1993-99; Governor,

# DICTIONARY OF INTERNATIONAL BIOGRAPHY

Reaseheath College of Agriculture, 1969-92; Chairman, Manchester International Airport Consultative Committee, 1986-2002; General Commissioner of Taxes, North Manchester, 1985-2003; Chairman, North West Regional Children's Planning Committee, 1977-81; Deputy Lieutenant for Cheshire, 1987-; Chairman, Cheshire Rural Community Council, 1988-96; Vice-Chairman, David Lewis Centre for Epilepsy, 1993-98; Member, Runcorn New Town Development Corporation, 1975-81; Parish Councillor, Nether Alderley, 34 years. Honours: Lady Patroness, 1996-97, Cheshire Agricultural Society; North of England Woman of the Year, 1985; Cheshire Woman of the Year, 1986; Deputy Lieutenant of Cheshire, 1987, Honorary Alderman, Cheshire County Council, 2001-. Memberships: President, Macclesfield Conservative Association, 1987-2000; Vice-President, 2001-, Tatton Conservative Association; Vice-President, Cheshire Agricultural Society, 1984-. Address: The Coach House, Stamford Road, Alderley Edge, Cheshire SK9 7NS, England. E-mail: margaret@mmelrose.freeserve.com.uk

**MELVIN-BURNS Betty,** b. 29 July 1921, Chicago, Illinois. Registered Nurse. m. George L Burns, deceased 1993, 7 sons, 1 daughter. Education: Diploma, School of Nursing, Loyola University, 1945; Certificate, Psychology and Neurology, University of Illinois, 1945; Cadet Nurse, US Naval Hospital, Chelsea, Massachusetts, 1945-46. Appointments: Clinical Instructor, Oak Park Hospital, Oak Park, Illinois; Night Supervisor, McHenry Hospital, McHenry, Illinois; Director of Nursing, City Hospital, Lancaster, Wisconsin; Occupational Health Nurse at Sherwin Wms Company; Occupational Health Nurse at Rockwell International, Carpentersville, Illinois. Memberships: Board of Directors, Suburban Chicago Association of Occupational Health Nurses; Vice-President, Board of Directors, Chateau Lake San Marcos, California. Address: 1682 Circa del Lago A109, Lake San Marcos, CA 92078, USA.

**MELZER John T S,** b. 9 September 1938, Ashland, Ohio, USA. Translator. Education: AB, Auburn University, USA, 1961; AM, University of Virginia, USA, 1964; PhD, Tulane University, USA, 1978; Appointments: Professor, Georgetown College, Kentucky, USA, 1964; Professor, Columbus State University, Georgia, USA, 1964-67; Professor, University of West Alabama, 1977; Director of Historical Research, Saint Augustine Restoration Commission, Saint Augustine, Florida, 1968; Drilling Fluids, Consultant, 1979-; Scholar-in-Residence, Professor, English Translex Institute, Miraflores, Lima, Peru, 1985-92; Investigador Ad Honorem, National Institute of Culture, Peru, 1989; Editor-in-Chief, Oakbowery Books, Auburn, Alabama, 1994. Publications: 4 journal articles; 18 newspaper articles on Peru and 3 newspaper articles on the Persian Gulf; Books: Fourteen Days to Field Spanish, 1985; Bastion of Commerce in the City of Kings the Consulado de Comercio de Lima 1593-1887, 1991; Oilfield Spanish, Thousands of Words and Terms, A Vocabulary of Walk-Around Rig-Spanish, 1997. Honours: Tau Kappa Alpha, National Forensics Honor Fraternity; Investigador Ad Honorem, National Institute of Culture of Peru; Honorary Diploma, University National Federico Villarreal, Lima, Peru, 1990; Consejo Nacional de Ciencia y Tecnologia Peru, Grant for publication of book Bastion of Commerce in the City of Kings in English, Spanish and German, 1991. Memberships: SAR; Alpha Phi Omega; Delta Tau Delta; Tau Kappa Alpha. Address: 74 Curtis Street, Camp Hill, AL 36950, USA. E-mail: drjohnmelzer@hotmail.com

**MEMOS Constantine Demetrius,** b. 26 November 1946, Patras, Greece. Civil Engineer. m. Maria Antonopoulou, 2 sons. Education: MEng, Civil Engineering, National Technical University of Athens, Greece, 1969; Diploma, Mathematics, University of Patras, Greece, 1972; DIC, PhD, University of London, Imperial College, 1977. Appointments: Educator, Civil Engineering Department, National Technical University of Athens, 1978-; Professor, Maritime Hydraulics and Port Engineering, 2004-; Engineer, Consultant, Port Planning and Design, 1978-. Publications: Over 80 articles in journals and conference proceedings, including Journal of Fluid Mechanics, Coastal Engineering, ASCE Journal of Ports and Waterways, Coastal Engineering Conference, Journal of Hydraulic Research. Honours: Unwin Prize, Imperial College, 1977; Embeirikeio Prize of Technological Science, with Award, Greece, 1988; David Hislop Award, Institution of Civil Engineers, London, 2004. Memberships: Fellow, ASCE; Member, PIANC; IAHR; New York Academy of Sciences. Address: National Technical University of Athens, 5 Heroon Polytechneiou, 15780 Zografos, Greece. E-mail: memos@hydro.ntua.gr

**MENA-ABRAHAM Josefina,** b. 23 November 1941, Mérida, Yucatán, México. Architect; Regional Planner. m. Antonio Marta Conseiçao, 1 daughter. Education: Architect, Instituto Tecnológico y de Estudios Superiores de Monterrey, México, 1957-65; Urban Sociology, La Sorbonne, France, 1966-67; MSc, Regional Planning, University College London, 1969-72; ARCUK Certificate, London, 1973. Appointments: Working experience as an Architect in Paris, London, Portugal (Europe) Cabo Verde (Africa) and México; Expertise: Waste Recycling systems for housing; Methodology "Planning for recycling" with IDRC, Canada, in 3 Mexican communities co-ordinating a team of 25 professionals, 1989-92; Municipal Development Urban Planning of South East Mexican States (Maya Zone), 1978-83; Design and development of several models of the SIDRO (integral system for recycling organic waste), 1978-2004. Publications: Quién decide el futuro de Mérida?, 1980; Community management of recycling SIDRO, 1983-84; Articles in numerous books: La Agorindustria en México, Chapingo,1987; Tecnología alternativa, transformación de desechos y Desarrollo Urbano, Colegio de México, 1988. Honours: Premio al Saber, ITSEM, 1965; Certificado de Invención No 6758 for the SIRDO technology, SECOFI, 1986; International Achievement Award, National Wildlife Federation, USA, 1999; International Dean of Project Water at the, International Women University, IFU, Hannover, Germany, 1998-2000. Membership: Who's Who Historical Society, 2004-2005. Address: Alamo 8-16, Col Los Alamos, Naucalpan de Juárez, Edo de México CP 53230, México. E-mail: gtasc2004@yahoo.com.mx Website: www.sirdo.com.mx

**MENDES Nilton Oliveira,** b. 11 November 1943, Rio de Janeiro, Brazil. Medical Doctor. m. Joana Darc Mendes, 1 son, 1 daughter. Education: MD, Riogrande do Norte University, 1969; Cardiologist sponsored by Hospital do Servidor Publico de São Paulo, 1976. Appointments: Chairman, Orthomolecular Medicine, Rio Grande do Norte University. Publications: Stress Management Strategy, 1999; Cardiology. Orthomolecular Therapy. Honours: Academia Brasileira de Medicina Militar Brasilia Federal District, 1985; Man of the Year 2004, American Biographical Institute. Memberships: American College for Advanced Medicine; International Society for Orthomolecular Medicine. Address: Av Miguel Castro 1275, ap 401 Natal 59075 RN-Brazil. E-mail: niltonortho@bol.com.br

**MENDES Sam,** b. 1 August 1965, England. Theatre Director. m. Kate Winslet, 1 son. Education: Magdalen College School; Oxford University; Peterhouse, Cambridge University. Appointments: Artistic Director, Minerva Studio Theatre, Chichester; Artistic Director, Donmar Warehouse, 1992-2002. Creative Works: Plays directed include: London Assurance,

Chichester; The Cherry Orchard, London; Kean, Old Vic, London; The Plough and the Stars, Young Vic, London, 1991; Troilus and Cressida, RSC, 1991; The Alchemist, RSC, 1991; Richard III, RSC, 1992; The Tempest, RSC, 1993; National Theatre debut with The Sea, 1991; The Rise and Fall of Little Voice, National and Aldwych, 1992; The Birthday Party, 1994; Othello (also world tour); Assassins, Translations, Cabaret, Glengarry Glen Ross, The Glass Menagerie, Company, Habeas Corpus, The Front Page, The Blue Room, To the Green Fields Beyond, (all at Donmar Warehouse) 1992-2000; Uncle Vanya and Twelfth Night, Donmar Warehouse, 2002; Oliver!, London Palladium; Cabaret, The Blue Room, Broadway, New York; Gypsy with Bernadette Peters, Broadway. Films: American Beauty, 1999; The Road to Perdition, 2002; Jarhead, 2005. Honours include: Commander of the British Empire; Critics' Circle Award, 1989, 1993, 1996; Olivier Award for Best Director, 1996; Tony Award, 1998; LA Critics' Award, Broadcast Critics' Award, Toronto People's Choice Award, Golden Globe Award, 1999; Shakespeare Prize, Academy Award for Best Director (also Best Film) for American Beauty, 2000; The Hamburg Shakespeare Prize; Oliver Award for Best Director (also Special Award), 2003. Address: 26-28 Neal Street, London, WC2H 9QQ, England. E-mail: mleigh@scampltd.com

**MÉNDEZ RODRÍGUEZ José Manuel,** b. 19 March 1955, Reinosa, Spain. Professor of Logic. 2 sons. Education: BA, History, 1978; BA, Philosophy, 1979; PhD, 1983. Appointments: Assistant Lecturer, 1980, Associate Professor, 1981, Professor, 1988-. Publications: Several articles in professional journals. Honours: 1st Class Distinction 1979; Special Distinction, 1983. Member of the Association for Symbolic Logic. Address: Departmento de Filosofia, Universidad de Salamanca, Edificio FES, Campus Unamuno, 37007 Salamanca, Spain.

**MENEM Carlos Saul,** b. 2 July 1935, Anillaco, La Rioja, Argentina. Politician. m. (1) Zulema Fatima Yoma, 1966, divorced, 1 son, deceased, 1 daughter, (2) Cecilia Bolocco, 2001. Education: Cordoba University. Appointments: Founder, Juventud Peronista, Peron Youth Group, La Rioja Province, 1955; Defended political prisoners following 1955 Coup; Legal Advisor, Confederacion General del Trabajo, La Rioja Province, 1955-70; Candidate, Provincial Deputy, 1958; President, Partido Justicialista, La Rioja Province, 1963-; Elected Govenor, La Rioja, 1973, re-elected, 1983, 1987; Imprisoned following military coup, 1976-81; Candidate for President, Argentine Republic for Partido Justicialista, 1989; President of Argentina, 1989-2001; Vice President, Conference of Latin-American Popular Parties, 1990-; Arrested for alleged involvement in illegal arms sales during his presidency, June 2001, charged, July 2001, placed under house arrest for five months; Presidential Candidate, 2003. Publications: Argentine, Now or Never; Argentina Year 2000; The Productive Revolution, with Eduardo Duhalde. Address: Casa de Gobierno, Balcarce 50, 1064 Buenos Aires, Argentina.

**MENKEN Alan,** b. 22 July 1949, New York, USA. Composer. Education: New York University. Creative Works: Theatre music including: God Bless You Mr Rosewater, 1979; Little Shop of Horrors, with Howard Ashman; Kicks; The Apprenticeship of Duddy Kravitz; Diamonds; Personals; Let Freedom Sing; Weird Romance; Beauty and the Beast; A Christmas Carol; Film music includes: Little Shop of Horrors, 1986; The Little Mermaid, 1988; Beauty and the Beast, 1990; Lincoln, 1992; Newsies, 1992; Aladdin, 1992; Life with Mikey, 1993; Pocahontas, with Stephen Schwartz, 1995. Honours include: Several Academy Awards, 1989, 1993, 1996; Golden Globe Award, 1996. Address: The Shukat Company, 340 West 55th Street, Apt 1A, New York, NY 10019, USA.

**MENNEN Ulrich,** b. 1 July 1947, Barberton, Mpumalanga, South Africa. m. Johanna Margaretha Louw, 2 sons, 1 daughter. Education: MBChB, University of Pretoria, 1970; FRCS, Glasgow, 1978, Edinburgh, 1978; FCS (SA) Ortho, 1979; MMed, Orthopaedics, University of Pretoria, 1979; PhD, Orthopaedics, 1983. Appointments include: Senior Surgeon, 1980, Principal Surgeon, 1981; Associate Professor and Principal Surgeon, 1983, Orthopaedics, Pretoria Academic Hospital; Microsurgery Fellow, Duke University Medical Centre, Durham, North Carolina, 1983; Professor and Head, Department of Hand- and Microsurgery, Medical University of Southern Africa, 1985-; Honorary Head, Hand Surgery Unit, Pretoria Academic Hospital; Head, Department of Orthopaedic Surgery, Medical University of Southern Africa, 1990-91; Visiting Professor, Hong Kong, Australia, USA, Vietnam, Iran, South Korea, Botswana, Ethiopia, Uganda, Tanzania; Private Hand Surgery Practice, 1992-; Founder and Member, Pretoria Hand Institute, Jakaranda Hospital, 1997-. Publications: Chirurgiese Sinopsis, 1978; Co-author, Surgical Synopsis, 1983; Editor, The Hand Book, 1988, second edition, 1994; Co-editor, Principles of Surgical Patient Care, vols 1 and 2, 1990, second edition, 2003; The History of South African Society for Surgery of the Hand 1969-1994, 1994; Numerous articles in professional journals and book chapters. Honours include: Registrar's Prize for Best Paper, 1978, 1979; G F Dommisse Orthopaedic Registrar Prize, 1979; Mer-National Literary Prize, for article, 1982; Smith and Nephew Literary Award, South African Orthopaedic Association, 1985; Chamber of Mines Research Grant, 1987; Glaxo Literary Award, 1990; Finalist, Wellcome Medal for Medical Research, 1990; Research Excellence Award, Faculty of Medicine, MEDUNSA, 1997; Masimanyane Award, Engineering Association, 1997; South African Bureau of Standards Design Institute Award, Overall Chairman's Award for Excellence, 1997; Numerous other literary prizes; Originator and developer of the Mennen Clamp-on Bone Fixation System. Memberships include: South African Medical Association; SA Orthopaedic Association; SA Association for Arthritis and Rheumatic Diseases; Cripples Research Association of South Africa; International Member, American Society for Surgery of the Hand; Executive Member and Past President, South African Society for Surgery of the Hand; Founding Member, South African Society for Hand Therapy; Executive Member, Secretary-General, International Federation of Societies for Surgery of the Hand. Address: 374 Lawley Street, Waterkloof, 0181, Pretoria, South Africa.

**MENTE Elena,** b. 13 June 1969, Thessaloniki, Greece. Academic. m. Ionnie Theodossiou. Education: BSc, Aristotle University of Thessaloniki, Greece; PhD, University of Aberdeen, Scotland. Appointments: Research Fellow, Department of Zoology, University of Aberdeen, 1999-2004; Assistant Professor, Department of Animal Production and Aquatic Environment, University of Thessaly, Greece, 2004-. Publications: Articles in scientific journals including: Journal of Experimental Biology; American Journal of Physiology; Journal of Experimental Zoology; Marine Ecology Progress Series; Aquaculture Journal; Journal of the Marine Biological Association, UK. Honours: European Community, 5th Framework Programme, Aquaculture Sustainability; Honorary Research Fellow, University of Aberdeen; Best Poster on Crustacean ; European Community Research Training Grant. Memberships: World Aquaculture Society; European Marie Curie Fellowship Association; Fisheries Society of the British Isles. Address: Department of Zoology, University of Aberdeen, Tillydrone Avenue, Aberdeen AB24 2TZ, Scotland and Department of Animal Production and Aquatic Environment, University of Thessaly, Greece.

**MEREDITH William (Morris),** b. 9 January 1919, New York, New York, USA. Poet; Retired Professor of English. Education: AB, Princeton University, 1940. Appointments: Instructor in English and Woodrow Wilson Fellow in Writing, Princeton University, 1946-50; Associate Professor in English, University of Hawaii, 1950-51; Associate Professor, 1955-65, Professor in English, 1965-83, Connecticut College, New London; Instructor, Bread Loaf School of English, Middlebury College, Vermont, 1958-62; Consultant in Poetry, Library of Congress, Washington, DC, 1978-80. Publications: Poetry: Love Letters from an Impossible Land, 1944; Ships and Other Figures, 1948; The Open Sea and Other Poems, 1958; The Wreck of the Thresher and Other Poems, 1964; Winter Verse, 1964; Year End Accounts, 1965; Two Pages from a Colorado Journal, 1967; Earth Walk: New and Selected Poems, 1970; Hazard, the Painter, 1975; The Cheer, 1980; Partial Accounts: New and Selected Poems, 1987. Non-Fiction: Reasons for Poetry and the Reason for Criticism, 1982; Poems Are Hard to Read, 1991. Editor: Shelley: Poems, 1962; University and College Poetry Prizes, 1960-66, 1966; Eighteenth-Century Minor Poets (with Mackie L Jarrell), 1968; Poets of Bulgaria (with others), 1985. Translator: Guillaume Apollinaire: Alcools: Poems, 1898-1913, 1964. Honours: Yale Series of Younger Poets Award, 1943; Harriet Monroe Memorial Prize, 1944; Rockefeller Foundation Grants, 1948, 1968; Oscar Blumenthal Prize, 1953; National Institute of Arts and Letters Grant, 1958, and Loines Prize, 1966; Ford Foundation Fellowship, 1959-60; Van Wyck Brooks Award, 1971; National Endowment for the Arts Grant, 1972, and Fellowship, 1984; Guggenheim Fellowship, 1975-76; International Vaptsarov Prize for Literature, Bulgaria, 1979; Los Angeles Times Prize, 1987; Pulitzer Prize in Poetry, 1988. Memberships: Academy of American Poets, chancellor; National Institute of Arts and Letters. Address: 6300 Bradley Avenue, Bethseda, MD 20817, USA.

**MERI Lennart,** b. 29 March 1929, Tallinn, Estonia. Former President of the Republic of Estonia; Professor. m. Helle Meri, 2 sons, 1 daughter. Education: Graduate, Historian, cum laude, Tartu University, 1953. Appointments: Dramatist, Vanemuine Theatre, 1953-55; Professor, Tartu Art School; Producer, Estonian Radio, 1955-61; Script Writer, 1963-68; Producer, 1968-71, 1986-88, Tallinnfilm; Foreign Relations Secretary, Estonian Writers Union, 1985-87; Estonian Popular Front and National Heritage Preservation Association, 1980's; Founder, Director, Estonian Institute, 1988-90; Ministry of Foreign Affairs, Estonia, 1990-92; Ambassador of Estonia to Finland, 1992; President, Republic of Estonia, 1992-96, re-elected, 1996-2001. Publications include: Kobrade ja karakurtide jälgedes (Following the Trails of Cobras and Black Widows), 1959; Virmaliste väraval (At the Gate of Northern Lights), 1974; Tulen maasta, jonka nimi on Viro (Coming From the Country Called Estonia), 1995. Address: Haabneeme, 74001 Vilmsi Vald, Harjummaa, Estonia.

**MERKEL Angela,** b. 17 July 1954, Hamburg, Germany. Chancellor of Germany. Education: Physics doctorate, 1978. Appointments: Chemist, scientific academy, East Berlin; Joined the Christian Democratic Union (CDU), 1990; Minister for Women and Youth, 1991-94; Minister for Environment, Nature Protection and Reactor Safety, 1994-98; General Secretary, 1993-2000, Chairman, 1998-2000, CDU Deutschlands; Chairman, CDU/CSU-Bundestagsfraktion, 2002-; Chancellor of Germany, 2005-. Address: Office of the Federal Chancellor, Willy-Brandt-Strasse 1, D-10557, Berlin, Germany.

**MESSENGER George C,** b. 20 July 1930, Bellows Falls, USA. Scientist. m. Priscilla Messenger, 2 sons, 1 daughter. Education: BS, Physics, Worcester Polytechnical Institute, 1951; MS, Electrical Engineering, University of Pennsylvania, 1958; PhD, Engineering, California Coast University, 1986. Appointments: Senior Engineer, Philco Corporation, 1951-59; Engineering Manager, Hughes Semiconductor, 1959-61; Vice President, Transistor Division, Transitron, 1961-63; Engineering Fellow, Northrop, 1963-68; Vice President, Messenger and Associates, 1968-. Publications include: The Effects of Radiation on Electronic Systems, 1986; Single Event Phenomena, 1997; Nonvolatile Semiconductor Memory Technology, 1998; 50 professional papers in refereed scientific journals. Honours: Robert H Goddard Award for Outstanding Professional Achievement, Worcester Polytechnic Institute, 1966; Fellow, IEEE, 1976; Berman Award, Naval Research Laboratory, 1982; Best Paper Award, Heart Conference, 1983; IEEE Annual Merit Award, 1986; Peter Haas Award, 1992. Memberships: Research Society of America; IEEE. Address: 3111 Bel Air Drive #7F, Las Vegas, NV 89109, USA. E-mail: gpmessenger@cox.net

**MEYER Conrad John Eustace,** b. 2 July 1922, Bristol, England. Retired Roman Catholic Priest. m. Mary Wiltshire. Education: Pembroke College, Cambridge; Westcott House, Cambridge; Ordained Priest in the Roman Catholic Church, 1995. Appointments: War Service, 1942-46; Lieutenant (S), Chaplain, RNVR, retired 1954; As Anglican: Diocesan Secretary for Education, 1960-69; Archdeacon of Bodmin, Truro Diocese, 1969-79 Honorary Canon, Truro Cathedral, 1960-79; Provost, Western Division of Woodard Schools, 1970-92; Examining Chaplain to the Bishop of Truro, 1973-79; Area Bishop of Dorchester, Oxford Diocese, 1979-87; Honorary Assistant Bishop, Truro Diocese, 1990-94; As Roman Catholic: Honorary Canon, Plymouth Roman Catholic Cathedral, 2001. Memberships: Formerly Chairman of Appeal Committee, Vice-Chairman of Society, 1989-90, Vice-President, 1990-, Society for Promoting Christian Knowledge (SPCK); Chairman, Cornwall Civil Aid and County Commissioner, 1993-96; Honorary Fellow, Institute for Civil Defence and Disaster Studies. Address: Hawk's Cliff, 38 Praze Road, Newquay, Cornwall TR7 3AF, England.

**MEYER Wieland,** b. 31 October 1962, Zwickau, Germany. Molecular Biologist. Education: MSc, Biology, 1986, PhD, Genetics, 1992, Humboldt University of Berlin, Germany. Appointments: Research Associate, Department of Genetechnology and Microbiology, Research Centre of Biotechnology, 1986-1988; Research Associate, HUB Department of Biology, Institute of Genetics, Biochemistry and Microbiology, IFZ Research and Developing Society Ltd, Berlin, Germany, 1989-92; Research Associate, Postdoctoral Fellow, Department of Microbiology, Duke University Medical Center, Durham, USA, 1992-95; Senior Scientific Officer, Head of Molecular Mycology, 1995-96, Senior Hospital Scientist, Head of Molecular Mycology, 1996-, Center for Infectious Diseases and Microbiology, University of Sydney at Westmead Hospital, Sydney; Senior Research Fellow, Department of Medicine, University of Sydney, 1996-; Postronge, Centre National de la Recherche (CNRS), University Paul Sabatiar, Toulouse, France, 2004-05. Publications: DNA fingerprinting of plants and fungi, Co-author, 1995; 54 articles in refereed journals; Associate Editor, Medical Mycology Journal, 1999-. Honours: Janssen-Cilag/ASM Mycology Award, 2001; Listed in several Who's Who and biographical publications. Memberships: International Trichoderma Study Group, 1992-; International Society for Human and Animal Mycology, 1994-; Vice-President, 1998-2002, President, 2002-, Australasian Mycological Society; Australian Society for Microbiology, 1998-; Deutschsprachige Mykologische Gesellschaft, 2001-; Convener, Mycology Interest Group, Australasian Society for Infectious Diseases, 2002-; British Mycological Society,

2002-. Address: Molecular Mycology Laboratory, University of Sydney at Westmead Hospital, Darcy Road, Westmead, NSW 2145, Australia. E-mail: w.meyer@usyd.edu.au  Webpage: www.mmrl.med.usy.edu.au

**MICHAEL George (Georgios Kyriacos Panayiotou),** b. 25 June 1963, Finchley, London, England. Singer; Songwriter; Producer. Career: Singer, The Executive, 1979; Singer, pop duo Wham! with Andrew Ridgeley, 1982-86; Solo artiste, 1986-; Worldwide appearances include: Live Aid, with Elton John, Wembley, 1985; Prince's Trust Rock Gala, 1986; Wham's 'The Final' concert, Wembley, 1986; Nelson Mandela's 70th Birthday Tribute, 1988; Rock In Rio II Festival, Brazil, 1991; A Concert For Life, tribute to Freddie Mercury, Wembley Stadium, 1992; Elizabeth Taylor AIDS Foundation Benefit, Madison Square Garden, New York, 1992; Dispute with Epic record label, and parent company Sony Entertainment, 1992-95; Television special, Aretha Franklin: Duets, 1993. Recordings: Albums: with Wham!: Fantastic, 1983; Make It Big, 1984; The Final, 1986; Solo albums: Faith, 1987; Listen Without Prejudice, Vol 1, 1990; Older, 1996; Older and Upper, 1998; Ladies and Gentlemen: The Best of George Michael, 1998; Songs from the Last Century, 1999; Patience, 2004; Contributor, Duets, Elton John, 1991; Two Rooms, 1992; Hit singles include: with Wham!: Wham Rap, 1982; Young Guns (Go For It), 1982; Bad Boys, 1983; Club Tropicana, 1983; Wake Me Up Before You Go Go, 1984; Last Christmas, 1984; Careless Whisper, 1984; Everything She Wants, 1984; Freedom, 1985; I'm Your Man, 1985; The Edge Of Heaven, 1986; Solo: A Different Corner, 1986; I Knew You Were Waiting For Me, duet with Aretha Franklin, 1987; I Want Your Sex, 1987; Faith, 1987; Father Figure, 1988; One More Try, 1988; Monkey, 1988; Kissing A Fool, 1988; Praying For Time, 1990; Freedom 90, 1990; Don't Let The Sun Go Down On Me, duet with Elton John; Too Funky, 1992; Five Live EP, 1993; Somebody To Love, with Queen, 1993; Jesus To A Child, 1995; Fast Love, 1996; Star People, 1997; You Have Been Loved, 1997; Outside, 1998; As, with Mary J Blige, 1999; If I Told You That, with Whitney Houston, 2000; Freeek!, 2002; Shoot the Dog, 2002; Amazing, 2004; Contributor, Do They Know It's Christmas?, Band Aid, 1985; Nikita, Elton John, 1985. Publication: Bare, with Tony Parsons (autobiography). Honours include: BRIT Awards: Best British Group, 1985; Outstanding Contribution to British Music, 1986; Best British Male Artist, 1988; Best British Album, 1991; Ivor Novello Awards: Songwriter Of The Year, 1985, 1989; Most Performed Work (Careless Whisper), 1985; Hit Of The Year (Faith), 1989; Grammy, with Aretha Franklin, 1988; Nordoff-Robbins Silver Clef Award, 1989; American Music Awards: Favourite Pop/Rock Male Artist, Soul R&B Male Artist, Favourite Album, 1989; ASCAP Golden Note Award, 1992. Address: c/o Connie Filipello Publicity, 17 Gosfield Street, London W1P 7HE, England.

**MICHAEL (H M King),** b. 25 October 1921, Romania. King of Romania. m. Princess Anne of Bourbon-Parma, 1948, 5 daughters. Appointments: Declared heir apparent, ratified by Parliament 1926; Proclaimed King, 1927, deposed by his father, 1930; Succeeded to the throne of Romania following his father's abdication, 1940; Led coup d'etat against pro Nazi dictator Ion Antonescu, 1944; Forced to abdicate following communist takeover of Romania, 1947; Subsequently ran chicken farm in Hertfordshire, England; Went to Switzerland as a Test Pilot, 1956; Worked for Lear Incorporated; Founder, Electronics Company; Stockbroker; Deported from Romania on first visit since exile, 1990; Returned to Romania, 1992; Romanian citizenship and passport restored, 1997; Undertook official mission for Romania's integration into NATO and EU 1997. Honours: Order of Victoria, USSR, 1945; Chief Commander,

Legion of Merit, USA, 1946; Honorary KCVO. Address: 17 La Croix-de-Luisant, 1170 Aubonne, Vaud, Switzerland.

**MIDDLEBURGH Charles Hadley,** b. 2 October 1956, Hove, East Sussex, England. Rabbi. m. Gilly Blyth. Education: BA (Hons) Ancient and Medieval Hebrew and Aramaic, 1979, PhD, Aramaic, 1982, University College, London. Rabbinic Ordination, Leo Baeck College, 1986. Appointments: Reader, Brighton and Hove, Progressive Synagogue, 1975-77; Minister, Kingston Liberal Synagogue, 1977-83; Rabbi, Harrow and Wembley Progressive Synagogue, 1983-97; Executive Director, Union of Liberal and Progressive Synagogues, 1997-2002; Rabbi, Dublin Jewish Progressive Congregation, 2002-; Rabbi, Progressive Judaism in Denmark, 2002-; Rabbi, Cardiff Reform Synagogue, 2005-; Lecturer in Aramaic, Bible and Practical Rabbinics, 1984-2002, Senior Lecturer in Rabbinics, 2003-, Leo Baeck College; Lecturer, Irish School of Ecumenics, Trinity College, Dublin, 2003-. Publications: Siddur Lev Chadash, Daily, Sabbath and Festival Liturgy, Union of Liberal and Progressive Synagogues (associate editor), 1995; Machzor Ruach Chadashah, High Holyday Liturgy, Union of Liberal and Progressive Synagogues (joint editor), 2003; Book reviews in the Jewish Chronicle, Church Times, Expository Times. Memberships: Fellow, Royal Society of Arts; Fellow, Zoological Society of London. Address: c/o Leo Baeck College, Centre for Jewish Education, The Sternberg Centre, 80 East End Road, Finchley N3 2SY, England. E-mail: charles@middle burgh.co.uk Website: www.middleburgh.co.uk

**MIDDLETON Roger,** b. 19 May 1955. Reader in the History of Political Economy; Writer. Education: BA, First Class Honours, Victoria University of Manchester, 1976; PhD, Cambridge University, 1981. Appointments: Lecturer in Economic History, University of Durham, 1979-87; Senior Lecturer in Economic History, University of Bristol, 1987-90; Reader in the History of Political Economy, 1997-. Publications: Towards the Managed Economy, 1985; Government Versus the Market, 1996; Charlatans or Saviours?, 1998; The British Economy Since 1945, 2000; Exemplary Economists (editor with R E Backhouse), 2000; Economic Policy under the Conservatives (with A Ringe & N Rollings), 2004. Contributions to: Economic, history and computing journals. Honours: T S Ashton Prize, Economic History Society, 1980; Choice Outstanding Academic Book, 1996, 1998; Royal Historical Society, fellow; Academician of the Social Sciences. Memberships: Royal Economic Society; Economic History Society; Political Studies Association; Institute of Fiscal Studies. Address: Department of Historical Studies, University of Bristol, Bristol BS1 1TB, England.

**MIDDLETON Stanley,** b. 1 August 1919, Bulwell, Nottingham, England. Novelist. m. Margaret Shirley Charnley, 22 December 1951, 2 daughters. Education: University College, Nottingham; BA, London University; Cert Ed, Cambridge University; MEd, Nottingham University. Appointments: H M Forces, 1940-46; Head of English, High Pavement College, Nottingham; Judith E Wilson Visiting Fellow, Emmanuel College, Cambridge. Publications: A Short Answer, 1958; Harris's Requiem, 1960; A Serious Woman, 1961; The Just Exchange, 1962; Two's Company, 1963; Him They Compelled, 1964; The Golden Evening, 1968; Wages of Virtue, 1969; Brazen Prison, 1971; Holiday, 1974; Still Waters, 1976; Two Brothers, 1978; In a Strange Land, 1979; The Other Side, 1980; Blind Understanding, 1982; Entry into Jerusalem, 1983; Daysman, 1984; Valley of Decision, 1985; An After Dinner's Sleep, 1986; After a Fashion, 1987; Recovery, 1988; Vacant Places, 1989; Changes & Chances, 1990; Beginning to End, 1991; A Place to Stand, 1992; Married Past Redemption, 1993; Catalysts, 1994; Toward the Sea, 1995; Live and Learn, 1996; Brief Hours, 1997; Against the Dark, 1997; Necessary Ends, 1999; Small Change, 2000; Love in the Provinces, 2004; Sterner Stuff, 2005. Honours: Co-Recipient, Booker Prize, 1974; Honorary MA, Nottingham University; Honorary MUniv, Open University; Honorary DLitt, De Montfort University; FRSL; Honorary DLitt, Nottingham Trent University, 2000. Membership: PEN. Address: 42 Caledon Road, Sherwood, Nottingham NG5 2NG, England.

**MIDLER Bette,** b. 1 December 1945, Paterson, New Jersey, USA. Singer; Actress; Comedienne. m. Martin von Haselberg, 1984, 1 daughter. Education: Theatre studies, University of Hawaii. Career: As actress: Cast member, Fiddler On The Roof, Broadway, 1966-69; Salvation, New York, 1970; Rock opera Tommy, Seattle Opera Company, 1971; Nightclub concert performer and solo artiste, 1972-; Numerous television appearances include: Ol' Red Hair Is Back, NBC, 1978; Bette Midler's Mondo Beyondo, HBO, 1988; Earth Day Special, ABC, 1990; The Tonight Show, NBC, 1991; Now, NBC, 1993; Films include: Hawaii, 1965; The Rose, 1979; Jinxed!, 1982; Down And Out In Beverly Hills, 1985; Ruthless People, 1986; Outrageous Fortune, 1987; Big Business, 1988; Beaches, 1988; Stella, 1990; Scenes From A Mall, 1990; For The Boys (also co-producer), 1991; Hocus Pocus, 1993; Own company, All Girls Productions, 1989-. Recordings: Albums include: The Divine Miss M, 1972; Bette Midler, 1973; Songs For The New Depression, 1976; Broken Blossom, 1977; Live At Last, 1977; Thighs And Whispers, 1979; The Rose, film soundtrack, 1979; Divine Madness, film soundtrack, 1980; No Frills, 1984; Beaches, film soundtrack, 1989; Some People's Lives, 1991; Best Of, 1993; Bette Of Roses, 1995; Experience the Divine, 1997; Bathhouse Betty, 1998; From a Distance, 1998. Singles include: The Rose; Wind Beneath My Wings (Number 1, US), from Beaches soundtrack, 1989; From A Distance, 1991. Publications: A View From A Broad; The Saga Of Baby Divine. Honours: After Dark Award, Performer Of The Year, 1973; Grammy Awards: Best New Artist, 1973; Best Female Pop Vocal Performance, The Rose, 1981; Record Of The Year, Song Of The Year, Wind Beneath My Wings, 1990; Special Tony Award, 1973; Emmy, Ol' Red Hair Is Back, 1978; Golden Globe Awards: The Rose, 1979; For The Boys, 1991; Oscar Nomination, Best Actress, The Rose, 1980; Contributor, We Are The World, USA For Africa, 1985; Oliver And Company, 1988. Address: c/o All Girls Productions, Animation Bldg #3B-10, 500 South Buena Vista, Burbank, CA 91521, USA.

**MIERS Christopher John Penrose,** b. 26 September 1941, Belfast, Northern Ireland. Artist. m. (1) Judith Mary Caroline Hoare, 1 son, 1 daughter (2) Liza Georgetta Thynne. Education: Wellington College and Royal Military Academy, Sandhurst (Sword of Honour); Staff College. Appointments: Served as regimental officer, Royal Green Jackets including active service in Borneo, Northern Ireland and with the United Nations Force in Cyprus; Commanded 4th Volunteer Battalion The Royal Green Jackets, 1982-84; Military Assistant to the Quartermaster General, Ministry of Defence, 1984-85; Retired as Lieutenant Colonel, 1985; Secretary, The Arts Club, London, 1986-90; Professional Artist, 1991-; Exhibitions: RA most years from 1985; RBA; NEAC; 21 one-man exhibitions of paintings include: The Minories, Colchester, 1964; Ansdell Gallery, Kensington, 1967, 1968; Fortescue Swann, Brompton Road, 1976; C D Soar & Son, Launceston Place, 1986, 1988; Sally Hunter Fine Art, 1990, 1993, 1995; Mall Galleries, 1991; Jerram Gallery, 1994, 1996; Grosvenor House, 1996; Tryon & Swann Gallery, 1998; Rafael Valls Ltd, 2000, 2002, 2004; Paintings in the collections of: The Imperial War Museum; House of Commons; H M Sultan of Oman. Honour: Mentioned in despatches for service in Borneo, 1964. Memberships: Royal Society of British Artists; The Arts Club; The Chelsea Arts Club;

The Fadeaways. Address: 114 Bishop's Mansions, Bishop's Park Road, Fulham, London SW6 6DY, England.

**MIHAYLOVA Lyudmila Stoyanova,** b. 17 October 1965, Stara Zagora, Bulgaria. m. Dragomir Jelev, 1 son. Education: MSc, Systems and Control Engineering, 1989, MSc, Informatics & Applied Mathematics, 1991, PhD, Systems and Control Engineering, 1996, Technical University of Sofia, Bulgaria. Appointments: Part time Assistant Professor, Technical University of Sofia, 1996-2000; Research Assistant, Bulgarian Academy of Sciences, 1996-2000; Research Assistant, Catholic University of Leuven, Belgium, 2000-02; Research Fellow, University of Ghent, Belgium, 2002-04; Research Fellow, University of Bristol, England, 2004-. Publications: 11 articles in journals; 36 conference papers; 6 book chapters; 41 citations. Honours: Young Scientist Award, XXIVth General Assembly of the International Union of Radio Science, Kyoto, Japan, 1993. Memberships: IEEE Member, Signal Processing Society, 1998-; International Science of Information Fusion, 1999-. Address: Department of Electrical and Electronic Engineering, University of Bristol, Merchant Venturers Building, Woodland Road, Bristol BS8 1UB, England. E-mail: mila.mihaylova@ieee.org

**MIKHAILUSENKO Igor Georgievich,** b. 20 April 1932, Moscow, Russia. Translator; Poet; Journalist. Education: Graduate, Maurice Thorez Foreign Languages Institute, Moscow, 1958; Higher Education Diploma, Translator from Russian into English. Appointments: Various posts as translator and English-language speaker; USSR Travel Agency, Intourist; Various assignments as a free-lance journalist; Poetry writer. Publications: Contributor to numerous publications including Dostoinstvo newspaper, 1995-2004; Many poems set to music, which became popular songs; Articles include: Tribute to Third Millennium (book), 2001; Memoirs of Moscow's Man (book); Poet's Dreams (book), 2001; A Peaceful Travel – USA Through Foreign Eyes, (book), 2001; What I Wish (Oh I Wish) I Had Said (book), 2002; Poems That Mirror My Soul (book), 2003; Poems about Flowers (book), 2004; The Will of Baron De Couberten – International Olympic Museum through the eyes of Moscow's poet (book), 2004. Honours: Many awards and citations for international peace efforts, including Badge of Honour, Moscow Peace Committee, 1982; Recognised by the United Poets Laureate International, 1987; Award, Editors of Fine Arts Press, Knoxville, USA, for noteworthy contribution to book: Rainbows and Rhapsodies and his excellence in poetry, 1988; Laureate Man of Letters, awarded the Laurel Wreath, 1997; Listed in several prestigious international biographical directories. Memberships: Laurel Leaves, Official Organ of the United Poets Laureate International; Board of Directors, International Writers and Artists Association. Address: Bolshaya Gruzinskaya Street, House 63, Apartment 87, Moscow 123056, Russia. E-mail: vitaigor@list.ru Website: http:remdate.narod.ru/mikhailusenko.htm

**MIKHAYLOVA Maria V,** b. 17 January 1946, Moscow, Russia. Philologist. Education: Student, Philological Faculty, Moscow State University, 1964-69; Postgraduate Course, 1969-72; PhD, 1974; DH, 1996. Appointments: Lecturer, Russian Literature of the end of the XIXth Century – the beginning of the XXth Century, 1969-82, Assistant Professor, 1982-98, Professor, 1998-, Philological Faculty, Department of Russian Literature of the XXth Century, Moscow State University. Publications: History of Russian Literary Criticism of the end XIXth Century – the beginning of the XXth Century, 1985; The Fate of Women Writers in Literature at the Beginning of the XXth Century, 1996; Articles in the Dictionary of Russian Women Writers, 1994; Prefaces and commentaries to books of fiction; Editor, feminist magazine: Preobrazhenie, 1993-99.

Honour: The Best Philologist of Moscow State University, 1996. Memberships: Moscow Union of Writers; Member of numerous dissertation boards. Address: Malaya Gruzinskaya Str. 28, Flat 162, 123557 Moscow, Russia. E-mail: mary12@rol.ru

**MIKKOLA Kari Juhani,** b. 13 May 1959, Salla, Finland. Process Operator; Writer on Science; Diplomat. Education includes: Short course in Theology, State Church Facility ERSTA, Stockholm, Sweden, 1976; Degree in Electricity Automation, 1977; Deacon's Studies, Swedish State Church, 1 year; Home Nurse School, Härnösand, 1979; Short course in Theology, Lekmanna School, Sigtuna, 1980; Manufacturing course, Forest Industry Centre, Markaryd, 1980; Russian History, University of Linköping, 1996; Currently studying Russian and Latin. Appointments: Currently Process Operator, Smurfit Aspa Bruk AB, Sweden; Independent Researcher in Astronomy, Astrophysics. Cosmology, Archaeology, Quantum Physics, Social Anthropology, Culture, Chemistry, Theology, Bible history; Diplomatic Councillor of the London Diplomatic Academy; Co-Founder, American Order of Excellence Society. Publications: Numerous, especially in theology and science. Honours: His Excellency Ambassador, Knight, International Order of Ambassadors; Citation of Meritorious Achievements in Natural Science; Citation of Meritorious Achievements in Astronomy and Astrophysics; Member, London Diplomatic Academy (LDA); Co-founder, Diplomatic Council, LDA; American Order of Excellence, 2000; International Peace Prize Award, 2003; Cabinet Member, World Peace and Diplomacy Forum, UK, 2003; Legion of Honor, United Cultural Convention, 2005; Many others. Memberships: National Geographic Society, USA; Society for Popular Astronomy, England; American Association for the Advancement of Science; New York Academy of Sciences; Member, London Diplomatic Academy (LDA); Co-founder, Diplomatic Council, LDA; European Life Scientists' Organization; Community of Scientists, USA; Member, Global Benefits Administration Corporation, USA, 2002; Swedish American Association, Sweden, 2004; Scandinavian Association for American Studies, Sweden, 2004; Nordic Association for American Studies, Sweden, 2004; European Association for British-American Studies, Sweden, 2004; Swedish Association for American Studies, Sweden, 2004. Address: Parkvägen 3, 69673 Aspa Bruk, Sweden. E-mail: kari.mikkola@swipnet.se

**MIKLOS Tomás,** b. 29 May 1938, Mexico City. Management and Planning Consultant; Future Studies. m. Monique, 1 son, 1 daughter. Education: Chemical Engineer (UNAM), 1959; PhD, Mathematics, Sorbonne, 1963; Master Degree in Psychoanalysis (CIEP), 1978. Appointments: Consultant, Government Human and Social Council; Latin American Institute for Educational Communication; General Coordinator, Adult Forming Network, RED-RED and RE.FORM.AD; General Director, CREFAL, International Agency: UNESCO, OEA, Mexican Government, General Director, Fund Javier Barros Sierra, Prospective Research Centre; General Director, National Institute for Advanced Assessment. Publications: Prospective Planning, 1991; Interactive Planning, 1994; Basics for Planning, 1999; Alternative Learning and Competency Based Education, 1999. Honours: Benito Juarez Medal; Honorary Mention, National Institute for Public Administration. Memberships: WFS; NYAAS; SMGH; ANHG; ANI. Address: Cerrada Del Rayo 20, La Herradura, 11002 Mexico City, Huixquilucan, Mexico.

**MILAM Diane Joy,** b. 8 October 1925, Jacksonville, Florida, USA. Architect. m. Thomas Gordon Dennis, deceased 1999. Education: BA, Bennington College, 1947; BA, 1956, M Arch, 1975, Columbia University School of Architecture. Appointments include: TAMS, 1945-47; Architecture,

Time Magazine, 1949-50; Edward Durrell Stone, 1952-60. Membership: American Institute of Architects. Address: 47 East 64th Street, Apt 10A, New York, NY 10021, USA.

**MILES Sarah,** b. 31 December 1941, England. Actress. m. Robert Bolt, 1967, divorced 1976, re-married 1988, deceased 1995. Education: Royal Academy of Dramatic Art, London. Creative Works: Films include: Those Magnificent Men in Their Flying Machines, 1964; I Was Happy Here, 1966; The Blow-Up, 1966; Ryan's Daughter, 1970; Lady Caroline Lamb, 1972; The Hireling, 1973; The Man Who Loved Cat Dancing, 1973; Great Expectations, 1975; Pepita Jiminez, 1975; The Sailor Who Fell From Grace With the Sea, 1976; The Big Sleep, 1978; Venom, 1981; Hope and Glory, 1987; White Mischief, 1988; The Silent Touch; Theatre appearances include: Vivat! Regina!; Asylum, 1988; TV appearances: James Michener's Dynasty; Great Expectations; Harem; Queenie; A Ghost in Monte Carlo; Dandelion; Dead Ring Around the Moon; The Rehearsal. Publications: Charlemagne, play, 1992; A Right Royal Bastard, memoirs, 1993; Serves Me Right, memoirs, 1994; Bolt From the Blue, memoirs, 1996.

**MILICHOVSKY Miloslav,** b. 13 February 1945, Babice, near Havlickuv Brod, Czech Republic. Senior Lecturer. m. Svatava Dostalova, 2 sons. Education: MS, Physical Chemistry, Institute of Chemical Technology, Pardubice, 1968; Organic Chemistry, ICT, Prague, 1975; CSc, Macromolecular Chemistry, ICT Pardubice, 1977; DrSc, Wood Chemistry and Technology, 1989. Appointments: Graduate Technologist, South Bohemian Papermill Vetrni, 1968; Assistant Professor, ICT Pardubice, 1976; Full Professor, Chemistry and Technology of Wood, Pulp and Paper, ICT Pardubice,2003; Head of Department, Wood, Pulp, Paper, University of Pardubice. Publications: More than 100 scientific articles in more than 8 scientific and professional journals. Memberships: Technical Association of Pulp and Paper Industry TAPPI; Association of Pulp and Paper Industry SPPaC; Czech and Slovak Papermaking Association SPPC. Address: University of Pardubice, Department of Wood, Pulp and Paper, Studentska 95, CZ 53210 Paradubice, Czech Republic.

**MILLAR Jack Ernest,** b. 28 November 1921, London, England. Artist. m. (1) 1 son, 2 daughters, (2) Pamela Izzard. Education: 1st Class Degree, Andrew Lloyd Scholarship for Landscape Painting, Royal College of Art, 1950. Appointments: Visiting Lecturer, Royal Academy Schools, 1964-92; Head of Fine Art, Walthamstow School of Art, 1966-73; Head of Fine Art, Kingston University, 1973-86. Publications: Light, Lucy Willis, 1989; Painting Flowers, Jenny Rodwell, 1993; Still Life in Oils, Jenny Rodwell, 1994. Honours: GLC Spirit of London Rowney Prize, 1979; GLC Prize, 1983; RBA 1st Prize, Daler Rowney, 1986; Hunting Group Prize Winner, 1987; De Lazolo Medal, 1989; Winsor & Newton Prize Winner, 2001. Memberships: RBA; NEAC. Address: 10 Overhill Road, East Dulwich, London SE22 0PH, England.

**MILLER (James) David Frederick,** b. 5 January 1935, Wolverhampton, England. Retired Company Director. m. Saffrey Blackett, 3 sons, 1 deceased, 1 daughter. Education: MA, Emmanuel College, Cambridge, Diploma, IPM, London School of Economics. Appointments: Director, J & P Coats Ltd, 1972-79, Coats Patons plc, 1977-92, Royal Scottish National Orchestra, 1985-93, Outward Bound Trust, Ltd, 1985-95, Coats Viyella plc, 1986-92, The Wolverhampton & Dudley Breweries plc, 1984-2001, (chairman 1992-2001), Scottish Life Assurance Co, 1995-2001, J&J Denholm Ltd, 1997-2005, Scottish Enterprise Forth Valley, 1994-2003 (vice-chairman, 1996-2003). Honours: Freeman City of London, 1983; Freeman, Worshipful Company of Needlemakers, 1983; Honorary DUniv: University of Stirling,

1984, University of Paisley, 1997; CBE, 1997. Memberships: Chairman: Scottish Vocational Education Council, 1992-97, Court, University of Stirling, 1992-99, Scottish Examination Board, 1995-97, Scottish Qualifications Authority, 1996-2000, Fairbridge in Scotland, 1998-, Clackmannon College of Further Education, 2004-; Director, Edinburgh Military Tattoo, 1990-2000. Address: Blairuskin Lodge, Kinlochard, Aberfoyle, by Stirling FK8 3TP, Scotland.

**MILLER Jeanne-Marie,** b. 18 February 1937, Washington DC, USA. Graduate Professor Emerita of English. m. Nathan J Miller. Education: BA, 1959, MA, 1963, PhD, 1976, English, Howard University. Appointments: Instructor, 1963-76, Graduate Assistant Professor, 1976-79, Graduate Associate Professor, 1979-92; Assistant Director, Institute for the Arts and the Humanities, 1973-75, Assistant for Academic Planning, Office of the Vice President for Academic Affairs, 1976-90; Director, Graduate Studies Program in English, 1991-97; Graduate Professor of English, 1992-97; Professor Emerita of English, 1997-, Howard University. Publications: 80 articles in variety of academic books and journals. Honours: Fellow, Ford Foundation, 1970-72; Fellow, Southern Fellowships Fund, 1972-74; Grantee, Howard University Faculty Research Grant, 1975, 1976-77, 1994-95, 1996-97; Grantee, American Council of Learned Societies, 1978-79; National Endowment for the Humanities, 1981-84; Pi Lambda Delta. Memberships: American Association of Higher Education; American Studies Association; College Language Association; National Council of Teachers of English; Modern Language Association; American Association of University Women; Corcoran Gallery of Art Association; Founder Member, John F Kennedy Memorial Centre for the Performing Arts; Washington Opera Society; Associate, Metropolitan Museum of Art; Metropolitan Opera Guild; Ibsen Society of America; Drama League of New York; Folger Shakespeare Library; Shakespeare Theatre Guild. Address: 504 24th Street, NE, Washington DC 20002-4818, USA.

**MILLER Jonathan (Wolfe),** b. 21 July 1934, London, England. Theatre, Film, and Television Director; Writer. m. Helen Rachel Collet, 1956, 2 sons, 1 daughter. Education: MB, BCh, St John's College, Cambridge, 1959. Appointments: Theatre, film, and television director; Resident Fellow in the History of Medicine, 1970-73, Fellow, 1981-, University College, London; Associate Director, National Theatre, 1973-75; Visiting Professor in Drama, Westfield College, London, 1977-; Artistic Director, Old Vic, 1988-90; Research Fellow in Neuropsychology, University of Sussex. Publications: McLuhan, 1971; Freud: The Man, His World, His Influence (editor), 1972; The Body in Question, 1978; Subsequent Performances, 1986; The Don Giovanni Book: Myths of Seduction and Betrayal (editor), 1990. Honours: Silver Medal, Royal Television Society, 1981; Commander of the Order of the British Empire, 1983; Albert Medal, Royal Society of Arts, 1990; Honorary Doctor of Letters, University of Cambridge. Memberships: Royal Academy, fellow; American Academy of Arts and Sciences. Address: c/o IMG Artists, Media House, 3 Burlington Lane, London W4 2TH, England.

**MILLER Keith John,** b. 12 January 1932. Emeritus Professor of Mechanical Engineering. Education: ScD (Camb); PhD; MA; BSc; FREng; FIMechE; FIMMM; FIMarETS; FCGI; FIEEE; FIMfgE; FRGS. Appointments: Lecturer in Engineering, University of Cambridge, 1968-77; Editor-in-Chief, International Journal Fatigue and Fracture of Engineering Materials and Structures, 1977-2001; Head, Department of Mechanical Engineering, 1982-87, Dean, Faculty of Engineering, 1987-89, University of Sheffield; Consultant to several industrial organisations in the UK, USA

and Australia. Publications: Over 250 publications. Honours: Founder's Gold Medallist, Royal Geographical Society; Doctor of Engineering, Honoris Causa, University of Waterloo, Canada; Doctor of Engineering, Honoris Causa, University of Sheffield, England; Mungo Park Silver Medallist, Royal Scottish Geographical Society; Bernard Hall Prize, Institution of Mechanical Engineers; Back Award, Royal Geographical Society; ESIS Award of Merit, 2004; Wohler Medal, The European Structural Integrity Society; Mechanics and Materials Award, Japanese Society of Mechanical Engineers; American Society for Testing and Materials Award for Achievements in Fatigue Research; Honorary Visiting Professor, Tsinghau University, Beijing, China; Visitor to Japan Award, The Japanese Society for the Promotion of Science. Memberships: Fellow, Trinity College, Cambridge, 1971-; Fellow, Royal Academy of Engineering; Foreign Member, Russian Academy of Sciences; Foreign Member, Ukrainian National Academy of Sciences; Fellow, Imperial College, London; Fellow, University of Central Lancashire; Fellow, City & Guilds Institute; Foreign Member, Belarussian Academy of Engineering & Technology; Honorary President, International Conference on the Mechanical Behaviour of Materials; Honorary Fellowship, International Congress on Fracture; Honorary Fellow, International Fatigue Congress; Honorary Fellow, DVM; Eminent Speaker, Institution of Engineers, Australia. Address: 40 Stumperlowe Park Road, Fulwood, Sheffield, S10 3QP, England. E-mail: k.j.miller@sheffield.ac.uk

**MILLER Patrick Figgis,** b. 22 March 1933, Calcutta, India. College Principal; Priest. m. (1) Margaret Bruzelius, 1 son, 1 daughter, (2) Susanne Oberholzer. Education: St John's School, Leatherhead, Surrey, 1945-51; Christ's College, Cambridge, 1953-56; Cuddesdon College, Oxford, 1956-58; PhD, Surrey University, 1995. Appointments: National Service, 1951-53; Parish Priest, St Cuthbert's Church, Portsmouth, 1958-61; Parish Priest, SCM Chaplain, Great St Mary's, Cambridge, 1961-63; Head of Religious Studies, Manchester Grammar School, 1963-69; Canon Residentiary, Southwark Cathedral, 1969-72; Director of Social Studies, Queen Mary's College, Basingstoke, 1972-79; Principal, CEO, Esher College, Surrey, 1980-98; Project Director, Learning for Living, a Templeton Foundation Project, 2000-04. Publications: Creeds and Controversies, 1969; New Movements in RE, 1975; Book reviews. Honours: Korean and UN medals. Memberships: London Flotilla; HMS President, Retired Officers' Association; British Legion. Address: 9 Fairfax Ave, Epsom, Surrey KT17 2QN, England. E-mail: patrickmiller@ewell3.freeserve.co.uk

**MILLER Stanley Lloyd,** b. 7 March 1930, Oakland, California, USA. Chemist. Education: Graduated, University of California, 1951; PhD, University of Chicago, 1954. Appointments: Postdoctoral Jewett Fellow, California Institute of Technology, 1954-55; Instructor in Biochemistry, Assistant Professor, Department of Biochemistry, Columbia College of Physicians and Surgeons, 1955-60; Assistant Professor, Associate Professor, Professor of Chemistry, University of California at San Diego, 1960-. Publications: The Origins of Life on the Earth, with L E Orgel, 1974. Memberships: NAS; Honorary Councillor, Higher Council of Scientific Research of Spain; Oparin Medal, International Society for the Study of Origin of Life. Address: University of California, San Diego, Department of Chemistry, La Jolla, CA 92093-0317, USA.

**MILLETT, Baron of St Marylebone in the City of Westminster, Peter Julian Millett,** b. 23 June 1932, London, England. Judge. m. Ann Mireille Harris, 2 sons. Education: Double First in Classics and Law, Trinity Hall, Cambridge. Appointments: Junior Counsel, Chancery Bar, 1958-73;

Standing Counsel to Department of Trade and Industry, 1967-73; Queen's Counsel, 1973-86; Member Insolvency Law Review Committee, 1976-82; High Court Judge, Chancery Division, 1986-94, Lord Justice of Appeal, 1994-98; Lord of Appeal in Ordinary, 1998-2004; Non-Permanent Judge, Court of Final Appeal, 2000-; Editor-in-Chief, Encyclopaedia of Forms and Precedents, 1990-. Publications: Various in legal journals. Honours: Knighted, 1986; Privy Counsellor, 1992; Honorary Fellow, Trinity Hall, Cambridge, 1992; Baron Millett of St Marylebone, 1998; Honorary LLD, London University, 2000. Memberships: Bencher Lincoln's Inn, 1980 (Treasurer, 2004); Home House. Address: 18 Portman Close, London W1H 9BR, England. E-mail: lord.millett@btinternet.com

**MILLINGTON Barry (John)**, b. 1 November 1951, Essex, England. Music Journalist; Writer. Education: BA, Cambridge University, 1974. Appointments: Music Critic, Times, 1977-2001; Reviews Editor, BBC Music Magazine; Artistic Director, Hampstead and Highgate Festival. Publications: Wagner, 1984, revised edition, 1998; Selected Letters of Richard Wagner (translator and editor with S Spencer), 1987; The Wagner Compendium: A Guide to Wagner's Life and Music (editor), 1992; Wagner in Performance (editor with S Spencer), 1992; Wagner's Ring of the Nibelung: A Companion (editor with S Spencer), 1993. Contributions to: Articles on Wagner to New Grove Dictionary of Opera, 1992, New Grove Dictionary of Music and Musicians, 2nd edition, 2001; Newspapers and magazines. Membership: Critics' Circle. Address: 50 Denman Drive South, London NW11 6RH, England.

**MILLIS Susan Mary (Lemon)**, b. 14 November 1953, Tidworth, Hampshire, England. Artist; Conservator; Expert in Pyrographic Techniques. m. Gareth Hughes Millis, 1 son, 1 daughter. Education: BA (1st class honours), Conservation and Restoration, De Montfort University, Lincoln, 1999-2002. Appointments: Professional Artist, 1977-; Voluntary work at The Victoria & Albert Museum, 2001; Smith Herbarium Conservator, National Museums, Liverpool, 2002-03. Publications: Article, A Burning Art, 1989; Pyrography: A Guide, 2004. Memberships: The Society of Women Artists; Society of Equestrian Artists; Artist Member, Miniature Art Society of Florida; Associate Member, Royal Society of Miniature Painters, Sculptors and Gravers; Fellow, Royal Society for the Encouragement of Arts, Manufactures & Commerce; Institute for Conservation. Address: 26 Doglands Farm, Newton by Toft, Market Rasen, Lincolnshire LN8 3NG, England. E-mail: susan@millis5080.fsnet.co.uk

**MILLOT Jean-Louis**, b. 21 August 1947, Noisy-le-Sec, France. Medical Advisor. Widower. Education: MD, Faculty of Medicine, Lyon, 1973; Maitrise Biomathematics and Statistics, Faculty of Medicine, Kremlin-Bicêtre, France, 1985-. Appointments: Private Practitioner, France, 1976-80; Medical Advisor, EDF Gaz de France, Annecy, France, 1980-. Publications: La place du lithium dans le traitement de l'hyperthyroïdie, 1977; Les accidents de sport chez les salariés d'EDF Gaz de France des régions Rhône-Alpes et Bourgogne-Fréquence et Gravité, 2000; Reduced efficiency of influenza vaccine in prevention of influenza-like illness in working adults: a 7-month prespective survey in EDF Gaz de France employees in Rhône-Alpes 1996-97, 2002. Address: EDF Gaz de France Distribution, 5 bd Decouz, BP 2334, 74011 Annecy Cedex, France. E-mail: jean-louis.millot@edfgdf.fr

**MILLS Hayley Catherine Rose Vivien**, b. 18 April 1946, London, England. Actress. m. Roy Boulting, 1971, divorced 1977, 2 sons. Education: Elmhurst Ballet School; 1st Alpine Vidamanette. Creative Works: Films include: Tiger Bay, 1959; Pollyanna, 1960; The Parent Trap, 1961; Whistle Down the Wind, 1961; Summer Magic, 1962; In Search of the Castaways, 1963; The Chalk Garden, 1964; The Moonspinners, 1965; The Truth About Spring, 1965; Sky West & Crooked, 1966; The Trouble with Angels, 1966; The Family Way, 1966; Pretty Polly, 1967; Twisted Nerve, 1968; Take a Girl Like You, 1970; Forbush and the Penguins, 1971; Endless Night, 1972; Deadly Strangers, 1975; The Diamond Hunters, 1975; What Changed Charley Farthing?, 1975; The Kingfisher Caper, 1975; Appointment with Death, 1987; After Midnight, 1992; TV appearances include: The Flame Trees of Thika, 1981; Parent Trap II, 1986; Good Morning Miss Bliss; Murder She Wrote; Back Home; Tales of the Unexpected; Walk of Life, 1990; Parent Trap III, IV, Amazing Stories; Numerous stage appearances. Publication: My God, 1988. Honours include: Silver Bear Award, Berlin Film Festival, 1958; British Academy Award; Special Oscar, USA; Golden Globe Award. Address: c/o Chatto & Linnit, Prince of Wales Theatre, Coventry Street, London W1V 7FE, England.

**MILLS Ian (Sir)**, b. 19 November 1935, Hampshire, England. Chartered Accountant. m. Elizabeth Dunstan, 1 son, 1 daughter. Education: Taunton's Grammar School, Southampton, 1946-54; Beal, Young & Booth, Chartered Accountants, Southampton, 1954-60. Appointments: Financial Consultant, World Bank team, Pakistan, 1962; Chief Accountant, University of Ibadan, Nigeria, 1965-68; Manager, Price Waterhouse, London, 1960-65, 1968-70; Partner, then Senior Partner, Price Waterhouse, London, 1973-92, (i/c Management Consultancy Services (MCS), Newcastle-upon-Tyne & Scotland, 1970-73; MCS, Africa, 1973-83; Central Government Services, 1983-85; Business Development, Europe, 1988-92); Director of Finance, NHS Excessive, 1985-88; Chair, Lambeth, Southwark & Lewisham Health Authority, 1991-96; Chair, North Thames Region of NHS, 1996-98; Chair, London Region of NHS, 1998-2001; Appointments Commissioner, London Region of NHS, 2001-03. Publications: Numerous articles on management, information systems and financial planning and control in professional journals, 1965-88; Numerous pamphlets and brochures on heritage issues, 1984-; Rebirth of a Building: the story in pictures of a 16-year programme of renovation, 2000; Craftsmen of St Margaret: illustrations of the work of 12 Victorian architects and craftsmen, forthcoming. Honours: Knighted, 2001; Fellow, Royal Society of Arts, 1994-; Fellow, Institute of Health Service Management, 1985-; Fellow, Chartered Institute of Management Consultants, 1963-; Fellow, Institute of Chartered Accountants, 1960-. Memberships: Chair, Independent Remuneration Panel, London Borough of Lewisham, 2001; Chair, Blackheath Historic Buildings Trust, 2003-. Address: 60 Belmont Hill, London SE13 5DN, England. E-mail: ianmills@mysector.co.uk

**MILNER Arthur David**, b. 16 July 1943, Leeds, England. Professor of Cognitive Neuroscience. Education: BA, 1965, MA, 1970, University of Oxford, England; Dip Psych, London, 1966; PhD, Experimental Psychology, University of London, 1971. Appointments: Research Worker, Institute of Psychology, London, 1966-70; Lecturer and Senior Lecturer in Psychology, 1970-85, Reader in Neuropsychology, 1985-90, Head Department of Psychology, 1983-88, 1994-97, Professor of Neuropsychology, 1990-2000, Dean, Faculty of Science, 1992-94, Honorary Professor of Neuropsychology, 2000-, University of St Andrews, Scotland; Professor of Cognitive Neuroscience, University of Durham, 2000-, Academic Director of Applied Psychology, 2000; Honorary Research Fellow, North Durham Health Care Trust, 2002-. Publications: Co-author and/or editor or co-editor of 6 books; Author and co-author of over 100 chapters in books and articles in refereed journals; Numerous invited lectures and workshops. Honours: Fellow, Royal Society of Edinburgh, 1992; Leverhulme Trust Research Fellow, 1998-2000; FC Donders Lecturer, Max-Planck-Institut, Nijmegen, 1999; Member, Scientific Council, Helmholtz Instituut, Netherlands, 2002-. Memberships: Experimental Psychology Society; International Neuropsychological Symposium; International Association of Attention and Performance; Royal Society of Edinburgh; European Brain and Behaviour Society. Address: Wolfson Research Institute, University of Durham, Queen's Campus, Stockton-on-Tees TS 17 6BH, England. E-mail: a.d.milner@durham.ac.uk

MIŁOSZ Czesław, b. 30 June 1911, Szetejnie, Lithuania. (US citizen, 1970). Poet; Novelist; Critic; Essayist; Translator; Professor of Slavic Languages and Literatures Emeritus. m. (1) Janina Dlusta, 1943, deceased 1986, (2) Carol Thigpen, 1992, deceased 2002. Education: M Juris, University of Wilno, 1934. Appointments: Programmer, Polish National Radio, Warsaw, 1934-39; Diplomatic Service, Polish Ministry of Foreign Affairs, 1945-50; Visiting Lecturer, 1960-61, Professor of Slavic Languages and Literatures, 1961-78, Professor Emeritus, 1978-, University of California at Berkeley. Publications: Poetry: Poems, 1940; Poems, 1969; Selected Poems, 1973, revised edition, 1981; Selected Poems, 1976; The Bells in Winter, 1978; The Separate Notebooks, 1984; Collected Poems, 1990; Provinces: Poems 1987-1991, 1991; Facing the River: New Poems, 1995; Roadside Dog, 1998. Novels: The Seizure of Power, 1955; The Issa Valley, 1981. Non-Fiction: The Captive Mind (essays), 1953; Native Realm: A Search for Self-Definition (essays), 1968; The History of Polish Literature, 1969, revised edition, 1983; Emperor of the Earth: Modes of Eccentric Vision, 1977; Nobel Lecture, 1981; Visions From San Francisco Bay, 1982; The Witness of Poetry (lectures), 1983; The Land of Ulro, 1984; The Rising of the Sun, 1985; Unattainable Earth, 1986; Beginning With My Streets: Essays and Recollections, 1992; Striving Towards Being (correspondence), 1997; Collected Works, 1999; It, 2000; Poetic Treatise with Author's Commentary, 2001; The Second Space, 2002; Orpheus and Euridice, 2002. Editor and Translator: Postwar Polish Poetry: An Anthology, 1965, revised edition, 1983. Honours: Prix Littéraire Européen, Les Guildes du Livre, Geneva, 1953; Marian Kister Literary Award, 1967; Guggenheim Fellowship, 1976; Neustadt International Literary Prize, 1978; Nobel Prize for Literature, 1980; National Medal of Arts, 1990; Order of the White Eagle, Poland, 1994; Order of Gedyminas, Lithuania, 1997; Several honorary doctorates. Memberships: American Academy and Institute of Arts and Letters; American Academy of Arts and Sciences; American Association for the Advancement of Slavic Studies; Polish Institute of Letters and Sciences in America. Address: c/o Department of Slavic Languages and Literatures, University of California at Berkeley, Berkeley, CA 94720, USA.

MILSOM Gerald Martin William, b. 28 August 1930, Halifax, Yorkshire, England. Hotelier and Restaurateur. 2 sons, 1 daughter. Education: Epsom College. Appointments: Lieutenant, Army Catering Corps, 1949-52; Chairman, Milsom Hotels Ltd, 1952-. Honours: OBE; Honorary Doctor, Anglia Polytechnic University; Master Innholder (MI); Fellow, HCIMA; Fellow, BHA. Memberships: Past Master and Member of the Court, Worshipful Company of Distillers; Chevalier de Tastevin; Member, Order Coteaux de Champagne. Address: Le Talboth, Dedham, Essex CO7 6HP, England.

MIN Byung-Woo, b. 26 December 1959, South Korea. Associate Professor of Orthopaedic Surgery. m. Hee-Jung Lee, 2 sons. Education: MD, 1980-84 MS, 1992-95, PhD, 1989, Kyungpook National University, South Korea; Korean Board of Medical Doctor; Korean Board of Orthopaedic Surgery.

Appointments: Internship, 1984-85, Residency, Department of Orthopaedic Surgery, 1986-89 Keimyung University, Dongsan Medical Centre; Military Service, Lieutenant Commander, Medical Corps, Yechon Air Base, 1989; Instructor, 1992-94, Assistant Professor, 1995-98, Associate Professor of Orthopaedic Surgery, 1999-, Keimyung University School of Medicine; Chief, Orthopaedic Department, Military Hospital of Yechon, 1989-91; Staff, Orthopaedic Department, Keimyung University Dongsan Medical Centre, 1992-.Publications: More than 90 articles in medical journals including: Journal of the Korean Orthopaedic Society; Journal of Arthoplasty; CORR. Honour: Fellowship, USC Center for Arthritis & Joint Implant Surgery, University of Southern California, Joint Implant Surgery, 1996-98. Memberships: Korean Orthopaedic Association; Korean Hip Society; Korean Traumatology Association; Western Pacific Orthopaedic Association; SICOT; Editorial Board, Journal of the Korean Orthopaedic Association; Editorial Board, Journal of Korean Hip Society. Address: Department of Orthopaedic Surgery, Keimyung University, Dongsan Medical Centre, 194 Dongsan-dong, Joongu, Daegu 700-712, South Korea.

MINGHELLA Anthony, b. 6 January 1954, Isle of Wight, England. Director; Playwright. m. Carolyn Choa, 1 son, 1 daughter. Education: St John's College; University of Hull. Appointments: Drama Lecturer, University of Hull. Creative Works: TV include: Inspector Morse, 1st series, screenplay; Films directed include: Truly Madly Deeply; Mr Wonderful; The English Patient, 1997; The Talented Mr Ripley, 2000. Honours include: Hon DLitt, University of Hull, 1997; First Honorary Freeman, Isle of Wight, 1997.Publications: Whale Music, 1983; Made in Bangkok, 1986; Jim Henson's Storyteller, 1988; Interior-Room, Exterior-City, 1989; Plays: One, 1992; Driven to Distraction: A Case for Inspector Morse, 1994; Two, 1997; The English Patient, screenplay, 1997. Website: www.bfi.org.uk

MINGORANCE RODRIGUEZ Maria del Carmen, b. 14 March 1960, Santa Cruz de Tenerife, Canary Islands. Spain. Professor. m. Alfonso Hernandez Padron, 2 daughters. Education: Degree in Biological Science, Zoology, Universidad de la Laguna, 1982; Diploma of Advanced Studies, 2004. Appointments: Professor, 1984-, Director, 1998-, Head of Studies, 1987-98, Marine Fisheries Institute, Santa Cruz de Tenerife. Publications: More than 35 articles in scientific journals and papers and posters presented at conference include most recently: Surface Swarms of Thysanopoda Monacantha on the East Coast of Tenerife, 2004; La Tragedia del Erika: Accidente y Consecuencias, 2004; Aplicacion de las Nuevas Tecnologias con un Grupo de Alumnos de Ciclo Formativo de Grado Medio, 2005; 3 book chapters. Honour: Diploma of Expertise, American Biographical Institute. Membership: Socia de la Asociacion Hispana de Documentalistas en Internet. Address: Pasaje de San Pedro, no 4-Edificio Veracruz C, 1° Derecha (B° Toscal), 38001 Santa Cruz de Tenerife, Canary Islands, Spain. E-mail: mminrod@gobiernodecanarias.org

MINNELLI Liza, b. 12 March 1946, USA. Singer; Actress. m. (1) Peter Allen, 1967, (2) Jack Haley Jr, 1974, (3) Mark Gero, 1979, divorced 1992, (4) David Gest, 2002, divorced. Creative Works: Films: Charlie Bubbles, 1968; The Sterile Cuckoo, 1969; Tell Me That You Love Me; Junie Moon, 1971; Cabaret, played Sally Bowles, 1972; Lucky Lady, 1976; A Matter of Time, 1976; New York, New York, 1977; Arthur, 1981; Rent-a-Cop, 1988; Arthur 2: On the Rocks, 1988; Sam Found Out, 1988; Stepping Out, 1991; Parallel Lives, 1994; TV specials: Liza; Liza With a Z, 1972; Goldie and Liza Together, 1980; Baryshnikov on Broadway, 1980; A Time to Live, 1985; My Favourite Broadway: The Leading Ladies, 1999; Theatre: The Best Foot Forward, 1963; Flora, the Red Menace, 1965; Chicago, 1975;

The Act, 1977-78; Liza at the Winter Garden, 1973; The Rink, 1984; Victor-Victoria, 1997; Recordings: Liza with a Z; Liza Minnelli: The Singer; Liza Minnelli: Live at the Winter Garden; Tropical Nights; The Act; Liza Minnelli: Live at Carnegie Hall; The Rink; Liza Minnelli at Carnegie Hall; Results, 1989; Maybe This Time, 1996; Minelli on Minelli, 2000. Honours include: Academy Award, Best Actress; Hollywood Foreign Press Golden Globe Award; British Academy Award; David di Donatello Award. Address: Angel Records, 810 7th Avenue, Floor 4, New York, NY 10019, USA.

**MINOGUE Kylie (Ann),** b. 28 May 1968, Melbourne, Victoria, Australia. Singer; Actress. Appointments: Actress, Australian TV dramas: Skyways, 1980; The Sullivans, 1981; The Henderson Kids, 1984-85; Neighbours, 1986-88; Film Appearances: The Delinquents, 1989; Streetfighter, 1994; Biodome, 1995; Sample People, 1998; Cut, 1999; Moulin Rouge, 2001; As Singer, biggest selling single of decade in Australia, Locomotion, 1987; Highest UK chart entry for female artist, Locomotion, 1988; Highest debut album chart entry, Australia, UK, Kylie, 1988; First ever artist with 4 Top 3 singles from an album; First female artist with first 5 singles to receive Silver discs; Performances worldwide. Creative Works: Albums: Kylie, 1988; Enjoy Yourself, 1989; Rhythm of Love, 1990; Let's Get To It, 1991; Kylie - Greatest Hits, 1992; Kylie Minogue, 1994; Kylie Minogue, 1997-98; Light Years, 2000; Fever, 2001; Body Language, 2004. Singles: Locomotion, 1987; I Should Be So Lucky, 1988; Je Ne Sais Pas Pourquoi, 1988; Especially For You, 1988; Never Too Late, 1989; Confide In Me, 1994; Put Yourself in My Place, 1995; Where Is The Feeling, 1995; Where The Wild Roses Grow, 1995; Some Kind of Bliss, 1997; Did it Again; Breathe, 1998; GBI (German Bold Italic), 1998; Spinning Around, 2000; On A Night Like This, 2000; Please Stay, 2000; Can't Get You Out of My Head, 2001; In Your Eyes, 2002; Love at First Sight, 2002; Red Blooded Woman, 2004. Honours: Numerous Platinum, Gold and Silver Discs; 6 Logies (Australia); 6 Music Week Awards (UK); 3 Smash Hits Awards (UK); 3 Australian Record Industry Association Awards; 3 Japanese Music Awards; Irish Record Industry Award; Canadian Record Industry Award; World Music Award; Australian Variety Club Award; MO Award (Australian Showbusiness); Amplex Golden Reel Award; Diamond Award, (Belgium); Woman of the Decade (UK); MTV, Australian Female Artist of the Year, 1998; Pop Release of the Year, Light Years, ARIA; Best International Solo Female Artist and Best International Album, 2002. Address: c/o Terry Blamey Management, P O Box 13196, London SW6 4WF, England.

**MIR Mohammad Afzal,** b. 6 May 1936, Kashmir. Physician. m. Lynda, 1 son, 2 daughters. Education: MBBS, 1962; DCH, 1965; MRCP, 1972; FRCP, 1985. Appointments: Senior House Officer, Alder Hey Children's Hospital, Liverpool; Medical Registrar, North Ormesby Hospital, Middlesborough; Resident Medical Officer, Queen Mary's Hospital, Sidcup; Medical Registrar, Manchester Royal Infirmary; Senior Medical Registrar, Manchester Royal Infirmary; Senior Lecturer and Consultant Physician, University of Wales, College of Medicine. Publications: Numerous papers in acute leukaemia, metabolic disorders, sodium transport and obesity; 10 books on basic clinical skills, PLAB and MRCP; 38 video tapes on basic clinical skills. Honours: Young Research Investigator's Award, British Cardiac Society, 1976; British Heart Foundation, European Travelling Fellowship, 1977. Memberships: British Cardiac Society; British Diabetic Association; British Hypertension Society; Medical Research Society; British Hyperlipidaemia Association. Address: Iscoed, Old Mill Road, Lisvane, Cardiff CF4 5XB, Wales. E-mail: afzal.mir@virgin.net

**MIROSHNYCHENKO Dmitri,** b. 7 April 1976, Simferopol, Crimea, USSR. Academic. Education: BSc, 1st Class Honours, Mathematics and Mechanics, 1993-97, MSc, Distinction, Mechanics, 1997-98, PhD, Physics and Mathematics, 1998-2000, Kiev University; MPhil, Mathematics, Loughborough University, 2000-2001. Appointments: Postdoctoral Research Associate, Department of Chemistry, University of Durham, 2001-2003; Postdoctoral Research Assistant, Department of Mathematics, University of Glasgow (studying Liquid Crystal Pre-patterning in Cell Division), 2003-2005. Publications: Articles in journals including: Kiev University Bulletin (x2); Dinamicheskie Sistemy; Journal of Mathematical Sciences; Physical Review E (x2); Journal of Mechanics and Physics of Solids; Molecular Crystals and Liquid Crystals; Journal of Fluid Mechanics. Honours: Silver Medal, Physics and Mathematics School of Simferopol, 1993; George Soros Student Grant, International Soros Support Educational Programme in Ukraine, 1994-95; Scholarship Awarded by the Cabinet of Ministers, Crimea, Ukraine, 1992-93; A number of prizes at Mathematics and Physics School Olympiads at the Crimean and Ukranian levels, 1991-93; Chess Under 16 Champion of Crimea, Ukraine, 1992. Memberships: Elected Fellow, Mathematics Division of Junior Academy of Sciences, Crimea, Ukraine, 1992; Junior Member, Isaac Newton Institute for Mathematical Sciences, Cambridge, 2000-; Bearsden Chess Club, Glasgow, Scotland, 2003-; International Liquid Crystal Society, 2004-. Address: Department of Mathematics, University of Glasgow, 15 University Gardens, Glasgow G12 8QW, Scotland. E-mail: dm@maths.gla.ac.uk

**MIRREN Helen,** b. 26 July 1945, London, England. Actress. m. Taylor Hackford, 1997. Creative Works: Roles include: The Faith Healer, Royal Court, 1981; Antony & Cleopatra, 1983, 1998; The Roaring Girl, RSC, Barbican, 1983; Extremities, 1984; Madame Bovary, 1987; Two Way Mirror, 1989; Sex Please, We're Italian, Young Vic, 1991; The Writing Game, New Haven, Connecticut, 1993; The Gift of the Gorgon, NY, 1994; A Month in the Country, 1994; Orpheus Descending, 2001; Dance of Death, New York, 2001; Films include: Age of Consent, 1969; Savage Messiah, O Lucky Man!, 1973; Caligula, 1977; The Long Good Friday, Excalibur, 1981; Cal, 1984; 2010, 1985; Heavenly Pursuits, 1986; The Mosquito Coast, 1987; Pascali's Island, 1988; When the Whales Came, 1988; Bethune: The Making of a Hero, 1989; The Cook, the Thief, his Wife and her Lover, 1989; The Comfort of Strangers, 1989; Where Angels Fear to Tread, 1990; The Hawk, The Prince of Jutland, 1991; The Madness of King George, 1995; Some Mother's Son, 1996; Killing Mrs Tingle, 1998; The Pledge, 2000; No Such Thing, 2001; Greenfingery, 2001; Gosford Park, 2001; TV include: Miss Julie; The Apple Cart; The Little Minister; As You Like It; Mrs Reinhardt; Soft Targets, 1982; Blue Remembered Hills; Coming Through; Cause Celebre; Red King, White Knight; Prime Suspect, 1991; Prime Suspect II, 1992; Prime Suspect III, 1993; Prime Suspect: Scent of Darkness, 1996; Painted Lady, 1997; The Passion of Ayn Rand, 1998. Honours include: BAFTA Award, 1991; Emmy Award, 1996; Screen Actor's Guild Award for Best Supporting Actress, 2001. Address: c/o Ken McReddie Ltd, 91 Regent Street, London W1R 7TB, England.

**MIRYALA Muralidhar,** b. 26 November 1963, Karvena, India. Scientist. m. Radha Rani, 1 son, 1 daughter. Education: BSc, 1984, MSc, 1987, BEd, 1998, PhD, 1992, Osmania University, India. Appointments: Post doctoral Research fellow, 1993-94, Part-time Lecturer in Physics, 1993-95, Young Scientist, 1995, Department of Physics, Osmania University, India; Visiting Scientist, 1996-97, Chief Research Scientists, 1998-, SRL-ISTEC, Japan. Publications: 170 Research Publications; 8 articles in edited books; 25 invited talks; Patentee in field (6); Reviewer for number of superconductivity journals; Evaluated PhD theses, others. Honours: Young Scientist Award, 1995; Director's Award SRL-ISTEC, 1998; PASREG Award for Excellence, 1999; Best Presentation Award, IWCCII, 2003; Director's Award, SRL-ISTEC, 2003; Listed in several biographical publications. Memberships: Minerals, Metals and Materials Society (TMS) USA; Founder member of ASSSI, India. Address: Superconductivity Research Laboratory SRL-ISTEC, 3-35-2 Iiokashinden, Morioka, Iwate 020-0852, Japan. E-mail: miryala1@istec.or.jp

**MIRZA Qamar, b.** 19 March 1927, Ferozepur, India. Librarian. Education: BA, 1947; Certificate in LSc, 1951; Registration Exam Library Association, London, 1953-54; Masters degree in LSc, 1968-69. Appointments: Assistant Librarian, Northumberland County Library, 1954-62; Deputy Librarian, University of Peshawar, Pakistan, Teacher at Department of LSc, 1962-68, 1971-74; Graduate Librarian, Western Institute of Technology, Australia, 1975-76; Librarian, Umm Al-Qura University, Makkah, Saudi Arabia, 1977-98. Publications: Perspective of Past, Present and Future of L-Services in the University of Peshawar, in Pakistan Librarianship, 1963-64; Islamic Subject Headings in LC Subject Headings, 1992. Honours: Beta Phi Mu. Memberships: Life Member, Pakistan Library Association. Address: 17/46 Wahdat Colony, Disposal Road, Gujranwala, Pakistan.

**MIRZOEFF Edward, b.** 11 April 1936, London, England. Television Producer. m. Judith Topper, 3 sons. Education: MA (Oxon), Open Scholarship in Modern History, The Queen's College, Oxford. Appointments: Market Researcher, Social Surveys (Gallup Poll) Ltd, 1959-58; Public Relations Executive, Duncan McLeish and Associates, 1960-61; Assistant Editor, Shoppers' Guide, 1961-63; BBC Television, 1963-2000; Executive Producer, Documentaries, 1983-2000; Freelance TV Producer, Director, 2000-; Director and Producer of many film documentaries including: Metro-land, 1973; A Passion for Churches, 1974; The Queen's Realm: A Prospect of England, 1977; The Front Garden, 1977; The Ritz, 1981; The Englishwoman and the Horse, 1981; Elizabeth R, 1992; Torvill and Dean: Facing the Music, 1994; Treasures in Trust, 1995; John Betjeman - The Last Laugh, 2001; Series Editor: Bird's-Eye View, 1969-71; Year of the French, 1982-83; In at the Deep End, 1983-84; Just Another Day, 1983-85; Editor, 40 Minutes, 1985-89; Executive Producer of many documentary series including: The House, 1992, Full Circle with Michael Palin, 1997; The 50 Years War: Israel and the Arabs, 1998; Children's Hospital, 1998-99; Queen Elizabeth The Queen Mother, 2002; The Lords'Tale, 2003; A Very English Village, 2005. Honours: CVO, 1993; CBE, 1997; BAFTA Award for Best Documentary, 1981; BAFTA Awards for Best Factual Series, 1985, 1989; BFI TV Award, 1988; Samuelson Award, Birmingham Festival, 1988; British Video Award, 1993; BAFTA Alan Clarke Award for Outstanding Creative Contribution to Television, 1995; International EMMY, 1996; Royal Philharmonic Society Music Award, 1996; British Press Guild Award for Best Documentary Series, 1996. Memberships: Vice-Chairman TV, 1991-95, Chairman, 1995-97, Trustee, 1999-, British Academy of Film and Television Arts (BAFTA); Trustee, 1999-, Vice Chair, 2000-02, Chair, 2002-06, Grierson Trust; Board Member, Director's and Producer's Rights Society, 1999-; Salisbury Cathedral Council, 2002-. Address: 9 Westmoreland Road, London, SW13 9RZ, England.

**MISETIC Bosiljko, b.** 10 September 1945, Grabovnik, Croatia. Attorney-at-Law. Divorced, 1 son, 1 daughter. Education: Law School, University of Zagreb. Appointments: Attorney-at-Law, 1980; Political Career, 1990; Minister of Justice

and Administration of the Republic of Croatia, 1991-92; Ambassador and special representative delegated by President of Republic of Croatia for relations with the Federation of Bosnia and Herzegovina, 1994; Vice Premier for Domestic Politics, 1995; Member of Parliament and Chairman of Justice Board, 1996-2000; Attorney-at-Law, 2000-. Publications: Numerous articles published in daily newspapers. Honours: Numerous honours and awards from President of Republic of Croatia for Outstanding Achievements and Contributions. Memberships: Bar Council (Association); Political Party (HDZ); Many other different foundations. Address: Petrinjska 31, 10000 Zagreb, Croatia. E-mail: oavjetnikbmisetic@zghtnet.hr

**MISHIMA Hiroyuki, b.** 8 January 1952, Koriyama, Fukushima, Japan. Professor. m. Amiko Tanaka, 1 son, 2 daughters. Education: BSc, Tokai University, Tokyo, 1974; PhD, Nihon University, Tokyo, 1986. Appointments: Teacher, High School, Shimizu, Japan, 1974-75; Prefectural High School, Gyoda, Japan, 1975-77; Assistant, 1977-78, Instructor, 1978-95; Assistant Professor, 1995-2003, Nihon University School of Dentistry at Matsudo; Visiting Assistant Professor, University of South Carolina, 1991-92; Professor, Kochi Gakuen College, 2003-. Publications: (in journals and proceedings) Tooth Enamel IV, 1984; Tooth Enamel V, 1989; Mechanisms and Phylogeny of Mineralization in Biological Systems, 1992; Biomineralization 93, 1994; Dental Morphology 98, 1999; Neanderthal Burials Excavations of the Dederiyeh Caves, Afrin, Syria, 2002; Biomineralization (BIOM 2001). Memberships: International Association for Dental Research; Japanese Association of Anatomists; Japanese Association of Oral Biology; Microscopy Society of America; New York Academy of Sciences; Society of Vertebrate Palaeontology. Address: Kochi Gakuen College, 292-26 Asahitenjinmachi, Kochi, 780-0955 Japan.

**MISHRA Arun Kumar, b.** 20 July 1945, Motihari, India. Eye Surgeon. m. Kalawati, 2 sons, 1 daughter. Education: MBBS; DO; DORCP & SI; FRCSI; FRCOphth; FEBO. Appointments: Senior Lecturer, Queen's Medical Centre, Nottingham NHS Trust and Honorary University Lecturer; Consultant Ophthalmic Surgeon, Rotherham DGH, South Yorkshire, Dewsbury National Health Trust, West Yorkshire. Publications: Entropion Correction by Fascia Lata Sling, British Journal of Ophthalmology. Honours: Former Justice of the Peace, West Yorkshire; Director of Public Instruction Merit Award. Memberships: British Medical Association; Royal College of Ophthalmology; European Society of Cataract and Refractive Surgeons; Life Member: West Yorkshire Magistrates Association, All India Ophthalmic Society, BIDA; Bihar Ophthalmic Society. Address: 214 Woodlands Road, Batley, West Yorkshire WF17 0QS, England. E-mail: amishra@yahoo.com

**MISHRA Raghu Nath (HEH Mt Hon Lord Sir), b.** 7 April 1947, Amwa Digar, UP, India. Philosopher. m. Miss Abha, 30 January 1973, 2 sons. Education: BSc Electrical Engineering, 1st Class Honours I, 1969; MTech, 1971; PhD, 1975; MA, Engineering Education, 1985; DCTech, 1988; DSc, DCS Business Management, DD, LLD, DIL magna cum laude, 1992; DSc, Telematics and Communication, DSc Cybernetics, DCE, 1993; MUniv, 1994. Appointments: Senior Research Assistant, Electrical Engineering, Indian Institute of Technology (IIT), Kanpur, 1973-75; Assistant Professor, Electrical Engineering, 1975-87, University Professor, 1977-, Associate Professor, Electrical Engineering (Computer Science), 1987-97, Professor, Computer Engineering, 1997-, Head, Computer and Information Technology, 2002-2004, Head Computer Engineering Department, 2005-, College of Technology, GBUAT, PantNagar. Publications include: Application of Memory Gradient Methods to Economic Load Dispatching

Problem, 1972; Univariate or One-Dimensional Search Techniques for Power Flow Optimisation Problems, 1973; Estimation, Detection and Identification Methods in Power System Studies, 1975; International System of Units, 1978; Memory Gradient Method via Bridge Balance Convergence, 1979; Assumptions in Theory of Ballistic Galvanometer, Hybrid Algorithm for Constrained Minimisation, Convergence of Nonlinear Algorithms, 1980. Honours: National Scholarship, Board of High School and Intermediate Education, Uttar Pradesh, 1963-69; Trainee as Student Engineer, Hindustan Steel Limited (now, Steel Authority of India Limited), summer vacations, 1967, 1968; Lala Balak Ramji Kohinoor Memorial Gold Medal; The RBG Modi Medal; NVR Nageswar Iyer Prize, BH University, 1969; Institute Scholarship, IIT Kanpur, 1969-73; International Register of Profiles Certificate, 1982, Medal, 1991; International Biographical Roll of Honour, 1983, 1984, 1985; CSIR registration as Instrumentation/Technologist, 1983; Men of Achievement, certificate of merit, 1984, Medal, 1991; First Five Hundred medal, plaque, 1985; Commemorative Medal of Honour, Pewter, 1986, Gold, 1993, Research Fellow Gilt Silver Coins, 1994, 1995; IBC Paperweight and Letter Opener, 1987; IBC Certificate of Appreciation, Member of Merit for Life, Confederation of Chivalry, 1988; International Leaders in Achievement, medal, International Who's Who of Intellectuals, Dictionary of International Biography, medals, 1990; Who's Who in Australasia and Far East, medals, Count of San Ciriaco, 1991; KLUO, KtT, 1992; Baron of Bohemian Crown (Royal Order), General Knighthood (NOBLE, JUST and CHILVALROUS) Medal for merit for life, CSC, CU, MIDI pins, Coptic Cross, Capt AM, 1993; KHG, 1994; Bharat Gaurav, 1998; Eminent Personalities of India, proclamation, 1999; Expert, Union Public Service Commission in Electrical Engineering for Civil Services (preliminary) and Engineering Services Examinations, 1994-2001; Dictionary of International Biography 30th Anniversary Edition Certificate, 2002; Uttaranchal Public Service Commission Specialist in Computer Science for Civil Services (preliminary) examinations, 2002, syllabus Revision, 2004; Invitation for founding membership of the Academic Council of the London Diplomatic Council of the London Diplomatic Academy, Best Citizens of India Award, 2002; Expert, Union Public Service Commission in Electronics and Telecommunication Engineering for Engineering Services Examinations, 2003-04; Nominations for Lifetime of Scientific Achievement Award, Dictionary of International Biography 31st Edition, Order of Excellence, Man of the Year for Strength of Character and Achievement, World Medal of Honor for Strong Character and personal dignity, International Peace Prize for Positive Peace and Justice, 2003; Top 100 Scientist, 2005; The World Book of Knowledge; Member of the Board of Studies of Vikram University, Ujjain, 2004. Listed in numerous international biographical publications including 1000 Great Scientists, 2000 Outstanding Scientists of the 20th Century, 2000 Outstanding Scientists of the 21st Century; The Cambridge Blue Book; Great Minds of the 21st Century; Who's Who in Engineering. Memberships: Deputy, International States Parliament for Safety and Peace, 1992-2002; Lifelong Member, World Academy Association of the Masters of the Universe; Lifelong Fellow, Australian Institute for Co-ordinated Research; ABI; ABI Research Association; International Advisor, Life Member, Indian Society for Technical Education; IIT Kanpur Alumni Association; Indian Alumni of the World University; Academy of Ethical Science; Indian Citizens Association; International Cultural Correspondence Institute; MIDI. Address: College of Technology Computer Department, GBP University of Agriculture and Technology, PantNagar, Uttaranchal-263 145, India.

**MITCHEL Joyce,** b. 14 February 1949, Dallas, Texas, USA. Investment Company President. 1 son. Education: Associate Degree, Business College, 1969; Extensive real estate courses and related continuing education; Investment and Finance; Diploma of Fellowship, American Biographical Institute, 2005. Appointments: President, Pay Dirt Investments; Honorary State Chairman, Congressional Business Commission, 2003; Chairman of the Board, Religious Organization, 2005. Honours: National Leadership Award, 2001; Oregon Businessman of the Year, 2002; Gold Medal Recipient, Business Advisory Council, 2003; Woman of the Year, 2005; International Peace Prize, 2005; The Key Award, 2005; Outstanding Female Executive Award, 2005; Listed in Who's Who publications and biographical dictionaries. Memberships: Dun & Bradstreet; Active Church Member; Porsche Club of America. Address: 3972 Carman Drive, Lake Oswego, Oregon 97035-2472, USA. E-mail: pdi@ifriendly.com

**MITCHELL Adrian, (Volcano Jones, Apeman Mudgeon, Gerald Stimpson),** b. 24 October 1932, London, England. Poet; Writer; Dramatist, Lyricist. 2 sons, 3 daughters. Education: Christ Church, Oxford, 1953-55. Appointments: Granada Fellow, University of Lancaster, 1968-70; Fellow, Wesleyan University, 1972; Resident Writer, Sherman Theatre, 1974-75; Unicorn Theatre for Children, 1982-83; Judith Wilson Fellow, University of Cambridge, 1980-81; Fellow in Drama, Nanyang University, Singapore, 1995; Dylan Thomas Fellow, UK Festival of Literature, Swansea, 1995. Publications: Novels: If You See Me Coming; The Bodyguard; Plays: Plays with Songs, 1995; Out Loud; Heart on the Left; Blue Coffee; All Shook Up; For children: Robin Hood and Maid Marian; Nobody Rides the Unicorn; Maudie and the Green Children; also adaptions of numerous foreign plays; Television: Man Friday, 1972; Daft as a Brush, 1975; Glad Day, 1978; Pieces of Piece, 1992; Poetry: Paradise Lost and Paradise Regained; 5 programmes of Brecht's poetry, 1998; Radio plays: Animals Can't Laugh; White Suit Blues; Anna on Anna; Plays: Tyger Tyger Two; Man Friday; Mind Your Head; A Seventh Man, White Suit Blues; Uppendown Money; Hoagy; In the Unlikely Event, Satie Day/Night; The Pied Piper; The Snow Queen; Jemima Puddleduck; The Siege; The Heroes; The Lion, The Witch and the Wardrobe; The Mammoth Sails Tonight; Who Killed Dylan Thomas; Films: Man Friday, 1975; The Tragedy of King Real, 1982; Music: The Ledge, opera libretto, 1961; Houdini, opera libretto, 1977; Start Again, oratorio, 1998. Contributions to: Newspapers, magazines, and television. Honours: Eric Gregory Award; PEN Translation Prize; Tokyo Festival Television Film Award; Honarary Doctorate, North London University, 1997. Memberships: Royal Society of Literature; Society of Authors; Writers Guild. Address: c/o Peters, Fraser and Dunlop Group Ltd, Drury House, 34-43 Russell Street, London WC2B 5HA, England.

**MITCHELL David John,** b. 24 January 1924, London, England. Writer. m. 1955, 1 son. Education: Bradfield College, Berkshire; MA, Honours, Modern History, Trinity College, Oxford, 1947. Appointment: Staff Writer, Picture Post, 1947-52. Publications: Women on the Warpath, 1966; The Fighting Pankhursts, 1967; 1919 Red Mirage, 1970; Pirates, 1976; Queen Christabel, 1977; The Jesuits: A History, 1980; The Spanish Civil War, 1982; Travellers in Spain, 1990; The Spanish Attraction, editor, 2001. Contributions to: Newspapers and magazines. Membership: Society of Authors. Address: 20 Mountacre Close, Sydenham Hill, London SE26 6SX, England.

**MITCHELL Enid G D,** b. 7 February 1931, London, England. Sculptor; Ceramist. 1 son, 2 daughters. Education: Intermediate Arts and Crafts, Ealing School of Art, 1947-50; Diploma of

Retail Furnishing, College of Distributive Trades, 1951-52; Study of Sculpture with Robert Thomas, Ealing School of Art, 1964-68; Visual Arts Diploma, London University (Extra Mural), 1967-71; Diploma in Art and Design with Merit, Ceramics, Chelsea School of Art, 1976-79. Career: Independent Sculptor and Ceramist; Exhibitions: Regular exhibitor, Society of Portrait Sculptors, 1967-78; Exhibitor, Royal Society of British Sculptors, 1974-; RBS Exhibitions include: Scone Palace, Scotland; Taliesin Centre, Swansea University; Work in permanent collection, Leamington Spa Museum; Work in private collections in England, Eire, Israel, Holland, Australia, Brunei (ceramics), USA and Wales. Honour: Gilchrist Prize, London University, 1971. Memberships: Society of Portrait Sculptors, 1967-78; Associate, 1974, Fellow, 1983, Royal Society of British Sculptors. Address: Medmenham 2, 32 Stanier Street, Swindon, Wiltshire SN1 5QX, England.

**MITCHELL George John,** b. 20 August 1933, Waterville, USA. Politician; Lawyer. 1 daughter. Appointments: Called to Bar, 1960; Trial Attorney, US Department of Justice, Washington, 1960-62; Executive Assistant to Senator Edmund Muskie, 1962-65; Partner, Jensen & Baird, Portland, 1965-77; US Attorney for Maine, 1977-79; US District Judge, 1979-80; US Senator from Maine, 1980-85; Majority Leader, US Senate, 1988-95; Special Advisor to President Clinton for Economic Initiatives in Ireland, 1995; Chancellor designate, Queen's University, Belfast, 1999-; Adviser, Thames Water, 1999-. Memberships: Chair, Maine Democratic Committee, 1966-68; Member, National Committee, Maine, 1968-77; Chair, Committee on Northern Ireland, 1995. Honours: Hon LLD, Queens University, Belfast, 1997; Honorary KBE, 1999; Shared, Honphouet-Boigny Peace Prize, 1999; Presidential Medal of Freedom, 1999; Tipperary International Peace Award, 2000. Address: c/o Verner, Liipfert, Bernhard, 901 15th Street, NW, #700, Washington, DC 20005, USA.

**MITCHELL J J,** b. 2 January 1965, Hampshire, England. Musician; Graphic Artist. m. Runi Delgado, divorced. Education: BA, Creative Arts, Plymouth Brethren Community College, 1986; Postgraduate Course, Graphic Art and Production, New York. Appointments: Typesetter, Leftfield Publishing and Printing, New Orleans, Louisiana, 1988-89; Bass Guitarist, Melonheads, 1989; Singer, Bass Guitarist, Plankton, 1990-91; Graphic Designer, Metro Publications, 1991-94; Chief Designer, X-L Art Publications, 1995-98; Director, Chief Designer, Plasma Comix. Memberships: Musicians Union; Equity; Star Trek Fan Club. Address: 4357 Sunscape Lane, Raleigh, NC 27613, USA.

**MITCHELL Jonathan Stuart,** b. 29 January 1947, Purley, Surrey, England. Barrister. m. Ute, 1 son, 1 daughter. Education: BA, Economics, Philosophy, English, MA, Trinity College, Dublin. Eire. Appointments: Treasurer, European Criminal Bar Association; Chair, Dulwich and West Norwood Liberal Democrats Constituency Party; Committee Member, Liberal Democrats Lawyers Association. Publications: Submission to the EU Network on Independent Experts in Fundamental Rights on their 2002 Report, 2003; Legal Aid in Europe, Council of Europe The Hague Conference on Access to Justice, 2004; Numerous articles on legal and political subjects in The Legal Democrat; Responses to the EU Commission and the UK Government on legislation. Memberships: Liberal Democrat Party; European Criminal Bar Association; Thames Rowing Club. Address: 35 Pickwick Road, London SE21 7JN, England. E-mail: mitchbrief@hotmail.com

**MITCHELL Joni (Roberta Joan Anderson),** b. 7 November 1943, Fort Macleod, Alberta, Canada. Singer; Songwriter. m. (1) Chuck Mitchell, 1965, (2) Larry Klein, 1982, 1 daughter by Brad McGrath. Education: Alberta College. Creative Works: Albums include: Song to a Seagull; Clouds; Ladies of the Canyon, 1970; Blue, 1971; For the Roses; Court and Spark, 1974; Miles of Aisles; The Hissing of Summer Lawns, 1975; Hejira, 1976; Don Juan's Reckless Daughter; Mingus, 1979; Shadows and Light, 1980; Wild Things Run Fast, 1982; Dog Eat Dog, 1985; Chalk Mark in a Rain Storm, 1988; Night Ride Home, 1991; Turbulent Indigo, 1994; Hits, 1996; Misses, 1996; Taming the tiger, 1998; Both Sides Now, 2000; Travelog, 2002; Songs include: Both Sides Now; Michael From Mountains; Urge for Going; Circle Game; TV includes: Joni Mitchell: Intimate and Interactive. Publication: Joni Mitchell: The Complete Poems and Lyrics. Honours include: Jazz Album of the Year, Rock-Blues Album of the Year, Downbeat Magazine, 1979; Juno Award, 1981; Century Award, Billboard Magazine, 1996; Polar Music Prize, Sweden, 1996; Governor General's Performing Arts Award, 1996; National Academy of Songwriters Lifetime Achievement Award, 1996; Rock and Roll Hall of Fame, 1997; National Academy of Popular Music-Songwriters Hall of Fame, 1997. Address: c/o S L Feldman & Associates, 1505 West 2nd Avenue, Suite 200, Vancouver, BC V6H 3Y4, Canada.

**MITCHELL Julian,** b. 1 May 1935, Epping, Essex, England. Author; Dramatist. Education: BA, Wadham College, Oxford, 1958. Appointment: Midshipman, Royal Naval Volunteer Reserve, 1953-55. Publications: Imaginary Toys, 1961; A Disturbing Influence, 1962; As Far as You Can Go, 1963; The White Father, 1964; A Heritage and Its History (play), 1965; A Family and a Fortune (play), 1966; A Circle of Friends, 1966; The Undiscovered Country, 1968; Jennie Lady Randolph Churchill: A Portrait with Letters (with Peregrine Churchill), 1974; Half-Life (play), 1977; Another Country (play), 1982, (film), 1984; Francis (play), 1983; After Aida (play), 1985; Falling Over England (play), 1994; August (adaptation of Uncle Vanya) (play), 1994, (film), 1995; Wilde (film script), 1997. Contributions to: Welsh History Review; Monmouthshire Antiquary. Address: 47 Draycott Place, London SW3 3DB, England.

**MITCHELL Lucille Anne,** b. 19 October 1928, Dayton Corners, Illinois, USA. Retired Elementary School Educator. m. Donald L Mitchell, 1 son, 3 daughters. Education: BS, Education, Augustana College, 1966; MS, Education, Western Illinois University, 1972; Education Specialist, 1974. Appointments: Teacher, Carbon Cliff, Elementary School, Illinois, 1962-65; Moline Board of Education, Illinois, 1967-92; Board Representative and Member, Illinois Network for School Development, Springfield, Illinois, 1973; Member, Textbook Selection Committee, Moline Board of Education, 1967-84; Teacher of Gifted, Moline Board of Education, 1985-87; Counsellor to Pastor, Community of Christ, 2001-2002; Elder in priesthood. Publications: Contributor of poetry: Footprints Through the Forest, 2000; Best Poems and Poets of 2001, 2001; Best Poems and Poets of 2004, 2004; International Who's Who in Poetry, 2004. Honours: Master Teacher, State of Illinois, 1984; Listed in Who's Who publications and biographical dictionaries. Memberships: Various committees, Illinois Education Association; Various committees, Moline Education Association; Programme Chairman, 1978-79, Recording Secretary, 1980-81, Delta Kappa Gamma. Address: 3214 55th Street Ct, Moline, IL 61265-5740, USA.

**MITCHELL (Raymond) Bruce,** b. 8 January 1920, Lismore, New South Wales, Australia. Academic. m. Mollie Miller. Education: MA (Melb), 1952; MA (Oxon), 1955; DPhil (Oxon), 1959; DLitt (Oxon), 1986. Appointments: Teacher, Education Department of Victoria, 1936-40; Commissioned

Service, Australian Imperial Force, 1941-46; Manager, Firm of Typesetters, Stereotypers and Lithographers, Melbourne, 1946-47; Student, Tutor, Lecturer, University of Melbourne, 1947-52; Australian National University Scholarship, Oxford University, 1952-54; Fellow and Tutor, St Edmund Hall, 1955-87; University Lecturer, Oxford University, 1955-87; Visiting Professor or Lecturer in 17 countries including Brown University, 1966-67. Publications include: A Guide to Old English, 1965, 2nd edition, 1968, reprinted 1971, 1975, 1978, 1981; A Guide to Old English Revised with Texts and Glossary 3rd edition (with Fred C Robinson), 1982, reprinted 1983, 1984; Old English Syntax, 2 volumes, 1985, reprinted 1985, 1985, 1997-98; A Guide to Old English Revised with Prose and Verse Texts and Glossary, 4th edition (with Fred C Robinson), 1986, reprinted 1987, 1988; On Old English: Selected papers, 1988; A Critical Bibliography of Old English Syntax to the End of 1984, 1990; A Guide to Old English, 5th edition (with Fred C Robinson), 1992, reprinted 1992 (twice), 1995, 1995, 1996 (twice), 1997 (twice), 1998, 1999, 2000; An Invitation to Old English and Anglo Saxon England, 1995, reprinted 1996 (twice), 1997 (twice), 1998, 2000; Beowulf : An Edition (with Fred C Robinson), 1998, reprinted 2000; Graham St Edmund Hall Oxford 1941-1999 (with Reggie Alton), 2000; Beowulf Repunctuated (with Susan Irvine), 2000; A Guide to Old English, 6th edition (with Fred C Robinson), 2001; over 80 articles in academic journals. Honour: Phil Dr honoris causa, Turku, 1986. Memberships: Finnish Academy of Arts and Sciences, 1989; Honorary Member, International Society of Anglo Saxonists, 1989; Honorary Fellow, Australian Academy of Humanities, 2002. Address: 39 Blenheim Drive, Oxford OX2 8DJ, England.

**MITCHELL Ross Galbraith,** b. 18 November 1920. Physician. m. June Phylis Butcher, 1 son, 3 daughters. Education: MB, CHB, 1944, MD, 1954, University of Edinburgh; Fellow, Royal College of Physicians of Edinburgh, 1956; Fellow, Royal College of Paediatrics and Child Health, 1996. Appointments: Lecturer, Child Health, University of St Andrews, 1952-55; Consultant Paediatrician, Dundee Royal Infirmary, 1955-63; Professor of Child Health, University of Aberdeen, 1963-72; Professor of Child Health, 1973-85, Dean of Medicine, 1978-81, University of Dundee. Publication: 7 Textbooks; 16 Chapters and 100 articles in Scientific Journals. Honours: Burma Star, 1945; Rockefeller Research Fellowship, Mayo Clinic, USA, 1952-53. Memberships: Association of Physicians of Great Britain and Ireland; British Medical Association. Address: Craigard, Abertay Gardens, Broughty Ferry, Dundee, DD5 2RR, Scotland.

**MITCHELL Valerie Joy,** b. 2 March 1941, São Paulo, Brazil. Educator (Charitable). m. (1) Henri Pierre Eschauzier, 1962, dissolved, 1970, 2 sons, (2) Graham Rangeley Mitchell, 1972, 1 daughter. Education: BA, McGill University, Montreal, Canada, 1958-62. Appointments: PA to Assistant Dean of Arts and Science, McGill University, Montreal, Canada, 1962-64; Public Relations Consultant, Mayer Lismann Opera Workshop for 3 years, Lecturer in Opera at luncheon clubs throughout UK, listed Foyles speaker, 1970-80; Assistant, Education Department, 1980-83, Director, Branches and Cultural Affairs, 1983-94, Deputy Director-General, 1989-94, English-Speaking Union; Director-General of the English-Speaking Union of the Commonwealth, 1994-; Secretary-General of the International Council for the English-Speaking Union, 1994-. Honours: Fellow, Royal Society of Arts, 1987; 2000 Certificate, European Union of Women, British Section for Women of Achievement Awards, 2000; OBE, 2001. Memberships: Education Committee of the Royal Academy of Dance, 1998-; International Committee, Shakespeare's Globe Theatre, 2000-; Pilgrims Society, 2001. Address: The English-Speaking Union,

Dartmouth House, 37 Charles Street, London W1J 5ED, England. E-mail: international@esu.org

**MITCHELL William Joseph,** b. 4 January 1936, Bristol, England. Catholic Priest. Education: MA, Jurisprudence, Corpus Christi College, Oxford, 1956; Seminaire S. Sulpice, Paris France, 1956-61; Ordained Priest, 1961; License in Canon Law, Pontifical Gregorian University, Rome, 1963. Appointments: Curate, Pro-Cathedral, Bristol, 1963-64; Secretary to the Bishop of Clifton, 1964-75; Parish Priest, St Bernadette, Bristol, 1975-78; Rector, Pontifical Beda College, Rome, 1978-87; Parish Priest, St John's, Bath, 1988-90; Parish Priest St Anthony's, Bristol, 1990-96; Parish Priest, St Mary-on-the-Quay, Bristol, 1996-97; Dean of Clifton Cathedral, 1997-2000; Parish Priest, St Michael's Tetbury, Gloucestershire, 2001-; Judicial Vicar and Episcopal Vicar for Matrimonial Matters, 2002-. Honours: Prelate of Honour (Monsignor), Pope John Paul I, 1978-; Canon of Cathedral Chapter, 1987-, Vicar General, 1987-2001, Diocese of Clifton; Judicial Vicar and Episcopal Vicar for Matrimonial Matters, 2002-. Membership: Chaplain to the Knights of the Holy Sepulchre, 2003. Address: St Michael's Presbytery, 31 Silver Street, Tetbury, Gloucestershire, GL8 8DH, England. E-mail: billmitchell@tetbury31.freeserve.co.uk

**MITKOVA Tatyana,** b. 13 September 1957, Moscow, Russia. Journalist. m. Vsevolod Solovyev, 1 son. Education: Degree in Journalism, Moscow Lomonosov State University. Appointments: Editor, Sunday TV programme; Anchor, 120 Minutes, -1991; Co-author, numerous documentaries, 1991; Freelance Journalist, ARD TV Co, Germany, 1991; Returned to all-Russian TV; Anchor, Segodnya (Today) evening news programme, NTV Independent Television Co, 1993-2004; Editor-in-Chief, 2001-, Acting Deputy General Director of Information Service, 2004-, NTV. Honours: Best News Programme Anchor, 1997. Memberships: Russian Television Academy, 2001-. Address: c/o NTV, ul Akademika Koroleva 12, R-127427, Moscow.

**MITROVIĆ Ljubiša,** b. 16 February 1943, Mokra, Bela Palanka, Serbia. Sociologist; Professor. m. Svetlana, 2 daughters. Education: Graduate, Sociology, Faculty of Philosophy, University of Belgrade, 1970; Master's Degree, Political Sciences, University of Belgrade, 1975; PhD, Sociological Sciences (General Sociology), University of Niš, 1977. Appointments include: Assistant Teacher, Faculty of Philosophy, 1971, Dean of the Faculty of Philosophy, 1983-87, Full-time Professor, Faculty of Philosophy, 1987, Vice-Rector, 1987-89, University of Niš; Professor, by invitation, World University Association "Plato", Greece, 2001; Director, Centre for Balkan Studies, 2002-. Publications: 27 books; Over 300 papers and articles; Most important books: Sociology and Contemporary Times, 1984; Sociology of Development, 1992; Contemporary Society – Strategies of Development and Their Actors, 1996; Contemporary Balkans within the Context of the Sociology of Social Change, 2003; General Sociology, Theory and Modern Society, 2003. Honours: October Prize of the City of Niš, 1987; University Rewards, 1985, 1987; Medal for Deserving Citizens of the Socialist Federative Republic of Yugoslavia, 1988. Memberships: Sociological Association of Serbia; Association for Political Sciences; Centre for Balkan Studies. Address: Oblačića Rada 24/4, 18000 Niš, Serbia and Montenegro.

**MIYAKE Issey,** b. 22 April 1939, Tokyo, Japan. Fashion Designer. Education: Tama Art University; Tokyo and La Chambre Syndicale de la Couture Parisienne, Paris. Appointments: Assistant Designer to Guy Laroche, Paris, 1966-68, to Hubert de Givenchy, Paris, 1968-69; Designer, Geoffrey

Beene (ready-to-wear firm), New York, 1969-70; Founder, Miyake Design Studio, Tokyo, 1970; Director, Issey Miyake International, Issey Miyake and Associates, Issey Miyake Europe, Issey Miyake USA, Issey Miyake On Limits, Tokyo; Executive Advisor, Planner, First Japan Culture Conference, Yokohama, 1980. Creative Works: Works exhibited in Paris, Tokyo and MIT, appears in collections of Metro Museum of Art, New York and Victoria and Albert Museum, London. Honours: Japan Fashion Editors Club Awards, 1974, 1976; Mainichi Design Prize, 1977; Pratt Institute Award, New York, 1979; Dr.h.c. Royal College of Art, 1993.

**MIYOSHI Isao,** b. 15 July 1932, Tokushima, Japan. Physician; Educator. m. Shigeko Kagawa, 3 sons. Education: MD, 1957, PhD, 1965, Okayama University, Japan. Appointments: Intern US Army Hospital, Tokyo, 1957-58; Resident Ohio State University, Columbus, 1958-59; Fellow, University of Texas, Houston, 1959-60; Member, Okayama University Hospital, Japan, 1966-81; Associate Professor, Kochi Medical School, Japan, 1981-82; Professor of Medicine, 1982-98; Professor Emeritus, 1998-. Publications: Numerous articles published in Medical Journals, 1961-2002. Honours: Recipient Hideyo Noguchi Prize, 1983; Princess Takamatsu Cancer Prize, 1984; Hammer Prize, 1985; Asahi Prize, 1987; Medal with Purple Ribbon, 1996. Memberships: Japanese Cancer Association; American Association of Cancer Research. Address: Kochi Medical School, Kochi 783-8505, Japan.

**MIZRAHI Isaac,** b. 14 October 1961, Brooklyn, New York, USA. Fashion Designer. Education: Parsons School of Design. Appointments: Apprenticed to Perry Ellis, 1982, full-time post, 1982-84; Worked with Jeffrey Banks, 1984-85, Calvin Klein, 1985-87; Founder, own design firm in partnership with Sarah Hadad Cheney, 1987; First formal show, 1988, First spring collection, 1988; First menswear line launched, 1990, Announced closure of firm, 1998.

**MIZUNO Hirobumi,** b. 28 April 1931, Ureshino, Saga Prefecture, Japan. Professor. Education: BSc, Mathematics, Waseda University, Japan; MSc, 1955, DSc, 1965, Mathematics, University of Tokyo. Appointments: Lecturer, Meiji University, Tokyo, 1959-66; Associate Professor, 1966-70, Professor, 1970-97, University of Electro-Communication; Professor, Meisei University, 1998-2003. Publications: Fundamentals of Information Algebra, 1980; Fundamentals of Information Mathematics, 1996; Articles in professional journals. Memberships: The Mathematical Society of Japan; American Mathematical Society. Address: 3-6-6-105 Iwadokita, Komae-shi, Tokyo 201-0004, Japan.

**MLINARIC-GALINOVIC Gordana,** b. 15 February 1950, Fuzine, Croatia. Microbiologist. m. Mili Galinovic, 1 son, 1 daughter. Education: MD, 1973, MSc, 1978, DSc, 1985, Medical School, University of Zagreb; Specialist of Medical Microbiology, Ministry of Health of Croatia, 1978. Appointments: Assistant to Professor, 1975-2002, Chief, WHO Virus Collaboration Centre, 1988-; Chief Investigator, Ministry of Science, Zagreb, project: Respiratory Syncytial Virus Infections, 1986-; Head, Microbiology Service, Croatian National Institute of Public Health, 2004. Publications: In medical journals. Honours: Fellowship, British Council, Royal Victoria Infirmary, Newcastle upon Tyne, 1985; Fellowship, University of Texas Medical Branch, Galveston, Texas, USA, 1991-92; Listed in several Who's Who and biographical publications. Memberships: European Society of Clinical Virology; Croatian Medical Academy; Croatian Medical Society. Address: Department of Virology, Croatian National

Institute of Public Health, Rockefellerova 12, 10 000 Zagreb, Croatia. E-mail: gordana.galinovic@hzjz.hr

**MO Timothy (Peter),** b. 30 December 1950, Hong Kong. Writer. Education: Convent of the Precious Blood, Hong Kong; Mill Hill School, London; BA, St John's College, Oxford. Publications: The Monkey King, 1978; Sour Sweet, 1982; An Insular Possession, 1986; The Redundancy of Courage, 1991; Brownout on Breadfruit Boulevard, 1995; Renegade or Halo², 1999. Contributions to: Periodicals. Honours: Gibbs Prize, 1971; Geoffrey Faber Memorial Prize, 1979; Hawthornden Prize, 1983; E M Forster Award, American Academy of Arts and Letters, 1992; James Tait Black Memorial Prize, 1999. Address: c/o Chatto & Windus, 20 Vauxhall Bridge Road, London SW1V 2SA, England.

**MOAGĂR-POLADIAN Gabriel,** b. 23 September 1965, Bucharest, Romania. Senior Researcher Physics. Education: MSc, 1985-90, PhD, 1992-99, Faculty of Physics, Bucharest University. Appointments: Research Scientist, SC Optoelectronica SA, work on infrared detectors, 1990-92; Research Scientists, SC Biotechnos, SA work on physical characterization of cells suspensions 3, 1992-94; Senior Researcher, National Institute of Microtechnology, work on optoelectronics, sensors and microsystems, 1994-. Publications: 23 articles and papers published/presented in international journals and conferences. Honours: Invited to join IEEE, American Association for the Advancement of Science, New York Academy of Sciences. Memberships: Romanian Physical Society; European Physical Society, European Optical Society, Optical Society of America. Address: Aleea Fuiorului Nr 6 bloc Y3A sc 1 et 6 ap 27, Sector 3, Bucharest, Romania.

**MOAT John,** b. 11 September 1936, India. Author; Poet. m. 1962, 1 son, 1 daughter. Education: MA, Oxford University, 1960. Publications: 6d per Annum, 1966; Heorot (novel), 1968; A Standard of Verse, 1969; Thunder of Grass, 1970; The Tugen and the Toot (novel), 1973; The Ballad of the Leat, 1974; Bartonwood (juvenile), 1978; Fiesta and the Fox Reviews and His Prophecy, 1979; The Way to Write (with John Fairfax), 1981; Skeleton Key, 1982, complete edition, 1997; Mai's Wedding (novel), 1983; Welcombe Overtunes, 1987; The Missing Moon, 1988; Firewater and the Miraculous Mandarin, 1990; Practice, 1994; The Valley (poems and drawings), 1998; 100 Poems, 1998; Rain (short stories), 2000; Hermes & Magdalen (poems and etchings), 2004; The Moment of Arvon (belles lettres), 2005. Address: Crenham Mill, Hartland, North Devon EX39 6HN, England.

**MOBERLEY Gary Mark,** b. Sydney, New South Wales, Australia. Musician (keyboards); Composer; Writer; Programmer. Musical Education: Grade 6, Australian Conservatory of Music, New South Wales. Career: Left Australia for London, 1971; Musical Director for soul acts with American Promotions Bureau, 1973; Recorded and toured with Tina Charles, 1974-76; Joined John Miles touring GB, Europe, USA and Canada, supporting Elton John, 1976; Joined The Sweet, 1978; Session work in Florida, USA recording with many Spanish artists, 1981; Returned to London and become involved with major recording studios and recording labels as a session musician, 1982; Live work/recorded with: The Sweet; John Miles Band; Terence Trent D'Arby; Prefab Sprout; Wet Wet Wet; The Damned; The Alarm; Hipsway; The The (Infected Album); Jodie Watley; Girlschool; Drum Theatre; Sigue Sigue Sputnik; Little Richard; Haywoode; Nicole; Big Country (remix); Loose Ends; The Associates; Talk Talk; Kiki Dee; Band Of Holy Joy; Dangerous Grounds; Funkadelia; Steel Pulse; Trevor Horn; The JBs; Red Beans and Rice; ABC; Fine

Young Cannibals; The Foundations; Jean Jacques Perrey; Live work with: Bee Gees; Paul Rodgers; Bonnie Tyler; Wilson Pickett; Eddie Floyd; Rufus Thomas; Ben E King; Arthur Conley; Andrew 'Junior Boy' Jones; Cookie McGhee; Texas Blues Summit; Memphis Blues Summit; 34 European tours; 9 American tours; 3 world tours; 5 albums of radio and TV themes used world-wide. Address: 43 High Street, Haddenham, Bucks, HP17 8ET, England. E-mail: gm@musicworld.fsbusiness.co.uk

**MOCKLER Robert J,** b. 23 May 1932, St Louis, Missouri, USA. Professor of Strategic Management. Education: BA, 1954, MBA, 1959, Harvard University; PhD, Columbia University, 1961. Appointments: Joseph F Adams Professor of Management, St John's University. Publications: 55 books and monographs, and over 200 case studies, articles, book chapters and presentations in professional journals. Honours include: Best Application Paper Award, Decision Sciences Institute, 1993; St Vincent de Paul Teacher/Scholar Award, St John's University (highest faculty award), 1995; Best Case Study Award's, Decision Sciences Institute, 1996 and Northeast Business and Economics Association, 2001; Concordia University Case Study Competition Award, 1998, 1999, 2000, 2003; Best Paper Award, Information Resources Management Association, International Conference, 1999; Distinguished Best Paper Award, Association for Small Business and Entrepreneurship, 2002. Memberships: several professional organisations. Address: Department of Management, St John's University, 114 East 90th Street (1B), New York, NY 10128, USA.

**MOCUMBI Pascoal Manuel,** b. 10 April 1941, Maputo, Mozambique. Medical Doctor. m. Adelina Isabel Bernadino Paindane, 3 January 1966, 2 sons, 2 daughters. Education: MD, University of Lausanne, 1973; Diploma, Health Planning, Institut Planification Sanitaire, University of Dakar, 1975. Appointments: Chief Medical Officer, Sofala Province, 1976-80; Minister of Health, 1980-87; Foreign Minister, 1987-94; Prime Minister, 1994-. Publications: Co-author, Manual de Obstetricia Pratica, Intervencoes Obstétricas; Health for All by the Year 2000?, 1996. Honours: National decorations; International decorations, Brazil, Chile. Memberships: Mozambique Medical Association; Mozambique Public Health Association; Mozambique Family Development Association. Address: Praça da Marinha, Maputo, Mozambique. E-mail: dgpm.gov@teledata.mz

**MOFFAT Gwen,** b. 3 July 1924, Brighton, Sussex, England. Author. m. Gordon Moffat, 1948, 1 daughter. Education: Hove County School for Girls, 1935-41. Appointments: Mountain Guide, 1953-73; Broadcaster, journalist and author, 1949-. Publications: Space Below My Feet, 1961; Two Star Red, 1964; On My Home Ground, 1968; Survival Count, 1972; Lady With a Cool Eye, 1973; Deviant Death, 1973; The Corpse Road, 1974; Hard Option, 1975; Miss Pink at the Edge of the World, 1975; Over the Sea to Death, 1976; A Short Time to Live, 1976; Persons Unknown, 1978; Hard Road West, 1981; The Buckskin Girl, 1982; Die Like a Dog, 1982; Last Chance Country, 1983; Grizzly Trail, 1984; Snare, 1987; The Stone Hawk, 1989; The Storm Seekers, 1989; Rage, 1990; The Raptor Zone, 1990; Pit Bull, 1991; Veronica's Sisters, 1992; The Outside Edge, 1993; Cue the Battered Wife, 1994; The Lost Girls, 1998; A Wreath of Dead Moths, 1998; Running Dogs, 1999; Private Sins, 1999; Quicksand, 2001; Retribution, 2002. Contributions to: Newspapers and magazines. Memberships: Crime Writers Association; Pinnacle Club. Agent: c/o Juliet Burton, 2 Clifton Avenue, London W12 9DR, England. E-mail: juliet.burton@virgin.net

**MOH Sangman,** b. 20 February 1963, Republic of Korea. Professor. m. Keumsook Yoon, 2 sons. Education: PhD, Information and Communications University, Republic of Korea, 2002. Appointments: Project Leader, Electronics and Telecommunications Research Institute, Republic of Korea, 1991-2002; Professor, Chosun University, Republic of Korea, 2002-. Publications: Professional papers and articles contributed to professional journals; Overseas and domestic patents in field. Honours: Registered Professional Engineer, Republic of Korea, 1993; Best Paper Award, Institute of Electronics Engineers of Korea, 1995; Ministerial Award, Ministry of Information and Communications, Republic of Korea, 2001; Listed in Who's Who publications and biographical dictionaries. Memberships: Institute of Electrical and Electronics Engineers; Association for Computing Machinery. Address: Department of Internet Engineering, Chosun University, 375 Seoseok-dong, Dong-gu, Gwangju 501-759, Republic of Korea. E-mail: smmoh@chosun.ac.kr

**MOHAN Chander,** b. 8 October 1939, Jehlum, Pakistan. Professor. m Tripta Kumari, 1 son, 1 daughter. Education: BA Honours, Mathematics, 1957, MA, Mathematics, 1960, Panjab University, Chandigarh, India; PhD, Mathematics, Roorkee University, Roorkee, India, 1967. Lecturer, Mathematics, Multanimal Modi College, Modinagar, India, 1961-64; Lecturer, 1964-70, Reader, 1970-85, Professor, 1985-2000, Head, Mathematics Department, 1994-1999, Roorkee University, Roorkee, India; Professor and Dean, Amity School of Computer Science, Noida (UP), India, 2000-02; Professor and Head, Mathematics Department, IILM College of Engineering and Technology, Greater NOIDA, (UP) India 2002-04; Professor, Department of Computer Science, Ambala College of Engineering & Applied Research, Ambala (Haryana), 2004-. Publications: Over 80 research publications in national and international research journals; Book: Optimization Techniques in Systems Analysis and Operations Research. Honours: Khosla Research Award, 1990; Millennium Award of Honour American Biographical Institute; Listed in Who's Who publications. Memberships: International Astronomical Union; Operations Research Society of India; Founder Member Indian Astronomical Society; Founder Member, Executive Committee Member, Indian Society for Industrial and Applied Mathematics. Address: 2821, Iqbal Gunj Road, Ambala Cantt, (Haryana), India. E-mail: chander_mohan2@rediff.mail.com

**MOHSIN Shamimul Hasnain,** b. 4 January 1938, Gorakhpur, India. Professor of Engineering. m. Shirin Mohsin, 1 son, 1 daughter. Education: BSc, Mechanical Engineering, BHU, India, 1958; Dr-Ing, Mechanical Vibrations, Technical University, Dresden, Germany, 1966. Appointments: Lecturer, Aligarh University, India, 1958-63; Doctoral Fellow, Germany, 1963-66; Design Engineer, Germany, 1966-68; Reader, 1968-71, Professor, 1971-98, Dean, 1988-90, Acting Vice-Chancellor, 1990-98 (off and on), Aligarh University; Professor: Tabriz University, Iran, Aden University, Yemen, Tripoli University, Libya; Professor, Dean and Director, SS Institute of Technology and Management, Aligarh, 2000-. Publications: More than 25 papers in Indian and foreign journals; Many papers presented in conferences in countries including India, Germany, Canada, Australia. Honours: Senior Post-doctoral Fellowship, Humboldt Foundation of Germany, 1974; Listed in Who's Who publications and biographical dictionaries. Memberships: Fellow, Institution of Engineers, India; Chairman, Institution of Engineers, India, Aligarh Local Centre, 1998-2000. Address: Mallah-Nagla Road, Dodhpur, Aligarh-202001 (UP), India. E-mail: shm@mohsinvilla.com

**MOHTA Vallabhdas A,** b. 26 April 1933, Akola (MS), India. Senior Advocate Supreme Court. m. Kamla, 3 sons. Education: BA, DAV College, Kanpur; LLB, Law College, Nagpur. Appointments: Judge, Bombay High Court, 1979-94; Chief Justice, Orissa High Court, 1994-95; Elected Member, 1968, 1973, Vice-Chairman, 1974, Bar Council of Maharastra; Founder, President, Radhadevi Goenka Women's College, Akola, 1976; President, Berar General Education Society, which runs four colleges and a school in Akola and Kanjara; Chairman of Court of Inquiry to investigate the causes of accident to Indian Airways aircraft at Aurangabad, 1993; Member of the Committee for Implementing Legal Aid Scheme, Government of India, 1993; President, India International Maheshwari Society, New Delhi, 2001-2005; Delegate, Indo-Soviet Cultural Society Study Tour of the USSR; Study Tour in China. Publications: Author: Books: Arbitration and Conciliation; Trade Marks, Passing Off & Franchising. Honours: Listed in Who's Who publications and biographical dictionaries. Memberships: President, Rotary Club of Akola, 1966-77; Governor's Group Representative for Akola, Amravati, Khamgon, Bhusabal and Jalgaon, 1968-69; Foreign Correspondents Club of South Asia, New Delhi; Supreme Court Bar Association. Address: A/207 "Priyadarshini", 17 IP Exnt. Delhi-110 092, India. E-mail: vamohta@hotmail.com

**MOIR (Alexander) (Thomas) Boyd,** b. 1 August 1939, Bolton, Lancashire, England. Medical Practitioner; Scientist. m. Isobel May Shechan, deceased, 1 son, 2 daughters. Education: MBChB, BSc, PhD, Edinburgh University. Appointments: Rotating Intern, New York City, USA; 1964-65; Scientific Staff, 1965-67, Clinical Scientific Staff, 1968-73, Medical Research Council; Senior Medical Officer, 1972-77, Principal Medical Officer, 1977-85, Director of Chief Scientist Organisation, 1986-96, Scottish Health Department; Currently, Honorary Appointments, Edinburgh and Glasgow Universities; Consultancy and Clinical Services. Publications: Publications on Neuroscience, Pharmacology, Biochemistry, Toxicology, Research Management, Public Health. Honours: FRCP (Edin); FRCP (Glasgow); FRCPath; FFPHM; FIBiol; FIFST; MFOM; MFPM; FRSS. Memberships: UK Royal Colleges of Physicians and their Faculties; Royal College of Pathologists; Institute of Biology; Association of Chemists and Biochemists; Pharmacology Society. Address: 23 Murrayfield Gardens, Edinburgh EG 12 6DG, Scotland. E-mail: boyd_moir@msn.com

**MOK Young Sun,** b. 17 November 1966, Kyungki Do, Korea. Chemical Engineering Educator. m. Heejung Kim, 1 son, 1 daughter. Education: BS, Department of Chemical Engineering, Yonsei University, 1989; MS, 1991, PhD, 1994, Department of Chemical Engineering, Korea Advanced Institute of Science and Technology, Korea. Appointments: Senior Researcher, Research Institute of Industrial Science and Technology, Korea, 1995-2000; Advisory Committee Member, Korea Electric Power Research Institute, Korea, 2000-2001; Assistant Professor, Cheju National University, Korea, 2000-. Publications: Articles in scientific journals include: Nonthermal Plasma – Enhanced Catalytic Removal of Nitrogen Oxides, 2003; Effect of Reaction Temperature on NOx Removal and Formation of By-products in Nonthermal Plasma Process Combined with Selective Catalytic Reduction, 2004. Honours: Bumseok Best Paper Award, Korean Institute of Chemical Engineers, 2002; Excellent Paper Award, Korean Society of Environmental Engineers, 2003; Listed in Who's Who publications and biographical dictionaries. Memberships: Life Member, Korean Institute of Chemical Engineers; Fellow, Korean Society of Environmental Engineers. Address: Department of Chemical Engineering, Cheju National University, Ara-dong, Jeju Do, Jeju 690-756, Korea. E-mail: smokie@cheju.ac.kr

**MOKRÝ Jaroslav,** b. 14 October 1964, Czech Republic. Histologist. m. Michaela Mokra, 1 son. Education: MD, 1990; PhD, 1995; Associate Professor, 1999. Appointment: Head, Department of Histology and Embryology, Charles University, Medical Faculty, Hradec Králové. Honours: Rector's Prize, Charles University, 1987, 1990; Young Histochemist Award, IFSHC, Kyoto, 1996; Eastern European Award, European Tissue Culture Society, Mainz, 1997. Memberships: Czech Anatomical Society; Czech Society for Histochemistry and Cytochemistry; Czech Society of Neuroscience; Czech Medical Chamber; Czechoslovak Biological Society; International Society for Stem Cell Research. Address: Department of Histology and Embryology, Charles University, Simkova 870, 500 38 Hradec Králové, Czech Republic.

**MOLDEN Nigel Charles,** b. 17 August 1948, Oxford, England. Company Director. m. Julia, 3 sons. Education: BSc (Hons), London University, 1970; MSc, Brunel University, 1986; PhD, Fairfax University, 1996. Appointments: General Manager, Warner Bros. Records, 1976-78; International General Manager, WEA Records, 1978-80; Head of International Marketing, Thorn EMI Screen Entertainment, 1980-84; Chairman, Magnum Music Group, 1984-97; Chairman, Magnum America Inc, 1995-97; Chief Executive, Synergie Logistics, 1997-. Publications: Enemies Within, 1993; Research Provides no Scapegoat, 1993; Thinking Positive, 1994; Adrift on the Waves, 1995. Honours: Fellow, Chartered Institute of Marketing, 1988; Freeman of the City of London, 1990; Fellow, Institute of Directors, 1994; Fellow, Royal Society of Arts, 1995; Fellow, British Management Institute, 1995. Address: Ashcombe House, Deanwood Road, Jordans, Buckinghamshire HP9 2UU, England. E-mail: synergielogistics@btconnect.com

**MÖLDER Leevi,** b. 4 July 1933, Tudulinna, Estonia. Professor of Chemical Engineering. m. Maila Vägi, 1961, 2 sons, 1 daughter. Education: MSc, Chemical Engineering, 1957, PhD, 1963, Tallinn Technical University. Appointments: Researcher, 1957-62, Associate Professor, 1962-73, Professor, 1973-85, 1992-2000, Emeritus Professor, 2001-, Tallinn Technical University; Head of Department, Institute of Chemistry, Estonian Academy of Sciences, 1983-97; Vice Chairman, Council Oil Shale, Estonian Academy of Sciences, 1989-99; Chairman, Commission on Liquid Fuels Quality Specification, Ministry of Economics, Tallinn, 1994-97; Consultant, RAS Kiviter Chemical Co, Kohtla-Jarve, Estonia, 1995-98. Publications: Technology of Heavy Chemicals, co-author, 1970; English-Estonian-Russian Dictionary of Chemistry, co-author, 1998; 203 articles in professional journals; 11 inventions. Honours: Mente et manu Medal, Tallinn Technical University, 1983, 1993; Paul Kogerman Medal, Estonian Academy of Sciences, 1987; White Star Order of Merit, 2004; Listed in numerous biographical publications. Memberships: American Society for Testing and Materials; Estonian Chemical Society; Union of Estonian Scientists; Estonian Society for Nature Conservation. Address: Tallinn Technical University, 5 Ehitajate tee, Tallinn 19086, Estonia. E-mail: leevi.molder@ttu.ee

**MOLIN Yury,** b. 3 February 1934, Romodanova Village, USSR. Chemist. m. Galina Jakovleva, 2 daughters. Education: MA, Moscow Institute of Physics and Technology, 1957; Candidate (PhD), 1962, Doctor, 1971, Institute of Chemical Kinetics and Combustion, Novosibirsk. Appointments: Researcher Institute of Chemical Physics, Moscow, 1957-59; Researcher, 1959, Head of Laboratory, 1967, Director, 1971, Head of Laboratory, 1993, Advisor of Russian Academy of Sciences, 2004-, Institute of Chemical Kinetics and Combustion, Novosibirsk; Lecturer, 1966, Professor, 1974-, Novosibirsk State University. Publications: Spin Exchange,

1980; Spin Polarization and Magnetic Effects in Radical Reactions, 1984; Infrared Photochemistry, 1985; 300 articles in scientific journals. Honours: National (Lenin) Prize, 1986; Mendeleev Lecturer, 1992; Fellow of EPR/ESR Society, 1998. Memberships: Corresponding Member, 1974, Full Member, 1981, USSR (Now Russian) Academy of Sciences; Editorial boards of journals. Address: Institute of Chemical Kinetics and Combustion, 3 Institutskaya Str, Novosibirsk 630090, Russia. E-mail: molin@ns.kinetics.nsc.ru

**MOLNÁR Gábor,** b. 17 July 1951, Debrecen, Hungary. Psychiatrist; Neurologist; Researcher. m. Jelena Aseva, 2 sons, 1 daughter. Education: Medical Diploma, Sechenow Medical School, Moscow, Russia, 1975; Specialist in Psychiatry, Debrecen Medical School, 1979; Specialist in Neurology, National Institute of Neurology and Psychiatry, 1982; Psychotherapeutical Education, Debrecen and Budapest, 1980-83. Appointments: Senior Assistant Professor, Debrecen Medical School, 1975-90; Senior Registrar, County Hospital, Debrecen, 1990-94; Consultant for numerous organizations, Debrecen, 1994-98; Psychiatrist-Neurologist, Researcher, Budapest Social Centre, 1998-. Publications: 100 papers and summaries; 7 expert reports. Honours: Award, Hungarian Medical Association, 1995; Award, National Institute of Psychiatry and Neurology, 1996; 2000 Achievement Diploma, 1998; International Man of the Millennium, 1999; Millennium Medal of Honour, 1999; Study Award, Hungarian Academy of Sciences, 2002; Listed in international biographical dictionaries. Memberships: International Society of Psychoneuroendocrinology, 1988; Collegium Internationale Neuro-Psychopharmacologicum, 1990; New York Academy of Sciences, 1994; WPA Section on Women's Mental Health, 1997. Address: Solymárvölgyi ut 78, Budapest H-1037, Hungary.

**MOLNÁR Imre,** b. 22 March 1941, Timár, Hungary. Professor. m. Ildikó Dobai. 1 daughter. Education: MSC, University Agriculture, Debrecen, Hungary, 1963; Specialist MSc, 1966, PhD, 1969, CSc, 1989, University Agriculture, Gödöllö, Hungary. Appointments: Centre Plant and Soil Health of Hajdu-Bihar County, 1964-90; H/D Co, Budapest, 1992; Ujtélet Agricultural Co-op Farm, Hencida, Hungary, 1992-98; University Szeged College Agriculture, Hungary, 1998-. Publications: Changes of the diversity (species cover) of weed communities in maize fields in Eastern Hungary, 1994-95; Weed flora of large and small maize fields in Bihar region of Eastern Hungary, 1994-95; Soil-plant relation as a communication system, No 5, 2000; Pattern of weed communities in wheat and maize fields No 6, 2003. Address: 16/A Postakert utca, 4025 Debrecen, Hungary. E-mail: molnar@mfk.u–szeged.hu

**MOLNÁR Péter Pál,** b. 2 March 1951, Pécs, Hungary. Physician; Pathologist; Neuropathologist. Divorced. Education: BS, 1969; MD, 1975; Board Certification, Pathology, 1979; PhD, Medicine, 1987; Board Certification, Neuropathology, 1989; Dr Sci, Hungarian Academy of Sciences, 1999. Appointments: Postdoctoral Fellow, Pathology, University Medical School, Department of Pathology, Debrecen, Hungary, 1975-79; Full Professor, 1995-; Visiting Fellow, NCI, NIH, Bethesda, Maryland, 1979-82; Visiting Professor, Northwestern University, Chicago, USA, 1992-95, 2000-; Director, Professor Tadashi Hirano Centre, Hungarian-Japanese Electron Microscopic Centre, University Medical School, Debrecen, 1994-. Publications: Numerous articles in professional journals; Several abstracts and book chapters. Honours: University Educational Award, 1975; Arányi Lajos Memorial Note; Outstanding Educator, 1994; Dr Med Habil, 1995; Selected as a member of the American Association for Cancer Research; Honorary Board Member, (for distinguished standing)

Research Board 2000, American Biographical Institute, 2000; Listed in 2000 Outstanding Intellectuals of the 20th Century, International Biographical Centre, Cambridge; Co-ordinator, Hungarian National Paediatric Neuro-Oncology Program, 2001. Memberships include: Hungarian Society of Biophysics; Hungarian Society of Pathology, Board of Directors, 1995; European Society of Clinical Investigation; European Society of Pathology; International Society of Neuropathology, Councillor, Hungarian Section, 1995; Hungarian Society of Biology; Hungarian Society for Microscopy; European Association of Neuro-Oncology, Board of Directors, 1996; International Academy of Pathology, Board of Directors, Hungarian Division, 1996; Society for Ultrastructural Pathology, Alabama, USA; New York Academy of Sciences; Society of Neuro-Oncology, USA; Research Board of Advisors of the American Biographical Institute; American Association for the Advancement of Science; Association for Neuro-Oncology, USA; Society for Neuro-Oncology of Hungary; British Society of Neuropathology; Editorial Board, Journal of Neuro-Oncology; Member, IBRO; The Hungarian Society of Paediatric Oncology. Address: University of Debrecen, Clinical and Health Sciences Centre (DE-OEC), Department of Pathology, Hungarian-Japanese EM Centre (HJEMC), Debrecen, Nagyerdei krt 98, POB 24, H-4012 Hungary. E-mail: molnarp@jaguar.dote.hu

**MOMOSE-SATO Yoko,** b. 2 May 1964, Tokyo, Japan. Senior Assistant Professor. m. Katsushige Sato, 1 son. Education: MD, School of Medicine, 1983-89, PhD, Graduate School, 1989-93, Tokyo Medical and Dental University. Appointments: Assistant Professor, 1993-98, Senior Assistant Professor, School of Medicine, 1998-99, Senior Assistant Professor, Graduate School, 1999-, Tokyo Medical and Dental University. Publications: Articles in scientific medical journals including, Progress in Neurobiology, Journal of Neuroscience. Honour: Research Award, The Physiological Society of Japan, 2000. Membership: The Japan Neuroscience Society. Address: Department of Physiology, Tokyo Medical and Dental University, Graduate School and Faculty of Medicine, 1-5-45, Yushima, Bunkyo-ku, Tokyo 113-8519, Japan. E-mail: yoko.phy2@tmd.ac.jp

**MONREAL ACOSTA Antonio,** b. 16 July 1975, Murcia, Spain. Composer. Education: Degrees on Piano, Composition and Music Theory. Appointments: Series of Compositions and their concerts under the same name of "Pane Lucrando"; Invention of a new system of musical notation; Acroamatical and written·teaching of his own new philosophy of music. Publications: Brachilogus; Propaedeuticon to my "Opus primum et ultimum", On Some Features of my Father Idiolect. Memberships include: EGO. Address: c/Princesa, 8 – 2o DCHA, 30.002 Murcia, Spain.

**MONTAGU OF BEAULIEU Edward John Barrington Douglas-Scott-Montagu, 3rd Baron,** b. 20 October 1926, London, England. Museum Administrator; Author; Elected Peer. m. (1) Elizabeth Belinda, 1959, divorced, 1974, 1 son, 1 daughter, (2) Fiona Herbert, 1974, 1 son. Education: St Peter's Court, Broadstairs; Ridley College, St Catharines, Ontario; New College, Oxford. Appointments: Founder, Montagu Motor Car Museum, 1952, world's first Motor Cycle Museum, 1956, National Motor Museum, Beaulieu, 1972; Founder-Editor, Veteran and Vintage magazine, 1956-79; Chairman, Historic Buildings and Monuments Commission, 1983-92; Free-lance motoring journalist; Hereditary Peer, 1947-99, Elected Peer, 1999-, House of Lords. Publications: The Motoring Montagus, 1959; Lost Causes of Motoring, 1960; Jaguar: A Biography, 1961, revised edition, 1986; The Gordon Bennett Races, 1963; Rolls of Rolls-Royce, 1966; The Gilt and the Gingerbread, 1967; Lost Causes of Motoring: Europe, 2 volumes, 1969, 1971;

More Equal Than Others, 1970; History of the Steam Car, 1971; The Horseless Carriage, 1975; Early Days on the Road, 1976; Behind the Wheel, 1977; Royalty on the Road, 1980; Home James, 1982; The British Motorist, 1987; English Heritage, 1987; The Daimler Century, 1995; Wheels within Wheels, 2000. Memberships: Federation of British Historic Vehicle Clubs, president, 1989-; Federation Internationale des Voitures Anciennces, president, 1980-83; Historic Houses Association, president, 1973-78; Museums Association, president, 1982-84; Union of European Historic Houses, president, 1978-81; Guild of Motoring Writers. Address: Palace House, Beaulieu, Brockenhurst, Hants SO42 7ZN, England.

**MONTAGU-POLLOCK Sir Giles Hampden,** b.19 October 1928, Oslo, Norway. Management Consultant. m. Caroline Veronica Russell, 1 son, 1 daughter. Education: de Havilland Aeronautical Technical School. Appointments: Airspeed ltd, 1949-51; G P Eliot at Lloyd's, 1951-52; de Havilland Engine Co Ltd, 1952-56; Advertising Manager, Bristol Aeroplane Co Ltd, 1956-59; Advertising Manager, Bristol Siddley Engines Ltd, 1959-71; Associate Director, J Walter Thompson Co Ltd, 1961-69; Director: C Vernon & Sons Ltd, 1969-71, Acumen Marketing Group, 1971-74, 119 Pall Mall Ltd, 1972-78; Management Consultant in Marketing, 1974-; Associate: John Stork & Partners, Ltd, 1980-88, Korn/Ferry International, 1988-2002. Memberships: MCIM; MInstD. Address: The White House, 7 Washington Road, London SW13 9BG, England.

**MONTEREE-ZALESKI Elizabeth,** b. 9 April 1942, Warsaw, Poland. Artist; Painter; Gallery Curator. m. Anthony, 1 son. Education: Diploma, Portraiture and Design, Warsaw Academy of Fine Arts, 1964. Appointments: Valuer and Gallery Advisor, National and Mutual Gallery, 1967-72; Gallery Curator, Studio Art Gallery, 1972-84; Freelance Journalist, Art Criticism, for Polish Newspapers, 1972; Gallery Curator, Studio Art Gallery, Olinda, Victoria, Australia, 1984-2004; Gallery Curator, Walter Jona Gallery, Olinda Victoria, Australia, 2004-. Honour: Awarded Diploma of Merit by Committee for 500th Anniversary of Nicholas Copernicus for promoting and exhibiting Polish artists in Australia, 1973. Memberships: AICA International; NVAA, Australia. Address: 1486 Mt Dandenong Tourist Road, Olinda, Vic 3788, Australia.

**MONTGOMERIE Colin,** b. 23 June 1963, Glasgow, Scotland. Golfer. m. Eimear Wilson, 1 son, 2 daughters. Education: Baptist University, Texas, USA. Career: Professional Golfer, 1987-; Member, Walker Cup team, 1985, 1987, Ryder Cup team, 1991, 1993, 1995, 1997, 1999, 2002, 2004, Dunhill Cup Team, 1988, 1991-2000, World Cup Team, 1988, 1991, 1992, 1993, 1997, 1998, 1999; Leader, European Tour Order of Merit, 1993-99; 28 European Tour wins as at end December 2002; Signed contract to play Yonex Clubs from 2004. Honours: Winner: Scottish Stroke Play, 1985; Scottish Amateur Championship, 1987; European Tour Rookie of the Year, 1988; Portuguese Open, 1989; Scandinavian Masters, 1991, 1999, 2001; Heineken Dutch Open, 1993; Volvo Masters, 1993; Spanish Open, 1994; English Open, 1994; German Open, 1994; Volvo German Open, 1995; Trophee Lancome, 1995; Alfred Dunhill Cup, 1995; Dubai Desert Classic, 1996; Murphy's Irish Open, 1996, 1997, 2001; Canon European Masters, Million Dollar Challenge, 1996; World Cup Individual, 1997; Andersen Consulting World Champion, 1997; Compaq European Grand Prix, 1997; King Hassan II Trophy, 1997; PGA Championship, 1998, 1999, 2000; German Masters, 1998; British Masters, 1998; Benson and Hedges International Open, 1999; BMW International Open, 1999; Standard Life Loch Lomond Invitational, 1999; Cisco World Matchplay, 1999; Skins Game, US, 2000; Novotel Perrier Open de France, 2000; Ericsson Australian Masters, 2001;

Volvo Masters Andalucia, 2002; TCL Classic, 2002; Macan Open, 2003; Caltex Masters Singapore, 2004. Member: winning European Ryder Cup team, 1995, 1997, 2002, 2004. Address: c/o IMG, McCormack House, Burlington Lane, London W4 2TH, England.

**MOODY A David,** b. 21 January 1932, New Zealand. University Teacher; Writer. m. Joanna S Moody. Education: BA, 1951, MA, 1952, Canterbury College, University of New Zealand; BA, 1st Class Honours, Oxford University, 1955. Appointments: Assistant Information Officer, UNHCR, Geneva; Lecturer, Senior Lecturer in English, University of Melbourne, 1958-65; Member, Department of English and Related Literature, 1966-99, Emeritus Professor of English and American Literature, 1999-, University of York. Publications: Virginia Woolf, 1963; Shakespeare: The Merchant of Venice, 1964; The Waste Land in Different Voices (editor), 1974; Thomas Stearns Eliot: Poet, 1979, 1994; At the Antipodes: Homage to Paul Valéry, 1982; News Odes: The El Salvador Sequence, 1984; Cambridge Companion to T S Eliot (editor), 1994; Tracing T S Eliot's Spirit: essays on his poetry and thought, 1996. Honours: Shirtcliffe Fellow, University of New Zealand, 1953-55; Nuffield Foundation Travelling Fellow, 1965; British Academy/Leverhulme Visiting Professor, 1988; Honorary member, T S Eliot Society, USA; Fellow, English Association. Memberships: Association of University Teachers; National Poetry Foundation; Member of the Editorial Board: Paideuma: A Journal of Scholarship on British and American Modernist Poetry, 2002-. Address: Church Green House, Old Church Lane, Pateley Bridge, N. Yorks HG3 5LZ, England.

**MOOK Sarah,** b. 29 October 1929, Brooklyn, New York, USA. Chemist. Education: BA, Hunter College, 1952; Graduate Coursework, Columbia University, 1954-57; Coursework, University of Hartford, 1958-59; Language Course, Columbia University, 1962-65. Appointments: Cartographic Aide, US Geological Survey, 1952-54; Research Assistant, Columbia University, 1954-57; Analytical Chemist, Combustion Engineering, 1957-59; Research Scientist, Radiation Applications Inc, 1959-62; Chemist, Marks Polarised Corp, 1962-64; Senior Chemist, NRA Inc, 1964-74; Clinical Technologist, Coney Island Hospital, 1974-84; Supervisor, 1984-89, Principal Chemist, 1989-95, Bellevue Hospital; Retired, 1995-. Publications: Several professional articles. Memberships: American Chemical Society; American Association for the Advancement of Science; American Association for Clinical Chemistry; New York Academy of Science. Address: 2042 East 14th Street, Brooklyn, NY 11229, USA.

**MOOLLAN Cassam Ismael (Sir),** b. 26 February 1927, Port Louis, Mauritius. Legal Consultant; Arbitrator. m. Rassoolbibie Adam Moollan, 1 son, 2 daughters. Education: LLB, London School of Economics and Political Science, University of London, 1947-50; Barrister at Law, Lincoln's Inn, London, 1951. Appointments: Private Practice at Mauritian Bar, 1951-55; District Magistrate, 1955-58; Crown Counsel, 1958-64; Senior Crown Counsel, 1964-66; Solicitor General, 1966-70; Puisne Judge Supreme Court, 1970; Senior Puisne Judge, Supreme Court, 1978; Chief Justice of Mauritius, 1982-88; Acting Governor General on several occasions every year, 1984-88; Retired, 1989. Publications: Editor, Mauritius Law Reports, 1982-88. Honours: Queen's Counsel, 1969; Knight Bachelor, 1982; Chevalier dans l'Ordre National de la Legion d'Honneur, France, 1986. Address: 22 Hitchcock Avenue, Quatre Bornes, Mauritius. E-mail: sircassam@chambers.sirhamid.intnet.mu

**MOON Bong Kyo,** b. 8 September 1968, Seoul, Korea. Researcher. Education: BS, Computer Science, Sogang

University, Korea. 1992; MS, Information and Communications, GIST, Korea, 1998; PhD, Telecommunications, King's College, University of London, 2004. Appointments: Researcher, INEX Technologies, Korea and USA, 1992-95; Researcher, ETRI, Korea, 1998-99; Researcher, Mobile VCE, UK, 2000-2002; Senior Researcher, Samsung Electronics, Korea, 2003-. Publications: Articles in scientific journals: Diffserv Extension for Qos provisioning in IP mobility environment, 2003; Quality of service Mechanism in All-IP Wireless Access Networks, 2004. Honours: Listed in Who's Who publications and biographical dictionaries. Memberships: IEE; IEICE. Address: 2003 Ho, 212 Dong, LG XII 2nd, Shinbong-dong, Yongin, Gyeonggi-do, Korea 449-150. E-mail: bongkyo.moon@ieee.org

**MOORE Brian C J,** b. 10 February 1946. Professor of Auditory Perception. Education: BA, 1968, MA, 1971, Natural Sciences, PhD, Experimental Psychology, 1971, University of Cambridge, England. Appointments: Lecturer, Psychology, University of Reading, England, 1971-73; Fulbright-Hayes Senior Scholar and Visiting Professor, Department of Psychology, Brooklyn College of CUNY, 1973-74; Lecturer, Psychology, University of Reading, 1974-77; Lecturer, Experimental Psychology, University of Cambridge, 1977-89; Fellow, Wolfson College, Cambridge, 1983-; Visiting Researcher, University of California at Berkeley, USA, 1985; Reader in Auditory Perception, 1989-95; Professor of Auditory Perception, 1995-, University of Cambridge. Publications: Books include most recently: An Introduction to the Psychology of Hearing, 4th edition, 1997, 5th edition, 2003; Cochlear Hearing Loss, 1998; New Developments in Hearing and Balance (co-editor), 2002; Over 84 book chapters and papers in conference proceedings; Over 332 publications in refereed journals. Honours include: T S Littler Prize, British Society of Audiology, 1983; Honorary Fellow, British Society of Hearing Aid Audiologists, 1999; Invitation Fellowship, Japanese Society for the Promotion of Science, 2000; Carhart Memorial Lecturer, American Auditory Society, 2003; Silver Medal, Acoustical Society of America, 2003. Memberships: Experimental Psychology Society; Fellow, Acoustical Society of America; Cambridge Philosophical Society; British Society of Audiology; American Speech-Language-Hearing Association; Audio Engineering Society; Acoustical Society of Japan; American Auditory Society; Association for Research in Otolaryngology; American Academy of Audiology; Fellow, Academy of Medical Sciences; Fellow, Royal Society. Address: Department of Experimental Psychology, University of Cambridge, Downing Street, Cambridge CB2 3EB, England. Website: http://hearing.psychol.cam.ac.uk

**MOORE David Moresby,** b. 26 July 1933, Barnard Castle, County Durham, England. Professor Emeritus of Botany. m. Ida Elizabeth Shaw, 2 sons. Education: BSc, Honours, Botany, 1954, PhD, 1957, DSc, 1984, University College and Botany Department, University of Durham. Appointments: Research Officer, Genetics Section, Division of Plant Industry, CSIRO, Canberra, ACT, Australia, 1957-59; Research Fellow, Department of Botany, University of California at Los Angeles, 1959-61; Lecturer, Genetics, Department of Botany, University of Leicester, England, 1961-68; Reader, Plant Taxonomy, 1968-76, Professor of Botany, 1976-94, Reading University, England. Publications: About 100 articles on taxonomy, geography, cytogenetics of plants; 19 books include: Vascular Flora of the Falkland Islands, 1968; Plant Cytogenetics, 1976, Flora Europaea Check-List and Chromosome-Number Index, 1982; Green Planet, 1982; Flora of Tierra del Fuego, 1983; Garden Earth, 1991. Honours: Botany Field Prize, University of Durham, 1954; British Association Studentship, University of Durham; Plaque for services to Magellanic Botany, Instituto de la Patagonia, Punta Arenas, Chile, 1976; Premio Perito Francisco

P Moreno, Sociedad Argentina de Estudios Geográficos, 1985; Enrique Molina Gold Medal, University of Concepción, Chile. Memberships: Botanical Society of the British Isles; Editorial Committees: Webbia, Italy, Polish Botanical Journal, Anales del Instituto de la Patagonia, Flora de Chile. Address: 26 Eric Avenue, Emmer Green, Reading, Berks, RG4 8QX, England.

**MOORE Demi,** b. 11 November 1962, Roswell, New Mexico, USA. Actress. m. Bruce Willis, divorced 2000, 3 daughters. Career: Started in TV, also Model; Films include: Blame it on Rio; St Elmo's Fire; One Crazy Summer; About Last Night...; Wisdom; The Seventh Sign; Ghost; Mortal Thoughts, also co-producer; The Butcher's Wife; A Few Good Men; Indecent Proposal; Disclosure; The Scarlet Letter; Striptease, 1995; The Juror, 1996; GI Jane, 1996; The Hunchback of Notre Dame, 1996; Now and Then, produced & acted, 1996; Deconstructing Harry, 1997; Austin Powers: International Man of Mystery, producer, 1997; Passion of Mind, 2000; Airframe; Charlie's Angels: Full Throttle, 2003; Theatre: The Early Girl; TV: General Hospital, Bedroom. Honour: Theatre World Award for The Early Girl. Address: c/o Creative Artists Agency, 9830 Wilshire Boulevard, Beverly Hills, CA 90212, USA.

**MOORE Julianne,** b. 1961, USA. Actress. Education: Boston University School for Arts. Creative Works: Stage appearances include: Serious Money, 1987; Ice Cream with Hot Fudge, 1990; Uncle Vanya; The Road to Nirvana; Hamlet; The Father; Film appearances include: Tales From the Darkside, 1990; The Hand That Rocks the Cradle, 1992; The Gun in Betty Lou's Handbag, 1992; Body of Evidence, 1993; Benny & Joon, 1993; The Fugitive, 1993; Short Cuts, 1993; Vanya on 42nd Street, 1994; Roommates, 1995; Safe, 1995; Nine Months, 1995; Assassins, 1995; Surviving Picasso, 1996; Jurassic Park: The Lost World, 1997; The Myth of Fingerprints, 1997; Hellcab, 1997; Boogie Nights, 1997; The Big Lebowski, 1998; Eyes Wide Shut, The End of The Affair, 1999; Map of the World, 1999; Magnolia, 1999; Cookie's Fortune, 1999; An Ideal Husband, 1999; Hannibal, 2000; The Shipping News, 2000; Far From Heaven, 2002; The Hours, 2002; TV appearances include: As the World Turns, series; The Edge of Night, series; Money, Power Murder, 1989; Lovecraft, 1991; I'll Take Manhattan; The Last to Go; Cast a Deadly Spell. Honours: Best Actress, Venice Film Festival, 2002. Address: c/o Creative Artists Agency, 9830 Wilshire Boulevard, Beverly Hills, CA 90212, USA.

**MOORE Patrick Alfred Caldwell (Sir),** b. 4 March 1923, England. Astronomer; Broadcaster; Writer. Appointments: Served with RAF during World War II; Officer, Bomber Command, 1940-45; Presenter, TV Series, The Sky at Night, 1957-; Radio Broadcasts; Director, Armagh Planetarium, Northern Ireland, 1965-68; Freelance, 1968-; Composer, Perseus and Andromeda (opera), 1975; Play, Quintet, Chichester, 2002. Publications: Over 170 books and numerous articles include: Moon Flight Atlas, 1969; Space, 1970; The Amateur Astronomer, 1970; Atlas of the Universe, 1970; Guide to the Planets, 1976; Guide to the Moon, 1976; Can You Speak Venusian?, 1977; Guide to the Stars, 1977; Guide to Mars, 1977; Atlas of the Universe, 1980; History of Astronomy, 1983; The Story of the Earth, 1985; Halley's Comet, 1985; Patrick Moore's Armchair Astronomy, 1985; Stargazing, 1985; Exploring the Night Sky with Binoculars, 1986; The A-Z of Astronomy, 1986; Astronomy for the Under Tens, 1987; Astronomers' Stars, 1987; The Planet Uranus, 1988; Space Travel for the Under Tens, 1988; The Planet Neptune, 1989; Mission to the Planets, 1990; The Universe for the Under Tens, 1990; A Passion for Astronomy, 1991; Fireside Astronomy, 1992; Guinness Book of Astronomy, 1995; Passion for Astronomy, 1995; Stars of the Southern Skies, 1995; Teach Yourself Astronomy, 1996;

Eyes on the Universe, 1997; Brilliant Stars, 1998; Patrick Moore on Mars, 1999; Yearbook of Astronomy AD 1000, 1999; Data Book of Astronomy, 2001. Honours include: Officer of the Order of the British Empire, 1968; Numerous Honorary Degrees; Honorary Member, Astronomic-Geodetic Society of the Soviet Union, 1971; Royal Astronomical Society's Jackson-Gwilt Medal, 1977; CBE, 1987; Fellow, Royal Society, 2001; Knight Bachelor, 2001; Minor Planet No 2602 is named in his honour; BAFTA Special Award, 2002. Memberships: Royal Astronomical Society; Member, British Astronomical Association, President, 1982-84; Athenaeum; Life Member, Sussex Cricket Club; Lord's Taverners. Address: Farthings, 39 West Street, Selsey, Sussex PO20 9AD, England.

MOORE Roger, b. 14 October 1927, London, England. Actor. m. (1) Doorn van Steyn, divorced, (2) Dorothy Squires, 1953, divorced, (3) Luisa Mattioli, 2 sons, 1 daughter. Education: Royal Academy of Dramatic Arts. Appointment: Special Ambassador for UNICEF, 1991-. Creative Works: Films include: Crossplot, 1969; The Man With the Golden Gun, 1974; That Lucky Touch, 1975; Save Us From Our Friends, 1975; Shout At The Devil, 1975; Sherlock Holmes in New York, 1976; The Spy Who Loved Me, 1976; The Wild Geese, 1977; Escape to Athens, 1978; Moonraker, 1978; Esther, Ruth and Jennifer, 1979; The Sea Wolves, 1980; Sunday Lovers, 1980; For Your Eyes Only, 1980; Octopussy, 1983; The Naked Face, 1983; A View to a Kill, 1985; Key to Freedom, 1989; Bed and Breakfast, 1989; Bullseye!, 1989; Fire, Ice and Dynamite, 1990; The Quest, 1997; TV appearances include: The Alaskans; The Saint, 1962-69; The Persuaders, 1972-73; The Man Who Wouldn't Die, 1992; The Quest, 1995. Publication: James Bond Diary, 1973.

MOORE Terence, b. 24 December, 1931, London, England. Retired Businessman. m. Tessa Catherine, 2 sons, 1 daughter. Education: BSc, Economics, London; AMP, Harvard, USA. Appointments: Various positions, Shell International, 1948-64; Economics Analyst, Investment Banking, 1964-65; Various positions, 1965-87, Managing Director, Supply and Trading, 1979-87, Chief Executive Officer, Conoco Ltd, 1987-95; Currently, Trustee Energy Institute Pension Fund. Publications: Various technical and business articles. Honour: CBE. Memberships: Fellow, Energy Institute; Associate, Chartered Insurance Institute; Associate, Institute of Chartered Shipbrokers; Friend: Royal Academy of Art, Tate Gallery, Imperial War Museum, National Trust. Address: 67 Merchant Court, 61 Wapping Wall, London EW1 3SJ, England. E-mail: terrymoore@terrymoore.demon.co.uk

MOORE Willis Henry Allphin, b. 14 December 1940, New York, New York, USA. Educator. 2 sons, 1 daughter. Education: BA, Letters, University of Oklahoma, 1962; M Education Administration, University of Hawaii, 1971; Certificate in Church Music, Virginia Theological Seminary, Alexandria, Virginia. Appointments: Adjunct Faculty, Chaminade University, Honolulu, Hawaii; Instructor, Department of Public Safety, Hawaii; Editor and Manager, Hawaii Geographic Society; Education Co-Ordinator, Bernice P Bishop Museum, Honolulu, Hawaii; Lecturer on Geography and Natural History, US National Audubon Society and various other venues in USA and Canada. Publications: Hawaii Parklands: Guide to the Parks and Natural History of Hawaii, 1988; Total Solar Eclipse Over Hawaii, 1991; Christmas Comes to Hawaii: A History of the Anglican Church in Hawaii, 1999; Many articles in newspapers, magazines and newletters including: The Hololulu Advertiser; The Honolulu Star-bulletin; Honolulu Weekly; Sierra Magazine; The Historiographer (National Episcopal Historians and Archivists). Honours: Top 10 Senior Men, University of Oklahoma, 1962; President's Religious Leadership Award,

1962; Listed in Who's Who publications and biographical dictionaries. Memberships: National Society for Arts and Letters; Corrections Education Association; National Episcopal Historians and Archivists; Hawaiian Historical Society; Sierra Club; Professional Travel Film Lecturers Association. Address: PO Box 37214, Honolulu, HI 96837-0214, USA. E-mail: willishamoore@hotmail.com

MOORHOUSE (Cecil) James (Olaf), b. 1 January 1924, Copenhagen, Denmark. European Politician. m. (1) 1 son, 1 daughter, (2) Catherine Hamilton Peterson. Education: King's College, 1942-44 and Imperial College, 1945-46, University of London: BSc (Eng); DIC Advanced Aeronautics; C Eng. Appointments: Designer with De Havilland Aircraft Co, 1946-48; Project Engineer, BOAC, 1949-53; Technical Adviser, 1953-68, Environmental Conservation Adviser, 1968-72, Shell International Petroleum; Environmental Adviser, Shell Group of Companies in UK, 1972-73; Group Environmental Affairs Adviser, Rio-Tinto Zinc Corporation, 1973-80; Consultant, 1980-84; MEP for London South, 1979-84; MEP, London South and Surrey East, 1984-99. Publications: Righting the Balance: A New Agenda for Euro-Japanese Trade (with Anthony Teasdale), 1987; Numerous articles and papers on aviation. Memberships: Club: Sloane; University (Washington, DC); The English Speaking Union; President, Help Tibet Trust (UK). Address: 211 Piccadilly, London W1J 9HF, England. E-mail: jamesmoorhouse@aol.com

MOORHOUSE Geoffrey, b. 29 November 1931, Bolton, Lancashire, England. Author. m. (1) Janet Marion Murray, 1956, 2 sons, 2 daughters, 1 deceased, (2) Barbara Jane Woodward, 1974, divorced, 1978, (3) Marilyn Isobel Edwards, 1983, divorced, 1996. Appointments: Editorial Staff, Bolton Evening News, 1952-54, Grey River Argus, New Zealand, Auckland Star, and Christchurch Star-Sun, 1954-56, News Chronicle, 1957, Guardian, Manchester, 1958-70. Publications: The Other England, 1964; The Press, 1964; Against All Reason, 1969; Calcutta, 1971; The Missionaries, 1973; The Fearful Void, 1974; The Diplomats, 1977; The Boat and the Town, 1979; The Best-Loved Game, 1979; India Britannica, 1983; Lord's, 1983; To the Frontier, 1984; Imperial City: Rise and Rise of New York, 1988; At the George, 1989; Apples in the Snow, 1990; Hell's Foundations: Town, Its Myths and Gallipoli, 1992; Om: Indian Pilgrimage, 1993; A People's Game: Centenary History of Rugby League Football 1895-1995, 1995; Sun Dancing: Medieval Vision, 1997; Sydney, 1999; The Pilgrimage of Grace: the rebellion that shook Henry VIII's throne, 2002; Great Harry's Navy: How Henry VIII Gave England Seapower, 2005. Contributions to: Newspapers and magazines. Honours: Cricket Society Award, 1979; Fellow, Royal Society of Literature, 1982; Thomas Cook Award, 1984; Nominated Booker Prize, 1997. Address: Park House, Gayle, near Hawes, North Yorkshire DL8 3RT, England.

MORAES Dominic, b. 19 July 1938, Bombay, India. Writer; Poet. m. Leela Naidu, 1970. Education: Jesus College, Oxford. Appointments: Managing Editor, Asia Magazine, Hong Kong, 1972-; Consultant, United Nations Fund for Population Activities, 1973-. Publications: A Beginning, 1957; Gone Away, 1960; My Son's Father (autobiography), 1968; The Tempest Within, 1972-73; The People Time Forgot, 1972; A Matter of People, 1974; Voices for Life (essays), 1975; Mrs Gandhi, 1980; Bombay, 1980; Ragasthan: Splendour in the Wilderness, 1988; Collected Poems 1957-87, 1988; Serendip (poems), 1980; Never At Home (autobiography), 1994; In Cinnamon Shade (poems), 2001. Honour: Hawthornden Prize, 1957. Address: 12 Sargent House, Allan Marg, Mumbai 400039, India.

**MORAWIEC Henryk Zygmunt,** b. 14 September 1933, Katowice, Poland. Academic Lecturer. m. Jadwiga Grabowska. Education: MSc, Technical University, Gliwice, 1958; PhD, 1967, DSc, 1978, Technical University Silesia, Katowice. Appointments: Head of Workshop, Institute of Non-ferrous Metals, Gliwice, 1961-72; Head of Department, 1972-78, Dean of Faculty, Director of Institute, 1990, University of Silesia, Katowice. Publications: Several articles in professional journals. Honours: Award, Polish Academy of Sciences, 1961; Diploma, Technical University, Brno, 1985; Award, Foundation for Electron Microscopy, Polish Science Foundation, 1994. Memberships: Committee, Materials Science and Committee, Crystallography, Polish Academy of Sciences. Address: University of Silesia, Bankowa 12, 40-007 Katowice, Poland.

**MORCOM Christopher,** b. 4 February 1939, London, England. Barrister; Queens Counsel. m. Diane Toledo, 1 son, 2 daughters. Education: Sherborne School; Trinity College, Cambridge. Appointments: Called to Bar, Middle Temple, 1963; Barrister, Specialist in Intellectual Property Law, 1964; Appointed Queen's Counsel, 1991, Elected Bencher, Middle Temple, 1995. Publications: Service Marks – A Guide to the New Law, 1987; A Guide to the Trade Marks Act 1994; The Modern Law of Trade Marks, 2000; Many articles on legal publications, including Intellectual Property Review. Honours: Exhibitioner, Trinity College Cambridge; MA (Hons); Certificate of Honor (Bar Finals); Astbury Scholar of Middle Temple. Memberships: Mauritius Bar, 1979; International Trademark Association; ECTA; AIPPI, Vice President of UK Group; LIDC, President, 1996-98, Honorary President, 2000-; IPI, Board and Council of Experts; INTA's International Panel of Neutrals; WIPO's Arbitration & Mediation Centers Panel of Neutrals. Address: Hogarth Chambers, 5 New Square, Lincoln's Inn, London WC2A 3RJ, England. E-mail: cmorcom@hogarth chambers.com

**MOREIRA Alberto,** b. 29 June 1962, Sao Jose Dos Campos, Brazil. Scientist. m. 14 November 1992, 1 son, 1 daughter. Education: BSEE, ITA, Sao Jose dos Campos, Brazil, 1980-84; MSEE, 1985-86; PhD, Electrical Engineering, Technical University of Munich, Germany, 1988-93. Appointments: Consultant, Research Assistant, Technology Institute of Aeronautics, ITA, 1985-86; Scientist, German Aerospace Centre, Institute for Radio Frequency Technology, 1987-91; Leader of the Group SAR Signal Processing, 1992-95; Leader, Department SAR Technology, German Aerospace Centre, 1996-2001; Director, Microwaves and Radar Institute, 2001-. Publications: 150 publications in international journals, conference papers and technical reports; 11 patents. Honours: PhD thesis with honours; NASA Certificate in appreciation of an outstanding contribution; DLR Scientific Award; IEEE, Transactions Prize Paper Award; IEEE, Young Radar Engineer of the Year; IEEE Fellow. Memberships: Fellow, IEEE; VDE; The Electromagnetics Academy. Address: German Aerospace Centre, Microwaves and Radar Institute, Postfach 1116, D-82230 Wessling, Germany. E-mail: alberto.moreira@gmx.net

**MORGAN David Vernon,** b. 13 July 1941, Llanelli, Wales. Distinguished Research Professor. m. Jean, 1 son, 1 daughter. Education: BSc (Wales), 1963; MSc (Wales), 1964; PhD (Cambridge), 1967; DSc (Leeds). Appointments: University of Wales Fellow, Cavendish Laboratory Cambridge, 1966-68; Fellow, Harwell, 1968-70; Lecturer, 1970-77, Senior Lecturer, 1977-80, Reader, 1980-85, University of Leeds; Professor, 1985-, Head of School, 1992-2002, Distinguished Research Professor, Microelectronics, 2002-, Cardiff University. Publications: 230 papers published in scientific journals and international conferences; Authored and Edited 14 books including: An

Introduction to Semiconductor Microtechnology, 1983, 2nd edition, 1990. Honours: FREng, 1996; FCGI for Services to Higher Education, 1998; Papal Cross (Pro Ecclesia et Pontifice) Services to Academe, 2004. Memberships: FInstP; FIEE; Welsh Livery Guild. Address: 6 Berrymead Road, Cyncoed, Cardiff CF23 6QA, Wales. E-mail: morgandv@cf.ac.uk

**MORGAN Edward Patrick William,** b. 17 September 1927, Shorncliff, Kent, England. Retired. m. Nora Jane, 1 son, 1 daughter. Education: English, Honours, University of Birmingham, Teaching Diplomas, University of London, 1947-53; B Theol, Honours, University of South Africa, 1982-87; Diploma, Credit Management Institute of South Africa; Diploma, Public Relations Institute of South Africa. Appointments: Secondary School Teacher, Hertfordshire County Council, Barnet then at St Dominic's, Haverstock Hill, (LCC), 1953-57; Rhodesia Government High School Teacher, Chaplin High School, Gwelo, Southern Rhodesia, 1957-63; National Fund Raising Manager, Marist, South Africa, 1964-67; South African Government High School Teacher, Johannesburg, 1967-69; National Marketing Manager, then National Credit Manager in Johannesburg and Director of companies in Harare and Johannesburg, 1969-93; Retired 1993. Publications: Life of St Paul (series for Jesuit Magazine, Salisbury, Rhodesia), 1961; Regional Correspondent for weekly "Southern Cross", South Africa. Memberships: Member for Wexford, Irish Senior Citizens' Parliament; Public Relations Institute and Marketing Management Institute, South Africa; Founder-Treasurer, Catenian Association of South Africa; Catholic Theological Society of South Africa and Theology Associations of Great Britain and Ireland; European Society of Theologians. Address: 21 St Brendan's, Rosslare Harbour, County Wexford, Ireland. E-mail: patemorgan@eircom.net

**MORGAN Kenneth,** b. 9 June 1945, Llanelli, Wales. Professor. m. Elizabeth Margaret Harrison, 2 sons. Education: BSc, 1966, PhD, 1970, DSc (Eng), 1987, University of Bristol; CMath; CEng; FIMA, 1978; FICE, 1993; FREng, 1997. Appointments: Scientific Officer, Mathematical Physics Division, UKAEA, AWRE Aldermaston, 1969-72; Lecturer, Department of Mathematics, University of Exeter, 1972-75; Lecturer, 1975-84, Senior Lecturer, 1984-86, Reader, 1986-88, Professor, 1988-89, Department of Civil Engineering, University of Wales, Swansea; Zaharoff Professor of Aviation, Department of Aeronautics, Imperial College, London 1989-91; Professor, Department of Civil Engineering, 1991-2002, Head of Department, 1991-96, Dean of Engineering, 1997-2000, Professor, School of Engineering, 2002-, Head Civil and Computational Engineering Centre, 2003-, University of Wales, Swansea; Visiting Scientist, Joint Research Centre of the EC, Ispra, Italy, 1980; Visiting Research Scientist, Institute for Computer Applications in Science and Engineering, NASA, Langley Research Center, Virginia, USA, 1985; Visiting Research Professor, Old Dominion University, Norfolk, Virginia, 1986-87; Visiting Research Professor, University of Virginia, 1988-92; Council, International Association for Computational Mechanics, 1993-; Management Board, European Committee for Computational Methods in the Applied Sciences, 1993-; Inter Research Council High Performance Computing Management Committee, 1995-98; Governor, Ysgol Gynradd Gymraeg, Bryn-y-Môr, Swansea, 2000-. Publications: Finite Elements and Approximations (co-author), 1983; The Finite Element Method in Heat Transfer Analysis (co-author), 1996. Honours: Special Achievement Award, NASA, Langley Research Center, 1989; Computational Mechanics Award, International Association for Computational Mechanics, 1998; Honorary Fellow, International Association for Computational Fluid Dynamics, 2003; Fellow, International Association for Computational Mechanics, 2004. Address: 137

Pennard Drive, Southgate, Swansea SA3 2DW, Wales. E-mail: k.morgan@swansea.ac.uk

**MORGAN Rex Henry**, b. Devon, England. Educator; Author. m. Mary Elizabeth Cottrell, 29 March 1958, 2 sons, 1 daughter. Education: Commonwealth School, University of Sydney, Australia; DiptTG, Teachers Guild of New South Wales; ATCL; LTCL, Trinity College, London, England; Associate, Royal Photographic Society; Honorary MSc, Brooks Institute, California, USA. Appointments: Founder, Pittwater House Schools, New South Wales, 1962; Freelance Broadcaster, Lecturer, Author, Editor, Shroud News; Led Hermes expeditions, and to Jordan, Israel; Visiting Professor, Shenzhen University, China. Publications include: Perpetual Miracle, 1983; Jubilee Picture Book, 1987; Frank Mason's Churt, 1988; Shroud Guide, 1983; The Hermes Adventure, 1985; With Man and Beast on the Oregon Trail, 1993; The History of Bathurst 1815-1915 (ed), 1994; Byzantine Frescoes (ed), 1994; Cappadocian Frescoes (ed), 1996; Catacombs and the Early Church (ed), 1998; Castle, Kitbag and Cattle Truck (introduction), 2001; A New Way of Learning English (with Professor He Huimin), 2003. Contributor: to numerous booklets, papers, articles, broadcasts. Honours: Dux of Course, Teachers Guild of New South Wales; Justice of the Peace, New South Wales; Fellow, Australian College of Education; MBE, 1969; Commonwealth of Australia Recognition Award for Senior Australians, 2000; HRH Princess Sirindhorn Badge of Recognition, Thailand, 2000; Board Member, Winitsuksa School Thailand, 1999-; National President, Friends of the Duke of Edinburgh's Award, Australia, 2000-; Member of the Order of Australia, 2002; Australian Centenary Medal, 2003; Officer, Order of St Lazarus, 2004. Memberships include: Fellow, Royal Geographical Society; Fellow, Royal Society of Arts; President, South East Asia Research Centre for the Holy Shroud, 1986; President, Rex Morgan Festival Committee, 1992-; South East Asia Writers' Award Committee, Thailand, 1995; Rex Morgan Foundation, 1999-; Committee, Thai Australia Association, 2002-. Address: Abercrombie House, Bathurst, NSW 2795, Australia.

**MORGAN Trefor Owen**, b. 11 March 1936, New South Wales, Australia. Medical Researcher. m. Olive Lawson, 1 son, 1 daughter. Education: University of Sydney, 1953-59; BScMed, 1958; MBBS, 1960; MD, 1972; Fellow, Royal Australian College of Physicians, 1972; Charles Stuart University, 1987-91; BApplSci, Wine, 1992. Appointments: Intern, Resident, Registrar, Clinical Supervisor, Royal Prince Albert Hospital, 1960-66; Visiting Scientist, National Institutes of Health, USA, 1966-69; Renal Physician, Princess Alexandra Hospital, Australia, 1969-71; Assistant in Medicine, 1971-77, Professor of Physiology, 1984, University of Melbourne, Victoria; Visiting Professor, University of Munich, Germany, 1975; Foundation Professor of Medicine, University of Newcastle, Australia, 1977-81; Specialist in Charge of Medicine, Repatriation Hospital, 1981-84; Visiting Professor, University Lausanne 1996. Publications: 350 scientific papers; 3 books. Honour: Honorary Professor, Shandong Academy of Medical Sciences, China. Memberships: International Society of Hypertension; High Blood Pressure Research Council of Australia; Secretary, Asian Pacific Society of Hypertension. Address: Department of Physiology, University of Melbourne, Parkville 3052, Victoria, Australia.

**MORGAN William Richard**, b. 27 March 1922, Cambridge, Ohio, USA. Mechanical Engineer. m. Marjorie Eleanor Stevens, 17 February 1946, 1 son, 1 daughter. Education: BSME, Ohio State University, 1944; MSME, Purdue University, 1950; PhD, Mechanical Engineering, 1951. Appointments: Licensed

Professional Engineer, Ohio; Power Plant Design Engineer, Curtiss Wright Corp, Columbus, Ohio, 1946-47; Instructor and Westinghouse Research Fellow, Purdue University; West Lafayette Indiana, 1947-51; Supervisor, Experimental Mechanical Engineering, GE, Cincinnati, 1951-55; Manager, Controls Analysis Development, Aircraft Gas Turbine Division, GE, 1955-59; Manager, XV5A vertical take-off and landing aircraft programme, GE, 1959-65; Manager, Acoustic Engineering, Flight Propulsion Division, GE, 1965-69; Manager, quiet engine programme 1969-71; President, Cincinnati Research Corporation, 1971-73; Vice President, SDRC International, Cincinnati, 1973-79; Engineering and Management Consultant, Cincinnati, 1979-. Publications: Numerous papers presented in seminars and symposia and articles in professional journals. Memberships: ASME; Sigma Xi; Pi Tau Sigma; Pi Mu Epsilon. Address: 312 Ardon Ln, Cincinnati, OH 45215, USA.

**MORI Tetsuo**, b. 2 January 1959, Wakayama, Japan. Consultant. m. Masayo Sekita. Education: BA, Chuo University, 1987. Appointments: Senior Management Consultant, Ernst & Young, Tokyo, 1990-92; Vice President, Bozell, Tokyo, 1994-97; Director, Saatchi & Saatchi Bates, Tokyo, 1997-2000; Sales & Marketing Consultant, Kodak, Tokyo, 1998; Consultant, Universal Record, Tokyo, 1998; Consultant, HP, Tokyo, 1999; Partner, Mercatela, Tokyo, 2001; COO, Spike Ltd, Tokyo, 2002; E-bus, Consultant, GM, Tokyo, 2002; Manager, Relationship Management, Amway, Tokyo, 2003-. Publications: Monthly I M Press, 2004; CRM White Paper, 2005. Honours: Knight, Order of Iron Crown, Nice. Address: Mure 4-3-38, Lansa D-301, Mitaka, Tokyo 181-0002, Japan.

**MORIARTY Kieran John**, b. 31 May 1951, Cheshire, England. Consultant Gastroenterologist. m. Theresa Butler, 2 sons, 2 daughters. Education: Trinity College, Cambridge, 1979-72; The London Hospital Medical College, 1972-75. Appointments: Senior House Officer to Dr Mike Lancaster-Smith, General Medicine and Gastroenterology, Queen Mary's Hospital, Sidcup, Kent, 1976-77; Clinical Research Fellow in Gastroenterology to Sir Anthony Dawson, Dr Mike Clark and Dr Chris Williams, 1979-93; Tutor in Medicine to Professor Lord Leslie Turnberg, University Department of Medicine, Hope Hospital, Salford, 1983-90; Consultant Gastroenterologist, Royal Bolton Hospital, 1990-. Publications: Holy Communion Wafers and Celiac Disease (prompted the Vatican to change Canon Law and allow use of low gluten communion wafers), 1989; Understanding Irritable Bowel Syndrome (written for patients), 2001; Recording: CD: Dr Keiran Moriarty - Irish Songs and Ballads (to fund nurses going to Lourdes to help the sick and disabled), 2002. Honours: British Hospital Doctor of the Year for multidisciplinary care for alcoholic patients, 1999; Team Leader of Winning British Hospital Doctor Gastroenterology Team of the Year, 1999; CBE for services to medicine, 2002; Mayo Association of Manchester Award for caring for the sick and disabled, 2003. Memberships: English Member of International Medical Committee of Lourdes; Chief Medical Officer, Salford Diocesan Pilgrimage to Lourdes ; Adviser to Chief Medical Officer, Deputy Director of Strategy at the Ministry of Health; Fellow, Royal College of Physicians of London; British Society of Gastroenterology; American Gastroenterological Association; Helped formulate Italian Government's nutritional policy. Address: 20 Bramhall Park Road, Bramhall, Stockport SK7 3DQ, England. E-mail: kieran.moriarty@bolton-tr.nwest.nhs.uk

**MORINAGA Masahiko**, b. 20 August 1946, Osaka, Japan. Professor. m. Kazue, 1 son, 1 daughter. Education: BS, 1969, MS, 1971, Kyoto University, Japan; PhD, Northwestern University, USA 1978. Appointments: Lecturer, 1979-83,

Associate Professor, 1983-91, Professor 1991-94, Toyohashi University of Technology; Professor, Nagoya University, 1994-. Honours: The Meritorious Award of the Japan Institute of Metals, 1989; The Nagai Science Award, 1991; Memorial Lecture for the Korean Institute of Metals, 1997; The Science Award of the DV-Xa Society of Japan, 2001. Memberships: The Minerals, Metals and Materials Society; The Japan Institute of Metals, Vice-President, 2005-; Iron and Steel Institute of Japan; Physical Society of Japan; DV-Xa Society of Japan, President, 2004-. Address: Department of Materials Science and Engineering, Graduate School of Engineering, Nagoya University, Furo-cho, Chikusa-ku, Nagoya 464-8603, Japan. E-mail: morinaga@numse.nagoya-u.ac.jp

**MORISSETTE Alanis,** b. 1 June 1974, Ottawa, Canada. Singer. Career: Solo recording artiste; Appeared on Canadian cable TV, aged 10; Signed contract as songwriter with MCA Publishing aged 14; Concerts include: Twix Mix Jamboree, with David Bowie, Birmingham NEC, 1995; 16 million albums sold. Recordings: Albums: Alanis, 1991; Now Is The Time, 1992; Jagged Little Pill, 1995; Space Cakes (live), 1998; Supposed Former Infatuation Junkie, 1998; Alanis Unplugged (live), 1999; Under Rug Swept, 2002. Singles: Fate Stay With Me; You Oughta Know, 1995; One Hand In My Pocket, 1995; Ironic, 1996. Film: Dogma, 1999. Honour: BRIT Award, Best International Newcomer, 1996; Four Grammy Awards, including Album of the Year and Best Rock Album; Best Female Award, MTV European Music Awards, 1996.

**MORRELL David William James,** b. 26 July 1933, Glasgow, Scotland. University Administrator; Lawyer. m. Margaret Rosemary, 2 sons, 1 daughter. Education: MA (Hons), 1954, LLB, 1957, University of Edinburgh. Appointments: Apprentice Solicitor, Shepherd & Wedderburn WS, 1954-57; Administrative Assistant, King's College, University of Durham, 1957-60; Assistant Registrar, University of Exeter, 1960-64; Senior Assistant Registrar, University of Essex, 1964-66; Academic Registrar, 1966-73, Registrar and Secretary, 1973-89, University of Strathclyde; Consultant to Institutional Management in Higher Education Programme of OECD, Paris, 1989-90; Lay Observer for Scotland, 1989-91; Scottish Legal Services Ombudsman, 1991-94; Chairman, 1995-96, Vice-Chairman, 1996-99, Lomond Healthcare NHS Trust; Member, Argyll and Clyde Health Board, 1999-2001; Chairman of University of Paisley, 1997-2002. Publications: Various on management in higher education and on lawyer/client relationships. Honours: Honorary Degree, Doctor of the University, University of Paisley, 2005. Memberships: National Trust for Scotland; Historic Scotland; Church of Scotland.

**MORRIS Desmond John,** b. 24 January 1928, Purton, Wiltshire, England. Zoologist; Author; Broadcaster; Artist. m. Ramona Baulch, 30 July 1952, 1 son. Education: BSc, Birmingham University, 1951; DPhil, Oxford University, 1954. Appointments: Zoological Research Worker, University of Oxford, 1954-56; Head of Granada TV and Film Unit, Zoological Society of London, 1956-59; Curator of Mammals, Zoological Society of London, 1959-67; Director, Institute of Contemporary Arts, London, 1967-68; Privately engaged writing books, 1968-73; Research Fellow, Wolfson College, Oxford, 1973-81; Privately engaged writing books and making television programmes, 1981-2005. TV series: Zootime, 1956-67; Life, 1965-67; The Human Race, 1982; The Animals Roadshow, 1987-89; The Animal Contract, 1989; Animal Country, 1991-96; The Human Animal, 1994; The Human Sexes, 1997; Solo exhibitions (paintings): Art galleries across England and in Holland, Belgium, France, USA and Ireland. Publications include: The Biology of Art, 1962; The Big Cats,

1965; Zootime, 1966; The Naked Ape, 1967; The Human Zoo, 1969; Patterns of Reproductive Behaviour, 1970; Intimate Behaviour, 1971; Manwatching, 1977; Animal Days, 1979; The Soccer Tribe, 1981; Bodywatching: A Field Guide to the Human Species, 1985; Catwatching, 1986; Dogwatching, 1986; Catlore, 1987; The Human Nestbuilders, 1988; The Animal Contract, 1990; Animal-Watching, 1990; Babywatching, 1991; Christmas Watching, 1992; The World of Animals, 1993; The Naked Ape Trilogy, 1994; The Human Animal, 1994; Bodytalk: A World Guide to Gestures, 1994; Catworld: A Feline Encyclopaedia, 1996; The Human Sexes: A Natural History of Man and Woman, 1997; Illustrated Horsewatching, 1998; Cool Cats: The 100 Cat Breeds of the World, 1999; Body Guards: Protective Amulets and Charms, 1999; The Naked Ape and Cosmetic Behaviour (with Kaori Ishida), 1999; The Naked Eye, Travels in Search of the Human Species, 2000; Dogs: a Dictionary of Dog Breeds, 2001; Peoplewatching, 2002; The Silent Language (in Italian), 2004; The Nature of Happiness, 2004; The Naked Woman, 2004. Contributions to: Many journals and magazines. Honour: Honorary DSc, Reading University, 1998. Membership: Scientific Fellow, Zoological Society of London. Address: c/o Jonathan Cape, Random Century House, 20 Vauxhall Bridge Road, London SW1V 2SA, England.

**MORRIS Gareth Charles Walter,** b. 13 May 1920, Clevedon, Somerset, England. Flautist. m. Patricia Mary Murray, 1 son, 3 daughters. Education: Privately; Royal Academy of Music, London. Career: Soloist and Chamber Musician; Professor of Flute, Royal Academy of Music, London, 1945-85; Principal Flautist, Philharmonia Orchestra, London, 1948-72; International Adjudicator in flute playing; First performance of numerous works for flute. Publications: Flute Technique, 1991; Numerous articles in journals and dictionaries. Honours: Associate, Royal Academy of Music; Fellow, Royal Academy of Music; Fellow, Royal Society of Arts. Memberships: Royal Society of Musicians; Royal Society of Arts; Member of Council of Honour, Royal Academy of Music. Address: 4 West Mall, Clifton, Bristol, England.

**MORRIS Richard Francis Maxwell,** b. 11 September 1944, Sussex, England. Chief Executive. m. Marian Sperling, 9 April 1983, 2 daughters. Education: New College, Oxford, 1963-66; College of Law, London, 1967. Appointments: Solicitor, Farrer & Co, 1967-71; Banker, Grindlay Brandts, 1971-75; Director, Invicta Radio plc, 1984-92; General Manager, Corporate Finance, SG Warburg & Co, 1975-79; Managing Director, Edward Arnold Ltd. 1987-91; Finance Director, Joint Managing Director, Hodder & Stoughton, 1979-91; Founder, Almaviva Opera, 1989-; Trustee, Governor, Kent Opera, 1985-90; Director, Southern Radio plc, 1990-92; Chief Executive, Associated Board of the Royal Schools of Music, 1993-; Trustee, Director, Kent Music School, 2001-; Member, Executive Committee, Chairman, Music Education Council, 1995-; Trustee, Council for Dance Education and Training, 1999-2005; Governor, The Yehudi Menuhin School, 2004-. Honours: Honorary RCM; Honorary RNCM; MA (Oxon). Memberships: Incorporated Society of Musicians. Address: 24 Portland Place, London W1B 1LU, England. E-mail: rmorris@abrsm.ac.uk

**MORRIS Richard Graham Michael,** b. 27 June 1948, Worthing, Sussex, England. Neuroscientist. m. Hilary Ann Lewis, 2 daughters. Education: MA, Trinity Hall, University of Cambridge, 1966-69; DPhil, Sussex University, 1969-73. Appointments: Senior Scientific Officer, British Museum, Natural History, Researcher, BBC Television, Science and Features Department, 1973-75; Lecturer, Psychology, 1977-86; MRC Research Fellow, 1983-86, University of St Andrews; Reader in Neuroscience, 1986-93, Professor of Neuroscience,

1993-, Director, Centre for Neuroscience, 1993-97, Chairman, Department of Neuroscience, University of Edinburgh, 1998-2002; Co-Director, Edinburgh Neuroscience, 2005-; Editorial roles in various scientific journals, 1990-. Publications: Over 150 papers in academic journals; Neuroscience: The Science of the Brain (booklet for secondary school children); Parallel Distributed Processing: Implications for Psychology and Neurobiology (editor), 1989. Honours: Fellow, Academy of Medical Sciences, 1998-; Decade of the Brain Lecturer, 1998; Zotterman Lecturer, 1999; Forum Fellow, World Economics Forum, 2000; Life Sciences Co-ordinate OST Foresight Project on Cognitive Systems, 2002-03; Yngve Zotterman Prize, Karolinska Institute, 1999; Henry Dryerre Prize, Royal Society of Edinburgh, 2000. Memberships: Experimental Psychology Society, Honorary Secretary, 1984-88; British Neuroscience Association, Chairman, 1991-95; Society for Neuroscience, USA; European Brain and Behaviour Society. Address: Neuroscience, University of Edinburgh, 1 George Square, Edinburgh EH8 9JZ, Scotland.

**MORRIS William (Bill),** b. 1938, Jamaica. Trade Union General Secretary. m. Minetta, deceased 1990, 2 sons. Appointments include: Joined engineering company, Hardy Spicers, Birmingham; Joined T&G, 1958; Elected Shop Steward, Hardy Spicers, 1962; Involved in first industrial dispute, 1964; Elected Member, T&G's General Executive Council, 1972; District Officer, T&G, Nottingham/Derby District, 1973; Northampton District Secretary, T&G, 1976; National Secretary of the Passenger Service Trade Group, T&G, 1979; Deputy General Secretary, T&G, 1986-92; Elected General Secretary, 1991, re-elected, 1995-2003; Member, TUC General Council, 1988-2003; Member, TUC Executive Committee, 1988-; Member, Commission for Racial Equality, 1980-87; Member, Executive Board of the International Transport Worker's Federation, 1986; Member, New Deal Task Force, 1997-2000; Member, Court of the Bank of England, 1998-; Member of Committee for Integrated Transport, 1999-; Member, Governing Councils, Luton University and Northampton University; Chancellor, University of Technology, Jamaica, 1999-. Honours: Numerous Honorary Degrees; Honorary Professorship, Thames Valley University , 1997; Honorary Fellowship, Royal Society of Arts, 1992; Honorary Fellowship City & Guilds London Institute, 1992; Order of Jamaica, 2002; Public Figure of the Year, Ethnic Multicultural Media Awards, 2002. Memberships: Board of Fullemploy, 1985-88; Trustee, 1987-90, Advisory Committee, 1997- Prince's Youth Business Trust. Address: 156 St Agnells Lane, Grove Hill, Hemel Hempstead, Hertfordshire, HP2 6EG, England.

**MORRISON Anthony James (Tony Morrison),** b. 5 July 1936, Gosport, England. Television Producer; Writer. m. Elizabeth Marion Davies, 30 July 1965, 1 son, 1 daughter. Education: BSc, University of Bristol, 1959. Appointments: Partner, South American Pictures; Director, Nonesuch Expeditions Ltd. Publications: Steps to a Fortune (co-author), 1967; Animal Migration, 1973; Land Above the Clouds, 1974; The Andes, 1976; Pathways to the Gods, 1978; Lizzie: A Victorian Lady's Amazon Adventure (co-editor), 1985; The Mystery of the Nasca Lines, 1987; Margaret Mee: In Search of Flowers of the Amazon (editor), 1988; QOSQO: Navel of the World, 1997; Peru: Country of Contrasts, 2003. Address: 48 Station Road, Woodbridge, Suffolk IP12 4AT, England. E-mail: morrison@southamericanpictures.com

**MORRISON Marion,** b. 18 August 1939, Melton, Suffolk, England. m. Tony, 30 July 1965, 1 son, 1 daughter. Education: BA Hons, History, University of Wales, 1958-61. Publications: Let's Visit Uruguay, Indians of the Amazon, Indians of the

Andes, 1985; An Inca Farmer, Atahualpa and the Incas, 1986; Let's Visit Venezuela, Let's Visit Paraguay, 1987; Bolivia, People and Places Brazil, 1988; Venezuela, People and Places Argentina, People and Places Central America, 1989; Colombia, 1990; World in View Ecuador, Peru, Bolivia, 1991; Uruguay, World in View Central America, 1992; Paraguay, Fact File Brazil, Amazon Rainforest and Its People, 1993; French Guiana, Highlights Brazil, Focus on Mexico, Real World Mexico and Central America, 1995; Belize, Highlights Peru, Highlights Argentina, Discovering Mexico, Discovering Brazil, Country Insights Brazil, 1996; Country Insights Cuba, 1997; Costa Rica, Peoples of the Americas (major contributor), 1998; Cuba, Colombia, Highlights Costa Rica, 1999; Peru, Ecuador, 2000; El Salvador, 2001; Children's Press: EOW Nicaragua, 2001; EOW Guyana, 2004; EPW Uruguay, 2005; EOW Guatemala, 2005; World Almanac Library Great Cities of the World, Mexico City, 2003; Rio de Janeiro, 2004; Buenos Aires, 2005. Contributions: Various magazines and journals. Address: 48 Station Road, Woodbridge, Suffolk IP12 4AT, England. Email: morrison@south-american-pic.com

**MORRISON Susan Marie,** b. 22 September 1962, Boston, Massachusetts, USA. Attorney. Education: BA, College of New Rochelle, 1984; JD, Suffolk University Law School, 1988. Appointment: Senior Associate, Litigation Department, Fitzhugh, Parker & Alvaro LLP (formerly Fitzhugh & Associates). Publication: Fitzhugh & Associates Lead Paint Desk Handbook, Get the Lead Out: Litigating Lead Paint Claims in New England and New York. Honours: American Bibliography's Woman of the Year 2004; Listed in Who's Who publications and biographical dictionaries. Memberships: Massachusetts Bar; Federal Bar 1st District; 1st Circuit Court of Appeals Bar; Supreme Court Bar; Federal Bar Association; Massachusetts Association of Trial Attorneys; American Bar Association; Association of Trial Lawyers of American. Address: 89 Pellana Road, Norwood, MA 02062, USA. E-mail: smorrison@fitzhughlaw.com

**MORRISON Toni (Chloe Anthony),** b. 18 February 1931, Lorain, Ohio, USA. Novelist. m. Harold Morrison, 1958, divorced 1964, 2 children. Education: Howard University; Cornell University. Appointments: Teacher, English and Humanities, Texas Southern University, 1955-57, Howard University, 1957-64; Editor, Random House, New York, 1965-; Associate Professor of English, State University of New York, 1971-72; Schweitzer Professor of the Humanities, 1984-89; Robert F Goheen Professor of the Humanities, Princeton University, 1989-. Publications: The Bluest Eye, 1970; Sula, 1974; Song of Solomon, 1977; Tar Baby, 1983; Beloved, 1987; Jazz, 1992; Playing in the Dark: Whiteness and the Literary Imagination, 1992; Nobel Prize Speech, 1994; Birth of a Nation'hood: Gaze, Script and Spectacle in the O J Simpson Trial, 1997; The Big Box (poems), 1999. Honours include: Pulitzer Prize and Robert F Kennedy Book Award, for Beloved, 1988; Nobel Prize for Literature, 1993; Commander, Ordre des Arts et des Lettres; National Medal of Arts, 2000. Membership: Council, Authors' Guild. Address: c/o Suzanne Gluck, International Creative Management, 40 57th Street West, NY 10019, USA.

**MORRISON Van (George Ivan Morrison),** b. 31 August 1945, Belfast, Northern Ireland. Singer; Songwriter; Composer; Musician. 1 daughter. Career: Founder, lead singer, Them, 1964-67; Solo artiste, 1967-; Appearances include: Knebworth Festival, 1974; The Last Waltz, The Band's farewell concert, 1976; Played with Bob Dylan, Wembley Stadium, 1984; Self Aid, with U2, Dublin, 1986; Glastonbury Festival, 1987; Prince's Rock Trust Gala, 1989; Performance, The Wall, by

Roger Waters, Berlin, 1990; Concert in Dublin, with Bono, Bob Dylan, 1993; Phoenix Festival, 1995. Recordings: Singles include: Gloria; Brown-Eyed Girl; Moondance; Domino; Wild Night; Albums include: Blowin' Your Mind, 1967; Astral Weeks, 1968; Moondance, 1970; His Band And Street Choir, 1973; Tupelo Honey, 1971; St Dominic's Preview, 1972; Hard Nose The Highway, 1973; It's Too Late To Stop Now, 1974; TB Sheets, 1974; Veedon Fleece, 1974; This Is Where I Came In, 1977; A Period Of Transition, 1977; Wavelength, 1978; Into The Music, 1983; Bang Masters, 1990; Common One, 1980; Beautiful Vision, 1982; Inarticulate Speech Of The Heart, 1983; Live At The Opera House Belfast, 1984; A Sense Of Wonder, 1984; No Guru, No Method, No Teacher, 1986; Poetic Champions Compose, 1987; Irish Heartbeat, 1988; Best Of..., 1990; Avalon Sunset, 1989; Enlightenment, 1990; Hymns To The Silence, 1991; Too Long In Exile, 1993; Best Of..., Vol 2, 1993; A Night in San Francisco, 1994; Days Like This, 1995; Songs of the Mose Allison: Tell Me Something, 1996; The Healing Game, 1997; The Skiffle Sessions: Live in Belfast, 1998, 2000; Brown Eyed Girl, 1998; The Masters, 1999; Super Hits, 1999; Back on Top, 1999. Also recorded on albums: with The Band: Cahoots, 1971; The Last Waltz, 1978; with John Lee Hooker: Folk Blues, 1963; Mr Lucky, 1991; with Bill Wyman: Stone Alone, 1976; with Jim Capaldi: Fierce Heart, 1983; with Georgie Fame: How Long Has This Been Going On, 1996. Honours include: Inducted into Rock And Roll Hall Of Fame, 1993; BRIT Award, Outstanding Contribution to British Music, 1994; Q Award, Best Songwriter, 1995.

**MORT Graham Robert,** b. 11 August 1955, Middleton, England. Poet. m. Maggie Mort, 12 February 1979, 3 sons. Education: BA, University of Liverpool, 1977; PGCE, St Martin's College, Lancaster, 1980; PhD, University of Glamorgan, 2000. Appointment: Creative Writing Course Leader, Open College of the Arts, 1989-2000. Publications: A Country on Fire; Into the Ashes; A Halifax Cider Jar; Sky Burial; Snow from the North; Starting to Write; The Experience of Poetry, Storylines; Circular Breathing; A Night on the Lash. Contributions to: Numerous literary magazines and journals. Honours: 1st Prizes, Cheltenham Poetry Competition, 1979, 1982; Duncan Lawrie Prizes, Arvon Poetry Competition, 1982, 1992, 1994; Major Eric Gregory Award, 1985; Authors Foundation Award, 1994. Memberships: Society of Authors; National Association of Writers in Education. Address: 2 Chapel Lane, Burton-in-Lonsdale, Carnforth, Lancs LA6 3JY, England.

**MORTENSEN Finn Hauberg,** b. 26 July 1946, Copenhagen, Denmark. Professor. m. Ella Bredsdorff, 3 sons, 2 daughters. Education: Cand. Phil. 1972, Mag. Art. 1975, Lic. Phil. 1979, Copenhagen University, Denmark. Appointments: Research Fellow, 1972-74, Assistant Professor, 1974-76, Associate Professor, 1976-89, Docent, 1989-91, Professor, 1991-, University of Southern Denmark; Research Professor, Copenhagen University, 1994-91; Guest Professor, Kwansei Gakuin University, 1997, 2002; Research Fellow, University of California, Berkeley, 2003, 2004; Chair, Institute of Philosophy, Education and the Study of Religions. Publications: Litteraturfunktion og symbolnorm 1-2, 1973; Danskfagets didaktik 1-2, 1979; Kierkegaards Either/Or, 1989; A Tale of Tales – H C Andersen, 1989; Funderinger over faget dansk, 1993; Kierkegaard Made in Japan, 1996; Villy Sørensen: Talt, 2002; Abe and Søko, Uddannelsesdebat 1969-2001, 2002; Bibliografi over Villy Sørensens Forfatterskab, 2003; Laeselist, Litteraturpaedagogiske essays 1-2, 2003. Honours: Gold Medal, Copenhagen University, 1969; Knighted by the Queen of Denmark. Memberships: Royal Danish Academy of Sciences and Letters; Chairman, Society for Danish Language and Literature; Chairman, Commission on Canonization of Literature, Ministry of Culture. Address: Laessøegade 26, DK-5000 Odense C, Denmark.

**MORTIMER John (Clifford), Sir,** b. 21 April 1923, Hampstead, London, England. Author; Barrister; Playwright. m. (1) Penelope Fletcher, 1949, 1 son, 1 daughter, (2) Penelope Gollop, 2 daughters. Education: Brasenose College, Oxford. Appointments: Called to the Bar, 1948; Master of the Bench, Inner Temple, 1975; Member, Board of National Theatre, 1968-; Chairman, Council Royal Society of Literature, 1989; Chairman, Council Royal Court Theatre, 1990-; President, Howard League for Penal Reform, 1991-. Publications: Novels: Charade, 1947; Rumming Park, 1948; Answer Yes or No, 1950; Like Men Betrayed, 1953; Three Winters, 1956; Will Shakespeare, 1977; Rumpole of the Bailey, 1978; The Trials of Rumpole, 1979; Rumpole's Return, 1981; Rumpole and the Golden Thread, 1983; Paradise Postponed, 1985; Rumpole's Last Case, 1987; Rumpole and the Age of Miracles, 1988; Rumpole a la Carte, 1990; Clinging to the Wreckage (autobiography), 1982; In Character, 1983; Character Parts (interviews), 1986; Summer's Lease, 1988; The Narrowing Stream; Titmuss Regained, 1990; Dunster, 1992; Rumpole on Trial, 1992; The Best of Rumpole, 1993; Murderers and Other Friends (autobiography), 1993; Rumpole and the Angel of Death, 1995; Rumpole and the Younger Generation, 1996; Felix in the Underworld, 1997; Rumpole's Return, 1997; The Third Rumpole Omnibus, 1997; The Sound of Trumpets, 1998; The Summer of a Dormouse (autobiography), 2000; Rumpole Rests His Case, 2001; Rumpole and the Primrose Path, 2002; Numerous plays and translations. Honours include: British Academy of Writers' Award, 1979, 1980.

**MOSES John Henry,** b. 12 January 1938, London, England. Clerk in Holy Orders. m. Susan Elizabeth, 1 son, 2 daughters. Education: Gladstone Memorial Prize, 1958, BA, History, 1959, PhD, 1965, Nottingham University; Certificate in Education, Trinity Hall, Cambridge, 1960; Deacon, 1964, Priest, 1965, Lincoln Theological College. Appointments: Assistant Curate, St Andrew, Bedford, 1964-70; Rector, Coventry East Team Ministry, 1970-77; Examining Chaplain to the Bishop of Coventry, 1972-77; Rural Dean of Coventry East, 1973-77; Archdeacon of Southend, 1977-82; Provost of Chelmsford, 1982-96; Dean of St Paul's Cathedral, 1996-; Visiting Fellow, Wolfson College, Cambridge, 1987; Member, General Synod, 1985-2005; Church Commissioner, 1988-; Member, ACC, 1997-2005; Chairman Council Centre for Study of Theology, Essex University, 1987-96; Rector, Anglia Poly University, 1992-96; Select Preacher, Oxford University, 2004-2005; Vice-President, City of London Festival, 1997-. Publications: The Sacrifice of God, 1992; A Broad and Living Way, 1995; The Desert, 1997; One Equall Light: an anthology of the writings of John Donne, 2003. Honours: Freeman City of London, 1997; Liveryman, Feltmakers' Company, 1998-; Plaisterers' Company, 1999-; Honorary Freeman, Water Conservators' Company, 2000; Honorary Liveryman, Masons' Company, 2005; Honorary Doctor Anglia Poly University, 1997; Order of Al Istiqal of Hashemite King of Jordan, 2002; Order of St John, 2003. Membership: Athenaeum. Address: The Deanery, 9 Amen Court, London EC4M 7BU, England. E-mail: thedean@stpauls cathedral.org.uk

**MOSIMANN Anton,** b. 23 February 1947, Switzerland. Chef; Restaurateur. m. Kathrin Roth, 1973, 2 sons. Appointments: Apprentice, Hotel Baeren, Twann; Worked in Canada, France, Italy, Sweden, Japan, Belgium, Switzerland, 1962-; Cuisinier, Villa Lorraine, Brussels, Les Prés d'Eugénie, Eugénie-les-Bains, Les Frères Troisgros, Roanne, Paul Bocuse, Collonges au Mont d'Or, Moulin de Mougins; Joined Dorchester Hotel,

London, 1975, Maitre Chef des Cuisines, 1975-88; Owner, Mosimann's, 1988-, Mosimann's Party Service, 1990-, The Mosimann Academy, 1995-, Creative Chefs, 1996-; Numerous TV appearances. Publications: Cuisine a la Carte, 1981; A New Style of Cooking: The Art of Anton Mosimann, 1983; Cuisine Naturelle, 1985; Anton Mosimann's Fish Cuisine, 1988; The Art of Mosimann, 1989; Cooking with Mosimann, 1989; Anton Mosimann – Naturally, 1991; The Essential Mosimann, 1993; Mosimann's World, 1996. Honours: Freedom of the City of London, 1999; Royal Warrant from HRH the Prince of Wales for Caterers, 2000; OBE, 2004; Numerous others. Address: c/o Mosimann's, 11B West Halkin Street, London SW1X 8JL, England.

**MOSS Kate,** b. 16 January 1974, Addiscombe, England. Model. 1 daughter. Career: Modelled for Harpers and Queen; Vogue; The Face; Dolce & Gabana; Katherine Hamnett; Versace, Yves St Laurent; Exclusive world-wide with Calvin Klein, 1992-99. Publication: Kate, 1994. Film: Unzipped, 1996; Honour: Female Model of the Year, VH-1 Awards, 1996. Address: Storm Model Management, 1st Floor, 5 Jubilee Place, London SW3 3TD, England.

**MOSS Norman Bernard,** b. 30 September 1928, London, England. Journalist; Writer. m. Hilary Sesta, 21 July 1963, 2 sons. Education: Hamilton College, New York, 1946-47. Appointments: Staff Journalist with newspapers, news agencies and radio networks. Publications: Men Who Play God - The Story of the Hydrogen Bomb, 1968; A British-American Dictionary, 1972, 5th edition, revised, 1994; The Pleasures of Deception, 1976; The Politics of Uranium, 1982; Klaus Fuchs: The Man Who Stole the Atom Bomb, 1987; Managing the Planet, 2000; 'Nineteen Week. America, Britain and the Fateful Summer of 1940', 2003 Honour: Magazine Writer of the Year, Periodical Publishers Association, 1982. Memberships: International Institute of Strategic Studies; Society of Authors. Address: 21 Rylett Crescent, London W12 9RP, England.

**MOSS Stirling,** b. 17 September 1929, London, England. Racing Driver. m. (1) Katherine Stuart Moson, 1957, dissolved 1960, (2) Elaine Barbarino, 1964, 1 daughter, dissolved 1968, (3) Susie Paine, 1980, 1 son. Education: Haileybury and Imperial Service College. Appointments: British Champion, 1951; Built Own Car, The Cooper-Alta, 1953; Drove in HWM Formula II Grand Prix Team, 1950, 1951, Jaguar Team, 1955; Leader, Maserati Sports & Grand Prix Teams, 1956, Aston Martin Team, 1956; Member, Vanwall, Aston Martin, Maserati Teams, 1958; Events include New Zealand, Monaco Grand Prix, Nurburgring 1,000km, Argentine 1,000km. UK, Pescara, Italy, Moroccan Grand Prix; Managing Director, Stirling Moss Ltd; Director, 28 companies; Journalist; Lecturer; President, Patron, 28 Car Clubs. Publications: Stirling Moss, 1953; In the Track of Speed, 1957; Le Mans 59, 1959; Design and Behaviour of the Racing Car, 1963; All But My Life, 1963; How to Watch Motor Racing, 1975; Motor Racing and All That, 1980; My Cars, My Career, 1987; Stirling Moss: Great Drives in the Lakes and Dales, 1993; Motor Racing Masterpieces, 1995; Stirling Moss, autobiography, 2001. Honours include: Honorary FIE, 1959; Gold Star, British Racing Drivers Club, 10 times, 1950-61; Driver of the Year, Guild of Motoring Writers, 1954; Sir Malcolm Campbell Memorial Award, 1957. Address: c/o Stirling Moss Ltd, 46 Shepherd Street, Mayfair, London W1Y 8JN, England. E-mail: stirlingmossltd@aol.com

**MÖSSBAUER Rudolf Ludwig,** b. 31 January 1929, Munich, Germany. Physicist. Education: Graduated, Munich Institute of Technology, 1952; PhD, 1958; Postgraduate Research, Max Planck Institute for Medical Research, Heidelberg, 1958.

Appointments: Professor of Physics, California Institute of Technology, Pasadena; Concurrent Professorship, Munich Institute of Technology; Discovered the Mössbauer Effect. Publications: Papers on Recoilless Nuclear Resonance Absorption and on Neutrino Physics. Honour: Nobel Prize for Physics, 1961. Address: Fachbereich Physik, Physik Department E 15, Technische Universität Menchen, D-85747 Garching, Germany. E-mail: beatrice.vbellen@ph.tum.de

**MOSZCZYNSKI Paulin,** b. 3 January 1936, Janów, Lubelski, Poland. Haematologist. m. Maria Otto, 1 son, 1 daughter. Education: University Medical School, Cracow, Poland, 1960; MD, 1968; Full Professor of Medicine, 1991. Appointments: Head, Department of Medicine, L Rydygier Hospital, Brzesko, Poland, 1975-; Head, Province Immunology Laboratory, Brzesko, 1978-; Consultant Haematologist, 1975-; President, International Institute of University Medicine, Tarnow, Poland, 1996-2003; Chair, many scientific sessions in international conferences in Poland and abroad; Lecturer, Technical Open University, Cracow, 1995-; Lecturer, Cracow University of Promotion of Health, Cracow, 2005-. Publications: Over 1,500 publications to professional and popular journals. Honours: Chivalry Cross of Order of the Rebirth of Poland, 1999; Individual Prize Ministry of Health and Social Welfare, 1989; Gloria Medicinae Medal, 1994; A Schweitzer Golden Medal, 1996, 1999. Memberships: Polish Academy of Medicine; New York Academy of Sciences; Albert Schweitzer World Academy of Medicine. Address: Wyzwolenia 7, 32-800 Brzesko, Poland.

**MOTION Andrew,** b. 26 October 1952, England. Biographer; Poet; Poet Laureate of the United Kingdom, 1999-. m. (1) Joanna J Powell, 1973, dissolved 1983, (2) Janet Elisabeth Dalley, 1985, 2 sons, 1 daughter. Education: Radley College and University College, Oxford. Appointments: Lecturer in English, University of Hull, 1977-81; Editor, Poetry Review, 1981-83; Poetry Editor, Chatto & Windus, 1983-89, Editorial Director, 1985-87; Professor of Creative Writing, University of East Anglia, Norwich, 1995-2004; Professor of Creative Writing, Royal Holloway, University of London, 2004-; Chair, Literary Advisory Panel Arts Council of England, 1996-98; Poet Laureate of the United Kingdom, 1999-. Publications: Poetry: The Pleasure Steamers, 1978; Independence, 1981; The Penguin Book of Contemporary British Poetry (anthology), 1982; Secret Narratives, 1983; Dangerous Play, 1984; Natural Causes, 1987; Love in a Life, 1991; The Price of Everything, 1994; Selected Poems, 1996-97, 1998; Salt Water, 1997; Here to Eternity, anthology, 2000; Public Property, 2001; Criticism: The Poetry of Edward Thomas, 1981; Philip Larkin, 1982; William Barnes Selected Poems (ed), 1994; Biography: The Lamberts, 1986; Philip Larkin: A Writer's Life, 1993; Keats, 1997; Wainewright the Poisoner, novel, 2000; The Invention of Dr Cake, novel, 2003. Honours include: Rhys Memorial Prize, 1984; Somerset Maugham Award, 1987; Whitbread Biography Award, 1993; Honorary DLitt, Hull, 1996, Exeter, 1999, Brunel, 2000, APU, 2001, Open University, 2002; Sheffield Hallam, 2003; Sheffield, 2005. Address: c/o Faber & Faber, 3 Queen Square, London WC1, England.

**MOULE Ros,** b. 18 March 1941, Swansea, Wales. Lecturer and Writer. 1 son, 1 daughter. Education: BA, University College of Swansea, 1962; PGCE, London Institute of Education, 1963. Appointments: Lecturer, American and European Studies, University of London, 1970-75; Lecturer, Kingston College of Further Education, Surrey, 1975-87, Swansea College, 1991-2001. Contributions to: Poetry Wales; Poetry Digest; Merlin; Westwords; Anglo Welsh Review. Honours: West Wales Writers Umbrella Annual Competition; Swansea Writers Circle Competition; Currently Chairperson of the Tibetan Yungdrung

Bön Study Centre (UK) SCO 23439 (Charity Number). Address: 15 Admirals Walk, Sketty, Swansea, West Glamorgan SA2 8LQ, Wales.

**MOUNT William Robert Ferdinand,** b. 2 July 1939, London, England. Novelist; Journalist; Editor. m. Julia Lucas, 20 July 1968, 2 sons, 1 daughter. Education: BA, Christ Church, Oxford, 1961. Appointments: Political Editor, 1977-82, 1985, Literary Editor, 1984-85, Spectator; Head of Prime Minister's Policy Unit, 1982-84; Political Columnist, The Times, 1984-85, Daily Telegraph, 1985-90; Editor, Times Literary Supplement, 1991-2002; Fellow, 1991, Council, 2002-, RSL; Senior Columnist, The Sunday Times, 2002-. Publications: Very Like a Whale, 1967; The Theatre of Politics, 1972; The Man Who Rode Ampersand, 1975; The Clique, 1978; The Subversive Family, 1982; The Selkirk Strip, 1987; Of Love and Asthma, 1991; The British Constitution Now, 1992; Umbrella, 1994; The Liquidator, 1995; Jem (and Sam), 1998; Fairness, 2001; Mind the Gap, 2004; Heads You Win, 2004. Contributions to: Spectator; Encounter; National Interest; London Review of Books. Honour: Hawthornden Prize, 1992; Honorary Fellow, University of Wales, Lampeter, 2002. Address: 17 Ripplevale Grove, London N1 1HS, England.

**MOURA Marcelo Francisco de Sousa Ferreira de,** b. 12 February 1962, Lourenço Marques, Mozambique. Auxiliary Professor. m. Ana Cristina Moura, 1 daughter. Education: Graduate, Mechanical Engineering, 1985; Doctor's Diploma, 1996, Faculty of Engineering, University of Porto, Portugal. Appointments: Assistant, 1986-96, Auxiliary Professor, 1996-, Faculty of Engineering, University of Porto, Portugal. Publications: More than 60 publications including papers in international scientific journals, international and national conferences, technical reports, dissertations and lecture notes. Memberships: Mecanica Experimental e Novos Materias, Research Group; Instituto de Engenharia Mechanica e Gestao Industrial; International Association of Computational Mechanics. Address: Faculdade de Engenharia da Universidade do Porto, R Dr Roberto Frias s/n, 4200-465 Porto, Portugal. E-mail: mfmoura@fe.up.pt

**MOWAT David,** b. 16 March 1943, Cairo, Egypt (British citizen). Playwright. Education: BA, New College, Oxford, 1964. Publications: Jens, 1965; Pearl, 1966; Anna Luse, 1968; Dracula, 1969; Purity, 1969; The Normal Woman, and Tyypi, 1970; Adrift, 1970; The Others, 1970; Most Recent Least Recent, 1970; Inuit, 1970; The Diabolist, 1971; John, 1971; Amalfi (after Webster), 1972; Phoenix-and-Turtle, 1972; Morituri, 1972; My Relationship with Jayne, 1973; Come, 1973; Main Sequence, 1974; The Collected Works, 1974; The Memory Man, 1974; The Love Maker, 1974; X to C, 1975; Kim, 1977; Winter, 1978; The Guise, 1979; Hiroshima Nights, 1981; The Midnight Sun, 1983; Carmen, 1984; The Almas, 1989; Jane, or The End of the World, 1992. Radio Plays. Honour: Arts Council Bursaries. Address: 7 Mount Street, Oxford OX2 6DH, England.

**MOXLEY Raymond James (Ray),** b. 28 June 1923, Sheffield, England. Chartered Architect. m. Ann March, 1 son, 2 daughters. Education: Oxford School of Architecture, 1939-42; War service, 1942-46; Demobilised as Captain Royal Engineers; Dipl Arch, Oxford School of Architecture, 1946-49. Appointments: Assistant Architect, Bristol City Architects Department, 1949-51; Own Practice, 1953; Senior Partner, Moxley, Jenner and Partners, 1970-95; Founder, Chairman of the Society of Alternative Methods of Management; Co-Founder, Association of Consultant Architects; Commodore, Cargreen Yacht Club, Cornwall, 2002-2004. Publications: Architects Eye; Building Management by Professionals; An Architects Guide to Fee

Negotiation. Honours: Honorary Fellow, University of the West of England; First Honorary Librarian of the Royal Institute of British Architects. Memberships: Fellow, Past Vice President, Royal Institute of British Architects; Past President, Association of Consultant Architects; Fellow, Royal Society of Arts; The Worshipful Company of Chartered Architects; Academician, Royal West of England Academy; The Royal West of England Yacht Club; Cargreen Yacht Club, Cornwall. Address: 10 The Beldevere, Chelsea Harbour, London SW10 0XA, England.

**MOYNIHAN Daniel Patrick,** b. 16 March 1927, Tulsa, Oklahoma, USA. Retired United States Senator; Writer. m. Elizabeth Therese Brennan, 29 May 1955, 2 sons, 1 daughter. Education: City College of New York, 1943; BA, Tufts University, 1948; MA, 1949, PhD, 1961, Fletcher School of Law and Diplomacy. Appointments: Special Assistant, 1961-62, Executive Assistant, 1962-63, to the US Secretary of Labor; Assistant Secretary of Labor, 1963-65; Fellow, Center for Advanced Studies, Wesleyan University, 1965-66; Professor of Education and Urban Politics, 1966-73, Senior Member, 1966-77, Professor of Government, 1973-77, Kennedy School of Government, Harvard University; Assistant for Urban Affairs, 1969-70, Counsellor, 1969-70, Consultant, 1971-73, to the President of the US; US Ambassador to India, 1973-75; US Permanent Representative to the United Nations, 1975-76; US Senator (Democrat) from the State of New York, 1977-2001. Publications: Beyond the Melting Pot (with Nathan Glazer), 1963; The Defenses of Freedom: The Public Papers of Arthur J Goldberg (editor), 1966; Equal Educational Opportunity (co-author), 1969; On Understanding Poverty: Perspectives for the Social Sciences (editor), 1969; The Politics of a Guaranteed Income, 1973; Coping: On the Practice of Government, 1974; Ethnicity: Theory and Experience (editor with Nathan Glazer), 1975; A Dangerous Place (with S Weaver), 1978; Counting Our Blessings: Reflections on the Future of America, 1980; Loyalties, 1984; Family and Nation, 1986; Came the Revolution: Argument in the Reagan Era, 1988; On the Law of Nations, 1990; Pandaemonium: Ethnicity in International Politics, 1993; Miles to Go: A Personal History of Social Policy, 1996; Secrecy: The American Experience, 1999. Contributions to: Professional journals. Honours: Meritorious Service Award, US Department of Labor, 1965; Centennial Medal, Syracuse University, 1969; International League for Human Rights Award, 1975; John LaFarge Award for Interracial Justice, 1980; Medallion, State University of New York at Albany, 1984; Henry Medal, Smithsonian Institution, 1985; SEAL Medallion, Central Intelligence Agency, 1986; Laetare Medal, University of Notre Dame, 1992; Thomas Jefferson Award, 1993; Numerous honorary doctorates. Address: c/o United State Senate, 464 Russell Senate Building, Washington, DC 20510, USA.

**MTHENGA Nyandoro (Stanley),** b. 17 February 1973, Blantyre, Malawi. Musician. m. Jane, 2 daughters. Education: Diploma in Administration; Self taught traditional artist. Appointments: Musician; Poet; Pioneer of Sena Jive Music (Seji Music); Only musician in Malawi playing pure, traditional music using electric equipment; Founder, Seji Vibrations musical group; Performed at two international festivals in Zimbabwe, 2000 and Durban, South Africa, 2002. Publications: Four traditional albums: Misozi Ya Ng'Ona; Nyakabusa; Mtchona; Moto Mdambo; Poem: Life is the Sun. Memberships: Musicians Association of Malawi. Address: c/o Box 1071, Lilongwe, Malawi. E-mail: stanmthenga@yahoo.com

**MUELLER Kathryn Lucile,** b. 14 February 1951, Lincoln, Nebraska, USA. Occupational Medicine Physician. m. Rex Logemann, 1 son, 1 daughter. Education: BA, MD, 1977, University of Nebraska; MPH, Medical College of Wisconsin,

1994. Appointments: Assistant Professor, 1987-98, Associate Professor, 1998-2005, Professor 2005-, Emergency Medicine and Preventive Medicine, University of Colorado, Health Sciences Center; Medical Director, Colorado Division of Worker's Compensation, 1991-; Residency Director, Occupational Medicine, University of Colorado. Publications: Acceptance and self-reported use of national occupational practice guidelines (co-author), 2000; numerous other book chapters on practice guidelines. Honours: President, Rocky Mountain Academy of Occupational Medicine; National Leadership Award, Central State Occupational Medicine Association. Membership: Fellow and Board of Directors, 2000-04, Secretary-Treasurer, 2004-, American College of Occupational and Environmental Medicine. Address: University of Colorado Health Sciences Center, 4200 E 39th Avenue B119, Denver, CO 80122, USA. E-mail: kathryn.mueller@uchsc.edu

**MUGGESON Margaret Elizabeth, (Margaret Dickinson, Everatt Jackson),** b. 30 April 1942, Gainsborough, Lincolnshire, England. Writer. m. Dennis Muggeson, 19 September 1964, 2 daughters. Education: Lincoln College of Technology, 1960-61. Publications: Pride of the Courtneys, 1968; Brackenbeck, 1969; Portrait of Jonathan, 1970; The Road to Hell (as Everatt Jackson), 1975; Abbeyford Trilogy, 1981; Lifeboat!, 1983; Beloved Enemy, 1984; Plough the Furrow, 1994; Sow the Seed, 1995; Reap the Harvest, 1996; The Miller's Daughter, 1997; Chaff Upon the Wind, 1998; The Fisher Lass, 1999; The Tulip Girl, 2000; The River Folk, 2001; Tangled Threads, 2002; Twisted Strands, 2003; Red Sky in the Morning, 2004; Without Sin, 2005. Membership: Romantic Novelists Association.

**MUIR Richard,** b. 18 June 1943, Yorkshire, England. Author; Photographer. Education: 1st Class Honours, Geography, 1967, PhD, 1970, University of Aberdeen. Appointment: Editor, National Trust Regional Histories and Countryside Commission National Park Series. Publications: Over 40 books, including: Modern Political Geography, 1975; Hedgerows: Their History and Wildlife (with N Muir), 1987; Old Yorkshire, 1987; The Countryside Encyclopaedia, 1988; Fields (with Nina Muir), 1989; Portraits of the Past, 1989; The Dales of Yorkshire, 1991; The Villages of England, 1992; The Coastlines of Britain, 1993; Political Geography: A New Introduction, 1997; The Yorkshire Countryside: A Landscape History, 1997; Approaches to Landscape; New Reading the Landscape, 2000; Landscape Detective, 2002; Encyclopaedia of Landscape, 2004; Ancient Trees, Living Landscapes, 2005; Valley of Ghosts, forthcoming. Contributions to: Academic journals and general periodicals. Honour: Yorkshire Arts Literary Prize, 1982-83; Honorary Research Fellow, Department of Geography and Environment, University of Aberdeen. Address: 20 Stray Walk, Harrogate, North Yorkshire HG2 8HU, England.

**MUIR WOOD David,** b. 17 March 1949, Folkestone, Kent, England. Civil Engineer. m. Helen Rosamond Piddington, 2 sons. Education: Royal Grammar School, High Wycombe, 1959-66; BA, 1970, MA, 1974, Peterhouse, Cambridge; PhD, Cambridge University, 1974. Appointments: William Stone Research Fellow, Peterhouse, Cambridge, 1973-75; Royal Society Research Fellow, Norwegian Geotechnical Institute, Oslo, 1975; Fellow, Emmanuel College, Cambridge, 1975-87; University Demonstrator in Soil Mechanics, Cambridge University Engineering Department, 1975-78; Geotechnical Engineer, Scott, Wilson, Kirkpatrick and Partners, Hong Kong, 1978; University Lecturer in Soil Mechanics, Cambridge University Engineering Department, 1978-87; Associate, Geotechnical Consulting Group, 1983-; Visiting Research Associate, University of Colorado, Boulder, USA, 1986; Cormack Professor of Civil Engineering, University of Glasgow,

Scotland, 1987-95; Elder, Cairns Church of Scotland, Milngavie, 1993-98; Royal Society Industry Fellow, Babtie Group, 1995-96; Professor of Civil Engineering, University of Bristol, 1995-; Consultant, Babtie Group, Glasgow, 1997-; Head, Department of Civil Engineering, University of Bristol, 1997-2002; MTS Visiting Professor of Geomechanics, University of Minnesota, 2000; Foundation for Industrial Science Visiting Professor, Institute for Industrial Science, University of Tokyo, 2003; Dean, Faculty of Engineering, University of Bristol, 2003-. Publications: 52 papers in journals; 102 papers in academic conferences. Honours: Rex Moir Prize, 1969; Archibald Denny Prize, 1970; British Geotechnical Society Prize, 1978; Fellow, Royal Academy of Engineering, 1998. Memberships: American Society of Civil Engineers; British Geotechnical Society; Remote Sensing and Photogrammetry Society; Society for Earthquake and Civil Engineering Dynamics; Fellow, Institution of Civil Engineers. Address: Leigh Lodge, Church Road, Abbots Leigh, Bristol BS8 3QP, England. E-mail: d.muir-wood@bristol.ac.uk

**MUKHERJEE Tara Kumar,** b. 20 December 1923, Calcutta, India. Retired. Education: Scottish Church College; Calcutta University, India. Appointments: Shop Manager, Bata Shoe Company, India, 1941-44; Buyer, Brevitt Schoes, 1951-56; Sundries Buyer, British Shoe Corporation, 1956-66; Production Administrator, Priestly Footwear Ltd, 1966-68; Head Store Manager, British Shoe Corporation, 1968-70; District Manager, 1970-78, Branch Manager, 1978-84, Save and Prosper Group; Area Manager, Guardian Royal Exchange, 1985-88; Managing Director, OWL Financial Services, 1988. Honours: Honorary Doctor of Philosophy, Middlesex University; FLIA; FRSA. Memberships: First Class Cricketer, Ranjy Trophy, Bihar, India; Leicestershire County Cricket Club; Indian National Club; Chairman, European Multicultural Foundation; President, Confederation of Indian Organisations (UK); President, European Union Migrants Forum; Royal Commonwealth Society; European Movement; President, India Film Society. Address: 51 Viking Way, Brentwood, Essex CM15 9HY, England. E-mail: emf@mbebrentwood.co.uk

**MULDER Johannes (Jan) W F,** b. 28 June 1919, Arnhem, The Netherlands. Emeritus Professor of Linguistics. m. Dora Kodong, deceased 15 July 2001, 2 sons. Education: Student of Sinology, University of Djakarta, Indonesia, 1950-51; BA (equivalent), Chinese and Japanese Linguistics and Literature, University of Leiden, The Netherlands, 1954; Doctoral Degree, 1958; MA Oxon, 1962; DPhil, Oxon, 1966; Fellow of St Cross College, Oxon. Appointments: Bibliographical Secretary, The Linguistic Survey of Asia, sponsored by the American State Department, 1959-61; Far Eastern Librarian, 1961-64, Senior Librarian, 1964-68, Oriental Institute, Oxford, England; Concurrently, Lectured in Linguistics at Oxford University and supervised research students; Senior Lecturer, 1968-72, Personal Chair in Linguistics, 1972-84, Emeritus Professor, 1984-, St Andrews University, Scotland; Visiting Professorships: Mahidol University, Thailand, 1984-85, Albert Ludwigs Universität, Freiburg, West Germany, 1985-86, 1989-90. Publications: Books: Sets and Relations in Phonology: an axiomatic approach to the description of speech, 1968; The Strategy of Linguistics: Papers on the theory and methodology of axiomatic functionalism ( in collaboration with SGJ Hervey), 1980; Theory of the linguistic sign (in collaboration with SGJ Hervey), 1972; Foundations of axiomatic linguistics, 1989; Ontological Questions in Linguistics (in collaboration with Dr Paul Rastall), 2005; Author and co-author of numerous articles in professional journals and conference proceedings; Initiator of the Linguistic Theory called Axiomatic Functionalism. Honours: Member Queen's College Oxford; Fellow, St Cross

College, Oxford; Honorary President, Societé Internationale de Linguistique Fonctionelle, 1984; 21st Century Award for Achievement, IBC, Cambridge, 2000-2001; American Medal of Honor for contribution to functional linguistics, ABI, USA, 2003. Memberships: Leiden Linguistic Circle, Chairman, 1959-61; Member Editorial Board, La Linguistique, 1976-; Societé Internationale de Linguistique Fonctionelle; President 1977-84. Address: Winterdijkweg, 4A, 3950 Kaulille, Belgium. E-mail: jfwmulder@yahoo.co.uk

**MULDOON Paul,** b. 20 June 1951, Portadown, County Armagh, Northern Ireland. Poet; Writer; Dramatist; Professor in the Humanities. m. Jean Hanff Korelitz, 1987. Education: BA, English Language and Literature, Queen's University, Belfast, 1973. Appointments: Producer, 1973-78, Senior Producer, 1978-85, Radio Arts Programmes, Television Producer, 1985-86, BBC Northern Ireland; Judith E Wilson Visiting Fellow, University of Cambridge, 1986-87; Creative Writing Fellow, University of East Anglia, 1987; Lecturer, Columbia University, 1987-88; Lecturer, 1987-88, 1990-95, Director, Creative Writing Programme, 1993-, Howard G B Clark Professor in the Humanities, 1998-, Princeton University; Professor of Poetry, University of Oxford, 1999-04; Writer-in-Residence, 92nd Street Y, New York City, 1988; Roberta Holloway Lecturer, University of California at Berkeley, 1989; Visiting Professor, University of Massachusetts, Amberst, 1989-90, Bread Loaf School of English, 1997-. Publications: Poetry: Knowing My Place, 1971; New Weather, 1973; Spirit of Dawn, 1975; Mules, 1977; Names and Addresses, 1978; Immram, 1980; Why Brownlee Left, 1980; Out of Siberia, 1982; Quoof, 1983; The Wishbone, 1984; Meeting the British, 1987; Madoc: A Mystery, 1990; Incantata, 1994; The Prince of the Quotidian, 1994; The Annals of Chile, 1994; Kerry Slides, 1996; New Selected Poems, 1968-94, 1996; Hopewell Haiku, 1997; The Bangle (Slight Return), 1998; Hay, 1998; Poems 1968-98, 2001; Moy Sand and Gravel, 2002. Theatre: Monkeys (television play), 1989; Shining Brow (opera libretto), 1993; Six Honest Serving Men (play), 1995; Bandanna (opera libretto), 1999. Essays: To Ireland, I, 2000. Translator: The Astrakhan Cloak, by Nuala Ni Dhomhnaill, 1993; The Birds, by Aristophanes (with Richard Martin), 1999. Editor: The Scrake of Dawn, 1979; The Faber Book of Contemporary Irish Poetry, 1986; The Essential Byron, 1989; The Faber Book of Beasts, 1997. Children's Books: The O-O's Party, 1981; The Last Thesaurus, 1995; The Noctuary of Narcissus Batt, 1997. Contributions to: Anthologies and other publications. Honours: Eric Gregory Award, 1972; Sir Geoffrey Faber Memorial Awards, 1980, 1991; Guggenheim Fellowship, 1990; T S Eliot Prize for Poetry, 1994; American Academy of Arts and Letters Award, 1996; Irish Times Poetry Prize, 1997; Pulitzer Prize for Poetry, 2002; Shakespeare Prize, 2004. Memberships: Aosdana; Poetry Society of Great Britain, president, 1996-; Royal Society of Literature, fellow; American Academy of Arts and Sciences, 2000. Address: Creative Writing Programme, Princeton University, Princeton, NJ 08544, USA.

**MULINDI-KING Luzili Ruth,** b 21 July 1947, Maragoli, Kenya. Music Educator; Choral Director; Ethnomusicologist. m. Roger P King, 2 daughters. Education: GNSM, Northern School of Music, 1972; Cert Ed, Music, Drama, Bretton Hall College, 1973; MA, Social Anthropology, Ethnomusicology, Queen's University, Belfast, 1984; Piano with Julia Moss and Margaret Gifford; Choral Training with Graham Hyslop and Maggie Burton-Page; Ethnomusicology with Professors John Blacking and John Baily. Appointments: Head of Music, AGHS, Kenya, 1973-77; Lecturer, Music Department, Kenyatta University, Nairobi, 1977-91; Head of Music, Lucton School, 1993-2004; Head of Music, St Richard's School, Bredenbury, England, 1999-; Visiting Lecturer, Goshen College, Indiana, USA,

Manchester University, UK. Publications: Editor, Music Time, 1991; Music in Logoli Culture, 1998; After the Bomb (in The Friend), 1999; Song: Chunga Maji Yasipungue, 1986; Report: Towards an Inclusive Singing Culture, 2004; British Council Scholarship for Postgraduate study at QUB; CD: Music Safari, 2004. Honour: First African Kenyan to win the KMF Leonard Machin Cup for the Bach Class (Prelude and Fugue), Best KMF Choral Director, 1976; Herefordshire Choir of the Year, 1999; Winston Churchill Fellow, 2002. Memberships: Incorporated Society of Musicians; Association of British Choral Directors; National Association of Music Educators; Kenya Music Trust. Address: Brick Cottage, Yarpole, Leominster, Herefordshire, HR6 0BA, England.

**MÜLLER Kurt Bernel,** b. 3 September 1943, Blens/Eifel, Germany. Professor of American Literature. m. Rosa Gomez Cagigal, 1 son, 1 daughter. Education: State Exam, English and German Philology, University of Cologne, Germany, 1970; PhD, 1976, Habilitation, 1988, University of Freiburg, Germany. Appointments: Academic Councillor, University of Freiburg, Germany, 1979-90; Deputy Professor, University of Trier, Germany, 1990-92; Professor and Chair of American Studies, University of Jena, Germany, 1992-. Publications: Books: Konventionen und Tendenzen der Gesellschaftskritik im expressionistischen amerikanischen Drama der zwanziger Jahre, 1977; Identität und Rolle bei Theodore Dreiser: Eine Untersuchung des Romanwerks unter rollentheoretischem Aspekt, 1991; Inszenierte Wirklichkeiten: Die Erfahrung der Moderne im Leben und Werk Eugene O'Neills, 1993; Ernest Hemingway: Der Mensch, der Schriftsteller, das Werk, 1999; Numerous articles as author and co-author in professional journals. Memberships: Deutscher Anglistenverband; Deutsche Gesellschaft für Amerikastudien; Gesellschaft für Kanadastudien. Address: Ernst-Abbe-Platz 8, D-07743 Jena, Germany. E-mail: X6muku@rz.uni-jena.de

**MUNDA Ivka Maria,** b. 7 July 1927, Ljubljana, Slovenia. Scientific Official. Education: Diploma, Biology, Chemistry; PhD, Marine Biology, University of Ljubljana, 1963; PhD, Marine Botany, University of Gothenbourg, Sweden, 1963. Appointments: Assistant, Biological Institute, Medical Faculty, University of Ljubljana; National Research Association, University of Trondheim; Water Research Institute, Oslo; Yearly Grants, Icelandic Research Foundation, Reykjavík, Iceland, for Algological Research, 1963-80; Scientific Official, Hydrobiologist Instituute, Yerseke, Holland, 1964-65; Scientific Official, Biological Institute, Centre for Scientific Research of the Slovene Academy of Science and Arts, 1966-; Grants from the Alexander von Humboldt Foundation, Bonn, Germany, 1975-76. Publications: 125 scientific papers, marine algal ecology, geographic distribution and biochemistry, international journals. Honours: Slovene Award, Boris Kidrič; 20th Century Achievement Award, International Biographical Centre; New Century Award, The Europe 500; 1000 Leaders of World Influence; Leading Intellectuals of the World, 2000-2001; Presidential Award, 500 Great Minds; Order of International Ambassadors; American Medal of Honour, Profiles of Excellence. Memberships: British Phycological Society; Phycological Society of America; International Phycological Society; COST; CIESM; Deutsche Botanische Geselschaft; The New York Academy of Sciences; Board of Governors, American Biographical Institute; Research Board of Advisors, ABI; The Planetary Society; Deputy Director General, Biographical Centre, Cambridge; Secretary General, United Cultural Convention, USA; Scientific Advisor to the Director General, IBC; The BWW Society, USA. Address: Centre for Scientific Research, Slovene Academy of Science and Arts, Novi trg 2, 1000 Ljubljana, Slovenia.

# DICTIONARY OF INTERNATIONAL BIOGRAPHY

**MUNN Bob (Robert William),** b. 16 January 1945, Bath, Somerset, England. Academic. m. Patricia Lorna Moyle, 1 son, 1 daughter. Education: BSc, Chemistry, 1965, PhD, Theoretical Chemistry, 1968, Bristol University; DSc, Manchester University, 1982. Appointments: Postdoctorate Fellow, National Research Council of Canada, 1968-70; ICI Postdoctoral Fellow, Edinburgh University, 1970-71; Lecturer in Chemistry, 1971-80, Reader in Chemistry, 1980-84, Professor of Chemical Physics, 1984-2004, Vice Principal for Finance, 1987-90, Dean, 1994-99, UMIST; Visiting Fellow, Australian National University, 1982; Vice President for Teaching and Learning, The University of Manchester, 2004-. Publications: Over 200 research-based publications; 2 co-authored books; 2 co-edited books. Memberships: Fellow, Royal Society of Chemistry; Chartered Chemist; Fellow, Institute of Physics; Chartered Physicist; Member, Institute for Learning and Teaching; Chartered Scientist. Address: The University of Manchester, Manchester M13 9PL, England. E-mail: bob.munn@manchester.ac.uk

**MUÑOZ Juan de Dios,** b. 2 November 1947, Paraná, Argentina. Agricultural Engineer. Education: Agricultural Engineer, 1973, Doctor of Pharmacobotany and Pharmacognosy, 2003, University of Buenos Aires. Appointments: Professor of Systematic Botany; Director, Oro Verde Botany Garden and Herbarium, Faculty of Agricultural Sciences, National University of Entre Ríos; Botanist, Entre Ríos Soil Survey Project; Director, Antiviral, Antibacterial; Antifungal and Antigouty Research Projects. Publications: Co-author, Trees and Shrubs of Entre Ríos, 1983; Co-author, Flora of Paraguay, 1990; Catalogue of Argentinian Vascular Plants, 1999; Argentine Phanerogamic Flora, 2000; Collaborator, Darwin Manual for Botanic Gardens, 1998; International Agenda for Botanic Gardens in Conservation, 2000. Honours: British Council Prize for Progress, 1965; College of Agricultural Engineers Gold Medal, 1975; Prize for Academic Excellence, IADE, 1996; Prize for Human Excellence, IADE, 1997; First National Prize for Human Excellence, IADE, 2001; Freeman of City, Paraná, 2001; Listed in national and international biographical dictionaries; Argentine Association of Natural Sciences Diploma of Honour, 2001; Entre Ríos National University Diploma of Honour, 2001; Organization of American States Award, 1983, 1990. Memberships: Argentine Society of Botany; American Society of Plant Taxonomists; Botanic Gardens Conservation International. Address: Facultad de Ciencias Agropecuarias, Universidad Nacional de Entre Ríos, CC24, 3100 Paraná, Entre Ríos, Argentina. E-mail: botanica@fca.uner.edu.ar

**MUNRO Alice,** b. 10 July 1931, Wingham, Ontario, Canada. Author. m. (1) James Armstrong Munro, 29 December 1951, divorced 1976, 3 daughters, (2) Gerald Fremlin, 1976. Education: BA, University of Western Ontario, 1952. Publications: Dance of the Happy Shades, 1968; A Place for Everything, 1970; Lives of Girls and Women, 1971; Something I've Been Meaning to Tell You, 1974; Who Do You Think You Are?, 1978, US and British editions as The Beggar Maid: Stories of Flo and Rose, 1984; The Moons of Jupiter, 1982; The Progress of Love, 1986; Friend of My Youth, 1990; Open Secrets, 1994; Selected Stories, 1996; The Love of a Good Woman, 1998; Hateship, Friendship, Courtship, Loveship, Marriage, 2001. Honours: Governor-General's Awards for Fiction, 1968, 1978, 1986; Guardian Booksellers Award, 1971; Honorary DLitt, University of Western Ontario, 1976; Marian Engel Award, 1986; Canada-Australia Literary Prize, 1994; Lannan Literary Award, 1995; W H Smith Literary Award, 1996; National Book Critics Circle Award, 1998. Address: The Writers Shop, 101 5th Avenue, New York, NY 10003, USA.

**MUNTEANU Ioan,** b. 23 June 1938, Igris, Romania. Physician. m. Gina Munteanu, 2 daughters. Education: Graduated, University of Medicine and Pharmacy, Timisoara, 1961; Doctor's degree as Physician, 1972. Appointment: Professor of Obstetrics and Gynaecology, Bega, University Clinic of Obstetrics and Gynaecology. Honours: Gh Marinescu Award, Romanian Academy, 1987; 1st in Romania to perform IVF, 1995. Memberships: Chief, Romanian Society of Human Reproduction; President, Romanian Society of Human Assisted Reproduction; New York Academy of Sciences; UPIGO; European Association of Gynaecology and Obstetrics; ESHRE; Obstetrics and Gynaecology Gestosis; International Federation of Gynaecology and Obstetrics; SOFIGO. Address: Bega, University Clinic of Obstetrics and Gynaecology, Boulevard Victor Babes Nr 12, 1900 Timosoara, Romania.

**MURAYAMA Yoko,** b. 16 August 1962, Kurume, Fukuoka, Japan. Physician. Education: MD, Shimane Medical University, Japan, 1988; PhD, Osaka University, 1997. Appointments: Resident, Toyonaka Municipal Hospital, Osaka, 1988-90; Researcher, Osaka University, 1990-98; Gastroenterologist, Ikeda Municipal Hospital, Osaka, 1998-99; Postdoctoral Fellow, 1999-2003, Assistant Professor, 2003-05, Osaka University Graduate School of Medicine, Department of Internal Medicine and Molecular Science; Directorate of Gastroenterology, Itami City Hospital, Hyogo, 2005-. Publications: Numerous articles in professional medical journals. Memberships: Japanese Society of Internal Medicine; Japanese Society of Gastroenterology; Japan Gastroenterological Endoscopy Society. Address: Kamishinden 1-19-1-906, Toyonaka City, Osaka, Japan. E-mail: yohkokiss@hotmail.com

**MURDOCH Keith Rupert,** b. 11 March 1931, Melbourne, Australia (American citizen, 1985-). Publishing and Broadcasting Executive. m. (1) Patricia Booker, divorced, 1 daughter, (2) Anna Maria Torv, 28 April 1967, divorced, 2 sons, 1 daughter, (3) Wendy Deng, 1999, 2 daughters. Education: MA, Oxon, Worcester College, Oxford, England, 1953. Appointments: Chief Executive Officer, 1979-, Chairman, 1991-, News Corporation; Owner, numerous newspapers, magazines and TV operations in UK, US, Italy, Asia and Australia. Honours: AC, 1984; Commander of the White Rose, First Class, 1986; Knight of St Gregory the Great, 1998. Address: News Corporation, 1211 Avenue of the Americas, New York, NY 10036, USA.

**MURDOCH Lachlan Keith,** b. 8 September 1971, Australia (American citizen). Business Executive. m. Sarah O'Hare, 1999. Education: Princeton University. Appointments: Reporter, San Antonio Express News, The Times (UK); Sub-Editor, The Sun (UK); General Manager, Queensland Newspapers Pty Ltd, 1994-95; Executive Director, News Ltd, 1995; Director, Beijing PDN Xinren Information Technology Co Ltd, 1995-; Deputy Chair, Star Television, 1995-; Deputy Chief Executive, News Ltd, 1995-96; Director, The Herald & Weekly Times Ltd, 1996-, News Corporation, 1996-; Deputy COO, 2000-, Independent Newspapers Ltd (NZ), 1997-; Executive Chair, Chief Executive Officer, News Ltd, 1997; Senior Executive Vice-President, US Print Operations News Corporation, 1999-. Address: News Ltd, 2 Holt Street, Surry Hills, NSW 2010, Australia.

**MURIN Gustav,** b. 9 April 1959, Bratislava, Slovakia. Author. m. Jana, 2 daughters. Education: BSc, 1983, MSc, 1984, PhD, 1991, Comenius University, Bratislava. Publications: Author: The Case of a Buried Cemetery, in Czech, 1989; Summer Favors Lovers, 1990; Comebacks from Light, 1990; Substitutional End of the World, 1992; Instinct Contra Culture, 1994; Orgasmodromes, 1997; How Are You, 1998; Animals, Me and Other, 1998; Sex Contra Culture, in Czech, 1999;

Substitutional End of the World, in Czech, 1999; Just Like the Gods, 2001; You Will Become Gods, in Czech, 2002; Co-author, 10 different story collections in Slovakia and 6 abroad; Author, 11 radio-dramas, TV documents, TV play and script for art movie; Author of more than 990 articles in 39 major Slovak, Czech and international newspapers and magazines; Numerous translations. Honours: Best Slovak story, 1979; Best Czech and Slovak story, 1981; Best Czech and Slovak novella, 1986; Special prize in Slovak radio drama, 1988; Honorary Fellow in Writing, University of Iowa, 1995; E E Kisch Award, 2003; Active participation in international literary conferences. Memberships: Member, 1993-, Secretary, 1995-97, President, 2000-04, Slovak Centre of the PEN International; Member, Slovak Centre of Roma Club, 1994-; Member, Slovak Syndicate of Journalists, 1995-. Address: J Hagaru 17, 831 51 Bratislava, Slovak Republic. E-mail: murin@m2.fedu.uniba.sk

**MURPHY Eddie (Edward Regan)**, b. 3 April 1951, Brooklyn, New York, USA. Film Actor. m. (2) Nicole Mitchell, 2 sons, 1 daughter. Creative Works: Films include. 48 Hours, 1982; Trading Places, 1983; Delirious, 1983; Best Defence, 1984; Beverly Hills Cop, 1984; The Golden Child, 1986; Beverly Hills Cop II, 1987; Eddie Murphy Raw, 1987; Coming to America, 1988; Harlem Nights, 1989; 48 Hours 2, 1990; Boomerang, 1992; Distinguished Gentleman, 1992; Beverly Hills Cop III, 1994; The Nutty Professor, 1996; Dr Dolittle, 1998; Holy Man, 1998; Life, 1998; Bowfinger, 1999; Toddlers, 1999; Pluto Nash, 1999; Nutty Professor II: The Klumps; Dr Dolittle 2, 2001; Showtime, 2002; I-Spy, 2003; Daddy Day Care, 2003; The Haunted Mansion, 2003; Shrek 2 (voice), 2004; Tours with own comedy show; Comedy Albums: Eddie Murphy, 1982; Eddie Murphy: Comedian, 1983; How Could It Be, 1984; So Happy, 1989; Recorded 7 albums of comedy and songs. Honours include: Numerous awards and nominations. Address: c/o Jim Wiatt, ICM, 8942 Wilshire Boulevard, Beverly Hills, CA 90211, USA.

**MURPHY Michael**, b. 2 May 1951. Consultant Haematologist. m. (Elizabeth) Sarah Green, 1 son, 1 daughter. Education: Medical School, St Bartholomew's Hospital Medical College, London, 1968-73. Appointments: Research Registrar, Haematology, 1978; Registrar, Haematology, Senior Registrar, Haematology, 1980-84, Senior Lecturer, Honorary Consultant, Haematology, 1985-96, St Bartholomew's Hospital London; Consultant Haematologist, National Blood Service and Department of Haematology, Oxford Radcliffe Hospitals NHS Trust, Oxford, 1996-; Senior Clinical Lecturer in Blood Transfusion, 1998-2004, Professor of Blood Transfusion Medicine, 2004-, University of Oxford; Secretary, Chief Medical Officer's National Blood Transfusion Committee, Department of Health, 2001-; Member, Scientific Committee, 1999-, Co-Chair, Transfusion Safety Group, 2001-, Biomedical Excellence for Safer Transfusion Collaborative; Member, Working Group for vCJD, UK Blood Services, 2001-; Co-Chair, Platelet Immunology Scientific Sub-committee, International Society of Haemostasis and Thrombosis, 2002-. Publications: Over 65 articles as first author and co-author in medical journals; 23 book chapters; Book: Practical Transfusion Medicine (co-editor), 2001, 2nd edition in press. Honours: Kenneth Goldsmith Award, British Blood Transfusion Society, 1994; Numerous research grants. Memberships include: British Society for Haematology; Royal College of Physicians; American Association of Blood Banks; International Society of Blood Transfusion. Address: National Blood Transfusion Service, John Radcliffe Hospital, Oxford OX3 9BQ, England. E-mail: mike.murphy@nbs.nhs.uk

**MURPHY Michael T**, b. 6 March 1955, Buffalo, New York, USA. Teacher. Education: BSEd, Industrial Arts, 1979; MSEd, Technical Education, 1990, Co-opEd, Vocational Certification, 1990, SUNY at Buffalo; Vocational Education, Carpentry Building Trades, 1991; Vocational Education, Drafting Certification, 1995. Appointments: Technology Education, Mayville Central, 1987-90; Drafting/CAD Instructor, Triangle Tech, Pittsburgh, 1990-91; Auto-CAD Instructor, Allegeheny Community College, Pittsburgh, 1990-91; CADD/Drafting Instructor, WD Ormsby Center, Erie 2, Architectural Chair – Regional Skills, USA, 1994-. Publications: Some work displayed in Better Homes & Gardens, 1981-; Films: Our Schools: Education in a Changing World; Western New York Schools; Hide in Plain Sight, Buffalo, mid Seventies; Gone in Sixty Seconds, Dunkirk, New York version. Honours: Nominated three times for Walt Disney Teacher of the Year, 1999, 2000, 2001; Listed in Who's Who publications and biographical dictionaries. Memberships: Northern Chautauqua Conservation Club; Loyal Order of Moose; Master Instructor, Hunter Safety, New York State, DEC; Western New York Technology; Pistol Instructor, New York State, Chautauqua County. Address: 7956 Keene Road, Derby, NY 14047, USA.

**MURRAY Bill**, b. 21 September 1950, Evanston, Illinois, USA. Actor; Writer. m. Margaret Kelly, 1980, 2 son. Education: Loyola Academy; Regis College, Denver; Second City Workshop, Chicago. Appointments: Performer, Off-Broadway National Lampoon Radio Hour; Regular Appearances TV Series Saturday Night Live; Appeared in Radio Series Marvel Comics' Fantastic Four; Co-Producer, Director, Actor, Quick Change, 1990; Writer, NBC-TV Series Saturday Night Live, 1977-80; Films: Meatballs, 1977; Mr Mike's Mondo Video, 1979; Where the Buffalo Roam, 1980; Caddyshack, 1980; Stripes, 1981; Tootsie, 1982; Ghostbusters, 1984; The Razor's Edge, 1984; Nothing Lasts Forever, 1984; Little Shop of Horrors, 1986; Scrooged, 1988; Ghostbusters II, 1989; Quick Change, 1990; What About Bob?, 1991; Mad Dog and Glory, 1993; Groundhog Day, 1993; Ed Wood, 1994; Kingpin, 1996; Larger Than Life, 1996; Space Jam, 1996; The Man Who Knew Too Little, 1997; With Friends Like These, 1998; Veeck as in Wreck, 1998; Rushmore, 1998; Wild Things, 1998; The Cradle Will Rock, 1999; Hamlet, 1999; Company Man, 1999; Charlie's Angels, 2000; The Royal Tenenbaums, 2001; Osmosis Jones, 2001; Lost in Translation, 2003. Honours include: Emmy Award, Best Writing for Comedy Series, 1977; BAFTA Award for Best Actor, 2004. Address: c/o William Carroll Agency, 139 N San Fernando Road, Suite A, Burbank, CA 91502, USA.

**MURRAY Dermot Patrick**, b. 26 August 1938, Wallasey, Cheshire, England. Medical Practitioner. Elizabeth Hanly. Education: MB ChB, University of Liverpool, 1957-62; PGMO Course, Army Medical College, 1967; MRCP (UK), 1974; Dip Ven, 1976; Management Certificate, Derby University, 1993; BA, Open University, 1999. Appointments: Pre-Registration, United Liverpool Hospitals, 1962-63; Ships Surgeon, P&O, 1963-64; Senior House Officer and Registrar, United Liverpool Hospitals, 1964-67; Captain, General Duties Medical Officer, RAMC, 1967-72; Major, Specialist progressing to Consultant Genito-Urinary Physician, RAMC, 1972-75; Lieutenant Colonel, Genito-Urinary Physician, RAMC, 1975-83; Consultant Genito-Urinary Physician, Derby Royal Infirmary, 1983-97; Self-employed, Genito-Urinary Physician and Lecturer, 1997-. Publications: 8 articles in medical press; 17 letters in medical press; 15 papers read to professional bodies. Honours: Territorial Decoration (TB), 1990; Bar to Territorial Decoration, 1996. Memberships: British Association; Association for Sexual Health; Derby Scientific Club, President 2003-2004, 2004-2005; Nottinghamshire Diocese for Social Care, Chairman, 2002-2004. Address: 10 Old Vicarage Lane, Quarndon, Derby DE22 5JB, England.

**MURRAY Raymond Laurence,** b. 5 September 1938, Newtownhamilton, County Armagh, Northern Ireland. Catholic Priest. Education: St Patrick's College, Maynooth, County Kildare (Seminary), 1955-62; BA, National University of Ireland, Maynooth, 1958; BD, Pontifical University of Maynooth, 1961; MA, 1964, PhD, 1993, Queen's University, Belfast. Appointments: Curate, St Teresa's Parish, Belfast, 1962-63; Curate, Clonoe, County Tyrone, 1963-64; Chaplain, Good Shepherd Convent, Newry, 1964-65; Curate, Monasterboice, County Louth, 1965-67; Curate, St Patrick's Parish, Armagh, 1967-85; Administrator, St Patrick's Cathedral, Armagh, 1985-93; Chaplain, Women's Prison, Armagh, 1967-86; Sabbatical year in Nürnberg, Germany and Rome, Italy, 1993-94; Assistant Acting Parish Priest, Killcluney, Assistant in Derrynoose, 1994-95; Parish Priest of Moneymore, 1995-96; Parish Priest of Holy Trinity, Cookstown, 1996-. Publications: Poetry in Irish: Athphreabadh na hÓige, 1964; Arán ar an Tábla, 1970; Lampaí Dearga, 2005; History: Irish Church History Today (editor), 1990; Lámhscríbhinn Staire an Bhionadaigh, 1994; Archdiocese of Armagh - A History (author), 2000; The Burning of Wildgoose Lodge, 2005; Ulster Local Studies (editor), 1975-84; Seanchas Ard Mhacha - Journal of the Armagh Diocesan Historical Society (editor), 1986-; Human Rights: The SAS in Ireland, 1990 (revised and updated, 2005); State Violence: Northern Ireland 1969-1997, 1998; Hard Time: Armagh Gaol 1971-1986, 1998; Author with Monsignor Denis Faul of 33 books and pamphlets on human rights in Northern Ireland. Honour: Honorary Prelate (Monsignor), 1995. Memberships: Association for Legal Justice, 1971-80; Founder Member and Chairperson, Die Irisch-Fränkische Gesellschaft (The Irish-Frankonian Society), 1983-87; Founder Member and Chairperson, Relatives for Justice, 1990-2002. Address: Parochial House, 1 Convent Road, Cookstown, County Tyrone BT80 8QA, Northern Ireland. E-mail: raylmurray@aol.com

**MURRAY Richard Henry,** b. 20 September 1936, St Paul, Minnesota, USA. Senior Executive. Education: Harvard University, USA, 1958; Harvard Law School, 1961. Appointments: Partner and Head of the Litigation Department of Oppenheimer Law Firm, St Paul, Minnesota, USA, 1961-73; General Counsel, Touche Ross, New York, USA, 1973-86; Executive Director, Touche Ross International, New York, 1986-89; Chairman and Chief Executive Officer, Minet Professional Services, London, England, 1989-94; General Counsel, Deloitte Consulting, New York, 1994-2002; Global Director of Legal and Regulatory Affairs, Deloitte Touche Tohmatsu, New York, 1994-2002; Chief Claims Strategist, Swiss Re, New York and Zürich, 2002- Present; Supervisory Board of the Centre for the Study of Financial Innovation (London); Advisory Board of Oxford Analytica (Oxford); Special Advisor to the Asia Business Council (Hong Kong); Member of APEP, Institute of International Insurance (Washington) and Republican Presidential Roundtable (Washington); Formerly, Chairman of the Professional Responsibility Committee, 1999-2002; Member of Lloyd's (London); British Insurance Association (London), 1989-94; Risk and Insurance Management Society, 1985-98; Task Force Member, Group of Thirty (Washington), 1994, 1996; Advisory Board Member of the Princess Grace Foundation (Monaco), 1983-90; Director, Executive Committee and Lecturer, Institute of Management Development (Lausanne). Address: Swiss Re, 55 East 52nd Street, 44th Floor, New York, NY 10055, USA E-mail: richard_murray@swissre.com

**MURRAY-LYON Iain Malcolm,** b. 28 August 1940, Edinburgh, Scotland. Consultant Physician. m. Teresa, 1 son, 1 daughter. Education: University of Edinburgh, 1958-64. Appointments: Consultant Physician and Gastroenterologist, Charing Cross Hospital and Chelsea and Westminster Hospital, London, 1974-2002; Honorary Consultant Physician and Gastoenterologist, Chelsea and Westminster Hospital, 2002-; Honorary Senior Lecturer in Medicine, Imperial College School of Medicine, 1993-. Publications: More than 200 articles on topics in gastroenterology and liver disease and the medical effects of chewing Khat (Qat) leaves. Honours: BSc (Hons), 1962; MB ChB, 1964; MD, 1973; FRCP, 1980; FRCPE, 1980; International Fellowship, National Institute of Health (NIH), USA, 1971-72. Memberships: British Society of Gastroenterology; British Association for the Study of the Liver; European Association for the Study of the Liver; International Association for the Study of the Liver; Brooks's; Hurlingham Club. Address: 149 Harley Street, London W1G 6DE, England.

**MURSELL (Alfred) Gordon,** b. 4 May 1949, Guildford; England. Priest in Church of England. m. Anne. Education: Pontifical Institute of Sacred Music, Rome, 1966-67; Brasenose College, Oxford, 1967-71; Cuddesdon College, Oxford, 1971-73; BA, History; BA, Theology; ARCM, Organ Performance; BD, Theology. Appointments: Curate, Walton, Liverpool, 1973-77; Vicar, St John's East Dulwich, London, 1977-86; Tutor, Salisbury-Wells Theological College, Salisbury, 1986-91; Team Rector, Stafford, 1991-99; Provost, 1999-2002, Dean, 2002-, Birmingham Cathedral. Publications: The Theology of Carthusian Life, 1989; Out of the Deep: Prayer as Protest, 1989; The Wisdom of the Anglo-Saxons, 1997; The Story of Christian Spirituality (editor), 2001; English Spirituality (2 volumes), 2001. Address: 103a Selly Park Road, Birmingham, B29 7LH, England. E-mail: gordonmursell@beeb.net

**MURTA Kenneth Hall,** b. 24 September 1929, Sunderland, England. Professor Emeritus. m. Joan Wilson, 2 sons, 2 daughters. Education: Dip Arch, B Arch, Kings College, University of Durham. Appointments: Assistant Architect, S W Milburn & Partners, Sunderland, 1954-56, Principal Architect, Newcastle City, 1956-59; Senior Lecturer, Ahmadu Bello University, Nigeria, 1959-62; Lecturer then Senior Lecturer, 1962-74, Professor of Architecture, 1975-94, Professor Emeritus, 1994-, Dean, Faculty of Architectural Studies, 1974-77, 1984-88, University of Sheffield; Designs include: Anglican Cathedral, Kaduna, Northern Nigeria; St John Park, Sheffield; St Lukes Lodgmoor, Sheffield; All Saints Church, Dewsbury; St Laurence Church, Heanor; Christ Church, Pitsmoor, Sheffield; All Saints Church, Denaby Main; St Mary the Less, University of Durham; Christ Church, Stannington, Sheffield; St Lawrence, Frodingham, Scunthorpe; All Saints, Totley, Sheffield; St Laurence, Thryberg; Pilgrims, Fordcombe, Kent. Publications: Contributions to: Architectural Review, Architects Journal, RIBA, Journal, Church Building, Publications by CIB, Rotterdam. Honours: Chairman, Board of Architectural Education, 1992-97; Honorary Secretary, The Ecclesiological Society, 1991-2000; Associate, 1954, Fellow, 1967, Royal Institute of British Architects; Architects Design Council, 1954-; Chairman, Sheffield Cathedral, Fabric Advisory Committee, 1990-. Address: Underedge, Back Lane, Hathersage, Hope Valley, Derbyshire S32 1AR, England.

**MUSAYEV Kamran Kazimoglu,** b. 30 October 1973, Amasya, Armenia. Cardiovascular Surgeon. m. Hanife Karagül, 3 daughters. Education: Medical Studies, Azerbaijan Medical University, 1990-92. Appointments: Medical School, Istanbul Medical Faculty, Turkey, 1992-96; Resident, Cardiovascular Surgery, Cerrahpasa Medical Faculty and Florence Nightingale Hospital, Istanbul, Turkey, 1996-2002. Publications: Vascular echinococcosis, 2002; The use of antologous perscardium for complicated mitral valve annulus, 2004; The role of antioxidant supplementation in cardiac transplantation, 2004. Honours: Founder and President, Azerbaijanian Society of Cardiovascular

Surgery. Memberships: Turkish Society of Cardiovascular Surgery; European Society for Cardiovascular Surgery. Address: Parlament Ave 76, Central Clinical Hospital, Baku, Azerbaijan. E-mail: kamrancan@yahoo.com

**MUSIL Rudolf,** b. 5 May 1926, Brno, Czech Republic. University Professor. m. Ing Liba Kochová, 26 July 1952, 2 sons. Education: RNDr, 1952, CSc, 1960, Habil, 1966, DSc, 1968, Full Professor, 1980, Education, Masaryk University, Charles University. Appointments: Full Professor, Institute of Geological Sciences, Faculty of Science, Masaryk University, Brno. Publications: Personalities of the Faculty of Science, 1997; Climatic Comparison of Terrestrial and Marine Sediments, 1997; Ende des Pliozäns und Unteres bis Mittleres Pleistozän, 1997. Honours: Silver Medal, National Museum, 1968; Silver Medal, Humboldt Universität, Berlin; Medal, Moravian Museum, 1968; Medal, Slaskie University, Poland, 1983; Medal, Velkopolskie Towarzystwo, 1983; Silver Medal, Academy, 1986; Gold Medal, Masaryk University, 1997. Memberships: Czech Society of Geology and Mineralogy; Czech Society of Speleology; National Committee, INQUA; Czech Committee of Stratigraphy; International Commission on History of Geological Sciences. Address: Kotlárska Str 2, 61137 Brno, Czech Republic. E-mail: rudolf@sci.muni.cz

**MUSKER Alison Awdry Chalmers,** b. 9 September 1938, Southampton, England. Watercolour Painter. m. Roger, 1 son, 2 daughters. Education: Sherborne School for Girls; SRN, The Middlesex Hospital, London; Studied under Jacqueline Groag and Edward Wesson, Ecole des Arts, Paris 1956; Studied under Leslie Orriss, Reading College of Art, 1968. Career: Solo exhibitions: Brotherton Gallery, Walton Street, London, 1981; King Street Gallery, St James's, London, 1983, 1985; The Royal Geographical Society, London, 1986, Richmond Gallery, Cork Street, London, Italy and Albania, 1990; Numerous group exhibitions include: Royal Institute of Painters in Watercolours, 1958, 1977-91; Singer and Friedlander Exhibition, Mall Galleries, 1998, 1999, 2000; Royal Academy, 1999, 2002, 2003; New English Art Club, Mall Galleries, 1993-98, 2003; The Small Paintings Group, Century Gallery, 2003; W H Patterson and Select Seven Exhibition, 1995-2004; Works in collections including: John Julius Norwich, Lady Dashwood, Barry Munn, Martin Vandersteen, The Landmark Trust, HRH The Prince of Wales; Peter Boizot Collection, The late Queen Mother, The late Shah of Persia; Charity work includes: Guest Lecturer for National Trust, 1993; Wardour Chapel Appeal, Christies, London, 1994; British Red Cross Society, 1994, 1995; Friends of the City Churches, London, 1995; APA, Mall Galleries, London, 1995; Music in Country Churches, 1996-2004; Painswick House, Rococco Garden Exhibition, 1998; Watercolour donated to North Hampshire Hospital, 2002; Painting given to Koestler Award Trust, 2002. Publications: Works mentioned in numerous articles and reference works; The Artist's Manual, 1995; The Drawing and Painting Course Book, 1996; Creative Watercolour Techniques; Complete Guide to Drawing and Painting. Honours: Agnes Reeve Memorial Prize, 1989, 1991; Award, International Watercolour Biennale, Mexico, 2000; The William-Powlett Prize, 2001. Memberships: Chelsea Art Society, 1980; The Small Paintings Group, 2000; Associate Member, 2000, Full member, 2003, Royal Watercolour Society; Music in Country Churches, succeeding Sir Hugh Casson PPRA. Address: Rose Cottage, Beech Hill, Reading, Berkshire RG7 2AZ, England.

**MUSTAFA Walid Said,** b. 10 October 1942, Al-Bireh, Palestine. Geographer; Educator. m. Valentina Korenda, 2 sons, 1 daughter. Education: BA, Geography, Damascus University, 1965; PhD, Kiev State University, Ukraine, 1972. Appointments: Lecturer, Department of Geography, Jordan University, Amman, Jordan, 1973-78; Acting Head, Department of Geography, Al-Najah University, Nablus, Palestine, 1979-80; Head, Research Centre, Department of Occupied Territory, Palestinian Liberation Organisation, Amman, Jordan, 1980-94; Senior Researcher and Lecturer, Department of History, Geography and Political Science, Bir Zeit University, Palestine, 1994-95; Dean of Students, 1996-2001, Lecturer, Department of Humanities, 2001-03, Dean, Faculty of Arts, Bethlehem University, Palestine, 2004-. Publications: Author: Bethlehem, The Story of the City, 1990; Jerusalem, Population and Urbanization, 1850-2000, English edition, 2000; Co-author: Collective Destruction of Palestinian Villages and Zionist Colonization, 1881-1982, 1987; Collective Books: Palestinian Encyclopaedia – General Edition, 1984; Toward Palestinian Strategy for Jerusalem, 1998; Palestinian Perspectives, 1999; Editor: Abu-Shusheh Village, 1995; Biet Jibreen Village, 1995; Biet-Nabala Village, 1998; Translator: The Death of a Little Girl and Other Stories, 1980; Gorbachev, MC, Perestroika – For Us and The World, 1990. Honours: Assistant Professor, 1973; Associate Professor, 1999. Memberships: Palestinian National Council, 1987-; Central Committee, Palestinian People's Party, 1982-98; Vice-President, Board of Trustees, Arab Thought Form, Jerusalem, 1998-; Board of Trustees, Applied Research Institute, Jerusalem, 1999-; Board of Trustees, Palestinian Human Rights Monitoring Group, 2000. Address: Bethlehem University, Frier Street, PO Box No 9, Bethlehem, Palestine. E-mail: wshmustafa@yahoo.com

**MUTH Richard Ferris,** b. 14 May 1927, Chicago Illinois, USA. Economist. m. Helene Louise Martin, 2 daughters. Education: US Coast Guard Academy, 1945-47; AB, 1949, MA, 1950, Washington University, St Louis; PhD, Chicago University, 1958; Master of Theology Studies, Emory University, 1995. Appointments: Associate Professor, University of Chicago, 1959-64; Professor of Economics, Washington University St Louis, 1966-70; Professor, Stanford University, 1970-83; Professor, 1983-2001, Chair, 1983-90, Professor Emeritus, 2001-, Emory University. Publications: With others: Regions, Resources & Economic Growth, 1960; Cities & Housing, 1969; Public Housing, 1974; Urban & Economic Problems, 1975; The Economics of Housing Markets (with Allen C Goodman), 1989. Honour: Phi Beta Kappa. Address: Department of Economics, Emory University, Atlanta, GA 30322-2240, USA. E-mail: rmuth@emory.edu

**MWANGOMBE Nimrod Juniahs,** b. 25 August 1951, Mombasa, Kenya. Professor of Neurosurgery. m. Agnes Wakesho, 1 daughter. Education: PhD, Neuro-oncology (London University), MBCHB, University of Nairo, 1976; MMEd (Surgery), University of Nairobi, 1980. Appointments: Registrar, National Hospital for Neurology and Neurosurgery, Institute of Neurology, London, 1984-88; Professor of Neurosurgery, University of Nairobi Medical School, Kenyatta National Hospital, Program Director, MMed Neurosurgery Program, 1988-2005. Publications: Many articles on tropical neurosurgery, tuberculosis, brain abscess and head injury. Honours: George Abun International Fellow, Congress of Neurology Surgeons, USA, McMaster University, Canada, 2002. Memberships: Fellow, College of Surgeons of East, Central and Southern Africa; Kenya Medical Association. Address: PO Box 74004, 00200 Nairobi, Kenya. E-mail: juniahs@yahoo.com

**MWENDA Kenneth Kaoma,** b. 5 January 1969, Livingstone City, Zambia. Lawyer; Diplomat. Education: LLB, Zambia, 1990; BCL/MPhil, Oxford, 1994, Gr Dip, LCCI, 1991; Adv Dip, IoC; AHCZ; MBA, Hull, 1995; DBA, Pacific Western, 1996; PhD, Pacific Western, 1999; DCL, Trinity; Gr Cert, Warwick, 1998; PhD, Warwick, 2000; FCI; FRSA; Rhodes

Scholar; Professor of Corporate Law. Appointments: Staff Development Fellow, Lecturer in Law, University of Zambia, 1991-95; Lecturer in Law, University of Warwick, UK, 1995-98; Visiting Professor of Law, University of Miskolc, Hungary, 1997; Young Professional, Counsel, Legal Department, 1998-99; Projects Officer, 2000-2003, Senior Projects Officer, 2003-04, Senior Counsel, 2004-, The World Bank; Visiting Professor, University of Zambia School of Law, Lusaka, 2001-02. Publications: Books: Legal Aspects of Corporate Capital and Finance, 1999; Banking Supervision and Systemic Bank Restructuring: An International and Comparative Legal Perspective, 2000; The Dynamics of Market Integration: African Stock Exchanges in the New Millennium, 2000; Contemporary Issues in Corporate Finance and Investment Law, 2000; Zambia's Stock Exchange and Privatisation Programme: Corporate Finance Law in Emerging Markets, 2001; Banking and Micro-Finance Regulation and Supervision: Lessons from Zambia, 2002; Principles of Arbitration Law, 2003; Frontiers of Legal Knowledge: Business and Economic Law in Context, 2003; More than 60 published journal and law review articles. Honours: Law Association of Zambia Best Student in Jurisprudence Prize, 1990; Selected to World Bank's Young Professionals Programme, 1998; University of Yale Law Faculty Fellowship, 1998; International Cultural Diploma of Honour, American Biographical Institute, 2001; Outstanding Professional Award in Corporate Law, ABI, 2001; International Commendation of Achievement and Success in Corporate Law, ABI, 2001; Listed in numerous biographical dictionaries and Who's Who publications. Memberships: Fellow, Royal Society of Arts of England; Fellow, Institute of Commerce of England; International Bar Association; Law Association of Zambia; British Association of Lawyers for the Defence of the Unborn. Address: The World Bank, 1818 H Street NW, Washington DC 20433, USA. E-mail: kmwenda@worldbank.org

**MYERS Mike**, b. 25 May 1963, Toronto, Ontario, Canada. Actor; Writer. m. Robin Ruzan, 1993. Creative Works: Stage appearances: The Second City, Toronto, 1986-88, Chicago, 1988-89; Actor and Writer, Mullarkey & Myers, 1984-86; TV show, Saturday Night Live, 1989-94; Films: Wayne's World, 1992; So I Married an Axe Murderer, 1992; Wayne's World II, 1993; Austin Powers: International Man of Mystery, 1997; Meteor, 1998; McClintock's Peach, 1998; Just Like Me, 1998; It's A Dog's Life, 1998; 54, 1998; Austin Powers: The Spy Who Shagged Me, 1998; Pete's Meteor, 1999; Austin Powers: Goldmember, 2002; Shrek (Voice), 2003; Cat in the Hat, 2003; Shrek 2 (Voice), 2004. Honours: Emmy Award for outstanding writing in a comedy or variety series, 1989; MTV Music Award, 1998; Canadian Comedy Award, 2000; American Comedy Award, 2000; Blockbuster Entertainment Award, 2000; Teen Choice Award, 2000; MTV Music Award, 2003; AFI Star Award, 2003. Address: c/o Creative Artists Agency, 9830 Wilshire Boulevard, Beverly Hills, CA 90212, USA.

**MYRONOVYCH Lyudmyla Maksymova**, b. 8 April 1949, Dyatlovo, Byelorussia. Chemist; Researcher. 1 daughter. Education: Engineer, Chemist-technologist, Dnipropetrovsk Chemistry-Technological Institute named by Dzerzhynskyy, 1972; Candidate of Chemical Scientists, All-Union Scientific Research Institute of Plants Protection Means, Moscow, Russia, 1988; Assistant Professor, General Chemistry Chair, Sumy State University, Kyiv, Ukraine, 1995; Doctor of Chemical Sciences, Russian Chemical-Technological University named by D I Mendeleyeyev, Moscow, Russia, 2003; Doctor of Chemical Sciences, Institute of Organic Chemistry, Kyiv, Ukraine, 2004. Appointments: Teacher, Technical School No 98 of Chemists, Mogilyov, Byelorussia, 1973-77; Production Training Officer, College of Chemists, Yaroslavl, Russia, 1977-

80; Junior Research Assistant, Research Assistant, Chernigiv Technological Institute, Chernigiv, Ukraine, 1980-90; Lecturer, Poltave Co-operative Institute, Poltave, Ukraine, 1990-94; Assistant Professor, 1994-2003, Professor, 2003-2005, Sumy State University, Sumy, Ukraine. Publications: 1 Monograph (co-author), 1990; Articles as co-author in professional journals including: Chemistry of Heterocyclic Compounds, 1986, 1987, 1989, 1994, 1996, 1998, 2001, 2003; Ukrainian Chemical Journal, 1989, 1992, 1993 (2), 1994, 1996, 1997 (2), 1998, 2000; Information HEI. Chemistry and Chemical Technology (Russia), 1992, 1994, 1996, 1997 (6), 1998, 1999 (2), 2000, 2003 (2), 2004; Journal of Applied Chemistry (Russia), 1992, 1994, 1995, 1996, 1999; Journal of General Chemistry (Russia), 1999, 2001, 2003; Journal of Organic Chemistry (Russia), 1998, 2002. Honour: Corresponding Member of the Academy, International Academy of Authors of Scientific Discoveries and Inventions, Moscow, 2003. Memberships: All-Union Chemical Association named by D I Mendelyeyev, Russian Federation, 1980-2004; Professional Associations of Ukraine, 1967-. Address: Zalivna Street 7, Apt 45, Sumy, Ukraine 40035. E-mail: myronovych@ua.fm

# N

**N'DOUR Youssou, b.** 1959, Dakar, Senegal. Musician; Singer; Songwriter. Career: Member, Sine Dramatic, 1972; Orchestre Diamono, 1975; The Star Band (houseband, Dakar nightclub, the Miami Club), 1976-79; Founder, Etoile De Dakar, 1979; Re-formed as Super Etoile De Dakar, 1982-; International tours include support to Peter Gabriel, US tour, 1987. Recordings: Albums: A Abijan, 1980; Xalis, 1980; Tabaski, 1981; Thiapathioly, 1983; Absa Gueye, 1983; Immigres, 1984; Nelson Mandela, 1985; The Lion, 1989; African Editions Volumes 5-14, 1990; Africa Deebeub, 1990; Jamm La Prix, 1990; Kocc Barma, 1990; Set, 1990; Eyes Open, 1992; The Best Of Youssou N'Dour, 1994; The Guide, 1995; Gainde - Voices From The Heart Of Africa (with Yande Codou Sene), 1996; Immigrés/Bitim Rew, 1997; Inedits 84-85, 1997; Hey You : The Essential Collection, 1988-1990; Best of the 80's, 1998; Special Fin D'annee Plus Djamil, 1999; Joko: From Village to Town, 2000; Batay, 2001; Le Grand Bal, Bercy, 2000; Le Grand Bal 1 & 2, 2001; Birth of a Star, 2001; Et Ses Amis, 2002; Nothing's in Vain, 2002; Hit Single: Seven Seconds, duet with Neneh Cherry, 1995; How Come Shakin' the Tree, 1998; Recorded with: Paul Simon, Graceland, 1986; Lou Reed, Between Thought and Expression, 1992; Otis Reading, Otis! The Definitive Otis Reading, 1993; Manu Dibango, Wafrika, 1994; Cheikh Lo, Ne La Thiass, 1996; Alan Stivell, I Dour, 1998. Address: Youssou N'Dour Head Office, 8 Route des Almadies Parcelle, BP 1310, Dakar, Senegal. E-mail: yncontact@yahoo.fr Website: www.youssou.com

**NABADE Mohammad Kabir, b.** 11 November 1960, Birnin Kebbi, Nigeria. Architect. m. Saratu Ibrahim and Maryam Ibrahim, 5 sons, 3 daughters. Education: BSc (Hons), Architecture, 1985; MSc, Architecture, 1988. Appointments: Pupil Architect, 1985; Assistant Lecturer, 1988, Senior Lecturer, 1992, Director, 1994, Deputy Rector, 1996, Rector, 1999-, Waziri Umaru Polytechnic, Birnin Kebbi, Kebbi State, Nigeria. Publications: Active and Passive Design Principles in Solar Architecture and Building Performance. Overview of Energy Utilisation and Biogas Digester; Emerging Issues and Challenges, Design and Construction of 10m³ Biogas Digester. Honours: Merit Award, Youth Council, NASU; NANS (North West); MESA, Rotaract; NACES. Memberships: ANIA; MARCHES; MNIM; MNISEARTH; FICEN. Address: Waziri Umaru Polytechnic, Birnin Kebbi, PMB 1034 Birnin Kebbi, Kebbi State, Nigeria.

**NAHUM Peter John, b.** 19 January 1947, London, England. Art Dealer; Academic. m. Renate Angelika Meiser. Education: Sherborne School, Dorset. Appointments: Initiated Victorian Painting Department, Head of British Painting Department, Senior Director on Chairman's Committee, Sotheby's, 1966-84; Adviser to British Rail Pension Fund on Victorian Paintings; Opened own gallery, The Leicester Galleries, 1984; Adviser to major private collections and museums around the world; Celebrity auctioneer for charities; Appears regularly on BBC TV's Antiques Roadshow. Publications: Books include: Fairy Folk in Fairy Land, 1998; Pre-Raphaelite – Symbolist – Visionary, 2001; Medieval to Modern, 2003; The Brotherhood of Ruralists and The Pre-Raphaelites, 2005; Contributions to daily press and antiques magazines. Memberships: British Antique Dealers' Association; The Society of London Art Dealers. Address: 5 Ryder Street, London SW1Y 6PY, England. E-mail: peternahum@leicestergalleries.com

**NAHYAN Zayed bin Sultan an- (Sheikh), b.** 1926. Ruler of Emirate of Abu Dhabi. m. Appointments: Appointed as personal representative to Ruler of Abu Dhabi (his brother), Al Ain, 1946; Ruler of Abu Dhabi, 1966-; President, Federation of United Arab Emirates, 1971-; Helped establish Gulf Co-operative Council. Address: Presidential Palace, Abu Dhabi, United Arab Emirates.

**NAIPAUL V(idiadhar) S(urajprasad) (Sir), b.** 17 August 1932, Chaguanas, Trinidad. Author. m. (1) Patricia Ann Hale, 1955, deceased 1996, (2) Nadira Khannum Alvi, 1996. Education: Queen's Royal College, Trinidad; BA, Honours, English, University College, Oxford, 1953. Publications: Novels: The Mystic Masseur, 1957; The Suffrage of Elvira, 1958; Miguel Street, 1959; A House for Mr Biswas, 1961; Mr Stone and the Knights Companion, 1963; The Mimic Men, 1967; A Flag on the Island, 1967; In a Free State, 1971; Guerrillas, 1975; A Bend in the River, 1979; The Enigma of Arrival, 1987; A Way in the World, 1994. Other: The Middle Passage, 1962; An Area of Darkness, 1964; The Loss of El Dorado, 1969; The Overcrowded Barracoon, and Other Articles, 1972; India: A Wounded Civilization, 1977; The Return of Eva Perón, 1980; Among the Believers, 1981; Finding the Centre, 1984; A Turn in the South, 1989; India: A Million Mutinies Now, 1990; A Way in the World, 1994; Beyond Belief: Islamic Excursions Among the Converted Peoples, 1998; Letters Between a Father and Son, 1999; Reading and Writing: a Personal Account, 2000; Half a Life, 2001. Contributions to: Journals and magazines. Honours: John Llewelyn Rhys Memorial Prize, 1958; Somerset Maugham Award, 1961; Hawthornden Prize, 1964; W H Smith Award, 1968; Booker Prize, 1971; Honorary Doctor of Letters, Columbia University, New York City, 1981; Honorary Fellow, University College, Oxford, 1983; Honorary DLitt, University of Cambridge, 1983, University of Oxford, 1992; Knighted, 1990; British Literature Prize, 1993; Nobel Prize for Literature, 2001. Memberships: Royal Society of Literature, fellow; Society of Authors. Address: c/o Gillon Aitken Associates, 29 Fernshaw Road, London SW10 0TG, England.

**NAIR Govindapillai Achuthan, b.** 17 February 1946, Trivandrum, India. Teacher; Researcher; University Professor. m. P Lakshmi Nair, 1 son, 2 daughters. Education: MSc, Zoology, Birla Institute of Technology and Science, Pilani, India, 1969; PhD, Aquatic Biology, 1981; DSc, Ecology, Kerala University, India, 2001. Appointments: CSIR, Government of India, Junior, Senior and Postdoctoral Fellow; Research Associate, Department of Ocean Development and US PL (480) Smithsonian Project; Deputy Director and Project Co-ordinator, ERRC, India; Assistant Professor, Associate Professor, Professor, Department of Zoology, University of Garyounis, Benghazi, Libya. Publications: 97 papers published on the subjects of general biology/ecology, breeding and population biology, feeding and nutritional biology, haematobiology, parasitology, biometrics, toxicology, pollution biology. Honours: Sri Chitra Prize, Kerala University for best research publications; Best Academician 2001-2002, University of Garyounis, Benghazi, Libya; Listed in Who's Who publications and biographical dictionaries. Memberships: Fellow, Linnean Society of London; New York Academy of Sciences; Asian Fisheries Society, Philippines. Address: Easwari Villas, Sasthamangalam, Thiruvananthapuram-695010, Kerala State, India. E-mail: gachu@wmcmail.com

**NAKAKUKI Shoichi, b.** 11 January 1940, Ibaraki, Japan. Retired Lecturer in Veterinary Anatomy. Education: Bachelor of Agriculture, Veterinarian, 1967; Master of Agriculture (Veterinary Medicine), 1969, Tokyo University of Agriculture and Technology; Doctor of Science, Comparative Anatomical Studies on the Mammalian Lung, Kyoto University, 1978. Appointments: Assistant Professor of Veterinary Anatomy,

1969-82, Lecturer of Veterinary Anatomy, 1982-2003, Tokyo University of Agriculture and Technology; Retired, 2003. Publications: More than 40 papers in scientific journals include: The New Interpretation of the Bronchial Tree, 1975; The Bronchial Tree and Pulmonary Artery of the Tamandua (Tamandua tetradactyla) Lung – An Important Example Supporting the Fundamental Scheme for the Bronchial Ramification of the Mammalian Lung, 1996. Honours: Member, New York Academy of Sciences, 1994-. Memberships: New York Academy of Sciences; American Association for the Advancement of Science; Japanese Association of Anatomists; The Japanese Society of Veterinary Science; Primate Society of Japan. Address: 281-2 Oosonoki Chiyokawa-mura, Yuki-gun, Ibaraki, 304-0801 Japan.

**NAKANISHI Yasuhiko,** b. 4 June 1967, Toyama, Japan. Retired Associate Professor; Engineering Educator. m. Tomoko Hasegawa. Education: Bachelor's Degree in Engineering, Kanazawa University, Kanazawa, Japan, 1986-90; Master's Degree in Engineering, 1990-92, PhD in Engineering, 1992-95, University of Tokyo, Minato-ku, Tokyo, Japan; Student, Hamamatsu University School of Medicine, Hamamatsu, Shizuoka, Japan, 2004-. Appointments: Research Associate, Toyohashi University of Technology, Toyohashi, Aichi, Japan, 1995-2000; Research Associate, 2000-2002, Assistant Professor, 2002-2004, Associate Professor, 2004, Gunma University, Kiryu, Gunma, Japan. Publications: Articles in scientific journals including: Japan Society of Mechanical Engineers International Journal (Series A), 1996 x 2; 1997, 2000; Computer Methods in Applied Mechanics and Engineering, 2001. Honour: Hatakeyama Award, The Japan Society of Mechanical Engineers, 1990. Memberships: Society of Powder Technology, Japan; The Japan Society of Mechanical Engineers. Address: 18-5 Mukaiyama-nishi-machi, Toyohashi, Aichi, 440-0861 Japan. E-mail: zan73024@nifty.com

**NAKASHIMA Toshio,** b, 6 September 1920, Japan. Professor. m. Sumiko Asakura, 1 son, 1 daughter. Education: DAgric, Hokkaido University, 1952; Exchange Program, University of Massachusetts, USA, 1959-60. Appointments: Assistant, Faculty of Agriculture, 1950, Lecturer, 1959, Assistant Professor, 1961, Professor, 1972-84, Member of University Senate, 1977-79, Hokkaido University; Professor, Hokkaido Musashi Women's Junior College, 1984-93. Publications: Over 50 scientific papers on ecology of Scarabaeidae and Ambrosia beetles; New Applied Entomology, textbook; Photographic Explanation of the Habits of Several Ambrosia Beetles, textbook. Honours: Emeritus Professor, Hokkaido University, 1984; The Order of the Rising Sun, 3rd Class, The Emperor of Japan, 1995. Memberships: Japanese Society of Applied Entomology and Zoology; Past Member of Senate, Japanese Society of Applied Entomology and Zoology, The Entomological Society of Japan; Japanese Society of Sericultural Science; Vice-Chairman, Drainage Canal of Chitose River; Past Vice-Chairman, Development of Tokachi River; Committee of Environmental Impact Assessment on Otarunai Dam. Address: D-206 Fureaino Machi, Noukendai, 3-51-1, Kanazawa-Ku, Yokohama, 236-0057, Japan.

**NAKASHIMA Tsutomu,** b. 22 March 1950, Ichinomiya City, Japan. Professor of Otorhinolaryngology. m. Mikiko, 1 son, 1 daughter. Education: Graduate, Nagoya University School of Medicine, 1974. Appointment: Professor of Otorhinolaryngology, Nagoya University School of Medicine, Japan, 1994-. Publication: Disorders of cochlear blood flow, 2003. Address: Department of Otorhinolaryngology, Nagoya University School of Medicine, 65, Tsurumaincho, Shomo-ku, Nagoya 466-8550, Japan.

**NAKAYAMA Tomohiro,** 22 April 1963, Mie, Japan. Medical Doctor. Education: MD, 1988, Postgraduate, 1990-94, PhD, 1994, Nihon University, Tokyo. Appointments: Medical Doctor II, Internal Medicine, Nihon University, Tokyo, 1988-90; Researcher II, Physiology, 1991, Researcher, Medical Research Institute, 1993-94, Nihon University School of Medicine, Tokyo; Chief, Internal Medicine Division, Nishi-Kofu National Hospital, Kofu, 1994-95; Senior Resident, Nihon University Hospital, Tokyo, 1995-2001; Assistant, Advanced Medical Research Centre, 2001-2003; Associate Professor, Advanced Medical Research Centre, 2003-. Publications: Sequence of the 5'-flanking region of the gene encoding human muscle glycogen synthase, 1994; Organisation of the human prostacyclin synthase gene, 1996; Nonsense mutation of human prostacyclin synthase gene in a family, 1997; Functional deletion mutation of the 5'-flanking region of the type A human natriuretic peptide receptor gene and its association with essential hypertension and left ventricular hypertrophy in the Japanese, 2000. Honours: Finalist, Research Award, Tanabe Biomedical Conference, Japan, 1997; 1st Prize, Nihon University School of Medicine Alumni Association Young Research Award, 1997, 2001; Finalist, Research Award, Tokyo Medical Doctors Association, 1998; 1st Prize Nihon University School of Medicine Alumni Association Research Award, 2001. Memberships: American Association for the Advancement of Science, 1996-; New York Academy of Sciences, 1998-; American Diabetes Association, 1999-; American Heart Association, Councillor, 2000-. Address: Nihon University School of Medicine, Advanced Medical Research Centre, Ooyaguchi kamimachi 30-1, Itabashi-ku, Tokyo 173-8610, Japan. E-mail: tnakayam@med.nihon-u.ac.jp

**NAKIB Khalil Adib,** b. 10 August 1944, Sidon, Lebanon. Lecturer. m. Joumana Shammaa', 1 son, 1 daughter. Education: BA, Public Administration, American University of Beirut, 1966; Master of Public Administration, New York University, USA, 1968; PhD, Public Administration, Florida State University, USA, 1972. Appointments: Executive Director, Lebanon Family Planning Association, 1973-76; Lecturer and Assistant Professor, American University of Beirut, 1976-80, 1986-; Lecturer in Management, The Lebanese University, 1976-77, 1979-80, 1985-87; Lecturer in Management, Beirut University College, 1977-78, 1986-94; Technical Specialist, 1977-84; Head of Section, 1984-90, Secretary of the Board, 1990-2003, Investment Co-ordinator, 2003-, Council for Development and Reconstruction. Publications: Bureaucracy and Development, A Study about the Lebanese Administration (in Arabic), 1976; Traditionalism and Change among Lebanese Bureaucrats, 1976. Memberships: Vice President, National Institute for Investment Guarantee, 1993-; Member: Development Studies Association, Makassed Philanthropic Islamic Association in Sidon. Address: Yasminah Building, Jal-al-Bahr, Ras Beirut, Beirut, Lebanon. E-mail: khalilnakib@hotmail.com

**NAM Charles Benjamin,** b. 25 March 1926, Lynbrook, New York, USA. Demographer; Sociologist. m. Marjorie Tallant, deceased, 1 son, 1 daughter. Education: BA, Applied Statistics, New York University, 1950; MA, Sociology, 1957, PhD, Sociology, 1959, University of North Carolina. Appointments: Staff, 1950-53, Branch Chief, 1957-63, US Bureau of the Census; Professor, Florida State University, 1964-95; Professor Emeritus and Author, Research Associate, Centre for Demography and Population Health, Florida State University, 1995-. Publications: 12 books; Over 100 articles and chapters. Honours: Fellow, American Association for the Advancement of Science; Fellow, American Statistical Association. Memberships: American Association for the Advancement of Science; Population Association of America, Past President; American Statistical Association; Society for the Study of Social

Biology; American Sociological Association; International Union for the Scientific Study of Population. Address: 820 Live Oak Plantation Road, Tallahassee, FL 32312-2413, USA. E-mail: charlesnam2@earthlink.net

**NAM Ki Min,** b. 28 January 1949, Chungbuk, Korea. Professor. m. Young Ja Jeon, 1 son, 1 daughter. Education: Bachelor of Social Work, 1969-73, MPA; Public Administration, 1977-79; PhD, Social Welfare, 1982-89, Seoul National University, Korea. Appointments include: Military Service, Korean Army, 1973-75; Full-time Lecturer, 1980-83, Assistant Professor, 1983-87, Associate Professor, 1987-92, Professor, 1992-, Department of Social Welfare, Cheongju University; Visiting Scholar, School of Social Work, University of Michigan, 1986-87; Visiting Scholar, School of Social Work, University of Wisconsin-Madison, 1993-94; Visiting Professor, School of Social Work and Family Studies, University of British Columbia, 2003-2004; Member, Welfare Advisory Committee, Chungbuk Province, 1995-96; Advisory Member, Welfare Fund for the Elderly, Chungbuk Province, 1995-2000; Advisory Member and Chairman, World Vision Yongnam Social Welfare Centre, 1995-; Vice-Chairman, Living Security Committee, Cheongju City, 2000-; Council Member, Hangeon Welfare Corporation, 2003-. Publications in Korean: Books include: Social Welfare Organization and Leadership, 1990; Social Welfare Administration (co-author), 1993; Understanding Modern Social Welfare, 2001; Modern Elderly Education (co-author), 2003; Social Welfare Administration in Korea (co-author), 2003; Social Welfare Policy, 2004; Introduction to Social Welfare, 2005; Numerous articles in social welfare journals. Honours: Minster Award, Ministry of Education, Korea, 1995; Chungsuk Academic Award, 2002; President Award, World Vision, 2002. Memberships: Korea Gerontological Society, 1979-, Council Member, 2000-2003; Korea Association for Social Welfare Studies, 1981-; Korean Academy of Social Welfare, 1984-, Vice-President, 2005, President, 2006; Korean Academy of Child Welfare, 1998-, Council Member and Editorial Member, 1998-2000; Korean Academy of Welfare for the Aged, 1998-, Council Member, 2002-; Academy of Korean Social Welfare Administration, 1999-, President, 1999-2001; Chungcheong Society of Welfare Development for the Aged, 2001-, President, 2001-. Address: 203-1205 Kukwha Apt, Samcheon-dong, Seo-ku, Tae Jeon City, 302-782, Korea. E-mail: km0128@hanmail.net

**NAM Taek-Jeong,** b. 20 April 1954, Masan, South Korea. Professor. m. Mee-Young Kim, 1 son. Education: BS, 1979, MS, 1981, Pukyong National University; PhD, Tokyo University, Japan, 1989. Appointments: Director, Seafood and Marine Bioresources Development Centre, 2002-2003; Vice-Director, Marine Bioprocess Research Centre, 2004-; Elder, Seomoon Presbyterian Church, Busan, Korea, 2000-. Publications: Articles in scientific journals as co-author: Thrombosponidin and Osteopontin Bind to Insulin-like Growth Factor (IGF) – Binding Protein-5 Leading to an Alteration in IGF-1-Stimulated Cell Growth, 2000; The complement component C1s is the protease that accounts for cleavage of insulin-like growth, 2000; Vitronectin Binding to IGF Binding Protein-5(1GFBP-5) Alters IGFBP-5 Modulation of IGF-1 Actions, 2002. Memberships: Endocrine Society, USA; Korean Society of Fisheries. Address: Pukyong National University, 599-1 Daeyeon-dong, Nam-gu, Pusan 608-737, Korea. E-mail: namtj@pknu.ac.kr

**NANDEDKAR Deepak Prabhakar,** b. 26 January 1944, Indore, Madhya Pradesh, India. Educator. m. Tarala, 1 son. Education: BSc, 1st Class with V Rank/Merit, Vikram University, 1963; MSc, Physics with Electronics and Radio Physics, 1st Class with II Rank/Merit, Indore University, 1965; MTech,

Electrical Engineering with specialisation in Electron-Devices Technology, 1967, PhD, 1970, IIT Mumbai. Appointments: Lecturer, 1969-76, Assistant Professor, 1976-2001, Associate Professor, 2001-, Department of Electrical Engineering, IIT, Powai, Mumbai, India. Publications: Numerous articles as co-author in enginneering/scientific journals including Journal of the Institution of Telecommunication Engineers, India, 1968; International Journal of Electronics, London, 1968, 1970. Honours: Distinguished Leader Medal, 2002; Certification and American Medal of Honor in the Field of Plasma and Electromagnetics (with Medal Number 53 out of 100 only worldwide), 2002; World Laureate of India and Proclamation in the Field of Education, 2002-2003; Teaching Excellence Award, 2003; Outstanding Professional Award in the field of Microelectronics and Communication, 2004, American Biographical Institute, USA; International Peace Price, 2003, 2005, United Cultural Convention, USA; International Educator of the Year for contribution to Teaching in Electrical Engineering, 2004, International Biographical Centre, England; Listed in Who's Who publications and biographical dictionaries. Memberships: Research Board of Advisors, 2002-; Life Fellow, 2002-; Consulting Editor, Contemporary Who's Who, ABI, 2002-2003; Life Member, Fellow, Institution of Electronics and Telecommunication Engineers, New Delhi, 2004-; Life Member, Indian Society for Technical Education, New Delhi, 2004-. Address: Department of Electrical Engineering, Indian Institute of Technology, IIT, Powai, Mumbai-400076, India.

**NAPIER Douglas Herbert,** b. 23 August 1923, Sidcup, Kent, England. Retired University Professor; Consultant. m. Jean Allen, 1 son. Education: BSc, Chemistry, 1944, MSc, Electrochemistry, 1947, Sir John Cass College, University of London; PhD, Chemical Engineering, Imperial College of Science and Technology, University of London, 1951. Appointments: Scientist-in-Charge of Combustion Department, British Coal Utilisation Research Association, 1951-57; Head, Chemical Projects Section, Vickers Research Limited, 1957-65; Senior Lecturer in Industrial Hazards, Department of Chemical Engineering and Chemical Technology, Imperial College of Science and Technology, 1965-80; Professor of Industrial Hazard Control, Department of Chemical Engineering and Applied Chemistry,, 1980-89, Emeritus Professor, 1989-, University of Toronto; Technical Director, Hazard and Risk Control, Concord Environmental, 1987-91; Industrial Hazard and Risk Consultant, Educator in Engineering Topics, 1991-; Assessor at numerous public inquiries and expert witness in actions involving fires, explosions and hazardous materials. Publications: Author or co-author of some 110 papers and numerous technical reports. Honour: Hans R Belliger Memorial Lecturer, Society of Chemical Industry. Memberships: Eur.Ing. (European Engineer) and Chartered Engineer, UK; Fellow, Institute of Energy; Chartered Chemist; Fellow, Royal Society of Chemistry; American Institute of Chemical Engineers; Society of Chemical Industry; Combustion Institute; British Occupational Hygiene Society; Institute of Risk Research. Address: Valencia Towers PH2, 335 Mill Road, Toronto, ON M9C 1Y6, Canada.

**NAPIER William McDonald, (Bill Napier),** b. 29 June 1940, Perth, Scotland. Astronomer. m. Nancy Miller Baillie, 7 July 1965, 1 son, 1 daughter. Education: BSc, 1963; PhD, 1966. Publications: The Cosmic Serpent, 1982; The Cosmic Winter, 1990; The Origin of Comets, 1990; Nemesis (novel), 1998; Revelation (novel), 2000; The Lure (novel), 2002; Shattered Icon (novel), 2003. Contributions to: New Scientist; Astronomy Today. Honour: Joint recipient, Arthur Beer Memorial Prize, 1986-87. Membership: Royal Astronomical Society, fellow;

International Astronomical Union; Spaceguard UK; Committee on Space Research. Address: County Cork, Ireland.

**NARAGHI Akhtar**. Writer. m. Javad Ebadi, deceased, 1 son, 1 daughter. Education: PhD, English Literature, McGill University, Canada, 1991. Appointments: Teacher at Teachers Training College, Tehran; Teacher, McGill University. Publications: Legacy: Selected Poems, 1992; The Big Green House: A Novel in Twelve Short Stories (translated into German, French and Persian), 1994, 5th edition, 2001; Solitude: Selected Poems, 1996; Blue Curtains: A Novel in Six Stories, 1999; With Mara That Summer: A Novel in Four Stories, 2004; Ghazal: The Poems of Safai Naraghi (editor), 1972; Contributor of forewords, articles, short stories and poems to numerous journals. Honours: The Big Green House shortlisted for the 1995 QSPELL Hugh MacLennan Prize for Fiction; Several interviews for newspapers, radio and television Listed in Who's Who publications and biographical dictionaries. Memberships: Founding President, International Organisation of the Helen Prize for Women, 1987; Member, Quebec Writers' Association. Address: PO Box 781, Place du Parc, Montreal, QC H2X 4A6, Canada. E-mail: persica@sypatico.ca

**NARASIMHA RAO Sabnavis**, b. 21 December 1949, Bangalore, India. Teacher. m. M Vimala, 1 daughter. Education: BSc (Hons), 1969; MSc, 1971; DBA, 1972; BASM, 2002; MD (AM), 2003. Appointments: Research Assistant, Department of Physiology, St John's Medical College, Bangalore, 1971-72; Lecturer in Zoology, 1972-, Professor, 1988-, Head of the Department, 2003-, MES College of Arts, Commerce and Science, Bangalore, India. Publications: Presented papers at various national conferences. Honours: Certificate of Appreciation, Government of Karnataka for Russian Festival in India; Dasara State Sports Award. Memberships: Zoological Society of India; Ethological Society of India; Institute of Holistic Therapy, Mexico; Fellow, World Society of Alternative Medicine, USA. Address: #42, Kanakapura Road, Basavanagudi, Bangalore, Karnataka, India. E-mail: narasirao@gmail.com

**NARAYANAN Arumugakannu**, b. 31 December 1938, Nagercoil, India. m. Kamala Devi, 2 sons, 1 daughter. Education: BSc, Chemistry, 1958; BSc, Agriculture, 1961; MSc, 1963; PhD, 1966. Appointments: Attache de Recherch, CNRS, Paris; Plant Physiologist, USAID, New Delhi; Pool Officer, TNAU, Coimbatore; Plant Physiologist, ICRISAT, Hyderabad; Professor, Crop Physiology, Acharya NGR Agricultural University, Hyderabad; Principal, Agricultural College, Bapatla; Professor, University Head, Plant Physiology; Retired; Emeritus Scientist, ICAR, Sugarcane Breeding Institute, Coimbatore; Secretary, Organic Agriculture Scientific Society for Integrated Services (OASIS); Project Adviser, TIFAC.DST Vision 2020 Mission, Agriculture Project at Kaucheepuram, Tamil Nadu, 2000-. Publications: 69 articles in professional journals. Honours: Fellow, Indian Society of Plant Physiology; AP State Best Teacher Award; Academy of Agricultural Science Award. Memberships: Patron, Plant Physiology Club, APAU; Member, Indian Society of Plant Physiology; Member, Society of Plant Physiology and Biochemistry; Editor, Organic India and Nara's Notepad. Address: D No 19, Phase 5 Maharani Ave, Vadavalli, Coimbatore 641041, Tamil Nadu, India. E-mail: prof_narayanan_a@hotmail.com

**NARAYANAN Kocheril Raman**, b. 27 October 1920, Uzhavoor, Kottayam, Kerala, India. President of India. Education: MA, Engl Literature, University of Travancore; BSc, Economics, 1st class honours, London School of Economics. Appointments: Lecturer, University of Travancore, 1943; Journalist, The Hindu, Madras & Times of India, Bombay; Indian

Foreign Service, 1949, serving in Indian Embassies in Rangoon, Tokyo, London, Canberra and Hanoi; Educator, Economic Administration, Delhi School of Economics, 1954-55; Joint Director, Orientation Centre for Foreign Technicians; India's Ambassador to Thailand, 1967-69, Turkey, 1973-75, China, 1976-78; Secretary, Ministry of External Affairs, 1976, retired, 1978; Vice Chancellor, Jawaharlal Nehru University, 1979-80; India's Ambassador to USA, 1980-84; MP, 1985-92; Union Minister of State for Planning, 1985, External Affairs, 1985-86, Science and Technology, Atomic Energy, Space, Electronics and Ocean Development and Vice-President, Council of Science and Industrial Research, 1986-89; Vice-President of India, 1992-97; President of India, 1997-2002. Publications include: India and America: Essays in Understanding; Images and Insights; Non-Alignment in Contemporary International Relations. Honours: Several honorary degrees. Memberships include: President, Indian Council for Cultural Relations, Indian Institute of Public Administration, Ramakrishna Mission Institute of Cultures, Calcutta; Patron, International Award for Young People, India. Address: Office of the President, Rashtrapati Bhavan, New Delhi 110 004, India.

**NARELL Penzik Irena**, b. 17 September 1923, Sanok, Poland. Freelance Writer. m. Murray, 2 sons. Education: BS, Columbia University, 1969. Appointments: Assistant, Polish United Nations Delegation, New York City, 1948-51; Owner, Art Originals Gallery, New York City, 1961-63, 1964-69; Co-Manager, The Steel Bandits, Musical Group; Project Director, San Francisco Jews Old Traditions on a New Frontier, Bicentennial Exhibition Judah L Magnes Museum, 1976; Project Director: Oral History and Photographic Exhibit, Community and Diversity – The Six Bay Area Families, Institute for Historical Study and the San Francisco Foundation, 1989. Publications: Ashes to The Taste, 1961; The Invisible Passage, 1969; Joshua Fighter for Bar Kochba, 1978; Our City, The Jews of San Francisco, 1981; History's Choice, 1996; Contributor, Numerous short stories; Reviews and articles to professional journals and magazines; Numerous translations. Honours: Agnon Prize, for short story; National Jewish Book Award, 1979. Memberships: Institute for Historical Study; Editorial Board, Western States Jewish History. Address: 1325 Santa Fe Ave, Berkeley, CA 94702-1047, USA.

**NARENDRAN T C**, b. 24 February 1944, Thrissur, Kerala, India. Retired Professor and Department Head. m. Mangala Bai, 2 sons. Education: MSc; PhD. Appointments: Postdoctoral Researcher, UK, 1980, USA, 1986; Research Officer, 1969-72, Lecturer, 1972-81, Reader, 1981-88, Professor, Head of Department, 1988-2004, Professor Emeritus, 2004-, Department of Zoology, University of Calicut, Kerala, India; Retired, 2004. Publications: 256 research papers; 6 books. Honours: Elected Fellow, Indian Academy of Sciences, Bangalore; Elected Fellow, Indian Academy of Entomology, Chennai; Vice-President, Ethological Society of India, 2002. Memberships: Life Member of 12 professional scientific societies. Address: Sruti, Kohinoor, Tenjipalam, PO 673635, Kerala, India.

**NAROTZKY Norman D**, b. 14 March 1928, Brooklyn, New York, USA. Artist; Painter; Printmaker. m. Mercedes Molleda, 2 daughters. Education: High School of Music and Art, 1945; BA, Brooklyn College, 1949; Art Students League, New York City, 1945-49; Cooper Union Art School, 1952; Atelier 17, Paris, 1954-56; Kunstakademie, Munich, 1956-57; New York Institute of Fine Arts, 1957-58; BFA, Cooper Union Art School, 1979. Appointments: 53 solo exhibitions in Europe and USA; Group shows: Brooklyn Museum of Art; National Gallery, Oslo; Salon de Mai and Salon des Réalités Nouvelles, Paris; Vi Bienal Sao Paulo, Brazil; Museum of Modern Art, New York; Baltimore

Museum of Art; San Francisco Museum of Art; Whitney Museum of Art, New York; Palazzo Strozzi, Florence; Haus der Kunst, Munich; Fundació Miro, Barcelona; Work in collections of museums in USA and Europe. Publications: The Raven Edgar Allan Poe: limited edition Artists Book with 9 original colour etchings, 1993; Various articles in professional journals and magazines. Honours: Wooley Foundation Fellowship, 1954; French Government Fellowship, 1955; Fulbright Fellowship, 1956; First Prize, Hebrew Educational Society, Brooklyn, New York, 1959; Painting Grant, Generalitat de Catalunya, 1983; Grand Prize, II Bienal D'Art FC, Barcelona, 1987. Memberships: Life Member, Art Students League of New York; Catalan Association of Visual Artists, Barcelona; Cercle d'Art Sant Lluc, Barcelona. Address: Putxet 84, 08023 Barcelona, Spain. E-mail: narotzky@compuserve.com Website: www.narotzky-art.com

**NASIR Babar Murad,** b. 25 October 1955, Karachi, Pakistan. Consultant. Education: BSc, 1st Class Honours, Electronics, 1975, D Phil, 1979, University of Sussex, England. Appointments: Lecturer, University of Ibadan, Nigeria, 1979-80; Principal System Analyst, NWDB, Nigeria, 1981; Researcher A, University of Greenwich, England, 1984-86; Postdoctoral Research Fellow, King's College, University of London, England, 1986-88; Research Fellow, Birkbeck College, University of London, 1989-90. Publications: Sole author 1994-98 of: 14 Colloquium Digest Articles, IEE; 1 UK Patent; 4 International conference proceedings articles. Honours: Nominated Man of the Year 2003, American Biographical Institute; Nominated as recipient of American Medal of Honor, 2003; Listed in Who's Who publications and biographical dictionaries. Membership: IEE. Address: 14 Cool Oak Lane, London NW9 7BJ, England. E-mail: bmnasir@talk21.com

**NASR Seyyed Hossein,** b. 7 April 1933, Tehran, Iran. University Professor. m. Soussan Daneshvary, November 1958, 1 son, 1 daughter. Education: BS, MIT, 1954; MSc, 1956, PhD, History of Science and Philosophy, 1958, Harvard University. Appointments: Professor of Philosophy and History of Science, 1958-79, Dean of Faculty of Letters, 1968-72, Vice Chancellor, 1970-71, Tehran University; Visiting Professor, Harvard University, 1962, 1965; Aga Khan Professor of Islamic Studies, American University of Beirut, 1964-65; President, Aryamehr University, 1972-75; Founder, 1st President, Iranian Academy of Philosophy, 1974-79; Distinguished Visiting Professor, University of Utah, 1979; Professor of Religion, Temple University, 1979-84; University Professor, The George Washington University, 1984-; A D White Professor-at-Large, Cornell University, 1991-97. Publications: Over 30 books and 500 articles in magazines and journals throughout the world. Honours: Royal Book Award of Iran, 1963; Honorary Doctorate, University of Uppsala, 1977; Honorary Doctorate, Lehigh University, 1996. Address: The George Washington University, Gelman Library, 709-R, 2130 H Street, NW Washington, DC 200152, USA.

**NASSER Sami,** b. 1 July 1952, Baghdad, Iraq. University Senior Lecturer. m. Ghina, 2 sons. Education: Diploma, Physics, Department of Physics, College of Science, Baghdad, 1973; BSc(Eng), Mechanical Engineering, Department of Mechanical Engineering Baghdad University of Technology, 1976; Postgraduate Diploma in Fuel and Energy Engineering, Department of Fuel Engineering, 1980, MSc, Combustion and Energy Sciences, 1981, PhD, Mechanical Engineering, Department of Mechanical Engineering, 1986, University of Leeds. Appointments: Lecturer, Thermal Sciences, Department of Mechanical Engineering, Baghdad Institute of Technology, 1976-79; Research Assistant in Combustion and Emission,

Department of Mechanical Engineering, University of Leeds Postdoctoral Research Fellow in Fluid Mechanics, Department of Mechanical Engineering, University of Surrey, 1985-88; Postdoctoral Research Associate in Aerodynamics, Department of Engineering, University of Cambridge, 1988-90; Senior Lecturer in Thermal and Energy Engineering, Faculty of Engineering and Information Sciences, University of Hertfordshire, 1990-. Publications: Author and co-author of more than 50 technical articles published in international journals and conference proceedings in the areas of aerodynamics, automotive and energy engineering. Memberships: Fellow, Institute of Energy; Royal Aeronautical Society; American Society of Automotive Engineers; Chartered Engineer; Permanent Member, Wind Energy Technical Committee, World Renewable; Energy Congress. Address: Department of Aerospace, Automotive and Design Engineering, Faculty of Engineering and Information Sciences, University of Hertfordshire, College Lane, Hatfield, Herts AL10 9AB, England. E-mail: s.nasser@herts.ac.uk

**NASSIUMA Dankit Katasi,** b. 5 September 1958, Kenya. Professor of Statistics. m. Elizabeth, 2 sons, 4 daughters. Education: BSc, Mathematics and Statistics, University of Nairobi, Kenya, 1981; MSc, Statistics, 1985, PhD, Time Series Analysis, Econometrics, University of Manitoba, Canada. Appointments: Consultant, 1985-; Lecturer in Statistics, 1992-96, Director of Graduate School, 1997-2004; Professor of Mathematics and Statistics, 1997-, Egerton University, Kenya; Editor in Chief, Egerton Journal; Project Manager, Kenya Integrated Household Budget Survey, 2004-2006. Publications: Books: Survey Sampling: Theory and Methods; Statistical Methods for Information Analysis; Articles in professional journals including: Time Series Journal (2); Communication in Statistics (3); EAJS (1); JAST (3); Egerton Journal (3); East African Medical Journal (1). Honours: CIDA Scholarship; Commonwealth Scholarship; IDRC Team Award. Memberships: Biometrics Society; Fellowship of Christian Unions; Kenya Mathematical Society. Address: Egerton University, PO Box 536, Njoro, Kenya. E-mail: dknassiuma@yahoo.com

**NASTASE Ilie,** b. 19 July 1946, Bucharest, Romania. Tennis Player. m. (1) 1 daughter, (2) Alexandra King, 1984. Appointments: National Champion (13-14 age group), 1959, (15-16 age group) 1961, (17-18 age group) 1963, 1964; Won, Masters Singles Event, Paris, 1971, Barcelona, 1972; Boston, 1973, Stockholm, 1975; Winner, Singles, Cannes, 1967, Travemunde, 1967, 1969, Gauhati, 1968, Madras, 1968, 1969, New Delhi, 1968, 1969, Viareggio, 1968, Barranquilla, 1969, Coruna, 1969; Budapest, 1969, Denver, 1969, Salisbury, 1970, Rome, 1970, Omaha, 1971, 1972, Richmond, 1971, Hampton, 1971, Nice, 1971, 1972, Monte Carlo, 1971, 1972, Baastad, 1971, Wembley, 1971, Stockholm, 1971, Istanbul, 1971, Forest Hills, 1972, Baltimore, 1972; Madrid, 1972, Toronto, 1972, S Orange, 1972, Seattle, 1972, Roland Garros, 1973, US Open, 1973; Winner, Doubles, Roland Garros (with Ion Tiriac), 1970; Played 130 matches for the Romanian team in the Davis Cup. Publication: Breakpoint, 1986. Honours: ILTF Grand Prix, 1972, 1973; Best Romanian Sportsman of the Year, 1969, 1970, 1971, 1973. Address: Clubul Sportiv Steaua, Calea Plevnei 114, Bucharest, Romania.

**NATANI Kirmach,** b. 5 June 1935, Milwaukee, Wisconsin, USA. Psychologist. 1 son. Education: MSc, Oklahoma University, Norman, 1971; PhD, Oklahoma University Health Science Center, 1977; NRC Postdoctoral, USAFSCH Aerospace Medicine, San Antonio, 1977-79. Appointments: Private Practice, Bi-State Neurometric Services, 1993-; Program Director, Institutional Treatment Center, Missouri Department of Corrections, 1999-2002. Publications include: Long Term

Changes in Sleep Stage Patterns on the South Polar Plateau, 1970; The Phoenix Effect; Ethnological Aspects of Small Group Behaviour During Extended Isolation/Confinement, 1991; The Psychophysiology of Adaptation and Competence: Altered States of Consciousness During Antarctic Wintering, 1991. Memberships: American Psychological Association; International Society for Clinical Neuroscience and Research; International Organisation of Psychophysiology; Fellow, American College of Forensic Examiners; International American Association of Disability Analysts; Missouri State Psychological Association; Board Certificates: Forensic Neuropsychology; Forensic Medicine, Senior Disability Analyst. Address: BI-State Neurometric Services, 2838 Gainsboro Court, St Louis, MO 63121-4717, USA. E-mail: knat3@juno.com

**NATARAJAN Maruthappa,** b. 23 October 1944, Tamilnadu State, India. Editor; Publisher. m. N Sasikala. Education: BSc, 1966; MA, 1969; Diploma in Journalism, PhD; 7 years' research on Women's Development, PhD degree awarded by the University of Madras, India, 2001. Appointments: Government Public Relations Officer, 1970-84; Assistant Director, 1984-86; Public Relations Manager, MMWSS Board and Deputy Director, 1986-88; Developed TamilWord Processor, Tamil Word, 2001. Publications: Energy; Arasi Pathilkal - Answers to Questions; Erisakthi; Nenjem Sumakkum Ninaivukal; Peraringer Anna Pesukirar Part-I, II, III; Peraringar Annavin Peruraigal Part-I, II, III, IV; Several articles in various journals and Tamil dailies. Honours: MOIF, 20th Century Award of Achievement. Memberships: Cosmopolitan Club, No N281, Chennai; Kodaikanal Boat and Rowing Club; Golf Club; All India Tamil Writers' Association; National Geographic Society. Address: H6/5 Arundale Beach Road, Kalachetra Colony, Besant Nagar, Chennai - 600 090, Tamil Nadu State, India. E-mail: mnindia@yahoo.com

**NATHAN Peter Geoffrey,** b. 27 July 1929, London, England. Solicitor. m. Caroline Mullen, 2 sons, 2 daughters. Education: MA, Oriel College, Oxford; Diplôme Etudes de Civilisation Française, University of Paris. Appointments: Writer RN, 1948-49; Admitted Solicitor, 1958 Herbert Oppenheimer Nathan & Vandyk, 1954-88, Partner, 1959-88; Consultant: Boodle Hatfield, 1988-92, Wood & Awdry (formerly Wood Awdry Wansbroughs), 1992-2000; Governor, Sports Aid Foundation, 1999-2002; Chairman, 1999-2002 Honorary President, 2003-, Sports Aid London; Chairman, 1984-97, Vice-President, 1997-, Deputy Chairman Peter May Memorial Appeal, 1995-97, London Playing Fields Society; Vice-President, Croydon Playing Fields Society, 1996-; National Heritage Secretary's Ministerial Nominee, London Council for Sport and Recreation, 1992-95; Trustee until 1996, Patron, 1996-, Oriel College Development Trust; Chairman, Oriel Law Society until 1996; Chairman, Oriel Law Fellowship Appeal until 1996; Chairman, Chiddingfold Branch of the Farnham Conservative Association, 1965-70. Honours: Freeman City of London, 1961; Master Worshipful Company of Gold and Silver Wyre Drawers, 1989; DL, Greater London, 1991; National Playing Fields Association President's Certificate, 1992; OBE, 1999. Memberships include: Community Health Council for Kensington, Chelsea and Westminster representing Royal Borough of Kensington and Chelsea, 1974-78; Council, British Heart Foundation, 1976-93; Council, Anglo-Swiss Society, 1988-; Court, City University, 1989-93; Livery Consultative Committee, Corporation of London, 1994-97; Law Society; Honorary Member, Geographical Association; Clubs: MCC; Vincent's (Oxford); Oriental; City University. Address: Kites Nest House, Bourton, Dorset SP8 5AZ, England.

**NAUGHTIE (Alexander) James,** b. 9 August 1951, Aberdeen, Scotland. Journalist. m. Eleanor Updale, 1986, 1 son, 2 daughters. Education: University of Aberdeen; Syracuse University. Appointments: Journalist, The Scotsman (newspaper), 1977-84, The Guardian, 1984-88, Chief Political Correspondent; Presenter, The World at One, BBC Radio, 1988-94, The Proms, BBC Radio and TV, 1991-, Today, BBC Radio 4, 1994-, Book Club, BBC Radio 4, 1998-. Publication: The Rivals, 2001. Honour: LLD, Aberdeen. Membership: Council, Gresham College, 1997-. Address: BBC News Centre, London W12 7RJ, England.

**NAVICKIENE Violetta,** b. 13 March 1957, Klaipeda, Lithuania. Lecturer. m. Antinas Navickas, 2 sons. Education: Masters Degree, Lecturer in English, 1974-79; PhD, Doctor of Philology Sciences, 1985-88; Bachelor's Degree, Business Administration, 2000-2005. Appointments: Lecturer, English, Associate Professor, English Philology, Director, English Language Centre, Klaipeda University, Lithuania. Publications: Two aspects of teaching vocabulary, 2001; Authentic Materials for the Classroom, 2001. Honours: Certificate of Honour for achievements at work; Silver Medal Award for achievements and long-term work. Memberships: Lithuanian Association of North American Studies; Klaipeda Junior Inner Wheel Club. Address: Pasvalio 16, Klaipeda, Lithuania. E-mail: akc@hmf.ku.lt

**NAVRATILOVA Martina,** b. 18 October 1956, Prague, Czech Republic (now American Citizen). Tennis Player. Career: Defected to the US in 1975, professional Player since; Titles: Wimbledon Singles, 1978, 1979, 1982, 1983, 1984, 1985, 1986, 1987, 1990; Doubles: 1976, 1979, 1982, 1983, 1984, 1985; Avon, 1978, 1979, 1981; Aust, 1981, 1983, 1985; France, 1982, 1984; US Open, 1983, 1984, 1986, 1987; Finalist at Wimbledon, 1988, 1989; Federation Cup for Czechoslovakia, 1973, 1974, 1975; 54 Grand Slam Titles (18 Singles, 37 Doubles); World Champion, 1980; Ranked No 1, 1982-85; 8 Wimbledon Titles, 1993; Women's Record for Consecutive wins, 1984; 100th Tournament win, 1985; only player to win 100 Matches at Wimbledon, 1991; Record 158 singles victories, 1992; 1,400 Victories, 1994; 167 Singles Titles, 1994; Made comeback in 2000 (in doubles only); Winner, Mixed Doubles, Australian Open, 2003 (oldest winner of a grandslam title). Appointments: President, Women's Tennis Association, 1979-80; Designs own fashionwear. Publications: Being Myself, 1985; The Total Zone (with Liz Nickles, novel, 1994); The Breaking Point (with Liz Nickles), 1996; Killer Instinct, (with Liz Nickles), 1998. Address: IMG, 1360 E 9th Street, Cleveland, OH 44114, USA.

**NAWAR Nagwa,** b. 7 August 1957, Mansoura, Egypt. Professor of Inorganic Chemistry. m. Hamad H Yehia, 2 sons. Education: BSc, Chemistry, 1979, MSc, Inorganic Chemistry, 1983, Mansoura University, Egypt; PhD, Inorganic and Organometallic Chemistry, Liverpool University, England, 1989. Appointments: Demonstrator, 1979-83, Assistant Lecturer, 1983-85, Lecturer, 1989-95, Associate Professor, 1995-2001, Professor, 2001-, Mansoura University, Egypt; Postgraduate Research Fellowship, 1983-85, Scientific Visitor, 1995, Liverpool University, England; Fulbright Fellowship, 1995, Assistant Research Scientist, 1996, Texas A&M University, USA; IMG (Tempus-Mech) Programme, UK, France, Austria, 2003. Articles in scientific journals including: Journal of Organometallic Chemistry, 2000 (2); Transactions of Metallic Chemistry, 2001 (2). Honours: Shuman Foundation Prize, Kingdom of Jordan, 1996; Masoura University Prize of Distinction, 2001. Memberships: Egyptian Chemical Society, 1982; American Chemical Society; WISE (Texas A&M University), 1995-; Associate Member, European Chemistry Thematic Network. Address: Chemistry Department,

Faculty of Science, Mansoura University, Mansoura 35516, PO Box 79, Egypt. E-mail: nnawar@mans.edu.eg

**NEAL Anthony James,** b. 18 October 1961, London, England. Consultant Oncologist (special interest in Breast Cancer). Education: Bachelor of Medicine, Bachelor of Surgery, 1985, Doctor of Medicine, 1995, University of London; Member, Royal College of Physicians (UK), 1988; Fellow, Royal College of Radiologists, 1992. Appointments: Consultant, Clinical Oncology, Royal Marsden NHS Trust, 1996-2000; Consultant, Clinical Oncology, St Luke's Cancer Centre, Guildford, Surrey, 2000-. Publications: Clinical Oncology, Basic Principles and Practice (co-author), 1st edition, 2nd edition, 3rd edition. Honours: Junior Investigator Award, British Oncological Association, 1994; ESTRO Physics Prize, 1994. Address: St Luke's Cancer Centre, Royal Surrey County Hospital, Guildford, Surrey GU2 5XX, England.

**NEASOM Norman,** b. 7 November 1915, Parish of Tardebigge, Worcestershire, England. Artist; Art Teacher. m. Jessie Mary Davis, 2 daughters. Education: Drawing, Painting, Composition and Illustration, Birmingham College of Arts and Crafts, 1931-35. Career: Teacher, Painting School Birmingham College of Art, 1946-54; Teacher, Redditch School of Art, 1954-80; Retired, 1980; Artist since childhood; Exhibitions: Royal Academy, 1970, 1974, 1976; Royal Watercolour Society; Royal Birmingham Society of Artists; Stratford Art Society; Mall Galleries; Work in collections: West Midlands Arts Council, Birmingham City Arts Collection and various private collections. Publications: Works reproduced by firms including Medici prints; Articles for Leisure Painter; Covers for Readers Digest; Illustrations for local history books. Honours: Twice winner James Priddy Award, Royal Birmingham Society of Arts. Memberships: Patron and Honorary Member, Stratford-on-Avon Art Society; Royal Watercolour Society; Royal Birmingham Society of Artists. Address: 95 Bromfield Road, Redditch, Worcestershire, B97 4PN, England.

**NEBE Michael,** b. 28 July 1947, Nordenbeck, Waldeck, Germany. Cellist; Conductor. Education: Educational Diploma and Teaching Qualifications, Dortmund Conservatorium; MMus, King's College, University of London, England, studied under Thurston Dart, Brian Trowell, Antony Milner, Geoffrey Bush; Licentiate, Royal Academy of Music, studying with Florence Hooton and Colin Hampton; Conducting, private studies in Germany and at Morley College, London under Lawrence Leonard; International Conductors' Seminar, Zlin, Czech Republic, 1991 and 1993 under Kirk Trevor, Jiri Belohlavek, Georg Tintner and Zdenek Bilek. Debut: Wigmore Hall, London, 1977. Career: Member, London Piace Consort, London Piace Duo, both until 1987, Plaegan Piano Quartet; Numerous performances as soloist and chamber music player throughout UK; Tours in Germany, Netherlands, USA, Canada, Australia; Conductor and Musical Director of Whitehall Orchestra (The Orchestra of the British Civil Service), 1990-; Associated Conductor, Surrey Sinfonietta until 1994; Founder and Musical Director, Fine Arts Sinfonia of London, 1994-; Appearances as conductor in the UK, Germany Spain, Turkey; Teacher, conductor, freelance musician, soloist, translator, writer, lecturer and adjudicator; Made numerous live and recorded radio and television appearances, CD recordings; Conducted over 150 British and world Premieres. Publications: Translation into German, Eta Cohen's Violin Tutor, 1979; Cello Tutor, 1984; Articles for British newspapers and magazines. Membership: Dvorak Society; Incorporated Society of Musicians; Musicians' Union. Address: c/o Thornton Management, 24 Thornton Avenue, London SW2 4HG, England.

**NEELEY G Steven,** b. Cincinnati, Ohio, USA. Professor of Philosophy; Attorney at Law; Philosophical Psychotherapist. Education: BS BA, Magna Cum Laude, Xavier University, 1980; JD, University of Cincinnati School of Law, 1985; MA, 1987, PhD, 1989, University of Cincinnati. Appointments: Law Clerk, Law Offices of T D Shackleford, 1982-84; Attorney-At-Law, Private Practice, 1985-; Adjunct Professor, Union Institute (Union for Experimenting Colleges and Universities), 1989-; Visiting Assistant Professor of Philosophy, Xavier University, 1989-92; Adjunct Professor of Philosophy, College of Mount St Joseph, 1992-93; Assistant Professor of Philosophy, 1993-97, Associate Professor of Philosophy, 1997-2003, Saint Francis College; Professor of Philosophy, Saint Francis University, 2003-; Philosophical Psychotherapist, Private Practice, 1997-. Publications: Books: The Constitutional Right to Suicide: A Legal and Philosophical Examination, 1994, 2nd edition, 1996; Schopenhauer: A Consistent Reading, 2003; Numerous articles in professional journals. Honours include: Swatsworth Faculty Award, Saint Francis, 1997; American Philosophical Association, Excellence in Teaching Award, 1998; Finalist, Saint Francis College Honor Society Distinguished Faculty Award, 1998, 1999, 2000, 2001, 2002, 2003; 2004; Student Government Association Teacher of the Year Award, 2004. Address: Saint Francis University, PO Box 6000, Loretto, PA 15940, USA.

**NEELY William Robert Nicholas (Bill),** b. 21 May 1959, Belfast, Northern Ireland. TV Journalist. m. Marion Kerr, 2 daughters. Education: BA Honours, Queens University, Belfast. Appointments: Reporter, BBC, Northern Ireland, 1981-87; Reporter, BBC Network, 1987-88; Reporter, Presenter, Sky TV, 1989 (January to June); Reporter, 1989-90, Washington Correspondent and US Bureau Chief, 1990-97, Europe Correspondent, 1997-2002, International Editor and Newscaster, 2002-, ITN. Honours: Royal TV Society News Award, 1999, 2001; Golden Nymph Trophy, Monte Carlo TV Festival, 2000. Address: 200 Gray's Inn Road, London WC1X 8X2, England. E-mail: bill.neely@itn.co.uk

**NEESON Liam,** b. 5 June 1952, Ballymena, Northern Ireland. Actor. m. Natasha Richardson, 1994, 1 son. Education: St Mary's Teachers College, London. Appointments: Forklift Operator; Architect's Assistant. Creative Works: Theatre includes: Of Mice and Men, Abbey Theatre Co, Dublin; The Informer, Dublin Theatre Festival; Translations, National Theatre, London; The Plough and the Stars, Royal Exchange, Manchester; The Judas Kiss; Films include: Excalibur; Krull; The Bounty; The Innocent; Lamb; The Mission; Duet for One; A Prayer for the Dying; Suspect Satisfaction; High Spirits; The Dead Pool; The Good Mother; Darkman; The Big Man; Under Suspicion; Husbands and Wives; Leap of Faith; Ethan Frome; Ruby Cairo; Schindler's List; Rob Roy; Nell; Before and After; Michael Collins; Les Misérables, 1998; The Haunting; Star Wars: Episode 1 – The Phantom Menace; Gun Shy, 1999; Gangs of New York, 2000; K19: The Widowmaker, 2002; Love Actually, 2003; TV includes: Arthur the King; Ellis Island; If Tomorrow Comes; A Woman of Substance; Hold the Dream; Kiss Me Goodnight; Next of Kin; Sweet As You Are; The Great War. Honours include: Best Actor, Evening Standard Award, 1997. Address: c/o ICM, 8942 Wilshire Boulevard, Beverly Hills, CA 90211, USA.

**NEGI Gorkhu Ram,** b. 1 April 1960, Suroo 15/20, India. Lecturer in Indian and European History. Education: MA, History, 1982; Postgraduate Diploma in Adult Education, 1985; MPhil, History, 1986; PhD, History, 2003. Appointments: Lecturer in History (ad-hoc), Government College, Rampur Bushahr, 1985-86; Lecturer in History (10+2), Senior

Secondary School, 1986-87; Lecturer in History, College Cadre, Government Post Graduate College, Rampur Bushahr HP, 1987-. Publications: Research paper, History of Christian Missionary Activities and their Impact on Himachal Pradesh 1840-1947 AD, 1995; The Himalaya Mission with Special Reference to the Contribution of American Missionaries and Samuel Evans Stokes, 1997; The Moravian Missionaries and their Contribution to the cause of tribals in Himachal Pradesh, published in the book, Tribal Development: Appraisal and Alternatives by Institute of Tribal Studies, Himachal Pradesh University, Shimla, 1998; The Moravian Brethren in India: with Special Emphasis on their Activities in the North-Western Himalayas', 2000; Christianity in Punjab: with Special Emphasis on Christian Missionaries Activities in Kangra and Lahaul, AD 1854-1940, 2002. Memberships: Life Member, Himachal Pradesh, History Congress; Life Member, American Studies Research Centre, Library Osmania University Campus, Hyderabad, India; Church History Association of India; Governing Body Member, Indian Confederation of Indigenous and Tribal People; Member, Rotary Club, Rampur Bushahr, Rotary International District 3080; Secretary (Elect), Rampur Bushakr Rotary Club, 2005-06; Attended Conference organised by the Society for Threatened Peoples, Bonn, Germany, 1995; Visits to Netherlands, Belgium, Luxembourg. Address: Government Post Graduate College, Rampur Bushahr, District Shimla, Himachal Pradesh-172001, India.

**NEGRI SEMBILAN Yang di-Pertuan Besar, Tuanku Jaafar ibni Al-Marhum Tuanku Abdul Rahman,** b. 19 July 1922, Malaysia. Malaysian Ruler. m. Tuanku Najihar binti Tuanku Besar Burhanuddin, 1943, 3 sons, 3 daughters. Education: Malay College; Nottingham University. Appointments: Entered Malay Administrative Service, 1944; Assistant District Officer, Rembau, 1946-47; Parti, 1953-55; Chargé d'Affaires, Washington DC, 1947; 1st Permanent Secretary, Malayan Permanent Mission to UN, 1957-58; 1st Secretary, Trade Counsellor, Deputy High Commissioner, London, 1962-63; Ambassador to United Arab Republic, 1962; High Commissioner, concurrently in Nigeria and Ghana, 1965-66; Timbalan Yang di-Pertuan Agong (Deputy Supreme Head of State), 1979-84, 1989-94; Yang di-Pertuan Agong (Supreme Head of State), 1994-99.

**NÉHER-NEUMANN Erzsébet,** b. 20 February 1935, Rábatamási, Hungary. Retired Chemical Engineer; Researcher in Solution Chemistry. Education: Diploma of Chemical Technician, Chemical Technical School, 1953; Diploma of Honour in Chemical Engineering, 1958, Technical Dr, 1964, University of Chemical Industries, Veszprèm, Hungary; Technical Dr, equivalent to PhD, Royal Institute of Technology, Stockholm, Sweden, 1987. Appointments: Assistant, 1958-64, 1st Assistant to Professor, 1965-67, University of Chemical Industries, Veszprèm, Hungary; Assistant, 1967-77, Research Engineer, 1977-2000, Department of Inorganic Chemistry, Royal Institute of Technology, Stockholm, Sweden; Retired, 2000. Publications: Articles in scientific journals including Acta Chemica Scandinavica, 1979, 1984, 1985, 1992, 1994, 1997, 1998, 1999; Journal of Solution Chemistry, 2003. Honour: 21st Century Award for Achievement with Illuminated Diploma of Honour, International Biographical Centre, Cambridge, England. Address: Smedsbacksgatan 7, 3tr, 115 39 Stockholm, Sweden.

**NEHORAI Arye,** b. 10 September 1951, Haifa, Israel. Professor. m. Shlomit, 1 son, 1 daughter. Education: BSc, Technion, Israel, 1976; MSc, Technion, Israel, 1979; PhD, Stanford University, 1983. Appointments: Research Engineer, Systems Control Technology Inc, 1983-85; Assistant Professor, Yale University, 1985-89; Associate Professor, Yale University,

1989-95; Professor, University of Illinois, Chicago, 1995-. Publications: More than 90 journal papers; 140 conference papers. Honours: University Scholar, University of Illinois; IEEE Signal Processing Society Senior Award for Best Paper, 1989; Magazine Paper Award, 2004; Fellow, IEEE; Fellow, Royal Statistical Society; Editor in Chief, IEEE Transactions on Signal Processing, 2000-2002; Vice President, Publications, IEEE Signal Processing Society, 2003-. Memberships: IEEE; Royal Statistical Society. Address: ECE Department, University of Illinois at Chicago, 851 S Morgan Street, Chicago, IL 60607, USA. E-mail: nehorai@ece.uic.edu

**NEIL Andrew,** b. 21 May 1949, Paisley, Scotland. Publisher; Broadcaster; Editor; Columnist; Media Consultant. Education: MA, University of Glasgow. Appointments: Conservative Party Research Department, 1971-73; Correspondent, The Economist, 1973-83; UK Editor, 1982-83, Editor, Sunday Times, 1983-94; Executive Chairman, Sky Television, 1988-90; Executive Editor and Chief Correspondent, Fox News Network, 1994; Contributing Editor, Vanity Fair, New York, 1994-; Freelance Writer and Broadcaster, 1994-97; Publisher, (Chief Executive and Editor-in-Chief), The Scotsman, Edinburgh, The Business, London, 1996-; Chief Executive, The Spectator and Apollo magazines, handbag.com, London, 2004; Anchorman, BBC TV's Despatch Box, ITV's Thursday Night Live; BBC Radio's Sunday Breakfast, 1998-2000; BBC TV's This Week with Andrew Neil; BBC TV's Daily Politics, 2003-; Lord Rector, University of St Andrews, 1999-2002; Fellow, Royal Society for Arts, Manufacture and Commerce. Publications: The Cable Revolution, 1982; Britain's Free Press: Does It Have One?, 1988; Full Disclosure (autobiography), 1996: British Excellence, 1999, 2000, 2001. Address: Glenburn Enterprises Ltd, PO Box 584, London SW7 3QY, England.

**NEILL John Robert Winder,** b. 17 December 1945, Dublin, Ireland. Archbishop. m. Betty Anne Cox, 3 sons. Education: Foundation Scholar, 1965, First Class Moderatorship, 1966, Trinity College, Dublin, 1962-66; Theological Tripos, 1968, Jesus College, Cambridge, 1966-69; General Ordination Examination, 1969, Ridley Hall, Cambridge, 1968-69. Appointments: Ordained Deacon, 1969, Priest, 1970, Bishop, 1986; Curate of Glenageary, Dublin, 1969-71; Bishop's Vicar, St Canice's Cathedral, Ossory, 1971-74; Rector of Abbeystrewry, Cork, 1974-78; Vicar of Saint Bartholomew's, Dublin, 1978-84; Dean of Waterford, 1984-86; Bishop of Tuam, 1986-97; Bishop of Cashel and Ossory, 1997-2002; Archbishop of Dublin and Primate of Ireland, 2002-. Honours: BA, University of Dublin, 1966; BA, University of Cambridge, 1968; MA, University of Dublin, 1969; MA, University of Cambridge, 1972; LLD (Honoris Causa), National University of Ireland, 2003. Address: The See House, 17 Temple Road, Dublin 6, Ireland. E-mail: archbishop@dublin.anglican.org

**NEILL Sam,** b. 14 September 1947, Northern Ireland. Actor. m. Noriko Watanabe, 1 daughter. 1 son by Lisa Harrow. Education: University of Canterbury. Creative Works: Toured for 1 year with Players Drama Quintet; Appeared with Amamus Theatre in roles including Macbeth and Pentheus in The Bacchae; Joined New Zealand National Film Unit, playing leading part in 3 films, 1974-78; Moved to Australia, 1978, England, 1980; TV appearances include: From a Far Country; Ivanhoe; The Country Girls; Reilly: Ace of Spies; Kane and Abel (mini-series); Submerged (film), 2001; Framed (film), 2002; Dr Zhivago (mini-series), 2002; Films: Sleeping Dogs, 1977; The Journalist; My Brilliant Career; Just Out of Reach; Attack Force Z; The Final Conflict (Omen III); Possession; Enigma; Le Sand des Autres; Robbery Under Arms; Plenty; For Love Alone; The Good Wife; A Cry in the Dark; Dead Calm; The

French Revolution; The Hunt for Red October; Until the End of the World; Hostage; Memoirs of an Invisible Man; Death in Brunswick; Jurassic Park; The Piano; Sirens; Country Life; Restoration; Victory; In the Month of Madness; Event Horizon; The Horse Whisperer; My Mother Frank; Molokai; The Story of Father Damien; Bicentennial Man; The Dish, 2000; Monticello; The Zookeeper, 2001; Jurassic Park III, 2001; Dirty Deeds, 2002; Perfect Strangers, 2002. Address: c/o ICM, 8942 Wilshire Boulevard, Beverly Hills, CA 90211, USA.

**NELSON Nigel David,** b. 16 April 1954, London, England. Journalist; Writer; Broadcaster. 3 sons, 2 daughters. Education: Sutton Valence School, Kent, England; Department of Journalism, Harlow College. Appointments: Crime Reporter, Kent Evening Post; Reporter, Daily Mail; Royal Correspondent; Daily Mail; New York Correspondent; Daily Mail; Feature Writer, TV Critic, Sunday Mirror; Political Editor, Sunday People. Publications: If I Should Die, film biography of Rupert Brooke For Burfield-Bastable Productions, 1986; The Porton Phial, a political thriller, 1991; The Honeytrap, short story, 1991. Honour: Commended, Young Journalist of the Year, 1974. Address: Sunday People, 1 Canada Square, Canary Wharf, London E14 5AP, England.

**NENASHEV Alexander Andreevich,** b. 12 June 1932, Kuibyshev, Russia. Clinical Therapist; Physiologist. m. Marinina Tamara Petrovna. Education: Graduate, Medical University Kuibyshev, 1962-65; Candidate of Medical Science, 1966; Doctor of Medicine, 1973. Appointments: Head of Department of Hyperbolic Oxygination Medicine, University of Kuibyshev, 1965-73; Head of Department of Normal and Pathologic Physiology, Medicine Department, Kabardino-Balkaria University, 1973-93; Professor Department of Medical Diagnostic Systems, Samara State Aerospace University, Samara, 1994-. Publications: Treatment of the anaerobic infections by the oxygen increased pressure (doctoral thesis), 1973; About 40 articles in medical journals; Monograph: Functional features and characteristics of erythrocytes of patients with hemorrhagic hemostathiapathies, 2003; 6 inventions include: Method of Investigation of erythrocytes' mechanical resistance, 1980; A device for investigation of erythrocytes' mechanical resistance, 1987; Method of decrease of chronic hypoxia of tissues, 1999. Honours: Gold Medal, Eureka 1999, Brussels; Silver Medal, Paris, 2000; Gold Medal, Moscow. Address: Samara State Aerospace University, Moskovskoe shosse 34, Ru Ramara, 443086 Russia. E-mail: bundov@mail.radiant.ru

**NERMUT Milan Vladimir,** b. 19 March 1924, Kyjov, Czech Republic. Divorced, 4 daughters. Education: Medical Bacteriology, 1956, CSc degree, 1958, Medical Faculty, Readership in Cytology, 1965, Faculty of Science, Purkyne University, Brno. Appointments: Department of Biology, Medical Faculty, Brno, 1947-62; Institute of Microbiology, Czechoslovak Academy of Sciences, Prague, 1962-65; Head of Electron Microscopy Laboratory, Institute of Virology, Czechoslovak Academy of Sciences, Bratislava, 1965-70; Max-Planck Institute for Virus Research, Tubingen, Germany, 1970-71; National Institute for Medical Research, MRC, London, 1971-89; National Institute for Biological Standards and Control, South Mimms, UK, 1991-2005; Visiting Scientist in UK, France, Canada, USA, Australia, Switzerland and Spain. Honours: Hlavka Memorial Medal, Czechoslovak Academy of Sciences, 1992; J E Purkyne Gold Medal, Medical Faculty, Masaryk University, Brno, 1992; Honorary Degree (DSc), Slovak Academy of Sciences, Bratislava, 1995; Memorial Medal, Masaryk University, Brno, 2003; Babak Medal, Biological Society, Brno, Czech Republic; Listed in national and international biographical dictionaries. Memberships:

Society of General Microbiology; Editorial Board Member: Micron; Veterinary Medicine; Microscopy and Analysis; Scripta Medica. Address: 12 Milton Road, London NW7 4AX, England. E-mail: mvnermut@nibsc.ac.uk

**NESTERENKO Tatyana,** b. 5 August 1959, Vladivostock, Russia. Government Official. m. Sergey, 2 daughters. Education: Degree in Economics, Khabarnovsk Institute of National Economy. Appointments: Economist, Auditor, Head of Budgetary Inspection, Financial Department, Anadyr Territorial Executive Committee, Chukotka, 1981-89; Head, Financial Department, Chukotka Territorial Executive Committee, Deputy Head of Administration, Head of Financial Directorate, Administration of Chukotka Autonomous Area, 1989-93; State Duma Deputy, Member, Committee for the Budget, Taxes, Banks and Finance, 1993-98; Head Federal Treasury and Deputy Minister of Finance, 1998-2004; Head, Federal Treasury (Federal Service), 2005-. Publications: About 80 publications in specialised periodicals. Honours: Distinguished Economist of the Russian Federation; Medal to Rank II Order for Service to the Fatherland; Honorary Diploma from the Russian Government; Awards from Russian Ministry of Finance. Address: Federal Treasury, ul. Ilyinka 9, 103097 Moscow, Russia. Website: www.roskazna.ru

**NETANYAHU Benjamin,** b. 21 October 1949. Politician; Businessman. m. 3 children. Education: BSc, 1974, MSc, 1976, MIT. Appointments: Managing Consultant, Boston Consulting Group, 1976-78; Executive Director, Jonathan Institute, Jerusalem, 1978-80; Senior Manager, Rim Inds, Jerusalem, 1980-82; Deputy Chief of Mission, Israeli Embassy, Washington DC, 1982-84; Permanent Representative to UN, 1984-88; Deputy Minister of Foreign Affairs, 1988-91, Deputy Minister, PM's Office, 1991-92; Leader, Likud, 1993-99; Minister of Foreign Affairs, 2002-03, of Finance, 2003-. Publication: A Place Among the Nations: Israel and the World, 1993; Fighting Terrorism, 1995; A Durable Peace, 2000. Address: Ministry of Finance, POB 13191, 1 Rehov Kaplan, Kiryat Ben-Gurion, Jerusalem 91008, Israel.

**NETANYAHU Benzion,** b. 25 March 1910, Warsaw, Poland. Historian; Educator; Editor. m. Cela Segal, 3 sons. Education: MA, Hebrew University, Jerusalem, 1933; Ph.D., Dropsie College, Philadelphia, Pennsylvania, USA, 1947. Appointments: Editor, Hebrew daily Hayarden, 1934-35; Editor, Political Library, 1936-39; Member, Jabotinsky Delegation to US, 1940; Head, public campaign and political activities, New Zionist Organisation of America, 1941-48; General Editor, Editor-in-Chief, ten volumes, Encyclopaedia Hebraica, 1949-62; Professor of Modern Hebrew Literature and Medieval Jewish History, Dropsie College, 1962-68; Professor of Jewish History and Hebrew Literature, Denver University, 1968-71; Professor of Judaic Studies, Cornell University, 1971-78; Professor Emeritus, Judaic Studies, 1978-. Publications include: Max Nordau, 4 studies, 1937-54; Theodor Herzl, two studies, 1937, 1962; Israel Zangwill, 1938; Leo Pinsker, 1944; Vladimir Jabotinsky, 3 Studies, 1981-2004; Don Isaac Abravanel: Statesman and Philosopher, 1953, 1998 (Spanish edition 2004, Hebrew edition 2005); The Marranos of Spain, 1966, 1999; The Cabbalistic Works ha-Kanah and ha-Peliah, 1975; The Origins of the Inquisition in Fifteenth Century Spain, 1995, 2001 (Spanish edition 1999); Toward the Inquisition: Essays on Jewish and Converso History in Late Medieval Spain, 1998; The Old-New Controversy about Spanish Marranism, 2000; Causas y fines de la Inquisición española, 2001; The Founding Fathers of Zionism (Hebrew), 2004; Numerous editorial works. Memberships: American Academy for Jewish Research, Fellow, 1965-; Real Academia de Bellas Artes y Ciencias Históricas de Toledo, Académico; The University of Valladolid, Doctor Honoris Causa, 2001. Address: 4 Haportzim Street, Jerusalem 93662, Israel.

**NEUBAUER Peter B,** b. 5 July 1913, Krems, Austria. Psychoanalyst. Education: MD, 1938; Child Analyst, 1964. Appointments: Clinical Professor of Psychiatry, New York University, 1970-; Former Director, Child Development Center; Chairman Emeritus, Center for Psychoanalytic Training and Research. Publications: Numerous articles in professional journals. Memberships: Sigmund Freud Gesellschaft, Vienna; Sigmund Freud Archives; American Psychoanalytic Association; International Psychoanalytic Association; American Academy of Child Psychiatry. Address: 33 East 70th Street, New York, NY 10021, USA.

**NEUFELD Karl H,** b. 16 February 1939, Warendorf, Germany. Professor of Theology. Education: Lic phil, 1965, Lic Theol, 1970, Lyon-Fouvière; Dr theol, Catholic Institute of Paris, 1975; Dr theol habil, Innsbruck University, 1980; Dr phil, München-Hochschule für Philosophie, 1983. Appointments: Assistant of K Rahner, 1971-73; Professor of Theology, Rome Pont University Gregoriana, 1978-1989; Professor of Theology, Innsbruck, 1990-. Publications: Books and articles about French Theology; Studies about the work of Ad Von Harnack, Philosophy and Theology, History of Thought and History of Theology, Theology of Religions. Honours: Honorary member, Direct Committee of Istituto di Scienze Religiouse, Trento, Italy. Memberships: ASS Internationale Card Henri de Lubac, Paris; German Cercle of Theologians, Dt Hochschulverband. Address: Sillgasse 6, P'fach 569 A- 6021, Innsbruck, Austria.

**NEW Anthony Sherwood Brooks,** b. 14 August 1924, London, England. Retired Architect; Writer. m. Elizabeth Pegge, 11 April 1970, 1 son, 1 daughter. Education: Northern Polytechnic School of Architecture, 1941-43, 1947-51. Publications: Observer's Book of Postage Stamps, 1967; Observer's Book of Cathedrals, 1972; A Guide to the Cathedrals of Britain, 1980; Property Services Agency Historic Buildings Register, Vol II (London), 1983; A Guide to the Abbeys of England and Wales, 1985; New Observer's Book of Stamp Collecting, 1986; A Guide to the Abbeys of Scotland, 1988. Memberships: Society of Antiquaries, fellow; Royal Institute of British Architects, fellow; Institution of Structural Engineers. Address: 45A Woodbury Avenue, Petersfield, Hants, GU32 2ED, England

**NEWBY Richard Mark (Baron of Rothwell in the County of West Yorkshire),** b. 14 February 1953, UK. Member of the House of Lords. m. Ailsa Ballantyne Thomson, 2 sons. Education: BA, Philosophy, Politics and Economics, 1971, MA, St Catherine's College, Oxford. Appointments: Private Secretary to Permanent Secretary, 1977-79, Principal Planning Unit, 1979-81, HM Customs and Excise; Secretary, SDP Parliamentary Committee, 1981; National Secretary, SDP, 1983-88; Executive, 1988-90, Director, 1991, Corporate Affairs, Rosehaugh plc; Director, Matrix Communications Consultancy Ltd, 1992-99; Chairman, Reform Publications, 1993-; Liberal Democrat, Treasury Spokesman, House of Lords, 1997-; Member, Centre for Reform Advisory Board; Director, Flagship Group, 1999-2001; Chief of Staff to Charles Kennedy MP, 1999-; Chairman Live Consulting, 2001-. Honour: OBE, 1990. Memberships: Trustee, Allachy Trust; Trustee, Coltstaple Trust; Reform; MCC. Address: House of Lords, London SW1A 0PW, England. E-mail: newbyr@parliament.uk

**NEWELL Mike,** b. 1942, St Albans, England. Film Director. m. Bernice Stegers, 1979, 1 son, 1 daughter. Education: University of Cambridge. Appointments: Trainee Director, Granada TV,

1963. Creative Works: TV work includes: Big Breadwinner Hog (series), 1968; Budgie (series); Thirty Minute Theatre and other TV plays; Director, European Premiere of Tennessee Williams' The Kingdom of the Earth, Bristol Old Vic; Films: The Man in the Iron Mask, 1976; The Awakening, 1979; Bad Blood, 1980; Dance with a Stranger, 1984; The Good Father, 1985; Amazing Grace and Chuck, 1986; Soursweet, 1987; Common Ground, 1990; Enchanted April, 1991; Into the West; Four Weddings and a Funeral, 1994; An Awfully Big Adventure, 1994; Donnie Brasco, 1997; Pushing Tin, 1998; Photographing Fairies (executive producer), 1997; 200 Cigarettes, 1999; Best Laid Plans, 1999; High Fidelity, 2000; Traffic, 2000. Honours include: BAFTA Award, Best Director, 1995.

**NEWEY Jon Wilton,** b. 12 January 1951, London, England. Editor; Publisher. m. Jill Newey, 1 son, 1 daughter. Education: Graphic Art Diploma Course, Kennington College. Appointments: Professional Musician, 1970-74; Department Head, Dalton's Weekly, 1974-77; Advertisement Manager, Sounds Magazine, 1977-91; Publisher, Top Magazine, 1991-99; Editor and Publisher, Jazzwise Magazine, 2000-. Publications: Books: The Tower Jazz Guide (editor); Tapestry of Delights (consultant editor); Music Mart Drum Guide (author); Jazz-Rock – A History (discographer); Articles in magazines including: Sounds, Music Mart, Mojo, Record Collector, Jazzwise, Jazz on CD, Jazz at Ronnie Scotts, Music Business, MI PRO. E-mail: jonnewey@jnal.com

**NEWING Peter,** b. 10 May 1933, Littlebourne, Canterbury, England. Clerk in Holy Orders. m. Angela Newing. Education: Cert Ed, Birmingham, Worcester College of Education, 1953-55; BA and Long Prize (Proxime Accesit), St John's College, Durham, 1960-65; B Ed, Bristol University, 1976; BSc, State University of New York, USA, 1985; Ed D, Pacific Western University, USA, 1988; Diploma, Religious Studies, Cambridge University, 1991. Appointments: National Service, RAF, London, 1951-53; Science Teacher, Bedfordshire County Council, 1955-60; Curate of Blockley with Aston Magna, 1965-69; Deacon, 1965, Priest, 1966, Gloucester; Priest in Charge of Taynton and Tibberton, 1969-75; Lecturer, Gloucestershire College of Arts and Technology, University of Gloucestershire, 1972-82; Tutor, Open University, 1975-76; Rector of Brimpsfield, Elkstone and Syde, 1975-95; Rector of Brimpsfield, Daglingworth, The Duntisbournes, etc., 1995-2001; Curate of Redmarley, Bromesberrow, Dymock etc., 2001-03, Honorary Curate, 2003-. Publications: Pamphlet, The Literate's Hood and Hoods of the Theological Colleges of the Church of England, 1959; Various articles on church bells. Honours: Fellow Society of Antiquaries, Scotland, 1959; Fellow Royal Society of Arts, London, 1960; Fellow The College of Preceptors, London, 1995. Memberships: Bishop of Gloucester's Visitor to Church Schools, 1976-94; Member of Court, University of Bristol, 1977-; Member, Gloucester Diocesan Synod, 1982-2001, re-elected 2003-; Member, Gloucester Diocesan Board of Finance, 1982-; Member, Gloucester Diocesan Board of Patronage, 1985-93, 2001-; Member, Panel of Advisers Incumbents (Vacation of Benefices) Measure 1977, 1985-; Member, Central Council of Church Bellringers, 1985-. Address: The Rectory, Albright Lane, Bromesberrow, Ledbury, Herefordshire HR8 1RU, England.

**NEWKIRK Herbert William,** b. 23 November 1928, Jersey City, New Jersey, USA. Materials Scientist. m. Madeleine Dorothy, 2 sons, 1 daughter. Education: AA, Pre-Engineering, Jersey City Junior College, 1948; BSc, Polytechnic Institute of Brooklyn, 1951; PhD, Ohio State University, 1956. Appointments: Chemist, General Electric, Hanford Research Laboratories, 1956-59; Chemist, RCA, David Sarnoff Research

Center, 1959-60; Group Leader, Materials Scientist, Lawrence Livermore National Laboratory, 1960-92; Consultant and Participating Guest, Environmental Restoration Division, Lawrence Livermore National Laboratory; Visiting Research Professor, Aachen Technical Institute and Philips Laboratories, Aachen, Germany, Philips Laboratories, Eindhoven, Netherlands, 1969-71. Publications: Over 50 publications and articles on various topics of materials science; 2 inventions. Honours: First Prize and Best of Show – Ceramographic Exhibit, American Ceramic Society, 1965; Research and Development 100 Magazine Award for Technologically Most Significant Invention, 1991; William L Dickinson High School Scholastic Hall of Fame, 2001. Memberships: American Association of Crystal Growth, Treasurer, Northern California Section; Phi Lambda Upsilon; Sigma Xi Fraternity. Address: 1141 Madison Avenue, Livermore, CA 94550, USA. E-mail: newkirk01@aol.com

**NEWMAN Elsie Louise,** b. 25 March 1943, Bowling Green, Ohio, USA. Mathematics Educator. m. Lawrence Joseph, 1 son, 1 daughter. Education: BS, Mathematics Education, Bowling Green State University, 1968; Master of Education, Mathematics, University of Toledo, 1992. Appointments: Mathematics Educator, Owens Community College; Professor; Co-Editor, Journal of Teaching and Learning; Treasurer, Owens Faculty Association; Mathematics Educator, Ohio Bureau of vocational Rehabilitation; Residential Crusade Chairman, American Cancer Society; Christman Clearing Bureau Assistant; Office Manager, Knights of Columbus; Supervisor, After School Study Programme, First United Methodist Church. Publications: Teaching multiplication with a model; Predicting grades in basic algebra. Honours: Phi Kappa Phi; Kappa Delta Pi; Honorary University Scholarships; Deans List; Kidney Foundation of NWO, High Individual Award. Memberships: National Council of Teachers of Mathematics; Ohio Association of Developmental Educators; University Choral Society, Bowling Green State University. Address: 328 South Summit Street, Bowling Green, OH 43402, USA.

**NEWMAN Nanette,** b. Northampton, England. Actress. m. Bryan Forbes, 2 daughters. Education: Italia Conti School; Royal Academy of Dramatic Art. Appointments: Varied Career in Films, Stage and TV. Creative Works: Appearances in Films including: The Wrong Box; The Stepford Wives; The Raging Moon; International Velvet; The Endless Game; The Mystery of Edwin Drood; Talk Show, The Fun Food Factory; TV Series, Stay With Me Till Morning; Comedy Series, Let There Be Love, Late Expectations. Publications: God Bless Love, That Dog, The Pig Who Never Was, Amy Rainbow, The Root Children; The Fun Food Factory; Fun Food Feasts; My Granny Was a Frightful Bore; The Cat Lovers Coffee-Table Book; The Dog Lovers Coffee-Table Book; The Cat and Mouse Love Story; The Christmas Cookbook; Pigalev; The Best of Love; Archie; The Summer Cookbook; Small Beginnings; Bad Baby; Entertaining with Nanette Newman and Her Two Daughters Sarah and Emma; Charlie The Noisy Caterpillar; Sharing; Cooking for Friends; Spider the Horrible Cat; There's A Bear in the Bath; A Bear in the Classroom; Take 3 Cooks; To You With Love, 1999; Up to the Skies and Down Again, 1999; Bad Baby Good Baby, 2002. Honours include: Best Actress Award, Variety Club; Best Actress, Evening News. Address: Chatto & Linnit Ltd, 123 King's Road, London SW3 4PL, England.

**NEWMAN Paul,** b. 26 January 1925, Cleveland, USA. Actor. m. (1) Jacqueline Witte, 1949, 1 son (deceased 1978), 2 daughters, (2) Joanne Woodward, 1958, 3 daughters. Education: Kenyon College; Yale University School of Drama. Appointments: Military Service, 1943-46. Creative Works: Stage appearances

include: Picnic, 1953-54; Desperate Hours, 1955; Sweet Bird of Youth, 1959; Baby Want a Kiss, 1964; Films include: The Rack, 1955; Somebody Up There Likes Me, 1956; Cat on a Hot Tin Roof, 1958; Rally Round the Flag, Boys, 1958; The Young Philadelphians, 1958; From the Terrace, 1960; Exodus, 1960; The Hustler, 1962; Hud, 1963; The Prize, 1963; The Outrage, 1964; What a Way to Go, 1964; Lady L, 1965; Torn Curtain, 1966; Hombre, 1967; Cool Hand Luke, 1967; The Secret War of Harry Frigg, 1968; Butch Cassidy and the Sundance Kid, 1969; WUSA, 1970; Pocket Money, 1972; The Life and Times of Judge Roy Bean, 1973; The Mackintosh Man, 1972; The Sting, 1973; The Towering Inferno, 1974; The Drowning Pool, 1975; Buffalo Bill and the Indians, 1976; Silent Movie, 1976; Slap Shot, 1977; Absence of Malice, 1981; The Verdict, 1982; Harry and Son (director), 1984; The Color of Money, 1986; Fat Man and Little Boy, 1989; Blaze, 1989; Mr and Mrs Bridge, 1990; The Hudsucker Proxy, 1994; Nobody's Fool, 1994; Message in a Bottle, 1999; Director: Rachel, Rachel, 1968; The Effect of Gamma Rays on Man in the Moon Marigolds, 1973; The Shadow Box, 1980; When Time Ran Out, 1980; Fort Apache: The Bronx, 1981; The Glass Menagerie, 1987; Super Speedway, 1997; Where the Money Is, 1998; Twilight, 1998; Where the Money Is, 2000; The Road to Perdition, 2001. Honours include: Best Actor, Academy of Motion Pictures, Arts and Sciences, 1959, 1962, 1964; Honorary Academy Award, 1986. Address: Newman's Own Inc, 246 Post Road East, Westport, CT 06880, USA.

**NEWSTEAD Charles George,** b. 8 April 1956, London, England. Clinical Director. m. Catherine Lucy McEwen, 3 sons, 1 daughter. Education: Davenant Foundation Grammar School, 1967-74; Guy's Hospital Medical School, 1974-81; BSc, 1st class honours, Basic Medical Sciences and Physiology, University of London, 1978; MB BS, University of London, 1981; MRCP (UK), 1986; MD, University of London, 1991; FRCP (London), 1997; Diploma in Health Services Management, University of York, 1998. Appointments: House Physician, Lewisham Hospital, 1981-82; House Surgeon, Guy's Hospital, 1982; Senior House Officer/Registrar Training Scheme, The Royal London Hospital, 1982-86; Lecturer in Renal Medicine, The Royal London Hospital Medical College (University of London), Honorary Registrar, The London Hospital, 1986-89; Honorary Lecturer Medical Unit, The Royal London Hospital Medical College, supported by The Medical Research Council, 1989-90; Clinical Lecturer in Medicine, University of Manchester, Honorary Senior Registrar (Renal and General Medicine), Manchester Royal Infirmary, 1990-93; Lead Clinician, Renal Services Leeds Teaching Hospitals NHS Trust, Consultant Renal Physician, St James's University Hospital, Leeds, Honorary Senior Lecturer, University of Leeds, 1990-93; Lead Clinician, Renal Services Leeds Teaching Hospitals NHS Trust, Consultant Renal Physician, St James's University Hospital, Leeds; Honorary Senior Lecturer, University of Leeds, 1993-2001; Clinical Director and Chair of Clinical Management Team, Renal Services Leeds Teaching Hospitals NHS Trust, 2003-. Publications: Co-author or author of over 30 peer-reviewed papers; More than 15 editorials, reviews and book chapters; Over 100 short reports or conference abstracts; Principal editor of 6 sets of clinical guidelines. Honours: Ian Howat Memorial prize; British Nutrition Foundation/Nestle Bursary Award; MRC Project Grant; National Kidney Research Fund Grant. Memberships: The Physiological Society; The Renal Association; European Dialysis and Transplant Association; European Renal Association; International Society of Nephrology; British Transplantation Society; The Royal College of Physicians of London; The Transplantation Society. Address: Renal Unit, St James's Hospital, Leeds LS9 7TF, England. E-mail: chas.newstead@leedsth.nhs.uk

**NEWTON-JOHN Olivia,** b. 26 September 1948, Cambridge, England. Singer; Actress. m. Matt Lattanzi, 1984, 1 daughter. Career: Moved to Australia, aged 5; Singer in folk group as teenager; Local television performer with Pat Carroll; Winner, National Talent Contest, 1964; Singer, actress, 1965-; Represented UK in Eurovision Song Contest, 1974; Music For UNICEF Concert, New York, 1979; Film appearances include: Grease, 1978; Xanadu, 1980; Two Of A Kind, 1983; It's My Party, 1995; Sordid Wives, 1999; Own clothing business, Koala Blue, 1984-. Recordings: Albums: If Not For You, 1971; Let Me Be There, 1974; Music Makes My Day, 1974; Long Live Love, 1974; If You Love Me Let Me Know (Number 1, US), 1974; Have You Ever Never Been Mellow, 1975; Clearly Love, 1975; Come On Over, 1976; Don't Stop Believin', 1976; Making A Good Thing Better, 1977; Greatest Hits, 1978; Grease (film soundtrack), 1978; Totally Hot, 1979; Xanadu (film soundtrack), 1980; Physical, 1981; 20 Greatest Hits, 1982; Olivia's Greatest Hits Vol 2, 1983; Two Of A Kind, 1984; Soul Kiss, 1986; The Rumour, 1988; Warm And Tender, 1990; Back To Basics: The Essential Collection 1971-92, 1992; Gaia - One Woman's Journey, 1995; More than Physical, 1995; Greatest Hits, 1996; Olivia, 1998; Back with a Heart, 1998; Highlights from the Main Event, 1999; Greatest Hits: First Impressions, 1999; Country Girl, 1999; Best of Olivia Newton John, 1999; Love Songs: A Collection: Hit singles include: If Not For You, 1971; What Is Life, 1972; Take Me Home Country Roads, 1973; Let Me Be There, 1974; Long Live Love, 1974; If You Love Me (Let Me Know), 1974; I Honestly Love You (Number 1, UK), 1974; Have You Never Been Mellow (Number 1, US), 1975; Please Mr Please, 1975; Something Better To Do, 1975; Fly Away, duet with John Denver, 1976; Sam, 1977; You're The One That I Want, duet with John Travolta (Number 1, US and UK, third-best selling single in UK), 1978; Summer Nights, duet with John Travolta (UK Number 1, 9 weeks), 1978; Hopelessly Devoted To You (Number 2, UK), 1978; A Little More Love, 1979; Deeper Than The Night, 1979; I Cant Help It, duet with Andy Gibb, 1980; Xanadu, with ELO (Number 1, UK), 1980; Magic (Number 1, US), 1980; Physical (US Number 1, 10 weeks), 1981; Make A Move On Me, 1982; Heart Attack, 1982; Twist Of Fate, from film soundtrack Two Of A Kind, 1983; Back with a Heart, 1998; Grease (Remix), 1998; I Honestly Love You, 1998; Physical Remix 1999, 1999. Honours include: OBE; Grammy Awards: Record of the Year, 1974; Best Country Vocal Performance, 1974; Best Pop Vocal Performance, 1975; Numerous American Music Awards, 1975-77, 1983; CMA Award, Female Vocalist Of Year (first UK recipient), 1975; Star on Hollywood Walk Of Fame, 1981; Numerous other awards from Record World; Billboard; People's Choice; AGVA; NARM; Goodwill Ambassador, UN Environment Programme, 1989. Address: MCA, 70 Universal City Plaza, North Hollywood, CA 91608, USA.

**NGUYEN Khue Vu,** b. 24 September 1952, Hanoi, Vietnam. Research Scientist. m. Martine Françoise Juilleret, 2 sons, 1 daughter. Education: Bachelor of Science, Biochemistry, 1979, Master of Science, Molecular Biology, 1980, PhD, Macromolecular Physical Chemistry, 1983, PhD, Physical Sciences, 1986, Université Louis Pasteur, Strasbourg, France. Appointments: Research Scientist, Ecole Européenne des Hautes Etudes des Industries Chimiques, Strasbourg, France, 1983-86; Research Scientist, Institut de Bacteriologie de la Faculté de Médecine, Strasbourg, France, 1986-87; Research Scientist, Anda Biologicals Company, Strasbourg, France, 1987-97; Research Scientist, Neurofit Company, Strasbourg, France, 1997-99; Research Scientist, Department of Biochemical Genetics and Metabolism and Mitochondrial Disease Center, University of California, San Diego, USA, 1999-. Publications: Numerous research articles in the areas of biopolymer chemistry,

physical and analytical chemistry, enzymology, immunology and molecular biology in scientific journals including: Journal of Polymer Science, 1986; Journal of Medical Microbiology, 1990; Biochemical Biophysical Research Communications, 2002; Annals of Neurology, 2004; Many patents. Honours: Listed in numerous Who's Who publications and biographical dictionaries. Memberships: American Chemical Society; American Society for Microbiology; American Association for the Advancement of Science; New York Academy of Sciences. Address: Biochemical Genetics and Metabolism, The Mitochondrial and Metabolic Disease Center, UCSD School of Medicine, 214 Dickinson Street, Building CTF, Room C-103, San Diego, CA 92103-8467, USA. E-mail: k25nguyen@ucsd.edu

**NGUYEN Kieu,** b. 7 May 1944, Vinhlong, Vietnam. Professional Engineer. m. My-yen T Pham, 3 sons, 2 daughters. Education: Bachelor of Technology, University of North Florida, USA, 1984. Appointment: Senior Civil Project Engineer, Township of Cherry Hill, New Jersey, USA. Membership: American Society of Civil Engineers. Address: 8821 Fairfield Street, Philadelphia, PA 19152, USA. E-mail: kieu1975@yahoo.com

**NGUYEN Phuong,** b. 30 June 1950, Saigon, Vietnam. Mechanical Engineer. Divorced, 1 son, 1 daughter. Education: BS, Mechanical Engineering, Dalat University, Vietnam, 1974; MS, Mechanical Engineering, Bristol University, England, 1983; PhD, Applied Mechanics, Cranfield Institute of Technology, Bedford, 1987. Appointments: Lecturer, Department of Mechanical Engineering, Cantho University, Vietnam, 1978-80; Pipe Stress Engineer, Santa Fe Brown (UK) Ltd, Milton Keynes, England, 1988; Structural Assessment Group, BNFL Magnox Generation and predecessor organisations, Gloucestershire, England, 1989-. Publications: The Historical Battles of the Vietnam War 1963-75, 1993; The Vietnam War Collection: From the First Battle Until the Last, 2001. E-mail: phuong. d.nguyen@magnox.co.uk

**NICHOLS Mike (Michael Igor Peschowsky),** b. 6 November 1931, Berlin, Germany. Stage and Film Director. m. (1) Patricia Scot 1957, (2) Margot Callas, 1974, 1 daughter, (3) Annabel Nichols, (4) Diane Sawyer, 1988. Education: University of Chicago. Creative Works: Shows Directed: Barefoot in the Park, New York, 1963; The Knack, 1964; Luv, 1964; The Odd Couple, 1965; The Apple Tree, 1966; The Little Foxes, 1967; Plaza Suite, 1968; Films Directed: Who's Afraid of Virginia Woolf?, 1966; The Graduate, 1967; Catch-22, 1969; Carnal Knowledge, 1971; Day of the Dolphin, 1973; The Fortune, 1975; Gilda Live, 1980; Silkwood, 1983; Heartburn, 1985; Biloxi Blues, 1987; Working Girl, 1988; Postcards From the Edge, 1990; Regarding Henry, Wolf, 1994; Mike Nicholas, 1995; The Birdcage, 1998; Primary Colors, 1998; What Planet Are You From?, 2000; All the Pretty Horses, 2000; Plays Directed: Streamers, 1976; Comedians, 1976; The Gin Game, 1978; Lunch Hour, 1980; The Real Thing, 1984; Hurlyburly, 1984; Waiting for Godot, 1988; Death and the Maiden, 1992; Blue Murder, 1995; The Seagull, 2001; Producer, Annie, 1977. Honours include: Tony Awards; National Association of Theatre Owners' Achievement Award. Address: c/o Mike Ovitz, CAA, 9830 Wilshire Boulevard, Beverly Hills, CA 90212, USA.

**NICHOLSON Bryan Hubert (Sir),** b. 6 June 1932, Rainham, Essex, England. Chairman. m. Mary, 1 son, 1 daughter. Education: Politics, Philosophy and Economics, Honours, Oriel College, Oxford, 1952-55. Appointments include: Unilever Management Trainee then District Manager, 1955-60; Sales Manager, Jeyes Group, 1960-64; Sales Director, UK, General Manager, Australia, Managing Director, UK and

France, 1964-72; Director, Operations, 1972-76, Executive Main Board Director, 1976-79, Chairman, UK, Chairman, Germany, Supervising Director, France and Italy, Executive Main Board Director, 1979-84, Rank Xerox Ltd; Chairman, Manpower Services Commission, 1984-87; Chairman, The Post Office, 1987-92; Chairman, Council for National Academic Awards, 1988-91; Chairman, National Council for Vocational Qualifications, 1990-93; Chancellor, Sheffield Hallam University, 1992-2001; Chairman, 1992-2001, Vice-president, 2001-, BUPA; Chairman, Varity Europe Ltd, 1993-96; President, Confederation of British Industry, 1994-96; Chairman, Cookson Group plc, 1998-2003; Pro-Chancellor and Chair of the Council of the Open University, 1996-2004; Chairman, 2001-2003, Deputy Chairman, 2003-2004, Chairman, 2004-2005, Goal plc (renamed Educational Development International plc);; Chairman, Financial Reporting Council, 2001-; Current Non-Executive Directorships: Equitas Holdings plc, 1996-, Education Development International plc, 2005-; President, Wakefield Trinity Wildcats, 2000-. Honours: KB, 1987; GBE, 2005; Companion of the Institute of Management, 1985-; FRSA, 1986-; Honorary FGCI, 1989; Honorary Fellow: Oriel College, Oxford, Manchester Metropolitan University, 1990, Scottish National Vocational Council, 1994-, Scottish Qualifications Authority, 1997; Elected Fellow, Chartered Institute of Marketing, 1991; Hon D Ed, Council for National Academic Awards, 1992; Honorary Doctor, Open University, 1994; Honorary Companion, Chartered Institute for Personnel and Development, 1994; Honorary Doctor of Letters, Glasgow Caledonian University, 2000; Honorary Doctor, Sheffield Hallam University. Membership: Oxford and Cambridge Club. Address: The Financial Reporting Council, 5th Floor, Aldwych House, 71-91 Aldwych, London WC2B 4HN, England. E-mail: b.nicholson@frc.org.uk Website: www.frc.org.uk

**NICHOLSON Geoffrey Joseph,** b. 4 March 1953, Sheffield, England. Writer. Education: MA, English, Gonville and Caius College, Cambridge, 1975; MA, Drama, University of Essex, Colchester, 1978. Publications: Street Sleeper, 1987; The Knot Garden, 1989; What We Did On Our Holidays, 1990; Hunters and Gatherers, 1991; Big Noises, 1991; The Food Chain, 1992; Day Trips to the Desert, 1992; The Errol Flynn Novel, 1993; Still Life with Volkswagens, 1994; Everything and More, 1994; Footsucker, 1995; Bleeding London, 1997; Flesh Guitar, 1998; Female Ruins, 1999; Bedlam Burning, 2000; The Hollywood Dodo, 2004. Contributions to: Ambit magazine; Grand Street; Tiger Dreams; Night; Twenty Under 35; A Book of Two Halves; The Guardian, Independent; Village Voice; New York Times Book Review; L.A. Weekly, Bookforum, Daily Telegraph; Salon.Com. Honour: Shortlisted, Yorkshire Post 1st Work Award, 1987; Shortlisted, The Whitbread Prize, 1998. Address: c/o A P Watt, 20 John Street, London EC1N 2DR, England.

**NICHOLSON Jack,** b. 22 April 1937, Neptune, New Jersey, USA. Actor; Film Maker. m. Sandra Knight, 1961, divorced 1966, 1 daughter. Career: Films include: Cry-Baby Killer, 1958; Studs Lonigan, 1960; The Shooting; Ride the Whirlwind; Hell's Angels of Wheels, 1967; The Trip, 1967; Head, 1968; Psych-Out, 1968; Easy Rider, 1969; On a Clear Day You Can See Forever, 1970; Five Easy Pieces, 1971; Drive, He Said, 1971; Carnal Knowledge, 1971; The King of Marvin Gardens, 1972; The Last Detail, 1973; Chinatown, 1974; The Passenger, 1974; Tommy, 1974; The Fortune, 1975; The Missouri Breaks, 1975; One Flew Over the Cuckoo's Nest, 1975; The Last Tycoon, 1976; Goin' South, 1978; The Shining, 1980; The Postman Always Rings Twice, 1981; Reds, 1981; The Border, 1982; Terms of Endearment, 1984; Prizzi's Honor, 1984; Heartburn, 1985; The Witches of Eastwick, 1986; Ironweed, 1987; Batman, 1989; The Two Jakes, 1989; Man Trouble, 1992; A Few Good

Men, 1992; Hoffa, 1993; Wolf, 1994; The Crossing Guard, 1995; Mars Attacks! The Evening Star, Blood and Wine, 1996; As Good As It Gets, 1997; The Pledge, 2000; About Schmidt, 2002; Anger Management, 2003. Honours: Academy Award, Best Supporting Actor, 1970, 1984; Academy Award, Best Actor, 1976; Cecil B De Mille Award, 1999; Kennedy Center Honor, 2001; Commander des Arts et des Lettres; Golden Globe for Best Dramatic Actor, 2003. Address: 12850 Mulholland Drive, Beverly Hills, CA 90210, USA.

**NICHOLSON John William,** b. 9 February 1955, Hampton Court, Middlesex, England. University Lecturer. m. Suzette, 2 sons, 2 daughters. Education: BSc, Kingston University, 1977; PhD, South Bank University, 1981. Appointments: Research Fellow, South Bank University, 1981-83; Higher Scientific Officer, Senior Scientific Officer, Principal Scientific Officer, Laboratory of the Government Chemist, 1983-94; Senior Lecturer in Biomaterials Science, King's College, London, 1995-97; Reader in Biomaterials Science, King's College, London, 1997-2002; Head of School of Science, Medway Campus and Professor of Biomaterials Chemistry, University of Greenwich, 2002-. Publications: Approximately 135 scientific articles; 4 books: The Chemistry of Polymers, 1991, 2nd edition, 1996; Acid Base Cements (with A D Wilson), 1993; Polymers in Dentistry (with M Braden, R Clarke and S Parker), 1996; The Chemistry of Medical and Dental Materials, 2002 . Honours: EurChem; CChem; FRSC; Jordan Award, Oil and Colour Chemists Association, 1987; President, 2001, Treasurer, 2003-, UK Society for Biomaterials. Memberships: Fellow, Royal Society of Chemistry; Royal Institution; UK Society for Biomaterials; European Society for Biomaterials; International Association for Dental Research. Address: School of Science, University of Greenwich, Chatham, Kent ME4 4TB, England. E-mail: j.w.nicholson@gre.ac.uk

**NICKLAUS Jack William,** b. 21 January 1940, Columbus, Ohio, USA. Professional Golfer. m. Barbara Jean Bash, 1960, 4 sons, 1 daughter. Education: Ohio State University. Career: Professional, 1961-; Winner: US Amateur Golf Championship, 1959, 1961; US Open Championship, 1962, 1967, 1972, 1980; US Masters, 1963, 1965, 1966, 1972, 1986; US Professional Golfers' Association, 1963, 1971, 1973, 1975, 1980; British Open Championship, 1966, 1970, 1978; 6 times, Australian Open Champion; 5 times, World Series winner; 3 times individual winner, 6 times on winning team, World Cup; 6 times, US representative in Ryder Cup matches; 97 tournament victories; 76 official tour victories; 58 times second, 36 times third; Won US Senior Open, USA; 136 tournament appearances, 1996; Played in 154 consecutive majors, 1999; Designer of golf courses in USA, Europe, Far East; Chairman, Golden Bear International Inc; Captain, US team which won 25th Ryder Cup, 1983 Co-chair, The First Tee's Capital Campaign, More Than A Game, 2000. Publications: My 55 Ways to Lower Your Golf Score, 1962; Take a Tip From Me, 1964; The Greatest Game of All, autobiography, 1969; Lesson Tee, 1972; Golf My Way, 1974; The Best Way to Better Your Golf, vols 1-3, 1974; Jack Nicklaus' Playing Lessons, 1976; Total Golf Techniques, 1977; On and Off the Fairway, autobiography, 1979; The Full Swing, 1982; My Most Memorable Shots in the Majors; My Story, 1997. Honours: Athlete of the Decade Award, 1970s; Hon LLD, St Andrew's, 1984; 5 times US PGA Player of the Year; Golfer of the Century, 1988. Address: 11780 US Highway #1, North Palm Beach, FL 33408, USA.

**NICKS Stevie (Stephanie Nicks),** b. 26 May 1948, California, USA. Singer; Songwriter. Appointments: Songwriter with Lindsey Buckingham; Recorded album, Buckingham Nicks, 1973; Joined Group, Fleetwood Mac, 1973. Creative Works:

Albums with Fleetwood Mac: Fleetwood Mac, 1975; Rumours, 1977; Tusk, 1979; Fleetwood Mac Live, 1980; Mirage, 1982; Tango in the Night, 1987; Behind the Mask, 1990; 25 Years - The Chain, 1992; Solo albums include: Bella Donna, 1981; The Wild Heart, 1983; Rock a Little, 1985; Time Space, 1991; Street Angel, 1994; Composer of Songs Rhiannon, Landslide, Leather and Lace, Dreams, Sara, Edge of Seventeen, If Anyone Falls (with Sandy Stewart), Stand Back (with Prince Rogers Nelson), I Can't Wait (with others), The Other Side of the Mirror, Time Space, Street Angel, Seven Wonders (with Sandy Stewart). Address: WEA Corporation, 79 Madison Avenue, Floor 7, New York, NY 10016, USA.

**NICOL Donald MacGillivray,** b. 4 February 1923, Portsmouth, England. Historian; Professor Emeritus. m. Joan Mary Campbell, 1950, 3 sons. Education: MA, 1948, PhD, 1952, Pembroke College, Cambridge. Appointments: Scholar, British School of Archaeology, Athens, 1949-50; Lecturer in Classics, University College, Dublin, 1952-64; Visiting Fellow, Dumbarton Oaks, Washington, DC, 1964-65; Visiting Professor of Byzantine History, Indiana University, 1965-66; Senior Lecturer and Reader in Byzantine History, University of Edinburgh, 1969-70; Koraës Professor of Modern Greek and Byzantine History, Language and Literature, 1970-88, Assistant Principal, 1977-80, Vice Principal, 1980-81, Professor Emeritus, 1988-, King's College, University of London; Editor, Byzantine and Modern Greek Studies, 1973-83; Birbeck Lecturer, University of Cambridge, 1976-77; Director, Gennadius Library, Athens, 1989-92. Publications: The Despotate of Epiros, 1957; Meterora: The Rock Monasteries of Thessaly, 1963, revised edition, 1975; The Byzantine Family of Kantakouzenos (Cantacuzenus) ca 1100-1460: A Genealogical and Prosopographical Study, 1968; Byzantium: Its Ecclesiastical History and Relations with the Western World, 1972; The Last Centuries of Byzantium 1261-1453, 1972, 2nd edition, 1993; Church and Society in the Last Centuries of Byzantium, 1979; The End of the Byzantine Empire, 1979; The Despotate of Epiros 1267-1479: A Contribution to the History of Greece in the Middle Ages, 1984; Studies in Late Byzantine History and Prosopography, 1986; Byzantium and Venice: A Study in Diplomatic and Cultural Relations, 1988; Joannes Gennadios - The Man: A Biographical Sketch, 1990; A Biographical Dictionary of the Byzantine Empire, 1991; The Immortal Emperor: The Life and Legend of Constantine Palaiologos, Last Emperor of the Romans, 1992; The Byzantine Lady: Ten Portraits 1250-1500, 1994; The Reluctant Emperor: A Biography of John Cantacuzene, Byzantine Emperor and Monk c. 1295-1383, 1996; Theodore Spandounes: On the Origin of the Ottoman Emperors (translator and editor), 1997. Contributions to: Professional journals. Membership: British Academy, fellow. Address: 4 Westberry Court, Pinehurst, Grange Road, Cambridge, CB3 9BG, England.

**NICOLOPOULOS Adamantios,** b. 23 January 1959, Athens, Greece. Banker. m. Lisa, 1 son, 1 daughter. Education: BS, Mechanical Engineering, Columbia University, 1980; MS, Mechanical Engineering, University of California, Berkeley, 1981; MBA, Finance/International Business, New York University, 1986. Appointments: Engineer, Corporate Engineering Department, Kaiser Aluminium and Chemical Corporation, California, 1982-84; Summer Intern/Consultant, Investment Banking Group, Citibank NA, New York, 1985-86; Internal Consultant, Operations Management, American International Group Inc, New York, 1986-87; Assistant Treasurer, Project Finance Group, New York, 1987-90, Assistant Vice President, International Project Finance, Zurich, 1990-91, Assistant Vice President, Project Capital Finance, New York, 1991-92, Swiss Bank Corporation; Finance Director, Finance Department, Copelouzos Group, Athens,

Greece, 1992-93; Associate Director, Investment Bank, Project Finance Advisory Group, Swiss Bank Corporation (SBC), London, 1993-94; Associate Director, Investment Banking, Project Finance Advisory, Natwest Markets, London, 1994-97; Executive Director, Corporate Finance, Transport Infrastructure, UBS Investment Bank, London, 1997-. Publications: Various articles in professional journals; Invited speaker at international and European conferences. Honours: Scholarship, Columbia University, 1979; Teaching programme assistantship for outstanding performance in mathematics, 1980; New York University Scholarship and Chancellor's Service Award for Leadership, 1986; Istrian Motorway Project, Deal of the Year Award, 1998, Best European Roads Deal, 2003. Memberships: Japan Karate Association; Stern School of Business Alumni Association; International Project Finance Association; Honour Students' Society, University of California, Berkeley; American Society of Mechanical Engineers. Address: 53 Swan Court, Flood Street, London SW3 5RT, England. E-mail: adam.nicol opoulos@ubs.com

**NIDDRIE Robert Charles,** b. 29 January 1935, Southampton, England. Chartered Accountant. m. Maureen Joy, 1 son, 2 daughters. Education: Brockenhurst Grammar School. Appointments: National Service 1959-61; Whittaker, Bailey & Co, 1952-59, 1962-75, Partner, 1963-75; Senior Partner in Charge, Southampton Office, Price Waterhouse, 1975-92; Trustee, Duphar Pension Scheme, 1992-2003; Local Director, Coutts & Co, 1992-2002; Non-Executive Director: Bournemouth Orchestras, 1986-96, Meridian Broadcasting Charitable Trust, 1993-2000, Sovereign Employee Benefits Ltd, 1993-95, Chairman, Southampton Cargo Handling plc, 1993-98, Hotel du Vin Ltd, 1994-2004; Founder Chairman, Hampshire Branch of Institute of Directors, 1980-86, Member, Institute of Directors Council, 1980-86; Trustee, Mayflower Theatre Trust, 1988-99; Governor King Edward VI School, Southampton, 1989-2003; Winchester Cathedral Guild of Voluntary Guides, 1995-; Trustee, Deputy Chairman, Royal Marines Museum, 1996-. Memberships: Fellow, Institute of Chartered Accountants; Associate, Chartered Institute of Taxation; Associate, Institute of Directors. Address: Morestead House, Morestead, Winchester, Hampshire SO21 1LZ, England.

**NIELSEN Andreas,** b. 20 July 1941, Denmark. Managing Director. m. Anne-Lise, 2 sons, 1 daughter. Education: B Com, Marketing, 1969; B Com, Organisation and Psychology, 1976. Appointments: Director of Daloon until 1989; Director of Tulip until, 1991; Owner of ANBO Foods, 1991-. Publications: Articles in Danish marketing papers. Honours: Listed in Who's Who publications and biographical dictionaries. Memberships: Danish Food Club; Danish Vikings. Address: Lundsvej 6, 5800 Nyborg, Denmark. E-mail: nyborg@email.dk

**NIEUW AMERONGEN Arie van,** Professor of Oral Biochemistry. Education: MSc, Biochemistry, 1970; PhD, Biochemistry, 1974, Vrije Universiteit, Amsterdam. Appointments: Assistant Professor, Dental Faculty, Department of Oral Biochemistry, 1974-78, Associate Professor, 1974-90, Chairman of Department, 1984, Professor of Oral Biochemistry, 1990-, Vrije Universiteit, Amsterdam; Head of the Subdepartment of Oral Biochemistry, 1984-; Chairman, Department of Basic Dental Sciences, 1999-; Chairman, Dutch Dental Research School, 2000-; Supervisor of 22 PhD Students; Organised 3 international congresses: 5th, 6th, 7th, European Symposium on the Application of Saliva in Clinical Practice and Research, Egmond aan Zee, 1999, 2002, 2005. Publications: First author, 100 papers; Co-author 200 papers; Books: Saliva and Salivary Glands, 1988; Saliva and Oral Health, 1994; Saliva and Dental Elements, 1999; Faith and Science, 2001; Saliva,

Salivary Glands and Oral Health, 2004. Memberships: Member of the Editorial Boards: Journal of Dental Research, 1998-2001; Journal of Odontology, 2000-2002; Oral Biosciences Medicine, 2003; 8 Patents. Address: Vrije Universiteit, Department of Oral Biochemistry, Van Der Boechorststraat 7, 1081 BT Amsterdam, The Netherlands.

**NIGAM Prakash Kumar,** b. 10 October 1923, Bhainsdahi, M.P. India. Electrical Engineer/Writer. m. Kanta Nigan, 2 sons, 1 daughter. Education: Bachelor of Science, Nagpur University, India, 1944; BS in Electrical Engineering, University of Wisconsin, USA, 1948. Appointments: Testing Engineer, G.E., USA, 1948-49; Electrical Engineer, Assistant Superintendent, Tata Electric Co. Bombay, India, 1950-60; Chief Power Engineer, HEC, Ranchi, India, 1968; Electrical Engineer with United Engineers, Crawford and Russel, Ebasco, New York, Commonwealth Associates, Bechtel Giffels in USA, 1968-81; Consulting Engineer, Accro and ADSC in US, 1983. Conference: Thermo Electric Plants as complement to Hydro-Electric Development in Bombay-Poona Region for World Power Conference, 1952. Publications include: Book, Reflections on History of the World in 20th Century, to be published 2005; 40 articles in newspapers, 1994-2004. Honours: Scholarship for Advance Studies in USA from J N Tata Endowment, Bombay, India. Memberships: Rotary International Club; Lions Club; A.I.E.E. Address: 43/44 Vijay Nagar Colony, Lalghati, Bhopal 462630, India.

**NIGHY William (Bill) Francis,** b. 12 December 1949, Caterham, Surrey, England. Actor. m. Diana Quick, 1 daughter. Education: St John Fischer School, Purley, Surrey, England. Career: National Theatre: A Map of the World and Skylight by David Hare; Pravda by David Hare and Howard Brenton; The Seagull by Chekov; Arcadia by Tom Stoppard; Mean Tears by Peter Gill; Blue Orange by Joe Benhall; A Kind of Alaska and Betrayal by Harold Pinter; Films: Still Crazy; Lawless Heart; Lucky Break; Love Actually; Underworld; Capture the Castle; TV: Absolute Hell; The Maitlands; The Lost Prince; The Men's Room; Numerous radio performances. Honours: Evening Standard Peter Sellars Comedy Award, 1998; Barclays Bank Theatre Award, Best Actor; BAFTA Award for Best Supporting Actor, 2004. Address: c/o Markham & Froggatt Ltd, Julian House, 4 Windmill Street, London W1P 1HF, England.

**NIKITENKO Leonid,** 19 April 1972, Irkutsk, Russia. Researcher. Education: BSc, Honours, 1997, MSc, 1994, University of Irkutsk, Russia; PhD, Russian Academy of Medical Sciences, 1997; MA, Linacre College, Oxford, England, 2002. Appointments: Research Assistant, The Babraham Institute, Cambridge, England, 1996-97; Postdoctoral Senior Research Assistant, University of Liverpool, England, 1997-98; Postdoctoral Research Fellow, University of Oxford, England, 1999-2002; Postdoctoral Research Fellow, The Wellcome Trust, 2002-2005; Tutor, Keble College, Oxford, England, 2003-. Publications: Articles as author in scientific journals including: Molecular Human Reproduction, 2000, 2001; Trends in Pharmaceutical Science, 2002; The FASEB Journal, 2003. Honours: PhD Studentship, President of the Russian Federation Fund, 1996; EPA Cephalosporin Junior Research Fellow, Linacre College, Oxford, 2002-2004; University of Oxford Merit Award, 2003. Memberships: Fellow, Royal Microscopical Society, UK; Biochemical Society, UK; Endocrine Society, USA; National Geographical Society, UK. Address: The University of Oxford, NDOG, Medical Sciences Division, John Radcliffe Hospital, Headington, Oxford OX3 9DS, England. E-mail: leonid.nikitenko@obs-gyn.ox.ac.uk

**NIKS Inessa,** b. 6 November 1938, St Petersburg, Russia. Piano Teacher; Musicology Teacher. m. Mikhail Niks, deceased, 1 son, 1 daughter. Education: Studied Piano, Special Music School for Gifted Children, St Petersburg, 1948-56; Master in Musicology, Diploma with Distinction, St Petersburg Conservatory, 1956-61. Career: Teacher of Musicology and Piano, Music College, Novgorod, Russia, 1961-64; Teacher of Musicology and Piano, Music School, St Petersburg, 1966-76; Head of Musicology Department, Pskov Music College, 1976-79; Owner, piano and musicology studio, Redlands, California, 1983-; Co-Founder, Niks Hand Retraining Center, 1991-. Publications: Numerous articles in specialist music journals concerning newly developed piano technique; Co-Inventor of Hand Guide, piano training device, 1991; Manual, Play Without Tension, supplement to piano training device, 1998; Manual, Type Without Tension, 2000. Honours: Silver Medal, 1983, Bronze Medal, 1984, International Piano Recording Competition; Finalist, Audio-Visual Piano, 1995. Memberships: Music Teachers' Association of California, 1983-; European Piano Teachers' Association, 1985-; The National League of American Pen Women, 2002-. Address: Niks Hand Retraining Centre, 1434 Fulbright Ave, Redlands, CA 92373, USA. Website: www.nikstechnique.com

**NIMMO Ian Alister,** b. 14 October 1934, Lahore, Pakistan. Journalist. m. Grace, 11 July 1959, 2 sons, 1 daughter. Education: Royal School of Dunkeld; Breadalbane Academy. Appointments: Lieutenant, Royal Scots Fusiliers, 1956; Editor, Weekly Scotsman, 1962; Editor, Evening Gazette, Teesside, 1970; Editor, Evening News, Edinburgh, 1976-89; Publishing Consultant, 1989-. Publications: Robert Burns, 1968; Portrait of Edinburgh, 1969; The Bold Adventure, 1969; Scotland at War, 1989; The Commonwealth Games, 1989; Edinburgh The New Town, 1991; Edinburgh's Green Heritage, 1996; Walking With Murder, 2005; Rhythms of the Celts, stage musical, 1997; Numerous articles and radio programmes. Membership: Vice President, Scottish Arts Club, 1995-2001; Chairman, Robert Louis Stevenson Club; Vice-President, Newspaper Press Fund. Address: The Yett, Whim Farm, Lamancha, By West Linton, Peebleshire EH46 7BD, Scotland. E-mail: iannimmoscotland@aol.com

**NIMOY Leonard,** b. 26 March 1931, Boston, Massachusetts, USA. Actor; Director. m. (1) Sandi Zober, 1954, divorced, 1 son, 1 daughter. (2) Susan Bay, 1988. Education: Boston College; Antioch University. Appointments: US Army, 1954-56; TV appearances include: Star Trek, 1966-69; Eleventh Hour; The Virginian; Rawhide; Dr Kildare; Film appearances include: Old Overland Trail, 1953; Satan's Satellites, 1958; Valley of Mystery, co-producer, 1967; Catlow, co-producer, 1971; Invasion of the Bodysnatchers, co-producer, 1978; Star Trek - The Motion Picture, co-producer, 1979; Star Trek: The Wrath of Khan, co-producer, 1982; Star Trek III: The Search for Spock, Director, 1984; Star Trek IV: The Voyage Home, Director, 1986; Star Trek V: The Final Frontier, 1989; Star Trek VI: The Undiscovered Country; Director, Three Men and a Baby, 1987, The Good Mother, 1988, Funny About Love, 1990, Holy Matrimony, 1994; The Pagemaster (voice), 1994; Carpati: 50 Miles, 50 Years, 1996; A Life Apart: Hasidism in America (voice), 1997; David, 1997; Brave New World, 1998; Sinbad, 2000; Atlantis: The Lost Empire, 2001. Publications: I Am Not Spock, autobiography, 1975; We Are All Children, 1977; Come Be With Me, 1979; I am Spock, 1995. Address: c/o Gersh Agency Inc, 222 North Cannon Drive, Beverly Hills, CA 90210, USA.

**NIRENBERG Marshall Warren,** b. 10 April 1927, New York, New York, USA. Biochemist. Education: Graduated, Biology, 1948, Master's Degree, 1952, University of Florida;

PhD, Biological Chemistry, University of Michigan, 1957. Appointments: National Institute of Health (Arthritic and Metabolic Diseases), 1957-62, Head, Laboratory of Biochemical Genetics, 1962-; Laboratory of Biochemical Genetics, National Heart, Lung and Blood Institute, Bethesda, Washington, DC; Work in deciphering the chemistry of the genetic code. Honour: Honorary Member, Harvey Society; Molecular Biology Award, National Academy of Sciences, 1962; Medal, Department of Health, Education and Welfare, 1963; Modern Medicine Award, 1964; National Medal for Science, President Johnson, 1965; Joint Winner, Nobel Prize for Physiology or Medicine, 1968; Louisa Gross Horwitz Prize for Biochemistry, 1968. Memberships: New York Academy of Sciences; AAAS; NAS; Pontifical Academy of Sciences, 1974; Deutsche Leopoldina Akademie der Naturforscher; Foreign Associate, Academy des Sciences, France, 1989. Address: Laboratory of Biochemical Genetics, National Heart, Lung and Blood Institute, Building 36, Room IC06, Bethesda, MD 20892, USA.

**NISH Ian Hill,** b. 3 June 1926, Edinburgh, Scotland. Retired Professor. m. Rona Margaret Speirs, 29 December 1965, 2 daughters. Education: University of Edinburgh, 1943-51; University of London, 1951-56. Appointments: University of Sydney, New South Wales, Australia, 1957-62; London School of Economics and Political Science, England, 1962-91. Publications: Anglo-Japanese Alliance, 1966; The Story of Japan, 1968; Alliance in Decline, 1972; Japanese Foreign Policy, 1978; Anglo-Japanese Alienation 1919-52, 1982; Origins of the Russo-Japanese War, 1986; Contemporary European Writing on Japan, 1988; Japan's Struggle with Internationalism, 1931-33, 1993; The Iwakura Mission in America and Europe, 1998; Japanese Foreign Policy in the Inter-War Period, 2002. Honours: Commander of the Order of the British Empire, 1990; Order of the Rising Sun, Japan, 1991. Memberships: European Association of Japanese Studies, president, 1985-88; British Association of Japanese Studies, president, 1978. Address: Oakdene, 33 Charlwood Drive, Oxshott, Surrey KT22 0HB, England.

**NISHIIKE Suetaka,** b. 21 July 1965, Oita, Japan. Otolaryngologist; Researcher. Education: MD, 1990, PhD, 1996, Osaka University. Appointments: Resident, Osaka University Hospital, Suita, 1990-91; Medical Staff, Public Health, Kinan General Hospital, Tanabe, 1991-92; Assistant Professor, Osaka University, Suita,1996-98; Chief, Osaka Prefectural Habikino Hospital, Habikino, 1998-2000; Assistant Professor, Osaka University, Suita, 2000-2001; Chief, Suita Municipal Hospital, 2001-2005; Assistant Professor, Kawasaki Medical School, 2005-. Publications: Numerous articles in professional journals. Honours: Fellow, German Academic Exchange Service, 1996; Listed in Who's Who publications and biographical dictionaries. Memberships: Council Member, Japan Society of Equilibrium Research; Fellow, Oto-Rhino-Laryngological Society of Japan; Member, Baranay Society, Sweden. Address: Department of Otolaryngology, Kawasaki Medical School, 577 Matsushima, Kurashiki, Okayama 701-0192, Japan. E-mail: nishiike@med.kawasaki-m.ac.jp

**NISHIKAWA Atsushi,** b. 5 August, 1967, Osaka, Japan. Associate Professor. m. Junko Nakamura, 2 sons. Education: BSc, Faculty of Engineering Science, 1990, MSc, Graduate School of Engineering Science, 1992, PhD, Graduate School of Engineering Science, 1995, Osaka University. Appointments: Research Fellow, Japan Society for the Promotion of Science, 1994-96; Visiting Researcher, Institute for Robotics and Intelligent Systems, University of Southern California, Los Angeles, 1995-96; Assistant Professor, 1996-2005, Associate Professor, 2005-, Osaka University, Toyonaka, Japan.

Publications: Books: Introduction to Robotics, 2000; Robust Vision for Vision-Based Control of Motion, 2000; Major articles: IEEE Transactions on Robotics and Automation, Special Issue on Medical Robotics; Advanced Robotics, Special Issue on Surgical Assistant Robotics. Honours: CARS 2003 Poster Award, 17th International Congress on Computer Assisted Radiology and Surgery, 2003; Biomedical Engineering Symposium 2004 Best Research Award, The Japan Society for Medical and Biological Engineers, 2004. Memberships: Institute of Electronics, Information and Communication Engineers; International Society for Computer Aided Surgery; Japan Society of Computer Aided Surgery; Robotics Society of Japan. Address: Osaka University, 1-3 Machikaneyama-cho, Osaka, Toyonaka 560-8531, Japan. E-mail: atsushi@me.es.osaka-u.ac.jp Website: http://robotics.me.es.osaka-u.ac.jp/~atsushi/

**NISHIKAWA Masao,** b. 15 July 1933, Tokyo, Japan. University Professor. m. Junko Monna, 1 son. Education: Graduate, University of Tokyo, 1956; Graduate, Graduate School, University of Tokyo, 1962; Studied at the Graduate Schools of the Universities of Pennsylvania and Columbia University, 1959-62. Appointments: Assistant, University of Tokyo, 1962-66; Professor, Tokyo Woman's Christian University, 1966-68; Professor, University of Tokyo, 1968-94, emerited, 1994-; Professor, Senshu University, 1994-2004. Publications: Der Erste Weltkrieg und die Sozialisten, 1999; Nationalisme et post-nationalisme du Japon, 2002; Numerous publications in Japanese. Honour: Viktor-Adler-Preis, Austrian State Award. memberships: AHA; HS. Address: Kichijoji Minami-cho 3-2-10, Musashino-shi, Tokyo, 180-0003 Japan. E-mail: nismamus@parkcity.ne.jp

**NISHIMATSU Yuichi,** b. 16 January 1932, Japan. Consultant Engineer; Professor Emeritus, University of Tokyo. m. Teiko Kawaguchi, 2 daughters. Education: Graduate, Department of Mining, University of Tokyo, 1954; DEng, University of Tokyo, 1969. Appointments: Research Engineer, Coal Research Institute, Tokyo, 1957; Professor, Department of Mining, University of Tokyo, 1976; Professor Emeritus, 1992-. Publications: Several articles in professional journals. Honours: 4 Prizes, Excellent Research Papers. Membership: Engineering Academy of Japan. Address: 31-9-1003 Honcho, Wako City, Saitama 351-0114, Japan.

**NISHIURA Hiroyuki,** b. 15 February 1953, Itami, Hyogo Prefecture, Japan. Scientist; Professor. Education: BS, 1976, MS, 1978, DS, 1981, Osaka University, Japan. Appointments: Postdoctoral Fellow, Soryushi Shogakukai Foundation, 1981-82; Postdoctoral Fellow, Japan Society for the Promotion of Science, Kyoto University, 1982-83; Postdoctoral Fellow, Johns Hopkins University, 1983-85; Associate Professor, 1991-2000, Professor, 2000-2005, Osaka Institute of Technology, Junior College; Professor, Faculty of Information Science and Technology, Osaka Institute of Technology, 2005-. Membership: Physical Society of Japan. Address: Faculty of Information Science and Technology, Osaka Institute of Technology, 1-79-1 Kitayama, Hirakata-city, Osaka 573-0196, Japan. E-mail: nishiura@is.oit.ac.jp

**NISHIZAWA Jun-ichi,** b. 12 September 1926, Sendai, Japan. Electrical Engineer; Educator. m. Takeko Hayakawa, 1 son, 2 daughters. Education: BEngineering, 1948, DEngineering (in old system), 1960, Emeritus Professor, 1990, Tohoku University; Honorary Doctor's degree, Humboldt University, 1989; Honorary Doctor's degree, Novosibirsk State University, 1996. Appointments: Assistant Professor, Tohoku University, 1954-62; Professor, 1962-90, Director, 1983-86, 1989-90, Research Institute of Electrical Communication, President,

1990-96, Tohoku University; Director, 1968-2004, Emeritus Director, 2004-, Semiconductor Research Institute; President, Iwate Prefectural University, 1998-2005; President, Tokyo Metropolitan University, 2005-. Publications: About 25 written and 7 edited including: Semiconductor Devices, 1961; Semiconductor Materials, 1968; Optoelectronics, 1977; Human Being Perish from the Earth in Eighty Years, 2000; Fundamentals and Application of Terahertz Electromagnetic Waves, 2005 et al. Honours: Japan Academy Prize, 1974; Jack A Morton Award, IEEE, 1983; Person of Cultural Merits, 1989; IOCG Laudise Prize, 1989; Kenneth J Button Prize, 1993; IEEE Edison Medal, 2000; Established IEEE Jun-ichi Nishizawa Medal, 2002. Memberships: Foreign Member, Russian Academy of Sciences; Foreign Member, Polish Academy of Sciences; Member, Japan Academy; Honorary Foreign Member, Korean Academy of Science and Technology; Foreign Member, Academy of Engineering Sciences of Serbia and Montenegro; Foreign Member, Engineering Academy of Czech Republic. Address: Semiconductor Research Institute, 519-1176, Aoba, Aramaki, Aoba-ku, Sendai 980-0845, Japan.

**NISSEL Siegmund (Walter),** b. 3 January 1922, Munich, Germany. Violinist. m. Muriel, 5 April 1957, 1 son, 1 daughter. Education: External Matriculation, Honours Degree, London University; Private violin study with Professor Max Weissgarber until 1938, then with Professor Max Rostal in London. Debut: With Amadeus Quartet at Wigmore Hall in London, 1948. Career: Founder Member of the Amadeus Quartet; innumerable BBC Radio and TV and ITV appearances; International concert career; Quartet disbanded in 1987 after the death of the violist Peter Schidlof. Recordings: Mozart, Beethoven, Schubert and Brahms Quartets; Benjamin Britten; Brahms Sextets; etc. Honours: Honorary DMus, London and York Universities; OBE; Verdienstkreuz für Musik in Germany and Austria; Honorary LRAM. Memberships: ISM; ESTA. Address: 11 Highgrove Point, Mount Vernon, Frognal Rise, London NW3 6PZ, England.

**NIVARTHI Raju,** b. 16 June 1964, India. Researcher. m. Aparna, 1 son, 1 daughter. Education: BS, 1984; MS, 1986; PhD, 1996. Appointments: Doctoral Fellow, School of Life Sciences, University of Hyderabad, India, 1987-93; Research Scientist, Department of Anesthesiology, New York University Medical Centre, New York, 1993-99; Scientist, Wyeth-Ayerst Research, Pearl River, New York, 1999-2001; Senior Scientist, Manager, Analytical Biochemistry, 2001-05, Manager, Biologics Quality Control, 2005-, Bristol-Myers Squibb, Syracuse, New York. Publications: Numerous articles in professional journals. Honours include: Junior Research Fellowship, CSIR, India, 1987, Senior Research Fellowship, 1990; Certificate of Merit, Pharmacia Biotech and Science Prize for Young Scientists, 1998; Post Doctoral Training Fellowship, National Institute of Drug and Abuse (National Institute of Health), 1998; cGMPs for Pharmaceutical QC and R and D laboratories, School of Pharmacy, University of Wisconsin, 1999; Listed in numerous Who's Who and biographical publications. Memberships: American Association for the Advancement of Science; American Chemical Society; American Society of Anesthesiologists; American Society for Biochemistry and Molecular Biology; International Anaesthesia Research Society; International Society for the Study of Xenobiotics; New York Academy of Sciences. Address: 161 North Way, Camillus, NY 13031, USA.

**NIXDORFF Uwe,** b. 12 June 1958, Hofheim/Ts, Germany. Cardiologist. m. Sigrid Nixdorff, 1 son, 1 daughter. Education: MD degree, Johann Wolfgang Goethe University, Frankfurt, 1985; Approbation, Licence for practising medicine, 1985;

Doctoral Thesis, Johann Wolfgang Goethe University, 1986; Specialisation as Internist, 1993; Subspecialisation as Cardiologist, 1995; Subspecialisation in Sports Medicine, 2003; Habilitation, Johannes Gutenberg University, Mainz, Germany, 1998; Security in Radiation Exposure qualification, 1998. Appointments: Study of Medicine, Johann Wolfgang Goethe University, 1978-85; Internal Department, Military Hospital, Giessen, Germany, 1985-86; Clinic for Heart and Circulatory Diseases, German Heart Centre, Munich, 1986-87; Resident, Johannes Gutenberg University Clinic, Mainz, Germany, 1987-98; Research Fellow, Michael Reese Hospital, Chicago, USA, 1988; Research Fellow, University of Virginia School of Medicine, Charlottesville, USA, 1989; Research Fellow, Harvard Medical School, Boston, USA, 1989; Consultant, Friedrich-Alexander University Clinic, Erlangen, Germany, 1998-. Publications: 52 original papers; 14 casuistic reports; 14 reviews; 144 abstracts; 28 articles in books; 294 lectures and posters. Honours: Young Investigator's Award, International Council on Electrocardiology, 1988; Best Abstract Award, Honourable Mention, International Society of Cardiovascular Ultrasound, 1996; Award for Increasing the Stature and Contributing to the Success of the 2nd World Congress of Echocardiography and Vascular Ultrasound, Beijing, 1996; Best Poster Award, 8th Essen-Mayo-Mainz Symposium, 1996; Fellow, European Society of Cardiology, 2000; Honourable Knight of the Order of St John, 2000; Listed in national and international biographical dictionaries. Memberships: American Heart Association; European Society of Cardiology; German Society of Cardiology; Chairman of Cluster of Working Groups of Cardiovascular Ultrasound, Nuclear Medicine, MRT and Cardio CT; Chairman of Working Group of Cardiovascular Ultrasound; American Society of Echocardiography; New York Academy of Science; German Society of Internal Medicine; Confederation of German Internists; German Society of Ultrasound Medicine; German Heart Foundation, Member of the Editorial Board; German Society of Sport's Medicine. Address: Turmhügelweg 22, D-91058 Erlangen, Germany. E-mail: uwe.nixdorff@t-online.de

**NIXON John,** b. 25 September 1952, Hemsworth, Yorkshire, England. Health Economist. m. Yumi Nixon, 2 sons, 2 daughters. Education: Certificate in Education (Cert Ed) 1983; BA (Hons), Social Policy, 1995; MSc Health Economics, 1996; PhD, Economics, 2002. Appointments: Lieutenant, Royal Navy, 1968-92; Tutor, Economics, 1996-98, Fellow, Centre for Reviews and Dissemination, 1998-2005, University of York. Publications: Numerous articles in peer-reviewed journals including most recently: How do we judge the quality of economic evaluations, 2003; The European Network of Health Economic Evaluation Databases, 2004; The usefulness of the NHS Economic Evaluation Database to researchers undertaking Health Technology Assessment Reviews, 2004. Memberships: International Health Economics Association; UK Health Economics Study Group; Society for Social Medicine. E-mail: jn105@york.ac.uk

**NOAKES Vivien,** b. 16 February 1937, Twickenham, England. Writer. m. Michael Noakes, 9 July 1960, 2 sons, 1 daughter. Education: MA, D Phil, English, Senior Scholar, Somerville College, Oxford. Appointments: Guest Curator, Exhibition: Edward Lear 1812-1888, Royal Academy of Arts, London and The National Academy of Design, New York, 1985; Consultant of Lear's paintings and manuscripts to all major auction houses; Honorary Governor, Harris Manchester College, Oxford, 1994-; Member, Governing Committees, Quintin Kynaston School, 2001-2003; LEA, Governor, 2004-; Judge, The Royal Society of Literature W H Heinemann Award, 1999-2004; Judge, The Winifred Holtby Prize for Regional Writing, 1999-2003.

Publications: Edward Lear: The Life of a Wanderer, 1968, 4th edition, 2004; For Lovers of Edward Lear, 1978; Scenes from Victorian Life, 1979; Edward Lear 1812-1888, The Catalogue of the Royal Academy Exhibition, 1985; The Selected Letters of Edward Lear, 1988; The Painter Edward Lear, 1991; The Imperial War Museum Catalogue of Isaac Rosenberg, 1998; The Daily Life of the Queen: An Artists Diary, 2000. The Poems and Plays of Isaac Rosenberg, 2004. Contributions to: Times; Times Literary Supplement; Daily Telegraph; New Scientist; Punch; Harvard Magazine; Tennyson Research Bulletin. Honours: Philip and Francis Hofer Lecturer, Harvard University, 1988; The Tennyson Society Memorial Address, Lincoln, 1988; Guest Lecturer, Yale Center for British Art, 2000; Lecturer, Somerville College, Oxford, 1995-96. Memberships: Fellow, Royal Society of Literature; Member, Society of Authors; PEN. Address: 146 Hamilton Terrace, London NW8 9UX, England. E-mail: mail@vivien-noakes.co.uk

**NOBBS David Gordon,** b. 13 March 1935, Orpington, Kent, England. Writer. m. (1) Mary Jane Goddard, 18 November 1968, 2 stepsons, 1 stepdaughter, divorced 1998, (2) Susan Sutcliffe, 4 August 1998, 1 stepdaughter. Education: Marlborough College, 1948-53; BA, English, St John's College, Cambridge, 1955-58. Publications: Novels: The Itinerant Lodger, 1965; Ostrich Country, 1967; A Piece of the Sky is Missing, 1968; The Fall and Rise of Reginald Perrin, 1975; The Return of Reginald Perrin, 1977; The Better World of Reginald Perrin, 1978; Second From Last in the Sack Race, 1983; A Bit of a Do, 1986; Pratt of the Argus, 1988; Fair Dos, 1990; The Cucumber Man, 1994; The Legacy of Reginald Perrin, 1995; Going Gently, 2000; Sex and Other Changes, 2004; TV: The Fall and Rise of Reginald Perrin; Fairly Secret Army; A Bit of a Do; Rich Tea and Sympathy; The Life and Times of Henry Pratt; Love On a Branch Line; Gentlemen's Relish. Address: c/o Jonathan Clowes Ltd, 10 Iron Bridge House, Bridge Approach, London NW1 8BD, England.

**NOBRE Marcos Augusto de Lima,** b. 26 March 1965, Votuporanga SP, Brazil. Assistant Professor. m. Silvania Lanfredi. Education: BScEd, Physics, 1993, MSc, Chemistry, 1995, PhD, Physical Chemistry, 1999, Federal University of Sao Carlos, Brazil. Appointments: Postdoctoral Associate, Metallurgical and Materials Engineering, 2000, Postdoctoral Associate, Materials Physic and Materials Chemistry, 2001, University of Sao Paulo, Brazil; Researcher, Materials Physic and Materials Chemistry, 2002, Assistant Professor, Physics, 2003, Universidade Estadual Paulista, Brazil. Publications: Articles published in professional scientific journals. Honours: Listed in international biographical dictionaries; International Scientist of the Year, IBC, 2003, 2004. Memberships: Associacao Brasileira de Ceramica; Associacao Brasileira de Quimica. Address: FCT-UNESP/DFQB, Rua Roberto Simonsen – 305, PO Box 467, CEP 19060-900, Presidente Prudente – SP, Brazil.

**NOIVILLE-HIRSCH Florence,** b. 23 July 1961, Paris, France. Journalist. m. Martin Hirsch, 3 daughters. Education: HEC, Institut d'Etudes Politiques de Paris; Master in Law, University of Paris. Appointments: Financial Analyst; Journalist, Co-editor of Literary Supplement, Le Monde; Participant in cultural TV show on I-TV. Publications: Isaac B Singer, a Biography; Many books for children. Honours: Fellowship, Onassis Foundation; Fellowship, Greek Ministry of Culture; Fellowship, Villa Mont-Noir for Writers; Grand Prize of the Biography, 2004. Memberships: Member, HEC Culture Group. Address: 28 avenue d'Eylau, 75116 Paris, France. E-mail: noiville@lemonde.fr

**NOJIRI Hideyuki,** b. 16 December 1943, Hokkaido, Japan. Professor. m. Mitsuko, 2 sons, 1 daughter. Education: Master of Engineering, Waseda University, Tokyo, 1969; Doctor of Engineering, Tokyo Institute of Technology, 1981. Appointments: Researcher, Nomura Research Institute, Tokyo, 1969-71; Assistant, Ibaraki University, 1971-74; Researcher, Aachen University of Technology, Germany, 1974-78; Researcher, Tokyo Institute of Technology, Tokyo, 1978-82; Assistant, Hosei University, Tokyo, 1980-82; Assistant Professor, 1982, Chief, Data Processing Center, 1984-87, Kumamoto University of Commerce; Professor, 1983-2005, Chief, Academic Computing Center, 1992-94, Kumamoto Gakuen University; Visiting Scholar, University of California at Berkeley, USA, 1988-89; Member of Advisory Board, Kumamoto Science and Technology Promotion Club, 1990-2000; Lecturer, Prefectural University of Kumamoto, 1996-2005; Lecturer, Kumamoto University, 2002-05; Exchange Scholar, The University of Montana, USA, 2005-06. Publications: Main author, 10 papers; Co-author, 3 books. Honours: Scholarship, Konrad Adenauer Foundation, 1974-78. Memberships: Japan Industrial Management Association; Operations Research Society of Japan; Society of Instrument and Control Engineers. Address: Kumamoto Gakuen University, 2-5-1 Oe, Kumamoto 862-0971, Japan.

**NOLTE Nick,** b. 1942, Omaha, USA. Film Actor. m. Rebecca Linger, 1984, divorced 1995, 1 son. Education: Pasadena City College; Phoenix City College. Creative Works: Films: Return to Macon County, 1975; The Deep, 1977; Who'll Stop the Rain, 1978; North Dallas Forty, 1979; Heartbeat, 1980; Cannery Row, 1982; 48 Hours, 1982; Under Fire, 1983; The Ultimate Solution of Grace Quigley, 1984; Teachers, 1984; Down and Out in Beverly Hills, 1986; Weeds, 1987; Extreme Prejudice, 1987; Farewell to the King, 1989; New York Stories, 1989; Three Fugitives; Everybody Wins; Q & A, 1990; Prince of Tides, 1990; Cape Fear, 1991; Lorenzo's Oil, 1992; Blue Chips, 1994; I'll Do Anything, 1994; Love Trouble, 1994; Jefferson in Paris, 1994; Mulholland Falls, 1996; Mother Night, 1996; Afterglow, 1997; Affliction, 1998; U-Turn; Breakfast of Champions, 1998; The Thin Red Line, 1998; The Golden Bowl, 2000; Investigating Sex, 2001; Double Down, 2001; The Good Thief, 2003; Northfork, 2003; Hulk, 2003; Numerous TV and theatre appearances. Address: 6153 Bonsall Drive, Malibu, CA 90265, USA.

**NOOR AL-HUSSEIN, H.M. Queen of Jordan,** b. Lisa Najeeb Halaby, 23 August 1951. m. King Hussein I of Jordan, 1978, deceased 1999, 4 children. Education: Princeton University. Appointments: Architechtural and Urban Planning Projects, Australia, Iran, Jordan, 1974-78; Founder, Royal Endowment for Culture and Education, Jordan, 1979, Annual Arab Childrens Congress, Jordan, 1980, Annual International Jerash Festival for Culture and Arts, Jordan, 1981, Jubilee School, Jordan, 1984, Noor Al-Hussein Foundation, Jordan, 1985, National Music Conservatory, Jordan, 1986; Chair, National Task Force for Children; Advisory Committee, UN University International Leadership Academy, Amman; Patron, General Federation of Jordanian Women, National Federation of Business and Professional Womens Clubs, Royal Society for Conservation of Nature and various cultural, sporting and national development organisations. Publication: Leap of Faith: Memoirs of an Unexpected Life, 2002. Honours: Numerous honorary doctorates, international awards and decorations. Memberships include: Honorary President, Jordan Red Crescent; Founding Member, International Commission on Peace and Food, 1992; President, United World Colleges, 1995. Address: Royal Palace, Amman, Jordan.

**NORDLANDER Nils Brage**, b. 29 October 1919, Piteå, Sweden. Physician. m. Brita Redin, 2 daughters. Education: Medical Studies in Stockholm and Uppsala, Licensed Physician, 1946; Honorary Doctor of Medicine, University of Uppsala, 1985. Appointments: Assistant Pathologist, Uppsala, 1945-47; Intern, Assistant Lecturer, Clinic of Internal Medicine, University Hospital of Uppsala, 1947-56; Head of Clinic of Internal Medicine and Geriatrics, Ulleråker Hospital, Uppsala, 1957-84; Retired, 1984; Private Practice, 1984-96. Publications: Several articles in internal medicine, medical history and medical politics. Honours: Knight of the Order of the Northern Star, 1986; The Royal Medal, 1990; Honorary Member, Students Association, Södermanlands-Nerikes Nation, Uppsala. Memberships: County Council of Uppsala, 1952-92, Chairman, 1974-80, 1989-92; Member, Federation of Swedish County Councils, 1970-82, Party Group Chairman; Chairman, Swedish Council for Information on Alcohol and Drugs, 1977-85; Vice-Chairman, Museum of Medical History, Uppsala. Address: Torsgatan 6 B, 753 15 Uppsala, Sweden.

**NORDSTRØM Hans-Henrik**, b. 26 June 1947, Nakskov, Denmark. Composer. m. Anne Kristine Smith, 1 son. Education: Royal Danish Academy of Music, Copenhagen, 1965-70. Debut: Copenhagen, 1990. Compositions include most recently: Mouvements (piano trio), 2000; Land of Shadows (bass clarinet and percussion), 2000; Light (flute and guitar), 2000; Fluctuations (4 guitars), 2000; Night Glow and Dawn Frosting (soprano and guitar), 2000; Chac (organ), 2000; Lost Traces (saxophone and percussion), 2001; In the Woods (violin and sinfonietta), 2001; The Twelve Bens (string trio, 2001); Imaginations (harpsichord), 2002; ...if a Tone in the Night (recorder and accordion, 2002; Growth (brass quintet), 2002; Fair Isle (violoncello, 12 woodwinds, 4 French horns), 2002; Riverrun (Septet), 2002; Quarks (string trio), 2002; Tingsominggenting (guitar), 2003; ALP (flute, clarinet, guitar, percussion and violin), 2003; Following the Wake (piano trio), 2003; Sketches from Iceland (piano quartet), 2003; Mourning Knight (mezzo, recorder, saxophone & percussion), 2003; ALP Too (viola and Guitar), 2003; Nuage d'Automne (trombone and sinfonietta), 2003-2004; Nuvole Italiane (piano), 2004; Nuages Élégiaques (trombone), 2004; Triskele (wind quintet), 2004; Ante Discum Solis (saxophone and harp), 2004; Røst (clarinet, bassoon and piano), 2004; Diecieis Fragmentos (mezzo, guitar and percussion), 2004; Sjúrður (soprano and saxophone), 2004; Infinite Water (clarinet and tape), 2005; Finnegan's (sinfonietta), 2005; "Stalingrad" (4 saxophones and 2 percussion), 2005; The Place That Is Not (saxophone and organ, 2005; Endro Karnag (flute & cello), 2005. Recordings: Hans-Henrik Nordstrøm 1 (Portrait CD), 1997; Hans-Henrik Nordstrøm 2 (Portrait CD), 1999; Hans-Henrik Nordstrøm 3 (Portrait CD), 2001; No 4: In the Woods (Portrait CD), 2003; No 5: North West (Portrait CD), 2005. Honours: Grant, Danish Art Foundation, 1990-; Danish Composer's Society's Grant, 2001; Artistic Co-Director, Contemporary Music in Susaa Festivals, held in August every year since 1993-; Composer of the Year, 2002, Bornholm Music Festival; Composer of the Year, Birkeroed, 2004. Membership: Danish Composers Society. Address: Skovmarksvej 52, Vetterslev, DK-4100 Ringsted, Denmark. E-mail: hans-henrik@nordstroem.dk Website: www.nordstroem.dk

**NORMAN Barry Leslie**, b. 21 August 1933, London, England. Writer; Broadcaster. m. Diana Narracott, 1957, 2 daughters. Appointments: Entertainments Editor, Daily Mail, London, 1969-71; Weekly Columnist, The Guardian, 1971-80; Writer and Presenter, BBC 1 Film, 1973-81, 1983-88, The Hollywood Greats, 1977-79, 1984, The British Greats 1980, Omnibus, 1982, Film Greats, 1985, Talking Pictures, 1988; Barry Norman's Film Night, BSkyB, 1998-2001; Radio 4 Today, 1974-76, Going

Places, 1977-81, Breakaway, 1979-80. Publications: Novels: The Matter of Mandrake, 1967; The Hounds of Sparta, 1968; End Product, 1975; A Series of Defeats, 1977; To Nick a Good Body, 1978; Have a Nice Day, 1981; Sticky Wicket, 1984. Non-Fiction: Tales of the Redundance Kid, 1975; The Hollywood Greats, 1979; The Movie Greats, 1981; Talking Pictures, 1987; 100 Best Films of the Century, 1992, 1998; And Why Not? 2002. Thriller: The Birddog Tape, 1992; The Mickey Mouse Affair, 1995; Death on Sunset, 1998. Honours: British Association of Film and Television Arts Richard Dimbleby Award, 1981; Magazine Columnist of the Year, 1991; Honorary DLitt, University of East Anglia, 1991, University of Hertfordshire, 1996; Magazine Columnist of the Year, 1991; Commander of the Order of the British Empire, 1998.

**NORMAN Geraldine (Lucia), (Geraldine Keen, Florence Place)**, b. 13 May 1940, Wales. U.K. Representative of the State Hermitage Museum. m. Frank Norman, July 1971. Education: MA, Honours, Mathematics, St Anne's College, Oxford, 1961; University of California at Los Angeles, USA, 1961-62. Publications: The Sale of Works of Art (as Geraldine Keen), 1971; 19th Century Painters and Paintings: A Dictionary, 1977; The Fake's Progress (co-author), 1977; The Tom Keating Catalogue (editor), 1977; Mrs Harper's Niece (as Florence Place), 1982; Biedermeier Painting, 1987; Top Collectors of the World (co-author), 1993; The Hermitage: The Biography of a Great Museum, 1997. Contributions to: The Times, The Independent, The Daily Telegraph and other Newspapers. Honour: News Reporter of the Year, 1976. Address: 5 Seaford Court, 220 Great Portland Street, London W1, England.

**NORMAN Gregory John**, b. 10 February 1955, Queensland, Australia. Professional Golfer. m. Laura, 1 July 1981, 1 son, 1 daughter. Career: Professional, 1976-; Numerous major victories including: Doral Ryder Open, 1990, 1993, 1996; South African Open, 1996; Players Championship, 1994; PGA Grand Slam of Golf, 1993, 1994; British Open, 1986, 1993; Canadian Open, 1984, 1992; Australian Masters, 1981, 1983, 1984, 1989, 1990; New South Wales Open, 1978, 1983, 1986, 1988; Australian Open, 1980, 1985, 1987; European Open, 1986; World Match-Play, 1980, 1983, 1986; Australian Team, Dunhill Cup, 1985, 1986. Publications: My Story, 1982-83; Shark Attack, 1987-88; Greg Norman's Instant Lessons, 1993; Greg Norman's Better Golf, 1994. Honours: Inducted into World Golf Hall of Fame, 2001. Address: Great White Shark Enterprises Inc, PO Box 1189, Hobe Sound, FL 33475-1189, USA.

**NORODOM RANARIDDH Prince**, b. 2 January 1944, Cambodia. m. 1968, 2 sons, 1 daughter. Appointments: President, United National Front for an Independent, Neutral, Peaceful & Co-operative Cambodia; Co-Chair, Provisional National Government of Cambodia; Minister of National Defence, Interior and National Security, 1993; Member, National Assembly, 1993-; Co-Prime Minister, Member, Throne Council, 1993; 1st Prime Minister of Royal Government of Cambodia, 1993-97; Chair, National Development Council, 1993-97; Found guilty of conspiracy with Khmer Rouges to overthrow the government, sentenced to 30 years imprisonment; In Exile; Returned from exile 1998; Professor of Public Law.

**NORODOM SIHANOUK Samdech Preah**, b. 31 October 1922, Cambodia. King of Cambodia. m. Princess Monique, 14 children (6 deceased). Education: Saigon; Vietnam; Paris; Military Training, Saumur, France. Appointments: Elected King, 1941, Abdicated, 1955; Prime Minister, Minister of Foreign Affairs, 1955, 1956, 1957; Permanent Representative to UN, 1956; Elected Head of State, 1960; Took Oath of Fidelity to Vacant Throne, 1960; Deposed by Forces of Lon Nol, 1970;

Resided, Peking; Established, Royal Government of National Union of Cambodia, (GRUNC) 1970; Restored as Head of State when GRUNC forces overthrew Khmer Republic, 1975, Resigned, 1976; Special Envoy of Khmer Rouge to UN, 1979; Founder, National United Front for an Independent Neutral, Peaceful and Co-operative Kampuchea, 1981-89; President, Tripartite National Cambodian Resistance, in exile 13 years, retured to Cambodia, 1991-93; Crowned King of Cambodia, 1993-; Colonel in Chief, Armed Forces, 1993-. Publications: L'Indochine vue de Pékin (with Jean Lacouture), 1972; My War With the CIA (with Wilfred Burchett), 1973; War and Hope: The Case for Cambodia, 1980; Souvenirs doux et amers, 1981; Prisonnier des Khmers Rouges, 1986; Charisme et Leadership, 1989. Address: Khemarindra Palace, Phnom Penh, Cambodia.

**NORTON Hugh Edward,** b. 23 June 1936, London, England. Business Executive. m. (1) Janet M Johnson, 1965, deceased, 1 son, (2) Joy Harcup, 1998. Education: Winchester College; Trinity College, Oxford. Appointments: Joined British Petroleum Company, 1959, Exploration Department, 1960, in Abu Dhabi, Lebanon & Libya, 1962-70, subsequently held appointments in Supply, Central Planning; Policy Planning, Regional Directorate Mid E & International & Government Affairs departments; Managing Director, BP's Associate Companies, Singapore, Malaysia, Hong Kong, 1978-81, Director of Planning, 1981-83, Regional Director for Near East, Middle East & Indian Sub-Continent, 1981-86, Director of Administration, 1983-86, Managing Director, CEO, BP Exploration Co, 1986-89, Chair, 1989-95, Managing Director, British Petroleum Co PLC, 1989-95; Chair, BP Asia Pacific Private Co Ltd, 1991-95; Director, Inchcape PLC, 1995-, Standard Chart PLC, 1995-, Lasmo PLC, 1997-. Memberships: Council, Royal Institute of Economic Affairs, 1991-. Address: c/o BP Asia Pacific Pte Ltd, BP Tower, 25th Storey, 396 Alexandra Road, 0511 Singapore.

**NORWICH John Julius (The Viscount Norwich),** b. 15 September 1929, London, England. Writer; Broadcaster. m. (1) Anne Clifford, 5 August 1952, 1 son, 1 daughter, (2) Mollie Philipps, 14 June 1989. Education: University of Strasbourg, 1947; New College, Oxford, 1949-52. Appointments: Writer, Royal Navy, 1947-49; Foreign Office, 1952-64; Third Secretary, British Embassy, Belgrade, 1955-57; Second Secretary, British Embassy, Beirut, 1957-60; First Secretary, Foreign Office, London, 1961; British delegation to Disarmament Conference, Geneva, 1960-64; Writer, Broadcaster, 1964-; Chairman: British Theatre Museum, 1966-71; Venice in Peril Fund, 1970-; Executive Committee, National Trust, 1969-95; Franco-British Council, 1972-79; Board, English National Opera, 1977-81. Publications: Mount Athos, 1966; Sahara, 1968; The Normans in the South, 1967; The Kingdom in the Sun, 1970; A History of Venice, 1977; Christmas Crackers 1970-79, 1980; Glyndebourne, 1985; The Architecture of Southern England, 1985; A Taste for Travel, 1985; Byzantium: The Early Centuries, 1988; More Christmas Crackers 1980-89, 1990; Venice: A Traveller's Companion (editor), 1990; The Oxford Illustrated Encyclopaedia of the Arts (editor), 1990; Byzantium, the Apogee, 1991; Byzantium: The Decline and Fall, 1995; A Short History of Byzantium, 1997; Shakespeare's Kings, 1999; Still More Christmas Crackers 1990-99, 2000; Paradise of Cities, 2003. Honours: Commander, Royal Victorian Order; Commendatore, Ordine al Merito della Repubblica Italiana; Award, American Institute of Architects. Memberships: Fellow, Royal Society of Literature; Fellow, Royal Geographical Society; Fellow, Royal Society of Arts. Address: 24 Blomfield Road, London W9 1AD, England.

**NOURSE Christopher Stuart,** b. 13 August 1946, Salisbury, Wiltshire, England. Arts Director. Education: LLB, University of Edinburgh, 1965-68; Middle Temple/Inns of Court School of Law, 1968-69. Appointments: Royal Opera House, English Opera Group, Royal Ballet New Group, 1972-76; General Manager, Sadler's Wells Royal Ballet, 1976-89; Administrative Director, Birmingham Royal Ballet, 1989-91; Assistant to the General Director, Royal Opera House, 1991-96; Executive Director, Rambert Dance Company, 1997-2001; Managing Director English National Ballet, 2001-2003; Trustee, National Youth Dance Trust, 2002-; Trustee, Youth Dance, England, 2004-. Membership: Fellow, Royal Society of Arts, 1998. Address: 55 Queen's Gate, South Kensington, London SW7 5JW, England.

**NOVAK Pavel,** b. 7 September 1918, Stribro, Czech Republic. Civil Engineer; University Teacher. m. R Elizabeth Maurer, 1 son, 1 daughter. Education: BSc (Hon), University of London (external), 1941; Ing Dr, 1949, CSc (PhD), 1958, Czech Technical University, Prague; Dr Sc, Technical University, Brno, 1965. Appointments: Assistant Engineer, Trent Navigation Co, Nottingham, 1941-42; Assistant Lecturer, University College, Nottingham, 1942-45; Scientific Officer to Principal Scientific Officer, Hydraulic Research Institute, Prague, 1945-67; Director, Institute of Hydrodynamics, Academy of Sciences, Prague, 1967-68; Senior Lecturer, Department of Civil Engineering, 1968-70, Professor of Civil and Hydraulic Engineering, 1970-83, Head of Department of Civil Engineering, 1981-83, Head of School of Civil & Mining Engineering, 1982-83, University of Newcastle. Publications: Over 100 papers in refereed journals and at international conferences; Author, Co-author and editor of 20 books. Honours: Corresponding Member, Academy of Science, Toulouse, 1967; James Hardie Speaker, Institution of Engineers, Australia, 1987; Honorary Member, International Association for Hydraulic Engineering and Research, 1989; Hlavka Medal, 1992, Bechyne Gold Medal, 1994, Czechoslovak Academy of Sciences; Hydraulic Structures Medal, American Society of Civil Engineers, 2003. Memberships: Fellow, Institution of Civil Engineers, UK; Fellow, Chartered Institution of Water and Environmental Management; Honorary Member, International Association for Hydraulic Engineering and Research. Address: 5 Glendale Avenue, Whickham, Newcastle upon Tyne, NE16 5JA, England. E-mail: pavel.novak@ncl.ac.uk

**NOVOTNA Jana,** b. 2 October 1968, Brno, Czech Republic. Tennis Player. Appointments: Won US Open Junior Doubles, 1986; Turned Professional, 1987; Won 1st Title, Adelaide, 1988; Olympic Silver Medal, Doubles wih Helena Sukova, 1988; Won Australian and US Open Mixed Doubles with Pugh, 1988; Won 6 Women's Doubles Titles, 1989; With Sukova, won Australian Open, French Open, Wimbledon Doubles, 1990; Reached Quarter Finals, French Open, 1991; Won 7 Doubles Titles with Savchenko Neiland, 1992; Won Singles Titles, Osaka and Brighton, 1993; Singles Titles, Leipzig, Brighton, Essen, 1994; Won Wimbledon Singles and Doubles, 1998; Announced retirement, 1999. Honours: Olympic Bronze Medal in Singles, Silver Medal in Doubles, Atlanta, 1996.

**NOWACKI Zbigniew,** b. 19 January 1940, Kutno, Poland. Professor; Electrical Engineer. m. Maria, 1 son. Education: MSc, Electrical Engineering, 1962; PhD, Electrical Drive Control, 1970; DSc, 1982, Professor, 1991. Appointments: Electrical Engineer, Factory of Transformers and Traction Apparatus, 1962-65; Teacher, 1966, Vice Dean, Electrical Faculty, 1987-93, Head, Electrical Drive Division, 1983-, Technical University of Lodz; Council for Science at Ministry of Scientific Research and Information Society Technologies, 2004-. Publications: Over 80 articles, 3 books: Suboptimal Control of an Induction Motor with Respect to a Modified Quadratic Performance Index, 1981; Electrical Drive in Question and Answers, 1986; Pulses

Width Modulation in Variable Frequency Drives, 1991; 4 books for students. Honours: 2 Awards, Ministry of Education, 1970, 1981. Memberships: Senior Member, Institute of Electrical and Electronic Engineers; European Power Electrics and Drive Association; PTETiS. Address: Konstytucyina 9/43, 90-155 Lodz, Poland.

**NUNN Trevor Robert,** b. 14 January 1940, Ipswich, England. Theatre Director. m. (1) Janet Suzman, 1969, 1 son, (2) Sharon Lee Hill, 1986, 2 daughters, (3) Imogen Stubbs, 1994, 1 son, 1 daughter. Education: Downing College, Cambridge. Appointments: Trainee Director, Belgrade Theatre, Coventry; Associate Director, Royal Shakespeare Company, 1964-86; Director Emeritus, 1986-; Founder, Homevale Ltd, Awayvale Ltd; Artistic Director, Royal National Theatre, 1996-2001. Creative Works: Productions include: The Merry Wives of Windsor, 1979; Once in a Lifetime, 1979; Juno and the Paycock, 1980; The Life and Adventures of Nicholas Nickleby, 1980; Cats, 1981; All's Well That Ends Well, 1981; Henry IV (pts I and II), 1981, 1982; Peter Pan, 1982; Starlight Express, 1984; Les Misérables, 1985; Chess, 1986; The Fair Maid of the West, 1986; Aspects of Love, 1989; Othello, 1989; The Baker's Wife, 1989; Timon of Athens, 1991; The Blue Angel, 1991; Measure for Measure, 1991; Heartbreak House, 1992; Arcadia, 1993; Sunset Boulevard, 1993; Enemy of the People, 1997; Mutabilitie, 1997; Not About Nightingales, 1998; Oklahoma, 1998; Betrayal, 1998; Troilus and Cressida, 1999; The Merchant of Venice, 1999; Summerfolk, 1999; Love's Labour's Lost, 2002; TV: Antony and Cleopatra, 1975; Comedy of Errors, 1976; Every Good Boy Deserves Favour, 1978; Macbeth, 1978; Shakespeare Workshops Word of Mouth, 1979; The Three Sisters, Othello, 1989; Porgy and Bess, 1992; Oklahoma!, 1999; Films: Hedda, Lady Jane, 1985; Twelfth Night, 1996; Operas: Idomeneo, 1982; Porgy and Bess, 1986; Cosi Fan Tutte, 1991; Peter Grimes, 1992; Katya Kabanova, 1994; Sophie's Choice, 2002. Publications: British Theatre Design, 1989. Honours: Numerous. Address: Royal National Theatre, Upper Ground, South Bank, London SE1 9PX, England.

**NUNOO Jonathan Nii Ahele,** b. 2 October 1941, Accra, Ghana. Water Engineer. m. Regina Efua, 1 son, 1 daughter. Education: Achimota School, Ghana, 1956-62; BSc in Civil Engineering, Kware Nkrumah University of Science and Technology, 1962-66; Postgraduate diploma in Public Health Engineering, Imperial College of Science and Technology, 1971-72. Appointments: Area Engineer, Greater Accra Region, 1977-80, Regional Director, Upper Region, 1980-88; Regional Director, Bronce Ahafo Region, 1988-96, Deputy Managing Director, 1986-99, Regional Director, Western Region, 1999-2001, Managing Director, 2001-03, Ghana Water Company Ltd. Publications: Eutrophification of Surface Waters, 1972. Honours: British Council Fellowship to study Public Health Engineering at Imperial College, University of London, 1971-72. Memberships: Chartered Civil Engineer, UK , ICE; Fellow, Ghana Institute of Engineers; Member, British Institute of Management; Member, Ghana Institute of Management; Member, Chartered Institute of Water and Environmental Management, UK; Associate, Chartered Institute of Arbitrators, UK. Address: P O Box 11624, Accra, North Ghana. E-mail: jean@africaonline.com.gh

**NUORTEVA Pekka Olavi,** b. 24 November 1926, Helsinki, Finland. Professor of Environmental Science. m. Sirkka-Liisa Welling-Vuontela, 1 son, 2 daughters. Education: MSc, Biology, 1951, DrSc, Zoology, 1955, Docent, Entomology, 1955, Competence for Chief of Zoological Museum, 1972, Professor, 1975, Helsinki University. Appointments: Research Worker, Finnish Agricultural Research Institute, Tikkurila, Finland, 1952; Demonstrator, Anatomy, Medical Faculty, Assistant,

Department of Ecology and Morphology, Institute of Zoology, 1954, Docent (Lecturer), Institute of Zoology, 1955; Lecturer in Parasitology, Veterinary High School, Helsinki, 1967; Intendent of the Zoological Museum of Helsinki University, 1958; Chief of the Department of Entomology, Zoological Museum, Helsinki University, 1972; Professor of Environmental Science, Helsinki University, 1975-. Publications: More than 300 scientific publications from a field including ecophysiology of insects, agricultural and forest phytopathology, medical entomology and parasitology, subarctic biology, methylmercury pollution of fish, cadmium bioaccumulation and cadmium resistance in ants, circulation of toxic metals and their antagonists in forest biota, blowflies as transmitters of disease germs, tick transmission by migratory birds; More than 650 popularisations about the above themes including 10 books; The Atlas of Finnish Animals. Honours: Chairman in numerous international congresses on environmental science, entomology and forensic science; National Prize for polularisation of science in Finland, 1974, 1977; Portrait in the Galleria Academica, Helsinki University, 1986; 2 First Class Medals, Finnish White Rose Order; 3 Golden Medals, Finnish League for Environmental Protection; 3 Medals from Scientific Societies. Memberships: Finnish Water Protection Committee, 1969-71; Committee for Environmental Protection in Finland, 1970-73; Finnish Energy Committee, 1987-89; Numerous scientific and environmental societies; Co-ordinator of scientific collaboration with some former socialist countries on behalf of Helsinki University. Address: Department of Environmental Science, Helsinki University, Caloniuksenk 6 C 64, FIN-00100 Helsinki, Finland.

**NURUDEEN Mohammed Ibrahim,** b. 2 July 1968, Juabenma-Ashanti, Ghana. Chief Executive Officer; Researcher. m. Fatema Nurudeen, 2 sons, 1 daughter. Education: Diploma, Communication Studies, Ahmadu Bello University Zaria, Nigeria, 1991-93; Degree in Social Sciences and Economics, East Carolina University, USA, 1994-96. Appointments: Founder, Foundation for Investment Research in Africa, Regional Administrator, United National Association in Kumasi-Ghana, 1996-97, Area Councillor, Ejisu Juaben District Assembly, 1998-2001; Abstract Presenter, Sixth International Congress on Aids in Asia, Pacific and Australia, 2001; Assistant Programme Officer, Non-Formal Education Division, Ministry of Education, Kumasi, 2003. Publications: Analysis of Ghana's Economy, 1999-2000; Let Us Attack Risk to Economic, Social and Cultural Rights, 2000; The Problem of Oil Price in World Market, 2000. Honours: Consulting Editor, American Biographical Institute; Award, Government Scholarship in Ghana, 1985-90. Memberships: United Nations Association, Ghana; International Investment Promotion Agencies, USA; Social Security and National Insurance Trust. Address: PO Box KS 9057, Kumasi, Ghana, West Africa. E-mail: nurumoha2000@yahoo.com

**NUTTING Cherie,** b. 24 April 1949, Newton, Massachusetts, USA. Photographer. Divorced. Education: Graduated, Spanish Literature, magna cum laude, University of Massachusetts, 1977; Graduate Courses, School of Visual Arts, New York, 1982-83; New England School of Photography, 1978-80. Appointments: Teacher, Brimmer and May School, Chestnut Hill, Massachusetts, 1977-80; Worked in collaboration with the late Paul Bowles on a book of text and photographs published November 2000, 1986-99; Manager and Photographer for The Master Musicians of Jajouka, 1988-96; Organised and co-ordinated the recording of the Rolling Stones, Continental Drift for Steel Wheels CD and BBC film: The Rolling Stones in Morocco, 1989; Photographer, manager and location assistant for recording: Apocalypse Across the Sky by The Master Musicians of Jajouka, 1991; Photographer, manager, design assistant and co-producer for Pipes of Pan CD and book with The Rolling Stones; Organised music for Bernardo Bertolucci's Sheltering Sky and Croneberg's Naked Lunch (Jajouka Music); Photographer, manager, locations assistant and co-producer for Peter Gabriels recording: Jajouka Between the Mountains, 1996; Exhibition: Rizzoli Gallery, San Francisco, 2000; The June Bateman Gallery, New York, NY, 2002. Publications: Pipes of Pan, in collaboration with Polygram and the Rolling Stones; Paul Bowles: Yesterday's Perfume; Book with Bachir Attar, The Master Musicians of Jajouka, in progress; Contributions to numerous magazines; Designs for several album covers. Honour: NEH Adviser, study of Haitian girls under Duvalier, 1980. Commissions and Creative Works: Photographs of Paul Bowles in Kunst Museums in Berne and Zurich. Address: PO Box 1691, New York, NY 10009, USA.

**NYBERG Tore Samuel,** b. 4 January 1931, Uppsala, Sweden. Professor Emeritus. m. Nurbaiti Pamuntjak. Education: fil. kand., Uppsala, 1956; fil. lic., Lund, 1960; fil.dr., Lund, 1965; exam. theol. Munich, 1969; dr phil. habil., Augsburg, 1981. Appointments: Alexander von Humboldt Research Fellow, Munich, 1967-69; Lecturer, Assistant Professor, Professor of Medieval History, Odense University (now University of Southern Denmark), 1970-2001; Professor Emeritus, 2001-; Visiting Professor, Augsburg, 1984; Director, International Birgittine Center, Farfa, Italy, 1993-94. Publications: Birgittinische Klostergründungen des Mittelalters, 1965; Dokumente und Untersuchungen zur inneren Geschichte der drei Birgittenklöster Bayerns 1420-1570, 1972-74; Die Kirche in Skandinavien, 1986; Monasticism in North-Western Europe 800-1200, 2000. Honours: Birgitta-Price, Birgittastiftelsen, Vadstena, Sweden; teol.dr.hc, Uppsala University, Sweden, 2003. Memberships: Commission International d'Histoire Ecclésiastique Comparée; Det Kongelige Samfund for Fædreneslandets Historie, Copenhagen. Address: Centre for History, University of Southern Denmark, Campusvej 55, DK-5230 Odense M, Denmark. E-mail: tny@hist.sdu.dk

**NYE Robert,** b. 15 March 1939, London, England. Author; Poet; Dramatist; Editor. m. (1) Judith Pratt, 1959, divorced 1967, 3 sons, (2) Aileen Campbell, 1968, 1 daughter. Publications: Fiction: Doubtfire, 1967; Tales I Told My Mother, 1969; Falstaff, 1976; Merlin, 1978; Faust, 1980; The Voyage of the Destiny, 1982; The Facts of Life and Other Fictions, 1983; The Memoirs of Lord Byron, 1989; The Life and Death of My Lord Gilles de Rais, 1990; Mrs Shakespeare: The Complete Works, 1993; The Late Mr Shakespeare, 1998. Children's Fiction: Taliesin, 1966; March Has Horse's Ears, 1966; Wishing Gold, 1970; Poor Pumpkin, 1971; Out of the World and Back Again, 1977; Once Upon Three Times, 1978; The Bird of the Golden Land, 1980; Harry Pay the Pirate, 1981; Three Tales, 1983; Lord Fox and Other Spine-Chilling Tales, 1997. Poetry: Juvenilia 1, 1961; Juvenilia 2, 1963; Darker Ends, 1969; Agnus Dei, 1973; Two Prayers, 1974; Five Dreams, 1974; Divisions on a Ground, 1976; A Collection of Poems, 1955-1988, 1989; 14 Poems, 1994; Henry James and Other Poems, 1995; Collected Poems, 1995, 1998. Plays: Sawney Bean (with Bill Watson), 1970; The Seven Deadly Sins: A Mask, 1974; Penthesilea, Fugue and Sisters, 1976. Translator: Beowulf, 1968. Editor: A Choice of Sir Walter Raleigh's Verse, 1973; The English Sermon, 1750-1850, 1976; The Faber Book of Sonnets, 1976; PEN New Poetry 1, 1986; First Awakenings: The Early Poems of Laura Riding (co-editor), 1992; A Selection of the Poems of Laura Riding, 1994. Contributions to: Magazines and journals. Honours: Eric Gregory Award, 1963; Guardian Fiction Prize, 1976; Hawthornden Prize, 1977. Membership: Royal Society of Literature, fellow.

**NYEKO Paulinus,** b. January 1941, Gulu District, Uganda. Teacher. m. Veronica Akelo Nyeko, 6 sons, 10 daughters. Education: B Ed Honours, Former University of East Africa, Makerere University College, 1962-67. Appointments: Careers Teacher, House Master, Examination Master, 1968-72; Deputy Headmaster, 'A'-level Secondary School, 1972-73; Headmaster, 'A'-level Boarding School, 1974-2001; Retired from teaching, 2001; Chairman, Board of Directors, Human Rights Focus, 1994-. Publications: Accessing the Law by IDP's, presented at a workshop on the Rights of Internally Displaced Persons in Uganda; Politics and Religion: A Symbiotic Relationship or Mutual Suspicion; The Dynamics in the Northern War; Leadership Qualities for Political Stability, Mobilisation and Good Governance; An Overview of Human Rights; Women's Rights as Human Rights; Children's Rights; Protecting the Human Rights of Internal Displaced Persons and Promoting their Organisational Processes, a paper presented at a Human Rights Seminar, Luxembourg, July 2005. Honour: Honorary Member, Research Board of Directors, American Biographical Institute. Memberships: Family Planning Association of Uganda (affiliated to IPPF); Uganda Red Cross (affiliated to ICRC); Chairman, Parents Teachers Association, St Joseph's College, Layibi; Chairman, Parents Teachers Association, Sir Samuel Baker School; Vice Chairman, Parents Teachers Association, Sacred Heart Secondary School. Address: Human Rights Focus, Airfield Road, Plot 5/7, PO Box 970 Gulu, Uganda, East Africa. E-mail: paulinusnyeko@yahoo.com

**NYIRI Ferenc (Baron),** b. 25 August 1964, Hodmezovasarhely, Hungary. Basstrombone Player. Education: Academy of Music, Franz Liszt, Szeged, 1985. Appointment: Symphony Orchestra of Pec, 1985. Publications: Journal of Hungarian Trombone-Tuba Association. Honours: Competition of Trombone, III Prize, 1984, II Prize, 1985; Price of Artisjus, 2001. Address: Ipoly sor 11/B. H 6724 Szeged, Hungary.

**NYUNT U Soe,** b. 18 April 1932, Meiktila, Myanmar. Retired Deputy Minister for Culture. m. Daw Hla Yin Yin Soe, 3 sons, 5 daughters. Education: Arts, University of Adult Education, Yangon, 1952-54; PhD, Poetry, Dublin Metropolitan University, Ireland, 2004. Appointments: Enrolled, No 1 Field Artillery Regiment, 1950; 2nd in Command, Ordnance Depot North Burma, Mandalay, 1961-62; Officer on Special Duty, posted to Office of Revolutionary Council Chairman, Ministry of Culture, 1962-63; Company Commander, No 26 Burma Regiment, 1963-65; Chairman, Township Security Council, Kyaikhto, posted to Ministry of Home Affairs, 1965-67; Major, 2nd in Command, No 47 Burma Regiment, 1967; 2nd in Command and Additional Commander, No 23 Burma Regiment, 1968; Officer on Special Duty, State Timber Board, Yangon, posted in Ministry of Agriculture and Forest, 1968-70; Lieutenant Colonel Commanding Officer, No 50 Burma Regiment, 1970-74; General Staff Grade 1, Defence Service, Psychological Warfare and Public Relations, 1974-76; General Staff Officer Grade 1 and Acting Deputy Commander in part time in Central Command, 1976-78; Chief Editor, Mirror Daily (NPE), posted to Ministry of Information, 1978-84; Director General, Fine Arts Department, promoted and posted to Ministry of Culture, 1984-88; Elected member, Pyithu Hluttaw (People's Parliament), by Myothit Township, 1984-88; Managing Director, News and Periodical Enterprise, transferred to Ministry of Information, 1988-92; Deputy, Ministry of Culture, 1993-2003; Retired, 2003. Publications: Over 1000 poems; 1500 articles; 88 books including: 24 books of poetry, 11 novels, 11 works of literary criticism and appreciation; 34 books of collected articles; 8 books on political affairs; 20 books translated into English, French, Chinese and German; Most recent works include: Myanmar Classical Poetry, 1998; The Epic Poems of

Conquering of Haing Gyi Island and Panwa, 1999; I Shall Never Forget Him, novelettes and short stories, 1999; My Precious Pearl, 2002; Appreciation of Myanmar Patriotic poems, 2004; A review of Myanmar History 1920-1962, 2004; O Sound of Bell from Nagasaki, epic poem, 2004. Honours include: State Military Service Medal, 1952; The People Militia Combating Medal; Medal of the Victory of Foreign Enemy Divisions Agression Battle (KMT); Medal for Excellent Administrative Field (1st class); Medal for Public Service; Medal for State Peace and Tranquility, 1990; Medal for State Law and Order Restoration, 1990; Sarpay Beikman Poem Award, 1962; National Literary Award, 1992; The Great Poet Laureate, Japan, 1996; Honourable Member, Min On Concert Association, Japan, 2000; The Literary Messenger of Friendship Award, China, 2001; Award for Excellent Performance in Literature, Myanmar, 2003; Decree of Prime Minister for Friendship Medal Decoration and Government Medal of LAO Democratic Republic, 2003; DPhil, Poetry, Dublin Metropolitan University, 2004. Memberships: Founder, Chairman, Myanmar Writers and Journalists Association; Patron, Myanmar Music Association; Patron of Arts and Crafts Association. Address: #152-2nd 45th Street , Botahtaung Township, Yangon, Myanmar.

# O

**O'BRIEN Conor Cruise, (Donat O'Donnell)**, b. 3 November 1917, Dublin, Ireland. Writer; Editor. m. (1) Christine Foster, 1939, divorced 1962, 1 son, 1 daughter, (2) Máire MacEntee, 1962, 1 adopted son, 1 adopted daughter. Education: BA, 1940, PhD, 1953, Trinity College, Dublin. Appointments: Member, Irish diplomatic service, 1944-61; Vice-Chancellor, University of Ghana, 1962-65; Albert Schweitzer Professor of Humanities, New York University, 1965-69; Member, Labour Party, Dublin North-east, Dail, 1969-77, Senate, Republic of Ireland, 1977-79; Visiting Fellow, Nuffield College, Oxford, 1973-75; Minister for Posts and Telegraphs, 1973-77; Pro-Chancellor, University of Dublin, 1973-; Fellow, St Catherine's College, Oxford, 1978-81; Editor-in-Chief, The Observer, 1979-81; Visiting Professor and Montgomery Fellow, Dartmouth College, New Hampshire, 1984-85; Senior Resident Fellow, National Humanities Center, North Carolina, 1993-94. Publications: Maria Cross, 1952; Parnell and His Party, 1957; The Shaping of Modern Ireland (editor), 1959; To Katanga and Back, 1962; Conflicting Concepts of the UN, 1964; Writers and Politics, 1965; The United Nations: Sacred Drama, 1967; Murderous Angels (play), 1968; Power and Consciousness, 1969; Conor Cruise O'Brien Introduces Ireland, 1969; Albert Camus, 1969; The Suspecting Glance (with Máire Cruise O'Brien), 1970; A Concise History of Ireland, 1971; States of Ireland, 1972; King Herod Advises (play), 1973; Neighbours: The Ewart-Biggs Memorial Lectures 1978-79, 1980; The Siege: The Saga of Israel and Zionism, 1986; Passion and Cunning, 1988; God Land: Reflections on Religion and Nationalism, 1988; The Great Melody: A Thematic Biography and Commented Anthology of Edmund Burke, 1992; Ancestral Voices, 1994; On the Eve of the Millennium, 1996; The Long Affair: Thomas Jefferson and the French Revolution, 1996; Memoir: My Life and Themes, 1998. Honours: Valiant for Truth Media Award, 1979; Honorary doctorates. Memberships: Royal Irish Academy; Royal Society of Literature. Address: Whitewater, Howth Summit, Dublin, Ireland.

**O'BRIEN Denis Patrick**, b. 24 May 1939, Knebworth, Hertfordshire, England. Economist. m. (1) Eileen Patricia O'Brien, deceased, 1985, 1 son, 2 daughters (2) Julia Stapleton, 1 daughter. Education: BSc, Economics, 1960, University College, London; PhD, Queen's University, Belfast, 1969. Appointments: Assistant Lecturer, 1963-65, Lecturer, 1965-70, Reader, 1970-72, Queen's University, Belfast; Professor of Economics, 1972-97, Emeritus Professor, 1998-, Durham University. Publications: J R McCulloch, 1970; The Correspondence of Lord Overstone (3 volumes), 1971; Competition in British Industry (jointly), 1974; The Classical Economists, 1975; Competition Policy, Profitability and Growth (jointly), 1979; Pioneers of Modern Economics in Britain (jointly), 1981; Authorship Puzzles in the History of Economics (jointly), 1982; Lionel Robbins, 1988; Thomas Joplin and Classical Macroeconomics, 1993; Methodology, Money and the Firm (2 volumes), 1994; The Classical Economists Revisited, 2003. Honours: FBA, 1988; Distinguished Fellow, History of Economics Society, 2003. Address: c/o Dr Julia Stapleton, Department of Politics, 48 Old Elvet, Durham DH1 3LZ, England.

**O'BRIEN Edna**, b. 15 December 1936, Tuamgraney, County Clare, Ireland. Author; Dramatist. m. 1954, divorced 1964, 2 sons. Education: Convents; Pharmaceutical College of Ireland. Publications: The Country Girls, 1960; The Lonely Girl, 1962; Girls in Their Married Bliss, 1963; August is a Wicked Month, 1964; Casualties of Peace, 1966; The Love Object, 1968; A Pagan Place, 1970; Night, 1972; A Scandalous Woman, 1974; Mother Ireland, 1976; Johnnie I Hardly Knew You, 1977; Mrs

Reinhardt and Other Stories, 1978; Virginia (play), 1979; The Dazzle, 1981; Returning, 1982; A Christmas Treat, 1982; A Fanatic Heart, 1985; Tales for Telling, 1986; Flesh and Blood (play), 1987; Madame Bovary (play), 1987; The High Road, 1988; Lantern Slides, 1990; Time and Tide, 1992; House of Splendid Isolation, 1994; Down by the River, 1997; James Joyce: A Biography, 1999; Wild Decembers, 1999; In the Forest, 2002; Iphigenia (play), 2003. Honours: Yorkshire Post Novel Award, 1971; Los Angeles Times Award, 1990; Writers' Guild Award, 1993; European Prize for Literature, 1995; American National Arts Gold Medal. Address: David Godwin Associates, 14 Goodwin Court, Covent Garden, London WC2N 4LL, England.

**O'BRIEN Francis J, Jr**, b. 7 December 1946, Providence, Rhode Island, USA. Scientist. m. Julianne Jennings, 1 son, 2 daughters. Education: BA, Rhode Island College, 1973; MA, Med, MPhil, Columbia University, 1977; PhD, Columbia University, 1980. Appointments: Statistician, US Government Research, 1980-87; Senior Scientist, US Navy, 1987-; Former President, Aquid Neck Indian Council, 1996-2002. Publications: 23 US patents; Numerous articles and proceedings papers; 6 Books. Honours: Who's Who in the East; Who's Who in Science and Engineering; Kappa Delta Pi; Pi Lambda Theta. Memberships: Mensa; Intertel; New York Academy of Sciences; Rhode Island Historical Society; Rhode Island Indian Council. Address: 12 Curry Avenue, Newport, Rhode Island, 02840-1412, USA. E-mail: moondancer_nuwc@hotmail.com

**O'BRIEN Keith Patrick**, b. 17 March 1938, Ballycastle, County Antrim, Northern Ireland. Cardinal in Catholic Church. Education: BSc, University of Edinburgh, 1955-59; St Andrew's College, Drygrange, Melrose, 1959-65; Dip Ed, Moray House College of Education, 1965-66. Appointments: Teacher and Chaplain, St Columba's Secondary School, Fife, 1966-71; Priest, St Patrick's Kilsyth, 1972-75; Priest, St Mary's, Bathgate, 1975-78; Spiritual Director, St Andrew's College, Drygrange, Melrose, 1978-80; Rector, Blairs College, Aberdeen, 1980-85; Archbishop of St Andrew's and Edinburgh, 1985-, Cardinal, 2003-. Honours: Cardinal in Catholic Church, 2003; Honorary LLD, University of St Francis Xavier, Antigonish, Nova Scotia, 2004; Honorary DD, University of St Andrew's, 2004; Honorary DD, University of Edinburgh, 2004. Address: 42 Greenhill Gardens, Edinburgh EH10 4BJ, Scotland.

**O'BRIEN Stephen**, b. 1 April 1957, East Africa. Member of Parliament. m. Gemma, 2 sons, 1 daughter. Education: MA (Hons) Law, Emmanuel College, Cambridge, 1976-79; Final Professional Examination, College of Law, Chester, 1979-80. Appointments: Solicitor, Senior Managing Solicitor, Freshfields Solicitors, City of London, 1981-88; Executive Assistant to the Board, 1988-89, Director of Corporate Planning, 1989-94, Director, International Operating Group, 1994-98, Deputy Chairman, Director, Redland Tile & Brick Ltd (Northern Ireland), 1995-98, Group Committee Member, 1990-98, Group Secretary and Director, Corporate Affairs, 1991-98, Redland PLC; International Business Consultant, 1998-; Member of Parliament for Eddisbury, South West Cheshire, 1999-; Parliamentary Private Secretary to the Chairman of the Conservative Party, 2000-2001; Opposition Whip (Front Bench), 2001-2002; Shadow Paymaster General, 2002-03; Shadow Secretary of State for Industry, 2003-05; Shadow Minister for Skills and Higher Education, 2005-. Memberships: CBI, Elected Member, South East Regional Council, 1995-98; Scottish Business in the Community, Council of Members, 1995-98; BMP Construction Products Association, 1995-99. Address: House of Commons, London SW1A 0AA, England. E-mail: obriens@parliament.uk

**O'CONNOR Sinead,** b. 8 December 1966, Dublin, Ireland. Singer. m. John Reynolds, divorced, 1 son, 1 daughter. Education: Dublin College of Music. Appointments: Band Member, Ton Ton Macoute, 1985-87. Creative Works: Singles include: Heroin, 1986; Mandinka, 1987; Jump in the River, 1988; Nothing Compares 2 U, 1990; Three Babies, 1990; You Do Something to Me, 1990; Silent Night, 1991; My Special Child, 1991; Visions of You (with Jan Wobble's Invaders of the Heart), 1992; Emperor's New Clothes, 1992; Secret Love, 1992; Success Has Made a Failure of Our Home, 1992; Albums include: The Lion and the Cobra, 1987; I Do Not Want What I Haven't Got, 1990; Am I Not Your Girl?, 1992; Universal Mother, 1994; Gospeloak, 1997; Sean-Nós Nua, 2002; Video films: Value of Ignorance, 1989; The Year of the Horse, 1991; TV film: Hush-a-Bye-Baby. Honours include: MTV Best Video, Best Single Awards, 1990; Grammy Award, Best Alternative Album, 1991. Address: c/o Principle Management, 30-32 Sir John Rogerson Quay, Dublin 2, Ireland.

**O'DONNELL Augustine Thomas (Gus),** b. 1 October 1952, London, England. Economist. m. Melanie, 1 daughter. Education: BA, First Class, Economics, University of Warwick, 1973; M Phil, Nuffield College Oxford, 1975. Appointments: Lecturer, Department of Political Economy, University of Glasgow, 1975-79; Economist, H M Treasury, 1979-85; First Secretary, British Embassy, Washington DC, USA, 1985-88; Senior Economic Advisor, H M Treasury, 1988-89; Press Secretary to the Chancellor of the Exchequer (Nigel Lawson then John Major), 1989-90; Press Secretary to the Prime Minister, 1990-94; Deputy Director, H M Treasury, UK Representative to the EU Monetary Committee, 1994-97; UK Executive Director to the International Monetary Fund and the World Bank, Minister (Economic), British Embassy, Washington DC, 1997-98; Head of the Government Economic Service with professional responsibility for 730 economists, 1998-2003; Director, 1998-99, Managing Director, 1999-2002, H M Treasury, Macroeconomic Policy and Prospects; Permanent Secretary to H M Treasury, 2002-. Publications: Adding It Up (PIU report), 2000; Reforming Britain's Economic and Financial Policy (co-editor), 2002; UK Policy Coordination: The Importance of Institutional Design, 2002; Microeconomic Reform in Britain (co-editor), 2004. Honours: Honorary Fellow, Nuffield College, Oxford; Honorary Degrees: Warwick University, Glasgow University. Memberships: Chairman, Treasury Gym Club; Member of World Economics International Advisory Board. Address: H M Treasury, 1 Horse Guards Road, London SW1A 2HQ, England.

**O'DONNELL Chris,** b. 1970, Winnetka, Illinois, USA. Actor. m. Caroline Fentress, 1997, 1 daughter. Creative Works: Films include: Men Don't Leave, 1990; Fried Green Tomatoes, 1991; Scent of a Woman, 1992; School Ties, 1992; The Three Musketeers, 1993; Blue Sky, 1994; Circle of Friends, 1995; Mad Love, 1995; Batman Forever, 1995; The Chamber, In Love and War, Batman and Robin, Cookie's Fortune, 1998; The Bachelor, 1998; Vertical Limit, 2000; 29 Palms, 2002; Kinsey, 2004. Address: c/o Kevin Huvane, CAA, 9830 Wilshire Boulevard, Beverly Hills, CA 90212, USA.

**O'DONOGHUE (James) Bernard,** b. 14 December 1945, Cullen, County Cork, Ireland. University Teacher of English; Poet. m. Heather MacKinnon, 23 July 1977, 1 son, 2 daughters. Education: MA in English, 1968, BPhil in Medieval English, 1971, Lincoln College, Oxford. Appointments: Lecturer and Tutor in English, Magdalen College, Oxford, 1971-95; Fellow and University Lecturer in English Wadham College, Oxford, 1995-. Publications: The Courtly Love Tradition, 1982; Razorblades and Pencils, 1984; Poaching Rights, 1987; The

Weakness, 1991; Seamus Heaney & the Language of Poetry, 1994; Gunpowder, 1995; Here Nor There, 1999; Outliving, 2003. Contributions to: Norton Anthology of Poetry; Poetry Ireland Review; Poetry Review; Times Literary Supplement. Honours: Southern Arts Literature Prize, 1991; Whitbread Poetry Award, 1995. Memberships: Poetry Society, London, 1984-; Fellow, Royal Society of Literature, 1999; Fellow, English Society, 1999; Association of University Teachers. Address: Wadham College, Oxford OX1 3PN, England.

**O'DONOGHUE Rodney (Rod) Charles,** b. 10 June 1938, Woodford , Essex, England. Retired Director; Historian; Writer. m. Kay Patricia Lewis, 2 sons, 1 daughter. Education: Merchant Taylor's School, 1951-56; Fellow of the Institute of Chartered Accountants. Appointments: Accounting Profession, 1956-63; To Finance and Administration Director, Kimberly-Clark Ltd, 1963-72; To Group Controller, Rank Xerox Group, 1963-72; Group Finance Director (Finance and IT), Pritchard Services Group plc, 1983-86; Main Board and Group Finance Director (Finance and IT), 1986-97, Main Board Director, 1997-1998, Inchcape plc; Retired 1998; Historian, Genealogist and Writer, Founder of The O'Donoghue Society, 1998-. Publications: The O'Donoghue Trail, 1990-95; O'Donoghue People and Places, 1999; Quarterly Journal for the O'Donoghue Society, 2000-; 2 books in progress. Memberships: Society of Genealogists; Irish Genealogical Research Society; Guild of One Name Studies; Highgate Golf Club; The National Trust; RSPB. Address: 30 Canonbury Park South, London N1 2FN, England. E-mail: rod@odonoghue.co.uk Website: www.odonoghue.co.uk

**O'FERRALL Patrick Charles Kenneth,** b. 27 May 1934, Wrecclesham, Surrey, England. Clerk in Holy Orders (Non-Stipendiary). m. (1) Mary Dorothea Lugard, deceased, 1 son, 2 daughters, (2) Wendy Elizabeth Barnett. Education: MA, New College, Oxford, 1954-58; Advanced Management Program, Harvard Business School, USA, 1983. Appointments: Various positions, Iraq Petroleum Group, 1958-70; BP Area Co-ordinator for Abu Dhabi Marine Areas Ltd and BP Eastern Agencies, 1971-73; Total CFP, Paris, 1974-77; Commercial Manager, 1977-82, Alwyn North Co-ordination Manager, 1983-85, Projects Co-ordination Manager, 1985-90, Total Oil Marine, London; Director, Total Oil Marine (Engineering Construction) Ltd, 1983-89; Deputy Chairman, 1991-93, Chairman, 1993-99, Lloyd's Register of Shipping; Member, Offshore Industry Advisory Board, 1991-94; Lay Reader, Church of England, 1961-2000; Ordained, Deacon, 2000, Priest, 2001; Curate, Saints Peter and Paul, Godalming, 2000-. Honours: Longstaff Exhibition, New College, Oxford; Fellow, Royal Society of Arts; Honorary Fellow, Royal Academy of Engineering; Companion, Chartered Management Institute. memberships: Past master, Worshipful Company of Coachmakers and Coach Harness Makers, 1993-94; Liveryman, Worshipful Company of Shipwrights; Member of Court of Common Council, City of London, 1996-2001; Chairman, City Branch Outward Bound Association, 1993-97; President Aldgate Ward Club, 1998, currently Honorary Chaplain; Retired Member of Baltic Exchange, currently Honorary Chaplain. Address: Catteshall Grange, Catteshall Road, Godalming, Surrey GU7 1LZ, England.

**O'HAGAN Antony Richard,** b. 3 October 1942, Nyeri, Kenya. Chartered Accountant. m. (1) Caroline Franklin, 1975, dissolved 1999, 1 son, 1 daughter, (2) Julia Sutherland, 2001. Education: Pembroke House School, Gil-Gil, Kenya; Wellington College, Crowthorne, Berkshire. Appointments: Articled Clerk, Senior, Supervisor, Manager, Coopers & Lybrand, Chartered Accountants, 1962-73; Group Accountant, Hays Wharf Group, 1973-76; Development Accountant, 1976-77, Group Financial

Accountant, 1977-82, Freemans Mail Order Group, London; Chief Accountant, St Martin's Property Corporation Ltd, 1982-86; Group Finance Director, St Martins Property Group, 1986-2001. Honours: Territorial Decoration, 1977; First Clasp to TD, 1983; Second Clasp to TD, 1989; Appointed Serving Brother, The Order of St John of Jerusalem, 2003. Memberships: Honourable Artillery Company, 1961-; Associate of the Institute of Chartered Accountants in England and Wales (ACA), 1969, Fellow (FCA), 1978; Liveryman, Foreign Warden, Fan Makers Company, London, 1982-; Lieutenant, Captain, Major, Territorial Army, 1961-91; Trustee, Chindits' Old Comrades Association, 1989-; Member, 1997, Member of London Council, 2000-, St John Ambulance, London District; Civilian Committee Chairman, London Wing, Air Training Corps, 1997-; Trustee, London Bridge Museum Trust, 1999-; Trustee, Vitalise, formerly Winged Fellowship Trust, 2003-; Deputy Lieutenant for the London Borough of Barking and Dagenham, 2004-. Address: 50 Dunbar Wharf, 124 Narrow Street, London E14 8BB, England. E-mail: arohagan@hotmail.com

**O'HALLORAN James**, b. 12 July 1932, Callan, County Kilkenny, Ireland. Priest; Educator. BA, London University, 1959; Post Graduate Diploma, Education, Oxford University, 1967; B Div, St Patrick's College, Maynooth, Ireland, 1979; MA, La Salle University, Philadelphia, USA, 1989. Appointments: Principal and Teacher, St Patrick's Primary and Secondary School, Malta, 1963-66, Salesian High School, Manzini, Swaziland, 1967-71; Curriculum Consultant, Amalgamated University of Botswana, Lesotho and Swaziland, Examining Board, 1967-71; Professor of English Literature and Education, Catholic University, Quito, Ecuador, 1972-78; Latin American Delegate, World Congress of Salesian Co-operators, 1976; Member, Ecuadorian Preparatory Team Puebla CELAM Conference, 1978; Visiting Lecturer, Theology: Kenya: Karen College, Nairobi, 1981; Kenyatta College, Nairobi, 1981, GABA Pastoral Centre, Eldoret, 1994-95, Tangaza Seminary, Nairobi, 1994; Sierra Leone: Kenema Pastoral Centre, 1981-91, Milton Margay College, Freetown, 1982; Fourah Bay University, 1982; England: Selly Oak Colleges, Birmingham University, 1982; Ushaw College, 1990; Ireland: Dundalk Catechetical Centre, 1982; Australia: Notre Dame University, Perth, 1992; Thailand: Tamkaenjam Buddhist Centre, 1992; South Africa: Ave Maria Pastoral Centre, Tzaneen, 1997-; Malawi: St John the Baptist Seminary, Mangochi, 2003; Lecturer, Theology, All Hallows College, Dublin, Ireland, 1993-; Milltown Institute, Dublin, Ireland, 1993-; Church of Ireland Theological College (Anglican), Dublin, 1996-; Kimmage Missionary Institute, Dublin, Ireland, 1980-81, 1997-98; Lecturer worldwide in Theology in parishes and missions, 1981-; Co-ordinator, Ecumenical European Team Third International Consult. Small (Basic) Christian Communities, Cochabamba, Bolivia, 1999; Animating Team, European Conference Small Christian Communities, Iona, Scotland, 1999. Principal publications: Living Cells, (theology) 1984; The Least of These (short stories), 1991; When the Acacia Bird Sings (novel), 1999; Remember José Inga (novel), 2003; Small Christian Communities, Vision and Practicalities (theology), 2003; The Brendan Book of Prayer, 2003; In Search of Christ: A Prayer Book for Seekers, 2004; Saving the Fish from Drowning: Reflections from the Barrio, forthcoming; Columnist, Irish Sunday Independent, 1984; Articles in professional journals. Honours: Swaziland Independence Medal, Government of Swaziland, 1969; Honorary Chieftanship, Sunyani, Ghana, 1982; Research Grant, Misereor, 1987-88; Listed in Who's Who publications and biographical dictionaries. Memberships: Irish Missionary Union; Conference of Religious of Ireland; Affiliated, National Council of Priests of Ireland. Address:

Salesian House, St Teresa's Rd, Crumlin, Dublin 12, Ireland. E-mail: ohallo@gofree.indigo.ie

**O'MEARA Mark**, b. 13 January 1957, Goldsboro, North Carolina, USA. Golfer. Education: Long Beach State University. Career: Professional Golfer, 1980-; Ryder Cup Team, 1985, 1989, 1991, 1997; Won US Amateur Championship, 1979, Greater Milwaukee Open, 1984, Bing Crosby Pro-American, 1985, Hawaii Open, 1985, Fuji Sankei Classic, 1985, Australian Masters, 1986, Lawrence Batley International, 1987, AT&T Pebble Beach National Pro-American, 1989, 1990, 1992, 1997, H-E-B TX Open, 1990, Walt Disney World/Oldsmobile Classic, 1991, Tokia Classic, 1992, Argentine Open, 1994, Honda Classic, 1995, Bell Canada Open, 1995, Mercedes Championships, 1996, Greater Greensboro Open, 1996, Brick Invitational, 1997, US Masters, 1998, British Open, 1998, World Matchplay 1998; Best Finish 2002, 2nd in Buick Invitational and 2nd in Buick Open. Honour: All-American Rookie of the Year, Long Beach State University, 1981; PGA Tour Player of the Year, 1998. Address: c/o PGA, Box 109601, Avenue of Champions, Palm Beach Gardens, FL 33410, USA.

**O'NEAL Ryan**, b. 20 April 1941, Los Angeles, USA. m. (1) Joanna Moore, divorced, 1 son, 1 daughter, (2) Leigh Taylor-Young, divorced, 1 son, 1 son with Farrah Fawcett. Career: Numerous TV appearances; Films include: The Big Bounce, 1969; Love Story, 1970; The Wild Rovers, 1971; What's Up, Doc? 1972; The Thief Who Came To Dinner, 1973; Paper Moon, 1973; Oliver's Story, 1978; The Main Event, 1979; So Fine, 1981; Partners, 1982; Irreconcilable Differences, 1983; Fever Pitch, 1985; Tough Guys Don't Dance, 1986; Chances Are, 1989; Faithful, 1996; Hacks, 1997; Burn Hollywood Burn, 1997; Zero Effect, 1998; Coming Soon, 1999; Epoch, 2000; People I Know, 2002; Malibu's Most Wanted, 2003.

**O'NEAL Shaquille Rashaun**, b. 6 March 1972, Newark, USA. Basketball Player. m. Shaunie Nelson, 2 children, 2 children from previous relationships. Education: Los Angeles University. Appointments: Center Orlando Magic, 1992-96; Los Angeles Lakers, 1996-. Creative Works: Films: Blue Chips, 1994; Kazaam, 1996; Music: has released five rap albums; Own record label, Twism. Memberships: National Basketball Association All-Star Team, 1993; Dream Team 11, 1994. Address: c/o Los Angeles Lakers; 3900 West Manchester Boulevard, Inglewood, CA 90306, USA.

**O'SULLEVAN Peter John (Sir)**, b. 3 March 1918. Racing Correspondent; Commentator. m. Patricia Duckworth, 1951. Education: Hawtreys, Charterhouse, College Alpin, Switzerland. Appointments: Chelsea Rescue Service, 1939-45; Editorial work and manuscript reading with Bodley Head Publisher; Racing Correspondent, Press Association, 1945-50, Daily Express, 1950-86, Today, 1986-87; Race Broadcaster, 1946-98; Chair, Osborne Studio Gallery, 1999-. Publication: Calling the Horses: A Racing Autobiography, 1989. Honours include: CBE; Derby Award, Racing Journalist of the Year, 1971, 1986; Racehorse Owner of the Year Award, Horserace Writers Association, 1974; Sport on TV Award, Daily Telegraph, 1994; Services to Racing Award, Daily Star, 1995; Media Awards Variety Club of Great Britain, 1995; Lester's Award, Jockeys' Association, 1996; Special Award, TV and Radio Industries Club, 1998. Address: 37 Cranmer Court, London SW3 3HW, England.

**O'SULLIVAN Maggie**, b. 20 July 1951, Lincoln, England. Poet. Publications: Concerning Spheres, 1982; An Incomplete Natural History, 1984; A Natural History in 3 Incomplete Parts, 1985; Un-Assuming Personas, 1985; Divisions of Labour, 1986; From the Handbook of That and Furriery, 1986; States of Emergency,

1987; Unofficial Word, 1988; In the House of the Shaman, 1993; Ellen's Lament, 1993; Excla (with Bruce Andrews), 1993; That Bread Should Be, 1996; Out of Everywhere (editor), 1996. Contributions to: City Limits; Reality Studios; Poetry Review; Slow Dancer; Writing Women; Angel Exhaust; Archeus; Palpi; Responses; Critical Quarterly; Inkblot; Writing; Sink; Raddle Moon; Ligne; Avec. Address: Middle Fold Farm, Colden, Hebden Bridge, West Yorkshire HX7 7PG, England.

**O'SULLIVAN Sonia,** b. 28 November 1969, Cobh, Ireland. Athlete. Education: Accounting Studies, Villanova, USA. Career: Gold Medal 1500m, Silver Medal 3000m, World Student Games, 1991; Holds 7 national (Irish) records; Set new world record (her first) in 2000m, TSB Challenge, Edinburgh, 1994, new European record in 3000m, TSB Games London, 1994; Gold Medal in 3000m European Athletic Championships, Helsinki, 1994; Winner, Grand Prix 3000m, 2nd overall, 1993; Silver Medal, 1500m World Championships, Stuttgart, 1993; Gold Medal, 5000m World Championships, Gothenburg, 1995; Gold Medal, World Cross Country Championships 4km, 8km, 1998; Gold Medal, European Championships 5000m, 10,000m, 1998; Silver Medal, 5,000m 2000 Olympic Games; Silver Medal, 5,000m, 10,000m European Championships, 2002. Publications: Running to Stand Still. Honours: Female Athlete of the Year, 1995; Texaco Sports Star of the Year (Athletics), 2002. Address: c/o Kim McDonald, 201 High Street, Hampton Hill, Middlesex TW12 1NL, England.

**O'TOOLE Peter Seamus,** b. 2 August 1932, Eire, Ireland. Actor. 1 son, 2 daughters. Education: RADA (Diploma), Associate, RADA. Career: Joined Bristol's Old Vic Theatre, played 73 parts, 1955-58; West End debut in Oh My Papa, 1957; Stratford Season, 1960; Stage appearances in, Pictures in the Hallway, 1962; Baal, 1963; Ride a Cock Horse, Waiting for Godot, 1971; Dead Eye Dicks, 1976; Present Laughter, 1978; Bristol Old Vic Theatre Season, 1973; Macbeth Old Vic, 1980; Man and Superman, 1982-83; Pygmalion, 1984, 1987; The Applecart, 1986; Jeffrey Barnard is Unwell, 1989, 1991, 1999; Films include: Kidnapped, 1959; The Day They Robbed the Bank of England, 1959; Lawrence of Arabia, 1960; Becket, 1963; Lord Jim, 1964; The Bible, 1966; What's New Pussycat?, 1965; Night of the Generals, 1967; Great Catherine, 1967; The Lion in Winter, 1968; Goodbye Mr Chips, 1969; Brotherly Love, 1970; Country Dance, 1970; Murphy's War, 1971; Under Milk Wood, 1972; The Ruling Class, 1972; Man of La Mancha, 1972; Rosebud, 1974; Man Friday, 1975; Foxtrot, 1975; Caligula, 1977; Power Play, 1978; Stuntman, 1978; Zulu Dawn, 1978; The Antagonists, 1981; My Favourite Year, 1981; Supergirl, 1984; Club Paradise, 1986; The Last Emperor, 1986; High Spirits, 1988; On a Moonlit Night, 1989; Creator, 1990; King Ralph, 1990; Wings of Fame, 1991; Rebecca's Daughters, 1992; Our Song, 1992; Civies, 1992; Fairytale: the True Story, 1997; Coming Home, 1998; The Manor, 1998; Molokai: The Story of Father Damien, 1999; Global Heresy, 2002; The Final Curtain, 2002; Bright Young Things, 2003; Troy, 2004. Publications: The Child, 1992; The Apprentice, 1996. Honours: Commander of the Order of Arts and Letters, France; Outstanding Achievement Award, 1999. Address: c/o William Morris Agency, Stratton House, Stratton Street, London, W1X 5FE, England.

**OAKES Philip,** b. 31 January 1928, Burslem, Staffordshire, England. Author; Poet. Appointments: Scriptwriter, Granada TV and BBC, London, 1958-62; Film Critic, The Sunday Telegraph, London, 1963-65; Assistant Editor, Sunday Times Magazine, 1965-67; Arts Columnist, Sunday Times, London, 1969-80; Columnist, Independent on Sunday, London, 1990, Guardian Weekend, London, 1991-. Publications: Unlucky Jonah: Twenty Poems, 1954; The Punch and Judy Man (with

Tony Hancock), screenplay, 1962; Exactly What We Want (novel), 1962; In the Affirmative (poems), 1968; The God Botherers, US edition as Miracles: Genuine Cases Contact Box 340 (novel), 1969; Married/Singular (poems), 1973; Experiment at Proto (novel), 1973; Tony Hancock: A Biography, 1975; The Entertainers (editor), 1975; A Cast of Thousands (novel), 1976; The Film Addict's Archive, 1977; From Middle England (memoirs), 1980; Dwellers All in Time and Space (memoirs), 1982; Selected Poems, 1982; At the Jazz Band Ball (memoirs); Shopping for Women (novel), 1994. Address: Fairfax Cottage, North Owersby, Lincolnshire LN8 3PX, England.

**OAKLEY Ann (Rosamund),** b. 17 January 1944, London, England. Professor of Sociology and Social Policy; Writer. 1 son, 2 daughters. Education: MA, Somerville College, Oxford, 1965; PhD, Bedford College, London, 1974. Appointments: Research Officer, Social Research Unit, Bedford College, London, 1974-79; Wellcome Research Fellow, Radcliffe Infirmary, National Perinatal Epidemiology Unit, Oxford, 1980-83; Deputy Director, Thomas Coram Research Unit, 1985-90; Director, Social Science Research Unit, 1990-, Professor of Sociology and Social Policy, 1991-, University of London. Publications: Sex, Gender and Society, 1972; The Sociology of Housework, 1974; Housewife, 1974, US edition as Women's Work: A History of the Housewife, 1975; The Rights and Wrongs of Women, 1976; Becoming a Mother, 1980; Women Confined, 1980; Subject Women, 1981; Miscarriage, 1984; Taking It Like a Woman, 1984; The Captured Womb: A History of the Medical Care of Pregnant Women, 1984; Telling the Truth about Jerusalem, 1986; What Is Feminism, 1986; The Men's Room, 1988; Only Angels Forget, 1990; Matilda's Mistake, 1990; Helpers in Childbirth: Midwifery Today, 1990; The Secret Lives of Eleanor Jenkinson, 1992; Social Support and Motherhood: The Natural History of a Research Project, 1992; Essays on Women, Medicine and Health, 1993; Scenes Originating in the Garden of Eden, 1993; Young People, Health and Family Life, 1994; The Politics of the Welfare State, 1994; Man and Wife, 1996; The Gift Relationship by Richard Titmuss, 1997; Who's Afraid of Feminism? 1997; Welfare Research: A critical review, 1998; Experiments in Knowing: Gender and Method in the Social Sciences, 2000; Welfare and Wellbeing: Richard Titmuss's contribution to social policy, 2001; Overheads, 2000; Gender on Planet Earth, 2002; Private Complaints and Public Health: Richard Titmus on the National Health Service, 2004; The Ann Oakly Reader: Gender, women and social science, 2005. Contributions to: Professional journals; Many chapters in academic books. Honours: Hon DLitt, Salford, 1995; Honorary Professor, University College, London, 1996-; Honorary Fellow, Somerville College, Oxford, 2001-. Address: c/o The Sayle Agency, 8B Kings Parade, Cambridge, CB2 1SJ, England.

**OAKLEY Peter,** b. 7 August 1935, Stafford, England. Artist; Educator. 4 sons, 5 daughters. Education: NDD, 1956; ATD, 1959; MA, 1987. Appointments: Artist, Designer, 1959; Head of Art, Beaumont Leys School, Leicester, 1959-67; Head of Art, Collegiate Girls School, Leicester, 1967-70; Senior Lecturer, Art and Design, Edge Hill College, Ormskirk, 1970-91; Set and costume designer, Andante Theatre Company and Vocal Chord Productions, 1991-93. Creative Works: Numerous exhibitions in London, Liverpool, Manchester, Stafford, Southport, Wigan, Belgium, Germany, Bristol, Accrington, Bury, Leigh, York. Honours: Listed in national and international biographical dictionaries. Memberships: Manchester Academy of Fine Arts, Vice President, 1990-93, President, 1993-97; Chairman, Warrington Visual Artists Forum. Address: Crab Lane House, Crab Lane, Cinnamon Brow, Warrington WA2 0WJ, England.

# DICTIONARY OF INTERNATIONAL BIOGRAPHY

**OAKLEY Robin Francis Leigh,** b. 20 August 1941, Kidderminster, Worcestershire, England. Journalist. m. Carolyn, 1 son, 1 daughter. Education: MA, Brasenose College, Oxford. Appointments: Liverpool Daily Post, 1964-70; Crossbencher Columnist and then Assistant Editor, Sunday Express, 1970-79; Assistant Editor, Now! Magazine, 1979-81; Assistant Editor, Daily Mail, 1981-86; Political Editor, The Times, 1986-92; Political Editor, BBC, 1992-2000; European Political Editor, CNN, 2000-; Turf Columnist, The Spectator, 1996-; Racing Correspondent, Financial Times, 2003-; Trustee, Thompson Foundation, 2001. Publications: Valley of the Racehorse – a portrait of the racing community of Lambourn, 2000; Inside Track – thirty years of political reporting, 2001. Honour: OBE, 2001. Membership: RAC. Address: 17 West Square, London SE11 4SN, England. E-mail: robin.oakley@cnn.com

**ODA Tarek Fathy,** b. 13 March 1965, Egypt. Assistant Professor of Mechanical Engineering. m. Wafaa Ahmed, 1 son, 1 daughter. Education: BSc, Mechanical Engineering, 1987, MSc Mechanical Engineering, 1994, PhD, 2000, Mechanical Engineering, Alexandria University, Egypt. Appointment: Assistant Professor, Mechanical Engineering, Mechanical Engineering Department, Higher Technological Institute, Egypt. Publications: Articles include: Secondary currents assessment for non-circular ducts; heater performance characteristics of direct gas fired heater; The use of exhaust gases for the absorption refrigeration cycles (a project in co-operation with the University of Florida, USA). Honours: Alexandria University Award, 1995; Alexandria University Award for Scientists, 2001. Address: 2 Mahmoud Maklad Street, Sidi Bishr, Alexandria, Egypt. E-mail: tarekrok@yahoo.com

**ODELL Robin Ian,** b. 19 December 1935, Totton, Hampshire, England. Writer. m. Joan Bartholomew, 19 September 1959. Publications: Jack the Ripper in Fact and Fiction, 1965; Exhumation of a Murder, 1975; Jack the Ripper: Summing-up and Verdict (with Colin Wilson), 1977; The Murderers' Who's Who (with J H H Gaute), 1979; Lady Killers, 1980; Murder Whatdunit, 1982; Murder Whereabouts, 1986; Dad Help Me Please (with Christopher Berry-Dee), 1990; A Question of Evidence, 1992; Lady Killer, 1992; The Long Drop, 1993; Landmarks in Twentieth Century Murder, 1995; The International Murderer's Who's Who, 1996. Contributions to: Crimes and Punishment; The Criminologist. Honours: FCC Watts Memorial Prize, 1957; International Humanist and Ethical Union, 1960; Edgar Award, Mystery Writers of America, 1980. Memberships: Our Society; Police History Society. Address: 11 Red House Drive, Sonning Common, Reading RG4 9NT, England.

**ODUARAN Akpovire Bovadjera,** b. 20 March 1955, Ughelli, Delta State, Nigeria. Professor of Adult Education. Education: B Ed (Honours), History, University of Benin, Benin City, Nigeria, 1978; MA, Adult Education, University of Ife (now Obafemi Awolowo University) Ile-Ife, Nigeria, 1983; PhD, Adult and Community Education, University of Ibadan, Nigeria, 1986; Certificate in Advanced Christian Leadership, Haggai Institute, Hawaii, USA, 1997. Appointments include: Graduate Assistant, 1981-83, Assistant Lecturer, 1983-85, Lecturer II, 1985-87, Lecturer I, 1987-90, Senior Lecturer, 1990-93, Professor of Adult and Community Education, 1993-97, University of Benin, Nigeria; Associate Professor of Adult Education, 1997-2000, Professor of Adult Education, 2000-, Head, Department of Adult Education, 2002-, University of Botswana, Gaborone, Botswana. Publications: Books as author: An Introduction to Community Development, 1994; Social Welfare and Social Work Education for Africa, 1996; The Essentials of Adult Learning, 1996; Effective Adult Learning and Teaching, 2000;

Literacy Programmes Development and Evaluation Process in Africa (co-author), 1995; 20 contributions to books and monographs; Over 40 articles in refereed journals; Numerous conference and seminar papers. Honours: Federal Government of Nigeria Scholar, 1980-88; Distinguished Alumnus Award, University of Benin; Professional Associate, The Continuum, Centre for Continuing Education, University of East London, UK, 2003; Listed in Who's Who publications and biographical dictionaries. Memberships: International Association for Community Development; Nigerian National Council for Adult Education; Nigerian Institute on Substance Abuse; Curriculum Organisation of Nigeria; Community Education and Research Society of Nigeria; Botswana Educational Research Association; International Consortium for Intergenerational Program (ICIP); Botswana Adult Education Association. Address: Department of Adult Education, University of Botswana, Gaborone, Botswana. E-mail: oduarana@mopipi.ub.bw

**OFFER Clifford Jocelyn,** b. 10 August 1943, Ightham, Kent, England. Clerk in Holy Orders. m. Catherine, 2 daughters. Education: St Peter's College, Oxford (sent down); BA, Exeter University; Westcott House, Cambridge. Appointments: Curate, Bromley Parish Church, 1969-74; Team Vicar, Southampton (City Centre), 1974-83; Team Rector of Hitchin, 1983-94; Archdeacon of Norwich and Canon; Librarian, Norwich Cathedral, 1994-. Publications: King Offa in Hitchin, 1992; In Search of Clofesho, 2002. Membership: FRSA. Address: 26 The Close, Norwich NR1 4DZ, England. E-mail: archdeacon. norwich@4frontmedia.co.uk

**OFUYA Thomas Inomisan,** b. 4 November 1954, Kano, Nigeria. Teacher; Researcher. m. Olayinka Oshinowo, 2 daughters. Education: BSc, Agriculture, 1976, PhD, Plant Science, Entomology, 1984, University of Ife, Nigeria. Appointments: Lecturer II, 1985 to Full Professor, 1999-, Federal University of Technology, Akure, Nigeria. Publications: Over 70 articles in peer-reviewed science journals; Editor, 1 book; Editor-in-chief, international journal, 1996-. Honours: Alexander Von Humboldt Research Fellowship, 1991; Royal Society London Research Fellowship, 1993; COSTED Research Fellowship, 1998; IFS/DANIDA Award, 1998. Memberships: Entomological Society of Nigeria; Science Association of Nigeria; Nigerian Society for Plant Protection. Address: Department of Crop, Soil and Pest Management, The Federal University of Technology, PMB 704, Akure, Nigeria. E-mail: tomofuya@yahoo.com

**OGG Wilson Reid,** b. 26 February 1928, Alhambra, California, USA. Social Scientist; Academician; Philosopher; Lawyer; Poet; Lyricist; Educator. Education: AA, 1947; AB, 1949; JD, University of California, 1952; Hon DD, University of Life Church, 1969; Doctorate, Religious Humanities, 1970. Appointments: Psychology Instructor, US Armed Forces Institute, Taegu, Korea, 1953-54; English Instructor, Taegu English Language Institute, 1954; Trustee Secretary, 1st Unitarian Church of Berkeley, 1957-58; Research Attorney, Continuing Education of the Bar, University of California, 1958-63; Vice President, International House Association, 1961-62; President, Board Chairman, California Society for Psychical Study, 1963-65; Private Law Practitioner, 1955-; Director, Admissions, International Society for Philosophical Enquiry, 1981-84. Publications: Poetry publications in numerous journals and anthologies; Author: The Unified Theory. Honours: Commendation Ribbon W Medal Pendant; Cultural Doctorate, World University; The International Peace Prize, United Cultural Convention, USA; Commemorative Medal, Medal of Science and Peace, 50th Anniversary of the Nobel Prize of Peace, 1953-2003. Memberships: American Mensa; Emeritus

Member, Faculty Club, University at Berkeley; The Triple Nine Society; International House Association; New York Academy of Sciences; London Diplomatic Academy; Scientific Faculty, Cambridge, England; Laureate, Top 100 Scientists for the Year, 2005; International Platform Association; San Francisco Bar Association; American Society of Composers, Authors and Publishers; American Bar Association; State Bar of California. Address: Pinebrook at Bret Harte Way, 1104 Keith Avenue, Berkeley, CA 94708, USA. E-mail: wilsonogg@alum.calberkeley.org; www.wilsonogg.com

**OGRAM Geoffrey Reginald,** b. 14 October 1937, Ealing, England. Retired College Principal Lecturer. m. Margaret Mary, 3 daughters. Education: BSc (Hons) Industrial Metallurgy, 1958, PhD, 1961, University of Birmingham. Appointments: Research Fellow, University of Birmingham, 1960-62; Research Metallurgist, GKN Group Research Centre, Wolverhampton, 1962-65; Lecturer, Senior Lecturer, Principal Lecturer in Metallurgy, Sandwell College, West Midlands, 1965-95. Publications: Articles in scientific journals: Effect of Alloying Additions in Steel, 1965; Directionality of Yield Point in Strainaged Steel, 1967; Magical Images – A Handbook of Stereo Photography (author's publication); The Music of Gordon Jacob (in preparation). Honours: MIMMM; C Eng. Memberships: British Magical Society, 1975, President, 1989-90; Magic Circle, 1978-; Catenian Association (Stafford Circle), President, 1980-85, 2001-2002, Provincial Councillor, 1985-91; Birmingham Japan Society, 1991-, Chairman, 1999-2001; Stereoscopic Society, 1997-; Governor St Anne's Roman Catholic Primary School, Stafford, 1997-; Organist, St Anne's Roman Catholic Church, Stafford, 1970-; Stafford Recorded Music Society, Secretary, 2004-. Address: 6 Silverthorn Way, Wildwood, Stafford ST17 4PZ, England. E-mail: geoff.ogram@virgin.net

**OGUCHI Takashi,** b. 13 March 1963, Matsumoto, Japan. Associate Professor. m. Chiaki, 1 son, 1 daughter. Education: BA, 1985, DSc, 1996, University of Tokyo, Japan. Appointments: Assistant Professor, Department of Geography, Faculty of Science, University of Tokyo, 1991-97; Visiting Scholar, Department of Hydrology and Water Resources, University of Arizona, USA, 1997; Visiting Scholar, Institute of Hydrology, UK, 1997-98; Associate Professor, Center for Spatial Information Science, University of Tokyo, 1998-; Member, Editorial Board, Catena, 1997-, Geomorphology, 1999-2002; Co-Editor-in-Chief, Geomorphology, 2003-; Member, International Advisory Board, Geographical Research, 2004-. Publications: Articles in scientific journals as author and first author include: River water quality in the Humber Catchment: An introduction using GIS-based mapping and analysis, 2000; Fluvial geomorphology and paleohydrology in Japan, 2001; Geomorphology and GIS in Japan: background and characteristics, 2001; An online database of Polish towns and historical landscapes using an Internet map server, 2002; Identification of an active fault in the Japanese Alps from DEM-based hill shading, 2003; Late Quaternary rapid talus dissection and debris-flow deposition on an alluvial fan in Syria, 2004. Honours: Excellent Paper Award for Young Geographers, Association of Japanese Geographers, 1995; A Leading Scientist of the World, Top 100 Scientists Pinnacle of Achievement Award, Salute to Greatness Award, IBC, 2005; Order of International Ambassadors, A Great Mind of the 21st Century, ABI, 2005. Memberships: Commission Member, International Geographical Union; Steering Committee Member: Association of Japanese Geographers, Japanese Geomorphological Union, GIS Association of Japan; Deputy Director General, IBC; Deputy Governor, ABI. Address: Centre for Spatial Information Science, University of Tokyo, 5-1-5 Kashiwanoha Kashiwa 277-8568, Japan. E-mail: oguchi@csis.u-tokyo.ac.jp

**OGUN Oluremi,** b. 10 October 1957, Owo Nigeria. Economics Educator. Education: BSc (Honours), Economics, 1981, MSc, Economics, 1983, PhD, Economics, 1990, University of Ibadan, Nigeria; ACIB, London, 1991. Publications: Several journal articles, 1 book. Honours: African Economic Research Consortium (AERC) Research Grant, 1992, 1994, 1996; Research Fellowship, 1994; Special Service Award, Institute for New Technology, UN University, Maastricht, 1992; Visiting Senior Economist, Financial Insitutions Training Centre, Lagos, 1994; Visiting Research Scholar, University of California at Santa Barbara, 1994-96; African Technology Policy Studies (ATPS) Research Grant, 1995; Listed in numerous biographical dictionaries. Memberships: Nigerian Economics Society, Life Member and Secretary Oyo State Chapter, 1993; AERC; ATPS; West African Economics Association; Chartered Institute of Bankers, London; Economic Development Association; Association of Third World Studies. Address: Department of Economics, University Ibadan, Nigeria.

**OGUNSANYA Elizabeth Adetokunbo,** b. 1 January 1948, Abeokuta, Ogun State, Nigeria. Teacher. m. Samuel Adewale Ogunsaya, 1 son, 1 daughter. Education: BA Ed, English, French, University of Ife (now Obafemi Awolowo University), 1972; M Ed, Guidance and Counselling/Psychology, Loyola University Chicago, Illinois, USA, 1979; PhD, Rehabilitation Counselling (Educational Studies), University College Cardiff, Wales, UK, 1988. Appointments include: English Teacher, Our Lady of the Apostles Secondary School, Ijebu-Ode, 1972-76; English Teacher, Community Secondary School, Ogamminana, 1976-77; Vice-Principal, Methodist Teachers Training College, Sagamu, 1980-81; Principal, Anglican Girl's Grammar School, Ijebu-Ode, 1981-85; Principal, Moslem Comprehensive High School, Impepe, Ijebu-Ode, 1989-95; Visiting Lecturer, 1997, Lecturer, 2002-, Faculty of Education, Olabisi Onanbanjo University, Ago-Iwoye, Nigeria. Publications: Books: Death in the Family, 1993; Total Youth, 1993; Knowledge is Power, 1993; English without Stress: Learning about Words and Sentences, 2002; Rehabilitating the Counsellor, 2002; Monograph: The Challenges and Blessings of Education: The Power for Effective Living, 2000; Numerous contributions to books, articles in professional journals and papers presented at workshops and conferences. Honours include: British Award for the best teacher at the University of Ife, 1972; Federal Scholarship, 1979; Hero of Adolescent Lovers Award, Counselling Association of Nigeria, 2001; Gold Award for meritorious sevice as Principal at Anglican Girl's Grammar School, Ijebu-Ode, 2004. Memberships: Girl Guides of Nigeria; Mothers' Union; Obanta Special Marshal Unit 104 Zone RS4; Counselling Association of Nigeria; State Population Education Committee. Address: Faculty of Education, Olabisi Onanbanjo University, Ago-Iwoye, Nigeria.

**OGUNSHAKIN Alex Abimola,** b. 2 February 1956, Omdo, Nigeria. Chartered Marketer. m. Joy Ogechi, 1 son, 1 daughter. Education: Diploma in Mass Communication, School of Journalism and TV, Frilsham Hermitage, Berkshire, England, 1976; Diploma in Commerce, Institute of Commerce, London, 1979; HND, Business Studies, Management Services Division, West Bromwich College of Commerce and Technology, England, 1977-80; Diploma in Marketing, Chartered Institute of Marketing, London, 1980. Appointments: Assistant Lecturer and Lecturer III, Marketing, Federal Polytechnic, Bida, Niger State, Nigeria, 1981-85; Merchandiser, Domino Stores Ltd, Yaba, Nigeria, 1985-87; Group Manager, Merchandising, UTC Stores, Lagos, Nigeria, 1987-90; Sales and Marketing Manger, John Holt PLC, Shipping Services Division, Nigeria, 1990-92; Cargo Sales Manger then National Cargo Sales Manager, United Parcel Services, Cargo Logistics Division, 1993-98;

Commercial Consultant, Folabim Commercial Services, Ikeja, Lagos, Nigeria, 1999-; Marketing Consultant, Bakafaj International (Freight) Ltd, 1998-2001; General Manager, Logistics, TNT Logistics Division, 2001-2002; National Sales and Marketing Manger, Bemil Nig Ltd, Lagos, 2003; General Manager, Alarm Centre Ltd, 2003; Executive Director, Grand Security Nigeria Ltd, 2003-. Publications: Concorde Plane Effect of British Aviation Industry, 1979; Sales Promotion - An Effective Marketing Tool, 1980. Honour: Presidential Merit Award, National Institute of Marketing, Nigeria, 2004. Memberships: Member, Chartered Institute of Marketing, UK; Fellow, British Society of Commerce; Member Institute of Commercial Management, UK; Fellow and Council Member, National Institute of Marketing of Nigeria. Address: PO Box 15056, Ikeja, Lagos, Nigeria.

**OGUTI Takasi,** b. 31 March 1930, Nagano-ken Japan. Professor. m. Yoko, 1 son, 1 daughter. Education: BS, Graduate, University of Tokyo, 1953; Doctor of Science, 1962. Appointments: Professor, Geophysics, University of Tokyo, 1970; Director, Geophysics Research Laboratory, University of Tokyo, 1985; Director, Solar Terrestrial Environment Laboratory, Nagoya University, 1989-. Publication: Metamorphoses of Aurora. Honours: Tanakadate Prize, 1962; Hasegawa Prize, 1993. Memberships: Society of Geomagnetism and Earth Planetary and Space Sciences. Address: Shakujiicho 7-33-9, Nerimaku, Tokyo 177-0041, Japan.

**OH Myuongho,** b. 11 December 1960, Pusan, Korea. Professor. m. Kyungyoon Shim, 1 son, 1 daughter. Education: BS, Korea Military Academy, 1984; MS, Oregon State University, 1988; PhD, Korea Advanced Institute of Science and Technology, 1996. Appointments: Lieutenant Colonel, Korea Army; Associate Professor, Korea Military Academy; Assistant Manager of Academic Board, 1990-91, Assistant Director of Computer Centre, 1997-99, Chairman of Department of Computer Science, 2000-2004, Korea Military Academy. Publications: Many articles to professional journals; Introduction to Computer Science; Improvement of Computer Efficiency; Differential Equations; Computer Network; C Language; Practical Use of Computers. Honours: Best Achievement Professor, Korea Military Academy, 2002, 2003; True Soldier of the Year 2003, Korea Army; Universal Award of Accomplishment, ABI, 2005. Memberships: Korea Information Society; Korea Mathematical Society; Korea Institute of Military Science and Technology. Address: Department of Computer Science, Korea Military Academy, Gong-Nung Dong, No-Won Gu, Seoul, Republic of Korea 139-799. E-mail: mhoh@kma.ac.kr

**OHASHI Tetsuya,** b. 21 August 1951, Sapporo, Japan. Materials Scientist. m. Yoshie Yokouchi, 26 March 1977. Education: BS, 1974, MS, 1976, PhD, 1981, Hokkaido University. Appointments: Researcher, 1982, Senior Researcher, 1991, Hitachi Research Laboratory, Hitachi Ltd; Research Fellow, National Research Institute of Metals, 1997; Professor, Kitami Institute of Technology, 1999-. Publications: Numerical Modeling of Plastic Multislip in Metal Crystals of FCC Type, 1994; Finite Element Analysis of Plastic Slip and Evolution of the Geometrically Necessary Dislocations, 1997. Memberships: Japan Society of Mechanical Engineering; Japan Institute of Metals; Materials Research Society; American Association for the Advancement of Science. Address: 3-367-1 Tanno, Tokoro, 099-2103, Japan.

**OHHIRA Iichiroh,** b. 6 February 1936, Osaka, Japan. Researcher. m. Masumi Ohhira. Education: Bachelor's Degree, Agriculture, 1960, Master's Degree, Agriculture, 1973, Doctorate, Natural Science, 1990, Okayama University, Japan;

Doctorate of Science in Health Science, Adam Smith University, USA, 2000; Doctorate in Veterinary Medical Science, Azabu University, Japan, 2000. Appointments: Securities Dealer, Ohi Securities Corporation, Okayama, 1960-71; Representative Director, Ohhira Gardens and Parks Design Office, Okayama, 1973-85; Representative Director, Ohhira Plant Pathology Research Centre, Okayama, 1973-85; Representative Director, Bio Activity Research and Development Centre, Okayama, 1974-2000; Founder, BIOBANK CO LTD, Okayama, 2000-; Researcher, Graduate School of Natural Science and Technology, Okayama University; Technical Adviser, Agriculture and Environmental Issues, Chengdu, Suchuan, China; Lecturer Chugoku Junior College, Okayama; Professor, Kangnung National University, Korea; Professor, Pusan Fisheries College, Korea. Publications: Articles in scientific journals include most recently: The Influences of Lactic Acid Bacteria (OM-X) on Bone Structure, 1999; Purification of Anti-Escherichia coli O-157 Components Produced by Enterococcus faecalis TH10, an Isolate from Malaysian Fermented Food, Tempeh, 2000; Antifungal Activity of the Fermentation Product of Herbs by Lactic Acid Bacteria against Tinea, 2002. Honours include: Okayama Nichinichi Newspaper Prize, 1981; Japanese Dairy Science Association Prize, 1991; Presidential Citation, Philippine Medical Association, 2002; Presidential Citation, International College of Surgeons, Philippine Section, 2004; Gusi Peace Prize, Philippines, 2004; Discovery of Enterococcus faecalis TH10, highly active and useful lactic acid bacterium, isolated and identified from Tempeh, a fermented food in Southeast Asia. Memberships include: American Association for the Advancement of Science; New York Academy of Sciences; American Society for Microbiology; Japanese Health Food & Nutrition Food Association; Japanese Dairy Science Association; Japanese Society for Bacteriology; The Japanese Society for Virology. Address: BIOBANK CO LTD, 601 Park Square SHOWA 1-7-15, Omote-cho, Okayama, 700-0822 Japan. E-mail: biobank@omx.co.jp

**OHKUCHI Akihide,** b. 12 December 1962, Himi City, Toyama, Japan. Obstetrician. m. Satomi, 1 daughter. Education: PhD, Jichi Medical School, Dr Ohkuchi, 2001. Publications: Over 20 articles in his field. Honours: International Scientist of the Year, IBC, 2003; Universal Award of Accomplishment, ABI, 2004; Lifetime Achievement Award; Da Vinci Diamond; Listed in national and international biographical records. Memberships: Japan Society of Obstetrics and Gynaecology; Japan Society of Perinatal and Neonatal Medicine; Japan Society for the Study of Toxaemia of Pregnancy; International Society of Ultrasound in Obstetrics and Gynaecology. Address: Department of Obstetrics & Gynaecology, Jichi Medical School, 3311-1 Yakushiji, Minamikawachi-machi, Tochigi, Japan 329-0498.

**OHLSSON Bertil Gullith,** b 24 July 1954, Malmö, Sweden. Scientist. Education: BS, Biology and Chemistry, 1979, PhD 1987, University of Lund, Sweden; Postdoctoral Fellow, Rockefeller University, New York, New York, 1987-90. Appointments: Assistant Professor, Department of Molecular Biology, Göteborg University, Sweden, 1991-92; Associate Professor, 1993-96, Research Associate, 1997-2004, Associate Professor, 2004-, Wallenberg Laboratory, Sahlgren's University Hospital, Göteborg, Sweden. Publication: Article in Journal of Clinical Investigation, 1996. Membership: Swedish Society of Medicine. Address: Wallenberg Laboratory, Sahlgren's University Hospital, SE-41345 Göteborg, Sweden. E-mail: bertil.olsson@wlab.gu.se

**OJHA Ek Raj,** b. 23 September 1957, Mauwa, Dotee, Nepal. Education: BSc, Agriculture, University of Agricultural Sciences,

1984; BA, English, Tribhuvan University, 1985; MSc, 1990, PhD, 1995, Rural and Regional Development Planning, Asian Institute of Technology. Appointments: Assistant Agriculture Officer, Department of Agriculture, Kathmandu, 1985-86; Agriculture Officer, Nepal Rastra Bank, Kathmandu, 1986-90; Research Associate, Asian Institute of Technology, 1991-95; United Nations Researcher, United Nations Centre for Regional Development, 1995-97; Senior Instructor, Banker's Training Centre, 1998-2000, Research Officer, Research Department, 2000, Central Bank of Nepal; Development Economist, United States Agency for International Development (USAID), Kathmandu, 2000; Visiting Scholar, Indiana University, USA, 2001; Associate Professor (and Associate Director, Human and Natural Resources Studies Centre), Kathmandu University, 2000-02; Faculty Member (rural development), Tribhuvan University, 2003-; Contract Faculty (human dimensions of development), Kathmandu University, 2004; Resource Person/Faculty Member (economic development), Kathmandu College of Management, 2004. Publications: Co-author: 1 monograph; 1 working paper; 3 institutional reports; Author: 4 books; Numerous articles in professional journals. Memberships: World Futures Studies Federation; Aaroyga Aashram; Pakistan Futuristics Foundation and Institute; Kirateshwar Sangeetashram. Address: GPO Box 13313, Kathmandu, Nepal. E-mail: ero@wlink.com.np

**OKAZAKI Motoaki,** b. 17 July 1937, Tokyo, Japan. Researcher. m. Keiko Yamaguchi, 3 daughters. Education: BS, Keio University, 1961. Appointments: Staff, Yokoyama-Kogyo Kanagawa-ken, 1961-63; Senior Engineer, Japan Atomic Energy Research Institute, Tokai-mura, Japan, 1963-97. Publications: Development of Two-Phase Flow Analysis Code by 2V2T Model, Derivation of Basic Equations, 1986; Analysis of Density Wave Instability in a Boiling Flow Using a Characteristic Method, 1994. Honours: Listed in several biographical publications. Memberships: Fellow, Japan Society of Mechanical Engineers. Address: 29-10 Ichigaya Sanai-cho, Shinjuku-ku, Tokyo, F162-0846, Japan.

**OKAZAWA Hidehiko,** b. 18 October 1961, Nagano, Japan. Radiologist; Nuclear Medicine Specialist. m. Chiseko, 1 son, 2 daughters. Education: MD, 1988, Faculty of Medicine, PhD, 1996, Graduate School of Medicine, Kyoto University. Appointments: Resident, Kyoto University Hospital, 1988-89; Radiologist, Shiga Medical Centre, Moriyama, Japan, 1989-92; Postdoctoral Fellow, Brain Imaging Centre, Montreal Neurological Institute, Canada, 1996-98; Medical Imaging Researcher, Shiga Medical Centre, 1999-2002; Associate Professor, University of Fukui, 2003-. Publications: Co-author of articles in professional medical journals including: Journal of Cerebral Blood Flow and Metabolism; Journal of Nuclear Medicine; Journal of Neurochemistry; Brain. Honour: 40th Annual Award, Japanese Society of Nuclear Medicine. Memberships: Society of Nuclear Medicine; International Society for Cerebral Blood Flow and Metabolism; European Association of Nuclear Medicine; Japanese Society of Nuclear Medicine; Japan Radiological Society. Address: Biomedical Imaging Research Centre, University of Fukui, 23-3 Shimaizuki, Matsuoka-cho, Fukui, 910-1193, Japan. E-mail: okazawa@fms rsa.fukui.med.ac.jp

**OKEN Robert J,** b. 15 October 1929, New York, USA. Neuroscientist; Researcher; Consultant. Divorced. Education: BA, 1949, PhD, 1958, New York University. Appointments: Vice President, Director, Oken Fabrics Inc, 1959-68, 1971-73; Researcher, Consultant, US Army and Navy, 1955-56; Researcher, Consultant, Teller Environmental Systems, 1969-70; Scientific Advisor, Lifer Environmental Group, 1984-87; Businessman, R A Siegel Galleries, New York, 1978-87;

Volunteer, Dover Medical Center, 1989-90; Researcher and Consultant, to Director, New York State Institute for Basic Research, 1991-93; Researcher, Consultant, Gerex Biotech Inc, 1994-98; Neuroscience Research, 1998-. Publications: Research papers in numerous medical journals and reviews. Honours: Phi Beta Kappa; Achievement Award, Dover Medical Center; Listed in several biographical dictionaries. Memberships: New York Academy of Sciences; New York Neuropsychology Group; American Chemical Society; American Association for Advancement of Science; MENSA; INTERTEL. Address: PO Box 412, Hopatcong, NJ 07843, USA. E-mail: robertjoken@nac.net.

**OKOKO Enobon Etim,** b. 11 May 1962, Ikot Eyo, Akwa Ibom State, Nigeria. Town Planner. m. Peace Okoko, 3 sons, 1 daughter. Education: Bachelor of Science, First Class Honours, University of Maiduguri, Nigeria, 1984; Master of Urban and Regional Planning, University of Ibadan, Nigeria, 1987; PhD, Federal University of Technology, Akure, Nigeria, 2002. Appointments: Lecturer, Town and Regional Planning Department, Federal Polytechnic, Nasarawa, Nigeria, 1988-91; Senior Lecturer, Urban and Regional Planning Department, Federal University of Technology, Akure, Nigeria, 1991-. Publications: Book: Quantitative Techniques in Urban Analysis, 2001; 3 book chapters; Over 20 articles in learned journals. Honours: Principal's Prize for Best Student of the Year in WASCE Examination, 1978; Dean's Prize for Best Student of the Year, Faculty of Social and Management Sciences, University of Maiduguri, 1984; Listed in Who's Who publications and biographical dictionaries. Memberships: Associate Member, Royal Geographical Society, London; Member, Society for Environment Management and Planning; Corporate Member, Nigerian Institute of Town Planners; Member, International Geographical Union, Commission on Modelling Geographical Systems (United Kingdom); Registered Town Planner, 2000. Address: Department of Urban and Regional Planning, School of Environmental Technology, Federal University of Technology, PMB 704, Akure, Ondo State, Nigeria. E-mail: enookoko@yahoo.com

**OKRI Ben,** b. 15 March 1959, Minna, Nigeria. British Author; Poet. Education: Urhobo College, Warri, Nigeria; University of Essex, Colchester. Appointments: Broadcaster and Presenter, BBC, 1983-85; Poetry Editor, West Africa, 1983-86; Fellow Commoner in Creative Arts, Trinity College, Cambridge, 1991-93. Publications: Flowers and Shadows, 1980; The Landscapes Within, 1982; Incidents at the Shrine, 1986; Stars of the New Curfew, 1988; The Famished Road, 1991; An African Elegy, 1992; Songs of Enchantment, 1993; Astonishing the Gods, 1995; Birds of Heaven, 1995; Dangerous Love, 1996; A Way of Being Free, 1997; Infinite Riches, 1998; Mental Fight, 1999; In Exilus (play), 2001. Contributions to: Many newspapers and journals. Honours: Commonwealth Prize for Africa, 1987; Paris Review/ Aga Khan Prize for Fiction, 1987; Booker Prize, 1991; Premio Letterario Internazionale Chianti-Ruffino-Antico-Fattore, 1993; Premio Grinzane Cavour, 1994; Crystal Award, 1995; Honorary DLitt, Westminster, 1997, Essex, 2002; Premio Palmi, 2000. Memberships: Society of Authors; Royal Society of Literature; Vice-president, English Centre, International PEN, 1997-; Board, Royal National Theatre of Great Britain, 1999-. Address: c/o Vintage, Random House, 20 Vauxhall Bridge Road, London SW1 2SA, England.

**OKUMURA Yoshihiro,** b. 17 August 1961, Usa City, Oita, Japan. Radiology; Nuclear Medicine. Education: Diploma in Medicine, University of Occupational and Environmental Health, Kitakyushu City, Japan, 1989; PhD, Okayama University School of Medicine, 2000. Appointments: Resident, Internal Medicine,

II, University of Occupational and Environmental Health, Japan, 1989-90; Resident, Internal Medicine, Toshiba Hospital, Shinagawa-ku, Japan, 1990-91; Staff Physician, Clinic of Toshiba Himeji, Japan, 1991-99; Researcher, 1992-99, Clinical Fellow, 2000-02, Assistant, 2003-04, Department of Radiology, Okayama University School of Medicine; Chairman, PET/RI Centre, Okayama Kyokuto Hospital, Japan, 2004-. Publications: Articles include research in comparison of diagnostic capabilities of Tl-201 Scintigraphy and fine-needle aspiration biopsy of thyroid nodules, 1999; Quantitative evaluation by Tl-201 Scintigraphy in the diagnosis of thyroid follicular nodules, 2003; The usefulness of serum thyroglobulin levels and Tl-201 Scintigraphy in differentiating between benign and malignant thyroid follicular lesions, 2002. Honours: Listed in national and international biographical dictionaries. Memberships: Japan College of Radiology; Japan Society of Nuclear Medicine; Society of Nuclear Medicine; The Radiological Society of North America. Address: Okayama City, Okayam Province, 800-0921, Japan. E-mail: yokumura@kyokuto.or.jp

**OLAIYA Samuel Ayodele,** b. 8 August 1938, Ode-Ekiti, Nigeria. Researcher. m. Adefunke Olaiya, 4 sons, 2 daughters. Education: MSc, Industrial Planning, 1969, PhD, Economics, 1972, Kiev Institute of National Planning, USSR; Certificate in Industrial Training, North East London Polytechnic, England 1979; Certificate in Management and Training, Leeds, England, 1991. Appointments: Director (Training), Industrial Training Fund, Nigeria; Director, Special Duties, The Presidency, Nigeria; Currently, Senior Lecturer, University of Ado-Ekiti, Nigeria. Publications: Training for Industrial Development in Nigeria; Prerequisites for a Profitable Business. Honours: Citation, Department of Industrial Organisation, Kiev Institute of National Planning, 1972; Citation for Good Service Award, Industrial Training Fund, Nigeria; Award as Effective Manager of the Year, 1990/91, University of Jos, Nigeria. Memberships: Nigerian Institute of Management; Nigerian Economic Society; Nigerian Institute for Training and Development. Address: Department of Economics, University of Ado-Ekiti, PMB 5363, Ado-Ekiti State, Nigeria.

**OLARU Radu,** b. 12 February 1949, Botosani, Romania. Electrical Engineer. m. 26 July 1978, 2 sons. Education: University degree, Faculty of Electrical Engineering, 1972, PhD, 1994, Technical University, Iasi. Appointments: Engineer in industry, Suceava, 1972-74; Engineer, Scientific Researcher, Institute of Research and Development of Technical Physics, Iasi, 1974-79; Assistant Professor, 1979-87, Lecturer, 1987-95, Associate Professor, 1995-99, Professor, 1999-, Technical University, Iasi. Publications: 3 books, 1997, 2003, 2004; 8 papers in world's leading journals; 60 papers published in Romania and abroad; 19 patents. Honours: 2 Silver Medals, International Exhibition of Inventions, Iasi, 1992, 1996; Biographical listing in several who's who publications. Memberships: Romanian Association of Measurements, 1990-94; Fellow, Faculty of Electrical Engineering Council, 1996-2000. Address: Technical University of Jasi, Faculty of Electrical Engineering, 53 Mangeron Blvd, 6600 Jasi, Romania.

**OLAZABAL Jose Maria,** b. 5 February 1966, Spain. Professional Golfer. Career: Member, European Ryder Cup team, 1987, 1989, 1991, 1993, 1997, Kirin Cup Team, 1987, Four Tours World Championship Team, 1989, 1990, World Cup Team, 1989, Dunhill Cup Team, 1986, 1987, 1988, 1989, 1992; Winner, Italian Amateur Award, 1983, Spanish Amateur Award, 1983, European Masters-Swiss Open, 1986, Belgian Open, 1988, German Masters, 1988, Tenerife Open, 1989, Dutch Open, 1989, Benson & Hedges International, 1990, Irish Open, 1990, Lancome Trophy, 1990, Visa Talhoyo Club Masters,

1990, California Open, 1991, Turespana Open de Tenerife, 1992, Open Mediterrania, 1992, US Masters, 1994, 1999, Dubai Desert Classic, 1998; Benson & Hedges International Open 2000, French Open, 2001, Buick Invitational, 2002; Tour victories include: NEC World Series of Golf, 1990; The International, 1991; US Masters, 1994, 1999; Dubai Desert Classic, 1998; Golf course designer. Address: PGA Avenue of Champions, Palm Beach Gdns, FL 33418, USA. Website: www.aboutgolf.com/jmo

**OLDFIELD Bruce,** b. 14 July 1950, England. Fashion Designer. Education: Sheffield City Polytechnic; Ravensbourne College of Art; St Martin's College of Art. Appointments: Founder, Fashion House, Producing Designer Collections, 1975; Couture Clothes for Individual Clients, 1981; Opened Retail Shop, Couture & Ready-to-Wear, 1984; Managing Board, British Knitting & Clothing Export Council, 1989; Designed for films, Jackpot, 1974, The Sentinel, 1976; Vice-President, Barnardo's, 1998; Govenor, London Institute, 1999-; Trustee, Royal Academy, 2000-. Publication: Seasons, 1987. Exhibition: Retrospective, Laing Galleries, Newcastle-upon-Tyne, 2000. Honours: Fellow, Sheffield Polytechnic, 1987, Royal College of Art, 1990, Durham University, 1991; Hon DCL (Northumbria), 2001. Address: 27 Beauchamp Place, London SW3, England.

**OLISA Kenneth Aphunezi,** b. 13 October 1951. Businessman. m. Julia Olisa, 2 daughters. Education: IBM Scholarship, Master of Arts, Natural, Social and Political and Management Sciences, Fitzwilliam College, Cambridge, 1971-74. Appointments include: Systems Engineer, GSD Large Account Salesman, Series /1 Salesman, Series/1 Product Marketing Manager, IBM (UK) Ltd, 1974-81; Manager, Director, UK Product Marketing; District Sales Manager, London City and South East, Director of Marketing, Europe, Africa and Middle East, Vice-President, US Marketing, Vice-President, World-Wide Marketing, Vice-President, Application Engineering (R&D), Président, Directeur Général, Wang France SA, Managing Director, Wang(UK), Senior Vice-President and General Manager, Europe Africa and Middle East, Wang Laboratories Inc, 1981-92; Director: Restoration Ltd (aka Interregnum Ltd), 1992-, Open Text Corporation, Canada, 1998-, Interregnum Investment Partners Ltd, 2000-, Adaptive Inc (US Based), 2002-, Yospace Technologies Ltd, 2003-, Interregnum Advisory Partners, 2003-, Biowisdom, 2004-; Chairman: Metapraxis Ltd, 1993-, Thames Reach Broadway, 1994-; Interregnum plc,2000, Managing Director, Fitzwilliam Society Trust Ltd, 1994-; Governor, Peabody Trust, 1998-; Commissioner, Postal Service Commission, 2000-. Honour: BVCA/Real Deals Private Equity Personality of the Year Award, 2003. Memberships: Freeman, City of London; Fellow, Royal Society of the Arts; Liveryman, Worshipful Company of Information Technologists. Address: Interregnum plc, 22-23 Old Burlington Street, London W19 2JJ, England. E-mail: ken.olisa@interregnum.com

**OLIVEIRA Carlos A,** b. 1 December 1942, Barras-Piauí, Brazil. Medical Doctor. Widowed, 3 daughters. Education: MD, Faculdade Nacional de Medicina, Rio de Janeiro, 1966; Specialist in Otolanyngology, American Board of Otolaryngology, Chicago Illinois, 1979; Doctor of Philosophy, Otolaryngology, University of Minnesota Graduate School, Minneapolis, Minnesota, USA, 1977; Postdoctoral Fellowship, Harvard Medical School, Boston, Massachusetts, USA, 1989. Appointments: Associate Professor, 1977-97, Professor and Chairman, Department of Otolanryngology, 1997-, Brasilia University Medical School, Brasilia, Brazil. Publications: 82 scientific articles published in Brazil, 14 scientific articles in international journals including, Annals of Otology, Rhinology & Laryngology; Archives of Otolaryngology; Laryngoscope;

International Tinnitus Journals. Honours: Physician Recognition Award, American Medical Association, 1977; International Scientist of the Year, IBC. Memberships: Prosper Menière Society; Schuknecht Society, Boston, Massachusetts, USA; Neuroquilibriumetric Society, Bad Kinssingen, Germany; Brazilian Otolaryngology Society; American Otological Society. Address: Avda W-3 Sul Quadra 716, Bloco E, Sala 202, Brasilia DF, Brazil. E-mail: oliv@abordo.com.br

**OLIVER (James) Michael (Yorrick)**, b. 13 July 1940, Worthing, England. Director; Chairman. m. Sally, 2 daughters. Education: Brunswick School; Wellington College. Appointments: Partner, Director, Kitcat & Aitken & Co, 1970-90; Managing Director, Carr Kitcat & Aitken, 1990-93; Director, 1994, 1996, Director of Investment Funds, 1996-2001, Scottish Widows Investment Partnership Ltd; Numerous directorships and trusteeships. Honours: LLD (Hon), University of East London, 1999; DLitt (Hon), City University, 2001; Knight of St John, 2001; Knight Bachelor, 2003. Memberships: Alderman, The City of London, 1987-; Justice of the Peace, City of London Bench, 1987-; Deputy Lieutenant of Cambridgeshire, 2004-; Chairman, St John Ambulance, City of London Centre, 1994-; Trustee, Museum of London, 2003-; Joint Chairman, Museum in Docklands, 2003-. Address: Paradise Barns, Bucks Lane, Little Eversden, Cambridge CB3 7HL, England.

**OLIVER John**, b. 14 April 1935, London, England. Retired Bishop. m. Meriel, 2 sons, 1 daughter (deceased). Education: Gonville and Caius College, Cambridge, 1956-59; Westcott House, Cambridge, 1959-60, 1964. Appointments: Curate in the Hilborough Group of parishes, 1964-68; Chaplain of Eton College, 1968-72; Team Rector of South Molton, 1973-82; Team Rector of Central Exeter, 1982-85; Archdeacon of Sherborne, 1985-90; Bishop of Hereford, 1990-2003; Member of the House of Lords, 1997-2003. Publications: The Church and Social Order, 1968; Contributor to: The Crisis in the Countryside (editor Leslie Francis), 2004; Contributions to: Theology; Crucible and occasional journalism. Address: The Old Vicarage, Glascwm, Powys LD1 5SE, Wales.

**OLLERENSHAW Kathleen Mary (Dame)**, b. 1 October 1912, Manchester, England. Mathematician. m. Robert G W Ollerenshaw, deceased, 1 son, 1 daughter both deceased. Education: Open Scholarship, Mathematics, Somerville College, Oxford, 1931-34; Oxford D Phil, Mathematics, 1945. Appointments: Chairman: Association of Governing Bodies of Girls' Public Schools, 1963-69, Manchester Education Committee, 1967-70, Manchester Polytechnic, 1968-72; Elected to Manchester City Council, 1956-81: Alderman, 1970-74, Lord Mayor, 1975-76, Deputy Lord Mayer, 1976-77, Leader of the Conservative Opposition, 1977-79, Honorary Alderman, 1981; Honorary Freeman of the City of Manchester, 1984-; Vice-President, British Association for Commercial and Industrial Education; Member: Central Advisory on Education in England, 1960-63, CNAA, 1964-74, SSCR, 1971-75, Layfield Committee of Enquiry into Local Government Finance, 1974-76; President, St Leonards School, St Andrews, 1976-2003; Deputy Pro Chancellor, University of Lancaster, 1978-91; Pro Chancellor, University of Salford, 1983-89; Director, Manchester Independent Radio Ltd, 1972-83; Deputy Lieutenant, Greater Manchester, 1987-; Honorary Colonel, Manchester and Salford Universities' Officer Training Corps, 1977-81. Publications: Books: Education of Girls, 1958; The Girls Schools, 1967; Returning to Teaching, 1974; The Lord Mayor's Party, 1976; First Citizen, 1977; Most-Perfect Pandiagonal Magic Squares, their Construction and Enumeration (with David Brée), 1998; To Talk of Many Things (autobiography), 2004; Numerous research papers in mathematical journals, 1940-2004. Honours:

Mancunian of the Year, Junior Chamber of Commerce, 1977; DStJ, 1983; Honorary Fellow: Somerville College, Oxford, 1978; Honorary Fellow, City and Guilds, London, 1980; Honorary Fellow, Institute of Mathematics and Its Applications, 1990, Fellow, 1964, Member, Council, 1972-, President, 1979-80; Honorary Fellow, UMIST, 1987; Freeman City of Manchester, 1984-; Honorary DSc Salford, 1975; Honorary LLD, Manchester, 1976; Honorary Colonel, Manchester and Salford Universities Officer Training Corps, 1977-81;Honorary DSc, CNAA; Honorary DSc, Lancaster, 1992; Honorary LLD, Liverpool, 1994; Honorary FIMA, 1988. Memberships: President: Manchester Technological Association, 1981, Manchester Statistical Society, 1983-85; Patron, Museum of Science and Technology, Manchester, 2003-; Vice President, Manchester Astronomy Society, 1998-; Chairman, Council Order of St John, Greater Manchester, 1974-89; Member, Chapter General Order of St John, 1978-96; Chartered Mathematician. Address: 2 Pine Road, Manchester M20 6UY, England. E-mail: kmo@mighty-micro.co.uk

**OLURINOLA Philip Folaranmi**, b. 4 October 1939, Iwo, Isin Local Government Area, Kwara State, Nigeria. Professor of Pharmaceutical Microbiology. m. Dorcas Omowumi Taiwo, 2 sons, 3 daughters. Education: Pharmaceutical Chemist Diploma, Chemists and Druggists Diploma, ABUZ, Nigeria, 1966; Bachelor of Science, Pharmacy, ABUZ, Nigeria, 1974; Doctor of Philosophy, Pharmacy, Bradford, UK, 1979; Diploma in Ministerial Studies, GRBTI, Zaria, 2000. Appointments: Staff, Superintendent Pharmacist, Northern Nigeria Civil Service, Kaduna, 1966-68, Kano, 1968-74; Lecturer in Pharmacy to Reader, 1975-92, Head, Pharmaceutics Department, 1985-91, Dean, Faculty of Pharmaceutical Sciences, 1988-92, Professor of Pharmaceutical Microbiology, 1992-, Ahmadu Bello University, Zaria, (ABUZ), Nigeria; Voluntary retirement of tenure appointment, 2004. Publications: Over 80 academic, research and professional articles in journals and conference proceedings, mostly on antimicrobial agents and chemotherapy; Latest book: The Pharmacy Profession: A Focus on Nigeria. Honours: Fellow, West African Postgraduate College of Pharmacists, 1994; Kaduna State PSN Merit Award, 1994; Fellow, Pharmaceutical Society of Nigeria, 1997; Iwo Community Highest Merit Award, 2003; Merit Award, Nigerian Association of Academic Pharmacists, 2004; Faculty Merit Award, 2004. Memberships: Pharmaceutical Society of Nigeria, 1966-; Nigerian Association of Academic Pharmacists, 1980-; Gideons International, 1982-; Society for Applied Bacteriology, UK, 1988-94; American Society for Microbiology, 1991-94. Address: Department of Pharmaceutics and Pharmaceutical Microbiology, Faculty of Pharmaceutical Sciences, Ahmadu Bello University, Zaria, Nigeria. E-mail: pfolurinola@yahoo.com

**OMAE Iwao**, b. 7 August, 1939, Takao, Japan. Chemist; Researcher. m. Junko Hasegawa, 1 son, 2 daughters. Education: BA, Japan National College, 1962; MA, 1965, PhD, Organotin Chemistry, 1968, Osaka University. Appointments: Assistant Professor, Osaka University, 1968-70; Researcher, Teijin Central Research Institute, 1970-77; Adviser, Teijin Technical Information Ltd, 1977-97; Lecturer, Osaka City University, 1997; Professor, Tsuzuki Integrated Education Institute, 1997-; Founder and Head, Omae Research Laboratories, 1998-. Publications: Books as author: Organometallic Intramolecular-coordination Compounds, 1986; Organotin Chemistry, 1989; Applications of Organometallic Compounds, 1998; Global Warming and Carbon Dioxide, 1999; Plastic Recycles, 2000; Associate Editors, Research Journal of Chemistry and Environment, Indore, India, 2003-. Honour: Prize for Outstanding Paper on Organotin Antifouling Paints, 6th International Conference for Maritime Safety and the

Environment, NEVA 2001, Russia. Memberships: Chemical Society of Japan; Society of Synthetic Organic Chemistry, Japan; American Chemical Society. Address: 335-23, Mizuno, Sayama, Saitama 350-1317, Japan. E-mail: um5i-oome@asahi-net.or.jp

**OMELCHENKO Nickolay Victorovich,** b. 26 June 1951, Kazakhstan, USSR. Professor of Philosophy. m. Svetlana, 2 daughters. Education: Diploma, Philosophy, 1978, Postgraduate studies, 1978-81, PhD, 1984, Moscow State University by the name of MV Lomonosov. Appointments: Assistant Professor, 1982-87, Senior Lecturer, 1987-92, Associate Professor, 1992-99, Philosophy Department, Dean, History and Philosophy Faculty, 1996-2000, Full Professor, Social Philosophy Department, 1999-, Dean, Philosophy and Social Technologies Faculty, 2000-, Volgograd State University, Russia. Publications: 65 including: Human Creativity and the Teaching of Philosophy, The Mansfield-Volgograd Anthology, 2000; participation in conferences. Honours: Exchange Professor, Mansfield University, Pennsylvania, USA, 1997; Academician of Academy for Humanities, St Petersburg, Russia, 1998-; Fulbright Scholar-in-Residence, Mansfield University, Pennsylvania, USA, 2001-02; included in international biographical directories. Memberships: Russian Philosophical Society, 1978-; International Erich Fromm Society, Germany, 1993-; Society for Philosophy of Creativity, USA, 1998-. Address: Volgograd State University, 2nd Prodolnaya Street 30, Volgograd 400062, Russia. E-mail: nomelchenko1@yandex.ru

**OMIDVAR Hedayat,** b. 3 January 1966, Abadan, Iran. Senior Expert. Education: BSc, 1995, MSc, 2001, Industrial Engineering. Appointments: Project Management, 1995-2001; Senior Expert, 2001-; National Iranian Gas Company. Publications: Articles in international journals. Memberships: Institute of Industrial Engineers, 1992; American Industrial Hygiene Association, 1994. Address: No 6 Arghavan Alley, Sabory St, Kashanak, Tehran 1978975981, Iran. E-mail: hedayatomidvar@yahoo.com

**OMOEGUN Olugbemisola Mopelola,** b. 29 May 1951, Ipetu-Ijesha, Oshun State, Nigeria. Lecturer. m. Z O Omoegun, 3 sons, 1 daughter. Education: Teachers' Grade II Certificate, 1969; National Certificate in Education, 1974; Bachelor's Degree in Education and English, 1978; Master's Degree in Education, 1983; Doctorate Degree, PhD, in Guidance and Counselling, 1988. Appointments: Senior Lecturer, Faculty of Education, Head of Department (Educational Foundations with Educational Psychology), University of Lagos; President, Counselling Association of Nigeria, Lagos Chapter; Chairman, Board of Governors of Eric Moore High School, Suru-Lere, Lagos; Staff Adviser, Student Counsellors' Association of Nigeria, Umilag Chapter; Co-ordinator, PGDE Programme, Umilag. Publications: The Adolescent and You; Career Guidance for Nigerian Students; A Functional Approach to Practicum in Guidance and Counselling. Honours: Merit Award as President of the Counselling Association of Nigeria for Meritorious Service. Memberships: Counselling Association of Nigeria; Nigeria Institute of Management; Nigeria Association of University Women; University of Lagos Women's Association; Mothers Union; Anglican Communion Lagos Diocese. Address: Department of Educational Foundations, Faculty of Education, University of Lagos, Akoka, Nigeria. E-mail: omoegun@unilag.online.com

**OMOTOSHO Grace Oluremi,** b. 17 February 1941, Lagos, Nigeria. Nurse. m. Michael D Omotosho, 3 sons, 2 daughters. Education: State Registered Nurse and Midwife, University College Hospital, Ibadan, Nigeria, 1964-68 (NMC

UK Registration - Nursing); Nephrology Training Observer, Hammersmith Hospital, London, 1974-75; Observer, Peritoneal Dialysis and Dialysis Transplantation, Georgetown University, Washington DC, 1983. Appointments: First Nephrology Nurse Practitioner in West Africa; Started the first dialysis centre in Nigeria, Lagos University Teaching Hospital, 1981; Chief Nursing Officer in charge of specialities, Lagos University Teaching Hospital, 1996-2000; Past President, Reagan Memorial Baptist Girls Secondary School (Old Girls Association) for 10 years. Publication: Frontiers in Dialysis (co-author). Honours: State Registered Nurse (England and Wales), 1964; Award for Excellence Plaque and Cash, Lagos University Teaching Hospital; Paul Harris Fellow. Memberships: Chairman, National Association of Nigerian Nurses and Midwives, LUTH Branch, Nigeria, 1989-93; Member, Nigerian Institute of Management, 1992; Fellow, West African College of Nursing, 1998; Past District 911 Chairman/Deputy Board Member and First National Representative/President of International Inner Wheel, Nigeria; President, International Women's Society, Nigeria, 2005-2006. Address: 11, Olabisi Street, Ilupeju Estate, Lagos, Nigeria. E-mail: gomotosho@yahoo.com

**ONDAATJE Michael,** b. 12 September 1943, Colombo, Sri Lanka. Author. 2 sons. Education: Dulwich College, London; Queen's University; University of Toronto. Publications include: Poetry: The Dainty Monsters, 1967; The Man With Seven Toes, 1968; There's a Trick with a Knife I'm Learning to Do, 1979; Secular Love, 1984; Handwriting, 1998; Fiction: The Collected Works of Billy the Kid; Coming Through Slaughter; Running in the Family; In the Skin of a Lion; The English Patient; Handwriting; Anil's Ghost, 2000. Honour: Booker Prize for Fiction, 1992; Prix Medicis, 2000. Address: 2275 Bayview Road, Toronto, Ontario N4N 3MG, Canada.

**ONEGA JAÉN Susana,** b. 17 November 1948, Madrid, Spain. Professor of English Literature. m. Francisco Curiel Lorente, 2 sons. Education: Degree, 1975, PhD, 1979, English Philology, University of Zaragoza; Numerous certificates for aptitude in English, French, Italian and German, Madrid, Cambridge, Heidelberg, 1967-77. Appointments: Teacher of English, Official School of Languages, Madrid, 1968-69; Untenured Lecturer, 1975-77, Untenured Associate Professor, 1977-83; Tenured Associate Professor, 1983-86, Full Professor, 1986, Vice-Head of Department, 1989-90, 1995-97, 2000-03Head of Department, 1987-89, 1991-93, 1993-95, 1997-99, Department of English, University of Zaragoza; Head of Research Team (financed by the Ministry of Education) 1991-95, 1995-98, 1998-2001, (financed by the Ministry of Science and Technology), 2002-04, 2005-07; Research Manager for The Philologies and Philosophy, Ministry of Science and Technology, 2001-03. Publications: Books include: Análisis estructural, método narrativo y "sentido" de The Sound and the Fury de William Faulkner, 1980; Estudios literarios ingleses II: Renacimiento y barroco (editor and author of introduction), 1986; Form and Meaning in the Novels of John Fowles, 1989; Telling Histories: Narrativizing History/Historicizing Literature (editor and author of introduction), 1995; Narratology: An Introduction (co-editor and co-author of introduction), 1996; Peter Ackroyd. The Writer and his Work, 1998; Metafiction and Myth in the Novels of Peter Ackroyd, 1999; London in Literature: Visionary Mappings of the Metroplis (co-editor and co-author of introduction), 2002; Refracting the Canon in Contemporary British Literature and Film (co-editor and co-author of introduction), 2004; Numerous articles in professional journals, book chapters, conference papers and translations. Honours: Extraordinary Prize for Degree in Philosophy and Letters, University of Zaragoza, 1976; Extraordinary Prize for Doctorate in Philosophy and Letters, University of Zaragoza,

1980; Enrique García Díez Award, 1990; Honorary Research Fellowship, Birkbeck College, University of London, 1995-96. Memberships: Spanish Association for Anglo-American Studies, 1977-; European Association for American Studies, 1977-; European Society for the Study of English, 1990-; International Association of University Professors of English, 1995-; National Federation of Associations of Spanish University Professors, 1997-2002; Corresponding Fellow, The English Association, 2003-; Association of Women Researchers and Technologists, 2003-. Address: Dpto de Filología Inglesa y Alemana, Facultad de Filosofía y Letras, 50009 Universidad de Zaragoza, Spain. E-mail: sonega@unizar.es

**ONG Hean-Choon,** b. 10 November 1945, Malaysia. Doctor. Education: MBBS, University of Malaya, 1970; MRCOG, 1975; MMEd, University of Singapore, 1982; FICS, USA, International College of Surgeons, 1983; FRCOG, UK, 1989; FAMM, Academy of Medicine of Malaysia, 1997; FRCP I, 1999. Appointments: Consultant, Obstetrician and Gynaecologist, Pantai Medical Centre; Past Chairman, Malaysian Representative Committee, RCOG, UK; Member, Executive Council, Malaysian Menopause Society; Member, National Estrogen Deficiency Awareness, Faculty of Malaysia. Publications: Over 75 scientific papers in local, regional and international journals. Honours: Many honours. Memberships: Royal College of Obstetrics-Gynaecology, UK; International College of Surgeons; Malaysian Medical Association. Address: 14, Jalan Desa Ria Satu, Taman Desa, Jalan Klang-Lama, 58100 Kuala Lumpur, Malaysia.

**ONG HIXSON Patricia,** b. 2 August 1969, Singapore. Research Associate. m. Richard Hixson. Education: BSc, National University of Singapore, 1991; MSc, Medical Science, 1993, PhD, Medical Genetics, 1996, University of Glasgow. Appointments: Postdoctoral Research Fellow, Montreal Children's Hospital Research Institute, Montreal, Quebec, Canada, 1996-98; Scientific Officer, Department of Pathology, Singapore General Hospital, Singapore, 1998-2000; Postdoctoral Associate, 2000-03, Postdoctoral Fellow, 2003-2005, Department of Paediatrics, Section of Leukocyte Biology, Research Associate, Department of Molecular and Human Genetics, 2005-, Baylor College of Medicine, Houston, Texas, USA. Publications: Articles in scientific journals including: Molecular and Cellular Probes, 1996, 1997, 1998; Human Heredity, 1998; Kidney International, 1998; Cancer Genetics, Cytogenetics, 2000; Blood, 2004; Veterinary Immunology and Immunopathology, 2005. Honour: Recipient, Glasgow University Postgraduate Research Scholarship, 1994-96. Memberships: American Society of Human Genetics; British Society of Human Genetics; Human Genome Organisation. Address: Baylor College of Medicine, One Baylor Plaza, Room T936, Houston, TX 77030, USA. E-mail: phixson@bcm.tmc.edu

**ONIFADE Ademola,** b. 26 May 1956, Osogbo, Nigeria. University Teacher. m. Toyin Oluyede, 1 son, 3 daughters. Education: B Ed (Hons), University of Ibadan, 1978; MPE, University of New Brunswick, Canada, 1980; PhD, University of Maryland, College Park, USA, 1983. Appointments: Head, Department of Physical and Health Education, Adeyemi College, Ondo State, Nigeria, 1985-86; Head, Department of Physical and Health Education, 1988-90, 1999-2000, Professor, 2000-, Dean, Faculty of Education, 2000-2004, Lagos State University. Publications: Psycho-Social Perspective of Sports, 1993; History of Physical Education in Nigeria, 2001; Emergent Issues in Sociology of Sports, 2001; Britain, Sport and Nation Building in Nigeria, 2004. Honours: Listed in Who's Who publications and biographical dictionaries. Memberships: Nigeria Academy

of Education; Nigerian Association for Physical and Health Education and Recreation. Address: Department of Physical and Health Education, Lagos State University, PMB 1087, Apapa, Lagos, Nigeria. E-mail: ademolaonifade@yahoo.com

**ONO Setsuko,** b. 5 February 1953, Tokyo, Japan. Restaurateur. m. Hiromi, 1 son, 1 daughter. Education: High School. Career: Restaurateur. Honour: Listed in Who's Who publications and biographical dictionaries. Address: 3102 Washington Road, Augusta, GA 30901, USA.

**ONODA Hiroaki,** b. 6 July 1974, Japan. Researcher; Inorganic Chemist. Education: Bachelor of Engineering, 1997; Master of Engineering, 1999; Doctor of Engineering, 2002, Kobe University, Japan. Appointments: Lecturer, Kobe Medical College, Japan, 1998-2004; Research Associate, 2002-2005, Guest Researcher, 2005-, Ritsumeikan University, Japan; Researcher, Kyoto University, Japan, 2005-. Publications: Many articles in the field of inorganic materials chemistry. Honours: Listed in Who's Who publications and biographical dictionaries; International Scientist of the Year 2005; Top 100 Scientists Pinnacle of Achievement Award; Order of International Ambassadors. Memberships: Chemical Society of Japan; Japanese Association of Inorganic Phosphorus Chemistry; Rare Earth Society of Japan; Society of Inorganic Materials, Japan; Ceramic Society of Japan; International Association of Ecotechnology Research. Address: Department of Materials Science and Engineering, Faculty of Engineering, Kyoto University, Yoshida-Honmachi, Sakyo-ku, Kyoto 606-8501, Japan. E-mail: h.onoda@materials.mbox.media.kyoto-u.ac.jp

**ONONO-ONWENG Nelson,** b. 26 January 1945, Lukome, Gulu, Uganda. Bishop of the Diocese of Northern Uganda, Church of Uganda (Anglican). m. Brenda Abong, 3 sons, 3 daughters. Education: Diploma in Education, Diploma in Theology, Makerere University, Uganda; Diploma in Conflict Resolution, Uppsala University, Sweden; Advanced Diploma in Community Development, Manchester University, England; BA, Pastoral Studies, International Bible College, USA. Appointments: Teacher, Abalokodi Primary School, Gulu Public Primary School, Awoo Primary School, Kweyo Primary School, Gulu, Uganda; Chaplain, Kitgum High School; Tutor, Unyama Teachers College, Gulu; Headmaster, Gulu Primary School, Gulu; Inspector of Schools, Kamapala City Council, Kampala; Chaplain, Makerere Business School, Kampala; Director, Lweza Training and Conference Centre, Kampala; Bishop, Diocese of Northern Uganda, Church of Uganda, Gulu; Founder, Jamii Yakupata Jamii Yakupatanisha, Acoli Religious Leaders Peace Initiative, Gulu; Founder, Community Vocational School, Gulu. Honours: Honorary MA in Systemic Theology, Anglican Theological College, Tokyo, Japan; Guinness Power of Goodness Award for peace initiative in Northern Uganda; Uganda Peace Award, 2000; UNESCO Award for Peace Education (The first African), 2001. Address: PO Box 232, Gulu, Uganda. E-mail: ononobp@yahoo.co.uk

**ONYEWADUME Ignatius Ugo,** b. 13 September 1956, Agbor, Delta State, Nigeria. University Lecturer. m. 3 children. Education: Teachers' Grade Two Certificate, St Thomas' Teacher Training College, Ibusa, 1975; Sports Teachers' Certificate, College of Physical Education, Afuze, 1978; BSc (Hons), University of Nigeria, Nsukka, 1982; MEd (Exercise Physiology), 1984, PhD (Exercise Physiology), University of Ibadan; Post Doctoral MEd (Special/Adapted Physical Education), University of Birmingham, UK, 1993. Appointments: Lecturer, Oyo State College of Education, Iwo, 1984-85; Graduate Assistant, University of Ibadan, 1986-87; Lecturer, 1988, Senior Lecturer, 1991, Head of Physical

Education Department and Director of Sports, 1989-93, Federal College of Education, Oyo; Lecturer I, 1993-96, Senior Lecturer, 1996-98, University of Benin; Senior Lecturer, University of Botswana, 1998-. Publications: Books: Physical Education and Sports in Africa, 1999; Who's Who in Physical Education, Health Education, Recreation, Sport and Dance Training Institutions in Africa, 1999; Over 29 refereed journal articles in scholarly and scientific journals; Over 13 chapters in books and edited conference proceedings. Memberships: African Representative and Board Member, International Federation for Adapted Physical Activity; International Federation of Sports Medicine; International Council of Sports Science and Physical Education; International Association of Sports Kinetics; African Association for Health Physical Education, Recreation, Sport and Dance; International Council for Alcohol and Addiction; Nigeria Association for Sport Science and Medicine; Nigeria Association for Physical, Health Education and Recreation; Botswana Association for Physical, Health Education, Recreation and Dance; Nigeria School Health Association Address: Department of Physical Education & Recreation, Faculty of Education, University of Botswana, Private Bag 0022, Gaborone, Botswana. E-mail: onyewadu@mopipi.ub.bw

**OPANUGA Emmanuel Adedoyin**, b. 2 September 1944, Ikenne, Nigeria. Physician. m. Abigeal Morounkeji, 3 sons, 4 daughters. Education: MB BS, College of Medicine, University of Ibadan, Nigeria, 1967-72; Residency and Chief Residency in General Surgery, Homer G Phillips Hospital, St Louis, Missouri, USA, 1975-79. Appointment: Practice in General Surgery and Emergency Medicine. Honours: Fellowship, Royal College of Surgeons of Ireland; Diplomate, American Board of Surgery; Fellowship, West African College of Surgeons; Fellowship, International College of Surgeons. Membership: American Medical Association. Address: 9080 Retreat Pass, Jonesboro, GA 30236, USA. E-mail: doyin@mindspring.com

**OPIE Iona**, b. 13 October 1923, Colchester, England. Writer. m. Peter Opie, 2 September 1943, deceased, 2 sons, 1 daughter. Publications: A Dictionary of Superstitions (with Moira Tatem), 1989; The People in the Playground, 1993; With Peter Opie: The Oxford Dictionary of Nursery Rhymes, 1951, new edition, 1997; The Oxford Nursery Rhyme Book, 1955; The Lore and Language of Schoolchildren, 1959; Puffin Book of Nursery Rhymes, 1963; A Family Book of Nursery Rhymes, 1964; Children's Games in Street and Playground, 1969; The Oxford Book of Children's Verse, 1973; Three Centuries of Nursery Rhymes and Poetry for Children, 1973; The Classic Fairy Tales, 1974; A Nursery Companion, 1980; The Oxford Book of Narrative Verse, 1983; The Singing Game, 1985; Babies: an unsentimental anthology, 1990; Children's Games with Things, 1997. Honours: Honorary MA, Oxon, 1962, Open University, 1987, DLitt, University of Southampton, 1987, University of Nottingham, 1991, Doctorate, University of Surrey, 1997; CBE, 1998; FBA, 1998. Address: Mells House, Liss, Hampshire GU33 6JQ, England.

**OPIK Lembit**, b. 2 March 1965, Bangor, County Down, Northern Ireland. Member of Parliament. Education: BA, Philosophy, Bristol University. Appointments: President, Bristol Students Union, 1985-86; Member, National Union of Students National Executive, 1987-88; Brand Assistant, 1988-91, Corporate Training and Organisation Development Manager, 1991-96, Global Human Resources Training Manager, 1997, Proctor and Gamble; Elected to Newcastle City Council, 1992; Elected as MP for Montgomeryshire, 1997; Party Spokesperson on Northern Ireland and Young People, 1997; Spokesperson for Wales, Leader of the Welsh Liberal Democrats, Member of Shadow Cabinet, 2001-. Publications: Articles on politics in newspapers and magazines; Weekly column in Shropshire Star,

The Week in Politics. Honours: Nominated for Channel 4 House Magazine New MP of the Year, 1998; Nominated for Country Life Rural MP of the Year, 1999. Memberships: Agriculture Select Committee, 1998-2001; Co-Chair, All Parliamentary Middle Way Group; Member, Spinal Injuries Association; Speaks on behalf of British Gliding Association; Chair, All Party Parliamentary Motorcycle Group; President, Shropshire, Astronomical Society. Address: House of Commons, London, SW1A 0AA, England. E-mail: opikl@parliament.uk

**OPOČENSKÝ Milan**, b. 5 July 1931, Hradec Králové. Professor Emeritus; General Secretary. m. Jana Jurankova, 2 sons, 1 daughter. Education: MDiv, 1950-54; ThD, 1965. Appointments: Junior Lecturer, 1954-60, Senior Lecturer, 1960-73, WSCF Europe Secretary, 1967-73, Professor of Christian Social Ethics, 1973-1999, General Secretary, World Alliance of Reformed Churches, Geneva, 1989-2000. Publications: Christians and Revolutions, 1977; Revolution und Widerstand, 1982; Faith Challenged by History, 2000. Honours: Several honorary degrees. Memberships: Societas Ethica; American Academy of Religion. Address: Nepomucka 1025, CZ-15000 Praha 5, Czech Republic.

**ORESCU Michaela Al**, b. 6 February 1927. Author; Researcher. m. George Tomescu, deceased, 1 son. Education: Fine Arts, History, Vocal Classical Music, Journalism; Doctor in Dacology. Appointments: Editor-in-Chief, Comterra Review; First Vice-President Dacromanian Academy; President, Pluridisciplinary Circle Dacoromania; President, Pluridisciplinary Circle Romanian Thinking; Co-operator in scientific and therapeutic work in bioenergotherapy in the ancient Romanian tradition; Participant, Dacology International Congress, 2000, 2001, 2002, 2003, 2004. Publications: About 60 publications, poetry, fiction, literary prose, scientific prose, essays, features, book and art reviews which include most recently: European Ancestral Medical Science and its Contribution to Ancient Asiatic Science, 1996; The Zone Mures-Transilvania-Romania, Ancestral Dwelling of Dacic and Indo-European Civilisation, 1997; Europe and Americas Civilisation, 2000; The Earth Mother in Dacic and Roman Cult, 2001; The Belagines Law, 2002; The Peahen – Romanian Mythology and Heraldry, 2002; Nicolae Miulescu and the Indo-European Problem, 2002; European Ancient Civilisations: Crete, 2002; Translation of historical novel, The Knight of Ronsard and the Ban Mărăcine; Haiku published in Leonid Storm Research, NASA Ames Research Center, USA. Honours include: Discovery of symbols not emphasised on the Plaites of Tărtăria and presentation at IV Congress of Dacology, Bucharest, 2003; First study, interpretation and presentation of the Plaite of Homorâciu; Honour Diploma, Romanian Writers Society for Science and Technology; Diploma, Mircea Eliade, Dacoromania Academy for the Promotion of Romanian Values; Honour Diploma, for contribution to the history of the Savarsin area, Ethnography and Art Museum; Honour Diploma, Romanian Meteors Society. Memberships: Fellow, Romanian Writers Society; Fellow, Romanian Writers Society for Science and Technology; Fellow, Astronomical Society of Meteors; Fellow, Scientific Society Getica; Founder, President, Pluridisciplinary Circle, Bogdan Petriceicu Hasdeu. Address: Str Valea Oltului nr 20, Bl A 43, sc A, et.2, ap.7, sector 6, cod 77426 Bucharest, Romania.

**ORING Stuart August**, b. 1932, Bronx, New York, USA. Photographer; Writer; Researcher. Education: MA, American University; BFA, Rochester Institute of Technology. Appointments: Photography Assistant, Commercial Advertising Photography, 1959-61; Industrial Photographer, 1962-64; Visual Information Specialist, Agricultural Research Service, 1967-69; AV Specialist, National AV Center, 1969-71; Visual

Information Specialist, Office of Economic Opportunity, 1971-74; United States Department of Agriculture, 1979-94; Manager, Founder, Isis Visual Communications, 1992-; Achievements include research and development of new approaches for analysing and interpreting art and photographs. Publications: Understanding Pictures: Theories, Exercises and Procedures; A Beginners Guide to Pictures; A Teachers Planning Guide; Articles published include: Composition - The Vocabulary of Photography, 1978; The I Ching and Dreams, 1985; Using the I Ching in the Fine Arts; Experiencing the Photograph, 1974; Photographs published in advertising, books, brochures, magazines, pamphlets, and others. Honours: Certificate of Recognition, Eastman Kodak Company. Memberships: National Art Education Association; Division of Visual Arts; American Psychological Association; Elected to board, American Society of Psychopathology of Expression; Institute for the Psychological Study of the Arts; Listed in national and international biographical dictionaries. Address: 2570 Redbud Lane, Owings, MD 20736, USA.

**ORLOFF Harold David**, b. 24 November 1915, Winnipeg, Manitoba, Canada. Chemist. m. Leah Orloff, 1 son, 2 daughters. Education: BSc, Honours, 1937, MSc, 1939, University of Manitoba; PhD, McGill University, 1941. Appointments: Research Chemist, Canadian Board of Grain Commissioners, 1938; Research Scientist, H Smith Paper Mills, 1941-48; Associate Director of Research, Ethyl Corporation, 1948-82; Adjunct Professor of Chemistry, University of Detroit, Michigan, USA, 1957. Publications include: Articles and papers in Pulp and Paper Magazine, Canada, 1946; Journal of the American Chemical Society, 1951, 1953, 1954; Chemical Reviews, 1954; Industrial Engineering and Chemistry, 1961; Botyu Kagaku, 1956; Proceedings of the 7th World Petroleum Congress, 1967; Zeolites, 1984; Poultry Science, 1985; Over 50 patents; Co-inventor, Arborite Plastics, also Secondary Chemical Recovery System for use in kraft pulp production. Honours: Isbister Scholar, University of Manitoba, 1934-37; Research Fellow, McGill University, 1940-41; Weldon Memorial Gold Medal, Senior Award of Canadian Pulp and Paper Association, 1948. Memberships: American Chemical Society; Sigma Xi; Pulp and Paper Associations, USA, Canada. Address: 2903 Victoria Circle, Apt D3, Coconut Creek, FL 33066, USA.

**ORLOVA Vera**, b. 17 May 1951, Blagoveschensk, Russia. Psychiatrist; Psychotherapist. m. Vladimir Kulkov, 2 daughters. Education: Diploma of Physician with excellent honours, 2nd Moscow Medical Institute, 1974; Candidate of Medical Sciences, 1984; Doctor of Medical Sciences, 2000. Appointments: Junior Researcher, Mental Health Research Centre, Russian Academy of Medical Sciences, 1977-97; Head of Psychiatric Expert Commission, Moscow, 1987-88; Senior Researcher, 1988-91, Leading Researcher, 1991-2005, Head of Genetic Unit (equivalent to Professor), 2001-, Mental Health Research Centre, Russian Academy of Medical Sciences. Publications: More than 120 articles as author and co-author in medical journals in the fields of clinical and biological psychiatry and genetics of schizophrenia. Honours: Gold Medal for Secondary education Diploma, 1968; Grant of British Council, 2000; Grant of Russian Foundation for Basic Investigations, 2002; Grant of Royal Society, 2004; Travel Grants for: 8th World Congress of Psychiatric Genetics, 1998; XI World Congress of Psychiatry, 1999; 7th and 8th World Congresses of Biological Psychiatry, 2001, 2005; Listed in Who's Who publications and biographical dictionaries. Memberships: Society of Neuropathologists and Psychiatrists, Russia; Society of Medical Genetics, Russia; World Federation of Societies of Biological Psychiatry. Address: Mental Health Research Centre, RAMS, Zagorodnoe Shosse 2, 113152, Moscow, Russia. E-mail: vorlova@yandex.ru

**ORMAN Stanley**, b. 6 February 1935, London, England. Consultant. m. Helen Hourman, 1 son, 2 daughters. Education: BSc, 1st Class Honours, Chemistry and Physics, 1957, PhD, Chemistry, 1960, Kings College, London; Fulbright Fellow, Brandeis University Massachusetts, USA, 1960-91. Appointments: Scientist Ministry of Defence, 1961-82, positions held include: Chief Weapons Systems Engineer Chevaline, 1980-82, Minister, British Embassy, Washington, USA, 1982-84, Deputy Director Atomic Weapons research Establishment, 1984-86, Founding Director General, SDI Participation Office, 1986-90; Under Secretary of State, UK Ministry of Defence, 1982-90; Chief Executive Officer, General Technology Systems, USA, 1990-96; Chief Executive Officer, Orman Associates, 1996-. Publications: Author book: Faith in G.O.D.S – Stability in Nuclear Age, 1991; 150 published papers and articles on chemistry, corrosion science, adhesion and defence issues including over 90 articles on missile defence; Participation in workshops and presentations at over 70 international conferences on defence issues. Honours: Captained London University Track Team, 1956-57; Represented Britain in World Student Games, 3rd in 100m and 7th in Long Jump, 1956; Jelf Medalist, King's College, London, 1957. Address: 17825 Stoneridge Drive, North Potomac, MD 20878, USA. E-mail: or2withdog@comcast.net

**ORME Michael Christopher L'Estrange**, b. 13 June 1940, Derby, England. University Professor; Medical Practitioner. m. (Joan) Patricia Orme, 1 son. Education: MA, MB, BChir (Cantab), 1964-65; MD, 1975; MRCP, 1967; FRCP, 1980. Appointments: Senior Lecturer, Clinical Pharmacology, 1975, Professor, 1984, Dean, Faculty of Medicine, 1991-96, University of Liverpool; Director of Education and Training, North West Regional Office, NHS Executive, 1996-2001; Retired 2001; Currently Professor Emeritus, University of Liverpool; Consultant Physician Emeritus, Royal Liverpool Hospital. Publications: 275 peer reviewed publications in journals; Books and book chapters on drug interactions, clinical pharmacology of oral contraceptives, drugs in tropical disease, anticoagulants and anti-rheumatic drugs. Honours: FRCGP (Hon), 1996; F Med Sci, 1998; DSc (Hon), Salford, 2000; FFPHM, 2000; Honorary Fellow, University of Central Lancashire, 2001. Memberships: Association of Physicians; British Pharmacological Society. Address: Lark House, Clapton-on-the-Hill, Cheltenham, Gloucestershire GL54 2LG, England. E-mail: morme@eandth ome.demon.co.uk

**ORMEROD Janette Louise**, b. 23 September 1946, Western Australia. Author and Illustrator. 2 daughters. Education: Associateship in Design, 1966, Associateship in Art Teaching, 1974, Western Australian Institute of Technology. Appointments: Secondary School Art Teacher, 1966-71; Tutor in Art Education, Mt Lawley College of Further Education, 1972-73; Senior Tutor in Design and Drawing, Western Australian Institute of Technology, 1974-79; Author and Illustrator of children's books based in the UK, 1980-; Publicity tours in Australia, USA, Canada and UK involving TV, radio and magazine interviews, workshops and presentations; Numerous presentations in libraries, bookshops, colleges and festivals for teachers, librarians, parents and students; Committee Member, Children's Writers and Illustrators Group, Society of Authors; Lecturer and Guest Lecturer, Leicester Polytechnic, Nene College Northampton, Anglia Polytechnic University Cambridge, Homerton College Cambridge. Publications: 74 children's books published in 21 countries; Numerous seminar and conference papers presented nationally and internationally. Honours include most recently: Child Study Children's Book Committee Children's Books of the Year Award for Sky Dancer, 1997; The Top 100 Books of 1998 You've Got to

Have in Your Library Collection, USA for Peek-A-Boo, CCBC Choices for Who's Whose?, American Booksellers "Pick of the Lists", for One Two Three...Jump! 1999; Shortlisted 1980-1999 Millennium Children's Book Award SLA YLG SLG, UK for One Two Three...Jump! 2000; ABA Pick Of the List, Oppenheim Platinum Award for Miss Mouse Takes Off, Miss Mouse's Day, Oppenheim Gold Award for Goodbye Mousie, Parent's Guide Children's Media Award for Goodbye Mousie, 2001. Memberships: UK Society of Authors - Children's Writers and Illustrators Group; USA Authors Guild; UK and USA Societies of Children's Book Writers and Illustrators; International Board on Books for Young People. Address: c/o Laura Cecil, Literary Agent, 17 Alwyne Villas, London N1 2HG, England. E-mail: lauracecil@mac.com

**ORMOND Julia,** b. 1965, England. Actress. m. Rory Edwards, divorced. Education: Farnham Art School; Webber Douglas Academy. Appointments: Worked in Repertory, Crucible Theatre, Sheffield, Everyman Theatre, Cheltenham; On tour with Royal Exchange Theatre, Manchester; Appeared in Faith, Hope and Charity, Lyric, Hammersmith; Treats, Hampstead Theatre; West End Debut in Anouilh's The Rehearsal; My Zinc Bed, 2000. Creative Works: TV appearances: Traffik (Channel 4 series); Ruth Rendell Mysteries; Young Catherine, 1990; Films: The Baby of Macon; Legends of the Fall; First Knight; Sabrina; Smilla's Sense of Snow, 1997; The Barber of Siberia, 1998; The Prime Gig, 2000; Resistance, 2003. Address: c/o CAA, 9830 Wilshire Boulevard, Beverly Hills, CA 90212, USA.

**ORMSBY Frank,** b. 30 October 1947, Enniskillen County, Fermanagh, Northern Ireland. Poet; Writer; Editor. Education: BA, English, 1970, MA, 1971, Queen's University, Belfast. Appointment: Editor, The Honest Ulsterman, 1969-89. Publications: A Store of Candles, 1977; Poets from the North of Ireland (editor), 1979, new edition, 1990; A Northern Spring, 1986; Northern Windows: An Anthology of Ulster Autobiography (editor), 1987; The Long Embrace: Twentieth Century Irish Love Poems (editor), 1987; Thine in Storm and Calm: An Amanda McKittrick Ros Reader (editor), 1988; The Collected Poems of John Hewitt (editor), 1991; A Rage for Order: Poetry of the Northern Ireland Troubles (editor), 1992; The Ghost Train, 1995; The Hip Flask: Short Poems from Ireland (editor), 2000. Address: 33 North Circular Road, Belfast BT15 5HD, Northern Ireland

**ÖRVELL Claes Gunnar,** b. 22 April 1945, Stockholm, Sweden. Physician; Virologist. m. Eva Reimert, 2 sons, 3 daughters. Education: MD, 1973, PhD, 1977, Karolinska Institute. Appointments: Researcher, Department of Virology, Karolinska Institute, 1978-79; Researcher, Virology, National Bacteriological Laboratory, 1980-92; Associate Professor, Karolinska Institute, 1988-; Senior Physician, Stockholm County Council, 1992-. Publications: Numerous scientific articles on the subjects structural, clinical and epidemiological studies on viruses. Honours: International Order of Merit, 2000, Order of International Fellowship, Adviser to Director General, Deputy Director General, IBC, 2001; Presidential Seal of Honor, World Biographic Day, ABI, 2001; Continental Governor, ABI, 2001; Founding member, American Order of Excellence, 2001; Hall of Fame, ABI, 2002; Ambassador of Grand Eminence, ABI, 2002; Minister of Culture, ABI, 2003; Order of Distinction, IBC, 2004. Memberships: Society General Microbiology. Address: Department of Clinical Virology, F68, Huddinge University Hospital, S-14186, Stockholm, Sweden. E-mail: claes.orvell@karolinska.se

**ORYAN Shahrbanoo,** b. 2 April 1947, Tehran, Iran. University Professor; Senior Lecturer. Education: BSc, Biology, University of Teachers Education, Tehran, Iran, 1970; PhD, Endocrinology, Sheffield University, England, 1974. Appointments: Assistant Professor, Head of Biology Department, 1975-79, Associate Professor, 1979-85, Full Professor, 1985-, University of Teachers Education, Tehran, Iran; General Secretary, Iranian Society of Physiology and Pharmacology, 1990-95. Publications: 12 titles of books in the field of Physiology; Published more than 55 journal articles. Honours: Outstanding Senior Lecturer of the Year 1999, University of Teachers Education. Memberships: International Union of Physiological Sciences; Federation of Asian and Oceanian Physiological Sciences; Iranian Society of Physiological Sciences; Project Director, Tracing petroleum contaminants in commercial fish resources of Persian Gulf, United Nation Compensation Committee. Address: University of Teachers Education, Department of Biology, 49 Dr Mofateh Avenue, PO Box 15815-1455 Tehran, Iran. E-mail: sh_oryan@yahoo.com

**OSBORN John Holbrook (Sir),** b. 14 December 1922, Sheffield, England. Semi-retired: Politician; Industrialist; Scientist; Soldier. m. (1) Molly Suzanne Marten, divorced 2 daughters, (2) Joan Mary Wilkinson, deceased, (3) Patricia Felicity Read. Education: MA Cantab, Part II Tripos Metallurgy, Trinity Hall, Cambridge University, England, 1943; Diploma in Foundry Technology, National Foundry College, Wolverhampton Technical College, 1949. Appointments: Royal Corps Signals, 1943-47; Battery Commander, Royal Artillery TA, 1948-55; Assistant Works Manager, Production Controller, Cost Controller, 1947-51, Company Director, 1951-79, Samuel Osborn and Company Limited, Sheffield, England; Conservative Candidate and Member of Parliament, Sheffield Hallam, 1959-87; Parliamentary Private Secretary to Minister for Commonwealth Relations, 1962-64; Joint Honorary Secretary, Conservative 1922 Committee, 1968-87; Former Chairman, Conservative Transport Committee, All-Party Road Study Group, Parliamentary Group Energy Studies; All-Party Channel Tunnel Group; Member of the European Parliament, 1975-79; Former Member of the Interim Licensing Authority; Friends of Progress. Publications: Co-author: Conservative publications: Export of Capital; Trade not Aid; Change or Decay; A Value Added Tax; European Parliamentary publications: Help for the Regions; Energy for Europe; Also Chairman of a Parliamentary and Scientific Committee report on Information Storage and Retrieval. Honours: Knight Bachelor, Birthday Honours 1983, for Public and Political Services; Chairman, Business in Development Committee, UK Chapter of Society of International Development, 1990-1995, attached to Worldaware; Member Executive, 1968-75, 1979-82, Life Member, 1987, IPU, UK branch; Life Member, CPA, UK branch, 1987-; Officer, 1960-87, Life Member, 1987, Parliamentary and Scientific Committee; European Atlantic Group Committee, 1990-; Member, Royal Institute of International Affairs, 1985-; Member, Conservative Group for Europe, European Movement, 1975-; Council Member, 1963-79, Life Member, Industrial Society; Junior Warden-Searcher, Assistant Searcher, Freeman, 1987-, Company of Cutlers in Hallamshire. Memberships: Fellow, Royal Society for Encouragement of the Arts, Manufacture and Commerce, 1966-; Trustee of many Sheffield Charitable Trusts; President, 1960-96, Honorary Patron, Sheffield Institute of Advanced Motorists; Fellow, Institute of Directors, 1955-; Fellow, Institute of Materials (now IM3), 1947-. Address: Newlands, 147 Hawton Road, Newark, Nottinghamshire, NG24 4QG, England. E-mail: j.h.osborn147@ntlworld.com

**OSBORNE Margaret Elizabeth Brenda,** b. 21 December 1931, Clifton, Bristol, England. Artist; Painter; Poet. m. Stuart John Osborne, 1 daughter. Education: Intermediate

Certificate in Arts and Crafts, West of England College of Art, 1950; National Diploma in Design, 1952; Art Teacher's Diploma, Painting, 1953; Ministry of Education Certificate in Education, 1953. Career: Art Teacher in Schools and Art College for 26 years; Currently, Professional Freelance Painter in oils, gouache painting figurative portraits to commission and domestic pets; Worked for Galleries, Tarmac, Cadbury's and Glynweb for retiring directors and for private collectors; Over 100 commissions; Exhibitions: The Young Contemporaries Exhibition, London, 1952; Works sent to the Pastel Society in the Mall Gallery in London, selected to tour in the provinces in the 1960's. Honours: Intermediate Art Scholarship, 1948; City Senior Scholarship, Bristol Education Committee, 1950; Senior Drawing Prize, West of England College of Art, 1952; Listed in Who's Who publications and biographical dictionaries. Membership: The Fawcett Society, 2003-. Address: 64 Burton Manor Road, Stafford ST17 9PR, England.

**OSBORNE Roy,** b. 15 July 1948, Bristol, England. Artist; Writer. Education: Bachelor of Arts, 1970, Postgraduate Certificate, 1971, Brighton Polytechnic; Postgraduate Diploma, Chelsea College of Art and Design, 1991; Master of Arts, University of London, 1994. Career: Part-time and visiting lecturer in art and design in 150 art schools world-wide, 1978-2002, including: Roehampton Institute, London; Westminster Adult Education Service, London; American College, London; Akron University, Ohio, USA; Slade School of Art, London; Artworks in private and public collections. Publications: Lights and Pigments, 1980; From Prism to Paintbox, 1989; The Color Compendium (contributor), 1989; Designing with Colour (contributor), 1991; Colour Teaching in Art, 1995; On Colour 1528 Thylesius (editor), 2003; Colour and Humanism (editor), 2003; Books on Colour 1500-2000, 2004; Color Influencing Form, 2004. Honour: Turner Medal of the Colour Group, 2003. Memberships: Society of Authors; National Artists' Register; Colour Group (Great Britain); Colour Association of the United States. Address: 15 Westerleigh Road, Bristol BS16 6UY, England. E-mail: art.school@virgin.net

**OSTOJIĆ Negoslav,** b. 9 September 1948, Ivanjica, Yugoslavia. Economist. m. Olga Dondur, 1 daughter. Education: BA, MA, Faculty of Economics, Belgrade. Appointments: Director, RCCDC Agency for Economic Co-operation among Developing Countries, Ljubljana, Slovenia; Editor-in-Chief, International Economic Journal, Development and South-South, Ljubljana; General Co-ordinator of World Scientific Banking Meeting, Belgrade (WSBM), Belgrade. Adviser, Institute for International Scientific Educational, Cultural and Technical Co-operation, Republic of Serbia, Belgrade; Editor-in-Chief, International Economic Journal, Development and South-South, Ljubljana; Executive Director, European Centre for Peace and Development of the University for Peace, established by United Nations, Belgrade; Publications include: Debt and Development; International Financing of Economic Development; Doing Business with Yugoslavia; Yugoslav Potentials for Scientific and Technical Co-operation; Directory, Corporate Research, Consulting and Engineering; Small and Medium-Size Enterprises in Developing Countries; SMEDC, Technical-Technological Development Marketing; Francois Perroux – l'homme et l'oeuvre (1903-1987); Co-author: Future of International Monetary, Financial and Trade Co-operation for Development; International Economic Trends and Policies. Their Effects on Eastern European Economies; Co-editor: Financial and Banking System of Yugoslavia; Privatization in the Economies of Transition (edited by Norman Scott and Negoslav P Ostojic); Experiences and Results of Privatization in the Economies in Transition (edited by Norman Scott and Negoslav P Ostojic); Recent Lessons From Transition and Privatization,

Problems of Institutions and Corporate Governance (edited by Norman Scott and Negoslav P Ostojic); Sustainable Strategy of the Ecological State of Montenegro (edited by Paul-Marc Henri and Negoslav P Ostojic); Numerous articles in the field of economics, international relations, banking, financing and contemporary management. Honour: PhD, honoris causa, International Economic Relations. Memberships: Society of International Development; Scientific Society of Economists of Serbia and Montenegro; President, Crvena Zvezda (Red Star) Chess Club, Belgrade. Address: European Centre for Peace and Development, Terazije 41/II, 11000 Belgrade, Yugoslavia. E-mail: ecpd@Eunet.yu

**OSWALD (William Richard) Michael (Sir),** b. 21 April 1934, Walton-on-Thames, Surrey. Racehorse Stud Manager. m. Lady Angela Oswald, 1 son, 1 daughter. Education: MA, King's College Cambridge. Appointments: 2nd Lieutenant, King's Own Regiment, BAOR, Korea, 1953-54; Captain, Royal Fusiliers (TA), 1955-60; Manager, Lordship and Egerton Studs, Newmarket, 1962-69; Director, Royal Studs, 1970-98; Racing Manager for H M Queen Elizabeth, The Queen Mother, 1970-2002; National Hunt Advisor to H M The Queen, 2002-; Member, Council of Thoroughbred Breeder's Association, 1964-2001, President, 1997-2001; Chairman, Bloodstock Industry Committee, Animal Health Trust, 1986-2002; Liveryman, Worshipful Company of Shipwrights. Honours: LVO, 1979; CVO, 1988; KCVO, 1998; Honorary DSc, De Montfort University, 1997; Honorary Air Commodore, 2620 Sqdn Royal Auxiliary Air Force, 2001-. Memberships: Jockey Club; Army and Navy Club. Address: The Old Rectory, Weasenham St Peter, King's Lynn, Norfolk PE32 2TB, England.

**OSWALD Angela Mary Rose (Lady),** b. 21 May 1938, London, England. Lady-in-Waiting. m. Sir Michael Oswald, 1 son, 1 daughter. Appointments: Extra Woman of the Bedchamber to H M Queen Elizabeth the Queen Mother, 1981-83; Woman of the Bedchamber to H M Queen Elizabeth the Queen Mother, 1983-2002. Honours: LVO, 1993; Freeman of the City of London, 1995; CVO, 2000. Address: The Old Rectory, Weasenham St Peter, King's Lynn, Norfolk, PE32 2TB, England.

**OTTOVÁ-LEITMANNOVÁ Angela,** b. 14 January 1952, Slovakia (former Czechoslovakia). Professor in Biophysics. m. H Ti Tien, deceased, 1 son, 1 daughter. Education: MSc, Humboldt University, Berlin, Germany, 1974; PhD, Biophysics, 1977; Associate Professor, 1989; DrSc, 1995, Professor, 2001. Appointments: Humboldt University, 1972-77; Slovak Academy of Sciences, 1977-81; Slovak Technical University, 1981-; Visiting Associate Professor, 1991-2001, Visiting Professor, Biophysics, Michigan State University, East Lansing, 2001-. Publications: Over 150 in professional journals. Honours: Several. Memberships: Union of Slovak Mathematicians and Physicists; Slovak Medical Society; Slovak Cybernetic Society at Slovak Academy of Sciences. Address: Department of Physiology, Michigan State University, Biomedical and Physical Sciences Building, East Lansing, MI 48824, USA.

**OUWEKERK Anita H. Van,** Educator. Education: BA, Northwestern State University, Natchitas, Louisiana; M Ed, University of New Orleans. Appointments: Teacher, Headstart, to all grades through to college freshman; Director, Greater Orange Literacy Services and Trainer of Tutors for Literacy organisations, 20 years; Currently Reading Teacher, Co-ordinator of Parallel Studies, Blinn College, Bryan, Texas; Continuing work as a literacy volunteer; Vice-President, 2002, President, 2003, College Academic Support Programmes. Memberships: President, Theta Chapter of Delta Kappa Gamma, Texas College Reading and Learning Association, 1996-2000;

Co-Chair, Convention Program, 2002, Co-Chair of Convention, National Level, 2003; Exhibits Co-Chair, National Conference, Austin, 2002, National Association of Developmental Education; Member, National Election and Awards Committees, Co-Chair, Teaching Excellence Special Interest Group, College Reading and Learning Association; President, Church Board of Trustees, Unitarian Universalist Fellowship of Brazos Valley. Address: 1506 Bennett Street, Bryan, TX 77802, USA.

**OUZTS Eugene Thomas,** b. 7 June 1930, Thomasville, Georgia, USA. Minister; Secondary Educator. m. Mary Olive Vineyard. Education: MA, Harding University, 1957; Postgraduate: Murray State University, University of Arkansas, Arizona State University, University of Arizona; Northern Arizona University. Appointments: Certificated Secondary Teacher, Arkansas, Missouri, Arizona; Ordained Minister Church of Christ, 1956; Minister in various Churches in Arkansas, Missouri, Texas, -1965; Teacher, various public schools, Arkansas, Missouri, 1959-65; Teacher, Arizona, 1965-92; Minister in Arizona Church of Christ, Clifton, Morenci, Safford and Duncan, 1965-. Honours: Civil Air Patrol, Arizona Wing Chaplain of Year, 1984; Thomas C Casaday Unit Chaplain, 1985; Arizona, Wing Safety Officer, 1989; Arizona Wing Senior Member, 1994; Meritorious Service Award, 1994; Southwestern Region Senior Member, 1995; Exceptional Service Award, 1997; Life Fellowship, IBA, Cambridge, England. Memberships: Military Chaplains Association; Disabled American Veterans; Air Force Association; American Legion; Elks; Board, Arizona Church of Christ Bible Camp; Airport Advisory Board, Greenlee County, Arizona; Civil Air Patrol/Air Force Auxiliary (Chaplain, 1982, 1st Lieutenant advanced through grades to Lieutenant Colonel, 1989); Assistant Wing Chaplain. Address: 739 E Cottonwood Road, Duncan, Arizona 85534-8108, USA.

**OVENDEN John Anthony,** b. 26 May 1945, Epping, Essex, England. Clergyman. m. Christine, 2 sons, 1 daughter. Education: BA, Open University; MA, Kings College, London. Appointments: Precentor and Sacrist, Ely Cathedral; Vicar of St Mary's, Primrose Hill, London; Canon of St George's Chapel, Windsor; Chaplain in the Royal Chapel, Windsor Great Park; Chaplain to H M The Queen. Address: Chaplain's Lodge, The Great Park, Windsor, Berkshire SL4 2HP, England.

**OVODOV Yury S,** b. 28 August 1937, Kharkov, Ukraine, USSR. Chemist; Immunochemist. m. Raisa G Ovodova, 1 son. Education: Lomonosov State University, Moscow, 1959; Candidate of Chemical Sciences, 1963; Doctor of Chemical Sciences, 1972; Professor in Bioorganic Chemistry, 1973. Appointments: Senior Laboratory Worker, Novosibirsk Institute of Organic Chemistry, Siberian Branch of the USSR Academy of Sciences, 1959-62; Intern, Institute of Chemistry of Natural Compounds, the USSR Academy of Sciences, Moscow, 1960-62; Junior Scientist, Laboratory of Chemistry of Natural Substances, Vladivostok, 1962-64; Deputy Director, 1967-87, and concurrently Head of Department, 1975-94, Head of Laboratory, 1964-75 and 1979-94, Pacific Institute of Bioorganic Chemistry, Far Eastern Branch, Academy of Sciences, Vladivostok; Elected Corresponding Member of the USSR Academy of Sciences, 1990; Full Member, Russian Academy of Sciences, 1992; Head, Department of Molecular Immunology, 1994-2004, Director, 2004-, Institute of Physiology, Komi Science Centre, the Urals Branch of the Russian Academy of Sciences, Syktyvkar; Concurrently, Director, Educational Scientific Centre, Syktyvkar State University, 2000-; Chief Scientist, Institute of Chemistry, Komi Science Centre, The Urals Branch of the Russian Academy of Sciences, Syktyvkar, 2002-. Publications: Triterpenic Glycosides of Gypsophila spp; Bioglycans-immunomnodulators; Bacterial Lipopolysaccharides; Oncofetal Antigens and Oncoprecipitins; The Chemical Foundations of Immunity; Selected Chapters of Bioorganic Chemistry; Structural Features and Physiological Activities of Plant Polysaccharides. Honours: Lenin Komsomol Prize, 1972; I I Mechnikov Award, 1993; Y A Ovchinnikov Award, 2003. Memberships: The Slav Academy of Science; New York Academy of Sciences; International Endotoxin Society; American Association for the Advancement of Science; Russian Biochemical Society; The Urals Immunology Society; Russian Physiological Society; Society of Biotechnologists of Russia. Address: Institute of Physiology, Komi Science Centre, The Urals Branch of the Russian Academy of Sciences, 50, Pervomaiskaya str, 167982 Syktyvkar, Russia.

**OVSTEDAL Barbara Kathleen, (Rosalind Laker),** b. England. Writer. m. Inge Ovstedal, 1945, 1 son, 1 daughter. Education: West Sussex College of Art. Publications: As Rosalind Laker: The Smuggler's Bride, 1976; Ride the Blue Ribbon, 1977; The Warwyck Trilogy, 1979-80; Banners of Silk, 1981; Gilded Splendour, 1982; Jewelled Path, 1983; What the Heart Keeps, 1984; This Shining Land, 1985; Tree of Gold, 1986; The Silver Touch, 1987; To Dance With Kings, 1988; Circle of Pearls, 1990; The Golden Tulip, 1991; The Venetian Mask, 1992; The Sugar Pavilion, 1993; The Fortuny Gown, 1995; The Fragile Hour, 1996; New World, New Love, 2002; To Dream of Snow, 2004. Contributions to: Good Housekeeping; Country Life; Woman; Woman's Own; Woman's Weekly. Honour: Winner, Elizabeth Goudge Historical Award, 1989. Memberships: Society of Authors; Romantic Novelists Association. Address: c/o Juliet Burton Literary Agency, 2 Clifton Avenue, London W12 9DR, England.

**OWEN Gordon P,** b. 28 June 1953, London, England. Voluntary Sector Fundraising Consultant; Trust Company Secretary. m. Janice Joel, 2 sons. Education: Diploma in Psychology; HND, Business Studies; NVQ Desktop Publishing and Word Processing; NVQ Level 4, Training Trainees. Appointments include: Principal, Messrs G Owen & Co, 1972-; Part-time Proprietor, Rent-A-Bar Service, 1981-2003; Principal Administrative Officer, London Borough of Newham, 1976-93; Projects/Fundraising Administrator and PR Officer, 1993-2002, Newham Youth Trust (Limited); London; Founder and Developer, Newnham Youth Lodge Hostel Project, 1979-94; Never-Land (Children's Adventure), 1993-; Corporate Customer Services Manager, Technologic LSI (Europe) Limited, London, 1998; Customer Services Executive, Barclays Bank Corporate International and Offshore, 1999; Office Utilisation Consultant, 1999; Regional Administrator, CSV Volunteering Partners, 1999-2002; Senior Co-ordinator, Newham Night Shelter, 1998-2003; Fundraising and Development Officer, CVS, 2002-2004. Honour: Queens Jubilee Award, 2002-03. Memberships include: Chairman, St Bartholomew's Social Club, 1976-79; St Bartholomew's Development Committee, 1977-84; St Bartholomew's District Church Council, 1977-87, 1998-; Parish Councillor, 1978-; Newham Deanery Synod, London, 1980-81, 1982-84; Chairman, Newham Youth Leaders Association, 1979-85; London Borough of Newham Education Committee Youth Panel, 1983-84, 1985-88; Newham Voluntary Agencies Council, Children and Young People Steering Committee, 1981-83; Founder, Developer, Newham Youth Lodge Hostel Project, 1979-94; Metropolitan Police Newnham Volunteer Cadet Corps, 1996-2004; Parochial Church Council, Parish of East Ham, London, 1977-87, 2000-; Parish Warden, 1999- Fete Chairperson and Co-ordinator, Friends of Barking Church of England School PTA, 1993-94; Institute of Charity Managers; British Apple Systems Users Group Royal Horticultural Society; Cyclists Touring Club; British Mountain Bike Federation; CoachVille; TrainingZone; Former memberships: National Youth Bureau;

National Association of Youth Clubs; London Union of Youth Clubs; Individual and Commercial Member, The Carnival Guild; The National Camping and Caravanning Club; Conway Owners Club; National Union of Licensed Victuallers Association; Shop Steward, 1982-84, 1986-93, Convenor, Branch Officer/ Information Technology Officer and Metropolitan Regional Representative, UNISON formerly NALGO, Newham Branch; The London Bungee Club. Address: Owen House, Barking, Essex IG11 9HY, England. E-mail: gordonowen1@yahoo.com Website: http://clik.to/messrsgowenco

**OWEN Nicholas David Arundel**, b. 10 February 1947, United Kingdom. Journalist; Television Presenter. m. Brenda, 2 sons, 2 daughters. Appointments: Journalist: Surrey Mirror, 1964, London Evening Standard, 1968-70, Daily Telegraph, 1970-71, Financial Times, 1972-79, Now! Magazine, 1979-81; Reporter and Presenter, BBC Television News, 1981-84; Presenter, ITN, 1984-; Royal Correspondent, ITV News, 1994-2000; Channel 4 News Business and Economics Correspondent; Presented ITV1's live hour and a half Budget Programme, 2004; Anchor, Parliament Programme, Channel 4's first daytime political series; Currently Presenter of ITV Lunchtime News, 2002-. Publications: History of the British Trolleybus, 1972; Diana – The People's Princess. Address: c/o Independent Television News, 200 Gray's Inn Road, London WC1X 8XZ, England. E-mail: nicholas.owen@itn.co.uk

**OWENS John Robin**, b. 26 May 1939, Shillong, Assam, India. Chartered Accountant. m. Margaret Ann Overton, 1 son, 1 daughter. Education: Wellington College, 1953-55; Welbeck College, 1956-57; Royal Military Academy, Sandhurst, 1958-59; Mechanical Sciences Tripos with Honours, 1960-63, MA, 1965, Emmanuel College, Cambridge. Appointments: British Regular Army, 1958-68, retired in rank of Captain; Price Waterhouse, 1968-73; Qualified ACA, 1971, FCA, 1975; Midland Bank Group, 1974-84; Director, Midland Montagu Leasing, 1978; Director, Forward Trust, 1979; Director, GATX Finance, 1984-85; Managing Director, Park Place Finance, 1985-86; Managing Director, Medens, 1986-89; Director, Brown Shipley & Co, 1989-1995; Chairman, Willhire Ltd, 1991; Chief Executive, The Building Centre Group, 1996-2001; Retired, 2001. Memberships: Royal Engineers Yacht Club; Medway Yacht Club. Address: Park Cottage, Livesey Street, Teston, Maidstone, Kent ME18 5AY, England. E-mail: robin@jrowens.co.uk

**OXLEY William**, b. 29 April 1939, Manchester, England. Poet; Writer; Translator. m. Patricia Holmes, 13 April 1963, 2 daughters. Education: Manchester College of Commerce, 1953-55. Publications: The Dark Structures, 1967; New Workings 1969; Passages from Time: Poems from a Life, 1971; The Icon Poems, 1972; Sixteen Days in Autumn (travel), 1972; Opera Vetera, 1973; Mirrors of the Sea, 1973; Eve Free, 1974; Mundane Shell, 1975; Superficies, 1976; The Exile, 1979; The Notebook of Hephaestus and Other Poems, 1981; Poems of a Black Orpheus, 1981; The Synopthegms of a Prophet, 1981; The Idea and Its Imminence, 1982; Of Human Consciousness, 1982; The Cauldron of Inspiration, 1983; A Map of Time, 1984; The Triviad and Other Satires, 1984; The Inner Tapestry, 1985; Vitalism and Celebration, 1987; The Mansands Trilogy, 1988; Mad Tom on Tower Hill, 1988; The Patient Reconstruction of Paradise, 1991; Forest Sequence, 1991; In the Drift of Words, 1992; The Playboy, 1992; Cardboard Troy, 1993; The Hallsands Tragedy, 1993; Collected Longer Poems, 1994; Completing the Picture (editor), 1995; The Green Crayon Man, 1997; No Accounting for Paradise (autobiography), 1999; Firework Planet (for children), 2000; Reclaiming the Lyre: New and Selected Poems, 2001; Namaste: Nepal Poems, 2004; London Visions, 2005. Contributions to: Anthologies and periodicals. Address:

6 The Mount, Furzeham, Brixham, South Devon TQ5 8QY, England.

**OYAMA Munetaka**, b. 5 September 1963, Fukuoka, Japan. Associate Professor. m. Mieko Oyama, 2 sons. Education: Master of Science, 1988, Doctor of Science, 1991, Kyoto University, Japan. Appointments: Research Associate, Nagoya University, Japan, 1991-94; Research Associate, 1994-99, Associate Professor, 1999-, Kyoto University, Japan. Publications: Over 80 articles in scientific journals including: Journal of Physical Chemistry A, 2002; Chemistry Communications, 2002; Perkin 2, 2001, 2002. Honour: Sano Award, Japan Electrochemical Society, 1998. Memberships: Electrochemical Society; International Electrochemical Society. Address: International Innovation Center, Kyoto University, Sakyo-ku, Kyoto 606-8501, Japan. E-mail: oyama@iic.kyoto-u.ac.jp

**OYLER Edmund John Wilfrid**, b. 8 February 1934, London, England. Chartered Accountant. m. Elizabeth Kathleen Larkins, 1961, 2 sons, 1 daughter. Education: Trinity College, Cambridge, 1953-56; BA, 1956; MA 1960; University College, London, 1970-72; LLM, 1972; Heythrop College, London, 1997-2000; MTh, 2000. Appointments: National Service, 2nd Lieutenant, Royal Signals, 1951-53; Chartered accountant in public practice, ACA, 1961, FCA, 1972; Articled – Pannell Crewdson and Hardy, 1956-60; Whinney Smith and Whinney, 1961; Partner, Whinney Murray and Co, 1967-79; Partner, Ernst and Whinney, 1979-89; Partner, Ernst and Young, 1989-97; Partner specialising in taxation of insurance companies, 1967-92; National tax partner, 1978-81; Partner with national responsibility for trusts, 1985-89; National compliance partner, 1988-97; Sole Practitioner, 1997-99. Memberships: Athenaeum; Madrigal Society; Georgian Group; Royal Geographical Society; Activities for ICAEW include: Co-opted Member of Council, 1996-99, Chairman, Financial Services Authorisation Committee, 1995-2001, Chairman, Joint Investment Business Committee, 1995-2001, Chairman, London Society of Chartered Accountants, 1996-97, Chairman, Joint Monitoring Unit Limited, 1997-2001. Address: 20 Bedford Gardens, London, W8 7EH, England.

**OZ Amos**, b. 4 May 1939, Jerusalem, Israel. Author; Professor of Hebrew Literature. m. Nily Zuckerman, 5 April 1960, 1 son, 2 daughters. Education: BA cum laude, Hebrew Literature, Philosophy, Hebrew University, Jerusalem, 1965; MA, St Cross College, Oxford, 1970. Appointments: Teacher, Literature, Philosophy, Huldah High School and Givat Brenner Regional High School, 1963-86; Visiting Fellow, St Cross College, Oxford, England, 1969-70; Writer-in-Residence, Hebrew University, Jerusalem, 1975-76, 1990; Writer-in-Residence, University of California, Berkeley, USA, 1980; Writer-in-Residence, Professor of Literature, The Colorado College, Colorado Springs, 1984-85; Writer-in-Residence, Visiting Professor of Literature, Boston University, Massachusetts, 1987; Full Professor of Hebrew Literature, Ben Gurion University, Beer Sheva, Israel, 1987-2005; Writer-in-Residence, Tel Aviv University, 1996; Writer-in-Residence, Visiting Professor of Literature, Princeton University, (Old Dominion Fellowship), 1997; Weidenfeld Visiting Professor of European Comparative Literature, St Anne's College, Oxford, 1998. Publications include: Where the Jackals Howl (stories), 1965, My Michael (novel), 1968; Under This Blazing Light (essays), 1978; Black Box (novel), 1987; Don't Call It Night (novel), 1994; All Our Hopes (essays) 1998; The Same Sea, 1999; A Tale of Love and Darkness (novel), 2002. Honours include: Holon Prize, 1965; Wingate Prize, London, 1988; Honorary Doctorate, Tel Aviv University, 1992; Frankfurt Peace Prize, 1992; Knight's Cross of the National Legion D'Honneur, France, 1997; Honorary

Doctorate, Brandeis University, USA, 1998; Israel's Prize for Literature, 1998; My Michael selected by Bertelsmann international publishers' panel as one of the greatest 100 novels of the 20th Century, 1999; Freedom of Expression Prize, Writers' Union of Norway, 2002; Goethe Cultural Award for his life's Work, 2005. Address: c/o Deborah Owen Ltd, 78 Narrow Street Limehouse, London E14 8BP, England.

**OZAWA Takeo,** b. 14 February 1932, Yokohama, Japan. Material Scientist. m. Hisae, 30 June 1957, 1 son, 1 daughter. Education: BSc 1955, MSc 1957, DSc 1980, University of Tokyo. Appointments: Researcher, 1957-70, Section Chief, 1970-87, Electrotech Laboratory, AIST, MITI; General Manager, Tsakuba Research Center, Daicel Chemical Industries Ltd, 1987-97; Professor, Chiba Institute of Technology, Department of Electrical Engineering, 1997-2002; Retired 2002; Part-time Professor, Chiba Institute of Technology Department of Electrical Engineering, 2002-03. Publications: Over 100 original papers. Honours: Mettler Award, North American Thermal Analysis Society, 1981; Best Energy Storage Paper, American Society of Mechanical Engineering, 1986; Kurnakov Medal, Kurnakov Institute of General and Inorganic Chemistry, 1984; ICTAC-TA Instruments Award, 2000. Memberships: President, International Confederation for Thermal Analysis and Calorimetry, 1992-96; Japan Society for Chemistry; Japan Institute for Electrical Engineers; Japan Society for Polymer Science. Address: 18-6 Josuishin-machi 1-chome, Kodaira, Tokyo 187-0023, Japan.

**OZICK Cynthia,** b. 17 April 1928, New York, New York, USA. Author; Poet; Dramatist; Critic; Translator. m. Bernard Hallote, 7 September 1952, 1 daughter. Education: BA, cum laude, English, New York University, 1949; MA, Ohio State University, 1950. Appointment: Phi Beta Kappa Orator, Harvard University, 1985. Publications: Trust, 1966; The Pagan Rabbi and Other Stories, 1971; Bloodshed and Three Novellas, 1976; Leviation: Five Fictions, 1982; Art and Ardor: Essays, 1983; The Cannibal Galaxy, 1983; The Messiah of Stockholm, 1987; Metaphor and Memory: Essays, 1989; The Shawl, 1989; Epodes: First Poems, 1992; What Henry James Knew, and Other Essays on Writers, 1994; Portrait of the Artist as a Bad Character, 1996; The Cynthia Ozick Reader, 1996; Fame and Folly, 1996; The Puttermesser Papers, 1997; The Best American Essays, 1998; Quarrel and Quandary, 2000. Contributions to: Many anthologies, reviews, quarterlies, journals, and periodicals. Honours: Guggenheim Fellowship, 1982; Mildred and Harold Strauss Living Award, American Academy of Arts and Letters, 1983; Lucy Martin Donnelly Fellow, Bryn Mawr College, 1992; PEN/Spiegel-Diamonstein Award for the Art of the Essay, 1997; Harold Washington Literary Award, City of Chicago, 1997; John Cheever Award, 1999; Lotos Club Medal of Merit, 2000; Lannan Foundation Award, 2000; National Critics' Circle Award for Criticism, 2001; Koret Foundation Aard for Literary Studies, 2001; Many honorary doctorates. Memberships: American Academy of Arts and Letters; American Academy of Arts and Sciences; Authors League; Dramatists Guild; PEN; Phi Beta Kappa. Address: c/o Alfred A Knopf Inc, 201 East 50th Street, New York, NY 10022, USA.

**ÖZSOYLU N Şinasi,** b. 29 August 1927, Erzurum, Turkey. Physician. m. F Selma, 2 sons, 1 daughter. Education: Istanbul University, 1951; Ankara University, 1959; Washington University, 1960, 1961; Harvard University, 1963. Appointments: Associate Professor, Paediatrics, Hacettepe University; Professor of Paediatrics and Haematology, 1969; Head, Paediatrics Department, 1976; Head, Haematology and Hepatology Departments, 1973-94. Publications: 855 in professional journals. Honours include: İhsan Dogramaci Award,

1979; Mustafa N Parlar Award, 1989; Hacettepe University Excellence in Science Achievement Award, 1991; TUSAV Honorary Award, 2002. Memberships: American Academy of Paediatrics, Honorary Fellow; American Paediatrics Society, Honorary Member; Islamic Academy of Sciences; Turkish Paediatric Society. Address: Fatih University Medical Faculty, Alparslan Türkeş Cad No 57 Emek, Ankara 06510, Turkey.

**OZVEREN Ali Evrenay,** b. 6 October 1945, Ankara, Turkey. Architect. m. Susan, 1 son. Education: Bachelor of Architecture Degree, Middle East Technical University, Ankara, Turkey, 1971. Appointments: Associate, 1979-84, Partner, 1984-91, Senior Partner, 1991-, GMW Architects, London; Managing Director, GMW Mimarlik, Turkey, 2000-. Honours: Award-winning projects include: The new international passenger terminals at Istanbul Atatürk Airport, Turkey; Ankara Esenboga Airport, Turkey; Mugla Dalaman Airport, Turkey. Memberships: Chamber of Architects of Turkey; Fellow, Royal Society of Arts, UK; Fellow, Chartered Society of Designers, UK. Address: GMW Architects, PO Box 1613, 239 Kensington High Street, London W8 6SI., England. E-mail: ali.ozveren@gmw-architects.com

# P

**PÄÄSUKE Mati**, b. 2 April 1954 Viljandi, Estonia. Professor. m. Maive Pääsuke, 1 son. Education: Diploma Physical Education, 1976, PhD, Physiology, University of Tartu, Estonia. Appointments: Researcher, 1981-88, Associate Professor, 1989-2001, Dean of Faculty of Exercise and Sports Sciences, 1989-98, Head, Institute of Exercise Biology and Physiotherapy, 1998-2004, Professor of Kinesiology and Biomechanics, 2002-, University of Tartu, Estonia. Publications: Over 40 articles in international refereed journals including: Acta Orthopaedica Scandinavica; Acta Physiologica Scandinavica; Annals of Anatomy, Ageing: Clinical and Experimental Research; European Journal of Applied Physiology; Electromyography and Clinical Neurophysiology; Pediatric Exercise Science. Honours: Listed in Who's Who publications and biographical dictionaries. Memberships: Estonian Physiological Society; Estonian Federation of Sports Medicine; International Society of Biomechanics in Sports. Address: Institute of Exercise Biology and Physiotherapy, University of Tartu, 5 Jakobi Street, 51014 Tartu, Estonia. E-mail: mati.paasuke@ut.ee Website: www.ut.ee/KKKB

**PACINO Al (Alfredo James)**, b. 25 April 1940, New York, USA. Actor. Education: The Actors Studio. Appointments: Messenger, Cinema Usher; Co-Artistic Director, The Actors Studio Inc, New York, 1982-83; Member, Artistic Directorate Globe Theatre, 1997-. Creative Works: Films include: Me, Natalie, 1969; Panic in Needle Park, 1971; The Godfather, 1972; Scarecrow, 1973; Serpico, 1974; The Godfather Part II, 1974; Dog Day Afternoon, 1975; Bobby Deerfield, 1977; And Justice For All, 1979; Cruising, 1980; Author! Author!, 1982; Scarface, 1983; Revolution, 1985; Sea of Love, 1990; Dick Tracy, 1991; The Godfather Part III, 1990; Frankie and Johnny, 1991; Glengarry Glen Ross, 1992; Scent of A Woman, 1992; Carlito's Way, 1994; City Hall, 1995; Heat, 1995; Donny Brasco, 1996; Looking For Richard, 1996; Devil's Advocate, 1997; The Insider, 1999; Chinese Coffee, 1999; Man of the People, 1999; Any Given Sunday, 1999; Insomnia, 2002; Simone, 2002; People I Know, 2002; The Recruit, 2003; Gigli, 2003. Honours include: Tony Award, 1996; British Film Award; National Society of Film Critics Award. Address: c/o Rick Nicita, CAA, 9830 Wilshire Boulevard, Beverly Hills, CA 90212, USA.

**PACKER Kerry Francis Bullmore**, b. 17 December 1937, Sydney, New South Wales, Australia. Publishing and Broadcasting Executive. m. Roslyn Weedon, 30 August 1963, 1 son, 1 daughter. Appointments: Chairman, Consolidated Press Holdings Ltd, 1974-; Director, Publishing & Broadcasting Ltd, 1994-. Memberships: Royal Sydney Golf Club; Australian Golf Club; Elanora Co Club; Tattersall's Athaeneum (Melbourne) Club. Address: Consolidated Press Holdings Ltd, 54 Park Street, Sydney, NSW 2000, Australia.

**PACKER William John**, b. 19 August 1940, Birmingham, England. Artist; Critic. m. Clare Winn. Education: Wimbledon School of Art, 1959-63; Brighton College of Art, 1963-64. Career: First exhibited Royal Academy 1963, many group exhibitions since then; Teacher in art schools, 1967-77; External Examiner, Visitor and Advisor at various art schools, 1979-; Art Critic, Art and Artists, 1969-74; Art Critic, Financial Times, 1974-; Recent Solo Exhibitions: Piers Feetham Gallery, 1996, 2001, 2004; Exhibitions curated include: British Art Show I, 1979-80; Elizabeth Blackadder Retrospective, 1984; Martin Fuller Retrospective, 2002. Publications: Books include: The Art of Vogue Covers, 1980; Fashion Drawing in Vogue, 1983; Henry Moore, 1986; John Houston, 2003; Numerous freelance

reviews, articles and catalogue essays. Honours: Honorary Fellow, Royal College of Art; Honorary RBA; Honorary FRBS; Honorary PS; Inaugural Henry Moore Lecturer, British Institute Florence, 1986; Artist Fellow, Ballinglen Foundation, Co Mayo, Ireland, 1995. Memberships: Crafts Council, 1980-87; Government Art Collection Advisory Committee, 1977-84; Fine Art Board, National Council for Academic Awards, 1976-83; International Association of Arts Critics; Chelsea Arts Club; Academy Club, Soho; The Garrick Club. Address: 39 Elms Road, London SW4 9EP, England.

**PACOLD Astra Paula**, b. 6 December 1957, Chicago, Illinois, USA. Doctor of Dental Surgery; Artist; Insurance Agent. Education: Illinois Benedictine College, Lisle, Illinois, 1975-76; Bachelor of Arts Degree, Mount St Mary's College, Los Angeles, California, 1979; Doctor of Dental Surgery, Northwestern Dental School, Chicago, Illinois, 1987; Continuing education certificate diplomas from Harvard medical School, CME, 2002, 2003, 2004. Appointments: Chief Executive Officer, Q-Arts, 1981-; Designer and manufacturer of dental and medical devices including Dropper Holder Caddy, forceps with disposable tips, Dental Aperture Asthma Twist Top; Graphic Designer; Sole Practitioner, Dental Practice, 1987-97; Insurance Agent, Owner of Alpine and Associates Financial Services. Publications: Articles in professional journals including: Contemporary Esthetics and Restorative Materials Magazine; Dental Products Report; Dental Economics Magazine; Poetry Book: The Colors of Life, 2003. Honour: CEO Leadership Achievement Award, 2003-2004. Memberships: International Association of Dental Research; American Association of Dental Research; Delta Sigma Delta Etu (Dental Fraternity); National Rifle Association; North American Hunting Club; Aircraft Owners and Pilots Association. Address: 14015 Cambridge Circles, Plainfield, IL 60544, USA. E-mail: qvpido@aol.com Website: http://qvpido.com

**PADFIELD Peter Lawrence Notton**, b. 3 April 1932, Calcutta, India. Author. m. Dorothy Jean Yarwood, 23 April 1960, 1 son, 2 daughters. Publications: The Sea is a Magic Carpet, 1960; The Titanic and the Californian, 1965; An Agony of Collisions, 1966; Aim Straight: A Biography of Admiral Sir Percy Scott, 1966; Broke and the Shannon: A Biography of Admiral Sir Philip Broke, 1968; The Battleship Era, 1972; Guns at Sea: A History of Naval Gunnery, 1973; The Great Naval Race: Anglo-German Naval Rivalry 1900-1914, 1974; Nelson's War, 1978; Tide of Empires: Decisive Naval Campaigns in the Rise of the West, Vol I 1481-1654, 1979, Vol II 1654-1763, 1982; Rule Britannia: The Victorian and Edwardian Navy, 1981; Beneath the Houseflag of the P & O, 1982; Dönitz, The Last Führer, 1984; Armada, 1988; Himmler, Reichsführer - SS, 1990; Hess: Flight for the Führer 1991, revised, updated edition, Hess: The Führer's Disciple, 1993; War Beneath the Sea: Submarine Conflict 1939-1945, 1995; Maritime Supremacy and the Opening of the Western Mind: Naval Campaigns that Shaped the Modern World 1588-1782, 1999; Maritime Power and the Struggle for Freedom: Naval Campaigns that Shaped the Modern World 1788-1851, 2003. Novels: The Lion's Claw, 1978; The Unquiet Gods, 1980; Gold Chains of Empire, 1982; Salt and Steel, 1986. Honour: Winner Mountbatten Maritime Prize, 2003. Membership: Society for Nautical Research. Address: Westmoreland Cottage, Woodbridge, Suffolk, England.

**PADMANABHAN Krishnan**, b. 11 May 1964, Trivandrum City, India. Research and Development Officer. Education: MSc, Eng, Materials Engineering, Indian Institute of Science, Bangalore, 1991; PhD, Materials Engineering, Indian Institute of Science, Bangalore, 1995. Appointments: Postdoctoral Fellow, Nanyang Technological University, Singapore, 1996-98; Guest

Researcher, University of Delaware and National Institute of Standards and Technology, USA, 1998-99; Guest Faculty, IIT, Madras, 1999; Research Fellow, Singapore MIT Alliance, 2000-02; Consultant, CEO, KALPANA. Publications: Over 50 articles in international refereed journals; Proceedings at international conferences and workshops; Many oral and poster presentations, short articles, lectures and seminars. Address: New No 40, 14th Cross Street, New Colony, Chromepet, Chennai 600044, India.

**PAE Chi-Un,** b. 1 May 1967, Pusan, Republic of Korea. Psychiatrist. m. You-Jeong Lee, 1 daughter. Education: MD, The Catholic University of Korea, 1992; MS, 2002, PhD, 2005, The Catholic University of Korea Graduate Medical School. Appointment: Assistant Professor, Department of Psychiatry, Kangnam St Mary's Hospital, The Catholic University of Korea College of Medicine. Publications: Articles in leading medical journals including: Psychiatric Genetics; Clinical Psychopharmacology; Biological Psychiatry in the Schizophrenia Research; International Journal of Neuropsychopharmacology; Journal of Clinical Psychiatry; Journal of Affective Disorders and other leading journals worldwide. Honours: Young Investigator Award, Korean Neuropsychiatric Association, 2002; Young Investigator Award, Korean College of Neuropsychopharmacology, 2003. Memberships: Korean Neuropsychiatric Association; Korean College of Neuropsychopharmacology; Korean Society of Biological Psychiatry. Address: Department of Psychiatry, Kangnam St Mary's Hospital, 505 Bampo-Dong, Seochi-Gu, Seoul 137-701, South Korea. E-mail: pae@catholic.ac.kr

**PAGE (Arthur) John (Sir),** b. 16 September 1919, London, England. Retired MP and Company Chairman. m. Anne Micklem, 4 sons. Education: Harrow School; Magdalene College, Cambridge, 1938-39. Appointments: World War II: Served with Norfolk Yeomanry in Middle East and Europe, 1939-45; MP, Conservative, Harrow West, 1960-87; Chairman, 3 Valleys Water, Hatfield, 1986-2001. Publications: A Page at a Time (autobiography), 2000; Numerous articles. Honours: Knighthood, 1984; Council of Europe Medal, 1988. Memberships: Brooks's; MCC. Address: Hitcham Lodge, Taplow, Buckinghamshire SL6 0HG, England.

**PAGEL Bernard E J,** b. 4 January 1930, Berlin, Germany. Astronomer. m. Annabel, 2 sons, 1 daughter. Education: Sidney Sussex College, Cambridge, 1947-50; The Observatories, Cambridge, 1950-54; University of Michigan, USA, 1952-53. Appointments: Research Fellow, Sidney Sussex College, 1953-56; Staff, Royal Greenwich Observatory, Herstmonceux, 1956-90; Professor of Astrophysics, NORDITA, Copenhagen, Denmark, 1990-98; Visiting Professor of Astronomy, University of Sussex, 1970-. Publications: Books: Théorie des Atmosphères Stellaires, 1971; Nucleosynthesis and Chemical Evolution of Galaxies, 1997; Research papers in scientific journals including: Nature, Monthly Notices of the RAS, conference proceedings. Honours: Kelvin Lecturer, BAAS, Manchester, 1962; Royal Astronomical Society Gold Medal, 1990; Fellow of the Royal Society, 1992. Memberships: Royal Astronomical Society; International Astronomical Union; Royal Society. Address: Groombridge, Lewes Road, Ringmer, East Sussex BN8 5ER, England. E-mail: bejp@sussex.ac.uk

**PAGET Henry James,** b. 2 February 1959, Wegberg, Germany. Senior Partner. m. Margrete Lynner, 1 son, 1 daughter. Education: Radley College, Oxfordshire. Appointments: Coldstream Guards; Provident Mutual; Barclays Bank plc; Hill Samuel; Senior Partner, St James's Place plc. Membership: Cavalry and Guards Club. Address: Summerfield, Little London, Heathfield, Sussex TN21 0NU, England.

**PAGET Julian Tolver (Lt. Col. Sir),** b. 11 July 1921, London, England. Army Officer. m. Diana Farmer, 1 son, 1 daughter. Education: MS, Modern Languages, Christ Church Oxford, 1939-40. Appointments: Commission in Coldstream Guards, 1940-68; Served Northwest Europe, 1944-45; Retired as Lieutenant Colonel, 1968; Author, 1967-; Gentleman Usher to H M The Queen, 1971-91. Publications: Counter Insurgency Campaigning, 1967; Last Post, Aden 1964-67, 1969; The Story of the Guards, 1976; The Pageantry of Britain, 1979; The Yeoman of the Guard, 1984; Wellington's Peninsular War, 1990; Hougoumont, 1992; The Coldstream Guards 1650-2000, 2000. Honours: Succeeded as 4th Baronet, 1972; CVO, 1984. Memberships: Cavalry and Guards Club; Flyfishers Club.

**PAGLIA Camille (Anna),** b. 2 April 1947, Endicott, New York, USA. Professor of Humanities; Writer. Education: BA, State University of New York at Binghamton, 1968; MPhil, 1971, PhD, 1974, Yale University. Appointments: Faculty, Bennington College, Vermont, 1972-80; Visiting Lecturer, Wesleyan University, 1980; Visiting Lecturer, Yale University, 1980-84; Assistant Professor, 1984-87, Associate Professor, 1987-91, Professor of Humanities, 1991-2000, Philadelphia College of the Performing Arts, later the University of the Arts, Philadelphia; Columnist, Salon.com, 1995-2001; University Professor and Professor of Humanities and Media Studies, University of the Arts, 2000-; Contributing Editor, Interview magazine, 2001-. Publications: Sexual Personae: Art and Decadence from Nefertiti to Emily Dickinson, 1990; Sex, Art, and American Culture: Essays, 1992; Vamps and Tramps: New Essays, 1994; Alfred Hitchcock's "The Birds", 1998; Break, Blow, Burn: Camille Paglia Reads Forty-Three of the World's Best Poems, 2005. Contributions to: Journals and periodicals and Internet communications. Address: University of the Arts, 320 South Broad Street, Philadelphia, PA 19102, USA.

**PAHANG H.R.H. Sultan of,** b. 24 October 1930, Istana Mangga Tunggal, Pekan, Malaysia. m. Tengku Hajjah Afzan binti Tengku Muhammad, 1954. Education: Malay College, Kuala Kangsar; Worcester College, Oxford; University College, Exeter. Appointments: Tengku Mahkota (Crown Prince), 1944; Captain, 4th Battalion, Royal Malay Regiment, 1954; Commander, 12th Infantry Battalion of Territorial Army, 1963-65, Lieutenant-Colonel; Member, State Council, 1955; Regent, 1956, 1959, 1965; Succeeded as Sultan, 1974; Timbalan Yang di Pertuan Agong (Deputy Supreme Head of State), Malaysia, 1975-79, Yang di Pertuan Agong (Supreme Head of State), 1979-84, 1985; Constitutional Head, International Islamic University, 1988. Honours include: DLitt, Malaya, 1988, LLD, Northrop, USA, 1993. Address: Istana Abu Bakar, Pekan, Pahang, Malaysia.

**PAICHADZE Sergei A,** b. 7 June 1936, Batumi, Georgia. Bibliologist. m. Larisa A Kozhevnikova, 1 son, 1 daughter. Education: Library Institute, 1956-61; Postgraduate, 1967-70; PhD, 1971; DSc, 1992; Professor, 1994. Appointments: Instructor, Dean, Proctor, Institute of Culture, Chabarovsk, 1971-86; Researcher, 1986-93; Head, Bibliology Group, 1995-2002; Senior Researcher, State Public Scientific Technician Library of the Siberian Branch of the Russian Academy of Sciences, 2002-; Member, Editorial Board of 2 scientific journals; Deputy Head of the PhD Council; Member, Committee on Complex Book Study, World Culture Council, RAS. Publications: More than 200 publications, monographs and articles in professional journals; 15 successful PhD students. Honour: Laureate, All-Russian Competitions of Scientific Works. Membership: Research Board of Advisors, American Biographical Institute, 2005-. Address: ul Voschod 15, 630200 Novosibirsk, Russia.

**PAIGE Elaine,** b. 5 March 1948, Barnet, England. Singer; Actress. Education: Aida Foster Stage School. Creative Works: West End theatre appearances in Hair, 1968, Jesus Christ Superstar, 1973, Grease (played Sandy), 1973, Billy (played Rita), 1974, Created roles of Eva Peron in Evita, 1978 and Grizabella in Cats, 1981, Abbacadabra (played Carabosse), 1983, Chess (played Florence), 1986, Anything Goes (played Reno Sweeney), 1989, Piaf, 1993-94, Sunset Boulevard (played Norma Desmond), 1995-96, The Misanthrope (played Célimène), 1998; The King and I, 2000; 14 solo albums, 4 multi-platinum albums, 8 consecutive gold albums. Honours include: Society of West End Theatres Award, 1978; Variety Club Award, 1986; British Association of Songwriters, Composers & Authors Award, 1993; Lifetime Achievement Award, National Operatic and Dramatic Association, 1999. Address: c/o EP Records, M M & M Pinewood Studios, Pinewood Road, Iver, Bucks SL10 0NH, England.

**PAISLEY Ian Richard Kyle,** b. 6 April 1926, Ireland. Politician; Minister of Religion. m. Eileen E Cassells, 1956, 2 sons, 3 daughters. Education: South Wales Bible College; Reformed Presbyterian Theological College, Belfast. Appointments: Ordained, 1946; Minister, Martyrs Memorial Free Presbyterian Church, 1946-; Moderator, Free Presbyterian Church of Ulster, 1951; Founder, The Protestant Telegraph, 1966; Leader (co-founder), Democratic Unionist Party, 1972; MP (Democratic Unionist), 1974-, (Protestant Unionist 1970-74), resigned seat, 1985 in protest against the Anglo-Irish Agreement; Re-elected, 1986; MP (Protestant Unionist) for Bannside, Co Antrim, Parliament of Northern Ireland (Stormont), 1970-72, Leader of the Opposition, 1972, Chair, Public Accounts Committee, 1972; Member, Northern Ireland Assembly, 1973-74, elected to Second Northern Ireland Assembly, 1982; Member, European Parliament, 1979-; MP for Antrim North, Northern.Ireland Assembly, 1998-2000; Member, Political Committee European Parliament Northern Ireland Assembly, 1998-. Publications include: Jonathan Edwards, The Theologian of Revival, 1987; Union with Rome, 1989; The Soul of the Question, 1990; The Revised English Bible: An Exposure, 1990; What a Friend We Have in Jesus, 1994; Understanding Events in Northern Ireland: An Introduction for Americans, 1995; My Plea for the Old Sword, 1997; The Rent Veils at Calvary, 1997; A Text a Day Keeps the Devil Away, 1997. Address: The Parsonage, 17 Cyprus Avenue, Belfast BT5 5NT, Northern Ireland.

**PAIVA Melquíades Pinto,** b. 6 March 1930, Lavras da Mangabeira, Brazil. Agronomist Engineer; University Professor. m. Maria Arair Pinto Paiva, 2 sons, 2 daughters. Education: School of Agronomy of Ceará, 1949-52; Agronomist Engineer; Specialisation in Ichthyology, National Museum of Natural History, Rio de Janeiro, 1956-57; University of São Paulo, 1969-72; Doctor of Biological Sciences. Appointments: Retired Full Professor, Federal University of Ceará, 1954-87; Visiting Professor, Researcher, Federal University of Rio de Janeiro, 1992-2004. Publications: 258 scientific papers, 31 scientific and technical books. Honours: Honorary Citizen of Fortaleza City, 1982; Medal, Presidente Castelo Branco of Ceará State Government, 1984; Medal, Scientific Merit, Federal University of Ceará, 1987; Medal Francisco Gonçalves de Aguiar of Ceará State Government, 1999; Honor Merit Certificate, Brazilian Society of Zoology, 2000; Trophy Sereia de Ouro of Organizations Vendes Mares (radio, journal and television) of Cearia, 2004; Emeritus Director, Marine Sciences Institute, Federal University of Ceará. Memberships include: Brazilian Society for the Advancement of Science; New York Academy of Sciences; American Fisheries Society; American Society for the Advancement of Science. Address: Rua Baronesa de Poconé, 71/701 Lagoa, 22471-270 Rio de Janeiro, Brazil. E-mail: mappaiva@uol.wm.br

**PAKENHAM Michael (The Honourable Sir),** b. 3 November 1943, Oxford, England. Company Director. m. Meta, 2 daughters. Education: MA (Cantab), Trinity College, Cambridge, 1964; Rice University, Houston, Texas, USA. Appointments: Ambassador to Luxembourg, 1991-94; Minister, British Embassy, Paris, 1994-97; Chairman, Joint Intelligence Committee and Intelligence Co-ordinator, 1997-2000; Ambassador to Poland, 2001-2003; Chairman, Pakerwest International, 2004-; International Adviser, Firecrest Hambro, 2004-; Director, Signet Management, 2004-; Senior Advisor, Access Industries, 2004-. Honours: CMG, 1993; KBE, 2003. Memberships: MCC; Garrick Club; Beefsteak Club; Rye Golf Club. Address: 34 Aldridge Road Villas, London W11 1BW, England.

**PAL Dulal Chandra,** b. 25 October 1940, Bangladesh (East Pakistan). Scientist; Indian Medicinal Plants Expert; Expert on Tribal Medicine, Plant Taxonomy and Indian Grasses; Social Worker. 1 son, 1 daughter. Education: MSc; FBS; FEs; FIAT; MNASc; MA Soc; FIAcd Soci Sc; BA (Special); German (Cert), Russian (Cert), Hindi (Pragya). Appointments: Lecturer, Botany, Degree College; Scientist, Government of India; Guest Professor, Botany, Vidya Sagar University, WB; Advisor, Compendium Government WB; Advisor, India Agri-Hort Society; Member, IPR India Chapter. Publications: 15 books; 186 scientific papers; 20 popular articles. Honours: Fellow: Botanical Society; Ethnobotanical Society; Indian Angiosperm; Taxonomy; Hersberger Medal, 2003. Memberships: National Academy of Science; Indian Botanical Society; Indian Science Congress Association; Indian Academy of Social Science; Asiatic Society.

**PAL Satyabrata,** b. 5 April 1945, Calcutta, West Bengal, India. University Professor; Dean of Post-Graduate Studies. m. Sm Swastika Pal, 1 son, 1 daughter. Education: BSc, Honours, 1964, MSc, 1966, PhD, Statistics, 1979, Calcutta University. Appointments: Lecturer, Ashutosh College, Calcutta, 1967-69; Lecturer, Assistant Professor, Kalyani University, 1969-74, Bidhan Chandra Krishi Viswavidyalaya, 1974-75; Reader, Associate Professor, 1975-82, Professor, 1983-, Head, 1979-82, 1985-88, 1995-98, Department of Agricultural Statistics, Faculty of Agriculture, Bidhan Chandra Krishi Viswavidyalaya, BCKV. Publications: 90 papers in international and national journals; 2 books on statistics, forthcoming. Honours: Elected Member, International Statistical Institute, Permanent Officer: Netherlands; Fellow: Academy of Science and Technology, West Bengal, Calcutta, India; Inland Fisheries Society of India, Barrackpore, West Bengal, India; Indian Association of Hydrologists, Roorkee, India; Senior Post Doctoral Fellow, International Rice Research Institute, Manila, Philippines. Memberships: Governing Body Member, Life Member of 6 societies and associations; Member, Finance Committee, International Biometric Society, USA; Governing Body Member, International Biometric Society, Indian Region. Address: 101/B Bakul Bagan Road, Kolkata 700025, West Bengal, India. E-mail: satbrpal@vsnl.net

**PALELLA Thomas Daniel,** b. 1 February 1951, Chicago, Illinois, USA. Physician; Rheumatologist. m. Julia Blackburn, 1 son, 1 daughter. Education: BS, Physics, Magna Cum Laude, John Carroll University, Cleveland, Ohio, 1969-73; MD (Hons), University of Illinois College of Medicine, Chicago, 1973-77. Appointments include: Intern, Internal Medicine, Michael Reese Hospital, Chicago, 1977-78; Research Fellow, Rackham Arthritis Research Unit and Human Purine Research Center,

1978-80, Resident, Internal Medicine, 1980-82, Chief Resident, Department of Internal Medicine, 1982-83, Assistant Professor of Internal Medicine (Rheumatology), 1983-89, Chief, Division of Rheumatology, Department of Internal Medicine, 1988-91, Director, Rackham Arthritis Research Unit, 1988-9, Associate Professor of Internal Medicine (Rheumatology), 1989-91, University of Michigan Medical Center, Ann Arbor, Michigan; Staff Physician, Veterans Administration Medical Center, Ann Arbor, Michigan, 1986-91; Faculty, Resident Training Programmes, Internal Medicine and Family Practice, Lutheran General Hospital, Park Ridge, Illinois, 1990-; Consultant to: SmithKline Beecham, Speakers Bureau, 1994-, G D Searle & Co, Medical Advisory Board (Arthritis Centers), 1995-; Pfizer US Pharmaceutical Group, Medical Advisory Board, 1996-; Rheumatologist, Private Practice, 1990-. Publications: 34 articles in peer-reviewed medical journals; 12 non peer reviewed articles; 44 abstracts; 12 book chapters include: Gout remedies, 1989; Disorders of purine and pyrimidine metabolism, 1990; Rheumatoid Arthritis, 1990; Gout and other disorders of purine metabolism, 1990. Honours include: James Scholar, University of Illinois College of Medicine, 1973-77; Alpha Omega Alpha, 1977; The Upjohn Award, 1977; Arthritis Foundation Investigator Award, 1984-87; Establishment of the Thomas D Palella Award for Excellence in Teaching, The University of Michigan Division of Rheumatology, 1990. Elected to The Best Doctors in America, 1996. Memberships include: Fellow, American Rheumatism Association; American College of Rheumatology, President, Central Region, 1996-97; American College of Physicians; American Federation for Clinical Research; American Society of Human Genetics; William D Robinson Society, University of Michigan, President, 1996; Society for Inherited Metabolic Diseases. Address: 150 N River Road, Suite #270, Des Plaines, IL60016, USA.

**PALEY Grace,** b. 11 December 1922, New York, New York, USA. Author; Poet; Retired University teacher. m. (1) Jess Paley, 20 June 1942, divorced, 1 son, 1 daughter, (2) Robert Nichols, 1972. Education: Hunter College, New York City, 1938-39; New York University. Appointments: Teacher, Columbia University, Syracuse University, Sarah Lawrence College, City College of the City University of New York. Publications: Fiction: The Little Disturbances of Man: Stories of Women and Men at Love, 1968; Enormous Changes at the Last Minute, 1974; Later the Same Day, 1985; The Collected Stories, 1994. Poetry: Long Walks and Intimate Talks (includes stories), 1991; New and Collected Poems, 1992. Other: Leaning Forward, 1985; Three Hundred Sixty-Five Reasons Not to Have Another War: 1989 Peace Calender (with Vera B Williams), 1988; Just as I Thought, 1998; Begin Again (poems), 2000. Contributions to: Books, anthologies and magazines. Honours: Guggenheim Fellowship, 1961; National Institute of Arts and Letters Award, 1970; Edith Wharton Citation of Merit as the first State Author of New York, New York State Writers Institute, 1986; National Endowment for the Arts Senior Fellowship, 1987; Vermont Governor's Award for Excellence in the Arts, 1993. Membership: American Academy of Arts and Letters. Address: Box 620, Thetford Hill, VT 05074, USA.

**PALIN Michael Edward,** b. 5 May 1943, Sheffield, Yorkshire, England. Freelance Writer and Actor. m. Helen M Gibbins, 1966, 2 sons, 1 daughter. Education: BA, Brasenose College, Oxford, 1965. Appointments: Actor, Writer: Monty Python's Flying Circus, BBC TV, 1969-74; Ripping Yarns, BBC TV 1976-80; Writer, East of Ipswich, BBC TV, 1986; Films: Actor and Joint Author: And Now for Something Completely Different, 1970; Monty Python and the Holy Grail, 1974; Monty Python's Life of Brian, 1978; Time Bandits, 1980; Monty Python's The Meaning of Life, 1982; Actor, Writer, Co-Producer, The Missionary,

1982; Around the World in 80 Days, BBC, 1989; Actor: Jabberwocky, 1976; A Private Function, 1984; Brazil, 1984; A Fish Called Wanda, 1988; Contributor, Great Railway Journeys of the World, BBC TV, 1980; Actor, Co-Writer, American Friends, film, 1991; Actor, GBH, TV Channel 4, 1991; Actor, Fierce Creatures, 1997; Michael Palin's Hemingway Adventure, BBC, TV, 1999. Publications: Monty Python's Big Red Book, 1970; Monty Python's Brand New Book, 1973; Dr Fegg's Encyclopaedia of All World Knowledge, 1984; Limericks, 1985; Around the World in 80 Days, 1989; Pole to Pole, 1992; Pole to Pole - The Photographs, 1994; Hemingway's Chair, 1995; Full Circle, 1997; Full Circle - The Photographs, 1997; Michael Palin's Hemingway Adventure, 1999; Sahara, 2002; For Children: Small Harry and the Toothache Pills, 1981; The Mirrorstone, 1986; The Cyril Stories, 1986. Honours: Writers Guild, Best Screenplay Award, 1991; Dr hc (Sheffield), 1992, (Queen's, Belfast), 2000. Address: 34 Tavistock Street, London WC2E 7PB, England.

**PALMER Arnold Daniel,** b. 10 September 1929, Latrobe, USA. Golfer; Business Executive. m. Winifred Walzer, 1954, 2 daughters. Education: Wake Forest University, North Carolina. Appointments: US Coast Guard, 1950-53; US Amateur Golf Champion, 1954; Professioanl Golfer, 1954-;Winner, 92 professional titles, including British Open 1961, 1962, US Open 1960, US Masters 1958, 1960, 1962, 1964, Candadian PGA 1980, US Seniors Championship 1981; Member, US Ryder Cup Team, 1961, 1963, 1965, 1967, 1971, 1973, Captain 1963, 1975; President, Arnold Palmer Enterprises; Board of Directors, Latrobe Area Hospital. Publications: My Game and Yours, 1965; Situation Golf, 1970; Go for Broke, 1973; Arnold Palmer's Best 54 Golf Holes, 1977; Arnold Palmer's Complete Book of Putting, 1986; Playing Great Golf, 1987; A Golfer's Life (with James Dodson), 1999; Playing by the Rules, 2002. Honours: LLD, Wake Forest National College of Education; DHL, Florida Southern College; Athlete of the Decade, Associated Press, 1970; Sportsman of the Year, Sports Illustrated, 1960; Hickok Belt, Athlete of the Year, 1960. Address: PO Box 52, Youngstown, PA 15696, USA.

**PALMER Beverly B,** b. 22 November 1945, Cleveland, Ohio, USA. Professor; Clinical Psychologist. m. Richard C Palmer, 1 son. Education: BA, Psychology, University of Michigan, 1964-66; Teaching Credential, English, Ohio State University, 1966-67; MA, Counselling, Ohio State University, 1967-69; PhD, Counselling, Psychology, Ohio State University, 1969-72. Appointments: Research Assistant, Department of Psychiatry, Ohio State University, 1966-68; Teacher, Secondary Education, Southwestern City Schools, Grove City, Ohio, 1967-69; Administrative Associate, Admissions Department, Ohio State University, 1969-70; Research Psychologist, Health Services Research Center, University of California, Los Angeles, 1971-77; Clinical Psychologist, Private Practice, California, 1985-; Chair of Psychology Graduate Program, 1986-, Professor, 1973-, Department of Psychology, California State University, Dominguez Hills. Publications include: Career Choices in Psychology and the Helping Professions, 1979; An Evaluation of Traditional and Alternative Mental Health Faculties, 1979; Instructor's Manual for Sexuality, 1984; Love and Death: The End of the Sexual Smokescreen, 1989; Love: Magill's Survey of Social Science: Psychology, 1993; Teaching Social Skills Through Face-to-Face Versus Computerized Instruction, 1996; Interpersonal Skills for Helping Professionals: An Interactive Internet-Based Guide, 2003. Honours: Proclamation from County of Los Angeles for community activities, 1972; Proclamation from County of Los Angeles for public health activities, 1981; Outstanding Professor Award, California State University, 1995; Fulbright Fellowship to Malaysia, 2001 and

2004; Fulbright Fellowship to Barbados, 2005; Fulbright Senior Scholar, 2002-07. Memberships: American Psychological Association; Association for Humanistic Psychology; Association for Women in Science; Psychologists for Social Responsibility; Phi Kappa Phi National Honor Society; Fulbright Fellowship to Barbados, 2005. Address: California State University, Dominguez Hills, Department of Psychology, Carson, CA 90747, USA.

**PALMER Frank Robert,** b. 9 April 1922, Westerleigh, Gloucestershire, England. Retired Professor; Linguist; Writer. m. Jean Elisabeth Moore, 1948, 3 sons, 2 daughters. Education: MA, New College, Oxford, 1948; Graduate Studies, Merton College, Oxford, 1948-49. Appointments: Lecturer in Linguistics, School of Oriental and African Studies, University of London, 1950-52, 1953-60; Professor of Linguistics, University College of North Wales, Bangor, 1960-65; Professor and Head, Department of Linguistic Science, 1965-87, Dean, Faculty of Letters and Social Sciences, 1969-72, University of Reading. Publications: The Morphology of the Tigre Noun, 1962; A Linguistic Study of the English Verb, 1965; Selected Papers of J R Firth, 1951-1958 (editor), 1968; Prosodic Analysis (editor), 1970; Grammar, 1971, 2nd edition, 1984; The English Verb, 1974, 2nd edition, 1987; Studies in the History of Western Linguistics (joint editor) 1986; Semantics, 1976, 2nd edition, 1981; Modality and the English Modals, 1979, 2nd edition, 1990; Mood and Modality, 1986, 2001; Grammatical Roles and Relations, 1994; Grammar and Meaning, 1995 (editor) 1995; Modality in Contemporary English (joint editor), 2003. Contributions to: Professional journals. Memberships: Academia Europaea; British Academy, fellow; Linguistic Society of America; Philological Society. Address: Whitethorns, Roundabout Lane, Winnersh, Wokingham, Berkshire RG41 5AD, England.

**PALTROW Gwyneth,** b. 1973, Los Angeles, USA. Actress. m. Chris Martin, 2003, 1 daughter. Education: University of California, Santa Barbara. Creative Works: Films include: Flesh and Bone, 1993; Hook; Moonlight and Valentino; The Pallbearer; Seven; Emma, 1996; Sydney; Kilronan; Great Expectations, 1998; Sliding Doors, 1998; A Perfect Murder, 1998; Shakespeare in Love, 1998; The Talented Mr Ripley, 1999; Duets, 1999; Bounce, 2000; The Intern, 2000; The Anniversary Party, 2001; The Royal Tenenbaums, 2001; Shallow Hal, 2001; Possession, 2002; View From the Top, 2003; Sylvia, 2003. Honours include: Academy Award, Best Actress, 1998. Address: c/o Rick Kurtzman, CAA, 9830 Wilshire Boulevard, Beverly Hills, CA 90212, USA.

**PALVA Ilmari Pellervo,** b. 5 May 1932, South Pirkkala, Finland. Physician; Haematologist. m. Seija Kaivola, 9 June 1956, 1 son, 3 daughters. Education: MD, 1956, PhD, 1962, University of Helsinki. Appointments: Registrar, 1959-63, Consultant, 1964-65, Department of Medicine, University Hospital, Helsinki; Instructor, University of Helsinki, 1963-64; Associate Professor, Internal Medicine, University of Oulu, 1965-74; Professor, Internal Medicine, University of Kuopio, 1974; Acting Professor, Medical Education, University of Tampere, 1975-76; Consultant, City Hospitals, Tampere, 1976-92, Retired, 1992. Publications: Over 250 scientific papers in professional journals. Honours: Knight of 1st Order, Finnish White Rose, 1986; Honorary Member, Finnish Society of Haematology, 1992. Memberships: Finnish Medical Association; Finnish Society of Internal Medicine; Finnish Society of Haematology; International Society of Haematology; American Society of Hematology. Address: Oikotie 8, FIN 33950 Pirkkala, Finland.

**PAN Chai-fu,** b, 8 September 1936, Loshon, Szechwan, China. Emeritus Professor. m. Maria C Shih, 1 son, 1 daughter. Education: BS, Chemical Engineering, National Taiwan University, 1956; PhD, Physical Chemistry, University of Kansas, USA, 1966. Appointments: Associate Professor, 1966-71, Professor, 1971-91, Emeritus Professor of Chemistry, 1991-, Alabama State University, USA. Publications: Contributions to Journal of Physical Chemistry, Journal of Chemical and Engineering Data, Canadian Journal of Chemistry, Journal of Chemical Society, Faraday Transaction 1, other professional journals. Honours: Phi Lambda Upsilon, 1963; Fellowship, American Institute of Chemists, 1971; Alabama State University Research Award, 1985; More than 30 listings. Memberships: American Chemical Society; Fellow, American Institute of Chemists. Address: 2420 Wentworth Drive, Montgomery, AL 36106, USA. E-mail: ppan@charter.net

**PANAYOTOV Panayot Petrov,** b. 14 March 1943, Elena, Bulgaria. Lecturer of Instrument Playing/Methodology. Education: MA, Musical Pedagogy, Weimar, Germany, 1977; MA, School Pedagogy and Management Education, 1996; Doctor of Philosophy, St Kliment Ohridsk University of Sofia, Bulgaria, 2000. Appointments: Lecturer, Music College of Weimar, Germany and Concert Performer, 1977-82; Teacher of Instrument Playing, Chamber Music, Classical and Electric Guitar, New Bulgarian University, Sofia, 1995-; Associate Professor and Doctor of Philosophy, Lecturer of Instrument Playing/ Methodology and Leader of Guitar Class, St Kliment Ohridski University of Sofia, 2000-. Publications: Author of more than 20 pedagogical books and articles on the methodology of instrument playing including: Etudes for Guitar 1 & 2, 2000, 2002; Methodik des Gitarrenunterrichts, 2003; Scales and Technical Exercises for Guitar, 2004. Memberships: Bulgarian Panel for Music Competitions; Bulgarian Inspecting Council of the Art Schools. Address: Block 85, Suha Reka, Entr E, App 19, Sofia 1517, Bulgaria. E-mail: panstil@internet.bg.net

**PANCHENKO Yurii Nikolayevich,** b. 6 April 1934, Kharkov, Ukraine. Chemist. m. Larisa Grigoriyevna Tashkinova, 1 son. Education: Department of Chemistry, MV Lomonosov Moscow State University, 1959; PhD, Chemistry (Molecular Spectroscopy), 1970. Appointments: Junior Researcher, Karpov Physico-Chemical Institute, 1959-61; Junior Researcher, 1961-77, Senior Researcher, 1977-, Department of Chemistry, Moscow State University. Publications: More than 200 scientific works in numerous scientific journals. Honours: Silver Medal, Medal of Eötvös Lorand Budapest University. Membership: Fellow, World Association of Theoretically Oriented Chemists. Address: Laboratory of Molecular Spectroscopy, Division of Physical Chemistry, Department of Chemistry, MV Lomonosov Moscow State University, Vorobiovy gory, Moscow 119899, Russia. E-mail: panchenk@physch.chem.msu.su

**PANDEY Jagdish,** b. 9 February 1928, Bararhi, PS Dehri-on-Sone Dist Rohtas, Bihar, India. Retired Chief Engineer, Irrigation Department, Government of Bihar. m. Smt Manorma, 4 sons, 3 daughters. Education: Fellow, Institution of Engineers, India, FIE, 1987; Chartered Engineer, India, 1988. Appointments: Assistant Engineer, Executive Engineer, Superintending Engineer, Chief Engineer, Irrigation Department, Government of Bihar, India. Publications: Rural Development and Small Scale Industries; Bihar and Small Scale Industries; Problem of Pollution and Science of the Modern Age; Sanskrit Language and Indian Civilisation; Saint Tulsidas and His Devotion; Problem of Unemployment and its Solution in India; Condition of Women and their Problem in India. Honours: Best Citizen of India Award; Man of Achievement Award, International Publishing House, New

Delhi; Man of the Year 1998, American Biographical Institute, ABI, USA; Distinguished Leadership Award, Research Board of Advisors, ABI, 1999; Rising Personalities of India Award for Outstanding Services, Achievements and Contribution, International Penguin Publishing House; 20th Century Bharat Excellence Award, Glory of India Award, Friendship Forum of India, New Delhi; National Udyog Excellence Award, International Institute of Education and Management; National Gold Star Award, International Business Council; Jewel of India Award, International Institute of Education and Management; Outstanding Intellectuals of the 20th Century, International Biographical Centre, Cambridge, England; The Millennium Achiever 2000, All India Achievers' Conference, New Delhi; Mahamana Madan Mohan Malvia Samman; Honour by Sanatan Brahman Samaj North Bihar Muzaffarpur (India); Eminent Personalities of India Award, Board of Trustees of International Biographical Research Foundation India in Recognition of Superb Achievements within the Community of Mankind during 20th Century; Vijay Rattan Award and Certificate of Excellence, India International Friendship Society; Bibhuti Bhushan Award, Jagatguru-Shankaracharya of Gobardhan Pith Puri; Sajio Maha Manav Award, National President Sanatan Samaj; Bharat Jyoti Award for outstanding services achievements and contribution, International Institute of Success Awareness, Delhi; Rashtriya Nirman Award, International Business Council; Honorary Member, Research Board of Advisors, ABI, USA, 1999; Life Time Achievement Award, National and International Compendium Delhi; Gold Medals, Friendship Forum of India; Rashitriya Ratan Shiromani Award, Modern India International Society; Gold Medal and Man of the Year, 2003; Great Achiever of India Award, FNP; Pride of India Award, International Institute of Education and Management; 21st Century Excellence Award, International Business Council; Rashtra Shresth Nidhi Award, Delhi; Eminent Citizen of India Award for outstanding achievements in chosen field of activity, NIC; International Gold Star Award, Taranath Ranabhat M P, Rt Hon Speaker, Pratinidhi Sabha (House of Representatives of Nepal), Kathmandu, 2004; Vijay Shree Award for most religious and spiritual activities, International Business Council; Goswami Tulsidal Award for excellent achievements and selfless services to the nations, Industrial Technology Foundation; Prominent Citizens of India Award, 2004; Vikas Shree Award for outstanding achievements in chosen Field of Activity, IIEM; Rashtra Prabha Award for Meritorious Accomplishments in Diverse Fields of Activities that immensely Contributed for the Nation's Progress; Rashtra Nirman Ratna Award for unmatched services to Mother India to enhance her prestige and honour; Indira Gandhi Excellence Award, Delhi; Golden Heart Award, Delhi; Noble Son of India Award, Delhi; Rajdhani Rattan Gold Medal Award, International Business Council, New Delhi; Golden Lifetime Achievement Award, Industrial Technology Foundation, Delhi. Memberships: Fellowship of Institution of Engineers, India; Chartered Engineer, India; President, Sanskrit Sanjivan Samaj; President, Jagjiwan Sanatorium Shankerpuri; President, Sur Mandir; President, Durga Puja Samiti Patna; President, Sanatan Brahman Samaj Bihar; Vice President, Sanatan Brahman Samaj India; President, Hindi Sahitya Sammelan Bihar Patna; Chief Patron, Subordinate Engineers Association, Bihar, Patna, India; Patron, Sangrakshak Mandal Pragya Samiti, Bihar, Patna; Member, International Bhojpuri Sammelan, Bihar, Patna; President, Ganga Sewa Sangh, Bihar, Patna; Patron, Bihar, Nepal Sanskritik Munch; Patron, Bihar, Kerala Sanskritik Munch. Address: Rajendra Nagar, Road No 6/C, Patna 800 016, Bihar, India.

**PANG Shiu Fun,** b. 22 February 1945, Hong Kong. Biologist; Biotechnologist. m. Celia Sook Fun Ho, 2 sons. Education: BSc, Biology, The Chinese University of Hong Kong, 1969;

MA, Biology, California State University, USA, 1971; PhD, Biology, University of Pittsburgh, USA, 1974. Appointment: Vice-President, Chief Technology Officer, CK Life Sciences Limited, Hong Kong, 2000-. Publications: More than 230 papers; Books include: Receptor and Non-receptor Mediated Actions of Melatonin; Recent Progress of Pineal Research – 40 Years After Discovery of Melatonin; Melatonin – Universal Photoperiodic Signal with Diverse Actions. Honours: Editor-in-Chief and Managing Editor, Biological Signals, Switzerland, 1990-97; Editor-in-Chief and Managing Editor, Biological Signals & Receptors, Switzerland, 1998-2001. Memberships: European Pineal Society, 1981-; International Brain Research Organisation, 1985-; Chinese Association of Physiological Sciences, China, 1988-. Address: CK Life Sciences Limited, 2 Dai Fu St, Tai Po Industrial Estate, Tai Po N.T., Hong Kong. E-mail: sf.pang@ck-lifesciences.com

**PANKOV Yuri,** b. 10 February 1930, Leningrad, USSR. Biochemist; Molecular Biologist. m. Svetlana Chumachenko, 1 son, 1 daughter. Education: Biochemist, Leningrad State University, 1953; PhD, 1963; DSc, 1968; Biophysicist, Moscow State University, 1972; Academician of the USSR Academy of Medical Sciences, 1986; Professor, 1987, MOIF, 2000. Appointments: Senior Scientist, Institute of Experimental Endocrinology and Hormone Chemistry (IEEHC), 1965-70; Deputy Director, IEEHC, 1970-83; Director of IEEHC, 1983-90; Director of Moscow WHO Collaborating Center on Human Reproduction, 1984-97; Director, Moscow WHO Collaborating Center on Diabetes, 1984-90; Head of Laboratory Molecular Endocrinology Endocrine Research Centre, 1990-. Publications: Biochemistry of hormones and hormonal regulation, 1976; Several articles in Nature; Biochemistry; Molecular Biology; Problem Endocrinology. Honours: Honorary member, Cuban Society of Endocrinology Metabolism, 1984; Honorary Citizen of Lexington, Kentucky, USA, 1987; Listed in numerous international biographical publications. Memberships: Endocrine Society; Planetary Society; European Association for the Study of Diabetes; American Diabetes Association; Adjunct Professor, Special Educational Programme on Biochemistry, Immunology, Molecular and Cellular Biology, A N Belozersky Institute, Moscow State University, 1999. Address: Endocrine Research Centre, Moscvorechye Str 1, 115478, Moscow, Russian Federation. E-mail: yuri-pankov@mtu-net.ru

**PANNICK David Philip,** b. 7 March 1956, London, England. Barrister. m. (1) Denise, deceased 1999, 2 sons, 1 daughter, (2) Nathalie. Education: Hertford College, Oxford, 1974-78. Appointments: Fellow, All Souls College Oxford, 1979-; Barrister, 1980-. Publications: Judges, 1992; Advocates, 1997; Human Rights Law and Practice (with Lord Lester of Herne Hill), 1999, 2nd edition 2004. Honours: QC, 1992; Honorary Doctorate, University of Hertfordshire, 1997; Honorary Fellow of Hertford College, Oxford, 2004. Address: Blackstone Chambers, Temple, London EC4Y 9BW, England. E-mail: davidpannick@blackstonechambers.com

**PAPACHRISTOU-PANOU Evangelia,** b. 5 April 1923, Athens, Greece. Author; Poet. Education: Literature and Philosophy. Publications: 24 poetry books, 1970-2004; 9 essay books, 1974-96; Numerous translations into English, French, Italian, Arabian and Persian. Honours: 1 Gold Medal, Mayor of Corinth, Greece; 2 Gold and 1 Silver Medals, Italy; 2 Silver Medals, France; 4 prizes for poetry; 1 prize for essay. Address: PO Box 204, 20100 Corinth, Greece.

**PAPADEMOS Lucas,** b. 11 October 1947, Athens, Greece. Bank Executive. Education: BSc, Physics, 1970, MSc, Electrical Engineering, 1972, PhD, Economics, 1977, Massachusetts

Institute of Technology. Appointments: Research Assistant, Teaching Fellow, Massachusetts Institute of Technology, 1973-75; Lecturer, Economics, 1975-77, Assistant and Associate Professor of Economics, 1977-84, Columbia University, New York; Senior Economist, Federal Reserve Bank of Boston, 1980; Visiting Professor of Economics, Athens School of Economics and Business, 1984-85; Professor of Economics, University of Athens, 1988-; Economic Counsellor (Chief Economist), 1985-93, Head, Economic Research Department, 1988-93, Deputy Governor, 1993-94, Governor, 1994-2002, Bank of Greece; Vice-President, European Central Bank, 2002-; Member, Greece's Council of Economic Experts. Publications: Numerous articles in professional journals and books chapters as author and co-author. Honour: Grand Commander of the Order of Honour, Greece, 1999-. Memberships include: Governor, International Monetary Fund for Greece, 1994-; General Council, 1999-, Governing Council, 2001-, European Central Bank; Chairman, Governor's Club, 2001-. Address: European Central Bank, Kaiserstr 29, D-60211 Frankfurt am Main, Germany.

**PAPADOPOULOS Stylianos G,** b. 4 May 1933, Corinth, Greece. Professor of Patrology. m. Soteria Tektonidou, 1 son, 2 daughters. Education: BD, School of Theology, University of Athens, 1955; Ecole Pratique des hautes Etudes, Sorbonne, Paris, 1956-57; Institut Catholique, Paris, 1956-57; Institut Russe de Théologie Orthodoxe, Paris, 1956-57; Faculty of Philosophy, Munich, 1957-59; Theological Faculty, Munich, 1957-59; PhD, School of Theology, University of Athens, 1967. Appointments: Assistant Professor, 1970, Associate Professor of Patrology, 1972, Full Professor of Patrology, 1978, Head of Faculty of Theology, School of Theology, 1986-87, 1997-99, University of Athens; Visiting Professor, Faculties of Theology, Bucharest, Sibiu, Romania, Moscow, St Petersburg, Russia, Beograd, Presov, Slovakia, Beyrouth, Liban, Sofia, Bulgaria, Coptic School of Theology, Egypt. Publications include: 35 books, 600 articles, Greek translations of Thomas Aquinas; Contribution to History of Byzantine Theology; Theology and Language, 1987; Patrology, vol I, 1987, Vol II, 1999; The Orthodox March: Church and Theology in the Third Millennium, 2000; J Chrysostomus, Vol I: His Life, His Activities, His Works and Vol II: His Theology, 1999; St Cyril of Alexandria: His Life, His Theology, His Christology, His Exegesis, 2004. Honours: Dr hc (Oradea); Listed in Who's Who and biographical publications. Address: Sifnou 23, Agia Paraskevi, Athens, Greece.

**PAPADOPULOS Nikolaos A,** b. 10 March 1966, Zevgolatio, Serres, Greece. Plastic Surgeon; Assistant Medical Director; Researcher; Physician. Education: MD, University of Naples and Perugia, Italy, 1991; Dr Med, 1999, Specialist in Plastic Surgery, 2001, Privat Docent (PhD), 2003, Technical University of Munich, Germany. Appointments: Guest MD, Department of Surgery, State Clinics Neuss, Germany, 1992-93; Resident MD, Department of Traumatology, Paracelsus Clinic Neuss, 1993-94; Resident MD, Department of Plastic Surgery, 1994-96, Resident MD, 1997-2000, Scientific Collaborator, 2000-02, Assistant Medical Director, 2002-, Technical University of Munich; Research Fellow, Centre of Surgical Techniques, Catholic University of Leuven, Belgium, 1996-97; Assistant Medical Director, Department of Plastic Surgery, Klinikum Dachau, Germany, 2001-02. Publications: Articles in scientific journals. Honours: Numerous awards including: Golden Award, 2nd International Congress of Quality of Life and Medical Practice, Greece, 2004; Annual Scientific Award, 2004, Golden Camera of Plastic Surgeons Award, 2004, Association of German Plastic Surgeons. Memberships include: Association of German Plastic Surgeons; Association of Bavarian Surgeons; Balkan Association of Plastic, Reconstructive and Aesthetic Surgery; German Medical Association; German Society of Surgery;

Hellenic Medical Association; International Fetal Medicine and Surgery Society. Address: Department of Plastic Surgery, Technical University of Munich, Ismaningerstr 22, D-81675 Munich, Germany. E-mail: n.papadopulos@lrz.tum.de

**PAPINEAU David Calder,** b. 30 September 1947, Como, Italy. Philosopher. m. Rose Wild, 6 July 1986, 1 son, 1 daughter. Education: BSc, Honours, University of Natal, 1967; BA, Honours, 1970, PhD, 1974, University of Cambridge. Appointment: Professor, King's College, London, 1990-. Publications: For Science in the Social Sciences, 1978; Theory and Meaning, 1979; Reality and Representation, 1987; Philosophical Naturalism, 1993; Introducing Consciousness, 2000; Thinking about G-sciousness, 2002; The Roots of Reason, 2003. Membership: British Society for the Philosophy of Science, President, 1993-95. Address: Department of Philosophy, King's College, London WC2R 2LS, England.

**PARAVICINI Nicolas Vincent Somerset,** b. 19 October 1937, London, England. Private Banker. m. Susan Rose Phipps. 2 sons, 1 daughter. Education: Royal Military College Sandhurst. Appointments: British Army, The Life Guards, 1957-69, retired as Major; Director, Joseph Sebag & Co, 1972-79; Chairman and Chief Executive, Sarasin Investment Management Ltd, 1980-89; Consultant, Bank Sarasin & Co, 1990-; Chief Executive, Ely Place Investments Ltd, 1992-98; Chairman, Harmony Management Ltd, 2003-. Memberships: London Stock Exchange, 1972-80; Freeman City of London, 1984; President, Becknockshire Agricultural Society, 1998-99; SSAFA Powys, 2002-; Clubs: White's; Pratt's; Corviglia Ski. Address: Glyn Celyn House, Brecon, Powys LD3 0TY, Wales. E-mail: glyncelyn@hotmail.com

**PARIS Richard Bruce,** b. 23 January 1946, Bradford, England. University Academic. m. Jocelyne Marie-Louise Neidinger, 1 son, 1 daughter. Education: BSc, 1967, PhD, 1971, DSc, Mathematics, 1999, University of Manchester. Appointments: Postdoctoral Fellow, Royal Society of London, 1972-73; Foreign Collaborator, 1973-74, Research Scientist, Euratom, Theory Division, Controlled Thermonuclear Fusion, 1974-87; Commissariat à l'Energie Atomique, France; Senior Lecturer, University of Abertay Dundee, 1987-99; Honorary Readership, University of St Andrews, 1998-; Reader in Mathematics, University of Abertay Dundee, 1999-. Publications: Books: Asymptotics of High Order Differential Equations (with A D Wood), 1986; Asymptotics and Mellin-Barnes Integrals (with D Kaminski), 2001; Author of over 100 papers and technical reports; Publications in Proceedings A Royal Society, Journal of Computational and Applied Mathematics, Physics of Fluids; Author of 2 chapters in Handbook of Mathematical Functions, forthcoming revised edition. Honours: Fellow of the Institute of Mathematics and Applications, 1986; CMath, 1992, DSc, 1999. Memberships: Institute of Mathematics and its Applications; Edinburgh Mathematical Society; Mathematical Association. Address: University of Abertay Dundee, Dundee DD1 1HG, Scotland. E-mail: r.paris@abertay.ac.uk

**PARISESCU Vasile, (Parizescu),** b. 25 October 1925, Braila, Romania. Fine Artist; Officer Engineer. m. Victoria, 1 daughter. Education: Bachelor of Art, Faculty of Philology and Philosophy, University of Bucharest, 1949; The Military School of Artillery, 1947; The Military technical Academy, 1953, The Fine Art School, Bucharest, 1973; Independent study of paintings with Dumitru Ghiata, Rudolph Schweitzer Cumpana and Gheorghe Vanatoru. Career: Painter; Scientist; General of the Brigade, Romanian Army; Command appointments in the Romanian Army in the field of armours and auto-drivers technology; 17 personal exhibitions in Romania and abroad;

Several national and group exhibitions; Many participations at international exhibitions including: Moscow, 1987, Rome, 1990, 1999, Tokyo, Osaka, Yokohama, 1994-95, Paris 2000, Wiene, 2003; Paintings in collections and museums in Romania, Austria, England, Canada, Switzerland, France, Germany, Netherlands, USA, Greece, Cyprus, Sweden, Turkey, Japan, Yugoslavia, Italy. President of the Society of Art Collectors of Romania; Director of the magazine, Pro Arte. Publications: 26 books in the field of science and technology; Over 1000 articles on science, technology and art; Monography Albums, Vasile Parizescu, 1995, 2001; The Encyclopaedia of Romanian Contemporary Artists, 1999, 2003; The Encyclopaedia of Great Personalities from Romanian History, Science and Culture, 5th volume, 2004; Several TV and Radio appearances. Honours: Laureate of the National First Prize for Science, 1979; The First National Prize, Republican Art Exhibitions, 1981, 1983, 1985, 1987; Laureate with diploma and medal, International Art Festival, Moscow, 1987; First Prize, National Salon of Art, Botosani, Romania, 1988; Cultural Diploma and Plaquette, City of Bucharest, 1988; Honoured Citizen of the city of Brăila, 1994; Albo D'Oro Prize and selected as Effective Senator of the International Academy of Modern Art, Rome, 1999. Memberships: President of Honour, Fine Arts Society, Bucharest; Member of the National Commission of Museums and Collections; National expert for modern and contemporary art. Address: Bd Nicole Balcescu nr 3, Bloc Dunarea 3, scara 1, ap 12, cod 70111, sector 1 Bucharest, Romania. Website: www.stdb.ro/arta/EVPARIZ.HTM

**PARK Hen Suh,** b. 27 February 1938, Seoul, Korea. Business and Management. m. Inhee Won, 1 son, 1 daughter. Education: MS in Electrical Engineering, Virginia Polytechnic Institute, Blackburg, Virginia, USA, 1966; Graduate Studies in Department of Electrical Engineering, MIT, Cambridge, Massachusetts, USA, 1966-68; PhD in E E, School of Electrical Engineering, Cornell University, Ithaca, New York, USA, 1972. Appointments: Senior Engineer, Applied Research Lab GTE, Watham, Massachusetts, USA, 1966-68; Senior Specialist in Data Transmission, TRW Systems Group, Redondo Beach, California, USA, 1972-75; Director of Security Data Processing Center, Agency of Defense Development, Seoul, 1975-77; Managing Director, Korea Telecommunications Company, 1977-80; Executive Director, Acting President, Korea Institute of Electronics Technology, Seoul, 1980-82; Invited Professor of Electrical Engineering, Korea University, Seoul, 1985; Senior Vice President, Oriental Telecommunications Co Ltd, Seoul, 1983-86; Representative Director, AirTouch Korea Ltd, 1985-96; Chairman and CEO, Korea Information and Communications Co Ltd, 1996-. Publications: 1 patent, Method and Apparatus for Automatically Generating Korean Character Fonts. Honours: Republic of Korea National Medal for Industrial Service Merit, 1993. Address: #601, Enigma Ville, 94 Cheong Dam-dong, Gang Nam-ku, Seoul, Korea. E-mail: hspark@kicc.co.kr Website: www.kicc.co.kr

**PARK In Suh,** b. 27 May 1937, Seoul, Korea. Medical Doctor; Professor. m. Soon Doe Lee, 1 son, 1 daughter. Education: MD, 1962, M. Med. Sci., 1967, PhD, 1978, Yonsei University, Seoul, Korea. Appointments: Intern, Resident, Severance Hospital, Seoul, 1962-66; Professor, Yonsei University College of Medicine, Seoul, 1970-2002, Professor Emeritus, 2002-; President, Korean Society of Gastrointestinal Endoscopy, Seoul, Korea, 1993-94; President, Korean Society of Gastroenterology, Seoul, 1998-99; President, Korean Society of Gastrointestinal Motility, Seoul, 1997-99; President, Korean College of H. pylori Research, Seoul, 1999; Fellow Medical Cancer Institute Hospital, Tokyo, Japan, 1972; Visiting Professor, Technical University, Munich, Germany, 1991; Chief of Gastroenterology, University Medical Centre, Yonsei University, Seoul, 1992-

97. Publications: Books: Gastritis (editor) and another 12 books; 474 published articles. Honours: Academic Awards, Korean Society of Internal Medicine, 1977, 1989; Order of Services Merit, Aquamarine Stripes, Government of Korea, 2002. Memberships: Korean College of H pylori Research; Korean Society of Gastrointestinal Motility; Korean Society of Gastroenterology; Korean Society of Gastrointestinal Endoscopy; American Gastroenterology Association; Vice-Chair of Research Committee, 1998-2002, World Organisation of Gastroenterology; International Society of Gastric Cancer. Address: #327-1 Sukyo-dong, Mapo-gu, Seoul 121-836, South Korea.

**PARK Kwangsung,** b. 4 January 1960, Suncheon, Korea. Professor of Urology. m. Sulhyun Kim, 1 daughter. Education: MD, Chonnam National University Medical School, 1983; PhD, Chonnam National University Graduate School, 1993. Appointments: Professor of Urology, Chonnam University Hospital, Korea; Board of Directors, International Society for the Study of Women's Sexual Health, 2001-2003; Editorial Board, International Journal of Impotence Research, 2003; Editorial Board, The Journal of Sexual Medicine, 2004. Publications: Diabetes induced alteration of clitoral hemodynamics and structure in the rabbit (co-author), 2002; Textbook of Andrology (Korean) (a chief editor), 2003. Honours: Jean-Paul Ginestie Prize, 1996, Newman Zorgniotti Prize, 2000, International Society for Impotence Research. Memberships: Korean Medical Association; Korean Urological Association; Korean Andrological Society; American Urological Association; International Society for Impotence Research. Address: Department of Urology, Chonnam University Hospital, 8 Hak-dong, Dong-ku, Gwangju 501-757, Republic of Korea. E-mail: kpark@chonnam.ac.kr

**PARK Kyeongsoon,** b. 25 December 1958, Incheon, Korea. Associate Professor. m. Mijin Han Park, 1 son, 1 daughter. Education: BS, Inha University, Korea, 1980; PhD, University of Maryland, USA, 1992. Appointments: Researcher, Agency for Defense Development, Daejeon, Korea; Research Associate, University of Massachusetts, Lowell, USA; Associate Professor, Chairman, Department of Advanced Materials Engineering, Sejong University, Seoul, Korea; Director, Centre for Advanced Materials, Seoul, Korea. Publications: Chemical Ordering in Semiconductor Thin Films; Electrical Properties of Ni-Mn-Co-(Fe) Oxide Thick-Film NTC Thermistors Prepared by Screen Printing; Microstructure and Mechanical Properties of Silicon Carbide Fiber-reinforced Aluminum Nitride Composites. Honours: President's Awards, Inha University; President's Awards, Agency for Defense Development. Korea. Memberships: Korea Institute of Metals and Materials; Korea Ceramic Society. Address: Department of Advanced Materials Engineering, Sejong University, 98 Kunja-Dong, Kwangjin-Ku, Seoul 143-747, Korea. E-mail: kspark@sejong.ac.kr

**PARK Myungkark,** b. 24 July 1950, Kangwon-do, Korea. Publisher; Physicist. m. Hyunmi Suh, 1 son. Education: BS, Physics, Seoul National University, 1972; MS, Physics, Wayne State University, 1979; PhD candidate, Physics, Washington State University, 1979-83; PhD Student, Physics, Kent State University, 1983-85; PhD Student, Physics, University of Cincinnati, 1985-87; Computing, SOC, 1987-88. Appointments: Publisher; President and Owner, Prompter Publications; US Publisher. Publications: Numerous books, journals, articles, notebooks, etc; ...Electron Emission...1981. Honours: Who's Who Medal, 2000; Great Minds of the 21st Century, 2005 (and its dedication); Man of the Year, 2005; many others. Memberships: AAAS; Inactive Member: APS, AMS, AVS,

KPS. Address: PO Box 167, Chongnyangni, Tongdaemoon-gu, Seoul 130-650, Korea.

**PARK Nicholas W,** b. 1958, Preston, Lancashire, England. Film Animator. Education: Sheffield Art School; National Film & TV School, Beaconsfield. Appointments: Aardman Animations, 1985, partner, 1995-. Creative Works: Films include: A Grand Day Out, 1989; Creature Comforts, 1990; The Wrong Trousers, 1993; A Close Shave, 1995; Chicken Run (co-director), 2000. Honours: BAFTA Award, Best Short Animated Film, 1990; Academy Award, 1991, 1994. Address: Aardman Animations Ltd, Gas Ferry Road, Bristol BS1 6UN, England.

**PARK Sehie,** b. 28 November 1935, Seoul, Korea. University Professor Emeritus. m. Cha Gyoung Park, 2 sons. Education: BS, 1959, MS, 1961, Seoul National University, Seoul, Korea; PhD, Indiana University, Bloomington, Indiana, USA, 1975. Appointments: Assistant, Instructor, Assistant Professor, 1963-75, Associate Professor, 1975-81, Professor, 1981-2001, Professor Emeritus, 2001-, Seoul National University; President, Korean Mathematical Society, 1982-84. Publications: Fixed point theory of multifunctions in topological vector spaces, 1992; Foundations of the KKM theory, 1996; Ninety years of the Brouwer fixed point theorem, 1999; The KKM principle implies many fixed point theorems, 2004; Fixed points of multimaps in the better admissible class, 2004. Honours: Culture Prize Seoul Metropolitan Government, 1981; Dongbaeg Medal of Civil Merit, 1987; National Academy of Sciences Prize, 1994. Memberships: National Academy of Sciences, Republic of Korea; Korean Academy of Science and Technology; Korean Mathematical Society; American Mathematical Society. Address: Centreville 103-1104, Dae Chi Dong, Gang Nam Gu, Seoul, Korea.

**PARK Seong-Joo,** b. 28 February 1966, Kyongju, South Korea. Registered Nurse. Education: B, Sulin University, Department of Nursing, 1984-87; M, Dongguk University, Department of Social Welfare, 2000-02. Appointments: Intensive Care Unit, Dongang Hospital, 1987-91; Intensive Care Unit, 1991-2002, Dialysis Unit, 2002-, Dongguk University Medical Centre. Publications: The Empirical Study on The Work Satisfaction of the Medical Agency Worker, 2002; Using Reagent Strips for Rapid Diagnosis of Peritonitis in Peritoneal Dialysis Patients, Advances in Peritoneal Dialysis, 2005. Honours: Best Abstract Award, Annual Dialysis Conference, US, 2005. Memberships: Korea Nurses Association; Korea Social Welfare Association. Address: Hyundai Apt 102-1203, Hwangsung-dong, Kyongju 780-130, South Korea.

**PARK She-Jik,** b. 18 September 1933, Kumi City, South Korea. Educator; Former Military Commander; Government Official. m. Suk-Ja Hong, 2 sons, 1 daughter. Education: BS, Science, Korea Military Academy, 1956; BA, Art, Seoul National University, 1959; Graduate, School of Public Administration, Seoul National University MA, 1985, Ed D, 1991, University of Southern California, USA. Appointments: Military: Special Assistant for Security to the President, 1975; Professor, Korea Military Academy; Commander, 3rd Infantry Division, Republic of Korea Army, 1979; Commander, Seoul Capital Security Command (Major General Retired), 1981; Minister of Government Administration; Minister of Sports; President, '86 Seoul Asian Games Organising Committee; President, '88 Seoul Olympic Organising Committee; Mayor of Seoul Metropolitan City, 1990-91; Director of National Security Planning Agency (equivalent to CIA); Member, National Assembly 14th-15th Session, 1992-2000; Member, Standing Committee for Labour and Environment, National Assembly; President, Korean Organising Committee for the 2002 FIFA World Cup, Korea/

Japan, 1998; Chairman, National Breakfast Prayer Meetings. President, Rice for Love Campaign. Publications: Books and Essays: Leadership Theory and Practice; Enriching National Strength; Heaven and Earth, East and West in Oneness (in Korean, Japanese and Chinese); The Seoul Olympics; PES Movement for Happiness of Humankind; 2002 World Cup and the Future of Korea, Japan and the World; A Bridge to the Future and Peace; Korean Peninsula, its Security Situation and the Way to Approach Peaceful Unification. Honours: Distinguished Military Medal, Wharang; Medal for National Security, Chunsu; Medal of Government Service World Class; Legion d'Honneur, France; Grand Officier de l'ordre de Leopold, Belgium; Olympic Order in Gold, IOC; Paralympics Gold Medal, ICC; Alumni Merit Award, USC, 1989; Man of the Year, 1990, UNESCO; Distinguished Award, Christian Ministership, World Evangelism, Korea. Memberships: President, Korea Overseas Veteran's Association; President Korea Youth Village; Chairman, Korea Military Academy Alumni Association. Address: #484-6 Pyong-chang-dong, Jong-no-ku, Seoul 110-848, Korea.

**PARK Ta-Ryeong,** b. 20 January 1961, Dongkwangyang, Korea. Professor. m. Hyung-Ji Kim, 3 sons. Education: BS, 1983, MS, 1985, Seoul National University; PhD, Michigan State University, 1991. Appointments: Senior Lecturer, 1991-93, Assistant Professor, 1993-97, Associate Professor, 1997-2002, Professor, 2002-, Hoseo University, Korea. Publications: Articles and papers to professional journals. Memberships: American Physical Society; Korean Physical Society. Address: Hoseo University, Department of Physics, Asan Choongnam 336-795, Korea.

**PARK Won Ho,** b. 25 September 1962, Seoul, Korea. Professor. m. Beob Hyang Ko, 2 sons, 1 daughter. Education: BS, 1985, MS, 1987, PhD, 1993, Textile Engineering, Seoul National University, Korea. Appointments: Postdoctoral, University of Massachusetts, 1996-97; Associate Professor, Kumoh National University, 1993-99; Professor, Chungnam National University, 1999-. Honours: Best Research Award, Kumoh National Institute of Technology, 1999; Scientific Award, Korean Fibre Society, 2004. Address: Department of Textile Engineering, Chungnam National University, 220 Gungdong, Yusungku, Daejeon 303-764, Korea. E-mail: parkwh@cnu.ac.kr Website: http://web.cnu.ac.kr/~bdal

**PARK Young W,** b. 21 February 1946, Kyung-Nam, South Korea. Professor. m. Eun Y Park, 2 sons. Education: BS, Kon Kuk University, 1973; MS, University of Minnesota, USA, 1976; PhD, Utah State University, 1981; MDiv, Houston Theological Seminary, 1989; DMin, Northern Baptist Theological Seminary, 1998. Appointments: Postdoctoral Research Associate, Utah State University, USA, 1981-82; Research Specialist, 1982-84, Associate Professor, 1984-97, Prairie View A&M University, Texas A&M System; Pastor, Bethany Korean Baptist Church, Houston, Texas, 1990-97; Professor, Fort Valley State University, Georgia, 1997-; Adjunct Professor, The University of Georgia, 2001-; Pastor, Warner Robins Korean Baptist Church, Georgia, 1999-. Publications: More than 50 scientific research papers in American and international refereed scientific journals; Editor, 1 book; More than 20 symposium papers; 13 book chapters; More than 150 abstract papers in proceedings of professional conferences. Honours include: Distinguished Faculty Award, Research Leader Award, Prairie View A&M University, 1985; 1st Place Scientist Paper Award, ARD Symposium, 1989, 1992; Member, Editorial Board, Small Ruminant Research Journal, 1990-; President, Sigma Xi, Prairie View A&M Chapter; Listed in numerous Who's Who and biographical publications. Memberships: Sigma

Xi; Institute of Food Technologists; American Dairy Science Association; International Goat Association; Federation of American Societies for Experimental Biology; Southern Baptist Convention. Address: Agricultural Research Station, College of Agriculture, Home Economics and Allied Programs, Fort Valley State University, Fort Valley, GA 31030-4313, USA. E-mail: parky@fvsu.edu

**PARKER Alan William (Sir),** b. 14 February 1944, London, England. Film Director; Writer. m. Annie Inglis, 1966, divorced 1992, 3 sons, 1 daughter. Education: Owen's School, Islington, London. Appointments: Advertising Copywriter, 1965-67; TV Commercial Director, 1968-78; Writer, Screenplay, Melody, 1969; Chair, Director's Guild of Great Britain, 1982-, British Film Institute, 1998-; Member, British Screen Advisory Council, 1985-. Creative Works: Writer, Director: No Hard Feelings, 1972; Our Cissy, 1973; Footsteps, 1973; Bugsy Malone, 1975; Angel Heart, 1987; A Turnip Head's Guide to the British Cinema, 1989; Come See the Paradise, 1989; The Road to Wellville, 1994; Director: The Evacuees, 1974; Midnight Express, 1977; Fame, 1979; Shoot the Moon, 1981; The Wall, 1982; Birdy, 1984; Mississippi Burning, 1988; The Commitments, 1991; Evita, 1996; Angela's Ashes, 1998; The Life of David Gale, 2003. Publications: Bugsy Malone, 1976; Puddles in the Lane, 1977; Hares in the Gate, 1983; Making Movies, 1998. Honours include: BAFTA Michael Balcon Award for Outstanding Contribution to British Film; National Review Board, Best Director Award, 1988; Lifetime Achievement Award, Director's Guild of Great Britain; BAFTA Award, Best Director, 1991; CBE. Address: c/o Creative Artists Agency, 9830 Wilshire Boulevard, Beverly Hills, CA 90212, USA.

**PARKER Anthony Wayne,** b. 3 February 1953, Little Rock, Arkansas, USA. m. Lisa Ann Laird, 3 sons. Education: BA, Magna Cum Laude, History, 1990, MA, American History, 1992, University of Georgia, Athens; PhD, Scottish/ American History, University of St Andrews, Scotland, 1996. Appointments: Teaching Fellow, 1996-98, Course Co-ordinator, Lecturer and Tutor, 1998-, Department of History and School of American Studies, Director, School of American Studies, 2000-, Director, University of Transatlantic Student Exchange & Study Abroad Programmes, 2001-, Associate Director of Administration and Undergraduate Programmes, Institute for Transatlantic, European and American Studies, 2003-, University of Dundee; Consultant, Emigration Exhibit Project, New Museum of Scotland, Edinburgh, Scotland, 1998-99; Convenor, Scottish Confederation of University and Research Libraries, North American Studies Group, Scotland, 1999-; Editorial Board, Journal of Transatlantic Studies, Scotland; Co-Conference Secretary, Council Member, Economic and Social History Society of Scotland, Scotland; External Academic Reviewer, National Museums of Scotland, Museum of Scotland International, Edinburgh, 2001-02; Consultant, ETL Project, University of Edinburgh collaborating with Universities of Coventry and Durham, 2001-; Consultant, National Library of Scotland Stakeholder Research and the new Draft Strategy for the National Libraries of Scotland, 2003-04. Publications: Book, Scottish Highlanders in Colonial Georgia: the Recruitment, Emigration and Settlement in Darien 1735-1748, 1997, reprinted 2002; Articles in professional journals; Various conference and seminar papers, and book reviews. Honours: Fellow, Institute of Contemporary Scotland; Fellow, Charles Warren Center for Studies in American History, Harvard University, International Seminar on the History of the Atlantic World, 1996; elected Phi Kappa Phi and National Honour Society, USA. Memberships: British Association for American Studies; Centre for Enterprise Management, College of Internal Affiliates; Scottish Association for the Study of America; Institute for Learning and Teaching

in Higher Education; Organisation of American Historians; Southern Historical Society; Eighteenth Century Scottish Studies Society; Transatlantic Studies Association; Scottish Trans-Atlantic Relations Project; Economic and Social History Society of Scotland. Address: School of American Studies, The University of Dundee, Dundee, DD1 4HN, Scotland. E-mail: a.w.parker@dundee.ac.uk

**PARKER James Mavin (Jim),** b. 18 December 1934, Hartlepool, England. Composer. m. Pauline Ann, 3 daughters. Education: Guildhall School of Music. Career: Composer. Compositions include: A Londoner in New York, 10 brass; Mississippi Five, woodwind quintet; The Golden Section, 5 brass; Clarinet Concerto; Follow the Star, musical with Wally K Daly; Film and TV music includes: Mapp and Lucia; Wynne and Penkovsky; Good Behaviour; The Making of Modern London; Girl Shy (Harold Lloyd); The Blot; Wish Me Luck; Anything More Would be Greedy; House of Cards; Parnell and the Englishwoman; Soldier Soldier; The House of Elliott; Body and Soul; Goggle Eyes; The Play the King; The Final Cut; Moll Flanders; Tom Jones; A Rather English Marriage; Lost for Words; Foyle's War; The Midsomer Murders. Honours: BAFTA Awards for Best TV Music for: To Play the King, 1993, Moll Flanders, 1997, Tom Jones, 1997, A Rather English Marriage, 1998; GSM Silver Medal, 1959; LRAM, 1959; Honorary GSM, 1985. Membership: BAFTA. Address: 16 Laurel Road, London SW13 0EE, England. E-mail: jimparker@fairads.co.uk

**PARKER John Richard,** b. Great Britain. Chartered Architect; Chartered Town Planner; Urban Designer. Education: Polytechnic of Central London and University College London; PhD, DipArch, DipTP; ARIBA; FRTPI; FRSA. Appointments: Job Architect, Department of Architecture and Civic Design, Schools Division, London County Council, 1961-64; Group Leader, Directorate of Development Services, London Borough of Lambeth, 1964-70; Head of Central Area Team, Department of Transportation and Development, Greater London Council, 1970-86; Consultant Planning Inspector, Department of the Environment, 1986-88; Founding Partner and Managing Director, Greater London Consultants Limited (and Partnership), 1986-96; Principal, John Parker Associates, 1996-; Director, Greater London Consultants, 1996-; Consultant, Council of Europe and Editor of Revised European Urban Charter, 2004-; Chairman, International Development Forum, 2000-04; Leader, RTPI International Development Network, 2004-; Trustee, Jubilee Walkway Trust, 2002-. Publications: Over 50 publications and public lectures, most recently: Character of Cities, 2002; Built Environment of Towns: Towards a Revised Urban Charter, 2002. Honours: 3 prize-winning entries in architectural competitions; Winston Churchill Fellow, 1967; RIBA Pearce Edwards Research Award, 1969; BALI Landscape Award, 1980; Edwin Williams Memorial Award, 1980; RICS/ Times Conservation Award, 1985; British Council Anglo/ Soviet Exchange Award, 1989. Memberships: Associate, Royal Institute of British Architects; Fellow, Royal Town Planning Institute; Fellow, Royal Society of Arts. Address: 4, The Heights, Foxgrove Road, Beckenham, Kent BR3 5BY, England. E-mail: jpa@btinternet.com

**PARKER Peter Robert Nevill,** b. 2 June 1954, Hereford, England. Education: BA, Honours, University College, London, 1977. Appointments: Executive Committee, English PEN, 1994-97; Trustee, 1994-, Chair, 1998-2000, PEN Literary Foundation; Associate Editor, Oxford D.N.B., 1996-2004; Trustee, London Library, 1998-; Council, Royal Society of Literature, 2004-. Publications: The Old Lie, 1987; Ackerley, 1989; The Reader's Companion to the Twentieth-Century Novel (editor), 1994; The Reader's Companion to Twentieth-Century Writers (editor),

1995; Isherwood, 2004. Contributions to: Daily Telegraph; Independent; Sunday Times; Hortus; TLS. Honour: FRSL, 1997. Literary Agent: Rogers, Coleridge and White ltd. Address: 20 Powis Mews, London, W11 1JN, England.

**PARKER Sarah Jessica,** b. 25 March 1965, Nelsonville, Ohio, USA. Actress. m. Matthew Broderick, 1997, 1 son. Creative Works: Stage appearances include: The Innocents, 1976; The Sound of Music, 1977; Annie, 1978; The War Brides, 1981; The Death of a Miner, 1982; To Gillian on Her 37th Birthday, 1983-84; Terry Neal's Future, 1986; The Heidi Chronicles, 1989; How to Succeed in Business Without Really Trying, 1996; Once Upon a Mattress, 1996; Film appearances include: Rich Kids, 1979; Somewhere Tomorrow, 1983; Firstborn, 1984; Footloose, 1984; Girls Just Want to Have Fun, 1985; Flight of the Navigator, 1986; LA Story, 1991; Honeymoon in Vegas, 1992; Hocus Pocus, 1993; Striking Distance, 1993; Ed Wood, 1994; Miami Rhapsody, 1995; If Lucy Fell, 1996; Mars Attacks!, 1996; The First Wives Club, 1996; Extreme Measures, 1996; Til There Was You, 1997; A Life Apart: Hasidism in America, 1997; Isn't She Great, 1999; Dudley Do-Right, 1999; State and Main, 2000; Numerous TV appearances include: Equal Justice, 1990-91; Sex and the City, 1998-2003. Honours: Golden Globe for Best Actress in a TV Series, 2001. Address: Creative Artists Agency, 9830 Wilshire Boulevard, Beverly Hills, CA 90212, USA.

**PARKES Roger Graham,** b. 15 October 1933, Chingford, Essex, England. Novelist; Scriptwriter. m. Tessa Isabella McLean, 5 February 1964, 1 son, 1 daughter. Education: National Diploma of Agriculture. Appointments: Staff Writer, Farming Express and Scottish Daily Express, 1959-63; Editor, Farming Express, 1963; Staff Script Editor, Drama, BBC-TV, London, 1964-70. Publications: Death Mask, 1970; Line of Fire, 1971; The Guardians, 1973; The Dark Number, 1973; The Fourth Monkey, 1978; Alice Ray Morton's Cookham, 1981; Them and Us, 1985; Riot, 1986; Y-E-S, 1986; An Abuse of Justice, 1988; Troublemakers, 1990; Gamelord, 1991; The Wages of Sin, 1992. Contributions to: Daily Express; Sunday Express. Honour: Grand Prix de Littérature, Paris, 1974. Memberships: Writers Guild of Great Britain; Magistrates Association. Address: Cartlands Cottage, Kings Lane, Cookham Dean, Berkshire SL6 9AY, England.

**PARKINSON Michael,** b. 28 March 1935, Yorkshire, England. TV Presenter; Writer. m. Mary Heneghan, 3 sons. Appointments: The Guardian, Daily Express, Sunday Times, Punch, Listener; Joined Granada TV Producer, Reporter, 1965; Executive Producer and Presenter, London Weekend TV, 1968; Presenter, Cinema, 1969-70, Tea Break, Where in the World, 1971; Hosted own chat show "Parkinson", BBC, 1972-82, 1998-, "Parkinson One to One", Yorkshire TV, 1987-90; Presenter, Give Us a Clue, 1984-, All Star Secrets, 1985, Desert Island Discs, 1986-88, Parky, 1989, LBC Radio, 1990; Help Squad, 1991, Parkinson's Sunday Supplement, Radio 2, 1994, Daily Telegraph, 1991-; Going for a Song, 1997-; Parkinson's Choice, Radio 2, 1999-2000. Publications: Football Daft, 1968; Cricket Mad, 1969; Sporting Fever, 1974; George Best: An Intimate Biography, 1975; A-Z of Soccer, co-author, 1975; Bats in the Pavilion, 1977; The Woofits, 1980; Parkinson's Lore, 1981; The Best of Parkinson, 1982; Sporting Lives, 1992; Sporting Profiles, 1995; Michael Parkinson on Golf, 1999; Michael Parkinson on Football, 2001. Honours: Sports Feature Writer of the Year, British Sports Journalism Awards, 1995, 1998; Yorkshire Man of the Year, 1998; BAFTA Award for Best Light Entertainment, 1999; Media Society Award for Distinguished Contribution to Media, 2000. Address: J W International, 74 Wimpole Street, London W1M 7DD, England.

**PARNHAM Michael John,** b. 13 March 1951, London. Pharmacologist. m. Elaine Whitehead, 3 sons, 1 daughter. Education: BSc, London, 1973; PhD, Bristol, 1976; MIBiol, UK, 1978; Habilitation, Pharmacology and Toxicology, Frankfurt am Main, 1990. Appointments: Research Fellow, Department of Pharmacology, Erasmus University, Rotterdam, 1976-80; Head, Immunopharmacology, Head, General Biology, A Nattermann, Rhone-Poulenc, Cologne, 1980-90; President, Parnham Advisory Services, Bonn, 1990-98; Adjunct Professor, University of Frankfurt am Main, 1990-; Managing Editor, Inflammation Research, 1992-; Director, Pharmacology and Toxicology, Senior Scientific Advisor, Pliva, Zagreb, 1998-; Director, Mixis France, Paris, 1999-2004. Publications: Author or co-author of over 250 scientific publications; Author, Ethical Issues in Drug Research; Series Editor, Progress in Inflammation Research, Milestones in Drug Therapy. Honours: Gosling Prize, Netherlands; Claudius Galenus Prize, Germany; Man of the Year, American Biographical Institute; Pliva Award, 2000, 2004; International Scientist of the Year, 2002, IBC; Inclusion into various Who's Who publications. Memberships: British Pharmacology Society; German Society for Pharmacology and Toxicology; European Association of Science Editors; Croatian Society of Pharmacologists; Society for Leukocyte Biology, USA. Address: Pliva Research Institute Ltd, Prilaz Baruna Filipovica 29, HR-10000 Zagreb, Croatia. E-mail: michael.parnham@pliva.hr

**PARR John Brian,** b. 18 March 1941, Epsom, England. University Researcher. m. Pamela Harkins, 2 daughters. Education: BSc (Econ), University College London, University of London, 1959-62; PhD, University of Washington, Seattle, USA, 1962-67. Appointments: Assistant Professor of Regional Science, 1967-72, Associate Professor of Regional Science, 1972-75, University of Pennsylvania, USA; Lecturer, Senior Lecturer in Urban Economics, 1975-80, Reader in Applied Economics, 1980-89, Professor of Regional and Urban Economics, 1989-, University of Glasgow. Publications include: Regional Policy: Past Experience and New Directions (co-edited book), 1979; Market Centers and Retail Location: Theory and Applications (co-authored book), 1988; Numerous refereed articles in professional journals include: Outmigration and the depressed area problem, 1966; Models of city size in the urban system, 1970; Models of the central place system: a more general approach, 1978; A note on the size distribution of cities over time, 1985; The economic law of market areas: a further discussion, 1995; Regional economic development: an export-stages framework, 1999; Missing elements in the analysis of agglomeration economies, 2002. Honours: Guest, Polish Academy of Sciences, Warsaw, Poland, 1977; Speaker, August Lösch Commemoration, Heidenheim an der Brenz, Germany, 1978; Speaker at the Ehrenpromotion (award of honorary doctorate) of Professor Dr Martin Beckmann, University of Karlsruhe, Germany, 1981; Participant in Distinguished Visitors Program, University of Pennsylvania, Philadelphia, 1983; Academician, Academy of Learned Societies for the Social Sciences, 2002; Moss Madden Memorial Medal, 2003. Memberships: Royal Economic Society; Scottish Economic Society; Regional Science Association International and British and Irish Section; Regional Studies Association; Member of various editorial boards of scientific journals. Address: Department of Urban Studies, University of Glasgow, Glasgow G12 8QQ, Scotland.

**PARR Robert G,** b. 22 September 1921, Chicago, Illinois, USA. Professor. m. Jane Bolstad, 1 son, 2 daughters. Education: AB, magna cum laude, Brown University, 1942; PhD, Physical Chemistry, University of Minnesota, 1947; Dhc, University of Leuven, 1986; Jagiellonian University, 1996. Appointments include: Assistant Professor, Chemistry, University of Minnesota, 1947-48; Assistant Professor, Professor, Chemistry, Carnegie Institute of Technology, 1948-62; Visiting Professor, Chemistry, Member, Center of Advanced Study, University of Illinois, 1962; Professor of Chemistry, Johns Hopkins University, 1962-74, Chairman, Department of Chemistry, 1969-72; William R Kenan Junior Professor of Theoretical Chemistry, University of North Carolina; Wassily Hoeffding Professor of Chemical Physics, 1990-. Publications: Over 200 scientific articles, 2 books. Honour: Langmuir Award, American Chemical Society; Award in Chemical Sciences, National Academy of Sciences. Memberships include: International Academy of Quantum Molecular Science; National Academy of Sciences; American Academy of Arts and Sciences; Indian National Science Academy. Address: Chemistry Department, University of North Carolina, Chapel Hill, NC 27599, USA.

**PARRINDER (John) Patrick,** b. 11 October 1944, Wadebridge, Cornwall, England. Professor of English; Literary Critic. 2 daughters. Education: Christ's College, 1962-65, Darwin College, 1965-67, Cambridge; MA, PhD, Cambridge University. Appointments: Fellow, King's College, Cambridge, 1967-74; Lecturer, 1974-80, Reader, 1980-86, Professor of English, 1986-, University of Reading. Publications: H G Wells, 1970; Authors and Authority, 1977, 2nd edition, enlarged, 1991; Science Fiction: Its Criticism and Teaching, 1980; James Joyce, 1984; The Failure of Theory, 1987; Shadows of the Future, 1995. Editor: H G Wells: The Critical Heritage, 1972; Science Fiction: A Critical Guide, 1979; Learning from Other Worlds, 2000. Contributions to: London Review of Books; Many academic journals. Honour: President's Award, World Science Fiction, 1987; Fellow, English Association, 2001. Memberships: H G Wells Society; Science Fiction Foundation; Society of Authors. Address: School of English and American Literature, University of Reading, PO Box 218, Reading, Berkshire RG6 6AA, England.

**PARROTT Andrew Haden,** b. 10 March 1947, Walsall, England. Conductor; Scholar; Director of Music. m. Emily Van Evera, 1 daughter. Education: Open Postmastership, BA, Merton College, Oxford, 1966-71. Appointments: Founder and Director, Taverner Choir, Consort and Players, 1973-; Music Director and Principal Conductor, London Mozart Players, 2000-; Music Director, New York Collegium, 2002-. Publications: Numerous recordings; Articles include those on Monteverdi, Purcell, Bach in scholarly journals; The New Oxford Book of Carols (co-editor); The Essential Bach Choir, 2000, German edition, 2003. Honours: Honorary Research Fellow, Royal Holloway, University of London, 1995-; Honorary Senior Research Fellow, University of Birmingham, 2000-. Address: c/o Allied Artist, 42 Montpelier Square, London SW7 1JZ, England. E-mail: name@alliedartists.co.uk

**PARRY Roger George,** b. 4 June 1953, London, England. Chief Executive. m. Johanna, 1 son. Education: BSc Geology, Bristol University, 1972-76 (sabbatical year: Vice-President of Student Union); MLitt, Economics, Jesus College, University of Oxford, 1976-79. Appointments: Personal Assistant to Charles and Maurice Saatchi, 1976; Freelance Journalist, BBC, Sunday Times, Observer, Broadcast, Campaign, Punch, Vogue, 1977-85; Reporting, Presenting, Producing, BBC TV and Radio, ITV, LBC, 1977-85; Consultant, McKinsey & Co, 1985-88; Development Director, WCRS Group plc, 1988-90; Development Director, Aegis Group plc, 1990-94; Marketing Advisor to KPMG, 1993-95; Founder London Radio, 1993-94; President, Carat North America Inc, 1994-95; Chief Executive, More Group plc, 1995-98, Chairman, Clear Channel International, 1998-; Non-Executive Directorships: Trustee,

Shakespeare's Globe Trust, 1987-; Chairman, Johnston Press plc, 1997-, Chairman, Future plc, 1999-, iTouch plc, 2000-05. Publications: People Businesses, 1991; Enterprise: The Leadership Role, 2003; Making Cities Work (co-author), 2003. Honour: Gold Medal, New York Film and TV Festival. Address: Clear Channel International, 1 Cluny Mews, London SW5 9EG, England. E-mail: rogerparry@clearchannelint.com

**PARSONS Charles Andrew (Charlie),** b. 7 August 1958, Tonbridge, Kent. TV Producer. Education: MA, English Language and Literature, Pembroke College, Oxford. Appointments: Journalist, Ealing Gazette Series, 1980-82; Programme Researcher, Producer, Current Affairs Department, London Weekend Television, 1982-90; Series Editor, Network 7, 1988; Managing Director and Director of programmes, Planet 24 UK: Creator/Executive Producer, The Word, Executive Producer, Hotel Babylon, Executive Producer, Handel's Messiah in Dublin, 1992, Creator, The Big Breakfast, Creator and Executive Producer, Survivor, 1992-99; Consultant, Carleton Television Productions, 1999-2001; Chief Executive Officer, Castaway Television Productions Ltd (owners of global rights to Survivor), 1999-; Executive Producer, Survivor (CBS) 2005, from 2001. Publications: Columnist, Independent on Sunday. Honours include: BAFTA for Network 7, 1987; RTS Award for The Big Breakfast, 1993; EMMY Award for Survivor, 2003. Memberships: Founder Member, Soho House; BAFTA. Address: c/o Castaway Television Productions, 4th Floor Aldwych House, London WC2E 4HN, England.

**PARSONS Jack,** b. 6 December 1920, Greasley, Nottinghamshire, England. Author; Consultant; Lecturer. m. Barbara June Barker, 1 son, 1 daughter. Education: Degree in Philosophy and Politics, Keele University, 1955. Appointments: Boy labourer; Engineering apprentice; Skilled craftsman, 1934-41; RAF pilot, UK, Africa, India, 1941-46; Aeronautical draftsman, site engineer in civil engineering, 1946-51; Sociological researcher, National Coal Board; Nuffield Research Associate, Lecturer in Sociology, Brunel University, 1955; Senior Lecturer in Population Studies, Deputy Director, Sir David Owen Population Centre, Cardiff University, 1975; Independent Researcher, Consultant, 1981-; Founder, Director, Population Policy Press, 2001-. Publications include: Population Versus Liberty, 1971; Population Fallacies, 1977; Human Population Competition, 1998. Honours: State Scholarship for Mature Students, 1951; Honorary Associate, the Rationalist Press, 1995; Honorary Life Member, Centre for Alternative Technology, 2000. Address: Treferig Cottage Farm, Llantrisant, CF72 8LQ, Wales. E-mail: jp@popolpress.com Website: www.populationparsons.com

**PARTINGTON Brian Harold,** b. 31 December 1936, Manchester, England. Clergyman. m. Valerie, 2 sons, 1 daughter. Education: St Aidan's Theological College, Birkenhead. Appointments: Curate, Emmanuel, Didsbury, 1963-66, Curate, St Mary's, Deane, 1966-68, Diocese of Manchester; Vicar of Kirk Patrick, 1968-96, Bishop's Youth Officer, 1968-77, Vicar of St Paul's, Foxdale, 1976-96, Vicar of St John's, 1977-96, Rural Dean of Peel, 1976-96, Canon of St Patrick St German's Cathedral, 1985-96, Vicar of St George's, Douglas, 1996-2004, Archdeacon of the Isle of Man, 1996-2005, Diocese of Sodor and Man. Honour: OBE, 2002; Memberships: Executive Chairman, Isle of Man Sports Council; Chairman, 1988-96, Vice-President, 1996-, Hospice Care; President, Isle of Man Hockey Association, 1997-; President, Isle of Man Cricket Association, 1998-; Vice-Chairman, 2001-2005,Chairman, 2005-, International Island Games Association, 2005-; Vice-Captain, Peel Golf Club, 2005; Douglas Rotary Club; Royal Commonwealth Society; Ecclesiastical Law Society. Address:

Brambles, Patrick Village, Isle of Man, IM5 3AN. E-mail: bpartington@mcb.net

**PARTON Dolly Rebecca,** b. 19 January 1946, Sevier County, Tennessee, USA. Singer; Composer. m. Carl Dean, 1966. Creative Works: Films include: Nine to Five, 1980; The Best Little Whorehouse in Texas, 1982; Rhinestone, 1984; Steel Magnolias, 1989; Straight Talk, 1991; The Beverly Hillbillies; Albums include: Here You Come Again, 1978; Real Love, 1985; Just the Way I Am, 1986; Heartbreaker, 1988; Great Balls of Fire, 1988; Rainbow, 1988; White Limozeen, 1989; Home for Christmas, 1990; Eagle When She Flies, 1991; Slow Dancing with the Moon, 1993; Honky Tonk Angels, 1994; The Essential Dolly Parton, 1995; Just the Way I Am, 1996; Super Hits, 1996; I Will Always Love You and Other Greatest Hits, 1996; Hungary Again, 1998; Grass is Blue, 1999; Best of the Best –Porter 2 Doll, 1999; Halos and Horns, 2002. Composed numerous songs including: Nine to Five. Publication: Dolly: My Life and Other Unfinished Business, 1994. Honours include: Vocal Group of the Year Award (with Porter Wagoner), 1968; Vocal Duo of the Year, All Music Association, 1970, 1971; Nashville Metronome Award, 1979; Female Vocalist of the Year, 1975, 1976; Country Star of the Year, 1978; Peoples Choice, 1980; Female Vocalist of the Year, Academy of Country Music, 1980; East Tennessee Hall of Fame, 1988. Address: RCA, 6 West 57th Street, New York, NY 10019, USA.

**PARTRIDGE Derek William,** b. 15 May 1931. London, England. Retired Diplomat. Appointments: HM Diplomatic Service: Foreign Office, London, England, 1951-54, Oslo, 1954-56, Jedda, 1956, Khartoum, 1957-60, Sofia, 1960-62, Manila, 1962-65, Djakarta, 1965-67, FCO, 1967-72, Brisbane, 1972-74, Colombo, 1974-77; Head, Migration and Visa Department, FCO, 1981-83; Head, Nationality and Treaty Department, FCO, 1983-86; British High Commissioner, Freetown, Sierra Leone, 1986-91; Liberal Democrat Councillor, London Borough of Southwark, 1994-2002. Honours: CMG, 1987. Memberships: National Liberal Club. Address: 16 Wolfe Crescent, Rotherhithe, London SE16 6SF, England.

**PARVEZ Tariq,** b. 5 April 1952, Multan, Pakistan. Oncologist. m. Kaniz Akhter, 2 sons, 1 daughter. Education: BSc, 1975, MBBS, 1976, MCPS, 1988, DMRT, 1988, MD, 1994. Appointments: GDMO Pakistan Army, 1976-79; Demonstrator, AIMC, Lahore, 1979-85; SMO Radiotherapy Mayo Hospital, Lahore, 1987-88; Head of Radiotherapy and Oncology, SGRH Lahore and AIMC, Lahore, 1988-97; Head of Radiotherapy and Oncology Services, Hospital Lahore, 1997-2001; Consultant Oncologist, KFH, Almadina Almunawra, KSA, 2001-. Publications: 7 books on cancer; 55 research papers; 1 booklet on breast cancer; 150 articles. Honour: President of Pakistan Gold Medal for Cancer Research; Year 2000 Millennium Medal of Honour; Medal Outstanding People of the 20th Century; Award and Dedication, Who's Who of Intellectuals; Distinguished Leadership Award; Certificate of Merit; Medal, Outstanding People of the 20th Century; Hall of Fame Award. Memberships: PSCP; Fellow, Association of UICC Fellows; Several national and international organizations and associations. Address: PO Box 3643, King Fahad Hospital, Al Medina Al Munawarah, Kingdom of Saudi Arabia. E-mail: tariq_parvez52@hotmail.com

**PASCALLON Pierre,** b. 12 November 1941, Gap, France. Economist; Educator. m. (1) Laurette Gaulin, 1968, deceased, (2) Christine-Claire Fourgeaud, 1999, 1 daughter. Education: Licence University, Aix en Provence, France, 1967; Doctorate, 1970. Appointments: Professor, Economic Sciences, Faculte de Sciences, Economics, Clermont-Ferrand, France, 1970-;

Adjunct Director, 1970-76; Vice-President, 1976. Publications: Contributor, articles to professional journals. Honours: Order Palmes Academiques; Chevalier dans l'ordre de la Legion d'Honneur. Memberships: Rotary Club; Club Participation et Progres. Address: 9 Place Saint-Avit, 63500 Issoire, France.

**PASCOE Frank Diggory (Digs),** b. 28 March 1939, Pietermaritzburg, South Africa. Engineer; Conservationist. m. Anne, 1 son, 4 daughters, 1 foster daughter. Education: Diploma, Industrial Welfare and Psychology, 1961; Degree, Electrical Engineering, 1962; Diploma, Conservation, Ecology, 1982; Diploma, National Engineers. Appointments: Developed self help schemes, small mining and tourism ventures, Zambia, 1964-71; Discovered world's largest deposit of emeralds, Zambia, 1966; Developed Jewellery Manufacturing and Exports SA, 1972-84; Travelled to USA and Brazil to study self-help schemes and community projects, 1984-85; Property Developer, shopping centre and office complex in "whites only" area for black business men, South Africa, 1986-96; Developed Lake Game viewing and Gemstone/Geology trails to assist local communities to create tourism ventures and related businesses, 1996-99. Publications include: Thesis: Automatic Control of Tumbling Ball Mills; Paper: Development of Information Lay-byes along a National Heritage Route; Present research: Origin of Man sites in Northern KwaZulu Natal/Museum of The Elephant – Africa's Power Icon. Honours: President, Zululand Agricultural & Industrial Show Society, 1998; Chairman, Provincial Roads & Tourism Committee; Eshowe Tourism Association; Regional Honorary Conservation Officers Group; Vice Chairman, Maputaland Tourism & Development Association; Executive; Regional Council Development Committee, Maputaland Biosphere reserve; Board Member, Community Radio Station, Eshowe Career Guidance College, Tourism Association of KwaZulu Natal Province; Space for Elephants Founding Trustee; Chief Executive Officer, Space for Elephants Foundation; Development of Museum & Research Centre for Post Graduate Students; Delegate, Africa Tourism Conference, Lusaka, Zambia, 1994; Trans Frontier Parks – Kingdom of KwaZulu Natal; Outstanding work in the Tourism Community; Promoting Tourism "Off the Beaten track"; TANK Provincial Tourism Development Award. Membership: Rotary International. Address: PO Box 86, Eshowe 3815, Kwa Zulu Natal, Republic of South Africa. E-mail: digspascoe@zulukin gdom.co.za

**PASCOE Jane,** b. 9 May 1955, Bristol, England. Artist. 1 son. Education: Foundation Course, Art and Design, 1973-74, BA Hons, Fine Art, 1st Class, 1977, Bristol Polytechnic Faculty of Art and Design; Art Teacher's Certificate, Brighton Polytechnic School of Art Education, 1977-78. Appointments: Art Teacher, Highbury School, Salisbury, 1979-84; Art Teacher, Blandford Upper School, 1984-86; Head of Art, Bournemouth School for Girls, 1986-88; Head of Art, Kingdown School, Warminster, 1988-89; Head of Art, The Atherley School, Southampton, 1989- ; Work exhibited in: Royal West of England Academy of Art; The Festival Gallery; The Victoria Gallery; Beaux Arts Gallery, Bath; Wessex Artists Exhibition, Salisbury; The Eye Gallery, Bristol; The Manor House Gallery, Cheltenham; Parkin Fine Art, London; The Mall Gallery, London; Work also included in numerous private collections including The Cheltenham and Gloucester Building Society and the Public Collection of the RWA, Bristol. Honour: Listed in several Who's Who and biographical publications. Memberships: Associate Member, 1983, Full Member, 1987, Royal West of England Academy of Art. Address: Honeysuckle Cottage, Charmus Road, Old Calmore, Southampton, Hampshire SO40 2RG, England.

**PATERSON Howard Cecil,** b. 16 March 1920, Edinburgh, Scotland. Retired. Widower, 1 son. Education: Daniel Stewart's College, Edinburgh, 1925-36; Edinburgh College of Art, 1937-39. Appointments: Army Service, Royal Artillery, 1939-45; Personnel Section Officer, 1945-49; TA, 1949-70: Retired as Lieutenant Colonel, 1970; Assistant Personnel Manager, Jute Industries Ltd, 1949-51; Deputy Director, Scottish Country Industries Development Trust, 1951-66; Senior Director, Scottish Tourist Board, 1966-81; Independent Tourism Consultant, Tourism Advisory Services, 1981-2000; Chairman, Taste of Scotland Scheme, 1984-86; Chairman, Scottish International Gathering Trust, 1981-91; Vice-Chairman, 1982-89, Chairman, 1989-90, Scottish Aircraft Collection Trust; Vice-Chairman, John Buchan Society, 1990-95; Chairman, 1990-2003, Honorary Life President, 2003-, Trekking and Riding Society of Scotland. Publications: Tourism in Scotland, 1969; The Flavour of Edinburgh, 1986. Honours: Territorial Decoration (TD) with two clasps; Front Line Britain Medal; Polish Medal, Custodian of Places of National Remembrance. Memberships: Royal Scots Club, Edinburgh; Scottish Reserve Forces and Cadets Association; Royal Artillery Association; Royal Artillery Institution; Founder Member, Firepower; Royal Artillery Museum, Woolwich; City of Edinburgh Artillery Officers Association; 52 Lowland Division Officers Club; Reserve Forces Association; Friend of Historic Scotland; Life Fellow, Royal Society for the Protection of Birds; Fellow, Society of Antiquaries in Scotland; Life Member, National Trust for Scotland; Friend, National Botanic Gardens of Scotland; Art Fund; Friend of the National Galleries of Scotland; Member, Scottish Borders Music and Arts Guild; The Scottish Rural Property and Business Association; Countryside Alliance; British Association for Shooting and Conservation; Scottish Association of Country Sports; World Wildlife Fund; Country Club UK; West Linton Historical Association; West Linton Music Society. Address: Dovewood, Carlops Road, West Linton, Peeblesshire EH46 7DS, Scotland.

**PATERSON Michael Hugh Orr,** b. 7 December 1927, Chiswick, Middlesex, England. Retired Museum Curator; Conservator; Educationist. m. Gillian Maureen Robinson. Education: BA, Manchester, 1951; Diploma of the Museums Association including Conservation of Easel Paintings, Courtauld Institute of Art, 1954. Appointments: Trainee, City Art Gallery and Museums, Birmingham, 1953-54; Successively Curator: City Art Gallery, Hereford; Municipal Art Gallery, Oldham; City Art Gallery, Leicester; Russell-Cotes Art Gallery and Museums, Bournemouth; London Borough of Enfield; RAF Museum, Hendon (part-time). Publications: Various guides to art galleries and historic houses; Art and the Theatre; The Bible in Art: Painters of Wessex, 1958-66. Honour: Honorary Curator/Archivist, Foundling Hospital Museum (part-time), 1982-94. Fellow, Royal Society of Arts; Fellow, Museums Association. Address: 24 Adamsrill Close, Enfield, Middlesex EN1 2BP, England.

**PATON David Romer,** b. 5 March 1935, Grandhome, Aberdeen, Scotland. Chartered Surveyor. m. Juliette Burney, 2 sons. Education: London School of Economics; Keble College, Oxford. Appointments: Chartered Surveyor, 1970-. Honours: OBE; CStJ; DL; Honorary degree, DBA; Fellow, Royal Institution of Chartered Surveyors; Fellow, Society of Antiquaries, Scotland. Memberships: Aberdeen Harbour Board; Scottish Council Development and Industry; North East Scotland Preservation Trust; Order of St John; Prince's Scottish Youth Business Trust; Aberdeen Civic Society; Macmillan Cancer Relief; Scottish Civic Trust; Aberdeen Foyer; Aberdeen and Grampian Chamber of Commerce; Many others. Address:

Grandhome, Danestone, Aberdeen AB22 8AR, Scotland. E-mail: davidpaton@btconnect.com

**PATRIARCA Eduardo Luis,** b. 22 April 1970, Oporto, Portugal. Composer; Teacher. m. Angela, 1 son, 1 daughter. Education: Piano studies, Curso de Música Silva Monteiro, 1985-90; Composition, Escola Superior de Música do Instituto Politécnico do Porto, 1990; Bachelor degree, Escola Superior de Música do Instituto Politécnico do Lisboa. Appointments: Teacher of Analysis and Compostion Technique and Theory, Escola de Música dos Carvalhos, 1990-91, 1991-92; Teacher of Analysis and Compostion Technique, Música de Santa Cecilia de Espinho, 1990-91; Teacher of Analysis and Compostion Technique and Acoustics, Música de Escola Municipal da Póvoa do Varzim, 1992-95; Teacher of Analysis and Compostion Technique, Conservatorio Calouste Gulbenkian de Braga, 1995-96; Teacher of Analysis and Compostion Technique and Acoustics and Theory, Escola Profissional de Arte de Mirandela, 1993-98; Teacher of Analysis and Compostion Technique and Acoustics, 1991-, Theory 1997-, Music History, 1998-, Academia de Música de S Pio X de Vila do Conde; Numerous compositions and recitals throughout Portugal and abroad. Publications: Essay, Work + Sound = Music; Score, Pour que une fée s'enchante; Score, Berceuse's for Morgana; Suite for String Orchestra; As Quatro Portas de Céu, childrens opera. Honours: Mention in Prague Festival with Taurus (orchestral version). Memberships: Portuguese Society of Authors. Address: Rua Luis de Camoes, 19, Touguinha, 4480-537 Vila do Conde, Portugal. E-mail: eduardo.patriarca@quantitas.pt

**PATTEN Brian,** b. 7 February 1946, Liverpool, England. Poet; Writer. Appointment: Regents Lecturer, University of California at San Diego. Publications: Poetry: The Mersey Sound: Penguin Modern Poets 10, 1967; Little Johnny's Confession, 1967; The Home Coming, 1969; Notes to the Hurrying Man: Poems, Winter '66-Summer '68, 1969; The Irrelevant Song, 1970; At Four O'Clock in the Morning, 1971; Walking Out: The Early Poems of Brian Patten, 1971; The Eminent Professors and the Nature of Poetry as Enacted Out by Members of the Poetry Seminar One Rainy Evening, 1972; The Unreliable Nightingale, 1973; Vanishing Trick, 1976; Grave Gossip, 1979; Love Poems, 1981; New Volume, 1983; Storm Damage, 1988; Grinning Jack: Selected Poems, 1990; Armada, 1996; The Utterly Brilliant Book of Poetry (editor), 1998. Editor: Clare's Countryside: A Book of John Clare, 1981; The Puffin Book of 20th Century Children's Verse, 1996; The Story Giant, 2001. Children's Books: Prose: The Jumping Mouse, 1972; Mr Moon's Last Case, 1975; Emma's Doll, 1976; Jimmy Tag-along, 1988; Grizzelda Frizzle, 1992; Impossible Parents, 1994; Beowulf, a version, 1999. Poetry: Gargling With Jelly, 1985; Thawing Frozen Frogs, 1990; The Magic Bicycle, 1993; The Utter Nutters, 1994; The Blue and Green Ark, 1999; Juggling with Gerbils, 2000; Little Hotchpotch, 2000; Impossible Parents Go Green; The Monsters Guide to Choosing a Pet (with Roger McGough), 2004. Contributions to: Journals and newspapers. Honour: Special Award, Mystery Writers of America, 1977; Arts Council of England, Writers Award, 1998; The Cholmondeley Award for Poetry, 2001; Freedom of the City of Liverpool, 2000; Honorary Fellow, John Moores University, 2002. Membership: Chelsea Arts Club. Address: c/o Rogers, Coleridge and White, 20 Powis Mews, London W11 1JN, England.

**PATTEN, Baron of Wincanton in the County of Somerset, John Haggitt Charles Patten,** b. 17 July1945, United Kingdom. Peer of the Realm; Company Director and Advisor. m. Lady Louise Alexandra Virginia Patten, 1 daughter. Education: MA, PhD, Sidney Sussex College, University of Cambridge; MA, University of Oxford. Appointments: Fellow and Tutor, Hertford College, Oxford, 1972-94; Member of Parliament (Conservative), Oxford, 1979-83, Oxford West and Abingdon, 1983-97 (retired); Parliamentary Private Secretary to Ministers of State at the Home Office, 1980-81; Parliamentary Under Secretary of State, Northern Ireland Office, 1981-83, Department of Health and Social Security, 1983-85; Minister of State: for Housing, Urban Affairs and Construction, 1985-87, Home Office, 1987-92; Secretary of State for Education, 1992-94; Non-executive Deputy Chairman, CCF Charterhouse plc, 2000-2001; Senior Advisor, Charterhouse Development Capital, 2001-; Non-executive Director: Energy Power Resources Ltd, 1997-, Lockheed Martin Holdings UK Ltd, 1999-; Senior Adviser, Lockheed Martin Overseas Corporation, 1997-; Member, Advisory Board, Thomas Goode & Co Ltd, 1997-. Publications: Books: The Conservative Opportunity (with Lord Blake); Things to Come: The Tories in the 21st Century; 4 other books. Honours: Privy Counsellor, 1990; Honorary Fellow, Manchester College, Oxford, 1996 Life Peer, 1997; Liveryman, Worshipful Company of Drapers. Address: House of Lords, London SW1A 0PW, England.

**PATTERSON Percival Noel James,** b. 10 April 1935, Dias Hanover, Jamaica. Politician; Lawyer. 1 son, 1 daughter. Education: BA, English, University of West Indies, 1958; BLL, London School of Economics, 1963. Appointments: Joined People's National Party, 1958; Party Organiser, People's National Party, 1958; Vice President, People's National Party, 1969; Minister of Industry, Trade and Tourism, 1972; Deputy Prime Minister and Minister of Foreign Affairs and Foreign Trade, 1978-80; Chairman, People's National Party, 1983; Deputy Prime Minister and Minister of Development, Planning and Production, 1989-90; Deputy Prime Minister and Minister of Finance and Planning, 1990-99; President and Party Leader, People's National Party, 1992; Prime Minister, 1992-. Honours: Sir Hughes Parry Prize for excellence in the Law of Contract; Leverhulme Scholarship, London School of Economics; Appointed to Privy Council of the United Kingdom, 1992; Honorary Doctor of Letters, Northeastern University, 1994; Honorary Degree of Doctor of Laws, Brown University, 1998; Numerous foreign awards include: Order of Jose Marti, Cuba, 1997; Order of the Volta, Ghana, 1999; Food and Agriculture Organisation Agricola Medal, Jamaica, 2001; Juan Mora Fernandez Great Silver Cross, Costa Rica, 2001. Address: Office of the Prime Minister, 1 Devon Road, Kingston 6, Jamaica. E-mail: jamhouse@cwjamaica.com

**PAUK Gyorgy,** b. 26 October 1936, Budapest, Hungary. Concert Violinist. m. Susan, 1 son, 1 daughter. Education: Franz Liszt Academy, Hungary. Career: London debut with the London Symphony Orchestra, under Lorin Maazel and recital debut, Wigmore Hall, 1962; Appearances with the world's leading orchestras; American debut with the Chicago Symphony Orchestra at the invitation of Sir George Solti, 1971; Soloist with most of the major orchestras of America; Performances with all London orchestras and in the provinces, at the Henry Wood Promenade seasons and at festivals including: Bath, Edinburgh, Cheltenham, City of London and Orkney; Performances regularly broadcast by the BBC; First performances of works by: Lutoslawski, Penderecki, Schnittke, Maxwell Davies and Michael Tippet; Jury member in most of the biggest violin competitions in the world; Ede Zathureczky Professor, Royal Academy of Music, London; Professor, Winterthur-Zurich Conservatory of Music, Switzerland; Plays the Massart Stradivarius of 1714. Recordings include: Most of the violin repertory and a number of award winning releases. Honours: First Prize, Paganini Competition, Genova; Premier Priz, Jaques Thibaud, Paris; First Prize, Munich Sonata Competition; Hungarian Order of the Republic, President of Hungary, 1998.

Address: c/o Royal Academy of Music, Marylebone Road, London NW1 5HT, England.

**PAUL Ashok Samuel,** b. 12 May 1959, Madurai, India. Physician. m. Elaine Ann Paul, 1 son, 1 daughter. Education: MBBS, Madras, 1983; FRCS (Ed), 1987; FRCS (Ed) Orthopaedics, 1994; MRCME, 2004. Appointments: Registrar, Orthopaedics, Northwest England, 1988-91; Senior Registrar, Manchester, 1991-94; Fellowship, Upper Limb Surgery, Wrightington, 1994; Consultant Orthopaedic and Trauma Surgeon, Manchester Royal Infirmary, 1994-. Publications: Over 100 publications. Honour: Charnley Prize for Orthopaedics. Memberships: BOA; BASK; BOSTA; BSSH; MRCME. Address: Wildacre, 19 Broad Lane, Hale Cheshire WA15 0DG, England. E-mail: ashok@paul2548.fsnet.co.uk

**PAUL Dieter,** b. 22 September 1938, Freital, Germany. Chemist. m. Christa, 2 sons. Education: Graduated as Chemist, 1962; Dr rer nat, TH Leuna-Merseburg, 1966; Dr habil, University of Leipzig, 1972. Appointments: Scientist, Institute of Polymer Chemistry, Teltow, 1964-91; Visiting Scientist, Instituto de Quimica y Biologia La Habana, 1979-83; Scientist, GKSS Research Centre Geestacht, Germany, 1992-; Director, Institute of Chemistry, GKSS, and Professor, University of Hamburg, Germany, 1994-2002; Professor Emeritus, 2003-. Publications: Author and co-author of about 200 publications and 60 patent applications in the field of applied polymer research, membranes and biomaterials. Honour: Order of Merit of the Federal Republic of Germany. Memberships: German Society of Chemistry; European Society of Membranes; Member of various scientific boards. Address: Wolfswerder 25, 14 532 Kleinmachnow, Germany.

**PAUL Jeremy,** b. 29 July 1939, Bexhill, Sussex, England. Writer. m. Patricia Garwood, 26 November 1960, 4 daughters. Education: King's, Canterbury and St Edmund Hall, Oxford. Publications: Numerous TV plays, series and adaptations, 1960-, including: Upstairs, Downstairs, 1971-75; Country Matters, 1972; The Duchess of Duke Street, 1976; Danger, UXB, 1977; A Walk in the Forest, 1980; The Flipside of Dominick Hide (with Alan Gibson), 1980; Sorrell and Son, 1983; The Adventures, Return and Memoirs of Sherlock Holmes, 1984-94; Lovejoy, 1991-94; Hetty Wainthropp Investigates, 1996-98; Midsomer Murders, 2001. Theatre: David Going Out, 1971; Manoeuvres, 1971; Visitors (with Carey Harrison), 1980; The Secret of Sherlock Holmes, 1988; The Watcher, 1989. Film: Countess Dracula, 1970. Membership: Writers Guild of Great Britain. Address: c/o Eben Foggitt Associates. E-mail: eben.foggitt@b tinternet.com.

**PAULAUSKAS Rytis,** b. 24 May 1969, Vilnius, Lithuania. Diplomat; Ambassador. m. Rūta Paulauskienė, 1 son. Education: LLM, Vilnius Law School, Vilnius, Lithuania, 1987-92; Training Courses, Academy of International Law, The Hague, Netherlands, 1992; MA, Fulbright Scholar, The Fletcher School of Law and Diplomacy, Tufts University, USA and J F Kennedy School of Government Harvard University, 2000-2001. Appointments include: Attaché the Acting Head, International Organisations Division, Ministry of Foreign Affairs of the Republic of Lithuania, 1991-93; First Secretary, Permanent Representation of the Republic of Lithuania, 1993-94, Deputy Permanent Representative of Lithuania, 1994-95, Council of Europe, Strasbourg, France; Counsellor, Permanent Mission of the Republic of Lithuania to the United Nations, New York, USA, 1995-96; Deputy Permanent Representative of the Republic of Lithuania to the United Nations, Legal Counsellor of the Mission, 1996-99; Rapporteur of the Sixt Committee (Legal Affairs), UN, 1998; Head, Security Policy Division,

Ministry of Foreign Affairs of the Republic of Lithuania, Head of the Secretariat of Lithuanian NATO Integration Commission to the Government, 1999-2000; Director, Multilateral Relations Department, Ministry of Foreign Affairs, Deputy Head of the Working Group on the Lithuanian Presidency of the Council of Europe, 2001-2003; Director, Security Policy Department, Ministry of Foreign Affairs, Executive Secretary of the Lithuanian Delegation for Negotiations on Accession to NATO, Member of the Working Group on the Preparation of National Security Strategy, 2003; Ambassador, Permanent Representative of the Republic of Lithuania to the UN, OSCE and other international organisations in Vienna, Austria, 2003-. Honours: Cross of the Commander of the Order of Merits to Lithuania; NATO Commemorative Insignia. Address: Doblhoffgasse 3/4, A-1010 Vienna, Austria. E-mail: rytis paulauskas@lithuanian mission.at

**PAVAROTTI Luciano,** b. 12 October 1935, Modena, Italy. Singer (Tenor). m. (1) Adua Veroni, 1961, 3 daughters, (2) Nicoletta Mantovani, 2003, 1 daughter. Education: DMus, Istituto Magistrale; Tenor Range. Career: Debut, Rodolfo in La Bohème, Reggio nell' Emilia, 1961; Edgardo in Lucia di Lammermoor, Miami, USA, 1965; Appearances incl: Staatsoper Vienna, Royal Opera House of London, 1963, La Scala European tour, 1963-64, La Scala, 1965, Metropolitan Opera House, New York, 1968, Paris Opéra and Lyric Opera of Chicago, 1973; Many recitals and concerts worldwide, 1973-; Appeared in MGM film, Yes, Giorgio, 1981; Sang Manrico in TV simulcast from the Metropolitan Opera House, 1988; New production of Rigoletto, 1989, Nemorino in L'Elisir d'Amore at Covent Garden, 1990; Concert at Glasgow, 1990; Sang Manrico at 1990 Maggio Musicale Florence and appeared with 2 other tenors at World Cup Concert, Caracalla; Concert performances of Otello at Chicago, 1991; Sang Otello and Nemorino in New York, 1991-92; Debut as Verdi's Don Carlos at opening of 1992-93 season, La Scala; Returned to Covent Garden as Cavaradossi, 1999; Radames, 2001; Tosca at Covent Garden, 2002; Metropolitan Opera as Arvino in I Lombardi 1994; Sang Gustavus (Ballo in Maschera) at Covent Garden, 1995, Metropolitan Opera House, 1997. Creative works: Recordings include: La Bohème, Madame Butterfly, Beatrice di Tenda, Lucia di Lammermoor, La Fille du Régiment, Maria Stuarda, Un Ballo in Maschera, Luisa Miller, Macbeth, Mefistofele, Idomeneo, Aida, Norma, Tosca, Otello. Publication: Pavarotti: My Own Story, with William Wright. Honours include: Honorary Degree, Pennsylvania, 1979; Grand Officier, Italy; Noce d'Oro National Prize; Luigi Illica International Prize; First Prize Gold Orfeo (Academie du Disque Lyrique de France); Kennedy Center Honor, 2001. Address: Via Giardini 941, 41040 Saliceta, Modena, Italy.

**PAVLICHENKOV Igor Mikhailovitch,** b. 4 December 1934, Reutov City, Moscow Region, Russia. Physicist; Theoretician. m. Olga Yavorskaya, 11 November 1972, 1 son. Education: Physics, Moscow University, 1958; Candidate of Physics, JINR, Dubna, 1964; DPhys, Kurchatov Institute, 1982. Appointments: Junior Researcher, 1958-83, Senior Researcher, 1983-87, Leading Researcher, 1987-93, Principal Researcher, 1993-, Kurchatov Institute. Publications: Several research papers in professional journals. Honours: I V Kurchatov Annual Prize, 1988, 1994. Memberships: Russian Nuclear Research Programme Committee, Moscow, 1986-90; Several scientific boards. Address: Russian Research Centre, Kurchatov Institute, 123182 Moscow, Russia.

**PAVLOVSKI Radovan,** b. 23 November 1937, Nish, Yugoslavia. Poet; Essayist; Travelogue-writer. Education: Law and Literature, St Cyril and Methodius University, Skopje.

Appointments: Lived and wrote in Zagreb, Croatia, 1964-82; Lived and wrote in Belgrade, Serbia, 1982-85; Returned to Skopje and Macedonia, 1985-; Presently lives and writes in Skopje. Memberships: Macedonian Writers Association; Macedonian PEN Centre; Writers Union of Croatia; Writers Union of Serbia. Publications: Author, several books of poetry: Drought, Weddings and Migrations, 1961; Korabia, 1964; High Noon, 1966; Through the Crack of the Sword, 1971; The Sun the Serpent Knows Nothing About, in Croatian, 1972; The Feast, in Croatian, 1973; Grains, 1975; Lightnings, 1978; Guards, 1980; Plague, 1984; Keys, 1986; Marena, selection, 1986; Foundation, 1988; Grains, Lightnings and Keys, trilogy, 1989; The God of the Morning, 1991; The Children of the Universe, poetry for children, 1993; The Rider of the Sound, 1995; The Son of the Sun, 1999; Shield, 2001; One Eyed, 2002; Numerous essays, manifestos and travelogues. Honours: Braka Miladinovci, 1965; 11 Oktomvri, 1971; Koco Racin, 1975; Povelba na pecalbarite, 1990; Goceva povelba, 1991; Mladost, 1961; Zlatna struna, 1973; 24 Disova prolet, 1978; Risto Ratovic, 1988; Award for The Feast, poetry competition, Croatia, 1972; Best Book for Grains poetry collection, JRT, Yugoslav Radio and TV's section for culture, 1975; The Man of the Year, ABI, 1997; Listed in internationally and nationally recognised biographical works. Address: Drustvo Na Pisatelite na Macedonia, 91000 Skopje, Macedonia.

**PAXMAN Jeremy Dickson,** b. 11 May 1950, Leeds, England. Journalist; Author. Education: St Catherine's College, Cambridge. Appointments: Journalist, Northern Ireland, 1973-77; Reporter, BBC TV Tonight and Panorama Programmes, 1977-85; Presenter, BBC TV Breakfast Time, 1986-89; Newsnight, 1989-, University Challenge, 1994-, Start the Week, Radio 4, 1998-2002. Publications: A Higher Form of Killing (co-author), 1982; Through the Volcanoes, 1985; Friends in High Places, 1990; Fish, Fishing and the Meaning of Life, 1994; The Compleat Angler, 1996; The English, 1998; The Political Animal, 2002; Numerous articles in newspapers and magazines. Honours include: Royal TV Society Award, International Reporting; Richard Dimbleby Award, BAFTA, 1996, 2000; Interview of the Year, Royal TV Society, 1997, 1998; Voice of the Viewer and Listener Presenter of the Year, 1994, 1997; Dr h c, Leeds, Bradford, 1999; Variety Club Media Personality of the Year, 1999; Fellow, St Edmund Hall, Oxford, St Catharine's College, Cambridge, 2001. Address: c/o BBC TV, London W12 7RJ, England.

**PAYMASTER Nalin Jagmohandas,** b. 13 April 1933, Bombay, India. Consultant Anaesthetist. m. Marjorie Elaine, 1 son, 1 daughter. Education: MBBS, Seth G S Medical College, University of Bombay; DA, KEM Hospital, University of Bombay; DA, University of London; FRCA, Royal College of Anaesthetists; ECFMG Certification, USA. Appointments: Resident Physician, St Georges Hospital, Bombay, 1955-56; House Physician, 1956-57, Resident Anaesthetist, 1957-59, KEM Hospital, Bombay; Senior House Officer in Anaesthesia, United Liverpool Hospitals, England, 1959-60; Anaesthetic Registrar, Liverpool Regional Hospital Board, England, 1960-61; Senior Anaesthetic Registrar, Newcastle Regional Hospital Board, England, 1961-62; Fellow in Anaesthesiology, University of Pennsylvania, Philadelphia, USA, 1962-63; Fellow in Anaesthesiology, University of Washington, Seattle, 1963-64; CSIR Scientists Pool Officer, KEM Hospital, Bombay, India, 1964-65; Consultant Anaesthetist, Mersey Regional Health Authority, England, 1965-94; Consultant Anaesthetist, Wirral and West Cheshire Community NHS Trust, 1994-2001. Publications: Author of articles on: anaesthetic equipment, induction of anaesthesia in children, muscle relaxants in anaesthesia, dental anaesthesia, induced hypotension in anaesthesia, local anaesthetic toxicity, pre-medication, intravenous nutrition, post-operative pain, magnesium metabolism, intracellular pH; Numerous papers presented at national and international medical conferences. Honours: Past Chairman Division of Anaesthesia, Past Chairman, Theatre Users Committee, Clatterbridge Hospital, Wirral; Past Member of Scientific and Medical Committees, Clatterbridge Hospital and Arbowe Park Hospital, Wirral; Past Member, Medical School chess, cricket, table tennis and swimming teams; Winner, Sunday Times Chess Competition; Listed in biographical dictionaries. Memberships: The Debrett Society; Birkenhead Medical Society; Gayton Probus Club; Heswall Duplicate Bridge Club; Wirral Duplicate Bridge Club; Pensby Chess Club. Address: The Close, Chantry Walk, Lower Heswall, Wirral, Merseyside, CH60 8PX, England. E-mail: nalin_paymaster@hotmail.com

**PAYNE Anthony G,** b. 17 August 1955, Lubbock, Texas, USA. m. Sachi Tsujii. Education: BS, Paleoanthropology, Columbia Pacific University, 1982; Diploma, Cornell University, 1984; Diploma, Natural Medicine, Werner Hoeferlin Institute, Germany, 1985; MA, Physical Anthropology, Columbia Pacific University, 1987; NMD, Aksem Oriental Medical School, Hearts of Jesus and Mary College, 1991; PhD, Pastoral Psychology, Romano Byzantine Catholic College, 1995; MD (Honorary), Open I University, 1998. Appointments: Science Advisor, Central Health Network, 1986-88; Scientific & Technical Consultant, PCT Company Inc, 1986-; Staff Naturopath, Steenblock Medical Clinic, 1989-90; Product Development, Human Sciences Research, 1990-95; Technical Adviser, Global Vision, Inc, 1991-94; Bench Research, BioProducts, Inc, 1994; Bench Research, Inter-Cal, Inc, 1994; Supt of Academic Affairs, RBES, 1995-99; Educator, Japan, 1999-2003; Staff Researcher, Steenblock Res. Institute, San Clemente, CA. USA, 2003-. Publications: Author: Naturopathic Medicine: A Primer for Laypersons; Natural Medicine: Remedies and Resources; Human Umbilical Cord Stem Cell Therapy: The Gift of Healing from Healthy Newborn Babies, 2006; Multiple AOL Alternative Medicine Board articles; Numerous articles published in popular press and professional journals. Honours: Royal Order of Physicians, Gold Medal, 1997; Scientist of the Year, 1997; Numerous awards for non-fiction writing. Memberships: Tribal Member, Choctaw Nation of Oklahoma; NYAS; MENSA. Address: 240 Avenida Vista Montanta #8B, San Clemente, CA 92672, USA. E-mail: dragpayne@yahoo.com Website: www.stemcelltherapies.org

**PAYNE Keith Attwood,** b. 28 May 1946, Cape Town, South Africa. Anaesthetist. m. Elizabeth M C Luyt, 2 sons. Education: MBChB, University of Cape Town, 1969; FFARACS, Royal College of Surgeons Australia, 1978; MD, University of Stellenbosch, 1990; FANZCA, Australian and New Zealand College of Anaesthetists, 1992. Appointments: Tutor Specialist, Anaestheia, Auckland Hospital, New Zealand, 1979; Principal Specialist, Anaesthesia, Tygerberg Hospital, Cape Town, South Africa, 1980-99; Chief Specialist, Anaesthesia, 2 Military Hospital, Cape Town, South Africa, 1999-. Publications: 30 research journal articles; 11 review journal articles, 6 other journal publications; Chapter on paediatric anaesthsia in Textbook: Introduction to Anaestheia. Honours: Pro Patria Medal, 1977; Critikon Travel and Lecture Scholarship, 1992. Memberships: South African Society of Anaesthetists; Australian and New Zealand College of Anaesthetists. Address: 36 Elizabeth Avenue, Pinelands, 7450 Western Cape, South Africa. E-mail: dpayne@telkomsa.net

**PAYNE Margaret Allison,** b. 14 April 1937, Southampton, England. Artist; Educationalist. Education: NDD, Painting,

Etching, Relief Printmaking, Harrow School of Art, 1955-59; ATC, Goldsmith's College, London University, 1959-60; BA (Hons), History of Art, Birkbeck College, London University, 1977-81; MA, Institute of Education, London University, 1981-83. Appointments: Art Teacher: Haggerston School, London, 1960-61, Harrow Art School, 1961-62, St Hilda's School, Bushey, 1965-68, Sarum Hall School, 1995-97; Senior Lecturer, University of Surrey, Roehampton, 1968-94; Exhibitions include: Annually with the Royal Society of Painter-Printmakers, 1962-90; Royal Academy Summer Exhibition: 1958, 1959, 1960, 1961, 1973, 1977; Young Contemporaries, 1960-61; Paris Salon, 1962-63; Norwich Art Gallery, 1964; Harrogate Art Gallery, 1977; Cardiff Art Gallery, 1978, 1979; Arts Club, London, 1987; Dickens Gallery, Bloxham, 1990; Many Educational Displays include: Art and Appreciation in a Multicultural Nursery School, 1989; Eastwood Nursery School at the Tate, 1989; Works in Sheffield City Art Gallery; Nottinghamshire and Sheffield Pictures for Schools. Publications: Articles in journals include: Under Fives at the Tate, 1989; Teaching Art Appreciation, 1990; Games Children Play, 1993; Froebelian Principles and the Art National Curriculum, 1993; What's in a Picture, 1994; Take Another Look, 1995. Membership: Fellow, Royal Society of Painter Etchers. Address: 11A Wallorton Gardens, East Sheen, London SW14 8DX, England.

**PEARCE John Allan Chaplin,** b. 21 October 1912, Sidcup, Kent, England. Solicitor. m. Raffaella Baione, 2 sons. Education: BA, Brasenose College, Oxford, 1931-35. Appointments: Commissioned 4th County of London Yeomanry, served North Africa and Italy, 1941-44; Major, Military Mission to Italian Army, Rome, 1945-46; Admitted Solicitor, 1947; Senior Partner, Sandilands, Williamson Hill & Co, 1952-70; Assistant, Legal Department, Church Commissioners for England, 1970-78. Honours: Liveryman, Worshipful Company of Skinners, 1937; Freeman of the City of London; Cavaliere of the Order of Merit of the Italian Republic, 1978. Memberships: Committee: British Italian Society, 1967-92, Venice in Peril Fund, 1970-99; Founder Member and First Chairman, 1975-77, Vice-President, 1980-, Turner Society; Club: Hurlingham. Address: 32 Brompton Square, London SW3 2AE, England.

**PEARCE Leslie Dennis,** b. 20 April 1945, Bow, East London, England. Factory Worker; Road Worker; Security Officer; Local Government Officer; Retired. m. Anne Black, 21 December 1990. Appointments: J Compton Sons & Webb, Uniform Clothing, Cap Cutter; R M Turner and Hunter, Timber Merchants, Trainee Sales; Poplar Borough Council, Road Labourer; United Dairies, Milk Roundsman; Securicor, Brinks Mat, Security Express, Cash In Transit Security Guard; London Borough of Hackney, Cashier, 1975-95, early retired. Publications include: Making Matters Verse; Pre-Conception, poem, 1997; Travellers Moon, 1997; Mirrors of the Soul, 1996; Voices in the Heart, 1997; Expressions, 1997; Tibby, 1998; Winter Warmer, 1998; What Love, 1998; Science, 1998; A Moving Sonnet, 1998, 1999; Three Cheers (poem), 1999; The Love Verses, 2004;. Honour: Editors Choice Award, 1996. Membership: International Society of Poets, Distinguished Member. Address: 29 Eastwood Road, Bexhill-on-Sea, East Sussex, TN39 3PR, England.

**PEARSALL Derek Albert,** b. 28 August 1931, Birmingham, England. Emeritus Professor of English. m. Rosemary Elvidge, 30 August 1952, 2 sons, 3 daughters. Education: BA, 1951, MA, 1952, University of Birmingham. Appointments: Assistant Lecturer, Lecturer, King's College, University of London, 1959-65; Lecturer, Senior Lecturer, Reader, 1965-76, Professor, 1976-87, University of York; Visiting Professor, 1985-87, Gurney Professor of English, 1987-2000, (Emeritus), Harvard University, Cambridge, Massachusetts, USA. Publications: John

Lydgate, 1970; Landscapes and Seasons of the Medieval World (with Elizabeth Salter), 1973; Old English and Middle English Poetry, 1977; Langland's Piers Plowman: An Edition of the C-Text, 1978; The Canterbury Tales: A Critical Study, 1985; The Life of Geoffrey Chaucer: A Critical Biography, 1992; John Lydgate (1371-1449): A Bio-bibliography, 1997; Chaucer to Spenser: An Anthology of Writings in English 1375-1575, 1999; Gothic Europe 1200-1450, 2001; Arthurian Romance: A Short Introduction, 2003. Memberships: Early English Text Society, council member; Medieval Academy of America, fellow; New Chaucer Society, president, 1988-90; American Academy of Arts and Sciences, fellow. Address: 4 Clifton Dale, York YO30 6LJ, England.

**PEARSON David C,** b. 14 June 1950, Great Britain. Chief Executive. m. 1 son, 1 daughter. Education: Blake School, Minnesota, USA (1 year); MA, Law, New College, Oxford. Appointments: Sales roles, Procter & Gamble Ltd, 1971-75; Mars Inc: Sales and marketing roles, Pedigree Petfoods, 1976-80, International Marketing Manager, Kal Kan Foods Inc, Los Angles, USA, 1980-81, General Manager, Effem Chile Limitada, Santiago, Chile, 1981-83; Partner in start-up food brokerage, Crombie Eustace Ltd, 1984-84; Director, General Manager, Greens of Brighton, Pillsbury UK Ltd, 1984-88; Sony UK Ltd: Managing Director, UK Consumer Products, 1988-98, Regional Director, UK and N Europe Consumer Products, 1993-95, Managing Director, UK Electronics, 1995-98, Country Manager, Sony UK Ltd, 1997-98; Managing Director, International Brands ( Speedo, Ellesse, Berghaus, Lacoste, etc), Pentland Group plc, 1998-99; Chief Executive Officer, NXT plc, 2000-. Honours: Elected Fellow, Marketing Society, 1995; UK Marketing Hall of Fame Award, 1995; FRSA, 1995-; Freeman, Worshipful Company of Marketors, 2004-. Memberships: CBI Market Strategy Group, 1988-93; CBI National Council, 1997-98; Duchy of Cornwall Marketing Advisory Board, 1991-96; Editorial Board, Journal of Brand Management; ISBA Council; Marketing Group of Great Britain. Address: 9 The Warren, Harpenden, Herts AL5 2NH, England. E-mail: dcpearson@btclick.com

**PECKOVER Richard Stuart,** b. 5 May 1942, Kings Lynn, Norfolk, England. Semi-retired Scientist. m. Elizabeth, 2 stepsons. Education: MA, Wadham College Oxford; PhD, Corpus Christi College, Cambridge. Appointments: Research Scientist, Culham Laboratory, 1969-81; Research Associate, MIT, 1973-74; Branch Head, 1983-87, Group Leader, 1982, Safety and Reliability Directorate; Assistant Director, 1987, Deputy Director, 1989, Site Director, 1990-92, Winfrith Technology Centre; Corporate Safety and Environment Director, United Kingdom Atomic Energy Authority, 1992-2000. Publications: Articles in professional journals, conference proceedings, reports and book chapters as author and co-author include: Symbolic programming for plasma physicists, 1971; Fuel coolant interactions in submarine vulcanism, 1973; Difference methods for time-dependent two-dimensional convection, 1973; Convective rolls driven by internal heat sources, 1974; Self-triggering of small-scale fuel-coolant interactions, 1976; On the dynamic interaction between magnetic fields and convection, 1978; On the mutual interaction between rotation and magnetic fields for axisymetric bodies, 1979; Melting front phenomena – analysis and computation, 1979; The stability of planar melting fronts in two-phase thermal Stefan problems, 1980; Non-uniform grid generation for boundary-layer problems, 1980; A simple electromagnetic catastrophe, 1981; Ex-vessel post accident heat removal, 1981; The rotation of solid cylinders in transverse magnetic fields, 1982; The evolution and validation of internal core debris retention devices in the UK LMFBRs, 1982; Debris Relocation Studies, 1982; An overview of external

hazard assessment, 1985; Regulatory Issues for the Nuclear Industry, 1994; Radiation Protection at low doses – Benefits and challenges, 2002; Should we discount low dose radiation risk? 2004. Honour: Honorary Doctorate, University of Middlesex, 2002. Memberships: FIMA; FInstP; FRAS; FRMetS; FCMI; FSaRS; MRSP; Member, American Nuclear Society; Vice-Chairman, Purbeck Standards Committee, 2001-2005. Address: The Barn, Pallington, Dorchester, Dorset DT2 8QU, England.

**PEDERSEN Charlotte Sejer,** b. 20 May 1965, Aars, Denmark. Editor; Journalist; Writer. m. Raúl Oliver Duran, 1 son. Education: Law Studies, 1984-85; Studies of Creative Writing, 1985-86; School of Journalism (DJH), 1987-91; Tutored studies associated with the Danish School of Authors, 1993-94; Literature studies, University of Copenhagen, 1993-95. Appointments: Journalist at DR, the Danish national radio, 1991-93; Freelance Journalist, 1993-95; Editing Staff, News Desk, Politiken Danish daily, 1995-96; Editor of I byen, the weekly cultural guide, Politiken, 1996-99; Feature Editor of the cultural section, Politiken; Cuba, November 1999-February 2000; Journalist, cultural section of Politiken, 2000; Cuba, Summer 2000-January 2001; Project Developer (based in Cuba) of a new feature magazine Magasinet for Politiken, 2000-2001; Editor of various supplements in Politken, 2001; Editor of Fredag, new quality guide of Politiken, 2002-2003; Project Manager of The European Exhibition in Politiken (newspaper project presenting all 25 countries of the New European Union), concurrently Editor of the weekly cultural guide Fredag of Politiken, 2003-2004; Editor, Literary Supplement of Politiken, 2004-. Publications: Numerous articles and columns in Politiken on cultural subjects; Lyrical children's books: I den syvende himmel, 1995; Fra ø til ø, 2003; Kuglehulens Hemmelighed (radio series for children), 1993. Honours: Edvard-prisen – Politiken Award for creativity and multi-talent, award for excellence of editing and coaching, 1998; International awards for best presentation of newspaper guide product, 1998, 2003. Memberships: Member of various professional female networks among them "Cybersisters" (www.cybersisters.dk.). Address: Politiken, Raadhuspladsen 37, DK-1745 Copenhagen V, Denmark. E-mail: charlotte.sejer.pedersen@pol.dk

**PEDERSEN K George,** b. 13 June 1931, Alberta, Canada. Educator. m. Penny, 1 son, 1 daughter. Education: Diploma, BC Provincial Normal School, 1952; BA, University of British Columbia, 1959; MA, University of Washington, 1964; PhD, University of Chicago, 1969. Appointments: Teacher, Vice President and Principal, various public schools, 1952-65; Academic appointments at University of Toronto, 1968-70, University of Chicago, 1970-72; Dean and Academic Vice President, University of Victoria, 1972-79; President, Simon Fraser University, 1979-83; President, University of British Columbia, 1983-85; President, University of Western Ontario, 1985-94; Interim President, University of Northern British Columbia, 1995; Founding President, Royal Roads University, 1995-96. Publications: The Itinerant Schoolmaster; Several book chapters; Innumerable articles. Honours: 10 major scholarships; Fellow, Canadian College of Teachers, Commonwealth Medal, 1992; Officer, Order of Canada, 1993; Order of Ontario, 1994; Order of British Columbia, 2002; Queens Jubilee Medal, 2002; LLD, McMaster University, 1996; D.Litt, Emily Carr Institute of Art and Design, 2003; LLD, Simon Fraser University, 2003; LLD, University of Northern British Columbia; Fellow, Royal Society for the Advancement of the Arts; many others. Address: 2232 Spruce St, Vancouver, BC V6H 2P3, Canada.

**PEKER Elya,** b. 15 June 1937, Moscow. Artist; Painter. m. Katrina Friedman, 1 son. Education: Diploma, Theater Decoration, Moscow Art Institute, 1956. Appointment:

Freelance Artist. Publications: Large series of posters and reproductions of Flower and Still Life paintings published and distributed world-wide. Honours: Cross of Order of International Ambassadors, title His Excellency, ABI, 1996; Listed in: Asian/American Who's Who, 1999, and numerous other Biographical Publications. Memberships: LIMA Licensing Industry Merchandisers' Association; International Platform Association. Commissions and Creative Works: Paintings. Address: 1610 East 19. Street No 297-196, Brooklyn, NY 11229, USA.

**PELARGONIO Salvatore,** b. 5 December 1927, Taranto, Italy. Medical Doctor. m. Eleonora Cassinari, 1 son, 2 daughters. Education: MD, University of Rome, Italy, 1952; MD, Maryland, USA, 1962; Diploma, Specialist in Cardiology, University of Turin, Italy, 1966; National Board for Professor in Paediatrics, 1972; Associate Professor, Paediatric Cardiology, 1981. Appointments: Intern, Istituto di Semeiotica Medica, Rome University, 1948-52; Rotating Intern, Newton-Wellesley Hospital, Massachusetts, USA, 1953-54; Resident, Paediatrics, Children's Hospital of Michigan, Wayne University, Detroit, USA, 1954-56; Resident, Paediatrics, Boston City Hospital, USA, 1956-57; Chief Resident, Paediatric Cardiology and Cardio-rheumatology, House of the Good Samaritan, Children's Hospital Medical Centre, Harvard Medical School, Boston, USA, 1957-58; Teaching Fellow, Paediatric Cardiology, Johns Hopkins Hospital Medical School, Baltimore, USA, 1958-59; Teaching Fellow in Medicine, Research Fellow, Assistant in Paediatrics and Paediatric Cardiology, Children's Hospital Medical Centre, Harvard Medical School, 1959-60, 1961-63; Assistant, Paediatric Cardiology, Institute of Paediatrics, University of Rome, Italy, 1960-72; Chief of Autonomous Section of Paediatric Cardiology, Catholic University of Rome, Italy, 1972-95. Publications: 176 articles concerning paediatric cardiology. Memberships: Founding member, Association of European Paediatric Cardiologists; Emeritus, American College of Cardiology; Italian Society of Cardiology; Italian Society of Paediatric Cardiology; Italian Society of Sport Cardiology; Italian Society of Medicine for Migration; Association of Doctors Against Torture, Italy; The New York Academy of Sciences. Address: Via Amantea 89, IT-000178, Rome, Italy.

**PELÉ (Edson Arantes do Nascimento),** b. 23 October 1940, Tres Coracoes, Minas Gerais State, Brazil. Football Player; Author. m. Rosemeri Cholbi, 1966, divorced 1978, 1 son, 2 daughters. Education: Santos University. Appointments: Football Player at Bauru, Sao Paulo, Bauru Athletic Club; Joined Santos FC, 1955; 1st International Game v Argentina; Played in World Cup, 1958, 1962, 1966, 1970; Retired with New York Cosmos; Chair, Pelé Soccer Camps, 1978-; Director, Santos FC, 1993-; Special Minister for Sports, Government of Brazil, 1994-; Director, Soccer Clinics. Publications: Eu Sou Pelé, 1962; Jogando com Pelé, 1974; My Life and the Beautiful Game, 1977; Pelé Soccer Training Program, 1982; The World Cup Murders (novel), 1988. Honours: 3 World Cup Winner medals; 2 World Club Championship medals; 110 international caps; 97 goals for Brazil; 1,114 appearances for Santos, 1,088 goals; 9 league championship medals; 4 Brazil Cup medals; Goodwill Ambassador for 1992; UN Conference on Environment and Development, Rio De Janeiro; International Peace Award, 1978; WHO Medal, 1989; Honorary KBE, 1997; FIFA World Footballer of the Century, 2000. Address: 75 Rockefeller Plaza, New York, NY 10019, USA.

**PELLEW Robin Anthony,** b. 27 September 1945, Corbridge, Northumberland, England. Conservationist. m. Pamela Daphne Gibson MacLelland, 1 son, 1 daughter. Education: BSc, Honours, Forestry and Natural Resources, University of Edinburgh, 1964-69; MSc, Distinction, Conservation, University College,

London, 1972-73; PhD, Zoology, University of London, 1982. Appointments: Senior Editor, Biological Sciences, Cambridge University Press, 1982-87; Chief Executive, World Conservation Monitoring Centre, Cambridge, 1987-93; Chief Executive, World Wide Fund for Nature UK, 1993-98; Chief Executive, Animal Health Trust, Newmarket, 1998-2001; Chief Executive, National Trust for Scotland, 2001-. Publications: Approximately 50 scientific papers and newspaper articles. Honour: Busk Medal for Scientific Discovery and Research, Royal Geographical Society, 1994. Memberships: British Ecological Society; Fellow Zoological Society of London; Fellow, Royal Society of Arts. Address: 32 Selwyn Gardens, Cambridge CB3 9AY, England. E-mail: rpellew@nts.org.uk

**PELLOW Andrew Charles Henry (Newman),** b. 29 September 1944, Nettlestone, Isle of Wight, England. Musician; Writer. Education: Diploma, History of Church Music, Williams School, 1986. Appointments: Organist, Nettlestone Methodist Chapel, 1956-93; Clerk, Legal Cashier, John Robinson & Jarvis, 1961-66, Robinson, Jarvis & Rolf, 1967-90; Freelance Piano Teacher, Accompanist, Calligrapher, 1990-; Organist, Choir Master, St Helen's (IW) Parish Church, 1993; Organist, Choir Master, Sandown Parish Church, Christ Church, Broadway, 1994-97; Director of Music, Organist, Choir Master, Parish and Priory Church of St Mary-the-Virgin, Carisbrooke, 1997-99; Freelance Organist, 1999-; Sub-Deacon with Traditional Anglican Church in Britain, St Barnabas Mission, Isle of Wight, 2004-. Publications: Robella Ruby (poems), 1985; Numerous poems in anthologies; Several articles in professional magazines and newsletters; Periodic letters and concert critiques in local press. Honours: AILCA, 1984; Winner, Piano, Organ, Composition, Speech, Poetry and Prose, Isle of Wight and Portsmouth Musical Competition Festivals, 1989-2003 and 2005; Twice winner, four times runner-up Isle of Wight County Press/Tritone Singers Annual Carol Competition, 1996, 1998, 2000, 2001, 2002 and 2004; LGMS, 1996; 1st Prize, Poetry, Poetry Today, 1998; Elected a Fellow of the Academy of St Cecilia, 2001; Granted Life Membership of the Central Institute, London (MCIL), 2002; Piano-Oxford Music Festival, 2003, 2004; Ceremonially admitted to CIL, 2003. Memberships: Executive Trustee, 1998-2003, Official Accompanist, 1994-2004, Isle of Wight Musical Competition Festivals; Friend of Winchester Cathedral; Guild of Musicians and Singers; Isle of Wight Organists' Association; St Thomas's (Ryde) Heritage Centre Friends and Trust (Hon Secretary), 1985-2005; Zion Chapel Trust; Isle of Wight Morris Minor Owners' Club, 1998-; Company Secretary, Primary Flats (Carisbrooke) Management Company Ltd, 1999-; Committee, Royal School of Church Music, Isle of Wight, 1999-; Parochial Church Council, St Michael and All Angels, Swanmore, 2000-03; Ryde Arts Festival (Planning Group), 2002-; The Guild of Church Musicians, 2004; Cornwall Family History Society, 2005; Amateur Actor, Bembridge (IW) Little Theatre Club, 2005. Address: 2 Radley Cottages, Nettlestone Hill, Nettlestone, Nr Sea View, Isle of Wight, PO34 5DW, England.

**PENA Lorenzo,** b. 29 August 1944, Alicante, Spain. University Professor. m. Teresa Alonso, 19 February 1969. Education: American Studies Diploma, Liège University, Belgium, 1978; PhD, Philosophy, Liège University, 1979; Master of Law, Spanish Open University, Madrid, Spain, 2004. Appointments: Professor of Philosophy, Pontifical University of Ecuador, 1973-75, 1979-83; Professor, University of Léon, Spain, 1983-87; Senior Science Researcher, CSIC (Spanish Institute of Advanced Study), 1987-; Visiting Position, Australian national University, Research School of Social Sciences, 1992-93. Publications: Rudiments of Mathematical Logic (Madrid), 1991; Philosophical Findings, 1992. Honours: National Prize for Literary Creation in the Humanities, Madrid,

1988. Memberships: Australian Association of Philosophy; Mind Association; Aristotelian Society; European Society of Analytical Philosophy. Address: Spanish Institute for Advanced Study, Department of Philosophy, Pinar 25, E28006 Madrid, Spain.

**PENHALE Bridget,** b. 29 August 1955, Holsworthy, Devon, England. Senior Lecturer. m. Dan Smith, 2 sons. Education: BA (Hons) Psychology, University of Nottingham, 1974-77; MSc, Social Work/CQSW, London School of Economics, University of London, 1980-81. Appointments: Student Community Action Co-ordinator, University of Nottingham, 1977-78; Residential Social Worker, Nottinghamshire Social Services, 1978-79; Social Worker, Sandwell Metropolitan Borough Council, 1979-80; Social Worker, Staffordshire Social Services, 1981-85; Social Worker, Norfolk Social Services, 1986-89; Lecturer in Social Work, University of East Anglia, joint appointment with Norfolk County Council, 1990-92; Team Manager, Norfolk Social Services, 1992-95; Lecturer in Social Work, 1996-2003, Senior Lecturer, 2003-2004, University of Hull; Senior Lecturer in Gerontology, University of Sheffield, 2004-. Publications include: Books as co-author: The Dimensions of Elder Abuse, 1997; Forgotten People: Positive Practice in Dementia Care, 1998; Stroke at your fingertips, 2000, 2nd edition, 2005; Child Protection and Maternal Mental Health, 2003; Adult Protection, forthcoming, 2006; Numerous book chapters and peer reviewed articles in professional journals. Honour: European Regional Representative, International Network for Prevention of Elder Abuse. Memberships: International Network for the Prevention of Elder Abuse; British Society of Gerontology; Action on Elder Abuse; British Association for Service to Elderly; British Association of Social Workers; Registered Social Worker with General Social Care Council; Child Poverty Action Group. Address: Community Ageing and Rehabilitation Department, University of Sheffield, 301 Glossop Road, Sheffield S10 2HL, England. E-mail: b.penhale@sheffield.ac.uk

**PENICK John Edgar,** b. 2 January 1944, Langley, Virginia. Educator. m. Nell Ann Inman, 1 son, 1 daughter. Education: BS, Zoology and Chemistry, 1966, MA, Junior College Teaching of Biology, 1969, University of Miami; PhD, Science Education, Biology, Florida State University, 1973. Appointments: Head, Science Department, Miami Jackson High, 1967-70; Teacher, Biology and Botany, Miami-Dade Junior College, Summer 1968; Science Methods, Plant Physiology, Florida State University, 1970-73; Assistant Professor and Director of Teacher Education, Loyola University, Chicago, 1973-75; Professor, 1982, Chair, 1981-82, 1990-92, University of Iowa, 1975-97; Professor and Head of Mathematics, Science and Technology Education, North Carolina State University, 1998-; Consultant, Lecturer, international institutions including, UNESCO, World Bank, in countries including Taiwan, Indonesia, Belize, Venezuela, Europe, New Zealand, Trinidad, USSR, Malaysia, Thailand, Philippines, Singapore, Australia, Jamaica. Publications: 193 articles, 39 books and monographs; 50 reviews; Numerous presented papers. Honours: Fellowships, awards include: Outstanding Science Educator in the United States, AETS, 1987; President, National Association of Biology Teachers, USA, 1989, Honorary Member, 2004; Burlington Northern Foundation Faculty Achievement Award, University of Iowa, 1992; AETS Award for Outstanding Mentor, 1997; President, AETS, 2002; Epsilon Pi Tau; Distinguished Service Citation, 2003; President, National Science Teachers Association, USA, 2003-04; Listed in Several Biographical Dictionaries. Memberships include: Board of Directors, National Science Teachers Association; Association for the Education of Teachers of Science; Sigma Xi; Board of Directors of ICASE, NABT, NSTA and Council of Scientific Society Presidents (CSSP). Address: 326 Poe Hall, Box 7801, North Carolina State University, Raleigh, NC 27695-7801, USA.

**PENN Sean,** b. 17 August 1960, Burbank, California, USA. Actor. m. (1) Madonna, 1985, (2) Robin Wright, 1996, 2 children. Creative Works: Theatre appearances include: Heartland; Slab Boys; Hurlyburly, 1988; Film appearances: Taps, 1981; Fast Times at Ridgemont High, 1982; Bad Boys, 1983; Crackers, 1984; Racing with the Moon, 1984; The Falcon and the Snowman, 1985; At Close Range, 1986; Shanghai Surprise, 1986; Colors, 1988; Judgement in Berlin, 1988; Casualties of War, 1989; We're No Angels, 1989; State of Grace, 1990; Carlito's Way, 1993; Dead Man Walking, 1996; U Turn, 1997; She's So Lovely, 1997; Hurlyburly, 1998; As I Lay Dying, 1998; Up at the Villa, 1998; The Thin Red Line, 1998; Sweet and Lowdown; Being John Malkovich; The Weight of Water; The Pledge, 2000; Up at the Villa, 2000; I am Sam, 2001; Mystic River, 2004; Director, Writer: The Indian Runner, 1991, The Crossing Guard, 1995. Honours include: Best Actor Award, Berlin Film Festival, 1996; Oscar for Best Actor, Mystic River, 2004. Address: William Morris Agency, 151 South El Camino Drive, Beverly Hills, CA 90212, USA.

**PENROSE Roger,** b. 8 August 1931, Colchester, Essex, England. Mathematician. Education: University College, London; Doctorate, Cambridge University, 1957. Appointments: Worked with father in the devising of seemingly impossible geometric figures; Lecturing and Research posts in Britain and the USA; Professor of Applied Mathematics, Birkbeck College, London, 1966-73; Rouse Ball Professor of Mathematics, Oxford University, 1973-98; Professor Emeritus, 1998- Important contributions to the understanding of astrophysical phenomena, especially Black Holes. Publications: Techniques of Differential Topology in Relativity, 1973; Spinors and Space-time, with W Rindler, volume I, 1984, volume II, 1986; The Emperor's New Mind, 1989; The Nature of Space and Time, with S Hawking, 1996; The Large, the Small and the Human Mind, 1997; White Mars, with B Aldiss, 1999; articles in scientific journals. Honours: Adams Prize, 1966-67; Dannie Heinemann Prize, 1971; Eddington Medal, 1975; Royal Medal, 1985; Wolf Foundation Prize for Physics, 1988; Dirac Medal and Prize, Institute of Physics, 1989; Einstein Medal, 1990; Science Book Prize, 1990; Naylor Prize, London Mathematical Society, 1991; 8 Dr h c; Hon D University, 1998. Memberships: London Mathematical Society; Cambridge Philosophical Society; Institute for Mathematics and its Applications; International Society for General Relativity and Gravitation; Fellow, Birkbeck College, 1998; Institute of Physics, 1999; Foreign Associate, National Academy of Sciences, USA, 1998. Address: Mathematical Institute, 24-29 St Giles, Oxford, OX1 3LB, England.

**PENZAR Ivan,** b. 17 December 1928, Gola, Koprivnica, Croatia. Professor. m. Branka, 2 sons, 1 daughter. Education: BSc, 1951, MSc, 1962, PhD, 1970, Physics of Atmosphere, Faculty of Sciences, University of Zagreb. Appointments: Research Assistant, 1951, Assistant Professor, 1972, Associate Professor, 1984, Full Professor, 1986, Physical Meteorology, Physics of Atmosphere, Dynamics of Atmosphere, Measurements in Meteorology, Basics of Geophysics at Faculty of Sciences, Agroclimatology, University of Zagreb and Osijek, Croatia and University of Mostar, Bosnia and Herzegovina. Publications: 81 scientific papers; 99 other papers; 7 books dealing with solar irradiation, climatology, interaction between the physics of the sea and atmosphere and history of Croatian Meteorology. Honours: The Order of Croatian Danica, with figure of Ruger Boschovich. Memberships: International Solar Energy Society; European Association for Atmosphere

Pollution; Croatian Committee for Geodessy and Geophysics; Scientific Council on Energetic, Croatian Academy of Science and Arts. Address: Grskoviceva 9, 10000 Zagreb, Croatia.

**PENZIAS Arno Allan,** b. 26 April 1933, Munich, Germany (US Citizen). Radio Engineer. m. (1) Anne Barras, 1954, 1 son, 2 daughters, (2) Sherry Chamovelevit, 1996. Education: Bachelor of Physics, City College of New York, 1954; Master's Degree, 1958, Doctorate, 1962, Columbia University, New York. Appointments: Staff Member, Radio Research Department, 1961-72, Head, Technical Research Department, 1972-74, Head, Radiophysics Research Department, 1974-76, Executive Director of Research and Communication Science, Radio Research Laboratories, Bell Telephone Company; Lecturer, Department of Astrophysical Science, Princeton University, 1967-82; Associate, Harvard College Observatory, 1968; Visiting Professor, Princeton University, 1972; Adjunct Professor, State University of New York at Stony Brook, 1975; Trustee, Trenton State College, New Jersey, 1976; First to detect Isotropic cosmic microwave background radiation. Honours: Henry Draper Medal, National Academy of Sciences, 1977; Herschel Medal, Royal Astronomical Society, 1978; Joint Winner, Nobel Prize for Physics, 1978; Pender Award, 1992; International Engineering Consortium Fellow Award, 1997; Numerous other prizes and awards. Memberships: National Academy of Engineering; American Astronomical Society; World Academy of Arts and Science; Fellow, AAAS; American Physical Society. Address: AT&T Bell Laboratories, 600 Mountain Avenue, Murray Hill, NJ 07974, USA.

**PEPE Frank A,** b. 22 May 1931, Schenectady, New York, USA. Emeritus Professor. Education: BS, Chemistry, Union College, 1953; PhD, Physical Chemistry, Yale University, 1957. Appointments: Instructor, 1957-60, Associate, 1960-63, Assistant Professor, 1963-65, Associate Professor, 1965-70, Professor, 1970-92, Department of Anatomy, School of Medicine, University of Pennsylvania, Chairman, Department of Anatomy, 1977-90, Professor, Department of Cell and Development Biology, 1992-96, Emeritus Professor, 1996-. Publications: Numerous articles in professional journals; Editor, Motility in Cell Function, 1979. Honours: Fellow, AAAS, 1987; Raymond C Truex Distinguished Lecture Award, Hahneman University, 1988. Memberships: American Association of Anatomists; American Chemical Society; AAAS; Sigma Xi; Micro Society of America. Address: 4614 Pine Street, Philadelphia, PA 19143-1808, USA. E-mail: fpepe@mail.med.upenn.edu

**PEPPÉ Rodney Darrell,** b. 24 June 1934, Eastbourne, East Sussex, England. Author; Artist. m. Tatjana Tekkel, 16 July 1960, 2 sons. Education: Eastbourne School of Art, 1951-53, 1955-57; London County Council Central School of Art, 1957-59; NDD, Illustration (special subject) and Central School Diploma. Appointments: Art Director, S H Benson Ltd, 1960-64; J Walter Thompson & Co Ltd, 1965-65; Consultant Designer to Ross Foods Ltd, 1965-72; Free-lance Graphic Designer, Illustrator, 1965-98; Children's Author and Illustrator, 1968; Toymaker and Automatist. Publications: The Alphabet Book, 1968; Circus Numbers, 1969; The House That Jack Built, 1970; Hey Riddle Diddle!, 1971; Simple Simon, 1972; ·Cat and Mouse, 1973; Odd One Out, 1974; Henry series, 1975-78; Rodney Peppé's Moving Toys, 1980; The Mice Who Lived in a Shoe, 1981; Run Rabbit, Run!, 1982; The Kettleship Pirates, 1983; Little Toy Board Book series, 1983; The Mice and the Flying Basket, 1985; The Mice and the Clockwork Bus, 1986; Thumbprint Circus, 1988; Huxley Pig series, 1989-90; The Animal Directory, 1989; The Mice on the Moon, 1992; The Mice and the Travel Machine, 1993; The Magic Toybox, 1996; Gus and Nipper, 1996; Hippo Plays Hide and Seek, 1997;

Angelmouse Series, 2000; Automata and Mechanical Toys, 2002; Toys and Models, 2003; Making Mechanical Toys, 2005. Contributions to: Periodicals. Membership: Society of Authors. Address: Stoneleigh House, 6 Stoneleigh Drive, Livermead, Torquay, Devon TQ2 6TR, England.

**PERAK H.H. Sultan of, Sultan Azlan Muhibbuddin Shah ibni Al-Marhum Sultan Yussuf Ghafarullahu-Lahu Shah,** b. 19 April 1928, Batu Gajah. Malaysian Ruler. m. Tuanku Bainun Mohamed Ali, 1954, 2 sons, 3 daughters. Education: Malay College; University of Nottingham. Appointments: Called to Bar, Lincoln's Inn; Magistrate, Kuala Lumpur; Assistant State Secretary, Perak; Deputy Public Prosecutor; President, Sessions Court, Seremban and Taiping; State Legal Advisor, Pahang and Johre; Federal Court Judge, 1973; Chief Justice of Malaysia, 1979; Lord President, 1982-83; Raja Kechil Bongsu (6th in line), 1962, Raja Muda (2nd in line), 1983; Sultan of Perak, 1984-; Yang di-Pertuan Agong (Supreme Head of State), 1989-94; Pro-Chancellor, University of Saina Malaysia, 1971, Chancellor, University of Malaya, 1986; Honorary Colonel-in-Chief, Malaysian Armed Forces Engineers Corps; Manager, Malaysian Hockey Team, 1972; President, Malaysian Hockey Federation, Asian Hockey Federation; Vice-President, International Hockey Federation, Olympic Council of Malaysia.

**PEREGOY Matthew E,** b. 2 October 1964, Virginia, USA. Company President. 1 son. Education: Attended Virginia Commonwealth University transferred to Oklahoma State University. Appointments: USAF Veteran; Creator and President, Financial Enterprise Inc, 1997; Chief Executive Officer, Lexington Heritage, 2002. Publications: Regular articles in local press, 1995-; Editor, Publisher, Newsletter "Solutions Great and Small...". Honours: Business Man of the Year 2003; American Medal of Honor, 2004; Listed in Who's Who publications and biographical dictionaries. Membership: Presidents Business Advisory Council. Address: 775 Downey Avenue, Brick, NJ 08723, USA. E-mail: www.financialenterprise.net

**PEREIRA Gerson Alves Jr,** b. 20 January 1968, São José do Rio Preto, Brazil. Trauma and Emergency Physician. m. Rejane Maira Goes, 1 son. Education: Graduate, Emergency Physician, Trauma Surgeon, Educator, São Paulo University, 1991; Certificates: General Surgery Specialist, 1996, Trauma Surgery Specialist, 1999, Brazilian College of Surgeons; Certificate, Digestive Surgery Specialist, Brazilian College of Digestive Surgery, 1996; Certificate, Intensive Care Specialist, Brazilian Intensive Care Association, 1997. Appointments: Medical Supervisor, Intensive Care, São Paulo University, São Paulo, Brazil, 1998-2003; Medical Co-ordinator, Intensive Care Unit, Santa Casa, Sertaozinho, Brazil, 2002-; Professor of Emergency Medicine, 2000-, Professor of Surgical Technique, 2002-, Medical Supervisor, Habilities Laboratory, 2002-, University of Riberão Preto, São Paulo, Brazil; Medical Co-ordinator, Emergency Medicine, Trauma and Intensive Care League, Riberão Preto, 2002-. Publications: Research into renal trauma, trauma scores, emergency medicine, medical management and intensive care. Honours: Rui Rerreira-Santos Prize, Best Medicine Student of the Surgery Department, University of São Paulo, Riberão Preto, Brazil, 1991; Good Services to Riberão Preto City, 2002; Listed in Who's Who publications and biographical dictionaries. Address: Av. Costabile Romano 2201, CEP 14096-900, Ribeirania, Riberão Preto, São Paulo, Brazil. E-mail: gersonapj@netsite.com.br

**PERHAM Michael Francis,** b. 8 November 1947, Dorchester, Dorset, England. Bishop of Gloucester. m. Alison Jane Grove, 4 daughters. Education: Hardye's School, Dorchester, 1959-

65; BA, 1974, MA, 1978, Keble College, Oxford; Cuddesdon Theological College, Oxford, 1974-76. Appointments: Ordained Deacon in Canterbury Cathedral, 1976; Assistant Curate, St Mary's Addington, Croydon, 1976-81; Ordained Priest in Canterbury Cathedral, 1977; Domestic Chaplain to Bishop of Winchester (Bishop John Taylor), 1981-84; Rector, Oakdale Team Ministry, Poole, 1984-92; Canon Residentiary and Precentor, Norwich Cathedral, 1992-98; Vice Dean of Norwich, 1995-98; (Last) Provost of Derby, 1998-2000; (First) Dean of Derby, 2000-04; Ordained Bishop in St Paul's Cathedral, 2004; (40th) Bishop of Gloucester, 2004-. Publications include: A New Handbook of Pastoral Liturgy, 2000; Signs of Your Kingdom, 2003; Glory in our Midst, 2005. Honours: Honorary Fellow, Royal School of Church Music, 2003-. Memberships: Member, Governing Body of SPCK, 2002-, Vice Chairman, 2005-; President, Alcuin Club, 2005-; Bishop Protector of the Society of St Francis, 2005. Address: Church House, College Green, Gloucester, GL1 2LY, England. E-mail: bshpglos@glosdioc.org.uk

**PERINA Jan,** b. 11 November 1936, Mestec Kralove. Professor of Physics. m. Vlasta Perinova, 1 son, 1 daughter. Education: Palacky University, 1964; PhD, Palacky University, 1966; RNDr, Palacky University, 1967; DSc, Charles University, 1984; Professor, 1990. Appointments: Laboratory of Optics and Joint Laboratory of Optics, Palacky University Olomouc, 1964-; Department of Optics, Palacky University Olomouc, Czech Republic, 1990-. Publications: About 300 publications on coherence and statistics of light; Books: Van Nostrand, 1972; Mir, 1974, 1987; Kluwer, 1984, 1985, 1991, 1994; World Scientific, 1998; J. Wiley, 2001. Honours: Awards of: Columbia University, 1983; Ministry of Education, 1991; Slovakia Academy of Science, 1996; Town of Olomouc, 2001; State Award of the Czech Republic, 2002. Memberships: Fellow of American Optical Society, 1984; Learned Society Bohemica, 1995. Address: Kmochova 3, 77900 Olomouc, Czech Republic.

**PEŘINOVÁ Vlasta Anna,** b. 16 October 1943, Ostravice, Czech Republic. Professor. m. Jan Peřina, 1 son, 1 daughter. Education: Graduate, Faculty of Natural Sciences, 1965, Rerum Naturalium Doctor, Mathematical Analysis, 1967, PhD, Mathematical Analysis, 1981, Associate Professor, 1992, Professor, General Physics and Mathematical Physics, 1995; Palacký University Olomouc, Czech Republic; DSc, General Physics and Mathematical Physics, Charles University, Prague, Czech Republic, 1990. Appointments: Research Worker, Computational Centre, 1966-68, Scientific Worker, Laboratory of Optics, 1968-84, Senior Scientific Worker, Joint Laboratory of Optics of Palacký University and Czechoslovak Academy of Sciences, 1984-90; Leading Scientific Worker, Laboratory of Quantum Optics, 1990-95; Professor, Department of Optics, 1995-, Faculty of Natural Sciences, Palacký University, Olomouc, Czech Republic. Publications: Monograph: Phase in Optics, 1998; Book Chapters in Modern Nonlinear Optics, 1993, Progress in Optics volume 33, 1994, volume 40, 2000, volume 43, 2002; Modern Nonlinear Optics part 1, 2001; Numerous articles in professional scientific journals. Honour: Collective Prize, Ministry of Education, Prague, 1991. Memberships: Union of Czech Mathematicians and Physicists, 1967-; International Society of Optical Engineering - SPIE, 1991. Address: Department of Optics, Faculty of Natural Sciences, Palacký University, Třída Svobody 26, 771 46, Olomouc, Czech Republic. E-mail: perinova@optnw.upol.cz

**PERLMAN Kato Lenard,** b. 18 July 1928, Budapest, Hungary. Research Chemist; Senior Scientist. m. David Perlman, deceased. Education: Dipl Chem, Eotvos Lorand University, Budapest, Hungary, 1950; PhD, Organic Chemistry, Eotvos Lorand University, Budapest, Hungary, 1960. Appointments: Research Chemist, Chinoin Pharmaceutical Company, 1950-54; Research Staff Member, Research Institute for Pharmaceutical Industry, Budapest, Hungary, 1954-62; Research Associate, Research Staff Member, Princeton University, New Jersey, USA, 1963-68; Research Associate, McArdle Laboratories, University of Wisconsin, USA, 1968-69; Research Associate, School of Pharmacy, University of Wisconsin, USA, 1969-72; Associate Scientist, School of Pharmacy, University of Wisconsin, USA, 1972-81; Research Associate, Biochemistry Department, University of Wisconsin-Madison, USA, 1981-87; Senior Scientist, Biochemistry Department, University of Wisconsin-Madison, USA, 1987-95; Distinguished Service Emerita, 1995-. Publications: 49 scientific publications; 40 US patents; 6 Hungarian patents. Memberships: American Chemical Society; British Chemical Society. Address: 1 Chippewa Ct, Madison, WI 53711, USA. E-mail: kperlman@wisc.edu

**PEROT (Henry) Ross,** b. 27 June 1930, Texarkana, Texas, USA. Industrialist. m. Margot Birmingham, 1956, 4 children. Education: US Naval Academy. Appointments: US Navy, 1953-57; IBM Corporation, 1957-62; Founder, Electron Data Systems Corporation, 1962, Chair of Board, CEO, 1982-86; Director, Perot Group, Dallas, 1986-; Founder, Perot Systems Corporation, WA, 1988-, Chair, 1988-92, 1992-, Board Member, 1988-; Chair, Board of Visitors, US Naval Academy, 1970-; Candidate for President of USA, 1992, 1996; Founder, Reform Party, 1995. Publications: Not For Sale at Any Price, 1993; Intensive Care, 1995. Address: The Perot Group, PO Box 269014, Plano, TX 75026, USA.

**PERRETT Bryan,** b. 9 July 1934, Liverpool, England. Author; Military Historian. m. Anne Catherine Trench, 13 August 1966. Education: Liverpool College. Appointment: Defence Correspondent to Liverpool Echo, during Falklands War and Gulf War. Publications: The Czar's British Squadron (with A Lord), 1981; A History of Blitzkrieg, 1983; Knights of the Black Cross: Hitler's Panzerwaffe and its Leaders, 1986; Desert Warfare, 1988; Encyclopaedia of the Second World War (with Ian Hogg), 1989; Canopy of War, 1990; Liverpool: A City at War, 1990; Last Stand: Famous Battles Against the Odds, 1991; The Battle Book: Crucial Conflicts in History from 1469 BC to the Present, 1992; At All Costs: Stories of Impossible Victories, 1993; Seize and Hold: Master Strokes of the Battlefield, 1994; Iron Fist: Crucial Armoured Engagements, 1995; Against All Odds! More Dramatic Last Stand Actions, 1995; Impossible Victories: Ten Unlikely Battlefield Successes, 1996; The Real Hornblower: The Life and Times of Admiral Sir James Gordon, GCB, 1998; The Taste of Battle, 2000; The Changing Face of Battle, 2000; Gunboat!, 2000; Last Convoy, 2000; Beach Assault, 2000; Heroes of the Hour, 2001; Trafalgar, 2002; Crimea, 2002; Waterloo, 2003; For Valour – Victoria Cross and Medal of Honor Battles, 2003; D Day, 2005; U-Boat Hunter, 2005. Contributions to: War Monthly; Military History; World War Investigator; War in Peace (partwork); The Elite (partwork). Memberships: Rotary Club of Ormskirk; Army Records Society; Society for Army Historical Research. Address: 7 Maple Avenue, Burscough, Nr Ormskirk, Lancashire L40 5SL, England.

**PERRI Yitzhak (Ernest Friedman),** b. 7 June 1927, Siebenburgen, Transylvania. Professor; Lecturer; Researcher; Director. m. Zipora Sternberg, 1 son, 1 daughter. Education: Teachers' and Rabbis' Seminar, Rome; BA, Erdstein College, Haifa, Israel; BA, PhD, Tel-Aviv University, Israel; MA, Hebrew University, Jerusalem, Israel; EdD, New York University, USA; Professorial nomination, NP University, California. Appointments: Teacher, Elementary School, Haifa,

1950-53; Headmaster, High School, Rishon Le Zion, 1954-57; Education Officer, Israel Defence Army, 1958-63; Principal, Teacher Training Institute for Academics, Tel Aviv, 1973-86; Senior Pedagogical Instructor, Ministry of Education and Culture, 1980-85; Supervisor, Inspector of Teacher Training, Ministry of Education and Culture, 1984-88; Lecturer in History and Historical Research Fellow, Tel Aviv University, 1984-88; Supervisor, Academic and Judaic Studies, New Port University, Israel, 1992-97; Scientific Leader of Postgraduate Research Students, Anglia Polytechnic University, Haifa, 1995-98; Principal, Holon City Academic College, 1987-99; Students' instructor for educational research, Open University, Israel, 1995-2005 and on. Publications: 28 books and 36 articles including: History of the Jews in Transylvania-Siebenburgen from the 13th to the 17th century, 1982; History of the Jews in Transylvania-Siebenburgen during the Middle Ages, 1984; History of the Jews in Transylvania-Siebenburgen during the 20th century two vol, 1995; History of the Jews in Transylvania-Siebenburgen during the 18th-19th centuries, 2000; History of the Conversion from Christianity to Judaism and the Judaistic Movement in Transylvania between the 16th and the 20th Centuries, 2001; History of the Jews in Hungary from their beginning until their collapse after the Holocaust, Vol I-VI, 2000, 2001, 2002, 2003, 2004, 2005. Honours: Special Award, Hungarian Jewish Research Organisation; Herzl Prize, The Culture Department – Hungarian Jewish Research Organisation. Memberships: Executive Branch, Israeli Teachers and Lecturers Trade Union; Teacher Training and Instructors Organisation; Teacher Training Institutes Principal, (Director); Public and voluntary activity in the field of developing High Education; Hungarian-Jewish Historical Research Association; Forum of the Hungarian Jewish Historical Researchers. Address: 64/5 Moshe Dayan St, Kiryat Ben-Gurion, Holon 58671, Israel.

**PERRIE Walter,** b. 5 June 1949, Lanarkshire, Scotland. Author; Poet; Critic; Travel Writer. Education: MA (Hons), Mental Philosophy, University of Edinburgh, 1975; MPhil, English Studies, University of Stirling, 1989. Appointments: Editor, Chapman, 1970-75; Scottish-Canadian Exchange Fellow, University of British Columbia, 1984-85; Managing Editor, Margin - International Arts Quarterly, 1985-90; Stirling Writing Fellow, University of Stirling, 1991; Strathkelvin District Creative Writing Fellow, 1992-93. Publications: Books: Poem on a Winter Night, 1976; A Lamentation for the Children, 1977; By Moon and Sun, 1980; Out of Conflict: Essays on Literature and Ideas, 1982; Concerning the Dragon, 1984; Roads that Move: a Journey through eastern Europe, 1991; Thirteen Lucky Poems, 1991; From Milady's Wood and Other Poems, 1997; Caravaserai (poems), 2004; Decagon: Selected Poems 1995-2005, 2005; Pamphlets: several pamphlets of poetry, 1970-77; 3 pamphlets of poetry and 3 of philosophical notes published for private circulation, 1999-2003. Other Publications: various long essays on literary and philosophical themes. Contributions to: Lines Review; New Edinburgh Review; Chapman; Margin; Cencrastus. Honours: Scottish Arts Council Writers Bursaries, 1976, 1983, 1994; Scottish Arts Council Annual Book Award, 1978; Eric Gregory Prize for Poetry, 1978; Ingram Merrill Foundation Award for Poetry, New York, 1987; Society of Authors Travelling Scholarship, 2000. Memberships: PEN, Scotland; Society of Authors. Address: 10 Croft Place, Dunning PH2 0SB, Scotland.

**PERRY Helen,** b. 4 March 1927, Birmingham, Alabama, USA. Nurse; Teacher. m. George Perry, deceased, 3 sons, 1 daughter. Education: Student, LaSalle Extension University, Chicago, 1968; Georgetown University, 1979; Doctorate, Mayanuis Mosaic Society, Duke University, San Antonio, 1979; Certified Paramedic. Appointments include: LPN Teacher, Wenona High School, City Board of Education, Birmingham, 1977-; Notary Public, Alabama, 1975-; Home Health Nurse, University of Alabama Birmingham Hospital, 1988-; Trustee, National Crime Watch, 1989; Member, Advisory Board, American Security Council, Virginia, 1969-91; Member, Coalition for Desert Storm; Volunteer, ARC, Birmingham, 1970; Member, Crime Watch American Police, Washington, 1989; Member, Hall of Fame, Presidential Task Force, Washington, 1983-91; Image Development Advisory Board; Nominee, National Republican Committee, Washington, 1991, 1992; Selected VIP Guest Delegate, Republican National Convention, Houston, 1992; Life Member Presidential Task Force, Washington, 1992; Member, Jefferson Committee, 2001; Nominated, Jefferson County Board of Education; Member, Advisory Board, National Congressional Committee, Washington; Member, Finance Committee Fundraiser, Middleton for Congress Campaign, 1994; Delegate, Commonwealth of Ky So Republican Leadership Conference, 2000; Minister, Greater Emmanuel Holiness Church, Birmingham, 1957-. Honours include: Named Good Samaritan, Law Enforcement Officers; Award, Alabama Sheriff Association, 1989; Award, Navy League, 1989-91; Certificate of Appreciation, Presidential Congressional Task Force, 1990, Republican National Committee, 1994; Diamond Award, USA Serve America, 1992; Republican Presidential Award, Legion of Merit, 1994; Royal Proclamation, Royal Highness Kevin, Prince Regent of Hutt River Province; Service Award, Alabama Board of Nursing; Outstanding Senior Citizens Certificate of Recognition. Memberships: Alabama Nurses Association; Unknown Players; National Republican Women Association; Life Member, LaSalle Extension University Alumni; Alabama Sheriff Association. Address: 2021 10th Avenue South, Apt 513, Birmingham, AL 35205, USA.

**PERRY Walter Laing Macdonald, (Lord Perry of Walton)** b. 16 June 1921, Dundee, Scotland. Physician; Scientist. m. (1) Anne Grant, 1946, 3 sons, (2) Catherine Crawley, 1971, 2 sons, 1 daughter. Education: MB, ChB, 1943, MD, 1948, DSc, 1958, St Andrews University. Appointments: Staff, Medical Research Council, 1947-52; Director, Department of Biological Standards, 1952-58; Professor of Pharmacy, 1958-68, Vice Principal, 1967-68, University of Edinburgh; Founding Vice Chancellor, Open University, 1969-81; Chairman, 1980-96, Pres, 1996- Videotel International. Publications: Open University, 1975; A Short Guide to Distance Education, 1987; Numerous articles in learned journals. Honours: OBE, 1957; Sykes Gold Medal, 1958; Knighted, 1974; FRCP; FRCPE; FRSE; FRS; Welcome Gold Medal, 1995; Fellow, University College, London and Open University; 10 Honorary Doctorates. Memberships: British Pharmaceutical Commission, 1952-68; British Pharmaceutical Society, 1948-; President, Research Defence Society, 1994-; Royal Society of Edinburgh, 2000. Address: 2 Cramond Road South, Edinburgh EH4 6AD, Scotland.

**PESCI Joe,** b. 9 February 1943, USA. Film Actor. Creative Works: Films include: Death Collector, 1976; Raging Bull, 1980; I'm Dancing as Far as I Can, 1982; Easy Money, 1983; Dear Mr Wonderful, 1983; Eureka, 1983; Once Upon a Time in America, 1984; Tutti Dentro, 1984; Man On Fire, 1987; Moonwalker, 1988; Backtrack, 1988; Lethal Weapon II, 1989; Betsy's Wedding, 1990; Goodfellas, 1999; Home Alone, 1990; The Super, 1991; JFK, 1991; Lethal Weapon III, 1992; Home Alone II, 1992; The Public Eye, 1992; My Cousin Vinny, 1992; A Bronx Tale, 1993; With Honours, 1994; Jimmy Hollywood, 1994; Casino, 1995; 8 Heads in a Duffel Bag, 1997; Gone Fishing, 1997; Lethal Weapon 4, 1998. Honours include: Academy Award, Best Supporting Actor, 1991.

**PESEK Jiri R V,** b. 19 April 1936, Prague, Czech Republic. Geologist. m. Jarmila Dobiasova, 2 daughters. Education: Graduate, Faculty of Science, Charles University, 1959; Postgraduate Study, 1962-66; PhD, 1967. Appointments: Institute of Geology Exploration, 1959-60; Assistant Professor, 1967-88, Associate Professor, 1988-91, Professor of Economic Geology, 1991-, Faculty of Science, Charles University. Publications: 16 books and textbooks, about 295 papers in professional journals. Honours: Gold Medal, Faculty of Science; Commemorative Medal, Charles University. Memberships include: Czech Geological Society, Sub-Commission on Carboniferous Stratigraphy. Address: Charles University Prague, Faculty of Science, 12843 Prague 2, Albertov 6, Czech Republic.

**PET'KOV Vladimir Ilyich,** b. 30 September 1956, Gorky, Russia. Science Educator; Researcher. m. Sidorova Tanyana Ivanovna, 1 son, 1 daughter. Education: Candidate of Chemical Sciences Diploma, Highest Certifying Commission, 1985; Associate Professor Certificate, USSR State Committee of National Education, 1991. Appointments: Postgraduate, Chemistry Department, 1981-84, Science Worker, Chemistry Institute, 1978-87, Associate Professor, 1987-2002, Doctoral Degree Student, 2002-2004, Nizhniy Novgorod State University, Russia. Publications: More than 80 articles as co-author in scientific journals include: Immobilisation of nuclear waste materials containing different alkali elements into single-phase NZP-based ceramics, 2003; Calorimetric study of sodium rich zirconium phosphate, 2003; Crystal chemical approach to predicting the thermal expansion of compounds in the NZP family, 2003. Honours: International Soros Science Educational Program, 1999, 2000, 2001; Listed in Who's Who publications and biographical dictionaries. Address: Nizhniy Novgorod State University, Prospect Gagarina 23, Nizhniy Novgorod 603950, Russia. E-mail: petkov@uic.nnov.ru

**PETANOVIĆ Mirna,** b. 29 January 1951, Slavonski Brod, Croatia. Microbiologist; Consultant. m. Zvonko Petanović, 2 sons. Education: MD, 1974, Specialist, Medical Microbiology with Parasitology, 1979, MSc, 1983, Consultant, 1991, PhD, 1998, Zagreb School of Medicine, Croatia. Appointments: Head, Serological Division, Microbiological Service, Medical Centre, Slavonski Brod, Croatia, 1979-90; Head Department of Microbiology, 1990-94; Research Assistant, Zagreb School of Medicine, 1988-; Head, Department of Microbiology, Public Health Institute of the Brod-Posavina County, Slavonski Brod, Croatia, 1994-. Publications: 33 papers include: The significance of asymptomatic bacteremia for the newborn, 2001; Detection of mycobateria using MGIT in Slavonski Brod, 2002; Specimens and isolated strains of mycobacterias during five years, 2004. Honours: HLZ Diploma, Croatian Medical Association, 1992, 1999. Memberships: HLZ; Croatian Microbiology Society; Chairman, Croatian Association of University Women; HLK; Apua Croatica. Address: Public Health Institute of the Brod-Posavina County, V Nazora BB, Slavonski Brod 35000, Croatia.

**PETER Gernot,** b. 26 April 1942, Linz, Donau, Austria. Chemist. m. Agnes, 1 son, 1 daughter. Education: Diploma in Organic, Inorganic and Physical Chemistry, Dr phil nat in Biochemistry, Physical Chemistry and Clinical Chemistry, Faculty of Biochemistry and Pharmacy, Johann-Wolfgang-von-Goethe-University, Frankfurt, Germany. Appointments: Scientific Assistant, Centre of Biological Chemistry, Johann-Wolfgang-von-Goethe-University, 1973-81; Part-time Scientific Assistant, Institute of Laboratory Diagnostics and Haematological Paternity Testing, Giessen, 1973-78; Head, Laboratory of Pharmacokinetics, ASTA Medica AG, Frankfurt,

1981-90; Head, Group of Nonclinical Pharmacokinetics, ASTA Medica, 1990-2000; Manager, Senior Scientist, Preclinical Sciences, ADME (since 2002: VIATRIS GmbH & Co KG), 2001-03; Retired. Publications: 30 scientific articles and meeting abstracts; Patents in field of cytostatics; Contribution of pharmacokinetic parts to more than 10 expert opinions in connection with the international approval of drugs; International study reports. Memberships: Society of German Chemists; German Cancer Society; Society of Laboratory Animal Science; European Society for Autoradiography; German Society of Natural Scientists and Physicians; New York Academy of Science; ADME panel in IPACT I and II. Address: Dr-Carl-Henss-Str 28, D-61130 Nidderau, Germany.

**PETER Roland,** b. 13 March 1940, Vienna, Austria. Biologist; Educator. m. Hedwig Kocko, 25 March 1972. Education: Studies in Biology, Chemistry and Biochemistry, University of Vienna, Thesis in Zoology, PhD, 1971. Appointments: Tutor, University of Vienna; Assistant Professor, 1972-81, Associate Professor (Oberrat), 1982-2001, University Professor of Cell Biology and Genetics, 2001-, Department of Cell Biology, University of Salzburg. Publications: Several articles on electrophoresis, stem cells, regeneration and reproduction in flatworms in scientific journals including: Zeitschrift für zoologische Systematik und Evolutionsforschung, Progress in Zoology, Verhandlungen der Deutschen Zoologischen Gesellschaft, Hydrobiologia, Marine Ecology, Belgian Journal of Zoology. Memberships: Freshwater Biological Association of the UK (Life Member); New York Academy of Sciences; Österreichische Biochemische Gesellschaft; Deutsche Gesellschaft für Zellbiologie. Address: Department of Cell Biology, University of Salzburg, Hellbrunnerstrasse 34, A-5020 Salzburg, Austria. E-mail: roland.peter@sbg.ac.at

**PETERS Manfred Nikolaus Josef,** b. 18 July 1943, Crombach, Belgium. Dean of Faculty of Arts. m. Monique Martin, 1 daughter. Education: BA, University Notre-Dame de la Paix, Namur, Belgium, 1964; MA, State University Liège, Belgium, 1966; PhD, State University, Ghent, 1970. Appointments: Faculty Assistant, University Notre-Dame de la Paix, Namur, 1966; Lecturer, 1976; Professor, 1984; Visiting Professor, University of Paderborn, 1994; Head, German Department, 1986; Dean of Faculty of Arts, 1997; President of the Association des Facultés ou Etablissements de Lettres et Sciences Humaines/ Agence universitaire de la Francophonie, 2003. Publications: Contributor, over 50 books and articles in French, German, English, Portuguese and Japanese. Honours: Officier de l'Ordre de Léopold, 1990; Verdienstkreuz am Bande des Verdienstordens der Republik Deutschland, 1991; International Cultural Diploma of Honor, 1995; Commandeur de l'Ordre de la Couronne, 2000. Memberships: Paulo-Freire-Gesellschaft; European Academy for Sciences and Arts; Association Belge de Linguistique Appliquée; Association pour la promotion de l'allemand en wallonie; Centre Mondial d'Information sur l'Education Bilingue; Deutsche Gesellschaft für Angewandte Linguistik; Deutsche Gesellschaft für Sprachwissenschaft; Societas Linguistica Europaea; International Pragmatic Association; Société Française d'Etude du Seizième Siècle; Lions Club Andenne; Table Ronde Liège 63; Table Ronde Andenne 99. Address: Rue de Bruxelles 61, B-5000 Namur, Belgium.

**PETERSON Richard Byron,** b. 10 May 1933, Sioux City, Iowa, USA. University Professor. m. Barbara B Peterson, 1 son, 1 daughter. Education: BA, Augustana College, Illinois, 1955; MA, University of Illinois, 1957; PhD, University of Wisconsin, 1966. Appointments: Ekco-Alcoa Containers Inc Personal Assistant, 1959-63; Assistant Professor, 1966-71; Associate

# DICTIONARY OF INTERNATIONAL BIOGRAPHY

Professor, 1971-78, Professor, 1978-, School of Business, University of Washington, Seattle, Washington 98195-3200, USA. Publications: Books include: The Modern Grievance Procedure in the United States, 1988; Managers and National Culture: A Global Perspective (editor), 1993; Advances in International Comparative Management (co-editor), 1998, 2000; Numerous research publications and articles and papers. Honours include: Phi Kappa Phi; Chair, International Management Division of Academy of Management, 1986-87; Distinguished Visiting Professor, Australian Graduate School of Management, University of New South Wales, 1988; Editorial Board, Journal of International Business Studies, 1987-88, 1989-90, 1991-92, 1993-94, 1995-96, 1997-98, 1999-2000. Memberships: Academy of Management; Industrial Relations Research Association (IRRA); Academy of International Business; International Industrial Relations Association. Address: 4737-49th NE, Seattle, WA 98105, USA.

**PETROBELLI Pierluigi,** b. 18 October 1932, Padua, Italy. University Teacher. Education: Laurea in Lettere, University of Rome, 1957; Master of Fine Arts, Princeton University, USA, 1961. Appointments: Librarian-Archivist, Istituto di studi verdiani, Parma, 1964-69; Professor of Music History, Conservatory "G L Rossini", Pesaro, 1970-73; Assistant Professor of Music History, University of Parma, 1970-73; Lecturer in Music, 1973-77, Reader in Musicology, 1978-80, Faculty of Music, King's College, University of London; Director, Istituto Nazionale di studi verdiani, Parma, 1980-; Professor of Music History, University of Perugia, 1981-83; Professor of Music History, University of Rome "La Sapienza", 1983-2005. Publications: Books: Tartini- Le fonti biografiche, 1968; Tartini, le sue idee e il suo tempo, 1992; Music in the Theatre, 1994; Some 120 articles in scholarly periodicals on music history, main topics: 1300 Italian Ars Nova; 17th Century Italian Opera; Mozart; Italian Opera of the 19th Century, mainly Verdi and Bellini. Honours: Chair of Italian Culture, University of California, Berkeley, 1988; Lauro de Bosis Lecturer in the History of Italian Civilisation, Harvard University, USA, 1996; Visitante distinguido, Universidad Nacional de Cordoba, Argentina, 1996; Foreign Honorary Member, Royal Musical Association, 1997; Corresponding Member of the American Musicological Society, 1989. Memberships: Member, Advisory Committee, Répertoire Internationale des sources musicales, 1973-; Member, Zentralinstitut für Mozartforschung, Internationale Stiftung Mozarteum, Salzburg, 1991; Accademia Europaea, 1992; Corresponding Member, Accademia Nazionale dei Lincei, 2000; National Member, 2005. Address: via di S. Anselmo 34, I-00153 Rome, Italy.

**PETROV Alexander Alexandrovich,** b. 3 February 1934, Orekhovo-Zuevo City, USSR. Applied Mathematician. m. Valentina Alexeevna Golovanova, 1 son. Education: Master's Degree, Moscow Institute of Physics and Technology, 1957; PhD, 1964; Professor, 1973. Appointments: Junior Researcher, 1963-68, Chief of Department, 1968-2005, Computing Centre, Academy of Sciences of USSR (since 1992 Russian Academy of Sciences, since 2004 Dorodnicin Computing Centre of Russian Academy of Sciences). Publications: More than 200 publications in scientific issues including more than 10 monographs; From Gosplan to Market Economy: Mathematical Analysis of the Evolution of the Russian Economic Structures (with I G Pospelov and AA Shaninin). Honours: Order of Friendship, State Prize of the USSR; The Peter the Great Medal (National). Membership: Academician, Russian Academy of Sciences. Address: Ul Vavilova 40, Moscow 119991, Russia. E-mail: petrov@ccas.ru

**PETROV Lachezar Angelov,** b. 2 February 1939, Sofia, Bulgaria. Chemical Engineer. 1 son, 1 daughter. Education: MS, Oil Chemistry, Chemical Engineering, University of Chemical Technology and Metallurgy, Sofia, 1962; PhD, Catalysis, Institute of Organic Chemistry, 1969, DSc, Catalysis, Institute of Kinetics and Catalysis, 1988, Bulgarian Academy of Sciences. Appointments: Research Fellow, Senior Research Fellow, Institute of Organic Chemistry, 1962-77, Scientific Secretary, Center of Chemical Sciences, 1978-83, Head, Laboratory of Kinetics of Catalytic Reactions, 1983-93, Deputy Director, 1983-89, Director, 1989-93, Institute of Kinetics and Catalysis, Head, Laboratory of Kinetics of Catalytic Reactions, 1995-, Deputy Director, 1995-97, Director, 1997-, Institute of Catalysis, Bulgarian Academy of Sciences. Publications: Numerous articles in professional journals. Honours include: Gold Medal, Plovdiv International Fair, 1980; Silver Medal, Ministry of Science and Development, 1981; Memorial Medal, Twenty Five Years Technological University of Bourgas, 1987; Memorial Medal, Ain Shams University, Cairo, Egypt, 1997; Gold Medal "Prof A Zlatarov", 2000, Gold Medal, 2001, Federation of Unions in Science and Engineering in Bulgaria. Memberships include: Bulgarian Catalysis Club; Russian Academy of Natural Sciences; Vice President, Union of Chemists in Bulgaria; President, Academy for Environmental Sciences; Vice President, Balkan Environmental Association. Address: Institute of Catalysis, Bulgarian Academy of Sciences, ul Acad G Bonchev Bl 11, Sofia 1113, Bulgaria.

**PETROV Valery Danilovich,** b. 13 February 1946, Moscow, Russia. Consultant; Educator; Researcher; Lecturer. Education: Honoured Diploma in Physics of Semiconductors, Moscow Technical University, Moscow Power Institute, 1970. Appointments: Engineer, Chief Engineer, Scientist, Chief Scientist, Head of Laboratory, Moscow, 1971-89; Consultant, Educator, Researcher, Lecturer, West Europe, 1992-; Made outstanding contributions to several scientific fields: Physics, Photochemistry, Volumic Imaging, Human Vision; Holography; Research in Extra-Terrestrial Environments; Lectures on computer- and laser-based systems of volumic and quasi-volumic imaging; Proposed a novel concept and mechanism of volumic human and animal vision drastically different from traditional one based on stereoscopic approach, 1995; Some elements of his concept can be traced in Leonardo da Vinci's work "A Treatise on Painting" and in the works of prominent early researchers; Postulated the conceptual notion of volumic view as a basis of volumic data acquisition, 1995; Proposed the unified concept of physical volumic spaces, their artificial imitations and hypothetical computer-generated spaces, 1997; Invented momental holography, 1976-78, the technique was used in space flights, resulting in the first ever holograms and interferograms made in microgravity conditions, 1981-83; Obtained first holograms outdoors, 1978; Recorded first holograms in violet part of visible spectrum and in the near ultra-violet range with semiconductor lasers, 1999; Inventor, several devices for volumic imaging and for measurement of deformations and vibrations, including those capable of working outdoors in unpromising natural environments, 1996-2002; Proposed holographic minirobot for investigations of Mars, 2003; Invented novel bathless techniques for ultra-high resolution silver-halide media, 1996-97; Introduced instantaneous spray-jet holography and holographic interferometry, 1990-2002; Invented dynamic – sliding holographic method permitting to process tremendous amounts of data – over 100 GB per second, 2001-03; In photochemistry field, devised monobath chemical solution for ultra-high resolution silver-halide media, 1976-78. Publications: 110 research articles published in refereed journals and conference proceedings; Over 60 communications at international scientific conferences and invited lectures.

Honours: Several Diplomas and Medals from IBC and from Marquis Who's Who in the World; Best Paper Award, from Toyota, 1999; Listed in more than 20 biographical books. Membership: FIBA. Address: Postfach 3350, D-89023, Ulm, Germany.

**PETTY William Henry,** b. 7 September 1921, Bradford, Yorkshire, England. Retired Educator; Poet. m. Margaret Elaine Bastow, 31 May 1948, 1 son, 2 daughters. Education: Peterhouse, Cambridge, 1940-41, 1945; MA, Cantab, 1950; BSc, London, 1953; D Litt, Kent, 1983. Appointments: Administrative, Teaching, and Lecturing posts, London, Doncaster, North and West Ridings of Yorkshire, Kent, 1945-73; Chief Education Officer, Kent, 1973-84; Chairman of Governors, Christ Church University College, Canterbury, 1992-94. Publications: No Bold Comfort, 1957; Conquest, 1967; Springfield: Pieces of the Past, 1994; Genius Loci (with Robert Roberts), 1995; The Louvre Imperial, 1997; Interpretations of History, 2000; No-One Listening, 2002; Breaking-time, 2005. Contributions to: Various anthologies, 1954-2005, reviews, quarterlies, and journals. Honours: Cheltenham Festival of Literature Prize, 1968; Camden Festival of Music and the Arts Prize, 1969; Greenwood Prize, Poetry Society, 1978; Lake Aske Memorial Award, 1980; Commander of the Order of the British Empire, 1981; Swanage Festival of Literature Prize, 1995; Ali Competition Prize, 1995; Kent Federation of Writers Prize, 1995; White Cliffs Prize, 2000; Otaker/Faber Competition, 2003 and 2004; Envoi Competition, 2004. Membership: Poetry Society; English Association. Address: Willow Bank, Moat Road, Headcorn, Kent TN27 9NT, England.

**PEYTON Kathleen Wendy, (Kathleen Herald, K M Peyton),** b. 2 August 1929, Birmingham, England. Writer. m. Michael Peyton, 1950, 2 daughters. Education: ATD, Manchester School of Art. Publications: As Kathleen Herald: Sabre, the Horse from the Sea, 1947; The Mandrake, 1949; Crab the Roan, 1953. As K M Peyton: North to Adventure, 1959; Stormcock Meets Trouble, 1961; The Hard Way Home, 1962; Windfall, 1963; Brownsea Silver, 1964; The Maplin Bird, 1964; The Plan for Birdsmarsh, 1965; Thunder in the Sky, 1966; Flambards Trilogy, 1969-71; The Beethoven Medal, 1971; The Pattern of Roses, 1972; Pennington's Heir, 1973; The Team, 1975; The Right-Hand Man, 1977; Prove Yourself a Hero, 1977; A Midsummer Night's Death, 1978; Marion's Angels, 1979; Flambards Divided, 1981; Dear Fred, 1981; Going Home, 1983; The Last Ditch, 1984; Froggett's Revenge, 1985; The Sound of Distant Cheering, 1986; Downhill All the Way, 1988; Darkling, 1989; Skylark, 1989; No Roses Round the Door, 1990; Poor Badger, 1991; Late to Smile, 1992; The Boy Who Wasn't There, 1992; The Wild Boy and Queen Moon, 1993; Snowfall, 1994; The Swallow Tale, 1995; Swallow Summer, 1995; Unquiet Spirits, 1997; Firehead, 1998; Swallow the Star, 1998; Blind Beauty, 1999; Small Gains, 2003; Greater Gains, 2005. Honours: New York Herald Tribune Award, 1965; Carnegie Medal, 1969; Guardian Award, 1970. Address: Rookery Cottage, North Fambridge, Chelmsford, Essex CM3 6LP, England.

**PFEFFER Philip E,** b. 8 April 1941, New York, NY, USA. Biophysicist. m. Judith Stadlen, 2 sons, 1 daughter. Education: BS Chemistry, Hunter College of the City University of New York, 1962; MS, Chemistry, 1964, PhD, Chemistry, 1966, Rutgers University, New Brunswick, NJ. Appointments: Teaching Assistant, 1962-64, Research Assistant, 1964-66, Department of Chemistry, Rutgers University, New Brunswick, NJ; NIH Postdoctoral Research Fellow with Gerhardt Closs, University of Chicago, 1966-68; Research Chemist, Lipid Research Lab, Eastern Regional Research Center, 1968-76; Physical Leader, Physical Chemistry Lab, 1976-80; Lead Scientist, Microbial Biophysics and Biochemistry Lab, 1980-; Visiting Scientist, Department of Plant Physiology, Centre d'Etudes Nucleaires de Grenoble, 1986; Oxford Research Fellow, Department of Plant Science, Oxford University, 1989; Visiting Professor, Insititut de Biologie Vegetale Moleculaire, Universite Bordeaux, 1998; Adjunct Full Professor, Department of Bioscience and Biotechnology, Drexel University, Philadelphia, 1996-. Publications: Author and Co-author of 156 publications. Honours include: Bond Award, American Oil Chemists Society, 1976; Philadelphia Federal Service Award for Scientific Achievement, 1979; Philadelphia American Chemical Society Award, 1982; USDA Science and Education Award, 1982; Agricultural Research Service North Atlantic Area Scientist of the Year, 1986; Competitive ARS Postdoctoral Research Associate Grants, 1986-1989; New Orleans ACS Award, 1987; Oxford University Visiting Scientist Stipend, 1989; OECD Fellowship, 1995, 1996; National Research Initiative Grant, Awardee, 1997-2000, 2002-2004. Memberships: American Society of Plant Biologists; American Chemical Society; International Society for Plant Microbial Interactions; AAAS. Address: USDA/ARS/Eastern Regional Research Center, Microbial Biophysics and Residue Chemistry, 600 E Mermaid Lane, Wyndmoor, PA 19038, USA.

**PFEIFFER Michelle,** b. 29 April 1957, Santa Ana, California, USA. Actress. m. (1) Peter Horton, divorced 1987, 1 adopted daughter, (2) David E Kelly, 1993, 1 son. Career: Films include: Grease 2; The Witches of Eastwick; Scarface; Married to the Mob; The Fabulous Baker Boys; Tequila Sunrise; Dangerous Liaisons, 1989; Frankie and Johnnie, 1990; Batman Returns, 1992; The Age of Innocence, 1993; Wolf, 1994; Dangerous Minds, 1997; Up Close and Personal, 1997; To Gillian on Her 37th Birthday, 1997; One Fine Day, 1997; A Thousand Acres, 1997; Privacy, 1997; The Story of US, 1999; The Deep End of the Ocean, 1999; A Midsummer Night's Dream, 1999; Being John Malkovitch, 1999; What Lies Beneath, 2000; I am Sam, 2001; White Oleander, 2002; Sinbad: Legend of the Seven Seas (voice), 2003; TV includes: Delta House; Splendour in the Grass. Address: c/o ICM, 8942 Wilshire Boulevard, Beverly Hills, CA 90211, USA.

**PHAN Giuong Van,** b. 2 February 1943, Le Thuy, Vietnam. Linguist; Educator. m. Dung Kim Pham, 4 children. Education: BA, University of Saigon, Vietnam, 1971; M Ed, University of Sydney, Australia, 1985; PhD, Linguistics; DipEd (Vietnam); Dip TEFL, Sydney University, Australia. Appointments: Vietnamese and English Teacher in High Schools, 1964-67; Cabinet Officer, Ministry of Education, Vietnam, 1969-72, 1974-75; Lecturer in English, English Language Centre, Vietnam, 1974-75; Lecturer, English, Polytechnic Institute, Vietnam, 1979-80; Part-time English Teacher for adult migrants, NSW-AMES, Australia, 1981-84; Lecturer, Vietnamese, Department of Humanities, 1985-92, Senior Lecturer, Vietnamese, 1992-95, Associate Professor, 1995-, Department of Asian Studies and Languages, Victoria University of Technology, Australia; General Co-ordinator, Vietnamese Language Faculty, Victoria School of Languages, 1987-; Numerous visiting lectureships in Vietnam, China, USA, 1991-; Editor-in-Chief, Vietnam Times Newspaper, Sydney, 1982; Editor-in-Chief, Viet Literature Magazine, Australia, 1998-; Chair, Setting and Marking for International Baccalaureate, Vietnamese, 2002-; Director, Vietnamese Heritage Project, 2002-. Publications: 22 books include: Vietnamese for Beginners, 1991; Vietnamese Phrase book, 2002; Vietnamese English Dictionary, 2002; 5 book chapters; More than 50 articles to Vietnamese newspapers and magazines in Vietnam, Australia, Canada, USA; Numerous papers presented at national and international conferences. Honours: Medal for educational and cultural services, Minister of Education of Vietnam, 1974; Victorian Achiever of the Year Award, Australia Day Committee, Victoria, 1991; Order of Australia Medal, 2000. Memberships: Australian Journalists' Association; International PEN, Melbourne Centre; Fellowship of Australian Writers; Linguistics Society of Australia; Modern Language Teachers' Association; Return Services League, Australia; Vietnamese Teachers' Association of Victoria; The Order of Australia Association, Australia. Address: Victoria University, Faculty of Arts, PO Box 14428 MCMC, Melbourne 8001 VIC, Australia. E-mail: giuong.phan@vu.edu.au

**PHILBERT Georges,** b. 1 May 1922, Paris, France. Retired University Professor. 1 daughter. Education: Bachelor of Science and Bachelor of Letters, 1938; Licencié es Sciences, 1941; Docteur es Sciences, University of Paris, France, 1957. Appointments: Delegate from French Government at KWI für Physik, Hechingen, Germany, 1966-; Chargé de Recherches, Collége de France, Paris; Maitre de Conferences (Associate Professor), 1958, Full Professor, 1960, University of Lyon, France; Retired through illness, 1994 Publications: Papers on: High Energy Physics, 1956-65, Superconductivity, 1957-58, Mass Spectrometry, 1957; Nuclear Physics, 1957-58. Honour: Officier des Palmes Academiques. Memberships: New York Academy of Sciences; American Association for the Advancement of Science. Address: 7 rue Chalgrin, 75116 Paris, France.

**PHILLIPS Anthony Charles Julian,** b, 2 June 1936, Falmouth, Cornwall, England. Headmaster. m. Victoria Ann Stainton, 2 sons, 1 daughter. Education: Solicitors Articled Clerk, 1953-58; Qualified as a Solicitor, 1958; Law Society's Honours Examination, 1958; BD First Class, AKC First Class, King's College, London, 1963; PhD, Gonville & Caius College, Cambridge, 1967; Pre-ordination, The College of the Resurrection, Mirfield, 1966. Appointments include: Solicitor, London, 1958-60; Curate, The Good Shepherd, Arbury, Cambridge, 1966-69; Dean, Chaplain and Fellow, Trinity Hall, Cambridge, 1969-74; Honorary Chaplain to the Bishop of Norwich, 1970-71; Chaplain and Fellow, St John's College, Oxford, 1975-86; Lecturer, Theology, Jesus College, Oxford, 1975-86; Examining Chaplain to the Bishop of Oxford, 1979-86; Examining Chaplain to the Bishop of Manchester, 1980-86; Domestic Bursar, St John's College, Oxford, 1982-84; Chairman, Faculty of Theology, 1983-85; S A Cook Bye Fellowship, Gonville and Caius College, Cambridge, 1984; Lecturer, Theology, Hertford College, Oxford, 1984-86; Archbishops of Canterbury and York Interfaith Consultant for Judaism, 1984-85; Examining Chaplain to the Bishop of Wakefield, 1984-86; Canon Theologian of the Diocese of Truro, 1985-2002; Headmaster, The King's School, Canterbury, 1986-96; Honorary Canon of Canterbury Cathedral, 1987-96; County Chaplain to St John Ambulance, 1996-2002; Chapter Canon of Truro Cathedral, 2001-2002, Emeritus Canon, 2002-; The Royal Cornwall Polytechnic Society, Board Member, 2003-, Chairman, 2004-; Governor, SPCK, 1998-, Chair of Publishing, 2000-. Publications: Books: Ancient Israel's Criminal Law, 1970; Deuteronomy, 1973; God BC, 1977; Lower than Angels: Questions raised by Genesis 1-11, 1983, 1996; Preaching from the Psalter, 1988; The Passion of God, 1995; Entering into the Mind of God, 2002; Essays on Biblical Law, 2002, paperback, 2004; Standing Up to God, 2005; Numerous articles in academic journals and newspapers. Honours: Archibald Robertson Prize, 1962, Junior McCaul Hebrew Prize, 1963, King's College, London; Serving Brother to the Order of St John, 2003. Memberships: Society of Old Testament Study; Worshipful Company of Broderers. Address: The Old Vicarage, 10 St Peter's Hill, Flushing, Nr Falmouth, Cornwall TR11 5TP, England.

**PHILLIPS Daniel Anthony,** b. 24 February 1938, Boston, Massachusetts, USA. Private Trustee. m. Diana Walcott Phillips, 1 son, 1 daughter. Education: AB Cum Laude, Harvard College, 1960; MBA, Harvard Business School, 1963. Appointments: Assistant to President, 1963-69, Vice-President, 1970-92, President, Chief Executive Officer, Director, 1992-2002; Former Chairman, President and Director, 2002-2003; Past Chair, Board of Directors, 1994-96, Director, 1991-, Alliance for Children and Families; President, 1988-98, Treasurer, 2002-, American Memorial Hospital, Rheims, France; Trustee and Member of Finance Committee, Cambridge Homes; Board of Directors, 1996-, Chair, 1997-98, Secretary Treasurer, Ways to Work, 1999-, Families International Inc; Past President, 1986-89, Honorary Trustee, Family Service of Greater Boston; Trustee, French Library and Cultural Center, 2003-; Treasurer and Director, Grime-King Foundation for the Elderly, Inc; Member, Corporate Advisory Board, Jobs for the Future; Governor and Trustee, Co-Chair of Capital Campaign, New Bedford Oceanarium; Corporator, George H and Irene L Walker Home for Children, Inc; Vice-President and Treasurer, Frederick E Weber Charities Corporation; Vice-Chair and Director, member, Executive Committee, Chair, Community Investments Committee, Chair, Foundations, Member, Leadership Council for Children and Youth, United Way of Massachusetts Bay. Honours: Recipient, HHA Award, Harvard Alumni Association, 1995; Grand Medal of Reims, 1998; Regional Champagne-Ardenne Medal, 1998; Chevalier, Legion of Honour, 2002. Memberships: Member, Advisory Board of the Corporate Resource Committee, The Boston Club; Past President and Treasurer, Charles Square Condominium Association; Member, Advisory Board, CEO's for Fundamental Change in Education; Elected Director, 1986-89, Vice-President, 1989093, Member, Executive Committee, 1989-93, 1996-2002, First Vice-President, 1996-97, President, 1997-98, Harvard Alumni Association; Secretary, Harvard College Class of 1960; Treasurer and Member of Executive Committee, Association of Harvard College Secretaries and Treasurers; Treasurer and Director, Land a Hand Society; Treasurer, Garden Under Glass Council, Massachusetts Horticultural Society; Member Executive Corporate Council, YWCA Boston. Address: Fiduciary Trust Company, 175, Federal Street, Boston, MA 02110, USA.

**PHILLIPS Francis Douglas,** b. 19 December 1926, Dundee, Scotland. Artist; Painter. m. Margaret Parkinson, 1 daughter. Education: DA, Dundee College of Art, 1951. Career: Military service with Army; Illustrator, D C Thomson & Co Ltd; Full time painter, 1966-; Illustrator, over 100 books; Taught water colour painting, Dundee Art Centre; Taught illustration, Dundee College of Commerce; Several paintings reproduced as Limited Edition Prints; Over 1077 covers for magazine, Peoples Friend; Cover work for British and French Readers Digest and Scottish Field; TV interviews, 1991, 1992, 1993, 1996; Radio Tay interview, 1995; Exhibited widely in commercial galleries including: Group Exhibitions: The Royal Scottish Academy; The Royal Glasgow Institute of Fine Art; The Royal Scottish Society of Painters in Watercolour; The Royal Institute of Painters in Watercolour, London; One Person Exhibitions: Stables Gallery, Bathgate, 1986; Dundee Art Galleries, 1987; Step Gallery, Edinburgh, 1989; Cornerstone Gallery, Stirling, 1998; Two Person Exhibitions: Victoria Art Galleries-Albert Institute, Dundee, 1955; Cornerstone Gallery, Dunblane, 1992; Cornerstone Gallery, Stirling, 1995, 1998; Queens Gallery, Dundee, 2002; Leith Gallery, Edinburgh, 2002; Numerous Four Person Exhibitions, Collections, Private Collections and Group Exhibitions. Publications: Contributions to several magazines including: The Artist Magazine; The International Artists Magazine; The Scots Magazine. Membership: Life Member,

Royal Glasgow Institute of Fine Art. Address: 278 Strathmore Avenue, Dundee, DD3 6SJ, Scotland.

**PHILLIPS Fred (Sir),** b. 14 May 1918, St Vincent. Queen's Counsel. m. Gloria, 3 sons, 2 daughters. Education: Barrister, Middle Temple, 1956; LL.B, London, 1957; MCL (Master of Civil Law), McGill University, 1968; LLD, Hon, University of the West Indies, 1989. Appointments: Cabinet Secretary, Federal Government of the West Indies, 1960-62; Administrator, St Kitts, Nevis, Anguilla, 1966-67; Governor, St Kitts, Nevis, Anguilla, 1967-69; Chief Legal Adviser in the Caribbean for Cable and Wireless, 1969-97. Publications: Freedom in the Caribbean: A Study in Constitutional Change, 1977; The Evolving Legal Profession in the Commonwealth, 1978; West Indian Constitutions: Post Independence Reforms, 1985; Caribbean Life and Culture: A Citizen Reflects, 1991; Numerous papers in journals. Honours: Commander of the Royal Victorian Order, (CVO); Knight Bachelor, 1967.

**PHILP Peter,** b. 10 November 1920, Cardiff, Wales. Writer. m. 25 September 1940, 2 sons. Publications: Beyond Tomorrow, 1947; The Castle of Deception, 1952; Love and Lunacy, 1955; Antiques Today, 1960; Antique Furniture for the Smaller Home, 1962; Furniture of the World, 1974; The Real Sir John (play), 1995. Contributions to: Times; Antique Dealer and Collectors Guide; Antique Collecting; Antique Furniture Expert (with Gillian Walkling), 1991; Antiques Trade Gazette, 1992-. Honours: Arts Council Award, 1951; C H Foyle Award, 1951. Membership: Society of Authors. Address: 77 Kimberley Road, Cardiff CF23 5DP, Wales.

**PHYSICK John Frederick,** b. 31 December 1923, London, England. Museum Curator. m. Eileen Mary Walsh, 1 sons, 1 daughter. Education: Battersea Grammar School; Dr of the Royal College of Art; D Litt, Lambeth. Appointments: Royal Navy, 1942-46; Victoria and Albert Museum, 1948-84, retired as Deputy Director; Currently, Vice-Chairman, Rochester Cathedral Advisory Committee. Publications: The Engravings of Eric Gill, 1965; Designs for English Sculpture 1680-1960, 1969; The Wellington Monument, 1976; Marble Halls, 1975; The Victoria and Albert Museum: the history of its building, 1982; Sculpture in Britain (editor 2nd edition), 1988; The Albert Memorial (contributor), 2000; Westminster Abbey, Henry VII's Chapel (contributor), 2003. Honours: CBE; Fellow, Society of Antiquaries. Memberships: Victorian Society; Society of Architectural Historians; Vice-President, Public Monuments and Sculpture Association; Vice-President, Church Monuments Society. Address: 14 Park Street, Deal, Kent CT14 6AG, England.

**PIANOWSKI Luiz Francisco,** b. 25 May 1957, Castro, Paraná, Brazil. Pharmacist; Biochemist. m. Isanira Fortes Pianowski, 1 son, 2 daughters. Education: Graduate, Pharmacy and Biochemistry, Universideade Estadual de Ponta-Grassa, Brazil, 1979; Doctorate in Pharmaceutical Technology, Faculdade de Farmacia do Porto, Porto, Portugal, 2001. Appointments: Chemistry and Biology Teacher, Christian Institute, Castro, Brazil, 1979-85; Owner and Director, Pianowski Laboratory of Clinical Analysis, Castro, Brazil, 1985-92; Industrial Director, Hebron Pharmaceutical Laboratory, SA, Caruaru, Brazil, 1994-2001; Research and Development Director, Aché-Pharmaceutical Laboratory SA, Guarulhos, Brazil, 2001-2002; Consultant on research and development for several companies. Publications: Book chapter: Pharmaceutical Gossypol from Brazil in Reproductive Medicine – A Millennium Review, 1999; Co-author: Desenvolvimento Technológico de Fitoterapicos, 2003; Many other articles and the development of several Phytomedicines. Honour: "Citizen Who Shines", Castro City,

Paraná, Brazil, 2000. Memberships: American Association of Pharmaceutical Scientists; Scientific Council, Aché Laboratory and Centroflora Industry. Address: Rua Setúbal 15, Residential Euroville, 12917-025 Bragança Paulista, São Paulo, Brazil. E-mail: luiz@pianowski.com.br

**PICARD Barbara Leonie,** b. 4 December 1917, Richmond, Surrey, England. Author. Publications: Ransom for a Knight, 1956; Lost John, 1962; One is One, 1965; The Young Pretenders, 1966; Twice Seven Tales, 1968; Three Ancient Kings, 1972; Tales of Ancient Persia, reprinted, 1993; The Iliad, 1991; The Odyssey, reprinted 2000; French Legends, Tales and Fairy Stories, 1992; German Hero-sagas and Folk-tales, 1993; Tales of the Norse Gods, 1994; Selected Fairy Tales, 1994; The Deceivers, 1996; The Midsummer Bride, 1999; Numerous other publications. Address: Oxford University Press, Great Clarendon Street, Oxford, England.

**PICCARDI Luigi,** b. 3 December 1961, Prato, Italy. Geologist. m. Cristina Poccianti, 1 son, 1 daughter. Education: BSc, Geology, cum laude, University of Firenze, Italy, 1988; Professional Habilitation Geologist, Italy, 1988; European School of Tectonics, ICTP Trieste, Italy, 1991; PhD, Tectonics, University of Firenze, Italy, 1993. Appointments: Consulting Geologist, 1988-94; Researcher, Italian National Research Council, Firenze, 1994-; Chairman, European COST Action 625, 2003-. Publications: Articles as author and co-author in scientific journals and conference proceedings including: Geophysical Journal International, 1999; Geology, 2000; 1st Joint GSA-GSL Meeting, 2001; Tectonophysics, 2004 in press. Honours: Visiting Professor, University of St Joan, Argentina, 1993; Listed in Who's Who publications and biographical dictionaries. Memberships: Ordine Nazionale Geologi, 1989; Italian Group of Structural Geology, 1992; Ordine Geologi Toscana, 1993; International Quaternary Association, 1995. Address: CNR Institute of Geosciences and Earth Resources, via G La Pira 4, 50121 Firenze, Italy.

**PICK Stepan,** b. 26 December 1949, Prague, Czech Republic. Physicist. Education: Graduate, 1973, RNDr, 1976, Charles University; CSc, Czechoslovak Academy of Sciences, 1981. Appointments: J Heyrovsky Institute of Physical Chemistry, 1974, Senior Researcher, 1986-; Visiting Professor, University of Nancy, France, 1992. Publications: Over 100 articles in professional journals. Memberships: Union of Czech Mathematicians and Physicists; Czech Union of Nature Conservation. Address: J Heyrovsky Institute of Physical Chemistry, Academy of Sciences of the Czech Republic, Dolejskova 3, CZ 18223 Prague 8, Czech Republic.

**PICKERING Alan Michael,** b. 4 December 1948, York, England. Pension Consultant. m. Christine. Education: BA (Hons), Politics and Social Administration, University of Newcastle, 1969-72. Appointments: British Rail Clerical Officer, 1967-69; Head of Membership Services, Electrical, Electronics, Telecommunications and Plumbing Union, 1972-92; Partner, Watson Wyatt, 1992-; Member Occupational Pensions Board, 1992-97; Chairman, National Association of Pension Funds, 1999-2001; Chairman, European Federation for Retirement Provision, 2001-04; Chairman, Plumbing Industry Pension Scheme, 2001-; Non-Executive Director, The Pension Regulator, 2005-. Trustee, Pre-Retirement Association, 2005-. Publication: A Simpler Way to Better Pensions, HMSO, 2002. Honour: CBE; Memberships: Blackheath and Bromley Harriers, President, 1992; Pensions Management Institute. Address: Watson Wyatt, 21 Tothill Street, London SW1H 9LL, England.

**PICKWOAD Michael Mervyn**, b. 11 July 1945, Windsor, Berkshire, England. Film Designer. m Vanessa Orriss, 3 daughters. Education: BSc, Honours, Civil Engineering, Southampton University. Career: Exhibitor, Director's Eye, MOMA, Oxford, 1992; Design of Eastern Art Gallery, Ashmolean Museum, Oxford, 1996; Films: Comrades, 1985; Withnail & I, 1986; The Lonely Passion of Judith Hearne, 1987; How to Get Ahead in Advertising, 1988; The Krays, 1989; Let Him Have It, 1990; Century, 1992; Food of Love, 1996; Honest, 1999; High Heels, 2000; Television: Running Late, 1992; The Dying of the Light, 1994; Cruel Train, 1994; Cider With Rosie, 1998; A Rather English Marriage, 1998; David Copperfield, 1999; Last of the Blonde Bombshells, 1999; Hans Christian Andersen, 2001; Death in Holy Orders, 2002; The Deal, 2003; Death on the Nile, 2003; Archangel, 2004. Publications: Architectural paper models for the National Trust, 1972; Landmark Trust, 1973; St Georges Chapel, 1974; Architectural drawings for Hugh Evelyn Prints, 1973. Memberships: BAFTA; GBFD; BECTU. Address: 3 Warnborough Road, Oxford OX2 6HZ, England.

**PIERCE Mary**, b. 15 January 1975, Montreal, Canada. Tennis Player. Career: Turned Professional, 1989; Moved to France, 1990; Represented France in Federation Cup, 1991; 1st Career Title, Palermo, 1991; Runner-up, French Open, 1994; Winner, Australian Open, 1995, Tokyo Nichirei, 1995; Semi-Finalist, Italian Open, Candian Open, 1996; Finalist, Australian Open singles, 1997, doubles with Martina Hingis, 2000; Winner of singles and doubles, with M Hingis, French Open, 2000; Highest singles ranking No 3; Winner of doubles, with M Hingis, Pan Pacific; French Federation Cup team, 1990-92, 1994-97; French Olympic team, 1992, 1996; 24 WTA Tour singles and doubles titles (by end 2002); France's (rising star) Burgeon Award, 1992; WTA Tour Comeback Player of the Year, 1997. Address: c/o WTA, 133 First Street North East, St Petersburg, FL 33701, USA.

**PIERCE Tish (Thresia Korte)**, b. 15 September 1928, Maize, Kansas, USA. Teacher; Writer. 2 sons, 1 daughter. Education: Friends University, 1955; MS, University of Nevada, 1978; Postgraduate, Wichita State University. Appointments: Teacher, Wichita, Kansas Public Schools, 1960-69, Clark County School District, 1970-2000. Publications: Numerous short stories; Contributor of articles to professional journals and newspapers. Honours include: Board of Directors, Kansas Newman University, 1966-68; Nominated, Wichita, Kansas Woman of the Year, 1967. Memberships: Clark County Education Association; National Education Association. Address: 1600 So. Valley View Blvd, Bldg 6, Apt 1106, Las Vegas, NV 89102, USA.

**PIERSCIONEK Barbara Krystyna**, b. 20 October 1960, London, England. Academic; Professor. 1 son. Education: BSc (optom), 1983, PhD, 1988, University of Melbourne. MBA, University of Bradford, 2000; Postgraduate Diploma (Law), 2001; Postgraduate Diploma, Legal Practice, 2003, LLM, 2004, Leeds Metropolitan University. Appointments: Schultz Research Fellow, 1991-97; Senior Lecturer, 1998-2000, Senior Research Fellow, 2000-2004, University of Bradford; Professor of Optometry and Vision Science, University of Ulster, 2004-. Publications: Over 80 articles and conference abstracts; 1 book chapter; 1 encyclopaedia article; Numerous articles in professional magazines. Memberships: Society of MBAs; Law Society; Australian Optometric Association. Address: Department of Biomedical Sciences, University of Ulster, Cromore Road, Coleraine BT52 15A, Northern Ireland. E-mail: b.pierscionek@ulster.ac.uk

**PIGOTT-SMITH Tim (Timothy Peter)**, b. 13 May 1946, Rugby, England. Actor; Director. m. Pamela Miles, 1 son. Education: Wyggeston Boys Grammar School, Leicester; KES Grammar School, Stratford-upon-Avon; BA (Hons), Bristol University, 1964-67; Bristol Old Vic Theatre School, 1967-69. Career: Theatre work includes: Bristol Old Vic, Royal Shakespeare Company, etc, 1969-; Television work includes: Dr Who, 1970; Jewel in the Crown, 1984; North & South, 2004; Film work includes: Aces High, 1975; Escape to Victory, 1981; Life Story, 1986, Remains of the Day, 1993; Alexander, 2004; V for Vendetta, 2005; Entente Cordiale, 2005; Flyboys, 2005. Publications: Out of India, anthology, 1986. Honours: Best TV Actor, TV Times Award, BPG Best Actor, (Jewel in the Crown), 1984; BAFTA Best TV Film (Life Story), 1986; Best Actor, Lisbon Film Festival, 2002. Memberships: Special Lecturer, Bristol University Drama Department. Address: Actual Management, 7 Gt Russell Street, London WC1B 3NH, England.

**PIKE Edward Roy**, b. 4 December 1929, Perth, Western Australia. Physicist. Education: BSc, Mathematics, 1953, BSc, Physics, 1954, PhD, Physics, 1957, University College, Cardiff, Wales. Appointments: Fellow, American Society for Testing Materials, University College, Cardiff, 1954-58; Research Assistant, University of Wales, Cardiff, 1957-58; Instructor, Massachusetts Institute of Technology, USA, 1958-60; Senior Scientific Officer to Chief Scientific Officer, Royal Signals and Radar Establishment, Malvern, England, 1960-86; Visiting Professor of Mathematics, Imperial College of Science and Technology, London, 1984-85; Non-Executive Director, Richard Clay plc (Printers), 1984-86; Clerk Maxwell Professor of Theoretical Physics, King's College, London, 1986-; Head of School of Physical Sciences and Engineering, King's College, London, 1991-94; Chairman, Stilo Technology Ltd (Publishing and World Wide Web software), 1995-2002; Chairman, 2000-02, Non-Executive Director, 2002-04, Stilo International plc; Director, Phonologica Ltd, 2004-. Publications: 300 papers and 10 books in the fields of theoretical physics, X-Ray diffraction, statistics, imaging and optics, inverse problems, compact disc technology. Honours: Charles Parsons Prize, Royal Society, 1975; McRobert Award, Confederation of Engineering Institutions, 1977; Annual Achievement Award, Worshipful Company of Scientific Instrument Makers, 1978; Civil Service Award to Inventors, 1980; Guthrie Medal and Prize, Institute of Physics, 1995; Fellow, University College Cardiff; Fellow King's College London; Fellow of the Institute of Mathematics and Applications; Fellow of the Institute of Physics; Fellow of the Optical Society of America; Fellow of the Royal Society. Address: Physics Department, King's College London, Strand, London WC2R 2LS, England.

**PIKE Lionel John**, b. 7 November 1939, Bristol, England. University Professor; Organist. m. Jennifer Marguerite Parkes, 2 daughters. Education: BA, Class I, Music, B Mus, MA, D Phil, Pembroke College, Oxford; FRCO; ARCM. Appointments: Organist, 1969-, Lecturer in Music, 1965-80, Senior Lecturer in Music and College Organist, 1980-2004, Professor of Music, 2004-, Royal Holloway College (University of London), UK. Publications: Beethoven, Sibelius and "The Profound Logic", 1978; Hexachords in Late Renaissance Music, 1998; Vaughan Williams and the Symphony, 2003; The Works of Henry Purcell, volumes 14 and 17 (editor); Many articles, compositions, reviews and CD's. Honours: Book: Beethoven, Sibelius and "The Profound Logic", named by Choice Magazine as one of the three best academic books in any subject for the year 1978-79; Limpus Prize for FRCO. Memberships: Royal College of Organists; Havergal Brian Society; Robert Simpson Society; RVW Society; Chaine des Rotisseurs. Address: Music

Department, Royal Holloway (University of London), Egham Hill, Egham, Surrey TW20 0EX, England. E-mail: lionel.pike @rhul.ac.uk

**PIMLOTT Steven Charles,** b. 18 April 1953, United Kingdom. Theatre Director. m. Daniela Bechly, 2 sons, 1 daughter. Education: MA, Cambridge University, 1971-74. Appointments: Staff Producer, English National Opera, 1976; Joined Opera North, 1978; Associate Director, Crucible Theatre, 1987-88, Royal Shakespeare Company, 1996-;2002 Artistic Director, The Other Place, Royal Shakespeare Company, 1998-2001; Currently Artistic Director, Chichester Festival Theatre with Martin Duncan and Ruth MacKenzie; Theatre includes: Ring Around the Moon, Manchester; Entertaining Mr Sloane, Harrogate; On the Razzle, Leeds Playhouse; Amadeus, Harrogate; The Daughter in Law, Sheffield; For RSC: Julius Caesar, 1991; Murder in the Cathedral, 1993; Measure for Measure, 1994; Richard III, 1995; As You Like It, 1996; Les Femmes Savantes, 1996; Camino Real, 1997; Anthony and Cleopatra, 1999, Richard II, 2000; Hamlet, 2001; Three world premieres of plays by Phyllis Nagy; Molière's The Miser for Royal National Theatre; Musicals include: Sunday in the Park with George; Joseph and the Amazing Technicolor Dreamcoat, West End, Broadway, UK Tour, Canada, Australia, 1991; Doctor Dolittle, 1998; Bombay Dreams, Apollo Victoria, Broadway; Opera includes: Productions for Opera North: Tosca; Nabucco; Bartered Bride; Werther; Prince Igor; Der Freischütz; La Bohème; Cavalleria Rusticana; Other productions: The Pearl Fishers, Scottish Opera; Don Giovanni, Victoria State Opera; Manon Lescaut, Australian Opera; La Traviata, Jerusalem Festival; Macbeth, Hamburg State Opera; Arena production of Carmen, 1988, Earls Court, Tokyo, Melbourne, Sydney, Birmingham, Dortmund, Zurich, Munich, Berlin; The Coronation of Poppea, English National Opera, 2000; Acting roles include: Mozart in Amadeus, Sheffield Crucible; The Duke of Plaza-Toro in The Gondoliers, Carl Rosa Opera Company; Sir Joseph Porter in HMS Pinafore, D'Oyly Carte at the Savoy Theatre; TV includes: Midsomer Murders. Honours: Associate Artist, Royal Shakespeare Company; Winner Olivier Award for Best Musical for Sunday in the Park with George. Address: c/o Harriet Cruikshank, 97 Old South Lambeth Road, London SW8 1XU, England.

**PIMPLE Gajendra Haridas,** b. 25 April 1964, Washim, India. Architectural Planner, Interior Designer; Vaastushastra Consultant. m. Manisha, 1 son, 1 daughter. Education: Diploma in Architecture, 1987; Vaastushastra Visharad (Bachelor of Vaastu-Science), 2000; Vaastushastra Pandit, (Master of Vaastu-Science), 2001. Appointments: Architectural Assistant to Mr Vishawas N Dikhole, Nagpure, 1987; Visiting Lecturer, Maharashatra Kala Vidhyalaya, Nagpur, 1988-92; Architectural and Interior Designer, own private practice, 1992-; Vaastushastra Consultant, own practice, 2000-. Publications: Research papers presented at conferences and seminars; Articles published in popular and professional journals. Honours: Special Guest of Honour, Pune, 1999; Vastu-Shiromani, Raipur, 1999; Vastu-Sadhak, Khajuraho, 2000; Scholar Guest of Honour, Nagpur, 2000; Special Guest of Honour, Moka, Mauritius, 2001; Vastu-Aaditya, Haridwar, 2001; Vastu-Manishi, Surat, 2001; Special Honour, Colombo, Sri Lanka, 2002; Vastu-Alankar, 2002. Memberships: Life Member, PACE International Astro-medical Academy; Life Member, International Federation of Astrology & Spiritual Science; Member, Shri Shankar Jyotir-Vidhyalay, Poona; Member, Asian Astrologers Congress, Calcutta; Member, International Vastu Association, Jodhpur; Member, Bhavsar Jyoti, Pune; Sadbhav, Khamgaon; Executive Member, President, Founder Member, Shri Swami Samartha Sewa Trust, Wardha; Executive Member, Vice President, Bhavsar Society,

Wardha; Executive Member, Vice President and Founder Member, Designers and Planners Association, Wardha. Address: 74, Isaji Layout, Gandhinagar, Near Vikas Vidhyalaya, Wardha, Maharashatra State, India.

**PINCHER (Henry) Chapman,** b. 29 March 1914, Ambala, India. Author. m. (1), 1 daughter, 1 son, (2) Constance Wolstenholme, 1965. Education: BSc Honours, Botany, Zoology, 1935. Appointments: Staff, Liverpool Institute, 1936-40; Royal Armoured Corps, 1940; Defence, Science and Medical Editor, Daily Express, 1946-73; Assistant Editor, Daily Express, Chief Defence Correspondent, Beaverbrook Newspapers, 1972-79. Publications: Breeding of Farm Animals, 1946; A Study of Fishes, 1947; Into the Atomic Age, 1947; Spotlight on Animals, 1950; Evolution, 1950; It's Fun Finding Out (with Bernard Wicksteed), 1950; Sleep and How to Get More of It, 1954; Sex in Our Time, 1973; Inside Story, 1978; Their Trade is Treachery, 1981; Too Secret Too Long, 1984; The Secret Offensive, 1985; Traitors - the Labyrinth of Treason, 1987; A Web of Deception, 1987; The Truth about Dirty Tricks, 1991; One Dog and Her Man, 1991; Pastoral Symphony, 1993; A Box of Chocolates, 1993; Life's a Bitch!, 1996; Tight Lines!, 1997. Novels: Not with a Bang, 1965; The Giantkiller, 1967; The Penthouse Comspirators, 1970; The Skeleton at the Villa Wolkonsky, 1975; The Eye of the Tornado, 1976; The Four Horses, 1978; Dirty Tricks, 1980; The Private World of St John Terrapin, 1982; Contamination, 1989. Honours: Granada Award, Journalist of the Year, 1964; Reporter of the Decade, 1966; Honorary DLitt, University of Newcastle upon Tyne, 1979; King's College, London, fellow, 1979. Address: The Church House, 16 Church Street, Kintbury, Near Hungerford, Berkshire RG15 0TR, England.

**PINKHAM Daniel W,** b. 31 January 1952, Los Angeles, California, USA. Artist. m. Victoria. Education: Los Angeles Art Center College of Design; Sergei Bongart School of Art, 1981-85. Appointments: California Art Club, Signature Designation, 1996-; Founder, Portuguese Bend Artist Colony, 1996-; Oil Painters of America, Signature Designation, 1998-; Board of Directors, California Art Club (established 1909), 2003-; Exhibitions in: Haggin Museum, Stockton, California, 2001; Edenhurst Gallery, Los Angeles, 2001; Hollis Gallery, Pasadena, California, 2003; Autry Museum, Los Angeles, 2003. Publications: Articles and work published in numerous professional and popular journals. Honours: Upcoming Artist Invitation, Los Angeles Museum of Art, 1978; Wrigley Award, Best of Show, 1983, Invitational Best of Show, 1984, Catalina Island, California; Tivoli Gallery Award, Springville Museum of Art, Springville, Utah, 1985; Top 20 American Plein Air Artist Award, San Jose Museum of Art, California, 1988; Permalba Award, Oil Painters of America, 1992. Memberships: California Art Club; Oil Painters of America; Portuguese Bend Artist Colony. Address: 1 Narcissa Drive, Rancho Palos Verdes, CA 90275, USA. E-mail: info@danielpinkham.com

**PINNEY Lucy Catherine,** b. 25 July 1952, London, England. Author; Journalist. m. Charles Pinney, 14 June 1975, divorced, 2000, 2 sons, 1 daughter. Education: BA, Honours, English, Education, York University, 1973. Publications: The Pink Stallion, 1988; Tender Moth, 1994; A Country Wife, 2004. Contributions to: Sunday Times; Observer; Daily Mail; Telegraph; Company; Cosmopolitan; Country Living; Country Homes and Interiors; She; The Times, columnist, 1998-2003. Honour: Runner-up, Betty Trask Prize, 1987. Address: Egremont Farm, Payhembury, Honiton, Devon EX14 0JA, England.

**PINSON William Meredith Jr,** b. 3 August 1934, Fort Worth, Texas, USA. Minister; Pastor; Executive. m. Bobbie

Judd Pinson, 2 daughters. Education: BA, University of North Texas, 1955; Miv, 1959, ThD, 1963, Southwestern Baptist Seminary; Postdoctoral Study, Columbia University, 1969-70; Postgraduate study, University of Edinburgh, Scotland, 1956-57. Appointments: Associate Director, Christian Life Commission, Baptist General Convention of Texas, 1957-63; Professor of Christian Ethics, Southwestern Baptist Seminary, 1963-75; Pastor, First Baptist Church, Wichita Falls, Texas, 1975-77; President, Golden Gate Seminary, Mill Valley, California, 1977-82; Executive Director, Baptist General Convention of Texas, 1982-2000; Executive Director Emeritus, BGCT, 2000-; Distinguished University Professor, Dallas Baptist University, 2000-; Director, Texas Baptist Heritage Centre, 2000-; Distinguished Visiting Professor, Baylor University, 2001-. Publications include: The Local Church in Ministry; Ready to Minister; How to Deal with Controversial Issues; The Biblical View of the Family; Co-author: Decision Making. Honours: Outstanding Alumnus Award, University of North Texas; Outstanding Alumnus Award, Southwestern Baptist Seminary; Several honorary doctorates; Listed in numerous biographical dictionaries. Memberships include: Association of Baptist Schools and Colleges; Baptist World Alliance. Address: Baptist General Convention of Texas, 333 North Washington, Dallas, TX 75246, USA.

**PIPPARD Alfred Brian (Sir)**, b. 7 September 1920, London, England. Physicist. m. Charlotte Frances Dyer, 3 daughters. Education: Clare College Cambridge, 1938-41. Appointments: Demonstrator, Lecturer, Reader in Physics, 1946-60, John Humphrey Professor of Physics, 1960-71, Cavendish Professor of Physics, 1971-82, Cambridge University; President, Clare Hall, Cambridge, 1966-73. Publications: Elements of Classical Thermodynamics, 1957; Cavendish Problems in Classical Physics, 1962; Dynamics of Conduction Electrons, 1965; Forces and Particles, 1972; Physics of Vibration, 2 volumes, 1978, 1983; Response and Stability, 1985; Magnetoresistance, 1989; Many papers in Proceedings of the Royal Society and other journals. Honours: Hughes Medal, Royal Society, 1959; Holweck Medal, 1961; Dannie-Heinemann Prize, 1969; Guthrie Prize, Institute of Physics, 1970; Knight Bachelor, 1975. Memberships: Fellow, Clare College, Cambridge, 1947-66; Fellow of the Royal Society, 1956-; Honorary Fellow, Clare College, 1973-; Honorary Fellow, Clare Hall, 1973; President, Institute of Physics, 1974-76; Honorary Fellow, Institute of Physics. Address: 30 Porson Road, Cambridge CB2 2EU, England.

**PIQUET Nelson**, b. 17 August 1952, Rio de Janeiro, Brazil. Racing Driver. m. (1) Maria Clara, (2) Vivianne Leao, 1 son. Appointments: 1st Grand Prix, Germany, 1978; Member, Ensign Grand Prix Team, 1978, BS McLaren Team, 1978, Brabham Team, 1978-85, Williams Team, 1986-87, Lotus Team, 1988-89, Benetton Team, 1990; Winner of 23 Grand Prix; Formula One World Champion, 1981, 1983, 1987.

**PISARCHIK Alexander N**, b. 3 June 1954, Minsk, Belarus. Physicist. m. Liudmila Kotashova, 1 son, 4 daughters. Education: MS, Belorussian State University, 1976; PhD, Institute of Physics, Minsk, 1990. Appointments: Visiting Professor, University Libre, Brussels, 1992; Visiting Professor, Universitat Autonoma de Barcelona, 1993-94, 1997-99; Visiting Professor, University of Iceland, Reykjavik, 1995; Senior Researcher, Institute of Physics, Minsk, 1996-99; Research Professor, Centro de Investigaciones en Optica, Leon, Gto, Mexico, 1999-. Publications: Contributor, articles to professional journals including Physics review A and E; Physics review Letters; Physica D; Physics Letters A; Optical Communications. Honours: First Prize, National Academy of Science, Minsk,

1999. Memberships: European Physical Society, 1994-; Academia Mexicana de Optica, 2000-; Society for Industrial and Applied Mathematics, 2001-; Mexican National System of Researchers (SNI, level 3), 2001-; Mexican National System of Evaluators on Science and Technology (SINECYT), 2002-. Address: Centro de Investigaciones en Optica AC, Loma del Bosque # 115, Col Lomas del Campestre, 37150 Leon, Guanajuato, Mexico. E-mail: apisarch@foton.cio.mx

**PISPAS Asterios (Stergios)**, b. 16 October 1967, Athens, Greece. Chemist. m. Tserepa Charikleia, 1 son. Education: BS, Chemistry, 1989, PhD, Polymer Chemistry, 1994, University of Athens, Greece. Appointments: Post Doctoral Fellow, Department of Chemistry, University of Alabama, Birmingham, USA, 1994-95; Research Associate, Department of Chemistry, University of Athens, Greece, 1997-2004; Associate Researcher, Theoretical and Physical Chemistry Institute, National Hellenic Research Foundation, 2004-. Publications: Over 80 research publications in refereed journals; Over 90 announcements in Scientific Conferences; Co-author, 1 book on Block Copolymers. Honours: American Institute of Chemists Foundation Award for Outstanding Postdoctoral Fellow, 1995; ACS-PMSE Doolittle Award for Best Paper, 2003. Memberships: Greek Chemists Association; Greek Polymer Society. Address: Theoretical and Physical Chemistry Institute, National Hellenic Research Foundation, 11635 Athens, Greece. E-mail: pispas@eie.gr

**PITCHER Harvey John**, b. 26 August 1936, London, England. Writer. Education: BA, 1st Class Honours, Russian, University of Oxford. Publications: Understanding the Russians, 1964; The Chekhov Play: A New Interpretation, 1973; When Miss Emmie was in Russia, 1977; Chekhov's Leading Lady, 1979; Chekhov: The Early Stories, 1883-1888 (with Patrick Miles), 1982; The Smiths of Moscow, 1984; Lily: An Anglo-Russian Romance, 1987; Muir and Mirrielees: The Scottish Partnership that became a Household Name in Russia, 1994; Witnesses of the Russian Revolution, 1994; Chekhov: The Comic Stories, 1998. Contributions to: Times Literary Supplement. Address: 37 Bernard Road, Cromer, Norfolk NR27 9AW, England.

**PITCHES Douglas Owen**, b. 6 March 1930, Exning, Suffolk, England. Poet & Artist. m. Barbara Joyce Budgen, 7 August 1954. Education: BA, Honours, Open University, 1979. Publications: Poems, 1965; Prayer to the Virgin Mary (Chaucer Translation), 1965; Man in Orbit and Down to Earth, 1981; Art Demands Love Not Homage, 1992. Contributions to: Orbis; Outposts; Envoi; Tribune; Anthologies: Responding; New Voices; Another 5th Poetry Book and others. Address: 14 Linkway, Westham, Pevensey, East Sussex BN24 5JB, England.

**PITMAN Jennifer Susan**, b. 11 June 1946, England. Racehorse Trainer. m. (1) Richard Pitman, 1965, 2 sons, (2) David Stait, 1997. Career: National Hunt Trainer, 1975-99; Director, Jenny Pitman Racing Ltd, 1975-99; Racing and Media Consultant, 1999-; Winners include: Corbiere, Welsh National, 1982, Grand National, 1983; Burrough Hill Lad, Welsh National, 1984, Cheltenham Gold Cup, 1984, King George VI Gold Cup, 1984, Hennessy Gold Cup, 1984; Smith's Man, Whitbread Trophy, 1985; Gainsay, Ritz Club National Hunt Handicap, 1987; Sporting Life Weekend Chase, 1987; Garrison Savannah, Cheltenham Gold Cup, 1991; Wonderman, Welsh Champion Hurdle, 1991; Don Valentino, Welsh Champion Hurdle, 1992; Royal Athlete, Grand National, 1995; Willsford, Scottish National, 1995. Publications: Glorious Uncertainty (autobiography), 1984; Jenny Pitman: The Autobiography, 1999; On the Edge, 2002; Double Deal, 2002; The Dilemma, 2003. Honours include: Racing Personality of the Year, Golden

Spurs, 1983; Commonwealth Sports Award, 1983, 1984; Piper Heidsieck Trainer of the Year, 1983-84, 1989-90; Variety Club of Great Britain Sportswoman of the Year, 1984. Address: Owls Barn, Kintbury, Hungerford, Berkshire, RG17 9XS, England.

**PITT Brad,** b. 18 December 1963, Shawnee, Oklahoma, USA. Film Actor. m. Jennifer Aniston, 2000, divorced, 2005. Creative Works: TV appearances include: Dallas (series); Glory Days (series); Too Young to Die? (film); The Image (film); Films include: Cutting Glass, 1989; Happy Together, 1989; Across the Tracks, 1990; Contact, 1991; Thelma and Louise, 1991; The Favor, 1992; Johnny Suede, 1992; Cool World, 1992; A River Runs Through It, 1992; Kalifornia, 1993; Legend of the Fall, 1994; 12 Monkeys, 1995; Sleepers, 1996; Mad Monkeys, 1996; Tomorrow Never Dies, 1996; Seven Years in Tibet, 1997; The Devil's Own, 1997; Meet Joe Black, 1998; Fight Club, 2000; Snatch, 2000; The Mexican, 2001; Spy Game, 2001; Ocean's Eleven, 2001; Confessions of a Dangerous Mind, 2002; Sinbad: Legend of the Seven Seas (voice), 2003; Troy, 2004; Ocean's Twelve, 2004; Mr & Mrs Smith, 2005. Address: Creative Artists Agency, 9830 Wilshire Boulevard, Beverly Hills, CA 90212, USA.

**PITTAWAY Neil John,** b. 14 August 1973, Wakefield, England. Artist. Education: BA (Hons) Fine Art, University of Gloucestershire, 1992-96; City & Guilds Teacher's Certificate, Dewsbury College, 1997-98; MA, Printmaking, University of Bradford, 1996-98; Postgraduate Diploma in Fine Art, The Royal Academy Schools, London, 1998-2001; PGCE, University of Huddersfield, 2004. Career: Various art education teaching posts at Dewsbury, Reigate, Kingston upon Thames and York Colleges; Work held in many private and public collections including: The Ashmolean Museum, Oxford; British Museum (RWS Collection), London; St Paul's Cathedral, London; Victoria and Albert Museum, London; Guildhall Art Library, London; St Thomas's Hospital, London; Dover Street Arts Club, London; D H Lawrence Museum and Birthplace, Nottingham; Work for: Great Artists, Channel 5 TV, 2001. Publications: Longitude: Printmaking Today, 2001; Drawings for "London in Poetry and Prose", Enitharmon Press, London, 2003; The RWS, The Watercolour Expert, 2004; Illustration Magazine, 2005. Honours: Selected Awards include: The Dover Street Arts Club Excellence in Drawing Award; The Gwen May Re Award; John Smith Award; British Institution prize for printmaking and drawing; Elizabeth Scott Moore Award. Memberships: Elected Associate Member, 2000, Full Member, 2005, Royal Society of Painter-Printmakers; Elected Associate Member, 2002, Full Member, 2005, Royal Watercolour Society; Elected Artist Member, Dover Street Arts Club, London, 2001-. Address: 1 Glenfields, Netherton, Wakefield, West Yorkshire WF4 4SH, England. E-mail: njpittaway@hotmail.com

**PIUNOVSKIY Alexei,** b. 16 March 1954, Moscow, Russia. Mathematician. m. Galina Piunovskaya, 2 daughters. Education: MSc, Electrical Engineering, 1971-76, MSc, Applied Mathematics, 1980, PhD, Applied Mathematics, 1981, Moscow Institute of Electronic Technology. Appointments: Engineer, Researcher, Moscow Institute of Electronic Technology, 1976-84; Head of Group, Moscow Institute of Physics and Technology, 1984-2000; Senior Lecturer, Reader, University of Liverpool, 2000-. Publications: 64 publications in total; Optimal Control of Random Sequences in Problems with Constraints, Kluwer, 1997; Articles in journals including: Mathematics of Operational Research; Journal of Mathematical Analysis and Applications. Honours: Multiple grants from Russian Fund of Basic Research, EPSRC, Royal Society, LMS, British Council. Membership: Moscow Mathematical Society. Address: Department of Mathematical Sciences, M & O Building, Peach

Street, The University of Liverpool, Liverpool L69 7ZL, England.

**PIZZEY Erin Patricia Margaret,** b. 18 February 1939, United Kingdom. International Author; Social Reformer. 1 son, 1 daughter, 7 adopted sons. Education: Lewiston Manor, Sherbourne, Dorset, England. Career includes: Author; Published Poet and Playwright; Founder, International Shelter Movement for Battered Men, Women and Children; 2 world tours lecturing on domestic violence and setting up refuges; Resident Expert on family violence, Phil Donahue Show, 1982; Patron of Care and Comfort Romania, 1998; Six weeks speaking tour of Canada, 2002. Publications: Fiction: The Watershed; In the Shadow of the Castle; The Pleasure Palace; First Lady; The Consul General's Daughter, 1988; The Snow Leopard of Shanghai, 1989; Other Lovers, 1991; Morningstar, 1992; Swimming with Dolphins, 1993; For the Love of a Stranger, 1994; Kisses, 1995; The Wicked World of Women, 1996; The Fame Game, 2000; Non-Fiction: Scream Silently or the Neighbours Will Hear, 1974; Infernal Child, 1978; Slut's Cookbook, 1981; Erin Pizzey Collects, 1982; Prone to Violence, 1982; All in the Name of Love; Wild Child (autobiography) TV Documentaries include: Scream Quietly or the Neighbours Will Hear, 1975; Chiswick Women's Aid, 1977; That Awful Woman, 1987; Cutting Edge: Sanctuary, 1991; Who's Failing the Family, 1999; Numerous contributions to newspapers, journals and magazines. Honours: International Order of Volunteers Diploma of Honour, 1981; Nancy Astor Award for Journalism, 1983; World Congress of Victimology Distinguished Leadership Award, San Francisco, 1987; St Valentino Palm d'Oro International Award for Literature, Italy, 1994. Memberships: Royal Society of Literature; Authors Club. Address: Flat 5, 29 Lebanon Park, Twickenham TW1 3DH, England. E-mail: erin.pizzey@blueyonder.co.uk

**PLATER Alan Frederick,** b. 15 April 1935, Jarrow on Tyne, County Durham, England. Writer; Dramatist. m. (1) Shirley Johnson, 1958, divorced 1985, 2 sons, 1 daughter, (2) Shirley Rubinstein, 1986, 3 stepsons. Education: King's College, Durham, 1953-57; University of Newcastle. Career: Full time writer, for stage, screen, radio, television, anthologies and periodicals, 1960-; Written extensively for radio, TV, films and theatre, also for The Guardian, Listener, New Statesman, etc; Plays include: The Fosdyke Saga; Films include: It Shouldn't Happen to a Vet; Keep the Aspidistra Flying; TV series include: Z Cars; Softly Softly; TV adaptions include: Barchester Chronicles; The Fortunes of War; A Very British Coup; Campion; A Day in Summer; A Few Selected Exits; Oliver's Travels; Dalziel and Pascoe. Publications: The Beiderbecke Affair, 1985; The Beiderbecke Tapes, 1986; Misterioso, 1987; The Beiderbecke Connection, 1992; Oliver's Travels, 1994; and others. Honours: Various stage, radio and television drama awards; Honorary Fellow, Humberside College of Education, 1983; Honorary DLitt (Hull), 1985; Hon DCL (Northumbria), 1997; Royal TV Society Writers' Award, 1988; BAFTA Writers' Award, 1988. Memberships: Royal Society of Literature, fellow; Royal Society of Arts, fellow; Co-chair, 1986-87, President, 1991-95, Writer's Guild of Great Britain. Address: c/o 200 Fulham Road, London SW10 9PN, England.

**PLAZEK Donald John,** b. 12 January 1931, Milwaukee, USA. Professor, Materials Science. m. Patricia Lenore Filkins, 4 sons, 3 daughters. Education: BS, Chemistry, 1953; PhD, Physical Chemistry, 1957. Appointments: Postdoctoral Research, University of Wisconsin, 1957-58; Fellow, Mellon Institute, 1958-67; Advisory Board, Journal of Polymer Science, 1991-98; Associate Editor, Rubber Chemistry and Technology, 1993-99. Publications include: The Frequency and Temperature

Dependence of the Dynamic Mechanical Properties of a High Density Polyethylene, 1961; An Instrument for Measuring Torsional Creep and Recovery, 1963; Co-author, Temperature Dependences of the Viscoelastic response of Polymer Systems, 1996; The Glass Temperature, 1996. Honours: George Stafford Whitby Award, The Rubber Division, American Chemical Society, 1993; The Bingham Medal, The Society of Rheology, 1995. Memberships: American Chemical Society; Fellow, American Physical Society; The Society of Rheology. Address: University of Pittsburgh, Materials Science Engineering Department, Pittsburgh, PA 15261, USA.

**PLEKHANOV Anton Yurievič,** b. 28 June 1966, Leningrad, USSR. Biologist; Biochemist. Education: Biology, Leningrad State University, 1988; Psychotherapy, St Petersburg Technical University, 1995; PhD, Biochemistry, St Petersburg State University, 2000. Appointment: Researcher, Petersburg Nuclear Physics Institute. Publications: 30 publications in professional journals and books. Honours: Russian Government Grant, 1997-2000; St Petersburg Administration Grant, 1997, 1999, 2000; FEBS Grant, 1999; French Government Grant, 1999, 2005; Russian Biochemical Society Prize, 1999; IBRO Grant, 1999, 2000, 2001; IUPS Grant, 2001; ISN Grant, 2001; RFBR Grant, 2001, 2003. Memberships: Russian Biochemical Society, 1995-; Russian Neurochemical Society, 1998-. Address: Peterburgskij Institut Jadernoj Fiziki, 188300 Gatchina Leningradskoj Oblasti, Russia. E-mail: ayplekhanov@mail.ru

**PLENDER Richard Owen,** b. 9 October 1945, Epsom, Surrey, England. Barrister; Author. m. Patricia Clare Ward, 2 daughters. Education: Open Exhibition, BA, 1967, LLB, 1968, Queen's College, Cambridge; MA, 1970, PhD, 1971, University of Sheffield; LLM summa cum laude, 1971, JSD, 1983, University of Illinois, USA; LLD, University of Cambridge, 1993. Appointments: Assistant Lecturer, University of Sheffield, 1968-70, University of Illinois, 1971-72, University of Exeter, 1972-74; Called to Bar, Inner Temple, 1974; Lecturer, Reader, Director Centre of European Law, King's College London, 1974-88; Visiting Professor, University of Paris II, 1988-89; Legal Advisor to UN High Commissioner for Refugees, 1976-78; Référendaire, European Court of Justice, 1980-83; Queens Counsel, 1988-. Publications: Books include: International Migration Law, 1972, 2nd edition, 1988; Fundamental Rights, 1973; Cases and Materials on the Law of the European Communities, 1980, 3rd edition, 1993; A Practical Introduction to European Community Law, 1980; Introduccion al Derecho Comunnario, 1985; Basic Documents in International Migration Law, 1988, 2 edition, 1996; Legal History and Comparative Law, 1990; The European Contracts Convention – The Rome Convention on the Choice of Law for Contracts, 1991, 2nd edition, 2001. Honours: Rebecca Squires Prize, University of Cambridge, 1967; College of Law Prize, University of Illinois, 1973; Berridale-Keith Prize, 1972; QC, 1988; Honorary Senior Member, Robinson College, Cambridge; Honorary Visiting Professor, City University. Membership: World Trade Organisation List of Panellists. Address: 20 Essex Street, London WC2R 3AL, England.

**PLESCH Gerta Regine (Traudi),** b. 4 December 1921, Vienna, Austria. m. (1) divorced, 1961, (2) Peter H Plesch, 1963, 2 sons, 1 deceased. Education: Berridge House, London University, 1939. Appointments: Volunteer work for Chairman of Hampstead ARP, 1939-41; Red Cross Nurse and volunteer work, 1941; Administrative Officer, consultancy firm, Stoke on Trent, 1961-63; Voluntary work and fundraiser for various charities, 1963-. Honours: MBE for services to medical and children's charities, 1987; OBE for services to the county of Staffordshire, 1999; Honorary Degree of Master of the

University, University of Keele, 2004. Memberships: Honorary Member, Stoke-on-Trent Medical Institute; Vice President, local Hospice; President, Ceramic City Choir. Address: 19 Sutherland Drive, Newcastle-under-Lyme, North Staffordshire, ST5 3ND, England. E-mail: traudi.plesch@virgin.net

**PLESKO Ivan,** b. 13 June 1930, Selpice, Slovakia. Physician. m. Anna, 2 daughters. Education: MD, Comenius University, Bratislava, 1955; PhD, 1964; DSc, Slovak Academy of Sciences, Bratislava, 1987; Associate Professor, 1968. Appointments: Research Assistant, 1955-68; Assistant Professor, Epidemiology, Comenius University, Bratislava, 1968-76; Host Researcher, Institute Pasteur, Paris, 1968-; Assistant Professor, University of Constantine, Algery, 1971-73; Head, Department of Epidemiology, Cancer Research Institute, Slovak Academy of Sciences, 1976-; Head, National Cancer Registry of Slovakia, 1996-. Publications: Atlas of Cancer Occurrence in Slovakia; Epidemiology of Lung Cancer; Atlas of Cancer Mortality in Central Europe; More than 130 papers in professional journals. Honours: Jesenius Medal, Research in medical sciences; Golden Medal, Research and Art; Gold medal of Health Promotion Foundation, Warsaw, Poland; Gold medal of the Slovak Medical Society; others. Memberships: League Against Cancer, Slovakia; International Association of Cancer Registries; Science Council; Czech National Cancer Registry; European Institute of Oncology. Address: Pri Suchom mlyne 62, 811 04 Bratislava, Slovakia.

**PLESKOV Vladimir Mikhailovich,** b. 25 February 1942, Usviaty, Russia. Biochemist. m. Natalya Lysova, 1 daughter. Education: MD, 1st State Medical Institute, 1965; PhD, Institute of Experimental Medicine, Leningrad, 1987. Appointments: Chief, Clinical Laboratory, Marine Hospital, Health Ministry, Leningrad, 1987-89; Currently Senior Scientist, Laboratory of Pathomorphology, Influenza Research Institute, Russian Academy of Sciences, St Petersburg. Publications: Author experimentally argumented hypothesis of pathogenesis of autoimmune demielinizating diseases of nervous system, mechanism of viral persistence in atherosclerotic plaques decreasing based on the restriction of transport into cells of some metabolites which take part in cell membranes formation; More than 100 in scientific journals. Honours: Member, National Geographic Society; Member, New York Academy of Sciences; Academic of Russian Academy of Sciences. Address: Ispytatelei pr 11-164, 197341 St Petersburg, Russia.

**PLESNIČAR Stojan Josip,** b. 5 February 1925, Gorica, Italy. Oncologist; Educator; Consultant; Editor. m. Ljudmila Mila Gec, 2 sons. Education: MD, University of Ljubljana, Slovenia, 1954. Appointments: Intern, General Hospital, Koper, 1955-57; Resident, Institute of Oncology, Ljubljana, 1958-63; Assistant Professor, The Faculty of Medicine, Ljubljana, 1964-72; Research Fellow, Karolinska Sjukhuset, Stockholm, Sweden, 1973-76; Professor of Oncology, Chairman of Oncology, 1982-95, University of Ljubljana, 1976-; Head, Department of Oncology and Radiotherapy, 1976-80; Founder and Head, Department of Tumour Biology, 1982-95; Lecturer, European School of Oncology, Milan, Italy, 1985-90; Visiting Professor and Fulbright Senior Researcher, University of Nebraska Medical School, Omaha, USA, 1981, 1982; Research Experience: Study of Tumour Metastases; Director, Institute of Oncology, Ljubljana, 1982-86; Lecturer and Member of the Senate, School of Environmental Sciences, University Polytechnic, Nova Gorica, Slovenia, 1997-. Publications: Cancer – A Preventable Disease, 1990, honourable mention, 1994; Textbook of Oncology and Radiotherapy, in Slovenian, 1977; Guest Editor in Seminars in Oncology: Cancer in the

Emerging World, 2001; Co-founder, Editor-in-Chief, Member of Editorial Board, Radiology and Oncology, 1990-, recognition of merits Federative Cancer Society, 1990; Co-ordinating Editor, Challenge-ESO Newsletter, 1994-; Lecturer in field; Member of the Editorial Board, Cancer Letter, Oxford, England; Seminars in Oncology, Philadelphia, USA. Honours: Recipient, Golden Medal, Slovenian Cancer Society, 1992; Listed in Who's Who publications and biographical dictionaries. Memberships: The Djerba Group, 1995; American Association for Cancer Research; New York Academy of Sciences; European Society of Medical Oncology; Medical Association of Slovenia; Slovenia Cancer Research Foundation, co-founder, 1993; Academic Association for Third University in Slovenia, president; Member of the Senate, newly founded Faculty of Medicine, University of Maribor, Slovenia, 2002; Nomination for Membership of the Slovenian Academy of Sciences and Arts, 2001;Lion's Club District 129, Slovewnia, Ljubljana, district governor, 1998-99. Address: Tesarska St, No 6, 1001 Ljubljana, Slovenia. E-mail: stojan.plesnicar@mf.uni-lj.si

**PLISCHKE Le Moyne W,** b. 11 December 1922, Greensburg, Pennsylvania, USA. Research Chemist. m. Joan Harper. Education: BS, Waynesburg College, Pennsylvania, 1948; MS, West Virginia University, 1952. Appointments: Instructor, Waynesburg College, Pennsylvania, 1948-49; Research Chemist, US Naval Ordnance Test Station, California, 1952-53; Assistant Professor of Chemistry, Commonwealth University, Virginia, 1953-54; Research Chemist, E I Dupont, New Jersey, 1955-57; Research Chemist, Monsanto, Florida, 1957-. Publications: 18 US patents; 51 foreign patents. Honours: Monsanto Achievement Award. Memberships: American Chemical Society. Address: 2100 Club House Drive, Lillian, AL 36549-5402, USA. E-mail: plis123@gulftel.com

**PLOMMET Michel Georges,** b. 24 September 1927, St Fons, France. Director. m. Anne Marie Laurent. Education: DVM, Alfort, Paris, 1951; Dairy Technology, Institute National Agronomic, Paris, 1953; Microbiology, Institute Pasteur, Paris, 1954. Appointments: Institute National Research Agronomique, Jouy en Josas,1953-63, at Tours-Nouzilly 1963-80; Director of the Laboratory, Tours Nouzilly, 1966-80; Co-Founder, First Administrator of the Nouzilly Centre, 1968-72; Co-founder and First President of the Scientific Committee of the National Federation of Animal Diseases, 1979-87. Publications: Over 200 papers in professional journals on animal infections, experimental pathology, immunity, vaccination, diagnostic and control, particularly staphylococcal mastitis in ewes, bovine and ovine brucellosis, Q fever, milk hygiene, staphylococcal toxins; Editor of 2 books on brucellosis and contributor to six. Honour: Officer Merite Agricole. Memberships: French Society of Microbiology; American Association for the Advancement of Science; New York Academy of Sciences. Address: 10 Avenue Champleroy, 89000 Auxerre, France.

**PLOWRIGHT Joan Anne,** b. 28 October 1929, Brigg, Lancashire, England. Actress. m. (1) Roger Gage, 1953, (2) Sir Laurence (later Lord) Olivier, 1961, 1 son, 2 daughters. Education: Old Vic Theatre School. Appointments: Member, Old Vic Company, toured South Africa, 1952-53. Creative Works: Plays and films include: Richard Wagner, 1982; Cavell, 1982; Britannia Hospital, 1981; Brimstone and Treacle, 1982; The Cherry Orchard, 1983; The Way of the World, 1984; Mrs Warren's Profession, 1985; Revolution, 1985; The House of Bernardo Alba, 1986; Drowning by Numbers, 1987; Uncle Vanya, 1988; The Dressmaker, 1988; The Importance of Being Earnest, 1988; Conquest of the South Pole, 1989; And a Nightingale Sang, 1989; I Love You to Death, 1989; Avalon, 1990; Time and the Conways, 1991; Enchanted April, 1991;

Stalin, 1991; Denis the Menace, 1992; A Place for Annie, 1992; A Pin for the Buterfly, 1993; Last Action Hero, 1993; Widow's Peak, 1994; On Promised Land, 1994; Return of the Natives, 1994; Hotel Sorrento, 1994; A Pyromaniac's Love Story, 1994; The Scarlet Letter, 1994; Jane Eyre, 1994; If We Are Women, 1995; Surviving Picasso, 1995; Mr Wrong, 1995; 101 Dalmatians, 1996; The Assistant, 1996; Shut Up and Dance, 1997; Tom's Midnight Garden, 1997; It May Be the Last Time, 1997; America Betrayed, 1998; Tea with Mussolini, 1998; Return to the Secret Garden, 1999; Frankie and Hazel, 1999; Bailey's Mistake, 2000; Global Heresy, 2000. Publications: And That's Not All, autobiography, 2001. Honours include: Best Actress, Tony Award, 1960; Best Actress, Evening Standard Award, 1964; Variety Club Award, 1976; Variety Club Film Actress of the Year Award, 1987; Golden Globe Award, 1993; 18th Crystal Award for Women in Film, USA, 1994. Address: c/o The Malthouse, Horsham Road, Ashurst, Steying, West Sussex BN44 3AR, England.

**POCOCK Tom, (Thomas Allcot Guy Pocock),** b. 18 August 1925, London, England. Author; Journalist. m. Penelope Casson, 26 April 1969, 2 daughters. Publications: Nelson and His World, 1968; Chelsea Reach, 1970; Fighting General, 1973; Remember Nelson, 1977; The Young Nelson in the Americas, 1980; 1945: The Dawn Came Up Like Thunder, 1983; East and West of Suez, 1986; Horatio Nelson, 1987; Alan Moorehead, 1990; The Essential Venice, 1990; Sailor King, 1991; Rider Haggard and the Lost Empire, 1993; Norfolk, 1995; A Thirst for Glory, 1996; Battle for Empire, 1998; Nelson's Women, 1999; Captain Marryat, 2000; The Terror Before Trafalgar, 2002; Stopping Napoleon, 2004. Contributions to: Numerous newspapers and magazines. Honour: Runner-up, Whitbread Biography Award (Horatio Nelson), 1987; Anderson Prize for naval history, 2001; Mountbatten Maritime Prize, 2004. Membership: Society of Authors. Address: 22 Lawrence Street, London SW3 5NF, England.

**PODGORSAK Ervin B,** b. 28 September 1943, Vienna, Austria. Medical Physicist. m. Mariana, 2 sons. Education: Dipl Eng, Physics, University of Ljubljana, Slovenia, 1968; MSc, Physics, 1970; PhD, Physics, 1973, University of Wisconsin, Madison, Wisconsin; Postgraduate training, University of Toronto, Ontario Cancer Institute, 1973-74. Appointments: Teaching Assistant, University of Ljubljana, Slovenia, 1966-68; Research Assistant, Nuclear Institute Jozef Stefan, Ljubljana, Slovenia, 1968; Research Assistant, University of Wisconsin, Madison, Wisconsin, 1969; Research Assistant, University of Wisconsin, Madison, Wisconsin, 1969-71; Teaching Assistant, University of Wisconsin, Madison, Wisconsin, 1971-72; Research Assistant, University of Wisconsin, Madison, Wisconsin, 1972-73; Post-doctoral Fellow, University of Toronto, 1973-74; Clinical Physicist, Ontario Cancer Institute, 1974; Assistant Professor, 1975-79, Director, Department of Medical Physics, 1979-, Associate Professor, 1979-85, Professor, 1985-, Director, Medical Physics Unit, 1991-, McGill University, Montréal, Québec. Publications: Over 120 peer-reviewed publications. Honours: Honorary Visiting Professor, University of Ljubljana; Fellowship, American Association of Physicists in Medicine; Canadian College of Physicists in Medicine; Sylvia Fedoruk Prize in Medical Physics; Farrington Daniels Award. Memberships: American Association of Physicists in Medicine; American College of Medical Physics; American Society of Therapeutic Radiology and Oncology; Association des Physiciens et Ingenieurs Biomedicaux du Québec; Canadian Association of Physicists; Canadian Organisation of Medical Physicists; Canadian Association of Radiation Oncologists; Canadian Radiation Protection Association; International Stereotactic Radiosurgical Society.

Address: Department of Medical Physics, McGill University Health Centre, 1650 avenue Cedar, Montréal, Québec H3G 1A4, Canada. E-mail: epodgorsak@medphys.mcgill.ca

**PODSIADLO Elzbieta,** b. 9 August 1938, Doly Opacie, Kielce voivodship, Poland. Lecturer. Education: MS, Natural Sciences, University of Wroclaw, 1962; PhD, Agricultural Sciences, 1972, Assistant Professor in Agricultural Sciences, 1987, The Agricultural University of Warsaw. Appointments: Teacher, secondary school, 1962-63; Laboratory Assistant, Senior Research Assistant, Assistant Professor, Professor, Department of Zoology, Agricultural University of Warsaw, 1963-. Publications include: Morpho-biological studies on primary parasites of scale insects from the genus of Asterodiaspis Signoret in Poland, 1986; Concept of the species of Asterodiaspis variolosa, 1990; A note on the position of thoracic spiracles in Diaspididae, 2002. Memberships: The Polish Entomological Society. Address: Department of Zoology, Agricultural University of Warsaw, Ciszewskiego 8, 02-786 Warsaw, Poland. E-mail: podsiadlo@alpha.sggw.waw.pl

**POITIER Sidney,** b. 20 February 1927, Miami, Floria, USA. Actor. m. (1) Juanita Hardy, 4 daughters, (2) Joanna Shimkus, 2 daughters. Appointments: Army service, 1941-45; Actor with American Negro Theatre, 1946; Member, 1994-2003, President, 1994-2003, Board of Directors, Walt Disney Company; Ambassador to Japan from the Commonwealth of the Bahamas; Actor, films including: Cry the Beloved Country; Red Ball Express; Go, Man, Go; Blackboard Jungle, 1955; Goodbye My Lady, 1956; Edge of the City, Something of Value, 1957; The Mark of the Hawk, The Defiant Ones, 1958; Porgy and Bess, 1959; A Raisin in the Sun, Paris Blues, 1960; Lilies of the Field, 1963; The Long Ships, 1964; The Bedford Incident, 1965; The Slender Thread, A Patch of Blue, Duel at Diablo, 1966; To Sir With Love, In the Heat of the Night, 1967; Guess Who's Coming to Dinner, 1968; For the Love of Ivy, 1968; The Lost Man, 1970; They Call Me Mister Tibbs, 1970; The Organization, 1971; The Wilby Conspiracy, 1975; Shoot to Kill, 1988; Deadly Pursuit, 1988; Separate But Equal, TV, 1992; Sneakers, Children of the Dust, TV, 1995; To Sir With Love II, TV, 1996; Actor, director, Buck and Preacher, 1972; Warm December, 1973; Uptown Saturday Night, 1974; Let's Do It Again, 1975; A Piece of the Action, 1977; One Man, One Vote, 1996; Director, Stir Crazy, 1980; Hanky Panky, 1982; Got For It, 1984; Little Nikita, 1987; Ghost Dad, 1990; Sneakers, 1992; The Jackal, 1997. Publication: This Life, 1980. Honours: Silver Bear Award, Berlin, 1958; NT Film Critics Award, 1958; Academy Award, Oscar, Best Actor of 1963; Cecil B De Mille Award, 1982; Life Achievement Award, American Film Institute, 1992; Kennedy Centre Honours, 1995; Honorary KBE; Honorary Academy Award for Lifetime Achievement, 2002. Address: c/o CAA, 9830 Wilshire Boulevard, Beverly Hills, CA 90210, USA.

**POLAK Julia Margaret,** b. 29 June 1939, Buenos Aires, Argentina. Professor of Endocrine Pathology. m. Daniel Catovsky, 2 sons, 1 daughter. Education: MD, 1964, Diploma, Histopathology, 1966, University of Buenos Aires; DSc, London University, 1980; MRCPath, England, 1974; FRCPath, England, 1986; MRCP, England, 1992; FRCP, England, 1999; FMedSci, England, 1999; ILT, England, 2002. Appointments include: Demonstrator, 1961-62, Senior House Officer in Surgery and Medicine, 1962, Registrar and Senior Registrar, 1963-67, Buenos Aires; Research Assistant, Department of Histochemistry, 1968-69, Assistant Lecturer, 1970-73, Lecturer, 1973-79, Senior Lecturer, 1979-82, Reader, 1982-84, Imperial College School of Medicine at Hammersmith Hospital; Honorary Consultant, 1979, Professor of Endocrine Pathology, 1984, Deputy Director, 1988-91, Head of department of Histochemistry, 1991, Department of

Histopathology, Hammersmith Hospital; Director of the Tissue Engineering Centre, London, 1998-; Editorial Board member of 36 journals. Publications: 23 books include most recently: Diagnostic Histopathology of Neuroendocrine Tumours, 1993; Clinical Gene Analysis and Manipulation – Tools, Techniques and Troubleshooting (jointly), 1996; Future Strategies for Tissue and Organ Replacement (jointly), 2002; More than 950 original articles in professional journals. Honours include: Beneti de Udaondo Cardiology Prize, 1967; Medal, Society of Endocrinology, 1984; Cable and Wireless Sir Eric-Sharpe Prize for Oncology, 1986/87; Honorary Doctorate, University of Computense, Spain, 1997; Medal, Swedish Society of Medicine, 1998; Dame Commander of the British Empire, 2003; Medal, Royal Society of Medicine, 2004; Honorary Doctor of Science, University of Sheffield, 2005. Memberships include: American Thoracic Society; British Cardiac Society; British Neuroendocrine Group; Commonwealth Association for Development; British Medical Association; Royal Society of Medicine; American Association of Pathologists. Address: Tissue Engineering and Regenerative Medicine Centre, Faculty of Medicine, Imperial College, 3rd Floor, Chelsea & Westminster Hospital, 369 Fulham Road, London SW10 9NH, England. E-mail: julia.polak@ic.ac.uk

**POLIAKOFF Stephen,** b. 1952, London, England. Dramatist; Director. m. Sandy Welch, 1983, 1 son, 1 daughter. Education: Westminster School; University of Cambridge. Theatre: Clever Soldiers, 1974; The Carnation Gang, 1974; Hitting Town, 1975; City Sugar, 1976; Strawberry Fields, 1978; Shout Across the River, 1978; The Summer Party, 1980; Favourite Nights, 1981; Breaking the Silence, 1984; Coming into Land, 1987; Playing with Trains, 1989; Sienna Red, 1992; Sweet Panic, 1996; Blinded by the Sun, 1996; Talk of the City, 1998; Remember This, 1999; Films: Hidden City, 1992; Close My Eyes, 1992; Century, 1995; The Tribe, 1998; Food of Love, 1998; TV plays include: Caught on a Train; She's Been Away; Shooting the Past, 1999; Perfect Strangers, 2001; The Lost Prince, 2003. Publications: Plays One, 1989; Plays Two, 1994; Plays Three; Sweet Panic; Blinded by the Sun; Talk of the City; Shooting the Past; Remember This. Honours include: Best British Film Award, 1992; Critic's Circle Best Play Award; Prix Italia; BAFTA Award; Venice Film Festival Prize. Address: 33 Donia Devonia Road, London N1 8JQ, England.

**POLLACK Sydney,** b. 1 July 1934, Lafayette, Indiana, USA. Film Director. m. Claire Griswold, 1958, 1 son, 2 daughters. Education: Neighbourhood Playhouse Theatre School, New York. Appointments: Assistant to Sanford Meisner, 1954; Acting Instructor, 1954-57, 1959-60; Army service, 1957-59; Executive Director, The Actors Studio, West Coast branch; Theatre appearances: The Dark is Light Enough, Broadway, 1954; A Stone for Danny Fisher, 1955; TV appearances include: Aloa Presents; Director, The Chrysler Theatre, Ben Casey, for TV, 1962-63; Director, films: The Slender Thread, 1965; This Property is Condemned, 1966; The Scalphunters, 1967; Castle Keep, 1968; They Shoot Horses Don't They, 1969-70; Jeremiah Johnson, 1971-72; The Way We Were, 1972-73; The Yakuza, 1974; Three Days of the Condor, 1974-75; Bobby Deerfield, 1976; The Electric Horseman, 1978-79; Absence of Malice, 1981; Tootsie, 1982; Producer, Song Writer, 1984; Out of Africa, producer, 1985; Havana, 1989; The Firm, 1993; Sabrina, 1996; Producer: The Fabulous Baker Boys, 1989; The Last Ship, 1990; King Ralph, co-executive producer; Dead Again, executive producer; Presumed Innocent, 1990; Sense and Sensibility executive producer; The Talented Mr Ripley, 1999; Co-producer: Bright Lights, Big City, 1988; Actor: The Player; Death Becomes Her; Husbands and Wives; A Civil Action; Eyes

Wide Shut. Address: Mirage Enterprises, De Mille Bldg, 110, 5555 Melrose Avenue, Los Angeles, CA 90212, USA.

**POLLOCK John (Charles)**, b. 9 October 1923, London, England. Clergyman; Writer. m. Anne Barrett-Lennard, 4 May 1949. Education: BA 1946, MA 1948, Trinity College, Cambridge; Ridley Hall, Cambridge, 1949-51. Appointments: Captain, Coldstream Guards, 1943-45; Assistant Master (History and Divinity), Wellington College, Berkshire, 1947-49; Ordained Anglican Deacon, 1951, Priest, 1952; Curate, St Paul's Church, Portman Square, London, 1951-53; Rector, Horsington, Somerset, 1953-58; Editor, The Churchman (quarterly), 1953-58; Chaplain to the High Sheriff of Devon, 1990-91. Publications: Hudson Taylor and Maria, 1962, new edition, 1996; Moody Without Sankey, 1963, new edition, 1995; The Keswick Story, 1964, new edition, 2005; The Christians from Siberia, 1964; Billy Graham, 1966, revised edition, 1969; The Apostle: A Life of Paul, 1969, revised edition, 1985, new edition as Paul the Apostle, 1999; Victims of the Long March, 1970; A Foreign Devil in China: The Life of Nelson Bell, 1971, new edition, 1988; George Whitefield and the Great Awakening, 1972, new edition as Whitfield: The Evangelist, 2000; Wilberforce, 1977, new edition as Wilberforce: God's Statesman, 2001; Billy Graham: Evangelist to the World, 1979; The Siberian Seven, 1979; Amazing Grace: John Newton's Story, 1981, new edition as Newton: The Liberator, 2000; The Master: A Life of Jesus, 1984, new edition as Jesus: The Master 1999; Billy Graham: Highlights of the Story, 1984; Shaftesbury: The Poor Man's Earl, 1985, new edition as Shaftesbury: The Reformer, 2000; A Fistful of Heroes: Great Reformers and Evangelists, 1988, new combined edition with On Fire for God, 1998; John Wesley 1989, new edition as Wesley: The Preacher, 2000; On Fire for God: Great Missionary Pioneers, 1990; Fear No Foe: A Brother's Story, 1992; Gordon: The Man Behind the Legend, 1993, new edition, 2005; Kitchener: The Road to Omdurman, 1998; Kitchener: Saviour of the Nation, 2000; Kitchener (comprising The Road to Omdurman and Saviour of the Nation), 2001; The Billy Graham Story, 2003-. Contributions to: Reference works including Oxford DNB and religious periodicals. Honours: The John Pollock Award for Christian Biography (annual) founded by Samford University, USA, 1999; Clapham Prize, Gordon College, USA, 2002; Honorary Doctor of Letters, Samford University, USA, 2002. Membership: English Speaking Union Club. Address: Rose Ash House, South Molton, Devonshire EX36 4RB, England.

**POLYAKOV Kirill Valentinovich**, b. 17 September 1973, Leningrad, USSR. Lawyer. m. Yulia, 2 sons. Education: Leningrad Technological Institute of Refrigerating Industry, 1995; North-West Academy of Governmental Service, 2004. Appointments: Involved in the Standing Commission for Agriculture, Processing Industry and Comsumer Market and Commission for Environment Safety and Environment Management; Deputy, Leningrad Region Legislative Assembly, 32nd Lomonosovsky Electoral District; Chairman, Management Board, Agrosoyux Regiony, 1995-2001; Chairman, Russian Parliament, 2001-; Nominated candidate for position of Chairman and elected, Leningrad Regional Legislative Assembly, 2003; Speaker, Russian Parliament, 2003-; Chairman, Regional Policy Council of United Socialistic Party of Russia, 2004-. Memberships: Leningrad Regional Chamber of Commerce and Industry. Address: 67 Suvorovsky av, 191 311 St Petersburg, Russia. E-mail: mail@lenoblzaks.ru Website: www.lenoblzaks.ru

**POMBEIRO Armando José Latourrette**, b. 9 June 1949, Porto, Portugal. Professor of Chemistry. 2 sons, 1 daughter. Education: Chemical Engineering, Instituto Superior Tecnico,

Portugal, 1971; DPhil, University of Sussex, England, 1976. Appointments: Assistant, 1971, Auxiliary Professor, 1975, Associate Professor, 1979, Full Professor, 1989, Instituto Superior Tecnico. Publications: 3 books; 40 book chapters and review articles; Over 260 articles in scientific journals; 10 patents; 10 didactic publications; 17 other publications including science and technology systems, biographies. Memberships: Full Member, Academy of Sciences of Lisbon, 1988-, Vice President of Class of Sciences, 1999-2000, Vice General Secretary, 1998, Secretary of Class of Sciences, 1998-2001, Directorate, 1998-, Commission for Publications; Secretary General, Academy of Sciences, 2001-; European Academies' Science Advisory Council (EASAC), 2001-; Fellow, Royal Society of Chemistry, 1986-; Higher Council for Science and Technology, 1995; Higher Council for Science, Technology and Innovation, 2004-; Physical and Engineering Science and Technology Panel, 1999, Advisory Panel on ASI Programme, 1995-98, NATO Science Programme; Member, European Academies Science Advisory Council, 2001-; Member, External Evaluation Commission of the Portuguese Universities, 2002-; Member and Co-Founder, Portuguese Electrochemical Society, President, 1988-89, 1994-95, Vice President, 1990-91, Secretary, 1983-87; Member and Co-Founder, Iberoamerican Society of Electrochemistry and National Representative, 1992-96; International Society of Electrochemistry; Affiliate Member, IUPAC; Portuguese Chemical Society. Address: Centro de Quimica Estutural, Complexo Interdisciplinar, Instituto Superior Tecnico, Av Rovisco Pais, 1049-001 Lisboa, Portugal. E-mail: pombeiro@ist.ut.pt

**PONCE DE LEAO POLICARPO Armando José**, b. 30 April 1935, Portugal. Professor. m. Maria Isabel, 2 sons, 1 daughter. Education: Graduated in Science, Physics and Chemistry, University of Coimbra, Portugal, 1957; Diploma of Advanced Studies in Science, 1960, PhD, University of Manchester, 1963; Doctor of Physics, University of Coimbra, Portugal, 1964. Appointments: Assistant, 1957-63, Associate Professor, 1968, Professor, 1979, Head of Department of Nuclear Physics Studies, University of Coimbra, Portugal; Research Fellow, CERN, Geneva; Research Fellow, Institute of Nuclear Studies, Tokyo; Head of the Physics Department; Director of the Physics Museum; Director, LIP, Particles Laboratory. Publications: Over 250 papers contributed to refereed scientific journals; Milestone papers on GPSC, gas proportional scintillation counters. Honours: Grã-Cruz da Ordem Nacional do Merito Cientifico da República Federativa do Brasil. Memberships: Academia de Ciencias de Lisboa, International Radiation Physics Society; European Physics Society; Committee of Science and Technology Policy (OCDE); ECFA. Address: Department of Physics, University of Coimbra, 3004-516, Coimbra, Portugal. E-mail: policarpo@lipc.fis.uc.pt

**PONG David Bertram Pak-Tang**, b. 28 September 1939, Hong Kong. Professor. m. Barbara Mar, 3 daughters. Education: St Paul's College, Hong Kong, 1951-60; BA, Hons, School of Oriental and African Studies, University of London, 1963; PhD, School of Oriental and African Studies, 1969. Appointments: Research Fellow, Institute of Historical Research, University of London, 1965-66; Fellow, Far Eastern History, School of Oriental and African Studies, University of London, 1966-69; Assistant Professor, History, University of Delaware, 1969-73; Associate Professor, History, 1973-89; Research Fellow, Research School of Pacific Studies, Institute of Advanced Studies, Australian National University, 1978-82; Professor, 1989-; Chair, Department of History, 1992-98; Director, East Asian Studies Programme, 1989-. Publications: Taiwan haifang bing kaishan riji; A Critical Guide to the Kwangtung Provincial Archives Deposited at the Public Record Office of London;

Ideal and Reality: Social and Political Change in Modern China, 1860-1949; Shen Pao-chen and China's Modernization in the Nineteenth Century; Shen Baozhen pingzhuan: Zhongguo Jindaihua de changshi; Resisting Japan: Mobilization for War in China, 1935-45; Many Articles. Honours: Research Fellowship, Institute of Historical Research, University of London, 1965-66; American Council of Learned Societies Research Fellowship, 1973-74; Research Fellow, Research School of Pacific Studies, Institute of Advanced Studies, Australian National University, 1978-82; Phi Kappa Phi Honor Society, 1999; Honorary Research Fellow, Modern History Research Centre, Hong Kong Baptist University, 2002-. Memberships: Association for Asian Studies; Society for Qing Studies; History Society of 20th-Century China; Modern Chinese History Society of Hong Kong; Chinese Military History Society; Phi Kappa Phi Honor Society. Address: Department of History, University of Delaware, Newark, DE 19716, USA.

**PONIATOWSKA Irena**, b. 5 July 1933, Góra Kalwaria, Poland. Musicologist. m. Andrzej Poniatowski, 14 November 1953, deceased 1994, 1 daughter. Education includes: Diploma, Musicology, Warsaw University, 1962; PhD, 1970; Qualification to Assistant Professor, 1983; Habil; Qualification to Professor, 1994. Career: Tutor, 1970, Vice Director, 1974-79; Assistant Professor, 1984, Extraordinary Professor, 1991, Ordinary Professor, 1996, Institute of Musicology, Vice Dean, Faculty of History, 1986-90, 1993-99, Warsaw University; President, Council, 1976-86, Vice President, 1986-91, Chopin Society; President: Congress, Musica Antiqua Europae Orientalis, Poland, 1988, 1991, 1994, 1997, 2000, 2003; Polish Chopin Academy, 1994-; Chopin Congress, 1999; President, Programm Council of Institut Fryderyk Chopin, 2001-; Editor of many encyclopaedias including: Polish Encyclopaedia of Music, Volumes I, II, III, IV, 1979; Various offices in Union of Polish Composers, Section of Musicologists. Publications: Beethoven Piano Texture, 1972; The Chronicle of the Important Musical Events in Poland 1945-72, 1974; Piano Music and Playing in XIX Century Artistic and Social Aspects, 1991; Dictionary of Music for Schools, 1991, 2nd edition, 1997; History and Interpretation of Music, 1993, 2nd edition, 1995; Editor, Musical Work: Theory History, Interpretation, 1984; Maria Szymanowska 25 Mazurkas, 1993; Editor, Chopin in the Circle of his Friends, Vols I-V, 1995-99; 24 Préludes de Frédéric Chopin op 28; Facsimile edition with commentaries, 1999; I Polonaise Brillante op 4 (violin and piano) of H Wieniawski, urtext and critical edition, 2000; Chopin and his Work in the Context of Culture, Vols 1-2, 2003; Many articles in collective works. Contributions to: Muzyka; Ruch Muzyczny; Rocznik Chopinowski; Chopin Studies; Res Facta; Barok; Hudobny Život; Quadrivium; Music Towards Tradition: Ideas, work, reception, (studies edited by Sz Paczkowski, 2004), dedicated to I Poniatowska for her 70th anniversary. Address: Filtrowa 63-38, 02-056 Warsaw, Poland.

**POOL Adam de Sola**, b. 5 November 1957, Palo Alto, California, USA. Venture Capitalist. m. Kristina Gjerde, 1 son. Education: BA, University of Chicago, 1981; MA, University of California, 1982; MBA, Massachusetts Institute of Technology. Economist, First National Bank of Chicago, 1980; Research Officer, 1982-83, International Officer, 1983-86, Assistant Vice President, 1986, Industrial Bank of Japan, New York; Associate, Corporate Finance, Salomon Brothers Inc, New York, 1987, 1988-92; Principal Banker, 1992-94, Senior Banker, 1994-95, European Bank for Reconstruction and Development; Chief Investment Officer, Yamaichi Regent ABC Polska, 1995-97; Owner, PP Investments, 1998-. Publications: Published photographer. Memberships: Board member: Relpol Centrum SA; Finesco SA; Korte-Organica RT; Honorary Member, Yale

Club. Address: ul Piaskowa 12c, 05-510 Konstanin, Poland. E-mail: pool@eip.com.pl

**POOLE Charles P**, b. 7 June 1927, Panama. Physicist. m. Kathleen, 2 sons, 3 daughters. Education: BA, Fordham University, 1950; MS, Physics, 1952; PhD, Physics, University of Maryland, 1958. Appointments: Physicist, Westinghouse Electronic Corporation, 1952-53; Physicist, Gulf Research Corporation, 1958-64; Associate Professor, Physics, University of South Carolina, 1964-66; Professor, Physics, 1966-94; Professor Emeritus, 1994-. Publications: 15 books; 16 review articles; 135 research publications; Electron Spin Resonance; Relaxation in Magnetic Resonance; Theory of Magnetic Resonance; Superconductivity; The New Superconductors; others. Honours: Russell Award, University of South Carolina; Jesse W Beams Award, American Physical Society; Fellow, EPR/ESR Society; Fellow, American Physical Society. Memberships: International Society of Magnetic Resonance. Address: Department of Physics, University of South Carolina, Columbia, SC 29208, USA.

**POOLEY Graham H J**, b. 11 March 1949, London, England. 1 son, 1 daughter. Education: Brentwood School, 1956-67; Oriel College, Oxford, 1967-70. Appointments: Director, Barclays de Zoete Wedd, Ltd, 1986-89; Managing Director, Chase Manhattan Limited, 1989-92; Self-employed Training Consultant and Life Coach, 1993-; Chelmsford Borough Councillor, 1995-2003. Memberships: Liberal Democrats; Friends of the Earth; Voting Reform Group/Make Your Vote Count; National Campaign for Nursery Education; National Trust; Woodlands Trust. Address: 49 Lockside Marina, Hill Road South, Chelmsford, Essex CM2 6HF, England.

**POPESCU Casin**, b. 17 August 1921, Husi, County F Iciu, Romania. Civil and Building Engineer. m. Mioara Popescu, 1 daughter. Education: Diploma in Civil Engineering, College for Building and Construction, Bucharest, Romania, 1942. Appointments: Assistant Professor, 1943-47, Honorary Secretary, 1945-47, Hydraulics Department, Polytechnic College, Bucharest (relieved of post for political reasons); Emigrated to Germany for political reasons, 1980; Research in the history of antiquity, 1980-2004; Freelance Engineer, Project Inspector, Atomic Energy Research Laboratories, Babcock-Braun-Bowery, Mannheim, Germany, 1982; Member, Centre Roumain de Recherches Etablissement libre d'enseignement supérior declare à l'Académie de Paris, 1984; Co-Founder (with wife), quarterly magazine: Paths of Fate in Balance, 1991; Officially recognised as a scientist and mathematical physicist in Romania, 2004. Publications: Numerous publications include, 1946-80: The Effect of Seismic Force on Metal Railroad Bridges - Shock Absorption and Resonance Phenomena, 1958; New Solution for Calculating the Vibration of Circular Concrete Plates, 1964; Fundamental historical works, 1980-2004: The Bridges over the Istru in the 1st Millennium Before Christ, 1984; The Legends of the Argonaut Saga – Historical Events, 1989; Who are the Etruscans, 1989, 2nd edition, 2004; Danubian Neolithic Writing, 1989; Leuce, the Achilles Island – Localisation and Historical References, 2000; The Romanian People and Their Christian Roots, 2004; Doctrina Chistiana – Prolegumene, 2004; Numerous papers for international symposiums on energy and the environment, 1987-90: Sonic Impulses – the Available Clean Energy, 1988; About the Recuperation of Wind Energy by means of Aeroturbosomites, 1988; The Mechanics of Hydrofoil Profiles and a New Generation of Turbines, 1989; Numerous patents: Founder, Theory of Hydrosonicity; Founder, Theory of Compressible Bodies or Sonic Geometry (includes Euclidian geometry, particularly in the case of $b_{p,t} = 0$, where $b_{p,t}$ is the coefficient of compressibility); Studies concerning the force of gravity resulting from the rotation of natural bodies around their axis; Studies concerning The Nature of Space and Time (Stephen Hawking/Roger Penrose) in the hypothesis of the compressibility of space and time. Address: Goldgasse 12, D-77652 Offenburg, Germany.

**POPIELA Tadeusz,** b. 23 May 1933, Nowy Sącz, Poland. Surgeon. m. Mieczysława Popiela, 1 son, 1 daughter. Education: Medical Faculty, Jagiellonian University, 1950-55; Dr Deg, 1961; Habilitation, 1965; Professor of Medicine, 1972. Appointments: Research Assistant, Department of Surgery, 1955-65; Assistant Professor, 1965-71; Head, Surgical Unit of Gastroenterology, 1971-76; 3rd Department and Clinic of General Surgery, Jagiellonian University; Rector, Medical Faculty, Jagiellonian University, 1972-81; Professor, Head, 1st Department of General and GI Surgery, Jagiellonian University, 1976-2003; Head, Intraoperative Radiotherapy and Chemotherapy Ward of the 1st Department of General and GI Surgery, 2003-. Publications: 21 monographies; 405 articles; 749 contributions at congresses. Honours: President's Best Poster Prize; CICD World Congress, Jerusalem, 1986; 2 First Prizes, International Gastric Cancer Congress, Kyoto, 1995; Doctor Honoris Causa, Pomeranian Medical University, 2002, Wroclaw Medical University, 2003. Memberships: Honorary member, JE Purkyne Czech Medical Association; Honorary member, German Society of Surgery; President, ESS, 2000; National delegate, ISS, CICD; Deputy Secretary, Executive Office Member, EAES; AGA; Society of Polish Surgeons; American College of Surgeons; IGSC; EDS; IGCA, council member; IHPE; ESES; Polish Academy of Sciences; Polish Academy of Arts and Sciences; State Committee for Scientific Research. Address: 1st Department of General and GI Surgery, Jagiellonian University, 40 Kopernika St, 31-501 Kraków, Poland. E-mail: mspopiel@cyf-kr.edu.pl

**POPOVIC Daniel John Brisbane,** b. 15 July 1945, Philadelphia, Pennsylvania, USA. Lector; Functioning Sub-Deacon; Author; Writer. Education: High School, St John Neumann, 1964; 2 Certificates, La Salle University, 1971; Accredited Interpreter, Government of Italy, 1975; Certified Lector, Commentator, 1980; Official Recognition, State of Pennsylvania, 1989, St Charles Seminary, 1980; Expertise on East Europe. Appointments: Relocation Specialist, City Philadelphia; Cashier; House Painter; Graphologist; Lecturer; Practical Nursing; Advisor, Counsellor, to Church and State, 25 years; Private Tutor, Europe; Functioning Sub-Deacon, 5 Rites. Publications: Prolific articles in various US newspapers and magazines; 5 articles, International Loreto Magazine; Author of a book and poems, MSO. Honours: US National Honour; Chapel 4 Chaplains Award; Legion of Honour; Honoured 50 times by 8 US Presidents and Foreign Dignitaries, Distinguished Leadership Award, 1996, 20th Century Achievement Award, 1999, IBC; Ninth generation direct descendant American Rev Forbear – Captain John Brisban, Sr (1730-1822). Memberships: Democratic National Committee; Academy Political Science; Carmelites; Blue Army of Fatima; Spiritual Child of Padre Pio; Library of Congress, Research Board Advisor: IBC and ABI; Philadelphia Rose Society; Associate, Woodrow Wilson International Centre Scholars; National Trust Historic Preservation. Address: 1519 South Hollywood Street, Philadelphia, PA 19146-3515, USA.

**POPPEL Emanuel S,** b. 25 December, 1925, Romania. Professor of Chemical Engineering. m. Mica-Claire Poppel, 1950. Education: MSc, Chemical Engineering, 1950, PhD, 1958, Doctor in Science, 1971, Polytechnic Institute, Iaşi, Romania. Appointments: Assistant, Professor, 1949-52, Lecturer, 1952-60, Associate Professor, 1960-70, Professor, 1970-96, Professor

Emeritus, 1996-, Technical University of Iaşi, Romania; Visiting Professor, Dresden and Darmstadt, Germany, 1972, 1974, Graz, Austria, 1995; Lecturer in Hungary, Holland, Poland, Russia, USA, England, Israel, Austria; Supervisor of more than 550 graduate students and 19 PhD theses. Publications: 220 scientific works and 10 licences in the field of fibre structures and rheology, electrokinetics in pulp and paper technology, processes and equipment in the pulp and paper industry; 8 books and monographs. Memberships: Fellow, International Academy of Wood Science; Honorary member, PITA/PIRA, England; New York Academy of Science; International Association of Scientific Papermakers. Address: Technical University of Iaşi, Department of Paper Science, Mangeron Str. 71, RO-700050 Iaşi, Romania. E-mail: epoppel@omicron.ch.tuiasi.ro

**PORTEOUS Ian Robertson,** b. 9 October 1930, Crossgates, Fife, Scotland. Mathematician. m. Shiona, 2 sons, 1 daughter. Education: MA, Edinburgh University, 1952; BA, 1956, PhD, 1960, Trinity College, Cambridge. Appointments: Lecturer, 1959-72, Senior Lecturer, 1972-98, University of Liverpool; Visiting Professor, Columbia University, New York City, 1961-62; Involvement with "Mathematical Education on Merseyside" from its inception, pioneering various ways of providing enrichment activities for pupils keen on mathematics in schools in the North-West of England and North Wales, 1976-; Creation and development of the Liverpool Mathematical Society's Funmaths Roadshow, 1999-; Liverpool City Councillor, 1974-78, Deputy Chairman of the Education Committee, 1974-76. Publications: Books: Topological Geometry, 2nd edition, 1981; Clifford Algebras and the Classical Groups, 1995; Geometric Differentiation, 2nd edition, 2001; Articles in scientific journals. Memberships: London Mathematical Society; Liverpool Mathematical Society. Address: Department of Mathematical Sciences, University of Liverpool, Liverpool L69 7ZL, England. E-mail: porteous@liverpool.ac.uk

**PORTER George (Lord Porter of Luddenham),** b. 6 December 1920, Stainforth, Yorkshire, England. Physical Chemist. m. Stella Brooke, 2 sons. Education: Graduated, Leeds University, 1941; Emmanuel College, Cambridge. Appointments: Radar Officer, Royal Navy, 1941-45; Demonstrator, Physical Chemistry, 1949-52, Assistant Director of Research, 1952-54, University of Cambridge; Professor of Physical Chemistry, 1955-63, Firth Professor and Head of Department of Chemistry, 1963-66, University of Sheffield; Professor of Chemistry, 1963-66, Director, 1966-85, Fullerian Professor of Chemistry, 1966-88, The Royal Institution, London; Professor Emeritus, 1988-. Publications: Chemistry for the Modern World, 1962; Progress in Reaction Kinetics; Numerous scientific papers; BBC TV series: Laws of Disorder, 1965; Time Machines, 1969-70; Natural History of a Sunbeam, 1976; Chemistry in Microtime, 1996. Honours include: Nobel Prize for Chemistry, shared with Professor R G W Norrish, 1967; Life Peerage, Lord Porter of Luddenham, 1990; Longstaff Medal of RSC, 1981; Michael Faraday Award, 1991. Address: Departments of Chemistry and Biochemistry, Imperial College, London, SW7 2AY, England.

**PORTILLO Michael Denzil Xavier (Rt Hon),** b. 26 May 1953. Broadcaster; Journalist. m. Carolyn C Eadie, 1982. Education: Peterhouse, Cambridge University, England. Appointments: Ocean Transport and Trading Co, 1975-76; Conservative Research Department, 1976-79; Special Adviser to Secretary of State for Energy, 1979-81; Kerr McGee Oil (UK) Ltd, 1981-83; Special Adviser to Secretary of State of Trade and Industry, 1983, to Chancellor of Exchequer, 1983-84; Member of Parliament for Enfield, Southgate, 1984-97 and for Kensington and Chelsea, 2000-05; Social Security, 1987-88, Minister of

State, Department of Transport, 1988-90; Minister of State for Local Government and Inner Cities, 1990-92; Chief Secretary to the Treasury, 1992-94; Secretary of State for Employment, 1994-95, for Defence, 1995-97; Shadow Chancellor, 2000-01; Freelance writer and broadcaster, 1997-; Adviser to Kerr McGee Corporation, 1997-2000; Director (non-executive), BAE Systems, 2002-; Member, International Commission for Missing Persons in former Yugoslavia. Publications: Clear Blue Water, 1994; Democratic Values and the Currency, 1998. Address: c/o 2nd Floor, 55 Grosvenor Street, London W1K 3HY, England.

**PORTWAY Christopher (John),** b. 30 October 1923, Halstead, Essex, England. Writer. m. Jaroslava Krupickova, 4 April 1957, 1 son, 1 daughter. Publications: Journey to Dana, 1955; The Pregnant Unicorn, 1969; All Exits Barred, 1971; Corner Seat, 1972; Lost Vengeance, 1973; Double Circuit, 1974; The Tirana Assignment, 1974; The Anarchy Pedlars, 1976; The Great Railway Adventure, 1983; Journey Along the Spine of the Andes, 1984; The Great Travelling Adventure, 1985; Czechmate, 1987; Indian Odyssey, 1993; A Kenyan Adventure, 1993; Pedal for Your Life, 1996; A Good Pair of Legs, 1999; The World Commuter, 2001; Flat Feet & Full Steam, forthcoming. Contributions to: Motoring and Leisure Magazine; Glasgow Herald; Saga Magazine; Heathrow International Traveller. Honour: Winston Churchill Fellow, 1993. Membership: Fellow, Royal Geographical Society; Founder Member, British Guild of Travel Writers. Address: 22 Tower Road, Brighton BN2 2GF, England.

**POSPÍŠIL Jaroslav,** b. 19 February 1935, Charváty, Czech Republic. Professor. Education: MSc, 1957; MEng, 1964; RNDr, 1968; PhD, 1968; DSc, 1992; Graduated in Physics and Mathematics, Palacký University, Electrical Engineering, University of Technology, Brno. Appointments: Researcher, Optics, Institute of Industrial Sciences, Tokyo University; Professor, Optics and Quantum Electronics, Head, Department of Applied Physics, Palacký University, Olomouc. Publications: Over 250 research papers in professional journals mainly in the field of transfer, statistical, digital and informational properties of optical, electrooptical, photographical, optoelectrical and human vision systems. Honours: Gold Medal, Palacký University, 1995; Merit Member and Honorary Member, Union of Czech Mathematicians and Physicists, 1996 and 2002. Memberships: International Society for Optical Engineering; Union of Czech Mathematicians and Physicists; Czech Committee, International Commission for Optics; Optics and Electronics Division of European Physical Society; Czech and Slovak Society for Photonics; Czech Society for Metrology. Address: Ovesná 10, 77900 Olomouc, Czech Republic.

**POSSAMAI Adam M,** b. 7 January 1970, Auvelais, Belgium. Senior Lecturer. m. Alpha Possamai-Inesedy, 1 son, 1 daughter. Education: BSS (Hons), GDIP Ed, Leuven, Belgium; PhD, La Trobe University, Australia. Appointments: Lecturer in Sociology, 1999-2004, Senior Lecturer in Sociology, 2004-, University of Western Sydney. Publications: Religion and Popular Culture, 2005; In Search of New Age Spiritualities, 2005; Articles in Journal of Consumer Culture and Culture and Religion. Memberships: President, Australian Association for the Study of Religions; Vice President, Research Committee 22 for the Sociology of Religion from the International Sociological Association; Co-editor, The Australian Religion Studies Review. Address: SASHS (Bankstown Campus), University of Western Sydney, Locked Bag 1737, Penrith South Dr, NSW 1737, Australia. E-mail: a.possamai@uws.edu.au

**POSTGATE John Raymond,** b. 24 June 1922, London, England. Microbiologist. m. Mary Stewart, 3 daughters. Education: First Class Honours, Chemistry, D Phil, Chemical Microbiology, Balliol College, Oxford; DSc, Oxford. Appointments: Senior Research Investigator to Principal Scientific Officer, Microbiology Group, Chemical Research Laboratory, 1948-59; Principal to Senior Principal Scientific Officer, Microbiological Research Establishment, 1959-63; Assistant Director, 1963-80, Director, 1980-87, AFRC Unit of Nitrogen Fixation, Professor now Emeritus of Microbiology, 1965-, University of Sussex; Visiting Professor, University of Illinois, Champaign-Urbana, USA, 1962-63; Visiting Professor, Oregon State University, Corvallis, USA, 1977-78. Publications include: Scientific books: The Sulphate-Reducing Bacteria, 1979, 1984; The Fundamentals of Nitrogen Fixation, 1982; Nitrogen Fixation, 1978, 1987, 1998; Microbes and Man, 1969, 1986, 1992, 2000; The Outer Reaches of Life, 1994, 1995; Other books: A Plain Man's Guide to Jazz, 1973; Lethal Lozenges and Tainted Tea, 2001; A Stomach for Dissent (with Mary Postgate), 1994; Over 200 research papers; 30 articles on popular science; Numerous record reviews and writings on jazz music. Honours: Williams Exhibition to Balliol College, Oxford; Honorary DSc, University of Bath, 1990; Honorary LLD, University of Dundee, 1997. Memberships: Fellow, Institute of Biology, 1965, President, 1982-84; Elected Fellow, Royal Society, 1977; President, Society for General Microbiology, 1984-87, Honorary Member, 1988; Honorary Member, Society for Applied Microbiology, 1988; Honorary Associate, Rationalist Press Association, 1995. Address: 1 Houndean Rise, Lewes, East Sussex BN7 1EG, England. E-mail: johnp@sussex.ac.uk

**POSTLETHWAITE Pete,** b. 16 February 1946, Lancashire, England. Actor. Career: Theatre includes: Macbeth, Bristol; Films include: The Last of the Mohicans; In the Name of the Father; Romeo and Juliet; Alien 3; Dragonheart; Distant Voices; Still Lives; Brassed Off; The Lost World; Jurassic Park; Amistad; The Serpent's Kiss; Among Giants; The Divine Ryans; TV includes: Between the Lines; Lost for Words; Butterfly Collectors. Address: c/o Markham and Froggart Ltd, 4 Windmill Street, London, W1P 1HF, England.

**POUND Keith Salisbury,** b, 3 April 1933, London, England. Clergyman. Education: BA, MA, St Catharine's College, Cambridge, 1951-54; Cuddesdon College, Oxford, 1955-57. Appointments: Curate, St Peter, St Helier, Morden, 1957-61; Training Officer, 1961-64; Warden, 1964-67, Hollowford Training Centre, Sheffield; Rector, Holy Trinity, Southwark, 1968-78; Rector, Thamesmead, 1978-86; Chaplain General and Archdeacon to H M Prison Service, 1986-93; Chaplain, Grendon and Springhill Prisons, 1993-98; Chaplain to H M The Queen, 1990-2003. Publication: Creeds and Controversies, 1965. Membership: Civil Service Club. Address: Adeleine, Pett Road, Pett, East Sussex TN35 4HE, England.

**POUNTNEY David Charles,** b. 9 March 1951, Wolverhampton, England. Lecturer. m. Janet, 3 sons. Education: BSc (Hons), Applied Mathematics, 1972, PhD, Rheology, 1976, University College of Wales, Aberystwyth. Appointments: Lecturer I, North Trafford Further Education College, Manchester, 1975-79; Lecturer II, 1979-83, Senior Lecturer, 1983-88, Liverpool Polytechnic; Principal Lecturer, 1988-, Mathematics and Statistics Leader, Teaching and Learning Co-ordinator, School of Computing and Mathematical Sciences, 2001-, Liverpool Polytechnic/John Moores University. Publications: 27 articles in scientific journals and textbooks as author and co-author, 1990-; 27 conference papers and invited lectures, 1990-. Honours: JMU Teaching Fellowship, 1995; Mathematics in Sport, multi-media based module for the MATHWISE consortium (number of universities led by CTI Centre, University of Birmingham), TLTP Funded, 1996. Memberships: British Society for Research into Learning Mathematics; 1996-; Secretary, Liverpool Mathematical Society, 1999-2004; Youth Activities Co-ordinator, Mathematical Association, 2000-; Secretary Mathematical Association Branches Committee, 2001-2003. Address: School of Computing and Mathematical Sciences, Liverpool John Moores University, Liverpool L3 3AF, England. E-mail: d.c.pountney@livjm.ac.uk

**POWELL Michael Peter,** b. 24 July 1950, Oxford, England. Consultant Neurosurgeon. m. Jennifer Shields, 3 daughters. Education: BA, MA, 1980, New College, Oxford, 1968-72; MB BS, Middlesex Hospital Medical School, University of London, 1972-75; FRCS, Royal College of Surgeons, England, 1980. Appointments: Registrar, Neurosurgery, 1980-82, Research Registrar, 1982-83, Bristol; Senior Registrar, National Hospital for Nervous Diseases, 1983-85; Consultant Neurosurgeon, National Hospital for Neurology and Neurosurgery, UCLH (Trust), 1985-. Publication: The Management of Pituitary Tumours (first edition 1996 with Professor S Lightman, second edition, 2003 with Professors S Lightman and E R Laws). Memberships: RCS England; BMA. Address: The National Hospital, Queen Square, London WC1N 3BG, England. E-mail: michael.powell@uclh.org

**POWELL Robert,** b. 1 June 1944, Salford, Lancashire, England. Actor. m. Barbara Lord, 1975, 1 son, 1 daughter. Career: TV roles include: Doomwatch, 1970; Jude the Obscure, 1971; Jesus of Nazareth, 1977; Pygmalion, 1981; Frankenstein, 1984; Hannay (series), 1988; The Sign of Command, 1989; The First Circle, 1990; The Golden Years, 1992; The Detectives, 1992-97; Theatre roles include: Hamlet, 1971; Travesties (RSC), 1975; Terra Nova, 1982; Private Dick, 1982; Tovarich, 1991; Sherlock Holmes, 1992; Kind Hearts and Coronets, 1998; Film include: Mahler, 1974; Beyond Good and Evil, 1976; Thirty Nine Steps, 1978; Imperative, 1981; Jigsaw Man, 1982; Shaka Zulu, 1985; D'Annunzio, 1987; The Mystery of Edwin Drood, 1993; The Sign of Command; Once on Chunuk Bar. Honours: Best Actor, Paris Film Festival, 1980; Venice Film Festival, 1982; Hon MA, 1990, Hon DLitt (Salford), 2000. Address: c/o Jonathan Altans Associates Ltd, 13 Shorts Gardens, London, WC2H 9AT, England.

**POWELL Sandy,** b. 7 April 1960. Costume and Set Designer. Education: St Martin's College of Art and Design, Central School of Art, London. Career: Costume designer for Mick Jagger on Rolling Stones European Urban Jungle tour, 1990, all shows by The Cholmondeleys and the Featherstonehaughs; Stage sets include: Edward II (RSC); Rigoletto (Netherlands Opera); Dr Ox's Experiment (ENO); Costumes for films include: Cobachan; The Last Of England; Stormy Monday; The Pope Must Die; Edward II; Caraveggio; Venus Peter; The Miracle; The Crying Game; Orlando; Being Human; Interview with a Vampire; Rob Roy; Michael Collins; The Butcher Boy; The Wings of the Dove; Felicia's Journey; Shakespeare in Love; Velvet Goldmine; Hilary and Jackie; The End of the Affair; Miss Julie; Gangs of New York; Far From Heaven. Honours: Best Technical Achievement Award, Evening Standard Awards, 1994; Academy Award, 1998; BAFTA Award, 1998. Address: c/o PFD, Drury House, 34-43 Russell Street, London, WC2B 5HA. E-mail: lmamy@pfd.co.uk

**POWLES Trevor J,** b. 8 March 1938, United Kingdom. Lead Clinician; Consultant. m. Penny, 2 sons, 1 daughter. Education: BSc, Physiology, London, 1961; MRCS, England, LRCP, London, 1964; MB BS, London, 1964; MRCP (UK), 1969, PhD, London, 1975; FRCP, London, 1983; Specialist: Endocrinology,

Medical Oncology, Recognised Teacher, University of London. Appointments: Consultant Medical Oncologist, 1978-2003, Chairman, Division of Medicine, 1988-90, Chairman, Clinical Research Committee, Member, Ethics Committee, 1991-94; Head of Breast Unit, 1994-2003, Royal Marsden Hospital; Member of the Research Directorate, 1991-2004, Member, Joint Research Directorate, 2000-2002, Royal Marsden Hospital and Institute for Cancer Research; Royal College of Physicians College Tutor, 1997-2000; Professor of Breast Oncology, 1998-2003, Emeritus Professor of Breast Oncology, 2003-, Institute of Cancer Research, London; Currently: Lead Clinician and Consultant, Breast Oncology, Parkside Oncology Clinic, London; Visiting Professorships: MD Anderson Cancer Center, Houston, Texas, USA, 1993; Dana-Faber Cancer Institute, Harvard Medical School, Boston, USA, 1995; Tom Baker Cancer Centre, University of Calgary, Canada, 1998. Honours: CBE, 2003; Special Award for Outstanding Achievement, All Party Parliamentary Breast Cancer Group, 2003. Memberships: Vice-President, International Society for Cancer Chemoprevention; American Association for Cancer Research; British Breast Group; British Association of Cancer Research; Association for Cancer Physicians; European Society for Medical Oncology; American Association of Clinical Oncology; Royal Automobile Club; National Charities: Trustee, Breast Cancer Research Trust; Patron, Breast Cancer Care; Scientific Advisory Board, National Osteoporosis Society. Address: Parkside Oncology Clinic, 49 Parkside, Wimbledon, London SW19 5NB, England.

**PRAGAY Desider A,** b. 12 August 1921, Clausenburg-Kolozsvar. Scientist, Professor. m. Dr Eva Bakay. Education: Agricultural Academy, Hungary, 1945; BS, University Clausenburg Political Economy, 1947; Chemistry University Budapest, 1950; MS, Biochemistry Budapest-Washington, 1961; PhD, Certified in Clinical Chemistry, 1969; Secretary, 22nd National Meeting American Association of Clinical Chemistry, Buffalo, New York, 1970; New York State Special License for Laboratory Directors, 1972. Appointments: Student Leader during Hungarian Revolution, 1956; Assistant Professor, University Medical School, Offical Distinction for Teaching, Budapest; Instructor, Assistant Professor, University of Utrecht, 1956-60; Research Associate, Buffalo, New York, 1960-63; Postdoctoral Fellow, Massachusetts General Hospital, Harvard, 1964-66; Assistant Professor, State University of New York, Buffalo, 1966-70; Associate Professor, Biochemistry and Pathology State University of New York Medical School, Buffalo, 1970-86; Professor, Chemistry, d'Youville College, 1975-86; Director, Chemistry Laboratory, University Hospital Buffalo Medical School, 1970-86; Emeritus Professor, Buffalo, Emeritus Academy Clinical Laboratory Physicians & Scientists; Emeritus, Clinical Chemists, Emeritus American Chemical Society; Emeritus Sigma Xi. Publications: Numerous articles on the field; Co-author, author, 4 books on Chemistry; Author: 12 books on History, Science History and Geography; Creator of SI Laboratory Values Converter, 1982. Honours: 2 postdoctoral fellowships; NIH Teaching Grant; Certificate of Merit, International Biographical Centre, 1972; Visiting Professor, China, Thailand, Kuwait, Caribbean, South America, 1975-83-; Fisher Science Award, 1975; American Clinical Chemistry Award, 1985; Somogyi Award, 1984-; Sigma Xi. Memberships: American Chemical Society; American Association of Clinical Chemistry Committee President for Laboratory Safety and Introduction of Laboratory pollution Control, 1973-75; Canadian Society Clinical Chemistry; Fellow, American Institute of Chemistry; Member, American Public Health Association; New York Academy of Sciences; Charter Member, Academy of Clinical Laboratory Science; Several Cultural Awards in Hungary, 1990-2000; Charter member,

Robert Boyle Society. Address: c/o Dr G Roland Hauzenberger str 13, 80687, München, Germany.

**PRANDOTA Jozef,** b. 4 June 1941, Czersk, near Warsaw, Poland. Physician. m. Lydia Pankow-Prandota, 1 daughter. Education: Physician, 1965, Doctor of Medicine, 1970, PhD, 1980, Professor of Medical Sciences, 1990, Full Professor, 2005, University Medical School, Wroclaw, Poland; Specialisation in Paediatrics, 1969, 1973; Specialist in Clinical Pharmacology, 1981. Appointments: Assistant-Adjunct, Department of Pharmacology, Medical School, Wroclaw; Adjunct, Clinical Paediatric Nephrology, 1975-77, Vice-Chief, Chief, 1978-2002, Department of Paediatrics, Korczak Memorial Hospital, Wroclaw; Member of Staff, Faculty of Public Health, Faculty of Medicine and Dentistry, University Medical School, Wroclaw, 2002-; Visiting Scientist: Department of Paediatrics, Emory University Medical School, Atlanta, USA, 1973-75, Department of Paediatrics and Pharmacology, Louisiana State University, Shreveport, USA, 1986, Department of Clinical Pharmacology, University Medical School, University of Paris XII, 1977-78; Department of Paediatrics/Paediatric Nephrology, Hannover, Germany, 1993. Publications: Articles in scientific journals including: Clinical Pharmacology and Therapeutics, 1975; International Urology and Nephrology, 1977, 1991, 1996; Pediatric Research, 1983; The International Journal of Pediatric Nephrology, 1984; Developmental Pharmacology and Therapeutics, 1986; Pediatric Infectious Diseases Journal, 1987; Drugs, 1988; European Journal of Clinical Pharmacology, 1988, 1991; Xenobiotica, 1991; Autoimmunity, 2001; Allergology and Immunopathology (Madrid), 2002; Several articles in The American Journal of Therapeutics, 2000-2005. Honours: Award for the Best Research Work in 1993, Polish Paediatric Society; Individual Award, Minister of Health, 2004. Memberships: European Society of Paediatric Nephrology; European Society for Paediatric and Perinatal Pharmacology; New York Academy of Sciences; Polish Paediatric Association. Address: University Medical School, Faculty of Public Health, 5 Bartla Street, 51-618 Wroclaw, Poland. E-mail: jzef.854735@pharmnet.com.pl

**PRASAD Braj Kishore,** b. 24 January 1956, Bekobar, Jharkhand, India. Research and Development. m. Meera, 1 daughter. Education: BSc Engg, Metallurgical Engineering, BIT, Sindri, 1981; MTech, Metallurgical Engineering, IIT, Kanpur, 1983; PhD, Metallurgical Engineering, University of Roorkee, 1994. Appointments: Research Officer, RRL, Bhopal, 1983-84; Lecturer, Metallurgical Engineering Department, REC Durgapur, 1984-85; Scientist B, 1985-90, Scientist C, 1990-95, Scientist EI, 1995-2000, Scientist EII, 2000-, RRL, Bhopal. Publications: 106 papers in international journals; 46 papers in conference proceedings. Honours: Best Paper Award, 1995; Khosla Research Award, 1997; Maximum Publications Impact Award, RRL Bhopal, 2002-03; Listed in national and international biographical dictionaries. Memberships: IIM; SAEST; MSI; MRSI; IE(I); ISE; ISNT; IIME. Address: Regional Research Laboratories, Habibganj Naka, Bhopal 462 026, India. E-mail: braj_kprasad@yahoo.com

**PRASANNA Sivaprakasam,** b. 5 November 1978, Chennai, India. Research Assistant. Education: B Pharm, Bachelor of Pharmacy, 1997-2001; M Pharm, Master of Pharmacy, Medicinal and Pharmaceutical Chemistry, 2001-03; PhD, Medicinal Chemistry, 2004-. Appointments: PhD Student and Research Assistant, University of Mississippi, USA. Publications: 10 articles in scientific journals; 1 book chapter in progress. Address: 417 Faser Hall, Department of Medicinal Chemistry, School of Pharmacy, University of Mississippi, MS 38677, USA. E-mail: psivapra@olemiss.edu

**PRASHAR Usha Kumari (Baroness of Runnymede),** b. 29 June 1948, Nairobi, Kenya. Member of the House of Lords. m. Vijay Sharma, July 1973. Education: BA, Honours, University of Leeds, 1967-70; Dip Soc, University of Glasgow, 1970-71. Appointments include: Conciliation Officer, Race Relations Board, 1971-76; Director, Runnymede Trust, 1976-84; Fellow, Policy Studies Institute, 1984-86; Director, National Council for Voluntary Organisations, 1986-91; Numerous activities from 1992-96 include: Membership of the Royal Commission on Criminal Justice, Lord Chancellors Advisory Committee on Legal Education and Conduct; The Arts Council; Chairman Parole Board of England and Wales, 1997-2000; First Civil Service Commissioner, 2000-; Chairman, National Literacy Trust, 2001-04; Chancellor, De Montfort University, 2000-; Chairman, Royal Commonwealth Society, 2001-; Board Member, Salzburg Seminar, 2000-04. Publications include: Contributed to: Britain's Black Population, 1980; The System: a study of Lambeth Borough Council's race relations unit, 1981; Scarman and After, 1984; Sickle Cell Anaemia, Who Cares? A survey of screening, counselling, training and educational facilities in England, 1985; Acheson and After: primary health care in the innercity, 1986. Honours: CBE 1994; Peerage, 1999; Honorary LLD: De Montfort, 1994; South Bank University, 1994; Greenwich, 1999; Leeds Metropolitan, 1999; Ulster, 2000; Oxford Brookes, 2000. Address: House of Lords, London SW1A 0PW, England. E-mail: prasharu@parliament.uk

**PRATCHETT Terry,** b. 28 April 1948, Beaconsfield, Buckinghamshire, England. Author. m. Lyn Marian Purves, 1 daughter. Appointments: Journalist; Writer. Publications: The Carpet People, 1971, revised 1992; The Dark Side of the Sun, 1976; Strata, 1981; The Colour of Magic, 1983; The Light Fantastic, 1986; Equal Rites, 1987; Mort, 1987; Sourcery, 1988; Wyrd Sisters, 1988; Pyramids, 1989; Eric, 1989; The Unadulterated Cat, 1989; Co-author, Good Omens: The Nice and Accurate Predictions of Agnes Nutter, 1989; Truckers, 1989; Guards! Guards!, 1989; Moving Pictures, 1990; Diggers, 1990; Wings, 1990; Reaper Man, 1991; Witches Abroad, 1991; Small Gods, 1992; Only You Can Save Mankind, 1992; Johnny and the Dead, 1993; Lords and Ladies, 1993; Men at Arms, 1993; Co-author, The Streets of Ankh-Morpork, 1993; Soul Music, 1994; Co-author, Interesting Times, 1994; The Discworld Companion, 1994; Maskerade, 1995; Co-author, The Discworld Map, 1995; Johnny and the Bomb, 1996; Feet of Clay, 1996; Hogfather, 1996; The Pratchett Portfolio, 1996; Jingo, 1997; The Last Continent, 1998; Co-author, A Tourist Guide to Loncre, 1998; Carpe Jugulum, 1998; Co-author, Death's Domain, 1999; Co-author, The Science of Discworld, 1999; The Fifth Elephant, 1999; Co-author, Nanny Ogg's Cookbook, 1999; The Truth, 2000; Thief of Time, 2001; The Amazing Maurice and His Educated Parents, 2002; Night Watch, 2002. Honours: OBE, 1998; Hon DLitt, (Warwick), 1999; Carnegie Medal. Address: c/o Colin Smythe, PO Box 6, Gerrards Cross, Buckinghamshire SL9 8XA, England.

**PREBBLE Richard,** b. 7 February 1948, Kent, England. Leader and List Member of Parliament, ACT New Zealand Party. m. (1) Nancy Prebble, 1970, (2) Doreen Prebble, 1991. Education: BA, LLB honours, Legal-economic problems, Auckland University; Lizzie Rathbone Scholar, 1967-70. Appointments: Admitted to Supreme Court as Barrister and Solicitor, 1971; Admitted to the Fiji Supreme Court Bar, 1973; Chair, Cabinet Committee, 1983-84; Headed privatisation programme; Key Minister, Labour Government, 1984-87; Elected Member of Parliament, Auckland Central, 1975-90; Professional Company Director, Works and Development Corporation, 1994-96; Elected Member of Parliament, Wellington Central, 1996-99; Leader and List Member of Parliament for ACT New Zealand

# DICTIONARY OF INTERNATIONAL BIOGRAPHY

Party, 1996-; Speaker and Advisor on regulatory, public sector, labour market, communications and transport reform; Speaking engagements in Europe, UK, USA, Indonesia, Australia and South America. Publications: I've Been Thinking, 1996; What Happens Next, 1997; I've Been Writing. Address: Parliament Buildings, Wellington 1, New Zealand. E-mail: richard.prebble @parliament.govt.nz

**PRENDERGAST Francis Joseph,** b. 13 July 1933, Ireland. Retired. m. Mary Sydenham, 3 sons, 1 deceased, 3 daughters, 1 deceased. Education: Christian Brothers School, Limerick; Diploma, Social and Economic Science, University College, Cork, Ireland; MA, Industrial Relations, Keele University, England. Appointments: Baker, Keane's Bakery, Limerick, 1950-73; General President, Irish Bakers and Confectioners and Allied Workers Union, 1967-70; Branch Secretary, ITGWU, Shannon, Clare County Branches, 1973-77; Regional Secretary, ITGWU, Limerick, Clare, 1977-82; Head Office Representative, ITGWU, Clare County, Limerick No 2 Branches, 1987-88; District Secretary, SIPTU, Limerick, 1990-93; Member, Board of Management, Crescent College Comprehensive SJ, 1973-91; Member, Governing Body, University of Limerick, 1974-79; President, Christian Brothers School Past Pupils Union, Limerick, 1995-99; Member, Limerick City Council, 1974-79; Mayor of Limerick, 1977-78, 1984-85; Dáil Eireann (Irish Parliament), Labour Party TD (Member of Parliament), Limerick East Constituency, 1982-87; Vice-President, Bureau of Consultative Council for Regional and Local Authorities Europe, 1990-94; Alternate Member, Committee of Regions, European Union, 1994-98; Chairman, Assembly of Regional Authorities, Ireland, 1995-96; Chairman, General Council of County Councils, Ireland, 1996-97; Chairman, Mid-West Regional Authority, Ireland, 1995-96; Member, Irish Language Steering Group, Department of Local Government and Environment, Ireland, 1984-99; Member, Irish Language Television Council, 1994-2000; Member, Governing Body, School of Celtic Studies, Dublin Institute of Advanced Studies, Dublin, 1996-2000; Member, Irish Place Names Commission, 1997-; Member, Executive Trust, Hunt Museum, Limerick, 2000-; Member, Irish Parliament Trust, 1985-; Chairman, Board of Management, Árd Scoil Ris Christian Brothers School, Limerick, 2003-. Publications: History of St Michael's Parish, Limerick, 2000; Limerick's Glory: From Viking Settlement to the New Millennium (co-author), 2002; Articles in: Remembering Limerick – Historical Essays, 1997, North Munster Antiquarian Journal, Old Limerick Journal, AMDG Publications, Ireland, Made in Limerick – Historical Essays, 2003; Dála an Scéil, a book of published newspaper articles; Weekly column in Irish for the Anois and Limerick Leader newspapers. Memberships: Garryowen Football Club; Voice of Limerick Choir; Thomond Archaeological Society; Limerick Thomond Probus Club. Address: "Avondonn", Cratloe Road, Mayorstone Park, Limerick, Ireland.

**PRESCOTT John Leslie,** b. 31 May 1938, Prestatyn, Wales. Politician; Trade Unionist. m. Pauline Tilston, 1961, 2 sons. Education: Ruskin College, Oxford; Hull University. Appointments: Trainee Chef, 1953-55; Steward, Merchant Navy, 1955-63; Recruitment Officer, General and Municipal Workers Union, 1965; Contested Southport for Labour, 1966; Full-time officer, National Union of Seamen, 1968-70; Member of Parliament, Kingston upon Hull East, 1970-83, Hull East, 1983-97, Kingston upon Hull East, 1997-; Member Select Committee, Nationalised Industries, 1973-79; Council of Europe, 1972-75; European Parliament, 1975-79; Personal Private Secretary to Secretary of State for Trade, 1974-76; Opposition Spokesman on Transport, 1979-81, Regional Affairs and Devolution, 1981-83, on Transport, 1988-89, on Employment, 1993-94; Member,

Shadow Cabinet, 1983-97; Member, National Executive Deputy Council, 1989-; Deputy Leader, Labour Party, 1994-; Deputy Prime Minister and Secretary of State for the Environment, Transport and the Regions, May 1997-2001; Deputy Prime Minister and First Secretary of State, 2001-. Publications: Not Wanted on Voyage: report of 1966 seamen's strike, 1966; Alternative Regional Strategy: A framework for discussion, 1982; Planning for Full Employment, 1985; Real Needs - Local Jobs, 1987; Moving Britain into the 1990s, 1989; Moving Britain into Europe, 1991; Full Steam Ahead, 1993; Financing Infrastructure Investment, 1994; Jobs and Social Justice, 1994. Address: House of Commons, London, SW1A 0AA, England.

**PRESCOTT Mark (Sir),** b. 3 March 1948, London, England. Racehorse Trainer. Education: Harrow. Appointment: Trainer at Newmarket, 1970-; Training over 1,700 winners including: Pivotal, Alborada, Albanova. Publications: The Waterloo Cup – The First 150 Years (co-author); Occasional contributor to publications including: The Racing Post and Horse and Hound. Address: Heath House, Newmarket, Suffolk CB8 8DU, England

**PRESCOTT Richard Chambers,** b. 1 April 1952, Houston, Texas, USA. Poet; Writer. m. Sarah Elisabeth Grace. Education: Self-taught. Publications: The Sage, 1975; Moonstar, 1975; Neuf Songes (Nine Dreams), 1976, 2nd edition, 1991; The Carouse of Soma, 1977; Lions and Kings, 1977; Allah Wake Up, 1978, 2nd edition, 1994; Night Reaper, 1979; Dragon Tales, 1983; Dragon Dreams, 1986, 2nd edition, 1990; Dragon Prayers, 1988, 2nd edition, 1990; Dragon Songs, 1988, 2nd edition, 1990; Dragon Maker, 1989, 2nd edition, 1990; Dragon Thoughts, 1990; Tales of Recognition, 1991; Kings and Sages, 1991; Dragon Sight: A Cremation Poem, 1992; Three Waves, 1992; Years of Wonder, 1992; Dream Appearances, 1992; Remembrance Recognition and Return, 1992; Spare Advice, 1992; The Imperishable, 1993; The Dark Deitess, 1993; Disturbing Delights: Waves of the Great Goddess, 1993; The Immortal: Racopa and the Rooms of Light, 1993; Hanging Baskets, 1993; Writer's Block and Other Gray Matters, 1993; The Resurrection of Quantum Joe, 1993; The Horse and The Carriage, 1993; Kalee Bhava: The Goddess and Her Moods, 1995; Because of Atma, 1995; The Skills of Kalee, 1995; Measuring Sky Without Ground, 1996; Kalee: The Allayer of Sorrows, 1996; The Goddess and the God Man, 1996; Living Sakti: Attempting Quick Knowing in Perpetual Perception and Continuous Becoming, 1997; The Mirage and the Mirror, 1998; Inherent Solutions to Spiritual Obscurations, 1999; The Ancient Method, 1999; Quantum Kamakala, 2000. Contributions to: Articles and essays to professional publications. Address: 8617 188th Street South West, Edmonds, WA 98026, USA.

**PRESS John Bryant,** b. 11 January 1920, Norwich, England. Retired Officer of the British Council; Writer. m. Janet Crompton, 20 December 1947, 1 son, 1 daughter. Education: Corpus Christi College, Cambridge, England. Publications: The Fire and the Fountain, 1955; The Chequer'd Shade, 1958; A Map of Modern English Verse, 1969; The Lengthening Shadows, 1971; John Betjeman, 1974; Poets of World War ll, 1984; A Girl with Beehive Hair, 1986. Contributions to: Encounter; Southern Review; Art International. Honours: Royal Society of Literature Heinemann Award, 1959; 1st Prize, Cheltenham Poetry Festival, 1959. Membership: Royal Society of Literature, Fellow. Address: 5 South Parade, Frome, Somerset BA11 1EJ, England.

**PRESS Vello,** b. 13 October 1934, Tallinn, Estonia. Scientific Worker. m. Lubomira Maria Broniarz. Education: Graduate Engineer, Technical University of Tallinn, 1957; PhD, Academy of Sciences, 1970; Diploma of Senior Researcher, 1974.

Appointments: Heat Power Engineer, The Shipyard and the Factory Building Materials, Tallinn, 1957-60; Junior Researcher, Institute of Thermal Physics and Electrophysics, 1960-70; Senior Researcher, 1970-93; Senior Lecturer, Poznan University of Technology, 1994-2004. 2004 Retired. Publications: About 50 papers and reports, in the fields of combustion of fuels and the mass transport in multicomponent media. Honours: Medal of Honour 2000 Millennium, American Biographical Institute. Memberships: Board of Advisors, American Biographical Institute. Address: Brzoskwiniowa Str 4, PL 62-031, Lubon, Poland.

**PRESSER Cary,** b. 20 June 1952, Brooklyn, New York, USA. Research Engineer. m. Karen Leslie, 2 daughters. Education: BSc, Aerospace Engineering, Polytechnic Institute of Brooklyn, New York, 1974; MSc, Aeronautical Engineering, Polytechnic Institute of Brooklyn, Farmingdale, New York, 1976; DSc, Aeronautical Engineering, Technion, Israel Institute of Technology, Haifa, Israel, 1980. Appointments: Engineering Assistant, Student Internship Program, Hypersonic Vehicles Division, Langley Research Center, Langley, Virginia, 1973; Teaching Fellow, Department of Aeronautical Engineering, Polytechnic Institute of Brooklyn, Farmingdale, 1975-75; Teaching Instructor, Department of Aeronautical Engineering, Technion, Israel Institute of Technology, Haifa, Israel, 1975-80; Research Engineer, 1980-94, Group Leader, High Temperature Processes Group, 1994-99, Group Leader, Thermal and Reactive Processes Group, 1999-2004, Research Engineer, 2004-, Process Measurement Division, Chemical Science and Technology Laboratory, National Institute of Standards and Technology, Gaithersburg, Maryland. Publications: Numerous articles as author and co-author include most recently: Phase Doppler Measurements of Liquid Agent Transport over a Heated Cylinder, 2003; A Phenomenological Droplet Impact Model for Lagrangian Spray Transport, 2003; Phase Doppler measurements of Liquid Fire-Suppressants over a Heated Cylinder, 2004. Honours include: Silver Medal Award for Meritorious Federal Service, 1991, SMART Bonus Award, 1992, US Department of Commerce; AIAA Terrestrial Energy Systems Technical Committee Best Paper Award, 1994; Listed in Who's Who publications and biographical dictionaries. Memberships include: American Institute of Aeronautics and Astronautics; Instrumentation Society of America; Fellow, American Society of Mechanical Engineers; American Institute of Chemical Engineers; American Society for Testing and Materials; American Association for Aerosol Research; American Chemical Society; American Association for the Advancement of Science; New York Academy of Science; Sigma Xi; Sigma Gamma Tau. Address: Thermal and Reactive Processes Group, Process Measurements Division, Chemical Science and Technology Laboratory, National Institute of Standards and Technology, 100 Bureau Drive, Stop 8360, Gaithersburg, MD 20899-8360, USA. E-mail: cpresser@nist.gov

**PRESSINGER Selwyn Philip Hodson,** b. 9 December 1954, Guildford, Surrey, England. Writer; Company Director. Education: Graduate, Aix-en-Provence University France; Graduate, Oxford Brookes University; Postgraduate, The College of Law, Chancery Lane, London, 1973-78. Appointments: Management Consultancy (Company Law, Marketing and Trade Finance), 1981-2005:- SCF (UK), SCT Lille (France), Tennant FM International Ltd, Maygrove Consulting Ltd, Wilton & Partners; Legal Training and Practice, 1977-80:- Solicitors Professional Course and Thicknesse Hull Solicitors, Westminster. Publications: Books: Rupert Pressinger OSB 1688-1741, Benedictine Prior, 1998; Major W.S.R. Hodson 1821-1858 – In Memoriam, 2001; Military & Equine Works of Captain Adrian Jones, 2005; The Knights of St John & Torphichen Scotland, 2005; Contributions to national newspapers and literary magazines including: The Times, The Financial Times, The Universe, The Literary Review, 1990-2004; Articles in military and historical journals including: Army Quarterly and Defence Journal, Soldiers of the Queen, Journal of the Victorian Military Society, Journal of the Society for Army Historical Research, 1998-2005. Honours: Fellow, Royal Geographical Society, 1993; Honorary Member, Hodson's Horse Officers' Association, 1997; Fellow, Royal Society of Arts, 1999. Memberships: Associate, Law Society, 1978; British Institute of Management, 1985; Institute for the Management of Information Systems, 1990; Chartered Institute of Marketing, 1994; Catholic Writers' Guild, 1996. Address: c/o 28 Old Brompton Road, South Kensington, London SW7 3SS, England.

**PRESTON-GODDARD John,** b. 5 May 1928, Liverpool, England. Painter. Partner, Kathleen Preston-Goddard. Education: Croydon School of Art. Career: Own studios since 1948; Freelance painter in oils and watercolour; Works sold in UK, USA, Europe, South Africa, Canada and South America. Publications: Numerous international publications. Address: The Studio House, Selborne Road, Park Hill Village, Croydon, Surrey CR0 5JQ, England.

**PREVIN André George,** b. 6 April 1929, Berlin, Germany. Conductor; Pianist; Composer. m. (1) Betty Bennett, divorced, 2 daughters, (2) Dory Langan, 1959, divorced 1970, (3) Mia Farrow, 1970, divorced 1979, 3 sons, 3 daughters, (4) Heather Hales, 1982, 1 son; (5) Anne-Sophie Mutter, 2003. Education: Berlin and Paris Conservatories. Appointments: Music Director, Houston Symphony, USA, 1967-69; Music Director, Principal Conductor, London Symphony Orchestra, 1968-79, Conductor Emeritus, 1979-; Composer, conductor, approximately 50 film scores; Guest Conductor, Guest Conductor most major world orchestras also, Royal Opera House, Covent Garden, Salzburg, Edinburgh, Osaka, Flanders Festival; Music Director, London South Bank Music Festival, 1972-74; Pittsburgh Symphony Orchestra, 1976-84, Los Angeles Philharmonic Orchestra, 1984-89; Music Director, Royal Philharmonic Orchestra, 1985-86, Principal Conductor, 1987-92; Conductor Laureate, London Symphony Orchestra, 1992-; Series of TV specials for BBC and American Public Broadcasting Service. Publications: Compositions, major works include: Every Good Boy Deserves a Favour (text by Tom Stoppard), 1977; Pages from the Calendar, 1977; Peaches, 1978; Principals, 1980; Outings, 1980; Reflections, 1981; Piano Concerto, 1984; Triolet for Brass, 1987; Variations for Solo Piano, 1991; Six Songs for Soprano and Orchestra, 1991; Sonata for Cello and Piano, 1992; The Magic Number, 1995; Trio for Bassoon, Oboe and Piano, 1994; Sonata for Violin, 1996; Sonata for Bassoon and Piano, 1997; Streetcar Named Desire (opera), 1998; Books: Music Face to Face, 1971; Orchestra (editor), 1977; Guide to Music, 1983; No Minor Chords: My Days in Hollywood, 1991. Honours include: TV Critics Award, 1972; Academy Awards for Best Film Score, 1959, 1960, 1964, 1965; Honorary KBE, 1995. Address: c/o Columbia Artists, 165 W 57th Street, New York, NY 10019, USA.

**PRICE (Alan) Anthony,** b. 16 August 1928, Hertfordshire, England. Author; Journalist; Editor. m. (Yvonne) Ann Stone, 1953, 2 sons, 1 daughter. Education: Exhibitioner, MA, Merton College, Oxford, 1952. Appointment: Editor, The Oxford Times, 1972-88. Publications: The Labyrinth Makers, 1970; The Alamut Ambush, 1971; Colonel Butler's Wolf, 1972; October Men, 1973; Other Paths to Glory, 1974; Our Man in Camelot, 1975; War Game, 1976; The '44 Vintage, 1978; Tomorrow's Ghost, 1979; The Hour of the Donkey, 1980; Soldier No

More, 1981; The Old Vengeful, 1982; Gunner Kelly, 1983; Sion Crossing, 1984; Here Be Monsters, 1985; For the Good of the State, 1986; A New Kind of War, 1987; A Prospect of Vengeance, 1988; The Memory Trap, 1989; The Eyes of the Fleet, 1990. Honours: Silver Dagger, 1970, Gold Dagger, 1974, Crime Writers Association; Swedish Academy of Detection Prize, 1978. Address: Wayside Cottage, Horton cum Studley, Oxford OX33 1AW, England.

**PRICE Barrie,** b. 13 August 1937, Bradford, England. Chartered Accountant. m. Elizabeth, 4 sons, 1 daughter. Education: St Bede's Grammar School, Bradford, 1948-53; ACA, 1959; FCA, 1968; ACCA, 1974; FCCA, 1980; MCMI, 1979; FCMI, 1980. Appointments: Trainee Accountant, 1953-58; Partner, 1962, Senior Partner 1974-, Lishman Sidwell Campbell and Price; Chairman and Managing Director, Lishman Sidwell Campbell & Price Ltd (formerly Slouand Ltd), 1968-; Director, Eura Audit International, 1999-; Senior Partner, LSCP LLP, 2003-; Senior Partner, ABS LLP, 2004-; Senior Partner, Eura Audit UK, 2005-; Director: Lishman Sidwell Campbell & Price Trustees Ltd, Lishman Sidwell Campbell and Price Financial Services Ltd, Tywest Investments Ltd, Slouand Ltd, Yorks Accountants Ltd, Yorks Consultants Ltd, Yorks Accountants and Auditors Ltd, Financial Centres Ltd, A1 Accountants Ltd, Ripon Accountants Ltd, Ripon Improvement Trust Ltd, Lyons St John Ltd, LSCP Ltd, Yorks Image Ltd, LSCP Properties Ltd, LSCP Nominees Ltd, Accountant UK On Line Ltd, A2Z Financial Services Ltd; Director, Eura Audit International, 1999-; Senior Partner, Eura Audit, UK, 2005-; Various appointments: AUKOL Ltd, Development Sharing (High Skellgate) Ltd, Gibsons Hotel (Harrogate) Ltd, Online Administrator Ltd; Board Member, Eura Audit International Paris, 2001-; Councillor, 1968-91, Mayor, 1980-81, Deputy Mayor, 1974-75, 1982-83, 1987-88, Ripon City Council; Councillor, 1974-91, Deputy Leader, 1987-88, 1990-91, Chairman, Economic Development Committee, Harrogate Borough District Council; Chairman: Ripon Life Care and Housing Trust, Ripon City and District Development Association, 1969-90, Harrogate Theatre Appeal, 2001-, Harrogate Theatre Forward Appeal, 2002-; President, Ripon City Conservative Association; Trustee: City of Ripon Festival, Chairman, 1981-, York Film Archive, Chairman, 1981-91, Ripon Cathedral Appeal, 1994-97, Ripon Museum Trust Appeal, Chairman, 1998-2000. Memberships: Ripon Chamber of Trade and Commerce, 1962-83, President, 1975-77, Life Member, 1983-; Roman Catholic Diocese of Leeds Finance Committee and Board, 1989-94; Ripon Tennis Centre; RSC; Ripon Civic Society; Life Member, Yorkshire Agricultural Society; Life Member, National Trust; Skipton and Ripon Conservative Association; ACA, 1959; FCA, 1968; FCCA; FCMI. Address: Prospect House, 54 Palace Road, Ripon, North Yorkshire HG4 1HA, England. E-mail: b.price@euraudituk.com

**PRICE Janet,** b. 5 February 1938, Abersychan, Pontypool, Gwent, South Wales. Singer (Soprano). m. Adrian Beaumont. Education: BMus (1st class honours) and MMus, University of Wales, Cardiff, 1956-62; LRAM (Singing Performer); ARCM (Piano Performer); LRAM (Piano Accompanist); Studied singing with Olive Groves, 1962-64; Special Study of French Vocal Music with Nadia Boulanger, France, 1966. Appointments: Singing career encompassing opera, concerts and recitals throughout the UK and Western Europe, parts of Canada and USA; Worked with leading orchestras and conductors including Haitink, Rozhdestvensky, etc; Sang opera with Glyndebourne Festival Opera, Welsh National Opera, Opera Rara, Kent Opera Co, Handel Opera Society, Northern Ireland Opera Trust, San Antonio Grand Opera Texas, BBC TV, etc; Specialty of resurrecting neglected heroines of the Bel Canto period in operas by Mercadante, Donizetti, Bellini, etc;

Numerous important premieres including Belgian premiere of Tippett's 3rd Symphony, Festival of Flanders, 1975; Adjudicator at competitions including Arts Council's Young Welsh Singers' Competition, RTE's Musician of the Future Competition, Dublin, Grimsby International Singers' Competition, Llangollen International Eisteddfod; Singing Professor at Royal Welsh College of Music & Drama, 1984-2004, and at Royal Academy of Music, London, 1997-. Publications: Commercial recordings for EMI, Argo, Philips, Decca, Opera Rara, etc; Role of Hecuba in video of Tippett's opera, King Priam, 1985; Article entitled Haydn's Songs from a Singer's Viewpoint, Haydn Yearbook, 1983. Honours: Winner, Arts Council's first Young Welsh Singers' Competition, 1964; Honorary ARAM, 2000; FRWCMD, 2004. Memberships: Royal Society of Musician of Great Britain. Address: 73 Kings Drive, Bishopston, Bristol BS7 8JQ, England.

**PRICE Margaret (Berenice) (Dame),** b. 13 April 1941, Tredegar, Wales. Singer (Soprano). Education: Trinity College of Music, London. Debut: Operatic debut with Welsh National Opera in Marriage of Figaro, 1963. Career: Renowned for Mozart Operatic Roles; Has sung in world's leading opera houses and festivals; Many radio broadcasts and television appearances; Major roles include: Countess in Marriage of Figaro, Pamina in The Magic Flute, Fiordiligi in Così fan tutte, Donna Anna in Don Giovanni, Constanze in Die Entführung, Amelia in Simon Boccanegra, Agathe in Freischütz, Desdemona in Otello, Elisabetta in Don Carlo, Aida and Norma; Sang: Norma at Covent Garden, 1987, Adriana Lecouvreur at Bonn, 1989, Elisabeth de Valois at the Orange Festival; Sang Amelia Grimaldi in a concert performance of Simon Boccanegra at the Festival Hall, 1990; Season 1993-94 in Ariadne auf Naxos at Opera de Lyon and Staatsoper Berlin. Recordings: Many recordings of opera, oratorio, concert works and recitals including, Tristan und Isolde, Le nozze di Figaro, Elgar's The Kingdom, Don Giovanni, Così fan tutte, Judas Maccabeus, Berg's Kingdom, Don Giovanni, Così fan tutte, Judas Maccabeus, Berg's Altenberglieder, Mozart's Requiem and Die Zauberflöte; Jury Member, Wigmore Hall International Song Competition, 1997. Honours: CBE; DBE, 1993. Memberships: Fellow of The College of Wales, 1991; Fellow of The College of Music and Drama of Wales, 1993. Address: c/o Stefan Hahn, Artist Management HRA, Sebastianplatz 3, 80331 Munich, Germany.

**PRICE Nick,** b. 28 January 1957, Durban, South Africa. Professional Golfer. m. Sue, 1 son, 1 daughter. Career: Professional Golfer, 1977-; Winner, PGA Championship, 1992, 1994, British Open, 1994, 3rd PGA Tour Money Leader, 1992; PGA Tour Money Leader, 1993; Zimbabwe Open, 1995; MCI Classic, 1997; Suntory Open, 1999; CVS Charity Classic, 2001; Mastercard Colonial, 2002; Founder, Nick Price golf course design, 2001; 10 US PGA victories, 25 world-wide victories. Honours: Vardon Trophy, 1993; Named Player of the Year, 1993. Address: c/o PGA Tour, 100 Avenue of the Champions, Palm Beach, FL 33410, USA.

**PRICE Richard,** b. 15 August 1966, Reading, England. Poet; Librarian. m. Jacqueline Canning, 6 December 1990, 2 daughters. Education: BA, Honours, English and Librarianship, PhD, The Novels and Plays of Neil M Gunn, 1926–1941. University of Strathclyde, Glasgow. Appointments: Curator, Modern British Collections, The British Library, London, 1992-2003; Head, Modern British Collections, 2003-. Publications: The Fabulous Matter of Fact: The Poetics of Neil M Gunn, 1991; César Vallejo: Translations, Transformations, Tributes (co-editor with Stephen Watts), 1998; La nouvelle alliance: influences francophones sur la litterature ecossaise (co-editor with David Kinloch), 2000; The

Star You Steer By: Basil Bunting and British Modernism (co-editor with James McGonigal), 2000; Novel: A Boy in Summer, 2002; Poetry Collections: Sense and a Minor Fever, 1993; Tube Shelter Perspective, 1993; Marks & Sparks, 1995; Hand Held, 1997; Perfume and Petrol Fumes, 1999; Frosted, Melted, 2002; Lucky Day, 2005. Contributions to: Comparative Criticism; Independent; Scotland on Sunday; New Writing Scotland; Verse; Poetry Scotland; Parenthesis; Edinburgh Review; Object Permanence; Guardian. Memberships: Poetry Society, 1998-. Address: c/o Modern British Collections, The British Library, 96 Euston Road, London NW1 2DB, England.

**PRICE Richard (John),** b. 15 August 1966, Reading, England. Librarian. m. Jacqueline Canning, 6 December 1990, 2 daughters. Education: BA, Honours, English Studies and Librarianship, 1988, PhD, 1994, University of Strathclyde. Appointments: Curator, Cataloguing, 1988, Information Officer, 1990, Curator, Modern British Collections, 1992-2003, Head Modern British Collections, 2003-, The British Library. Publications: Sense and a Minor Fever, 1993; Tube Shelter Perspective, 1993; Marks & Sparks, 1995; Hand Held, 1997; Perfume & Petrol Fumes, 1999; A Boy in Summer, 2002; Lucky Day, 2005. Contributions to: Independent; Verse; Europ; Journal of Comparative Criticism; Object Permanence; New Writing Scotland; Forward Anthology; Angel Exhaust; Poetry Scotland. Honour: 1st Prize, STV, Glasgow and Strathclyde Universities, 1988. Memberships: Poetry Society. Address: c/o Modern British Collections, The British Library, 96 Euston Road, London NW1 2DB, England.

**PRICE Roger (David),** b. 7 January 1944, Port Talbot, Wales. Professor of Modern History; Writer. Education: BA, University of Wales, University College of Swansea, 1965. Appointments: Lecturer, 1968-82, Senior Lecturer, 1982-83, Reader in Social History, 1984-91, Professor, European History, 1991-94, University of East Anglia; Professor of Modern History, University of Wales, Aberystwyth, 1993-. Publications: The French Second Republic: A Social History, 1972; The Economic Modernization of France, 1975; Revolution and Reaction: 1848 and The Second French Republic (editor and contributor), 1975; 1848 in France, 1975; An Economic History of Modern France, 1981; The Modernization of Rural France: Communications Networks and Agricultural Market Structures in 19th Century France, 1983; A Social History of 19th Century France, 1987; The Revolutions of 1848, 1989; A Concise History of France, 1993, second edition, 2005; Documents on the French Revolution of 1848, 1996; Napoleon III and the French Second Empire, 1997; The French Second Empire: an Anatomy of Political Power, 2001; People and Politics in France, 1848-1870, 2004. Contributions to: Numerous Magazines and journals. Honour: DLitt, University of East Anglia, 1985. Membership: Fellow, Royal Historical Society, 1983. Address: Department of History and Welsh History, University of Wales, Aberystwyth, Ceredigion SY23 3DY, Wales.

**PRIDEAUX Humphrey Povah Treverbian,** b. 13 December 1915, London, England. Soldier; Businessman. m. Cynthia Birch Reynardson, 4 sons. Education: BA, Hons, 1936, MA, 1945, Trinity College Oxford, 1933-36. Appointments: Regimental and Staff appointments, Regular Army, 1936-53; Director, 1956-73, Chairman, 1963-73, NAAFI; Director, 1964-68, Chairman, 1973-88, London Life; Director, 1968-81, Chairman, 1972-81, Brooke Bond Liebig; Director, 1969-81, Vice-Chairman, 1977-81, W H Smith; Director, 1981-93, Chairman, 1983-93, Morland & Co. Honours: Kt, 1971; OBE; DL. Memberships Cavalry and Guards Club. Address: Kings Cottage, Buryfields, Odiham, Hook, Hampshire RG29 1NE, England. E-mail: hptprideaux@aol.com

**PRIEST Graham George,** b. 14 November 1948, London, England. Philosopher. m. Anne Catherine Priest, divorced 2001, 1 son, 1 daughter. Education: BA, 1970, MA, 1974, St John's College, Cambridge University; MSc with distinction, Mathematical Logic, Bedford College, London University, 1971; PhD, Mathematics, London School of Economics, 1971-74; LittD, University of Melbourne, 2002. Appointments: Lecturer, Department of Logic and Metaphysics, University of St Andrews, Scotland, 1974-76; Lecturer, 1976-79, Senior Lecturer, 1979-87, Associate Professor, 1987-88, Department of Philosophy, University of Western Australia; Professor, Department of Philosophy, University of Queensland, 1988-2000; Visiting Professorial Fellow, University of St Andrews, Scotland, 2000-; Boyce Gibson Professor of Philosophy, University of Melbourne, 2001-. Publications: Over 100 papers; Books include: In Contradiction: a study of the transconsistent, 1987; Beyond the Limits of Thought, 1995; Introduction to Non-Classical Logic, 2001; Editor, 6 works; 26 reviews; Numerous papers at conferences and learned societies. Honours: President, Australasian Association for Logic, 1988; President, Australasian Association of Philosophy; Elected Life Member, Clare Hall, Cambridge, 1991; Elected Fellow, Australian Academy of Humanities, 1995; Chair of the Council, Australasian Association of Philosophy; 1st Vice-President, International Union for Logic, Methodology and Philosophy of Science, 1998-2003. Memberships: Australian Association of Philosophy; Australasian Association for Logic. Address: Department of Philosophy, University of Melbourne, Australia 3010.

**PRIEST Jean Hirsch,** b. 5 April 1928, Chicago, Illinois, USA. Professor Emeritus. m. Robert Eugene, deceased, 1 son, 2 daughters. Education includes: PhB Hons, 1947, BS, 1950, MD Hons, 1953, University of Chicago; MD, Illinois, 1957-1970; MD, Washington, 1959-1965; MD, Georgia, 1971-; MD, Montana, 1991-97. Appointments include: Clinical Instructor, Department of Pediatrics, Epidemiologist, Laboratory Bacteriologist, 1957-58, University of Illinois, Chicago, Illinois; Staff Physician, Respiratory Center, Columbus Hospital, Chicago Illinois, 1957-58; Clinical Instructor, Department of Pediatrics, University of Washington, Seattle, 1960-62; Instructor, Department of Pediatrics, 1963-65, Director, Birth Defects Clinic, 1964-67, Assistant Professor, Department of Pediatrics and Pathology, 1965-71, University of Colorado Medical Center, Denver, Colorado; Visiting Member of staff, Department of Zoology, University of St Andrews, Scotland, 1969-70; Visiting Professor, Department of Community Health, Research Cytogeneticist, University of Auckland, New Zealand, 1980-81; Director, Prenatal Diagnosis Program, 1973-90, Professor Emeritus, 1990-, Emory University, Atlanta, Georgia; Director, Genetics Laboratory, Physician, Shodair Hospital, Helena, MT, 1990-95; Professor Emeritus, Faculdade de Medicina de Marilla, SP, Brasil, 2000-. Publications: 3 books; 8 book chapters; 7 book reviews; 27 abstracts; 86 refereed. Memberships: American Society for Cell Biology; Chair, Social Issues Committee, 1976-80, American Society of Human Genetics; American Board of Medical Genetics; Tissue Culture Association; Vice-President, 1977-81, American Dermatoglyphics Society; International Dermatoglyphics Society; Association of Cytogenetic Technologists; Sigma Xi; American Medical Association. Address: 843 Barton Woods Road NE, Atlanta, GA 30307, USA. E-mail: jpriest517@aol.com

**PRIMDAHL Soren,** b. 16 July 1967, Skanderborg, Denmark. Chemical Engineer. 1 son, 1 daughter. Education: MSc, Chemical Engineering, Technical University of Denmark, 1993; PhD, University of Twente, The Netherlands, 1999. Appointments: Research Scientist, 1993-98, Senior Research

Scientist, 1998-2001, Risoe National Laboratory, Denmark; Development Engineer, OFS Fitel Denmark, 2001-04; Project Leader, Rockwool International A/S, 2004;. Publications: Patents and several articles in professional scientific journals. Address: Straedet 7, DK-3550 Slangerup, Denmark. E-mail: soeren.primdahl@rockwool.com

**PRINCE (Prince Rogers Nelson)**, b. 7 June 1958, Minneapolis, Minnesota, USA. Singer; Songwriter; Producer. m. Mayté Garcia, 1996, 1 son (deceased). Appointments: Leader, Prince and The Revolution; Singer, New Power Generation, 1991-; Numerous tours and concerts. Creative Works: Singles: 1999; Alphabet Street; Controversy; I Could Never Take The Place; If I Was Your Girlfriend; Let's Go Crazy; Little Red Corvette; Purple Rain; Raspberry Beret; Sign O' The Times; U Got The Look; When Doves Cry; Cream; Gold. Albums: For You, 1978; Dirty Mind, 1979; Controversy, 1979; Prince, 1979; 1999, 1983; Purple Rain, 1984; Around the World in a Day, 1985; Parade, 1986; Sign of the Times, 1987; Lovesexy, 1988; Batman, 1989; Graffiti Bridge, 1990; Diamond and Pearls, 1991; Come, 1995; The Gold Experience, 1995; The Rainbow Children, 2002; One Nite Alone – Live! 2002; Musicology, 2004. Honours: Academy Award, Best Original Score, 1984; 3 Grammy Awards, 1985; Brit Awards, 1992, 1993, 1995; Q Award, Best Songwriter, 1990. Address: Warner Bros Records, 75 Rockefeller Plaza, New York, NY 10019, USA.

**PRINGLE Charles Norman Seton (Air Marshal Sir)**, b. 6 June 1919, Dublin, Ireland. Retired Engineer. m. Margaret Sharp, 1 son. Education: BA, MA, St John's College, Cambridge. Appointments: Royal Air Force, 1941-76, final appointment, Controller of Engineering Supply and Chief Engineer; Senior Executive, Rolls-Royce (1971) Ltd, 1976-78; Non-Executive Director, Hunting Engineering, 1976-78; Chairman, Council of Engineering Institutions, 1977-78; The Director, Chief Executive, Society of British Aerospace Companies Ltd, 1978-84; Non-Executive Director, Cobham plc, 1985-89. Publications: Technical papers, Royal Aircraft Establishment, 1949. Honours: CBE 1967; KBE, 1973; Honorary Fellow (President, 1975-76), Royal Aeronautical Society; Fellow, Royal Academy of Engineering; Life Fellow, Wildfowl & Wetland Trust; Life Fellow, RSPB. Address: Appleyards, Fordingbridge, Hampshire SP6 3BP, England

**PRINGLE Jack Brown**, b. 13 March 1952, Cambuslang, Glasgow, Scotland. Architect. 2 daughters. Education: BA Honours, Bristol University, 1970-73; DipArch, 1974-75; RIBA Pt II, 1977. Appointments: Powell and Moya, 1973-81; Jack Pringle Architects, 1981-86; Pringle Brandon, 1986-; Royal Institute of British Architects, Council, 1980-86, 2003-, Vice-President, 2003-2005, President Elect, 2004-.Honours: RIBA; FRSA; FICPD. Memberships: RIBA; FRSA. Address: 10 Bonhill Street, London EC2A 4QT, England.

**PRIOR Allan**, b. 13 January 1922, Newcastle upon Tyne, England. Author. Education: Newcastle upon Tyne; Blackpool. Publications: A Flame in the Air, 1951; The Joy Ride, 1952; The One-Eyed Monster, 1958; One Away, 1961; The Interrogators, 1965; The Operators, 1966; The Loving Cup, 1968; The Contract, 1970; Paradiso, 1972; Affair, 1976; Never Been Kissed in the Same Place Twice, 1978; Theatre, 1981; A Cast of Stars, 1983; The Big March, 1983; Her Majesty's Hit Man, 1986; Führer - the Novel, 1991; The Old Man and Me, 1994; The Old Man and Me Again, 1996. Address: 11 Cokers Lane, Croxted Road, London SE21 8NF, England

**PRITZKER Andreas E M**, b. 4 December 1945, Baden, Switzerland. Physicist. m. Marthi Ehrlich, (1970) deceased

1998. M. Ursula Reist, (2003). Education: PhD, Physics, Swiss Federal Institute of Technology (ETH), Zurich, Switzerland. Appointments: Scientist, Alusuisse, 1975-77; Consulting Engineer, Motor Columbus, 1977-80; Scientist, Swiss Institute for Nuclear Research, 1980-83; Assistant to President Board of Swiss Federal Institutes of Technology, 1983-87; Head Administration, Paul Scherrer Institute, 1988-98; Head, Logistics and Marketing, Paul Scherrer Institute, 1998-2002. Publications: Filberts Verhangnis, 1990; Das Ende der Tauschung, 1993; Eingeholte Zeit, 2001; Several short stories. Memberships: Swiss Writers Association; PEN Swiss-German Centre. Address: Rebmoosweg 55, CH 5200 Brugg, Switzerland. E-mail: apritzker@bluewin.ch

**PROCHASKA Charles Roland**, b. 8 December 1941, Nampa, Idaho, USA. Aerospace Engineer. m. Judith Diane Armstrong, 3 sons, 1 stepson, 1 stepdaughter, deceased. Education: Graduated in Aerospace Engineering, University of Michigan, 1965. Appointments: Specialist Engineer, BCAC-BMS-BAC, Renton and Kent, Washington, 1965-79; Senior Specialist Engineer, 767 Division, Boeing Co, Everett, Washington, 1979-82, Boeing Marine Systems, Renton, 1982-87; Principal Engineer, Sea Lance, Boeing Aerospace and Electronics, Kent WA, 1987-90; Principal Engineer, 777 Division, Boeing Co Cargo Systems, Renton, 1990-91; Manager, 777 Division Boeing Co Cargo Furnishings, Everett, 1991-95, 777 Division Boeing Co Insulation, Everett, 1994-95, Payloads, Boeing Co Insulation-New Process, Everett, 1995-97; Option Management, Boeing Co, Everett, 1997-98; Manager, Payloads, Boeing Co Emergency Equipment-Narrow Bodies, Everett, 1998-99; Principal Engineer, Emergency Equipment, 767 Airplane Cabin Interiors, 1999; Principal Engineer, Payloads Concept Center, Boeing Co, Everett, 1999-2002; Owner, Whidstar Construction, 2002-. Publications: Project POSSUM, Polar Orbiting Satellite System-University of Michigan, 1965; National Aerospace Standard 3610, Cargo Unit Load Devices, 1968; Blueprints for Skyriders, 1968; Minuteman Stage III Hardening Review, Silo Equipment, 1972; Sea Lance Production Readiness Review, 1987; 777 Cargo Systems Critical Design Review, 1992; Option Management, the TBS Project Overview, 1997; Certification Plan, 767-400 Emergency Equipment, 1999; 3 Patents. Honours include: National Merit Award, 1960; East Quadrant Award, University of Michigan, 1964; Dean's List, University of Michigan, 1965; Outstanding Performance Award, Boeing, 1979; Employee of the Month, Boeing, 1989; Vice-President's Award for Working Together, Alan Mulally et al, 1995; District Award of Merit, Green River District Chief, Seattle Council, Boy Scouts of America; Listed in several Who's Who and biographical publications. Memberships: Society of Professional Engineering Employees in Aerospace; Washington State Grange; Quadrants Society; National Merit Society. Address: 3499 Smugglers Cove Road, Greenbank, WA 98253-9764, USA. E-mail: whidstar@whidbey.com

**PROCTER (Mary) Norma**, b. 15 February 1928, Cleethorpes, Lincolnshire, England. Opera and Concert Singer. Education: Wintringham Secondary School, Grimsby; Vocal and Music studies in London with Roy Henderson, Alec Redshaw, Hans Oppenheim and Paul Hamburger. Career: London debut, Southwark Cathedral, 1948; Operatic debut, Aldeburgh Festival in Britten's Rape of Lucrecia, 1959, 1960; Royal Opera House, Covent Garden in Gluck's Orpheus, 1961; Specialist in concert works, oratorios and recitals; Performed at festivals and with major orchestras in France, Germany, Netherlands, Belgium, Spain, Italy, Portugal, Norway, Denmark, Sweden, Finland, Austria, Luxembourg, Israel, South America; Performances with conductors including: Bruno Walter, Leonard Bernstein, Jascha Horenstein, Bernard Haitink, Raphael Kubelik, Karl

Richter, Pablo Casals, Malcolm Sargent, Charles Groves, David Willcocks, Alexander Gibson, Charles Mackerras, Norman del Mar. Recordings include: The Messiah; Elijah; Samson; Second, Third and Eighth Symphonies and Das Klagende Lied by Mahler; First Symphony by Hartmann; Scenes and Arias by Nicholas Maw; Le Laudi by Hermann Suter; Brahms and Mahler Ballads with Paul Hamburger; Songs of England with Jennifer Vyvyan, 1999; The Rarities by Britten including world premier release of 1957 recording of Canticle II – Abraham and Isaac with Peter Pears and Benjamin Britten, 2001. Honour: Honorary RAM, 1974. Membership: President, Grimsby Philharmonic Society. Address: Nor-Dree, 194 Clee Road, Grimsby, Lincolnshire DN 32 8NG, England.

**PROST Alain Marie Pascal,** b. 24 February 1955, Lorette, France. Motor Racing Team Owner; Former Racing Driver. 2 sons. Education: College Sainte-Marie, Saint-Chamond. Career: French and European Champion, Go-Kart racing, 1973; French Champion, 1974-75; French and European Champion, Formula Three Racing, 1979; Joined Marlboro MacLaren Group, 1980; Winner, French, Netherlands and Italian Grand prix, 1981; World Champion, 1985, 1986, 1989, 1993; Winner, Brazilian, French, Mexican, Spanish and British Grand Prix, 1990; South African, San Marino, Spanish, European, Canadian, French, British, German Grand Prix, 1993; Silverstone Grand Prix, 1993; Estoril Grand Prix; 51 Grand Prix wins; Technical consultant to McLaren Mercedes, 1995; Founder and President, Prost Grand Prix team, -. Publication: Vive ma vie, 1993. Honours: Officer, Legion d'honneur; Honorary OBE, 1994. Address: Prost Grand Prix, 7 avenue Eugène Freyssinet, 78286 Guyancourt Cedex, France.

**PROUDFOOT (Vincent) Bruce,** b. 24 September 1930, Belfast, Northern Ireland. Geographer. m. Edwina V W Field, 2 sons. Education: BA, 1951, PhD, 1957, Queen's University, Belfast. Appointments: Research Officer, Nuffield Quaternary Research Unit, 1954-58; Lecturer, 1958-59, Queen's University, Belfast; Lecturer, 1959-67, Tutor, 1960-63, Librarian, 1963-65, Hatfield College, University of Durham; Associate Professor, 1967-70, Professor, 1970-74, University of Alberta, Canada; Professor of Geography, 1974-93, Emeritus Professor of Geography, 1993-, University of St Andrews; Member of Council, 1975-78, 1992-93, Honorary Editor, 1978-92, Chairman of Council, 1993-99, Vice-President, 1993-, Royal Scottish Geographical Society. Publications: Books: Frontier Settlement Studies (joint editor with R G Ironside et al), 1974; Site, Environment and Economy (editor), 1983; The Downpatrick Gold Find, 1955; Author and co-author of numerous papers in geographical, archaeological and soils journals and book chapters. Honours: Lister Lecturer, British Association for the Advancement of Science, 1964; Estyn Evans Lecture, Queens University Belfast, 1985; Bicentenary Medal, Royal Society of Edinburgh, 1997; FSA, 1963; FRSE, 1979; FRSGS, 1991; OBE, 1997. Memberships: Fellow Royal Society of Arts; Fellow Royal Anthropological Institute; Fellow Royal Geographical Society with Institute of British Geographers; Fellow Society of Antiquaries Scotland. Address: Westgate, 12 Wardlaw Gardens, St Andrews, Fife KY16 9DW, Scotland.

**PROULX E(dna) Annie,** b. 22 August 1935, Norwich, Connecticut, USA. Writer. m. James Hamilton Lang, 22 June 1969, divorced 1990, 3 sons, 1 daughter. Education: BA (cum laude), University of Vermont, 1969; MA, Sir George Williams University (now Concordia University), Montreal, 1973; Doctoral orals passed, thesis abandoned mid-stroke. Publications: Books: Heart Songs and Other Stories, 1988; Postcards, 1992; The Shipping News, 1993; Accordion Crimes, 1996; Close Range: Wyoming Stories, 1999; The Old Ace in

the Hole, 2002; Close Range: Wyoming Stories 2, 2004; Short story: The Half-Skinned Steer, 1998; Editor: Best American Short Stories of 1997. Contributions to: Periodicals. Honours include: Guggenheim Fellowship, 1992; PEN/Faulkner Award, 1993; National Book Award for Fiction, 1993; Chicago Tribune Heartland Award, 1993; Irish Times International Fiction Award, 1993; Pulitzer Prize in Fiction, 1994; Alumni Achievement Award, University of Vermont, 1994; New York Public Library Literary Lion, 1994; Dos Passos Prize for Literature, 1996; Honorary Doctor of Laws, Concordia University, Montreal, 1999; Book Award, The New Yorker, 2000; Ambassador Book Award, English Speaking Union, 2000; Willa Award 2000, 2000; Borders Original Voices Award in Fiction, 2000; San Francisco Chronicle 100 Best of the West Novelists, 2000; Honorary Doctor of Letters, University of Toronto, 2000; Evil Companions Literary Award, Denver, 2001; Best American Novel, Best Foreign Language Novels Award, Chinese Publishing Association and People's Literature Publishing House, China, 2002; Mary McCarthy Award, Bard College, 2005; Aga Khan Award, Paris Review, 2005. Memberships: Phi Alpha Theta; Phi Beta Kappa. Address: PO Box 230, Centennial, WY 82055, USA. E-mail: aproulx@wyoming.com

**PRUSINSKI Antoni,** b. 23 June 1925, Czestochowa, Poland. Physician; Professor of Neurology. m. Maria Bryniarska, 2 daughters. Education: MD, Medical Faculty, Medical University of Lodz, Poland, 1947-52; Specialist in Neurology, 1956; PhD, Medical University of Lodz, 1960; DSc, Medical University of Lodz, 1962. Appointments: Assistant and Senior Assistant, Department of Neurology, Medical University of Lodz, 1952-63; Assistant Professor (docent), 1962-74; Extraordinary Professor of Neurology, 1974-83; Ordinary Professor of Neurology, 1984; Chairman, Head of the Chair and Department of Neurology, Medical University of Lodz, 1963-95; Retired, 1995. Publications: 400 articles and communications in field of clinical neurology and headache in various journals (mainly in Polish); 42 books (author, co-author or editor) include: Migrena (Migraine), 2 editions, 1976-82 (Russian and Czech translations); Principles of clinical neurology (in Polish), 5 editions, 1970-89. Honours: 1st degree award of Ministry of Health, 4 times, 1973-90; Honorary member, Polish Neurological Society, 1996; Copernicus Medal, Polish Academy of Sciences, 1996; Doctor honoris causa, Medical University of Lodz, 1997; Listed in several biographical dictionaries. Memberships: International Headache Society, Board Member, 1980-96; European Headache Federation, Board Member, 1990-97; Polish Neurological Society, President, 1991-97; Polish Headache Society, President, 1997-99. Address: 41 Bracka Street 91-709, Lodz, Poland.

**PRUSTY Rabin,** 6 October 1939, Cuttack, India. Scientist; Engineer. Education: MSCE, Masters in Science and Masters in Environmental Engineering, West Virginia University, 1979. Appointments: Environmental Engineer, specialising in pollution control projects, such as analysis of effects of toxic chemicals on humans, and the establishment of health-based safe disposal limits for toxic waste, 1979-. Main research interests: 12 years' research into Multiple Chemical Sensitivity (MCS), Electromagnetic Fields (EMF) Sensitivity; Genetic engineering and the alteration of gene and cell structures due to exposure to toxic chemicals. Publications: Numerous articles contributed to specialist scientific and computer journals; MCS website, www.nettally.com/prusty/mcs.htm. Honours: International Scientist of the Year, 2001; Man of the Year 2004; Listed in numerous Who's Who publications and biographical dictionaries. Membership: The Institute of Electrical and Electronics Engineers, 1993-94. Address: PO Box 20517, Tallahassee, FL 32316-0517, USA. E-mail: rprusty@yahoo.com

**PRYBYLA Jan S,** b. 21 October 1927, Poland. Professor Emeritus. m. Jacqueline Meyer, 1 son, 1 daughter. Education: BComm, 1949; MEconSc, 1950; PhD, 1953. Appointments: Professor of Economics, Pennsylvania State University, 1958-95; Visiting Professor of Economics, Nankai University, Tianjin, China, 1987-88; Visiting Scholar, Institute of International Relations, National Chengchi University, Taipei, Taiwan. Publications: Co-author, Russia and China on the Eve of a New Millennium, 1997; Contributor, The Chinese Communist State in Comparative Perspective, 2000. Honours: Lindback Award for Distinguished Teaching, Pennsylvania State University, 1971; Distinction in the Social Sciences Award, Pennsylvania State University, 1979; Adjunct Faculty, US Department of State, Foreign Service Institute, Washington, DC, USA. Memberships: President, Conference on European Problems; Member, American Association for Chinese Studies; Member, Association for Comparative Economic Studies. Address: 5197 N Spring Pointe Pl, Tucson, AZ 85749, USA. E-mail: jprybyla@prodigy.net

**PRYCE John Derwent,** b. 29 January 1941, Bowness on Windermere, England. University Lecturer. m. (1) Christine, 1967, divorced 1988, 2 sons, 1 daughter, (2) Kate, 1990, 1 daughter. Education: Dragon School, Oxford; Eton College; BA, Mathematics, Trinity College, Cambridge, 1962; PhD, Mathematics, University of Newcastle Upon Tyne, 1965; Cert Ed, University of Bristol, 1966. Appointments: Mathematics Teacher, 1966-68; Lecturer, University of Aberdeen, 1968-75; Lecturer, University of Bristol, 1975-88; Sabbatical Professor, University of Toronto, Canada, 1982-83; Lecturer, Senior Lecturer, Royal Military College of Science, Cranfield University, 1988-. Publications: Books: Basic Methods of Linear Functional Analysis, 1973; Numerical Solution of Sturm-Liouville Problems, 1993; 51 articles in refereed journals/conference proceedings. Honours: Co-director, Uniben International Conferences on Scientific Computing, Benin City, Nigeria, 1992, 1994; Guest Editor, Volume on Differential Equations, Special Millennium Edition of Journal Computational and Applied Mathematics, 2000. Memberships: Fellow, Institute of Mathematics and Applications; Chartered Mathematician. Address: 142 Kingshill Road, Old Town, Swindon, Wiltshire, SN1 4LW, England.

**PRYCE Jonathan,** b. 1 June 1947, North Wales. Actor. Partner, Kate Fahy, 2 sons, 1 daughter. Education: Royal Academy of Dramatic Art. Career: Stage appearances include: The Comedians, 1975, 1976; Hamlet, Royal Court, London, 1980; The Caretaker, National Theatre, 1981; Accidental Death of an Anarchist, Broadway, 1984; The Seagull, Queen's Theatre, 1985; Macbeth, RSC, 1986; Uncle Vanya, 1988; Miss Saigon, Drury Lane, 1989; Oliver!, London Palladium, 1994; My Fair Lady, 2001; TV appearances include: Roger Doesn't Live Here Anymore (series), 1981; Timon of Athens, 1981; Martin Luther, 1983; Praying Mantis, 1983; Whose Line is it Anyway?, 1988; The Man from the Pru, 1990; Selling Hitler, 1991; Mr Wroe's Virgins, 1993; Thicker Than Water, 1993; Films include: Something Wicked This Way Comes, 1982; The Ploughman's Lunch, 1983; Brazil, 1985; The Doctor and the Devils, 1986; Haunted Honeymoon, 1986; Jumpin' Jack Flash, 1987; Consuming Passions, 1988; The Adventures of Baron Munchausen, 1988; The Rachel Papers, 1989; Glen Garry Glen Ross, 1992; The Age of Innocence, 1993; A Business Affair, 1993; Deadly Advice, 1994; Carrington, 1995; Evita, 1996; Tomorrow Never Dies, 1997; Regeneration, 1997; Ronin, 1998; Stigmata, 1999; Very Annie Mary, 2001; Unconditional Love, 2001; The Affair of the Necklace, 2001; Bride of the Wind, 2001; Recordings: Miss Saigon, 1989; Nine-The Concert, 1992; Under Milkwood, 1992; Cabaret, 1994; Oliver!, 1995; Hey! Mr

Producer, 1998; My Fair Lady, 2001. Honours: Tony Award, 1976; Oliver and Variety Club Awards, 1991; Tony and Drama Desk Awards, 1994; Best Actor, Cannes Film Festival, 1995; Best Actor, Evening Standard Film Awards, 1996. Address: c/o Julian Belfrage Associates, 46 Albemarle Street, London W1X 4PP, England.

**PUCKETT Richard Edward,** b. 9 September 1932, Klamath Falls, Oregon, USA. Artist; Consultant; Retired Recreation Executive. m. Velma Faye Hamrick, 14 April 1957 (deceased 1985), 1 son, 3 daughters. Education: Southern Oregon College of Education, 1951-56; Lake Forest College, Illinois, 1957-58; Hartnell Junior College, Salinas; College Major, Fine Arts and Education; San Jose State University, California, 1973; BA, Public Service, University San Francisco, 1978. Appointments: Acting Arts and Crafts Director, Ft Leonard Wood, Missouri, 1956-57; Arts and Crafts Director; Assistant Special Services Officer (designed and opened 1st Ft Sheridan Army Museum), Ft Sheridan, Illinois, 1957-59; Arts and Crafts Director, Ft Irwin, California, 1959-60; Arts and Crafts Director, Ft. Ord, California (directed and opened 1st Presidio of Monterey, California, Army Museum), 1960-; Artist, Consultant, Retired Recreation Executive, Ft Ord, California, 1986; Directed and built the largest and most complex arts and craft program in the Department of Defense; Had the model program for the army; Taught painting classes and workshops for 30 years. Creative Works: Exhibitions: One-Man Shows at Seaside City Hall, 1967-86, 2002, Ft Ord Arts and Crafts Centre Gallery, 6 times, 1967-86, Presidio of Monterey Art Gallery, Del Messa Gallery, Carmel, California, 1998; Southern Oregon Art Gallery, Medford, 2000, Country Rose Gallery, Hollister, California, 2001-03, Walter Avery Gallery Seaside City Hall, 2002; Sasoontsi Gallery, 2004; Works in private collections in USA, Canada and Europe; Designed and opened first Ft Sheridan Army Museum, Presidio of Monterey Museum, exhibited in group shows at Salinas Valley Art Gallery, Del Messa Gallery, 2001-03, 2001-04; Glass on Holiday, Gatlinburg, Tennessee, 1981-82. Donated over 4,000 items, slides, scrapbooks, paintings, arts and crafts items, etc to University of Monterey Bay, Ft Ord; Donated photo collection, Hartnell Junior College. Honours: 1st Place, Department of Army Programming Award, 6 times, 1975-84; 5 USA Army Forces Command 1st Place Awards for Programming and Publicity, 1979-84; 1st and 3rd Place, Modern Sculpture, Monterey, California Fair, Fine Arts Exhibition, 1979; 19 Awards for Outstanding Performance; Commanders Award Medal, 1987. Memberships: Salinas Fine Arts Association; Monterey Peninsula Art Association; Southern Oregon Art Association; President, Salinas Valley Art Association; Ford Ord Alumni Association; IBA; ABA; Listed in various Biographical Dictionaries including: Life Fellow, Institute of Biographical Association; Who's Who in America; Who's Who in the World. Address: 210 San Miguel Ave, Salinas, CA 93901, USA.

**PULLMAN Bill,** b. 1955, Hornell, New York, USA. Actor. Education: University of Massachusetts. m. Tamara, 3 children. Appointments: Former drama teacher, building contractor, director of theatre group; Started acting in fringe theatres, New York; Moved to Los Angeles; Films include: Ruthless People; A League of Their Own; Sommersby; Sleepless in Seattle; While You Were Sleeping; Caspar; Independence Day; Lost Highway, 1997; The End of Violence, 1997; The Thin Red Line, 1998; Brokedown Palace, 1998; Zero Effect, 1998; A Man is Mostly Water, 1999; History is Made at Night, 1999; The Guilt, 1999; Lake Placid, 1999; Coming to Light: Edward S Curtis and the North American Indians (voice), 2000; Titan AE, 2000; Numbers, 2000; Ignition, 2001; Igby Goes Down, 2002; 29

Palms, 2002; Rick, 2003. Address: c/o J J Harris, 9560 Wilshire Boulevard, Suite 50, Beverly Hills, CA 90212, USA.

**PULLMAN Philip,** b. 19 October 1946, Norwich, England. Author. m. Jude Speller, 15 August 1970, 2 sons. Education: BA, Oxford University, 1968. Appointments: Teacher, Middle School, 1972-86; Lecturer, Westminster College, Oxford, England, 1986-96. Publications: The Ruby in the Smoke, 1986; The Shadow in the North, 1987; The Tiger in the Well, 1990; The Broken Bride, 1992; The White Mercedes, 1992; The Tin Princess, 1994; Northern Lights, 1995; The Golden Compass, 1996; Spring-Heeled Jack, 1997; Puss in Boots, 1997; The Subtle Knife, 1997; Count Karlstein, 1998; Clockwork, 1998; I Was a Rat! 2000; The Amber Spyglass, 2000; Lyra's Oxford, 2003. Contributions to: Reviews in Times Educational Supplement; The Guardian. Honours: Carnegie Medal, 1996; Guardian Children's Fiction Award, 1996; British Book Awards Children's' Book of the Year, 1996; British Book Awards WH Smith Children's Book of the Year, 2000; Whitbread Children's Book of the Year Prize, 2001; Whitbread Book of the Year Award, 2001; BA/Book Data Author of the Year Award, 2001; Booksellers' Association Author of the Year, 2001, 2002; British Book Awards Author of the Year Award, 2002; Whitbread Book of the Year Award, 2002. Address: c/o A P Watt Ltd, 20 John Street, London, WC1N 2DR, England.

**PUMPENS Paul,** b. 21 October 1947, Riga, Latvia. Molecular Biologist. Education: Biochemist Diploma, Latvian University, 1970; Candidate in Biology, Latvian Academy of Science, Riga, 1975; Doctor in Biology, Institute of Molecular Biology, 1988; Doctor habil Biology, Latvian Council of Science, Riga, 1991; Professor, 1992. Appointments: Research Fellow, Institute of Organic Synthesis, 1973-89; Head of Laboratory, Institute of Organic Synthesis, 1989-90; Head of Department, Biomedical Research and Study Centre, University of Latvia, 1991-. Publications: Over 200 articles in scientific press. Honours: All-Union Comsomol's Prize; Latvian Academic Science Award; Grindel Medal; Minister Council Award. Membership: Latvian Academy of Sciences. Address: Biomedical Research and Study Centre, University of Latvia, Ratsupites Str 1, Riga, LV-1067, Latvia. E-mail: paul@biomed.lu.lv

**PUÑA Marcos Javier,** b. 23 August 1977, Oruro, Bolivia. Performer; Teacher of Classical Guitar. m. Leticia Mérola. Education: Degree, "Vincente Ascone" School of Music, Montevideo, Uruguay, studied with Abel Carlevaro, Uruguay, 1996-99. Appointments: Professor of Classical Guitar; Many concerts in Bolivia, Venezuela, Chile, Peru, Brazil, Argentina and Uruguay, 1993-2005. Recordings: Compact Discs: Concierto Espagñol (Spanish Concert), 1998; Paseo Sudamericano, 2004. Honours: First Prize, National Guitar Competition, Tarija, Bolivia, 1994; First Prize, Musical Competition of "Juventudes Musicales", Uruguay, 1996; First Prize, "César Cortinas" International Competition of Music, Montevideo, Uruguay, 2003. Address: c/ Daniel Albornoz 1645, Cochabamba, Bolivia. E-mail: marcos@marcospuna.com Website: www.marcospuna.com

**PUNCOCHAR Pavel,** b. 20 March 1944, Pelhrimov, Czech Republic. Biologist; Ecologist. m. Marcela, 1 daughter. Education: MSc, Faculty of Life Sciences, Charles University, Prague, 1966; RNDr, Hydrobiology, 1969; PhD, Hydromicrobiology, 1972; Appointments: Czech Academy of Sciences, Hydrobiological Laboratory, 1967; Institute of Landscape Ecology, Prague, 1985-86; Water Research Institute, Prague, 1986-97; Director, 1990-97; Ministry of Agriculture, Gen.Dir. Section of Watermanagement Policy, 1998. Publications; More than 300 papers, contributions in Czech and or

international journals. Memberships: International Commission for Elber River Protection; International Commission for Danube River Protection; International Commission for Oder River Protection; Member, Research Board, Ministry of the Environment; Czech Academy of Sciences, Hydrobiological Institute; Vice Chairman, ICID; Others. Address: Zitkova 225, 15300 Prague 5, Czech Republic.

**PUNTER David Godfrey,** b. 19 November 1949, London, England. Professor of English; Writer; Poet. m. Caroline Case, 5 December 1988, 1 son, 2 daughters. Education: BA, 1970, MA, 1974, PhD, 1984, University of Cambridge. Appointments: Lecturer in English, University of East Anglia, 1973-86; Professor and Head of Department, Chinese University of Hong Kong, 1986-88; Professor of English, University of Stirling, 1988-2000; Professor of English, University of Bristol, 2000-. Publications: The Literature of Terror, 1980; Blake Hagel and Dialectic, 1981; Romanticism and Ideology, 1982; China and Class, 1985; The Hidden Script, 1985; Introduction to Contemporary Cultural Studies (editor), 1986; Lost in the Supermarket, 1987; Blake: Selected Poetry and Prose (editor), 1988; The Romantic Unconscious, 1989; Selected Poems of Philip Larkin (editor), 1991; Asleep at the Wheel, 1997; Gothic Pathologies, 1998; Spectral Readings (editor), 1999; Selected Short Stories, 1999; Companion to the Gothic (editor), 2000; Writing the Passions, 2000; Postcolonial Imaginings, 2000. Contributions to: Hundreds of articles, essays, and poems in various publications. Honours: Fellow, Royal Society of Arts; Fellow, Society of Antiquaries (Scotland); Scottish Arts Council Award; Founding Fellow, Institute of Contemporary Scotland; DLitt, University of Stirling. Address: Department of English, University of Bristol, Bristol BS8 1TB, England.

**PURI Kailash,** b. 17 April 1926, Rawalpindi, Pakistan. Writer. m. Gopal Singh Puri, 1 son, 2 daughters. Appointments: Chief Editor, Subagwati, first women's magazine in Punjabi, 1956; Editor, Kirna Weekly and Roopvati monthly, 1968-73; Consultant, Marks & Spencer, 1972-76; Director, East West Family Advisory Centre; Manager/Teacher, Crosby Yoga Centre, 1972-95; TV Presenter and counselling appearances on BBC TV, ITV, Granada, Asian TV channels, Zee and Channel East; Weekly Columnist; Visiting Lecturer, Leith's School of Food & Wine, 1984-90; Presented papers in international cultural and religious conferences in USA, India, Korea, Japan and Cairo. Publications: Author of 35 books, many translated into several languages. Honours: Bhai Mohan Sing Vaid Literary Award, 1985; Shromani Sahitkar Award, Language Department, Patiala, 1988; Institute of Sikh Studies Award, 1988; Ambassador for Peace Award; Personality of the Year Award, Khalsa College, London, 1989; Women of Achievement Award, 1999; Millennium Women's Award, 2000; Lifetime Achievement Award, International Panjabi Society, 2001; Lifetime Achievement Award, 2004; Mayor of Ealing. Memberships: President, UK Asian Women's Association, Merseyside, 1975-95; Patron, Women of the Year Lunch and Assembly, 1989; President, Inner Wheel Club, Merseyside, 1980-82; Governor, Woodlands School; Executive Member, Governors' Consultative Committee; President, Punjabi Women's Social and Cultural Society; UK Adviser, Puthohar Association; Vice-President, Women's Federation for World Peace; Director, Women's Aid;. Address: 6 Haven Green Court, London W5 2UZ, England.

**PURI Sanjay,** b. 23 November 1961, Rampur, India. Physicist. m. Bindu Puri, 2 sons. Education: MS Physics, IIT Delhi, India, 1982; PhD, Physics, University of Illinois at Urbana-Champaign, USA, 1987. Appointments: Assistant Professor, 1987-93, Associate Professor, 1993-2001, Professor, 2001-,

Jawaharlal Nehru University (JNU), New Delhi. Publications: Approximately 115 papers and books on statistical physics and nonlinear dynamics. Honours: Young Scientist Medal, Indian National Science Academy, 1993; Satyamurthy Medal, Indian Physics Association, 1995; Birla Science Award, Birla Science Centre, 2001; Homi Bhabha Fellowship, Bhabha Fellowships Council, 2003. Address: School of Physical Sciences, Jawaharlal Nehru University, New Delhi 110067, India. E-mail: puri@mail.jnu.ac.in

**PURKIS Andrew James,** b. 24 January 1949, London, England. Charity Director. m. Jennifer Harwood Smith, 1 son, 1 daughter. Education: 1st Class Honours Modern History, Corpus Christi College, Oxford, 1967-70; St Antony's College, Oxford, 1971-74; Doctor of Philosophy, 1978. Appointments: Administrative Trainee, 1973-76, Private Secretary, 1976-77, Principal, 1977-80, Northern Ireland Office; Head of Policy Analysis, 1980-84, Head of Policy Planning, 1984-86, Assistant Director, 1986-87, National Council for Voluntary Organisations; Director, Council for the Protection of Rural England, 1987-91; Public Affairs Secretary to the Archbishop of Canterbury, 1992-98; Chief Executive, Diana, Princess of Wales Memorial Fund, 1998-. Publications: Housing and Community Care (with Paul Hodson), 1982; Health in the Round (with Rosemary Allen), 1983. Honours: OBE; DPhil; MA. Membership: FRSA, 1989. Address: 38 Endlesham Road, Balham, London SW12 8JL, England.

**PURSER Philip John,** b. 28 August 1925, Letchworth, England. Journalist; Author. m. Ann Elizabeth Goodman, 18 May 1957, 1 son, 2 daughters. Education: MA, St Andrews University, 1950. Appointments: Staff, Daily Mail, 1951-57; Television Critic, Sunday Telegraph, 1961-87. Publications: Peregrination 22, 1962; Four Days to the Fireworks, 1964; The Twentymen, 1967; Night of Glass, 1968; The Holy Father's Navy, 1971; The Last Great Tram Race, 1974; Where is He Now?, 1978; A Small Explosion, 1979; The One and Only Phyllis Dixey, 1978; Halliwell's Television Companion (with Leslie Halliwell), 1982, 2nd edition, 1986; Shooting the Hero, 1990; Poeted: The Final Quest of Edward James, 1991; Done Viewing, 1992; Lights in the Sky, 2005. Contributions to: Numerous magazines and journals. Memberships: Writers Guild of Great Britain; British Academy of Film and Television Arts. Address: 10 The Green, Blakesley, Towcester, Northamptonshire NN12 8RD, England.

**PURVES Libby, (Elizabeth Mary Purves),** b. 2 February 1950, London, England. Journalist; Broadcaster; Writer. m. Paul Heiney, 2 February 1980, 1 son, 1 daughter. Education: BA, 1st Class Honours, University of Oxford, 1971. Appointments: Presenter-Writer, BBC, 1975-; Editor, Tatler, 1983. Publications: Adventures Under Sail (editor), 1982; Britain at Play, 1982; The Sailing Weekend Book, 1984; How Not to Be a Perfect Mother, 1987; One Summer's Grace, 1989; How Not to Raise a Perfect Child, 1991; Casting Off, 1995; A Long Walk in Wintertime, 1996; Home Leave, 1997; More Lives Than One, 1998; Holy Smoke, 1998; Regatta, 1999; Passing Go, 2000; A Free Woman, 2001; Acting Up, 2004. Contributions to: Newspapers and magazines. Honours: Best Book of the Sea, 1984; OBE, Services to Journalism, 1999; Columnist of the Year, 1999; Desmond Wettern Award, 1999. Membership: RSA. Address: c/o Rogers Coleridge White, 20 Powis Mews, London W11 1JN, England.

**PUTIN Vladimir Vladimirovich,** b. 7 October 1952, Leningrad, USSR. Lawyer. m. Ludmila A Putina, 2 daughters. Education: Graduate, Faculty of Law, Leningrad State University, 1975. Appointments: Soviet State Security Service, 1975-90; Assistant Rector, International Affairs, Leningrad State University, Adviser to Chairman, Leningrad City Council, 1990; Head,

International Committee, St Petersburg Mayor's Office, 1991-96, concurrently, First Deputy Chairman of the Government of St Petersburg, 1994-96; Deputy Property Manager, under President Yeltsin, Moscow, 1996; Deputy Chief of Staff, Main Control Department of the Administration of the Russian Federation, 1997; First Deputy Chief of Staff in Charge of Russian Regions and Territories, 1998; Director, Russian Federal Security Service, 1998; Secretary, Russian Security Council, 1999; Prime Minister of the Russian Federation, 1999; Acting President, 1999, President of the Russian Federation, 2000-. Honours: Master of Sports in sambo wrestling, 1973; Master of Sports in judo, 1975; Won sambo championships in St Petersburg many times; Candidate of Economic Sciences. Address: The Kremlin, Moscow, Russia. E-mail: president@kremlin.ru

**PUTTNAM David Terence (Baron),** b. 25 February 1941, London, England. Film Producer. m. Patricia Mary Jones, 1 son, 1 daughter. Appointments: Advertising, 1958-66; Photography, 1966-68; Film production, 1968-; Chairman, Enigma Productions Ltd, 1978-, Spectrum Strategy Ltd, 1999-; Director, National Film Finance Corporation, 1980-85, Anglia TV Group, 1982-99, Village Roadshow Corporation, 1989-99, Survival Anglia, 1989-, Chrysalis Group, 1993-96; Chairman, CEO, Columbia Pictures, USA, 1986-88; President, Council for Protection of Rural England, 1985-92; Visiting Lecturer, Bristol University, 1984-86; Visiting Industrial Professor, 1986-96; Governor, Lecturer, LSE, 1997-; Governor, 1974-, Chair, 1988-96, National Film and TV School; Chair, Teaching Council, 2000-02; Productions include: That'll Be the Day; Mahler; Bugsy Malone; The Duellists; Midnight Express; Chariots of Fire; Local Hero; The Killing Fields; Cal; Defence of the Realm; Forever Young, 1984; The Mission, 1985; Mr Love, 1986; Memphis Belle, 1989; Meeting Venus, 1990; Being Human, 1993; War of the Buttons, 1993; Le Confessional, 1995; My Life So Far, 2000. Publications: Rural England: Our Countryside at the Crossroads, 1988; Undeclared War: The Struggle to Control the World's Film Industry, 1997; My Life So Far, 1999. Honours: Honorary FCSD; Honorary degrees (Bristol, Leicester, Manchester, Leeds, Bradford, Westminster, Humberside, Sunderland, Cheltenham and Gloucester, Kent, London Guildhall Universities, Royal Scottish Academy, Imperial College London; Special Jury prize for the Duellist, Cannes, 1977; 2 Academy Awards, 4 BAFTA Awards for Midnight Express, 1978; 4 Academy Awards, 3 BAFTA Awards for Chariots of Fire, 1981; 3 Academy Awards and 9 BAFTA Awards for The Killing Fields, 1985; Michael Balcon Award, BAFTA, 1982; Palme d'Or, Cannes, 1 Academy Award, 3 BAFTA Awards for The Mission, 1987; Officier, Ordre des Arts et des Lettres, 1986. Memberships include: Vice President, BAFTA; Chancellor, University of Sunderland; Chairman, National Endowment for Science, Technology and the Arts, National Museum of Photography, Film and TV; Education Standards Task Force, 1997-2000. Address: Enigma Productions, 29A Tufton Street, London, SW1P 3QL, England.

**PYBUS Rodney,** b. 5 June 1938, Newcastle upon Tyne, England. Writer; Poet. m. Ellen Johnson, 24 June 1961, 2 sons. Education: BA, Honours, Classics, English, MA, 1965, Gonville and Caius College, Cambridge. Appointments: Journalist, TV producer, 1962-76; Lecturer, Macquarie University, Australia, 1976-79; Literature Officer, Cumbria, 1979-81; Co-editor, Stand, 1993-98. Publications: In Memoriam Milena, 1973; Bridging Loans, 1976; At the Stone Junction, 1978; The Loveless Letters, 1981; Talitha Cumi, 1985; Cicadas in Their Summers: New and Selected Poems, 1988; Flying Blues, 1994. Contributions to: London Review of Books; New Statesman; London Magazine; Kenyon Review; Ambit; Iowa Review; Sydney Morning Herald; Equivalencias; Poetry Review; Stand; Times Literary Supplement; Critical Survey; Guardian; Independent; Rialto.

Honours: Alice Hunt Bartlett Award, Poetry Society, 1974; Arts Council Writer's Fellowships, 1982-85; National Poetry Competition Awards, 1984, 1985, 1988; 1st Prize Peterloo Poetry Competition, 1989; Hawthornden Fellowship, 1988. Memberships: Society of Authors; Poetry Society. Address: 21 Plough Lane, Sudbury, Suffolk CO10 2AU, England.

# Q

**QAFMOLLA Luan,** b. 16 January 1950, Tirana, Albania. Chemical Engineer. m. Luljeta Qafmolla, 1 son, 1 daughter. Education: Diploma for Nuclear Chemical Engineer, Natural Science Faculty, University of Tirana, 1972-77. Appointments: Lecturer, Radiation Protection, Medical Faculty, Tirana, 1987; Lecturer, General Chemistry, Skanderberg Army Faculty, 1991; Leader of several diploma students, Natural Science Faculty, 1996; Currently, Chemical Engineer, Department of Human and Environment Protection, Chief, Radioactive Waste Management Laboratory, Institute of Nuclear Physics, Tirana. Publications: Author and co-author, over 50 articles in professional journals; Participant in numerous scientific conferences, seminars and congresses. Honour: Medal of Work, 3rd Class, 1987; Honorary Member, SOROS Foundation, Tirana, 1998; Honorary Member, Research Council, IBC, 2003. Memberships: Albanian Physics Union; Albanian Chemical Engineering Union; Balkan Physical Union; Czech-Slovak Hygienists Society; Edinburgh 98 Club. Address: Institute of Nuclear Physics, Rruga Alexander Moisiu 80, PO Box 85, Tirana, Albania. E-mail: l_qafmolla@hotmail.com

**QUAID Dennis,** b. 9 April 1954, Houston, Texas, USA. Actor. m. (2) Meg Ryan, 1991, divorced, 1 son. Education: University of Houston. Career: Stage appearances in Houston and New York; Performances with rock band The Electrics; Songwriter for films: The Night the Lights Went Out in Georgia; Tough Enough; The Big Easy; TV appearances: Bill: On His Own; Johnny Belinda; Amateur Night at the Dixie Bar and Grill; Everything That Rises; Films: September 30 1955, 1978; Crazy Mama; Our Winning Season; Seniors; Breaking Away; I Never Promised You a Rose Garden; Gorp; The Long Riders; All Night Long; Caveman; The Night the Lights Went Out in Georgia; Tough Enough; Jaws 3-D; The Right Stuff; Dreamscape; Enemy Mine; The Big Easy; Innerspace; Suspect; DOA; Everyone's All-American; Great Balls of Fire; Lie Down With Lions; Postcards from the Edge; Come and See the Paradise; A 22 Cent Romance; Wilder Napalu; Flesh and Bone; Wyatt Earp; Something To Talk About, 1995; Dragonheart, 1996; Criminal Element, 1997; Going West, 1997; Gang Related, 1997; Savior, 1997; Switchback, 1997; The Parent Trap, 1998; On Any Given Sunday, 1999; Frequency, 2000; Traffic, 2000; The Rookie, 2002; Far From Heaven, 2002; Cold Creek Manor, 2003; The Alamo, 2004; The Day After Tomorrow, 2004.

**QUANT Mary,** b. 11 February 1934, London, England. Fashion, Cosmetic and Textile Designer. m. Alexander Plunket Greene, 1957, deceased 1990, 1 son. Education: Goldsmith's College of Art, London, England. Career: Started in Chelsea, London, 1954; Director, Mary Quant Group of Companies, 1955-; Joint Chair, Mary Quant Ltd; Design Council, 1971-74; UK-USA Bicentennial Liaison Committee, 1973; Retrospective exhibition of 1960s fashion, London Museum, 1974; Victoria and Albert Museum Advisory Council, 1976-78; Senior Fellow, Royal College of Art, 1991; Director (non-executive), House of Fraser, 1997-. Publications: Quant by Quant, 1966; Colour by Quant, 1984; Quant on Make-up, 1986; Mary Quant Classic Make-up and Beauty Book, 1996. Honours: Honorary Fellow, Goldsmiths College, University of London, 1993; Honorary FRSA, 1995; Sunday Times International Fashion Award, Rex Award, USA, Annual Design Medal, Society of Industrial Artists and Designers, Piavolo d'Oro, Italy, Royal Designer for Industry, Hall of Fame Award, British Fashion Council (for outstanding contribution to British fashion), 1990; Dr hc, Winchester College of Art, 2000. Address: Mary Quant Ltd, 3 Ives Street, London SW3 2NE, England.

**QUEIROZ Francisco Manuel Monteiro de,** b. 7 June 1951, Kuito-Bie, Angola. Lawyer; Professor of Economic Law. 1 son, 2 daughters. Education: Degree in Law, Agostinho Neto University, Luanda, Angola, 1984; Postgraduate in International Economic Law, Agostinho Neto University, Angola and São Paulo University, Brazil, 1986; Master in Law, Economic Law Sciences, Classic University, Lisbon, Portugal, 1996. Appointments: Magistrate of Public Prosecution, 1979-84; Professor of Economic Law, 1085-, Director of Faculty of Law, 1986-2000, Agostinho Neto University; Parliamentary Affairs Consultant/Advisor, Cabinet of the President of Angola, 2005-; Analyst of Macroeconomics and Political Economics, Angola. Publications: Articles, book chapters and conference papers include: The Constitution Angolan Economic, 1992; The Economic Role of the Angolan State, 1996; Informal Sector of Economy in Angola: Contributes for Understanding and Framing Juridical-Economic (Master's Dissertation), 1996; No Official Sector of Economy in Angola: Juridical Perspective – Economic, 1996; The Importance of the Traditional Economy, 1996; The International Juridical Personality of the Organisations that Follow the Armed Road to Conquer the Power — The Case of UNITA, 1998; The Responsibilities of Angola in Peace in the Process of Economic Integration of SADC, 2002; The Penal Economic Right, 2003; The Rights of Foreign Investor Vis a Vis to the Angolan Investment Law, 2003. Honour: Certificate of Best Professor of the Year 2001, Faculty of Law. Memberships: Angolan Strategic Studies Association; Angolan Lawyers Association; Portuguese Lawyers Association; Canadian Association of African Studies until 2003. Address: Rua Marien N'Gouabi, 101 R/C (Lawyers Office) Luanda, Angola. E-mail: f.queiroz@ebenet.net

**QUEL Eduardo Jaime,** b. 12 January 1940, Mar del Plata, Argentina. Professor. m. Maria Silvia, 2 sons, 1 daughter. Education: Graduate, Physics, University of La Plata, Argentina, 1962; Doctor, Physical Sciences, University of Louvain, Belgium, 1970; Doctor, Physics, University of La Plata, Argentina, 1973. Appointments: Professor, National Technical University, 1964; Head, Laser Group, Citefa, Argentina, 1972-1980; Director, Ceilap Investigation Centre for Lasers and Applications, 1980-; Professor, National University of San Martin, 1995. Publications include: Laser scientific works presented at international and national Congresses; Papers and articles published in important international and national magazines; Co-Author of 2 books; Co-Editor of 1 book. Honour: Recorrido Dorado Award, 1992. Memberships: Sociedad Cientifica Argentina; Asociacion Fisica Argentina; Optical Society of America; American Geophysical Union. Address: Sucre 3774, 1430 Buenos Aires, Argentina. E-mail: quel@citefa.gov.ar

**QUIGLEY Stephen Howard,** b. 29 May 1951, Boston, Massachusetts, USA. Executive Editor. m Suzanne Elizabeth Daley, 2 sons, 1 daughter. Education: BA, French and International Relations, Dartmouth College, Hanover, New Hampshire, 1973. Appointments: College Sales Representative, Acquisitions Editor, Regional Sales Manager, Addison-Wesley Publishing Co Inc, Boston, Chicago and DC, 1973-84; Acquisitions Editor, Scott, Foresman and Company, Chicago, 1985-88; Senior Mathematics Editor, PWS Publishing Company, Boston, 1988-95; Executive Editor, John Wiley & Sons Inc, Hoboken, New Jersey and Marblehead, 1995-. Honours: Editor of the Year, 1990; Man of Achievement Award, 2002; Listed in Who's Who publications and biographical dictionaries; Dartmouth Club of the Year, 1990; Association of American Publishers Professional/Scholarly Publications Book of the Year, 2001 and 2002. Memberships include: American Mathematical Society; MAA; National Council of Teachers of Mathematics; American Statistical Association; Association for Supervision and Curriculum Development; Geological Society of America; Massachusetts Bar Association; Boston Rotary International; American Red Cross; Boy Scouts of America. Address: John Wiley & Sons Inc, Two Hooper Street, Marblehead, MA 01945, USA. E-mail: squigley@wiley.com

**QUIGLEY Vlad,** b. 17 April 1969, London, England. Celebrity Artist. Education: Southampton Institute of Art and Design; Northbrook College; Joe Orlando (EC Comics). Career: Artist and portraitist in monochrome, linear, Art Nouveau, Pop Art; Baroque; Art of (and in collaboration with) celebrity models, actresses, Gothic models; Collaborators include: Nikki Diamond, Evelyne Bennu, Red Vamp and Terri Summers; Private portraits for clients, models actresses and model agencies; Book illustrations; Pop Art Exhibitions in Britain, Europe and world-wide. Publications: Varney the Vampire; Black Planet; Carnopolis; Nymphos from Oz; Viola D'Amour; Dracula's Guest; Bride of Dracula; Taloola, Eulalie; Official Monster Raving Loony Party; Time Machine; Space Vampires. Honours: Lenape Sacred Pipe Ceremony; Adopted Lenape native American; Adopted Okibwa Native American; Awarded Bronze Sculpture, Funded by French Government; Listed in Who's Who publications and biographical dictionaries. Membership: Action for ME. Address: 276A Lower Addiscombe Road, Croydon, Surrey CR0 7AE, England. Website: www.vladquigley.com

**QUIN Louis DuBose,** b. 5 March 1928, Charleston, South Carolina, USA. Professor of Chemistry. m. Gyöngyi Szakal Quin, 2 sons, 1 daughter (by previous marriage). Education: BS, The Citadel, 1947; MA, 1949, PhD, 1952, University of North Carolina. Appointments: Chemical Industry and US Army, 1952-56; Department of Chemistry, Duke University, 1956-86, Assistant Professor to J B Duke Professor, Chair, 1970-76; Department Chemistry, University of Massachusetts, 1986-96, Head, 1986-94; Chemistry Department, University of North Carolina at Wilmington, Distinguished Visiting Professor, 1997-.99 Publications: 247 research publications, 8 authored or edited books. Honours: AE and BA Arbusov Award in Phosphorus Chemistry, 1997; North Carolina Distinguished Lecturer, 1999; Fellow, American Association for the Advancement of Science. Membership: American Chemical Society, Sigma Xi. Address: 124 White Oak Bluffs, Stella, NC 28582, USA.

**QUINN Aiden,** b. 8 March 1959, Chicago, USA. Actor. m. Elizabeth Bracco, 1987, 2 daughters. Career: Worked with various theatre groups, Chicago; Off-Broadway appearances in Sam Shepard plays: Fool for Love; A Lie of the Mind; Hamlet, Chicago; TV film: An Early Frost; Films: Reckless, 1984; The Mission; All My Sons; Stakeout; Desperately Seeking Susan; Crusoe; The Handmaid's Tale; At Play in the Fields of the Lord; Avalon; Legends of the Fall; Mary Shelley's Frankenstein, 1994; The Stars Fell on Henrietta, 1994; Haunted, 1994; Michael Collins, 1996; Looking for Richard, 1996; Commandants, 1996; The Assignment, 1997; Wings Against the Wind, 1998; This is My Father, 1998; Practical Magic, 1998; Blue Vision, 1998; The Imposters, 1998; 50 Violins, 1999; In Dreams, 1999; Two of Us, 2000; See You In My Dreams, 2000; Evelyn, 2002; A Song for a Raggy Boy, 2003; Bobby Jones: Stroke of Genius, 2004. Address: CAA, 930 Wilshire Boulevard, Beverly Hills, CA 90212, USA.

**QUINN Sheila Margaret (Dame Sheila Quinn),** b. 16 September 1920, Blackpool, Lancashire, England. Nurse. Education: SRN, Lancaster Royal Infirmary, Lancaster, 1943-47; SCM, Lordswood Maternity Hospital, Birmingham, 1948-49; Nurse Tutor Diploma, London University and Royal College of Nursing, 1955-57; BSc (Hons) Economics, London

University, 1960-63; Henley Management College, 1968. Appointments: Various Hospital Posts, 1949-57; Principal Nurse Tutor, Prince of Wales Hospital, London, 1957-61; Director, Social and Economic Welfare Division, 1961-66, Executive Director, International Council of Nurses, Geneva, 1966-70; Chief Nurse, Southampton University Hospitals, 1970-74; Chief Area Nurse, Hampshire, 1974-78; Chief Regional Nurse, Wessex, 1978-83; Chief Nursing Advisor, British Red Cross, 1983-89; International Nursing Consultant, 1989-; Advisory Committee on Nursing of European Union, 1979-87, President, 1979-82; Standing Committee of Nurses of the European Union, 1975-89, President, 1983-89. Publications: Nursing in the European Community, 1980; Caring for the Carers, 1981; ICN Past and Present, 1993; Nursing, The European Dimension, 1993; A Dame Abroad (Memoir Club), 2004; Numerous articles in national and international nursing journals. Honours: Fellow Royal College of Nursing, 1977; CBE, 1978; Hon DSc (Soc Sc), Southampton University, 1986; DBE, 1987; Christiane Reimann International Award for Nursing, 1993. Memberships: Life Vice President and Fellow Royal College of Nursing; Fellow, Royal Society of Medicine; Vice Chair, Brendon Care Foundation for the Total Care of Elderly, Winchester; Trustee and Former Chair, SCA Community Care Services, Southampton. Address: 23 Albany Park Court, Winn Rd, Southampton SO17 1EN, England. E-mail: dsmq@hotmail.co.uk

**QUINSEY Vernon Lewis,** b. 10 October 1944, Flin Flon, Manitoba, Canada. Professor and Head of Psychology. m. Jill L Atkinson, 4 sons, 1 daughter. Education: BSc, University of North Dakota at Grand Forks, 1966; MSc, 1969, PhD 1970, University of Massachusetts at Amherst. Appointments: Director of Research, Penetanguishene Mental Health Centre, 1976-84 and 1986-88; Visiting Scientist, Institut Philippe Pinel, 1984-86; Professor of Psychology, 1988-, Psychiatry, 1994-, Biology, 2003-, Queen's University, Kingston, Ontario, Canada. Publications: 8 books; Over 150 articles and chapters. Honours: Senior Research Fellowship, Ontario Mental Health Foundation, 1997-2001. Memberships: Human Behavior and Evolution Society; Association for the Treatment of Sexual Abusers; International Academy of Sex Research; Fellow, Canadian Psychological Association. Address: Psychology Department, Queen's University, Kingston, Ontario, Canada, K7L 3N6.

**QUINT David Paul,** b. 24 July 1950, Iowa, USA. Investment Banker. m. Kathleen Svern, 2 sons, 2 daughters. Education: Bachelor of Arts, 1972, Juris Doctorate, 1975, University of Notre Dame. Appointments: Attorney, Arter & Hadden, 1975-83; Managing Director, Belden & Blake (UK) Inc., 1983-92; Chief Executive, RP&C International, 1992-. Publications: Articles, Notre Dame Law Review. Honours: Member, Notre Dame Law Review; Fellow, Rotary International. Membership: Ohio State Bar Association. Address: 31A St James's Square, London, SW1Y 4JR, England. E-mail: dquint@rpcint.co.uk

**QUIRK Sir Randolph (Baron Quirk of Bloomsbury),** b. 12 July 1920, Isle of Man, England. Emeritus Professor of English Language and Literature; Writer. m. (1) Jean Williams, 1946, divorced 1979, 2 sons, (2) Gabriele Stein, 1984. Education: BA, 1947, MA, 1949, PhD, 1951, DLitt, 1961, University College, London. Appointments: Lecturer in English, 1947-54, Professor of English Language, 1960-68, Quain Professor of English Language and Literature, 1968-81, University College, London; Commonwealth Fund Fellow, Yale University and University of Michigan, 1951-52; Reader in English Language and Literature, 1954-58, Professor of English Language, 1958-60, University of Durham; Vice Chancellor, 1981-85, University of London; President, British Academy; Independent Peer, House of Lords. Publications: The Concessive Relation in Old English Poetry,

1954; Studies in Communication (with A J Ayer and others), 1955; An Old English Grammar (with C L Wrenn), 1955, enlarged edition (with S E Deskis), 1994; Charles Dickens and Appropriate Language, 1959; The Teaching of English (with A H Smith), 1959, revised edition, 1964; The Study of the Mother-Tongue, 1961; The Use of English, 1962, enlarged edition, 1968; Prosodic and Paralinguistic Features in English (with D Crystal), 1964; A Common Language (with A H Marckwardt), 1964; Investigating Linguistic Acceptability (with J Svartvik), 1966; Essays on the English Language: Mediaeval and Modern, 1968; Elicitation Experiments in English (with S Greenbaum), 1970; A Grammar of Contemporary English (with S Greenbaum, G Leech, and J Svartvik), 1972; The English Language and Images of Matter, 1972; A University Grammar in English (with S Greenbaum), 1973; The Linguist and the English Language, 1974; Old English Literature: A Practical Introduction (with V Adams and D Davy), 1975; A Corpus of English Conversation (with J Svartvik), 1980; Style and Communication in the English Language, 1982, revised edition, 1984, A Comprehensive Grammar of the English Language (with S Greenbaum, G Leech and J Svartvik), 1985; English in the World (with H Widdowson), 1985; Words at Work: Lectures on Textual Structure, 1986; English in Use (with G Stein), 1990; A Student's Grammar of the English Language (with S Greenbaum), 1990, revised edition 1997; An Introduction to Standard English (with G Stein), 1993; Grammatical and Lexical Variance in English, 1995. Contributions to: Scholarly books and journals. Honours: Commander of the Order of the British Empire, 1976; Knighted, 1985; Life Peerage, 1994; Numerous honorary doctorates; Various fellowships. Memberships: Academia Europaea; American Academy of Arts and Sciences; British Academy, President, 1985-89. Address: University College London, Gower Street, London WC1E 6BT, England.

# R

**RAATH Andries W G,** b. 15 December 1954, Klerksdorp, Republic of South Africa. Senior Professor. m. Marianda Raath, 1 son, 1 daughter. Education: B Juris, LLB, PU for CHE; MA and D Phil, University of the Free State, South Africa. Appointments: Admitted as Advocate of the Supreme Court of South Africa, 1979; Advocate of the Supreme Court of Baphuthatswana, 1982; Senior Lecturer in Jurisprudence, University of Baphuthatswana, 1980; Senior Lecturer, 1984, Professor, 1994, Senior Professor, 2004, University of the Free State. Publications: More than 300 researched academic articles and popular academic treatises; More than 30 books on subjects including law and history. Memberships: More than 20 national and international organisations. Address: Faculty of Law, University of the Free State, PO Box 339, Bloemfontain, Republic of South Africa. E-mail: raatha.rd@mail.uovs.ac.za

**RACZKA Tony,** b. 16 January 1957, Pottsville, Pennsylvania. Artist; Educator. m. Patricia G Martinez, 1 daughter, 1 step-daughter. Education: BFA, Northern Arizona University, Flagstaff, USA, 1978; MFA, Northern Illinois University DeKalb, USA, 1980; Postgraduate Studies, University of California, San Diego, USA, 1991-92. Appointments: Instructor of Art, Southwestern College, Chula Vista, California, 1981-84; Instructor of Art, Northern Arizona University, Flagstaff, Arizona, 1983; Registrar, Mingei International Museum of Folk Art, San Diego California, 1985-86; Instructor of Art, San Diego State University, 1987; Senior Museum Preparator, University Art Gallery, University of California, San Diego, California, 1989-95. Publications: To Consociate and Foster the Self, 2000; Words of Wonder, Wit, and Well?....Well Being, 2000; The Blending of Natures and the Perception of the Real, 2000. Honours: Exhibitions at commercial galleries: Quint Gallery, La Jolla, 1982, San Diego, 1983; Printworks, Chicago, 1982, 1984; One-Person Show: Queens College Art Center, CUNY, Flushing, New York, 1999-; Recipient, Pollock-Krasner Foundation Award, 2001. Memberships: International Society of Phenomenology and the Sciences of Life; San Diego Museum of Art. Address: 4430 42nd Street #2, San Diego, CA 92116, USA. E-mail: raczkatony@aol.com

**RADIC Njegomir,** b. 17 September 1943, Vrgorac, Croatia. Professor of Chemistry. m. Ksenija, 1 son. Education: Graduate, Faculty of Chemical Technology, University of Split, 1969; MS, 1974, PhD, 1978, Chemical Sciences, University of Zagreb; Postdoctoral Fellow, University of Cincinnati, USA, 1981-82. Appointments: Teaching Assistant, Assistant Professor, Associate Professor, Professor, 1996-, Faculty of Chemical Technology, Split. Publications: Over 50 papers mostly in international journals; Main research interests include the preparation and application of potentiometric sensors. Memberships: American Chemical Society; Croatian Chemical Society. Address: Sizgoriceva 20, 21000 Split, Croatia.

**RADONS Jürgen,** b. 21 February 1960, Lünen, Germany. Biologist. m. Vera Beatrix Langhammer, 9 September 1999. Education: Diploma, Biology, 1985; PhD, Biochemistry, 1991; Habilitation, Experimental Medicine, 2004. Appointments: Postgraduate Fellow, Cellular and Molecular Immunology, Biochemistry, 1986-91; Postdoctoral Fellow, Immunology and Biochemistry, 1991-92, Diabetology, 1992-96; Research Fellow, Rheumatology, 1996-98, Molecular Immunology, 1998-; Lecturer, Senior Scientist, Experimental Medicine, 2004-. Publications: Several articles in professional journals. Honours: International Scientist of the Year 2001; Leader of Science, Technology and Engineering, 2001; Great Minds

of the 21st Century; One of 500 Leaders of Influence; 2000 Outstanding Scientists of the 20th Century; 2000 Outstanding Scientists of the 21st Century; 2000 Outstanding Intellectuals of the 21st Century; 2000 Eminent Scientists of Today; Five Hundred Leaders of Influence. Membership: The American Biographical Institute, Research Board of Advisors. Address: Arnulf-Enders-Strasse 5, D-93059 Regensburg, Germany.

**RADOUKANOV Svetlozar,** b. 28 December 1952, Veliko Tarnovo, Bulgaria. Cellist. m. Nelli, 1 daughter. Education: Graduate, Cello, Music Academy, Sofia, Bulgaria, 1979; Master class training with Professor Sigfrid Palm, Bayreuth, Germany. Career: Solo cello player and leader of a group, Sofia National Opera, 1979-; Solo player in chamber orchestras; Participant in national and international competitions; Has recorded compact discs with famous Bulgarian singers including: Don Carlos with Nicola Ghiuselev; Ein Maskenball with Maria Hristova; Other recordings with foreign opera orchestras; CD Recital, Bulgarian National Radio, 2003: Golden Fond, Teleman, Sarabande, Korelli, Adagio, Brahms - Mina, Sleeping Song, Kassado - To My Daughter; Artin Poturlian - Voices and Steps for Solo Cello, 2003. Honour: National Competition "Svetoslav Obretenov", 1978. Address: Dobrotic Str 43, vh B ap 31, Sofia-1330, Bulgaria.

**RADULESCU Elena,** b. 14 May 1927, Rosiorii-de-Vede, Romania. Professor; Senior Specialist in Haematology. m. Alexandru A Matusa, divorced 1969, 1 child. Education: Faculty of General Medicine, Cluj, 1950s; MD, PhD, Medical Sciences, University of Medicine and Pharmacy "Iuliu Hateganu", 1977; Postgraduate studies in London, England; Certificate as a University Professor, Romanian Medical Sciences Academy, 1999. Appointments: Laboratory Physician, Oradea Hospital, -1957; Laboratory Specialist, CFR Hospital; Researcher, Department of Haematology, Oncologic Institute "Ion Chiricuta", Cluj, 1966-91; Senior Researcher, Cluj-Napoca branch of Biotehnos SA, Bucharest, 1991-93; Senior Researcher, 2nd Paediatric Clinic, Cluj, 1993-2002; Senior Specialist, Clinical Laboratory, Polyclinic, 2002-. Publications: Numerous papers and articles; Contributions to the study of leukaemia, lymphomas and myelodysplastic syndromes. Honours: Honorary Member, Professor's Council of University Medicine and Pharmacy, 1992; First degree Diplomas of Excellence; Listed in national and international biographical dictionaries. Memberships: International Federation of Researchers for Science and Technology; World Society of Cellular and Molecular Biology; International Society of Haematology. Address: Henri Coandă Nr 1, Ap 16, Cluj-Napoca, 400417, Romania.

**RAE John Malcolm,** b. 20 March 1931, London, England. Writer; Educationist. Education: MA, Sidney Sussex College, Cambridge, 1955; PhD, King's College, London. Appointment: Headmaster, Westminster School, London, 1970-86. Publications: The Custard Boys, 1960; Conscience and Politics, 1970; The Golden Crucifix, 1974; The Treasure of Westminster Abbey, 1975; Christmas is Coming, 1976; Return to the Winter Place, 1979; The Third Twin: A Ghost Story, 1980; The Public School Revolution, 1981; Letters from School, 1987; Too Little, Too Late?, 1989; Delusions of Grandeur, 1993; Letters to Parents, 1998; Sister Genevieve, 2001. Contributions to: Encounter; Times Literary Supplement; Times Educational Supplement; Times; Sunday Telegraph. Honour: United Nations Award for Film Script, 1962. Address: 25 Cedar Lodge, Lythe Hill Park, Haslemere, Surrey GU27 3TD, England.

**RAE John William,** b. 16 December 1938, UK. Lawyer. Education: MA, Queen's College Oxford. Appointments: Territorial Army: 2nd Lieutenant, 5 Battalion Queen's Royal

Regiment, 1959-60, Lieutenant, 3 Battalion Queen's Royal Surrey Regiment, 1961-63, TA Reserve of Officers, 1963-67; Regular Army Reserve of Officers II, 1967-85, 1988-; Hon. Artillery Co (HSF), 1985-88; Called to the Bar, Inner Temple, 1961; Worked way around world, 1962-64; International Commercial Lawyer (German speaker), 1965-78; Practising Barrister, 1979-95; Director, Campden Hill Court Ltd, 1995-98, 2001-. Memberships: Committee, Campden Hill Residents' Association; Oxford University Society (Chairman West London Branch, 1968-96); Aldersgate Ward Club; Friends of the City Churches; Friends of Holland Park, Kensington; Notting Hill Gate Advisory Group (RBK&C); Countryside Alliance; Freeman City of London; Master, Worshipful Company of Plumbers, 1982-83, Member, Court of Assistants; Trustee: St Michael's Trust, St Magnus the Martyr Church; Freeman, Worshipful Company of Painter-Stainers; Clubs: Athenaeum; Coningsby. Address: 16a Campden Hill Court, Campden Hill Road, London W8 7HS, England.

**RAIMONDI Ruggero,** b. 3 October 1941, Bologna, Italy. Singer (Bass). m. Isabel Maier. Education: Student: Theresa Pediconi, Rome, 1961-62, Armando Piervenanzi, 1963-65. Debut: Spoleto, 1964. Career: Appeared Rome Opera; Principal opera houses in Italy; Metropolitan Opera, 1970; Munich; La Scala; Lyric Opera; Chicago; Paris Opera; Sang Don Giovanni at Gyndebourne, 1969 and throughout the world; Covent Garden, 1972 as Fiesco in Simon Boccanegra; Vienna Staatsoper, 1982 as Don Quichotte; Hamburg, 1985 as Gounod's Mephistopheles; Sang Selim in Il Turco in Italia; Chicago, 1987, as Mozart's Count; Pesaro, 1985 and Vienna as Don Profundo in Il Viaggio a Reims; Sang in the opening concert at the Bastille Opéra, 1989; 25th Anniversary Celebration at the Barbican Hall, 1990; Scarpia in a televised Tosca from Rome, 1992; Il Barbiere di Siviglia, 1992; Sang Rossini's Mosè at Covent Garden, 1994; Donizetti's Don Pasquale; Iago in Otello, Salzburg, 1996; Don Quichotte at Rome and throughout the world; Sang Thomas Becket in Pizetti's Murder in the Cathedral, 2000; Sang his first Don Alfonso in Cosi fan Tutti, 2004; Opera production since 1986. Films: Sang Don Giovanni in Joseph Losey's film of Mozart's opera; Sang Escamillo in Francesco Rosi's Carmen; Boris in Zulawsky's film Boris Godunov; Appears in the movie Tosca directed by Benoît Jacquot, 2001; Recordings: 2 Verdi Requiems; Complete operas: Attila, I Vespri Sicilliani, La Bohème, Aida, Don Carlos, Forza de Destino, Il Pirata, Norma, Don Giovanni, Carmen, Nozze di Figaro, Italiana in Algeri, Boris Godunov; Pelléas et Mélisande, Turandot, Barbiere di Siviglia, Cenerentola, Simon Boccanegra, Macbeth, Nabucco, I Lombardi, Tosca. Honours: Recipient, Competition Award, Spoleto; Commandeur des Arts et Lettres, France; Officier de la Légion d'Honneur, France; Grand Ufficiale Della Republica, Italy; Chevalier de l'Ordre de Malte; Citizen of Honour, City of Athens; Commandeur du Mérite Culurel, Monaco. Address: 140 bis, rue Lecourbe, F-75015 Paris, France.

**RAINE Craig (Anthony),** b. 3 December 1944, Shildon, County Durham, England. Poet; Writer. m. Ann Pasternak Slater, 27 April 1972, 3 sons, 1 daughter. Education: Honours Degree in English Language and Literature, 1966, BPhil, 1968, Exeter College, Oxford. Appointments: Lecturer, Exeter College, Oxford, 1971-72, Lincoln College, Oxford, 1974-75, Christ Church, Oxford, 1976-79; Books Editor, New Review, London, 1977-78; Editor, Quarto, London, 1979-80; Poetry Editor, New Statesman, London, 1981, Faber & Faber, London, 1981-91; Fellow, New College, Oxford, 1991-; Editor, Arete magazine, 1999-. Publications: Poetry: The Onion, Memory, 1978; A Journey to Greece, 1979; A Martian Sends a Postcard Home, 1979; A Free Translation, 1981; Rich, 1984, 1953: A Version of Racine's Andromaque, 1990; History: The Home

Movie, 1994; Clay. Whereabouts Unknown, 1996; A la recherche du temps perdu, 2000; Collected Poems 1978-99, 2000. Other: The Electrification of the Soviet Union (libretto), 1986; A Choice of Kipling's Prose (editor), 1987; Haydn and the Valve Trumpet (essays), 1990; In Defence of T S Eliot (essays), 2000; Collected Poems 1978-1999, 2000; Rudyard Kipling: The Wish House and Other Stories (editor), 2002. Contributions to: Periodicals. Honours: 1st Prizes, Cheltenham Festival Poetry Competition, 1977, 1978; 2nd Prize, National Poetry Competition, 1978; Prudence Farmer Awards, New Statesman, 1979, 1980; Cholmondeley Poetry Award, 1983; Sunday Times Award for Literary Excellence, 1998. Memberships: PEN; Royal Society of Literature. Address: c/o New College, Oxford OX1 3BN, England.

**RAITT Bonnie,** b. 8 November 1949, Burbank, California, USA. Musician (guitar, piano). Education: Radcliffe College. Career: Performer, blues clubs, US East Coast; Concerts include: MUSE concert, Madison Square Garden with Bruce Springsteen, Jackson Browne, Carly Simon, The Doobie Brothers, 1979; Roy Orbison Tribute Concert with artists including: Whoopi Goldberg; kd lang; Bob Dylan; B B King, 1990; Performances with artists including: Stevie Wonder, Bruce Springsteen, Aretha Franklin, Willie Nelson, Elton John. Recordings: Albums include: Bonnie Raitt, 1971; Give It Up, 1972; Takin' My Time, 1973; Streetlights, 1974; Home Plate, 1975; Sweet Forgiveness, 1977; The Glow, 1979; Green Light, 1982; Nine Lives, 1986; Nick Of Time, 1989; The Bonnie Raitt Collection, 1990; Luck Of The Draw, 1991; Road Tested, 1995; Fundamental, 1998; Singles include: Something to Talk About, 1991; Not the Only One, 1992; Burning Down the House, 1996. Honours include: 4 Grammy Awards: Album of Year; Best Rock Vocal Performance; Best Female Pop Vocal Performance; Best Traditional Blues Performance (with John Lee Hooker), and numerous nominations. Address: PO Box 626, Los Angeles, CA 90078, USA.

**RAJ Mariapragasam Arputha,** b. 24 May 1944, Mullanvilai, Tamil Nadu. Worker in vineyard of Jesus. m. Boomadevi Maria Packiam, 3 sons, 1 daughter. Education: Diploma in Company Law; Diploma in Labour Law and Administrative Law; Diploma in Taxation Laws; Diploma in Theology; Diploma in D T P; P G Diploma in Personnel Management and Industrial Relations; BA; Bachelor of General Law; Bachelor of Law; Graduate in Theology; BTh, Master of Biblical Studies; Master of Religious Education; Doctor of Divinity; Doctor of Ministry; LLD; PhD; DLitt; ThD. Appointments: Catechist, Itinerant Evangelist; Cup-bearer in C.S.I; Assistant to Presbyter, Sunday Class Teacher; Vacation Bible School Teacher, Director; Preacher, Bible Teacher; Youth Leader; Christian Leader; Tracts and Bibles Distributor; Prayer Partner; Bible Hymns and Lyrics Composer; Writer in Christian Journals; Director of Bible Institute and Library. Publications: Biblical Essays; Christian Songs; Sermons; Biblical Poems; Publisher in many Christian journals. Honours: Divine Dazzle; Philanthropic Devotee; Man of Religious Education; Awards from Christian Arts and Literature League; Biblical Leader Award, Call Christian Society, Madras. Memberships: Associate Minister, Restoration Fellowship International; Association of Theologians; Amen Prayer Army; Indian Prayer Force; Prayer Partner of Evangelical Literature Service; Research Board of Advisors, American Biographical Institute. Address: Director of Miracle Centre Bible Institute and Universal Christian Unit, 66 – Alagapuri Nagar, Devakottai Extension, PO 630303 Tamil Nadu State, South India.

**RAJASEKARAN Ekambaram,** b. 5 November 1966, Thanjavur, India. Bioinformaticist. m. R Meenal, 1 son, 1 daughter. Education: DMLT, 1984, BSc, 1987, MSc, 1989, PhD,

1995. Appointments: Laboratory Technician, Cholan Clinical Laboratory, Thanjavur, India, 1984-87; Scientist-in-Charge, Calyx Software Ltd, New Delhi, 1997-99. Research interests include: Biostatistics, thermodynamics, electrostatics, software use in chemical research, theoretical studies on biological systems. Publications: Numerous papers and articles contributed to peer-reviewed journals, including, Solvation Thermodynamics of Amino Acids: An Assessment of the Electrostatic Contribution and Force Field Dependence, 1997 (co-author); Counterion Condensation in DNA systems: The cylindrical Poisson-Boltzmann model revisited, 1994; Conference papers include, Computer Simulations of Atomic Force Microscope: Frictional Anisotropy and the Role of Surface Relaxation, 1996; Role of Software Tools in Chemical Research, 1999. Honours: Listed in several international biographical directories. Memberships: Indian Biophysical Society; Biotechnological Society of India. Address: Umbalapadi Post, Papanasam Taluk, Thanjavur 614203, Tamil Nadu, India. E-mail: scindu@sancharnet.in

**RAKOWSKI Andrzej,** b. 16 June 1931, Warsaw, Poland, Musicologist; Acoustician. m. Magdalena Jakobczyk, 1 son, 2 daughters. General Education: MA, 1957, DSc, 1963, Upper PhD (habilitation), 1977, Warsaw University. Musical Education: MA, State College of Music in Warsaw, 1958. Appointments: Music Producer, Polish Disc Recording Company, 1956-58; Acoustic Consultant, Opera National Theatre, 1966-70; Assistant, Associate, Professor of Musical Acoustics, 1955-2001-, Deputy Rector, 1972-75, Rector (President), 1981-87, Head of the Chair of Music Acoustics, 1968-2001, Chopin Academy of Music, Warsaw; Part-time Professor, Institute of Musicology, Warsaw University, 1987-2003, A Mickiewicz University, Poznan, 1997-; Visiting Professor: Central Institute for the Deaf and Washington University St Louis, USA, 1977-78, McGill University, Montreal, 1985, Hebrew University, Jerusalem, 1991, New University of Lisbon, 2004. Publications: Books: Selected Topics on Acoustics, 1959; Categorical Perception of Pitch in Music, 1978; The Access of Youth to Musical Culture, 1984; Studies on Pitch and Timbre of Sound in Music (editor), 1999; Creation and Perception of Sound Sequences in Music (editor), 2002; Over 120 articles to scientific journals including: Acustica; Acta Acoustica; Journal of the Acoustical Society of America; Psychology of Music; Musicae Scientiae; Perception Psychophysics, Muzyka. Honours: Awards of the Minister of Culture in Poland, 1966, 1968, 1982, 1987; Polish State Awards, Silver Cross of Merit, 1981, Golden Cross of Merit, 1973; Order of the Revival of Poland, Bachelor's Cross, 1982, Officers Cross, 2002. Memberships: Polish Music Council, Vice President, 1984-89; Union of Polish Composers; Polish Academy of Sciences, 1994-, Acoustical Committee President, 1996-; European Society for Cognitive Sciences of Music, President, 2000-2003; Honorary Member, Polish Acoustical Society; Honorary Member, Polish Phonetic Association; Fellow, Acoustical Society of America. Address: Pogonowskiego 20, Warsaw 01564, Poland. E-mail: rakowski@chopin.edu.pl

**RALPH Philip Pyman,** b. 4 August 1931, Walton on Thames, England. Accountant; Merchant Banker. m. Joan Frances Scott Brown, 2 sons. Education: Clare College, Cambridge, 1952-55; Articles, Albert Goodman & Co, 1955-58; Peat, Marwick Mitchell & Co, 1958-62. Appointments: Non-Executive Director, Chamberlin & Hill, 1971-98; Hill Samuel & Co Ltd, 1962-71; Director, 1968-71; Director, Head of Corporate Finance, William Brandt & Co Ltd, 1973-76; Director, Head of Corporate Finance, Charterhouse Japhet Ltd, 1976-81; Associate Director of Corporate Finance, The General Electric Company plc, 1981-88; Executive Vice Chairman, 1988-96; Non-Executive Director, 1996-99, The Summit Group plc;

Non-Executive Director, Olim Convertible Trust, 1989-99; Non-Executive Director, Northgate Info Solutions, 1996-2000; Member of Council, The Girls Day School Trust, 1997-2003. Memberships: Fellow, Institute of Chartered Accountants, 1958-; Currently trustee and/or committee member for several charities. Address: Oak Tree House, Warboys Road, Kingston on Thames, Surrey KT2 7LS, England. E-mail: philip.ralph@oaktreehouse.co.uk

**RALPH Richard Peter,** b. 27 April 1946, London, England. Diplomat. (1) Margaret Elizabeth Coulthurst, 1970, divorced 2001, 1 son, 1 daughter, (2) Jemma Victoria Elizabeth Marlor, 2002. Education: Honours Degree, Politics, Edinburgh University, Scotland. Appointments: Joined, HM Diplomatic Service, 1969; Third Secretary, Foreign and Commonwealth Office (FCO), 1969-70; Third, then Second, Secretary, Laos, 1970-74; Second, then First, Secretary, Portugal, 1974-77; First Secretary, FCO, 1977-81; First Secretary and Head of Chancery, Zimbabwe, 1981-85; First Secretary, then Counsellor, FCO, 1985-89; Counsellor, Washington, USA, 1989-93; Ambassador, Latvia, 1993-95, Governor, Falkland Islands, Commissioner for South Georgia and the South Sandwich Islands, 1996-99; Ambassador, Romania (also accredited to Moldova), 1999-2002; Ambassador to Peru, 2003-. Honours: Companion of the Order of St Michael and St George (CMG); Commander of the Royal Victorian Order(CVO). E-mail: richard.ralph@fco.gov.uk

**RAMDIN Ronald Andrew,** b. 20 June 1942, Union Park Road, Marabella, Trinidad. Historian; Biographer; Novelist; Writer; Lecturer. m. Irma de Freitas, 1969, divorced 1983, 1 son. Education: School Leaving Certificates, Harmony Hall Canadian Mission School, Trinidad; Diploma in Speech and Drama, New Era Academy of Drama and Music, 1963; Diploma in Industrial Relations and Trade Union Studies, University of Middlesex, 1977; BSc, Economics, London School of Economics and Political Science, 1982; DLitt, University of London, 1995. Publications: From Chattel Slave to Wage Earner, 1982; Introductory Text: The Black Triangle, 1984; The Making of the Black Working Class in Britain, 1987; Paul Robeson: The Man and His Mission, 1987; World in View: West Indies, 1990; The Other Middle Passage, 1995; Reimaging Britain: 500 years of Black and Asian History, 1999; Arising From Bondage: A History of the Indo-Caribbean People, 2000; Post-War Immigration, in the Folio Society's England, 1945-2000; Martin Luther King Jr, 2004; Rama's Voyage: A Novel, 2004; Mary Seacole, 2005; Freelance journalist with BBC World Service; Guest appearances and interviews over many years as author on BBC Radios Four and Two and on BBC and ITV television programmes including the double award-winning "The Unknown Soldiers"; Lectured extensively in libraries, schools and universities across Britain and internationally, including Seville and Sorbonne; Invited to give presitigious Whitbread Cardiff Lecture in 1997; Appeared on first day of 2000 Cheltenham Festival with Professor Richard Hoggart, Professor Felipe Fernandez-Armesto and Peter Jay, former British Ambassador of the United States; Contributions to: Anglo-British Review; City Limits; Dragon's Teeth; Race Today; Caribbean Times; West Indian Digest; History Workshop Journal. Honours: Scarlet Ibis Medal, Gold Award, Trinidad and Tobago High Commission, London, 1990; Hansib, Caribbean Times, Community Award, Britain, 1990. Memberships: Society of Authors; Fellow, Royal Historical Society; Fellow, Royal Society of Arts. Address: 22 Plympton Road, Kilburn, London NW6 7EG, England. E-mail: ron@ronramdin.com

**RAMOS Theodore Sanchez de Pina,** b. 30 October 1928, Oporto, Portugal. Portrait Painter. m. Julia Nan Rushbury, separated, 4 sons, 1 deceased. Education: Colegio Araujo

Lima, Oporto; The Northern Polytechnic, London; Hornsey School of Art; RAS Dip, Royal Academy Schools, 1949-54. Appointments: Portrait painter; Former Visiting Lecturer, Harrow School of Art; Brighton College of Art; Royal Academy Schools. Publications: Numerous illustrations for Penguin books and other publishers. Memberships: East India Club; Marylebone Cricket Club; Reynolds Club. Address: Studio 3, Chelsea Farm House, Milmans Street, London SW10 0DA, England.

**RAMOS-SOBRADOS Juan I,** b. 28 January 1953, Bernardos, Segovia, Spain. Professor of Mechanical Engineering. m. Mercedes Naveiro, 2 sons. Education; B Aeronautical Engineering, 1975, Dr Engineering, 1983, Madrid Polytechnic University, Spain, 1975; MA, Mechanical and Aerospace Engineering, 1979, PhD, Mechanical and Aerospace Engineering, 1980, Princeton University, USA. Appointments: Research Engineer, Helicopter Design, Madrid, 1976-77; Research Assistant, 1977-78, Teaching Assistant, 1979, Department of Mechanical and Aerospace Engineering, Princeton, New Jersey, USA; Instructor, 1979-80, Assistant Professor, 1980-85, Faculty Member of Center for Energy and Environmental Studies, 1980-91, 1991-93, Associate Professor, 1985-89, Professor, 1989-93, Department of Mechanical Engineering, Carnegie Mellon University, Pittsburgh, Pennsylvania; Visiting Professor, Universita degli Studi di Roma Tor Vergata, Rome, 1988-89; Visiting Professor, 1990-91, Professor, 1992- E T S Ingenieros Industriales, Universidad de Malaga, Spain. Publications: Book: Internal Combustion Engine Modelling, 1989; Over 250 papers in journals, proceedings of international conferences on fluid mechanics, combustion and applied mathematics. Honours: Prize Francisco Arranz, Association of Aeronautical Engineers, Madrid, 1975; Aeronautical Engineering Medal, Ministry of Education and Science, Madrid, 1977; National Award in Aeronautical Engineering, King Juan Carlos I of Spain, 1977; Daniel and Florence Guggenheim Fellow, Princeton University September 1977 - January 1978, honorary May to August, 1978; George Van Ness Lothrop Fellowship in Engineering, Princeton, 1979-80; Ralph R Teetor Award, Society of Automotive Engineers, 1981. Address: ETS Ingenieros Industriales, Universidad de Malaga, Plaza El Ejido s/n, 29013 Malaga, Spain.

**RAMPLING Charlotte,** b. 5 February 1946, London, England. Actress. m. (2) Jean Michel Jarre, 1978, 2 sons, 1 step daughter (1 son from previous marriage). Career: Films include: The Knack, 1963; Rotten to the Core, Georgy Girl, The Long Duel, Kidnapping, The Damned, 1969; Skibum, Corky, 1970; 'Tis Pity She's a Whore, Henry VIII and His Six Wives, 1971; Asylum, 1972; The Night Porter; Giordano Bruno, Zardoz, Caravan to Vaccares, 1973; The Flesh of the Orchid, Yuppi Du, 1974-75; Farewell My Lovely, Foxtrot, 1975; Sherlock Holmes in New York, Orca – The Killer Whale, The Purple Taxi, 1976; Stardust Memories, 1980; The Verdict, 1983; Viva la Vie, 1983; Beauty and Sadness, 1984; He Died with His Eyes Open, 1985; Max mon Amour, Max My Love, 1985; Angel Heart, 1987; Paris by Night, 1988; Dead on Arrival, 1989; Helmut Newton, Frames from the Edge, Hammers Over the Anvil, 1991; Time is Money, 1992; La marche de Radetsky, TV Film, 1994; Asphalt Tango, 1995; Wings of a Dove, 1996; The Cherry Orchard, 1998; Signs and Wonders, 1999; Aberdeen, 1999; Fourth Angel, Under the Sand, Superstition, 2000; See How They Run, 2002; TV: numerous appearances. Honours: Chevalier Ordre des Arts et des Lettres, 1986; Cesar d'honneur, 2001; Chevalier, Legion d'honneur, 2002. Address: c/o Artmédia, 20 avenue Rapp, 75007 Paris, France.

**RANDLE Peter,** b. 16 April 1951, Warwickshire, England. Director; Computer Consultant. Education: BSc (Hons),

London University, 1973; MSc, Queen's University, Canada, 1975; Doctorand, Max-Planck-Institute, Heidelberg, Germany, 1975-78; Chartered Chemist, 1976; Chartered Engineer, 1990; Chartered Mathematician, 1996; Chartered Scientist, 2004; Chartered IT Practitioner, 2004 Certified Qualified Teacher, UK, 1979. Appointments: Managing Director, Global ICT Consultancy Ltd; Head of Computing, Standard Telephones &Cables/ITT Inc, 1982-84; Director Computing and Order Processing, Micro Business Systems plc, 1985-86; Partner, Principal, Nova Consultancy, England, 1980-92; IP Advisor: Council of European Professional Information Societies (CEPIS), 1997-, EURIM, 1996-99, electronic working groups including, Health Informatics, World Health Organisation and G-8 Standards and IEEE WWW Best Practice; Member, UK's DTI Encryption Group; Founder Member, British Computer Society, Software Copyright Committee, 1983-98. Publications: Articles in professional journals and government and G-8 reports. Honour: Fellow Royal Society of Medicine as a Distinguished Scientist, 2004. Memberships include: New York Academy of Sciences; Institute of Directors, UK; Royal Society of Chemistry, UK; Computer Society of IEEE, USA; Canadian Information Processing Society; Associate Member, Incorporated Society of Musicians; Charitable work with Pituitary Foundation (UK), Awareness representative for Dorset. Address: c/o 180 Grays, Weymouth, Dorset DT4 9SW, England. E-mail: peter_randle@computer.org

**RANDLE CLINTON Dorothy Louise,** b. 4 June 1925, Des Moines, Iowa, USA. Writer. m. Moses Clinton, 1 son. Education: Bachelor of Fine Arts, Drake University, 1949. Appointments: Bookkeeper; Recreation Leader; Teacher; Government Worker. Publications: Numerous; Poems include: Masks in a Strange Wind; Without the Bubbling; Parting Thoughts; It's Not Always Red; Arrant Bullet; The Look and the See; Bizarre Responses; Temporary Symphony; Then and Now; Memory Lapse; A Human Viper; The Comics Double Mouth; A Cruise. Honours: Inducted into International Poetry Hall of Fame; Several Editor's Choice Awards; Two Editor's Preference Awards of Excellence. Membership: International Society of Poets. Address: 1530 Maple, Des Moines, IA 50316, USA.

**RANE Ganesh P,** b. 5 July 1943, Karwar, India. Businessman; UN Consultant. m. Suchita, 1 daughter. Education: ADV DME, 1964; Graduate, Adv Engg, 1965; PGDIM (Bom), 1974; DOM, (Bom), 1975; EDP-Prof Mgt (USA), 1976; EDP-Prod Mgt (Bom), 1975; PhD (California, USA), 1995. Appointments: Design and Development Engineer, 1865-76; Production Manager, 1976-80; Management Educator, Entrepreneurship Trainer to Management Institutes in Mumbai and overseas, 1976-82; Chief Chartered Engineer and Management Consultant in Somalia, 1980-82; UNIDO Chief Technical Advisor to PDR Yemen, 1982-88; UNIDO Consultant, Somalia, 1986; UNIDO Consultant to Syrian Arab Republic, 1990-91; ILO Consultant to LDC Programme, 1990-91; UNDP/UNIDO Chief Technical Advisor (CTA) to Vietnam, 1990-94; Chief Executive Director, President, Entrepreneur, RRR Industries, 1987-; RANE Consultancy Services Pvt Ltd, 1988-; ULTRA-EDM Tools and Components Co Pvt Ltd, 1994-; MITSUCHI EDM Technologies Pvt Ltd, 1996-. Publications: Papers presented at international and national conferences and in journals. Honours: Presidents Honour, Somalia, 1982; Honour of Merit, Ministry of Industry and Trade of Government, Yemen, 1988; Vijaya Shree Award, Enriching Human Life and Outstanding International Achievement, 1994; The Best Citizens of India Award, 1999; District Chairman, Rotary UNAIDS Co-operation Programme on HIV/AIDS, Rotary International District 3140, 1998-; RRR Industries, a SMI leader of business initiative to "Break the Silence", active on care economy at the world of work, workplace awareness to unorganised and SMI Sector, 1998-; Numerous Rotary International Awards include: RI Presidential Citation Award, 1997, 1998, 1999. Memberships: Licensed Professional Engineer, ASME International (USA), 1974-; Licensed Industrial Engineer, European Institute of Industrial Engineers, 1974-; Institute of Management Services, UK; Institute of Mechanical Engineers, UK; International Golfing Fellowship of Rotary. Address: RRR Industries, A/109 Ansa Industrial Estate, Saki-Vimar Road, Mumbai 400072, India.

**RANSFORD Tessa,** b. 8 July 1938, Bombay, India. Poet; Writer; Editor. m. (1) Iain Kay Stiven, 29 August 1959, divorced 1986, 1 son, 3 daughters, (2) Callum Macdonald, 7 December 1989, (deceased). Education: MA, University of Edinburgh, 1958; Teacher Training, Craiglockhart College of Education, 1980. Appointments: Founder, School of Poets, Edinburgh, 1981-; Director, Scottish Poetry Library, 1984-99; Editor, Lines Review, 1988-98Retired, 1999; Freelance Poetry Practitioner and Adviser, 1999-; Royal Literary Fund Writing Fellow, 2001-04. Publications: Light of the Mind, 1980; Fools and Angels, 1984; Shadows from the Greater Hill, 1987; A Dancing Innocence, 1988; Seven Valleys, 1991; Medusa Dozen and Other Poems, 1994; Scottish Selection, 1998; When it Works it Feels Like Play, 1998; Indian Selection, 2000; Natural Selection, 2001; Noteworthy Selection, 2002; The Nightingale Question: five poets from Sarong, 2004. Contributions to: Anthologies, reviews, and journals. Honours: Scottish Arts Council Book Award, 1980; Howard Sergeant Award for Services to Poetry, 1989; Heritage Society of Scotland Annual Award, 1996; OBE, New Years Honours, 2000; Society of Authors Travelling Scholarship, 2001. Memberships: Fellow, 1994; Saltire Society, honorary member 1993; Scottish Library Association, honorary member, 1999; Scottish Poetry Library, ex-officio honorary member, 1999; Fellow and Director, Centre for Human Ecology, 2002; Honorary Doctorate, Paisley University (DUniv), 2003; Scottish International PEN, President, 2003-; Institute of Contemporary Scotland, Honorary Fellow, 2005. Address: 31 Royal Park Terrace, Edinburgh EH8 8JA, Scotland. Website: http://www.wisdomfield.com

**RANTZEN Esther,** b. 22 June 1940. Television Presenter. m. Desmond Wilcox, 1977, deceased 2000, 1 son, 2 daughters. Education: MA, Somerville College, Oxford. Appointments: Studio manager, making dramatic sound effects, BBC Radio, 1963; Presenter, That's Life, BBC TV 1973-94; Scriptwriter, 1976-94; Producer, The Big Time (documentary series), 1976; Presenter: Esther Interviews..., 1988; Hearts of Gold, 1988, 1996; Drugwatch; Childwatch; The Lost Babies (also producer); Esther (talk show), 1994-; The Rantzen Report, 1996-. Publications: Kill the Chocolate Biscuit (with D Wilcox), 1981; Baby Love, 1985; The Story of Ben Hardwick (with S Woodward), 1985; Once Upon a Christmas, 1996; Esther: The Autobiography, 2000; A Secret Life, 2003. Honours include: BBC TV Personality of 1975, Variety Club of Great Britain; Richard Dimbleby Award, BAFTA, 1988; Snowdon Award for Services to Disabled People, 1996; Royal TV Society Hall of Fame Award, 1998; Champion, Community Legal Service, 2000; Hon DLitt, South Bank University, 2000. Memberships: National Consumer Council, 1981-90; Health Education Authority, 1989-95; Chairman, Childline. Address: BBC TV, White City, 201 Wood Lane, London, W12 7RJ, England.

**RANU Harcharan Singh,** b. 5 February 1939, Lyallpur, India. Biomedical Scientist; Professor; Biomedical Engineer. Education: BSc, Leicester Polytechnic, Leicester, England, 1963; MSc, University of Surrey, Guildford, Surrey, England, 1968; PhD, University of Westminster and Middlesex Hospital Medical School, London, England, 1976. Appointments:

Professor and Director, Louisiana Technical University, USA; Consultant, Columbia University College of Physicians and Surgeons, New York, USA, 1988-; Professor and Chairman, Department of Biomechanics, New York College of Osteopathic Medicine, USA, 1989-93; Professor and Executive Assistant to President and Director, Life University, 1993-; President, American Orthopaedic Biomechanics Research Institute, Atlanta, Georgia, USA, 1997-. Publications: Numerous articles in professional medical journals and conference proceedings include most recently: Laserectomy of the Herniated Spinal Discs: A New Treatment Technique; Relief From Low-Back Pain in Sports By Infusion of Saline into the Human Nucleus Pulposus and Establishing the Pressure-Volume Relationship (Ranu's Principle), 1999; In Vivo Micro-Fracture Simulation In Olympic Field Hockey Players, 1999; Simulation of Micro-Fracture Injury in Female Gymnasts – An in Vivo Study, 2002; 3-D Foot Pressure Measurements in Normal and Diabetic Persons, 2005. Honours: Edwin Tate Award, University of Surrey, England, 1967; James Clayton Award, Institution of Mechanical Engineers, London, England, 1974-76; Hilliburton Award, Louisiana Technical University, 1983; President's Prize, The Biological Engineering Society of Great Britain, 1984; Third International Olympic Committee World Congress on Sports Sciences Award, Atlanta, USA, 1995. Memberships include: Fellow, American Society of Mechanical Engineers; Fellow, Institution of Mechanical Engineers, London; Fellow, The Biological Engineering Society (Institute of Physics and Engineering in Medicine), London; American Society of Biomechanics; Orthopaedic Research Society of USA; American Association for the Advancement of Science; Charted Scientist; The Science Council, UK; American College of Sports Medicine. Address: PO Box 724441, Atlanta, GA 31139-1441, USA.

**RAO M V M Satyanarayana,** b. 22 January 1946, Ramachandrapuram, India. Geophysicist. m. Meenakshi, 1 son, 1 daughter. Education: BSc, 1963, MS, Physics, 1965, PhD, Geophysics, 1974, Osmania University. Appointments: Scientific Assistant, DLRL, 1965-66; Scientific Assistant, 1966-71, Scientist, 1971-92, NGRI; Deputy Director, NIRM, 1992-95, NGRI, 1995-. Publications: 95 research publications. Honours include: DAAD Fellowship, 1976; AP Akademi Young Scientist Award, 1981; US Fulbright Fellowship, 1987; Japan STA Fellowship, 1990; AEWG Gold Medal, 1997; ISNT National Award for Best Technical Paper in Research and Development in NDT, 1999; JSPS Invitation Fellowship from Japan, 2004; Listed in Who's Who publications and biographical dictionaries. Memberships: AEWG India; International Society of Rock Mechanics; AP Akademi of Sciences; Indian Geophysical Union; Life Fellow, Ultrasonic Society of India, ISNT, India; Fellow, Geological Society of India. Address: National Geophysical Research Institute (CSIR), Uppal Road, Hyderabad 500 007, India.

**RAO Nagaraja B K,** b. 23 March 1934, Bangalore, India. Professor; Editor; Publisher. m. 2 daughters. Education: BSc, University of Mysore, India, 1955; MSc, University of Southampton, England, 1971; DIISc, The Indian Institute of Science, India, 1963; PhD, 1963, PhD, 1978, University of Birmingham, England; DTech, University of Sunderland, England, 2004. Appointments: Head of Packaging, LRDE, Bangalore, India, 1956-64; Head of Packaging, Hairlok Co, Bedford, England, 1965-67; Research Fellow, University College London, 1969-70; Post Doctoral Research Fellow, University of Birmingham, England, 1971-79; Senior Lecturer, Birmingham Polytechnic, 1980-89; Reader/Professor, Southampton Institute, 1990-96. Publications: Over 120 technical papers in well-known journals; Editor and author, Handbook of Condition Monitoring;

Contributed chapters in The Handbook of Condition Monitoring, and Infrasound & Low Frequency Vibration; Editor in chief and publisher, International Journal of Condition Monitoring and Diagnostic Engineering Management. Honours: Visiting Professor, University of Glamorgan, Wales; External Examiner, University of Wales Institute of Cardiff, Wales; Visiting Lecturer: Vaxjo University, Sweden; Lulen University of Technology, Sweden; Vellore Institute of Technology, India. Address: 307 Tiverton Road, Selly Oak, Birmingham, B29 6DA, England. E-mail: rajbkrao@btinterner.com

**RAO Talasila Prasada**, b. 2 June 1955, Munipalle, India. Scientist; Deputy Director and Head. m. Sarada, 1 son, 1 daughter. Education: BSc, Chemistry, 1971-74, MSc, Chemistry, 1974-76, Andhra University; PhD, Indian Institute of Technology, Madras, 1977-81. Appointments: Manager, R&D, Purex Laboratories, Bangalore, 1981-82; Scientist B, IICT, Hyderabad, 1982-83; Scientist B, CECRI, Karakudi, 1983-86; Scientist C, 1986-89, Scientist $E_1$, 1989-94, Scientist $E_2$, 1994-99, Scientist F, 1999-, Regional Research Laboratory, Trivandrum. Publications: 1 article in Encyclopaedia of Analytical Science, 2nd edition; Chapters in 2 books; 21 reviews; 142 research papers; 6 patents; PhDs awarded under supervision: 7. Honours: Professor T L Ramachar Award for Best Paper in Electrochemical Science, 1987; Andhra University Medal in the field of Chemistry, 1994. Memberships: Kerala Academy of Sciences (KAS), Trivandrum; Society for the Advancement of Electrochemical Science and technology (SAEST), Karaikudi; Chemical Research Society of India (CRSI), Bangalore; Indian Society of Analytical Scientists, Mumbai; Indian Society for Electroanalytical Chemistry (ISEAC), Mumbai; ABI's Research Board of Advisors; New York Academy of Sciences. Address: Inorganic and Analytical Chemistry Group, Regional Research Laboratory (CSIR), Trivandrum-695019, India.

**RAOOF Mohammed**, b. 19 November 1955, Tehran, Iran. University Professor. m Mojgan Etemad. Education: BSc (Eng), Civil Engineering, 1975-78, MSc, Concrete Structures and Technology. 1978-79, PhD, Structural Analysis, 1979-83, DSc (Eng), Structural Engineering and Mechanics, 2002, Imperial College, London University. Appointments: Research Assistant, Imperial College, 1981-85; Structural Engineer, Wimpey Offshore Engineers and Constructors Ltd, 1985-86; Lecturer II, 1986, Senior Lecturer, 1988, Bridon Reader, 1991, Bridon Professor of Structural Mechanics, 1992, South Bank University, London, 1986-94; Professor of Structural Engineering, Civil and Building Engineering Department, Loughborough University, 1994-. Publications: Sole author of 21 international journal and 19 refereed international conference papers; Co-author of 54 international and 16 refereed national journal and 49 refereed international conference papers; Papers presented in 54 international conferences with 42 of them having been held outside the UK in 20 different countries across 4 continents. Honours: T K Hsieh Award, Institution of Civil Engineers in Conjunction with the Society of Earthquake and Civil Engineering Dynamics, 1985; James Watt Gold Medal, Institution of Civil Engineers, 1991; CEGB Prize, Institution of Mechanical Engineers, 1991; Trevithick Premium, Institution of Civil Engineers, 1993; Henry Adams Award (Diploma), Institution of Structural Engineers, 1993; First winner of the 14th Khwarizmi International Award 2000-2001, Endorsed by UNESCO and presented personally by the President of Iran, 2001. Memberships: Diploma of Membership of Imperial College, 1979; Member, 1995-2000, Fellow, 2000-, Institution of Structural Engineers; Fellow, Institution of Civil Engineers, 2002-. Address: Civil and Building Engineering Department, Loughborough University, Loughborough, Leicestershire LE11 3TU, England. E-mail: m.raoof@lboro.ac.uk

**RAPEANU Sevastian**, b. 24 July 1932, Richitele, Judetul Arges; Romania. Physicist. m. Doina Constantin Rapeanu, 2 sons. Education: MSc, Mathematics and Physics Faculty, Bucharest University, 1957; Specialization in Sweden, "Atomic motion in solids and liquids by thermal neutrons" through stipend from IAEA, Vienna, Royal Institute of Technology, 1962-63; PhD in Physics, Institute of Atomic Physics, Romanian Academy, Bucharest, 1969; PhD degree supervisor, Reactor Physics and Nuclear Data, 1970, and Condensed Matter Physics, 1990; Doctor Docent in Physics, Senate of Bucharest University, 1976. Appointments include: Head of Laboratory and Deputy Director, Atomic Physics Institute, 1969-70; Specialty Inspector, Nuclear Power Section – Ministry Council, 1970-71; General Inspector, State Committee for Nuclear Energy, 1971-77; Professor, Machinery Engineering Technology Faculty, Pitesti University, 1978-81; Scientific Director, Nuclear Power Reactors Institute, Pitesti, 1977-82; General Director of National Agency for Atomic Energy, 1994-97; President of Interministerial Council of NAAE, Co-ordinator, Realization of Nuclear National Program, 1996-2010; Member of Board of Directors, National Institute for Electrostatics and Electrotechnologies, Bucharest, 1997-2000; Currently Member, Consultative Council, Nuclear Regulatory Body and Member, Technology Committee, Romanian Academy; Co-ordinator, The Explanatory Dictionary – Nuclear Energy (Romanian, English, French), 1999, 2004, 2005; Research activities in fields including: Neutron physics, total reflection of neutrons, neutron polarisation, neutron spectrometry, neutron elastic and inelastic scattering, condensed matter and physics, statics and dynamics of simple liquids and molecular, hydrogen in metals, water, heavy water and water solution, nuclear materials and nuclear energetics. Publications: Over 200 papers in national and international speciality journals; Co-author: Tables and Formulae for Mathematics, Physics and Chemistry, 1964; Atomic and Nuclear Physics, 1976; Techniques and Measurements at Nuclear Reactors, 1983; Translator, Reactor Physics by Shulten and Guth (from English), 1975; Translator, Course of Dosimetry by VI Ivanov, 1999; Co-author: Elemente Suport pentru Dezafectarea Reactorului Nuclear de Cercetare VVR-S, Vol 1, 2003; Participant in numerous national and international conferences; Numerous scientific articles for professional journals. Honours: IAEA, Vienna, 1995; INP Pitesti, 1996, 1999; RANE-Bucharest, 1996; JINR Dubna, Russia, 1996; Jubilee Medal, 1996; International Man of the Year, IBC, 2000-2001; Man of the Year, ABI, 2001; American Diploma of Honor, ABI, 2002; International Diploma of Honour, IBC, 2003; Romania - The United States of America Medal, 30 Years of Co-operation in The Peaceful Use of Nuclear Energy, 1974-2004; Top 100 Scientists, IBC, 2005; Noteworthy Personality in Science, Special Commission of the Romanian Academy of Science; Listed in numerous biographical dictionaries. Memberships: Numerous Professional Societies, including: International Committee for Nuclear Data-IAEA, 1976-79; Chairman of Organising Committee of the 10th ICND Session, Bucharest, 1978; Condensed Matter Physics, JINR-Dubna, Russia, 1994-97; Academy of Romanian Scientists; Romanian Physical Society; European Physical Society. Address: Terasei Alley 8, bl R12A, sc2, et 3, ap 54, PO 82, Sector 4, 041774 Bucharest, Romania.

**RAPHAEL Frederic Michael**, b. 14 August 1931, Chicago, Illinois, USA. Writer. m. 17 January 1955, 2 sons, 1 daughter, deceased 2001. Education: St John's College, Cambridge, England. Publications: Obbligato, 1956; The Earlsdon Way, 1958; The Limits of Love, 1960; The Trouble With England, 1962; The Graduate Wife, 1962; Lindmann, 1963; Darling, 1965; Orchestra and Beginners, 1967; Two for the Road (film script with preface), 1968; Like Men Betrayed, 1970; Who Were You With Last Night?, 1971; April, June and November, 1972;

Richard's Things, 1973; California Time, 1975; The Glittering Prizes, 1976; Somerset Maugham (biography), 1977; Sleeps Six (short stories), 1979; Cracks in the Ice: Views and Reviews, 1979; Oxbridge Blues (short stories), 1980; Byron (biography), 1982; Heaven and Earth, 1985; Think of England, 1990; A Double Life, 1993; Of Gods and Men (Greek mythology revisited), 1993; The Latin Lover (short stories), 1994; Old Scores, 1995. Translations (with Kenneth McLeish): The Poems of Catullus, 1978; The Plays of Aeschylus, 2 volumes, 1991; Euripides: Bacchae, Medea, Hippolytus; Sophocles, Ajax , 1992, 1993, 1996; Coast to Coast, 1998; All his Sons (short stories), 1999; Eyes Wide Open (A Memoir), 1999; Personal Terms, 2001; Petronius: Satyricon (translation), 2001; The Benefits of Doubt (essays), 2002; A Spoilt Boy, 2003; Rough Copy, 2004; Becket by Jean Anouilh (translation with Stephen Raphael), 2004; Some Talk of Alexander, 2006; Cuts and Bruises, 2006. Contributions to: Sunday Times; Times Literary Supplement; Spectator; Poetry Nation Review; Areté. Honours: Lippincott Prize, 1961; Best Screenplay Writers' Guild, 1964, 1965; USA Academy Award, 1966; British Academy Award, 1966; Royal TV Society Award, 1976; ACE (US Cable TV) Awards, 1985, 1991; Prix Génevois, 2000. Membership: Royal Society of Literature, Fellow. Address: c/o Deborah Rogers, Rogers, Coleridge and White, 20 Powis Mews, London W11 1JN, England.

**RASHBA Emmanuel Iosif,** b. 30 October 1927, Kiev, Ukraine. Physicist. m. Erna Kelman, 1 son, deceased, 1 daughter. Education: Diploma with Honour, Kiev, 1949; PhD, Kiev, 1956; Doctor of Sciences, Ioffe Institute for Physics and Technology, Leningrad, 1963; Professor of Theoretical and Mathematical Physics, Landau Institute for Theoretical Physics, Moscow, 1967. Appointments: Junior and Senior Scientist, Institute of Physics, Kiev, 1954-60; Head of Theoretical Department, Institute for Semiconductors, Kiev, 1960-66; Head of Department and Principal Scientist, Landau Institute for Theoretical Physics, Moscow, 1966-97; Research Professor, University of Utah, Salt Lake City, 1992-2000; Research Professor, SUNY at Buffalo, 2001-2003; Research Professor, Harvard University, Cambridge, 2004-. Publications: Collection of Problems in Physics, in Russian, 1978, 1987, in English 1986, in Japanese, 1989; Spectroscopy of Molecular Excitons, in Russian, 1981, in English, 1985; About 220 contributed and review papers in professional journals. Honours: National Prize in Science, USSR, 1966; Ioffe Prize of the Academy of Sciences of the USSR, 1987; ICL Prize, Conference of Lumin. and Optical Spectroscopy, 1999; Arkady Aronov Memorial Lecture, 2005; Sir Nevill Mott Lecture, 2005. Membership: Fellow American Physical Society. Address: Department of Physics, Harvard University, Cambridge, MA 02138, USA. E-mail: erashba@physics.harvard.edu

**RASHKOVA Tsetska Grigorova,** b. 16 May 1952, Rousse, Bulgaria. Mathematician; Researcher. m. Petar Ivanov Rashkov, 2 daughters. Education: MSc, Mathematics, Sofia University, St Kl Ohridski, 1971-76; PhD, Mathematics, Algebra and Number Theory, 1997. Appointments: Assistant Professor, 1976-79, Senior Assistant Professor, 1979-89, Chief Assistant Professor, 1989-2000, Associate Professor, 2000-, University of Rousse, A Kanchev. Publications: Varieties of metabelian Jordan algebras, co-author, 1989; Varieties of algebras having a distributive lattice of subvarieties, 1995; Identities in algebras with involution, 1999; Matrixalgebras with involution and central polynominals, 2002. Memberships: Union of Bulgarian Mathematicians; Union of Scientists in Bulgaria. Address: Department of Algebra and Geometry, Centre of Applied maths and Informatics, Pedagogical Faculty, University of Rousse

"Angel Kanchev", Studentska str 8, Rousse 7017, Bulgaria. E-mail: tcetcka@ami.ru.acad.bg

**RATAN John,** b. 23 September 1960, Arunachal Pradesh, India. Consultant Paediatric Surgeon. m. Simmi K Ratan, 1 son, 1 daughter. Education: MBBS, 1985, MS, 1989, Jimper, Pondicherry; MCh, Paediatric Surgery, All India Institute of Medical Sciences, 1992. Appointments: Senior Resident, Paediatric Surgery, 1989-92; Consultant, Paediatric Surgery, Jain Medical Centre, Sitaram Bhartiya Institute of Science and Research, Delhi. Publications: More than 30 articles in reputed medical journals. Honours: Best Student of Science at State Level; First Surgeon in India to report surgically treated survivor of Type 3 Laryngotracheal Cleft using conservative approach. Memberships: Indian Medical Association; Indian Association of Paediatric Surgeons. Address: E-13/13, Khirki Extension, Malviya Nagar, New Delhi, 110017, India. E-mail: drjohnsimmi@yahoo.com

**RATAN Simmi,** b. 30 December 1965, Delhi, India. Doctor; Paediatric Surgeon. m. John Ratan, 1 son, 1 daughter. Education: MBBS, Maulana Azad Medical College, Delhi University, 1987; MCh, Paediatric Surgery, All India Institute of Medical Sciences, 1994; Diplomate of National Board, Paediatric Surgery, 2003. Appointments: Senior Resident, Paediatric Surgery, All India Institute of Medical Sciences, New Delhi; Senior Research Associate, Council of Scientific and Industrial Research, India, 1997-2000; Lecturer, Paediatric Surgery, PT BD Sharma Postgraduate Institute of Medical Sciences, Rohtak, Haryana, India, 2001-. Publications: About 55 published articles in many international journals of repute; Contributed more than 10 chapters for different books and websites. Honours: Many Merit Certificates in secondary school and undergraduate medical career, distinction in anatomy, first position in preventive and social medicine, second position in physiology college level; Rashtriya Gaurav Award for Meritorious Service, 2003; Selected Professionals of 2004, IBC; Leading Professional of 2005, IBC; Listed in Who's Who publications and biographical dictionaries. Memberships: Indian Medical Association; Indian Association of Paediatric Surgeons; Indian and Asian Society of Paediatric Urology. Address: E-13/13, Khirki Extension, Malviya Nagar, New Delhi-110017, India. E-mail: drjohnsimmi@yahoo.com

**RATCLIFFE Eric Hallam,** b. 8 August 1918, Teddington, Middlesex, England. Retired Physicist and Information Scientist; Writer; Poet; Editor. Appointment: Founder-Editor, Ore, 1955-95. Publications: Over 30, including: The Visitation, 1952; The Chronicle of the Green Man, 1960; Gleanings for a Daughter of Aeolus, 1968; Leo Poems, 1972; Commius, 1976; Nightguard of the Quaternary, 1979; Ballet Class, 1986; The Runner of the Seven Valleys, 1990; The Ballad of Polly McPoo, 1991; Advent, 1992; The Golden Heart Man, 1993; Fire in the Bush: Poems, 1955-1992, 1993; William Ernest Henley (1849-1903): An Introduction, 1993; The Caxton of Her Age: The Career and Family Background of Emily Faithfull (1835-1895), 1993; Winstanley's Walton, 1649: Events in the Civil War at Walton-on-Thames, 1994; Ratcliffe's Megathesaurus, 1995; Anthropos, 1995; Odette, 1995; Sholen, 1996; The Millennium of the Magician, 1996; The Brussels Griffon, 1996; Strange Furlongs, 1996; Wellington- A Broad Front, 1998; Capabilities of the Alchemical Mind, 1999; Cosmologia, 2000; Loyal Women, 2000; No Jam in the Astrid, 2002; The Divine Peter, 2002; On Baker's Level, 2002; Selected Long Poems, 2003; Desert Voices, 2003; The Ruffian on the Stairs, 2005; Going for God, 2005. Contributions to: Anthologies and journals. Honour: Baron. Royal Order of the Bohemian Crown, 1995. Address: 7 The Towers, Stevenage, Hertfordshire SG1 1HE, England.

**RATHER Dan,** b. 31 October 1931, Wharton, Texas, USA. Broadcaster; Journalist. m. Jean Goebel, 1 son, 1 daughter. Education: BA, Journalism, Sam Houston State College, Huntsville, Texas, 1953; University of Houston; South Texas School of Law. Appointments: Staff, United Press International, Houston Chronicle, KTRH Radio, Houston, KHOU-TV, Houston; White House Correspondent, 1964-65, 1966-74, Chief, London Bureau, 1965-66, CBS-TV; Anchorman-Correspondent, CBS Reports, 1974-75; Co-Editor, 60 Minutes, CBS-TV, 1975-81; Anchorman, Dan Rather Reporting, CBS Radio, 1977-; Anchorman and Managing Editor, CBS Evening News with Dan Rather, 1981-; CBS News special programmes. Publications: The Palace Guard (with Gary Gates), 1974; The Camera Never Blinks Twice (with Mickey Herskowitz), 1977; Memoirs: I Remember (with Peter Wyden), 1991; The Camera Never Blinks Twice: The Further Adventures of a Television Journalist, 1994; Deadlines and Datelines: Essays at the Turn of the Century, 1999. Honours: Many Emmy Awards; Dan Rather Communications Building named in his honour, Sam Houston State University, Huntsville, Texas. Address: c/o CBS News, 524 West 57th Street, New York, NY 10019, USA.

**RATTLE Simon (Sir),** b. 19 January 1955, Liverpool, England. Conductor. m. (1) Elise Ross, 2 sons, (2) Candace Allen, 1996. Education: Royal Academy of Music. Career: Has conducted orchestras including: Bournemouth Symphony, Northern Sinfonia, London Philharmonic, London Sinfonietta, Berlin Philharmonic, Los Angeles Philharmonic, Stockholm Philharmonic, Vienna Philharmonic, Philadelphia Orchestra, Boston Symphony; Début: Queen Elizabeth Hall, 1974, Royal Festival Hall, 1976, Royal Albert Hall, 1976, Assistant Conductor, BBC Symphony Orchestra, 1977; Associate Conductor, Royal Liverpool Philharmonic Society, 1977-80; Glyndebourne début, 1977, Royal Opera, Covent Garden, 1990; Artistic Director London Choral Society, 1979-84; Principal Conductor and Artistic Advisor, City of Birmingham Symphony Orchestra (CBSO), 1980-90, Music Director, 1990-98; Artistic Director, South Bank Summer Music, 1981-83; Joint Artistic Director, Aldeburgh Festival, 1982-93; Principal Guest Conductor, Los Angeles Philharmonic, 1981-94, Rotterdam Philharmonic, 1981-84; Principal Guest Conductor, Orchestra of the Age of Enlightenment, 1992-; Chief Conductor and Artistic Director, Berlin Philharmonic Orchestra, 2002-. Publications: Over 30 recordings with CBSO. Honours: Edison Award, 1987; Grand Prix du Disque, 1988; Grand Prix Caecilia, 1988; Gramophone Record of the Year Award, 1988; Gramophone Opera Award, 1989; International Record Critics' Award, 1990; Grand Prix de l'Academy Charles Cros, 1990; Gramophone Artist of Year, 1993; Montblanc de la Culture Award, 1993; Toepfer Foundation Shakespeare Prize, 1996; Gramophone Award for Best Concerto recording, Albert Medal (RSA), 1997; Choc de l'Année Award, 1998; Gramophone Award for Best Opera Recording, 2000; Gramophone Awards for Best Orchestral Recording and Record of the Year, 2000; Officier des Arts et des Lettres, 1995. Address: c/o Askonas Holt Ltd, Lonsdale Chambers, 27 Chancery Lane, London, WC2A 1PF, England.

**RAVENALL Suzanne,** b. 7 August 1968, Hertfordshire, England. Chief Executive Officer. Appointments: UK Area Sales Manager, National Training, National Accounts, Stena Sealink; Contractor, Consultant, Transnet, South Africa; Contractor, Consultant, Vodacom, South Africa; Chief Executive Officer, IDCS Beyond Outsourcing™, South Africa. Honours: Business Woman of the Year Finalist, South Africa, African Investor; Business Woman of the Year Runner-Up with Commendation. Memberships: YPO; Institute of Directors. Address: PO Box 99, Rivonia 2128, Johannesburg, South Africa. Website: www.beyondoutsourcing.com.za

**RAVERTY Aaron (Thomas Donald),** b. 13 March 1950, Stillwater, Minnesota, USA. Benedictine Monk; Anthropologist; Editor. Education: BA, Anthropology, 1972, MA, Anthropology, 1979, PhD, Sociocultural Anthropology, 1990, University of Minnesota, Minneapolis; MA, Systematic Theology, St John's University, Collegeville, Minnesota, 1979. Appointments: Preparatory School Instructor, St John's Preparatory School, Collegeville, Minnesota, 1975-76; University Instructor, St John's University, Collegeville, 1975-90; Editor, The Liturgical Press, Collegeville, 1991-; General Editor, Worship Magazine, 1993-94; Book Review Editor, Monastic Interreligious Dialogue Bulletin. Publications: Contributions to newsletters and journals; Editor, The Modern Catholic Encyclopedia, 1994, 2004; The Encyclopedia of American Catholic History, 1997. Honours: Certificate of Merit, St John's University, 1987; Fellowship Status in the American Anthropological Association, 1993; Choice Editorial Award, The Encyclopedia of American Catholic History, 1998. Memberships: American Benedictine Academy; American Association of Physical Anthropologists, 1972-79; Fellow, American Anthropological Association, 1980-; Board Member, Monastic Interreligious Dialogue; Secretary of the Board of Monastic Interreligious Dialogue, 1994-99; International Graphoanalysis Society, 1996-; Communications Committee Member, St John's University Alumni Board of Directors, 1999-2003; Member, St John's Abbey Spiritual Life Program Board of Advisors, 2002-04. Address: PO Box 2015, St John's Abbey, Collegeville, MN 56321-2015, USA.

**RAVICHANDRAN Veerasamy,** b. 19 May 1975, Pattukkottai, Tamil Nadu, India. Teacher. Education: BPharm, K M College of Pharmacy, Madurai, 1992-96; MPharm, Pharmaceutical Chemistry, Dr H S Gour Vishwavidyalaya, Sagar, 1997-98. Appointments: Lecturer, Fathima College of Pharmacy, Kadayanallur, 1999-2001; Assistant Professor, KMCH College of Pharmacy, Kovai Estate, Coimbatore, 2001-. Publications: 5 international papers; 12 national papers. Honours: Listed in biographical dictionaries; Reviewer, Indian Journal of Chemistry, 2004-. Address: 1/109 West Street, Moothakurichi (PO), Pattukkottai (TK), Thanjavur (Dt), Tamil Nadu, India 614 906. E-mail: phravi75@rediffmail.com

**RAWAT Nirmala,** b. 9 August 1946, Jaipur, Rajasthan, India. Social Worker. m. Laxman Rawat, 3 daughters. Education: Master of Arts, 1963. Appointments: Patron, Sports Control Board of India for the Disabled; Patron, Rajasthan Cricket Association for the Disabled; Patron, Global Common Society International, Jaipur; Chief Adviser, Indian Cultural Preservation and Development Trust, Jaipur. Honours: Jaipur Samaroh Samiti, 1996; Alek Bharti Samman, Jaipur, 1996; Bharat Vikas Parishad, Ahemdabad, 1996; Award, Government of Rajasthan, Department of Social Welfare, 1997; Shri KVHS, 1997; JSVP, 1997; Great Woman of the 21st Century, 2004. Address: White Rose Building, C-91, Lal Kothi Scheme, Janpath Jonk Road, Jaipur, Rajasthan, India 302015. E-mail: typhoon_mines@yahoo.co.in

**RAWNSLEY Andrew Nicholas James,** FRSA (Fellow of the Royal Society of Arts) b. 5 January 1962, Leeds, England. Journalist; Broadcaster; Author. m. Jane Hall, 1990, 3 daughters. Education: Sidney Sussex College, Cambridge; MA, History, Cambridge. Appointments: BBC, 1983-85; Reporter, Feature Writer, 1985-87, Political Columnist, 1987-93, The Guardian; Writer, Presenter, A Week in Politics, 1989-97, Bye Bye Blues, 1997, Blair's Year, 1998, Channel 4 series; Associate Editor, Chief Political Commentator, The Observer, 1993-; Writer,

Presenter, The Agenda, ITV series, 1996, The Westminster Hour, Radio 4 series, 1998-; The Unauthorised Biography of the United Kingdom, 1999. Publication: Servants of the People: The Inside Story of New Labour, 2000. Honours: Student Journalist of the Year, 1983; Young Journalist of the Year, 1987; Columnist of the Year, What the Papers Say Awards, 2000; Book of the Year, Channel 4/House Magazine Political Awards, 2001; Jounalist of the year, Channel 4 Awards, 2003. Address: The Observer, 119 Farringdon Road, London EC1R 3ER, England. E-mail: andrew.rawnsley@observer.co.uk

**RAY Asim Kumar,** b. 6 October 1937. Teacher; Researcher. m. Parul Basu, 1 daughter. Education: BSc (honours), Physics, University of Calcutta, 1956; MSc, Physics, University of Calcutta, 1958; PhD, Particle Physics, Carnegie Mellon University, 1969. Appointments: Trainee, Atomic Energy Establishment, Trombay, Bombay, 1959-60; Research Associate, Tata Institute of Fundamental Research, Bombay, 1960-63; Lecturer, 1969-76, Reader, 1976-84, Professor, 1984-, Head of Department of Physics, 1981-87, Dean of Faculty of Science, 1990-92, Professor in Charge, Computer Centre, 1991-97, Registrar, 1992-93, Retired, 2002, Visva-Bharati University, India; Visiting Scientist, USA, Japan and Italy, 1980-95; Senior Associate, IUCAA, Pune, India, 1994-97; Currently Visiting Faculty, S N Bose National Centre for Basic Sciences, Salt Lake Sector III, Kolkata, India. Publications: Editor and co-editor, Dirac and Feynman, Pioneers in Quantum Mechanics; Editor and co-editor, Proceedings of XI DAE Symposium on High Energy Physics; Over 40 professional research papers. Honours: Fulbright Scholar. Memberships: Indian Physics Association; Indian Physical Society; Indian Association of Cultivation Science; Indian Association of General Relativity and Gravitation. Address: Uttaran, Purva Palli (North), Santiniketan 731235, India. E-mail: asimkray@yahoo.co.in

**RAY Malabika,** 30 October 1936, Bankura, West Bengal, India. University Teacher; Researcher. m. Subroto, 1 son. Education: BSc Honours, Botany, Calcutta University, 1955; MSc, Botany, 1957; PhD, Botany, 1965; Specialisation: Cytology, Genetics and Environmental Toxicology. Appointments: JRF, ICAR, 1958-64; SRF, CSIR, 1964-66; Lecturer, Botany, Visva, Bharati University, 1966; Reader, Botany, 1983; Professor, Botany, 1991-; Invented techniques for rapid assessment of phytotoxicity of water using plants as indicators of environmental pollution; Pioneer, Environmental Stress Genetical Studies on Cereals; Proposed (with Subroto Ray) a new theory for the Origin and Evolution of Life. Publications: 70 research papers; 2 Editorial books; Invited lectures in India and abroad; Chaired International and National Seminars. Honours: Fellow, Indian Society of Genetics and Plant Breeding; Fellow, Indian Association for Biological Studies; Woman of the Year, American Biographical Institute, 1997; Rising Personalities of India Gold Medal and commemorative gold-centred plaque, International Penguin Publishing House, 2004. Address: A-1/5, Ishwar Chandra Nibas, 68/1, Bagmari Road, Kolkata-700054, West Bengal, India.

**RAYNER Claire Berenice, (Sheila Brandon, Ann Lynton, Ruth Martin),** b. 22 January 1931, London, England. Writer; Broadcaster. m. Desmond Rayner, 23 June 1957, 2 sons, 1 daughter. Education: State Registered Nurse, Gold Medal, Royal Northern Hospital, London, 1954; Midwifery, Guy's Hospital. Publications: Over 90 books, ranging from medical to fiction, 1961-97. Contributions to: Professional journals, newspapers, radio, and television. Honours: Freeman, City of London, 1981; Medical Journalists Association Award, 1987; Honorary Fellow, University of North London, 1988; Best Specialist Consumer Columnist Award, 1988; Order of the British Empire, 1996; Honorary Doctorate from Oxford Books'

University, 2000; Honorary Doctorate, Middlesex University, 2002. Memberships: Royal Society of Medicine, fellow; Society of Authors; President, Patients Association; President, Gingerbread; President, Humanist Society; Council member, Charter 88; Video Appeals Committee, British Board of Film Classification. Address: Holly Wood House, Roxborough Avenue, Harrow-on-the-Hill, Middlesex HA1 3BU, England.

**RAYNER Desmond,** b. 31 October 1928, London, England. Artist; Writer; Actor. m. Claire Rayner, 2 sons, 1 daughter. Education: Certificate in Acting, LGSM, Guildhall School of Music and Drama, 1950-51. Career: RAF, 1946-49; Numerous advertising and public relations posts, 1957-69; Agent and manager to wife Claire Rayner. Creative works: Designed productions: Heaven and Charing Cross Road; A Murder Has Been Arranged; The Boy With A Cart; Lady Windermere's Fan; Numerous art exhibitions, 1975-2002, including Art Deco in Egypt, London – Another Perspective; and many others; Private collections in Australia, Canada, USA and UK. Publications: Novels: The Dawlish Season, 1984; The Husband; Encore. Memberships: Equity; Royal Academy of Fine Art; Actors Centre. Address: Holly Wood House, Roxborough Avenue, Harrow-on-the-Hill, Middlesex, HA1 3BU, England.

**RE Edward Domenic,** b. 14 October 1920, Santa Marina, Salina, Italy. Retired Federal Judge. m. Margaret A Corcoran, 5 sons, 7 daughters. Education: BS, 1940, LLB, 1943, St John's University; JSD, New York University Law School, 1950. Appointments: Colonel (retired), US Air Force; Judge Advocate General's Department; Emeritus Distinguished Professor of Law, St John's University School of Law; Chairman, Foreign Claims Settlement Commission of the US, by appointments of President John F Kennedy and President Lyndon B Johnson; Assistant Secretary of State for educational and Cultural Affairs by appointment of president Lyndon B Johnson; Judge, United States Customs Court, by President Lyndon B Johnson; Chief Judge, United States Customs Court, by President Jimmy Carter; First Chief Judge of the United States Court of International Trade; Member, Judicial Conference of the United States; Member of the Executive Committee of the Judicial Conference of the United States. Publications: Books include: Foreign Confiscations in Anglo-American Law, 1951; Brief Writing and Oral Argument, 8th edition, 2000; Cases and Materials on the Law of Remedies, 5th edition, 2000; Selected essays on Equity, 1955; Freedom's Prophet (Writings of Zechariah Chafee, Jr), 1981; Numerous articles on international law, human rights, legal education, the judiciary and the legal profession. Honours: US Air Force Commendation Medal; Distinguished Service Award; First recipient "Pro Patria" Award, US Junior Chamber of Commerce; LI General Assembly, Knights of Columbus; Liberty Medal of City of New York, Mayor Koch; Highest Rank( Cavaliere Gran Croce) Legion of Merit, Republic of Italy; Trinacria Award, British-Italian Law Association, London, UK. Memberships: American Bar Association; International president, International Association of Jurist, Italy-USA; American Society for Legions of Merit of the Republic of Italy; Representative at the United Nations for International Association of Judges (NGO). Address: 305 Beach 147 Street, Neponsit, NY 11694, USA.

**READ Anthony,** b. 21 April 1935, Staffordshire, England. Writer; Dramatist. m. Rosemary E Kirby, 29 March 1958, 2 daughters. Education: Central School of Speech and Drama, London, 1952-54. Publications: The Theatre, 1964; Operation Lucy (with David Fisher), 1980; Colonel Z (with David Fisher), 1984; The Deadly Embrace (with David Fisher), 1988; Kristallnacht (with David Fisher), 1989; Conspirator (with Ray Bearse), 1991; The Fall of Berlin (with David Fisher), 1992;

Berlin: The Biography of a City (with David Fisher), 1994; The Proudest Day: India's Long Road to Indendence (with David Fisher), 1997; The Devil's Disciples, 2003; The Baker Street Boys, 2005. Other: Over 200 television films, plays, series and serials. Honours: Pye Colour TV Award, 1983; Wingate Literary Prize, 1989. Membership: Trustee, Past Chairman, Writers Guild of Great Britain. Address: 7 Cedar Chase, Taplow, Buckinghamshire, England.

**READE John Brian,** b. 4 July 1938, Wolverhampton, England. University Lecturer. m. Suzanne, 3 sons, 2 daughters. Education: 1st Class Honours (Wrangler), 1961, Part III Distinction, 1962, PhD, 1962-65, Trinity College, Cambridge. Appointments: Lecturer in Mathematics, Birmingham University, 1965-67; Lecturer in Mathematics, University of Manchester, 1967-2003. Publications: Books: Introduction to Mathematical Analysis, 1986; Calculus with Complex Numbers, 2003; Various research papers on mathematics. Honours: MA, PhD, Cambridge University. Memberships: London Mathematical Society; Cambridge Philosophical Society. Address: 123 Andover Avenue, Middleton, Manchester M24 1JQ, England. E-mail: suzanne.reade@virgin.net

**REAGAN Nancy Davis (Anne Francis Robbins),** b. 6 July 1921, New York, USA. Former American First Lady. m. Ronald Reagan, 1952, deceased 2004, 1 son, 1 daughter, 1 step-son, 1 step-daughter. Education: BA, Smith College, Massachusetts, USA. Appointments: Contract actress, Metro-Goldwyn-Mayer, 1949-56; Former author, syndicated column on prisoners-of-war and soldiers missing in action; Civic worker active on behalf of Vietnam War veterans, senior citizens, disabled children and drug victims; Member, Board of Directors, Revlon Group Inc, 1989-; Honorary National Chairman, Aid to Adoption of Special Kids, 1977; Actress in films including: The Next Voice You Hear, 1950; Donovan's Brain, 1953; Hellcats of the Navy, 1957. Publications: Nancy, 1980; To Love a Child (with Jane Wilkie); My Turn (memoirs), 1989. Honours: One of Ten Most Admired American Women, Good Housekeeping Magazine, 1977; Woman of Year, Los Angeles Times, 1977; Permanent member, Hall of Fame of Ten Best Dressed Women in US, Lifetime Achievement Award, Council of Fashion Designers of USA, 1988. Address: 2121 Avenue of the Stars, 34th Floor, Los Angeles, CA 90067, USA.

**REAMSBOTTOM Barry,** b. 4 April 1949, Nairn, Scotland. A Senior Secretary to Speaker of the House of Commons. Education: St Peter's Roman Catholic Secondary School, Aberdeen, 1959-64; Aberdeen Academy, 1964-66. Appointments: Scientific Assistant, Isaac Spencer & Co, Aberdeen, Scotland, 1966-69; Social Security Officer, DHSS, Aberdeen, 1969-76; Area Officer, National Union of Public Employees, Edinburgh, 1976-79; Head of Education Department, 1979-87, Press Officer, Journal Editor, 1987-92, General Secretary, 1992-2002, Civil and Public Services Association, London, then Public and Commercial Services Union; Currently, a Senior Secretary to the Speaker of the House of Commons. Honour: Fellow, Centre for American Studies, Salzburg, Austria. Memberships: Amnesty International; Labour Party. Address: 156 Bedford Hill, London SW12 9HW, England. E-mail: breams@onetel.com

**REARDON Raymond (Ray),** b. 8 October 1932, Tredegar, Wales. Snooker Player. m. (1) Susan Carter, divorced, 1 son, 1 daughter. (2) Carol Lovington, 1987. Career: Welsh Amateur Champion, 1950-55; English Amateur Champion, 1965; Turned professional, 1967; Six times World Snooker Champion, 1970-78; Benson & Hedges Masters Champion, 1976; Welsh Champion, 1977, 1981, 1983; Professional Players Champion, 1982; Retired, 1992; Active in running World

Professional Billiards and Snooker Association; Occasional TV appearances. Publications: Classic Snooker, 1974; Ray Reardon (autobiography), 1982. Honour: MBE.

**REDFORD Robert,** b. 18 August 1937, Santa Monica, California, USA. American Actor. m. Lola Van Wegenen, divorced, 3 children. Education: University of Colorado. Creative Works: Films include, War Hunt, 1961; Situation Hopeless But Not Serious, 1965; Inside Daisy Clover, 1965; The Chase, 1965; This Property is Condemned, 1966; Barefoot in the Park, 1967; Tell Them Willie Boy is Here, 1969; Butch Cassidy and the Sundance Kid, 1969; Downhill Racer, 1969; Little Fauss and Big Halsy, 1970; Jeremiah Johnson, 1972; The Candidate, 1972; How to Seal a Diamond in Four Uneasy Lessons, 1972; The Way We Were, 1973; The Sting, 1973; The Great Gatsby, 1974; The Great Waldo Pepper, 1974; Three Days of the Condor, 1975; All the President's Men, 1976; A Bridge Too Far, 1977; The Electric Horseman, 1980; Brubaker, 1980; The Natural, 1984; Out of Africa, 1985; Legal Eagles, 1986; Havana, 1991; Indecent Proposal, 1993; The Clearing, Sacred Planet, 2004, Director, Ordinary People, 1980; Milagro Beanfield War (also producer), 1988; Promised Land (executive producer), 1988; Sneakers, 1992; A River Runs Through it (also director), 1992; Quiz Show (director), 1994; The River Wild, 1995; Up Close and Personal, 1996; The Horse Whisperer, 1997; The Legend of Bagger Vance, (also director, producer), How to Kill Your Neighbour's Dog (executive producer), 2000; The Last Castle, 2001; Spy Game, 2001. Honours: Academy Award, Golden Globe Award, Best Director, 1981; Audubon Medal, 1989; Dartmouth Film Society Award, 1990; Screen Actors' Guild Award for Lifetime Achievement, 1996; Honorary Academy Award, 2002. Address: c/o Creative Artists Agency, 9830 Wilshire Boulevard, Beverly Hills, CA 90212, USA.

**REDGRAVE Lynn,** b. 8 March 1943. Actress; Playwright. m. John Clark, 1967, 1 son, 2 daughters. Education: Central School of Speech and Drama. Career: Films include: Girl With The Green Eyes; Tom Jones; Georgy Girl; Smashing Time; The Virgin Soldiers; The Deadly Affair; The National Health; Every Little Crook and Nanny; The Happy Hooker; Sunday Lovers; Getting It Right; Morgan Stewart's Coming Home; Everything You Always Wanted to Know About Sex; The Big Bus; Midnight; Shine; Strike; The Simian Line; Touched; The Annihilation of Fish; The Next Best Thing, 2000; My Kingdom, 2001; Unconditional Love, 2001; TV includes: Pygmalion; Egg on the Face of the Tiger; The Bad Seed; Whatever Happened to Baby Jane; Gauguin the Savage; White Lies; Gods and Monsters; Rude Awakening; Stage work includes: Hamlet; Much Ado About Nothing; Andorra; Hay Fever; Slag; My Fat Friend; Shakespeare for My Father; California Suite; Saint Joan; Les Liaisons Dangereuses; The Cherry Orchard; Mrs Warren's Profession; Don Juan in Hell; Notebook of Trigorin; Moon Over Buffalo, 1996; The Mandrake Root, 2001; Noises Off, 2001; Radio includes: As You Like It; Vile Bodies; Tales for Halloween. Honours include: Sarah Siddons, Chicago and Jefferson Awards (Misalliance). Publications: This is Living, 1991; Named President of the Players, 1994. Address: c/o John Clark, PO Box 1207, Topanga, CA 90290, USA,

**REDGRAVE Steve,** b. 23 March 1962, Marlow, England. Oarsman. m. Ann, 1 son, 2 daughters. Education: Doctor Civil Law, honoris causa. Appointments: Represented, UK at Junior World Championships, 1979; Silver medal, 1980; Stroke, British Coxed 4, Gold Medal Winners, Los Angeles Olympic Games, 1984; Gold Medals, Single Scull, Coxless Pair (with Andy Holmes) and Coxed 4, Commonwealth Games, 1986; Coxed Pair (with Holmes), World Championships, 1986; Coxless Pair Gold Medal and Coxed Pair Silver Medal (with Holmes), World

Championships, 1987; Gold Medal (with Holmes), Coxless Pair and Bronze Medal, Coxed Pair, Olympic Games, Seoul, 1988; Silver Medal (with Simon Berrisford), Coxless Pairs, World Championships, 1989; Bronze Medal, Coxless Pair (with Matthew Pinsent), World Championships, Tasmania, 1990; Gold Medal, Coxless Pair (with Pinsent), World Championships, Vienna, 1991; Gold Medal, Olympic Games, Barcelona, 1992; Gold Medals at World Championships, Czech Republic, 1993, USA, 1994, Finland, 1995; Gold Medal, Olympic Games, Atlanta, 1996; Winners of World Cup, Gold Medal, Coxless 4, France, (with Pinsent, Foster, Cracknell), 1997; Gold Medal Winners, Coxless 4, World Championships, Cologne, 1998; Gold Medal Winners, Coxless 4, St Catherines (with Pinsent, Coode, Cracknell), 1999; Gold Medal, Olympic Games, Sydney, 2000. Publications: Steven Redgrave's Complete Book of Rowing, 1992; A Golden Age (autobiography), 2000; You Can Win At Life, 2005. Honours: Sports Personality of the Year, 2000; British Sports Writers; Association Sportsman of the Year, 2000; Laurens Lifetime Achievement Award, 2001; Honorary DSc (Buckingham, Hull), 2001. Address: c/o British International Rowing Office, 6 Lower Mall, London W6 9DJ, England.

**REDGRAVE Vanessa,** b. 30 January 1937, England. Actress. m. Tony Richardson, 1962, divorced 1967, deceased 1991, 2 daughters, 1 son by Franco Reio. Education: Central School of Speech and Drama. Career: Films include: Morgan – A Suitable Case for Treatment; Sailor from Gibraltar, 1965; Charge of the Light Brigade; The Seagull; Isadora Duncan, 1968; The Devils, 1970; Mary Queen of Scots, 1971; Murder on the Orient Express, 1974; Julia, 1977; Playing for Time, 1980; Wetherby, 1984; Howard's End, 1992; Breath of Life, The Wall, Sparrow, They, The House of the Spirits, Crime and Punishment, Mother's Boys, Little Odessa, A Month by the Lake, 1996; Mission Impossible, 1996; Looking for Richard, 1997; Wilde, 1997; Mrs Dalloway, 1997; Bella Mafia (TV), 1997; Deep Impact, 1998; Cradle Will Rock, 2000; The House of the Spirits; Crime and Punishment; Little Odessa; Produced and narrated documentary film The Palestinians, 1977; Theatre includes: A Midsummer Night's Dream, 1959; The Prime of Miss Jean Brodie, 1966; Cato Street, 1971; Threepenny Opera, 1972; Macbeth, 1975; Ghosts, 1986; A Madhouse in Goa, 1989; Heartbreak House, 1992; Antony and Cleopatra, Houston, Texas (also directed), 1996; John Gabriel Borkman, 1996; Song at Twilight, 1999; The Cherry Orchard, 2000; The Tempest, 2000; Lady Windermere's Fan, 2002. Publications include: An Autobiography, 1991. Honours: Variety Club Award; Evening Standard Award for Best Actress, 1961; Cannes Film Festival Best Actress (Morgan-A Suitable Case for Treatment, 1966); UK Film Critic's Guild and National Society of Film Critics Leading Actress Award (Isadora Duncan,) 1969; Academy Award Best Supporting Actress (Julia, 1978); TV Award for Best Actress (Playing for Time, 1981); Laurence Olivier Award, 1984; Dr hc, Massachusetts, 1990. Memberships: Co-Founder Moving Theatre, 1974; Workers' Revolutionary Party (Candidate for Moss Side, 1979); Fellow, BFI, 1988.

**REDMAN Christopher Willard George,** b. 30 November 1941, Pretoria, South Africa. Clinical Professor of Obstetric Medicine. m. Corinna Susan Page, 4 sons, 1 daughter. Education: MB BChir, Cambridge University, 1967; MRCP, London, 1972; FRCP, London, 1981. Appointments: Training in Baltimore, USA, Oxford and Sheffield UK, 1967-70; Lecturer in Medicine, Oxford University, 1970-76; University Lecturer, 1976-89, Clinical Reader, 1989-92, Clinical Professor, 1992-, Obstetric Medicine, University of Oxford. Publications: More than 200 research and review articles on pre-eclampsia and medical disorders of pregnancy, 1973-. Honours: Chesley

Award, International Society for the Study of Hypertension in Pregnancy; Barnes Award, International Society of Obstetric Medicine. Memberships: Fellow of the Royal College of Physicians, London; Fellow of Lady Margaret Hall, Oxford. Address: Nuffield Department of Obstetrics and Gynaecology, John Radcliffe Hospital, Oxford OX3 9DU, England.

**REDTENBACHER Andreas Gottlieb,** b. 8 May 1953, Vienna, Austria. Roman Catholic Priest. Education: Mag. Theol., University of Vienna, Austria, 1977; Lic. Theol., 1979, Dr. Theol., 1983, Gregorian University, Rome; Postgraduate Student for Habilitation, University of Trier, Germany, 2002-. Appointments: Ordained Priest, 1978; Religions Professor and Rector for Students, 1979; University Assistant in Liturgy and Lecturer in Liturgy, University of Vienna, Austria, 1981; Parish Priest in St Vitus, 1990; Nominated President, Committee for Liturgy in the Episcopal-Vikariat of the City of Vienna, Austria, 1981; Nominated President of the Conference of Liturgists in the Austrian Roman Catholic Church, 1995. Publications: Presbyter und Presbyterium, 1980; Zukunft aus dem Erbe, 1983, second edition, 2003: Wo Sich Wege Kreuzen, 1985; Liturgie und Leben, 2002; Reike: Pices – Parsch Fluodrien, bisher Bel I-II; Die Zukunft der Liturgie, 2004; Liturgie in der Stadl, 2005; Many published articles. Honour: Archiepiscopal Konsistorialrat. Memberships: International Societas Liturgica; Editorial Board, Heiliger Dienst; Corresponding Member, Editorial Board, Bibel und Liturgie. Address: Stiftplatz 1, A-3400 Klosterneuburg, Austria. E-mail: a.redtenbacher@stift-klosterneuburg.at

**REDWOOD John Alan (Rt Hon),** b. 15 June 1951, Dover, England. Member of Parliament. m. Gail Chippington, 14 June 1974, 1 son, 1 daughter. Education: BA, Honours 1971, MA, DPhil, 1975, Oxford University. Appointments: Manager, then Director, NM Rothschild & Sons, 1977-89; Chairman Norcros Plc, 1987-89; MP for Wokingham, 1987-; Minister, UK Government, 1989-95; Shadow President, Board of Trade, 1997-99; Shadow Front Bench Spokesman on the Environment, 1999-2000; Chair, Murray Financial Corporation, 2002-04; Chairman Concentric plc, 2003-. Publications: Reason, Ridicule and Religion, 1976; Public Enterprise in Crisis, 1980; Co-author, Value for Money Audits, 1981; Co-author, Controlling Public Industries, 1982; Going for Broke, 1984; Equity for Everyman, 1986; Popular Capitalism, 1989; Global Marketplace, 1994; The Single European Currency, with others, 1996; Our Currency, Our Country, 1997; The Death of Britain? 1999; Stars and Strife, 2001; Just Say No, 2001; Third Way – Which Way, 2002; Singing the Blues, 2004; Superpower Struggles, 2005. Honours: Parliamentarian of the Year Awards, 1987, 1995, 1997. Address: House of Commons, London, SW1A 0AA, England.

**REED Lou,** b. 2 March 1942, Brooklyn, New York, USA. Musician. m. Sylvia Morales, 1980. Education: BA, Syracuse University. Songwriter and recording artist, 1965-; Founder member, Velvet Underground band, 1966-70; Toured with Andy Warhol's The Exploding Plastic Inevitable; Poet; Film actor. Publications: Recordings, solo albums include: Lou Reed, 1972; Rock'n'Roll Animal, 1972; Berlin, 1973; Sally Can't Dance, 1974; Metal Machine Music, 1975; Lou Reed Live, 1975; Coney Island Baby, 1976; Walk on the Wild Side; Street Hassle, 1978; Live, Take No Prisoners, 1978; Vicious, 1979; The Bells, 1979; Growing Up in Public, 1980; Rock 'n' Roll Diary, 1967-80; Blue Mask, Legendary Hearts, 1983; New York, 1989; Songs for Drella (with John Cale), 1990; Magic and Loss, 1992; Set the Twilight Reeling, 1996; Perfect Night Live in London, 1998; Ecstasy, 2000; Several albums with Velvet Underground. Publication: Between Thought and Expression (selected lyrics), 1991; Pass Thru Fire, 2000. Honour: Rock and

Roll Hall of Fame, 1996. Address: c/o Sister Ray Enterprises, 584 Broadway, Room 609, New York, NY 10012, USA.

**REES David Benjamin,** b. 1 August 1937, Wales. Minister of Religion; Lecturer; Author. m. 31 July 1963, 2 sons. Education: BA, BD, MSc, University of Wales; MA, University of Liverpool; PhD, University of Salford; FRHisS. Appointments: Minister, Presbyterian Church of Wales, Cynon Valley, 1962-68, Heathfield Road, Liverpool, 1968-; Part-time Lecturer, University of Liverpool, 1970-99; Editor, Angor, Liverpool, 1979-; Editor, Peace and Reconciliation Magazine, 2000-02. Publications: Wales: A Cultural History, 1980; Preparation for a Crisis: Adult Education in England and Wales 1945-1980, 1981; Liverpool, Welsh and Their Religion, 1984; Owen Thomas: A Welsh Preacher in Liverpool, 1991; The Welsh of Merseyside, 1997; Local and Parliamentary Politics in Liverpool from 1800 to 1911, 1999. Contributions to: Magazines and newspapers such as Independent and Guardian. Honour: Ellis Griffith Prize, 1979. Memberships: Cymmrodorion Society; Welsh Academy. Address: 32 Garth Drive, Liverpool L18 6HW, England. E-mail: ben@garthdrive.fsnet.co.uk

**REES Peter Wynford Innes (Baron of Goytre in the County of Gwent),** b. 9 December 1926. Life Peer; Barrister; Politician. m. Anthea Peronelle Wendell. Education: Christ Church, Oxford. Appointments: Served in Scots Guards, 1945-48; Called to the Bar, Inner Temple, 1953; Bencher; Practised Oxford circuit; Contested, as a Conservative, Abertillery, 1964, 1965, Liverpool, West Derby, 1966; Elected MP (Conservative), Dover, 1970-74, Dover and Deal, 1974-83, Dover, 1983-87; PPS to Solicitor General, 1972; Minister of State, HM Treasury, 1979-81; Minister of Trade, 1981-83; Chief Secretary to the Treasury and Member of Cabinet, 1983-85. Honours: QC, 1969; PC, 1983. Memberships: Former Member, Court and Council, Museum of Wales, Museum and Galleries Commission; Liveryman, Worshipful Company of Clockmakers. Address: Goytre Hall, Abergavenny, Monmouthshire NP7 9DL, Wales.

**REES-MOGG Lord William, Baron Rees-Mogg of Hinton Blewitt,** b. 14 July 1928, Bristol, England; Journalist; Writer. m. Gillian Shakespeare Morris, 1962, 2 sons, 3 daughters. Education: Balliol College, Oxford. Appointments: Staff, The Financial Times, 1952-60; City Editor, 1960-61, Political and Economic Editor, 1961-63, Deputy Editor, 1964-67, The Sunday Times; Editor, 1967-81, Columnist, 1992-, The Times; Columnist, The Mail on Sunday, 2004-; Director, The Times Ltd, 1968-81, GEC, 1981-97, EFG Private Bank, 1993-, Value Realisation Trust, 1996-99; Vice-Chairman, Board of Governors, BBC, 1981-86; Chairman, Arts Council of Great Britain, 1982-89, Pickering and Chatto Ltd, 1983-, Sidgwick and Jackson, 1985-89, Broadcasting Standards Council, 1988-93, International Business Communications plc, 1994-98; Chairman, Fleet Street Publications, 1995-. Publications: The Reigning Error: The Crisis of World Inflation, 1974; An Humbler Heaven, 1977; How to Buy Rare Books, 1985; Blood in the Streets (with James Dale Davidson), 1988; The Great Reckoning (with James Dale Davidson), 1991; Picnics on Vesuvius: Steps Toward the Millennium, 1992; The Sovereign Individual: How to Survive and Thrive During the Collapse of the Welfare State (with James Dale Davidson), 1997. Honours: Honorary LLD, University of Bath, 1977; Knighted, 1981; Life Peerage, 1988. Address: 17 Pall Mall, London SW1Y 5LU, England.

**REEVE Jonathan,** b. 5 January 1943, Pembury, Kent, England. Physician. m. Caroline, 2 sons, 3 daughters. Education: Oriel College, Oxford and Guy's Hospital, London, 1961-68, 1965-68; MA, BM, BCh, 1976; DM, 1976; FRCP (Lond), 1983; DSc (Oxon), 1984. Appointments: MRC Clinical Research Fellow, Clinical Research Centre, Harrow, 1973-76; Fogarty-NIH International Travelling Fellow, Massachusetts General Hospital, 1976-77; MRC Clinical Scientific Staff, CRC, Harrow, 1977-93, (Head Bone Research, 1985-93); MRC ESS and Consultant Physician, Addenbrooke's Hospital, Cambridge, 1994-. Publications: 200 peer reviewed articles in scientific literature, principally concerning diseases of the skeleton; 117 other articles including reviews and book chapters. Honours: André Lichtwitz Prize for Research on Calcified Tissues, INSERM, France, 1984; Kohn Award for Excellence in Osteoporosis, National Osteoporosis Society, 2001. Memberships: Academy of Medical Sciences; Royal College of Physicians, London; Association of Physicians; Bone and Tooth Society; American Society of Bone and Mineral Research. Address: Box 157, Department of Medicine, Addenbrooke's Hospital, Cambridge CB2 2QQ, England.

**REEVE Marion José,** b. 26 September 1926, Watford, England. Artist. m. Albert Edward Butcher, 6 November 1968, deceased. Education: St Joan of Arc School, Rickmansworth, England, 1937-44; Intermediate Examination, Art and Crafts, 1950; National Diploma, Design, 1953. Career: Landscape Painter and Sculptor. Honour: Stations of the Cross, St Michael and All Angles Church West Watford, England. Address: 10 Kelmscott Crescent, Watford, Hertfordshire, WD18 0NG, England.

**REEVES Keanu,** b. 2 September 1964, Beirut, Lebanon. Actor. Education: Toronto High School for Performing Arts; Training at Second City Workshop. Career: Stage appearances include: Wolf Boy; For Adults Only; Romeo and Juliet; with rock band Dogstar, 1996-; TV films: Letting Go, 1985; Act of Vengeance, 1986; Babes in Toyland, 1986; Under the Influence, 1986; Brotherhood of Justice, 1986; Save the Planet (TV special), 1990; Films: Prodigal, Flying, 1986; Youngblood, 1986; River's Edge, 1987; Permanent Record, 1988; The Night Before, 1988; The Prince of Pennsylvania, 1988; Dangerous Liaisons, 1988; I Love You to Death, 1990; Tune in Tomorrow, 1990; Bill and Ted's Bogus Journey, 1991; Point Break, 1991; My Own Private Idaho, 1991; Bram Stoker's Dracula, 1992; Much Ado About Nothing, 1993; Even Cowgirls Get the Blues, Little Buddha, 1993; Speed, 1994; Johnny Mnemonic, 1995; A Walk in the Clouds, 1995; Chain Reaction, Feeling Minnesota, The Devil's Advocate, 1996; The Last Time I Committed Suicide, 1997; The Matrix, 1998; The Replacements, 2000; The Watcher, 2000; The Gift, 2000; Sweet November, 2001; The Matrix: Reloaded, 2003; The Matrix: Revolutions, 2003; Something's Gotta Give, 2003. Address: c/o Kevin Houvane, 9830 Wilshire Boulevard, Beverly Hills, CA 90212, USA.

**REGIS John,** b. 13 October 1966, Lewisham, London, England. Athlete. Career: Winner, UK 200m (tie), 1985; 100m, 1988, Amateur Athletics Association 200m, 1986-87; UK record for 200m, Silver Medal, Olympic Games Seoul, 1988; 300m indoor record holder Commonwealth Games, 1990; Silver Medal 200m, 1991; Gold medal 4 x 100m relay, 1991; Gold Medal 200m 4 x 400m relay, 4 x 400m relay, 1993; Gold Medal World Cup, 1994; Member, British team Olympic Games, Atlanta, 1996; Retired, 2000; Member, Great Britain bobsleigh training team, 2000-; Founder, Stellar Athletes Ltd, 2001; Coach, UK Athletics sprint relay team, 2001-. Address: c/o Belgrave Harriers Athletic Club, Batley Croft, 58 Harvest Road, Englefield Green, Surrey, England.

**REGNARD Thomy Maxime Christian,** b. 7 October 1958, Curepipe, Mauritius. Company Managing Director. m. M A Alexandra Pitot, 3 sons. Education: SC; HSC. Appointments: Marketing Manager, Ferney Textiles, 1983-89; Managing Director, Associated Textiles, 1989-. Honours: Certificate of

Award Department Management, 1980; Certificate of Merit, 1980; Certificate in Marketing Management, 1980; Diploma in Marketing Management, 1981. Memberships: Mauritius Turf Club; Dodo Club; Institute of Marketing Management, South Africa. Address: Bois Cheri Road, Moka, Mauritius. E-mail: tichris@intnet.mu

**REID Christina,** b. 12 Mar 1942, Belfast, Northern Ireland. Playwright. Education: Queen's University, Belfast, 1982-83. Appointments: Writer-in-Residence, Lyric Theatre, Belfast, 1983-84, Young Vic Theatre, London, 1988-89. Publications: Did You Hear the One About the Irishman?, 1980; Tea in a China Cup, 1983; Joyriders, 1986; The Last of a Dyin' Race, 1986; The Belle of The Belfast City, 1986; My Name? Shall I Tell You My Name?, 1987; Les Miserables (after Hugo), 1992; Clowns, 1996; The King of the Castle, 1999. Christina Reid: Plays One, 1997; The Gift of the Gab, 2004. Plays produced in England, Ireland, Europe (in translation), Australia and USA. Honours: Ulster TV Drama Award, 1980; Giles Cooper Award, 1986; George Devine Award, 1986. Address: 6th floor, Fairgate House, 78 New Oxford Street, London WC1A 1HB, England

**REID Graham Charles,** b. 29 August 1945, Finchley, England. Chartered Accountant. m. Gaye, 1 son. Education: Kings College, London University, 1963-66. Appointments: Articled Clerk, Legg London & Co, 1966-69; Chartered Accountant, Grant Thornton (formerly Thornton Baker), London Office, 1970-77, Manager, Founded Ipswich Office, 1977-79, Partner, Ipswich Office, 1979-2002; Retired, Tax Planning Consultant, 2002-. Memberships: Treasurer, Suffolk Branch of the Institute of Directors; Chairman, Suffolk Board, The Prince's Trust; Member, Eastern Regional Council, The Prince's Trust. Address: Mitchery Farmhouse, Rattlesden, Bury St Edmunds, Suffolk, IP30 0SS, England. E-mail: grahamcreid@msn.com

**REID John,** b. 8 May 1947, Bellshill, Lanarkshire, Scotland. Politician. m. (1) Cathie, deceased 1998, 2 sons, (2) Carine Adler. Education: PhD, History, Stirling University; PC, 1998. Appointments include: Research Officer, Labour Party in Scotland, 1979-83; Political Adviser to Labour Leader, Neil Kinnock, 1983-85; Scottish Organiser, Trade Unionists for Labour, 1986-87; Member of Parliament representing Motherwell North and then Hamilton North and Bellshill for the past 17 years; Parliamentary Posts: Opposition Spokesman on Children, 1989-90; Opposition Spokesman in Defence, 1990-97; Minister of Defence, 1997-98; Minister for Transport, 1989-99; Secretary of State for Scotland, 1999-2001; Secretary of State for Northern Ireland, 2001-2002; Party Chair and Minister without Portfolio, 2002-2003; Leader of the House of Commons, 2003; Secretary of State for Health, 2003-. Address: House of Commons, London, SW1A 0AA, England.

**REID SCOTT David Alexander Carroll,** b. 5 June 1947, Ireland. Company Chairman. m. (1) 3 daughters, (3) Clare Straker, 1 son. Education: MA, Lincoln College, Oxford. Appointments: Vice-President, White Weld & Co, 1969-77; Seconded Senior Advisor, Saudi Arabian Monetary Agency, 1978-83; Managing Director, Merrill Lynch & Co, 1983-84; Managing Director, DLJ Phoenix Securities Ltd, 1984-98; Vice Chairman, Donaldson Lufkin & Jenrette, 1998-2000; Vice-Chairman, CSFB, 2000-2001; Chairman, Hawkpoint Partners, 2001-. Honours: BA, MA, Modern History. Memberships: Turf Club; Kildare Street Club, Dublin; Irish Georgian Society; Lloyd's of London; Advisor to the Board, The Cabo Delgado Biodiversity and Tourism Project, Mozambique. Address: 2 Cottismore Gardens, London W8 5PR, England. E-mail: david.reidscott@hawkpoint.com

**REIF Stefan Clive,** b. 21 January 1944, Edinburgh, Scotland. Professor; Writer. m. Shulamit Stekel, 19 September 1967, 1 son, 1 daughter. Education: BA, Honours, 1964, PhD, 1969, University of London; MA, 1976, LittD, 2002, University of Cambridge, England. Appointments: Professor of Medieval Hebrew Studies and Director of Genizah Research, University of Cambridge; Editor, Cambridge University Library's Genizah Series, 1978-. Publications: Shabbethai Sofer and his Prayer-book, 1979; Interpreting the Hebrew Bible, 1982; Published Material from the Cambridge Genizah Collections, 1988; Genizah Research after Ninety Years, 1992; Judaism and Hebrew Prayer, 1993; Hebrew Manuscripts at Cambridge University Library, 1997; A Jewish Archive from Old Cairo, 2000; Why Medieval Hebrew Studies, 2001; The Cambridge Genizah Collections, 2002. Contributions to: Over 250 articles in Hebrew and Jewish studies. Memberships: Fellow, Royal Asiatic Society; Council, Jewish Historical Society of England, ex-president, 1991-92; Honorary Fellow, Mekize Nirdamim Society, Jerusalem; British Association for Jewish Studies, ex-president, 1992; Society for Old Testament Study; Theological Society, Cambridge, ex-president, 2002-04. Address: Taylor Schechter Genizah Research Unit, Cambridge University Library, West Road, Cambridge CB3 9DR, England.

**REILLY-DEAS Anne,** b. 28 November 1950, Mullingar, Ireland. Artist; Poet; Accounting Executive. m. Arthur Deas, divorced. Education: Loreto College; Bloomfield College; Business Studies, Rosse Business College and Christie Business College. Career: Accounting Executive in the private and public sectors, 1967-83; Volunteer work, campaign work, 1983-86; Artist, 1986-; Exhibitions: Invited to exhibit: Tullynally Castle, 1986; Caley House, 1988; Granard Library, 1989; Longford Library, 1989; Mullingar Library, 1989; Cheltenham Show, 1990; Irish Council Against Blood Sports Art Exhibition, 1990; ArtUs, Mullingar Arts Resource Centre, 1992; Art Horizons, New York, USA, 1992; Art 54 Gallery, New York, 1993; International Lions Club Art Auction, 1993; Townley Hall, Drogheda, 1996; Allen Manor, 1997-98; Mullingar Arts Centre, 1999; Christie Wild International, Florida and Harrogate, 2000; DFN Gallery, New York, 2000; International ArtExpo, New York, 1997-2001; International ArtExpo, San Francisco, 2000-2001; Special Olympic Games Art Exhibition, 2003; Orchard House, 2002-2004; Greenville, 1989-92, 2001-2004. Publications: Features in: Westmeath Examiner Newspaper; Longford Leader Newspaper; Modern Woman Magazine; Events Programme Alliance Française; Brochures; Catalogues; Poems published in newspapers and magazines. Honours: Prize Winner, Athlone Agricultural Show Art Section, 1986; Selected, Royal Hibernian Academy Summer Exhibition, Dublin, 1992; Selected/Commended Certificate National Irish Bank Exhibition, Dublin, 1994; Sponsored/Selected Solo Exhibition "Through Time," Alliance Française, Dublin, presented with a book "Art Contemporain En France," 1996; Invited/Selected New York Prestige Artists Debut, 2000; Listed in Who's Who publications and biographical dictionaries. Membership: Qualified for Mensa Membership. Address: Greenville, Dublin Road, Castlepollard, Co. Westmeath, Ireland.

**REINER Rob,** b. 6 March 1947, New York, USA. Actor; Writer; Director. (1) Penny Marshall, 1971, divorced, (2) Michele Singer, 1989. Education; University of California at Los Angeles. Career: Appeared with comic improvisation groups: The Session; The Committee; Scriptwriter for Enter Laughing, 1967; Halls of Anger, 1970; Where's Poppa, 1970; Summertree, 1971; Fire Sale, 1977; How Come Nobody's on Our Side, 1977; TV appearances: All in the Family, 1971-78; Free Country, 1978; Thursday's Game, 1974; More Than Friends, 1978; Million Dollar Infield, 1972; Director, This is

Spinal Tap, 1984; The Sure Thing, 1985; Stand By Me, 1986; The Princess Bride, 1987; Misery, 1990; Co-producer, director, When Harry Met Sally, 1989; A Few Good Men, 1992; North, The American President, 1995; Ghosts of the Mississippi, 1996; The Story of Us, 1999; Alex and Emma, 2003; Rumor Has It ..., 2005. Address: c/o Castle Rock Entertainment, 335 North Maple Drive, Suite 135, Beverly Hills, CA 90212, USA.

**REINL Harry Charles,** b. 13 November 1932, Germany (US Citizen). Economist; Researcher. Education: BS, Fordham University, 1953; Certificate, Graduate School, United State Department of Agriculture, Washington, 1966; MA, George Washington University, 1968; Certificate, Massachusetts Institute of Technology, 1972; Certificate, Modern Digital Communication, George Washington University School of Engineering and Applied Science, 1974. Appointments: Head, Market Research, Timex Manufacturing, Waterbury Connecticut, 1955-58; Junior Observer, Sperry Rand Corporation, New York City, 1958-62; Labour Economist, Manpower Administration, United States Department of Labor, Washington, 1962-68; Labour Economist, Office of Personnel Management, United States Civil Service Commission, Washington, 1968-; Manager, New York Branch, Willmark Service, New York City, 1971; Neurology Testing, Veterans Administration Medical Center, Washington DC, 1989-; Research Professor, Haute Ecole de Recherché, 1992; Founding Partner, Hudson Institute Competitiveness Center, 1993-; Deputy Director General, International Biographical Centre, 1997; Member, Academic Council, London Diplomatic Academy, 2004. Publications: Several professional publications include: Entry in the New York Law Journal, 1984; Author (on microfilm) The Story of My Life, 1984; Author of an Inspirational Essay in the IBC's Millennium Time Capsule, 2000. Honours: HHD, London Institute of Applied Research, 1992; Honorary Doctorate, Brownell University, 1993; Republican Majority Medal, 1997; Medal of Freedom, Republican National Senatorial Inner Circle, 1999; Da Vinci Diamond Award, 2003; Certificate of Service George Bush Presidential Library Foundation, 2003; International Peace Prize, 2005. Memberships: Life Member, Republican National Committee, Washington, 1979-; Member, Republican National Senatorial Committee, Washington, 1990; Founding Member, World Peace and Diplomacy Forum, Cambridge, 2003; Founding Member, National Tolerance Campaign, Montgomery, Alabama, 2004; New York Academy of Sciences; Family Immigration History Center, Ellis Island (Contributor); President's Club; Fordham University Club, Washington. Address: 2425 Mt Vernon Avenue, Alexandria, VA 22301, USA.

**REITMAN Ivan,** b. 27 October 1946, Komarno, Czechoslovakia. Film Director and Producer. m. Genevieve Robert, 1 son, 2 daughter. Education: MusB, McMaster University. Career: Producer, stage shows: The Magic Show, 1974; The National Lampoon Show, 1975; Merlin (also director), 1983; Director and Executive Producer, films: Cannibal Girls, 1973; They Came From Within, 1975; Death Weekend, 1977; Blackout, 1978; National Lampoon's Animal House, 1978; Heavy Metal, 1981; Stop! Or My Mom Will Shoot, 1992; Space Jam, 1996; Private Parts, 1996; Producer and Director: Foxy Lady, 1971; Meatballs, 1979; Stripes, 1981; Ghostbusters, 1984; Legal Eagles, 1986; Twins, 1988; Ghostbusters II, 1989; Kindergarten Cop, 1990; Dave, 1993; Junior, 1994; Executive Producer: Rabid, 1976; Spacehunter: Adventures in the Forbidden Zone, 1983; Big Shots, 1987; Casual Sex?, 1988; Feds, 1988; Beethoven, 1992; Beethoven's 2nd, 1993; Commandments, 1996; Road Trip, 2000; Producer and director, TV series: The Late Shift, 1996; Father's Day, 1997. Membership: Director's Guild of America.

Address: c/o CAA, 9830 Wilshire Boulevard, Beverly Hills, CA 90212, USA.

**REMNICK David J,** b. 29 October 1958, Hackensack, New Jersey, USA. Journalist; Writer. m. Esther B Fein, 2 sons, 1 daughter. Education: AB, Princeton University, 1981. Appointments: Reporter, Washington Post, 1982-91; Staff writer, 1992-, Editor-in-Chief, 1998-, The New Yorker. Publications: Lenin's Tomb: The Last Days of the Soviet Empire, 1993; The Devil Problem (and Other True Stories), 1996; Resurrection: The Struggle for a New Russia, 1997; King of the World: Muhammad Ali and the Rise of an American Hero, 1998; Life Stories: Profiles from The New Yorker (editor), 1999; Wonderful Town: Stories from The New Yorker (editor), 1999. Contributions to: Newspapers and periodicals. Honours: Livingston Award, 1991; Pulitzer Prize for General Non-Fiction, 1993; Helen Bernstein Award, New York Public Library, 1994; George Polk Award, 1994. Address: The New Yorker, Four Times Square, New York, NY 10036, USA.

**REMOVILLE Jacques Robert Philippe,** b. 17 December 1934, Hanoï, Vietnam. Chemical Engineer. m. Nicole Dramas, 1 son, 2 daughters. Education: Ingenieur, Ecole Centrale des Arts et Manufactures de Paris, 1959. Appointments: Scientific Officer, then Acting Head of Unit, Post-Irradiation Service, Joint Research Centre, Karlsruhe and Petten, 1962-68; Research Coordinator, Luxatom, 1969-84; Scientific Officer, Torus Remote Operations, Joint European Torus, Culham, UK, 1984-89; Senior Administrative Officer, Commission of the European Communities, DG Research, Brussels, 1990-99. Publications: 33 international presentations or publications, including 16 nuclear, 2 solar and 15 on science policy; 29 EC reports. Honour: Médaille de Reconnaissance, FLSG, 1985. Memberships: Association des Centraliens. Address: 1157 Avenue du Golf, La Tour de Mare, F 83600, Fréjus, France.

**RENCYS Sigitas,** b. 8 November 1948, Siauliai City, Lithuania. Scientist; Writer; Manager. m. Ina, 2 daughters. Education: Diploma, Philology and Lithuanian Language and Literature Teaching, Vilnius University, 1966-71; Postgraduate Studies, Doctor of Humanities, Academy of Public Sciences, Moscow, Russia, 1977-80. Appointments: Consultant on Literature, Lithuanian Writer's Union, 1970-74; Instructor, Assistant Head, Head, Culture Division, Central Committee, Lithuanian Communist Party, 1974-87; Assistant Head, Culture Division, Head, Arts Sector, Assistant Head, Division of Humanities, Central Committee of Soviet Union Communist Party, 1987-91; Deputy Director General, Publishing Firm "Marathon", 1991-92; Editor-in-Chief, Private Company "Fodio", 1992; Country Director in Lithuania, MBA Enterprise Corps, USA, 1993-97; State Counsellor on Science and Development, Government of the Republic of Lithuania, 1994; Program Head, Business Training Centre in Vilnius, Business Institute of Kaunas University and Norwegian Management Institute, 1997-99; Administrator, Vilnius Branch, International School of Management, 1999-2000; Director, Baltic Management Foundation, 1993-2002; Director, Lithuanian State Science and Studies Foundation, 2002-. Publications: Author of books: Fidelity to the Human being, 1979; Tragedy: History and Today, 1983; The Abyss of Hope, 1998; Boy's Poems, 2004; Co-author of several books about Lithuanian literature; About 200 publications in periodicals, including publications on culture, literature, management and economy education. Honours: Listed in Who's Who publications and biographical dictionaries. Memberships: Council Member, Governing Council of European Science Foundation; Lithuanian Writer's Union; Council Member, Lithuanian Society of Management; Board Member, Lithuanian Association of Scientific and Technical

Societies; Council Member, Lithuanian-Ukrainian Friendship Society; Board Member, Lithuanian Concordia Fund; Council Member, Vilnius Branch, Lithuanian Social Democratic Party. Address: J Basanaviciaus g 17-25, LT-2009 Vilnius, Lithuania. E-mail: sigitas@ktl.mii.lt

**RENDELL Ruth Barbara (Baroness Rendell of Babergh), (Barbara Vine),** b. 17 February 1930, England. Writer. m. Donald Rendell, 1950, divorced 1975, 1 son, remarried Donald Rendell, 1977, deceased 1999. Publications: From Doon with Death, 1964; To Fear a Painted Devil, 1965; Vanity Dies Hard, 1966; A New Lease of Death, 1967; Wolf to the Slaughter, 1967 (televised 1987); The Secret House of Death, 1968; The Best Man to Die, 1969; A Guilty Thing Surprised, 1970; One Across Two Down, 1971; No More Dying Then, 1971; Murder Being Once Done, 1972; Some Lie and Some Die, 1973; The Face of Trespass, 1974 (televised as An Affair in Mind, 1988); Shake Hands for Ever, 1975; A Demon in My View, 1976 (film 1991); A Judgement in Stone, 1977; A Sleeping Life, 1978; Make Death Love Me, 1979; The Lake of Darkness, 1980 (televised as Dead Lucky, 1988); Put on by Cunning, 1981; Master of the Moor, 1982 (televised 1994); The Speaker of Mandarin, 1983; The Killing Doll, 1984; The Tree of Hands, 1984 (film 1989); An Unkindness of Ravens, 1985; Live Flesh, 1986; Heartstones, 1987; Talking to Strange Men, 1987; A Warning to the Curious: The Ghost Stories of M R James (editor), 1987; The Veiled One, 1988 (televised 1989); The Bridesmaid, 1989; Ruth Rendell's Suffolk, 1989; Undermining the Central Line (with Colin Ward), 1989; Going Wrong, 1990; Kissing the Gunner's Daughter, 1992; The Crocodile Bird, 1993; Simisola, 1994; The Reason Why (editor), 1995; The Keys to the Street, 1997; Road Rage, 1997; The Chimney Sweeper's Boy, 1998; A Sight for Sore Eyes, 1999; Harm Done, 1999; The Babes in the Wood, 2002; As Barbara Vine: A Dark-Adapted Eye, 1986 (televised 1994); A Fatal Inversion, 1987 (televised 1992); The House of Stairs, 1988; Gallowglass, 1990; King Solomon's Carpet, 1981; Asta's Book, 1993; No Night is Too Long, 1994; The Brimstone Wedding, 1996; Grasshopper, 2000; Piranha to Scurfy and Other Stories, 2000; Short Stories: The Fallen Curtain, 1976; Means of Evil, 1979; The Fever Tree, 1982; The New Girl Friend, 1985; Collected Short Stories, 1987; The Copper Peacock, 1991; Blood Linen, 1995. Honours: Arts Council National Book Award for Genre Fiction, 1981; Royal Society of Literature, Fellow, 1988; Sunday Times Award for Literary Excellence, 1990; Cartier Diamond Dagger Award, Crime Writers Association, 1991; Commander of the Order of the British Empire, 1996; Life Peerage, 1997. Memberships: Royal Society of Literature, Fellow. Address: 26 Cornwall Terrace Mews, London, NW1 5LL, England.

**RENFREW (Andrew) Colin (Baron Renfrew of Kaimsthorn),** b. 25 July 1937, Stockton-on-Tees, England. Educator; Archaeologist; Author. m. Jane M Ewbank, 1965, 2 sons, 1 daughter. Education: St John's College, Cambridge; BA Honours, 1962, MA, 1964, PhD, 1965, ScD, 1976, Cambridge University; British School of Archaeology, Athens. Appointments: Lecturer, 1965-70, Senior Lecturer in Prehistory and Archaeology, 1970-72, Reader, 1972, University of Sheffield; Head of Department, Professor of Archaeology, University of Southampton, 1972-81; Head of Department, Disney Professor of Archaeology, University of Cambridge, 1981-; Master, Jesus College, Cambridge, 1986-97; Director, McDonald Institute for Archaeological Research, 1990-; Guest Lecturer, universities, colleges; Narrator, television films, radio programmes, British Broadcasting Corporation. Publications include: The Emergence of Civilisation: The Cyclades and the Aegean in the Third Millennium B.C., 1972; Before Civilisation: The Radiocarbon Revolution and Prehistoric Europe, 1973;

Problems in European Prehistory, 1979; Approaches to Social Archaeology, 1984; The Archaeology of Cult: The Sanctuary at Phylakopi, 1985; Archaeology and Language: The Puzzle of Indo-European Origins, 1988; The Idea of Prehistory, co-author, 1988; Archaeology: Theories, Methods, and Practice, co-author, 1991, 2nd edition, 1996; The Cycladic Spirit: Masterpieces from the Nicholas P Goulandris Collection, 1991; The Ancient Mind: Elements of Cognitive Archaeology, co-editor, 1994; Loot, Legitimacy and Ownership, 2000; Archaeogenetics (editor), 2000; Contributor to: Journals including Archaeology; Scientific American. Honours: Rivers Memorial Medal, Royal Anthropological Institute, 1979; Fellow, St John's College, Cambridge, 1981-86; Sir Joseph Larmor Award, 1981; DLitt, Sheffield University, 1987; Huxley Memorial Medal and Life Peerage, 1991; Honorary Degree, University of Athens, 1991; DLitt, University of Southampton, 1995; Foreign Associate, National Academy of Sciences, USA, 1997; Fyssen Prize, 1997. Memberships include: Fellow, British Academy; Ancient Monuments Board for England, 1974-84; Royal Commission on Historical Monuments, 1977-87; Historic Buildings and Monuments Commission for England, 1984-86; Ancient Monuments Advisory Committee, 1984-; British National Commission for UNESCO, 1984-86; Trustee, British Museum, 1991-. Address: McDonald Institute for Archaeological Research, Downing Street, Cambridge, CB2 3ER, England.

**RENO Janet,** b. 21 July 1938, Miami, Florida, USA. Lawyer. Education: BA, Cornell University; LLB, Harvard University. Appointments: Florida Bar, 1963; Associate, Brigham & Brigham, 1963-67; Partner, Lewis & Reno, 1971-72; Administrative Assistant State Attorney, 11th Judicial Circuit Florida, Miami, 1973-76, State Attorney, 1978-93; Partner, Steel, Hector & Davis, Miami, 1976-78; US Attorney-General, 1993-2001. Memberships: American Bar Association; American Law Institute; American Judicature Society. Honours: Women First Award, YWCA, 1993; National Women's Hall of Fame, 2000. Address: Department of Justice, 10th Street and Constitution Avenue, NW Washington, DC 20530, USA.

**RENO Jean,** b. 30 July 1948, Casablanca, Morocco. Actor. m. (1) divorced, 1 son, 1 daughter, (2) Nathalie Dyszkiewicz, 1996, 1 son, 1 daughter. Career: Films: Clair de Femme, 1979; Le Dernier Combat, 1983; Signes Extérieurs de Richesse, 1983; Notre Histoire, 1984; Subway, 1985; I Love You, 1986; The Big Blue, 1988; L'Homme au Masque d'Or, 1990; La Femme Nikita, 1991; L'Operation Corned Beef, 1991; Loulou Graffitti, 1991; The Visitors (also wrote screenplay), 1993; Leon, 1994; French Kiss, 1995; Roseanna's Grave, 1997; Les Couloirs du Temps, 1998; Godzilla, 1998; Les Rivieres pourpres, 2000; Just Visiting, 2001; Wasabi, 2001; Decalage horaire, 2002; Rollerball, 2002; Tais-toi, 2003; Les Rivieres pourpres 2 – Les anges de l'apocalypse, 2004; Onimusha 3, 2004. Address: Chez Les Films du Dauphin, 25 rue Yves-Toudic, 75010 Paris, France.

**RENTON, Baron (Life-Peer) of Huntingdon in the County of Cambridgeshire, David Lockhart-Mure Renton,** b. 12 August 1908, Dartford, Kent, England. Barrister; QC. m. Clare Duncan, 3 daughters. Education: MA, BCL, University College, Oxford, 1927-31. Appointments: Called to Bar, Lincoln's Inn, 1933; South Eastern Circuit; Junior, 1938, Elected to General Council of the Bar, 1939; QC, 1954; Bencher, Lincoln's Inn, 1962, Treasurer, 1979; Major RA, served in SE England, 1939-42, Egypt and Libya, 1942-45; MP, Huntingdonshire, 1945-79, National Liberal, 1945-50, National Liberal and Conservative, 1950-68, Conservative, 1968-79; Parliamentary Secretary, Ministry of Fuel and Power, 1955-57, Ministry of Power, 1957-58; Joint Parliamentary Under-Secretary of State, Home Office,

1958-61; Minister of State, Home Office, 1961-62; Chairman, Select Committee for Revision of Standing Orders, House of Commons, 1963, 1970; Deputy Chairman, Special Select Committee on House of Commons Procedure, 1976-79; Member, Committee of Privileges, 1963-68; Recorder of Rochester, 1963-68, Guildford, 1968-71; Vice-Chairman, Council of Legal Education, 1968-70, 1971-73; Member of Senate of Inns of Court, 1967-69, 1970-71, 1975-79; Royal Commission on the Constitution, 1971-73; Chairman, Committee on Preparation of Legislation, 1973-75; A Deputy Speaker of the House of Lords, 1982-88. Publications: Occasional articles in legal journals and in the Parliamentary House Magazine. Honours: QC, 1954; Privy Counsellor, 1962, KBE, 1964; Deputy Lieutenant, Huntingdonshire, 1962, Huntingdon and Peterborough, 1964, Cambridgeshire, 1974; Life Peer, 1979. Memberships: President, Conservation Society, 1970-71; President, Statute Law Society, 1980-2000; President, MENCAP, 1982-88; President, National Council for Civil Protection (formerly National Council for Civil Defence), 1980-91; President, All Party Arts and Heritage Group, 1989; Patron: Huntingdon Conservative Association, 1979-, Ravenswood Foundation, 1979, Huntingdonshire RBL, 1984-, Greater London Association for the Disabled, 1986-; Design and Manufacture for Disablement, 1986-; Carlton Club; Pratts. Address: 16 Old Buildings Lincoln's Inn, London WC2A, England.

**RESENDE Marcelo,** b. 26 August 1963, Rio de Janeiro, Brazil. Researcher; Lecturer. Education: BA, Economics, 1985, BS, Psychology, 1990, State University of Rio de Janeiro; MSc, Pontifical Catholic University, 1989; MA, Economics, University of Pennsylvania, 1993; DPhil, Economics, University of Oxford, 1997. Appointments: Lecturer, Pontifical Catholic University, 1987-89; Assistant Professor, State University of Rio de Janeiro, 1990; Assistant Professor, 1990-98, Associate Professor, 1998-, Federal University of Rio de Janeiro; Visiting Fellow, European University Institute, Italy, 2005-06. Publications: Several articles in professional journals. Honours include: Listed in Who's Who and biographical publications; Scholarships, Ministry of Science and Technology and Ministry of Education, Brazil. Membership: Brazilian Society of Econometrics. Address: Av Pasteur 250, URCA, 22290-240 Rio de Janeiro, Brazil. Email: mresende@ie.ufrj.br

**RETNEV Vladimir Mikhailovich,** b. 4 May 1926, Yaroslavl, Russia. Professor, Occupational Medicine. m. Retneva Elena Nickolaevna, 1 son, 1 daughter. Education: Doctor of Medicine, 1965. Appointments: Doctor, Occupational Medicine, 1950-51; Postgraduate Course, 1951-54; Assistant, 1954-59, Lecturer, 1963-68, Professor, 1968-74, Head, 1974-94, Professor, 1994-, Occupational Health Department, Saint Petersburg Medical Academy of Postgraduate Education; Deputy Director of Research, Scientific Research Institute of Industrial Hygiene and Occupational Diseases, 1959-63; St Petersburg Medical Academy of Postgraduate Studies, 1965-76. Publications: About 600 articles, including 18 monographs and guidelines. Honours: Professor; Honoured Scientist; Numerous orders and medals of Russia. Memberships: Academician, International Academy of Sciences in Ecology and Safe Lifestyle; Academician, Russian Academy of Natural Sciences. Address: 195027, PO Box N10, Saint Petersburg, Russia.

**REYMOND Claude Jean-Marie,** b. 21 November 1923, Yverdon, Switzerland. Professor of Law. m. Claire, deceased 1995, 2 sons, 1 daughter. Education: Diploma, State Classical College, Lausanne, Switzerland 1941; Dr en droit (LLM), 1948; State Bar Examination, 1950. Appointments: Partner, 1952-76, Senior Partner, 1979-96, of Counsel, 1996-2002, Baudat et Reymond, Barristers and Solicitors; Professor, Lausanne

University School of Economics, 1965-82; Associate Professor, Geneva University School of Law, 1971-89; Professor Emeritus, Lausanne University, 1982. Publications: Essai sur l'acte fiduciaire, 1948; Le trust et le droit suisse, 1955; Co-author, Swiss National and International Arbitration Law, 1989; Numerous articles on commercial law and the law of arbitration. Honours: Holder of Paul Foriers Chair, Free University of Brussels, School of Law, 1983; Correspondant de L'Institut de France, Académie des Sciences morales et politiques, 2001. Memberships include: Vaud and Swiss Lawyers Associations; International Law Association; Comité français de droit international privé; Chartered Institute of Arbitrators, London. Address: 15 chemin de Passiaux, CH-1008 Prilly, Switzerland. E-mail: reymond@grand-chene.ch

**REYNOLDS Albert,** b. 3 November 1935, Rooskey, County Roscommon, Ireland. Politician; Company Director. m. Kathleen Coén, 2 sons, 5 daughters. Education: Notre Dame University; Stoney Hill College, Boston; National University of Ireland; University of Philadelphia, Jesuits; University of Melbourne; University of Aberdeen. Appointments: Company Director, own family business: C&D Foods, Edgeworthstown, Co Longford, Ireland; Director, many Irish and international companies; Political Career: Entered national politics, 1977, Elected to Dáil; Minister for Posts and Telegraphs and Transport, 1979-81; Minister for Industry and Energy, 1982; Minister for Industry and Commerce, 1987-88; Minister for Finance and Public Service, 1988-89; Minister of Finance, 1989-91; Vice-President, 1983-92, President, 1992-94, Fianna Fáil Party; Elected Taoiseach (PM), 1992-94; Chair, Bula Resources, 1999-2002, Longford Recreational Devt Centre. Memberships: Board of Governors: European Investment Bank; World Bank International Monetary Fund. Honour: Hon LLD (University College, Dublin), 1995. Address: Leinster House, Dáil Éirann, Kildare Street, Dublin 2, Ireland.

**REYNOLDS Elbert Brunner,** b. 17 September 1924, Bryan, Texas, USA. Associate Professor. m. Louise K Reynolds, 1 son, 1 daughter. Education: BS, Mechanical Engineering, 1947; MS, Mechanical Engineering, 1948; PhD, Mechanical Engineering, 1957. Appointments: Instructor, Mechanical Engineering, 1948-52, Assistant Professor, 1952-53, Pennsylvania State University; Part-time Instructor, Mechanical Engineering, University of Wisconsin, 1954-55; Service Engineer, E I, Du Pont de Nemours and Company, 1957-61; Associate Professor of Mechanical Engineering, University of Virginia, 1961-64; Consultant, US Naval Weapons Laboratory, 1963-64; Associate Professor of Mechanical Engineering, 1967-69, Coordinator of Mechanical Engineering Technology, 1979-90, of Mechanical Engineering Technology, 1983-90, Texas Technical University. Publications include: The Influence of Method of Junction Formation and Heat Treatment on the Electromotive Force, 1957; Compressible Fluid Flow, 1963; Heat Transfer and Thermodynamics, 1964. Memberships: American Society of Mechanical Engineers; Society of Automotive Engineers; American Society of Engineering Education; Sigma Xi; Phi Kappa Phi; Pi Tau Sigma. Address: 5437 8th Street, Lubbock, TX 79416, USA.

**REYNOLDS Graham** b. 10 January 1914, Highgate, London, England. Writer; Art Historian. Education: BA, Honours, Queens' College, Cambridge. Publications: Nicholas Hilliard and Isaac Oliver, 1947, 2nd edition, 1971; English Portrait Miniatures, 1952, revised edition, 1988; Painters of the Victorian Scene, 1953; Catalogue of the Constable Collection, Victoria and Albert Museum, 1960, revised edition, 1973; Constable, The Natural Painter, 1965; Victorian Painting, 1966, revised edition, 1987; Turner, 1969; Concise History of Watercolour Painting, 1972; Catalogue of Portrait Miniatures, Wallace Collection,

1980; The Later Paintings and Drawings of John Constable, 2 volumes, 1984; English Watercolours, 1988; The Earlier Paintings of John Constable, 2 volumes, 1996; Catalogue of European Portrait Minatures, Metropolitan Museum of Art, New York, 1996; The Miniatures in the Collection of H.M. the Queen, The Sixteenth and Seventeenth Centuries, 1999. Contributions to: Times Literary Supplement; Burlington Magazine; Apollo; New Departures. Honours: Mitchell Prize, 1984; Officer of the Order of the British Empire, 1984; Commander of the Victorian Order, 2000; British Academy, fellow, 1993; Honorary Keeper of Minatures, Fitzwilliam Museum, Cambridge, 1994. Address: The Old Manse, Bradfield St George, Bury St Edmunds, Suffolk IP30 0AZ, England.

**REYNOLDS Keith Ronald, (Kev Reynolds),** b. 7 December 1943, Ingatestone, Essex, England. Author; Photojournalist; Lecturer. m. Linda Sylvia Dodsworth, 23 September 1967, 2 daughters. Publications: Walks and Climbs in the Pyrenees, 1978, 3rd edition, 1993; Mountains of the Pyrenees, 1982; The Weald Way and Vanguard Way, 1987; Walks in the Engadine, 1988; The Valais, 1988; Walking in Kent, 1988; Classic Walks in the Pyrenees, 1989; Classic Walks in Southern England, 1989; The Jura, 1989; South Downs Way, 1989; Eye on the Hurricane, 1989; The Mountains of Europe, 1990; Visitors Guide to Kent, 1990; The Cotswold Way, 1990; Alpine Pass Route, 1990; Classic Walks in the Alps, 1991; Chamonix to Zermatt, 1991; The Bernese Alps, 1992; Walking in Ticino, 1992; Central Switzerland, 1993; Annapurna, A Trekkers' Guide, 1993; Walking in Kent, Vol II, 1994; Everest, A Trekkers' Guide, 1995; Langtang: A Trekkers Guide, 1996; Tour of the Vanoise, 1996; Walking in the Alps, 1998; Kangchenjunga: A Trekkers' Guide, 1999; Walking in Sussex, 2000; 100 Hut Walks in the Alps, 2000; Manaslu: A Trekkers' Guide, 2000; Tour of Mont Blanc, 2002; Alpine Points of View, 2004; The Pyrenees, 2004. Contributions to: The Great Outdoors; Climber and Hill Walker; Environment Now; Trail Walker; Country Walking; High. Membership: Outdoor Writers' Guild. Address: Little Court Cottage, Froghole, Crockham Hill, Edenbridge, Kent TN8 6TD, England.

**REYNOLDS Vernon,** b. 14 December 1935, Berlin, Germany. Professor Emeritus, Oxford University. m. Frances Glover, 5 November 1960, 1 son, 1 daughter. Education: BA, PhD, London University; MA, Oxford University. Publications: Budongo: A Forest and its Chimpanzees, 1965; The Apes, 1967; The Biology of Human Action, 1976, 2nd edition, 1980; The Biology of Religion (with R Tanner), 1983; Primate Behaviour: Information, Social Knowledge and the Evolution of Culture (with D Quiatt), 1993; The Cimpanzees of the Budongo Forest, 2005. Memberships: Fellow, Royal Anthropological Institute; Chairman, Biosocial Society; Primate Society of Great Britain; Society for the Study of Human Biology. Address: School of Anthropology, Oxford University, 51 Banbury Road, Oxford OX2 6PE, England.

**REZNIK Nadezhda I,** b. 26 September 1945, Svobodny, Russia. Physicist; Methodologist. Alexander Reznik, 2 sons, 2 daughters. Education: Graduate, Physics, Far East State University, 1969; PhD, Candidate, State Pedagogical University, Chelyabinsk, 1989, Moscow, 1990; Docent, Radioelectronics, State Education Committee, Moscow, 1992; Certificate, International Association of Humanistic Psychology, San Francisco, CA/ Moscow, Russia, 1994; Doctor of Pedagogical Science, State Higher Attestation Committee, Moscow, 1997; Professor of Radioelectronics, Ministry of General Education, Moscow, Russian Federation, 1998. Appointments: Engineer, 1969-70, Lecturer, 1970-90, Assistant Professor, 1990-97, Professor, 1997-99, Department of Radio Electronics, Pacific Higher

Naval Academy, Vladivostok, Russia; Consultant Professor, Institute of New Forms of Education, Tel Aviv Branch, Israel, 1999-2001; Scientific Research Worker, Ben Gurion University of the Negev, Israel, 2001-. Publications: Over 70 publications in pedagogy and psychology of education, methodology and methods of education, among which: 2 monographs, 2 manuals; Invariant Basis of Intersubject and Innersubject Connections: Methodological and Methodical Aspects (monograph), 1998; Co-ordination of educational systems: Psychological aspects (journal article), 2003. Honours: Award for Excellence in the field of higher education, Moscow, 1991; Grant and Bonus as a best teacher on behalf of the Governor, Primorsk Region, 1997. Memberships: Editorial Council of the Science, Culture, Education Journal, Ministry of Higher Education; Science Council on Doctoral Theses, Far East Technical University; Maslan Women's Support Centre; Israel Crisis Centre; Fund for Needy Immigrants, Israel. Address: Lui Pikard Street 38/9, Be'er Sheva, Israel 84710. E-mail: nadreznik@hotmail.com

**RHIMES Richard David,** b. 2 June 1947, Dromana, Victoria, Australia. Engineer. m. Heather Marie, 3 sons. Education: Diploma, Civil Engineering, 1971; Graduate Diploma, Industrial Management, 1974; Bachelor of Engineering, 1980. Appointments: Manager, Crisis and Risk Management, Mobil Oil Australia, 1995-99; Risk Management Co-ordinator Downstream, Asia-Pacific and ExxonMobil, 1999-2000; General Manager, Quality and Risk, Qantas Airways Limited, 2000-. Publications: Many Risk and Safety publications for a variety of conferences in Asia Pacific, Malaysia, Singapore, Sydney and Melbourne, Australia. Honours: Chartered Professional Engineer, Australia; Certified Safety Professional, USA. Memberships: Associate Fellow, Australia Institute of Management; Member, Institution of Engineers, Australia; Member, Risk Management Institute of Australasia; Fellow, American Society of Civil Engineers; Member, Chartered Institute of Transport. Address: Qantas Airways Ltd, Qantas Jet Base, Bldg MB8, Mascot, NSW 2020, Australia.

**RHODES Richard (Lee),** b. 4 July 1937, Kansas City, Kansas, USA. Writer. m. Ginger Untrif, 1993, 2 children by previous marriage. Education: BA, cum laude, Yale University, 1959. Publications: Non-Fiction: The Inland Ground, 1970; The Ozarks, 1974; Looking for America, 1979; The Making of the Atomic Bomb, 1988; A Hole in the World, 1990; Making Love, 1992; Dark Sun, 1995; How to Write, 1995; Deadly Feasts, 1997; Trying to get some Dignity (with Ginger Rhodes), 1996; Visions of Technology, 1999; Why They Kill, 1999; Masters of Death, 2001; Fiction: The Ungodly, 1973; Holy Secrets, 1978; The Last Safari, 1980; Sons of Earth, 1981. Contributions to: Numerous journals and magazines. Honours: National Book Award in Non-Fiction, 1987; National Book Critics Circle Award in Non-Fiction, 1987; Pulitzer Prize in Non-Fiction, 1988. Membership: Authors Guild. Address: c/o Janklow and Nesbit Associates, 455 Park Avenue, New York, NY10021, USA.

**RHODES Zandra Lindsey,** b. 19 September 1940. Fashion Designer. Education: Royal College of Art. Career: Designer (textile, 1964-); Print Factory/Studio with A McIntyre, 1965; Fashion Industry, 1966-; Produced dresses from own prints in partnership with S Ayton, shop on Fulham Rd, 1967-68; US solo collection, 1969; annual fantasy shows in US, founded Zandra Rhodes (UK) Ltd; with A Knight & R Stirling, 1975-86; now world-wide, currently works in: interior furnishings, fine art with various collections in US and England, Speaker. Honours include: English Designer of the Year, 1972; Emmy for Best Costume (Romeo and Juliet, US, 1984); Lifetime Achievement at the British Fashion Awards, 1995. Publication: The Art of Zandra Rhodes, 1984; The Zandra Rhodes Collection by Brother, 1988. Address: 79-85 Bermondsey Street, London, SE1 3XF, England.

**RHYEE Jong-Soo,** b. 1 July 1975, Cheong-Won, Chung-buk, South Korea. Physicist; Materials Scientist; Poet. m. Eun-Hye Sun. Education: BS, Physics, Chung-buk National University, 1998; MS, Condensed Matter Physics, Pohang University of Science and Technology, 2000; PhD, Magnetic Materials, Gwangju Institute of Science and Technology, Materials Science and Engineering, 2005. Appointments: Leader of Global Association of Culture and Peace in Gwang-Ju, 2002-03; Journalist in Korean Composers, Poem Criticism, 2003-; Senior Referee of Journal of Applied Physics, 49th Conference on Magnetism and Magnetic Materials, 2004; Research Fellow, Posco Research Lab, 2005-. Publications: 20 articles in professional scientific journals. Honours: Seo-Nam Fellowship, 1994-98; Best Poster Award, Korean Physical Society, 2003; Literature Award, Monthly Journal of the Literature World, 2000; Brain Korea Academic Award, GIST, 2005. Memberships: Korean Physical Society; American Physical Society; Korean Institute of Metals and Materials; World Literature Society in Korea Poem Division. Address: Electrical Steel Research Group, POSCO Technical Research Laboratory, 1 Goedong-dong Nam-gu, Gyeongbuk, Pohang 780-785, South Korea. E-mail: soflee@posco.co.kr

**RHYS David Garel,** b. 28 February 1940, Swansea, Wales. Economist. m. Charlotte Mavis, 1 son, 2 daughters. Education: University of Wales, Swansea; University of Birmingham. Appointments: Lecturer and Assistant Lecturer, University of Hull; Lecturer and Senior Lecturer, University College, Cardiff; Professor of Motor Industry Economics and Director of the Centre for Automotive Research, Cardiff University Business School. Publications: The Motor Industry: An Economic Survey, 1972; The Motor Industry in the European Community, 1989; Contributions to: Journal of Industrial Economics; Journal of Transport History; Journal of Transport Economics; Bulletin of Economic Research; Scottish Journal of Political Economy; Journal of Economic Studies; Journal of Accounting and Business Research; World Economics. Honours: OBE, 1989; Castrol – IMI Gold Medal, 1989; Welsh Communicator of the Year, 1993; Neath Port Talbot Business Award, 1999; Motortrader Outstanding Achievement in the Motor Trade, 2001; Honorary Fellow, University of Wales Swansea Institute, 2003. Memberships: Royal Automobile Club, Pall Mall; Fellow, Royal Society for Arts Commerce and Manufacture; Fellow, Institute of Transport Administration; President, Institute of the Motor Industry; Freeman of the City of London and Liveryman, Carmen's Company. Address: Cardiff University Business School, Aberconway Building, Colum Drive, Cardiff CE10 3EU, Wales. E-mail: rhysg@cardiff.ac.uk

**RIACHI Antoine Ayoub,** b. 11 November 1933, Zahlé, Lebanon. Expert Socio-Economist. m. Sabah Adib Moawad, 3 children. Education: Oriental College, Zahlé, Lebanon; Collège des Apôtres, Jounieh, Lebanon; DEA, Ecole Practique des Hautes Etudes, Paris, France; PhD, Socio-Economics, University of Paris, Sorbone, France. Appointments: Analyst/ Statistician, Ministry of Social Affairs, Lebanon; Journalist, Arabic Programmes at ORTF, Paris; Researcher, Expert for Middle East and African Affairs, Arnold Bergstrasse Institute, Freiburg, Germany; Expert Committee Delegate to Congo, Africa; Director, Economics Research Group, Lebanon; Lecturer, Lebanese Civic Council; Director, ECOGROUP FRANCE, Paris; Editor-in-Chief, Eco Press Review and various socio-economic studies; Chairman, Société d'études, recherches et dévloppement industriels (SERDI). Publications: Author: Disparity of Social Classes in Lebanon; Social Structure

of Confessions in Lebanon; The New Trend of Socialism in the World; Security in the Gulf; A Conflict of Antagonism: nationalism and globalisation; Metaphysics of Social Ages, under publication. Address: ECOGROUP, 23 rue Washington, Paris 75008, France. E-mail: ecof@animail.net

**RIBADU Abdullahi Yusufu,** b. 2 September 1960, Fufore, Adamawa State, Nigeria. Veterinarian; Lecturer. m. Aisha Mohammed Abba, 2 daughters. Education: DVM, 1979-84, MSc, 1986-88 Ahmadu Bello University, Zaria, Nigeria; PhD, University of Liverpool, England, 1990-93; Postdoctoral Studies, Rakuno Gakuen University, Ebetsu, Hokkaido, Japan, 1997-99. Appointments: Assistant Lecturer, 1985, Lecturer II, 1989, Lecturer I, 1993, Senior Lecturer, 1996, Associate Professor, 1999, Professor, 2002, Head, Department of Veterinary Surgery and Reproduction and Member of the Senate, University of Maiduguri, Nigeria, 2000-2004; Vice-Chancellor, Federal University of Technology, Yola, Nigeria, 2004-. Publications: Over 25 publications mainly in the area of ultrasonography and endocrinology of ovarian cysts in cattle published in professional journals including: Veterinary Record; British Veterinary Journal; Animal Reproduction Science; Animal Science; Journal of Reproduction and Fertility. Honours: Commonwealth Scholarship Commission, UK, 1990-93; Japan Society for the Promotion of Science, 1997-99. Memberships: Nigeria Veterinary Medical Association; Society for the Study of Reproduction, Cambridge, UK; Nigerian College of Veterinary Surgeons. Address: Vice-Chancellor's Office, Federal University of Technology, Yola, Nigeria. E-mail: ayaribadu@yahoo.com

**RICCI Cristina,** b. 12 February 1980, Santa Monica, California, USA. Film Actress. Career: Actor in commercials then in films: Mermaids, 1990; The Hard Way, 1991; The Addams Family, 1991; The Cemetery Club, 1993; Addams Family Values, 1993; Casper, 1995; Now and Then, 1995; Gold Diggers: The Secret of Bear Mountain, 1995; That Darn Cat, 1996; Last of the High Kings, 1996; Bastard Out of Carolina, 1996; Ice Storm, 1997; Little Red Riding Hood, 1997; Fear and Loathing in Las Vegas, 1998; Desert Blue, 1998; Buffalo 66, 1998; The Opposite Sex, 1998; Small Soldiers, 1998; Pecker, 1999; 200 Cigarettes, 1999; Sleepy Hollow, 1999; The Man Who Cried, 2000; Monster,2003: Address: c/o ICM, 8942 Wilshire Boulevard, Beverly Hills, CA 90211, USA.

**RICE Susan Ilene,** b. 7 March 1946, Providence, Rhode Island, USA. Banker. m. C Duncan Rice, 2 sons, 1 daughter. Education: BA, Wellesley College; M Litt, Aberdeen University. Appointments: Medical Researcher, Yale University Medical School, 1970-73; Dean of Saybrook College, Yale University, 1973-79; Staff Aide to the President, Hamilton College, 1980-81; Dean of Students, Colgate University, 1981-86; Senior Vice President, NatWest Bancorp, 1986-96; Head of Branch Banking, then Managing Director, Personal Banking, Bank of Scotland, 1997-2000; Chief Executive, Lloyds TSB, Scotland, 2000-; Member, HM Treasury Policy Action Team on Access to Financial Services, 1997-2000; Member, Aberdeen Common Purpose Advisory Board, 1999-; Member, Foresight Sub-Committee on Retail Financial Services, 2000; Trustee, David Hume Institute, 2000-; Member, Scottish Advisory Task Force on the New Deal, 2000-05; Chair, Edinburgh International Book Festival, 2001-; Treasurer, The March Dialogue, 2001-; Director, Scottish Business in the Community, 2001-; Director, UK Charity Bank, 2001-; Chair, Committee of Scottish Clearing Bankers, 2001-2003; Chair, Advisory Committee of the Scottish Centre for Research on Social Justice, 2002-; Member, BP Scottish Advisory Board, 2002-2003; Director, Scottish and Southern Energy plc, 2003-; Member, HMT Financial Inclusion

Taskforce, 2005-. Publications: Articles on banking, insurance, business, marketing, diversity, corporate responsibility and financial exclusion published in The Scotsman, The Herald, Scotland on Sunday, Insurance Day, New Statesman, Finance and Ethics Quarterly, Scottish Banker, Scottish Homes, Business AM, Holyrood Magazine, Business Insider Magazine, Being Scottish and in the proceedings of several conferences; Co-author of several articles published in medical journals, early 1970's. Honours: CBE; Chartered Banker; FCIBS; CCMI; FRSA; FRSE; Spirit of Scotland Annual Business Award, 2002; Corporate Elite Business Award, 2002; DBA (Hon), The Robert Gordon University; Dr honoris causa, Edinburgh University; DLitt (Hon), Heriot Watt University; DUniv (Hon), Paisley University. Address: Lloyds TSB Scotland, Henry Duncan House, 120 George Street, Edinburgh EH2 4TS, Scotland. E-mail: susan.rice@lloydstsb.co.uk

**RICE Tim (Sir) (Miles Bindon)**, b. 10 November 1944, Amersham, Buckinghamshire, England. Songwriter; Broadcaster. m. Jane Artereta McIntosh, 1974, 1 son, 1 daughter. Education: Lancing College. Career: EMI Records, 1966-68; Norrie Paramor Organisation, 1968-69; Founder, Director, GRRR Books Ltd, 1978-, Pavilion Books Ltd, 1981-97. Appearances on TV and radio including Just A Minute, Radio 4; Creative Works: Lyrics for stage musicals (with Andrew Lloyd Webber): Joseph and the Amazing Technicolor Dreamcoat, 1968; Jesus Christ Superstar, 1970; Evita, 1976; Cricket, 1986; Other musicals: Blondel, with Stephen Oliver, 1983; Chess, with Benny Andersson and Bjorn Ulvaeus, 1984; Tycoon, with Michel Berger, 1992; Selection of songs, Beauty and the Beast, with Alan Menken, 1994; Heathcliff, with John Farrar, 1996; King David, with Alan Menken, 1997; Aida, with Elton John, 1998; Lyrics for musical films: Aladdin, with Alan Menken, 1992; The Lion King, with Elton John, 1994, theatre version, 1997; Aida, with Elton John, 1998; El Dorado, with Elton John, 1999; Lyrics for songs with other composers including Paul McCartney, Mike Batt, Freddie Mercury, Graham Gouldman, Marvin Hamlisch, Rick Wakeman, John Barry. Publications: Songbooks from musicals; Co-author of over 20 books in the series Guinness Book of British Hit Singles, Albums, etc; Fill Your Soul, 1994; Cricket Writer, National Newspapers and Cricket Magazines; Treasures of Lords, 1989; Oh, What a Circus, autobiography, 1995. Honours: Oscar, Golden Globe, Best New Song, A Whole New World, 1992, for Can You Feel The Love Tonight, with Elton John, 1994, and for You Must Love Me with Andrew Lloyd Webber, 1996; Gold and platinum records in numerous countries; 11 Ivor Novello Awards; 2 Tony Awards; 5 Grammy Awards; Kt, 1994. Memberships: Chairman, Stars Organisation for Spastics, 1983-85; Shaftesbury Avenue Centenary Committee, 1984-86; President, Lords Taverners, 1988-90; Dramatists' Saints and Sinners, Chairman, 1990; Cricket Writers; Foundation for Sport and the Arts, 1991-; Garrick Club; Groucho Club; Main Committee, 1992-94, 1995-, President, 2002-03, MCC. Address: c/o Lewis & Golden, 40 Queen Anne Street, London, W1M 0EL, England.

**RICH Adrienne (Cecile)**, b. 16 May 1929, Baltimore, Maryland, USA. Poet; Writer. m. Alfred H Conrad, 1953, deceased 1970, 3 sons. Education: AB, Radcliffe College, 1951. Appointments: Visiting Poet, Swarthmore College, 1966-68; Adjunct Professor, Columbia University, 1967-69; Lecturer, 1968-70, Instructor, 1970-71, Assistant Professor, 1971-72, Professor, 1974-75, City College of New York; Fannie Hurst Visiting Professor, Brandeis University, 1972-73; Professor of English, Douglass College, New Brunswick, New Jersey, 1976-78; A D White Professor-at-Large, Cornell University, 1981-85; Clark Lecturer and Distinguished Visiting Professor, Scripps College, Claremont, California, 1983; Visiting Professor, San Jose State University, California, 1985-86; Burgess Lecturer, Pacific Oaks College, Pasadena, California, 1986; Professor of English and Feminist Studies, Stanford University, 1986-94; Board of Chancellors, Academy of American Poets, 1989-91; Clark Lecturer, Trinity College, Cambridge, 2002. Publications: Poetry: A Change of World, 1951; (Poems), 1952; The Diamond Cutters and Other Poems, 1955; Snapshots of a Daughter-in-Law: Poems 1954-1962, 1963; Necessities of Life: Poems 1962-1965, 1966; Selected Poems, 1967; Leaflets: Poems 1965-1968, 1969; The Will to Change: Poems 1968-1970, 1971; Diving into the Wreck: Poems 1971-1972, 1973; Poems Selected and New, 1975; Twenty-One Love Poems, 1976; The Dream of a Common Language: Poems 1974-1977, 1978; A Wild Patience Has Taken Me This Far: Poems 1978-1981, 1981; Sources, 1983; The Fact of a Doorframe: Poems Selected and New 1950-1984, 1984; Your Native Land, Your Life, 1986; Time's Power: Poems 1985-1988, 1989; An Atlas of the Difficult World: Poems 1988-1991, 1991; Collected Early Poems 1950-1970, 1993; Dark Fields of the Republic: Poems 1991-95, 1995; Midnight Salvage: Poems 1995-1998, 1999; Arts of the Possible: Essays and Conversations, 2001; Fox: Poems 1998-2000, 2001; The Fact of a Doorframe: Poems 1950-2000, 2002; The School Among the Ruins: Poems, 2000-04; Other: Of Woman Born: Motherhood as Experience and Institution, 1976; On Lies, Secrets and Silence: Selected Prose 1966-1978, 1979; Blood, Bread and Poetry: Selected Prose 1979-1985, 1986; What Is Found There: Notebooks on Poetry and Politics, 1993, revised 2003; Arts of the Possible: Essays and Conversations, 2001. Honours: Yale Series of Younger Poets Award, 1951; Guggenheim Fellowships, 1952, 1961; American Academy of Arts and Letters Award, 1961; Bess Hokin Prize, 1963; Eunice Tietjens Memorial Prize, 1968; National Endowment for the Arts Grant, 1970; Shelley Memorial Award, 1971; Ingram Merrill Foundation Grant, 1973; National Book Award, 1974; Fund for Human Dignity Award, 1981; Ruth Lilly Prize, 1986; Brandeis University Creative Arts Award, 1987; Elmer Holmes Bobst Award, 1989; Commonwealth Award in Literature, 1991; Frost Silver Medal, Poetry Society of America, 1992; Los Angeles Times Book Award, 1992; Lenore Marshall/Nation Award, 1992; William Whitehead Award, 1992; Lambda Book Award, 1992; Harriet Monroe Prize, 1994; John D and Catharine T MacArthur Foundation Fellowship, 1994; Academy of American Poets Dorothea Tanning Award, 1996; Lannan Foundation Lifetime Achievement Award, 1999; Bollingen Prize for Poetry, 2003; Editor, Muriel Rukeyser, Selected Poems, 2004; National Book Critics Circle Award, 2005; Honorary doctorates. Address: c/o W W Norton & Co, 500 Fifth Avenue, New York, NY 10110, USA.

**RICH David Z**, b. 11 May 1940, Detroit, Michigan, USA. Economist. Publications: Contemporary Economics; The Dynamics of Knowledge; The Economics of Welfare; The Economics of International Trade; The Economic Theory of Growth and Development; Crisis Theory; Order and Disorder, 2001. Memberships: Society for a Beautiful Israel; Association for the Promotion of Human Rights; Society for the Prevention of Cruelty to Animals; American Association for Americans and Canadians in Israel. Address: PO Box 3382, Tel Aviv 61033, Israel.

**RICH Frank Hart**, b. 2 June 1949, Washington, District of Columbia, USA. Journalist. m. (1) Gail Winston, 1976, 2 sons, (2) Alexandra Rachelle Witchel, 1991. Education: BA, Harvard University, 1971. Appointments: Co-Editor, Richmond Mercury, Virginia, 1972-73; Senior Editor and Film Critic, New York Times Magazine, 1973-75; Film Critic, New York Post, 1975-77; Film and Television Critic, Time Magazine, 1977-80; Chief Drama Critic, 1980-93, Op-Ed Columnist, 1994-, New

York Times; Columnist, New York Times Sunday Magazine, 1993. Publications: The Theatre Art of Boris Aronson (with others), 1987; Hot Seat: Theater Criticism for the New York Times 1980-93, 1998; Ghost Light, 2000. Contributions to: Newspapers and periodicals. Address: c/o The New York Times, 229 West 43rd Street, New York, NY 10036, USA.

**RICH Nigel Mervin Sutherland,** b. 30 October 1945, Somerset, England. Company Director. m. Cynthia Elizabeth Davies, 2 sons, 2 daughters. Education: MA, Law, New College, Oxford. Appointments: Articled Clerk, Deloitte Plender Griffiths, London, 1967-71; Qualified Accountant, Deloitte Haskins & Sells, New York, 1971-73; Jardine Matheson Holdings South Africa, Hong Kong,, 1974-94, Managing Director, 1989-94; Group Chief Executive, Trafalgar House PLC, London, 1994-96; Currently: Chairman: Exel plc, Chairman, Hamptons Group Limited; Non-executive Director: CP Ships Limited, John Armit Wines Ltd, Matheson & Co Ltd, Pacific Assets Trust plc; Co-chairman, Philippine British Business Council; Chairman of Governors, Downe House School. Honour: CBE, 1995. Memberships: Freeman of the City of London; 4th Warden of the Court of the Worshipful Company of Tobacco Pipemakers and Blenders; Fellow, Institute of Chartered Accountants of England and Wales. Address: Sutherland Corporate Services Limited, 7 Lower Sloane Street, London SW1W 8AY, England.

**RICHARD Cliff (Harry Webb) (Sir),** b. 14 October 1940, Lucknow, India. Singer. Appointments: Leader, Cliff Richard and The Shadows; Solo Artist; International Concert Tours, 1958-; Own TV Show; Numerous TV and radio appearances. Creative Works: Films: The Young Ones; Expresso Bongo; Summer Holiday; Wonderful Life; Musicals: Time, 1986-87; Heathcliff, 1996-97; Albums include: 21 Today, 1961; The Young Ones, 1961; Summer Holiday, 1963; 40 Golden Greats, 1977; Love Songs, 1981; Private Collection, 1988; The Album, 1993; Real as I Wanna Be; Something's Goin' On, 2004; Over 120 singles. Publications: Questions, 1970; The Way I See It, 1972; The Way I See It Now, 1975; Which One's Cliff, 1977; Happy Christmas from Cliff, 1980; You, Me and Jesus, 1983; Mine to Share, 1984; Jesus, Me and You, 1985; Single-Minded, 1988; Mine Forever, 1989; My Story: A Celebration of 40 Years in Showbusiness, 1998. Honours: OBE, 1980; Knighted, 1995; Numerous music awards. Membership: Equity. Address: c/o PO Box 46C, Esher, Surrey KT10 0RB, England.

**RICHARD Theodoor Arnoldus Maria,** b. 10 January 1966, Heumen, Holland. Lawyer. m. Hui-Chuan Pai, 1 son. Education: LLM University of Nijmegen, Nijmegen, Holland, 1988; Postgraduate, University of Poitiers, France, 1989; MA (unfinished), Journalism, University of Mississippi, 1990. Appointments: Clifford Chance, Amsterdam, 1990-94; Junior Partner, Van der Koft Advocates, Amsterdam, 1994-97; Senior Partner, Theodoor Richard Advocate, 1997-. Publications: Articles in professional journals: Auteursrecht, het internet en de infornatiesnelweg, 1995; Naar een economische benadering van het Autersrecht, 1996; Verdeling van Radio-omroepfrequenties: het axioma van de tijdelijkheid, 2002; Report: Auteursrechten en naburige rechten in de informatiemaatschappij, 2001; Regular column in Telecombrief. Honours: Guest Tutor, Maurits Binger Film Institute; Listed in Who's Who publications and biographical dictionaries. Memberships: Dutch Copyright Association; Dutch Media Law Association; Dutch Ballet Association; Dutch Friends of the Opera Association; Arti et Amicitiae, De Kring, Amsterdam. Address: Herengracht 529, 1017 BV Amsterdam, Holland.

**RICHARDS Hubert John,** b. 25 December 1921, Weilderstadt, Germany. Lecturer; Writer. m. 22 December 1975, 1 son, 1 daughter. Education: STL (Licence in Theology), Gregorian University, Rome; LSS (Licence in Scripture), Biblical Institute, Rome. Publications: The First Christmas: What Really Happened?, 1973; The Miracles of Jesus: What Really Happened?, 1975; The First Easter: What Really Happened?, 1977; Death and After: What Will Really Happen?, 1979; What Happens When You Pray?, 1980; Pilgrim to the Holy Land, 1985; Focus on the Bible, 1990; The Gospel According to St Paul, 1990; God's Diary, 1991; Pilgrim to Rome, 1994; Quips and Quotes, 1997; Anthology for the Church Year, 1998; Philosophy of Religion, 1998, 2nd edition, 2000; The Bible: What Does It Really Say?, 1999; Who's Who and What's What in the Bible, 1999; More Quips and Quotes, 2000; Jesus, Who Did He Think He Was?, 2000; Plain English Bible: 160 Readings, 2001; 1600 Quips and Quotes, 2003. Contributions to: Regular articles and reviews in various publications. Membership: Norfolk Theological Society. Address: 59 Park Lane, Norwich, Norfolk NR2 3EF, England.

**RICHARDS Isaac Vivian Alexander (Sir) (Viv),** b. 7 March 1952, St John's, Antigua. Cricketer. m. Miriam Lewis, 1 son, 1 daughter. Career: Right-hand batsman, off-break bowler; Played for Leeward Islands, 1971-91 (Captain 1981-91), Somerset, 1974-86, Queensland, 1976-77, Glamorgan, 1990-93; 121 tests for West Indies, 1974-91, 50 as Captain, scoring 8,540 runs (average 50.2) including 24 hundreds and holding 122 catches; Scored 36, 212 first-class runs (114 hundreds, only West Indian to score 100 hundreds); Toured England, 1976, 1979 (World Cup), 1980, 1983 (World Cup), 1984, 1988 (as Captain), 1991 (as Captain); 187 limited-overs internationals scoring 6, 721 runs (11 hundreds including then record 189 not out v England at Old Trafford, 1984; Chair, Selectors, West Indies Cricket Board, 2002-. Publication: Co-author, Viv Richards (autobiography); Hitting Across the Line (autobiography), 1991; Sir Vivian, 2000. Honour: Wisden Cricketer of the Year, 1977; One of Wisden's Five Cricketers of the Century, 2000; Cricket Hall of Fame, 2001; Dr hc (Exeter), 1986. Address: West Indies Cricket Board, PO Box 616, St John's, Antigua.

**RICHARDS Keith (Keith Richard),** b. 18 December 1943, Dartford, Kent, England. Musician; Vocalist; Songwriter. m. (1) Anita Pallenberg, 1 son, 1 daughter, (2) Patti Hansen, 1983, 2 daughters. Education: Sidcup Art School. Career: Member, The Rolling Stones, 1962-; Co-Writer (with Mick Jagger) numerous songs and albums, 1964-. Creative Works: Albums: The Rolling Stones, 1964; The Rolling Stones No 2, 1965; Out of Our Heads, 1965; Aftermath, 1966; Between the Buttons, 1967; Their Satanic Majesties Request, 1967; Beggar's Banquet, 1968; Let it Bleed, 1969; Get Yer Ya-Ya's Out, 1969; Sticky Fingers, 1971; Exile on Main Street, 1972; Goat's Head Soup, 1973; It's Only Rock'n'Roll, 1974; Black and Blue, 1976; Some Girls, 1978; Emotional Rescue, 1980; Still Life, 1982; Steel Wheels, 1989; Flashpoint, 1991; Voodoo Lounge, 1994; Stripped, 1995; Bridges to Babylon, 1997; No Security, 1999. Singles: It's All Over Now; Little Red Rooster; (I Can't Get No) Satisfaction; Jumping Jack Flash; Honky Tonk Women; Harlem Shuffle; Start Me Up; Paint It Black; Angie; Going to a Go-Go; It's Only Rock'n'Roll; Let's Spend the Night Together; Brown Sugar; Miss You; Emotional Rescue; She's So Cold; Undercover of the Night. Films: Sympathy for the Devil, 1970; Gimme Shelter, 1970; Ladies and Gentlemen, the Rolling Stones, 1974; Let's Spend the Night Together, 1983; Hail Hail Rock'n'Roll, 1987; Flashpoint, 1991. Honours: Grammy, Lifetime Achievement Award, 1986; Rock'n'Roll Hall of Fame, 1989; Q Award, Best Live Act, 1990; Ivor Novello Award, Outstanding Contribution to British Music, 1991; Songwriters Hall of Fame, 1993. Address: c/o Jane Rose, Raindrop Services, 1776 Broadway, Suite 507, New York, NY 10019, USA.

**RICHARDS Rex Edward (Sir),** b. 28 October 1922, Colyton, Devon, England. Academic. m. Eva Vago, 2 daughters. Education: BA (Oxon), 1945; FRS, 1959, DSc (Oxon), 1970; FRIC, 1970; FRSC, FBA (Hon), 1990; Hon FRCP, 1987; Hon FRAM 1991. Appointments: Fellow of Lincoln College, Oxford, 1947-1964; Dr Lee's Professor of Chemistry, Oxford, 1964-70; Warden of Merton College, Oxford, 1969-84; Vice-Chancellor, Oxford University, 1977-81; Chairman, Oxford Enzyme Group, 1969-1983; Chancellor, University of Exeter, 1982-98; Commissioner, Royal Commission for Exhibition of 1851, 1984-1997; Director, The Leverhulme Trust, 1984-94; Chairman, British Postgraduate Medical Federation, 1986-93; President, Royal Society of Chemistry, 1990-92; Retired, 1994. Publications: Numerous in scientific journals. Honours: Corday-Morgan, Chemical Society, 1954; Fellow of the Royal Society, 1959; Tilden Lecturer, Chemical Society, 1962; Davy Medal, The Royal Society, 1976; Theoretical Chemistry and Spectroscopy, Chemical Society, 1977; Knight Bachelor, 1977; EPIC, 1982; Medal of Honour, University of Bonn, 1983; Royal Medal, The Royal Society, 1986; President's Medal, Society of Chemical Industry, 1991; Associé étranger, Académie des Sciences, Institut de France, 1995; Honorary degrees: East Anglia, 1971; Exeter, 1975; Dundee, 1977; Leicester, 1978; Salford, 1979; Edinburgh, 1981; Leeds, 1984; Kent, 1987; Cambridge, 1987; Thames Polytechnic (University of Greenwich) Centenary Fellow, 1990; Birmingham, 1993; London, 1994; Oxford Brookes, 1998; Warwick, 1999. Memberships: Trustee: National Heritage Memorial Fund, 1980-84, Tate Gallery, 1982-88, 1991-93, National Gallery, 1982-88, 1989-93; National Gallery Trust, 1996-, Chairman, 1996-99; National Gallery Trust Foundation, 1997-, (Chairman, 1997-1999); Henry Moore Foundation 1989-, (Chairman, 1994-2001). Address: 13 Woodstock Close, Oxford, OX2 8DB, England. E-mail: rex.richards@merton.oxford.ac.uk

**RICHARDS Sonia Elizabeth,** b. 3 February 1939, Exeter, Devon, England. Housewife. m. Michael John, 30 November 1957, 1 son, 2 daughters. Education: Shorthand, Typing, Bookkeeping, Proof Reading. Appointments: Shorthand Typist, British Rail Space Market Research. Publications: The Other Side of the Mirror, 1996; Voices in the Heart, 1997; Womens Words, 1997; Quiet Moments', 1997; We Can Achieve Our Dream, 1998; The Ultimate Villanelle Collection, 1998; The Mind Behind the Face, 1998; Crystal Moments, 1999; Changing Seasons, 1999; Seasons of the Mind, 1999; Refreshing Thoughts, 2003; Inspirations from the Heart, 2003; Windows of the Mind, 2004. Honour: Special Commendation, 1997. Address: 67 Iolanthe Drive, Exeter EX4 9DZ, Devon, England.

**RICHARDSON Ian William,** b. 7 April 1934, Edinburgh, Scotland. Actor. m. Maroussia Frank, 2 sons. Education: Edinburgh, Royal Scottish Academy of Music and Drama; Glasgow University. Career: Stage appearances in major roles, especially in Shakespeare, including: Proteus, Two Gentlemen of Verona, 1970; Prospero, The Tempest, 1970; Tom Wrench (Trelawny), Sadlers Wells, 1971-72; Richard II/Bolingbroke, 1973; Berowne, Love's Labours Lost, 1973; Iachimo, Cymbeline, 1974; Shalimov, Summer Folk, 1974; Henry Higgins, My Fair Lady, Broadway, 1974; Ford, Merry Wives of Windsor, 1975; Richard III, 1975; Jack Tanner (Man and Superman), Shaw Festival Theatre, Niagara-on-the Lake, Canada, The Government Inspector, Romeo and Juliet, Old Vic, 1979; Lolita, New York, 1981; The Miser, Chichester, 1995; The Magistrate, Chichester and London, 1997; The Seven Ages of Man, Guildford, 1999; The Hollow Gown, Australia and Canada, 2002-04. Film appearances include: The Darwin Adventure, 1971; Man of La Mancha, 1972; Marat/Sade, Hound of the Baskervilles, 1982; The Sign of Four, 1982; Whoops Apocalypse, 1986; The Fourth Protocol, 1986;

Asking For Trouble, 1986; Burning Secret, 1988; Rosencrantz and Guildenstern are Dead, 1990; The Year of the Comet, 1991; Words Upon a Window Pane, 1993; Baps, 1996; Dark City, 1996; From Hell, 2002; TV includes: The Gravy Train Goes East, 1991; House of Cards, 1991; An Ungentlemanly Act, 1992; To Play the King, 1993; Remember (USA), 1993; Catherine the Great, 1994; Savage Play, 1994; The Final Cut, 1995; The Canterville Ghost, 1997; The Magicians House, 1999; Murder Rooms, 2000; Gormenghast, 2000; Murder Rooms II, 2001; Strange, 2001-02; Booze Cruise 2 & 3, 2005. Publications: Preface to Cymbeline, 1976; Preface to the Merry Wives of Windsor, 1988. Honours: James Bridies Gold Medal, RSAMD; Tony nomination, New York; Drama Desk Award, New York, Royal TV Society Award, 1981-82, 1991; Broadcasting Press Guild Award, 1990; BAFTA Award, 1991; Doctor of Drama (DDr). Address: c/o London Management, 2-4 Noel Street, London, W1V 3RB, England.

**RICHARDSON Joely,** b. 1958, Lancashire, England. Actress. m. Tim Bevan, divorced, 1 daughter. Education: The Thacher School, Ojai, California; Royal Academy of Dramatic Art. Career: London stage debut in Steel Magnolias, 1989; TV appearances include: Body Contact, Behaving Badly, 1989; Heading Home, Lady Chatterly's Lover, 1993; The Tribe, Echo; Films: Wetherby, 1985; Drowning by Numbers, 1988; Shining Through, 1991; Rebecca's Daughters, 1992; Lochness, 1994; Sister, My Sister, 1995; 101 Dalmatians, 1995; Believe Me, 1995; Hollow Reed, 1996; Event Horizon, 1996; Wrestling with Alligators, Under Heaven, The Patriot, Maybe Baby, Return to Me, 2000; The Affair of the Necklace, 2001; Shoreditch, 2003: Address: c/o ICM, Oxford House, 76 Oxford Street, London, W1N 0AX, England.

**RICHARDSON Miranda,** b. 3 March 1958, Southport, England. Actress. Education: Old Vic Theatre School, Bristol. Career: Theatre appearances include: Moving, 1980-81; All My Sons; Who's Afraid of Virginia Woolf?; The Life of Einstein; A Lie of the Mind, 1987; The Changeling; Mountain Language, 1988; Etta Jenks; The Designated Mourner, 1996; Aunt Dan and Lemon, 1999; Film appearances: Dance With a Stranger, 1985; The Innocent; Empire of the Sun; The Mad Monkey; Eat the Rich; Twisted Obsession; The Bachelor, 1992; Enchanted April, 1992; The Crying Game, 1992; Damage, 1993; Tom and Viv, 1994; La Nuit et Le Moment, 1994; Kansas City; Swann, 1995; Evening Star, 1996; The Designated Mourner, 1996; Apostle, 1996; All for Love; Jacob Two Two and the Hooded Fang; The Big Brass Ring, 1998; Sleepy Hollow, 1998-99; Get Carter, 1999; Snow White, 2001; The Hours, 2001; Spider, 2001; Rage on Placid Lake, 2001; The Actors, 2002; Falling Angels, 2002; The Prince and Me, 2003; Phantom of the Opera, 2003; Wah-Wah, 2004; Harry Potter and the Goblet of Fire, 2004; Gideon's Daughter, 2005; Provoked, 2005; TV appearances include: The Hard Word; Sorrel and Son; A Woman of Substance; After Pilkington; Underworld; Death of the Heart; Blackadder II and III; Die Kinder (mini series), 1990; Sweet as You Are; Fatherland; Saint X, 1995; Magic Animals; Dance to the Music of Time, 1997; The Scold's Bridle; Merlin, 1997; Alice, 1998; Ted and Ralph, 1998; The Lost Prince, 2003. Honours: Golden Globe Award for Best Comedy Actress, 1993; BAFTA Award for Best Supporting Actress, 1993; Golden Globe Award, 1995; Royal TV Society's Best Actress. Address: c/o ICM, 76 Oxford Street, London, W1N 0AX, England.

**RICHARDSON Natasha Jane,** b. 11 May 1963. Actress. (1) Robert Fox, 1990, divorced, 1994, (2) Liam Neeson, 1994, 2 sons. Education: Central School of Speech and Drama. Career: Theatre includes: A Midsummer Night's Dream; Hamlet; The Seagull, 1985; China, 1986; High Society, 1986; Anna Christie,

1990, 1992; Cabaret, 1998; Closer, 1999; The Lady from the Sea, 2003; Film appearances include: Every Picture Tells a Story, 1985; Gothic, 1987; A Month in the Country, 1987; Patty Hearst, 1988; Fat Man and a Little Boy, 1989; The Handmaid's Tale, 1990; The Comfort of Strangers, 1990; The Favour, The Watch and the Very Big Fish, 1992; Past Midnight, 1994; Widows Peak, 1994; Nell, 1994; The Parent Trap, 1998; Blow Dry, 2000; Waking up in Reno, 2000; Maid in Manhattan, 2003; TV includes: In a Secret State, 1985; Ghosts, 1986; Hostages, 1992; Suddenly Last Summer, 1993; Zelda, 1993; Tales From the Crypt, 1996; Haven, 2000. Honours: Most Promising Newcomer Award, 1986; Plays and Players Award, 1986, 1990; Best Actress, Evening Stand Film Awards, 1990; London Theatre Critics Award, 1990; Tony Award, 1998.

**RICHMOND Douglas,** b. 21 February 1946, Walla Walla, Washington, USA. History Professor. m. Belinda González, 1 daughter. Education: BA, 1968, MA, 1971, PhD, 1976, University of Washington. Appointments: Assistant Professor, 1976-82, Associate Professor, 1982-92, Professor of History, 1992-, Department of History, University of Texas, Arlington. Publications: Venustiano Carranza's Nationalist Struggle, 1983; Carlos Pellegrini and the Crisis of the Argentine Elites, 1880-1916, 1989; The Mexican Nation: Historical Continuity and Modern Change, 2001. Honour: Harvey P Johnson Award, 1985 and 2004; Capitán Alonso de León Medalla, 2004. Memberships: Southwest Council on Latin American Studies; Southern Historical Association; Conference on Latin American History. Address: Department of History, Box 19529, University of Texas, Arlington, TX 76019-0529, USA.

**RICHMOND, LENNOX AND GORDON, Duke of, Charles Henry Gordon Lennox,** b. 19 September 1929. London, England. Chartered Accountant. m. Susan Monica Grenville-Grey, 1 son, 4 daughters. Education: Eton, 1944-48; William Temple College, Rugby, 1956-58; Chartered Accountant, 1956. Appointments: 2nd Lieutenant, KRRC (60th Rifles), 1949-50; Lieutenant, Queen's Westminsters (KRRC) TA, 1951-54; Financial Controllers Department, Courtaulds Ltd, Coventry, 1959-64; Director of Industrial Studies, William Temple College, 1964-68; Member, West Midlands Regional Economic Planning Council, 1965-68; Member, West Sussex Economic Forum Steering Group, 1996-2002; Chairman, Rugby Council of Socil Service, 1961-68; Chairman, Goodwood Group of Companies, 1969-, Dexam International (Holdings) Ltd, 1965-, Trustees of Sussex Heritage Trust, 1978-2001; Sussex Rural Housing Partnership, Action in Rural Sussex, 1993-2005, Wiley Europe Limited, 1993-98; Boxgrove Priory Trust, 1994-, and Member, Boxgrove Almshouses Trust, 1955-; Chairman, Chichester Cathedral Development Trust, 1985-1991; Chairman, West Sussex Coastal Strip Enterprise Gateway, 2000-05; Member, 1960-80, Chairman, Board for Mission and Unity of the General Synod, 1969-78, Church of England General Synod/Church Assembly; Church Commissioner, 1963-76; Member, Central and Executive Committees, World Council of Churches, 1968-75; Chairman, Christian Organisations Research and Advisory Trust, 1965-87; Lay Chairman, Chichester Diocesan Synod, 1976-79; Vice-Chairman, Archbishops' Commission on Church and State, 1966-70; Treasurer, 1979-82, Chancellor, 1985-98, University of Sussex; Deputy Lieutenant, 1975-1990, Lord Lieutenant, 1990-94, West Sussex. Honours: Honorary LLD Sussex University, 1986; Medal of Honour, British Equestrian Federation, 1983; Winner, FT Arts and Business Award for Individuals, 2000. Memberships: Institute of Chartered Accountants, 1956-; Companion, Institute of Management, 1982-; Honorary Treasurer, 1975-82, Deputy President, 1982-86, Chairman South East Region, 1975-78, Historic Houses Association; Chairman, Bognor Regis Regeneration and Vision Group, 2002-; Member, Joint Steering Group on Bognor Regis Regeneration, 2002-; President: Sussex Rural Community Council (Action in Rural Sussex), 1973-; Chichester Festivities, 1975-; South East England Tourist Board, 1990-2004; Sussex County Cricket Club, 1994-2000, Patron, 2000-; President, British Horse Society, 1976-78; African Medical and Research Foundation UK, 1996-. Address: Molecomb, Goodwood, Chichester, West Sussex PO18 0PZ, England. E-mail: richmond@goodwood.co.uk

**RICKARD John Anthony,** b. 12 July 1945, Birmingham, England. Vice Chancellor; President. m. Veronica Jane, 1 son. Education: BSc (Hons), 1966; PhD, Mathematics, 1970. Appointments: Lecturer, 1969-76, Senior Lecturer, Mathematics Department, 1976-77, Senior Lecturer, Mathematics Department and Graduate School of Business Administration, 1977-80, University of Melbourne; Professor, 1980-84, Vice Chairman, 1981-82, Chairman, 1984, School of Social and Industrial Administration, Griffith University; Professor, Graduate School of Management, University of Melbourne, 1984-92; Henty Corporation Ltd, 1987-92; Credit Co-op, Reserve Board, 1988-90; Chairman/Director, University of Melbourne Credit Co-op Ltd, 1988-92; Friendly Society Reserve Board, 1990-92; Member, CI La Trobe University, 1991-2000; Branchnet Pty Ltd, 1991-92; Director, Graduate School of Management, 1992-94; Professor, Management, Deakin University, Victoria, 1992-94; Deputy Chairman, Australian Financial Institutions Commission (AFIC), 1992-95; Chairman, Caval Ltd, 1992-2000; Managing Director, Deakin Australia, 1993-94; Former Head, Sir John Monash Business Centre Pty Ltd, 1995-97; Director, Auseon Ltd, 1995-97; Director, Information Central Australia Ltd, 1993-2000; Director, Monash Mt Eliza Business School Ltd, 1994-2000; Pro Vice Chancellor and Dean, Faculty of Business and Economics, Monash University, Victoria, 1994-2000; Director, UniSuper Ltd, 2000-; Vice Chancellor and President, Southern Cross University, 2000-04; Director, UniSuper Ltd, Deputy Chairman, BioProspect Ltd, 2001-02. Publications: Co-author: Problems Problems, 1980; Borrowing Money, Lending Money, 1983; Statistics for Business and Economics, 1989. Honours: Centenary Medal, 2003. Memberships: Board of Directors, Australian Vice Chancellors Committee; Board of Directors, UniSuper Ltd. Address: Central Queensland University, Bruce Highway, Rockhampton, Queensland 4701, Australia. E-mail: vc@cqu.edu.au

**RICKETTS Herbert,** b. 17 August 1924, Arequipa, Peru. Business Administrator. m. Angela Bustamante, 2 sons, 4 daughters. Education: BA, Rollins College, USA, 1944-47; MBA, Harvard Graduate Business School, Boston, USA, 1948-49; Economic Seminar, Oxford University, England, 1948. Appointments: General Manager, President of the Board, Ricketts and Co; Director, Co-founder, Banco Del Sur Peru; Member of Board of Directors of: Inca Tops SA, Sur Motors SA, Regesur SA, Ricketts Turismo SA, CIA San Juan SA, Inmobiliaria Magnopata SA, Servi Autos SA. Honours: Honorary Consul of The Netherlands; Membership of the Royal order of Orange Nassau. Memberships: Camara de comercio e industrias de Arequipa, Ex-President; Club Arequipa, Ex-President. Address: Avenida parra #218, PO Box #1, Arequipa, Peru.

**RICKMAN Alan,** Actor. Education: Chelsea College of Art; Royal College of Art; Royal Academy of Dramatic Art (RADA). Career: 2 seasons with Royal Shakespeare Company, Stratford; Stage Appearances include: Bush Theatre, Hampstead and Royal Court Theatre; Les Liasons Dangereuses (RSC, Stratford, London and Broadway); The Lucky Chance, The Seagull, (Royal Court); Tango at the End of Winter (Edinburgh Festival and Piccadilly), 1991; Hamlet, 1992; Antony and Cleopatra (National Theatre), 1998; TV appearances include: Obadiah Slope, The Barchester Chronicles, 1982; Pity in History, 1984; Revolutionary Witness, Spirit of Man, 1989; Rasputin (USA), 1995; Private Lives, 2001-02; Films include: The January Man; Close My Eyes; Truly Madly Deeply; Die Hard; Robin Hood: Prince of Thieves; Bob Roberts, 1992; Mesmer, 1993; An Awfully Big Adventure, 1994; Sense and Sensibility, 1995; Michael Collins, 1996; Rasputin, 1996; Mesmer; Dark Harbour, 1997; The Judas Kiss, 1997; Dogma, 1998; Galaxy Quest, 1999; Blow Dry, 1999; Play, 2000; The Search for John Gissing, 2000; Harry Potter and the Philosopher's Stone, 2001; Harry Potter and the Chamber of Secrets, 2002; Love Actually, 2003; Harry Potter and the Prisoner of Azkaban, 2004; Director, The Winter Guest, 1997. Honours: Time Out Award, 1991; Evening Standard Film Actor of the Year, 1991; BAFTA Award, 1991; Golden Globe Award, 1996; Emmy Award, 1996; Variety Club Award, 2002. Address: c/o ICM, Oxford House, 76 Oxford Street, London, W1N 0AX, England.

**RICKS Christopher (Bruce),** b. 18 September 1933, London, England. Professor of the Humanities; Writer; Editor. m. (1) Kirsten Jensen, 1956, divorced 1975, 2 sons, 2 daughters, (2) Judith Aronson, 1977, 1 son, 2 daughters. Education: BA, 1956, BLitt, 1958, MA, 1960, Balliol College, Oxford. Appointments: Lecturer, University of Oxford, 1958-68; Visiting Professor, Stanford University, 1965, University of California at Berkeley, 1965, Smith College, 1967, Harvard University, 1971, Wesleyan University, 1974, Brandeis University, 1977, 1981, 1984; Professor of English, University of Bristol, 1968-75; University of Cambridge, 1975-86; Professor of the Humanities, Boston University, 1986-; Co-Director, Editorial Institute, 1999-; Andrew W Mellon Distinguished Achievement Award, 2004-07. Publications: Milton's Grand Style, 1963; Tennyson, 1972, revised edition, 1987; Keats and Embarrassment, 1974; The Force of Poetry, 1984; Eliot and Prejudice, 1988; Beckett's Dying Words, 1993; Essays in Appreciation, 1996; Reviewery, 2002; Allusion to the Poets, 2002; Decisions and Revisions in T S Eliot, 2003; Dylan's Visions of Sin, 2003. Editor: Poems and Critics: An Anthology of Poetry and Criticism from Shakespeare to Hardy, 1966; A E Housman: A Collection of Critical Essays, 1968; Alfred Tennyson: Poems, 1842, 1968; John Milton: Paradise Lost and Paradise Regained, 1968; The Poems of Tennyson, 1969, revised edition, 1987; The Brownings: Letters and Poetry, 1970; English Poetry and Prose, 1540-1674, 1970; English Drama to 1710, 1971; Selected Criticism of Matthew Arnold, 1972; The State of the Language (with Leonard Michaels), 1980, new edition, 1990; The New Oxford Book of Victorian Verse, 1987; Inventions of the March Hare: Poems 1909-1917 by T S Eliot, 1996; Oxford Book of English Verse, 1999; Selected Poems of James Henry (editor), 2002. Contributions to: Professional journals. Honour: Honorary DLitt, Oxford, 1998; Honorary D Litt, Bristol, 2002. Memberships: American Academy of Arts and Sciences, fellow; British Academy, fellow; Tennyson Society, vice-president; Housman Society, vice-president. Address: 39 Martin Street, Cambridge, MA 02138, USA.

**RIDLEY Brian Kidd,** b. 2 March 1931, Newcastle upon Tyne, England. Physicist. m. Sylvia Jean Nicholls, 1 son, 1 daughter. Education: BSc 1st Class Honours, Physics, 1953, PhD, 1957, University of Durham. Appointments: The Mullard Research Laboratory, Redhill, 196-64; Lecturer, 1964-67; Senior Lecturer, 1967-71, Reader, 1971-84, Professor, 1984-90, Research Professor, 1990-; Department of Physics, University of Essex, Colchester; Visiting appointments: Distinguished Visiting Professor, 1967, Research Fellow, 1976, 1990-; Visiting Professorships: Stanford, 1967, Danish Technical

University, 1969, Princeton, 1973, Lund, 1977, Santa Barbara, 1981, Eindhoven Technical University, 1983, Hong Kong University of Science and Technology, 1997, 1999, Cornell, 3 months annually, 1990-; Current consultancies: UK Ministry of Defence, Great Malvern; British Telecom (now Corning), Office of Naval Research. Member: Programme Committee International Conference on Hot Carriers, 1986-89; Honorary Editorial Board, Solid State Electronics, 1990-95; Advisory Editorial Board of Journal of Physics Condensed Matter, 1996-2000; Executive Board, Journal of Physics, 2000-2003; Physics College of Engineering and Physical Sciences Research Council of the UK. Publications: Over 200 research papers; Books include: Time, Space and Things, 1976, 3rd edition, 1995, reprinted 2000; The Physical Environment, 1979; Quantum processes in Semiconductors, 1982, 4th edition, 1999; Electrons and Phonons in Semiconductor Multilayers, 1997; On Science, 2002; 7 book chapters. Honours: Fellow of the Royal Society; Paul Dirac Medal and Prize; Fellow of the Institute of Physics. Membership: American Physical Society. Address: Department of Electronic Systems Engineering, University of Essex, Colchester, Essex CO4 3SQ, England.

**RIDPATH Ian (William),** b. 1 May 1947, Ilford, Essex, England. Writer; Broadcaster. Publications: Over 30 books, including: Worlds Beyond, 1975; Encyclopedia of Astronomy and Space (editor), 1976; Messages From the Stars, 1978; Stars and Planets, 1978; Young Astronomer's Handbook, 1981; Hamlyn Encyclopedia of Space, 1981; Life Off Earth, 1983; Collins Guide to Stars and Planets, 1984; Gem Guide to the Night Sky, 1985; Secrets of the Sky, 1985; A Comet Called Halley, 1985; Longman Illustrated Dictionary of Astronomy and Astronautics, 1987; Monthly Sky Guide, 1987; Star Tales, 1989; Norton's Star Atlas (editor), 1989; Book of the Universe, 1991; Atlas of Stars and Planets, 1992; Oxford Dictionary of Astronomy (editor), 1997; Eyewitness Handbook of Stars and Planets, 1998; Gem Stars, 1999; Times Space, 2002; Times Universe, 2004. Membership: Fellow, Royal Astronomical Society; Member, Society of Authors, Association of British Science Writers. Address: 48 Otho Court, Brentford Dock, Brentford, Middlesex TW8 8PY, England. Website: www.ianridpath.com

**RIESENHUBER Klaus,** b. 29 July 1938, Frankfurt am Main, Germany. Professor of Philosophy; Jesuit Priest. Education: Study of Philosophy, St Georgen, Frankfurt, 1957-58; Study of Philosophy, Berchmanskolleg Pullach, 1960-62; Lic Phil, 1962; Study of Philosophy, Universität München, 1962-67; Dr Phil, 1967; Study of Japanese Culture, Kamakura, Japan, 1967-69; Study of Theology, Sophia University, 1969-72; Master of Theology, 1972; Dr of Theology, 1989. Appointments: Lecturer, Philosophy, Sophia University, 1969; Assistant Professor, 1974; Director, Institute of Medieval Thought, Sophia University, 1974-2004; Professor, 1981-; Director, Zen-Hall Shinmeikutsu, Tokyo, 1990-; Part time Guest Professor, Tokyo University; Kyushu University; Tohoku University; Japanese Broadcast University; Keio University; Waseda University; Tokyo Metropolitan University. Publications: Die Transzendenz der Freiheit zum Guten; Existenzerfahrung und Religion; History of Ancient and Medieval Philosophy (in Japanese); Freedom and Transcendence in the Middle Ages (in Japanese); Fountain Streams of Medieval Philosophy (in Japanese); History of Medieval Thought (in Japanese); Man and Transcendence (in Japanese); Editor and co-author of 58 books in Japan; Co-editor of Nishida Kitaro Collected Works (24 volumes, in Japanese, in progress). Memberships: Japanese Society of Medieval Philosophy; Japanese Society of Philosophy; Japanese Fichte Society; 5 other philosophical associations. Address: S J House,

Sophia University, 7-1 Kioicho, Chiyoda-ku, Tokyo 102-8571, Japan.

**RIGG (Enid) Diana (Elizabeth) (Dame),** b. 20 July 1938, Doncaster, England. Actress. m. (1) Manahem Gueffen, 1973, divorced 1976, (2) Archibald Hugh Stirling, 1982, divorced 1993, 1 daughter. Education: RADA. Career: Professional début as Natella Abashwilli, The Caucasian Chalk Circle, York Festival, 1957; Repertory Chesterfield and Scarborough 1958; Films include: A Midsummer Night's Dream, 1969; On Her Majesty's Secret Service, 1969; Julius Caesar, 1970; The Hospital, 1971; Theatre of Blood, 1973; A Little Night Music, 1977; The Great Muppet Caper, 1981; Evil Under the Sun, 1982; A Good Man in Africa, 1993; TV appearances include: Emma Peel in the Avengers, 1965-67; Women Beware Women, 1965; Married Alive, 1970; Diana (USA), 1973; In This House of Brede, 1975; Three Piece Suite, 1977; Clytemnestra in The Serpent Son, 1979; The Marquise, 1980; Hedda Gabler, 1981; Rita Allmers in Little Eyolf, 1982; Reagan in King Lear, 1983; Witness for the Prosecution, 1983; Bleak House, 1984; Host Held in Trust, A Hazard of Hearts, 1987; Worst Witch, 1987; Unexplained Laughter, 1989; Mother Love, 1989; Host Mystery! (USA), 1989; Zoya, 1995; Rebecca, 1996; Many leading roles with RSC and with theatres in UK and USA. Publications: No Turn Unstoned, 1982; So To The Land, 1994; Honours include: Plays and Players Award for Best Actress, 1975, 1978; Honorary doctorates, Stirling University, 1988; Leeds, 1991, South Bank, 1996; BAFTA Award, Best Actress, 1990; Evening Stand Award, 1993, 1996, 1996; Tony Award, Best Actress, 1994; Emmy, Best Supporting Actress, 1997; BAFTA, 2000. Memberships include: Vice-President, Baby Life Support Systems (BLISS), 1984-; Chancellor, University of Stirling, 1997-.

**RILEY Patrick Anthony,** b. 22 March 1935, Neuilly-Sur-Seine, France. Pathologist. m. Christine E Morris, 1 son, 2 daughters. Education: MB, BS (Lond), 1960; PhD (Lond), 1965; DSc (Lond), 1990; FRCPath, 1985; FIBiol, 1976. Appointments: Rockefeller Scholar, 1962-63; MRC Junior Clinical Research Fellow, 1963-66; Beit Memorial Research Fellow, 1966-68; Wellcome Research Fellow, 1968-70; Lecturer in Clinical Pathology, University College Hospital Medical School, London, 1970-73; Senior Lecturer in Biochemical Pathology, 1974-76, Reader in Cell Pathology, 1976-84, Professor of Cell Pathology, 1984-2000, Emeritus Professor, 2000-, University College, London; Currently, Director, Totteridge Institute for Advanced Studies and Honorary Research Associate, Gray Cancer Institute. Publications: Reviews and chapters in books; Dictionary of Medicine; More than 250 substantive research contributions to learned journals. Honours: Myron Gordon Award, 1993; Centenary Medal, Charles University, Prague, Czech Republic, 1996. Memberships include: Linnean Club; Athenaeum Club; Royal Society of Medicine; NCUP. Address: 2 The Grange, Grange Avenue, London N20 8AB, England.

**RIMAN Joseph Vavrinec Prokop,** b. 30 January 1925, Horni Sucha. Biochemist; Scientist. m. Vera Tomek. Education: MD, Charles University, Prague, 1950; PhD, Chemistry, CS Academy of Science, 1955; DSc, Chemistry, 1967; Associate Professor, Habil Doc, Medical Faculty, Charles University, 1967; Full Professor, Biochemistry, Science Faculty, 1984; DSc, Biology h c, Purkynje University, 1987. Appointments: Research Physician, 1st Clinic Pediatrics, Medical Faculty, Charles University, Prague, 1950-51; Scientist, Senior Scientist, Institute of Organic Chemistry and Biochemistry, CS Academy of Sciences, Prague, 1951-74; Founder, Director, Institute of Molecular Genetics, 1975-91. Publications: Published in various international journals; 128 original experimental papers,

Biochemistry of retroviruses and growing vertebrate cells. Honours include: Laureate of the State Prize for Science of Czechoslovakia, 1969 and 1977, and Soviet Union, 1978; Gold Plaque of J G Mendel, Czechoslovak Academy of Science, 1980; Silver Medal, Charles University, 1985; Gold Einstein-Russel Pugwash Medal, 1987; Skrjabin's Medal, 1987; J E Fogarty NIH Medal, 1987; Hippocrates Medal, Kyoto University Medical School, 1988; Gold Lomonosov Medal, 1986; Gold Medal, Slovak Academy of Science for Merits, 1989; Gold Medal, Meidji University, Nagoya, 1990; K Yagis Gold Memorial Medal, 1990; Gold Plaque for Merits for Science and Mankind; Gold Pin, G W Leibniz Society. Memberships include: Honorary Member, Hungarian Academy of Science; Foreign Member, Bulgarian Academy; Foreign Member, Russian Academy of Science; Foreign Fellow, Indian National Science Academy; Foreign Member G W Leibniz Society, Germany; Foreign Member German Society of Biological Chemistry; Full Member Central European Academy of Science and Art, 1997-; Science Secretary, 1977-, Vice-President Biological Sciences, 1982-, President, 1986-90, Czechoslovak Academy of Sciences. Address: Institute of Molecular Genetics, Academy of Science, Fleming n 2, Prague 6 16637 Czech Republic.

**RINGELSTEIN Erich Bernd,** b. 9 January 1948, Boppard on the Rhine, Germany. Physician; Professor; Educator. m. Hannelore Wirz, 2 sons. Education: Johannes Gutenberg University, Mainz, 1973; Diplomate, Board of Psychiatry and Neurology, Germany. Appointments: Intern, various hospitals, Mainz, Wiesbaden, Germany, 1973-75; Research Fellow, Department of Neuropathology, University Hospital Mainz, 1976-77; Fellow, State of Hessia, Psychiatry Hospital, Hadamar, 1977-79, Department of Neurology, University Hospital Aachen, 1980-82, Department of Neuroradiology, 1982-83; Attending Physician, Neurology, University Hospital Aachen, 1983-86; Research Fellow, Scripps Clinic and Research Foundation, La Jolla, California, USA, 1987; Vice Chairman, Senior Attending Neurologist, Associate Professor, 1988-92; Professor, Chairman, Department of Neurology, University Hospital WWU, Munster, 1992-. Publications: Numerous articles in professional journals. Honours: Prize, Best Article, 1990; Hugo Spatz Prize, German Neurological Society, 1992; Reward, Best Teacher, University Hospital Munster, 1993, 2002. Memberships: European Neurological Society; German Society of Neurology; German Society of Neuroradiology; German Society of Neurophysiology; Stroke Fellow, AHA; President, European Society on Neurosonology and Cerebral Hemodynamics, 2001-; President, German Stroke Society, 2004-. Address: University Hospital of the Westfälische Wilhelms University, Department of Neurology, Albert Schweitzer Str 33, 48129 Münster, Germany.

**RIPPON Angela,** b. 12 October 1944, Plymouth, Devon, England. Television and Radio Presenter; Writer. m. Christopher Dare, 1967, divorced. Education: Grammar School, Plymouth, England. Appointments: Presenter, Reporter, BBC TV Plymouth, 1966-69; Editor, Presenter, Producer, Westward Television, 1967-73; Reporter, BBC TV National News, 1973-75, Newsreader, 1975-81; Founder, Presenter, TV-am, 1983; Arts Correspondent, WNETV (CBS), Boston, 1983; Reporter, Presenter, BBC and ITV, 1984; TV appearances: Angela Rippon Meets...; Antiques Roadshow; In the Country; Compere, Eurovision Song Contest, 1976; The Morecombe and Wise Christmas Show, 1976, 1977; Royal Wedding, 1981; Masterteam, 1985, 1986, 1987; Come Dancing, 1988-; What's My Line? 1988-; Healthcheck; Holiday Programme; Simply Money, 2001-; Channel 5 News, 2003-; Radio: Angela Rippon's Morning Report for LBC, 1992; Angela Rippon's Drive Time Show, LBC, 1993; The Health Show, BBC Radio 4; Friday

Night with Angela Rippon, BBC Radio 2; LBC Arts Programme, 2003-. Publications: Riding, 1980; In the Country, 1980; Mark Phillips: The Man and His Horses, 1982; Angela Rippon's West Country, 1982; Victoria Plum, 1983; Badminton: A Celebration, 1987; Many recordings. Honours: Dr hc, American International University, 1994; New York Film Festival Silver Medal, 1973; Newsreader of the Year, Radio and Television Industries Awards, 1976, 1977, 1978; Television Personality of the Year, 1977; Emmy Award, 1984; Sony Radio Award, 1990; New York Radio Silver Medal, 1992; Royal TV Society Hall of Fame, 1996; European Woman of Achievement, 2002. Memberships: Vice-President, International Club for Women in Television; British Red Cross; NCH Action for Children; Riding for the Disabled Association; Director, Nirex, 1986-; Chair, English National Ballet, 2000-. Address: Knight Ayton, 114 St Martin's Lane, London, WC2N 4AZ, England.

**RITBLAT Jillian Rosemary (Jill),** b. 14 December, 1942, United Kingdom. Barrister. m. (1), 1 son, 1 daughter, (2) John Ritblat. Education. DA, Westfield College, London. Appointments: Called to the Bar, Gay's Inn, 1964; Pupillage to Robin Simpson, QC, Victor Durand and Jeremy Hutchinson's Chamber, 1964-65; Alternate Delegate for International Council of Jewish Women, UN, Geneva, 1977-79; Events Organiser, 1984-87, Chairman, 1987-90, Member Acquisitions Sub-Committee, 1992-93, International Council Member, 1995-, Patrons of New Tate Art Gallery; Member, 1995-, Vice-Chairman, 1996-2001, Member, Steering Group, -2001, International Council Tate Gallery; Co-Curator: The Curate's Egg, Anthony Reynolds Gallery, 1994, One Woman's Wardrobe, Victoria and Albert, 1998-99; Executive Producer, Normal Conservative Rebels: Gilbert & George in China, Edinburgh Film Festival, 1996; Member, Arts Council Appraisal for West Midlands Arts, 1994; Board Member: British Telecom New Contemporaries, 1991-, Vice-Chair, 1991-; Jerusalem Music Centre, 1991; Design Trustee, Public Art Commissioners Agency, 1996-99; Jury Member: Painting in the Eighties, 1987, Turner Prize, 1988, British Airways New Artist Award, 1990, Swiss Bank Corporation Euro Art Competition, 1994, 1995, NatWest 90's Prize for Art 1995, 1995, Financial Times Arts and Business Awards, 2000, 2001; Building Commission RIBA Regni Award, 2001. Honours: V&A Catalogue Design and Art Direction Silver Award for Graphic Design, 1999; Gold Medal, Chicago Film Festival, 1996. Memberships: Member, 1986-, Council Member, 1993-, Association of Museum of Modern Art, Oxford; International Council, Jerusalem Museum, 1987; Advisory Council Friends of the Tate Gallery, 1990; Special Events Committee, National Art Collections Fund, 1991-92; William Townsend Memorial Lectureship Committee, 1991-; Patron, National Alliance for Art, Architecture and Design, 1994-; Royal Academy of Music Development Committee, 2002-. Address: 10 Cornwall Terrace, London NW1 4QP, England.

**RITCHIE Lewis Duthie,** b. 26 June 1952, Fraserburgh, Scotland. Academic General Practitioner. m. Heather Skelton. Education: BSc, Chemistry, 1978, MBChB, Commendation, 1978, University of Aberdeen; MSc, Community Medicine, University of Edinburgh, 1982; MD, University of Aberdeen, 1993; Vocational Training in General Practice, 1979-82; Specialist Training in Public Health Medicine, 1982-87. Appointments: General Practice Principal, Peterhead Health Centre, 1984-; Consultant in Public Health Medicine, Grampian Health Board, 1987-92; Honorary Consultant in Public Health Medicine, Grampian Health Board, 1993-; Sir James Mackenzie Professor of General Practice, University of Aberdeen, 1993-; Membership of a number of national medical advisory committees on behalf of the Scottish Executive Health Department and the Department of Health England, 1989-. Publications: Book: Computers in Primary Care, 1986; Over 100 publications on computing, cardiovascular prevention, lipids, hypertension, immunisation, oncology, intermediate care, community hospitals, and fishermen's health. Honours: Munday and Venn Prize, University of Aberdeen, 1977; John Watt Prize, University of Aberdeen, 1977; Kincardine Prize, North East Faculty, Royal College of General Practitioners, 1978; John Perry Prize, British Computer Society, 1991; Ian Stokoe Memorial Award, Royal College of General Practitioners, 1992; Blackwell Prize, University of Aberdeen, 1995; OBE, 2001. Memberships: Diploma of the Royal College of Obstetricians and Gynaecologists, 1980; British Computer Society, 1985; Fellow, Royal Society of Medicine, 1987; Member Royal Environmental Health Institute for Scotland, 1991; Fellow, Faculty of Public Health Medicine, 1993; Fellow Royal College of General Practitioners, 1994; Fellow, Royal College of Physicians of Edinburgh,1995; Fellow, British Computer Society, 2004; Chartered Computer Engineer, 1993; Fellow, Royal Society of the Arts, 2001; Founding Fellow of the Institute of Contemporary Scotland, 2001; Chartered Information Technology Professional, 2004. Address: Department of General Practice and Primary Care, University of Aberdeen, Foresterhill Health Centre, Westburn Road, Aberdeen AB25 2AY, Scotland. E-mail: l.d.ritchie@abdn.ac.uk

**RITTNER Luke Philip Hardwick,** b. 24 May 1947, Bath, Somerset, England. Chief Executive. m. Corinna Edholm, 1 daughter. Education: City of Bath Technical College; Acting Course, Dartington College, 1 year; London Academy of Music and Dramatic Art. Appointments: Administrative Director Bath International Festival, 1968-76; Founder and Director, Association for Business Sponsorship of the Arts (now renamed Arts & Business), 1976-83; Secretary General, Arts Council of Great Britain, 1983-90; Director of Marketing, Communications and Public Affairs, Sotheby's, 1992-99; Chief Executive, Royal Academy of Dance, 1999-. Honour: Honorary Dr of Arts, University of Bath. Membership: Garrick. Address: Royal Academy of Dance, 36 Battersea Square, London SW11 3RA, England. E-mail: lrittner@rad.org.uk

**RIVERS Ann,** b. 26 January 1939, Texas, USA. Poet. Education: BA, 1959. Appointments: Editor-Publisher, SHY, 1974-79; Guest Editor, As-Sharq, 1979; Contributing Editor, Ocarina, 1979-82. Publication: Samos Wine, 1987; A World of Difference, 1995; Pilgrimage and Early Poems, 2000; Pluto Probe, 2003. Contributions to: Ore; Iotà; Orbis; Poetry Nottingham; Pennine Platform. Address: Hydra, GR 180 40 Greece.

**ROBBINS John Francis Whiting,** b. 5 November 1921, Balham, London, England. Mechanical Engineer. m. (1) Joan Young, deceased, 1984, 1 son, 1 daughter, (2) Virginia Huntington, deceased, 2004. Education: BSc (Eng) Mechanical Engineering, City and Guilds College, London, 1941; Higher National Certificate, Electrical Engineering, Kingston Technical College, Surrey, England, 1951. Appointments: Engineer Officer, final rank Flight Lieutenant RAF, responsible for maintenance of Hurricane and Lancaster Aircraft and motor transport, 1941-46; Mechanical Engineer, Research and Development Department, supervised machine, fitting and welding shops, pressure vessel work and laboratory installation, Distillers Co Ltd, Epsom, England, 1946-57; Mechanical Design Engineer, design of various parts for flight simulators and preparing proposals for various contracts, Canadian Aviation Electronics, Montreal, Canada, 1957-62; Engineer to Project Engineer, mechanical and some electrical design of ultracentrifuges, including refrigeration systems and associated biomedical instrumentation, Beckman

Instruments Inc (now Beckman Coulter), 1962-88. Honours: Defence Medal 1939-45; General Service Medal, 1939-45; US Patent, 1971. Memberships: C.Eng.M.I.Mech.E.; Ordre des Ingénieurs du Québec. Address: 921 Campbell Avenue, Los Altos, CA 94024, USA. E-mail: jfrvhr@earthlink.net

**ROBBINS Tim,** b. 16 October 1958, New York, USA. Actor; Director; Screen Writer. 2 sons with Susan Sarandon. Education: University College of Los Angeles. Career: Member, Theatre for the New City; Founder, Artistic Director, The Actor's Gang; Theatre includes: Ubu Roi, 1981; Director, A Midsummer Night's Dream, 1984; The Good Woman of Setzuan, 1990; Co-writer with Adam Simon: Alagazam, After the Dog Wars, Violence; The Misadventures of Spike Spangle; Farmer; Carnage – A Comedy (Represented USA at Edinburgh International Festival, Scotland); Films: Bull Durham, 1988; Cadillac Man; Jacob's Ladder; Five Corners; Tapeheads; Miss Firecracker; Eric the Viking; Jungle Fever; The Player; The Shawshank Redemption; Short Cuts; The Hudsucker Proxy; IQ; Actor, writer, director, Bob Roberts; Dead Man Walking; Writer, director, Nothing to Lose; Director, actor, The Moviegoer, Arlington Road, The Cradle Will Rock, 1999; Austin Powers: The Spy Who Shagged Me, 1999; Mission to Mars, 2000; High Fidelity, 2000; The Truth About Charlie, 2002; Mystic River, 2003; Code 46, 2003. Honours: Best Supporting Actor Oscar for Mystic River, 2004.

**ROBERT Leslie (Ladislas),** b. 24 October 1924, Budapest, Hungary. Biochemist. m. Jacqueline Labat, 3 daughters. Education: MD, Paris, 1953; PhD, Lille, 1977; Postdoctoral Training, Department of Biochemistry, University of Illinois, Chicago; Columbia University, New York; Honorary Research Director, French National Research Center (CNRS), 1994-. Appointment: Research Director, Department of Ophthalmic Research, Hotel Dieu Hospital, Paris, France. Publications: 6 books on ageing biology; 1 book on time-regulations in biology; 12 books on connective tissues; 900 publications in international journals. Honours: Honorary doctorate, Semmelweis Medical University, Budapest, 1972; Verzar Medal for Gerontology Research, University of Vienna, 1994; Novartis Prize, International Gerontological Association, 1997. Memberships: Academy of Sciences of Hungary and Germany (Nordrheim-Westfalie); French and International Biochemical Societies; Past president, French Society for Connective Tissue Research; Past president, French Society of Atherosclerosis. Address: 7 Rue J B Lully, 94440 Santeny, France. E-mail: lrobert5@wanadoo.fr

**ROBERTS Brian,** b. 19 March 1930, London, England. Writer. Education: Teacher's Certificate, St Mary's College, Twickenham, 1955; Diploma in Sociology, University of London, 1958. Appointments: Teacher of English and History, 1955-65. Publications: Ladies in the Veld, 1965; Cecil Rhodes and the Princess, 1969; Churchills in Africa, 1970; The Diamond Magnates, 1972; The Zulu Kings, 1974; Kimberley: Turbulent City, 1976; The Mad Bad Line: The Family of Lord Alfred Douglas, 1981; Randolph: A Study of Churchill's Son, 1984; Cecil Rhodes: Flawed Colossus, 1987; Those Bloody Women: Three Heroines of the Boer War, 1991. Address: 7 The Blue House, Market Place, Frome BA11 1AP, Somerset, England.

**ROBERTS Denys Tudor Emil,** b. 19 January 1923, London, England. Judge. m. Fiona Alexander, 10 February 1985, 1 son. Education: MA, Wadham College, Oxford 1948; BCL, 1949; Bar, London, 1950. Appointments: Crown Counsel, Nyasaland, 1953-59; Attorney General, Gibraltar, 1960-62; Solicitor General, Hong Kong, 1962-66; Attorney General, Hong Kong, 1966-73; Chief Secretary, Hong Kong, 1973-78; Chief Justice, Hong Kong, 1979-88; Chief Justice, Brunei Darussalam, 1979-

2001; Member, Hong Kong Court of Final Appeal, 1997-2003; President, Court of Appeal, Brunei Darussalam, 2002-03. Publications: Books: Smuggler's Circuit, 1954; Beds and Roses, 1956; The Elwood Wager, 1958; The Bones of the Wajingas, 1960; How to Dispense with Lawyers, 1964; I'll Do Better Next Time, 1995; Yes Sir, But, 2000. Honours: OBE, 1960; CBE, 1970; KBE, 1975; SPMB, Brunei, 1984. Memberships: Honorary Fellow, Wadham College, Oxford; Honorary Bencher, Lincoln's Inn; President, MCC, 1989-90; Garrick Club. Address: The Grange, North Green Road, Pulham St Mary, Norfolk IP21 4QZ, England.

**ROBERTS Dorothy (Elizabeth),** b. Brisbane, Queensland, Australia. Concert Pianist; Abstract Artist. Divorced, 1 son. Education: Studies at Sydney Conservatorium of Music, including Piano, Harmony, History of Music, Form of Music, Chamber Music; Clara Schumann technique with Adelina de Lara, London. Career: Music concerts at Balliol College, Oxford, Purcell Room, South Bank, London; Performed Liszt's Piano Concerto in E Flat with London Symphony Orchestra at Royal Albert Hall, London; Other concerto performances with the Hallé Orchestra, Northern Sinfonia Orchestra and London Bach Players; Recitals in London, UK provinces, Glasgow, Germany, Australia, France, Netherlands, Canada; TV appearance with the Hallé Orchestra; Other TV appearances with Richard Bonynge, 2 pianos, including playing with the BBC Orchestra; Many one man shows as abstract painter including London, Provinces, New York; Works in collections in UK, Europe, Canada, USA and Australia as Dorothy Lee Roberts. Honours: AMusA; LMus; Honorary DLit, Bradford University, 1995; Recently confirmed as the only Grand Pupil of the Clara Schumann piano-playing tradition; Winner, 95 Art International, New York. Address: Alveley House, 17 Lindum Road, Lincoln LN2 1NS, England.

**ROBERTS Ian,** b. 21 May 1953, South Africa. Medical Doctor. m. Georgina Louise, 2 daughters. Education: Bachelor of Science, Biochemistry (1st class honours), 1975, Master of Science, Clinical Biochemistry, 1982, Surrey University; MB ChB, Dundeed University, 1979; MSc, Management, London Business School, 1994. Appointments: NHS Medical Doctor, 1979-85; International Medical Adviser, Roussel Laboratories, London and Paris, 1985-88; Director, Clinical Research, Boehringer Ingelheim, London, 1988-89; Chief Executive Officer, Clinical Research Foundation, London, 1989-92; International Medical Director, Laboratories Almirall, Barcelona, 1992-95; Senior Management Consultant, Monitor Company, 1995-96; Special Adviser to the Minister of Health, Government of South Africa, 1996-2000; Consultant, Pfizer, New York, 2000-01; Consultant, World Bank, Washington, 2000-01; Non-Executive Director, Vaccine Research International plc, England, 2001-02; Consultant, Charles Street Securities Investment Bank, England, 2001-02; Consultant, Adam Smith Institute, England, 2001-04; Medical Director, Sedac Therapeutics, France, 2002-03; Director of Research & Development, SR Pharma, England, 2003-; Consultant, Midatech, England, 2005-. Publications: Numerous articles in professional medical journals. Memberships: British Medical Association; Royal College of Pathologists. Address: 12 Huron Drive, Liphook, Hampshire GU30 7TZ, England. E-mail: ianroberts21@doctors.org.uk

**ROBERTS (Priscilla) Jane (Stephanie) (Hon Lady Roberts),** b. 4 September 1949. Curator. m. Hugh Ashley Roberts, 2 daughters. Education: BA (Hons), Westfield College, University of London; MA, Courtauld Institute of Art, University of London. Appointments: Curator of the Print Room, Royal Library, Windsor Castle, Berkshire, England, 1975-; Librarian, Windsor Castle, 2002-. Publications: Holbein, 1979; Leonardo: a Codex

# DICTIONARY OF INTERNATIONAL BIOGRAPHY

Hammer, 1981; Master Drawings in the Royal Collection, 1985; Royal Artists, 1987; A Dictionary of Michaelangelo's Watermarks, 1988; Leonardo da Vinci (joint author), 1989; A Souvenir Album of Sandby Views of Windsor, 1988; A King's Purchase: King George III and the Collection of Consul Smith, 1993; Holbein and the Court of Henry VIII, 1993; Views of Windsor: Watercolours by Thomas and Paul Sandby, 1995; Royal Landscape: the Gardens and Parks of Windsor, 1997; Ten Religious Masterpieces: a Millennium Celebration, 2000; Royal Treasures (editor), 2002; George III & Queen Charlotte (editor), 2004; Articles in Burlington Magazine; Report of the Society of Friends of St George's. Address: Royal Library, Windsor Castle, Windsor, Berkshire SL4 1NJ, England.

**ROBERTS Julia,** b. 28 October 1967, Georgia, USA. Actress. m. (1) L Lovett, 1993, divorced 1995, (2) Daniel Moder, 2002, 1 son, 1 daughter. Career: Films include: Blood Red; Mystic Pizza; Steel Magnolias; Flatliners; Sleeping with the Enemy; Pretty Woman; Hook; Batman; The Pelican Brief, 1993; Pret á Porter; I Love Trouble, 1994; Something to Talk About, 1996; Michael Collins, 1996; Everyone Says I Love You, 1996; My Best Friends Wedding, 1997; Conspiracy Theory, 1997; Notting Hill, 1998; Stepmom, 1998; Runaway Bride, 1999; Erin Brockovich, 2000; The Mexican, 2001; America's Sweethearts, 2001; Ocean's Eleven, 2001; Full Frontal, 2002; Confessions of a Dangerous Mind, 2003; Mona Lisa Smile, 2003; Closer, 2004; Ocean's Twelve, 2004; UNICEF Goodwill Ambassador, 1995. Honour: Golden Globe (Steel Magnolias, 1990). Address: ICM, 8942 Wilshire Boulevard, Beverly Hills, CA 90211, USA.

**ROBERTS Mary Belle,** b. 27 September 1923, Akron, Ohio, USA. Social Worker. Education: Bachelor of Psychology, University of Michigan, 1948; MSW, 1950; New York School of Social Work, Third Year Social Work, 1953-54. Appointments: Instructor of Alabama Medical School, Department of Psychiatry, 1951-53; ALA, Department of Public Health, Division of Mental Hygiene, 1950-53; Bur MH, Div Com Serv, Pennsylvania Department of Public Welfare, 1954-55; DHEW, PHS, NIMH, Com Services, 1955-64; Private practice, 1964-68; Family Counseling Service of Miami and prior organisations, 1968-90; Private practice, 1990-; Apogee, 1994-96. Publications: JPSW Effective Mental Health by Activation of Community's Potential; Edit the Vocational Rehabilitation of the Mentally Ill; Leadership Training for Mental Health Promotion; Editorials, Alabama Mental Health Bulletin. Honours: Phi Kappa Phi; Licensed MD and Fl; Life Fellow, Royal Society Health; Diplomate, NASW; AAUW named gifts, 1978 and 1981. Memberships: NASW; ACSW; Royal Society of Health; ABECSW; DAR; USD of 1812; AAUW; YWCA; IBC; ABI; University of Michigan Alumni Association; Smithsonian; AARP. Address: 8126 SW, 105th Place, Ocala, FL 34481-9132, USA.

**ROBERTS Michael Victor,** b. 23 September 1941, High Wycombe, England. Librarian. m. Jane Margaret, deceased, 1 son, 1 daughter. Education: Bachelor of Arts, Clare College, Cambridge, 1960-63; Loughborough Technical College, 1963-64; Master of Arts, 1966. Appointments: Various junior professional posts in Loughborough, Leeds and City of London, 1964-70; Principal Cataloguer, 1970-73, Keeper of Enquiry Services, 1973-82, Guildhall Library, City of London; Deputy Director, City of London Libraries and Art Galleries, 1982-95. Publications: Numerous articles in professional and academic journals; Editor, Guildhall Studies in London History, 1973-82; Editor, Branch Journal of the Library Association Local Studies Group, 1996-98; Editor, Archives and the Metropolis, 1998; Editor, Framlingham Historical Society, 1997-. Honours: Associate of the Library Association, 1967; Chartered Librarian,

1967; Member, Chartered Institute of Library and Information Professionals, 2002. Memberships: Governor, Bishopsgate Foundation, 1996-; Deputy Chairman, Bishopsgate Foundation, 1999-2002; Chairman, Bishopsgate Foundation, 2002-; Member, Council of British Records Association, 1987-; Member, East of England Regional Archives Council, 1999-; Member, Shadow East of England Museums, Libraries and Archives Council, 2001-02; Trustee, Housing the Homeless Central Fund, 1997-; Officer/Trustee of various local societies and charities. Address: 43 College Road, Framlingham, Suffolk IP13 9ER, England.

**ROBERTS Robert (James),** b. 11 January 1931, Penrith, Cumbria, England. Retired Headmaster; Poet. m. Patricia Mary Milbourne, 8 August 1959, 1 son, deceased, 1 daughter. Education: MA, Pembroke College, Cambridge, 1951-55. Appointments: Assistant Master, Fettes, 1955-75; Housemaster, 1970-75; Headmaster, Worksop, 1975-86. Publications: Amphibious Landings, 1990; First Selection, 1994; Genius Loci, 1995; Second Selection, 1995; Worm's Eye View, 1995; Third Selection, 1996; Fourth Selection, 1997; Fifth Selection, 1998; Flying Buttresses, 1999. Contributions to: Spectator; Countryman; Poetry Review; Acumen; Envoi; Orbis; Outposts; Poetry Nottingham; Staple; Westwords; First Time; Iota; Doors; Otter; Nutshell; Literary Review; Poetry Wales; Seam. Honours: Many awards. Address: Ellon House, Harpford, Sidmouth, Devon EX10 0NH, England.

**ROBERTSON Angus Struan Carolus,** b. 29 August 1969, Wimbledon, England. Member of Parliament. Partner: Carron Rita Grace Anderson. Education: Master of Arts, Politics and International Relations, Aberdeen University. Appointments: News Editor, Austrian Broadcasting Corporation, 1991-99; Reporter, BBC Austria, 1992-99; Contributor: National Public Radio, USA; Radio Telfís Eireann, Ireland; Deutsche Welle, Germany; Consultant in Media Skills, Presentation Skills and Political Affairs, Communications Skills International, 1994-2001; MP for Moray, 2001; Scottish National Party Spokesperson on Foreign Affairs and Defence. Memberships: Select Committee on European Scrutiny, 2001; Vice-Chair, All Party Offshore Oil and Gas Industry Group, 2001; Scotch Whisky Group, 2001; Austria Group, 2002; All Party South Caucasus Group, 2004; Vice-Convenor, All Party Royal Airforce Group, 2004-. Address: 9 Wards Road, Elgin, Moray IV30 1NL, Scotland. E-mail: info@moraymp.org

**ROBERTSON George Islay McNeill (Lord Robertson of Port Ellen),** b. 12 April 1946. Politician. m. Sandra Wallace, 1970, 2 sons, 1 daughter. Education: MA honours, Economics, University of Dundee, 1968. Appointments: Research Assistant Tayside Study, 1968-69; Scottish Organiser, General and Municipal Workers Union, 1969-78; MP for Hamilton, 1978-97, for Hamilton South, 1997-99; Parliamentary Private Secretary to Secretary of State for Social Services, 1979; Opposition Spokesman on Scottish Affairs, 1979-80, on Defence, 1980-81, On Foreign and Commonwealth Affairs, 1981; Principal Spokesman for Scotland, 1994-97; Secretary of State for Defence, 1997-99; Secretary General, NATO, 1999-. Honours: Grand Cross; Order of Merit (Germany, Hungary, Italy, Luxembourg, etc); Joint Parliamentarian of the Year, 1993; Received life peerage, 1999; Grand Cross of the Order of the Star of Romania, 2000; Knight, Order of the Thistle, UK, 2004; Knight Grand Cross, Order of St Michael and St George, UK, 2004; Honorary Regimental Colonel of the London Scottish Volunteers; Honorary Doctorates: University of Dundee, St Andrews; University of Bradford; Cranfield University-Royal Military College of Science; Baku State University, Azerbaijan; The French University, Yerevan, Armenia; Academy of Sciences, Azerbaijan and Kirgyz Republic; National School of

Politics and Administration Studies, Bucharest. Memberships: Vice-Chairman, Board British Council, 1985-94; Governor, Ditchley Foundation, 1989-; Member, Her Majesty's Privy Council, 1997; President, Royal Institute of International Affairs, 2001-; Elder Brother, Trinity House, 2002-; President, Hamilton Burns Club, 2002-. Address: House of Lords, London, SW1A, England.

**ROBERTSON George Wilber,** b. 20 December 1914, Alberta, Canada. Agrometeorologist. m. Lucille Eileen Davis, 1 son, 1 daughter. Education: BSc, Mathematics and Physics, University of Alberta, 1939; MA, Physics and Meteorology, University of Toronto, 1948. Appointments: Meteorological Assistant, Meteorological Service of Canada, 1938; Officer in Charge, Meteorological Section, No 2 Air Observer School, British Commonwealth Air Training Plan, Edmonton, 1940; Meteorologist, MSC Meteorological Office, Edmonton Airport, 1945; Meteorologist, Central Meteorological Analysis Office of MSC, Ottawa, 1950; Agrometeorologist, Field Husbandry, Soils and Agricultural Engineering Division of Experimental Farms Service, Canada Department of Agriculture, Ottawa, 1951; Expert in Agrometeorology and Climatology, World Meteorological Organization, Philippines, 1969; Senior Scientist, Head of Environment Section, Research Station, Swift Current, Saskatchewan, 1971; Consultant, Food and Agriculture Organisation, Rome, Italy, 1972; Retired from Government Service, 1973; Consultant, Canadian Wheat Board, Winnipeg, 1973; Consultant, WMO, Geneva, 1974; Project Manager, FAO/UNDP Technical Assistance Project with Malaysia Federal Land Development Authority, 1975; Private Consultant in Agrometeorology, several short term projects in developing countries with various international agencies, 1977-98. Publications: Numerous scientific papers, technical reports, feasibility studies and press articles. Honours: Literary A Pin, University of Alberta, 1938; President's Award, 1951, Darton's Prize, 1953, Canadian Branch, Royal Meteorological Society; Accredited as Consulting Meteorologist, Canadian Meteorological and Oceanographic Society, 1987; Elected Fellow, Canadian Society of Agrometeorology, 1987; John Patterson Medal, Atmospheric Environmental Service, Canada, 1992; Honouree, Baier & Robertson Symposium on Modeling and Measurement of Soil Water Content, 1995. Memberships: American Meteorological Society; Royal Meteorological Society, London; Agricultural Institute of Canada; Canadian Society of Agronomy; Ontario Institute of Professional Agrologists; Canadian Meteorological and Oceanographic Society; American Association for the Advancement of Science; The New York Academy of Sciences; Canadian Society of Agrometeorology. Address: 1604-3105 Carling Avenue, Ottawa, ON K2H 5A6, Canada. E-mail: georger400@aol.com

**ROBERTSON Grace,** b. 13 July 1930, Manchester, England. Photographer; Painter; Writer; Lecturer;. m. Godfrey Thurston Hopkins, 1 son, 1 daughter. Education: Maria Grey Teachers Training College, Twickenham; Self taught photographer. Appointments: Photojournalist, Picture Post, 1949-57; Freelance Photographer, 1957-60; Teacher 1956-78; Exhibitions: National Museum of Photography, Film and TV, 1986; Photographers Gallery, 1987; Zelda Cheatle Gallery, London, 1989; National Museum of Wales, Cardiff, 1989; Gardner Centre, University of Sussex, 1990; Cathleen Ewing Gallery, Washington DC, 1992; Royal National Theatre (retrospective exhibition), 1993; Watershed, Bristol, 1993; University of Brighton, Sussex, 1994; Towner Gallery, 1994; Leica Gallery, New York, 1998; A Sympathetic Eye (retrospective exhibition), University of Brighton, Aberdeen Art Gallery and The Lowry, 2002; Works in collections including: Victoria and Albert Museum; National Museum of Photography, Film and TV, Bradford; Helmut Gernsheim Collection, University of Texas, National Gallery of Australia; Hulton Getty Collection, London. Publications: Grace Robertson: Picture Post Photographer, 1989; Into the Nineties, 1992; Grace Robertson: A Sympathetic Eye, 2002; Articles in newspapers and magazines. Honours: Distinguished Photographer's Award, American Women in Photography International Magazine, 1992; Hon DLitt, University of Brighton, 1995; Honorary Fellow of the Royal Photographic Society, 1996; OBE, 1999. Address: Wilmington Cottage, Wilmington Road, Seaford, East Sussex BN25 2EH, England.

**ROBERTSON Thomas John McMeel,** b. 10 January 1928, Nagpur, India. Chartered Engineer. m. Maureen Enca, 12 June 1954, 2 sons. Education: BSc, Mechanical Engineering, Glasgow University, 1952; Member, Institute of Mechanical Engineers, 1961; European Engineer, 1988; Member, Institute of Patentees & Inventors, 1988. Appointments: Royal Air Force, Engineering Officer, English Electric Test & Design Engineer; Cowley Concrete - Works Manager, Sir W G Armstrong Whitworth Equipment Co, Development Engineer, UKAEA, Reactor Operations & Project Engineer. Publications: Anthologies: Crime Against the Planet, 1994; To You With Love, 1997; A Variety of Verse, 1997; Timeless Exposures, 1998; Isis Valley Verses, 1999; National Poetry Anthology, 2002; National Poetry Anthology, 2003. Contribution to: Creative Writing (Pamphlet), 1996. Membership: Sinodun Writing Group. Address: The Popars, School Lane, Milton, Abingdon, Oxon OX14 4EH, England.

**ROBINSON Anne Josephine,** b. 26 September 1944, Crosby, Liverpool, England. Journalist; Broadcaster. m. John Penrose, 1 daughter. Education: Farnborough Hill Convent, Hampshire; Les Ambassadrices, Paris. Appointments: Reporter, Daily Mail 1967-68; Reporter, Sunday Times, 1968-77; Women's Editor, 1979-80, Assistant Editor, 1980-93, Columnist, 1983-93, Daily Mirror; Columnist, Today, 1993-95; Columnist, The Sun, 1995-97; Columnist, The Express 1997-98; Columnist, The Times, 1998-2001; Columnist, Daily Telegraph, 2003-; Television: Afternoon Plus, Thames TV, 1986; Breakfast Time, BBC TV, 1987; Presenter and Writer, Points of View, BBC TV, 1988-98; Presenter and Editor, The Write Stuff, Thames TV, 1990; Presenter, Questions, TVS, 1991; Presenter, Watchdog, BBC TV, 1993-2001; Presenter, Going for a Song, BBC TV, 2000; Presenter, The Weakest Link, BBC TV, 2000-; Presenter, The Weakest Link, NBC Television, 2001-2002; Presenter, Test the Nation, BBC TV, 2002- Presenter, Guess Who's Coming to Dinner, BBC TV, 2003; Presenter, Out Take TV, BBC TV, 2003-; Travels with My Unfit Mother, 2004; Radio: Presenter, The Anne Robinson Show, BBC Radio 2, 1988-93. Honour: Honorary Fellow, Liverpool John Moores University, 1996. Membership: Vice-President Alzheimer's Society. Address: c/o Drury House, 34-43 Russell Street, London WC2B 5HA, London. E-mail: tracey.chapman@css-stellar.com

**ROBINSON (Alfred) Christopher,** b. 18 November 1930, York, England. Soldier; Charity Worker. m. Amanda Boggis-Rolfe, dissolved, 2 sons, 2 daughters. Education: Royal Military Academy, Sandhurst. Appointments: Major, 16th/5th The Queen's Royal Lancers, 1951-65; Trade Indemnity Company Ltd. 1066-70; Glanvill Enthoren Ltd, 1970-73; The Spastic's Society, now Scope, 1973-91; Ferriers Barn Centre for Young Disabled People, 1973-, President, 1987; The Little Foundation, 199-, Chairman, 1996; The Mother & Child Foundation, 1994-, Chairman, 2001. Memberships: Institute of Fundraising, Welfare Committee Chairman, Royal British Legion, Bures Branch; Executive Committee, Dedham Vale Society; Vice-Chairman, Colne Stow Countryside Association; Fundraising Committee Chairman, British Red Cross, Suffolk Branch; Lay

Chairman, Sudbury Deanery Synod; Member, St Edmundsbury and Ipswich Diocesan Synod. Address: Water Lane Cottage, Bures, Suffolk CO8 4DE, England.

**ROBINSON Derek, (Dirk Robson),** b. 12 April 1932, Bristol, England. Writer. m. Sheila Collins, 29 April 1968. Education: MA, Downing College, Cambridge, England. Publications: Goshawk Squadron, 1971; Rotten With Honour, 1973; Kramer's War, 1977; The Eldorado Network, 1979; Piece of Cake, 1983; War Story, 1987; Artillery of Lies, 1991; A Good Clean Fight, 1993; Hornet's Sting, 1999; Kentucky Blues, 2002; Damned Good Show, 2002; Invasion, 1940, 2005. Honour: Shortlisted for Booker Prize, 1971. Address: Shapland House, Somerset Street, Kingsdown, Bristol BS2 8LZ, England.

**ROBINSON John Martin,** b. 10 September 1948, Lancashire, England. Architectural Historian. Education: Fort Augustus Abbey School; University of St Andrews, 1966-70; Oriel College, Oxford, 1970-73; MA, 1st Class Honours, 1970; D. Phil, 1973; D Litt, 2002; Appointments: GLC, Historic Buildings Division, 1974-86; Architectural Editor, Survey of London, 1978-80; Partner, Historic Building Consultants, 1988-; Architectural Writer, Country Life, 1973-; Librarian to Duke of Norfolk, 1978-. Publications: The Wyatts; Observations of Humphry Repton; Georgian Model Farms; The Dukes of Norfolk; The Latest Country Houses; The Country House At War; Cardinal Consalvi; Architecture of Northern England; Country Houses of North West; Oxford Guide to Heraldry (with T Woodstock). Honours: FSA; Knight of Malta; Maltravers Herald of Arms Extraordinary. Memberships: Travellers; Pratts; Beefsteak; XV; Pitt; Roxburghe. Address: Beckside House, Barbon, Via Carnforth, Lancashire LA6 2LT, England. E-mail: mentmore@historical-buildings.co.uk

**ROBINSON Karen,** b. 15 August 1958, New Brunswick, New Jersey, USA. Dietician. m. Richard A Robinson. Education: BS, Home Economics, Montclair State College, New Jersey, 1980; Certified Food Services Sanitation Manager, New Jersey, 1984; Dietetic Internship, Veterans Affairs Medical Center, Virginia, 1991; Masters Degree, Health Sciences, Dietetics, James Madison University, Virginia, 1992. Appointments: Temporary Sales Secretary, Banquet preparation Staff, Boar's Head Inn, Charlottesville, Virginia, 1986-88; Head Diet Counsellor, Diet Center, Charlottesville, Virginia, 1986-90; Public Health Nutritionist, Central Shenandoah Health District, Waynesboro, Virginia, Health Department, 1993-97; Dietetic Intern Mentor, 1993-97; Consulting Dietician, Hebrew Hospital Home, Bronx, New York, 1998; Food Service Manager, Sodexho Marriot Services, Morningside House Nursing Home, Bronx, New York, 1998-99; Clinical Dietician, Yonkers General Hospital, Yonkers New York, 1999-2001; Community Services Instructor, Westchester Community College, Valhalla, New York, 2001; Inpatient/Outpatient Dietician, Park Care Pavilion (formerly Yonkers General Hospital, 2001-); Clinical Dietician, St John's Riverside Hospital, Yonkers, New York, 2002-. Publications: Abstract as co-author: The psychological predictors of successful weight loss, 1992; Contributed articles to local newspapers and journals. Honours: Recipient, New York State Dietetic Association Grant. Listed in Who's Who publications and biographical dictionaries. Memberships: American Dietetics Association; Dieticians in Nutrition Support; Gerontological Nutritionists Practice Group; Consulting Dieticians in Health Care Facilities; American Association Family and Consumer Sciences; Westchester Rockland Dietetic Association; Virginia Dietetics Association, 1993-97; Virginia Public Health Association, 1995-97. Address: 10-02 Hunter Lane, Ossining, NY 10562, USA.

**ROBINSON Sir Kenneth (Ken),** b. 4 March 1950, Liverpool, England. Educator. m. Marie Thérése, 1 son, 1 daughter. Education: B Ed (with Honours), English and Drama, University of Leeds, 1972; Certificate of Education (with Distinction); Doctor of Philosophy, University of London, 1980. Appointments: Co-ordinator, Drama 10-16, National Development Project , Schools Council of England and Wales, 1974-77; Freelance lecturer, writer, 1977-79; Director, Calouste Gulbenkian Foundation National Committee of Inquiry on The Arts in Schools, 1979-81; Director, Gulbenkian Foundation/ Leverhulme Inquiry: The Arts and Higher Education, 1981-82; Director, Calouste Gulbenkian Foundation, Arts Education Development Programme, 1981-83; Publisher, Managing Editor, Arts Express, national monthly magazine, 1983-85; Director, National Curriculum Council's, Arts in Schools Project, 1985-89; Professor of Arts Education, 1989-2001, Professor Emeritus, 2001-, University of Warwick; Currently, Senior Adviser, J Paul Getty Trust, Los Angeles, California, USA. Publications: 18 books and monographs; 17 book chapters and journal papers; Numerous newspaper features and interviews and appearances on radio and television. Honours: Knighted for services to the arts, June 2003. Memberships include: Member of Board and Chairman, Education Committee, Birmingham Royal Ballet; Education Adviser, Chairman Education Policy Group, Arts Council of Great Britain; Education Advisory Council, Independent Television Commission; Director, British Theatre Institute; Adviser to Outreach Programme, The Royal Academy. Address: J Paul Getty Trust, 1200 Getty Center Drive, Los Angeles, 90049, USA.

**ROBINSON Mary,** b. 21 May 1944, Ballina, County Mayo, Ireland. International Civil Servant; Former Head of State. m. Nicholas Robinson, 1970, 2 sons, 1 daughter. Education: Trinity College, Dublin; King's Inns, Dublin; Harvard University, USA. Appointments: Barrister, 1967, Senior Counsel, 1980; Called to English Bar (Middle Temple), 1973; Reid Professor of Constitutional and Criminal Law, Trinity College, Dublin, 1969-75, Lecturer, European Community Law, 1975-90; Founder, Director, Irish Centre for European Law, 1988-90; Senator, 1969-89; President, Ireland, 1990-97; UN High Commissioner for Human Rights, 1997-. Honours include: LLD honoris causa (National University of Ireland; Cambridge; Brown; Liverpool; Dublin; Montpellier; St Andrews; Melbourne; Columbia; National University of Wales; Poznan; Toronto; Fordham; Queens University, Belfast); Dr honoris causa Public Services (Northeastern University); Honorary Docteur en Sciences Humaines (Rennes), 1996; Honorary LLD (Coventry), 1996; Berkeley Medal, University of California; Medal of Honour, University of Coimbra; Medal of Honour, Ordem dos Advogados, Portugal; Gold Medal of Honour, University of Salamanca; Andrés Bello Medal, University of Chile; New Zealand Suffrage Centennial Medal; Freedom Prize, Max Schmidheiny Foundation (Switzerland); UNIFEM Award, Noel Foundation, Los Angeles; Marisa Bellisario Prize, Italy, 1991; European Media Prize, The Netherlands, 1991; Special Humanitarian Award, CARE, Washington DC, 1993; International Human Rights Award, International League of Human Rights, New York, 1993; Liberal International Prize for Freedom, 1993; Stephen P Duggan Award (USA), 1994; Freedom of the City of Cork; Honorary AO; Council of Europe North South Prize, Portugal, 1997; Collar of Hussein Bin Ali, Jordan, 1997; F D Roosevelt Four Freedoms Medal, 1998; Erasmus Prize, Netherlands, 1999; Fulbright Prize, USA, 1999; Garrigues Walker Prize, Spain, 2000; William Butler Prize, USA, 2000; Indira Gandhi Peace Prize, India, 2000; Sydney Peace Prize. Memberships include: Royal Irish Academy; Honorary Bencher Kings Inns, Dublin, Middle Temple, London.

Address: Palais des Nations, United Nations, 1211 Geneva 10, Switzerland.

**ROBINSON Robert Henry,** b. 17 December 1927, Liverpool, England. Writer; Broadcaster. m. Josephine Mary Richard, 1958, 1 son, 2 daughters. Education: Raynes Park Grammar School; MA, Exeter College, Oxford. Publications: Landscape With Dead Dons, 1956; Inside Robert Robinson, 1965; The Conspiracy, 1968; The Dog Chairman, 1982; Everyman Book of Light Verse (editor), 1984; Bad Dreams, 1989; Prescriptions of a Pox Doctor's Clerk, 1991; Skip All That: Memoirs, 1996; The Club, 2000. Contributions to: Newspapers, radio and television. Address: 16 Cheyne Row, London SW3, England.

**ROBINSON Tony,** b. 13 August 1946, London, England. Actor; Writer; TV Presenter. 1 son, 1 daughter. Education: Central School of Speech and Drama. Career: Theatre: Numerous appearances as a child actor including the original stage version of the musical Oliver!; Several years in repertory theatre; Theatre director, 2 years, then Chichester Festival Theatre, Royal Shakespeare Company and National Theatre; Touring in 1 man show, Tony Robinson's Cunning Night Out, 2005; Television: Ernie Roberts in Horizon's Joey; Baldrick in Black Adder (4 series, BBC); Sheriff of Nottingham in Maid Marian and Her Merry Men (also writer, 4 series); Alan in My Wonderful Life (3 series, Granada); Leading role in Channel 4 series, Who Dares Wins; As presenter: Points of View; Stay Tooned; Time Team (Channel 4,); Social history series: The Worst Jobs in History, 2004; Historical Documentaries for Channel 4 on: The Peasants Revolt, the Roman Emperors, Macbeth, Robin Hood, the Holy Grail. Publications: Children's television programmes include: 30 episodes of Central TV's Fat Tulips Garden; 13 part BBC series based on Homer's Iliad and Odyssey: Odysseus – The Greatest Hero of Them All; 26 episodes of the Old Testament series Blood and Honey; 17 children's books include: Tony Robinson's Kings and Queens; Adult books include most recently: The Worst Jobs in History; Archaeology is Rubbish – A Beginners Guide (with Professor Mick Aston); In Search of British Heroes; Currently putting the entire works of Terry Pratchett onto audio tape. Honours: 2 Royal Television Society Awards; BAFTA Award; International Prix Jeunesse; Honorary MA: Bristol University, 1999, University of East London, 2002; Honorary Doctorate: University of Exeter, 2005; Open University, 2005. Memberships: British Actors Equity, Vice-President, 1996-2000; President, Young Archaeology Club; National Executive Committee, Labour Party, 2000-2004. Address: c/o Jeremy Hicks Associates, 11-12 Tottenham Mews, London W1T 4AG, England.

**ROBINSON William Peter,** Professor Emeritus. Education: MA, D Phil (Oxon); Fellow, Australian and British Psychological Societies; Chartered Psychologist; CSCE Qualified Interpreter in Russian. Appointments: Academic positions at Universities of Hull, London, Southampton; Chairs of Education at Macquarie and Bristol Universities; Chair of Social Psychology, Bristol University; Currently, University and Leverhulme Senior Research Fellow and Professor Emeritus, Bristol University; Trustee: College of St Paul and St Mary, Cheltenham; Chair, Deaf Studies Trust; Chair and Vice-Chair, The Red Maid's School, Bristol; Bristol Municipal Charities. Publications: 4 authored books; 2 technical reports; 5 edited books; 4 edited series; More than 100 journal articles and chapters; Including most recently: Books: The New Handbook of Language and Social Psychology (co-editor), 2001; Language in Social Worlds, 2003; Book chapters: Language in communication: frames of reference, 2001; The contemporary cultural context for deception and malingering in Britain, 2003; Articles as author and co-author: Language use and education in relation to social class and gender, 2000; Similarities and differences in perceptions and evaluations of the communications styles of American and British managers, 2002; Single sex teaching and achievement in science, 2003. Honours include: DSIR (ESRC) Postgraduate Award; Honorary Professor, Instituto Superior de Psicologia Aplicada, Lisbon; Visiting Professor, Monash University, Cheltenham CHE; Fellow, Japanese Society for the Promotion of Science; Visiting Scholar, Wolfson College, Oxford; JV Smyth Memorial Lecturer, Melbourne; Centenary Lecturer, University of Hanover; 13 funded research projects. Memberships: Various committees, SSRC/ESRC; Chair and Committee Member Social Psychology Section, Member of Council, British Psychological Society; Co-founder and Foundation President, International Association of Language and Social Psychology; Research Committee, International Communication Association; Co-founder triennial international conferences on language and social psychology, 1979-. Address: Department of Experimental Psychology, University of Bristol, 8 Woodlands Road, Bristol BS8 1TN, England.

**ROBISON Victor James,** b. 29 April 1920, Youngstown, Ohio, USA. Retired US Naval Officer. Education: BS, 1942, MA, 1948, Case Western Reserve University, Cleveland , Ohio; Continued studies in American Culture at Sorbonne University, Paris, 1949-50, and Philosophy, Columbia University, New York City, 1950-51. Appointments: Communications Officer, USS Taylor (DD468), Pacific, 1943-46; Training Officer, US Naval Reserve Training Center, Baltimore, Maryland, 1952-55; Assistant Operations Officer, USS Worcester (CL144), 1956-57; US Naval Attaché and Naval Attaché for Air, American Embassy, Warsaw, Poland, 1957-58; Officer-in-Charge, Naval Liaison Group and Chief, Plant Engineering and Maintenance Division, Alternative Joint Communication Agency, Ft Richie, Maryland, 1958-61; US Naval Attaché and Naval Attaché for Air, American Embassy, Brussels, Belgium, 1962-66; Assistant Curator for the US Navy, Washington DC, 1967-69; Appraiser of Naval Memorabilia and Artefacts, 1970-76. Honours: Awarded Naval Unit Commendation and Asian-Pacific Medal with 13 Battle Stars and other medals for service during WWII on Taylor; Decorated Order of Leopold II, Belgian Minister of Defence, 1966. Memberships: Beta Theta Pi Fraternity; Veterans of Foreign Wars; American Legion; Smithsonian Institution; Navy League. Address: 423 Seventh St SE, Washington DC 20003, USA.

**ROBSON Bryan,** b. 11 January 1957, Chester-le-Street, England. Footballer. m. Denise Robson, 1979, 1 son, 2 daughters. Career: Professional footballer with Manchester United, FA Cup winners, 1983, 1985, 1990; European Cup Winners' Cup, 1991; Player, Manager, Middlesborough Football Club, 1994-; Assistant Coach English National Team, 1994-; Winner, League Championship, 1992-93, 1993-94; 90 caps (65 as captain), scoring 26 international goals. Honours: OBE; Hon MA (Salford), 1992, (Manchester), 1992.

**ROCCA Costantino,** b. 4 December 1956, Bergamo, Italy. Golfer. m. 1 son, 1 daughter. Career: Former factory worker and caddie; Turned professional, 1981; Qualified for PGA European Tour through 1989 Challenge Tour; Won Open V33 Da Grand Lyon and Peugeot Open de France; First Italian Golfer to be member European Ryder Cup team, 1993; Member, winning European Ryder Cup team, 1995.

**ROĆEN Milan,** b. 23 November 1950, Rasova, Zabljak, Montenegro. Diplomat. m. Stana Roćen, 1 son. Education: Journalism, Faculty of Political Science, Belgrade University. Appointments: Journalist, weekly magazine: Economic Politic, Belgrade, 1976-79; Staff Member, Information and

Propaganda Department of the Presidency of the Central Committee of the League of Communists of Montenegro, 1979-82; Chief of Staff of President of the Central Committee of the League of Communists of Montenegro, 1982-88; Deputy Minister of Foreign Affairs of Montenegro, 1988-92; Minister-Counsellor for Political Affairs at the Former Republic of Yugoslavia Embassy, Moscow, 1992-97, (Chargé d'Affaires of the Yugoslav Embassy in Moscow, 1993-94); Foreign Policy Advisor to the Prime Minister of the Republic of Montenegro, 1997-98; Foreign Policy Adviser to the President of the Republic of Montenegro, Special Envoy of President Djukanovic in talks in Paris, London, Bonn, Berlin, Vienna and Moscow, Chairman of the International Co-operation Commission of the Democratic Party of Socialists of Montenegro, 1998-2003; Chief Political Adviser to the Prime Minister of the Republic of Montenegro; Extraordinary and Plenipotentiary Ambassador of Serbia and Montenegro in the Russian Federation, 2003-. Publications include: Articles in the weekly magazine: Economic Politic; Student Magazine; Daily newspaper: Pobjeda. Membership: Democratic Party of Socialists of Montenegro. Address: 13 Jula 2/11, Podgorica, Montenegro.

**ROCHE DE COPPENS Peter G,** b. 24 May 1938, Vevey, Switzerland. Professor, Author. m. Maria Teresa Crivelli. Education: BS, Columbia University, New York, 1965; MA, 1966, PhD, 1972, Fordham University, New York. Appointments: Professor of Sociology/Anthropology, East Stroudsburg University of Pennsylvania, 1970-; Created TV program: Soul Sculpture, East Stroudsburg University, 1991-; Consultant, United Nations, PNUCID, 1997; Adjunct Professor, Department of Culture and Values in Education, McGill University, Montreal, 1998. Publications: Divine Light and Fire and Divine Light and Love, 1992, 1994; L'Alternance Instinctive and La Voie Initiatique de l'An 2000 (Louise Courteau). Honours: Phi Beta Kappa; Woodrow Wilson Fellow; Knight Commander of Malta; American Biographical Institute's Commemorative Medal of Honor. Memberships: American Sociological Association; American Orthopsychiatric Association; New York Academy of Sciences; American Association for the Advancement of Science. Address: 124 S Kistler Street, East Stroudsburg, PA 18301 2604, USA.

**ROCHETTE Jean-François,** b. 15 March 1939, Paris, France. Banker; Economist. m. Veronique Turrettini, 1 son, 2 daughters. Education: Ecole Superieure Commerce Maturité, 1960; Licence es Sciences Economiques, 1964; Licence es Sciences Politiques, 1966; Certificate of Finance, New York, USA, 1970. Appointments: Manager, Lombard Odier Bankers, Geneva; Deputy President, United Overseas Bank, Geneva; Investment Counsellor, Rochette Associates, Geneva; Board of Directors, Barclays Bank, Switzerland; Vice-Chairman, B C P Bank, Geneva. Address: La Lezardiere, 290 B rte Lausanne, 1293 Bellevue-Geneva, Switzerland. E-mail: rochette.assoc@b luewin.com

**ROCK David Annison,** b. 27 May 1929, Sunderland, England. Architect. m. (1) Daphne Elizabeth Rock, 3 sons, 2 daughters, (2) Lesley Patricia Rock. Education: B Arch Hons (Dunelm), School of Architecture, Kings College, University of Durham, 1947-52; Cert TP (Dunelm), Department of Town Planning, Kings College, University of Durham, 1950-52; School of Town Planning, University of London, 1952-53. Appointments: 2nd Lieutenant, Royal Engineers, 1953-55; Basil Spence & Partners, 1952-53, 1955-59; David Rock Architect, 1958-59; Partner, Building Design Partnership, 1959-71; Chairman, Managing Director, Rock Townsend, 1971-92; Head, Lottery Architecture Unit, Arts Council of England, 1995-99; Partner, Camp 5, 1992-; Chairman, Dryden Street, 1971-80; Chairman, Barley Mow

Workspace, 1973-92; Lottery Awards Panel, Sports Council of England, 1995-97; Vice-President, 1987-88, 1995-97, President, 1997-99, Royal Institute of British Architects; Vice-President, 2000, President, 1997-99, 2002-, Architects Benevolent Society; Trustee, Montgomery Sculpture Trust, 2000-2004; Trustee, South Norfolk Building Preservation Trust, 2002-2005; Finance Director, Huguenot Court Limited, 2003-. Publications: Books: Vivat Ware! 1974; The Grassroots Developers, 1980; Numerous articles in building press, 1960-. Honours: Department of the Environment Housing Medals, RIBA Architecture Awards, Civic Trust Awards, 1965-; Glover Medal, 1949; HB Saint Award, 1950; Crown Prize,1951; Soane Medallion, 1954; Owen Jones Studentship, 1960; RIBA/Building Industry Trust Fellow, 1979; President's Medal, AIA, 1998; Honorary Fellow, American Institute of Architects, 1998. Memberships: Past President, RIBA; Fellow, Chartered Society of Designers. Address: The Beeches, 13 London Road, Harleston, Norfolk IP20 9BH, England. E-mail: david.rock1@btinternet.com

**RODAHL Kaare,** b. 17 August 1917, Rodal, Norway. Retired. m. Joan Hunter, 1 son, 1 daughter. Education: MD, 1948, DSc, 1950, Oslo University; USA Medical Degree, 1957. Appointments: Special Consultant, US Air Force, 1949; Chief, Department of Physiology, Arctic Aeromedical Laboratory, Fairbanks, Alaska, 1950-52; Assistant Professor of Physiology, Oslo University, 1952-54; Director of Research, Arctic Aeromedical Laboratory, Fairbanks, Alaska, 1954-57; Director of Research, Lankenau Hospital, Philadelphia, 1957-65; Director, Institute of Work Physiology, Oslo, Norway, 1965-87; Professor, Norwegian College of Physical Education, Oslo, Norway, 1966-87; Retired. Publications include: Textbook of Work Physiology, 2003; The Physiology of Work, 1989; Stress Monitoring in the Workplace, 1994. Honours include: Honorary member, staff and faculty, US Army Command and General Staff College, Fort Leavenworth, Kansas, 1960; Knight of the Royal Norwegian Order of St Olav, 1988. Memberships: American Physiological Society; Norwegian Medical Association. Address: Maaltrostveien 40, 0786 Oslo, Norway.

**RODDICK Anita Lucia,** b. 23 October 1942, Littlehampton, England. Business Executive. m. Gordon Roddick, 1970, 2 daughters. Education: Newton Park College of Education, Bath. Appointments: Teacher, English and History; Worked in library of International Herald Tribune, Paris and Women's Rights Department of ILO, based at UN, Geneva; Owner, Manager, restaurant and hotel; Opened first branch of the Body Shop, Brighton, Sussex, 1976; The Body Shop International floated on Unlisted Securities Market, 1984; Group Manager, Director, -1994, Chief Executive Officer, 1994-98, Joint Chairman, 1998-2002, Director (non-executive), internal consultant, 2002-, The Body Shop International PLC; Trustee of the Body Shop Foundation, 1990-, New Academy of Business, 1996; Patron of various organisations. Publications: Body and Soul (autobiography), 1994; Business as Unusual, 2000. Honours: Veuve Cliquot Businesswoman of Year, 1984; British Association of Industrial Editors Communicator of Year, 1988; Co NatWest Retailer of Year Award, 1988; Hon D University (Sussex), 1989, (Open University), 1995; Global 55 Environment Award, 1989; Hon LLD (Nottingham), 1990, (New England College), 1991, (Victoria, Canada), 1995; Business Leader of Year, National Association of Women Business Owners (USA), 1992; Botwinick Prize in Business Ethics, 1994; Business Leadership Award, University of Michigan, 1994; 1st Annual Womanpower Award, Women's Business Development Centre, 1995; USA Women's Center Leadership Award, 1996; American Dream Award, Hunter College, 1996; Philanthropist of Year, Institute of Fundraising Managers, 1996. Address: The

Body Shop International, Watersmead, Littlehampton, West Sussex, BN17 6LS, England.

**RODMAN Dennis Keith,** b. 13 May 1961, Trenton, New Jersey, USA. Basketball Player. Education: Cooke County Junior College; Southeastern Oklahoma State University. Career: West Detroit Pistons, 1986-93; Forward San Antonio Spurs, 1993-95, Chicago Bulls, 1995-99; L A Lakers, 1999; NBA Defensive Player of Year, 1990, 1991; NBA Championship Team, 1989-90, 1996; All-Defensive First Team, 1989-93, All-Defense Second Team, 1994; All Star Team, 1990, 1992. Film appearances: Cutaway; Simon Sez; Double Team. Publications: Bad as I Wanna Be, 1997; Walk on the Wild Side, 1997; Words from the Worm: An Unauthorised Trip Through the Mind of Dennis Rodman, 1997. Address: L A Lakers, 3900 West Manchester Boulevard, Inglewood, CA 90306, USA.

**RODNA Alexandru Leonte,** b. 3 January 1951, Bucharest, Romania. Physicist. m. Marieta Rodna. Education: License Diploma in Physics (MS), University of Bucharest, Romania, 1975; Diploma, Mathematics, University "Babes Bolyai", Cluj-Napoca, Romania, 1991. Appointments: Radiation Protection Officer for X-ray and gamma radiography, 1975-84; Design Physicist for ultrasonic control equipment for radiography rooms, 1984-85 Teacher of Physics in secondary schools, 1985-91, Radiation Protection Expert, 1991-97, Section Head, 1997-2004, Director, 2004-, National Commission for Nuclear Activities Control, Bucharest. Publications: Papers presented at conferences and reports include most recently as co-author: New Romanian Radiation Protection Regulatory Framework, IAEA-CN-91, 2002; Implemantation of Romanian NPP Spent Fuel Management Strategy – A Regulatory Approach, 2003; New Romanian regulation for issuing practice permits for nuclear activities and for designation of radiological protection qualified experts, 2003. Membership: Group of Experts of Central Commission for Nuclear Accidents and Dropping of Cosmic Objects. Address: National Commission for Nuclear Activities Control, Blvd Libertatii 14, PO Box 42-2, Bucharest 4, Romania 761061. E-mail: alexandru.rodna@cncan.ro

**RODRIGUES Christopher John,** b. 24 October 1949, London, England. Financial Services. m. Priscilla, 1 son, 1 daughter. Education: Cambridge University; Harvard Business School. Appointments: Spillers Foods, 1971-72; Foster Turner & Benson, 1972-74; McKinsey & Co, 1976-79; American Express, 1978-88; Chief Executive Officer, Thomas Cook, 1988-95; Non-Executive Director, Energis, 1997-2002; Chief Executive Officer, Bradford & Bingley plc, 1996-2004; Executive Committee, National Trust, 1994-2004; Non-Executive Director, Financial Services Authority, 1997-2003; Non-Executive Director, Hilton Group, 2003-; President & Chief Executive Officer, VISA International, 2004-. Honours: BA with Honour in Economics and Economics History; MBA with distinction. Memberships: Fellow, Royal Society for the Encouragement of Arts, Manufactures and Commerce. Address: VISA International, PO Box 8999, San Francisco, CA 94128-8999, USA.

**RODWELL (His Honour) Daniel Alfred Hunter,** b. 3 January 1936, Bombay, India. Lawyer. m. Veronica Cecil, 2 sons, 1 daughter. Education: Munro College, Jamaica; Worcester College, Oxford. Appointments: National Service, 1954-56: 2nd Lieutenant, The West Yorkshire Regiment, 1955; Captain and Adjutant, 3rd Battalion, Prince of Wales Own Regiment of Yorkshire, 1962-66; Called to Bar, Inner Temple, 1960; Assistant Recorder, 1976; Recorder, 1980; Queen's Counsel, 1982; Circuit Judge, 1986-2002; Resident Judge, Luton Crown Court, 1993-2000; Resident Judge, Aylesbury Crown Court,

1999-2002; Deputy Circuit Judge, 2002-05. Publications: Journal article: Applications for Third Party Material Where Public Interest Immunity is Likely to be Claimed, 1998; Problems with the Sexual Offences Act, 2003. Honour: Queen's Counsel 1982. Memberships: Royal Institution of Great Britain; Bar Yacht Club; Pegasus Club; Inner Temple. Address: Roddimore House, Winslow Road, Great Horwood, MK17 0NY, England. E-mail: dan.rodwell@btinternet.com

**ROGERS Howard Dennis,** b. 20 March 1948, Miami, Florida, USA. Attorney. m. Mary Kathleen Rogers, 1 son, 1 daughter. Education: BA with Honors, Florida State University, 1970; JD, University of Florida, 1979. Appointments: Blake & Associates P.A., 1981-84; Jacobs, Robbins, Gaynor et al. P.A., 1984-86; Foley & Lardner P.A., 1986-93; Carey & Florin, P.A., 1993-96; Mitchell & Rogers P.A., 1996; Florin, Roebig, Walker Huddlestun & Rogers, 1996-2000; H Dennis Rogers, P.A., 2000-. Honours: The Bar Register of Pre-eminent Lawyers; Listed in Who's Who publications and biographical dictionaries. Memberships: National Lawyer Honor Society; Million Dollar Advocates Forum; American Mensa Society, 1971-80; Florida Bar; Association of Trial Lawyers of America; Academy of Florida Trial Lawyers; Clearwater Bar Association. Address: 28163 US Hwy 19 North, Suite 200, Clearwater, FL 33761-2696, USA.

**ROGOZKIN Victor,** b. 23 February 1928, Leningrad, Russia. Biochemist. m. Komkova Antonina. Education: AB, Military Institute of Physical Culture, Leningrad, 1953; State University, Leningrad, 1958; BD (Hon) State University, Leningrad, 1960; DSc, Institute of Physiology, Leningrad, 1966. Appointments: Researcher, Research Institute of Physical Culture, Leningrad, 1959-65; Professor of Biochemistry, 1966-70; Director of the Institute, 1970-2003. Publications: Current Research in Sport Science, 1996; Co-editor: Nutrition, Physical Fitness and Health, 1978; Author: Physical Activity in Disease Prevention and Treatment, 1985; Metabolism of Anabolic Andorgenic Steroids, 1991; Over 360 papers; Current major research interests relate to exercise biochemistry and sports nutrition. Honours: Honoured Scientist of Russian Federation, 1989; Award, United States Sports Academy, 1991. Memberships: Research Group on Biochemistry of Exercise UNESCO; Editorial Board, International Journal Sport Nutrition. Address: Research Institute of Physical Culture, Dynamo Ave 2, 197110 St Petersburg, Russia.

**ROH Moo-hyun,** b. 6 August 1946, Gimhae, Gyeongsangnam-do, Korea. President of the Republic of Korea. m. Kwon Yang-sook, 1 son, 1 daughter. Education: Graduate, Busan Commercial High School, 1966; Passed 17th National Bar Examination, 1975. Appointments: Judge, Daejeon District Court, 1977; Practising Attorney, 1978-; Human Rights Lawyer, 1981-; Chairman and Director, Busan Headquarters, Citizens' Movement for a Democratic Constitution, 1987; One of Leaders of June Democratisation Struggles, 1987; Elected to 13th National Assembly in Busan's Eastern District, 1988; Member, Special Committee to Investigate Political Corruption during the Fifth Republic, 1988; Spokesman, 1991, Senior Member, Central Committee, 1993, United Democratic Party; Director, Research Centre for Local Autonomy, 1993; Standing Committee Member, Committee for the Promotion of National Reconciliation and Unity, 1996; Vice-President, National Congress for New Politics, 1997; Elected to 15th National Assembly, 1998; Minister of Maritime Affairs and Fisheries, 2000-2001; Advisor and Senior Member, Central Committee, Millennium Democratic Party, 2000; Elected President of the Republic of Korea, 2002; Sworn in as President for a 5 year term of office, 2003. Publications: Honey, Please Help Me! 1994;

Roh Moo-hyun Meets Lincoln, 2001; Thoughts on Leadership, 2002.

**ROHATGI Pradip Krishna (Roy),** b. 10 November 1939, Calcutta, India. Professor; Consultant. m. Pauline Mary Rohatgi. Education: Bachelor of Commerce, Calcutta University, 1960; Bachelor of Science, Economics, University of London, 1964; Associate Examinations of the Institute of Taxation (UK), 1967; Associate Member, 1969, Fellow, 1974, Institute of Chartered Accountants of England and Wales; Fellow, Institute of Chartered Accountants of India, 1980. Appointments: Senior Economist and Statistician in industrial market research, London, 1963-66; Articled and qualified as a Chartered Accountant, Mann Judd & Co, London, 1966-70; Arthur Andersen Worldwide Organisation, 1970-94, London Office Manager, 1974, Partner 1980, Head of Accounting and Audit Division for Gulf Countries, Dubai Office, 1980-84, Managing Partner for South Asia, Mumbai, India, 1980-89; Senior Partner and Consultant, London, 1990-94, retired as Partner, 1994; International Taxation and Strategy Advisor, 1994-2004; Visiting Professor in International Taxation, RAU University, South Africa, 1996; Advisor to the Mauritius Offshore Business Activities Authority and Ministry of Economic Affairs, Financial Service and Corporate Affairs, 2000-; Professor of International Tax Planning, St Thomas University School of Law, Miami, USA, 2002-; Conference Director, Annual International Taxation Conference, Mumbai, India, 1995-. Publications: Book: Basic International Taxation, 2001, 2nd edition, 2005; More than 300 articles and over 1,000 presentations. Memberships: International Fiscal Society; International Tax Planning Association. Address: 43 Great Brownings, College Road, London SE21 7HP, England. E-mail: roy@itpa.org

**ROHEN Edward, (Bruton Connors),** b. 10 February 1931, Dowlais, South Wales. Poet; Writer; Artist. m. Elizabeth Jarrett, 4 April 1961, 1 daughter. Education: ATD, Cardiff College of Art, 1952. Appointments: Art Teacher, Ladysmith High, British Columbia, Canada, 1956-57; Head of Art, St Bonaventures, London, 1958-73; Ilford County High for Boys, Essex, 1973-82. Publications: Nightpriest, 1965; Bruised Concourse, 1973; Old Drunk Eyes Haiku, 1974; Scorpio Broadside 15, 1975; Poems/Poemas, 1976; A 109 Haiku and One Seppuku for Maria, 1987; Sonnets for Maria Marriage, 1988; Sonnets: Second Sequence for Maria, 1989. Contributions to: Poetry Wales; Anglo-Welsh Review; Irish Press; Mabon; Tribune; Argot; Edge; Little Word Machine; Second Aeon; Planet; Carcanet; Poetry Nippon; Riverside Quarterly; Littack; Wormwood Review; Twentieth Century Magazine. Memberships: Korean War Veterans Writers and Arts Society; Academician, Centro Cultural Literario e Artistico de o Jornal de Felgeiras, Portugal; Welsh Academy; Poet's Society of Japan. Address: 57 Kinfauns Road, Goodmayes, Ilford, Essex IG3 9QH, England.

**RÖHSER Günter,** b. 27 July 1956, Rothenburg ob der Tauber, Germany. m. Hedwig Röhser, 3 sons. University Professor. Education: Studies in Protestant Theology in Erlangen, Heidelberg and Neuendettelsau, 1975-81; Doctor of Theology, 1986; Habilitation in New Testament Theology, 1993. Appointments: Director of Studies, Ecumenical Institute, University of Heidelberg, 1982; Pastor, Lutheran Church, Bavaria, 1987; Associate Professor, University/GHS Siegen, 1994; Professor for Bible Studies, RWTH Aachen, 1997; Professor for the New Testament, University of Bonn, 2003. Publications: Metaphorik und Personifikation der Sünde, 1987; Prädestination und Verstockung, 1994; Stellvertretung im Neuen Testament, 2002. Memberships: Studiorum Novi Testamenti Societas; Academic Society for Theology; Society for Protestant Theology; Society of Biblical Literature; International Society for the Study of Deuterocanonical and Cognate Literature. Address: Faculty of Protestant Theology, Section for the New Testament, University of Bonn, Am Hof 1, D-53113 Bonn, Germany. E-mail: g.roehser@ev-theol.uni-bonn.de

**RONAY Egon,** b. Pozony, Hungary (UK citizen). Publisher; Journalist. m. (1) 2 daughters, (2) Barbara Greenslade, 1967, 1 son. Education: LLD, University of Budapest; Academy of Commerce, Budapest; Trained in kitchens of five family restaurants and abroad. Appointments: Manager, 5 restaurants within family firm; Emigrated from Hungary, 1946; General Manager, 2 restaurant complexes in London before opening his Marquee Restaurant, 1952-55; Founder, The Egon Ronay Guides, 1957, Publisher, 1957-85; Gastronomic and good living weekly columnist, Sunday Times, 1986-91; Sunday Express, 1991. Publications: The Unforgettable Dishes of My Life, 1989; Weekly columnist on eating out, food, wine and tourism, Daily Telegraph and later Sunday Telegraph, 1954-60; Weekly column, the Evening News, 1968-74; Editor-in-Chief, Egon Ronay Recommends (Heathrow Airport Magazine), 1992-94. Honours: Médaille de la Ville de Paris, 1983, Chevalier de l'Ordre du Mérite Agricole, 1987. Memberships: Academie des Gastronomes (France), 1979 Founding Vice-President, International Academy of Gastronomy; Founder, President, British Academy of Gastronomes. Address: 37 Walton Street, London SW3 2HT, England.

**ROOKE Denis Eric,** b. 2 April 1924, London, England. Chemical and Mechanical Engineer. m. Elizabeth Brenda, 1 daughter. Education: Westminster City School; Addey and Stanhope School; BSc (Eng) Diploma, Mech Eng and Chem Eng, University College, London; Chancellor, Loughborough University, 1989-2003. Appointments: Military Service, REME UK and India, 1944-49; Staff of South Eastern Gas Board on Coal Tar By Products, 1949; Deputy Manager, Tar Works, 1954; Seconded to North Thames Gas Board for work on LNG 1957; Member, Technical Team on Methane Pioneer, world's first demonstration of LNG transfer across ocean; Development Engineer, South Eastern Gas Board, 1959; Development Engineer, Gas Council, 1960; Member, Production and Supplies, Gas Council, 1966-71; Deputy Chairman, British Gas Corporation, 1972-76; Chairman, British Gas, 1976-89. Publications: Papers to Institution of Gas Engineers, World Power Conference and World Petroleum Conference. Honours: Prince Philip Medal, Royal Academy of Engineering, 1992; Rumford Medal, Royal Society, 1986; CBE, 1970; Knight Bachelor, 1977; Order of Merit, 1997; Numerous honorary degrees. Memberships: Former Fellowship of Engineering, 1977-, President, 1986-91, Royal Academy of Engineering; Royal Society, 1978-; Penultimate Line-Commissioner, 1984, Chairman, 1987-2001, Royal Commission for Exhibition of 1851. Address: 23 Hardy Road, Blackheath, London SE3 7NS, England.

**ROONEY Mickey (Joe Yule Jr),** b. 23 September 1920, Brooklyn, USA. Actor. m. (1) Ava Gardner, (2) Betty J Rase, 2 sons, (3) Martha Vickers, (4) Elaine Mahnken, (5) Barbara Thomason, 4 children, (6) Margie Lang, (7) Carolyn Hockett, 2 sons, (8) Jan Chamberlin, 2 stepsons. Education: Pacific Military Academy. Career: Served AUS, World War II; TV programmes including series: The Mickey Rooney Show; Films include: Judge Hardy's Children; Hold That Kiss; Lord Jeff; Love Finds Andy Hardy; Boys Town; Stablemates; Out West With the Hardys; Huckleberry Finn; Andy Hardy Gets Spring Fever; Babes in Arms; Young Tom Edison; Judge Hardy and Son; Andy Hardy Meets Debutante; Strike up the Band; Andy Hardy's Private Secretary; Men of Boystown; Life Begins for Andy Hardy; Babes on Broadway; A Yank at Eton; The Human

Comedy; Andy Hardy's Blonde Trouble; Girl Crazy; Thousands Cheer; National Velvet; Ziegfeld Follies; The Strip; Sound Off; Off Limits; All Ashore; Light Case of Larceny; Drive a Crooked Road; Bridges at Toko-Ri; The Bold and the Brave; Eddie; Private Lives of Adam and Eve; Comedian; The Grabbers; St Joseph Plays the Horses; Breakfast at Tiffany's; Somebody's Waiting; Requiem for a Heavyweight; Richard; Pulp; It's a Mad Mad Mad Mad World; Everything's Ducky; The Secret Invasion; The Extraordinary Invasion; The Comic; The Cockeyed Cowboys of Calico Country; Skidoo; BJ Presents; That's Entertainment; The Domino Principle; Pete's Dragon; The Magic of Lassie; Black Stallion; Arabian Adventure; Erik the Viking; My Heroes Have Always Been Cowboys, 1991; Little Nimo: Adventures in Slumberland (Voice), 1992; Silent Deadly Night 5; The Toymaker; The Milky Life; Revenge of the Baron; That's Entertainment II; The Legend of OB Taggart, 1995; Kings of the Court, 1997; Killing Midnight, 1997; Boys Will Be Boys, 1997; Animals, 1997; Sinbad: The Battle of the Dark Knights, 1998; Babe: Pig in the City, 1998; The Face on the Barroom Floor, 1998; The First of May, 1998; Holy Hollywood, 1999; Internet Love, 2000; Lady and the Tramp II: Scamp's Adventure, 2001; Topa Topa Bluffs, 2002; Paradise, 2003; Strike the Tent, 2004; A Christmas Too Many, 2004. Address: PO Box 3186, Thousand Oaks, CA 91359, USA.

**ROONEY Patrick Joseph,** b. 8 December 1943, Coatbridge, Scotland. Physician. m. Katherine Boyle, 3 sons, 1 daughter. Education: MB, ChB, 1966, Doctor of Medicine, 1976, Glasgow University; Member, Royal College of Physicians, UK, 1970; Fellow, Royal College of Physicians and Surgeons of Glasgow, 1979; Fellow, Royal College of Physicians of Edinburgh, 1983; Licentiate, Medical College of Canada, 1986. Appointments: Senior House Officer and Registrar in Medicine, Southern General Hospital, Glasgow, Scotland, 1967-70; Registrar of Medicine, Royal Infirmary of Edinburgh, Scotland, 1970-72; Associate Clinical Fellow, National Institute of Arthritis, Metabolism and Digestive Diseases, National Institutes of Health, Bethesda, Maryland, USA, 1975-67; Senior Registrar in Medicine, Centre for Rheumatic Disease and University Department of Medicine, Royal Infirmary, Glasgow, 1973-77; Consultant Physician and Honorary Clinical Lecturer, Western District Teaching Hospitals, Glasgow, Scotland, 1977-81; Director, Rheumatic Diseases Unit, Chedoke Division of Chedoke-McMaster Hospitals; Director of Medical-Surgical Service, Hamilton Psychiatric Hospital, 1986-91; Director, Standardized Patient Program, McMaster University, 1989-91; Professor and Head, Centre for Medical Sciences Education, The University of the West Indies, Trinidad, 1991-93; Professor of Medicine, McMaster University, Hamilton, Ontario, 1981-94; Professor of Medicine, St George's University School of Medicine, Grenada, West Indies, 1994-. Publications: Over 40 publications of original research; Major collaborative or directive role in over 50 articles; Numerous editorial and review articles, communications, chapters in books and monographs. Honours: Awarded Copeman Fellowship, Arthritis and Rheumatism Council of Great Britain, 1975; Schering Travelling Award, Canadian Society for Clinical Investigation, 1989. Memberships: British Society of Rheumatology; Canadian Rheumatism Association; European Society for Clinical Investigation; Canadian Society for Clinical Investigation; International Back Pain Society; American College of Rheumatology; New York Academy of Sciences, Caribbean Academy of Sciences; Founding fellow, American Rheumatism Association. Address: Department of Educational Services, St George's University, School of Medicine, PO Box 7, St George's, Grenada, West Indies.

**ROSARIO Luis Bras,** b. 21 November 1964, Lisbon, Portugal. Physician. Education: Medical degree, University of Lisbon, 1988. Appointments: Resident, 1989-90, Cardiology Fellow, 1991-95, Hospital Santa Marta, Lisbon; Clinical and Research Fellow, Visiting Physician, Brigham and Women's Hospital, Harvard Medical School, Boston; Cardiologist, Head, Heart Failure Unit, 1999-, Hospital Garcia de Orta, Lisbon; Physiology Research Fellow, University College, London; Assistant, Physiology Department, University of Lisbon; Research Fellow, Institute of Molecular Medicine, Lisbon. Publications: Articles in professional journals. Honours: Research Award on Heart Failure; Portuguese Health Ministry; European Society Fellowship for Intervention Cardiology; Listed in national and international biographical dictionaries. Memberships: Portuguese Society Biology; Secretary to the Board, 2001-03, Portuguese Society of Cardiology; American Society Echocardiography; American Society Nuclear Cardiology; Fellow of European Society of Cardiology. Address: R Quinta Grande, 8 r/c 2780-186, Oeiras, Portugal.

**ROSE, Rt Hon Lord Justice, Rt Hon Sir Christopher Dudley Roger,** b. 10 February 1937, Hyde, England. Lord Justice of Appeal. m. Judith, 1 son, 1 daughter. Education: Morecambe Grammar School, Repton; LLB, Hughes Prize, Leeds University, 1954-57; BCL, 1959, Eldon Scholar, 1959, Wadham College, Oxford. Appointments: Law Lecturer, Wadham College Oxford, 1959-60; Teaching Fellow, University of Chicago, 1960-61; Called to Bar, Middle Temple, 1960; Practised, Northern Circuit, 1961-85; Queen's Counsel, 1974; High Court Judge (QBD), 1985-92; Presiding Judge, Northern Circuit, 1987-90; Lord Justice of Appeal, 1992-; Chairman, Criminal Justice Consultative Council, 1994-2000; Vice-President, Court of Appeal (Criminal Division), 1997-. Honours: Middle Temple, Bencher, 1983, Treasurer, 2002; Kt, 1985; Privy Counsellor, 1992. Address: Royal Courts of Justice, Strand, London WC2A 2LL, England.

**ROSE John Luke,** b. 19 July 1937, Northwood, Middlesex. Composer; Lecturer; Pianist; Author. Education: B Mus, 1957, LMusTCL, 1957, PhD, 1963, University of London, Trinity College of Music. Appointments: Lecturer (Extra-Mural Studies), Oxford University, 1959-66; Examiner, Trinity College of Music, London, 1960-63; Teacher (part-time), St Marylebone Grammar School, 1963-66; Overseas Examiner, Trinity College in USA, Newfoundland, Canada, Fiji, New Zealand, Australia, India Compositions: BBC World premiers of Symphony No 1 "The Mystic"; Piano Concerto; Violin Concertos; Macbeth Overture; Cantata "The Pleasures of Youth"(Boosey & Hawkes). Publications: Various compositions, poems and articles; Wagner's Music Dramas (book); The Himalayan Dream (novel); Odysseus (opera); St Francis (musical drama); Mystic Celebration (hymns and anthems). Honours: Honorary Fellow, Trinity College London; Royal Philharmonic Prize for Symphony No 1, 1957 and Symphony No 2, 1958. Memberships: Association of University Tutors; British Academy. Address: c/o Portland Wallis Direct, 31 Mill Road, Ringmar, Sussex, BW8 5HZ, England.

**ROSE Justin,** b. 30 July 1980, Johannesburg, South Africa (British National). Professional Golfer. Education: Robert May's School; Coached by David Leadbetter in UK and at his American Academy. Amateur Career: Teams: England Under 18, 1995; Great Britain and Ireland Under 18, 1996; England, 1996-98; Great Britain and Ireland Walker Cup (youngest ever player), 1997; European Mens, 1998; Professional Career: Teams: World Cup, England, 2002, 2003; Seve Trophy, Great Britain and Ireland, 2003; Playing History: 11th, Beazer Homes Challenge Tour Championship, 15th,

Scottish PGS Championship, 1999; 21st, Italian Open, 11th, BMW International Open, 2000; 7th, BMW International Open, 9th, Via Digital de España, 2nd, Mercedes-Benz South African Open, 2nd, Alfred Dunhill Championship, 2001; T4th, Dunlop Phoenix, T4th, Visa Taiheiyo Masters, 1st, Dunhill Championship, 1st, Nashua Masters, South African Tour, 1st, Chunichi Crowns, Japan, 3rd, Deutsche Bank, SAP Open TCP of Europe, 1st Victor Chandler, British Masters, 5th, Scottish Open, 5th WGC-NEC Invitational, 2002; 2nd, WGC World Cup, 3rd, Deutsche Bank Championship, T3rd, Open de France, T5th, US Open Championship, T5th, Deutsche Bank, SAP Open TCP of Europe, T4th, Johnnie Walker Classic, T7th, Dunhill Championship, 2003; T4th, Bell Canadian Open, T5th HP Classic of New Orleans, 4th Memorial Tournament, T7th MCI Heritage, 1st, Bilt Skins, India, 2004. Honours: Amateur Victories: McGregor Trophy (youngest ever winner and record score), 1995; Carris Trophy (youngest ever winner), 1995; Open regional Pre Qualifier at North Hants, 1995; St Andrews Links Trophy, 1997; Daily Telegraph UK Under 19 Finals, 1997; Peter McEvoy Trophy, 1998; Silver Medal, Open Championship (equals lowest round by an amateur), 1998; Professional Victories: See above; First man in the world to win 4 times, 2002. Address: c/o Rob Alter, IMG, McCormack House, Burlington Lane, Chiswick, London W4 2TH, England.

**ROSE Kenneth Vivian**, b. 15 November 1924, Bradford, Yorkshire, England. Writer. Education: Repton School; Scholar, MA, New College, Oxford, 1948. Appointments: Assistant Master, Eton College, 1948; Editorial Staff, Daily Telegraph, 1952-60; Founder, Writer, Albany Column, Sunday Telegraph, 1961-97. Publications: Superior Person: A Portrait of Curzon and his Circle in Late Victorian England, 1969; The Later Cecils, 1975; William Harvey: A Monograph, 1978; King George V, 1983; Kings, Queens and Courtiers: Intimate Portraits of the Royal House of Windsor, 1985; Harold Nicolson,1992; Elusive Rothschild: The Life of Victor, Third Baron, 2003. Contributions to: Dictionary of National Biography. Honours: Fellow, Royal Society of Literature, 1976; Wolfson Award for History, 1983; Whitbread Award for Biography, 1983; Yorkshire Post Biography of the Year Award, 1984; Commander of the Order of the British Empire, 1996. Address: 38 Brunswick Gardens, London W8 4 AL, England.

**ROSEANNE (Roseanne Barr)**, b. 3 November 1952, Salt Lake City, USA. Actress. m. (1) Bill Pentland, (2) Tom Arnold, divorced 1994, 3 children from previous marriage, (3) Ben Thomas, 1994, 1 son. Appointments: Former window dresser, cocktail waitress; Comic in bars and church coffee-house, Denver; Producer, forum for women performers Take Back the Mike, University of Boulder, Colorado; Performer, The Comedy Store, Los Angeles; Featured, TV special Funny and The Tonight Show; TV special, On Location: The Roseanne Barr Show, 1987; Star, TV series, Roseanne ABC, 1988-97; Host, Roseanne Show, 1998-; Actress in films: She Devil, 1989; Freddy's Dead, 1991; Even Cowgirls Get the Blues, 1994; Blue in the Face, 1995; Unzipped, 1995; Meet Wally Sparks, 1997. Publications: My Life as a Woman, 1989; Roseanne: My Lives, 1994. Honours: Emmy Award, Outstanding Actress in a Comedy Series, 1993.

**ROSEN Michael**, b. 17 October 1927, Dundee, Scotland. Medical Practitioner. m. Sally Cohen, 2 sons, 1 daughter. Education: MB ChB, St Andrew's University, 1949; FFARCS, 1957. Appointments: House appointments, Bolton, Portsmouth, Bradford, 1949-53; RAMC, 1953-55; Registrar, Anaesthesia, Royal Victoria Infirmary, Newcastle upon Tyne, 1954-57; Senior Registrar, Cardiff, 1957-60; Fellow, Case Western University, Ohio, USA, 1960-61; Consultant Anaesthetist,

Cardiff Hospitals, 1961-94; Honorary Professor in Anaesthetics, 1986; Member, GMC, 1989-92. Publications: Percutaneous Cannulation of Great Veins, 1981, 2nd edition, 1991; Obstetric Anaesthesia Safe Practice, 1982; Patient-Controlled Analgesia, 1984; Tracheal Intubation, 1985; Awareness and Pain in General Anaesthesia, 1987; Ambulatory Anaesthesia, 1991; Quality Measures Emergency, 2001. Honours: CBE, 1990; Honorary Member, French and Australian Societies of Anaesthesia; Honorary FFARCSI, 1990; Honorary Fellow, Academy of Medicine, Malaysia; Honorary LLD, Dundee, 1996; FRCOG, 1989; FRCS, 1994. Memberships: President, Association of Anaesthetists, 1986-88; President, Royal College of Anaesthetists, 1988-91. Address: 45 Hollybush Road, Cardiff CF 23 6TZ, Wales. E-mail: rosen@mrosen.plus.com

**ROSEN Norma**, b. 11 August 1925, New York, New York, USA. Writer; Teacher. m. Robert S Rosen, 1960, 1 son, 1 daughter. Education: BA, Mt Holyoke College, 1946; MA, Columbia University, 1953. Appointments: Teacher, Creative Writing, New School for Social Research, New York City, 1965-69, University of Pennsylvania, 1969, Harvard University, 1971, Yale University, 1984, New York University, 1987-95. Publications: Joy to Levine!, 1962; Green, 1967; Touching Evil, 1969; At the Center, 1982; John and Anzia: An American Romance, 1989; Accidents of Influence: Writing as a Woman and a Jew in America (essays), 1992; Biblical Women Unbound: Counter-Tales (narratives), 1996. Contributions to: Anthologies and other publications; Commentary, New York Times Book Review & Magazine, MS, Raritan, etc. Honours: Saxton, 1960; CAPS, 1976; Bunting Institute 1971-73. Memberships: PEN; Authors Guild; Phi Beta Kappa. Address: 133 East 35th Street, New York, NY 10016, USA.

**ROSENTHAL Barbara**, b. 17 August 1948, The Bronx, New York City. Photographer; Conceptual Artist; Video Artist; Writer; Avante-garde Artist. 2 daughters. Education: BFA Painting, Carnegie-Mellon University, Pittsburgh, Pennsylvania, 1970; MFA, Painting, Queens College, City University of New York, 1973. Appointments: Parsons School of Design, New School University; CUNY; Fellow, College of Staten Island; Nassau Community College; University of Bridgeport; Jersey City State College; School of Visual Arts; Stephens College; Manhattan College. Civic Activities: Co-Director, eMediaLoft.org (collaborating with artists to realize their projects). Publications: Soul & Psyche; Homo Futurus; Sensations; Clues to Myself. Commissions and Creative Works: Installations, Performances, Photography; Video; Collections: Museum of Modern Art; Whitney Museum of American Art. Gallery: Monique Goldstrom Gallery, NYC. Honours: CAPS Grant; Experimental Video Center Finishing Funds; Harvestworks Finishing Fund; Visual Studies Workshop Artist-in-Residence Media Access; Adapters Creative Projects Grant. Address: 463 West St, #A-629, New York, NY 10014-2035, USA. Website: www.the-artists.org

**ROSS Alexander (Sandy)**, b. 17 April, 1948, Grangemouth, Scotland. Television Producer. m. Alison Joyce, 2 sons, 1 daughter. Education: LLB, Edinburgh University, 1970; Certificate in Community Work, Moray House College, 1975. Appointments: Solicitor; Lecturer in Law; Producer, Grampian TV, 1976-86; Head of Entertainment, 1980-99, Managing Director, 1999-2004, Managing Director, International Development, 2004-, Scottish TV. Memberships: BAFTA; Glen Golf Club; Haunted Major Golf Society. Address: 200 Renfield Street, Glasgow G2 3PR, Scotland. E-mail: sandy.ross@smg.plc.uk

**ROSS Diana,** b. 26 March 1944, Detroit, Michigan, USA. Singer; Entertainer; Actress; Fashion Designer. m. (1) Robert Ellis Silberstein, 1971, 3 daughters; (2) Arne Ness, 23 October 1985, 1 son. Career: Backing singer, the Temptations, Marvin Gaye, Mary Wells; Lead singer, Diana Ross and The Supremes; Solo artiste, 1969-; Appearances include: Opening ceremonies, Football World Cup, USA, 1994; Rugby World Cup, South Africa, 1995; Film appearances: Lady Sings The Blues, 1972; Mahogany, 1975; The Wiz, 1978; Television specials: An Evening With Diana Ross, 1977; Diana, 1980; Christmas In Vienna, 1992; Business ventures: Diana Ross Enterprises Inc; Anaid Film Productions; RTM Management Corp; Chondee Inc. Recordings: Albums include: Diana Ross, 1970; Lady Sings The Blues, 1972; Touch Me In The Morning, 1973; The Boss, 1979; Why Do Fools Fall In Love?, 1981; Eaten Alive, 1984; Silk Electric, 1982; Chain Reaction, 1986; Ain't No Mountain High Enough, 1989; The Force Behind The Power, 1991; Motown's Greatest Hits, 1992; Live...Stolen Moments, 1993; One Woman - The Ultimate Collection, 1993; The Remixes, 1994; Take Me Higher, 1995; Very Special Christmas, 1998; Every Day is a New Day, 1999. Publication: Secrets Of A Sparrow (autobiography), 1993. Honours include: Citations: Vice-President Humphrey; Mrs Martin Luther King, Rev Abernathy; Billboard award: Record World award, World's Outstanding Singer; Grammy Award, 1970; Female Entertainer Of The Year, NAACP, 1970; Golden Globe, 1972; Antoinette Perry Award, 1977; Nominated Rock and Roll Hall Of Fame, 1988. Address: RTC Management, PO Box 1683, New York, NY 10185, USA.

**ROSS Donald Nixon,** b. 4 October 1922, Kimberley, South Africa. Surgeon. m. Barbara Cork, 1 daughter. Education: BSc, 1942, MB Ch B, First Class Honours, University of Cape Town, 1946; FRCS Eng., 1949; FACS, 1966; FACC, 1982; FRCS Hon Ireland, 1984; FRCS Hon Thailand, 1989; FACS Hon USA, 1993. Appointments: Senior Registrar, Thoracic Surgery, Bristol, 1952; Research Fellow, 1953, Senior Thoracic Registrar 1954, Guy's Hospital; Consultant Thoracic Surgeon, 1958, Senior Surgeon, 1967, National Heart Hospital; Director, Department of Surgery, Institute of Cardiology, 1970; Consultant Surgeon, Middlesex Hospital, 1978. Publications: More than 250 publications include: Books: A Surgeon's Guide to Cardiac Diagnosis. Part I. The Diagnostic Approach, 1962; A Surgeon's Guide to Cardiac Diagnosis. Part II. The Clinical Picture, 1967; Medical and Surgical Cardiology (co-author), 1969; Surgery and Your Heart (with Barbara Hyams), 1982; Cardiac Valve Allografts (co-editor), 1988; Principles of Cardiac Diagnosis and Treatment (with Terence English and Roxanne McKay), 1992. Honours include: University Gold Medal, University of Cape Town, 1946; National Heart Hospital Lecturer, 1971; St Cyres Lecturer, 1974; Order of Cedars of Lebanon, 1975; Order of Merit, Federal Republic of Germany, 1975; Guest Lecturer, Association of Thoracic Surgeons, USA, 1980; Honorary DSc, Council for National Academic Awards, Guildhall, London, 1982; Clement Price Thomas Award, Royal College of Surgeons, 1983; Guest Lecturer, Southern Thoracic Surgeons, USA, 1984; Denton Cooley Award, 1984; Thomas Burford Lecturer, St Louis, USA, 1986; Tudor Edwards Lecturer, Royal College of Surgeons, 1988; John Kirkland Lecturer, Mayo Clinic, 1992; Visiting Professor, Cleveland Clinic, 1992; Order of Thailand, 1994; Honorary Fellow, Royal Society of Medicine, 1995. Memberships include: Thoracic Surgical Societies of: India, Australasia, Thailand, Greece, Chile, Spain, Florida, Pennsylvania; Fellow, Royal Society of Medicine; Past President, Society of Thoracic Surgeons of Great Britain and Ireland; Honorary Fellow, Society of Thoracic Surgeons of America and the American Association of Thoracic Surgery. Address: 25 Upper Wimpole Street, London W1G 6NF, England. E-mail: donald.ross@ukonline.co.uk

**ROSS James Magnus,** b. 3 March 1972, United Kingdom. Orchestra Conductor. Education: MA, History, 1993, MST, Music, 1994, D Phil, Music, 1998, Christ Church, Oxford University. Appointments: Music Director: Christ Church Festival Orchestra, 1993-, Chorus and Orchestra, Royal College of Paediatricians, 1994-, Northampton University Orchestra, 2001-, Welwyn Garden City Music Society, 2000-, St Albans Symphony Orchestra, 2001-; Oxford Unib Sinfonietta, 2005-; Guest Conductor: Sarajevo Philharmonic Orchestra, Bosnia, 1998, 1999, Oxford University Philharmonia, UK, 1999, Camden Chamber Orchestra, UK, 1999, Oxford Opera Society, UK, 1999; Bologna University Chamber Choir, Italy, 2002, Harbin Symphony Orchestra, China, 2002; Nis Symphony Orchestra, Serbia, 2002, Symphony Orchestra of Sri Lanka, Sri Lanka, 2001, 2003, 2005. Publications: Book chapters: Music in the French Salon in French Music since Berlioz (eds. C Potter and R Langham Smith), 2005; Republican Patriotism in the Third Republic Opera in Nationalism and Identity in Third Republic France (ed. B Kelly), 2005; Vincent d'Indy l'interpreté in Vincent d'Indy et son temps, 2005; Articles and reviews in professional journals include: D'Indy's Fervaal: Reconstructing French Identity at the Fin de Siècle, 2003. Honours include: British Academy Studentship, 1993-97; Osgood Award, 1996; Sir Donald Tovey Memorial Prize, 1998. Memberships: Performers and Composers Section, Incorporated Society of Musicians, UK; Conductors Guild, USA. E-mail: conductor@saso.org.uk Website: www.james-ross.com

**ROSS Nicholas David (Nick),** b. 7 August 1947, London, England. Broadcaster. m. Sarah Patricia Ann Caplin, 3 sons. Education: BA (Hons), Psychology, Queen's University Belfast. Appointments: Broadcaster and Moderator; Freelance 1971-; Television: Northern Ireland's main news, 1971-72; Man Alive, BBC2, 1976-83; Out of Court, BBC2, 1981-84; Breakfast Time & Sixty Minutes, BBC1, 1983-85; Crimewatch UK, BBC1 1984-; A Week in Politics, Channel 4, 1985-87; Star Memories, BBC1, 1985; Crimewatch File, BBC1, 1986-; Watchdog, BBC1, 1985-86; Crime Limited, BBC1, 1992-95; Westminster with Nick Ross, BBC2, 1994-97; Party Conferences live coverage, BBC2, 1997; Election Campaign, BBC2, 1997; Trail of Guilt, BBC1, 1999; Nick Ross, BBC2, 1999; Destination Nightmares, BBC1, 1999-2000; Storm Alert, BBC1, 1999; The Syndicate, BBC1, 2000; The Search, BBC1, 1999-2000; British Bravery Awards, BBC1, 2000; So You Think You Know How to Drive, BBC1, 1999-2002; Radio: Call Nick Ross, 1986-97; The Commission, 1998-. Publications: Various newspaper and magazine articles. Honours: Radio Broadcaster of the Year, Broadcasting Press Guild Awards, 1996; Winner, Best TV Documentary, Celtic Film Festival, 1999; Winner, Best Factual Programme, TV Quick Awards, 2001; Honorary Doctorate, Queen's University, Belfast. Memberships: Fellow, Royal Society of Arts, Fellow Royal Society of Medicine; Ambassador World Wildlife Fund; Chairman, Jill Dando Institute of Crime Science, University College London; Nuffield Council of Bioethics; Royal College of Physicians Committee on Medical Ethics; Academy of Medical Sciences Study on the Use of Non-Human Primates; President, Healthwatch; Advisory Board, Victim Support; Director, UK Stem Cell Foundation; Patron: Saneline, National Missing Persons Helpline, Apex Trust, National Depression Campaign, Prisoners Abroad, Simon Community Northern Ireland; Reynaud & Scleroderma Association; Tacade; Myasthenia Gravis Association; Animal Care Trust; British Wireless for the Blind Fund. Address: PO Box 999, London W2 4XT, England. E-mail: nickross@lineone.net

**ROSS-MACDONALD M(alcolm) J(ohn), (Malcolm Macdonald, Malcolm Ross, M R O'Donnell),** b. 29 February 1932, Chipping, Sodbury, Gloucestershire, England. Freelance

Writer; Editor; Designer. m. Ingrid Giehr, 2 daughters. Education: Falmouth School of Art, 1950-54; Slade Diploma, University College, London, 1958. Appointments: Lektor, Folk University, Sweden, 1959-61; Executive Editor, Aldus Books, 1962-65; Visiting Lecturer, Hornsey College of Art, 1965-69. Publications: The Big Waves, 1962; Macdonald Illustrated Encyclopaedia (executive editor), 10 volumes, 1962-65; Spare Part Surgery (co-author), 1968; Machines in Medicine, 1969; The Human Heart, 1970; World Wildlife Guide, 1971; Beyond the Horizon, 1971; Every Living Thing, 1973; World from Rough Stones, 1974; Origin of Johnny, 1975; Life in the Future, 1976; The Rich Are With You Always, 1976; Sons of Fortune, 1978; Abigail, 1979; Goldeneye, 1981; The Dukes, 1982; Tessa'd'Arblay, 1983; In Love and War, 1984; Mistress of Pallas, 1986; Silver Highways, 1987; The Sky with Diamonds, 1988; A Notorious Woman, 1988; His Father's Son, 1989; An Innocent Woman, 1989; Hell Hath No Fury, 1990; A Woman Alone, 1990; The Captain's Wives, 1991; A Woman Scorned, 1991; A Woman Possessed, 1992; All Desires Known, 1993; To the End of Her Days, 1993; Dancing on Snowflakes, 1994; For I Have Sinned, 1994; Kernow and Daughter, 1994; Crissy's Family, 1995; Tomorrow's Tide, 1996; The Carringtons of Helston, 1997; Like a Diamond, 1998; Tamsin Harte, 2000; Rose of Nancemellin, 2001. Contributions to: Sunday Times; New Scientist; Science Journal; Month; Jefferson Encyclopaedia. Memberships: Authors Guild; Society of Authors. Address: c/o David Higham Ltd, 5-8 Lower John Street, London W1R 4HA, England.

**ROSSE 7 Earl of, Sir Brendan Parsons, 10th Bart,** also: Baron Ballybritt and Oxmantown. Lord of the Manors of Womersley and Woodhall in England and Parsonstown, Newtown and Roscomroe in Ireland, b. 21 October 1936 (Irish National). Director. m. Alison Cooke-Hurle, 2 sons, 1 daughter. Education: Grenoble University; MA, Christ Church, Oxford University. Appointments: United Nations Official, 1963-80; Successively, UNDP and UNESCO Representative, UN Volunteer Field Director, Iran; UN Disaster Relief Co-Ordinator, Bangladesh; Director, Historic Irish Houses and Gardens Association, 1980-91; Director, Agency for Personal Service Overseas, 1981-89; Appointed to Irish Government's Advisory Council in Development Co-Operation, 1983-88; Founding Director, Birr Scientific and Heritage Foundation, responsible for Ireland's Historic Science Centre. Honours: LLD, Honoris causa, Dublin; Honorary FIEI; Honorary Life Member, RDS. Memberships: RAS; RNS; Royal Society for Asian Affairs. Address: Birr Castle, Co. Offaly, Ireland.

**ROSSELLINI Isabella,** b. 18 June 1956, Rome, Italy (US citizen). Actress; Model. m. (1) M Scorsese, 1979, divorced 1982, (2) J Wiedemann, divorced, 1 daughter. Education: Rome Academy of Fashion and Costume; New York School for Social Research. Career: Costume Designer for Roberto Rossellini (father), New York, 1972; Journalist for Italian TV; Vogue Cover Girl, 1980; Contracted to Lancome Cosmetics, 1982-95; Vice President, Marketing Department, Lancaster Cosmetics GPs, 1995-; As Actress: Films include: A Matter of Time, 1976; Blue Velvet, 1986; Cousins, 1989; Wild at Heart, 1990; Death Becomes Her, 1994; Immortal Beloved, 1994; Wyatt Earp, 1994; The Innocent, 1995; The Funeral, 1996; Big Night, 1996; Crime of the Century, 1996; Left Luggage, 1998; The Imposters, 1998; The Real Blonde, 1998; Don Quixote, 2000; Il Cielo cade, 2000; Empire, 2002; Roger Dodger, 2002; The Tulse Luper Suitcases: The Moab Story, 2003; The Saddest Music in the World, 2003; The Tulse Luper Suitcases, Episode 3, Antwerp, 2003. Address: c/o United Talent Agency, 9560 Wilshire Boulevard, Floor 5, Beverly Hill, CA 90212, USA.

**ROSSWICK Robert Paul,** b. 1 June 1932. Consultant, General and Endocrine Surgery. Education: MB BS (Lond), The London Hospital Medical College, 1955; D Obst, RCOG, 1957; FRCS (Eng), 1961; MS (Surgery), Illinois, 1963; MAE, 1997. Appointments: House Surgeon, Poplar Hospital, London, England, 1955-1956; House Physician, Swindon Hospital, Wiltshire, 1956; Obstetric SHO, Greenwich Hospital, London, 1957; Lecturer in Anatomy, Kings College, London, 1957-59; Surgical SHO, 1959-1960, Locum SHO, 1963, The London Hospital; Surgical Registrar, St Andrew's, Bow, London, 1961-62; Surgical Registrar, Harold Wood Hospital, Essex, 1963-64; Surgical Registrar, 1964-66, Senior Registrar, 1966-70, St George's Hospital, London; Senior Registrar, Winchester and Royal Marsden Hospital, 1966-1970; Consultant-in-Charge, Accident and Emergency Department, 1970-74, Consultant Surgeon, 1970-93, Honorary Senior Lecturer in Surgery, St George's Hospital Medical School, 1970-93, St George's Hospital, London; Surgeon, The Royal Masonic Hospital, 1975-1993; Examiner in Surgery: The University of London; The Society of Apothecaries; PLAB. Publications: Numerous papers on abdominal surgery, thyroid surgery; Letters in medical journals; Addresses to medical societies; Presidential address, The Medical Society of London, a review of 1000 thyroidectomies, 1990. Honours: Robertson-Exchange Fellow in Surgery, Rush-Presbyterian-St Luke's Hospital, Chicago, USA, 1962-63; Past member of Council, Section of Surgery, Royal Society of Medicine; Chairman, Wandsworth Division, 1984-87, Delgate, ARM, etc, British Medical Association; Councillor, Hunterian Society, 1987-1995; Editor, 1984-1989, President, 1990-1991, Treasurer and Trustee, 1994-, The Medical Society of London. Memberships: Fellow: The Association of Surgeons; The British Association of Endocrine Surgeons; The CRC Multiple Endocrine Neoplasia Group; The British Society of Gastroenterology; The Collegium Internationale of Chirurgicae Digestiva; The Chelsea Clinical Society; Liveryman: The Worshipful Society of Apothecaries, Treasurer, Livery Committee, 1992-96; Member: Independent Doctors Forum; Medical Appeals Tribunals, Independent Tribunal Service; The Academy of Experts; UK Register of Expert Witnesses. Address: 5 Staffordshire House, 50 Broughton Avenue, London N3 3EG, England.

**ROTENBERG Vadim,** b. 5 August 1941, Kirov, USSR. Physician; Scientist. m. Samarovich Nataly, 2 daughters. Education: MD, 1st Moscow Medical Institute, 1964; Postgraduate Student, Academy of Sciences, USSR, 1966-69; PhD, 1970; DSc, 1979. Appointments: Junior Doctor, City Hospital, Moscow, 1964-66; Junior Scientist, 1st Moscow Medical Institute, 1969-78, Senior Scientist, 1978-88, Head of Laboratory, 1988-90; Emigration to Israel, 1990; Head Laboratory Abarbanel Mental Health Centre Bat-Iam, Israel, 1992-2001; Senior Lecturer, Tel Aviv University, 1995-; Head Psychologic Project Zionist Forum, 1996-2002. Publications: Over 150 scientific articles in professional journals; Books: The Adaptive Function of Sleep, 1982; Search Activity and Adaption, 1984; Self Image and Behaviour, 2001; Dreams, Hypnosis and Brain Activity, 2001. Honours: Best Annual Science Publication, Moscow Medical Institute, 1982, 1984; Wolfsson Grant for Outstanding Scientists, Tel-Aviv, 1992; Listed in Who's Who publications. Memberships: European Society Sleep Research; International Psychophysiological Society; New York Academy of Sciences. Address: Abarbanel Mental Health Centre, Keren Kayemet 15, Bat-Yam, Israel.

**ROTH Andrew,** b. 23 April 1919, New York, New York, USA. Political Correspondent. m. (1) Mathilda Anna Friederich, 1949, divorced 1984, 1 son, 1 daughter (2) Antoinette Putnam, 2004. Education: BSS, City College of New York, 1939; MA,

Columbia University, 1940; Harvard University; Honorary PhD, Open University, 1992. Appointments: Reader, City College, 1939; Research Associate, Institute of Pacific Relations, 1940; Editorial Writer, The Nation, 1945-46; Foreign Correspondent, Toronto Star Weekly, 1946-50; London Correspondent, France Observateur, Sekai, Singapore Standard, 1950-60; Director, Parliamentary Profiles, 1955-; Political Correspondent, Manchester Evening News, 1972-84; New Statesman, 1984-96. Publications: Japan Strikes South, 1941; French Interests and Policies in the Far East, 1942; Dilemma in Japan, 1945; The Business Background of MPs, 1959, 7th edition, 1980; The MPs Chart, 1967, 6th edition, 1987; Enoch Powell: Tory Tribune, 1970; Can Parliament Decide..., 1971; Heath and the Heathmen, 1972; Lord on the Board, 1972; Sir Harold Wilson: Yorkshire Walter Mitty, 1977; Parliamentary Profiles, Vols I-IV, 1984-85, 2nd edition, 1988-90; 4th edition, 1998; New MPs of '92, 1992; Mr Nice Guy and His Chums, 1993; New MPs of '97, 1997; New MPs of 2001, 2001. Address: 34 Somali Road, London NW2 3RL, England.

**ROTH Barbara**, b. 9 June 1916, Milwaukee, Wisconsin, USA. Organic Medicinal Chemistry. Education: BS, Chemistry, Beloit College, 1937; MS, Organic Chemistry, 1939, PhD, Organic Chemistry, 1941, Northwestern University. Appointments: Instructor, Chemistry, Lake Forest College, Illinois, 1940-41; Research Chemist, Calco Div, American Cyanamid Co, 1941-51; Research Supervisor, Toni Div, The Gillette Co, 1951-55; Senior Research Chemist, 1955-70, Group leader, Organic Chemistry, 1970-86, Burroughs Wellcome Co; Head, Dihydrofolate Reductase Program, 1980-86; Consultant, 1986-87; Adjunct Professor, University of North Carolina, School of Pharmacy, 1971-86, Chemistry Department, 1986-92. Publications: Articles in professional journals on heterocyclic chemistry, especially pyrimidines and condensed pyrimidines, 2,4-diamino derivatives as antimicrobial and anticancer agents, folic acid analogues, leucovorin rescue from toxicity, receptor-based drug design of dihydrofolate reductase enzyme inhibitors; Chapters in several books in field; 27 US Patents in field and non-equivalent foreign patents. Honours: Fellow, AAAS Chemistry; Distinguished Service Award, Beloit College, 1982; Chairman, Medicinal Chemistry Division, American Chemical Society, 1977, Secretary, 1975-76; Alumni Trustee, Beloit College, 1986-89. Memberships: American Chemical Society (Medicinal Chemistry Division); AAAS. Address: 347 Carolina Meadows Villa, Chapel Hill, NC 27517, USA.

**ROTH Gabriel**, Civil Engineer; Transport Economist. Appointments: Ministry of Transport's Panel on Road Pricing, 1961-63; Served in World Bank, 1967-86; President of the Services Group, 1987-89. Publications: Paying for Parking, 1996; Paying for Roads: The Economics of Traffic Congestion, 1967; The Private Provision of Public Services in Developing Countries, 1987; Roads in a Market Economy, 1996; Editor, Paving the Way for Private Roads, forthcoming. Address: 4815 Falstone Avenue, Chevy Chase, MD 20815, USA. Website: http://home.earthlink.net/~roths/

**ROTH Hans Walter**, b. 1944, Worms, Germany. Ophthalmologist. m. Katharina, 3 sons. Education: Medical Degree, 1970; Ophthalmic Surgeon, 1975; Visiting Professor, 1992. Appointments: Physician, Head Physician, University Eye Hospital, Ulm, Germany and German Army Hospital, 1970-82; Lecturer in Ophthalmology and Contactology, University of Ulm Medical School, Ulm; National Representative of ECLSO; Vice President, Chairman, President, International Contact Lens Council of Ophthalmology. Publications: Author and Co-Author, 590 papers; 28 books of physiology, contactology and optics. Honours: HKSCV Scientific Award,

1970; Fick-Kalt Muller Medal, ECLSO, 1990; Distinguished Visiting Lecturer, CLAO, 1990; Javal Pin, 1990; BVA Scientific Award, 1992; Ehrenkreuz des DFV, 1993; Javal Silver Award, 1994; BVA Honorary Award, 1996; Javal Gold Award, 1996; Bundesverdienstkreuz, 1996; Halberg Medal, 1997; Györffy Medal, 2004. Memberships: DOG; BVA; IAK; ICLCO; CLAO; ECLSO; AER; JAPCLSOC; Honorary Member: Hungarian Contact Lens Society; Austrian Contact Lens Society; European Contact Lens Society. Address: Im Wiblinger Hart 48, D-89079 Ulm, Germany.

**ROTH Tim**, b. 1961, Dulwich, England. Actor. Education: Brixton and Camberwell College of Art. m. Nikki Butler, 1993, 2 sons (1 son from previous relationship). Career: Fringe groups including: Glasgow Citizens Theatre, The Oval House and the Royal Court; Appeared on London stage in Metamorphis; Numerous TV appearances; Films: The Hit; A World Apart; The Cook, The Thief, His Wife and Her Lover; Vincent and Theo; Rosencrantz and Guildenstern are Dead; Jumpin at the Boneyard; Resevoir Dogs; Bodies Rest and Motion; Pulp Fiction; Little Odessa; Rob Roy; Captives; Four Rooms; Hoodlums; Everyone Says I Love You; Liar; The War Zone (director); The Legend of 1900, Vatel; Lucky Numbers; Planet of the Apes; Invincible; The Musketeer; Emmett's Mark; Whatever We Do; To Kill A King; With It. Address: Ilene Feldman Agency, 8730 West Sunset Boulevard, Suite 490, Los Angeles, CA 90069, USA.

**ROTHSCHILD Evelyn de (Sir)**, b. 29 August 1931. Banker. m. (1) Victoria Schott, 1972, dissolved 2000, 2 sons, 1 daughter, (2) Lynn Forester, 2000. Education: Trinity College, Cambridge. Appointments: Chairman, Economist Newspaper, 1972-89, United Racecourses Ltd, 1977-94, British Merchant Banking and Securities Houses Association (formerly Accepting Houses Committee), 1985-89; Chairman, N M Rothschild and Sons Ltd, 1976-. Address: N M Rothschild & Sons Ltd, New Court, St Swithin's Lane, London, EC 4, England.

**ROTTE Karl Heinz**, b. 18 October 1933, Pasewalk, Germany. Retired Radiologist. m. Ursula Kambach, 1 son. Education: Studies at Humboldt University, Berlin, Germany, 1953-58; MD, 1958; Resident, General Hospital Prenzlau, Germany, 1959-62. Appointments: Specialisation in Diagnostic Radiology, Robert-Rössle Cancer Research Institute, Berlin-Buch, 1962-77; Habilitation, 1974; Chairman, Department Diagnostic Radiology, Lung Research Institute Berlin-Buch, 1977-80; Chairman, Department of Computed Tomography and Department of Diagnostic Radiology, Cancer Research Institute, Berlin-Buch, 1980-96; Interim Chairman, Department of Diagnostic Radiology, Kuwait Cancer Control Centre, 1984-86; Professor of Diagnostic Radiology, Academy of Sciences, Berlin, 1987. Publications: 2 monographs: Computer aided diagnosis of peripheral bronchial cancer, 1977; Computed tomography in oncology, 1989; 200 publications in scientific journals and book contributions. Honours: Leibnitz Medal, Academy of Sciences, Berlin, 1974; W-Friedrich Award, Society of Radiology of Germany, 1976. Memberships: German Roentgen Society; Roentgen Society of Berlin. Address: Grabbe-Allee 14, D-13156 Berlin, Germany. E-mail: krotte5025@aol.com

**ROURKE Mickey Philip Andre**, b. 1956, New York, USA, Actor; Boxer. m. (1) Debra Fuer, (2) Carre Otis, divorced. Education: Actor's Studio, New York, USA. Career: Film appearances include: Fade to Black, 1941, 1979; Heaven's Gate, 1980; Body Heat, 1981; Diner, 1982; Eureka, 1983; Rumblefish, 1983; Rusty James, 1983; The Pope of Greenwich Village, 1984; 9½ Weeks, 1984; Year of the Dragon, 1985; Angel Heart, 1986; A Prayer for the Dying, 1986; Barfly, 1987; Johnny Handsome, 1989; Homeboy, 1989; Francesco, 1989; The Crew, 1989; The

Desperate Hours, 1990; Wild Orchid, 1990; On the Sport, 1990; Harley Davidson and the Marlboro Man, 1991; White Sands, 1992; FTW; Fall Time; Double Time; Another 9½ Weeks; The Rainmaker, 1997; Love in Paris, 1997; Double Team, 1997; Buffalo '66, 1997; Thursday, 1998; Shergar, 1999; Shades, 1999; Out in Fifty, 1999; The Animal Factory, 2000; Get Carter, 2000; The Pledge, 2001; The Hire: Follow, 2001; Picture Claire, 2001; They Crawl, 2001; Spun, 2002; Masked and Anonymous, 2003; Once Upon A Time in Mexico, 2003; Driv3r (voice), 2004; Man on Fire, 2004.

**ROUX Albert Henri,** b. 8 October 1935, Smur-en-Broinnais, France. Chef; Restaurateur. m. Monique Merle, 1959, 1 son, 1 daughter. Appointments: Military service, Algeria; Founder (with brother Michel Roux), Le Gavroche Restaurant, London (now co-owner with son Michel J), 1967-; The Waterside Inn, Bray (now sole owner), 1972-; Opened 47 Park Street Hotel, 1981; Opened Le Poulbot, le gamin, Gavvers, Les Trois Plats and Rouxl Britannia (all as part of Roux Restaurants Ltd), 1969-87; Began consultant practice, 1989. Publications: (with Michel Roux) New Classic Cuisine, 1983; The Roux Brothers on Pâtisserie, 1986; The Roux Brothers on French Country Cooking, 1989; Cooking for Two, 1991. Honours: Maître Cuisinier de France, 1968; Honorary Professor, Bournemouth University, 1995-; Chevalier du Mérite Agricole; Honorary DSc (Council for National Academic Awards), 1987. Memberships: Founder Member, Academy Culinaire de Grande Bretagne. Address: Le Gavroche, 43 Upper Brook Street, London, W1Y 1PF, England.

**ROUX Michel André,** b. 19 April 1941. Chef; Restaurateur. m. (1) Francoise Marcelle Becquet, divorced 1979, 1 son, 2 daughters. (2) Robyn Margaret Joyce, 1984. Appointments: Commis Patissier and Cuisinier, British Embassy, Paris, 1955-57; Commis Cook to Cécile de Rothschild, 1957-59, Chef, 1962-67; Military Service, 1960-62; Proprietor: Le Gavroche, 1967, The Waterside Inn, 1972, Le Gavroche, Mayfair, 1981. Publications: New Classic Cuisine, 1983; Roux Brothers on Patisserie, 1986; At Home With the Roux Brothers, 1987; French Country Cooking, 1989; Cooking for Two, 1991; Desserts, A Lifelong Passion, 1994; Sauces, 1996; Life is a Menu, autobiography, 2000; Only the Best, 2002; Eggs, 2005. Honours: Numerous Culinary Awards including: Gold Medal, Cuisiniers Français, Paris, 1972; Laureate Restaurateur of the Year, 1985; Chevalier, Ordre National du Mérite, 1987; Ordre des Arts et des Lettres, 1990; Honorary OBE, 2002; Chevalier de la légion d'Honneur, 2004; Numerous other awards and decorations. Memberships: Academician, Culinaire de France, English Branch; Association Relais et Desserts; Association Relais et Chateaux. Address: The Waterside Inn, Ferry Road, Berkshire SL6 2AT, England.

**ROWE John Richard,** b. 1 August 1942, Woodford, Essex. Film and Television Producer and Director. m. Rosa Mary Balls. Education: Royal Society of the Arts Education Certificate in English Literature. Appointments: Cutting Rooms and Film Library, 20th Century Fox, 1958-61; Film Researcher, Associated Redifusion, 1962-65; Film Researcher first major ITV documentary series, The Life and Times of Lord Mountbatten, 1965-69; Film Researcher, Thames television, 1965-69; Principal Film Researcher, The World at War, 1971-74; Head of Production Research, Thames Television, 1972-82; Head of Programming, Sky Television, 1982-84; Head of Production, British Sky Broadcasting, 1984-93; Executive Producer and set up television side of QVC, The Shopping Channel, 1993-95; Producer and Director TV commercials for various clients, 1995-96; Producer, Director for Screeners, 13 half hour shows on the cinema, 1997; Producer, Director,

children's series, Blue's Clues, 1997-2002; Producer, Director, children's comedy show, Havakazoo, 65 half hour shows, 2001; Director, Documentary on Anthony Quinn, Reflections in the Eye, 2001; Director, Monkey Makes, 2003; Director, Big Cook Little Cook, 2004; Currently, Chief Executive John Rowe Productions. Publications: In depth interview, Televisual, 1983; Contributor to: Satellite Wars, Channel 4, 1993. Honour: Part of the Emmy Award winning team for The World at War. Address: 24 Long Hill, Mere, Warminster, Wiltshire, BA12 6LR, England.

**ROWLANDSON Maurice Leonard,** b. 15 August 1925, London, England. Administrator. m. Marilyn Yvonne, 2 sons, 1 deceased, 2 daughters, 1 deceased. Education: College of Estate Management, 1943-46; Northwestern College, Minneapolis, Minnesota, USA, 1947-49. Appointments include: Articled to the Borough Engineer and Surveyor of Wembley, 1943-45; Managing Director, 1945-46, Chairman, 1946-74, Messrs Chas. Davy & Co Ltd; Estate Manager, Hildenborough Hall, 1946-50; Boys' Administrative Chief, The Campaigners Youth Organisation, 1950-52; Extension Secretary, 1952-61, The Evangelical Alliance, Personal Assistant to the Director, 1960-61; Lieutenant Commander, Royal Naval Reserve, 1956-75; Chairman, Trans World Radio (Monte Carlo), 1963-93; Chairman of HRE Ltd and 5 associated companies, 1958-85; Director, Billy Graham Evangelistic Association UK, 1960-87; Organiser of Earls Court Crusades, 1961-67; Livelink Secretary for 250 satellite relays, 1988-89; National Co-ordinator for Global Mission, 1992-94; Appointed as Consultant to the Billy Graham Evangelistic Association UK, 1996; Justice of the Peace, 1971-95 (Chairman, Tendring Bench, 1993-95); Crown Court Magistrate, 1995-98; Extension Consultant to United Christian Broadcasters, 1997-2001. Publications: Unexpected Adventure, 1953; Let's Have A Film, 1961; Life With Billy, 1992; Life with the Venturers, 1995; I'm Going to Ask You...., 1997; Life at the Keswick Convention, 1997. Honours: Member, Royal Institute of Chartered Surveyors; Royal Naval Reserve, Reserve decoration. Memberships: Founder of the Venturer Norfolk Broads Cruise, 1946 (still running); Associate of the Inner Magic Circle; Member of the Council of Reference of the Evangelisation Society; Chairman, Walk Thru the Bible UK, 1987-2001. Address: PO Box 292, Swindon, Wilts SN5 5XQ, England. E-mail: mauricerow@aol.com

**ROWLEY Rosemarie (Rose Mary, Rosemary) Teresa,** b. 7 October 1942, Dublin, Ireland. 1 son. Writer; Poet; Essayist. Education: BA, 1969, MLitt, 1984, Trinity College, Dublin, Ireland; Dip Psych, National University of Ireland, 1996. Career: Civil secretarial work, Green Activist, 1983-87; Poet and Essayist. Publications: The Broken Pledge, 1985; The Sea of Affliction, 1987; Betrayal into Origin, 1987, revised 1996; The Wake of Winter, 1987, revised 1996; Freedom & Censorship – why not have both?, 1987, reprinted 1996; Flight into Reality, 1989, issued on cassette tape 1996; The Puzzle Factory, 2001; Hot Cinquefoil Star, 2002; Fasting Festival, 2004; In Memory of Her, forthcoming; Co-editor, Seeing the Wood and the Trees, 2003. Honours: Image/Maxwell House Award, 1988; Scottish International Open Poetry Competition, Long Poem Award, 1996, 1997, 2001, 2004. Memberships: MENSA, UK and Ireland; Irish Byron Society and Shaw Society at United Arts Club; Trinity College Dublin Alumni; Long Poem Group, UK. Address: Booterstown, Co Dublin, Ireland. E-mail: rosemariero wley@yahoo.co.uk

**ROWLING J(oanne) K(athleen),** b. 1965, Bristol, England. Writer. (1) divorced, 1 daughter, (2) Neil Murray, 2001, 1 son, 1 daughter. Education: Graduated, University of Exeter, 1986. Publications: Harry Potter and the Philosopher's Stone, 1997;

Harry Potter and the Chamber of Secrets, 1998; Harry Potter and the Prisoner of Azkaban, 1999; Harry Potter and the Goblet of Fire, 2000; Quidditch Through the Ages, 2001; Fantastic Beasts and Where to Find Them, 2001; Harry Potter and the Order of the Phoenix, 2003; Harry Potter and the Half-Blood Prince, 2005. Honours: British Book Award Children's Book of the Year, 1997; Rowntree Nestle Smarties Prizes, 1997, 1998; Officer of the Order of the British Empire, 2000. Address: c/o Christopher Little Literary Agency, Ten Eel Brook Studios, 125 Moore Park Road, London SW6 4PS, England. Website: www.jkrowling.com

**ROWSELL Joyce (Joyce Gwyther)**, b. 20 November 1928, Mardy, Glamorgan, South Wales. Artist. m. Geoffrey Norman Rowsell, 2 sons. Education: BA, University of London, History of Art, 1988. Career: Draughtswoman, British Telecom, 1947-60; Freelance Illustrator; Self Employed artist exhibiting in UK and abroad; Miniaturist, USA and UK; Permanent Collections: Miniature Artists of America; The Dutch Foundation of Miniature Art; The Hilliard Collection. Publications: Somerset Magazine, 2001; The Artist (UK), 2001; West Country Life, 2001; Countryman, 2005. Honours: 47 awards for miniature painting; Title, Miniature Artist of America. Memberships: Founder Member, Hilliard Society; Miniature Art Society, Florida; Miniature Painters, Sculptors and Gravers Society of Washington DC; Associate of Royal Society of Miniature Painters, Sculptors and Gravers; Cider Painters of America; Roswell Fine Art Society, NM. Address: Spring Grove Farm, Milverton, Somerset, TA4 1NW, England. E-mail: joyce@rowsell.net Website: www.spring-grove-gallery.com

**ROXMAN (Pia) Susanna (Ellinor)**, b. 29 August 1946, Stockholm, Sweden. Writer; Poet; Literary Scholar. Education: King's College, London University; BA, hons, Comparative Literature, Philosophy, Lund University, Sweden, 1973; PhD, hons, Comparative Literature, Gothenburg University, Sweden, 1984. Appointments: Visiting Lecturer, Lund University and elsewhere, 1976-; Critic on Swedish National Newspapers, 1977-; Head, Centre of Classical Mythology, Lund University, 1996-; Lecturer, Classical Mythology, Department of Classics, Lund University, 2003-04. Publications: Written in English: Guilt and Glory: Studies in Margaret Drabble's Novels 1963-80, 1984; Goodbye to the Berlin Wall, 1991; Broken Angels, 1996; Emblems of Classical Deities in Ancient and Modern Pictorial Arts, 2003; Several books written in Swedish; Numerous English poems in Cimarron Review, USA, Crab Orchard Review, USA, The Fiddlehead, Canada, Orbis, UK, Pembroke Magazine, USA, Prairie Schooner, USA, The Spoon River Poetry Review, USA, Staple, UK, Wascana Review, Canada, and many other magazines world-wide; Also more than a couple of thousand arts articles world-wide and scholarly contributions to academic journals, anthologies and encyclopaedias. Honours: Arts Award, County Council of Malmo, Sweden, 1984; Swedish Balzac Prize, 1990; Editor's Choice Prize, Marjorie Lees Linn Poetry Award, USA, 1994, 1995; Arts Award, City of Lund, for Broken Angels, 1996; Whitbread nomination, UK, for Broken Angels, 1997; Second Prize, for short story, Vigil in Berlin, New Fiction Award Contest, New York, 2001; Susanna Roxman is one of the internationally best known Scandinavian poets. Memberships: Authors' Centre South, Sweden; Conservatory of American Letters. Address: Lagerbrings Vag 5B, SE-224 60 Lund, Sweden. E-mail: susanna.roxman@telia.com

**ROY Arundhati**, b. 1961, Bengal, India. Writer. m. (1) Gerard da Cunha, divorced, (2) Pradeep Krishen. Education: Delhi School of Architecture. Appointments: Artist; Actress; Film and Television Writer. Publication: The God of Small Things, 1997; The End of Imagination, essay, 1998; The Great Common

Good, essay, 1999; The Cost of Living, collected essays, 2002; The Algebra of Infinite Justice, collected essays, 2002; Screenplays: In Which Annie Gives It Those Ones; Electric Moon. Contributions to: Periodicals. Honour: Booker Prize, 1997. Address: c/o India Ink Publishing Co Pvt Ltd, C-1, Soami Nagar, New Delhi 110 017, India.

**ROY Michael Presley-Roy**, b. 20 April 1928, London, England. Artist (Drawing and Painting). Education: Oxford School Certificate, 1944; Newland Park College, Bucks, 1967-70; Teacher's Certificate, Art Advanced Level, Distinction, Reading University; Hornsey College of Art, Postgraduate Department, Diploma in Art Education, London University, 1973-76. Appointments: From 1950, various teaching and commercial positions including: Head of Art Department, Orchard School, Slough; Art Lecturer, Langley College, Berkshire; Semi-retirement, 1984-; The State Apartments, Windsor Castle, 1985-88; A professional artist in multi-media (landscapes, religious themes, figurations, flower-pieces and abstract/fantasy idiomatic motifs); Originator of "Art Lark" monoprint series from original works by Michael Roy, selected "Art Lark" images available from Leeds Metropolitan University, www.axisartists.org.uk ref 5238; Group exhibitions of Wessex Biennial and exhibitions curated by/at Southampton Civic AG (viz: Aquarium, Le Coq dans la Boîte, The Artist's Chair, Art From Words – Self Portrait, 2001). Publications: Author: The Rôle of the Art Teacher, 1976; The Art Lark, 1992; Featured in: British Contemporary Art, 1993; International Panorama of Contemporary Art, 1998; Ahoy Clausentum, 1994; Who's Who in Art, 2005; Sotheby's charity auction catalogues. Commissions and Creative Works: In various private and public collections in UK and abroad including: Flight of the Holy Family, Allington Castle, Kent, 1958; Mary Magdalene, Crowmarsh Church, Oxon, 1959; Carisbrooke Halt, Trustees, Carisbrooke Castle Museum, Isle of Wight, 1957; Calvary, Windsor Parish Church, Berks, 1967; Flamingo Dancers, Red Swans, Reading AG, Berks, 1980; Quarr Abbey from the South, Quarr Abbey, Isle of Wight 1970; Crucifixion, Madonna with Child Jesus, paintings in Holy Trinity Church, Gosport, Hants (www.holytrinitygosport.co.uk); Sailing into the Millennium, presented by Gosport Borough Council, Hants, 2005. Honours: Los Peroquitos (Diploma Award, international section, visual poetry Biennial) Mexico City, 1996; Bronze Medal, Best Poetry of 1996, International Society of Poetry, Maryland, USA, 1996. Address: "La Palette", 31 Bedford Street, Gosport, Hants, PO12 3JL, England.

**ROY Raymond R Jr**, b. 29 December 1965, New Bedford, Massachusetts, USA. Organic Chemist. Education: BS cum laude, Chemistry, Cameron University, 1998; MS, Organic Chemistry, 2001, PhD, Organic Chemistry, 2002, University of Oklahoma. Appointments: Served in US Navy; Cameron University, 1994-98; Graduate Student, Research Assistant, Teaching Assistant, Laboratory Instructor, Organic Chemistry Lecturer, University of Oklahoma, 1998-2002; Senior Research Chemist, Tyco Healthcare, 2002-2004; Chemist, Shelf Life Team Leader, Food and Drug Administration, 2004-. Publications: Articles in scientific journals include: Conversion of N-Aromatic Amines and Amindes to O-Aromatic Esters, Phenols, Biphenyls, Aromatic Halides and Energetic Materials via Nirtosomide Intermediate, US copyright TX5-752-122. Honours: National Dean's List, 1994-95, 1995-96, 1996-97, 1997-98; Inducted into Phi Lambda Upsilon, 2001; Listed in Who's Who publications and biographical dictionaries. Memberships: Veterans of Foreign Wars; Disabled American Veterans; Phi Eta Sigma; Phi Lambda Upsilon; American Chemical Society; University of Oklahoma Alumni Society.

Address: Food and Drug Administration, Detroit District, 300 River Place, Suite 5900, Detroit, MI 48207, USA.

**ROY Salil Kumar,** b. 1 March 1939, Vatia, India. University Professor. m. Snigdha, 1 daughter. Education: BSc (Hons), 1958, MSc (Tech), 1961, Calcutta University, India; ScD, Massachusetts Institute of Technology, USA, 1966. Appointments: Research Scientist, American Standard, Piscataway, New Jersey, USA, 1966-72; Lecturer (Scale A), 1972-74, Senior Lecturer, 1975-94, Associate Professor, 1995-99, National University of Singapore; Sole Proprietor, Roy Materials Consultancy, 1999-2001; Professor, Petra Christian University, Surabaya, Indonesia, 2001-. Publications: Over 280 papers, articles and patents. Honours: John Marquis Memorial Award for publishing the most useful paper for industry, American Ceramics Society, 1978. Memberships: Fellow, Institute of Diagnostic Engineers, UK; American Ceramic Society. Address: Petra Christian University, Postgraduate Program in Civil Engineering, JL Siwalankerto 121-131, Surabaya 60236, Indonesia, E-mail: matscitechroy@yahoo.com

**ROZGONYI Ferenc,** b. 21 September 1938, Tarcal, Hungary. MD; Specialist for Medical Microbiology. m (1) Gertrúd Maria Szécsi (deceased), (2) Katalin Szitha. Education: Student, Medical University of Debrecen, 1957-63; Medical Doctor, summa cum laude, 1963; Specialist for Laboratory Medicine, diploma, 1967; Specialist for Medical Microbiology, diploma, 1979. Appointments: PhD, 1978; Dr Med Sciences, 1988; Dr Med/Habil, Debrecen, 1995; University Professor in Debrecen, 1995; Director, Chairman, Institute of Medical Microbiology, Semmelweis University, Budapest, 1996-2003 (retired from this position); University Professor, 2003-. Publications: Over 140 articles and other publications on antibiotic resistance and pathogenicity of bacteria; About 350 lectures and posters presented in national and international conferences; Author: (manual) Rapid Microbiology Diagnostic Methods for General Practitioner. Honours: Doubly awarded by Hungarian Academy of Sciences, 1972, 1985; Honoured twice for excellent teaching, Ministry of Public Health, 1980, Ministry of Welfare, 1991; L Batthyány – Strattmann Award, Minister of Public Health, Welfare and Family Affairs of Hungary, 2003, in recognition of his outstanding professional activity and achievement of several decades; Recipient, Doctoral School Medal, Semmelweis University, 2000; Honourable Certification, Hungarian Association for Innovation, 2003; Gold Seal-Ring, Ignác Semmelweis plaquette, Semmelweis University, 2003; Rezso Manninger plaquette, Hungarian Society for Microbiology, 2003. Memberships: Chairman, Curators Board for the Foundation of Struggle for Health, Hungary, 1990-; Executive Board: Hungarian Society of Chemotherapy, 1991-, Hungaria Helvetia Association, Debrecen, 1991-; Editorial Boards: Acta Microbiologica et Immunologica Hungarica, 1996-; Hungarian Venerology Archive, 1998-; Board of Advisors, Focus Medicinae, 1999-; Member, Hungarian Medical Chamber, 1992-; European Society for Clinical Microbiology and Infectious Diseases, 1992-, Hungarian Representative at its European Council, 2001-; World-wide Hungarian Medical Academy, 1999-. Address: Institute of Medical Microbiology, Faculty of Medicine, Semmelweis University, Nagyvárad tér 4, Budapest, H-1089, Hungary.

**ROZSÍVAL Pavel,** b. 27 September 1950, Cheb, Czech Republic. Ophthalmologist; Surgeon; Educator. m. Iva Fišerová, 1 son, 1 daughter. Education: MD, Charles University, Prague, 1974; Diploma in Nuclear Chemistry, Czech Technical University, 1977; PhD, 1979; Board Certified, 1981; Associate Professor, 1991; Professor, 1996. Appointments: Scientific Worker, Charles University, Hradec Králové, 1979-84; Head,

District Department, Ophthalmology, Teplice, 1984-86; Head of Regional Department, Ophthalmology, Ústí nad Labem, 1986-93; Head of Department, Ophthalmology, Charles University, 1993-; Consultant, National Medical Library, Prague, 1978-92. Publications: Over 200 articles in professional journals; Over 500 lectures; Ophthalmology for Family Physicians; Modern Cataract Surgery; Diabetic Macro and Microangiopathy; Eye Infections. Honour: Medal, 650th Anniversary of Charles University. Memberships: Czech Ophthalmological Society, President, 1997-; Scientific Advisory Board, Czech Ministry of Health, 1998-; Czech Glaucoma Society; Czech Society for Cataract and Refractive Surgery; American Academy of Ophthalmology; American Society of Cataract and Refractive Surgery; International Society for Cataract Surgery (Binkhorst Society); Deutschesprachigen Gesellschaft für Intraokularlins enimplantationen; New York Academy of Sciences. Address: Department of Ophthalmology, Charles University, 500 05 Hradec Králové, Czech Republic.

**RUBENS Bernice Ruth,** b. 26 July 1923, Cardiff, Wales. Author. m. Rudi Nassauei, 1947, 2 daughters. Education: BA, University of Wales, 1944. Appointments: Author, Director, documentary films on Third World subjects. Publications: Novels: Set on Edge, 1960; Madame Sontsatzka, 1962; Mate in Three, 1964; The Elected Member, 1968; Sunday Best, 1970; Go Tell the Lemming, 1972; I Sent a Letter to My Love, 1974; Ponsonby Post, 1976; A Five-year Sentence, 1978; Spring Sonata, 1979; Birds of Passage, 1980; Brothers, 1982; Mr Wakefield's Crusade, 1985; Our Father, 1987; Kingdom Come: A Solitary Grief, 1991; Mother Russia, 1992; Autobiopsy, 1993; Yesterday in the Back Lane, 1995; The Waiting Game, 1997; I, Dreyfus, 1999; Milwaukee, 2001; Nine Lives, 2002; The Sergeant's Tale, 2003. Honours: Booker Prize, 1970; American Blue Ribbon, for Documentary film, 1972; Honorary DLitt, University of Wales. Membership: Fellow, University College, Cardiff. Address: 213A Goldhurst Terrace, London NW6 2ER, England.

**RUBINSTEIN Julius B,** b. 10 October 1940, Kiev, USSR. Metallurgical Engineer. m. Eugenia Ilyinichna Feldman, 1 daughter. Education: BS, MS, Metallurgical Engineering, Institute of Steels and Alloys, Moscow, 1957-62; PhD, Mineral Processing Research and Design, Mining Institute, Moscow, 1967; Doctor of Science, 1982; Professor of Science, 1985; Academician of the Russian Academy of Mining Science, 1995. Appointments: Scientist, 1862-68, Chief Scientist, 1968-70, Research and Design Mining Institute, Moscow; Chief Scientist, 1970-83, Head of Department, Flotation Equipment and Technological Processes Optimisation, 1983-99, Head of Department of Mineral Processing Processes and Apparatus, 1999-, Research and Design Institute of Solid Fossil Fuels Preparation, Moscow; Consulting assignments with Israeli, German and American companies, 1992-; Visiting Professor, Wuxan University, Wuxan, China, 1992; Principal Collaborating Scientist of the Research Project and Visiting Scholar, Nottingham University, England, 1994-98. Publications: 9 books; 10 brochures; 59 patents; More than 140 articles in scholarly journals; 20 papers at international conferences and congresses. Honours: 2 Awards, Russian Complex of National Achievements, 1977, 1984; Award, Russian Society of Authors and Inventors, 1989; Award, Russian Ministry of Energy for Outstanding Achievements in the Field, 2002. Memberships: President, Science Committee, Institute of Solid Fossil Fuels Preparation , Moscow; Member, Science Committee, Russian Academy of Sciences, Moscow; Russian Academy of Mining Science, Moscow, Russia. Address: Sireneviy Bulvar 36 Apt 20 Moscow, Russia 105077. E-mail: julius40@mail.ru

**RUBINSTEIN Shimon,** b. 21 January 1941, Berlad, Romania. Historian. m. Gretty Rotman-Rubinstein, deceased, 1 son. Education: BA General Modern History and Political Sciences, 1965, Secondary School Teacher's Certificate, 1966, Certified Historical Archivist, 1968, Hebrew University of Jerusalem. Appointments: High School Teacher of History, Dimona, Israel, 1966-68; Director, Historical Archives of Yad Ben-Zvi Institute, Jerusalem, 1970-2001. Publications include: At a Close Perspective: Reflections on the Centenary of David Ben-Gurion, 1986; German Atrocity or British Propaganda: The Seventieth Anniversary of a Scandal – German Corpse Utilisation Establishments in WW1, 1987; The Negev – The Great Zionist Blunder 1919-1929, 4 volumes, 1988; Crisis and Change, Petah-Tikva in the Transition Period from Turkish to British Rule, 5 volumes, 1988-90; German-Turkish Endeavours in the Field of Engineering, Water Exploration and Agriculture in the Sinai and the Negev during WW1 and the Part Played Therein by the (Jewish) Yishuv, 1989; At the Height of Expectations: The Land Policy of the Zionist Commission in 1918, 1993; From Berlad to the Maabarah of Rosh Pina: The First Years of an Immigrant Family in the Galilee 1950-1956, 1993; Coinage, Measures and Weights in Eretz-Israel from the Beginning of the 19th Century to the Period of Transition from Ottoman to British Rule, 1997; A Personal Exchange of Letters with a Hebrew Patriot [Abraam Thomi], in the Diaspora 1985-1991, 2 volumes, 1999; Personal Tragedies as a Reflection to a Great Tragedy Called Struma, 2003; Annotated Bibliography on the Transition Period from Turkish to British Rule in Eretz-Israel, 3 volumes, 2004. Honours: Shulamit and Professor Kalugai Award, Institute for Eretz-Israel Research of Yad Ben-Zvi, 1980. Memberships: Israel Association of Graduates in the Social Sciences; World Union of Jewish Studies. Address: Haavtaha St 14, P O Box 7360, Jerusalem 91072, Israel.

**RUBINSZTEIN David Chaim,** b. 14 March 1963, Cape Town, South Africa. Medical Scientist. m. Judy, 1 son, 2 daughters. Education: MB ChB, 1981-86; BSc (Med) Hons, 1988; PhD, 1993; DipRCPath, 1996; MRCPath, 1997; FRCPath, 2005. Appointments: Senior Registrar, Genetic Pathology, Addenbrooke's Hospital, Cambridge, 1993-98; Glaxo Wellcome Research Fellow, Honorary Consultant in Medical Genetics, 1998-2002, Wellcome Trust Senior Research Fellow, Honorary Consultant in Medical Genetics, 2002-, Reader in Molecular Neurogenetics, 2003-2005, Professor in Molecular Neurogenetics, 2005-, University of Cambridge. Publications: More than 140 research papers in international journals including: Nature Genetics; Nature Medicine; Proceedings of the National Academy of Science, USA; American Journal of Human Genetics; Human Molecular Genetics. Honours: GA Reynolds Scholarship, 1981-86; MRC Post-Intern Award, Guy Elliott Fellowship, 1988; MRC Post-graduate Bursary, Marion Beatrice Waddell Award, University of Cape Town Research Associateship, Stella and Paul Loewenstein Research Scholarship, 1989-93; Glaxo Wellcome Research Fellowship, 1998; Wellcome Trust Senior Clinical Fellowship, 2002; Fellow of the Academy of Medical Sciences, 2004. Memberships: Clinical Genetics Society; British Society for Human Genetics; World Federation of Neurology Research Group on Huntington's Disease. Address: Cambridge Institute for Medical Research, Addenbrooke's Hospital, Hills Road, Cambridge CB2 2XY, England. E-mail: dcr1000@hermes.cam.ac.uk

**RUCKMAN Robert Julian Stanley,** b. 11 May 1939, Uxbridge, Middlesex, England. Chartered Engineer; Civil Servant. m. Josephine Margaret Trentham, 1 son, 1 daughter. Education: ONC, Electrical Engineering, 1957-60, HNC, Electrical and Electronic Engineering, 1960-62; IERE Endorsements, 1963, Harrow Technical College; MSc Transport Studies, Cranfield

Institute of Technology, 1974-75. Appointments: Computer Testing and Commissioning, Elliott Bros Ltd, Borehamwood, Hertfordshire, 1961-64; Logic and Systems Designer, Serck Controls, Leamington Spa, Warwickshire, 1964-66; Technical Staff, System Sciences Corporation, Falls Church, USA, 1966-67; Transitron Electronic Corporation, Boston, USA, 1967-68; J Langham Thompson Ltd, Luton, Bedfordshire, 1968-70; Ministry of Transport, 1970-74; Birmingham Regional Office, Department of Transport, 1975-78; Cost Benefit Analyst, Computer Analyst, Department of Transport Road construction Unit, 1978-87; Computer Manager (Senior Professional Technical Officer), Department of Transport, West Midlands Region, Birmingham, 1987-95; Assessor, British Computer Society Professional Review Panel. Publications: Articles in scientific journals include: A Data Logger Scaler and Alarm Limit Comparator, 1967; Alarm Detection Using Delay Line Storage, 1966; Integral Alarms for Data Loggers, 1967; The Effects of Trip Characteristics on Interurban Model Choice, 1975; Guide for WMRO Geographical Information System, 1991. Honour: Department of Transport Award in recognition of work for development of Accident Analysis Geographical Information System, 1991. Memberships: Member of the Institution of Electrical Engineers; Member of The British Computer Society; Fellow, Institution of Analysts and Programmers; Member, Institute of Logistics and Transport; Chartered Engineer (C.Eng); European Engineer (Eur-Ing); Cranfield Society. Address: 'Flamingo', 13 Alexander Avenue, Droitwich Spa, Worcestershire WR9 8NH, England. E-mail: robert_ruckman@tinyworld.co.uk

**RUDKIN James David,** b. 29 June 1936, London, England. Dramatist. m. Alexandra Margaret Thompson, 3 May 1967, 2 sons, 1 deceased, 2 daughters. Education: MA, St Catherine's College, Oxford, 1957-61. Appointment: Judith E Wilson Fellow, University of Cambridge, 1984; Visiting Professor, University of Middlesex, 2004-. Publications: Afore Night Come (stage play), 1964; Schoenberg's Moses und Aron (translation for Royal Opera), 1965; Ashes (stage play), 1974; Cries From Casement as His Bones are Brought to Dublin (radio play), 1974; Penda's Fen (TV film), 1975; Hippolytus (translation from Euripides), 1980; The Sons of Light (stage play), 1981; The Triumph of Death (stage play), 1981; Peer Gynt (translation from Ibsen), 1983; The Saxon Shore (stage play), 1986; Rosmersholm (translation from Ibsen), 1990; When We Dead Waken (translation from Ibsen), 1990. Opera Libretti: The Grace of Todd, music by Gordon Crosse, 1969; Inquest of Love, music by Jonathan Harvey, 1993; Broken Strings, music by Param Vir, 1994. Contributions to: Drama; Tempo; Encounter; Theatre Research Journal. Honours: Evening Standard Most Promising Dramatist Award, 1962; John Whiting Drama Award, 1974; Obie Award, New York, 1977; New York Film Festival Gold Medal for Screenplay, 1987; European Film Festival Special Award, 1989; Sony Silver Radio Drama Award, 1994. Memberships: Hellenic Society. Address: c/o Casarotto Ramsay Ltd, National House, 60-66 Wardour Street, London W1V 4ND England.

**RUDOLF (Ian) Anthony,** b. 6 September 1942, London, England. Literary Critic; Poet; Translator; Publisher. Divorced, 1 son, 1 daughter. Education: BA (Modern Languages Tripos, Part One; Social Anthropology Part Two) Trinity College, Cambridge, 1964; Diploma, British Institute, Paris, 1961. Appointments: Co-Founder and Editor, Menard Press, London, 1969; Adam Lecturer, Kings' College, London, 1990; Pierre Rouve Memorial Lecturer, University of Sofia, 2001; Visiting Lecturer, Arts and Humanities, London Metropolitan University, 2001-2003; Royal Literary Fund Fellow, University of Hertfordshire, 2003-2004, 2004-2005; Royal Literary Fund

Fellow, University of Westminster, 2005-2006. Publications: The Same River Twice, 1976; After the Dream: Poems 1964-79, 1980; Primo Levi's War Against Oblivion (literary criticism), 1990; Mandorla (poetry), 1999; The Arithmetic of Memory (autobiography), 1999; Translations include: Yesterday's Wilderness Kingdom (poetry) by Yves Bonnefoy, 2001; Blood from the Sky (novel) by Piotr Rawicz, 2004; Contributions to periodicals. Honours: Chevalier de l'Ordre des Arts et des Lettres, 2004; Fellow, Royal Society of Literature, 2005. Address: 8 The Oaks, Woodside Avenue, London N12 8AR, England. E-mail: anthony.rudolf@virgin.net

**RUDY Dorothy L**, b. 27 June 1924, Ohio, USA. Professor of English and Creative Writing; Poet. m. Willis Rudy, 31 January 1948, 1 son, 2 daughters. Education: BA, Queens College, 1945; MA, Philosophy, Columbia University, 1948. Appointments: Professor of English and Creative Writing, Montclair State University, 1964-88; Lecturer, Fairleigh Dickinson University, 1988-90, 1996-2002, Bergen Community College, 1991-96, YMHA Wayne, Humanities Scholar of the Arts, 1993-. Publications: Quality of Small and Other Poems, 1971; Psyche Afoot and Other Poems, 1978; Grace Notes to the Measure of the Heart, 1979; Voices Through Time and Distant Places, 1993. Contributions to: Passaic Herald News; Letters; Poem; Laurel Review; Just Pulp; Composers; Authors and Artists Quarterly; Scimiter and Song; Bitterroot; Cellar Door; Pet Gazette; Black Buzzard Press. Honour: American Poets Fellowship, 1971; New Jersey Literary Society Hall of Fame, 1994; Certificate of Achievement in the Arts, Literature, Contemporary Women's Club of Bergenfield, 1997. Memberships: Composers, Authors and Artists of America; PEN Women; Bergen Poets; New York Poetry Forum; Browning Society; New England Small Press Association, Women's Board; Scambi International. Address: 161 West Clinton Avenue, Tenafly, NJ 07670, USA.

**RUDY Mikhail**, b. 3 April 1953, Tashkent, USSR. Pianist. 1 son, 1 daughter. Education: Moscow Tchaikovsky Conservatory under Professor Jacob Flier, 1969-76. Career: World-wide international pianist; Conductors include: Karajan, Maazel, Tilson Thomas, Temirbauer, Tieleman, Jurowsko, Senderling, Jarvi; Regular guest with major orchestras and festivals; Founder, Artistic Director, St Riquier Festival. Works: Complete transcription of the Ballet "Pertrushka". Honours: First Prize, Moscow Tchiakovsky Conservatory; Prize Winner, Bach Competition, Leipzig, 1972; First Grand Prix, Marguerite Long, Paris with Felicitations by Arthur Rubenstein, 1975; Chevalier Arts et Lettres, 1994; Grand Prix du Disque, Academie Charles Gros for Scriabine integrale; Grand Prix du Disc Liszt in Budapest; Deutsche Schallplatten Kritik Preis for Schostakovich Concerto; Grand Prix, Academie Française du Disque for Tchaikovsky/Rachmaninov Concerti with Jansens. Address: 3 Villa Flore, 75016 Paris, France. E-mail: mabousq@club-internet.fr

**RUKIEH Mohamad**, b. 1 June 1951, Tartous, Syria. Geologist; Director General. m. Amal Ibrahim, 2 sons, 3 daughters. Education: Bachelor, Geological Sciences, Damascus University, 1973; Diploma, Mining Geological Engineering, 1977; PhD, Geology and Mineralogy, Moscow Geological Prospecting Institute. Appointments: Director of Prospecting, General Establishment of Geology and Mineral Resources, Ministry of Petroleum, 1980-86; General Supervisor of Marble Quarries, Marble Company; Director of Field Studies, 1986-, Director General, 2002-, General Organisation of Remote Sensing; Exploration of sites of hyrothermal iron accompanied with Sulphid of minerals (copper, lead and zinc) in Sirghaya area, Syria, Oolitic iron in Addmeir area, Syria; Important sites to the deep xenoliths in the volcanic rocks in Aldqadmous area, Syria;

Most recent areas of research include: Using remote sensing techniques for natural disasters monitoring and mitigation; New data about the tectonic structure of the Arabian Plate; The tectonics and topography of the Arabian Rift and its impact on water; The annular structures in Lebanon and the Western Part of Syria; Physiographic analysis and littology mapping from space images (case study from Syria). Publications: More than 40 researches, articles, and papers in professional technical journals include most recently: Tectonics of Lebanon and Western Part of Syria Using Space Imagery Interpretation, 1997; Annular Structures in the Space Images: Kinds, Distribution, Study Method and their Economic Importance, 2000; The Annular Structures in Lebanon and the Western Part of Syria, 2001. Honour: Man of the Year, 2002, American Biographical Institute, 2002; Man of Achievements, 2005. Memberships include: Academy of Engineering Sciences of the Russian Federation; Syrian Geological Society; Syrian Scientific Society for Information; Editor, Remote Sensing Journal; Editorial Board, Syrian Journal of Geology; Editor-in-Chief, Geological Sciences Review; Member of Scientific Committees in many International Conferences Address: General Organisation of Remote Sensing, PO Box 12586, Damascus, Syria. E-mail: gors@mil-sy. Website: www.gors-sy.r.org

**RUMANE Abdul Razzak**, b. 8 June 1948, Chandve, India. Electrical Engineer; Consultant. m. Noor Jehan, 1 son, 1 daughter. Education: BE, Electrical Engineering, Government College of Engineering, Marathwada University, Aurangabad, India, 1972; Diploma in Modern Management, British Career Training College, 1981; Diploma in International Trade, British Management Association, 1982; MS, General Engineering, Kennedy-Western University, USA, 2002; PhD, Kennedy-Western University, USA, 2005. Appointments include: Senior Electrical Engineer, Pan Arab Consulting Engineers, Kuwait, 1991-99; Senior Electrical Engineer, Dar Al Handsasah, (Shair and Partners), Kuwait, 1999-2004; Senior Electrical Engineer, Pan Arab Consulting Engineers, Kuwait, 2004-. Honours: Twentieth Century Achievements Award, ABI; Global Award of Accomplishment, Who's Who Institute; International Order of Merit, IBC; The World Order of Science-Education-Culture with title of "Cavalier", European Academy of Informatisation; Medal of Science and Peace, Albert Schweitzer International University Foundation; Bharat Gaurav Award, Gem of India, India International Friendship Society. Memberships: Kuwait Society of Engineers; Fellow, The Institution of Engineers (India); Senior Member, IEEE, USA; Associate Member, American Society of Civil Engineers; MEW (Kuwait) Registration (Supervisor First Class); Member, American Society for Quality; Member, SAVE International; London Diplomatic Academy; International Benevolent Research Forum. Address: At & PO Chandve, Talk – Mahad, Dist. Raigad, Maharashtra, India 402301. E-mail: rarazak@yahoo.com

**RUS Ioan A**, b. 28 August 1936, Ianosda, Bihor, Romania. Mathematics Educator; Researcher. m. Ileana Moga, 1 son, 1 daughter. Education: BS, Mathematics, 1960, PhD, Mathematics, 1968, Babes-Bolyai University. Appointments: Assistant Professor, 1960-67, Lecturer, 1967-72, Associate Professor, 1972-77, Professor, 1977-, Vice-Rector, 1976-84, 1992-96, Babes-Bolyai University. Publications: Principles and Applications of Fixed Point Theory, 1979; Differential Equations, Integral Equations and Dynamical Systems, 1996; Fixed Point Theory 1950-2000, 2002; Editor, Fixed Point Theory Journal; Contributor of articles to professional journals. Honours: Doctor honoris causa, University of Baia Mare, 2004; Consulting Editor, Contemporary Who's Who, ABI. Memberships: American Mathematical Society; Japanese

Association of Mathematical Scientists. Address: Babes-Bolyai University, Kogalniceanu Nr 1, Cluj-Napoca, Romania.

**RUSH Alan de Lacy,** b. 16 July 1936, Esher, England. Writer; Research Historian. Education: MA, University of Glasgow, Scotland, 1971; MA, University of Essex, England, 1973. Appointments: Lecturer, Riyadh University, Saudi Arabia, 1971-72; King Abdul-Aziz University, Jeddah, Saudi Arabia, 1973-75; Kuwait University, Kuwait, 1975-82. Publications: Al-Sabah, History and Genealogy of Kuwait's Ruling Family, 1987; Records of Kuwait, 1989; Ruling Families of Arabia, 1991; Records of the Hashemites, 1995; Records of Iraq, 2001. Contributions to: Burke's Royal Families of the World, 1982; Middle East Economic Digest; Financial Times; Arabic newspapers; Journal of Royal Society for Asian Affairs. Address: 8 Upper Addison Gardens, London W14 8AL, England.

**RUSH Geoffrey,** b. 6 July 1951, Toowoomba, Queensland, Australia. Actor. m. Jane Menelaus, 1988, 1 son, 1 daughter. Education: Jacques Lecoq of Mime, Paris. Career: Began with Queensland Theatre Company; Films include: The Wedding, 1980; Starstruck, 1982; Twelfth Night, 1986; Midday Crisis, 1994; Dad and Dave on our Selection, 1995; Shine; Children of the Revolution, 1996; Elizabeth, 1998; Shakespeare in Love, 1998; The Magic Pudding, 1999; Mystery Men, 1999; House on Haunted Hill, 1999; Quills, 1999; The Tailor of Panama, 2000; Lantana, 2001; Frida, 2002; Theatre includes; Hamlet; The Alchemist; The Marriage of Figaro; The Small Poppies; TV includes: Menotti, 1980-81; The Burning Piano, 1992; Mercury, 1995; Bonus Mileage, 1996. Honours: Academy and BAFTA Awards, Australian Film Institute Award, Golden Globe Award for Shine; BAFTA Award for Best Supporting Actor, for Shakespeare in Love. Address: C/o Shanahan Management, PO Box 478, Kings Cross, NSW 2011, Australia.

**RUSHDIE (Ahmed) Salman,** b. 19 June 1947, Bombay, India. Writer. m. (1) Clarissa Luard, 1976, dissolved 1987, died 1999, 1 son, (2) Marianne Wiggins, 1988, divorced 1993, 1 stepdaughter, (3) Elizabeth West, 1997, 1 son. Education: MA, King's College, Cambridge. Appointments: Actor, Fringe Theatre, London, 1968-69; Advertising Copywriter, 1969-73; Part-time Copywriter, 1976-80. Publications: Grimus, 1975; Midnight's Children, 1981; Shame, 1983; The Jaguar Smile: A Nicaraguan Journey, 1987; The Satanic Verses, 1988; Haroun and The Sea of Stories, 1990; Imaginary Homelands (essays), 1991; The Wizard of Oz, 1992; The Ground Beneath Her Feet, 1999; Fury, 2001; Step Across the Line: Collected Non-Fiction 1992-2002, 2002; TV Films: The Painter and The Pest, 1985; The Riddle of Midnight, 1988; Contributions to professional journals. Honours: Booker McConnell Prize for Fiction, 1981; Arts Council Literary Bursary, 1981; English Speaking Union Literary Award, 1981; James Tait Black Memorial Book Prize, 1981; Prix du Meilleur Livre Etranger, 1984; Nominated for Whitbread Prize, 1988; Booker Prize, 1993; Commander of the Order of Arts and Letters of France, 1999. Memberships: PEN; Production Board, British Film Institute; Advisory Board, Institute of Contemporary Arts; FRSL; Executive, Camden Committee for Community Relations, 1975-82. Address: c/o Aitken & Stone Ltd, 29 Fernshaw Road, London SW10 0TG, England.

**RUSHMAN Geoffrey Boswall,** b. 20 August 1939, Northampton, England. Medical Practitioner. m. Gillian Mary, 3 daughters. Education: MB BS, St Bartholomew's Hospital, 1957-62; Conjoint Diploma (MRCS LRCP), 1962; Royal College of Anaesthetists (FFARCS), 1970. Appointments: Trainee Anaesthetist, St Bartholomew's Hospital, 1968-73; Consultant Anaesthetist, Southend Hospital, 1974-99; Examiner

Royal College of Anaesthetists, 1991-99; Council Member, 1985-88, Secretary, 1991-92, President, 1999-2000, Section of Anaesthetics, Royal Society of Medicine; Council Member, Royal Society of Medicine, 2001-2005. Publications: Parenteral Nutrition for the Surgical Patient (jointly), 1971; Synopsis of Anaesthesia (jointly), 8th, 9th, 10th, 11th and 12th editions, 1977, 1982, 1987,1993, 1999 (with Greek, Polish, Spanish, Italian and German Editions); Short History of Anaesthesia (jointly), 1996; Short Answer Questions in Anaesthesia, 1997. Honours: Hichens Prize (jointly), 1962; Police Award for Bravery, 1969; Association of Anaesthetists Prize for contributions to anaesthesia (jointly), 1971. Address: Godbegot, Aylesbury Road, Thame, Oxon, England.

**RUSPOLI Francesco,** b. 11 December 1958, Paris, France. Artist; Painter. Education: MA, Set and Costume design, Central St Martin, England, 1995. Career: Abstract figurative painter and colourist; Theatre designer of set and costumes; Exhibitions: Numerous exhibitions in UK and abroad 1983- include most recently: Group shows: Galiere d'Art, Nice, 2000; Agora Gallery, New York, 2000, 2001; Llewellyn Alexander Gallery, London, 2000, 2001; Hay's Gallery, London, 2001; Royal Free Hampstead Hospital, London, 2001; Nobleart Gallery, Cambridge, 2001; Salon des Arts, London, 2002; Plus One Plus Two Galleries, London, 2002; Artlands, Norfolk, 2002; DACS, London, 2002; Colouris, London, 2003; One man shows: Sylvia White Gallery, New York, 2000; Ministere des Finances, Paris, 2000; Mayfair Festival, London, 2000, 2003; Hay's Gallery, London, 2001; Artlands, London, 2003, 2004; Set and Costume Design: Shakespeare's Universe, Barbican, 1994; Loves Labours Lost, Cochrane Theatre, 1994; Triangle, Cochrane Theatre, 1995; Commercial, CTVC Studios, 1995; Snuff, London Film Festival, 1995; The May, Barons Court Theatre, 1997; Mind the Gap, Canal Café Theatre, 1999; Commissions: Painting, The Rating and Evaluation Association, London; Painting, Temple, Barristers, London; Mural, Le Cigale Restaurant, London; Mural, Insurance MGA, Nice, France; Painting, Hotel Grau Roig, Andorra; Private collections and museums: Robert Hardy; Dame Felicity Lott; Delia De Pau; Gauguin Museum, Tahiti; Works in private collections in London, Paris, Tel-Aviv, Barcelona, Rome, Milan, Glasgow, Deauville, Cannes, Nice, Lille, Lyon, New York. Publications: Works featured in Exhibit A Magazine; Observer Magazine. Honours: Silver Medal, Grand Prix of Rome, 1985; Bronze Medal, Biennial, Villeneuve-Loubet, 1985; Golden Painting, 1986, Silver Medal, 1986, Gold Medal, 1988, Institute of French Culture; Eugene Frometin, Federation Latin, France, 1987; Bronze Medal, Mairie 17e Arrond Paris, France, 1991; Academician, 1994, Knight of the Art, 1998, Academy Geci-Marino, Italy. Address: 54 Chestnut Grove, Balham, London SW12 8JJ, England. E-mail: francesco. ruspoli@virgin.net Website: www.francesco-ruspoli.com

**RUSSELL Anthony Patrick,** b. 11 April 1951, Wirral, England. Circuit Judge. Education: MA, Pembroke College, Oxford. Appointments: Called to the Bar, 1974; Queen's Counsel, 1999; Circuit Judge, 2004-. Membership: Honorary Fellow, 2002, Vice-President, 2004, Guild of Church Musicians. Address: The Law Courts, Openshaw Place, Ring Way, Preston PR1 2LL, England.

**RUSSELL John,** b. 22 January 1919, Fleet, England. Art Critic; Writer. Education: MA, Magdalen College, Oxford, 1940. Appointments: Honorary Attaché, Tate Gallery, 1940-41; Staff, Ministry of Information, 1941-43, Naval Intelligence Division, Admiralty, London, 1943-46; Contributor, 1945-49, Art Critic, 1949-74, The Sunday Times; Art Critic, 1974-82, Chief Art Critic, 1982-91, The New York Times. Publications: Shakespeare's Country, 1942; British Portrait Painters, 1945;

Switzerland, 1950; Logan Pearsall Smith, 1950; Erich Kleiber, 1956; Paris, 1960, 2nd edition, 1983; Seurat, Private View (with Bryan Robertson and Lord Snowdon), 1965; Max Ernst, 1967; Henry Moore, 1968; Ben Nicholson, 1969; Pop Art Redefined (with Suzi Gablik), 1969; The World of Matisse, 1970; Francis Bacon, 1971; Édouard Vuillard, 1971; The Meanings of Modern Art, 1981, new and enlarged edition, 1990; Reading Russell, 1989; London, 1994; Matisse: Father and Son, 1999. Contributions to: Various publications including New York Review of Books, 1999-2000. Honour: Honorary Member, Century Association, New York, 2000. Membership: American Academy of Arts and Letters, 1966; Guggenheim Fellow, 2000-2001. Address: 166 East 61st Street, New York, NY 10021, USA.

**RUSSELL Ken,** b. 3 July 1927, Southampton, England. Film Director. m. (1) Shirley Russell, 4 sons, 1 daughter, (2) Vivian Jolly, 1 son, 1 daughter, (3) Hetty Baines, 1992, 1 son. Education: Nautical College, Pangbourne, England. Career: Former actor, freelance magazine photographer; Director, numerous TV documentaries for BBC, shown all over world; Documentaries include: Elgar; Bartok; Debussy; Hebri Rousseau; Isadora Duncan; Delius; Richard Strauss; Clouds of Glory; The Mystery of Dr Martini; The Secret Life of Arnold Bax; TV series: Lady Chatterly's Lover; Director, films: French Dressing, 1964; Billion Dollar Brain, 1967; Women in Love, 1969; The Music Lovers, 1970; The Devils, 1971; The Boyfriend, 1971; Savage Messiah, 1972; Mahler, 1973; Tommy, 1974; Lisztomania, 1975; Valentino, 1977; Altered States, 1981; Gothic, 1986; Aria (segment), 1987; Salome's Last Dance, 1988; The Lair of the White Worm, 1988; The Rainbow, 189; Whore, 1990; Prisoners of Honour, 1991; Lion's Mouth, 2002; Actor, film: The Russia House, 1990; The Rake's Progress (Stravinsky), 1982; Die Soldaten (Zimmerman), 1983; Opera: Princess Ida, 1992; Salome, Bonn, 1993. Publications: A British Picture: An Autobiography, 1989; Altered States: The Autobiography of Ken Russell, 1991; Fire Over England, 1993. Address: c/o Peter Rawley, ICM, 8942 Wilshire Boulevard, Beverly Hills, CA 90021, USA.

**RUSSELL Kurt von Vogel,** b. 17 March 1951, Springfield, Massachusetts, USA. Actor. m. Season Hubley, 1979, divorced, 1 son, 1 son with Goldie Hawn. Career: Child actor, Disney shows and films; Professional baseball player, 1971-73; Films include: It Happened at the World's Fair, 1963; Unlawful Entry, 1992; Captain Ron, 1992; Tombstone, 1993; Stargate, 1994; Executive Decision, 1996; Escape from LA, 1996; Breakdown, 1997; Soldier, 1998; Vanilla Sky, 2001; Interstate 60, 2002; Dark Blue, 2002; Miracle, 2004; TV series include: lead role in Travels With Jamie McPheeters, 1963-64; The New Land, 1974; The Quest, 1976; TV films include: Search For the Gods, 1975; The Deadly Tower, 1975; Christmas Miracle in Caulfield USA, 1977; Elvis, 1979; Amber Waves, 1988; Numerous guest appearances. Honours: 5 acting awards; 10 baseball awards; 1 golf championship. Memberships: Professional Baseball Players' Association; Stuntman's Association. Address: Creative Artists' Agency, 9830 Wilshire Boulevard, Beverly Hills, CA 90212-1825, USA.

**RUSSELL Martin James,** b. 25 September 1934, Bromley, Kent, England. Writer. Publications: No Through Road, 1965; The Client, 1975; Mr T, 1977; Death Fuse, 1980; Backlash, 1981; The Search for Sara, 1983; A Domestic Affair, 1984; The Darker Side of Death, 1985; Prime Target, 1985; Dead Heat, 1986; The Second Time is Easy, 1987; House Arrest, 1988; Dummy Run, 1989; Mystery Lady, 1992; Leisure Pursuit, 1993. Memberships: Crime Writers' Association; Detection Club.

Address: 15 Breckonmead, Wanstead Road, Bromley, Kent BR1 3BW, England.

**RUSSELL Norman Atkinson,** b. 7 August 1943, Belfast, Northern Ireland. Anglican Priest. m. Victoria Christine Jasinska, 2 sons. Education: MA, Churchill College, Cambridge; BD, London. Appointments: Articled Clerk, Cooper Brothers & Company, London, 1966-67; Curate, Christ Church with Emmanuel, Clifton, Bristol, 1970-74; Curate, Christ Church, Cockfosters, London and Anglican Chaplain, Middlesex Polytechnic, 1974-77; Rector of Harwell with Chilton, 1977-84; Priest in Charge of Gerrrards Cross, 1984-88 and Fulmer, 1985-88; Rector of Gerrards Cross and Fulmer, 1988-98; Archdeacon of Berkshire, 1998-. Honour: Honorary Canon, Christ Church, Oxford, 1995-98. Address: Foxglove House, Love Lane, Donnington, Newbury, Berkshire RG14 2JG, England. E-mail: archdber@oxford.anglican.org

**RUSSELL Willy, (William Martin Russell),** b. 23 August 1947, Liverpool, England. Dramatist; Writer. m. Ann Seagroatt, 1969, 1 son, 2 daughters. Education: Certificate of Education, St Katherine's College of Education, Liverpool. Appointments: Teacher, 1973-74; Fellow, Creative Writing, Manchester Polytechnic, 1977-78. Publications: Theatre: Blind Scouse, 1971-72; When the Reds (adaptation), 1972; John, Paul, George, Ringo and Bert (musical), 1974; Breezeblock Park, 1975; One for the Road, 1976; Stags and Hens, 1978; Educating Rita, 1979; Blood Brothers (musical), 1983; Our Day Out (musical), 1983; Shirley Valentine, 1986; The Wrong Boy (novel), 2000; Songs and poetry. Television Plays: King of the Castle, 1972; Death of a Young Young Man, 1972; Break In (for schools), 1974; Our Day Out, 1976; Lies (for schools), 1977; Daughter of Albion, 1978; Boy With Transistor Radio (for schools), 1979; One Summer (series), 1980. Radio Play: I Read the News Today (for schools), 1979. Screenplays: Band on the Run, 1979; Educating Rita, 1981. Honours: Honorary MA, Open University; Honorary Director, Liverpool Playhouse. Address: c/o Margaret Ramsay Ltd, 14A Goodwin's Court, St Martin's Lane, London WC2, England.

**RUSSO Carlo Ferdinando,** b. 15 May 1922, Naples, Italy. University Professor. m. Adele Plotkin. Education: Degree in Filologia antica, University of Pisa, 1943; Diploma, Scuola Normale, Pisa, 1945. Appointments: Assistant Editor, 1946-62, Managing Editor, 1962-, Belfagor journal; Instructor, University of Florence, Italy, 1946-48; Instructor, University of Cologne, Germany, 1948-50; Libero Docente, Greek and Latin Philology, Rome, 1951; Professor, University Bari, Italy, 1950-62; Professor tenure, 1962-97; Professor Emeritus, 1999. Publications: Senecae, Apocolocyntosis, 1948, 6th edition, 1985; Hesiodi, Scutum, 1950, 3rd edition, 1968; La Coppa di Nestore di Pitecusa-Ischia, (Monumenti Antichi, Accademia dei Lincei), 1955-92; Aristofane Tautore di teatro, 1962, 3rd edition, 1992, English edition, 1994, paperback, 1997; Die Gestalt einer archaischen Handschrift und einer kyklischen Ilias, 1983; Omero e il Disco di Festo, 1995; Omero nasce con le Olimpiadi (Olimpiade seconda), 1999; L'anno poetico XXXVI, 2003; I dolori di Omero omicida, 2004; Curator of works by H Fränkel, G Pasquali and E Fraenkel, 1969-83, 1992, 1994. Address: Casa ed Olschki, Casella post 66, 50100 Florence, Italy. E-mail: cf.russo@lgxserve.ciseca.uniba.it

**RUSSO René,** b. 1955, California, USA. Actress. m. Dan Gilroy, 1992, 1 daughter. Career: Formerly model Eileen Ford Agency; Film appearances include: Major League, 1989; Mr Destiny; One Good Cop; Freejack; Lethal Weapon 3; In the Line of Fire; Outbreak; Get Shorty; Tin Cup; Ransom; Buddy; Lethal Weapon 4, 1998; The Adventures of Rocky and Bullwinkle,

1999; The Thomas Crown Affair, 1999; Showtime, 2002; Big Trouble, 2002; TV appearance: Sable (series). Address: c/o Progressive Artists Agency, 400 South Beverly Drive, Suite 216, Beverly Hills, CA 90212, USA.

**RUSTAN Peter Agne,** b. 21 February 1941, Köping, Västmanland, Sweden. Mining Engineer. m. Brita Järvhammar, divorced 2002, 1 son, 3 daughters. Education: Mining Engineer, 1965; Technical Licentiate, 1973; Technical Dr, Mining, 1995; Associate Professor, Mining, 1995. Appointments: Stockholm Assistant in Mining, Royal Institute of Technology, 1965-70; Mine Planning Engineer, Luossavaara-Kirunavaara, Malmberget, Sweden, 1971-74; Researcher and Teacher, Lulea University of Technology, Lulea, Sweden, 1974-98; Consultant, 1998-. Publications: Co-author, Underground Ventilation, Stiftelsen Bergteknisk Forskning, Sweden, 1984; Editor-in-Chief, Rock Blasting Terms and Symbols; A A Balkenna, Rotterdam, 1998. Memberships: International Society of Explosives Engineers, USA and International Society for Rock Mechanics. Address: Lagmansvagen 20, SE-954 32 Gammelstad, Sweden. E-mail: agne.rustan@spray.se

**RUSZCZYŃSKA-SZENAJCH Hanna,** b. 30 June 1930, Warsaw, Poland. Education: MS, Geology, 1955, PhD, Geology, 1964, Habilitation in Geology, 1975, University of Warsaw. Appointments: Assistant, 1955-64, Adjunct Professor, 1964-95, Associate Professor, 1995-2000, Department of Geology, University of Warsaw. Publications: Over 35 papers in scientific journals, mainly in the fields of glacial geology and quaternary geology; 2 books: monographs on glacial and quaternary geology of central and eastern Poland; Over 20 presentations to scientific conferences and meetings. Honours: Awards from the Ministry of Higher Education and the Rector of the University of Warsaw, for papers and books on glacial geology, 1966, 1978, 1979, 1983, 1998. Memberships: Polish Geological Society; International Union for Quaternary Research, INQUA, 1977-2003; Quaternary Research Association; Association of Polish Geomorphologists. Address: Department of Geology, University of Warsaw, Żwirki i Wigury 93, 02-089, Warszawa, Poland.

**RUTTER Michael Llewellyn,** b. 15 August 1933, Brummanna, Lebanon. Professor of Developmental Psychiatry; Writer. m. Marjorie Heys, 27 December 1958, 1 son, 2 daughters. Education: MB ChB, 1950-55, MD, 1963, University of Birmingham; DPM, University of London, 1961. Appointments: Professor of Developmental Psychopathology, University of London; Social, Genetic and Developmental Psychiatry Research Centre. Publications: Depression in Young People: Development and Clinical Perspectives (co-editor), 1986; Language Development and Disorders (co-editor), 1987; Treatment of Autistic Children (co-editor), 1987; Parenting Breakdown: The Making and Breaking of Intergenerational Links (co-author), 1988; Assessment and Diagnosis in Child Psychopathology, 1988; Straight and Devious Pathways From Childhood to Adulthood, 1990; Biological Risk Factors for Psychosocial Disorders, 1991; Developing Minds: Challenge and Continuity Across the Lifespan, 1993; Stress, Risk and Resilience in Children and Adolescents, Processes, Mechanisms and Interventions (co-editor), 1994; Child and Adolescent Psychiatry: Modern Approaches (co-editor), 3rd edition, 1994; Development Through Life: A Handbook for Clinicians (co-editor), 1994; Psychosocial Disorders in Young People: Time Trends and their Causes (co-editor), 1995; Behavioural Genetics (co-author), 3rd edition, 1997; Antisocial Behaviour by Young People (co-author), 1998. Contributions to: Numerous professional journals. Honours: 10 honorary doctorates; Knight Baronet, 1992; American Psychological Association Distinguished Scientific Contribution Award, 1995; Castilla

del Pino Prize for Achievement in Psychiatry, Cordoba, Spain, 1995; Royal Society of Medicine, honorary fellow, 1996; Royal College of Paediatrics and Child Health, honorary founding fellow, 1996; Society for Research in Child Development, president elect, 1997. Memberships: American Academy of Arts and Sciences, honorary foreign member; Royal College of Psychiatrists, fellow; Royal College of Physicians, fellow; Fellow, Royal Society, 1997-; President, Society for Research into Child Development, 1999-. Address: SGDP Research Centre, Institute of Psychiatry, De Crespigny Park, Denmark Hill, London SE5 8AF, England.

**RUTTY Jane Elizabeth,** b. 6 January 1964, Watford, England. Registered Nurse; Academic. m. Guy Nathan Rutty. Education: Registered General Nurse, Hedgecock School of Nursing, Barking Hospital, 1988; Intensive Care Nursing, SE Thames College of Nursing, The Brook Hospital, 1990; Diploma in Professional Studies in Nursing, University of Westminster, 1992; BSc (Hons) Education Studies (Nursing, University of Wolverhampton, 1994; MSc, Nursing, Royal College of Nursing Institute, London, 1998; PhD, University of Bradford, ongoing, 1998-. Appointments: Staff Nurse, Medicine, King George Hospital Ilford, 1988; Staff Nurse, Intensive Care and Coronary Care Unit, The Brook Hospital, Woolwich, 1988-89; Research Nurse, Thrombosis Research Unit, Medical School, King's College Hospital, London, 2089-90; Post Registration Student Nurse, SE Thames College of Nursing, The Brook Hospital, 1990; Staff Nurse, Intensive Care, Coronary Care and Theatre Recovery Unit, Northwick Park Hospital, Harrow, 1990-92; Staff Nurse, Intensive Care Unit, Groby Road Hospital, Leicester, 1992-93; Nurse Tutor Student,1993-94; Senior Lecturer, 1994-96, University of Wolverhampton; Lecturer, 1996-2000, Senior Academic Lecturer, Nursing, 2000-2002, University of Bradford; Principal Lecturer, Nursing, DeMontfort University, Leicester, 2002-. Publications: 15 articles as author and co-author on professional journals; 6 abstracts in journals; 4 book chapters. Honours: Medici Fellowship, 2004-2005; Member, Higher Education Academy. Memberships: International Association of Forensic Nursing; National Clinical Skills Network; Qualitative Research Network; British Association of Critical Care Nursing; Royal College of Nursing: Critical Care Forum, Research Society, Education Forum, Ethics Forum, History of Nursing Society. E-mail: jrutty@dmu.ac.uk

**RUZEVICIUS Juozas,** b. 19 March 1952, Lithuania. Professor; Business Consultant. m. Danguole, 2 daughters. Education: Degree, Commodity Science and Trade Organisation, Vilnius University, 1974; PhD, Moscow Institute of Co-operative Trade, 1978. Appointments: Chairman, Products Expert, Co-operative Trade of Radviliskis, 1973-74; Manager, Lithuanian Confederacy of Consumer Co-operatives, 1974-75; Teacher, Associate Professor, Lithuanian Academy of Management, Moscow Institute of Co-operative Trade, Vilnius University, 1978-88; Professor of Management Department, Head of Quality Management Department, Economics Faculty, Vilnius University, 1988-2004, 2005-; Expert of International Classifications, 1991-94, Member of Laws, 1992-98, Government of Lithuania; Consultant: Centre of European Law, Turin, 1996, World Trade Centre, Brussels, 1996, More than 60 companies in Lithuania, 1998-2005; Member of Council, Lithuanian Association of Consumers, 1995-; Scientific Expert, International Scientific Journal "Forum Ware", 1998-; Member of Council, "Best of Lithuania", Confederacy of Industrialists of Lithuania, 2003-2004; Accredited Representative, Lithuanian Standardisation Body, 2003-; Scientific Executive, Ministry of Health Care of Lithuania, 2003-2004; Scientific Leader, Ministry of Economy of Lithuania, 2003-2004. Publications: About 130 scientific publications. Memberships: President, Lithuanian

Society of Commodity Science; Vice President, 1997-2003, Member of Executive Board, 2004-, International Association of Commodity Science, Vienna. Address: Aitvaru 72, LT-08400 Vilnius, Lithuania. E-mail: juozas.ruzevicius@ef.vu.lt

**RUZICKA Marek Captain,** b. 29 August 1960, Sobeslav, Czech Republic. Naturalist. m. Magdalena Zhofova, 2 sons. Education: MSc, Environmental Engineering, 1984; Postgraduate course, Enzyme Engineering, 1988; Postgraduate studies, Applied Mathematics, 1987; PhD, Chemical Engineering, 1990; Partial study of Physics, Charles University, Prague, 1990-94. Appointments: Scientist, Institute of Chemical Process Fundamentals, Academy of Sciences, Prague, Czech Republic, 1990-. Publications: 15 articles in professional scientific journals. Honours: British Chevening Scholarship, University of Birmingham, 1994-95; Honorary Research Fellow, University of Birmingham. Memberships: Union of Czech Mathematicians and Physicists; Euromech. Address: Institute of Chemical Process Fundamentals, Rozvojova 135, 16502 Prague, Czech Republic. E-mail: ruzicka@icpf.cas.cz

**RYABOV Yuri,** b. 15 June 1923, Charkov City, Ukraine. Scientist; Teacher. m. Alla, 1 son, 2 daughters. Education: Graduated, 1950, Postgraduate, 1950-53, Candidate of Science, Physics and Mathematics, 1953, DrSc, 1963, Professor, 1965, Department of Celestial Mechanics, Moscow University. Appointments: Junior Researcher, Astronomy Institute, Moscow University, 1953-55; Docent, Moscow Energetic Institute (by correspondence), 1955-60; Docent, Department of Celestial Mechanics, Moscow University, 1960-65; Head, Department of Numerical Methods, Moscow Patric Lumumba University, 1965-71; Head, Department of Mathematics, 1971-93, Professor, 1993-, Moscow State Auto and Highway Construction University. Publications: Over 140 articles, monographs, science-for-laymen articles, books and scholarly texts on theory and applications of differential equations, nonlinear oscillations, numerical methods, celestial mechanics and astronomy. Honours: Honoured Scientist of Russia, 1992; Order of Patriotic War and other awards as participant of World War II; Twentieth Century Award for Achievement, IBC, 1993; Distinguished Leadership Award, ABI. Memberships: International Astronomical Union; European Astronomical Society; Editorial Board, Earth and Universe magazine. Address: Chernyachovsky str 12-81, Moscow 125319, Russia. Email: ryabov@vmat.madi.ru

**RYAN Meg,** b. 19 November 1961, Fairfield, Connecticut, USA. Actress. m. Dennis Quaid, 1991, divorced, 1 son. Education: New York University. Career: Formerly in TV commercials; TV appearances: As The World Turns; One of the Boys; Amy and the Angel; The Wild Side; Charles in Charge; Owner, Prufrock Pictures; Films: Rich and Famous, 1981; Amytyville III-D; Top Gun; Armed and Dangerous; Innerspace; DOA; Promised Land; The Presidio; When Harry Met Sally; Joe Versus the Volcano; The Doors; Prelude to a Kiss; Sleepless in Seattle; Flesh and Bone; Significant Other; When a Man Loves a Woman; IQ; Paris Match; Restoration; French Kiss, 1995; Two for the Road, 1996; Courage Under Fire, 1996; Addicted to Love, 1997; City of Angels, 1998; You've Got Mail, 1998; Hanging Up, 1999; Lost Souls, 1999; Proof of Live, 2000; Kate & Leopold, 2001; In the Cut, 2003; Against the Ropes, 2004. Address: c/o ICM, 8942 Wilshire Boulevard, Beverly Hills, CA 90211, USA.

**RYBICKI Jerzy,** b. 6 June 1953, Warsaw, Poland. Boxer. m. Urszula Kosztowny, 1 son, 2 daughters. Education: Master, Academy of Physical Education, Warsaw, 1981. Career: Polish Junior Champion, 1971; Polish Senior Champion, 1974, 1975, 1977, 1978, 1989, 1981; Bronze Medal, European

Championship, Katowice, 1975, Halle, 1977; Gold Medal, Olympic Champion, Montreal, 1976; Bronze Medal, European Championship, 1978; Olympic Bronze Medal, Moscow, 1980; Championship, France, 1980, 1982. Address: Uminskiego 10 m 7, 03-984, Warsaw, Poland

**RYDER Winona,** b. 29 October 1971, Minnesota, USA. Actress. Education: American Conservatory Theatre, San Francisco. Career: Films include: Lucas, 1986; Beetlejuice, 1988; Great Balls of Fire; Heathers, 1989; Edward Scissorhands, 1990; Bram Stoker's Dracula, 1992; Age of Innocence, 1993; Little Women; How to Make an American Quilt; The Crucible; Looking for Richard; Boys; Alien Resurrection; Girl Interrupted, 1999; Lost Souls, 1999; Autumn in New York, 1999; Mr Deeds, 2002; S1m0ne, 2002; The Day My God Died, voice, 2003. Honours: Golden Globe Best Supporting Actress, 1994. Address: 10345 W Olympic Boulevard, Los Angeles, CA 90064, USA.

**RYDYGIER Edward,** b. 17 November 1953, Warsaw, Poland. Physicist; Financial Analyst; Teacher. m. Hanna Rydygier. Education: Master of Science in Physics, Warsaw University, 1978; Postgraduate Studies, Statistical Methods Diploma, 1992; Computer Science Diploma, Polish Academy of Sciences, Mathematical Institute, 1992; Coud. For PhD, Technical Science, 2005; Krakow University of Technology, Krakow, Poland; Postgraduate Studies, Insurance and Banking Diploma, 2001, Warsaw Technical University. Appointments: Physicist, Institute of Nuclear Research, Otwock, Poland, 1978-82; Adjunct Lecturer, Institute for Nuclear Studies, Otwock, Poland, 1983-99; Inspector Warsaw District Labour Office, Warsaw, Poland, 2000; Consultant of the World Bank with the Ministry of the State Treasury, Warsaw, Poland, 2000; Lecturer, Education Centre, Vocational Studies of Business and Economics, Warsaw, Poland, 2001-; Inspector, Archive of Municipal Office of Warsaw, 2002-; Lecturer, University of Economics and Technology in Legionowo, Poland, 2004-. Publications: 90 scientific publications including 50 conference articles presented at international scientific conferences and workshops, Honours: European Vocational Title, European Physicist, conferred by President of European Physical Society on behalf of European Commission of EU, 1997; Member, Research Board of Advisors of the American Biographical Institute, 2001-. Memberships: Polish Physical Society; Founder Member, Polish Nuclear Society; Member General Revision Committee Polish Society of Universalism. Address: ul Narbutta 60 m. 8, 02-541 Warsaw, Poland. E-mail: erydygier@targowek.waw.pl

**RZEDOWSKI Jerzy,** b. 27 December 1926, Lwów, Poland. Botanist. m. Graciela Calderón, 3 daughters. Education: Biology, National School of Biological Sciences, National Polytechnic Institute, Mexico, 1954; Doctor of Biology, Faculty of Science, National University of Mexico, 1961. Appointments: Professor, San Luis Potosí University, 1954; Professor, Researcher, Postgraduate College, 1959; Professor, National School of Biological Sciences, National Polytechnic Institute, 1961; Researcher, Institute of Ecology, 1984-. Publications: 120 articles in scientific journals; 26 fascicles; 45 book chapters; 6 books. Honours: Diploma al mérito botánico; Ordre des palmes académiques; Doctorado honoris causa, Universidad Autónoma Chapingo; Doctorado honoris causa, Universidad Michoacana de San Nicolás de Hidalgo; Premio al mérito ecologico; Asa Gray Award; Botany Millennium Award; José Cuatrecasas Medal for Excellence in Tropical Botany. Memberships: Botanical Society of America; American Society of Plant Taxonomists; Sociedad Argentina de Botánica; International Association of Plant Taxonomy; Sociedad Botánica de México. Address: Apartado postal 386, 61600 Pátzcuaro, Michoacán, Mexico. E-mail: jerzy@inecolbajio.edu.mx

# DICTIONARY OF INTERNATIONAL BIOGRAPHY

# S

**SAAD Akram Saad,** b. 19 December 1956, Cairo, Egypt. Civil Engineer. m. Hanan, 1 son, 1 daughter. Education: BSc, Civil Engineering, Cairo University, 1979; MBA, Project Management, Missouri University, 2002; Certified Senior Corrosion Technologist, NACE International, USA. Appointments: Resident Engineer, Lahmeyer International; Resident Engineer, Hyder Consultants; Project and Follow-up Engineer, SPECO; Project Manager, RAMW; Project Manager, Al SaLama; Site Manager, TEKSIS; Site Engineer, Arab Swiss Engineering; Site Engineer, Cementation; Site Engineer, Aarding BV; Site Engineer. Publications: Report in Concrete Repair by the use of SFRS; Use of bonding Agent in Concrete Rehabilitation, Case Study. Memberships: ASCE; NACE; SEI; GROHE; Egyptian Engineering Syndicate. Address: PO Box 2413, Abu Dhabi, United Arab Emirates. E-mail: akramabdallh@hotmail.com

**SAAD Ali Samir,** b. 11 May 1964, Lebanon. Assistant Professor. m. Hoda Damaj, 2 sons, 2 daughters. Education: BS, Physics and Medical Instrumentation, University of St Etienne, France, 1985-89; Master in Digital Image Processing, Institute of Computer and Telecommunication, University of Rennes, France, 1990; Master in Electronics Systems, 1992, PhD, Electrical Engineering, Digital Image Processing, 1996, Polytechnic School of Engineering, Nantes, France. Appointments: Research Associate, National Center for Macromolecular Imaging, Baylor College of Medicine, Houston, Texas, USA, 1996-2000; Assistant Professor, King Saud University, College of Applied Medical Sciences, Department of Biomedical Technology, 2000-. Publications: Articles in scientific journals as author and co-author include most recently: Wavelets filtering for classification of very noisy electron microscopic single particles images – Application on structure determination of VP5-VP19C recombitant, 2003; Conformational Changes in Sindis virions Resulting from Exposure to Low pH and Interactions with Cells Suggest that Cell Penetration May Occur at the Cell Surface in the Absence of Membrane Fusion, 2004; Orientation determination by wavelets matching for 3D reconstruction of very noisy electron microscopic virus images, 2005. Honours: NIH Grant (New method for 3D reconstruction of Herpes virus), 1999; NSF Grant, 2000; Welch Foundation Grant, 2001; Listed in Who's Who publications and biographical dictionaries. Memberships: American Association for the Advancement of Science; Arab Association for Science and Technology; Saudi Radiology Association; Arriyadh Biomedical Engineering Association. Address: King Saud University, College of Applied Medical Sciences, Department of Biomedical Technology, PO Box 10219, Riyadh, Saudi Arabia. E-mail: asaad64@yahoo.com

**SAAIMAN Nolan,** b. 21 December 1960, Pretoria, South Africa. Internal Auditor. m. Anita, 2 sons. Education: B Comm, Accounting Sciences, 1982; B Comm, Honours, Accounting, 1988; Diploma, Datametrics, 1992; Certified Information Systems Auditor, 1992; Certified Financial Services Auditor, 1996; Computer Professional Qualifying Examination of the Computer Society of South Africa, 1996; Certified Internal Auditor, 1998; Certified Financial Consultant, 2001; Certified Business Manager, 2001. Appointments: Senior Internal Auditor, South African Post Office, 1985-88; Accountant Van Wyk and Louw, 1988-89; Manager's Assistant, Information Systems Audit Department, First National Bank, 1990-92; Manager, Computer Audit Services, SA Eagle, 1992-94; IT Audit Manager, SA Housing Trust, 1995-97; Audit Manager, Senior Auditor, Daimler Chrysler, South Africa, 1997-. Publications:

Articles about computer audit, membership matters and internal audit, in Newsletter of the Institute of Internal Auditors, South Africa, 1995-96; Article on internal audit in Institute of Directors Directorship Magazine, 1997. Honours: Completed Comrades Marathon (90kms), 1984, 1986; Served on Board of Institute of Internal Auditors, South Africa, 1996-97; 21st Century Award for Achievement, IBC, 2001; Listed in Who's Who Publications and biographical dictionaries. Memberships: Information Systems Audit and Control Association; Institute of Directors; Institute of Internal Auditors; Computer Society of South Africa; Institute of Financial Consultants, The Association of Professionals in Business Management, USA; Who's Who Historical Society. Address: 26 Retha Court, Veglaer Street, Pierre Van Ryneveld Park, 0157 South Africa. E-mail: nolan.s aaiman@daimlerchrysler.com

**SAATCHI Charles,** b. 9 June 1943. Advertising Executive. m. (1) Doris Lockhart, (2) Kay, 1990, divorced 2001, 1 daughter. Education: Christ's College, Finchley, London, England. Appointments: Former junior copywriter, Benton and Bowles (US advertising agency), London; Associate Director, Collett Dickinson Pearce, 1966-68; with Ross Cramer formed freelance consultancy, Cramer Saatchi, Director, 1968-70; Co-founder (with Maurice Saatchi) of Saatchi and Saatchi (advertising agency), 1970, Saatchi & Saatchi PLC, 1984, Director, 1970-93, President, 1993-95; Co-founder, Partner, M&C Saatchi Agency, 1995-; Founder, The Saatchi Gallery, 2003-. Address: 36 Golden Square, London, W1R 4EE, England.

**SAATCHI Baron (Life Peer) Maurice,** b. 21 June 1946. Advertising Executive. m. Josephine Hart, 1984, 1 son, 1 stepson. Education: BSc, London School of Economics. Appointments: Co-Founder, Saatchi & Saatchi Company, 1970; Chairman, Saatchi & Saatchi Company PLC, 1984-94, Director, 1994; Co-founder, Partner, M&C Saatchi Agency, 1995-; Chairman, Megalomedia PLC, 1995-; Director (non-executive) Loot, 1998-; Shadow Cabinet Office Minister, 2001-. Publications: The Science of Politics, 2001. Memberships: Governor, LSE; Council, Royal College of Art, 1997-; Trustee, Victoria & Albert Museum, 1988-. Address: 36 Golden Square, London, W1R 4EE, England.

**SABOLIC Ivan,** b. 15 January 1950, Kljuc. Scientific Adviser. m. Branka Sabolic, 2 daughters. Education: MD, School of Medicine, 1973, MSc, Biomedicine, 1976, PhD, Biomedicine, 1980, University of Zagreb, Zagreb, Croatia. Appointments: Assistant, 1973-84; Assistant Professor, 1984-87; Professor, 1987-91, Department of Physiology, School of Medicine, University of Zagreb, Croatia; Research Fellow, Massachusetts General Hospital/Harvard Medical School, Boston, USA, 1991-93; Scientific Adviser, Institute for Medical Research and Occupational Health, Zagreb, Croatia, 1994-. Publications: 195 Research articles in international and national scientific journals; 1800 citations. Honours: Fogarty International Research Collaborative Award, 1995 and 1999; Croatian State Award for Science, 1999. Memberships: The Croatian Biochemical Society; The Croatian Physiological Society; The American Physiological Society; The German Physiological Society. Address: Institute for Medical Research and Occupational Health, Ksaverska cesta 2, HR 10001 Zagreb, Croatia. E-mail: sabolic@imi.hr

**SACCO Rodolfo,** b. 21 November 1923, Fossano, Italy. Professor of Law. m. Amélie Gay, 2 daughters. Education: Doctor in Laws. Appointments: Professor in Comparative Law and Civil Law, Triest, Pavia, Turin; Dean in the Jammahadda Ummadda Soomaaliyed, Mogadishu, Somalia. Publications: La comparaison juridique au service de la connaissance du droit,

1991; Introduzione al diritto comparato, 5th edition, 1992; Il diritto africano, 1995; Sistemi guiridici comparati, 1996; Il contratto, 3rd edition, 2004. Honours: Socio Nazionale, Accademia Nazionale dei Lincei; Correspondant de L'Institut de France –Académie des Sciences Morales; President, International Association of Legal Sciences; Doctor Honoris Causa: University of Paris II, University of Geneva, and McGill University, Montreal. Address: 77 Corso San Maurizio, 10124 Turin, Italy.

**SACHS Horst,** b. 27 March 1927, Magdeburg, Germany. Mathematician: University Teacher. m. Barbara Nowak. Education: Diploma, 1953, Dr rer nat, 1958, Dr rer nat habil, 1963, Martin-Luther-University, Halle-Wittenberg, Halle (Saale), Germany. Appointments: Science Assistant, University Halle-Wittenberg, Germany, 1953-63; Professor of Mathematics, Technical University of Ilmenau, Ilmenau, Germany, 1963-92; Retired, 1992. Publications: Textbooks on graph theory, 1970-72; Monograph: Co-author, Spectra of Graphs, 1980, 1982, 1995; Scientific articles mainly of graph theory, 1956-2005. Honour: Founding Fellow, Institute of Combinatorics and its Applications, TICA, Winnipeg, 1991; Euler Medal, 2000. Memberships: TICA; Deutsche Mathematiker-Vereinigung; Mathematische Gesellschaft in Hamburg. Address: Grenzhammer 65, D-98693 Ilmenau, Germany. E-mail: horst.sachs@tu-Ilmenau.de

**SACHS Leo,** b. 14 October 1924, Leipzig, Germany. Scientist. m. Pnina Salkind, 1 son, 3 daughters. Education: BSc, University of Wales, Bangor, 1948; PhD, Trinity College, Cambridge University, England, 1951. Appointments: Research Scientist, Genetics, John Innes Institute, England, 1951-52; Research Scientist, 1952-, Founder, Department of Genetics and Virology, 1960, Professor, 1962, Head, Department of Genetics, 1962-89, Dean, Faculty of Biology, 1974-79, Otto Meyerhof Professor of Biology, Weizmann Institute of Science, Rehovot, Israel. Publications: Science papers in professional journals. Honours: Israel Prize, Natural Sciences, 1972; Fogarty International Scholar, National Institutes of Health, Bethesda, 1972; Harvey Lecture, Rockefeller University, New York, 1972; Rothschild Prize, Biological Sciences, 1977; Wolf Prize, Medicine, 1980; Bristol-Myers Award, Distinguished Achievement in Cancer Research, New York, 1983; Doctor Honoris Causa, Bordeaux University, France, 1985; Royal Society Wellcome Foundation Prize, London, 1986; Alfred P Sloan Prize, General Motors Cancer Research Foundation, New York, 1989; Warren Alpert Foundation Prize, Harvard Medical School, Boston, 1997; Doctor of Medicine Honoris Causa, Lund University, Sweden, 1997; Honorary Fellow, University of Wales, Bangor, 1999; Emet Prize for Life Sciences, 2002. Memberships: European Molecular Biology Organization; Israel Academy of Sciences and Humanities; Foreign Associate USA National Academy of Sciences; Fellow, Royal Society, London; Foreign Member, Academia Europaea; Honorary Life Member, International Cytokine Society. Address: Weizmann Institute of Science, Department of Molecular Genetics, Rehovot, Israel.

**SACKS Jonathan Henry,** b. 8 March 1948, London, England. Rabbi. m. Elaine Taylor, 1970, 1 son, 2 daughters. Education: Christ's College, Finchley; Gonville and Caius College, Cambridge; New College, Oxford; London University; Jews' College, London; Yeshivat Etz Hayyim, London. Appointments: Lecturer, Middlesex Polytechnic, 1971-73; Jew's College, London, 1973-76, 1976-82; Rabbi, Golders Green Synagogue, London, 1978-82, Marble Arch Synagogue, London, 1983-90; Chief Rabbi Lord Jakobvits Professor (1st incumbent), Modern Jewish Thought, 1982-; Director, Rabbinic Faculty, 1983-90, Principal, 1984-90, Chief Rabbi,

1991-, United Hebrew Congregations of the Commonwealth; Editor, Le'ela (journal), 1985-90; Presentation Fellow, King's College, London, 1993; Association President, Conference of European Rabbis, 2000-; Visiting Professor of Philosophy, Hebrew University, Jerusalem and of Theology and Religious Studies, King's College, London. Publications: Torah Studies, 1986; Tradition and Transition, 1986; Traditional Alternatives, 1989; Traditional in an Untraditional Age, 1990; The Persistence of Faith, 1991; Orthodoxy Confronts Modernity (Editor), 1991; Crisis and Covenant, 1992; One People? Tradition, Modernity and Jewish Unity, 1993; Will We Have Jewish Grandchildren? 1994; Faith in the Future, 1995; Community of Faith, 1995; The Politics of Hope, 1997; Morals and Markets, 1999; Celebrating Life, 2000; Radical Then Radical Now, 2001; The Dignity of Difference: How To Avoid the Clash of Civilizations, 2002; The Chief Rabbi's Haggadah, 2003; From Optimism to Hope, 2004; To Heal a Fractured World, 2005. Honours: Honorary degrees from the Universities of: Bar Ilan, Cambridge, Glasgow, Haifa, Middlesex, Yeshiva University New York, University of Liverpool, St Andrews University and Leeds Metropolitan University; Honorary Fellow, Gonville and Caius College, Cambridge, 1993; Kings College; Jerusalem Prize, 1995; Awarded Doctorate of Divinity by Archbishop of Canterbury, 2001; Knighted, Queen's Birthday Honours, 2005. Address: 735 High Road, London, N12 0US, England.

**SADANGI Amitabha,** b. 14 October 1959, Ganjan, Orissa, India. Business Executive. m. Basanti Mishra, 1 son. Education: Diploma in Disaster Management; BA, LLB, Arts and Law; MA, Labour and Social Welfare. Appointments: State Co-ordinator, Churches' Auxiliary for Social Action; Senior Project Officer, OXFAM UK; Deputy Country Director, India, International Development Enterprises – International; Country Director International Development Enterprises, Sri Lanka; Chief Executive Officer, International Development Enterprises, India. Publications: Integrating Poor into Market Systems; Low Cost Technology for Poverty reduction; Two Faces of Innovations. Honours: World Technology Network, Social Entrepreneurship Finalist, 2004; Listed in Who's Who publications and biographical dictionaries. Memberships: World Technology Network; International Network of Professionals. Address: C-5/43 Safdarjung Development Area, New Delhi 110016, India. E-mail: amitabha@ide-india.org; Website: www.ide-india.org

**SADGROVE Sidney Henry, (Lee Torrance),** b. 1920, England. Artist; Teacher; Writer. Publications: You've Got To Do Something, 1967; A Touch of the Rabbits, 1968; The Suitability Factor, 1968; Stanislaus and the Princess, 1969; A Few Crumbs, 1971; Stanislaus and the Frog, 1972; Paradis Enow, 1972; Stanislaus and the Witch, 1973; The Link, 1975; The Bag, 1977; Half Sick of Shadows, 1977; Bleep, 1977; All in the Mind, 1977; Icary Dicary Doc, 1978, Angel, 1978; Filling, 1979; First Night, 1980; Only on Friday, 1980; Hoodunnit, 1984; Pawn en Prise, 1985; Just for Comfort, 1986; Tiger, 1987; State of Play, 1988; Warren, 1989; Dear Mrs Comfett, 1990. Membership: Writers Guild of Great Britain. Address: Pimp Barn, Withyham, Hartfield, Sussex, TN7 4BB, England.

**SADIE Stanley (John),** b. 30 October 1930, Wembley, Middlesex, England. Musicologist; Lexicographer; Writer. m. (1) Adèle Bloom, 10 December 1953, deceased 1978, 2 sons, 1 daughter, (2) Julie Anne McCornack, 18 July 1978, 1 son, 1 daughter. Education: BA, 1953, Mus B, 1953, MA, 1957, PhD, 1958, University of Cambridge. Appointments: Faculty, Trinity College of Music, London, 1957-65; Music Critic, The Times of London, 1964-81; Editor, The Musical Times, 1967-87. Publications: Handel, 1962; The Pan Book of Opera (with Arthur

Jacobs), 1964, 3rd edition, 1984; Mozart, 1966; Beethoven, 1967, 2nd edition, 1974; Handel, 1968; Handel Concertos, 1972; The New Grove Dictionary of Music and Musicians (editor), 20 volumes, 1980, revised edition, 29 volumes, 2001; The New Grove Dictionary of Musical Instruments (editor), 1984; The Cambridge Music Guide (with Alison Latham), 1985; The New Grove Dictionary of American Music (editor with H Wiley Hitchcock), 4 volumes, 1986; Mozart Symphonies, 1986; The Grove Concise Dictionary of Music (editor), 1988; Handel Tercentenary Collection (editor with A Hicks), 1988; History of Opera (editor), 1989; Performance Practice (editor with Howard M Brown), 2 volumes, 1989; Man and Music (general editor), 8 volumes, 1989-93; Music Printing and Publishing (co-editor), 1990; The New Grove Dictionary of Opera (editor), 4 volumes, 1992; Wolfgang Amadè Mozart: Essays on His Life and Music (editor), 1995; New Grove Book of Operas (editor), 1996. Contributions to: Professional journals and general publications. Honours: Commander of the Order of the British Empire, 1982; Honorary LittD, 1982. Memberships: Critics Circle; International Musicological Society, president, 1992-97; Royal College of Music, fellow; Royal Academy of Music, honorary; Royal Musical Association, president, 1989-94; American Musicological Society. Address: The Manor, Cossington, Somerset TA7 8JR, England.

**SAFIRE William,** b. 17 December 1929, New York, New York, USA. Columnist; Writer. m. Helene Belmar Julius, 16 December 1962, 1 son, 1 daughter. Education: Syracuse University, 1947-49. Appointments: Reporter, New York Herald-Tribune Syndicate, 1949-51; Correspondent, Europe and the Middle East, WNBC-WNBT, 1951; Radio-TV Producer, WMBC, New York City, 1954-55; Vice-President, Tex McCrary Inc, 1955-60; President, Safire Public Relations, 1960-68; Special Assistant to President Richard M Nixon, 1969-73; Columnist, The New York Times, 1973-. Publications: The Relations Explosion, 1963; Plunging into Politics, 1964; Safire's Political Dictionary, 1968, 3rd edition, 1978, new edition as Safire's New Political Dictionary, 1993; Before the Fall, 1975; Full Disclosure, 1977; Safire's Washington, 1980; On Language, 1980; What's the Good Word?, 1982; Good Advice on Writing (with Leonard Safire), 1982, new edition, 1992; I Stand Corrected, 1984; Take My Word for It, 1986; You Could Look It Up, 1988; Language Maven Strikes Again, 1990; Leadership (with Leonard Safire), 1990; Fumblerules, 1990; The First Dissident, 1992; Lend Me Your Ears, 1992; Quoth the Maven, 1993; In Love with Norma Loquendi, 1994; Sleeper Spy, 1995; Watching My Language, 1997; Spread the Word, 1999; Scandalmonger, 2000; Let A Smile Be Your Umbrella, 2002. Contributions to: Newspapers and magazines. Honour: Pulitzer Prize for Distinguished Commentary, 1978. Membership: Pulitzer, Board, 1995-; Chairman, The Charles A Dana Foundation. Address: c/o The Dana Foundation, 900 15th St NW, Washington, DC 20005, USA.

**SAFRONOV Nikas (Nikolay),** b. 8 April 1955 Ulyanovsk, USSR. Artist; Painter. 3 sons. Education: Rostov Art School, 1972-74; Vilnius Academy of Fine Arts, 1979-82. Career: Free Lance Painter of portraits, landscapes, using various techniques and their combinations, experiments with them and works with texture and classical painting; Professor, Ulyanovsk University. Publications: 5 art albums in the last 5 years; Numerous articles in newspapers and journals. Honours: International Order of St Konstantin the Great; Order of St Stanislav; Order of St Anna; Knight of Science and Fine Arts, Russian Academy of Natural Sciences; Title of Prince Awarded by the Russian Assembly of Nobility; Gold Watch from Vladimir Putin, President of Russia; Honourable Citizen of Ulyanovsk and Saratov; Honourable Citizen of Baku, Republic of Azerbaijan; Honorary Doctor,

Azerbaijan State Art and Culture University; Listed in Who's Who publications and biographical dictionaries. Memberships: Academician, International Art Academy; Russian Professional Union of Artists, Moscow. Address: Flat 2, House 17, Brusov Side-Street, Moscow 125009, Russia.

**SAH Bindeshwar Prasad,** b. 3 September 1946, Chak Kusiyari, Bidupur R.S., Bihar, India. Lecturer; Teacher. m. Smt Sumitra, 3 sons. Education: BA, Honours, English, 1967; MA, English, 1969; LLB, 1971; MA, Hindi, Gold Medal; Bachelor of Teaching (BT); Master of Education (M.Ed); Diploma in Distance Education from IGNOU; PhD, English, English and Hindi Drama. Appointments: Postgraduate Teacher, 1972; Lecturer in English, 1981; Counsellor and Assistant Co-ordinator, IGNOU, 1987-94; Senior Lecturer in English, 1986; Reader in English, 1994; Guest Lecturer, Arunachal University, 1999. Publications: Poems in English and Hindi, 1962-; Articles in English and Hindi; Editor, 12 books; Institutional magazines; Presented research papers in professional seminars and workshops. Honours: Nehru Academic Award, 1964; National Merit Scholarship, 1964; University Topper in English Honours Exam, 1967; International Man of the Year, IBC, 1999-2000; Man of the Year, ABI, 1999; International Distinguished Leadership Award, ABI, 2000. Memberships: Life Member, ASRC, Hyderabad; The Quest, Ranchi; Board of Studies, English, of Arunachal Varsity; Secretary, Ar Pr College Teachers' Association; Fellow of the United Writers' Association of India, Chennai; Member, Research Board of Advisers, American Biographical Institute, 2000-; Deputy Governor, ABI; Deputy Director General, International Biographical Centre, England. Address: Head, Department of English, D N Government College, Itanagar 791113, Arunachal Pradesh, India.

**SAHA Manoranjan,** b. 8 January 1952, Manikganj, Dhaka, Bangladesh. Professor of Applied Chemistry and Chemical Technology. m. Kabita, 1 son, 1 daughter. Education: BS (Hons), Chemistry, Dhaka University, 1974; MS, Chemical Engineering, Azerbaijan Institute of Petroleum and Chemistry, Baku, USSR, 1977; PhD, Petroleum and Petrochemicals, 1982; Postdoctoral Studies, Indian Institute of Science, Bangalore, 1995, Indian Institute of Petroleum, Dehradun, 1996. Appointments: Assistant Professor, 1983-90, Associate Professor, 1990-94, Professor, 1994-, Chairman, Department of Applied Chemistry and Chemical Technology, 1998-2001, Dhaka University, Dhaka, Bangladesh. Publications: 125 publications in national and international journals. Honours: Listed in Who's Who publications and biographical dictionaries. Memberships: Asiatic Society Bangladesh; Bangladesh Association for the Advancement of Science; Bangladesh Chemical Society; Bangladesh Association of Scientists and Scientific Professions. Address: Department of Applied Chemistry and Chemical Technology, University of Dhaka, Dhaka-1000, Bangladesh. E-mail: msaha@udhaka.net

**SAHIN Ömer,** b. 7 May 1969, Elbistan, K. Maras, Turkey. Researcher. m. Ayse Sahin, 1 son, 2 daughters. Education: BSc, 1991, MSc, 1994, PhD, 1999, Chemical Engineering, Istanbul Technical University. Appointments: Research Assistant, 1994-99, Research fellow, 1999-2003; Assistant Professor, 2003, Associate Professor, 2003, Harran University, Turkey. Publications: Articles in scientific journals include: Dehydration kinetics of sodium perborate tetrahydrate to monohydrate in fluidized bed drier, 1999; Calcination kinetics of Ammonium pentaborate using the Coats-Redfern and Genetic algorithm method by thermal analysis, 2001; Production of high bulk density anhydrous borax in fluidized bed granulator, 2002; The role of transport processes in the crystallization kinetics of ammonium pentaborate, 2003. Honours: Recipient, Promotion for Publication, Turkish Science Council and Harran University. Address: Basbakanlik Toplu Konutlari, A2 blok 15 sok No 66, Eurensanayi – s.urfa, Turkey. E-mail: osahin@harran.edu.tr

**SAHNI Brij Bhushan,** b. 24 January 1962, Hyderabad, India. Computer Scientist. m. Shikha Sahni, 1 daughter. Education: Diploma in Journalism; PhD, Computer Science. Appointments: Research Scientist, Audio Visual Research Centre; Member of Faculty, Department of Computer Science, University of Hyderabad; Chairman and Managing Director, Infotrack Systems specialising in software products for human resources management. Honours: Stony Carter Award for Professional Excellence and Humanism; Listed in Who's Who publications and biographical dictionaries. Memberships: Life Member, American Studies Research Centre; Life Member, Indian Institute of Public Administration; President, Ustad Shaik Dawood Academy of Music. Address: 4-1-12/2 Tilak Road, Hyderabad 500001, India. E-mail: bhushan@info-track.com Website: www.info-track.com

**SAID Edward,** b. 1 November 1935, Jerusalem, Palestine. Professor; Writer. m. Mariam Cortas, 14 December 1970, 2 children. Education: AB, Princeton University, 1957; AM, 1960, PhD, 1964, Harvard University. Appointments: Instructor, 1963-65, Assistant Professor, 1965-67, Associate Professor, 1967-70, Professor, 1970-77, Parr Professor of English and Comparative Literature, 1977-89, Old Dominion Foundation Professor of Humanities, 1989-, University Professor, 1992-, Columbia University; Visiting Professor, Harvard University, 1974, Johns Hopkins University, 1979, Yale University, 1985; Fellow, Center for Advanced Study in the Behavioural Sciences, Palo Alto, California, 1975-76; Christian Gauss Lecturer in Criticism, Princeton University, 1977; Carpenter Professor, University of Chicago, 1983; T S Eliot Lecturer, University of Kent, Canterbury, 1985; Northrop Frye Chair, University of Toronto, 1986; Messenger Lecturer, Cornell University, 1986; Wilson Lecturer, Wellesley College, 1991; Amnesty Lecturer, University of Oxford, 1992; Lord Northcliffe Lecturer, University College, London, 1993; Reith Lecturer, BBC, London, 1993. Publications: Joseph Conrad and the Fiction of Autobiography, 1966; Beginnings: Intention and Method, 1975; Orientalism, 1978; The Question of Palestine, 1979; Literature and Society, 1979; Covering Islam, 1981; The World, the Text and the Critic, 1983; After the Last Sky, 1986; Blaming the Victims, 1988; Muscial Elaborations, 1991; Culture and Imperialism, 1993; Representations of the Intellectual, 1994; The Politics of Dispossession, 1994; Ghazzah-Arihah: Salam Amriki, 1994; Out of Place: A Memoir, 1999; The End of the Peace Process: Oslo and After, 2000; Reflections on Exile, essays, 2001. Contributions to: Professional journals and other publications. Honours: Guggenheim Fellowship, 1972-73; Social Science Research Fellow, 1975; Lionel Trilling Awards, Columbia University, 1976, 1994; René Wellek Award, American Comparative Literature Association, 1985; Spinoza Prize, 1999; Morton Dauwen Zabel Award, 2000. Memberships: American Academy of Arts and Sciences; American Comparative Literature Association; Association of Arab-American University Graduates; Council on Foreign Relations; Modern Language Association; PEN, executive board, 1989-. Address: c/o Department of English, Columbia University, New York, NY 10027, USA.

**SAIHO P Alphonse,** b. 8 August 1952, Nimindogum Village, Papua New Guinea. m. 1 son, 5 daughters. Education: Matriculated, Military School; Graduated Correctional Officer; Certified in Counselling and Training for Hiv/Aids. Appointments: Counsellor; HIV/AIDS Trainer and Counsellor; Church work Charismatic Leader and Communion Minister; Diocesan Co-ordinator for Charismatic Renewal in Catholic Church; Chairman, Mediation Committee in Courts Systems; Chairman, RFL Judiciary Committee; OTML Non-work Related Committee; OTML Housing Committee; High School and Primary School Board, Disciplinary Committee; Managing Director and Owner, Nimindogum Spice Producers Ltd; Co-ordinator of Social Services Drug and Alcohol Awareness. Publications: Articles in newspapers. Honours: OBE, 2000; UNIYF Honours for Family and Social Welfare. Memberships: AACP, USA; SIPCC, Germany; Papua New Guinea Institute of Personnel Management; Papua New Guinea NAC TOT and Counsellor of Hiv/Aids. Address: PO Box 626, THBUBIG, Papua New Guinea. E-mail: asaiho@online.net.pg

**SAINSBURY Roger Norman,** b. 11 June 1940, Hitchin, Hertfordshire, England. Civil Engineer; Company Director. m. Susan Higgs. Education: MA, Engineering Science, Keble College Oxford, 1969; Member, 1966, Fellow, 1978, resigned 2001, Institution of Civil Engineers (ICE); Fellow, Royal Academy of Engineering, 1986. Appointments: Trainee Engineer, Rendel Palmer & Triton, Consulting Engineers, 1962-66; Engineer, various companies in the Mowlem Group, 1966-76; Director, Mowlem Building Ltd, 1976-82; Director, John Mowlem and Company plc, 1982-95; Responsible for development, construction and operations of London City Airport, Corporate Development and special projects particularly those in the field of private finance initiative; Director, Greater Manchester Metro Ltd, 1989-95; UK Detention Services Ltd, 1989-95; Member of Council, Vice-President, 1995-98, President, 1998-99, resigned 2001, Institution of Civil Engineers; Executive Board, 1995-98, Chairman Working Group, Housing Grants Construction and Regeneration Act, 1995-99, Chairman, Adjudication Board, 2000-2003, Construction Industry Council; Various Committees and Working Parties, Royal Academy of Engineering; Senior Industrial Adviser to the Director General, 1997-2000, Member Regulatory Policy Committee, 2000-2002, OFWAT; Member, Advisory Board, Department of Engineering, University of Oxford, 2000-2004. Publications include most recently: London City Airport (co-author), 1993; Transport Infrastructure-Mobilising Private Investment (working party member and lead author), 1993; Sustainability and Acceptability in Infrastructure Development (working party member and lead author), 1996; Presidential Address, Institution of Civil Engineers, 1998. Honours: George Stephenson Medal, 1972, Reed and Mallik Medal, 1984; Telford Premium, 1984, Parkman Medal, 1994, ICE; Construction News Man of the Year Award, 1979. Memberships: Stewardship Recorder, St Michael's Church, Highgate; Secretary, Abbeyfield North London Society Ltd; President, The Keble Association, 2000-2004. Address: 88 Dukes Avenue, London N10 2QA, England. E-mail: rsainsbury@blueyonder.co.uk

**SAINT Dora Jessie, (Miss Read),** b. 17 April 1913, Surrey, England. Novelist; Short Story and Children's Fiction Writer. Education: Homerton College, 1931-33. Publications: Village School, 1955; Village Diary, 1957; Storm in the Village, 1958; Hobby Horse Cottage, 1958; Thrush Green, 1959; Fresh From the Country, 1960; Winter in Thrush Green, 1961; Miss Clare Remembers, 1962; The Market Square, 1966; The Howards of Caxley, 1967; Country Cooking, 1969; News from Thrush Green, 1970; Tyler's Row, 1972; Christmas Mouse, 1973; Battles at Thrush Green, 1975; No Holly for Miss Quinn, 1976; Village Affairs, 1977; Return to Thrush Green, 1978; The White Robin, 1979; Village Centenary, 1980; Gossip From Thrush Green, 1981; A Fortunate Grandchild, 1982; Affairs at Thrush Green, 1983; Summer at Fairacre, 1984; At Home in Thrush Green, 1985; Time Remembered, 1986; The School at Thrush

Green, 1987; The World at Thrush Green, 1988; Mrs Pringle, 1989; Friends at Thrush Green, 1990; Changes at Fairacre, 1991; Celebrations at Thrush Green, 1992; Farewell to Fairacre, 1993; Tales From a Village School, 1994; The Year at Thrush Green, 1995; A Peaceful Retirement, 1996. Honour: Member of the Order of the British Empire, 1998. Membership: Society of Authors. Address: c/o Michael Joseph, Peugain, 80 Strand Books, London WC2 0RL England.

**SAINT LAURENT Yves (Henri Donat),** b. 1 August 1936, Oran, Algeria. Couturier. Appointments: With Christian Dior, 1954-57, sucessor to Christian Dior, 1957-60; Shareholder Société Yves Saint Laurent, 1962-; Consultant to Chinese government, 1987-; Announced retirement, 2002; Designer, costumes for ballets: Cyrano de Bergerac, 1959; Adage et Variations, Notre-Dame de Paris, 1965; Sheherezade, 1973; Delicate Balance, 1967; Films: The Pink Panther, 1962; Belle de Jour, 1967; La Chamade, 1968; La Sirène du Mississippi, 1969; L'Affaire Stavisky, 1974; Designer, stage sets and costumes for Les Chants de Maldoror, 1962; Spectacle Zizi Jeanmaire, 1961, 1963, 1968; Exhibitions: Metropolitan Museum of Art, NY, 1983; Beijing Museum of Fine Arts, 1985; Musée des Arts de la Mode, Paris, 1986; House of Painters of USSR, 1986; Hermitage Museum, Leningrad, 1987; Art Gallery of NSW, Sydney, 1987; Sezon Museum, Tokyo, 1990; Espace Mode Méditerranée, Marseilles, 1993. Publication: La Vilaine Lulu, 1967. Honours: International Award of Council of Fashion Designers of America, 1982; Best Fashion Designer Oscar, 1985; Chevalier Légion d'honneur. Address: 5 avenue Marceau, 75116 Paris, France.

**SAJIENĖ Valiulytė Antanina,** b. 28 February 1931, Pakalniškiai, Šiauliai District, Lithuania. Primary Education Teacher. m. Kazimieras Sajus, 2 daughters. Education: Primary Education Pedagogics and Methods, Telšiai Pedagogical School, 1953-55; Masters Degree, Special School Teacher and Speech Therapy, Šiauliai Pedagogical Institute, Faculty of Defectology, 1969-76. Appointments: Teacher, Mickiškė Primary School, 1951-52; Head, Patausalė Primary School, 1952-53; Head, Vaitkaičiai Primary School, 1955-69; Teacher, Šiauliai 5th Secondary School, 1969-91; Teacher-Administrator, Šiauliai Catholic Primary School, 1991-93; Primary Education Teacher, Šiauliai Didždvaris Gymnasium, 1993-2001; Lecturer in quality evaluation of primary education changes, The Centre of Pedagogues' Professional Development of the Republic of Lithuania; Lecturer, Šiauliai University In-Service Training Institute for raising teachers' qualifications; lecturer, Centre of School Development of the Republic of Lithuania. Publications: Co-author, Integrated Education and Self-education in First Grade, 1997; Created a system of criterion evaluation by ideographic principle of individual advance and 1st-2nd and 3rd –4th year pupils' Achievement Books applied to this system, 1998; Created first level (primary) daybook suitable for ideographic evaluation that is used currently in Lithuania as an official document, 1999; Prepared and published, Integrated Education and Self-education in the Second Grade, 2002; Gives consultations in periodicals. Honours: The Remembrance Medal of the International Festival of Songs and Dances, 1960; The Seal of Work Veteran, 1973; Title of Primary Education Teacher Supervisor, 1996; The 2nd Degree Medal of Grand Duke of Lithuania Gediminas by the President of Lithuania, 1997; Jubilee Medal of Lithuanian School 1397-1997, 1997; Teacher of the Year 1999 and awarded a National Premium; Title, Primary Education Teacher, Expert. Membership: Lithuanian Association of Primary Education Pedagogues. Address: Dariaus ir Girėno 14-68, Š iauliai, LT-78249, Lithuania. E-mail: seltinis@takas.lt

**SAKAI Masahiro,** b. 1 April 1959, Sumoto, Hyogo, Japan. Professor. m. Takami Shimokawa, 1 son, 1 daughter. Education: BS, 1981, MS, 1983, Miyasaki University; PhD, University of Tokyo. 1992. Appointments: Assistant Professor, 1986-92, Associate Professor, 1993-94, Kitasato University; Associate Professor, 1995-2003, Professor and Chair, 2004-, Miyasaki University. Publications: More than 150 articles in scientific journals including: Journal of Fish Diseases; Applied and Environmental Microbiology; Fish Pathology; Fish and Shellfish Immunology; Journal of Endocrinology; Vaccine; Gene; Developmental and Comparative Immunology; Molecular Immunology . Honours: Scientific Promoing Award, Japanese Society of Fish Pathology, 2004; Miyazaki Bunko Syou, Miyasaki Prefectural Government, 2004. Memberships: Japanese Society of Fish Pathology; Japanese Society of Fisheries Sciences; American Society for Microbiology. Address: University of Miyasaki, Gakuenkibanadi nishi, 1-1 Miyazaki City, Miyazaki 8892192, Japan. E-mail: m.sakai@cc.miyasaki-u.ac.jp

**SAKAKIBARA Kuniki,** b. 17 August, 1944, Nagoya, Japan. Professor. m. Kunie Matsumoto, 1 son, 1 daughter. Education: Master of Education, 1970, PhD, 2003, Nagoya University, Japan. Appointments: Sectional Chief, Nippon Recruit Centre Co Inc, Tokyo, 1976-83; Assistant Professor, 1983-88, Professor, 1988-91, Toyohashi Junior College; Professor, Aichi Shukutoku Junior College, 1991-96; Professor, Aichi Shukutoku University, Aichi Gun, 1996-. Publications: Author, Psychology of People and Organizations, 1999; The Process of Job Performance Skills Development among the Local Government Employees, 2004; Co-author: Organizational Psychology, 1988; Nagoya Towards the 21st Century, 1998; Handbook of Personnel Assessment, 2000. Memberships: Academy of Management; Japanese Association of Industrial and Organizational Psychology; Japanese Psychology Association; Japanese Academy of Human Resource Development. Address: 6-12-6 Oshizawadai Kasugai, Aichi Pref, 487-0005 Japan. E-mail: saki@asu.aasa.ac.jp

**SAKAMOTO Yoshikazu,** b. 16 September 1927, Los Angeles, California, USA. Political Scientist. m. Kikuko Ono, 2 daughters. Education: Hogakushi, Faculty of Law, University of Tokyo, 1951. Appointments: Associate Professor, Faculty of Law, 1954, Professor of International Politics, Faculty of Law, 1964-88, Professor Emeritus, 1988-, University of Tokyo; Professor, Meiji-Gakuin University, 1988-93; Senior Research Fellow, International Christian University, 1993-96. Publications: Editor: Asia: Militarization and Regional Conflict, 1988; Global Transformation, 1994; Author, The Age of Relativization, 1997; Nuclearism and Humanity, 2 volumes (editor), 1999; Selected Works, 6 Volumes, 2004-2005. Honours: Rockefeller Fellow, 1956-57; Eisenhower Fellow, 1964; Special Fellow, United Nations Institute for Research and Training; Mainichi National Book Award, 1976. Memberships: Secretary-General, International Peace Research Association, 1979-83; American Political Science Association; Japanese Political Science Association. Address: 8-29-19 Shakujii-machi, Nerimaku, Tokyo 177-0044, Japan.

**SALA PARCERISAS Robert,** b. 8 September 1949, Torà, Spain. Physician. Education: Student, University of Barcelona, 1966-75; Physician, 1976; Professional Degree, 1977; Master in Tropical Medicine, 1992, Medical Doctor, 1995, University of Barcelona. Appointments: Adjunct Physician, Residència Sanitària, Hospital Arnau de Vilanova, Lleida, 1976; Clinical Physician: FERS (Spain), Mbini, Guinea Ecuatorial, 1997; Médicus Mundi Asturias (Spain), Ntita, Burundi, 1994; Médicos sin Fronteras (Spain), N'Giva, Angola, 1992; Ministério da Saúde, Tete and Quelimane, Moçambique, 1982-84; JOSPICE (United Kingdom), Morazán, Honduras, 1978; Assistant, Unitat d'Eritropatologia (Eritropathology Unity), Hospital Clínic i Provincial of Barcelona, Spain, 2003-. Publications: Functional Aspects of Granulocytic Leukocytes, Mainly Neutrophils, Related With Effects of the Heroin (doctoral thesis), 1995; Oxygen-derived germicide metabolites and ultraviolet radiation in the neutrophilic leukocyte phagosome, 1998; Concomitant factors influencing a measles epidemic in Ondgiva, 1998; Annotation concerning the initial energy in the phagosome oxidative burst of the segmented neutrophil, 1999; A Perspective on the Oxidative Burst in the Phagosome of the Leukocyte and its Neoplastic Transformation, 2002. Honours: Scholar, Sociedad Española de Patología del Aparato Respiratorio, 1989-90. Address: Plaça del Pati, N° 5 2n 4a, 25750 Torà (Lleida), Spain. E-mail: jsala126@yahoo.com

**SALEEM Mohammad Abdul,** b. 1 July 1948, Hyderabad, Pakistan. Businessman. m. Merle Ann Saleem, 1 November 1979, 2 sons, 1 daughter. Education: Civil Engineering. Appointments: Managing Director, Mayfair Hotel, Dubai and Fujairah, United Arab Emirates; Planinng Engineer, Al Azam Ltd, Karachi, 1968-72; Tarmac Overseas Ltd, Muscat, Oman, 1973-78; Managing Partner, Abu Shabi Property Management, United Arab Emirates, 1978-87; Managing Director, Emirated Plaza Hotel, Abu Dhabi, 1987-; Managing Director, Al Hamra Plaza Resn, Abu Dhabi, 1987-; Managing Dir, Fujairah Intl Hotel, Fujairah, 1987-; Managing Director, Sparkle Laundry, Abu Dhabi, 1987-; Managing Director, Mascot Overseas, Isle of Man, 1987. Memberships: Business Community Abu Dhabi; Pakistan Engineers Club; Hotel Association. Address: PO Box 4604, Al Wadha Tower, Salam Street, Abu Dhabi, United Arab Emirates.

**SALIM Muhammad Khurram,** b. 23 June 1967, Dhaka, Bangladesh. m. Fateha Begum, 28 August 1994. Education: BA, English and European Studies, Phillips University, 1989; Diplomas in Journalism, London School of Journalism. Contributions to: Bangladesh Observer; Asian Times; Phillips University Publication; Buckingham University Publication. Address: 116 Ewhurst Road, Crofton Park, London SE4 1SD, England.

**SALINGER J(erome) D(avid),** b. 1 January 1919, New York, USA. Author. m. Claire Douglas, divorced, 1 son, 1 daughter. Education: Military college. Career: Travelled in Europe, 1937-38; Army service with 4th Infantry Division (Staff Sergeant), 1942-46. Publications include: Novels: The Catcher in the Rye, 1951; Franny and Zooey; Raise High the Roof Beam; Carpenter and Seymour - An Introduction, 1963; Stories: For Esme with Love and Squalor, 1953; Numerous stories, mostly in the New Yorker, 1948-; Hapworth 16, 1924, 1997. Address: c/o Harold Ober Associates Inc, 425 Madison Avenue, New York, NY 10017, USA.

**SALISBURY-JONES Raymond Arthur,** b. 31 July 1933, Camberley, England. Director of Music. Education: MA (Hons), Modern History, Christ Church, Oxford, 1953-56. Appointments: Executive, Rolls Royce Ltd/Rolls Royce Motors Ltd, 1956-75; Director, Rolls Royce Motors International, 1973-75; Chairman, Hambledon Vineyards Ltd, 1974-85; Managing Director, RSJ Aviation International Ltd, 1976-91; Non-executive Director Daniel Thwaites plc, 1974-98; Senior Consultant, Middle East Consultants Ltd, 1995-98; Consultant to mi2g Ltd (Internet Security Specialists), 1997-2000; Organist, St Mark's, Islington, 2002-. Honours: Rowe Piano Competition, 1948; Harford Lloyd Organ Prize, 1950; MA (Hons), Oxon. Memberships: Royal College of Organists. Address: The Charterhouse, Charterhouse Square, London EC1M 6AN, England. E-mail: rsj100@talk21.com

**SAMBROOK Richard Jeremy,** b. 24 April 1956, Canterbury, England. Journalist; Broadcasting Executive. m. Susan Jane Fisher, 1 son, 1 daughter. Education: BA (Hons) Reading University; MSc, Birkbeck College, London University. Appointments: Trainee Journalist, Thomson Regional Papers, 1977-80; BBC Radio News, 1980-84; BBC TV News, 1984-92; News Editor, 1992; Head of Newsgathering, 1996-2000; Deputy Director, BBC News, 2000-2001; Director, BBC News, 2001-2004; Director, World Service and Global News, 2004-. Honours: Fellow, RTS; Fellow, RSA. Address: BBC, Bush House, The Aldwych, London WC2B 4PM, England.

**SAMPRAS Pete,** b. 12 August 1971, Washington DC, USA. Tennis Player. m. Brigette Wilson, 1 son. Career: US Open Champion, 1990, 1993, 1995, 1996; Grand Slam Cup Winner, 1990; IBM/ATP Tour World Championship - Frankfurt Winner, 1991; Member, US Davis Cup Team, 1991, 1995; US Pro-Indoor Winner, 1992; Wimbledon Singles Champion, 1993, 1994, 1995, 1997, 1998, 1999, 2000; European Community Championships Winner, 1993, 1994; Ranked No 1, 1993; Winner, Australian Open, 1994; RCA Championships, 1996, ATP Tour World Championships, 1996, Australian Open, 1997; Winner, San José Open, 1997; Philadelphia Open, 1997; Cincinnati Open, 1997; Munich Open, 1997; Paris Open, 1997; Hanover Open, 1997; Advanta Championship, 1998; Winner of 63 WTA Tour singles titles and 2 doubles. Address: ATP Tour, 420 West 45th Street, New York, NY 10036, USA. Website: www.petesampras.com

**SAMRA Jorge José H,** b. 25 November 1920, Republic of Lebanon. Naturalised Argentinean. Mechanical and Electrical Engineer; Investigator. Education: Graduated as Mechanical and Electrical Engineer, La Plata National University, Argentina. Appointments: Positions in leading companies, more than 30 years, including Chief Engineer, Pilkington PLC subsidiary, 22 years; About 22 European and US visits regarding projects. Publications: Papers: Astronomical Contributions on the Solar System; Cosmic Rays Velocities Exceed Considerably the Speed of Light: Firm evidence of the Newtonian constancy of Length, Time and Mass. Honours: Best Graduate, High School (at the University entrance year); 1 of Best Graduates, La Plata National University; Letter of Congratulation for paper on Astronomical contributions to the solar system, National Research Council, Canada, 1992. Membership: COSPAR Associate. Address: Universidad Nacional de La Plata, Suipacha 1274, 1011 Buenos Aires, Argentina.

**SAMSONOV Vasily,** b. 24 January 1948, Krasnodar, USSR. Physicist; Educator. m. Marina Samsonova, 1 son, 2 daughters. Education: Engineer-Physicist, Moscow Physical Technology Institute, 1972; PhD, Central Aerohydrodynamic Institute, Moscow, 1980; DSc, International Geological Academy, Moscow, 2002. Appointments: Aerodynamic Engineer, 1972-82, Chief of Group, 1982-93, Vice-Head of Division, 1985-93, Central Aerohydrodynamics Institute, Moscow; Associate Professor, Pontificia Universidad Catolica del Peru, Lima, Peru, 1993-. Publications: Articles in scientific journals: Computational method for supersonic aircraft aerodynamics, 1978; New results of investigations in wind turbine aerodynamics, 1992. Honours: International Award for the best research of 2000, Union de Universidades de America Latinas, 2000; Honorary Visitant of CUSCO, 2000. Address: PUCP, Ingenienia Mechanica, Av. Universitaria 18, San Miguel, Lima – 32, Peru. E-mail: vsamson@pucp.edu.pe

**SANABRIA Juan-Ramon,** b. 31 August 1962, Bogota, Colombia. Transplant Surgeon. m. Monica Parra, 1 son, 1 daughter. Education: MD, MSc, General Surgery, Fellowship in

Solid Organ Transplantation and Hepatobiliary and Pancreatic Surgery, University of Toronto, Canada. Appointments: Clinical Associate Attending, Toronto General Hospital, 2000-2001; Assistant Professor of Surgery, Division of Transplantation, Medical College of Ohio, 2001-2003; Assistant Professor of Surgery, Division of Transplantation, University Hospitals Health Systems, Case Western Reserve University, Cleveland, Ohio, 2004-. Publications: 25 papers in professional medical journals as co-author include most recently: Innominate artery interposition graft simplifies the portal venous drainage method of pancreas transplantation, 1999; Early laparacopic cholecystectomy for acute cholecystitis: a safe procedure, 1999; Hepatic venous outflow occlusion from subcapsular hematoma: evidence for an intrahepatic compartment syndrome, 2002; 2 book chapters. Honours include: Samuel Lunenfield Research Scholarship, 1992; A W Harrison Resident Teaching Award, 1997; Counsellor at Large, The Toledo Surgical Society, 2004. Memberships include: Fellow, Royal College of Physicians and Surgeons of Canada; Fellow, American College of Surgeons; American Society of Transplant Surgeons; American Hepato Pancreatic and Biliary Association; International Society for Digestive Surgery; European Society for the Study of Liver Diseases. Address: 11100 Euclid Avenue, Lakeside Building, 7504, Division of Transplantation, Department of Surgery, University Hospitals of Cleveland, Cleveland OH 44106, USA. E-mail: juan.sanabria@uhhs.com

**SANCHEZ-VICARIO Arantxa,** b. 18 December 1971, Barcelona, Spain. Tennis Player. Career: Coached Juan Nunez; Winner, 1st professional title at Brussels, 1988; Winner, French Open Women's title, 1989, 1994, 1998; International Championships of Spain, 1989, 1990, Virginia Slims Tournaments, Newport, 1991, Washington, 1991; Winner, Canadian Open, 1992, Australian Open, 1992, 1993, US Open, 1994, named International Tennis Federation World Champion, 1994; Silver Medal, doubles, Bronze Medal, singles, Olympics, 1992; Silver Medal, singles, Bronze Medal, doubles, Olympics, 1996; Spanish Federal Cup team, 1986-98, 2000-01; winner of 14 Grand Slam titles, 96 WTA Tour titles and over 16 million dollars in prize money at retirement November 2002. Honours: Infiniti Commitment to Excellence Award, 1992; Tennis Magazine Comeback Player of the Year, 1998; Principe de Asturiasi Award, Spain, 1998; International Tennis Federation Award of Excellence, 2001. Memberships: Spanish Olympic Committee, 2001. Addresss: International Management Group, 1 Erieview Plaza, Suite 1300, Cleveland, OH 4414, USA.

**SANCTUARY Gerald P,** b. 22 November 1930, Bridport, Dorset, England. Solicitor. Divorced, 3 sons, 2 daughters. Education: Law Society's School of Law London, 1949-53; Royal Air Force, qualified as pilot on jets (Vampire Mark V), awarded Wings, 1955. Appointments: Assistant Solicitor, Sherrards, Kingston-on -Thames, 1955-57; Partner, Hasties Solicitors, Lincoln's Inn Fields, London, 1957-63; Field Secretary, National Marriage Guidance Council, 1963-65; National Secretary, National Marriage Guidance Council, 1965-68; Executive Director, Sex Information and Education Council of the United States (SIECUS), 1969-71; Secretary, Professional and Public Relations, The Law Society, 1971-78; Executive Director, International Bar Association, London, 1978-79; Legal Adviser and Senior HQ Co-ordinator for regional and Local Affairs, MENCAP (Royal Society for Mentally Handicapped Children and Adults), London, 1979-84; Secretary, NUJ Provident Fund, London, 1985-95; Retired, 1995. Publications: Marriage Under Stress, 1968; Divorce - and After, 1970; Before You See a Solicitor, 1973; After I'm Gone - What Will Happen to my Handicapped Child? 1984, second edition, 1991; The Romans in St Albans, The Monastery at St Albans, Tudor St

Albans, Fishpool Street St Albans, historical booklets, 1984, 1985, 1986; Shakespeare's Globe Theatre, 1992; Running a Marriage Guidance Council; Local Society Handbook; Editor, 12 titles in the series: It's Your Law, 1973-78; Numerous articles in professional journals and newspapers and magazines. Memberships: The Law Society; The Guild of Air Pilots and Air Navigators of the City of London, Past Honorary Treasurer; The Institute of Public Relations. Address: 99 Beechwood Avenue, St Albans, Hertfordshire AL1 4XU, England.

**SANDER Louis Wilson,** b. 31 July 1918, San Francisco, California, USA. Professor of Psychiatry. m. Betty Thorpe, 2 sons, 1 daughter. Education: AB, 1939, MD, Medical School, 1942, University of California; Intern, University of California Hospital, 1942-43. Appointments: 2nd Lieutenant to Major, USAAF Medical Corps, 1943-46; Resident in Psychiatry to Professor of Psychiatry, School of Medicine, 1947-68, Principal Investigator, Longitudinal Study in Early Personality Development, 1963-87, Professor of Psychiatry, School of Medicine, 1968-78, Boston University; Professor of Psychiatry, Senior Scholar, School of Medicine, University of Colorado, 1978-87. Publications: Contributor, over 50 articles, book chapters; reviews to professional publications, 1962-2002. Honours: Recipient, Research Career Development Award, US Public Health Service, 1963-68; Research Scientist Awards, US Public Health Service, 1968-78; Research Grantee, US Public Health Service, March of Dimes, W Grant Foundation; MacArthur Foundation, Spencer Foundation, National Council on Alcoholism; other organisations; Honorary Membership Award, American Psychoanalytic Association, 2001. Memberships: American Medical Association; American Psychiatric Association; American College of Psychoanalysts; Boston Psychoanalytic Society; American Association for the Advancement of Science; Society for Research in Child Development; American Academy of Child Psychiatry; World Association for Infant Mental Health; Boston Change Process Study Group, 1995-; San Francisco Psychoanalytic Society and Institute. Address: 2525 Madrona Ave, St Helena, CA 94574-2300, USA.

**SANDERS Jeremy Keith Morris,** b. 3 May 1948, London, England. Chemist. m. Louise Sanders, 1 son, 1 daughter. Education: BSc, Chemistry, Imperial College, London; PhD, Chemistry, 1972, MA, 1974, ScD, 2001, University of Cambridge; FRSC, C Chem, 1978. Appointments: Research Associate, Pharmacology, Stanford University, USA, 1972-73; Demonstrator, then Lecturer, then Reader in Chemistry, 1973-96, Professor of Chemistry, 1996-, Head, Department of Chemistry, 2000-, University of Cambridge; Chair, Chemistry sub-panel, 2008 UK Research Assessment Exercise, 2004-. Publications: Book: Modern NMR Spectroscopy (with B K Hunter), 1987, 1992; Over 250 research papers on aspects of organic, inorganic and biological chemistry. Honours: Meldola Medal, Royal Institute of Chemistry, 1975; Hickinbottom Award, Royal Society of Chemistry, 1981; Pfizer Academic Award for work on nuclear Overhauser effect, 1984; Pfizer Academic Award for work on in vivo NMR, 1988; Josef Loschmidt Prize, Royal Society of Chemistry, 1994; Elected FRS, 1995; Elected FRSA, 1997; Pedler Medal and Prize, Royal Society of Chemistry, 1996; Visiting Fellow, Japan Society for the Promotion of Science, 2002; Izatt-Christensen Award in Macrocyclic Chemistry, USA, 2003. Membership: The Athenaeum. Address: University Chemical Laboratory, Lensfield Road, Cambridge CB2 1EW, England. E-mail: jkms@cam.ac.uk Website: www-sanders.ch.cam.ac.uk/

**SANDERS Roy,** b. 20 August 1937, England. Honorary Professor in Plastic Surgery; Honorary Consultant Plastic

Surgeon. Education: BSc Honours, Anatomy, 1959, MB, BS, 1962, University of London; FRCS England, 1967. Appointments: Gunner, 1957-62, Regimental Medical Officer, 1963-75; Member, Company of Pikemen & Musketeers, Honourable Artillery Company, 1981-, Honourable Artillery Company; Senior Lecturer, Institute of Orthopaedics, University of London, 1973-76; Honorary Consultant and Director, Regional Burns Centre, 1973-76, Trustee, Mount Vernon Hospital Reconstructive Plastic Surgery Trust, 1973-97, Member, Executive Board (or predecessor), 1986-98, Clinical Director and Consultant Plastic Surgeon, 1986-98, Trustee, Restoration and Appearance Function Trust (RAFT) 1989-92, Advisor to the Board of Trustees of RAFT, 1992-98, Director of RAFT Institute and Consultant Plastic Surgeon, 1998-2004, Currently Honorary Consultant Plastic Surgeon, Mount Vernon Hospital; Honorary Professor in Plastic Surgery, University College, London; Officer Commanding The Light Cavalry, Honourable Artillery Company, 1990-2004; Founder and Convenor of the European Conference of Scientists and Plastic Surgeons, 1997-. Publications: Numerous articles in medical journals. Memberships: Royal College of Surgeons of England; British Association of Plastic Surgeons; Academy of Experts; Vice-president, Honourable Artillery Company, 2004-2006. Address: The Consulting Suite, 82 Portland Place, London W1B 1NS, England. E-mail: roy.sanders@btclick.com

**SANDERSON Teresa (Tessa) Ione,** b. 14 March 1956. Athlete. Career: Represented Britain in javelin, 1974-; Commonwealth Games Gold Medallist, 1978, 1986, 1990; European Championship Gold Medallist, 1978; Olympic Games Gold Medallist, Olympic Record, 1984; World Cup Gold Medallist, 1992; Other achievements: Fourth Place at Barcelona Olympics, 1992; Several records including: UK Javelin record, 1976; Presenter, Sky News Sports, 1989-92; Involvement with various charities. Publications: My Life in Athletics, 1985. Honours: British Athletics Writers Association Female Athlete of the Year, 1977, 1978, 1984; Honorary BSc University of Birmingham; OBE; MBE. Memberships: Board member, English Sports Council, 1998-. Address: c/o Derek Evans, 68 Meadowbank Road, Kingsbury, London NW9, England. E-mail: tessa@tprmplus.freeserve.co.uk

**SANDFORD John Cyril (Lord),** b. 22 December 1920, Goring-on-Thames, Oxfordshire, England. Peer. m. Catharine Mary Hunt, 2 sons, 2 daughters. Education: Royal Naval College, Dartmouth, 1939; Westcott House Theological College, Cambridge, 1956. Appointments: Royal Navy: Midshipman, 1940, Eastern Mediterranean, 1940-41, North African and Sicily invasions, 1944, Signal Officer, 1945, House Officer, Royal Naval College, Dartmouth, 1947, Flag Lieutenant to Admiral Sir Charles Lambe, Flag Officer Commanding 3 Aircraft Squadron, 1949, Flag Officer Air (Home), 1951, on staff of Admiral Sir Charles Lambe, Commander-in-Chief Far East Station, 1953, Commander, Communications, SE Asia, 1953, commander in HMS Tyne (Home Fleet Flagship), 1954-56, retired from Navy 1956; Ordained 1958, Curate Parish of St Nicholas Harpenden, 1958-63; Member, House of Lords, 1959-88; Chairman, Hertfordshire County Council Social Service, 1966-69; Executive Chaplain to Bishop of St Albans, Mission and Ecumenical Affairs, 1965-68; Chairman, Board of Church Army, 1969-70; Opposition Whip, House of Lords, 1966-70; Parliamentary Under Secretary of State, Department of the Environment, 1970-73; Department of Education and Science, 1973-74; Member, Select Committee on European Community Directive, 1978-88; Member, Board of Ecclesiastical Insurance Office, 1978-89; Church Commissioner, Chairman, Redundant Churches, 1982-89; Chairman, Association of District Councils; Chairman, South East Regional Planning Council, 1981-89;

Suffered Stroke in 1988. Honours: Distinguished Service Cross for bravery in the Mediterranean, 1942; Honorary Fellow, Institute of Landscape Architects, 1971. Memberships: Conservative Party; Association of Conservative Peers; Friends of the Lake District; President, Camping and Caravan Club; Vikings Rowing Club; Offa's Dyke Association; Ski Club of Great Britain. Address: 27 Ashley Gardens, Ambrosden Avenue, London SW1P 1QD, England.

**SANDLER Adam,** b. 9 September 1966, Brooklyn, New York, USA. Actor; Screenwriter. m. Jackie Titone, 2003. Education: New York University. Career: Actor, films include: Shakes the Clown; Coneheads; Mixed Nuts; Airheads; Billy Madison; Happy Gilmore; Bullet Proof; Guy Gets Kid, 1998; The Wedding Singer, 1998; The Water Boy, 1998; Big Daddy, 1999; Little Nicky, 2000; Punch-Drunk Love, 2002; Mr Deeds, 2002; Anger Management, 2003; Fifty First Dates, 2004; Actor, writer, Saturday Night Live; TV appearances include: Saturday Night Live Mother's Day Special, 1992; MTV Music Video Awards, 1994; Saturday Night Live Presents President Bill Clinton's All-Time Favourites, 1994; 37th Annual Grammy Awards, 1995; ESPY Awards, 1996. Publications: Co-writer: Billy Madison; Happy Gilmore; The Water Boy; Recordings: Album: Stan and Judy's Kid; They're All Gonna Laugh at You! 1993. Honours: Peoples Choice Award, 2000. Address: c/o Ballstein-Grey, 9150 Wilshire Boulevard, Suite 350, Beverly Hills, CA 90212, USA.

**SANFORD Geraldine A Jones,** b. 1 August 1928, Sioux Falls, South Dakota, USA. Poet; Teacher; Editorial Assistant. m. Dayton M Sanford, 28 August 1948, deceased 1993, 4 sons, 1 daughter. Education: BA, English and Psychology, Augustana College, 1971; MA, English, University of South Dakota. Appointments: Editorial Assistant, South Dakota Review, 1973-99, Editor Yearly Issue, 1975-99; Instructor and Lecturer in English, University of South Dakota, 1978, 1979; Instructor, University of Minnesota, 1979-82; Extension Instructor, University of South Dakota, 1991. Publication: Unverified Sightings From Dakota East. Contributions to: Real Dakota; Vermillion Literary Project; Longneck; Mankato Poetry Review; Prairie Winds; South Dakota Magazine; Yearnings; Poets Portfolio; Spirits from Clay; South Dakota Review; North Country; Rocky Mountain Creative Arts Journal; North Country Anvil; Aspect; Sunday Clothes. Honours: Graduate Student Poetry Award, University of South Dakota, 1976; Gladys Haase Poetry Prize, 1977. Address: 306 West 36th Street, Apt 22, Sioux Falls, SD 57105, USA.

**SANTER Jacques,** b. 18 May 1937, Wasserbilig. Politician. m. Danièle Binot, 2 sons. Education: Athenée de Luxembourg; University of Paris; University of Strasbourg; Inst d'Etudes Politiques, Paris. Appointments: Advocate, Luxembourg Court of Appeal, 1961-65; Attaché, Officer of Minister of Labour and Social Security, 1963-65; Govt attaché, 1965-66; Parliament Secretary Parti Chrétien-Social, 1966-72, Secretary-General, 1972-74, President, 1974-82; Secretary of State for Cultural and Social Affairs, 1972-74; Member, Chamber of Deputies, 1974-79; Member, European Parliament, 1975-79, VP, 1975-77; Municipal Magistrate, City of Luxembourg, 1976-79; Minister of Finance of Labour and of Social Security, 1979-84; Prime Minister, Minister of State and Minister of Finance, 1984-89; Prime Minister, Minister of State, of Cultural Affairs and the Treasury and Financial Affairs, 1989-94; President, European Committee, 1994-99. Honour: Hon LLD (Wales), 1998. Address: 69 rue J-P Huberty, 1742 Luxembourg.

**SANTILLÁN ALDANA Julio Francisco,** b. 18 November 1972, Peru. Librarian. Education: Librarianship and Information Science, San Marcos University; Technical Education:

Programmes and Languages for Design and Development Web: Dreamweaver, Fireworks, Flash, PHP Nuke; Programmes for Information Units: WinIsis, GenIsis, WWWIsis. Appointments: Library Assistant, Library of Facultad de Letras, San Marcos University, 1995; Library Assistant, Central Library, Ricardo Palma University, 1996; Library Assistant, Library of Facultad de Derecho, San Marcos University, 1997; Adviser, Guatemala Library, Embassy of Guatemala in Peru, 1997; Reference Librarian, National Library of Peru, 1998-99; Technical Consultant, Care Peru, 2001-2002; Technical Consultant, Legal Library, Banco Continental (BBVA Bank), 2002; Librarian, Documentation Centre, Instituto Bartolemé de las Casas, 2003-; Librarianship workshops: Web Design for Libraries, National Library of Peru, 2001-2002; Search strategies and information recovery, National Library of Peru, 2001-2002; Editor, Biblios: Electronic Journal of Information Sciences; Co-ordinator, Theological and Philosophical Information Network; Editor (for Peru) E-prints in Library and Information Science. Publications: Articles in professional journals: Apuntes para la historia de la Biblioteca Central de la Universidad de San Marcos, 1999; Legislación bibliotecaria, 2000; Las referencias bibliográficas de recursos electrónicos y sus partes, 2000. Honour: Grantee, IFLA/ALP, 2004. Membership: Collaborator, Associación Hispana de Documentalistas en Internet. Address: Calle Andrés Alco 159, Comas, Lima 7, Peru. E-mail:santillan@peru.com

**SANTOS Nunos C**, b. 17 July 1972, Lisbon, Portugal. Biochemist; Researcher; Professor. m. Elisabete Santos, 1 son. Education: Degree in Biochemistry, 1995; PhD, Biochemistry, 1999, University of Lisbon. Appointments: Researcher, Technical University of Lisbon, 1994-99; Teaching Assistant, 1999-2000, Assistant Professor, 2000-, University of Lisbon (Lisbon Medical School). Publications: Author of more than 30 scientific articles and book chapters on molecular biophysics and biomembranes. Honour: Calouste Gulbenkian Foundation Award, 2001; Jose Luis Champalimaud Award (Basic Sciences, ex-aequo), 2004. Membership: Biophysical Society, USA. Address: Instituto de Biopatologia Quimica, Faculdade de Medicina de Lisboa, Av Prof Egas Moniz, 1649-028 Lisbon, Portugal. E-mail: nsantos@fm.ul.pt

**SARAMAGO José**, b. 16 November 1922, Azinhaga, Portugal. Author; Poet; Dramatist. Education: Principally self-educated. Publications: Fiction: Manual de Pintura e Caligrafia, 1977, English translation as Manual of Painting and Calligraphy, 1994; Objecto Quase (short stories), 1978, English translation as Quasi Object, 1995; Levantado do Chao (Raised from the Ground), 1980; Memorial do Convento, 1982, English translation as Baltasar and Blimunda, 1987; A Jangada de Pedra, 1986, English translation as The Stone Raft, 1994; O Ano da Morte de Ricardo Reis, 1984, English translation as The Year of the Death of Ricardo Reis, 1991; Historia do Cerco de Lisboa (The History of the Siege of Lisbon), 1989; O Evangelho segundo Jesus Cristo, 1991, English translation as The Gospel According to Jesus Christ, 1994; Ensaio Sobre A Cegueira, 1996, English translation as Blindness; All the Names, 2000. Other: Poems, plays, diaries, etc. Contributions to: Various publications. Honours: Several literary awards and prizes, including the Nobel Prize for Literature, 1998. Address: c/o Harcourt Brace & Co, 6277 Sea Harbor Drive, Orlando, FL 32887, USA.

**SARANDON Susan Abigail**, b. 4 October 1946, New York, USA. Actress. m. Chris Sarandon, divorced, 1 daughter, 1 daughter with Franco Amurri, 2 sons with Tim Robbins. Education: Catholic University of America. Career: Stage appearances include: A Coupla of White Chicks Sittin' Around Talkin'; An Evening with Richard Nixon; A Stroll in the Air; Albert's Bridge; Private Ear, Public Eye; Extremities; numerous

TV appearances; Actor, films include: Joe, 1970; Lady Liberty, 1971; The Rocky Horror Picture Show, 1974; Lovin' Molly, 1974; The Great Waldo Pepper, 1975; The Front Page, 1976; Dragon Fly, 1976; Walk Away Madden; The Other Side of Midnight, 1977; The Last of the Cowboys, 1977; Pretty Baby, 1978; King of the Gypsies, 1978; Loving Couples, 1980; Atlantic City, 1981; Tempest, 1982; The Hunger, 1983; Buddy System, 1984; Compromising Positions, 1985; The Witches of Eastwick, 1987; Bull Durham, 1988; Sweet Hearts Dance, 1988; Married to the Mob; A Dry White Season, 1989; The January Man, 1989; White Palace; Thelma and Louise, 1991; Light Sleeper, 1991; Lorenzo's Oil; The Client; Little Women, 1995; Safe Passage, 1995; Dead Man Walking, 1996; James and the Giant Peach, 1996; Illuminate, 1998; Twilight, 1998; Stepmom, 1999; Anywhere But Here, 1999; Cradle Will Rock, 1999; Rugrats in Paris, 2000; Joe Gould's Secret, 2000; Cats and Dogs, 2001; Igby Goes Down, 2002; The Banger Sisters, 2003. Honour: Academy Award for Best Actress, 1996. Address: c/o ICM, Martha Luttrell, 8942 Wilshire Boulevard, Beverly Hills, CA 90211, USA.

**SARGENT John Richard**, b. 22 March 1925, Birmingham, England. Economist. m. Hester, deceased 2004, 1 son, 2 daughters. Education: BA, First Class, Christ Church, Oxford, 1948. Appointments: Fellow and Lecturer in Economics, Worcester College, Oxford, 1951-62; Economic Consultant, H M Treasury, 1963-65; Professor of Economics, Founder Member of Department of Economics, 1965-73, Pro-Vice-Chancellor, 1970-72, University of Warwick; Group Economic Advisor, Midland Bank, 1974-84; Houblon-Norman Research Fellow, Bank of England. Publications: Numerous articles in economic journals include most recently: Roads to Full Employment, 1995; Towards a New Economy? Recent Inflation and Unemployment in the UK, 2002; Book, British Transport Policy, 1958. Honours: Rockefeller Fellow, USA, 1959-60; Honorary Professor of Economics, University of Warwick, 1974-81; Visiting Professor, London School of Economics, 1981-82. Memberships: Reform Club, 1965-; Member of Council, Royal Economic Society, 1969-74; Member, Doctors and Dentists Pay Review Body, 1972-75; Member, Armed Forces Pay Review Body, 1972-85; Member, Economic and Social Research Council, 1980-85. Address: 38 The Leys, Chipping Norton, Oxfordshire OX7 5HH, England.

**SASSOON Vidal**, b. 17 January 1928, London, England. Hair Stylist. m. divorced 1980, 2 sons, 2 daughters. Education: New York University. Career: Served with Palmach Israeli Army; Creator, hairdressing style based on Bahaus and geometric forms; Founder, Chairman, Vidal Sassoon Inc; President, Vidal Sassoon Foundation; Founder, Vidal Sassoon Centre for the Study of Anti-Semitism and Related Bigotries at Hebrew University, Jerusalem. Honours: Awards include: French Ministry of Culture Award; Award for services rendered, Harvard Business School; Intercoiffure Award, Cartier, London, 1978; Fellow, Hair Artists International.

**SATHULURI Ramachandra Rao**, b. 13 May 1969, Swarna, Andhra Pradesh, India. Postdoctoral Research Associate. m. Visali Sathuluri. Education: BSc, Chemistry, Andhra Pradesh, India, 1986-89; MSc, Biochemistry, Andhra Pradesh, India, 1990-92; PhD, Biochemistry, Central Food Technology Research Institute, Mysore, India, 1992-98; Computer Diploma in FORTRAN, Andhra Pradesh, India, 1997-97. Appointments: Junior Research Fellow, CSIR, India, 1992-95; Senior Research Fellow, 1995-98, Research Associate, 1998-99, CFTRI (CSIR), India; Monbukagakusho Post Doctoral Fellow, 1999-2001, Japan Society for the Promotion of Science Postdoctoral Fellow, 2001-2003, Monbukagakusho Postdoctoral Research Fellow,

2003-, Japan Advanced Institute of Science and Technology, Japan. Publications: 28 research publications in peer reviewed international journals; 9 patents filed and obtained, India and Japan; 3 chapters in text books; 2 popular articles in scientific magazines. Honours include: JSPS Fellowship; Monbukagakusho Fellowships; Young Scientist of the Year Award, AFST, India, 2001; Listed in Who's Who publications and biographical dictionaries. Memberships: Japan Society for Bioscience, Biotechnology and Agrochemistry; Society for Bioscience and Engineering, Japan; Japan Chemical Society; Phytochemical Society of Europe, 1996-99. Address: Japan Advanced Institute of Science and Technology, 1-1, Asahidai, Nomi City, Ishikawa 923-1292, Japan. E-mail: srrao@jaist.ac.jp

**SATO Kazuhiko,** b. 14 September 1959, Natori, Japan. Assistant Professor. Education: BA, Tohoku Gakuin University, 1982; MA, English Linguistics, University of Northern Iowa, 1991. Appointments: Teacher, Tohoku Gakuin Junior and Senior High School, Sendai, Japan, 1982-89; Instructor, 1994-99, Assistant Professor, 1999-, Miyagi National College of Technology, Natori, Japan. Publications: Several articles and research reports. Memberships: Teachers of English to Speakers of Other Languages; Linguistic Society of America; Linguistic Association of Great Britain; Cognitive Science Society. Address: 9-8 Kotobukiyama, Shiroishi, Miyagi 989-0241, Japan.

**SATO Kunitomo,** b. 19 August 1954, Osaka, Japan. Medical Doctor. Education: Graduate, Medical Department, National University of Osaka, 1978; Doctor of Health and Sport, Doctor of Industry, Certificate of Lifetime Education, Japan Medical Society; Approved doctor to handicapped people, heart, kidneys and limbs; Specialist of Internal Medicine approved by the Japanese Internal Medical Society. Appointments: Cardiovascular Division of the Institute of Internal Medicine, National Osaka University Hospital, 1978-; Chief, Sakurabashi-Watanabe Hospital, 1979-; Head, Cardiovascular division of both the North-Osaka Hospital and General Kanoh Hospital, 1980-; Chairman, President, General Hospital Centre, 1986-; President, Trustee, New Miyajima Hospital; Main Doctor of Oono town; Cardiovascular Specialist, Japanese Circulation Society; President, Cardiac Transplantation Centre of Kyushu; Councillor, WSTSC-JC; Councillor Member (Clinical Cardiology, Cardiac Surgery and Anaesthesia, High Blood Pressure Group); Premium Professional Member of AHA/ASA (American Heart Association, American Stroke Association); Active Member, Center's Kids' Non-Smoking Movement; Representative of Rugby Football in Japan, 18-42 years; Professional scuba diver; Professional tennis player; Professional in martial arts (Judo, Karate, Aikido – all black belts). Publications: Over 500 medical articles including: Clinical Significance of Human Plasma ANP, BNP measurements – Current and Future prospectives; Real Analysis of AMI ECGs; ECG's Series; All about Arhythmias; ES-cells: Current Topics and Future Prospectives, 2005; What decides the prognosis of ALC patients, 2005; Numerous books including: Sudden Death Occurs to People Who are in the Prime of Life!; Your Life Depends on the Selection of a Cardiac Doctor; The Ultimate Strategies for The Bland-White-Garland Syndrome; Histories of Cardiac Surgeons & My Ultimate Therapies, 2004; For Cancer, Heart Disease Patients and Families in End-Stage: The Ultimate & the 3rd Epoch-Making Medicines & The Most Modern Strategies of all Medical Fields, 2005; Newspaper columnist on arts (jazz and pictures), Peace, welfare, sports and Alzheimer's Disease. Honours: Distinguished Service Medal, 1998; Companion of Honour, 2001; Deputy Director General, IBC, 2001; Founder, The Scientific Faculty, 2001-02; Presidential Seal of Honor, 2001; Lifetime Achievement Award,

2002; Deputy Director General and Vice Consul to the IBC, 2002; International Honour Society, 2002; Deputy Governor, ABI, 2002; Key of Success as a Notable Author; World Citizen of the Year, ABI, 2002; Life Senator, WNC; Leading Intellectuals of the World, 2003; World Peace and Diplomacy Forum, IBC, 2003; Man of the Year, ABI, 2002-05. Listed in: 2000 Outstanding Intellectuals of the 21st Century, IBC, 2003; Who's Who in the 21st Century, IBC, 2003; 500 Founders of the 21st Century, IBC, 2001; One Thousand Great Asians of the 21st Century, IBC, 2002; The Lifetime of Achievement 100, IBC, 2004; International Order of Merit, 2004; Deputy Director General Inner Circle, IBC, 2004; Man of Achievement, ABI, 2005. Memberships: Japan Medical Society; Japan Circulation Society; Society of CV MRI (SCMR), Paris, France; American Heart Association; American Stroke Association; World Society of Cardio-Thoracic Surgeons - Japanese chapter; Pan-Pacific Surgical Association - Japanese chapter; Japanese Heart Rehabilitation Society; Japanese International Medical Society; Order of International Fellowship, IBC, 2003; Japanese Padry and ECG Society; Japanese Holter ECG Society; Governor, Chancellor, Japanese Intra-Hp Infection Society; Japanese Intensive Care Society; and others. Address: 505 1-6 3-Chome, Higashi-Tada, Kawanishi-City, Hyogo-Pref, 666-0122, Japan.

**SATPATHY Sashi,** b. 1 March 1956, Berhampur, India. Professor of Physics. m. Namita Satpathy, 2 sons, 1 daughter. Education: MSc, 1977; PhD, 1982. Appointments: Scientific Staff Member, Max-Planck Institute, Germany, 1982-86; Research Associate, Xerox, Palto Alto, California, 1986-87; Assistant Professor, 1987-93, Associate Professor, 1993-98; Professor, 1999-, University of Missouri. Publications: Over 75 papers in professional journals. Fellow of the American Physical Society. Address: University of Missouri, Department of Physics, Columbia, MO 65211, USA.

**SATSIOS Kostas,** b. 10 May 1971, Serres, Greece. Electrical Engineer. m. Maria Tsinari, 2 sons. Education: Diploma of Electrical Engineer, 1994, PhD, Electrical Engineering, 1999. Appointments: General Manager, NRG-ORION (An energy saving company); Consultant to Holy and Great Monastery of Vatopaidi, Mouth Athos. Publications: 17 articles in scientific journals and papers presented at international refereed conferences as co-author include most recently: The Influence of Nonhomogeneous Earth on the Inductive Interference Caused to Telecommunication Cables by Nearby AC Electric Traction Lines, 2000; A fuzzy logic system for calculation of the interference of overhead transmission lines on buried pipelines, 2001; Combined fuzzy logic and genetic algorithm techniques – application to an electromagnetic field, 2002. Honours: Listed in Who's Who publications and biographical dictionaries. Memberships: IEEE; Power Engineering Society; Magnetics Society. Address: Thomas Matopoulos S.A., NRG-ORION, Gavriilidi 5, 546 55 Thessaloniki, Greece. E-mail: drsatsios@nrg-orion.gr

**SATUBALDINA Zhannat Sagandykovna,** b. 5 February 1961, Almaty City, Kazakhstan. Company Vice-President. 1 son, 1 daughter. Education: Graduate, Almaty Institute of National Economy, 1982; Doctor of Economic Science, Moscow State University "Lomonosov", 1987; Management of Assets, Financial Institute of New York. Appointments: Laboratory Assistant, Almaty Research Institute of Economy, 1981-82; Junior Scholar, Automation Planning and Structures Improvement Processes, Government of Kazakhstan Scientific Research Institute, 1982-93;, Postgraduate, 1983-85, Junior Scholar, 1985-86, Economics Faculty, Moscow State University; Teacher, Subfaculty of Accountancy and Economic Analysis, Almaty Institute of State Economy, 1987-93; Head,

Deposits Section, Commercial Bank "Kazmetallbank", 1993-94; First Deputy Director, Investment and Privatisation Fund "Metallinvest", 1995-99; Head of Department of Licensing and Control, 1999-2000, Executive Director of Commission, 2000-2001, National Commission on Bonds of the Republic of Kazakhstan; Department of Regulation of the Securities Market, National Bank of the Republic of Kazakhstan, 2001-2002; Chief Accountant, 2002-2003, Vice-President, National Company "Kazakhstan Temir Zholy", 2003-. Membership: Corresponding Member, International Academy of Economy. Address: Kazakhstan Temir Zholy, 98 Pobeda Avenue, Asatna 473000, Kazakhstan.

**SATYAMURTI Carole,** b. 13 August 1939, Bromley, Kent, England. Poet; Writer; Lecturer. Education: BA, Honours, London University, 1960; Diploma in Social Work, University of Birmingham, 1965; MA, University of Illinois, 1967; PhD, University of London, 1979. Appointments: Lecturer, Principal Lecturer, University of East London, 1968-. Publications: Occupational Survival, 1981; Broken Moon (poems), 1987; Changing the Subject (poems), 1990; Striking Distance (poems), 1994; Selected Poems, 1998; Love and Variations (poems), 2000; Stitching the Dark: New and Selected Poems, 2005. Honours: 1st Prize, National Poetry Competition, 1986; Arts Council of Great Britain Writers Award, 1988; Cholmondeley Award, 2000. Address: 15 Gladwell Road, London N8 9AA, England.

**SAUNDERS Ann Loreille, (Ann Cox-Johnson),** b. 23 May 1930, London, England. Historian. m. Bruce Kemp Saunders, 4 June 1960, 1 son, 1 daughter. Education: Plumptre Scholar, Queen's College, London, 1946-48; BA Honours, University College, London, 1951; PhD, Leicester University, 1965. Appointments: Deputy Librarian, Lambeth palace, 1952-55; Archivist, Marylebone Public Library, London, 1956-63; Honorary Editor, Costume Society, 1967-; London Topographical Society, 1975-. Publications: London, City and Westminster, 1975; Art and Architecture of London, 1984, St Martin-in-the-Fields, 1989; The Royal Exchange, monograph, 1991; The Royal Exchange, editor and co-author, 1997. Contributions to: Magazines. Honours: Prize for Best Specialist Guide Book of the Year, British Tourist Board, 1984; Fellow, University College, London, 1992; MBE, 2002. Memberships: Society of Antiquaries, Fellow; Costume Society; London Topographical Society. Address: 3 Meadway Gate, London NW11 7LA, England.

**SAUNDERS Sally Love,** b. 15 January 1940, Bryn Mawr, Pennsylvania, USA. Poet; Poetry Therapist; Lecturer; Freelance Writer. Education: BS, George Williams College, Downers Grove, IL, 1965; Poetry Writing Course, The New School, 1968-69; Several other courses. Appointments: Poetry Therapist, Institute of Pennsylvania Hospital, Philadelphia, University of Louisville, Kentucky; Lectures, teaching at schools and other venues; Appearances on TV and radio; Numerous poetry writing workshops; Poetry readings. Publications: Past the Near Meadows, 1961; Pauses, 1978; Fresh Bread, 1982; Random Thoughts, 1992; Patchwork Quilt, 1993; Quiet Thoughts and Gentle Feelings, 1996; Word Pictures, 1998. Contributions to: Anthologies and journals. Honours: Honourable Mention, New American Poetry Contest, 1988; Silver Poet Award, World of Poetry, 1989; Nutmegger Book Award. Memberships: National Writers Club; Press Club of San Francisco; Poets and Writers Guild; Association for Poetry Therapy; Poetry Society of America; Ina Coolbirth Circle; Pen and Pencil Club, Philadelphia; Academy of American Poets; American Poetry Center. Address: 609 Rose Hill Road, Broomall, PA 19008, USA.

**SAVA Vasyl,** b. 16 May 1951, Zelene, Ukraine. Research Scientist. m. Alla Krivich, 2 sons. Education: BS, Odessa State University of Ecology, Ukraine, 1973; PhD, Institute of Bio-organic Chemistry, Academy of Sciences of USSR, Minsk, 1985. Appointment: Assistant Professor, Department of Neurology, University of South Florida, Tampa, Florida, USA. Publications: 78 research publications including 20 patents; As co-author: Rubratoxin-B elicits anti-oxidative and DNA repair responses in Mouse Brain, 2004; Effects of melanin and manganese in DNA damage and repair in PC12-derived neurons, 2004. Honours: Rank of Senior Scientist, Higher Certifying Board of Ukraine; International Research Programme INTAS. Memberships: International Society for Free Radical Biology and Medicine; Society for Neuroscience, USA; American Society for Neurochemistry. Address: 27614 Sky Lake Circle, Wesley Chapel, FL 33453, USA. E-mail: vsava@hsc.usf.edu

**SAVKOVIC-STEVANOVIC Jelenka,** 21 January 1946, Markovica, Serbia. Professor of Chemical Engineering. m. Miroljub Stevanovic. Education: BS, Degree,1970; MSc, Degree, 1975, Department of Chemical Engineering, University of Belgrade; PhD, Degree, Institut für Thermodynamik und Anlegentechnik, Technische Universität, West Berlin and Department of Chemical Engineering, University of Belgrade, 1981. Appointments: Researcher, Department of Chemical Catalysis, Institute for Chemical Technology and Metallurgy, Belgrade, 1970; Assistant, 1972, Assistant Professor, 1982, Associate Professor, 1988, Full Professor, 1993, Department of Chemical Engineering Faculty of Technology and Metallurgy, University of Belgrade, Yugoslavia. Publications: Author and co-author: Books, Information Systems in the Process Techniques, 1987; Artificial Intelligence in Chemistry and Chemical Engineering, 1989, Process Modeling and Simulation, 1995; Process Engineering Intelligent Systems, 1999; Informatics, 2001; Over 600 articles to professional journals, patentee in field. Honours: First Prize from Belgrade City for Bachelor of Science Thesis, 1970; DAAD Prize for Research Work, 1980; 2nd Prize TI, St Petersburg, 1989; The Gold Medal, Nikola Tesla, 1993. Address: Faculty of Technology and Metallurgy, University of Belgrade, Karnegijeva, 4, 11000 Belgrade, Yugoslavia. Website: www.tmf.bg.ac.yu

**SAWYER Roger Martyn,** b. 15 December 1931, Stroud, England. Author. m. Diana Harte, 30 August 1952, 2 sons. Education: BA Honours, Diploma in Education, University of Wales, 1958; PhD, History, University of Southampton, 1979. Publications: Casement: The Flawed Hero, 1984; Slavery in the Twentieth Century, 1986; Children Enslaved, 1988; The Island from Within (editor), 1990; 'We are but Women': Women in Ireland's History, 1993; Roger Casement's Diaries 1910: The Black and The White (editor), 1997. Contributions to: Anti-Slavery Reporter; BBC History; Immigrants and Minorities; South. Honour: Airey Neave Award, 1985. Memberships: Anti-Slavery International, council member, 1984-98; Research Fellow, Airey Neave Trust; Bembridge Sailing Club; Old Wycliffian Society. Address: Ducie House, Darts Lane, Bembridge, Isle of Wight PO35 5YH, England.

**SAXTON Robert Louis Alfred,** b. 8 October 1953, London, England. Composer; University Lecturer. Partner, Teresa Cahill. Education: BA, 1975, MA, St Catharine's College, Cambridge; B.Mus, Worcester College, Oxford, 1976; D.Mus, University of Oxford, 1992. Appointments: Lecturer, Bristol University, 1984-85; Fulbright Award, Visiting Fellow, Princeton University, USA, 1985-86; Head of Composition, Guildhall School of Music and Drama, London, 1991-97; Head of Composition, Royal Academy of Music, London, 1998-99; University Lecturer, Tutorial Fellow in Music, Worcester

College, Oxford, 1999-; Governor, South Bank Board, London, 1998-. Compositions: Over 40 published compositions; Works recorded on EMI, Sony, Hyperion, NMC and Signum labels. Publications: The Process of Composition, 1998; Darkness to Light – Cycles and Circles, 2003; The Orchestral Composer, 2003. Honours: 1st Prize, Gaudeamus Music Week, Holland, 1975; FGSM; Patron: The Society of English Singers and Speakers; Bristol University Musical Society. Memberships: Royal Overseas League; Royal Society of Musicians. Address: Worcester College, Oxford OX1 2HB, England.

**SAYERS Bruce McArthur,** b. 6 February 1928, Hampstead, London England. Emeritus Professor of Computing Applied to Medicine. m. Ruth Woolls Humphery. Education: BSc, MSc, University of Melbourne, Australia, 1944-48; PhD, DIC, DSc, University of London. Appointments: Biophysicist/ Electronic Engineer, Baker Medical Research Institute and Clinical Research Unit, Alfred Hospital Melbourne, 1949-54; Philips Electrical Limited Research Fellow in Human Auditory Communication, DSIR Research Assistant in Psychoacoustics, Telecommunications Section, 1954-58, Lecturer, Electrical Engineering, 1958-62, Senior Lecturer, Medical Electronics, 1962-65, Reader, 1965-68, Professor of Electrical Engineering Applied to Medicine, 1968-84, Head of Department of Electrical Engineering, 1979-84, Professor of Computing Applied to Medicine, 1984-90, Head of Department of Computing, 1984-89, Dean of City and Guilds College, 1984-85, 1985-88, 1991-93, Kobler Professor of the Management of Information Technology, 1990-93, Director, Centre for Cognitive Systems, 1990-98, Emeritus Professor of Computing Applied to Medicine, 1993-, Imperial College, London; Temporary Advisor, 1970-87, 1995-96, Member of Expert Panel on Health Research, 1988-2000, Member, 1988-94, Vice-Chairman, 1997-2000, Global Advisory Committee on Health Research, WHO. Publications: Publications on: Speech and hearing, Audiology and neuro-otology, biomedical signal and systems analysis, cardio-respiratory physiology, circulation and cardiology, epidemiological modelling, health technology, public health and health assessment, knowledge based health indicators; Co-editor and contributor, Understanding the Global Dimensions of Health, 2004. Honours: Travelling Lecturer, Nuffield Foundation and National Research Council of Canada, 1970-71; President, Section of Measurement in Medicine, Royal Society of Medicine, 1971-72; Visiting Professor, Birmingham, Alabama, McGill, Melbourne, Rio de Janeiro, Toronto; Freeman City of London, 1986; Liveryman, Worshipful Company of Scientific Instrument Makers, 1985; Honorary Foreign Member, Societa Medica Chirurgia di Bologna, 1965; Honorary Member: WHO Medical Society, 1974, Eta Kappa Nu, 1984; Honorary Fellow, World Innovation Foundation, 2002; Vice-President, International Commission on theme: Health and Medical Sciences, UNESCO Encyclopaedia of Life Support Systems, 2004-. Memberships: FIEE, 1980, FCGI, 1983, FREng, 1990, FIC, 1996. Address: Lot's Cottage, Compton Abbas, Shaftesbury, Dorset SP7 0NQ, England.

**SAZONOV Victor Fedorovich,** b. 26 November 1947, Saratov, USSR. Speaker of Samara Regional Duma. m. Natalia, 1 son, 1 daughter. Education: Diploma on Physical Culture, Saratov State Pedagogical University, 1971; Lawyer's Diploma, Academy of the Home Office, 1978. Appointments: Various positions in the Penitentiary System of Saratov Region, 1971-87; Head, Penitentiary Service, Samara Regional Department of the Interior, 1996-; Head, Samara Regional Pententiary Department of the Ministry of Justice of Russian Federation, 1999-2001; Deputy Speaker, Samara Regional Duma, 2001. Publications: Numerous publications in media on the legislative regulation, self-governance and legal enlightenment. Honours: Order of

Honour; The Deserved Worker of the Home Office medal; Memorable Medal of Koni; Silver Medal for Strengthening the Penitentiary System; Medal of St Prince Dahiil, Moscow Russian Orthodox Church. Memberships: Council of Legislators of the Council of the Federation, Federal Assembly; Deputy Chairman, Council of the Peoples of the Russian Assembly. Address: 187 Molodogvardeyskaya Str, Samara 443100, Russia. Website: www.duma.sam-reg.ru

**SCACCHI Greta,** b. 18 February 1960, Milan, Italy. Actress. 1 son, 1 daughter. Education: Bristol Old Vic Drama School. Career: Films include: Second Sight; Heat and Dust; Defence of the Realm; The Cocoa-Cola Kid; A Man in Love; Good Morning Babylon; White Mischief; Paura e Amore (Three Sisters); La Donna dell Luna (Woman in the Moon); Schoolmates; Presumed Innocent; Shattered; Fires Within; Turtle Beach; Salt on Our Skins; The Browning Version; Jefferson in Paris, 1994; Country Life, 1995; Emma, 1996; Cosi; The Serpent's Kiss, 1997; The Red Violin, 1998; Cotton Mary, 1998; Ladies Room, 1999; The Manor, 1999; Tom's Midnight Garden, 2000; Looking for Anbrandi, 2000; One of the Hollywood Ten, 2000; Festival in Cannes, 2001; Baltic Storm, 2003; Il Ronzio delle mosche, 2003; Sotto falso nome, 2004; Theatre includes: Cider with Rosie; In Times Like These; Airbase; Uncle Vanya; The Guardsman; TV includes: The Ebony Tower; Dr Fischer of Geneva; Waterfront (series); Rasputin; The Odyssey (series), 1996; Macbeth, 1998; Christmas Glory, 2000; Jeffrey Archer: The Truth, 2002. Honours: Emmy Award, 1996. Address: Susan Smith Associates, 121 San Vincente Boulevard, Beverly Hills, CA 90211, USA.

**SCALES Prunella M R West,** Actress. m. Timothy West, 1963, 2 sons. Education: Old Vic Theatre School, London; Herbert Berghof Studio, New York, USA; Repertory in Bristol Old Vic, Oxford, Salisbury, England; Chichester and Stratford, 1967-68; London Theatre Appearances include: The Promise, 1967; The Wolf, 1975; An Evening with Queen Victoria, 1979-99; Quartermaine's Terms, 1981; When We Are Married, 1986; Single Spies, National Theatre, 1988; School for Scandal, National Theatre, 1990; Long Day's Journey Into Night, National Theatre, 1991; At Leeds: Happy Days, 1993; The Birthday Party, 1999; The Cherry Orchard, 2000; The External, 2001; Too Far to Walk (King's Head), 2002; A Woman of No Importance, 2003; TV includes: Fawlty Towers, 1975, 1978; Mapp and Lucia (series), 1985-86; What the Butler Saw, 1987; After Henry, 1988-92; Signs and Wonders, 1995; Breaking the Code, 1997; Emma, 1997; Midsommer Murders, 1999; Silent Witness, 2000; Queen Victoria, 2003; Films: An Awfully Big Adventure, 1994; Stiff Upper Lips, 1997; An Ideal Husband, 1998; The Ghost of Greville Lodge, 2000; Numerous other areas of work including: Radio; Directing (Leeds, South Australia, National Theatre Studio, Nottingham Playhouse). Honours: CBE; Honorary DLitt, Bradford; Honorary DLitt, University of East Anglia. Address: c/o Conway Van Gelder, 18-21 Jermyn Street, London SW1Y 6HP, England.

**SCANLON Mary Elizabeth,** b. 25 May 1947, Dundee, Scotland. Member of Scottish Parliament. 1 son, 1 daughter. Education: MA, Economics, Political Science, University of Dundee; Fellow of the Institute of Professional Development. Appointments: Secretarial and Administrative posts in civil service and private sector, 1962-73; Full-time Mother (Part-time Evening Class Lecturer); Student, University of Dundee, 1979-83; Lecturer, Economics, Abertay University, Dundee and Perth College, 1983-94; Lecturer in Economics and Business Management, Inverness College (University of the Highlands and Islands Network), 1994-99; Member of the Scottish Parliament, Highlands and Islands, 1999-; Scottish Conservative Spokesman on Communities; Convenor of the Scottish Parliament Cross Party Group on Funerals and Bereavements; Vice Convenor of Cross Party Group on Kidney Disease. Address: (Constituency): 37 Ardconnel Terrace, Inverness IV2 3AE, Scotland. E-mail: mary.scanlon.msp@scottish.parliament.uk

**SCARFE Gerald A,** b. 1 June 1936, London, England. Cartoonist. m. Jane Asher, 2 sons, 1 daughter. Career: Contributor, cartoons to Punch, 1960-, Private Eye, 1961-, Daily Mail, 1966-, Sunday Times, 1967-, Time, 1967-; Animator and film director, BBC, 1969-; Group exhibitions at Grosvenor Gallery, 1969, 1970, Pavilion d'Humour, Montreal, 1969, Expo, 1970, Osaka, 1970; Solo exhibitions: Waddell Gallery, New York, 1968, 1970, Vincent Price Gallery, Chicago, 1969, Grosvenor Gallery, 1969, National Portrait Gallery, 1971, Royal Festival Hall, 1983, Langton Gallery, 1986, Chris Beetles Gallery, 1989, National Portrait Gallery, 1989-99; Comic Art Gallery, Melbourne; Gerald Scarfe in Southwark, 2000; Consultant designer and character designer for film: Hercules, 1997; Theatre design: Ubu Roi, Traverse Theatre, 1957; What the Butler Saw, Oxford Playhouse, 1980; No End of Blame, Royal Court, London, 1981; Orpheus in the Underworld, English National Opera, Coliseum, 1985; Who's A Lucky Boy, Royal Exchange, Manchester, 1985; Born Again, 1990; The Magic Flute, Los Angeles Opera, 1992; An Absolute Turkey, 1993; Mind Millie for Me, Haymarket, 1996; Fantastic Mr Fox, Los Angeles Opera, 1998; Peter and the Wolf, Holiday on Ice, Paris and world tour; Television: Director and presenter: Scarfe on Art; Scarfe on Sex; Scarfe on Class; Scarfe in Paradise; Subject of Scarfe and His Work with Disney, South Bank Special. Publications: Gerald Scarfe's People, 1966; Indecent Exposure, 1973; Expletive Deleted: The Life and Times of Richard Nixon, 1974; Gerald Scarfe, 1982; Father Kissmas and Mother Claus, 1985; Scarfe by Scarfe (autobiography), 1986; Gerald Scarfe's Seven Deadly Sins, 1987; Line of Attack, 1988; Scarfeland, 1989; Scarfe on Stage, 1992; Scarfe Face, 1993; Hades: the truth at last, 1997. Honours: Zagreb Prize for BBC film, Long Drawn Out Trip, 1973. Address: c/o ICM, Oxford House, 76 Oxford Street, London W1N 0AX, England.

**SCARFE Norman,** b. 1 May 1923, Felixstowe, England. Writer. Education: King's School, Canterbury, Senior King's Scholar, 1940; MA, Honours, History, Oxford, 1949. Appointments: Chairman, Centre of East Anglia Studies, University of East Anglia, 1989-96; Founder, Honorary General Editor, Suffolk Records Society, 1958-92. Publications: Assault Division: The 3rd British Infantry Division from D-Day to VE Day, 1947, new edition with foreword by Sir Michael Howard, 2004; Suffolk, 1960, 4th edition, 1988, Essex, 1968, 2nd edition, 1982; The Suffolk Landscape, 1972, 2nd edition, 1987, new edition, 2002; Cambridgeshire, 1983; Suffolk in the Middle Ages, 1986; A Frenchman's Year in Suffolk (1784), 1988; Innocent Espionage: The La Rochefoucauld Brothers' Tour of England in 1785, 1995; Jocelin of Brakelond, 1997; To the Highlands in 1786: The inquisitive journey of a young French aristocrat, 2001, (the 3rd book in the La Rochefoucauld Brothers in Britain trilogy); Contributions to: Proceedings, Suffolk Institute of Archaeology; Aldeburgh Festival Annual Programme Book; Country Life; The Book Collector; Dictionary of National Biography. Honours: Fellow, Society of Antiquaries, 1964; Honorary Litt D, University of East Anglia, 1989; Member of the Order of the British Empire, 1994; Citoyen d'Honneur, Colleville Montgomery, Basse-Normandie, 1994; East Anglia's History: Studies in Honour of Norman Scarfe, 2002. Memberships: International PEN; Suffolk Book League, founder chairman, 1982. Address: The Garden Cottage, 3 Burkitt Road, Woodbridge, Suffolk IP12 4JJ, England.

**SCATENA Lorraine Borba,** b. 18 February 1924, San Rafael, California, USA. Farmer-Rancher; Women's Rights Advocate. m. Louis G Scatena, 14 February 1960, deceased 1 November 1995, 1 son, 1 daughter. Education: BA, Dominican College, San Rafael, 1945; California Elementary Teacher Certificate, 1946; California School of Fine Arts, 1948; University California, Berkeley, 1956-57. Appointments: Teacher, Fairfax Elementary School, California, 1946-53; Assistant to Mayor Fairfax City Recreation, 1948-53; Teacher, Librarian, US Dependent Schools, Mainz am Rhine, Germany, 1953-56; Translator, Portugal Travel Tours, Lisbon, 1954; Bonding Secretary, American Fore Insurance Group, San Francisco, 1958-60; Rancher, Farmer, Yerington, Nevada, 1960-98; Member, Nevada State Legislative Commission, 1975; Co-ordinator, Nevadans for Equal Rights Amendment, 1975-78; Testifier, Nevada State Senate and Assembly, 1975, 1977; Member, Advisory Committee, Fleischmann College of Agriculture, University of Nevada, 1977-80, 1981-84; Speaker, Grants and Research Projects, Bishop, California, 1977, Choices for Tomorrow's Women, Fallon, Nevada, 1989; Trustee Wassuk College Hawthorne, Nevada, 1984-87; Travelled to AAUW South Pacific Conferences in Hawaii, to address women of Arizona, California, Hawaii and Nevada on women's study and action projects through networking and coalition, continued tour to Washington DC where she led discussion groups for AAUW presidents of North Dakota, Louisiana, Maine and Montana, states where women share the same problems of transportation, communication, employment and medical care, 1982; Attended and assisted with leadership meetings with AAUW elected officers from 16 states in Denver, Colorado, 1982. Honours include: AAUW Nevada State Humanities Award, 1975; Invitation to first all-women delegation to USA from People's Republic of China, US House of Representatives, 1979; AAUW branch travelship, Discovering Women in US History, Radcliffe College, 1981; NRTA State Outstanding Service Award, 1981; AAUW Future Fund National Award, 1983; Soroptimist International Women Helping Women Award, 1983; Fellow World Literary Academy, 1993; AAUW, Lorraine Scatena Endowment Gift named in her honour for significant contributions to AAUW National Educational Foundation, 1997. Memberships include: Marin Society of Artists, 1948-53; American Association of University Women, 1968-, Nevada State Convention General Chairman, 1976, 1987; Lyon County Museum Society, 1978-; Lyon County Retired Teachers' Association, Unit President, 1979-80, 1984-86; State Convention General Chairman, 1985; Participated in public panel with solo presentation, Shakespeare's Treatment of Women Characters, Nevada Theatre for the Arts hosting Ashland, Oregon Shakespearean actors local performance, 1987; Rural American Women Inc; AAUW, Branch President, 1972-74, 1974-76; President, AAUW, Nevada State, 1981-83; Nevada Representative for First White House Conference for Rural American Women, Washington, 1980; Italian Catholic Federation, Branch President, 1986-88; Charter Member, Eleanor Roosevelt Education Fund for Women and Girls, 1990, sustaining member, 1992-; Member, Nevada Women's History Project, University Nevada, 1996-; Poetry presenter, World Congress on Arts and Communication, Lisbon, Portugal, 1999; Washington, 2000; Cambridge University, St John's College, 2001; Vancouver, Canada, 2002; Dominican University of California, President's Circle, 1997-; American Association of University Women, Leaders Circle, 1998-; The National Museum of Women in the Arts, Washington DC, charter member, 1987, council member, 1999-; University of California, Berkeley, Bancroft, Librarian's Council, 2002. Address: PO Box 247, Yerington, NV 89447-0247, USA.

**SCHAEFER Henry,** b. 8 June 1944, Grand Rapids, Michigan, USA. Education: BS, Chemical Physics, Massachusetts Institute of Technology, 1966; Fellow, National Defense Education Act, 1969; PhD, Chemical Physics, Stanford University, 1969. Appointments include: Assistant Professor of Chemistry, 1969-74, Associate Professor of Chemistry, 1974-78, Professor of Chemistry, 1978-87, University of California at Berkeley; Director, Institute for Theoretical Chemistry, University of Texas, 1979-80; Wilfred T Doherty Professor of Chemistry, University of Texas, 1979-80; Director, Centre for Computational Chemistry, University of Georgia, 1987-; Graham Perdue Professor of Chemistry, University of Georgia, 1987-; Visiting Professor, Australia, Switzerland, Argentina and France. Publications: 1,000 journal articles; Book chapters; Books; Conference proceedings. Honours include: American Chemical Society Award in Pure Chemistry, 1979; Leo Hendrik Baekeland Award, 1983; Schrodinger Medal, World Association of Theoretical Organic Chemists, 1990; Centenary Medal, Royal Society of Chemistry, 1992; Lamar Dodd Award, University of Georgia, 1995; Professor Honoris Causa, St Petersburg State University, 1996; Doctor Honoris Causa, University of Plovdiv, 1998; Doctor Honoris Causa, Beijing Institute of Technology, 1999; Doctor Honoris Causa, University of Sofia, 1999; Professor Honoris Causa, Beijing Normal University, 1999; Gold Medal, Comenius University, 2000; Professor Honoris Causa, Fudan University, 2001; Professor Honoris Causa, Chinese Academy of Sciences, Shanghai, 2001; Doctor Honoris Causa, Huntington College, 2002; Professor Honoris Causa, Yunnan University, Kunming, 2002; Professor Honoris Causa, Guangxi Normal University, Guilin, China, 2003; Professor Honoris Causa, Chengdu University, Chengdu, China, 2003; American Chemical Society Award in Theoretical Chemistry, 2003; Ira M Remsen Award, American Chemical Society, 2003; Joseph O Hirschfelder Prize, University of Wisconsin, 2005; Professor Honoris Causa, Xinjiang University, Urumqi, China, 2004; Joseph O Hirschfelder Prize, University of Wisconsin, 2005; Guest lecturer at numerous universities, conferences and symposia; Several grants and research funding. Memberships include: Fellow, American Academy of Arts and Sciences; Fellow, American Physical Society; Fellow, American Association for the Advancement of Science; Fellow, Alfred P. Sloan Foundation; Fellow, John S. Guggenheim Foundation; Member, Editorial Board, Chemical Physics Letters; Member, Editorial Board, Advances in Quantum Chemistry; Fellow, American Scientific Affiliation; Fellow, American Institute of Chemists; Member, Editorial Board, Journal of Molecular Structure; Editor in Chief, Molecular Physics; President, World Association of Theoretically Oriented Chemists. Address: Centre for Computational and Quantum Chemistry, University of Georgia, Room 505 Computational Chemistry Building, 1004 Cedar Street, Athens, GA 30602-2525, USA. E-mail: hfsiii@uga.edu Website: www.ccqc.uga.edu/group/Dr.Schaefer.html

**SCHAEFFER Charles David Jr,** b. 14 June 1948, Allentown, Pennsylvania, USA. Professor. Education: BA, Chemistry, Franklin & Marshall College, Lancaster, Pennsylvania, 1966-70; PhD, Chemistry, State University of New York at Albany, Albany, New York, 1970-74. Appointments: Assistant Professor, 1976, Associate Professor, 1981, Faculty of the Department of Chemistry, Elizabethtown College, Elizabethtown, Pennsylvania; A C Baugher Associate Professor of Chemistry, 1987, 1990, Chairman, Department of Chemistry, 1989, 1992, A C Baugher Professor of Chemistry, 1991-, Elizabethtown College. Publications: Numerous scientific papers in professional journals. Honours: Recipient of many awards including: John Frederick Steinman Award for Excellence in Research, Elizabethtown College, 1985; Elected Historian of the Conventions of the Intercollegiate Student Chemists for an indefinite term. Memberships: Member of many professional organisations including: Sigma Xi, American Chemical Society; Royal Society of Chemistry. Address: Chemistry Department, Elizabethtown College, One Alpha Drive, Elizabethtown, PA 17022-2298, USA.

**SCHELLIN Thomas Erling,** b. 31 July 1939, Hamburg, Germany. Marine Engineer. m. Andrea Bielfeldt, 11 April 1984, 1 step son, 1 step daughter. Education: BS, Rensselaer Polytechnic Institute, Troy, New York, USA, 1962; MS, Massachusetts Institute of Technology, Cambridge, Massachusetts, USA 1964; PhD, Mechanical Engineering, Rice University, 1971. Appointments: Teaching Assistant, Department of Naval Architecture Massachusetts Institute of Technology, 1962-64; Mechanical Engineer, Shell Development Co, Houston, Texas, USA 1964-68; Research Assistant, Rice University, Houston, Texas, USA, 1968-71; Design Engineer, The Offshore Co, Houston, Texas, USA 1971-72; Research Scientist, GKSS, Geesthacht, Germany, 1972-75; Naval Architect, Germanischer Lloyd, Hamburg, 1976-. Publications include most recently as co-author: An Aid to Operating decisions Based on Nonlinear Response of a Crane Barge in Waves, 2001 Direct Computation of Wave-induced Design Loads for Ships, 2001; Assessment of Sloshing Loads for Tankers, 2001; Prediction of Wetdeck Slamming Loads for a Catamaran. Honours: Achievement Award, American Society of Mechanical Engineers, 1993; Listed in Who's Who publications and biographical dictionaries. Memberships include: American Society of Mechanical Engineers; Society of Naval Architects and Marine Engineers; Schiffbautechnische Gesellschaft; International Association of Classification Societies Ltd. Address: Abteistrasse 23, 20149 Hamburg, Germany. E-mail: schn@germanlloyd.org

**SCHIFFER Claudia,** b. 25 August 1970, Düsseldorf, Germany. Model. m. Matthew Vaughn, 2002, 1 son. Career: Worked for Karl Lagerfeld, 1990; Revlon Contract, 1992-; Appearances on magazine covers, calendars, TV; Released own exercise video; Appeared in films: Ritchie Rich; The Blackout, 1997; Desperate But Not Serious, 1999; The Sound of Claudia Schiffer, 2000; Black and White, 2000; Chain of Fools, 2000; In Pursuit, 2000; Life Without Dick, 2001; Love Actually, 2003; Retired from modelling, 1998; Owns share in Fashion Café. Publication: Memories. Memberships: US Committee, UNICEF, 1995-98. Address: c/o Elite Model Management, 40 Parker Street, London WC2B 5BH, England.

**SCHILD Rudolph Ernst,** b. 10 January 1940, Chicago, Illinois, USA. Astrophysicist. m. Jane Struss. Education: BS, 1962, MS, 1963, PhD, 1967, University of Chicago. Appointments: Research Fellow, Postdoctorate, California Institute of Technology, 1967-69; Scientist, Smithsonian Astrophysical Observatory, 1969-; Lecturer, Harvard University, 1977-82. Publications: Over 200 scientific papers in refereed journals; The Electronic Sky: Digital Images of the Cosmos, 1985; Voyage to the Stars, CD Rom, 1994; 2 patents. Honours: Discovered gravitational lens time delay, 1986; Discovered nature of missing mass, 1997. Memberships: American Astronomical Society, 1967-; International Astronomical Union, 1969-. Address: Centre for Astrophysics, 60 Garden Street, Cambridge, MA 02138, USA. E-mail: rschild@cfa.harvard.edu

**SCHILLING (Karl Friedrich) Guenther,** b. 16 August 1930, Leipzig, Germany. Agricultural Chemistry Educator. m. Gudrun Linschmann, 2 sons. Education: Studies in Agricultural Sciences and Chemistry, Friedrich-Schiller-University, Jena, Germany, 1951-56; Diploma in Agricultural Sciences, 1954, in Chemistry, 1956; Dr agr, 1957; Training in Radio Chemistry,

Moscow, USSR, 1958; Dr agr habilitatus, 1960. Appointments: Lecturer, Plant Nutrition, 1960-61, Full Professor, Plant Nutrition and Soil Science, Director, Institute of Agricultural Chemistry, 1961-70, Friedrich-Schiller-University, Jena, Germany; Full Professor, Physiology and Nutrition of Crop Plants, Martin-Luther-University Halle-Wittenberg, Germany, 1970-95; Professor Emeritus, 1995; Dean of Agricultural Faculty, 1983-90; Rector of Martin-Luther-University Halle-Wittenberg, 1990-93; Vice President, Rector's Conference of the Federal Republic of Germany, 1991-95. Publications: 230 contributions to scientific journals and books; 1 monograph; Author and editor, Pflanzenernährung und Düngung, university textbook, revised edition, 2000. Honours include: Medal and Diploma, 8th International Fertiliser Congress, Moscow, 1976; National Prize for Science and Technology, Berlin, 1982; Dr Heinrich Baur Prize, Munich, 1994; Golden Sprengel-Liebig-Medal, Leipzig, 1997. Memberships: Deutsche Akademie der Naturforscher Leopoldina; Matica Srbska; Verband Deutscher Landwirtschaftlicher Untersuchungs-und Forschungsanstalten, Vice-President, 1993-96. Address: Institute for Soil Science and Plant Nutrition of the Martin-Luther-University Halle-Wittenberg, Julius-Kuehn-Str 31, 06112 Halle (Saale), Germany. E-mail: schilling@landw.uni-halle.de

**SCHLESINGER Arthur M(eier) Jr,** b. 15 October 1917, Columbus, Ohio, USA. Historian; Retired Professor; Author. m. (1) Marian Cannon, 1940, divorced 1970, 2 sons, 2 daughters, (2) Alexandra Emmet, 1971, 1 son. Education: AB, Harvard University, 1938; Henry Fellow, University of Cambridge, 1938-39; Society of Fellows, Harvard University, 1939-42. Appointments: Associate Professor, 1946-54, Professor of History, 1954-61, Harvard University; Special Assistant to President John F Kennedy, 1961-63; Visiting Fellow, Institute for Advanced Study, Princeton, New Jersey, 1966; Schweitzer Professor in Humanities, City University of New York, 1966-95. Publications: Orestes A Brownson: A Pilgrim's Progress, 1939; The Age of Jackson, 1945; The Vital Center, 1949; The General and the President (with R H Rovere), 1951; The Age of Roosevelt, Vol I, The Crisis of the Old Order 1919-1933, 1957, Vol II, The Coming of the New Deal, 1958, Vol III, The Politics of Upheaval, 1960; Kennedy or Nixon: Does It Make Any Difference?, 1960; The Politics of Hope, 1963; The National Experience (with John Blum), 1963; A Thousand Days: John F Kennedy in the White House, 1965; The Bitter Heritage: Vietnam and American Democracy 1941-66, 1967; The Crisis of Confidence, 1969; The Imperial Presidency, 1973; Robert Kennedy and His Times, 1978; The Cycles of American History, 1986; The Disuniting of America, 1991; A Life in the 20th Century: I. Innocent Beginnings, 2000; War and the American Presidency, 2004. Editor: Paths to American Thought, 1963; The Promise of American Life, 1967; The Best and Last of Edwin O'Connor, 1970; The History of American Presidential Elections (with F L Israel), 1971, new edition, 1986; The Coming to Power, 1972; The Dynamics of World Power: A Documentary History of United States Foreign Policy 1945-1972, 1973; History of US Political Parties, 1973; Running for President, 1994. Contributions to: Professional journals. Honours: Francis Parkman Prize, Society of American Historians, 1957; Bancroft Prize, Columbia University, 1958; Pulitzer Prize in History, 1946, in Biography, 1966; National Book Awards, 1966, 1979; American Academy of Arts and Letters Gold Medal in History and Biography, 1967; Fregene Prize for Literature, Italy, 1983; National Humanities Medal, 1998; Grants, fellowships and honorary doctorates. Memberships: American Academy of Arts and Letters, president, 1981-84, chancellor, 1984-87; American Civil Liberties Union; American Historical Association; American Philosophical Society; Americans for Democratic Action, chairman, 1952-54; Massachusetts Historical Society;

Council on Foreign Relations; Franklin and Eleanor Roosevelt Institute, co-chairman, 1983-; Society of American Historians; Phi Beta Kappa. Address: 455 East 51st Street, New York, NY 10022, USA.

**SCHMEIDLER Felix,** b. 20 October 1920, Leipzig, Germany. m. Marion Pampe, 1 son, 1 daughter. Education: Universität München, Studium der Astronomie, 1938-41; Dr rer nat, Universität München, 1941; Habilitation für Astronomie an Universität München, 1950. Appointments: Assistant der Universitätssternwarte München, 1943; Professor für Astronomie an Universität München, 1957; Assistant Director, Universitätssternwarte, München, 1979-86; University Observatory Cambridge, England, 1950-51; Mt Stromlo Observatory, Canberra, Australia, 1954-55. Publications: More than 100 articles in scientific journals; Books: Alte und moderne Kosmologie, 1961; Nikolaus Copernicus, Serie Große Naturforscher, 1970; Edition, Works of the Astronomers Hevelius, 1969, Regiomontanus, 1972; Kommentar zu "De revolutionibus, 1998. Honours: Silberne Medaille der Universität Helsinki, 1968; Kulturpreis der Landsmannschaft Westpreußen, Münster, 1973; Honorary Citizen der Stadt Königsberg in Bayern, 1982; Ehrenschild Deutschordensland der Ost- und Westpreußenstiftung in Bayern, 1997. Memberships: Royal Astronomical Society London, 1951; International Astronomical Union, 1955; Altpreußische Gesellschaft für Wissenschaft, Kunst und Literatur, 1981. Address: Mauerkircher Strasse 17, D81679 München, Germany.

**SCHMID Rudi (Rudolf),** b. 2 May 1922, Glarus, Switzerland. Professor of Medicine. m. Sonja Wild, 1 son, 1 daughter. Education: Universities of Zurich, Lausanne and Geneva, 1939-47; MD, University of Zurich, 1947; PhD, Biology, University of Minnesota, USA, 1954; Postgraduate Medical Education, University of California, San Francisco and University of Minnesota, 1948-54; Senior Fellow, Columbia University, New York, 1954-55. Appointments: Assistant Professor of Medicine, Harvard University, 1957-62; Professor of Medicine, University of Chicago, 1962-66; Professor of Medicine, University of California, San Francisco, 1966-2004; Dean School of Medicine, 1982-89, Associate Dean, University of California, San Francisco, 1989-95; Senior Haematologist, National Institutes of Sciences, Bethesda, Maryland, 1955-57; Retired, 2005-. Publications: 130 scientific papers in top medical journals of USA, Switzerland, Germany; Member of American and Swiss Editorial Councils; Member of Chinese Editorial and Academy Councils. Honours include: Member, Japanese Advisory Board; President, American Association for the Study of Liver Disease, 1965; Association of American Physicians, 1987; Honorary Professor, Peking Union Medical College; Honorary Member, Leopoldina, German Academy of Medical Sciences. Memberships include: National Academy of Sciences, USA; International Association for the Study of the Liver; Swiss Academy of Medical Science; German-American Academic Council. Address: 211 Woodland Road, Kentfield, Marin County, CA 94904, USA. E-mail: s.d.schmid@worldn et.att.net

**SCHMIDKUNZ Heinz,** b. 3 October 1929, Graslitz, Sudetenland. Professor of Chemistry. m. Liselotte, 1 daughter. Education: Diploma, Master of Chemistry, 1959; PhD, Physical Chemistry, 1963; Professor of Chemistry, 1980. Appointments: Assistant, Physical Chemistry, University of Frankfurt/M, Germany, 1959; University Lecturer for Teacher Education at University, 1963-80; Professor of Chemistry, University of Dortmund, Germany, 1980-. Publications: 11 books; 200 articles in journals. Honour: Heinrich-Roessler-Award, German Chemical Society, 1989; Literary Award, Austrian Society of Chemistry Teachers, 2004; Honorary Member, German Chemical Society, 2005. Memberships: German Chemical Society; Austrian Society of Teachers in Chemistry. Address: Obermarkstr. 125, D-44267 Dortmund, Germany. E-mail: heinz.schmidkunz@uni-dortmund.de

**SCHMIDT Robert Milton,** b. 7 May 1944, Milwaukee, Wisconsin, USA. Physician; Scientist; Educator. m. Jessie Knight, 2 sons. Education: AB, Northwestern University, 1966; MD, Columbia University College of Physicians and Surgeons, 1966-70; Further studies at University of California (San Diego); Centers for Disease Control, Atlanta; Master Public Health, Harvard, 1974-75; PhD studies including Law, Emory Institute Liberal Arts, 1975-76, 1981-82; MA, Health and Ageing, San Francisco State University, 1989-99. Appointments: Hematology Division, US Public Health Service, Centers for Disease Control, Atlanta, Georgia, 1971-79; Special Assistant to Director, State Laboratory Institute of Massachusetts, Boston, 1974-75; President, Founder, Medical Director, Component Centers, International Health Resource Center of Hawaii, 1979-82; Director of California Pacific Medical Center, Health Watch Medical Center and Health Watch International, Director, Center for Preventive Medicine and Health Research, Senior Scientist, Institute of Cancer Research, 1983-; Institute of Epidemiology and Behavioral Medicine, 1983-88; Professor, Biomedical Science, Hematology and Preventive Medicine, Director of Health Professions Programs, Chair of the Health Professions Advising Committee, member Gerontology Faculty Council, San Francisco State University, 1983-99; Author or co-author over 300 reviewed publications in professional journals and conference proceedings; 17 major books and 28 technical manuals. Memberships include: Fellow, American Association for the Advancement of Science; American College of Physicians; American Society of Clinical Pathologists; American College of Pathologists; American College of Preventive Medicine; American Medical Informatics Association; International Society of Hematology; The Royal Society of Medicine; American Geriatrics Society; Knight of Malta; Cosmos Club; Alumni Regent, Columbia University of Physicians and Surgeons; Harvard Clubs of New York City and Northern California; Northwestern University; Emory University Graduate School of Arts and Sciences; Circle Club; National Gallery of Art, Washington, DC; Many others. Address: Whaleship Plaza, 25 Hinckley Walk, San Francisco, CA 94111-2303, USA. E-mail: rmschmidtmd@aol.com

**SCHMIED-KOWARZIK Wolfdietrich,** b. 11 March 1939, Friedberg, Germany. University Professor. m. Iris, 2 sons, 1 daughter. Education: Dr Phil, 1963; Habilitation, Bonn, 1970. Appointments: Professor of Philosophy, Pedagogy, University Kassel, 1971. Publications: 16 books; Edited, 36 books; 300 articles; Denken aus geschichtlicher Verantwortung. Honours: Kritik und Praxis; Bundesverdienstkreuz, Ehrenkreuz I. kl. Memberships: International Hegel Gesellschaft; Internationall Schelling Gesellschaft; International Fichte Gesellschaft; European Academy of Sciences and Arts. Address: Universitat Kassel, Nora Platiel Strasse 1, D 34109 Kassel, Germany. E-mail: schmiedk@uni-kassel.de Website: http://www.uni-kassel.de/~schmiedk

**SCHNAGL Roger Dieter,** b. 10 October 1944, Reitendorf, Austria. Microbiology Educator; Researcher in Virology. m. Heather York Syme. Education: BS (Hons), 1969, PhD, 1975, University of Melbourne. Appointments: Postdoctoral Research Fellow, University of Melbourne, 1975-78; Lecturer, 1979-86, Senior Lecturer, 1987-2004, Head of Department, 1993-95, 2000-2004, Deputy Head of Department, 1996-2000, Department of Microbiology, LaTrobe University, Melbourne;

Director, Advanced Electron Microscope Facility, La Trobe University, Melbourne, 2001-2002. Publications: Over 50 articles in numerous international science journals. Honours: Numerous research grants and awards, 1979-. Memberships: Fellow, Australian Society for Microbiology; New York Academy of Sciences. Address: Department of Microbiology, La Trobe University, Bundoora, Victoria 3083, Australia.

**SCHNEEWEISS Ulrich,** b. 25 March 1923, Potsdam, Germany. Doctor; Medical Microbiologist. m. Sigrid Schmilinsky, 1 son, 2 daughters. Education: Student, 1946-52, Dr.med., 1952, Dr. med. habil., 1960. Appointments: Scientific Assistant, 1952-55, Head Assistant, 1956-63, Department of Serology, University Lectureship, Medical Microbiology, Immunology, Epidemiology, 1961-68, Humboldt University, Berlin; Scientific Assistant, 1963-68, Professor, Head of Department of Diagnostic Research, 1968-88, German Academy of Sciences, Institute for Cancer Research, Robert Roessle Clinic. Publications: 90 research papers, textbooks, monographs: Reihenuntersuchung auf Syphilis..., 1963; Grundriss der Impfpraxis, 1964-68; Allgemeine/Spezielle Mikrobiologie, 1968; Transplantations- und Tumorimmunologie, 1973; Tumorforschung am biologischen Modell, 1980; Penicillin – eine medizinhistorische Perspektive, 1999. Honour: Robert Koch Medal, German Academy of Sciences, 1982. Honours: European Association for Cancer Research, 1982; German Academy of Scientists LEOPOLDINA, Halle (Saale), 1986. Address: Boenkestrasse 55, D-13125 Berlin, Germany.

**SCHOENHAGEN Paul,** b. 27 January 1964, Koblenz, Germany. Physician; Cardiovascular Imaging Specialist. m. Noelle Schoenhagen, 2 sons, 1 daughter. Education: Medical School Marburg, Germany, 1985-91, Tuebingen, Germany, 1991-92; MD, 1992; Doctoral Thesis, Cardiovascular Medicine, Marburg, Germany, 1995. Appointments: Residency, Internal Medicine and Radiology, Stuttgart, Germany, 1992-96; Residency, Internal Medicine, 1996-99, Fellowship, Cardiovascular Medicine, 1999-2002; Fellowship, Cardiovascular Tomography, 2002-2003, Staff, Department of Diagnostic Radiology and Cardiovascular Medicine, 2003-, The Cleveland Clinic Foundation, Cleveland, Ohio, USA. Publications: Articles in scientific journals include most recently: Extent and Direction of Arterial Remodeling in Stable versus Unstable Coronary Syndromes: An Intravascular Ultrasound Study, 2002; Relation of matrix-metalloproteinase 3 found in coronary lesion samples retrieved by directional coronary atherectomy to intravascular ultasound observations on coronary remodeling, 2002; Coronary Plaque Morphology and Frequency of Ulceration Distant from Culprit Lesions in Patients with Unstable and Stable Presentation, 2003. Honours: Postdoctoral Fellowship Grant, Ohio Valley, American Heart Association, 2001-2003; 2nd James E Muller Vulnerable Plaque Award, 2002. Memberships: European Society of Cardiology; Fellow American Heart Association; Radiologic Society of North America. Address: The Cleveland Clinic Foundation, Radiology H6-6, 9500 Euclid Avenue, Cleveland, OH 44195, USA. E-mail: schoenp1@ccf.org

**SCHOLEY Arthur (Edward),** b. 17 June 1932, Sheffield, England. Children's Writer; Playwright; Librettist; Lyric Writer. Publications: The Song of Caedmon (with Donald Swann), 1971; Christmas Plays and Ideas for Worship, 1973; The Discontented Dervishes, 1977; Sallinka and the Golden Bird, 1978; Twelve Tales for a Christmas Night, 1978; Wacky and His Fuddlejig (with Donald Swann), 1978; Singalive (with Donald Swann) 1978; Herod and the Rooster (with Ronald Chamberlain), 1979; The Dickens Christmas Carol Show, 1979; Baboushka (with Donald Swann) 1979; Candletree (with Donald

Swann), 1981; Five Plays for Christmas, 1981; Four Plays About People, 1983; Martin the Cobbler, 1983; The Hosanna Kids, 1985; Make a Model Christmas Crib, 1988; Who'll Be Brother Donkey?, 1990; Brendan Ahoy!, (with Donald Swann), 1994; The Journey of the Christmas Creatures (with Karen Bradley), 1998; The Discontented Dervishes, 2002; The Panagon Parrot, 2002. Address: 10 Chiltern Court, Pages Hill, London N10 1EN, England. E-mail: scholey@arthurscholey.co.uk

**SCHOMMERS Wolfram,** b. 15 January 1941, Wuppertal, Germany. Scientist; Professor of Physics. m. Gisela Anna, 1 daughter. Education: Diploma, Physical Technology, 1964; Diploma, Theoretical Physics, 1969; Dr rer nat (PhD), 1972. Appointments: Theoretical Physicist; Professor of Theoretical Physics; Editor, various physical journals; Editor, book series: Foundations of Natural Science and Technology; Editor-in-Chief, Journal of Computational and Theoretical Nanoscience. Publications: Books: Structure and Dynamics of Surfaces I, 1986; Structure and Dynamics of Surfaces II, 1987; Quantum Theory and Pictures of Reality, 1989; Space and Time, Matter and Mind, 1994; Symbols, Pictures and Quantum Reality, 1995; Zeit und Realität, 1997; The Visible and the Invisible, 1998; Elemente des Lebens, 2000; What is Life?, 2002; Formen des Kosmos, 2002. Honours: Academic Board, Humboldt Society; Professor of Theoretical Physics of the Chinese Academy of Sciences, honorary guest position; Twentieth Century Achievement Award; New Century Award. Membership: Academy Humboldt Society; Advisory Board, Medicinal Ethics; Deputy Governor, ABI. Address: Forschungszentrum Karlsruhe, Institut of Nanotechnology, PO Box 3640, 76021 Karlsruhe, Germany.

**SCHÖN Wilhelm,** b. 12 October 1951, Linz, Danube, Germany. Civilisation Critic; Novelist; Environmentalist; Amateur Cosmologist. Education: Studies in Philology, History and Philosophy, University of Vienna, 1972-76; Private studies, Frankfurt, Main and Zurich, Switzerland, 1976-77; Employment Instructions in plastics industry, 1978-79; Private forestry planning, early 1980s; Characterisation curriculum, Computer PC for MS/DOS Microsoft, 1994. Appointments: Adjunct in the physics laboratory of Dr Kofler, Foliplast in Tyrol and Chemielaborant at Chemo-Phos, 1980-84; Private projects, 1984; First book published, 1985. Publications: Sturmvögel ziehen nach Nirgendwo, novel, 1985; Im Schatten des Drachenflugs der Macht, documentary, 1986; Meine Nation heißt Würde, 1987; Urlaub vom Wort Zwei: Collected Papers, 1994; Articles: Systemterrorismus, 1986; The Ecological Manifesto, 1988; Charta des Analytischen Naturalismus, 1991; Dissidenten-Chronologie, 1994; Kinderfänger, 1999; Rudi and Wilhelm Schön: Teufel Emerich, 2002. Memberships: Amnesty International, 1983-95; Friends of the Earth, 1989-94; IGAA, 1991-2000; IGoöA, 1991-2001; IASCP and the International Society for Environmental Ethics, early 1990's; NPG and Argus, 1994-; WWF, 1996-; THWA, 1998-2000; ODV, 1998-; VCO; PRO GS. Address: orb Zentrum, Abensbergstr 51, A-4051 Pasching, Austria.

**SCHÖNFELDER Volker,** b. 5 October 1939, Barmstedt, Germany. Professor of Physics. m. Bärbel Schönfelder, 3 sons. Education: Diploma in Physics, 1966; Dr.rer.nat., 1970; Dr. rer. nat. habil., 1979; Professor of Physics, 1995. Appointment: Head, Gamma Ray Astronomy Group, Max-Planck-Institut für Extraterrestrische Physik, until October 2004. Publications: About 400 publications in scientific journals; Editor of the book: The Universe in Gamma Rays, 2001. Honours: NASA Exceptional Scientific Achievement Award, 1993; Deutscher Philip Morris Forschungspreis, 1997. Memberships: Deutsche Physikalische Gesellschaft; Astronomische Gesellschaft.

Address: Max-Planck-Institut für Extraterrestrische Physik, Postfach 1603, 85740 Garching, Germany. E-mail: vos@mpe.mpg.de

**SCHROEDER Gerhard Fritz Kurt,** b. 7 April 1944, Mossenberg, Germany. Politician. m. Doris Koepf, 1 child. Education: Degree in Law, Goettingen University, 1971. Appointments: Lawyer, Hanover, Germany, 1978-90; Chairman, Young Social Democrats, 1978-80; Legislator, German Bundestag, 1980-86; Leader of the Opposition, State Parliament of Lower Saxony, 1986-90; Prime Minister, Lower Saxony, 1990-98; Chancellor, Government of Germany, 1998-2005. Publications: Contributor of articles to numerous professional publications.

**SCHTEPA Vladimir Ilitch,** b. 30 September 1937, Novosibirsk, Russia. Astronomer. Education: Moscow State University, Fakultat of Physiks, Astronomical Division, 1961-67; Appointments: Junior Research Assistant, Sakhalin Komplex Science Research Institute, 1967-69; Owner, publisher and chief-redaktor for journal "Fakts", 1987 . Publications: Articles on: Essence of Economic Processes, 1990-98; Physics and astronomy and history, 1987-98 in "Fakts"; Books in Russian (soon to be published in English): How to build a spaceship/Physical principals of natural philosophy; Main categories of Economics/Logical paradigm, 2003-2004.. Honours: Distinguished Leadership Award, ABI, 1998; Gold Medal, International Who's Who of Intellectuals; Silver Medal, 2000 Outstanding Intellectuals of the 20th Century, IBC. Memberships: Russian Writers Organisation; Russian Physical Society. Address: Dahlborgsg 6, 38243 Nybro, Sweden. E-mail: vladimir.schtepa@telia.com Website: www.spaceship.ru

**SCHULBERG Budd,** b. 27 March 1914, New York, New York, USA. Author. m. (1) Virginia Ray, 23 July 1936, divorced 1942, 1 daughter, (2) Victoria Anderson, 17 February 1943, divorced 1964, 2 sons, (3) Geraldine Brooks, 12 July 1964, deceased 1977, (4) Betsy Anne Langman, 9 July 1979, 1 son, 1 daughter. Education: AB cum laude, Dartmouth College, 1936. Appointments: Founder-President, Schulberg Productions; Founder-Director, Watts Writers Workshop, Los Angeles, 1965-; Founder-Chairman, Frederick Douglass Creative Arts Center, New York City, 1971-. Publications: What Makes Sammy Run?, 1941; The Harder They Fall, 1947; The Disenchanted, 1950; Some Faces in the Crowd, 1953; Waterfront, 1955; Sanctuary V, 1969; The Four Seasons of Success, 1972; Loser and Still Champion: Muhammad Ali, 1972; Swan Watch, 1975; Everything That Moves, 1980; Moving Pictures: Memories of a Hollywood Prince, 1981; Love, Action, Laughter and Other Sad Tales, 1990; Sparring with Hemingway and Other Legends of the Fight Game, 1995. Editor: From the Ashes: Voices of Watts, 1967. Screenplays: Little Orphan Annie (with Samuel Ornitz), 1938; Winter Carnival (with F Scott Fitzgerald), 1939; Weekend for Three (with Dorothy Parker), 1941; City Without Men (with Martin Berkeley), 1943; Government Girl, 1943; On the Waterfront, 1954; A Face in the Crowd, 1957; Wind Across the Everglades, 1958. Contributions to: Leading magazines. Honours: Academy Award, 1954; New York Critics Circle Award, 1954; Screen Writers Guild Award, 1954; Venice Film Festival Award, 1954; Christopher Award, 1955; German Film Critics Award, 1957; B'hai Human Rights Award, 1968; Prix Literaire, Deauville Festival, 1989; Westhampton Writers Lifetime Achievement Award, 1989; World Boxing Association Living Legend Award, 1990; Southampton Cultural Center 1st Annual Literature Award, 1992. Memberships: American Civil Liberties Union; American Society of Composers, Authors and Publishers; Authors Guild; Dramatists Guild; Players' Club, founder member; PEN; Phi Beta Kappa; Writers Guild East.

Address: c/o Miriam Altschuler Literary Agency, RR1, Box 5, Old Post Road, Red Hook, NY 12571, USA.

**SCHULER Robert Jordan**, b. 25 June 1939, California, USA. Professor of English; Poet. m. Carol Forbis, 7 September 1963, 2 sons, 1 daughter. Education: BA, Honours, Political Science, Stanford University, 1961; MA, Comparative Literature, University of California, Berkeley, 1965; PhD, English, University of Minnesota, 1989. Appointments: Instructor in English, Menlo College, 1965-67; Instructor in Humanities, Shimer College, 1967-77; Professor of English, University of Wisconsin, 1978-. Publications: Axle of the Oak, 1978; Seasonings, 1978; Where is Dancers' Hill?, 1979; Morning Raga, 1980; Red Cedar Scroll, 1981; Floating Out of Stone, 1982; Music for Monet, 1984; Grace: A Book of Days, 1995; Journeys Toward the Original Mind, 1995; Red Cedar Suite, 1999; In search of "Green Dolphin Street", 2004; Dance into Heaven, 2005. Contributions to: Caliban; Northeast; Tar River Poetry; Longhouse; Dacotah Territory; Wisconsin Academy Review; Wisconsin Review; North Stone Review; Wisconsin Poetry 1991 Transactions; Hummingbird; Abraxas; Lake Street Review; Inheriting the Earth; Mississippi Valley Review; Coal City Review; Gypsy; Imagining Home, 1995. Honour: Wisconsin Arts Board Fellowship for Poetry, 1997; Awards from Wisconsin Humanities Council; Illinois Arts Council; NEA. Membership: Phi Kappa Phi; Land Commissioner, Land Use Planner, Dunn County, Menomonie Township. Address: E4549 479th Avenue, Menomonie, WI 54751, USA. E-mail: Schulerr@uw.stout.edu

**SCHULLER Gunther (Alexander)**, b. 22 November 1925, New York, New York, USA. Composer; Conductor; Music Educator; Publisher. m. Marjorie Black, 8 June 1948, deceased 1992, 2 sons. Education: St Thomas Choir School, New York City, 1937-40. Appointments: Teacher, Manhattan School of Music, New York City, 1950-63; Teacher, 1963-84, Artistic Co-Director, 1969-74, Director, 1974-84, Berkshire Music Center, Tanglewood, Massachusetts; Co-Director, Smithson Jazz Masterworks Orchestra, 1991-1997; Faculty, Yale School of Music, 1964-67; President, New England Conservatory of Music, Boston, 1967-77; Music Publisher, 1975-99; Record Producer, GM Recordings, 1980-; Artistic Director, Festival at Sandpoint, 1985-98. Publications: Horn Technique, 1962, 2nd edition, 1992; Early Jazz: Its Roots and Musical Development, 1968; Musings, 1985; The Swing Era, 1988; The Compleat Conductor, 1997. Contributions to: Various publications. Honours: Guggenheim Fellowship, 1962-63; ASCAP-Deems Taylor Award, 1970; Rodgers and Hammerstein Award, 1971; William Schuman Award, Columbia University, 1989; John D and Catharine T MacArthur Foundation Fellowship, 1991; Pulitzer Prize in Music, 1994; Honorary doctorates. Memberships: American Academy of Arts and Sciences; American Academy of Arts and Letters. Address: 167 Dudley Road, Newton Centre, MA 02159, USA.

**SCHULZE Hagen**, b. 31 July 1943, Tangier, Morocco. Historian. m. Ingrid Schulze-Bidlingmaier, 2 sons. Education: Political Science, Sociology, Philosophy, Rheinische Friedrich-Willhelms-Universität zu Bonn, Christian-Albrechts-Universität zu Kiel, 1963-67; Dr Phil, 1967; Habilitation, 1977, Privatdozent, 1977-79, Christian-Albrechts-Universität. Appointments: Research Staff, Edition Akten der Reichskanzlei, Bundesarchiv Koblenz, 1968-71; Research Staff, Stiftung Preussischer Kulturbesitz, Berlin, and Visiting Lecturer, Modern History, Christian-Albrechts-Universität, 1971-76; Professor of Modern History and Theory and Methodology of History, Friedrich-Meinecke-Institut, Freie Universität Berlin, 1979-89; Professor of Modern History and Director of the Institute of History,

Universität der Bundeswehr, Munich, 1988-93; Professor of Modern German and European History, 1994-; Director, German Historical Institute London, 2000-. Publications: Main monographs since 1990 include: Die Wiederkehr Europas, 1990; The Course of German Nationalism: From Frederick the Great to Bismark, 1763-1867, 1991; States, Nations and Nationalism: From the Middle Ages to the Present, 1996; Germany: A New History, 1998; Phönix Europa. Die Moderne Seit 1740, 1998; Deutsche Errinerungsorte 3 vols (co-author), 2001. Honours: Scholarships include: Heisenberg Fellowship, 1978-79; Volkswagen Fellow, St Antony's College, University of Oxford, 1985-86; Member, Herodotus Fellow, 1992, Visiting Fellow, 1996, Institute for Advanced Study, Princeton University; Visiting Fellow, 1998, Fellow Commoner, 2000-, Sidney Sussex College, University of Cambridge. Address: German Historical Institute London, 17 Bloomsbury Square, London WC1A 2NJ, England.

**SCHULZE-BELLI Paola**, b. 9 April 1939, Trieste, Italy. University Professor. m. Kristian Schulze, 1 son. Education: High School of Classical Studies, Latin and Ancient Greek; Conservatory Diploma in Piano Studies; Degree in Modern Literature and Languages, German, English, Catholic University of Milan, 1962; 2 Year Diploma in Translation, German English, Faculty for Translators and Interpreters, University of Trieste. Appointments: Assistant Professor, German Language and Literature, Department of Foreign Languages and Literature, 1969-79, University of Trieste, Udine (now an independent university); Associate Professor, German Language and Literature, Department of Humanities, 1980-, Associate Professor, Department of International and Diplomatic Services, 2002-, University of Trieste, Trieste; President and Founder, Association of Medieval Culture, Trieste, 1989-; Organiser of 5 international conferences in Trieste: Love and Adventure in Arthurian Romances, 1988; The Romans in Tristan, 1989; Medieval Women Mystics, 1991; Thomasin of Cividale and Medieval Didactic Literature, 1993; Men and the Sea in the Middle Ages, 2002. Publications: Publications on Austrian and German authors of the 19th and 20th centuries; Anthology of German Poets of WW1, 1985; First translation into Italian of a 13th century book: Mechthild of Magdeburg's The Flowing Light of the Godhead (La luce fluente della Divinità), 1991; First translation into Italian of the novel "Rodinka" by Lou Andreas-Salome, 1992; Publications on Medieval Culture in the German and English Language, and publications about myths such as Pandora; Editor: Mediaevalia Tergestina I, II, III, 2002, 2004; Speeches at International Center for Medieval Studies, Western Michigan University, USA and International Medieval Congress, University of Leeds, England. Memberships: Association of Medieval Culture; Lions Club "Alto Adriatico", Trieste. Address: Department of Humanities, University of Treiste, Piazzale Europa 1, 34123 Trieste, Italy. E-mail: schulzep@libero.it

**SCHUMACHER Joel**, b. 29 August 1939, New York, USA. Film Director. Education: Parson School of Design, New York. Appointments: Work in fashion industry aged 15; Owner boutique Paraphernalia; Costume designer, Revlon, 1970s; Set and production design; Writer, director for TV; Films include: The Incredible Shrinking Woman; DC Cab (also screenplay); St Elmo's Fire (also screenplay); The Lost Boys; Cousins; Flatliners; Dying Young; Falling Down; The Client; Batman Forever; A Time to Kill; Batman and Robin; Eight Millimeter; Flawless (also screenplay and producer); Gossip; Tigerland; Phone Booth; Bad Company. Publications: (screenplays) Sparkle; Car Wash; The Wiz. Address: Joel Schumacher Productions, 400 Warner Boulevard, Burbank, CA 91522, USA.

**SCHUMACHER Michael,** b. 3 January 1969. Motor Racing Driver. m. Corinna Betsch, 1995, 2 children. Appointments: Began Professional Career, 1983; 2nd Place, International German Formula 3 Championship, 1989; Driver for Mercedes, 1990; International German Champion Formula 3 Championship, 1990; European Formula 3 Champion, 1990; World Champion, Formula 3, Macau and Fiji, 1990; Formula 1 Contestant, 1991-; 1st Formula One Victory, Belgium, 1992; Other Grand Prix wins: Portuguese, 1993, Brazilian, 1994, 1995, 2000, 2002, Pacific, 1994, San Marino, 1994, 2000, 2002, Monaco, 1994, 1995, 1999, 2001, Canadian, 1994, 1998, 2000, French, 1994, 1995, Hungarian, 1994, 1998, 2001, European, 1994, 1995, 2000, 2001, Spanish, 1995, 2001, 2002, Italian, 1996, Japanese, 1997, Australian, 2000, 2001, 2002, Italian, 1996, 2000, American, 2000, Japanese, 1997, 2000, Malaysian, 2000, 2001, Austrian, 2002; Third Place, World Motor Racing Championship, 1992, Fourth Place, 1993; Formula One World Champion, 1994, 1995, 2000, 2001, 2002, 2003. Publication: Formula for Success (with Derick Allsop), 1996; Michael Schumacher (biography with Christopher Hilton), 2000. Address: c/o Weber Management GmbH, 70173 Stuttgart, Hirschstrasse 36, Germany. Website: www.mschumacher.com

**SCHUNK Werner (Walter),** b. 12 January 1938, Sundhausen/Gotha, Germany. Doctor; University Teacher. m. Christine Margarete Seyfert, 1 daughter. Education: Study of Medicine, Humboldt University, Berlin and Medical Academy in Erfurt; Doctor of Medicine, 1963; Dr Habilitatus, University of Halle, 1974; Specialist in Occupational Medicine. Appointments: Chief Doctor, Company Outpatients Department Gotha, 1968-72; Director of Occupational Medicine, 1972-92, Professor of Medicine, 1976, Pro-Rector, 1976-81 Medical Academy of Erfurt; Director of Institute of Science (Private), 1992-; Private Practice; Specialist in Toxicology and Internal Medicine; Research work in Medical Schools including: London, Birmingham, Paris, Karolinska Institute, Stockholm. Publications: Author: Schadstoffe in der Gummiindustrie, 1995, 1996, 1998, 2000; Arbeits und Gewerhetoxikologie, 1997, 1998, 1999, 2000, 2004; Eco-med edition: Stoffkataster für das Backgewerbe, 2002, 2003, 2004; 65 patents in the field of biomaterials: new polymers and your toxicology. Honours: Title: Medizinalrat; Science Prize of Academy in Germany, 1978, 1983. Membership: Gesellschaft of Arbeits und Umweltmedizin. Address: Gallettistrasse 2, 99867 Gotha/Thür. Germany. E-mail: werner.schunk@web.de Website: www.werner-schunk.de

**SCHUPP Ronald Irving,** b. 10 December 1951, Syracuse, New York, USA. Clergyman; Missionary; Civil and Human Rights Leader. Education: Certificates, Moody Bible Institute, 1986; 1988; Advanced Certificate, Evangelical Training Association, 1992; Certificate, Centre for Biblical Counselling, 2001; Certificates, Henry George School of Social Science, Chicago, Illinois, 2002, 2003. Appointments: Ordained Baptist Ministry, 1976; Ordained Ministry, The Old Country Church, 1972; Missionary, Assistant Pastor, The Old Country Church, Chicago, 1972-76; Field Organiser, Staff Person, Nite Pastor: Chicago, 1972-78, Southern Culture Exchange, 1973-76, Alternative Christian Training School, Chicago, 1974-78, The Great American Coffeehouse, Chicago, 1976-78, Chicago Area Conference on Hunger and Malnutrition, 1974-78; Assistant Director, Uptown Community Organisation, Chicago, 1974-76; Missionary, Solid Rock Baptist Church, Chicago, 1976-89; Director, Chicago Action Centre, 1978-80; Missionary, Church-Licensed Pastoral Counsellor, Marble Rock Missionary Baptist Church, Chicago, 1990-; Representative, Lakota Nation (Traditional), 1993-; American Indian Movement; Representative, League of Indigenous Sovereign Nations of the Western Hemisphere, 1993-; President, Citizens Taking Action

Inc, 1995-97. Honours: Appreciation Award, West Englewood United Organisation/Clara's House Shelter, Chicago, 1992; Named Wa-Kin-Ya-Wicha-Ho Thunder Voice by Traditional Lakota Elders, 1992; Named Kiyuyakki Northern Lights by Inuit Elder Etok, 1994; Tributes in US Congressional Record, Congressman Bobby Rush, 1993; Senator Carol Mosely Braun, 1994. Memberships include: Chicago Coalition for the Homeless, 1989-99; Homeless on the Move for Equality, 1990-92, Board of Directors, 1990-92; National Coalition for the Homeless, 1991-2000; National Union of the Homeless, 1992-95; Member, Steering Committee, 1st Congressional District Ministerial Association, 1993-95, Chair, Housing Committee, 1993-95, Chicago; United Nations Association USA, 1996-2000; Americans Disabled for Attendant Programs Today, 1997-2000; Steering Committee, Raising Issues to Demand Everyone's Right to Service, 1997-98. Address: 1246 W. Pratt Blvd, Apt 707, Chicago, IL 60626-4386, USA.

**SCHÜSSLER Elizabeth.** Professor. m. Francis Fiorenza, 1 daughter. Education: Classical Languages and Literature, 1949-58; Theology, Philosophy and German Literature, 1958-60, Theology, 1960-62, University of Würzburg; Theology, University of Münster, 1964-70. Appointments: Assistant Professor, 1970-75, Associate Professor, 1975-80, Full Professor, 1980-84, Theology, University of Notre Dame; Co-ordinator of Scripture, Notre Dame Institute for Clergy Education, 1976-76; Distinguished Theologian in Residence at the College of Wooster, 1982; Talbot Professor of New Testament, 1984-88, Director and Initiator of Feminist Liberation Theology and Ministry, Doctor of Ministry Program, 1986-88, The Episcopal Divinity School; Krister Stendahl Professor, Harvard University, The Divinity School, 1988-; Chair, Religion, Gender and Culture Program, HDS, 1996-2000. Publications: Numerous books, journals and articles. Honours include: First Annual Women's Ordination Conference Service Award, 1984; US Catholic of the Year Award, 1987; Theresa of Avila, Long Island Women's Ordination Conference Award, 1989; Continuum Book Award, 1994; Biblical Archeologist Award, 1995; SBL Excellence in Mentoring Award, 2001; Catholic Press Association First Place Award for Wisdom Ways, 2002. Memberships include: Society of Biblical Literature; Catholic Biblical Association; American Academy of Religion; College Theology Society; Studiorum Novi Testamenti Societas; Doctoral Fellow, Society for Values in Higher Education; American Theological Society; American Academy of Arts and Sciences. Address: Harvard Divinity School, 45 Francis Ave, Cambridge, MA 02138, USA.

**SCHWARZ Berthold Eric,** b. 20 October 1924, Jersey City, USA. Physician. m. 22 January 1955, 1 son, 1 daughter. Education: AB, Dartmouth College, 1945; Certificate, Dartmouth Medical School, 1945; MD, New York University College of Medicine, 1950; MS, Mayo Graduate School of Medicine, 1957. Appointments: Intern, Mary Hitchcock Memorial Hospital, Hanover, New Hampshire, 1950-51; Fellowship, Psychiatry, Mayo Foundation, Rochester, Minnesota, 1951-55; Private Practice, Psychiatry, Montclair, New Jersey, 1955-82; Consultant, Essex County Medical Centre, Cedar Grove, New Jersey, 1965-82; Private Practice, Vero Beach, Florida, 1982-2001; Research into parapsychiatry and ufology, 2001-. Publications include: Co-author, with B A Ruggieri, Parent Child Tensions; You Can Raise Decent Children; Author: Psychic Dynamics; The Jacques Romano Story; Parent Child Telepathy; Psychic Nexus; UFO Dynamics; Into the Crystal; Psychiatric and Paranormal Aspects of Ufology; More than 175 articles. Memberships: American Medical Association; American Psychiatric Association; American Association for the Advancement of Science; American Society for Psychical Research; Parapsychlogical Association; Academy of Religion and Psychical Research. Address: 642 Azalea Lane, Vero Beach, FL 32963, USA. E-mail: ardisps@aol.com

**SCHWARZENEGGER Arnold Alois,** b. 30 July 1947, Graz, Austria (US citizen, 1963). Actor; Author; Businessman; Former Bodybuilder; US Governor of California. m. Maria Owings Shriver, 1985, 2 sons, 2 daughters. Education: University of Wisconsin-Superior. Appointment: Elected Governor of California, 2003. Career: Film appearances include: Stay Hungry, 1976; Pumping Iron, 1977; The Jayne Mansfield Story, 1980; Conan the Barbarian, 1982; The Destroyer, 1983; The Terminator, 1984; Commando, 1985; Raw Deal, 1986; Predator, 1987; Running Man, 1987; Red Heat, 1988; Twins, 1989; Total Recall, 1990; Kindergarten Cop, 1990; Terminator II, 1991; Last Action Hero, 1993; Dave (cameo), 1993; True Lies, 1994; Junior, 1994; Eraser, 1996; Single All the Way, 1996; Batman and Robin, 1997; With Wings with Eagles, 1997; End of Days, 1999; The Sixth Day, 2001; Collateral Damage, 2002; Terminator 3: Rise of the Machines, 2003; The Rundown, 2003; Around the World in 80 Days, 2004. Publications: Arnold: The Education of a Bodybuilder, 1977; Arnold's Bodyshaping for Women, 1979; Arnold's Bodybuilding for Men, 1981; Arnold's Encyclopedia of Modern Bodybuilding, 1985; Arnold's Fitness for Kids (jointly), 1993. Honours: National Weight Training Coach Special Olympics; Bodybuilding Champion, 1965-80; Junior Mr Europe, 1965; Best Built Man of Europe, 1966; Mr Europe, 1966; Mr International, 1968; Mr Universe (amateur), 1969. Memberships: Volunteer, prison rehabilitation programmes; Chairman, President's Council on Physical Fitness and Sport, 1990. Address: PMK, Suite 200, 955 South Carillo Drive, Los Angeles, CA 90048, USA.

**SCHWARZKOPF Elisabeth (Dame),** b. 9 December 1915, Jarocin, Poland. Singer (Soprano). m. Walter Legge 1953, deceased 1979. Education: High School of Music, Berlin studied with Maria Ivogün-Raucheisen, Lula Mysz-Gmeiner and Dr. Heinrich Egenolf. Debut: Deutsches Opernhaus Berlin; appeared at Staatsoper Wien, Royal Opera House Covent Garden, London; La Scala Milan; San Francisco Opera; Reopening Bayreuth Festival, 1951; Salzburger Festspiele 1947-64; Film "Der Rosenkavalier", Salzburger Festspiele, 1960. Recordings: 16 complete Operas, various Symphonies; Songs and Arias with Orchestra, 6 complete Operettas, Leider with pianoforte: 21 LP's and 16 CD's. Publications: Editor, On and Off the Record: a memoire of Walter Legge. Honours: Recipient of numerous awards including: Cambridge MUsD; Lilli Lehmann Medal, Salzburg; MusD,(hc) University of Washington DC; Mozart Medal Frankfurt, Arts et Letters, Paris; Ehrensenatorin Hochschule für Musik Carl Maria von Weber, Dresden; DMus (hc) Glasgow. Address: Rebhusstrasse 29, CH 8126 Zumikon, Switzerland.

**SCOFIELD Paul (David),** b. 21 January 1922, King's Norton, England. Actor. m. Joy Parker, 1943, 1 son, 1 daughter. Education: London Mask Theatre Drama School, 1940's. Career: Actor, Member Birmingham Repertory Theatre, 1941, 1943-46, Stratford-upon-Avon, Shakespeare Memorial Theatre, 1946-48, Arts Theatre, 1946, Phoenix Theatre, 1947, W H M Tennent, 1949-56, Associate Director, National Theatre, 1970-71; 2 seasons in New York; Films include: The Train, 1963; A Man for All Seasons, 1967; King Lear, 1970; Scorpio, 1972; A Delicate Balance, 1972; 1919, Anna Karenina, 1984; When the Whales Came, 1988; Henry V, 1989; Hamlet, 1991; Quiz Show, 1993; The Little Riders, 1995; The Crucible, 1995; TV: The Ambassadors, 1977; The Potting Shed, 1981; If Winter Comes, 1981; Song at Twilight, 1982; Come into the Garden Maud, 1982; A Kind of Alaska, 1984; Summer Lightning, 1985; Only Yesterday, 1986; The Attic, 1988; Utz, 1991;

Martin Chuzzlewit, 1994; Theatre appearances include: Hamlet ( Moscow), 1955; Hamlet, The Power and the Glory, A Family Reunion at the Poenix Theatre, London, 1955-56; A Man for All Seasons, London, 1962-63; King Lear (Eastern Europe, Helsinki, Moscow, New York), 1963, 1964; Timon of Athens 1965; The Government Inspector (London), 1966; Staircase, 1967; Macbeth, 1968; Uncle Vanya, 1968; The Tempest, 1974; Amadeus, 1979; Othello, 1980. Honours: CBE, 1956; CH, 1999; Oscar for A Man for All Seasons (film), 1967; Honorary Degrees: Glasgow University, Kent University, 1973, Sussex University, 1985; St Andrew's University, Oxford University; Shakespeare Prize, Hamburg, 1972; Danish Film Academy Award; Tony Award, Evening Standard Drama Award for John Gabriel Borkman, 1996. Address: The Gables, Balcombe, West Sussex, RH17 6ND, England.

**SCORSESE Martin,** b. 17 November 1942, Flushing, New York, USA. American Film Director; Writer. m. (1) Laraine Marie Brennan, 1965, 1 daughter. (2) Julia Cameron, divorced, 1 daughter. (3) Isabella Rossellini, 1979, divorced 1983. (4) Barbara DeFina, 1985. Education: New York University. Appointments: Faculty Assistant, Instructor, Film Department, New York University, 1963-66; Instructor, 1968-70; Director, Writer of Films, including: What's a Nice Girl Like You Doing in a Place Like This?, 1963; It's Not Just You, Murray, 1964; Who's That Knocking At My Door?, 1968; The Big Shave, 1968; Director, Play, The Act, 1977-78; Director, Writer of Documentaries; Supervisor Editor, Assistant Director, Woodstock, 1970; Associate Producer, Post-Production Supervisor, Medicine Ball Caravan, 1971, Box Car Bertha, 1972; Director, Films: Mean Streets, 1973; Alice Doesn't Live Here Any More, 1974; Taxi Driver, 1976; New York, New York, 1977; King of Comedy, 1981; Actor, Director, The Last Waltz, 1978; Director, Raging Bull, 1980, After Hours, 1985, The Color of Money, 1986; Director, The Last Temptation of Christ, 1988, Goodfellas, 1989, Cape Fear, 1991, The Age of Innocence, 1993, Clockers, 1994, Casino, 1995; Kundun, 1997; Bringing Out the Dead, 1999; The Muse, 1999; The Gangs of New York, 2002; Executive Producer, The Crew, 1989; Producer, The Grifters, 1989; Co-Producer, Mad Dog and Glory, 1993. Publications: Scorsese on Scorsese, 1989; The Age of Innocence: The Shooting Script (with Jay Cocks), 1996; Casino (with Nicholas Pileggi), 1996; Kundun, 1997; Bringing Out the Dead, 1999; The Muse, 1999; Gangs of New York, 2002. Honours: Edward J Kingsley Foundation Award, 1963, 1964; 1st Prize, Rosenthal Foundation Awards of Society of Cinematologists, 1964; 1st Prize, Screen Producers Guild, 1965, Brown University Film Festival, 1965, Shared Rosellini Prize, 1990; Named Best Director, Cannes Film Festival, 1986; Courage in Filmmaking Award, Los Angeles Film Teachers Association, 1989; Award, American Museum of the Moving Image, 1996; Award for Preservation, International Federation of Film Wards, 2001; Golden Globe for Best Director, 2003. Address: c/o United Artists, 10202 West Washington Blvd, Culver City, CA 90230, USA.

**SCOTT James,** b. 8 December 1954, Croxdale, Durham, England. Cleric. Education: New College, Durham, 1971-75; Certificate, 1993, Diploma, 1994, Christian Studies, Westminster College, Oxford; BA, Theology, 1999, MA, Theology (Dogma and Church History), 2002; Greenwich School of Theology; Doctor of Letters (Church Ministry), Trinity College, 1998; PhD, Theology (Dogma and Pastoral Studies), Greenwich School of Theology, ongoing studies, 2005. Appointments: Durham County Treasury, 1973-76; Novitiate, Third Order of Franciscans (Church of England), 1976; Scargill House Community, 1977-79; Life Profession, Third Order of Franciscans (Church of England), 1979; Personal

# DICTIONARY OF INTERNATIONAL BIOGRAPHY

Assistant to the Prior of GCA, 1979; Disabled due to the effects of a spinal cord tumour, 1978-; Pastoral Assistant, Church of England, 1980-93; Received into the Catholic Church and Life Profession, transferred to Roman Catholic Franciscan Third Order, 1993; Personal Tutor, Greenwich School of Theology, 2002-; Personal Mentor for students at Brookes, Oxford and Westminster, Oxford, 2005-. Publications: The Problem of Evil for the Religious Believer (monograph), 1997; The Meaning of the Concept of Covenant in the Holy Scriptures (BA thesis), 1998; The Life of St Francis of Assisi: Is Franciscanism Relevant Today? (MA thesis), 2002. Honours: Serving Brother, Order of St John, 1986; Mensa Certificate of Merit, 1995; Knight of St Columba, 1995; Officer, Order of St John, 1996; Awarded Richardson Salver for exceptional service to the community in the face of great personal adversity, St John Ambulance, 1998. Memberships: St John Ambulance, 1971-2001: Divisional President, 1987-93, Area Vice-President, 1993-96, Northumbria County Vice-President, 1996-2001; Knights of St Columba, 1995-: Deputy Grand Knight, Council 549, 1996, Grand Knight, Council 549, 1997-99, Northumbrian Provincial Action Convenor, 1995, Deputy Grand Knight, Council 142, 2001-2004; Alumni: Westminster College, Oxford, 1994-, Greenwich School of Theology, 1998-, Brookes, Oxford, 2001-. Address: Wear Lodge, Manor Lane, Aisthorpe, Lincoln, LN1 2SG, England.

**SCOTT Paul Henderson,** b. 7 November 1920, Edinburgh, Scotland. Essayist; Historian; Critic; Former Diplomat. Education: MA, MLitt, University of Edinburgh. Publications: 1707: The Union of Scotland and England, 1979; Walter Scott and Scotland, 1981; John Galt, 1985; Towards Independence: Essays on Scotland, 1991; Scotland in Europe, 1992; Andrew Fletcher and the Treaty of Union, 1992; Scotland: A Concise Cultural History (editor), 1993; Defoe in Edinburgh, 1994; Scotland: An Unwon Cause, 1997; Still in Bed with an Elephant, 1998; The Boasted Advantages, 1999; A Twentieth Century Life, 2002; Scotland Resurgent, 2003. Contributions to: Newspapers and journals. Honours: Andrew Fletcher Award, 1993; Oliver Award, 2000. Memberships: International PEN, former president, Scottish Centre; Saltire Society; Association for Scottish Literary Studies; Scottish National Party. Address: 33 Drumsheugh Gardens, Edinburgh EH3 7RN, Scotland.

**SCOTT Ridley,** b. 30 November 1937, South Shields, England. Film Director. Education: Royal College of Art. Career: Director, numerous award-winning TV commercials, 1970-; Début as feature film director with The Duellists, 1978; Other films include: Alien; Blade Runner; Legend; Someone to Watch Over Me; Black Rain; Thelma and Louise, 1942; Conquest of Paradise, 1992; White Squall, 1995; G I Jane, 1997; Gladiators, 1999; Hannibal, 2000; Black Hawk Down, 2001; The Gathering Storm, 2002; Co-Producer, The Browning Version, 1994. Honour: Honorary D Litt, Sunderland; TV Emmy for Best Made-for-TV Film, 2002. Address: Scott Free 42/44 Beak Street, London, W 1R, 3DA, England.

**SCOTT Tony,** b. 21 June 1944, Newcastle upon Tyne, England. Film Director. Education: Sunderland College of Art; Leeds College of Art; Royal College of Art Film and TV Department. Career: Assistant Director, Dream Weaver, 1967; The Movement Movement, 1967; Cameraman: The Visit; Untitled; Compromise; Milian; Fat Man; Worked for Derrick Knight & Alan King Associates; Visual Director and Cameraman, pop promotional films, Now Films Ltd; TV cameraman, Seven Sisters, 1968; Co-producer, actor, Don't Walk; Assistant Director, Gulliver; Writer, Director, Editor, Loving Memory, 1969-70; Visual Director, Cameraman, publicity film for Joe Egg; Director, One of the Missing, 1989; Other films include:

Revenge; Top Gun; Beverly Hills Cop II; Days of Thunder; The Last Boy Scout; True Romance; Crimson Tide; The Fan; Enemy of the State; Director, Scott Free Enterprises Ltd; Director, TV and cinema commercials for Ridley Scott and Associates. Honours: Grand Prix, Mar del Plata Festival, Argentina; Prix de la TV Suisse, Nyon; 2nd Prize, Esquire Film Festival, USA; Diploma of Merit, Melbourne. Address: Totem Productions, 8009 Santa Monica Boulevard, Los Angeles, CA 90046, USA.

**SCOTT-THOMAS Kristin,** b. Redruth, England. Actress. m. François Oliviennes, 1 son, 1 daughter. Education: Central School of Speech and Drama; Ecole National des Arts et Technique de Théâtre, Paris. Career: Resident in France from age of 18; Stage appearances include: La Terre Etrangère; Naive Hirondelles and Yves Peut-Etre; Appearances on TV in France, Germany, Australia, USA, Britain include: L'Ami d'Enfance de Maigret; Blockhaus; Chameleon La Tricheuse; Sentimental Journey; The Tenth Man; Endless Game; Framed; Titmuss Regained; Look at it This Way; Body and Soul; Actress in films: Djamel et Juliette; L'Agent Troubé; La Méridienne; Under the Cherry Moon; A Handful of Dust, Force Majeure; Bille en tête; The Bachelor; Bitter Moon; Four Weddings and a Funeral; Angels and Insects; Richard III; The English Patient; Amour et Confusions; The Horse Whisperer; Random Hearts; Up at the Villa; Gosford Park; Life As a House; Petites Coupures, 2003. Honours include: BAFTA Award; Evening Stand Film Award.

**SCOWCROFT Philip Lloyd,** b. 8 June 1933, Sheffield, England. Retired Solicitor. m (Elsie) Mary Robinson, deceased, 2 daughters. Education: MA, LLM Cantab., Trinity Hall, Cambridge, 1953-56; Admitted Solicitor, 1959. Appointments: Solicitor to successive Doncaster Local Authorities, 1959-93; Retired 1993. Publications include: Cricket in Doncaster and District, 1985; Lines to Doncaster, 1985; Singing for Pleasure: A Centenary History of Doncaster Choral Society, 1988; British Light Music, 1997; Railways in British Crime Fiction, 2004; Numerous articles on music, transport, crime fiction, military history and sport for many different periodical publications and for Grove's Dictionary, 2001 edition and various Oxford Companions. Memberships: Many societies to do with music, transport, crime fiction, military history and sport including: Committee member: Spohr Society of Great Britain, Railway and Canal Historical Society, Dorothy L Sayers Society; Chairman, Doncaster Arts and Museum Society, 1968-; President, Doncaster Choral Society, 1992-. Address: 8 Rowan Mount, Doncaster DN2 5PJ, England.

**SCUDAMORE Peter,** b. 13 June 1958, Hereford, England. Jockey. m. Marilyn, 1980, 2 sons. Career: Former point-to-point and amateur jockey; Estate agency; Professional National Hunt Jockey, 1979-93; 1,677 winners; 7 times champion National Hunt Jockey, record 221 winners, 1988-89; Retired as Jockey, 1993; Director, Chasing Promotions, 1989-; Racing Journalist, Daily Mail, 1993-; Partner with Trainer Nigel Twiston-Davis. Publications: A Share of Success (co-author), 1983; Scudamore on Steeplechasing (co-author); Scu: The Autobiography of a Champion, 1993. Membership; Joint President, Jockeys Association.

**SCULLY Sean,** b. 30 June 1945, Dublin, Ireland. Artist. Education: Croydon College of Art, London, 1965-68; BA, 1st Class Honours, Fine Arts, University of Newcastle upon Tyne, 1968-71; Graduate Studies, Harvard University, Boston, USA, 1972-73. Appointments include: Lecturer, Chelsea College of Arts and Design, London, 1973-75; Lecturer, Goldsmith College of Art and Design, London, 1973-74; Visiting Art Professor, Princeton University, New Jersey, USA, 1978-82; Professor, Parsons School of Art, New York City, 1981-84; Professor for

Painting, Akademie der Bildenden Künste, Munich Germany, 2002-; Exhibitions: Numerous group exhibitions from 1969- include: Matrix Berkeley 1978-98, University of California Berkeley Art Museum, 1998; The Essl Collection: The First View, Vienna Austria, 1999; On Canvas: Contemporary Painting from the Collection, The Guggenheim Museum, New York, 2000; A Century of Drawing, National Gallery of Art, Washington DC, 2001; Color/Concept, National Gallery of Australia, Canberra, 2002; Divergent, Galerie Lelong, New York, 2003; A Vision of Modern Art, In Memory of Dorothy Walker, Irish Museum of Modern Art, Dublin, Ireland, 2004; Numerous solo exhibitions from 1973- include: Sean Scully on Paper, Metropolitan Museum of Art, New York, 2000; Sean Scully: Light and Gravity, Knoedler + Company, New York, 2001; Centro de Arte Oiticica, Rio de Janeiro, Brazil, 2002; Hotel des Arts, Toulon, 2003; Timothy Taylor Gallery, London, 2003; Gallerie Lelong, Paris, 2004; Sean Scully Prints, Irish Cultural Centre, Paris, 2004; Works in public collections in USA, South America, Europe, Australia and Japan. Publications: Numerous articles and reviews of his work and exhibitions in books, magazines and journals; New monographs: The Color of Time, The Photographs of Sean Scully, 2003; Sean Scully by David Carrier, 2004. Honours: Stuyvesant Foundation Prize, 1970; John Knox Fellowship, UK, 1972; Harkness Fellowship, New York City, 1975-77; Guggenheim Fellowship , New York City, 1983; National Endowment for the Arts Fellowship, USA, 1983; Honorary Doctor of Fine Arts Degree, Massachusetts College of Art, USA, 2003; Honorary Doctor of Fine Arts, National University of Ireland, 2003. Memberships: The London Institute of Arts and Letters, London, UK, 2000; Aosdána, Dublin, Ireland, 2001. Address: Neo Neo Inc, 447 West 17th Street, New York, NY 10011, USA.

**SEAGER (OLSON-STOKES) Dauna Gayle,** b. 22 September 1925, Logan, Cache Co, Utah, USA. Audiologist; Speech Pathologist. m. (1) Arch J Stokes, deceased 1970, 2 sons, 1 daughter, (2) Floyd W Seager, deceased 1996. Education: AS, Weber State University, 1964; BS, Utah State University, 1968; MS, Utah State University, 1969. Appointments: Clinic Supervisor, USU Speech/Hearing Clinic, 1966-69; Speech Pathologist, Weber County Schools and Davis County Schools, 1969-71; Speech Pathologist, St Benedict's Hospital, 1970; Homecare, St Benedict's and Mokay-Dee Hospitals, 1970-96. Publications: Articles in newspapers and magazines. Honours: Ogden Business and Professional Women's Woman of the Achievement Award, 1982; Ogden Business and Professional Women's Woman of the Year, 1984; Utah Governor's Silver Bowl Award, 1990; President George Bush's Point of Light Award, 1990. Memberships: Ogden Business and Professional Women's Organisation; Altrusa International; Daughters of Utah Pioneers; Daughters of the American Revolution; Womanise Legislative Council; Weber County Republican Women; Aglaia Charitable Club. Address: 4046 South 895 East, Ogden, Utah 84403-2416, USA.

**SEAGROVE Jennifer (Jenny) Ann,** b. Kuala Lumpur, Malaysia. Actress. Education: Bristol Old Vic Theatre School. Career: Theatre includes: Title role in Jane Eyre, Chichester Festival Theatre; Ilona in the Guardsman, Theatr Clwyd; Bett in King Lear in New York, Chichester Festival Theatre; Opposite Tom Conti in Present Laughter in the West End; Annie Sullivan in The Miracle Worker, UK tour and West End; Dead Guilty with Hayley Mills by Richard Harris, on tour and West End; The Dark Side, Thorndike Theatre, Leatherhead and on tour; Canaries Sometime Sing, Vertigo and Dead Certain, Theatre Royal, Windsor; Gertrude in Hamlet, Ludlow; Brief Encounter at the Apollo; The Female Odd Couple, Windsor and West End; Title role in The Constant Wife, Lyric Theatre, Shaftesbury

Avenue; David Hare's The Secret Rapture, Lyric Theatre, Shaftesbury Avenue. Television includes: Emma Harte in A Woman of Substance; Paula in Hold the Dream; The title roles in Diana and Lucy Walker; Laura Fairlie in The Woman in White; The heroines of The Hitch-Hiker Killer and In Like Flynn; Leading roles in The Betrothed with Burt Lancaster, Magic Moments, Some Other Spring, The Eye of the Beholder, Incident at Victoria Falls, Deadly Games; Judge John Deed. Films: To Hell and Back in Time for Breakfast; A Shocking Incident (Oscar for Best Film); Tattoo; Moonlighting; Sherlock Holmes' The Sign of Four; Savage Islands; Local Hero; Appointment with Death; A Chorus of Disapproval; The Guardian; Miss Beatty's Children; Don't Go Breaking My Heart; Zoe. Honour: The Michael Eliott Fellowship Award, 2004. Memberships: Equity; SAG. Address: c/o ICM, Oxford House, 76 Oxford Street, London W1N 0AX, England.

**SEARLE Geoffrey William,** b. 11 April 1914, London, England. m. Constance Tyrrell, 1940, deceased 1996, 1 son, 1 daughter. Education: Chartered Accountant, 1936. Appointments: Qualified Assistant, 1936-39, W B Keen & Co Chartered Accountants; Royal Navy, 1939-46, Lieutenant Commander RNVR; Joined BP, 1946, Director of Finance and Planning and Chairman of Executive Committee BP Trading, retired 1974; Chairman: Star Offshore Services Ltd, 1974-80, LASMO plc (formerly London & Scottish Marine Oil plc), 1978-85 (managing director, 1974-78), Association of British Independent Oil Exploration Companies (Brindex), 1982, Belden & Blake International Ltd, 1986-92; President, Reigate and Surrey Co LTC, 1980-88. Publication: At Sea Level, 1994. Honours: DSC, 1943; CBE, 1972. Memberships: Fellow, Institute of Petroleum, 1982; Clubs: Naval; RAC; City of London; Walton Heath Golf Club. Address: 20 Beech Road, Reigate, Surrey, RH2 9LR, England.

**SEBASTIAN Phylis Sue (Ingram),** b. 24 January 1945, Childersburg, Alabama, USA. Real Estate Broker; Real Estate Appraiser; Fine Art Appraiser. m. (1) Robert E Martin, 1965, divorced 1978, 2 sons, 2 daughters, (2) Thomas Haskell Sebastian III, 1985, 1 step son, 3 step daughters. Education: BS, Accounting and Business Administration, 1988; Real Estate Broker, Career Education Systems, 1988; Real Estate Appraisal Certificate, PREA, CIMA, International College of Real Estate Appraisal, Nashville, Tennessee; Computer Specialist, 1999. Appointments: Hostess, radio show, St Louis, Missouri, 1970s; Numerous feature articles published in St Louis Globe Democrat and Post Dispatch Newspapers, 1970s; Owner, Astrology Consultants, 1970-2003; Licensed Real Estate Broker, Owner, Broker Phylis Sebastian Real Estate, Farmington, Missouri, 1989-2003; US Auto Sales, Park Hills, Missouri, 1993-97; Owner, Business & Legal Services, Park Hills, 1993-2003; Partner La Femme Fine Antique Auction Service, Ironton, Missouri, Arcadia Valley Auction Co Inc, 1997-2003; Ordained minister, Progressive Universal Life Church, 2002; Numerous appearances on TV, St Louis. Publications: 5 books including: Marriages in Madison County Missouri for 1848-1868, 1998; 1910 Census for Madison County Missouri, 1998; Published poet; Many articles in various newspapers. Memberships: 1st Treasurer, Co-founder, Astrological Association of St Louis, 1976-77; Co-founder, Missouri Mental Health Consumer Network, Mineral Area Chapter, 1989-93; Member, National Gardening Club; Library of Congress; Smithsonian; National Historic Society; Founder, Genealogy Society of Madison County Missouri. Address: Arcadia Valley Auction Co Inc & Real Estate, 315 West Russell Street, Ironton, Missouri 63650-1316, USA. E-mail: phylis@phylissebastian.com

**SEDAGHATIAN Mohamad Reza,** b. 11 February 1938, Shiraz, Iran. Consultant Neonatologist. m. Nezhat Khalili, 3 sons, 1 daughter. Education: MD, Shiraz medical School, Iran, 1964; American Board of Pediatrics, USA, 1972; American Sub-Board of Neonatal and Perinatal Medicine, 1991, 1998. Appointments: Professor of Paediatrics, Shiraz Medical School, Shiraz, Iran, 1973-84; Senior Consultant, Head, Neonatal Department, 1985-, Acting Medical Director, 2003, Deputy Medical Director, 2003, Chairman, Department of Paediatrics, 2005, Mafraq Hospital, Abu Dhabi, United Arab Emirates; Professor of Paediatrics, Gulf Medical College, 2005. Publications: More than 40 articles in different medical journals. Honour: Physician Recognition Award, American Medical Association, 1998-2000. Membership: President, Emirates Perinatal Society; President, Emirates Neonatal Society; Emirate Medical Association; American Academy of Pediatrics; American Academy of Perinatal Medicine. Address: PO Box 2851, Abu Dhabi, United Arab Emirates. E-mail: reza@sedaghatian.net

**SEDAKA Neil,** b. 13 March 1939. Singer; Songwriter. m. Leba Margaret Strassberg, 11 September 1962, 1 son, 1 daughter. Musical Education: Graduate, Juilliard School of Music. Career: Solo performer, worldwide, 1959-; Television appearances include: NBC-TV Special, 1976. Compositions include: Breaking Up Is Hard To Do; Stupid Cupid; Calendar Girl; Oh! Carol; Stairway To Heaven; Happy Birthday Sweet Sixteen; Laughter In The Rain; Bad Blood; Love Will Keep Us Together; Solitaire; The Hungry Years; Lonely Night (Angel Face). Recordings: Albums include: In The Pocket; Sedaka's Back; The Hungry Years; Steppin' Out; A Song; All You Need Is The Music; Come See About Me; Greatest Hits, 1988; Oh! Carol And Other Hits, 1990; Timeless, 1992; Calendar Girl, 1993; Tuneweaver, 1995; The Immaculate, 1997; Tales Of Love, 1999. Honours: Songwriters' Hall Of Fame, 1980; Platinum album, Timeless, 1992; Numerous Gold records; Various industry awards. Memberships: AGVA; AFofM; AFTRA. Address: c/o Neil Sedaka Music, 201 East 66th Street, Suite 3N, New York, NY 10021, USA.

**SEED Michael Joseph Steven,** b. 16 June 1957, Manchester, England. Clergyman. Education: Washington Theological Union, Washington DC; MDiv, The Catholic University of America, Washington DC, 1984; Heythrop College, London; STL, 1987, STD, 1989, Pontifical Lateran University, Rome; PhD, Polish University, London, 1991. Appointments: Entered Franciscan Friars of the Atonement, 1978; Final Profession, 1985; Ordained Deacon, 1985; Chaplain, Westminster Cathedral, 1985-; Ordained Deacon, 1986; Chaplain, Westminster Hospital, 1986-90; Secretary for Ecumenism to the Archbishop of Westminster, 1988-; Officiating Chaplain to the Forces, Wellington Barracks, 1990-2000; Chaplain, Society of Useless Information, 1998; Foreign Corresponding Academician, Historical Institute of Dom Luiz I, Portugal, 1998. Publications: I Will See You in Heaven, 1991; Sons and Mothers (contributor), 1996; Faith Hope and Chastity (contributor), 1999; Will I See You in Heaven?, 1999; Assurance, 2000; Letters from the Heart, 2000; Catholic Lives (contributor), 2001; The Gift of Assurance, 2003. Honours: Cross of Merit in Gold, Poland, 1988; Order of Orthodox Hospitallers, Cyprus, 1988; Ecclesiastical Knight Commander of Grace, Sacred and Military, Constantinian Order of St George, Naples, 1989; Cross Pro Ecclesia et Pontifice, Holy See, 2004. Memberships: Beefsteak Club; Ben Nicolson/Philip Toynbee Club. Address: Clergy House, 42 Francis Street, London SW1P 1QW, England.

**SEFF Karl,** b. 23 January 1938, Chicago, USA. Professor. Education: BS, Chemistry, Berkeley, 1955-59; PhD, Physical Chemistry, 1959-64, Postdoctoral work, Zeolite powder crystallography, 1964, Massachusetts Institute of Technology; Postdoctoral work, Single-crystal crystallography, University of California at Los Angeles, 1964-66. Appointments: Assistant Research Chemist, UCLA, 1966-68; Assistant Professor, University of Hawaii, 1968-73; Associate Professor, University of Hawaii, 1973-75; Visiting Scholar, Princeton, 1974-75; Professor, University of Hawaii, 1975-; Associate Researcher, University of Mexico, 1981-82; Visiting Scholar, Oxford, UK, 1988; Visiting Professor, Dartmouth, 1989; Visiting Scholar, Korean universities, 1996; Chair, University of Hawaii, 2000-2003. Publications: Numerous articles. Memberships: American Crystallographic Association; American Chemical Society; Sigma Xi. Address: Chemistry Department, University of Hawaii, 2545 The Mall, Honolulu, HI 96822-2275, USA. E-mail: seff@hawaii.edu

**SEHERR-THOSS Hans Christoph,** b. 13 October 1918, Potsdam, Nr Berlin, Germany. Mechanical Engineer; Historian. Biographer,. m. Therese Kunath. Appointments: Design Work, ZF Friedrichshafen, 1947-49; Librarian, German Automobile Club, 1954 83; Vice President, FIA Historical Commission, 1983-98; Consulting Engineer; Registrar; Author, Independence, 1984-. Publications: Die Entwicklung der Zahnradtechnik, 1965; Die deutsche Automobilindustrie, 1974, 1979; FIA - Automobile World Records, 1988; Oldtimer, 1965; 75 Years ADAC, 1978; FIA, Dictionary of Famous Personalities in the Automobile World, 2000, 2002; Co-author: Sport – Ueberblick, 1951; Forum der Technik, 1966; 50 Years of BMW, 1966, 1972; 160 Biographies in NDB; Raederwerk, 1989; Yearbook Presse u Sport, 1958; H Buessing, 1986; MAN Nutzfahrzeugbau, 1991; Universal Joints and Driveshafts, 1992; Editor: Zwei Maenner – ein Stern, 1984. Memberships: German Units: ADAC; German Archivists Association (VdW); FIA Historical Commission, 1983-, Chairman Personalities, 1988-. Address: Habichtstreet 39, Unterhaching Nr Munich, D-82008, Germany.

**SEINFELD Jerry,** b. 29 April 1955, Brooklyn, USA. Comedian. Education: Queens College, New York. Career: Former Salesman; Stand-up Comedian, 1976-; Joke-writer, Benson (TV series), 1980; Actor, Seinfeld (TV series), 1989-97, also co-writer, producer; The Ratings Game, film, 1984; The Seinfeld Chronicles, 1990; I'm Telling You for the Last Time, 1999. Publication: Sein Language, 1993. Honours: 2 American Comedy Awards; Emmy Award for Outstanding Comedy Series (Seinfeld), 1993. Address: c/o Lori Jonas Public Relations, 417 South Beverly Drive, Suite 201, Beverly Hills, CA 90212, USA.

**SEK Danuta,** b. 8 December 1935, Katowice, Poland. Chemist; Scientist. m. Mieczyslaw Sek, 1 son. Education: MS, 1958; PhD, 1967; DSc, 1983; Professor, 1999. Appointments: Head of Laboratory, Cefarm, Katowice, 1958-64; Assistant, Technical University, Gliwice, 1964-67; Head of Laboratory, 1967-74, Deputy Director, 1974-, Director, 1998-2002, Head of Department, 2002-, Institute of Polymer Chemistry, Zabrze. Publications: Over 100 articles in scientific journals. Honours: Award, Scientific and Technical Committee, Warsaw, 1967; Award, Scientific Secretary, Polish Academy of Sciences, 1973. Memberships: New York Academy of Sciences; International Eurasian Academy of Sciences. Address: Centre of Polymer Chemistry, Polish Academy of Sciences, 34 M Curie-Sklodowska Street, PO Box 20, 41-819 Zabrze, Poland.

**SEKINE Yoshimoto,** b. 19 November 1968, Japan. Physician. m. Yuko Sekine, 1 son. Education: MD, University of Ryukyus Faculty of Medicine, 1989-95; PhD, Postgraduate School, Hamamatsu University School of Medicine, 1996-2000. Appointments: Trainee Psychiatrist, 1995-96, Assistant

Professor, 2000-, Hamamatsu University School of Medicine. Publications: Articles in medical journals including: American Journal of Psychiatry; Neuropsychopharmacology; Journal of Clinical Psychopharmacology. Honours: Research Award, Kenjiro Takayanagi, 2001; Travel Award, 2001, Research Award, 2002, Japanese Society of Biological Psychiatry; Research Award, Dr Paul Janssen, 2002; Research Award, Public Health Research Centre, 2003; Research Award, Japan Brain Science Society, 2004. Memberships: American Association for the Advancement of Science; Japanese Society of Biological Psychiatry; Japan Brain Science Society. Address: Department of Psychiatry and Neurology, Hamamatsu University School of Medicine, Hamamatsu, Shizuoka 431-3192, Japan.

**SELBOURNE David,** b. 4 June 1937, London, England. Writer; Playwright. Publications: The Play of William Cooper and Edmund Dew-Nevett, 1968; The Two-Backed Beast, 1969; Dorabella, 1970; Samson and Alison Mary Fagan, 1971; The Damned, 1971; Class Play, 1973; Brook's Dream: The Politics of Theatre, 1974; What's Acting? and Think of a Story Quickly!, 1977; An Eye to India, 1977; An Eye to China, 1978; Through the Indian Looking Glass, 1982; The Making of a Midsummer Night's Dream, 1983; Against Socialist Illusion: A Radical Argument, 1985; In Theory and In Practice: Essays on the Politics of Jayaprakash Narayan, 1986; Left Behind: Journeys into British Politics, 1987; A Doctor's Life: The Diaries of Hugh Selbourne MD 1960-63, 1989; Death of the Dark Hero: Eastern Europe 1987-90, 1990; The Spirit of the Age, 1993; Not an Englishman: Conversations With Lord Goodman, 1993; The Principle of Duty, 1994; The City of Light, 1997; One Year On: The 'New' Politics and Labour, Centre for Policy Studies, 1998; Moral Evasion, 1998; The Losing Battle with Islam, 2005. Translation: The City of Light, by Jacob d'Ancona, 1997. Honour: Member, Academy of Savignano, Italy, 1994; Officer, Order of Merit of the Italian Republic, 2001. Memberships: Society of Authors, London; United Oxford and Cambridge Club, London. Address: c/o Christopher Sinclair-Stevenson, 3 South Terrace, London SW7, England.

**SELEŠ Monica,** b. 2 December 1973, Novi Sad, Yugoslavia (US Citizen, 1994). Tennis Player. Career: Winner of: Sport Goofy Singles, 1984; Singles and Doubles, 1985; French Open, 1990, 1991, 1992; Virginia Slims Championships, 1990, 1991, 1992; Australian Open, 1991, 1992, 1993, 1996; US Open, 1991, 1992; Canadian Open, 1995, 1996, 1997; Los Angeles Open, 1997; Tokyo Open, 1997; Semi-finalist at: French Open, 1989; Quarter-finalist at: Wimbledon, 1990; Member, winning US Federal Cup team, 1996, 1999, 2000; 59 WTA Tour titles, 9 Grand Slam titles and over $14million in prize money, -2002. Publication: Monica: From Fear to Victory, 1996. Honours: Named youngest No 1 ranked player in tennis history for women and men, at 17 years, 3 months and 9 days; Ted Tinling Diamond Award, 1990; Associated Press Athlete of the Year 1990-91; Tennis Magazine Comeback Player of the Year, 1995; Flo Hyman Award, 2000. Address: IMG, 1 Erieview Plaza, Cleveland, OH 44114, USA.

**SELF Will,** b. 26 September 1961. Author; Cartoonist. m. (1) Katherine Sylvia Anthony Chancellor, 1989, divorced 1996, 1 son, 1 daughter, (2) Deborah Jane Orr, 1997, 1 son. Education: Christ's College; Exeter College, Oxford. Appointments: Cartoon illustrator, New Statesman, City Limits; Columnist: The Observer, 1995-97; The Times, 1997-; Independent on Sunday, 2000-. Publications: Collected cartoons, 1985; Short stories: Quantity Theory of Insanity, 1991; Grey Area, 1994; Tough Tough Toys and Tough Tough Boys, 1998; Novellas: Cock and Bull, 1992; The Sweet Smell of Psychosis, 1996; Novels: My Idea of Fun, 1993; Great Apes, 1997; How the

Dead Live, 2000; Perfidious Man, 2000; Feeding Frenzy, 2001; Dorian, 2002; Junk Mail (selected journalism), 1995; Sore Sites, collected journalism, 2000.

**SELKIRK OF DOUGLAS, Baron of Cramond in the City of Edinburgh, James Alexander Douglas Hamilton,** b. 31 July 1942, United Kingdom. Life Peer. m. Priscilla Susan (Susie) Buchan, 4 sons. Education: MA, Balliol College, Oxford; LLB, University of Edinburgh. Appointments: Officer TA 6/7 Battalion Cameronians Scottish Rifles, 1961-66, TAVR, 1971-74, Captain, 2nd Battalion Lowland Volunteers; Advocate, 1968-76; MP, Conservative, Edinburgh West, 1974-97; Scottish Conservative Whip, 1977; A Lord Commissioner of the Treasury, 1979-81; Parliamentary Private Secretary to Malcolm Rifkind MP, as Foreign Office Minister, 1983-86, as Secretary of State for Scotland, 1986-87; Parliamentary Under Secretary of State for Home Affairs and Environment, 1987-92 (including, local government at the Scottish Office, 1987-89, additional responsibility for local government finance, 1989-90 and for the arts in Scotland, 1990-92); Parliamentary Secretary of State for Education and Housing, Scottish Office, 1992-95; Disclaimed Earldom of Selkirk, 1994 (prior to succession being determined, 1996) Heir to Earldom of Selkirk (son), John Andrew Douglas-Hamilton, Master of Selkirk); Minister of State for Home Affairs and Health (with responsibility for roads and transport and construction) Scottish Office, 1995-97; Scottish Parliament: Business Manager and Chief Whip, Conservative Group, 1999-2000, Spokesman on Home Affairs, 2001-2003, on Education, 2003-. Publications: Motive for a Mission: The Story Behind Hess's Flight to Britain, 1971; The Air Battle for Malta: the Diaries of a Fighter Pilot; Roof of the World: Man's First Flight Over Everest, 1983; The Truth About Rudolf Hess, 1993. Honours: Oxford Boxing Blue, 1961; President, Oxford Union, 1964; Privy Counsellor, 1996; QC (Scotland), 1996; Life Peer, 1997. Memberships: Honorary President, Scottish Amateur Boxing Association, 1975-98; President, Royal Commonwealth Society Scotland, 1979-87, Scottish National Council, UN Association, 1981-87, International Rescue Corps, 1995; Royal Company of Archers (Queen's Body Guard for Scotland); Honorary Air Commodore No 2 (City of Edinburgh) Maritime HQ Unit, 1994-99; 603 (City of Edinburgh) Squadron RAAF, 1999-; Life Member, National Trust for Scotland; Patron, Hope and Homes for Children, 2002-; President, Scottish Veterans Garden City Association Inc, 2003-. Address: c/o House of Lords, London SW1A 0PW, England.

**SELLECK Tom,** b. 29 January 1945, Detroit, Michigan, USA, Actor. Education: University of Southern California. m. (1) Jackie Ray, 1 step son, (2) Julie Mack, 1 daughter. Career: Actor, films include: Myra Beckinridge; Midway; Coma; Seven Minutes; High Road to China; Runaway; Lassiter; Three Men and a Baby; Her Alibi, 1988; Quigley Down Under; An Innocent Man, 1989; Three Men and a Lady, 1991; Folks, 1991; Mr Baseball, 1991; Christopher Columbus: The Discovery, 1992; Folks!, 1992; Mr Baseball, In and Out; The Love Letter, 1999; Running Mates, 2000; TV includes: Returning Home; Bracken's World; The Young and the Restless; The Rockford Files; The Sacketts; Role of Thomas Magnum in Magnum PI; Divorce Wars; Countdown at the Super Bowl; Gypsy Warriors; Boston and Kilbride; The Concrete Cowboys; Murder She Wrote; The Silver Fox; The Closer (series), 1998; Last Stand at Saber River; Friends, 1996, 2000; Ruby Jean and Joe; Broken Trust, 1995; Washington Slept Here, 2000; Louis l'Amour's Crossroads Trail, 2000. Address: c/o Esme Chandlee, 2967 Hollyridge Drive, Los Angeles, CA 90068, USA.

**SELSNICK Frances,** b. 23 December 1922, New York, USA. Surgeon. Education: New York State Board of Medicine, 1946;

MD, Glasgow University, Scotland; Fellowship of Royal College of Surgeons, England, 1956; ChM, Master of Surgery, University of Liverpool, 1959. Appointments: Attending Surgeon, VA Medical Center, Reno, Nevada; Associate Chief of Staff, Womens Veteran Health Program, Reno, Nevada; Medical Center, Department of Veterans' Affairs, USA. Honours: John D Chase Award; Mark Wallcott Award; Martha Washington Medal; Hands and Heart Award. Memberships: Fellow, Royal College of Surgeons; Member, Royal Society of Medicine. Address: Post Office Box 7826, Reno, NV 89510, USA.

**SELTZER Gilbert L**, b. 11 October 1914, Toronto, Ontario, Canada. Architect. m. Molly, deceased, 1 son, 1 daughter. Education: B Arch, University of Toronto, Canada, 1937. Appointments: Partner, Gehron & Seltzer, New York, New York, 1952-58; Sole Proprietor, Gilbert L Seltzer Associates, New York, New York and West Orange, New Jersey, specialising in governmental and institutional projects, 1958-; Representative work includes: Projects at US Military Academy, US Merchant Marine Academy, Denison University, Rutgers University, William Paterson University, New Jersey City University, University of Medicine and Dentistry of New Jersey, Utica Memorial Auditorium, Veterans Administration Medical Centers. Publications: Numerous articles in Architectural Journals. Honours: Awards including: Henry Hering Medal of National Sculpture Society. Memberships: American Institute of Architects; New Jersey Society of Architects. Address: 80 Main Street, West Orange, NJ 07052, USA.

**SEN Amartya Kumar**, b. 3 November 1933, Santiniketan, India. Professor of Economics and Philosophy; Writer. m. (1) Nabaneeta Dev, 1960, divorced 1974, 2 daughters, (2) Eva Colorni, 1977, deceased 1985, 1 son, 1 daughter, (3) Emma Rothschild, 1991. Education: BA, Presidency College, Calcutta, 1953; BA, 1955, MA, PhD, 1959, Trinity College, Cambridge. Appointments: Professor of Economics, Jadavpur University, Calcutta, 1956-58; Fellow, Trinity College, Cambridge, 1957-63, All Souls College, Oxford, 1980-88; Professor of Economics, Delhi University, 1963-71, London School of Economics and Political Science, 1971-77; Professor of Economics, 1977-80, Drummond Professor of Political Economy, 1980-88, University of Oxford; Andrew D White Professor at Large, Cornell University, 1978-85; Lamont University Professor and Professor of Economics and Philosophy, Harvard University, 1988-98; Master Trinity College, Cambridge, 1998-. Publications: Choice of Techniques, 1960; Collective Choice and Welfare, 1970; Guidelines for Project Evaluation (with P Dasgupta and Stephen Marglin), 1972; On Economic Inequality, 1973; Employment, Technology and Development, 1975; Poverty and Famines: An Essay on Entitlement and Deprivation, 1981; Choice, Welfare and Measurement, 1982; Resources, Values and Development, 1984; Commodities and Capabilities, 1985; On Ethics and Economics, 1987; The Standard of Living (with others), 1987; Hunger and Public Action (with Jean Dreze), 1989; Jibanayatra o arthaniti, 1990; The Political Economy of Hunger (editor with Jean Dreze), 3 volumes, 1990-91; Money and Value: On the Ethics and Economics of Finance/Denaro e valore: Etica ed economia della finanza, 1991; Inequality Reexamined, 1992; The Quality of Life (editor with Martha Nussbaum), 1993; Economic Development and Social Opportunity (with Jean Dreze), 1995; Development as Freedom, 1999. Contributions to: Professional journals. Honours: Mahalanobis Prize, 1976; Honorary Doctor of Literature, University of Saskatchewan, 1979; Nobel Prize in Economic Science, 1998; Honorary CH, 2000; Grand Cross, Order of Scientific Merit, Brazil, 2000. Memberships: American Academy of Arts and Sciences; American Economic Association, president, 1994-; British Academy, fellow; Development Studies Association;

Econometric Society, fellow; Indian Economic Association; International Economic Association, president, 1986-88, honorary president, 1988-; Royal Economic Society. Address: c/o Trinity College, Cambridge CB2 1TQ, England.

**SEN Asim Kumar**, b. 2 January 1939, Kolkata, West Bengal, India. Scientist. m. Tapati Sen (Das Gupta), 1 daughter. Education: BSc (Hons), Physics, 1958, MSc (Tech) Radio Physics and Electronics, 1961, PhD (Sci), Radio Physics and Electronics, 1967, University of Calcutta. Appointments: Lecturer, University of Kalyani, India, 1965-67; Consultant, Communications Research Centre, Government of Canada, 1972; President and Scientist, Synchrosat Ltd, 1973-; Lecturer, Adjunct Professor, University of Ottawa, Canada, 1975-86, 1999. Publications: Books: Gyrolite Stabilization: A Breakthrough of the Seventies, 1982; Dynamics of Gyroscopic Bodies, 1987; Patents: Attitude Stabilization and Control of Dual Spin Aircraft, 1977; Generation of Electricity using Gravitational Energy, 1988; Gravitational Energy System (Momentum Turbine), 2002; 5 reports; 40 papers. Honours: Postdoctoral Fellow, University of Manitoba, 1967-69; NASA Research Associate, Goddard Space Flight Center, USA, 1969-71. Memberships: Registered Member, Association of Professional Engineers of Ontario; Life Senior Member, Institute of Electrical and Electronics Engineers (USA); Associate Fellow, American Institute of Aeronautics and Astronautics; Fellow, Institute of Electronics and Telecommunications Engineers of India. Address: 1100 Ambleside Drive, Unit 102 Ottawa, Canada K2B 8G6. E-mail: aksen@synchrosat.com Website: www.synchrosat.com

**SEN Tapas Kumar**, b. 1 March 1933, Calcutta, India. Teacher; Manager. m. Sondra Kotzin Sen, 1 son, 1 daughter. Education: MSc, Applied Psychology, Calcutta University, 1954; PhD, Psychology, Johns Hopkins University, 1963. Appointments: Member, Technical Staff, Bell Laboratories, 1963-72; Human Resources Director, AT&T, 1973-96; Executive Director, Workforce Development, Rutgers University, New Brunswick, New Jersey, USA, 1999-; Executive Committee Member, Governor's State Employment and Training Commission, New Jersey, 2000-; Chair, Governance Committee, State Employment and Training Commission, 2004-. Publications: 15 papers in professional publications include: Building the Workplace of the Future in A Blueprint for Managing Change, A Conference Board Report; Advisory Editor, Work in America Encyclopedia, 2003. Honours: The Mayflower Group Leadership Award, 1985; Toastmasters International, Area Governor of the Year, public speaking, 1970. Memberships: Fellow, Human Factors and Ergonomics Society; American Psychological Association; The Dearborn Group. Address: 29 Arden Road, Mountain Lakes, NJ 07046, USA. Website: tsitsi@att.net

**SENGENDO Kawesa Ahmad**, b. 24 September 1958, Mbarara, Uganda. Educator. m. Fatuma and Zulaikh, 3 sons, 3 daughters. Education: BSc, Honours, 1982, Postgraduate Diploma in Education, First Class, 1983, Makerere University; MScEd, PhD, Education, 1987, University of Kansas, USA. Appointments: Teaching Assistant, Makerere University; Research Assistant, 1985-86, Graduate Teaching Assistant, 1986-87, University of Kansas; Lecturer, School of Education, Makerere University, 1987; Part-time Lecturer, University Secretary, Islamic University, Uganda, 1988-2000; Director, 2001-03, Kampala Campus, Vice Rector, 2003-04, Rector, 2004-, Islamic University in Uganda. Publications: Articles: The Amic University in Uganda; Educational Challenges in the New South Africa; Challenges of Inter-Faculty Cooperation and Coordination. Honour: AFGRAD Fellow, 1984-87. Memberships: Uganda National Council for Science and Technology; Board of Governors Gombe Secondary School and Kawempe Muslim Secondary School; Secretary Uganda Muslims' Scholarship Board; Uganda Muslims' Welfare Association; Patron, Uganda Muslims' Students' Association. Address: Islamic University in Uganda, PO Box 2555, Mbale, Uganda. E-mail: aksengendo@yahoo.com

**SENNAROGLU Alphan,** b. 10 November 1966, Nicosia, Cyprus. Physicist, Professor. m. Figen Ecer Sennaroglu, 1 daughter. Education: BS, 1988, MS, 1990, PhD, 1994, Electrical Engineering, Cornell University, Ithaca, New York. Appointments: Assistant Professor, 1994-99; Associate Professor, 1999-, Associate Professor, 1999-2004; Full Professor, 2004-, Koc University, Istanbul, Turkey. Publications: Over 70 journal and conference articles in the field of ultrashort lasers, nonlinear optics and spectroscopy. Honours: Several, including Werner Von Siemens Excellence Award, 2001; Distinguished Young Scientist Award, 2001, Turkish Academy of Science. Memberships: IEEE; OSA. Address: Department of Physics, Koc University, Rumelifeneri Yolu, Sariyer 80910 Istanbul, Turkey. E-mail: asennar@ku.edu.tr

**SEREBRIER José,** b. 3 December 1938, Montevideo, Uruguay. Musician; Conductor. m. Carole Farley, 29 March 1969, 1 daughter. Education: Diploma, National Conservatory, Montevideo, 1956; Curtis Institute of Music, 1958; BA, University of Minnesota, 1960; Studied with Aaron Copland, Antal Dorati, Pierre Monteux. Career: Debut, Carnegie Hall; Independent Composer and Conductor, 1955-; Apprentice Conductor, Minnesota Orchestra, 1958-60; Associate Conductor, American Symphony Orchestra, New York, 1962-66; Musical Director, American Shakespeare Festival, 1966; Composer-in-Residence, Cleveland Orchestra, 1968-71; Artistic Director, International Festival of Americas, Miami, 1984-; Opera Conductor, United Kingdom, USA, Australia and Mexico; Guest Conductor, numerous orchestras; International tours in USA, Latin America, Australia and New Zealand. Compositions: Published over 100 works; Variations on a Theme from Childhood, for chamber orchestra; Symphony for Percussion; Concerto for Violin and Orchestra; Concerto for Harp and Orchestra; Symphonie Mystique, 2003; Orchestration and recording of George Gershwin's Three Piano Preludes and the Lullaby; Also works for chorus, voice, keyboard; Over 180 recordings for major labels with orchestras from United Kingdom, Germany, Oslo, Spain, Italy, Sicily, Belgium, Czechoslovakia and Australia. Honours: Ford Foundation Conductors Award; Alice M Ditson Award, 1976; Deutsche Schallplatten Critics Award; Music Retailers Association Award; Guggenheim Fellow, 1958-60; 2 Guggenheim awards; Rockfeller Foundation Grants; Commissions, National Endowment for the Arts and Harvard Musical Association; BMI Award; Koussevitzky Foundation Award; 8 Grammy Nominations, 1975-2004; Subject of book by Michel Faure, 2002; 5 Grammy Nominatinos in 2004, including Best New Composition for 3rd symphony, Symphonie Mystique; Winner, Latin Grammy for Best Classical Album for recording of Carmen Symphony by Bizet-Serebrier with Barcelona Symphony Orchestra, 2004. Memberships: American Symphony Orchestra League; American Music Center; American Federation of Musicians. Address: 270 Riverside Drive, New York, NY 10025, USA.

**SEREGIN Artur Alexandrovich,** b. 27 December 1941, Voronezh, USSR. Physicist. m. 1967, 2 daughters. Education: Physicist, University of Voronezh, 1964; Candidate of Physics-maths Science, University of Moscow, 1970; Doctor of Physics-maths Science, JINR of Dubna, 1990. Appointments: Senior Laboratory Assistant IPPE, Obninsk, Russia, 1965-69; Junior Scientific Worker, 1969-73; Senior Scientific Worker, 1973-93; Chief Scientific Worker, 1993-. Publications: Author and

co-author of 104 scientific works, articles, on nuclear physics and laser physics. Honours: Senior Scientific Worker. Address: Institute of Physics and Power Engineering, Bondarenko Sq 1, Obninsk 249 033, Russia. E-mail: seregin@ippe.obninsk.ru

**SEREGINA Eleena Andreevna,** b. 24 July 1945, Taganrog, Rostov Region, USSR. Physicist. m. 2 daughters. Education: Physicist, University of Voronezh, 1967; Post Graduate Course, Institute of Physics and Power Engineering of Obninsk, 1970; Candidate of Physics-Maths Science, JINR of Dubna, 1987; Doctor of Physics-Maths Science, Institute of Physics and Power Engineering of Obninsk, 2003. Appointments: Engineer, 1971-81, Junior Scientific Researcher, 1981-86, Senior Scientific Researcher, 1989-96, Chief Scientific Researcher, 1996-. Publications: Author and co-author of 120 scientific works on nuclear physics, spectroscopy and laser physics; 2 patents. Honour: Senior Scientific Worker. Address: Institute of Physics and Power Engineering, Bondarenko Sq. 1, Obninsk 249033, Russia. E-mail: sergina@ippe.ru

**SERIANNI Luca,** b. 30 October 1947, Rome, Italy. Professor of the History of the Italian Language. Education: Laurea in Lettere, 1970. Appointments: Assistant Professor, University of Rome, 1973; Lecturer, University of Siena, Arezzo, 1974-75; Lecturer, University of L'Aquila, 1975-76; Lecturer, University of Messina, 1976-80; Full Professor of History of the Italian Language, University of Rome "La Sapienza", 1980-. Publications include: Grammatica italiana (with A Castelvecchi), 1988; Saggi di storia linguistica italiana, 1989; Storia della lingua italiana: il primo Ottocento, 1989; Storia della lingua italiana: il secondo Ottocento, 1990; Lezioni di grammatica storica italiana, 1998; Introduzione alla lingua poetica italiana, 2001; Viaggiatori, musicisti, poeti. Saggi di storia della lingua italiana, 2002; Italiani scritti, 2003. Honours: Visiting Professor, University of Santiago de Compostela, Spain, 1996; Honoris causa, University of Valladolid, Spain, 2002; Award for Linguistics and Philology, Italian Ministry of National Heritage and Culture, 2004. Memberships: Accademia Nazionale dei Lincei, Rome; Accademia della Crusca, Florence. Address: via C Marenco di Moriondo 45, I-00121 Rome, Italy.

**SERIU Masafumi,** b. 23 September 1964, Kyoto, Japan. Theoretical Physicist. Education: BS, 1987, MSc, 1989, DSc, 1992, Kyoto University. Appointments: Research Fellow, Department of Physics, Kyoto University, 1992-93; Postdoctoral Fellow, Inter-University Centre for Astronomy and Astrophysics, Pune, 1993-95; Yukawa Memorial Fellow, Yukawa Institute for Theoretical Physics, Kyoto University, 1996; Research Fellow, Japan Society for Promotion of Sciences, 1996; Associate Professor, Fukui University, 1996-; Visiting Research Associate, Institute of Cosmology, Tufts, University, USA, 1999-2000. Publications: Several articles in professional journals. Honours: Prize, Silver Jubilee Essay Competition, Indian Association for Research Award, 1993; Honda Heihachiro Memorial Scholarship, Japan Association for Mathematical Sciences, 1994, 1995; Yukawa Memorial Fellowship, 1995; Research Fellowship, Japan Society for the Promotion of Sciences, 1996; Grant-in-Aid, Inamori Foundation, 1998. Memberships: Japan Physical Society; Japan Astronomical Society; Seiwa Scholars Society. Address: Fukui University, Bunkyo 3-9-1, Fukui 910-8507, Japan.

**SERNICKI Jan Kazimierz,** b. 7 April 1943, Warsaw, Poland. Electronic Engineer - Nuclear Electronics. m. Krystyna Elzbieta Łysakowska-Sernicka. Education: Master's degree, 1969, Postgraduate training, 1971-75, Doctor of Engineering, 1976, Warsaw Technical University. Appointments: Electronic Engineer, 1969-71, Research Engineer, 1976-78, Institute of

Nuclear Research, Świerk; Scientific Worker, Joint Institute of Nuclear Research, Dubna, Russia, 1978-81; Specialist, Department of Nuclear Spectroscopy and Technique, The Andrzej Soltan Institute for Nuclear Studies, Świerk, 1981-. Publications: Author, papers in Progress in Medical Physics, 2 in 1977, 3 in 1978; Co-author, paper in Nukleonika, 1981; Author, papers in Nuclear Instruments and Methods in Physics Research A, 1983, 2 in 1985, 1986, 2 in 1988, 1990, 1997, in Nukleonika, 1995, 2000. Address: Saska 99-4, 03-914 Warsaw, Poland.

**SEROK Shraga, b.** 10 April 1929, Poland. Psychotherapist. m. Fryda, 3 daughters. Education: Diploma in Social Work, 1959; MA, Psychology, Israel, 1970; PhD, School of Applied Social Science, Case Western Reserve University, Cleveland, Ohio, USA, 1975; Postgraduate Study, Gestalt Institute of Cleveland, 1975. Appointments: Lecturer, Psychopathology, Human Development and Gestalt Therapy; Founder, Faye Ratner Gestalt Programme; Director, Tel Aviv University, for 20 years; Professor, Ben Gurion University, Beer Sheva; Private practice, individual, couples, group, family psychotherapy; Professor Emeritus. Publications: 45 articles in English and Hebrew in various areas of human behaviour; Books: Human Fulfilment (Hebrew), 1984; Innovative Applications of Gestalt Therapy (English), 2000. Memberships: American Psychological Association, 1982-2000; Israel Psychotherapy Association; Israeli Association of S W; International Group Psychotherapy; Israeli Association of Family Therapy; Member of Board of Director of International Gestalt Therapy Association. Address: 8 Shimshon str, Rishon le Zion 75270, Israel.

**SERRA-BROOKS Beverly, b.** 27 July 1957, Azusa, USA. Concert Pianist. m. Education: AA degree, Santa Barbara City College; BFA Degree, California Institute of the Arts; MM Degree, California State University Northridge; American Conservatory at Fontainbleau, France; Scholarship Fellow, The Music Academy of the West, Santa Barbara, California; DMA, Claremont Graduate University, 2003; Major teachers: James Shearer in Pasadena, Reginald Stewart at the Music Academy of the West, Jorg Demus in Austria, Leonid Hambro at Cal-Arts, Michel Beroff in France and Jerome Lowenthal in the USA. Debut: Recital, Japan-America Theater, Los Angeles, 1993; Solo piano recital, Carnegie Hall, New York, 1998. Career: Professor of Piano, Mount St Mary's College, Los Angeles, California; National Public Radio, Performance Today; Classic King Radio, Seattle; KUSC, Los Angeles; Guest artist, John Hopkins University special event series; Carmel Performing Arts series; Clara Schuman at the Piano, Starring as Clara in the One-Woman Histro-drama Broadway production; Recording Artist for EROICA Classical Recordings and CD's, 2000-; Recitals in Paris and Boston, San Diego Museum of Art, 2000-02; Appointed, Bethune-Cookman College Music Department; Solo recitals, Leipzig and Zwickau, Germany, 2005. Recordings: From the Musical Tree: Music of Beethoven, Bach and Debussy, 2001; Romantic Variations; Music of Clara Schuman, Robert Schuman and Chopin; CD, Song of a Country Priest, 2005. Honours: Winner, Artists International Competition, 1997; Gold medal, Music Arts Award; James Irvine Music Award, 1985-86; Pillsbury Foundation Music Award, 1983-86; Fellowships, International Institute for Chamber Music; California Association of Professional Music, 1998; One of the Top 100 Classical Musicians, 2005. Memberships: Teachers Board Member; The College Music Society and American College of Musicians. Address: 2056 Anne Circle, S Daytona Beach, FL 32119 USA.

**SERVADEI Annette, b.** 16 October 1945, Durban, Natal. Pianist. m. 1972-1981, 1 son, 1 daughter. Education: Began studies with concert pianist mother, 1949; Also Violin and Organ studies, diploma level; Further studies Milan, Detmold, Salzburg, London, with Deckers, Schilde, Kabos, Zecchi, W Kempff; LTCL (T), 1964; LRSM (P), 1965; UPLM, 1965; FTCL, 1970; BMus, 1979, UNISA; Fine Arts Diploma KIAD, 2000; HND in Sound Production UKC, 2003; BA (Hons) in Fine Art, University of Kent, 2005. Debut: Wigmore Hall, London, 1972. Career: Started broadcasting, age 10; Concerto debut with Durban Symphony Orchestra, age 12; Recitals and concertos, very wide repertoire, UK, West Europe, Africa, USA; Frequent live radio and TV broadcasts; University Senior Piano Tutor; Lecture recitals, Masterclasses; Eisteddfod Adjudicator; Outstanding performer of Liszt, Ravel and 20th century American music, Played world premiere, Taverner's Palintropos, London, 1980; took Sabbatical specialising in Mozart, 1997; Returned to concert platform 2003. Recordings: Britten and Khachaturian Piano Concertos with London Philharmonic Orchestra; Mendelssohn, Schumann and Brahms piano pieces; Complete piano music of Sibelius, 5 CDs and 2 CDs of Dohnanyi piano music. Honours: Scholarships, Oppenheimer Trust and UNISA, 1963-70; UNISA, 1974; Letter of recommendation from Wilhelm Kempff for Beethoven interpretation, 1974; Artist of the Year, UK Sibelius Society, 1993. Membership: Incorporated Society of Musicians. Address: 3 Bournemouth Drive, Herne Bay, Kent CT6 8HH, England. Website: www.pwd.uk.com. E-mail: annetteservadei@tiscali.co.uk

**SERVICE Alastair Stanley Douglas, b.** 8 May 1933, Hampstead, London, England. Writer; Campaigner. m. (1) Louisa Anne Hemming, 1 son, 1 daughter, (2) Zandria Madeleine Pauncefort. Education: The Queen's College, Oxford, 1953-55. Appointments: Midshipman, RNR, 1951-53; Lazards (London), Brazil and Washington DC, 1955-64; Director, Seeley Service & Co (Publishers), 1964-79; Hon Campaign organiser for MP's and Peers' support of law reforms (Divorce, Family Planning, Abortion, Civic Amenities, et al), 1964-75; National Chief Executive/Chairman, Family Planning Association of UK, 1975-89; Deputy Chairman, Health Education Authority/Council, 1976-89; Regional Chairman, Wessex Region NHS, 1993-94; Chairman, Wiltshire Health Authority NHS, 1992-2000; Committee Member, Victorian Society, 1975-95; Trustee, The Prince's Foundation, 1999-2002; Chairman, The Avebury Society, 2002-; Chairman, Judging Panel for the Prince's Crafts Scholarships, 2002-. Publications: Books: A Birth Control Plan for Britain, 1972; Edwardian Architecture and its Origins, 1975; Edwardian Architecture, 1977; The Architects of London 1066 to now, 1979; London 1900, 1979; Lost Worlds, 1981; Edwardian Interiors, 1982; Megaliths of Europe, 1979 (revised 2nd edition, 1993 as Standing Stones of Europe); Anglo-Saxon and Norman Buildings, 1982; Victorian and Edwardian Hampstead, 1989; Libretto for The Angel Cantata (music by Robin Nelson), 2003; Brunel's Kingdom (concert, music drama with music by Robin Nelson as part of I K Brunel's second centenary celebrations), forthcoming, 2006. Honour: CBE, 1995. Memberships: Garrick Club. Address: Swan House, Avebury, Wiltshire, SN8 1RA, England.

**SESÉ Luis M, b.** 18 September 1955, Madrid, Spain. Chemistry Educator; Researcher. m. Mercedes Mejias, 1 son. Education: BS, University Complutense Madrid, 1976; MSc, honours, 1978; PhD, 1983. Appointments: Ayudante, 1978-80, Encargado, 1980-81, University Complutense; Encargado, 1981-82, Colaborador, 1982-84, Titular, 1985-87, Titular Numerario, 1987-, University National Educational Distance, Madrid. Publications: Research papers in professional journals; Books; Educational Video: Fifteen minutes in the life of the electron, 2002. Honours: Premio Extraordinario de Licenciatura, University Complutense, 1979; 3rd Prize, X Bienal Internacional de Cine y Video Cientifico, Spain, 2001; 2nd Prize, XXII Bienal

Internacional de Cine Cientifico, Spain, 2002; 2nd Prize, Fisica en Acción 3 (RSEF), Spain, 2002; Listed in several Who's Who and biographical publications. Memberships: New York Academy of Sciences; Planetary Society; Spanish Royal Society of Physics, 2002-; Einsteinian Chair of Science, World Academy of Letters; American Association for the Advancement of Science. Address: Facultad de Ciencias, University National Educational Distance, Senda del Rey 9, 28040 Madrid, Spain.

**SETHI Rajinder Singh,** b. 1 February 1938, Nowshera, Peshawar District, India (now Pakistan). Research Chemist. m. Harbans Ahuja, 1969, 2 daughters. Education: BSc (Hons) Chemistry, 1960, MSc Chemistry, 1962, Research Fellow, Chemistry Department, 1962-66, PhD, Physical Chemistry, Delhi University. Appointments: Postdoctoral Research Fellow, Imperial College, London, England, 1966; Extraction Metallurgy, Nuffield Research Group, 1966-70; Senior Scientist, 1970-73, Principal Scientist, 1973-76, Senior Principal Scientist, 1976-84, Chief Chemist, 1984-98, Plessey Company Ltd (later GEC-Marconi Materials Technology Ltd, Northampton); Senior Research Associate, Cambridge University, 1998-. Publications: Research activities patented and presented at national and international conferences; Research reports for government agencies; Peer-reviewed publications in: Analyst, Appl Phys Letters, Biosensors & Bioelectronics, Analytical Chemistry, Anal Chim Acta, Electrochim Acta, J Mol Recognition, J Matr Sci, Matr in Electronics, Thin Solid Films, Chemtronics, Trans of Faraday Soc, etc. Honours: Listed in national and international biographical dictionaries. Memberships: Chartered Chemist; Fellow, Royal Society of Chemistry, UK; Electrochemical Society, USA. Address: 68 Westone Avenue, Northampton, NN3 3JQ, England. E-mail: rss2600@aol.com

**SEVERIN Irina,** b. 8 March 1964, Brasov, Romania. Engineer; Associate Professor. m. Romulus Severin, 1 daughter. Education: PhD, Mechanical Engineering, 1987, Doctoral Thesis, Materials Technology, Metals Matrix Composites, presented Politehnica University Bucharest, Catholic University Louvain La Neuve, Belgium, 1997, Quality Systems and Internal Audit, Politehnica University, Bucharest, 1994; Training Stages: France 1996, Belgium, 1997, UK, 1999, France and UK, 2000. Appointments: Computer Enterprise Bucharest, Romania, 1987-90; University Assistant, 1990-95, Lecturer, 1995-99, Assistant Professor, 1999-; Invited Professor, University of Rennes I, France, 2000-; Co-ordination Expert, 2001-2004, Deputy, 2004-, National Agency, Leonardo da Vinci. Romania; Head of Department, Quality Audit, National Agency for Community Programmes, Education and Vocational Training, Romania; Evaluator Expert, DG Research CE, Brussels, Belgium, 2001-; Evaluator, Expert, National Agency Socrates, Romania, 2004. Publications: Metal Matrix Composites Professing Technologies, 2000; Quality Engineering, 2000, 2003; 2005 Articles in Metals Research and New Materials, 1994, 1994, 1996, 1998; Materials Science Forum, 1996; Politehnica University Science Bulletin; Science and Engineering of Composite Materials, 1997, 1998, 2000. Honours: Aurel Vlaicu Award for research on metal matrix composites, Romanian Academy, 1995. Memberships: Deutsche Gesellschaft für Materialkunde; Romanian Association for Nonconventional Technologies; Romanian Association for Consumer Protection, Directorate Council. Address: Politehnic University of Bucharest, 313 Splaiul Independentei, Bucharest, Romania. E-mail: irana.severin@leonardo.ro

**SEVERTSEV Vladimir Nikolaevich,** b. 15 May 1948, Smolensk region, Russia. Electronics Engineer. m. Tatiana Nikolaevna Severtseva, 1 son, 1 daughter. Education: Higher Education, Moscow Institute of Steel and Alloys; PhD, 1999. Appointments: Chief of Research Department of R&PA "Orion";

Chief Designer of FGUP "Alpha"; Director General, Chief Designer JSC "Niimikropriborov". Publications: More than 100 scientific articles, among them 32 inventions and patents. Memberships: Academician, Laser Academy of Sciences of the Russian Federation. E-mail: vnsevertsev@zelao.ru

**SEWELL Rufus Frederick,** b. 29 October 1967. Actor. m. Yasmin Abdallah, 1999, 1 son with Amy Gardner. Career: Actor; Films include: Twenty-One; Dirty Weekend; A Man of No Importance; Carrington; Victory; Hamlet; The Woodlanders; The Honest Courtesan; Martha Meet Frank; Daniel and Laurence; Illuminata; Dark City; Bless The Child; A Knight's Tale; The Extremists; Tristan and Isolde; TV appearances include: The Last Romantics; Gone To Seed; Middlemarch; Dirty Something; Citizen Locke; Cold Comfort Farm; Henry IV; Charles II: The Power and the Passion; Helen of Troy; Stage appearances include: Royal Hunt of the Sun; Comedians; The Last Domain; Peter and the Captain; Pride and Prejudice; The Government Inspector; The Seagull; As You Like It; Making it Better; Arcadia; Translations; Rat in the Skull; Macbeth; Luther; Taste. Address: c/o Julian Belfrage Associates, 46 Albermarle Street, London, W1X 4PP, England.

**SEWER Martin,** b. 19 November 1971, Zurich, Switzerland. Kung Fu Teacher. Education: Studied and practised Judo, 13 years; Studies in Karate, Jiu-Jitsu, Boxing; Studies of Wushu, Choy Lay Fat, Kong Style Tai Chi Chuan, Wu Family Hung Gar with Chinese Martial Arts Masters in China and Hong Kong; Studies in Chinese Culture; Examination for Master, 1992; 5th Dan/Tuan through Grand Master Dr Chiu Chi Ling, head of Hung Gar Kung Fu system, 2001; Honorary PhD, Martial Science, ACMS, 2002; Honorary PhD, Martial Arts, World Martial Art League, Germany, 2002; Honorary PhD, Martial Arts, International University of Martial Arts Science, Florida, 2002; Honorary CMD, Chinese Martial Arts, ACMS, 2003; 5th Tuan, World Kuoshu Foundation, 2004. Career: Founder, Kung Fu School Martin Sewer, Zurich Switzerland, 1993; Owner and Publisher of "Kung Fu" Swiss Martial Arts News Magazine; Speaker on Martial Arts at European seminars; Referee for national and international tournaments; Licensed International Referee by World Kuoshu Federation; President, Swiss Branch, International Chiu Chi Ling Hung Gar Kung Fu Association. Publications: Articles on martial arts in magazines. Honours: Numerous titles and awards at national and international tournaments; Represented in the Wong Fei Hung Museum, Foshan, China; Presidential Silver Award, US President, George W Bush, 2004. Memberships: European Chief Co-ordinator, International Chiu Chi Ling Gar Kung Fu Association; Executive Committee and Ranking Committee, The World Kuoshu Federation; Swiss Representative, European Hung Gar Association; Hong Kong Martial Arts Association; American Traditional Chinese Medical and Traumatology Association; Co-Founder Swiss GONG FU. Address: Wilenstrasse 59, CH-9500 Wil SG, Switzerland.

**SEYMOUR David,** b. 24 January 1951, Surrey, England. Lawyer. m. Elisabeth, 1 son, 2 daughters. Education: MA, Jurisprudence, The Queen's College, Oxford, 1969-72; LLB, Fitzwilliam College, Cambridge, 1973-74; Gray's Inn, Called to the Bar, 1975. Appointments: Law Clerk, Rosenfeld, Meyer & Susman (Attorneys), Beverly Hills, California, 1972-73; Legal Adviser's Branch, Home Office, 1975-97; Legal Secretary to the Attorney General, 1997-2000; Legal Adviser, Home Office and Northern Ireland Office, 2000-. Honours: Open Exhibition, The Queen's College, Oxford, 1969-72; Holt Scholar, Gray's Inn, 1974; Elected Bencher, Gray's Inn, 2001; CB, New Year Honours List, 2005. Address: Home Office, 2 Marsham Street,

# DICTIONARY OF INTERNATIONAL BIOGRAPHY

London SW1P 4DF, England. E-mail: david.seymour@homeoffice.gov.uk

**SHAFAEDDIN Mehdi,** b. 21 July 1945, Iran. Economist; Educator. m. Shahnaz, 28 August 1970, 2 daughters. Education: BA, Economics, Tehran University, 1969; MA, Economics, Tehran University, 1971; DPhil, Economic Development, Oxford, 1980. Appointments: In charge of Macroeconomic and Development Polices Branch, UNCTAD; Senior Economist, Co-ordinator, Economic Co-operation Among Developing Countries; Chief, Enterprise Development Strategy; Chief, Policy Development; Senior Adviser, Trade Policy; Lecturer, Webster University, Geneva; Editor, UNCTAD Bulletin; Assistant Professor, University of Abureyhan, Tehran; Acting Chief, Industrial Research and Programmes, Institute of Standards and Industrial Research, Tehran. Publications: Trade Policy at the Crossroads, 2005 and many articles in professional journals. Honours: Scholarship, British Counsel for B Lit, Oxford; Scholarship, Tehran University, D Phil and BA; Listed in National and International Biographical Who's Who Publications. Memberships: Development Study Association, UK. Address: United Nations, Geneva, Switzerland. E-mail: shafaeddin@bluewin.ch

**SHAFFER (Sir) Peter (Levin),** b. 15 May 1926, Liverpool, England. Dramatist. Education: BA, Trinity College, Cambridge, 1950. Appointments: Literary Critic, Truth, 1956-57; Music Critic, Time and Tide, 1961-62; Cameron Mackintosh Visiting Professor of Contemporary Theatre and Fellow, St Catherine's College, Oxford, 1994. Publications: Plays: Five Finger Exericse, 1958; The Private Ear and the Public Eye, 1962; The Merry Roosters Panto (with Joan Littlewood), 1963; The Royal Hunt of the Sun, 1964; Black Comedy, 1965; White Lies, 1967; The White Liars, 1968; The Battle of Shrivings, 1970; Equus, 1973; Amadeus, 1979; Yonadab, 1985; Lettice and Lovage, 1987; The Gift of the Gorgon, 1992. Contributions to: Radio and television. Honours: Evening Standard Drama Awards, 1958, 1979, 1988; New York Drama Critics Cricle Awards, 1959, 1976; London Theatre Critics Award, 1979; Plays and Players Award, 1979; Tony Awards, 1979, 1980; Drama Desk Award, 1980; Academy Award, 1985; Golden Globe Award, 1985; Los Angeles Film Critics Association Award, 1985; Premi David di Donatello, 1985; Commander of the Order of the British Empire, 1987; Shakespeare Prize, Hamburg, 1989; William Inge Award for Distinguished Achievement in the American Theatre, 1992. Membership: Royal Society of Literature, fellow.

**SHAFIK Ahmed,** b. 10 May 1933, Shebin-el-Kom, Menoufia Governorate, Egypt. Surgeon. m. Olfat Elsibai, 2 sons. Education: Undergraduate studies, 1951-57, MD, 1962, Cairo University Faculty of Medicine. Appointments at Cairo University Faculty of Medicine, Kasr elAini Teaching Hospital: House Officer, 1957-58; Lecturer of Surgery, 1962-70; Assistant Professor of Surgery, 1970-75; Full Professor of Surgery, 1975; Head, Emergency Division, 1980-84; Head, Surgical Divisions 27 and 29, 1984-90; Chairman, Department of Surgery and Experimental Research, 1990-. Publications: Over 700 contributions to medical research, introducing new anatomical, physiological, pathological and therapeutical findings in coloproctology, gastroenterology, urology, andrology, gynaecology and others, describing amongst other entities over 80 hitherto unknown reflexes there by enhancing the understanding of mechanisms that regulate and co-ordinate anal and vesical continence and evacuation, or are responsible for deglutition or control genital functions and sexual performance including coitus in both sexes; Also created an immunostimulating antiviral drug, MM1, which has proved very successful in the combat of AIDS. Honours: State Award

for Science and Arts, 1st Class, 1977; Nomination for Nobel Prize in Medicine, 1981. Memberships include: International Society of University Colon and Rectal Surgeons; The American Society of Colon and Rectal Surgeons; American Association of Anatomists; New York Academy of Sciences; Society of Experimental Biology and Medicine; Academy of Surgical Research; International Pelvic Floor Dysfunction Society; Mediterranean Society of Pelvic Floor Disorders; Mediterranean Society of Coloproctology. Address: 2 Talaat Harb Street, Cairo, Egypt. E-mail: shafik@ahmed-shafik.org

**SHAH Natubhai K,** b. 16 September 1932, India (British Citizen). Academic; Retired Medical Practitioner. m. Bhanumati Shah, 1 son, 1 daughter. Education: MBBS, 1957; PhD, Jain Religion, 1998. Appointments include: General Practitioner, India, 1957-68, Leicester, UK, 1968-96; Retired, 1996-; Fellow, Royal Society of Medicine, 1998-; Visiting Professor, Faculty of Comparative Religions, Antwerp, Belgium, 1999; Honorary Fellow, University of Birmingham, 2002; Established Jain Centre and Jain Studies, Leicester, London and Mumbai; Established, Ahimsa for Quality of Life, Welfare International Charity; President, Jain Samaj Europe, 1977-89, 1991-93; Chairman, Jain Sangha of Europe; Secretary General, World Council of Jain Academies; Co-Chairman, Jain-Christian Association, Jain-Jewish Association; Co-ordinator, London Council of Jain Organisations; Trustee, Inter-Faith Network, UK; Member, Ethnic Minorities Higher Education Advisory Committee, Leicester University; Member, Shitenoji International Interfaith Dialogue Group, 1996-; Represents Jainism at the highest level in UK government, local authorities and other institutions; Jain Representative, Commonwealth Day Observance, Westminster Abbey, 1993-; Member of Faith Advisory Committee, Golden Jubilee Celebration, Buckingham Palace, 2002; Director, Faith Based Regeneration Network, Vice-Chairman, Barnet Multi-Faith Forum; Member, Barnet SACRE; Faith Advisor, UNICEF. Publications: Executive Editor, Jain quarterly magazine, 1982-91; Jainism: The World of Conquerors, 2 volumes (author), 1998; Numerous articles in community publications and 2 in academic journals. Honours: Award from Delhi Jain Mahasabha, Vice-President of India, 1987; Honoured by Jain Organisations of UK, 1988; Honoured by Jain Community, 1989; International Leader in Achievement, International Biographical Centre, Cambridge England, 1990; Man of the Year 1991, American Biographical Institute; Private Luncheon with HM Queen Elizabeth II, Buckingham Palace, 2000; Jain Ratna Award, Prime Minister of India, 2001. Address: 20 James Close, London NW11 9QX, England.

**SHAH Samir Ramnik,** b. 2 August 1956, Mumbai, India. Medical Doctor. m. Nalini Shah. Education: MBBS, 1978; MD (Medicine), 1982; DM (Gastroenterology), 1986. Appointments: Consultant Gastroenterologist, Sir H N Hospital, 1986, Jaslok Hospital, 1995; Head, Division of Liver Disease, Bhatia Hospital, 2000; Secretary, Indian Association for the Study of the Liver; Honorary General Secretary National Liver Foundation. Publications: Textbook chapter: Parasitic Diseases of the Liver, 2003; Articles in scientific journals: Prevalence and significance of HBV genotype in patients with chronic hepatitis B from Western India (co-author), 2004; Treatment of Hepatitis C (author), 2005. Honour: Hargobind Foundation Scholar 1996-97. Memberships: Indian Society of Gastroenterology; Indian Association for the Study of the Liver; Asia Pacific Association for Study of the Liver. Address: 303, Doctor House, Peddar Road, Mumbai 400026, India. E-mail: shahsamir@vsnl.com

**SHAH Syed Muzammil Hussain,** b. Chapman Kot, Azad Kashmir. Public Relations Officer; Journalist. Education: BA, University of the Punjab, Lahore, 1986; BA (Hons)

Media, Higher Institute of Islamic Da'wah and Journalism, Muhammad Bin Saud University, Riyadh, Saudi Arabia, 1988; Master in Arabic, Punjab University, Lahore, 1988; Master in Mass Communication, Allama Iqbal Open University, Islamabad, 2000. Appointments: Programme Producer, Da'wah Academy, 1989, In Charge Public Relations, 1989-, In Charge Public Relations to the Rector, 1997, International Islamic University, Islamabad; Additional appointments include: Social Worker, Chapman Kot, Azad Kashmir, 15 years; Editorial Board Member, Higher Institute of Islamic Da'wah, Madina Munawwara's Magazine, 3 years; Urdi-Arabic, Arabic-Urdu Translator with Kashmir-ul-Muslima Magazine, 1990-95; Prepared and presented a number of programmes on Kashmir in Radio Pakistan Islamabad Series Kashmir Ki Awaz, 1995-97; Participated in the coverage of activities of the First International Islamic Arts and Crafts Exhibition in Islamabad, 1997; Worked with Pakistan Television Corporation as a resource person and desk editor, 2000-2001; Engaged with OIC Standing Committee of Scientific and Technological Co-operation in the preparation of an Arabic Newsletter, 2003-. Publications: Articles in journals and newspapers and translations. Memberships: Historical and Archaeological Association of Pakistan; DAIRA (Literary and Cultural Association of Pakistan); AA Translators Inc, Canada; Shah-e-Hamdan International Islamic Association; Honorary Member, Board of Governors, American Biographical Institute. Address: PO Box 1485. Islamabad, Pakistan. E-mail: muzammil58@yahoo.com

**SHAHJAHAN Munir,** b. 23 July 1962, Dhaka, Bangladesh. Medical Researcher; Physician Scientist. m. Sabrina Sultana, 1 son, 1 daughter. Education: MBBS (MD), University of Dhaka, 1990; MPH (Master of Public Health), University of Texas, Houston, School of Public Health, 1996; Dr PH (Doctor of Public Health), University of Texas, Houston, 2004. Appointments: House Physician, Dhaka Medical College Hospital, Bangladesh, 1991-93; Lecturer and Medical Officer, Medical College for Women, Dhaka, Bangladesh, 1993-94; Research Assistant, University of Texas Houston, School of Public Health, USA, 1994-97; Research Assistant, AIDS Educational and Training Center for Texas and Oklahoma, 1997-98; Senior Research Assistant, Clinical Research Protocol Co-ordinator, Data Manager, Senior Data Analyst, M D Anderson Cancer Center, Houston, Texas, USA, 1998-. Publications: Co-author, Ethnic Differences in HIV Testing, 1999; Non-Adherence to Protease Inhibitors, 2000; Nonablative Stem Cell Transplantation for Older Patients with AM L/MDS, 2002. Honour: Recipient of Scholarship Award for Academic Excellence, Bangladesh Government, 1983-90; Travel Grant Award for best Abstract, American Society of Blood and Marrow Transplantation, 2004. Memberships: American Public Health Association; American Society of Blood and Marrow Transplantation; American Society of Clinical Oncology; American Society of Hematology; Association of Clinical Research Professionals. Address: 7900 Cambridge #9-2G, Houston, TX 77054, USA. E-mail: msjahan@hotmail.com

**SHAKHOVSKY Victor Ivanovich,** b. 9 January 1939, Vikolaevsk, Volgograd Region, Russia. Teacher of English; Linguist. 1 daughter. Education: Graduate, Volgograd Pedagogical University, 1963; Doctor of Linguistics; Full Professor. Appointments: Chair of SLJ, 1974-85; Professor and Chair of Linguistics, Head, Laboratory "Language and Personality", Volgograd State Pedagogical University, Russia, 1988-. Publications: 250 publications on language and emotions; 21 books include: Categorization of emotions by lexico-semantic system of the language; Text and its Cognitivo-emotive transformations; Emotions in Business Communication. Honour: Honoured Scientist of the Russian Federation. Address:

Titov Street 32, Apt 8, Volgograd 400123, Russia. E-mail: shakhov@vspu.ru

**SHAMS Hoda Zaky,** b. 26 January 1943, Cairo, Egypt. Professor of Organic Chemistry. m. Kadry Youssef Dimian, 2 sons. Education: BSc, Chemistry, 1963, MSc, Organic Chemistry, 1970, PhD, Organic Chemistry, Cairo University. Appointments: Professor, Organic Chemistry, Helwan University, Helwan, Cairo, Egypt, 1993-; Examiner, Cairo University; Visitor Researcher, Rutgers University, USA; Participator, NIH, 1990; Director, PhD and MSc students, Helwan and Cairo Universities. Publications: Pigment and Resin Technology; Phosphorus, Sulfur and Silicon; Numerous articles in scientific journals. Honours: Listed in several Who's Who and biographical dictionaries. Memberships: Literati Club; MCB University, Bradford, UK. Address: Department of Chemistry, Faculty of Science, Helwan University, Helwan, Cairo, Egypt. E-mail: shamshoda@hotmail.com

**SHAN Jesse Chienhua,** b. 23 March 1962, Taiwan. Semiconductor Scientist. m. Ichen Virginia Lin, 3 sons. Education: BS, Materials Science and Engineering, National Cheng Kung University, Taiwan, 1985; MS, Materials Engineering, Auburn University, 1989; PhD, Materials Science and Engineering, University of California at Davis, 1994. Appointments: Lead Engineer, Mitsubishi Silicon America; Senior Process Development Engineer, Wafertech LLC; Operations Manager, Symmorphix Inc; Director of Product Development, Integrated Optics Communication Corp., Founder and Chief Executive Officer, Acrux Technologies Inc. Publications: 12 technical publications; 5 US patents. Honours: Listed in Who's Who publications and biographical dictionaries. Memberships: IEEE; MRS; ION. Address: 1701 Oak Avenue, Los Altos, CA 94024, USA. E-mail: jesse@acruxinc.com Website: www.acruxinc.com

**SHAND William Stewart,** b. 12 October 1936, Derby, England. Surgeon. m. Caroline, deceased 2005, 2 sons, 1 step-son, 2 step-daughters. Education: Repton School; St Johns College, Cambridge; The Medical College of St Bartholomew's Hospital London; MA, 1962; MD Cantab, 1970; FRCS, 1969; FRCS Ed, 1970. Appointments include: Consultant Surgeon, King Edward VII's Hospital for Officers, London; Honorary Consultant Surgeon, St Mark's Hospital for Diseases of the Colon and Rectum, London; Consultant Surgeon to Hackney and Homerton Hospitals, London; Honorary Consultant, St Luke's Hospital for the Clergy, London; Penrose May Tutor, Royal College of Surgeons of England, London, 1980-85; Governor of the Medical College of St Bartholomew's Hospital; Governor of the British Postgraduate Medical Federation; Member of the Court of Examiners of the Royal College of Surgeons of England, 1985-91; Consultant Surgeon, St Bartholomew's Hospital London, 1973-96; Currently: Penrose May Teacher, Royal College of Surgeons of England, London, 1985-; Governor of Sutton's Hospital in Charterhouse, 1989-; Trustee, 1995-2000, Vice President, 2001-, Phyllis Tuckwell Hospice, Farnham, Surrey; Member, Honorary Medical Panel of the Artists' General Benevolent Institution, 1979-; Honorary Consulting Surgeon to St Bartholomew's Hospital and the Royal London Hospital, London. Publications: Articles in various journals and contributions to books on surgery, colorectal disease, Chronic Inflammatory Bowel Disease in children and oncology; Book: The Art of Dying – The Story of Two Sculptors' Residency in a Hospice (co-author), 1989. Honour: National Art Collections Fund Award, 1992. Memberships: Member of the Court of Assistants of the Worshipful Society of Apothecaries of London, Master, 2004-2005; Member of the Court of Assistants of the Worshipful Company of Barbers of London, Master, 2001-

2002; Travelling Surgical Society of Great Britain and Northern Ireland, President, 1994-97; Fellow, Association of Surgeons of Great Britain and Ireland; President, Cambridge Medical Graduates Club; Fellow, Hunterian Society; Fellow, Harveian Society of London; Chairman, Homerton Hospital Artwork Committee, 1985-92; Honorary Curator of Ceramics, Royal College of Surgeons, England, 1980-. Address: Dan-y-Castell, Castle Road, Crickhowell, Powys NP8 1AP, Wales.

**SHANGGUAN Dongkai,** b. 12 December 1963, Henan Province, China. Materials Scientist. m. Guilian Gao, 2 sons. Education: BSc, Tsinghua University, China, 1984; DPhil, University of Oxford, England, 1989; MBA, San Jose State University, 2003. Appointments: Postdoctoral Visiting Fellow, University of Cambridge, England, 1989; Postdoctoral Research Fellow, The University of Alabama, USA, 1989-91; Manufacturing Engineer, Technical Specialist, Senior Technical Specialist, Supervisor, Ford Motor Co, USA, 1991-2001; Senior Director of Advanced Technology, Flextronics, 2001-. Publications: Book, "Cellular Growth of Crystals"; Over 150 technical papers; 20 US and international patents. Honours: St Edmund Hall Brockhues Graduate Awards, Oxford University, 1986, 1987; Outstanding Young Manufacturing Engineer Award, Society of Manufacturing Engineers, 1998; Soldertec Lead-Free Soldering Award, 2002; Total Excellence in Electronics Manufacturing Award, SME, 2005. Memberships: Board of Review, Metallurgical and Materials Transactions; Board of Advisors, Association of Forming and Fabricating Technologies - Society of Manufacturing Engineers; SAE Transactions Review Committee; Senior Member, SME. E-mail: dshangguan@yahoo.com

**SHANKAR Ravi,** b. 7 April 1920, Varansi, India. Musician (sitar); Composer. m. Sukanya, 23 January 1989, 1 son, 2 daughters. Musical Education: Studied under Ustad Allaudin Khan of Maihar. Career: International career as solo sitarist; Former director of music, All-India Radio; Founded National Orchestra, All India Radio; Founder, Director, Kinnara School of Music, Bombay, 1962, Los Angeles, 1967; Currently Regents professor, University of California; Concerts worldwide (except East and South Africa); Major festivals include: Edinburgh; Woodstock; Monterey. Compositions include: 2 Concertos, sitar and orchestra, 1971, 1981; Swagathan Su Swagathan, 1982; Arpan (in honour of George Harrison); Film scores: Pather Panchali; Charlie; Chappaqua; Ghandhi; Music for television production, Alice In Wonderland; Opera-ballet, Ghanashayam, 1989. Recordings: Over 50 albums include: Concertos 1 and 2 for Sitar and Orchestra, Raga Jageshwari, 1981; Homage To Mahatma Ghandhi, 1981; West Meets East (with Yehudi Menuhin and others); Chants of India; Full Circle: Carnegie Hall 2000. Publications: My Music My Life (autobiography), 1968; From India, 1997; Mantram: Chant of India, 1997; Raga Jogeshwari, 1998; In London [live], 1999l; Concerto for Sitar and Orchestra, 1999. Honours: Fellow, Sangeet Natak Academy, 1976; Padma Vibushan, 1981; Elected to Rajya Sabha (Indian Upper House), 1986; Magisaysay; Grand Prize, Fukuoka, Japan; Praemium Imperiale Arts Award; Juliet Hollister Award; The Polar Music Prize, given by the King of Sweden; Bharat Ratna The Jewel of India; Commandeur de la Legion d'Honneur, France; Honorary Knight Commander of the Order of the British Empire, 2001; 12 honorary doctorates worldwide. Address: The Ravi Shankar Foundation, 132 N El Camino Real, Suite 316, Encinitas, CA 92024, USA.

**SHARIF Omar (Michael Chalhoub),** b. 10 April 1932, Cairo, Egypt. Actor. m. (1) Faten Hamama, 1 son, (2) 1973. Education: Victoria College, Cairo. Career: Salesman, lumber-import firm; 24 Egyptian films and 2 French co-production films; Films include: Lawrence of Arabia; The Fall of the Roman Empire; Behold a Pale Horse; Genghis Khan; The Yellow Rolls Royce; DoctorZhivago; Night of the Generals; Mackenna's Gold; Funny Girl; Cinderella-Italian Style; Mayerling; The Appointment; Che; The Last Valley; The Horseman; The Burglars; The Island; The Tamarind Seed; Juggernaut; Funny Lady; Ace Up My Sleeve; Crime and Passion; Bloodline; Green Ice; Top Secret; Peter the Great (TV); The Possessed; Mountains of the Moon; Michaelangelo and Me; Drums of Fire; Le Guignol; The Puppet; The Rainbow Thief; 558 rue Paradis; Gulliver's Travels (TV); Heaven Before I Die; The 13th Warrior; The Parole Officer; Shaka Zulu: The Citadel (TV); Monsieur Ibrahim et les fleurs de Coran; Soyez prudents… (TV); Urban Myth Chillers (TV); Hidalgo; Theatre: The Sleeping Prince, England, 1983. Publications: The Eternal Male (autobiography), 1978. Address: c/o William Morris Agency, 151 El Camino Drive, Beverly Hills, CA 90212, USA.

**SHARON Ariel,** b. 1928. Politician; Army Officer - retired. m. 2 sons. Education: Studies at Hebrew University, 1952-53; Studies Staff College, Camberley UK, 1957-58. Appointments: Active in Hagana since early youth; Instructor Jewish Police units, 1947; Platoon Commander Alexandroni Brigade; Regimental Intelligence Officer, 1948; Company Commander, 1949; Commander Brigade Reconnaissance Unit, 1949-50; Intelligence Officer Central Command and Northern Command, 1951-52; In charge of Unit 101 on numerous reprisal operations until 1957; Commander Paratroopers Brigade Sinai Campaign, 1956; Training Commander General Staff, 1958; Commander Infantry School, 1958-69; Commander Armoured Brigade, 1962; Head of Staff Northern Command, 1964; Head Training Department of Defence Forces, 1966; Head Brigade Group during Six-Day War, 1967; Resigned from Army, July 1973; Recalled as Commander Central Section of Sinai Front during Yom Kippur War, October1973; Forged bridgehead across Suez Canal; Adviser to Prime Minister, 1975-77; Minister of Agriculture in charge of Settlements, 1977-81; Minister of Defence, 1981-83; Minister without Portfolio, 1990-92; Minister of Trade and Industry, 1984-90; Minister of Construction and Housing, 1990-92; Minister of National Infrastructure, 1996-99; Chairman Cabinet Committee to oversee Jewish immigration from USSR, 1991-96; Prime Minister of Israel, 2001-. Publication: Warrior (autobiography), 1989. Memberships: Founder Member Likud Front, 1973; Member Knesset - Parliament - 1973-74, 1977-; Member Ministerial Defence Committee, 1990-92. Address: Ministry of National Infrastructure, P O Box 13106, 234 Jaffa Street, Jerusalem 91130, Israel.

**SHARP Dennis Charles,** b. 30 November 1933, Flitwick, Bedford, England. Architect. m. Yasmin A Shariff, 1 son, 1 daughter. Education: Luton School of Art, 1951-54; AA Dipl., AA School, London; MA, Leverhulme Fellow, School of Architecture, Liverpool University, 1960-63; Registered Architect (ARB); Chartered Architect (RIBA). Appointments: Architect with British Rail Moderisation Group; Bedfordshire County Architects Department, 1958-60; Architect and Research Officer, Civic Trust for the North West, 1963064; Lecturer, University of Manchester, 1964-68; Senior Lecturer and AA General Editor, AA School, London, 1968-82; Dennis Sharp Architects, London and Hertford, 1982-. Publications: Modern Architecture and Expressionism, 1966; The Picture Palace, 1968; The Rationalists, 1978, new edition, 2000; Santiago Calatrava, 1992, 1995; 20th Century Architecture, 1994, 3rd edition, 2001; The Bauhaus, 1994; Connell, Ward & Lucas, 1995. Honours: Professor International Academy of Architects, 1987; Medaille D'Argent, Academie d'Architecture, Paris, 1991; UIA Jean Tschumi Award, 1993; Various Architecture Research Awards including: RIBA, AA, RSA. Memberships: Director,

International Architectural Critics Committee; International Academy of Architecture; Architectural Association; RIBA; FBUA; Architecture Club; Society of Authors. Address: 1 Woodcock Lodge, Epping Green, Hertford SG13 8ND, England. E-mail: dsharp@sharparchitects.co.uk

**SHARP Lindsay,** b. 22 August 1947, Bromley, Kent, England. Museum Director. m. (1) Maggie Sommi, 1968, divorced 1980, 1 son, (2) Robyn Sharp, 1981, 1 daughter. Education: Scholarship, Modern History, Wadham College, Oxford, 1966; First Class Honours, Modern History, Oxford University, 1969; Clifford Norton Research Fellowship in the History of Science, Queen's College, Oxford, 1972-75; Doctorate in History, Oxford University, 1970-76. Appointments: Assistant Keeper, Pictorial Collection, Science Museum, London, 1976-78, Deputy Director, Museum of Applied Arts and Sciences, 1978-79; Foundation Director, Powerhouse Museum (Museum of Applied Arts and Sciences), Australia, 1978-88; Director, Entertainment and Leisure, Merlin International Properties, Australia, 1988-90; Managing Director of Communication and Recreation Expertise Pty Ltd, Australia, 1990-95; Project Director, then Senior Museum Consultant, Auckland Institute and Museum, New Zealand, 1990-94; Director, Executive Consultant, The Earth Exchange, Sydney, Australia, 1990-93; Senior Museum Consultant, Deputy Director, Milken Family Foundation, Santa Monica, California, 1993-96; President and Board Member, Foundation of the Royal Ontario Museum, Canada, 1996-2000; President and Chief Executive Officer, The Royal Ontario Museum, Canada, 1996-2000; Director, National Museum of Science and Industry incorporating: National Museum of Photography, Film and Television, Bradford; National Railway Museum, York; Science Museum, London; National Collections Centre, Wiltshire; Locomotion: NRM at Shildon, County Durham, 2000-05. Publications: Articles in academic journals include: Walter Charlton's Early Life 1620-1659 and Relationship to Natural Philosophy in Mid-Seventeenth Century England, 1973; Timber, Science and Economic Reform in the Seventeenth Century, 1975; The Royal College of Physicians and Interregnum Politics, 1975. Memberships: American Association of Museums; Museums Australia; Museums Association UK; Trustee, Beacon Fellowship Charitable Trust. Address: Magdalene House, High Street, Templecombe, Somerset BA8 0JD, England.

**SHARPE David Thomas,** b. 14 January 1946, Kent, England. Consultant Plastic Surgeon. m. (1) Patricia Lilian Meredith, 1971, dissolved 2002, 1 son, 2 daughters, (2) Tracey Louise Bowman, 2004. Education: Grammar School for Boys, Gravesend; MA, Downing College, Cambridge; MB BChir, Clinical Medical School, Oxford; FRCS, 1975; House Surgeon, Radcliffe Infirmary, Oxford, 1970-71; Senior House Officer, Plastic Surgery, Churchill Hospital, Oxford, 1971-72; Accident Service, Radcliffe Infirmary, 1972; Pathology, Radcliffe Infirmary, 1972-73; General Surgery, Royal United Hospital, Bath, 1973-75; Plastic Surgery, Welsh Plastic Surgery Unit, Chepstow, 1976. Appointments: Registrar, Plastic Surgery, Chepstow, 1976-81; Canniesburn Hospital, Glasgow, 1978-80; Senior Registrar, Plastic Surgery, Leeds and Bradford, 1980-84; Visiting Consultant Plastic Surgeon, Yorkshire Clinic, Bradford, 1985-; BUPA Hospital Elland, West Yorkshire, 1985-; Cromwell Hospital, London, 1985-; Chairman, Breast Special Interest GP, British Association of Plastic Surgeons, 1997-; President, British Association of Aesthetic Plastic Surgeons, 1997-99; Chairman, Yorkshire Air Ambulance, 2001-03; Inventor and Designer of medical equipment and surgical instruments and devices; Exhibitor, Design Council, London, 1987. Publications: Chapters, leading articles and papers on plastic surgery topics, major burn disaster management , tissue expansion and breast

reconstruction. Honours: OBE, 1986; British Design Award, 1988; Prince of Wales Award for Innovation & Production, 1988. Memberships: British Association of Plastic Surgeons; British Association of Aesthetic Plastic Surgeons; Fellow, Royal College of Surgeons of England; International Society of Aesthetic Plastic Surgeons. Address: Hazelbrae, Calverley Lane, Calverley, Leeds LS28 5QQ, England. E-mail: profsharpe@hotmail.com

**SHARPE Tom (Thomas Ridley),** b. 30 March 1928, London, England. Novelist. m. Nancy Anne Looper, 1969, 3 daughters. Education: Pembroke College, University of Cambridge. Appointments: Social Worker, 1952; Teacher, 1952-56; Photographer, 1956-61; Lecturer in History at Cambridge College of Arts and Technology, 1963-71; Full-time novelist, 1971-. Publications: Riotous Assembly, 1971; Indecent Exposure, 1973; Porterhouse Blue, 1974; Blott on the Landscape, 1975; Wilt, 1976; The Great Pursuit, 1977; The Throwback, 1978; The Wilt Alternative, 1979; Ancestral Vices, 1980; Vintage Stuff, 1982; Wilt on High, 1984; Grantchester Grind, 1995; The Midden, 1996; Wilt in Nowhere, 2005. Address: 38 Tunwells Lane, Great Shelford, Cambridge, CB2 5LJ, England.

**SHATNER William,** b. 22 March 1931, Montreal, Quebec, Canada. Actor. m. (1) Gloria Rosenberg, 1956, divorced 1969, 3 children, (2) Marcy Lafferty, 1973, divorced 1996, (3) Nerine Kidd, 1997, deceased 1999, (4) Elizabeth Anderson, 2001. Education: BA, McGill University. Career: Appeared, Montreal Playhouse, 1952, 1953; Juvenile roles, Canadian Repertory Theatre, Ottawa, 1952-53, 1953-54; Shakespeare Festival, Stratford, Ontario, 1954-56; Broadway appearances include: Tamburlaine the Great, 1956; The World of Suzie Wong, 1958; A Shot in the Dark, 1961; Numerous TV appearances; Films include: The Brothers Karamazov, 1958, The Explosive Generation, 1961, Judgement at Nuremberg, 1961, The Intruder, 1962, The Outrage, 1964, Dead of Night, 1974, The Devil's Rain, 1975, Star Trek, 1979, The Kidnapping of the President, 1979, Star Trek: The Wrath of Khan, 1982, Star Trek III, The Search for Spock, 1984, Star Trek IV: The Voyage Home, 1986, Star Trek V: The Final Frontier, 1989, Star Trek VI: The Undiscovered Country, 1991, National Lampoon's Loaded Weapon, 1993; Star Trek: Generations, 1994; Ashes of Eden, 1995; Star Trek: Avenger, 1997; Tek Net, 1997; Free Enterprise, 1999; Miss Congeniality, 2000; Groom Lake (also director and co-writer), 2002. Publications: Ashes of Eden; Star Trek: Avenger, 1997; Step into Chaos, 1999; Get a Life, 1999; The Preserver, 2000; Spectre, 2000. Address: c/o Melis Productions, 760 North La Cienega Boulevard, Los Angeles, CA 90069, USA.

**SHAW Carolyn Janet,** b. 24 April 1947, Cheshire, England. Head Mistress. m. Charles Shaw, 1 son, 1 daughter. Education: BA (Hons), English, London University; PGCE, Liverpool University. Appointments: English Teacher, La Sainte Union Convent, Bath, 1972-74; Head of English, Mount St Agnes Academy, Bermuda, 1974-78; Marketing Manager, Eastern Europe, Instapro International, 1985-89; English Teacher, University Advisor, The Cheltenham Ladies' College, 1989-96; Head Mistress, St Mary's School, Calne, 1996-2003; Head Mistress, Roedean School, 2003-. Memberships: Boarding Schools Association; Girls' Schools Association; Vice-Chairman, Independent Schools Examinations Board. Address: Roedean School, Brighton BN2 5RQ, England. E-mail: headmistress@roedean.co.uk

**SHAW Dorothy E.** Scientist. Education: PhD, University of Manitoba, 1953. Appointments: Demonstrator, 1948, Teaching

Fellow, 1949-53, University of Sydney; Plant Pathologist, Chief Plant Pathologist, Department of Primary Industry, Papua New Guinea, 1955-76; Consulting Plant Pathologist for PNG, Department of Primary Industries in Australia, 1977; Visiting Scientist, Department of Primary Industries, Indooroopilly, Australia, 1978-. Publications: Numerous articles in professional journals. Honours: Commonwealth of Australia Scholarships, 1943-47; Thomas Lawrance Pawlett Scholar, University of Sydney, 1953; Rockefeller Grant, 1955; MBE, 1971; Fellow, Australian Institute of Agricultural Science and Technology, 1974; Independence Medal, PNG, 1975; Daniel McAlpine Memorial Lecturer, Australasian Plant Pathology Society, Canberra, 1999. Address: Plant Pathology, Department of Primary Industries, Meiers Road, Indooroopilly, Q 4068, Australia. E-mail: carrie.wright@dpi.qld.gov.au

**SHAW Sen-Yen,** b. 26 March 1945, Taiwan. Professor of Mathematics. m. Tsui Yueh Chen, 2 daughters. Education: BS, Fu-Jen University, 1967; MA, 1972, PhD, 1977, University of Illinois, Chicago. Appointments: Associate Professor, National Central University, Chung-Li, Taiwan, 1977-82; Professor, 1982-2003, Head, Department of Mathematics, 1987-90; Professor, Lunghwa University of Science and Technology, 2003-. Publications: Over 80 papers in professional mathematical journals or books. Honour: Sun Yat-Sen Prize, 1985. Memberships: American Mathematical Society; Mathematical Society of Taiwan. Address: F13, 309, Wenhua Road Sec 2, Panchiao City, Taiwan.

**SHCHERBAN Vladimir G,** b. 16 May 1939, Nizhny Novgorod, Russia. Engineer; Mechanic. m. Ludmila Shcherban, 2 daughters. Education: Graduate, Technical University, Nizhny Novgorod, 1961. Appointments: Chief of Technical Department "Mashinostroitelnyi zavod" Ltd, Nizhny Novgorod, Russia. Publication: Book: The dynamic theory of physical space, primary physical structures and fields. The system of basic concepts, 2004. Address: 5 Piskunova Str of 47, 603005 Nizhny Novgorod, Russia. E-mail: vgshcherban@mail.ru (summertime: doronin@mail.ru)

**SHE Jin-Hua,** b. 23 May 1963, Jinshi, Hunan, China. University Professor. m. Yoko Miyamoto. 1 son. Education: Masters Degree, 1990, PhD, 1993, Tokyo Institute of Technology, Japan. Appointments: Lecturer, 1993-2001, Associate Professor, 2001-, Tokyo University of Technology, Japan; Guest Lecturer, Toyota Techno Service Corporation, Japan, 2001-; Guest Professor, Central South University, China, 2002-. Publications: Articles in scientific journals including: IEEE Trans. On Automatic Control, Automatica, Systems and Control Letters, Transactions of ASME; Control Engineering Practice; Engineering Application of Artificial Intelligence; IEE Proceedings. Honour: Prize Paper Award, International Federation of Automatic Control. Memberships: IEEE; Institute of Electrical Engineers of Japan; Society of Instrument and Control Engineers. Address: School of Bionics, Tokyo University of Technology, 1404-1 Katakura, Hachioji, Tokyo 192-0982, Japan. E-mail: she@cc.teu.ac.jp Website: www.teu.ac.jp/Rougi/hp037/she.htm

**SHEARER Alan,** b. 1970, Gosforth, Newcastle upon Tyne. Footballer. Career: Coached as child at Wallsend Boys' Club; Striker; Played for Southampton, 1987-92, Blackburn Rovers, 1992-96; Signed by Newcastle United for world record transfer of £15 million (Captain), 1996; First played for England, 1992, Captain 1996-2000. Address: Newcastle United Football Club, St James Park, Newcastle Upon Tyne, NE1 4ST, England.

**SHEEN Charlie,** b. 3 September 1965, New York, USA. Actor. m. Donna Peele, 1995. Actor, TV films include: Silence of the

Heart; The Boys Next Door; Films include: Apocalypse Now; Grizzly II; The Predator; The Red Dawn; Lucas; Platoon; The Wraith; Day Off; Young Guns; Wall Street; Eight Men Out; Major League; Backtrack; Men at Work; Courage Mountain; Navy Seals; The Rookie; Stockade (director); Secret Society; Hot Shots; Dead Fall; The Three Musketeers; The Chase; Major League II, 1994; Terminal Velocity, 1994; The Shadow Conspiracy, 1995; Shockwave, 1995; All Dogs Go to Heaven (voice), The Arrival, 1996; Money Talks, 1997; No Code of Conduct, 1998; Free Money, 1998; Letter From Death Row, 1998; Being John Malkovich, 1999; Cared X; Good Advice, 2000; Lisa Picard is Famous, 2001. Address: c/o Jeffrey Ballard Public Relations, 4814 Lemara Avenue, Sherman Oaks, CA 91403, USA.

**SHEEN Martin (Ramon Estevez),** b. 3 August 1940, Dayton, Ohio, USA. Actor. m. Janet Sheen, 1961, 3 sons, 1 daughter. Career: Actor, films include: The Incident; Catch 22; Rage; Badlands; Apocalypse Now; Enigma; Gandhi; The King of Prussia; The Championship Season; Man, Woman and Child; The Dead Zone; Final Countdown; Loophole; Wall Street; Night Beaker; Da, 1988; Personal Choice, 1989; Cadence (also director), 1990; Judgement in Berlin, 1990; Limited Time; The Maid, 1990; Cadence (also director), 1990; Hear No Evil; Hot Shots part Deux (cameo); Gettysburg, 1993; Trigger Fast; Hit!; Fortunes of War; Sacred Cargo; The Break; Dillinger and Capone; Captain Nuke and the Bomber Boys; Ghost Brigade; The Cradle Will Rock; Dead Presidents; Dorothy Day; Gospa; The American President; The War At Home; Spawn; Storm; Monument Avenue, Free Money; Lost & Found, 1999; Apocalypse New Redux, 2001; Catch Me If You Can, 2003; TV appearances include: The Defenders; East Side/West Side; My Three Sons; Mod Squad; Cannon; That Certain Summer; Missiles of October; The Last Survivors; Blind Ambition; Shattered Spirits; Nightbreaker; The Last POW?; Roswell; The West Wing; Stage appearances: The Connection (New York and European tours); Never Live Over A Pretzel Factory; The Subject was Roses; The Crucible. Honours include: Honorary Mayor of Malibu, 1989-; Golden Satellite Award, 2000; Golden Globe Award, 2000. Address: c/o Jeff Ballard, 4814 Lemara Avenue, Sherman Oaks, CA 91403, USA.

**SHELDON Sidney,** b. 11 February 1917, Chicago, Illinois, USA. Author. m. (1) Jorja Curtright, deceased 1985, 1 daughter (2) Alexandra Kostoff, 1989. Education: Northwestern University. Appointments: Served USAAF WWII; Former reader, Universal and 20th Century Fox Studios; Creator, writer and producer: Nancy; The Patty Duke Show; I Dream of Jeannie; Creator, Hart to Hart (TV) show. Publications: Screenplays include: Billy Rose's Jumbo; The Bachelor and the Bobby Soxer, 1947; Easter Parade; Annie Get Your Gun; Dream Wife (also director); Buster Keaton Story (also director); Plays include: Roman Candle; Jackpot; Dream With Music; Alice in Arms; Redhead; Novels: The Naked Face, 1970; The Other Side of Midnight, 1975; A Stranger in the Mirror, 1976; Bloodline, 1977; Rage of Angels, 1980; Master of the Game, 1982; If Tomorrow Comes, 1985; Windmills of the Gods, 1987; Memories of Midnight, 1991; The Doomsday Conspiracy, 1991; The Stars Shine Down, 1992; Nothing Lasts Forever, 1994; Morning Moon and Night, 1995; The Best Laid Plans, 1997; Tell Me Your Dreams, 1998; The Sky is Falling, 2000. Honours: Academy Award for The Bachelor and the Bobby Soxer, 1947; Writers Guild of America Award for Easter Parade, 1948. Address: c/o William Morrow & Co, 1350 Avenue of the Americas, New York, NY 10019, USA.

**SHEPARD Sam, (Samuel Shepard Rogers),** b. 5 November 1943, Fort Sheridan, Illinois, USA. Dramatist; Actor. m. O-

Lan Johnson Dark, 9 November 1969, divorced, 1 son; 1 son, 1 daughter with Jessica Lange. Education: Mount San Antonio Junior College, Walnut, California, 1961-62. Career: Plays: Cowboys, Rock Garden, 1964; 4-H Club, 1965; Up to Thursday, 1965; Rocking Chair, 1965; Chicago, 1965; Icarus's Mother, 1965; Fourteen Hundred Thousand, 1966; Red Cross, 1966; Melodrama Play, 1966; La Turista, 1967; Cowboys #2, 1967; Forensic and the Navigators, 1967; The Holy Ghostly, 1969; The Unseen Hand, 1969; Operation Sidewinder, 1970; Shaved Splits, 1970; Mad Dog Blues, 1971; Terminal, 1971; Cowboy Mouth (with Patti Smith), 1971; Black Bog Beast Bait, 1971; The Tooth of Crime, 1972; Blue Bitch, 1973; Nightwalk (with Megan Terry and Jean-Claude van Itallie), 1973; Geography of a Horse Dreamer, 1974; Little Ocean, 1974; Action, 1974; Killer's Head, 1974; Suicide in B-Flat, 1976; Angel City, 1976; Curse of the Starving Class, 1977; Buried Child, 1978; Tongues, 1979; Savage/Love, 1979; Seduced, 1979; True West, 1981; Fool for Love, 1983; Superstitions, 1983; The Sad Lament of Pecos Bill on the Eve of Killing his Wife, 1983; A Lie of the Mind, 1985; States of Shock, 1991; Simpatico, 1993; TV: Lily Dale, 1996; Purgatory, 1999; Hamlet, 2000; Films: Days of Heaven; Frances; The Right Stuff; Country; Crimes of the Heart; Baby Boom; Defenceless, 1989; Voyager; Thunderheart, 1992; The Pelican Brief, 1994; Safe Passage, 1995; The Good Old Boys, 1995; Curtain Call, 1997; The Only Thrill, 1997; Snow Falling on Cedars, 1999; One Kill, 2000; Shot in the Heart, 2001; Swordfish, 2001; The Pledge, 2001. Publications: A Murder of Crows, novel, 1996; Cruising Paradise, short stories, 1996. Honours: Obie Awards, 1966, 1966, 1966, 1968, 1973, 1975, 1977, 1979, 1984; Rockefeller Foundation Grant, 1967; Guggenheim Fellowships, 1968, 1971; National Institute and American Academy of Arts and Letters Award, 1974; Creative Arts Award, Brandeis University, 1975; Pulitzer Prize in Drama, 1979; New York Drama Critics' Circle Award, 1986. Memberships: American Academy of Arts and Letters; Theater Hall of Fame. Address: c/o International Creative Management, 8942 Wilshire Boulevard, Beverly Hills, CA 90211, USA.

**SHEPHARD Gillian Patricia (Rt Hon)**, b. 22 January 1940, Great Britain. Politician. m. Thomas Shephard, 1975, 2 step sons. Education: St Hilda's College, Oxford. Appointments: Schools Inspector and Education Officer, 1963-75; Cambridge University Extra Mural Board Lecturer, 1965-87; Norfolk County Council, 1977-89; For Norfolk County Council: Chair of Social Services Committee, 1978-83; Education Committee, 1983-85; Chair, West Norfolk and Wisbech Health Authority, 1981-85; Norwich Health Authority, 1985-87; Conservative MP South West Norfolk, 1987-97, Norfolk South West, 1997-; Parliamentary Private Secretary to Economic Secretary to the Treasury, 1988-89; Parliamentary Under Secretary of State, Department of Social Security, 1989-90; Treasury Minister of State, 1990-92; Employment Secretary of State, 1992-93, for Agriculture, Fisheries and Food, 1993-94, For Education, 1995; For Education and Employment, July 1995; Women's National Commission Co-Chair, 1990-91. Publication: Shephard's Watch, 2000. Memberships: Council Member, University of Oxford, 2000-. Honour: Honorary Fellow, St Hilda's College, Oxford, 1991. Address: House of Commons, London SW1A 0AA, England.

**SHEPHERD John Alan (Sir)**, b. 27 April 1943, Edinburgh, Scotland. m. Jessica Nichols, 1 daughter. Education: MA, Selwyn College, Cambridge, 1961-64; MA, Stanford, 1964-65. Appointments: HM Diplomatic Service, 1965-2003 including: Ambassador, Bahrain, 1988-91; Minister, Bonn, 1991-95; Director, Middle East, Foreign and Commonwealth Office, 1996-97; Deputy Under Secretary, Foreign and Commonwealth Office, Member of Boards of Foreign and Commonwealth

Office, BOTB later BTI, 1997-2000; Member, Review Committee of Government Export Promotion Services, 1998-99; Ambassador to Italy, 2000-2003; Currently: Secretary-General, Global Leadership Foundation; Chairman, Norbert Brainin Foundation; Deputy-Chairman, Trustees of Prince's School for Traditional Arts. Publication: Rhine Tasting in Motor Boat and Yachting, 1996. Honours: CMG, 1988; KCVO, 2000. Membership: Oxford and Cambridge Club. Address: GLF, 14 Curzon Street, London W1J 5HN, England.

**SHEPPARD David (Stuart) (Lord Sheppard of Liverpool)**, b. 6 March 1929, Reigate, Surrey, England. Retired Bishop; Writer. m. Grace Isaac, 19 June 1957, 1 daughter. Education: MA, Trinity Hall, Cambridge. Appointments: Ridley Hall Theological College Assistant Curate, St Mary's, Islington, 1955-57; Warden, Mayflower Family Centre, Canning Town, 1957-69; Bishop Suffragan, Woolwich, 1969-75; Bishop of Liverpool, 1975-97; Chairman, Martin Luther King Foundation, 1970-75, General Synod Board for Social Responsibility, 1991-96; Chairman, Churches' Enquiry into Unemployment and the Future of Work, 1995-97; President, Sussex County Cricket Club, 2001-03. Publications: Parson's Pitch, 1964; Built as a City, 1974; Bias to the Poor, 1983; The Other Britain, 1984; Better Together (with D Worlock), 1988; With Christ in the Wilderness (with D Worlock), 1990; With Hope in Our Hearts (with D Worlock), 1994; Steps Along Hope Street, 2002. Honours: Honorary LLD, University of Liverpool, 1981; Honorary Fellow, Trinity Hall, Cambridge, 1983; Honorary DTech, Liverpool Polytechnic, 1987; Honorary DD, University of Cambridge, 1991; Honorary DD, University of Exeter, 1998; Freedom, City of Liverpool, 1995; Life Peerage, 1998; Honorary DUniv, Open University 1999; Honorary DD, University of Wales, 2000. Address: Ambledown, 11 Melloncroft Drive, West Kirby, Merseyside L48 2JA, England.

**SHER Antony**, b. 14 June 1949, Cape Town, South Africa. Actor; Artist; Author. Career: Films: Shadey; the Young Poisoner's Handbook; Alive and Kicking; Mrs Brown; Shakespeare in Love; TV appearances include: The History Man; Collision Course; The Land of Dreams; Genghis Cohn; The Moon Stone; Plays include: John, Paul, Ringo and Bert; Teeth n' Smiles; Cloud Nine; A Prayer for My Daughter; Goosepimples; King Lear; Tartuffe; Richard II; Merchant of Venice; The Revenger's Tragedy; Hello and Goodbye; Singer; Tamburlaine the Great; Travesties; Cyrano de Bergerac; The Winter's Tale; Torch Song Trilogy; True West; Arturo Ui; Uncle Vanya; Titus Andronicus; Stanley; Mahler's Conversion; ID, 2003; The Malcontent. Publications: Year of the King, 1986; Middlepost, 1988; Characters, 1989; Changing Steps (Screenplay), 1989; The Indoor Boy, 1991; Cheap Drives, 1995; Woza Shakespeare! (co-author), 1996; The Feast, 1998; Beside Myself (autobiography), 2001. Honours: Best Actor Awards, Drama Magazine, London Standard Awards, 1985; Olivier Award for Best Actor, Society of West End Theatres, 1985, 1997; Best Actor Award, Martini TMA Awards, 1996; Peter Sellers Evening Standard Film Award, 1998; Honorary D Litt (Liverpool), 1998. Address: c/o ICM, Oxford House, 76 Oxford Street, London W1N 0AX, England.

**SHER Emmanuil Moiseyevich**, b. 29 March 1929, Port Khorly, Ukraine. Physicist Researcher. m. Elena, 1 son. Education: BS, Moscow State University, 1951; Physicist, St Petersburg State University, 1952; PhD, Physical Electronics, 1967; DSc, Physics of Semiconductors and Dielectrics, 1983. Appointments: Senior Engineer, Vacuum Technology, 1952-59; Researcher, Senior Scientific Researcher, Leading Scientific Researcher, Physics of Thermoelectricity, Electron Emission, High Temperature Superconductors and Thin Solid Films, 1959-. Publications: 100

articles, 21 patents, scientific editor of 2 books. Honours: Bronze Medal, 1963, Silver Medal, 1983; Honorary Academician, International Academy of Refrigeration, 1999. Memberships: AF Ioffe Physico-Technical Institute, Russian Academy of Sciences, 1959-; International Thermoelectric Society, 1991; New York Academy of Sciences, 1996. Address: 20 Orbely Str, apt 73, 194223 St Petersburg, Russia. E-mail: em.sher@mail.ioffe.ru

**SHERBET Gajanan Venkatramanaya,** b. 25 March 1935, Bantval, Karnataka, India. Pathologist; Cell Biologist; Research Scientist. m. Madurai Subramanyam Lakshmi. Education: BSc, 1956, MSc, 1958, PhD, 1962, University of Pune, India; MSc, 1967, DSc, 1978, University of London. Appointments: Research Scientist, Chester Beatty Research Institute, London, 1964-69; Research Fellow, Harvard University, USA, 1966; Research Scientist, University College Hospital Medical School, University of London, 1970-77; Research Scientist, Cancer Research Unit, 1977-81; Acting Director, Cancer Research Unit, 1988-89, Deputy Director, 1981 2000, Reader in Experimental Oncology, Cancer Research Unit, 1988-2000, Member of Communication and Signal Processing Research Group, School of Electrical, Electronic & Computer Engineering, 2001-, University of Newcastle upon Tyne; Adjunct Professor, Institute for Molecular Medicine, Huntington Beach, California, USA, 1999-; Associate Editorships: Anticancer Research, 1998-; Journal of European Citizen's Quality of Life, 2003; Cancer Genomics and Proteomics, 2004-; Editorial Board, Current Cancer Therapy Review, 2005-. Publications: Books: The Biophysical and Biochemical Characterisation of Cell Surface, 1977; The Biology of Tumour Malignancy, 1982; The Metastic Spread of Cancer, 1987; The Genetics of Cancer: Genes Associated with Cancer Invasion, Metastasis and Cell Proliferation, 1997; Calcium Signalling in Cancer, 2001; Genetic Recombination in Cancer, 2003; Editor of 4 books; Numerous articles to professional journals. Honours: The Lord Dowding Fund Award, London University, 1969-73; Beit Memorial and Williams Fellow, London University, 1969-3; Felix Wankel and Ernst Hutzenlaub Prize, 1977; Cancer Research Campaign Fellow, University of Newcastle upon Tyne, 1985-2000. Memberships: Fellow, Royal College of Pathologists; Fellow Royal Society of Chemistry; Fellow, Institute of Biology; American Association for Cancer Research; British Association for Cancer Research; British Neuro-Oncology Group; Life Member, Indian Association for Cancer Research. Address: School of Electrical, Electronic and Computer Engineering, University of Newcastle upon Tyne, Merz Court, Newcastle upon Tyne NW1 7RU, England. E-mail: gajanan.sherbet@ncl.ac.uk

**SHERIFF Bat-Sheva,** b. 28 June 1937, Tel-Aviv, Israel. Professor, Chairman, Israel Postal and Philatelic Museum. m. Mordechai Manfred Segal, 1962, 2 sons. Education: Teacher's Diploma, University of Tel Aviv; Graduated, Philosophy and Literature, Hebrew University, Jerusalem. Appointments: Teacher, Secondary School, 1956-71; Director, Cultural Project for Underprivileged Youth in Development Areas, 1971-86; Editor, Monthly Journal for Inspectors; Inspector, Ministry of Education and Culture. Publications: Poems, 1956; Not All the Rivers, 1964; Love Poems, 1972; Persuasive Words, 1974; Man That is Honour – Psalm 49, 1978; Festive Poems, 1981; Ashes Instead of Bread, 1982; By Necessity and By Right, 1986; Letters to Bat-Sheva, 1990; Ancient People, 2002; The Soul is the Matter, 2003; Wilderness of the Eagle-Owl, 2004. Numerous videos; Contributions to newspapers and periodicals, radio and television broadcasts. Memberships: Executive Committee, Hebrew Writers' Association; Press Council of Israel; PEN Israel; Israeli Council of Arts and Culture; Society of Authors,

Composers and Music Publishers; International Confederation of Societies of Authors and Composers. Address: 10 Emek Rafaim, PO Box 7353, Jerusalem 91072, Israel.

**SHERLOCK (Thomas) Harley,** b, 3 March 1926, Croydon, England. Architect. m. Fionnuala Boyd, 2 sons, 1 daughter. Education: Architectural Association School of Architecture. Appointments: Partner Planning Design Team, 1953-; Partner, Andrews Emmerson & Sherlock, 1960-; Partner, Andrews Sherlock & Partners, 1965-; Consultant, 1991-; Public sector work in low-rise, high-density housing and the rehabilitation of 19th century streets in London; Chairman, London Amenity and Transport Association, 1972-80; Chairman, Transport 2000, 1980-85; Chairman, Royal Institute of British Architects London Region, 1984-86; Chairman, Islington Society; Advisory Member, Islington Council's Planning Committee, 17 years. Publications: Cities Are Good For Us, 1991; The Compact City (co-author), 1996; Villagers Five Shillings, 2002; Articles and lectures on urbanism: Institute of Housing 1993, Christ's College Cambridge, 1993, Green College, Oxford, 1994, Cambridge (postgraduates), 1997-2002. Honours: MA, Honoris Causa, London Metropolitan University for services to architecture and planning in London, 2003; Awards to Andrews Sherlock & Partners: Department of the Environment Awards for Good Design in Housing, 1965, 1970; 6 Commendations for Good Design in Housing, 1970-83; Civic Trust Commendation, 1970. Memberships: Royal Institute of British Architects; Architectural Association; Fellow Royal Society for the Arts; Vice-President, Transport 2000; President, Islington Society. Address: 13 Alwyne Place, London N1 2NL, England. E-mail: harley@andrewssherlock.demon.co.uk

**SHERRIN Ned, (Edward George Sherrin),** b. 18 February 1931, Low Ham, Somerset, England. Director; Producer; Writer. Education: MA, University of Oxford; Barrister-at-Law. Publications: Cindy-Ella (with Caryl Brahms), 1962; Rappel 1910 (with Caryl Brahms), 1964; Benbow Was His Name (with Caryl Brahms), 1967; Ooh La (with Caryl Brahms), 1973; After You Mr Feydeau (with Caryl Brahms), 1975; A Small Thing Like an Earthquake, 1983; Song by Song (with Caryl Brahms), 1984; Cutting Edge, 1984; 1956 and All That (with Neil Shand), 1984; The Metropolitan Mikado (with Alistair Beaton), 1985; Too Dirty for the Windmill (with Caryl Brahms), 1986; Loose Neds, 1990; Theatrical Anecdotes, 1991; Ned Sherrin in His Anecdotage, 1993; The Oxford Dictionary of Humorous Quotations, 1994; Sherrin's Year, diary, 1996; Scratch an Actor, novel, 1996; I Wish I'd Said That (collection of quotations), 2004. Honour: Commander of the Order of the British Empire. Address: 4 Cornwall Mansions, Ashburnham Road, London SW10 0PE, England.

**SHEYNOV Victor Pavlovich,** b. 23 May 1940, Yaroslavl, Russia. Psychologist; Sociologist. m. Ludmila V Davidenko, 1 daughter. Education: Diploma with Honours, Moscow Regional Pedagogical Institute, 1958-63; Doctor of Mathematics, 1968; Docent, 1971; PhD, Biology, 2000; Professor, 2003. Appointments: Docent, Senior Lecturer, Belarusian Technical University, 1987-90; Director, Founder, "Manager I" Innovation Enterprise, 1990-94; Professor of Psychology, Minsk Management University, 1994-96; Professor of Psychology, Minsk Management Institute, 1996-99; Professor, Belarusian State University, Minsk, Belarus, 1999-. Publications: 30 books and about 150 scientific articles and publications on psychology, sociology, conflictology, management, advertising, physics and mathematics. Honours: Doctor of Mathematics, 1968; Docent, 1971; PhD, Sociology, 2000; Professor, 2003. Membership: Academician, International Academy for Information

Technologies. Address: av Prospekt Gazety Pravda 54, Apt 22, Minsk, 220116 Belarus. E-mail: sheinov1@mail.ru

**SHI Feng,** b. 1 July 1949, Tianjin, China. Linguistics. m. Meihua Tian, 1 son. Education: Harbin Normal University, 1979; MA, Chinese People University, Beijing, 1982; PhD, Nankai University, 1990. Appointments: Faculty, Tianjin Foreign Language College, 1982-85; Teacher, Nankai University, 1985, Professor, Chinese Linguistics and Phonetics, Nankai University, 1993; Professor, Beijing Language and Culture University, 1993; Research Fellow, City University of Hong Kong, 1995; Professor, Nagoya Gakuin University, Japan, 1998; Dean, International College of Chinese Studies, Nankai University, 2001-. Publications: 8 books and over 60 articles in professional journals. Address: International College of Chinese Studies, Nankai University, Tianjin, China.

**SHIBATA Hiroshi,** b. 9 February 1958, Fukuoka, Japan. Associate Professor. Education: BS, Physics, 1981, MS, 1983, Condensed Matter Theory, ScD, 1992, Statistical Physics, Kyushu University, Japan. Appointments: Full-time Teacher, Nakamura Gakuen Female High School, 1984-86; Teacher, Fukuoka Prefectural Moji High School, 1986-87; Lecturer, Associate Professor, Kumamoto Institute of Technology, 1996 (Kumamoto Institute of Technology changed to Sojo University, 2000). Publications: Articles as author and co-author in scientific journals including: Physica A, 1993, 1998, 2000, 2004. Memberships: European Physical Society; American Physical Society; Physical Society of Japan; Japan Society of Fluid Mechanics; American Association for the Advancement of Science. Address: Sojo University, Ikeda 4-22-1, Kumamoto, 860-0082, Japan. E-mail: shibata@ed.sojo-u.ac.jp Website: www.ed.sojo-u.ac.jp/~shibata/

**SHIBATA Yo,** b. 25 January 1972, Aichi, Japan. Researcher. Education: Qualification of Dentist, Showa University School of Dentistry, 1996; PhD, Showa University School of Dentistry Graduate School, 2000. Appointment: Assistant Professor, Department of Oral Biomaterials and Technology, Showa University School of Dentistry, 2000-. Publications: Articles in scientific medical journals including: International Journal of Oral and Maxillofacial Implants, 2002, 2004; Journal of Dental Research, 2002, 2004, 2005; Biomaterials, 2004. Honours: Listed in Who's Who publications and biographical dictionaries. Membership: International Association for Dental Research; Japanese Society for Dental Materials and Devices; Japanese Society for Biomaterials. Address: 1-5-8 Hatanodai, Shinagawa-ku, Tokyo 142-8555, Tokyo, Japan. E-mail: yookun@dent.showa-u.ac.jp

**SHIBUE Yasuhiro,** b. 9 September 1955, Osaka, Japan. University Professor. m. Yumiko Yanai, 1 son, 1 daughter. Education: BSc, 1979, MSc, 1981, PhD, 1986, University of Tokyo. Appointments: Research Assistant, 1987-88, Assistant Professor, 1988-90, Associate Professor, 1990-99, Professor, 1999-, Hyogo University of Teacher Education. Publications: Mineralization and Transportation of Tungsten in Hydrothermal Solution: Some Studies on Several Japanese Tungsten Deposits; Cation Exchange Properties of Phillipsite: The Difference Between Si-rich and Si-poor Phillipsites. Memberships: The Geochemical Society; American Geophysical Union; The Japanese Association of Mineralogists, Petrologists and Economic Geologists. Address: Geoscience Institute, Hyogo University of Teacher Education, Yashiro, Kato-gun, Hyogo 673 1494 Japan. E-mail: yshibue@sci.hyogo-u.ac.jp

**SHIEH Wung Yang,** b. 22 September 1956, Taipei, Taiwan. Professor. m. Jiin Jiun Leu, 2 sons, 1 daughter. Education:

Master's Degree, University of Tokyo, 1986; Doctor's Degree, 1989. Appointments: Associate Professor, 1989-94, Professor, 1994- Institute of Oceanography, National Taiwan University, Taipei. Publications: Contribution of articles to professional journals including International Journal of Systemic and Evolutionary Microbiology and Canadian Journal of Microbiology. Memberships: The Japanese Society of Microbial Ecology; The Chinese Society of Microbiology. Address: Institute of Oceanography, National Taiwan University, PO Box 23-13, Taipei, Taiwan. E-mail: winyang@ntu.edu.tw.

**SHIEH Ying-Hua,** b. 19 January 1958, Taipei, Taiwan. Doctor. Education: Taipei Medical University, Taiwan; George Washington University, USA. Appointments: Chief of Department of Family Medicine, Taipei Medical College Hospital, Taipei; President, Chinese Association of Travel Medicine; President, Chinese Association of Health Care of the Elderly; Congress Chairperson, The Second Asia-Pacific Travel Health Congress, 1998; Congress Chairperson of the World Congress of Travel Medicine, 2000. Publications: 29 articles in professional journals including: Arterial blood pressure and blood lipids as cardiovascular risk factors and occupational stress in Taiwan International Journal of Cardiology 81, 2001; Estimating Stature from Knee Height for Adults in Taiwan, 2001; Evaluation of the Hepatic and Renal-protective Effects of Ganoderma lucidum in Mice, 2001; Systematic Immunity-Enhancing Effects in Healthy Subjects Following Dietary Consumption of the Lactice Acid Bacterium Lactobacillusrhamnosus IIN001, 2001; Associations of Smoking, Lack of Exercise and Body Mass Index with Occupational Stress Factors in a Population of Male White-Collar Workers in Taipei, Taiwan, 2001; Work Related Psychosocial Factors and the Risk of Musculoskeletal Disorders, 2002. Honours: Outstanding Ten Physicians in Taiwan; Hsin-Lin Award, Taiwan; Huans' Award, USA. Memberships: Member: Family Medicine Association; Emergency Medicine Association; Chinese Association of Health Care of The Elderly; Endocrine Medicine Association; Chinese Association of Travel Medicine; Taipei Medicine University Hospital, Family Medicine; President, Chinese Association of Care of Elderly; Chinese Association of Travel Medicine; Asia-Pacific Travel Medicine Society; Taiwan Association of Family Medicine. Address: No 2-1, Lane 92, Sec 2, Min-Chuan E Rd, Taipei, Taiwan, ROC. E-mail: clarejchw@yahoo.com.tw

**SHIH Frank Yeong-Chyang,** b. 11 June 1957, Taiwan. Professor. m. An-Ling Huang, 1 son, 1 daughter. Education: BS, National Cheng-Kung University, Taiwan, 1980; MS, State University of New York, Stony Brook, 1984; PhD, Purdue University, 1987. Appointments: Systems Engineer, China Steel Incorporated, 1982-83; Research Assistant, Purdue University, 1984-87; Assistant Professor, 1988-93, Associate Professor, 1993-98, New Jersey Institute of Technology; Visiting Research Fellow, Air Force Rome Laboratory, New York, 1995; Guest Professor, Project Co-ordinator, National Taiwan University, 1995-96; Professor, New Jersey Institute of Technology, 1998-. Publications: Over 130 articles in professional journals and conferences. Honours include: Merit Awards, New Jersey Institute of Technology, 1988-98; Research Initiation Award, National Science Foundation, 1991. Membership: IEEE. Address: 153 Sun Valley Way, Morris Plains, NJ 07950-2017, USA.

**SHIH Ming-Hsiang,** b. 15 January 1963, Taichung, Taiwan. Professor. m. Pei-Ju Liao, 1 son, 1 daughter. Education: Bachelor, National Chung-Hsing University, 1985; Master, National Taiwan University, 1987; PhD, Rheinisch Westfälische Technische Hochschule, Aaachen, Germany, 1996. Appointments: Engineer: Sinotech Engineering Consultant Inc,

1989-90; Assistant Professor, Chao-Yang University of science and Technology, 1997-98; Assistant Professor, 1998-2002, Associate Professor, 2002-, National Kaohsiung First University of Science and Technology. Publications: 20 international journal papers; 17 papers presented at international conferences; 2 US patents; 1 Japanese patent; 6 Taiwanese patents. Honours: Visiting Scholar, DAAD, Germany, 2002; Honour Member, Phi-Tao-Phi Association; Award for Research Article, Society of Structural Engineering, 2003. Memberships: Life Member, Taiwan Association of Earthquake Engineering. Address: No 1 University Road, Yen-Chao, Kaohsiung County, 824 Taiwan. E-mail: mhshih@ccms.nkfust.edu.tw

**SHIH Tso-Min,** b. 4 April 1935, Ying-Cheng, Shantung, China. Mining Engineering Educator. m. Ching-Ch'i Hsia Shih, 1 June 1961, 1 son, 2 daughters. Education: BSc, National Cheng-Kung University, Taiwan, 1958; MSc, McGill University, Montreal, Canada, 1965. Appointments: Research Assistant, Nova Scotia Technical College, Halifax, Canada, 1965-66; Lecturer, 1968 72, Associate Professor, 1972-74, Professor, Department Chairman, 1974-80, Professor, 1980-, National Cheng-Kung University, Tainan, Taiwan, China. Publications: Diamond, book (in Chinese), 1996; The Exploitation and Utilization of Graphite, book (in Chinese); More than 50 publications in journals and conference proceedings. Honours: Chinese Institute of Mining and Metal Engineering, Taipei, 1972, 1991; Pi Epsilon Tau National Petroleum Engineering Honor Society, Los Angeles, 1989; Department of Reconstructions, Taiwan Provincial Government, 1993; Mining Association of China, 1996. Memberships: Chinese Institute of Petroleum Engineers; Chinese Institute of Mining and Metal Engineering, Director, 1976-78; Mining Association of China, Director 1988-96; Chinese Institute of Engineers; Retired, 2000; Part time Professor, National Cheng-Kung University, 2000-; Full Professor, Diwan University, Tainan County, 2003-. Address: No 74 Fl 1 Tung-Ning Road, Tainan, Taiwan, 701, China.

**SHIKHMURZAEV Yulii Damir,** b. 12 September 1957, Ryazan, USSR. Mathematician. m. Zimfira Gallyamova, 1 daughter. Education: MSc, Applied Mathematics and Mechanics, 1980, PhD, Physics and Mathematics, 1985, Moscow State University. Appointments: Junior Research Scientist, 1984-88, Research Scientist, 1989-92, Senior Research Scientist, 1992-96, Moscow State University; Lecturer, University of Leeds, UK, 1996-98; Senior Lecturer, 1999-2001, Reader, 2001-, School of Mathematics, University of Birmingham, UK; Visiting Researcher, University of Naples, Italy, 1988-89; Visiting Professor, University of Pierre and Marie Curie, France, 2002; Associate Editor, Continuum Mechanics & Thermodynamics, 2005-. Publications: More than 40 articles; 2 patents. Memberships: International Society of Coating Science and Technology; European Mechanics Society; German Society for Applied Mathematics and Mechanics; London Mathematical Society. Address: School of Mathematics, University of Birmingham, Edgbaston, Birmingham B15 2TT, England. E-mail: yulii@for.mat.bham.ac.uk

**SHIM Chan Shik,** b. 11 March 1962, Seoul, South Korea. Medical Doctor. m. In-kyung Shin, 1 son, 1 daughter. Education: MD, 1987; MA, 1994; PhD, 2003; Board Certified, Korean Board of Neurological Surgery, 1996. Appointments: Vice-President, Medical Affairs, Wooridul Spine Hospital, Seoul, Korea, 2002-2003; Visiting Professor, Department of Neurosurgery, Kyung-Hee University, College of Medicine, Seoul, Korea, 2000-; Vice-President, Academic Affairs, Wooridul Spine Hospital, Seoul, Korea, 2005-. Publications: Articles in medical journals include: Partial disc replacement with PDN prosthetic disc nucleus device: Early clinical results,

2003; Fluoroscopically assisted percutaneous translaminar facet screw fixation following anterior lumbar interbody fusion: Technical report, 2005. Memberships: Spine Arthroplasty Society; Korean Neurosurgical Society; International Society of Minimal Intervention for Spine Surgery. Address: 47-4 Chungdam-Dong, Kangnam-Gu, Seoul, South Korea 135-100. E-mail: shimcs@wooridul.co.kr

**SHIM Jae-Goo,** b. 24 August 1966, Daegu, Korea. Researcher. m. Jung-Mi Jang, 2 sons. Education: BA, Yeungnam University, Korea, 1992; MS, Kyungpook National University, Korea, 1994; PhD, Tohoku University, Japan, 1999. Appointment: Senior Member, Technical Staff, Korea Electric Power Research Institute. Publications: Papers in scientific journals including: Journal of American Chemical Society; Chemical Communications. Honours: Listed in Who's Who publications and biographical dictionaries. Address: 110-401 Purun Apt, Jeonmin-Dong, Yusung-Gu, Daejeon 305-727, Korea.

**SHIMADA Yasuyuki,** b. 12 May 1960, Kyoto, Japan. Medical Doctor. m Rika Shimada, 3 sons, 1 daughter. Education: MD, 1985, PhD, 1996, Kyoto Prefectural University of Medicine. Appointments: Research Fellow, Rayne Institute, St Thomas Hospital, London, England, 1993-95; Registrar, Cardiothoracic Surgery, St George Hospital, Australia, 1996-98; Senior Lecturer, Kyoto Prefectural University of Medicine, 1999-2002; Director, Cardiovascular Surgery, Saiseikai Suota Hospital, 2003-2004; Director, Cardiovascular Surgery, Yuri Kumiai General Hospital, 2005-;Fellowship, Japanese Association for Thoracic Surgery, 2000; Active Member of the International Society for Cardiovascular Surgery, 2002-; Board Certified Surgeon, The Japanese Board of Cardiovascular Surgery, 2004-. Publications: Does Angiotension Converting Enzyme Inhibitor Protect the Heart?; From Laboratory to Operating Room; Clinical Application of Experimental Study; Current Pharmaceutical Design, in press, 2005. Memberships: American Heart Association; American Stroke Association. Address: Cardiovascular Surgery, Yuri Kumiai General Hospital, 38 Ieno-ushiro Aza, Kawaguchi, Honjo, Akita 015-8511, Japan. E-mail:yasuyuki.shimada@ma8.seikyou.ne.jp

**SHIMAZU Seiichiro,** b. 26 January 1961, Ashiya-shi, Hyogo-ken, Japan. Researcher. Education: BSc, 1983, MSc, 1985, Kagoshima University, Japan; PhD, Kyoto University, Japan, 2003. Appointments: Kagoshima University, Japan, 1985-86; Fujimoto Diagnostics Inc, Habikino Institute, Japan, 1986-93; Fujimoto Pharmaceutical Corporation, Research Institute, Japan, 1993-97; Kyoto University, Japan, 1997-99; Fujimoto Pharmaceutical Corporation, Research Institute, Japan, 1999-. Publications: Articles as co-author in scientific journals including: Japanese Journal of Pharmacology, 1998; European Journal of Pharmacology, 2000; Journal of Neurochemistry, 2001; Journal of Neural Transmission, 2003; Annals of Neurology, 2003. Honours: The Japanese Journal of Pharmacology Prize Award, 1999; Listed in Who's Who publications and biographical dictionaries. Memberships: Movement Disorder Society; Japan Bioindustry Association; Japanese Pharmacological Society. Address: Matsuoka 4-11-18-208, Matsubara-shi, Osaka 580-0042, Japan.

**SHIMBO Satoru,** b. 28 November 1948, Japan. Professor. m. 1 daughter. Education: Graduate, Foreign Linguistics Department, Dokkyo University, 1972; MC, Philosophy (Western and Oriental), 1974 Dr C in Philosophy, Japanese Intellectual Thought and History, 1977, Chuo University. Appointments: Full-time Lecturer, Foreign Linguistics Department, Himeji Dokkyo University, 1989-2002; Professor, Faculty of Liberal Arts and Sciences, Bunka Women's University, 2003-.

Publications: 24 volumes include: Shinran: His Nembatsu and Thanks to Aminda Budda, 1985; The Japanese Intellectual Thought and History, 1989; Zen Thought in Japan, 1992; The Shobogenzo of Dogen, 2000; Japanese View on Life and Ethics, 2001. Honours: Honorary Doctor of Philosophy, IONO University, 2001; Award of Academic Study, Association for Study of Japanese Spiritual Culture, 2002; 21st Century Award, Illuminated Diploma of Honour, IBC, Cambridge, England; 2005 International Peace Prize, USA; Doctor of Literature, Tsukuba University, Japan, 2005. Memberships: Japanese Association for Comparative Philosophy, 1974-; Japanese Association for Religious Studies, 1975-. Address: 1-12-43 Akitu-cho, Higashi-Murayama-shi, 189-0001 Tokyo, Japan.

**SHIMODAIRA Hisashi,** b. 5 May 1941, Kamiinagun, Nagano, Japan. Information Scientist; Educator. m. Mitsuko Shimodaira, 1 son. Education: Bachelor of Engineering, 1969, Master of Engineering, 1971, Doctor of Engineering, 1982, Tokyo Metropolitan University. Appointments: Senior Manager, Nippon Telegraph and Telephone Corporation, 1986-92; Senior Research Engineer, Nihon MECCS Co Ltd, Thuoo-ku, Tokyo, Japan, 1992-96; Professor, Faculty of Information, Bunkyo University, Chigasaki, Kanagawa, Japan, 1996-. Publications: More than 50 refereed research papers on information technology including, computer vision, artificial and computational intelligence and evolutionary computation in international journals and conferences, include: Time series prediction (book chapter), 2001; Model-based process fault diagnosis (book chapter), 2001; A Method of Selecting Similar Learning Data Based on Correlation Coefficients in the Prediction of Time Series Using Neural Networks, 1996; An empirical performance comparison of niching methods for genetic algorithms (journal article), 2002; A Shape-from-Shading Method of Polyhedral Objects Using Prior Information, forthcoming. Honours: Universal Award of Accomplishment, 2005; Listed in Who's Who publications and biographical dictionaries. Memberships: IEEE; IEICE; IPSJ; JSAI; Member of Programme Committee for genetic and Evolutionary Computing Conference, 200-2002. Address: 2-2-16 Katsuradai, Aoba-ku, Yokohama-City, Kanagawa 227-0034, Japan. E-mail: shimo-hi@hi-ho.ne.jp Website: www.hi-ho.ne.jp/shimo-hi/hmpg.htm

**SHIN Dong Hoon,** b. 1 January 1966, Kimhae, Korea. Professor. m. Eunju Lee, 1 daughter. Education: MD, 1994, PhD, 1999, Seoul National University, Seoul, Korea; Certification for Specialist of Geriatrics, 2003. Appointments: Assistant Professor, Dankook University College of Medicine, Chonan, Korea, 1999-2001; Assistant Professor, Seoul National University, Seoul, Korea, 2001-. Publications: Articles in scientific journals: FAS ligand in RNA expression in the mouse central nervous system; Radiological analysis on a mummy from a medieval tomb in Korea; Histological analysis on the medieval mummy in Korea. Honour: Listed in Who's Who publications and biographical dictionaries. Memberships: American Society for Cell Biology; Korean Society for Anatomists. Address: Department of Anatomy, Seoul National University College of Medicine, 28 Yongon-Dong, Chongno-Gu, Seoul 110-799, Korea. E-mail: drdoogi@snu.ac.kr

**SHIN Dong-Keun,** b. 13 June 1959, Incheon, South Korea. Independent Researcher in Computer Science. m. Helen Chang, 2 sons. Education: UC Berkeley, USA; George Washington University, USA. Publications: A Comparative Study of Hash Functions for a New Hash-Based Relational Join Algorithm, 1991; A Sorting Method by Dong-Keun Shin, 1998; Writing letters to the world's academic communities, Dr Dong-Keun Shin has challenged to be the greatest computer scientist in the

world since 1997. Address: Hwa Shin Building, Suite 701, 705-22 Yuksam-dong, Kangnam-gu, Seoul 135-080, Korea.

**SHIN Geh-Ryeun,** b. 13 August 1954, Hampyeong, South Jeolla Province, Korea. Member of National Assembly. 2 sons. Education: College of Law, Korea University, 1974-85; Graduate School of Journalism and Mass Communication, Korea University, 1998. Appointments: President of Student Council, Korea University; Vice-Mayor for Political Affairs, Seoul Metropolitan City, 1998; Advisor to President Elect, Roh Moo-Hyun for Personnel Affairs, 2003; Chief Secretary to President Elect, Roh Moo-Hyun, 2003; Member of the 17th National Assembly (Lawmaker, 14th, 16th and 17th National Assemblies). Publication: Translator, Russian Revolution by E H Carr, 1983. Honour: Yellow Stripes Order of Service Merit. Memberships: Advisor of Korean Speech and Debate Association; President, Korea Professional Fishing Association; Honorary President, Shinssine Movie Club; Advisor of the Medical Association for the Public. Address: 102-1102 SK Apt, 104-1 Jongam 2-Dong, Seongbuk-Ku, Seoul, Korea. Website: www.sgr21.or.kr

**SHIN Jae Cheol,** b. 17 December 1975, Seoul, Korea. Researcher. Education: BS, Physics, 1994-2001, MS, Physics, 2001-2003, Kyung Hee University, Korea; PhD, Electrical Engineering, University of Wisconsin, Madison, USA, 2005-. Appointments: Drill Instructor, Army Recruiting Training Centre, Republic of Korea Army, 1996-98; Research Assistant, Kyung Hee University, Korea, 2001-2003; Commissioned Researcher, Nano Device Research Centre KIST, Seoul, Korea, 2003-2005. Publication: Spectral Response Change in Quantum Well Infrared Photodetector by Using Quantum Well Intermixing (journal article), 2003. Honour: Prize awarded by a Division Commander of the Republic Korea Army. Address: 17-7 Gahyun-dong, Kyungki-do, Anseong 456-020, Korea. E-mail: cheory75@hanmail.net

**SHIN Sang-Chul,** b. 12 July 1947, Gwangju City, Korea. Professor. m. 1 son, 2 daughters. Education: BS, College of Pharmacy, 1965-69, MS, Department of Pharmaceutics, 1971-73, PhD, 1974-79, Seoul National University. Appointments: Senior Researcher, Dean, Central Research Laboratory, Ilyang Pharmaceutical Company Ltd, 1979-85; Professor, College of Pharmacy, Chonnam National University, 1985-; Visiting Professor, College of Pharmacy, Wisconsin University, USA, 1993-94; Dean, College Pharmacy, Chonnam National University, 2000-2002; President, The Korean Society of Pharmaceutical Sciences and Technology, 2004-2005. Publications include: High-Performance Liquid Chromatic Determination of Trimebutine and its Metabolite, N-Monodesmethyl Trimebutine, in Rat and Human Plasma, 1999; Percutaneous Absorption of Piroxicam From Poloxamer 407 Gels in Rats, 1999; Release of Adriamycin From Poly(r-benzyl-L-glutamate)/poly(ethylene oxide) Nanoparticles, 1999; Mucoadhesive and Physicochemical Characterization of Carbopol-Poloxamer Gels Containing Triamcinolone Acetonide, 1999. Honours: Academic Awards, Korean Society of Pharmaceutics, 1995; Excellent Science Thesis Award, Korean Federation of Science and Technology, 1997. Memberships: Korean Society of Pharmaceutics; Pharmaceutical Society of Korea; American Association of Pharmaceutical Scientists. Address: College of Pharmacy, Chonnam National University, 300 Yongbongdong, Buggu, Gwangju 500-757, Korea.

**SHINAWATRA Thaksin,** b. 26 July 1949, Chiangmai Province, Thailand. Prime Minister of Thailand. m. Khunying Potjaman Shinawatra, 1 son, 2 daughters. Education: Graduate, Police Academy, Thailand, 1973; Master Degree in Criminal

Justice, Eastern Kentucky University, USA, 1975; Doctorate Degree in Criminal Justice, Sam Houston State University, USA, 1978. Appointments: Royal Thai Police Department, 1973-87; Founder, Shinawatra Computer and Communications Group, 1987-94; Founder, THAICOM Foundation, long distance satellite education programme, 1993; Established Thai Rak Thai Party and Leader of Thai Rak Tai Party, 1998-; 23rd Prime Minister of Thailand, 2001-. Honours: Royal Decorations: Knight Grand Cordon (Special Class) of the Most Noble Order of the Crown of Thailand, 1995; Knight Grand Cordon (Special Class), Most Exalted Order of the White Elephant, 1996; Knight Grand Cross (First Class), Most Admirable Order of the Direkgunabhorn, 2001; Knight Grand Commander, Most Illustrious Order of Chula Chom Klao, 2002; Foreign Decorations: The Royal Order of Sahametrei (Grand Cross), Kingdom of Cambodia, 2001; Ahmed Al Fateh, Kingdom of Bahrain, 2002; The Most Blessed Order of Setia Negara Brunei (First Class), Brunei Darussalam, 2002; Commander Grand Cross of the Royal Order of the Polar Star of the Kingdom of Sweden, 2003; Numerous other awards include: Honorary Doctorate, Thammasat University, 1994; Sam Houston Humanitarian Award, Sam Houston State University, USA, 2002; Honorary Doctorate, Tokyo Institute of Technology, Japan, 2003. Memberships: President, Northerners Association of Thailand, 1998-. Address: Office of the Prime Minister, Government House, Thanon Nakhon Pathem, Bangkok 10300, Thailand.

**SHINTANI Yasushi,** b. 18 May 1958, Yokohama, Japan. Molecular and Cellular Biologist. m. Kiyoko Mizuno, 1 son, 1 daughter. Education: BSc, 1982, MSc, 1984, PhD, 1993, Kyoto University, Japan. Appointments: Takeda Chemical Industries Ltd, Japan, 1984-89, 1992-93; Assistant Research Head, 1994-96, Research Head, 1997-2003; Associate Researcher, Harvard Medical School, Boston, USA, 1990-91; Research Head, Takeda, Pharmaceutical Company Limited, 2004-. Publications: Scientific papers concerning serum-free cell culture, anti-cancer drugs, G-protein-coupled receptors and novel cytokines published in scientific journals including: Nature, JBC, BBRC, and others. Honours: Listed in Who's Who publications and biographical dictionaries. Memberships: Japanese Association for Animal Cell Technology; Japanese Biochemical Society; American Society for Biochemistry and Molecular Biology. Address: 291-501, Nishi-Midorigaoka, Toyonaka, 560-0005 Japan. E-mail: shintani-yasushi@takeda.co.jp

**SHIPLEY Jenny,** b. 1952, New Zealand. Politician. m. Burton, 1 son, 1 daughter. Appointments: Former School Teacher; Farmer, 1973-88; Joined National Party, 1975; Former Malvern County Councillor; MP for Ashburton (now Rakaia), 1987-; Minister of Social Welfare, 1990-93, Womens Affairs, 1990-98, Health, 1993-96, State Services, 1996-97, State Owned Enterprises, Transport, Accident Rehabilitation and Compensation Insurance; Minister Responsible for Radio New Zealand; Minister in Charge of New Zealand Security Intelligence Services, 1997-; Prime Minister of New Zealand, 1997-99; Leader of the Opposition, 2000-2001. Address: Parliament Buildings, Wellington, New Zealand. E-mail: hq@national.org.nz

**SHIRLEY, Dame (Vera) Stephanie, (Steve),** b. 16 September 1933, Dortmund, Germany. Company President. m. Derek George Millington Shirley, 1 son, deceased. Education: BSc (Spec.), Sir John Cass College, London, 1956; FBCS, 1971; CEng, 1990; CITP, CIMgt. Appointments: PO Research Station, Dollis Hill, 1951-59; CDL, Subsidiary of ICL, 1959-62; Founder and Chief Executive, 1962-87, Director, 1962-93, Life President, 1993-, Xansa Plc; Director, Tandem Computers Inc,

1992-97; Director, AEA Technology Plc, 1992-2000; Director, John Lewis Partnership, 1999-2001; European Advisory Board, Korn/Ferry International, 2001-2004. Publication: The Art of Prior's Court School, 2002. Honours: DBE, 2000; OBE, 1980; CCMI (CBIM, 1984); FREng, 2001; Honorary FCGI, 1989; Honorary Fellow: Manchester Metropolitan University, 1989, Staffordshire University, 1991, Sheffield Hallam University, 1992, IMBC, 1999, Birkbeck, 2002, New Hall, Cambridge, 2002; Foundation Fellow, Balliol College, Oxford, 2001; Honorary DSc: Buckingham, 1991, Aston, 1993, Nottingham Trent, 1994, Southampton Institute, 1994, Southampton, 2003, Brunel, 2005; Honorary DTech: Loughborough, 19991, Kingston, 1995; DUniv: Leeds Metropolitan, 1993, Derby, 1997, London Guildhall, 1998, Stirling, 2000; Honorary DLitt, de Montfort, 1993; Honorary DBA: West of England, 1995, City, 2000; Honorary Dr, Edinburgh, 2003; Recognition of Information Technology Achievement Award, 1985; Gold Medal Institute of Management, 1991; Mountbatten Medal, IEE, 1999; Beacon Award for Start-ups, 2003; British Computer Society Lifetime Achievement Award, 2004; US National Woman's Hall of Fame, 1995. Memberships include: Council, Industrial Society, 1984-90; NCVQ, 1986-89; President, British Computer Society, 1989-90; Vice-President, C&G, 2000-05; Member, Council, Duke of Edinburgh's Seventh Commonwealth Study Conference, 1991-92; British-North American Committee, 1992-2001; Chairman, Women of Influence, 1993; Trustee, Help the Aged, 1987-90; Patron: Disablement Income Group, 1989-2001; Centre for Tomorrow's Co, 1997-; Member, Oxford University Court of Benefactors; Founder: The Kingwood Trust, 1993, The Shirley Foundation, 1996, Prior's Court Foundation, 1998, Autism Cymru, 2001; Trustee, National Alliance for Autism Research, 2004; Chair, National Alliance for Autism Research (UK), 2004; Master, Information Technologists Company, 1992, Liveryman, 1992; Freeman, City of London, 1987. Address: 47 Thames House, Phyllis Court Drive, Henley on Thames, Oxfordshire RG9 2NA, England. E-mail: steve@steveshirley.com

**SHISHKINA Olga Dmitrievna,** b. 23 August 1963, Nizhny Novgorod, Russia. Hydrophysicist. m. George Kondratiyev. Education: Master of Science, Mechanical Engineering, Gorky Polytechnical Institute, 1986; PhD, Technical Science, St Petersburg State Marine Technical University 1995. Appointments: Engineer Probationer ( design of the stratified tank and laboratory equipment; study of the effect of internal waves on the drag force of a submerged body), 1986-88, Research Associate, 1988-95, Research Scientist, 1995-2000, Senior Research Scientist, 2000-, Institute of Applied Physics, Russian Academy of Sciences, Nizhny Novgorod, Russia. Publications: Articles in scientific journals include: Resonant generation of solitary wave in thermocline, 1995; Internal waves and their influence on the drag of submerged bodies (PhD Thesis), 1995; Comparison of the drag coefficients...., 1996; Editor and Translator: Dynamics of Internal Gravity Waves in the Ocean by Yu Miropolsky, 2001. Honours: Diploma of Academician A N Krylov Scientific-Technical Society, 1989; Individual Grant, Soros Foundation, 1995. Address: Institute of Applied Physics, Russian Academy of Sciences, GSP-120, 46 Ul'janov Str, 603950 Nizhny Novgorod, Russia. E-mail: ol.sh@hydro.appl.sci-nnov.ru

**SHITTU Gaffar Mola,** b. 24 June 1948, Kano, Nigeria. Consultant Paediatrician. m. Gabriella Hulicsko, 3 sons. Education: MD, Medical University of Debrecen, Hungary, 1970-76; Paediatric Institute, 1980-82; Member Hungarian College of Physicians. Appointments: Medical Officer, National Stadium, Surulere, Lagos, 1976-77; FIFA Registers Sports Medicine Doctor, 1977; Health Services Management Board,

Kano, 1977-80; Medical Officer Grade I, Asmau Memorial Hospital, Kano, 1982-84; Consultant Paediatrician. Honours: National Treasurer, then Social Secretary, Guild of Medical Directors; President, Rotary Club of Bompai, Kano, Nigeria; Chairman, Kano Chapter, GM Directors and Nigerian Medical Association. Memberships: Hungarian College of Paediatricians; Nigerian Paediatric Association; Guild of Medical Directors. Address: Classic Clinics Ltd, 1A Abbas Road, Arakan Avenue, PO Box 244, Kano, Nigeria. E-mail: piu1948@yahoo.co

**SHKOLNIKOVA Nelli,** b. 8 July 1928, Zolotonosha, Ukraine. Violinist. Education: Music studies, BMus, MMus, Moscow Conservatory, 1949-57; Honours degree in Violin. Career: Concert tours in USSR, Austria, Australia, Bulgaria, Czechoslovakia, France, Finland, Hungary, East Germany, Canada, USA, Norway, New Zealand, Japan, 1953-; Appeared with conductors such as Kondrashin, Rozhdestvensky, Munch, Cluytens, Sanderling, Masur, Ormandy; Currently Professor of Violin at Indiana University School of Music, USA. Recordings: Tchaikovsky - Concerto in D op 35; Mozart - Concerto No 4 in D K218; Mendelssohn - Concerto in E Minor; Beethoven - Sonata No 2 in A major op 12 No 2, Sonata No 8 in G major op 30 No 3; Copland - Sonata in G major; Handel - Sonata No 1 in A major, Sonata No 3; Pieces by Paganini, Prokofiev and others. Contributions to: Reviews in Le Figaro, New York Post, Berliner Morgenpost, Arbeiderbladet, Pravda, others. Honours: Grand Prix at Marguerite Long-Jacques Thibaud Competition, Paris, France, 1953; Honoured Artist of Russian Republic, 1978. Membership: American String Teachers' Association. Address: 2814 St Remy Circle, Bloomington, IN 47401, USA.

**SHLYGIN Victor Victorovich,** b. 30 June 1950, Smolensk, Russia. Biophysicist. m. Timoshina Valentina, 1 son, 1 daughter. Education: Graduate, Department of Automotive and Apparatus Building, Kharkov Polytechnic Institute, 1973; Doctor of Physico-Mathematics, Moscow State University, 1992. Appointments: Scientific Collaborator, Institute of Biophysics, Academy of Science, USSR, 1973-86; Scientific Collaborator, All Union Institute of Biotechnology, Moscow, 1986-88; Scientific Collaborator, Intersectional Research and Technology Complex, "Eye Microsurgery", 1988-2002; Director, Private Liceum, Moscow, 1993-94; Institute of Informatic Problems, Russian Academy of Science, 1999-2005. Publications: 20 patents; 65 articles include: Possible Change in the Blood Vessel on Electromagnetic Exposure; Identifiability of an Enzyme Network, 1990; Effect of Magnetic Field on the Excitation Transmission along Nerve Fibers Innervating a Blood Vessel, 2001. Honour: Award for Biophysics, 1975. Membership: New York Academy of Sciences. Address: Taininskaja 26, A 79, 129345 Moscow, Russia.

**SHNITKA Theodor Khyam,** b. 21 November 1927, Calgary, Alberta, Canada. Physician; Pathologist. m. Toby Garfin. Education: BSc. 1948, MSc, 1952, MD, 1953, University of Alberta, Edmonton; Resident in Pathology, University of Alberta Hospital, Edmonton, 1954-58; Speciality Certification, Royal College of Physicians and Surgeons of Canada, 1958; Postdoctoral Fellow in Surgery, Histochemistry, Johns Hopkins University School of Medicine, USA, 1959-60; Fellow, Royal College of Physicians and Surgeons of Canada, 1972. Appointments: Lecturer, 1958-59, Assistant Professor, 1959-62, Associate Professor, 1962-67, Professor, 1967-87, Chairman, Department of Pathology, 1980-87, Professor Emeritus of Pathology, 1987-, Faculty of Medicine, University of Alberta, Edmonton, Canada. Publications: Enzymatic histochemistry of gastrointestinal mucous membrane, 1960; Co-author, Macroscopic identification of early myocardial infarcts, by alterations in dehydrogenase activity, 1963; Co-

editor, Gastric Secretion - Mechanisms and Control, 1967; Author, co-author, 45 scientific articles and 7 book chapters, on diagnostic pathology and electron microscopy, cell biology and pathobiology of lysosomes and peroxisomes, and neurobiology. Honours: Annual Outstanding Achievement Award, Medical Alumni Association, University of Alberta, Edmonton, 1983; Honorary Affiliate Membership, Canadian Society of Laboratory Technologists, 1988; Outstanding Physician Award, Edmonton Academy of Medicine, 1988. Memberships: Life Member: New York Academy of Sciences; Alberta and Canadian Medical Associations; Emeritus Member: Microscopy Society of America; Histochemical Society Inc; Canadian Association of Pathologists; American Society for Cell Biology; Active, Microscopical Society of Canada, Alpha Omega Alpha, Honour Medical Society. Address: 12010 87th Avenue NW, Edmonton, Alberta, T6G 0Y7, Canada.

**SHORT Clare (Rt Hon),** b. 15 February 1946, Birmingham, England. Politician. m. (1) 1964, divorced 1974, (2) A Lyon, 1981, deceased 1993, 1 son. Education: BA Honours, Political Science, Universities of Leeds and Keele. Appointments: Civil Service, Home Office, 1970-75; Director, All Faith for One Race, 1976-78; Youthaid, 1979-83; Labour MP, Birmingham Ladywood, 1983-; Shadow Employment Spokesperson, 1985-89, Social Security Spokesperson, 1989-91, Environmental Protection Spokesperson, 1992-93, Spokesperson for Women, 1993-95; Shadow Secretary of State for Transport, 1995-96, for Overseas Development, 1996-97; Secretary of State for International Development, 1997-2003; Select Committee Home Affairs, 1983-85; Chair, All Party Group on Race Relations, 1985-86; NEC, 1988-98; Vice-President, Socialist International Women, 1992-96; Chair, Women's Committee National Executive Committee, 1993-97; Chair, NEC International Committee, 1996-98; Party Representative, Social International Congress, 1996. Membership: UNISON. Address: House of Commons, London SW1A 0AA, England.

**SHORT Nigel,** b. 1 June 1965, Leigh, Lancashire, England. Chess Player. m. Rea Karageorgiou, 1987, 1 daughter. Appointments: At age of 12 beat Jonathan Penrose in British Championships; International Master, 1980; Grand Master, 1984; British Champion, 1984, 1987; English Champion, 1991; President, Grand Masters Association, 1992; Defeated Anatoly Karpov, 1992; Defeated by Kasparov, 1993; Ranked 7th Player in World; Chess Columnist, The Daily Telegraph, 1991; Stripped of International Ratings by World Chess Foundation, 1993, reinstated, 1994; Resigned from FIDE and formed Professional Chess Association with Gary Kasparov, 1993, left PCA, 1995; Ranked 17th in the world by FIDE, January 2003. Publications: Learn Chess with Nigel Short, 1993. Honours: Honorary Fellow, Bolton Institute, 1993-; Honorary MBE, 1999. Address: c/o The Daily Telegraph, 1 Canada Square, London, E14 5DT, England. E-mail: ndshort@hotmail.com

**SHORTER John,** b. 14 June 1926, Redhill, Surrey, England. Chemist. m. Mary Patricia Steer, 28 July 1951, 2 sons, 1 daughter. Education: BA, 1947, BSc, 1948, DPhil, 1950, Exeter College, Oxford. Appointments: Assistant Lecturer, 1950-52, Lecturer in Chemistry, 1952-54, University College, Hull; Lecturer in Chemistry, 1954-63, Senior Lecturer, 1963-72, Reader, Physical Organic Chemistry, 1972-82, Emeritus Reader in Chemistry, 1982-, University of Hull; RT French Visiting Professor, University of Rochester, New York, USA, 1966-67. Publications include: Correlation Analysis in Organic Chemistry, 1973; Correlation Analysis of Organic Reactivity, 1982; Co-editor: Advances in Linear Free Energy Relationships, 1972; Correlation Analysis in Chemistry, 1978; Similarity Models in Organic Chemistry, Biochemistry and

Related Fields, 1991. Honour: 75th Anniversary Medal, Polish Chemical Society, 2001. Memberships: Fellow, Royal Society of Chemistry; Secretary, International Group for Correlation Analysis in Chemistry (formerly organic chemistry), 1982-2004; International Union of Pure and Applied Chemistry. Address: 29A Meadowfields, Whitby, North Yorkshire YO21 1QF, England.

**SHRIMPTON Michael,** b. 9 March 1957, Ely, Cambridgeshire, England. Barrister; Part-time Immigration Judge. Education: LLB (Hons), Wales, 1981; Inns of Court School of Law, 1982-83; Called to the Bar by Gray's Inn, 1983. Appointments: Barrister specialising in national security law; Assisted General Pinochet following his arrest in the UK; Part-time Chairman, Immigration Appeal Tribunal, 1992; Part-time Immigration Adjudicator, 1995; Part-time Immigration Judge, 2005; Speaker, Intelligence Conference (INTELCON), Washington DC, 2005. Publications: Law of War, Journal of International Security, 2002; Various articles in The Times and legal journals. Honours: General Election Candidate, 1987; European Parliament Candidate, 1989. Memberships: Midland Circuit; Administrative Law Bar Association; American Trial Lawyers Association; Military Commentators Circle; Defence and Security Forum; United States Naval Institute; International Institute for Strategic Studies; RUSI; RIIA (Chatham House); European Atlantic Group. Address: 7 Willow Herb, Watermead, Buckinghamshire HP19 0FH, England. E-mail: michael@mshrimpton.co.uk

**SHU Peter H C,** b. 2 June 1948, Nanjing, China. New Business Development Manager. m. Chun Wan Liu Shu, 1 daughter. Education: BS, National Taiwan University, 1970; MS, The Ohio State University, USA, 1974; PhD, Rensselaer Polytechnic Institute, 1978; Post Doctoral Research Fellow, University of Massachusetts at Amherst, Massachusetts, 1978-79; MBA, State University of New York at Albany, 1982. Appointments: Project Leader, General Electric Corporation, Selkirk, New York, 1979-85; Materials Specialist, Bayer Corporation, Pittsburgh, Pennsylvania, 1985-90; Deputy Technical General Manager, Bayer Taiwan Co Ltd, 1990-99; Regional Technical Manager, Asia Pacific Region, Bayer Polymers Co Ltd, Hong Kong, 1999-2001; Manager, New Business Development, NAFTA, Bayer Material Science LLC, Pittsburgh, USA, 2001-. Publications: 14 papers; 1 book chapter; 25 patents; 50 talks. Honours: Taiwan Ministry of Education, Merit Scholarship, 1966-70; Chinese Army Academy, Teaching Officer of the Year, 1971; General Electric Management Award, 1983. Memberships: ACS; SPE; SAE; Chairman, Chinese School Board, Pittsburgh, 1984; Board Member, Overseas Chinese Association, 1984. Address: 206 Doubletree Drive, Venetia, PA 15367, USA. E-mail: peter.shu @bayermaterialscience.com

**SHUBIK Martin,** b. 24 March 1926, Manhattan, New York, USA. Economics Educator. m. Julia Kahn, 1 daughter. Education: BA, 1947, MA, 1949, University of Toronto, Canada; AM, Political Economy, 1951, PhD, 1953, Princeton University, New Jersey, USA. Appointments: Part-time Demonstrator, Physics, University of Toronto, 1948-49; Part-time Research Assistant, 1950-51, Research Assistant, 1951-53, Research Associate, 1953-55, Economics Research Project, Princeton University; Fellow, Center for Advanced Study in Behavioural Sciences, Palo Alto, California, 1955-56; Consultant, Management Consultation Services, General Electric Company, 1956-60; Adjunct Research Professor, Pennsylvania State University, 1957-59; Visiting Professor of Economics, Yale University, 1960-61; Staff, T J Watson Research Laboratories, IBM, 1961-63; Professor of Economics of Organization, Yale University, 1963-75; Visiting Professor, Escuela de Estudios Economicos, University of Chile, 1965;

Institute for Advanced Studies, Vienna, Austria, 1970; Consultant, RAND Corporation, California, 1970-71; Visiting Professor, Department of Economics, University of Melbourne, Australia, 1973; Director, Cowles Foundation for Research in Economics, 1973-76, Seymour H Knox Professor of Mathematical Institutional Economics, 1975-, Yale University. Publications: Books include: Readings in Game Theory and Political Behaviour, 1954; Strategy and Market Structure, 1959; Editor, Essays in Mathematical Economics in Honour of Oskar Morgenstern, 1967; Uses and Methods of Gaming, 1975; The War Game, co-author, 1979; The Mathematics of Conflict, 1983; The Theory of Money and Financial Institutions, Volumes I and II, 1999; Numerous articles in professional journals. Honours: Lanchester Prize, 1984; Koopman Prize, Military Application Section, INFORMS, 1995; International Insurance Society Shin Research Excellence Award, 1999; Numerous scholarships. Memberships include: Fellow, Center for Advanced Study in the Behavioural Sciences, 1955; Fellow, Econometric Society, 1971; Fellow, World Academy of Arts and Sciences, 1975; Fellow, American Academy of Arts and Sciences, 1985; Fellow, Connecticut Academy of Arts and Sciences, 1993; Science Board, Santa Fe Institute, 1997-2003. Address: Cowles Foundation for Research in Economics, Yale University, PO Box 208281, New Haven, CT 06520, USA.

**SHUCKBURGH Julian John Evelyn,** b. 30 July 1940, Ottawa, Canada. Publisher. 2 sons, 3 daughters. Education: Law Tripos, Peterhouse, Cambridge, 1958-61. Appointments: Editor, Methuen & Co, 1961-65; Senior Editor, Weidenfeld & Nicolson Ltd, 1965-72; Editorial Director, W H Allen Ltd, 1972-75; Publishing Director and Managing Director, Pitkin Pictorials Ltd, Garrod & Lofthouse (Printers), 1975-78; Managing Director and Founder, Shuckburgh Reynolds Ltd, 1978-87; Publishing Director, Condé Nast Books, 1992-97; Associate Publisher, Ebury Press, 1992-2000; Managing Director, Barrie & Jenkins Ltd, 1987-2000. Publications: The Bedside Book, 1979; The Second Bedside Book, 1981; London Revealed, 2003. Memberships: The Garrick Club; The Bach Choir. Address: 22 Ellingham Road, London W12 9PR, England. E-mail: julianshu ckburgh@22ellingham.com

**SHUKMAN David Roderick,** b. 30 May 1958, London, England. Journalist. m. Jessica Pryce-Jones, 2 sons, 1 daughter. Education: Durham University, 1977-80. Appointments: Coventry Evening Telegraph, 1980-83; News Trainee, 1983-85; Reporter, BBC Northern Ireland, 1985-87; Defence Correspondent, 1987-95, European Correspondent, 1995-99, World Affairs Correspondent, 1999-, BBC News. Publications: All Necessary Means: Inside the Gulf War (with Ben Brown), 1991; The Sorcerer's Challenge, 1995 (US edition, Tomorrow's War, 1996); Various newspapers and magazines. Memberships: Royal Institute for International Affairs; International Institute for Strategic Studies. Address: World Affairs Unit, BBC TV Centre, London W12 7RJ, England. E-mail: david.shukman@bbc.co.uk

**SHUREY Richard,** b. 22 September 1951, Wales. Factory Worker. m. Christine, 6 May 1972, 2 sons, 1 daughter. Publications: Jewels of the Imagination, 1997; By the Light of the Moon, 1997; On Reflection, 1997; Never Forget, 1998; From the Hand of a Poet, 1999; Open Minds, 1999. Contributions to: South Wales Echo; Celtic Press; Rhondda Leader. Honours: Editor's Choice Award for Outstanding Achievement in Poetry, International Library of Poetry, 1997. Memberships: Poetry Guild. Address: 107 Tylacelyn Road, Penygraig, Tonypandy, Rhondda-Cynon-Taff CF40 1JR, South Wales.

**SICHIK Vasily,** b. 14 June 1937, Bereza, Belarus. Professor. 2 sons. Education: Higher Education. Appointments:

Professor of the Belarussian National Technical University; Vice-President, International Academy on Information Technologies. Publications: An experimental substantiation of magnetodynamics forces, 1989; Measuring converters of ionizing radiation on the basis at semiconductor instrument structures, 1991; Computer simulation of dialectic spectrum of GaASm 1998; Electronic phonedoscope, 2000; Effective control of electrostatic fields, 2002; Contactless control of constant voltage over high voltage circuits, 2002; Electric models of active components of sensing measuring device, 2003; Principles of contruction of simulator on instrument structures of measuring converters, 2004; 20 patents. Honour: Honours of the International Academy of Information Technologies. Memberships: Academician, International Academy of Information Technologies; Academician of the Belarussian Engineering Academy. Address: 49-18 Pr Rokossovskogo, Minsk 220094, Republic of Belarus.

**SIDIBE El Hassane**, b. 12 May 1951, Thilene, Dagana, Saint Louis, Senegal. Doctor of Medicine; Teacher; Researcher. m. Amsatou Sow, 2 sons, 2 daughters. Education: Threefold Excellence Prize and Sevenfold registered in Honor Table, Bachelor of Science, Lycee Charles de Gaulle, St Louis, 1970; Medical Doctor, Dakar University, 1984; Internship, Dakar, 1977; Medical Assistant, Paris, 1984; Resident, Paris, 1986; Registered candidate in Academie Nationale de Medicine, 2000. Appointments: Assistant, Endocrinology Faculty of Medicine, Dakar, 1986-98; Certificate in Internal Medicine and Endocrinology, Metabolism and Nutrition, 1994; Aggregate Professor in Endocrinology, Metabolism, Nutrition, 1998; Master of Medical Sciences, 2000, Proposed Emeritus Professor, 2005, Paris VII University. Publications: African Diabetic microangiopathy, 1979; Primary hypothyroidism in Senegal, 1984; Major diabetes mellitus complications in Africa, 2000; Sheehan disease African experience, 2000; Pheochromocytoma in Africa, 2001. Honours: LS Senghor Foundation Grant, 1984; Medal, Societe Medicale des Hopitaux de Paris 150th Birthday, 1999; Chevalier des Palmes Academiques Françaises, 2001. Memberships: New York Academy of Sciences, 1995; SMHP; SNFMI; ALFEDIAM; SFE; Endocrine Society; Panafrican Diabetes Study Group; MDSG; SPE; ADA; ARCOL; Société Québecoise de l'HTA; SNFBMN; Member, European Academy of Sciences; Art and Humanities Candidate in Academie des Sciences and Academie Française, Paris. Address: Villa 2A, Rue 1xC Point E, BP 5062, Fann, Dakar, Senegal.

**SIEFKEN Hinrich Gerhard**, b. 21 April 1939, Cologne, Germany. University Teacher. m. Marcia Corinne Birch, 1 son, 1 daughter. Education: German and English, University of Tübingen (Vienna and Newcastle); Dr Phil, magna cum laude, 1964; Staatsexamen, 1964. Appointments: Tutor, University of Tübingen, 1962-65; Lektor, University College of North Wales, Bangor, 1965-66; Wissenschaftlicher Assistent, University of Tübingen, 1966-67; Lecturer, Senior Lecturer, German, Saint David's University College, Lampeter, 1969-79; Professor of German, Head of Department, 1979-97, Head of School of Modern Languages, 1986-88, Dean of Faculty of Arts, 1988-89, Director, Institute of German, Austrian and Swiss Affairs, 1991-93, University of Nottingham. Publications: Books include: Kafka. Ungeduld und Lässigkeit, 1997; Thomas Mann – Goethe "Ideal der Deutschheit", 1981; Die Weisse Rose und ihre Flugblätter (editor), 1994; Theodor Haecker, Leben und Werk (co-editor), 1995; Experiencing Tradition: Essays of Discovery. For Keith Spalding, with A Bushell, 2003; Numerous articles in academic journals. Honours: D Litt, University of Nottingham, 1990; Ehrengabe zum Theodor Haecker-Preis der Stadt Esslingen, 1995; Emeritus Professor, University of Nottingham, 1997; Professor of Modern Languages, University of Wales Bangor. Address: 6 Mountsorrel Drive, West Bridgford, Nottingham NG2 6LJ, England. E-mail: hinrichsiefken@hotmail.com

**SIEGEL Robert (Harold)**, b. 18 August 1939, Oak Park, Illinois, USA. Professor of English. m. Roberta Ann Hill, 19 August 1961, 3 daughters. Education: BA, Wheaton College, 1961; MA, Johns Hopkins University, 1962; PhD, Harvard University, 1968. Appointments: Assistant Professor, Dartmouth College, 1968-75; Visiting Lecturer in Creative Writing, Princeton University, 1975-76; Poet-in-Residence, McManes Visiting Professor, Wheaton College, 1976; Visiting Professor, J W v Goethe Universitat, Frankfurt, 1985; Coordinator, Graduate Program in Creative Writing, University of Wisconsin-Milwaukee, 1977-80 and 1992-94; Professor of English, University of Wisconsin-Milwaukee, 1983-. Publications: Poetry: The Beasts and The Elders, 1973; In A Pig's Eye, 1980. Fiction: Alpha Centauri, 1980; Whalesong, 1981; The Kingdom of Wundle, 1982; White Whale, 1991; The Ice At the End of the World, 1994. Contributions to: Anthologies and journals. Honours: Honorable Mention, Merit Awards, Atlantic Monthly College Poetry Contest, 1960; Margaret O'Loughlin Foley Award, 1970; The Cliff Dwellers' Arts Foundation Award, 1974; Chicago Poetry Prize, Society of Midland Authors, 1974; Prairie Schooner Poetry Prize, 1977; Jacob Glatstein Memorial Prize, 1977; Ingram Merrill Award, 1979; National Endowment for the Arts Fellowship, 1980; ECPA Gold Medalion, 1981; Book of the Year Award, Campus Life Magazine, 1981; 1st Prize for Juvenile Fiction, Council for Wisconsin Writers, 1981; 1st Prize for Poetry, Society of Midland Authors, 1981; Matson Award, 1982; Golden Archer Award, 1986; Pushcart Prize Nominations, 1990, 1995; Milton Center Poetry Prize, 1994. Memberships: Author's Guild; Association of Scholars and Critics. Address: University of Wisconsin, PO Box 413, Milwaukee, WI 53201, USA.

**SIEGEL Stuart Elliott**, b. 16 July 1943, Plainfield, New Jersey, USA. Paediatrician. m. Linda, 1 child. Education: Bachelor of Arts, Summa Cum Laude, Boston University, 1967; Doctor of Medicine, Magna Cum Laude, 1967. Appointments: Associate Haematologist, Attending Physician, Consultant, Clinic Laboratories, Children's Hospital Los Angeles, 1972-76; Assistant Professor of Paediatrics, USC School of Medicine, 1972-76; Head, Division of Haematology, Oncology, Department of Paediatrics, Children's Hospital Los Angeles, USC School of Medicine, 1976-; Co-ordinator, Paediatric Oncology, USC School of Medicine, 1976-; Associate Professor of Paediatrics, USC School of Medicine, 1976-81; Professor of Paediatrics, 1981-; Head, Division of Oncology, County, USC Medical Center, 1986-; Deputy Physician in Chief, Children's Hospital Los Angeles, 1987-91; Acting Physician in Chief, Acting Chairman, Department of Paediatrics, 1987; Associate Director, Paediatric Oncology, Kenneth Norris Jr Comprehensive Cancer Centre, 1989-; Associate Chair, Department of Paediatrics, Children's Hospital Los Angeles, 1994-96; Vice Chairman, Department of Paediatrics, USC School of Medicine, 1994-; Director, Children's Centre for Cancer and Blood Diseases, Children's Hospital, Los Angeles, 1995-. Publications: 193 reviewed journals; 4 non-reviewed journals; Paediatrics 1, Hematology and Oncology; Desk Reference of Paediatrics Oncology; 28 Chapters in Books; 3 Invited Articles; others. Honours: Boston University Collegium of Distinguished Alumni; National Alumni Council; Massachusetts Medical Society; Alpha Omega Alpha; Stuart E Siegel Endowed Chair in Paediatric Oncology, Keck School of Medicine of the University of Southern California; National Caring Award, The Caring Institute; Cited in Best Doctors in America; Many others. Memberships: Los Angeles County

Medical Association; American Association for Cancer Research; Many others. Address: Children's Hospital, Los Angeles Div, Haematology and Oncology MS#54, PO Box 54700, Los Angeles, CA 90054-0700, USA.

**SIJANOVIC Sinisa,** b. 4 September 1967, Vukovar, Croatia. Obstetrician; Gynaecologist; Assistant Professor. m. Ivanka. Education: MD, Medical School, Zagreb, 1992; Master of Biomedicine Science, University of Zagreb, 1997; Graduate, Obstetrician and Gynaecologist, Medical School, Zagreb, 1999; Doctor of Philosophy, Medical School, Zagreb, 2003. Appointments: Practice in Clinical Hospital, 1992-93; Assistant in Anatomy, Medical School, Zagreb, 1992-94; Residency Training, Gynaecology and Obstetrics, 1994-99; Fellowship, Laparoscopic and Open Gynaecological Surgical Procedures, Department of Obstetrics and Gynaecology, Friedrich-Schiller University, Jena, Germany, 2000; Fellowship, Department of Obstetrics and Gynaecology, Dartmouth Hitchcock University, New Hampshire, USA, 2000; Fellowship, Department of Obstetrics and Gynaecology, University Hospital, Ljubljana, Slovenia, 2003; Assistant Professor, Obstetrics and Gynaecology, Medical School, Osijek, Croatia, 2004. Publications: Articles in medical journals as co-author include: Bone loss in premenopausal women on long-term suppressive therapy with thyroid hormone, 2001; Laparoscopic treatment of primary ovarian pregnancy, 2002; Assessment of reliability endometrial brush cytology in detection etiology of late postmenopausal bleedings, 2004. Honour: Award, International Federation of Gynecology and Obstetrics, 2000. Memberships: ISGE; Croatian Medical Association; Croatian Medical Chamber; Croatian Society of Gynaecologic Endoscopy; Croatian Society for Gynaecology and Obstetrics; Croatian Society for Menopausis. Address: Clinical Hospital of Osijek, Obstetrics and Gynaecology Department, 3100 Osijek, Croatia. E-mail: sinisa.sijanovic@os.htnet.hr

**SIKDAR Malay Kanti,** b. 1 January 1948 Brahmachal, Bangladesh. Writer; Scientist; Scholar; Manager. m. Susmita, 1 daughter. Education: BSc (Physics with honours), Calcutta University; MSc (Physics), PhD (Physics), Kalyani University. Appointments: UGC Junior, Senior Fellow, 1973-77, CSIR Senior/PD Fellow, 1977-79; District Manager, Food Corporation of India, NPD Kolkata. Publications: Many research papers and articles including: Higher Order of Lives in the Universe; 1 novel and several short stories; More publications forthcoming. Honours: Bal Sahayog Award, 2000; Bharat Excellency Award with Gold Medal, 2001; Secular India Harmony Award, 2001; UWA Lifetime Achievement Award, 2002; Indian Growing Personalities Award with Gold Medal, 2002; Man of the Year, 2002; American Medal of Honor, 2003; ABI World Lifetime Achievement Award, 2003; International Peace Prize, 2003; Eminent Personality of India, International Biographical Research Foundation, Nagpur, India, 2003; Great Indian Achievement Award Gold Medal, 2004; FFI Lifetime Achievement Award and Gold Medal, 2004; Da Vinci Diamond Award, IBC; FFI Udyog Gaurav Award, 2005; Bharat Yogyta Award, 2005; Rashtray Jyoti Award. Memberships: Indian Association for the Cultivation of SC; Indian Science Congress, Nikhi; Bharat Banga Sahitya Sanmelan; Institute of Commercial Management, UK. Address: C/27, Navadarsha Co-operative Housing Society Ltd, Birati, Kolkata 700134, India.

**SIKI Bela,** b. 21 February 1923, Budapest, Hungary. Pianist; Professor. m. Yolande Oltramare, 1 son, 1 daughter. Education: Franz Liszt Academy, Budapest, 1945; Prix De Virtuosite Avec Distinction, Geneva, 1948. Appointments: Adjunct Professor, Geneve, 1951-53; Professor, University of Washington, Seattle, 1965-93; Professor, University of Cincinnati, 1980-

85. Publications: Piano Repertoire, 1981; Worldwide concert tours, numerous recordings. Honour: Concours International D'Execution Musicale. Address: 5424 Elleray Lane NE, Seattle, WA 98105, USA.

**SILBERSTON (Zangwill) Aubrey,** b. 26 January 1922, London, England. Economist. m. Michèle Ledic, 1 son. Education: London School of Economics; Jesus College Cambridge. Appointments: War Service, Royal Fusiliers, Iraq, Egypt, Italy, 1941-45; Economist, Courtaulds Limited, 1946-50; Research Fellow, St Catharine's College, Cambridge, 1950-53; Lecturer in Economics, University of Cambridge, 1951-71; Fellow, St John's College, Cambridge, 1958-71; Chairman, Faculty Board of Economics and Politics, University of Cambridge, 1966-70; Official Fellow in Economics, 1971-78, Dean, 1972-78, Nuffield College, Oxford; Professor of Economics, Imperial College London, 1978-87; Professor Emeritus of Economics, University of London, Senior Research Fellow, Tanaka Business School, Imperial College, 1987-. Publications: Education and training for industrial management, 1955; The motor industry (jointly), 1959; The patent system (jointly), 1967; The economic impact of the patent system (jointly), 1973; The future of the multi-fibre arrangement (with Michèle Ledic), 1989; Environmental economics,(editor), 1995; The changing industrial map of Europe (jointly), 1996; Articles in academic journals. Honours: Rockefeller Fellow, University of California, Berkeley, 1959-60; CBE, 1987. Memberships: Monopolies Commission, 1965-68; Non-Executive Board Member, British Steel Corporation, 1967-76; Departmental Committee on the Patent System (Banks Committee), 1967-70; Royal Commission on the Press, 1974-77; Secretary-General, Royal Economic Society, 1979-92; Royal Commission on Environmental Pollution, 1986-96; Lay-Judge, Restrictive Practices Court, 1986-92; President, Confederation of European Economic Associations, 1987-89; Vice-President, Royal Economic Society, 1992-; Council of Experts, Intellectual Property Institute, London, 1996-. Address: Tanaka Business School, Imperial College, London SW7 2AZ, England.

**SILLITOE Alan,** b. 4 March 1928, Nottingham, England. Writer; Poet; Dramatist. m. Ruth Fainlight, 19 November 1959, 1 son, 1 daughter (adopted). Education: Principally self-taught. Appointments: Writer, 1948-. Publications: Without Beer or Bread (poems), 1957; Saturday Night and Sunday Morning (novel), 1958; The General (novel), 1960; The Rats and Other Poems, 1960; Key to the Door (novel), 1961; Road to Volgograd (travel), 1964; A Falling Out of Love and Other Poems, 1964; The Death of William Posters (novel), 1965; A Tree on Fire (novel), 1967; A Start in Life (novel), 1967; Shaman and Other Poems, 1968; Love in the Environs of Voronezh and Other Poems, 1968; Travel in Nihilon (novel), 1971; Raw Material (memoir), 1972; The Flame of Life (novel), 1974; Storm and Other Poems, 1974; Barbarians and Other Poems, 1974; Mountains and Caverns: Selected Essays, 1975; The Widower's Son (novel), 1976; The Storyteller (novel), 1979; Snow on the North Side of Lucifer (poems), 1979; Her Victory (novel), 1982; The Lost Flying Boat (novel), 1983; Down from the Hill (novel), 1984; Sun Before Departure (poems), 1984; Life Goes On (novel), 1985; Tides and Stone Walls (poems), 1986; Out of the Whirlpool (novel), 1987; The Open Door (novel), 1989; Lost Loves (novel), 1990; Leonard's War, 1991; Snowstop, 1993; Collected Poems, 1994; Collected Stories, 1995; Leading the Blind (travel), 1995; Life Without Armour (autobiography), 1995; Alligator Playground (stories), 1997; Collected Stories, 1997; The Broken Chariot (novel) 1998; The German Numbers Woman (novel), 1999; Birthday, novel, 2001; Flight of Arrows, essays, 2003; A Man of His Time, novel, 2004. Other: Short stories; Plays. Honours: Author's Club Prize, 1958; Hawthornden Prize, 1960; Honorary Fellow, Manchester

Polytechnic, 1977; Honorary Degrees, Nottingham Polytechnic, 1990, Nottingham University, 1994; Visiting Professor, Honorary Doctorate, 1998, De Montfort University, Leicester. Memberships: Royal Geographical Society, fellow; Society of Authors; Writers Action Group. Address: 14 Ladbroke Terrace, London W11 3PG, England.

**SILVA Christopher P,** 17 March 1960, Fortuna, California, USA. Electrical Engineer. Education: BSc, Electrical Engineering, 1982, MSc, Electrical Engineering, 1985, PhD, Engineering, 1993, University of California at Berkeley. Appointments: Member of Technical Staff, 1989, Senior Member of the Technical Staff, 1995, Engineering Specialist, 1999, Senior Engineering Specialist, 2003-, The Aerospace Corporation, El Segundo, California. Publications: Technical conference and professional journal papers, book contributions, and technical presentations in various professional, academic and industrial venues. Honours: BSEE with highest honours distinction, UC Alumni Scholar, National Science Foundation Fellowship; Lockheed Leadership Fellowship; Fellowship, Institute for Electrical and Electronic Engineers; Senior Membership, American Institute of Aeronautics and Astronautics; Corporate Division Team and Individual Achievement Awards; Corporate President's Award; Listed in several Biographical Publications. Memberships include: American Association for the Advancement of Science, American Mathematical Society; Mathematical Association of America; Society of Industrial and Applied Mathematics; Eta Kappa Nu; Phi Beta Kappa; Tau Beta Pi. Address: 26766 Menominee Place, Rancho Palos Verdes, CA 90275, USA. E-mail: chris.p.silva@aero.org

**SILVER Peter John,** b. 8 September 1949, Birmingham, England. Chartered Accountant. m. Marylyn Anne, 2 sons, 1 daughter. Education: Solihull School, Solihull, 1958-68; Lanchester Polytechnic (now University of Coventry), 1968-69. Appointments: Articled Clerk, Whinney Murray & Co (now Ernst & Young), 1968-73; Senior, Vincent Vale & Co (now BDO Stoy Hayward), 1973-74; Senior, Tranter Lowe & Co, 1974-78; Partner, Holyoak Southgate & Co, 1978-89; Partner, Silver & Co, 1989-; Director, Broad Oaks Investments Ltd, 1999-; Director, Sastak Ltd, 2001-; Director, Dudley and West Midlands Zoological Society Ltd, 2003-. Honours: Fellow, Institute of Chartered Accountants; Fellow, Royal Society of Arts. Memberships: Federation of Small Business; Talyllyn Railway Society; Severn Valley Railway Company; Great Western Railway Society; Shropshire Chamber of Agriculture; National Farmers Union. Address: The Hollies, 16 St John Street, Bridgworth, Shropshire WV15 6AV, England.

**SILVERSTONE Alicia,** b. 4 October 1976, California, USA. Actress. Appointments: Stage Debut in Play, Carol's Eve, Metropolitan Theatre, Los Angeles; Stared in 3 Aerosmith Videos including: Cryin; Formed own production company, First Kiss Productions; Films: The Crush, 1993; The Babysitter, 1995; True Crime, 1995; Le Nouveau Monde, 1995; Hideaway, 1995; Clueless, 1995; Batman and Robin, 1997; Excess Baggage (also Producer), 1997; Free Money, 1998; Blast from the Past, 1999; Love's Labour Lost, 2000; Scorched, 2002; Global Heresy, 2002; Scooby Doo: Monsters Unleashed, 2004; TV: Torch Song, 1993; Shattered Dreams, 1993; The Cool and the Crazy, 1994; The Wonder Years, 1997. Address: c/o Premiere Artists Agency, Suite 510, 8899 Beverly Boulevard, Los Angeles, CA 90048, USA.

**SIMIC Charles,** b. 9 May 1938, Belgrade, Yugoslavia (US citizen, 1971). Associate Professor of English; Poet; Writer. m. Helen Dubin, 1964, 1 son, 1 daughter. Education: University of Chicago, 1956-59; BA, New York University, 1967.

Appointments: Faculty, California State College, Hayward, 1970-73; Associate Professor of English, University of New Hampshire, 1973-. Publications: Poetry: What the Grass Says, 1967; Somewhere Among Us a Stone is Taking Notes, 1969; Dismantling the Silence, 1971; White, 1972, revised edition, 1980; Return to a Place Lit by a Glass of Milk, 1974; Biography and a Lament, 1976; Charon's Cosmology, 1977; Brooms: Selected Poems, 1978; School for Dark Thoughts, 1978; Classic Ballroom Dances, 1980; Shaving at Night, 1982; Austerities, 1982; Weather Forecast for Utopia and Vicinity: Poems: 1967-1982, 1983; The Chicken Without a Head, 1983; Selected Poems 1963-1983, 1985, revised edition, 1990; Unending Blues, 1986; The World Doesn't End: Prose Poems, 1989; In the Room We Share, 1990; The Book of Gods and Devils, 1990; Hotel Insomnia, 1992; A Wedding in Hell, 1994; Walking the Black Cat, 1996; Jackstraws, 1999. Other: The Uncertain Certainty: Interviews, Essays and Notes on Poetry, 1985; Wonderful Words, Silent Truth, 1990; Dimestore Alchemy, 1992; Unemployed Fortune Teller, 1994; Orphan Factory, 1998; A Fly in the Soup, 2000. Editor: Another Republic: 17 European and South American Writers (with Mark Strand), 1976; The Essential Campion, 1988. Translator: 12 books, 1970-92. Honours: PEN Awards, 1970, 1980; Guggenheim Fellowship, 1972; National Endowment for the Arts Fellowships, 1974, 1979; Edgar Allan Poe Award, 1975; American Academy of Arts and Letters Award, 1976; Harriet Monroe Poetry Award, 1980; Fulbright Fellowship, 1982; Ingram Merrill Foundation Fellowship, 1983; John D and Catharine T MacArthur Foundation Fellowship, 1984; Pulitzer Prize in Poetry, 1990; Academy of American Poets Fellowship, 1998. Address: c/o Department of English, University of New Hampshire, Durham, NH 03824, USA.

**SIMION Ionel,** b. 28 November 1957, Fieni, Dambotiva, Romania. Professor. m. Maria Carmen, 1 son, 1 daughter. Education: M Eng Degree, Faculty of Machine Manufacturing Technology, University Politehnica, 1977-82; PhD, Technical Sciences, Computer Aided Fixture Design, 1995. Appointments: Engineer, Mechanical Company Plopeni, Danubia Company, Bucharest, 1982-84; Assistant Professor, Associate Professor, 1984-2001, Professor, Head of Department of Descriptive Geometry and Engineering Graphics, 2001-, University Politehnica, Bucharest; Director, Instruction Centre for Engineering Graphics, 2002-; Director, Multimedia Laboratory for Engineering Graphics, 2002-. Publications: 87 scientific papers in Romanian and foreign journals; 18 books. Memberships: International Society for Geometry and Graphics; Romanian Society for Engineering. Address: 36 Nitu Vasile St, bl 1, ap 17, sector 4, Bucharest, Romania. E-mail: isimion@geom.desc.pub.ro

**SIMM Robert James,** b. 2 March 1948, Manchester, England. Art Consultant. 2 sons, 1 daughter. Education: Politics and Economics, Honours, Lancaster University, 1971. Appointments: Head of Management Development, Marks and Spencer; Head of Human Resources, Management Consulting, Price Waterhouse; Senior Partner and UK Chairman, KPMG Management Consulting. Publications: Cabinet Office Performance Appraisal Techniques; Numerous articles in many publications including: Cranfield University; London Business School; Oxford Templeton College; INSEAD; IMEDE; The Times. Honours: MATA; FIMC; MITD; QIO; FRSA; FIBM. Address:77 Greenhill, Prince Arthur Road, Hampstead, London NW3 5TZ, England.

**SIMMONS Michael,** b. 17 October 1935, Watford, England. Writer. m. Angela Thomson, 20 April 1963, 2 sons. Education: BA, Honours, Russian, Manchester University, 1960; Birkbeck College, 1998-. Appointments: Parliamentary Correspondent,

Glasgow Herald, 1964-67; East Europe Correspondent, Financial Times, 1968-72; Deputy Editor, Society, East Europe Correspondent, Third World Editor, The Guardian, 1977-97; Freelance Writer and Editor, 1997-. Publications: Berlin: The Dispossessed City, 1988; The Unloved Country; A Portrait of the GDR, 1989; The Reluctant President, A Life of Vaclav Havel, 1992; Landscapes of Poverty, 1997; On the Edge, 2001; Essays on: Church and Community, 2000; Getting a Life, 2002. Membership: Trinity Cricket Club. Address: 24 Rodney Road, New Malden, Surrey KT3 5AB, England. E-mail: micsimmo@compuserve.com

**SIMMONS Sherwin P**, Lawyer. Education: AB, 1952, LLB, 1954 (replaced by JD, 199), Columbia University. Appointments: Bar and Court Admission: Tennessee, 1954; Florida, 1957; US Supreme Court; US Tax Court, Court of Federal Claims; Attorney Adviser, US Tax Court, 1954-56; Associate, 1956-60, Partner, 1960-70, Fowler, White, Collins, Gillen Humkey & Barkin; Founding Partner, Trenam, Simmons, Kemker, Scharf & Barkin, 1970-77; Stockholder, President, Chairman of the Executive Committee, Trenam, Simmons, Kemker, Scharf, Barkin, Frye & O'Neill, 1977-94; Chair of the Tax Group, Steel Hector & Davis LLP, 1994-; Adjunct Professor of Law, University of Miami School of Law, 1995-. Publications: Author of more than 800 books and articles on tax law in a variety of tax, business and estate planning publications. Honours include: The Best Lawyers in America, 1987, 1989-90, 1991-92, 1993-94, 1995-96, 1997-98; The Best Trust and Estates lawyer in the United States, Town and Country Magazine, 1998; leading Florida Attorney. American Research Corporation, 1995, 1996, 1997, 1998, 1999; Distinguished Service Award, ABA Section of Taxation, 2001; Ranked among the leading tax attorneys in the US by Chambers and Partners, 2003; Listed in Who's Who publications and biographical dictionaries. Memberships include: Professional: American Bar Association, 1958-, Commission on Multidisciplinary Practice, 1998-; Florida Bar, 1957, Executive Council, 1958-; American Law Institute, 1966-; Fellow, American College of Trust and Estate Counsel, 1969; Fellow, American College of Tax Counsel, 1981; Fellow, American College of Employee Benefits Counsel, 2001; Fellow, American Bar Foundation; Federal Bar Association; International Bar Association; American Judicature Society; Community: Florida Orchestra, Tampa; Tampa Bay Performing Arts Center Inc; Tampa Bay International Trade Council; Tampa Rotary Club. Address: Steel Hector & Davis LLP, 200 South Biscayne Boulevard, Miami, FL 33131-2398, USA. E-mail: sptax@steelhector.com

**SIMON Neil**, b. 4 July 1927, New York, USA. Playwright. m. (1) Joan Baim, 1953, deceased, 2 daughters, (2) Marsha Mason, 1973, divorced, (3) Diane Lander, 1987, 1 daughter. Education: New York University. Appointments: Wrote for various TV programmes including: The Tallulah Bankhead Show, 1951; The Phil Silvers Show, 1958-59; NBC Special; The Trouble with People, 1972; Plays: Come Blow your Horn, 1961; Little Me (musical), 1962; Barefoot in the Park, 1963; The Odd Couple, 1965; Sweet Charity (musical), 1966; The Star-Spangled Girl, 1966; Plaza Suite, 1968; Promises, Promises (musical), 1968; Last of the Red Hot Lovers, 1969; The Gingerbread Lady, 1970; The Prisoner of Second Avenue, 1971; The Sunshine Boys, 1972; The Good Doctor, 1973; God's Favourite, 1974; California Suite, 1976; Chapter Two, 1977; They're Playing Our Song, 1979; I Ought to be in Pictures, 1980; Fools, 1981; Little Me (revised version), 1982; Brighton Beach Memoirs, 1983; Biloxi Blues, 1985; The Odd Couple Female Version, 1985; Broadway Bound, 1986; Rumors, 1988; Lost in Yonkers, 1991; Jake's Women, 1992; The Goodbye Girl (musical), 1993; Laughter on the 23rd Floor, 1993; London

Suite, 1995; Screenplays include: After the Fox, 1966; Barefoot in the Park, 1967; The Odd Couple, 1968; The Out of Towners, 1970; Plaza Suite, 1971; The Last of the Red Hot Lovers, 1972; The Heartbreak Kid, 1973; The Prisoner of Second Avenue, 1975; The Sunshine Boys, 1975; Murder by Death, 1976; The Goodbye Girl, 1977; The Cheap Detective, 1978; California Suite, 1978. Honours: Many awards and nominations include: Emmy Award; Antoinette Perry (Tony) Awards for The Odd Couple; Writers Guild Screen Award for the Odd Couple, 1969; American Comedy Award for Lifetime Achievement, 1989; Pulitzer Prize, 1991. Publication: Rewrites: A Memoir, 1996; Individual Plays. Address: c/o A DaSilva, 502 Park Avenue, New York, NY 10022, USA.

**SIMON Norma**, b. 24 December 1927, New York City, USA. Children's Book Author. m. Edward Simon, 7 June 1951, 1 son, 2 daughters. Education: BA, Economics, Brooklyn College, 1943-47; MA, Early Childhood Education, Bank St College of Education, 1968; Graduate Work, New School of Social Research. Appointments: Clerical Worker, Frances I duPont & Co, New York City, 1943-46; Teacher, Vassar Summer Institute, Poughkeepsie, New York, Department of Welfare, Brooklyn, New York, 1948-49; Downtown Community School, New York City, 1949-52; Thomas School, Rowayton, Connecticut, 1952-53; Founder, Director, Teacher, Norwalk Community Cooperative Nursery School, Rowayton, Connecticut, 1953-54; Teacher, Norwalk Public Schools, Connecticut, 1962-63; Group Therapist, Greater Bridgeport Child Guidance Center, Connecticut, 1965-67; Special Teacher, Mid-Fairfield Child Guidance Center, Connecticut, 1967-69; Consultant, Stamford Pre-School Program, Connecticut, 1965-69; Consultant, School Division, Macmillan Publishing Co, Inc, New York City, 1968-70; Consultant to Publishing Division, Bank Street College of Education, 1967-74, Follow-Through Program, 1971-72; Consultant, Davidson Films Inc, 1969-74, Aesop Films, 1975-79, San Francisco, California; Consultant, Children's Advertising, Dancer-Fitzgerald-Sampler Inc, New York City, 1969-79; Volunteer, Wellfleet Elementary School, 1972-2000; Consultant, Fisher-Price Toys, East Aurora, New York, 1978. Publications include: Firefighters, 1995; The Baby House, 1995; Wet World, 1995; The Story of Hanukkah, 1997; The Story of Passover, 1997; Looking Back at Wellfleet, 1997; All Kinds of Children, 1999; All Families are Special, 2003. Honours include: Jeremiah Cahir Friend of Education Award, Barnstable County Education Association, 1987; Parents' Council on Books Choice, 1998. Memberships: Authors Guild; Delta Kappa Gamma; AAUW. Address: PO Box 428, South Wellfleet, MA 02663-0428, USA.

**SIMON Paul**, b. 13 October 1941, Newark, New Jersey, USA. Singer; Composer. m. (1) Peggy Harper (divorced), 1 son, (2) Carrie Fisher (divorced), (3) Edie Brickell, 30 May 1992, 2 sons, 1 daughter. Education: BA, Queens College; Postgraduate, Brooklyn Law School. Career: Duo, Simon And Garfunkel, with Art Garfunkel, 1964-71; Appearances with Garfunkel include: Monterey Festival, 1967; Royal Albert Hall, 1968; Reunion concerts: Central Park, New York, 1981; US, European tours; Solo artiste, 1972-; Apperances include: Anti-war Festival, Shea Stadium, New York, 1970; Farm Aid V, 1992; Hurricane Relief concert, Miami, 1992; Born At The Right Time Tour; Tour, Europe and Russia; Television includes: Paul Simon Special, 1977; Paul Simon's Graceland - The African Concert, 1987; Paul Simon - Born At The Right Time, 1992; Film appearances: Monterey Pop, 1968; Annie Hall, 1977; All You Need Is Cash, 1978; One Trick Pony, 1980; Steve Martin Live, 1985. Compositions include: The Sound Of Silence; Homeward Bound; I Am A Rock; Mrs Robinson; The Boxer; Bridge Over Troubled Water; Cecilia; Slip Slidin' Away; Late

In The Evening; You Can Call Me Al; The Boy In The Bubble; Graceland; Paul Simon - Songs From The Capeman, 1997. Albums: with Art Garfunkel: Wednesday Morning 3AM, 1964; Sounds Of Silence, 1965; Parsley Sage Rosemary And Thyme, 1967; The Graduate (film soundtrack), 1967; Bookends, 1968; Bridge Over Troubled Water, 1970; Simon and Garfunkel's Greatest Hits, 1972; Breakaway, 1975; Watermark, 1978; Collected Works, 1981; The Concert In Central Park, 1982; Various compilation albums; Solo albums: Paul Simon, 1972; There Goes Rhymin' Simon, 1973; Live Rhymin': Paul Simon In Concert, 1974; Still Crazy After All These Years, 1975; Greatest Hits Etc, 1977; One-Trick Pony, 1980; Hearts And Bones, 1983; Graceland, 1986; Negotiations and Love Songs, 1988; Rhythm Of The Saints, 1990; Paul Simon's Concert In The Park, 1991; Paul Simon 1964-1993, 1993; Paul Simon - Songs From The Capeman, 1997; You're the One, 2000. Publications: The Songs of Paul Simon, 1972; New Songs, 1975; One-Trick Pony (screenplay); 1980; At The Zoo (for children), 1991. Honours include: Grammy awards: two for The Graduate soundtrack, 1968, six for Bridge Over Troubled Water, 1970, two for Still Crazy After All These Years, 1986, one for Graceland, 1987; Emmy Award, Paul Simon Special, NBC-TV, 1977; Inducted into Rock And Roll Hall Of Fame, with Art Garfunkel, 1990; Antoinette Perry Award, The Capeman, Best Original Score Written For The Theatre 1997-98; Honorary Doctorate of Music, Berkelee College of Music, 1986, Yale University, 1996, Queens College, 1997; Numerous Grammy Awards. Address: Paul Simon Music, 1619 Broadway, Suite 500, New York, NY 10019, USA.

**SIMPSON John (Cody Fidler),** b. 9 August 1944, Cleveleys, England. Broadcaster; Writer. m. (1) Diane Jean Petteys, 1965, divorced 1995, 2 daughters, (2) Adèle Krüger, 1996. Education: MA, Magdalene College, Cambridge. Appointments: Various positions, BBC, 1966-82; BBC Diplomatic Editor, 1982-88; Foreign, later World Affairs Editor, 1988-; Associate Editor, The Spectator, 1991-95; Columnist, The Sunday Telegraph, 1995-. Publications: The Best of Granta (editor), 1966; Moscow Requiem, 1981; A Fine and Private Place, 1983; The Disappeared: Voices From a Secret War, 1985; Behind Iranian Lines, 1988; Despatches From the Barricades, 1990; From the House of War: Baghdad and the Gulf, 1991; The Darkness Crumbles: The Death of Communism, 1992; In the Forests of the Night: Drug-Running and Terrorism in Peru, 1993; The Oxford Book of Exile (editor), 1995; Lifting the Veil: Life in Revolutionary Iran, 1995; Strange Places, Questionable People (autobiography), 1998; A Mad World, My Masters, 2000; News from No Man's Land: Reporting the World, 2002. Honours: Fellow, Royal Geographical Society, 1990; Commander of the Order of the British Empire, 1991; BAFTA Reporter of the Year, 1991, 2001; RTS Richard Dimbleby Award, 1991; Columnist of the Year, National Magazine Awards, 1993; Honorary DLitt, De Montfort University, 1995; RTS Foreign Report Award, 1997; Peabody Award, USA, 1997; Dr hc, Nottingham, 2000. Address: c/o BBC Television Centre, Wood Lane, London W12 7RJ, England.

**SIMPSON O J (Orenthal James),** b. 9 July 1947, San Francisco, USA. Former Professional Football Player; Actor; Sports Commentator. m. (1) Marguerite Whitley, 1967, divorced, 1 son, 1 daughter, (2) Nicole Brown, 1985, divorced 1992, deceased 1994, 2 sons. Education: University of Southern California; City College, San Francisco. Appointments: Member, World Record 440 yard relay team (38.6 sec), 1967; Downtown Athletic Club, 1968; Halfback, Buffalo Bills, 1969-75; San Francisco 49'ers, 1978-79; American Football League All-Star team, 1970; ProBowl Team, 1972-76; Sports Commentator, ABC Sports, 1979-86; Analyst, ABC Monday Night Football Broadcasts, 1984-85; co-host, NFL Live on NBC, 1990; Has appeared in several TV films; Acquitted of two charges of murder, 1995; Found responsible for the deaths of Nicole Brown Simpson and Ronald Goldman by civil jury, 1997; Films include: The Towering Inferno, 1974; Killer Force, 1976; The Cassandra Crossing, 1977; Capricorn One, 1978; Firepower, 1979; Hambone and Hillie, 1984; The Naked Gun, 1988; The Naked Gun 2 ½: The Smell of Fear, 1991; The Naked Gun 33 ½: The Final Insult. Publication: I Want to Tell You, 1995. Honours: Recipient of various football awards.

**SINCLAIR Andrew Annandale,** b. 21 January 1935, Oxford, England. Writer; Historian. m. Sonia Melchett, 25 July 1984, 2 sons. Education: Major Scholar, BA, PhD, Trinity College, Cambridge, 1955-59; Harkness Fellow, Harvard University,1959-61; American Council of Learned Societies Fellow, Stanford University, 1964-65. Appointments: Founding Fellow, Churchill College, 1961-63; Lecturer, University College, London, 1966-68; Publisher, Lorrimer Publishing, 1968-89; Managing Director, Timon Films Limited, 1968-2004. Publications: The Breaking of Bumbo, 1959; My Friend Judas, 1959; Prohibition: The Era of Excess, 1961; Gog, 1967; Magog, 1972; Jack: A Biography of Jack London, 1977; The Other Victoria, 1981; King Ludd, 1988; War Like a Wasp, 1989; The War Decade: An Anthology of the 1940's, 1989; The Need to Give, 1990; The Far Corners of the Earth, 1991; The Naked Savage, 1991; The Strength of the Hills, 1991; The Sword and the Grail, 1992; Francis Bacon: His Life and Violent Times, 1993; In Love and Anger, 1994; Jerusalem: The Endless Crusade, 1995; Arts and Cultures: The History of the 50 Years of the Arts Council of Great Britain, 1995; The Discovery of the Grail, 1998; Death by Fame: A Life of Elisabeth, Empress of Austria, 1998; Guevara, 1998; Dylan the Bard: A Life of Dylan Thomas, 1999; The Secret Scroll, 2001; Blood and Kin, 2002; An Anatomy of Terror, 2003; Rosslyn, 2005. Contributions to: Sunday Times; Times; New York Times; Atlantic Monthly. Honours: Somerset Maugham Prize, 1967; Venice Film Festival Award for Under Milk Wood, 1971. Memberships: Royal Literary Society, fellow, 1968; Society of American Historians, fellow 1970. Address: Flat 20, Millennium House, 132 Grosvenor Road, London SW1V 3JY, England.

**SINCLAIR David Mackenzie,** b.9 October 1937, Glasgow, Scotland. Artist. m. Anitra, 2 sons. Education: Studied drawing and painting under the tutelage of William and Mary Armour and David Donaldson, Glasgow School of Art; Awarded a Post Diploma and major travelling scholarship; Studied in Holland, Paris and London. Career: Solo exhibitions: London: The Duncan Campbell Gallery, Piano Nobile Gallery; Atlanta, USA: Tom Deans Gallery; Edinburgh: Bourne Fine Art, The Open Eye Gallery, The Printmaker's Gallery, Randolph Gallery; Glasgow: Ewan Mundy Fine Art, Cyril Gerber Gallery, The Kelly Gallery; South-West Scotland: Gracefield Arts Centre; McGill Duncan Gallery; Borders: Mainhill Gallery, Maltings Art Centre, Broughton Gallery, Shire Gallery, Alnwick; Public Shows: Islington Art Fair; Mall Galleries; The Glasgow Art Fair; Compass Gallery (Cyril Gerber associated), Glasgow; Royal Scottish Academy, Edinburgh; Royal Glasgow Institute. Honours: Murray Thompson Award, RSA, 1995; Morrison Portrait Award in the RSA, 1997; Windsor and Newton Award, Royal Scottish Society of Painters in Watercolours Shows, 2004. Membership: Elected Member, Royal Scottish Society of Painters in Watercolours, 2001, member of Council, 2002. Address: Rosebank Cottage, Paxton, Berwick upon Tweed TD15 1TE, United Kingdom.

**SINCLAIR, 18th Lord, Matthew Murray Kennedy St Clair,** b. 9 December 1968, Dumfries, Scotland. Surveyor.

Education: Glenalmond College; Royal Agricultural College, Cirencester. Appointments: Associate, Smiths Gore Surveyors; Director, Saint Property Ltd. Honour: MRICS. Memberships: RICS; MRAC; New Club. Address: Knocknalling, Dalty, Castle Douglas, Kirkcudbrightshire, DG7 3ST, Scotland. E-mail: mstc@saintproperty.com

**SINCLAIR Olga Ellen, (Ellen Clare, Olga Daniels),** b. 23 January 1923, Norfolk, England. Writer. m. Stanley George Sinclair, 1 April 1945, 3 sons. Publications: Gypsies, 1967; Hearts By the Tower, 1968; Bitter Sweet Summer, 1970; Dancing in Britain, 1970; Children's Games, 1972; Toys, 1974; My Dear Fugitive, 1976; Never Fall in Love, 1977; Master of Melthorpe, 1979; Gypsy Girl, 1981; Ripening Vine, 1981; When Wherries Sailed By, 1987; Gretna Green: A Romantic History, 1989; as Olga Daniels: Lord of Leet Castle, 1984; The Gretna Bride, 1995; The Bride From Faraway, 1987; The Untamed Bride, 1988; The Arrogant Cavalier, 1991; A Royal Engagement, 1999; An Heir for Ashingby, 2004; The Countess and the Miner, 2005. Memberships; Society of Authors; Romantic Novelists Association; Society of Women and Journalists; Norwich Writer's Circle, president. Address: Sycamore, Norwich Road, Lingwood, Norfolk NR13 4BH, England.

**SINCLAIR Robert Charles,** 21 July 1958, Canada. Research Scientist. m. Kelly Lynn. Education: BA, Honours, Psychology, University of Western Ontario, 1981; MS, Psychology, 1984, PhD, Psychology, 1988, The Pennsylvania State University, USA. Appointments: Assistant Professor, Psychology, Central Michigan University, USA, 1987-91; Associate Professor, Psychology, University of Alberta, 1991-2001; President, Sinclair & Associates, 1997-; Vice President, Oraclepoll Research, 2001-; Full Professor, Psychology, Laurentian University, 2003-. Publications: Numerous papers in scientific journals including: Nature; The Bulletin of the World Health Organization; Organizational Behavior and Human Decision Processes; Journal of Applied Social Psychology, Social Cognition; Personality and Social Psychology Bulletin and others. Memberships: Society for Experimental Social Psychology; The Midwestern Psychological Association. Address: Professor of Psychology, Laurentian University, A226C, 935 Ramsey Lake Road, Sudbury, ON P3E 2C6, Canada. E-mail: rsinclair@laurentian.ca

**SINDEN Donald (Sir),** b. 9 October 1923, Plymouth, Devon, England. Actor; Writer. m. Diana Mahony, 1948, 2 sons. Appointments: Professional Actor, 1942-; Films for the Rank Organisation, 1952-60; Associate Artist, Royal Shakespeare Company, 1967-. Publications: A Touch of the Memoirs, 1982; Laughter in the Second Act, 1985; Everyman Book of Theatrical Anecdotes (editor), 1987; The English Country Church, 1988; The Last Word (editor), 1994. Honour: Commander of the Order of the British Empire, 1979; Knighted, 1997. Memberships: Council of British Actors Equity, 1966-77, trustee, 1988-2004; Arts Council, Drama Panel, 1973-77, Advisory Board, 1982-86 Federation of Playgoers' Societies, president, 1968-93; Royal Theatrical Fund, president, 1983-; Royal Society of Arts, fellow, 1966-; Green Room Benevolent Fund, president, 1998-2004. Address: Number One, NW11 6AY, England.

**SINGER Nicky Margaret,** b. 22 July 1956, Chalfont-St-Peter, England. Novelist. m. James King-Smith, 2 sons, 1 daughter. Education: University of Bristol. Appointments: Associate Director of Talks, ICA, 1981-83; Programme Consultant, Enigma Television, 1984-85; Chair, Brighton Festival Literature Committee, 1988-93; Member of Ace Literary Magazines Group, 1993-96; Co-Founder, Co-Director, Performing Arts Labs, 1987-96; Board Member, Printer's Devil, 1993-97; Presenter,

BBC2's Labours of Eve, 1994-95; Board Member, South East Arts, 2000-03. Publications: Novels: To Still the Child, 1992; To Have and To Hold, 1993; What She Wanted, 1996; My Mother's Daughter, 1998. Non-Fiction: The Tiny Book of Time (with Kim Pickin), 1999; The Little Book of the Millennium (with Jackie Singer), 1999; Children's Fiction: Feather Boy, 2002; adapted for TV, 2004; Doll, 2003; The Innocent's Story, forthcoming. Honours: Winner, Blue Peter Book of the Year Award (Feather Boy), 2002; Winner, BAFTA Best Drama (Feather Boy), 2004); Shortlisted, Book Trust Teenage Prize (Doll), 2003. Address: c/o Conville and Walsh, 2 Ganton Street, London WIF 7QL, England.

**SINGH Ashok Kumar,** b. 29 June 1945, Bihar, India. Geologist; Geotech Engineer. m. Pushpalata, 3 daughters. Education: BSc (Hons), Applied Geology, 1964, MSc, AISM, Applied Geology, 1965, Indian School of Mines; MSc, DIC, Engineering Rock Mechanics, Imperial College, London, 1972. Appointments: Geologist, Head of Rock Mechanics, Hindustan Copper, India, 1966-79; Rock Mechanics Engineer, Chief Geologist, Zambia Consolidated Copper Mines Ltd, 1980-99; Mine Manager, Manager Mining Services, Mopani Copper Mines plc, Zambia, 2000-2001; Group Hydrogeological Engineer, Manager, Mineral Resources & Hydrogeology, Konkola Copper Mines plc, Zambia, 2002-. Publications: 12 technical papers in various symposia, seminars and technical magazines. Honours: Commonwealth Fellowship to Australia for research in the field of geomechanics, 1977. Memberships: The Institute of Materials, Minerals and Mining, UK; Chartered Engineer, Council of Engineers, UK; Engineering Institution of Zambia; Registered Engineer, Zambia. Address: No 66, 9th Street, Post Box 10100, Chingola, Zambia. E-mail: ashoks@zamtel.zm

**SINGH Gurbachan,** b. 10 April 1938, Punjab, India. Retired Education Advisor. m. Surjit Kaur, 1 son, 2 daughters. Education: BA (Hons); BEd; MPhil; PhD; FRSA. Appointment: Teacher until 1984; Education Advisor to Local Education Authorities, UK, 1984-94; Retired, 1994. Publications: Main books: Language, Race & Education; Equality and Education. Various papers and articles on minority and pluralist educational issues in Britain. Honour: Fellow of the Royal Society of Arts, UK. Address: "Briar Cottage", 53 The Hollow, Littleover, Derby DE 23 6GH, England.

**SINGH Indarjit,** b. 17 September 1932, Rawalpindi, Pakistan. Broadcaster; Journalist. m. Kanwaljit Kaur, 2 daughters. Education: Chartered Engineer, Miningin Engineer and Management Consultant. Appointments: Broadcaster and Journalist, BBC Radio 4's Thought for the Day, Radio 2's Pause for Thought, Any Questions, The Moral Maze, Agenda, Book Programme and other current affairs and religious programmes on radio and television, 1974-; Subject of a number of TV documentaries; Consultant for and presenter of several programmes on TV and radio; Mine Manager; Management Consultant in industry and local government; Lecturer on Sikhism, interfaith understanding and race relations, UK, USA, Canada, Austria, Italy, Germany and Poland. Publications: Editor, Sikh Messenger, 1984-; Translator, Sikh Reyal Maryada; Contributor, Times, Guardian, Independent and many other national and international newspapers and magazines. Honours: National Templeton Prize, 1989; Interfaith Medallion, 1991; Order of the British Empire, 1996; Doctor of Letters, Coventry University, 2002; Doctorate of Law, Leicester University, 2004. Memberships: MI MinE; CEng; MComm; MBA. Address: 43 Dorset Road, Merton Park, London, SW19 3EZ, England. E-mail: sikhmessenger@aol.com

**SINGH Raj Kumar Prasad,** b. 2 July 1947, Sheotar, Bihar, India. Metallurgical Engineer. m. Chintamani, 1 son, 1 daughter. Education: BSc, Engineering, Bihar Institute of Technology, Sindri, 1970; M Tech, Indian Institute of Technology, Bombay, 1975; PhD, Indian Institute of Technology, Madras, 1994. Appointments: Deputy Manager, Bokard Steel Plant, SAIL, 1972-79; Assistant General Manager, Research and Development Centre for Iron and Steel, Steel Authority of India, 1980-94; General Manager, Quality Control, Research and Development, Lloyds Steel Industries Ltd, 1994-99; Professor, VNIT, Nagpur, 2000-2003; Director General, Institute for Steel Development and Growth, 2003-. Publications: Over 30 national and international publications, including, EDD Quality Steels Al-Deoxidation Techniques; Sulphide Shape Control in HSLA Steels; Combined Blowing of Converters; Failure Analysis. Honours: Listed in several international biographical directories. Memberships: Life Fellow, Indian Institute of Metals; Life Member, Indian Society of Non-Destructive Testing. Address: Ispat Niketan, 1st Floor, 52/1A Ballygunge Circular Road, Kolkata 700 019, India. E-mail: rkpsingh@hotmail.com

**SINGH Tej P,** b. 20 October 1949, Moradabad, India. Researcher; Teacher. m. Meera Singh, 1 daughter. Education: MSc, 1971; PhD, 1975. Appointments: Post-doctoral Fellow, 1976; Lecturer, Indore University, 1977; Humboldt Foundation Fellow, 1978-80; Reader, Sardar Patel University, 1980-83; Professor, Head, All India Institute of Medical Sciences, New Delhi, 1984-. Publications: 250 articles in professional journals. Honour: K. K. Foundation National Award for Science and Technology, 2001. Memberships: Indian Biophysical Society; Max-Planck Society, Germany; Indian Crystallographic Association; Fellow of Indian Academy of Sciences; Fellow of the National Academy of Sciences; Fellow of the Indian National Science Academy; Fellow of the Third World Academy of Sciences. Address: Department of Biophysics, All India Institute of Medical Sciences, New Delhi 110 029, India. E-mail: tps@aiims.aiims.ac.in

**SINGLETON Valerie,** b. 9 April 1937, England. Education: Arts Educational School London, RADA. Appointments: Broadcast Personality and Writer; Bromley Rep, 1956-57, subsequently, No 1 Tour, Cambridge Arts Theatre, Theatre work, TV appearances, Compact and Emergency Ward 10 and others, top voice over commentator for TV commercials and advertising magazines; BBC 1: Continuity Announcer, 1962-64, Presenter, Blue Peter, 1962-72, Nationwide, 1972-78, Val Meets the VIPs (3 series), Blue Peter Special Assignment (4 series), Blue Peter Royal Safari with HRH The Princess Anne, Tonight and Tonight in Town, 1978-79, Blue Peter Special Assignments Rivers Yukon and Niagara, 1980; BBC 2: Echoes of Holocaust, 1979, The Migrant Workers of Europe, 1980, The Money Programme, 1980-88; Radio 4: PM 1981-93, several appearances Midweek; Freelance Broadcaster and Travel Writer, 1993-; Channel 4: Presenter, Back-Date (daily quiz programme), 1996; Playback, History Channel, 1998, second series, 1999; Numerous appearances in TV advertising. Honour: OBE. Membership: Equity. Address: c/o Arlington Enterprises, 1-3 Charlotte Street, London W1, England.

**SINHA Neeti,** b. 29 June 1970, Lucknow, India. Scientist. m. Sandeep Kumar, 1 daughter. Education: PhD/DPhil, University of Oxford England; Post-doctoral Research, NCI, National Institutes of Health, USA, 1998-2003. Appointment: Associate Research Scientist, Johns Hopkins University, Baltimore, USA, 2003-. Publications: 14 research articles on protein thermodynamics and structure in top-rated scientific journals such as: PNAS, USA; Structure, Folding and Design; Biophysical Journal; Protein Engineering; and invited reviews.

Honours: Felix Scholarship Award, Oxford; Radhakrishnan Bequest at Oxford; Post-doctoral Visiting Fellowship, NIH, USA; Outstanding Scientist Category in USA; JR Fellowship and Lecturership, CSIR, India. Memberships: American Association for the Advancement of Science; The Protein Society; International Society for Computational Biology. Address: Biocalorimetry Center, Biology Department, Johns Hopkins University, 3400 N Charles Street, Baltimore, MD 21218, USA. E-mail: nsinha@jhu.edu

**SINNATHURAY Arasa Raj,** b. 16 July 1969, Kuala Lumpur, Selangor, Malaysia. Otolaryngologist; Researcher. m. Claire Quinn. Education: MB BCh, National University of Ireland, Dublin, Ireland, 1994; Doctor of Medicine, Queen's University, Belfast, Northern Ireland, ongoing; Fellow of the Royal College of Surgeons in Ireland (General Surgery); Fellow of the Royal College of Surgeons in Ireland (Otolaryngology). Appointments: Registered Physician with Irish Medical Council and General Medical Council, United Kingdom; Senior House Officer, General Surgical Training, Belfast, 1996-98; Otolaryngology Senior House Officer Training, Northern Ireland, 1998-2000; Research Fellow, Medical Genetics Department and Regional Cochlear Implant Centre, Queen's University, Belfast, 2000-; Specialist Registrar in Otolaryngology, 2003-. Publications: Contributory author to professional journals in otolaryngology. Invited reviewer (Ad Hoc), Journal of Public Health Medicine; Invited speaker to Cochlear Implant Departments: South Thames, England and Belfast; Ongoing research in genetic screening of cochlear implant recipients and creation of a database. Honours: 2nd Place Bronze Medal and 1st Class Honours in Physics, 1989 and Microbiology, 1992; 3rd Prize, Medical Audit Competition, Sperrin Lakeland Hospital Trust, Northern Ireland, 1999; Grantee: Cochlear Europe Ltd, 2001-2003, Mason Medical Foundation, England, 2002; Listed in Who's Who publications and biographical dictionaries. Memberships: Medical Protection Society, UK; British Association of Otolaryngologists, Head and Neck Surgeons; European Academy of Otology and Neurotology. Address: Belfast City Hospital, Cochlear Implant Centre, Lisburn Road, Belfast BT9 7AB, Northern Ireland. E-mail: rajsinn@aol.com

**SINNOTT Jan Dynda,** b. 14 June 1942, Cleveland, Ohio. Psychologist. Life partner: Lynn Johnson, 2 sons, 2 daughters. Education: BS, St Louis University, 1964; MA, 1973, PhD, 1975, Catholic University of America. Appointments: Workshop Lecturer, 1971-; Social Rehabilitation Services Research Trainee, 1971-74; Research Assistant, 1971-72, Teaching Assistant, 1973, Catholic University of America; Research Associate, Human Sciences Research, Virginia, 1975; Lecturer, 1975-77, Research Associate, 1975-77, Catholic University of America; Founder and Director, Human Development Research, 1977-80; Principal Investigator, Centre on Ageing, University of Maryland, 1977-80; Guest Scientist, Gerontology Research Centre, National Institute on Ageing, NIH, 1980-89; Director, Centre for Study of Adult Development and Ageing, 1989-91, Associate Director, Institute for Cognition and Teaching, 2001-, Tenured Professor of Psychology, 1978-, Towson University, Maryland. Publications: The Development in Logic in Adulthood: Postformal Thought and Its Application; Plus numerous other reviews, books, articles, book chapters and papers. Honours: Towson University Faculty Excellence Award; Listed in Who's Who publications and biographical dictionaries. Memberships: Fellow, American Psychological Association; Fellow, Gerontological Society of America; Fellow, American Psychological Society; many others. Address: 9923 Cottrell Terrace, Silver Spring, Maryland 20903, USA. E-mail: jsinnott@towson.edu

**SIO Jimmy Ong**, b. 9 March 1954, Manila, Philippines. Education: BS, Biology, California State College in Bakersfield, California, USA, 1976; PhD, Cell Biology, University of Texas Health Science Center, Dallas, 1985; MD, Emory University School of Medicine, Atlanta, Georgia, 1985. Appointments: PGY-1 Resident in Anatomical Pathology, Emory University School of Medicine, 1985-86; Resident in Internal Medicine, Kern Medical Center, Bakersfield, 1990-93; Physician, Southern California Permanente Medical Group, Bakersfield, 1993-. Publications: Article for the book, Immunological Aspects of Infertility and Fertility Regulation, 1980; Article for the journal, Biology of Reproduction, 1982. Honours: Outstanding Physician of the Year 2002, Southern California Permanente Medical Group; Universal Award of Accomplishment 2003, ABI. Memberships: InterNet Associates; New York Academy of Sciences. Address: 8800 Ming Avenue, Bakersfield, CA 93311, USA.

**SÎRBU Valeriu**, b. 25 February 1950, Cladova, Romania. Archaeologist; Researcher. m. Livia Sîrbu, 2 sons. Education: History Studies, University of Bucharest, 1970-74; Doctors degree, University of Jassy, 1993. Appointments: Museologist, 1975-81, First Museologist, 1981-91, Department Chief, 1991-93, Manager Assistant, 1993-96, Senior Researcher, 1993-2004, Department Chief, 1996-99, Manager Assistant, 1999-2005, Museum of Brăila, Romania; Senior Researcher, Romanian Institute of Archaeology, 1996-2005; Professor, University "Constantin Brâncoveanu", Brăila, 2000-2002; Visiting Professor, Sorbonne University, 2004; Archaeological excavations in 14 settlements and necropolises, Bronze Age and Iron Age in Romania, 2 sites in Ukraine, other sites in the Republic of Moldavia. Publications: 10 books, 6 co-authored; 122 studies and articles, some co-authored in the field of history and archaeology of the Thracian world in Hallstatt and La Tène; Numerous lectures at international symposia and conferences. Honours: Prize "Nicolae Bălcescu", Romanian Academy, 1993. Memberships: National Commission of Archaeology, Romania; President, Funerary Archaeology Studies Association; President, XXXth Commission of the International Union of Prehistoric and Protohistoric Sciences. Address: Museum of Brăila, 3 Square Traian, 810153 Brăila, Romania. E-mail: valeriu_sirbu@yahoo.co.uk

**SIRIK Yury**, b. 13 May 1946, Dnepropetrovsk, Ukraine. Aerospace Engineer. m. Tatiana Sirik, 1 son, 1 daughter. Education: Hydroaerodynamics, Mechanical Mathematical Faculty, State University of Dnepropetrovsk, Ukraine, 1965-70;Scientific Research Energy Institute, Moscow, Russia, 1969; Increased Qualification Course, Central Scientific Research Institute Machine-building, Kaliningrad, Russia, 1979; Theory of Design, State Design Office "Yuzshnoe", Dnepropetrovsk, Ukraine, 1980. Appointments: Engineer, Research Institute of Machine-building Technology, Zlatoust, Russia, 1970-73; Engineer, Design Office Mechanical Engineering, Miass, Russia, 1973-80; Engineer, State Design Office "Yuzshnoe", Pavlograd, Ukraine, 1980-; Senior Investigator, Physical-Technical Group, Pavlograd, Ukraine, 1991-. Publications: More than 10 research reports; 11 articles; 5 patents. Address: Balashovskaya Street 14, 33, Pavlograd, Dnepropetrovsk oblast, 51413, Ukraine.

**SIROTA Nicolay Nicolaevich**, b. 2 November 1913, Saint Petersburg, Russia. Physics Researcher; Educator. m. Irina Mironovna Sirota, 1 son. Education: Diploma, Engineer, 1936, Postgraduate Student, Doctor of Technology, 1936-39, Moscow Institute of Steel and Alloys; Senior Scientific Researcher, Presidium Academy of Sciences, USSR, 1948; Doctor of Science, Physical-Mathematics, Moscow State University, 1951. Appointments: Education, Physics Faculty, Moscow State University, 1939-50; Head of Chair, Institute of Metallurgy, Marinpol, Ukraine, 1940-41; Soviet Army, 1942-43; Senior Scientific Researcher, Institute of Inorganic Chemistry, Academy of Sciences, USSR, 1944-54; Head of Chair of Physics, Institute of Nonferrous Metals, Moscow, 1954-57; Director, Scientific Leader, Institute of Physics of Solids and Semiconductors of National Academy of Sciences, Minsk, Belorussia, 1957-75; Head of Chair, Physics of Solids and Semiconductors, State University, Minsk, 1957-62; Head of Chair, Theoretical Physics, Pedagogical University, Minsk, 1963-75; Head of Ostwalds Chair (Visiting Professor), K-M University Leipzig, Germany, 1980; Head of Chair of Physics, Moscow State University of Nature Improvement, 1978-89; Professor, 1989-. Publications: Thermodynamic and Statistical Physics, 1969; Physical-Chemical Nature of Changeable Composition Phases, 1970; Chemical Bonds in Semiconductors, 1967; Certain Problems of Polymorphism, Part I, 1982, Part II, 1987; Physics and Physical-Chemical Analysis of Condensed Matters (Collected works), Part I, 2001, Part II, 2002, Part III, 2003; Analytical Expression of the Kapiza Magnetoresistance Low, 2004; Bibliography NN Sirota, 1998. Honours: Orders of the Labour Red Banner, 1967, 1973; Medals, 1947, 1954, 1970, 1988, Supreme Soviet USSR, 1995, 1997, 1999, Government of the Russian Federation; Honorary Decoration, Supreme Soviet BSSR, Academy of Sciences USSR, Belorussia, 1963-2003; Prize, Council of Ministers, USSR, 1950; Honorary Scientist, Supreme Soviet BSSR, 1968; Honorary Scientist, President of the Russian Federation, 2004. Memberships: Academician, National Academy of Sciences, Belorussia, 1956-; Member Scientific Councils including: Physics of Solids, Semiconductors, Magnetism, Low Temperature, Academy of Sciences, USSR, 1963-79; Member, International Committee of Electron Spin Density, International Union of Crystallography, 1969-79. Address: Leninsky Prosp. 123-1-741, Moscow 117513, Russia. E-mail: n.sirota@ru.net

**SISK Fred Dean**, b. 26 May 1940, Johnson City, Tennessee, USA. Retired Cartographer. m. Martha Lynn Robinson Sisk. Education: BS, Geography, East Tennessee State University, 1962; MS, Cartography, George Mason University, 1984. Appointments: Artillery Officer, United States Army Battery Commander, Fort Sill, Oklahoma, 1962-65; Cartographer, Army Map Service, US Army Topographic Command, Defense Mapping Agency, Washington DC, 1965-79; Senior Cartographer, Course Manager, Deputy Division Chief, Senior Instructor, Master Instructor, Defense Mapping School, Fort Belvoir, Virginia, 1979-88; Training Co-ordinator, 1988-89, Cartographer, Security Officer, 1989-95, Defense Mapping Agency, Reston, Virginia; Retired, 1995; Security Officer, Notary Public, State of Virginia, Officer of Election, City of Fredericksburg, 1996-. Honours: Sustained Superior Performance Award, US Army Topographic Command, 1971; Outstanding Performance Award, Defense Mapping School, 1985, 1986; Lifetime Achievement Award in Photography, International Freelance Photographers Organization, 2004; Master Photographer Regnant, Honorary Degree of Excellence, International Freelance Photographers Org, 2004; Listed in Who's Who publications and biographical dictionaries. Memberships: President, Fox Run Homeowners Association, Fredericksburg, Virginia, 1996-; Past Chairman, Memorial Advisory Commission, City of Fredericksburg, Virginia; Board of Directors, Fredericksburg Regional Transit System; Master Photographer, International Freelance Photographers Organization; Life Member, National Rifle Association, Washington DC; Civil War Round Table, Fredericksburg, Virginia; Republican National Committee, Washington DC; Republican Presidential Task Force, Washington DC; The

Heritage Foundation, Washington DC. Address: 18 Devonshire Drive, Fredericksburg, VA 22401, USA

**SISSONS Peter George,** b. 17 July 1942. Television Presenter. m. Sylvia Bennett, 1965, 2 sons, 1 daughter. Education: University College Oxford. Appointments: Graduate Trainee, ITN, 1964, General Reporter, 1967, Industrial Correspondent, 1970, Industrial Editor, 1972-78, Presenter, News at One, 1978-82; Presenter, Channel 4 News, 1982-89; Presenter, 6 O'Clock News, 1989-93, 9 O'Clock News, 1994-2000, 10 O'Clock News, 2000-03, News 24, 2003-, BBC TV News; Chair, BBC TV Question Time, 1989-93. Honours: Broadcasting Press Guild Award, 1984; Royal TV Society Judges' Award, 1988; Honorary Fellow, Liverpool John Moores University, 1997; Hon LLD, University of Liverpool, 2002. Address: BBC Television Centre, Wood Lane, London, W12 7RJ, England.

**SJÖRS Hugo M,** b. 1 August 1915, Stora Skedvi, Sweden. Emeritus Professor. m. Gunnel Thelander, 1 son, 2 daughters. Education: Fil Mag, 1942, Fil Lic, 1945, Fil Dr, 1948, Uppsala University. Appointments: Docent, 1948, Professor of Ecological Botany, 1962-80, Emeritus, 1980, Uppsala University; Deputy Assistant Professor, Lund University, 1952-55; Assistant Professor, School of Forestry, Stockholm, 1955-62. Publications: 2 Textbooks: Nordic Plant Geography, Ecological Botany (both in Swedish); About 200 papers on Plant Ecology and Peatlands. Honours: Linnaeus Gold Medal, Royal Physiographic Society, Lund; Nature Conservation Prize, Species Data Bank, Swedish Agricultural University. Memberships: Royal Swedish Academy of Sciences; Foreign Member, Finnish Academy of Sciences; Honorary Member, British Ecological Society; Honorary Member, Swedish Botanical Society. Address: Stenbrohultsvägen 103, 75758 Uppsala, Sweden.

**SKÅRDERUD Finn,** b. 27 October 1956, Tynset, Norway. Psychiatrist. m. Marianne Røed, 1 son, 2 daughters. Education: Medical Doctor, 1982; Diploma in Family Therapy, 1989; Specialist in Psychiatry, 1997; Diploma in Psychoanalytic Psychotherapy, 1996; Supervisor in Psychotherapy, 1999. Appointments: MD, Department of Psychiatry, Ullevål Hospital, Oslo, 1984-89; Psychotherapeutic Private Practice, 1988-; Psychiatrist, National Centre for Child and Adolescent Psychiatry, Oslo, 1990-97; Psychiatrist for the Norwegian Olympic Committee, 1999-; Professor in Health and Social Work, Lillehammer University College, 2005-. Publications: 12 books; 45 book chapters, 20 scientific articles in referee based journals and 140 additional publications covering the fields of psychiatry, psychotherapy, film, literature, art and culture. Honours: 2 awards for health information; 1 prize for non-fictional authorship. Memberships: Norwegian Medical Association; Norwegian Psychiatric Association. Address: Gaustadveien 155, 0372 Oslo, Norway. E-mail: finns@online.no; Website: www.skarderud.no

**SKÁRMETA Antonio,** b. 7 November 1940, Antofagasta, Chile. Writer. Education: Graduated, University of Chile, 1963; MA, Columbia University, 1966. Appointments: Ambassador to Germany, 2000-01. Publications: El entusiasmo, 1967; Desnudo en el tejado, 1969; El ciclista del San Cristóbal, 1973; Tiro libre, 1973; Soñé que la nieve ardía, 1975, English translation as I Dreamt the Snow Was Burning, 1985; Novios y solitarios, 1975; La insurrección, 1980, English translation as The Insurrection, 1983; No pasó nada, 1980; Ardiente paciencia, 1985, English translation as Burning Patience, 1987; Match Ball, 1989; Watch Where the Wolf is Going, 1991. Contributions to: Periodicals. Honours: Premio Casa de las Américas, 1969; Guggenheim

Fellowship, 1986; Academy Award Nomination, 1996. Address: Chilean Embassy, 53173 Bonn, Kronprinzenstr 20, Germany.

**SKARSGÅRD J Stellan,** b. 13 June 1951, Goteborg, Sweden. Actor. m. My Gunther, 1976, 5 sons, 1 daughter. Appointments: With Royal Dramatic Theatre, Stockholm, 1972-87; Films Include: Simple Minded Murderer, 1982; Serpent's Way, 1986; Hip Hip Hurrah, 1987; The Unbearable Lightness of Being, 1988; Good Evening Mr Wallenberg, 1990; The Ox, 1992; Wind, 1992; The Slingshot, 1993; Zero Kelvin, 1994; Breaking the Waves, 1995; Insomnia, 1997; Amistad, 1997; Good Will Hunting, 1997; Ronin, 1998; Deep Blue Sea, 1998; Passion of Mind, 1999; For TV, Hamlet, 1984. Honours: Best Actor, Berlin Film Festival, 1982; Twice Best Film Actor in Sweden; Best Actor, Rouen Film Festival, 1988, 1992; Best Actor, Chicago Film Festival, 1991; Jury's Special Prize, San Sebastian Film Festival, 1995; European Film Award.

**SKIFF Warner Mason,** b. 11 December 1955, Oxnard, California, USA. Physical Chemist. Education: BA, Chemistry, 1977, PhD, Chemistry, 1985, Arizona State University. Appointments: Research Associate, Centre for Solid State Science, Arizona State University, 1985-88; Senior Research Chemist, Shell Oil Company, Houston, Texas, 1988-99; Assistant Professor, University of Alaska, Fairbanks, 1999-2004; Vice President, General Molecular Inc, Fort Collins, Colorado, USA, 1999-. Publications: About a dozen articles; Research contributions: Electron energy loss spectroscopy, force field development and application, theoretical catalysis. Honours: Burton Medal, Microscopy Society of America; Visiting Scientist, Shell Research and Technology Centre, Amsterdam, The Netherlands. Address: P O Box 271, Dillingham, Alaska 99576, USA.

**SKINNER Sandford Lloyd,** b. 6 August 1933, Clare, South Australia. Physiologist. 1 son, 3 daughters. Education: Matriculation, 1951; MBBS, Adelaide, 1957; MD, Adelaide, 1962. Appointments: Reader, Physiology, University of Melbourne, 1968-98; Assistant Physician, Austin Hospital, Melbourne, Australia, 1977-2001; Principal Fellow, Department of Physiology, University of Melbourne, 1999-. Publications: Over 120 articles in professional medical journals. Honours: Travelling CJ Martin Research Fellowship, NH and MRC, 1962-64; Grant, Danish Government, 1973; Stipend, French Government, 1980. Memberships: Australian Physiological and Pharmacological Society; Australian Society of Endocrinology; International Society of Hypertension; Australasian Society of Nephrology; Fellow, Royal Australian College of Physicians. Address: 50 Molesworth Street, North Melbourne, Vic 3051, Australia.

**SKOPINSKY Vadim Nikolaevich,** b. 3 May 1946, Moscow. Higher School Professor. m. Elena, 2 sons. Education: Graduate, 1970; Post Graduate, 1970-73; Candidate of Technical Sciences, 1974; Doctor of Technical Sciences, Moscow Engineer Construction Institute, 1989. Appointments: Research Worker, 1973-76; Associate Professor, 1976-89; Professor, 1989-90; Head of Material Strength Chair, 1990-. Publications: Articles to professional journals and proceedings at conferences. Honours: Science Grantee, Academy of Transport Sciences, Moscow; Fundamental Research Grantee, Russian State Commission in Higher Education, 1996. Memberships: Member Academic Board; Member, Research Board of Advisors, ABI, USA; Member, Special Science Council, Institute of Technology and Mechanical Engineering; Member, Science Council, Moscow. Address: Alleya Zhemchugovoy 1-1-127, 111402 Moscow, Russia.

**SKOROBOGATOV German,** b. 10 January 1937, Datsan Cheata Region, Siberia. Physics-Chemistry Educator. m. Eugeniaja Nadeoshkeana, 3 daughters. Education: Magister, 1959, PhD, 1967, Department of Chemistry, Leningrad State University; Professor of Chemistry, St Petersburg State University, 1996. Appointments: Researcher, Institute of Silicate Chemistry, 1960-61; Researcher, Department of Physics, 1966-67, Chief of Photochemistry Laboratory, Department of Chemistry, 1968-2004, Professor, Department of Chemistry, 1984-2004, St Petersburg (Leningrad) State University. Publications: Radiochemistry and Chemistry of Nuclear Reactions, 1960; Orthodoxical and Paradoxical Chemistry, 1985; Co-author, book: Theoretical Chemistry, 2000; Take Care! Tap Water!, 2003; Foundations of Theoretical Chemistry, 2003; Articles in professional journals. Honours: Research Fellow, Coin, ABI, Bronze edition, 1993, Silver edition, 1996; Listed in national and international biographical dictionaries. Memberships: Mendeleev's Chemical Society (Moscow), 1975-2003; American Mathematical Society, 1988-98; Planetary Society, 1992 99. Address: Department of Chemistry, St Petersburg State University, Universitetskii prosp 26, 198504 St Petersburg, Russia. E-mail: gera.skor@pobox.spbu.ru

**SKROMNE-KADLUBIK Gregorio,** b. 9 April 1939, Mexico City. Nuclear Medicine Physician. m. Blanca Sofia Castillo, 1 son. Education: MD, National University, 1962; Nuclear Medicine, MD University of Sao Paulo, Brazil, 1968; MSc, National University, 1972. Appointments: Professor, Physiology, 1965; Head, Section, Nuclear Medicine, 1969-; Researcher, Faculty of Medicine, Mexico City, 1972; Coordinator, Nuclear Medicine, National Polytechnic Institute, 1978-88; Head, Nuclear Medicine, ISSSTF Mexico, 1974-88. Publications: 320 articles in nuclear medicine. Honours: Golden Medal, Sao Paulo, Brazil; G Soberan Medal, Health Society of Mexico. Memberships: AAAS; New York Academy of Sciences; International Brain Organisation. Address: Holbein 65 # 101, Mixcoac, DF, Mexico.

**SKRZYPCZYNSKA Małgorzata Cecylia,** b. 26 December 1940, Wadowice, Poland. Professor. m. Andrzej, 1 daughter. Education: MA, Faculty of Biology and Earth Science, Jagiellonian University, Kraków, 1958-63; Dr of Forest Sciences, 1971, Dr Sc, 1979, Professor Dr Sc, Forest Entomology, 1994, Agricultural University of Kraków. Appointments: Assistant Professor, 1964-71, Adjunct Professor, 1971-79, Assistant Professor, 1979-94, Professor, 1994-, Agricultural University of Kraków. Publications include: 265 publications including 106 monographs, studies and dissertations; 2 Books, 1 with Professor J Křistek; Numerous articles in magazines and journals dealing with forest entomology with particular reference to seed insect pests of conifers and zoocecidology/plant galls. Honours: Stypendist, Czechoslovak Academy of Science, 1974; Stipendist, University of Bodenkultur, Vienna, Austria, 1979, 1981; Złoty Krzyż Zasługi, 1986; Krzyż Kawalerski Orderu Odrodzenia Polski, 2000. Memberships: Deputy, Working Party IUFRO, 1992-2004; Polish Entomological Society; Polish Forest Society. Address: Agricultural University of Kraków, Department of Forest Entomology, 31-425 Kraków, Al 29 Listopada 46, Poland. E-mail: rlbozek@cyf-kr.edu.pl

**SKULJ Jola Jozica,** b. 8 December 1947, Slovenia. Senior Research Fellow. m. Madzarevic Branko, 1 daughter. Education: Diploma, Comparative Literature, Literary Theory, 1980; MA, Comparative Literature, Literary Theory, 1991. Appointments: Free Lance Critic, several literary magazines, 1968-74; Students Assistant, Department of Comparative Literature, 1973-78; Part time Research Work, Institute of Literature, 1979-81; Research Assistant, 1981-91; Senior Research Fellow, 1991-96; Senior

Specialist Adviser, 1996-. Publications: The Modern Novel, 1990; Dialogism as a non finalized concept of truth, 1997; Comparative Literature and Cultural Identity, 1999; Literature as Repository of Historical Consciousness: Reinterpreted Tales of Mnemosyne, 2000; Multilingualism as Strategy of Modern Dialogism, 2002; Modernism and the Crisis of Consciousness, 2003; The Novel and Its Terrain(s) of Reinterpreted Identities in the Age of Globalisation, 2004; Literature and Space: Spaces of Transgressiveness, 2004; others. Honour: Salzburg American Seminar Fellowship. Memberships: International Comparative Literature Association; Slovene Comparative Literature Association; ICLA Research Committee on Eastern and South-Eastern Europe, 2003-; Executive Board, European Network of Comparative Literary Studies, 2003-; Executive Council of International Comparative Literature Association, 2004-. Address: Tavcarjeva 1, 1000 Ljubljana, Slovenia.

**SKURATOV Yuri,** b. 3 June 1952, Ulan-Ude, USSR. Lawyer. m. Elena Skuratova, 1 son, 1 daughter. Education: University of Law, Sverdlovsk City, USSR, 1973. Appointments: Director, Scientific Research Institute, General Prosecutor's Office, 1993-95; General Prosecutor of the Russian Federation, 1995-2000; Professor, Russian State Social University, 2000-; President, Charity Foundation, Legal Technologies of the XXI Century, 2001-. Publications: Articles in professional journals include: The freedom of meetings and demonstrations: theory and practice; State border of the Russian Federation: basis of the legal regulation, 1993; Parliament and President in the Constitution of the Russian Federation, 1994; Books as co-author: Commentary to the Law of the Russian Federation, "About the Prosecutor's Office", 1996; Commentary to the Criminal Code of the Russian Federation, 2002; Constitutional Law of the Russian Federation, 2004. Honours: Doctor of Law; Professor; Honoured Lawyer of the Russian Federation. Memberships: International Association of Prosecutors; International Association of Criminal Law; International Informatization Academy; International Academy of Ecology and Life Protection Sciences. Address: kv 434 d 36 ul Garibaldi, Moscow, Russia.

**ŠLAPAL Josef,** b. 21 December 1955, Brno, Czech Republic. Mathematician. m. Ivana Rybárová, 2 daughters. Education: MA Pure Mathematics, 1975-80, PhD Algebra, 1989-92, Masaryk University, Brno. Appointments: Lecturer, 1981-82, Senior Lecturer, 1982-86, Technical University of Ostrava; Senior Lecturer, 1986-94, Associate Professor, 1994-2000, Professor, 2000-, Technical University of Brno. Publications: Over 60 research papers in renowned mathematical journals. Honours: German Academy of Sciences Fellowship, 1994; DAAD Fellowship, Germany, 1998; Dr Jiri Nehnevajsa Memorial Award, University of Pittsburgh, 1999; NATO-CNR Outreach Fellowship, Italy, 2002. Memberships: American Mathematical Society; New York Academy of Sciences; Union of Czech Mathematicians and Physicists; National Geographic Society. Address: Department of Mathematics, Technical University of Brno, 616 69 Brno, Czech Republic. E-mail: slapal@fme.vutbr.cz Website: http://at.yorku.ca/h/a/a/a/10.htm

**SLATER Edward Charles,** b. 16 January 1917, Melbourne, Australia. Biochemist. m. Marion Winifred Hutley, 1 daughter. Education: MSc, University of Melbourne, 1935-39; PhD, DSc, Cambridge University, England, 1946-48. Appointments: Biochemist, Australian Institute of Anatomy, Canberra, Australia, 1939-46; Research Fellow, Molteno Institute, Cambridge University, 1946-55; Professor of Biochemistry, University of Amsterdam, 1955-85; Honorary Professor, Southampton University, 1985-90. Publications: About 450 articles in scientific journals and books; 1 monograph: The Story of a Biochemical Journal, 1986; Co-editor several publications.

Honours include: Dixon Scholarship, Major James Cuming Memorial Scholarship in Chemistry, University of Melbourne, 1937; British Council Scholarship, 1946; Rockefeller Foundation Fellowship, 1949; University of Brussels Medal, 1956; Gold Medal, University of Bari, Italy, 1965; Medal of the Societe de Chimi Biologiqie, France, 1966; Keilin Medal, Biochemical Society, 1974; Knighthood in the Order of the Netherlands Lion, 1984; Honorary DSc, University of Southampton, 1993; Honorary D Biol. Sci., University of Bari, 1997. Memberships: Royal Netherlands Academy of Science, 1964; Dutch Company of Science, 1970; Corresponding Member, National Academy of science of Argentina, 1973; Honorary Member, Japanese Biochemical Society, 1973; Fellow of the Royal Society, 1975; Honorary Member, Biochemical Society, 1987; Fellow World Innovation Foundation, 2001. Address: 9 Oaklands, Lymington, Hants SO41 3TH, England. E-mail: ecslater@btinternet.com

**SLAVITT David R(ytman), (David Benjamin, Henry Lazarus, Lynn Meyer, Henry Sutton),** b. 23 March 1935, White Plains, New York, USA. Novelist; Poet; Translator; Lecturer. m. (1) Lynn Nita Meyer, 27 August 1956, divorced 1977, 2 sons, 1 daughter, (2) Janet Lee Abrahm, 16 April 1978. Education: BA, magna cum laude, Yale University, 1956; MA, Columbia University, 1957. Appointments: Instructor in English, Georgia Institute of Technology, Atlanta, 1957-58; Staff, Newsweek magazine, 1958-65; Assistant Professor, University of Maryland, College Park, 1977; Associate Professor of English, Temple University, Philadelphia, 1978-80; Lecturer in English and Comparative Literature, Columbia University, 1985-86; Lecturer, Rutgers University, 1987-; Lecturer in English and Classics, University of Pennsylvania, 1991-97; Faculty Member, Bennington College, 2000-; Visiting Professorships; Many university and college poetry readings. Publications: Novels: Rochelle, or Virtue Rewarded, 1966; Anagrams, 1970; ABCD, 1972; The Outer Mongolian, 1973; The Killing of the King, 1974; King of Hearts, 1976; Jo Stern, 1978; Cold Comfort, 1980; Alice at 80, 1984; The Agent, 1986; The Hussar, 1987; Salazar Blinks, 1988; Lives of the Saints, 1989; Turkish Delights, 1993; The Cliff, 1994; Get Thee to a Nunnery: Two Divertimentos from Shakespeare, 1999. Henry Sutton: The Exhibitionist, 1967; The Voyeur, 1969; Vector, 1970; The Liberated, 1973; The Sacrifice: A Novel of the Occult, 1978; The Proposal, 1980. As Lynn Meyer: Paperback Thriller, 1975. As Henry Lazarus: That Golden Woman, 1976. As David Benjamin: The Idol, 1979. Non-Fiction: Understanding Social Life: An Introduction to Social Psychology (with Paul F Secord and Carl W Backman), 1976; Physicians Observed, 1987; Virgil, 1991; The Persians of Aeschylus, 1998; Three Amusements of Ausonius, 1998; Re-Verse: Essays on Poets and Poetry, forthcoming. Other: Editor: Adrien Stoutenburg: Land of Superior Mirages: New and Selected Poems, 1986; Short Stories Are Not Real Life: Short Fiction, 1991; Crossroads, 1994; A Gift, 1996; Epigram and Epic: Two Elizabethan Entertainments, 1997; A New Pleade: Seven American Poets, 1998. Translator: The Eclogues of Virgil, 1971; The Eclogues and the Georgics of Virgil, 1972; The Tristia of Ovid, 1985; Ovid's Poetry of Exile, 1990; Seneca: The Tragedies, 1992; The Fables of Avianus, 1993; The Metamorphoses of Ovid, 1994; The Twelve Minor Prophets, 1999; The Voyage of the Argo of Valerius Flaccus, 1999; Sonnets of Love and Death of Jean de Spande, 2001; The Elegies of Propertius, 2001. Contributions to: Various other books as well as periodicals. Honours: Pennsylvania Council on the Arts Award, 1985; National Endowment for the Arts Fellowship, 1988; American Academy and Institute of Arts and Letters Award, 1989; Rockefeller Foundation Artist's Residence, 1989. Address: 523 South 41st Street, Philadelphia, PA 19104, USA.

**SLECHTA Jiri,** b. 26 April 1939, Havlikuv Brod, Czechoslovakia. Theoretical Physicist; Cyberneticist. 1 daughter. Education: RNDr, Charles University, Prague, Czechoslovakia, 1957-62. Appointments: Lecturer, 1964-65, Senior Lecturer, 1965-69, Department of Theoretical Physics, Charles University, Prague; Research Fellow, Department of Physics, University of Warwick, England, 1969-71; Senior Research Associate, School of Mathematics and Physics, University of East Anglia, England, 1971-74; Research Fellow, Physics Department, University of Leeds, England, 1976-77. Publications: Numerous articles in professional scientific journals. Honours: Listed in national and international biographical dictionaries. Memberships: American Physical Society; Institute of Physics, London; European Physical Society; Institute of Mathematics and its Applications, UK; New York Academy of Sciences; British Cybernetic Society; Czechoslovak Mathematics and Physics Society; International Association of San Marino; TAKIS. Address: 5 Beckhill Chase, Leeds 7, LS7 2RQ, England. E-mail: jiri.slechta@hotmail.com

**SLEEP Wayne,** b. 17 July 1948, Plymouth, England. Dancer; Actor; Choreographer. Education: Royal Ballet School (Leverhulme Scholar). Appointments: Joined Royal Ballet, 1966; Soloist, 1970; Principal, 1973; Roles in: Giselle; Dancers at a Gathering; The Nutcracker; Romeo and Juliet; The Grand Tour; Elite Syncopations; Swan Lake; The Four Seasons; Les Patineurs; Petroushka (title role); Cinderella; The Dream; Pineapple Poll; Mam'zelle Angot; 4th Symphony; La Fille Mal Gardee; A Month in the Country; A Good Night's Sleep; Coppelia; Also roles in operas: A Midsummer Nights Dream; Aida; Theatre Roles: Ariel in the Tempest; title role in Pinocchio; Genie in Aladdin; Soldier in The Soldiers Tale; Truffaldino in the Servant of Two Masters; Mr Mistoffelees in Cats; Choreography and lead role, The Point; co-starred in Song and Dance, 1982, 1990; Cabaret, 1986; formed own company, DASH, 1980; Dancer and Joint Choreographer, Bits and Pieces, 1989; Film: The Virgin Soldiers; The First Great Train Robbery; The Tales of Beatrix Potter; Numerous TV appearances include: Series, The Hot Summer Show, 1983, 1984. Publications: Variations on Wayne Sleep, 1983; Precious Little Sleep, 1996. Honours: Show Business Personality of the Year, 1983. Address: c/o Nick Thomas Artists, Event House, Queen Margaret's Road, Scarborough, YO11 2SA, England.

**SLOAM Nigel Spencer,** b. 17 December 1950, London, England. Actuary. m. Elizabeth, 1 son, 1 daughter. Education: MA, Corpus Christi College, Oxford; Fellow, Institute of Actuaries (FIA); Chartered Mathematician (C Math); Associate of the Society of Actuaries (ASA). Appointments: Trainee Actuary, Messrs Bacon & Woodrow, 1972-76; Actuary, Sahar Insurance Co of Israel, 1976-77; Manager, Actuarial Department, Charterhouse Magna Insurance Co, 1977-78; Director, Messrs Bevington Lowndes Ltd, 1978-79; Senior Partner, Nigel Sloam & Co, 1979-. Publications: Numerous articles on small self administered pension schemes; on retirement provisions for entrepreneurs and on employment provision without liability. Honours: Chairman, Association of Consulting Actuaries, SSAS Committee; Pensioneer Trustee. Memberships: Institute of Actuaries; Association of Consulting Actuaries; Association of Pensioneer Trustees; Institute of Mathematics and its Applications; Worshipful Company of Actuaries; The Maccabaeans. Address: Roman House, 296 Golders Green Road, London NW11 9PY, England. E-mail: nigel@nigelsloam.co.uk

**SLOANE J P,** b. 1942, Hollywood, California, USA. Biblical Scholar; Lecturer; Author. Education: Certificate in TU Production, Purdue University, 1981; Graduate of Oral

Roberts Institute of Charismatic Studies, Tulsa, Oklahoma, 1985; Institute of Jewish-Christian Studies, Dallas, Texas, 1992; Moody Blue Institute, Chicago, Illinois, 1998; IBEX Campus, Abu Gosh, Israel, 2001; Graduate, BA, Summa Cum Laude, 2003, Master in Nouthetic Counseling, The Masters College, Los Angeles, California; Doctorate of Theology, Trinity Theology Seminary, in progress; Studied: Religions of the Middle East, Jewish Thought and Culture, Physical Geography of Israel and Archeology. Appointments: In addition to lectures around the USA, Christian TV appearances include The PTL Club; Lester Sumrall Today; Richard Roberts Live; The 700 Club; LeSea Broadcasting's World Harvest and Trinity Broadcasting's Praise The Lord. Publications: Author of children's series: Awesome Animal Adventures; Kingdom of the Butterflies; Do Our Pets Go To Heaven and Do Animals Go To Heaven? Contributor to Focus on the Family's; Adventures in Odyssey; Alexander Scourby's Dramatized Version of the Bible; Word, Inc; Co-author (with daughter), Yes – You Can Be A Virgin Again!, 2005. Honours: Featured in the 1998-99, 1999-2000 publications of The National Dean's List, representing only the top ½ of 1% of the United States college students; The National Scholars Honor Society (Life), 2005; Appeared in the Smithsonian and Who's Who in the World, Millennium edition, also current editions of Who's Who in the World and Who's Who in America, Providence, New Jersey; Dictionary of International Biography, Cambridge, England; recipient of three international Angel awards; Medal of Merit, President Ronald Reagan; Keys to the Cities of New Orleans, Louisiana; Nashville, Tennessee; Monticello, Indiana. Governor's Commendation and appointment as Honorary Lieutenant Governor for the State of Indiana; Honorary Kentucky Colonel; Honorary Colonel and Aide-de-Camp of Governor Treen and Governor Edwards and, State of Louisiana; Honorary Sheriff of Los Angeles County. Address: Ste 407, 2219 East Thousand Oaks Blvd, Thousand Oaks, CA 91362-2930, USA. Website: www.jpsloane.com

**SMALLWOOD John Frank Monton**, b. 12 April 1926. Church Commissioner. m. Jean Margaret Lovell, 1 son, 2 daughters. Education: City of London School; MA, Classics, Peterhouse, Cambridge, 1951. Appointments: Japanese translation and interrogation, RAF, 1944-48; Private Secretary to Governors, 1959-62, Adviser, 1967, Auditor, 1969, Deputy Chief Accountant, 1974-79, Bank of England; Member, Church Assembly/General Synod, 1965-2000 (Standing Committee, 1971-96); Numerous ad hoc committees, etc over years including: Working Party on State Aid for Churches in use, 1971-96; Central Board of Finance, 1965-98 (Deputy Vice Chairman, 1972-82); Pensions Board, 1985-96; Anglican Consultative Council, 1975-87 (Trinidad, 1976, Lambeth Conference, 1978, Canada, 1979, Newcastle, 1981, Singapore, 1987); Trustee: City Parochial Foundation, 1969-99 (Vice Chairman, 1977-81; Chairman, 1981-92); Trust for London, 1986-99 (Chairman, 1986-92); Overseas Bishoprics Foundation, 1977-99 (Chairman, 1992-99); Lambeth Palace Library, 1978-98. Memberships: Southwark Diocesan Board of Finance, 1962-2000 (Chairman, 1975-2000); Southwark Ordination Course Council, 1960-74 and 1980-94 (Vice Chairman, 1980-94); Corporation of Church House Council, 1986-96; Churches' Main Committee, 1987-96; BCC, 1987-90; Lee Abbey Council, 1969-74; Lay Reader, 1983-. Address: The Willows, Parkgate Road, Newdigate, Dorking, Surrey RH5 5AH, England.

**SMELLIE Jean McIldowie**, b. 14 May 1927, Liverpool, England. Paediatrician. m. Ian Colin Stuart Normand, 1 son, 2 daughters. Education: Huyton College, Liverpool; St Hugh's College, Oxford; University College Hospital, London; Degrees and Diplomas: BA Hons Physiology Oxon, 1947; BM Oxon, 1950; DCH England, 1953; MRCP London, 1954; MA Oxon,

1957; FRCP London, 1975; DM Oxon, 1981. Appointments include: House appointments, 1951-54; Paediatric Registrar, 1955-56, Paediatric First Assistant, 1956-60, University College Hospital, London; Lecturer, Infant Nutrition and Dietetics, Queen Elizabeth College, University of London, 1957-60; Lecturer, Paediatrics, Nuffield Department of Medicine, Oxford, 1960-61; Fellow in Pathology, Johns Hopkins Hospital, Baltimore, USA, 1964-65; Locum Consultant Paediatrician, 1961-63 and 1968-69, Honorary Consultant Paediatrician (part-time), 1970-93, University College Hospital, London; Part-time appointments: Senior Lecturer, Paediatrics, Department of Clinical Sciences, University College, London, 1976-93; Senior Clinical Medical Officer, Southampton and SW Hampshire District, 1977-92; Honorary Senior Clinical Lecturer, University of Southampton, 1987-93; Honorary Consultant Paediatric Nephrologist, Guy's Hospital, London, 1984-93, Honorary Consultant Paediatric Nephrologist, Hospital for Sick Children, Great Ormond Street, London, 1984-; Emeritus Consultant Paediatrician, University College Hospitals, 1993-; Scientific Adviser, International Reflux Study in Children (Europe and USA), 1974-; Member, Medical Advisory Committee, Sir Jules Thorn Charitable Trust, 1987-97. Publications: More than 120 original articles, approximately 56 in peer reviewed journals, on urinary tract infections, vesico-ureteric reflux, renal scarring, neonatal, general and metabolic paediatric conditions; 16-18 book chapters. Honours: Open Scholarship, St Hugh's College, Oxford, 1944-48; Honorary Member: European Society for Paediatric Urology, 1993; British Paediatric Association, 1995; British Association for Paediatric Nephrology, 1995; American Urological Association, 1998; Honorary Fellow, Royal College of Paediatrics and Child Health, 1996. Memberships: European Society of Paediatric Nephrology; Renal Association; International Paediatric Nephrology Association; Founder Member: British Association for Paediatric Nephrology; Neonatal Society. Address: 23 St Thomas Street, Winchester, Hampshire S023 9HJ, England.

**SMENDZIANKA Regina**, b. 9 October 1924, Toruń, Poland. Pianist; Teacher. Education: MA, (Diploma with Highest Distinction) Academy of Music in Cracow, Poland, 1948. Appointments: Concert-pianist debut with Cracow Philharmonic Orchestra, 1947; Numerous concert tours in Poland and 33 countries of Europe, Asia and the Americas as recitalist and as soloist with orchestras, 1947-; Numerous gramophone records in Poland, Japan, Holland, Italy, Germany; Numerous radio and TV records, films in Poland and abroad; Large repertoire from 16th century to contemporary music; Teacher, Cracow Academy of Music, 1964; Assistant Professor, 1967; Rector, 1972, 1973; Head of Chair of Piano, 1972-96, Professor, 1977-96, Honorary Member of Chair of Piano, 1996-, Honorary Professor, 1997-, Doctor honoris causa, 2002, F Chopin Academy of Music, Warsaw; Numerous courses of interpretation, lectures and concert lectures in Poland, Denmark, Germany, Finland, Japan, France, Venezuela and Mexico; Member of Piano Competition Juries in Poland, Japan, Russia, Finland, Germany, Italy and Sweden. Publications: Editor, music publications and records; Articles on music in Poland, USA and Japan; Papers on scientific issues of Warsaw F Chopin Academy of Music; Introductions and articles to concert-programmes; Book, How to Play Chopin – an attempt to answer, 2000. Honours include: Prize winner, IV International F Chopin Competition, Warsaw, 1949; Composers Association Medal, 1971; Badge of Merit Culture Worker, 1971 Minister of Culture Prizes, 1955, 1959, 1965, 1977, 1987, 1994; Chevalier Cross, 1959, Officer Cross, 1964, Commander Cross with Star, 2004, Polonia Restituta Order; Primate Gold Medal: Ecclesiae Populoque Servitium Praestanti, 2005; Tadj Order, Shah of Iran, 1968, Banner of the Labour Order II class, 1975, I class, 1985; Aguilla de Tlatelolco Medal of the Foreign Affaires

Minister of Mexico, 1978; Minister of Culture Team Prize, 1979; Excellentia International Order of Merit, IBC Cambridge, 1990; Listed in numerous Who's Who publications and biographical dictionaries. Memberships include: F Chopin Society, Warsaw, 1947-; Polish Musicians Association (SPAM), 1958-; Member Correspondent, Mexico Institute of Culture, 1978-; Iberian Culture Society, Warsaw, 1978-; President of own Foundation (Regina Smendzianka Foundation) in support of Polish music culture and young Polish pianists, 1988-; Honorary Vice-President of EPTA Society (Polish section of European Pianist Teachers Association in London), 1991; Honorary Friend of PTNA (Piano Teachers National Association of Japan), 1999-. Address: 02-529 Warszawa, Narbutta 76/10, Poland.

**SMETANA Karel,** b. 28 October 1930, Prague, Czech Republic. Physician; Scientist. m. Vlasta Smetanova, 24 October 1953, 1 son. Education: MUDr (MD), Charles University, Prague, Czech Republic, 1955; CSc, (PhD), 1962; DrSc (DSc), 1967. Appointments: Lecturer, Dept of Histology, Charles University, Prague, 1955-62; Scientific Officer, Head, Senior Scientific Officer, Department of Blood Cytology, Laboratory of Ultrastruct Research, Czechoslovak Academy of Science, 1962-84; Research Fellow, Department of Pharmacology, Baylor College of Medicine, Houston, Texas, USA, 1962; Visiting Associate Professor, 1963; Professor, 1970; Director, Institute of Hematology and Blood Transfusion, Prague, 1984-90; Senior Scientific Officer, 1990-, Head of Laboratory, Cytology and Electron Microscopy, 1990-2000; Head, Chair of Hematology and Transfusion Service, 1985-93; Lecturer, Hematology and Transfusion Service, Institute of Postgraduate Medical Study, Prague, 1993-; Chairman, Board of Postgraduate Scientific Studies in Cell Biology and Pathology, Charles University, Prague, 1994-. Publications: 270 articles on cell nucleus, nucleolus, malignant cells; 1 monograph with H Busch, The nucleolus; 6 Monographic Chapters in various science monographs; Chapters in 7 textbooks. Honours: State Prize; Scientific Prize, Minister of Health; State Purkynje Medal; Purkynje Medal; Honorary Medals; Wilhelm Bernhard's Medal; Honorary Membership, Czech Hematological Society, Czech and Slovak Biological Society; Czech Histochemical Society; Science Prize; Many others. Memberships: Czech Histochemical Society; Czech Hematological Society; Czech Histochemical Society; Austrian Hematological Society; Society of Clinical Cytology; New York Academy of Sciences. Address: Prague 4, Puchovska 2, Czech Republic 141 00.

**SMIRNOVA Alfia,** b. 10 June 1951, Russia. Philologist. m. V Smirnov, 1 daughter. Education: Graduate,1976, Postgraduate Course, Candidate of Philological Science, Russian Literature of the XXth Century, PhD, Russian Literature of the XXth Century, 1991-94, Philological Department, State University of Bashkiria. Appointments: Head of Literature Sub-Faculty, Head of Philological Department, Professor, Chief Editor of scientific magazine "Vestnik", series of philological journalism, Volgograd State University, 1981-2004; Author and Presenter of TV programme about literature, 1990-2000; Currently, Professor, Moscow State Pedagogical University. Publications: Monograph, Nature isn't what you mean. Russian philosophical nature prose of 1960-1980; 120 articles in scientific magazines, books and conference proceedings. Honours: Certificate, Ministry of Education, Russian Federation, 2000; Silver Medal, Volgograd State University, 2001; Included in the book of Successful Professional Women, 2003. Memberships: PhD Board, Council of Volgograd State University; Member of Candidate Degree Board on Russian Literature, Astrakhan University. Address: Sergeya Makeeva 1-151, 123100 Moscow, Russia. E-mail: igor.sheim@g23.relcom.ru

**SMITH Andrew Benjamin,** b. 6 February 1954, Dunoon, Scotland. Palaeontologist. m. Mary Patricia Cumming Simpson, 2 daughters. Education: BSc, Geology, 1st Class Honours, University of Edinburgh, 1976; PhD, Biological Sciences, University of Exeter, 1979; DSc, University of Edinburgh, 1989. Appointments: Lecturer, Department of Geology, University of Liverpool, 1981-82; Research Scientist, Department of Palaeontology, The Natural History Museum, London, 1982-. Publications: More than 200 monographs and scientific papers. Honours: Linnean Society Bicentenial Medal, 1993; Geological Society Bigsby Medal, 1995; Geological Society Lyell Medal, 2002; Elected Fellow of the Royal Society of Edinburgh, 1996; Elected Fellow of the Royal Society, 2002; Linnean Medal for Zoology, 2005. Memberships: Fellow of the Linnean Society; Fellow of the Geological Society; Fellow of the Royal Society of Edinburgh; Fellow of the Royal Society. Address: Department of Palaeontology, The Natural History Museum, Cromwell Road, London SW7 5BD, England. E-mail: a.smith@nhm.ac.uk

**SMITH C Philip,** b. 10 June 1928, Southport, Lancashire, England. Book Artist; Binder; Inventor; Author. m. Dorothy Mary Weighill, 3 sons. Education: Southport School of Art, 1949-51; Royal College of Art, London, (Roger Powell), 1951-54, ARCA (1st Class), 1954. Career: MDE (Meister der Einbandkunst), 1970; Fellow, Designer Bookbinders, President, 1977-79; Editor, The New Bookbinder, 1980-95; Teacher of Drawing, Modelling (sculpture), Bookbinding at Malvern School of Art, 1955-57; Assistant to Sydney Cockerell (Bookbinder), 1957-61; Own studio, 1961-; British Museum team for Florence Flood Disaster, 1966-67; Bindings in many public and private collections world-wide include: Victoria and Albert Museum, British Library, Royal Collection, Royal Library, Holland, New York Public Library, HRHRC, Texas; 150 book arts exhibitions, several painting exhibitions include: John Moores, RBA. Publications: The Lord of the Rings and Other Bookbindings of Philip Smith, 1970; New Directions in Bookbinding, 1974; The Book: Art & Object, 1982; A Book Art: Concept & Making in preparation; Numerous articles, reviews, exhibition catalogues internationally. Honours: Gold Medal, 2nd International Biennale, Sao Paulo, 1972; Presidium of Honour, Czechoslovakia, 1989; Silver Medal, Paris International Bookbinding Art, 1992; Gold Medal EEC Bookbinding Prize, 1993; Patents for Maril, 1971; Lap-Back Book- structure, UK and USA, 1994; MBE for Services to Art, 2000; Silver Medal, International Exhibition of Books as Art, Italy, 2000, 2002. Memberships: Designer Bookbinders; Meister der Einbandkunst, Germany; Canada of B and B Artists Guild (CBBAG); Society of Bookbinders, UK; Center for Book Arts, New York. Address: The Book House, Yatton Keynell, Chippenham, Wiltshire SN14 7BH, England.

**SMITH Chris(topher) Robert (Rt Hon) (Lord Smith of Finsbury),** b. 24 July 1951. Politician. Education: Pembroke College, Cambridge; Harvard University (Kennedy Scholar 1975-76). Appointments: Development Secretary, Shaftesbury Society Housing Association, 1977-80; Development Co-ordinator, Society for Co-operative Dwellings, 1980-83; Councillor, London Borough of Islington, 1978-83; Chief Whip, 1978-79; Chair, Housing Committee, 1981-83; Labour, MP for Islington South and Finsbury, 1983-2005; Opposition Spokesman on Treasury and Economic Affairs, 1987-92; Principal Opposition Spokesman on Environmental Protection, 1992-94; National Heritage, 1994-95; Social Security, 1995-96; Health, 1996-97; Secretary of State for Culture, Media and Sport, 1997-2001; Chairman, Millennium Commission, 1997-2001; Created Life Peer, 2005; Member, Committee on Standards in Public Life, 2001-05; Chairman, Classic FM Consumer Panel, 2001-; Senior Adviser to The Walt Disney Company

Ltd on UK film and television work; Visiting Professor in Culture and Creative Industries, University of the Arts, London, 2002-; Member of Board of Royal National Theatre; Chairman, Donmar Warehouse; Chairman of Wordsworth Trust; Member of Advisory Council of London Symphony Orchestra; Senior Associate of Judge Institute in Management Studies, Cambridge University; Honorary Fellow, Pembroke College, Cambridge; Director of Clore Leadership Programme, 2003-; Chairman of Judges, Man Booker Prize, 2004; Chair, London Cultural Consortium, 2004-; Formerly: Chair, Labour Campaign for Criminal Justice, 1985-88; Tribune Group of MP's, 1988-89; President, Socialist Environmental and Resources Association, 1992-; Member, Executive of the Fabian Society, 1990-97 (Chair, 1996-97); Member of the Board of Shelter, 1986-92; Has held positions in several other organisations. Publication: Creative Britain, 1998. Address: House of Lords, London, SW1A 0PW, England.

**SMITH David John,** b. 10 October 1948, Melbourne, Australia. Physicist; Educator. m. Gwenneth Bland, 1971, divorced 1992, 2 daughters. Education: BSc, Honours, University Melbourne, 1970; PhD, University Melbourne, 1978; DSc, University Melbourne, 1988. Appointments: Postdoctoral Scholar, University Cambridge, England, 1976-78; Senior Research Associate, 1979-84; Associate Professor, 1984-87, Arizona State University; Professor, 1987-, Regents' Professor, 2000-. Publications: Author, 15 book chapters, 400 professional journal articles; Editor, 15 conference proceedings. Honours: Fellow, Institute of Physics, England, 1981; Charles Vernon Boys Prize, Institute Physics, England, 1985; Faculty Achievement Award, Burlington Resources Foundation, 1990; Director, Cambridge University High Resolution Electron Microscope, 1979-84; NSF Center for High Resolution Electron Microscopy, 1991-96; ASU Centre for High Resolution Electron Microscopy, 1996-; Director, Center for Solid State Science, Arizona State University, 2001-2004; Fellow, American Physical Society, 2002. Memberships: American Physical Society; Microscopy Society of America; Material Research Society; Institute of Physics, UK. Address: Department of Physics and Astronomy, Arizona State University, Tempe, AZ 85287-1504, USA.

**SMITH David Lawrence,** b. 3 December 1963, London, England. Historian. Education: Eastbourne College, 1972-81; BA 1st Class Hons, 1985, MA, 1989, PhD, 1990, Selwyn College, Cambridge. Appointments: Fellow, 1988-, Director of Studies in History, 1992-, Admissions Tutor, 1992-2003, Praelector, 1996-, Tutor for Advanced Students, 2004-, Selwyn College, Cambridge; Affiliated Lecturer in History, 1995-, University of Cambridge; Visiting Assistant Professor, University of Chicago, 1991; Visiting Professor, Kyungpook National University, South Korea, 2004. Publications: Books: Oliver Cromwell, 1991; Louis XIV, 1992; Constitutional Royalism and the Search for Settlement, 1994; The Theatrical City (with R Strier and D Bevington), 1995; A History of the Modern British Isles, 1603-1707: The Double Crown, 1998; The Stuart Parliaments, 1603-1689, 1999; The Early Stuart Kings (with G Seel), 2001; Crown and Parliaments (with G Seel), 2001; Cromwell and the Interregnum (editor), 2003; Contributions to Oxford Dictionary of National Biography, 2004, also contributions to academic journals. Honours: Alexander Prize, Royal Historical Society, 1991; Thirlwall Prize, University of Cambridge, 1991. Membership: Fellow, Royal Historical Society, 1992; President, Cambridge History Forum, 1997-. Address: Selwyn College, Cambridge CB3 9DQ, England. E-mail: dls10@cam.ac.uk

**SMITH Delia,** b. 18 June 1941. m. Michael Wynn Jones. Cookery Writer; Broadcaster. m. Michael Wynn Jones. Appointments: Several BBC TV Series; Cookery Writer,

Evening Standard, (later Standard), 1972-85; Columnist, Radio Times; Director, Norwich City Football Club; Canary Catering. Publications: How to Cheat at Cooking, 1971; Country Fare, 1973; Recipes From Country Inns and Restaurants, 1973; Family Fare, book 1, 1973, book 2, 1974; Evening Standard Cook Book, 1974; Country Recipes From "Look East", 1975; More Country Recipes From "Look East", 1976; Frugal Food, 1976; Book of Cakes, 1977; Recipes From "Look East", 1977; Food For Our Times, 1978; Cookery Course, part 1, 1978, part 2, 1979, part 3, 1981; The Complete Cookery Course, 1982; A Feast For Lent, 1983; A Feast For Advent, 1983; One is Fun, 1985. Editor: Food Aid Cookery Book, 1986, A Journey into God, 1988, Delia Smith's Christmas, 1990, Delia Smith's Summer Collection, 1993; Delia Smith's Winter Collection, 1995; Delia's Red Nose Collection, Comic Relief, 1997; How to Cook, Book 1, 1998; How to Cook Book 2, 1999; How to Cook Book 3, 2001; Delia's Chocolate Collection, Comic Relief, 2001; Delia's Vegetarian Collection, 2002; The Delia Collection: Soup, Chicken, Chocolate, Fish, 2003; Italian, Pork, 2004. Honours: OBE, 1995; Honorary Degree, Nottingham University, 1996; Fellowship, Royal TV Society, 1996; Honorary Degree, UEA, 1999; Honorary Fellow, Liverpool John Moores, 2000. Address: c/o Deborah Owen Ltd, 78 Narrow Street, London E14 8BP, England.

**SMITH Donald Frederick,** b. 30 January 1945, Chicago, Illinois, USA. m. Helle B Smith, 2 sons. Education: BSc, Psychology, Duke University, Durham, North Carolina, 1967; MA, Physiology and Psychology, McMaster University, Hamilton, Ontario, Canada, 1968; PhD, Biopsychology, Pritzker School of Medicine, University of Chicago, Illinois, 1971; Dr.med, University of Copenhagen, Denmark, 1980. Appointments include: Research Assistant, Division of Behavioral Sciences, Department of Psychology, University of Chicago, 1968-71; Senior Lecturer, Health Psychology and Psychobiology, University of East London, Department of Psychology, 1992-93; Consultant, Health Psychology, Committee on Social Health Services, Aarhus Municipality; Psychotherapist, Clinic for Applied Psychology, Private Practice, Arhus, 1986-; Senior Scientist, Institute for Basic Research in Psychiatry, Department of Biological Psychiatry and PET Centre of Aarhus University Hospital, Denmark. Publications include: Monoaminergic mechanisms in stress-induced analgesia, 1982; Stereoselective effects of tranylcypromine enantiomers on brain serotonin, 1982; Lithium and carbamazepine: Effects on locomotion of planaria, 1983; Role of 5-HT and NA in spinal dopaminergic analgesia, 1983; Handbook of Stereoisomers: Drugs in Psychopharmacology, 1984; Handbook of Stereoisomers: Therapeutic Drugs, 1989; PET neuroimaging of clomipramine challenge in humans: focus on the thalmus, Brain Research, 2001. Memberships: Several societies and associations. Address: Psychiatric Hospital, Aarhus University, Skovagervej 2, 8240 Risskov, Denmark.

**SMITH Hamilton Othanel,** b. 23 August 1931, New York, New York, USA. Microbiologist. m. Elizabeth Anne Bolton, 1957, 4 sons, 1 daughter. Education: Graduated, Mathematics, University of California at Berkeley, 1952; MD, Johns Hopkins University, 1956. Appointments: Junior Resident Physician, Barnes Hospital, 1956-57; Lieutenant, USNR, Senior Medical Officer, 1957-59; Resident, Henry Ford Hospital, Detroit, 1959-62; Postdoctoral Fellow, Department of Human Genetics, 1962-64, Research Associate, 1964-67, University of Michigan; Assistant Professor, 1967-69, Associate Professor, 1969-73, Professor of Microbiology, 1973-81, Professor of Molecular Biology and Genetics, 1981-, Johns Hopkins University; Sabbatical year with Institut fur Molekular-Biologie, Zurich University, 1975-76. Honour: Guggenheim Fellow, 1975-76;

Joint Winner, Nobel Prize for Physiology or Medicine, 1978. Memberships: NAS; AAAS. Address: Department of Molecular Biology, Johns Hopkins University School of Medicine, 720 Rutland Avenue, Baltimore, MD 21205, USA.

**SMITH Ivor Ramsey,** b. 8 October 1929, Birmingham, England. University Professor. m. Pamela Mary. Education: BSc, 1954, PhD, 1957, DSc, 1973, University of Bristol. Appointments: Design & Development Engineer, GEC, Witton, Birmingham, 1956-59; Lecturer, Senior Lecturer, Reader, Birmingham University, 1959-74; Professor of Electrical Engineering, 1974-, Head of Department of Electronic & Electrical Engineering, 1980-90, Dean of Engineering, 1983-86, Pro-Vice Chancellor, 1987-91, Loughborough University. Publications: 350 articles in learned society journals and at international conference proceedings in his field. Memberships: Fellow, Institution of Electrical Engineers; Fellow, Royal Academy of Engineering. Address: Department of Electronic & Electrical Engineering, Loughborough University, Loughborough, Leicestershire, LE11 3TU, England. E-mail: i.r.smith@lboro.ac.uk

**SMITH Jacqueline Mitchell,** b. 7 July 1930, Reading, Pennsylvania, USA. Artist. m. Calvin E Smith, 2 sons, 1 daughter. Education: Pennsylvania State University, 1951-52; Art League of Alexandria, Virginia, 1970's-; Bachelor of Arts, Albright College, 1971; Master of Education, Temple University, 1976; Master of Education in Spanish, Millersville University, 1989. Career: Commissioned to paint local historical scenes, seascapes and figurative works, 1950's-; Works exhibited at William Ris Galleries, Stone Harbor, New Jersey, 1993-2004; Numerous exhibitions include most recently: Miniature Art Society of Florida, St Petersburg, Florida, 2005; Berks Art Alliance Juried Art Exhibition, Reading Museum, Pennsylvania, 2002-2004; The Hilliard Society, Wells, Somerset, England, 2003, 2004; The Royal Miniature Society, Westminster Gallery, London, England, 2003; The MPSGS of Washington DC, 1998-2004; Philadelphia Watercolour Society Exhibit, The Hill School, Pottstown, Pennsylvania, 2004; Phoebe Berks Village, Wernersville, Pennsylvania (one-woman show), 2004; World Federation of Miniaturists, Smithsonian, Washington, DC, 2004; SAMAP-FRANCE International Exhibition, Chateau de Bernicourt, France, 2004; Cider Painters of America, Dallas, Pennsylvania, 2004. Publications: Articles about her works include: Berks In Focus, 1977; The Reading Eagle, 1979; The Butler Eagle, 1999; The Derrick, Venango Newspaper, 1999. Honours: Honourable Mention Doylestown Art League Exhibition, 1999; Second Place in Portraiture Award, The Miniature Painters, Sculptors and Gravers Society of Washington, DC Exhibition, 2003; Best New Exhibitor Award, The Hilliard Society Exhibition, Somerset, England, 2003. Memberships: Miniature Painters, Sculptors and Gravers Society of Washington, DC; World Federation of Miniaturists; Cider Painters of America; Doylestown Art League; Berks Art Alliance; The Hilliard Society. Address: 113 East Penn Avenue, Wernersville, PA 19565-1611, USA. E-mail: jmsces@comcat.com

**SMITH James Cuthbert,** b. 31 December 1954, London, England. m. 3 children. Chairman; Professor. Education: First Class honours degree, Natural Sciences (Zoology), Christ's College, Cambridge, England, 1976; PhD, London University, 1979. Appointments: NATO Postdoctoral Fellow, Sidney Farber Cancer Institute and Harvard Medical School, 1979-1981; ICRF Postdoctoral Fellow, 1981-1984; National Institute for Medical Research, 1984-1990; Head, Laboratory of Developmental Biology, 1991, Head Genes and Cellular Controls Group, 1996, NIMR; Member of Zoology Department, Senior Group Leader and Chairman-designate, Wellcome/CRC Institute, Cambridge,

2000; Fellow, Christ's College, Cambridge, 2001; Chairman, Wellcome Trust/Cancer Research UK Institute, Cambridge, 2001-; Humphrey Plummer Professor of Developmental Biology, University of Cambridge, 2001-. Publications: Numerous co-authored papers and articles to professional journals. Honours: Zoological Society's Scientific Medal, 1989; Otto Mangold Prize, German Society for Developmental Biology, 1991; Wellcome Visiting Professor, Basic Medical Sciences, 1991-1992; Elected member, European Molecular Biology Organisation, 1992; Howard Hughes Medical Institute International Research Scholar, 1993-98; Elected Fellow, Royal Society, 1993; EMBO Medal, 1993; Honorary Senior Research Fellow, Department of Anatomy and Developmental Biology, University College, London, 1994; Jenkinson Lecture, Oxford University, 1997; Marshal R Urist Lecture and Award, 1997; Elected Fellow, Institute of Biology, 1997; Visiting Professor, Queen Mary and Westfield College, University of London, 1997-; Founder Fellow, Academy of Medical Sciences, 1998; Feldberg Foundation Award, 2000; Member, Academia Europaea, 2000; William Bate Hardy Prize, 2001. Memberships: Numerous committees including: HFSPO Review Committee – Molecular Approaches, 1997-2000; Council, Royal Society, 1997-1999; Council, Academy of Medical Sciences; 1998-2001. Address: Wellcome Trust/Cancer Research UK Institute of Cancer and Developmental Biology, University of Cambridge, Tennis Court Road, Cambridge CB2 1QR, England.

**SMITH Kenneth George Valentine,** b. 11 March 1929, Birmingham, England. Retired Entomologist. m. Alma Vera Thompson, 2 sons. Education: Birmingham Central College of Technology, 1945-47; University of Keele, 1952-54. Appointments: Field Assistant Entomologist, Ministry of Agriculture, Fisheries and Food, 1950-52; Senior Technician, Hope Department of Entomology, Oxford University, 1954-62; Principal Scientific Officer, British Museum (Natural History), 1962-89; Editor in Chief, Entomologist's Monthly Magazine, 1982-. Publications: Over 300 papers on entomology in scientific journals including books: Empididae of South Africa, 1969; Insects and Other Arthropods of Medical Importance, 1973; A Bibliography of the Entomology of the Smaller British Offshore Islands, 1983; Manual of Forensic Entomology, 1986; Darwin's Insects, 1987; An Introduction to the Immature Stages of British Flies, 1989. Memberships: Chartered Biologist; C Biol; F I Biol; FRES; FLS. Address: 31 Calais Dene, Bampton, Oxfordshire OX18 2NR, England.

**SMITH Maggie Natalie (Dame),** b. 28 December 1934, Ilford, Essex, England. Actress. m. (1) Robert Stephens, 1967, divorced 1975, deceased 1995, 2 sons, (2) Beverley Cross, 1975, deceased 1998. Career: Theatre appearances include: With Old Vic Company, 1959-60; Rhinoceros, 1960; The Private Ear and the Public Eye, 1962; With the National Theatre played in The Recruiting Officer, 1963; Othello, 1964; Much Ado About Nothing 1965; The Beaux' Stratagem, 1970; Private Lives, 1972; 1976, 1977, 1978, 1980 seasons, Stratford Ontario Canada; Lettice and Lovage, London, 1987, New York, 1990; The Importance of Being Earnest, 1993; Three Tall Women, 1994-95; Talking Heads, 1996; The Lady in the Van, 1999; Films include: The VIP's 1963; The Pumpkin Eater, 1964; Young Cassidy, 1965; Othello, 19666; The Honey Pot, 1967; Hot Millions, 1968; The Prime of Miss Jean Brodie, 1969; Travels with My Aunt, 1972; Love and Pain and the Whole Damn Thing, 1973; Murder by Death, 1975; Death on the Nile, 1978; California Suite, 1978; Quartet, 1980; Clash of the Titans, 1981; Evil Under the Sun, 1982; The Missionary, 1982; A Private Function, 1984; A Room with a View, 1986; The Lonely Passion of Judith Hearn, 1987; Hook, 1991; The Secret Garden, 1993; Richard III, 1995; First Wives Club, 1996; Washington Square,

1998; Tea with Mussolini, 1999; The Last September, 2000; Harry Potter and the Philosopher's Stone, 2001; Gosford Park, 2002; Harry Potter and the Chamber of Secrets, 2002; Harry Potter and the Prisoner of Azkaban, 2004. Honours include: Honorary D Lit, St Andrew's and Leicester Universities, 1982, Cambridge, 1993; Evening Standard Best Actress Award, 1962, 1970, 1982, 1985, 1994; Best Actress Award, Film Critics' Guild, USA, 1969; BAFTA Award, Best Actress,1984, 1987, 1989; BAFTA Award for Lifetime Achievement, 1992; Tony Award, 1990. Address: c/o Write on Cue, 29 Whitcomb Street, London, WC2H 7EP, England.

**SMITH Stanley Desmond,** b. 3 March 1931, Bristol, England. Physicist. m. Gillian Anne Parish, 1 son, 1 daughter. Education: BSc, Physics Department, University of Bristol, 1949-52, PhD, Physics Department, University of Reading, 1952-56; DSc, University of Bristol, 1966. Appointments: Senior Scientific Officer, Royal Aircraft Establishment, Farnborough, 1956-58; Research Assistant, Department of Meteorology, Imperial College, 1958-59; Research Assistant, Lecturer, Reader, Physics Department, University of Reading, 1959-70; Professor of Physics, Head of Department, Dean of Science Faculty, Heriot-Watt University, Edinburgh, 1970-96; Chairman and Chief Executive Officer, Edinburgh Instruments Ltd, 1996-(previously part-time Chairman and Founder, Director, 1971-). Publications: Books: Infrared physics, 1966; Optoelectronic Devices, 1995; Some 215 scientific papers and review articles on semiconductors, IR spectroscopy, interference filters, tunable lasers, optical computing, satellite meteorology; Chairman, Scottish Optoelectronics Association, 1996-98. Honours: C V Boys Prize, Institute of Physics, 1976; EPIC Award (Education in Partnership with Industry or Commerce) 1st Prize, 1982; TOBIE Award (Technical or Business Innovation in Electronics), Department of Trade and Industry, 1986; James Scott Prize, Royal Society of Edinburgh, 1987; OBE, 1998; Hon DSc, Heriot-Watt University, 2003. Memberships: Fellow, Royal Society of Edinburgh, 1973; Fellow, Royal Society, 1976; Fellow, Institute of Physics, 1976; Advisory Council on Science and Technology, Cabinet Office, 1985-88; Defence Scientific Advisory Council, 1985-91. Address: Treetops, 29D Gillespie Road, Edinburgh EH13 0NW, Scotland. E-mail: des.smith@edinst.com

**SMITH Troy Alvin,** b. 4 July 1922, Sylvatus, Virginia. Aerospace Research Engineer. m. Grace Marie (Peacock) Dees, 24 November 1990. Education: BCE degree, University of Virginia, 1948; MSE degree, University of Michigan, 1952; PhD degree, University of Michigan, 1970; Registered Professional Engineer, Virginia, Alabama. Appointments: US Navy Reserve, Pacific Theatre of Operations, 1942-46; Structural Engineer, Corps of Engineers, US Army, 1948-59; Chief Structural Engineer, Brown Engineering Company Inc, Huntsville, Alabama, 1959-60; Structural Research Engineer, US Army Missile Command, Redstone Arsenal, Alabama, 1960-63; Aerospace Engineer, US Army Missile Command, 1963-80; Aerospace Research Engineer, US Army Missile Command, 1980-96; Aerospace Engineer Emeritus, US Army Aviation and Missile Command, Redstone Arsenal, Alabama, 1996-2003; Aerospace Engineer Emeritus, US Army Research, Development, and Engineering Command, Aviation and Missile Research, Development, and Engineering Center, Redstone Arsenal, Alabama, 2003-. Publications: Numerical Solution for the Dynamic Response of Rotationally Symmetric Shells of Revolution under Transient Loadings, (doctoral dissertation, University of Michigan, 1970); Articles in AIAA Journal and Journal of Sound and Vibration on analysis of shells; 17 major US Army technical reports on analysis of shells and other structures. Honour: Awarded Secretary of the Army Research

and Study Fellowship for Graduate Study at the University of Michigan, 1969. Memberships: Sigma Xi; New York Academy of Sciences; Association of US Army. Address: 2202 Yorkshire SE, Decatur, AL 35601-3470, USA.

**SMITH Will, (Willard C Smith II),** b. 25 September 1968, Philadelphia, Pennsylvania, USA. Singer; Rap Artist; Actor. m. (1) Sheree Zampino, 1 son, (2) Jada Pinkett, 1997, 1 son. Career: Formed duo, DJ Jazzy Jeff and the Fresh Prince; Star of TV sitcom, The Fresh Prince of Bel Air; Film appearances, Six Degrees of Separation, 1993, Bad Boys, 1995, Independence Day, 1996, Men in Black, 1997, Enemy of the State, 1998; Wild Wild West, 1999; Men in Black: Alien Attack, 2002; Legend of Bagger Vance, 2000; Ali, 2002. Recordings: With DJ Jazzy Jeff: Singles: Parents Just Don't Understand; I Think I Could Beat Mike Tyson; Summertime, 1991; Boom! Shake the Room, 1993; Albums: Rock the House, 1997; He's the DJ, I'm the Rapper, 1988; And In This Corner..., 1989; Homebase, 1991; Code Red, 1993; Greatest Hits, 1998; Solo: Singles: Just Cruisin', 1997; Men in Black, 1997; Gettin' Jiggy With It, 1998; Miami, 1998; Wild Wild West, 1999; Albums: Big Willie Style, 1997; Willennium, 1999. Honours: Grammy Awards, with DJ Jazzy Jeff, Best Rap Performance, 1988, 1991; Grammy Award, Best Rap Solo Performance, 1998; MTV Music Video Awards, Best Male Video, Best Rap Video, 1998; American Music Awards, Favorite Male Artist, Favorite Album, Favorite Male Soul/R&B Artist, 1999.

**SMITH OF CLIFTON (Lord), Professor Sir Trevor Arthur Smith,** b. 14 June 1937, London, England. Politician. m. Julia, 2 sons, 1 daughter. Education: London School of Economics, 1955-58. Appointments: Lecturer in Politics, University of Exeter, England, 1959-60; Lecturer in Politics, University of Hull, England, 1962-67; Lecturer, Senior Lecturer, Professor of Politics, 1967-91, Deputy Principal, 1985-90, Queen Mary, London; Vice-Chancellor, University of Ulster, 1991-99; Liberal Democrat Front Bench Spokesman on Northern Ireland, 2000-. Publications: The Fixers; The Politics of Corporate Economy; Anti-Politics; Direct Action & Representative Democracy; Town & County Hall; Town Councillors; Training Managers; Numerous articles. Honours: Knighted, 1996; Life Peer, 1997; Honorary LLD, Dublin, Hull, Belfast, National University of Ireland; Honorary DHL, Alabama; Honorary DLitt, Ulster; Honorary Fellow, Queen Mary, London. Memberships: Fellow Royal Historical Society; AcSS; Vice-President, Political Studies Association. Address: House of Lords, London SW1A 0PW, England. E-mail: smitht@parliament.uk

**SMITHERS Alan George,** b. 20 May 1938, London, England; Professor of Education; Author; Broadcaster. 2 daughters. Education: BSc, First Class Honours, Botany, 1959, PhD, Plant Physiology, 1966 King's College London; MSc, Psychology and Sociology of Education, 1973, PhD, Education, 1974, Bradford; MEd, Manchester, 1981; Chartered Psychologist, 1988. Appointments: Lecturer in Biology, College of St Mark and St John, Chelsea, 1962-64; Lecturer in Botany, Birkbeck College, University of London, 1964-67; Research Fellow in Education, 1967-69, Senior Lecturer in Education, 1969-76, University of Bradford; Professor of Education, University of Manchester, 1977-96; Professor of Policy Research, Brunel University, 1996-98; Sydney Jones Professor of Education, University of Liverpool, 1998-2004; Professor of Education and Director, Centre for Education and Employment Research, University of Buckingham, 2004-; Royal Society Committee on Teacher Supply, 1990-94; National Curriculum Council, 1992-93; Beaumont Committee on National Vocational Qualifications, 1995-96; Special Adviser to House of Commons Education and Skills Committee, 1997-. Publications: Numerous publications include most recently: Teacher Qualifications, 2003; The Reality of School Staffing, 2003; England's Education, 2004; Teacher Turnover, Wastage and Movements Between Schools, 2005; Over 100 research papers in botany, psychology and education; Columnist, Times Educational Supplement, 1995-97; Columnist, The Independent, 1997-; Panellist, The Times ed forum, 2001-04; Regular broadcaster, speaker and contributor to the print media. Honours: Fellow, Society for Research into Higher Education. Memberships: British Psychological Society; Society for Research into Higher Education. Address: Centre for Education and Employment Research, Department of Education, University of Buckingham, Buckingham MK18 1EG, England. E-mail: alan.smithers@buckingham.ac.uk

**SMITHSON Simon,** b. 28 June 1954, London, England. Architect. Education: BA (hons), 1976, Dip Arch, 1979, Corpus Christi College, Cambridge; MA, Urban Design, Harvard University, 1982. Appointments: Architect, George Candelis, Paris, France, 1976-77; Foster Associates, London, 1979-80; Teaching Assistant, Harvard University, 1981-82; Cambridge Seven Associates, Cambridge, USA, 1982-85; Civitas Inc, Denver, Colorado, USA, 1985-88; Visiting Design Critic, University of Colorado, 1987-88; Nicholas Hare Architects, London, 1989-91; Architect, 1991-, Associate, 1996-, Richard Rogers Partnership, London; Lecturer, Leeds Metropolitan University, 2000; Visiting Lecturer, Madrid University, Spain, 2002-03; Lecturer, University of Utah, USA, 2003. Memberships: London Rowing Club. Address: Richard Rogers Partnership, Thames Wharf, Rainville Road, London W6 9HA, England.

**SMOLYAR Edward Josef,** b. 18 August 1935, Ostrov, Russia. Mechanic; Mathematician. m. Ulitina Izolda, deceased, 1 son. Education: Degree, Mechanical Engineering, St Petersburg University, 1957; Mathematics Degree, 1965; Postgraduate, 1968; PhD, Agrophysical Research Institute. Appointments: Engineer, Researcher, Leading Researcher, various engineering firms, St Petersburg, 1957-65; Senior Scientist Agrophysical Research Institute. St Petersburg, 1969-. Publications: About global stability dynamical systems: the solution to A J Lurie and M A Izerman's problems; Creation of frequence-integral criteria stability non-stationary linear systems, 1966-2004; Dynamics fluid and turbulence into inhomogeneous boundary layer 1976-2004; Transfer substance into system blood-fabric, 2002-2004. Honours: Listed in Who's Who publications and biographical dictionaries. Address: Agrophysical Research Institute, Gradansky pr 14, 195220 St Petersburg, Russia. E-mail: office@agrophys.mail.ru

**SNÆDAL Magnús,** b. 17 April 1952, Akureyri, Iceland. Linguist; Philologist; Educator. 1 son. Education: BA, Icelandic Language and Literature, 1978, Cand. mag. Degree, Icelandic Linguistics, 1982, University of Iceland, Reykjavík. Appointments: Language Consultant for the Terminological Committee of the Icelandic Medical Association, 1984-96; Lecturer, General Linguistics, 1989-94, Associate Professor of General Linguistics, 1994-, University of Iceland, Reykjavík. Publications: Book: A Concordance to Biblical Gothic, Volumes I and II, 1998; 19 articles, 7 of them on the Gothic language written in English; Editor of 5 books/dictionaries in the field of Icelandic medical terminology. Address: Ránargata 35a, 101 Reykjavík, Iceland. E-mail: hreinn@hi.is

**SNELL Lawrence Silvester,** b 18 December 1914, Newlyn, Cornwall, England. Historian; University Teacher. m. Elizabeth Iris James, 1 son, 2 daughters. Education: Penzance School of Art; St Augustine's College, Canterbury; Exmouth College of Education (University of Exeter); Institute of Historical

Research, University of London; University of Leicester; MA; PhD; FSA; FRHistS; FRGS; FRSA. Appointments: Served with Duke of Cornwall's Light Infantry, 1939-46; Head of the History Department, Acland School, London, 1948-64; Head of History, Wood Green Grammar School, 1965-69; Tutor in History, University of London Department of Extra Mural Studies, 1960-69; Senior Lecturer in History, Newman College, University of Birmingham, 1969-81; Tutor in History, University of Birmingham Department of Extra Mural Studies, 1970-82; Tutor in History, Open University, 1972-82; For the past 35 years became well known as a guide to the ecclesiastical art and architecture of France, Belgium, Germany, Austria, Spain, Portugal, Yugoslavia, Italy and Greece; Senior Guide/ Lecturer in the cathedrals of St Mark, Venice and Santa Maria Assunta, Torcello, 1980-2003. Publications include: History of the Duke of Cornwall's Light Infantry, 1945; The Edwardian Inventories of Church Goods for Cornwall, 1951; The Chantry Certificates for Cornwall, 1953; The Chantry Certificates for Devon and the city of Exeter, 1961; The Suppression of the Religious Foundations of Devon and Cornwall, 1967; London Chantries and Chantry Chapels, 1978; The Mosaics of San Marco, Venice, 1986; Numerous book reviews and articles; Editor of numerous historical and archaeological bulletins, transactions and newsletters. Honours: Jenner Award, Royal Institution of Cornwall, 1957; Elected Bard of the Gorsedd of Cornwall, 1956; Schoolmaster Fellow, Wadham College, Oxford, 1967; Gave the John Stow Commemoration Address, 1977; Gave the Convocation Lecture, University of Leicester, 1985. Memberships: Honorary Secretary, North London Branch, Historical Association, 1955-70; Member, National Council, Historical Association, 1960-76; Council Member, Publications Editor, 1968-84, Vice President, 1985-, London and Middlesex Archaeological Society; President, Midland Cornish Association, 1976-90; Member, Royal Institution of Cornwall. Address: Peard's Acre, South Zeal, Okehampton, Devon EX20 2JR, England. E-mail: ystoryoraneglos@aol.com

**SNIEDZE Ojars Andrejs,** b. 19 January 1930, Latvia. Inventor; Researcher. m. Janet Mary Pearce, 2 sons, 1 daughter. Education 1st Class Certificate in Wireless Telegraphy, 1958; Certificate, Marine Radar, 1959; Part of Dip Tech, Business Administration, 1969; Technical and Further Education Certificate in Occupational Health and Safety. Appointments: Chief Radio Officer, R&K Shipping, New York City, 1959-66; Project Engineer, E&C Engineering, Adelaide, South Australia, 1969-74; Senior Technical Officer, Telecom, Australia, 1987-93; Manager, Research and Development, SA Safety Engineering, Lonsdale, South Australia, 1993-97; Owner Manager, SA Safety Engineering, Tranmere, South Australia, 1997-; Director, Payneham Table Tennis Academy, Firle, South Australia, 2000-. Publications: Various publications on occupational health and safety and on home security for neighbourhood watch schemes; Energy absorbing bollards for protection of outdoor diners, pedestrians and property from out of control vehicles (own invention). Honours: Meritorious Service Award, 1994; Member of Management Committee, Communications Workers Union, Adelaide, South Australia; Various Certificates in Occupational Health and Safety. Memberships: Life Member, IEEE; Ex-Member, Safety Institute of Australia and Ergonomics Society of Australia and New Zealand; Joined Latvian Air Force, Volunteer, October 1944. Address: 47 Hallett Avenue, Tranmere, South Australia 5073. E-mail: sniedze@picknowl.com.au

**SNIPES Wesley,** b. 31 July 1962, Orlando, USA. Actor. (1) April, 1985, divorced 1990, 1 child, (2) Nikki Park, 2003, 2 children. Education: High School for Performing Arts, New York; State University of New York. Appointments: Telephone Repair Man, New York; Broadway Appearances include Boys

# DICTIONARY OF INTERNATIONAL BIOGRAPHY

of Winter; Execution of Justice; Death and King's Horseman; Waterdance; Appeared in Martin Scorsese's video Bad, 1987; Films Include: Wildcats; Streets of Gold; Major League; Mo Better Blues, 1990; Jungle Fever, 1991; New Jack City; White Men Can't Jump; Demolition Man; Boiling Point; Sugar Hill; Drop Zone; To Wong Foo: Thanks for Everything, Julie Newmar, 1995; The Money Train; Waiting to Exhale; The Fan, 1996; One Night Stand; Murder at 1600; Blade, 1997; The Vampire Slayer, 1997; US Marshals, 1998; Down in the Delta, 1998; The Art of War, 2000; Blade 2, 2002; Undisputed, 2002; Unstoppable, 2004; Blade: Trinity, 2004; 7 seconds, 2005; The Marksman, 2005; Co-Founder, Struttin Street Stuff Puppet Theatre, mid 1980's. Honours: ACE Award for Best Actor for Vietnam War Stories, 1989. Address: Amen RA Films, 9460 Wilshire Boulevard, Beverly Hills, CA 90212, USA.

**SNODGRASS W D (S S Gardons, Will McConnell, Kozma Prutkov),** b. 5 January 1926, Wilkinsburg, Pennsylvania, USA. Poet; Writer; Dramatist; m. (1) Lila Jean Hank, 6 June 1946, divorced December 1953, 1 daughter, (2) Janice Marie Ferguson Wilson, 19 March 1954, divorced August 1966, 1 son, (3) Camille Rykowski, 13 September 1967, divorced 1978, (4) Kathleen Ann Brown, 20 June 1985. Education: Geneva College, 1943-44, 1946-47; BA, 1949, MA, 1951, MFA, 1953, University of Iowa. Appointments: Instructor in English, Cornell University, 1955-57; Instructor, University of Rochester, New York, 1957-58; Assistant Professor of English, Wayne State University, Detroit, 1959-67; Professor of English and Speech, Syracuse University, New York, 1968-77; Visiting Professor, Old Dominion University, Norfolk, Virginia, 1978-79; Distinguished Professor, 1979-80, Distinguished Professor of Creative Writing and Contemporary Poetry, 1980-94, University of Delaware, Newark; Various lectures and poetry readings. Publications: Poetry: Heart's Needle, 1959; After Experience, 1967; As S S Gardons, Remains: A Sequence of Poems, 1970, revised edition, 1985; The Fuehrer Bunker, 1977; If Birds Build With Your Hair, 1979; D D Byrde Calling Jennie Wrenne, 1984; A Colored Poem, 1986; The House the Poet Built, 1986; A Locked House, 1986; The Kinder Capers, 1986; Selected Poems, 1957-87, 1987; W D's Midnight Carnival (with DeLoss McGraw), 1988; The Death of Cock Robin (with DeLoss McGraw), 1989; Each in His Season, 1994; The Fuehrer Bunker: The Complete Cycle, 1995. Essays: In Radical Pursuit, 1975; After-Images, 1999. Play: The Fuehrer Bunker, 1978. Other: Translations of songs; Selected Translations, 1998; Criticism: De/Compositions: 101 Good Poems Gone Wrong, 2001; To Sound Like Yourself: Essays on Poetry (criticism), 2002; Make-Believes: Verses and Visions, 2004. Contributions to: Essays, reviews, poems to many periodicals. Honours: Ingram Merrill Foundation Award, 1958; Longview Foundation Literary Award, 1959; National Institute of Arts and Letters Grant, 1960; Pulitzer Prize in Poetry, 1960; Yaddo Resident Awards, 1960, 1961, 1965; Guinness Poetry Award, 1961; Ford Foundation Grant, 1963-64; National Endowment for the Arts Grant, 1966-67; Guggenheim Fellowship, 1972-73; Government of Romania Centennial Medal, 1977; Honorary Doctorate of Letters, Allegheny College, 1991; Harold Morton Landon Translation Award, Academy of American Poets, 1999; Doctor of Humane Letters, University of Delaware, 2005. Memberships: National Institute of Arts and Letters; Academy of American Arts & Sciences; Poetry Society of America; International PEN. Address: 3061 Hughes Road, Erieville, NY 13061, USA.

**SNOW Peter John,** b. 20 April 1938, Dublin, Ireland. Television Presenter; Reporter; Author. m. (1) Alison Carter, 1964, divorced 1975, 1 son, 1 daughter, (2) Ann Macmillan, 1976, 1 son, 2 daughters. Education: Wellington College and Balliol College, Oxford. Appointments: 2nd Lieutenant,

Somerset Light Infantry, 1956-58; Newscaster, Reporter, ITN, 1962-79; Diplomatic and Defence Correspondent, 1966-97; Presenter, BBC Newsnight, 1979-97; Tomorrows World, 1997-2001; BBC Election Programmes, 1983-; BBC Radio 4 Mastermind, 1998-2000; Radio 4 Random Edition, 1998-; Radio 4 Masterteam, 2001. Publications: Leila's Hijack War (co-author), 1970; Hussein: a biography, 1972. Honours: Judges Award, Royal TV Society, 1998. Address: c/o BBC TV Centre, Wood Lane, London W12 7RJ, England. E-mail: peter.snow@bbc.co.uk

**SNOW Philip,** b. 7 September 1947, Altrincham, Cheshire. Wildlife Painter; Book Illustrator. Education: Northwich College of Art, 1964-67; BA 1st Class Honours, Manchester Polytechnic, 1980-83; CNNA Graphics. Career: Self-employed Painter and Illustrator, 1983-; Wildlife and Landscape Painter; Exhibitions include: Mall Galleries; Tryon; South Bank; Barbican; Association of Illustrators Gallery ; Design Centre; In Focus Gallery; Royal Opera Arcade; Royal Academy Exhibition of British Art in the Gulf States; Royal Cambrian Gallery; National Eisteddfod; Anglesey Heritage Gallery; Beaumaris Arts Festival; Nature in Art, Gloucester, 2004; National Exhibition of Wildlife Art, Gordale, Wirral, yearly; Tegfryn Gallery, Menai Bridge, North Wales, Biannual Exhibition; Works in private and public collections world-wide. Publications: Illustrations for over 50 books including: Collins Field Notebook of British Birds; River Birds; A Wandering Voice; The Cottage Book; The Marsh Harrier; The Falcon Folio; Collins Birds by Behaviour, 2003; Birds of Anglesey, 2004; The Design & Origin of Birds and Hebridean Wildlife and Landscape Sketchbook (author and illustrator of both), 2005. Many articles about his work include: North Wales Life, 1992; Cheshire Life, 2004. Honours: BA 1st Class Honours; CNNA Graphics. Address: 2 Beach Cottages, Malltreath, Anglesey LL62 5AT, North Wales. E-mail: philip snow@snow4083.freeserve.co.uk

**SNOWDON Antony Charles Robert Armstrong-Jones (1st Earl of)** b. 7 March 1930, London, England. Photographer. m. (1) HRH The Princess Margaret, 1960, divorced 1978, deceased 2002, 1 son, 1 daughter, (2) Lucy Lindsay-Hogg, 1979, 1 daughter. Education: Jesus College, Cambridge. Appointments: Consultant, Council of Industrial Design, 1962-89; In charge of design of Investiture of HRH the Prince of Wales, Caernarfon, 1969; Editorial Adviser, Design Magazine, 1961-67; Artistic Adviser to The Sunday Times, Sunday Times Publications Ltd, 1962-90; Photographer, Telegraph Magazine, 1990-96; Constable of Caernarfon Castle, 1963-; President, Civic Trust for Wales, Contemporary Art Society for Wales, Welsh Theatre Company; Vice President, University of Bristol Photographic Society; Senior Fellow, Royal College of Art, 1986; Provost, 1995-; Fellow, Institute of British Photographers, British Institute of Professional Photographers; Chartered Society of Design; Royal Photographic Society; Royal Society of Arts; Manchester College of Art and Design; Member, Faculty Royal Designers for Industry; South Wales Institute of Architects; Chair Snowdon Report on Integrating the Disabled, 1972; Member, Council, National Fund for Research for the Crippled Child; Founder, Snowdon Award Scheme for Disabled Students, 1980; President, International Year of Disabled People, 1981; Patron, British Disabled Water Ski Association; Member, Prince of Wales Advisory Group on Disability, 1983; Metropolitan Union of YMCAs; British Water Skiing Federation; Welsh National Rowing Club; Circle of Guide Dog Owners. Publications: London, 1958; Malta, 1958; Private View, 1965; Assignments, 1972; A View of Venice, 1972; Photographs by Snowdon: A Retrospective, 2000; Many others. Honours include: Honorary Member, North Wales Society of Architects; Dr hc, Bradford, 1989; LLD, Bath, 1989; Dr hc, Portsmouth, 1993; Art Directors

Club of New York Certificate of Merit, 1969; Society of Publication Designers Certificate of Merit, 1970; The Wilson Hicks Certificate of Merit for Photocommunication, 1971; Society of Publication Designers Award of Excellence, 1973; Designers and Art Directors Award, 1978; Royal Photographic Society Hood Award, 1979. Address: 22 Launceston Place, London, W8 5RL, England.

**SOBOLEV Konstantin,** Research Consultant; Professor. Education: BS/MS (honor), Moscow State Civil Engineering University, Russia, 1988; PhD, Research Institute of Concrete and Reinforced Concrete, Russia, 1993. Appointments: Assistant Professor of Civil Engineering, Head, Department of Civil Engineering, European University of Lefke; Part time Lecturer, Gazi University, Turkey; Manager, Research and Development, NIGBAS-Precast, ISIKLAR Holding, Turkey; Head, Department of Fine Grinding and Powder Materials, Institute of Materials Research and Effective Technologies, Russia; Research Consultant, numerous organisations in USA, Turkey, Russia and China, currently SCI Con Technologies, Turks and Caicos Islands; Professor of Civil Engineering, Universidad Autónoma de Nuevo León, México. Publications: Many articles published in professional journals and presented at conference. Honours: RD MNTS Grant for Research of Cement Based Materials with Low Thermal Expansion, Russia, 1995; NATO-TUBITAK Post-Doctoral Fellowship for Research on High-Performance Cement and Concrete, Turkey, 1996; Turkish Technology Development Foundation Grant for Development of Double Wall Precast Panel at NIGBAS-Precast, Turkey, 1999; YOK Equivalency Certificate in Materials Science, Turkey, 2003. Memberships: ACI International, USA; National Scientific Network, SNI, Mexico; Scientific and Technical Society KNOWLEDGE, Russia. Address: Doctorate Program on Materials and Structures, Facultad de Ingeniería Civil, Universidad Autónoma de Nuevo León, Apartado Postal #17, Ciudad Universitaria, San Nicolás de los Garza NL, México 66450. E-mail: k_sobolev@yahoo.com

**SODERBERGH Steven,** b. 14 January 1963, Atlanta, USA. Film Director. m. Elizabeth Jeanne Brantley, 1989, divorced 1994. Education: high school and animation course, Louisiana State University. Appointments: Aged 15 made short film Janitor; Briefly editor, Games People Play (TV show); Made short film Rapid Eye Movement while working as coin-changer in video arcade; Produced video for Showtime for their album 90125; Author, Screenplay for Sex, Lies and Videotape, 1989; Kafka, 1991; The Last Ship, 1991; King of the Hill, 1993; The Underneath, 1996; Schizopolis, 1996; Out of Sight, 1998; Executive Producer: Suture, 1994; The Daytrippers, 1996; Writer Mimic, 1997; Nightwatch, 1998; The Limey, 1999; Erin Brockovich, 1999; Traffic, 2000; Ocean's Eleven, 2001; Solaris, 2002. Honours: Academy Award for Best Director, Traffic, 2000. Address: P O Box 2000, Orange, VA 22960, USA.

**SOKOTO Malam Abdullahi Alhaji Shehu,** b. 12 December 1953, Sabon-Birni area in Sokoto Town, Nigeria. Teacher and Researcher. m. 2 wives, 8 sons, 4 daughters. Education: Grade II, TC 11, 1974; NCE, 1978; BA Ed, 1983; MA, in Islamic Studies, 1988; Doctoral Candidate; PhD in Islamic Studies, Law and Jurisprudence. NB: The PhD was awarded subject to corrections. Appointments: Primary Schoolteacher, 1974-78; Secondary College Teacher, 1978-87; University Lecturer, 1987-2001, rising through the ranks as Assistant Lecturer 1987-89, Lecturer II, 1989-1991; Lecturer I, 1991-93; Senior Lecturer, 1994-; Head of Department; Vice Principal; Principal; Inspector of Education; Executive Director of Sokoto State History Bureau, now Waziri Junaidu History and Culture Bureau. Publications: 21 articles and chapters published in various academic research

journals; Books and national dailies such as the Path Newspaper, Sokoto, Nigeria; 9 book drafts and monographs; Most current papers: Implementation of Sharicah in Nigeria: An Outline of its Meaning, Philosophy, Application, Obstacles and Challenges, presented at NATAIS National Conference, Ibadan, 2001; The Life, Times and Contribution of Malam Umar Al-Kammu to the Nineteenth Century Jihad in Nigeria, 1754-1815, translated into Hansa, presented at Sakkwato Historical Projects Seminar, 2002; 32 completed academic and intellectual research works; 44 seminar and conference papers, 21 published. Honours: Five Merit Awards centring on Education, Teaching and Research, Community Services, Administration. Memberships: ASUU; NATAIS; NASR; NUT; NDCC; Nigerian Int-Religious Council, Sokoto, Nigeria; Membership and chairmanship to committees, boards and parastatals within and outside University. Address: PO Box 1627, Sokoto, Sokoto State, Nigeria.

**SOLANDT Jean Bernard,** b. 23 December 1936, France. Banker. m. Sheila Hammill, 1 son, 1 daughter. Education: Collège Technique Commercial, Strasbourg, France. Appointments: Banker, Société Générale, Strasbourg, Paris and London, 1954-68. Schroder Group: Joined Group, 1968, Director, IBJ Schroder Bank & Trust Co Inc, 1984-86, Director, Schroders Japan Ltd, 1984-95, Group Managing Director, Finance Markets Division, Schroders plc, 1984-97, Chairman, Schroder Securities (1984) Ltd, 1985-89, Director, Schroder & Co Inc, 1986-96, Director, Schroder Wertheim & Co Inc, 1986-97, Director, Schroder Wertheim Holdings Inc, 1986-97, Director, Schroders Asia Ltd, 1991-97, Chairman, Schroder France SA, 1992-97, Director J Henry Schroder Bank AG, 1993-97, Chairman, Schroder Structured Investments Inc, 1995-97, Director, 1973-97, Chairman, 1996-97, J Henry Schroder & Co, Director, Schroders plc, 1982-97; Adviser to Royal Trustees Investment Committee, 1993-97; Non-Executive Director: Royal Trust of Canada (London), 1978-82, Woolwich Building Society (now Woolwich plc), 1993-98, Banc Woolwich SpA Banque Woolwich, 1994-98. Member, British Bankers Association Executive Committee, 1990-94. Honour: Honorary FCIB. Address: 27 Heathgate, London NW11 7AP, England.

**SOLBRIG Ingeborg Hildegard,** b. 31 July 1923, Weissenfels, Germany. (US Citizen). Professor Emerita. Education: Diploma, Chemist, University of Halle, Germany, 1948; BA, summa cum laude, German Studies, San Francisco State University, 1964; Graduate Studies, German Literature, University of California at Berkeley, 1964-65; MA, 1966, PhD, Humanities and German Studies, 1969; Stanford University. Appointments include: Assistant Professor, University of Rhode Island, Kingston, 1969-70; Assistant Professor, University of Tennessee, Chattanooga, 1970-72; Assistant Professor, University of Kentucky, Lexington, 1972-75; Associate Professor, 1975-81; Professor, 1981-93, Professor Emerita, 1993-, University of Iowa, Iowa City. Publications: Books: Hammer-Purgstall and Goethe, 1973; Rilke Heute. Beziehungen und Wirkungen, 1975; Reinhard Goering. Seeschlacht/Seabattle, translator, editor, 1977; Momentaufnahmen, 2000; Essay: Orient-Rezeption, 1996, 2000; Numerous book chapters and scholarly articles in professional journals; Reports, interviews, poems, observations, stories and travelogues published in various journals, magazines and newspapers, 1955-75. Honours: Fellow, Austrian Ministry of Education, 1968; Dissertation Fellow, Stanford University, 1968-69; Gold Medal "pro rebus orientalibus", 1974; Old Gold Fellow, University of Iowa, 1977; Grantee, American Council of Learned Societies and DAAD, 1980; Senior Faculty Research Fellow, University of Iowa, 1983; National Endowment for the Humanities Grantee, 1985; Fellow, May Brodbeck Faculty Research Grant, 1989; 2000 Millennium Medal of Honor; IBC Medal of Honor; Listed in Who's Who publications and biographical dictionaries. Memberships: Delta Phi Alpha, 1973; Deutsche Ehrenverbindung; Life Member, Modern Language Association; Founding Member, Goethe Society of North America; Honorary Member, Egyptian Society for Literary Criticism; Member, Society for the History of Alchemy and Chemistry; Canadian and American Societies for Eighteenth Century Studies; Goethe Society of Weimar; Deutsche Schiller-Gesellschaft; Founding Member, International Herder Society; Active member, Trinity Episcopal Church. Address: 1126 Pine Street, Iowa City, IA 52240, USA. E-mail: hsolbrig@blue. weeg.uiowa.edu Website: www.avalon.net/~hilreier

**SOLIMAN Mostafa Mohamed,** b. 13 December 1928, Cairo, Egypt. Professor Emeritus. m. Soad M., 2 daughters. Education: BSc, Civil Engineering, Cairo University, Egypt, 1953; MSc, Civil Engineering, Colorado State University, USA, 1957; PhD, Civil Engineering, Utah State University, USA, 1959. Appointments: Civil Engineer, Ministry of Public Works, 1953-59; Lecturer, 1960-67, Assistant Professor, 1967-72, Professor, 1972-88, Professor Emeritus, 1988-, Ain Shams University, Egypt; Consultant, 1972-. Publications: Numerous papers on irrigation, hydraulics and hydrology in many conferences; Author, many books in same field most recently, Environmental Hydrology. Honours: Ideal Engineer Medal, Egyptian Syndicate, 1984; Honorary Member ASCE; Arid Land Hydrology Award, ASCE; A S Award. Memberships: ASCE; Egyptian Syndicate; Egyptian Society of Engineers; President, Egyptian Society of Irrigation Engineers. Address: 24 Mohamed Mahmoud Kassim, Heliopolis, Cairo, Egypt. E-mail: msoliman1@hotmail.com

**SOLIMANDO Dominic A, Jr,** b. 4 April, Brooklyn, New York, USA. Pharmacist; Medical Writer; Consultant. Education: BSc Pharmacy, Philadelphia College of Pharmacy and Science, 1976; AMEDD Officer Basic Course, US Army Academy of Health Sciences, Fort Sam, Houston, Texas, 1976; MA, Management and Supervision: Healthcare Administration, Central Michigan University, Mt Pleasant, 1980; AMEDD Officer, Advanced Course, US Army Academy of Health Sciences, Fort Sam, Houston, Texas, 1982; US Army Command and General Staff College, Fort Leavenworth, Kansas, 1985; PhD Candidate, Clinical Pharmacy, Purdue University, West Lafayette, Indiana, 1986-89. Appointments: Staff Pharmacist, Walter Reed Army Medical Centre, Washington, DC, 1977; Chief, Pharmacy Service, Andrew Rader Army Health Clinic, Fort Myer, Virginia, 1977-79; Clinical Pharmacist, Haematology-Oncology Service, Walter Reed Army Medical Centre, 1979-82; Clinical Preceptor, College of Pharmacy, Medical College of Virginia, Virginia Commonwealth University, 1982; Chief, Oncology Pharmacy Section, Tripler Army Medical Centre, Honolulu, Hawaii, 1983-86; Clinical Preceptor, 1983, Adjunct Professor, 1984-86, 1989-90, College of Pharmacy, University of the Pacific; Chief, Haematology-Oncology Pharmacy, Letterman Army Medical Centre, San Francisco, 1989-90, 1991-92; Clinical Preceptor, Oncology, ASHP Residency in Pharmacy Practice, Letterman Army Medical Centre, 1989-90; Chief, Pharmacy Service, Operation Desert Shield/Desert Storm, Saudi Arabia/Iraq, 1990-91; Chief, Haematology-Oncology Pharmacy Section, Walter Reed Army Medical Centre, 1992-96; Clinical Assistant Professor, School of Pharmacy, University of Maryland, 1992-96; Clinical Preceptor, School of Pharmacy and Pharmacal Sciences, Howard University, 1992-96; Clinical Preceptor, Oncology, ASHP Residency in Pharmacy Practice, Walter Reed Army Medical Centre, 1992-96; Programme Director, ASHP Speciality Residency in Oncology Pharmacy, Walter Reed Army Medical Centre, 1992-96, 2001-02; Clinical Associate Professor, School of Pharmacy, University of Arkansas, 1995, 2001; Oncology Pharmacist, Department of Pharmacy, Thomas Jefferson University Hospital, Philadelphia,

1996-98; Clinical Preceptor (Oncology), ASHP Residency in Pharmacy Practice, Thomas Jefferson University Hospital, Philadelphia, 1996-98; Clinical Preceptor, College of Pharmacy, Temple University, 1998; Clinical Associate Professor, 1998, Clinical Preceptor, 1996-98, Philadelphia College of Pharmacy, University of the Sciences in Philadelphia; Oncology Pharmacy Manager, Lombardi Cancer Centre, Georgetown University Medical Centre, Washington, 1998-99; Director of Oncology Drug Information/Consultant, cancereducation.com, New York, 1999-2000; Oncology Pharmacy Consultant/Medical Writer, Arlington, Virginia, 1999-; Oncology Pharmacist, Department of Pharmacy, Walter Reed Army Medical Centre, 2000-; President, Oncology Pharmacy Services Inc, Arlington, Virginia, 2000-; Assistant Professor, School of Pharmacy, Howard University, Washington, DC, 2003-. Publications: Numerous articles in scientific journals; Drug Information Handbook for Oncology, 1999, 2000, 2003. Honours include: 'A' Proficiency Designator, Office of the Surgeon General, Department of the Army, 1994; WMSHP-Bayer Recognition Award, Washington Metropolitan Area Society of Health System Pharmacists, 2000; Board Certified Oncology Pharmacist, 2000-; Distinguished Achievement Award in Hospital and Institutional Practice, Academy of Pharmacy Practice and Management, American Pharmaceutical Association, 2001. Memberships: American College of Clinical Pharmacy; American Institute of the History of Pharmacy; American Medical Writers Association; American Pharmacists Association; American Society of Health-System Pharmacists; Federation Internationale de Pharmaceutique; International Society of Oncology Pharmacy Practitioners. Address: Oncology Pharmacy Services Inc., 4201 Wilson Boulevard # 110-545, Arlington, VA 22203, USA. E-mail: oncrxsvc@aol.com

**SOLOVYEV Valery,** b. 1 June 1952, Kazan, Russia. University Teacher. m. Venera Bairasheva, 1 son. Education: High Education Diploma, Applied Mathematics, Kazan State University, 1974; PhD, Mathematical Logic, Novosibirsk State University, 1980; Full Doctor Degree, Computer Science, Russian Academy of Science, 1996. Appointments: Professor, Department of Computer Science, Kazan State University, 1998-; Vice-Director, Institute of Informatics, Kazan, 2000-; Chief of Cognitive Science Laboratory, Kazan, 2001-; Executive Director, Russian Association for Cognitive Science, 2005. Publications: Abstract theory of computability: program approach, 1993; Algebras of recurvive functions, 1999. Honours: Academic of the International Informatization Academy, 1997; Honorary President, Russian Go Federation, 1998-; Man of the year, 2002; Distinguished Leadership Award, American Biographical Institute, 2002. Memberships: Association for Computational Linguistics; European Association for Artificial Intelligence; Slavic Cognitive Linguistics Association. Address: Karbysheva str, 63/1-17, Kazan, 420101, Russia. E-mail: solovyev@mi.ru

**SOMASEKHAR Nethi,** b. 6 July 1967, Khammam, India. Research Scientist. m. Vani, 1 son. Education: BS, Agriculture, Andhra Pradesh Agricultural University, 1988; MS, Nematology and Plant Pathology, 1990, PhD, Nematology and Molecular Biology, 1993, Indian Agricultural Research Institute. Appointments: Junior Research Fellow, 1988-90, Senior Research Fellow, 1990-93, Department of Nematology, Indian Agricultural Research Institute; Scientist, ARS, Indian Council of Agricultural Research, 1993-99; Post-doctoral Research-Scientist, Entomology, Ohio State University, USA, 2000-01; Scientist (SS), ARS, Indian Council of Agricultural Research, 2002-. Publications: 30 research articles; 5 research reviews; 5 popular articles; 10 abstracts. Honours include: Gold Medal, Outstanding Performance in BS, 1988; Gold Medal, Outstanding

Performance in MS, 1990; Lakshmi Mills Award, Best Project in PG Diploma in Electronic Data Processing, 1996; Invited to lecture on Soil Biodiversity, Academy of Environmental Biology, 1998; Benerjee Gold Medal, Best Research Paper in Environmental Biology, 1998; Professor D J Raski Young Scientist Award, Nematological Society of India, 1998; Fellow, Afro-Asian Society of Nematologists, 1998; Fellow, Nematological Society of India, 2002. Memberships: Society of Nemotologists, USA; Afro-Asian Society of Nematologists, UK; Australasian Society of Nemotologists; Life Member, Nematological Society of India; Life Member, Indian Science Congress Association; Founder Life Member, Society for Plant Biochemistry and Biotechnology; Life Member, Environmental Protection Society of India; Academy of Environmental Biology. Address: Department of Nematology, Sugarcane Breeding Institute, Coimbatore, 641007, India. E-mail: nssekhar@hotmail.com

**SOMEKAWA Mina,** Concert Pianist; Piano Teacher. Education: Bachelor of Arts, English, Sophia University, 1981; Postgraduate Musical Studies, University of Missouri-Columbia, 1990-92; Bachelor of Music in Piano Performance, 1993; Master of Music in Piano Performance, 1995, Doctor of Musical Arts in Piano Performance, in progress, University of Illinois at Urbana-Champaign. Appointments: Teaching: Teaching Assistant, University of Illinois at Urbana-Champaign, 1994-96; Faculty, Blue Lake Fine Arts Camp, Twin Lake, Michigan, 1998; Visiting Assistant Professor of Music, Millsaps College, Jackson, Mississippi, 2002; Private piano instructions, various cities in Illinois, 1996-2001, various cities in Mississippi, 2002-; Adjudication: National Federation of Music Clubs, Springfield, Illinois, 1998; Mississippi Symphony Orchestra Young Artists' Competition, 2002; Mississippi Music Teachers Association – Bach Festival, 2004; Performance Activities: Associate Keyboardist: Civic Orchestra of Chicago, 1995-96; Principal Keyboardist: Sinfonia da Camera, Urbana, Illinois, 1995-2001; Champaign-Urbana Symphony, Illinois, 1996-2004; Illinois Symphony Orchestra, Springfield, Illinois, 1997-; Fresno Philharmonic, California, 1998-; Major Solo Piano Recitals: Artist Presentation Society Recital Series, St Louis, 1993; Dame Myra Hess Memorial Concert Series, Chicago, 1998 (live radio broadcast); Concerto Solo on Piano and Harpsichord: University of Illinois Summer Festival Orchestra, 1994; Illinois Chamber Orchestra, 2000, 2003. Publications: Ballet Class I played by Mina Somekawa (cassette tape), 1989; The Snowman, Easy Piano Picture Book Series, 1989; The Snowman, piano reduction score, 1987, translated Japanese editions from Zen-on, reprinted annually. Honours: Numerous prizes in piano competitions, 1991-95; Honour for Highest Academic Performance, Sophia University, 1978; Phi Beta Kappa, 1991; Sigma Alpha Iota/ Ruth Melcher Allen Memorial Award, University of Missouri, 1991; Golden Key National Honor Society, 1991; University Fellowship, Music, University of Illinois, 1993-94; Recognition as an Excellent Teaching Assistant, University of Illinois, 1995, 1996, Pi Kappa Lambda, 1996. Memberships: College Music Society; Mississippi Music Teachers Association; American Federation of Musicians – Local #12, Sacramento, California. Address: 1315 N Jefferson St #214, Jackson, MS 39202, USA. E-mail: msomekawa@msn.com

**SOMER Ljiljana,** b. 13 April 1947, Subotica, Yugoslavia. Professor of Histology and Embryology; Specialist in Pathology. m. Tibor Somer, 2 sons, 1 daughter. Education: MD, Faculty of Medicine, Novi Sad, Serbia and Montenegro, 1967-73; MSc, Faculty of Natural Sciences, Novi Sad, 1980; PhD, Faculty of Medicine, Novi Sad, 1984; Certified Pathologist, Clinical Centre, Novi Sad, 1993. Appointments: Assistant Researcher, Histology and Embryology, 1975-86, Assistant Professor, 1986-91, Associate Professor, 1991-96, Professor, 1996-, Head of the Institute of Histology and Embryology, 1998-, Faculty of Medicine, Novi Sad. Publications: 137 scientific papers and articles in domestic and international scientific journals; Master's thesis: Histophysiological Characteristics of the Pineal Gland in Experimental Diabetes, 1980; Doctoral thesis: Hypophysis under the Influence of Alcohol, 1984. Memberships: Association of Anatomists of Serbia and Montenegro; Association of Pathologists of Serbia and Montenegro. Address: Institute of Histology and Embryology, Faculty of Medicine, Hajduk Veljkova 3, 21000 Novi Sad, Serbia and Montenegro. E-mail: biblmf@uns.ns.ac.yu

**SOMMARIVA Corrado,** b. 5 April 1962, Genoa, Italy. Consultant. 1 son, 1 daughter. Education: PhD, Chemical Engineering, University of Genoa; Diploma in Management, University of Leicester; Ashridge Leadership Course. Appointments: Director of Water Projects, Ansaldo Energia; Research Director, Middle East Research Center; Head of Desalination Department, Mott MacDonald Ltd; Vice President, International Desalination Association; President, European Desalination Society. Publications: Numerous articles and papers published in professional scientific journals; Book, Desalination Management. Honours: High Quality Treatise Award, High Quality Essay Award, IDA, 1995; Best Paper Award, 2001, 2002, 2003, Technology Innovation Award, 2003, Mott MacDonald. Memberships: Board of Directors, IDA; Board of Directors, European Desalination Association; Powergen Advisory Board; Waste Water Europe. Address: Mott MacDonald Ltd, PGB, Victory House, Trafalgar Place, Brighton, East Sussex BN1 4FY, England.

**SONDHEIM Stephen Joshua,** b. 22 March 1930, New York, New York, USA. Composer; Lyricist. Education: BA, Williams College, 1950. Compositions: Incidental Music: The Girls of Summer, 1956; Invitation to a March, 1961; Twigs, 1971; Lyrics: West Side Story, 1957; Gypsy, 1959; Do I Hear A Waltz?, 1965; Candide, (additional lyrics) 1973; Music and Lyrics: A Funny Thing Happened on the Way to the Forum, 1962; Anyone Can Whistle, 1964; Evening Primrose, 1966; Company, 1970; Follies, 1971; A Little Night Music, 1973; The Frogs, 1974; Pacific Overtures, 1976; Sweeney Todd, 1979; Merrily We Roll Along, 1981, 1997; Sunday in the Park With George, 1984; Into the Woods, 1987; Assassins, 1991; Passion, 1994; Anthologies: Side by Side by Sondheim, 1976; Marry Me A Little, 1980; You're Gonna Love Tomorrow, 1983; Putting It Together, 1992; Company ...In Jazz, 1995; A Little Night Music, 1996. Film: Stavisky, 1974; Reds, 1981; Dick Tracy, 1990. Honours: Antoinette Perry Award, 1971, 1972, 1973, 1979; Drama Critics' Award, 1971, 1972, 1973, 1976, 1979; Evening Standard Drama Award, 1996; Grammy Award, 1984, 1986. Memberships: President, Dramatists Guild, 1973-81; American Academy and Institute of Arts and Letters. Address: c/o Flora Roberts, 157 West 57th Street, New York, NY 10019, USA.

**SONG Kwang Soon,** b. 13 February 1955, Daegu, Korea. Surgeon; Educator; Professor. m. Hye Young Jeong, 2 sons. Education: Bachelor, KyungPook National University School of Medicine, 1979; Master, 1982, PhD, 1986, KyungPook National University. Appointments: Director and Chief of Staff, Department of Orthopaedic Surgery, School of Medicine, 2000-2004, Director of Department of Education and Research, Dongsan Medical Center, 2005-, Keimyung University. Publications: Book: The Ilizarov Method for treatment of complex fracture (co-author); More than 90 articles in journals listed at Science Citation Index, Medicus Index including: JBJS, JPO, JOT, JPOB and orthopaedic journals in Korea.

Honours: Prize for excellency of scientific achievement, Korean Orthopaedic Association, 1986, 2003; Award for excellency of scientific achievement, Korean Paediatric Orthopaedic Association, 2002; Prize for scientific achievement, Korean Medical Doctor Association, 2004; 2005 Universal Award of Accomplishment, American Biographical Institute, 2005. Memberships: Corresponding Member, Paediatric Orthopaedic Society of America; Board of Directors, Korean Orthopaedic Association; Board of Directors, Korean Paediatric Orthopaedic Society. Address: 201-402 Metro Palace, Manchondong, Daegu, Korea. E-mail: skspos@dsmc.or.kr

**SONG Yeong Wook**, b. 13 February 1956, Taejon, Korea. Physician. m. Hee Jeong Kwon, 20 December 1982, 1 son, 2 daughters. Education: MD, 1980, PhD, 1990, Seoul National University, 1980. Appointments: Intern, 1980-81, Resident, 1981-84, Seoul National University Hospital; Captain, Korean Army, 1984-87; Instructor, 1988-90, Assistant Professor of Medicine, 1992-95, Associate Professor of Medicine, 1995-2000, Professor, Chief of Division of Rheumatology, 2000-, Seoul National University; Clinical Fellow, Rheumatology, University of California Medical Center, Los Angeles, 1990-92. Publications: Abnormal Distribution of Fcg Receptor Type IIA Polymorphisms in Korean Patients with Systemic Lupus Erythematosus, 1998; Paclitaxel Reduces Anti-DNA Antibody Titer and BUN Prolonging Survival in Murine Lupus, 1998. Honour: Ellis Dressner Award, Southern California Chapter, Arthritis Foundation, 1992; Young Investigator Award, Seoul National University Hospital, 2000. Memberships: Fellow, American College of Rheumatology; Korean Association of Internal Medicine; Korean Rheumatism Association. Address: Seoul National University Hospital, Chongno-ku 28 Yongun-dong, Seoul 110-744, Korea.

**SONNENFELD Barry**, b. 1 April 1953, New York. Cinematographer; Film Director. Appointments: Cinematographer (Films): Blood Simple, 1984; Compromision Positions, 1985; Three O'Clock High, 1987; Raising Arizona, 1987; Throw Momma from the Train, 1987; Big, 1988; When Harry Met Sally..., 1989; Miller's Crossing, 1990; Misery, 1990; TV: Out of Step, 1984; Fantasy Island, 1998; Secret Agent Man, 2000; The Crew, 2000; Director (films): The Addams Family, 1991; Addams Family Values, 1993; Get Shorty, 1995; Men in Black, 1997; Wild Wild West, 1999; Chippendales, 2000; Director, Co-producer, For Love of Money, 1993. Honours: Emmy Award for best cinematography. Address: Gersh Agency, 232 North Canon Drive, Beverly Hills, CA 90210, USA.

**SONNTAG Philipp**, b. 28 December 1938, Halle/Saale, Germany. Writer; Physicist. m. Mechthild Sonntag, 1 son from first marriage. Education: Physicist Diploma, University of Munich, Germany, 1964; Dr.rer.nat., Technical University, Hanover, Germany, 1969; Copywriter Diploma, Axel Andersson Academy, 1998. Appointments: Member of Staff, Max Planck Institute on the Conditions of Life, 1964-78; Active Member, Expert Committees of the Liberal Party (FDP), 1975-; Main political impact for avoiding nuclear armament and warfare until 1983; Science Centre, Berlin, 1979-86; Founding Member, Institute for Interdisciplinary and Alternative Technology Development, Styria, Austria; Shareholder and Innovation Manager of several technically oriented firms; Author, short stories, essays, science fiction. Publications: More than 200 publications in science, politics and literature include: Mathematical Analysis of the Impact of Nuclear Weapons, 1970; Stability and Deterrence regarding Nuclear Weapons (with H Afheldt), 1971; Verhinderung und Linderung atomarer Katastophen, 1981; Wege in die Informationsgesellschaft (co-author Peter Otto), 1985; Key Technologies, 1988; The Role of

Technology Transfer Agencies for Establishing European Co-operation, 1995. Honours: Publicist Award on "Town Ecology" Banking Consortium, 1978; Award as Human Rights Promoter, German Group of Citizens Commission on Human Rights. Memberships: Association of German Scientists; Association of Technical Communication; Society for New Literature, Berlin; Liberal Party, Germany; Institute for Interdisciplinary and Alternative Technology Development, Styria, Austria; Society for Wood Research; Jewish Culture Association; Lichtblick (support of prisoners' journalism); Network Future; c-base (unification of media artists). Address: Lepsiusstr. 45, D-12163 Berlin, Germany. E-mail: phil.sonntag@t-online.de Website: www.philipp-sonntag.de

**SØRENSEN Bent Erik**, b. 13 October 1941, Copenhagen, Denmark. Professor of Physics. m. Kirsten Inger, 1 son, 1 daughter. Education: PhB, University of Copenhagen, 1961; MS, Maths and Physics, 1965, PhD, Physics, 1974, Niels Bohr Institute, Denmark; Advanced Management Diploma, INSEAD, France, 1991. Appointments: Research Fellow, Nordic Institute of Atomic Physics, 1965-67; Associate Professor Niels Bohr Institute, 1967-80; Professor of Physics, Roskilde University, Denmark, 1980-; Technical Director, COWI Consulting, Denmark, 1988-91; President, NOVATOR Advanced Technical Consulting, Denmark, 1991-; Sabbatical Appointments: Yukawa Institute, Kyoto, Japan, 1967, Lawrence Berkeley Laboratory, USA, 1968-71, Yale University, USA, 1974, National Renewable Energy Laboratory, Golden, 1980, Centre Nationale de Recherche, Grenoble, France, 1975, 1976, 1979, University of New South Wales, Sydney, Australia, 1982, 1986; Consultant to: Department of Commerce and Department of Environment and Energy, Denmark, 1975-, Ministry of Trade and Industry, Japan, 1975, UN Environment Programme, Kenya, 1979-82, UN Department of International Economic and Social Affairs, USA, 1979-92, International Atomic Energy Agency, Austria, 1979-92, Department of the Environment, Australia, 1991, Organisation for Economic Co-operation and Development, 1992-93, International Energy Agency, 1993-96, Intergovernmental Panel on Climate Change, 1993-96; Head, Hydrogen Committee, 1998-2002, Head, Danish Solar Energy Committee, 1998, Hydrogen Strategy Committee, 2004, Danish Department for Energy and Environment. Publications: Over 30 books include: Superstring Theory, Lifecycle Analysis of Energy Systems, 1997; Renewable Energy, 3rd edition, 2004; Hydrogen and Fuel Cells, 2005; Over 500 articles in professional journals and project reports. Honours: Citizen of Honour, San Salvador, 1979; Australian-European Award for Distinguished Scholars, 1982; Knighted by the Queen of Denmark, 1989; Danish Solar Energy Prize, 2002; European Solar Prize, Berlin, 2002. Memberships: American Association for the Advancement of Science; New York Academy of Science. Address: Roskilde University Institute 2, Energy and Environment, Bldg 27, Universitetsvej 1, PO Box 260, DK-4000 Roskilde, Denmark. Website: http://mmf.ruc.dk/energy

**SORVINO Mira**, b. 28 September 1968. Actress. Education: Harvard University. Career: Film appearances include: Amongst Friends, 1993; The Second Greatest Story Ever Told, 1993; Quiz Show, 1994; Parallel Lives, 1994; Barcelona, 1994; Tarantella, 1995; Sweet Nothing, 1995; Mighty Aphrodite, 1995; The Dutch Master, 1995; Blue in the Face, 1995; Beautiful Girls, 1996; Norma Jean and Marilyn, 1996; Jake's Women, 1996; Romy and Michele's High School Reunion, 1997; The Replacement Killers, 1997; Mimic, 1997; Summer of Sam, 1999; At First Sight, 1999; Joan of Arc: The Virgin Warrior, 2000; Television: The Great Gatsby, 2000. Honours: Academy Award, Best Supporting Actress, Mighty Aphrodite. Address: The William

Morris Agency, 1325 Avenue of the Americas, New York, NY 10019, USA.

**ŠOŠA Tomislav,** b. 29 October 1948, Šibenik, Croatia. Professor of General and Vascular Surgery. Education: School of Medicine, Zagreb University, Croatia, 1967-72; Research Fellow, 1969-72; Master of Medical Science, 1979; General Surgery Board Certification, 1979; Doctor of Medical Science, 1981. Appointments: Intern, 1973, Chief, General Practice Division, 1974, Dubrovnik Medical Centre; Assistant Lecturer in Surgery, Department of Surgery, Zagreb University School of Medicine, 1975; Residency in General Surgery, 1975; Research Assistant, Department of Surgery, Zagreb University School of Medicine, 1979; Associate Professor in Surgery, 1984; Advanced training in practice, theory and experimental work in vascular surgery, Montefiore Medical Center, Albert Einstein College of Medicine, New York, USA, 1991; Head of Department of Surgery, Merkur Clinical Hospital, 1991; Member of the 4th Eschelon, Main Croatian Health Care Headquarters during the Croatian Homeland War, 1991-95; Professor, Zagreb University School of Medicine, 1992-; Specialist in Vascular Surgery, Ministry of Health, Republic of Croatia, 1995; Organised and performed the first successful liver transplant in Croatia, 1998. Publications: 77 scientific papers and 28 chapters in textbooks which include: Operative reconstruction with femoral artery bypass, arterial patch plasty and operative dilations of the blood vessels in Operative Surgery, 1987; Complicanze delle protesti nelle recostruzione del tratto femero-popliteo-tibiale, in Le Protesti Vascolari, 1987; Surgery (editor), 1991. Honours: First May Day Award, Dean of the University of Zagreb, 1971, 1972; 2nd Award for Experimental Research, Meeting of Croatian and Slovenian Surgeons, 1976; Award for exceptional activity and contribution to the work and development of Zagreb University School of Medicine, 1983; Diploma of Gratitude, Croatian Medical Association, 1996; City of Zagreb Prize, 2002. Memberships include: Croatian Medical Association; Croatian Chamber of Physicians; International Society for the Study of Vascular Anomalies; European Society of Vascular Surgery; Croatian Phlebotic Society; Croatian Society for Vascular Surgery; New York Academy of Sciences; Croatian Neurological Society. Address: University Hospital Merkur, Zajčeva ul. 19, 10000 Zagreb, Croatia. E-mail: klinika-bolnika-merkur1@zg.hinet.hr

**SOTIROV Vassil,** b. 31 May 1947, Sofia, Bulgaria. Writer. m. Svetla Sotirova, 1 son, 1 daughter. Education: Graduate, French Language School, Sofia, 1966. Appointments: Editor at: The Bulgarian National Radio, 1971-79; Caricature Magazine, 1981-84; Cartoons Film Studio, 1985-89; Pardon Newspaper, 1991-93; Couma Newspaper, 1993-2001; Republika Newspaper, 2001-2002. Publications include: Lions Never Cry (stories), 1981; Murder of a Cricket (poetry), 1982; Death Leap (poetry), 1989; There is for Some and There isn't for Others (poetry), 1990; Shooing Away Evil Spirits (poetry), 1991; Patting a Hedgehog (poetry for children), 1991; 45 Poems are Enough (poetry), 1993; We Were Alive to Meet Each Other (poetry), 1997; Light Cavalry in the Subway (stories), 2000; The Heart of the Group (poetry), 2004; Translations include: The Big Will by François Villon (poetry), 1992, 1993, 2000; Night Vigils by Leopold Saingor (poetry), 2003. Honours: Silver Date Award for a comic story, the Town of Bordiguerra, Italy, 1978; South Spring Award for a debut book of poetry, 1983; Silver Honours, 1981 and Golden Honours, 1986, for comic stories, Aleko International Competition, Sofia; Lamar Award for Poetry, 1991; Translators' Union of Bulgaria Award, 1993; Golden Plaquette Award for Satire, 3rd National Poetical Competition "For a More Human World", 2003. Membership: Bulgarian

Writers' Union. Address: 1, Velchova Zavera Sq, Apt 13, 1164 Sofia, Bulgaria.

**SOUDAN Jean Pol, (Soudan Lord John's)** b. 2 July 1953, Louise-Marie, Belgium. Flemish Artist; Painter. Divorced, 1 son. Education: Academy of Tournai, 1968-70; Academy of London, 1972-73; Academy of Lille, 1973-74; Academy of Brussels, 1974-76. Career to date: Painter, originally inspired by the Ardennes countryside and the North Sea; Later work in more fantastic and symbolic style, oriented towards an austral painting looking for high colours; Puts finishing touches to his paintings by scraping with a palette knife, which is an expression of excellence; Represented in many different museums in Belgium and several other countries; Architect, Industrial Design Draughtsman, concentrated on making projects concerning various ancient and new villas styles or luxury buildings; Involved with projects on Belgian power stations, Brussels Underground system and many building companies in Brussels; Signs paintings under the name of Lord John's. Publications: Featured in many reference publications and other books. Memberships: Royal Association and Royal Foundation of the Professional Belgian Artists Painters; Royal Association and Royal Foundation, Sabam of Belgium; Authors Rights Copyright and Preservations for the Belgian Artists; Member, Accadémia del Verbano. Address: 95 rue de la Lorette, The Old Memphis, Renaix 9600, Belgium. Website: www.artpartnerscenter.com

**SOUSA Isabel Maria Nunes,** b. 2 February 1960, Lisbon, Portugal. Professor. m. Luis Manuel Gomes Boavida-Portugal, 2 daughters. Education: Graduate, Food Engineering, Instituto Superior de Agronomia, Technical University of Lisbon, 1984; PhD, Food Science, University of Nottingham, England, 1994; Habilitation (with unanimous approval), Technical University of Lisbon, 2001. Appointments: Product Development of Quick Frozen Foods, Iglo Ice Cream Industries SA, Lisbon, Portugal, Assistant Lecturer, 1985, Lecturer, 1994, Professor with habilitation, 2001- Instituto Superior de Agromonia, Technical University of Lisbon. Publications: 5 chapters in books on food engineering/food rheology; Over 30 papers in peer-reviewed international periodicals and 10 in technical periodicals; Over 50 papers to international congresses; 40 oral presentations at international symposia, 7 of which were plenary or invited. Honour: Title of Expert in Food Engineering, Professional Association of Portuguese Engineers. Memberships: Founding Member, Portuguese Society of Rheology; Ordem Engenheiros Portugueses; Portuguese Society of Chemistry, Agricultural Sciences. Address: ISA, Daiat Tapada da Ajuda, 1349-017, Lisbon, Portugal. E-mail: isabelsousa@isa.utl.pt

**SOUSA-PINTO Alexandre,** b. 13 September 1936, Porto, Portugal. General Practitioner. m. Carmen, 1 son, 2 daughters. Education: MD, 1960, PhD, 1971, Associate Professor, 1978, University of Oporto; Family Medicine Specialist, Portuguese Medical Association, 1993. Appointments: Docent, Anatomy 1960-79, Full Professor of Anatomy, 1979-84, Full Professor of General Practice, 1984-2005, Chairman, Department of General Practice, 1984-2004, Medical School of Oporto; State Secretary of Scientific Research, Portuguese Government, 1978; Dean of Medical School of Oporto, 1984-92; Manager, "Clinica ORMASA", Porto, 1997-2005. Publications: 50 papers on neuroanatomy research mainly in international journals; 60 papers on general practice, some in international journals; 14 papers on work medicine, a few in international journals. Honours: President, Department of General Practice of the Medical School of Oporto, 1984-2005; President of Portuguese Academy of Medicine, 2001-2005. Memberships: WONCA; Royal College of General Practitioners; Portuguese Academy of Medicine; Portuguese Association of General Practitioners;

Lisbon Society of Medical Sciences. Address: Quinta de S. Verissimo, Figueiredo, 4720 Amares, Portugal. E-mail: aspinto@med.up.pt

**SOUTHGATE Christopher Charles Benedict,** b. 26 September 1953, Exeter, Devon. Writer; Editor. m. Sandra Joyce Mitchell, 23 June 1981, 1 stepson. Education: BA, Honours, Natural Sciences, 1974, MA, PhD, Biochemistry, 1978, Christs College, University of Cambridge; GMC, South-West Ministerial Training course, Exeter, 1991. Appointments: Research Associate, Biochemistry, University of North Carolina; Research Officer, Bath University; Pastoral Assistant, University Chaplaincy, 1990-96, Director of Modular Studies, 1997-2001, Honorary University Fellow, School of Classics and Theology, 1999, Exeter University; Staff Tutor, South West Ministry Training Course, 2001. Publications: Landscape or Land?, 1989; Annotations: Stonechat - Ten Devon Poets (editor), 1992; Selected Early Poems, 1991; A Love and Its Sounding: Explorations of T S Eliot, 1997; God, Humanity and the Cosmos: A Textbook in Science and Religion, 1999; Beyond the Bitter Wind: Poems 1982-2000, 2000; God and Evolution: Theodicy in the Light of Darwin, 2002. Honours: South West Arts Literature Award, 1985; Iolaire Arts Prize, 1987; Sidmouth Arts Festival Prize, 1991; Southwest Open Poetry Commendation, 1991; Science and Templeton Foundation Award, 1996; Science and Religion Course Award, 1996; Science and Religion Course Development Award; Hawthornden Fellowship, 1999. Memberships: Editorial Board, Ecotheology; Committee, Science and Religion Forum; Trustee, King George VI and Queen Elizabeth Foundation of St Catharine's, Cumberland Lodge, Windsor; The Society of Authors; Christians in Science; Higher Education Academy Teaching; Marylebone Cricket Club; Hawk's Club. Address: Parford Cottage, Chagford, Devon TQ13 8JR, England.

**SPAARGAREN Albert Cornelis,** b. 27 February 1935, Leyden, The Netherlands. Retired Linguist. Appointments: Commercial Administration, -1952; Horticultural activities, Great Britain, France, Netherlands and Switzerland, -1964; Linguistic activities within Gemeente Universiteit of Amsterdam, -1996. Memberships: IEEE; International Broadcasting Convention; Protection of Nature; Friends of the Earth. Address: Karel Doormanstraat 111, 1st Stock, 1055 VE Amsterdam, Netherlands.

**SPACEY Kevin,** b. 26 July 1959, South Orange, New Jersey, USA. Actor. Education: Juilliard Drama School, New York. Career: Stage debut in Henry IV, Part 1; Broadway debut in Ghosts, 1982; Other theatre appearances include: Hurlyburly, 1985; Long Day's Journey into Night, London, 1986; Yonkers, New York; The Iceman Cometh, London, 1998; Films: Working Girl, 1988; See No Evil, Hear No Evil, 1989; Dad, 1989; Henry and June, 1990; Glengarry Glen Ross, 1992; Consenting Adults, 1992; Hostile Hostages, 1994; Outbreak, 1995; The Usual Suspects, 1995; Seven, 1995; Looking for Richard, 1996; A Time to Kill, 1996; LA Confidential, 1997; Midnight in the Garden of Good and Evil, 1997; American Beauty, 1999; Ordinary Decent Criminal, 2000; Pay It Forward, 2000; The Shipping News, 2001; The Life of David Gale, 2003; Director, Albino Alligator, 1997. Honours Tony Award, 1986; Academy Award for Best Actor, 1999. Address: William Morris Agency, 151 South El Camino Drive, Beverly Hills, CA 90212, USA.

**SPARK Dame Muriel Sarah,** b. 1 February 1918, Edinburgh, Scotland. Author; Poet. m. S O Spark, 1937, dissolved, 1 son. Education: James Gillespie's School for Girls; Heriot Watt College, Edinburgh. Appointments: Political Intelligence Department, British Foreign Office, 1944-45; General Secretary,

Poetry Society, 1947-49; Editor, The Poetry Review, 1947-49; Founder, Forum literary magazine. Publications: Fiction: The Comforters, 1957; Robinson, 1958; The Go-Away Bird and Other Stories, 1958; Memento Mori, 1959; The Ballad of Peckham Rye, 1960; The Bachelors, 1960; Voices at Play, 1961; The Prime of Miss Jean Brodie, 1961; The Girls of Slender Means, 1963; The Mandelbaum Gate, 1965; Collected Stories I, 1967; The Public Image, 1968; The Very Fine Clock (for children), 1968; The Driver's Seat, 1970; Not to Disturb, 1971; The Hothouse by the East River, 1973; The Abbess of Crewe, 1974; The Takeover, 1976; Territorial Rights, 1979; Loitering with Intent, 1981; Bang-Bang You're Dead and Other Stories, 1982; The Only Problem, 1984; The Stories of Muriel Spark, 1985; A Far Cry from Kensington, 1988; Symposium, 1990; The French Window and the Small Telephone (for children), 1993; Omnibus I, 1993; Omnibus II, 1994; Reality and Dreams, 1996; Omnibus III, 1996; Omnibus IV, 1997; Aiding and Abetting, 2000; The Complete Short Stories, 2002; The Finishing School, 2004. Poetry: The Fanfarlo and Other Verse, 1952; Collected Poems 1, 1967; Going Up to Sotheby's and Other Poems, 1982; All the Poems of Muriel Spark, 2004. Play: Doctors of Philosophy, 1963. Non-Fiction: Child of Light: A Reassessment of Mary Wollstonecraft Shelley, 1951, revised edition as Mary Shelley, 1987; John Masefield, 1953, revised 1992; Curriculum Vitae (autobiography), 1992; The Essence of the Brontës, 1993. Editor: 1950; Selected Poems of Emily Brontë, 1952; The Brontë Letters, 1954. Honours: Prix Italia, 1962; FRSL, 1963; Yorkshire Post Book of the Year Award, 1965; James Tait Black Memorial Prize, 1966; Hon DLitt, Strathclyde, 1971, Edinburgh, 1989, Aberdeen, 1995, St Andrews, 1998, D University, Heriot Watt University, DLitt, University of Oxford, 1999, University of London, 2001; Honorary Doctor of Humane Letters, The American University of Paris, 2005; Honorary Member, American Academy of Arts and Letters, 1978; 1st Prize, FNAC La Meilleur Recueil des Nouvelles Etrangères, 1987; Saltire Scottish Book of the Year Award, 1987; CLit, 1991; Ingersoll Foundation T S Eliot Award, 1992; Honorary FRSE, 1995; Dame Commander of the Order of the British Empire, 1993; Commandeur de l'Ordre des Arts et des Lettres, France, 1996; David Cohen British Literature Prize, 1997; International PEN Gold Pen Award, 1998; 1st Enlightenment Award, Edinburgh, 2004; XXXIII Premio Letterario Internazionale Isola d'Elba-Raffaello Brignetti, 2005; Hon Doctor of Humane Letters, American University of Paris, 2005; Honorary Citizen of Civitella in Val di Chiana, 2005. Address: c/o David Higham Associates Ltd, 5-8 Lower John Street, Golden Square, London W1R 4HA, England.

**SPARR Brigitte,** b. 2 February 1958, Colmar, France. General Surgeon. Education: Residency in Surgery, 1983-87; Doctorate of Medicine, 1984; Clinical Chief-Assistant, 1987-91; Senior Registrar, 1991-98, Vascular Surgery, 1992-; War Surgery, 1992. Appointments: MBA, Master in real computer time, 1992-93; Health Business School ESSEc, 1993-94; Hospital of Paris Bordeaux, Montreal, London UK, USA Mayo Clinic, WDC, Houston; General Vascular Cardio-thoracic Surgeon. Publications: About Carotid Surgery; Ileo-Anal Pouch; Pancreatitis; Colic Fistulas; Total Artificial Heart Program. Honours include: New York Academy of Sciences, 1984; European Board of Surgery; Royal College of Surgeons of Scotland. Memberships: AFC; EDS. Address: 31 Avenue de la Brunerie, 77330 Ozoir-la-Ferriere, France.

**SPEAR Walter Eric,** b. 20 January 1921. Physicist. m. Hilda Doris King, 2 daughters. Education: BSc, PhD, DSc, University of London. Appointments: Lecturer then Reader, Physics, University of Leicester, 1953-68; Harris Professor of Physics, 1968-91, Professor Emeritus, 1991-, University of

Dundee. Publications: Author of numerous research papers on electronic and transport properties in crystalline solids, liquids and amorphous semi-conductors. Honours: Europhysics Prize, European Physical Society, 1977; Max Born Medal and Prize, Institute of Physics and German Physical Society, 1977; Makdougall-Brisbane Medal, Royal Society of Edinburgh, 1981; Maxwell Premium, Institute of Electrical Engineers, 1981, 1982; Rank Prize for Optoelectronics, 1988; Mott Award, 1989; Rumford Medal, Royal Society, 1990. Memberships: FInstP, 1962; Fellow of the Royal Society of Edinburgh, 1972; Fellow of the Royal Society, 1980. Address: 20 Kelso Place, Dundee DD2 1SL, Scotland.

**SPEARING Ruth Lilian,** b. 7 January 1952, England. Haematologist. m. Leslie Snape, 1 son, 1 daughter. Education: MB, ChB, University of Bristol, 1977; FRACP, FRCPA (Haematology). Appointments: Intern, Christchurch Hospital (Surgery), New Zealand, and Professor A E Read, Bristol, UK (Medicine), 1977-78; Registrar, Internal Medicine, Christchurch Hospital, 1978-81; Registrar, Internal Medicine (part-time), 1981-82, Haematology (part-time), 1982-83, Dunedin Hospital, New Zealand; Registrar, Haematology (part-time), Plymouth General Hospital, UK, 1983-84; Senior Registrar, Haematology (part-time), Royal Liverpool Hospital, UK, 1984-87; Acting Director, Regional Blood Transfusion Service, Christchurch, 1987-89; Clinical Lecturer, Department of Pathology, University of Otago, 1987-96; Consultant Haematologist, Clinical and Laboratory Haematology, 1989-, Acting Clinical Director, when Clinical Director absent, 1993-98, Clinical Director, Haematology, 1998-2004, Christchurch Hospital; Senior Clinical Lecturer, Department of Pathology, University of Otago, 1996-; Member, 1996-, Chairman, 1996-2000, 2002-, Ceredase Treatment Panel; Member, Standing Advisory Committee for Higher Training in Haematology, Royal Australasian College of Physicans, 1998-; Member, New Zealand Cancer Treatment Working Party, 2001-; Member, Haematology Medical Oncology Subcommittee of the NZCTWP, 2001-; Chairman, Senior Medical Staff Association, Christchurch Hospitals, 2003-; Member, IT subcommittee, NZCTWP, 2002-; Chairman, IT subcommittee, NZCTWP, 2003-; Member, Clinical Board, Canterbury District Health Board, 2003-. Publications: Numerous articles in professional scientific journals, abstracts presented as oral presentations at professional meetings, invited presentations at professional meetings and abstracts presented as posters at professional meetings. Honours: Numerous successful grant applications. Memberships: Fellow, Royal Australasian College of Physicians; Fellow, Royal College of Pathologists of Australasia; Member, British Society of Haematology; Member, Haematology Society of New Zealand and Australia; Member, Australian and New Zealand Bone Marrow Transplant Society. Address: Department of Haematology, Christchurch Hospital, Private Bag, Christchurch, New Zealand. E-mail: ruth.spearing@adhb.govt.nz

**SPELLING Aaron,** b. 22 April 1923, Dallas, Texas, USA. Television Producer; Writer. m. Carole Gene Marer, 1968, 1 son, 1 daughter. Education: University of Paris, Sorbonne; Southern Methodist University. Appointments: Served, USAAF, 1942-45; Co-owner, Thomas-Spelling Productions, 1969-72; Co-President, Spelling-Goldberg Productions, 1972-76; President, Aaron Spelling Productions Inc, Los Angeles, 1977-86; Chairman and Chief Executive Officer, 1986-; Producer, numerous TV programmes including: Dynasty; The Colbys; Love Boat; Hotel; Beverly Hills 90210; Melrose Place; Sunset Beach; Pacific Palisades; Over 110 Movies of the Week for American Broadcasting Corporation; Films produced include: Mr Mom; 'Night; Mother; Surrender; Cross My Heart; Soapdish. Publications: Author of numerous TV plays and films;

Aaron Spelling: A Prime Time Life, 1996. Honours: Bronze Star Medal; Purple Heart with Oak Leaf Cluster; Eugene O'Neil Award, 1947, 1948; National Association for Advancement of Colored People Image Award, 1970, 1971, 1973, 1975; Man of the Year Award, Publicists' Guild of America, 1971; B'nai B'rith Man of the Year Award, 1985; NAACP Humanitarian of the Year, 1983. Memberships: Board of Directors, American Film Institute; Writer's Guild of America; Producers Guild of America; The Caucus, Hollywood Radio and TV Society; Hollywood TV Academy of Arts and Science. Address: Spelling Entertainment Group, 5700 Wilshire Boulevard, Floor 5, Los Angeles, CA 90036, USA.

**SPENCE Malcolm Hugh,** b. 23 March 1934, London, England. Barrister. m. (Jennifer) Jane Cole, 1 son, 1 daughter. Education: Law Degree and LLM, Gonville and Caius College, Cambridge, 1954-57; Student, Gray's Inn, 1957-58; James Mould Scholar; Holker Senior Exhibitioner; Lee Prizeman; Called to the Bar, 1958. Appointments: Chambers of John Widgery QC, later Lord Chief Justice; Pupil to Nigel Bridge, later Senior English Law Lord; Appeared in Divisional Court of Appeal repeatedly for Minister of Housing and Local Government; Local government practice, especially town and country planning and compulsory purchase; QC, 1979; Appeared in Singapore 5 times and Hong Kong 3 times, always, bar one, for the Government; Chartered Arbitrator; Bencher Gray's Inn, 1988. Publications: The Law and Practice of Rating and Valuation (co-author), 1961; Basic Principles of Compensation for Land Resumption, Hong Kong, 2000; Principles Governing the Valuation of Land in the Context of Arbitration (journal article), 2000; The Chambers of Marshall Hall – 125 Years, 2005. Honours: QC; MA; LLM; FCIArb. Memberships: Hawks Club; Caledonian Club. Address: 2-3 Gray's Inn Square, London WC1R 5JH, England. E-mail: chambers@2-3graysinnsquare.co.uk

**SPENCER Aida Besancon,** b. 2 January 1947, Santo Domingo, Dominican Republic. Professor; Minister. m. William David Spencer, 1 son. Education: BA, Douglass College, 1968; ThM, MDiv, Princeton Theological Seminary, 1973, 1975; PhD, Southern Baptist Theological Seminary, 1982. Appointments: Community Organiser, 1969-70; Campus Minister, 1973-74; Adjunct Professor, New York Theological Seminary, 1974-76; Academic Dean, Professor, Alpha-Omega Community Theological School, 1976-78; Professor of New Testament, Gordon-Conwell Theological Seminary, 1982-. Publications: God through the Looking Glass: Glimpses from the Arts; Global God; Prayer Life of Jesus; Beyond the Curse: Women Called to Ministry; Paul's Literary Style; Goddess Revival; Joy through the Night; 2 Corinthians; Latino Heritage Bible. Honours: Eternity Book of the Year, 1986; Christianity Today Book Award, 1996. Memberships: Society of Biblical Literature; Evangelical Theological Society; Christians for Biblical Equality; Institute for Biblical Research; Ašociacion para la Educacion Teologica Hispana. Address: Gordon-Conwell Theological Seminary, 130 Essex Street, S Hamilton, MA 01982, USA.

**SPENCER David A,** b. 7 November 1963, Stepney, London, England. Geologist. Education: BSc (Honours), Geology, University of Exeter, UK, 1983-86; Diploma of Imperial College, Structural Geology and Rock Mechanics, Royal School of Mines, Imperial College of Science and Technology, University of London, 1987-88; MSc, Structural Geology and Rock Mechanics, Royal School of Mines, London, 1987-88; Doctor of Natural Sciences, Swiss Federal Institute of Technology (ETH), Zurich, 1989-93. Appointments include: Hydrological Consultant, Partnerscaft Pro Aliminos, Philippines, 1992-94; Accepted as Senior Post-Doctoral Research Fellow (SNSF) at Universities of: Cambridge (UK), Stanford (USA),

California (Santa Barbara), Maine (USA), Punjab (Pakistan), Tokyo Institute of Technology, MIT, Boston, USA, 1997-99; Research Assistant Professor, Lecturer in Structural Geology, University of Maine, Orono, USA, 1997-98; Staff Geologist - Structural Geologist, Project Manager, Saga Petroleum ASA, Oslo, Norway, 1998-2000; Senior Reservoir Geologist, Roxar Software Solutions, London, 2003-. Publications: 24 scientific publications, 46 articles, 81 abstracts, 4 theses, 1 consultant report, 22 research reports, 6 expedition reports. Honours: Many scholarships and awards, also many athletic awards in a variety of sports. Memberships include: Fellow, Royal Geographic Society (with Institute of British Geographers); Fellow, Royal Astronomical Society; Fellow, American Geographical Society; Fellow, Geological Society; Fellow, Geological Association of Canada; Fellow, Geological Society of India; Fellow, Royal Society of Arts; Fellow, Linnean Society of London. Address: PO Box 30692, London E1 0TH, Great Britain. E-mail: DSpencer@online.no

**SPENCER Gillian Bryne White**, b. 22 July 1931, London, England. Museum Curator. 1 son. Education: BA, History, 1952, MA, 1956, Newnham College, Cambridge; Academic Postgraduate Diploma in Prehistoric Archaeology, Institute of Archaeology, London University, 1954. Appointments: Curator, Saffron Walden Museum, 1958-61; Museums Education Officer, City of Norwich Museums, 1969-74; Director, Wakefield MDC Art Gallery, Museums and Castles, 1974-90; First Chairman, Wakefield Cathedral Fabric Advisory Committee, 1991-96. Publications: A Beaker Burial at Weeke, Winchester; Excavation of the Battle Ditches, Saffron Walden (co-author); Discoveries in Old World Archaeology, Encyclopaedia Britannica Year Book, 1961; Museums in Education: Trends in Education, 1974. Honours: State Scholarship, 1949-52, 1952-54; Fellow of the Museums Association, 1990. Membership: Museums Association. Address: 12 Belgrave Mount, Wakefield, West Yorkshire WF1 3SB, England.

**SPERLICH Diether Johannes Telesphor**, b. 15 January 1929, Vienna, Austria. University Professor Emeritus. m. Eva Sebek, 3 sons, 1 daughter. Education: Biology and Physics, 1947-52, PhD, Genetics, 1952, Medicine, 1958-62, University of Vienna. Appointments: Assistant Professor, 1955-63, University of Vienna; Guest Investigator, The Rockefeller Institute, New York, 1964; Associate professor, University of Vienna, 1965-71; Professor, 1971-76, Full Professor and Head of Department of Population Genetics, 1976-97, Professor Emeritus, 1998-, University of Tuebingen, Germany. Publications: Books: Populationsgenetik, 1973, 1978; Chromosomal Polymorphism in Natural and Experimental Populations – Genetics in Drosophila (co-author), 1986; Beitraege zur Evolutionstheorie (co-author), 1980; Biologie für Medizine, 1995; Editor-in-Chief, J Zool Syst Evol Res, 1995-2005. Honours: Theodor Koerner Preis, Austria, 1960, 1964; Kardinal Initzer Preis, Austria, 1967; Honorary Professor, University of Salzburg, 1982; Foreign Member, Finish Academy of Science, 1983; Honorary Doctoral Degree, University of Oulu, Finland, 1995. Memberships: Genetische Gesellschaft; Deutsche Zoologische Gesellshaft; European Society of Evolutionary Biology; Gesellschaft für Biologische Systematik. Address: Goesstr 82, D72070 Tuebingen, Germany. E-mail: diether.sperlich@uni-tuebingen.de

**SPICER (William) Michael (Hardy) (Sir)**, b. 22 January 1943, United Kingdom. Member of Parliament. m. Patricia Ann Hunter, 1 son, 2 daughters. Education: MA, Economics, Emmanuel College, Cambridge. Appointments: Assistant to Editor, The Statist, 1964-66; Conservative Research Department, 1966-68; Director, Conservative Systems Research, 1968-70; Managing Director, Economic Models Ltd, 1970-80;

Member of Parliament, South Worcestershire, 1974-97, West Worcestershire, 1997-; PPS, Department of Trade, 1979-81; Parliamentary Under Secretary of State (Minister for Aviation, 1985-87), Department of Transport, 1984-87; Parliamentary Under Secretary of State (Minister for Coal and Power), Department of Energy, 1987-90; Minister of State (Minister for Housing and Planning), Department of the Environment, 1990; Member, Treasury Select Committee, 1997-2001; Chairman, Treasury Sub-Committee, 1999-2001. Publications: A Treaty Too Far, 1992; The Challenge from the East, 1996; Novels: Final Act, 1981; Prime Minister Spy, 1986; Cotswold Manners, 1989; Cotswold Murders, 1990; Cotswold Mistress, 1992; Cotswold Moles, 1993; Contributor, Royal Institution Public Administration. Honour: Knighted, 1996. Memberships: Vice-Chairman, Deputy Chairman, 1983-84, Conservative Party; Chairman: Parliamentary Office of Science and Technology, 1990, Parliamentary and Scientific Committee, 1996-99, European Research Group, 1994-2001, Congress for Democracy, 1998-; President, 1996-, Chairman, 1991-96, Association of Electricity Producers; Governor, Wellington College, 1992-2004; Chairman and Captain, Lords and Commons Tennis Club, 1996-; Member, 1997-99, Chairman, 2001-, 1922 Committee; Member of Board, Conservative Party, 2001. Address: House of Commons, London SW1A 0AA, England.

**SPIELBERG Steven**, b. 18 December 1947, Cincinnati, Ohio, USA. Film Director; Producer. m. (1) Amy Irving, 1985, divorced 1989, 2 sons, (2) Kate Capshaw, 1 daughter, 1 adopted daughter. Education: California State College, Long Beach. Career: Film Director, Universal Pictures; Founder, Amblin Entertainment; Co-founder, Dreamworks SKG Inc, 1995-; Founder, Starbright Foundation. Creative Works: As Film Director: Duel (for TV), 1971; Something Evil (for TV), 1972; The Sugarland Express, 1974; Jaws, 1975; Close Encounters of the Third Kind, 1977; 1941, 1979; Raiders of the Lost Ark, 1981; E.T. (The Extra Terrestrial), 1982; Twilight Zone - The Movie, 1983; Indiana Jones and the Temple of Doom, 1984; The Color Purple (also producer), 1985; Empire of the Sun, 1988; Always, 1989; Hook, 1991; Jurassic Park, 1992; Schindler's List, 1993; Some Mother's Son, 1996; The Lost World, 1997; As Producer: I Wanna Hold Your Hand, 1978; Poltergeist (also co-writer), 1982; Gremlins, 1984; Young Sherlock Holmes (executive producer), 1985; Back to the Future (co-executive producer), 1986; The Goonies (writer, executive producer), 1986; Batteries Not Included (executive producer), 1986; The Money Pit (co-producer), 1986; An American Tail (co-executive producer), 1986; Who Framed Roger Rabbit, 1988; Gremlins II (executive producer), 1991; Joe Versus the Volcano (executive producer), 1991; Dad (executive producer) 1991; Cape Fear (co-executive producer), 1992; The Flintstones, 1994; Casper, 1995; Twister (executive producer), 1996; Men in Black, 1997; The Lost World: Jurassic Park, 1997; Amistad, 1997; Deep Impact, 1998; Saving Private Ryan, 1998; The Last Days (documentary), 1999; AI; Artificial Intelligence, 2001; Minority Report, 2002; Catch Me If You Can, 2002; The Terminal, 2004; The Legend of Zorro, 2005; Memoirs of a Geisha, 2005; Director, TV episodes, including Columbo; E.R; Band of Brothers, 2000; Semper Fi, 2000; Taken, 2002. Publication: Close Encounters of the Third Kind (with Patrick Mann). Honours include: Directors Guild of America Award Fellowship, 1986; BAFTA Awards; Irving G Thalberg Award, 1987; Golden Lion Award, Venice Film Festival, 1993; Academy Awards; John Huston Award, 1995; Dr hc, University of Southern California, 1994; Lifetime Achievement Award, Directors' Guild of America, 1999; Britannia Award, 2000; Grosses Bundesverdienstkreuz, 1998; Hon KBE. Address: CAA, 9830 Wilshire Boulevard, Beverly Hills, CA 90212, USA.

**SPILLER Andres,** b. 24 December 1946, Buenos Aires, Argentina. Oboist; Conductor. m. Marcela Magin, 2 sons, 1 daughter. Education: Conservatorio Nacional; Private studies, Hochschule für Musik Köln, Germany; Summer courses with Heinz Holliger, Bruno Maderna, Franco Ferrara, Michael Gielen, Volker Wangenheim. Career: Assistant Conductor, National Symphony Orchestra and Oboe Soloist; Oboe Soloist, Camerata Bariloche and Soloist of Bach Academy, Buenos Aires; Conductor, La Plata Chamber Orchestra; Performed with Koeckert Quartet in Munich; Other European appearances include Madrid, Rome and Radio Zürich; Toured America and Europe with Camerata Bariloche; Professor of Oboe and Chamber Music. Recordings: Death of an Angel; Tango. Honours: DAAD Fellowship for study in Germany; Sociedad Hebraica Prize; 2nd Prize, Promaciones Musicales; Premio Konex, 1989, 1999. Address: Medrano 47, 5øA, 1178 Buenos Aires, Argentina.

**SPITALNIK Jorge,** b. 17 September 1933, Montevideo, Uruguay. Engineer. m. Susana Nathan, 1 son, 1 daughter. Education: Industrial Engineer, University of Uruguay, 1958; Ingenieur en Genie Atomique, INSTN Saclay, University of Paris, France, 1959; Diploma, Imperial College, Nuclear Power, University of London, 1960; Mechanical Engineer, Federal University, Rio de Janeiro, Brazil, 1976. Appointments: Head, Steam Generation Department, University of Uruguay, 1958-64; Officer, International Atomic Energy Agency, 1964-68; Director, Nuclear Research Centre, Uruguay, 1969-73; Department Head, Nuclebras, Brazil, 1973-77; National Director, UNDP-Nuclebras Nuclear Project, 1978-85; Assistant Advisor to Director, Nuclen, 1985-96; Superintendent, Nuclen, 1996-97; Technical Advisor to Director, Electronuclear, 1997-98; Deputy Manager, Nuclear Technology and Safety, Eletronuclear, 1998-2000; Member, Board of Directors, ANS, 1995-99, 2000-2003; Technical Director, FEBRAE, 1998-2006; Executive Director, UPADI, 2001-; Vice President WFEO, 2003-07; Chairman, Energy Task Group, WFEO-COMTECH, 2002-2003; Chair, Energy Committee WFED, 2003-07; Chair, International Nuclear Societies Council, 2003-04; Chair, International Nuclear Energy Academy, 2005-06. Publications: More than 100. Honours: Fellow, American Nuclear Society; Best Publication Award of Latin American Section of American Nuclear Society, 1995, 1998. Memberships: Institute of Mechanical Engineering; American Nuclear Society; International Nuclear Energy Academy; Pan American Academy if Engineering; Brazilian Federation of Engineering Societies; Latin American Section of ANS; WFEO-COMTECH. Address: Av Epitacio Pessoa, 2900/ Apt 1001, 22471-001 Rio de Janeiro, Brazil.

**SPOONER David Eugene,** b. 1 September 1941, West Kirby, Wirral, England. Writer; Naturalist. m. Marion O'Neil, 9 March 1986, 1 daughter. Education: BA, hons, University of Leeds, 1963; Diploma in Drama, University of Manchester, 1964; PhD, University of Bristol, 1968. Appointments: Lecturer, University of Kent, 1968-73; Visiting Professor, Pennsylvania State University, 1973-74; Lecturer, Manchester Polytechnic, 1974-75; Head of Publishing Borderline Press, 1976-85; Director, Butterfly Conservation, East Scotland. Publications: Unmakings, 1977; The Angelic Fly: The Butterfly in Art, 1992; The Metaphysics of Insect Life, 1995; Creatures of Air: Poetry 1976-98, 1998; Insect into Poem: 20th Century Hispanic Poetry, 1999, 2001; Thoreau's Insects, 2001; The Insect-Populated Mind: how insects have influenced the evolution of consciousness, 2005. Contributions to: Iron; Interactions; Tandem; Weighbauk; Revue de Littérature Comparée; Bestia (Fable Society of America); Margin; Corbie Press; Butterfly Conservation News; Butterfly News; Field Studies. Honours: American Medal of Honor for Natural History admitted to American Hall of Fame.

Memberships: The Welsh Academy Associate; Association Benjamin Constant. Address: 96 Halbeath Road, Dunfermline, Fife KY12 7LR, Scotland.

**SPRATT Brian Geoffrey,** b. 21 March 1947. Professor. m. Jiaji Zhou, 2 sons. Education: BSc, 1st class honours, 1968, PhD, 1972, Microbiology, University College, London. Appointments: Research Associate, University College, London, 1972-73; Research Fellow, Princeton University, USA, 1973-75; Research Fellow, University of Leicester, 1975-80; Lecturer in Biochemistry, 1980-87; Reader in Molecular Genetics, 1987-89; Professor of Molecular Genetics, 1990-97; University of Sussex; Professor of Biology, University of Oxford, 1997-2001; Professor of Molecular Microbiology, Imperial College of Science, Technology and Medicine, 2001-; Honorary Professor, London School of Hygiene and Tropical Medicine, 2002-. Publications: Author and co-author of over 170 articles on biochemistry, genetics and microbiology in academic journals. Honours: Fleming Award, Society for General Microbiology, 1982; Pfizer Award, 1983; Fellow, Royal Society of London, 1993; Hoechst-Roussel Award of the American Society for Microbiology, 1993; Kitasato Medal for Microbial Chemistry, Kitasato Institute, Japan, 1995; Fellow, Academy of Medical Sciences, 1998; Fellow American Academy of Microbiology, 2003; Leeuwenhoek Award, Royal Society, 2004. Address: Department of Infectious Disease Epidemiology, Faculty of Medicine, Imperial College, St Mary's Hospital Campus, Norfolk Place, London W2 1PG, England. Email: b.spratt@ic.ac.uk

**SPRIGGE Timothy Lauro Squire,** b. 14 January 1932, London, England. Emeritus Professor of Philosophy; Writer. m. Giglia Gordon, 4 April 1959, 1 son, 2 daughters. Education: BA, 1955, MA, PhD, 1961, Cantab. Appointment: Professor of Philosophy, University of Edinburgh. Publications: The Correspondence of Jeremy Benthan (editor), 1968; Facts, Words and Beliefs, 1970; Santayana: An Examination of His Philosophy, 1974; The Vindication of Absolute Idealism, 1983; Theories of Existence, 1984; The Rational Foundation of Ethics, 1987; James and Bradley: American Truth and British Reality, 1993. Contributions to: Professional journals. Honour: Fellow, Royal Society of Edinburgh. Memberships: Mind Association; Scots Philosophical Club. Address: 5 King Henry's Road, Lewes, East Sussex, BN7 1BT, England.

**SPRINZ Detlef Friedrich,** b. 2 December 1960, Saarbrücken, Germany. Education: MA, Economics, University of the Saarland, Germany; AM, 1986, PhD, 1992, Political Science, The University of Michigan, USA. Appointments: Senior Fellow, Potsdam Institute for Climate Impact Research, Germany, 1992-; Partner, Ecologic-Institute for International and European Environmental Policy, 1995-2002; Adjunct Position, University of Potsdam, Germany; Visiting Fellow, Max-Planck Institute, 2000-03; Fellow, University of Essex, England, 2001; Ruhrgas Fellow, University of Oslo, Norway, 2004; Scientific Committee, European Environment Agency, 2005-. Publications: Co-editor, Models, Numbers, Cases: Methods for Studying International Relations; Co-editor, International Relations and Global Climate Change; Measuring the Effect of International Environmental Regimes; The Interest-Based Explanation of International Environmental Policy. Honours: European Academy, Bad Neuenahr-Ahrweiler; Listed in Who's Who publications and biographical dictionaries. Memberships include: American Political Science Association; International Studies Association; German Political Science Association; German Council on Foreign Relations. Address: Pasewaldtstrasse 6A, 14169 Berlin, Germany. E-mail: sprinz@sprinz.org Website: http://www.sprinz.org

**SPROT Aidan Mark,** b. 17 June 1919, Lilliesleaf, Scotland. Soldier; Farmer. Education: Stowe School, Buckinghamshire. Appointments: Commissioned Scots Greys, 1940; Served in Palestine, Egypt, Libya, Italy, France, Belgium, Holland, Germany, WWII; Served Libya, Egypt, Jordan, Germany, retired as Lieutenant Colonel, 1962; Adjutant of Regiment, 1945-46, Commanding Officer, 1959-62; Inherited Haystoun Estate in Peeblesshire, 1965; Farmed 3 farms (hill sheep and cattle); Retired, 2003; County Councillor, Peeblesshire, 1963-75; County Director, 1966-74, Patron, 1983-, Peeblesshire Red Cross; County Commissioner, 1968-73, President, 1973-99, Peeblesshire Scout Association. Publication: Swifter than Eagles, War Memoirs 1939-45, 1998. Honours: Military Cross, 1944; Scout Association Medal of Merit, 1993; British Red Cross Association Badge of Honour, 1998; JP, Peeblesshire, 1966-; Deputy Lieutenant, Peeblesshire, 1966-80; Lord Lieutenant, Tweeddale (formerly Peeblesshire), 1980-94; Honorary Freeman, County of Tweeddale, 1994-. Memberships: Queen's Bodyguard for Scotland, Royal Company of Archers, 1950-; Member, 1970-89, President, 1986-89, Lowlands of Scotland TA and VRA; Service Chaplains' Committee, Church of Scotland, 1974-82, 1985-92; Member, 1947-, Secretary, 1964-74, Royal Caledonian Hunt; President, 1988-96, Lothian Federation of Boys Clubs; Trustee, 1989-98, currently Honorary Vice-President, Royal Scottish Agricultural Benevolent Institution; Honorary Member, Rotary Club of Peebles, 1986-; Honorary President, 1990-, Peebles Branch, Royal British Legion; Honorary President, 1994-, Tweeddale Society. Address: Crookston, by Peebles EH45 9JQ, Scotland.

**SPUFFORD Peter,** b. 18 August 1934, Hutton, Somerset, England. m Margaret Spufford, 1 son, 1 daughter, deceased. Education: BA, 1956, MA, 1960, PhD, 1963, LittD, University of Cambridge. Appointments: Research Fellow, Jesus College, Cambridge, 1958-60; From Assistant Lecturer to Reader, University of Keele, 1960-79; From Lecturer to Professor of European History, now Emeritus, Faculty of History, University of Cambridge, 1979-2001; Fellow, Queens' College, Cambridge, 1979-. Publications include: Handbook of Medieval Exchange; Money and its use in Medieval Europe (also in Spanish); Power and Profit. The Merchant in Medieval Europe (also in Spanish, German and Italian). Memberships include: Fellow of the British Academy; Fellow of the Society of Antiquaries; FRNS; FSG. Address: Queens' College, Cambridge CB3 9ET, England.

**SPURWAY Marcus John,** b. 28 October 1938, Surrey, England. Retired Insurance Broker and Director. m. Christine Kate Townshend, 2 sons. Appointments: National Service, 4 Regiment, Royal Horse Artillery; Insurance Broker, Director, Morgan Reid & Sharman, Ltd (Lloyd's Brokers, formerly B&C Aviation Insurance Brokers); Specialist in Aviation Insurance; Retired 1999. Publications: Aviation Insurance Abbreviations, Organisations and Institutions, 1983; Aviation Insurance. The Market and Underwriting Practice, 1991; Aviation Law and Claims, 1992. Address: Lomeer, Common Road, Sissinghurst, Kent TN17 2JR, England.

**SPYROPOULOS Christos-Christopher,** b. 11 December 1937, Rododafni Aegiou, Greece (American citizen, 1975). Conductor; University Professor. m. Georgia Meintanas, 1971, 1 son, 2 daughters. Education: Theological School, Corinth, 1949-54; Theology and Philosophy, University of Athens, 1954-58; Byzantine Music, Advanced Theory in Classical Music, Athens Conservatory, 1953-60; Instrumentation and Orchestral Conducting with Professor Hans Swarowski, Music Academy, Vienna, 1962-64; Advanced Training in International Law, University of Vienna, 1962-64. Appointments: NATO Alliances Officer, Greek Royal Airforce, 1958-60; Reserve (current rank

of Brig General), USAF, 1964; Professor of Music, National Academy of Music, Athens, 1960-62, 1979-85; Professor, Orfio Conservatory of Music, Athens, 1960-62; Education Director, Professor, The Hellenic-American Schools, New York, 1963-68; Inspector, US Civil Aviation, 1972-74; Advisor to President Richard M Nixon, Washington DC, 1971-74; Chairman Examining Committee, American Federation of Musicians, New York, 1973-77; Marketing Advisor, Aramco, Saudi Arabia and Nigeria, 1987-89; Professor of International Law, Worcester University, Massachusetts, USA, 1989-91; Marketing Director, Olympic Airways, Boston, 1989-91; Guest Conductor of symphony orchestras in Vienna, Salzburg, Moscow, Paris, Geneva, Sydney, Minneapolis, Philadelphia, Los Angeles, Chicago, 1964-2002. Publications: The Philosophical Approach of Leadership, Leaders Toward Government, Organizations and Business Establishments, 1975; Sociological Approach to an Interpretation of Religious Phenomena, 1976. Membership: International Musicians Association of America, President, 1973; The Air Line Pilots Association International; The Greek American Organization (ΛΗΕΡΛ), 1966; Member, Greek Literature Association. Honours: Award in Flight Safety, 1970; Distinction (Flag) for 200 years of American Independence, US Government, 1976; Award, Greek Literature Association, 1995. Address: 32 Rododafnis Str, Glyka Nera, AG Parakevis, Athens 15344, Greece.

**SRIDHARAN Varadachari,** b. 2 July 1960, Chennai, Tamil Nadu, India. Assistant Professor. m. Sudha Sridharan, 1 daughter. Education: BSc, 1982; MSc, 1984; PhD, 1990; PDF, 1990. Appointments: Lecturer, International Institute of Population Sciences, Bombay; Lecturer, Vellore Engineering College, Vellore; Lecturer, Anna University, Chennai; Currently, Assistant Professor, Anna University, Chennai. Publications: 40. Honour: 3rd Rank in BSc (Statistics) Degree. Memberships: Indian Society for Technical Education; Operations Research Society of India. Address: Department of Mathematics, College of Engineering, Anna University (Main Campus), Chennai 600025, India.

**SRIVASTAVA Chandrika Prasad,** b. 8 July 1920, Unnao, India. Retired Diplomat. m. Nirmala Salve, 2 daughters. Education: BA, First Class, 1940, BA, First Class Honours, 1941, MA, First Class, 1942, Bachelor of Laws First Class, 1944, Lucknow, India. Appointments include: Officer on Special Duty, 1946-48, Under Secretary, 1948-49, Ministry of Commerce, Government of India; City Magistrate, Lucknow, 1950; Additional District Magistrate, Meerut, 1951-52; Officer on Special Duty, Directorate General of Shipping, 1953; Deputy Director-General of Shipping, 1954-57; Deputy Secretary, Ministry of Transport, Private Secretary to the Minister of Transport and Communications/Minister of Commerce and Industry, 1958; Senior Deputy Director-General of Shipping; Managing Director, Shipping Corporation of India Limited, Bombay, 1961-64; Joint Secretary to the Prime Minister of India, 1964-66; Chairman of the Board of Directors and Managing Director, Shipping Corporation of India Ltd, 1966-73; Chairman, Board of Directors, Mogul Line Limited, 1967-73; Secretary General, 1974-89, Secretary General Emeritus, 1990-, International Maritime Organisation, United Nations; Chancellor, 1983-91, Founding Chancellor Emeritus, 1991-, World Maritime University; Specialisation in national and international maritime affairs. Publications: Lal Bahadur Shashtri Prime Minister of India 1964-66, 1995; Corruption: India's Enemy Within, 2001; World Maritime University – First Twenty Years, 2003. Honours: Over 30 world-wide decorations and honours include: Honorary Member, The Honourable Company of Master Mariners, UK, 1978-89; Commander du Merite Maritime, France, 1982; Order of Prince Henry, the Navigator (Commander), Portugal, 1983; Commander's Cross of the Order of Merit, Poland, 1986; Seatrade Award for Achievement, Seatrade Organisation, 1989; Honorary Knight Commander of the Most Distinguished Order of St Michael and St George, UK, 1990; Similar decorations and honours from India, Italy, Germany, Norway, Spain, Sweden and several other countries; International Maritime Prize, IMO, United Nations, 1992; Doctor of Laws, Honoris Causa: Bhopal University, 1984, University of Wales, 1987. University of Malta, 1988. Memberships: Life Governor, The Maritime Society, UK; Life Member, Board of Governors, World Maritime University; Anglo-Belgian Club, London; India International Centre, New Delhi; Willingdon Club, Mumbai; Poona Club, Pune, India. Address: c/o International Maritime Organisation, 4 Albert Embankment, London SE1 7SR, England.

**SRIVASTAVA Radhey Shyam,** b. 7 June 1931, Bahadurganj (UP), India. Scientist. m. Vijay Laxmi, 1 son, 2 daughters. Education: BSc, 1951, MSc, 1953, PhD, 1963, Lucknow University; Certificate in Proficiency in French, 1957. Appointments: Research Fellow, Lecturer, 1954-58, Lucknow University; Junior Scientific Officer, 1958-61, Senior Scientific Officer, 1961-71, Principal Scientific Officer, 1971-80, Deputy Chief Scientific Officer, 1980-91, Defence Science Centre, New Delhi, India. Publications: Books: Turbulence (pipe Flows), 1977; Interaction of Shock Waves, 1994; Research papers and reports. Honours: Postdoctoral Royal Society Research Fellow, Imperial College of Science and Technology, London, 1965-67; Visiting Scientist: Institute for Aerospace Studies, University of Toronto, 1980-81; Materials Research Laboratories, Melbourne, 1983; Chiba University, Japan, 1991; Visiting Professor, Ernst Mach Institute, Freiburg, Germany, 1995; Visiting Professor, Chiba University, Japan 2000; Visiting Professor, Tohoku University, Japan, 2000; Visiting Professor, Tokyo Denki University, Japan, 2001; Visiting Professor, Aachen University, Germany, 2002; 2000 Millennium Medal of Honor, ABI, USA, 2000; 20th Century Award for Achievement, 1998. Memberships: Fellow, National Academy of Science, India; Life Member, Bharat Ganita Parishad, India; Indian Science Congress; Kothari Centre for Science, Ethics and Education (KCSEE); Fellow, United Writers' Association of India. Address: A-3/260, Janakpuri, New Delhi 110058, India.

**ST CLEMENT Pamela,** b. 11 May 1942. Actress; Presenter. m. Andrew Louis Gordon, 1970, divorced 1979. Education: The Warren, Worthing; Rolle College, Devon; Rose Bruford College of Drama, Kent. Career: Television appearances include: Wild at Heart; BBC Animal Awards: Zoo Chronicles; Adopt-a-Wild-Animal; BBC Eastenders, 1986-; Whipsnade, (2, 13 part wildlife series); Not for the Likes of Us (Play for Today); The Tripods; Cats Eyes; Partners in Crime; Shoestring; Emmerdale Farm; Horseman Riding By (BBC series); Shall I See You Now (BBC play); Within these Walls (2 series); Theatre includes: Joan Littlewood's Theatre Royal, Stratford; Royal Shakespeare Company; Prospect Theatre Company (Strindberg and Chekov); Thorndike Theatre (Macbeth); Yvonne Arnaud Theatre (I am a Camera); Leeds Playhouse (Once a Catholic); Victoria Theatre/Dome Brighton (The Music from Chicago); Films include: Hedda; Dangerous Davies; The Bunker; Scrubbers. Honour: Presented Duke of Edinburgh Awards, St James' Palace, 2000. Memberships: President, West Herts RSPCA; Vice-President, Scottish Terrier Emergency Care Scheme; Patron: London Animal Day; Tusk Trust; Africat (UK); Pets as Therapy; Leicester Animal Aid Association; Ridgeway Trust for Endangered Cats; Pro-Dogs; Other charities involved with: PDSA; Blue Cross; National Animal Welfare Trust; Battersea Dogs Home; Environmental Investigation Agency; Hearing Dogs for Deaf People; International League for the Protection of

Horses; Kennel Club Good Citizens Dog Scheme; Project Life Line; Earth Kind; WSPA; Humane Education Trust; Member, Institute of Advanced Motorists. Address: c/o Saraband Associates, 265 Liverpool Road, London N1 1LX, England.

**STACK Steven,** b. 20 December 1947, Providence, Rhode Island, USA. College Professor. 3 sons. Education: Assistant Professor of Sociology, Alma College, 1976-79; Assistant Professor of Sociology, Indiana University, 1979-81; Associate Professor of Sociology, Penn State University, 1981-85; Associate, Full Professor, Sociology, Auburn University, 1985-90; Full Professor of Criminal Justice, Wayne State University, 1990-. Publications include: 175 articles in professional journals; 33 book chapters; 249 papers read in professional meetings. Honours: Grant, National Institute of Mental Health; grants, Henry Frank Guggenheim Foundation; Edwin Shneidman Award, American Association of Suicidology; Louis Dublin Award, American Association of Suicidology. Memberships: American Association of Suicidology; American Sociological Association; National Council on Family Relations; American Society of Criminology; Academy of Criminal Justice Sciences. Address: Department of Criminal Justice, Wayne State University, Detroit, MI 48292, USA. E-mail: aa1051@wayne.edu

**STAFFORD Francis Melfort William Fitzherbert (Lord),** b. 13 March 1954, Rhynie, Scotland. Landowner. m. Katharine, 2 sons, 2 daughters. Education: Reading University, England; RAC, Cirencester, England. Appointments: Non Executive Director, Tarmac Industrial Products, 1985-94; Chair, Governor, Swynnerton School, 1986-; Non Executive Director, NHS Foundation Trust, 1990-99; Vice Chairman, Harper Adams University College, 1990-; Vice Chairman, Hanley Economic Building Society, 1993-; Pro Chancellor, Keele University, 1993-; Landowner. Honours: Deputy Lieutenant, 1994-. Memberships: Army and Navy Club; Lord's Taverners; Sunningdale Golf Club; Patron and President various organisations mainly in Staffordshire. Address: Swynnerton Park, Stone, Staffordshire, ST15 0QE, England. E-mail: ls@lo rdstafford.demon.co.uk

**STAFFORD-CLARK Max,** b. 17 March 1941. Theatre Director. m. (1) Carole Hayman, 1971, (2) Ann Pennington, 1981, 1 daughter. Education: Trinity College, Dublin. Appointments: Artistic Director, Traverse Theatre, Edinburgh, 1968-70; Director, Traverse Workshop Company, 1970-74; Artistic Director, Joint Stock, 1974-79; English Stage Company, Royal Court Theatre, 1979-93; Out of Joint, 1993-; Visiting Professor, Royal Holloway and Bedford College, University of London, 1993-94; Maisie Glass Professor, University of Sheffield, 1995-96; Visiting Professor, University of Hertfordshire, 1999-; Visiting Professor, University of York, 2003-; Principal Productions: Fanshen; Top Girls; Tom and Viv; Rat in the Skull; Serious Money; Our Country's Good; The Libertine; The Steward of Christendom; Shopping and Fucking; Blue Heart; Drummers; Some Explicit Polaroids; Rita, Sue and Bob Too/A State Affair; A Laughing Matter; The Permanent Way; Macbeth. Publication: Letters to George 1989. Honours: Hon Fellow, Rose Bruford College, 1996; Hon DLitt, Oxford Brookes, 2000; Hon DLitt, Hertfordshire, 2000. Address: 7 Thane Works, Thane Villas, London N7 7PH, England.

**STAGNARO Sergio,** b. 7 December 1931, Sestri Levante, Genoa. Medical Doctor. m. Marina Neri, 1 son, 1 daughter. Education: MD, Genoa University, 1956; Haematology, Gastroenterology, Metabolic Diseases, Pavia University. Appointments: Retired General Practitioner; Researcher in Physical Semiotics; Founder, Biophysical Semeiotics.

Publications: 150 articles on Biophysical Semeiotics; Books: Introduzione Alla Semeiotica Biofisica Terreno Oncologico; Nuovi Aspetti e Fondamentali Sviluppi di un Importante Metodo Diagnostico Clinico; Le Costituzione Semeiotiche-Biofisiche; La Melatomina nella Prevenzione Primaria dei Tumori; Single Patient Based Medicine. Honour: Listed in several Who's Who and biographical publications. Address: Via E Piaggio 23/8, 16037 Riva Trigoso, Genoa, Italy. E-mail: dottsergio@semeio ticabiofisica.it

**STAHL Alexander Hans Joachim,** b. 27 April 1938, Netzschkau, Vogtland. Official. m. Bärbel Schultheis, 2 sons. Education: Diploma in Politics, Free University, Berlin, 1965. Appointments: Adviser in informal education for the young at the Arbeitskreis deutscher Bildungsstätten, Bonn, 1965-67; Lecturer, Political Education, Jugenhof Vlotho, 1967-69; Youth Officer, Land Youth Office Westfalen-Lippe, Landschaftsverband Westfalen-Lippe, 1972-; Deputy-in-Chief, board of film censors, (Freiwillige Selbstkontrolle der Filmwirtschaft) Wiesbaden, 1989-. Publications: Editor, journal: Mitteilungen des Landesjugendamtes Westfalen-Lippe, Landschaftsverband Westfalen-Lippe, Landeshaus Münster, 1969-; Honour: Councillor, Stadt Münster, 1975-79; Honorary Member, Bavarian Association of Youth Officers. Address: Von-Humboldt-Str 33, D48159 Münster, Germany.

**STALDER-STRAUB Henry Joseph,** b. Hilterfingen, Switzerland, Canadian and Australian citizen. Philosopher. Education: BSc, DBA, Pacific Western University; PhD, Pacific Southern University, Research Professor, Habilitation at Canadian School of Management. Appointments: Numerous postings to international banks, including American Express, Zurich; UBS, Toronto and Sydney; VR Hottinger, New York, Luxembourg; Zurich, London, Netherlands and Austria, 1987-. Publications: Numerous books and papers on various subjects, including leadership, risk philosophy, corporate survival strategies and rational realism, including Precise Conclusive Thinking; Risk Philosophy; Make Peace with Time; Leadership Capacity; Critical Intellectual Expansion; Essentialism; The Counterworld; Dichotomy and Interdependence. Honours include: Grand Cross of St John; Grand Cross of St George; KCCM; KCSA; KCLJ; Lipper Awards No 1. Memberships: SVFV; AIMR; Swiss Holdings and Finance Corporation; Swiss Bankers' Association; National Club, Toronto; Union Club, Sydney. Address: Rotelstrasse 3, 8413 Neftenbach, Switzerland.

**STALLONE Sylvester Enzio,** b. 6 July 1946, New York, USA. Actor; Film Director. m. (1) Sasha Czach, 1974, divorced, 2 sons, (2) Brigitte Nielsen, 1985, divorced 1987, (3) Jennifer Flavin, 1997, 2 daughters. Education: American College of Switzerland; University of Miami. Appointments: Has had many jobs including: Usher; Bouncer; Horse Trainer; Store Detective; Physical Education Teacher; Now Actor, Producer, Director of own films; Founder, White Eagle Company; Director, Carolco Pictures Inc, 1987-; Film appearances include: Lords of Flatbush, 1973; Capone, 1974; Rocky, 1976; FIST, 1978; Paradise Alley, 1978; Rocky II, 1979; Nighthawks, 1980; Escape to Victory, 1980; Rocky III, 1981; First Blood; Rambo, 1984; Rocky IV, 1985; Cobra, 1986; Over the Top, 1986; Rambo II, 1986; Rambo III, 1988; Set Up, 1990; Tango and Cash, 1990; Rocky V, 1990; Isobar, 1991; Stop or My Mom Will Shot, 1991; Oscar, 1991; Cliffhanger, 1992; Demolition Man, 1993; Judge Dredd, 1994; The Specialist, 1994; Assassins, 1995; Firestorm, 1996; Daylight, 1996; Cop Land, 1997; An Alan Smithee Film: Burn Hollywood Burn, 1998; Get Carter, 2000; Producer, Director, Staying Alive, 1983. Publications: Paradise Alley, 1977; The Rocky Scrapbook, 1997. Honours: Oscar for best film, 1976;

Golden Circle Award for best film, 1976; Donatello Award, 1976; Christopher Religious Award, 1976; Honorary Member, Stuntmans' Association; Officier Ordre des Arts et des Lettres. Memberships: Screen Actors' Guild; Writers' Guild; Directors' Guild. Address: William Morris Agency, 151 El Camino Drive, Beverly Hills, CA 90212, USA.

**STAMP Terence,** b. 22 July 1938, London. Actor. Career: Theatre work before film debut in Billy Budd, 1962; Other films include: Term of Trial, 1962; The Collector, 1965; Modesty Blaise, 1966; Far From the Madding Crowd, 1967; Poor Cow, 1967; Blue, 1968; Theorem, 1968; Tales of Mystery, 1968; The Mind of Mr Soames, 1969; A Season in Hell, 1971; Hu-man, 1975; The Divine Creature, 1976; Striptease, 1977; Meetings With Remarkable Men, 1978; Superman, 1978; Superman II, 1979; Death in the Vatican, 1980; The Bloody Chamber, 1982; The Hit, 1984; Link, 1985; Legal Eagles, 1986; The Sicilian, 1986; Wall Street, 1988; Alien Nation, 1988; Young Guns, 1988; Prince of Shadows, 1991; The Real McCoy, 1992; The Adventures of Priscilla Queen of the Desert, 1994; Bliss, 1995; Limited Edition, 1995; Mindbender; Love Walked In, 1996; Kiss the Sky, 1997; The Limey, 1999; Bow Finger, 1999; Red Planet, 2000; Theatre: Dracula; The Lady from the Sea. Publications: Stamp Album, 1988; Coming Attractions, 1988; Double Feature, 1989; The Night, 1992; Stamp Collection, 1997. Honours: Hon Dr of Arts, University of East London, 1993. Address: c/o Markham and Froggatt, 4 Windmill Street, London, W1P 1HF, England.

**STANDISH Norman Weston,** b. 4 April 1930, Marion, Iowa, USA. Chemist; Chemical Engineer. m. Ingrid C J Jueschke, 1 son, 2 daughters. Education: BS, Beloit College, Beloit, Wisconsin, 1952; MS, 1958, PhD, 1960, Purdue University, Lafayette, Indiana. Appointments: Research Chemist, 1961-68, Manager, Technical Services, 1968-82, Standard Oil, Ohio; Laboratory Director, Exploration and Production, Sohio-BP American Inc, 1982-85; Manager, Strategic Planning, BP Exploration and Production Company, 1985-88; Executive Director, EPIC Polymer Lifecycle Center, 1992-94; International Business Consultant, 1995-; Currently President, Standish House Inc and Standish House Consulting Inc. Publications: Reinforced Plastics, chapter in Tool and Manufacturing Engineers Handbook; 24 US patents; 37 published papers; 87 technical presentations; 15 invited papers. Honours include: Commercial Solvents Fellowship; Science Advisory Board, Texas A and M University, 1985-; DAR Citizenship Award, 2004; Listed in national and international biographical dictionaries. Memberships: American Men and Women of Science, Advisory Board, Holyoke Community College, 1965-67; Lt Governor, Cleveland Mayflower Society, 1979; American Chemical Society, Career Consultant, 2000-, Chair, Employment Services Advisory Board, 1997, committees including Committee on Economic and Professional Affairs, 1997-, Chair, Sub-Committee on Employment Services, also regional and divisional offices; Society of Manufacturing Engineers; Society of Petroleum Engineers; Society of Plastic Engineers, Plastic Recycling Committee; Past Chair, Cleveland Technical Societies Council; President, North American Manx Association, 2003-04; President, Soule Kindred in America, 2003-04. Address: PO Box 105, 540 West Carroll Street, Lanark, IL 61046-0105. E-mail: nstandish@aeroinc.net

**STANKIEWICZ Anna,** b. 11 September 1958, Szczecinek, Poland. Educating Engineering. Education: MSc, Computer Science and Control Systems, Institute of Engineering Cybernetics, Technical University of Wroclaw, Poland. Appointments: Assistant in the Institute of Engineering Cybernetics, Technical University of Wroclaw, Poland,

1983-85; Assistant Professor, Technical University of Lublin, Department of Automation, Poland, 1988-94; Lecturer, Institute of Technical Sciences, Agricultural Academy of Lublin, Poland, 1996-. Publications: Over 40 articles and papers in specialist scientific journals. Honours: Award of the Polish Academy of Sciences, 1981, 1982; Award from the Rector of Wroclaw Technical University, 1985; 1986. Memberships: Institute of Electrical and Electronics Engineers, Control Systems Society, 1999-. Address: Institute of Technical Sciences, Agricultural Academy, Doswiadczalna 50A 20-282 Lublin, Poland. E-mail: anna.stankiewicz@ar.lublin.pl

**STANOULOV Nicolay Spassov,** b. 9 July 1923, Sofia, Bulgaria. Radio/Communication Engineer; Cybernetician; System Analyst. m. Anne Christova, 1 son. Education: BS, Mathematics, Sofia University 1948; MS, Radio Engineering, Technical University, Sofia, 1952; Candidate of Science Degree, 1976, Doctor of Science Degree, 1979, Bulgarian Academy of Sciences, Sofia. Appointments at the Bulgarian Academy of Sciences: Junior Research Fellow, Senior Research Fellow, Associate Professor, 1961-63; Central Laboratory of Control Systems and Institute of Engineering Cybernetics, 1963-79; Central Computing Institute, Automatic Programming Division, 1979-82; Head of System Analysis Division, Central Laboratory of Control Systems, 1982-89; Scientific Consulting, Institute of Computer Technologies, 1989-90. Publications: 2 books; Over 150 professional publications. Honours: Numerous awards, Bulgarian Academy of Sciences; Award, Polish Academy of Sciences. Membership: International Society of Multiple Criteria Decision Making. Address: Ul Czar Assen 100, 1463 Sofia, Bulgaria.

**STAPLETON Carlos,** b. 27 January 1939, Long Island, New York, USA. Law Enforcement. m. Barbara, 2 sons, 2 daughters. Education: Graduate, High School of Commerce, New York. Appointments: New York Police Department, retired; Emergency Medical Technician; New York State Motor Vehicle Road Test Inspector. Publications: Articles in: New York NewsDay Paper; New York Daily News Paper; Queens Chronicle News Paper; Queens Village Community District Representative. Honours: Accomplishment and Honor Award, New York City Police Department; Certificate of Achievement, NYS Emergency Medical Technician. Memberships: Wayanda Civic Association; Queens Village Community Group Association; Queens Village Community Representative. Address: 88-12 Parsons Blvd, Jamaica, NY 11432, USA.

**STARITSKY Yuri Grigorievich,** b. 28 October 1913, St Petersburg, Russia. Geologist. m. Staritskaya (Morozova) M, 2 daughters. Education: Engineer Geologist, Mining Institute, St Petersburg, 1947; Candidate of Science, 1951; DSc, 1969. Appointments: Senior Researcher, 1946-51, Head of Department, 1955-73, Leading Researcher, 1973-, All Russian Geological Research Institute, St Petersburg; Assistant Professor, Mining Institute, Krivoi Rog, Ukraine, 1951-53; Researcher, Academy of Sciences, St Petersburg, 1953-55; Head of Regional Departments of Ostsiberia and West Russia; Leading Research, 1975-. Publications: Minerageny of the Siberian Platform Cover, 1970; History of Development and Minerageny of the Russian Platform Cover, 1987; Metallogenic Map of the Russian Platform Cover, 1985; Metallogenic Map of the West-Siberian Platform Cover, 1985; Life of the Expanding Earth, 1998; Map of Ore-Bearing Formations and Ore Zones of the East-European Platform Cover, 2000; Mineral deposits of the European Russia, 2003; Co-author, Russian Metallogenic Dictionary, 2003; Co-author, Geological-Mineragenical Map of the World, 2004; More than 250 articles in professional journals; Member, editorial boards of all metallogenic maps

of the former USSR and Russian Federation. Honours: Order of Great Patriotic War, President of Supreme Soviet of Russian Federation, 1990; Scholar Emeritus of Russian Federation, 1990. Memberships: Russian Mineralogy Society; St Petersburg Scientists Club. Address: Apt 54, 82/11 Moika Embankment, 190000 St Petersburg, Russia. E-mail:dashak@mail.line.ru

**STARK Ian David,** b. 22 February 1954, Galashiels, Scotland. Equestrian. m. Jenny, 1 son, 1 daughter. Education: Galashiels Academy. Career: 4 Olympic Silver Medals, 1984, 1988, 1992, 1996, 2000; 3 times winner, Badminton, 1986, 1988, 1999; Team Gold, World Championships, 1986; 6 team Gold Medals, European Championships; Individual Gold Medal, European Championships, 1991. Publications: Flying Scot, 1988; Glenburnie & Murphy Himself, 1992; Stark Approach, 1998; Walking a Cross Country Course, 1999; Stark Reality, 2000. Honours: MBE, 1989; OBE, 2001; Fellow, British Horse Society, 2005. Memberships: British Horse Society; British Eventing; British Show Jumping Association. Address: Haughhead, Ashkirk, Selkirk, TD7 4NS, Scotland. E-mail: haughhead@yahoo.co.uk

**STARK Richard James,** b. 6 October 1950, Melbourne, Australia. Medical Practitioner (Neurologist). m. Janet Keys-Brown, 15 December 1972, 1 son, 1 daughter. Education: MB BS (Hons), Monash University, 1973; FRACP, Royal Australasian College of Physicians, 1980; MACLM, Australian College of Legal Medicine, 1999. Appointments: RMO/Neurology Registrar, 1974-79, Visiting Neurologist, 1982-, Alfred Hospital, Melbourne; Neurology Registrar, The London Hospital, 1979-81; Neurology Registrar, National Hospitals for Nervous Diseases, London, 1981-82; Visiting Neurologist, Caulfield Hospital, Melbourne, 1982-; Visiting Neurologist, Peter MacCallum Cancer Institute, Melbourne, 1982-; Hon Senior Lecturer, 1993-2004, Hon Clin Assoc Prof, 2005-, Department of Medicine, Monash University; Senior Examiner, Australian Medical Council, 1996-; External Examiner, M Med, Malaysia, 1997. Publications: More than 50 articles in various medical scientific journals. Honours: Sophie Davis Prize, Monash University, 1973; HH Green Scholarship in Medicine, 1973; H Power Scholarship in Surgery, 1973; Bushell Fellowship, 1979; AAN appointee, NHQS, 1981. Memberships: Member, 1980-, Council member, 1984-90, 1997-, Hon secretary, 1984-87, Hon treasurer, 1997-, Chair Victorian state committee, 1989-92, Australian Association of Neurologists; Fellow, 1980-, Committee for examinations, 1992-98, Specialist advisory committee in Neurology, 1984-87, 1992-, Royal Australasian College of Physicians; Australian Medical Association; Australian College of Legal Medicine; Victoria Medical Panels; Australian Brain Foundation, 1985-91; Migraine Foundation of Australia, vice president, 1996-; IN Group, Patron, 1992-. Address: 15 Collins Street, Melbourne, Victoria 3000, Australia.

**STARKEY Lawrence Harry,** b. 10 July 1919, Minneapolis, Minnesota, USA. Synoptic Philosopher. m. (1) 1 son, 2 daughters, (2) Hallie Jean Hughes. Education: BA, honours, University of Louisville, 1942; MDiv, Southern Baptist Theological Seminary, 1945; MA, 1951, PhD, 1960, University of Southern California. Appointments: Engineering Draftsman, Electromotive Division, General Motors, 1937-39; Instructor, Assistant Professor, Registrar, Los Angeles Baptist College and Seminary, 1945-51; Science Film Writer, Moody Institute of Science, 1955-57; Associate Professor, Bethel College, St Paul, 1958-62; Associate Professor, Department Chair, Linfield College, 1962-63; Engineering Writer, Convair Division, General Dynamics, 1963-66; Associate Professor, Alma College, 1966-68; Associate Editor, Principal Editor,

Philosophy, Encyclopaedia Britannica, 1968-72; Associate Professor, Department Chair, Jamestown College, 1973-75; Part-time Lecturer, Program Co-ordinator, Television Producer, North Dakota State University, 1976-79; Draftsman, Designer, Concord Inc, North Dakota, 1977-85; Instructor, Moorhead State University, 1985-86; Lecturer, University of Missouri, Rolla, 1986-88. Publications: Red River of Life (film); Several articles in professional journals, a children's encyclopaedia, the World Congress of Philosophy Web Site; Abstracts of the Particles Conference, Sweden; The Vorträge of the Leibniz-Kongress, Germany. Honours: Speed Junior Scholarship; University Graduate Scholarship; Citizen Ambassador to Russia, Hungary. Memberships include: American Philosophical Association; Section President, American Scientific Affiliation, 1954, 1970, 1971; Metaphysical Society of America. Address: 1325 North 63rd Street, Wauwatosa, WI 53213-2919, USA.

**STARODETKO Eugeniy,** b. 1 April 1933, Borisov, Belarus (former USSR). Mechanical Engineer. m. Galina Budkevich, 2 sons. Education. Leningrad Polytechnic University, 1951 57; 1st PhD Degree in Engineering, 1967, 2nd PhD Degree in Engineering, 1976, MHPS, Moscow. Appointments: Design Engineer, Zhodino Road Construction Machine Plant, Zhodino, Belarus, 1957-58; Design Engineer, Leading Designer-Engineer, Designers Team Leader, Izhora Heavy Machine Plant, City of Leningrad, USSR (now St Petersburg, Russia), 1958-63; Team Leader, Deputy Department Head, Department Head, Gorky Technology-Design and Scientific Research Institute of Mechanisation and Automation for the Automotive Industry, Gorky City, USSR (now Nizhniy Novgorod, Russia), 1964-77; Senior Scientific Researcher, Leader of CAD Systems Laboratory, 1977-99, Senior Scientific Researcher, 1999-2004, Institute of Engineering Cybernetics, Belarusian Academy of Sciences, Minsk City, Belarus; Professor, Belarusian State University, 1988-; Retired, 2004-. Publications: Over 150 publications on computer graphics, CAD and internal-combustion engine design; 5 monographs include: Some Elements of Computer Geometry; Super Engine; Student aid manuals; Scientific articles, USSR national standards on geometrically oriented computer languages; Over 20 patents issued in Belarus, Russia, Ukraine, USA. Honours: PhD, Engineering, 1967; PhD, Engineering, 1976; Professor, 1988; Academician, International Academy of Information Technologies, 1996. Memberships: Doctoral Scholar Council on Computer Graphics and Computer Engineering, Belarusian Academy of Sciences. Address: 1509 Kulman St, Minsk, 220100 Belarus.

**STARR Kenneth Winston,** b. 21 July 1946, Vernon, Texas, USA. Lawyer. m. Alice J Mendell, 1970, 1 son, 2 daughters. Education: George Washington University; Brown University; Duke University. Appointments: Law Clerk, Court of Appeals, Miami, 1973-74; Supreme Court, 1975-77; Associate, Gibson, Dunn and Crutcher, Los Angeles, 1974-75; Associate Partner, 1977-81; Counsellor to Attorney General, Justice Department, Washington, DC, 1981-83; Solicitor General, 1989-93; Judge, Court of Appeals, 1983; Partner, Kirkland and Ellis, Washington, DC, 1993-94; Independent Counsel for Whitewater Investigations as well as any collateral matters arising out of any investigation of such matters including obstruction of justice or false statements, 1994-. Publications: Contributor, articles to legal journals. Memberships: Several law organisations. Address: Kirkland and Ellis, 655 15th Street, Suite 1200, Washington, DC 2005, USA.

**STARR Ringo (Richard Starkey),** b. 7 July 1940, Dingle, Liverpool, England. Musician. m. (1) Maureen Cox, 1965, divorced, 2 sons, 1 daughter, (2) Barbara Bach, 1981. Career:

Member, Rory Storm and The Hurricanes; Member, The Beatles, 1962-70; Worldwide tours, 1963-; Attended Transcendental Meditation Course, Maharishi's Academy, Rishkesh, India, 1968; Co-Founder, Apple Corps Ltd, 1968; Solo Artiste, 1969-; Narrator, Thomas The Tank Engine, (children's TV). Creative Works: Recordings by the Beatles include: Please, Please Me, 1963; With the Beatles, 1963; A Hard Day's Night, 1964; Beatles for Sale, 1965; Help!, 1965; Rubber Soul, 1966; Revolver, 1966; Sergeant Pepper's Lonely Hearts Club Band, 1967; The Beatles (White Album), 1968; Yellow Submarine, 1969; Abbey Road, 1969; Let it Be, 1970; Films by the Beatles: A Hard Day's Night, 1964; Help!, 1965; Yellow Submarine (animated colour cartoon film), 1968; Let it Be, 1970; Individual appearance in films: Candy, 1968; The Magic Christian, 1969; 200 Motels, 1971; Blindman, 1971; That'll Be the Day, 1973; Born to Boogie (also directed and produced), 1974; Son of Dracula (also produced), 1975; Lisztomania, 1975; Ringo Stars, 1976; Caveman, 1981; The Cooler, 1982; Give My Regards to Broad Street, 1984; Singles as solo artist: It Don't Come Easy; Back Off Boogaloo; Photograph; You're Sixteen; Oh My My; Snookeroo; Only You. Honours: BPI Awards; Rock'n'Roll Hall of Fame, 1988. Address: c/o Mercury Records, 825 8th Avenue, New York, NY 10019, USA.

**STARY Frank E,** b. 3 January 1941, St Paul, Minnesota, USA. Professor. m. Education: Bchem, University of Minnesota, 1963; PhD, Inorganic Chemistry, University of Cincinnati, 1969; Appointments: Undergraduate Research, University of Minnesota, 1960-63; Graduate Research, University of Cincinnati, 1964-68; Postdoctoral Research, University of California Irvine, 1968-72; Research Associate, University of Missouri-St Louis, 1972-74; Assistant Professor, Professor, Maryville University-St Louis, Missouri, 1974-. Publications: 15 articles. Honours: Distinguished Teaching Award, 1981. Memberships: American Chemical Society; Phi Lambda Upsilon, Sigma Xi. Address: Maryville University, 13550 Conway Road, St Louis, MO 63141-7299, USA. E-mail: fstary@maryville.edu

**STAUFFER John Eugene,** b. 16 September 1932, Bronxville, New York, USA. Chemical Engineer. m. Valerie, 2 daughters. Education: BS, Princeton University, 1954; ChE, Massachusetts Institute of Technology, 1957; PhD, Worcester Polytechnic Institute, 1960. Appointments: Stauffer Chemical Company, 1960-1983; Stauffer Technology, 1983-. Publications: Quality Assurance of Food; Fuel Pellets for Thermonuclear Reactions, US Patent. Memberships: American Chemical Society; Sigma Xi. Address: 6 Pecksland Road, Greenwich, CT 06831, USA. E-mail: stauftek@aol.com

**STAUNTON Imelda Mary Philomena Bernadette,** b. 9 January 1956. Actress. m. Jim Carter, 1983, 1 daughter. Appointments: Repertory Exeter, Nottingham, York, 1976-81; Stage appearances include: Guys and Dolls, 1982, 1996; Beggar's Opera, 1985; She Stoops to Conquer; Chorus of Disapproval, 1985; The Corn is Green, 1985; Fair Maid of the West, 1986; Wizard of Oz, 1986; Comrades, 1987; Uncle Vanya, 1988; Into the Woods, 1990; Phoenix, 1990; Life x 3, 2000; TV appearances include: The Singing Detective, 1986; Yellowbacks, 1990; Sleeping Life, Roots, Up the Garden Path, 1990; Antonia and Jane; David Copperfield, 1999; Victoria Wood Xmas Special, 2000; Murder, 2001; Cambridge Spies, 2002; Strange, 2002; Film appearances include: Peter's Friends, 1992; Much Ado About Nothing, 1993; Deadly Advice, 1994; Sense and Sensibility; Twelfth Night; Remember Me, 1996; Shakespeare in Love, 1998; Another Life, 1999; Rat, 1999; Crush, 2000; Bright Young Things, 2002; Virgin of Liverpool, 2002; Blackball, 2002; Family Business, 2002. Honours: Oliver

Award, Best Supporting Actress; Oliver Award, Best Actress in a Musical.

**STAVANS Ilan,** b. 7 April 1961, Mexico. Critic; Writer; Professor. m. Alison Sparks, 19 June 1988, 2 sons. Education: BA, Universidad Autónoma Metropolitana, 1984; MA, The Jewish Theological Seminary, 1987; MA, 1988, MPhil, 1989, PhD, 1990, Columbia University. Appointments: Series Editor, Jewish-Latin America; Series Editor, Latino Voices; Lewis-Sebring Professor in Latin American and Latino Culture, Amherst College, Department of Spanish, 1993-; 5-College 40th Anniversary Professor, 2005-2008; Research Fellow, Institute of Latin American Studies, University of London, 1998-99; Host of television show La Plaza: Conversations with Ilan Stavans, 2001-. Publications include: The Hispanic Condition; Art and Anger; The Riddle of Cantinflas; The One-handed Pianist; Mutual Impressions; The Oxford Book of Jewish Stories; The Essential Ilan Stavans; Latino USA: A Cartoon History; The Inveterate Dreamer: Essays and Conversations on Jewish Literature; On Borrowed Words: A Memoir of Language; The Schocken Book of Modern Sephardic Literature. Octavio Paz: A Meditation; The Poetry of Pablo Neruda; Spanglish: The Making of a New American Language; Isaac Barhevis Singer: Collected Stories (3 vols), Encyclopedia Latina (4 vols), Dictionary Days; Ruben Dario: Selected Writings; Conversations with Ilan Stavans. Honours include: National Endowment for the Humanities, 1991-92; Latino Literature Prize, 1992; Bernard M Baruch Excellence in Scholarship Award, 1993; Nomination to the Nona Balakian Excellence in Reviewing Award, National Book Critics Circle, 1994; Guggenheim Fellowship, 1998-99; Chile's Presidential Medal; Emmy Nomination; Antonia Pantoja Award; Latino Hall of Fame, 2001; Commonwealth Humanities Scholar, 2005. Address: Department of Spanish, Amherst College, Amherst, MA 01002, USA.

**STEAD C(hristian) K(arlson),** b. 17 October 1932, Auckland, New Zealand. Poet; Writer; Critic; Editor; Professor of English Emeritus. m. Kathleen Elizabeth Roberts, 8 January 1955, 1 son, 2 daughters. Education: BA, 1954, MA, 1955, University of New Zealand; PhD, University of Bristol, 1961; DLitt, University of Auckland, 1982. Appointments: Lecturer in English, University of New England, Australia, 1956-57; Lecturer, 1960-61, Senior Lecturer, 1962-64, Associate Professor, 1964-67, Professor of English, 1967-86, Professor Emeritus, 1986-, University of Auckland; Chairman, New Zealand Literary Fund Advisory Committee, 1972-75, New Zealand Authors' Fund Committee, 1989-91. Publications: Poetry: Whether the Will is Free, 1964; Crossing the Bar, 1972; Quesada: Poems 1972-74, 1975; Walking Westward, 1979; Geographies, 1982; Poems of a Decade, 1983; Paris, 1984; Between, 1988; Voices, 1990; Straw Into Gold: Poems New and Selected, 1997; The Right Thing, 2000; Dog: Poems, 2002; The Red Tram, 2004. Fiction: Smith's Dream, 1971; Five for the Symbol, 1981; All Visitors Ashore, 1984; The Death of the Body, 1986; Sister Hollywood, 1989; The End of the Century at the End of the World, 1992; The Singing Whakapapa, 1994; Villa Vittoria, 1997; The Blind Blonde with Candles in her Hair (stories), 1998; Talking about O'Dwyer, 2000; The Secret History of Modernism, 2002; Mansfield, 2004; Non-fiction: The New Poetic: Yeats to Eliot, 1964, revised, 1987, 2005; In the Glass Case: Essays on New Zealand Literature, 1981; Pound, Yeats, Eliot and the Modernist Movement, 1986; Answering to the Language: Essays on Modern Writers, 1990; The Writer at Work, 2000; Kin of Place: Essays on Twenty New Zealand Writers, 2002. Editor: World's Classics: New Zealand Short Stories, 1966, 2nd edition, 1975; Measure for Measure: A Casebook, 1971, revised edition, 1973; Letters and Journals of Katherine Mansfield, 1977, 2004; Collected Stories of Maurice Duggan, 1981; The New Gramophone Room: Poetry and Fiction

(with Elizabeth Smither and Kendrick Smithyman), 1985; The Faber Book of Contemporary South Pacific Stories, 1994; Werner Forman, New Zealand, 1994. Contributions to: Poetry, fiction and criticism to various anthologies and periodicals. Honours: Katherine Mansfield Prize, 1960; Nuffield Travelling Fellowship, 1965; Katherine Mansfield Menton Fellowship, 1972; Jessie Mackay Award for Poetry, 1972; New Zealand Book Award for Poetry, 1975; Honorary Research Fellow, University College, London, 1977; Commander of the Order of the British Empire, 1984; New Zealand Book Award for Fiction, 1985 and 1995; Queen Elizabeth II Arts Council Scholarship in Letters, 1988-89; Queen's Medal for services to New Zealand literature, 1990; Fellow, Royal Society of Literature, 1995; Senior Visiting Fellow, St John's College, Oxford, 1996-97; Hon DLitt, University of Bristol, 2001; Fellow, English Association, 2004. Membership: New Zealand PEN, chairman, Auckland branch, 1986-89, national vice president, 1988-90. Address: 37 Tohunga Crescent, Auckland 1, New Zealand.

**STEADMAN Alison,** b. 26 August 1946, Liverpool, England. Actress. m. Mike Leigh, 2 sons. Education: Drama School, Loughton, Essex. Appointments: Began career in repertory theatre, Lincoln, Bolton, Liverpool Worcester and Nottingham; Stage appearances include: Sandy in the Prime of Miss Jean Brodie; Beverley in Abigail's Party; Mae-Sister Woman in Cat on a Hot Tin Roof, National Theatre; Mari Hoff in The Rise and Fall of Little Voice; David Edgar's Maydays, Royal Shakespeare Company, Joking Apart; Kafka's Dick, Royal Court; Marvin's Room, 1993; The Plotters of Cabbage Patch Corner; The Provoked Wife, Old Vic, 1997; When We Are Married; The Memory of Water; Entertaining Mr Sloane; Bette in Cousin Bette; TV Appearances: Z Cars; Hard Labour; Abigail's Party; Nuts in May; The Singing Detective; Virtuoso; Newshounds; The Short and Curlies; Gone to Seed; Selling Hitler; Pride and Prejudice; The Wimbledon Poisoner; Karaoke; No Bananas; The Missing Postman; Let Them Eat Cake; Fat Friends; The Cappuccino Years; Films: Champions; Wilt; Shirley Valentine; Life is Sweet; Blame it on the Bellboy; Topsy Turvy; Happy Now. Honours: Honorary MA, University of East London; Evening Standard Best Actress Award, 1977; Olivier Award for Best Actress, 1993.

**STEED Theresa Jean,** b. 10 March 1932, Grapeland, Texas, USA. Retired. m. Jarvis L Steed, 3 daughters. Education: Bachelor of Music Education, Southern College of Fine Arts, Texas, 1956; Postgraduate work, University of Texas, 1961; Sul Ross University, Texas, 1962; University of Wisconsin, 1962. Appointments: Executive Secretary, Hughes Tool Corporation, Houston, 1950-53; Executive Secretary, Cactus Petroleum Corporation, Houston, 1954; Executive Secretary to the Director of Piesner Research, Stouffer Chemical Co, Houston, 1956-57; Elementary School Teacher, Rosenburg Independent School District, 1957-58; Kindergarten, Elementary Music Educator, Sonora Independent School District, 1959-65; Elementary School Teacher, Houston Independent School District, 1965-67; Co-founder, Co-owner, Steed Tile and Manufacturing Co, Texas, 1965-; Executive Secretary Conoco Oil Company, Houston, 1967-68; Elementary School Teacher, Conroe Independent School District, 1968-70; Publications: Author, Audio-Visual Curriculums for Music Education; Kindergarten through Eighth Grade, 1962. Honours: Honorary Master of Rhymes, Duke University, 1961. Memberships: Order of the Eastern Star, 1960-; Delta Kappa Gamma Honorary Sorority, 1962-; Women in Construction, Charter Member, 1970-75; Democratic National Committee, Washington DC, 1993-; Democratic Senatorial Campaign, Washington DC, 1997; World War Two Museum, Charter Member, New Orleans, 2002; National Trust for Historic Preservation, Charter Member, 2002; National

Democratic Committee, 2004. Address: 17595 FM 1097 West, Montgomery, TX 77356, USA. E-mail: tsteed@txucom.net

**STEEL Danielle,** b. 14 August 1950, New York, USA. Writer. m. (2) Bill Toth, 1977; (3) John A Traina Jr, 4 sons, 5 daughters. Education: Lycee Francais; Parsons School of Design, New York; University of New York. Appointments: Public Relations and, Advertising Executive, Manhattan, New York; Published first novel, 1973, then wrote advertising copy and poems for women's magazines; Wrote first bestseller, The Promise, 1979. Publications: Going Home, 1973; Passion's Promise, 1977; Now and Forever, 1978; Seasons of Passion, 1978; The Promise, 1979; Summer's End, 1980; The Love Again, 1981; Palomino, 1981; Loving, 1981; Rememberance, 1981; A Perfect Stranger, 1982; Once in a Lifetime, 1982; Crossings, 1982; Thurston House, 1983; Full Circle, 1984; Having a Baby, 1984; Family Album, 1985; Wanderlust, 1986; Fine Things, 1987; Kaleidoscope, 1987; Zoya, 1988; Star, 1989; Daddy, 1989; Heartbeat, 1991; Message from Nam, 1991; No Greater Love, 1991; Jewels, 1992; Mixed Blessings, 1992; Vanished, 1993; Accident, 1994; The Gift, 1994; Wings, 1995; Lightning, 1995; Five Days in Paris, 1995; Malice, 1995; Silent Honor, 1996; The Ranch, 1996; The Ghost, 1997; Special Delivery, 1997; The Ranch, 1998; The Long Road Home, 1998; The Klone and I, 1998; Mirror Image, 1998; Bittersweet, 1999; The Wedding, 2000; The House on Hope Street, 2000; Journey, 2000; Lone Eagle, 2001; Answered Prayers, 2002; Dating Game, 2003; Johnny Angel, 2003; Safe Harbour, 2003; Ransom, 2004; Second Chance, 2004, Echoes, 2004; Impossible, 2005; Miracle, 2005; Eight Children's Books; One Book of Poetry. Address: c/o Dell Publishing, 1745 Broadway, New York, NY 10019, USA.

**STEEL OF AIKWOOD David Martin Scott Steel (Baron) (Life Peer),** b. 31 March 1938, Kirkcaldy, Scotland. Politician; Journalist; Broadcaster. m. Judith Mary MacGregor, 1962, 2 sons, 1 daughter. Education: Prince of Wales School, Nairobi, Kenya; George Watson's College; Edinburgh University. Appointments: President, Edinburgh University, Liberals, 1959; Member, Students Representative Council, 1960; Assistant Secretary, Scottish Liberal Party, 1962-64; Member of Parliament for Roxburgh, Selkirk and Peebles, 1965-83; for Tweeddale, Ettrick and Lauderdale, 1983-97; Scottish Liberal Whip, 1967-70; Liberal Chief Whip, 1970-75; Leader, Liberal Party, 1976-88; Co-Founder Social and Liberal Democrats, 1988; President, Liberal International, 1994-96; Member of Parliament delegate to UN General Assembly, 1967; Former Liberal Spokesman on Commonwealth Affairs: Sponsor, Private Member's Bill to Reform law on abortion, 1966-67; President, Anti-Apartheid Movement of UK, 1966-69; Chair, Shelter, Scotland, 1969-73; Countryside Movement, 1995-97; BBC TV Interviewer in Scotland, 1964-65; Presenter of Weekly Religious Programmes for Scottish TV, 1966-67; for Granada, 1969; for BBC, 1971-76; Director, Border TV, 1991-98; Rector, University of Edinburgh, 1982-85; Chubb Fellow, Yale University, USA, 1987; D L Ettrick and Lauderdale and Roxburghshire. Publications: Boost for the Borders, 1964; No Entry, 1969; A House Divided, 1980; Border Country, 1985; Partners in One Nation, 1985; The Time Has Come, 1987; Mary Stuart's Scotland, 1987; Against Goliath, autobiography, 1989. Honours: Freedom of Tweeddale, 1989; KBE, 1990; Ettrick and Lauderdale, 1990; Hon Dr, Stirling, 1991; German Grand Cross, 1992; Hon D Litt: Buckinghamshire, 1994, Heriot Watt, 1996; Hon LLD: Edinburgh, 1997, Strathclyde, 2000, Aberdeen, 2001; Bronze Medal, London-Cape Town Rally, 1998; D Univ, Open University, 2001; LL D, St Andrews, 2003; Legion d'Honneur, 2003; KT, 2004; LL D, Glasgow-Caledonian, 2004. Address: House of Lords, London, SW1A 0PW, England.

**STEELE Tommy (Thomas Hicks),** b. 17 December 1936, Bermondsey, London, England. Actor; Singer. m. Ann Donoghue, 1960, 1 daughter. Career: First stage appearance, Empire Theatre, Sunderland, 1956; First London appearance, Dominion Theatre, 1957; Major roles include: Buttons, Rodgers and Hammerstein's Cinderella, Coliseum, 1958; Tony Lumpkin, She Stoops To Conquer, Old Vic, 1960; Arthur Kipps, Half A Sixpence, Cambridge Theatre, 1963-64; The same, Broadhurst Theatre, New York, 1965; Truffaldino, The Servant Of Two Masters, Queen's, 1969; Dick Whittington, London Palladium, 1969; Meet Me In London, Adelphi, 1971; Jack Point, The Yeoman Of The Guard, City Of London Festival, 1978; The Tommy Steele Show, London Palladium, 1973; Hans Andersen, 1974, 1977; One-man show, Prince of Wales, 1979; Singing In The Rain (also director), 1983; Some Like It Hot, 1992; What A Show, Prince of Wales Theatre, 1995; Film appearances: Kill Me Tomorrow, 1956; The Tommy Steele Story; The Duke Wore Jeans; Tommy The Toreador; Light Up The Sky; It's All Happening; The Happiest Millionaire; Half A Sixpence; Finian's Rainbow; Where's Jack?; Television: Writer, actor, Quincy's Quest, 1979. Compositions: Composed, recorded, My Life My Song, 1974; A Portrait Of Pablo, 1985; Publications: Quincy, 1981; The Final Run, 1983; Rock Suite - An Elderly Person's Guide To Rock, 1987. Honour: OBE, 1979.

**STEENBURGEN Mary,** b. 8 February 1953, Newport, Arizona, USA. Film Actress. m. (1) Malcolm McDowell, 1980, divorced, 1 son, 1 daughter, (2) Ted Danson, 1995. Education: Neighborhood Playhouse. Appointments: Films include: Goin' South, 1978; Time After Time, 1979; Melvin and Howard, 1980; Ragtime, 1981; A Midsummers Night's Sex Comedy, 1982; Romantic Comedy, 1983; Cross Creek, 1983; Sanford Meidner - Theatre's Best Kept Secret, 1984; One Magic Christmas, 1985; Dead of Winter, 1987; End of the Line, 1987; The Whales of August, 1987; The Attic: The Hiding of Anne Frank, 1988; Parenthood, 1989; Back to the Future Part III, 1989; Miss Firecracker, 1989; The Long Walk Home, 1990; The Butcher's Wife, 1991; What's Eating Gilbert Grape, 1993; Philadelphia, 1993; Pontiac Moon, 1994; Clifford, 1994; It Runs in the Family, 1994; Pontiac Moon; My Family; Powder; The Grass Harp; Nixon; Gulliver's Travels, 1996; About Sarah, 1998; Trumpet of the Swan, 2001; Nobody's Baby, 2001; I Am Sam, 2001; Life as a House, 2001; The Trumpet of the Swan (voice), 2001; Sunshine State, 2002; Wish You Were Dead, 2002; Hope Springs, 2003; Casa de los babys, 2003; Elf, 2003; Marilyn Hotchkiss' Ballroom Dancing and Charm School, 2005; Theatre appearances include: Holiday, 1987; Candida, 1993. Address: c/o Ames Cushing, William Morris Agency Inc, 151 El Camino Drive, Beverly Hills, CA 90212, USA.

**STEFANILE Felix Neil,** b. 13 April 1920, New York, New York, USA. Retired Professor; Poet. m. Selma Epstein, 17 January 1953. Education: BA, City University of New York, 1944. Appointments: Visiting Poet, Lecturer, 1961-62, Assistant Professor, 1962-64, Associate Professor, 1964-69, Professor, 1969-87, Purdue University; Chairman, Editorial Board, Purdue University Press, 1964-69; Editor, Publisher, Sparrow Press, 1954-89. Publications: If I Were Fire; In That Far Country; The Blue Moustache; Umberto Saba; East River Nocturne; A Fig Tree in America; The Dance at St Gabriel's, 1995; The Country of Absence, 2000. Contributions to: New York Sunday Times Book Review; Sewanne Review; Virginia Quarterly Review; Poetry; Parnassus; TriQuarterly; Hudson Review; New York Times. Honours: Pushcart Press Prize; Standard Oil of Indiana Foundation Award; Virginia Quarterly Review Emily Clark Balch Award; Nathan Haskell Dole Prize; National Endowment for the Arts Prize; John Ciardi Award for Lifetime Achievement in Poetry, 1997. Memberships: Poetry Society of

America; American Literary Translators Association. Address: 103 Waldron Street, West Lafayette, IN 47906, USA.

**STEGNIY Oleksandr,** b. 25 January 1961, Kyiv City, Ukraine. Sociologist. m. Darina Kovach, 1 son, 1 daughter. Education: Diploma, History and Social Science, State University of Kyiv, 1979-85; Preparing dissertation in the Europe and Northern America Department, Institute for Social and Economical Problems of Foreign Countries, Academy of Sciences of Ukraine, 1986-90; Preparing dissertation for Doctor Degree, Institute of Sociology, Academy of Sciences of Ukraine, 1999-2002. Appointments: Research Fellow, Western Ukrainian Laboratory, Institute of Sociology, Ukrainian National Academy of Sciences, Uzhgorod, 1991-92; Research Fellow, Public Opinion Research Department, Institute of Sociology, Ukrainian National Academy of Sciences, 1992-93; Research Fellow, Social Diagnostic Department, Institute of Sociology, Ukrainian National Academy of Sciences, 1993-94; Head, Department of Social and Political Research, Centre of Social and Marketing Research (SOCIS), a full member of the Gallup International Association, 1994-2001; Deputy Director, Centre of Political and Electoral Studies, SOCIS, 2001-. Publications: Over 80 publications including 4 monographs: Non-Governmental Environmental Organisations in Ukraine – Present State and Trends of Development, 1996; The Regionalism in Ukraine as a Subject of Sociological Research (co-author), 1998; The Environmental Movement in Ukraine: Sociological Analysis, 2001; Institutionalisation of Environmental Interests in the Society of Sociogenic Risks, 2002. Membership: Sociological Association of Ukraine. Address: Flat 104, Kioto-5, Kyiv – 156, 02156 Ukraine. E-mail: steg@socis.kiev.ua

**STEIN Robert A,** b. 5 August 1933, Duluth, Minnesota, USA. Writer; Educator. m. Betty L Pavlik, 1955, 3 sons. Education: MA, Writing, 1986, MA, Counselling/Education, 1968, BSc, Industrial Management, 1956, University of Iowa; Permanent Professional Counselling/Teaching Certificate, Iowa Board of Public Instruction, 1968; US Air Force Squadron Officers' School, 1960; US Air Force Command and Staff College, 1966; Air Force Academic Instructor School, with Honors, 1966; Industrial College of the Armed Forces, with Honors, 1973. Appointments: Officer and Pilot, USAF, 1956-77, Retired as Colonel; Assistant Professor of Aerospace Studies, 1964-66, University of Iowa; Associate Professor, 1966-68; Professor, 1975-77; Member, Faculty Division of Writing, Kirkwood Community College, Iowa City and Cedar Rapids, Iowa, 1984-89; Instructor, Creative Writing Program, Iowa City/Johnson County Senior Center, 1994-. Publications: Novels: Apollyon: A Novel, 1985; The Chase, 1988; The Black Samaritan, 1997, 2nd edition, 2000; The Vengeance Equation, 2000, 2nd edition, 2001, Screenplay, 2001; Fiction: Death Defied, 1988; Non-Fiction: Statistical Correlations, 1967; Engineers Vs. Other Students: Is There A Difference?, 1967; WhatEVER Happened to Moe Bushkin?, 1967; Quest for Viability: One Way!, 1976; Threat of Emergency, 1988. Honours: 5 Wartime Decorations, 9 Merit Awards; All-American Swimming, 1950; Outstanding Faculty Award, University of Iowa, 1967-68; Iowa Authors' Collection, 1985; Minnesota Authors' Collection, 1987; International Literary Award, 1988; Lifetime Achievement Award, University of Iowa, 1999; Entered in Iowa Athletics Hall of Fame, 2002. Memberships: The Authors Guild; The Authors League of America.

**STEINEM Gloria,** b. 25 March 1934, Toledo, Ohio, USA. Feminist; Political Activist; Lecturer; Editor; Writer. Education: BA, Smith College, 1956; Chester Bowles Asian Fellow, India, 1957-58. Appointments: Contributing Editor, Glamour Magazine, 1962-69; Co-Founder and Contributing Editor, New

York Magazine, 1968-72; Co-Founder and Member of the Board of Directors, Women's Action Alliance, 1970-; Co-Founder and Editor, 1971-87, Columnist, 1980-87, Consulting Editor, 1987-, Ms Magazine; Convenor and Member of the National Advisory Committee, Women's Political Caucus, 1971-; Co-Founder and President of the Board of Directors, Ms Foundation for Women, 1972-; President, Voters for Choice, 1979-. Publications: The Thousand Indias, 1957; The Beach Book, 1963; Wonder Woman, 1972; Outrageous Acts and Everyday Rebellions, 1983; Marilyn: Norma Jeane, 1986; Revolution from Within: A Book of Self-Esteem, 1992; Moving Beyond Words, 1994. Contributions to: Anthologies and magazines. Honours: Penney-Missouri Journalism Award, 1970; Ohio Governor's Award for Journalism, 1972; Woman of the Year, McCall's Magazine, 1972; D Human Justice, Simmons College, 1973; Bill of Rights Award, American Civil Liberties Union of Southern California, 1975; Woodrow Wilson International Center for Scholars Fellow, 1977; National Woman's Hall of Fame, 1993. Memberships: American Foundation of Television and Radio Artists; Authors Guild; National Organization for Women; National Press Club; Phi Beta Kappa; Society of Magazine Writers. Address: c/o Ms Magazine, 230 Park Avenue, 7th Floor, New York, NY 10169, USA.

**STELLWAAG Michael Karl,** b. 8 March 1951, Landau/Pfalz, Germany. Physician; Cardiologist. m. Ute Stellwaag, 1 son. Education: Study of Chemistry, 1970-76, Diplom Chemiker Hauptprüfung, 1976, Study of Medicine, 1975-80, Medical Doctor, 1985, University of Göttingen, Germany. Appointments: Internship, Städtische Kliniken Oldenburg, 1980-81; Resident in Radiology, Oncology and Surgery, 1982-85; Resident in Internal Medicine and Cardiology, 1986-92, Chief Resident in Cardiology, 1992-93, University of Marburg; Consultant in Cardiology, Deutsche Klinik für Diagnostik, Wiesbaden, 1993-99; Private Practice, 2000-. Address: Burgstr 6-8, D-65183 Wiesbaden, Germany

**STEPASHIN Sergey Vadimovich,** b. 2 March 1952, Port Arthur. Security Official. m. 1 son. Education: Higher Political College, USSR Ministry of Internal Affairs; Military Academy; Financial Academy under the Russian Federation Government; LLD, Candidate Degree in History, Professor; Russian Federation State Councillor of Justice. Military Rank: Colonel-General. Appointments: Service in Interior Forces, 1973-90; Lecturer, Higher Political College, Leningrad, 1981-90; Deputy to RSFSR Supreme Soviet, Head, Committee on Defence and Security, Russian Federation Supreme Soviet, 1990-93; Chief, Leningrad Federal Security Agency Branch and Deputy Chair, Russian Federation Federal Security Agency, 1991-92; First Deputy Director, 1993-94, Director, 1994-95, Federal Counter-Intelligence Service (later Federal Security Service); Head of Administration, Department of Government, 1995-97; Minister of Justice, 1997-98, of Internal Affairs, 1998-99; First Deputy Chairman of Government, 1999; Chair of Government (Prime Minister), 1999; Member, State Duma (Parliament), 1999-2000; Chair, Accounts Chamber of Russian Federation, 2000- (re-appointed 2005); President, European Organisation of Supreme Audit Institutions, 2002-05. Publications: Personal and Social Security (Political and Legal Issues), St Petersburg, 1994. Honours: Order of Fortitude, 1998; Order "For Merits Before Fatherland", 3rd degree, 2002; French Order of Legion of Honour, Commodore Degree, 2005. Address: Accounts Chamber of the Russian Federation, Zubovskaya Str 2, Moscow 119992, Russian Federation. E-mail: info@ach.gov.ru Website: www.ach.gov.ru

**STEPHENS Frederick Oscar,** b. 7 August 1927, Sydney, Australia. Professor of Surgery. m. Sheilagh Kelly, 2 sons, 3

daughters. Education: MBBS, The University of Sydney, 1951; FRCS (Edinburgh), 1958; FACS, 1965; FRACS, 1967; MD, 1970, MS, 1970, The University of Sydney. Appointments: Senior Professorial Registrar, The University of Aberdeen, 1958-60; Joyce Fellow in Surgical Research, Portland Oregon, USA, 1960-61; Senior Lecturer in Surgery, 1961, Associate Professor in Surgery, 1963, Professor and Head of the Department of Surgery, 1988, The University of Sydney; Currently, Emeritus Professor. Publications: Over 200 publications in medical and surgical journals; Books: Cancer Explained, 1997; All About Prostate Cancer, 2000; All About Breast Cancer, 2001; The Cancer Prevention Manual, 2002. Honours: Wellcome Travelling Fellow, 1960; Joyce Fellow in Surgical Research, 1960-61 Fulbright Fellow and Visiting Professor, San Francisco, 1969-70; US Founders Lecturer, 1972; Queen's Jubilee Medal, 1978; Foundation President, The International Society for Regional Cancer Therapy, 1991-98; Order of Australia, 1993; Surgeon to the Queen and other visiting royalty and the visiting President of the USA during their visitis to New South Wales; Many Visiting Professorships in Australia, UK, USA, Germany, Israel and Japan. Memberships: Australian Medical Association; Edinburgh, Australian and American Colleges of Surgeons; International Society for Regional Cancer Therapy; Director, The Sporting Chance Foundation for Cancer Research. Address: 16 Inkerman Street, Mosman, NSW 2088, Australia. E-mail: sheilagh.kelly@uts.edu.au

**STEPHENS Jack,** b. 1 December 1936, Huntington Park, California, USA. Writer; Photographer. m. Kristi Kellogg Stephens. Education: BA, Journalism, Washington State University, 1962. Appointments: Editor-Reporter, Ferndale Record, 1961; Reporter Maui News, 1963-67; Reporter, Pacific Business News, 1969-72; Journalism Instructor, Maunaolu College, 1967-73; Owner, Aquarius Enterprises, 1968-. Publications: Contributions to a variety of magazines. Honours: Bay League Long Jump Champion, 1953-54; Southern California Long Jump Champion, 1954; Martin Relays Long Jump Champion, 1960. Memberships: Society of Professional Journalists, 1959-; Maui's Maunaolu College Journalism Instructor and Publications Director, 1967-73. Address: 3-3400 Kuhio Highway A-103, Lihue, HI 96766-1051, USA.

**STETTLER Simon (Simon de Beauvalleé),** b. 2 June 1944, Arni, Switzerland. Writer. m. Brunhilde Tritten, 1 son, 1 daughter. Education: Vocational School; Master Course; Pilotenbrevet. Appointments: Self-employed writer; Freelance journalist, Radio DRS. Publications: Poetry: Geistesblitze, 1981; Literarische Wirtinnenverse, 1997; Last-Minute-Gedichte, 1999; Thousands of letters to the editor and newspaper articles; Iron Sculptures, including at Thun station. Memberships: Schweiz Schriftstellerverein; Bernischer Schriftstellerverein; ProLitteris. Address: Bahnhofstrasse 2, CH 3507 Biglen, Switzerland. E-mail: simon.stettler@bluewin.ch

**STEVEN Stewart Gustav,** b. 30 October 1935, Hamburg, Germany. Journalist. m. Inka Sobieniewska, 1 son. Education: Mayfield College, Sussex. Appointments: Political Reporter, Central Press Features, 1961-63; Political Correspondent, Western Daily Press, 1963-64; Political Reporter, 1964-65, Diplomatic Correspondent, 1965-67, Foreign Editor, 1967-72, Daily Express; Assistant Editor, 1972-74, Associate Editor, 1974-82, Daily Mail; Editor, 1982-92, Columnist, 1996-, Mail on Sunday; Director, Associated Newspapers Holdings Ltd, 1989-95; Editor, Evening Standard, 1992-95. Publications: Operation Splinter Factor, 1974; The Spymasters of Israel, 1976; The Poles, 1982. Memberships: Chair, Liberty Publishing and Media Ltd, 1996-97; Chair, Equity Theatre Commission, 1995-96; National Campaign for the Arts, 1996-; Member, Board for

Better English Campaign, 1995-97; Thames Advisory Group, 1995-97; London Film Commission, 1996-; Honorary Perpetual Student, Bart's Hospital, 1993. Address: 29 Priory Avenue, Chiswick, London, W4 1TZ, England.

**STEVENS Geoffrey,** b. 4 June 1942, West Bromwich, England. Chemist; Poet. m. (1) Barbara C Smith, 20 Feb 1965, 1 daughter, (2) Geraldine M Wall, 6 July 1996. Education: HNC, Chemistry, Wolverhampton Polytechnic. Appointments: Director of Industrial Archaeology, Black Country Society; Editor, Purple Patch Poetry Magazine, 1976-. Publications: Ecstasy, 1992; Field Manual for Poetry Lovers, 1992; A Comparison of Myself With Ivan Blatny, 1992; The Surreal Mind Paints Poetry, 1993; The Complacency of the English, 1995; Skin Print, 1995; For Reference Only, 1999; The Phrenology of Anaglypta, 2003. Contributions to: Magazines and periodicals. Honour: Award for Service to Poetry, Hastings Poetry Festival, 1997. Address: 25 Griffiths Road, West Bromwich B71 2EH, England.

**STEVENS Jocelyn Edward Greville (Sir),** b. 14 February 1932, London, England. Publisher. m. Jane Armyne Sheffield, 1956, dissolved 1979, 1 son, deceased, 2 daughters. Education: Cambridge University. Appointments: Military Service, Rifle Brigade, 1950-52; Journalist, Hulton Press, 1955-56; Chair and Managing Director, Stevens Press Ltd, Editor, Queen Magazine, 1957-58; Personal Assistant to Chair, 1968, Director, 1971-81, Managing Director, 1974-77, Beaverbrook Newspapers; Managing Director, Evening Standard Co Ltd, 1969-72; Managing Director, Daily Express, 1972-74; Deputy Chair and Managing Director, Express Newspapers, 1974-81; Editor and Publisher, The Magazine, 1982-84; Director, Centaur Communications, 1982-84; Governor, Imperial College of Science, Technology and Medicine, 1985-92; Governor, Winchester School of Art, 1986-89; Rector and Vice Provost, RCA, 1984-92; Chair, The Silver Trust, 1990-93; English Heritage, 1992-2000; Deputy Chair, Independent TV Commission, 1991-96; Non Executive Director, The TV Corporation, 1996, Asprey & Co, 2002, Garrad & Co, 2002; President, The Cheyne Walk Trust, 1989-93; Trustee, Eureka! Children's Museum, 1990-2000; Chair, The Phoenix Trust; Director, The Prince's Foundation, 2000. Honours: Hon D Litt, Loughborough, 1989, Buckingham, 1998; Hon FCSD, 1990; Senior Fellow, RCA, 1990. Address: 14 Cheyne Walk, London, SW3 5RA, England.

**STEVENS Shakin' (Michael Barratt),** b. 4 March 1948, Ely, Cardiff, South Wales. Singer; Songwriter. Career: Enjoyed much success touring for many years with his band, the Sunsets; Starred in the multi-award-winning West End musical, Elvis, which ran for 19 months from 1977; Signed as solo artist with Epic Records world-wide in 1978; First UK Top 30 single, Hot Dog, charted in 1980; First European chart entry, Marie Marie, in 1980; First UK Number 1, later a major international hit, This Ole House, 1981; 38 hit singles, 36 of which were consecutive, throughout the 1980s and 1990s; UK hits: Four No.1s, three No.2s, 12 Top 5 hits, 15 Top 10 hits, 25 Top 20 hits, 30 Top 30 hits and 32 Top 40 hits; Musical collaborations include Bonnie Tyler, Roger Taylor, Hank Marvin and Albert Lee; Tours, personal appearances and television performances world-wide; Headlining to an audience of 200,000 in Vienna in 2003; Most successful hit-maker of the 1980s in the UK, with more weeks in the charts (254 in the 80's alone) than any other international recording artist; His work has been covered by many artists including Eddie Raven (A Letter To You) and Sylvia (Cry Just A Little Bit), No 1 and No 9 in the Nashville charts, and Barry Manilow (Oh Julie), US hit in 1982. Recordings: Hit singles, albums and songs have sold millions of copies, earning numerous honours and awards, including many Gold and Platinum discs world-wide; Hit albums include (UK): Shakin' Stevens Take One!; This Ole House; Shakin' Stevens; Shaky; Give Me Your Heart Tonight; The Bop Won't Stop; Greatest Hits; Lipstick, Powder and Paint; Let's Boogie; A Whole Lotta Shaky; There's Two Kinds Of Music - Rock'n'Roll; The Epic Years; UK hit singles include: Hot Dog; Marie Marie; This Ole House; You Drive Me Crazy; Green Door; It's Raining; Oh Julie; Shirley; I'll Be Satisfied; The Shakin' Stevens EP; It's Late; Cry Just A Little Bit; A Rockin' Good Way (To Mess Around And Fall In Love), duet with Bonnie Tyler; A Love Worth Waiting For; A Letter To You; Teardrops; Breaking Up My Heart; Lipstick Powder And Paint; Merry Christmas Everyone; Turning Away; Because I Love You; A Little Boogie Woogie (In The Back Of My Mind); What Do You Want To Make Those Eyes At Me For?; Love Attack; I Might; The Best Christmas Of Them All; Radio. Honours include: 30 Top 30 hits in a decade, unsurpassed by any other artist; Best singer/performer, MIDEM; Chartmaker Award for 4 simultaneous singles in the German chart; Gold and Platinum discs world-wide; First double platinum single ever to an international artist, Sweden; Most weeks in UK charts for international recording artist; Gold Badge Award from the British Academy of Composers and Song Writers; Number One Gold Award from The Guinness Book of British Hit Singles; In 2004 ranked as the 16th highest selling artist in the UK ever. Address: c/o Sue Davies, The HEC Organisation, PO Box 184, West End, Woking, Surrey GU24 9YY, England. E-mail: suedavies@shakinstevens.com

**STEVENSON Juliet**, b. 30 October 1956, England. Actress. 1 son, 1 daughter, 2 stepsons. Education: Hurst Lodge School, Berkshire; St Catherine's School, Surrey; Royal Academy of Dramatic Arts. Appointments: Plays include: Midsummer Night's Dream; Measure for Measure; As You Like It; Troilus and Cressida; Les Liaisons Dangerouses; Caucasian Chalk Circle; No I; Footfalls; Other Worlds; Yerma; Hedda Gabler; Death and the Maiden; Duchess of Malfi; Films include: Drowning by Numbers; Ladder of Swords; Truly Madly Deeply; The Trial; The Secret Rapture; Emma; The Search for John Gissing; Who Dealt?; Beckett's Play; Bend It Like Beckham; Food of Love; Several TV roles include: The Politician's Wife; Cider with Rosie; The Politician's Wife; A Doll's House; Life Story; Antigone; The March; Maybury; Thomas and Ruth; Aimée; The Mallens; Living With Dinosaurs; Wrote and fronted BBC documentary Great Journeys; Radio includes: To the Lighthouse; Volcano; Albertina; House of Correction; Hang Up; Cigarettes and Chocolate; A Little Like Drowning; Victory. Publications: Clamourous Voices, 1988; Shall I See You Again?; Players of Shakespeare. Honours: Bancroft Gold Medal, Royal Academy of Dramatic Arts, 1977; Time Out Award for Best Actress, 1991; Evening Standard Film Award for Best Actress, 1992; Lawrence Olivier Theatre Award for Best Actress, 1992. Address: c/o Markham and Froggatt Ltd, Julian House, 4 Windmill Street, London, W1P 1HF, England.

**STEWART Alec James**, b. 8 April 1963, Merton, London, England. Cricketer. m. Lynn, 1 son, 1 daughter. Education: Tiffin Boys' School, Kingston Upon Thames. Appointments: Right-hand opening Batsman; Wicket Keeper; Surrey, 1981- (Captain 1992-97); 126 Tests for England, 1989-90 to 2 Jan 2003, 14 as Captain, scoring 8187 runs (average 40.13) including 15 hundreds; Scored 25,438 first class runs (48 hundreds) to end of 2002; Held 11 catches, equaling world first-class record, for Surrey v Leicestershire, Leicester, 19-22 August, 1989; Toured Australia, 1990-91, 1994-95 and 1998-99 (captain); 161 limited-overs internationals to 7 January 2003; Overtook record (118) of Graham Gooch to become England's most-capped cricketer, Lords July 2002. Publications: Alec Stewart: A Captain's Diary, 1999. Honour: Wisden Cricketer of the Year, 1993. Address:

c/o Surrey Cricket Club, Kennington Oval, London, SE11 5SS, England.

**STEWART Dave**, b. 9 September 1952, Sunderland, Tyne and Wear, England. Musician (guitar, keyboards); Songwriter; Composer. m. Siobhan Fahey, 1 August 1987, divorced, 1 son. Career: Musician, Harrison and Stewart (with Brian Harrison); Longdancer; The Catch, 1977; Renamed The Tourists, 1979-80; Formed Eurythmics with Annie Lennox, 1980-89; Worldwide concerts include Nelson Mandela's 70th Birthday Tribute, Wembley, 1988; As solo artiste: Nelson Mandela Tribute concert, Wembley, 1990; Amnesty International Big 30 concert, 1991; Founder, Spiritual Cowboys, 1990-92; Vegas, with Terry Hall, 1992-93; Founder, own record label Anxious Records, 1988; Owner, The Church recording studio, 1992; Producer, session musician, for artistes including Bob Dylan; Mick Jagger; Tom Petty; Daryl Hall; Bob Geldof; Boris Grebenshikov. Compositions: All Eurythmics songs co-written with Lennox; Theme for Jute City, BBC1; Co-writer, film score Motorcycle Mystics; Co-writer with Gerry Anderson, music for children's series GFI, 1992. Recordings: Albums: with The Tourists: The Tourists; Reality Affect; Luminous Basement; with Eurythmics: In The Garden, 1982; Sweet Dreams (Are Made Of This), 1983; Touch (Number 1, UK), 1984; 1984 (For The Love Of Big Brother), film soundtrack, 1984; Be Yourself Tonight, 1985; Revenge, 1986; Savage, 1988; We Too Are One (Number 1, UK), 1989; Eurythmics Greatest Hits (Number 1, UK), 1991; Eurythmics Live 1983-89, 1992; with the Spiritual Cowboys: Dave Stewart And The Spiritual Cowboys, 1990; with Vegas: Vegas, 1992; Solo: Greetings From The Gutter, 1994; Film directed: Honest, 2000; Film soundtrack: De Kassiere, with Candy Dulfer, 1990; Hit singles include: with the Tourists: I Only Want To Be With You, 1979; So Good To Be Back Home, 1979; with Eurythmics: Sweet Dreams (Are Made Of This) (Number 1, US), 1983; Love Is A Stranger, 1983; Who's That Girl?, 1983; Right By Your Side, 1983; Here Comes The Rain Again, 1984; Sex Crime (1984), 1984; Would I Lie To You?, 1985; There Must Be An Angel (Playing With My Heart), 1985; It's Alright (Baby's Coming Back), 1986; When Tomorrow Comes, 1986; Thorn In My Side, 1986; Missionary Man, 1986; You Have Placed A Chill In My Heart, 1988; Love Is a Stranger, 1991; Sweet Dreams, 1991; I Saved the World, 1999; 17 Again, 1999; Solo: Lily Was Here, with Candy Dulfer, 1990; Contributor, Rock The World, 1990; Give Peace A Chance, Peace Choir, 1991; Videos: Eurythmics Live; Sweet Dreams; Savage. Honours: MTV Music Awards, Best New Artist Video, Sweet Dreams, 1984; BRIT Awards: Best Producer, 1986, 1987, 1990; Grammy, Best Rock Performance, Missionary Man, 1987; Ivor Novello Awards: Songwriters of the Year (with Annie Lennox), 1984, 1987; Best Song, It's Alright, 1987. Current Management: Miss Management, 16101 Ventura Blvd, Suite 301, Encino, CA 91436, USA. Address: c/o East West Records, Electric Lighting Station, 46 Kensington Court, London W8 5DP, England.

**STEWART David**, b. 27 January 1964, Dartford, Kent, England. Solicitor. 2 daughters. Education: BA, Repton York University; CPE, 1986, LSF, 1987, Chester College of Law. Appointments: Solicitor, Blyth Dutton, London, 1987-90; Attorney, Miller and Simons, British West Indies, 1990-92; Solicitor, 1992-95, Partner, 1995-97, S J Berwin, London; Partner and Head of Commercial Litigation, Olswang, 1997-. Address: 90 High Holborn, London WC1V 6XX, England. E-mail: david.stewart@olswang.com Website: www.olswang.com

**STEWART Gordon Thallon**, b. 5 February 1919, Paisley, Scotland. Physician; University Professor. m. (1) Joan Kego, deceased (2) Georgina Walker, 2 sons, 2 daughters. Education:

BSc, 1939, MB, ChB, 1942., MD 1949, University of Glasgow; DTM and H, University of Liverpool, 1947. Appointments: House Surgeon then House Physician, Glasgow, Scotland, 1942-43; Medical Officer, Royal Navy (Surgeon Lieutenant, RNVR), 1943-46; Hospital and research appointments in UK (Aberdeen, Liverpool, London), 1947-63; Professor of Epidemiology, Schools of Medicine and Public Health, University of North Carolina at Chapel Hill, USA, 1963-68; Watkins Professor and Head, Department of Epidemiology and Professor of Medicine, Tulane University, New Orleans Louisiana, USA, 1968-72; Consultant Physician, Epidemiology and Preventive Medicine, National Health Service, UK and Mechan Professor of Public Health, University of Glasgow, 1972-84; Emeritus Professor, 1984-. Publications: Books: Chemotherapy of Fungal Infection (with R W Riddell), 1955; Penicillin Group of Drugs, 1965; Penicillin Allergy (with J McGovern), 1970; Editor: Trends in Epidemiology, 1972; Chapters on epidemiology, control of infectious diseases and education in other books; Articles on same and on drug abuse and public health subjects in mainline medical journals, articles on liquid crystals and ordered structures in biology and medicine. Honours: High Commendation for MD Thesis, University of Glasgow, 1949; WHO Visiting Professor, Dow Medical College, Karachi, Pakistan, 1953; Senior Visiting Foreign Fellow, US National Science Foundation, 1963-64; Visiting Professor, Cornell University Medical College, New York, USA, 1971; Emeritus Fellow, Infectious Diseases Society of America; Visiting Lecturer and Consultant at various hospitals and colleges in Europe, Canada, America, India, Pakistan, Middle East, Africa; Consultant WHO; New York City Health Department; US Navy (Camp Lejeune, North Carolina). Memberships: Fellow: Royal College of Physicians, Glasgow; Royal College of Pathology, London; Faculty of Public Health of the Royal College of Physicians; Royal Statistical Society; Medical Society of London; Royal Society of Medicine; Member, British Medical Association. 29/9 Inverleith Place, Edinburgh EH3 5QD, Scotland.

**STEWART Ian,** b. 28 August 1950, Blantyre, Scotland. Member of Parliament. m. 2 sons, 1 daughter. Education: Stretford Technical College; Manchester University. Appointments: Regional Office, Transport and General Workers Union, 1978-97; Member of Parliament for Eccles, 1997-; Fellow, Industry and Parliament Trust; Member, Deregulation Select Committee, 1998-2001; Member, Information Select Committee, 1998-2001; Backbench PLP Groups: Education and Employment, 1997-, Trade and Industry, 1997-, Foreign Affairs, 1997-2001; Treasury, 2001-; All Party Groups: Chemical Industry Group, Retail Industry Group, Regeneration Group. Occupational Health & Safety Group, Parliamentary Information Technology Committee (executive member); United Nations Association, Commonwealth Parliamentary Association, Vice-Chair, All Party China Group; Vice Chair, APPG on Kazakhstan; Chair, Group for Vaccine Damaged Children; Chair, All Party Community Media Group; Parliamentary Private Secretary to Brian Wilson MP, Minister for Industry and Energy (Stephen Timms), 2001-; PPS at DTI, 2005. Address: London Parliamentary Office, House of Commons, London SW1A 0AA, England. E-mail: ianstewartmp@parliament.uk

**STEWART Jane,** b. Ontario, Canada. Minister for Human Resources Development. 2 sons. Education: Bachelor of Science (Hons), Trent University, 1978. Appointments: Imperial OI Ltd; Human Resources professional working with small and large companies across Canadaand the USA; Chair, National Liberal Caucus, 1994-96; Member, Standing Committee on Finance; Member of Parliament, Ontario Federal Riding of Brant, 1993-; Minister, National Revenue, 1996-97; Minister, Indian Affairs and Northern Development, 1997-99; Minister, Human

Resources Development, 1999-. Address: 140 Promendae du Portage, Phase IV, 14th Floor, Hull, Quebec K1A 0J9, Canada. E-mail: min.hrdc-drhc@hrdc-drhc.gc.ca

**STEWART M Dee,** b. 8 October 1935, Indianapolis, USA. Musician (trombonist); Professor. m. Rozella, 1 son, 1 daughter. Education: BS, Music Education, Ball State University, 1957; MM Music Education, 1962, Northwestern University. Appointments: Philadelphia Orchestra, 1962-80; Indiana University, 1980-. Publications: Books: Arnold Jacobs: Legacy of a Master; Philip Farker: Legacy of a Master; CDs: Trombone Under a Tree; Stewart Sounds. Honours: Neill Humfeld Award for Excellence in Teaching, 1998; Teaching Excellence Award, Indiana University. Memberships: International Trombone Association; American Federation of Musicians. Address: School of Music, Indiana University, Bloomington, IN 47405, USA.

**STEWART Lady Mary Florence Elinor,** b. 17 September 1916, Sunderland, England. Writer; Poet .m. Frederick Henry Stewart, 24 September 1945. Education: BA, 1938, DipEd, 1939, MA, 1941, University of Durham. Publications: Madam, Will You Talk?, 1954; Thunder on the Right, 1957; My Brother Michael, 1959; The Ivy Tree, 1961; The Moonspinners, 1962; The Crystal Cave, 1970; A Walk in Wolf Wood, 1970; The Little Broomstick, 1971; The Hollow Hills, 1973; Touch Not the Cat, 1976; The Last Enchantment, 1979; The Wicked Day, 1983; Thornyhold, 1988; Frost on the Window and Other Poems, 1990; Stormy Petrel, 1991; The Prince and the Pilgrim, 1995; Rose Cottage, 1997. Contributions to: Magazines. Honours: Frederick Niven Prize; Scottish Arts Council Award; Honorary Fellow, Newnham College, Cambridge. Memberships: PEN. Address: House of Letterawe, Loch Awe, Dalmally, Argyll PA33 1AH, Scotland.

**STEWART Paul,** b. 4 June 1955, London, England. Author. m. Julie, 1 son, 1 daughter. Education: English, 1st class honours, Lancaster University, 1974-77; Creative Writing with Malcolm Bradbury, UEA, 1978-79; German, University of Heidelberg, 1980-82. Appointments: EFL Teacher, Germany, 1980-82; EFL Teacher, Sri Lanka, 1982-83; EFL Teacher, Brighton, 1984-90; Writer, Child Carer (of own children), 1990-. Publications include: Stormchaser, 1999; The Birthday Presents, 1999; The Blobheads, series of 8 books, 2000; Midnight Over Sanctaphrax, 2000; Rabbit's Wish, 2001; The Curse of the Gloamglozer, 2001; The Were-pig, 2001; Muddle Earth, 2003, VOX, 2003; Freeglader, 2004; Fergus Crane, 2004. Honours: Gold Medal; Winner of Smarties Prize.

**STEWART Rod (Roderick David),** b. 10 January 1945, Highgate, North London, England. Singer. m. (1) Alana Collins, 1 son, 1 daughter, 1 daughter with Kelly Emberg, (2) Rachel Hunter, 1990, 1 son, 1 daughter. Career: Singer with: Steampacket; Shotgun Express; Jeff Beck Group, 1967-69; Concerts include: UK tour with Roy Orbison, 1967; US tours, 1967, 1968; The Faces, 1969-75; Appearances include: Reading Festival, 1972; UK, US tours, 1972; Solo artiste, 1971-; Solo appearances include: Rock In Rio, Brazil, 1985; Vagabond Heart Tour, 1991-92. Recordings: Singles include: Reason To Believe; Maggie May; (I Know) I'm Losing You; Handbags And Gladrags; You Wear It Well; Angel; Farewell; Sailing; This Old Heart Of Mine; Tonight's The Night (Gonna Be All Right); The Killing Of Georgie (Parts 1 and 2); Get Back; The First Cut Is The Deepest; I Don't Want To Talk About It; You're In My Heart; Hot Legs; D'Ya Think I'm Sexy?; Passion; Young Turks; Tonight I'm Yours; Baby Jane; What Am I Gonna Do; Infatuation; Some Guys Have All The Luck; Love Touch; Every Beat Of My Heart; Downtown Train; Rhythm Of My Heart; This

Old Heart Of Mine; Have I Told You Lately; Reason To Believe; Ruby Tuesday; You're The Star; Albums include: 2 with Jeff Beck; 4 with the Faces; Solo albums: Every Picture Tells A Story, 1971; Never A Dull Moment, 1972; Atlantic Crossing, 1975; A Night On The Town, 1976; Foot Loose And Fancy Free, 1977; Blondes Have More Fun, 1978; Foolish Behaviour, 1980; Tonight I'm Yours, 1981; Camouflage, 1984; Love Touch, 1986; Out Of Order, 1988; The Best Of, 1989; Downtown Train, 1990; Vagabond Heart, 1991; Lead Vocalist, 1992; Unplugged... And Seated, 1993; A Spanner In The Works, 1995; When We Were the New Boys, 1998; It Had To Be You: The Great American Songbook, 2002; Numerous compilations. Honours include: BRIT Awards, Lifetime Achievement Award, 1993; First artist to top US and UK singles and album charts simultaneously, 1971. Address: c/o Warner Music, 28 Kensington Church Street, London, W8 4EP, England.

**STEWART William Gladstone,** b. 15 July 1933, Lancaster, England. Television Producer; Presenter; Writer. m. Laura Calland Stewart, 2 daughters, 3 other children. Education: Shooters Hill Grammar School, London, 1945-50; Woolwich Polytechnic, 1951-52. Appointments: Royal Army Educational Corps, 1952-55; Served with Kings African Rifles in Kenya; Worked with BBC, 1958-67; Independent and Freelance, Producer, Director, 1967-; Productions include: Eric Sykes, Bless this House with Sid James; Father Dear Father with Patrick Cargill; Entertainment Series and one off "specials" with Max Bygraves, Tommy Cooper, Frankie Howerd, Bruce Forsyth; Major long-running series with David Frost, The Frost Programme, David Frost Live from London; With Johnny Speight, Lady is a Tramp, 'Till Death, The 19th Hole; Major drama series for Channel 4, Tickets for the Titanic; Co-Founder (with Colin Frewin), Sunset and Vine Productions, 1976; Founder, Regent Productions, 1980-; Currently, Presenter Channel 4 programme, Fifteen-to-One, 1988-. Publications: Regular contributor of articles on media matters to national newspapers and journals including, Independent, RTS Journal, Broadcast, The Listener, The Producer, Televisual, Evening Standard, Impact; Lectures on the return of cultural artefacts, especially the Parthenon Marbles to Athens, at The European Parliament in Strasbourg, UNESCO in Paris, The Smithsonian in Washington, in Athens, London and New York; Institute of Art and Law Annual Lecture, 2000; 5 city lecture tour across USA and Canada, 2003. Memberships: Fellow, Royal Television Society; British Academy Film and Television Arts; Royal Horticultural Society; Hall of Fame of the Royal Television Society; President, The Media Society 2003-2005. Address: 6 Putney Common, London SW15 1HL, England. E-mail: haybohan@aol.com

**STEWARTBY Baron, Sir (Bernard Harold) Ian (Halley) Stewart,** b. 10 August 1935, United Kingdom. m. Deborah Charlotte Buchan, 1 son, 2 daughters. Education: MA, Jesus College Cambridge, 1956-59; D Litt, University of Cambridge, 1978. Appointments include: National Service: Sub-Lieutenant, RNVR, 1954-56, later Lieutenant Commander, RNR; Brown Shipley & Co Ltd, Merchant Bankers, 1960-82, Director, 1971-83; MP, Conservative, North Hertfordshire (Hitchin), 1974-92; Parliamentary Private Secretary to Chancellor of the Exchequer, 1979-83; Parliamentary Under-Secretary of State for Defence Procurement, 1983; Economic Secretary to the Treasury, 1983-87; Minister of State for the Armed Forces, 1987-88; Minister of State, Northern Ireland, 1988-89; Non-Executive Director, 1990-93, Deputy Chairman, 1993-2004, Standard Chartered plc; Non-Executive Director, Diploma plc, 1990-; Chairman, The Throgmorton Trust PLC, 1990-2005; Member, Financial Service Authority, 1993-97; Deputy Chairman, Amlin plc, 1995-; Non-Executive Director, Portman Building Society,

1995-2002; Chairman, Brazilian Smaller Companies Investment Trust PLC, 1998; President, Sir Halley Stewart Trust, 2000-. Publications: The Scottish Coinage, 1955, 2nd edition, 1967; Coinage in Tenth Century England (joint author), 1989. Honours: RD, 1972; FBA, 1981; FRSE, 1986; PC, 1989; Kt, 1991; Baron, 1992; K St J, 1992; Sanford Saltus Gold Medal, British Numismatic Society, 1971; Medallist, Royal Numismatic Society, 1996. Memberships: Director, British Numismatic Society, 1965-75; County Vice-President, St John Ambulance, Hertfordshire, 1978-; British Academy Committee for Sylloge of Coins of the British Isles, 1967-, Chairman, 1993-2003; Member of Council, Haileybury, 1980-95; Chairman, Treasure Valuation Committee, 1996-2001. Address: House of Lords, Westminster, London SW1A 0AA, England.

**STEYER Rolf,** b. 1 December 1950, Fulda, Germany. m. Anna-Maria, 1 son, 1 daughter. Education: Military Service, Bundesgrenzschutz border police, 1969-71; Diploma in Psychology, Göttingen, 1977; PhD, Psychology, Frankfurt am Main, 1982; Habilitation, Psychology, University of Trier, 1989. Appointments: Research Assistant, University of Göttingen, 1977; Assistant, University of Frankfurt am Main, 1977-82; Assistant Professor, University of Trier, 1982-94; Director of Methodology Research, ZUMA, Mannheim, 1994; Associate Professor, Methodology and Assessment, University of Magdeburg, 1995; Full Professor, Methodology and Evaluation Research, University of Jena, 1996-; General Secretary, European Association of Psychological Assessment, 1996-99; Co-Editor in Chief, European Journal of Psychological Assessment; Prorektor, University of Jena, 2002-04; President, Center for Human Resources, Research, Development and Training; 2002-04; President, European Association of Methodology. Publications: Theory of causal regression models, 1992; Measuring and Testing, co-author, 1993; Probability and Regression, author, 2002; Editor of several newsletters. Memberships: German Society for Psychology; European Association of Methodolgy; European Association of Personality Psychology; European Mathematical Psychology Group; European Association of Psychological Assessment; Psychometric Society. Address: Institute of Psychology, Am Steiger 3, Haus 1, D-07743 Jena, Germany. E-mail: rolf.steyer@uni-jena.de

**STICH Michael,** b. 18 October 1968, Pinneberg, Germany. Tennis Player. m. Jessica Stockmann, 1992. Appointments: National Junior Champion, 1986; Turned professional, 1988; Semi-finalist, French Open, 1990; Member, West German Davis Cup Team, 1990; Won first professional title, Memphis, 1990; Winner, Men's Singles Championship, Wimbledon, 1991; Men's Doubles (with John McEnroe), 1992; Won ATP World Championship, 1993; Retired, 1997; Won 28 professional titles; UN Ambassador, 1999-; German Davis Cup team Captain, 2001-2002. Address: Ernst-Barlach-Strasse 44, 2200 Elmshorn, Germany.

**STIEGLER Drago,** b. 24 October 1919, Zagreb, Croatia. Mathematician. m. Hildegard Sarko, 1 daughter. Education: Study of mathematics and theoretical physics, University of Zagreb, 1938-46; Study of philosophy, 1946-49; UNESCO Research Fellow, Institut Henri Poincaré, Paris, 1954-55; Active Participant in Séminaire de Recherches Louis de Broglie, and Séminaire Bourbaki, University of Paris, 1954-55; Research Scholarship, Balokovich Foundation, Harvard University, USA, 1961-63; PhD, Relativity, 1963. Appointments: Professor of Mathematics, School of Engineering, Zagreb, 1946-50; Researcher in Optics, Ghetaldus, Optical Industry Zagreb, 1950-59; Constructed all sorts of eyeglasses for correction of Myopia, Hypermetropia and Astigmatismus, produced since 1957 in

Ghetaldus and exhibited at the International Trade Exhibition for Ophthalmic Optics in Cologne, 1984; AGFA, Optics, Munich, 1960; T University Munich, 1964-84. Publications: Research in Relativity; Quantum Theory; Cosmology; Optics; History and Philosophy of Mathematical Sciences including: Proof that the velocity of light is equal in all galilean systems of reference, Paris (1952), and London (1958); Correspondence with Albert Einstein concerning the Axiomatic Foundations of Special Theory of Relativity, 1951 (Einstein Archives, Boston, Jerusalem, Collected Papers of Albert Einstein) Discovered: the law of anomalous (differential) rotation of spherical cosmical bodies with application to the Sun, Jupiter and Saturn, communicated at the International Congress of Mathematicians, Nizza, 1970, published in Academy of Sciences, Paris, 1971, 1972; Right and Left in the electrodynamics of moving bodies are physically no equivalent, 1972, 1978 (London-New York); Showed that the velocity of expanding matter in Einstein Friedmann theory in the case of the model of the universe with constant negative curvature is in the neighbourhood of the beginning greater than the velocity of light in vacuo, 1967. Honours: DMathPhys, honoris causa; Twentieth Century Award for Outstanding Achievement in Physics and Cosmology. Memberships: Different academies of sciences; Fellow, Royal Astronomical Society, London.

**STIGWOOD Robert Colin**, b. 16 April 1934, Adelaide, Australia. Business Executive. Education: Sacred Heart College, Adelaide. Appointments: Established Robert Stigwood Organisation (RSO), 1967; Formed RSO Records, 1973; Founder, Music for UNICEF; Producer of films: Jesus Christ Superstar; Bugsy Malone; Gallipoli; Tommy; Saturday Night Fever; Grease; Sergeant Pepper's Lonely Hearts Club Band; Moment by Moment; Times Square; The Fan; Grease 2; Staying Alive; Evita; Gallipoli; Producer of stage musicals: Hair; Oh! Calcutta; The Dirtiest Show in Town; Pippin; Jesus Christ Superstar; Evita; Grease, 1993; Saturday Night Fever; TV producer in England and USA: The Entertainer; The Prime of Miss Jean Brodie; Chair of Board, Stigwood Group of Companies. Honours: Key to City of Los Angeles; Tony Award, 1980, for Evita; International Producer of the Year, ABC Interstate Inc. Address: c/o Robert Stigwood Organization, Barton Manor, Wippingham, East Cowes, Isle of Wight, PO32 6LB, England.

**STILES Frank**, b. 2 April 1924, Chiswick, London, England. Composer; Conductor; Violist. m. (1) Estelle Zitnitsky, 23 December 1969, 4 daughters, (2) Elizabeth Horwood, 1 September 1988. Education: BSc, Imperial College, 1949; BMus, Durham University, 1952; Postgraduate studies, Paris Conservatoire, 1955; LGSM; AGSM. Appointments: Composer; Conductor Violist; Principal Conductor, Priory Concertante of London; Director, Holland Music School, 1982-92; Composer in Residence, Protoangel Visions Festival, Normandy by Spital, Lincolnshire. Publications: 5 symphonies; Dramatic Cantata Masada; Song Cycle for Tenor and Orchestra and for Baritone and Piano Mans 4 Seasons; 7 Concertos for violin, viola (2), guitar, clarinet, cello, piano; 6 string quartets; Trios; Duos; 2 violin and piano sonatas; 2 viola and piano sonatas; among others. Honours: City of London Award for Composition, 1955; ABI Medal of Honour, 2000; ABI Stature of Universal Accomplishment, 2001. Memberships: Composers' Guild of Great Britain; Incorporated Society of Musicians; British Academy of Composers and Songwriters; Musicians Union; PRS; MCPS; Royal Society of Musicians. Address: 43 Beech Road, Branston, Lincoln LN4 1PP, England. E-mail: frankstiles @callnetuk.com Website: www.impulse.music.co.uk/stiles.htm

**STING (Gordon Matthew Sumner)**, 2 October 1951, Wallsend, Newcastle-Upon-Tyne, England. Singer; Musician (bass); Actor. m. (1) Frances Tomelty, 1 May 1976, divorced 1984, 1 son, 1 daughter; (2) Trudie Styler, 20 August 1992, 2 sons, 2 daughters. Career: School teacher, Newcastle, 1975-77; Singer, songwriter, bass player, The Police, 1977-86; Solo artiste, 1985-; Numerous worldwide tours, television and radio, with the Police and solo; actor in films: Quadrophenia, 1980; Secret Policeman's Other Ball, 1982; Brimstone And Treacle, 1982; Dune, 1984; The Bride, 1985; Plenty, 1985; Julia And Julia, 1988; Stormy Monday, 1988; The Adventures Of Baron Munchausen, 1989; Stormy Monday, 1989; Rosencrantz and Guildenstern are Dead; Resident Alien; The Music Tells You; The Grotesque; Mercury Falling, 1996; Broadway Performance, Threepenny Opera, 1989. Recordings: Hit singles include: Walking On The Moon; Message In A Bottle; So Lonely; Roxanne; De Do Do Do, De Da Da Da; Every Little Thing She Does; Every Breath You Take; Invisible Sun; Can't Stand Losing You; Don't Stand So Close To Me; If You Love Somebody; Englishman In New York; If I Ever Lose My Faith In You; Fields Of Gold; Love Is Stronger Than Justice; Cowboy Song (with Pato Banton); Let The Soul Be Your Pilot; Roxanne 97; Brand New Day; After the Rain has Gone, 2000; Albums: with the Police: Outlandos D'Armour, 1977; Regatta De Blanc, 1979; Zenyatta Mondatta, 1980; Ghost In The Machine, 1981; Synchronisity, 1983; Bring On The Night, 1986; Solo albums: The Dream Of The Blue Turtles, 1985; Nothing Like The Sun, 1987; The Soul Cages, 1991; Ten Sumner's Tales, 1994; Mercury Falling, 1996; Brand New Day, 1999; After the Rain has Gone, 2000; Contributor, Tower Of Song (Leonard Cohen tribute), 1995. Publications: Jungle Stories: The Fight for the Amazon, 1989. Honours include: 10 Grammy Awards (with Police and solo); Ivor Novello Award for Best Song They Dance Alone, 1989; Q Award, Best Album, 1994; BRIT Award, Best Male Artist, 1994; 4 songwriting awards (BMI), 1998; Brit Award for Outstanding Contribution to Music, 2002; Emmy Award for Best Performance (Sting in Tuscany…. All This Time), 2002. Membership: PRS.

**STIPE Michael**, b. 1960, Decatur, Georgia, USA. Rock Musician. Education: University of Georgia. Appointments: Lead singer and song writer with REM band, 1980-; Owner OO (film co). Albums include: (for IRS): Murmur, 1982-83; Document; (for Warner): Green, 1988; Out of Time, 1991; Automatic for the People, 1992; Monster, 1994; New Adventures in Hi-Fi, 1996; Up, 1998; Reveal, 2001. Address: c/o Warner Bros Records, 3300 Warner Boulevard, Burbank, CA 91505, USA.

**STIRES Midge**, b. 5 April 1943, Orange, New Jersey, USA. Painter. m. Peter D Schnore, 2 sons. Education: Bachelor of Fine Art, Syracuse University, USA. Honours: Pollock and Krasner Foundation Grant; Elizabeth Foundation for the Arts Grant; Artists for the Environment Residency Grant. Publications: Painting Panoramas, The Artists Magazine, 1990. Memberships: National Association of Painters in Casein and Acrylic. Address: 144 Red Oak Dr, Boyertown, PA 19512 8963, USA.

**STÖCKER Michael Wilhelm**, b. 25 January 1948, Kassel, Germany. Principal Scientist; Professor. m. Wencke Ophaug, 17 September 1994, 1 son. Education: Dr.rer.nat, 1979, Diploma, Chemistry, 1975, University of Münster, Germany. Appointments: Research Assistant, University of Bergen, Norway, 1980-82; Research Scientist, 1982-89, Senior Scientist, 1989-92, Principal Scientist, 1992-, Centre for Industrial Research (SINTEF Materials and Chemistry), Oslo, Norway; Professor of Chemistry, University of Bergen, Norway, 1999-2004, Norwegian University of Science and Technology,

Trondheim, Norway, 2004-. Publications: 120 scientific papers, 6 review papers, Book Editor: Advanced Zeolite Sciences and Applications, 1994. Honours: Councillor, International Zeolite Association; Chairman, International Zeolite Association Catalysis Committee; Member, International Zeolite Association Synthesis Committee. Memberships: Editor-in-Chief, Journal, Microporous and Mesoporous Materials. Address: SINTEF Materials and Chemistry, PO Box 124, Blindern, N-0314 Oslo, Norway.

**STOCKTON Eric Sidney,** b. 5 December 1924, London, England. Chemist; Philosopher. m. (1) Ruth Abrahams, (2) Catherine Pye, deceased, 1 son, 1 daughter, (3) Myra Scott. Education: BSc (London), Chemistry (main) and Physics (subsidiary), Imperial College, London, 1944. Appointments: Junior Scientist in the metallurgical industry working on the Manhattan Project, 1943-44; Chemist, electrical power generating industry working on corrosion problems in power station boiler plant; Lecturer in charge of Laboratory Technicians Training, Isleworth Polytechnic; Philosophical studies under the auspices of the University of Aberdeen; Producer of website in the form of a monthly essay "Atheist Thought"; Pioneered local island website in Orkney; President, Environmental Concern Orkney (founder of their website); Founder/Editor, The Scottish Humanist (now called Humanism Scotland), -1996. Publications: Lady Godiva, satirical net magazine, now discontinued: Over 90 articles on atheism on the internet; Several articles in print publications including: Life and Work, Church of Scotland, Humanist, Canada. Honours: BSc (London), 1944; Associateship of the Royal College of Science, 1944. Memberships: Humanist Society of Scotland; National Secular Society; South Place Ethical Society. Address: West Cott, Sanday, Orkney KW17 2BW, Scotland. E-mail: stockton.sanday.orkney@zetnet.co.uk

**STOCKTON William M Jr,** b. 22 March 1956, McKeesport, Pennsylvania, USA. Cosmetic Dentist. Education: BS, Howard University, 1983; DDS, Howard University College of Dentistry, 1988. Appointments: Staff Dentist, Syracuse Community Health Center, 1989-90; Private Practice focusing on cosmetic dentistry, 1990-. Honours: Congressional Businessman's Advisory Council, 1998, Honorary Chairman, 2000; Gold Medal for Community Service and Mentoring, US Congress, 2001; Congressional Business Advisory Council Businessman of the Year, State of New York, 1999, 2000, 2001; Named as One of the Top Cosmetic Dentists in North America, 2000-; Listed in Who's Who publications and biographical dictionaries. Memberships: American Dental Association; Congressional Businessman's Advisory Council; Life member, Republican National Committee; President's Inner Circle Club. Address: 2323 Main Street, Buffalo, NY 14214, USA.

**STODDART Alexander John,** b. 30 May 1959, Edinburgh, Scotland. Sculptor. m. Catriona, 3 daughters. Education: John Neilson High School, Paisley, Scotland; BA (Hons) 1st Class, Glasgow School of Art; PhD (research not yet written up), Glasgow University. Career: Statues and Monuments: Robert Burns/John Wilson Monument, Kilmarnock, Scotland, 1995; David Hume Statue, Edinburgh, 1997; John Witherspoon Statue (casts at University of Paisley, Scotland and Princeton University, New Jersey, USA), 2000; Sculptor to the New Queen's Gallery, Buckingham Palace (completed 2002); Statue of Immanuel Kant (Private Collection), 2004; Robert Louis Stevenson Monument, Edinburgh, 2004; Sculptor to Millennium Monument, Atlanta, Georgia, USA (in progress); Adam Smith Statue, Edinburgh, commenced 2005; Exhibitions: Busts of Men, Leeds City Art Gallery, 2002, Kirkintilloch Auld Kirk Museum, 2004; Various radio and television appearances.

Honours: Honorary Doctorate (D Univ), University of Paisley, 1998; Arthur Ross Award of Classical America for Public Statuary, 2001; Honorary Professorship, Department of Media Studies, University of Paisley, 2003. Memberships: Brother of Art Workers Guild, London; Paisley Society of Hammermen; Committee of Honour, INTBAU. Address: C/o The University of Paisley, High Street, Paisley PA1 2BE, Scotland. E-mail: sandy@stoddart.com

**STOKES Daniel Patrick,** b. 7 September 1945, Dublin, Ireland. Writer; Poet. Education: MA, English and Philosophy, Trinity College, Dublin, 1968; HDipEd, National University of Ireland, 1969. Appointments: Teacher, 1969-78; Vice Principal, St Patrick's Cathedral School, 1976-80; Full-time Writer, 1980-. Publications: Keepsake Poems, 1977; Poems for Christmas, 1981; Interest and Other Poems, 1982. Contributions to: New Poetry; Lines Review; Poetry Ireland Review; Sunday Tribune; Journal of Irish Literature; Irish Times; Ariel; Atlantic Review; Dekalb Literary Arts Journal; Studies; Cyphers; Ulster Tatler; Cork Examiner; Connacht Tribune; Prism International. Honours: Yorkshire Poets Award, 1977; New Poetry Competition, 1978; Poetry Athlone Award, 1980; Edinburgh Fringe First Award, 1982. Address: 4 Newbridge Drive, Sandymount, Dublin 4, Ireland.

**STOLL David (Michael),** b. 29 December 1948, London, England. Composer. m. Erika Eigen, 25 July 1980, 1 stepson. Education: Worcester College, Oxford, 1967-70; MA (Oxon); Royal Academy of Music, London, 1970-71. Career: Music Director, Greenwich Young People's Theatre, 1971-75; Subsequently freelance as Composer and Music Producer working in concert music, theatre and media. Compositions include: Piano Quartet, 1987; Sonata for 2 Pianos, 1990; Piano Sonata, 1991; String Trio, 1992; Fanfares and Reflections, 1992; String Quartet no 1, 1994; Monument, 1995; The Bowl of Nous, 1996; False Relations, 1997; Motet in Memoriam, 1998; Midwinter Spring, 1998; String Quartet no 2, 1999; Cello Concerto, 2000; Octave Variations, 2001; Teller of Tales (co-composer), musical; The path to the River, octet, 2001; Cello Sonata, 2001; Fools by Heavenly Compulsion, 2002; Sonnet, string orchestra, 2002; Theatre Dreams, brass quintet, 2003; A Colchester Suite, pipes, 2003; Also much production music and music and songs for children; Consultant in Music and Creativity for Primary Schools. Recordings: Chamber Music, 1993, re-issued 2001; The Shakespeare Suite, 2000; The String Quartets, 2001; Fools by Heavenly Compulsion, string quartet, 2005. Honours: Hadow Open Scholarship in Composition to Worcester College, Oxford, 1967; Fellow of the Royal Society of Arts; Director of British Music Rights; Associate, Royal Academy of Music, 2002. Memberships: British Academy of Composers and Songwriters (former Chairman). Address: 26 Belgrave Heights, Belgrave Road, Wanstead, London E11 3RE, England. E-mail: davidstoll@btconnect.com

**STOMP Frank Alwin,** b.22 July 1957, Gorssel, The Netherlands. Professor. Education: BS, Mathematics, 1981, MS, Mathematics, 1984, University of Utrecht, The Netherlands; PhD, Computer Science, 1989, Eindhoven University of Technology, The Netherlands. Appointments: Scientific Collaborator, University of Nijmegen, The Netherlands, 1984-90; Assistant Professor, Åbo Akademi, Turku, Finland, 1990-91; Visitor, The Weizmann Institute of Science, Rehovot, Israel, 1991; Visiting Scientist, The Technion, Haifa, Israel, 1991-92; Assistant Professor, University of Kiel, Germany, 1992-93; Member of Technical Staff, AT&T Bell Laboratories, New Jersey, USA, 1993-96; Research Associate, Royal Military College of Canada, 1996; Adjunct Professor, University of California, Davies, USA, 1997-98; Assistant Professor, Wayne

State University, Detroit, Michigan, USA, 1998-2001; Associate Professor, Oakland University, Rochester, Michigan, USA, 2001-2002; Associate Professor, Wayne State University, Detroit, Michigan, USA, 2002-. Publications: Articles as author and co-author in refereed scientific journals include most recently: Specification and Correctness of Cache Coherency in SCI, 1999; Cache Coherency in SCI: Specification and a Sketch of Correctness, 1999; Correctness of Substring-Preprocessing in Boyer-Moore's Pattern Matching Algorithm, 2003; Safety Assurance via On-Line Monitoring, 2003; A Complete Mechanization of Correctness of a String Preprocessing Algorithm, 2004. Honours: MS Degree cum laude; Listed in Who's Who publications and biographical dictionaries. Memberships: IEEE; ACM; EATCS. Address: Department of Computer Science, Wayne State University, Detroit, MI 48202, USA. E-mail: fstomp@cs.wayne.edu

**STONE Carole,** b. 30 May 1942, Maidstone, Kent, England. Media Consultant; Journalist. m. Richard Lindley, 1999. Education: Ashford County Grammar School for Girls; Southampton Technical College. Appointments: Newsroom Secretary, BBC South, 1963; Station Assistant, BBC Radio Brighton, 1967; Regional News Producer, BBC Bristol, 1970; Network Radio Talks Producer, producing regular editions of Radio 4's Woman's Hour, Down Your Way, You and Yours, BBC, based Bristol, 1972; Editor, BBC Radio 4's current affairs series, Any Questions? and Any Answers? 1977-1989; Deputy Editor, BBC1 Topical Features, 1989; Originated and presented, Mother of Mine for BBC 1, 1990; Reporter, BBC 1, Bite Back, 1991-93; Host of Carole Stone and Company, Viva! 963 am, 1996-96; Mental health manager, Camden and Islington Community Health Services, 1995-98; Currently: Partner, London Debating Forum Intelligence Squared; Media Consultant to Chairs and Chief Executives of public companies; Journalist, Author; Director, Lindley Stone Ltd, independent television production company. Publications: Networking – the Art of Making Friends, 2001; The Ultimate Guide to Successful Networking, 2004; Articles published in the national press magazines and specialist business publications; Columnist, The Church of England Newspaper. Honours: Award Winner, London Businesswomen's Network Achievers Awards, 1983; President's Award, European Federation of Black Women Business Owners. Memberships include: Life Member, Bristol Business Ladies Club; Fellow, Royal Society of Arts; Council Member, Royal Television Society, 1991-94; Board, London Press Club; Council, Women in Journalism; President, The Media Society, 1997-99; Vice Patron, National Missing Persons' Helpline; Patron SANE; Patron, Triumph Over Phobia; Council Member, Central Council for Education and Training in Social Work , 1996-99; Trustee, Facial Surgery Research Foundation; Trustee, The Wallace Collection. Address: Flat 1, 19 Henrietta Street, London WC2E 8QH, England. E-mail: carole@carolestone.com

**STONE Oliver William,** b. 15 September 1946, New York, USA. Screenwriter; Director. Education: BFA, Yale University; New York University Film School. Appointments include: Teacher, Cholon, Vietnam, 1965-66; US Merchant Marine, 1966; Served, US Army, Vietnam, 1967-68; Taxi Driver, New York City, 1971; Screenwriter, Seizure, 1973, Midnight Express, 1978, The Hand, 1981, Conan the Barbarian, with J Milius, 1982, Scarface, 1983, Year of the Dragon, with M Cimino, 1985, 8 Million Ways to Die, with D L Henry, 1986, Salvador, with R Boyle, 1986; Writer, Director, Platoon, 1986; Co-writer and Director: Wall Street, 1987; Talk Radio, 1988; The Doors, 1991; Screenwriter, Producer and Director: Born on the Fourth of July, 1989; JFK, 1991; Heaven and Earth, 1993; Natural Born Killers, 1994; Nixon, 1995; Director, U-Turn, 1997; Co-Writer,

Evita, 1996; Producer: South Central, 1992; Zebrahead, 1992; The Joy Luck Club, 1993; New Age, 1994; Wild Palms, TV mini-series, 1993; Freeway, 1995; The People vs Larry Flynt, 1996; Any Given Sunday, 2000; Comandante (documentary), 2003; Executive Producer: Killer: A Journal of Murder, 1995; (HBO)Indictment: The McMartin Preschool, 1995. Honours: Winner of numerous awards including: 2 Academy Awards for Platoon and Born of the Fourth of July; BAFTA Award, Directors Guild of America Award, for Platoon; Purple Heart with Oak Leaf Cluster; Bronze Star. Memberships: Writers' Guild of America; Directors' Guild of America; Academy Motion Pictures Arts and Sciences. Address: Ixtlan, 201 Santa Monica Boulevard, 6th Floor, Santa Monica, CA 90401, USA.

**STONE Ronald William,** b. 27 March 1959, Merseyside, England. Record Producer; Engineer; Programmer; Musician (guitar); Songwriter. Education: Art College. Career: Member, Afraid Of Mice, 1978; Backing musician for China Crisis, 1982; Formed Freeze Frame, 1984 (hits in Europe, Japan, Australia); Producer/Engineer for: Easterhouse; Throwing Muses; The Pixies; Oceanic; River City People; Audioweb; Pete Wylie; Shack; Sara Cracknell; Mansun; Christians; Connie Lush; Sian James; Lotus eaters; TNT; Marli (Singer Fame Academy, BBC TV) Live sound: Easterhouse; Jason Donovan; WOMAD 1996, 1997; Consultant A&R for major record labels; Music production/composition for BBC TV series, Birdman, 1999. Compositions: Composer/producer for TV/Cinema commercials: Commonwealth Games, 2002; Morrisons Supermarkets, 2003/2004/2005; Co-op Banking; Yorkshire Tourist Board; Philips CD/DVD players; Yves St Laurent; Circulon Pans; Alminox metals (Germany); Krazy Fretes (Germany, award winning); BMG/Zomba, USA; George Lopez Show (Theme); Music for the MTV Awards, 2004; TV/Film soundtracks albums; Film Music: Hope, 2003; Max-N, 2004. Recordings: Producer/engineer for Say Something Good, River City People; All works by Oceanic, 1991-93; Mansun, Singles including Wide Open Space and album: Attack of the Grey Lantern (Gold Disc); Connie Lush, Blues Album of the Year, 2003; TNT Best New Band, 2003. Address: Audio 5.1, 5A Shrewsbury Road, Prenton, Mersyside CH43 1UU, England. E-mail: studio@rsopro51.plus.com

**STONE Sharon,** b. 10 March 1958, Meadville, USA. Actress. m. (1) Michael Greenburg, 1984, divorced 1987, (2) Phil Bronstein, 1998, 1 adopted son. Education: Edinboro College. Career: Films include: Star Dust Memories (debut); Above the Law; Action Jackson; King Solomon's Mines; Allan Quatermain and the Lost City of Gold; Irreconcilable Differences; Deadly Blessing; Personal Choice; Basic Instinct; Dairy of a hit Man; Where Sleeping Dogs Lie; Sliver; Intersection; The Specialist; The Quick and the Dead; Casino; Last Dance; Diabolique, 1996; Sphere; The Might, 1999; The Muse, 1999; Simpatico, 1999; TV includes: Tears in the Rain; War and Remembrance; Calendar Girl Murders; The Vegas Strip Wars. Honour: Chevalier, Ordre des Arts et des Lettres. Address: c/o Guy McElwaine, PO Box 7304, North Hollywood, CA 91603, USA.

**STOPPARD Tom (Sir), (Thomas Straussler),** b. 3 July 1937, Zin, Czechoslovakia (British citizen). Dramatist; Screenwriter. m. (1) Jose Ingle, 1965, divorced 1972, 2 sons, (2) Dr Miriam Moore-Robinson, 1972, divorced 1992, 2 sons. Publications: Plays: Rosencrantz and Guildenstern are Dead, 1967; The Real Inspector Hound, 1968; Albert's Bridge, 1968; Enter a Free Man, 1968; After Magritte, 1971; Jumpers, 1972; Artists Descending a Staircase, and, Where Are They Now?, 1973; Travesties, 1975; Dirty Linen, and New-Found-Land, 1976; Every Good Boy Deserves Favour, 1978; Professional Foul, 1978; Night and Day, 1978; Undiscovered Country, 1980; Dogg's Hamlet, Cahoot's

Macbeth, 1980; On the Razzle, 1982; The Real Thing, 1983; The Dog It Was That Died, 1983; Squaring the Circle, 1984; Four Plays for Radio, 1984; Rough Crossing, 1984; Dalliance and Undiscovered Country, 1986; Largo Desolato, by Vaclav Havel (translator), 1987; Hapgood, 1988; In the Native State, 1991; Arcadia, 1993; Indian Ink, 1995; The Invention of Love, 1997; The Seagul, 1997; The Coast of Utopia: Ttrilogy: Part One: Voyage, Part Two: Shipwreck, Part Three: Salvage, 2002; The Television Plays 1965-1984, 1993. Fiction: Introduction 2, 1964; Lord Malquist and Mr Moon, 1965. Other: 8 screenplays; Various unpublished state, radio, and television plays. Honours: John Whiting Award, Arts Council, 1967; New York Drama Critics Award, 1968; Italia Prize, 1968; Tony Awards, 1968, 1976, 1984; Evening Standard Awards, 1968, 1972, 1974, 1978, 1993, 1997; Olivier Award, 1993; Knighted, 1997; Order of Merit, 2000.

**STOREY David (Malcolm),** b. 13 July 1933, Wakefield, England. Writer; Dramatist; Screenwriter; Poet. m. Barbara Rudd Hamilton, 1956, 2 sons, 2 daughters. Education: Diploma, Slade School of Art, 1956. Publications: This Sporting Life, 1960; Flight into Camden, 1960; Radcliffe, 1963; Pasmore, 1972; A Temporary Life, 1973; Edward, 1973; Saville, 1976; A Prodigal Child, 1982; Present Times, 1984; Storey's Lives: Poems 1951-1991, 1992; A Serious Man, 1998. Honours: Macmillan Fiction Award, 1960; John Llewellyn Memorial Prize, 1960; Somerset Maugham Award, 1960; Evening Standard Awards, 1967, 1970; Los Angeles Drama Critics Award, 1969; Writer of the Year Award, Variety Club of Great Britain, 1969; New York Drama Critics Award, 1969, 1970, 1971; Geoffrey Faber Memorial Prize, 1973; Fellow, University College, London, 1974; Booker Prize, 1976. Address: c/o Jonathan Cape Ltd, Random Century House, 20 Vauxhall Bridge Road, London SW1V 2SA, England.

**STRAKHOV Vladimir Vitalievich,** b. 12 June 1951, Yaroslavl, Russia. Ophthalmologist. m. 2 daughters. Education: Graduate, Yaroslavl State Medical Academy, 1974; Practical Ophthalmologist, 1974-79; Postgraduate course, 1979-82; Bachelor of Medicine Degree, 1983; Professor, 1995, Doctor of Medicine, 1997, Germany. Appointments: Assistant, Eye Diseases Clinic, 1988-92, Head of the Eye Diseases Department, 1992-, Regional Hospital, Yaroslavl, Russia. Publications: 82 articles. Honour: Honoured Doctor of the Russian Federation. Memberships: Chairman, Regional Ophthalmological Association; Member, Government of Russia Ophthalmological Association. Address: Regional Hospital, Eye Diseases Clinic, Yakovlevskaya Str 5, Yaroslavl, 150062, Russia. E-mail: strakhov51@mail.ru

**STRANGE Curtis,** b. 30 January 1955, Norfolk, Virginia, USA. Professional Golfer. m. Sarah Jones, 2 sons. Education: Wake Forest University. Career: Professional, 1976-; First joined PGA tour, 1977; Won Pensacola Open, 1979; Won Sammy Davis Jr Greater Hartford Open, 1983; Won LaJel Classic, 1984; Won Honda Classic, Panasonic-Las Vegas International, 1985; Won Canadian Open, 1985; Won Houston Open, 1986; Won Canadian Open, Federal Express – St Jude Classic, NEC Series of Golf, 1987; Won Sandway Cove Classic, Australia, 1988; Won Industry Insurance Agent Open, Memorial Tournament, US Open, Nabisco Championships, 1988; Won US Open, Palm Meadows Cup, Australia, 1989; Won Holden Classic, Australia, 1993. Memberships: Member, PGA Tour Charity Team, Michelob Championship, Kingsmill, 1996. Honours: Captain US Ryder Cup Team after playing on five Ryder Cup Teams, 2002; Golf Analyst, ABC Sports, 1997-; Golfer of the Year, 1986, 1987. Address: c/o IMG, 1 Erieview Plaza, Suite 1300, Cleveland, OH 44114, USA.

**STRÁNSKÝ Karel Josef,** b. 18 December 1931, Brno, Czech Republic. Scientific Research Worker. m. Dana Böhmová, 1 son, 1 daughter. Education: Dipl Ing, 1958, PhD (CSc), 1965, Brno University of Technology; Dr Sc, Military Academy Brno, 1976; Assistant Professor, 1991, Professor, 1992, Technical University VSB Ostrava. Appointments: Technician and Researcher, Šmeral Works Foundry, 1958-66; Scientific Research Worker and Head of Materials Department, Military Academy Brno 1967-96; Professor, Brno University of Technology, 1996-. Publications: More than 1150 published articles mostly in Czech but also in English, German, French and Russian include most recently as co-author: Structural stability of deposits and welded joints in power engineering, 1998. Honours: National Prize of Czech Republic, 1977; Silver Medal of František Křižik, Czechoslovak Academy of Science, 1987. Memberships: Honorary Member, Czech Foundry Association; Member of Central Head Committee, Czech Scientific Association of Materials. Address: Bystřinova 3, 67200 Brno, Czech Republic. E-mail: stranskyk@umi.fme.vutbr.cz

**STRAUSS Botho,** b. 2 December 1944, Naumberg-an-der-Saale, Germany. Author; Poet; Dramatist. Education: German Language and Literature, Drama, Sociology, Cologne and Munich. Publications: Bekannte Gesichter, gemischte Gefühle (with T Bernhard and F Kroetz), 1974; Trilogie des Wiedersehens, 1976; Gross und Klein, 1978; Rumor, 1980; Kalldeway Farce, 1981; Paare, Passanten, 1981; Der Park, 1983; Der junge Mann, 1984; Diese Erinnerung an einen, der nur einen Tag zu Gast War, 1985; Die Fremdenführerin, 1986; Niemand anderes, 1987; Besucher, 1988; Kongress: Die Kette der Demütigungen, 1989; Theaterstücke in zwei Banden, 1994; Wohnen Dammern Lügen, 1994. Honours: Dramatists' Prize, Hannover, 1975; Schiller Prize, Baden-Württemberg, 1977; Literary Prize, Bavarian Academy of Fine Arts, Munich, 1981; Jean Paul Prize, 1987; Georg Büchner Prize, 1989. Membership: PEN. Address: Keithstrasse 8, D-17877, Berlin, Germany.

**STRAW Jack (John Whitaker Straw) (Rt Hon),** b. 3 August 1946, Buckhurst Hill, Essex, England. Politician; Lawyer. m. (1) Anthea L Watson, 1968, divorced 1978, 1 daughter, deceased, (2) Alice E Perkins, 1978, 1 son, 1 daughter. Education: University of Leeds. Appointments: President, National Union of Students, 1969-71; Member, Islington Borough Council, 1971-78; Inner London Education Authority, 1971-74; Deputy Leader, 1973-74; Called to bar, Inner Temple, 1972; Bencher, 1997; Practised as Bar, 1972-74; Special Adviser to Secretary of State for Social Services, 1974-76; To Secretary of State for Environment, 1976-77; On Staff of Granada TV (World in Action), 1977-79; Member of Parliament for Blackburn, 1979-; Opposition Treasury Spokesman, 1980-83; Local Government Spokesman, 1982-87; Member of Parliament, Committee of Labour Party (Shadow Cabinet), 1987-97; Shadow Secretary of State for Education, 1987-92; For the Environment (Local Government), 1992-94; Shadow Home Secretary, 1994-97; Home Secretary, 1997-2001; Secretary of State for Foreign and Commonweath Affairs, 2001-; Member, Council Institute for Fiscal Studies, 1983-2000; Lancaster University, 1988-92; Vice President, Association of District Councils; Visiting Fellow, Nuffield College, Oxford, 1990-98; Governor, Blackburn College, 1990-; Pimlico School, 1994-2000 (Chair 1995-98); Fellow, Royal Statistics Society, 1995-; Labour; Hon LLD, 1999; Labour Publications: Contributions to pamphlets, newspaper articles, Policy and Ideology, 1993. Address: House of Commons, London, SW1A 0AA, England.

**STRAWSON Galen John,** b. 5 February 1952, Oxford, England. Philosopher. m. (1) Jose Said, 20 July 1974, dissolved 1994, 1 son, 2 daughters, (2) Anna Vaux, 6 January 1997, 2

sons, dissolved 2003. Education: BA, Philosophy, 1973, MA, 1977, University of Cambridge; BPhil, 1977, DPhil, 1983, University of Oxford. Appointments: Assistant Editor, 1978-87, Consultant, 1987-, Times Literary Supplement, London. Publications: Freedom and Belief, 1986; The Secret Connection, 1989; Mental Reality, 1994. Contributions to: Times Literary Supplement; Sunday Times; Observer; London Review of Books; Independent on Sunday; Guardians; Mind; American Philosophical Quarterly; Inquiry; Financial Times; Journal of Consciousness Studies; Analysis, Philosophical Studies etc. Honours: R A Nicholson Prize for Islamic Studies, Cambridge, 1971; T H Green Prize for Moral Philosophy, Oxford, 1983; Fellow, Jesus College, Oxford, 1987-2000; Visiting Fellow, Australian National University, 1993; Visiting Professor, New York University, 1997; Visiting Professor, Rutgers University, 2000; Professor of Philosophy, University of Reading , 2001-; Distinguished Professor of Philosophy, City University of New York, 2004- . Membership: Mind Association. Address: Philosophy Department, Reading University, RG6 6AA, England.

**STRAWSON Peter (Frederick) (Sir),** b. 23 November 1919, London, England. Retired Professor of Metaphysical Philosophy; Author. m. Grace Hall Martin, 1945, 2 sons, 2 daughters. Education: Christ's College, Finchley; St John's College, Oxford. Appointments: Assistant Lecturer in Philosophy, University College of North Wales, 1946; John Locke Scholar, 1946, Reader, 1966-68, Waynflete Professor of Metaphysical Philosophy, 1968-87, University of Oxford; Lecturer in Philosophy, 1947, Fellow and Praelector, 1948, Fellow, 1948-68, Honorary Fellow, 1979-, University College, Oxford; Visiting Professor, Duke University, 1955-56; Fellow of the Humanities Council and Visiting Associate Professor, 1960-61, Visiting Professor, 1972, Princeton University; Fellow, 1968-87, Honorary Fellow, 1989, Magdalen College, Oxford; Woodbridge Lecturer, Columbia University, 1983; Immanuel Kant Lecturer, University of Munich, 1985; Visiting Professor, Collège de France, 1985. Publications: Introduction to Logical Theory, 1952; Individuals, 1959; The Bounds of Sense, 1966; Philosophical Logic (editor), 1966; Studies in the Philosophy of Thought and Action (editor), 1968; Logico-Linguistic Papers, 1971; Freedom and Resentment, 1974; Subject and Predicate in Logic and Grammar, 1974; Scepticism and Naturalism: Some Varieties, 1985; Analyse and Métaphysique, 1985, English translation as Analysis and Metaphysics, 1992; Entity and Identity, 1997. Contributions to: Scholarly journals. Honours: Knighted 1977; Honorary Doctorate, Munich, 1998. Memberships: Academia Europaea; American Academy of Arts and Sciences, honorary member; British Academy, fellow. Address: Magdalen College, Oxford, OX1 4AU, England.

**STREEP Meryl (Mary Louise),** b. 22 June 1949, Summit, New Jersey, USA. Actress. m. Donald Gummer, 1978, 1 son, 3 daughters. Education: Singing Studies with Estelle Liebling; Studied Drama, Vassar; Yale School of Drama. Appointments: Stage debut, New York, Trelawny of the Wells; 27 Wagons Full of Cotton, New York; New York Shakespeare Festival, 1976 in Henry V and Measure for Measure; Also in Happy End (musical); The Taming of the Shrew; Wonderland (musical); Taken in Marriage; Numerous other plays; Films include: Julia, 1976; The Deer Hunter, 1978; Manhattan, 1979; The Seduction of Joe Tynan, 1979; The Senator, 1979; Kramer vs Kramer, 1979; Still of the Night, 1982; Silkwood, 1983; Plenty, 1984; Falling in Love, 1984; Ironweed, 1987; A Cry in the Dark, 1988; The Lives and Loves of a She Devil, 1989; Hollywood and Me, 1989; Postcards from the Edge, 1991; Defending Your Life, 1991; Death Becomes Her, 1992; The House of the Spirits; The River Wild, 1994; The Bridges of Madison County, 1995;

Before and After; Marvin's Room; One True Thing, 1998; Dancing at Lughnasa, 1999; Music of the Heart, 1999; The Hours, 2002; Adaptation, 2003; Many others; TV appearances include: The Deadliest Season; Uncommon Women; Holocaust; Velveteen Rabbit; First Do No Harm, 1997; Many others. Honours: Academy Award for Best Supporting Actress for Kramer vs Kramer, 1980; Best Supporting Actress Awards from National Society of Film Critics for the Deer Hunter; New York Film Critics Circle for Kramer vs Kramer, The Seduction of Joe Tynan and Sophie's Choice; Emmy Award for Holocaust; British Academy Award, 1982; Academy Award for Best Actress for Sophie's Choice, 1982; Hon Dr, Yale, 1983; Dartmouth, 1981; Lafayette, 1985; Bette Davis Lifetime Achievement Award, 1998; Special Award Berlin International Film Festival, 1999; Golden Globe for Best Supporting Actress, Adaptation, 2003. Address: c/o Creative Artists Agency, 9830 Wilshire Boulevard, Beverly Hills, CA 90212, USA.

**STREET Brian Frederick,** b. 2 June 1927, United Kingdom. Retired Chemical Engineer. m. (1) Margaret Carleton, 1951, deceased 1998, 1 son, 5 daughters, (2) Sally Ann May, 2003. Education: BSc, Chemical Engineering, University of Birmingham; AMP, Harvard Business School. Appointments: Refinery Technologist, Shell Refining (UK), 1948-51; Chief Chemist, Sarawak Oil Fields Ltd, 1950's; Chief Technologist, Shell Chemicals UK, 1960's; Chief Executive, Plastics Division BCL, 1970-75; Managing Director, Chairman, Air Products PLC and Chief Scientific Officer, Air Products Europe, 1976-92; Honorary Professor, Member of Council, Pro-Chancellor and Chairman of Council, University of Surrey, 1991-98; Retired, 1998. Honours: Fellow, Royal Academy of Engineering; Honorary Doctor of the University, University of Surrey. Memberships: FIChemE, Former President; FREng, Former Senior Vice-President. E-mail: brisas17@hotmail.com

**STREET-PORTER Janet,** b. 27 December 1946, England. Journalist; TV Presenter; Producer; Editor. m. (1) Tim Street-Porter, 1967, divorced 1975, (2) A M M Elliot, 1976, divorced 1978, (3) Frank Cvitanovich, divorced 1988, deceased 1995. Education: Architectural Association. Career: Petticoat Magazine Fashion Writer and Columnist, 1968; Daily Mail, 1969-71; Evening Standard, 1971-73; Own Show, LBC Radio Programme, 1973; Presenter, London Weekend Show, London Weekend Television (LWT), 1975; Producer, presenter, Saturday Night People (with Clive James and Russell Harty), The Six O'Clock Show (with Michael Aspel), Around Midnight, 1975-85; Network 7 for Channel 4, 1986-; BBC Youth and Entertainment Features Head, 1988-94; Head, Independent Production for Entertainment, 1994; Managing Director, Live TV, Mirror Group plc, 1994-95; TV Presenter, Design Awards, Travels with Pevsner, Coast to Coast, The Midnight Hour, 1996-98, As the Crow Flies (series), 1999; Cathedral Calls, 2000; J'Accuse, Internet, 1996; Janet Save the Monarchy, 2005; So You Think You Can Teach, 2004; Editor, The Independent on Sunday, 1999-2001; Editor-at-Large, 2001-. Publications: Scandal, 1980; The British Teapot, 1981; Coast to Coast, 1998; As the Crow Flies, 1999; Baggage, 2004. Honours: Prix Italia for the Vampyr, 1992; BAFTA award for originality for Network 7, 1998. Memberships: Vice President, Ramblers' Association; President, Globetrotters Club, 2003-; Fellow, Royal Television Society. Address: c/o Emma Hardy, Princess Television, Princess Studios, Whiteley, 151 Queensway, London WC2 4SB, England. E-mail: emma.hardy@princesstv.com

**STREETEN Paul Patrick,** b. 18 July 1917, Vienna, Austria. Retired Professor. m. Ann H Higgins, 9 June 1951, 1 stepson, 2 daughters. Education: MA, University of Aberdeen, 1944; BA, 1947 MA, 1952, Oxon; DLitt, 1976. Appointment: Chairman of the Board of World Development, 1972-2003. Publications: Economic Integration, 1961, 2nd edition, 1964; Frontiers of Development Studies, 1972; Development Perspectives, 1981; First Things First, 1981; What Price Food?, 1987; Mobilizing Human Potential, 1989; Thinking About Development, 1995, paperback, 1997; Globalisation: Threat or Opportunity, 2001. Contributions to: Magazines, journals and books. Honours: Honorary Fellow, Institute of Development Studies, 1980; Honorary Fellow, Balliol College, 1986; Essays in Honour of Paul Streeten: Theory and Reality in Development, (edited by Sanjaya Lall and Frances Stewart), 1986; Development Prize, Justus Liebig University, 1987; Honorary LLD, University of Aberdeen, 1980; Honorary DLitt, University of Malta, 1992; Silver Sign of Honour for Services to the Land of Vienna; Wassily Leontief Award, Tufts University. Memberships: Royal Economic Society; American Economic Association; Society for International Development Address: Box 92, Spencertown, NY 12165, USA.

**STREISAND Barbra Joan,** b. 24 April 1942, Brooklyn, New York, USA. Singer; Actress; Director; Producer; Writer; Composer; Philanthropist. m. (1) Elliott Gould, 1963, divorced 1971, 1 son, (2) James Brolin, 1998. Education: Erasmus Hall High School. Career: Began recording career with Columbia records, 1963; Appeared in musical play Funny Girl, New York, 1964, London, 1966; TV programme My Name is Barbra shown in England, Holland, Australia, Sweden, Bermuda and the Philippines; Films: Funny Girl, 1968; Hello Dolly, 1969; On a Clear Day You Can See Forever, 1969; The Owl and the Pussycat, 1971; What's Up Doc?, 1972; Up the Sandbox, 1973; The Way We Were, 1973; For Pete's Sake, 1974; Funny Lady, 1975; A Star is Born, 1977; The Main Event, 1979; All Night Long, 1981; Yentl, 1934; Nuts, 1987; Sing 1989; The Prince of Tides, 1990; The Mirror Has Two Faces, 1996; Numerous albums, singles, TV and concert appearances. Honours: New York Critics Best Supporting Actress Award, 1962; Grammy Awards for Best Female Pop Vocalist, 1963, 64, 65, 77, 86; GB Variety Poll Award, Best For Actress, 1966; Golden Globe Academy Award, 1968; Special Tony Award, 1970; Golden Globe, Best Picture, Best Director, 1984; 5 Emmy Awards; Peabody Award; 3 Cable Ace Awards; 37 Gold and 21 Platinum Albums. Address: c/o Jeff Berg, ICM, 8942 Wilshire Boulevard, Beverly Hills, CA 90211, USA.

**STRONG Roy (Colin) (Sir),** b. 23 August 1935, London, England. Writer; Historian; Lecturer. m. Julia Trevelyan Oman, 1971, deceased, 2003. Education: Queen Mary College, London; Warburg Institute, London. Appointments: Assistant Keeper, 1959, Director, Keeper and Secretary, 1967-73, National Portrait Gallery, London; Ferens Professor of Fine Art, University of Hull, 1972; Walls Lecturer, J Pierpoint Morgan Library, New York, 1974; Director, Victoria and Albert Museum, London, 1974-87; Director, Oman Publications Ltd; Andrew Carnduff Ritchie Lecturer, University of Yale, 1999. Publications: Portraits of Queen Elizabeth I, 1963; Holbein and Henry the VIII, 1967; The English Icon: Elizabethan and Jacobean Portraiture, 1969; Tudor and Jacobean Portraits, 1969; Van Dyck: Charles I on Horseback, 1972; Splendour at Court: Renaissance Spectacle and the Theatre of Power, 1973; Nicholas Hilliard, 1975; The Renaissance Garden in England, 1979; Britannia Triumphans: Inigo Jones, Rubens and Whitehall Palace, 1980; Henry, Prince of Wales and England's Lost Renaissance, 1986; Creating Small Gardens, 1986; Gloriana: Portraits of Queen Elizabeth I, 1987; A Small Garden Designer's Handbook, 1987; Cecil Beaton: The Royal Portraits, 1988; Creating Small Formal Gardens, 1989; Lost Treasures of Britain, 1990; A Celebration of Gardens (editor), 1991; The Garden Trellis, 1991; Small Period Gardens, 1992; Royal Gardens, 1992; A Country Life, 1994; Successful

Small Gardens, 1994; William Larkin: Vanitù giacobite, Italy, 1994; The English Vision: Country Life 1897-1997; The Story of Britain, 1996; The Tudor and Stuart Monarchy, 3 volumes, 1995-97; The Story of Britain, 1996; The English Vision: Country Life 1897-1997, 1997; The Roy Strong Diaries 1967-1987, 1997; The Spirit of Britain. A Narrative History of the Arts, 1999, re-issued as The Arts in Britain, 2004; Garden Party, 2000; The Artist and the Garden, 2000; Ornament in the Small Garden, 2001; Feast – A History of Grand Eating, 2002; The Laskett – The Story of a Garden, 2003; Passions Past & Present, 2005; Coronation: A History of Kingshill and the British Monarchy, 2005. Co-Author: Leicester's Triumph, 1964; Elizabeth R, 1971; Mary Queen of Scots, 1972; Inigo Jones: The Theatre of the Stuart Court, 1973; An Early Victorian Album: The Hill-Adamson Collection, 1974; The English Miniature, 1981; The English Year, 1982; Artists of the Tudor Court, 1983. Honours: Fellow, Queen Mary College, 1976; Knighted, 1982; Senior Fellow, Royal College of Arts, 1983; High Bailiff and Searcher of the Sanctuary of Westminster Abbey, 2000; Honorary doctorates: Leeds 1983; Keele, 1984; Worcester, 2004; Honorary Fellow, Royal Society of Literature, 1999; President of the Royal Photographic Society's Award, 2003. Memberships: Arts Council of Great Britain, chairman, arts panel, 1983-87; British Council, Fine Arts Advisory Committee, 1974-87; Royal College of Arts Council, 1979-87; Westminster Abbey Architectural Panel, 1975-89; President, Garden History Society, 2000-. Address: The Laskett, Much Birch, Herefordshire HR2 8HZ, England.

**STUART Jessica Jane,** b. 20 August 1942, Ashland, Kentucky, USA. Retired; Teacher; Poet; Writer. Divorced, 2 sons. Education: AB, Western Reserve University, Cleveland, Ohio, 1964; MA, 1967, MA, 1969, PhD, 1971, Indiana University, Bloomington, Indiana. Appointments: Teaching, University of Florida, 1986-88, Santa Fe Community College, Gainesville, Florida, 1986-88; Flagler College and St Johns River Community College, St Augustine, Florida, 1989-90. Publications: Eyes of the Mole, 1968; White Barn, 1971; A Year's Harvest, 1956; Transparencies (with prose), 1986; Novels: Yellowhank, 1973; Passerman's Hollow, 1974; Land of the Fox, 1975; A Peaceful Evening Wind, 2002; Short stories: Gideon's Children, 1976; Chapbooks: Finding Tents, 2002; Celestial Moon, 2003; Spanish Moss, 2003; Mardi Gras, 2004; The Turning Year, 2005; Along the River's Shore, 2004. Honours: Grand Prix, KSPS Kentucky State Poetry Society, 1993; Cameo Chapbook Contest Award (Poetry), 1998; State Poetry Contests Award; Mississippi Poetry Society First Place, 2002. Memberships: MPS (Mississippi); OSPS (Oregon); APS (Arizona). Address:225 Stuart Lane, Greenup, KY 41144, USA.

**STUBBS Imogen Mary,** b. 20 February 1961, Rothbury, England. Actress. m. Trevor Nunn, 1994, 1 son, 1 daughter. Education: Exeter College, Oxford; Royal Academy of Dramatic Arts. Appointments: Appeared with RSC in The Rover; Two Noble Kinsmen; Richard II, 1987-88; Othello, 1991; Heartbreak House, 1992; St Joan, 1994; Twelfth Night, 1996; Blast from the Past, 1998; Betrayal, 1998; The Relapse, 2001; TV appearances include: The Rainbow; Anna Lee; After the Dance; Films include: Nanon; A Summer Story; Erik the Viking; True Colours; A Pin for the Butterfly; Fellow Traveller; Sandra c'est la vie; Jack and Sarah; Sense and Sensibility, 1995; Twelfth Night, 1996. Honours: Gold Medal, Chicago Film Festival. Address: c/o Michael Foster, ICM, Oxford House, 76 Oxford Street, London, W1N 0AX, England.

**STUBBS Jean,** b. 23 October 1926, Denton, Lancashire, England. Author. m.(1) Peter Stubbs, 1 May 1948, 1 son, 1 daughter, (2) Roy Oliver, 5 August,1980. Education: Manchester School of Art, 1944-47; Diploma, Loreburn Secretarial College,

Manchester, 1947. Appointments: Copywriter, Henry Melland, 1964-66; Reviewer, Books and Bookmen, 1965-76; Writer-in-Residence for Avon, 1984. Publications: The Rose Grower, 1962; The Travellers, 1963; Hanrahan's Colony, 1964; The Straw Crown, 1966; My Grand Enemy, 1967; The Passing Star, 1970; The Case of Kitty Ogilvie, 1970; An Unknown Welshman, 1972; Dear Laura, 1973; The Painted Face, 1974; The Golden Crucible, 1976; Kit's Hill,1979; The Ironmaster, 1981; The Vivian Inheritance, 1982; The Northern Correspondent, 1984; 100 Years Around the Lizard, 1985; Great Houses of Cornwall,1987; A Lasting Spring, 1987; Like We Used To Be, 1989; Summer Secrets, 1990; Kelly Park, 1992; Charades, 1994; The Witching Time, 1998; I'm a Stranger Here Myself, 2004. Contributions to: Anthologies and magazines. Honours: Tom Gallon Trust Award, 1964; Daughter of Mark Twain, 1973. Memberships: PEN; Society of Women Writers and Journalists; Detection Club; Lancashire Writers Association; West Country Writers; Society of Authors. Address: Trewin, Nancegollan, Helston, Cornwall TR13 0AJ, England.

**STUDER Gerald C,** b. 31 January 1927, Smithville, Ohio, USA. Christian Minister. m. Marilyn Ruth Kreider, 2 daughters. Education: BA, Goshen College, 1947; ThB, Goshen Biblical Seminary, 1949; BD GBS, 1957, MDiv, GBS, 1971. Appointments: Pastor, Smithville (Ohio) Mennonite Church, 1947-61; Scottdale (PA) Mennonite Church, 1961-73; Plains Mennonite Church, Lansdale, Pennsylvania,1973-90; Conference Minister, Atlantic Coast Mennonite Conference, 1990-94. Publications: Numerous articles in magazines; Books: Christopher Dock: Colonial Schoolmaster, 1967; After Death, What?, 1976. Memberships: First President of the North American Mennonite Youth Fellowship, 1947-50; Mennonite Publication Board, 1956-59, 1965-68, 1993-01; General Mennonite Board, 1971-73; Mennonite Historical and Research Committee, 1960-71; International Society of Bible Collectors, 1965-, President, 1988-2002. Address: 1260 Orchard Lane, Lansdale, PA 19446, USA.

**STULTING Andries Andriessen,** b. 29 August 1948, Cape Town, South Africa. Ophthalmologist. m. Lemainé, 2 daughters. Education: MB ChB (Pret), 1973; MMed (Ophth) (Pret), 1981; FRCOphth, 1989; FCS (SA) (Ophth), 1993; FACS, 1995; FICS, 1996. Appointments: Professor and Chairman, Department of Ophthalmology, Faculty of Health Sciences, University of the Free State, South Africa, 1982-. Publications: 360 presentations at congresses; 50 articles. Honours: President, Ophthalmological Society of South Africa, 1989-91, 1997-99; President, Free State Branch, South African Medical Association, 1995, 2001, 2003; Best Clinical Lecturer at the Faculty of Medicine, University of the Orange Free State, 1982, 1985, 1989, 1991, 1993, 1996; Frik Scott Memorial Lecturer, 1989; D J Wood Memorial Lecturer, 1993; Bloemfonteiner of the Year, 1996; Vice-President, The Colleges of Medicine of South Africa, 1998-; Seven Star Merit Award, National Council of the Blind, 1999; President, College of Ophthalmologists, 2000-; Eddy Epstein Lecturer, 2001; Giel Kritzinger Safari Award Lecturer, 2001; Hennie Meyer Lecturer, 2001. Memberships: Vice Chairperson, South African Medical Association; Health Professions Council; Medical and Dental Professions Board; Past President, Honorary Secretary, Ophthalmological Society of South Africa; American Academy of Ophthalmology; Fellow, Royal College of Ophthalmologists; International Intraocular Implant Club; Southern African Cataract and Refractive Society; Past President, Vitreoretinal Association. Address: 50 Gascony Crescent, Bayswater, Bloemfontein 9301, Republic of South Africa. E-mail: stulting@doh.ofs.gov.za

**STUMMER Peter Olaf,** b. 1 June 1942, Jauernig, Czech Republic. Senior Lecturer. m. Anne Stummer-Schwegmann. Education: English, Romance Philology, Philosophy, 1961-66; Teacher's Diploma, 1966; PhD, 1969; 2nd Teacher's Diploma, 1970. Appointments: Tutor Students' Hall of Residence, 1965-70; Tutor, English Department, Munich, 1967-69; Secondary School Teacher and University Lectureship, 1979-71; Assistant Professor, University of Cologne, 1971-74; Assistant Professor, 1974-78, Lecturer (tenured), 1978-, Senior Lecturer, Literatures Written in English, 1980-, University of Munich. Publications: Author and editor of several books; Author of over 30 articles on various aspects of diverse literatures written in English, especially from Africa, India and Australia; Conference Convenor; Originator of Postgraduate Programme on English Speaking Countries. Honours: German Studies Association, University of Aberdeen; Visiting Professor, University of Trento; Lectureship, University of Passau. Memberships: One-time Vice President, ASNEL; EACLALS; ACLALS; EASA; ASAL; BASA; German Association for Australian Studies. Address: Edelweiss-strasse 115, D-82178 Puchheim, Germany. E-mail: peter.stummer@lmu.de

**SU Der-Ruenn,** b 11 March 1937, Chekiang, China. Physicist. Education: BS, Physics, National Taiwan University, Taipei; MS, University of Pennsylvania; PhD, State University of New York; Appointments: Assistant Instructor, University of Pennsylvania; Researcher, State University of New York; Visiting Professor, Fu-Jen University, Taiwan, the National Central University and the National Taiwan Normal University; Professor, National Taiwan University Taipei. Publications: Book chapter in Density Functional Methods in Chemistry (Springer-Verlag, NY, 1991); The Collected Papers of Der-Ruenn Su on Quantum Physics (Sciences & Technologies, Tai-Pei, 1999); Quantum Mechanics, an intermediate aspect, (Sciences & Technologies, Tai-Pei) and numerous papers in physics and other fields. Honours: 2 Government Prizes, 1973, 1978; Six-Arts Medal, Chinese Ministry of Education, 1983; Honorary DSc, Marquis Giuseppe Scicluna International University; Honorary DPhil, Albert Einstein International Academy. Memberships: Chinese Physical Society; American Physical Society; Former member, American Association for the Advancement of Science. Address: Physics Department, National Taiwan University; Taipei, Taiwan 10617, China.

**SUCHET David Courtney,** b. 2 May 1946, London, England. Actor. m. Sheila Ferris, June 1976, 1 son, 1 daughter. Appointments: Former Member, National Youth Theatre; Chester Repertory Company; RSC, 1973, Associate Artist. Creative Works: Roles includes: Tybalt in Romeo and Juliet, 1973, Orlando in As You Like It, 1973, Tranio in Taming of the Shrew, 1973, Zamislov in Summerfolk, 1974, 1975, Wilmer in Comrades, 1974, The Fool in King Lear, 1974, 1975, Pisanio in Cymbeline, 1974, Hubert in King John, Ferdinand King of Navarre in Love's Labour's Lost, 1975, Shylock in The Merchant of Venice, 1978, Gruio in Taming of the Shrew, 1978, Sir Nathaniel in Love's Labour's Lost, 1978, Glougauer in Once in a Lifetime, 1978, Caliban in The Tempest, 1978, Shylock in The Merchant of Venice, 1978, Sextus Pompey in Antony and Cleopatra, 1978, Angelo in Measure for Measure, 1979; Oleanna, 1993; What a Performance, 1994; Who's Afraid of Virginia Woolf?, 1997; Saturday, Sunday and Monday, 1998; Amadeus, 1998-2000; Man & Boy, 2004-05. Films include: Big Foot & The Hendersons, 1986; Crime of Honour, 1987; The Last Innocent Man, 1987; A World Apart, 1988; To Kill a Priest (also known as Popielusko), 1988; The Lucona Affair, When the Whales Came, 1990; Executive Decision, 1995; Deadly Voyage, 1995; Sunday, 1996; A Perfect Murder, 1998; Wing Commander, 1998; RKO, 1999; Sabotage, 1999; Live From

Baghdad, 2002; The Wedding Party, 2002; Foolproof, 2002; Numerous TV appearances including: Master of the Game, 1984; Reilly – Ace of Spies, 1984; Mussolini: The Untold Story, 1985; The Life of Agatha Christie, 1990; Hercule Poirot in Agatha Christie's Poirot, 7 Series including 100th Anniversary Special: The Mysterious Affair at Styles, 1990; Days of Majesty, 1994; The Cruel Train, Moses, 1995; Solomon, 1997; Seesaw, 1997; The Way We Live Now, 2001; National Crime Squad, 2001-02; Maggie, 2003; Several radio drama roles, audio recordings and voice overs. Publications: Author of essays in Players of Shakespeare, 1985. Honours: Brown Belt in Aikido; 1st Master of Japanese Samurai; Best Radio Actor of the Year for The Kreutzer Sonata (one-man show), 1979; Best Actor for Beria in Red Monarch, Marseilles Film Festival, 1983; Best Actor for Stress, British Industry/Science Film Association, 1986; Best Actor for Song for Europe, Freud, Blott on the Landscape, Royal TV Society Performance Awards, 1986; Best Actor, Variety Club Award for John in Oleanna and Salieri in Amadeus, 1998; 1994; Several BAFTA, SWET, Oliver and other nominations; Critics' Circle Award for Best Actor as George in Who's Afraid of Virginia Woolf?, 1997; Best Actor for Salieri in Amadeus, Backstage Theatre Award, LA, 2000; Best Actor for Melmotte in The Way We live Now, TV, Radio and Industry, Royal Television Society, Broadcasting Press Guild, 2002; OBE. Memberships: Fellow, Royal Society of Arts; Governor, Royal Shakespeare Company; Fight Dirs Association; Garrick Club, London; St James's Club, London. Address: c/o Ken McReddie, 21 Barrett Street, London W1U 1BD, England.

**SUDDABY Arthur,** b. 26 February 1919, Hull, East Yorkshire, England. Retired Polytechnic Director; Retired Scientific Consultant; Author. m. Elizabeth Bullin Vyse, 1944, deceased 1965, 2 sons. Education: BSc in Chemistry, Hull Technical College; BSc in Mathematics, MSc in Mathematical Physics, Chelsea College, London; PhD in Theoretical Physics, Queen Mary College, London; Professional Qualifications, CChem, FRSC, CEng MIChemE. Appointments: Organic chemist and biochemist in various industrial posts in pharmaceuticals, solvent manufacture, edible oil refining and research on therapeutic drug intermediates, 1937-47; Lecturer in Physical Chemistry and Chemical Engineering, West Ham College of Technology, 1947-50; Senior Lecturer in Physics, 1950-61, Head, Department of Physics, 1961-66, Principal, 1966-70, Sir John Cass College, London; Provost of the City of London Polytechnic, now London Metropolitan University, 1970-81; Retired, 1981-; Scientific Consultant on the carriage of goods by sea, 1981-90. Publications: Scientific research and review papers in various scientific journals; Contributions on educational matters; Articles in the press on educational matters. Honour: CBE, 1980. Memberships: Member, Education Committee of the Institute of Chemical Engineers, 1948-51; Member, various CNAA committees, 1969-81; Member, London and Home Counties Regional Advisory Council on Higher Education, 1971-81; Member, Court of the City University, 1967-81; Member, Oakes Committee on Management of Public Sector Higher Education, 1977-78; Member, Visiting Committee, Cranfield Institute of Technology; Chairman, Committee of Directors of Polytechnics, 1976-78; Chairman, Association of Navigation Schools, 1972; Member, Athenaeum. Address: Castle Hill House, Godshill Wood, Fordingbridge, Hampshire, SP6 2LU, England.

**SUDELEY, 7 Baron, Merlin Charles Sainthill Hanbury-Tracy,** b. 17 June 1939, London, England. Lecturer and Author. m (1) Elizabeth Villiers (2) Margarita Kellett. Education: History, Worcester College, Oxford, 1960-63. Appointments: Fellow of the Society of Antiquaries; Chairman, Conservative Monday Club; Lay Patron, Prayer Book Society; Patron,

Bankruptcy Association; Vice-Chancellor, Monarchist League; Chairman, Constitutional Monarchy Association; Introduced debates in the House of Lords on: Export of manuscripts, 1973; Cathedral finance, 1980; Teaching and use of the Prayer Book in theological colleges, 1987; Cleared the Prayer Book (Protection) Bill on second reading in the House of Lords, 1981; Lecture tours to the USA, 1983, 1996; Occasional Lecturer, Extra-Mural Department, University of Bristol; Appearances on radio and television, 1960-. Publications: Book: The Sudeleys – Lords of Toddington (joint author), 1987; Contributor to: Contemporary Review; Family History; London Magazine; Monday World; Quarterly Review; Vogue; The Universe; John Pudney's Pick of Today's Short Stories; Montgomeryshire Collections; Salisbury Review; Transactions of the Bristol and Gloucester Archaeological Society. Honour: FSA, 1989. Address: 25 Melcombe Court, Dorset Square, London NW1 6EP, England.

**SUGA Hiroyuki,** b. 4 October 1941, Japan. Director General. m. Atsuko, 2 daughters. Education: MD, Okayama University Medical School; PhD, University of Tokyo. Appointments: Assistant Professor, University of Tokyo and Johns Hopkins University, 1978; Director, National Cardiovascular Center Research Institute, Osaka, 1991; Professor of Physiology, Okayama University Medical School, 1991-2000; Director General, Research Institute, National Cardiovascular Center, Osaka, 2000-. Honours: Johns Hopkins Honor Award, 1982; Paul Dudley White International Lecturer, 1993; Upjohn Science Award, 1993; Konrad Witzig Lecturer, 1994. Memberships: American Physiology Society; American Heart Association. Address: 2-5-10 Uenosaka, Toyonaka, Osaka 560-0012, Japan.

**SUGIURA Takeyuki,** b. 20 October 1960, Kaizuka, Osaka, Japan. Pharmacist; Researcher; Research Manager. Education: BS, 1979-83, MS, 1983-85, PhD, Faculty of Pharmaceutical Science, 1992, University of Tokyo; Visiting Scientist, Molecular Biology Department, Harvard Medical School, Massachusetts General Hospital, 1994-96. Appointments: Research Scientist, Banyu Pharmaceutical, 1985-86; Project Leader, Hoechst Japan, 1987-98; Senior Research Scientist, Daiichi Pharmaceutical, 1999-. Publications: Articles in scientific journals including: Biotechnical Letters, 1990; Cytotechnology, 1991; Journal of Biotechnology, 1992, 2003; Biotechnology Bioengineering, 1992, 1996; Protein Expression and Purification, 1995; Enzyme and Microbial Technology, 1998; Biochemical Journal, 1999; Biochemical and Biophysical Research Communications, 1999, 2004; Bone, 2001. Address: Daiichi Pharmaceutical Co Ltd, 16-13 Kitakasai 1-chome, Edogawa-ku, Tokyo 134-8630, Japan. E-mail: sugiuy79@daiichipharm.co.jp

**SUH Zung-Shik,** b. 1 February 1960, Taegu, Kyungpook, Republic of Korea; College Professor. m. Zung-Souk Lee, 1 son. Education: BS, Electronics Engineering, Kyungpook National University, Taegu, Korea, 1984; MS, 1987, PhD, Electrical Engineering, 2002, Korea Advanced Institute of Science and Technology (KAIST). Appointments: Researcher, Gold Star Central Research Institute, 1988-91; Part-time Teacher, Kumoh National University of Technology and Kumi College, 1992-95; Currently, College Professor, Kumi College, Korea. Publications: Articles in scientific journals including: IEEE Journal of Quantum Electronics, 2003; Proceedings of SPIE, 2004. Honours: Listed in Who's Who publications and biographical dictionaries. Address: Kumi College, Bukok-Dong 407, Kyungpook Kumi, 730-711, Korea. E-mail: zssuh@kumi.ac.kr

**SUKUL Diwaker,** b. 5 April 1965, Delhi, India. Clinical Psychologist. m. Rakhi, 1 daughter. Education: BA (Honours); MA, Clinical Psychology; PhD (Psychology); MD (Alternative

Medicine); Diploma in Addictive Behaviour; Diploma in E. Hypnotherapy, Psychotherapy, NLP. Appointments: Director, Turning Point Alcohol Project, 1991-97; Founder, Director, Kamkus group of clinics in Harley Street, London, Birmingham, Dubai, India, 1997-; Dean, Kamkus Institute of Integrated Medicine, 2004-. Publications: Addiction; Alcohol Report – Complementary Therapy for the Treatment of Addiction; Several papers in international conferences on Addiction, Eastern Psychotherapy, Panchkarma Therapy (in publication). Honours: MD, Alternative Medicine; Listed in Who's Who publications and biographical dictionaries. Memberships include: Addiction Forum; Alcohol Concern; Hypnotherapy Register. Address: The Kamkus Clinic, 97 Harley Street, London W1, England. E-mail: dsukul@usa.net Website: www.kamkushealthcare.co.uk

**SULEIMAN Michael Wadie,** b. 26 February 1934, Tiberias, Palestine. University Professor. m. Penelope Ann Powers, 1 son, 1 daughter. Education: BA, Bradley University, 1960; MSc, 1962, PhD, 1965, University of Wisconsin-Madison, Wisconsin. Appointments: Assistant Professor, 1965-68, Associate Professor, 1968-72, Professor, 1972-90, University Distinguished Professor, 1990-, Kansas State University. Publications: Books, monographs and edited works include: Political Parties in Lebanon: The Challenge of a Fragmented Political Culture, 1967; American Images of Middle East Peoples: Impact of the High School, 1977; The Arabs in the Mind of America, 1988; Arab Americans: Continuity and Change (Co-editor, co-author), 1989; US Policy on Palestine from Wilson to Clinton, (editor and co-author), 1995; (Arabic translation) US Policy on Palestine from Wilson to Clinton, 1996; Arabs in America: Building a New Future (editor and co-author), 1999; Numerous journal articles, essays, papers. Honours: Ford Faculty Research Fellowship, 1969-70; American Research Centre in Egypt Fellowship, 1972-73; Center for International Exchange of Scholars (CIES) Islamic Civilization Grant, 1985; National Endowment for the Humanities (NEH) Grant, 1989-91; University Distinguished Professor, Kansas State University, 1990-; Faculty Research Abroad Program (Fulbright-Hayes) Fellowship, 1983-84, summers, 1991, 1993, 1994, 2004; Institute for Advanced Study Fellowship, Princeton, NJ, 1994-95. Address: Department of Political Science, Kansas State University, Manhattan, KS 66506-4030, USA. E-mail: suleiman@ksu.edu

**ŠULJAGIC Strahinja-Straja,** b. 16 January 1941, Belgrade, Serbia. Dramatist; Translator. 1 son. Education: High Journalist School; German Language. Career: Dramatist for theatre, radio and TV; Translator. Creative Works include: A Slow Steamboat for Shanghai (for Iskara Grabul, Architect); From the Old Days; Please Hold My Hand; Sister Helen; Rose Earli (drama for Rose and Patrick Earli); Love Letter of a Big Tragedy Actress, Mary Jaszai to her Young Lover Dr Janos Plese (for actress Eliza Gerner, La Dame); Good-By Abazia (Comedy) (for his mother, Greta Henzel); Autumn Passions (drama for two) (for actor Vlada Amidžić); England's Spring and Citizens of Calais (for Sara Kestelman); The Rockfellers Violin; Jelena Dimitriewna; Zinocka (for la Dame Zina Zrelza); Scream of Bird Turaku (for poet Bryan Govett); 3 books. Honours: Many awards for translations of Jewish poetry and prose. Memberships: NUNS (Free Journalists); Dramatists Alliance; Blood Donor. Address: Karadordeva St 49, 111 Entr., Apr 18/IX Floor, 11000 Belgrade, Serbia.

**SULLIVAN Wendy,** b. 18 May 1938, London, England. Painter; Poet. Education: Notre Dame High School, London. Career: Exhibitions: Brixton Gallery, 1981-97; Royal Academy Summer Shows, 1989,1990, 1997, 1998; South Bank Picture Show, 1990; Dagmar Gallerie, East Dulwich, 1990-92; Cooltan Arts, Brixton

and Camden, 1992-95; Brixton Gallery, Retrospective, 1995; 2 Solo Shows, West Norwood Library, 1997, 1999; 2 Solo Shows Ritzy Cinema, 2000, 2001, Solo Show, Brixton Library, 2000; Artist in Residence, ASC Studios, Brixton, 2000-01; Solo Show, Jacaranda Restaurant, Brixton, 2002-04; Solo Show, The Village Hall, Brixton, 2002; Brixton Open, 2003; Solo Show, Bettie Moreton Gallery, Brixton, 2004; 1st Annual Dulwich Art Fair, 2004; Works in collections: St Mark's Centre, Deptford; Lambeth Archives; St John's Church, Brixton; Breast Scanning Clinic, Camberwell; Dagmar Gallerie (now private), France; Movement for Justice. Publications: Contributions to poetry magazines for 40 years. Honours: Winner Brixton Open, 2003; Listed in Who's Who publications and biographical dictionaries. Address: 127 Crescent Lane, London SW4 8EA, England.

**SUMIYOSHI Tomiki,** b. 18 December 1964, Tokyo, Japan. Psychiatrist; Researcher. m. Sawako Suemasa. Education: MB, 1989, MD, 1989, PhD, 1993, Kanazawa University School of Medicine; Diplomate, National Medical Board of Japan, 1989. Appointments: Resident, Fukui Prefectural Psychiatric Hospital, Japan, 1990; Ward Administrator, Kanazawa University Hospital, Japan, 1991-93; Research Associate, Department of Psychiatry, Case Western Reserve University, Cleveland, 1993-95; Assistant Professor, Department of Psychiatry, Saitama Medical School, Japan, 1995-96; Assistant Professor, Department of Neuropsychiatry, Director, Neurochemistry Research, Toyama Medical and Pharmaceutical University, 1996-; Appointed Psychiatrist, Health and Welfare Ministry, Japan, 1996-; Associate Professor, Neuropsychiatry, University of Toyama School of Medicine, Japan, 2000-; Visiting Professor, Department of Psychiatry, Vanderbilt University School of Medicine, Nashville, USA, 2000-2002. Publications: Numerous articles as author and co-author in medical journals in English include most recently: Enhancement of cognitive performance in schizophrenia by addition of tandospirone to neuroleptic treatment, 2001; Plasma glycine and serine levels in schizophrenia compared to normal controls and major depression: Relation to negative symptoms, 2004; Prediction of changes in memory performance by plasma homovanillic acid levels in clozapine-treated patients with schizophrenia, 2004; Disorganization of semantic memory underlies alogia in schizophrenia: An Analysis of verbal fluency performance in Japanese subjects, 2005; 8 book chapters in English and Japanese. Honours: Research Award, Saburo Matsubara Memorial Fund for Psychiatric Research, 1993; Young Investigator Award, National Alliance for Research on Schizophrenia and Depression, Chicago, 1995, New York, 2001; Society Award, Japanese Society of Biological Psychiatry, 1996; Rotary Ambassadorial Scholarship, Rotary International, 1994-95; Japan Education and Science Ministry Fellowship for Long-term Research in Foreign Countries, 2000-2002; ACNP Memorial Travel Award, American College of Neuropsychopharmacology, 2001. Memberships: World Federation of Societies of Biological Psychiatry; Society for Neuroscience; Collegium Internationale Neuro-Psychopharmacologicum; Schizophrenia International Research Society; New York Academy of Sciences. Japanese Society of: Biological Psychiatry, Neuropsychopharmacology, Clinical Neuropsychopharmacology, Psychiatry and Neurology, Prevention of Psychiatric Diseases, Brain Sciences, Psychiatric Diagnosis. Address: Department of Neuropsychiatry, University of Toyama School of Medicine, 2630 Sugitani, Toyama, 930-0194 Japan. E-mail: sumiyo@med.u-toyama.ac.jp

**SUMMER Donna,** b. 31 December 1948, Boston, USA. Singer; Actress. m. (1) Helmut Sommer, divorced, 1 daughter, (2) Bruce Sudano, 1 son, 1 daughter. Appointments: Singer, 1967-; Appeared in German stage production, Hair, in Europe, 1967-75; Appearing in Vienna Folk productions of Porgy and Bess;

German production of The Me Nobody Knows; Has sold over 20 million records; Albums: The Wanderer; Star Collection; Love to Love You Baby; Love Trilogy; Four Seasons of Love; I Remember Yesterday; The Deep; Shut Out; Once Upon a Time; Bad Girls; On the radio; Walk Away; She Works Hard for the Money; Cats without Claws; All Systems Go, 1988; Another Time and Place, 1989; Mistaken Identity, 1991; Endless Summer, 1994; I'm a Rainbow, 1996; Live & More Encore, 1999. Honours: Best Rhythm and Blues Female Vocalist, National Academy of Recording Arts and Sciences, 1978; Best Female Vocalist, 1879; Favourite Female Pop Vocalist, American Music Awards, 1979; Favourite Female Vocalist of Soul Music, 1979; Ampex Golden Reel Award for single and album On the radio, 1979; Album Bad Girls, Soul Artist of Year, Rolling Stone Magazine, 1979; Best Rock Performance; Best of Las Vegas Jimmy Award, 1980; Grammy Award for Best Inspirational Performance, 1984; Several Awards for Best Selling Records. Address: 2401 Main Street, Santa Monica, CA 90405, USA.

**SUN Andy,** b. 23 November 1953, Taiwan, Republic of China. Doctor; Professor. m. Hsiung Shu-Yun, 1 son, 1 daughter. Education: DDS, School of Dentistry, Medical College, National Taiwan University, 1978; PhD, Immunology, Medical College, National Taiwan University, 1992. Appointments: Attending Physician, National Taiwan University Hospital, 1989-; Associate Professor, Fu-Jen Catholic University, 1993-94; Associate Professor, 1996-2003, Professor, 2003-, The Shih Hsin University; Visiting Professor, Tianjin Medical University, 1999-; Visiting Professor, Hu-Bei Traditional Chinese Medical College, 1999-; Visiting Associate Professor, Shanghai Traditional Chinese Medical University, 1999-2003; Visiting Professor, Shanghai Traditional Chinese Medical University. Publications: Articles in professional journals. Honours: Outstanding Immunology Research, Graduate of Medical College, 1987; Awards for papers, National Science Council, 1988-96, 1998, 2000. Memberships: Central Committee, 14th Plenary Session, KMT; President, University and College Lecturers Association; New York Science Council; President, Straits Academic and Cultural Exchange Association; President, Chinese Health and Spirit Research and Development Association; Chinese Society of Immunology. Address: National Taiwan University Hospital, Taipei, Taiwan, ROC.

**SUN Jie,** 21 April 1946, Qingdao, China. Professor. Education: MS, Chinese Academy of Science, People's Republic of China, 1981; MS, 1983, PhD, 1986, University of Washington, USA. Appointments: Assistant Professor, Northwestern University of USA, 1986-92; Senior Lecturer, 1993-97, Associate Professor, 1998-2001, Professor, 2002-, National University of Singapore. Publication: Advances in Optimization and Approximation, 1994. Honour: Outstanding University Researcher, 1999. Membership: Mathematical Programming Society. Address: Department of Decision Sciences, National University of Singapore, Republic of Singapore 119260. E-mail: jsun@nus.edu.sg

**SUN Ron,** b. 8 October 1960, Shanghai, China. Cognitive Scientist; Computer Scientist. Education: BSc in Computer Information Science, Fudan University, 1983; MSc in Mathematics and Computer Science, Clarkson University, USA, 1986; PhD in Computer Science, Brandeis University, 1991. Appointments: Assistant Professor of Computer Science and Psychology, 1992-98, Associate Professor of Computer Science and Psychology, 1998-99, Departments of Computer Science and Psychology, University of Alabama at Tuscaloosa; Adjunct Professor of Psychology, University of Alabama at Birmingham, 1998-2000; Visiting Scientist, NEC Research

Institute, Princeton, New Jersey, 1998-2003; Associate Professor of Computer Engineering and Computer Science, Department of Computer Engineering and Computer Science, University of Missouri-Columbia, Columbia, 1999-2002; Full Professor and James C Dowell Endowed Professor of CECS, Department of CECS, University of Missouri, Columbia, 2002-2003; Full Professor, Department of Cognitive Science, Rensselaer Polytechnic Institute, 2003-. Publications: Author, Integrating Rules and Connectionism for Robust Commonsense Reasoning, 1994; Duality of the Mind, 2002; Editor: Cognition and Multi-Agent Interaction, 2005; Co-editor: Computational Architectures Integrating Neural and Symbolic Processes, 1994; Connectionist Symbolic Integration, 1997; Hybrid Neural Systems, 2000; Sequence Learning: Paradigms, Algorithms, and Applications, 2001; Numerous book chapters, papers and articles in the field, especially in human and machine learning, reasoning and representation in neural networks, hybrid models, autonomous agents and multi-agent systems. Honours include: Graduate Fellowship and Scholarship in Computer Science, Brandeis University, 1988-91; David Marr Award in Cognitive Science, Cognitive Science Society, 1991; Senior Member, Institute of Electrical and Electronics Engineers, 1998; Member, European Academy of Science, 2002. Memberships: Institute of Electrical and Electronics Engineers; Cognitive Science Society; Life Member, American Association for Artificial Intelligence; International Neural Network Society; Upsilon Pi Epsilon. Address: Cognitive Science Department, Rensselaer Polytechnic Institute, 110 8th Street, Troy, NY 12180, USA.

**SUN Shi-Ying,** b. 11 March 1933, Shanghai, China. Professor in Microwave and Communication. m. Zhang Han-Yang, 1 daughter. Education: Graduate, Electronic Engineering, Shanghai Jiao Tong University, 1953; Graduate, Russian, Harbin Foreign Language Institute, 1955; Graduate Student, Microwave Devices and Techniques, University of Electronic Science and Technology, China, Chengdu, 1956-58. Appointments: Lecturer, Microwave Devices and Techniques, UESTC, 1961-; Joined, 1978-, Associate Professor, 1982-88, Full Professor, 1988-, Microwave Theory and Techniques, Shanghai Jiao Tong University; Co-chairman, MMIC session APMC'88, 1988; Director, 5 research projects sponsored by National Natural Science Foundation of China, 1983-; Director, research project sponsored by Electronic Scientific Academy of Electronic Industrial Ministry, 1988-89; Director, Research Project, Multimedia Visible Telephone Compression Coder Including ITU-T G723.1-Dual Rate Speech Coder for Multimedia Communication Transmitting at 5.3 & 6.3 kbps, 1997-2001; Director, Research Project, Video Compression Coder, 1999-2002; Co-director, Research Project, MPEG-4 Real Time Compression Encoder/Decoder and Real Time Video Transmission over IP Networks, 2002-04. Publications include: Over 50 scientific papers including: CAD and Performance of the Ultra Wide Band GaAs FET Amplifiers; Multiplier Method and Performance of the Developed Broadband Low Noise GaAs FET Amplifiers; A Variation Method of Predicting Resonant Frequency of Cylindrical Dielectric Resonator; Books: Author, Measurement of Microwave Devices; Co-author, Microwave Techniques, Microwave Electronic Devices, volumes I and II. Honours include: Award, State Council and Education Committee, China, 1960; 1st Class Prize, Excellent Advisor to Graduate Students, Shanghai Jiaotong University, 1986; World Lifetime Achievement Award, Gold Statue, American Biographical Institute, 1997; 3rd Prize and Diploma for Microwave Achievement, Pei-yuan Zhou Foundation, 1998; The Who's Who New Century Medal – Leaders for the New Century, Baron's Who's Who, USA, 2001; Listed in numerous Who's Who publications and biographical dictionaries. Memberships: Senior Member, IEEE; Senior Member, Chinese Institute of

Electronics; Board Member, Microwave Board of Shanghai Institute of Electronics, 1990-2002. Address: Department of Electronic Engineering, Shanghai Jiaotong University, No 1954 Hua Shan Road, Shanghai 200030, China.

**SUN Xue-Zhi,** b. 3 September 1963, Jilin Province, China. Researcher; Medical Doctor. m. Zhang Rui, 2 sons. Education: BMed, Medical Diploma, Norman Bethune University of Medical Sciences, Changchun, China 1985; PhD, School of Medicine, Nagoya University, Nagoya, Japan 1996. Appointments: Researcher, Doctor, Laboratory of Industry Hygiene, Ministry of Public Health, China, Beijing, China, 1985-91; Professor Assistant, School of Medicine, Tokushima University, Tokushima, Japan, 1996-97; Researcher, National Institute of Radiological Sciences, Chiba, Japan, 1997-; Visiting Professor, Nagoya University, Nagoya, Japan, 2000-; Research Adviser, National Institute of Radiological Sciences, Chiba, Japan, 2001-. Publications: Author, The World of Human Being; Contributor of articles to professional Journals. Honours: Recipient of numerous awards including: Academic Awards of the Japanese Teratology Society; Certificate of Recognition of Who's Who, 2000; Academic Awards of the Medical Society of China; Academic Awards of The Japan Radiation Research Society, 2002. Memberships: Japanese Teratology Society; Japanese Association of Anatomists; Japan Radiation Research Society; Medical Society of China; American Association for the Advancement of Science; New York Academy of Sciences; Japan Neuroscience Society. Address: National Institute of Radiological Sciences, 4-9-1 Anagawa, Inage-ku, Chiba-shi, Chiba 263-8555, Japan. E-mail: sun_s@nirs.go.jp

**SUNDARALINGAM Kandiah,** b. 15 January 1942, Jaffna, Sri Lanka. University Academic. m. Sivamalar Sundaralingam, 2 sons. Education: BSc Honours, University of Ceylon, Colombo, 1965; PhD, University of Durham, England, 1971; Advanced Certificate in Microcomputer Technology, CPTI, Melbourne, Australia, 1994. Appointments: Physics Staff, University of Sri Lanka, 1965-75; Physics Staff, University of Technology, Lae, Papua New Guinea, 1975-82; Physics Staff, University of the South Pacific, Fiji, 1982-90; Sessional Staff, Monash University, 1990-99, Swinburne University, Australia, 1991-; Member, International Lithospheric Program, University of California, Los Angeles. Publications: Crust and uppermost mantle structure of the arc regions of South West Pacific Islands, 1990; Shear velocity structure beneath the Western Australian region, 1997. Honours: Postdoctoral Fellow, University of California at Los Angeles; Associate, ICTP, Trieste, Italy; Research Scientist, BMR, Canberra, Australia. Memberships: Former Fellow, Royal Geological Society, London; AIP; ACS; ASEG. Address: 77 Camelot Drive, Glen Waverley, Victoria 3150, Australia. E-mail: sundak@hotmail.com

**SUNG Wen-Pei,** b. 20 January 1964, Nan-Ton, Taiwan. Professor; Professional Engineer. m. Hui-Tzu Chiu, 2 daughters. Education: Bs, 1986; MS, 1989; PhD, 2003. Appointments: Structural Engineer, Sinotech Engineering Consultants Inc, Taiwan, 1990-92; Engineering Consultant, Tai Fan Construction Co, Taiwan, 1992-2005; Associate Professor, 2001-2005, Professor, 2005-, National Chan-Yi Institute of Technology, Taiwan. Publications: 31 international papers; 41 Chinese journal papers, 9 international conference papers; 23 Chinese conference papers; 2 monographs in Chinese; 2 textbooks on Calculus. Honours: Outstanding Research Achievement Awards, 2002, 2003, 2004, 2005; Outstanding Research Award of Science and Technology, 2005; Outstanding Research, The Society of Chinese Structural Engineering, 2003. Memberships: Phi Kappa Phi Honor Society, North Carolina State University Chapter, USA; Phi Taur Phi Academic Honor Society; Society

of Chinese Structural Engineering. Address: No 35, Ln 215, Chung Suan Rd, Sect 1, Taiping, Taichung 4111, Taiwan. E-mail: sung809@ncit.edu.tw

**SUNKLODAS Jonas Kazys,** b. 28 September 1945, Užpaliai Town, Utena District, Lithuania. Mathematician, m. Janina Survilaitė, 1 son, 3 daughters. Education: Mathematics major, Vilnius University, 1963-68; Postgraduate studies, Institute of Physics and Mathematics, Lithuanian Academy of Sciences, 1972-74; Doctors degree, Mathematics, Vilnius University, 1979; Habilitated Doctors degree of Physical Sciences, Mathematics, Institute of Mathematics and Informatics, 1999; Title of Professor, Vilnius Gediminas Technical University, 2004. Appointments: Junior Research Fellow, Institute of Physics and Mathematics, Lithuanian Academy of Sciences, 1970-71; Instructor, Faculty of Mathematics and Mechanics, Vilnius University, 1973-78; Junior Research Fellow, 1975-81, Senior Research Fellow, 1982-2002, Chief Research Fellow, 2003-, Institute of Mathematics and Informatics, Lithuanian Academy of Sciences; Associate Professor, 1997-99, Professor, 1999-, Faculty of Fundamental Sciences, Vilnius Gediminas Technical University. Publications: Articles in science publications on probability theory; Author, over 50 scientific publications. Memberships: Lithuanian Mathematicians' Society. Address: Institute of Mathematics and Informatics, Akademijos 4, 220 cab, LT-08663 Vilnius, Lithuania.

**SURDIA PROBONEGORO Noer Mandsjoeriah,** b. 8 November 1932, Jakarta, Indonesia. Professor in Polymer Science and Surface Science. m. Tata Surdia, 2 sons, 1 daughter. Education: Sarjana S-1 degree, Physical Chemistry, Institute of Technology, Bandung, 1960; MSc, Chemistry (Surface Science), Rensselaer Polytechnic Institute, Troy, New York, USA, 1964; PhD, Chemistry (Surface Science), Faculty of Mathematics and Natural Sciences, Institute of Technology, Bandung, 1966. Appointments: Curriculum Builder, Indonesian Institute of Textile Technology, 1965-99; Head of Chemistry Department, Institute of Technology, Bandung, 1974-76; Co-ordinator of Polymer Co-operation, ITB-USTL Montpellier, France, 1976-79; Director of Women's College, 1979-83; National Point of Contact in Indonesia for ASEANCUPS, 1985-91; President, Indonesian Polymer Association; Head of Materials Science and Engineering Study Programme (Graduate), Institute of Technology, Bandung, 1991-2002; Student Research Advisor S-1 (200), S-2 (65); Doctor's theses S-3 (20) at ITB; Vice-Rector I, Bandung Raya University, 2000-2006; Research Panel Member of New Materials, Ministry of Research, 1992-2004; Research Evaluator of New Materials, National Integrated Supreme Research Programme, Ministry of Research, 1992-2004. Publications: Books: Bonding and Molecular Structure, 1993; Editor and Translator, Alberty R A, F Daniels, Kimia Fisika Vol 1 and 2, 1981; 35 articles in scientific journals and book chapters; 40 papers as keynote speaker and seminars. Memberships: Indonesian Chemical Society; Indonesian Polymer Association; Indonesian Society of Women Graduates. Address: Jl Dago Timur 2, Bandung 40135, Indonesia.

**SURYAVANSHI Arvind Krishnajirao,** b. 13 October 1957, Sirsi, Karnataka, India. Teaching; Researcher. m. Vani A Suryavanshi, 1 son, 1 daughter. Education: PhD, UMIST, England, 1991-94; MTech, IIT, Mumbai, 1986-88; BEng, Karnataka, India, 1974-79. Appointments include: Scientists-C, National Institute of Oceanography, (NIO), Goa, India, 1982-91; Research Associate, University of Sheffield, UK, 1995-97; Manager, Concrete Consultancy, The Associated Cement Company Ltd, India, 1997; Research Fellow, National University of Singapore, Singapore, 1997-99; Senior Engineer, Poh Cheong Concrete Products Pte Ltd, 1999-2001;

Teaching Fellow, Nanyang Technological University (NTU), Singapore. 2001-2003; Principal Engineer, Setsco Pte Ltd, Singapore, 2003-. Publications: 24 technical papers published in International Journals and International Conference proceedings related to Civil Engineering. Honours: Commonwealth Fellow, 1991-94. Listed in: Biographical Publication. Address: Blk116, #03-619, Yishun Ring Road, Singapore 760116.

**SUSUKI Yasufumi,** b. 22 June 1961, Fukui City, Japan. Associate Professor. Education: Master of Engineering, 1986, Doctor of Engineering, 1997, Kyoto University. Appointments: Scientific Associate, Faculty of Engineering, Kyoto University, 1986-96; Associate Professor, Faculty of Education, Osaka Kyoiku University, 1996-. Publications: Numerous articles in scientific journals including: European Physical Journal D, 1999; Physical Reviews A, 2000, 2004; Journal of the Physical Society of Japan, 2001, 2002. Address: Department of Physics, Osaka Kyoiku University, 4-698-1 Asahigaoka, Kashiwara 582-8582, Japan. E-mail: susuki@cc.osaka-kyoiku.ac.jp

**SUTCLIFFE Serena Gillian,** b. 21 May 1945, England. Expert on Wine; Author; Consultant. m. David Peppercorn. Education: England and Switzerland; Master of Wine Examination, 1976. Appointments: Translator, UNESCO; Director, Peppercorn and Sutcliffe, 1988-91; Senior Director, Member European Board, Head, International Wine Department, Sotheby's London, 1991-; Chairman, Institute of Wine, 1994-95. Publications: Books: Wines of the World; Great Vineyards and Winemakers; The Wine Drinker's Handbook; A Celebration of Champagne; Bollinger, 1994; The Wines of Burgundy, new edition, 2005; Contributor of articles to: Decanter; Quarterly Review of Wines; Planet Vins et Spiritueux. Honours: Chevalier dans l'Ordre des Arts et des Lettres; New York Institute of Technology's Professional Excellence Award; Book of the Year Award for A Celebration of Champagne, Decanter, 1988. Memberships: Institute of Masters of Wine; Académie Internationale du Vin. Address: c/o Sotheby's, 34-35 New Bond Street, London W1A 2AA, England. E-mail: serena.sutcliffe@sothebys.com

**SUTHERLAND Donald McNichol,** b. 17 July 1935, St John, Canada. Actor. m. (1) Lois May Hardwick, 1959; m. (2) Shirley Jean Douglas, 1966, divorced, 1 son, 1 daughter, (3) Francine Racette, 1971, 3 sons. Education: University of Toronto. Appointments: Appeared on TV (BBC and ITV) in Hamlet; Man in the Suitcase; The Saint; Gideon's Way; The Avengers; Flight into Danger; Rose Tattoo; March to the Sea; Lee Harvey Oswald; Court Martial; Death of Bessie Smith; Max Dugan Returns; Crackers; Louis Malle; The Disappearance; Films include: The World Ten Times Over, 1963; Castle of the Living Dead, 1964; Dr Terror's House of Horrors; Fanatic, 1965; Act of the Heart, 1970; M*A*S*H*, 1970; Kelly's Heroes, 1970; Little Murders, 1970; Don't Look Now, 1973; The Day of the Locust, 1975; 1900, 1976; The Eagle Has Landed, 1977; The Great Train Robbery, 1978; Lock Up, 1989; Apprentice to Murder, 1989; Los Angeles, 1989; The Railway Station Man, 1991; Scream from Stone, 1991; Faithful, 1991; JFK, 1991; Backdraft; Agaguk; Buffy the Vampire Slayer; Shadow of the Wolf, 1993; Benefit of the Doubt; Younger and Younger, 1993; Six Degrees of Separation, 1993; The Puppet Masters; Disclosure; Outbreak; Hollow Point; The Shadow Conspiracy; A Time To Kill; Virus, 1999; Instinct, 1999; Toscano, 1999; The Art of War, 2000; Panic, 2000; Space Cowboys, 2000; Uprising, 2001; The Big Herst, 2001; Final Fantasy: The Spirits Within, 2001; Plays: Lolita, 1981; Enigmatic Variations, 2000; President, McNichol Pictures Inc. Honours: TV Hallmark Hall of Fame; Officer, Ordre des Lettres; Order of Canada; Hon PhD; Golden Globe for Best Supporting Actor in a TV series or TV Movie,

2003. Address: 760 N La Cienega Boulevard, Los Angeles, CA 90069, USA.

**SUTHERLAND Peter Denis,** b. 25 April 1946, Dublin, Ireland. Lawyer. m. Maria Cabria Valcarcel, 2 sons, 1 daughter. Education: Gonzaga College; Degree in Civil Law, University College, Dublin, 1967. Appointments: Called to Bar, King's Inns, 1968; Middle Temple, 1976; Bencher, 1981; Attorney of New York Bar, 1981; Attorney and Counsellor of Supreme Court of USA, 1986; Tutor in Law, University College, Dublin, 1969-71; Practising Member, Irish Bar, 1969-81, 1981-82; Senior Counsel, 1980; Attorney General of Ireland, 1981-82, 1982-84; Member, Council of State, 1981-82, 1982-84; Commissioner for Competition and Commissioner for Social Affairs and Education, EEC, 1985-86, for Competition and Relations with European Parliament, 1986-89; Chairman, Allied Irish Banks, 1989-93; Director, GPA, 1989-93; Director, CRH plc, 1989-93; Director, James Crean plc, 1989-93; Chairman, Board of Governors, European Institute of Public Administration, 1991-96; Director, Delta Air Lines Inc, 1992-93; Director General, GATT, later WTO, 1993-95; Honorary Bencher, King's Inns, Dublin, 1995; Director, Investor, 1995-2005; Chairman, Goldman Sachs International, 1995-; Director, Telefonaktiebolaget LM Ericsson, 1996-2004; Goodwill Ambassador to the United Nations Industrial Development Organisation; Chairman, BP plc, 1997-; Director, Royal Bank of Scotland Group plc, 2001-; Chairman (Europe), Trilateral Commission, 2001-; The Federal Trust, President; Chairman, The Consultative Board of the DG of the WTO. Publications: Premier Janvier 1993 ce qui va changer en Europe, 1989; Numerous articles in law journals. Honours include: Honorary LLD: St Louis, 1986; NUI, 1990; Dublin City, 1991; Holy Cross, Massachusetts, 1994; Bath, 1995; Suffolk, USA, 1995; TCD, 1996; Reading, 1997; Nottingham, 1999; Exeter, 2000; DUniv, Open, 1995; Gold Medal, European Parliament, 1988; The First European Law Prize, Paris, 1988; New Zealand Commemorative Medal, 1990; Grand Cross: King Leopold II, Belgium, 1989; Order of Infante Dom Henrique, Portugal, 1998; Grand Cross of Civil Merit, Spain, 1989; Chevalier, Legion d'Honneur, France, 1993; Commander, Order of Ouissam Alaouite, Morocco, 1994; Order of Rio Branco, Brazil, 1996; The David Rockefeller International Leadership Award, 1998; UCD Foundation Day Medal. Memberships: The Stephen's Green Hibernian Club, Dublin; Fitzwilliam Lawn Tennis, Dublin; Lansdowne FC, Dublin; The Athenaeum, London; Marks Club, London. Address: Goldman Sachs International, Peterborough Court, 133 Fleet Street, London, EC4A 2BB, England.

**SUZMAN Janet,** b. 9 February 1939, Johannesburg, South Africa. Actress; Director. m. Trevor Nunn, 1969, divorced 1986, 1 son. Education: BA, University of Wittwatersrand; Graduate, London Academy of Music and Dramatic Arts, 1962. Career: For the RSC: The Wars of the Roses; Portia, Ophelia, Celia, Rosalind, Katherina; The Relapse; The Greeks, 1980; London Theatre includes: The Birthday Party; Three Sisters; Hedda Gabler; The Duchess of Malfi; Andromache; The Retreat from Moscow; Television includes: The Family Reunion; St Joan; Macbeth; Twelfth Night, Hedda Gabler; Three Men in a Boat; Clayhanger (serial), 1975-76; Mountbatten-Last Viceroy of India, 1985; The Singing Detective, 1986; The Miser, 1987; Revolutionary Witness, 1989; Masterclass on Shakespearean Comedy, 1990; Masterclass from Haymarket Theatre (Sky TV), 2001; White Clouds (BBC), 2002; Films include: A Day in the Death of Joe Egg, 1970; Nicholas & Alexandra, 1971; Nijinsky, 1978; The House on Garibaldi Street; The Priest of Love, 1981; The Black Windmill; Nuns on the Run, 1990; Leon the pig-Farmer, 1992; Max, 2001; Fairy Story, 2002; Numerous performances in South Africa; Wrote and Directed The Free State – a South African response to the Cherry Orchard, performed at the Birmingham Repertory Theatre, 1997 (revived for UK tour, 2000); Lectures include: The Spencer Memorial Lecture, Harvard University, USA, 1987; The Tanner Lectures, Brasenose College, Oxford, 1995; The Judith E Wilson Annual Lecture, Trinity Hall, Cambridge, 1996; The Draper's Lecture, Queen Mary and Westfield College, University of London. 1997. Publications: Hedda Gabler: The Play in Performance, 1980; Acting with Shakespeare – Three Comedies, 1996; The Free State, 2000; A Textual Commentary on Anthony and Cleopatra, 2001. Honours: Honorary Degrees: MA, Open University; D Lit, Warwick University; D Lit, Leicester University; D Lit, Queen Mary and Westfield College, London University; D Lit, University of Southampton, 2002; Vice-President of London Academy of Music and Dramatic Arts. Address: c/o Steve Kenis & Co, Royalty House, 72-74 Dean Street, London W1D 3SG, England. E-mail: sk@sknco.com

**SUZUKI Fujio,** b. 17 February 1933, Toyonaka, Osaka, Japan. Professor Emeritus m. Yuriko Nagai, 2 sons, 1 daughter. Education: BA, Department of Chemistry, Faculty of Science, 1955, PhD, Department of Bioorganic Chemistry, Graduate School of Science, 1960, Osaka University. Appointments: Instructor, 1960-61, 1964-65, Assistant Professor, 1965-66, Associate Professor, 1966-77, Professor, 1977-96, Councilor, 1979-81, Advisor, 1980-81, Director, Life Science Library, 1989-93, Professor Emeritus, 1996-, Department of Biochemistry, Faculty of Dentistry, Osaka University, Japan; Assistant Research Biochemist, University of California, Berkeley, 1961-64; Visiting Professor, SUNY Upstate Medical Center, 1974-75; Professor Emeritus, Norman Bethune Medical University, Changchun, China, 1993; Editor-in Chief, Journal Bone and Mineral Metabolism, 1994-. Publications: Regulation of cartilage differentiation and metabolism, 1994; Cartilage-derived growth factor and anti-tumour factor. Past, present and future studies. Breakthroughs and views, 1999. Honours: Fulbright Fellow, 1961-64; Young Investigators Award, Japan Biochemical Society, 1970; Award Asahi Press, 1984; Award, Japanese Society for Bone and Mineral Research, 1996; Kroc Foundation Lectureship, 1996. Memberships: Japan Biochemistry Society; Japan Society for Bone and Mineral Research; Japan Medical Library Association; New York Academy of Sciences; Japan Society for Connective Tissue Research; Japan Society for Cartilage Metabolism. Address: 2-13-11 Nakasakurazuka, Toyonaka, Osaka 561-0881, Japan. E-mail: fsuzuki@oak.ocn.ne.jp

**SUZUKI Toru,** b. 12 May 1967, Kamakura, Kanagawa, Japan. Cardiologist; Educator. m. Mitsuko Suzuki. Education: MD, The University of Tokyo School of Medicine, Japan, 1992; PhD, The University of Tokyo Graduate School of Medicine, Japan, 1998. Appointment: Faculty, Department of Clinical Bioinformatics, University of Tokyo, Japan, 2002-. Publications: Over 80 publications in scientific journals. Honours: Finalist, Samuel Levine Young Investigator Award, American Heart Association, 1995; IFCC/AVL Award, International Federation of Clinical Chemistry, 1996. Address: Department of Clinical Bioinformatics, Graduate School of Medicine, The University of Tokyo, 7-3-1 Hongo, Bunkyo-ku, Tokyo 113-8655, Japan.

**SUZUKI Yoshio,** b. 12 October 1931, Tokyo, Japan. Economist. m. Yukiko, 3 sons, 1 daughter. Education: Graduated, 1955, Doctor of Economics, 1976, Tokyo University. Appointments: Joined Bank of Japan, 1955; Visiting Lecturer, Tokyo University, 1972; Chief Manager, Special Research Division, 1974, Chief Manager, Domestic Division, 1976, Economic Research Department, Bank of Japan; General Manager,

Matumoto Branch, Bank of Japan, 1977; Visiting Lecturer, Shinshu University, 1978; Deputy Director, 1981, Director, 1984, Institute for Monetary and Economic Studies, Bank of Japan; Executive Director, Bank of Japan, 1988; Vice Chairman, 1989, Chairman, 1990, Board of Counsellors, Nomura Research Institute Ltd; Elected, Member of House of Representatives, Tokai District, Shadow Minister for Economy and Finance of the New Frontier Party, 1996; Vice Chairman, Policy Board of the Liberal Party, 1998; Re-elected, Member of the House of Representatives, Tokyo District, 2000; Chairman, Committee of Discipline, House of Representatives, 2002; Chairman, Suzuki Seikei Forum, 2004. Publications: Numerous books and papers published in English, German, Chinese and Korean. Honours: Nikkei Cultural Prize for Economic Literature, 1967; Economist's Prize, Mainichi Newspaper Company, 1975; Public Finance Fellowship, Institute of Fiscal and Monetary Policy, 1987; The Order of the Rising Sun, Gold Ray with Neck Ribbon, Emperor, 2004. Memberships: The Association of Economics and Econometrics; The Association of Money and Banking; The Mont Pelerine Society. Address: 2-5-8 Kamitakaido, Suginami-ku, Tokyo 168-0074, Japan. E-mail: info@suzuki.org

**ŠVEC Jan G,** b. 22 November 1966, Olomouc, Czech Republic. Voice Scientist. m. Hana Švecová. Education: MSc, Fine Mechanics and Optics, 1990, PhD, Biophysics, Palacký University, Olomouc, Czech Republic, 1996; PhD, Medical Sciences, University of Groningen, The Netherlands, 2000. Appointments: Assistant Professor, Institute of Postgraduate Medical Education, Department of Phoniatrics and Audiology, Prague, Czech Republic, 1995-99; Research Scientist, Centre for Communication Disorders, Medical Healthcom Ltd, Prague, Czech Republic, 1995-; Visiting Research Scientist, National Center for Voice and Speech, Denver Center for the Performing Arts, Denver, Colorado, USA, 2001-04; Research Scientist, Groningen Voice Research Laboratory, Department of Biomedical Engineering, University of Groningen, The Netherlands, 2004-. Publications: Over 80 scientific papers, over 25 as first author in journals and proceedings; over 170 presentations, over 80 personally presented at scientific congresses, symposia and seminars in Europe, North America, Africa and Australia; Video Programme: Introduction to Videokymography, 1997. Honours: Fulbright Commission Award, 1995; Silver Medal for Best Scientific Video, AVEC World Video Festival of the XVI World ORL Congress, Sydney Australia, 1997; Best Publication Award, Czech ORL Society, 2000; International Scientist of the Year 2002, International Biographical Centre; Best Publication Award, Institute of Thermomechanics, Academy of Sciences of the Czech Republic, 2003. Memberships: Czech Acoustical Society; International Association of Logopedics and Phoniatrics, Chair, Voice Committee, 2004-2007; The Voice Foundation, Associate; Acoustical Society of America, Associate; International Biographical Centre Research Council; Research Board of Advisors, American Biographical Institute, 2003-2004; Associate Editor, Logopedics, Phoniatrics, Vocology. Address: Groningen Voice Research Laboratory, Department of Biomedical Engineering, University of Groningen, Antonius Deusinglaan 1, NL 9713 AV Groningen, The Netherlands. E-mail: j.g.svec@med.rug.nl Website: http://www.ncvs.org

**SVENSSON Charles Robert Wilhelm,** b. 11 September 1947, Göteburg. Associate Professor; Scientist. Education: Associates Degree, Electronics, 1969; BSc, Physics, 1983, MSc, Physics, 1991, PhD, Thermionic Energy Converter Concept, 1994, Göteburg University. Appointments: Design Engineer, electronic temperature meters and heart beat monitors, -1981; Part-time teacher, 1981-83, Full-time Teacher, 1983-87, College of Applied Engineering and Maritime Studies, Chalmers

University of Technology; Graduate Student, Department of Physical Chemistry, Göteburg University and Chalmers University of Technology, 1987-94; Assistant Professor, Chalmers University of Technology, 1995-96; Associate Professor, Chalmers University of Technology, 1996-; Visiting Research Professor, West Virginia University, USA, 2004. Publications: Numerous articles and papers; 2 patents. Memberships: Society of Automotive Engineers; American Society of Mechanical Engineers. Address: Dörravägen 1, SE-43893 Landvetter, Sweden. E-mail: term@chl.chalmers.sc Website: www.chl.chalmers.se/~term

**SVIRIDOV Andrei Valentinovitsh,** b. 22 December 1946, Moscow, Russia. Entomologist. Education: Moscow Lomonosov State University, 1965-70. Appointments: Senior Laboratory Assistant, 1970-71, Junior Researcher, 1971-86, Researcher, 1987-92, Senior Researcher, 1992-, Moscow Lomonosov State University; Scientific degree, Candidate of Biological Sciences (Dr), 1984; Academic Studies, Senior Researcher, 1995. Publications: 318 scientific publications, 1970-, include books: Types of the Biodiagnostic Keys and Their Applications, 1994; Biodiagnostical Keys: Theory and Practice, 1994; Key to the insects of Russian Far East, Vol 5, Part 4, 2003. Memberships: Russian Entolomological Society; Moscow Society Naturalists; Society Europea Lepidopterology; Systematic Zoology/Biology; Hist-Genealogy Society, Moscow; Descendents Council of the Great War of 1812-1814 Vets; Commission of Red Book of Russia; Commission of Red Book of CIS. Address: Dr A V Sviridov, Zoological Museum, Moscow State Lomonosov University, Bolshaya Nikitskaya St 6, 125009 Moscow, Russia.

**SWAMINATHAN Monkombu Sambasivan,** b. 7 August 1925, Tamil Nadu, India. Director. Education: BSc, Travancore University, 1944; BSc, Agriculture, Coimbatore Agricultural College, Madras University, 1947; Associateship, Indian Agricultural Research Institute, New Delhi, 1949; UNESCO Fellow, Agricultural University, Wageningen, The Netherlands, 1949-50; PhD, School of Agriculture, University of Cambridge, England, 1952; Research Associate, Genetics, University of Wisconsin, USA, 1952-53. Appointments: Teacher, Researcher, Research Administrator, Central Rice Research Institute, Cuttack, Indian Agricultural Research Institute, New Delhi, 1954-72; Director General, Indian Council of Agricultural Research, Secretary, Government of India, Department of Agricultural Research and Education, 1972-80; Secretary, Government of India, Ministry of Agriculture and Irrigation, 1979-80; Acting Deputy Chairman, Planning Commission, Government of India, 1980; Member, Planning Commission, Government of India, 1980-82; Director General, International Rice Research Institute, Los Banos, Philippines, 1982-88; Honorary Director, Centre for Research on Sustainable Agricultural and Rural Development, Madras, 1989-; UNESCO Chair in Ecotechnology and President, Pugwash Conferences on Science and World Affairs. Publications: Numerous articles in professional journals. Honours include: 1st World Food Prize laureate, 1987; Tyler Prize, 1992; UNEP-Saskawa Environment Prize, 1994; V Gangadharan Award, Outstanding Contributions to National Development, 1997; BP Pal Memorial Award, Indian Science Congress Association, 1998; Volvo Environment Prize, 1999; UNESCO Gandhi Gold Medal, 1999; Franklin D Roosevelt Four Freedoms Award, 2000; Plant and Humanity Medal, 2000; Indira Gandhi Prize for Peace, Disarmament and Development, 2000; Millennium Alumnus Award, Tamil Nadu Agricultural University, 2000; Millennium Scientist Award, Indian Science Congress Association, 2001; 48 honorary doctorates from numerous universities world wide. Address: M S Swaminathan Research Foundation, 3rd Cross Street, Taramani Institutional Area, Chennai (Madras) 600 113, India.

**SWANGER David,** b. 1 August 1940, New Jersey, USA. Professor; Poet. m. Lynn Lundstrom, 5 April 1970, 1 son, 2 daughters. Education: BA, Swarthmore College, 1963; MAT, 1964, EdD, 1970, Harvard University. Appointments: Assistant Professor, Harvard University, 1970-71; Associate Professor, 1976-85, Professor 1985-, University of California, Santa Cruz. Publications: The Poem as Process, 1971; Lemming Song, 1976; The Shape of Waters, 1978; Inside the Horse, 1981; Essays in Aesthetic Education, 1991; Family, 1994; The Evolution of Education, 1995; This Waking Unafraid, 1995. Contributions to: Georgia Review; Malahat Review; Poetry Northwest; Chariton Review; America Post and Critic; Quarry West; New Letters; Mother Earth News; Negative Capability; Whetstone; Nimrod; Minnesota Review; Cutbank; Tendril; America; Reaper. Honours: National Endowment for the Arts Poetry Award, 1989; Foley Award, 1991. Memberships: Academy of American Poets; Poets and Writers. Address: Porter College, University of California, Santa Cruz, CA 95064, USA.

**SWAYZE Patrick,** b. 18 August 1954. Actor; Dancer. m. Lisa Niemi, 1976. Education: Harkness and Joffrey Ballet Schools. Appointments: Began as dancer in Disney on Parade on tour as Prince Charming; Appeared on Broadway as dancer in Goodtime Charley Grease; TV appearances in North and South: Books I and II; The New Season; Pigs vs Freaks; The Comeback Kid; The Return of the Rebels; The Renegades. Films include: Skatetown USA, 1979; The Outsiders; Uncommon Valor; Red Dawn; Grandview USA - also choreographer; Dirty Dancing - co-wrote song and sings She's Like the Wind; Steel Dawn; Tiger Warsaw; Road House; Next of Kin; Ghost; Point Break; City of Joy; Father Hood; Tall Tales; To Wong Foo - Thanks for Everything - Julie Newmar; Three Wishes; Letters from a Killer, 1997; Vanished, 1998; Black Dog, 1998; Without a Word, 1999; The Winddrinker, 2000; Wakin'Up In Reno, 2000; Forever Lulu, 2000; Donnie Darko, 2001. Address: c/o William Morris Agency, 151 South El Camino, Beverly Hills, CA 90212, USA.

**SWEENEY Ronald Terence,** b. 1 September 1932, Hull, England. Journalist; Company Director. m. Amy, 1 daughter. Education: Diplomate in Architectural Studies, Hull College (now University of Humberside); Institute of Practitioners in Advertising Postgraduate in Race Relations and Social Analysis, University of Bradford, 1987; Postgraduate, Church and Social Studies, Napier University, Edinburgh, 2000. Appointments: Journalist ; Editor; Director of Marketing, PR Company, Leeds, Manchester, London; Head of Marketing and Communications, Bradford University College; Lecturer at several universities in western-eastern Europe; Managing Director, International Travel and Conferences. Publications: Editor of Education News; Many articles in newspapers and trade professional press. Honours: Nationally Accredited Lay Preacher; Several awards for educational publications and public speaking. Memberships: Life Member, National Union of Journalists; International Federation of Journalists (Brussels); Several Travel/Conference Related Organisations. Address: "Tirconnell", 11 Endor Crescent, Burley-in-Wharfdale, West Yorkshire LS29 7QH, England.

**SWETCHARNIK Sara Morris,** b. 21 May 1955, Shelby, NC, USA. Artist; Sculptor; Painter; Writer. m. William Norton Swetcharnik, 2 August 1981. Education: The Art Students League of New York, 1979-81; Postgraduate, Schuler School of Fine Art, Baltimore, Maryland, 1973-78; Private Study, Melvin Gerhold Studio, Frederick, Maryland, 1970-73. Appointments: Instructor, Frederick Academy for the Arts, Frederick, Maryland, 1981-82; Workshop Instructor, Landon School, Washington DC, 1991-96; Invitational Lecturer, Arts Task Force, Fulbright Conference, 2000, 2001;

Guest Lecturer, The Institute, Mount Saint Mary's College, Emmitsburg, Maryland, 2001; Juror at several national and international exhibitions. Creative Works: Solo Exhibitions including: Catepetl Gallery, Frederick, Maryland, 1977; Holly Hills Country Club, Frederick, Maryland, 1991; Landon School Gallery, Washington DC, 1992; Frederick Community College Art Gallery, Maryland, 1993; Showcase of Terra-cotta Animal Sculpture, Weinberg Center for the Arts, Frederick, Maryland, 1994; Komodo Dragon Yearling and other Animal Sculptures, Reptile Discovery Center, National Zoological Park, Washington DC, 1995-2001; Jungle Tails: Narratives and Sculptures of Animals, http://www.marrder.com/htw/special/jungletails; Several group and two person exhibitions; Publications include: Glass Lizard, 1998; Marked for Life, 1998; Birthday Burro, 1998; Alfredo's Tigrillo, 1998. Honours include: IIE Fulbright Fellowship, Sculpture, Spain, 1987-88, 1988-89; Artist in Residence Fellowship, American Numismatic Association Conference, 1994; Fellowship, Virginia Center for the Creative Arts. Memberships: Delaplaine Visual Art Centre, Frederick, Maryland; Fulbright Association. Address: National Capitol Post Office Station, PO Box 77794, Washington, DC 20013, USA. E-mail: saraswetcharnik@fulbrightweb.org

**SWIFT Graham Colin**, b. 4 May 1949, London, England. Writer. Education: Dulwich College; Queens' College, Cambridge; University of York. Publications: The Sweet Shop Owner, 1980; Shuttlecock, 1981; Waterland, 1983; Out of This World, 1988; Ever After, 1992; Last Orders, 1996; The Light of Day, 2003; Short Stories: Learning to Swim and Other Stories, 1982; The Magic Wheel, 1986. Honours: Geoffrey Fabor Memorial Prize; Guardian Fiction Prize; Royal Society of Literature Winifred Holtby Award, 1983; Premio Grinzane Cavour, Italy, 1987; Prix du Meilleur livre etranger, France, 1994; Booker Prize, James Tait Black Memorial Prize, 1996; Hon LittD, East Anglia, 1998; Hon DUniv, York, 1998. Address: c/o A P Watt, 20 John Street, London, WC1N 2DR, England.

**SWINBURNE Richard Granville**, b. 26 December 1934, Smethwick, Staffordshire, England. Professor of Philosophy; Author. m. Monica Holmstrom, 1960, separated 1985, 2 daughters. Education: BA, 1957, BPhil, 1959, Dip Theol, 1960, MA, 1961, University of Oxford. Appointments: Fereday Fellow, St John's College, Oxford, 1958-61; Leverhulme Research Fellow in the History and Philosophy of Science, University of Leeds, 1961-63; Lecturer to Senior Lecturer in Philosophy, University of Hull, 1963-72; Visiting Associate Professor of Philosophy, University of Maryland, 1969-70; Professor of Philosophy, University of Keele, 1972-84; Distinguished Visiting Scholar, University of Adelaide, 1982; Nolloth Professor of the Philosophy of the Christian Religion, 1985-2002, Emeritus Nolloth Professor, 2002-, University of Oxford; Visiting Professor of Philosophy, Syracuse University, 1987; Visiting Lecturer, Indian Council for Philosophical Research, 1992; Visiting Professor of Philosophy, University of Rome, 2002; Visiting Professor of Philosophy, Catholic University of Lublin, 2002; Visiting Professor of Divinity, Yale University, 2003; Visiting (Collins) professor of Philosophy, St Louis University, USA, 2003. Publications include: Space and Time, 1968, 2nd edition, 1981; The Concept of Miracle, 1971; An Introduction to Confirmation Theory, 1973; The Coherence of Theism, 1977, revised edition, 1993; The Existence of God, 1979, 2nd edition, 2004; Faith and Reason, 1981, 2nd edition, 2005; Personal Identity (with S Shoemaker), 1984; The Evolution of the Soul, 1986, revised edition, 1997; Responsibility and Atonement, 1989; Revelation, 1992; The Christian God, 1994; Is There a God?, 1996; Providence and the Problem of Evil, 1998; Epistemic Justification, 2001; The Resurrection of God Incarnate, 2003. Honour: Fellow, British Academy, 1992. Address: 50 Butler Close, Oxford OX2 6JG, England. E-mail: richard.swinburne@oriel.ox.ac.uk

**SYDDALL Thomas Harold**, b. 23 December 1938, Auckland, New Zealand. Patent Attorney. m. Ann Antrobus. Education: BSc, University of New Zealand, 1960; LLB, Victoria University of Wellington, 1966. Appointments: Registered Patent Attorney, 1963; Bar and Solicitor, High Court of New Zealand, 1966; Partner, A J Park (formerly A J Park & Son), Intellectual Property Lawyers, 1966-2004; Consultant, 2004-; Notary Public, 1995. Publications: Contributor to professional journals; New Zealand chapter in Katzarov's Manual on Industrial Property all over the World. Honour: International Order of Merit, 1997. Memberships: Fellow, New Zealand Institute of Patent Attorneys, President, 1980-82, Exam Board, 1991-2003; Wellington District Law Society; New Zealand Group, Asian Patent Attorneys Association, Executive, 1985-2003; New Zealand Institute of Chemistry; New Zealand Association of Scientists, Council Member, 1992-2004; New Zealand Group, International Association for the Protection of Industrial Property; New Zealand Section, International Federation of Industrial Property Attorneys; British Overseas Member, Chartered Institute of Patent Agents. Address: A J Park, Huddart Parker Building, Post Office Square, Wellington, New Zealand.

**SYKES Alfred Geoffrey**, b. 12 January 1934. Professor Emeritus of Inorganic Chemistry. m. Elizabeth Blakey, 2 sons, 1 daughter. Education: Huddersfield College; BSc, PhD, 1958, DSc, 1973, University of Manchester; CChem, FRSC, 1972. Appointments: Lecturer, 1961-70, Reader, 1970-80, University of Leeds; Professor of Inorganic Chemistry, University of Newcastle upon Tyne, 1980-99, Professor Emeritus, 1999-; Visiting Scientist, Argonne National Laboratories, USA, 1968; Visitor or Visiting Professor: Heidelberg University, 1975; Northwestern University, USA, 1978; University of Berne, 1980; University of Sydney, 1984; University of Kuwait, 1989; Universities of Adelaide and Melbourne, 1992; University of Newfoundland, 1995; Universities of the West Indies, 1997; University of Lausanne, 1998; University of Stellenbosch, Cape Town and Bloemfontein, 1999, University of La Laguna, Spain, 2000, City University of Hong Kong, 2001/2; Denmark Technical University, 2002; Troisième Cycle Lecturer, Les Rasses, 1971, Les Diablerets, 1987 Champéry, 2000, French-speaking Swiss Universities. Publications: Editor: Advances in Inorganic and Bio-inorganic Mechanisms, volumes 1-4, 1982-86; Advances in Inorganic Chemistry, volumes 32-53, 1988-2002; Book: Kinetics of Inorganic Reactions, 1966; Over 470 papers and reviews in scientific journals. Honours: Tilden Lecturer, Medal and Prize, RSC, 1984; Fellow, Japanese Society for the Promotion of Science, 1986; Fellow, Royal Society, 1999; Royal Society, Kan Tong Po Fellow, Hong Kong, 2002; Honorary DSc, Free State University, South Africa, 2003. Address: Department of Chemistry, University of Newcastle, Newcastle upon Tyne NE1 7RU, England. E-mail: a.g.sykes@ncl.ac.uk

**SYKES Eric**, b. 4 May 1923, England. Actor; Writer; Director. m. Edith Eleanor Milbradt, 1 son, 3 daughters. Education: Ward St School, Oldham. Appointments: Long running TV comedy show Sykes (with Hattie Jacques); Many other TV appearances; Films include: actor: Orders are Orders; Watch Your Stern; Very Important Person; Heavens Above; Shalako; Those Magnificent Men in Their Flying Machines; Monte Carlo or Bust!; The Boys in Blue; Absolute Beginners; The Others, 2000; Plays include: Big Bad Mouse, 1977-78; A Hatful of Sykes, 1977-78; Run for your Wife, 1992; The 19th Hole, 1992; Two of a Kind, 1995; Fools Rush In, 1996; The School for Wives, 1997; Kafka's

Dick, 1998-99; Caught in the Wet, 2001-02; Radio includes: (as writer) Educating Archie; The Goon Show, Co-wrote 24 episodes with Spike Milligan including 2 specials; The Frankie Howerd Show. Publications: The Great Crime of Grapplewick, 1996; UFO's Are Coming Wednesday, 1995; Smelling of Roses, 1997; Sykes of Sebastopol Terrace, 2000. Honours: OBE, 1986; Freeman City of London, 1988; Lifetime Achievement Award, Writer's Guild, 1992; CBE, 2005. Address: 9 Orme Court, London, W2 4RL, England.

**SYMS Sylvia**, b. 6 January 1934, London, England. Actress; Director. m. Alan Edney, 1957, divorced 1989, 1 son, 1 daughter. Education: Royal Academy of Dramatic Art. Appointments: Founder Member, Artistic Director, Arbela Production Company; Numerous lectures include: Dodo White McLarty Memorial Lecture, 1986; Member, The Actors' Centre, 1986-91; Films include: Ice Cold in Alex, 1953; The Birthday Present, 1956; The World of Suzie Wong, 1961; Run Wild Run Free, 1969; The Tamarind Seed, 1974; Chorus of Disapproval, 1988; Shirley Valentine, 1989; Shining Through, 1991; Dirty Weekend, 1992; Staggered, 1994; Food for Love, 1996; Mavis and the Mermaid, 1999; TV includes: Love Story, 1964; The Saint, 1967; My Good Woman, 1972-73; Nancy Astor, 1982; Ruth Rendell Mysteries, 1989; Dr Who, 1989-90; May to December, 1989-90; The Last Days of Margaret Thatcher, 1991; Natural Lies; Mulberry; Peak Practice; Ruth Rendell Mysteries, 1993, 1997-98; Ghost Hour, 1995; Heartbeat, 1998; At Home with the Braithwaites, 2000, 2001; Theatre includes: Dance of Death; Much Ado About Nothing; An Ideal Husband; Ghosts; Entertaining Mr Sloane, 1985; Who's Afraid of Virginia Woolf?, 1989; The Floating Lightbulb, 1990; Antony and Cleopatra, 1991; For Services Rendered, 1993; Funny Money,1996; Ugly Rumours, 1998; Radio includes: Little Dorrit; Danger in the Village; Post Mortems; Joe Orton; Love Story; The Change, 2001; Plays and TV Director: Better in My Dreams, 1988; The Price, 1991; Natural Lies, 1991-92. Honours: Variety Club Best Actress in Films Award, 1958; Ondas Award for Most Popular Foreign Actress, Spain, 1966. Address: c/o Barry Brown and Partners, 47 West Square, London, SE11 4SP, England.

**SYNEK Jiri (George), (Frantisek Listopad)**, b. 26 November 1921, Prague, Czechoslovakia. University Teacher; Poet; Writer. 1 son, 5 daughters. Education: Dr Phil. Publications: Malelasky, 1945; Slava urknuti, 1945; Vzduch, 1946; Prvni veta, 1946; BojoVenezuel, 1947; Jarmark, 1947; Svoboda a jine ovoce, 1960; Tristao ou a Traiçao de um Intelectual, 1960; Cerny bily nevim, 1973; Contos Carcomidos, 1974; Secos & Molhados, 1982; Estreitamento Progressivo, 1983; Primeiro Testamento, 1985; Mar-Seco-Gelado-Quente, 1986; Os Novos Territórios, 1986; Album de Família, 1988; Outubro Oriente, 1992; Biografia de Cristal, 1992; Nastroje Pameti, 1992; Final Rondi, 1992; Blizko Daleko, 1993; Meio Conto, 1993; Oprava houslí a kytar, 1996; Prvni vety, 1997; Tristan z mesta do mesta, 1998; Krles, 1998; Milostná stehování, 2001; Prísti poezie; Em Chinatown com a Rosa, 2001; Chinatown S Rózou, 2001; Fruta tocada por falta de jardiniero, 2003; O jardim fecha as 18:30, 2004. Contributions to: Czech, Portuguese, American and French newspapers and reviews. Honours: Academy of Fine Arts, Prague, 1948; Swedish Academy, Lund, 1949; Christian Academy, Rome, 1950; Prize, Radio Free Europe, 1952; Critic's Prizes, Lisbon, 1968, 1970, 1980; Doctor honoris causa, CSFR, 1992; Franz Kafka Prize and Medal, 2000; Medal of Merit for Extraordinary Artistic Achievement, Prague, 2001; Prize Gracias Agit, Prague, 2004. Memberships: PEN Club International; Society of Portuguese Writers. Address: Rua Joao Dias 15, Lisbon 1400, Portugal.

**SYNEK Miroslav**, b. 18 September 1930, Czechoslovakia. Physicist; Chemist; World Affairs Independent Consultant. 1 son, 1 daughter. Education: Certificate, Industrial Chemistry Technical School, Prague, 1946-50; Analytical Chemist, Industrial Medicine Institute, 1950-51; Certificate in Liberal Arts, 1951; MS, Physics with distinction, Charles University, 1956; PhD, University of Chicago, 1963. Appointments: Research Physicist, Academy of Sciences, Prague, 1956-58; Assistant to Associate Professor, De Paul University of Chicago, 1962-67; Professor, Texas Christian University, Fort Worth, 1967-71; Lecturer, Researcher, University of Texas, Austin, 1971-75; Faculty tenure, University of Texas San Antonio, 1975-95; Scientific advisor to various institutions and organisations. Publications: Articles in numerous scientific journals, abstracts to presentations; Reviewer for several professional publications. Honours: Fellow, American Association for the Advancement of Science; Texas Academy of Science; American Institute of Chemists; Life Fellow, American Physical Society; Listed in a number of Who's Who and biographical publications. Memberships include: American Association of University Professors; National Education Association; Texas State Teachers Association; Emeritus Member, The American Association of Physics Teachers; American Chemical Society; American Museum of Natural History; Distinguished Member, International Society of Poets; Diplomat Member, World Affairs Council, SA. Address: PO Box 5937, San Antonio, TX 78201, USA. E-mail: m.synek@juno.com

**SYRISTOVA Eva**, b. 7 November 1928, Prague. Professor Emeritus of Psychopathology and Psychotherapy. m. Syriste Jaroslav MD, 1 son. Education: PhD, 1951, C Scientiarum in Psychopathology and Psychotherapy, Charles University, 1962. Appointments: Editor, SPN Publications, Prague, 1951-53; Clinical Psychologist, Institute of Psychiatry, Prague, 1953-57; Lecturer, 1957-67, Professor 1967-94, Prodean for Scientific Research, 1992-94, Professor Emeritus, 1994-, Psychopathology, Psychotherapy, Charles University, Prague; Pioneer of psychotherapy and art-therapy of schizophrenic psychosis in the Czech Republic. Publications: The Possibilities and Limitations of the Psychotherapy of Schizophrenic Diseases, 1965; The Imaginary World, 1973; Normality of the Personality, 1973; The Cracked Time, 1988; The Group Psychotherapy of Psychoses, 1989; Man in Crisis, 1994; The Poem as a Home in the Homelessness of Paul Celan, 1994. Honours: Honorary Appreciation Czech Medical Society for contribution to Czech Sciences, 1978; Honorary Prize for Translation of Celan's Poetry, 1983. Memberships: IAAP; IBRO; World Phenomenology Institute, International Association of Phenomenology and Sciences of Life; New York Academy of Sciences; Czech Medical, Psychiatric and Artistic Association; Director, White Rawen for Non-professional Art in Prague. Address: Sluknovska 316, 190 00 Prague 9, Czech Republic.

**SYRKIN Alexander**, b. 16 August 1930, Ivanovo, USSR. Philologist; Professor Emeritus. Education: Graduate (MA), Moscow State University, 1953; Candidate of History (PhD), 1962; Doctor of Philology, 1971. Appointments: Junior Research Associate, Institute of History, Academy of Science of USSR, Moscow, 1955-61; Junior Research Associate, 1961-71, Senior Research Associate, 1971-77, Institute of Oriental Studies, Academy of Science of USSR, Moscow; Research Fellow, Associate Professor, Institute of Asian and African Studies, 1978-98, Professor Emeritus, 1998-, Hebrew University, Jerusalem. Publications: Books, articles, commented translations of classical texts, essays on subjects including: Indology, Byzantine Studies, Russian Literature, etc; Examples include: Poem about Digenes Akritas, Moscow, 1964; Certain Problems Regarding the Study of the Upanishads, Moscow,

1971; To Descend in Order to Rise, Jerusalem, 1993; Upon Re-reading the Classics, Jerusalem, 2000; Upanishads, 3rd edition, Moscow, 2003. Former Memberships include: FRAS of Great Britain and Ireland; International Association of Buddhist Studies; International Association of Semiotic Studies. Address: Dov Gruner Str 236, Apt 17, Talpiot Mizrah, Jerusalem 91291 (POB 29278), Israel.

**SZABÓ Zoltán,** b. 18 March 1957, Tirgu-Mures, Romania. Anaesthesiologist. m. Márta Hanangi, 1 son, 1 daughter. Education: MD, Institutul de Medicina si Farmacie, Tirgu-Mures, Romania. 1983; Specialist in Anaesthesia and Intensive Care, Hungarian Board of Anaesthesia, Hungary, 1988; PhD, Thoracic and Cardiovascular Anaesthesia, Linköping, Sweden, 2001. Appointments: Resident, Sitalul Clinic, Judetean Mures, Romania, 1983-86; Resident 2, Sebészeti Klinika, 1986-88, Specialist in Anaesthesia, 1988-95, Debrecen University, Hungary; Doctor and Specialist in Anaesthesia, 1995-2001, Consultant Anaesthetist, 2001-, University Hospital, Linköping Heart Centre. Publications: Articles in scientific journals as co-author include most recently: Neurological injury after surgery for ischemic heart disease: risk factors, outcome and role of metabolic interventions, 2001; Early postoperative outcome and medium term survival in 540 diabetic and 2239 nondiabetic patients undergoing coronary artery bypass grafting, 2002; Simple intra operative method to rapidly pass a pulmonary artery flotation catheter into the pulmonary artery, 2003; High Dose Glucose-Insulin-potassium after cardiac surgery: a retrospective analysis of clinical safety issues, 2003. Honour: First Prize for Best Poster, Congress of Cardiac Anaesthesia, Budapest, EACTA, 1990. Memberships: EACTA; S AI; Founding Member, Rotary, Debrecen. Address: Department of Cardothoracic and Vascular Anaesthesia, Östergötlands Heart Centre, S-58185 Linköping, Sweden.

**SZAMBORSKI Jozef J,** b. 24 June 1921, Warsaw, Poland. Physician. m. Wanda Ustaszewska, 1 son. Education: Graduate Faculty of Medicine, University of Lodz; PhD, Medical School, Warsaw, Poland, 1967; Professor of Pathology, Medical School, 1980. Appointments: Professor, Pathology, Medical School, Warsaw, Poland, 1973-91; Head, Department of Pathology Institute of Gynaecology Medical School, Warsaw. Honours: Vice Dean, Faculty of Medicine, Warsaw, 1981-84; Honorary Member, Polish Society of Pathologists, 1995. Memberships: International Society of Gynaecological Pathologists; International Academy of Pathology. Address: Department of Pathology, Institute of Obstetrics-Gynaecology, Medical School, Warsaw, Karowa 2, 00-315 Warszawa, Poland.

# T

**TABER Roger Noel**, b. 21 December 1945, Gillingham, Kent, England. Librarian; Poet; Writer. Education: BA, English and American Literature, University of Kent, 1973; Postgraduate Diploma, Library and Information Science, Ealing School of Librarianship, 1975. Appointments: Freelance Writer/Librarian, 1964-. Publications: (major) inclusion in How Can You Write a Poem When You're Dying of Aids, 1993; Visions of the Mind, 1998. Own collections: Love and Human Remains, 2000; First Person Plural, 2002; The Third Eye, 2004. Contributions to: Numerous poetry magazines and anthologies. Honours: Placed in National Competitions. Address: Flat C, Hammond House, 45A Gaisford Street, London NW5 2EB, England. E-mail: rogertab@aol.com.

**TABOR David**, b. 23 October 1913, London, England. m. Hannalene Stillschweig, 2 sons. Physicist. Education: BSc, Physics, Royal College of Science, London, 1934; Researched with George Thomson, 1934-36, Frank Bowden, 1936-39; PhD, 1939. Appointments: Division of the Commonwealth Scientific Research Organisation, Melbourne, 1940-46; Assistant Director of Research, 1946-61, Lecturer in Physics, 1961-64, Reader in Physics, 1964-73, Professor of Physics, 1973-81, Emeritus Professor of Physics, 1981-, Physics and Chemistry of Solids, Cavendish Laboratory, Cambridge Studied the effects between solid surfaces (tribology). Publications: Hardness of Metals, 1951; Gases, Liquids and Solids, 1969; Friction and Lubrication of Solids, Part I, 1959, 1986, Part II, 1964; Friction – An Introduction to Tribology, 1973; Contributions to learned journals on friction and adhesion. Honours include: Guthrie Medal, Institute of Physics, 1974; Royal Medal, Royal Society, 1992. Address: Cavendish Laboratory, Madingley Road, Cambridge, CB3 0HE, England.

**TADLIP Marilou Palicte**, b. 16 May 1946, Asturias, Cebu, Philippines. Library Director. Widow, 5 children. Education: BSE, Magna Cum Laude, Library Science and English, University of San Carlos, 1967; Master in Library Science, University of Hawaii, 1971; Master of Arts in English Language Teaching (lacks thesis), 1987, Doctor in Education, 1995, University of San Carlos. Appointments: Director of Libraries, University Library System, University of San Carlos, Cebu City, Philippines, 1976-; Assistant Professor, Graduate Centre for Library Science, University of San Carlos, Cebu City, 1976-. Publication: Doctoral Dissertation: Training Needs of Library Personnel in SVD Schools of the Philippine Southern Province: Proposed Guidelines for Staff Development Training Designs, 1995. Honours include: Outstanding Alumnae Award, University of San Carlos Girls High School Alumni Association, 1982; Special Award, Share a Child Movement, 1990; Loyalty Award, University of San Carlos, 1998; Outstanding Academic and Research Librarian, Philippine Association of Academic and Research Libraries, 1998; Most Outstanding Alumna Award in the field of Library Science, University of San Carlos Alumni Association, 1999; James J Meany Award, PAASCU Hall of Fame Philippine Accrediting Association of Schools, Colleges and Universities, 2004. Memberships include: National Committee on Libraries and Information Service, 2004-; Philippine Library Association; Philippine Association of Teachers in Library Science; Philippine Association of Academic and Research Libraries; Cebu Librarians Association; American Library Association; East-West Alumni Association, Honolulu; Phi Delta Kappa. Address: St Jude Acres Phase II, Bulacao, Pardo, 6000 Cebu City, Philippines. E-mail: direklib@usc.edu.ph

**TAEL Kaja**, b. 24 July 1960, Tallinn, Estonia. Diplomat. Education: Estonian Language and Literature, Tartu University, 1978-83; PhD, Institute for Language and Literature of the Academy of Sciences of Tallinn, 1989. Appointments: Researcher, Department of Grammar, Institute for Language and Literature, Academy of Sciences, Tallinn, 1984-89; Guest Scholar, Chair of Finno-Ugric Languages, Uppsala University Sweden, 1990-91; Director, Estonian Institute Tallinn (non-governmental institution for informational and cultural exchange in co-operation with the Foreign Ministry), 1991-95; Lecturer, Chair of Nordic Languages, Tallinn Pedagogical University, 1995-2000; Foreign Policy Advisor to the President of Estonia, Mr Lennart Meri, 1995-98; Joined the Estonian Foreign Ministry, 1998; Executive Secretary of the Estonian-Russian Intergovernmental Commission, 1998-99; Director General, Policy Planning Department, Estonian Ministry of Foreign Affairs, 1999-2001; Ambassador Extraordinary and Plenipotentiary of the Republic of Estonia at the Court of St James, London, 2001. Publications: Computer Analysis of the Estonian Word Order (PhD thesis), 1989; An Approach to Word Order Problems in Estonian, 1990; Book chapter in The scientific Grammar of the Estonian Language, 1993, 1996; Articles on information structure and word order; Translations into Estonian: John Stuart Mill "On Liberty", 1996; Henry Kissinger "Diplomacy", 2000; Eric Hobsbawm "The Age of Extremes", 2002. Honours: Swedish Polar Star, 1995; Finnish Lion, 1995; Mexican Aguila Azteca, 1996; Estonian Order of the White Star, 2000. Memberships: Chairman of the Board, Estonian Institute; Farmers Club, London. Address: The Estonian Embassy, 16 Hyde Park Gate, London SW7 5DG, London.

**TAHERZADEH Mohammad J**, b. 22 March 1965, Isfahan, Iran. Biotechnologist. m. Arezoo Keivandarian, 2 sons. Education: BSc, Chemical Engineering, 1989; MSc, Chemical Engineering, 1991; PhD, Biochemical Engineering, 1999. Appointments: Vice Director, Jahad Daneshgahi, Isfahan University of Technology, Iran, 1988-91; Lecturer, Chemical Engineering, Isfahan University of Technology, 1992-94; Assistant Professor, Chemical Reaction Engineering, Chalmers University of Technology, Sweden, 1999-2001; Assistant Professor, Chemical Engineering, Lund University of Technology, Sweden, 1999-2001; Associate Professor, Chemical Reaction Engineering, Sweden, 2002-04; Professor, School of Engineering, University of Boras, Sweden, 2004-. Honours: Prize for the Excellent Rank among the Graduated MSc students by Iran's President; Listed in biographical publications. Address: School of Engineering, University of Boras, 50190 Boras, Sweden.

**TAIT Andrew**, b. 4 November 1958, Wallsend, nr Newcastle upon Tyne, England. Poet; Music Teacher. Education: Science A Levels, Tynemouth Sixth Form College, 1975-77; French Horn, Guildhall School of Music and Drama, 1977-81. Publications: Poetry Collections: On the Sea I Spied Him, 21 Pre-Metaphysical Poems, 2005; Songs: 12 albums of songs released via the music page of Viz magazine including: Songs From The Heart of the Primal Goat, 1989; Why Do Hamsters Look At You Like That? 1994; My Love is Like a Whirling Elephant, 1997; Back Off! There's a Lobster Loose! 2001; Autobiography: Me and Peter Beardsley; Poetry in periodicals: The Sunday Times, The Independent, The Big Issue, Other Poetry, Morden Tower Poets; Interviews: Features in many publications, including The Sunday Times Magazine, Time Out, Get Rhythm, Viz, The Independent, Poetry Now; Poems: Going Back Over The Wasteland; Everyone's a Fruit and Nutcase; Damson in Distress; Robert's Oriental Tea Garden; The Little Leafy Lane Off To The Left; Metaphysical Experiences; Thursdays; Suspense Account; Television and radio appearances. Honours: Winner, Bloodaxe

Poetry Competition; Winner, Iron Press 30th Anniversary Haiku Competition. Memberships: Morden Tower Poetry Society. Address: PO Box 1041, Newcastle Upon Tyne, NE99 2TY, England.

**TAIWO Kehinde Adekunbi**, b. 3 October 1962, Kano, Nigeria. Associate Professor in Food Process Engineering; Researcher. m. Oluwafemi Taiwo, 3 sons. Education: BSc, University of Ife, Ile-Ife, Nigeria, 1985; MSc, 1988, PhD, 1997, Obafemi Awolowo University, Ile-Ife, Nigeria. Appointments: Junior Research Fellow, 1989-91, Research Fellow II, 1991-93, Research Fellow I, 1993-96, Senior Research Fellow, 1996-2001, Technology, Planning and Development Unit, Senior Lecturer, 2001-2002. Associate Professor (Reader), 2002-, Department of Food Science and Technology, Obafemi Awolowo University, Ile-Ife, Nigeria. Publications: 42 articles in scientific journals and conference proceedings as co-author include most recently: A study on the Nigerian food industry and the impact of technological changes on the small scale food enterprises, 2002; Comparative evaluation of the effects of pulsed electric field and freezing on cell membrane permeabilization and mass transfer during dehydration of red bell peppers, 2003; Osmotic dehydration of strawberry halves: Influence of osmotic agents and pretreatment methods on mass transfer and product characteristics, 2003; Drying and storage characteristic of pepper, 2003; Moving women from subsistence farming to commercialisation: Issues and Policy imperatives, 2003 Gender, Technology and Poverty: Issues in post harvest crop processing technologies, 2003. Honours include: Postgraduate Fellowship, Obafemi Awolowo University, 1986-89; DAAD Fellowship, Germany, 1992-93; Alexander von Humboldt Fellowship, Goethe Institute Berlin, 1999 and Technical University Berlin, 2000-2001. Memberships: Nigerian Society of Engineers; Nigerian Society of Agricultural Engineers; Third World Organisation of Women in Science; Nigerian Institute of Food Scientists and Technologists; Fellow, Centre for Gender Studies, Obafemi Awolowo University. Address: Department of Food Sciences and Technology, Obafemi Awolowo University, Ile Ife, Nigeria. E-mail: kehindetaiwo3@yahoo.com

**TAK Woo-Taek**, b. 8 March 1968, Seoul, South Korea. Doctor. m. So-Ra Kim, 1 son, 1 daughter. Education: B, Dongguk University, 1987-94; M, Dankook University, 1999-2001; PhD, Dankook University, 2002-05. Appointments: Fellowship, Division of Nephrology, Dankook University Hospital, 2002-03; Instructor, Dongguk University Medical Centre, 2003-04; Assistant Professor, 2005-. Publications: Pulse wave velocity for access arterial compliance in ESRD patients, 2004; Rapid diagnosis of peritonitis in peritoneal dialysis patients, 2005; Expression of aquaporin-1 in peritoneal membrane is regulated by osmotic stimuli and corticosteroids in rat model of peritoneal dialysis, 2005; Altered expression of peritoneal aquaporin-1 and water transport during long-term peritoneal dialysis in rats, 2005. Honours: Best Abstract Award, Annual Dialysis Conference, US, 2005. Memberships: Korean Association of Internal Medicine; Korean Society of Nephrology; ERA-EDTA. Address: Division of Nephrology, Dongguk University Medical Centre, Jukdo2-dong 646-1, Pohang, Gyeongbuk, Korea 791-707.

**TAKAMURA Seishi**, b. 29 June 1968, Nagoya, Japan. m. Sawako Takamura, 1 son, 1 daughter. Education: BS, Engineering, 1991, MS, Engineering, Graduate School, 1993, PhD, Engineering, Graduate School, 1996, Faculty of Engineering, Electronic Engineering, University of Tokyo. Appointments: Chief Research Engineer, 1998-2004, Senior Research Engineer, 2004-; Human Interface Laboratories, Visual Communication Laboratory, Video Coding Group (currently

NTT Cyberspace Laboratories, Image Media Communication project, Video Coding Group), Nippon Telegraph and Telephone Corporation; ITSCJ Technical Committee SC29/WG11/VIDEO Subcommittee Member, 1998-, SC29/WG11/MEPEG-4 Subcommittee Member, 1998-; Research Fellow, NICT Natural Vision Project, 2000-; Referee, ITE Paper Publication Committee, 2002-; OB Referee, 2004-; Board Member, IEICE Image Engineering Technical Group; PCSJ/IMPS Organisation Committee, 2002-; Board Member, IPSJ Audio Visual, Audio visual and multimedia information processing, 2003-2005; PCM Program Committee Member, 2004-; ITE Senator, 2004-. Publications: 21 international conference papers; 43 domestic conference papers, 7 journal papers, 4 books, 13 commentaries, 39 patent applications, domestic and international; 12 ISO/IEC JTC 1/SC 29 WG (MPEG) Standardisation contributions. Honours include: Pre-Business Award, Director of NTT Human Interface Laboratories, 1999; Research Promotion Award, Institute of Image Electronics Engineers of Japan, 2001; Niwa-Takayanagi Memorial Award (Best Paper Award), Institute of Image Information and Television Engineers, 2002; Pest Poster Award, 2002, 2003, Frontier Award, 2004, Picture Coding Symposium of Japan; Telecom System Technology Award, Telecommunication Advancement Foundation, 2004. Memberships: Institute of Image Electronics Engineers of Japan; Institute of Image Information and Television Engineers. Address: 1-9-20 Yuigahama, Kamakura, Kanagawa 248-0014, Japan.

**TAKAOKA Akinori**, b. 29 July 1967, Japan. Researcher. Education: PhD, 1996, MD, 1996, Internal Medicine, Sapporo University, Japan; Postdoctoral, Immunology, University of Tokyo, Japan, 1996-97. Appointments: Research Associate, 1997-2000, Assistant Professor, 2000-2002, Lecturer, 2002-, Department of Immunology, Graduate School of Medicine and Faculty of Medicine, University of Tokyo. Publications: Articles in scientific journals as co-author include: Cross talk between interferon g and a/b signalling components in caveolar membrane domains, 2000; IRF family of transcription factors as regulators of host defense, 2001; A weak signal for strong responses: interferon – revisited, 2001; Integration of IFN-a/b signalling to p53 responses in tumor suppression and antiviral defense, 2003; Integral role of IRF-5 in the gene induction programme activated by Toll-like receptors, 2005. Honours: Ohno Award, Sapporo Medical University, 1992; Young Investigator Award, International Cytokine Society, 2000; Research Award, Japanese, Cancer Association, 2001; Milstein Young Investigator Award, International Society for Interferon and Cytokine Research, 2003; The Princess Takamatsu Cancer Research Fund, 2003. Memberships: International Society for Interferon and Cytokine Research; Japanese Cancer Association; Japanese Society for Immunology; Japanese Society of Internal Medicine; Japanese Society of Gastroenterology; Japan Gastroenterological Endoscopy Society; Molecular Biology Society of Japan. Address: Department of Immunology, Graduate School of Medicine and Faculty of Medicine, University of Tokyo, Hongo 7-3-1, Bunkyo-ku, Tokyo 113-0033, Japan. E-mail: takaoka9@m.u-tokyo.ac.jp

**TAKEMURA Hiroshi**, b. 23 June 1962, Komagane, Nagano, Japan. Anaesthesiologist. m. Yoshiko Takemura, 1 son, 1 daughter. Education: MD, 1988, PhD, 1998, Showa University School of Medicine, Shinagawa-ku, Tokyo, Japan. Appointments: Resident, Department of Anaesthesiology, Showa University Hospital, Shinagawa-ku, 1988-90; Medical Staff, Sempo Tokyo Takanawa Hospital, Minato-ku, 1990-91; Assistant, Department of Anaesthesiology, Showa University Toyosu Hospital, Koutou-ku, 1991-93, Showa University Hospital, Shinagawa-ku, 1993; Medical Expert (Technical Co-operation), Cairo University Paediatric Hospital, Cairo, 1993-94; Assistant, Department of Anaesthesiology, Showa University Hospital, Shinagawa-ku, 1994-2003; Medical Practitioner, Pain Management Office TA, Yokohama, Japan, 2003-. Publications: Articles in medical journals: Correlation of cleft type with incidence of perioperative respiratory complications in infants with cleft lip and palate (clinical investigation, author), 2002; Mandibular nerve block treatment for trismus associated with hypoxic-ischemic encephalopathy (case report, author) , 2002. Memberships: American Society of Regional Anesthesia and Pain Medicine; Japan Society of Pain Clinicians; Japanese Society of Anesthesiologists. Address: Pain Management Office TA, 13-74 Kakinokidai Aoba-ku, Yokohama, 227-0048 Japan. E-mail: hy-take@msd.biglobe.ne.jp

**TALVET Jüri,** b. 17 December 1945, Pärnu, Estonia. Professor of Literature. m. Margit Oja, 1 son, 2 daughters. Education: MA, University of Tartu, Estonia, 1972; PhD, University of St Petersburg, Russia, 1981. Appointments: Lecturer of Western Literature, 1974-86, Associate Professor of Western Literature, 1986-91, Chair of Comparative Literature, 1992-, Tartu University, Estonia. Editor, Interlitteraria, annual international journal of comparative literature of the Estonia Association of Comparative Literature. Publications: In Estonian: Awakenings (poetry), 1981; A Travel to Spain, 1986; The Archer and the Cry (poetry), 1986; Soul's Progress and Surprises of Climate (poetry), 1990; From Spain to America (essays about Spain, Mexico, Cuba and Nicaragua), 1993; The Spanish Spirit ( a collection of articles on Spanish and Catalan literature), 1995; Estonian Elegy and Other Poems, 1997, Spanish translation, 2002; American Notes or Contemplations of Estonia (essays), 2000; Do You Also Have Grapes? (poetry), 2001; A Call for Cultural Symbiosis (essay, in English), 2005. Honours: Prize of Estonian Literature for essay genre, 1986; Order of Isabel the Catholic of Spain, 1992; Order of White Star of 4th Class of the Republic of Estonia, 2001. Memberships: Estonian Writers Union, 1984; Chairman, Estonian Association of Comparative Literature, 1994-; International Comparative Literature Association, 1994-, Member of Executive Committee, 2000-2003. Address: Pikk 100-12, 50606, Tartu, Estonia. E-mail: talvet@ut.ee

**TAM Bit-Shun,** b. 21 February, 1951. Professor; Mathematician. Education: BA, Mathematics, 1973, PhD, Mathematics, 1977, University of Hong Kong. Appointments: Teaching Assistant, University of Hong Kong, 1973-78; Postdoctoral Fellow, University of Waterloo, Canada, 1978-79; Instructor, Auburn University, Alabama, USA, 1979-81; Associate Professor, 1981-84, Professor, 1984-, Research Professor, 1995-2003, Tamkang University, Taiwan, Lady Davis Visiting Professor, 2004, Technion, Israel. Publications: About 50 research papers in international mathematical journals. Honours: Editor, Tamkang Journal of Mathematics, 1982-; Associate Editor, Linear Algebra and Its Applications, 1991-; Associate Editor, Applied Mathematics E-Notes, 2001-; Associate Editor, Electronic Journal of Linear Algebra, 2002-. Memberships: American Mathematical Society; Mathematical Society of Republic of China; International Linear Algebra Society; Chinese Linear Algebra Society, Vice-President, 1996-. Address: Department of Mathematics, Tamkang University, Tamsui, Taiwan 251, Republic of China. E-mail: bsm01@mail.tku.edu.tw

**TAMAGAKE Keietsu,** b. 12 May 1939, Japan. Professor of Physical Chemistry. m. 1 daughter. Education: Bachelor's degree, 1964, Doctor's degree, 1969, Pharmaceutical Sciences, Tokyo University. Appointments: Research Associate, Tokyo University, 1964-75; Postdoctoral Researcher, Kansas State University, USA, 1975-77; Associate Professor, 1978-91,

Professor, 1991-2005, Okayama University, Japan. Publications: Numerous articles in scientific journals. Memberships: The Chemical Society of Japan; The Pharmaceutical Society of Japan; Spectroscopical Society of Japan; Society of Computer Chemistry, Japan. Address: Faculty of Pharmaceutical Sciences, Okayama University, 1-1-1 Tsusima-naka, Okayama 700-8530, Japan. E-mail: tamagake@pharm.okayama-u.ac.jp

**TAMARI Shmuel,** b. 16 June 1937, Jerusalem, Israel. Iconotextologist. m. Miryam, 1 son. Education: BA, Institutes of Archaeology and Asian and African Studies, The Hebrew University, 1960; MG Environmental Studies, Muslim Medieval Urbanisation, Faculty of Architecture and Urbanism, Technion, Haifa, Israel, 1962; PhD, Oriental School, Rome University, 1966; Postdoctoral specialisation in restoration and preservation of historical monuments, Faculty of Architecture, Rome University. Appointments: Lecturer, 1968-72, Senior Lecturer, 1972-76, Professor, 1976-2000, Professor Editor, 2000-, Director department of Arabic, 1972-80, Bar-Ilan University, Ramat-Gan, Israel; Lecturer, 1968-72, Senior Lecturer, 1972-76, Tel Aviv University, Israel; Directorship, The Israeli Oriental Society, 1972-86. Publications: Numerous articles and books including the following in English: Qalᶜat al-Tīna in Sinai: a historical and architectural analysis; Darb al-hajj in Sinai: an archaeological and historical study; Topological studies in the "Masālik al absār fī mamālik al-amsār" of Ibn Fadlallāh al-ᶜUmarī; Iconotextual studies in mid-eastern Islamic religious architecture and urbanism in the early Middle Ages; Iconotextual studies in the Muslim ideology of Umayyad architecture and urbanism; Iconotextual studies in the Muslim vision of paradise; A comprehensively annotative edition of KITĀB ᶜAjā'ib AL-MALAKŪT of Abū Jaᶜfar Muhammad b. ᶜAbīdallāh al-Kisā'ī. Membership: The International Centre for the Study of Preservation and Restoration of Cultural Property. Address: 15 Nordau Street, Ramat Gan 52464, Israel.

**TAMOŠAITIS Romualdas,** b. 17 June 1959, Kuršėnai, Lithuania. Building Engineer. m. Aušra Tamošaitienė, 4 daughters. Education: Bachelor of Science, Vilnius Institute of Civil Engineering, Lithuania, 1982; PhD, Dnepropetrovsk Institute of Civil Engineering, Russia, 1991. Appointments: Executive Manager, Kaunas Building Trust, 1982-85; Lecturer, Vilnius Institute of Civil Engineering, 1985-93; Minister's Assistant, Ministry of Building and Urban Development of Lithuania, 1993-95; Deputy Director, Cash Department, Bank of Lithuania, 1995-97; Director, Vilnius Gediminas Technical University Research Board, 1998-2004; Currently Associate Professor, Vilnius Gediminas Technical University. Publications: Author of over 50 publications in the area of building technology and management in Lithuanian, Russia and English. Memberships: Lithuania Building Engineers Association; Lithuanian Standards Technical Committee "Security". Address: Saulatekio Alėja 11, Vilnius, Lithuania. E-mail: roma@adm.vtu.lt

**TAMTOMO Didik Gunawan,** b. 13 March 1948, Surakarta, Indonesia. Lecturer; Physician; Businessman. m. Dwi Yanti Hastuti, 3 daughters. Education: Physician, Diponegoro University, Semarang, 1969-76; Master of Management, Jakarta Management Institute, Jakarta, 1993-95; Master of Health, Sebelas Maret University, Surakarta, 1999-2001. Appointments: Physician, Indonesian Doctors Association, Surkarta, Indonesia, 1976-; Lecturer: Faculty of Medicine, Sebelas Maret University, Surakarta, 1976-, Hygiene and Work Safety Academy, Surakarta, 1980-; Anatomist, Anatomist Association, Surakarta, 1980-; Family Physician, Indonesian Doctors Association, Surakarta, 1999-; Lecturer, Master of Family Health, Sebelas Maret University, Surakarta, 2000.

Publications: Book: Cardio Anatomy, Female Reproductive Organ; Article: Bio Smart. Honours: International Golden Citra Award, Kharisma Indonesia International Foundation, 1999; Indonesia Development Award, Kharisma, Indonesia International Foundation, 1999; Insan Penggerak Pembangunan, Indonesia, Anugerah Pretasi Indonesia, 1999; Listed in Who's Who publications and biographical dictionaries. Memberships: Indonesian Medical Association; Indonesian Anatomy Association; Indonesian Family Medicine Association. Address: Jl.Margorejo 11/3 Surakarta, Midle of Java, Indonesia.

**TAN Amy,** b. 19 February 1952, Oakland, California, USA. Writer. m. Lou DeMattei, 6 April 1974. Education; BA, 1973, MA, 1974, San Jose State College; Postgraduate studies, University of California at Berkeley, 1974-76. Publications: The Joy Luck Club, novel, 1989, film, 1993; The Kitchen God's Wife, novel, 1992; The Moon Lady, children's book, 1992; The Chinese Siamese Cat, children's book, 1994; The Hundred Secret Senses, novel, 1995; The Bonesetter's Daughter, 2000; Numerous short stories and essays. Contributions to: Various periodicals. Honours: Commonwealth Club Gold Award for Fiction, San Francisco, 1989; Booklist Editor's Choice, 1991; Marian McFadden Memorial Lecturer, Indianapolis-Marion County Public Library, 1996. Address: c/o Ballantine Publications Publicity, 201 East 50th Street, New York, NY 10022, USA.

**TAN Boen Hie,** b. 14 December 1926, Padangan, Java, Indonesia. Analytical Chemist; Biomedical Scientist. Education: BS, 1952, MS, 1955, ScD, 1962, University of Leyden, Netherlands; Nuclear Medicine Specialist. Appointments: Fellow, Assistant Professor, University of Leyden, 1953-55, 1962-64; Fellow, Research Associate, Max Planck Institute, Göttingen, Germany, 1961-62, University of Minnesota, Minneapolis, USA, 1955-61, 1964-68, 1971-72; Research Associate, New York Hospital, Cornell Medical Center, New York City, 1968-72; Research Associate, University of Groningen, Maastricht, Netherlands, 1973-81; Research Associate, University of South Alabama, Mobile, USA, 1982-92; Analytical Chemist, Alabama State Environmental Management, Montgomery, 1992-. Publications: Over 55 articles in professional journals, including research on sulfhydryl, disulphide groups in denatured and renatured proteins; purification, QA/QC analyses of environmental pollutants, pharmacokinetic, pharmacological activities of new drugs; alpha-1-antitrypsin, plasma proteins, enzymes, inhibitors, fibrin formation and lysis; vanadate-sulfhydryl complexes and PDE activities; diabetes and the heart; DNA damage and repair. Honours: Research Fellow, University of Minnesota, 1955-61, 1964-65, 1972; Research Fellow, Max Planck Institute of Biophysical Chemistry, 1961. Memberships: American Association for the Advancement of Science; American Chemical Society; American Association for Clinical Chemistry, Nederlandse Vereniging voor Nucleaire Geneeskunde; New York Academy of Sciences; Alabama Academy of Science. Address: PO Box 230451, Montgomery, AL 36123, USA.

**TAN Kok Kiong,** b. 25 August 1967, Singapore. Lecturer. m. Po Lean Chee, 1 son, 1 daughter. Education: Bachelor of Engineering (1st Class), 1992; PhD, Electrical Engineering, 1995. Appointments: Research Fellow, Singapore Institute of Manufacturing Technology, 1995-96; Lecturer, 1996-2000, Associate Professor, 2000-, Department of Electrical and Computer Engineering, National University of Singapore. Publications: More than 100 journal article; 6 books; 10 book chapters. Honours: Shortlisted for Young Scientist Award, 2000; Shortlisted for Singapore Youth Award, 2001. Memberships: IEEE; ISA; SME. Address: Department of Electrical and Computer Engineering, 4 Engineering Drive 3, National University of Singapore, Singapore 117576, Singapore. E-mail: eletankk@nus.edu.sg

**TAN Lihua,** b. 22 October 1955, Jiangsu, China. Conductor. m. Lumin Qiao, October 1980, 1 daughter. Education: Graduated, Shanghai Conservatory of Music. Debut: Conducting Bruch's Violin Concerto and Dvorák Symphony No 9, Wuhan Orchestra, China, 1980. Career: Conductor, China Central Philharmonic Symphony Orchestra, 1990-96; Music Director, Principal Conductor, Beijing Symphony Orchestra, 1993-; Guest Conductor, Russian State Academic Symphony Orchestra, 2000-2001; Chinese premieres include: Pines of Rome, Dvorák Symphony No 7, Prokofiev Symphony No 5, Tchaikovsky Manfred Symphony; Guest conducting appearances include: New York Youth Symphony, Seattle Federal Way Symphony, Russian National Symphony, China Philharmonic Orchestra, Novosibirsk Symphony Orchestra, London Philharmonic Orchestra, Britain Royal Philharmonic Orchestra, Trier Opera House (Germany), International Philharmonic (Germany), Australian Youth Orchestra, Australian Tasmania Symphony, Israel Symphony Orchestra, Panama State Symphony Orchestra, Bogota Philharmonic Orchestra, Orquestra Sinfónica Uanl (Mexico), Seoul Symphony Orchestra; Venues include: New York City's Avery Fisher Hall, Lincoln Center, Moscow's Tchaikovsky Conservatory of Music, Sydney Town Hall, Beijing Forbidden City Concert Hall, Munich Philharmonic Concert Hall, Lisinski Concert Hall, Congress Centre Villach. Recordings: Beethoven Symphony No 5, Brahms Symphony No 4 with Beijing Symphony Orchestra, Dvorák Symphony Nos 8 and 9, Haydn Symphony No 94, Mendelssohn, Saint-Saëns and Tchaikovsky's violin concertos with China Central Philharmonic Symphony Orchestra. Publication: Article, Conducting Technique and Instrumental Performance, 1988. Honour: Professor Laureate, Tian Jin Conservatory of Music. Memberships: Chairman, Beijing Musicians Association; Vice Chairman, China Musicians Association; Standing Committee, China Symphony Development Foundation. Address: Beijing Symphony Orchestra, No A-1 Eight Poplar, Shuang Jing, Chao-Yang District, Beijing 100022, China.

**TAN Sinforosa,** b. 7 July 1943, Lugait, Misamis Oriental, Philippines. College Professor. m. William H P Kaung. Education: BS, Chemical Engineering, University of San Carlos, Philippines, 1965; MST, Mathematics, Cornell University, USA, 1970; PhD, Curriculum Development, Syracuse University, USA, 1975. Appointments: Teacher, Iligan Capitol College, 1965-68; Mathematics Chairperson, 1967-68; Counsellor, Advanced Placement Programme, Cornell University, summer 1970; Resident Assistant, Crouse-Irving Memorial Hospital School of Nursing, 1970-73; Graduate Assistant, Syracuse University, 1973-75; Math Consultant, Mount Vernon Board of Education, 1975-76; Director, Metric Programme, Bronx Community College, 1976-77; Adjunct Mathematics Faculty, Mercy College, 1976-78; Teacher, Westchester Community College, 1977-; Professor, Mathematics, 1991-; Sophia and Joseph C Abeles Distinguished Professorial Chair in Mathematics. Publications: Revitalising Mathematics with problem solving, collaborative learning and the TI graphing calculators; Implementing the crossroads in mathematics as a pilot programme; Transforming the teaching of mathematics, technology recharging faculty, and reforming the mathematics curriculum; Calculators in education: A survey of calculator technology in the Westchester and Putnam high schools; Implementing Reform Methods of Teaching Mathematics in a Traditional and Conservative Department, 2001; many others. Honours: New York State Mathematics Association of Two Year Colleges, Outstanding Contributions to Mathematics Education Award; Pi Lambda Theta, Region

1 Outstanding Educator Award for Teaching Excellence; State University of New York, Chancellor's Excellence in Teaching Award; University of San Carlos Most Outstanding Alumnus; Outstanding Contributor Award, Westchester Community College Student Senate, 1999; Outstanding Achievement Award in Education, Philippine Chinese Association of America (Northeast), Inc, 2001; Outstanding Achievement Award in the field of Education, YWCA of White Plains and Central Westchester, 2002; Numerous other outstanding service awards. Memberships: Pi Lambda Theta International Honour and Professional Association in Education; American Mathematical Association of Two Year Colleges; New York State Mathematics Association; National Council of Teachers of Mathematics; Association of Filipino Teachers of America; Numerous others. Address: Mathematics Department, Westchester Community College, 75 Grasslands Road, Valhalla, NY 10595-1636, USA.

**TANAKA-AZUMA Yukimasa**, b. 7 March 1964, Sakai, Japan. Pharmacologist; Biochemist; Researcher. m. Hiromi Tanaka, 31 March 1991, 1 son, 1 daughter. Education: BSc, Biology, 1982-86, MSc, Biology, 1986-88, Konan University, Kobe, Japan; PhD, Pharmacology, Okayama University, Okayama, Japan, 2000. Appointments: Central Research Institute, Nissin Food Products Co Ltd, 1988-2002; Research Student, Japan Collection of Microorganisms, RIKEN, Wako, Japan, 1999-2000; Food Safety Research Institute, Nissin Food Products Co Ltd, 2002-. Publications: 19 papers in scientific journals include: Cholesterol-lowering effects of NTE-122, a novel acyl-CoA: cholesterol acyltransferase (ACAT) inhibitor, on cholesterol diet-fed rats and rabbits, 1998; Effects of NTE-122, a novel acyl-CoA:cholesterol acyltransferase inhibitor, on cholesterol esterification and secretions of apoliprotein B-containing lipoprotein and bile acids in HepG2, 1999; Effects of NTE-122, a novel acyl-CoA:cholesterol acyltransferase inhibitor, on cholesterol esterification and high-density lipoprotein-induced cholesterol efflux in macrophages, 1999; Effects of NTE-122, an acyl-CoA:cholesterol acyltransferase inhibitor, on cholesterol esterification and lipid secretion from CaCo-2, and cholesterol absorption in rats, 1999; Biological evaluation of styrene oligomers for endocrine-disrupting effects (II), 2000; Effects of NTE-122, an acyl-CoA:cholesterol acyltransferase inhibitor, prevents the progression of atherogenesis in cholesterol-fed rabbits, 2001; Lactobacillus casei NY1301 increases the adhesion of Lactobacillus gasseri NY0509 to human intestinal Caco-2 cells, 2001. Honours: Listed in Who's Who publications and biographical dictionaries. Memberships: Member, Scientific Council, The Japanese Pharmacological Society; Member, The Japanese Society for Food Science and Technology. Address: Food Safety Research Institute, Nissin Food Products Co Ltd, 2247 Noji, Kusatsu, Shiga 525-0055, Japan. E-mail: y-azuma@mb1.nissinfoods.co.jp

**TANDALE Tukaram**, b. 1 June 1949, Kolhapur, India. Engineering Geologist. m. Meghna Hawal, 1 son, 1 daughter. Education: BSc, 1972; MSc, 1974; PhD, 1986. Appointment: Geological Unit Pune, Koyana Project, Jalsampatti Bhavan Kothrud, Pune, Maharashtra, India, 1991-. Publications: Over 35 research papers in engineering geology, conjunctive use of groundwater and surface water, Laterites and Laterite profiles, coastal studies, Maharashtra, Laterites, Quaternary geology, remote sensing. Memberships: Geological Society; Indian Society for Rock Mechanics and Tunnelling Technology. Address: Geological Unit Pune, Koyana Project, Kothrud, Pune 411038, Maharashtra, India.

**TANDBERG Erik**, b. 19 October 1932, Oslo, Norway. Consultant; Writer. Divorced, 1986, 1 son, 1 daughter. Education. BSME, University of Santa Clara, California,

1957; MS, Metallurgy, Stanford University, California, 1959; Postgraduate Studies, Rocket Propulsion, Princeton University, New Jersey, 1965. Appointments: Royal Norwegian Air Force, 1959-71, Major, 1966; Consultant, Hartmark & Co, 1972-74; Chief Engineer, Director, Norconsult, 1974-80. Publications: 4 Books; Numerous articles in professional journals on Space related matters; Several TV and radio programs. Memberships: Oslo City Council, 1971-90; American Institute of Aeronautics and Astronautics; Fellow, British Interplanetary Society; Norwegian Association for Chartered Engineers. Address: PO Box 5267 Majorstuen, 0303 Oslo, Norway.

**TANG Yin Sheng**, b. 23 October 1962, Anhui, China. Physicist; Engineer. m. Hua Chun Shi, 1 son, 1 daughter. Education: BSc, Electronics and Electrical Engineering, Hefei University of Technology, China, 1983; MSc, Applied Physics, Xidian University, China; PhD, Solid State Physics, University of Science and Technology of China, 1988. Appointments: Scientist, Chinese Academy of Sciences, 1986-88; Visiting Fellow Surrey University, UK, 1988-90; Faculty Research Fellow, Glasgow University, Scotland, 1990-96; Senior Scientist, University of California, Los Angeles, 1996-99; Director of Photonics/Senior Photonics Engineer, R & D Laboratories, Culver City, California, 1999-2002; President, Ortus Systems Corp, Irvine, California, 2002-. Publications: Over 80 refereed journal articles; Over 70 conference papers published in international professional journals including: Journal of Applied Physics; Physical Review, IEEE Transactions. Address: 201 Rockview, Irvine, CA 92612-3234, USA.

**TANIMURA Makoto**, b. 24 October 1966, Kunitachi, Tokyo, Japan. Solid-State Physicist. m. Fumika Ayakoji, 2 sons. Education: Bachelor of Engineering, 1990, Master of Engineering, 1992, PhD, Engineering, 1998, Waseda University, Japan. Appointments: Senior Researcher, NISSAN ARC, LTD, 1992-; Visiting Researcher, Yokohama City University, 2000-; Part-time Teacher, Waseda University, 2003-. Publications: Articles in scientific journals including: Physical Review, 1995, 1996, 1997, 2003; Journal of Chemical Society Faraday Transaction, 1998; Applied Physics Letters, 2001; Journal of Physics Condensed Matter, 2002. Honour: Best Poster Award, Japan Institute of Metals, 2003. Memberships: Physical Society of Japan; Japan Institute of Metals. Address: Research Department, NISSAN ARC LTD, 1 Natsushima-cho, Yokosuka, Kanagawa 237-0061, Japan. E-mail: tanimura@nissan-arc.co.jp

**TANNINEN Seppo Johannes**, b. 9 June 1948, Alavus, Painter; Poet; Critic. 1 son, 1 daughter. Education: Finnish Art Academy, 1968-70. Appointments: Artists Association of Finland; Seinajoki Art Museum Association. Creative Works: Amos Anderson Museum; Vaino Aaltonen Museum; Nelimarkka Museum; Collection of the State of Finland; Merita Collections; Collections of the Finnish Post and Tele; Pohjola Collections; K H Renlund Museum; Ostrobothnian Museum. Publications: Krunoja, Visual Poems, WSOY, 1977; Italy Diary, poems, 1983; Articles and Art Critics. Honours: 3 Years Artist Scholarship, State of Finland, 1989; 5 years Artist Scholarship, State of Finland, 1993. Memberships: Finnish Painters Union; Ostrobothnian Artists Association; Seinajoki Artists Association; Non Art Group; Union of Finnish Critics; International Association of Art Critics. Address: Villenraitti 8, 60200 Seinajoki, Finland.

**TARAKANOV Boris Vasiljevich**, b. 19 April 1933, Wichuga, Russia. Microbiologist. m. Ludmilla Isaeva, 23 May 1959, 2 daughters. Education: DVM, Agricultural Institute, Ivanovo, 1956; D in Biological Sciences, All Russian Research Institute of Animal Physiology, Biochemistry and Nutrition,

1985; Professor, 1996. Appointments: Veterinarian, Sovkhoz, Chitinsky, Russia, 1956-62; From Aspirant to Chief, Department of Biotechnology of Micro-organisms, All Russian Research Institute of Animal Physiology, Biochemistry and Nutrition, Borovsk, Russia, 1962-; Chairman, Council, Agricultural Science, Scientific Centre, Kaluga, Russia, 1993-97; Assessor, Australian Research Council, Canberra, 1996-. Publications: Study of the Microflora in Forestomachs of Ruminants, 1977; Microbiology of the Digestion of Ruminants, 1982; Methods of Study of the Digestive Tract Microflora in Farm Animals and Poultry, 1998; Using of Probiotics in Animal Husbandry, 1998; Perspectives of Creation of New Probiotics on the Base of Recombinant Strains of Bacteria Expressing Eucaryotic Genes, 2002; Chapter in Reference Book: Normal the Microflora of the Forestomachs of Ruminants, 2002. Honours: Meritorious Scientific Worker, Russian Federation, 1995; Gold Medal, All Russian Exhibition Centre, 1997; Medal, 2000 Outstanding Scientists of the 21st Century, 2002; Listed in national and international biographical dictionaries. Memberships: Russian Society of Microbiology; Russian Society of Physiology. Address: All Russian Research Institute of Animal Physiology, Biochemistry and Nutrition, 249013, Borovsk, Russia.

**TARANTINO Quentin,** b. 1963, Los Angeles, USA. Film Director. Appointments: Worked in Video Archives, Manhattan Beach; Actor; Producer: Killing Zoe; Red Rain, 1995; Four Rooms, 1995; From Dusk Till Dawn, 1996; Curdled, 1996; Ying xiong, 2002; Director: Reservoir Dogs; Pulp Fiction, 1994; Jackie Brown, 1997; 40 Lashes (also writer), 2000; Kill Bill: Vol 1 (also writer), 2003; Kill Bill: Vol 2 (also writer), 2004 Appearances include: Sleep With Me, 1994; Destiny Tunes on the Radio, 1995; Desperado, 1995; Girl 6, 1996; From Dusk Till Dawn, 1996; Little Nicky, 2000. Publications: Screenplays: True Romance, 1995; Natural Born Killers, 1995; Jackie Brown, 1998; Kill Bill (novel), 2003. Honours: Golden Palm, Cannes Film Festival, 1994. Address: WMA, 151 El Camino Drive, Beverly Hills, CA 90212, USA.

**TAREFDER Rafiqul A.** Education: BS, Civil Engineering, Bangladesh Engineering University, Dhaka, 1995; MS, Geotechnical Engineering, Asian Institute of Technology, Bangkok, Thailand, 1998; PhD, Civil Engineering, University of Oklahoma, Norman, Oklahoma, 2003. Appointments include: Design Engineer, DTI, Dhaka, Bangladesh, 1995-96; Graduate Research Assistant, 1996-98, Research Associate, 1998 Asian Institute of Technology, Thailand, 1996-98; Teaching Assistant, University of Calgary, Canada, 1999; Consultant, Surbec-ART Environmental LLC, Oklahoma, 1999-2000; Engineer Intern, Oklahoma Department of Transportation, 2001-2002; Research Assistant, Instructor, University of Oklahoma, Norman, 2000-03; Visiting Assistant Professor, Texas Southern University, Houston, 2003-04; Assistant Professor, Idaho State University, Pocatello, 2004-. Publications: Book chapter, Design of Neural Networks for Pavement Rutting (co-author), November 2004; Articles in refereed journals as author or co-author include recently: Formulation of Mix Design and Asphaltic Encapsulation of Hydrocarbon Contaminated Soil, 2003; A Laboratory and Statistical Evaluation of Factors Affect Rutting, 2004; An Alternate Method of Determination of Asphalt Content, 2004. Honours include: Dean's List, Bangladesh University of Engineering and Technology, 1991; Government of Japan Scholarship for Higher Education, Asian Institute of Technology, 1996; Cleo Cross Scholarship for Academic Accomplishments, 2001, Graduate College Travel Grant, 2002, Outstanding Graduate Research Assistant, 2002, Sooner Heritage Scholarship, Office of the President, 2003, University of Oklahoma; Faculty Development Travel Grant, Texas Southern University, 2004. Memberships: Institute of Engineers

of Bangladesh; Association of Asphalt Paving Technologists; American Society for Testing Materials; Member, Institute of Transportation Engineers; Associate Member, American Society of Civil Engineers; Idaho State University Representative, Transportation Research Board (TRB). Address: College of Engineering, Idaho State University, Campus Box 8060; Pocatello, Idaho 83209, USA. E-mail: tarerafi@isu.edu

**TARUSCHIO Franco Vittorio,** b. 29 March 1938, Montefano (MC), Italy. Former Chef and Restaurateur. m. Ann, 1 daughter. Career: Restaurateur. Formerly at: Hotel Spendide Lugano; Restaurant La Belle Meunière Clermont-Ferrand, Three Horseshoes Hotel, Rugby; Proprietor (now retired), Walnut Tree Inn, Llandewi, Skirrid, Abergavenny, Wales for 37 years; Currently President of St Anne's Hospice, Malpas, Newport, Gwent, Wales. Publications: Leaves from the Walnut Tree-Recipes of a Lifetime, 1993; Bruschetta, Crostoni, Crostini, 1995; Franco and Friends (Food from the Walnut Tree), 1997; Ice Creams and Semi Freddi, 1997; 100 Great Pasta Dishes. Honours: Gold Medal for services to tourism in Wales, 1985; Egon Ronay Restaurant of the Year Award, 1987; Premio Portonovo for Excellence in Italian Gastronomy, 1995; 4 out of 5 Good Food Guide, 1996, 8 out of 10 Good Food Guide, 1999; Honorary OBE, 2003. Address: The Willows, 26 Pen-Y-Pound, Abergavenny, Mon NP7 7RN, Wales.

**TATARKIN Alexander,** b. 11 March 1946, Port-Arthur Village, Chelyabinsk Region, Russia. Economist; Lawyer; m. Tatiana Nikolaevna, 1 son. Education: Planner-Accountant, Troitsk Agricultural Technical School, 1964; Lawyer, Sverdlovsk Law Institute, 1972; Candidate Degree in Economics, Associate Professor, 1981; Doctorate Degree in Economics, Professor, 1990; Corresponding Member, Russian Academy of Sciences, 1997. Appointments: Economist, Chief Economist, Berezinsky Grain Growing State Farm, Chelyabinsk Region, 1964-65; Army Service, 1965-68; Assistant, Holder of Chair, Dean of Faculty, Sverdlovsk Law Institute, 1972-87; Deputy and Scientific Director, 1987-90, Acting Director, 1990-91, Director, Member of the Presidium, 1991-, Institute of Economics, Ural Branch, Academy of Sciences of the USSR (since 1991, Russian Academy of Sciences); Member of the Bureau, Faculty of Social Sciences, Russian Academy of Sciences, 2002-. Publications: Author and co-author of more than 530 publications of scientific papers and guidance manuals including 69 monographs. Honours: Gold Medal, USSR Exhibition of Economic Achievement, 1989; Torch of Birmingham, 1999; Honoured Scientist, 1996 Laureate of State Prize in Science and Technology, 1999; Laureate of International Prize "Crystal Dragon", 2002; Order of Friendship, 2002; Kosygin Prize Laureate, 2002; The Institute of Economics was the winner of the 9th regional contest "Leader in Business", 2005. Memberships: Chairman, Associate Academic Council for Economic Sciences, Ural Branch, Russian Academy of Sciences; Expert Council for Russian State Commission for Academic Degrees and Titles; Scientific-Methods Council for monitoring threats of energy preparedness, RF Department of Industry; Scientific-Methods Council for Regional Economy, RF Department of Economy; Board Member, Ural Chamber of Commerce and Industry. Address: 29 Moskovskaya St, Yekaterinburg, Russia 620014. E-mail: navra@mail.ru Website: www.uran.ru/structura/institutes/ieconom.htm

**TAYLOR Alison,** b. 20 April 1944, Stockport, Cheshire, England. Author; Journalist. 1 son, 1 daughter. Education: Certificate of Qualification in Social Work; Diploma in Social Work. Appointments: Psychiatric social work and probation; Senior childcare posts, Gwynedd County Council, 1976-86; Claim for unfair dismissal settled, 1989; Author; Journalist;

Conference guest speaker. Publications: 5 novels: Simeon's Bride; In Guilty Night; The House of Women; Unsafe Convictions; Child's Play; Papers on child care, ethics and social issues; Lectured and written on 18th and 19th century Welsh and German literature, music and poetry. Honours: Community Care Readers Award, 1996; Campaign for Freedom of Information Award, 1996; Pride of Britain Award, 2000. Memberships: Elected, Welsh Academy, 2001; Elected Fellow, Royal Society of Arts, 2003; Member, American Beethoven Society. Address: c/o Larinia Trevor Literary Agency, 7 The Glasshouse, 49a Goldhawk Road, London W12 8QP, England.

**TAYLOR Anna,** b. 14 July 1943, Preston, Lancashire, England. Teacher; Writer; Artist; Translator. m. John E Coombes, 22 December 1967, divorced 1982, 1 son. Education: BA (Honours), German and English, University of Bristol, 1965; CertEd, University of York, 1967; MA, Modern German Literature (incomplete) Manchester University, 1967-68; MA, Sociology of Literature, University of Essex, 1980. Career: Intermittent Teacher, 1964-94; Artistic Collaborator to French Sculptor, Michael Serraz, Paris, 1969-90; Since 1984, published writer of poetry, also several theatre credits; Published reviews and essays in diverse publications. Publications: Poetry: FAUSTA, 1984; Cut Some Cords, 1988; Both And: A Triptych, 1995; Out of the Blues, 1997; INTER-, 1998; Bound-un-bound, 2003; Novella: Pro Patria: a private suite, 1987. Honours: Scholarship to Manchester University, 1967; RedBeck Press Short Collection, Joint 1st Prize, 1995; 1st prize for Poem: Chthonia, Second Light Poetry Competition, 2002; 2nd, 3rd prizes and several short-listings in poetry competitions since 1980. Membership: Writers Guild of Great Britain; Founder Member, Yorkshire Playwrights. Address: 82 Blackhouse Road, Fartown, Huddersfield, West Yorkshire HD2 1AR, England.

**TAYLOR Harris C,** b. 30 April 1940, Brooklyn, New York, USA. Physician; Endocrinologist. m. Diana Kahn Taylor, 1 son, 1 daughter. Education: BS, Queens College, City University of New York, 1961; MD, University of Chicago School of Medicine, 1965. Appointments: Director, Endocrinology Laboratory, 1978-96, Director, Internal Medicine Residency, 1985-94, Lutheran Hospital, Cleveland, Ohio; Currently Clinical Professor of Medicine-Endocrinology, Case Western Reserve University School of Medicine, Cleveland. Publications: 33 papers in peer reviewed journals; 2 book chapters. Honours include: Phi Beta Kappa; Best Doctors in America, 1998, 2001-02, 2003-04; Master Teacher Award, American College of Physicians, 2001. Memberships: Fellow, American College of Physicians; Fellow, American College of Endocrinology; Endocrine Society; President, Diabetes Association of Cleveland, 1982-84. Address: 3166 Huntington Road, Shaker Heights, OH 44120, USA.

**TAYLOR John,** b. 22 August 1925, Atherton, Lancashire, England. Retired University Reader. Education: Scholar, MA, Balliol College, Oxford, 1943-44, 1947-50. Appointments: Lecturer and Senior Lecturer, 1950-70, Reader in Medieval History, 1970-90, Chairman School of History, 1979-82, Leeds University; Visiting Associate Professor, Princeton University, USA, 1961-62; President, Yorkshire Archaeological Society, 1984-89; President, Leeds Philosophical and Literary Society, 1972-74. Publications include: English Historical Literature in the Fourteenth Century, 1987; Rymes of Robin Hood (co-author), 3rd edition, 1997; The St Albans Chronicle 1376-94 (co-author), 2003; Many articles. Honours: Leverhulme Research Fellow, 1982-83; FRHistSoc. Memberships: Royal Historical Society; Yorkshire Archaeological Society. Address: Storey Cottage, Main Street, Kirkby Overblow, Harrogate, North Yorkshire HG3 1HD, England. E-mail: storeycottage@tesco.net

**TAYLOR Judy, (Julia Marie Hough),** b. 12 August 1932, Murton, Swansea, Wales. Writer. m. Richard Hough, 1980. Appointments: Bodley Head Publishers, 1951-81; Director, Bodley Head Ltd, 1967-84, Chatto, Bodley Head and Jonathan Cape Ltd, 1973-80, Chatto, Bodley Head & Jonathan Cape Australia Pty Ltd, 1977-80; Consultant to Penguin, Beatrix Potter, 1981-87, 1989-92. Publications: Sophie and Jack, 1982; My First Year: A Beatrix Potter Baby Book, 1983; Sophie and Jack in the Snow, 1984; Dudley and the Monster, 1986; Dudley Goes Flying, 1986; Dudley in a Jam, 1986; Dudley and the Strawberry Shake, 1986; That Naughty Rabbit: Beatrix Potter and Peter Rabbit, 1987; Beatrix Potter 1866-1943, 1989; Beatrix Potter's Letters: A Selection, 1989; So I Shall Tell You a Story, 1993. Play: Beatrix (with Patrick Garland), 1996; Edward Ardizzone's Sketches for Friends: A Selection, 2000. Contributions to: Numerous professional journals. Honour: Member of the Order of the British Empire, 1971. Memberships: Publishers Association Council; Book Development Council; UNICEF International Art Committee; UK UNICEF Greetings Card Committee; Beatrix Potter Society; Royal Society of Arts, fellow. Address: 31 Meadowbank, Primrose Hill Road, London NW3 3AY, England.

**TE KANAWA Kiri Jeanette Claire (Dame),** b. 6 March 1944, Gisborne, New Zealand. Singer (Soprano). m. Desmond Park, 1967, divorced, 1997, 1 son, 1 daughter. Education: St Mary's College, Auckland; London Opera Centre. Appointments: Debut, Royal Opera Covent Garden, 1970; La Scala, Milan, debut 1978; Sang at Salzburg Festival in 1979, with San Francisco Opera Company in 1980, and at Edinburgh and Helsinki Festivals, 1980; Operas include: Boris Godunov; Parsifal; The Marriage of Figaro; Otello; Simon Boccanegra; Carmen; Don Giovanni (also film version 1979); Faust; The Magic Flute; La Bohème (5 times); Eugene Onegin; Cosi Fan Tutte; Arabella; Die Fledermaus; La Traviata; Der Rosenkavalier; Manon Lescaut; Sang at the wedding of HRH The Prince of Wales, London, 1981; Sang the Countess in Capriccio at San Francisco, 1990, and Covent Garden; Sang the premiere of Paul McCartney's Liverpool Oratorio, at Liverpool Cathedral and in London, 1991; Sang Amelia in new production of Simon Boccanegra at Covent Garden, 1991; Season 1992 with Mozart's Countess at Metropolitan Opera, and Desdemona at Covent Garden; Appeared on 2000 Today from Gisborne, New Zealand, 1 January 2000; Sang at Queen's Jubilee Prom, 2002. Creative works: Recordings include: Elvira in Don Giovanni; Fiordiligi in Cosi Fan Tutte; Otello; Micaela in Carmen; Mozart Vespers and C Minor Mass; Pamina in The Magic Flute; The Marriage of Figaro; Hansel and Gretel; Strauss' Songs with Orchestra; Die Fledermaus; Woodbird in Siegfried; Recitals records. Publications: Land of the Long White Cloud, 1989; Opera for Lovers, 1997. Honours: OBE; DBE; ONZ, 1995; Honorary Degrees, Oxford, Cambridge, Dundee, Nottingham, Auckland, Durham, Bath, Sunderland, Chicago, Waikato Universities and Post University in USA. Address: c/o Talent Financial, Drury House, 34-43 Russell Street, London WC23 5HA, England.

**TEBBIT, Baron of Chingford in the London Borough of Waltham, Norman Beresford Tebbit,** b. 29 March 1931, Enfield, England. Politician. m. Margaret Elizabeth Daines, 1956, 2 sons, 1 daughter. Education: Edmonton County Grammar School. Appointments: RAF Officer, 1949-51; Commercial Pilot and holder of various posts, British Air Line Pilots' Association, 1953-70; Member of Parliament for Epping, 1970-74; Chingford, 1974-92; Parliamentary Private Secretary, Department of Employment, 1972-73; Under Secretary of State, Department of Trade, 1979-81; Ministry of State, Department of Industry, 1981; Secretary of State for Employment, 1981-83; Trade and Industry, 1983-85; Chancellor of the Duchy of

Lancaster, 1985-87; Chairman, Conservative Party, 1985-87; Director, BET Plc, 1987-96; British Telecom Plc, 1987-96; Sears PLC, 1987-99; Spectator Ltd, 1989-2005; Advisor, JCB Excavators, 1991-; Co-Presenter, Target, Sky TV, 1989-97; Columnist, The Sun, 1995-97; Columnist, Mail on Sunday, 1997-2001. Publications: Upwardly Mobile, 1988; Unfinished Business, 1991; Weekly Columnist, The Sun, 1995-97 and The Mail on Sunday, 1997-2001; Numerous political booklets, newspapers and magazine articles. Honours: Life Peer, Baron Tebbit of Chingford; Companion of Honour. Memberships: Association of Conservative Peers; Liveryman of the Guild of Air Pilots and Navigators; Council Member of the Air League; Companion of the Royal Aeronautical Society; Chairman, Nuffield Orthopaedic Centre Appeal, 1990-2005; Chairman, Battle of Britain London Monument Appeal, 2003-. Address: House of Lords, Westminster, London, SW1A 0PW, England.

**TEBBS Margaret Cecilia,** b. 5 September 1948, Hillingdon, Middlesex, England. Botanical Illustrator. Education: Manor School, Ruislip, Middlesex. Appointments: Curator and Botanist, Department of Botany, Natural History Museum, London, 1967-91; Freelance Botanical Illustrator; Commissions mostly from staff and visitors to the Herbarium, Royal Botanic Gardens, Kew, England. Publications: Illustrator of books including most recently: Airplants – a study of the genus Tillandsia. New Plantsman vol 2 by A Rodriguez, 1995; Flora of Egypt, vols 1-3, by L Boulos, 1999-2002; Blepharis, a taxonomic study by K Vollesen, 2000; The Leguminosae of Madagascar by D Du Puy et al, 2002; Studies in the genus Hypericum by NKB Robson, 2002. Address: 2 Furzey Corner, Shipton Lane, Burton Bradstock, Dorset DT6 4NQ, England. E-mail: tebbsatfurzey@aol.com

**TECSON Antonio P,** b. 25 August 1932, Manila, Philippines. Financial Executive. m. Shui Shian Lily, 2 sons, 2 daughters. Education: BSc, Commerce, Far Eastern University, 1956. Appointments: Section Chief, 1962-65, Assistant Manager, 1965-68, Assistant Vice President, 1970-72, Vice President, 1972-81, China Banking; President, Phil-Solid Finance and Credit Corp, 1981-91; President and Chairman, Mandarin Credit Ventures Inc, 1991-; Chairman, Richmond Capital Inc, 1993-. Honours: Most Outstanding Alumni, FEU Institute of Accounts, Business and Finance Alumni Foundation Inc, 1997; 75th Founding Anniversary Diamond Jubilee Award, 2003; Outstanding Manilan, 2003; Outstanding PICPA Member, 2003; Lion of the Year with a Golden Heart Award, 2003; Most Outstanding Alumnus, Chiang Kai Shek Institute University, 2003; Hall of Fame Award, Board of Trustees of FEU IABF, 2003; Certificate of Excellence, The Manila Times, 2004; Elected National Board of Directors, Philippine Institute of Certified Public Accountants, 2005. Memberships: Philippine Chinese Charitable Association Inc; Chinese General Hospital and Medical Center; Filipino-Chinese General Chamber of Commerce Inc; Manila Host Lions Club; Philippine Institute of Certified Public Accountants Western Chapter; FEU-IABF Alumni Foundation Inc; Metro Manila Regional Council; Philppine Institute of Certified Public Accountants; Philippine Sun Yat Sen High School Alumni Association; Philippine Council for the Promotion of Peaceful Reunification of China; Chan Wing Chung Tong Family Association Inc; Philippine Federation of Filipino Cantonese Association Inc; Quezon City Filipino Chinese Businessmen Inc; Mandarin Management Corp; Mandarin Credit Ventures Inc; Richmond Capital Inc. Address: Rm 620 Equitable PCI Bank Bldg, 262 Juan Lunastreet, 1006 Binondo Manila, Philippines.

**TEJMAN Chaim Henry,** b. 11 May 1935, Poland. Medical Doctor. m. Roth, 1 son, 1 daughter. Appointments: Surgery and

Orthopaedics; Skin and Allergy; Physics and Natural Sciences; Philosophy. Publications: 2 books: United Nature Theory: Wave Theory (Grand Unified Theory), 2001; Thoughts on Wave Theory, Vol II, 2003. Address: The Hebrew University of Jerusalem, Givat Ram, PO Box 39035, Jerusalem 91390, Israel. E-mail: chaimt@12.net.il

**TEKAVČIĆ Pavao,** b. 23 August 1931, Zagreb, Croatia. University Professor. m. Zorica Živković-Tekavčić. Education: Graduate, Romance Linguistics, 1954, PhD, Istro Romance Linguistics, 1963, Zagreb University. Appointments: Assistant Professor of Italian Linguistics, 1957; Ordinary Professor of Italian Linguistics, 1973; Retired, 1983. Publications: 3 books; 360 articles including scientific papers and review articles. Honours: Award, Italian Government, 1979; Award, Italian Institute in Zagreb, 2001; Commendatore dell'Ordine della Stella della Solidarietà Italiana Award, Italian Government, 2004. Memberships: Society of Romance Linguistics; Society of Italian Linguistics. Address: Berislaviceva 12, 10000 Zagreb, Croatia.

**TEML Jiri,** b. 24 June 1935, Vimperk, Bohemia. Composer. m. 1969, 1 son. Education: Economic Qualification; Theory and Composition lessons with Bohumil Dusek and Jiri Jaroch, 1966-76. Career: Producer and Head of Music, Czech Radio Plzen, 1976-80; Producer of Classical Music Programmes, Czech Radio Prague, 1980-2000; Retired 2000; External work for Czech Radio Prague, 2000-; Collaborations with the Plzen Radio Folk Ensemble Compositions include: Orchestral works: Suita Giocosa for small orchestra, 1973; 1st Symphony, People and Springs for strings, harp and timpani, 1976; Concert for violin and orchestra, 1979; Fantasia – concert for violin, harp and orchestra, 1983; Concerto Grosso, Tribute to Handel, 1984; Symphony No 2, War with the Newts, 1987; Jubilee Variations, 1989; Epitaph for strings and percussion, 1992; Symphony No 3, Kafka, 1994; Concertino, Hommage a Vivaldi, oboe and strings, 1995; Vocal: Little Sun, children's songs, 1976; 3 Short Songs for a Hen-Pecked Husband (Moravian Folk Texts), 1980; Circus Noise, songs for children, 1984; Water Music, 1984; Chamber Music and Solo Instruments: Chamber Music for oboe and piano, 1971; Fantasia Appassionata for organ, 1972; 4 Interventions for violin and guitar, 1977; Triptych for French horn and organ, 1983; Alchymists, 6 compositions for organ, 1984; Pantomima for flute and piano, 1987; String Quartet No 4, Divertimento, 1996. Honours: Third Prize, Prague Spring Festival with Fantasia Appasionata for organ, 1972; Prizes for Little Sun, 1978, Circus Noise, 1984, OIRT. Memberships: The Association of Czech Composers; The B Martinu Foundation, Prague. Address: Jordana Jovkova 3261, 14300 Prague 4, Czech Republic.

**TEMPEST Henry Roger,** b. 2 April 1924, London, England. Landowner. m. Janet Evelyn Mary Laughton, 2 sons, 3 daughters. Education: Christ Church College, Oxford. Appointments: Scots Guards, 1943-47, served North West Europe (wounded 1945); Appointed to Q Staff HQ Guards Division, 1945; Staff Captain, 1946; Britannia Rubber Co Ltd, 1947-51; Emigrated to Lusaka, Northern Rhodesia, 1952; Incorporated Cost Accountant (AACWA), South Africa, 1959; Returned to UK, 1961; Financial Officer, University of Oxford Department of Nuclear Physics, 1962-72; Inherited Broughton Hall Estate, 1970; Lord of the Manors of Broughton, Coleby, Burnsall and Thorpe, and of Coleby, Lincolnshire. Honours: Knight of Malta, 1949; Deputy Lieutenant of North Yorkshire, 1981. Memberships: North Yorkshire County Council, 1973-85; Skipton Rural District Council, 1973-74; Executive Committee, Country Landowners Association, Yorkshire, 1973-87; Council, Order of St John, North Yorkshire, 1977-97; President Skipton

Branch Royal British Legion, 1974-91; Governor: Craven College of Further Education, 1974-85, Skipton Girls' High School, 1976-85; Member Pendle Forest and Craven Harriers Hunt Committee, 1973-98; ACIS, 1958; FCIS, 1971; British Computer Society, 1973-; Clubs: Lansdowne; Pratt's. Address: Broughton Hall, Skipton, N Yorks BD23 3AE, England. E-mail: henrytempest@hormail.com

**TENNANT Emma,** b. 20 October 1937. Author. 1 son, 2 daughters. Publications: Hotel de dream, 1976; The Bad Sister, 1978; Wild Nights, 1979; Faustine, 1992; Two Women of London, 1993; Pemberley, 1994; Strangers: A Family Romance, 1998; Girlitude, 1999; Burnt Diaries, 1999; Felony, 2002. Honour: Honorary DLitt, Aberdeen, 1996. Membership: Fellow, Royal Society of Literture, 1984. Address: c/o Marsh Agency, 11-12 Dover St, London, W.I. England.

**TEPFERS Ralejs,** b. 28 December 1933, Rezekne, Latvia. Professor Emeritus. m. Ira Majors, 1 son, 2 daughters. Education: Civ Eng (MSc), , 1958, Tekn lic degree, 1966, Tekn dr, 1973, Docent, Reinforced Concrete Structures, 1973, Chalmers University of Technology, Göteborg; Dr. ing hc, Latvian Academy of Sciences, 1996. Appointments: Worked on building sites, Sweden and Switzerland; Military service, 1959; Assistant, Department of Building Technology, 1960, Development of Structural Laboratory, 1967-69, Associate Professor, Building Materials and House Building Techniques, 1969, Professor, Building Technology, 1995, Professor Emeritus, 2001-, Chalmers University of Technology. Publications: Numerous articles in professional journals. Honours: JSPS Fellowship, Tohoku University, Sendai, Japan, 1988. Memberships: Swedish Concrete Association; Latvian Concrete Association; Nordic Concrete Federation; Life Honorary Membership, Comité Euro-Internationale du Béton-fédération internationale du béton; RILEM Committee; American Concrete Institute. Address: Department of Structural Engineering, Chalmers University of Technology, S-412 96 Göteborg, Sweden. E-mail: ralejs.te pfers@ste.chalmers.se Website: http://www.bm.chalmers.se/ bm9707/Division/Dindex.htm

**TERASHIMA Takeshi,** b. 13 October 1963, Japan. Internist; Educator. m. Sanae, 1 son, 1 daughter. Education: Diplomate, School of Medicine, 1988, Resident, Department of Internal Medicine, 1988-95, Keio University, Tokyo, Japan; Postdoctoral Fellow, University of British Columbia, Vancouver, Canada, 1995-97. Appointments: Assistant Professor, Tokyo Dental College, Ichikawa General Hospital, Japan, 1999-. Publications: Papers in scientific journals including: Chest; American Journal of Respiratory and Critical Medicine. Honours: Grantee, Pfizer Health Research Foundation, 1995; Grantee, Japanese Ministry of Education, Science and Culture, 2001. Memberships: Japanese Society of Internal Medicine; Japanese Respiratory Society; American Thoracic Society. Address: Tokyo Dental College, Ichikawa General Hospital, 5-11-13 Sugano, Ichikawa, Chiba 272-0824, Japan. E-mail: terashima@1988.jukuin.keio.ac.jp

**TERPSTRA Vern,** b. 20 August 1927, Wayland, Michigan, USA. Emeritus Professor. m. Bonnie Fuller, 1 son, 1 daughter. Education: BBA, 1950, MBA, 1951, PhD, 1965, University of Michigan. Appointments: Director, Normal School, Belgian Congo, 1953-61; Professor, Wharton School, University of Pennsylvania, 1964-66; Professor, University of Michigan, 1966-92; Professor Emeritus, 1992-. Publications: Books: International Marketing, 8th edition; Cultural Environment of International Business, 3rd edition; International Dimensions of Marketing, 4th edition; American Marketing in Common Market; Over 75 articles in professional journals. Honours: President, 1971-72, Fellow, 1976, Academy of International

Business; Global Marketing Award, American Marketing Association, 2004. Memberships: Academy of International Business; American Marketing Association. Address: Business School, University of Michigan, Ann Arbor, MI 48109, USA. E-mail: vterp@umich.edu

**THABIT JONES Peter,** b. 18 May 1951, Swansea, Wales. Poet; Writer. m. Hilary, 4 sons, 2 daughters. Education: Diploma in Higher Education, University of Wales; Diploma in Office Studies; Higher National Certificate in Leisure/Conservation Management; Postgraduate Certificate in Education (Further and Higher Education). Appointment: Editor, SWAG Magazine, 1995-99; Chairman and Treasurer, Swansea Writers and Artists Group, 1996-99; Tutor, Part-time Degree Programme, University of Wales, Swansea. Publications: Tacky Brow, 1974; The Apprenticeship, 1977; Clocks Tick Differently, 1980; Visitors, 1986; The Cold Cold Corner 1995; Ballad of Kilvey Hill, 1999; Selected Poems (USA), 2003. Contributions to: 2Plus2; Poetry Wales; Poetry Review; Anglo-Welsh Review; Planet; Outposts Poetry Quarterly; Poetry Nottingham; NER/ BLQ; Urbane Gorilla; Docks; Cambrensis; Orbis; White Rose; Exile; Iota; Krax; Weyfarers; Western Mail; South Wales Evening Post; Momentum; Asp; Children's poetry included in many anthologies; Work translated into Russian and published throughout Russia in a British Council Moscow schools project. Honours: Eric Gregory Award for Poetry, 1979; Grants, Royal Literary Fund, 1987, Society of Authors, 1987, Welsh Arts Council, 1990; Commendations, National Poetry Competition, 1983, 1988, Bridport Arts Festival, 1984, Welsh Arts Council (prose), 1986, (poetry), 1987; Outposts Competition Winner, 1988; Workshop Writer, St Thomas School Workshop for Prince Charles, Swansea, 1995.Memberships: Poetry Society, London; Swansea Writers and Artists Group, Chairman and Treasurer; The Welsh Academy, full member, 1995-; Founder and Editor, The Seventh Quarry, Swansea poetry magazine, 2004. Address: Dan y Bryn, 74 Cwm Level Road, Brynhyfryd, Swansea SA5 9DY, Wales.

**THAMBIRATNAM David Pathmaseelan,** b. 12 August 1943, Sri Lanka. Professor of Structural Engineering. m. Sulogini Vethanayagam, 2 sons, 1 daughter. Education: BSc (Engin) First Class Honours, 1968; MSc (Struct), 1975; PhD (Struct), 1978. Appointments include: District, Construction Engineer, Department of Buildings and PWD, Government of Sri Lanka, 1968-73; Chief Construction Engineer, (Colombo South) Department of Buildings, Government of Sri-Lanka, 1978-79; Senior Structural Engineer, Department of Buildings, Government of Sri Lanka, 1979-80; Lecturer, 1980-81, Senior Lecturer 1981-87, 1988-90; Department of Civil Engineering, National University of Singapore; Lecturer, 1990-91, Senior Lecturer, 1991-93, Associate Professor, 1993-96, Professor, 1996-, Structural Engineering, School of Civil Engineering, Queensland University of Technology; Major research areas: Structural dynamics, disaster mitigation and impact attenuation of structural systems, dynamics of flexible structures and health monitoring of bridges Publications: 150 articles in international journals and conference proceedings. Honours: Canadian Commonwealth Scholarship, 1973-78; Graduate Fellowship, University of Manitoba, 1975-78; Commendation by Prime Minister of Sri Lanka, 1979. Memberships: Fellow, American Society of Civil Engineers; Fellow, Institution of Engineers, Australia, Fellow, Institution of Civil Engineers, UK. Address: School of Urban Development Faculty of Built Environment and Engineering, Queensland University of Technology, GPO Box 2434, Brisbane, QLD 4001, Australia.

**THATCHER, Baroness of Kesteven in the County of Lincolnshire, Margaret Hilda Thatcher,** b. 13 October

1925, Grantham, England. Barrister; Politician; Former Prime Minister. m. Dennis Thatcher, 1951, deceased 2003, 1 son, 1 daughter. Education: Somerville College, Oxford. Appointments: Research Chemist, 1947-51; Entered Bar, Lincoln's Inn, 1953; Conservative Member of Parliament, Barnet, Finchley, 1959-92; Minister of Pensions and National Insurance Parliamentary Secretary, 1961-64; Opposition Spokesperson for Education, 1969-70; Secretary of State for Education and Science, 1970-74; Leader of Her Majesty's Opposition, 1975-79; First Lord of the Treasury and Minister for Civil Service, 1979-90; Conservative Party Leader, 1975-90; Prime Minister, 1979-90; Retired from public life, 2002. Publications: In Defence of Freedom, 1986; The Downing Street Years, 1979-90, 1993; The Path to Power, 1995; The Collected Speeches of Margaret Thatcher, 1997; Statecraft, 2002. Honours: Honorary Fellow, Royal Institute of Chemistry, Freedom of the Royal Borough of Kensington and Chelsea, 1979; Freedom of the London Borough of Barnet, 1980; Freedom of the Falkland Islands, Honorary Master of the Bench at Gray's Inn, 1983; Freedom of the City of London, 1989; Freedom of The City of Westminster, 1990; Hon LLD, Buckingham, 1986; Dr hc, Rand Afrikaans, 1991; Presidential Medal of Freedom, USA, 1991; Order of Good Hope, South Africa, 1991; Dr hc, Weizman Institute of Science, 1992; MacArthur Foundation Fellowship, 1992; Hon Citizen of Gorasde, 1993; Dr hc, Mendeleyev, 1993; Hilal-i-Imitaz, 1996; LG; OM; PC; FRS; Life Peer, created 1992. Memberships: Honorary Bencher, Gray's Inn, 1975; No Turning Back Group President, 1990-; Bruges Group Honorary President, 1991-; International Advisory Board, British American Chamber of Commerce; Worshipful Company of Glovers (Member); Chancellor, University of Buckingham, 1993-; Advisory Board Chair University of London Institute of US Studies, 1994-; Royal Society of St George Vice President, 1999-; Conservative Companion of Guild of Cambridge Benefactors, 1999-. Address: The House of Lords, Westminster, London SW1A 0PW, England.

**THEOBALD-HICKS Barry John Frederick,** b. 25 October 1945, Lockington Hall, Castle Donnington, Derbyshire. Company Director; Administrator; Amateur Historian; Genealogist; Archivist; 19th Lord of the Manor of Danbury with Bretton, County of Essex. m. Sharon Ann Friend. Education: Morely College, London, 1960-65; London College of Art and Printing, 1963-66; University of London, 1986-88; Certificate of Safety Management, British Institute of Management, 1992. Appointments: Deputy Manager to Lady Tara Heffler, Catalogue Department, Manager, Printing and Stationary, Fire, Health and Safety Manager (UK), Sotheby's Auctioneers, Mayfair, London, 1978-93; Senior Museum Assistant, Leighton House Museum and Art Gallery, Royal Borough of Kensington and Chelsea, 1993-96; Director, Parke Morrison Construction Ltd, 1994-98; Director, Consolidated Land Ltd, 1995-98; Managing Director, Theobald-Hicks, Morris & Gifford Ltd, 1999-. Publications: History of the Lords of the Manor of Danbury in Essex (unpublished); History of Heather Parish Church, Leicestershire, 1986; Now I Know Where You Are Granddad, 1998; Contributor to: The Millennium Book of All Saints Church, Kent, 2000; A Theobald History (The Faversham Connection), 2004; Newsletter of the St John Historical Society. Honours include: St John Ambulance Long Service Medal, 1975 with 3 bars, 1980, 1985, 2002; Freeman, City of London, 1985; Officer, The Venerable Order of St John of Jerusalem, 1988; Commander, Orthodox Order of Hospitallers, 1989; Officer, 1992, Commander, 1995, Knight of Justice, 2000, Officer, Companionate of Merit, 2001, Order of St Lazarus; Knight Grand Cross of Justice, Order of St Stanislas, 2000; Knight Commander, Order of St Gregory the Great, 2004; Knight of Justice, Order of the Collar of St Agatha of Paterno,

2005; Liveryman of the Worshipful Company of Scriveners. Memberships include: Fellow: Royal Microscopical Society, Royal Society of Art, Society of Antiquaries of Scotland; British Institute of Management, Institute of Administrative Management; Museums Association, Associate, Ambulance Service Institute; The Royal British Legion (Sidcup & Foots Cray Branch); Royal Army Medical Corps Association; St John Historical Society; St John Ambulance. Address: 3 Leechcroft Avenue, Blackfen, Kent DA15 8RR, England.

**THEODOROU Stavroula,** b. 6 March 1973, Ioannina, Greece. Physician; Radiologist. Education: MD, University of Ioannina School of Medicine, Ioannina, Greece, 1997; Speciality in Radiology, University of Ioannina Medical Centre, 1998-2003; Clinical duties and research in Musculoskeletal Imaging and Quantitative Bone Densitometry, University of California San Diego Medical Center, San Diego, California, USA, 1999, 2000-2001. Appointments: Department of Radiology, University of Ioannina Medical Centre, Ioannina, Greece, 1998-2003; Department of Radiology, University of California, San Diego, California, USA, 1999, 2000-2001; Department of Radiology, Thornton Hospital, University of California San Diego, California, USA, 1999. Publications: 23 original articles; Co-author, 5 books. Honours: Award of Excellence in University Studies, Greek National Scholarship Foundation, 1992, 1994; Award of Excellence in Pathology, University of Ioannina Medical Centre, 1996; Support in Research, Veterans Affairs, San Diego Medical Center Grant, California, USA; Certificate of Merit for Educational Exhibit, Radiological Society of North America, 1999, 2000; Certificate of Merit for Educational Exhibit, American Roentgen Ray Society, Washington DC, 2000; Best Scientific Exhibit, American Society of Spine Radiology, Florida, 2001. Memberships: American College of Radiology, Radiological Society of North America; Society for Clinical Densitometry; American Society for Bone Mineral Research; Los Angeles Radiological Society; National Osteoporosis Foundation. Address: 13 Papadopoulos Street, Ioannina 45444, Greece. E-mail: rjtheodorou@hotmail.com

**THEODORU Stefan Gheorghe,** b. 11 June 1921, Braila, Romania. Civil Engineer; Writer; Editor. m. Nina Bogos, 2 sons. Education: MS, Civil Engineering, Politechnic Institute of Bucharest, Romania, 1947. Appointments: Civil Engineer, Bucharest, Vienna, New York; Inventor, Writer, Editor, New York and Bucharest; Co-inventor, Pattern Recognition System. Publications include: Poetry: Versuri Vol I, 1973; Versuri Vol II, 1988; La Lumina, 1993; Odiseea Unui Cuget, 1993; Meeting in Twilight, 1994; The Bag of Stars, 1995; Centum, 1997; The Whispers of the Old Walnut Tree, 2001; Drama: Un Drac de Fata, 1952; Ciclu, 1954; Teatru, 1993; Doamna, 1995; Duminica la Ora Sase, 1997; Cersetorul, 1998; TATI, 2002; Prose: Fata Fara Glas, 1993; Un Milionar Nebun, 1996; Genius, 1996; Nascuta in Castelul lui Dracula, 1997; Adam si Sotiile Sale, 1998; Iac'asa, 1999; Marul din Poveste, 1998; Refugiatii, 2002; History: Lupta de la Nicopole, 1975; A Wallachian Flag, 1977; Transylvania, 1995; Drapelul de Margine, 1999; Contributions to numerous anthologies; Numerous articles in magazines and newspapers. Honours: Poetry: Daily Yomiuri Award, Tokyo, 1995; Pantheon Publishing House Semn Award, 1997; Romanian-Japanese Magazine Award, 1997; Orion Award, 1997; International Ashiya Haiku Festa Award, Hyogo, Japan, 2000; The British H S J W Hackett International Haiku Award, 2000; Prose: Tempus Foundation Award, Best Novel of the Year, 1998; Literary Circle V Carlova Award, 1995-98; Drama: Romanian Cinematography Award, 1952; Dacoromanian Academy Award, Best Theatre Play, 1998, 1999. Memberships include: Engineering Association of Romania, 1948; Romanian Academic Society, München, 1966; Society of

American Inventors, 1981; New York Academy of Sciences; Union of Romanian Journalists; Haiku Society of America; International Association of Romanian Writers and Artists, Georgia; American Legion; Romanian Vexilologic Society. Address: 28-18 29th St, Long Island City, NY 11102, USA.

**THERON Charlize,** b. 7 August 1975, South Africa. Actress. Education: Trained as a ballet dancer. Appointments: Model, Milan, 1991; Actress, Los Angeles, 1992-; Films include: Children of the Corn III, 1994; Two Days in the Valley, 1996; That Thing You Do! 1996; Trial and Error, 1997; Hollywood Confidential, 1997; Devil's Advocate, 1997; Cop Lane/The Yards, 1997; Might Joe Young, 1998; Celebrity, 1998; The Cider House Rules, 1999; The Astronaut's Wife, 1999; The Yards, 2000; Reindeer Games, 2000; Men of Honour, 2000; The Legend of Bagger Vance, 2000; Navy Diver, 2000; Sweet November, 20001; The Curse of the Jade Scorpion, 2001; 15 Minutes, 2001; The Yards/Nightwatch, 2002; Waking Up in Reno, 2002; Trapped, 2002; 24 Hours, 2002; Executive Producer, Sweet Home Alabama, 2002; The Italian Job, 2003; Monster, 2003. Honours: Best Actress Oscar for Monster, 2004. Address: c/o Spanky Taylor, 3727 West Magnolia, Burbank, CA 91505, USA.

**THEROUX Paul Edward,** b. 10 April 1941, Medford, Massachusetts, USA. Writer. m. (1) Anne Castle, 4 December 1967, divorced 1993, 2 sons, (2) Sheila Donnelly, 18 November 1995. Education: BA, University of Massachusetts. Appointments: Lecturer, University of Urbino, Italy, 1963, Soche Hill College, Malawi, 1963-65; Faculty, Department of English, Makerere University, Uganda, 1965-68, University of Singapore, 1968-71; Visiting Lecturer, University of Virginia, 1972-73. Publications: Fiction: Waldo, 1967; Fong and the Indians, 1968; Girls at Play, 1969; Murder in Mount Holly, 1969; Jungle Lovers, 1971; Sinning with Annie, 1972; Saint Jack, 1973; The Black House, 1974; The Family Arsenal, 1976; The Consul's File, 1977; Picture Palace, 1978; A Christmas Card, 1978; London Snow, 1980; World's End, 1980; The Mosquito Coast, 1981; The London Embassy, 1982; Half Moon Street, 1984; O-Zone, 1986; My Secret History, 1988; Chicago Loop, 1990; Millroy the Magician, 1993; My Other Life, 1996; Kowloon Tong, 1997; Collected Stories, 1997; Fresh-Air Fiend, 1999; Hotel Honolulu, 2000; Dark Star Safari: Overland from Cairo to Cape Town, 2002; Non-Fiction: V S Naipaul, 1973; The Great Patagonian Express, 1979; The Kingdom by the Sea, 1983; Sailing Through China, 1983; Sunrise with Sea Monsters, 1985; The White Man's Burden, 1987; Riding the Iron Rooster, 1988; The Happy Isles of Oceania, 1992; The Pillars of Hercules, 1995; Sir Vidia's Shadow: A Friendship Across Five Continents, 1998. Honours: Editorial Awards, Playboy magazine, 1972, 1976, 1977, 1979; Whitbread Award, 1978; James Tait Black Award, 1982; Yorkshire Post Best Novel Award, 1982; Thomas Cook Travel Prize, 1989; Honorary doctorates. Memberships: Royal Geographical Society; Royal Society of Literature, fellow; American Academy of Arts and Letters.

**THIAN Bob,** b. 1 August 1943, South Africa. Chief Executive Officer; Chairman. m. Liselotte Von Borges, 2 daughters. Education: Licence en Droit, Geneva, Switzerland, 1967; Barrister, Gray's Inn, London, 1968-71. Appointments: Legal Advisor, Glaxo Group Ltd, Project Development Executive, Glaxo-Allenburys Export Ltd, Managing Director, Glaxo Farmaceutica Lda, 1968-80; European Business Development Director, Abbott International, European Regional Director, Abbott Laboratories, 1980-87; Vice president, International Operations, Novo Industri A/S, 1987-89; Group Chief Executive, North West Water Group plc, 1990-93; Non-Executive Director, Celltech Group plc, 1992-99; Founder and Chief Executive,

Renex Ltd, 1993-; Non-Executive Director, Medeval Ltd, 1995-98; Group Chief Executive, The Stationery Office Group, ex HMSO, 1996-99; Chairman, Imo Group Ltd, 1999-2000; Chairman, Tactica Solutions Ltd, 1999-2000; Chairman, Astron Group Ltd, 2001-05; Chairman, Orion Group Ltd, 2001-04; Chairman, Whatman Plc, 2002-; Chairman, Southern Water Services Ltd, 2003-. Memberships: Chantilly Golf; Lansdowne Club. Address: 16 Princes Gate Mews, London SW7 2PS, England. E-mail: bob.thian@renex.net

**THIENE Gaetano,** b. 1 July 1947, Longare (VI), Italy. Medical Doctor; Professor. m. Marialuisa Valente, 2 sons, 1 daughter. Education: Medical Degree, 1972; ECMG, 1972; Postgraduate Diploma, Cardiology, 1975; Postgraduate Diploma, Pathological Anatomy, 1978. Appointments: Assistant Professor, 1972-77, Assistant Professor-Chief Resident, 1977-80, Associate Professor in Cardiovascular Pathology, 1980-90, Professor in Cardiovascular Pathology, 1990-, Director, PhD Course on Cardiosciences, 1991-, Director, Institute of Pathological Anatomy, 1998-, University of Padua Medical School, Padua, Italy; President, Society for Cardiovascular Pathology, USA and Canadian Academy of Pathology, 2003-. Publications: 628 (462 Index Medicus); 642 abstracts; 632 papers at congresses and lectures; 12 monographs. Honours: Giovanni e Silvio Cagnetto, 1972; NATO Jr CNR, 1977; Giacomo Binda, 1980; Furio Cicogna, 1981; Mannheim Lecture, 1985. Memberships: AECVP; AEPC; EACTS; ESC; IAP; SCVP; SHVD; SIC; SICP. Address: University of Padua Medical School, Institute of Pathological Anatomy, Via A Gabelli N 61, 35121 Padua, Italy. E-mail: cardpath@unipd.it

**THILL Georges Emile André,** b. 30 November 1935, Bullange, Belgium. University Emeritus Professor. Education: Mathematics, Belgian Licence and Agregation enseignement secondaire, University of Louvain, Philosophy, BA; Doctorate, Theological Sciences, Paris; Postgraduate Studies, High Energy Physics. Appointments: Researcher, Laboratoire de Physique Nucléaire, Collège de France, Paris, 1966-67 and Institut Interuniversitaire belge des sciences nucléaires, Laboratoire des Hautes Energies, Brussels, 1962-73; Scholar, University of Namur, Belgium, 1973-2001; Director of the interdisciplinary Department for Sciences, Philosophies, Societies, Faculty of Natural Science, Namur, 1976-88; Member of the Executive Committee, Course Director in the Field, Science Technology Society, Inter-University Centre of Postgraduate Studies, Dubrovnik, 1986-94; Senior Fellow, EC Programme Monitor/FAST, Science Research Development, Brussels, 1991-94; Chair Professor, Professeur Ordinaire, 1986-2001, Emeritus Professor, University of Namur, 2001-; Emeritus Professor, Faculty of Human Sciences, State University of Haiti, Port-au-Prince, Haiti, 2002-; Visiting or Invited Professor in different universities: Dakar, Louvain, Brussels, Copenhagen, Donetsk National Technical University and others; Director of the Scientific Co-ordination, PRELUDE, International Networking Programme of Research and Liaison between Universities for Development, Research and Educational Network for sustainable co-development, NGO of UNESCO Collective Consultation on Higher Education implemented on the five continents (72 countries), 1985-; Responsible for the UNESCO-PRELUDE Chair of Sustainable Development, 2001-. Publications: 26 books including: La fête scientifique, 1973; Technologies et sociétés, 1980; Plaidoyer pour des universités citoyennes et responsables, 1998; Le dialogue des savoirs, 2001; L'eau, patrimoine commun mondial, 2002; Femmes, Savoirs, Sciences et Développement Durable, 2004. Over 100 scientific articles. Honours: Director of the Scientific Co-ordination of PRELUDE; Scientific Director, UNESCO Unitwin-PRELUDE Chair; President, Institut Interuniversitaire Belge de la Vie,

Sciences et Qualité de Vie, Brussels; 2003 International Peace Prize, United Cultural Convention, USA. Memberships: Notably Scientific Society of Brussels; Steering Committee, International Network on the Role of the Universities for Developing Areas; Deontological Committee, Service Public Federal (SPF) de Belgique, Sante Publique, Sécurité del la Chaîne Alimentaire et Enviroment Division Bien-Être Animal et CITES; Joint Committee of Bioéthics of the Centre d'etudes et de recherches vétérinaires et agronomiques (CERVA), Institut Pasteur, Institut Scientifique de Santé Publique (ISP), Brussels; Editing Board, La Revue Nouvelle, PRELUDE Review and Newsletter. Address: 65, Rue Saint-Quentin, B-1000, Brussels, Belgium.

**THISTLETHWAYTE (John) Robin,** b. 8 December 1935, London, England. Land Owner; Chartered Surveyor. m. Mary Katharine Grasett, 2 sons, 1 daughter. Education: Royal Agricultural College, Cirencester. Appointments: Partner, Savills, 1961-86; Consultant to Savills plc, 1986-96; Mayor of Chipping Norton, 1964, 1965; Justice of the Peace; Chairman, Chipping Norton Petty Sessional Division, 1985, 1985; Chairman North Oxfordshire and Chipping Norton Petty Sessional Division, 1989-91. Memberships: Fellow of the Royal Institution of Chartered Surveyors; Clubs: Boodle's, St James's. Address: Sorbrook Manor, Adderbury, Oxfordshire OX17 3EG, England.

**THOMAS Donald Michael,** b. 27 January 1935, Redruth, Cornwall, England. Poet; Writer; Translator. 2 sons, 1 daughter. Education: BA, 1st Class Honours, English, MA, New College, Oxford. Appointment: English teacher, Teignmouth, Devon, 1959-63; Lecturer, Hereford College of Education, 1963-78; Full-time author, 1978-. Publications: Poetry: Penguin Modern Poets 11, 1968; Two Voices, 1968; Logan Stone, 1971; Love and Other Deaths, 1975; The Honeymoon Voyage, 1978; Dreaming in Bronze, 1981; Selected Poems, 1983; Puberty Tree, 1992. Fiction: The Flute Player, 1979; Birthstone, 1980; The White Hotel, 1981; Ararat, 1983; Swallow, 1984; Sphinx, 1986; Summit, 1987; Lying Together, 1990; Flying into Love, 1992; Pictures at an Exhibition, 1993; Eating Pavlova, 1994; Lady With a Laptop, 1996; Alexander Solzhenitsyn, 1998; Charlotte, 2000. Translator: Requiem, and Poem Without a Hero, by Akhmatova, 1976; Way of All the Earth, by Akhmatova, 1979; The Bronze Horseman, by Pushkin, 1982. Honours: Gollancz/Pan Fantasy Prize; Pen Fiction Prize; Cheltenham Prize; Los Angeles Times Fiction Prize. Address: The Coach House, Rashleigh Vale, Tregolis Road, Truro TR1 1TJ, England. E-mail: dmthomas@btconnect.com

**THOMAS Iwan,** b. 5 January 1974, Farnborough, Hampshire. Athlete. Education: Brunel University. Appointments: Fourth-ranked BMX rider, Europe, 1988; Fifth Olympic Games 400m, 1996; Silver Medal, 4 x 400m relay; Gold Medal Amateur Athletics Association, Championships 400m, 1997, British records, 44.36 seconds, 1998; Silver Medal World Championships 4 x 400m relay, 1997; Gold Medal European Championships 400m, 1998; Gold Medal, World Cup 400m, 1998; Gold Medal Commonwealth Games 400m, 1998. Honours: British Athletics Writers Male Athlete of the Year, 1998; Patron Norwich Union Startract Scheme. Address: c/o UK Athletics, Athletics House, 10 Harbourne Road, Edgbaston, Birmingham, B15 3AA, England. Website: www.iwanthomas.com

**THOMAS Kenneth G,** b. 25 June 1944, Llanelli, Wales. Executive Vice President, Operations and Chief Operating Officer. m. Beth, 2 daughters. Education: BSc Honours, Metallurgy, University College, Cardiff, Wales, 1970; MSc and DIC, Management Sciences, Imperial College, University of London, 1971; PhD, Technical Sciences, Delft University of Technology, Delft, The Netherlands, 1994; Chartered Engineer, UK. Appointments: Mill Superintendent, Giant Yellowknife Mines Limited, Gold Producer, Northwest Territories, Canada, 1985-87; Vice-President, Metallurgy, 1987, Vice-President, Metallurgy and Construction, 1989, Senior Vice-President, Metallurgy and Construction, 1990, Senior Vice-President, Technical Services, 1995, Barrick Gold Corporation, Gold Producer, Ontario, Canada, 1987-2001; Global Managing Director, Mining and Mineral Processing, 2001, Managing Director, Western Australia, 2002-2003, Hatch, Consulting Engineers and Construction Managers, Mississauga, Ontario, Canada; Executive Vice President, Operations and Chief Operating Officer, Crystallex International Corporation, International Gold Company, Toronto, Canada, 2003-. Publications: Numerous technical and management papers internationally. Book: Research, Engineering Design and Operation of a Pressure Hydrometallurgical Facility for Gold Extraction. Honours: Mill Man of the Year Award, 1991, Airey Award, 1999, Selwyn G Blaylock Medal, 2001, Canadian Institute of Mining, Metallurgy and Petroleum. Memberships: Association of Professional Engineers of Ontario, Canada; Fellow, Institute of Mining, Metallurgy and Mining, UK; Fellow, Canadian Institute of Mining, Metallurgy and Petroleum; Fellow, Canadian Academy of Engineering. Address: 2005, Heartwood Court, Mississauga, Ontario L5C 4P7, Canada.

**THOMAS Lindsey Kay Jr,** b. 16 April 1931, Salt Lake City, Utah, USA. Research Ecologist Emeritus; Consultant; Educator. m. Nancy Ruth Van Dyke, 2 sons, 2 daughters. Education: BS, Utah State Agricultural College, Logan, Utah, 1953; MS, Brigham Young University, Provo, Utah, 1958; PhD, Duke University, Durham, North Carolina, 1974. Appointments: Park Naturalist, National Capital Parks, National Park Service, 1957-62; Park Naturalist (Research), Region 6, 1962-63; Research Park Naturalist, National Capital Region, 1963-66; Instructor, Department of Agriculture Graduate School, 1964-66; Research Biologist for Southeast Temperate Forests, 1966-71; Research Biologist, National Capital Parks, 1971-74; Research Biologist, National Capital Region, 1974-93; Guest Lecturer, Washington Technical Institute (University of the District of Columbia), 1976; Adjunct Professor, George Mason University, 1988-; Adjunct Professor, George Washington University, 1992-98; Research Biologist, National Biological Service, 1993-96; Resource Management Specialist, Baltimore-Washington Parkway, National Park Service, 1996, National Capital Parks East, 1996-98; Member, Board of Directors, Prince William County (Virginia) Service Authority, 1996-2004; Ecological and Resource Management Consultant, National Capital Region, 1998-. Publications: Numerous articles in professional journals. Honours include: Superior Performance Award for Conduct and Progress in the Exotic Plant Management Research Programme; Incentive Award for Safety Feature at Overlook; Incentive Award for Interpretive Information to be placed on C&O Canal Location Map. Memberships: American Association for the Advancement of Science; Botanical Society of Washington; Ecological Society of America; George Wright Society; The Nature Conservancy; Society for Early Historic Archaeology; Sigma Xi the Scientific Research Society; Southern Appalachian Botanical Society; Washington Biologists' Field Club; National Trust for Historic Preservation; Maryland Native Plant Society. Address: 13854 Delaney Road, Woodbridge, VA 22193, USA.

**THOMAS Patrick,** b. 27 July 1960, Oxford, England. Musician; Composer; Producer. Education: BA, hons, Psychology, Open University; Private Classical Piano Lessons; Studied with Mary Howell-Pryce, St Edmund Campion School, Oxford. Career: Paris with Chuck Berry, Continental Drift, 1989; London with Derek Bailey, Eugene Chadbourne, Keith Rowe, 1990; London with John Zorn, Bucket Head, Paul Lovens, 1991; Germany with Tony Oxley, Sirone, Larry Stabbins, Manfred Schoof, 1992; Glasgow with Lol Coxhill, 1993; Berlin Jazz Festival with Bill Dixon, 1994; London Jazz Cafe with Thurston Moore, Lee Renaldo, 1996; Solo, Copenhagen, 1997; Austria Graz Music Protocol, with And, 1997; CMN Tour, with Butch Morris; London Sky Scraper; Vancouver Jazz Festival, with Eugene Chadborne and Alex Ward, 1998; Cologne, Germany with Celebration Orchestra, 1998; Uncool Festival, Switzerland, with Scatter, 1999; Konigsberg Festival with Eugene Chadbourne and Jimmy Carl Black, 2003. Compositions: Ensemble WX7e Turntables Dialogue (with interruptions); Pulse, for drum machine and two percussionists; Reflex, for ensemble and computers. Recordings: With Tony Oxley Quartet, Incus, 1992; Lol Coxhill, Halim Nato, 1993; One Night in Glasgow, Scatter, 1994; Company 91, 3 volumes, 1994; Mike Cooper Island Songs, 1995; Celebration Orchestra, The Enchanted Messenger, 1996; Tones of Life, Guidance, 1997; Solo Album, Remembering, 1998; Total Tuesday, Hellington Country, 1998; And, Intakt, 1998; Hard Edge, with Rhys Chatham, 1999; Powerfield, EEE, 1999. Publications: Islam's Contribution to Jazz and Improvised Music, 1993; Upside Down (The Myth of Jazz History), 1998. Honours: Arts Council of Great Britain Jazz Bursary for 3 Electro-acoustic Compositions. Membership: Performing Rights Society. Address: 5 Saint Omer Road, Cowley, Oxford OX4 3HB, England.

**THOMAS Richard Stephen,** b. 13 June 1943, London, England. National Health Service Confederation Director. m. Sandra Thomas, 1 son, 1 daughter. Education: University of Wales Institute of Science and Technology; Member of the Institute of Health Service Management. Appointments: Various NHS Management Posts in Wales, 1961-78; Area Personnel Officer, Dyfed Health Authority, Wales, 1978-86; Assistant General Manager, East Dyfed Health Authority, 1986-93; Chief Executive, Carmarthen NHS Trust, 1993-97; Chief Executive, Morriston Hospital NHS Trust, 1997-99; Director, The Welsh NHS Confederation, 1999-. Memberships: Past Chairman, South West Branch, Institute of Health Service Management; Former Honorary Secretary, Welsh Association of Health Authorities; Non-Executive Director, College of Sir Gar Carmarthen; Past Chairman and Past President, Carmarthen Round Table; Past Chairman, Carmarthen Ex-Round Tablers Club; Member and Past Chairman, Carmarthen Tywi Rotary Club. Address: Underhill, 7 Llygad-yr-Haul, Llangunnor, Carmarthen SA31 2LB, Wales. E-mail: richard.thomas@confed.wales.nhs.uk

**THOMAS Zdenek,** b. 11 May 1929, Opava, Czechoslovakia. Civil Engineer. m. Jitka Kadlecova, 1 son. Education: Civil Engineer, 1954; PhD, 1967; Doctor of Sciences, 1992. Appointments: Water Research Institute, Prague, 1954-91; Delft Hydraulic Laboratory, The Netherlands, 1968-69; Institute for Water Structures, University of Stuttgart, Germany, 1989; Institute of Hydrodynamics, Czech Academy of Sciences, 1992; Engineering Institute, Mexican Autonomous University, 1996-97; Mexican Petroleum Institute, 1999-2004. Publications: 32 scientific papers including 3 monographs. Honours: Listed in Who's Who publications and biographical dictionaries. Memberships: Scientific-Technical Society, Prague; Union of Czech Mathematics and Physicists; Czech Association for Chemical Technology. Address: Kladenska 19, 16000 Prague 6, Czech Republic. E-mail: ZThomas@seznam.cz

**THOMPSON Barnaby,** b. 29 March 1961, London, England. Film Producer. m. Christina Robert, 1 son, 1 daughter. Education: BA (Hons), Theology and Philosophy, Oxford University. Appointments: Co-producer, Broadway Pictures, USA; Producer, Fragile Films, 1996-; Head of Ealing Studios,

2001-. Honours: Dear Rosie (short film) Oscar and BAFTA nominations; An Ideal Husband, Golden Globe, and BAFTA nominations. Memberships: BAFTA; Academy of Motion Picture Arts and Sciences. Address: Ealing Studios, Ealing Green, London W5 5EP, England. E-mail: info@ealingstudios.com Website: www.ealingstudios.com

**THOMPSON Daley,** b. 30 July 1958, Notting Hill, London, England. Athlete. m. Tisha Quinlan, 1987, 1 child. Appointments: Sussex Schools 200m title, 1974; First competitive decathlon, Welsh Open Championship, 1975; European Junior Decathlon Champion, 1977; European Decathlon Silver Medallist, 1978; Gold Medallist, 1982, 1986; Commonwealth Decathlon Gold Medallist, 1978, 1982, 1986; Olympic Decathlon Gold Medallist, Moscow, 1980, LA, 1984; World Decathlon Champion, 1983; Established new world record for decathlon (at Olympic games, LA); Set four world records and was undefeated between 1978 and 1987; Retired, July 1992; Invited to run leg of the Olympic Torch relay at the opening of Sydney Olympic Games, 2000. Publications: Going for Gold, 1987; The Greatest, 1996. Address: Church Row, Wandsworth Plain, London, SW18, England.

**THOMPSON David Morgan,** b. 9 July 1929, Ryde, Isle of Wight, England. Art Critic. m. Freda Dowie. Education: BA, Corpus Christi, Oxford. Appointments: Art Critic, The Times, 1956-64; Founder, Director, Stage Sixty theatre company, Theatre Royal, Stratford East, 1964-66; Director, Institute of Contemporary Arts, London, 1969-72. Publications: Scripted 10 BBC TV art programmes, 1980-86; Monograph, Becker, 2003. Honours: Council of Europe Award; Blue Ribbon Award, New York Film Festival; BAFTA Best Specialist Film Award. Memberships: British Council Fine Art Committee; Arts Council Exhibitions Committee; Hayward Gallery Advisory Committee; Greater London Arts Association; Lloyd Committee for a National Film School. Address: Hollies, Love Lane, Westleton, Nr Saxmundham, Suffolk IP17 3BA, England.

**THOMPSON Emma,** b. 15 April 1959, England. Actress. m. (1) Kenneth Brannagh, 1989, divorced, (2) Greg Wise, 1 daughter. Education: Newnham College, Cambridge, England. Career: Cambridge Footlights while at University; Films include: Henry V, 1989; Howards End, Dead Again, 1991; Cheers, 1992; Peter's Friends, 1992; Much Ado About Nothing; In the Name of the Father, Remains of the Day, 1993; My Father the Hero, 1994; Junior, 1994; Sense and Sensibility, wrote screenplay and acted, 1996; The Winter Guest, 1997; Primary Colors, 1997; Judas Kiss, 1997; Imagining Argentina, 2002; Love Actually, 2003; Harry Potter and the Prisoner of Azkaban, 2004; Nanny McPhee, in progress; TV includes: Carrott's Lib; Saturday Night Live; Tutti Frutti; Fortunes of War; Thompson; Knuckle; The Winslow Boy; Look Back in Anger; Blue Boy; Ellen; Wit; Angels in America, 2002; Stage appearances include: Me and My Girl, 1984-85; Look Back in Anger, 1989; A Midsummer Night's Dream, 1990; King Lea, 1990. Honours: Best TV Actress Awards: Tutti Frutti and Fortunes of War; Evening Standard Awards: Howards End, 1992; Remains of the Day, 1994; Academy Awards: Howards End, 1994; Sense and Sensibility (for Best Screenplay Adaptation, 1996); BAFTA Award: Howards End, 1994. Address: Hamilton Hodell Ltd, 1st Floor, 24 Hanway Street, London W1T 1UH, England.

**THOMPSON Ernest Victor,** b. 14 July 1931, London, England. Author. m. Celia Carole Burton, 11 September 1972, 2 sons. Publications: Chase the Wind, 1977; Harvest of the Sun, 1978; The Music Makers, 1979; Ben Retallick, 1980; The Dream Traders, 1981; Singing Spears, 1982; The Restless Sea, 1983; Cry Once Alone, 1984; Polrudden, 1985; The Stricken Land,

# DICTIONARY OF INTERNATIONAL BIOGRAPHY

1986; Becky, 1988; God's Highlander, 1988; Lottie Trago, 1989; Cassie, 1990; Wychwood, 1991; Blue Dress Girl, 1992; Mistress of Polrudden, 1993; The Tolpuddle Woman, 1994; Ruddlemoor, 1995; Moontide, 1996; Cast no Shadows, 1997; Mud Huts and Missionaries, 1997; Fires of Evening, 1998; Somewhere a Bird is Singing, 1999; Here, There and yesterday, 1999; Winds of Fortune, 2000; Seek a New Dawn, 2001; The Lost Years, 2002; Paths of Destiny, 2003; Tomorrow is For Ever, 2004. Various books on Cornish and West Country subjects. Contributions to: Approximately 200 short stories to magazines. Honour: Best Historical Novel, 1976. Memberships: Society of Authors; West Country Writers Club, vice president; Mevagissey Male Choir, vice patron; Royal Society of Literature; Cornish Literary Guild, president, 1998. Address: Mira la Costa, Avenida de Malta N23, Casab, 03500 Benidorm, Alicante, Spain.

**THOMPSON Francis George,** b. 29 March 1931, Isle of Lewis, Scotland. Retired Senior Lecturer; Poet. m. Margaret Elaine Pullar, 23 April 1960, 1 son, 3 daughters. Education: Fellow, Institution of Electrical Incorporated Engineers. Appointments: Technical Writer; Technical College Lecturer; Senior Lecturer. Publications: Void, 1975; First Light, 1977; Touchlines, 1978; Reflections, 1985. Contributions to: Lines Review; Chapman; Prospice; Northwords; Orbis; Words. Honour: Hugh McDiarmid Memorial Cup, Scottish Open Poetry Competition, 1979. Address: 5 Rathad na Muilne, Stornoway, Isle of Lewis, Scotland.

**THOMPSON Olaniran Anthony,** b. 16 August 1971, Akure, Ondo State, Nigeria. Economist; Clergyman. m. Aderonke Favour-Betty, 1 daughter. Education: BSc, Economics and Statistics, University of Benin, Benin City, Nigeria; National Diploma in Accountancy, Yaba College of Technology, Yaba, Lagos, Nigeria. Appointments: Auditor, 1995; Sales Executive, 2000; Currently, Administrator. Publications: Understanding Your Time and Season; Managing Your Courtship; Maximise Your Friendship. Honour: International School of Ministry. Membership: Associate Member, Nigeria Institute of Management. Address: Way of Peace Ministries, PMB 652, Akure, Ondo State, Nigeria. E-mail: ronkeniran@yahoo.com

**THOMPSON Terence,** b. 19 January 1928, Staffordshire, England. Composer; Teacher; Clarinettist; Saxophonist. Education: ABSM, performer and teacher; ABSM, (T T D), Birmingham School of Music, after Military Service in the South Staffordshire Regiment. Career: Music Master, West Bromwich Technical High School, 1950-59; Part-Time Clarinet Tutor, Birmingham School of Music, 1954-55; Head of Music, March End School, Wednesfield, 1960-66; Part-Time Lecturer, West Midlands College of Higher Education, 1965-89; Senior Teacher, Wolverhampton Music School, 1968-93. Compositions: Boogie and Blues; Suite Chalumeau Swing; Suite City Scenes; Back to Bach; Two syncopated dances; Something Blue; 36 other arranged works published; 17 other compositions self published; 37 other arranged works self published. Recordings: London Saxophone Quartet in digital; Two Light Pieces, 1999; A Cumbrian Voluntary, 2000 Music for a While; Music for the New Millennium; Variations on The Young May Moon. Memberships: Performing Right Society; British Academy of Composers and Songwriters; The Light Music Society; National Union of Teachers; Mechanical-Copyright Protection Society; Birmingham Conservatoire Association. Address: 58 Willenhall Road, Bilston, West Midlands WV14 6NW, England.

**THOMPSON-CAGER-STRAND Chezia Brenda.** Poet; Director; Artist; Educator. Education: BA, 1973, MA, 1975, Washington University; Doctorate of Arts, Carnegie-Mellon University, 1984. Appointments: Assistant Professor of English, Clarion State College, 1980-82; Site Reviewer, National Endowment for the Arts Expansion Arts Program, 1984; Assistant Professor, Afro-American Studies, University of Maryland, Baltimore, 1982-85; Associate Professor, Theater/African –American Studies, Mendenhall Center for the Performing Arts, Smith College, 1985-88; Artist in Residence, Theater Department, University of Pennsylvania; Consultant, African American Newspaper Archives and Research Center, 1989-92; Artist in Residence, Albany (Georgia) State College, 1994; Consultant, Baltimore City Public Schools Multicultural Initiative, 1992-94; Professor of Language and Literature, 1994-, Director, Spectrum of Poetic Fire Reading Series, 1999-, Maryland Institute College of Art. Publications: 2 books; 3 poetry chapbooks; Teaching Jean Toomer's 1923 Cane, 2004; When Divas Dance, poetry, 2004; Regional Poetry CD, The Road Less Taken: The Saint Valentine Sunday Poetry Marathon, 2001; Contributor of poems, reviews and articles in professional and public journals. Honours include: Distinguished Black Marylander Award in the Arts, Towson University, 2000; Maryland State Arts Council Individual Artist Award in Poetry, 1999, 2001; Lucus Grant in Teaching, MICA, 2001; Associate Fellowship in Poetry, Atlantic Center for the Arts, 2002; Tuition Grant in Poetry, Bread Loaf, 2002; Finalist in 2002 Naomi Madgett Long Poetry Competition for Lotus Press. Memberships: Board of Directors, LINK: A Journal of the Arts in Baltimore and the World; Modern Language Association; Poetry Society of America; Academy of American Poets; National Council of Teachers of English. Address: 1300 Mount Royal Avenue, Baltimore, MD 21217, USA. E-mail: spectrum@mica.edu Website: www.spectrumofpoeticfire.com.

**THOMPSON Wendy,** b. 28 October 1953, Montreal, Canada. Government Official. 1 adopted daughter, 2 step sons. Education: Diploma Collegial Studies, Bachelor of Social Work, Master of Social Work, McGill University, Canada; PhD, Bristol University. Appointments: Part-time Sessional Lecturer, McGill University, 1977-81; Executive Director, Head and Hands, Montreal, 1976-80, West Island Association for People with Learning Disabilities, Quebec, 1981-82; Senior Programmes Officer, Greater London Council, 1985-86; Head of Finance and Programmes, London Strategic Policy Unit, 1986-87; Assistant Chief Executive, Islington Council, 1987-93; Chief Executive, Turning Point Charity, 1993-96; Chief Executive, London Borough of Newnham, 1996-99; Director of Inspection, Audit Commission; Chief Executive, Office of Public Service Reform, Cabinet Office, 2001-; Former Member, Government's Urban Task Force and Better Regional Task Force; Board Member, Work Foundation. Publications: Books: Bureaucracy and Community (contributor), 1990; Citizen's Rights in a Modern Welfare System (contributor), 1992; Management for Quality in Local Government (contributor), 1992; Fitness for Purpose: Shaping New Patterns for Organisations and Management (co-author), 1993; Contributor to other publications and author of numerous conference papers. Address: Office of Public Service Reform, 22 Whitehall, London, SW1A 2WH, England. E-mail: wendy.thompson@cabinet-office.x-gsi.gov.uk

**THORNTON Billy Bob,** b. 4 August 1955, Hot Springs, Arizona, USA. Actor. m. Angelina Jolie, 2000, 1 adopted son. Appointments: Films include: Sling Blade, 1996; U-Turn, 1997; A Thousand Miles, 1997; The Apostle, 1997; A Gun a Car a Blonde, 1997; Primary Colours, 1997; Homegrown, 1998; Armageddon, 1998; A Simple Plan, 1998; Pushing Tin, 1998; The Man Who Wasn't There, 2001; Bandits, 2001; TV: The 1000 Chains; Don't Look Back; The Outsiders; Hearts Afire. Honours: Academy Award for Best Actor, Independent Spirit Awards. Address: c/o Miramax, 7966 Beverly Boulevard, Los Angeles, CA 90048, USA.

**THORNTON Frank (Frank Thornton Ball),** b. 15 January 1921, Dulwich, London. Actor. m. Beryl Jane Margaret Evans. 1 daughter. Education: Alleyn's School, Dulwich; London School of Dramatic Art, Scholarship, 1938-39; Qualified as Navigator, RAFVR, 1944; Demobbed as Flying Officer, 1947. Appointments: Council Actors' Benevolent Fund, Vice-President, 1982-90; Actor; Theatre includes: Laertes, Bassanio, Lysander, Catesby, Bardolph, Mosca in Jonson's Volpone, Donald Wolfit's Shakespeare Company, Strand and St James's Theatres, 1941-42; John Gielgud's Macbeth, Piccadilly Theatre, 1942; Flare Path, Apollo Theatre, 1942-43; Post-war several tours and repertory; Meals on Wheels, Royal Court, 1965; Alibi for a Judge, Savoy, 1966-67; The Young Visiters, Piccadilly, 1969; When We are Married, Strand, 1970; Eeyore in Winnie-the-Pooh, Phoenix, 1971-72; Aguecheek in Twelfth Night, Duncan in Macbeth, RSC, Stratford and Aldwych, 1974-75; Sir Patrick Cullen in The Doctor's Dilemma, Mermaid; The Chairs, Royal Exchange, Manchester, 1980; Sir John Tremayne in Me and My Girl, Adelphi, 1984-85; John of Gaunt in Richard II, Ludlow Festival, 1987; The Tutor, Old Vic, 1988; Ivanov and Much Ado About Nothing, Strand, 1989; George Bernard Shaw in The Best of Friends, 1990 and 1991; The Major General in The Pirates of Penzance, London Palladium, 1990; It Runs in the Family, Playhouse, 1993; Harvey, Shaftesbury, 1995; Hobson in Hobson's Choice, Lyric, 1995-96; Cash on Delivery, Whitehall, 1996-97; The Jermyn Street Revue, J S Theatre, 2000; Television: Many dramas and situation comedies include: It's a Square World; The World of Beachcomber; HMS Paradise; Scott on....; The Taming of the Shrew; Captain Peacock in Are You Being Served?, 1972-84; Truly in Last of the Summer Wine, 1997-; Films include: The Bed-Sitting Room; A Funny Thing Happened on the Way to the Forum; A Flea in her Ear; Great Expectations; The Old Curiosity Shop; Gosford Park; Back in Business; Radio includes: Propaganda broadcasts, 1942-43; The Embassy Lark; The Big Business Lark; Mind Your Own Business. Membership: The Garrick Club. Address: c/o David Daly Associates, 586A King's Road, London SW6 2DX, England.

**THORNTON Leslie Tillotson,** b. 26 May 1925, Skipton, North Yorkshire, England. Sculptor; Principal Art Lecturer (Retired). m. Constance Helen Billows, 1 son, 1 daughter. Education: Keighley Art School, 1940-42; Conscripted for Mines, 1943-45; National Diploma of Art and Design, Leeds College of Art, 1945-48; Sculpture School, Royal College of Art, 1948-51; Associate of RCA. Appointments: Part-time Lecturer in London Art Colleges: Bromley, Hammersmith and Central School, 1951-65; Senior Lecturer in Charge of Sculpture, University of Sunderland, 1965-70; Principal Lecturer in Charge of Sculpture, University of Stafford, 1970-89; Exhibitions include: Arts Council Contemporary British Sculpture, 1957/58; 10 Young British Sculptors, IV Sao Paulo Biennale, Brazil, 1957; CAS Religious Theme Exhibition, Tate Gallery, 1958; 10 Young British Sculptors, British Council Touring Exhibition, Rio de Janeiro, Montevideo, Santiago, Lima, Caracas, 1958; 5th and 10th International Biennale Middleheim Park, Antwerp, 1959, 1969; British Artists Craftsmen Exhibition touring America, 1960; English Painters and Sculptors, Zurich, 1963; Art Sacre, Museum of Modern Art, Paris, 1965; Northern Sculptors Exhibition, Newcastle, 1967; One man Exhibitions, Gimpel Fils Gallery, London, 1957, 1960, 1969; Sion House, London, 1970; Royal Academy, London, 1974/76, 1978/79; Solihull Annual Exhibition, 1979; Retrospective Exhibition, Holden Gallery, Manchester, 1981; Royal Academy, 1987; 100 Years of Sculpture, Moore Institute, Leeds, 2004; Commissions: Daily Mirror Building, London, 1961; Crucifix, St Louis Priory, Missouri, 1965; Crucifix, St Ignatious College, Enfield, 1968; Works in collections including: Museum of Modern Art, New York; Peggy Guggenheim Collection, Venice; Arts Council of Great Britain; Victoria and Albert Museum; Leeds City Art Gallery; National Gallery of Scotland; Private collections in UK North and South America, Sweden and Belgium. Publications: Works reviewed in books and journals including: 20th Century Steel Sculptures US, 2002; Handbook of 20th Century British Sculpture, 2004. Honours: Panel Member, Council for National Academic Awards; Fellow, Royal Society of Arts; Associate, Royal Society of British Sculptors. Address: Stable Cottage, 45 Chatsworth Place, Harrogate HG1 5HR, England.

**THORPE David Richard,** b. 12 March 1943, Huddersfield, England. Political Biographer. Education: BA, Honours, 1965, MA, 1969, Selwyn College, Cambridge. Appointment: Appointed Official Biographer of Lord Home of the Hirsel, 1990; New Authorised Biographer of Sir Anthony Eden, 1996. Publications: The Uncrowned Prime Ministers: A Study of Sir Austen Chamberlain, Lord Curzon and Lord Butler, 1980; Selwyn Lloyd, 1989; Alec Douglas-Home, 1996; Eden: The Life and Times of Anthony Eden, 1st Earl of Avon 1897 1977, 2003. Contributions to: The Blackwell Biographical Dictionary of British Political Life in the 20th Century, 1990; Telling Lives: From WB Yeats to Bruce Chatwin (edited by Alistair Horne), 2000; The Oxford Dictionary of National Biography, 2004. Memberships: Johnson Club; Oxford and Cambridge University Club; Archive Fellow, Churchill College, Cambridge, 1986; St Antony's College, Oxford, Alistair Horne Fellow, 1997-98; Brasenose College, Oxford, Senior Member, 1998-. Address: Brasenose College, Oxford OX1 4AJ, England.

**THRING Meredith Wooldridge,** b. 17 December 1915, Melbourne, Australia. Retired Professor. m. Margaret Hooley, 2 sons, 1 daughter. Education: BA 1st Class (Hons) Part II Physics, Trinity College Cambridge, 1937; ScD, Cambridge University. Appointments: Senior Scientific Officer, British Coal Utilisation Research Association, 1937-46; Head of Physics Department, British Iron and Steel Research Association, 1946-53; Professor of Fuel Technology and Chemical Engineering, Sheffield University, 1953-64; Professor of Mechanical Engineering, Queen Mary College, London University, 1964-81. Publications: Books: The Science of Flames and Furnaces, 2nd edition, 1960; Pilot Plants, Models and Scale Up Methods in Chemical Engineering, 1957; Man Machines and Tomorrow, 1973; How to Invent (with E R Laithwaite), 1975; The Seven Riddles of the Universe, 2005. Memberships: Athenaeum; Founder Fellow, Royal Academy of Engineering; FIMechE; SFInstE. Address: Bell Farm, Brundish, Suffolk IP13 8BL, England.

**THRUSH Brian Arthur,** b. 23 July 1928, Hendon, England. Retired University Professor. m. Rosemary Catherine Terry, 1 son, 1 daughter. Education: BA, MA, PhD, ScD, Emmanuel College, Cambridge. Appointments: Lecturer, Assistant Director of Research, Demonstrator in Physical Chemistry, 1953-69, Reader in Physical Chemistry, 1969-78, Professor of Physical Chemistry, 1978-95, Professor Emeritus, 1995-, University of Cambridge; Fellow, 1960, Vice Master, 1986-90, Emmanuel College, Cambridge; Visiting Professor of Chinese Academy of Sciences, 1980-90. Publications: Many original papers in learned scientific journals. Honours: Tilden Lecturer, Chemical Society , 1965; Michael Polanyi Medallist, Royal Society of Chemistry, 1986; Rank Prize for Opto-Electronics, 1992. Memberships: Fellow Royal Society, 1976, Council Member, 1990-92; Fellow, Royal Society of Chemistry, 1977; Lawes Trust Committee, 1979-89; National Environment Research Council, 1985-90; Member, Academia Europaea, 1990, Council Member, 1992-98. Address: Brook Cottage, Pemberton Terrace, Cambridge, CB2 1JA, England.

**THUBRON Colin Gerald Dryden,** b. 14 June 1939, London, England. Writer. Publications: Mirror to Damascus, 1967; The Hills of Adonis: A Quest in Lebanon, 1968; Jerusalem, 1969; Journey Into Cyprus, 1975; The God in the Mountain (novel), 1977; Emperor (novel), 1978; The Venetians, 1980; The Ancient Mariners, 1981; The Royal Opera House Covent Garden, 1982; Among the Russians, 1983; A Cruel Madness, 1984; Behind the Wall: A Journey Through China, 1987; Falling, 1989; Turning Back the Sun, 1991; The Lost Heart of Asia, 1994; Distance (novel), 1996; In Siberia, 1999; To the Last City (novel), 2002. Contributions to: Times; Times Literary Supplement; Independent; Sunday Times; Sunday Telegraph; New York Times; Granta. Honours: Fellow, Royal Society of Literature, 1969; Silver Pen Award, 1985; Thomas Cook Award, 1988; Hawthornden Prize, 1989; RSGS Mungo Park Medal, 2000; RSAA Lawrence of Arabia Memorial Medal, 2001; Vice-President, Royal Society of Literature, 2003. Membership: PEN. Address: Garden Cottage, 27 St Ann's Villas, London W11 4RT, England.

**THWAITE Ann,** b. 4 October 1932, London, England. Writer. m. Anthony Thwaite, 4 August 1955, 4 daughters. Education: MA, Dlitt, Oxford University (St Hilda's College). Appointments: Visiting Professor, Tokyo Women's University; Contributing Editor, Editorial Board, Cricket Magazine (US). Publications: Waiting for the Party: A Life of Frances Hodgson Burnett; Edmund Gosse: A Literary Landscape; A A Milne: His Life; Emily Tennyson: The Poet's Wife; Glimpses of the Wonderful, The Life of Philip Henry Gosse. Honours: Duff Cooper Prize, 1985; Whitbread Biography Award, 1990. Memberships: Fellow, Royal Society of Literature; Society of Authors; PEN. Address The Mill House, Low Tharston, Norwich NR15 2YN, England.

**THWAITE Anthony Simon,** b. 23 June 1930, Chester, Cheshire, England. Poet; Critic; Writer; Editor. m. Ann Barbara Harrop, 4 August 1955, 4 daughters. Education: BA, 1955, MA, 1959, Christ Church, Oxford. Appointments: Visiting Lecturer in English, 1955-57, Japan Foundation Fellow, 1985-86, University of Tokyo; Producer, BBC, 1957-62; Literary Editor, The Listener, 1962-65, New Statesman, 1968-72; Assistant Professor of English, University of Libya, 1965-67; Henfield Writing Fellow, University of East Anglia, 1972; Co-Editor, Encounter, 1973-85; Visiting Professor, Kuwait University, 1974, Chairman of the Judges, Booker Prize, 1986; Director, 1986-92, Editorial Consultant, 1992-95, André Deutsch, Ltd; Poet-in-Residence, Vanderbilt University, 1992. Publications: Poetry: Home Truths, 1957; The Owl in the Tree, 1963; The Stones of Emptiness, 1967; Inscriptions, 1973; New Confessions, 1974; A Portion for Foxes, 1977; Victorian Voices, 1980; Poems 1953-1983, 1984, enlarged edition as Poems 1953-1988, 1989; Letter from Tokyo, 1987; The Dust of the World, 1994; Selected Poems, 1956-1996, 1997; A Different Country, 2000. Other: Contemporary English Poetry, 1959; Japan (with Roloff Beny), 1968; The Deserts of Hesperides, 1969; Poetry Today, 1973, 3rd edition, revised and expanded, 1996; In Italy (with Roloff Beny and Peter Porter), 1974; Twentieth Century English Poetry, 1978; Odyssey: Mirror of the Mediterranean (with Roloff Beny), 1981; Six Centuries of Verse, 1984. Editor: The Penguin Book of Japanese Verse (with Geoffrey Bownas), 1964 revised and expanded, 1998; The English Poets (with Peter Porter), 1974; New Poetry 4 (with Fleur Adcock), 1978; Larkin at Sixty, 1982; Poetry 1945 to 1980 (with John Mole), 1983; Collected Poems of Philip Larkin, 1988; Selected Letters of Philip Larkin, 1992; Further requirements: Philip Larkin, 2001; A Move in the Weather, 2003. Honours: Richard Hillary Memorial Prize, 1968; Fellow, Royal Society of Literature, 1978; Cholmondeley Prize, 1983; Officer of the Order of the British Empire, 1990. Address: The Mill House, Low Tharston, Norfolk NR15 2YN, England.

**TIEN Hwei-Fang,** b. 24 June 1952, Taipei, Taiwan. Professor. m. Hsian-Fu Hung, 1 son, 1 daughter. Education: MD, PhD, Institute of Clinical Medicine, Medical College, National Taiwan University. Appointments: Professor, Visiting Staff, Department of Medicine, Medical College, National Taiwan University Hospital. Publications: Marrow matrix matelloproteinases (MMPS) and tissue inhibitors of MMP in acute leukaemia, 2002; SOCS-1 Methylation in patients with newly diagnosed acute myeloid leukaemia, Gene Chromosome Cancer, 2003. Honours: Award for Outstanding Research, National Science Council, 1992, 1998; Award for Outstanding Medical Research in Oncology, Chinese Oncology Society, 1995. Memberships: American Society of Hematology; International Society of Hematology; Hematology Society of Taiwan; Chinese Oncology Society; Chinese Society of Internal Medicine. Address: National Taiwan University Hospital 7, Chung Shan S Road, Taipei 1000, Taiwan.

**TIJARDOVIĆ Ivica,** b. 1 September 1960, Šibenik, Croatia. Shipmaster. Divorced, 1 daughter. Education: Officer Certificate, Slovenia, 1980; Bachelor of Science, Navigation, Croatia, 1983; Master Mariner Certificate, Croatia, 1986; Master of Science, Technology of Transport, Croatia, 1989; Instructor for ARPA and Bridge Team Training, Norway, 1990; PhD, Navigation, Naval Academy, Gdynia, Poland, 1994. Appointments: Sea experience: Cadet, 1979; Officer, 1981, Captain, 1990; Since 1998 has been sailing again as Captain; Supervisor of Commercial and Technical Management for Vessels with the Shipbuilding Company of Split, Croatia, 1986-87; Assistant of Navigation, 1987, Lecturer in Navigation, 1990-98, Assistant Professor of Navigation, Maritime Faculty, Split, Croatia; Assistant Professor of Navigation, 2000; Specialist for GPS and AIS receiver application in practice; Expert in Ship Stability, visited more than 150 vessels and met more than 300 captains and officers. Publications: Numerous articles in Brown's Nautical Almanac (www.skipper.co.uk), 3 articles in Journal of Navigation (www.rin.org.uk), The Simplest and Fastest Star Finder; Articles on the commercial and technical management of ships; Numerous books for students in Croatia; Draft Survey Book for International Market (www.iims.org.uk). Honours: One of 3 captains nominated for Shipmaster of the Year 2004, Lloyds List and Institute of Navigation, UK; According to USA Notice to Mariners, the Observer No 1 with the most acknowledged reports for Safety of Navigation, 1998-2003; Received a recognition for his contributions to navigation from the hands of HRH The Duke of Edinburgh KG KT, 2004. Memberships: Fellow, Royal Institute of Navigation; Nautical Institute, UK; Singer, 1st Tenor in Split, Croatia. Address: Nazorov Prilaz 37, 21000 Split, Croatia. E-mail: ivica.tijardovic@st.t-com.hr

**TILAK Kolluru Sambasiva,** b. 12 February 1951. Professor of Zoology. Education: BSc, 1971, MSc, 1974, PhD, 1980, Andhra University. Appointments: Lecturer, 1977-92, Associate Professor, 1992-2000, Professor, 2000-, Nagarjuna University; Head, Department of Zoology, 2000-02, Board of Studies Chairman (PG) Zoology, 2003-05, Co-ordinator, MSc Zoology Course, Distance Education, 2003-05, Acharya Nagarjuna University; Member, External PG Board of Studies, Kakatiya University, Warangal, 2003-05; Subject Committee Expert Member, Board of Intermediate Education, AP Government, Hyderabad, 2003-05. Publications: 43 papers published; Editor, 4 books. Honours: UGC Junior Research Fellowship, AUPG Centre, Guntur, 4 years. Memberships: Fellow, Academy of Environmental Biology; Associated Member in Chemistry and Conservation of Environment; Academic Council Member,

Institute of Applied Sciences, Technology and Management, Rushikesh. Address: Department of Zoology, Nagarjuna University, Nagarjunanagar 522 510, AP, India. E-mail: kstilak@yahoo.com

**TILLION Diana.** Artist. Education: Art-related and composition courses at various universities and colleges. Appointments: Artist; Instructor, art classes, 1988-98; Commissions include two 57' murals, NBA Bank Building, Homer, Alaska, 1997. Publications: Numerous articles in professional journals; Article, Octopus Ink Painting, 1966; Novel, Guardians of the Great North Pacific Casino, 2000. Memberships: Former vice chairman, Alaska State Council on the Arts; Alaska Poetry Society; National League of American Pen Women. Address: Box 6409, Halibut Cove, AK 99603, USA.

**TINDLE David,** b. 29 April 1932, Huddersfield, Yorkshire, England. Education: Coventry School of Art. Career: Artist: Designed and painted set for Iolanta (Tchaikovsky), Aldeburgh Festival, 1988; Visiting Tutor, 1973-83, Fellow, 1981, Honorary Fellow, 1984, Royal College of Art; Ruskin Master of Drawing, St Edmund Hall, Oxford, 1985-87; Now lives and works in Italy; Numerous exhibitions in London and the provinces, 1952-, include: First one-man exhibition, London, 1953, regular one-man shows, Piccadilly Gallery, 1954-83, Hamburg Gallerie XX, 1974-85, Los Angeles and San Francisco, 1964, Bologna and Milan, 1968, One-man show, Fischer Fine Art, 1985, 1989, 1992, Redfern Gallery, London, 1994, 1996, 1998-99, 2000, 2001, 2003, 2005, St Edmund Hall, Oxford, 1994, The Shire Hall Gallery, Stafford, 1994; Numerous group exhibitions and international biennales in Europe; Works in many public and private collections including the Tate Gallery, National Portrait Gallery. Honours: Elected Associate of the Royal Academy (ARA), 1973; Elected Full Royal Academician (RA), 1979; Honorary Fellow, St Edmund Hall, Oxford, 1988-; Honorary Member, Birmingham Society of Artists; Honorary MA, St Edmund Hall, Oxford, 1985; RA Johnson Wax Award, 1983. Address: Via C Barsotti 194, S. Maria del Giudice, 55058 Lucca, Italy.

**TING Joseph Y S,** b. 15 July 1969. Physician. Education: Bachelor of Medical Science, with Distinction, Bachelor of Medicine and Bachelor of Surgery, University of Queensland, Brisbane, Australia; Fellowship of the Australasian College for Emergency Medicine. Appointments: Clinical Associate Lecturer, University of Queensland Medical School, Faculty of Health Sciences, Brisbane, 1997-2001; Ship's Physician, MV Grigory Mikheev, Falklands, Sub-Antarctic Islands and Antarctic Peninsula, 2002; Ship's Physician, Clipper Odyssey Yale Stanford Alumni Cruise, South Island, New Zealand, 2002; Currently Staff Specialist Emergency Physician, Mater Public Adult and Children's Hospitals, South Brisbane; Clinical Senior Lecturer, Division of Anaesthesiology and Critical Care, School of Medicine, University of Queensland. Publications: Articles in medical journals as author and co-author: Ciguatera poisoning: example of a public health challenge, 1998; Hyperosmolar diabetic non-ketotic coma, hyperkalaemia and an unusual near death experience, 2001; Rhabdomyolysis and psychogenic polydipdia, 2001; Ciguatera poisoning: a global issue with common management problems, 2001; Blunt traumatic aortic injury: A review of initial diagnostic modalities and a proposed diagnostic algorithm, 2003; 4 papers presented at conferences. Honours: Mayne Undergraduate Research Scholarship, University of Queensland, 1991; University of Queensland and Queensland Sudden Infant Death Research Foundation Research Grants, 1991. Memberships: President, Trainee's Subcommittee, Australian Society for Emergency Medicine; Scenario Project Core Team, Australian Scenario Project; Community Advisory Council, Special Broadcasting Services (Australia), 2002-. Address: 54 Bentley St, Balmoral 4171, Brisbane, Queensland, Australia. E-mail: jysting@mailbox.uq.edu.au

**TIRIMO Martino,** b. 19 December 1942, Larnaca, Cyprus. Concert Pianist; Conductor. m. Mione J Teakle, 1973, 1 son, 1 daughter. Education: Royal Academy of Music, London; Vienna State Academy. Debut: Recital, Cyprus, 1949. Career: Conducted La Traviata 7 times at Italian Opera Festival, Cyprus, 1955; London debut, 1965; Concerto performances with most major orchestras, and recitals, TV and radio appearances in Britain, Europe, USA, Canada, South Africa and the Far East from 1965; Gave public premiére of complete Schubert Sonatas, London, 1975, 1985; Public premiére of Beethoven concertos directing from the keyboard, Dresden and London, 1985, 1986; Gave several premiéres of Tippett Piano concerto since 1986; Four series of performances of complete Beethoven piano sonatas, 2000; Two series devoted to the major piano works of Robert and Clara Schumann, 2001; Six-concert series devoted to the major piano works of Chopin, 2002; Founded Rosamunde Trio 2002; Professor. Trinity College of Music, 2003-; Performed at special Athens Festival during Olympic period with Vienna Philharmonic in 2004. Compositions include: film score for the Odyssey in 8 episodes for Channel 4 TV, 1998. Recordings: Brahms Piano Concertos; Chopin Concertos; Tippett Piano Concerto (with composer conducting); Rachmaninov Concertos; Complete Debussy piano works; Complete Janacek piano works; Complete Schubert Piano Sonatas; Various other solo recordings with mixed repertoire. Publications: Schubert: The Complete Piano Sonatas, 3 volumes, edited for Wiener Unitext Edition (with own completions to the unfinished movements), 1997-99. Honours: Gold Medal, Associated Board of the Royal Schools of Music; Liszt Scholarship, Royal Academy of Music; 11 other Prizes at Royal Academy of Music including Macfarren Medal; Boise Foundation Scholarship, 1965; Gulbenkian Foundation Scholarship, 1967-69; Joint Winner, Munich International Competition, 1971; Winner, Geneva International Competition, 1972; ARAM, 1968; FRAM, 1979; Silver Disc, 1988; Gold Disc, 1994; Ran with the Olympic Torch, 2004. Address: 1 Romeyn Road, London SW16 2NU, England. E-mail: martino@tirimo.fslife.co.uk

**TLÁSKAL Tomáš,** b. 2 April 1950, Prague, Czech Republic. Paediatric Cardiac Surgeon. m. Květa Laurinová, 1 daughter. Education: MD, Charles University, Prague, 1974; General Surgery Diploma, 1978, Cardiac Surgery Diploma, 1984, Institute for Postgraduate Medical Education, Prague; CSc, PhD, Medicine, 1991, Associated Professor of Surgery Diploma, 1997, Charles University, Prague; Fellow, European Board of Thoracic and Cardiovascular Surgery Diploma, 1998. Appointments: Senior House Officer, Hospital Novy Bydzov, 1974-76; Senior House Officer, 1976-1978, Senior Registrar, 1979-84, Staff Cardiac Surgeon, 1985-90, Consultant Paediatric Cardiac Surgeon and Deputy Chief, 1991-2004, Chief of Division of Cardiac Surgery, 2004-, Kardiocentrum, University Hospital Motol, Prague; Consultant Paediatric Cardiac Surgeon, Cardiocentro, Hospital W Soller, Habana, Cuba, 1987-88; Teacher, 2nd School of Medicine, Charles University, 1992-; Associate Professor of Surgery, Charles University, Prague, 1997-; Associate Professor of Surgery, Institute of Postgraduate Education in Medicine, 1999-; Consultant, Institute for Mother and Child Care, 1998-. Publications: Over 100 articles published in professional journals. Memberships: Association for European Paediatric Cardiology; European Association for Cardio-Thoracic Surgery; Czech Medical Society; Czech Society of Cardiology; Czech Society of Cardiovascular Surgery; Czech Paediatric Society; Czech Society of Paediatric Surgery; Czech Society of Surgery; Movement for Life (Czech

Republic); International Society of Cardio-Thoracic Surgeons; CTS Net. Address: Nad Palatou 3, 150 00 Prague 5, Czech Republic. E-mail: tomas.tlaskal@lfmotol.cuni.cz Website: www.ctsnet.org/home/ttlaskal

**TOBIAS Edward Spencer,** b. 13 December 1965, Paisley, Scotland. Clinician; Scientist. m. Ruth Tobias. Education: BSc (1st Class Honours), Molecular Biology, 1987; MBChB with Commendation, 1990; PhD, Biochemistry and Molecular Biology, 1997, University of Glasgow; MRCP UK (Royal College of Physicians UK), 1993; CCST in Medical Genetics, 2001; FRCP, Royal College of Physicians and Surgeons, Glasgow, 2004. Appointments include: Senior House Officer, Glasgow Western/Gartnavel Hospitals General Medical Rotation, 1991-93; MRC Training Fellow, Division of Biochemistry and Molecular Biology, University of Glasgow, 1993-96; Clinical Research Scientist, Cancer Genetics Laboratory, Beatson Institute for Cancer Research, 1996-97; Specialist Registrar in Medical Genetics, Duncan Guthrie Institute of Medical Genetics, Yorkhill Hospital, Glasgow, 1997-2001; Currently: GlaxoWellcome Senior Clinical Research Fellow, University of Glasgow; Honorary Consultant in Medical Genetics, Yorkhill Hospital, Glasgow; Discovered the TES gene on human chromosome 7. Publications: Articles in medical journals as first author and co-author include most recently: The TES gene at 7q31.1 is methylated in tumours and encodes a novel growth-suppressing LIM domain protein, 2001; Cataplexy in the Prader-Willi syndrome, 2002; Identification and functional assessment of novel and known insulin receptor mutations in five patients with syndromes of severe insulin resistance, 2003; Selected book chapter: The Molecular Biology of Cancer, 2005, in Principles and Practice of Medical Genetics, 5th Edition. Honours: MRC Training Fellowship, 1993; Glaxo Wellcome Clinical Research Fellowship, 2001. Memberships: Scottish Cancer Foundation Research Committee; British Society for Human Genetics; Cancer Genetics Group (UK); British Association for Cancer Research; European Association for Cancer Research; Glasgow Southern Medical Society; Royal Medico-Chirurgical Society of Glasgow; British Medical Association. Address: Section of Medical Genetics, Division of Developmental Medicine, University of Glasgow, Yorkhill Hospital, Glasgow G3 8SJ, Scotland. E-mail: gbcv55@udcf.gla.ac.uk

**TOBIAS Phillip Vallentine,** b. 14 October 1925, Durban, Natal, South Africa. Retired University Professor. Education: BSc, 1946, BSc Hons, 1947, MBBCh, 1950, PhD, 1953, DSc, 1967, University of Witwatersrand, Johannesburg. Appointments: Lecturer, 1951-52, Senior Lecturer, 1953-58, Professor, 1959-93, Head of Department, 1959-90, Dean of Faculty of Medicine, 1980-82, Member of Council, 1971-74, 1975-84, Professor Emeritus, 1994-; Honorary Professorial Research Fellow, 1994-, School of Anatomical Sciences, University of Witwatersrand; Past Chairman, Kalahari Research Committee; Past Director, Palaeo-Anthropology Research Unit; Past Director, Sterkfontein Research Unit; Past President, International Association of Human Biologists; Former President, Royal Society of South Africa; Founder and Sometime President, Institute for the Study of Mankind in Africa, Anatomical Society of Southern Africa, South African Society for Quaternary Research; Former President, South African Science Writers Association. Publications: Over 1100 including 40 books, 90 chapters in books; Notable works Chromosomes, sex cells and evolution in a mammal, 1956; Australopithecus boisei, 1967; The Bushmen, San Hunters and Herders of the Kalahari, 1978; Hominid Evolution Past Present and Future, 1985; The Brain in Hominid Evolution, 1971; Man's Anatomy, 1963-88; The Meaning of Race, 1961-72; Homo habilis, 1991; Humanity from African Naissance to Coming Millennia, 2001. Honours:

Rivers Memorial Medal, 1978; Balzan Prize, 1987; LSB Leakey Prize, 1991; Carmel Award of Merit, 1992; Order of Meritorious Service of South Africa, 1992; Fellow of the Royal Society London, 1996; Charles Darwin Lifetime Achievement Award, 1997; Commander of the National Order of Merit of France, 1998; Order of the Southern Cross of South Africa, 1999; Hrdlicka Medal, 1999; Commander of the Order of Merit of Italy, 2000; UNESCO Medal, 2001; ISMS Medal, 2001; Honorary Cross for Science and Arts, First Class, Austrian Federal Government, 2002. Memberships: Academy of Science of South Africa; Royal Society, London; Royal Society of South Africa; South African Medical Association; South African Archaeological Society; American Association of Physical Anthropologists; National Academy of Sciences, USA; American Philosophical Society; American Academy of Arts and Sciences; American Anthropological Association; Royal Anthropological Institute of Great Britain and Ireland; Royal College of Physicians, London; Linnean Society, London; South African Institute of Race Relations; Anatomical Society of Southern Africa; Anatomical Societies (hon) of USA, Great Britain and Ireland, Canada, Israel. Address: School of Anatomical Sciences, University of the Witwatersrand Medical School, 7 York Road, Parktown, Johannesburg 2193, South Africa. E-mail: tobiaspv@anatomy.wits.ac.za

**TOMALIN Claire,** b. 20 June 1933, London, England. Author. m. (1) Nicholas Osborne Tomalin, deceased 1973, 2 sons (1 deceased), 3 daughters (1 deceased), (2) Michael Frayn, 1993. Education: MA, Newnham College, Cambridge, 1954. Appointment: Literary Editor, New Statesman, 1974-77; Literary Editor, The Sunday Times, London, 1979-86. Publications: The Life and Death of Mary Wollstonecroft, 1974; Shelley and His World, 1980; Parents and Children, 1981; Katherine Mansfield: A Secret Life, 1987; The Invisible Woman: The Story of Nelly Teran and Charles Dickens, 1990; The Winter Wife, 1991; Mrs Jordan's Professions, 1994; Jane Austin: A Life, 1997; Maurice by Mary Shelley, 1998; Several Strangers: writing from three decades, 1999; Samuel Pepys: The Unequalled Self, 2002; Exhibitions: Mrs Jordan, English Heritage Kenwood, 1995; Hyenas in Petticoats: Mary Wollstonecraft and Mary Shelley, Wordsworth Trust and National Portrait Gallery, 1997-98; Play: The Winter Wife, 1991. Honours: Whitbread First Book Prize, 1974; James Tait Black Memorial Prize, 1990; Hawthornden Prize, 1991; NCR Prize, 1991; Trustee, National Portrait Gallery, 1992-; Theatre Literary Award, New York 1995; Whitbread Awards for Book of the Year and Best Biography. Membership: PEN, Vice-president, 1998; Member, London Library Committee, 1997-2000; Advisory Committee for the Arts, Humanities and Social Sciences, British Library, 1997-; Council, Royal Society of Literature, 1997-2000. Address: 57 Gloucester Crescent, London NW1 7EG, England. E-mail: clairetomalin@dial.pipex.com

**TOMASELLI Keyan Gray,** b. 31 August 1948, Johannesburg, South Africa. Director; Professor. m. Ruth Teer-Tomaselli, 1 son, 1 daughter. Education: BA, honours; MA, Dramatic Art; PhD. Appointments include: Demonstrator in Geography, 1972; Instructor, Sussex Study and Speed Reading Course, Educational Technology Unit, 1973; Tutor, School of Dramatic Art, 1978-79, Senior Tutor, 1981, University of Witwatersrand; Lecturer, Department of Journalism and Media Studies, Rhodes University, 1981-84; Professor, Director, Cultural and Media Studies, University of Natal, Durban, 1985-. Publications include: Action Research, Participatory Communication: Why Governments Don't Listen, 1997; Cultural Studies and Theoretical Impoverishment, 1998; Die Volgen der Apartheid und ihre Uberwindung durch Zeichenanaluse Semiotik Sudafrika, 1998; Cultural Studies in Africa, 1998. Honours:

Nominated, International Journalism Scholarship Award, Rotary South Africa, 1984; Honorary Member, South Africa Film and Television Technicians' Association, 1988; Africa Network's (Chicago) KW ANZAA Award, 1988; Fellow, University of Natal, 1995. Memberships include: International Visual Sociology Association; International Association for Media and Communication Research. Address: University of Kwazulu-Natal, King George V Avenue, Durban 4041, South Africa.

**TOMITA Ken-ichi,** b. 5 June 1928, Nagasaki, Japan. Professor Emeritus. m. Namie Tokuhisa, 1 son, 1 daughter. Education: BSc, Hiroshima University, 1953; DSc, Osaka University, 1959. Appointments: Research Associate, Massachusetts Institute of Technology, 1959-64; Research Associate, Institute of Protein Research, 1964-65, Professor, Faculty of Pharmaceutical Science, 1965-92, Osaka University. Publications include: Nucleic Acid Structure. Honour: Scientific Award, Pharmaceutical Society of Japan, 1989. Memberships: Crystallographic Society of Japan; Pharmaceutical Society of Japan. Address: 1-82 Hagiwaradai Higashi, Kawanishi 666-0005, Japan.

**TOMLINSON, Hon Mr Justice, Hon Sir Stephen Miles,** b. 29 March 1952, Wolverhampton, England. Justice of the High Court. m. Joanna Greig, 1 son, 1 daughter. Education: Scholar, Worcester College, Oxford; Eldon Law Scholar, MA; Called to the Bar, Inner Temple, 1974. Appointments: Barrister in practice, 1975-2000; QC, 1988; A Recorder of the Crown Court, 1995-2000; Judge of the High Court of Justice, 2000. Honour: Knighted, 2000. Address: Royal Courts of Justice, Strand, London WC1A 2LL, England.

**TOMOVA Malina,** b. 21 January 1950, Plovdiv, Bulgaria. Poet; Script Writer. m. Ivan Tzanev, 3 daughters. Education: Russian Language and Literature, Slavic Languages Department, Sofia University "St Clement Ohridsky", 1976. Appointments: Editor, Narodna Mladezh Newspaper, 1976-78; Free-lance Translator, 1978-80; Editor, Yantra Literary Magazine, 1980-89; Editor, Literary Newspaper, 1989-2003; Editor-in-Chief, Romano Ilo Newspaper, 1994-99; Director and Editor, Stigmati Publishing House, 1996-2003. Publications: Books: Poetry: Dusha, 1978; Ezheliubov, 1987; Stigmati, 1994; Translations: 14 books by Russian authors; Films: Burn, burn, little flame, 1994; Vasilitsa (documentary), 1996; The Story of a Hat, 2003. Honours: The Critics' Award at the Varna Film Festival "Golden Rose" for humanitarian ideas for film Burn, burn, little flame, 1994; Award for Creative Works, Ministry of Culture of Bulgaria, 2002. Memberships: Union of Bulgarian Writers, 1986-95; Association of Bulgarian Writers, 1995-; Association of Bulgarian Film Makers, 1996-. Address: 41 Skobelev Blvd, Sofia 1606, Bulgaria. E-mail: stigmati@abv.bg

**TONDL Aleš,** b. 31 July 1925, Znojmo, Czechoslovakia. Retired Scientist. m. Henrieta Tondl, 1 son. Education: MSc, 1950, PhD, 1950, Faculty of Mechanical Engineering, Technical University, Brno; Candidate of Sciences, 1956, Doctor of Sciences, 1967, Faculty of Engineering, Technical University, Prague. Appointments: Faculty of Mechanical Engineering, Technical University, Brno, 1949-50; National Research Institute for Machine Design, Prague, 1950-55; Slovak Academy of Sciences, Bratislava, 1956; National Research Institute for Machine Design, Prague, 1957-90. Publications: Author or co-author of more than 200 articles, 17 mongographs and 11 books which include most importantly: Some Problems of Rotor Dynamics, 1965, Russian and Japanese translation, 1971; Non-linear Vibrations (with G. Schmidt), 1991; Quenching of Self-Excited Vibrations, 1991. Honours: State Prize for Rotordynamics, 1963; Honorary Professor, Technical University, Vienna, 1994; Honorary Member, IFToMM,

1995; Dr honoris causa, Technical University, Brno, 1999. Memberships: Gesellschaft für angewandte Mathematik und Mechanik; Society for Mechanics, Czech Academy of Sciences. Address: Zborovská 41, CZ-150 00 Prague 5, Czech Republic.

**TONIOLO Antonio Quirino,** b. 13 March 1948, Siena, Italy. Physician; Medical Educator. m. Amelia Giuditta Tremolanti, 2 sons. Education: MD, University of Pisa, 1972; Specialist in Medical Microbiology, 1976; School of Military Medicine, Florence, 1976; Visiting Fellow, Experimental Medicine Laboratory, National Institutes of Health, Bethesda, Maryland, USA, 1978-81; Department of Microbiology, University of Galveston, Texas, 1984; Visiting Scientist, Department of Molecular Immunology, University of Tokyo, Japan, 1997. Appointments: Lieutenant, Italian Army, 1976-77; Professor, Medical Microbiology, Italian universities of Sassari (1985-89), Pisa (1990-91), Pavia (1991-98), and Insubria (1998-); Consultant Virologist, Ospedale Santa Chiara, Pisa, 1989-91; Consultant Microbiologist, Institute for Pharmacokinetic Analysis, Ligornetto, Switzerland, 2000-; Director, Department of Clinical and Biological Sciences, University of Insubria, 2001-; Director, Clinical Pathology Department, Ospedale di Circolo e Fondazione Macchi, Varese, 2001-. Publications: Over 200 scientific publications. Honours: Director, Socrates-Erasmus Program, European Community, 1988-90; President, Rotary Club Varese-Verbano, 1999-2000; Scientific Director, Giornale Italiano di Microbiologia Medica, 2001-; President, Italian Society of Medical, Dental and Clinical Microbiology, 2001-05. Memberships: Life Member, Italian Society of Microbiology; Board of Directors, Italian Society of Laboratory Medicine; Corresponding Member, American Society of Microbiology; Corresponding Member, International AIDS Society; Corresponding Member, NIH Alumni Association; Swiss Society for Microbiology; Senior Member, Rotary Club Varese-Verbano. Address: Laboratory of Medical Microbiology, University of Insubria and Ospedale di Circolo, Viale Borri 57, 21100 Varese, Italy. E-mail: antonio.toniolo@uninsubria.it

**TOOTHMAN Carl Delano,** b. 19 July 1940, Panama, Republic of Panama. Photo Artist. 1 son. Education: Santa Monica City College, 1961-64. Appointments: Freelance Artist. Publication: Internet homepage, www.geocities.com/toothowl/, 1997-. Honours: Festival Award, Madonna Festival, Los Angeles, California, 1963; Rochester Festival, Rochester, New York, 1964; Culture Prize, Sodertalje, Sweden, 1974. Memberships: Fellow, North American Academy of Arts and Sciences. Address: A-Ringen 103 9tr, 302 55 Halmstad, Sweden. E-mail: carl@halmstad.net Website: www.geocities.com/toothowl/

**TOOVEY Stephen,** b. 29 November 1953, London, England. Physician. m. Linda, 1 daughter. Education: MB BCh, University of the Witwatersrand, 1978; Certified in Clinical Tropical Medicine and Travellers' Health, American Association of Tropical Medicine and Hygiene. Appointments: Clinical Consultant, Tropix Healthcare Ltd; Tutor, Royal Free Medical School, London; Managing Director, SAA-Netcare Travel Clinics; Managing Director, British Airways Travel Clinics, South Africa. Publications: 47 articles in professional journals. Honours: Kurt Gilles Memorial Award in Psychiatry. Memberships: Fellow, Australasian College of Tropical Medicine; Fellow, Faculty of Travel Medicine; American Society of Tropical Medicine and Hygiene; International Society of Travel Medicine. Address: Burggartenstrasse 32, Bottmingen, CH-4103, Switzerland.

**TOPORKOV Victor Vasilievich,** b. 24 September 1956, Lepel, Vitebsk, Belarus. Computer Scientist. m. Anna S Anikushina. Education: Graduate, 1979, PhD, 1985, Doctor of

Technical Sciences, 2000, Moscow Power Engineering Institute. Appointments: Researcher, Moscow Power Engineering Institute, 1979-1987; Head of Laboratory, Ministry of Aviation Industry, Moscow, 1987-96; Head of Computer Science Department, Moscow Power Engineering Institute, 1996-. Publications: Book: Models of Distributed Computations, 2004; Articles to professional journals including: Journal of Computer and Systems Sciences International; Programming and Computer Software; Automation and Remote Control; Automatic Control and Computer Sciences. Honours: Senior Researcher, High Attestation Commission, 1990-; Professor, Ministry of Education, Russia, 2001-. Membership: Russian Academy of Electrotechnical Sciences. Address: Moscow Power Engineering Institute, ul. Krasnokazarmennaya 14, Moscow, 111250, Russia. E-mail: toporkovvv@mpei.ru Website: http: //www.mpei.ru/vt.mpei.ac.ru

**TORO-HARDY Alfredo,** b. 22 May 1950, Caracas, Venezuela. Ambassador. m. (1) 2 sons, 1 daughter, (2) Gabriela Gaxiola. Education: Lawyer, Central University of Venezuala, Caracas, 1973; Diploma in Public Administration, Ecole National d'Administration, Paris, France, 1974; Attestation in Comparative Petroleum Law, University of Paris II, Institute of Comparative Law, Paris, France, 1974; Magister Scientiarum, International Trade Law, Central University of Venezuela, 1977; Legum Magister, Corporate Law, University of Pennsylvania Law School – Wharton School, Philadelphia, USA, 1979. Appointments include: Assistant to the Director of Petroleum Energy, Ministry of Energy and Mines, Caracas, 1975-76; Joint Legal Advisor, International Trade Institute, Caracas, 1976-77; Adviser on International Legal Affairs and Member of the Board of several of its companies, Vollmer Organisation, 1979-82; Adviser, Foreign Affairs Committee, Chamber of Deputies, Congress of the Republic of Venezuela, 1985-92; Adviser to the Minister, Foreign Affairs Ministry, Caracas, 1992; Director, "Pedro Gual" Institute for Higher Diplomatic Studies, Foreign Affairs Ministry, 1992-94; Ambassador to Brazil, 1994-97; Ambassador to Chile, 1997-99; Non-resident Ambassador to the Commonwealth of the Bahamas, 2000-2001; Ambassador to the White House, Washington DC, 1999-2001; Ambassador to the Court of St James's, London, 2001-; Concurrently, Non Resident Ambassador to the Republic of Ireland, 2002-. Publications: Author of 14 books including: The Age of Villages: The small village vs the global village, 2002; Irak y la Reconfiguración del Orden Mundial, 2003; Tiene Futuro América Latina, 2004; Co-author of 11 books; Numerous articles in academic magazines including: Cambridge Review of International Affairs (UK); Politica Externa (Brazil); Revista del Parliamento Latinoamericano (Latin America). Honours: Several Venezuelan and foreign decorations. Memberships include: Royal Institute for Foreign Affairs, UK; Windsor Energy Group, UK; The Chairmans Club, UK; Global Dimensions, UK; Inter American Dialogue, USA; Comisión Interamericana de Justicia y Paz, Chile; Fundación de Estudios del Futuro, Caracas, Venezuela; Asociación Política Internacional, Caracas, Venezuela. Address: Venezuelan Embassy, 1 Cromwell Road, London SW7 2HR, England. E-mail: alfredotorohardy@hotmail.com

**TORPHICHEN The Rt Hon Lady (Pamela Mary),** b. 11 July 1926, Middlesex, England. Musician; Composer. m. (1) Thomas Philip Hodson Pressinger, deceased 1961, 1 son, 1 daughter, (2) James Bruce Sandilands, 14th Lord Torphichen, deceased 1975. Education: Old Palace Convent, Mayfield; LRAM, Royal College of Music, London, 1940-43. Appointments: Nurse, The Red Cross & VAD, Royal Navy, 1944-46; elected Borough Councillor for Hampstead, Conservative Party, 1949-52; Honorary Secretary, The Catholic Prisoners Aid Society, 1961-65; Honorary Secretary, The Wiseman Society, 1965-

75; President, The Ladies of Charity of St Vincent de Paul, Westminster, 1975-. Publications: Various musical compositions for piano, 1976-2000. Honours: Catholic Woman of the Year, 1996; Companion of the Sovereign Military Order of Malta, Delegation of Scotland, 1990. Memberships: Catholic Union of Great Britain; Latin Mass Society; The Ladies of Charity of St Vincent de Paul; The European-Atlantic Group, Ladies Committee; The Turf Club, Lady Associate Member; Aid to the Church in Need; British Academy of Composers & Songwriters. Address: 69 Cornwall Gardens, London SW7, England.

**TORRANCE Sam,** b. 24 August 1953, Largs, Scotland. Golfer. m. Suzanne, 1 son, 2 daughters. Appointments: Professional Golfer, 1970-; Has played in 8 Ryder Cups and represented Scotland on numerous occasions; Winner, Scottish PGA Championship, 1978, 1980, 1985, 1991, 1993; Member, Dunhill Cup Team (8 times); World Cup Team (11 times); Hennessy Cognac Cup Team (5 times); Double Diamond Team (3 times); Captain, European Team in Ashai Glass Four Tours Championships, Adelaide, 1991; Captain, Ryder Cup Team, 2001; Winner of 28 tournaments world-wide since 1972 including: Italian Open, 1987; Germany Masters, 1990; Hersey Open, 1991; Kronenbourg Open, 1993; Catalan Open, 1993; Honda Open, 1993; Hamburg Open, 1993; British Masters, 1995; French Open, 1998. Address: c/o Katrina Johnston, Carnegie Sports International, The Glassmill, 1 Battersea Bridge Road, London, SW11 3BZ, England.

**TORRANCE Thomas F(orsyth),** b. 30 August 1913, Chengdu, China. Minister of Religion; Professor of Theology. m. Margaret Edith Spear, 2 October 1946, 2 sons, 1 daughter. Education: MA, 1934; BD, 1937; DrTheol, 1946; DLitt, 1971. Appointments: Founder-Editor, Scottish Journal of Theology, 1948-88; Moderator, General Assembly, Church of Scotland, 1976-77. Publications: The Doctrine of Grace, 1949; Calvin's Doctrine of Man, 1949; Kingdom and Church, 1956; Conflict and Agreement in the Church, 2 volumes, 1959-60; Theology in Reconstruction, 1965; Theological Science, 1969; God and Rationality, 1971; Theology in Reconciliation, 1975; Space, Time and Resurrection, 1976; Space, Time and Incarnation, 1979; The Ground and Grammar of Theology, 1980; Christian Theology and Scientific Culture, 1980; Divine and Contingent Order, 1981; Reality and Scientific Theology, 1984; The Hermeneutics of John Calvin, 1987; The Trinitarian Faith, 1988; The Christian Frame of Mind, Reason, Order and Openness in Theology and Natural Science, 1989; Karl Barth, Biblical and Evangelical Theological Theologian, 1990; Senso del divino e scienza mnoderna, 1992; Theological Dialogue between Orthodox and Reformed Churches (editor), 1993; Royal Priesthood, 1993; Divine Meaning: Studies in Patristic Hermeneutics, 1994; Trinitarian Perspectives: Toward Doctrinal Agreement, 1994; The Christian Doctrine of God, One Being Three Persons, 1996; Scottish Theology: From John Knox to John McLeod Campbell, 1996. Contributions to: Numerous publications. Honours: Honorary doctorates; Honorary DD, Edinburgh, 1996. Memberships: British Academy; International Academy of Religious Sciences, president, 1972-81; International Academy of the Philosophy of Sciences; Center of Theological Inquiry, Princeton, New Jersey; Royal Society of Edinburgh. Address: 37 Braid Farm Road, Edinburgh EH10 6LE, Scotland. E-mail: ttorr@globalnet.co.uk

**TORRES Rosa Maria Fernandes,** b. 22 May 1952, Fragoso-Barcelos, Portugal. Education: High Degree in Piano, Music Conservatory of Braga and Musical Education, University of Minho; Postgraduate studies, Zoltán Kodály Pedagogical Institute of Music, Kecskemét, Hungary; Teacher's Former about Musical Education and Kodály Methodology, Portugal and Spain. Appointments: Music Teacher, Conservatório de Música Calouste Gulbenkian, Braga. Publication: As Canções Tradicionais Portuguesas no Ensino de Música, Contribuição da Metodologia de Zoltán Kodály, 1998, 2nd edition, 2000. Membership: International Kodály Society; Associação Portuguesa de Educação Musical. Address: Rua Martins Sarmento, nº 202 1ºC, 4710 Braga, Portugal. E-mail: rosatorres@clix.pt

**TORVILL Jayne,** b. 7 October 1957, England. Ice Skater. m. Philip Christensen, 1990. Career: British Pair Skating Champion with M Hutchinson, 1971; Insurance Clerk, 1974-80; With Christopher Dean: British Ice Dance Champion, 1978-83, 1994; European Ice Dance Champion, 1981-82, 1984, 1994; World Ice Dance Champion, 1981-84; World Professional Ice Dance Champion, 1984, 1985, 1990, 1995, 1996; Olympic Ice Dance Champion, 1984; Olympic Ice Dance Bronze Medal, 1994; Tours include: Australia and New Zealand, 1984; Royal Variety Performance, London, 1984; World tour with own company of international skaters, 1985; Guest artists with IceCapades, 1987; World tour with company of skaters from Soviet Union, 1988; Guest of South Australian Government, 1991; Great Britain tour with company of Ukraine skaters, 1992; Torvill & Dean, Face the Music, World Tour, UK, Australia and North America, 1994; Stars on Ice Tour, USA and Canada, 1997-98; Torvill and Dean Ice Adventures, UK, 1997-98; Television: Path of Perfection, 1984; Fire & Ice, 1986; World Tour (video), 1988; Bladerunners (documentary), 1991; Great Britain Tour (TV special and video), 1992; The Artistry of Torvill and Dean, 1994; Face the Music (video), 1995; Torvill and Dean: The Story So Far (video), 1996; Bach Cello Suite (with Yo-Yo Ma), 1996. Publications: with Christopher Dean: Torvill and Dean: Autobiography, 1984; Torvill and Dean: Facing the Music, 1995. Honours: MBE, 1981; BBC Sports Personality of the Year with Christopher Dean, 1983-84; Olympic Ice Dance Gold Medal, 1984; Figure Skating Hall of Fame with Christopher Dean, 1989; Olympic Ice Dance Bronze Medal, 1994; Hon MA, Nottingham Trent University, 1994; OBE, 2000. Address: c/o Sue Young, PO Box 32, Heathfield, East Sussex TN21 0BW, England.

**TOWNES Charles Hard,** b. 28 July 1915, Greenville, South Carolina, USA. Physicist. m. Frances Brown, 4 daughters. Education: BA, BS, Furman University, 1935; MA, Duke University, 1937; PhD, California Institute of Technology, 1939. Appointments: Bell Telephone Laboratories, 1939-47; Associate Professor, 1948-50, Professor, 1950-61, Chairman, Department of Physics, 1952-55, Columbia University; Executive Director, Columbia Radiation Laboratory, 1950-52; Vice-President, Director of Research, Institute for Defense Analyses, 1959-61; Provost, Professor of Physics, 1961-66, Institute Professor, 1966-67, Massachusetts Institute of Technology; University Professor, 1967-86, Emeritus Professor, 1986-94, Professor, Graduate School, 1994-, University of California, Berkeley. Publications: Books: Microwave Spectroscopy, 1955; Making Waves, 1995; How the Laser Happened. Adventures of a Scientist, 1999. Honours: Thomas Young Medal and Prize, Institute of Physics and The Physical Society, England, 1963; Nobel Prize for Physics, 1964; Medal of Honour, Institute of Electrical and Electronics Engineers, 1966; Wilhelm Exner Award, Austria, 1970; Niels Bohr International Gold Medal, 1979; Officier de la Légion d'Honneur, France, 1990; Rabindranath Tagore Birth Centenary Plaque of the Asiatic Society, 1999; Founders Award of the National Academy of Engineering, 2000; Lomonosov Gold Medal of the Russian Academy of Science, 2001; Templeton Prize, 2005; 27 honorary doctorates, US and abroad; Numerous prizes, awards, lectureships, other honours. Memberships: Fellow, American Physical Society, Council, 1959-62, 1965-71, President, 1967; Life Fellow, Institute of

Electrical and Electronics Engineers; National Academy of Sciences; American Philosophical Society; Royal Society of London; National Academy of Engineering; Many more. Address: Department of Physics, University of California, Berkeley, CA 94720, USA. E-mail: cht@ssl.berkeley.edu

**TOWNSEND Sue,** b. 2 April 1946, Leicester, England. Author. Publications: The Secret Diary of Adrian Mole Aged Thirteen and Three-Quarters, 1982; The Growing Pains of Adrian Mole, 1984; The Diaries of Adrian Mole, 1986; Bazaar and Rummage, Groping for Words, Womberang: Three Plays, 1984; True Confessions of Adrian Albert Mole; Mr Bevan's Dream, 1989; Ten Tiny Fingers, Nine Tiny Toes, play, 1989; Adrian Mole From Minor to Major, 1991; The Queen and I, 1992; Adrian Mole – The Wilderness Years, 1993; Plays, 1996; Ghost Children, 1997; Adrian Mole: The Cappuccino Years, 1999; Number Ten, 2002; Adrian Mole and the Weapons of Mass Destruction, 2004; The Queen in Hell Close (chapbook), 2005. Memberships: Writers Guild; PEN. Address: Reed Books, Michelin House, 81 Fulham Road, London, SW3 6RB, England.

**TOWNSHEND Peter Dennis Blandford,** b. 19 May 1945, Isleworth, London. Composer; Performer of Rock Music; Author. m. Karen Astley, 1968, 1 son, 2 daughter. Education: Acton County Grammar School; Ealing Art College. Appointments: Contracted as member of The Who to Fontana Records, 1964; MCA Records, 1965; WEA Records, 1979; Retired from the Who, 1984; Contracted as solo artist to Atco Records, USA, 1979; To Virgin Records, 1986; Owner, Eel Pie Recording Ltd, 1972-83; Established, Eel Pie (bookshops and publishing co), 1976-83; Established Meher Baba Oceanic (UK archival library), 1976-81; Editor, Faber and Faber (publishers), 1983; Final tour with The Who, 1989; Recordings include: with The Who, I Can't Explain, 1965; My Generation; Tommy (rock opera); Quadrophenia (rock opera); The Iron Man, 1989; Solo, Empty Glass, 1980; Chinese Eyes, 1982; White City, 1985; Iron Man, 1989. Publications: The Story of Tommy (with Richard Barnes); Horse's Neck, 1985; Tommy: The Musical, 1995; London, 1996. Honours: Ivor Novello Award, 1981; British Phonographic Industry Award, 1983; Rock and Roll Hall of Fame, 1990; Oliver Award, 1997; Q Award for Lifetime Achievement, 1997; Ivor Novello Lifetime Achievement Award, 2001; PRS Awards for CSI and CSI Miami, 2004; Silver Clef, 30th Anniversary Award for The Who, 2005. Address: c/o Trinifold Management, 12 Oval Road, London, NW1 7DH, England.

**TRAN VAN TRUONG,** b. 28 July 1933, Hanoi, Vietnam. Professor; Physician. m. Ton Thi Ha, 3 sons. Education: Graduate, Faculty of Odonto-Stomatology, Hanoi University of Medicine, 1962; Scientific Study on Plastic Surgery, Beijing University of Medicine, China; PhD, Faculty of Stomatology, Bucharest, Romania, 1971; Scientific Study on Maxillo Facial and Plastic Reconstructive Surgery, Faculty of Stomatology, The Netherlands University of Medicine, 1977. Appointments: Head of Department of Dentistry, Hanoi Health Service, 1962-66; Deputy Director, Hanoi Vietnam-Cuba Hospital, 1972-80; Visiting Professor, Faculty of Dentistry, Phnom Penh, Cambodia, 1980-82; Head of Department of Odonto-Ophthalmological Otorhinolaryngology, Bach Mai Hospital, Ministry of Health, 1982-83; Visiting Professor, Faculty of Odonto-Stomatology, Madagascar, 1983-86; Director, 1989-, Associate Professor 1991, Institute of Odonto-Stomatology, Ministry of Health, Hanoi; Professor, Rector, University of Odonto-Stomatology, Hanoi, 2002-. Publications: 65 professional books, articles and scientific works on Odonto-Stomatology published in national and international journals and conference proceedings include: Relative Fluoradating efficacy of different fluoride system in Vietnamese dentifrices, 1997 Unilateral and Bilateral cleft lip repair, 1998; National Oral Health Survey of Vietnam 1999-2000; Observations on Odontomas in Vietnam, 2005. Honours: Medal of Resistance, 1962, 1988; Eminent Doctor, 1997; Labour Medal, 2002; People's Doctor, 2003. Memberships: FDI; President, Vietnam Odonto-Stomatology Association; Vice-President, Academic of Denistry International; Council Member, Mekong River Region Universities of Odonto-Stomatology. Address: University of Odonto-Stomatology, 40A Trang Thi Street, Hanoi, Vietnam. E-mail: isto.maxfahn@hn.vnn.vn

**TRAPPE Paul,** b. 12 December 1931, Trier/Moselle, Germany. Professor of Sociology. 2 sons, 1 daughter. Education: Prom. Dr. Phil, Mainz University, Germany, 1959; Habilitation, Bern University Switzerland, 1964; Language Examinations: Italian, Perugia, Italy; English, London, England; Spanish, Madrid, Spain, French, Frankfurt, Germany; Government Consultant, Field Research in Mediterranean and African countries. Appointments: Assistant, Law Faculty, Mainz, Germany, 1959-61; Assistant, Law and Economics Faculty, Bern, Switzerland, 1961-64; Docent for Sociology, Bern University, Switzerland, 1964-66; Ordinary Professor and Director, Institute for Sociology, Kiel University, Germany, 1966-69; Ordinary Professor and Director, Institute for Sociology, Basle University, Switzerland, 1968-2002; President, European Faculty for Land Use and Development, Strassburg, 1999-; Editor, Social Strategies, 1975-. Publications: Several books on sociology of law and socio-economic development; About 200 articles in professional journals. Honours: Triennial Jubilee Prize, International Co-operative Alliance, London, 1970; Man of the Year, ABI, 1990; Festschrift in Honour of P Trappe: Social Strategies, vol 35, Peter Lang AG, Bern, 2002; Hall of Fame, IBC, 2005. Memberships: International Association for Philosophy and Social Philosophy, President, 1979-83; International Sociological Association, 1964-; The Communitarian Network (SASE), Washington DC, 1990-; Academic Response to Antisemitism & Racism, 1997-; AAAS, Washington DC, 1998-; New York Academy of Sciences, New York, 1997-; The Order of International Fellowship, 2005-. E-mail: p.trappe@bluewin.ch

**TRATTNER Carola-Lotty,** b. 29 May 1925, Braila, Romania. Senior University Lecturer. m. Egon, 1 son. Education: Certificate, Philology Branch, Onescu College, Bucharest, Romania, 1943-44; MA, Language and Literature, Faculty of Philology, University of Bucharest, 1944-47; Certificate, Postgraduate Pedagogical Seminar, Bucharest, 1947-48; Certificate, Second Pedagogical Seminar, Tel Aviv, Israel, 1974. Appointments: English Assistant, Faculty of Philology, University of Bucharest, 1949-52; English Assistant, Reader, Senior Lecturer, Teacher Trainer and Examiner, Institute of International Relations, Bucharest, 1952-56; English Senior Lecturer, Teacher Trainer and Examiner, Academy of Economic Studies, Bucharest, 1956-73; English Teacher for New Immigrants, Academic Recycling Institute, Ramat Gan, Israel, 1974-77; Lecturer for Communication English, French, Business French, Tel Aviv-Jaffa People's University, Tel Aviv, 1974-86; Teacher, Head of English Department, Teacher Trainer and Examiner, Shazar High School, Bat Yam, Israel, 1976-89; Recycling courses Lecturer, Organiser and Examiner for potential English Teachers, Ministry of Education and Culture, 1989-90; Senior Lecturer, Organiser, Examiner for the Tel Aviv-Jaffa Chamber of Commerce, Ministry of Labour, 1978-2002; Senior Lecturer, Academic College, Holon, 1990-2005; International interpreter (simultaneous translation) for English, French, Romanian, German (more than 100 conventions for the United Nations, FAO, governmental bodies,

law/medicine/agriculture/various technical branches/journalism/ youth/women, etc from Oxford to China). Publications: Over 20 books in English, French, Romanian and Hebrew, 1952-2005, among them monolingual and bilingual Dictionaries, general and specific (English-Hebrew, Hebrew-English, Juridical and Economic; English-Romanian and English-Hebrew; Glossaries for the foreign trade, banking, diplomatic activities, the textile industry, motor-car technology) and University specialised textbooks; Translation into English of 10th grade World Geography textbook; Collections of texts for translation. Memberships: English Teachers' Association in Israel. Address: 52 Eilat St, 58364 Holon, Israel. E-mail: trattner@email.com

**TRAUTNER Christoph,** b. 22 May 1954, Munich, Germany. Physician; Scientist. Education: Doctor of Medicine, Ludwig-Maximilians-University, Munich, 1978; Master of Political Science, Free University of Berlin, Germany, 1986; Public Health Physician, Board of Physicians, Hamburg, Germany, 1989; Master of Public Health, Harvard University, Boston, USA, 1990-91; Certificate in Epidemiology, German Epidemiological Association, 1998; Habilitation, School of Public Health, University of Bielefeld, Germany, 2000. Appointments include: Scientific Assistant in Oncology, Department of Radiology, Ludwig-Maximilians-University, Munich, 1979-80; Locum positions in general practice, 1980-81; District Health Commissioner, District Office of Berlin-Tiergarten, Berlin, 1981-85; Director, Section of Prevention and Rehabilitation, Ministry of Health and Social Affairs, Hamburg, Germany, 1986-90; Research Assistant, Harvard University, USA, 1991; Scientific Assistant, Oncology, Department of Radiation Therapy, University of Ulm, 1991-92; Research Associate in Public Health, Heinrich-Heine-University, Düsseldorf, 1992-97; Research Associate and Deputy Director (Research) of the Institute, Institute of Occupational and Social Medicine and Epidemiology, Charité University Hospital, Berlin, 1997-2001; Research Associate, Project Manager, University of Applied Sciences, Magdeburg-Stendal, Department of Social Affairs and Public Health, Magdeburg, 2001-2002; Chair, Gesundheitsforschung e.V, Berlin, 1999-; Privatdozent, School of Public Health, University of Bielefeld, 2000-; Professor of Medicine, Public Health, University of Applied Sciences, Braunschweig/Wolfenbüttel, 2002-; Owner of MediSC – Medicine Science, Consulting, Berlin, 2003-. Publications: Book: Modellvorhaben zur Verbesserung der Versorgung bei Diabetes mellitus. Bestandsaufnahme und Sekundäranalyse (co-author), 1995; More than 20 original articles; Numerous abstracts and presentations. Honour: Bavarian State Scholarship for Talented Students, 1972-78. Memberships include: International Epidemiological Association; Society for Epidemiologic Research; International Biometric Society; European Association for the Study of Diabetes; German Diabetes Association. Address: Stephanstr 67, D-10559 Berlin, Germany. E-mail: trautner@healthresearch-online.org

**TRAVOLTA John,** b. 18 February 1954, Englewood, New Jersey, USA. Actor. m. Kelly Preston, 1991, 1 son. Appointments: Films: Carrie, 1976; The Boy in the Plastic Bubble (for TV), 1976; Saturday Night Fever, 1977; Grease, 1978; Moment by Moment, 1978; Urban Cowboy, 1980; Blow Out, 1981; Staying Alive, 1983; Two of a Kind, 1983; Perfect, 1985; The Experts, 1988; Chains of Gold, 1989; Look Who's Talking, 1989; Look Who's Talking Now, 1990; The Tender, 1991; All Shook Up, 1991; Look Who's Talking 3, 1994; Pulp Fiction, 1994; White Man's Burden, 1995; Get Shorty, 1995; Broken Arrow, 1996; Phenomenon, 1996; Michael, 1997; Face Off, 1997; She's So Lovely, 1997; Primary Colors, 1998; A Civil Action, 1998; The General's Daughter, 1999; Battlefield Earth, 2000; Lucky Numbers, 2000; Swordfish, 2001; Domestic

Disturbance, 2001; Austin Powers in Goldmember, 2002; Basic, 2003; The Punisher, 2004; A Love Song for Bobby Long, 2004; Ladder 49, 2004; Be Cool, 2005; TV Series: Welcome Back Kotter, 1975-77; l.p. records, 1976, 1977. Publication: Staying Fit, 1984. Honours: Billboard Magazine Best New Male Vocalist Award, 1976; Best Actor Award, National Board of Review, 1978; Male Star of the Year, National Association of Theatre Owners, 1983; Alan J Pakula Prize, 1998.

**TREANOR Frances,** b. Penzance, Cornwall. Artist; Author. Divorced, 1 daughter. Education: Fine Art, Goldsmiths College, London University; Postgraduate Studies, Middlesex University, 1966-67; ATC (Lon); Diploma in Geriatric Art Teaching, London University, 1972; Certificate in Psychotherapy Counselling. Appointments: Taught and lectured on art and design appreciation in various ILEA and adult establishments including: Erith College of Technology; American Intercontinental University; Blackheath Conservatoire of Music and the Arts; Twice Vice Chair, Blackheath Art Society; Freelance sponsored workshops; Private and corporate commissions; Artist in Residence, Royal Greenwich Park, 2005-06; Recent exhibitions include: The Pastel Society, Centenary Exhibition at FBA, 2000; English Heritage, Rangers House, Greenwich Artists Group, 2000; St Alphege Church, Open Studios Exhibition, 2000; Greenwich and Docklands, International Festival Open Studios, 2002, 2003, 2004; London Chamber of Commerce and Industry, selected artist, 2002; The Stephen Lawrence Gallery, University of Greenwich, mixed show, 2004. Honours: The Royal Drawing Society's Exhibit Prize, The Children's Royal Academy, London; Major County Scholarship, 1962; Twice winner, Law Society Art Group Special Prize, 1972, 1973; Dip d'Honneur, Salon d'Antony, Paris, 1975; Winner, L'Artiste Assoiffe Award, 1980; Exhibitor, The Lord Mayor's Award Exhibition, Guildhall, 1975, 1977; Represented Greenwich at twin town of Maribor, Yugoslavia, 1980; Lewisham art representative, Reinickendorf, Berlin, Germany, 1982; The George Rowney Pastel Award, Birmingham, 1982; The Frank Herring Award for Merit, 1984; Conte (UK) Award, 1986; Willi Hoffmann-Guth Award, 1988; Membership: London Press Club. Address: 121 Royal Hill, Greenwich, London SE10 8SS, England. E-mail: frances@treanor4778.fsbusiness.co.uk Website: www.axisweb.org/artist/francestreanor

**TREBY Ivor Charles,** b. Devonport, England. Poet. Education: MA, Honours, Biochemistry, Oxford. Publications: Poem Cards, 1984; Warm Bodies, 1988; Foreign Parts, 1989; Woman with Camellias, 1995; The Michael Field Catalogue: A Book of Lists, 1998; Translations From the Human, 1998; A Shorter Shīrazād, 101 poems of Michael Field chosen and annotated by Ivor C Treby, 1999; Awareness of the Sea, selected poems 1970-1995, 2000; Uncertain Rain, sundry spells of Michael Field chosen and annotated by Ivor C Treby, 2002. Contributions to: Windmill Book of Poetry; Bete Noire; Poetry Review; Staple; Anglo-Welsh Review; Contemporary Review; Honest Ulsterman; Literary Review; Rialto. Address: Parapets, 69 Redcliffe Close, RB Kensington and Chelsea, London SW5 9HZ, England.

**TREGLOWN Jeremy Dickinson,** b. 24 May 1946, Anglesey, North Wales. Professor of English; Biographer; Editor; Critic. m. (1) Rona Bower, 1970, divorced, 1982, 1 son, 2 daughters, (2) Holly Urquhart Eley, 1984. Education: MA, BLitt, Oxon; PhD, London. Appointments: Lecturer in English, Lincoln College, Oxford, 1974-77; University College, London, 1977-80; Assistant Editor, 1980-82, Editor, 1982-90, Times Literary Supplement; Chairman of Judges, Booker Prize, 1991; Ferris Professor of Journalism, Princeton University, USA, 1992; Professor of English, University of Warwick, England, 1993-; Chairman of the Judges, Whitbread Book of the Year Award,

1998; Leverhulme Research Fellow, 2001-03. Publications: Letters of John Wilmot, Earl of Rochester (editor), 1980; Spirit of Wit: Reconsiderations of Rochester (editor), 1982; Introduction, R L Stevenson, In the South Seas, 1986; Selection, and Introduction, The Lantern Bearers: Essays by Robert Louis Stevenson, 1987; Introductions to reprints of complete novels of Henry Green, 1991-98; Roald Dahl: A Biography, 1994; Grub Street and the Ivory Tower: Literary Journalism, and Literary Scholarship from Fielding to the Internet, (editor with Bridget Bennett), 1998; Romancing: The Life and Work of Henry Green, 2000; V S Pritchett: A Working Life, 2004. Contributions to: Numerous magazines and journals. Membership: Fellow, Royal Society of Literature. Address: Gardens Cottage, Ditchley Park, Enstone, Nr Chipping Norton, Oxford OX7 4EP, England.

**TRETTER Verena,** b. 10 October 1967, Vienna, Austria. Scientist. Education: Dipl Ing, Biotechnology, University of Agriculture, Vienna, Austria, 1991; PhD, Institute of Chemistry, University of Agriculture, Vienna, Austria, 1994. Appointments: Postdoctoral Fellow, University Clinic for Psychiatry, Vienna, 1994-2000; Postdoctoral Fellow (Marie Curie Fellowship), MRC-Laboratory for Molecular Cell Biology, University College London, 2000-. Publications: 15 original papers in scientific journals as co-author. Honour: Marie Curie Fellowship of the European Community; Listed in national and international biographical dictionaries. Memberships: Society of Neuroscience, USA; Neurowissenschaftliche Gesellschaft, Germany; Biochemical Society, Austria; Austrian Society for Biotechnology. Address: University College London, Gower Street, London WC1E 6BT, England. E-mail: v.tretter@ucl.ac.uk

**TRICHET Jean-Claude,** b. 20 December 1942, Lyon, France. President of the European Central Bank. Education: Ingénieur civil des Mines, Ecole nationale supérieure des Mines de Nancy, 1964; Economics, University of Paris, 1966; Graduate, Institut d'études politiques de Paris, 1966; Graduate, Ecole nationale d'administration, 1969-71. Appointments: Engineer in the competitive sector, 1966-68; Inspecteur adjoint de Finances, 1971; Assigned to the General Inspectorate of Finance, 1974; Assigned to the Treasury Department, 1975; Secretary General, Interministerial Committee for Improving Industrial Structures, 1976; Adviser to the Minister of Economic Affairs, 1978; Adviser to the President of the Republic on Industry, Energy and Research, 1978; Head, Development Aid Office, Deputy Director of Bilateral Affairs, 1981, Head, International Affairs, 1985, Chairman of the Paris Club - sovereign debt rescheduling (1985-93), Director, 1987, Treasury Department; Director, Private Office of the Minister for Economic Affairs, Finance and Privatisation, 1986; Alternate Governor, International Monetary Fund, -1993; Alternate Governor, World Bank, 1987; Censor, Banque de France, 1987; Chairman, European Monetary Committee, 1992-93; Governor, Banque de France, 1993; Member, Board of Directors of the Bank for International Settlements, 1993; Governor, World Bank, 1993-95; Chairman, Monetary Policy Council, Banque de France, 1994; Member, Council of the European Monetary Institute, 1994; Alternate Governor, International Monetary Fund, 1995-2003; Member, Governing Council of the European Central Bank, 1998; Governor of the Banque de France, 1999; Chairman, Group of Ten Governors, 2003; President, European Central Bank, 2003. Honours: Officier de l'Ordre national de la Légion d'honneur, France; Officer de l'Ordre national du Mérite, France; Commander or Grand Officer, National Orders of Merit in Argentina, Austria, Belgium, Brazil, Ecuador, Germany, Ivory Coast and Yugoslavia; Policy Maker of the Year, The International Economy magazine, 1991; Prize, Zerilli Marimo, Academie des Sciences morales et politiques,

1999; International Prize, Pico della Mirandola, 2002. Address: European Central Bank, Postfach 16 03 19, D-60066 Frankfurt am Main, Germany.

**TRIER Peter Eugene,** b. 12 September 1919, Darmstadt, Germany. Research Director; Consultant. m. (1) Margaret Holloway, deceased 1998, 3 sons (2) Teresa Watson. Education: Mathematical Wrangler MA, Trinity Hall, Cambridge, 1941; MSc, Mathematics, Open University, 1997. Appointments: Royal Naval Scientific Service, 1941-50; Mullard Research Laboratories (now Philips Research Laboratories), 1950-59, Director, 1953-69; Director, Philips Electronics and Subsidiaries, 1957-85, Director of Research, Philips UK, 1969-81; Director, Philips Electronics UK, 1969-85; Pro-Chancellor, Brunel University, 1980-99. Publications: Mathematics and Information, 1983; Many papers in scientific and technical journals. Honours: Honorary D.Tech., Brunel University, 1975; Fellow, Royal Academy of Engineering, 1978; CBE, 1980; Glazebrook Medal and Prize, Institute of Physics, 1984. Memberships: Institution of Electrical Engineers, Vice-President, 1974-77; Fellow Institute of Physics; Fellow, Institute of Mathematics, President, 1982-83; Council, 1969-99, Chairman, 1973-79, Brunel University; Chair, Electronics Research Council, 1976-80, Chair, Defence Scientific Advisory Council, 1981-85, Ministry of Defence; Committee of Management, The Wine Society, 1977-92. Address: 14 Mill View Gardens, Croydon, Surrey CR0 5HW, England.

**TRIFONOV Nikolai Yurievich,** b. 27 June 1948, Voronezh, Russia. Civil Servant; Valuer. m. Evgeniia Trifonova, 2 sons. Belarusian State University, Physics Faculty, Minsk, 1966-71; Honorary Diploma, Belarusian State University, Special Faculty Applied Mathematics, Minsk, 1972-75; Candidate of Science, Institute of Physics, Belarusian Academy of Science, Minsk, 1987; Centre Formation Realites Internationales, Paris, France, 1992. Appointments: Held posts in Ukrainian Academy of Science, Kharkov, Belarusian Academy of Science, Minsk, 1973-81; Posts in Belarusian Polytech Institute, Minsk, 1981-91; Council Co-Chairman, Minsk Exchange, 1991; Vice President, Western Real Estate Exchange, Minsk, Belarus, 1991-94; Council Member, Belarusbank, Minsk, 1993-95; President, Belarusian Real Estate Guild, Minsk, 1994-; President, Belarusian Society Valuers, Minsk, 1996-; Director East And Central European Relations, European Real Estate Society, 1998-; Managing Director, Council of Valuers' Associations of CIS, Minsk, 2003-; Professor, Belarusian State University, 2004-. Publications: Over 200 on economics, law, mathematics, physics, chemistry in Russian and English including Chapter 5 in: Real Estate Education throughout the World: Past, Present and Future, 2002. Honours: Honorary Member, Osteuropaische Sachverstandige Verein, OSV, 1995; Honorary Member, Associacao Portuguesa Avaliadores Activos Fixos, AAPOR, 1996; Union Kyrgyz Appraiser, OKO, 2000. Memberships: Belarusian Real Estate Guild, BREG, 1994; Osteuropaische Sachversandige Verein, OSV, 1995; European Real Estate Society, ERES, 1995; Belarusian Society of Valuers, BSV, 1996; International Club Directors, ICD, 2001; Fellow, Royal Institution of Chartered Surveyors, FRICS, 2003. Address: Belarusian Society of Valuers, 17A Kalvaryiskaya Street, Minsk 220004, Belarus. E-mail: guild@user.unibel.by

**TRIMBLE W David,** b. 15 October 1944. Politician. m. (1) Heather McComb, divorced, (2) Daphne Elizabeth Orr, 1978, 2 sons, 2 daughters. Education: LLB, 1st class, Queens University, 1968. Appointments: Bar at Law, 1969, Lecturer, Law, Senior Lecturer, 1977, Head of Department, Commercial and Property Law, 1981-89; Convention Member, South Belfast, 1975-76; Joined Ulster Unionist Party, 1977; Vice Chairman, Lagan Valley Unionist Association, 1983-85; Chairman, 1985, 1990-96, Honorary Secretary, Ulster Unionist Council; Chairman, UUP Legal Committee, 1989-95; Member of Parliament, Upper Bann, 1990-2005; Chairman, UUP Constitutional Development Committee, 1995; Leader, Ulster Unionist Party, 1995-2005; Member of the New Northern Ireland Assembly, Upper Bann Constituency, 1998-2002; First Minister until Assembly suspended, 2002. Honours: Shared Nobel Peace Prize, 1998; Honorary LLD, Queen's, 1999, New Brunswick, 2000, Wales, 2002. Memberships: Devolution Group, 1979-84; Founder, Chairman, Ulster Society, 1985-90; Chairman, Lisburn Ulster Club, 1985-86.

**TROFIMOV Boris Alexandrovich,** b. 2 October 1938, Tchita, Eastern Siberia, Russia. Chemist. m. Nina Ivanovna Vodyannikova, 1 son. Education: Graduate, 1961, PhD equivalent, 1964, Irkutsk State University; DSc Degree, St Petersburg (Leningrad) University, 1970. Appointments: Head of Laboratory, 1970, Professor, 1974, Vice-Director, 1990, Irkutsk Institute of Organic Chemistry, SB, USSR Academy of Sciences; Director, A E Favorsky Irkutsk Institute of Chemistry, SB, Russian Academy of Sciences, 1994-. Publications: More than 1800 publications include: 15 monographs, 700 major papers, more than 500 Russian and foreign patents; Promoter of 57 PhD students, 19 D Sci (habilitations). Honours: Basic Research in Siberian Chemical Science, 1984, 1990; Applied Research in Siberian Chemical Science, 1985; Gold, 1979, Silver, 1987 and 2 Bronze Medals, 1972, 1978, Russian Exhibition for Economic Achievements; Orders: Sign of Honour, 1986, Friendship, 1989; Butlerov Prize, Russian Academy of Sciences, 1997; Medal and Diploma of Mendeleev Reader, St Petersburg, 2003. Memberships: Academician, Russian Academy of Science; Editorial Board Member: Zh.Organ.Khim (Russia), Sulfur Letters, Sulfur Reports (Australia), Main Group Chemistry (USA); Presidium, Irkutsk Scientific Centre, Russian Academy of Sciences; Presidium, East Siberian Scientific Centre, Russian Academy of Medical Science; Asia-Pacific Academy of Materials; Council of Experts of the Supreme Commission on Scientific Qualification; National Committee of Russian Chemists; Interdepartmental Scientific Council on Chemical and Biological Weapon Convention at the Russian Academy of Sciences and Russian Agency of Ammunition; International Council for Main Group Chemistry, The Netherlands; Honorary Fellow, Florida Center for Heterocyclic Compounds; Bureau of Scientific Council on Organic and Elemento-Organic Chemistry, Russian Academy of Sciences; Council of the section "Organic Chemistry", D I Mendeleev Russian Chemical Society; Scientific Council, Research Centre of Energy Infrastructure "Asia-Energy". Address: A E Favorsky Irkutsk Institute of Chemistry SB RAS, 1, Favorsky Str, Irkutsk 664033, Russia. Website: www.inchemistry.irk.ru

**TROITSKI Yuri Vladimirovich,** b. 10 July 1928, Semipalatinsk, USSR. Researcher; Physicist. m. Galina S Rodyukova, 2 sons. Education: MS, University of Nizhni Novgorod, 1952; PhD, Tomsk Polytechnic Institute, 1960; DSc, 1972, Professor, 1990, Siberian Division of the USSR Academy of Sciences, Novosibirsk. Appointments: Researcher, Siberian Division of USSR Academy of Sciences, 1955-62, 1967-72; Head of Laboratory, Institute of Semiconductor Physics, 1963-66; Head of Laboratory, 1973-98, Chief Scientist, 1999-, Institute of Automation and Electrometry, Siberian Division of the Russian Academy of Sciences, Novosibirsk. Publications: Books: Single-frequency gas lasers, 1975; Reflection multiple-beam interferometers, 1985; Author and co-author of 200 published papers in microwave electronics, optics, lasers, interferometry, gravitational wave detectors; 14 registered inventions. Memberships: SPIE, 1993; OSA, 1995; New

York Academy of Sciences, 1996; Honoured Scientist of the Russian Federation, 2002. Address: Institute of Automation and Electrometry, Academician Koptyug Avenue 1, Novosibirsk, 630090, Russia. E-mail: troitski@iae.nsk.su

**TROLLOPE Andrew David Hedderwick,** b. 6 November 1948, York, England. Barrister. Divorced, 2 sons. Education: Charterhouse School, Godalming, Surrey; University of Nancy, France; Inns of Court School of Law. Appointments: Called to the Bar, 1971; Assistant Recorder, 1984, Recorder, 1989, Queen's Counsel, 1991, Bencher, Inner Temple, 2002. Memberships: International Relations Committee of the Bar Council; Council of Management; British Institute of International and Comparative Law. Address: 187 Fleet Street, London EC4A 2AT, England. Website: www.187fleetstreet.com

**TROLLOPE Joanna,** b. 9 December 1943. Author. m. (1) David Potter, 1966, 2 daughters, (2) Ian Curteis, 1985, divorced 2001, 2 step-sons. Education: MA, St Hugh's College, Oxford, 1972. Appointments: Information and Research Department, Foreign Office, 1965-67; Various teaching posts, 1967-79; Chair, Advisory Committee on National Reading Initiative, Department of National Heritage, 1996; Member, Advisory Committee on National Year of Reading, Department of Education, 1998; Trustee and Member, Joanna Trollope Charitable Trust, 1995-; Patron County of Gloucestershire Community Foundation, 1994-. Publications: Eliza Stanhope, 1978; Parson Harding's Daughter, 1979; Leaves from the Valley, 1980; The City of Gems, 1981; The Steps of the Sun, 1983; Britannia's Daughter: A Study of Women in the British Empire, 1983; The Taverner's Place, 1986; The Choir, 1988; A Village Affair, 1989; A Passionate Man, 1990; The Rector's Wife, 1991; The Men and the Girls, 1992; A Spanish Lover, 1993; The Country Habit, 1993; The Best of Friends, 1995; Next of Kin, 1996; Faith, 1996; Other People's Children, 1998; Marrying the Mistress, 2000; Girl From the South, 2002; Brother and Sister, 2004; Second Honeymoon, 2006; The Book Boy, 2006; As Caroline Harvey: Legacy of Love, 1992; A Second Legacy, 1993; The Brass Dolphin, 1997; Contributions to newspapers and magazines. Honours: Romantic Novelist of the Year, 1980; OBE, 1996; Deputy Lieutenant for the County of Gloucestershire, 2002; Memberships: Vice-President, Trollope Society; Council Member, Society of Authors; Council Member, West Country Writers Association. Address: c/o Peters Fraser and Dunlop, Drury House, 34-43 Russell Street, London, WC2B 5HA, England. Website: www.joannatrollope.net

**TROMMSDORFF Gisela,** b. 24 December 1941, Munster, Westfalia, Germany. Professor. m. H J Kornadt. Education: Diploma Degree, 1967; Dr Phil, 1970; Venia Legendi, 1975. Appointments: Studies in developmental and social psychology, University of Gottingen, FU Berlin, University of North Carolina, Chapel Hill; Cologne and Mannheim, 1963-1967; Research Assistant, 1967-68; Director of Administration, Sonderforschungsber 24, University of Mannheim, 1969-74; Professor, RWTH, 1978-87; Visiting Professor, Japan Society for the Promotion of Science, Tokyo and Nagoya, 1985; Chair of Developmental Psychology and Cross Cultural Psychology, Full Professor (tenure), 1987-, Department of Psychology, University of Konstanz, Germany, 1987-; Visiting Professor, Keio University, Tokyo, Japan, 1988, 1989, 1991, each three months. Publications: Numerous publications in international journals; Member of many professional national and international editorial and advisory boards. Honours: many. Memberships: German Society for Psychology; European Association for Experimental Social Psychology; German Society for Sociology; International Society for the Study of Behavioural Development; International Association for Cross-Cultural Psychology (IACCP); German Society for Sociology; German Association for Asian Studies; Vice-president, German-Japanese Society for Social Sciences. Address: University of Konstanz, Department of Psychology, Chair of Developmental Psychology and Cross-Cultural Psychology, Box D14, D-78457 Konstanz, Germany. E-mail: trommsdorff@uni-konstanz.de

**TRUBETSKOY Kliment Nikolayevich,** b. 3 July 1933, Moscow, USSR. Mining Engineer. m. 2 sons. Education: Moscow Institute of Non-Ferrous Metals and Gold, 1961; Doctor of Technical Sciences, 1981; Professor, 1982; Academician, RAS. Appointments: Manager of Mines, 1953-56; Associate, Mining Institute A A Skochinskii, 1961-67; Senior Associate, Institute of Earth Physics, 1967-77; Head of Laboratory, 1977, Deputy Director, 1987, Director, 1987-2003, Institute of Complex Exploitation of Mineral Resources; Member of the Presidium, RAS, 1996-2001; Adviser of the Presidium, Russian Academyof Sciences, 2001; Head of Chair, Russian State Geological Prospecting University, 2003. Publications: 650 publications; 30 monographs; Encyclopaedia of Life Support Systems, 2002; 4 learned books; 70 patents. Honours: USSR and Russian State Prizes; Prize of the President of Russian Federation; 2nd Prize of the Government of Russian Federation for the field of science, technics and education; B Krupinsky Medal, WMC; 300 Years of German-Russian Friendship in Mining Medal. Memberships: Academician, Russian Academy of Sciences; Foreign Member, Academy of Engineering Sciences of Serbia and Montenegro. Address: Kryukovski Tupik 4, Moscow 111020, Russia. E-mail: trubetsk@ipkonran.ru

**TRUBKO Sergey,** b. 26 September 1948, St Petersburg, Russia. Optical Designer; Scientist. m. Liza Trubko, 1 son, 1 daughter. Education: BS, University of Fine Mechanics and Optics, St Petersburg, 1971; MS, Honours, 1973; PhD, 1977. Appointments: Scientist, to Senior Scientist, D I Mendeleev Metrology Institute, S I Vavilov State Optical Institute, St Petersburg, 1977-94; Senior Optical Engineer, Symbol Tech, Holtsville, New York, USA, 1996-98; Senior Scientist, CycloVision Tech, New York, 1998-99; Vice President, Chief Scientist, RemoteReality, Westborough, Massachusetts, 2000-. Publications: Design of Cemented Doublets, 1984; Numerous articles in professional journals; 9 patents. Honours: Silver Medal, high school; Inventor and Rationalizer Medal. Membership: International Society of Optical Engineering. Address: RemoteReality 4 Technology Drive, Westborough, MA 01581, USA. E-mail: strubko@remotereality.com

**TRUETT Philip Arthur,** b. 14 October 1942, Croydon, Surrey. m. Juliet Macadam, 2 daughters. Education: Cranleigh School; Grenoble University. Appointments: Lloyd's, 1961, Member of Lloyd's, 1973-; Directorships: Furness-Houlder (Reinsurance) Ltd, Furness-Houlder (Overseas Insurance Services) Ltd, 1971-80; MWE Underwriting Agencies Ltd, 1980-83; Fenchurch Underwriting Agencies Ltd, 1983-93; Minories Ltd, 1993-97; Aberdeen Underwriting Agencies Ltd, 1997-99; Hampden Private Capital Ltd, 1999-; Chairman, Lloyd's Benevolent Fund, 2005. Publications: Heather and Heaven – Walton Heath Golf Club (Chief Research Assistant); Chapters in: Aspects of Collecting Golf Books, 1996 - Yearbooks and Annuals; Hazards, 1993 - To Rake or Not to Rake Bunkers. Honour: Heather and Heaven winner of USGA International Book Award, 2003. Memberships: Royal and Ancient Golf Club; Walton Heath Golf Club, Captain, 1993, Director, 1992-93, 1999-2000; Rye Golf Club; Royal Cinque Ports Golf Club; Clapham Common Golf Club, Lloyd's Golf Club, Honorary Secretary, 1985-95, Captain, 1996, President, 2000; British Golf Collectors Society, One of 5 Founding Members, Captain, 1992-93; Old Cranleighan Golf Society, Honorary Secretary, 1968-73, Captain, 1982; South

Eastern Junior Golf Society, Captain, 1968, Vice-President, 1975, President, 1991-; Golf Collectors Society (US), Board, 1997-2003; Senior Golfers' Society; Kadahar Ski Club; Ephemera Society; Private Libraries Association; Committee, Annual National Service for Seafarers; Walton-on-the-Hill and District Local History Society, President, 1998-. Address: Woodbine House, 12 Spencer Road, South Croydon, Surrey CR2 7EH, England. E-mail: philip@truett.co.uk

**TRUMP Donald John,** b. 14 June 1946, New York, USA. Property Developer. m. (1) Ivana Zelnicek, 1977, divorced 1991, 2 sons, 1 daughter, (2) Marla Maples, 1993, 1 daughter. Education: Fordham University; University of Pennsylvania. Appointments: President, Trump Organisation; Board of Directors, Police Athletic League; Advisory Board, Lenox Hill Hospital and United Cerebral Palsy; Director, Fred C Trump Foundation; Founder Member, Committee to complete construction of Cathedral of St John the Divine and Wharton Real Estate Centre; Former Co-Chair, New York Vietnam Veterans Memorial Fund. Publications: Trump: The Art of the Deal, 1987; Trump: Surviving at the Top, 1990; the Art of the Comeback, 1997. Address: Trump Organization, 725 Fifth Avenue, New York, NY 10022, USA.

**TRUTER Ilse,** b. 5 May 1964, Port Elizabeth, South Africa. Pharmacist; University Professor. Education: BCom, 1985, BCom Hons, 1987, MCom, 1988, DCom, 1993, BPharm, 1993, MSc, 1994, University of Port Elizabeth; PhD, Potchefstroom University for Christian Higher Education, 2000. Appointments: Temporary Lecturer, Department of Business Economics, University of Port Elizabeth, 1988; Pharmacist Intern, Westway Pharmacy, Port Elizabeth, 1993-94; Temporary Lecturer, Pharmacy Practice, Department of Pharmacy, 1993, Temporary part-time Lecturer, Pharmacy Practice, Department of Pharmacy, 1994-95, Researcher, Drug Utilisation Research Unit, 1994-, Permanent full-time Lecturer, Pharmacy Practice, Department of Pharmacy, 1995-97, Permanent full-time Senior Lecturer, Department of Pharmacy, 1998-2000, University of Port Elizabeth; Associate Professor, Department of Pharmacy, 2001-2004, Associate Professor, Department of Pharmacy, 2005-, Nelson Mandela Metropolitan University. Publications: Author, over 170 research publications; Author and co-author, 199 presentations at conferences and symposia; Author, 18 radio talks. Honours: Runner-up, 1985, Winner, 1986; AIESEC-Barclays National Essay Competition; Alfred Radis Memorial Award and Medal, 1990; Gencor S$_2$A$_3$ Bronze Medal, Best Masters study, 1994; Pharmacia and Upjohn Achievement Award winner, 1996, 1997; Euro Durg EACPT Poster Prize, Germany, 1998; ISPE Poster Prize, USA, 1999; Recipient of the Roche Best Publication Award, in conjunction with The Academy of Pharmaceutical Sciences in 2001 for the best publication in Pharmacy Practice in South Africa in 2000; Wellness Excellence Award, South African National Wellness Conference, University of Port Elizabeth, 2003; Pharmacy Teacher of the Year Award, South Africa, 2003; Listed in national and international biographical publications. Memberships: South African Pharmacy Council; Pharmaceutical Society of South Africa; South African Academy of Pharmaceutical Sciences; South African Association of Hospital and Institutional Pharmacists; International Society for Pharmacoepidemiology; Pharmacological Society of South Africa; Public Health Association of South Africa; Southern African Institute for Management Scientists. Address: Nelson Mandela Metropolitan University, PO Box 77000, Port Elizabeth 6031, South Africa. E-mail: ilse.truter@nmmu.ac.za

**TSAI Chon-Haw,** b. 24 March 1958, Chiayi, Taiwan. Neurologist. m. Wen-Li Lo, 2 sons, 1 daughter. Education: MB,

China Medical College, 1976-83; Doctor of Medical Sciences, Chang Gung University, 1991-95. Appointments: Neurologist, 1989; Lecturer in Neurology, 1994; Associate Professor, Neurology, CGMH, 1995; Associate Professor in Neurology, 2000, Head, Department of Neurology, 2001-, China Medical University Hospital. Publications: Two novel mutations of the glycine receptor gene in a Taiwanese hyperekplexia family (neurology), 2004; Kindling stimuli delivered at different times in the sleep-wake cycle (sleep), 2004; Pallidotomy effect on the cortical excitability in patients with severe Parkinson's disease (movement disorders), 2005. Honours: Best poster, annual meeting of Taiwan Neurological Society, 1987; Research Award, National Science Council, Taiwan, 1998. Memberships: Taiwan Neurological Society; Movement Disorder Society; American Academy of Neurology. Address: Department of Neurology, China Medical University Hospital, 2 Yuh-Der Road, Taichung 404, Taiwan. E-mail: d8079:www.cmuh.org.tw

**TSAO Vivian J Y,** b. 24 April 1950, Taipei, Taiwan (American Citizen). Artist; Art Professor; Author. m. Raymond Clyde Coreil. Education: BA, Fine Arts, National Taiwan Normal University, Taiwan, 1973; Master of Fine Arts in Painting, Carnegie Mellon University, Pittsburgh, Pennsylvania, USA, 1976. Appointments: Assistant Editor, Children's Art Page, Central Daily News, Taiwan, 1971-74; Art Instructor, National Taipei Teachers College, Taiwan, 1972-74; Worked on consignments for: Kingpitcher Gallery, Pittsburgh, Pennsylvania, USA, 1976-77; Nardin Galleries, New York City, USA, 1979-80; The Art Collaborative, New York City, USA, 1985-87; Correspondent, Hsiung Shih Art Monthly, Taiwan, 1980-96; Programme Auditor, Free-lance Reviewer of Exhibitions, 1990-96, Juror on Panel, 1996-99, New York State Council on the Arts, New York City; Adjunct Assistant Professor of Drawing and Design, Department of Fine Arts, Pace University, New York City, 1990-; Contributing writer in the USA, United Daily News, Literary Page, Taiwan; 14 solo and 49 group exhibitions include: American Academy of Arts and Letters; The Brooklyn Museum; Taipei Fine Arts Museum; Ceres Gallery; Biddington's Internet Gallery. Publications: Book: The Mark of Time: Dialogues with Vivian Tsao on Art in New York, 2003; Article: A Holistic Approach to Art Criticism: An Interview with Art Critic Michael Brenson, 1988; Black Velvet at Dusk (essay), 2000. Honours: Artist-in-Residence, New York State Council on the Arts; Certificate of Merit, Pastel Society of America; Scholarship Grant, Carnegie Mellon University. Memberships: Inducted Fellow, Society of Fellows, Dyson College, Pace University; Elected Full Member, Pastel Society of America; College Art Association of America. Address: 17 Fuller Place, Brooklyn, NY 11215-6006, USA. E-mail: viviantsao@earthlink.net

**TSAY Jyh-Shen,** b. 25 October 1969, Kinmen, Taiwan. Professor. Education: BSc, 1992, PhD, 1997, National Taiwan Normal University. Appointments: Postdoctoral Research Fellow, Academia Sinica, 1997-99; Visiting Research Fellow, Institute for Physical and Theoretical Chemistry, Bonn University, 1999-2000; Assistant Professor, Tunghai University, 2000-04; Associate Professor, National Chung-Cheng University, 2004-. Publications: 40 articles in scientific journals. Honours: Best Dissertation Award, Physical Society of Republic of China, 1998; Research Award, Taiwan Association for Magnetic Technology, 2003; Best Poster Award, Physical Society, Republic of China, 1997. Address: Department of Physics, National Chung-Cheng University, 160 Sang-Hsing Min-Hsiung, Chia-Yi 621, Taiwan. E-mail: jstsay@ccu.edu.tw

**TSITVERBLIT Naftali Anatol,** b. 29 October 1963, Kiev, Ukraine. Researcher. Education: MSc, Faculty of Mechanical and Power Engineering, Kiev Polytechnic Institute, 1987; PhD, Faculty of Mechanical Engineering, Tel-Aviv University, 1995. Appointments: Engineer, Scientific Research Institute of Robotics, Kiev, USSR, 1985-87; Teaching Assistant, Instructor, Tel-Aviv University, 1988-94; Visiting Scientist, Cornell University, 1994; Postdoctoral Research Fellow, Lamont-Doherty Earth Observatory of Columbia University, 1995-97; Postdoctoral Fellow, Geophysical Fluid Dynamics Summer Program, Woods Hole Oceanographic Institution, 1996; Visiting Scientist, Department of Fluid Mechanics and Heat Transfer of Tel-Aviv University, 1997-. Publications: In scientific journals, books and conference proceedings; Finite-Amplitude double-component convection due to different boundary conditions for two compensating horizontal gradients, 2000; Mechanism of finite-amplitude double-component convection due to different boundary conditions, 2004. Memberships: American Physical Society, 1995-2003; American Geophysical Union, 1995-; New York Academy of Science, 1995-2002; American Association for the Advancement of Science, 1999-2003. Address: 1 Yanosh Korchak Street, Apt 6, Kiryat Nordau, Netanya 42495, Israel. E-mail: naftali@eng.tau.ac.il

**TSUTSUI Toshinori,** b. 14 March 1952, Shiota, Saga, Japan. Anaesthesiologist. m. Kimiko Takeda. Education: Master of Science, 1978, Doctor of Medicine, 1986, Yamaguchi University, Japan. Appointments: Assistant Lecturer, Yamaguchi University, 1980-84; Senior Lecturer, Osaka City University, 1986-88; Chief Anaesthesiologist, Shimonoseki Welfare Hospital, 1988-96; Chief Anaesthesiologist, Saga National Hospital, 1996-2004. Memberships: Fellow, Japanese Society of Anaesthesiologists, 1978-; Fellow, Biomedical Fuzzy Systems Association, 1988-. Address: Department of Anaesthesiology, Saga National Hospital, 1-20-1, Hinode, Saga, Saga 849-8577 Japan. E-mail: ksikyoku@vega.ocn.ne.jp

**TSVETKOV Oleg Boris,** b. 7 September 1939, Leningrad, USSR. Professor of Thermophysical Properties of Fluids. m. Marianna Konstantin Utkina, 2 daughters. Education: Diploma in Engineering, Technological Institute of Refrigeration (TIR), Leningrad, 1961; PhD, TIR, 1965; DSc, TIR, 1983; Postgraduate, Northwestern University, Evanston, Illinois, USA, 1979-80; TIR, Leningrad, 1980-83; University of Maryland, Washington DC, 1987-88. Appointments: Research Assistant Professor, TIR, 1964-68; Associate Professor, Royal University, Phnom-Pehn, Cambodia, 1968-70; Acting Director, Research Department, TIR, 1970-79; Pro Rector of Research, State Academy of Refrigeration and Food Technology (SARFT former TIR), St Petersburg, Russia, 1983-98, Head of Department, State University of Refrigeration and Food Engineering (formerly SARFT), St Petersburg, 1991-. Publications: Numerous articles in professional journals. Honours include: Vice Chairman, 14th World Congress of Refrigeration, Moscow, 1975; Vice-President Com B1, International Institute of Refrigeration, 1972-75, 1995-; Medal, USSR Ministry of Higher Education, Moscow, 1981; President, Science and Technology Society of Food Industry, St Petersburg, 1990-98; Recipient, Excellence in Teaching and Research, 1993; Vice-President, International Academy of Refrigeration, 1998; Research Grantee, International Science Foundation, 1994; Medal, Fifty Years of Victory in Second World War, 1995; Deputy editor-in-chief Proc. of the International Academy of Refrigeration, 1997; Research Grantee, EU Contract, 1998-2002; Professor Emeritus, 1999; Medal, 300 Years of St Petersburg, 2003; Vice President, Programm Committee of XI Russian Thermophysical Properties Conference, 2004; Medal, 60 Years of the Liberation of Leningrad from the Blockade, 2004; Medal, Sixty Years of Victory in Second World War, 2005.. Memberships: International Academy of Sciences in Higher Education, 1992-;

Member, Editorial Board, Kholodilnaya Teknika, Moscow, 1992-; Member, International Academy of Refrigeration, 1993; Member, International Union of Pure and Applied Chemistry, 1994-; Member, Editorial Board, Refrigeration Business, 1995-; Member, National Committee on Thermophysics, Russian Academy of Sciences, 1997-. Address: 31 Moika Embankment, Apt 54, 191186 St Petersburg, Russia. E-mail: obereg@softrex.com

**TUBBS Charles A,** b. 21 October, 1953, Beloit, USA. Law Enforcement Officer. m. Cindy Olstead, 3 sons, 1 daughter. Education: Sociology, University of Wisconsin, Rock County, 1972-1974; Graduate, Police Academy, Blackhawk Technical College, 1974; Graduate, Special Studies, Wisconsin State Patrol Academy, 1978; Graduate, Senior Police Executive Institute, University of Wisconsin, OSKOSH, 1987; Graduate, Northwestern University School of Police Staff and Command, 1995; BS, Criminal Justice Administration, Mount Senario College, 1997. Appointments: Jr Police Officer, 1969-70; Field Patrol Officer, 1974-79; Police School Liaison Officer, 1979-80; Patrol Sergeant, 1980-83; Administrative Captain, 1983-87; Captain of the Records Bureau, 1987; Captain of Professional Standards and Training, 1987-88; Captain of Patrol, 1988-90; Interim Chief of Police, 1990-91; Captain of People and Public Issues, 1991-96; East Side Patrol Captain District Commander, 1996-98; Deputy Chief of Police, 1998-2004; Administrator, Division of Juvenile Corrections, 2004-. Honours: Numerous Awards and Honours include: Officer of the Year Award, Wisconsin Law Enforcement Officers Association, 1992, 1994; Distinguished Officer of the Year in USA, National United Law officers Association (Top Blacks in Law Enforcement), 1993; Outstanding Leadership Award, National Association for the Advancement of Coloured People, 1993; Honorable Mention, Top Cops, NAPO, 1994; One of the Top 100 Law Enforcement Official/Heroes in the USA, US President, 1994; Outstanding and Invaluable Service to the Community, US House of Representatives Special Congressional Award, 1994; Wisconsin Professional Police Association Certificate of Merit, 1996; Thrasher Award, National Gang Crime Research Center, 1996, 1998; Community Builders Award, Beloit, 1997; State of Wisconsin Certificate of Commendation, 1998; Distinguished Service Award for Appreciation, Brother Dutton Parochial School, 1998; Leadership Appreciation Certificate, Louis Porter Club, 1998; Inducted, Rock County Hall of Honor, 2003; Included in several who's who and biographical listing publications. Memberships include: National Black Police Officer Association; National Organization of Black Law Enforcement Executives; National Association of School Safety and Law Enforcement Officers; Wisconsin Law Enforcement Officers Association; Wisconsin Police Women Association; Wisconsin Association of Chiefs of Police; Former School Board member, School District of Beloit Board of Education; National Association for the Advancement of Coloured People; Central Christian Church; New Zion Baptist Church; Black Professional Role Models; Ambassador, Greater Beloit Chamber of Commerce; International Association of Chiefs of Police; Latino Coalition of Rock County; Optimist International. Address: 2690 Chatsworth Dr, Beloit, WI 53511-2306, USA. E-mail: charles.tubbs@doc.state.wi.us

**TUCKER Eva Marie,** b. 18 April 1929, Berlin, Germany. Writer. m. 11 March 1950 (widowed 1987), 3 daughters. Education: BA, Honours, German, English, University of London. Appointments: C Day-Lewis Writing Fellow, Vauxhall Manor School, London, 1978-79; Hawthornden Writing Fellowship, 1991. Publications: Contact (novel), 1966; Drowning (novel), 1969; Berlin Mosaic (novel), 2005; Radetzkymarch by Joseph Roth (translator), 1974. Contributions to: BBC Radio 3 and 4; Encounter; London Magazine; Woman's Journal; Vogue; Harper's; Spectator; Listener; PEN International. Memberships: English PEN; Society of Authors. Address: 63B Belsize Park Gardens, London NW3 4JN, England.

**TUCKER Helen,** b. 1 November 1926, Raleigh, North Carolina, USA. Writer. m. William Beckwith. Education: BA, Wake Forest University, 1946; Graduate Studies, Columbia University, 1957-58. Publications: The Sound of Summer Voices, 1969; The Guilt of August Fielding, 1972; No Need of Glory, 1973; The Virgin of Lontano, 1974; A Strange and Ill-Starred Marriage, 1978; A Reason for Rivalry, 1979; A Mistress to the Regent: An Infamous Attachment, 1980; The Halverton Scandal, 1980; A Wedding Day Deception, 1981; The Double Dealers, 1982; Season of Dishonor, 1982; Ardent Vows, 1983; Bound by Honor, 1984; The Lady's Fancy, 1991; Bold Impostor, 1991. Contributions to: Lady's Circle; Ellery Queen Mystery Magazine; Alfred Hitchcock Mystery Magazine; Ladies Home Journal; Crecent Review; Montevallo Review; Redbook Magazine. Honours: Distinguished Alumni Award, Wake Forest University, 1971; Franklin County Artist of the Year Award, 1992. Address: 2930 Hostetler Street, Raleigh, NC 27609, USA.

**TUKE Diana Rosemary,** b. 5 July 1932, Weymouth, Dorset, England. Lecturer; Freelance Journalist; Writer; Author. Education: British Horse Society Preliminary Instructor's Certificate, Porlock Vale Riding School, 1954. Appointments: Picture Editor, The Encyclopaedia of the Horse, 1973; Lectured, updated Equine Feeding Section of Instruction Manual, Metropolitan Police, 1986. Publications: A Long Road to Harringay, 1960; Bit-by-Bit, 1965; Riding Cavalcade, contributor, 1967; Tomorrow, short story, 1968; Stitch-by-Stitch, 1970; Horse-by-Horse, 1973; The Complete Book of the Horse (contributor), 1973; The Encyclopaedia of the Horse (contributor), 1973; Getting Your Horse Fit, 1977; The Rider's Handbook, 1977; Feeding Your Horse, 1980; Cottage Craft Guide to Aintree Bits, 1982; Horse Tack - The Complete Equipment Guide for Riding and Driving (contributor), 1982; The Country Life Book of Saddlery and Equipment (contributor), 1982; Clipping Your Horse, 1984; Feeding Your Horse and Pony, 2nd edition, 1988; Horse Trials Review No 2 - Feeding for Fitness, video, 1990; Clipping, Trimming and Plaiting Your Horse, 2nd edition, 1992; Nursing Your Horse, 1999, 2nd edition, 2002; Novels: Ravensworth, 2000, 2nd edition, 2005; When the Rivers Roared, 2000, 2nd edition, 2005; Away in the Mountains, 2001, 2nd edition, 2005; The Lonely Shore, 2001, 2nd edition, 2005; The Old Mill, 2004; Contributions to: Riding; Horse and Hound; The Daily Telegraph; The Field; The Cronical of the Horse, USA; Others. Honours: Trophies for sale of books: Bit-by-Bit, 25,000 copies, 1995; Getting Your Horse Fit, 25,000 copies, 1995; Clipping, Trimming and Plaiting Your Horse, 10,000 copies, 1998. Membership: British Equestrian Writer's Association. Address: Gallery House, Duddenhoe End, Saffron Walden, Essex CB11 4UU, England.

**TULASIEWICZ Witold,** b. Berlin, Germany. Part time Professor of Language Education; Researcher. Appointments: Fellow, Wolfson College Cambridge; Former Full-time University Teacher, University of Cambridge; Director and Co-director of several national and international projects including: Education as Dialogue; Europe East and West; Currently researching and practising the application of a language awareness approach to the study of language. Publications include: Index Verborum zur deutschen Kaiserchronik (author); Teaching the Mother Tongue in a Multilingual Europe (co-author); Education in a Single Europe (co-author). Memberships: Comparative Education Society in Europe;

Association of Language Awareness; Committee for Russian and East European Studies in Cambridge; Polish Academy of Sciences Abroad; Belarus Academy of Educational Studies; Corresponding Member, Brandenburg Berlin Academy; Consultant to EU Committee of the Regions. Address: Wolfson College, Barton Road, Cambridge CB3 9BB, England. E-mail: wft20@cam.ac.uk

**TULEEV Aman Gumirovich,** b. 13 May 1944, Krasnovodsk, Turkmenian Republic. Politician. m. Elvira Solovyeva, 2 sons, 1 deceased. Education: Novosibirsk Institute of Railway Engineering, 1973; Academy of Social Studies, 1989. Appointments: Assistant Station Master, 1964-69, Station Master, 1969-73, Railway Station, Moundebash; Station Master, Railway Station, Mezhdurechensk, 1973-78; Head, Novokuznetsk Line, Kemerovo Railway, 1978-85; Head, Transport Department, Kemorovo's Regional Committee of the CPSU, 1985-88; Head, Kemerovo Railway, 1988-90; Chairman. Kemerovo's Regional Council of People's Deputies, People's Deputy of RSFSR, 1990-93; Candidate for Presidency, 1991, 1996, 2000; Chairman, Legislative Assembly of Kemerovo Region, Member of the Council of Federations of the Federal Assembly of the Russian Federation, 1994-96; Minister, Russian Federation for collaboration with the States, Members of CIS, 1996-97; Governor, Kemerovo Region, 1997-. Publications: Author of more than 100 articles and books including: Power in hands of a man and man in hands of the power, 1993; State power in region: personal factor, social contacts, 1998; To remain yourself, 1999; Political leader and political leadership in regional conflicts, 1999; We have the only Russia, 1999; Political leadership in modern Russia, 2000. Honours: The Order of Honor, the highest award of Mongolia; The Order of the North Star. Memberships: Honorary Railwayman; Freeman of Kemerovo and Novokuznetsk; Honorary Doctor of Sciences, Ulan-Bator University of Mongolian Academy of Sciences; Full Member, International Academy of Informatization; Full Member, International Engineering Academy. Address: pr Sovetskiy, 62, 650099 Kemerovo, Russia. Website: www.mediakuzbass.ru

**TULLY (William) Mark,** b. 24 October 1935, Calcutta, India. Journalist; Broadcaster. m. Margaret Frances Butler, 13 August 1960, 2 sons, 2 daughters. Education: Marlborough College; MA, Trinity Hall, Cambridge, 1959. Appointments: Regional Director, Abbeyfield Society, 1960-64; Assistant, Appointments Department, 1964-65, Assistant, later Acting Representative, New Delhi, 1955-69, Programme Organiser and Talks Writer, Eastern Service, 1969-71, Chief of Bureau, Delhi, 1972-93, South Asia Correspondent, 1993-94, BBC; Freelance writer, broadcaster, journalist, 1994-. Publications: Amritsar: Mrs Gandhi's Last Battle (with Satish Jacob), 1985; From Raj to Rajiv (with Z Masani), 1988; No Full Stops in India, 1991; The Heart of India, 1995; The Lives of Jesus, 1996; India in Slow Motion (with Gillian Wright), 2002. Honours: Officer of the Order of the British Empire, 1985; Padma Shri, India, 1992; Honorary Fellow, Trinity Hall, Cambridge, 1994; Honorary Doctor of Letters, University of Strathclyde, 1997. Address: 1 Nizamuddin East, New Delhi 110 013, India. E-mail: tulwri@ndf.vsnl.net.in

**TURJANMAA Ville Mikael,** b. 8 March 1970, Helsinki, Finland. Computer Programmer. Education: University of Helsinki, 1991. Appointments: Programmer, 1998; Founder of Menuet OS, 2000. Publication: Dr Dobbs (Cover), 2001. Membership: International Who's Who. Address: Caloniuksenkatu 3A 19, 00100 Helsinki, Finland.

**TURK Austin Theodore,** b. 28 May 1934, Gainesville, Georgia, USA. Sociologist; Criminologist. m. Ruth-Ellen Marie Grimes. Education: BA, cum laude, University of Georgia, 1956; MA, University of Kentucky, 1959; PhD, University of Wisconsin, 1962. Appointments: Instructor, to Professor, Indiana University, 1962-74; Professor of Sociology, University of Toronto, 1974-88; Professor of Sociology, 1988-, Chair, 1989-94, University of California at Riverside. Publications: Criminality and Legal Order, 1969; Political Criminality: The Defiance and Defense of Authority, 1982. Honours: President, American Society of Criminology, 1984-85; Fellow, American Society of Criminology, 1978. Memberships: American Society of Criminology; American Sociological Association; Academy of Criminal Justice Sciences; Law and Society Association. Address: Department of Sociology, University of California, Riverside, CA 92521, USA.

**TURNER Amédée Edward,** b. 26 March 1929, London, England. Queens Counsel. m. Deborah Dudley Owen, 1 son, 1 daughter. Education: BA, 1951, MA, 1953, Christ Church, Oxford. Appointments: Practised at Patent Bar, Inner Temple, London, 1954-57; Counsel at Kenyon & Kenyon (Patent Attorneys) New York, USA, 1957-60; Practice at Patent Bar, London, 1960-; Contested General Elections (Conservative) Norwich North, 1964, 1966, 1970; Appointed Queens Counsel, 1976-; Elected to European Parliament for Suffolk and Harwich and Suffolk and Cambridgeshire (Conservative), European Democratic Group, European People's Party, 1979-94; Chief Whip, 1989-2002, Chairman, 2002-04, Civil Liberties Committee; Counsel, Oppenheimer Wolff & Donnelly, Brussels, 1994-2001; Senior Counsel, Apco Europe, 1995-98; Member Executive Committee European League for Economic Co-operation, 1996-; Director, CJA Consultants, 2001-, Chairman, 2005-; Phare Advisor to Macedonian Parliament on approximation of EU legislation, 2001-2002; Member, Advisory Council to the Anglican Observer to UN, 2002-. Publications: The Law of Trade Secrets, 1964; The Law of the New European Patent, 1979; Reports for the European Commission including Intellectual Property Law and the Single Market, 1997; Numerous political articles on behalf of the Conservative Party. Honours: Queens Counsel, 1976; Honorary Member of the European Parliament, 1994. Memberships: Carlton Club; The European Network; Conservative Group for Europe; Tory Reform Group; Kenya Society; African Society; International Association for the Protection of Industrial Property; Bar Association for Commerce and Industry. Address: Penthouse 7, Bickenhall Mansions, London W1U 6BS, England. E-mail: amedee.turner@btinternet.com

**TURNER Bryan Stanley,** b. 14 January 1945, Birmingham, England. Academic. m. Eileen H Richardson, 1 son, 2 daughters. Education: BA, 1966, PhD, 1970, University of Leeds; D Litt, Flinders University, 1986; MA, Cambridge University, 2002. Appointments: Lecturer in Sociology, University of Aberdeen, 1969-74; Lecturer in Sociology, University of Lancaster, 1974-78; Senior Lecturer in Sociology, 1989-80, Reader in Sociology, 1980-82, University of Aberdeen; Professor of Sociology and Head of Department of Sociology, 1982-88, Foundation Director, Centre for Multicultural Studies, 1986-87, Flinders University, South Australia; Professor of General Social Sciences and Chairman of the Department, University of Utrecht, The Netherlands, 1988-90; Professor of Sociology, University of Essex, 1990-93; Dean of Arts and Professor of Sociology, Deakin University, 1993-98; Professor of Sociology, 1998-, Head of Department, 1999-2001, University of Cambridge; Professorial Fellow, Fitzwilliam College, Cambridge, 2002-05; Professor of Sociology, Asia Research Institute, National University of Singapore; Honorary Professor,

Deakin University, 2004-; Faculty Associate, Yale University, Center for Cultural Sociology, 2004-. Publications: 19 books as sole author include most recently: Classical Sociology, 1999; The New Medical Sociology, 2004; 13 edited books include; Blackwell Companion to Social Theory, 2000; Islam. Critical Concepts in Sociology, 4 volumes, 2003; The Sage Handbook of Sociology, 2005; Cambridge Dictionary of Sociology, 2003 ongoing; Numerous book chapters and articles in scientific journals. Honours include: Fellow, Human Rights Centre, University of Essex, 1992; Distinguished Visiting Fellow, La Trobe University, 1992; Distinguished Visiting Professor, University of Helsinki, Finland, 1995 FRSA, 2002. Memberships include: Fellow, Academy of Social Sciences, Australia; Fellow Fitzwilliam College, Cambridge; Australian Sociological Association; International Sociological Association; American Sociological Association; American Political Science Association; British Sociological Association. Address: 40 Sunset View, Singapore 597202. E-mail: aribst@nus.edu.sg

**TURNER Lynette,** b. 28 May 1945, London, England. Graphic Artist. Education: BSc (Hons) Zoology, Manchester University, 1965-68; Etching, City and Guilds Art School, 1968-69; HNDD, Graphic Design, Manchester Polytechnic, 1970-71. Career: Set up etching workshop at home at the Oval in London and sold prints at Heal's and Liberty's, 1975-94; Moved to Cornwall 1994-; Exhibitions: Century Gallery, Henley, 1976; Margaret Fisher Gallery, 1976; RA, 1977; SE London Art Group, YMCA, Great Russell Street, 1983; RA Summer Show, 1987; Etchings and watercolours, The Crypt of St Martin-in-the-Fields, 1989. Publications: Works featured in the Observer, 1989; Currently working on comic strip adventures. Honour: 2nd Prize for Etching, City and Guilds Art School, 1969. Membership: Royal Cornwall Polytechnic Society. Address: Pendynas, Minnie Place, Falmouth, Cornwall TR11 3NN, England.

**TURNER Martin William,** b. 3 October 1940, Reading, Berkshire, England. Artist. Widowed. Education: Painting, Medway College of Art, Rochester, Kent, 1957-60; Passed entrance examination to Royal Academy Schools, 1961. Career: Teaching and Lecturing in Art, 1957-61; First exhibited at the Royal Academy Summer Exhibition, 1961; Mural painting, commissioned by the Ministry of Defence, 1969; Series of paintings commissioned by the National Savings Bank, 1972; Commissioned portrait of Sir Robert Neame, 1977; Mural painting commissioned by GEC Elliot Automation, 1978; Mural Painting commissioned by Rochester City Council for their Civic Centre, 1984; Series of paintings purchased by King's College London, 1987; Series of commissioned paintings of: The National Westminster Tower, Lloyds of London, The Stock Exchange, Tower Bridge, The Guildhall, 1987; Series of paintings commissioned by the Medici Society of London street scenes, 1994; Regular exhibitor at: Royal Academy Summer Exhibition; Royal Institute of Oil Painters of Painters in Watercolour. Works represented in many public and private collections in the UK and abroad. Honours: Bronze Medal, Royal Institute of Painters in Watercolour, 1976; 2nd Prize, Artist in Watercolour Competition, 1977; Finalist, Athena International Art Award Competition, 1986; Prize-winner, Laing Landscape Competition, 1989; 2nd Prize, Nature in Art Competition, sponsored by Chevron, 1996; 2nd Prize, Singer & Friedlander/Sunday Times Watercolour Competition, 1998; 3rd Prize, Pastel Society, 2000; 2nd Prize, Royal Watercolour Society, 2001; 2nd Prize, Over Sixties Art Competition 2001, 2001; 1st Prize, Laing Landscape/Seascape Competition, 2001. Memberships: Elected Member, Royal Institute of Oil Painters, 1975; Elected Member, National Society, 1976. Address: 126 O'Donnell Court, Brunswick Centre, London WC1N 1AQ, England.

**TURNER Neil Clifford,** b. 13 March 1940, Preston, England. Research Scientist. m. Jennifer Gibson, 3 sons. Education: BS (Hons), 1962; PhD, 1968; DSc, 1983. Appointments: Plant Physiologist, CT Agricultural Experimental Station, New Haven, USA, 1967-74; Senior Research Scientist, 1974-84, Research Leader, 1984-93, Chief Research Scientist, 1993-, CSIRO Plant Industry, Canberra and Perth, Australia; Adjunct Professor, University of Western Australia, Perth, Australia, 1998-. Publications: Adaption of Plants to Water and High Temperature Stress, 1980; Plant Growth, Drought and Salinity, 1986; Crop Production on Duplex Soils, 1992; The Role of Agroforestry and Perennial Pasture in Mitigating Waterlogging and Secondary Salinity, Special Issue, Agricultural Water Management, 2002. Honours: Fellow, American Society of Agronomy, 1982; Fellow, Crop Science Society of America, 1985; Fellow, Australian Academy of Technology Sciences and Engineering, 1992; Medallist, 1993, Fellow, 1995, Australian Institute of Agricultural Science and Technology; Institute for Scientific Information Australian Citation Laureate, 2001; Foreign Fellow, Indian Academy of Agricultural Sciences, 2003; Centenary Medal, Australia, 2003. Memberships: Australian Academy of Technology Science and Engineering; Australian Institute of Agricultural Science and Technology, ACT President, 1978-79. Address: CSIRO Plant Industry, Private Bag PO 5, Wembley (Perth), Western Australia 6913 Australia.

**TURNER R Chip,** b. 18 January 1948, Shreveport, Louisiana, USA. Television Network Executive. m. Sandra Aymond Turner, 2 sons. Education: BA, Communications, Louisiana College, 1970; Baptist Theological Seminary, New Orleans, 1973; Accredited in Public Relations (APR-PRSA), 1995. Appointments: State Director, ACTS Television Network, State Media Director, Louisiana Baptist Convention, 1981-85; Assistant Director of Development, Coordinator of Telecommunications, Northwestern State University, 1995-97; National Director of Local Programming, Odyssey Cable Network, 1997-99; Vice-President for Marketing and Distribution, Family Net Television, Fort Worth, Texas, 1999-; National President of the Association of Baptists for Scouting, 2005-. Publications: The Church Video Answer Book; The Church and Video; Why Not Baptist? A History of the Association of Baptists for Scouting; Managing Editor and Contributor, 75 Glorious Years, A History of Calvary Baptist Church; Author of articles in over 35 magazines. Honours: National Distinguished Eagle Scout Award; Named Senior Practitioner for Southern Public Relations Federation; National Outstanding Youth Leadership Award for Religious Heritage of America. Memberships: Public Relations Society of America; Baptist Communicators Council; National Cable Telecommunications Association; National Religious Broadcasters. Address: Family Net, 6350 West Freeway, Fort Worth, TX 76116, USA. E-mail: cturner@familynettv.com

**TURNER Ted (Robert Edward II),** b. 19 November 1938. American Broadcasting Executive; Yachtsman. m. (1) Judy Nye, divorced, 1 son, 1 daughter, m. (2) Jane S Smith, 1965, divorced 1988, 1 son, 2 daughters, (3) Jane Fonda, 1991, separated, 1999. Education: Brown University. Appointments: General Manager, Turner Advertising, Macon GA, 1960-63; President, CEO, Various Turner Companies, Atlanta, 1963-70; Chair of Board, President, Turner Broadcasting System Inc (merged with Time Warner to form Time Warner Inc), 1970-96; Vice Chair, Time Warner Inc, 1996; President, Atlanta Vraves, 1976; Now Owner; Chair of Board, Atlantic Hawks, 1977; Better World Society, WA, 1985-90; Founder and Chair, UN Foundation; Director, Martin Luther King Center, Atlanta; Acquired New Line Cinema Corporation, 1993; Sponsor, Creator, The Goodwill Games, Moscow, 1986; Winner, 1977 America's Cup in yacht

Courageous. Publication: The Racing Edge, 1979. Honours: Named Yachtsman of the Year 4 times; Numerous Awards. Address: Turner Broadcasting System Inc, One CNN Centre, Box 105336, Atlanta, CA 30348, USA.

**TURNER Tina (Annie Mae Bullock),** b. 26 November 1939, Brownsville, Tennessee, USA. Singer; Songwriter. m. Ike Turner, 1958, divorced 1978, 4 sons. Appointments: Member, Ike and Tina Turner, 1958-78; Numerous TV, films and concert appearances world-wide. Creative Works: Solo Recordings: Let's Stay Together, 1983; What's Love Got To Do With It?, 1984; Better Be Good To Me, 1984; Private Dancer, 1984; We Don't Need Another Hero, 1985; One of the Living, 1985; It's Only Love, 1985; Typical Mae, 1986; The Best, 1989; I Don't Wanna Lose You, 1989; Be Tender With Me Baby, 1990; It Takes Two, 1990; Way of the World, 1991; I Don't Wanna Fight, 1993; Goldeneye, 1995; Wildest Dreams, 1996; Films: Gimme Shelter, 1970; Soul to Soul, 1971; Tommy, 1975; Mad Max Beyond the Thunderdome, 1985; What's Love Got to Do with It , vocals, 1993; Last Action Hero, 1993. Publication: I, Tina (autobiography), 1985. Honours: Grammy Awards; Record of the Year; Song of the Year; Best Female Vocal Performance; Best Female Rock Vocal, 1985; Favourite Soul/R&B Female Artist & Video Artist, 1985; Best Female Pop/Rock Artist, 1986; MTV Music Video Award, 1985; Star on Hollywood Walk of Fame, 1986; Rock'n'Roll Hall of Fame (with Ike Turner), 1991; World Music Award, Outstanding Contribution to The Music Industry, 1993.

**TURNER-WARWICK Margaret,** b. 19 November 1924, London. Physician. m. Richard Turner-Warwick, 2 daughters. Education: MA, BM, BCh, Oxford University, 1950, DM, 1956; PhD, London University, 1961; Clinical Training, University College Hospital, Brompton Hospital, 1950-61; Consultant Physician: Elizabeth Garrett Anderson Hospital, 1961-67; Brompton and London Chest Hospitals, 1967-72; Professor of Medicine, Brompton and Cardiothoracic Institute, London, 1972-87; Dean, Cardiothoracic Institute, London, 1984-87; President, Royal College of Physicians, 1989-92; Chairman, Royal Devon Exeter Healthcare Trust, 1992-95. Publication: Book: Immunology of Lung, 1979. Honours: Dame Commander of the British Empire; Osler Medal, Oxford, 1996; Presidential Award, European Respiratory Society, 1997; President's Medal, British Thoracic Society, 1999; Honorary DSc: New York University, 1985, Exeter University, 1990, University of London, 1990, Hull University, 1991, University of Sussex, 1992, University of Oxford, 1992, University of Cambridge, 1993, University of Leicester, 1997; Fellowships: ACP (Hon.); Royal College of Radiology; Fellow, Academy of Medical Science, 1998; Royal College of Physicians, Ireland; Royal College of Physicians and Surgeons, Glasgow; University College, London; Faculty of Public Health Medicine; Faculty of Occupational Medicine; Royal Australian College of Physicians; Bencher, Middle Temple (Hon.); Royal College of Physicians and Surgeons, Canada (Hon.); Royal College of Anaesthetists (Hon.); College of Medicine of South Africa (Hon.); Royal College of Pathologists (Hon.); Imperial College London (Hon.); Royal College of General Practitioners (ad eundum); Royal College of Physicians of Edinburgh; Royal College of General Practitioners; Green College, Oxford (Hon.); Lady Margaret Hall, Oxford (Hon.); Girton College, Cambridge (Hon.). Memberships: British Thoracic Society, President, 1982; Academy of Malaysia; South German and Australasian Thoracic Societies (Hon.); Association of Physicians of Great Britain and Ireland (Hon.); Alpha Omega Alpha. Address: Pynes House, Thorverton, Nr Exeter, Devon EX5 5LT, England.

**TUTSSEL Mark Christopher,** b. 31 August 1958, Cardiff, Wales. Advertising Creative Director. m. Julie Elizabeth Tutssel, 1 son. Education: Cardiff College of Art and Design, 1976-80; Harrison Cowley Advertising Fellowship, 1979-80. Appointments: Junior Art Director, Saatchi & Saatchi, 1980-81; Art Director, MWK Advertising, 1981-86; Art Director, 1986-90, Creative Director, 1990-99, Executive Creative Director, 1999-2002, Leo Burnett, London; Vice-Chairman and Deputy Chief Creative Officer, Leo Burnett USA, 2002-2004; Vice-Chairman and Regional Chief Creative Officer, Leo Burnett North America, 2004-. Publications: Work appears in various books including: Design and Art Direction; The One Show; Eurobest; Communication Arts, USA; The Andy's; The Art Directors' Club of Europe; The Art Directors' Club of New York; Cannes Awards; The British Television Awards. Honours: Numerous advertising awards including: The Cannes Grand Prix; 8 Cannes Gold Lions; 2 Eurobest Grand Prix; 22 Eurobest Golds; 4 D&AD Silver Pencils; The Clio Grand Prix; The Andy Grand Prix, 10 Andy Awards; Former Welsh Schoolboys Champion, Football and Basketball; Most Awarded Advertising Creative Director in the World, 2001; Listed in biographical dictionaries. Memberships: Design and Art Direction; The One Club, New York; Fellow, Royal Society of Arts; Soho House, London and New York; East Bank Club, Chicago; Chicago Creative Club; London Welsh Rugby Club, London; Art Directors' Club of New York. Address: Leo Burnett, 35 West Wacker Drive, Chicago, IL 60601, USA. E-mail: mark.tutssel @chi.leoburnett.com

**TUTT Leslie William Godfrey,** b. London, England. Mathematical Statistician and Actuary. Education: MSc, PhD, London University. Appointments: Lecturer on financial, business statistical and actuarial topics to professional bodies and universities in UK, USA and throughout central and eastern Europe, 1970-; Consultant to a number of British companies, 1981-. Publications: Many research papers and technical articles on finance, pensions and insurance, modelling of mortality and morbidity trends, application of stochastic simulation to decision making, social policy issues associated with genetics, for UK and overseas actuarial, statistical and financial journals; Author, joint author of 17 books including: Private Pension Scheme Finance, 1970; Pension Scheme Investment, Communications and Overseas Aspects, 1977; Financial Advisers Competence Test, 1985; Financial Services Marketing and Investor Protection, 1988; Taxation and Trusts, 1989; Private Investment Planning, Corporate Investment Planning, 1990; Pensions and Insurance Administration, 1992; Personal Financial Planning, 1995; Pension Law and Taxation, 2002. Honour: Lectureship Diploma, Department of Mathematics, Moscow State University, Russia, 1995. Memberships: Fellow, Past Chairman, Institute of Statisticians of Royal Statistical Society; Fellow, Faculty of Actuaries, Member of Council, 1975-78; Board of Examiners, 1980-90; Associate, Society of Actuaries, USA, Fellow Society of Actuaries of Ireland, 1977; Chartered Insurance Institute, Examinations Assessor, 1980-2000; Fellow, Pensions Management Institute, 1976; Founder Member, Pensions Research Accountants Group, Member of Executive Committee, 1976-85; National Association of Pension Funds, Member of Council, 1979-83. Address: 21 Sandilands, Croydon, Surrey CR0 5DF, England.

**TUTT Sylvia Irene Maud,** b. London, England. Chartered Secretary and Administrator. Appointments: Chartered Secretary and Administrator in private practice; Writer; Senior Examiner, Chartered Insurance Institute, 1975-2004; Examiner, Society of Financial Advisers, 1992-2004. Publications: Author of numerous technical articles in professional and financial journals; Author or joint author of the following books: Private Pension Scheme Finance, 1970; Pensions and Employee Benefits, 1973; Pension Law and Taxation, 1981; Financial Aspects of Pension Business, 1985; Financial Aspects of Life Business, 1987; A Mastership of a Livery Company, 1988; Financial Aspects of Long Term Business, 1991; Pension Law and Administration, 2002. Memberships: Fellow and Past Member of Council, The Publications and Public Relations Committee, Education Committee, Benevolent Management Committee and Crossways Trust, Past President of its Women's Society and Past Chairman of London Branch, Institute of Chartered Secretaries and Administrators; Fellow Royal Statistical Society; Fellow Royal Society of Arts; Member of Court of City University London; Past President, Soroptimist International of Central London; Past President, United Wards Club of the City of London; Past President, Farringdon Ward Club, London; President, City Livery Club, London, 2001-2002; Past Chairman and currently Vice-President, Royal Society of St George, City of London Branch; Court Assistant, The Scriveners Company; Master, 1983-84, Worshipful Company of Chartered Secretaries and Administrators, Member of its Finance and General Purposes Committee, Managing Trustee of its Charitable Trust, 1978-; Freeman, Guild of Freemen of the City of London. Address: 21 Sandilands, Croydon, Surrey CR0 5DF, England.

**TUTTLE Lisa,** b. 16 September 1952, Houston, Texas, USA. Writer. Education: BA, Syracuse University, 1973. Publications: Windhaven, 1981; Familiar Spirit, 1983; Catwitch, 1983; Children's Literary Houses, 1984; Encyclopedia of Feminism, 1986; A Spaceship Built of Stone and Other Stories, 1987; Heroines: Women Inspired by Women, 1988; Lost Futures, 1992; Memories of the Body, 1992; Panther in Argyll, 1996; The Pillow Friend, 1996; Love on Line, 1998; Writing Fantasy and Science Fiction, 2001; The Mysteries, 2005. Contributions to: Magazines. Honour: John W Campbell Award, 1974; British Science Fiction Award, 1989. Address: C/O Abner Stein, 10 Roland Gardens, London SW7 3PH, England.

**TUTU Desmond Mpilo, (Most Rev),** b. 7 October 1931, Klerksdorp, South Africa. Archbishop Emeritus. m. Leah Nomalizo Tutu, 1955, 1 son, 3 daughters. Education: Bantu Normal College; University of South Africa; St Peter's Theological College, Rosettenville; King's College, University of London; LTh; MTh. Appointments: Schoolmaster, 1954-57; Parish priest, 1960-; Theology Seminary Lecturer, 1967-69; University Lecturer, 1970-71; Associate Director, Theology Education Fund, World Council of Churches, 1972-75; Dean of Johannesburg, 1975-76; Bishop of Lesotho, 1977-78; Bishop of Johannesburg, 1984-86; Archbishop of Cape Town, Metropolitan of the Church of the Province of Southern Africa, 1986-96; Chancellor, University of Western Cape, 1988-; President, All Africa Conference of Churches, 1987-; Secretary-General, South Africa Council of Churches, 1979-84; Visiting Professor, Anglican Studies, New York General Theology Seminary, 1984; Elected to Harvard University Board of Overseers, 1989; Director, Coca Cola, 1986-; Visiting Professor, Emory University, Atlanta, 1996-; Leader, Truth and Reconciliation Commission, 1995-; Archbishop Emeritus, Cape Town, 1996-; Robert R Woodruff Visiting Distinguished Professor, Candler School of Theology, 1998-99; William R Cannon Distinguished Visiting Professor, Emory University, 1999-2000. Publications: Crying in the Wilderness, 1982; Hope and Suffering, 1983; The Rainbow People of God, 1994; An African Prayer Book, 1996; The Essential Desmond Tutu, 1997; No Future without Forgiveness, 1999. Honours include: Numerous Honorary Degrees; Nobel Peace Prize, 1984; Carter-Menil; Human Rights Prize, 1986; Martin Luther King Junior Peace Award, 1986; Third World Prize, 1989; Order of

Jamaica; Freedom of Borough of Merthyr Tydfil, Wales; Order of Meritorious Service, South Africa, 1996; Order of Grand Cross, Germany; Nelson Mandela Award for Health and Human Rights, Florida, USA, 1998; Monismanien Prize, Uppsala University Sweden, 1999; MESB Service Award, Medical Education for South African Blacks, 1999; Athenagoras Award for Human Rights, 2000. Memberships: Third Order of Society of St Francis; President, All Africa Conference of Churches; Council for National Orders, Republic of South Africa. Address: c/o Truth and Reconciliation Commission, PO Box 3162, Cape Town 8000, South Africa.

**TVETEN Ulf,** b. 16 May 1934, Oslo, Norway. Senior Scientist. Divorced, 1 son. Education: Master of Science, Physics, Chemistry, Astronomy, University of Oslo, Norway, 1959. Appointments: Norwegian Defence Research Establishment, 1959-60; Leader, Radiation Shielding Group, Institute for Atomic Energy, Kjeller, Norway, 1960-67; Research Scientist, Rocket Engine Operations Nuclear Project, Aerojet-General Corporation, Sacramento, California, USA, 1967; Research Scientist, Stone & Webster Corporation, Boston, Massachusetts, USA, 1968; Senior Scientist, Institute for Energy Technology (former Institute for Atomic Energy), 1968-; Chairman, OECD/NEA Group of Experts on Reactor Accident Consequence Assessment, 1986-; Consultant, United States Nuclear Regulatory Commission, 1989, 1990; Epidemiological studies on Aircraft personnel/Cosmic radiation/Cancer, 1992-; Epidemiological studies on Aircraft personnel/Cosmic radiation/ Pregnancy outcomes, 2000-; Principal oboe and English horn player, University Symphony Orchestra of Oslo; Several exhibitions of tapestries in the Oslo area. Publications: Numerous publications as author and co-author include: Accident analyses performed for the Norwegian Government Commission on Nuclear Power, 1979; How the fall-out from Chernobyl was detected and measured in Nordic Countries, 1986; Environmental consequences of releases from nuclear accidents, 1990; Cancer incidence among Norwegian airline pilots, 2000; Comparing different methods of estimating cosmic radiation exposure of airline personnel, 2000; Aircraft Accidents and Other Causes of Death among Norwegian Commercial Pilots, 2002; Pregnancy outcome in offspring of airline pilots and cabin attendants, 2003. Memberships: Several Expert Groups at Organisation for Economic Co-operation and Development; Numerous Expert groups International Atomic Energy Agency; Board, International Union of Radioecology; SCOPE50 Work Group, (Scientific Committee on Problems of the Environment); Board, Gay Health Council; National and Nordic Associations against AIDS. Address: Munkedamsveien 100, N-0270 Oslo, Norway. E-mail: ulf.tveten@c2i.net

**TWAIN Shania,** b. 28 August 1965, Windsor, Toronto, Canada. Country Singer; Songwriter. m. Robert John Lange, 1 son. Appointments: Several TV performances on CMT and TNN; Songwriter with husband. Creative Works: Albums: Shania Twain: The Woman in Me; Come On Over; Up! 2002; Singles: Any Man of Mine; From This Moment On; That Don't Impress Me Much; Man! I Feel Like A Woman; Don't Be Stupid (You Know I Love You); I'm Gonna Get You Good, 2002; Up! 2003; Ka-Ching! 2003. Honour: CMT European Rising Video Star of the Year, 1993; Favourite New Country Artist, American Music Award, 1995; Female Vocalist Award, Canadian Country Music Awards, 1995; Female Artist of the Year; Country Music TV/Europe, 1996; numerous other awards. Address: Mercury Nashville, 54 Music Square E, Nashville, TN 37203, USA. Website: www.shaniatwain.com

**TWUM Michael Kyei,** b. 30 April 1954, Worawora, Ghana. Author; Poet. m. Maureen, 22 August 1986, 3 sons. Education:

Modern School of Commerce, Accountancy, Ghana, 1974; German Language and Culture, University of Bonn, 1984. Appointments: Author Poet, 1970-; Regional Accountant, Ministry of Agriculture, Ivory Coat, 1976-77; Bilingual Secretary, Chartered Accountants, Ivory Coast, 1978-79; Administrative Accountant, American Embassy, Ivory Coast, 1979-80. Publications: Golden Poems from Africa, 1982; Beyond Expectations, 1983; Great Adventures of an African, 1984. Contributions to: Newspapers and magazines. Honours: Certificates, IBC, England; Silver Medal, 1985, Gold Medal, 1987, Shield of Valor, ABI, USA. Memberships: ABIRA, Lifetime Deputy Governor, IBC; National Association of Writers; PEN International; World Institute of Achievement; Secretary General, United Cultural Convention, 2004. Address: 78 Acacia Road, Mitcham, Surrey CR4 1ST, England.

**TYLER Anne,** b. 25 October 1941, Minneapolis, Minnesota, USA. Writer. m. Taghi M Modaressi, 3 May 1963, 2 children. Education: BA, Duke University, 1961; Postgraduate Studies, Columbia University, 1962. Publications: If Morning Ever Comes, 1964; The Tin Can Tree, 1965; A Slipping Down Life, 1970; The Clock Winder, 1972; Celestial Navigation, 1974; Searching for Caleb, 1976; Earthly Possessions, 1977; Morgan's Passing, 1980; Dinner at the Homesick Restaurant, 1982; The Best American Short Stories, 1983 (editor with Shannon Ravenel), 1983; The Accidental Tourist, 1985; Breathing Lessons, 1988; Saint Maybe, 1991; Tumble Tower (juvenile), 1993; Ladder of Years, 1995; A Patchwork Planet, 1998; Back When We Were Grown-ups, 2001; Short stories in magazines. Honours: National Book Critics Circle Award for Fiction, 1985; Pulitzer Prize for Fiction, 1989. Memberships: American Academy of Arts and Letters; American Academy of Arts and Sciences. Address: 222 Tunbridge Road, Baltimore, MD 21212, USA. E-mail: atmBaltimore@aol.com

**TYLER Liv,** b. 1 July 1977, Portland, Maine, USA. Actress. m. Royston Langdon, 2003. Career: Film appearances include: Silent Fall; Empire Records; Heavy; Stealing Beauty; That Thing You Do!; Inventing the Abbotts; Plunkett and Macleane, 1999; Armageddon, 1998; Cookie's Fortune, 1999; Onegin, 1999; The Little Black Book, 1999; Dr T and the Women, 2000; The Lord of the Rings: The Fellowship of the Ring, 2001; One Night at McCool's, 2001; The Lord of the Rings: The Two Towers, 2002; The Lord of the Rings: The Return of the King, 2003; Jersey Girl, 2004; Lonesome Jim, 2004. Address: c/o CAA, 9830 Wilshire Boulevard, Beverly Hills, CA 90212, USA.

**TYMAN John Henry Paul,** b. 9 November 1923, London. Retired Academic. m. Barbara Eveline Hood Phillips, 2 sons. Education: BSc, Chemistry, Maths, University of London, 1943; PhD, 1960; FRSC, 1969; DSc, 1982. Appointments: Works and Development Chemist, May and Baker Ltd, Rhone, Poulenc, 1943-45; Research Scientist, Senior Scientist, Unilever Ltd, 1945-56; Research and Development Manager, Proprietary Perfumes, Quest International, 1956-62; Lecturer, Reader, Chemistry, Brunel University, 1963-89. Publications: Numerous academic papers to learned societies, educational videos, patents and contributions to international symposia on chemistry totalling 200 topics; 5 books. Honours: Several research grants. Memberships: Royal Society of Chemistry, 1944-; Society of Chemical Industry, 1951-. Address: 150 Palewell Park, East Sheen, London, SW14 8JH, England. E-mail: jhptyman@hotmail.com

**TYSON Mike G,** b. 30 June 1966, New York, USA. Boxer. m. Robin Givens, 1988, divorced 1989. Appointments: Defeated Trevor Berbick to win WBC Heavyweight Title, 1986; Winner WBA Heavyweight Title, 1987; IBF Heavyweight Title, 1987;

Former Undefeated World Champion, winner all 32 bouts, lost to James Buster Douglas, 1990; Defeated Donovan Ruddock, 1991; Sentenced to 6 years imprisonment for rape and two counts of deviant sexual practice, 1992; Appealed against sentence; Appeal rejected by US Supreme Court, 1994; released, 1995; Regained title of Heavyweight World Champion after defeating Frank Bruno, 1996; Lost to Evander Holyfield, 1996; License revoked by Nevada State Athletics Commission after disqualification from rematch against Holyfield, 1996; reinstated on appeal 1998; Sentenced to a years imprisonment for assault, 1999; released on probation, 1999; Fought Lennox Lewis, 2002 for the WBC and IBF titles, knocked out in eighth round. Honours: Honorary Chair Cystic Fibrosis Association, 1987; Young Adult Institute, 1987. Address: Don King Productions, 501 Fairway Drive, Deerfield Beach, FL 33441, USA.

**TZANEV Ivan,** b. 30 November 1941, Ostritza, Bulgaria. Poet. m. Malina Tomova, 3 daughters. Education: Slavic Languages Department, Sofia University "St Clement Ohridsky", 1968. Appointments: Editor, Studentska Tribuna Newspaper, 1967-69; Editor, Rodna Rech Literary Magazine, 1969-72; Editor, Plamak Literary Magazine, 1973-81; Editor, Bulgarian Artist Publishing House, 1981-82; Editor, Bulgarian Writer Publishing House, 1982-91; Editor-in-Chief, Children's Literary Supplement, Alf, of Literary Forum Newspaper, 1991-92; Free-lance Poet, 1992-99; Editor, Rodna Rech Literary Magazine, 1999-2000; Free-lance Poet, 2000-. Publications: 8 books of poetry; 14 books of poetry for children. Honours: National Literary Award "P R Slavejkov" for contribution to development of literature for children, 1994; National Literary Award, "Ivan Nikolov", 1997; Andrersen's Author Diploma, 1998; Award, International Art Academy, Paris, 1998; National Award "Hr G Danov" for the Best Children's Book, 2000; National Award, "Furnadjiev", 2000; National Award, "Yavorov", 2001; National Award, "Penjo Penev", 2002. Memberships: Union of Bulgarian Writers, 1972-95; Association of Bulgarian Writers, 1995-; International Art Academy, Sofia-Paris, 1998-. Address: 41 Skobelev Blvd, Sofia 1606, Bulgaria. E-mail: stigmati@abv.bg

# U

**UBUKATA Yuu,** b. 18 January 1945, Gumma, Japan. Professor. m. Yohko Ida, 2 sons, 1 daughter. Education: Master of Engineering, 1969, Doctor of Science, 1996, Tokyo Metropolitan University. Appointment: Department of Civil Engineering, Tokyo Metropolitan University, 1969-. Publications: Physiology of Phosphate-removing Bacteria; Fundamental Mechanisms in Biological Wastewater Treatment. Memberships: New York Academy of Sciences; International Water Association. Address: Tokyo Metropolitan University, Department of Civil & Environmental Engineering, 1-1 Minami-ohsawa, Hachiohji, Tokyo 192-0397, Japan. E-mail: ubukata@ecomp.metro-u.ac.jp

**UCHIDA Kazuo,** b. 31 October 1938, Kyoto, Kyoto-Fu, Japan. Technologist; Director. m. Akiko Terao, 1 son. Education: Kyoto University Medical Technology School, 1961; Japan Certified Clinical Chemist; Japan Certified Medical Technologist. Appointments: Chief Chemist, Kobe Steel Co Ltd Hospital, Kobe, Japan, 1961-72; Head Chemist, Japan Medical Laboratories, Ibaraki, Japan, 1972-84; Director, Kyoto Medical Science Laboratory, Kyoto, Japan, 1984-. Publications: Articles in medical journals include: Improving diagnostic information from urine analysis (co-author in Japanese), 2002; Measurements of cystatin-C and creatinine in urine, 2002. Honours: Recipient Ogata Tomio Award, Ogata Tomio Granting Body, 1993; Katoh Katuya Award, Nagoya Public Health Institute, 1995. Memberships: Japan Society for Clinical Chemistry, Japan Society of Laboratory Medicine. Address: 102-30-4-3 Morikitacho, Higashinada-ku, Kobe-City, Hyogo-ken, 658-0001 Japan. E-mail: uchidakz@mb.infoweb.ne.jp

**UENO Makato,** b. 2 December 1969, Matsue, Japan. Paediatrician; Neurologist. m. Noriko. Education: MD, 1995, PhD, 2003, Tottori University, Yonago, Japan. Appointments: Physician, Division of Child Neurology, Institute of Neurological Sciences, Faculty of Medicine, Tottori University, Yonago, Japan, 1995-96, 1997-2004; Physician, Department of Paediatrics, Faculty of Medicine, Kyushu University, Fukuoka, Japan, 1996-97. Publications: Books: Neural tube defect, congenital malformation of the brain, 2001; Congenital disorders of glycosylation, 2003; 7 articles in medical journals include most recently: High-dose ethosuximide for epilepsy in Angelman syndrome: implication of GABA (A) receptor subunit, 2001; Unilateral occlusion of the middle cerebral artery after varicella-zoster virus infection, 2002; Photosensitivity in electroencephalogram of child with 45, X/46, X, mar (X) Turner Syndrome, 2003. Memberships: Japan Paediatric Society; Japan Society of Human Genetics; Japan Society of Child Neurology; Japan Epilepsy Society. Address: Division of Child neurology, Institute of Neurological Sciences, Faculty of Medicine, Tottori University, 36-1 Nishi-Machi, Yonago 683-8504, Japan.

**UFODIKE Edochiem Ben Chidi,** b. 13 June 1946, Nnewi, Nigeria. University Professor. m. Chinyelu Ify, 3 sons. Education: BSc, University of Nigeria, 1975; PhD, University of Aston in Birmingham, England, 1981. Appointments: Teacher, Biology, St Louis Grammar School, Ibadan, 1975-76; Teacher, Biology, Federal Govt Girls College, Owerri, 1976-77; Lecturer, later Professor, University of Jos, 1977-; Visiting Professor, Universite Laval Quebec, Canada, 1990-91; Visiting Professor, Instituto Technologica de Sonora, Cuidad Obregon, Mexico on Third World Academy of Sciences Fellowship, 1991; Visiting Professor and Head, Department of Fisheries; Michael Okpara University of Agriculture, Umudike, Nigeria, 2000. Publications: Over 60 publications in scientific journals.

Honour: Fellow Nigerian Association for Aquatic Sciences, 1998; Service Diploma Award Olympic Federation, 2001, and others. Memberships: Nigerian Association for Aquatic Sciences; Biotechnology Society of Nigeria; American Fisheries Society; Japanese Society of Scientific Fisheries; Institute of Biology (UK); Rotary International; Full Gospel Business Mens Fellowship International. Address: Department of Zoology, University of Jos, Nigeria. E-mail: ufodike@unijos.edu.ng

**UGAJIN Ryuichi,** b. 17 June 1963, Tokyo, Japan. Physicist. Education: PhB, University of Tokyo, 1988; MS, 1990; PhD, 1997. Appointments: Research Scientist, Sony Research Centre, 1990-99; Frontier Science Laboratories, Sony Corporation, 1998-2002-; Fusion Domain Laboratory, Sony Corporation, 2002-; Senior Research Scientist, Head, Bio/Complex Area Laboratory, 2000; Leader Biomorphic Materials Initiative, 2001-2002; Editorial Board, J Nanosci Nanotechnology, 2001-. Publications: Physical Review Letters; Applied Physics Letters; Articles in various journals. Memberships: Physical Society of Japan. Address: Fusion Domain Laboratory, Sony Corporation, 5-21-15 Higashikojiya, Ota-ku, Tokyo 144 0033, Japan. E-mail: ryuichi.ugajin@jp.sony.com

**UKAEGBU David Okwukanmanihu,** b. 28 January 1939, Umuahia, Nigeria. Professional Accountant; MGT Scientist. Education: General Certificate of Education, Wolsey Hall, Oxford, Kings College, University College, Ibadan, 1958-66; Taxation, Foulks Lynch & Co Ltd, London; Chartered Secretaries and Administration, Metropolitan College, St Albans and Manchester College, England, 1962-70; Doctorate thesis, at Harvard University, Massachusetts Institute of Technology and Alexander Hamilton Institute Inc, through the Institute for International Research, London and New York, 1975-79; Degree in Management Sciences, MBIM, from the Institute of Management, UK and American Management Association, USA; BSc/MBA, Business Administration, California Coast University, Santa Ana, USA, 1982; Diploma, Kings College, Cambridge, 2000-01; Graduated with honours, Crossroads Bible Institute, USA, 2003; World Bible School, USA, 2004. Appointments: Chief Audit Clerk, 1958-60, Assistant Audit Manager, 1961-64, Audit Manager, 1964-66, Articled Clerk, 1967-70, Firms of Chartered Accountants; Professional Accountant and Management Consultant, 1971-2005; Professional Accountant, MGT Consultant, Charter House, 1971-2004; Chief Accountant, Consultant, Silver Shoes Manufacturing Company Ltd, 1974-99; Honorary Treasurer, Employers Association of Leather Footwear and Rubber Industries of Nigeria, 1990-94. Publications: Unpublished work in investment financing, 1986; Articles in professional financial journals. Honours: IBC Outstanding Speaker Award; ABI World Laureate; Recommended as Decision Maker in International Finance, Currencies and Foreign Exchange, International Reports, London; 2000 Scholars of the 20th Century; 2000 Scholars of the 21st Century; ABI International Peace Prize, 2003; 1000 Leaders of World Influence, Ambassador of Grand Eminence, Leading Intellectuals of the World, ABI; The Da Vinci Diamond for Inspirational Excellence, IBC; Certificate of Achievement, Crossroads Bible Institute, 2003; Certificate of Recognition, World Bible School, USA, 2004; World Medal of Freedom, ABI, 2005; Living Legends 2004/2005, International Professional of the Year, 2005, IBC. Memberships: New York Academy of Sciences; American Association for the Advancement of Science; Planetary Society; British Institute of Securities Laws; FFA; FCEA; AIPA, Dublin, Ireland; London Diplomatic Academy. Address: Charter House Auditors, No 9 Item St Umuahia, PO Box 998, Umuahia Abia State, Nigeria.

# DICTIONARY OF INTERNATIONAL BIOGRAPHY

**ULLMAN Susanne,** b. 15 May 1938, Copenhagen, Denmark. Physician; Professor of Dermatology; Doctor of Medical Science. Education: Medical Degree, University of Copenhagen, 1965; Postgraduate Training in Dermatology, Rigshospital, University of Copenhagen. Appointments: Visiting Professor, University of Minnesota, Minneapolis, USA, 1974-76; Professor of Dermatology, Rigshospital, University of Copenhagen, 1979; Visiting Professor, King Faisal University, Dahran, Saudi Arabia, 1981; Visiting Professor, Hunan Medical University, Changsa, Hunan, China, 1989; Professor of Dermatology, Bispebjerg Hospital and Rigshospital, University of Copenhagen, 1996; Co-ordinator, Education of Dermatologists in Denmark, 1983-90; Member, National Board of Health's Advisory Group on AIDS, 1984-89; Member, National Board of Health's Advisory Group on Sexually Transmitted Diseases, 1987-; Member, Committee for The Robert J Gorlin Conference on Dysmorphology, Minneapolis, 1996-. Publications: Author and Co-author, 90 publications in international and Danish journals. Address: Bispebjerg Hospital, Department of Dermatology, DK 2400, Copenhagen, Denmark.

**ULMANIS Guntis,** b. 13 September 1939, Riga, Latvia. Economist. m. Aina, 1 son, 1 daughter. Education: Diploma of Highest Education in Economy, The State University of Latvia, 1963. Appointments: Various positions and eventually Manager of Riga's Municipal Services; Member of the Board of the Bank of Latvia, 1971-92, 1992-93; Member of Parliament, 1993; President of Latvia, 1993-99; Director General of 2006 IIHF World Championship Organising Committee, 2002-2006. Publication: Autobiographical book: Notevis Jau Neprasa Daudz (subsequently translated into Russian). Membership: National Library of Latvia Support Foundation. Address: President's Chancery, Pils Laukums 3, Riga LV-1900, Latvia. E-mail: eva@president.lv

**UMEZULIKE Augustine Chibuzor,** b. 7 January 1960, Enugu, Nigeria. Medical Doctor. m. Clara Duchi, 1 son, 2 daughters. Education: School of Medicine, University of Benin, Benin City, Nigeria, 1980-86; University of Nigeria Teaching Hospital, Enugu, Nigeria, 1992-98; Chaim Sheba Medical Center, Tel Aviv University, Israel, 2003-2004. Appointments: House Officer, University of Nigeria Teaching Hospital, 1986-87; Youth Corps Doctor, Enugu Local Government Health Services, 1987-88; Doctor-in-Charge, Anambra State Prison Medical Service, 1988-92; Senior House Officer, Registrar, Senior Registrar, University of Nigeria Teaching Hospital, Enugu, 1992-98; Consultant Obstetrician and Gynaecologist, National Hospital Abuja, 1999-. Publications: 17 published articles or publications in both local and international journals in various aspects of obstetrics and gynaecology. Honours: Best Student in Medical Microbiology Examination, 1984; Ministerial Commendation for the First Surgical Operation in Enugu Prison, 1988; Rotaract Award for Selfless Services to Humanity, 1994; National Hospital Management Commendation for initiating and co-ordinating most successfully the First International Gynaecological Edoscopic Surgery Workshop in Nigeria, 2005; Listed in Who's Who publications and biographical dictionaries, 2004-05. Memberships: Nigerian Medical Association; Society of Gynaecologists and Obstetricians of Nigeria; Founder and Co-ordinator of "Women Health Issues" an NGO that surgically repairs VVF free of charge to patients; Medical Co-ordinator, Zarephat Foundation, an NGO working on HIV/AIDS, Rural Surgical Practice; Affiliated to Israeli Training Endoscopic Center. Address: Department of Obstetrics and Gynaecology, National Hospital Abuja, Nigeria. E-mail: acumezulike@yahoo.com

**UMLAUFOVA Miloslava,** b. 5 April 1939, Plana nad Luznici, Czech Republic. Consultant. m. Karel Umlauf, 1 son. Education: MSc, with honours, 1961; PhD, 1972. Appointments: Lecturer, 1960-64; Project Manager, 1964-65; Senior Lecturer, Czech Technical University, Prague, 1965-81; Vice Head, Department of Organisation and Managing, 1984-88; Vice Dean, Faculty of Civil Engineering, 1990-93; Associate Professor, 1981-94; Chief Executive, MC Triton, 1990-98; President, M C Triton, 1998-2004. Publications: More than 300 articles in field of management; Co-author, Organisation for success, 1991; Culture of Firm, 1993; Prevention and Management of Entrepreneurial Crisis, 1995. Honours: Successful Manager, Czech Republic, 1994; Award of Franz Kafka, 1999. Memberships: President, Czech Women's Business and Management Association; Chairman, Foundation Hospital Homolka. Address: Na Okraji 6, Praha 6, Czech Republic.

**UMODEN Gabriel Emmanuel,** b. 4 September 1954, Calabar, Nigeria. Educator; Publisher. m. Folasade Gab-Umoden, 2 sons, 2 daughters. Education: BA (Hons), Geography, University of Lagos, Lagos, Nigeria, 1977; Postgraduate Diploma, International Relations and Diplomacy, Nigerian Institute of International Affairs, Lagos, Nigeria, 1980. Appointments include: Accounts Officer, Ministry of Information, Calabar, 1973-74; NYCS Teacher, Government Secondary School, Mayo Belwa, Gongola State, 1977-78; Produce Officer, Federal Ministry of Trade, Lagos, 1978-80; Chairman, Chief Executive, Gabumo Group of Companies including: Gabumo Publishing Ltd, Accelerated Educational Services (Access) Ltd; Anjogab Graphic Equipment Co Ltd, Gabumo Investments Ltd, Vindes Properties Ltd, Galilee Seafoods Ltd, Access Books Distributors Ltd; Director, Manilla Insurance Co Ltd, Calabar, 1987-89; Vice-Chairman, Toro Petrochemicals Ltd, Lagos, 1988-; Vice-Chairman Obekpa Petrochemicals Ltd, Lagos, 1988- Chairman, Access Schools Governing Council, 1994-; Vice-Chairman, Obekpa Petroleum Ltd, Lagos, 1997-; LOC Board Member (Ghana-Nigeria, 2000, CAF Championship), 1999-2000. Publications: Books include: The Babangida Years (author), 1992; NYSC – Twenty years of National Service (co-author), 1993; Numerous books as publishing consultant include: International Peace and Security, 1997; National War College Yearbook, 1996-98; Capacity Building for Peace Keeping, 1998; Statecraft, Peace and Security, 1998; Bauchi State – The Making of a State, 1999; The UN Peace Mission in Angola, 1999; The Challenge of Peace, 1999; Nigeria: A People United, A Future Assured, Vol 1 & 2, 2000. Honours: Chieftancy Title "Ada Idaha Ke Efik Eburutu" by His Majesty The Obong of Calabar, 2001; Distinguished Citizen Award, Cross River State Government, 2002; Chieftancy Title "Ntufam Aseng Ekpeam" by HRM The Ndidem of the Quas and the Paramount Ruler of Calabar Municipality, 2003. Address: Gabumo House, Plot 5, North Industrial Estate, Esuk Utan, PO Box 389, Housing Estate Post Office, Calabar, CRS, Nigeria.

**UNSWORTH Barry (Forster),** b. 10 August 1930, Durham, England. Novelist. m. (1) Valerie Moor, 15 May 1959, divorced, 1991, 3 daughters, (2) Aira Pohjanvaara-Buffa, 1992. Education: BA, University of Manchester, 1951. Appointments: Lectureships in English; Writer-in-Residence, University of Liverpool, 1984-85, University of Lund, Sweden, 1988. Publications: The Partnership, 1966; The Greeks Have a Word for It, 1967; The Hide, 1970; Mooncrankers Gift, 1973; The Big Day, 1976; Pascalis Island, 1980, US edition as The Idol Hunter, 1980; The Rage of the Vulture, 1982; Stone Virgin, 1985; Sugar and Rum, 1988; Sacred Hunger, 1992; Morality Play, 1995; After Hannibal, 1996; Losing Nelson, 1999; The Songs of the Kings, 2002. Honours: Heinemann Award, Royal Society of Literature, 1974; Arts Council Creative Writing Fellowship,

1978-79; Literary Fellow, University of Durham and University of Newcastle upon Tyne, 1983-84; Co-Winner, Booker Prize, 1992; Hon LittD, Manchester, 1998. Address: c/o Hamish Hamilton, 22 Wrights Lane, London W8 5TZ, England.

**UPDIKE John (Hoyer),** b. 18 March 1932, Shillington, Pennsylvania, USA. Author; Poet. m. (1) Mary Entwistle Pennington, 26 June 1953, divorced 1977, 2 sons, 2 daughters, (2) Martha Ruggles Bernhard, 30 September 1977, 3 stepchildren. Education: AB, Harvard University, 1954; Ruskin School of Drawing and Fine Art, Oxford, 1954-55. Publications: Fiction: The Poorhouse Affair, 1959; The Same Door, 1959; Rabbit, Run, 1960; Pigeon Feathers and Other Stories, 1962; The Centaur, 1963; Of the Farm, 1965; The Music School, 1966; Couples, 1968; Bech: A Book, 1970; Rabbit Redux, 1971; Museums and Women and Other Stories, 1972; A Month of Sundays, 1975; Marry Me: A Romance, 1976; The Coup, 1979; Too Far to Go: The Maples Stories, 1979; Problems and Other Stories, 1979; Your Lover Just Called: Stories of Joan and Richard Maple, 1980; Rabbit is Rich, 1981; Bech is Back, 1982; The Witches of Eastwick, 1984; Roger's Version, 1986; Trust Me: Short Stories, 1987; S, 1988; Rabbit at Rest, 1990; Memories of the Ford Administration, 1992; Brazil, 1994; The Afterlife and Other Stories, 1994; Toward the End of Time, 1997; Bech at Bay, 1998; More Matter: Essays and Criticism, 1999; Gertrude and Claudius (novel), 2000; Licks of Love, 2001. Poetry: The Carpenter Hen and Other Tame Creatures, 1958; Telephone Poles and Other Poems, 1963; Midpoint and Other Poems, 1969; Seventy Poems, 1972; Tossing and Turning, 1977; Sixteen Sonnets, 1979; Jester's Dozen, 1984; Facing Nature, 1985; Collected Poems, 1953-1993, 1993. Non-Fiction: Picked Up Pieces, 1975; Hugging the Shore: Essays and Criticism, 1983; Just Looking: Essays on Art, 1989; Self-Consciousness: Memoirs, 1989; Odd Jobs, 1991; A Century of Arts and Letters (editor), 1998. Play: Buchanan Dying, 1974. Contributions to: Many publications. Honours: Guggenheim Fellowship, 1959; National Book Award for Fiction, 1966; Prix Medicis Etranger, 1966; O Henry Awards for Fiction, 1966, 1991; MacDowell Medal for Literature, 1981; Pulitzer Prizes in Fiction, 1982, 1991; National Book Critics Circle Awards for Fiction, 1982, 1991, and for Criticism, 1984; PEN/Malamud Memorial Prize, 1988; National Medal of Arts, 1989. Memberships: American Academy of Arts and Letters; American Academy of Arts and Sciences. Address: Beverly Farms, MA 01915, USA.

**URCH David Selway,** b. 10 February 1933, London, England. University Teacher. m. Patricia Maria Erszebet Hair, 4 sons, 1 daughter. Education: Drapers' Company's Scholar, 1951; BSc, 1st Class Honours, Chemistry, 1954, PhD, 1957, Queen Mary College, University of London. Appointments: Research Fellow, Yale University, USA, 1957-59; Lecturer, Birmingham University, England, 1960; Lecturer, Reader, Chemistry, Queen Mary and Westfield College, University of London, 1961-98; Senior Lecturer, Chemistry, Brunel University, 1998-2000; Chemistry Lecturer, New York University in London, 2000-. Publications: Over 200 papers in scientific literature; Book: Orbitals and Symmetry, 1970, revised, 1979. Honours: Fellow Royal Society of Chemistry; Chartered Chemist. Memberships: Royal Society of Chemistry; American Chemical Society; Mineralogical Society; Association of University Teachers; Catenian Association. Address: 56 Mount Ararat Road, Richmond, Surrey TW10 6PJ, England. E-mail: du3@nyu.edu

**UTHAMOCHOLAN,** b. 19 April 1944, Voimedu, Tamilnadu, India. Retired Government Officer. m. Saroja, 2 sons. Education: Bachelor of Arts, Political Science. Appointments: Tahsildar (Taluk Administrative Officer), Revenue Department, Government of India; Special Tahsildar, Gas Authority of India,

1996; Special Tahsildar, Oil and Natural Gas Corporation Ltd, 2000, 2001; Currently retired. Publications: Novels: Tholai Doora Velicham; Kasakkum Inimai, screened on TV; Poo Pookkum Kalam; Manasukkul Aayiram; Short story collections: Thunai Enroru Thodarkadhai, kept as lesson for Bachelor of Arts students, 1990-91; Arambam Ippadithan; Valkai Engum Vasalkal; Vallamai Tharoya; Sindhu Teacher; Manitha Theevukal; Kuruvi Marantha Koodu; Pamarasamy; Ore Oru Thuli; Thamacholan Short Stories. Honours: Tamil Ilakkia Mamani, Professor V Perumal Charitable Trust "KGF" Karnataka, India; Barathi Pani Selvar, All India Tamil Writers Association, Chennai; 20 Prizes for Best Short Story in competitions organised by various Tamil magazines; 2 Prizes for Best Mini Novel in literary association competitions; 2 Prizes for Best Novel in Tamil magazine competitions. Memberships: Honorary President, Member in Tamilnadu, Progressive Writers Association, Tamilnadu; All India Tamil Writers Association, Chennai, Tamilnadu; Joint Secretary, Lions Club of Thiruthuraipoondi (324-A2 Lions District), India. Address: 525 Sathya Illam, Mannai Road, Madappuram-614715, Thiruthuraipoondi, Tamilnadu, India.

**UYENO Teiso Edward,** b. 31 March 1921, Vancouver, British Columbia, Canada. Behavioural Psychopharmacologist. m. Mary Murata. Education: BA, 1947, MA, 1952, PhD, 1958, University of Toronto, Canada. Appointments: Research Assistant, University of Toronto, 1955-57; Research Associate, Stanford University, 1958-61; Behavioural Psychopharmacologist, Stanford Research Institute, 1961-77; Behavioural Psychopharmacologist, SRI International, 1977-. Publications: Over 90 scientific publications. Honours: National Institute of Health Grants, 1963-66, 1968-70, 1971-74. Memberships: American Society for Pharmacology and Experimental Therapeutics; American Psychological Association; Psychonomic Society; SRI International Alumni Association. Listed in: Several Biographical Publications. Address: 350 Valencia Drive, Los Altos, California 94022, USA.

**UZUNIDIS Dimitri Nicolas,** b. 24 May 1960, Alexandropolis, Greece. Professor; Economist. m. Sophie Boutillier, 1 son, 1 daughter. Education: Diploma, Journalism, Athens, Greece, 1979; Master in Sociology, 1985, PhD, Economics, 1987, University of Paris 10. Appointments: Associate Professor, Institute of Political Studies, Lille, France, 1991-96; Assistant Professor, University of Littoral, Dunkirque, France, 1992-; Professor, Postgraduate School, University of Littoral, Invited Professor, Institute of Social Management, Paris, 2002-; Director, Research Unit: Industry and Innovation, 1994-; Editor: Innovations, L'esprit economique. Publications: Le Travail brade, 1997; La Legende de l'entrepreneur, 1999; Mondialisation et Citoyennete, 1999; L'histoire des entrepreneurs, 2002; L'innovation et l'economie contemporaine, 2004: Firm Power In "Contemporary Post-Keynsian Analysis", 2005; John Kenneth Galbraith and the Future of Economics. Honours: Ministry of Industry, Athens, Greece, 1989; Ministry of National Education, Paris, 1999; Palmes Academiques, 2004. Memberships: French Council of Universities; Association of French Economists; The Society of Advancement of Socio-Economics; Observatory of Globalization; Vice-President, European Citizenship Association. Address: MRSH-Lab RII, 21 Quai de la Citadelle, F-59140 Dunkirque, France. E-mail: Uzunidis@univ-littoral.fr Website: www-heb.univ-littoral.fr/rii

# V

**VAGNORIUS Gediminas,** b. 10 June 1957, Plunge District, Lithuania. Politician. m. Nijole Vagnorienė, 1 son, 1 daughter. Education: D Econ Science, Institute of Engineering and Construction, Vilnius, Lithuania. Appointments: Engineer-Economist, Junior Researcher, Researcher, Institute of Economics, Lithuanian Academy of Sciences, 1989-90; Deputy to Lithuanian Supreme Soviet, Member, Presidium, 1990-91; Prime Minister of Lithuania, 1991-92, 1996-99; Member of Parliament, 1992-; Chair, Council of Ministers of Lithuania, 1991-92, 1996-99; Chair, Board, Homeland Union/Lithuanian Conservative Party, 1993-2000; Chair, Moderate Conservative Union, 2000-; Chair, Christian Conservative Social Union (CCSU). Address: CCSU, Odminiu Str 5, 01122 Vilnius, Lithuania. E-mail: sekretoriatas@nks.lt

**VAIDYA Sadashiv Satish,** b. 13 October 1961, Chalisgaon (MS), India. Electrical Engineer. m. Pushpalata, 1 son, 1 daughter. Education: IISS, Daly College, Indore (MP), India, 1979; BE, VRCE, Nagpur University, India, 1983. Appointments: Senior Design Engineer (Offshore Projects), Mazagon Dock Ltd, Mumbai, India, 1983-90; Electrical Design Engineer, M/S NPCC, Abu Dhabi, United Arab Emirates, 1991; Electrical Design Engineer, Offshore Engineering, M/S Abu Dhabi Marine Operating Company (ADMA-OPCO Oil and Gas Producing Company), 1992-; Associated with "Sri Sathya Sai Baba", India; Voluntarily building a school for poor students in Bhopal for higher secondary level education, fund-raising. Honours: Recognition Award for Y2K Project, ADMA-OPCO; Spot Recognition Award, ADMA-OPCO, 2001; Listed in Who's Who publications and biographical dictionaries. Address: ADMA-OPCO, ZKAU, 13E-1, PO Box 303, Abu Dhabi, United Arab Emirates. E-mail: vaidya@adma.co.ae

**VAIDYA Udaychandra.** Astrologer. Education: PhD, Astrology. Appointments: Jain Gospel Astrologer. Honours: MahaMahopadhyay, Gold Medallist, Sri Lanka; Jyotish Maharshi, Gold Medallist; Jyotish Chakravarti; Jyotish Vishwa Vidyacharya; Jyotish Mahasagar, Gold Medallist; Jyotish Bharat Bhushan; Jyotish Acharya; Jyotish Samrat; Jyotish Ratna; Honorary Research Advisor, ABI, USA; Man of the Year, ABI, USA, 2004. Memberships: MAIAS, USA; FMAFA, USA; PMIFA, Sri Lanka; MARP, CAL. Address: Om Astro Research Center, #494 Kulkarni Galli, Belgaum – 590 002, Karnataka, India. E-mail: udaychandra_vaidya@yahoo.com

**VAJPAYEE Atal Bihari,** b. 25 December 1924, Gwalior, Madhya Pradesh, India. Prime Minister of India. Education: Student of political science and law. Career: Journalist; Joined Bharatiya Jana Sangh, now Bharatiya Janata Party, 1951-; Elected to the Lok Sabha, House of the People, 9 times; Elected to the Rajya Sabha, House of the States, twice; Foreign Minister; Leader of the Opposition; Prime Minister of India, 1996, 1998-2004; Minister of Health and Family Welfare, Atomic Energy and Agriculture, 1998-. Publications: New Dimensions of India's Foreign Policy; Jan Sangh Aur Musalmans; Three Decades in Parliament; collections of poems and numerous articles. Honours: Hon PhD, Kanpur University, 1993; Padma Vibhushan; Best Parliamentarian, 1994. Memberships: Chair, National Security Council, 1998-; Member, National Integration Council, 1961-. Address: 7 Race Course Road, New Delhi 110011, India.

**VALDEIRA Maria Luísa,** b. Portugal. Cellular Biologist. Education: BSc, Pharmaceutical Sciences, 1975, PhD, Pharmacy, Microbiology, 1989, Lisbon University, Lisbon, Portugal; Postdoctoral, Enzimology, Virology, Gulbenkian Institute of Science, 1991. Appointments: Monitor of Microbiology, 1974-76, Assistant of General Cellular Biology and Pharmacognosy, 1976-89, Assistant Professor of Training of Structural Characterisation of Virus and/or Virusoids from Plants, Associate Professor of Cellular Biology, 2002-, Faculty of Pharmacy, University of Lisbon; Visiting Scientist: National Laboratory of Veterinary Research, Lisbon, Biochemistry Laboratory, University of Coimbra, Chemistry Department, University of Aveiro. Publications: Articles in scientific journals as co-author include most recently: Catechols from Abietic Acid. Synthesis and Evaluation as Antioxidants and Bioactive Compounds, 2003; Synthesis of Porphyrin Derivatives with Sugar Moieties and Evaluation of their Antiviral Activity Against HSV-1 and HSV-2, 2003; Study of antiviral activity of cationic porphyrins against Human Cytomegalovirus, 2003; Study of Antiviral Activity of porphyrin derivatives against herpes viruses, 2003; Evaluation of the Antiviral and Antimicrobial activities of Triterpenes isolated from Euphorbia Segetalis, 2003; An easy synthetic access to cationic -vinyl substituted meso-tetraphenylporphyrins: mass spectrometry studies and biological assays, 2004. Memberships: Portuguese Society of Electron Microscopy and Cellular Biology; Portuguese Society of Biotechnology; Portuguese Society of Biochemistry; Portuguese Society of Virology; Portuguese Pharmaceutical Society; Portuguese Scientific Workers. Address: University of Lisbon, Faculty of Pharmacy, Laboratory of Cellular and Molecular Biology, Av das Forcas Armadas. 1600-083 Lisbon, Portugal.

**VALERY Anne Catherine,** b. 24 February 1926, London, England. Scriptwriter; Autobiographer; Novelist; Theatre Playwright. Publications: Baron Von Kodak, Shirley Temple and Me, 1973; The Edge of a Smile, 1974; The Passing Out Parade (theatre), 1979; Tenko Reunion, 1984; Talking About the War... (non-fiction), 1991. Other: Over 50 television plays. Contributions to: Radio Times. Honours: Book of the Month, Telegraph; BAFTA Award, Tenko (TV Series), 1984; A chapter in the forthcoming book on Quentin Crisp: A Stately Homo. Memberships: PEN International; Fawcett Society. Address: Flat 3, 28 Arkwright Road, London NW3 6BH, England.

**VALIEV Ruslan Z,** b. 26 September 1949. Professor; Scientific Director. Education: Diploma, Physical Metallurgy, Ural State Technical University, Russia, 1971; Cand Sci (PhD), Solid State Physics, State University of Kharkov, Ukraine, 1977; Dr Sci, Solid State Physics, Institute for Materials Science, Academy of Sciences of the USSR, Kiev, 1984. Appointments: Research Associate and Instructor, Department of General Technology and Metals Science, Ufa Aviation Institute, now Ufa State Aviation Technical University, 1973-80; Research Director, Department of Physical Metallurgy, Ufa Aviation Institute, 1980-86; Deputy Director on Research, Professor and Head of Laboratory, Institute of Metals Superplasticity Problems, Russian Academy of Sciences, 1986-95; Professor and Scientific Director, Institute of Physics of Advanced Materials, USATU, 1995-; Head, Chair of General Physics, 2002-04, Head, Chair of Nanotechnologies, 2004-, Ufa State Aviation Technical University; Expert in modern materials science, pioneer and world authority in fabrication of bulk nanostructured metals by severe plastic deformation. Publications: Numerous invited talks and lectures presented at international conferences and meetings; 9 books; Over 350 papers in refereed journals; Over 10 patents (USSR, Russia and USA). Honours: Best Research Among Young Scientists, 1977; Silver Medal, Exhibition of USSR Achievements, 1988; Diploma, Scientific Discovery in the USSR, 1987; Corresponding Member, Bashkir Academy of Sciences, 1991; Medal, Institute of Material Science, Tokyo

State University, 1991; Outstanding Russian Scientists Award, 1994, 1997; COBASE Scholar in Northwestern University, USA, 1994; Professorship, INPG, France, 1992, 1993, 1995; Professorship, Doshisha University, Kyoto, Japan, 1996; International Science Foundation Award, USA-Russia, 1994; NSF Scholarship and Professorship, University of California, Davis, USA, 1997, 1998, 1999; NSF Scholarship, University of Southern California, USA, 1997, 1999; Professorship, University of Vienna, 2000; Humboldt Foundation Research Award, 2001; Gold Medal, All-Russia Exhibition of Achievements, 2002, 2003; #6 Most Cited Author Publishing in Materials Science, Institute for Scientific Information, USA, 2003-04. Memberships: Academic Committee for New Materials, Russia; Interstate Council on Strength and Plasticity, Russia; Bashkir Academy of Sciences, Russia; Council for Habitation Theses Defence, Russia; International Committee for Nanostructured Materials, Japan; The Minerals, Metals and Materials Society, USA; International Academy of Sciences for Institutions of Higher Learning, Russia; International Committee on Superplasticity, USA; International Committee on Strength and Plasticity, USA; International Committee on Physics of Strength and Ductility, Hungary; The Materials Research Society, USA; The Steering Committee "nanoSPD": Bulk Nanomaterials through Severe Plastic Deformation. Address: Institute of Physics of Advanced Materials, Ufa State Aviation Technical University, 12 K Marx St, Ufa 450000, Russia. E-mail: rzvaliev@mail.rb.ru

**VALLANCE-OWEN John,** b. 31 October 1920, Ealing, London, England. Physician. m. Reneé Thornton, 2 sons, 2 daughters. Education: Friars School, Bangor, 1930-36; Epsom College, 1936-39; St John's College Cambridge, 1939-43; MA, MB BChir Cantab, 1946, London Hospital, 1943-46; MD, Cantab, 1951; FRCP, 1962; FRCPath, 1971; FRCPI, 1973. Appointments include: Pathology Assistant and Medical First Assistant to Sir Horace Evans, London Hospital, 1946-51; Medical Tutor, Royal Postgraduate Medical School, Hammersmith Hospital, 1952-55, 1956-58; Consultant Physician and Lecturer in Medicine, King's College, University of Durham, 1958-64; Consultant Physician, Royal Victoria Infirmary and Reader in Medicine, University of Newcastle upon Tyne, 1964-66; Professor of Medicine, Queen's University, Belfast, 1966-82; Consultant Physician, Royal Victoria Hospital, Belfast, 1966-82, Belfast City Hospital, 1966-82, Foster Green Hospital, 1975-82; Foundation Professor and Chairman, Department of Medicine, 1983-88, Assistant Dean, 1984-88, The Chinese University of Hong Kong; Consultant in Medicine to Hong Kong Government, 1984-88, to British Army in Hong Kong, 1985-88; Medical Adviser on Clinical Complaints, North East Thames Regional Health Authority, 1989-96, Thames Regional Health Authority, 1995-96; Visiting Professor, Imperial College of Science Technology and Medicine, Hammersmith Hospital, 1989-; Consultant Physician, London Independent Hospitals, 1989-99 and Wellington Hospital, 1999-2003. Publications: Essentials of Cardiology, 1961, 2nd edition, 1968; Diabetes: Its Physiological and Biochemical Basis, 1976; Numerous papers in biochemical, medical and scientific journals. Honours: Rockefeller Fellowship, 1955-56; Oliver Sharpey Prize, Royal College of Physicians, 1976. Memberships: Life Member, Royal Society of Medicine; East India; United Services Recreation, Hong Kong. Address: 10 Spinney Drive, Great Shelford, Cambs, CB2 5LY, England.

**VALNERE Rita,** b. 21 September 1929, Bene, Latvia. Painter. m. Eduards Kalnins, 1 daughter. Education: Graduate, J Rozentala Art School, Riga, 1949; Graduate, Latvian Academy of Arts, Painting Department, under leadership of E Kalnins with diploma work, Puķu Veikalā, 1949-56; Professor, 1985; MA, 1992. Appointments: Exhibitions in Latvia and abroad,

1955-; Creative trip to France, 1965; Pedagogue, 1967-, Assistant Professor, 1978-, Professor, 1985-, Latvian Academy of Arts; Creative trip to Italy, 1970; Recent exhibitions include: One-man shows in Riga, 1977, 1980, Lapmežciemā (Tukuma district), 1983, Auce, 1985, Moscow, Artists of USSR Union House, 1987, "Nepārtrauktība", Latvian State Museum of Arts, 1996-97; Gallery M6 and Gallery Lita, Riga, 2000; Group exhibitions include: Moscow, 1980, Bremen (Germany), 1981, Luxembourg, 1983, Moscow, 1984, Berlin, 1984, Latvian Academy of Arts, Cologne, Dusseldorf, 1990; Works collected in State Art Museum of Latvia, Latvian Artists Union, Gekosso Gallery in Japan, Tretiakov Gallery in Moscow, Ministry of Culture of Russia, Tukums Art Museum and many private collections in Latvia, India, Germany, USA, Japan. Publications: Work appears in monographs, catalogues, books, albums, journals; Honours: Laureate, Baltics 2nd Painting triennial, Vilnius, 1972; Honorary Title of Latvia SSR, 1977; Diploma Latvian Artists Union, Medal and Prize, 1986; Peoples Artist of Latvia, 1987. Memberships: Latvian Artists Union, 1957; International Association of Arts B-13. Address: A Čaka iela 67/69, App 1, Riga, Latvia, LV 1001.

**VAMVUKA Despina,** b. 20 June 1958, Hania, Greece. Chemical Engineer. m. Theodore Kaloumenos, 2 sons. Education: Diploma in Chemical Engineering, 1982; MSc, Organic Chemical Technology, 1982; MSc, Advanced Chemical Engineering, 1983; PhD, Chemical Engineering, 1988. Appointments: Research Assistant, UMIST, UK, 1984-88; Postdoctoral, University of Patras, Greece, 1989-91; Associate Teaching Scientist, 1991-92, Professor, 1993-, Technical University of Crete. Publications: Book: Clean Use of Coals; University publications for students; About 55 articles in international scientific journals and conference proceedings. Honours: Invited Lecturer in universities; Member of Organising and Scientific Committees in conferences; Referee of international journals and research programmes. Memberships: Greek Association of Chemical Engineers; Greek Chamber of Technology; Combustion Institute; ACS. Address: Department of Mineral Resources Engineering, Technical University of Crete, Hania 73100, Greece.

**VAN ALLEN James Alfred,** b. 7 September 1914, Mount Pleasant, Iowa, USA. Physicist. Education: BS, Iowa Wesleyan College, 1935; MS, 1936, PhD, 1939, University of Iowa. Appointments: Research Fellow, Department of Terrestrial Magnetism, Carnegie Institute, Washington, DC, 1939-42; Ordnance and Gunnery Officer, US Navy, 1942-46; Supervisor, High Altitude Research Group and Proximity Fuse Unit, Applied Physics Department, Johns Hopkins University, 1946-50; Organised and led scientific expeditions to Peru, 1949, Gulf of Alaska, 1950, Greenland, 1952, 1957, Antarctica, 1957, to study cosmic radiation; Professor of Physics, Head of Physics Department, University of Iowa, 1951; Project Matterhorn, 1953-54; Research Associate, Princeton University, 1954; Helped organise International Geophysical Year, 1957-58; Professor of Physics, Head of Department, 1951-85, Carver Professor of Physics, 1985-92, Regent Distinguished Professor 1992-, Professor Emeritus, University of Iowa; Key figure in the development of the US space programme; Discovered the earth's magnetosphere, named the "Van Allen Belt". Publications: Physics and Medicine of the Upper Atmosphere; Rocket Exploration of the Upper Atmosphere; Origins of Magnetospheric Physics, 1983; 225 scientific papers. Honours: Numerous honorary DSc degrees; Distinguished Civilian Service Medal, US Army, 1959; NASA Medal for Exceptional Scientific Achievement, 1974; Distinguished Public Service Award, US Navy, 1976; Award of Merit, American Consulting Engineers Council, 1978; Space Science Award, American

Institute of Aeronautics and Astronautics, 1982; Crawford Prize, Swedish Royal Academy of Sciences, 1989. Address: Department of Physics and Astronomy, 701 Van Allen Hall, University of Iowa, Iowa City, IA 52242, USA.

**VAN ALLEN Veronica Elaine**, b. 6 May 1936, Queens, New York, USA. Director of Marketing. m. Ian Helsby, 2 daughters. Education: Bachelor of Education, University of Miami, 1963; Institute for Organisational Management Certificate, US Chamber of Commerce, 1990. Appointments: Teacher of English and Physical Education, 1963-67; Substitute Teacher, 1972-75; Executive Director, Royal Palm Festival (producing parades and airshows); Executive Vice President, Northern Palm Beaches Chamber of Commerce responsible for operation of chamber. Publications: Annual Chamber of Commerce "Guide to Northern Palm Beaches"; Royal Palm Festival Newspaper Supplement; "Airshow of the Palm Beaches" magazine; Regular column in local newspaper. Honours: Royal Palm Festival Newspaper Supplement Award; Royal Palm Festival Video Award. Memberships: International Festivals Association; Tourist Development Council of Palm Beach County; Leadership, Palm Beach County. Address: 170 Esperanza Way, Palm Beach Gardens, FL 33418, USA.

**VAN DE KAMP Alexandra**, b. 23 April 1965, Portchester, New York, USA. Poet; Editor; Professor. m. William D Glenn III. Education: BA, English, University College, London, Johns Hopkins University, Baltimore, USA, 1987; Master of Fine Arts, Poetry, University of Washington, Seattle, 1991. Appointments: Teaching Assistant, University of Washington, 1989-91; Reading Series Organiser, The Watermark Series, Seattle, 1990-91; Office Manager, Kaplan Educational Center, Seattle, 1992-93; Full-time ESL Instructor, Linguacenter, Madrid, Spain, 1993-94; Director of Studies, ESL Instructor, Linford Academy, Madrid, 1994-98; Founder, Madrid Writers Group, Spain, 1995-97; ESL Instructor, Eco 3, Madrid, 1998-99; Editor and co-founder, Terra Incognita magazine, Brooklyn, 1998-; ESL Instructor, Training Express, Madrid, 1999-2000; Adjunct Professor, English Language Center, New School University, New York, 2001; Adjunct Professor, Intensive English Program, Long Island University, 2000-; Curator, Latino and Latin American Reading Series, Cornelia Street Café, New York, 2003-. Publications: Prose, numerous poems and translations. Honours: Nominated, Pushcart Prize for Essay, 1994; 2001 Quentin R Howard Poetry Prize; Nominated, 2003 Pushcart Prize in Poetry. Memberships: Council of Literary Magazines and Presses, Terra Incognita. Address: 469 47th Street, Brooklyn, NY 11220, USA. E-mail: avandekamp65@yahoo.com

**VAN DEN BROEK Gerard J**, b. 18 July 1953, Netherlands. Director. m. Claudia Weertman, 1 son, 1 daughter. Education: BA, 1977, MA, 1980, Anthropology, Doctor of Social Sciences, 1986, Leiden University. Appointments: Director, Management, Moscow, St Petersburg Exhibitions and Conferences, 1993; Senior Consultant, Major Financial Institution; Account Manager, Public Relations; Science Journalist, Publicist, numerous periodicals; Research Associate, Leiden University; Managing Director, Bibliotheca Philosophica Hermetica, 1991-93; Director, Provincial Library of Friesland, 1996-2001; Director, Central Archives Selection Services, Home Office, 2001-. Publications: Numerous articles in professional international journals. Honours include: Grants, Netherlands Organization for Pure Scientific Research, 1983, 1984; Fulbright Grant, Netherlands-America Commission for Educational Exchange, 1984. Memberships include: American Board of Investigation, American Biographical Center; Netherlands Semiotic Society, Chair, 1991-94; Chair, Communal Commission of the Arts, 1997-2001; Board Member, Oldambt

Historiography Foundation, 2001-; Board Member, Memorial Foundation, Winschoten, 2004-. Address: Rijksstraatweg 124, 9752 BK Haren, The Netherlands.

**VAN DUYN Mona (Jane)**, b. 9 May 1921, Waterloo, Iowa, USA. Poet; Writer; Critic; Editor; Reviewer; Lecturer. m. Jarvis A Thurston, 31 August 1943. Education: BA, Iowa State Teachers College, 1942; MA, State University of Iowa, 1943. Appointments: Reviewer, Poetry magazine, 1944-70; Instructor in English, State University of Iowa, 1945, University of Louisville, 1946-50; Founder-Editor (with Jarvis A Thurston), Perspective: A Quarterly of Literature, 1947-67; Lecturer in English, 1950-67, Adjunct Professor, 1983, Visiting Hurst Professor, 1987, Washington University, St Louis; Poetry Advisor, College English, 1955-57; Lecturer, Salzburg Seminar in American Studies, 1973; Poet-in-Residence, Bread Loaf Writing Conferences, 1974, 1976; Poet Laureate of the USA, 1992-93; Numerous poetry readings. Publications: Valentines to the Wide World: Poems, 1959; A Time of Bees, 1964; To See, To Take, 1970; Bedtime Stories, 1972; Merciful Disguises: Poems Published and Unpublished, 1973; Letters From a Father and Other Poems, 1982; Near Changes: Poems, 1990; Lives and Deaths of the Poets and Non-Poets, 1991; If It Be Not I: Collected Poems, 1993; Firefall, 1993; Selected Poems, 2002. Contributions to: Many anthologies; Poems, criticism, reviews, and short stories in various periodicals. Honours: Eunice Tietjens Memorial Prize, 1956; National Endowment for the Arts Grants, 1966-67, 1985; Harriet Monroe Memorial Prize, 1968; Hart Crane Memorial Award, 1968; 1st Prize, Borestone Mountain Awards, 1968; Bollingen Prize, 1970; National Book Award for Poetry, 1971; Guggenheim Fellowship, 1972-73; Loines Prize, National Institute of Arts and Letters, 1976; Fellow, Academy of American Poets, 1981; Sandburg Prize, Cornell College, 1982; Shelley Memorial Award, Poetry Society of America, 1987; Ruth Lilly Prize, 1989; Pulitzer Prize in Poetry, 1991. Memberships: Academy of American Poets, chancellor, 1985; National Institute of Arts and Letters. Address: 7505 Teasdale Avenue, St Louis, MO 63130, USA.

**VAN GINNEKEN Andreas Johannes**, b. 1 January 1935, Wynegem, Belgium. Scientist. m. Lydia D Thompson, 1 son. Education: MSc, 1960, PhD, 1966, Chemistry, University of Chicago, USA. Appointments: Postdoctoral Fellow, Physics Department, McGill University, 1966-70; Staff Member, Fermilab, 1970-. Publications: Numerous articles in journals such as Physical Review and Physical Review Letters, Nuclear Instruments and Methods; Numerous presentations to conferences and workshops. Memberships: American Physical Society. Address: Fermilab, Box 500, Batavia, IL 60510, USA. E-mail: vangin@fnal.gov

**VAN MEERTEN Reinier Jan**, b. 2 July 1919, Kediri, Java. Retired Academic. m. Ans Van der Heide. Education: MSc, Biology and Chemistry, University of Wageningen, 1947, PhD, Physics, University of Nymegen, 1966; Self taught study of Decipherment. Appointments: Chemistry Teacher for 13 years; Head of Gas Research Laboratory and a Lung Function Department, Groesbeek/Nymegen for 20 years. Publications: Computer Guided Diagnosis of Asthma, Asthmatic Bronchitis, Chronic Bronchitis and Emphysema, 1971; Book: Creation (description of the creation of particles smaller than the electron, the structure of neutron, isoneutron and proton the origin of Life and the origin of Knossos), 2005. Honour: Summary of his book "Creation" featured in "Update", New York Academy of Sciences, 2005. Membership: Darwin Associate and Member, New York Academy of Sciences. Address: De Vyvers 12, 7991 BW, Dwingeloo, The Netherlands.

**VAN SANT Gus Jr,** b. 1952, Louisville, Kentucky, USA. Film Director; Screenwriter. Education: Rhode Island School of Design. Appointments: Former Production Assistant to Ken Shapiro. Films include: Mala Noche; Drugstore Cowboy, 1989; My Own Private Idaho, 1991; Even Cowgirls Get the Blues, 1993; To Die For, 1995; Kids, 1995; Ballad of the Skeletons, 1996; Good Will Hunting, 1997; Psycho, 1998; Finding Forrester, 2000. Publications: 108 Portraits, 1995; Pink, 1997. Honours: National Society of Film Critics Awards for Best Director and Screenplay, 1990; New York Film Critics and Los Angeles Film Critics Award for Best Screenplay, 1989; PEN Literary Award for Best Screenplay Adaptation, 1989. Address: c/o William Morris Agency Inc, 151 South El Camino Drive, Beverly Hills, CA 90212, USA.

**VAN TAMELEN Eugene Earle,** b. 20 July 1925, Zeeland, Michigan, USA. Chemist. m. Mary Houtman, 1 son, 2 daughters. Education: AB, Hope College, 1947; MS, 1949, PhD, 1950, Harvard University. Appointments: Instructor to Professor, 1950-61, Homer Adkins Professor, 1961-62, University of Wisconsin, Madison; Professor of Chemistry, 1962-87, Department Chairperson, 1974-78, Stanford University, CA; Professor Extraordinarius, University of Groningen, Netherlands, 1967-74. Publications: Over 200 research publications in areas of organic chemistry, inorganic chemistry, biochemistry, mostly in Journal of the American Chemical Society; Editor, Bioorganic Chemistry: An International Journal, 1971-82. Honours: American Chemical Society Award in Pure Chemistry, 1961; Leo Hendrick Baekeland Award, 1965; Guggenheim Fellow, 1965, 1973; Award for Creative Work in Synthetic Organic Chemistry, 1970; Various honorary DSc degrees; Listed in several Who's Who and biographical publications. Memberships: National Academy of Sciences; Advisory or Editorial Boards, Chemical and Engineering News, Synthesis, Bioinorganic Chemistry, Accounts of Chemical Research. Address: 23570 Camino Hermoso, Los Altos Hills, CA 94024-6407, USA. E-mail: vantamelen@aol.com

**VAN ZANTEN David Theodore,** Professor of Art History. Education: Visiting Student, Courtauld Institute of Art, University of London, England, 1963-64, BA, Princeton University, 1965; MA, 1966, PhD, 1970, Harvard University. Appointments: Assistant Professor, McGill University, Canada, 1970-71; Assistant Professor, promoted to Associate Professor, University of Pennsylvania, 1971-79; Associate Professor promoted to Professor, Northwestern University, 1979-; Visiting Professor: Cornell University, 1976, University of California, Berkeley, 1979, Columbia University (Mathews Lectures), 1980. Publications include: The Architecture of the Ecole des Beaux Arts (contributor), 1977; The Architectural Polychromy of the 1930's, 1977; The Beaux-Arts Tradition in French Architecture (editor), 1982; Louis Sullivan: The Function of Ornament (contributor), 1986; Designing Paris: The Architecture of Duban, Labrouste, Vaudoyer and Duc, 1987; Building Paris: Architectural Institutions and the Transformation of the French Capital, 1830-1870, 1995; Sullivan's City: The Meaning of Ornament for Louis Sullivan, 2000. Honours: Fulbright Fellowship, Paris, 1968-69; Prix Bernier, Académie des Beaux-Arts, Paris; Alice Davis Hitchcock Award (best book in architectural history that year), 1988; NEH Senior Fellowship, 1989-90, 1997-98; Named Chevalier of the Ordre des Arts et des Lettres, Minister of Culture, Republic of France, 1995; Guggenheim Fellowship, 2001-2002. Address: Department of Art History, Northwestern University, Evanston, IL 60208-2208, USA. E-mail: d-van@northwestern.edu

**VANDE KEMP Hendrika,** b. 13 December 1948, Voorthuizen, Gelderland, The Netherlands. Clinical Psychologist; Educator. Education: BA, Hope College, 1971; MS, 1974, PhD, 1977, University of Massachusetts/Amherst. Appointments: Internship, Clinical Psychology, Topeka State Hospital, 1975-76; Instructor in Psychology, 1976-77, Assistant Professor in Psychology, 1977-81, Associate Professor of Psychology, 1982-91, Professor of Psychology, 1992-2001, Graduate School of Psychology, Fuller Theological Seminary. Publications: Co-author: Femininity and Shame: Women and men giving voice to the feminine, 1997; Humanistic Psychology and Feminist Psychology, 1999; Introduction to the special issue on historical aspects of dreaming, 2000; Author: Christian Psychologies for the 21st Century: Lessons from History, 1998; Grieving the death of a sibling or the death of a friend, 1999; Mentoring as a witness to the way of exchange, 2000; Author and co-author of numerous articles. Honours include: National Honor Society, 1966; Valedictorian, Lakewood Public Schools, 1967; Eta Sigma Phi, National Honorary Classical Fraternity, 1968; Psi Chi, National Honor Society in Psychology, 1969; Pi Sigma Alpha, 1970; Phi Beta Kappa, Zeta of Michigan, 1971; Hope College Scholarship, Michigan Competitive Scholarship, Michigan Tuition Grant, 1967-1971; Fellow, American Psychological Association, Division 26, 1989; William Bier Award, 1990; C Davis Weyerhaeuser Award for Excellence, 1996; John Templeton Foundation Award, 1996; Distinguished Service Award, Theoretical and Philosophical Psychology, 2000; Distinguished Service Award, Psychology of Religion, 2001. Memberships: International Society for the History of the Behavioural and Social Sciences; American Psychological Association; American Association for Marriage and Family Therapy. E-mail: hendrika@cox.net

**VANDROSS Luther,** b. 20 April 1951, New York, USA. Singer; Songwriter; Arranger; Producer. Career: Member, Listen My Brother (musical theatre workshop), Harlem, 1973; Session singer (recordings and commercials), arranger, 1974-80; Leader, own group, Luther, 1976-77; Solo artiste, 1980-; Regular international concerts. Compositions include: Fascination, David Bowie; You Stopped Lovin' Me, Roberta Flack; Recordings: Albums: Luther, 1976; This Close To You, 1977; Solo albums: Never Too Much, 1981; Forever For Always For Love, 1982; Busy Body, 1984; Give Me The Reason, 1986; Any Love, 1988; The Best Of Luther Vandross, 1989; Power Of Love, 1991; Never Let Me Go, 1993; Songs, 1994; This is Christmas, 1995; Your Secret Love, 1996; I Know, 1998; Hit singles include: The Night I Fell In Love, 1985; Give Me The Reason, from film Ruthless People, 1986; Stop To Love, 1987; There's Nothing Better Than Love, duet with Gregory Hines, 1987; Any Love, 1989; She Won't Talk To Me, 1989; Here And Now, 1990; Power Of Love/Love Power, 1991; Don't Want To Be A Fool, 1991; The Best Things In Life Are Free, duet with Janet Jackson, from film Mo' Money, 1992; Love The One You're With, 1995; Going in Circles, 1995; I Can Make It Better, 1996; Are You Using Me?, 1998; Heart of a Hero, 1999; Sessions as backing singer include: Young Americans, David Bowie, 1974; Songs For The New Depression, Bette Midler, 1975; Sounds And Stuff Like That, Quincy Jones, 1978; Le Freak, Chic, 1978; We Are Family, Sister Sledge, 1978; Other sessions for Ringo Starr; Carly Simon; Chaka Khan; Average White Band; Vocal arranger, No More Tears, Donna Summer and Barbra Streisand, 1979; Producer, recordings by Aretha Franklin; Dionne Warwick; Diana Ross; Whitney Houston; Contributor, Voices That Care (Red Cross charity record), 1991; The Heart Of A Hero (AIDS research benefit record), 1992. Honours include: MVP Background Singer, 1977-80; Grammy Awards: Best R&B Vocal Performance, 1991, 1992; Best R&B Song, 1992; Grammy Nomination, Best R&B Vocal, 1987; Soul Train Music Awards: Best Male R&B Album, 1987, 1992; Best Male R&B Single, 1990; American Music Awards: Favourite

Soul/R&B Male Artist, 1988, 1990, 1992; Favourite Soul/R&B Album, 1992; NAACP Image Awards: Best Male Artist, 1990; Best Male Vocalist, Best Album, 1992; Luther Vandross Day, Los Angeles, 1991. Address: Epic Records, 550 Madison Avenue, New York, NY 10022, USA..

**VANDYK Neville David,** b. 6 September 1923, London, England. Retired Solicitor and Legal Journalist. m. Paula Borchert, 1 daughter. Education: B Com, 1947, PhD (Econ), 1950, School of Economics, London University; Admitted Solicitor, 1957. Appointments: HM Forces including service in India, Burma and Japan, 1942-46; Research Assistant, London School of Economics, 1951-52; With Herbert Openheimer, Nathan and Vandyk Solicitors, 1953-58; Assistant Editor, 1958-63, Managing Editor, 1963-68, Editor, 1968-88, Solicitors' Journal; Founder Member, West London Law Society, President, 1970-71; Honorary Professor of Legal Ethics, University of Birmingham, 1981-83. Publications: Tribunals and Inquiries, 1965; Accidents and the Law, 1975, 2nd edition, 1979; National Health Service in Halsbury's Laws of England, 3rd edition, 1959, 4th edition, 1982. Memberships: Burma Star Association; Law Society; British Legal Association. Address: 217 Strand, London WC2R 1AS, England.

**VANYUSHIN Boris,** b. 16 February 1935, Tula, Russia. Professor. m. Abrosimova Valeria Ivanovna. Education: MS, Biology Department, Moscow State University, 1957; PhD, Bakh Biochemistry Institute, Academy of Sciences, Moscow, 1961; DSci, Biology Department, Moscow State University, 1973. Appointments: Junior Research Scientist, Plant Biochemistry Department, 1960-64, Senior Research Scientist, Laboratory of Bio-organic Chemistry, 1965-73, Moscow State University; Postdoctoral Research Fellow, Virus Research Unit ARC, Cambridge, England, 1964-65; Head, Department of Molecular Bases of Ontogenesis, Belozersky Institute, Moscow State University, 1973-; Regent's Lecturer, Department of Biochemistry, University of California at Irvine, USA, 1976; UNESCO Expert in Molecular Biology, Lucknow University, India, 1978; Head, Laboratory of Hormonal Regulation of Plant Ontogenesis, Institute of Agricultural Biotechnology, Moscow, 1985-96; Visiting Professor, University of Catania, Italy, 1990; Visiting Research Fellow, National Centre for Toxicology Research, Arkansas, USA, 1994-95. Publications: Book, Molecular and Genetic Mechanisms of Ageing, 1977; Author of more than 400 papers in various journals. Honours: Award, Lomonosov Prize, 2002; Belozersky Prize, 2004; Grants, International Science Foundation, 1994-95; Russian Foundation of Fundamental Research, 1993-95, 1996-98, 1999-. Memberships: Russian Biochemical Society; Russian Society of Plant Physiologists; DNA Methylation Society; Corresponding Member, Russian Academy of Sciences. Address: Belozersky Institute of Physico-Chemical Biology, Moscow State University, 119992 Moscow, Russia. E-mail: vanyush@belozersky.msu.ru

**VARALLO Francis "Bob" V,** b. 28 June 1935, Chicago, Illinois, USA. US Army Colonel (Retired). 1 son, 2 daughters. Education: BSH, Loyola University, Chicago, 1958; US Army Command and General Staff College, 1971; National Security Management, National War College, 1972. Appointments: From Second Lieutenant to Colonel, US Army, 1958-88, Deputy Director for Intelligence Collection, Vietnam, 1967-68; Deputy Corps Advisor, Vietnam, 1971-72, G-2, 8th Infantry Division, 1972-74; US Army Attaché, 1974-75; Plans and Policy Intelligence Officer, 1975-78, Installation Commander, 1978-79, Duty Director for Intelligence, 1979-81, Defense Intelligence Agency; J-2, (Senior US Military Intelligence Officer) United States Forces, Japan, 1981-84; Director of Intelligence and

Security, Defense Nuclear Agency, 1985-88; Regional Security Manager, Unisys Corporation, Salt Lake City, Utah, 1988-90; President, Nevada Association of Manufactured Home Owners, Inc., 1997-. Honours: NRCC Nevada Businessman of the Year, 2002, 2004; Republican Gold Medal, 2002, 2003; Ronald Reagan Republican Gold Medal, 2004; Man of the Year 2004, American Biographical Institute, USA; Listed in Who's Who publications and biographical dictionaries. Memberships: American Legion; Veterans of Foreign Wars; Disabled American Veterans; Military Officers Association of America; Vietnam Veterans Association; National Rifle Association; Freedom Alliance; The Heritage Foundation; Selous Foundation; Young America's Foundation; The Ronald Reagan Foundation; Colonial Williamsburg Foundation; Senior Congress; Civil War Preservation Trust; NRCC Business Advisory Council; NRCC House Majority Trust; Vice-President, Western Region, Manufactured Home Owners Association of America Inc. Address: 2900 S Valley View Blvd, Suite 251, Las Vegas, NV 89102, USA.

**VARGA László,** b. 17 April 1927, Békéscsaba, Hungary. Engineer; Professor of Geotechnics. m. Maria Wellmann, 1 son, 1 daughter. Education: BS, Engineering, 1950; University Doctorate, 1960; Candidate of Technical Science (PhD equivalent), Hungarian Academy of Sciences, 1964. Appointments: Assistant Professor, 1950-59, Adjunct, 1959-65, Associate Professor, 1965-72, Technical University Budapest; Professor, Head of Department of Geotechnics, 1972-90, Technical College of Győr. Publications: 74 papers, reports; 23 lecture notes; Textbooks and 17 (mostly as co-author) technical books. Honours: Order of Labour, 1981; Pro Universitate Győr, 1995; Széchy Prize, 2000; Zielinski Prize, 2000. Memberships: International Society for Soil Mechanics and Geotechnical Engineering, 1966-; Hungarian Chamber of Engineers, 1990-. Address: H-9023 Győr, Tihanyi Árpád Street 58, Hungary.

**VARGAS-HERNÁNDEZ José Guadalupe,** b. 8 November 1951, Zapotiltic, Jalisco, México. Economist. m. Maria Elba González, 6 May 1976, 3 sons. Education: MBA, 1980; PhD, Economics, 1992; PhD, Public Management, 1998. Appointments: Professor, Instituto Tecnológico de Cd Guzmán, 1974-94; Director, Mass Media Communication, Presidencia Municipal Cd Guzmán, Jalisco, 1985-1990; Director, Patronato Instituto Tecnológico de Cd Guzmán, 1983-93; General Manager, Consejo de Colaboración Ciudadana, Cd Guzman, 1992-94; CEO, Novacal, 1994-95; Independent Consultant, 1980-2000; Research Professor, Instituto Tecnológico de Colima, 1994-2000; Research Professor, Universidad de Colima, 1994-2000; Research Professor, Instituto Tecnológico de Cd Guzmán, 2000-; Research Professor, Centro Universiario del Sur, Universidad de Guadalajara, 2000-; Research Professor, Doctorate in Management Studies, UASLP; Research Assistant, University of California at Berkeley. Publications: Over 300 essays and articles in professional scientific journals and reviews in the field of organisational economics; Books A Challenge to the Quest for Leadership and Managerial Effectiveness, 1980; La Culturocracia en México;. Honours include: Sommer Al Mérito; CONACYT Award; PSU Award; British Council Award, 1982. Memberships: Academy of Management; British Academy of Management; Eastern Region of Organisation of Public Administrators. Address: Cerrada Petronilo López 31, Cd Guzmán, Jalisco 49000, México. E-mail: jvargas@cusur.udg.mx

**VARGHESE Thomas,** b. 27 April 1965, Pallipad, Alleppey (Dt), Kerala, India. Lecturer. m. Susan Kurian, 1 son. Education: MSc (Physics), Mahatma Gandhi University, Kottayam, Kerala, 1987; BEd (Physical Science), Kerala University, Trivandrum,

1988; MPhil (Physics), 1992, PhD (Physics), 2003, Mangalore University, Karnataka. Appointments: Lecturer, Govt Model VHSE, Ambalapuzha, 1992-93; Lecturer, Govt Brennen College, Tellicherry, 1993-94; Lecturer, College of Applied Sciences, Calicut, 1995; Senior Gr Lecturer, Nirmala College, Muvattupuzha, 1995-. Publications: 9 articles in professional journals; Co-editor, Science and Society journal. Memberships: International Radiation Physics Society. Address: Department of Physics, Nirmala College, Muvattupuzha 686 661, Kerala State, India. E-mail: surajthomas@sancharnet.in

**VASCONCELLOS Josefina de,** b. 26 October 1904, Molesey-on-Thames, England. Independent Sculptor; Designer; Writer; Innovator. m. Delmar Banner, deceased. Education: Educated at home; Royal Academy Schools. Career: Sculptor; Works include: High Altar and Statue, Varengeville, Normandy; Pastoral Crook for Bristol Cathedral, 1948; National War Memorial, Battle of Britain, Aldershot, 1955; Life size Mary and Child, St Paul's Cathedral, 1955; The Flight into Egypt for St Martin in the Fields, now in Cartmel Priory, 1958; Winged Victory Crucifix, Clewer Church and Canongate Kirk, Edinburgh, 1964; Lord Denning (portrait in bronze), Magdelen College, Oxford, 1969; Life size Virgin and Child, Blackburn Cathedral, 1974; Reredos, Parish Church, Ambleside, Wordsworth Chapel, 1988; Life size bronzes Reconciliation, one in ruins of Coventry Cathedral, one in Peace Park, Hiroshima, 1995, also for the grounds of Stormont, Northern Ireland and a site on the remains of the Berlin Wall, 1999; Escape to Light, 2001; First Christian Stone Circle, Mongrisedale, 2003; Invited one-man exhibition, Manchester Cathedral, 1991. Publications: Book, She Was Loved: Memoirs of Beatrix Potter, 2003; Subject of Josefina de Vasconcellos: Her Life and Art by Dr Margaret Lewis, 2002. Honours: Honorary DLitt, University of Bradford, 1977; MBE, 1985; Jean Watson Davidson Medal, Society of Portrait Sculptors, 2000. Memberships: Founding Member, Society of Portrait Sculptors; Founder, Adventure Base for Disabled Youngsters; Founder, The Harriet Trust. Address: Top Floor Studio, 15 Rowan Court, Ambleside, Cumbria LA22 0EE, England.

**VASILENKO Tatyana F,** b. 18 July 1952, Atamanovo, Russia. Physiologist; Researcher. m. V Muravyev, 2 daughters. Education: Doctor in Biology, State University, St Petersburg, 1980. Appointments: Junior Researcher, Institute of Biology, Komi Department, Academy of Sciences of USSR, Syktyvkar, Russia, 1981-86; Researcher, 1986-91, Senior Researcher, 1991-98, Senior Researcher, 1998-2004, Head of Laboratory of Physiology of Ruminant Animals, 2004-, Institute of Physiology, Komi Science Centre, Ural Division, Russian Academy of Sciences, Syktyvkar, Russia. Articles in scientific journals including: ALCES, 1999, 2001; Zoological Journal of the Russian Academy of Sciences, 2000, 2002; 12 patents. Membership: Physiological Society named after J P Pavlov, Russian Academy of Sciences. Address: Institute of Physiology, Pervomayskaya St 50, Komi Republic, Syktyvkar 167982, Russia.

**VASILJEV Alexander V,** b. 21 June 1955, Kuragata, Kazakhstan. Economist; Metallurgy Engineer. m. Marina G Tuzovskaya, 31 December 1985, 2 daughters. Education: Diploma, Engineering, Metallurgy Institute, 1977; Candidate, Technical Sciences, Moscow, 1982; Top (Doctoran) Scholar Institute, Economic Industry NAS, Ukraine, Donetsk, 1991-93; High Science Employee, Sociology, Academy of Management, Moscow, 1992; PhD, Economics, Academy of Management, Moscow, 1993; Probationer, Institute IBMER, Poland, 2000-2001. Appointments: Junior then Senior scientific employee, Institute Mariupol, Ukraine, 1980-84; Manager,

Research Laboratory, Metallurgy Institute, Manager, Institute of Labour of Ukraine, Manager, Institute of Economic-Law Research, NAS, Ukraine, 1985-98; Chairman, Sectory Science Council, Institute Olga W Wasilievoy-Catholic of Economic and Social/ Cultural Research, Mariupol, 1989-; Lecturer, Donetsk University, Donetsk, 1990-91; Professor, PriAzov State Technical University, Mariupol, 1993-98; Professor, Mariupol Humanitary Institute, Donetsk University, Mariupol, 1994-95; Organiser, Mariupol branch, Institute of Economic-Law Research, NAS, Ukraine, Mariupol, 1995-97; Professor, Taganrog's Institute of Management and Economics, 2001-02; Vice-Chairman, Civil International Committee, 2001-; Chief Branch of Management of Mariupol's Department of Academy of Management Staff, 2002-2003; Professor, Department of Inter-regional Academy of Control of Staff, Mariupol, 2003-2004; Professor, Odessa I I Mechnikov National University, Odessa, 2004-. Publications: Problems of methodology perfecting parameters of expenditures of labour: social infrastructure (monograph), 1992; The highcromicarbon alloys for the castings instruments (the purpose of removing masses containing fuel the 1Y Chernobyl Nuclear Station), 1993; On frontier third thousand years, 1996 (monograph); The Labour of Many Thousand Years (from Gomers and Pontis Empire to EU), 1998; Theoretical and Methodological Basis of Concepts of Transformation and Preservations of Labour (articles on sociology and economic theory) (monograph), 1998; The Main Rules and Substatations of New Approaches: Second Report for Rume Club about Revolution of Effectiveness (monograph), 2001; Gothy in Europe, 2004; Management of foreign trade activities in Light of Law of Preservation of Labor and Law of Non-destructive intelligent & Spiritual Labour, 2004; Ukrainian Budget $128,100,000,000, 2005; 19% in Year – Will to develop in Ukraine, 2005; Beginnings Political Arithmetic of Ukraine, 2005; Problems of maintenance of reproduction of a labour in conditions of intensive development of integration processes, www.cic-wsc.org, Doc 189, 2005; Contributed articles to professional journals. Honours: Recipient, Certificate, Fredrick P Furth Foundation, 1990; Medal "Met Gotey & Cafa, St Ignatia", 1999; Certificate For Good Work to 140 years Odessa I I Mechnikov National University, 2005; Honorary Member, Academy of Economic Sciences and Entrepreneurship. Memberships: New York Academy of Sciences; 1817 Heritage Society, New York Academy of Sciences; American Association for the Advancement of Sciences; Research Board of American Biographical Institute; Union of Economists of Ukraine. Address: Fl 519, Dovzgenko 9B St, 65058 Odessa, Ukraine. E-mail: vasiljev@cic-wsc.org Website: www.cic-wsc.org

**VASILJEV Valery A,** b. 10 July 1929, vil. Novo-Ukainka, Ukraine. Economist; Metallurgical Engineer. m. Olga V Vasiljeva, 1 son. Education: Diploma, Engineering, Technical Institute, 1952; Degree in Economics, Moscow Institute of Management, 1978; High Science Employee, Institute, Mariupol, Ukraine, 1986; Dr Com, Academy of Economic Sciences and Entrepreneurship, Moscow, 1995. Appointments: Chief Technical Officer, Igorsky Plant, St Petersburg, Russia, 1952-54; Main Engineer, Collective Farms, Kuragata, Dgambul, Kazahstan, 1955-56; Chief Engineer, Metallurgy Plants of Ukraine, 1957-74; Chief Economic Department, Ukrgipramez Mariupol, 1975-87; Lecturer, Pri Azov, State Technical University, Mariupol, 1987-; Director, Institute of Economic, Social and Cultural Research, Mariupol, 1995-; President, Chairman, Azov (Ukrainian) Department, Academy of Economic Sciences and Entrepreneurship, 1999-; Chairman, Civil International Committee, 2001-. Publications: The Progressive Way of Production of Models, 1973; The Directory Founder, 2nd edition, 1983; Methodological priorities at valuations objective expenditures of labour in market economy (is devoted to light memory of outstanding scientist of America, Russia and Ukraine, Valery Ivanovich Tereshenko), 1995; The Base of Management in Light of Law of Preservation of Labour, 2002; Methodological fundamentals of social stabilization of economic development, 2004; Management of foreign trade activities in Light of Law of Preservation of Labour and Law of Non-destructive Intelligent & Spiritual Labour, 2004; Gothy in Europe, 2004; Fundamental organisation of Production and Management (monograph), 2004; Ukrainian Budget $128,100,000,000, 2005; 19% in Year – Will to develop in Ukraine, 2005; Beginnings Political Arithmetic of Ukraine, 2005, contributed articles to professional journals. Honours: Certificate Frederick P Furth Foundation, 1990; Medal "Met. Gotey & Cafa, St Ignatia", 1999; Medal, Auth: Law-Preservation-Labour, IBC, 2003. Memberships: International Biographical Centre; Academy of Economic Sciences and Entrepreneurship; Academy of Economic Sciences of Ukraine; Academy of Sciences of New York; 1817 Heritage Society, New York Academy of Sciences; Board Research, American Biographical Institute; Union Economic, Ukraine. Address: Fl 24, Nahimova, 122, St, 87534 Mariupol, Donetsk Region, Ukraine. E-mail: vasiljev@cic-wsc.org

**VASSILEV Hristo Stoynov,** b. 21 March 1969, Troyan, Bulgaria. Engineer. Education: Dip Eng; D Mitropolia, Bulgaria. Appointments: Served Bulgarian Air Force, 1993-94; Self-employed Engineer, 1995-99; Flight Navigator on AN-12 Air Sofia, 1999-. Address: Hristo Botev #9, Troyan 5600, Bulgaria. E-mail: hristo_vassilev@yahoo.com

**VAUGHAN Dindy Belinda,** b. 26 December 1938, Kogarah, New South Wales, Australia. Consultant in Arts Education and Environment. 1 daughter. Education: BA (honours), University of Sydney, Australia, 1967; MA, Flinders University, South Australia, 1970. Appointments: Tertiary Lecturer, Royal Melbourne Institute of Technology and Footscray Institute (now Victoria University of Technology); Academic Assessor, Deakin University; Community Arts Officer; Frequent contracts and commissions for music composition; Consultant in arts, education and environment; Established Gallery Without Walls. Publications: By-line Correspondent for local paper, 1979-81; Books and articles on environment and the arts; Musical composition scores including tutoring books. Honours: University of Sydney Alumni Association Award for achievements in community service; Listed in several biographical dictionaries. Memberships: Life Member, University of Sydney Alumni Association; Life Member, Sydney University Arts Association; Melbourne Composer's League; Australian Geographic; Candlebark Community Nursery; Life Member, Croydon Conservation Society; Life Member, Dandenong Ranges Community and Cultural Centre; Greenpeace; Australian Conservation Foundation; Australians for Native Title and Reconciliation (ANTAR); Initiator and Chief Co-ordinator for Focus on Water, Victoria, 2005. Address: PO 668 Ringwood, VIC 3134, Australia. E-mail: rondaf@vicnet.net.au

**VAUGHAN John Patrick,** b. 27 December 1937, Penzance, Cornwall, England. University Professor; Doctor of Medicine. m. Pauline Macaulay, 2 sons, 2 stepsons, 1 stepdaughter. Education: MBBS, Guy's Hospital, London, 1961; MRCP (Edin), 1965; FRCP (Edin), 1982; Diploma in Tropical Public Health, 1969, MD, 1978, University of London; Fellow, Faculty of Public Health (FFPH), 1988. Appointments: Overseas employment: Papua New Guinea, 1966-68, Tanzania, 1969-73, USA, 1989, Bangladesh, 1995-98, Switzerland, 2001-2002; Professor, London School of Hygiene and Tropical Medicine, 1988-98; Director, Public Health Sciences International Centre for

Diarrhoeal Disease Research, Bangladesh, 1995-98; Professor Emeritus, Epidemiology and Public Health, 1998-; Public Health Advisor, UK Cabinet Office, 2000-2001; International Consultant in public health to World Bank, Washington, World Health Organisation, Geneva, Department for International Development, London; International Advisor, BRAC School of Public Health, Bangladesh, 2004-. Publications: Over 120 scientific journal publications and 9 books on public health. Extensive journal editing and publishing experience. Honours: CBE "For services to public health overseas", 1998; Listed in Who's Who publications and biographical dictionaries. Memberships: Trustee, Malaria Consortium, 2002-; Trustee, BBC World Service Trust, 2003-. Address: Health Policy Unit, London School of Hygiene and Tropical Medicine, London WC1E 7HT, England. E-mail: jpatrickvaughan@aol.com

**VEERAKYATHIAH V D,** b. 25 June 1926, Vaddagere, India. Retired. m. V Rajamma, 25 June 1955, 2 sons. Education: BSc, Agriculture. Appointments: Village Level Worker, 1954-55; Agricultural Extension Officer, 1955-57; Block Development Officer, 1957-65; Principal, State Level Young Farmers Training Centre, 1 year; Instructor, Orientation and Study Centre, Government of India, Poona, 1 year; Assistant Development Commissioner, 1967-71; Assistant Director, Land Army, 1971-72; Principal, Rural Development Training Centre, Mandya, Karnataka, 1972-75; Secretary, Chief Executive Officer, State Khadi and Village Industries Board, Bangalore, 1976-77; Project Director, SFDA, Government of Karnataka, 1977-80; Selected for Indian Administrative Service, Government of India; Director, Special Economic Programmes, IRDP, Government of Karnataka, 1980-82; Director, Backward Classes and Other Weaker Sections, 1982-84. Publications: 3 professional papers in the Indian Science Congress Sessions. Memberships: Honorary Director, Asian Institute for Urban Development; Advisor, Ganga Rural Development Trust; Bangalore Zilla Aadhar Member, Age Foundation, Ministry of Social Welfare, Government of India; Honorary President, Vaddagere Temple Development Committee; Founder-President, Akhila Kunchitigara Mahal Mardal, Bangalore. Address: 596 IInd Stage 1 E Block, Rajajinagar, Bangalore 560010, India.

**VELINOV Milen T,** b. 29 July 1959, Bulgaria. Physician; Researcher. m. Milena Velinova, 1 son, 1 daughter. Education: MD, Higher Medical Institute, Sofia, 1986; PhD, Biomedical Institute, Sofia, 1995. Appointments: Postdoctoral Fellow, University of Connecticut Health Centre, USA, 1991-95; Resident in Paediatrics, New York Methodist Hospital, 1995-98; Staff Research Scientist, New York State Institute for Basic Research, Staten Island, 1998-; Fellow in Clinical Genetics, Maimonides Medical Centre, 1999-2003; Assistant Professor of Paediatrics, State University of New York, College of Medicine, 2004; Program Director, Comprehensive Genetic Services, Assistant Director, Speciality Clinical Laboratories, 2004-, NYS Institute for Basic Research. Publications: Co-author: Connective Tissue Research, 29:13, 1993; American Journal of Medical Genetics, 47:294, 1993; Nature Genetics, 6(3):314, 1994; Molecular Genetics and Metabolism, 69:81, 2000. Honours: Fellow's Clinical Research Award, Society for Paediatric Research, 1994; Resident Research Grant, American Academy of Paediatrics, 1997. Memberships: American Society of Human Genetics; American Academy of Paediatrics; American College of Medical Genetics. Address: New York State Institute for Basic Research, 1050 Forest Hill Road, Staten Island, NY 10314, USA. E-mail: velinovm@aol.com

**VELTCHEVA Albena Dimitrova,** b. 5 January 1964, Vabel, Bulgaria. Research Scientist. m. Lyoubomir Petkov Veltchev,

1 son, 1 daughter. Education: MSc, Physical Faculty, Sofia University, Sofia, Bulgaria. 1987. Appointments: Researcher, 1988-94, Junior Researcher, 1995-97, Institute of Oceanology, Bulgarian Academy of Sciences, Varna, Bulgaria; Fellow, Japan, Science and Technology Agency, 1998-2000; Transport Technical Researcher, Corporation for Advanced Transport and Technology, 2000-2002; Visiting Researcher, Port and Airport Research Institute, Japan, 2002-03; Visiting Researcher, ECOH Co, Yokohama, Japan, 2004-. Publications: Articles in scientific journals and papers presented at conferences as author and co-author include: Wave groupiness in the nearshore area by Hilbert spectrum, 2001; Wave and group transformation by a Hilbert spectrum, 2002; Effect of the distortion of typhoon pressure distribution on the storm surge estimation, 2002; Comparison of methods for calculation of wave envelope, 2003; Identification of the components of wave spectra by the HHT method, 2004. Honours: Gold Medal, Mathematical High School Diploma, 1982; Listed in Who's Who publications and biographical dictionaries. Address: ECOH Co, Portside-daya Bld 10-35, Sakae-cho, Kanagawa-ku, Yokohama 222-0052, Japan. E-mail: velchevi@bigfoot.com

**VENDLER Helen, (Helen Hennessy),** b. 30 April 1933, Boston, Massachusetts, USA. Professor; Poetry Critic. 1 son. Education: AB, Emmanuel College, 1954; PhD, Harvard University, 1960. Appointments: Instructor, Cornell University, 1960-63; Lecturer, Swarthmore College and Haverford College, Pennsylvania, 1963-64; Associate Professor, 1966-68, Professor, 1968-85, Boston University; Fulbright Lecturer, University of Bordeaux, 1968-69; Poetry Critic, The New Yorker, 1978-99; Overseas Fellow, Churchill College, Cambridge, 1980; Senior Fellow, Harvard Society of Fellows, 1981-93; Visiting Professor, 1981-85, Kenan Professor, 1985-90, Associate Academic Dean, 1987-92, Porter University Professor, 1990-, Harvard University; Charles Stewart Parnell Fellow, 1996, Honorary Fellow, 1996-, Magdalene College, Cambridge. Publications: Yeats's Vision and the Later Plays, 1963; On Extended Wings: Wallace Stevens' Longer Poems, 1969; The Poetry of George Herbert, 1975; Part of Nature, Part of Us: Modern American Poets, 1980; The Odes of John Keats, 1983; Wallace Stevens: Words Chosen Out of Desire, 1984; The Harvard Book of Contemporary American Poetry (editor), 1985; Voices and Visions: The Poet in America, 1987; The Music of What Happens, 1988; Soul Says, 1995; The Given and the Made, 1995; The Breaking of Style, 1995; Poems, Poets, Poetry, 1995; The Art of Shakespeare's Sonnets, 1997; Seamus Heaney, 1998; Coming of Age as a Poet, 2003; Poets Thinking, 2004; Invisible Listeners, 2005. Contributions to: Professional journals. Honours: Lowell Prize, 1969; Guggenheim Fellowship, 1971-72; American Council of Learned Societies Fellow, 1971-72; National Institute of Arts and Letters Award, 1975; Radcliffe College Graduate Society Medal, 1978; National Book Critics Award, 1980; National Endowment for the Humanities Fellowships, 1980, 1985, 1994, 2005; Keats-Shelley Association Award, 1994; Truman Capote Award, 1996; Jefferson Medal, American Philosophical Society, 2002; Jefferson Lecturer, NEH, 2004; Many honorary doctorates; Phi Beta Kappa. Memberships: American Academy of Arts and Letters; American Academy of Arts and Sciences, vice-president, 1992-95; American Philosophical Society; English Institute; Modern Language Association, president, 1980. Address: Harvard University, Department of English, Barker Center, Cambridge, MA 02138, USA.

**VENKATARAMANA Neelam K,** b. 27 February 1958, Tirupathi, India. Neurosurgeon. m. Shobha Venkat, 1 daughter. Education: MB BS, S V Medical College, 1980; MCh (Neurosurgery), National Institute of Mental Health and Neuroscience, 1986. Appointments: Assistant Professor, Neurosurgery, National Institute of Mental Health and Neurosciences, 1987-91; Consultant Neurosurgeon, Manipal Hospital, 1991-2001; Director, Manipal Institute for Neurosurgical Disorders, 2001-; Head Neurosurgery Department, Manipal Hospital, 2001-; Founder, Managing Trustee, Comprehensive Training Consortium, Bangalore, 2000-. Publications: Articles in medical journals as author and co-author include most recently: Deep Brain Stimulation - A Novel Therapy for Parkinson's Disease, 2000; Treatment of Parkinson's Disease, 2001; Endoscopic Neurosurgery, 2001; Pregnant Woman with Recurrent Metastasis, Clinical Case Report, 2002; Effect of intravenous corticosteroids on death within 14 days in 10008 adults with clinically significant head injury (MRC CRASH Trial): randomised placebo-controlled trial, CRASH Collaborators, 2004; Surgery for multiple intracranial aneurysms, 2005; Spontaneous spinal extradural haematoma, 2005; Numerous chapers in textbooks and papers presented at conferences. Memberships: Neurological Society of India; Indian Society for Sterotactic and Functional Neurosurgery; Indian Society for Paediatric Neurosurgery; Indian Society for Cerebro Vascular Surgery; American Association of Neurological Surgeons; International Society of Paediatric Neurosurgery; New York Academy of Sciences; Asian Congress of Neurological Surgeons; Commonwealth Association for Mental Handicap and Developmental Disabilities; Inter Academy Biomedical Science Forum; Indian Society of Oncology; Indian Society of Palliative Medicine; Bangalore Neurological Society; Andhra Pradesh Neuro Scientist Association; Surgical Society of Bangalore. Address: #105 Surya Apts, 98 Rustum Bagh Airport Road, Bangalore-560017, Karnataka, India. E-mail: mind99@vsnl.net

**VENN George Andrew Fyfe,** b. 12 October 1943, Tacoma, Washington, USA. Professor; Writer; Editor; Poet; Critic. m. Elizabeth Cheney, divorced, 1 son, 1 daughter. Education: BA, College of Idaho, 1967; MFA, Creative Writing, University of Montana, 1970; Central University, Quito, Ecuador; University of Salamanca, Spain; City Literary Institute, London. Appointments: Writer-on-Tour, Western States Arts Foundation, 1977; Foreign Expert, Changsha Railway University, Hunan, China, 1981-82; General Editor, Oregon Literature Series, 1989-94; Writer-in-Residence, Eastern Oregon University. Publications: Sunday Afternoon: Grande Ronde, 1975; Off the Main Road, 1978; Marking the Magic Circle, 1988; Oregon Literature Series, 1992-94; West of Paradise: New Poems, 1999; many poems, essays, stories. Contributions to: Oregon Humanities; Writer's Northwest Handbook; North West Review; Northwest Reprint Series; Poetry Northwest; Willow Springs; Clearwater Journal; Oregon East; Portland Review; Worldviews and the American West (book). Honours: Pushcart Prize, 1980; Oregon Book Award, 1988; Stewart Holbrook Award, 1994; Andres Berger Poetry Prize, Northwest Writers, 1995. Memberships: Oregon Council of Teachers of English; Fishtrap Gathering. Address: Department of English, Eastern Oregon University, La Grande, OR 97850, USA.

**VEREKER John (Michael Medlicott) (Sir),** b. 9 August 1944, UK. Governor of Bermuda. m. Judith Diane Rowen, 1 son, 1 daughter. Education: BA (Hons), University of Keele, 1967. Appointments: World Bank, Washington, 1970-72; Principal, Ministry of Overseas Development, 1972; Private Secretary to successive Ministers of Overseas Development, 1977-78; Prime Minister's Office, 1980-83; Under Secretary, 1983-88, Principal Finance Officer, 1986-88, Overseas Development Administration, Foreign and Commonwealth Office; Deputy Secretary, Department for Education, 1988-93; Permanent Secretary, Department for International Development, 1994-2002; Governor and Commander-in-Chief of Bermuda, 2002-.

Publication: Blazing the Trail (Journal of Development Studies), 2002. Honours: CB, 1992; CIMgt, 1995; Hon D Litt, University of Keele; KCB, 1999; FRSA, 1999, KStJ, 2001. Memberships: Chairman, Student Loans Co Ltd, 1989-91; Board Member, British Council, 1994-2001; Board Member, Institute of Development Studies, 1994-2000. Address: Government House, Hamilton, Bermuda.

**VERMA Rajan Kumar,** b. 25 August 1973, New Delhi, India. Research Scientist. m. Shikha Verma. Education: B Pharm, Pharmaceutical Sciences, University of Delhi, India, 1996; M Pharm, Pharmaceutics, Banaras Hindu University, India, 1998; PhD, Pharmaceutics and Drug Delivery, National Institute of Pharmaceutical Education and Research, India, 2002. Appointments: Senior Research Fellow, National Institute of Pharmaceutical Education and Research, Mohali, India, 1998-2002; Research Scientist, Ranbaxy Research Laboratories, Gurgaon, India, 2002-. Publications: 11 articles as co-author in professional journals include most recently: development and evaluation of extended release formulations of isosorbide mononitrite based on osmotic technology, 2003; Development and evaluation of osmotically controlled oral drug delivery system of glipizide, 2004; Compatibility studies between isosorbide mononitrite and selected excipients used in the development of extended release formulations, in press; 3 patents, 3 patents pending; 7 papers presented at national and international conferences. Honours: UGC Fellowship, 1996-97; Senior Research Fellowship, 1999-2002, Foreign Travel Grant, 2001, Council of Scientific and Industrial Research. Membership: Life Member, Indian Pharmaceutical Association. Address: House No 1366-A, Gali Sunaran, Najafgarh, New Delhi 110043, India. E-mail: vermarajan73@yahoo.com

**VERNICKAITÉ Ruslana,** b. 22 September 1934, Minsk, Belarus. Physician; Obstetrician-gynaecologist. Education: Doctor's Assistant-Obstetrician, Kaunas Paramedical and Obstetrical School, 1950-54; Diploma, 1954; Physician, Kaunas Medical Institute, 1960-67, Diploma, 1967; Candidate in Science degree, Diploma, 1984; DSc, Medicine, Vilnius, Lithuania, 1993. Appointments: Physician Obstetrician-Gynaecologist, Kretinga Maternity Clinic, 1967-68; Obstetrician-Gynaecologist and Chief Consultant, Obstetrical Department, Klaipéda City Hospital, 1968-89; Obstetrician-Gynaecologist, Women's Consultation No 3, Klaipéda City Hospital, 1989-97; Obstetrician-Gynaecologist, Unit No 2, Klaipéda City Primary Health Care Centre, 1997-. Publications: Monograph, SOS to the Life on Earth: The effect of environmental factors and atmospheric chemical pollutants on the human organism at certain periods of its ontogenesis, 1999; 95 scientific works on obstetrics, perinatology, chronomedicina, chronopharmacology, cytochemistry, clinical pathophysiology, human ontogenesis and ecology, published in Europe, Japan, USA, Canada, China, Denmark, Finland, Slovenia, Slovakia, Bulgaria, Ukraine, Russia; 1 invention. Honours: Fellow of the American Biographical Institute with Gold Medallion, International Cultural Diploma of Honour, 1996; Greatest and Great Minds of the 21st Century, ABI, USA, 2002; 2000 Outstanding Scientists of the 20th Century, IBC, 1999, The IBC Millennium Time Capsule, 1999, International Scientist of the Year, IBC, Gold Medal, 2001, IBC, England; Torch of Global Inspiration, ABI, 2000, Scientific Excellence Gold Medal, USA, 2001; The World Order Science – Education – Culture, The European Academy of Informatisation, Brussels, Belgium, 2002; Diploma, Greatest and Great Minds of the 21st Century, USA, 2002; Diploma, Ambassador of Grand Eminence, USA, 2002; Great Minds of the 21st Century Gold Medal, USA, 2002; Da Vinci Diamond, IBC, 2004; Albert Schweitzer International University Medal for Science and Peace, Spain, 2004; American Medal of Honor,

2004; Proclamation: The Genius Elite (Documented in Leading Intellectuals of the World, ABI, USA), 2004. Memberships: International Association of Biometeorology, Calgary, 1993; LFIBA, DDG, 1995; IBA, 1995; ABI Board of Governors, 1996; ABIRA, 1996; Secretary General, United Cultural Convention, USA, 2001; Founder Diplomatic Counsellor, London Diplomatic Academy, England, 2000; International Diplomatic Academy, London, 2002; Honourable Member, Bulgarian Association of Clinical and Experimental Pathophysiology, Sofia, 1997; Member of the Assembly of the International Diplomatic Academy, Geneva, 2002. Address: Rambyno 7-5, LT-93173 Klaipéda, Lithuania.

**VERSACE Donatella,** b. 1955, Reggio Calabria, Italy. Designer. m. Paul Back, 1 son, 1 daughter. Appointments: Joined Versace, 1978; Formerly overseer of advertising and public relations, accessories designer, children's collection designer, solo designer, Versus and Isante Lines; Creative Director, Gianni Versace Group, 1997-. Address: c/o Keeble Cavaco and Duka Inc, 450 West 15th Street, Suite 604, New York, NY 10011, USA.

**VESEY Sir Thomas Eustace (7th Viscount de Vesci, 8th Baron Knapton),** b. 8 October 1955, Dublin, Ireland. Managing Director. m. Sita-Maria de Breffny, 2 sons, 1 daughter. Education: Eton; St Benets Hall, Oxford. Appointments: Assistant to racehorse trainer, Vincent O'Brien, 1977-80; Bloodstock Agent, Los Angeles, USA, 1980-83; Director of Abbey Leix Estate Company Ltd, Ireland, 1980-95; Campaigner for end of extraction of peat moss for gardeners; Managing Director, Horticultural Coir Ltd, 1999-. Honours: 7th Viscount de Vesci; 8th Baron Knapton; 9th Baronet Vesey. Memberships: Amnesty International; Liberty; Whites Club. Address: 14 Rumbold Road, London, SW6 2JA, England.

**VICAR Jan,** b. 5 May 1949, Olomouc, Czech Republic. Musicologist; Composer. m. (1) Anna Vicarova, 2 sons, (2) Eva Vicarova, 1 son, 1 daughter. Education: MA, Palacky University Olomouc, 1972; Conservatory in Ostrava, 1972; PhD, 1974; MA, Academy of Music and Performing Arts, Prague, 1981; CSc, 1985. Appointments: Teacher, Department of Musicology, Palacky University, 1973-; Chair, 1990-98, 2000-2003; Teacher, Department of Music Theory and History, Academy of Music and Performing Arts, Prague, 1980-; Editor in Chief, Hudebni Rozhledy, 1986-89; Professor, Theory and History of Music, Prague, 1998-; Professor, Composition, Birmingham Southern College, Alabama, USA, 2005. Publications: The Accordion and its Musical Use; Vaclav Trojan; Music Criticism and Popularization of Music; Music Aesthetics; Imprints: Essays on Czech Music and Aesthetics; Compositions: String Quartet; Nonet; The Cry; Japanese Year; Preludes/Phantasms; Choruses and Songs for Children; Three Marches for Dr Kabyl; Vivat Universitas!; Towards the Mountains. Honours: Fulbright Scholar, 1998-99, USA. Memberships: Czechoslovak Society of Arts and Sciences. Address: Malostranske namesti 13, 118 00 Praha 1, Czech Republic.

**VIDAL Gore, (Edgar Box),** b. 3 October 1925, West Point, New York, USA. Writer. Education: Graduate, Phillips Exeter Academy, 1943. Publications: Novels: Williwaw, 1946; In a Yellow Wood, 1947; The City and the Pillar, 1948; The Season of Comfort, 1949; A Search for the King, 1950; Dark Green, Bright Red, 1950; The Judgment of Paris, 1952; Messiah, 1954; Julian, 1964; Washington, DC, 1967; Myra Breckinridge, 1968; Two Sisters, 1970; Burr, 1973; Myron, 1974; Kalki, 1978; Creation, 1981; Duluth, 1983; Lincoln, 1984; Empire, 1987; The Smithsonian Institution, 1998; The Golden Age, 2000. Stories: A Thirsty Evil, 1956. Play: Visit to a Small Planet, 1957.

Television and Broadway productions: The Best Man, 1960; Romulus, 1966; Weekend, 1968; An Evening with Richard Nixon, 1972; Gore Vidal's Lincoln, 1988. Essays: Rocking the Boat, 1962; Reflections upon a Sinking Ship, 1969; Homage to Daniel Shays, 1973; Matters of Fact and of Fiction, 1977; The Second American Revolution, 1982; Armageddon?, 1987; United States: Essays 1952-1992, 1993. Memoir: Palimpsest, 1995. Films: The Catered Affair, 1956; The Left-Handed Gun, 1958; The Best Man, 1964. Teleplays: The Death of Billy the Kid, 1958; Dress Gray, 1986. Honour: National Book Award, 1993. Membership: American Academy of Arts and Letters. Address: 84010 Ravello, Italy.

**VIDJAK Needa.** b. 29 January 1966, Split, Croatia. Psychotherapist for Drug Addicts. Education: Mathematician-Informatician, Mathematical-Informatical School, Split, Croatia, 1984; Doctor of Medicine, Medical University, Zagreb, Croatia, 1989; Theologian, Theological University, Split, Croatia, 1993; Master of Medical Services, Medical University, Zagreb, Croatia, 2001; Postgraduate study of Social Psychiatry, Group Analysis. Appointments: Doctor Trainee, Health's Home, Split, Croatia, 1989-90; Professor, Nursing School, Split, 1991-92; Psychotherapist for Drug Addicts, Leader of Counselling Centre, Meeting Community, Split, 1992-; Voluntary work: Telephone Psychotherapist, Tele-Apel Centre, Split, 1990-92; Psychotherapist for Refugees, Refugee Centre, Split, 1991; Psychotherapist for Drug Addicts in Prison, Split, 1992-93. Publication: Journal article: Treating Heroin Addiction: Comparison of Methadone Therapy, Hospital Therapy without Methadone and Therapeutic Community, 2003. Honours: Reviewer, CMJ (Croatian Medical Journal), 2003-; Listed in Who's Who publications and biographical dictionaries. Memberships: Mensa International, Split, 2002; Member of Advisory Council of Archbishop, Split, 2004-. Address: Rudera Boskovicka 12, Split 21000, Croatia. E-mail: neda.vidjak@st.htnet.hr

**VIDLÁKOVÁ Olga Anna,** b. 17 January 1928, Duchcov, Czech Republic. Associate Professor. m. Lubor Vidlák, 2 daughters. Education: LLD, Charles University, Prague, 1951; Candidate, Science in Administrative Law, Czechoslovak Academy of Sciences, 1975; Associate Professor of Environmental Law and Administrative Law, Charles University, 1988. Appointments: Research Group Leader, Institute of Landscape Ecology, Czechoslovak Academy of Sciences; Chief Resident Fellow, Deputy Director, Institute of State Administration; Director of Department, PMO, Czech Government, 1991-92; Director, Department of Public Administration, Office for Legislation and Public Administration of the Czech Republic, 1992-96; Senior Advisor to Deputy Minister of Interior, 1997-99; Head, Department of Law and Administrative Science, Faculty of Economics and Administration, University Pardubice, 2000-01; Independent consultant in Public Administration, Partner, Institute for Legal Education and Information, Prague, Head of Public Administration Section, 2002-; Appointed Expert-Evaluator by Council of Europe GRECO Project for 2nd evaluation round, 2003-2005. Publications: Author, 18 books; Contributor, 38 books; over 350 articles in national and international professional journals; 65 papers published in proceedings from various national and international congresses, conferences and seminars. Honours: Plaques, 1981, Golden Badge, 1988, Council for Environment, Czech Government; Commemorative Medals from Masaryk University, Brno, 1996 and Universitas Pardubiciensis, 2001; Presidential Seal of Honor for exemplary achievements in the field of law and administration, ABI, 2000; International Woman of the Year, IBC, 2001. Memberships: IUSSP, 1968-88; IIAS; Founding Member, Czechoslovak Demographic Association, 1965,

Member of its Ruling Committee until 1989, Elected Honorary Member, Czech Demographic Association, 1994;; Legislative Council of Czech Government, 1991-98; Delegate to PUMA Com/OECD, 1995-99; Member, Carolinum Association of Alumnorum et Amicorum Universitatis Carolinae Pragensis, 1991-, Member of its Ruling Committee, 2002-; Democratic Club, Prague, 1996; Fellow, ABI, 2004; NISPAcee Observer, 2004-. Address: Na Zvoničce 32/1014, 147 00 Prague 4, Czech Republic.

**VIERECK Peter (Robert Edwin),** b. 5 August 1916, New York, New York, USA. Historian; Poet; Professor. m. (1) Aanya de Markov, June 1945, divorced May 1970, 1 son, 1 daughter, (2) Betty Martin Falkenberg, 30 August 1972. Education: BS, 1937, MA, 1939, PhD, 1942, Harvard University; Graduate Study as a Henry Fellow, Christ Church, Oxford, 1937-38. Appointments: Instructor, Tutor, Harvard University, 1946-47; Assistant Professor of History, 1947-48; Visiting Lecturer in Russian History, 1948-49, Smith College, Northampton, Massachusetts; Associate Professor, 1948-55, Professor of Modern European and Russian History, 1955-65, Mount Holyoke Alumnae Foundation Chair of Interpretative Studies, 1965-79, William R Kenan Chair of History, 1979-, Mount Holyoke College; Whittal Lecturer in Poetry, Library of Congress, Washington, DC, 1954, 1963; Fulbright Professor in American Poetry and Civilization, University of Florida, 1955; Elliston Chair and Poetry Lecturer, University of Cincinnati, 1956; Visiting Lecturer, University of California at Berkeley, 1957, 1964, City College of the City University of New York, 1964; Visiting Research Scholar in Russian for the Twentieth Century Fund, 1962-63; Director, Poetry Workshop, New York Writers Conferences, 1965-67. Publications: History: Metapolitics: From the Romantics to Hitler, 1941, revised edition as Metapolitics: The Roots of the Nazi Mind, 1961, 2nd revised edition, 1965, updated edition, 1982; Conservatism Revisited: The Revolt Against Revolt, 1815-1949, 1949, 2nd edition as Conservatism Revisited and the New Conservatism: What Went Wrong?, 1962, 3rd edition, 1972; Shame and Glory of the Intellectuals: Babbitt, Jr Versus the Rediscovery of Values, 1953; The Unadjusted Man: A New Hero for Americans: Reflections on the Distinction Between Conserving and Conforming, 1956; Conservatism: From John Adams to Churchill, 1956, revised edition, 1962; Inner Liberty: The Stubborn Grit in the Machine, 1957; Conservatism from Burke and John Adams till 1982: A History and an Anthology, 1982. Poetry: Terror and Decorum: Poems 1940-1948, 1948; Strike Through Mask: Lyrical Poems, 1950; The First Morning: New Poems, 1952; Dream and Responsibility: The Tension Between Poetry and Society, 1953; The Persimmon Tree, 1956; The Tree Witch: A Poem and a Play (First of All a Poem), 1961; New and Selected Poems, 1932-1967, 1967; Archer in the Marrow: The Applewood Cycles of 1967-1987, 1987; Tide and Continuities: Last and First Poems, 1995-1938, 1995; Metapolitics from Wagner to Hitler, 2002. Play: Opcomp: A Modern Medieval Miracle Play, 1993. Contributions to: Monographs, essays, reviews and poems to numerous periodicals. Honours: Pulitzer Prize in Poetry, 1949; Guggenheim Fellowship, 1959-60; Rockefeller Foundation Research Grant, 1958; National Endowment for the Humanities Senior Research Fellowship, 1969; Poetry Award, Massachusetts Artists Foundation, 1978; Sadin Prize, New York Quarterly, 1980; Golden Rose Award, 1981, Varoujan Poetry Prize, 1983, New England Poetry Club; Ingram Merrill Foundation Fellowship in Poetry, 1985. Memberships: American Committee for Cultural Freedom, executive committee; American Historical Association; Committee for Basic Education, charter member; Oxford Society; PEN; Phi Beta Kappa; Poetry Society of America. Address: 12 Silver Street, South Hadley, MA 01075, USA.

**VIERTL Reinhard,** b. 25 March 1946, Hall in Tirol, Austria. Professor of Applied Statistics. m. Dorothea, 2 sons. Education: Dipl Ing, 1972; Dr techn. 1974. Appointments: Assistant, 1972-79; University Docent, 1979-80; Research Fellow, University of California, Berkeley, 1980-81; Visiting Docent, University of Klagenfurt, 1981-82; Full Professor, Vienna University of Technology, 1982-; Visiting Professor, University of Innsbruck, 1991-93; Seasonal Instructor, University of Calgary, summer 2003. Publications: 7 books, including Statistical Methods for Non-Precise Data, 1996; Over 100 scientific papers in mathematics, probability theory, life testing, regional statistics, Bayesian statistics, and statistics with non-precise data. Honours: Max Kade Fellow, 1980. Memberships: Royal Statistical Society, London; Austrian Statistical Society; International Statistical Institute; German Statistical Society; New York Academy of Sciences; Austrian Mathematical Society. Address: Department of Statistics, Vienna University of Technology, Wiedner Hauptstr 8/107, A-1040 Vienna, Austria. E-mail: r.viertl@tuwien.ac.at

**VIGILI Maurizio Giovanni,** b. 28 June 1957, Asmara, Ethiopia. Medical Doctor. m. Carmen Cattaneo, 1 daughter. Education: Degree in Medicine and Surgery, University of Padova, Italy, 1982; Speciality in Otorhinolaryngology, University of Verona, Italy, 1985; Speciality in Audiology, University of Verona, Italy, 1989. Appointments: Assistant, Ear, Nose and Throat Department, Desenzano Hospital, 1985-90; Assistant Doctor, National Cancer Institute "Regina Elena", Rome, 1990-98; Director, Ear, Nose and Throat Department, San Carlo Hospital, Rome, 1998-; Director of the course: Use of $CO_2$ Laser in ENT Surgery, 1999-. Publications: More than 100 articles published in national and international journals. Honour: G Teatini Award, 1997. Memberships: European Laryngological Society; Societa Italiana di Otorinolaringoiatria. Address: Divisione di Otorinolaringoiatria, Ospedale San Carlo, via Aurelia 275, 00165 Rome, Italy. E-mail: vigili@idi.it

**VIHLA Minna Liisa Johanna,** b. 18 July 1966, Lapua, Finland. m. Juha Kopu, 1 son. Education: Medical Doctor, 1991; Bachelor of Arts, 1993, Master of Arts, 1994, Doctor of Philosophy, 1999. Appointments: Physician, Espoo and Kirkkonummi, Finland, 1992-93; Assistant Researcher, Helsinki University, Finland, 1996-99; Researcher, Helsinki University of Technology, 1999-; Researcher, University of Konstanz, Germany, 2002. Publications: Book: Medical Writing: Modality in Focus, 1999; Articles in scientific journals, PNAS, 2000; Neuroscience Letters, 2002, 2003, 2004; Cognitive Brain Research, 2003; Speech Communication, 2005. Address: Brain Research Unit, Low Temperature Laboratory, Helsinki University of Technology, PO Box 2200, 0215 HUT Espoo, Finland. E-mail: vihla@neuro.hut.fi

**VIJAYARATNAM Kanapathipillai,** b. 10 May 1948, Analaitivu, Ceylon (Sri Lanka). Chartered Civil, Water, Environmental Engineer and Manager; Consultant; Educator. m. Sakuntala Mylwaganam, 31 October 1979. Education: BSc (Engineering), Honours (Ceylon), 1971; MEng (AIT), 1977; MSc, Eng (London), 1982; DIC (Imperial College, London), 1982; DSc (Eng), 2004; Certificate, Sustainable Business, World Business Council on Sustainable Development, 1999. Appointments: Instructor Civil Engineering, University of Ceylon, 1972; Civil Engineer Mahaveli (River) Development Board, 1972-75; Postgraduate Engineering Studies, Asian Institute of Technology, 1976-77; Civil Engineer, Renardet Engineering, Singapore, 1977-80; Postgraduate Engineering Studies, Imperial College, London, 1981-82; Engineer, Chanton Engineering Ltd, Middlesex, England, 1984-85; Engineer, S P Collins & Associates, Consulting Engineers,

Cambridge, 1985-86; Consulting Engineer, 1986-88; Senior Engineer, Neilcot Construction, 1988-90; Engineer, Clean Water Department, Binnie & Partners Consulting Engineers, 1990-94; Senior Engineer, Gr I, SMHB, Consulting Engineers, KL Malaysia, 1995-96; Principal Engineer (Deputy Project Manager), Resident Engineer, SSP Consulting Engineers, Malaysia, 1996-97; Engineering Consultant, England, 1998; Director, Rosebury Consulting Ltd, Engineering Consultants, 1999-; Executive Director, AITA – NET (Europe) Ltd, 2001-04; Executive President and Dean, London Engineering School, 2004-;Distinguished Participant, World Summit on Sustainable Development, South Africa, 2002; World Water Forum and Ministerial Conference, The Netherlands, 2000, Japan, 2003; Stockholm Water Symposium, 2002; Entrepreneur Workshop, Singapore, 2004; Adjunct Faculty, Professor and Dean, School of Engineering Management, Sustainable Development and Public Policy, American University of London, 2003; Original contributions to Integrated water resources development of river basins, World Water Resources Congress, 1977; Mathematical modelling, optimisation and simulation of water treatment systems, Dissertation/Thesis to Imperial College, London, 1982 and Conferences in USA (1986) and UK (1987); Assessment of Mathematical Methods of Multicriterion/Multiobjective methods for Water Resources Management, 1994; Sustainable development of dams and hydropower, 1995, 1998; Sustainable urban environmental management, 1999; Re-engineering of water supply organisations, 1996; Sustainable water supply system planning for Cities, 2001, Making waste work, UK, 2000; Sustainable Waste Management, USA, 2001; Broader education of civil, water resources and environmental engineers, 1986, 1995; Pioneer of multidisciplinary Faculty of Engineering Management and Environment, 2004. Publications: Conference Proceedings and Technical Reports, USA, England, Malaysia, Switzerland, Sweden and Egypt. Honours: UK Government Scholar, 1976-77; NATO - Advanced Study Institute Grantee, 1981; Grantee, UNESCO/Colorado State University, 1981; Cricket team Champions, UK Engineering Consultants Tournament, 1993; Elected as one of top 500 Leaders of 21st Century, 1999; Listed among 100 Eminent Tamils of 20th Century at website: www.tamilnation.org, 2000, Man of the Year, 2004, ABI, 2004; One of 100 Greatest Minds of 21st Century, 2005; One of 500 Greatest Geniuses of 21st Century, 2005; Vijayaratnam's paper on Engineering Education for Sustainable Development in New Millennium on MIT website, 2000-; Awarded several medals, prizes and accolades for pioneering contribution to Sustainable Engineering Environment; Listed in numerous biographical publications; Pilgrimage to 7 Hindu temples in South India, 1988 and 2004, and Varanasi, East India, 1988; Pilgrimage to 11 Hindu temples in Singapore, Sivarathri night, 2004. Memberships: CEng, MICE, 1977; MCIWEM, 1979; MASCE, 1986; MIWRA, 1992; MIAHR, 1993; MIWA, 1993; MIHA, 1998; Association of Environmental Engineering and Science Professors, 2005. Address: 1 Ashcroft Rise, Coulsdon Woods, Coulsdon, Surrey CR5 2SS, England. E-mail: president@londones.com

**VIKBERG Veli Valtteri,** b. 2 November 1936, Pyhäjärvi, Ul, Finland. Retired Physician; Amateur Entomologist. m. Marjatta Kurkela, 1 son, 3 daughters. Education: Licenciate of Medicine, 1961, Specialising in medical microbiology, 1967, University of Helsinki. Appointments: Senior Physician, Laboratory Department, Central Hospital of North Karelia, Joensuu, 1967-74; Senior Physician, Laboratory Department, 1974-87, Senior Physician, Department of Clinical Microbiology, 1988-95, Central Hospital of Kanta-Häme, Hämeenlinna; Retired, 1995. Publications: Numerous articles in scientific journals, 1960-2005. Memberships: The Entomological Society of Finland,

1959; The International Society of Hymenopterists, 1991. Address: Liinalammintie 11 as. 6, FI-14200 Turenki, Finland.

**VILLENEUVE Jacques,** b. 9 April 1971, Canada. Racing Car Driver. Appointments: Started racing in Italian Touring Car Championship Italian Formula 3, 1989, 1990; With Reynaud and Alfa Romeo, 1992; Japanese Formula 3, 1993; Formula Atlantic, 1993; IndyCar Driver, 1994-95; IndyCar Racing Champion, 1995; Drove Formula One Cars with Williams Renault Team, then British American Racing team, now with BAR-Honda; Grand Prix Winner, Britain, 1996, 1997, Brazil, 1997; Argentina, 1997; Spain, 1997; Hungary, 1997, Austria, 1997; Luxembourg, 1997; Formula One Champion, 1997.

**VINCENT John James,** b. 29 December 1929, Sunderland, England. Writer; Broadcaster; Methodist Minister; Writer. m. Grace Johnston Stafford, 4 December 1958, 2 sons, 1 daughter. Education: BD, Richmond College, London University, 1954; STM, Drew University, 1955; DTheol, Basel University, 1960. Appointments: Ordained Minister, Methodist Church, 1956; Leader, Ashram Community, 1967-; Director, Urban Theology Unit, 1969-97; Director Emeritus 1997-; Adjunct Professor, New York Theological Seminary, 1979-87; President, Methodist Church of Great Britain, 1989-90; Honorary Lecturer, Sheffield University, 1990-, Birmingham University, 2003-. Publications: Christ and Methodism, 1964; Here I Stand, 1967; Secular Christ, 1968; The Race Race, 1970; The Jesus Thing, 1973; Stirrings, Essays Christian and Radical, 1975; Alternative Church, 1976; Disciple and Lord, 1976; Starting all over Again, 1981; Into the City, 1982; OK Let's Be Methodists, 1984; Radical Jesus, 1986; Mark at Work, 1986; Britain in the 90's, 1989; Liberation Theology from the Inner City, 1992; A Petition of Distress from the Cities, 1993; A British Liberation Theology, bi-annual volumes, editor,1995-; The Cities: A Methodist Report, 1997; Hope from the City, 2000; Faithfulness in the City, 2003; Methodist and Radical, 2004; Using Mark's Gospel Today, 2006. Memberships: Studiorum Novi Testamenti Societas; Alliance of Radical Methodists; Urban Theologians International, Joint Chair, 1995-. Address: 178 Abbeyfield Road, Sheffield S4 7AY, England.

**VINENT-CANTORAL Aida,** b. 8 November 1948, Havana, Cuba. Mediator. Education: BA, Alverno College; MA, Certificate in Dispute Resolution, Marquette University; Additional courses in Dispute Resolution, Negotiation of Labour Contracts, Negotiations and teaching of such, Harvard University; Hamlin University; Northwestern University; University of Michigan, Ann Arbour; South Texas College of Law, Houston; Federal Mediation and Conciliation Institute, Washington DC; Programmes in Transformative Mediation, Hofstra and Pepperdine Universities (sponsored by the United States Postal Service); Coursework in themes relating to persons with disabilities, difficulties encountered by families, especially in educational, legal and social systems; Difficulties encountered by families of various ethnic roots in social immigration and cultural systems; Counselling problem gamblers. Appointments: Disability Division, Milwaukee County Department of Human Services; Mediator, Family Court, Milwaukee County; Mediator, United States Postal Service in cases pertaining to allegations of discrimination, pre and post legal; Neutral Third Party Opinions, Walworth County Family Court; Facilitator, Parenting Program for Education of Parents in Divorce Situations, Centro Legal; Neutral Third Party Opinion pertaining to cases of abuse or exploitation of children; Dispute resolution services between individuals, partners and associates in business; Mediator, Wisconsin Special Education Mediation System. Honours: Social Worker of the Year, Foster Parents Association of Wisconsin; Listed in Who's Who publications and biographical dictionaries. Memberships: Association for Conflict Resolution; Association of Family Courts; Wisconsin Association of Mediators; Wisconsin Association of Homicide Investigators; Wisconsin Council on Problem Gambling; Alumnae Association of Sacred Heart Schools. Address: PO Box 462, Greendale, WI 53129, USA. E-mail: avinent@aol.com

**VIRELLI Louis J Jr,** b. 4 November 1948, Philadelphia, Pennsylvania, USA. Attorney. m. Barbara Ann Rotella, 2 sons. Education: BE, Mechanical Engineering, Villanova University, 1970; JD, University of Tennessee, 1972. Appointments: Patent Attorney, Sperry New Holland Co., New Holland, Pennsylvania, 1973-74; Associate Counsel, Westinghouse Co., Pittsburgh, Pennsylvania, 1974-76; Associate, Paul & Paul, Philadelphia, PA, 1976-80; Partner, 1980-84; Patent Counsel, National Starch & Chemical & Co, Bridgewater, NJ, 1984-88, Assistant General Counsel, Intellectual Property, 1988-92, General Counsel, Intellectual Property, 1992-95; Assistant General Counsel Patents, Unilever US, Inc, Edgewater, NJ, 1988-95, Vice-President, General Patent Counsel, 1995-96, Senior Vice-President, General Patent Counsel, and Unilever PLC & NV, 1997-2003, Senior Vice-President, General Counsel, Intellectual Property, Unilever, Englewood Cliffs, New Jersey and Unilever PLC & NV, London, England and Rotterdam, Netherlands, 2003-. Memberships: ABA; Association Corporate Patent Counsel; Philadelphia Patent Law Association; New Jersey Patent Law Association; Intellectual Property Owners Association. Address: Unilever Intellectual Property Group, 700 Sylvan Ave, Englewood Cliffs, NJ 07632, USA.

**VISWESWARA Channarayapatna Sreekantaiah,** b. 27 November 1936, Mysore City, India. Chartered Engineer; Consultant. m. K Sudhamani, 3 daughters. Education: Intermediate Science, The Vijaya College, University of Mysore, 1953; BSc, The National College, University of Mysore, 1955; BE, Civil, The National Institute of Engineering, University of Mysore, 1959. Appointments: Junior Engineer, PWD, Mysore State; Assistant Inspecting Officer, DGS & D, India Government, 1963-66; Design Engineer, Chief Design Engineer, Metallurgical and Engineering Consultants Ltd, India, 1967-95; Consultant, Assistant Chief Consultant, Ajaokuta Steel Plant, Nigeria, 1988-90; Consultant, Advisor, Simplex Castings (Pvt) Ltd, Bangalore, 1996-97; Consultant, Civil and Structural works, Mysore, 1997-; Resident Engineer, Techno Arts Construction (Pvt) Ltd, Bangalore, Mysore, 2000-01; Consultant, Dalal Matt Macdonald (Pvt) Ltd, Mumbai, Mysore, 2003-04. Publications: Several articles for professional Seminars. Honours: Fellow of the Institute of Engineers, Civil Section, India, 1981; Best Citizen of India Award, 1998; Vikasa Rathna Award, 2004; Numerous entries in British and American biographical dictionaries. Address: No 1063/74, 2nd Main, 8th Cross Road, Vidyaranyapuram, Mysore, 570 008, Karnataka, India.

**VIZINCZEY Stephen,** b. 12 May 1933, Kaloz, Hungary. Writer. m. September 1963, 3 daughters. Education: University of Budapest, 1949-50; Academy of Theatre Arts, Budapest, 1951-56. Appointments: Editor, Exchange Magazine, 1960-61; Producer, Canadian Broadcasting Corporation, 1962-65. Publications: In Praise of Older Women, 1965; The Rules of Chaos, 1969; An Innocent Millionaire, 1983; Truth and Lies in Literature, 1986; The Man with the Magic Touch, 1994; Be Faithful unto Death (translation), 1995; Wishes, 2005. Contributions to: Currently; The Los Angeles Times Book Review. Memberships: PEN; Society of Authors; ALCS; Award, Premio Letterario Isola d'Elba R Brignetti, 2004. Address: 70 Coleherne Court, Old Brompton Road, London SW5 0EF, England.

**VLACHOPOULOS Lazaros Argiriou,** b. 1965, Drama, Greece. Doctor of Educational Psychology; Chevalier, OSJ. Education includes: BA, Honours, Psychology, 1995; MSc, Developmental Psychology, 1998; Psy D, School Psychology, 2000; Advanced Diploma in Psychotherapy, 2005; Training in: Career, Family and Marriage Counselling, Group Psychoanalytic Psychotherapy, Psychodrama, Psychodynamic Projection Tests; Teachers' Training College, Aegean University, 1989; PgCC, Special Education, University of Malta, 1993; Bilateral Diplomacy, 2004; Negotiating Skills, 2004; Public Diplomacy, 2005; Informatics in Education; European Co-ordinator, in-service training, University of Hull. Appointments: 6 years teaching experience as a primary school teacher of which: 2 in mainstream primary education, 2 in special education, 1 in cross-cultural education in Hungary, 1 year Headmaster, Special Education Unit of Lemnos, Greece; 2 years school psychologist, Lemnos, Greece; 1 year teaching experience in computer science; 1 semester teaching experience in vocational education, computers; 1 semester, teaching experience in vocational education, child psychology; 1 semester in vocational education in social psychology; Currently School Psychologist, Diagnostic, Assessment and Support Centre of Drama, Greek Ministry of Education; Scientific Associate of the Culture and Youth Centre of the Municipality of Drama, Greece. Publications: Rob, chapter in Children with Special Needs, some hopes, 1995; Special Education in Greece, 1996; School abilities evaluation in a Special Educational Unit, 1998; Burnout Syndrome, 1999; Children's Negative Behaviour as a Reaction to Parents' Behaviour, 1999; Bulling, 2001; Chaos Theory in Psychology, 2003; Towards a Greek Culture Diplomacy, 2004; Defining and Supporting Slow Learners, 2005. Memberships: International Association for Applied Psychology; International Family Therapy Association; Knight Commander of Grace, Sovereign Order of Saint John of Jerusalem. Address: Iras 1, 66100 Drama, Greece.

**VLASKO-VLASOV Konstantin Aleksandrovich,** b. 16 February 1920, USSR. Radio Engineer. m. Lidia Nikolaevna Vlasko-Vlasova, 1 son, 1 daughter. Education: Moscow Red Flag Military Aviation Technical School, 1938-1940; Military Air Engineering Academy "Mogaiski", 1944-50; Candidate of Science, 1957; Senior Science Collaborator, Senior Lecturer, 1997. Appointments: Senior Engineer, Construction Bureau-1, Third Chief Government of Soviet Ministers of USSR, 1950-51; Vice-Chief of the Laboratory of Construction Bureau-1, Technical Engineering Ministry, 1951-1954; Vice-Chief Constructor, Construction Bureau-1, State Committee of Radioelectronics, 1954-58; Chief of the Vice-Chief Constructor's Department of the Construction Bureau "Strela", Radio Industry Ministry, 1958-69; Chief of Construction Bureau, FGUP Research Institute "Cometa", 1969-99; Head of Collaboration of FGUP Research "Cometa", 1999-. Publications: Numerous scientific works mainly about: Creation of arming systems, developing and choosing methods of radio-guidance of airborne vehicles, processing of encrypted information received from space-ships and other questions of radio-guidance; Some articles published in scientific technical journals and periodicals including: News of Cosmonautics; Questions of Radio-Electronics; Basic and Applied Cosmonautics. Honours: Stalin Premium, 1953; Lenin Premium, 1972; State Premium of Russian Federation, 1997; 5 Orders; 23 Medals. Memberships: Honorary Member (Academician), Space Academy named after Tsiolkovsky; International Academy of Information. Address: App 15, Kosmonauta Volkova Street 25/2, Moscow 125299, Russia.

**VLASOV Anatoliy N,** b. 27 September 1946, Sergeevka, Belarus. Lawyer. m. Dana K Leshkovich, 2 sons. Education:

Faculty of Law, Bashkir State University. Appointments: Worker in Petrochemical Factory; Head of Housing Services; Assistant to Heads of Enterprises dealing with staff and legal maintenance; Adviser, Legal Department, Ministry of Transport, Belarus; Adviser, Legal Maintenance, BelRos Communication Association, Unitary Enterprise Telemix. Publications: Many articles in mass Belarussian media; Brochure, Legal and Economic Aspects of the State Ideology of a Civil Society in Belarus. Honours: Man of the Year, 2002; Doctor of Philosophy in the field of Information Technologies. Memberships: Corresponding Member, International Academy of Information Technologies. Address: Maja Kovskogo Str 20-117, Minsk 220006, Belarus. E-mail: andpas@tut.by

**VLASSOV Vasiliy V,** b. 15 June 1953, Novosibirsk, USSR. Physician. m. Irina, 23 November 1973, 1 daughter. Education: MD, Military Medical Academy, St Petersburg, Russia; Dr Medical Science; Professor. Appointments: Air Surgeon, 1976-79; Clinical Physiology Department Head, Irkutsk, Aviation Hospital, 1980-88; Professor, Head Department, Aerospace Medicine Saratov Military Medical Institute; Professor, Head Department, Social Science Saratov Medical University, 1995-2001; Professor, Moscow Physics-Technical University, 2001-; Chief Editor, Media Sphera Publishing Group, Moscow. Publications: Effectiveness of diagnostic tests; Aviat Space Environmental Medicine; Military Medicine. Memberships: Russian Medical Association, Cochrane Collaboration, Director of Russian Branch, 2001-. Address: PO Box 13, Moscow 109451, Russia.

**VOLLMAR James Anthony,** b. 8 January 1952, Wellingborough, Northamptonshire, England. Writer; Poet; Playwright. Education: Queen Mary College, University of London, 1970-72. Appointment: Founder, Editor, Greylag Press, 1977-. Publications: Circles and Spaces; Orkney Poems; Hoy: The Seven Postcards; Warming the Stones; Explorers Log Book. Contributions to: Agenda; Iron; Oasis; Joe Soaps Canoe; Ally; Pacific Quarterly; Ambit. Memberships: Writers' Guild of Great Britain. Address: 7 Moreton Way, Kingsthorpe. Northampton, NN2 8PD, England.

**VOLPOV Evgeni,** b. 20 February 1959, Donetzk Region, Ukraine. Electrical Research Engineer. m. Irena Volpov, 2 sons. Education: Masters Degree, St Petersburg State Technical University, 1976-82; PhD, Electrotechnical Institute of Russia, 1986-89. Appointments: R&D and Failure Analysis Engineer, Planning, Development and Technology Division, Israel Electric Corporation, Haifa, Israel; Specialising in electric field modelling, insulation co-ordination, and diagnostics of HV power apparatus. Publications: Articles in scientific journals include: HVDC Gas Insulated Apparatus: Electric Field Specificity and Insulation Design Concept, 2002; Electric Field Modeling and Field Formation Mechanism, 2003. Honours: Listed in Who's Who publications and biographical dictionaries. Address: Israel Electric Co, Planning, Development and Technology Division, Haifa 31000, Israel. E-mail: evgeni.volpov@gmx.net Website: http://www.geocities.com/evgeni_volpov

**VOLTTI Hilkka Annikki,** b. 6 December 1944, Mikkeli, Finland. Chemist. Education: MSc, Biochemistry, 1970; PhD, Biochemistry, 1974; Clinical Chemist, Clinical Chemistry, 1983. Appointments: Assistant, Department of Biochemistry, University Oulu, Finland; Research Assistant, Finnish National Research Council, Oulu, 1969-72; Reader, Associate Professor, Medical Biochemistry, University of Oulu, 1973-79; Lecturer, Biochemistry, 1980-81; Chemist, University Hospital, Oulu, 1982-84; Clinical Chemist, Central Hospital, Kymenlaakso, Kotka, 1985-2001; Retired, 2001. Publications: Contributions to professional journals. Honours: International Scientist of the Year, IBC, 2002; Woman of Achievement, IBC, 2002; Most Influential Scientist of the Decade, ABI, 2002; Woman of the Year, ABI, 2002, 2003; Universal Award of Accomplishment, ABI, 2002; Nomination to both the Companion of Honour Awards and the Honours List of 500 Founders of the 21st Century, IBC, 2002; The Global Award of Accomplishment, BWW, 2000; Listed in numerous biographical reference books. Memberships: Fellowship of the International Biographical Association, Cambridge, England; Member, Scientific Advisor to the President and Director of the BWW Society, USA; Member, ABI Research Association's Board of Governors, USA. Address: Tallinnankatu 6-8 A 3, 48100 Kotka, Finland.

**VON GIZYCKI Alkistis,** b. Famagusta, Cyprus. Educator; Scholar. m. (1) Nicholas Romanoff, deceased 1977, (2) Walter von Gizycki, divorced, 1 son, 1 daughter. Education: BA (Honours), Political Science, International Relations and Social Anthropology, 1971; MA, Psychology, New School University, USA. Appointments: Approximately 15 years in Education; Teacher, Professor, Counsellor, Researcher, Writer, Scholar, Freelance, Volunteer, Co-ordinator, Civic Leader, Church Board Officer, Refugee of War. Honours: Fulbright (after Senator) Scholarship; Pattilo Scholar, College Honours, General Excellence Award, Valed, Outstanding Performances; Woman of the Year (Millennium) and Outstanding Woman of the 21st Century by the American Biographical Institute; Community Volunteer Awards; Work Place awards; Great success in a scientific discovery implemented creating new trends (kept low key); Inclusion in 2000 Notable American Women; Who's Who in International, Professional and Business Women; Millennium Who's Who among American Women. Memberships: New York Academy of Sciences (NYAS); American Psychological Association (APA); American Association of University Women (AAUW); National Organisation of Women (NOW), American Association of Retired Professionals (AARP), American Civil Liberties Union (ACLU). Address: PO Box 230159, Brooklyn, NY 11223, USA

**VORA Bipin,** b. 1 April 1943, Harij, Gujarat, India. Chemical Engineer. m. Kalpi, 1 son, 2 daughters. Education: BSc honours, Chemistry, University of Mumbai, 1963; BS, 1965, MS, 1967, Chemical Engineering, University of New Mexico, USA. Appointments: Various Research and Development and Technical Services positions, UOP LLC, 1967-90; Associate Director, Olefins and Detergents Research and Development, 1990-94; Director, Olefins and Detergents Research and Development, 1994-2000; Senior Corporate Fellow, Development, UOP LLC, 2001-. Publications: Over 120 publications; Over 150 international patents. Honours: Distinguished Alumni, University of New Mexico, 1999; ACS National Award of Industrial Chemistry, 2002; AICHE National Award, in Chemical Engineering Practice, 2003. Memberships: Fellow, American Institute of Chemical Engineer; Member, American Chemical Society. Address: 1324 Kallien Court, Naperville, IL 60540, USA. E-mail: bipin.vora@uop.com

**VUKASOVIĆ Ante,** b. 9 January 1929, Osijek, Croatia. University Professor. m. Nada Vukasović, 1 son, 1 daughter. Education: Teachers' Academy Degree, Osijek, Croatia, 1950; Faculty of Philosophy, Department of Pedagogy, 1956, PhD, Scientific Degree, Faculty of Philosophy, 1965, Doctorate and Honorary Title of Scientific Advisor, 1979, University of Zagreb. Appointments: Teacher, Šestanovac Primary School near Split, 1950-51; Student, University of Zagreb, 1951-56; Teachers' Academy Professor, 1956-57; Director, Pedagogical Centre for primary and secondary school teacher training for the region of Eastern Slavonia, Osijek, 1957-60; Assistant Lecturer,

1960-66, Senior Lecturer, 1966-73, Associate Professor, 1973-78, Professor, 1978-93, Department of Pedagogy, Faculty of Philosophy, University of Zagreb; Director of Centre for Education and Research, 1971-79; Director, Scientific Research Project: System and programme of pre-service and in-service training of teachers for work in the field of family planning, UN Fund for Population Activity, 1979-83. Publications: Over 1400 publications including books as author, editor and co-author, scientific dissertations in conference proceedings and journals, newspaper articles and reviews, most notably: The Influence of the Contemporary Technology on the Concept of General Education (doctoral dissertation), 1964; Vocational and Technical Education, 1972; Moral Education, 1974; Intellectual Education, 1976; Moral Qualities of Our Students, 1977; Training Teachers for Educational Work in the Area of Humanization of Relations between the Sexes, 1982; Education for Humane Relationships and Responsible Parenthood, 1984; Pedagogy, 1990; Ethics – Morality – Personality, 1993; Family – the Source and Bearer of Life, 1999. Honours include: National Decoration: Work Medal with a Gold Wreath, 1971; Award for Improvement of Scientific Research Work, 1971; Several Jan Amos Komenský Medals, Danica Hrvatska Order of Merit, Republic of Croatia, 1996; National "Ivan Filipović Award" for lifetime achievement, 2002. Memberships include: Chairman, Society of Croatian-Slovakian Friendship, 1993-2003; World Association for Educational Research; Academy of Humanities, St Petersburg, Russia; Management Board, Croatian Victimological Society; Croatian Pedagogical Literary Association; Croatian Pedagogical Society; Croatian Society for Life and Family. Address: Gjure Szaba 13, 10 000 Zagreb, Croatia. E-mail: hkz@hkz-mi.hr

# W

**WABWAYA Frederick Mburi,** b. 24 April 1957, Kisumu City, Kenya. Telecommunications Engineer. m. Mary Aluoch, 1 son, 4 daughters. Education: HND, Electronics, Kenya, 1986; BSc, Telecommunications, USA, 2000; MBA, Telecommunications Management, USA, 2001; MSc, Data Communications, Brunel University, UK, 2004. Appointments: Assistant Engineer, 1983-86, Engineer-in-Charge, 1986-90, Voice of Kenya (Kenya Broadcasting Corporation);Telecommunications Engineer, 1990-92, Chief of Workshop, 1992-93, Assistant Centre Manager, 1993-94, Centre Manager, 1994-96, SITA (Airlines World-wide Telecommunication and Information Services); Electronic and Communications Engineer, United States Agency for International Development, Bureau for Africa, 1997-99; IT Executive, UN (UNAET), Australia and East Timor, IT Executive, UN (ONUB), 2000-. Publication: Asynchronous and synchronous digital design signal processor reducing microwave radiation for mobile handset users and in base stations. Honours: Diploma in Engineering, IEE, UK; MIEE, IEEE, USA; Superior Citation, US State Department; Management and Teamwork Skills, USAID. Memberships: MIEE, UK; MIEEE, USA; MERB, Kenya; MIEK, Kenya; MCS, USA; MIEC, USA. Address: PO Box 4884, New York, NY 10163-4884, USA. E-mail: frediwabwaya@hotmail.com

**WADDINGTON David James,** b. 27 May 1932, Edgware, Middlesex, England. University Professor. m. Isobel Hesketh, 2 sons, 1 daughter. Education: BSc, ARCS, DIC, PhD, Imperial College, University of London. Appointments: Senior Lecturer, 1965-78, Professor of Chemical Education, 1978-2000, Pro-Vice Chancellor, 1985-91, Professor Emeritus, 2000-, University of York; Visiting Professor, Institut für Pedagogik, University of Kiel, Germany, 2000-. Publications: Organic Chemistry, 1962; Organic Chemistry Through Experiment (with H S Finlay), 1965; Modern Organic Chemistry (with R O C Norman), 1972; Chemical Education in the Seventies (with A Kornhauser and C N R Rao), 1980; Teaching School Chemistry (editor), 1985; Education, Industry and Technology (jointly), 1987; Chemistry: the Salters Approach (jointly), 1990; Salters Advanced Chemistry (jointly), 1994, 2nd edition 2000; Science for Understanding Tomorrow's World (jointly), 1995; Partners in Chemical Education (with J N Laxonby), 1996; Salters Higher Chemistry (jointly), 1999; Essential Chemical Industry (jointly), 1999. Honours: Nyholm Medal, Royal Society of Chemistry, 1985; Brasted Award, American Chemical Society, 1988; National Order of Scientific Merit, Brazil, 1997; Honorary Professor, University of Chemical Technology, Moscow, 1998. Memberships: President, Education Committee, Royal Society of Chemistry, 1981-83; Chairman, Committee of Teaching of Chemistry, IUPAC, 1981-86; Chairman, Committee of Teaching of Science, ICSU, 1990-94; Liveryman, Salters Company, 2001-. Address: University of York, York YO10 5DD, England. E-mail: djw1@york.ac.uk

**WADE David,** b. 2 December 1929, Edinburgh, Scotland. Writer. Education: Queen's College, Cambridge, 1952. Appointments: Radio Critic, The Listener, 1965-67, The Times, 1967-89. Publications: Trying to Connect You; The Cooker; The Guthrie Process; The Gold Spinners; Three Blows in Anger; The Ogden File; The Carpet Maker of Samarkand; The Nightingale; Summer of 39; The Facts of Life; A Rather Nasty Crack; On Detachment; The Tree of Strife; Power of Attorney; Alexander. Membership: Society of Authors. Address: Willow Cottage, Stockland Green Road, Southborough, Kent TN3 0TL, England.

**WADE (Sarah) Virginia,** b. 10 July 1945, Bournemouth, England. Tennis Player. Education: University of Sussex. Appointments: Amateur player, 1962-68, professional, 1968-; British Hard Court Champion, 1967, 1968, 1973, 1974; USA Champion, 1968 (singles) 1973, 1975 (doubles); Italian Champion, 1971; Australian Champion, 1972; Wimbledon Ladies Champion, 1977; Played Wightman Cup for Great Britain, 1965-81, Captain 1973-80; Played Federation Cup for Great Britain, 1967-81, Captain, 1973-81; Commentator, BBC, 1980-. Publications: Courting Triumph (with Mary Lou Mellace), 1978; Ladies of the Court, 1984. Honours include: LLD, Sussex, 1985; International Tennis Hall of Fame, 1989. Membership: Committee, All England Lawn Tennis Club, 1983-91. Address: c/o International Management Group, Pier House, Strand on the Green, London W4 3NN, England.

**WAETZMAN Larry Samuel,** b. 11 December 1945, Reading, Pennsylvania, USA. Urban Planner. m. Bonnie Waetzman, 2 sons, 1 daughter. Education: BA, Franklin & Marshall College, 1967; MA, University of Wisconsin (Madison), 1969. Appointments: 1st Lieutenant, US Army, 1969-71; Borough Planner, Borough of Morristown, Pennsylvania, 1972-74; Director of Community Development, Haverford Township, Pennsylvania, 1974-78; Planner, Government Studies and Systems Inc., 1978-81; Partner, Tredinnick Waetzman Associates, 1981-87; Owner, Waetzman Planning Group, 1987-2000; President, Waetzman Planning Group Inc., 2000-. Publications: Various articles: Pennsylvania Department of Community Affairs Reports; New Jersey Municipalities; 8 professional education seminars: Corman Educational Services, Pennsylvania Bar Institute, International Council of Shopping Centers. Memberships: Practising Planner, American Institute of Certified Planners; Licensed Professional Planner, New Jersey; American Planning Association; New Jersey Planning Officials. Address: 1230 County Line Road, Bryn Mawr, PA 19010, USA. E-mail: lsw@waetzmanplanning.com Website: www.waetzmanplanning.com

**WAGONER David (Russell),** b. 5 June 1926, Massillon, Ohio, USA. Professor of English; Poet; Author. m. (1) Patricia Parrott, 1961, divorced 1982, (2) Robin Heather Seyfried, 1982, 2 daughters. Education: BA, Pennsylvania State University, 1947; MA, Indiana University, 1949. Appointments: Instructor, DePauw University, 1949-50, Pennsylvania State University, 1950-53; Assistant Professor, 1954-57, Associate Professor, 1958-66, Professor of English, 1966-, University of Washington, Seattle; Editor, Poetry Northwest, 1966-; Elliston Professor of Poetry, University of Cincinnati, 1968. Publications: Poetry: Dry Sun, Dry Wind, 1953; A Place to Stand, 1958; Poems, 1959; The Nesting Ground, 1963; Staying Alive, 1966; New and Selected Poems, 1969; Working Against Time, 1970; Riverbed, 1972; Sleeping in the Woods, 1974; A Guide to Dungeness Spit, 1975; Travelling Light, 1976; Collected Poems, 1956-1976, 1976; Who Shall be the Sun?: Poems Based on the Love, Legends, and Myths of Northwest Coast and Plateau Indians, 1978; In Broken Country, 1979; Landfall, 1981; First Light, 1983; Through the Forest: New and Selected Poems, 1977-1987, 1987; Traveling Light: Collected and New Poems, 1999. Fiction: The Man in the Middle, 1954; Money, Money, Money, 1955; Rock, 1958; The Escape Artist, 1965; Baby, Come on Inside, 1968; Where Is My Wandering Boy Tonight?, 1970; The Road to Many a Wonder, 1974; Tracker, 1975; Whole Hog, 1976; The Hanging Garden, 1980. Editor: Straw for the Fire: From the Notebooks of Theodore Roethke 1943-1963, 1972. Honours: Guggenheim Fellowship, 1956; Ford Foundation Fellowship, 1964; American Academy of Arts and Letters Grant, 1967; National Endowment for the Arts Grant, 1969; Morton Dauwen Zabel Prize, 1967; Oscar Blumenthal Prize, 1974; Fels Prize, 1975; Eunice Tietjens

Memorial Prize, 1977; English-Speaking Union Prize, 1980; Sherwood Anderson Prize, 1980; Pacific Northwest Booksellers Award, 2000. Membership: Academy of American Poets, chancellor, 1978. Address: University of Washington, 4045 Brooklyn Avenue NE, Seattle, WA 98105, USA.

**WAINWRIGHT Geoffrey,** b. 16 July 1939, Yorkshire, England. Professor of Systematic Theology; Methodist Minister. m. Margaret Wiles, 20 April 1965, 1 son, 2 daughters. Education: BA, 1960, MA, 1964, BD, 1972, DD, 1987, University of Cambridge; DrThéol, University of Geneva, 1969. Appointments: Editor, Studia Liturgica, 1974-87; Professor of Systematic Theology, The Divinity School, Duke University, Durham, North Carolina, 1983-. Publications: Christian Initiation, 1969; Eucharist and Eschatology, 1971, 2nd edition, 1981; The Study of Liturgy (co-editor), 1978, 2nd edition, 1992; Doxology, 1980; The Ecumenical Moment, 1983; The Study of Spirituality (co-editor), 1986; On Wesley and Calvin, 1987; Keeping the Faith: Essays to Mark the Centenary of Lux Mundi (editor), 1989; The Dictionary of the Ecumenical Movement (co-editor), 1991; Methodists in Dialogue, 1995; Worship With One Accord, 1997; For Our Salvation, 1997; Is the Reformation Over? Catholics and Protestants at the Turn of the Millennia, 2000; Lesslie Newbigin: A Theological Life, 2000; The Oxford History of Christian Worship (co-editor), 2005. Contributions to: Reference books and theological journals. Honours: Numerous named lectureships world-wide; Berakah Award, North American Academy of Liturgy, 1999; Received a Festschrift: Ecumenical Theology in Worship, Doctrine, and Life: Essays Presented to Geoffrey Wainwright on his 60th Birthday, 1999; Outstanding Ecumenist Award, Washington Theological Consortium, 2003. Memberships: American Theological Society, secretary, 1988-95, president, 1996-97; International Dialogue Between the World Methodist Council and the Roman Catholic Church, chairman; Societas Liturgica, president, 1983-85; World Council of Churches Faith and Order Commission, 1976-91. Address: The Divinity School, Duke University, Durham, NC 27708, USA.

**WAITE Terence Hardy,** b. 31 May 1939, Bollington, England. Writer and Broadcaster. m. Helen Frances Watters, 1964, 1 son, 3 daughters. Education: Church Army College, London. Appointments: Lay Training Advisor to Bishop and Diocese of Bristol, 1964-68; Advisor to Archbishop of Uganda, Rwanda and Burundi, 1968-71; International Consultant with Roman Catholic Church, 1972-79; Advisor, Archbishop of Canterbury on Anglican Communion Affairs, 1980-92; Iranian Hostages Mission, 1981; Libyan Hostages Mission, 1985; Kidnapped in Beirut, 1987, Released, 1991. Publications: Taken on Trust, 1993; Footfalls in Memory, 1995; Travels with a Primate, 2000. Honours include: Hon DCL, Kent, 1986, City of London, Durham, 1992; Hon DLL, Liverpool; Hon LLD, Sussex, 1992; Hon LHD, Wittenberg University, 1992; Hon Dr International Law, Florida Southern University, 1992; Dr hc, Yale University Divinity School, 1992; Roosevelt Freedom Medal, 1992; Man of the Year, England, 1985; Freeman, City of Canterbury, 1992, Borough of Lewisham, 1992; Hon DPhil, Anglia Polytechnic, 2001; Hon DLitt, Nottingham Trent, 2001. Memberships: Church of England National Association, 1966-68; Co-ordinator, Southern Sudan Relief Project, 1969-71; Butler Trust, Prison Officers Award Programme; President, Y-Care International (YMCA International Development Committee); President, Emmaus UK (for the Homeless), 1996-; Founder Chair, Friends of Victim Support, 1992-; Patron, Strode Park Foundation for the Disabled; Rainbow Trust; Fellow Commoner, Trinity Hall, Cambridge, 1992-; Honorary Chancellor, Florida Southern University, 1992; Chairman, Prison Video Trust; Trustee

Freeplay Foundation. Address: Trinity Hall, Cambridge, CB2 1TJ, England.

**WAKEHAM John (Baron Wakeham of Malden),** b. 1932. Chartered Accountant; Politician. m. Alison Bridget, 3 sons. Appointments: Chartered Accountant with own practice; Retired from business, 1977; Elected Conservative Member of Parliament for Maldon and Rochford, 1974, South Colchester and Maldon, 1983; Ministerial Appointments: Assistant Government Whip, 1979; Lord Commissioner of the Treasury, 1981; Parliamentary Under Secretary of State, Department of Industry, 1981; Minister of State, Treasury, 1982; Government Chief Whip, 1983; Appointed Member of the Privy Council, Lord Privy Seal and Leader of the House of Commons, 1987; Lord President of the Council and Leader of the House of Commons, 1988; Secretary of State for Energy, 1989; Lord Privy Seal and Leader of the House of Lords, 1992; Retired from Government, 1994; 6 Non-Executive Directorships; Chairman, Cothill House, 1998; Chairman, Alexandra Rose Day, 1998; Chairman, Vosper Thorneycroft Holdings Plc, 1995; Chairman, Press Complaints Commission, 1995-2002; Non-Executive Director, Enron Corporation, 1994-2002; Bristol and West PLC, 1995-2002; NM Rothschild & Sons Ltd, 1995-2002; Chairman, Royal Commission on House of Lords Reform, 1999-2000; Chairman, Michael Page International Plc, 2001-02;. Honours: JP; DL; FLA; Honorary PhD; Honorary D Univ. Memberships: Director, National Association for Gambling Care, Educational Resources and Training; Trustee and Committee of Management, RNLI; Trustee, HMS Warrior 1860; Clubs: Garrick, Carlton, Royal Yacht Squadron, Royal Southern Yacht Club. Address: House of Lords, London SW1, England.

**WAKELEY Amanda,** b. 15 September 1962, England. Fashion Designer. m. Neil David Gillon, 1992. Appointments: Fashion industry, New York, 1983-85; Designing, private clients, England, 1986; Launched own label, 1990; Retail, wholesale world-wide, bridal, high street brand Amanda Wakeley for Principles and corporate-wear consultancy. Honours: Glamour Award, British Fashion Awards, 1992, 1993, 1996. Membership: Co-Chair, Fashion Targets Breast Cancer Campaign, 1996, 1998, 2000, 2002.

**WAKOSKI Diane,** b. 3 August 1937, Whittier, California, USA. Poet; Professor of English. m. Robert J Turney, 14 February 1982. Education: BA, English, University of California at Berkeley, 1960. Appointments: Poet-in-Residence, Professor of English, 1975-, University Distinguished Professor, 1990-, Michigan State University; Many visiting writer-in-residencies. Publications: Poetry: Coins and Coffins, 1962; Discrepancies and Apparitions, 1966; The George Washington Poems, 1967; Inside the Blood Factory, 1968; The Magellanic Clouds, 1970; The Motorcycle Betrayal Poems, 1971; Smudging, 1972; Dancing on the Grave of a Son of a Bitch, 1973; Virtuoso Literature for Two and Four Hands, 1975; Waiting for the King of Spain, 1976; The Man Who Shook Hands, 1978; Cap of Darkness, 1980; The Magician's Feastletters, 1982; The Collected Greed, 1984; The Rings of Saturn, 1986; Emerald Ice: Selected Poems 1962-1987, 1988; Medea the Sorceress, 1991; Jason the Sailor, 1993; The Emerald City of Las Vegas, 1995; Argonaut Rose, 1998; The Butcher's Apron: New and Selected Poems, 2000. Criticism: Towards a New Poetry, 1980. Contributions to: Anthologies and other publications. Honours: Cassandra Foundation Grant, 1970; Guggenheim Fellowship, 1972; National Endowment for the Arts Grant, 1973; CAPS Grant, 1988, New York State, 1974; Writer's Fulbright Award, 1984; Michigan Arts Council Grant, 1988; William Carlos Williams Prize, 1989; Distinguished Artist Award, Michigan Arts Foundation, 1989; Michigan Library Association Author of the Year, 2004. Memberships: Author's

# DICTIONARY OF INTERNATIONAL BIOGRAPHY

Guild; PEN; Poetry Society of America. Address: 607 Division Street, East Lansing, MI 48823, USA.

**WALCOTT Derek (Alton),** b. 23 January 1930, Castries, St Lucia, West Indies. Poet; Dramatist; Visiting Professor. m. (1) Fay Moyston, 1954, divorced 1959, 1 son, (2) Margaret Ruth Maillard, 1962, divorced, 2 daughters, (3) Norline Metivier, 1982, divorced 1993. Education: St Mary's College, Castries, 1941-47; BA, University College of the West Indies, Mona, Jamaica, 1953. Appointments: Teacher, St Mary's College, Castries, 1947-50, 1954, Grenada Boy's Secondary School, St George's, 1953-54, Jamaica College, Kingston, 1955; Feature Writer, Public Opinion, Kingston, 1956-57; Founder-Director, Little Carib Theatre Workshop, later Trinidad Theatre Workshop, 1959-76; Feature Writer, 1960-62, Drama Critic, 1963-68, Trinidad Guardian, Port-of-Spain; Visiting Professor, Columbia University, 1981, Harvard University, 1982, 1987; Assistant Professor of Creative Writing, 1981, Visiting Professor, 1985-, Brown University. Publications: Poetry: 25 Poems, 1948; Epitaph for the Young: XII Cantos, 1949; Poems, 1951; In a Green Night: Poems 1948-1960, 1962; Selected Poems, 1964; The Castaway and Other Poems, 1965; The Gulf and Other Poems, 1969; Another Life, 1973; Sea Grapes, 1976; The Star-Apple Kingdom, 1979; Selected Poems, 1981; The Fortunate Traveller, 1981; The Caribbean Poetry of Derek Walcott and the Art of Romare Bearden, 1983; Midsummer, 1984; Collected Poems 1948-1984, 1986; The Arkansas Testament, 1987; Omeros, 1989; Collected Poems, 1990; Poems 1965-1980, 1992; Derek Walcott: Selected Poems, 1993. Plays: Cry for a Leader, 1950; Senza Alcun Sospetto or Paolo and Francesca, 1950; Henri Christophe: A Chronicle, 1950; Robin and Andrea or Bim, 1950; Three Assassins, 1951; The Price of Mercy, 1951; Harry Dernier, 1952; The Sea at Dauphin, 1954; Crossroads, 1954; The Charlatan, 1954, 4th version, 1977; The Wine of the Country, 1956; The Golden Lions, 1956; Ione: A Play with Music, 1957; Ti-Jean and His Brothers, 1957; Drums and Colours, 1958; Malcochon, or, The Six in the Rain, 1959; Jourmard, or, A Comedy till the Last Minute, 1959; Batai, 1965; Dream on Monkey Mountain, 1967; Franklin: A Tale of the Islands, 1969, 2nd version, 1973; In a Fine Castle, 1970; The Joker of Seville, 1974; O Babylon!, 1976; Remembrance, 1977; The Snow Queen, 1977; Pantomime, 1978; Marie Laveau, 1979; The Isle is Full of Noises, 1982; Beef, No Chicken, 1982; The Odyssey: A Stage Version, 1993; Tiepolo's Hound, 2000. Non-Fiction: The Antilles: Fragments of Epic Memory: The Nobel Lecture, 1993; What the Twilight Says (essays), 1998. Honours: Rockefeller Foundation Grants, 1957, 1966, and Fellowship, 1958; Arts Advisory Council of Jamaica Prize, 1960; Guinness Award, 1961; Ingram Merrill Foundation Grant, 1962; Borestone Mountain Awards, 1964, 1977; Heinemann Awards, Royal Society of Literature, 1966, 1983; Cholmondeley Award, 1969; Eugene O'Neill Foundation Fellowship, 1969; Gold Hummingbird Medal, Trinidad, 1969; Obie Award, 1971; Officer of the Order of the British Empire, 1972; Guggenheim Fellowship, 1977; Welsh Arts Council International Writers Prize, 1980; John D and Catharine T MacArthur Foundation Fellowship, 1981; Los Angeles Times Book Prize, 1986; Queen's Gold Medal for Poetry, 1988; Nobel Prize for Literature, 1992. Memberships: American Academy of Arts and Letters, honorary member; Royal Society of Literature, fellow. Address: c/o Faber & Faber, 3 Queen Square, London, WC1N 3AU, England.

**WALD Cem,** b. 20 May 1968, Ankara, Turkey. Business Executive. m. Monique Wald. Education: Master of Business Administration; Doctorate. Appointments: Chief Executive Officer and Managing Director: International Moving and Consulting Services Inc, New York, USA, 1999; Chief Executive Officer and Managing Director, European Moving Association GmbH, 2000; Chief Executive Officer and Managing Director, Prime Consulting Alliance, London, England, 2001; Chief Executive Officer and Managing Director, European Moving Association, Poland, 2002; Chief Executive Officer and Managing Director, Datix Beteiligungs AG and ConVest AG – Mergers and Acquisitions, 2004. Publication: Article in Focus Magazine about successful management. Honours: Manager of the Year 2003, German Economy; Listed in Who's Who publications and biographical dictionaries. Memberships: International Academic Society; European Commerce Association; Household Goods Forwarders of America. Address: Schwedenpfad 16, 61348 Bad Homburg, Germany. E-mail: cem.wald@primebank.net Website: www.primebank.net

**WALKER Alan Roland,** b. 9 October 1945, Oxford, England. m. Margaret Walker, 1 son, 3 daughters. Education: BSc, Honours, Zoology, London, 1967; MSc, Applied Entomology, Nairobi, Kenya, 1969; PhD, Veterinary Epidemiology, London External, 1976. Appointments: Research Demonstrator, Department of Zoology, University of Nairobi, Kenya, 1967-69; Veterinary Research Officer (Entomologist), Department of Veterinary Services, Government of Kenya, Veterinary Research Laboratory, Kabete, Kenya, 1970-76; Research Fellow, 1997-95, Senior Lecturer in Veterinary Parasitology, Royal (Dick) School of Veterinary Studies, 1996-, University of Edinburgh; Consultant on entomological and vector borne disease matters to: Food and Agriculture Organisation of the United Nations, Department for International Development of the UK, Scottish Executive Environment and Rural Affairs Department; Editorial Boards: Medical and Veterinary Entomology, Experimental and Applied Acarology, Tropical Animal Health and Production. Publications: 82 publications in formal literature on vector borne diseases, 1969-2005; Books: The Arthropods of Humans and Domestic Animals – a guide to preliminary identification (author), 1994; Ticks of Domestic Animals in Africa – a guide to identification of species (co-author), 2003. Membership: Chartered Biologist, Institute of Biology, 1979. Address: Royal (Dick) School of Veterinary Studies, University of Edinburgh, Roslin, EH25 9RG, Scotland. E-mail: alanw@staffmail.ed.ac.uk

**WALKER Alice (Malsenior),** b. 9 February 1944, Eatonton, Georgia, USA. Author; Poet. m. Melvyn R Leventhal, 17 March 1967, divorced 1976, 1 daughter. Education: BA, Sarah Lawrence College, 1966. Appointments: Writer-in-Residence and Teacher of Black Studies, Jackson State College, 1968-69, Tougaloo College, 1970-71; Lecturer in Literature, Wellesley College, 1972-73, University of Massachusetts at Boston, 1972-73; Distinguished Writer, Afro-American Studies Department, University of California at Berkeley, 1982; Fannie Hurst Professor of Literature, Brandeis University, 1982; Co-Founder and Publisher, Wild Trees Press, Navarro, California, 1984-88. Publications: Once, 1968; The Third Life of Grange Copeland, 1970; Five Poems, 1972; Revolutionary Petunias and Other Poems, 1973; In Love and Trouble, 1973; Langston Hughes: American Poet, 1973; Meridian, 1976; Goodnight, Willie Lee, I'll See You in the Morning, 1979; You Can't Keep a Good Woman Down, 1981; The Color Purple, 1982; In Search of Our Mother's Gardens, 1983; Horses Make a Landscape Look More Beautiful, 1984; To Hell With Dying, 1988; Living by the Word: Selected Writings, 1973-1987, 1988; The Temple of My Familiar, 1989; Her Blue Body Everything We Know: Earthling Poems, 1965-1990, 1991; Finding the Green Stone, 1991; Possessing the Secret of Joy, 1992; Warrior Marks (with Pratibha Parmar), 1993; Double Stitch: Black Women Write About Mothers and Daughters (with others), 1993; Everyday

Use, 1994; By the Light of My Father's Smile, 1998; The Way Forward is with a Broken heart, 2000. Editor: I Love Myself When I'm Laughing... And Then Again When I'm Looking Mean and Impressive, 1979. Honours: Bread Loaf Writer's Conference Scholar, 1966; Ingram Merrill Foundation Fellowship, 1967; McDowell Colony Fellowships, 1967, 1977-78; National Endowment for the Arts Grants, 1969, 1977; Richard and Hinda Rosenthal Pound Award, American Academy and Institute of Arts and Letters, 1974; Guggenheim Fellowship, 1977-78; Pulitzer Prize for Fiction, 1983; American Book Award, 1983; O Henry Award, 1986; Nora Astorga Leadership Award, 1989; Freedom to Write Award, PEN Center, West, 1990; Honorary doctorates. Address: c/o Random House, 201 E 50th Street, New York, NY 10022, USA.

**WALKER Catherine**, b. 27 June 1945, Pas de Calais, France. Couturier. m. John Walker, deceased, 2 daughters. Education: University of Lille; University of Aix-en-Provence. Appointments: Director, Film Department, French Institute, London, 1970; Lecturer, French Embassy, London, 1971, The Chelsea Design Company Ltd, 1978-; Founder Sponsor, Honorary Member of Board, Gilda's Club; Founder Sponsor, Haven Trust. Publication: Catherine Walker, an Autobiography by the Private Couturier to Diana Princess of Wales, 1998; Catherine Walker, Twenty Five Years 1977-2002. Honours: Designer of the Year for British Couture, 1990-91; Designer of the Year for Glamour Award, 1991-92. Address: 65 Sydney Street, Chelsea, London SW3 6PX, England.

**WALKER Miles Rawstron**, b. 13 November 1940, Colby, Isle of Man. Politician; Company Director. m. Mary L Cowell, 11 October 1966, 1 son, 1 daughter. Education: Shropshire College of Agriculture, 1959-60. Appointments: Member and Chairman, Arbory Parish Commissioners, 1970-76; Member of House of Keys, Isle of Man Government, 1976-; Elected to Chief Ministry, 1986-96, Member of Treasury, 1996-, Isle of Man Government. Publications: Isle of Man Government Policy Documents, 1987-96. Honours: CBE, 1991; Awarded LLD, Liverpool University, 1994; KB, 1997. Memberships: Member, Isle of Man Treasury, 1996-2000; Chair, Isle of Man Swimming Association; President, Rotary Club, 2000-01; Port St Mary Rifle Club. Address: Magher Feailley, Main Road, Colby, IM9 4AD, Isle of Man. E-mail: miles.walker@talk21.com

**WALKER OF WORCESTER, Baron of Abbots Morton in the County of Hereford and Worcester, Peter Edward Walker**, b. 25 March 1932, Harrow, Middlesex, England. Businessman; Politician. m. Tessa Joan Pout, 3 sons, 2 daughters. Education: Latymer Upper School, 1944-48. Appointments: Member, Conservative Party National Executive Committee, 1956; National Chairman, Young Conservatives, 1958-60; Parliamentary Candidate, Dartford, 1955, 1959; Member of Parliament, Worcester, 1961-92; Youngest Member of Shadow Cabinet, 1965; Youngest Member of the Cabinet, 1970; Member of all Conservative Cabinets, 1970-90; Minister for Housing and Local Government, 1970; Secretary of State for the Environment, 1970-72, for Trade and Industry, 1972-74; Opposition Spokesman on Trade and Industry and Consumer Affairs, 1974, Defence, 1975-75; Minister for Agriculture, Fisheries and Food, 1979-83; Secretary of State for Energy, 1983-87; Secretary of State for Wales, 1987-90; Non-Executive Director: British Gas plc, 1990-96, Dalgety plc, 1990-96, Tate & Lyle plc, 1990-2001; Caparo Group Limited, 1995; Chairman, Kleinwort Benson Group plc, 1996-98; Vice-Chairman, Dresdener Kleinwort Benson; Adviser to the Treuhand in Germany on the disposal of state owned assets in former Eastern Germany Currently Vice-Chairman Dresdener Kleinwort Wasserstein, Chairman, Allianz Cornhill Insurance plc, Non-Executive Director, LIFFE

Holdings plc, ITM Power. Publications: The Ascent of Britain, 1976; Trust the People, 1987; Staying Power (autobiography), 1991. Honours: MBE, 1960; PC, 1970; Venezuelan Order of Miranda, 1971; Commander's Cross of the Order of Merit of the Federal Republic of Germany, 1994; Chilean Order of Bernardo O'Higgins, Degree Gran Official, 1995; Rank of Grand Officer of the Order of May of the Argentine Republic, 2002; Freedom of the City of Worcester, 2003. Memberships: Former Chairman, English Partnerships; UK-China Forum; British-Mexican Business Network; President, 1999-2002, Current Vice-President, German-British Chamber of Industry and Commerce; Chairman, Carlton Club, 1998-2004; Worcester County Cricket Club. Address: Abbots Norton Manor, Gooms Hill, Abbots Norton, Worcester WR7 4LT, England.

**WALL Charles Terence Clegg**, b. 14 December 1936, Bristol, England. Mathematician. m. Alexandra Joy Hearnshaw, 2 sons, 2 daughters. Education: BA, 1957, PhD, 1960, Trinity College, Cambridge. Appointments: Fellow, Trinity College Cambridge, 1959-64; Harkness Fellow, IAS Princeton, 1960-61; Lecturer, Cambridge University, 1961-64; Reader, Oxford University, Fellow St Catherine's College, 1964-65; Professor of Pure Mathematics, 1965-99, Senior Fellow, 1999-2003, Emeritus Professor, 1999-, University of Liverpool; Royal Society Leverhulme Visiting Professor, Mexico, 1967; SERC Senior Fellow, 1983-88; JSPS Fellow, Tokyo Institute of Technology, 1987; Invited speaker at numerous international conferences. Publications: Books: Surgery on compact manifolds, 1970; A geometric introduction to topology, 1972; The geometry of topological stability (with A A du Plessis), 1995; Singular points of plain curves, 2004; About 160 papers in scientific journals. Honours: Numerous academic awards at school and university; Junior Berwick Prize, 1965; Whitehead Prize, 1976; Polya Prize, 1988; London Mathematical Society; Sylvester Medal, Royal Society, 1988. Memberships: Cambridge Philosophical Society; American Mathematical Society; London Mathematical Society; Fellow of the Royal Society, Council, 1974-76; Foreign Member, Royal Danish Academy; Honorary Member, Irish Mathematical Society. Address: 5 Kirby Park, West Kirby, Wirral, Merseyside CH48 2HA, England. E-mail: terry6.wall@which.net

**WALLACE-CRABBE Chris(topher Keith)**, b. 6 May 1934, Richmond, Victoria, Australia. Poet; Writer. m. (1) Helen Margaret Wiltshire, 1957, 1 son, 1 daughter, (2) Marianne Sophie Feil, 2 sons. Education: BA, 1956, MA, 1964, University of Melbourne; Reader in English, 1976-87, Professor of English, 1987-, Personal Chair, 1987-97, Professor Emeritus, 1998-, University of Melbourne; Visiting Chair in Australian Studies, Harvard University, 1987-88, USA. Publications: Poetry: No Glass Houses, 1956; The Music of Division, 1959; Eight Metropolitan Poems, 1962; In Light and Darkness, 1964; The Rebel General, 1967; Where the Wind Came, 1971; Act in the Noon, 1974; The Shapes of Gallipoli, 1975; The Foundations of Joy, 1976; The Emotions Are Not Skilled Workers, 1979; The Amorous Cannibal and Other Poems, 1985; I'm Deadly Serious, 1988; For Crying out Loud, 1990; Falling into Language, 1990; From the Republic of Conscience, 1992; Rungs of Time, 1993; Whirling, 1998; By and Large, 2001; Next, 2004; Selected Poems 1956-1994, 1995. Novel: Splinters, 1981. Other: Melbourne or the Bush: Essays on Australian Literature and Society, 1973; Falling into Language, 1990; Author! Author!, 1999. Editor: Volumes of Australian poetry and criticism. Honour: Masefield Prize for Poetry, 1957; Farmer's Poetry Prize, 1964; Grace Leven Prize, 1986; Dublin Prize, 1987; Christopher Brennan Award, 1990; Age Book of the Year Prize, 1995. Address: c/o The Australian Centre, University of Melbourne, Melbourne, Victoria 3010, Australia.

**WALMSLEY James Naylor,** b. 6 September 1929, Rockford, Illinois, USA. Hydroponic Farming Executive. m. (1) Ann Walmsley, divorced, 4 children, (2) Helga Walmsley, divorced, 2 children. Education: Student, George Washington University, 1950-52, Loyola University, 1953-55, Northwestern University, 1955. Appointments: With US Navy, 1949-53; Investment Banker, Hornblower & Weeks, Chicago, 1955-61; President, Manin International Inc, Chicago, 1961-72; President, Jinga Hydroponic Farms Ltd, Chicago, 1972-; President, Bahedeshar Ltd, Technical R&D, Clarksburg, West Virginia, 1995-; Managing Director, Manin International Inc, Las Vegas, Nevada, 2000-; Active: Points of Light Foundation, Children Defense Fund; West Virginia Representative, Republican Presidential Roundtable, 2001; Honorary Chairman, Grassroots campaign, Republican Headquarters, 2002. Honour: Recipient International American Award, 1987. Memberships: Royal Horticulture Society; American Horticultural Society; New York Academy of Sciences; The Heritage Foundation. Address: Bahedeshar Ltd, 728 Milford Street, Clarksburg, WV 26301, USA

**WALTERS Barbara,** b. 25 September 1931, Brookline, Massachusetts, USA. Television Broadcaster. m. (1) Lee Guber, 1963, divorced 1976, 1 adopted daughter, (2) Merv Adelson, 1986, divorced 1993. Education: Sarah Lawrence College, New York. Appointments: Writer, Producer, WNBC TV, Station WPIX, CBS TV Morning Broadcasts; Producer, NBC TV; Writer, Today Programme, NBC TV, 1961, Reporter, Panel Member, 1963-74, Co-Host, 1974-76; Moderator, Not for Women Only, 5 years; Correspondent, ABC News, Co-Anchor, Evening News Programme, 1976-78, Fascinating People, 1994-; Co-Executive Producer, The View ABC, New York, 1997-. Publications: How to Talk with Practically Anybody About Practically Anything, 1970; Contributor to several magazines. Honours include: Silver Satellite Award, American Women in Radio and TV, 1985; Named One of the 100 Most Important Women of the Century, Good Housekeeping, 1985; President Award, Overseas Press Club, 1988; Lowell Thomas Award for Journalism, 1990, 1994; Lifetime Achievement Award, International Women's Media Foundation, 1992. Address: 20/20 147 Columbus Avenue, 10th Floor, New York, NY 10023, USA.

**WALTERS Julie,** b. 22 February 1950, Birmingham, England. Actress. m. Grant Roffey, 1998, 1 daughter. Education: Manchester Polytechnic; School Governor, Open University. Creative Works: Films include: Educating Rita, 1983; She'll Be Wearing Pink Pyjamas, 1984; Personal Services, 1986; Prick Up Your Ears, 1986; Buster, 1987; Mack the Knife, 1988; Killing Dad, 1989; Stepping Out, 1991; Just Like a Woman, 1992; Sister My Sister, 1994; Intimate Relations, 1996; Titanic Town, 1997; Girls Night, 1997; All Forgotten, 1999; Dancer, 1999; Billy Elliot, 2000; Harry Potter and the Philosopher's Stone, 2001; Before You Go, 2002; Harry Potter and the Chamber of Secrets, 2002; Calendar Girls, 2003; Harry Potter and the Prisoner of Azkaban, 2004; Mickybo and Me, 2004; TV includes: Talent, 1980; Wood and Walters, 1981; Boys From the Blackstuff, 1982; Say Something Happened, 1982; Victoria Wood as Seen on TV, 1984, 1986, 1987; The Birthday Party, 1986; Her Big Chance, 1987; GBH, 1991; Stepping Out, 1991; Julie Walters and Friends, 1991; Clothes in the Wardrobe, 1992; Wide Eyed and Legless, 1993; Bambino Mio, 1993; Pat and Margaret, 1994; Jake's Progress, 1995; Little Red Riding Hood, 1995; Intimate Relations, 1996; Julie Walters in an Alien, 1997; Dinner Ladies, 1998-99; Jack and the Beanstalk, 1998; Oliver Twist, 1999; My Beautiful Son, 2001; Murder, 2002; The Canterbury Tales, mini-series, 2003; The Return, 2003; Several stage appearances. Publication: Baby Talk, 1990. Honours: Variety Club Best Newcomer Award, 1980; Best Actress Award, 1984; British

Academy Award for Best Actress, 1984; Golden Globe Award, 1984; Variety Club Award for Best Actress, 1991; Olivier Award, 2001. Address: c/o ICM, 76 Oxford Street, London W1N 0AX, England.

**WALTERS Sherwood George,** b. 9 May 1926, Detroit, Michigan, USA. Professor; Consultant. m. Alexandra Sielcken, 4 September 1952, 1 son, 3 daughters. Education: BA cum laude, Economics, History and Political Science, Western Maryland College, 1949; MS, International Trade, History, Columbia University, 1950; MBA with distinction, Columbia University Graduate School of Business, 1953; PhD honours scholar, New York University, 1960; Certificate Area Studies Specialist in Latin American Affairs, Institute of Public Affairs and Regional Studies, Government Department, New York University, 1960. Appointments: Private through 1st Lieutenant, Infantry/Quartermaster Corps, service in the European Theatre of Operations, 1944-47; Instructor through Associate Professor of Economics, Sociology and Marketing, College of Business Economics, Lehigh University, Bethlehem, Pennsylvania, 1950-60; Fellow, EI DuPont de Nemours, Wilmington, DE, summer 1951; President, Director, S G Walters Associates, management consultant firm, 1952-; Producer, Director and Co-presenter with wife, Breakfast with the Walters, commercially sponsored half-hour daily commentary/interview radio programme, WEST/NBC, Easton, Pennsylvania, 1953-57; Director Research Committee, US Council for Small Business Development, Co-Director, EI DuPont de Nemours Interdisciplinary Research Team and Ford Foundation Special Studies Scholar at Harvard University Business School, Cambridge, MA, summer 1956; Project Director, US Small Business Administration, Export potential for US small business in Latin America; Executive Vice President, Director of Centres, Retail Planning Manager, Development Projects Manager, Mobil Oil, New York City, 1960-65; Executive Officer, Marketing Director, General Tire and Rubber International Plastics Co, Manager, Commercial Marketing, Chemical Plastics Division, Akron, Ohio, 1965-70; Professor, Rutgers Business School, New Jersey, 1970-93; Professor Emeritus, Management Studies, Rutgers University, 1993-; Founding Director, Interfunctional Management Program, Rutgers University Business School, 1970-88; Founding Director, PhD Management Program; Chairman, Organization and Operations Management Department, Rutgers Graduate School of Business Administration; Director, various international programmes in management, banking and science in Romania, Puerto Rico, Sweden, France and Northern Ireland, for International Labor Organization (ILO), United Nations Industrial Development Organization (UNIDO), US State Department, National Science Foundation (NSF), 1971-2004; Evaluator/Emissary, US National Science Foundation Industry University Co-operative Research Centers Program, 1980-2004; Helped establish and sustain many Industry/University Co-operative Research Centers and International Tie Research Programs whilst working with National Science Foundation and the New Jersey Commission for Science and Technology at Rutgers University. Publications: Co-author, 7 books; 186 articles and government reports; 3 seminal books: Marketing Management Viewpoints Commentary and Readings, 2nd edition, 1970; Mandatory Housing Finance Programs, A Comparative International Analysis, 1975; Managing the Industry, University Co-operative Research Centres: A Guide for Directors and Other Stakeholders, 1998. Honours: President, Economics Society, Western Maryland College, 1948-49; Member, Aragonaut Honors Society, Western Maryland College, 1949; Founders Day Award, New York University, 1960; Professor of the Year (student selected), Rutgers Graduate School of Business, 1976; Christian R & Mary F Lindback Award for Excellence in Teaching, Rutgers University, 24 May

1983; Republican Presidential Legion of Merit, 11 February 1994; National Science Foundation Excellence Award for many years of dedicated service and significant contributions to the Nation and the NSF Industry University Co-operative Research Centers Program, 2004; Board of Trustees Alumni Award, McDaniel College (formerly Western Maryland College), 2005; Beta Gamma Sigma Honorary Society, Columbia University, 1953-; Secretary, Treasurer, President, Lehigh Chapter, 1953-60; Secretary, Treasurer, President, Rutgers Chapter, 1970-88; Presented to HRH Prince Charles, 6 May 1997 at Queen's University, Belfast, Northern Ireland to commenton the accomplishments of Industry University Co-operative Research Centres in the United Kingdom and the United States; 2004 Businessman of the Year Award Winner from North Carolina, 15 March 2005 by the Business Advisory Council of the National Republican Congressional Committee; Listed in national and international biographical dictionaries; Sons of the Revolution; Sons of the American Revolution; Appointed to New Jersey Governor's Commission Task Force on Energy; Judicial Committee on Energy Safety Standards; Committee on Liquefied Natural Gas; Chairman, Sub-Committee, Forecasting Demand and Supply for Liquefied Natural Gas, 1975, 1976. Memberships: Chairman, University/Industrial Partnerships, John Von Neumann Center, Princeton University, Princeton, New Jersey, 1986; Newcomen Society; Fellow, Academy of Political Science, 2005; Adviser, National Republican Congressional Commission on Tax Reform, 2001; Honorary Chairman, Business Advisory Council, National Republican Congressional Committee, 2003-04; Elder, Trustee, Co-Director Christian Education Committee, Topsail Presbyterian Church, Hampstead, North Carolina. Address: 110 Topsail Watch Lane, Hampstead, NC 28443-2728, USA.

**WALTON James Stephen,** b. 27 November 1946, Kingston upon Thames, Surrey, England. Research Scientist. m. Dorcas Ann Graham, 1 son, 1 daughter. Education: Diploma in Physical Education, 1968, Certificate of Education, 1968, Carnegie College of Physical Education, Leeds, England; MA, Education, Michigan State University, USA, 1970; MS, Applied Mechanics, Stanford University, California, USA, 1976; PhD, Physical Education, Biomechanics, Pennsylvania State University, USA, 1981. Appointments: Graduate Teaching Assistant, Michigan State University, 1968-69; Teacher, Gaynesford High School, Carshalton, Surrey, England, 1969-70; Graduate Teaching and Research Assistant, Pennsylvania State University, 1970-74; Graduate Teaching Assistant, Stanford University, California, 1974-76; Director of Engineering, Computerised Biomechanical Analysis, Amherst, Massachusetts, 1979; Associate Senior Research Scientist, 1979-81, Senior Research Scientist, 1981-85, Biomedical Science Department, General Motors Research Laboratories; Vice-President Applications Engineering, Motion Analysis Corporation, 1987-88; President/Owner, 4D Video, Sebastopol, California, 1988-; US National Delegate to the International Congress on High-Speed Photography and Photonics, 2005-2011. Publications: Numerous papers in scientific journals and presented at conferences including: Image-Based Motion Measurement: The Camera as a Transducer, 1997; Image-Based Motion Measurement: An Introduction to the Element of the Technology, 1998; Calibration and Processing of Image as an After Thought, 2000; A High-Speed Video Tracking System for Generic Applications, 2000; The Camera as a Transducer, 2000. Honours: Fellow, Society of Photo-optical Instrumentation Engineers (SPIE) Honorary Fellow, British Association for Physical Training. Memberships include: American Association for the Advancement of Science; American Society for Photogrammetry and Remote Sensing; New York Academy of Sciences; Sigma Xi; Society of Photo-Optical Instrumentation Engineers Address: 4D Video, 825 Gravenstein Highway North, Suite #4, Sebastopol, California 95472-2844, USA.

**WANAMAKER Zoë,** b. New York, USA. Actress. m. Gawn Grainger, 7 November 1994, 1 stepson, 1 stepdaughter. Education: Hornsey College of Art; Central School of Speech and Drama. Appointments: Actor; Theatre: A Midsummer Night's Dream, 1970; Guys and Dolls, 1972; The Cherry Orchard, 1970-71; Dick Whittington, 1971-72; Tom Thumb, Much Ado About Nothing, 1974; A Streetcar Named Desire, Pygmalion, The Beggar's Opera, Trumpets and Drums, 1975-76; Wild Oats, 1977; Once in a Lifetime, 1970-80; The Devil's Disciple; Wild Oats; Ivanov; The Taming of the Shrew; Captain Swing; Piaf; A Comedy of Errors, Twelfth Night and The Time of Your Life, 1983-85; Mother Courage; Othello; The Importance of Being Earnest 1982-83; The Bay at Nice and Wrecked Eggs, 1986-87; Mrs Klein; The Crucible; Twelfth Night, 1973-74; Cabaret, 1974; Kiss Me Kate, 1974; The Taming of the Shrew, 1975; Loot; Made in Bangkok, 1988; The Last Yankee, 1993; Dead Funny, 1994; The Glass Menagerie; Sylvia, 1996; Electra, 1997; The Old Neighbourhood, 1998; Electra, New York, 1998; Battle Royal, 1999; Boston Marriage, Donmar Warehouse, 2001; Boston Marriage, New Ambassadors, 2002; Hildy in His Girl Friday, National Theatre, 2003. TV: Sally for Keeps, 1970; The Eagle Has Landed, 1972; Between the Wars, 1973; The Silver Mask, 1973; Lorna and Ted, 1973; The Confederacy of Wives, 1974; The Village Hall, 1975; Danton's Death, 1977; Beaux Stratagem, 1977; The Devil's Crown, 1978-79; Strike, 1981; Baal, 1981; All the World's A Stage, 1982; Richard III, 1982; Enemies of the State, 1982; Edge of Darkness, 1985; Paradise Postponed, 1985; Poor Little Rich Girl, 1987; Once in a Lifetime, 1987; The Dog It Was That Died, 1988; Ball Trap on the Cote Sauvage, 1989; Othello, 1989; Prime Suspect, 1990; Love Hurts, 1991-93; Dance to the Music of Time, 1997; Gormenghast, Leprechauns, David Copperfield, 1999. Radio including: The Golden Bowl, Plenty, 1979; Bay at Nice, 1987; A February Morning, 1990; Carol, book reading, 1990; Such Rotten Luck, 1991, series I and TV films: The Blackheath Poisonings, Central, 1991; Memento Mori, BBC, 1991; Countess Alice, BBC, 1991; The English Wife, 1994; The Widowing of Mrs Holroyd, BBC, 1995; Wilde; Swept in By the Sea; TV: Adrian Mole, The Cappuccino Years, 2001; My Family, BBC Series 1-5, 2000-04; Miss Marple: A Murder is Announced, 2004; Commentary, Someone to Watch Over Me, 2004; Dr Who: The End of the World, 2005; Film: Harry Potter and the Philosopher's Stone, 2001; Five Children & It, 2003. Honours: SWET Award, 1979; Numerous Tony nominations; Drama Award, Mother Courage, 1985; Honorary DLitt, Southbank University, 1995; Variety Club of Great Britain Award, Best Actress, Electra, 1997; Olivier Awards including Best Actress for Electra, 1997; Calaway Award, New York, Best Actress, Electra; Best Actress, BAFTA for Love Hurts, Prime Suspects and Wilde; Honorary Doctorate Richmond American University of London; CBE; Boston Marriage, Oliver Nomination, Best Actress, 2002; Patron, Prisoners of Conscience; UK TV Mummies: Favourite UK TV Mum, 2004; Rose d'Or, Best Comedy Actress, My Family, 2005. Membership: Honorary Member, Voluntary Euthanasia Society; Trustee, Honorary President, Shakespeare's Globe. Address: c/o Conway Van Gelder, 18/21 Jermyn Street, London SW1Y 6HP, England. Website: www.geocities.com/zwsite

**WANG Haibo,** b. 28 June 1962, Guangdong, China. Anaesthesiologist; Microbiologist; Tropical Medicine Specialist. m. Chaoyin Han, 1 son, 1 daughter. Education: MD, Zhanjiang Medical College, China, 1984; Master in Medicine, Jinan University School of Medicine, China, 1987; PhD, Microbiology, Medical College of Virginia, USA, 1996.

Appointments: Lecturer, Jinan School of Medicine, China, 1987-91; House Officer and Fellow, 1996-2001, Assistant Professor, 2001- Louisiana State University School of Medicine, Shreveport, USA. Publications: As co-author, Phlebotomine sandflies in Zhejiang Province with the description of a new species sergentomyia zhongi, 1991; Cyclin dependent kinases in plasmodium falciparum, 1993; Cell cycle and regulation in Plasmodium falciparum (PhD Dissertation), 1996. Honours: ABA Diplomas. Memberships: AMA; ASA. Address: Department of Anesthesiology, Louisiana State University Health Science Center, Shreveport, LA 71130, USA. E-mail: hwang2@lsuhsc.edu

**WANG Jennie (Lin Jian),** b. 19 March 1952, Shanghai, China. Literature Educator. Education: BA, cum laude, San Francisco State University, California, USA, 1983; MA, English, Stanford University, California, 1984; PhD, English, State University of New York at Buffalo, Buffalo, New York, USA, 1992. Appointments: Instructor of English, Department of Foreign Languages, Shanghai Jiao-Tong University, Shanghai, China, 1977-79; Teaching Fellow, Department of English, State University of New York at Buffalo, Buffalo, New York, 1987-91; Preceptor, Expository Writing Program, Harvard University, Cambridge, Massachusetts, 1992-93; Research Associate, Department of Ethnic Studies, University of California at Berkeley, Summer 1996; Assistant Professor, 1993-98, Associate Professor, 1998-, Department of English Language and Literature, University of Northern Iowa, Cedar Falls, Iowa; Visiting Scholar, Department of English, University of California at Berkeley, 2000-01, 2003-04; Full Professor of Comparative Literature, Dissertation Director, Department of Chinese Language and Literature, Fudan University, Shanghai, China, 2004-. Publications: Author: Novelist Love in the Platonic Tradition: Fielding, Faulkner and the Postmodernists, 1997; Chinese Translator, Smiles on Washington Square: A Love Story of Sorts by Raymond Federman, 1999; The Iron Curtain of Language: Maxine Hong Kingston and American Orientalism, in progress; Numerous articles on Post-modern fiction and American Orientalism in literary journals and books. E-mail: linjian@fudan.edu.cn

**WANG Mingxing,** b. 18 January 1944, Shandong, China. Professor. m. Xuhui Niu, 1 son. Education: BS, Shandong University, Department of Physics, China, 1962-67; Department of Atmospheric Physics, Oxford University, England, 1974-78. Appointments: Professor, 1985-; Deputy Director, 1993-97, Director General, 1997-2001, Institute of Atmospheric Physics, Chinese Academy of Sciences. Publications: Atmospheric Chemistry, 1999; $CH_4$ emission from Chinese rice paddies, 2001. Honours: National Excellent Scientist, 2001; National Award of the Advances of Science and Technology, 2001. Membership: Vice President, Society of Particuology of China. Address: Institute of Atmospheric Physics, CAS, Beijing 100029. E-mail: wmx@mail.iap.ac.cn

**WANNER Sonia Viktoria,** b. 15 March 1931, Gothenburg, Sweden. Artist in Fine Arts. m. Sigvard Ulf, 2 sons. Appointments: Chalmers University of Technology and Architecture, Gothenburg, 1976-94; More than 100 exhibitions in Sweden, Norway, Geneva, Innsbruck, New York, Los Angeles, Paris and Vienna; Best known for marine oils of rough seas, also acclaimed for well-balanced landscapes and still life paintings. Publications: Author and editor: "Oceans" Sonia Wanner Art (book). Honours: Scholarship, Eva Ljungqvist's Scholarship Fund, 1992; Hall of Fame for Outstanding Achievements in the field of Fine Arts, USA, 2000; Toile D'Or de L'Année, Fédération Nationale de la Culture Française, France, 2001; Art-atlas of the World: 1001 Reasons to Love the Earth,

World Art Collection, Netherlands, 2001; Medaille D'Argent, Arts-Science-Lettres, Paris, 2005; Arts and Humanities Advisor to the Director General, International Biographical Centre, England, (AdVAh); Listed in numerous biographical publications. Memberships: Chamber of Commerce and Industry, Gothenburg; Regional Resource Centre for Women's Work and Development in Western Sweden, Gothenburg; Women's Art Library, London; National Museum of Women in the Arts, Washington; Metropolitan Museum of Arts, New York; Linos School, New York and Verona; Société Academique Arts-Science-Lettres, Paris France. Address: Haljerod 620, 442 96 Kode, Sweden. Website: www.wanner.net

**WANSELL (Stephen) Geoffrey,** b. 9 July 1945, Greenock, Scotland. Author; Journalist. Divorced, 1 son, 1 daughter. Education: BSc, Econ, London School of Economics, 1962-66; MA Student and Tutorial Assistant, University of Sheffield, 1966-67. Appointments: Reporter, Columnist, News Editor, Times Educational Supplement, 1967-70; Reporter, Feature Writer, The Times, 1970-73; Programme Controller, London Broadcasting Company and Independent Radio News, 1973-75; Pendennis Columnist, The Observer, 1977-78; Columnist, Now! Magazine, 1979-81; Columnist, Sunday Telegraph Magazine, 1981-85; Executive Producer, Motion Picture, When The Whales Came, 1989; Columnist, Sunday Express, 1993; Feature Writer, Daily Mail, 1999-2005. Publications: Author of 8 books. Honour: Shortlisted for the Whitbread Book of the Year, 1995. Membership: Garrick Club. Address: Flat 9, 1a Montagu Place, London W1H 2EP, England. E-mail: geoffreywansell@aol.com

**WARD Shirley Ann,** b. 25 September 1941, Peterborough, England. Teacher; Psychotherapist. Education: Teaching Diploma, Cambridge School of Education; Advanced Diploma in Education, Leicester University; MEd, Nottingham University. Appointments: Teacher, 1963-86; Pastoral consultant and Supervisor, 1978-; Self Employed Psychotherapist, 1978-; European Certificate in Psychotherapy; Director, Amethyst Resources for Human Development, 1982-; Trainer of Psychotherapists, 1985-; International Adviser, Association of Pre and Perinatal Psychology and Health, 1991-; International Workshops, Northern Ireland, Eire, France, Russia, USA, 1981-; United Nations, Vienna, 1993-97; Member, Killaloe RC Diocesan Child Protection Committee with Bishop Willie Walsh, 2003-; Currently majoring in Pre and Perinatal Psychology and Psychotherapy (based on work of late British psychiatrist, Dr Frank Lake, working in the field of 'from conception to birth'); Counselling individual clients suffering from post traumatic stress related to war, abuse and negative life situations. Publications: Numerous articles in learned journals including: Suicide and Pre and Perinatal Psychotherapy, 2004. Memberships: European Association for Psychotherapy; Irish Council for Psychotherapy; Irish Association for Humanistic and Integrative Psychotherapy; United Kingdom Council for Psychotherapy; United Kingdom Association of Humanistic Psychotherapy Practitioners; Grail Society. Address: Amethyst, Ballybroghan, Killaloe, Co Clare, Ireland. E-mail: shirleyward@eircom.net Website: www.holistic.ie/amethyst/

**WARD Simon,** b. 19 October 1941, Beckenham, England. Actor. m. Alexandra Malcolm, 3 daughters. Education: Royal Academy of Dramatic Art. Creative Works: Stage appearances include: Konstantin in The Seagull, Birmingham Repertory, 1964; Abel Drugger in The Alchemist and Hippolytus in Phèdre, Playhouse, Oxford, 1965-66; Dennis in Loot, Jeannetta Cochrane and Criterion, 1966; The Unknown Soldier in the Unknown Soldier and His Wife, Ferdinand in The Tempest and Henry in The Skin of Our Teen, Chichester Festival, 1968; Donald in Spoiled, Haymarket, 1971; Romeo in Romeo and

Juliet, Shaw, 1972; Troilus in Troilus and Cressida, Young Vic; Films include: I Start Counting, 1970; Young Winston, 1971; Hitler - The Last Ten Days, 1972; The Three Musketeers, 1973; The Four Musketeers, Deadly Strangers, All Creatures Great and Small, 1974-75; Aces High, 1975; Battle Flag, 1976; The Four Feathers, 1978; Zulu Dawn, 1979; Supergirl, Around the World in 80 Days, Double X, 1992; Wuthering Heights; Ghost Writers; TV includes: The Black Tulip; The Roads to Freedom; Holocaust (serial). Address: c/o Shepherd & Ford Associates Ltd, 13 Radner Walk, London SW3 4BP, England.

**WARFIELD John N(elson),** b. 21 November 1925, Sullivan, Missouri, USA. Researcher. m. Rosamond Howe, 2 sons, 1 daughter. Education: BA, Mathematics, 1948, BSc, Electrical Engineering, 1948, MSc, Electrical Engineering, 1949, University of Missouri; Army Specialised Training Program, 1944-46, Graduate Study, 1949-51, Pennsylvania State University; PhD, Electrical Engineering, Purdue University, 1952. Appointments: Instructor, Electrical Engineering, University of Missouri, 1949; Instructor, 1949-51, Assistant Professor, 1952-53, Associate Professor, 1953-55, Electrical Engineering, Pennsylvania State University; Assistant Professor, 1955-56, Associate Professor, 1956-57, University of Illinois, Urbana; Associate Professor, Associate Director of Computer Laboratory, Purdue University, Indiana, 1957-58; Associate Professor, 1958-59, Professor, 1959-66, University of Kansas; Visiting Professor, University of Colorado at Boulder, 1965; Adjunct Professor of Electrical Engineering, Ohio State University, Columbus, 1966-73; Senior Research Leader, Battelle Memorial Institute, 1966-74; Chairman, Department of Electrical Engineering, 1974-78, Harry Douglas Forsyth Professor of Electrical Engineering, 1974-83, Director, Centre for Interactive Management, 1980-81, University of Virginia at Charlottesville; Visiting Professor of Management, University of Northern Iowa, 1980-81; University Professor, 1984-2000, Emeritus, 2000-, George Mason University, Fairfax, Virginia. Publications: Co-translator, Synthesis of Linear Communications Networks; Introduction to Electronic Analog Computers, 1959; Principles of Logic Design, 1963; Societal Systems: Planning, Policy and Complexity, 1976; A Science of Generic Design: Managing Complexity Through Systems Design, 1994; Co-author, A Handbook of Interactive Management, 1994; Understanding Complexity: Thought and Behaviour, 2002; The Mathematics of Structure, 2003; Discovering Systems Science, 2003; Numerous articles in professional journals. Honours include: Western Electric Fund Award for Excellence in Instruction of Students, 1966; Eminent Scholar, University of Virginia, 1974-83, George Mason University, 1984-; Outstanding Contribution Award, IEEE Systems, Man and Cybernetics Society, 1977; Centennial Medal, IEEE, 1984; Peace Pipe Award, Americans for Indian Opportunity, 1987; Mayor's Certificate, City of Austin, Texas, 1993; Plaque of Recognition, Minister of Social Development, Governor of Guanajuato, 1994; Third Millennium Medal, IEEE, 2000; Laureate, George Mason University, 2002. Memberships include: IEEE; Association for Integrative Studies; Charles S Peirce Society; Society for Design and Process Science; Tau Beta Pi; Eta Kappa Nu; Sigma Xi; Panetics Society; Board of Advisers, Magic Circle Chamber Opera Company, New York; President, Integrative Sciences, Inc, 2001; President, AJAR Publishing Company, 2002. Address: 2673 Westcott Circle, Palm Harbor, FL 34684, USA. E-mail: jnwarfield@aol.com Website: http://jnwarfield.com

**WARNE Shane Keith,** b. 13 September 1969, Ferntree Gully, Melbourne, Australia. Cricketer. m. Simone, 1 son, 2 daughters. Appointments: Leg-Break and Googly Bowler; Right-Hand Lower-Order Batsman; 183 first-class matches for Hampshire took 70 wickets (average 23.1), 2000; Highest ever Australian

wicket taker in Tests; 107 Tests for Australia, 1991-92 to 2002, taking 491 wickets (average 25.71) and scoring 2,238 runs, took hat-trick v England, Melbourne, 1994; Took 850 wickets and scored 4,103 runs in 1st class cricket, to 2003; Toured England, 1993, 1997, 2001; 191 limited-overs internationals (11 as Captain), to 2003; Captain Victoria Sheffield Shield Team (Bushrangers), 1996-99; received 12 month ban for testing positive for a banned substance, 2003. Publications: Shane Warne: The Autobiography, 2001. Honours: Wisden Cricketer of the Year, 1994; Selected as one of five Wisden Cricketers of the Century, 2000. Address: c/o Victorian Cricket Association, 86 Jolimont Street, Victoria 3002, Australia.

**WARNER Margaret Anne (Megan),** b. 4 September 1943, Epsom, Surrey, England. Educator. Education includes: Teacher's Certificate, Mathematics, Froebel Educational Institute, London, 1964; Diploma, English as a Second Language, 1976, Diploma, School Management Studies, 1979, College of Preceptors; Master's Degree, Educational Studies, University of Surrey at Roehampton, 1990; Ofsted Registered Inspector, 1996; Performance Management Consultant, DfES/NPQH/Consortium, 2000. Appointments include: Assistant Teacher various schools, ILEA and Australia, 1964-72; Deputy Headteacher, Church of England Primary School, Oxfordshire, 1973-79; Headteacher, Church of England Primary School, ILEA, 1979-89; Teaching Practice Supervisor, primary and nursery classes, London Boroughs, 1990-91; SEN Co-ordinator, Mathematics Teacher, Girl's High School, Merton, 1991-92; Assistant Teacher, Merton Middle School, 1992-93; Head of Religious Education Departments, Wandsworth, 1993, 1994-95, i/c Pupils with Statements, 1994, Wandsworth Comprehensive School; Team Inspector, Primary, Secondary, Special, 1994-; Registered Primary Inspector, 1996-; Sole Trader trading as MAW Education, 1999-; DfES Trained Performance Management Consultant, 2000-. Publications: Headteachers perceptions of their role in spiritual education (book chapter, editor R Best), 1996; Reflections on Inspection (book chapter, editor R Best), 2000; 81 Ofsted Inspection Reports, 1996-2004. Honours: Listed in Who's Who publications and biographical dictionaries. Memberships: Institute for Registered Inspectors of Schools; National Association for Educational Inspectors and Consultants; Association for Supervision and Curriculum Development; Associate, College of Preceptors. Address: 50 Five Mile Drive, Oxford OX2 8HW, England. E-mail: M.A.Warner@technocom.com

**WARNER OF CRAIGENMADDIE Gerald,** b. 22 March 1945, Scotland. Author and Columnist. Education: St Aloysius' College, Glasgow; MA (Hons), Medieval and Modern History, University of Glasgow, 1968; Research in Irish History, 1968-71. Appointments: Parliamentary Candidate (Conservative) for Hamilton, 1974; Broadcaster, 1974-; Author, 1980-; Columnist and Social Diarist, The Sunday Times Scotland, 1989-95; Special Adviser to Secretary of State for Scotland, 1995-97; Leader Writer, Scottish Daily Mail, 1997-; Columnist, 1997-, Leader Writer, 2004-, Scotland on Sunday. Publications: Books: Homelands of the Clans, 1980; Being of Sound Mind, 1980; Conquering by Degrees, 1985; The Scottish Tory Party : A History (Foreword by the Rt Hon Margaret Thatcher), 1988; The Sacred Military Order of St Stephen Pope and Martyr, 2005. Honours: O St J, 1970; Knight of Grace and Devotion, Sovereign Military Order of Malta, 1979; Knight, Jure Sanguinis, Sacred Military Constantinian Order of St George, 1994. Membership: FSA Scot. Address: 17 Huntly Gardens, Glasgow G 12 9AT, Scotland.

**WARNOCK Helen Mary, (Baroness),** b. 14 April 1924, England. Philosopher; Writer. m. Sir Geoffrey Warnock, 1949, deceased 1995, 2 sons, 3 daughters. Education: MA, BPhil, Lady Margaret Hall, Oxford. Appointments: Fellow and Tutor in Philosophy, 1949-66, Senior Research Fellow, 1976-84, St Hugh's College, Oxford; Headmistress, Oxford High School, 1966-72; Talbot Research Fellow, Lady Margaret Hall, Oxford, 1972-76; Mistress, Girton College, Cambridge, 1985-91; Visiting Professor of Rhetoric, Gresham College, 2000-2001; Several visiting lectureships. Publications: Ethics Since 1900, 1960, 3rd edition, 1978; J-P Sartre, 1963; Existentialist Ethics, 1966; Existentialism, 1970; Imagination, 1976; Schools of Thought, 1977; What Must We Teach? (with T Devlin), 1977; Education: A Way Forward, 1979; A Question of Life, 1985; Teacher Teach Thyself, 1985; Memory, 1987; A Common Policy for Education, 1988; Universities: Knowing Our Minds, 1989; The Uses of Philosophy, 1992; Imagination and Time, 1994; Women Philosophers (editor), 1996; An Intelligent Person's Guide to Ethics, 1998; A Memoir: People and Places, 2000; Making Babies, 2002; Nature and Mortality, 2003; Utilitarianism (editor), 2003. Honours: 15 honorary doctorates; Honorary Fellow, Lady Margaret Hall, Oxford, 1984, St Hugh's College, Oxford, 1985, Hertford College, Oxford, 1997; Dame Commander of the Order of the British Empire, 1984; Life Peer, 1985; Albert Medal, RSA; Honorary Fellowship, British Academy, 2000. Address: 60 Church Street, Great Bedwyn, Wiltshire SN8 3PF, England.

**WARWICK (Marie) Dionne,** b. 12 December 1940, East Orange, New Jersey, USA. Singer. m. Bill Elliott, divorced 1975, 2 sons. Education: Hartt College of Music, Hartford, Connecticut; Masters Degree, Music. Appointments: Singer, Gospel Groups, The Drinkard Singers, The Gospelaires; Solo Singer, 1962-; Numerous concerts, tours and benefit shows worldwide. Creative Works: Singles: Anyone Who Had A Heart, 1964; Walk On By, 1964; A Message To Michael, 1966; Alfie, 1967; I Say A Little Prayer, 1967; Do You Know The Way To San José, 1968; This Girl's In Love With You, 1969; I'll Never Fall In Love Again, 1970; Then Came You, 1974; I'll Never Love This Way Again, 1979; Heartbreaker, 1982; All The Love In The World, 1983; That's What Friends Are For (AIDS charity record), 1985; Albums include: Greatest Hits, 1990; Dionne Warwick Sings Cole Porter, 1990; Hidden Gems: The Best of Dionne Warwick, Volume 2, 1992; Friends Can Be Lovers, with Whitney Houston, 1993; Dionne Warwick and Placido Domingo, 1994; Aquarela do Brasil, 1994; From the Vaults, 1995; Dionne Sings Dionne, 1998; I Say a Little Prayer For You, 2000. Honours: Top Selling Female Artist, NARM, 1964; Best Female Pop Vocal Performance, 1969, 1970, 1980; Best Contemporary Vocal Performance, 1971; Best Female R&B Vocal Performance, 1980; Best Pop Performance, Duo or Group, 1987; Song of the Year, 1987; Star on Hollywood's Walk of Fame, 1985; NAACP Key of Life Award, 1990; CORE Humanitarian Award, 1992; Nosotros Golden Eagle Humanitarian Award, 1992; City of New York Award, Contribution to AIDS Research, 1987; DIVA Award, 1992; Platinum and Gold Discs. Address: c/o Arista Records Inc, 6 West 57th Street, New York, NY 10019, USA.

**WASHINGTON Denzel,** b. 28 December 1954, Mount Vernon, New York, USA. Film Actor. m. Pauletta Pearson, 1983, 2 sons, 2 daughters. Education: Fordham University; American Conservatory Theatre, San Francisco. Creative Works: Off-Broadway appearances include: Ceremonies in Dark Old Men; When the Chickens Come Home to Roost; A Soldier's Play; Films include: A Soldier's Story, 1984; The Mighty Quinn, 1987; Cry Freedom, 1987; Heart Condition, 1989; Glory, 1990; Love Supreme, 1990; Mo' Better Blues, 1990; Ricochet, 1991; Mississippi Masala, 1991; Much Ado About Nothing, 1992; Malcolm X, 1992; The Pelican Brief, 1993; Philadelphia, 1993;

Devil in a Blue Dress, 1995; Courage Under Fire, 1996; The Preachers Wife, 1996; Fallen, 1997; He Got Game, 1998; The Siege, 1998; The Bone Collector, 1999; The Hurricane, 1999; Remember the Titans, 2001; John Q, 2002; Antwone Fisher, 2002; Out of Time, 2003; Man of Fire, 2004; Manchurian Candidate, in progress. Honours include: Academy Award, Best Supporting Actor, 1990; Awards for Best Actor, Supporting Actor and Director, National Association for the Advancement of Colored People Awards, 2003. Address: c/o ICM, 8942 Wilshire Boulevard, Beverly Hills, CA 90211, USA.

**WASSERSTEIN Wendy,** b. 18 October 1950, Brooklyn, New York, USA. Dramatist; Writer. Education: BA, Mount Holyoke College, 1971; MA, City College of the City University of New York, 1973; MFA, Yale University, 1976. Publications: Plays: Any Woman Can't, 1973; Happy Birthday, Montpelier Pizz-zazz, 1974; When Dinah Shore Ruled the Earth (with Christopher Durang), 1975; Uncommon Women and Others, 1975; Isn't it Romantic, 1981; Tender Offer, 1983; The Man in a Case, 1986; The Heidi Chronicles, 1988; The Sisters Rosensweig, 1992. Other: Miami (musical), 1986; Bachelor Girls (essays), 1990; Pamela's First Musical (children's picture book), 1996. Honours: Guggenheim Fellowship, 1983; American Playwrights Project Grant, 1988; Pulitzer Prize for Drama, 1989; Tony Award, 1989; New York Drama Critics Circle Award, 1989; Drama Desk Award, 1989; Outer Critics Circle Award, 1989; Susan Smith Blackburn Prize, 1989. Memberships: British American Arts Association; Dramatists Guild; Dramatists Guild for Young Playwrights. Address: c/o Royce Carlton Inc, 866 United Nations Plaza, Suite 4030, New York, NY 10017, USA.

**WASTERLAIN Claude,** b. 15 April 1935, Courcelles, Belgium. Neurologist. m. Anne Thomsin, 1 son. Education: CSc, 1957, MD, 1961, University of Liege; LSc, Molecular Biology, Free University of Brussels, 1969. Appointments: Resident, 1964-66, Chief Resident, 1966-67, Medical College, New York City; Assistant Professor, Cornell University, 1970-75; Associate Professor, Cornell University Medical College, 1975-76; Associate Professor, 1976-79, Professor of Neurology, 1979-, University of California, Los Angeles School of Medicine; Chair, VA Greater Los Angeles Health Care System, 1997-. Publications: Over 400 articles; Many books and book chapters; Status Epilepticus (book), 1984; Neonated Seizures (book). Honours: Milken Award for Basic Research in Epilepsy, American Epilepsy Association, 1992; Golden Hammer Teaching Award, University of California, Los Angeles. Memberships include: American Neurological Association; Fellow, American Academy of Neurology; American Epilepsy Society; American and International Societies for Neurochemistry. Address: Neurology Department (127), VA Medical Center, 11301 Wilshire Boulevard, West Los Angeles, CA 90073, USA.

**WATANABE Toru,** b. 2 May 1960, Niigata, Japan. Medical Doctor; Paediatrician. m. Chieko Hoshi, 2 sons, 2 daughters. Education: MD, Niigata University, 1985; PhD, Niigata University Graduate School of Medicine and Dental Science, 2002. Appointments: Resident, 1985-90, Staff, 1991-, Department of Paediatrics, Niigata City General Hospital. Publications: 62 articles in medical journals including: Pediatric Nephrology; Nephron; Clinical Nephrology; Journal of Clinical Endocrinology and Metabolism; Pediatrics International; Pediatrics; European Journal of Pediatrics. Honours: Plenary Presentation Award, 1994, Best Clinical Research Award, 1999, Japanese Society for Pediatric Nephrology; Listed in Who's Who publications and biographical dictionaries. Memberships: Japanese Society for Paediatric Nephrology; International

Pediatric Nephrology Association; Japan Pediatric Society; Japanese Society of Nephrology. Address: Department of Paediatrics, Niigata City General Hospital, 2-6-1 Shichikuyama, Niigata 950-8739, Japan. E-mail: twata@hosp.niigata.niigata.jp

**WATELAIN Eric, b.** 18 October 1971, France. Senior Lecturer. m. Laure de Thieny de Faletans, 1 son, 2 daughters. Education: Master, University of Lille, 1995; Certificate, Lifesavers France National Degree, 1996; PhD, Lille University, France, 1999. Appointments: Temporary Assistant Teaching and Research, 1999-2000, Senior Lecturer, Human Movement Analysis, Specialist in Adapted Physical Activity and Locomotion, 2000-, University of Valenciennes, France; Assistant Physician, Medicine, Central Hospital, Lille, France, 2002-. Publications: Articles on the evaluation and control of human locomotion in scientific medical journals including: Gait and Posture; Clinical Biomechanics; Archives of Physical Medicine and Rehabilitation. Memberships: French Association of Research in Physical Activity and Sport; Biomechanics Society, France; International Society of Gait and Posture Research. Address: LAMIH, University of Valenciennes le Mont Houy, 59313 Valenciennes, Cedex 9, France. E-mail: eric.watelain'unist.va lenciennes.fr

**WATERS, General Sir (Charles) John, b.** 2 September 1935, Rangoon, Burma. Retired Army Officer. m. Hilary Doyle Nettleton, 3 sons. Education: Royal Military Academy, Sandhurst; Army Staff College, Camberley, 1967; Royal College of Defence Studies, 1982. Appointments: Commissioned into Gloucestershire Regiment, 1955; Instructor Army Staff College, 1973-75; Commanding Officer, 1 Battalion The Gloucestershire Regiment, 1975-77; Colonel General Staff, 1 Armoured Division, 1977-79; Commanded 3 Infantry Brigade, 1979-81; Royal College of Defence Studies, 1982; Deputy Commander, Land Forces, Falklands, 1982; Commander 4 Armoured Division, 1983-85; Commandant, Staff College, Camberley, 1986-88; General Officer Commanding and Director of Operations, Northern Ireland, 1988-90 (dispatches 1990); Colonel, The Gloucestershire Regiment, 1985-91; Colonel Commandant, Prince of Wales Division, 1988-92; Commander-in-Chief, United Kingdom Land Forces, 1990-93; Deputy Supreme Allied Commander Europe, 1993-94; ADC General to HM The Queen, 1992-94. Honours: OBE, 1977; CBE, 1981; KCB, 1988; GCB, 1995; Honorary Colonel, Royal Devon Yeomanry, 1991-97, Wessex Yeomanry, 1991-97; Kermit Roosevelt Lecturer, 1992; Deputy Lieutenant, Devon, 2001. Memberships: Advisory Council, Victory Memorial Museum, Arlon, Belgium, 1988-97; Chairman of the Council, National Army Museum, 2002-; President, Officers' Association, 1997; County President, Devon Royal British Legion, 1997-2002; Admiral: Army Sailing Association, 1990-93, Infantry Sailing Association, 1990-93; Member of the Council, Cheltenham College, 1990-97; Governor, Colyton Primary School, 1996-2002; Magistrate, 1998-; President, Honiton and District Agricultural Society, 2004. Address: c/o Lloyds Bank, Colyton, Devon EX23 6JS, England.

**WATERS Brian Richard Anthony, b.** 27 March 1944, Liverpool, England. Architect. m. Myriam Leiva Arenas. Education: City of London School, 1958-63; Degree and Diploma in Architecture, St Johns, Cambridge, 1963-68; PCL Diploma in Town Planning, 1969-71; RIBA, 1972; MRTPI, 1973. Appointments: City Corporation Planning Department, 1968-70; Greater London Council Architects Department, 1969-70; Shankland Cox & Associates, 1970-72; Founder, The Boisot Waters Cohen Partnership, 1972. Publications: Joint Publishing Editor, Planning in London; International Building Press Award; 4 commendations for articles in Architect's Journal,

Building, RIBA Journal; 2 commendations for Magazine of the Year, Planning in London; Current Planning correspondent of Architects' Journal. Honours: Master, Worshipful Company of Chartered Architects, 2002-03. Memberships: RAC; Hurlingham Club. Address: 17 Lexham Mews, London W8 6JW, England. E-mail: brian@bwcp.co.uk

**WATHEN Julian Philip Gerard, b.** 21 May 1923, Cromer, England. Retired Banker. m. Priscilla Wilson, 1 son, 2 daughters. Education: Harrow School, 1937-42. Appointments: Captain, British Army, 60th Rifles, 1942-47; Third Secretary, British Embassy, Athens, 1947; Barclays Bank DCO, 1948-, Ghana Director, 1961-65, General Manager, 1965-75, Vice Chairman, 1975-80; Vice Chairman, Barclays Bank Ltd, 1980-84. Memberships: Fellow, Institute of Bankers. Address: Woodcock House, Owlpen, Dursley GL11 5BY, England.

**WATSON Emily, b.** 14 January 1967, London, England. Actress. Creative Works: Films: Breaking the Waves; Mill on the Floss; Metroland; The Boxer; Hilary and Jackie; Angela's Ashes, 1991; The Cradle Will Rock; Trixie; The Luzhin Defense; Gosford Park, 2001; Equilibrium, 2002; Red Dragon, 2002; Punch-Drunk Love, 2002; Blossoms and Blood, 2003; Life and Death of Peter Sellers, 2004; Separate Lies, 2004; Wah Wah, 2005; The Proposition, 2005; Corpse Bride, 2005; Crusade in Jean, 2005; Theatre includes: Uncle Vanya; Twelfth Night. Honours include: New York Society of Film Critics Award; National Society of Film Critics Award. Address: c/o ICM Ltd, Oxford House, 76 Oxford Street, London W1N 0AX, England.

**WATSON James Dewey, b.** 6 April 1928, Chicago, Illinois, USA. m. Elizabeth Lewis, 1968, 2 sons. Education: Graduated, Zoology, University of Chicago, 1947; Postgraduate Research, University of Indiana, PhD, 1950. Appointments: Research into viruses, University of Copenhagen, 1950; Cavendish Laboratory, Cambridge University, 1951; Senior Research Fellow, Biology, California Institute of Technology, 1953-55; Several positions, Department of Biology, Harvard University; Assistant Professor, 1955-58, Associate Professor, 1958-61, Professor, 1961-68; Director, 1968, President, 1994-, Quantitative Biology, Cold Spring Harbor Laboratory; Associate Director, NIH (USA), 1988-89; Director, National Center for Human Genome Research, NIH, 1989-92; Newton Abraham Visiting Professor, Oxford University, England, 1994; Research to help determine the structure of DNA. Publications: Molecular Biology of the Gene, 1965, 1970, 1976; The Double Helix, 1968; The DNA Story, 1981; Recombinant DNA: A Short Course, 1983; The Molecular Biology of the Cell, 1986; Recombinant DNA, 1992; Papers on the structure of DNA, on protein synthesis and on the induction of cancer by viruses. Honours: Joint Winner, Nobel Prize for Physiology or Medicine, 1962; John J Carty Gold Medal, 1971; Medal of Freedom, 1977; Gold Medal Award, National Institute of Social Sciences, 1984; Kaul Foundation Award for Excellence, 1992; Capley Medal of Royal Society, 1993; National Biotechnology Venture Award, 1993; Lomosonov Medal, 1994; National Medal of Science, 1997; Liberty Medal Award, 2000; Benjamin Franklin Medal, 2001. Address: Cold Spring Harbor Laboratory, PO Box 100, Cold Spring Harbor, New York NY 11724, USA.

**WATSON Ronald Eugene, b.** 9 February 1949, Hayward, California, USA. Soldier; Ichthyologist. m. Candace Elaine Roth, 1 son, 1 daughter. Education: Self-educated. Career: Collection and observation of marine and freshwater gobies, Hawaiian Islands, 1978-80; Ichthyological survey of freshwater streams, northern Virginia, USA, 1981-86; Ecology of fishes in freshwater streams and wetlands, Florida, USA, 1990-92; Ichthyological survey of freshwater streams, New Caledonia, with University of the Pacific, Noumea, 1997; Ichthyological survey of freshwater fishes, Guam, Mariana Islands with University of Guam Marine Laboratory and Division of Aquatic and Wildlife Resources, 1999; Surveying freshwater streams in North Province, New Caledonia with National Museum of Natural History Chloe II Expedition, 1999; Ichthyological survey of freshwater fishes, Pohnpei, Federated States of Micronesia, 1999. Publications: Numerous articles in professional journals; Presentations at international meetings; Referee of manuscripts for peer reviewed academic journals and proceedings. Honours: Lentipes watsoni, new species of freshwater goby named in his honour, 1997; Bavarian Academy of Sciences High Award, 1998. Memberships: Biological Society of Washington; American Society of Ichthyologists and Herpetologists. Address: 3658 NW 41st Lane, Gainesville, FL 32605-1468, USA. E-mail: rewatson@bellsouth.net

**WATSON Thomas Sturges (Tom),** b. 4 September 1949, Kansas City, USA. Golfer. m. Linda Tova Rubin, 1973, 1 son, 1 daughter. Education: Stanford University. Appointments: Professional, 1971-; British Open Champion, 1975, 1977, 1980, 1982, 1983; Record low aggregate for British Open of 268, record two single round scores of 65, lowest final 36-hole score of 130, Turnberry, 1977; Won US Masters Title, 1977, 1981; Won US Open, 1982; Won World Series, 1975, 1977, 1980; Winner, numerous other open championships, 1974-; First player ever to win in excess of $500,000 in prize money in one season, 1980; Ryder Cup Player, Captain, 1993-. Publication: Getting Back into Basics (jointly), 1992. Honours include: Top Money Winner on US PGA Circuit, 1977, 1978, 1979, 1980; US PGA Player of the Year, 1977, 1978, 1979, 1980, 1982; PGA World Golf Hall of Fame, 1988-. Address: PGA America, PO Box 109801, 100 Avenue of the Champions, Palm Beach Gardens, FL 33410, USA.

**WATTS Charlie (Charles Robert),** b. 2 June 1941, England. Musician. m. Shirley Anne Shepherd, 1964, 1 daughter. Appointments: Drummer, Rolling Stones, 1963-. Creative Works: Albums with The Rolling Stones include: The Rolling Stones, 1964; The Rolling Stones No 2, 1965; Out of Our Heads, 1965; Aftermath, 1966; Big Hits, 1966; Got LIVE if You Want It!, 1967; Between the Buttons, 1967; Their Satanic Majesties Request, 1967; Beggars Banquet, 1968; Let it Bleed, 1969; Get Yer Ya-Ya's Out!, 1970; Stone Age, 1971; Sticky Fingers, 1971; Goats Head Soup, 1973; It's Only Rock 'N' Roll, 1974; Black and Blue, 1976; Love You Live, 1977; Some Girls, 1978; Emotional Rescue, 1980; Tattoo You, 1981; Still Life, 1981; Dirty Work, 1986; Steel Wheels, 1989; Flashpoint, 1991; Voodoo Lounge, 1994; Solo albums include: Charlie Watts Orchestra - Live at Fulham Town Hall, 1986; From One Charlie, 1992; Warm and Tender, 1993; From One Charlie, 1995; Long Ago and Far Away, 1996; Films include: Sympathy For the Devil, 1969; Gimme Shelter, 1970; Ladies and Gentlemen, The Rolling Stones, 1977; Let's Spend the Night Together, 1983; Flashpoint, 1991. Publication: Ode to a High Flying Bird, 1965. Address: c/o Munro Sounds, 5 Church Row, Wandsworth Plain, London SW18 1ES, England.

**WAX Ruby,** b. 19 April 1953, Illinois, USA. Comedienne; Actress. m. Edward Richard Morison Bye, 1988, 1 son, 2 daughters. Education: Berkeley University; Royal Scottish Academy of Music and Drama. Appointments: With Crucible Theatre, 1976, Royal Shakespeare Company, 1978-82. Creative Works: TV includes: Not the Nine O'Clock News, 1982-83; Girls on Top, 1983-85; Don't Miss Wax, 1985-87; Hit and Run, 1988; Full Wax, 1987-92; Ruby Wax Meets..., 1996, 1997, 1998; Ruby, 1997, 1998, 1999; Ruby's American Pie, 1999, 2000; Hot Wax, 2001; The Waiting Game, 2001, 2002; Ruby, 2002; Films include: Miami Memoirs, 1987; East Meets Wax, 1988; Class of '69; Ruby Takes a Trip, 1992; Plays include: Wax Acts (one woman show), 1992; Stressed (one woman show), 2000. Publication: How Do You Want Me? (autobiography), 2002.

**WAY Danny,** b. 15 April 1974, Portland, Oregon, USA. Professional Skateboarder. m. Kari Way, 2 sons. Career: Started skateboarding 1988, Turned professional for Alein Workshop 1989. Film appearances include: The DC video, 2002; Alien Workshop – mosaic, 2003. TV appearances include: Legends or the Extreme, 2003. Honours: MTV Sports and Music Festival 1st Place in highest air, 1999; Holds the Guinness Book of World Records highest air on a skateboard at 18'+, and longest air on a skateboard at 65'; Thrasher Magazine Skater of the Year, 1992. Address: Carlsbad, California, USA.

**WEAVER Sigourney,** b. 8 October 1949, New York, USA. Actress. m. James Simpson, 1984, 1 daughter. Creative Works: Films include: Annie Hall, 1977; Tribute to a Madman, 1977; Camp 708, 1978; Alicn, 1979; Eyewitness, 1981; The Year of Living Dangerously, 1982; Deal of the Century, 1983; Ghostbusters, 1984; Une Femme ou Deux, 1985; Half Moon Street, 1986; Aliens, 1986; Gorillas in the Mist, 1988; Ghostbusters II, 1989; Aliens 3, 1992; 1492: Conquest of Paradise, 1993; Dave, 1993; Death and the Maiden, 1994; Jeffrey, 1995; Copycat, 1996; Snow White in the Black Forest, 1996; Ice Storm, 1996; Alien Resurrection, 1997; A Map of the World, 1999; Galaxy Quest, 1999; Get Bruce, 1999; Company Man, 1999; Airframe, 1999; Heartbreakers, 2001. Honours include: Golden Globe Best Actress Award, 1988; Best Supporting Actress Golden Globe Award, 1988.

**WEBB Robert Gravem,** 18 February 1927, Long Beach, California, USA. Retired Professor of Biological Sciences. m. Patricia A (Peden) Webb, 1 son. Education: BS, 1950, MS, 1952, University of Oklahoma; PhD, University of Kansas, 1960. Appointments: University of Texas at El Paso, 1962-93; Retired, 1993. Publications: 1 book: Reptiles of Oklahoma; 135 publications dealing with amphibians and reptiles. Honours: Faculty Research Award, University of Texas at El Paso, 1978; President, Society for the Study of Amphibians and Reptiles, 1980. Memberships: Herpetologists' League; American Society of Ichthyologists and Herpetologists; Society for the Study of Amphibians and Reptiles; Societas Europeae Herpetologica; Southwestern Association of Naturalists. Address: Department of Biological Sciences, University of Texas at El Paso, El Paso, TX 79968-0519, USA. E-mail: rgwebb@utep.edu

**WEBSTER Henry de Forest,** b. 22 April 1927, New York, USA. Neuroscientist. m. Marion Havas Webster, 4 sons, 1 daughter. Education: BA, Chemistry (cum laude), Amherst College, Massachusetts, 1948; MD, Harvard Medical School, Boston, Massachusetts, 1952. Appointments: Postgraduate training, Internal Medicine, Neurology, Neuropathology, 1952-59, Instructor, Neurology to Assistant Professor, Neuropathology, Harvard Medical School, 1959-66; Associate Professor, Professor, Neurology, University of Miami Medical School, 1966-69; Head, Section Cell Neuropathology, 1969-97; Chief, Laboratory Exp Neuropathology, 1984-97, Emeritus Scientist, 1997-, NINDS, National Institute of Health, Bethesda, Maryland, USA. Publications: Co-author, book: Fine Structure of the Nervous System, 1970, 1976, 1991; Book chapters, reviews, scientific articles. Honours: Weil Award, American Association of Neuropathologists, 1960; Superior Service Award, US Public Health Service, 1977; Alexander von Humboldt Foundation (Germany) Senior US Scientist Award, 1985; Honorary Professor, Norman Bethune University Medical Science, 1991; Scientific Award, Peripheral Neuropathy Association, 1994.

Memberships: American Association of Neuropathologists, President, 1978-79; International Society of Neuropathology, President, 1986-90; Honorary Member, International Society of Neuropathology and Japanese Society of Neuropathology; Fellow, Royal College of Medicine. Address: National Institutes of Health, Bldg 10, Rm 5B-16, Bethesda, MD 20892-1400, USA. E-mail: websterh@ninds.nih.gov

**WEBSTER John Barron, (Jack Webster),** b. 8 July 1931, Maud, Aberdeenshire, Scotland. Journalist. m. Eden Keith, 17 Feb 1956, 3 sons. Education: Maud School; Peterhead Academy; Robert Gordon's College, Aberdeen. Publications: The Dons, 1978; A Grain of Truth, 1981; Gordon Strachan, 1984; Another Grain of Truth, 1988; Alistair MacLean: A Life, 1991; Famous Ships of the Clyde, 1993. The Flying Scots, 1994; The Express Years, 1994; In the Driving Seat, 1996; The Herald Years, 1996; Webster's World (1997); From Dali to Burrell (1997); Reo Stakis Story (1999); The Auld Hoose (2005). Television Films: The Webster Trilogy, John Brown: The Man Who Drew a Legend, 1994. Honours: Bank of Scotland Awards, Columnist of the Year, 1996; UK Speaker of the Year, 1996. Address: 58 Netherhill Avenue, Glasgow G44 3XG, Scotland.

**WEBSTER Richard,** b. 6 May 1933, Derby, England. Scientist. m. Mary Buxton, 1 son, 2 daughters. Education: BSc, Chemistry, University of Sheffield, 1954; D Phil, Oxford University, 1966; DSc, Sheffield University, 1983. Appointments: Soil Chemist, Northern Rhodesia (Zambia) Government, 1957-61; Research Associate, Oxford University, 1961-68; Senior Scientific Officer, 1968-71, Principal Scientific Officer, 1971-79, Soil Survey of England and Wales; Senior Research Scientist, CSIRO Division of Soils, Australia, 1973-74; Senior Principal Scientific Officer, Soils Department, Rothamsted Experimental Station, 1979-90; Maître de Recherche, Ecole Nationale Supérieure des Mines de Paris, 1990; Chief Editor of Catena, 1990-95; Directeur de Recherche, Institut National de la Recherche Agronomique, France, 1990-91; Visiting Scientist, Rothamsted Experimental Station, 1991-92, 1993-94; Guest Professor, Swiss Federal Institute of Technology, 1992-94; Professor, Eidgenössische Forschungsanstalt für Wald, Schnee und Landschaft (WSL), Switzerland, 1994-95; Editor-in Chief, European Journal of Soil Science, 1995-2003; Visiting Professor in Soil Science, University of Reading, 1997-; Currently Deputy Editor, European Journal of Soil Science. Publications: Author of more than 200 papers in scientific journals, conference proceedings and other collected works; 3 text books; 3 atlases; 20 technical reports. Honour: Docteur Honoris Causa, Louvain, 1995. Membership: British Society of Soil Science. Address: Rothamsted Research, Harpenden, Herts AL5 2JQ, England. E-mail: richard.webster@bbsrc.ac.uk

**WEERASINGHE Arjuna,** b. 24 April 1963, Columbo, Sri Lanka. Surgeon. Education: MBBS, 1992; MRCP (UK), 1995; FRCS (Eng), 1997; PhD (Lond), 2003. Appointments: National Health Service, 1994-. Publications: Articles in professional medical journals including: Annals of Thoracic Surgery; Circulation; Journal of Thoracic and Cardiovascular Surgery. Honour: Honours in Surgery at MBBS. Memberships: Royal College of Physicians, UK; Royal College of Surgeons of England; Society of Cardiothoracic Surgeons of Great Britain and Ireland. Address: Department of Cardiothoracic Surgery, Hammersmith Hospital, Du Cane Road, London W12 0NN, England.

**WEIDNER Stanislaw Marian,** b. 22 March 1947, Wrzesnia. Biochemist; Plant Physiologist. Educator. m. Maria Minakowska, 1 son, 1 daughter. Education: Master, Olsztyn University of Agricultural Technology, Poland, 1971; Doctor,

1980. Appointments: Assistant, 1971-80, Adjunct, 1980-89, Assistant Professor, 1989-92, Associate Professor, 1992-2001, Olsztyn University of Agricultural Technology; Visiting Professor, Okayama University, 1998-99; Professor, 2001-, Head of Department of Biochemistry, 2005-, University of Warmia and Mazury, Olsztyn; Achievements include research in possible involvement of cytoskeleton in regulation of cereal caryopses dormancy and germination. Publications: 60 articles in professional journals; Co-Editor, Biochemistry of Vertebrates, 1998 and 2005. Honours: Silver and Gold Cross for Achievements in Science and Educational Fields, President of Poland, 1994, 2003; State Commission for Scientific Research Grantee, 1993-96, 1997-2001, 2004-07; COST project European Co-op, 1996-2001, 2003-09; Recipient of several research fellowships. Memberships: Federation of European Biochemical Societies; Federation of European Societies of Plant Biology; International Society for Seed Science; Polish Society for Experimental Biology; Polish Botanical Society; Editorial Council, Acta Physiologiae Plantarum, 2000-. Address: Iwaszkiewicza Street 41/3, PL-10089 Olsztyn, Poland. E-mail: weidner@uwm.edu.pl Website: www.geocities.com/stanislawweidner/

**WEIMANN Robert Karl,** b. 18 November 1928, Magdeburg, Germany. Scholar; Critic; Teacher. m. Maja Weimann, 2 sons, 3 daughters. Education: PhD, 1955, Phil Habil, 1962, Humboldt University, Berlin; Full Professor, 1968. Appointments: Professor, Humboldt University, 1965-68; Faculty member, Academy of Sciences, Berlin, 1968-91; Visiting Professor, University of Virginia, 1974; Visiting Professor, Toronto, 1982; Visiting Professor, Harvard University, 1984, 1989; Visiting Professor, Berkeley, 1986; Vice President, Akademie der Künste, Berlin, 1979-90; President, German Shakespeare Society, Weimar, 1985-93; Chair, Literaturwissenschaft, Max Planck Society Associate Institute, 1992-94; Professor, University of California, Irvine, 1992-2001. Publications: Books: New Criticism, 1962; Shakespeare und die Tradition des Volkstheaters, 1967; Literaturgeschichte und Mythologie, 1971; Structure and Society in Literary History, 1976, 1984; Shakespeare und die Macht der Mimesis, 1988; Authority and Representation in Early Modern Discourse, 1996; Author's Pen and Actor's Voice, 2000; Prologues to Shakespeare's Theatre: Performance and Liminality, 2004 (with Douglas Bruster); More than 40 essays and articles; Part of works translated into more than a dozen languages. Honours: Honorary Doctorate, 1988; Honorary Member, MLA, 1985-; American Medal of Honor for Contributions to Theatre History, 2002; Listed in national and international biographical dictionaries. Memberships: MLA; Deutsche Shakespeare Gesellschaft; International Shakespeare Association; International PEN; Akademie der Künste, Berlin; Academy of Sciences, New York; American Association for the Advancement of Science. Address: Muhlenbecker Str 22, 16352 Basdorf, Germany.

**WEINBERG Jerry L,** b. 2 December 1931, Detroit, Michigan, USA. Research Scientist, Astronomy and Space Science. m. Marcia Hawver, 2 sons. Education: BS, Physics and Mathematics, St Lawrence University, 1958; PhD, Astrophysics and Atmospheric Physics, University of Colorado, 1963. Appointments: Assistant Professor, Astrophysics, 1963-65, Supervisor, Haleakala Observatory, 1964-65, Associate Astrophysicist, 1965-68, University of Hawaii; Astronomer, 1968-70, Astronomer, Associate Director, 1970-73, Dudley Observatory; Research Professor, Astronomy and Space Science, Director, Space Astronomy Laboratory, SUNY, Albany, 1973-80; Research Professor, Astronomy, Director, Space Astronomy Laboratory, 1980-89, Director, Florida Space Science Institute, 1987-89, University of Florida; Research Director, 1988-89,

President, CEO, Chief Scientist, 1989-94, Institute for Space Science and Technology, Gainesville and Orlando, Florida; Vice President, Research and Development, Furon Incorporated, Indialantic, Florida and Newport Beach, California, 1990-; Senior Scientist, Vice President, Research, 1994-95; Corporate Vice President for Research and Development, Chief Operating Officer, 1996-97; MK Industries Incorporated; President, MK Research Inc, 1996-97; President, CEO, Technology Applications Group, Snellville, Georgia, 1997-; President, CEO, Technology Care Givers/Care Giving Worldwide Incorporated, Snellville, 1997-; Scientific Advisory Board, Layers of Light Inc, Irvine, California, 2003-; Founder, Chief Executive Officer, Coal Tek, LLC, 2004-. Publications include: Over 150 scientific and technical publications. Honours: NASA Skylab Achievement Award, 1974; NASA Medal for Exceptional Scientific Achievement, 1974; NASA Group Achievement Award, 1982. Memberships include: American Astronomical Society; American Geophysical Union; Chairman, Space Debris Working Group of American Institute of Aeronautics and Astronautics; Space Science Working Group, Association of American Universities; International Academy of Astronautics; Working Group on Photometry, Commission VII, International Association of Geomagnetism and Aeronomy; Optical Society of America; International Astronomical Union, Past President, Commission 21; International Committee on Space Research. Address: Care Giving Worldwide Inc, 3440 Quinn Ridge Drive, Snellville, GA 30039, USA.

**WEINBERG Steven,** b. 3 May 1933, New York, New York, USA. Professor of Science; Author. m. Louise Goldwasser, 6 July 1954, 1 daughter. Education: BA, Cornell University, 1954; Postgraduate Studies, Copenhagen Institute of Theoretical Physics, 1954-55; PhD, Princeton University, 1957. Appointments: Research Associate and Instructor, Columbia University, 1957-59; Research Physicist, Lawrence Radiation Laboratory, Berkeley, 1959-60; Faculty, 1960-64, Professor of Physics, 1964-69, University of California at Berkeley; Visiting Professor, 1967-69, Professor of Physics, 1979-83, Massachusetts Institute of Technology; Higgins Professor of Physics, Harvard University, 1973-83; Senior Scientist, Smithsonian Astrophysics Laboratory, 1973-83; Josey Professor of Science, University of Texas at Austin, 1982-; Senior Consultant, Smithsonian Astrophysics Observatory, 1983-; Various visiting professorships and lectureships. Publications: Gravitation and Cosmology: Principles and Application of the General Theory of Relativity, 1972; The First Three Minutes: A Modern View of the Origin of the Universe, 1977; The Discovery of Subatomic Particles, 1982; Elementary Particles and the Laws of Physics (with R Feynman), 1987; Dreams of a Final Theory, 1992; The Quantum Theory of Fields, Vol I, Foundations, 1995, Vol II, Modern Applications, 1996, Vol III, Supersymmetry, 2000; Facing Up, 2001; Glory and Terror, 2004. Contributions to: Books, periodicals and professional journals. Honours: 16 honorary doctoral degrees; J Robert Oppenheimer Memorial Prize, 1973; Dannie Heineman Prize in Mathematical Physics, 1977; American Institute of Physics-US Steel Foundation Science Writing Award, 1977; Nobel Prize in Physics, 1979; Elliott Cresson Medal, Franklin Institute, 1979; Madison Medal, Princeton University, 1991; National Medal of Science, National Science Foundation, 1991; Andrew Gemant Prize, American Institute of Physics, 1997; Piazzi Prize, Governments of Sicily and Palermo, 1998; Lewis Thomas Prize for the Scientist as Poet, Rockefeller University, 1999; Benjamin Franklin Medal of American Philosophical Society, 2004. Memberships: American Academy of Arts and Sciences; American Mediaeval Academy; American Philosophical Society; American Physical Society; Council on Foreign Relations; History of Science Society; International Astronomical Union; National Academy of Science; Phi Beta Kappa; Philosophical Society of Texas, president, 1994; Royal Society; Texas Institute of Letters. Address: c/o Department of Physics, University of Texas at Austin, Austin, TX 78712, USA.

**WEINSTEIN Harvey,** b. USA. Film Company Executive. Appointment: Co-Chair, Miramax Films Corporation, New York. Creative Works: Films produced jointly include: Playing for Keeps, 1986; Scandal, 1989; Strike it Rich, 1990; Hardware, 1990; A Rage in Harlem, 1991; The Crying Game, 1992; The Night We Never Met, 1993; Benefit of the Doubt, 1993; True Romance, 1993; Mother's Boys, 1994; Like Water for Chocolate, 1994; Pulp Fiction, 1994; Pret-A-Porter, 1994; Smoke, 1995; A Month by the Lake, 1995; The Crossing Guard, 1995; The Journey of August King, 1995; Things To Do In Denver When You're Dead, 1995; The Englishman Who Went Up A Hill But Came Down A Mountain, 1995; Blue in the Face, 1995; Restoration, 1995; Scream, 1996; The Pallbearer, 1996; The Last of the High Kings, 1996; Jane Eyre, 1996; Flirting with Disaster, 1996; The English Patient, 1996; Emma, 1996; The Crow: City of Angels, 1996; Beautiful Girls, 1996; Addicted to Love, 1997; Shakespeare in Love, 1998; Allied Forces, She's All That, 1999; My Life So Far, 1999; The Yards, 1999; Bounce, 2000; Scary Movie, 2000; Boys and Girls, 2000; Love's Labour Lost, 2000; Scream 3, 2000; About Adam, 2000; Chocolat, 2000; Spy Kids, 2001; Scary Movie 2, 2001; The Others, 2001; Lord of the Rings: The Fellowship of the Ring, 2001; Iris, 2001; Halloween: Resurrection, 2002; Spy Kids 2: Island of Lost Dreams, 2002; Lord of the Rings: The Two Towers, 2002; Gangs of New York, 2002; Chicago, 2002; Spy Kids 3-D: Game Over, 2003; Kill Bill: Vol 1, 2003; Scary Movie 3, 2003; Lord of the Rings: Return of The King, 2003; Cold Mountain, 2003; Kill Bill: Vol 2, 2004; Numerous other films in progress. Address: Miramax Films Corporation, 375 Greenwich Street, New York, NY 10013, USA.

**WEINSTEIN Robert,** b. 1954, USA. Film Producer; Executive. Appointment: Co-Chair, Miramax Films Corporation. Creative Works: Films produced include: Playing for Keeps (with Alan Brewer), 1986; Scandal (with Joe Boyd and Nik Powell), 1989; Strike it Rich, 1990; Hardware (with Nik Powell, Stephen Wooley, Trix Worrell), 1990; A Rage in Harlem (with Terry Glinwood, William Horberg, Nik Powell), 1991; The Night We Never Met (with Sidney Kimmel), 1993; Benefit of the Doubt, 1993; True Romance (with Gary Barber, Stanley Margolis, James G Robinson), 1993; Mother's Boys (with Randall Poster), 1994; Pulp Fiction (with Richard N Gladstein), 1994; Pret-A-Porter (with Ian Jessel), 1994; Smoke (with Satoru Iseki), 1995; A Month By the Lake (with Donna Gigliotti), 1995; The Crossing Guard (with Richard N Gladstein), 1995; The Journey of August King, 1995; Things To Do in Denver When You're Dead (with Marie Cantin), 1995; The Englishman Who Went Up a Hill But Came Down a Mountain (with Sally Hibbin, Robert Jones), 1995; Blue in the Face (with Harvey Keitel), 1995; Restoration (with Donna Gigliotti), 1995; Velvet Goldmine, 1998; Shakespeare in Love, 1998; Allied Forces, 1999; My Life So Far, 1999; The Yards, 1999; Music of the Heart, 1999; The Cider House Rules, 1999; Down To You, 2000; Boys and Girls, 2000; Scream 3, 2000; Love's Labour's Lost, 2000; Scary Movie, 2000; Chocolat, 2000; Spy Kids, 2001; Scary Movie 2, 2001; The Others, 2001; Lord of the Rings: The Fellowship of the Ring, 2001; Iris, 2001; Halloween: Resurrection, 2002; Spy Kids 2: Island of Lost Dreams, 2002; Lord of the Rings: The Two Towers, 2002; Gangs of New York, 2002; Chicago, 2002; Spy Kids 3-D: Game Over, 2003; Kill Bill: Vol 1, 2003; Scary Movie 2, 2003; Lord of the Rings: Return of the King, 2003; Cold Mountain, 2003; Kill Bill: Vol 2, 2004; Several other films in progress. Address: Miramax Films Corporation, 375 Greenwich Street, New York, NY 10013, USA.

**WEIR Kenneth Ross,** b. 23 May 1938, Dunblane, Scotland. Piano Performer. Education: BA, Classical Greek, English, Music, 1960, B Mus (Hons), 1961, Otago University, New Zealand. MM, Piano Performance, Indiana University, USA, 1972; A.Mus.D., Organ and Piano Performance, University of Michigan, Ann Arbor, USA, 1979. Appointments: Associate Instructor (part-time), Piano, Indiana University, 1970-72; Lecturer in Piano, Canterbury University, New Zealand, 1973-75; Part-time Tutor in Piano, University of Melbourne, Australia, 1981-83; Lecturer in Piano, West Australian Academy of Performing Arts, 1984-87; Head of Keyboard Studies, 1987-95, Visiting Specialist Teacher, Piano, 1995-, Sherborne School, Dorset, England; Concerts in the UK, Europe, USA, Asia, Australia and New Zealand including recitals with international soloists and ensembles; Broadcaster on ABC (Australia), Radio New Zealand and BBC. Publication: Research paper: Aspects of Rhythm in the Organ and Piano Music of Jehan Alain, 1986. Recordings: Choir and Organ, with Peter Godfrey, Conductor, New Zealand, 1970; Organ Music by Clérambault, Messiaen, Alain, New Zealand, 1975; Ginastera, Debussy, Granados, Haydn, 1992; Rachmaninoff, Debussy, Franck, 2001. Honours: James Clark Prize in Greek, Otago, 1959; Evans Travelling Scholarship in Music, Otago, 1963-65; International Prize, 3rd place, St Albans Organ Festival, 1967; Highest Distinction Award in Piano, Indiana University, 1972; Rackham Research Travel Grant, University of Michigan, 1978. Address: 28 Herrison House, Charlton Down, Dorchester, Dorset DT2 9XA, England. E-mail: kennethweir@cathedra.fsnet.co.uk

**WEIR Peter Lindsay,** b. 21 August 1944, Sydney, Australia. Film Director. m. Wendy Stites, 1966, 1 son, 1 daughter. Education: Sydney University. Appointments: Real Estate, 1965; Stagehand, TV, Sydney, 1967; Director, Film Sequences, Variety Show, 1968; Director, Amateur University Reviews, 1967-69; Director, Film Australia, 1969-73; Made Own Short Films, 1969-73; Independent Feature-Film Director, Writer, 1973-. Creative Works: Films: Cars That Ate Paris, 1973; Picnic at Hanging Rock, 1975; The Last Wave, 1977; The Plumber (TV), 1978; Gallipoli, 1980; The Year of Living Dangerously, 1982; Witness, 1985; The Mosquito Coast, 1986; The Dead Poets Society, 1989; Green Card, 1991; Fearless, 1994; The Truman Show, 1997; Master and Commander: The Far Side of the World, 2003. Honours include: BAFTA Award, Best Director, 1997; BAFTA Award, Best Director, 2004. Address: Salt Pan Films Pty Ltd, PO Box 29, Palm Beach, NSW 2108, Australia.

**WEISMAN Malcolm,** Barrister; Minister of Religion. m. Rosalie Spiro, 2 sons. Education: MA, St Catherine's College, Oxford. Appointments: Jewish Chaplain, RAF, 1956; Honorary Chaplain, University of Oxford, 1971-; Senior Chaplain, HM Forces, 1972-; Secretary General, 1980-92, Honorary President, 1993-, Allied Air Forces Chief of Chaplains Committee; Secretary, Former Chiefs of Air Forces Chaplains Association, 1994; Called to the Bar, Middle Temple, 1961; Assistant Commissioner, Parliamentary Boundaries, 1976-88; Recorder of the Crown Court, 1980; Head of Chambers, 1982-90; Special Immigration Adjudicator, 1998; Member, Bar Disciplinary Tribunal; Editor, Menorah Magazine; Adviser to small Jewish communities and Hillel Counsellor to Oxford and Cambridge Universities. Honours: Blackstone Pupillage Award, 1961; Man of the Year Award, 1980; Chief Rabbi's Award for Excellence, 1993; Honorary Chaplain to: Mayor of Westminster, 1992-93; Mayor of Barnet, 1994-95; OBE, 1997; Chaplain to Mayor of Redbridge, 2005-06; USA Military Chaplaincy Award for

Outstanding Service, 1998; Gold Medal, International Council of Christians and Jews, 2002; Rabbinical Council Award for Service, 2005. Memberships: MOD Advisory Committee on Military Chaplaincy; Cabinet of Chief Rabbi of Commonwealth; Member of Courts of Universities of: East Anglia, Sussex, Kent, Lancaster, Essex, Warwick; Member Senior Common Room Universities of: Kent, East Anglia, Lancaster; Fellow, University of Essex Centre for the Study of Theology; Governor and Trustee, Parmiter's School; Trustee, Multi-Faith and International Multi-Faith Chaplaincy Centre, University of Derby; Trustee, Jewish Music Heritage Trust; Patron, Jewish National Fund. Address: 1 Gray's Inn Square, London WC1R 5AA, England.

**WEISS Richard J,** b. 14 December 1923, New York City, New York, USA. Physicist. m. Daphne Watson, 1 son, 2 daughter. Education: BS, City University of New York, 1944; Ensign, US Naval Academy, Annapolis, Maryland, 1944; MA, University of California, 1947; PhD, New York University, 1950. Appointments: Physicist, Materials Laboratory, Watertown, MA, 1949-79; Research Assistant, Cavendish Laboratories, Cambridge, England, 1956-57; Research Scientist, Imperial College, London, 1962-63; Professor of Physics, King's College, London, 1979-89; Editor, World Scientific Series in Popular Science, 1985-; Secretary, Fakebusters (scientific detection of fakery in art). Publications: Books: Solid State Physics for Metallurgists, 1962; X-Ray Determination of Electron Distributions, 1966; X-Ray Diffraction, 1972; Compton Effect, 1976; Magic of Physics, 1987; A Brief History of Light, 1990; Fakebusters I, 1999; Fakebusters II, 2001. Honour: Rockefeller Public Service Award, 1956. Address: 4 Lawson Street, Avon, MA 02322, USA. E-mail: rjwboug@aol.com

**WEIZSÄCKER Carl Friedrich von,** b. 28 June 1912, Kiel, Germany. Theoretical Physicist. Education: PhD, University of Leipzig, 1933. Appointments: Assistant, Institute of Theoretical Physics, University of Leipzig, 1934-36; Kaiser Wilhelm Institute of Physics, Berlin-Dahlem; Lecturer, University of Berlin, 1936-42; Chair, University of Strasbourg, 1942; Kaiser Wilhelm Institute, 1944; Member of German research team investigating feasibility of nuclear weapons, but feared that such weapons may be used by the Nazi government; Director, Department, Max Planck Institute of Physics, Göttingen, 1946, with Honorary Professorship; Professor of Philosophy, University of Hamburg, 1957-69; Honorary Chair, University of Munich, 1969; Director, Max Planck Institute, 1970; Investigated the way in which energy is generated in the centre of stars; Devised theory on the origin of the solar system. Publications include: Bedingungen der Freiheit, 1990; Der Mensch in seiner Geschichte, 1991; Zeit und Wissen, 1992; Der bedrohte Friede-heute, 1994; Wohin gehen wir?, 1997. Address: Alpenstrasse 15, 82319 Starnberg, Germany.

**WELD Wilfrid Joseph,** b. 16 March 1934, East Wantley, Sussex, England. Landowner; Farmer; Company Director; Chartered Surveyor. m. Eleanor Sarah (Sally), 3 sons, 4 daughters. Education: Stonyhurst College; Royal Military Academy, Sandhurst; College of Estate Management. Appointments: Regular Commission in The Queen's Bays serving in BAOR, Jordan, Libya and UK; Qualified as Chartered Land Agent (transferring to RICS on amalgamation), 1959-65; Resident Agent to the Trustees of the Weld Estate and Colonel Sir Joseph Weld, 1959-70; Currently: Tenant for Life and Trustee of the Lulworth Estate – 5000 hectares of agricultural land, woodland, leisure, fishing and shooting; Director of Weld Enterprises Ltd – caravan park, car park, heritage centre and other leisure interests at Lulworth Cove; Partner in Lulworth Castle Farms – 1500 hectares of dairy, 1000 milking cows, arable and sheep; Partner in Lulworth Leisure – Lulworth Castle and park and ancillary leisure interests; Director: Weld Enterprises Ltd, Lulworth Leisure Ltd, Dorset Gardens Trust Ltd; Trustee, Lulworth Estate, Weld of Lulworth Charitable Trust; Weld Grandchildren's Education Trust; JP, 1981; Magistrate Central Dorset Bench, 1981-2002; Deputy Lieutenant for the County of Dorset, 1984; High Sheriff of Dorset, 1996-97. Honours: FRICS; Honorary Doctor of Arts, Bournemouth University, 1998. Memberships: General Committee, 1967, Executive Committee, 1970-2002, President, 1990-2002, Patron, 2002-, Hampshire Cricket Club; Former Executive Committee, Chairman, Current Vice-President, Dorset County Cricket Club; Worshipful Company of Farmers and Freeman of the City of London; President, Dorset Master Thatcher's Association, Former President, Dorset Working Spaniel Club, Lulworth Royal British Legion; Inaugural Chairman, 1988-94, Vice-President, 1994-2001, President, 2001-, Dorset Gardens Trust; Patron: Bournemouth & Poole College Foundation; Patron, Headway, Dorset; MCC, I Zingari, Leander, CLA; RASE; Game Conservancy; Dorset Wildlife Trust, Friend of the Royal Academy; National Arts Collection Fund; RHS. Address: Lulworth Castle House, Wareham, Dorset BH20 5QS, England. E-mail: wjweld@aol.com

**WELDON Fay,** b. 22 September 1931, Alvechurch, Worcestershire, England. Writer. m. (1) Ron Weldon, 12 June 1961, 4 daughters, (2) Nick Fox, 1994. Education: MA, St Andrews University, 1952; CBE. Career: Numerous theatre plays and over 30 television plays, dramatizations and radio plays. Publications: Fat Woman's Joke, 1968; Down Among the Women, 1971; Female Friends, 1975; Remember Me, 1976; Praxis, 1978; Puffball, 1980; The President's Child, 1982; Letters to Alice, 1984; Life and Loves of a She Devil, 1984; Rebecca West, 1985; The Shrapnel Academy, 1986; The Hearts and Lives of Men, 1987; Leader of the Band, 1988; Wolf of the Mechanical Dog, 1989; The Cloning of Joanna May, 1989; Party Puddle, 1989; Moon Over Minneapolis or Why She Couldn't Stay, (short stories), 1991; Life Force, 1992; Growing Rich, 1992; Affliction, 1994; Splitting, 1995; Worst Fears, 1996; Wicked Women, (short stories), 1996; Big Women, 1998; A Hard Time to be a Father (short stories), 1998; Rhode Island Blues, 2000; Godless in Eden (essays), 2000; Nothing to Wear, Nowhere to Hide, 2002; Auto-da-Fay (autobiography), 2002; Mantrapped, 2004; She May Not Leave, 2005; Contributor to numerous journals and magazines. Honours: DLitt, Universities of Bath, 1989 and St Andrews, 1992; Women in Publishing, Pandora Award, 1997. Memberships: Royal Society of Authors. Address: c/o Curtis Brown, 5th Floor, Haymarket House, 28-29 Haymarket, London SW1Y 4SP, England.

**WELDON Shelly,** b. 22 September 1960, London, England. Singer; Entertainer; Musician (piano, keyboard, guitar); Writer. Education: Pitman's College, London. Musical Education: Advanced studies with Professor Dora Zafransky, Hon Professor, Trinity College of Music. Career: 2 tours, Sweden; Swedish television and radio broadcasts, 1982, 1983; Writer, producer, presenter, Capitol Radio, 1982; Personal appearance, before HM The Sultan of Oman, 1983; Radio Tross, Amsterdam, 1984; Norwegian tour, radio broadcasts, 1985; Dorchester Hotel, London, 1987-88; Featured session singer, Heathrow Hotels, London; Winner, Alternative Eurovision Song Contest, London Newstalk Radio, with If Heaven Is A Kiss Away (own lyric), 1995; Live TV, 1996; Channel 5 TV, 1997; Talent Channel, 1997; Stars in Their Eyes as Carmen Miranda, Granada TV, 1998; BBC Choice, 1999; Currently writing book and lyrics with composer, Marie Francis for a new family musical project (original story). Compositions include: Lyricist, While There's A Song To Sing (composer, Marie Francis), signature tune

for tenor Wynford Evans, programmes, BBC Radio 2, 1993. Recordings include: The Touch of Love, 1983; Album: Shelly At The Sheraton, 1983; Let the Bells Ring, 1996. Theatre Debut: Wellington Womble in "The Wombles", Gate Theatre, Dublin, 1976. Honours: Presented to HRH Princess Alexandra, for highest single donation to Kingston Hospital Scanner Appeal, 1994; Lenny Beige, BBC Choice, 2000. Memberships: British Equity; PRS. Address: c/o British Equity, Guild House, Upper St Martin's Lane, London WC2H 9EG, England. E-mail: shelly@beeb.net

**WELLER Elizabeth Boghossian,** b. 7 August 1949, Beirut, Lebanon. Psychiatrist; Physician. m. Ronald A Weller, 1 son, 1 daughter. Education: BSc, 1971, MD, 1975; Resident in Psychiatry, Washington University, 1978; Fellow, Child Psychiatry, University of Kansas, 1979. Appointments: University of Kansas, 1979-85; OSU, 1985-96; Professor of Psychiatry and Pediatrics, University of Pennsylvania, 1996-. Publications: Papers in refereed journals. Honours include: Alpha Omega Alpha, 1975; American Academy, Clinical Psychiatry Research Award, 1982, 1984, 1988; Outstanding Young Woman in Psychiatry, 1985; Professor of Year, Department of Psychiatry, 1990; Distinguished Award, Program Chair, American Academy of Clinical Psychiatry, 1992; Outstanding Mentor Award, presented at annual meeting, American Academy of Child and Adolescent Psychiatry, Toronto, Canada, 1997. Memberships: Fellow, Academy of Child and Adolescent Psychiatry; President, Society of Biological Psychiatry, 1995; American College of Psychiatrists, 1995; Director, American Board of Psychiatry and Neurology, 1996-; President, American Board of Psychiatry and Neurology, 2004. Address: Children's Hospital, 34th and Civic Center Blvd, Philadelphia, PA 19104, USA.

**WELLER Paul,** b. 25 May 1958, Woking, Surrey, England. Singer; Songwriter; Musician (guitar, piano). m. Dee C Lee, December 1986. Career: Founder, singer, guitarist, The Jam, 1976-1982; Concerts include: Reading Festival, 1978; Great British Music Festival, 1978; Pink Pop Festival, 1980; Loch Lomond Festival, 1980; Founder, The Style Council, 1983-89; Appearances include: Miners benefit concert, Royal Albert Hall, London, 1984; Live Aid, Wembley Arena, 1985; Film: JerUSAlem, 1987; Founder, The Paul Weller Movement, 1990; Solo artiste, 1990-; UK and international tours; Phoenix Festival, 1995; T In The Park Festival, Glasgow, 1995; Own record label, Freedom High. Creative works: Compositions include: My Ever Changing Moods; Shout To The Top; The Walls Come Tumbling Down; Have You Ever Had It Blue, for film Absolute Beginners; It Didn't Matter; Wanted; Sunflower; Wild Wood; The Weaver; Recordings: Albums: with The Jam: In The City, 1977; This Is The Modern World, 1977; All Mod Cons, 1978; Setting Sons, 1979; Sound Affects, 1980; The Gift, 1982; Dig The New Breed, 1982; Snap!, 1983; Greatest Hits, 1991; Extras, 1992; Live Jam, 1993; with Style Council: Introducing The Style Council, 1983; Café Bleu, 1984; Our Favourite Shop, 1985; Home And Abroad, 1986; The Cost Of Loving, 1987; Confessions Of A Pop Group, 1988; The Singular Adventures Of The Style Council, 1989; Here's Some That Got Away, 1993; Solo albums: Paul Weller, 1992; Wild Wood, 1993; Live Wood, 1994; Stanley Road, 1995; Heavy Soul, 1997; Modern Classics, 1998; Heliocentric, 2000; Illumination, 2002. Honours include: Ivor Novello Award; BRIT Awards, 1995, 1996. Address: c/o Go'Discs Ltd, 72 Black Lion Lane, Hammersmith, London W6 9BE, England. Website: www.paulweller.com

**WELLS Martin John,** b. 24 Aug 1928, London, England. Zoologist; Educator. m. Joyce Finlay, 8 Sept 1953, 2 sons. Education: BA, 1952; MA, 1956; ScD, 1966. Publications: Brain and Behaviour in Cephalopods, 1962; You, Me and the Animal World, 1964; Lower Animals, 1968; Octopus: Physiology and Behaviour of an Advanced Invertebrate, 1978; Civilization and the Limpet, 1998. Contributions to: Several journals. Honours: Silver Medal, Zoological Society, 1968; Fellow, Churchill College, Cambridge. Memberships: Philosophical Society; Cambridge Drawing Society; Royal Highland Yacht Club. Address: The Bury Home End, Fulbourn, Cambridge, England.

**WELTY Eudora,** b. 13 April 1909, Jackson, Mississippi, USA. Author. Education: Mississippi State College for Women; BA, University of Wisconsin, 1929; Postgraduate Studies, Columbia School of Advertising, 1930-31. Publications: A Curtain of Green, 1941; The Robber Bridegroom, 1942; The Wide Net, 1943; Delta Wedding, 1946; Music From Spain, 1948; Short Stories, 1949; The Golden Apples, 1949; The Ponder Heart, 1954; The Bride of the Innisfallen, 1955; Place in Fiction, 1957; The Shoe Bird, 1964; Thirteen Stories, 1965; A Sweet Devouring, 1969; Losing Battles, 1970; One Time, One Place, 1971; The Optimist's Daughter, 1972; The Eye of the Story, 1978; The Collected Stories of Eudora Welty, 1980; One Writer's Beginnings, 1985; Eudora Welty Photographs, 1989; The Norton Book of Friendship (editor with Ronald A Sharp), 1991; A Writer's Eye: Collected Book Reviews, 1994; Monuments to Interruption: Collected Book Reviews, 1994; The First Story, 1999. Contributions to: The New Yorker. Honours: Guggenheim Fellowship, 1942; O Henry Awards, 1942, 1943, 1968; National Institute of Arts and Letters Grant, 1944, and Gold Medal, 1972; William Dean Howells Medal, American Academy of Arts and Letters, 1955; Christopher Book Award, 1972; Pulitzer Prize in Fiction, 1973; Presidential Medal of Freedom, 1980; National Medal for Literature, 1980; Notable Book Award, American Library Association, 1980; American Book Awards, 1981, 1984; Commonwealth Medal, Modern Language Association, 1984; National Medal of Arts, 1987; Chevalier de l'Ordre des Arts et Lettres, France, 1987. Membership: American Academy of Arts and Letters. Address: 1119 Pinehurst Street, Jackson, MS 39202, USA.

**WEN Shaojun,** b. April 1955, Beijing, China. Doctor; Researcher; Professor; Director. Education: MD, Capital University of Medical Sciences, 1989; Postdoctoral Studies, University of Paris 7, Denis Diderot, 1997. Appointments: Resident Physician, 1978-86, Attending Physician, 1989-92, Department of Cardiovascular Diseases, Xuanwu Hospital, Beijing; Vice-Researcher, Medical Research Centre of Geriatric Diseases, Beijing, 1992-95; Vice-Researcher, Key Laboratories of Brain Aging, Beijing, 1997-98; Director, Researcher, Professor, Department of Hypertension Research, Beijing Anzhen Hospital of the Capital University of Medical Sciences & Beijing Institute of Heart, Lung and Blood Vessel Diseases, Beijing, 1998-. Publications: 10 books; 120 articles. Honours: 3rd class technological and advanced award, Beijing, 1987; 2nd class technological award, Beijing Board of Health, 1989; 2nd class technological innovation award, Beijing Board of Health, 1989; 2nd class technological award, Beijing Board of Health, 1990; 1st class technological award, Beijing Board of Health, 1990; 2nd class technological award, Beijing Board of Health, 1990; 3rd class learned award, Beijing, 1993; 2nd class technological award, Beijing Board of Health, 1994; 3rd class technological and advanced award, Beijing, 2001. Memberships: Chinese Hypertension League; World Hypertension League; American Heart Association; Chinese Medical Association; Principal, Youth Worker Forum, Beijing; Secretary-General, Geriatric Sanitarian Committee, Cardiovascular Specialty. Address: Department of Hypertension Research, Beijing Anzhen Hospital of the Capital University of Medical Sciences & Beijing Institute of Heart, Lung and Blood Vessel Diseases,

Anzhen Li, Anding Men Wai, Beijing 100029, China. E-mail: wenshaojun@yahoo.com.cn

**WENDT Albert,** b. 27 October 1939, Apia, Western Samoa. Professor of English; Writer; Poet; Dramatist. 1 son, 2 daughters. Education: MA, History, Victoria University, Wellington, 1964. Appointments: Professor of Pacific Literature, University of the South Pacific, Suva, Fiji, 1982-87; Professor of English, University of Auckland, 1988-. Publications: Fiction: Sons for the Return Home, 1973; Pouliuli, 1977; Leaves of the Banyan Tree, 1979; Ola, 1990; Black Rainbow, 1992. Short Stories: Flying-Fox in a Freedom Tree, 1974; The Birth and Death of the Miracle Man, 1986; The Best of Albert Wendt's Short Stories, 1999. Plays: Comes the Revolution, 1972; The Contract, 1972. Poetry: Inside Us the Dead: Poems 1961-74, 1975; Shaman of Visions, 1984; Photographs, 1995. Honours: Landfall Prize, 1963; Wattie Award, 1980; Commonwealth Book Prize, South East Asia and the Pacific, 1991; Companion of the New Zealand Order of Merit, 2001. Address: c/o Department of English, University of Auckland, Private Bag 92019, Auckland 1, New Zealand. Website: www.auckland.ac.nz

**WENG Zhu Liang,** b. 14 September 1929, Jiande City, China. Painter; Professor. m. Wang Jin, 1 son, 1 daughter. Education: Zhejiang Academy of Fine Arts, 1952. Appointments: Senior Professional Painter, Zhejiang Painting Academy. Publications: Pictorial collection for Treasures of Contemporary Chinese Painting; Articles in several books. Honours: 3rd Prize, Paintings and Calligraphy Competition, Hong Kong. Memberships: Senior Member, Society of Lin Fen Mians Art Studies; Council Member, Zhejiang Society of Art Commentary Studies; Member, Chinese Artists' Association. Address: Zhejiang Painting Academy, Wu Lin Square, Hangzhou, Peoples Republic of China.

**WEPPEN Wolfgang von der,** b. 6 September 1943, Znojmo, Czechoslovakia. Freelance Author. m. Brigitte Vongehr, 3 daughters. Education: Philosophy, German Language and Literature; History; Politics; Psychology; History of the Arts, Universities of Vienna, Austria and Wuerzburg, Bavaria, Germany; Master of Arts, 1971; High School Teacher, 1971; Dr phil, 1983. Appointments: Assistant, Philosophy, University of Wuerzburg; University Expert of the Bavarian High School Association; High School Head Master; Freelance Author; Member of the Executive Committee of the Humboldt-Gesellschaft; Chairman, Socratic Society. Publications: Philosophy: Die existentielle Situation und die Rede; Articles to: Philosophy of Language and Philosophy of Culture; Ethics: W. von Humboldt, Wittgenstein, Karl Mannheim, Josef Pieper, Franz Vonessen; Philosophical Essays: Der Spaziergänger, Das verlorene Individuum; Lyrics (Metaphysische Gedichte) and narrative prose: Viktorsberg (novel); Tales. Honours: Preis des Kuratoriums der Unterfraenk. Gedenkjahrstiftung, University of Wuerzburg, 1984; Great Minds of the 21st Century, ABI, USA, 2004. Memberships: Sokratische Gesellschaft; Humboldt Gesellschaft; Gesellschaft für wissenschaftliche Phänomenologie; Forschungskreis für Metaphysik; Société Européene de Culture, Venice; Member, Research Board of Advisors, ABI, 2005; Life Fellowship, IBA, 2005. Address: Pfeffingerweg 33, D-83512 Wasserburg, Germany. E-mail: wolfgangvdweppen@gmx.de Website: www.sokratische-gesellschaft.de

**WERNER Helmut,** b. 19 April 1934, Mühlhausen, Germany. Professor of Chemistry. Widower, 1 son, 1 daughter. Education: Diploma, University of Jena, 1958; PhD, 1961, Habilitation, 1966, Technical University of Munich; Honorary Doctorate, University of Zaragoza, Spain, 2001. Appointments: Assistant Professor, 1968, Full Professor, 1970, University of Zürich,

Switzerland; Full Professor, Head of Department, 1975, Dean of Faculty, 1987-89, Chairman Interdisciplinary Research Unit, 1990-2001, University of Würzburg. Publications: 630; 1 monograph; 4 books edited. Honours: Fellow Royal Society of Chemistry, 1987; Member of the Academy Leopoldina, 1988; Alfred-Stock-Award, German Chemical Society, 1988; Max-Planck-Research Award, 1994; Centenary Medal and Lecturership, 1994; Alexander-von-Humboldt Award, 1995; Paulo-Chini-Memorial Lectureship, 1995. Memberships: Deutsche Chemische Gesellschaft; Swiss Chemical Society; Royal Society of Chemistry; American Chemical Society; Deutsche Gesellschaft für Naturforschung. Address: Institut für Anorganische Chemie, Am Hubland, D-97074 Würzburg, Germany. E-mail: helmut.werner@mail.uni-wuerzburg.de

**WESKER Arnold,** b. 24 May 1932, London, England. Dramatist; Playwright; Director. m. Dusty Bicker, 2 sons, 2 daughters. Appointments: Founder-Director, Centre Fortytwo, 1961-70. Publications: Chicken Soup with Barley, 1959; Roots, 1959; I'm Talking About Jerusalem, 1960; The Wesker Trilogy, 1960; The Kitchen, 1961; Chips with Everything, 1962; The Four Seasons, 1966; Their Very Own and Golden City, 1966; The Friends, 1970; Fears of Fragmentation (essays), 1971; Six Sundays in January (stories), 1971; The Old Ones, 1972; The Journalists, 1974; Love Letters on Blue Paper (stories), 1974, 2nd edition, 1990; Say Goodbye!: You May Never See Them Again (with John Allin), 1974; Words--As Definitions of Experience, 1976; The Wedding Feast, 1977; Journey Into Journalism, 1977; Said the Old Man to the Young Man (stories), 1978; The Merchant (renamed Shylock), 1978; Fatlips, 1978; The Journalists: A Triptych, 1979; Caritas, 1981; Distinctions (essays), 1985; Yardsale, 1987; Whatever Happened to Betty Lemon, 1987; Little Old Lady, 1988; Shoeshine, 1989; Collected Plays, 7 volumes, 1989-97; As Much As I Dare (autobiography), 1994; Circles of Perception, 1996; Break, My Heart, 1997; Denial, 1997; The Birth of Shylock and the Death of Zero Mostel (diaries), 1997; The King's Daughters (stories), 1998; Barabbas (play for TV), 2000; Groupie (play for radio), 2001; The Wesker Trilogy, 2001; One Woman Plays, 2001. Contributions to: Stage, film, radio and television. Honours: Fellow, Royal Society of Literature, 1985; Honorary DLitt, University of East Anglia, 1989; Honorary Fellow, Queen Mary and Westfield College, London, 1995; Honorary DHL, Denison University, Ohio, 1997. Memberships: International Playwrights Committee, president, 1979-83; International Theatre Institute, chairman, British Centre, 1978-82. Address: Hay on Wye, Hereford HR3 5RJ, England. Website: www.arnoldwesker.com

**WEST Timothy Lancaster,** b. 20 October 1934. Actor; Director. m. (1) Jacqueline Boyer, 1956, dissolved, 1 daughter, (2) Prunella Scales, 1963, 2 sons. Education: Regent Street Polytechnic, London, 1951-52. Appointments: Freelance Actor and Director, 1956-, Member, various times, Royal Shakespeare Company, National Theatre, Old Vic Company and Prospect Theatre Company; Artistic Director, Billingham Theatre Company, 1974-76, Old Vic Company, 1980-82; Director in Residence, University of Washington, 1982; Associate Director, Bristol Old Vic, 1991-; Film appearances include: The Looking Glass War; The Day of the Jackal; Oliver Twist; Cry Freedom; 102 Dalmatians; The Fourth Angel; Villa des Roses; Iris; Beyond Borders; TV appearances include: Why Lockerbie?; Framed; Smokescreen; Reith to the Nation; Eleven Men Against Eleven; Cuts; Place of the Dear; Midsomer Murders; Murder in Mind; Bedtime; Numerous theatre appearances. Publications: I'm Here I Think, Where Are You? 1997; A Moment Towards the End of the Play, 2001; Various articles in national newspapers, National Trust magazine, Times Literary Supplement. Honours: CBE, 1984; Honorary DUniv, Bradford, 1993; Honorary DLitt,

West of England, 1994; East Anglia, 1995; Honorary DLitt, University of Westminster, 1999. Memberships: FRSA, 1992-; Chairman, London Academy of Music and Dramatic Art, 1992-; Chairman, All Change Arts, 1986-99; At various times, member of Arts Council Drama and Touring Panels, various Theatre Boards; Director, National Student Drama Festival; President, Society for Theatrical Research.

**WESTBROOK Roger,** b. 26 May 1941, Surrey, England. Retired Diplomat. Education: MA, Modern History, Hertford College, Oxford. Appointments: Foreign Office, 1964: Assistant Private Secretary to the Chancellor of the Duchy of Lancaster and Minister of State, Foreign Office, 1965; Yaoundé, 1967; Rio de Janeiro, 1971; Brasilia, 1972; Private Secretary to Minister of State, Foreign Office, 1975; Head of Chancery, Lisbon, 1977; Deputy Head, News Department, 1980, Deputy Head, Falkland Islands Department, 1982, Overseas Inspectorate, Foreign and Commonwealth Office, 1984; High Commissioner, Brunei, 1986-91; Ambassador to Zaire, 1991-92; High Commissioner, Tanzania, 1992-95; Ambassador to Portugal, 1995-99, UK Commissioner, Expo 98, Lisbon; Chairman, Spencer House, 2000-; Chairman, Anglo Portuguese Society, 2000-2003; Council, Book Aid International, 2002-; Chairman, Foreign and Commonwealth Office Association, 2003-. Honour: CMG, 1990. Address: 33 Marsham Court, Marsham Street, London, SW1P 7JY, England.

**WESTERBERG Siv,** b. 11 June 1932, Borås, Sweden. Lawyer. m. Per Westerberg, 2 sons, 1 daughter. Education: Medicine Kandidat, 1954, Medicine Licentiat, 1960, University Uppsala; Juris kandidat, 1982, University of Lund. Appointments: Hospital Doctor, University Clinics in Gothenburg, Sweden, 1960-63; GP, Gothenburg, 1964-79; Lawyer, Gothenburg, 1982-; Specialised in medical and sociomedical cases; Tried and won several cases in the European Court of Human Rights. Publication: Books, To be a Physician, 1977; Punishment Without Crime, 2004. Address: Skårsgatan 45, SE-412 69, Göteborg, Sweden.

**WESTERLUND Elaine M,** b. 19 November 1945, Boston, Massachusetts, USA. m. Joseph F Doherty, 1 son. Education: BSc, Northeastern University, 1980; EdM, 1982, EdD, 1987, Boston University. Appointments: Founder, 1980, Peer Counsellor, Group Facilitator, 1980-82, Psychotherapist, 1982-88, Director, 1988-, Incest Resources Inc, 1st organisation in country and world for survivors of childhood sexual abuse, 1980; Psychology Trainee, Solomon Carter Fuller Mental Health Centre, Roxbury, Massachusetts, 1981-82, Laboure Centre Mental Health Clinic, South Boston, Massachusetts, 1982-83; Psychology Intern, South Shore Mental Health Centre, Quincy, Massachusetts, 1983-84; Psychologist in private practice, Cambridge, Massachusetts, 1988-; Consultant, Guest Lecturer in field; Pioneer of survivor self-help movement in USA; Developed original programme and treatment models for survivors. Publications: Author: Responding to Incest: In Memory of Nancy, 1987; Women's Sexuality After Childhood Incest, 1992; Articles including Thinking About Incest, Deafness and Counselling, 1993. Honours: Dean's Citation, Northeastern University, 1980; Teaching Fellowship, 1982-83, Practitioner-Teacher Award, 1982-83, School of Education Award, 1983-84, Boston University; Counselling Award and Academic Award, US Achievement Academy, 1987; Diplomate, American Board Psychological Specialties, 1999; Diplomate, American Psychotherapy Association, 1999; Outstanding Alumni Award for Health Sciences, Northeastern University, 1999; Psi Chi; Pi Lambda Theta; Sigma Epsilon Rho. Memberships: Massachusetts Psychological Association; American College of Forensic Examiners; American Psychotherapy Association;

# DICTIONARY OF INTERNATIONAL BIOGRAPHY

Massachusetts State Association of the Deaf; Founding Member, Deaf Women's Counselling Project, 1986. Address: One Arnold Circle, Cambridge, MA 02139-2250, USA.

**WESTMAN Carl E,** Lawyer. Education: BBA, Sam Houston State University, 1966; JD, 1969, LLM, Taxation, 1972, University of Miami; Master Licensed Captain, United States Coast Guard. Appointments: Bar and Court Admissions: Florida, 1969; US District Court, Southern District of Florida, 1969; US Tax Court, 1977; US District Court, Middle District of Florida, 1977; Partner, Frost & Jacobs, 1983-93; Partner, Roetzel & Andress, 1993-98; Partner, Administrative Partner, Steel Hector & Davis LLP, 1999-2004; Director, Cohen & Grigsby, 2004-. Honours: Listed in Who's Who publications and biographical dictionaries. Memberships include: Professional: Collier County Bar Association; Estate Planning Council of Naples; Florida Bar, Real Property, Probate and Trust Law Section and Health Law Section; Community: Chairman, Board of Trustees, Naples Community Hospital Inc; Chairman, Board of Trustees, NCH Healthcare System; Dean's Council, University of Miami, Rosensteil School of Marine and Applied Science; Chairman Southwest Florida Planned Giving Committee, Audubon of Florida; Board of Directors, Marco Island Yacht Club; Trustee, Pikeville College; Founding Member, Former Vice-president, Community Foundation of Collier County; Former Chairman, David Lawrence Mental Health Foundation; Former District Chairman, Eagle Board of Review, Southwest Florida Council, Boy Scouts of America. Address: Cohen & Grigsby, Collier Place 1, 3003 Tamiami Trail North, Suite 300, Naples, FL 34103-2714, USA. E-mail: cwestman@cohenlaw.com

**WESTMINSTER, Archbishop of (RC), His Eminence Cardinal Cormac Murphy-O'Connor,** b. 24 August 1932, Reading Berkshire, England. Education: The Venerable English College Rome; PhL, STL, Gregorian University, Rome. Appointments: Ordained Priest, 1956; Assistant Priest, Corpus Christi Parish, Portsmouth, 1956-63; Sacred Heart Parish, Fareham, 1963-66; Private Secretary, Chaplain to Bishop of Portsmouth, 1966-70; Parish Priest, Parish of the Immaculate Conception, Southampton, 1970-71; Rector, The Venerable English College, Rome, 1971-77; Bishop of Arundel and Brighton, West Sussex, 1977-2000; Archbishop of Westminster, 2000-; Created Cardinal Priest of the title Santa Maria sopra Minerva, 2001; Chairman: Bishops' Committee for Europe, 1978-83; Committee for Christian Unity, 1983-2000; Department for Mission and Unity Bishops' Conference of England and Wales, 1993-; Joint Chairman, ARCIC-II, 1983-2000; President, Catholic Bishops' Conference of England and Wales, 2000-; Vice-President, Council of the Episcopal Conferences of Europe, 2001-. Publications: The Family of the Church, 1984; At the Heart of the World, 2004. Honours: Honorary DD, Lambeth, 1999; Freeman of the City of London, 2001; Honorary Bencher of the Inner Temple, 2001; Bailiff Grand Cross of Sovereign Military Order of Malta, 2002; Prior of British and Irish Delegation of Constantine Order, 2002. Memberships: Presidential Committee of the Pontifical Council for the Family, 2001-; Congregation for Divine Worship and the Discipline of the Sacraments, 2001-; Administration of the Patrimony of the Holy See, 2001; Pontifical Council for Culture, 2002-; Pontifical Commission for the Cultural Heritage of the Church, 2002-; Pontifical Council for Promoting Christian Unity, 2002. Address: Archbishop's House, Westminster, London SW1P 1QJ, England. E-mail: archbishop@rcdow.org.uk Website: www.rcdow.org.uk/archbishop.

**WESTWOOD Vivienne Isabel,** b. 8 April 1941, England. Fashion Designer. 2 sons. Career: Developed Punk fashion in partnership with Malcolm McLaren, Chelsea, London, 1970-

83; Work produced for musicians including: Boy George; The Sex Pistols; Bananarama; Adam and the Ants; Bow Wow Wow; Solo avant-garde designer, 1984-; Also worked with S Galeotti, Italy, 1984; Launched Mini Crini, 1985; Produced collection featuring Harris tweed suits and princess coats; Pagan 5, 1989; Opened own shop in Mayfair, London, 1990; Launch of signature fragrance, Boudoir, 1998; Numerous fashion shows including: London; Paris Tokyo; New York. Honours: Professor of Fashion, Academy of Applied Arts, Vienna, 1989-91; Hochschule der Künste, Berlin, 1993-; Senior FRCA, 1992; British Designer of the Year, 1990, 1991; OBE, 1992; Queen's Award for Export, 1998. Address: Westwood Studios, 9-15 Elcho Street, London SW11 4AU, England.

**WHATELY Kevin,** b. 6 February 1951, Northumberland, England. Actor. m. Madelaine Newton, 1 son, 1 daughter. Education: Newcastle Polytechnic; The Central School of Speech and Drama, 1972-75. Career: Extensive television work including: Neville Hope in Auf Wiedersehen Pet, 1982-2004; Sergeant Lewis in Inspector Morse, 1986-2001; Steve in B & B, 1992; Dr Jack Kerruish in Peak Practice, 1992-95; Skallagrig, 1994; Trip Trap (BBC), 1996; Gobble, 1996; Jimmy Griffin in the Broker's Man, 1997-98; Pure Wickedness (BBC), 1999; What Katy Did (Tetra), 1999; Plain Jane (Carlton), 2001; Nightmare Neighbour (BBC), 2001; Hurst in Promoted to Glory, 2003; Dad, 2005; Belonging, ITV 2005; Footprints in the Snow, 2005; Theatre includes: Prince Hal in Henry IV Part 1 (Newcastle), 1981; Andy in Accounts (Edinburgh and London), 1982; Title Role in Billy Liar (national tour), 1983; John Proctor in The Crucible (Leicester), 1989; Daines in Our Own Kind (Bush), 1991; Twelve Angry Men (Comedy), 1996; Snake in the Grass (Pert Hall Co, Old Vic), 1997; How I Learned to Drive (Donmar), 1998; Film: Hardy in The English Patient (Miramax), 1996; Paranoid, 1999; Purely Belter, 2000; Silent Cry, 2001; The Legend of the Tamworth Two, 2003. Honours: Pye Comedy Performance of the Year Award, 1983; Variety Club Northern Personality of the Year, 1990; Honorary Doctor of Civil Law, Northumbria University. Memberships: Ambassador for the Prince's Trust; Ambassador for Newcastle and Gateshead; Ambassador for Sunderland; Vice-President, NCH; Patron, SPARKS; Patron, The Rose at Kingston Theatre; Patron Oesophageal Patients Association. Address: c/o CDA, 125 Gloucester Road, London SW7 4TE, England.

**WHEATER Roger John,** b. 24 November 1933, Brighton, Sussex, England. Conservationist. m. Jean Ord Troup, 1 son, 1 daughter. Education: Brighton, Hove & Sussex Grammar School, 1945-50; Brighton Technical College, 1950-51. Appointments: Assistant Superintendent of Police, Uganda, 1956-61; Chief Warden, Murchison Falls National Park, 1961-70; Director, Uganda National Parks, 1970-72; Director, Royal Zoological Society of Scotland, 1972-98; Chairman: Federation of Zoological Gardens of Great Britain & Ireland, 1993-96; Anthropoid Ape Advisory Panel, 1977-91; Editorial Board, World Zoo Conservation Strategy, 1991-93; European Association of Zoos & Aquaria, 1994-97; Access Forum, 1996-2000; Tourism and Environment Forum, 1999-2003; National Trust for Scotland, 2000-; Heather Trust, Deputy Chairman, 1999-2003; Scottish Natural Heritage, 1997-99; President: Association of British Wild Animal Keepers, 1984-99; International Union of Zoo Directors (now World Association of Zoos and Aquaria), 1988-91; Cockburn Trout Angling Club, 1997-. Publications: Wide range of publications on national park management, environmental education, captive breeding, animal welfare, access to countryside, National Trust for Scotland Properties, etc. Honours: OBE, 1991; Honorary Professor, Edinburgh University, 1993; Honorary Doctorate, DUniv, 2004; Honorary Fellow, RSGS, 1995; Honorary Fellow, RZSS, 1999;

Awards for outstanding achievement, World Association of Zoos and Aquaria, 2001; National Federation of Zoos in Great Britain and Ireland, 1998; European Association of Zoos and Aquaria, 2004. Memberships: Fellow: Royal Society, Edinburgh, 1991-; Royal Society of Arts, 1991-, Institute of Biology, 1987-; Trustee: Dian Fossey Gorilla Fund, 1993-; Dynamic Earth, Edinburgh, 1998-. Address: 26 Douecot Road, Edinburgh, EH12 7LE, England. E-mail: rj@wheater.fsworld.co.uk

**WHEELER Charles Selwyn**, b. 26 March 1923, Bremen, Germany. Journalist. m. Dip Singh, 2 daughters. Education: Tynemouth School; Cranbrook School. Appointments: Journalist, Daily Sketch, 1940-41; BBC News, 1946-50, BBC German Service correspondent, Berlin, 1950-53, Producer, Panorama, 1956-58, Staff correspondent, Berlin, Cyprus, South Asia, USA and Europe, 1959-75, Presenter, Panorama, 1975-76, BBC; Freelance journalist, 1977-; Newsnight correspondent; Documentaries for BBC, Channel 4 TV and BBC Radio 4. Honours: CMG; Hon Dr of Letters, University of Sussex; Hon Dr of the Open University. Address: 10A Portland Road, London W11 4LA, England.

**WHEELER (Henry) Neil George (Sir)**, b. 8 July 1917, Plymouth, Devon, England. Air Chief Marshal. m. Alice Elizabeth Weightman, 2 sons, 1 daughter. Education: RAF College Cranwell, 1935-37. Appointments: Royal Air Force, 1935-76; Retired as Air Chief Marshal; Director Rolls Royce Ltd, 1977-82; Director Flight Refuelling Ltd, 1977-85. Publications: Numerous articles on aeronautical matters mostly connected with operations during the 1939-45 war. Honours: DFC, 1941; Bar to DFC, 1943; DSO, 1943, OBE, 1949; AFC, 1954; CBE, 1957; ADC to H M The Queen, 1957-61; CB, 1967, KCB, 1969, GCB, 1975. Memberships: Fellow of the Royal Aeronautical Society; Companion of the British Institute of Management; Vice-President of the Air League; Past Master of the Guild of Air Pilots and Air Navigators. Address: Boundary Hall, Cooksbridge, Lewes, East Sussex BN8 4PT, England.

**WHELAN Peter**, b. 3 October 1931, Newcastle-under-Lyme, England. Playwright. Education: BA (Hons), University of Keele, Staffordshire, 1955. Appointments: Director, Garland Compton Ltd (Advertising Agency), 1977; Director, Reeves Robertshaw Ltd, 1982; Associate Writer, Royal Shakespeare Company, 1990-. Plays produced and published: Double Edge (co-author), 1975; Captain Swing (RSC), 1978; The Accrington Pals (RSC), 1981; Clay (RSC), 1982; The Bright and Bold Design (RSC), 1992; The School of Night (RSC), 1993; Shakespeare Country (BT/Little Theatre Guild), 1993; The Tinderbox (New Vic, Newcastle), 1994; Divine Right (Birmingham Rep), 1996; The Herbal Bed (RSC, Sydney and New York), 1997; A Russian In The Woods (RSC), 2001; The Earthly Paradise (Almeida Theatre), 2005. Honours: Writers Guild Best Play Nominations; Lloyds Private Banking Playwright of the Year, 1996; TMA Regional Theatre Awards, Best New Play, 1996; Nomination Best Play, Olivier Awards, 1997. Address: c/o The Agency, 24 Pottery Lane, Holland Park, London W11 4LZ, England.

**WHELAN Ruth**, b. 26 February 1956, Tullow, Co Carlow, Republic of Ireland. Education: BA (MoD), Trinity College, Dublin, 1977; Higher Diploma in Education, Trinity College, Dublin, 1978; MA, 1981; Diplôme d'études approfondies, University of Paris X, Nanterre, 1982; PhD, Trinity College, Dublin, 1984. Appointments: French language teacher, Rathdown School, Dublin, 1977-78; Instructor in English as a foreign language, Ecole d'Été de Dublin, 1978; Academic tutor, Department of French, Trinity College, Dublin, 1979-81; Instructor in English as a foreign language, École Normale

Supérieure, Paris, 1981-82; Instructor in English as a foreign language, École Nationale Supérieure de la Statistique et des Affaires Économiques, Paris, 1983-84; Student Mentor, 1991-97, Lecturer in French, 1984-96, Senior Lecturer in French, 1996-97, Trinity College, Dublin; Editorial Board, Correspondance de Pierre Bayle, Voltaire Foundation, Oxford, 1988-98; Editorial Board of the Oxford Encyclopaedia of the Enlightenment, 1996-2003; Professor of French and Head of Department, National University of Ireland, Maynooth, 1997-. Publications: 8 books; Over 50 articles and essays; 7 translations. Honours: Irish Government Scholarship, 1973-78; Dr Hely-Hutchinson Stewart Literary Scholarship, Trinity College, Dublin, 1977-79; Graduate Studentship, Research Award, Trinity College, Dublin, 1978-81; Visiting Studentship, École Normale Supérieure, Paris, 1981-84; French Government Scholarship, 1981-82; Research Fellowship, Collège de France, Paris and The Winifred Cullis Grant, The International Federation of University Women, Geneva, 1982-83; Arts (Letters) Faculty Research and Travel Award, 1987; Visiting Fellow, Herzog August Bibliothek, Wolfenbuttel, Germany, and Research Award, Faculty of Arts and Social Sciences Benefaction Fund, Trinity College, Dublin, 1988; Elected Fellow, Trinity College, Dublin, 1990; Senior Visitor, Linacre College, and the Voltaire Foundation, Oxford, 1992; Research Award, Provost's Fund, Trinity College, Dublin, and Research Award, Faculty of Arts and Social Sciences Benefaction Fund, Trinity College, Dublin, 1995; Elected Member, Royal Irish Academy, 2000; Research Professorship, NUI Maynooth, 2004-05; Listed in international biographical dictionaries. Memberships: Friends of the Library, Trinity College, Dublin; The Huguenot Society of Great Britain and Ireland; Society for French Studies, Great Britain and Ireland. Address: Department of French, National University of Ireland, Maynooth, Co Kildare, Ireland. E-mail: ruth.whelan@may.ie

**WHIPPLE Fred Lawrence**, b. 5 November 1906, Red Oak, Iowa, USA. Astronomer. m. (1) Dorothy Woods, 1 son, (2) Babette Frances Samelson, 2 daughters. Education: AB, University of California, Los Angeles, 1924-27; PhD, University of California, Berkeley, 1927-31; MS, honorary, Harvard University, 1945; DSc, honorary, American International College, 1958; DSc, honorary, Temple University, 1961; DLitt, honorary, Northeastern University, 1961; LLD, honorary, CW Post College of Long Island University, 1962; DSc, honorary, Univ Arizona. Appointments: Teaching Fellow, University of California, 1927-29; Instructor, Stanford University, 1929; Lick Observatory Fellow, 1930-31; Instructor, University of California, 1931; Staff Member, Harvard College Observatory, 1931-77; In Charge, Oak Ridge Station, Harvard College Observatory, 1932-37; Instructor, 1932-38, Lecturer, 1935-45, Harvard University; Research Associate, Radio Research Laboratory, OSRD, 1942-45; Associate Professor, 1945-50, Chairman, Committee on Concentration in the Physical Sciences, 1947-49, Chairman, Department of Astronomy, 1949-56, Professor, 1950-77, Harvard University; Director, Smithsonian Institution Astrophysical Observatory, 1955-73; Phillips Professor of Astronomy, 1968-77; Senior Scientist, Smithsonian Institution Astrophysical Observatory, 1973-; Phillips Professor of Astronomy, Emeritus, 1977-. Publications: Earth, Moon and Planets, 1942; Orbiting the Sun, 1981; The Mystery of Comets, 1985; Numerous scientific papers and several articles in professional journals. Honours include: Bruce Gold Medal, Astronomy Society of the Pacific, 1986; Phi Beta Kappa Award in Science, 1986; Henry Norris Russell Lecturer, 1988; Fred L Whipple Lecturer, American Geophysical Union, Planetary Division, 1990; Medal, University of California Los Angeles, 1997. Memberships include: American Astronomical Society; American Astronautical Society; American Geophysical Society; American Institute of Aeronautics & Astronautics.

Address: Smithsonian Astrophysical Observatory, 60 Garden Street, Cambridge, MA 02138, USA.

**WHIPPLE George,** b. 24 May 1927, St John, New Brunswick, Canada. Retired. Education: Vancouver Teacher's College, 1953. Publication: Life Cycle, 1984; Passing Through Eden, 1991; Hats Off to the Sun, 1996; Carousel, 1999; Tom Thomson and Other Poems, 2000; Origins, 2003; Fanfares, 2003; Footsteps on the Water, 2005; The Peaceable Kingdom, 2006. Contributions to: Poetry Canada Review; Canadian Forum; Fiddlehead; Writers Market (USA); Candleabrum (UK); Antigonish Review. Memberships: League of Canadian Poets; The Writers Union of Canada. Address: 2004-4390 Grange Street, St Burnaby, BC, V5H 1P6, Canada.

**WHITAKER (Baroness of Beeston in the County of Nottinghamshire); Janet Alison Whitaker,** Life Peer; Member of the House of Lords. Education: Major Scholar BA, Girton College, Cambridge; Farley Graduate Scholar, MA, Brynmawr College, USA; Radcliffe Fellow, Harvard, USA. Appointments: Commissioning Editor, André Deutsch Ltd, 1961-66; Speechwriter to Chairman of the Health and Safety Commission, 1976; Head of Gas Safety, Health and Safety Executive, 1983-86, Head of Nuclear Safety Administration, 1986-88; Head of Health and Safety, Department of Employment, 1988-92; Head of Sex Equality, 1992-96; Member, Employment Tribunals, 1995-2000; Consultant, CRE and Commonwealth Secretariat, 1996-99; Member: Immigration Complaints Audit Committee, 1998-99, European Union Select Committee Sub-Committee on Education, Social Affairs and Home Affairs, 1999-2003, Joint Committee on Human Rights, 2000-03, Joint Parliamentary Committee on the Draft Corruption Bill, 2003-, Friends Provident Committee of Reference; Chair, Camden Racial Equality Council, 1999; Chair, Working Men's College, 1998-2001; Non Executive Director, Tavistock and Portman NHS Trust, 1997-2001; Deputy Chair, Independent Television Commission, 2001-2003; Vice President, British Humanist Association, One World Trust; Trustee: UNICEF; Patron, British Stammering Association; SoS Sahel; Runnymede Trust. Memberships: Overseas Development Institute Council; Opportunity International; Advisory Council, Transparency International (UK); Interact Worldwide; Reform Club. Address: The House of Lords, London SW1A 0PW, England.

**WHITBREAD Fatima,** b. 3 March 1961, Stoke Newington, England. Athlete. m. Andrew Norman, 1997, 1 son. Appointments: UK International Debut as Javelin Thrower, 1977; European Junior Champion, 1979; European Cup Champion, 1983; European Cup Silver Medallist, 1985; European Champion, 1986; Commonwealth Games Bronze Medallist, 1982, Silver Medallist, 1986; Olympic Games Bronze Medallist, 1984, Silver Medallist, 1988; World Championships Silver Medallist, 1983; World Record Holder, 1986; World Champion, 1987; Retired, 1990; Founder Member, President, Chafford Hundred A.C; Marketing Consultant. Honours include: BBC Sports Personality of the Year, 1987; British Sports Writers Sportswoman of the Year, 1986, 1987; British Athletic Writers Woman Athlete of the Year, 1986, 1987. Memberships include: Voluntary Service Overseas Ambassador, 1992-93; President, Thurrock Harriers Athletic Club, 1993-; Governor, King Edward Grammer School, Chelmsford, 2000-02. Address: Chafford Hundred Information Centre, Elizabeth Road, Chafford Hundred, Grays, Essex RM16 6QZ, England. E-mail: champinternational@tinyworld.co.uk

**WHITE Edmund (Valentine III),** b. 13 January 1940, Cincinnati, Ohio, USA. Writer. Education: BA, University of Michigan, 1962. Appointments: Writer, Time-Life Books, New York City, 1962-70; Senior Editor, Saturday Review, New York City, 1972-73; Assistant Professor of Writing Seminars, Johns Hopkins University, 1977-79; Adjunct Professor, Columbia University School of the Arts, 1981-83; Executive Director, New York Institute for the Humanities, 1982-83; Professor, Brown University, 1990-92; Professor of Humanities, Princeton University, 1999-. Publications: Fiction: Forgetting Elena, 1973; Nocturnes for the King of Naples, 1978; A Boy's Own Story, 1982; Aphrodisiac (with others), stories, 1984; Caracole, 1985; The Darker Proof: Stories from a Crisis (with Adam Mars-Jones), 1987; The Beautiful Room is Empty, 1988; Skinned Alive, stories, 1995; The Farewell Symphony, 1997; The Married Man, 2000. Non-Fiction: The Joy of Gay Sex: An Intimate Guide for Gay Men to the Pleasures of a Gay Lifestyle (with Charles Silverstein), 1977; States of Desire: Travels in Gay America, 1980; The Faber Book of Gay Short Fiction (editor), 1991; Genet: A Biography, 1993; The Selected Writings of Jean Genet (editor), 1993; The Burning Library, essays, 1994; Our Paris, 1995; Proust, 1998; The Flâneur, 2001. Contributions to: Many periodicals. Honours: Ingram Merrill Foundation Grants, 1973, 1978; Guggenheim Fellowship, 1983; American Academy and Institute of Arts and Letters Award, 1983; Chevalier de l'ordre des arts et lettres, France, 1993; Officier Ordre des Arts et des Lettres, 1999. Address: c/o Amanda Urban, International Creative Management, 40 West 57th Street, New York, NY 10019, USA.

**WHITE Elvina,** b. 29 January 1966, Petersfield, Hampshire, England. Care Pathways Co-ordinator. m. Kevin Dunk, 2 sons. Education: BSc Biology, University of Sussex, England, 1987. Appointments: Research Assistant, Liverpool Congenital Malformations Registry, University of Liverpool, 1988-91; Medical Audit Administrator, St Helens & Knowsley Health Authority, 1991-92; Medical Audit Facilitator, Wigan & Bolton Health Authority, 1992-2000; Evaluation Co-ordinator, Department of Health Secondment, Bolton Community Healthcare NHS Trust, 1996-97; Care Pathways Co-ordinator, Royal Liverpool Children's NHS Trust, Alder Hey, 2000-. Publications: Using Integrated Care Pathways as an Effective Tool to Implement Guidelines, 2002; An Integrated Care Pathway for Burns, 2003. Address: Royal Liverpool Children's NHS Trust, Alder Hey Hospital, Eaton Road, Liverpool L12 2AP, England. E-mail: elvina.white@rlc.nhs.uk

**WHITE George Edward,** b. 19 March 1941, Northampton, Massachusetts, USA. Professor. m. Susan Davis White, 2 daughters. Education: BA, Amherst College, 1963; MA, PhD, Yale University, 1967; JD, Harvard Law School, 1970. Appointments: Law Clerk, Chief Justice Earl Warren, Supreme Court of United States, 1971-72; Assistant Professor of Law, University of Virginia Law School, 1972-74; Associate Professor, 1974-77; Professor, 1977-86; John B Minor Professor of Law and History, 1986-2003; University Professor, 1992-2003; David and Mary Harrison Distinguished Professor of Law, 2003-. Publications: The Eastern Establishment and the Western Experience, 1968; The American Judicial Tradition, 1976; Patterns of American Legal Thought, 1978; Tort Law in America, 1980; Earl Warren: A Public Life, 1982; The Marshall Court and Cultural Change, 1987; Justice Oliver Wendell Holmes: Law and the Inner Self, 1993; Intervention and Detachment: Essays in Legal History and Jurisprudence, 1994; Creating the National Pastime, 1996; The Constitution and the New Deal, 2000; Alger Hiss's Looking-Glass Wars, 2004. Honours: Fellow, National Endowment for the Humanities, 1977-78, 1982-83; Fellow, Guggenheim Foundation, 1982-83; Triennial Award for Distinguished Scholarship, Association of American Law Schools, 1996. Memberships: Phi Beta Kappa; American Academy of Arts and Sciences; Society of American

Historians; American Law Institute. Address: School of Law, University of Virginia, 580 Massie Road, Charlottesville, VA 22903, USA.

**WHITE Marco Pierre,** b. 11 December 1961, Leeds, England. Chef; Restaurateur. m. (1) Alexandra McArthur, 1988, divorced 1990, 1 daughter, (2) Lisa Butcher, 1992, divorced 1994, (3) Matilda Conejero-Caldera, 2000, 2 sons, 1 daughter. Appointments: Commis Chef, The Box Tree, Ilkley, 1978; Commis Chef de Partie, Le Gavroche, 1981, Tante Claire, 1983; Sous Chef, Le Manoir aux Quat' Saisons, 1984; Chef, Proprietor, Harveys, 1987-, The Restaurant, 1993-; Co-Owner, The Canteen, 1992-96; Founder, Criterion Restaurant with Sir Rocco Forte, 1995-; Re-opened Quo Vadis, 1996-; Oak Room, Le Meridien, 1997-99; MPW Canary Wharf, 1997-; Café Royal Grill Room, 1997-; Mirabelle Restaurant, Curzon Street, 1998-; L'Escargot Belvedere, 1999; Wheeler of St James, 2002. Publications: White Heat, 1990; White Heat II, 1994; Wild Food From Land and Sea, 1994; Canteen Cuisine, 1995; The Mirabelle Cookbook, 1999. Honours include: Restaurant of the Year, Egon Ronay (for The Restaurant), 1997. Address: Mirabelle Restaurant, 56 Curson Street, London W1Y 7PF, England.

**WHITE Susan Dorothea,** b. 10 August 1941, Adelaide, South Australia. Visual Artist; Painter; Sculptor; Printmaker. m. Brian Freeman, 2 sons, 1 daughter. Education: Full-time studies, South Australian School of Art, Adelaide, 1959-60; Full-time studies, Julian Ashton Art School, Sydney, 1960-61; Additional studies in sculpture, 1959-61, 1985-89 and printmaking, 1972, 1975, 1978. Career: Solo exhibitions, Australia, Europe, USA, 1962-98; Group exhibitions, Australia, Europe, USA, Asia, South America, 1959-2004. Collections held in: Hechinger Collection, Washington DC; National Gallery of Australia, Canberra; Dr Ulla Mitzdorf Collection, Munich; Museum of International Contemporary Graphic Art, Norway; FMK Gallery, Budapest; Gallery of Modern Art, Lublin; Mornington Peninsula Arts Centre, Victoria; Westmead Centre, Sydney. Publications: Artwork appears in numerous publications; Significant artwork: The First Supper, 1988; The Seven Deadly Isms, 1992; The Seven Deadly Sins of Modern Times, 1993; It Cuts Both Ways, 1998; Next-Door Neighbours, 2000; Menopausal Me in a Saucepan Lid, Warts 'n All, with Everything, including the Kitchen Sink, 2001; Lost for Words, 2003. Memberships: Viscopy; National Association for the Visual Arts. Address: 278 Annandale St, Annandale (Sydney), NSW 2038, Australia. E-mail: studio@sus andwhite.com.au Website: www.susandwhite.com.au

**WHITEHURST Brooks Morris,** b. 9 April 1930, Reading, Pennsylvania, USA. Chemical Engineer. m. Carolyn Boyer, 2 sons, 1 daughter. Education: BS, Chemical Engineering, Virginia Polytechnic Institute and State University, 1951. Appointments: Senior Process Assistant, American Enka Corporation, 1951-56; Process Research Engineer, Va-Cara Chemical Corporation, 1956-63; Project Engineering, Texaco Inc, 1963-66; Manager, Engineering Services, Special Project, Long-Range Planning, Texasgulf, 1967-81; President, Whitehurst Associates Inc, 1981-. Publications: Paper presented at Solar World Forum, Brighton, UK, 1981; Patents and current work on biodegradable chelate systems, development of environmentally friendly products for forest fertilization and seedling propagation, waste rubber recycling, micronutrients for agriculture; Use of waste products from saw mills and paper pulp production in agriculture. Honour: Recipient, Commendation from US President, 1981. Memberships: National Association of Professional Engineers; American Institute of Chemical Engineers. 1983 Hoods Creek Drive, New Bern, NC 28562, USA.

**WHITELEY Lucinda Jane,** b. 4 October 1961, London, England. Director. m. Michael Watts, 2 daughters. Education: BA, University of Newcastle upon Tyne. Appointments: Production Co-ordinator, Longman Video, 1983-84; Programme Manager, 1984-86, Head of Programme Planning, 1987-88, Children's Channel; Editor, Early Morning TV Service, Big Breakfast, C4 TV, 1988-92; Commissioning Editor, Children's Programmes C4 TV, 1993-97; Senior Vice President Production, Polygram Visual Programme, 1997-99; Freelance Executive Producer, 1999-2000; Director, Novel Entertainment: Fimbles, Roly Mo Show, Horrid Henry, Miriam Stoppard's Having a Baby, 2001-. Honours: 7 Baftas; 3 Emmys; 2 Prix Jeunesse; RTS Award; Peabody Award; Prix Europa; British Animation Award. Memberships: Board Member, BAFTA; Vice-Chair, World Summit on Children's Television, 1998. Address: Novel Entertainment, 39 Lonsdale Road, London NW6 6RA, England. E-mail: lucinda@novelentertainment.co.uk

**WHITNEY Stewart Bowman,** b. 15 November 1938, Buffalo, New York, USA. Professor Emeritus; Expedition Leader. m. Joan Noel Conti, 2 sons, 4 daughters. Education: BA, University of Buffalo, 1961; MA, 1965, PhD, 1972, SUNY, Buffalo. Appointments: Study Director, School of Medicine, SUNY, Buffalo, 1962-65; Assistant Professor, Ithaca College, 1965-69; Assistant Professor, Antioch College, 1970-73; Professor, Niagara University, 1973-. Publications: Several book and numerous articles in professional journals. Honours: Outstanding Achievement, International Wildlife; CFLE, National Council on Family Relations; FAACS, American Board of Sexology; Alpha Kappa Delta. Memberships: National Council on Family Relations; American Board of Sexology; American Sociological Association; World Future Society; Society for Scientific Study of Sexuality. Address: Space Settlement Studies, Department of Sociology, Timon Hall, Niagara University, NY 14109, USA. E-mail: swhitney@niagara.edu

**WHITTINGDALE John,** b. 1959. Member of Parliament. m. Ancilla, 2 children. Education: Economics Degree, University College, London. Appointments: Head, Political Section, Conservative Research Department, 1982-84; Special Advisor to three consecutive Secretaries of State for Trade and Industry, 1984-85; Political Secretary to the Prime Minister, 1988-90; Private Secretary to Baroness Thatcher, 1990-92; Elected Member of Parliament for South Colchester and Maldon, 1992; Member, House of Commons Select Committee on Health, 1993-97; Parliamentary Private Secretary to the Minister of State for Education and Employment, 1994-96; Elected Member of Parliament for Maldon and East Chelmsford, 1997; Opposition Whip, 1997; Frontbench Treasury Spokesman, 1998; Parliamentary Private Secretary to the Leader of the Opposition, 1999; Shadow Secretary of State for Trade and Industry, 2001; Shadow Secretary of State for Culture, Media and Sport, 2002; Shadow Secretary of State for Agriculture, Fisheries and Food, 2003-.

**WIDDECOMBE Ann Noreen,** b. 4 October 1947, Bath, Somerset, England. Member of Parliament. Education: University of Birmingham, 1966-69; University of Oxford, Lady Margaret Hall. Appointments: Member of Parliament, Maidstone and The Weald. 1987-; Parliamentary Under Secretary (1) Social Security (2) Employment, 1990-94; Minister of State, Employment, 1994-95; Minister of State, Home Office, 1995-97; Shadow Health Secretary, 1998-99; Shadow Home Secretary, 1999-2001. Publications: The Clematis Tree, 2000; An Act of Treachery, 2002; Father Figure, 2005; An Act of Peace, 2005. Honour: Privy Counsellor, 1997. Address: House of Commons, London SW1, England.

**WIDMER Winifred Ruth,** b. 25 January 1921, Herkimer, New York, USA. Law and Educational Research Administration. m. Francis E Downey, 1 step-son, 2 step-daughters. Education: LLB, cum laude, Albany Law School, Union University, 1954; BA, History and Government, Russell Sage College, 1958. Appointments: Admitted to practice, New York State Bar, 1954, United States Supreme Court, 1958; Officer, Assistant Director for Administration, Corporate Secretary, The Research Foundation of State University of New York, a non-profit educational corporation administering research and educational funds for the State University of New York, 1954-80; Retired, 1988. Honours: Honorary Juris Doctor, Albany Law School, Union University, 2003; Kate Stoneman Award, Albany Law School, 2003; Member, Justinian Society honorary legal society. Memberships: Former Member, Council on Governmental Relations, subcommittee of NACUBO, representing the Research Foundation; Former member, New York State Bar Association; Board of Trustees, Capital District Genealogical Society; The Essex Society for Family History; National Curtis/ Curtiss Society. Address: 3 Colonial Avenue, Albany, New York 12203-2009, USA. E-mail: fnwdowney@worldnet.att.net

**WIEMANN Marion R Jnr,** b. 7 September 1929, Chesterton, Indiana, USA. Biologist; Microscopist; Graphoanalyst. 1 daughter. Education: BSc, Biological Sciences, Indiana University, Bloomington, 1959; Certificates and Formal Training in Microscopy, McCrone Research Institute, Chicago, 1967-71; ScD Hons, The London Institute of Applied Research, 1994; ScD Hons, World Academy, Germany, 1995; Professor of Science, Australian Institute for Co-ordinated Research, Australia, 1995. Appointments: Histological Research Technician, 1959, Research Assistant, 1959-62, Research Technician, 1962-64, 1965-67, Senior Research Technician, 1967-70, Research Technologist, 1970-79, University of Chicago; Science Teacher, Westchester Township School Corporation, Chesterton, Indiana, 1964-66; Principal, Marion Wiemann and Associates, Consulting, Research and Development, Chesterton, Indiana, 1979-89; Consultative Faculty World University, 1991-. Publications: Tooth Decay, Its Cause and Prevention Through Controlled Soil Composition and Soil pH, 1985. Honours: Scholarships; Various awards of merit; Recipient, Scouter's Key, 1968, Arrowhead Honour, 1968, Boy Scouts of America; Henri Dunant Silver Medal with Silver Bars, 1995; Albert Einstein Silver Medal, Huguenin, Le Locke, Switzerland, 1995; Listed in national and international biographical dictionaries. Memberships: International Graphoanalysis Society; International Society of Soil Science; ABI Research Association; Field Museum of Natural History; Life Patron, IBA and ABI; Life Member, World Institute of Achievement; Life Fellow, World Literary Academy; Vice President, 1967-70, President, 1970-71, State Microscopal Society of Illinois; World Explorers Club; Enobled, Royal College Heraldry, Australia, 1991; National Weather Service. Address: PO Box 1016, Chesterton, IN 46304, USA.

**WIENER Marvin S,** b. 16 March 1925, New York City, USA. Rabbi; Editor; Executive. m. Sylvia Bodek, 1 son, 1 daughter. Education: BS, 1944; MS, 1945; BHL, 1947; MHL and Ordination, 1951; DD (Hon), 1977. Appointments: Registrar, Rabbinical School, Jewish Theological Seminary of America, 1951-57; Consultant, Frontiers of Faith, television series, NBC, 1951-57; Director, Instructor Liturgy, Cantors Institute-Seminary College Jewish Music, Jewish Theological Seminary of America, 1954-58; Faculty Co-ordinator, Seminary School and Womens Institute, 1958-64; Director, National Academy for Adult Jewish Studies, United Synagogue, New York City, 1958-78; Editor, Burning Bush Press, 1958-78, United Synagogue Review, 1978-86; Director, Committee on Congregational Standards, United Synagogue, 1976-86; Consultant, Community Relations and Social Action, 1981-82, Editor, Executive, Joint Retirement Board, 1986-. Publications: Editor of numerous volumes of Judaica; Author of articles in professional journals. Memberships include: American Academy of Jewish Research; Association of Jewish Studies. Address: 67-66 108th Street, Apt D-46, Forest Hills, NY 11375-2974, USA.

**WIESEL Elie(zer),** b. 30 September 1928, Sighet, Romania (US citizen, 1963). Author; Professor in the Humanities Religion and Philosophy. m. Marion Erster Rose, 1969, 1 son. Education: Sorbonne, University of Paris, 1948-51. Appointments: Distinguished Professor, City College of the City University of New York, 1972-76; Andrew W Mellon Professor in the Humanities, 1976-, Professor of Philosophy, 1988-, Boston University; Distinguished Visiting Professor of Literature and Philosophy, Florida International University, Miami, 1982; Henry Luce Visiting Scholar in the Humanities and Social Thought, Yale University, 1982-83. Publications: Un Di Velt Hot Geshvign, 1956, English translation as Night, 1960; L'Aube, 1961, English translation as Dawn, 1961; Le Jour, 1961, English translation as The Accident, 1962; La Ville de la chance, 1962, English translation as The Town Beyond the Wall, 1964; Les Portes de la foret, 1964, English translation as The Gates of the Forest, 1966; Le Chant des morts, 1966, English translation as Legends of Our Time, 1968; The Jews of Silence: A Personal Report on Soviet Jewry, 1966; Zalmen, ou, la Folie de Dieu, 1966, English translations as Zalmen, or, The Madness of God, 1974; And the Sea is Never Full: Memoirs, 1969-, English translation, 1999; Le Mendiant de Jerusalem, 1968, English translation as A Beggar in Jerusalem, 1970; Entre deux soleils, 1970, English translation as One Generation After, 1970; Célébration Hassidique: Portraits et légendes, 1972, English translation as Souls on Fire: Portraits and Legends of Haisdic Masters, 1972; Le Serment de Kolvillag, 1973, English translation as The Oath, 1973; Célébration Biblique: Portraits and Legends, 1975; Un Juif aujourd'hui: Recits, essais, dialogues, 1977, English translation as A Jew Today, 1978; Dimensions of the Holocaust (with others), 1977; Four Hasidic Masters and Their Struggle Against Melancholy, 1978; Le Proces de Shamgorod tel qu'il se droula le 25 fevrier 1649: Piéce en trois actes, 1979, English translation as The Trial of God (as It Was Held on February 25, 1649, in Shamgorod): A Play in Three Acts, 1979; Images from the Bible, 1980; Le Testament d'un poète Juif assassine, 1980, English translation as The Testament, 1981; Five Biblical Portraits, 1981; Somewhere a Master, 1982; Paroles d'étranger, 1982; The Golem: The Story of a Legend as Told by Elie Wiesel, 1983; Le Cinquieme Fils, 1983, English translation as The Fifth Son, 1985; Signes d'exode, 1985; Job ou Dieu dans la tempete, 1986; Le Crépuscule au loin, 1987, English translation as Twilight, 1988; The Six Days of Destruction (with Albert H Friedlander), 1989; L'Oublie: Roman, 1989; From the Kingdom of Memory, 1990; Evil and Exile (with Philippe-Michael de Saint-Cheron), 1990; The Forgotten, English translation, 1992; Monsieur Chouchani: L'enigme d'un Maitre du XX Siècle: Entretiens Avec Elie Wiesel, Suivis d'une Enquete, 1994; Tous les Fleuves Vont a la Mer: Mémoires, 1994, English translation as All Rivers Run to the Sea: Memoirs, 1995; Mémoire a Deux Voix (with Francois Mitterrand), 1995, English translation as Memoir in Two Voices, 1996; Et la mer n'est pas remplie, Memoirs Vol II, 1996; Celebration prophetique, 1998; King Solomon and his Magic Ring, 1999; The Judges, novel, 2002; After the Darkness, essays, 2002; Elie Wiesel: Conversation, 2002; Le temps des déracinés, novel, 2003; Wise Men and Their Tales (Portraits of Biblical, Talmudic and Hasidic Masters, 2003; Et où vas-tu (essays), 2004. Honours: Numerous, including: Prix Medicis, 1969; Prix Bordin, 1972; US Congressional Gold Medal,

1985; Nobel Prize for Peace, 1986; US Presidential Medal of Freedom, 1992; Grand-Croix of the French Legion of Honor, 2001. Memberships: American Academy of Arts and Sciences; Amnesty International; Author's Guild; European Academy of Arts and Sciences; Foreign Press Association, honorary lifetime member; Jewish Academy of Arts and Sciences; PEN; Writers Guild of America; The Royal Norwegian Society of Sciences and Letters; Founding President, Universal Academy of Cultures, Paris, 1993-; PEN New England Council, 1993-; Fellow, American Academy of Arts and Letters, Department of Literature, 1996-; Honorary Fellow, Modern Language Association of America, 1998; Honorary Member, Romanian Academy, 2001. Address: Boston University, 147 Bay State Road, Boston, MA 02215, USA.

**WIGGINS Christopher David,** b. 1 February 1956, Leamington Spa, England. Composer; Music Teacher. m. Karin Czok, 1985, divorced 1995. Education: University of Liverpool, 1974-77, Postgraduate, 1978-79; Bretton Hall College, University of Leeds, 1977-78; Goldsmiths College, London (part-time), 1980-82; University of Surrey (part-time), 1991-97; BA honours, Music, 1977, BMus, 1979, Liverpool University; PGCE, Bretton Hall, University of Leeds, 1978; MMus, London, 1982; FTCL, Composition, 1986; MPhil, Surrey, 1997. Career: Teacher of Music, Putteridge High School, Icknield High School, Luton Sixth Form College, Luton, 1979-95; GCSE Examiner, Music, 1989-95; Conducted various concerts by Central Music School String Orchestra, Tallinn, Estonia, 1990-93; Education Director, Classical Music Show, London, 1993-94; A Level Examiner, Music, 1995-; Head of Music and Examinations Co-ordinator, International School, Berlin-Potsdam, 1995-98; Co-founder and Vice Principal, Erasmus International School, Potsdam, 1999-2003; Co-ordinator, with Berliner Landesmusikakademie, visit to Berlin by string ensemble from University of Surrey, 2001-; Member of Senior Management Team, Schiller Academy, Potsdam, Germany, 2003-2004; Teacher of Music and English, Neues Gymnasium Potsdam, 2004; Schools Inspector for CIE, 2004-; I B Music Examiner, 2005-; Co-ordinator, 1st Potsdamer Hornfest, 2006; Major Compositions: About 150 compositions, over 110 performed; Over 90 published in USA, Netherlands, Germany and UK, including over 30 pieces for horn ensemble. Major Recordings include: Missa Brevis op 69; Ave Maria op 70; Soliloquy IX op 94 no 9; In Einem Kripplein Lag Ein Kind op 72; Elegy op 83, CD released in Estonia, 1995; Five Miniatures for 4 horns op 85; and others. Honours: Allsop Prize, Composition, Liverpool, 1977; Wangford Composers' Prize, 1991. Memberships: International Horn Society; PRS; MCPS; ESTA, UK; ABCD, Member of Convocation, University of London. Address: c/o Tilsdown Lodge, Dursley, Gloucestershire GL11 5QQ, England.

**WILBUR Richard (Purdy),** b. 1 March 1921, New York, New York, USA. Poet; Writer; Translator; Professor. m. Mary Charlotte Hayes Ward, 20 June 1942, 3 sons, 1 daughter. Education: AB, Amherst College, 1942; AM, Harvard University, 1947. Appointments: Assistant Professor of English, Harvard University, 1950-54; Associate Professor of English, Wellesley College, 1955-57; Professor of English, Wesleyan University, 1957-77; Writer-in-Residence, Smith College, 1977-86; Poet Laureate of the USA, 1987-88; Visiting Lecturer at various colleges and universities. Publications: Poetry: The Beautiful Changes and Other Poems, 1947; Ceremony and Other Poems, 1950; Things of This World, 1956; Poems, 1943-1956, 1957; Advice to a Prophet and Other Poems, 1961; The Poems of Richard Wilbur, 1963; Walking to Sleep: New Poems and Translations, 1969; Digging to China, 1970; Seed Leaves: Homage to R F, 1974; The Mind-Reader: New Poems, 1976; Seven Poems, 1981; New and Collected Poems, 1988; Bone

Key and other poems, 1998; Mayflies, 2000. For Children: Loudmouse, 1963; Opposites, 1973; More Opposites, 1991; A Game of Catch, 1994; Runaway Opposites, 1995; Opposites, More Opposites and Some Differences, 2000; The Pig in the Spigot, 2000. Non-Fiction: Anniversary Lectures (with Robert Hillyer and Cleanth Brooks), 1959; Emily Dickinson: Three Views (with Louise Bogan and Archibald MacLeish), 1960; Responses: Prose Pieces, 1953-1976, 1976. Editor: Modern American and Modern British Poetry (with Louis Untermeyer and Karl Shapiro), 1955; A Bestiary, 1955; Poe: Complete Poems, 1959; Shakespeare: Poems (with Alfred Harbage), 1966, revised edition, 1974; Poe: The Narrative of Arthur Gordon Pym, 1974; Witter Bynner: Selected Poems, 1978. Translator: Molière: The Misanthrope, 1955; Molière: Tartuffe, 1963; Molière: The School for Wives, 1971; Molière: The Learned Ladies, 1978; Racine: Andromache, 1982; Racine: Phaedra, 1986; Molière: The School for Husbands, 1992; Molière: The Imaginary Cuckold, 1993; Molière: Amphitryon, 1995; Molière: Don Juan, 2000; Molière: The Bungler, 2000. Honours: Harriet Monroe Memorial Prizes, 1948, 1978; Oscar Blumenthal Prize, 1950; Guggenheim Fellowships, 1952-53, 1963-64; Prix de Rome Fellowship, American Academy of Arts and Letters, 1954; Edna St Vincent Millay Memorial Award, 1957; Pulitzer Prizes in Poetry, 1957, 1989; National Book Award for Poetry, 1957; Ford Foundation Fellowship, 1960; Bollingen Prizes, 1963, 1971; Brandeis University Creative Arts Award, 1971; Shelley Memorial Award, 1973; Drama Desk Award, 1983; Chevalier, Ordre des Palmes Academiques, 1983; Los Angeles Times Books Prize, 1988; Gold Medal for Poetry, American Academy and Institute of Arts and Letters, 1991; Edward Mac Dowell Medal, 1991; National Medal of Arts, 1994. Memberships: Academy of American Poets, chancellor; American Academy of Arts and Letters, president, 1974-76, chancellor, 1976-78, 1980-81; American Academy of Arts and Sciences; American Society of Composers, Authors and Publishers; Authors League of America; Dramatists Guild; Modern Language Association, honorary fellow. Address: 87 Dodwells Road, Cummington, MA 01206, USA.

**WILBY Basil Leslie, (Gareth Knight),** b. 1930, Colchester, England. Writer. Education: BA, Hons, French, Royal Holloway College, University of London, 2000; Postgraduate Diploma, Imperialism and Culture, Sheffield Hallam University, 2002. Publications: A Practical Guide to Qabalistic Symbolism, 1965; The New Dimensions Red Book, 1968; The Practice of Ritual Magic, 1969; Occult Exercises and Practices, 1969; Meeting the Occult, 1973; Experience of the Inner Worlds, 1975; The Occult: An Introduction, 1975; The Secret Tradition in Arthurian Legend, 1983; The Rose Cross and the Goddess, 1985; The Treasure House of Images, 1986; The Magical World of the Inklings, 1990; The Magical World of the Tarot, 1991; Magic and the Western Mind, 1991; Tarot and Magic, 1991; Evoking the Goddess, 1993; Dion Fortune's Magical Battle of Britain, 1993; Introduction to Ritual Magic (with Dion Fortune), 1997; The Circuit of Force (with Dion Fortune) 1998; Magical Images and the Magical Imagination, 1998; Principles of Hermetic Philosophy (with Dion Fortune), 1999; Merlin and the Grail Tradition, 1999; Dion Fortune and the Inner Light, 2000; Spiritualism and Occultism (with Dion Fortune), 2000; Pytheness, the Life and Work of Margaret Lumley Brown, 2000; Dion Fortune and the Threefold Way, 2002; The Wells of Vision, 2002; The Abbey papers, 2002; Granny's Magic Cards, 2004. Contributions to: Inner Light Journal, 1993-2005. Address: c/o 38 Steeles Road, London NW3 4RG, England.

**WILBY David Christopher,** b. 14 June 1952, Leeds, England. Barrister at Law; Queen's Counsel. m. Susan Christine, 1 son, 3 daughters. Education: Roundhay School, Leeds; BA (Hons),

MA, Downing College, Cambridge. Appointments: Called to the Bar, Inner Temple, 1974; Silk, 1998; Recorder, 2000; Recorder in Civil, 2001; Bencher, 2002. Publications: Editor, Professor Negligence and Liability Law Reports, 1996-; Professor Negligence Key Cases, 1996; Author, The Law of Damages, Butterworths Common Law Series, 2002; Editor, Atkins Court Forms, Health and Safety, 2001. Honours: Member, Bar Council, 1997-99; Executive Committee, PNBA, 1995-; Chairman, North America Bar Council, 1998-2000; Chairman, Millennium Bar Conference, 2000. Memberships: Royal Overseas League; Pannal Golf Club; American Bar Association; International Association of Defense Counsel, USA. Address: 14 Temple House, Temple Avenue, London EC4Y 0ZF, England.

**WILCHEK Meir,** b. 17 October 1935, Warsaw, Poland. Biochemist. m. Esther Edlis, 1 son, 2 daughters. Education: BS, Bar-Ilan University, Ramat Gan, Israel, 1960; PhD, Weizmann Institute of Science, Rehovot, 1965. Appointments: Chief Chemist, Yeda Co, Rehovot, Israel, 1960-62; Chief Consultant, Miles-Yeda (Bio Makor), Rehovot, 1960-87; Research Associate, Department of Biophysics, 1965-66, Senior Scientist, 1968-71, Associate Professor, 1971-74, Professor, 1974-, Department Head, 1977-78, 1983-87, Dean of Biochemistry, 1995-99, Weizmann Institute of Science, Rehovot; Visiting Fellow, 1966-67, Research Associate, 1967-68, Visiting Scientist, 1972, 1974-75, Fogarty Scholar, 1981-82, National Institutes of Health, USA. Publications: 400 articles in professional journals. Honours: Rothschild Prize for Chemistry, Israel, 1984; Wolf Prize for Medicine, Israel, 1987; Pierce Prize, Rockford, Illinois, USA, 1987; Honorary DSc, University of Waterloo, Canada, 1989; Israel Prize in Biotechnology, Israeli Government, 1990; Sarstedt Prize for Analytical Biochemistry, 1990; Honorary PhD, Bar-Ilan University, Ramat Gan, 1995; Distinguished Clinical Chemist Award, International Federation of Clinical Chemistry, 1996; Honorary PhD, University of Jyvaskyla, Finland, 2000; Honorary PhD, Ben-Gurion University, Beer-Sheva, Israel, 2000; Anfinsen Award, Protein Society, USA, 2004; Wilhem-Exner-Medal, Austria, 2004; Listed in several Who's Who and biographical publications. Memberships: Honorary Member, American Society of Biological Chemists; American Chemical Society; Foreign Associate, Institute of Medicine, National Academy of Sciences, USA; European Molecular Biology Organisation; Israel Biochemistry Society; Israel Chemical Society; Israel Immunological Society; Israeli Academy of Sciences. Address: Ha-Avoda St 3Bm Rehovot, Israel.

**WILDER Gene,** b. 11 June 1935, Milwaukee, Wisconsin, USA. Film Actor; Director; Producer. m. (1) Mary Joan Schutz, 1967, divorced 1974, 1 daughter, (2) Gilda Radner, 1984, deceased, (3) Karen Boyer, 1991. Education: University of Iowa; Bristol Old Vic Theatre School. Appointment: US Army, 1956-58. Creative Works: Films include: Bonnie and Clyde, 1966; The Producers, 1967; Start the Revolution Without Me, 1968; Quackser Fortune Has a Cousin in the Bronx, 1969; Willy Wonka and the Chocolate Factory, 1970; The Scarecrow, 1972; Everything You Always Wanted to Know About Sex, But Were Afraid to Ask, 1971; Rhinoceros, 1972; Blazing Saddles, 1973; Young Frankenstein, 1974; The Little Prince, 1974; Thursday's Game, 1974; The Adventure of Sherlock Holmes's Smarter Brother, 1975; Silver Streak, 1976; The World's Greatest Lover, 1977; The Frisco Kid, 1979; Stir Crazy, 1980; Sunday Lovers, 1980; Hanky Panky, 1982; The Woman in Red, 1984; Haunted Honeymoon, 1986; See No Evil, Hear No Evil, 1989; Funny About Love, 1990; Another You, 1991; Stuart Little (voice), 1999; Murder in a Small Town, 1999; TV appearances include: The Scarecrow, 1972; The Trouble With People, 1973; Marlo Thomas Special, 1973; Thursday's Games, 1973; Something

Wilder, 1994-; Alice in Wonderland (film), 1999; The Lady in Question (film), 1999. Address: Ames Cushing, William Morris Agency, 151 El Camino Drive, Beverly Hills, CA 90212, USA.

**WILDGOOSE Jane,** b. 22 August 1954, England. Artist; Designer; Writer; Researcher. 1 daughter. Education: BA (Hons) Fashion & Textiles, Winchester School of Art, 1977. Appointments: Freelance costume and production designer for stage and film, 1979-2000; Visiting Lecturer, Winchester School of Art, 1994-; Founder, Keeper, The Wildgoose Memorial Library, 2003-; Co-devisor, On One Lost Hair, BBC Radio 4, with Gregory Whitehead and Neil McCarthy, 2004; Artists' Mentor, Commissions East, Cambridge, 2004-; Exhibitions in Manchester, Maidstone, London and Bexhill. Publications: Articles in professional and popular journals. Honours: Arts Council Year of the Artist Award with Sally Hampson, Upstream, 2000-01; Arts Council Year of the Artist Award with Mary Hooper, A Rose Flowering by the Sea, 2000-01; Wellcome Sciart Research Award with consultant gastroenterologist Dr Peter Isaacs and opera director Philip Parr, Viewing the Instruments, 2000-01; Victoria Rashbone Award, Manchester Letherium Ideas Competition, 2005; NESTA Dream Time Fellowship, 2005-06. Memberships: Costume Society. Address: 21A Topsfield Parade, London N8, England. E-mail: wildgoose@janewildgoose.co.uk

**WILFORD John Noble,** b. 4 October 1933, Murray, Kentucky, USA. Journalist; Writer. m. Nancy Watts Paschall, 25 December 1966, 1 daughter. Education: BS, Journalism, University of Tennessee, 1955; MA, Political Science, Syracuse University, 1956; International Reporting Fellow, Columbia University, 1961-62. Appointments: Science Reporter, 1965-73, 1979-, Assistant National Editor, 1973-75, Director of Science News, 1975-79, Science Correspondent, 1979-, New York Times, New York City; Mc Graw Distinguished Lecturer in Writing, Princeton University, 1985; Professor of Science Journalism, University of Tennessee, 1989-90. Publications: We Reach the Moon, 1969; The Mapmakers, 1981; The Riddle of the Dinosaur, 1985; Mars Beckons, 1990; The Mysterious History of Columbus, 1991; Cosmic Dispatches, 2000. Contributions to: Nature; Wilson Quarterly; New York Times Magazine; Science Digest; Popular Science. Honours: Westinghouse-American Association for the Advancement of Science Writing Award, 1983; Pulitzer Prizes for National Reporting, 1984, shared 1987; Ralph Coats Roe Medal, American Society of Mechanical Engineers, 1995; American Academy of Arts and Sciences, fellow, 1998. Memberships: Century Club, New York City; National Association of Science Writers; American Geographical Society, council member, 1994-. Address: New York Times, 229 West 43rd Street, New York, NY 10036, USA.

**WILHELMI Cynthia Joy,** b. 12 September 1946, Marshaltown, Iowa, USA. Information Technology Consultant. 1 son, 1 daughter. Education: BA, Art, University of Iowa, 1969; BA, Equivalent Degree in Journalism, 1993, MA, Communication, 1996, University of Nebraska. Appointments include: Editor, Publisher, Contributing Author, Salaam, Omaha, Nebraska, 1985-86; Master Artist-in-Residence, Nebraska Arts Council, 1985-91; Graduate Teaching Assistant, University of Nebraska, 1993-95; Program Co-ordinator, Family Friends of Easter Nebraska, Visiting Nurse Association, 1996-97; College Instructor, Midland Lutheran College, Fremont, 1997-99; Information Technology Consultant, Inacom Headquarters, Omaha, 1998; Information Technology Consultant, Bass and Associates, Omaha, 1999-2000; Information Technology Consultant, RHI Consulting, Omaha, 2000; Information Technology Consultant, TEKsystems, Omaha, 2000-; IT Business Analyst, Alegent Health, Omaha;

Test Engineer, Regression Test Development, Project Leader, IT Consultant, Ameritrade (Securities Trading); Senior Test Engineer, Third Party Vendor Interface Management, Lincoln Benefit Life Insurance Company, Lincoln, Nebraska; Senior Test Engineer, Ameritas Life Insurance Corporation, Omaha, Nebraska; US Airforce Data Manager (Contractor), Air Force Weather Agency (Secret Clearance), Bellvue Airforce Base, Nebraska. Publications: Numerous articles in professional journals. Honours: Outstanding Graduate Teaching Assistant Award, University of Nebraska at Omaha, 1995; Admiral in the Great Navy of Nebraska; Honorary Member, Society of Collegiate Journalists; Nebraska Republican Gubernatorial Re-election Campaign Committee; One Thousand Great Scientists, IBC, Cambridge, England; Listed in Who's Who publications and Biographical Dictionaries. Memberships: Phi Delta Gamma; Nebraska Admirals' Association; American Association of University Women; Advisory Council, Foster Grandparents; Society for Technical Communication; Friends of Art, University of Nebraska; Mensa (Nebraska-Western Iowa Executive Committee). Address: 2145 NW 86th Street, #43, Clive, IA 50325, USA. E-mail: cwi813@earthlink.net

**WILHELMI Zdzislaw Ludwik,** b. 20 September 1921, Lomza, Poland. Nuclear Physicist; Professor. m. Hanna Szmit, 2 daughters. Education: MSc, M Techn Sci, Technical University of Lodz, 1948; MSc, 1952, PhD, 1954, Docent, 1956, Extraordinary Professor, 1962, Ordinary/Full Professor, 1971, Warsaw University. Appointments: Director, Physics Division, Technical University, Lodz, 1953-54; Director, Nuclear Physics Division, Warsaw University, 1964-91; Director, Nuclear Physics Division, 1956-63, Director, Nuclear Reactions Division, 1963-70, Institute of Nuclear Research, Warsaw; Director, Nuclear Safety and Environmental Protection, International Atomic Energy Agency, Vienna, Austria, 1970-73; Organiser and Director of 18 successive International Summer Schools of Nuclear Physics, 1968-88; Director, Nation-wide Research Program on Interaction of Radiation and Matter, 1986-91. Publications: About 200 original articles on nuclear reaction and nuclear structure published in scientific journals; 25 monographs and textbooks in field; About 40 international conference contributions published in conference proceedings and scientific journals. Honours: Gold Cross of Merit with Swords, 1944; Cross of Valour, 1944; Order of Polonia Restituta, Knight Cross, 1964, Officer Cross, 1991; Commander Cross, 2003; Honor Title, Meritorious Teacher of Polish Peoples Republic; 1st prize, State Council of Nuclear Energy; 1st Prize, Minister of Science and Education. Memberships: Polish Physical Society, President, 1974-80; Fellow, American Physical Society; Fellow, Institute of Physics, Great Britain; European Physical Society, Member, Executive Committee, 1975-81; Ettore Majorana Centre for Science Culture. Address: Institute of Experimental Physics, Warsaw University, ul Hoza 69, 00-681 Warsaw, Poland. E-mail: wilhelmi@zfja-gate.fuw.edu.pl

**WILKES Maurice Vincent,** b. 26 June 1913, England. Mathematician. Education: Graduated, Mathematics, St John's College, Cambridge. Appointments: University Demonstrator, 1937; Radar and Operational Research, World War II; Lecturer, Acting Director, Mathematical Laboratory, Cambridge University, 1945, Director of Laboratory, 1946-70; Head, Computer Laboratory, 1970; Professor of Computer Technology, University of Cambridge, 1965-80; Staff Consultant, Digital Equipment Corporation, 1980-86; Adjunct Professor, MIT, 1981-85; Research Strategy, Olivetti Research Board, 1986-96; Adviser on Research Strategy, Olivetti and Oracle Research Laboratory, 1996-99; Staff Consultant, AT&T Laboratories, Cambridge, 1999-2002. Publications: Oscillations of the Earth's Atmosphere, 1949; Preparation of Programs for an Electronic Digital Computer, 1951, 1957; Automatic Digital Computers, 1956; A Short Introduction to Numerical Analysis, 1966; Time-Sharing Computer Systems, 1968; The Cambridge CAP Computer and its Operating System, 1979; Memoirs of a Computer Pioneer, 1985; Computing Perspectives, 1995. Honours: 9 honorary degrees; Harry Goode Memorial Award, 1968; Eckert-Mauchly Award, 1980; McDowell Award, 1981; Faraday Medal, 1981; Pender Award, 1982; C and C Prize, 1988; Italgas Prize, 1991; Kyoto Prize, 1992; John von Neumann Medal, 1997; Mountbatten Medal, 1997. Memberships include: Fellow, St John's College, Cambridge, 1950; Fellow, Royal Society, 1956; First President, British Computer Society, 1957; American Academy of Arts and Sciences; US National Academy of Engineering. Address: Computer Laboratory, University of Cambridge, William Gates Building, J J Thomson Road, Cambridge, CB3 0FD, England.

**WILKINS Maurice Hugh Frederick,** b. 15 December 1916, Pongaroa, New Zealand. m. Patricia Chidgey, 1959, 2 sons, 2 daughters. Education: Graduated, Physics, St John's College, Cambridge, 1938; Doctorate, University of Birmingham, 1940. Appointments: Ministry of Home Security and Aircraft Production; Manhattan Project, development of atomic bomb, University of California; Biophysics project, St Andrews University, Scotland, 1945; Biophysics Research Unit, King's College, London, 1946, Assistant Director, 1950, Deputy Director, 1955, Director, 1970-72; Professor of Biophysics, Head of Department, 1970-82, Fellow, 1973-, Professor Emeritus, 1981-, King's College. Publications: Papers on luminescence and topics in biophysics, eg, molecular structure of nucleic acids and structure of nerve membranes. Honours: Albert Lasker Award, American Public Health Association, 1960; Joint Winner, Nobel Prize for Physiology or Medicine, 1962; Honorary LLD, Glasgow, 1972; Honorary ScD, Birmingham, 1992; Honorary DSc, London, 1998. Memberships: Honorary Member, American Society of Biological Chemists, 1964; President, British Society for Social Responsibility in Science, 1969-91; Foreign Honorary Member, American Academy of Arts and Sciences, 1970; Russell Committee against Chemical Weapons, 1981; Food and Disarmament International, 1984-. Address: 30 St John's Park, London, SE3 7JH, England.

**WILLAMOWSKI Michael,** b. 23 November 1939, Brno, Czech Republic. Academic Librarian. m. Sibylle Zwirner-Willamowski, 2 sons, 1 daughter. Education: Degree in Physics, 1972; Doctor rerum naturalium, 1975. Appointments: Captain, German Airforce, 1961-62; Teacher, Hamburg, Germany, 1966-70; Information Broker, Universität der Bundeswehr, Hamburg, 1976-. Publications: Achievements include: Invention of semipermeable membranes for reverse osmosis. Memberships: Deutsche Gesellschaft für Schiffahrt-und Marinegeschichte; Verband der Elekrotechnik. Address: Gruener Bogen 10, D-22113 Oststeinbek, Germany. E-mail: tuscade@hotmail.com Website: www.topsurfen.de

**WILLCOCKS Michael (Sir),** b. 27 July 1944, Kent, England. Lieutenant General Retired; Gentleman Usher of the Black Rod. m. Jean, 1 son, 2 daughters. Education: Royal Military Academy, Sandhurst, 1962-64; BSc (Hons), London University, 1965-68; Army Staff College, 1975-76; Higher Command and Staff Course, 1988; Royal College of Defence Studies, 1991. Appointments: Regimental and Staff Appointments, 1965-83; Commanding Officer, 1st Regiment Royal Horse Artillery, 1983-85; Staff Posts, UK, 1985-89; Commander, Royal Artillery 4th Armoured Division, 1989-90; Chief of Staff, Land Operations, Gulf War, 1991; Director, Army Plans and Programme, 1991-93; Director General, Land Warfare, 1993-94; Chief of Staff, Allied Command Europe Rapid Reaction Corps, 1994-96;

Chief of Staff, Land Component Implementation Force, Bosnia-Herzegovina, 1995-96; Assistant Chief, UK Army, 1996-99; Deputy Commander (Operations) Stabilisation Force, Bosnia-Herzegovina, 1999-2000; UK Military Representative to NATO, the EU and WEU, 2000-2001; Retired 2001; Gentleman Usher of the Black Rod, Secretary to the Lord Great Chamberlain and Serjeant at Arms of the House of Lords, 2001-. Publication: Airmobility and the Armoured Experience, 1989. Honours: Meritorious Service Medal (USA), 1996, 2000; CB (Companion Order of Bath), 1997; KCB (Knight Commander Order of Bath), 2000. Memberships: Pilgrims; European Atlantic Group; Honourable Artillery Company; Honorary Colonel 1st Regiment Royal Horse Artillery; Colonel Commandant Royal Artillery; Commissioner, Royal Hospital Chelsea, 1996-99; Clubs: National Liberal, Pitt. Address: House of Lords, London SW1A 0PW, England. E-mail: willcocksm@parliament.uk

**WILLIAM SCOTT Seann,** b. 3 October 1976, Cottage Grove, Minnesota. Actor. Films include: Born into Exile, 1997; American Pie, 1999; Final Destination, 2000; Road Trip, 2000; Dude, where's my car?, 2000; Evolution, 2001; American Pie 2, 2001; Jay and Silent Bob Strike Back; 2001; Stark Raving Mad, 2002; Old School, 2003; Bulletproof Monk, 2003; American Wedding, 2003; The Rundown, 2003. TV Appearances include: Unhappily Ever After, 1996; Something so Right, 1998; The Big Breakfast, 2001; The Tonight Show with Jay Leno, 2001; Diary, 2003. Honours: MTV Movie Award, 2002; MTV Movie Award, 2004.

**WILLIAMES Lee,** b. 4 July 1942, Darby, Pennsylvania, USA. University Administrator; Professor. m. Frances Williames, 2 sons, 1 daughter. Education: BA, La Salle University, 1964; MA, European History, Niagara University, New York, 1966; Area Certificate, Soviet and East European Affairs, Soviet Institute, 1966; PhD, Russian and European History, State University of New York, Binghamton, 1981. Appointments: Professor of History, Director, Honours Program, College Misericordia, 1966-86; Professor, Assistant Provost for Academic Affairs, University of Scranton, Pennsylvania, 1986-92; Professor, Vice President for Academic Affairs, Secretary of the Board of Directors, University of St Thomas, Houston, 1992-2000; Secretary General, International Council Universities of St Thomas Aquinas, 1995-97; Acting President, summer 1997, currently Vice President, Academic Affairs Emeritus and Professor of History, University of St Thomas. Publications: Numerous articles on European/Russian History; Author, Anton Chekhov The Iconoclast. Honours: Jubilarian Medal, La Salle University; Centennial Medal, University of Scranton; Fellow, American Council on Education. Memberships: American Association for the Advancement of Slavic Studies; American Council on Education. Address: University of St Thomas, 3800 Montrose Boulevard, Houston, TX 77006, USA.

**WILLIAMS Bernard Arthur Owen (Sir),** b. 21 September 1929, Southend, Essex, England. Professor of Philosophy; Writer. m. (1) Shirley Vivienne Teresa Brittain Catlin, 1955, divorced 1974, 1 daughter, (2) Patricia Law Skinner, 1974, 2 sons. Education: BA, 1951, MA, 1954, Balliol College, Oxford. Appointments: Fellow, All Souls College, Oxford, 1951-54, 1997-; Fellow and Tutor in Philosophy, New College, Oxford, 1954-59; Lecturer in Philosophy, University College, London, 1959-64; Visiting Professor, 1963; Senior Fellow in the Humanities, 1978, Princeton University; Professor of Philosophy, Bedford College, London University, 1964-67; Knightbridge Professor of Philosophy, Cambridge University, 1967-79; Fellow, 1967-79, 1988-, Provost, 1979-87, King's College, Cambridge; Visiting Professor, Harvard University, 1973; Visiting Professor, 1986, Monroe Deutsch Professor

of Philosophy, 1988-, Sather Professor of Classics, 1989, University of California at Berkeley; White's Professor of Moral Philosophy, Oxford University, and Fellow, Corpus Christi College, Oxford, 1990-96; Visiting Fellow, Wissenschaftskolleg, Berlin, 1997. Publications: British Analytical Philosophy (editor with A C Montefiore), 1966; Morality, 1972; Utilitarianism: For and Against (with J J C Smart), 1973; Problems of the Self, 1973; Descartes: The Project of Pure Enquiry, 1978; Moral Luck, 1981; Utilitarianism and Beyond, (editor with A K Sen), 1982; Ethics and the Limits of Philosophy, 1985; Shame and Necessity, 1993; Making Sense of Humanity, 1995; Plato, 1998; Der Wert der Wahrheit, 1998; Truth and Truthfulness, 2002. Other: What is Truth? (writer and presenter), Channel 4 TV, UK, 1988. Contributions to: Scholarly books and journals. Honours: Honorary Fellow, Balliol College, Oxford, 1984, Corpus Christi College, Oxford, 1996; Dr Margrit Egner Stiftung Prize, Zürich, 1997; Knight, 1999; Hon DLitt, Yale, 2001; Hon DHL, Chicago, 1999; Hon LLD, Harvard, 2002. Memberships: American Academy of Arts and Sciences, honorary foreign member; Sadler's Wells Opera, later English National Opera, board, 1968-86; Chairman, Government Committee on Obscenity and Film Censorship, 1977-79; British Academy, fellow; Commission on Social Justice, Labour Party, 1992-94. Address: All Souls College, Oxford, OX1 4AL, England.

**WILLIAMS C(harles) K(enneth),** b. 4 November 1936, Newark, New Jersey, USA. Poet; Professor. m. (1) Sarah Dean Jones, 1966, divorced 1975, 1 daughter, (2) Catherine Justine Mauger, April 1975, 1 son. Education: BA, University of Pennsylvania, 1959. Appointments: Visiting Professor, Franklin and Marshall College, Lancaster, Pennsylvania, 1977, University of California at Irvine, 1978, Boston University, 1979-80; Professor of English, George Mason University, 1982; Visiting Professor, Brooklyn College, 1982-83; Lecturer, Columbia University, 1982-85; Holloway Lecturer, University of California at Berkeley, 1986; Professor, Princeton University, 1996-. Publications: A Day for Anne Frank, 1968; Lies, 1969; I Am the Bitter Name, 1972; With Ignorance, 1977; The Women of Trachis (co-translator), 1978; The Lark, the Thrush, the Starling, 1983; Tar, 1983; Flesh and Blood, 1987; Poems 1963-1983, 1988; The Bacchae of Euripides (translator), 1990; A Dream of Mind, 1992; Selected Poems, 1994; The Vigil, 1997; Poetry and Consciousness (selected essays), 1998; Repair (poems), 1999; Misgivings, A Memoir, 2000; Love About Love, 2001; The Singing, 2003. Contributions to: Akzent; Atlantic; Carleton Miscellany; Crazyhorse; Grand Street; Iowa Review; Madison Review; New England Review; New Yorker; Seneca Review; Transpacific Review; TriQuarterly; Yale Review; Threepenny Review. Honours; Guggenheim Fellowship; Pushcart Press Prizes, 1982, 1983, 1987; National Book Critics Circle Award, 1983; National Endowment for the Arts Fellowship, 1985; Morton Dawen Zabel Prize, 1988; Lila Wallace Writers Award, 1993; Berlin Prize Fellowship, 1998; PEN Voelker Prize, 1998; Pulitzer Prize, 2000; Los Angeles Times Book Prize, 2000; National Book Award, 2003; Ruth Lilly Prize, 2005. Memberships: PEN; American Academy of Arts and Science. Address: 245 Moore St, Princeton, NJ 08540, USA.

**WILLIAMS Christopher Maxwell John,** b. 25 September 1948, Sydney, Australia. Agricultural Scientist. m. Judith Barbara Spall, 1 daughter. Education: BScAgric Hons, Agriculture, University of Sydney 1970; PhD, Agronomy, University of Adelaide, 1978. Appointments: Senior Research Officer, South Australia Department of Agriculture, Naracoorte, South Australia 1975-79; Senior Lecturer, Massey University, Palmerston North, New Zealand 1979-81; Senior Agronomist, Department of Agriculture, Walpeup, Victoria, Australia

1981-82; Senior Research Scientist, Horticulture, South Australian Research and Development Institute, Adelaide, 1982-, including Convenor, Potatoes, 2000, Australian Potato Research and Development conference in Adelaide July 2000. Publications: Author or co-author of over 100 articles on potato, horticulture and viticulture crop agronomy; Potato Varieties for South Australia. Honours: Recipient, Howard Memorial Trust Scholarship, 1977; Best Paper Award, Australian Potato Industry Conference, 1990; Convenor, Australian Potatoes, 2000 Conference, Adelaide, July 2000; Research Team first to show Molybdenum deficiency can be a major cause of yield loss in grapevines. Memberships: Australian Institute of Agricultural Science and Technology; International and Australian Societies for Horticultural Science. Address: South Australian Research and Development Institute, Waite Precinct, GPO Box 397, Adelaide, SA 5001, Australia. E-mail williams.chrism@saug ov.sa.gov.au

**WILLIAMS Cynthia Ann,** b. 8 December 1959, Portsmouth, Virginia, USA. Nurse. 2 sons, 2 daughters. Education: Medical Specialist Diploma, 1982; Primary Leadership Development Diploma, 1984; Licensed Practical Nurse Diploma, 1986; Basic Non-Commissioned Officers Course Diploma, 1993; Associate Arts Degree, 1994; Bachelor of Arts in Theology Degree, 2004. Appointments: United States Army, 1981-2001; LPN, Home Health Care Pediatrics; Equal Opportunities Representative, 1996; Ordained Minister, Victory New Testament Fellowship, 2001-; Foster Parent, Prince William County, Virginia, USA, 2002. Publications: Marriage – Not Just a Simple "I Do" (commentary), 1999; One of Those Women (book), 2001; Monthly articles, Freewill Fellowship Ministry On-line, 2000-2001; Relationships On-line Producer Romauld Wells. Memberships: Presidential Prayer Team; Concerned Women of America; Non-Commissioned Officers Association; Partner, Aaron's Army, Paula White Ministries, KCM Ministries, BELL Ministries. Address: 2241 Sedgewick Drive, VA Beach, VA 23454, USA. E-mail: oneofthosewomen@yahoo.com

**WILLIAMS David Alexander,** b. 20 October 1940, Nottingham, England. Author; Professional Musician. m. Henriette, 2 sons, 2 daughters. Education: Becket School, Nottingham; Newcastle University; Fellow, Chartered Institute of Insurance. Appointments: Manager, Technical Insurance Adviser to Commercial and Industrial Companies, 1960-73; Organisation and Systems Consultant in UK and Holland, 1973-78; Management Training, 1978-80; New Computer Systems Project Manager, Royal Insurance (UK) Ltd, 1980-92; National Youth President, 1967-70, Member, 1978-87, Chairman, 1982-83, St Vincent de Paul; President, 1993-98, SVP Shrewsbury Central (Diocesan) Council; Member, Social Welfare Committee of the Bishops' Conference of England and Wales; Policy and Resources Committee (National), 1993-98; Recruitment and Training Committee, 1993-2005; National Vice President, St Vincent de Paul (England and Wales), 1997-2002; Vice President, St Vincent de Paul International Commission for the Revision of the General Principles and Statutes of the Society, 1999-2003; Responsible on the International Council General of the St Vincent de Paul Society for implementation of the Rule and Statutes, Aggregation of Conferences and Institution of Councils, 2003-. Publications: Alternative Prayers, 1970; Recruitment in the 70s; Visiting the Elderly at Home, Parts 1 & 2; The Mind & Heart of a Vincentian, 2001; Three additional sets of prayers for St Vincent de Paul Conferences, 2002; All publications of the Society of St Vincent de Paul; Articles for Vincentian Concern. Memberships: St Vincent de Paul Society; Time and Space Trustee; Family Tree (Carers Group) Trustee. Address: 7 Barrymore Way, Bromborough, Wirral, CH63 0HN, England. E-mail: da.w@ntlworld.com

**WILLIAMS Elisabeth Ann,** b. 13 January 1937, London, England. Lecturer. Education: BA Honours, History, 1960, PhD, 1964, Birkbeck College, University of London. Appointments: Lecturer, Senior Lecturer, Medieval History, Polytechnic of North London, 1965-88; Retired, 1988; Senior research fellow, University of East Anglia, 1997-. Publications: Books: The Domesday Survey and the Dorset Geld Rolls in Victoria History of the County of Dorset volume III (edited by R B Pugh), 1969; A biographical dictionary of Dark-Age Britain (with Alfred P Smyth and David Kirby), 1991; The English and the Norman Conquest, 1995; Kingship and government in pre-Conquest England, 1999; Æthelred "the Unready": the ill-counselled king, 2003; Numerous articles in academic journals and book chapters; Author of numerous entries in the New Dictionary of National Biography, 2004; Academic Editor, Great Domesday Book: a facsimile (with R W H Erskine and Geoffrey Martin), 6 volumes 1986-92; Academic Editor, Little Domesday (with Geoffrey Martin), 3 volumes, 2000. Memberships: Fellow of the Royal Historical Society; Fellow of the Society of Antiquaries. Address: 77 Gordon Road, London E11 2RA, England.

**WILLIAMS Herbert Lloyd,** b. 8 September 1932, Aberystwyth, Wales. Writer; Poet; Dramatist. m. Dorothy Maud Edwards, 13 November 1954, 4 sons, 1 daughter. Publications: The Trophy, 1967; A Lethal Kind of Love, 1968; Battles in Wales, 1975; Come Out Wherever You Are, 1976, new edition 2004; Stage Coaches in Wales, 1977; The Welsh Quiz Book, 1978; Railways in Wales, 1981; The Pembrokeshire Coast National Park, 1987; Stories of King Arthur, 1990; Ghost Country, 1991; Davies the Ocean, 1991; The Stars in Their Courses, 1992; John Cowper Powys, 1997; Looking Through Time, 1998; A Severe Case of Dandruff, 1999; Voices of Wales, 1999; The Woman in Back Row, 2000; Punters, 2002. Television Dramas and Documentaries: Taff Acre, 1981; A Solitary Mister, 1983; Alone in a Crowd, 1984; Calvert in Camera, 1990; The Great Powys, 1994; Arouse All Wales, 1996. Radio Dramas: Doing the Bard, 1986; Bodyline, 1991; Adaptations: A Child's Christmas in Wales, 1994; The Citadel, 1997. Contributions to: Reviews and journals. Honours: Welsh Arts Council Short Story Prize, 1972, and Bursary, 1988; Aberystwyth Open Poetry Competition, 1990; Hawthornden Poetry Fellowship, 1992; Rhys Davies Short Story Award, 1995. Memberships: Welsh Academy, fellow; The Powys Society; The William Barnes Society; The Society of Authors. Address: 63 Bwlch Road, Fairwater, Cardiff CF5 3BX, Wales

**WILLIAMS Hemine Weigel,** b. 4 February 1933, Sellersville, Pennsylvania, USA. College Teacher; Writer and Editor. Performing Musician. m. Jay Gomer Williams, 2 sons, 2 daughters. Education: AB, 1954, MA, 1956, Vassar College; PhD, Musicology, Columbia University, 1964. Appointments: Teacher of Music History: Vassar College, 1954-59; Hamilton College, 1964-65; Teacher, Religion and Arts, Hamilton College, 1972-93; Scholar in Residence, Hamilton College, 1994-; Assistant to Donald Jay Grout, The Operas of Scarlatti, 1980-87; Member, international editorial board for complete works edition of G B Pergolesi; Professional accompanist, organist, choral director, area churches; Organ soloist with Utica Symphony; Solo and ensemble recitals; Freelance writer and editor. Publications; The Operas of Scarlatti, vol 6, 1980; The Symphony 1720-1840, series B, 1983; Co-author, A Short History of Opera, 3rd edition, 1988, 4th edition (greatly expanded and revised), 2003; Co-author, Giovanni Battista Pergolesi: A Guide to Research, 1989; Sibelius and His Masonic Music, 1998; Francesco Bartolomeo Conti: His Life and Music, 1999; Thomas Hastings: An Introduction To His Life and Music (in press); Contributor to music books and journals. Honours: Maarston Fellowship; Theodore Presser Award, Composition;

Commission from San Francisco Opera, 1982; Fulbright Lecturer in Musicology; Council of International Exchange of Scholars, New Zealand, 1987; Dewitt Clinton Masonic Award for Community Service. Memberships: American Musicological Society; College Music Society; Fulbright Association. Address: 7153 College Hill Road, Clinton, New York 13323, USA.

**WILLIAMS Malcolm David,** b. 9 April 1939, South Wales. Author. Widower, 1 daughter. Education: Birmingham University Institute of Education, 1959-61. Publications: Yesterday's Secret, 1980; Poor Little Rich Girl, 1981; Debt of Friendship, 1981; Another Time, Another Place, 1982; Mr Brother's Keeper, 1982; The Stuart Affair, 1983; The Cordillera Conspiracy, 1983; The Girl from Derry's Bluff, 1983; A Corner of Eden, 1984; Sorrow's End, 1984; A Stranger on Trust, 1987; Shadows From the Past, 1989. Contributions to: Various publications, two Poetry Collections, 1998 and 2003. Honours: 1st Prize, Short Story Competition, 1961, 1969, 2005. Memberships: Society of Authors; West Country Writers Association; World Literary Academy, fellow; British Haiku Society. Address:17 Beaumont Road, Cheltenham, Glos, GL51 0LP, England.

**WILLIAMS Nigel,** b. 20 January 1948, Cheadle, Cheshire, England. Novelist; Playwright. Education: Oriel College, Oxford. Publications: Novels: My Life Closed Twice, 1977; Jack be Nimble, 1980; Charlie, 1984; Star Turn, 1985; Witchcraft, 1987; Breaking Up, 1988; Black Magic, 1988; The Wimbledon Poisoner, 1990; They Came from SW19, 1992; East of Wimbledon, 1993; Scenes from a Poisoner's Life, 1994; Forty Something, 1999; Hatchettxlycett, 2000. Plays: Double Talk, 1976; Snowwhite Washes Whiter, 1977; Class Enemy, 1978; Easy Street, 1979; Sugar and Spice, 1980; Line 'em, 1980; Trial Run, 1980; WCPC, 1982; The Adventures of Jasper Ridley, 1982; My Brother's Keeper, 1985; Deathwatch (after Genet), 1985; Country Dancing, 1986; As It Was, 1987; Nativity, 1989. Television plays include: Bertie and Elizabeth, 2002; Dirty Tricks, 2002; Uncle Addy, 2004. Honour: Somerset Maugham Award for Fiction, 1978; International Emmy, 2003. Address: c/o Judy Daish Associates, 2 St Charles Place, London, W10 6EG, England.

**WILLIAMS Robbie (Robert Peter),** b. 13 February 1974, Stoke-on-Trent, Staffordshire, England. Singer. Career: Member, UK all-male vocal group Take That, 1990-95; Solo artiste, 1995-; Television includes: Take That And Party, C4, 1993; Take That Away documentary, BBC2, 1993; Take That In Berlin, 1994. Recordings: Albums: Take That And Party, 1992; Everything Changes, 1993; Greatest Hits, 1996; Solo album: Life Thru A Lens, 1997; I've Been Expecting You, 1998; The Ego Has Landed, 1999; Sing When You're Winning, 2000; Swing When You're Winning, 2001; Escapology, 2002; Hit singles: with Take That: It Only Takes A Minute, 1992; I Found Heaven, 1992; A Million Love Songs, 1992; Could It Be Magic, 1993; Why Can't I Wake Up With You, 1993; Love Ain't Here Anymore, 1994; Never Forget, 1995; Pray, 1993; Relight My Fire (with Lulu), 1993; Babe, 1993; Everything Changes, 1994; Sure, 1994; Back For Good, 1995; Solo hit singles: Freedom, 1996; Old Before I Die, 1997; Lazy Days, 1997; South of the Border, 1997; Angels, 1997; I've Been Expecting You, 1998; Millennium, 1998; Let Me Entertain You, 1998; No Regrets, 1999; She's The One/It's Only Us, 1999; Strong, 1999; Rock DJ, 2000; Kids, with Kylie Minogue, 2000; Supreme, 2000; Let Love Be Your Energy, 2001; Eternity/Road To Mandalay, 2001; Better Man, 2001; Somethin' Stupid (with Nicole Kirman), 2001; Feel, 2002; My Culture, 2002; Come Undone, 2003; Something Beautiful, 2003; Sexed Up, 2003. Publications: F for English, 2000; Numerous videos, books, magazines. Honours

include: 7 Smash Hit Awards, 1992; 1 Smash Hit Award, 1996; BRIT Awards: Best Male Artist, Best Single, Best Video, 1998; MTV Award, Best Male, 1998; Smash Hits, Best Male, 1998; Nordoff-Robbins Music Therapy Original Talen Award, 1998; BRIT Awards: Best Video, Best Single, 1999. Memberships: Equity; Musicians' Union; MCPS; PRS; ADAMI; GVC; AURA. Address: c/o IE Music Ltd, 59 A Chesson Road, London, W14 9QS, England,

**WILLIAMS Robert Joseph Paton,** b. 25 February 1926, Wallasey, Cheshire, England. Scientist; Academic. m. Jelly Klara Büchli, 2 sons. Education: BA, 1948, DPhil, 1951, Chemistry, Merton College, Oxford University. Appointments: Junior Research Fellow, Merton College, Oxford, 1951-55; Tutor, Chemistry, Wadham College, Oxford, 1955-66; Lecturer, Chemistry, Oxford University, 1955-72; Commonwealth Fellow, Harvard Medical School, USA, 1965-66; Tutor, Biochemistry, Wadham College Oxford, 1966-72; Reader, Chemistry, 1972-74, Royal Society Napier Research Professor, 1974-91; Senior Research Fellow, 1991-93, Emeritus Fellow, 1993-, Wadham College, Oxford; Visiting Professor, Royal Free Hospital, London University, 1991-95. Publications: Books: Inorganic Chemistry (with C S G Phillips) volume 1 and 2, 1966; The Natural Selection of the Chemical Elements (with J R R Fràusto da Silva), 1996; Bringing Chemistry to Life (with J R R Fràusto da Silva), 1999; The Biological Chemistry of the Elements (with J R R Fràusto da Silva), 2nd edition, 2001; Editor of several books; Over 600 articles in chemical and biological journals. Honours include: Fellow of the Royal Society, 1972; Twice Medallist of the Biochemical Society; Twice Medallist of the Royal Society; Three times Medallist of the Royal Chemical Society; Twice Medallist of the European Biochemical Societies and the International Union of Biochemistry; Named Lecturer at Numerous colleges and universities in the UK, USA and Europe; Honorary Doctorates: Universities of Leicester, Keele, East Anglia and Lisbon. Memberships: Fellow Royal Society of Chemistry; Honorary Member, British Biophysics Society, Society for Biological Inorganic Chemistry, Society for the Study of Calcium Proteins; Member, Biochemical Society; Editor of several journals; Foreign Member, Academies of Belgium, Sweden, Portugal and Czechoslovakia. Address: Inorganic Chemistry Laboratory, Oxford University, South Parks Road, Oxford, OX1 3QR, England. E-mail: bob. williams@chem.ox.ac.uk

**WILLIAMS Robin,** b. 21 July 1951, Chicago, USA. Actor; Comedian. m. (1) Valerie Velardi, 1978, 1 son, (2) Marsha Garces, 1989, 1 son, 1 daughter. Education: Juillard School, New York. Creative Works: TV appearances include: Laugh-In; The Richard Pryor Show; America 2-Night; Happy Days; Mork and Mindy, 1978-82; Carol and Carl and Whoopi and Robin; Stage appearances include: Waiting for Godot; Films include: Popeye, 1980; The World According to Garp, 1982; The Survivors, 1983; Moscow on the Hudson, 1984; Club Paradise, 1986; Good Morning Vietnam, 1987; Dead Poets' Society, 1989; Awakenings, 1990; The Fisher King, 1991; Hook, 1991; Dead Again, 1991; Toys, 1992; Being Human, 1993; Aladdin (voice), 1993; Mrs Doubtfire, 1993; Jumanji, 1996; The Birdcage, 1996; Jack, Hamlet, Joseph Conrad's The Secret Agent, 1996; Good Will Hunting, 1997; Flubber, 1997; What Dreams May Come, 1998; Patch Adams, 1998; Jakob the Liar, 1999; Bicentennial Man, 1999; Get Bruce, 1999; One Hour Photo, 2001; Insomnia, 2002; Death to Smoochy, 2002; The Final Cut, 2004; House of D, 2004; Recordings: Reality, What a Concept, 1979; Throbbing Python of Love; A Night at the Met. Honours include: Several Emmy Awards; Several Grammy Awards; Golden Globe Award, 1988, 1991. Address: CAA, Creative Artists Agency, 9830 Wilshire Boulevard, Beverly Hills, CA 90212, USA.

# DICTIONARY OF INTERNATIONAL BIOGRAPHY

**WILLIAMS Roger Stanley,** b. 28 August 1931, Beckenham, Kent, England. Physician. m. (1) Lindsay Mary Elliot, 2 sons, 3 daughters, (2) Stephanie de Laszlo, 1 son, 2 daughters. Education: London Hospital Medical School, University of London; MRCS, LRCP, MBBS (Honours), 1953; MRCP (London), 1957; MD (London), 1960; FRCP, 1966. Appointments: Junior Medical Specialist, Queen Alexandra Hospital, Millbank, 1956-58; Medical Registrar and Tutor, Royal Postgraduate Medical School, 1958-59; Lecturer in Medicine, Royal Free Hospital, 1958-65; Consultant Physician, Royal South Hants and Southampton General Hospital, 1965-66; Director Institute of Liver Studies and Consultant Physician, King's College Hospital and Medical School, 1966-96; Professor of Hepatology, King's College London, 1994-96; Director, Institute of Hepatology, University College London, and Honorary Consultant Physician, University College London Hospitals, 1996-; Member Scientific Group on Viral Hepatitis, WHO Geneva, 1972; Consultant, Liver Research Unit Trust, 1974-; Member, Advisory Group on Hepatitis, DHSS, 1980-96; Member, Clinical Standards Advisory Committee, Department of Health, 1994-; Medical Director, Foundation for Liver Research. Publications: Author and co-author of approximately 2,500 papers articles, chapters and books. Honours: Honorary Fellowships: FRCPI, FRCP, FRCS, FRCPEd, FRACP, F MedSci; Nightingale Prize, International Federation of Medical and Biochemical Engineering (jointly), 1980; Gold Medal, Canadian Liver Foundation, 1992; Hospital Doctor of the Year Award for Gastoenterology, 1994; British Association for the Study of the Liver Lifetime Achievement Award, 2003; Wyeth Senior Achievement Award in Clinical Transplantation, American Society of Transplantation, 2004; Numerous named and invited lectures. Memberships include: Royal Society of Medicine; European Association for the Study of the Liver; President, 1989-90, British Society of Gastroenterology; Freeman City of London; Liveryman, Worshipful Society of Apothecaries. Address: Institute of Hepatology, Royal Free and University College Medical School, University College, London, 69-75 Chenies Mews, London WC1E 6HX, England. E-mail: roger.williams@ucl.ac.uk

**WILLIAMS Rowan Douglas (Most Reverend and Right Honourable the Lord Archbishop of Canterbury),** b. 14 June 1950, Swansea, Wales. Archbishop. m. Jane Paul, 1 son, 1 daughter. Education: BA, 1971, MA, 1975, Christ's College, Cambridge; D Phil, Wadham College, Oxford, 1975; College of the Resurrection, Mirfield, 1975; Deacon, 1977, Priest, 1978; DD, 1989. Appointments: Tutor, Westcott House, Cambridge, 1977-80; Honorary Curate, Chesterton St George, Ely, 1980-83; Lecturer in Divinity, Cambridge, 1980-86; Dean and Chaplain, Clare College, Cambridge, 1984-86; Canon Theologian, Leicester Cathedral, 1981-82; Canon Residentiary, Christ Church, Oxford, 1986-92; Lady Margaret Professor of Divinity, Oxford, 1986-92; Enthroned as Bishop of Monmouth, 1992; Enthroned as Archbishop of Wales, 2000; Enthroned as Archbishop of Canterbury, 2003. Publications: The Wound of Knowledge, 1979; Resurrection, 1982; The Truce of God, 1983; Arius, Heresy and Tradition, 1987, 2nd edition, 2001; Teresa of Avila, 1991; Open to Judgement (sermons), 1994; After Silent Centuries (poetry), 1994; On Christian Theology (essays), 2000; Lost Icons: Reflections on Cultural Bereavement, 2000; Christ on Trial, 2000; Remembering Jerusalem (poetry) 2001; Ponder These Things, 2002; Writing in the Dust, 2002; The Dwelling of the Light, 2003; Silence and Honey Cakes, 2003; Anglican Identities, 2004. Membership: Fellow of the British Academy. Address: Lambeth Palace, London SE1 7JU, England.

**WILLIAMSON (John) Ellis,** b. 28 October 1931, Galveston, Texas, USA. Certified Public Accountant. m. Betty Jean Lynch,

3 sons. Education: St Edward's University, Austin Texas, 1952-56; BS, Accounting, University of Houston, Texas, 1959-60; Galveston College, Galveston, Texas, 1987-88. Appointments: Ed Walsh Sr, CPA, Galveston, Texas, 1950-52, 1957-58; Price Waterhouse, CPA, Houston, Texas, 1956-57; Monsanto Co, Texas City, Texas, 1958-1985; The Little Store, Galveston, Texas, 1989-91; Fisherman's Wharf, Galveston, Texas, 1991-94; County of Galveston-Toll Collector, Galveston, Texas, 1992-94; Bishop's Palace, Galveston, Texas, 1994-95; Sacred Heart Church, Galveston, Texas, 1995-96; Founded first Stoke Club in Galveston, Texas, 1968; President, Stroke Clubs International, 1977-. Publications: Galveston Stoke Clubs Newsletter; International Stroke Clubs Bulletin; Various talks and presentations. Honours include: Ten Year St Edward's Alumni Award, 1966; Various Monsanto Employee Awards; Numerous awards from American Biographical Institute and International Biographical Centre, UK; Many letters of congratulations and citations; Honorary Member, Knights of Columbus, 1998. Memberships include: Former President, Galveston Stroke Club; Stroke Clubs International; Sacred Heart Men's Club; American Institute of Certified Public Accountants; St Edward's University Alumni Association; American Heart Association. Address: 805-12th Street, Galveston TX 77550, USA. E-mail: strokeclubs@earthlink.net

**WILLIAMSON Joel R,** b. 27 October 1929, Anderson County, South Carolina, USA. Professor; Writer. m. Anna Woodson, 18 November 1986, 1 son, 2 daughters. Education: AB, 1949, MA, 1951, University of South Carolina; PhD, University of California, Berkeley, 1964. Appointments: Instructor, 1950-64, Assistant Professor, 1964-66, Associate Professor, 1966-69, Professor, 1969-85, Lineberger Professor in Humanities, 1985-, Department of History, University of North Carolina, Chapel Hill. Publications: After Slavery: The Negro in South Carolina During Reconstruction, 1965; Origins of Segregation, 1968; New People: Miscegenation and Mulattoes in the US, 1980; The Crucible of Race, 1984; A Rage for Order, 1986; William Faulkner and Southern History, 1993. Honours: Parkman, Emerson, Owsley, Kennedy, Mayflower Awards; Mayflower Cup, 1994; Finalist, Pulitzer Prize in History, 1985, 1994. Memberships: Society of American Historians; Southern Association for Woman Historians; Southern Historical Association; Organisation of American Historians; American Historical Society. Address: 211 Hillsborough Street, Chapel Hill, NC 27514, USA. E-mail: william@email.unc.edu

**WILLIAMSON John Peter,** b. 19 January 1943, Amersham, Buckinghamshire, England. Businessman. m. Dorothy Shirley Esther Williamson, 2 sons. Education: Addey and Stanhope Grammar School; Hackney Technical College; Thames Polytechnic. Appointments include: Engineer and Production Development Manager, Rolex Watch Co, 1960-63 (founder Rolex Sports Club, founder Rolex Rocketry Society); Joint Managing Director and Financial Controller, Dynamic Reading Institute, 1968-69; Pioneering International Instructor in speed reading, memory, mind maps and mind training techniques (unofficial world speed reading record holder, 1967-68); Group Financial Controller, Company Secretary and Assistant Managing Director, Hunter-Print Group plc, 1971-74; Assistant to Company Comptroller ITT/STC, 1975 (responsibility for 26 Divisions); Manager, Corporate Planning; Manager, Operational Audit, Investigations, Operational Reviews and Manager, Computer Audits (1976-80), UK Chairman, ITT Bd (USA); Consultant, Liberty Life, Trident Life, Sun Life Unit Services, College of Taxation; C E Health & Co insurance brokers; Principal: Williamson Scrap and Waste Dealers, 1951-56, Williamson Light Vehicle Manufacturers, 1951-56, The Fun Weaponry Co, 1953-59; Williamsons Professional

Private Tuition Training, 1968-74; Williamson Business Consultancy and Turnround Specialists, 1968-74, Williamson & Co Chartered Accountants, 1973-2003; J P Williamson and Co Chartered Accountants, 1981-86; Partner, Williamson of Peckham (watchmakers and jewellers), 1954-64; Partner, Williamson Property Management, 1964-68; UK Managing Director, Odin Security and Surveillance, 1963-2003; Managing Director, Prestige Micro-Systems, 1976-2002; Founder Chairman & Managing Director, Guardian Financial Services (Guardian Independent plc), 1983-2004; Principal and Managing Director: Guardian Independent Property Services, 1983-93, Guardian Independent Wills and Trusts, 1994-2000, Guardian Independent Executors, 1994-2000, Guardian Independent Publishing Corporation, 1995-99; Guardian Independent Group International, 1995-2000, Guardian Independent General Insurance Services, 1995-2003, Guardian Independent Financial Corporation, 1995-2003; Guardian Independent Business Transfer Services, 1996-2001, Guardian Independent Debt and Arbitration Service, 1996-2003; Guardian Independent Eagles, 1996-2002; Guardian Independent Network Marketing, 1996-2002; Guardian Independent Corp Services, 1996-2002; Audits Incorporated, 1996-2002; GIANTS Corporation, 1996-2003; The Operational Audit Corporation, 1997-2000; Guardian Independent Taxation Solutions, 1997-2001; Guardian Independent Strategic Planners, 1997-2002; GIMAPS, 1997-2002; Guardian Independent Health and Wealth, 1999-2001; Guardian Independent Communications Corp, 1999-2001; Consultant and Coach: The Wealth Coach, 1983-, The Wealth Coach Ltd, 2003-; WOW! Windows, Display and Design, 2004-; Team Leader "The Product Factory", 2005-. Memberships: Founder, Chairman, British Institute of Management's Younger Managers Association, 1969-70; Founder, Chairman, SE London Micro-Computer Club (SELMIC) and consultant to several local and national computer clubs, 1975-80; Co-Founder, Association of London Hobby Computer Clubs, 1980; Chairman, SE London Area Society of Chartered Accountants, 1992-93; Founder Member, Institute of Financial Planning, 1987; Committees: Institute of Chartered Accountants, SIB Vetting Panel; ICA Ethics and Regulation Review Panel; London Business Board; Main Committee ICA London District Society of Chartered Accountants; Regional Committee Life Assurance Association, 1993-94; Member: College of Taxation (examiner); Institute of Internal Auditors (examiner, 1978); FIMBRA; PIA; FSA; Life Insurance Association; Institute of Financial Planning; NACFB; Corporation of Financial Brokers; FCA; CInstSMM; MCIM; FInstD; MIMgt; MIOM; AMBHI; MIIM; MLIA(Dip); ALIMA (Dip); ACFB; Certified Guerrilla Marketing Coach; Licensed Credit Broker; Member, National Association of Commercial Finance Brokers; Member, Corporation of Finance Brokers. Publications: Author, ITT/STC EDP Audit Manual; Creator "Warpspeed Learning Systems"; Author and Founder of the Wealth Coach systems and publications; Creator of the Rainmaker Masterclass. Honours: Freedom of the City of London, 1986; Rated as one of the top 2% Financial Advisers in the World, Million Dollar Round Table; Rated as one of the top 39 Financial Advisers in the UK, Life Insurance Association, Achievement Forum – Inner Circle, 1995, 1996; Rated as one of the top 366 Chartered Accountants in the UK, Institute of Chartered Accountants of England and Wales, 1995. Address: c/o The Wealth Coach Limited, PO Box 56, Eltham, London SE9 1PA, England. E-mail: john@thewealthcoach.org

**WILLIS Bruce Walter,** b. 19 March 1955, Germany. Actor; Singer. m. Demi Moore, divorced 2000, 3 daughters. Education: Montclair State College; Moved to USA, 1957; Studied with Stella Adler. Creative Works: Stage appearances: (off Broadway): Heaven and Earth, 1977; Fool for Love, 1984; The Bullpen; The Bayside Boys; The Ballad of Railroad William;

Films: Prince of the City, 1981; The Verdict, 1982; Blind Date, 1987; Sunset, 1988; Die Hard, 1988; In Country, 1989; Die Hard 2: Die Harder, 1990; Bonfire of the Vanities, 1990; Hudson Hawk, 1991; The Last Boy Scout, 1991; Death Becomes Her, 1994; Distance, 1994; Color of Night, 1994; North, 1994; Nobody's Fool, 1994; Pulp Fiction, 1994; Die Hard with a Vengeance, 1995; 12 Monkeys, 1995; Four Rooms, 1996; Last Man Standing, 1996; The Jackal, 1997; The Fifth Element, 1997; Mercury Rising, 1998; Armageddon, 1998; Breakfast of Champions, 1998; The Story of US, 1999; The Sixth Sense, 1999; Unbreakable, 2000; Disneys' The Kid, 2000; Bandits, 2001; Hart's War, 2002; Grand Champion, 2002; True West, 2002; Tears of the Sun, 2003; Rugrats Go Wild! (voice), 2003; Charlie's Angels: Full Throttle, 2003; The Whole Ten Yards, 2004; TV: Trackdown (film); Miami Vice (series); The Twilight Zone (series); Moonlighting (series), 1985-89; Friends (guest), 2000; Recordings: The Return of Bruno, 1987; If It Don't Kill You, It Just Makes You Stronger, 1989. Honours include: People's Choice Award, 1986; Emmy Award, 1987; Golden Globe Award, 1987.

**WILLIS Gladden Williams,** b. 26 March 1939, Minden, Louisiana, USA. Pathologist; Tree Farmer; Photographer. m. Lydia Hall, 2 sons. Education: BS, Centenary College, Shreveport, Louisiana, USA, 1957-60; MD, Tulane University School of Medicine, New Orleans, Louisiana, USA, 1960-64; Pathology Residency, LSU Medical Center, Shreveport, Louisiana, USA, 1964-69; Surgical Pathology Fellowship, Memorial Sloan-Kettering, New York, USA, 1969-71. Appointments: Private Practice Pathology, 1971-73; Pathologist, 1973-2005, Director, Anatomic Pathology, 1976-2003, Vice-Chair, Laboratory Medicine, 1996-2003, Ochsner Clinic Foundation, New Orleans, Louisiana, USA; Retired 2005. Publications: 28 scientific papers and presentations; 1,348 scientific photographs in biology and other textbooks. Honours: George Washington Honor Medal, Valley Forge Foundation; Listed in several Who's Who publications and biographical dictionaries. Memberships: Association of Directors of Anatomic Pathology; Arthur Purdy Stout Society; Royal Microscopical Society; International Academy of Pathology; New York Academy of Sciences; American Society of Media Photographers. Address: PO Box 719, Doyline, LA71023, USA. E-mail: gladdenwillis@direcway.com

**WILLSIE Sandra K,** b. 18 August 1953, Parsons, Kansas, USA. Physician. m. Thomas Syverson. Education: BS, Pittsburg State University, Pittsburg, Kansas, USA, 1975; Doctor of Osteopathic Medicine, Kansas City University of Medicine and Biosciences, College of Osteopathic Medicine, Kansas City, Missouri, 1983; Rotating Internship, 1983-84; Internal Medicine Internship, 1984-85; Internal Medicine Residency, 1985-87; Fellowship, Pulmonary Diseases and Critical Care Medicine, 1987-89. Appointments include: Assistant Professor of Medicine, 1989-94, Associate Professor of Medicine, 1994-99, Interim Chair, Department of Medicine, 1998-2000, Professor of Medicine, 1999-2000, UMKC School of Medicine, Kansas City Missouri; Professor of Medicine, 2000-, Vice-Dean of Academic Affairs, Administration and Medical Affairs, 2000-2002, Vice-President for Academic Affairs/Dean, 2002-, Kansas City University of Medicine and Biosciences, Kansas City, Missouri; Medical Director, Pulmonary Clinic, Truman Medical Center, 1991-2000; Medical Director, Kansas City Public Health Department Tuberculosis Clinic, 1996-2000; Pulmonologist, Affiliated with University Family Medical Care Center, Medical Center of Independence, Independence, Missouri, 2000-. Publications: Numerous articles as author and co-author in medical journals include most recently: Improved strategies and new treatment options for allergic rhinitis, 2001; Tumor necrosis alpha's role in lung injury following ischemia and reperfusion: model studies, 2003; Helicobacter pylori-related immunoglobulins in Sarcoidosis, 2004; 5 book chapters; Numerous published abstracts. Honours include: Numerous Research Grants; UMKC Chancellor's Teaching Enhancement Award, 1990; AMA, Physician Recognition Award, 1991; Young Investigator Award, American College of Chest Physicians, 1992; Harvard University's Macy Institute's Physician Educator Program, 2001, participated as invited "Returning Faculty Scholar", 2002, 2003, 2004. Memberships include: Fellow: American College of Physicians, American College of Chest Physicians; American Thoracic Society; Society of Critical Care Medicine; American Osteopathic Association; Greater Kansas City Bioterrorism Medical Advisory Panel; Medical Group Management Association. Address: Kansas City University of Medicine and Biosciences, 1750 Independence Avenue, Kansas City, MO 64106, USA. E-mail: swillsie@kmumb.edu

**WILSON A(ndrew) N(orman),** b. 27 October 1950, England. Author. m. (1) Katherine Duncan-Jones, 2 daughters, (2) Ruth Alexander Guilding, 1991, 1 daughter. Education: MA, New College, Oxford. Appointments: Lecturer, St Hugh's College and New College, Oxford, 1976-81; Literary Editor, The Spectator, 1981-83. Publications: The Sweets of Pimlico (novel), 1977; Unguarded Hours (novel), 1978; Kindly Light (novel), 1979; The Laird of Abbotsford, 1980; The Healing Art (novel), 1980; Who Was Oswald Fish (novel), 1981; Wise Virgin (novel), 1982; A Life of John Milton, 1983; Scandal (novel), 1983; Hilaire Belloc, 1984; Gentlemen in England (novel), 1985; Love Unknown (novel), 1986; The Church in Crisis (co-author), 1986; Stray (novel), 1987; Landscape in France, 1987; Incline Our Hearts (novel), 1987; Penfriends from Porlock: Essays and Reviews, 1977-86, 1988; Tolstoy: A Biography, 1988; Eminent Victorians, 1989; C S Lewis: A Biography, 1990; A Bottle in the Smoke (novel), 1990; Against Religion, 1991; Daughters of Albion (novel), 1991; Jesus, 1992; The Vicar of Sorrows (novel), 1993; The Faber Book of Church and Clergy, 1992; The Rise and Fall of the House of Windsor, 1993; The Faber Book of London (editor), 1993; Hearing Voices (novel), 1995; Paul: The Mind of the Apostle, 1997; Dream Children (novel), 1998; God's Funeral, 1999; The Victorians, 2002. Honours: Royal Society of Literature, fellow, 1981; Whitbread Biography Award, 1988. Address: 5 Regent's Park Terrace, London, NW1 7EE, England.

**WILSON Andrew Bray Cameron (Hon),** b. 3 June 1936, Adelaide, South Australia. Former Justice of the High Court of Fiji. m. Julie Elizabeth Pearce, 11 April 1987. 2 son, 6 daughters. Education: LLB, University of Adelaide, 1959. Appointments: Barrister and Solicitor, 1960-72; Judge, Adelaide Juvenile Court, 1972-76; Judge District Court of South Australia, 1972-99; Acting Justice of the Supreme Court of Papua New Guinea, 1973; Lecturer, Criminology, University of Adelaide, 1973; Justice of the National and Supreme Courts, Papua New Guinea, 1978-80; Justice of the Supreme Court of Samoa, 1999-2000; Justice of the High Court of Fiji, 2002-03; Auxiliary Judge, District Court of South Australia, 2003-. Honours: Churchill Fellowship, 1972; AM, 1998. Memberships: Member, Council, Law Society, South Australia, 1961-72; Chairman, Prisoners Aid Association, South Australia, 1966-73; Member, Social Welfare Advisory Council, 1970-72; Member, Australia and New Zealand Society of Criminology, 1971-; Member, Law Reform Committee, South Australia, 1972; Member Coalition Against Crime, 1990-94; Vice-President, 1973-77, 1991-93, President, 1993-95, Australian Crime Prevention Council; Chairman, McDouall Stuart Board, Burra Art Gallery, South Australia, 1995-97; President, Offenders Aid and Rehabilitation

Services, South Australia, 1997-99. Address: 114 Allinga Avenue, Glenunga, SA 5064, Australia.

**WILSON Colin Henry,** b. 26 July 1931, Leicester, England. Author. m. (1) Dorothy Betty Troop, 1 son, (2) Joy Stewart, 2 sons, 1 daughter. Appointments: Visiting Professor, Hollins College, Virginia, 1966-67, University of Washington, Seattle, 1967, Dowling College, Majorca, 1969, Rutgers University, New Jersey, 1974. Publications: The Outsider, 1956; Religion and the Rebel, 1957; The Age of Defeat, 1959; Ritual in the Dark, 1960; The Strength to Dream, 1962; Origins of the Sexual Impulse, 1963; Necessary Doubt, 1964; Eagle and the Earwig, 1965; The Glass Cage, 1966; Sex and the Intelligent Teenager, 1966; Voyage to a Beginning, 1969; Hermann Hesse, 1973; Strange Powers, 1973; The Space Vampires, 1976; Mysteries, 1978; Starseekers, 1980; Access to Inner Worlds, 1982; Psychic Detectives, 1983; The Essential Colin Wilson, 1984; Rudolf Steiner: The Man and His Work, 1985; An Encyclopedia of Scandal (with Donald Seaman), 1986; Spider World: The Tower, 1987; Aleister Crowley - The Man and the Myth, 1987; An Encyclopedia of Unsolved Mysteries (with Damon Wilson), 1987; Marx Refuted, 1987; Written in Blood (with Donald Seaman), 1989; The Misfits - A Study of Sexual Outsiders, 1988; Beyond the Occult, 1988; The Serial Killers, 1990; Spiderworld: The Magician, 1991; The Strange Life of P D Ouspensky, 1993; Unsolved Mysteries Past and Present (with Damon Wilson), 1993; Atlas of Holy Places and Sacred Sites, 1996; From Atlantis to the Sphinx, 1996; Alien Dawn, 1998; The Devil's Party, 2000; Atlantis Blueprint (with Rand Fle'math), 2000; Spiderworld: Shadowland, 2003; Autobiography Dreaming to some Purpose, 2004. Contributions to: The Times; Daily Mail. Membership: Society of Authors. Address: Tetherdown, Trewallock Lane, Gorran Haven, Cornwall, PL26 6NT, England.

**WILSON Sir Colin (Alexander) St John,** b. 14 March 1922. Architect; Emeritus Professor. m. (1) Muriel Lavender, 1955, dissolved 1971, (2) Mary Jane Long, 1 son, 1 daughter. Education: Felsted School; MA, Corpus Christi College, Cambridge, 1940-42; Dip Lond, School of Architecture, London University, 1946-49. Appointments: Served War, RNVR, 1942-46; Assistant in Housing Division, Architects Department, LCC, 1950-55; Lecturer, School of Architecture, University of Cambridge, 1955-69; Practised in association with Sir Leslie Martin, 1956-64; Visiting Critic, Yale University School of Architecture, 1960, 1964 and 1983; Fellow, Churchill College, Cambridge, 1962-71; Own private practice, 1964-; Bemis Professor of Architecture, MIT, USA, 1970-72; Exhibitions: Venice Biennale, 1996; retrospective, RIBA, 1997, Bristol and Glasgow, 1998; Architecture of British Library exhibition, tour, USA, 2000; Bishop Visiting Professor, 2000, Yale School of Architecture, USA; Consultant, Chicago City Library. Publications: Sundry reviews in journals in Japan, Italy, Norway and Spain; Work of practice appeared on Opus 1 and Opus 2 film surveys of the Arts in Britain, British Council, 1967 and 1986; Colin St John Wilson, 1997; The Architecture of the British Library at St Pancras, 2004; An Architecture of Invitation: Colin St John Wilson, 2005. Honours: SCONUL award for design excellence; Commander, Order of the Lion, Finland, 1992; FRSA, DUniv, Essex, 1998; Honorary Fellow, Corpus Christi College, 1998; Honorary LittD, Cambridge, 1999; Honorary LLD, Sheffield, 1999; Architects' Jl/Bovis/RA Grand Award, 2000. Memberships: Fitzwilliam Museum Syndicate, 1985-89; Arts Council of Great Britain, 1990-94 (Chair, Architecture Unit, 1992-94); Board of Advisers, MAArch, Helsinki University of Technology, Finland, 1994; Trustee: Tate Gallery, 1973-80; National Gallery, 1977-80; British Architectural Library, 2001-. Address: Colin St John Wilson & Associates, Clarendon Buildings, 27 Horsell Road, London N5 1XL, England.

**WILSON OF TILLYORN, Baron (Life Peer) of Finzean in the District of Kincardine and Deeside and of Fanling in Hong Kong, Sir David Clive Wilson**, b. 14 February 1935. m. Natasha Helen Mary Alexander, 2 sons. Education: Scholar, MA, Keble College, Oxford; University of Hong Kong; Visiting Scholar, Columbia University New York, USA; PhD, University of London. Appointments: HM Diplomatic Service: Joined SE Asia Department, Foreign Office, 1958; Third Secretary, Vientiane, 1959-60; Language Student, Hong Kong, 1960-62; Third then Second Secretary, Peking, 1963-65; First Secretary, Far Eastern Department, 1965-68, resigned 1968; Editor, The China Quarterly, Contemporary China Institute SOAS, University of London, 1968-74; Rejoined HM Diplomatic Service, 1974; Cabinet Office, 1974-77; Political Adviser, Hong Kong, 1977-81; Head, Southern European Department, Foreign and Commonwealth Office 1981-84; Assistant Under Secretary of State responsible for Asia and the Pacific, Foreign and Commonwealth Office, 1984-87; Governor and Commander in Chief of Hong Kong, 1987-92; Member of the Board, British Council, 1993-2002, Chairman, Scottish Committee, 1993-2002; Council, CBI Scotland, 1993-92; Prime Minister's Advisory Committee on Business Appointments, 2000-; Chairman, Scottish and Southern Energy (formerly Scottish Hydro-Electric), 1993-2000; Director, Martin Currie Pacific Trust plc, 1993-2003; Chancellor, University of Aberdeen, 1997-; Master, Peterhouse, Cambridge, 2002-. Honours: CMG, 1985; KCMG, 1987; GCMG, 1991; Life Peer, 1992; KT, 2000; Honorary Fellow, Keble College, Oxford, 1987; KStJ, 1987; Honorary LLD, University of Aberdeen, 1990, University of Abertay Dundee, 1995, Chinese University of Hong Kong, 1996; Honorary DLitt, University of Sydney, 1991; FRSE, 2000; Burgess of Guild, City of Aberdeen, 2003. Memberships: President: Bhutan Society of the UK, 1993-, Hong Kong Society, 1994-, Hong Kong Association, 1994-; Vice-President, RSGS, 1996; Chairman of Trustees, National Museums of Scotland, 2002-; Chairman, Council of Glenalmond College, 2000-05, Scottish Peers' Association, 2000-2002; Member, Carnegie Trust for the Universities of Scotland, 2000-; Registrar, Order of St Michael and St George, 2001-. Address: House of Lords, London SW1A 0PW, England or The Master's Lodge, Peterhouse, Cambridge, CB2 1QY, England.

**WILSON David Geoffrey**, b. 30 April 1933, Urmston, Lancashire, England. Retired Banker. m. Dianne. Education: Leeds Grammar School, 1944-46; Hulme Grammar School for Boys, 1947-50; Honorary MA, Manchester University, 1983; Honorary MA, Salford University, 1996. Appointments: Williams Deacon's Bank Ltd, 1952-70, Company Secretary, 1965-70; Merger into Williams & Glyn's Bank Ltd, 1970-86, Company Secretary, 1970-72, Manager (Mosley Street, Manchester), 1973-77, Superintendent of Branches, 1977-78, Area Director, 1978-82; Seconded as Regional Director, National Enterprise Board for North West, Yorkshire & Humberside (British Technology Group), 1982-85; Regional Director based in Manchester, British Linen Bank, 1985-91; Retired, 1991; High Sheriff of Greater Manchester, 1991-92; Part time Chairman, North Manchester Health Authority and North Manchester NHS Healthcare Trust, 1991-97. Honours: Honorary Consul for Iceland, 1981-; Deputy Lieutenant, Greater Manchester, 1985; OBE, 1986; Vice Lord-Lieutenant of Greater Manchester, 2003-. Memberships: Army & Navy Club, London; Lancashire County Cricket Club, Manchester. Address: 28 Macclesfield Road, Wilmslow, Cheshire SK9 2AF, England. E-mail: wilsondg@talk21.com

**WILSON Jim C**, b. 16 July 1948, Edinburgh, Scotland. Writer; Poet. m. Mik Kerr, 21 August 1971. Education: MA, Honours, English Language and Literature, University of Edinburgh, 1971. Appointments: Lecturer, English Telford College, Edinburgh, 1972-81; Writer-in-Residence, Stirling District, 1989-91; Creative Writing Tutor, University of Edinburgh, 1994-. Publications: The Loutra Hotel, 1988; Six Twentieth Century Poets; Cellos in Hell, 1993. Contributions to: Scotsman; Chapman; Lines Review; Radical Scotland; Times Educational Supplement; Cencrastus; Outposts; Orbis; Acumen; Rialto; Poetry Canada Review; Envoi; 2 Plus 2; Poet's Voice; Iron; Stand; Encounter; Literary Review; Imago (Australia). Honours: Scottish Arts Council Writer's Bursary, 1987, 1994; 1st Prize Scottish International Open Poetry Competition, 1997, 2005; Award, 1987; 1st Prize, Swanage Arts Festival Literary Competition, 1988, 1989, 1997; Hugh MacDiarmid Trophy for Poetry, 1997, 2005. Address: 25 Muirfield Park, Gullane, East Lothian EH31 2DY, Scotland.

**WILSON Kenneth Brian**, b. 10 April 1937, Bangor, Wales. College Principal; Teacher; Minister of Religion. m. Jennifer Rosemary Floyd, 1 son, 2 daughters. Education: MA, Trinity Hall, Cambridge, 1957-61; Bristol University, C Wesley College, Methodist Ordination, 1961-64; M Litt, (part-time) 1969, PhD, 1978 (part-time), Bristol University. Appointments: Assistant Minister, Hinde Street Methodist Church, London, Chaplain to London University Methodist Society and Middlesex Hospital, 1964-66; Assistant Chaplain, 1966-69, Chaplain, 1969-73, Kingswood School, Bath; Rowbotham Chair in Philosophy and Ethics, Wesley College, Bristol, Part-time Lecturer, University of Bristol, 1973-80; Principal Designate, Acting Vice-Principal, 1980-81, Principal, 1981-96, Westminster College, Oxford; Member of the Faculty of Theology, University of Oxford, 1993-2000; Director of Research, 1996-2001, Honorary Senior Research Fellow, 2000-, Queen's College, Birmingham; Honorary Lecturer, School of Historical Studies, University of Birmingham, 1996-; Visiting Fellow, University College, Chichester, 2004-; Montgomery Lecturer, Christian Education, 2005-. Publications include: Making Sense of It: An Essay in Philosophical Thought, 1973; Living It Out, 1976; The Experience of Ordination (editor), 1979; Focus on God (with F Young), 1986; Freedom and Grace (with I Jones), 1988; Governance and Authority in the Roman Catholic Church (editor with Noel Timms), 2000; Readings in Church Authority ( editor with G Mannion, R Gaillardetz and Jan Kerkhofs), 2003. Honours: Fernley Hartley Lecturer, British Methodist Conference, 1973; MA (Oxon), 1980; Fellow of the Royal Society of Arts, 1987; OBE, 1992; Hon DTh, Lycoming College, Pennsylvania, USA, 1994; Hon DLl, High Point University, North Carolina, USA, 1995. E-mail: 113061.3141 @compuserve.com

**WILSON Robert Woodrow**, b. 10 January 1936, USA. Radioastronomer. m. Elizabeth Rhoads Sawin, 1958, 2 sons, 1 daughter. Education: Bachelor's Degree, Rice University, 1957; PhD, California Institute of Technology, 1962. Appointments: Technical Staff, Bell Telephone Laboratory, Holmdel, New Jersey, 1963, Head, Radiophysics Department, 1976-94; Senior Scientist, Harvard-Smithsonian Center for Astrophysics, 1994-; Detected cosmic microwave background radiation, supposedly a residue of the Big Bang. Publications: Numerous articles in scientific journals. Memberships: NAS; American Astronomical Society; American Physical Society; International Astronomical Union. Honours: Henry Draper Award, National Academy of Sciences, 1977; Herschel Award, Royal Astronomical Society, 1977; Joint Winner, Nobel Prize for Physics, 1978. Address: Harvard-Smithsonian Center for Astrophysics, 60 Garden Street #42, Cambridge, MA 02138, USA.

**WILTON Christopher Edward John**, b. 16 December, 1951, Bahrain. Diplomat. m. Dianne, 1 son, 1 daughter. Education:

BA (Hons), Middle East Studies, University of Manchester, 1971-75. Appointments: Various posts in embassies in Bahrain, Tokyo and the Foreign and Commonwealth Office; Commercial Counsellor, British Embassy, Riyadh, 1990-94; HM Consul General, Dubai, 1994-97; Foreign and Commonwealth Office, 1997-99; Managing Director, International Marketing, BAE Systems, 1999-2001; Foreign and Commonwealth Office, 2001-2001; HM Ambassador, Kuwait, 2002-. Honour: Companion of the Order of St Michael and St George (CMG), 2004. Memberships: Athenaeum Club; Lansdowne Club. Address: FCO (Kuwait), King Charles Street, London SW1A 2AH, England.

**WINCH Donald Norman,** b. 15 April 1935, London, England. Professor of the History of Economics. m. Doreen Lidster, 5 August 1983. Education: BSc, London School of Economics and Political Science, 1956; PhD, Princeton University, 1960. Appointments: Visiting Lecturer, University of California, Berkeley, 1959-60; Lecturer in Economics, University of Edinburgh, 1960-63; Lecturer, 1963-66, Reader, 1966-69, Dean, School of Social Sciences, 1968-74, Professor of the History of Economics, 1969-, Pro-Vice-Chancellor, Arts and Social Studies, 1986-89, University of Sussex; Publications Secretary, Royal Economic Society, 1971-; Visiting Fellow, Institute for Advanced Study, Princeton, New Jersey, 1974-75, King's College, Cambridge, 1983, Australian National University, 1983, St Catharine's College, Cambridge, 1989, All Souls College, Oxford, 1994; Review Editor, Economic Journal, 1976-83; British Council Distinguished Visiting Fellow, Kyoto University, 1992; Carlyle Lecturer, University of Oxford, 1995. Publications: Classical Political Economy and Colonies, 1965; James Mill: Selected Economic Writings (editor), 1966; Economics and Policy, 1969; The Economic Advisory Council 1930-1939 (with S K Howson), 1976; Adam Smith's Politics, 1978; That Noble Science of Politics (with S Collini and J W Burrow), 1983; Malthus, 1987; Riches and Poverty, 1996. Contributions to: Many learned journals. Honours: British Academy, fellow, 1986-, vice president, 1993-94; Royal Historical Society, fellow, 1987-. Address: c/o Arts B, University of Sussex, Brighton BN1 9QN, England.

**WINEGARTEN Renee,** b. 23 June 1922, London, England. Literary Critic; Author. m. Asher Winegarten, deceased, 1946. Education: BA, 1943, PhD, 1950, Girton College, Cambridge. Publications: French Lyric Poetry in the Age of Malherbe, 1954; Writers and Revolution, 1974; The Double Life of George Sand, 1978; Madame de Staël, 1985; Simone de Beauvoir: A Critical View, 1988; Accursed Politics: Some French Women Writers and Political Life 1715-1850, 2003 Contributions to: Journals. Memberships: George Sand Association; Society of Authors; Authors Guild. Address: 12 Heather Walk, Edgware, Middlesex HA8 9TS, England.

**WINFREY Oprah,** b. 29 January 1954, Missouri, USA. Talk Show Host; Actress. Education: Tennessee State University. Career: Radio WVOL while at University in Tennessee, then on TV Stations: WTVF-TV Nashville as Reporter and Anchor, WJZ-TV Balt News, Co-anchor, 1976; People are Talking, Co-host, 1978; AM Chicago, Host, show re-named The Oprah Winfrey Show, 1985-; formed Harpo Productions, Owner/Producer, 1986; Founder, Editing Director, The Oprah Magazines, 2000-; Partner, Oxygen Media, 2000-; Producer of several TV films; Actress: The Color Purple, 1985; Native Son, 1986; The Woman of Brewster Place, TV, 1989; Throw Momma From the Train, 1988; Listen Up: The Lives of Quincy Jones, 1990; Beloved, 1998. Publications: Oprah, 1993; In the Kitchen with Rosie, 1996; Make the Connection, 1996. Honours: Numerous awards including: International Radio

and Television Society's Broadcaster of the Year Award, 1988; Lifetime Achievement Award, National Academy of TV Arts and Sciences, 1998. Address: Harpo Productions, 110 N Carpenter Street, Chicago, IL 60607, USA.

**WING Robert Farquhar,** b. 31 October 1939, New Haven, Connecticut, USA. Astronomer. m. Ingrid McCowen Wing, deceased, 2 sons, 1 daughter. Education: BS, Yale University, 1961; Attended Cambridge University, 1961-62; PhD, University of California, Berkeley, 1967. Appointments: Assistant Professor, 1967-71, Associate Professor, 1971-76, Professor, 1976-2002, Professor Emeritus, 2002-, Astronomy Department, Ohio State University. Publications: Approximately 150 research articles in journals of astronomy and astrophysics; The Carbon Star Phenomenon (editor), 2000. Honours: Various research grants from the NSF and NASA. Memberships: International Astronomical Union; Royal Astronomical Society; American Astronomical Society; Astronomical Society of the Pacific; American Association of Variable Star Observers; International Amateur Professional Photoelectric Photometry Association; International Dark Sky Association. Address: 400 Lenappe Drive, Columbus, OH 43214, USA. E-mail: wing@astronomy.ohio-state.edu

**WINGATE John Allan,** b. 15 March 1920, Cornwall, England. Author. 1 son, 1 daughter. Publications: Submariner Sinclair Series, 1959-64; Sinclair Action Series, 1968, 1969, 1971; HMS Belfast, In Trust for the Nation, 1972; In the Blood, 1973; Below the Horizon, 1974; The Sea Above Them, 1975; Oil Strike, 1976; Black Tide, 1976; Avalanche, 1977; Red Mutiny, 1977; Target Risk, 1978; Seawaymen, 1979; Frigate, 1980; Carrier, 1981; Submarine, 1982; William the Conqueror, 1984; Go Deep, 1985; The Windship Race, 1987; The Man Called Mark, 1996; The Fighting Tenth, 2005. Honour: Mentioned in Dispatches, 1942; Distinguished Service Cross, 1943. Membership: Nautical Institute. Address: c/o Lloyd Bank Plc, Waterloo Place, Pall Mall, London SW1Y 5NJ, England.

**WINGER Debra,** b. 16 May 1955, Cleveland, USA. Actress. m. Timothy Hutton, 1986, divorced, 1 son. Education: California University, Northridge. Appointments: Served, Israel Army, 1972; First Professional Appearance, Wonder Woman, tv series, 1976-77. Creative Works: Films include: Thank God Its Friday, 1978; French Postcards, 1979; Urban Cowboy, 1980; Cannery Row, 1982; An Officer and a Gentleman, 1982; Terms of Endearment, 1983; Mike's Murder, 1984; Legal Eagles, 1986; Black Widow, 1987; Made in Heaven, 1987; Betrayed, 1988; The Sheltering Sky, 1990; Everybody Wins, 1990; Leap of Faith, 1992; Shadowlands, 1993; A Dangerous Woman, 1993; Forget Paris, 1995; Big Bad Love, 2002; Radio, 2003; Eulogy, 2004. Address: c/o CAA, 9830 Wilshire Boulevard, Beverly Hills, CA 90212, USA.

**WINIARCZYK Marek,** b. 30 June 1947, Wrocław, Poland. Historian. Education: MA, 1970, PhD, 1976, Doctor habilitatus, 1982, Department of Classics, University of Wrocław, Poland. Appointments: Librarian, 1970-73, Lecturer, Department of Foreign Languages, 1973-83, Associate Professor of Classical Languages, 1983-93, Professor of Ancient History, 1993-, University of Wrocław. Publications: Diagorae Melii et Theodori Cyrenaei reliquiae, 1981; Euhemeri Messenii reliquiae, 1991; Bibliographie zum antiken Atheismus, 1994; Co-editor: Abkürzungen aus Personalschriften des XVI bis XVIII Jahrhunderts, 1993 (second edition, 2002); Author, dictionary: Sigla Latina in libris impressis occurrentia, 1995; Euhemeros von Messene. Leben, Werk und Nachwirkung, 2002. Honours: Listed in Who's Who publications and biographical dictionaries. Memberships: Wrocławskie Towarzystwo Naukowe; Polskie

Towarzystwo Filologiczne; Polskie Towarzystwo Historyczne; American School of Classical Studies at Athens, 1995. Address: Mianowskiego 25/2, 51-605, Wrocław, Poland.

**WINKEL Wolfgang,** b. 15 June 1941, Danzig, Germany. Zoologist. m. Doris Laux, 1 daughter. Education: Graduation (Dr rer nat), University Brunswick, 1968. Scientific Assistant, Institute of Avian Research, Wilhelmshaven, Germany, 1970-77; Head, Working group population ecology of Vogelwarte Helgoland, Brunswick, 1978-. Publications: Over 150 in scientific journals; (co-author) Eco-ornithological Glossary, 1983; (co-author) Die Vogelfamilien der Westpaläarktis, 1995; Editor-in-Chief, Die Vogelwelt, 1971-87; Co-editor, Die Vogelwarte, 1972-2004. Honours: Silberne Ehrennadel, Deutscher Bund für Vogelschutz, 1984; Förderpreis der Werner-Sunkel-Stiftung, Deutsche Ornithologen-Gesellschaft, 2001. Memberships: Deutsche Ornithologen-Gesellschaft; British Ornithologists Union; American Ornithologists Union. Address: Institut für Vogelforschung, Vogelwarte Helgoland, Arbeitsgruppe Populationsökologie Braunschweig, Bauernstr 14, D-38162 Cremlingen-Weddel, Germany. E-mail: w.winkel@tu-bs.de

**WINKELMAN Joseph William,** b. 20 September 1941, Keokuk, Iowa, USA. Artist; Printmaker. m. Harriet Lowell Belin, 2 daughters. Education: BA, English, University of the South, Sewanee, Tennessee, 1964; CFA, University of Oxford, 1971. Appointments: President, Royal Society of Painter-Printmakers, 1989-95; Artist-in-Residence, St John's College, Oxford, 2004. Honours: Honorary Member: Royal Watercolour Society, Oxford Art Society, Printmaker's Council of Great Britain. Memberships: Royal Society of Painter-Printmakers; Royal West of England Academy. Address: The Hermitage, 69 Old High Street, Headington, Oxford OX3 9HT, England.

**WINNER Michael Robert,** b. 30 October 1935, London, England. Producer; Director; Writer. Education: Downing College, Cambridge University. Appointments: Film Critic and Fleet Street Journalist; Contributor to: The Spectator, Daily Express, London Evening Standard; Columnist, The Sunday Times, The News of the World; Panellist on Any Questions, BBC Radio; Presenter, Michael Winner's True Crimes; Entered motion pictures, 1956 as Screen Writer, Assistant Director, Editor; Member of the Council and Trustee, Director's Guild of Great Britain, 1983-; Founder and Chairman, The Police Memorial Trust, 1984; Director, Scimitar Films Ltd. Films include: Play it Cool, 1962; The Cool Mikado, 1962; West Eleven, 1963; The System, 1963; You Must Be Joking, 1965; The Jokers, 1966; I'll Never Forget What's 'isname, 1967; Hannibal Brooks, 1968; The Games, 1969; Lawman, 1970; The Nightcomers, 1971; Chato's Land, 1971; The Mechanic, 1972; Scorpio, 1972; The Stone Killer, 1973; Death Wish, 1974; Won Ton Ton The Dog That Saved Hollywood, 1975; The Sentinel, 1976; The Big Sleep, 1977; Firepower, 1978; Death Wish Two, 1981; The Wicked Lady 1982; Scream for Help, 1984; Death Wish Three, 1985; Appointment with Death, 1988; A Chorus of Disapproval, 1989; Bullseye!, 1990; Dirty Weekend, 1993; Parting Shots, 1997; Actor: For the Greater Good, 1990; Decadence, 1993; Radio Play: The Flump, 2000; Theatre Productions: The Tempest, Wyndhams, 1974; A Day in Hollywood A Night in Ukraine, 1978; TV: Starring in and/or directing commercials including: Esure Insurance; Kenco, Doritos, Books for Schools. Publications: Winner's Dinners, 1999, revised edition, 2000; Winner Guide, 2002; Biography: Winner Takes All, 2004. Honour: MA (Cantab). Address: 219 Kensington High Street, London W8 6BD, England. E-mail: winner@ftech.co.uk

**WINSLET Kate,** b. October 1975, Reading, England. Actress. m. (1) Jim Threapleton, 1998, divorced 2001, 1 daughter, (2) Sam Mendes, 2003, 1 son. Education: Theatre School, Maidenhead. Creative Works: TV appearances: Get Back; Casualty; Anglo-Saxon Attitudes; Films: A Kid in King Arthur's Court; Heavenly Creatures, 1994; Sense and Sensibility, 1996; Jude, 1996; Hamlet, 1996; Titanic, 1997; Hideous Kinky, 1997; Holy Smoke, 1998; Quills, 1999; Enigma, 2000; Iris, 2001; The Life of David Gale, 2002; Plunge: The Movie, 2003; Eternal Sunshine of the Spotless Mine, 2004; Finding Neverland, 2004; Pride (voice), 2004: Romance & Cigarettes, 2005. Honours include: BAFTA Award; Best European Actress, European Film Academy, 1998; Film Actress of the Year, Variety Club of Great Britain, 1998.

**WINTERS Shelley,** b. 18 August 1922, St Louis, USA. Actress. m. (1) Vittorio Gassmann, 1 daughter, (2) Anthony Franciosa, 1957, divorced 1960. Education: Wayne University. Creative Works: Films include: A Thousand and One Nights; A Place in the Sun; Playgirl; Executive Suite; The Diary of Anne Frank, 1958; Odds Against Tomorrow; Let No Man Write My Epitaph; Lolita, 1962; Wives and Lovers, 1963; The Balcony, 1964; A House is Not A Home, 1964; A Patch of Blue, 1965; Time of Indifference, 1965; Alfie, 1965; The Moving Target, 1965; The Poseidon Adventure, 1972; Cleopatra Jones, 1973; Blume in Love, 1974; Whoever Slew Auntie Roo, 1974; Heaven Save Us From Our Friends, 1975; Diamonds, 1975; That Lucky Touch, 1975; Next Stop Greenwich Village, 1976; The Tenant, 1976; Pete's Dragon, 1977; The Magician, 1979; The Visitor, 1980; Over the Brooklyn Bridge, 1983; The Delta Force, 1985; Awakenings, 1990; Stepping Out, 1991; The Pickle, 1996; Portrait of a Lady, 1996; Gideon's Webb, 1998; La Bamba, 1999; Stage appearances include: A Hatful of Rain, 1955; Girls of Summer, 1957; The Night of the Iguana; Cages; Who's Afraid of Virginia Wolf?; Minnie's Boys; Marlon Brando: The Wild One, 1996; TV appearances include: The Vamp, 1972-73; Roseanne (TV series). Publications: Shelley also Known as Shirley (autobiography); One Night Stands of a Noisy Passenger (play), 1971; Shelley II: The Middle of My Century, 1989. Honours include: Academy Awards; Emmy Award, Best Actress, 1964; Monte Carlo Golden Nymph Award, 1964; International TV Award, Cannes Festival, 1965. Address: c/o Jack Gilliardi, ICM, 8942 Wilshire Boulevard, Beverly Hills, CA 90211, USA.

**WINTERTON Rosie,** b. 10 August 1958, Leicester, England. Member of Parliament. Education: BA (Hons), History 2:1, University of Hull, England, 1979. Appointments: Assistant to John Prescott MP, 1980-86; Parliamentary Officer, London Borough of Southwark, 1986-88; Parliamentary Officer, Royal College of Nursing, 1988-90; Managing Director, Connect Public Affairs, 1990-94; Head of Private office of John Prescott MP, Deputy Leader of the Labour Party; Entered Parliament as MP for Doncaster Central, 1997; Elected representative of Parliamentary Labour Party on the National Policy Forum of the Labour Party, 1997-2001; Chair of Transport and General Worker's Parliamentary Group, 1998-99; Leader of Leadership Campaign Team, 1998-99; Member on Standing Committee of Transport Bill, 2000; Intelligence and Security Committee, 2000; Member on Standing Committee of Finance Bill, 2000; Standing Committee of the Local Government Finance (Supplementary Credit Approvals) Bill and the Regional Development Agencies Bill; Member of the Labour Party Strategic Campaign; Parliamentary Secretary, Lord Chancellor's Office, 2001. Address: Guildhall Advice Centre, Old Guildhall Yard, Doncaster, South Yorkshire, DN1 1OW, England.

**WINWOOD Stephen Lawrence,** Birmingham, England. Musician; Composer. m. Eugenia Crafton, 1987, 1 son, 3 daughters. Career: Singer, Musician, Spencer Davis Group, 1964-67, Traffic, 1967-74, Blind Faith, 1970; Solo Artist, 1974-; Director, F S Ltd. Creative Works: Albums include: Arc of a Diver, 1980; Talking Back to the Night, 1982; Back in the Highlife, 1986; Roll With It, 1988; Chronicles, 1991; Refugees of the Heart, 1991; Traffic, Far From Home, 1994; Junction 7, 1997. Honours: 14 Gold Records; 4 Platinum Record Awards; 2 Grammy Awards. Address: c/o Trinity Cottage, Tirley, Gloucs GL19 4EU, England.

**WIRASINHA Anushka Hemamali,** Company Director; Computer Science Author and Researcher. Education: BSc (Hons), Economics, London School of Economics; Special Studies in Administration and Management, Harvard University, USA. Appointments: Junior Management Executive, Ceylon Shipping Lines, Sri Lanka; Assisting Lecturer, Micro Computers and Information Technology, Harvard University, USA, 1996-98; Technical Advisor/Computer Consultant, Ceylon Shipping Lines, Sri Lanka, 1998-2002; Computer Science Author, Prentice Hall, India, 2001-; Science Fiction Author, Publish America, 2004-; Director, Computer Literate Generation (Pvt) Ltd. Publications: Visually Learn PC; On Your Marks Net Set Go! Surviving in an E-World; Flash in a Flash: Web Development; Microchip Militant; Spread the Word Around: MS Word; Computer Tutor; Study Buddy; Who Owns the Alphabet?; Java Essence; Digital Art. Honours: Best Selling Author, India Times; Sigma Xi Honor Society; Who's Who Among Young Asian Americans; International Who's Who of Professionals; International Who's Who of Information Technology; First Sri Lankan to put forth varied combination of computer titles; Originator, Author, computer book in English, published in Sri Lanka; Initiator, introduction of Digital Art into Sri Lankan schools; Nominee, Marquis Who's Who in Science and Engineering, 2005-06. Address: 950 Massachusetts Avenue #401, Cambridge, MA 02139, USA. E-mail: anushkawirasinha@msn.com

**WITTICH John Charles Bird, (Charles Bird),** b. 18 February 1929, London, England. Retired Librarian; Writer. m. June Rose Taylor, 10 July 1954, 1 son, 1 daughter. Education: BA, 1951. Publications: Off Beat Walks In London, 1969, 2001; London Curiosities, 1975, 1997; London Villages, 1976, new expanded edition, 1992; London Street Names, 1976, 2003; Guide and Short History of St John's Church Hyde Park Crescent, 1980; London Parks and Squares, 1981; Catholic London, 1988; Churches, Cathedrals and Chapels, 1989, Guide to Bayswater, 1989, 2005; Exploring Cathedrals, 1992, 1996; Hidden World of Regent's Park, 1992, 2002; History and Guide to St Magnus the Martyr Church, Lower Thames Street, London EC3, 1994, new revised edition, 2005; Curiosities of Surrey, 1994; Explorers' London, 1995; Spot-it Guide to London, 1995; Walks Round Haunted London, 1996; London Bus Top Tourist, 1997; History and Guide: St Vedast-alias-Foster Church, London, EC2, 1999; Curiosities of London and Westminster, 2003; In preparation: Clerks' Churches (The 150 Churches of the Parish Clerks' Company); Sites of London; A Guide to Literary London; A Postcode Guide to Haunted London; Walks through London's Mews, Parks and Squares; Curiosities of the City of Canterbury, 2006; Contributions to: Periodicals and journals. Memberships: Life Member, City Livery Club; Life Member, Royal Society of St George, City of London Branch; Life Member, Royal Photographic Society; Fellow, Royal Society of Arts; Fellow, Life Member, Ancient Monuments Society; Member, Institute of Tourist Guiding; Liveryman Emeritus, Worshipful Company of Woolmen of the City of London; Liveryman of the Worshipful Company of Musicians; Past Master Emeritus of the Worshipful

Company of Parish Clerks of the City of London; Life Member, National Art Fund Collection; Member, Minor Order of the Readers of the Church of England, 1980-2005, Reader Emeritus, 2005-. Address: 88 Woodlawn Street, Whitstable, Kent CT5 1HH, England.

**WITTMANN-LIEBOLD Brigitte,** b. 28 March 1931, Gotha, Thüringen, Germany. Scientist. m. Heinz-Günter Wittmann, 1 son, 1 daughter. Education: Diploma in Chemistry, University of Tübingen, 1958; Dr rer nat, Chemistry, Biochemistry, University of Munich, 1959; Professor, Free University Berlin, 1984. Appointments: Scientific Assistant, Max Planck Institute of Biochemistry, Munich, 1960, Max Planck Institute of Biology, Tübingen, 1961- 1967; Group Leader, Max Planck Institute of Molecular Genetics, Berlin, 1967- 1991; Head of Protein Chemistry, Max Delbrück Centre, Berlin-Buch, 1992-2000. Publications: More than 400 articles. Honours: Award, Minister of Technology, Germany; Analytica Award, 1986; Edman Award, Sweden, 1991; Beckurts Award, Munich, 1997; Innovation Award, Berlin-Brandenburg 1997. Memberships: VAAM, Germany; German Society of Cell Biology; German Society of Biochemistry and Molecular Biology. Address: Wittmann Institute for Technology and Analysis of Biomolecules, WITA GmbH, Warthestrasse 21, D-14513 Teltow/Berlin, Germany. E-mail: wittmannliebold@wita.de Website: www.wita.de

**WOGAN Michael Terence (Terry),** b. 3 August 1938, Ireland. Broadcaster. m. Helen Joyce, 1965, 2 sons, 1 daughter. Education: Crescent College, Limerick; Belvedere College, Dublin. Appointments: Announcer, RTE, 1963, Senior Announcer, 1964-66; Various programmes for BBC Radio, 1965-67; Late Night Extra, BBC Radio, 1967-69; The Terry Wogan Show, BBC Radio 1, 1969-72, BBC Radio 2, 1972-84, 1993; Wake Up to Wogan, BBC Radio 2, 1995-. Creative Works: TV shows include: Lunchtime with Wogan, ATV; BBC: Come Dancing; Song for Europe; The Eurovision Song Contest; Children in Need; Wogan's Guide to the BBC; Blankety Blank; Wogan; Terry Wogan's Friday Night; Auntie's Bloomers; Wogan's Web; Points of View, 2000-01. Publications: Banjaxed, 1979; The Day Job, 1981; To Horse, To Horse, 1982; Wogan on Wogan, 1987; Wogan's Ireland, 1988; Bumper Book of Togs, 1995; Is It Me?, autobiography, 2000. Honours include: Radio Award, 1980; Radio Industry Award, 1982, 1985, 1987; Carl Alan Award, 3 times; Variety Club of Great Britain Special Award, 1982; Showbusiness Personality, 1984; Radio Personality of Last 21 years, Daily Mail National Radio Awards, 1988; Sony Radio Award, Barcelona Olympics, 1993; Best Breakfast Show, 1994. Address: c/o Jo Gurnett, 2 New Kings Road, London SW6 4SA, England.

**WOHLLEBEN Rudolf,** b. 4 June 1936, Bad Kreuznach, Germany. Retired Telecommunications and Antenna Engineer. Writer. m. Rosemarie, 2 sons, 1 stepson, 1 stepdaughter. Education: BSEE, University of Karlsruhe, 1957; MSEE, Dipl-Ing, Technical University, Munich; Dr Ing, 1969; RWTH, Aachen. Appointments: Lecturer, Radar, Antennas, Radioastronomy, Microwaves, University of Kaiserslautern, Germany, 1980-; Forschungsinst f HF-Physik, Rolandseck, 1961-64; Institut f Techn Elektronik, RWTH Aachen, 1964-70; Max-Planck Institute fuer Radioastronomie, Electronics Division, Bonn, 1971-99; Retired, 1999-; Writer, 1999-. Publications: 70 articles in professional journals; 8 books, including Interferometry in Radioastronomy and Radar Techniques, 1991; Fruehe Spaetlese, poems, 1997; (The Poet) Stefan George, for enthusiasts and scholars (in German), 2004. Honours: Sport Medal, town of Bonn, 2002. Memberships include: Informationstechnische Gesellschaft, Germany;

Verband deutschen Schriftsteller, Stefan-George-Gesellschaft/ Bingen, 4 WSC-Corps; Chairman, Verein für corpsstudent. Geschichtsforschung; Chairman, Verein d Freunde u Foerderer d Wachenburg b Weinheim. Address: Kurhausstr 1A, D-55543 Bad Kreuznach, Germany. E-mail: r.wohlleben@freenet.de

**WOLFE Tom, (Thomas Kennerly Wolfe Jr)**, b. 2 March 1930, Richmond, Virginia, USA. Writer; Journalist; Artist. m. Sheila Berger, 1 son, 1 daughter. Education: AB, Washington and Lee University, 1951; PhD, American Studies, Yale University, 1957. Appointments: Reporter, Springfield Union, Massachusetts, 1956-59; Reporter and Latin American Correspondent, Washington Post, 1959-62; Writer, New York Sunday Magazine, 1962-66; City Reporter, New York Herald Tribune, 1962-66; Magazine Writer, New York World Journal Tribune, 1966-67; Contributing Editor, New York magazine, 1968-76, Esquire magazine, 1977-; Contributing Artist, Harper's magazine, 1978-81. Publications: The Kandy-Kolored Tangerine-Flake Streamline Baby, 1965; The Electric Kool-Aid Acid Test, 1968; The Pump House Gang, 1968; Radical Chic and Mau-mauing the Flak Catchers, 1970; The Painted Word, 1975; Mauve Gloves and Madmen, Clutter and Vine, 1976; The Right Stuff, 1979; In Our Time, 1980; From Bauhaus to Our House, 1981; The Purple Decades: A Reader, 1982; The Bonfire of the Vanities, 1987; A Man in Full, 1998; Hooking Up, 2000; I am Charlotte Simmons, 2004. Contributions to: Newspapers and magazines. Honours: Various honorary doctorates; American Book Award, 1980; Harold D Vursell Memorial Award, American Academy of Arts and Letters, 1980; John Dos Passos Award, 1984; Theodore Roosevelt Medal, Theodore Roosevelt Association, 1990; St Louis Literary Award, 1990; Membership: American Academy of Arts and Letters. Address: c/o Janklow & Nesbit Associates, 445 Park Avenue, New York, NY 10022, USA.

**WOLFERS Michael**, b. 28 September 1938, London, England. Writer; Translator. Education: Wadham College, Oxford, 1959-62; South Bank Polytechnic, 1990-91. Appointments: Journalist, The Times, London, 1965-72; Visiting Senior Lecturer, African Politics and Government, University of Juba, 1979-82. Publications: Black Man's Burden Revisited, 1974; Politics in the Organisation of African Unity, 1976; Luandino Vieira: The Real Life of Domingos Xavier, 1978; Poems from Angola, 1979; Samir Amin, Delinking: Towards a Polycentric World, 1990; Hamlet and Cybernetics, 1991; Thomas Hodgkin: Letters from Africa, 2000. Contributions to: Numerous publications. Memberships: Royal Institute of International Affairs; Gyosei Institute of Management. Address: 66 Roupell Street, London SE1 8SS, England.

**WOLFF Tobias J A**, b. 19 June 1945, Birmingham, USA. Writer. m. Catherine Dolores Spohn, 1975, 2 sons, 1 daughter. Education: BA, Oxford University, 1972; MA, Stanford University, 1975; LHD (hon), Santa Clara University, 1996. Appointments: US Army, 1964-68; Reporter, Washington Post, 1972; Writing Fellow, Stanford University, 1975-78; Writer-in-Residence, Arizona State University, 1978-80, Syracuse University, 1980-97, Stanford University, 1997-; Director, creative writing programme, 2000-02. Publications: Hunters in the Snow, 1981; The Barracks Thief, 1984; Back in the World, 1985; This Boy's Life, 1989; In Pharaoh's Army: Memories of a Lost War, 1994; The Vintage Book of Contemporary American Short Stories, 1994; The Best American Short Stories, 1994; The Night in Question, 1996; Old School, 2003. Honours include: Guggenheim Fellow, 1983; National Endowment Fellow, 1978, 1984; PEN/Faulkner Award for Fiction, 1985; Rea Award, 1989; Whiting Foundation Award, 1989; Los Angeles Times Book Prize, 1989; Ambassador Book Award, 1990; Lila Wallace/

Readers Digest Award, 1993; Esquire-Volvo-Waterstone Award for Non-Fiction, 1994; Exceptional Achievement Award, American Academy of Arts and Letters, 2001; Fairfax Prize for Literature, 2003; PEN/Faulkner Award for Fiction nominee, 2004. Address: English Department, Stanford University, CA 94305-2087, USA.

**WONDER Stevie (Steveland Morris)**, b. 13 May 1950, Saginaw, Michigan, USA. Singer; Musician; Composer. m. Syreeta Wright, 1970, divorced 1972, (2) Yolanda Simmons, 3 children. Education: Michigan School for the Blind, 1963-68; Self-taught, harmonica and piano. Appointments: Motown Recording Artist, 1963-70; Founder, President, Black Bull Music Inc; Founder, Wonderdirection Records Inc and Taurus Productions; Numerous concerts worldwide. Creative Works: Fingertips Part 2, 1963; Uptight (Everything's Alright), 1966; I Was Made to Love Her, 1967; For Once in My Life, 1968; My Cherie Amour, 1969; Yester-Me, Yester-You, Yesterday, 1969; Signed Sealed Delivered I'm Yours, 1970; Superstition, 1973; You Are the Sunshine of My Life, 1973; Higher Ground, 1974; Living For the City, 1974; You Haven't Done Nothin', 1974; Boogie On Reggae Woman, 1975; I Wish, 1977; Sir Duke, 1977; Master Blaster, 1980; Lately, 1981; Happy Birthday, 1981; Ebony and Ivory, 1982; I Just Called To Say I Love You, 1984; Part-Time Lover, 1985; Don't Drive Drunk, 1985; Albums include: Music of My Mind, 1972; Innervisions, 1973; Songs in the Key of Life, 1976; Journey Through the Secret Life of Plants, 1979; Hotter than July, 1980; Original Musiquarium, 1981; Woman in Red, 1984; In Square Circle, 1986; Characters, 1987; Jungle Fever, 1991; Inner Peace, 1995; Motown Legends, 1995. Honours: Edison Award, 1973; Songwriters Hall of Fame, 1983; Numerous American Music Awards; Oscar, Best Song, 1984; Gold Ticket, Madison Square Garden, 1986; Soul Train Heritage Award, 1987; Rock'n'Roll Hall of Fame, 1989; Nelson Mandella Courage Award, 1991; IAAAM Diamond Award for Excellence, 1991; Lifetime Achievement Award, National Academy of Songwriters, 1992; NAACP Image Award, 1992; Numerous Grammy, Charity and Civil Rights Awards. Address: c/o Steveland Morris Music, 4616 W Magnolia Blvd, Burbank, CA 91505, USA.

**WONG Po-Keung**, b. 17 August 1954, Hong Kong. University Teacher. m. Lai-hor Lee, 1 son, 2 daughters. Education: BSc, Honours, Biology, 1977, M Phil, Biology and Microbiology, 1979, The Chinese University of Hong Kong; PhD, Microbiology, University of California, Davis, USA, 1983. Appointments: Lecturer, 1986-94, Senior Lecturer, 1994-96, Associate Professor, 1996-97, Professor, 1997-, The Chinese University of Hong Kong. Publications: More than 100 articles in journals of environmental science and technology. Honours: Council Member, HKQAA; Chairman, ISO 1400 Technical Committee, Hong Kong; Editor-in-Chief, Journal of Environmental Sciences. Memberships: Chartered Institution of Water and Environmental Management; American Chemical Society; International Water Association; Society of Toxicology. Address: Department of Biology, The Chinese University of Hong Kong, Shatin, NT, Hong Kong SAR, China. E-mail: pkwong@cuhk.edu.hk

**WOO John**, b. 1948, Guangzhou, China. Film Director. Education: Matteo Ricci College, Hong Kong. Appointments: Production Assistant, Assistant Director, Cathay Film Co, 1971; Assistant Director to Zhang Che, Shaw Bros. Creative Works: Films: The Young Dragons, 1973; The Dragon Tamers; Countdown in Kung Fu; Princess Chang Ping; From Riches to Rags; Money Crazy; Follow the Star; Last Hurrah for Chivalry; To Hell with the Devil; Laughing Times; Plain Jane to the Rescue; Sunset Warriors (Heroes Shed No Tears); The Time

You Need a Friend; Run Tiger Run; A Better Tomorrow; A Better Tomorrow II; Just Heroes; The Killer; Bullet in the Head; Once a Thief; Hard Boiled; Hard Target; Broken Arrow; Face/Off; Kings Ransom; Mission Impossible II; The Last Word (producer); Windtalkers, 2000; The Hire: Hostage, 2002; Red Skies (producer), 2002; Paycheck, 2003; Bullet Proof Monk (producer), 2003. Address: c/o MGM Studios Inc, 2500 Broadway Street, Santa Monica, CA 90404, USA.

**WOOD Charles (Gerald),** b. 6 August 1932, St Peter Port, Guernsey, Channel Islands. Playwright. Education: Birmingham College of Art, 1948-50. Publications: Prisoner and Escort, 1961; Cockade, 1963; Tie Up the Ballcock, 1964; Don't Make Me Laugh, 1965; Meals on Wheels, 1965; Fill the Stage with Happy Hours, 1966; Dingo, 1967; Labour, 1968; H, Being Monologues at Front of Burning Cities, 1979; Collier's Wood, 1970; Welfare, 1971; Veterans; or, Hair in the Gates of the Hellespont, 1972; The Can Opener, 1974; Jingo, 1975; The Script, 1976; Has "Washington" Legs?, 1978; The Garden, 1982; Red Star, 1984; Across for the Garden of Allah, 1986; The Plantagenets (after Shakespeare), 1988; Man, Beast and Virtue (after Pirandello), 1989; The Giants of the Mountain (Pirandello), 1991; The Tower (Dumas), 1993. Screenplays: The Knack, 1965; Help (co-author), 1965; How I Won the War, 1967; The Charge of the Light Brigade, 1968; The Long Day's Dying, 1968; The Bed-Sitting Room (co-author), 1968; Fellini Satyricon, 1969; Cuba, 1980; Vile Bodies, 1981; Tumbledown, 1988; Iris (co-author), 2002. Television scripts. Honours: WGGB Award, 1965; Evening Standard, 1963, 1972; Fellow of the Royal Society of Literature, 1984; Prix Italia, RAI, 1988; British Academy for Film and Television Arts Award, 1988; RTS Award, 1988; Humanities Award, 2002. Address: Long Barn, Sibford Gower, Near Banbury, Oxfordshire OX15 5RT, England.

**WOOD David Bernard,** b. 21 February 1944, Sutton, England. Playwright; Director; Actor; Magician. m. Jacqueline Stanbury, 2 daughters. Education: Chichester High School for Boys; BA (Hons) in English, Worcester College, Oxford, 1963-66. Appointments: Freelance actor, playwright, director, magician, children's book author. Publications: Many plays; Children's books. Honours: OBE, 2004; Honorary MA, University of Chichester, 2005. Memberships: Society of Authors; British Actors' Equity; The Magic Circle (MIMC); International Brotherhood of Magicians. Address: c/o Casarotto Ramsay Ltd, National House, 66 Wardour Street, London W1V 4ND, England. E-mail: agents@casarotto.uk.com

**WOOD Elijah,** b. 28 January 1981, Ceder Rapids, Iowa, USA. Actor. Education: Avent Studios, Modelling school. Films include: Back to the Future Part II, 1989; Internal Affairs, 1990; The Adventures of Huck Finn, 1993; The War, 1994; The Ice Storm, 1997; Oliver Twist, 1997; Deep Impact, 1998; The Faculty, 1998; Chains of Fools, 2000; The Lord of the Rings: The Fellowship of the Ring, 2001; The Adventures of Tom Thumb and Thumbelina, 2002; The Lord of the Rings: The Two Towers, 2002; The Lord of the Rings: The Return of the King, 2003; Eternal Sunshine of the Spotless Mind, 2004. TV Appearances include: Frasier, 1994; Adventures from the Book of Virtues, 1996; SM:TV Live, 2001; The Osbournes, 2002; The Buzz, 2002; Player$, 2002; The Tonight Show with Jay Leno, 2003; Saturday Night Live, 2003; NY Graham Norton, 2004; King of the Hill (voice), 2004. Honours: Young Artist Award, 1991; Saturn Award, 1994; Young Star Award, 1998; Empire Award, 2002; Young Hollywood Award, 2002. MTV Movie Award, 2003; National Board of Review, USA, 2003; Saturn Award, 2004; Broadcast Film Critics Association Award, 2004; Screen Actors Guild Award, 2004; Visual Effects Society

Awards, 2003. Address: c/o Nicole David 151 S El Camino Drive, Beverly Hills, CA 90212-2775, USA.

**WOOD James Albert,** b. 9 November 1949, Enterprise, Oregon, USA. Professor. m. Maritza Alvarez, 1 daughter. Education: BS, David Lipscomb University, 1975; BA, MA, Southern Oregon University, 1979; EdD, Texas A&M University, 1986; Postgraduate Studies, University of Tennessee and Sul Ross State University Rio Grande College. Appointments: Graduate Teaching Assistant, Texas A&M University at Kingsville, and University of Tennessee; Spanish ESL Teacher, Sheldon ISD, Texas, Galena Park, ISD, Texas, Rice Consolidated ISD, Texas, Jefferson Co ISD, Madras, Oregon; Senior Program Development Specialist, University of Oklahoma; Full Professor, Sul Ross State University Rio Grande College. Publications: 41 articles in refereed journals. Honour: Dean's Grant, Bilingual Fellowship; Listed in national and international biographical dictionaries. Memberships: National Association for Bilingual Education; Texas Association for Bilingual Education; TESOL; ASCD; TTE; Life Member, Non-Commissioned Officers Association; American Legion; Life Member, VFW; Masonic Lodge 472. Address: PO Box 1415, Uvalde, TX 78802, USA. E-mail: jawood@sulross.edu

**WOOD Mark William,** b. 28 March 1952. Chief Executive. m. Helen Lanzer, 1 son, 1 daughter. Education: BA (Honours), University of Leeds; MA, Warwick University; Certificate of Education, Oxford University. Appointments: Correspondent (Vienna, East Berlin, Moscow), 1977-85, Chief Correspondent (West Germany), 1985-87, Editor (Europe), 1987-89, Editor-in-Chief, 1989-2000, Head, Strategic Media Investments and Alliances, 2000-02, Reuters; Director, Reuters Holdings, 1990-96; Chairman, Reuters Television, 1992-2002; Director, 1993-, Chairman, 1998-, Chief Executive, 2003-, Independent Television News. Memberships: Member, 1995-2000, Vice Chairman, 1998-99, Chairman, 1999-2000, Library and Information Commission; Commonwealth Press Union, 1996-2000; Rathenau Gesellschaft, Germany, 1999-; Board Member, 2000-, Chairman, 2003-, MLA, Council for Museums, Archives and Libraries. Address: ITN, 200 Grays Inn Road, London WC1X 8XZ, England. Website: www.itn.co.uk

**WOOD Renate,** b. 5 February 1938, Berlin, Germany. Poet. m. William B Wood, 30 June 1961, 2 sons. Education: PhD, Stanford University, 1970; MFA Program for Writers, Warren Wilson College, North Carolina, 1985. Appointments: Lecturer, University of Colorado, Boulder, 1985-91; Faculty, Program for Writers, Warren Wilson College, North Carolina. Publications: Points of Entry, 1981; Raised Underground, 1991; The Patience of Ice, 2000. Contributions to: American Poetry Review; Massachusetts Review; New England Review; TriQuarterly; Virginia Review; Seneca Review; Prairie Schooner; Ploughshares. Honours: Nominee, Colorado Governor's Award for Excellence in the Arts, 1982; Grant, Colorado Council on the Arts, 1995. Memberships: Associated Writing Programs; Academy of American Poets. Address: 1900 King Avenue, Boulder, CO 80302, USA.

**WOOD Roger Holmes,** b. 26 April 1920, Corning, New York, USA. Educator; Financial Planner. m. Phyllis Anderson, 2 sons, 1 daughter. Education: AB, University of Pittsburgh, 1944; MS, Columbia University Graduate School of Journalism, 1945; MA, San Francisco State University, 1951; PhD, International College, 1978; American College CLU, ChFC, College of Financial Planning, CFP. Appointments: Educator, schools and colleges, 1947-; Agent, New York Life, 1954-; Journalist, 1944-47. Publications: When Tankers Collide, novel; A Forgiving at Assisi, autobiography; Life is a Four Letter Word. Memberships include: Numerous professional, historical, genealogical and learned affiliations, including, Sons of the American Revolution; Society of Genealogists, London; First Families of Ohio; San Francisco Estate Planning Council; Society of Financial Service Professionals; Chartered Life Underwriter (CLU); Chartered Financial Consultant (ChFC); College for Financial Planning; Certified Financial Planner (CFP); Accredited Estate Planner (AEP). Address: 65 Capay Circle, San Francisco, CA 94080, USA.

**WOOD Ronnie (Ronald),** b. 1 June 1947, England. Musician. m. (1) 1 son, (2) Jo Howard, 1985, 1 son, 1 daughter. Appointments: Guitarist, Jeff Beck Group, 1968-69, The Faces, 1969-75, The Rolling Stones, 1975-. Creative Works: Albums with Jeff Beck Group: Truth, 1968; Beck-Ola, 1969; with The Faces: First Step, 1970; Long Player, 1971; A Nod's As Good As A Wink...To A Blind Horse, 1971; Ooh La La, 1973; Coast to Coast Overtures and Beginners, 1974; with The Rolling Stones: Black and Blue, 1976; Love You Live, 1977; Some Girls, 1978; Emotional Rescue, 1980; Tattoo You, 1981; Still Life, 1981; Undercover, 1983; Rewind 1971-1984, 1984; Dirty Work, 1986; Steel Wheels, 1989; Flashpoint, 1991; Voodoo Lounge, 1994; Solo albums including: Slide on This, 1992; Films include: Let's Spend the Night Together, 1983; Flashpoint, 1991; Also played with Bo Diddley, Rod Stewart, Jerry Lee Lewis. Address: c/o Monroe Sounds, 5 Church Row, Wandsworth Plain, London SW18 1ES, England. Website: www.ronniewood.com

**WOODFORD Peggy,** b. 19 September 1937, Shillong, Assam, India. Writer. m. Walter Aylen, 1 April 1967, 3 daughters. Education: MA (Hons) English, St Anne's College, Oxford. Appointments: Research Assistant, BBC TV, 1962-64; Senior Tutor, Padworth College, Berkshire, 1965-68; Writer. Publications: Abraham's Legacy, 1963; Please Don't Go, 1972; Backwater War, 1975; The Real Thing, 1977; Rise of the Raj, 1978; See You Tomorrow, 1979; You Can't Keep Out the Darkness, 1980; The Girl With a Voice, 1981; Love Me, Love Rome, 1984; Misfits, 1984; Monster in Our Midst, 1987; Schubert, 2nd edition, 1989; Out of the Sun, 1990; Mozart, 2nd edition, 1990; Blood and Mortar, 1994; Cupid's Tears, 1995; On the Night, 1997; Jane's Story, 1998; One Son is Enough, 2006. Honours: Italian Government Research Scholarship, 1959-60. Address: c/o Laura Morris Literary Agency, 21 Highshore Road, London SE15 5AA, England.

**WOODRING Carl,** b. 29 August 1919, Terrell, Texas, USA. Educator. m. Mary Frances Ellis, 24 December 1942, deceased 2003. Education: BA, 1940, MA, 1942, Rice University; AM, 1947, PhD, 1949, Harvard University. Publications: Victorian Samplers, 1952; Virginia Woolf, 1966; Wordsworth, 1965, revised edition, 1968; Politics in English Romantic Poetry, 1970; Nature into Art, 1989; Table Talk of Samuel Taylor Coleridge (editor), 1990; Columbia History of British Poetry (editor), 1993; Columbia Anthology of British Poetry (co-editor), 1995; Literature: An Embattled Profession, 1999; Lucky Thirteen: USS Hopkins, DD 249, DMS 13 (co-author), 2000. Contributions to: Western Review; Virginia Quarterly Review; PMLA; Keats-Shelley Journal; Comparative Drama. Honours: Guggenheim Fellowship, 1955; American Council of Learned Societies, Fellow, 1965; Phi Beta Kappa Gauss Prize, 1971; PKB Visiting Scholar, 1974-75; Senior Mellon Fellow, 1987-88. Memberships: American Academy of Arts and Sciences; International Association of University Professors of English; Grolier Club. Address: 1034 Liberty Park Drive, Austin, TX 78746, USA.

**WOODS James,** b. 18 April 1947, Vernal, Utah, USA. Actor. m. (1) Kathryn Greko, 1980, (2) Sarah Owen, 1989. Education:

University of California, Los Angeles; Massachusetts Institute of Technology. Creative Works: Films include: The Visitors, 1971; The Way We Were, 1972; The Gambler, 1974; Distance, 1975; Alex and the Gipsy, 1976; The Choirboys, 1977; The Onion Field, 1979; Black Marble, 1980; Fast Walking, 1982; Split Image, 1982; Videodrome, 1983; Once Upon a Time in America, 1984; Against All Odds, 1984; Joshua Then and Now, 1985; Best Seller, 1987; Cop, 1987; The Boost, 1989; True Believer, 1989; Immediate Family, 1989; Straight Talk, 1992; Diggstown Chaplin, 1992; The Gateway, 1994; Curse of the Starving Class, 1994; Casino, 1995; Nixon, 1996; Killer: A Journal of Murder, 1966; Ghosts of Mississippi, 1996; Hercules (voice), 1997; Contact, 1997; Vampires, 1998; True Crime, 1999; Virgin Suicides, 2000; Race to Space, 2001; John Q, 2001; Riding in Cars with Boys, 2001; Scary Movie 2, 2001; Rudy: The Rudy Giuliani Story, 2003; TV films include: Holocaust, 1978; Promise, 1986; My Name is Bill W, 1989; Next Door, 1994; The Summer of Ben Tyler, 1996; Dirty Pictures, 2000; Showtime, 2000. Honours include: Emmy Award, 1989. Address: c/o Guttman Associates, 118 South Beverly Drive, Beverly Hills, CA 90212, USA.

**WOODS Philip Wells,** b. 2 November 1931, Springfield, Massachusetts, USA. Musician (Alto Saxophone, Clarinet); Composer. m. Jill Goodwin, 20 December 1985, 1 son, 2 daughters. Education: Lessons with Harvey Larose, Springfield; Manhattan School, New York, 1948; Juilliard Conservatory, 1948-52. Career: Appearances with Benny Goodman, Buddy Rich, Quincy Jones, Thelonious Monk, Michel Legrand, Dizzy Gillespie and others; Appearing with own bands, Phil Woods Quintet, Phil Woods Little Big Band, Phil Woods Big Band; Featured, soundtracks of films including It's My Turn; Bandleader, Composer, Arranger and Soloist. Compositions include: Three Improvisations for Saxophone Quartet; Sonata for Alto and Piano; Rights of Swing; The Sun Suite; Fill the Woods with Light; I Remember; Deer Head Sketches. Recordings include: Images, with Michel Legrand, 1976; I Remember, Phil Woods Quartet, 1979; Dizzy Gillespie Meets Phil Woods Quintet; Evolution, Phil Woods Little Big Band; An Affair to Remember, Phil Woods Quintet; The Rev & I, with Johnny Griffin; Elsa, 1998; Porgy and Bess, 1999. Honours: Down Beat Magazine New Star Award, 1956, Critics' Poll Winner, alto saxophone, 1975-79, 1981-90, 1992, Readers' Poll Winner, alto saxophone, 1976-95; Grammy Award, Images with Michel Legrand, 1976, for More Live, Phil Woods Quartet, 1982, 1983; National Association of Jazz Educators Poll Winner, alto saxophone, 1987, Phil Woods Quintet, 1987; East Stroudsburg University Honorary Degree, 1994; Induction into American Jazz Hall of Fame, 1994; Officier des Arts et des Lettres; Beacon Jazz Award, 2001. Memberships: Delaware Water Gap Celebration of the Arts; Board of Directors, Al Cohn Memorial Jazz Collection; American Federation of Musicians; International Association of Jazz Educators. Address: Box 278, Delaware Water Gap, PA 18327, USA.

**WOODS Tiger (Eldrick),** b. 30 December 1975, Cypress, California, USA. Golfer. Education: Stanford University. Appointments: Winner: International Junior World Championship, 1984-91; National Youth Classic, 1990; US Junior Championships, 1991 (youngest winner), 1992, 1993; US Amateur Championships, 1994 (youngest winner), 1995, 1996; Las Vegas Invitational Competition, 1996; Walt Disney Classic, 1996; Honda Asian Classic, 1997; Mercedes Championships, 1997, 2000; US Masters, 1997 (youngest winner, broke records for lowest score and greatest margin of victory), 2001, 2002; Bell S Classic, 1998; US PGA Championship, 1999, 2000; National Car Rental Golf Classic, 1999; WGC American Express Championship, 1999; AT&T Pebble Beach National

Pro-Am, 2000; Bay Hill Invitational, 2000, 2001, 2002; US Open, 2000, 2002; British Open, 2000; Winner, numerous other titles; Contract with Nike, 1999-. Memberships: Member, US Team World Amateur Team Championship, 1994, US Walker Cup Team, 1995. Honours include: Golf World Player of the Year, 1992; Man of the Year, 1994; Sports Illustrated Sportsman of the Year, 1996, 2000; PGA Tour Player of the Year, 1997, 1999-2002. Address: PGA, PO Box 109601, 100 Avenue of the Champions, Palm Beach Gardens, FL 33418, USA.

**WOODWARD Edward,** b. 1 June 1930, Croydon, Surrey, England. Actor; Singer. m. (1) Venetia Mary Collett, 1952, 2 sons, 1 daughter, (2) Michele Dotrice, 1987, 1 daughter. Education: Kingston College; Royal Academy of Dramatic Art. Creative Works: Stage appearances include: Mercutio in Romeo and Juliet, Laertes in Hamlet, Stratford, 1958; Rattle of a Simple Man, Garrick, 1962; Two Cities (musical), 1968, Cyrano in Cyrano de Bergerac; Flamineo in The White Devil, National Theatre Company, 1971; The Wolf, Apollo, 1973; Male of the Species, Piccadilly, 1975; On Approval, Theatre Royal, Haymarket, 1976; The Dark Horse, Comedy, 1978; Beggar's Opera, 1980; The Assassin, 1982; Richard III, 1982; The Dead Secret, 1992; 3 productions, New York; Films include: Becket, 1966; The File on the Golden Goose, 1968; Hunted, 1973; Sitting Target, 1974; Young Winston, 1974; The Wicker Man, 1974; Stand Up Virgin Soldiers, 1977; Breaker Morant, 1980; The Appointment, 1981; Comeback, 1982; Merlin and the Sword, 1982; Champions, 1983; A Christmas Carol, 1984; King David, 1984; Uncle Tom's Cabin, 1989; Mister Johnson, 1990; Deadly Advice, 1993; A Christmas Reunion, 1994; Gulliver's Travels, 1995-96; The Abduction Club, 2002; Over 2000 TV productions including title role in Callan, 1966-71; The New Professionals, 1998-99; Night Flight, 2002; 12 LP records as singer, 3 as poetry; 14 talking book recordings. Honours: Numerous international and national acting awards.

**WOOLFSON Michael Mark,** b. 9 January 1927, London, England. Emeritus Professor. m. Margaret Frohlich, 2 sons, 1 daughter. Education: Jesus College, Oxford, 1944-47; UMIST, 1949-52; MA (Oxon), 1951; PhD (Man), 1952; DSc (Man), 1961. Appointments: 2nd Lieutenant, Royal Engineers, National Service, 1947-49; Research Fellow, Cambridge, 1952-54; ICI Fellow, Cambridge, 1954-55; Lecturer, 1955-61; Reader, 1961-65, UMIST; Professor of Theoretical Physics, York, 1964-94, Emeritus Professor, 1994-. Publications: Direct Methods in Crystallography, 1960; An Introduction to X-ray Crystallography, 1970, 2nd edition, 1997; The Origin of the Solar System: The Capture Theory, 1989; Physical and non-physical methods of solving crystal structures, 1995; An introduction to computer simulation, 1999; The origin and evolution of the Solar System, 2000; Planetary Science, 2002; Articles in learned journals. Honours: C.Phys, 1961; FRAS, 1966; FRS, 1984; Hughes Medal, Royal Society, 1986; Patterson Award, American Crystallographic Association, 1990; Gregori Aminoff Medal, Royal Swedish Academy, 1992; Dorothy Hodgkin Prize, British Crystallographic Association, 1997; Honorary Fellow, Jesus College, Oxford, 2001; Ewald Prize, International Union of Crystallography, 2002. Memberships: Institute of Physics; Royal Astronomical Society; Royal Society; Yorkshire Philosophical Society, President, 1985-99. Address: Physics Department, University of York, York YO10 5DD, England. E-mail: mmw1@york.ac.uk

**WOOSNAM Ian Harold,** b. 2 March 1958, England. Golfer. m. Glendryth Pugh, 1983, 1 son, 2 daughters. Education: St Martin's Modern School. Appointments: Professional Golfer, 1976-. Creative Works: Tournament Victories: News of the World Under-23 Matchplay, 1979; Cacharel Under-25

Championship, 1982; Swiss Open, 1982; Silk Cut Masters, 1983; Scandinavian Enterprise Open, 1984; Zambian Open, 1985; Lawrence Batley TPC, 1986; 555 Kenya Open, 1986; Hong Kong Open, 1987; Jersey Open, 1987; Cepsa Madrid Open, 1987; Bell's Scottish Open, 1987, 1990; Lancome Trophy, 1987; Suntory World Match-Play Championship, 1987, 1990; Volvo PGA Championship, 1988; Million Dollar Challenge, 1988; Carrolls Irish Open, 1988, 1989; Panasonic Euro Open, 1988; Welsh Pro Championship, 1988; American Express Mediterranean Open, 1990; Torras Monte Carlo Open, 1990; Epson Grand Prix, 1990; World Cup Team and Individual Winner, 1987; World Cup Individual Winner, 1991; US Masters, 1991; USF+G Lassic, 1991; PGA Grand Slam, 1991; Fujitsu Mediterranean Open, 1991; Torras Monte Carlo Open, 1991; European Monte Carlo Open, 1992; Lancome Trophy, 1993; Murphy's English Open, 1993; British Masters, 1994; Cannes Open, 1994; Heineken Classic, 1996; Scottish Open, 1996; German Open, 1996; Johnnie Walker Classic, 1996; Volvo PGA Championships, 1997; Hyundai Motor Masters, 1997; Ryder Cup Member, 1983, 1985, 1987, 1989, 1991, 1993, 1995, 1997; European Ryder Cup Team Captain, 2006; Numerous team events. Publications: Ian Woosnam's Golf Masterpieces (with Peter Grosvenor), 1991; Golf Made Simple: The Woosie Way, 1997. Membership: President, World Snooker Associate, 2000-. Address: cc/o IMG, McCormack House, Burlington Lane, London W4 2TH, England. Website: www.woosie.com

**WORSLEY, Sir (William) Marcus John,** b. 6 April 1925, Hovingham, Yorkshire, England. Retired Landowner. m. Bridget Assheton, deceased 2004, 3 sons, 1 daughter. Education: New College Oxford. Appointments: JP, 1957-90 ( Chairman, Malton Bench 1983-90); Member of Parliament for Keighley, 1959-64; Member of Parliament for Chelsea, 1966-74; Second Church Estates Commissioner, 1970-74; Church Commissioner, 1976-84; Deputy Chairman, National Trust, 1986-92; High Sheriff, North Yorkshire, 1982; Lord Lieutenant, North Yorkshire,1987-99. Address: Park House, Hovingham, York, YO62 4JZ, England.

**WORSLEY William Ralph,** 12 September 1956, York, England. Chartered Surveyor. m. Marie-Noelle Dreesmann, 1 son, 2 daughters. Education: Royal Agricultural College. Appointments: Chairman, Hovingham Estates; Vice-Chairman, Scarborough Building Society; Director, The Brunner Investment Trust plc; Member, Executive Committee, Country Land and Business Association; Member, Forestry Commission's Advisory Panel; Vice-Chairman, Howardian Hills AONB JAC. Honour: Fellow, Royal Institution of Chartered Surveyors. Address: Hovingham Hall, York, England. E-mail: office@hovingham.co.uk.

**WORSTHORNE Sir Peregrine (Gerard),** b. 22 December 1923, London, England. Journalist; Editor; Writer. m. (1) Claude Bertrand de Colasse, 1950, deceased 1990, 1 daughter, (2) Lady Lucinda Lambton, 1991. Education: BA, Peterhouse, Cambridge; Magdalen College, Oxford. Appointments: Sub-editor, Glasgow Herald, 1946; Editorial Staff, The Times, 1948-53; Daily Telegraph, 1953-61; Deputy Editor, 1961-76; Associate Editor, 1976-86, Editor, 1986-89, Editor, Comment Section, 1989-91, Sunday Telegraph. Publications: The Socialist Myth, 1972; Peregrinations: Selected Pieces, 1980; By the Right, 1987; Tricks of Memory (autobiography), 1993; In Defence of Aristocracy, 2004. Contributions to: Newspapers and journals. Honours: Granada Columnist of the Year, 1980; Knighted, 1991. Address: The Old Rectory, Hedgerley, Buckinghamshire SL2 3VY, England.

**WORTON Michael John,** b. 20 July 1951, Luanshya, Zambia. Academic. Education: Dumfries Academy; MA, Gold Medal, F C Green Prize, PhD, University of Edinburgh. Appointments: Lecturer in French, University of Liverpool, 1976-80; Lecturer in French, 1980-90, Senior Lecturer in French, 1990-94, Professor of French, 1994-98, Fielden Professor of French Language and Literature, 1998-, Vice-Provost (Teaching and Learning), 1998-2004, Vice-Provost (Academic and International), 2004-, University College London. Publications: Intertextuality: Theories and Practices (editor and introduced with Judith Still); Tournier: La Goutte d'or, 1992, reprinted 1995; René Char: The Dawn Breakers/Les Matinaux (editor, Introduced and translated), 1992; Textuality and Sexuality: Reading Theories and Practice (with Judith Still), 1993; Michel Tournier (editor), 1995; Typical Men, 2001; Women's Writing in Contemporary France (with Gill Rye), 2002; National Healths: Gender, Sexuality and Health in a Cross Cultural Context (with Nana Wilson-Tagoe), 2004; Author of more than 60 book chapters and articles. Honour: Chevalier des Palmes Académiques. Memberships: HEFCE Strategic Committee on Quality, Assessment, Learning and Teaching; Member, Board of Management and Chair of Monitoring and Evaluation Committee, Arts and Humanities Research Board; Member, Higher Education Panel, Church of England Board of Education; Member, Council, Kings College London. Address: Vice-Provost's Office, UCL, Gower Street, London WC1E 6BT, England. E-mail: m.worton@ucl.ac.uk

**WÓRUM Ferenc,** b. 15 March 1936, Hungary. Professor of Medicine; Cardiologist. m. Erzsébet Mészáros, 2 sons. Education: MD, University Medical School of Debrecen, 1960; Specialist of Internal Diseases, 1965; Specialist of Cardiac Diseases, 1988; PhD, Hungarian Academy of Sciences, 1980; Széchenyi Professorial Scholarship, 1998. Appointments: Assistant Professor, Lecturer, Associate Professor, 1960-92, Professor, 1992-, Departments of Internal Medicine, Medical and Health Science Centre, University of Debrecen; Pioneer of Clinical Cardiac Electrophysiology and modern Arrhythmology in Hungary (His-Bundle ECG, Programmed Electro-stimulation); Head of the Research Working Group of Cardiac Arrthythmias, Cardiac Electrophysiology, Pacemaker and Implantable Defibrillator Therapy; Developed several new cardiologic instruments and methods; Reader of 4 medical journals. Publications: 185 publications (45 passages in books); 229 lectures in 18 countries; 69 European, World and International Congresses, 10 in USA, Canada, Australia and Hong Kong. Honours: 3 Governmental Awards: Award for Sporting Activity, 1976; Awards for University Teaching, 1980, 1986. Memberships: Hungarian Society of Internal Medicine, 1965-; Hungarian Society of Cardiology, 1975-; Board, Hungarian Society of Cardiology, 1990-98; Board, Hungarian Arrhythmia's and Pacemaker Working Group, 1990-98. Address: 1st Department of Medicine, Medical and Health Science Centre, University of Debrecen, Nagyerdei krt. 98, PO Box 19, H-4012 Debrecen, Hungary. E-mail: worum@internal.med.unideb.hu

**WRIGHT George T(haddeus),** b. 17 December 1925, New York, New York, USA. Professor Emeritus; Author; Poet. m. Jerry Honeywell, 28 April 1955. Education: BA, Columbia College, 1946; MA, Columbia University, 1947; University of Geneva, 1947-48; PhD, University of California, 1957. Appointments: Teaching Assistant, 1954-55, Lecturer, 1956-57, University of California; Visiting Assistant Professor, New Mexico Highlands University, 1957; Instructor, Assistant Professor, University of Kentucky, 1957-60; Assistant Professor, San Francisco State College, 1960-61; Associate Professor, University of Tennessee, 1961-68; Fulbright Lecturer, University of Aix-Marseilles, 1964-66, University of

Thessaloniki, 1977-78; Visiting Lecturer, University of Nice, 1965; Professor, 1968-89, Chairman, English Department, 1974-77, Regents' Professor, 1989-93, Regents' Professor Emeritus, 1993-, University of Minnesota. Publications: The Poet in the Poem: The Personae of Eliot, Yeats and Pound, 1960; W H Auden, 1969, revised edition, 1981; Shakespeare's Metrical Art, 1988; Aimless Life: Poems 1961-1995, 1999; Hearing the Measures: Shakespearean and Other Inflections, 2002. Editor: Seven American Literary Stylists from Poe to Mailer: An Introduction, 1973. Contributions to: Articles, reviews, poems and translations in many periodicals and books. Honours: William Riley Parker Prize, Modern Language Association, 1974, 1981; Guggenheim Fellowship, 1981-82; National Endowment for the Humanities Fellowship, 1984-85. Memberships: Minnesota Humanities Commission, 1985-88; Modern Language Association; Shakespeare Association of America; Phi Kappa Phi. Address: 2617 West Crown King Drive, Tucson, AZ 85741, USA.

**WRIGHT John MacNair Jr,** b. 14 April 1916, Los Angeles, California, USA. United States Army. m. Helene Tribit, 28 June 1940, 2 sons. Education: BSc, US Military Academy, West Point, New York, 1940; MBA, University Southern California, Los Angeles, California 1956; MSc, International Affairs, George Washington University, Washington DC, 1973. Appointments: Battery Executive Officer, Battery Sunset, 91st Coast Artillery, Corregidor, Philippine Islands, 1940-42; Battery Commander, Battery Wright, 1942; Prisoner of War of Japan, Philippine Islands, Japan, Korea, 1942-45; Intelligence Division, War Department General Staff, Washington, DC, 1946-48; Military Attaché, US Embassy, Asuncion, Paraguay, 1948-50; Executive Officer, 30th Infantry Regiment, Fort Benning, Georgia, 1950; Student Advanced Course, Infantry School, Fort Benning, Georgia, 1950-51; Commander, 3rd Battalion, 508th Airborne Regimental Combat Team, Fort Benning, Georgia, 1951-52; Student, Command and General Staff College, Fort Leavenworth, Kansas, 1952-53; Assistant Chief of Staff for Personnel, Assistant Chief of Staff for Logistics, 7th Infantry Division, Korea, 1953-54; Office of Deputy Chief of Staff, Logistics, Department of the Army, Washington, DC, 1956-58; Office of Chief of Staff, US Army, Washington, DC, 1958-60; Student, National War College, Washington, DC, 1960-61; Chief of Staff, 8th Infantry Division, Bad Kreuznach, Germany, 1961-62; Assistant Chief of Staff, Plans and Operations, VII Corps, Stuttgart, Germany, 1962-63; Assistant Chief of Staff, Plans and Operations, Seventh Army, Stuttgart, Germany 1963; Assistant Division Commander, 11th Air Assault Division, Fort Benning, Georgia, 1963-65; Assistant Division Commander, 1st Cavalry Division, Vietnam, 1965-66; Office of Assistant Chief of Staff, Force Development, Department of the Army, Washington, DC 1966-67; Commanding General, US Army Infantry Center and Commandant, US Army Infantry School, Fort Benning, Georgia, 1967-69; Commanding General, 101st Airborne Division, Vietnam, 1969-70; Comptroller of the Army, Washington, DC, 1970-72; Retired, 1972; National Director of Research and Development, National Director of Programs, National Director of Exploring, Boy Scouts of America, N Brunswick, New Jersey and Irving, Texas, 1973-81; Retired, 1981. Publication: Captured on Corregidor, 1988. Honours include: Distinguished Service Medal with two Oak Leaf Clusters; Silver Star with Oak Leaf Cluster; Legion of Merit with Oak Leaf Cluster; Distinguished Flying Cross; Bronze Star Medal with Oak Leaf Cluster; Purple Heart with Oak Leaf Cluster; Air Medal with 59 Oak Leaf Clusters; Army Commendation Medal; Prisoner of War Medal; American Defense Service Medal; Asiatic Pacific Campaign Medal; World War II Victory Medal; US Presidential Unit Citation with three Oak Leaf Clusters; National Defense Service Medal with Oak

Leaf Cluster; Korea Service Medal; United Nations Service Medal; Republic of Korea Presidential Unit Citation; Vietnam Service Medal; Philippine Defense Medal; Philippine Liberation Medal; Philippine Independence Medal; Philippine Presidential Unit Citation; Paraguayan Order of National Merit; Vietnamese Gallantry Cross with three Palms and Gold Star; Vietnamese Commendation Medal; Vietnamese National Order, 5th Class; Vietnamese Civic Actions Medal, 1st Class; Vietnamese Armed Forces Honor Medal, 1st Class; Vietnamese Rural Revolutionary Development Medal with Palm; Vietnamese National Police Honor Medal, 1st Class; Combat Infantryman Badge; Master Parachutist Badge (US, German and Vietnamese); Senior Army Aviator Badge; Freedoms Foundation at Valley Forge: George Washington Honour Medal; America's Freedom Festival: Freedom Award; Boy Scouts of America: Distinguished Eagle Scout Award; Silver Antelope; Silver Beaver. Memberships include: National Eagle Scout Association; Kentucky Colonels; National Flag Foundation; National Congress of Patriotic Organisations; Society of the Cincinnati; Baronial Order of Magna Charta; Order of the Crown of Charlemagne; many others. Address: 21227 George Brown Avenue, Riverside, CA 92518-2881, USA.

**WRIGHT John Robert,** b. 20 October 1936, Carbondale, Illinois, USA. Priest; Professor. Education: BA optime merens, University of the South, Sewanee, Tennessee, 1958; MA Honours, Mediaeval History, Emory University, Atlanta, Georgia, 1959; MDiv cum laude, General Theological Seminary, New York City, 1963; DPhil, Oxford University, England, 1967. Appointments: Ordained, 1963; Instructor in Church History, Episcopal Divinity School, Cambridge, Massachusetts, 1966-68; Assistant Professor of Church History, 1968-71, Professor of Church History, 1971-, St Mark's Professor of Ecclesiastical History, 1974-, General Theological Seminary, New York City; Several visiting positions including Visiting Professor, St George's College, Jerusalem, 1982, 1992, 1995, 1996; Provost's Visiting Professor in Divinity, Trinity College, University of Toronto, 1989. Publications: Author, co-author, editor, co-author, 16 books including: Episcopalians and Roman Catholics: Can They Ever Get Together?, 1972; Handbook of American Orthodoxy, 1972; A Communion of Communions: One Eucharistic Fellowship, 1979; The Church and the English Crown, 1305-1334: A Study based on the Register of Archbishop Walter Reynolds, 1980; Called to Full Unity: Documents on Anglican-Roman Catholic Relations 1966-1983, 1986; Prayer Book Spirituality, 1989; Readings for the Daily Office from the Early Church, 1991; The Anglican Tradition: A Handbook of Sources, 1991; On Being a Bishop: Papers on Episcopacy from the Moscow Consultation 1992, 1993; Saint Thomas Church Firth Avenue, 2001; Russo-Greek papers 1863-1874, 2002; Forthcoming: Anglican Commentaries on the 39 Articles; The Privilege of England 1231-1530; 3 booklets; 169 papers and articles. Honours include: Phi Beta Kappa, Pi Gamma Mu and Omicron Delta Kappa, 1958; Life Fellow, Royal Historical Society, London, 1981-; DD hc, Episcopal Theological Seminary of the Southwest, Austin, Texas, 1983; Honorary Canon Theologian to Bishop of New York, 1990-; DD hc, Trinity Lutheran Seminary, 1991; DCnL hc, University of the South, 1996; Dr. Theol. hc, University of Bern (Switzerland), 2000; Holy Crosses of the Orthodox Patriarchs of Constantinople, Jerusalem, Antioch and Moscow; Historiographer of the Episcopal Church, 2000-; Life Fellow, Society of Antiquaries, London, 2001. Memberships include: The Anglican Society, President, 1994-; North American Academy of Ecumenists, President, 1989-91; Conference of Anglican Church Historians, Convenor, 1995-; American Catholic Historical Association; American Society of Church History; Medieval Academy of America. Address: c/o General

Theological Seminary, 175 Ninth Avenue, New York, NY10011, USA. E-mail: wright@gts.edu

**WRIGHT Paul (Hervé Giraud),** b. 12 May 1915. Retired. m. Beatrice Frederika Rathbone, 1 daughter. Appointments: John Lewis Partnership Ltd, 1933-39; Served in HM Forces, 1939-45; Major, KRRC; HQ 21 Army Group, 1944-45 (despatches); Contested (L) NE Bethnal Green, 1945; Assistant Director, Public Relations, National Coal Board, 1946-48; Director, Public Relations, Festival of Britain, 1948-51; HM Foreign Service: Paris and New York, 1951-54; Foreign Office, 1954-56; The Hague, 1956-57; Head of Information, Policy Department in Foreign Office, 1957-60; Cairo, 1960-61; UK Delegation to North Atlantic Council, 1961-64; Minister for Information, Washington, 1965-68; Director General, British Information Services, New York, 1964-68; Ambassador to Congo (Kinshasa) and to Republic of Burundi, 1969-71; Ambassador to the Lebanon, 1971-75; Special Representative of the Secretary of State for Foreign and Commonwealth Affairs, 1975-78; Chairman, Irvin Great Britain Ltd, 1979-88; Chairman, British American Arts Association, 1983-88; Chairman, British Lebanese Association , 1987-90; Chairman, Member Council, Forte plc, 1987-96. Publications: A Brittle Glory, autobiography, 1986. Honours: OBE, 1952; CMG, 1960; KCMG, 1975; Honorary Secretary General, London Celebrations Committee for Queen's Silver Jubilee, 1977; Knight of the Order of the Cedar of Lebanon, 1990; Honorary RCM, 1990; KCSG, 1996; GCSG, 2000. Memberships: Vice Chairman, The American Festival, 1985; President, Elizabethan Club, 1988-95; Governor, 1981-2000, (Chairman, 1993-2000), Westminster Cathedral Choir School; Chairman, Westminster School Development Council, 1994-97; Trustee, Trusthouse Charitable Foundation, 1996-2000; Life Vice President, Hearing Dogs for Deaf People. Address: 62 Westminster Gardens, Marsham Street, London SW1P 4JG, England.

**WRIGHT Robert Alfred (Air Marshal Sir),** b. 10 June 1947, Hamble, Hampshire, England. Military Representative. m. Margaret, 1 son, 1 daughter. Education: Graduate, Royal Air Force Staff College, 1982. Appointments: Operational Requirements Division, Ministry of Defence, 1982-84; Directing Staff, Royal Air Force Staff College, 1984-87; Officer Commanding IX Squadron, RAF Brueggen, 1987-89; Personal Staff Officer to Chief of Air Staff, 1989-91; Station Commander, RAF Brueggen, 1992-94; Assistant Chief of Staff, Policy & Plans, NATO HQ, High Wycombe, 1994-95; Air Commander, Operations Headquarters Strike Command, 1995-97; Promoted to Air Vice Marshal, 1997; Military Advisor to High Representative, Sarajevo, 1997-98; Chief of Staff to Air Member for Personnel and Deputy Commander-in-Chief, Personnel & Training Command, RAF Innsworth, 1998-2000; Assistant Chief of Staff, Policy & Requirements, Supreme Headquarters Allied Powers Europe, 2000-02; Promoted to Air Marshal, 2002; UK Military Representative to NATO and EU Military Committees, 2002-. Honours: Air Force Cross, 1982; KBE, 2004. Memberships: Fellow, Royal Aeronautical Society; President: Combined Services Winter Sports Association; RAF Winter Sports Federation; RAF Athletics Association; Naval 8/ 208 Squadron Association. Address: UKMILREP, HQ NATO, Boulevard Leopold III, 1110 Brussels, Belgium.

**WRIGHT Theodore Paul Jr,** b. 12 April 1926, Port Washington, New York, USA. Professor. m. Susan J Standfast, 1 son, 2 daughters. Education: BA, Swarthmore College, 1949; MA, 1951, PhD, 1957, Yale University. Appointments: Instructor to Associate Professor, Bates College, Lewiston, Maine, USA, 1955-65; Associate Professor, Professor, Graduate School of Public Affairs, State University of New York at

Albany, Albany, New York, 1965-95; Emeritus Professor, 1995-. Publications: American Support of Free Elections Abroad, 1963; 67 articles on Muslim politics, India and Pakistan, 1963-2004. Memberships: Association for Asian Studies; Board Member, American Council for the Study of Islamic Society; Past President, now Newsletter Editor, South Asian Muslim Studies Association; Columbia University Faculty Seminar on South Asia, 1967-; Past President, New York Conference on Asian Studies; European Conference on Modern South Asian Studies, 1979-; Board Member, New Netherland Institute. Address: 17 Wellington Way, Niskayana, NY 12309, USA. E-mail: wright15@Juno.com

**WRONG Dennis Hume,** b. 22 November 1923, Toronto, Ontario, Canada. Emeritus Professor of Sociology. Education: BA, University of Toronto, 1945; PhD, Columbia University, New York City, 1956. Appointments: Instructor, Department of Economics and Social Institutions, Princeton University, 1949-50; Instructor in Sociology, The Newark College, Rutgers University, Newark, New Jersey, 1950-51; Research Associate and Lecturer, Department of Political Economy, University of Toronto, 1954-56; Assistant Professor and Associate Professor, Department of Sociology, Brown University, 1956-61; Associate Professor of Sociology, Graduate Faculty, The New School for Social Research, 1961-63; Professor and Chairman, Department of Sociology, University College, New York University, 1963-65; Professor of Sociology, University of Nevada, Reno, 1965-66; Professor of Sociology, 1966-94, Emeritus Professor of Sociology, 1994-, New York University. Publications: Author and editor: 11 books; Numerous articles in professional, intellectual and political journals. Honours: Visiting Fellow, Nuffield College, Oxford University, 1978; Guggenheim Fellow, 1984-85; Visiting Fellow, European University Institute, Florence, Italy, 1996-97. Memberships: Pre-doctoral Fellow, Canadian Social Science Research Council; Fellow, Woodrow Wilson International Center for Scholars, Washington DC, 1991-92. Address: 144 Drakes Corner Road, Princeton, NJ 08540, USA.

**WU Jiann-Kuo,** b. 25 February 1950, Taipei, Taiwan. University President. m. Li-Hwa, 1 son, 2 daughters. Education: Diploma, National Taipei Institute of Technology, 1971; PhD, University of Nebraska, 1984. Appointments: Professor, 1989-; Dean, Academic Affairs, 1993-97; President, National Taiwan Ocean University, 1997-2003; Board Chairman, Metal Industries Research and Development Centre, 2003-. Publications: Over 200 papers, materials science. Memberships: The Minerals, Metals and Materials Society. Address: National Taiwan Ocean University, 2 Pei-Ning Road, Keelung, Taiwan 20024, China.

**WU Ming-Lu,** b. 3 March 1963, Nanzhao County, Henan Province, China. Management Consultant. m. Chung Shing, 1 son, 1 daughter. Education: BEng, Applied Mathematics, Jihin University of Technology, Changchun, China, 1983; MSc, Operations Research and Cybernetics, 1986, PhD, Probability and Mathematical Statistics, 1994, Academia Sinica, Beijing, China. Appointments: Assistant Professor, 1986-91, Associate Professor, 1994-95, National Research Centre for Science and Technology for Development, Beijing; Research Fellow, Department of Management Sciences, City University of Hong Kong, 1995-. Publications: 14 recent papers for internationally refereed journals; Co-authored 2 books: China's Economic Development and Some Related Factors' Analysis, 1991; International Competitiveness, 1992. Address: Department of Management Sciences, City University of Hong Kong, 83 Tat Chee Avenue, Kowloon, Hong Kong. E-mail: msminglu@cityu.edu.hk

**WULSTAN David,** b. 18 January 1937, Birmingham, England. Research Professor. m. Susan Graham, 1 son. Education: Royal Masonic School, Bushey; BSc (Lond), College of Technology, Birmingham; MA, Magdalen College, Oxford; Studied under Egon Wellesz and Bernard Rose, also Lennox Berkeley and Peter Wishart; Composition: Clarence Raybould and Sir Adrian Boult (conducting). Appointments: Fellow and Lecturer, Magdalen College, Oxford, 1964-78; Visiting Professor, Department of N E Studies, Berkeley, USA, 1979; Statutory Lecturer and Professor of Music, University College, Cork, 1979-83; Gregynog Professor of Music, University of Wales, Aberystwyth, 1983-90; Research Professor, 1990-; Director, The Clerkes of Oxenford (founded 1961). Publications: Tudor Music, 1985; Editions of Gibbons & Sheppard; The Emperor's Old Clothes, 2001; The Poetic and Musical Legacy of Heloise and Abelard, 2003; The Play of Daniel (new edition), 2006; Music from the Paraclete, 2006; Appearances at BBC Proms and many festivals in Britain and Europe; Broadcasts and TV appearances. Memberships: Member of Council, Plainsong & Medieval Music Society; Consulting Editor, Spanish Academic Press; Fellow, Royal Society of Musicians; Musical Consultant, Centre for the Study of the Cantigas de Santa Maria, Oxford. Address: Ty Isaf, Llanilar, Aberystwyth, Cardiganshire, SY23 4NP, Wales.

**WYMAN Bill (William George),** b. 24 October 1941, London, England. Musician. m. (1) Diane Cory, 1959, divorced 1968, 1 son, (2) Mandy Smith, 1989, divorced 1991, (3) Suzanne Accosta, 1993, 3 daughters. Appointments: Bass-Player, The Rolling Stones, 1962-93; Owner, Ripple Records, Ripple Music, Ripple Publications, Ripple Productions; Bill Wyman Enterprises. Creative Works: Albums include: 12 x 5, 1964; New, 1965; Big Hits, 1966; Got Live If You Want It, 1967; Flowers, 1967; Sucking in the 70's, 1981; Still Life, 1981; Rewind, Dirty Work, 1986; Emotional Rescue, 1988; Steel Wheels, 1989; Flashpoint, 1991; Voodoo Lounge, 1994; Solo recordings include: Stone Alone, 1976; Monkey Grip, 1974; Bill Wyman, 1981; Willie & the Poor Boys, 1985; Stuff, 1993; Struttin' Our Stuff, 1997; Anyway the Wind Blows, 1998; Groovin', 2000; Double Bill, 2001; Blues Odyssey, 2001; Just for a Thrill, 2004; Single: (Si Si) Je Suis Un Rock Star; Films: Sympathy for the Devil, 1970; Gimme Shelter, 1970; Ladies and Gentlemen the Rolling Stones, 1974; Let's Spend the Night Together, 1982; Digital Dreams, 1983; Filmscore: Green Ice, 1981. Publications: Stone Alone: The Story of a Rock and Roll Band (with Ray Coleman), 1990; Wyman Shoots Chagall, 2000; Bill Wyman's Blues Odyssey (with Richard Havers), 2001; Rolling With The Stones (with Richard Havers), 2002. Honours include: Prince's Trust Award, 1991; Ivor Novello Award for Outstanding Contribution to British Music, 1991; Blues Foundation, Memphis Literary Award, 2002. Address: c/o Ripple Productions Ltd, 344 Kings Road, London SW3 5UR, England.

**WYNNE-PARKER Michael,** b. 20 November 1945, Willersley Castle, Derbyshire, England. Author; PR Consultant. m. (1) divorced, 1991, 2 daughters, (2) Mandana Farzaneh, 1995. Education: Lady Manners School. Appointments: Founder and Chairman, English Speaking Union of Sri Lanka, 1983-; Founder and President, English Speaking Union of South Asia, 1985-; Consultant to Public and Private Companies in 26 countries, also to governments, charities and individuals; Founder and President, Introcom International, 1989-; Chairman, Guild of Travel and Tourism, 1999-; Trustee, A Heart for Russia, 2005-. Publications: Healing and the Wholeness of Man, 1972; Bridge Over Troubled Water, 1989, 1998; The Mandana Poems, 1998; Impressions of Orthodoxy in Estonia, 2004; Reflections in Middle Years, 2005; Fifty Estonia Recipes, 2005 and others.

Honours: Papal Medal, Pope Paul VI, 1971; Miembro de Honor, Union Monarquica Espanola, 1974; Grand Cordon, Order of the Crown of Yemen, 1977; Knight Commander, Military and Hospitaller Order of St Lazarus of Jerusalem, 1980; Harpers and Queen Award for Excellence, Philanthropist of the Year, Runner-up to HRH Prince Charles, 1988. Memberships: Founder Patron, Pensthorpe Waterfowl Trust; Former Chairman, Council for the Advancement of Arab-British Understanding, Eastern Region, UK; Chairman, 1999 British Forces Foundation Ball; Co-Founder, Mencap City Foundation; Life Member, Royal Society of St George; Founder Member, Sri Lanka Friendship Association; Life Member, Norfolk Naturalists Trust. Address: Guild of Travel and Tourism, Suite 193, Temple Chambers, Temple Avenue, London EC4Y 0DB, England. E-mail: info@ introcominternational.com

# DICTIONARY OF INTERNATIONAL BIOGRAPHY

# X

**XADJIOANNOU Ioannis,** b. 7 January 1927, Kali, Pella, Greece. Retired Teacher. m. Efthimia, 2 sons. Education: BA, Teachers' Academy of Thessaloniki, Greece, 1952. Appointments: Currently retired Teacher; Writer of articles in literary newspapers and magazines in North Greece. Publications: Poems include: Waiting for the Dawn, 1975; Panorama, 1977; The Shadow and the Body, 1987; Recycling, 2000; Other books include: Spiritual Walks, 1977; Poetic Issues (A-B-C), 1994; Poetic Issues, 2001. Honours: Honours from the Authors' Union of North Greece, 1982; Honours from the Municipality of Athens, 1990; Award, Committee of Authors "Goddess Athena", 1996; Honours from the Publishers' Union, 1997. Memberships: Authors' Union of North Greece; Authors' Union of Greece. Address: 57 Analipseos Str., Thessaloniki, 546 44 Greece. E-mail: info@idrogios.gr

**XIA Jisong,** b. 15 May 1925. Professor in Modern Philosophy. m. 1 April 1956, 1 son, 1 daughter. Education: Bachelor in Politics, National Central University, Nanjing, 1943-48; MPhil, People's University of China, Beijing, 1952-54. Appointments: Assistant Lecturer, Department of Politics, National Central University, 1948-52; Lecturer, Department of Politics, Nanjing University, 1954-78; Associate Professor and Deputy Head of Department, Department of Philosophy, Nanjing University, 1978-82; Professor and Head of Department, Department of Philosophy, Nanjing University, 1982-90; Professor, Department of Philosophy, Hangzhou University and Zhejiang University, Hangzhou, 1990-. Publications: More than 10 books including: Course of the Modern Philosophy in the West, 1985; Mathematics Philosophy in the West, 1986; Review on Existentialism, 1987; Philosophy of Science in the West. Honour: Honorary Head of the Philosophy Department, Nanjing University. Memberships: Philosophy Division of the State Council's Academic Degree Committee in China; Vice Chairman, Society of Modern Foreign Philosophy Study in China; Chairman of the Society of Foreign Philosophy Study in China. Address: Department of Philosophy, College of Humanities, Zhejiang University, Hangzhou 310028, China.

**XING Qiwu,** b. 29 December 1953, Shanghai, China. Chemist. m. Hong Zhu, 1 son. Education: Anhui Normal University, Wuhu, China, 1975-78; Hangzhou University, Zhejiang, China, 1980-83; MSc, 1983; Julius-Maximilians-Universität, Würzburg, Bavaria, Germany, 1989-90; Universität Bayreuth, Germany, 1990-93; Dr.rer.nat, 1993. Appointments: Agricultural Labourer, Mechanic, Skilled Worker of Chemical Plant, Product Manager in Anhui, China, 1970-75; University Assistant, Anhui Normal University, 1978-80; University Assistant, 1984-86, Lecturer, 1986-89, Hangzhou University; Teaching Assistant, Universität Bayreuth, Germany, 1990-93; Researcher, Forschungsinstitut für Chemie und Erdöl, Technische Universität Wien, Austria, 1993; Researcher, Institut für Neue Materialien gem, GmbH, Saarbrücken, Germany, 1993-98; Chairman of Board of Directors, Society of Chinese Chemists and Chemical Engineers in Germany, 1997-98, Member of Board of Directors, 1998-99; Head of Development, Graf Papiere GmbH, Grimma, Saxony, Germany, 1998-2001; Managerial employee of Analytical Department, EnviroTex GmbH, Augsburg, Bavaria, Germany, 2001-. Publications: Several articles in professional journals. Memberships: Society of Chinese Chemists and Chemical Engineers in Germany. Address: Mőrikeweg 6 D-85080 Gaimersheim, Germany.

**XU Mingxing,** b. December 1932, Licheng, Shandong, China. Education: Wuhan Tongji Medical University, 1959.

Appointments: Department Director, Consultant Director, Shandong Sanitation and Epidemic Prevention Station; Member, Child and Adolescent Health Committee, Chinese Preventive Medical Association; Vice Chairman, Child and Adolescent Health Committee, Shandong Preventive Medical Association; Editor, Consultant, Chinese Journal of School Health; Retired, 1993. Publications: 30 academic papers; 16 articles on popular science; Editor, 4 books. Honours: Best Professional Personnel, Shandong Provincial Health Bureau, 1992; Special Subsidiary Award, State Council, 1994; 1st and 2nd prizes, Shandong Provincial Science and Technology Bureau; 1st prize, Shandong Provincial Health Bureau. Address: No 70 Jingshi Road, Jinan, Shandong, 250014, Peoples Republic of China.

**XUEREB Pierre Henri,** b. 23 March 1959, Birmandreis, Algeria. Musician; Professor of Viola. m. Anne Delord, 3 sons, 1 daughter. Education: Baccalauréat, Paris, 1975; 1st Prize, Viola, Conservatoire National Superieur de Musique de Paris, 1975; Bachelor of Arts cum laude, Boston University, USA, 1982. Appointments: Viola Soloist, Ensemble Intercontemporain (Pierre Boulez), Paris, 1978-80; Assistant Professor, 1983-90, Professor of Viola, 1990-, Conservatoire National Superieur de Musique, Paris; Professor of Viola, Ecole Normale de Musique de Paris, 2002-; Professor of Viola, Conservatoire Royal de Musique, Liège, Belgium, 2003-. Recordings: Numerous recordings for Deutsche Gramophon, Harmonia Mundi, Talent, 3D, Adda, Calliope, Timpani, Metronome. Honour: Grand Prix du Disque, Academie Charles Cros. Address: 95 rue Petit, 75019 Paris, France. E-mail: xueweb@aol.com Website: www.xuereb-viola.com

# DICTIONARY OF INTERNATIONAL BIOGRAPHY

## Y

**YABLANSKI Tsanko,** b. 9 September 1944, Biala Slatina, Bulgaria. Geneticist. m. Liliana, 1 son, 1 daughter. Education: Agronomist Bachelor, 1969, PhD, Animal Genetics, 1975, University of Agriculture, Sofia; Dr Sc, Animal Genetics and Breeding, Trakia University, Stara Zagora, 1988. Appointments: Assistant Professor, 1975-83, Associate Professor, 1983-90, Vice President of University, 1990-95, Full Professor, Head of Department of Genetics, 2003-, Trakia University; Editor-in-chief of Bulgarian Journal of Animal Science, 1990-95; Mayor of the City of Stara Zagora, 1995-99; Ambassador of the Republic of Bulgaria to State of Israel, 1999-2003. Publications: Over 60 articles and books in the field of genetics and animal breeding. Honours: Honorary Member, Union of Scientists in Bulgaria, 1997; Honorary Citizen, City of Durham, NK, USA, 1998; Outstanding Friend of Strasburg Medal, 1998; Listed in international biographical dictionaries. Memberships: Union of Scientists in Bulgaria; European Association for Animal Production, International Society for Animal Genetics; Rotary Club Stara Zagora. Address: bul Ruski 56, ap 11, 6000 Stara Zagoza, Bulgaria. E-mail: tsyab@hotmail.com

**YADUGIRI Kiran Kumar,** b. 9 June 1966, Hanumakonda, Andhra Pradesh, India. Company Executive. m. Y Brinda, 2 children. Education: M Com, LLB, Kakatiya University; P G Dip, Public Relations, Ambedkar University; Diploma in Computer and Commercial Practice, Government Polytechnic, Adilabad. Appointments: From Marketing Manager to Vice-President, Sreemitra Group, 1994-; Director, Mount Opera – Multi Theme Park; Executive Director, Sreemitra Developers Limited (Leading Realtor in Andhra Pradesh); Executive Director, Vishwabharathy Foundation. Publications: Books: Medha; Claim Your Time. Honours: Rashtritya Ratan Award, 2001; Bala Bandhu Puraskar, 2002; Life Time Achievement Award, 2003; National Citizen Award, 2003; Hall of Fame Award, USA Martial Arts Association; Rajiv Ghandi Sadbhavana Award; Lions International Presidents Leadership Medal. Memberships: Chairman, Indian Association of Friendship with Foreign Companies; District Chairman, Lions Clubs International; Vice Patron, Blue Cross; Life Member, Hyderabad Management Association; World Wide Fund for Nature, India; Chairman, Trishna India Foundation; All India Management Association; Indo-American Friendship Council; Chairman, Indo-American Friendship Association; Vice President and Advisory Council Member, Golden Dragons Academy of Martial Arts; Federation of Andhra Pradesh Chambers of Commerce and Industry; Advisory Member, Potti Sriramullu Telegu University; Hyderabad Golf Association; Kurnool Club. Address: C/o P Hanumantha Rao, 3-6-747/2 Street No 13, Himayathnagar, Hyderabad, 500 –029, AP, India.

**YAKOVLEV Valery Petrovitch,** b. 28 September 1940, Volgograd, Russia. Physicist. m. Margarita Yakovleva, 2 daughters. Education: MS, Distinction, 1963, PhD, 1967, DSc, 1987, Moscow Engineering Physics Institute. Appointments: Assistant Professor, 1967-69, Senior Lecturer, 1969-75, Associate Professor, 1975-88, Full Professor, 1988-, Moscow Engineering Physics Institute; Heraeus Professor, Universität Ulm, Germany, 1994-1996. Publications: Over 170 scientific papers on quantum electrodynamics of strong fields, physics of semiconductors, interferometry of atomic states and matter waves, subrecoil laser cooling and atom optics and strange kinetics; Monograph, Mechanical Action of Light on Atoms, 1990. Address: Theoretical Nuclear Physics Department, Moscow Engineering Physics Institute, Kashirskoe shosse 31, 115409 Moscow, Russia. E-mail: yakovlev@theor.mephi.ru

**YALOW Rosalyn,** b. 19 July 1921, New York, New York, USA. Medical Physicist. m. Aaron Yalow, 1943, 1 son, 1 daughter. Education: Graduated, Physics, Hunter College, New York, 1941; PhD, Experimental Nuclear Physics, University of Illinois, 1945. Appointments: Assistant in Physics, University of Illinois, 1941-43; Instructor, 1944-45; Lecturer and temporary Assistant Professor in Physics, Hunter College, New York, 1946-50; Physicist and Assistant Chief, 1950-70, Acting Chief, 1968-70, Chief Radioimmunoassay Reference Laboratory, 1969, Chief Nuclear Medicine Service, 1970-80, Senior Medical Investigator, 1972-92, Senior Medical Investigator Emeritus, 1992-, Director, Solomon A Berson Research Laboratory, Veterans Administration Medical Center, 1973-92, Radioisotope Service, Veterans Administration Hospital, Bronx, New York; Research Professor, 1968-74, Distinguished Service Professor, 1974-79, Department of Medicine, Mount Sinai School of Medicine, New York; Distinguished Professor at Large, 1979-85, Professor Emeritus, 1985-, Albert Einstein College of Medicine, Yeshiva University; Chair, Department of Clinical Sciences, Montefiore Hospital, Bronx, 1980-85; Solomon A Berson Distinguished Professor at Large, Mt Sinai School of Medicine, New York, 1986-; Harvey Lecturer, 1966; American Gastroenterology Association Memorial Lecturer, 1972; Joslyn Lecturer, New England Diabetes Association, 1972; Franklin I Harris Memorial Lecturer, 1973; 1st Hagedorn Memorial Lecturer, Acta Endocrinologia Congress, 1973; President, Endocrine Society, 1978-79; Honours: Over 60 honorary doctorates; Joint Winner, Nobel Prize for Physiology or Medicine, 1977; More than 30 other awards. Memberships: NAS; American Physics Society; Radiation Research Society; American Association of Physicists in Medicine; Biophysics Society; American Academy of Arts and Sciences; American Physiology Society; Foreign Associate, French Academy of Medicine; Fellow, New York Academy of Science; Radiation Research Society; American Association of Physicists in Medicine; Associate Fellow in Physics, American College of Radiology; American Diabetes Association; Endocrine Society; Society of Nuclear Medicine. Address: Veterans Administration Medical Center, 130 West Kingsbridge Road, Bronx, New York, NY 10468, USA.

**YAMAGATA Toshio,** b. 25 March 1948, Utsunomiya City, Japan. Physical Oceanographer. m. Yoko Yamagata, 1 son, 1 daughter. Education: Bachelor of Science, 1971, Master of Science, 1973, Doctor of Science, 1977, University of Tokyo. Appointments: Associate Professor, Research Institute for Applied Mechanics, Kyushu University, 1979; Associate Professor, 1991, Professor, 1995-, Graduate School of Science, University of Tokyo. Publications: About 100 publications in professional scientific journals including: Philosophical Transactions, Royal Society London, 1989; Bulletin of the American Meteorological Society, 1997; Nature, 1999. Honours: Okada Prize and Society Prize, Japan Oceanographic Society; Society Prize, Japan Meteorological Society; Burr Steinbach Scholar of Woods Hole Oceanographic Institution; The Sverdrup Gold Medal, American Meteorological Society; Medal with Purple Ribbon, The Emperor of Japan. Memberships: Japan Oceanographic Society; Japan Meteorological Society; American Geophysical Union; American Meteorological Society, (Fellow); The Oceanographic Society of the United States of America. Address: Department of Earth and Planetary Science, Graduate School of Science, The University of Tokyo, Tokyo 113-0033, Japan. Website: http://www-aos/eps.s.u-tokyo.ac.jp/~yamagata/indexj.html

**YAMAGUCHI Masashi,** b. 1 September 1948, Yamagata, Japan. Associate Professor. m. Naoko Terakawa, 2 sons, 1 daughter. Education: BS, Yamagata University, Yamagata,

Japan, 1971; MS, Tokyo Metropolitan University, Tokyo, Japan, 1974; DSc, 1978. Appointments: Visiting Research Fellow, Memorial Sloane-Kettering Cancer Center, New York, USA 1979; Associate Researcher, 1980; Staff Scientist, Monell Chemical Senses Center, Philadelphia, USA, 1980-81; Research Associate, The Jikei University School of Medicine, Tokyo, Japan, 1981-88; Lecturer, 1988-96, Associate Professor, 1996-, Chiba University, Chiba, Japan. Publications: Articles in medical journals include: Dynamics of hepatitis B virus core antigen in a transformed yeast cell, 1994; The spindle pole body duplicates in early G1 phase in a pathogenic yeast Exophiala dermatitidis, 2002; Quantitative three-dimensional structural analysis of Exophiala dermatidis yeast cells by freeze-substitution and serial ultrathin sectioning, 2003; Guide Book for Electron Microscopy (in Japanese), 2004. Honours: Best Paper Award, Japanese Society of Microscopy, 1996 and 2005; Best Paper Award, Japanese Society of Microscopy, 2005. Memberships: Japanese Society of Microscopy; Japanese Society of Medical Mycology; Mycological Society of Japan. Address: Research Centre for Pathogenic Fungi and Microbial Toxicosis, 1-8-1 Inohana, Chuo-ku, Chiba 260-8673, Japan. Website: http://www.pf.chiba-u.ac.jp/

**YAMAGUCHI Masayoshi,** b. 15 June 1947, Atami, Japan. Professor. m. Eiko Yamaguchi, 1 son, 1 daughter. Education: Bachelor, 1971, Master, 1973, PhD, 1976, Pharmaceutical Sciences, Shizuoka College of Pharmacy. Appointments: Research Associate, 1973-86, Assistant Professor, 1986-87, Shizuoka College of Pharmacy; Visiting Lecturer, University of Pennsylvania, 1981; Visiting Assistant Professor, Texas Tech University, 1985-86; Visiting Assistant Professor, University of Texas, 1988-89; Faculty, 1987-91, Associate Professor, 1991-93, Professor, 1993-, Life and Health Sciences, University of Shizuoka. Publications: Over 440 original scientific papers; Calcium and Life; Biometals; Prevention of Osteoporosis and Nutrition; Discoverer of regucalcin as a regulatory protein in intercellular signalling and a novel protein RGPR-p117 as transcription factor; 32 reviews and books; 6 international and 11 national patents. Honours: Award for Academy Encouragement in Tokai Branch of Pharmaceutical Society of Japan, 1981; Takeda Science Promotion Foundation, 1987; Sato Memorial Foundation Prize, 1992; Saito Prize, Chion Party, Japan, 1992; Encouragement Foundation in Pharmaceutical Research, 1994; Award, Mishima Kaiun Memorial Foundation, Japan, 1999; Bounty from Yamanouchi Foundation for Research in Metabolic Disorders, Japan, 2004; International Scientist of the Year, International Biographical Centre (IBC), 2004; Lifetime Achievement Award, IBC, 2004; International Order of Merit, IBC, 2004; Hall of Fame, IBC, 2004; Outstanding Professional Award, American Biographical Institute (ABI), 2004; American Hall of Fame, ABI, 2004; World Lifetime Achievement Award, ABI, 2004; International Peace Prize, United Cultural Convention, 2004; 2005 Lifetime Achievement Award, United Cultural Convention, USA; Lifetime Achievement Award, World Congress of Arts, Sciences and Communications, 2005; American Order of Excellence, ABI. Memberships: New York Academy of Sciences, 1996-2000, 2005-; European Society of Calcium, 1999-2004; American Society of Cell Biology; American Society for Bone and Mineral Research; International Society for Bone and Mineral; American Society for Biochemistry and Molecular Biology; Japan Society of Biochemistry, Councillor, 1992-; Councillor, The Japan Endocrine Society, 1988-; Councillor, Japanese Society for Bone and Mineral Research, 1988-; Councillor, Japan Society of Pharmacology, 1987-; Councillor, Japan Society for Biomedical Research on Trace Elements, 1990-; Councillor, Japan Society for Osteoporosis, 1999-; Editor, Biomedical Research on Trace Elements, Japan, 2002-2005; Editorial Academy Member of the

International Journal of Molecular Medicine, 2001-; Deputy Director General, IBC, 2004-; Research Board Advisor, ABI, 2004-; Deputy Governor, ABI, 2005-; Marquis's Who's Who in Science and Engineering 2003-04, 2005-06; Marquis' Who's Who in the World, 2005, 2006; Great Minds of the 21st Century, ABI, 2005; 2000 Outstanding Scientists of the 21st Century, IBC, 2005; 2000 Outstanding Intellectuals of the 21st Century, IBC, 2005; The Cambridge Blue Book Special, IBC, 2006. Address: Senagawa 1-chome, 15-5, Aoi-ku, Shizuoka City 420-0913, Japan. E-mail: yamaguch@u-shizuoka-ken.ac.jp

**YAMAMOTO Irwin Toraki,** b. 5 April 1955, Wailuku, Maui, Hawaii. Editor; Publisher. Education: YB, Business Administration, Marketing, Chaminade University, 1977. Appointments: President, Editor, Publisher, The Yamamoto Forecast, Kahului, Hawaii, 1977-. Publications: Book: Profit Making in the Stock Market, 1983; Columnist, The Hawaii Herald, 1978-. Honours: Named: Top Market Timer; Top Gold Timer; Top Bond Timer; Timer Digest Honor Roll, Timer Digest; Also honors by: Select Information Exchange; Rating the Stock Selectors. Address: PO Box 573, Kahului HI, 96733-7073, Hawaii.

**YAMAMOTO Kentaro,** b. 12 November 1969, Yokohama, Japan. Researcher. Education: Bachelor of Engineering, 1993, Master of Engineering, 1995, Doctor of Engineering, 1998, Kumamoto University, Japan. Appointments: Consulting Engineer, Kokusai Kogyo Co, Amagasaki, Japan, 1990-91; Research Associate, Kagoshima University, Kagoshima, Japan, 1998-. Publications: Articles in scientific journals including: Geotextiles and Geomembranes; Soils and Foundations. Memberships: Japan Society of Civil Engineers; Japanese Geotechnical Society. Address: Department of Ocean Civil Engineering, 1-21-40, Korimoto, Kagoshima, 890-0065 Japan. E-mail: yamaken@oce.kagoshima-u.ac.jp

**YAMANO Yoshiki,** b. 3 May 1936, Japan. Physician; Orthopaedic Surgeon. m. Kazuko, 1 son. Education: Graduate, Oska City Medical School, 1962; Medical Degree, Osaka City University, 1973; Specialist Orthopaedic Surgery, 1975. Appointments: Lecturer, Department of Orthopaedic Surgery, Osaka City University, 1971; Associate Professor, 1977, Professor, 1986, Kawasaki Medical School; Professor, 1993, Emeritus Professor, 2002, Osaka City Graduate University Medical School. Publications: Primary Care in Orthopaedics, 1995; Fracture and Trauma, 2000; Contributor: Oxford Textbook of Orthopaedics and Traumatology, 2002; Articles: Fingertip replantation, ultramicrosurgery; Nerve Grafting; Cervical Disc Herniation. Honours: Moriwake Prize, 1980; Kanae Prize, 2001. Memberships include: SICOT; International Society of Reconstructive Microsurgery; Emeritus Member, Japanese Orthopaedic Association; Japanese Society for Surgery for Hand. Address: 1-4-17 Ebarajicho, Sakaishi, Osaka, 593-8304, Japan.

**YAMASHITA Hitoshi,** b. 30 December 1964, Ehime, Japan. Acupuncturist. m. Atsuko Tanaka, 2 sons. Education: BS, Acupuncture, Meiji University of Oriental Medicine, 1987; PhD, Health Sciences, University of Tokyo, 2002. Appointments: Technician, Ehime Prefectural Institute of Oriental Medicine, 1987-92, Instructor, Tsukuba College of Technology Clinic, 1992-; Honorary Research Fellow, Complementary Medicine, University of Exeter, England, 1999-2002; Visiting Research Fellow, Department of Family Nursing, University of Tokyo, 1999-2004. Publications: 9 books, first author, 2 books including: Acupuncture a scientific appraisal (Japanese translation); 165 articles, first author, 114 articles including: Adverse events related to acupuncture, 1998; Incidence of adverse reactions associated with acupuncture, 2000; Safety of acupuncture: Incident reporting and feedback may reduce risks, 2002; Popularity of complementary and alternative medicine in Japan: a telephone survey, 2002. Honours: President's Award, Meiji University of Oriental Medicine, 1987; Ibaraki Foundation for International Conference, 1996; Grants for Scientific Research, 2001. Memberships: Chairman, Committee for Safe Acupuncture, Japan Society of Acupuncture and Moxibustion; Member, Executive Committee, Japanese Association for Alternative, Complementary and Traditional Medicine; Founding Member, Japanese Society of Integrative Medicine; International Editorial Board Member, Focus on Alternative and Complementary Therapies; Founding Member, International Society of Complementary Medicine Research. Address: Tsukuba College of Technology Clinic, 4-12-7 Kasuga, Tsukuba, 305-0821, Japan.

**YAMAZAKI Yoshio,** b. 7 September 1953, Hanno Saitama, Japan. Railman. Appointments: Seibu Railway Company, Kitatama Station, 1969; Iruma-shi Station, 1969; Eidan Subway Koishikawa Factory, 1970; Various, 1970-73, East Japan Railway Company, Okubo Station; Head Clerk, Tokyo Ticket Administration Centre, 2001-. Memberships: National Geographic Society; Highlander Club; International Air line Passengers Association; The Oxford Club; The Executive Club. Listed in: Several Biographical Publications. Address: 7-18 Iwasawa, Hanno-Shi Saitama-Ken, 3570023 Japan.

**YANG Czau-Siung,** b. 28 January 1922, Nan-Tou, Taiwan. Professor. Medical Microbiologist. m. Pi-Yun Lin, 1 son, 2 daughters. Education: MD, Imperial University College, Taihoku, Japan, 1945; D M Sc, Matsumoto Medical School, Japan, 1960. Appointments: Fellow in Virology, Baylor College of Medicine, Houston, Texas, USA, 1961-63; Professor of Microbiology, College of Medicine, National Taiwan University, Taipei, 1963-92, Professor Emeritus, College of Medicine, 1992-; Director, Institute of Microbiology, 1969-75; Fellow, International Union Against Cancer, 1972-73; Consultant, USN Medical Research Unit #2 Taipei, 1974-77; Director, National Institute of Preventive Medicine, Department of Health, Taipei, 1977-81; Dean, College of Medicine, National Taiwan University, 1985-87; President, Ching-Hsing Medical Foundation, 1988-; President, National Taiwan University Medical College Alumni Association, 2000-. Publications: Co-editor, Human Tumor Immunology, 1984; Epstein-Barr Virus and Human Diseases, 1990; Publisher, Journal of Microbiology, Immunology and Infection, 1998-2001; Contributor of articles to professional journals. Memberships: Chinese Society of Microbiology; Chinese Society of Immunology; Formosan Medical Association; American Society of Microbiology; New York Academy of Sciences. Address: 2F #38 Yun-Ho St., Taipei, 106 Taiwan. E-mail: csyang@ha.mc.ntu.edu.tw

**YANG Dal Mo,** b. 7 April 1963, Sang Ju, Republic of Korea. Radiologist. m. Gum-Hee Lee, 2 daughters. Education: MD, Kyung-Hee University, Seoul, Korea, 1988; National Medical Licence, Ministry of Health and Welfare of Korea, 1988; Korean Board of Diagnostic Radiology, Ministry of Health and Welfare of Korea, 1992. Appointments: Radiology Residency, Kyung-Hee University Hospital, Seoul, Korea, 1989-92; Director of Diagnostic Radiology, Gil Medical Centre, Incheon, Korea, 1992-99; Assistant Professor of Diagnostic Radiology, 1999-2001, Associate Professor of Diagnostic Radiology, 2001-, Gachon Medical School Gil Medical Centre. Publications: 20 articles in medical journals as author and co-author include most recently: Imaging findings of hepatic sinusoidal dilation, 2004; Acute necrotizing encephalopathy in Korean infants and children: imaging findings and diverse clinical outcome, 2004;

Unusual causes of tubo-ovarian abscess: CT and MR imaging findings, 2004; Cystic lesions in the posterosuperior portion of the humeral head on MR arthography: correlations with gross and histologic findings in cadavers, 2005; Tailgut cyst: MRI evaluation, 2005. Honours: Cum Laude Award, Radiological Society of North America, 2003; Certificate of Merit Award, American Roentgen Ray Society, 2003; Cum Laude Award European Congress of Radiology, 2004. Memberships: Korean Radiological Society; Korean Society of Abdominal Radiology. Address: Department of Radiology, Gachon Medical School, Gil Medical Centre, 1198 Guwol-Dong, Namdong-Gu, Incheon, 405-760 Republic of Korea. E-mail: dmyang@gilhospital.com

**YANG Dian-Qing,** b. 18 March 1956, Yichun, China. Research Scientist. m. Ya-Xue Lui, 1 son, 1 daughter. Education: BSc, Northeast Forestry University, China, 1978; MSc, Northeast Forestry University, China, 1981; PhD, University of Toronto, Canada, 1991. Appointments: Lecturer, Department of Forestry, Northeast Forestry University, Harbin, China, 1981-86; Research Fellow, Department of Forest Sciences, Laval University, Quebec, PQ, 1991-94; Mycologist and Research Scientist on Wood Protection, Forintek Canada Corp, Eastern Laboratory, Sainte-Foy, PQ, Canada, 1994-. Publications: 100 publications in forest pathology, mycology, fungal molecular biology, biological control and wood protection; 1 US and 1 Canadian patent in wood protection. Honours: 2nd Prize for excellent research on Forest Science, Forest Ministry of China; University of Toronto open fellowship; The Jeanne F Goulding Fellowship; University of Toronto departmental graduate student Research Assistant Award. Memberships: Various institutions including: British Mycological Society; American Wood Preservation Association; Forest Products Society. Address: Forintek Canada Corp, 319 rue Franquet, Sainte-Foy, Quebec, G1P 4R4, Canada.

**YANG Heung-Joon,** b. 1 June 1946, Kyungnam Province, Korea. Chief Executive Officer; Businessman. m. Hyesook Jhe Yang, 1 daughter. Education: BS, Chemical Engineering, Seoul National University, Seoul, Korea, 1969; PhD, Bioengineering, University of Washington, Seattle, Washington, USA, 1989; Advanced Management Programme, Business Administration School, Seoul National University, 2002. Appointments: Executive and Director, 1991-94, Vice-President and Chief Technology Officer, 1995-98, Senior Vice-President, Strategic Business Planning, 1999, Executive Vice-President and Chief Executive Officer, Life Sciences Unit, 2000-2002; President and Chief Executive Officer, LG Life Sciences, 2002-; Vice-Chairman, Board of Korean Pharmaceutical Manufacturers Association, 2003-; Vice-Chairman, Board of Korean Bioindustries Association, 2003-; Member of Advisory Board on Korea Biotechnology Policy, 2004-. Publication: Opportunities and Challenges for Life Science Industries in Developing Countries (conference paper), 2005. Honour: Awarded the Gold Tower Order of Industrial Service Merit on Korea's 39th Annual Inventions Day. Memberships: American Chemical Society; Korean Chemical Engineering Society; The National Academy of Engineering of Korea. Address: LG Twin Towers (East Tower), 20 Yoido-dong, Youngdungpo-gu, Seoul, 150-721 Korea. E-mail: hjyang@lgls.co.kr

**YANG Lian,** b. 22 February 1955, Bern, Switzerland. Poet. m. Liu You Hong, 19 October 1989. Appointments: Writer, Central Broadcasting, 1977-88; Visiting Scholar, Auckland University, 1989-90, Sydney University, 1992-93; Writer-in-Residence, Berlin, 1990-91; Fellowship, Amherst College, USA, 1993-94; Poet-in-Residence, Akademie Schloss Solitude. Publications include: Li Hun, 1985; Huang Hun, 1986; Pilgerfahrt, 1986; In Symmetry with Death, 1988; Huang, 1989; Ren de Zijue,

1989; Masks and Crocodile, 1990; The Death in Exile, 1990; Yi, 1991; Gedichte, 1992; Gui Hua, 1994; Non-Person Singular, 1994; Geisterreden, 1995; Where the Sea Stands Still, 1995; Der Ruhepunkt des Meeres, 1996; Yang Lian's Works, 1982-1997, 1998; Where the Sea Stands Still - New Poems, 1999; City of dead Poets, 2000; Yi, 2001; Notes of a Blissful Ghost, 2002. Contributions to: Times Literary Supplement; World Apart; Wild Peony; Die Zeit; Die Tageszeitung. Honours: Chinese Poetry Readers Choice, 1986; Flaiano International Prize, Italy, 1999; Poetry Books Society Recommended Translation, UK, 1999. Memberships: Survivors Poetry Club, founder; Today Literature Research Society, Councillor. Address: 22 Carlton Mansions, Holmleigh Road, London N16 5PX, England.

**YANG Lin-De,** b. 12 December 1939, Wuxi, China. Professor. m. Ruo-Lian Qian, 2 sons. Education: Graduated, Tongji University, 1963. Appointments: Assistant, 1963, Lecturer, 1978, Associate Professor, 1987, Professor, 1990-, Tongji University. Publications: Back Analysis of Rock tunnel Using Boundary Element Method, 1989; Back Analysis theory and its Application in Geotechnical Engineering, 1996; Back Analysis of Initial Rock Stresses and Time-dependent Parameters, 1996; The evaluation of the segment internal forces in the construction process of shield tunnel, 1999; A Calculation Method for Composite Lining in NATM, Frontiers of Rock Mechanics and Sustainable Development in the 21st Century, 2001; Shaking Table Test and Numerical Calculation on Subway Station Structures in Soft Soil, 2003; The Durability for Concrete Lining Structure of Highway-tunnel and the thickness of Concrete Cover, 2003; A Study on Risk Durability Failure of the Segments for Underwater Tunnel, 2004. Memberships: CSRME; CSCE. Address: 1239 Siping Road, Tongki University, Shanghai 200092, China. E-mail: yangldn@mail.tongi.edu.cn Website: http://geotec.tongji.edu.cn/selfpage/yang-linde.htm

**YANG Shian-Cherng,** b. 2 October 1954, Taipei, Taiwan. Chemical Engineer. m. Jenny Q Z Lee, 2 sons. Education: BS, Chemistry, National Taiwan Normal University, Taipei, Taiwan, 1978; MS, Chemical Engineering, National Tsing Hua University, Hsinchu, Taiwan, 1980; PhD, Chemical Engineering, University of Connecticut, USA, 1988. Appointments: Instructor , Lee-Ming Institute of Technology, Taipei, Taiwan, 1982-83; Research Scientist, Engineer, Stonehart Associates Inc., Madison, Connecticut, USA, 1988; Researcher, Industrial Technology Research Institute, Chutung, Hsinchu, Taiwan, 1989-2005. Publications: Articles in scientific journals including: Electrochimica Acta, 1992; Journal of Power Sources, 1994; Journal of Electrochemical Society, 2000. Honours: Listed in Who's Who publications and biographical dictionaries. Membership: Electrochemical Society, USA. Address: 14-3, Ln 64, Sec 2, Chungsiao E Road, Taipei, Taiwan 100, Republic of China. E-mail: syang8253@yahoo.com.tw

**YANG Xin-She,** b. 31 January 1965, Henan, China. Research Fellow. m. Haiyun Zhang, 1 son. Education: BSc, Computer Science, Beijing, 1982-86; MSc, Physics, Chinese Academy of Sciences, 1986-89; DPhil, Applied Mathematics, University of Oxford, 1994-97. Appointments: College Lecturer, Corpus Christi College, Oxford, 1995-96; Research Fellow, University of Leeds, 1998-2001; Senior Research Fellow, University of Wales, Swansea, 2001-2004; Research Associate, Department of Engineering, University of Cambridge, 2004-. Publications: 45 research papers in international journals and conference proceedings include: Chaos in small-world networks, 2001; Allais gravity and pendulum effect, 2003; Pattern formation, 2004. Honours: Distinguished Young Scientist, Chinese Academy of Sciences, 1992; Garside Senior Scholarship, 1995, 1996; Fellow of Royal Institution, 2005-. Memberships:

Royal Institution; American Mathematical Society. Address: Department of Engineering, University of Cambridge, Trumpington Street, Cambridge CB2 1PZ, England. E-mail: xy227@eng.cam.ac.uk

**YANG Xinjian (Sam),** b. 15 November 1954, Hunan, China. Environmental Engineer. m. Bing Shui, 1 son. Education: Bachelor of Engineering, Xiangtan University, China, 1982; Master of Science, University of Cincinnati, Cincinnati, Ohio, 1991. Appointments: Lecturer, Xiangtan University, China, 1982-86; Research Scholar, University of Cambridge, England, 1987-88; Research Assistant, Graduate Student, University of Cincinnati, part-time USEPA Contractor, Cincinnati, 1988-91; Senior Engineer, Process and Development, Preussag Noell Inc, Long Beach, California, 1991-97; Senior Engineer: Mitsubishi, 1997-2000, ABB-Alstan Inc, 2000-2001, ERM Inc, 2004-. Publications: Many published papers in China, England and United States authorised textbooks; Invented 7 patent applications and one privately owned patent. Honours: Chinese Education Committee Scholarship; Honorary Fellowship, Salford University; Visiting Scholar, University of Cambridge, England; Listed in national and international biographical dictionaries. Memberships: Air and Waste Management Association, USA; Chinese Science and Technology Association, China. Address: 12001 Cherry Street, Los Alamitos, CA 90720, USA.

**YANG Yun-Liang,** b. 30 March 1963, Tapei City, Taiwan, Republic of China. Molecular Geneticist. m. Hsiu-Jung Lo, 2 daughters. Education: BS, National Chung-Hsing University, Taichung, Taiwan, 1985; PhD, Indiana University, Bloomington, Indiana, USA, 1993. Appointments: Research Associate, Department of Biology, Indiana University, Bloomington, Indiana, USA, 1993-94; Research Fellow, Department of Medicine, Brigham and Women's Hospital, Harvard Medical School, Boston, Massachusetts, 1995-99; Assistant Professor, Department of Biological Science and Technology, National Chiao-Tung University, Hsin-chu, Taiwan. Publications: Articles in scientific journals include: Efg 1 involved in drug resistance through regulating the expression of ERG3 in Candida albicans; Receptors for polytropic and xenotropic mouse leukaemia viruses encoded by a single gene at RMC1; Suppression of ColE1-high-copy-number mutants by mutations in the polA gene of Escherichia coli. Honours: Ching-Er Medal, National Chung-Hsing University, 1985; Excellent Award for Graduate Advisor, National Chiao-Tung University, 2001; Secondary Award for Teaching, National Chiao-Tung University, 2002. Address: 75 Pao-Ai Street, Department of Biological Science and Technology, NCTU, Hsin-chu, Taiwan, ROC.

**YANTOVSKI Evgeny,** b. 13 May 1929, Kharkov, Ukraine. Mechanical Engineer. m. Alla Lomakina, 1 daughter. Education: Mechanical Engineer, Kharkov Aviation Institute, 1951; Candidate of Engineering Science, Kourchatov Atomic Energy Institute, 1963; Doctor of Engineering Science, Krjijanovski Energy Institute, Moscow, 1973; Professor, State Attest Committee, Moscow, 1989. Appointments: Technologist, Aviation Mill, Taganrog, 1951-53; Design Engineer, 1953-59, Head of MHD Laboratory, 1959-71, Electrotechnical Institute, Kharkov; Senior Researcher, Krjijanovski Energy Institute, Moscow, 1971-74; Senior Researcher, Institute for Industrial Energetics, Moscow, 1974-86; Chief Researcher, Energy Research Institute, Russian Academy of Science, Moscow, 1986-95; Numerous Visiting Lectureships throughout Europe and USA. Publications: Books: Theory of electrorockets for space propulsion, co-author, 1970, 1978; Magnetohydrodynamic Generators, 1972; Compressional Heat Pumps, 1982; Energy and Exergy Currents, 1988, 1994; Industrial Heat Pumps, 1989; Articles in English include: The thermodynamics of power plants without exhaust gases, 1991; Exergonomics in Education, 2000; Gas Power Zero Emission Convergency Complex, 2000; A version of Non-equilibrium Thermodynamics with Entropy and Information as Positive and Negative Thermal Charge, 2001; Zero Emission Ion Transport Membrane Oxygen Power Cycle (ZEITMOP), 2002; Toward a Live Sea near the Dead one, 2002; Zero Emission Membrane Piston Engine System (ZEMPES), 2003 and other articles in professional journals. Address: Elsass str 58, D-52068 Aachen, Germany. E-mail: iksvotnay@aol.com

**YAO Kui,** b. 14 October 1967, Huainan, China. Senior Scientist. Education: BS, Xi'an Jiaotong University, China, 1989; MS, Xidian University, China, 1992; PhD, Xi'an Jiaotong University, China, 1995. Appointments: Post Doctoral Fellow, 1995-97, Research Fellow, assigned by Institute of Materials Research and Engineering, 1997-98, Nanyang Technological University, Singapore; Research Associate, Pennsylvania State University, USA, 1998-99; Research Fellow, 1997-2001, Senior Research Fellow, 2002-2003, Senior Scientist, 2003-, Institute of Materials Research and Engineering (IMRE), Singapore. Publications: Many invention patents and technical publications in scientific journals. Memberships: IEEE; MRS. Address: Institute of Materials Research and Engineering, 3 Research Link, Singapore 117602, Singapore.

**YAPOR Wesley Yamil,** b. 3 July 1955, Chicago, Illinois, USA. Neurosurgeon; Divemaster. 3 sons, 1 daughter. Education: Abraham School of Medicine, University of Illinois, Chicago; Divemaster, Professional Association of Diving Instructors. Appointments: Assistant Professor of Neurosurgery, Northwestern University, Chicago; Private Practice, Northwestern Neurosurgical Associates specialising in brain and spine surgery; Divemaster, Elite Diving Charters specialising in Lake Michigan wreck diving charters; Captain, US Coastguard, Merchant Marine. Publications: Several articles in medical journals including: Neurosurgery; Journal of Neurosurgery; Neurological Surgery; Stroke; 2 books: Onsite Management of Diving and Boating Emergencies; Essentials of Diving Safety; Patent: The Cerebral Dilator, patents in USA, England, Germany, France and Japan. Memberships: American Medical Association; Illinois State Medical Association; Chicago Medical Association; Illinois Neurological Association; Chicago Neurological Association; American Association of Neurological Surgeons; Congress of Neurological Surgeons; United State Coastguard; US Merchant Marine and Licensed Captain. Address: Northwestern Neurosurgical Associates, 201 East Huron, Suite 9-160, Chicago, IL 60611, USA. E-mail: weslypap@aol.com

**YAQUB Pervez Raziq,** b. 15 December 1961, Peshawar, Pakistan. Engineer. m. Kiran Raziq, 1 son, 2 daughters. Education: BSc, University of Peshawar, 1981; BSc Engineering with honours, 1985, MSc Engineering with honours, University of Engineering and Technology, Peshawar; PhD, Keio University, Tokyo, Japan, 1998; MBA, FDU, New Jersey, USA. Appointments: Aircraft Engineer, Pakistan International Airlines, 1986-87; Shift Engineer, Pakistan Water and Power Development Authority, 1987-88; Assistant Divisional Engineer, Pakistan Telecommunication Corporation, 1988-93; English Teacher, YMCA and Minami Junior High School, Tsurugashima, Saitama, Japan, 1995-98; Research Engineer, NOKIA, 1998-99; Assistant Manager, DDI Corporation, Japan, 1999-2001; Research Director, Toshiba America Research Inc, 2001-. Publications: Research papers in professional journals, transactions and international conference proceedings; Editor, Writer, English Newspaper, Keio University. Honours: Scholarship, Rikkyo University, Tokyo, 1993-95; Scholarship,

Keio University, 1995-96; Scholarship, Ministry of Education, Government of Japan, 1996-98; Principal Nominee as Visiting Researcher, Rikkyo University. Memberships: IEICE; Christian Students Fellowship Pakistan; Anglican Church Peshawar; Operation Committee and Session Chair, IWDCCA; Chairman, Mobile Wireless Internet Forum, 2000-. Address: 15 Cook Court, Stewartsville, NJ 08886, USA.

**YASUFUKU Sachio,** b. 11 November 1929, Qingdao, China. Electrical Engineer. m. Yoko Kikutani, 16 December 1958. Education: BSc, 1952, DEng, 1979, Nagoya University. Appointments: Engineer, Furukawa Electric Co Ltd, Japan, 1952-72; Senior and Chief Specialists, Toshiba Corporation, Japan, 1972-89; Adjunct Professor, Tokyo Denki University, 1989-2005. Publications: 13 papers, on IEEE Transactions Electrical Insulation; 10 papers on IEEE Electrical Insulation Magazine; 13 papers on IEEE DEIS Sponsored Conference Proceedings; Altogether over 60 papers published; Over 10 patents (including US patents). Honours: National Award Invention, Japan, 1963; 23rd National Award for JEMA, about Progress of Electric Machinery, 1974; IEEE Fellow Award, 1993; Distinguished Service Award, IEEE DEIS, 1997; IEEE Life Fellow, 2001. Memberships: Society Polymer Science, Japan, 1952; IEEE, 1972; IEEJ, 1974. Address: 603, 2-5 2-chome, Katase, Fujisawa City, 251-0032 Japan.

**YE Minglu,** b. 13 April 1936, Fujian Province, China. Professor of Chemistry. m. Jingjuan Tang, 1 son, 1 daughter. Education: Graduated, Chemistry Department, Fudan University, Shanghai, China, 1958. Appointments: Worked in Department of Nuclear Science, 1958-96, then Department of Environmental Science and Engineering, 1996-98, Fudan University, Shanghai, 1958-98; Professor and Director of the Nuclear Chemistry Section, Fudan University; Lectures, Nuclear Chemistry and Application of Nuclear Technology and completed many science research projects; Visiting Scholar, Freie Universitat Berlin (Free University, Berlin), West Germany, 1984-85; Visiting Researcher, Japan Atomic Energy Research Institute, 1994; Retired, 1998. Publications: 5 books include: Radiochemistry Experiments, 1991; Introduction of Environmental Chemistry, 1997; 62 scientific papers. Honours: 5 science and technology prizes awarded by Shanghai Science Commission and Ministry of Nuclear Industry of China, 1984-96; Biography listed in several national and international biographical publications. Memberships: Council Member: Isotope Society of China, 1985-98, Nuclear and Radiochemistry Society of China, 1991-98. Address: 14 Sydney Road, Lindfield, NSW 2070, Australia. E-mail: mingluye@yahoo.com.au

**YELTSIN Boris Nikolayevich,** b. 1 February 1931, Sverdlovsk, Russia. Politician (Retired). Education: Urals Polytech Institute. Appointments: Foreman, Chief of Works, Chief Engineer, Head, Construction Administration, Yushgorstvoy Trust, 1955-63; Chief Engineer, Director, Sverdlovsk House Building Complex, 1963-68; Member, CPSU, 1961-90; Secretary, Sverdlovsk Provincial Committee, 1968-76; 1st Secretary, District Central Committee, Sverdlovsk, 1976-85; Member, Party Central Committee, 1981; Secretary, Central Committee, 1985-86; 1st Secretary, Moscow Party Committee, 1985-87; Candidate Member, Politburo, 1986-88; 1st Deputy Chairman, State Committee for Construction, 1987-89; Chairman, Committee for Construction and Architecture, 1989-90; Member, Congress of People's Deputies, 1989-91; Chairman, Supreme Soviet, RSFSR, 1990-91; President, Russian Federation, 1991-99; Resigned, 1999; Acting Head, Russian Federation Defence Ministry, 1992; Supreme Commander of Russian Army, 1992-99. Publications: Against the Grain, autobiography, 1990; Three Days, 1992; Memoirs: The View from the Kremlin, 1990, 1994,

2000. Honours: Olympic Gold Order, 1992; German Press Award, 1996.

**YENTOB Alan,** b. 11 March 1947, England. Television Administrator. 1 son, 1 daughter, by Philippa Walker. Education: University of Grenoble, France; University of Leeds. Appointments: BBC General Trainee, 1968; Producer, Director, 1970-, Head of Music & Arts, 1985-88, BBC TV; Controller, BBC 2, 1988-93, BBC 1, 1993-96, BBC Director of Programmes, 1996-97; BBC Director of TV, 1997-2000, of Drama, Entertainment and Children's Programmes, 2000-. Honours: Fellow, RCA, RIBA. Memberships: Board of Directors, Riverside Studios, 1984-88, British Film Institute Production Board, 1985-93; British Screen Advisory Council; Advisory Committee, Institute of Contemporary Arts; Council, Royal Court Theatre; Governor, National Film School, 1998-; South Bank Board, 1999-. Address: BBC Television, Television Centre, Wood Lane, London W12 7RJ, England.

**YEO Jung-Sou,** b. 10 May 1950, Gimcheon, Korea. Professor. m. Taesun Kim, 1 son, 1 daughter. Education: BS, Department of Animal Science, Yeungnam University, Korea, 1973; MS, 1978, PhD, 1981, Department of Animal Science, Seoul National University. Appointments: Postdoctoral, University of Minnesota, USA, 1984-85; Concurrent, Researcher, Rural Development Organisation, Korea, 1988-92, Director, Biotechnology Institute, Yeungnam University, Korea, 1987-99; Dean of Natural Resources College, Yeungnam University, Korea, 2001-. Publications: Animal Biotechnology and another 10 publications; Linkage Mapping and QTL on Chromosome 6 in Korean Cattle (Hanwoo) and another 80 articles. Honours: The Best Agricultural Research, Minister of Agriculture, Korea; The Best Researcher, Korean Society of Animal Science and Technology, Korea. Memberships: Korean Society of Animal Science and Technology; American Poultry Science. Address: School of Biotechnology, Yeungnam University, Gyeongsan, Gyeongbuk, 712-749 Korea. E-mail: jsyeo@yu.ac.kr

**YIN Ken-Ming,** b. 22 August 1958, Kaoshiung, Taiwan. Professor of Chemical Engineering. m. Li-Li Cheng, 2 sons. Education: BS, Chemical Engineering, National Taiwan University, 1980; MS, Chemical Engineering, University of New Mexico, USA, 1985; PhD, Chemical Engineering, Texas A&M University, USA, 1991. Appointments: Assistant Research Engineer, Texas A&M University, 1991-92; Professor, Yuan-Ze University, Taiwan, 1999. Publications: 27 articles in international scientific journals as author and co-author include most recently: An Annular Reactor Model for Copper Electrowinning under Laminar Flow, 2001; A Parametric Study on the Electrochemical Impedance Spectroscopy of Organic Coated Steels in Hydrochloric Acid Solutions, 2003; Mathematical Model of Galvanostatic Pulse with reverse Plating in the Presence of Surface Blocking Agent, 2003. Honours: Silver Medal Award, 1993, First-time Authors' Award, 1994, American Electroplaters and Surface Finishers Society. Membership: Electrochemical Society. Address: 13-9F, Alley 81, Yuan-Tung Road, Neili, Taoyuan, Taiwan 32026. E-mail: cekenyin@saturn.yzu.edu.tw

**YOELI Pinhas (Günther Aptekmann),** b. 1 July 1920, Bayreuth, Germany. Professor. m. Agi Izsakova, 2 sons. Education: Eidgenoessische Technische Hochschule, Switzerland, 1956. Appointments: Senior Lecturer, Technion, Israel, 1957-64; Associate Professor, 1964-68; Professor, Tel Aviv University, 1968-91; Professor Emeritus, 1991-. Publications: Cartographic Drawing with Computers, author, 1982; Contributions to articles in professional journals. Memberships: Israel Surveyors Association; Association of Engineers and Architects; Israel Cartographic Association, president, 1988-91. Address: Tel Aviv University, Ramat Aviv, Tel Aviv, Israel. E-mail: yoeli@post.tau.ac.il

**YOKOYAMA Kazunari K,** b. 11 March 1951, Hokkaido, Japan. Researcher. m. Tomoko Yokoyama, 2 sons. Education: PhD, Science, Tokyo University, 1979. Appointments: Division Head, Gene Engineering Division, RIKEN, Japan; Honorary Professor, China, Medical University, China; Adjunct Professor, University of Tennessee, Knoxville, USA; Visiting Professor, Fudan University, China. Publications: Articles in scientific journals including: Proceedings of the National Academy of Science, USA, 1981, 1987; EMBO Journal, 1992, 1995; Genes and Development, 1998; Nature, 1998, 2000; Molecular and Cellular Biology, 2002; Cancer Research, 2003, 2005; Science, 2005. Honours: Research Award, China Medical University, 1995; Research Award, Fudan University, 1997; Research Award, Shanghai Biotechnology Association, 1997. Memberships: American Association for Cancer Research; American Microbiology Society. Address: Gene Engineering Division, RIKEN, BioResource Center, 3-1-1 Koyadai, Tsukuba, Ibaraki 305-0074, Japan. E-mail: yokoyama@brc.riken.jp

**YOON Hyung-Joo,** b. 23 October 1962, Busan, Korea. Researcher. m. 1 son. Education: BS, Dong-A University, 1985; MS, 1987, PhD, 2001, Seoul National University. Appointments: Director of Pollinator Research Laboratory, Department of Agricultural and Technology, National Institute of Agriculture Science and Technology, Korea, 2003-; Visiting: Huazhong University, China, 2002, Division of Apiculture, Research Institute of Pomology and Floriculture, Poland, 2002; Copenhagen University Denmark, 2003, Tamagawa University, Japan, 2004, Chinese Academy of Agricultural Science, 2005. Publications: Over 20 papers in scientific journals as co-author include most recently: Colony developmental characteristics of the bumblebee, Bombus ignitus by the first ovipostion day, 2004; Influence of chilling duration on oxygen consumption and hatchability of eggs in silkworm, Bombyx mori, 2004; Phylogenetic relationships among some bumblebees (Hymenoptera:Apidae) common in Korea inferred from mitochondrial 16S rRNA sequences, 2004; A novel cellulase gene from the mulberry longicorn beetle, Apriona germari: Gene structure, expression and enzymatic activity, 2005; N-glycosylation is necessary for enzymatic activity of a beetle (Apriona germari) cellulase, 2005. Memberships: Editor, International Journal of Industrial Entomology, 2004-; Editor, Korean Journal of Applied Entomology, 2004-; Executive Director: Korean Society of Entomology, 2002-, Korean Society of Sericultural Science, 2002-, Korean Society of Apiculture, 2003-. Address: Department of Agricultural Biology, The National Institute of Agricultural Science and Technology, RDA, Suwon 441-100, Korea. E-mail: yoonhj@rda.go.kr

**YORK Michael (Michael York-Johnson),** b. 27 March 1942, Fulmer, England, Actor. m. Patricia McCallum, 1968. Education: University College, Oxford. Appointments: Dundee Repertory Co, 1964, National Theatre Company, 1965; Guest Lecturer, Chair, CA Youth Theatre. Creative Works: TV appearances include: The Forsyte Saga; Rebel in the Grave; True Patriot; Much Ado About Nothing; Jesus of Nazareth; A Man Called Intrepid; For Those I Loved; The Weather in The Streets; The Master of Ballantrae; Space; The Far Country; Are You My Mother, 1986; Ponce de Leon, 1987; Knot's Landing, 1987; The Four Minute Mile, 1988; The Lady and the Highwayman, 1988; The Heat of the Day, 1988; A Duel of Love, 1990; The Road to Avonlea, 1990; Teklab, 1994; September, 1995; A Young Connecticut Yankee in King Arthur's Court, 1995; Not of This Earth, 1995; The Ring, 1996; True Women, 1996; The Haunting of Hall House, 2000; The Lot, 2001; Founding Fathers, Founding Brothers; Films include: The Return of the Musketeers, 1988; Till We Meet Again, 1989; The Heat of the Day, 1989; The Night of the Fox, 1990; Eline Vere, 1990; Duel of Hearts, 1990; The Wanderer, 1991; The Long Shadow, 1991; Wide Sargasso Sea, 1991; Rochade, 1991; Discretion Assured, 1993; The Shadow of a Kiss, 1994; Fall From Grace, 1994; Gospa, 1995; Goodbye America, 1996; Austin Powers, 1996; Dark Planet, 1996; The Ripper, 1997; A Knight in Camelot, 1998; Perfect Little Angels, 1998; Wrongfully Accused, 1998; One Hell of a Guy, 1998; The Omega Code, 1999; Borstal boy, 2000; Megiddo, 2001; Austin Powers in Goldmember, 2002. Publications: The Courage of Conviction, 1986; Voices of Survival, 1987; Travelling Player (autobiography), 1991; Accidentally on Purpose (autobiography), 1992; A Shakespearian Actor Prepares, 2000; Dispatches From Armageddon, 2002. Honours: Numerous. Address: c/o Andrew Manson, 288 Munster Road, London SW6 6BQ, England. Website: www.michaelyork.net

**YORK Susannah,** b. 9 January 1942, London, England. Actress. m. Michael Wells, 1960, divorced 1976, 1 son, 1 daughter. Education: Royal Academy of Dramatic Art. Creative Works: Films include: Tunes of Glory, 1960; The Greengage Summer, 1961; Freud, 1962; Tom Jones, 1963; The Seventh Dawn, 1964; Act One Scene Nun, 1964; Sands of the Kalahari, 1965; Scruggs, 1966; Kaleidoscope, 1966; A Man for All Seasons, 1966; Sebastian, 1967; The Killing of Sister George, 1968; Duffy, 1968; Lock Up Your Daughters, 1969; They Shoot Horses, Don't They?, 1969; Country Dance, 1970; Jane Eyre, 1970; Zee and Co, 1971; Happy Birthday Wanda June, 1971; Images, 1972; The Maids, Gold, 1974; Conduct Unbecoming, 1974; That Lucky Touch, 1975; Skyriders, 1976; Eliza Fraser, 1976; The Shout, 1977; The Silent Partner, Superman II, 1980; Yellowbeard, Fatal Attraction, 1985; A Summer Story, 1987; Melancholia, 1988; Just Ask for Diamond, 1988; Princess, 1993; TV appearances: The Crucible; Fallen Angels; Second Chance; We'll Meet Again; The Other Side of Me; Macho; Trainer; Devices and Desires; Producer, The Big One, 1983; Numerous stage appearances. Publications: Childrens books: In Search of Unicorns; Larks Castle. Honours include: Best Actress Award, Cannes Film Festival.

**YORKE Margaret, (Margaret Beda Nicholson),** b. 30 January 1924, Surrey, England. Writer. 1 son, 1 daughter. Appointments: Assistant Librarian, St Hilda's College, Oxford, 1959-60; Library Assistant, Christ Church, Oxford, 1963-65; Chairman, Crime Writers Association, 1979-80. Publications: Summer Flight, 1957; Pray Love Remember, 1958; Christopher, 1959; Deceiving Mirror, 1960; The China Doll, 1961; Once a Stranger, 1962; The Birthday, 1963; Full Circle, 1965; No Fury, 1967; The Apricot Bed, 1968; The Limbo Ladies, 1969; Dead in the Morning, 1970; Silent Witness, 1972; Grave Matters, 1973; No Medals for the Major, 1974; Mortal Remains, 1974; The Small Hours of the Morning, 1975; Cast for Death, 1976; The Cost of Silence, 1977; The Point of Murder, 1978; Death on Account, 1979; The Scent of Fear, 1980; The Hand of Death, 1981; Devil's Work, 1982; Find Me a Villain, 1983; The Smooth Face of Evil, 1984; Intimate Kill, 1985; Safely to the Grave, 1986; Evidence to Destroy, 1987; Speak for the Dead, 1988; Crime in Question, 1989; Admit to Murder, 1990; A Small Deceit, 1991; Criminal Damage, 1992; Dangerous to Know, 1993; Almost the Truth, 1994; Pieces of Justice, 1994; Serious Intent, 1995; A Question of Belief, 1996; Act of Violence, 1997; False Pretences, 1998; The Price of Guilt, 1999; A Case to Answer, 2000; Cause for Concern, 2001. Honours: Swedish Academy of Detection, 1982; Cartier Diamond Dagger, Crime Writers Association, 1999 Address: c/o Curtis Brown Ltd, Haymarket House, 28/29 Haymarket, London SW1Y 4SP, England.

**YOSHIDA Fumitake,** b. 20 March 1913, Saitama, Japan. Professor Emeritus, Kyoto University. m. Kazuko, deceased, 1 son, 1 daughter. Education: BEng, 1937, Dr Eng, 1951, Kyoto University. Appointments: Chemical Engineer, Hitachi Ltd, 1937-45; Assistant Professor, 1945-51, Professor, 1951-76, Professor Emeritus, 1976-, Kyoto University; Visiting Fellow, Yale University, 1952; Research Fellow, University of Wisconsin, 1959; Visiting Professor, University of California, Berkeley, 1963; Visiting Professor, University of Pennsylvania, 1970; Guest Professor, University of Dortmund, 1987. Publications: Around 60 research papers; Book: Chemical Engineering and Artificial Organs, with Sakai, in Japanese, 1993. Honours: Distinguished Service Citation, University Wisconsin, 1988; Honorary Dr Ing, University of Dortmund, 1992. Memberships: National Academy of Engineering, USA; American Institute of Chemical Engineers; American Chemical Society; Society Chemical Engineers, Japan; Japanese Society of Artificial Organs. Address: 2 Matsugasaki-Yobikaeshi, Sakyo-ku, Kyoto 606-0912, Japan.

**YOSHIDA Hiroshi,** b. 5 August 1962, Sasebo, Nagasaki, Japan. Doctor; Educator; Scientist. m. Mayumi Watanabe, 1 son. Education: MD, 1987, PhD, 1999, National Defence Medical College; Medical Diplomate, Japan, 1987. Appointments: Lieutenant Colonel, Medical Department, Ground Staff Office, Japan Defence Agency, 2000-2001; Instructor, 2001-2003, Assistant Professor, 2003-, Department of Internal Medicine, Chief Physician of General Medicine, 2003-, Jikei University School of Medicine. Publications: Articles as first author and co-author in medical journals including: ATVB, 1997, 1998; Biochemical Journal, 1998; Atherosclerosis, 1998, 2005; Biochemical Pharmacology, 1999; Current Opinion in Lipidology, 2003; Journal of Lipid Research, 2003; Clinical Science, 2005; Clinica Chimica Acta, 2004, 2005. Honours: Award for Outstanding Publication Article, National Defence Medical Society, 2000; Encouragement Prize, Japanese Society of Laboratory Medicine, 2004. Memberships: Fellow, Japanese Society of Internal Medicine, 1993-; Fellow Japanese Circulation Society, 1994-; Councillor, Japan Atherosclerosis Society; American College of Physicians. Address: Division of General Medicine, Department of Internal Medicine, Kashiwa Hospital, Jikei University School of Medicine, 163-1 Kashiwashita, Kashiwa, Chiba, 277-8567 Japan. E-mail: hyoshida@jikei.ac.jp

**YOSHIDA Tsuguo,** b. 12 September 1952, Yokosuka City, Japan. Physician; Associate Professor. m. Shizue Komori, 1 son, 2 daughters. Education: Bachelor of Science, Tokyo University of Education, Tokyo, 1971-76; Doctor of Medicine, University of Tsukuba, Tsukuba City, 1979-86. Appointments: Systems Engineer, IBM, Tokyo, Japan, 1976-79; Physician Tsukuba University Hospital, 1986-92; Part-time Radiologist, Tsukuba Municipal Hospital Tsukuba City, 1986-2004; Associate Professor, Tsukuba College of Technology, Tsukuba City, 1992-2004. Publications: Articles in medical journals conference proceedings include: Evaluation on Surface and Deep Temperature of Phantom Irradiated by Pulsed or Continuous Microwaves, 1997; Mental health of the visually and hearing impaired students from the viewpoint of University Personality Inventory, 1998; Making Tactile Charts on a Personal Computer for Blind Students in the Allied Health Professions, 2002. Honours: Life Science Foundation, 1972 The Telecommunication Advancement Foundation, 1999. Memberships: MENSA International, London; Consultant, Tsukuba City Office, Tsukuba City, Ibaraki Prefecture, Japan, 2001-2004, Address: 2-15-30 Higashi, Tsukuba City, Ibaraki Prefecture, Japan 305-0046. E-mail: tyl@mx3.ttcn.ne.jp

# DICTIONARY OF INTERNATIONAL BIOGRAPHY

**YOSHIHARA Hiroshi,** b. 16 October 1963, Tokyo, Japan. Associate Professor. Education: Bachelor of Agriculture, 1987, Doctor of Philosophy, 1995, Forest Products Department, Faculty of Agriculture, University of Tokyo, Japan. Appointments: Research Associate, Faculty of Agriculture, University of Tokyo, Japan, 1988-96; Associate Professor, Faculty of Science and Engineering, Shimane University, Japan, 1996-. Publications: Articles in scientific journals include: Mode II R-curve of wood measured by 4-ENF test, 2004. Honours: Progress Award, 1994, Prize, 2001, Japan Wood Research Society. Memberships: Japan Wood Research Society; Wood Technological Association of Japan; Society of Materials Science, Japan. Address: Department of Natural Resources Process Engineering, Faculty of Science and Engineering, Shimane University, Nishikawazu-cho 1060, Matsue, Shimane, 690-8504, Japan. E-mail: yosihara@riko.shimane-u.ac.jp

**YOSHIKANE Hiroaki,** b. 25 December 1959, Aichi, Japan. Medical Doctor. m. Keiko Yoshikane, 2 daughters. Education: Medical Doctor, Nagoya University. Appointments: Handa City Hospital, 1986-90; Nagoya University School of Medicine, 1990-93; Kariya General Hospital, 1993-95; Handa City Hospital, 1995-2002; Yoshikane Clinic, 2002-. Publications: Articles in medical journals include: Carcinoid tumors of the gastrointestinal tract: evaluation with endoscopic unltrasonography, 1993; Sequential observation of gastric ulcer healing by endoscopic ultrasonography, 1994. Memberships: Japanese Society of Internal Medicine; Japanese Society of Gastroenterology; Japan Society for Gastroenterological Endoscopy; American Society for Gastrointestinal Endoscopy. Address: 3-13-3 Aoyama, Handa, Aichi, 475-0836 Japan. E-mail: winwin@cac-net.ne.jp

**YOSHINO Fumio,** b. 7 August 1925, Tokyo, Japan. Medical Doctor; Physician. m. Niwa Hisayo, 1 son, 1 daughter. Education: MD, Yokohama Medical College, 1951; Resident, Yokohama City University Hospital, 1952-57; Dr of Medical Science, Kyoto University, 1959. Appointments: Laboratory Physician, Kanagawa Cancer Institute Hospital, 1963-68; Professor of Medical Technology, Kanagawa Prefectural College of Nursing and Medical Technology, 1968-91; Certified Laboratory Physician, 1980. Publications include: Textbook of Medical Technology; Handbook for Diagnosis Using Clinical Laboratory Data; SI Units in Japan. Honours: Professor Emeritus; Emeritus Member, American Association for Clinical Chemistry; Emeritus Member, Japanese Society of Laboratory Medicine. Memberships: Japanese Association for Clinical Chemistry and others. Address: 174-44 Ooba-cho, Aoba-ku, Yokohama, 225-0023, Japan. E-mail: y_fum@msg.biglobe.ne.jp

**YOSHIOKA Shoichi,** b. 3 November 1962, Okayama, Japan. Geophysicist. m. Masako Kunita. Education: BSc, Kobe University, Japan, 1985; MSc, 1987, PhD, 1990, Kyoto University, Japan. Appointments: Postdoctoral Fellow, Kyoto University, Japan, 1990-91; Postdoctoral Fellow, University of Tokyo, 1991-92; Postdoctoral Fellow, Utrecht University, The Netherlands, 1992-94; Assistant Professor, Ehime University, Matsuyama, Japan, 1994-97; Associate Professor, Kyushu University, 1997-. Publications: Contributor of numerous articles to professional journals. Memberships: American Geophysical Union; Seismological Society of Japan. Address: Aquitaine 203, Maimatsubara 5-12-5, Higashi Ward, Fukuoka 813-0042, Japan.

**YOSHIYAMA Mitsuharu,** b. 26 August 1964, Sawara, Chiba, Japan. Physician. Education: MD, Showa University School of Medicine, 1989; PhD, Showa University Graduate School of Medicine, 1993. Appointments: Research Associate,

Department of Pharmacology, University of Pittsburgh School of Medicine, 1989-98; Instructor, 1998, Research Assistant Professor, 1998-2005, Department of Pharmacology, University of Pittsburgh, School of Medicine, USA; Showa University, Fujigaoka Hospital, 2000; Department of Neurology, Chiba University Graduate School of Medicine, 2000-2003; Asahi Hospital for Neurological Diseases, 2001-2003; Yamanashi Onsen Hospital, 2003-05; Adjunct Professor, Department of Urology, University of Yamanashi Interdisciplinary Graduate School of Medicine and Engineering, 2003-05. Memberships: Society for Neuroscience, 1990-; International Brain Research Organisation, 1990-; International Continence Society, 2004. Address: Yamanashi Onsen Hospital, 855 Komatsu, Kasugai-cho, Fuefuki, Yamanashi, 406-0004 Japan. E-mail: pxn15164@nifty.com

**YOSHIZAWA Masahito,** b. 29 September 1952, Niitsu, Niigata Prefecture, Japan. University Professor. m. Makiko Okuzumi Yoshizawa, 1 son, 2 daughters. Education: Doctor of Science, Condensed Matter Physics, Tohoku University, Japan. Appointments: Alexander-von-Humboldt Fellow, Frankfurt University, Germany, 1984-86; Guest Researcher, Max-Planck Institute, Grenoble, France, 1986-89; Professor, Iwate University, Japan, 1989-; Achievements include: Discovery of dynamic and static properties of vortices in superconductors by ultrasonic investigation; Research in first ultrasonic investigation on organic superconductors; Development of magneto-cadio graph apparatus with three-dimensional current distribution image for diagnosis of heart disease. Memberships: Physical Society of Japan; Japan Biomagnetism and Bioelectromagnetics Society. Address: Graduate School of Frontier Materials and Functional Engineering, Iwate University, 4-3-5 Ueda, Morioka 020-8551, Japan. E-mail: yoshizawa@iwate-u.ac.jp

**YOSHIZAWA Masayasu,** b. 18 June 1952, Osaka, Japan. University Professor. m. Yoko, 2 daughters. Bachelor of Economics, 1975, Master of Economics, 1977, Kobe University. Appointments: Lecturer, 1980, Associate Professor, 1985, Professor, 1991-, Dream of the Department of Economics, 2003-, Hiroshima University of Economics. Publications: Market Mechanism and Economic Policies, 1993; Monetary Theories and Economic Policies, 1999; Market, Foreign Trade, Income Distribution and Money, 2002; Macroeconomics and Japan's Economy, 2002. Address: 4-15-12 Bishamondai, Asaminami-ku, 731-0152 Hiroshima, Japan.

**YOUNG Ben,** b. 1 December 1967, Hong Kong. Assistant Professor. Education: BSc, 1990, BEng, 1992, PhD, 1997, University of Sydney, Australia. Appointments: Senior Researcher, University of Sydney Australia, 1997-98; Assistant Professor, Nanyang Technological University, Singapore,1998-2001; Assistant Professor, Hong Kong University of Science and Technology, 2001-. Publications: Papers presented at conferences. Honours: Highly Commendable Paper Award, 7th International Conference on Steel and Space Structures, 2002; Bechtel Foundation Engineering Teaching Excellence Award, 2003; Listed in Who's Who publications and biographical dictionaries. Memberships: Fellow, Hong Kong Institute of Steel Construction; Member, American Society of Civil Engineers. Address: Hong Kong University of Science and Technology, Clear Water Bay, Kowloon, Hong Kong. E-mail: byoung@ust.hk

**YOUNG Ian George,** b. 5 January 1945, London, England. Poet; Writer; Editor. Appointments: Director, Catalyst Press, 1969-80, Director, TMW Communications, 1990-. Publications: Poetry: White Garland, 1969; Year of the Quiet Sun, 1969; Double Exposure, 1970; Cool Fire, 1970; Lions in the Stream,

1971; Some Green Moths, 1972; The Male Muse, 1973; Invisible Words, 1974; Common-or-Garden Gods, 1976; The Son of the Male Muse, 1983; Sex Magick, 1986. Fiction: On the Line, 1981. Non-Fiction: The Male Homosexual in Literature, 1975, 2nd edition, 1982; Overlooked and Underrated, 1981; Gay Resistance, 1985; The AIDS Dissidents, 1993; The Stonewall Experiment, 1995; The Aids Cult, 1997; The Beginnings of Gay Liberation in Canada, 2005. Honours: Several Canada Council and Ontario Arts Council Awards. Membership: International Psychohistory Association. Address: 2483 Gerrard Street East, Scarborough, Ontario M1N 1W7, Canada.

**YOUNG John Riddington,** b. 19 October 1947, Sheffield, England. Consultant Surgeon. m. Elizabeth Anne Barnes, 2 sons, 4 daughters. Education: MB ChB, Sheffield University, 1970; DLO, 1974, FRCS, 1976, Royal College of Surgeons of England; M Phil, Open University, Brussels, 2000. Appointments: Senior Registrar, Manchester Royal Infirmary, 1974-81; Senior Consultant Surgeon, Otolaryngology, Head and Neck Surgery, 1981-; Commanding Officer (Subst.Colonel), 211 (Wessex) Field Hospital, RAMC (v); Area Surgeon, North Devon, St John Ambulance. Publications: Inns and Taverns of Old Norwich, 1975; Wessex Field Hospital and the Croix de Guerre, 1996; Interesting Otolaryngology, 1998; Offbeat Otolaryngology, 2002; St Michaels's Church, Horwood: An Illustrated History, 2000. Honours: Territorial Decoration, 1985, and Bar, 1997; Officer (Brother) Most Venerable Order of Hospital of St John of Jerusalem. Memberships: Mackenzie Society; Blaize Society. Address: West Barton, Horwood, Bideford, Devon EX39 4PB, England.

**YU Hyun-Kyu,** b. 31 July 1958, Daegu, Korea. Semiconductor Engineer. m. Jung-Hee Kim, 1 son, 1 daughter. Education: BS, 1981, MS, 1983, Department of Electronics Engineering, Kyungbook National University; PhD, Department of Electrical and Electronics Engineering, Korea Advanced Institute of Science and Technology (KAIST), 1994. Appointments: Principal Staff and Manager of RF/Analog SoC Design Team, ETRI, Korea; Head of National Research Laboratory on RF CMOS Technology Area, Ministry of Science and Technology, Korea; Visiting Professor, University of Florida, USA; Adjunct Professor, Chunpook National University, Korea; Founder and Chairman Committee of Silicon RF Integrated Circuit Technology Workshop; Technical Advisor, Korean Intellectual Property Office. Publications: 37 papers in international journals include most recently: Prescaler Using Complementary Clocking Dynamic Flip-Flop, 2003; Variable Inductance Multilayer Inductor with MOSFET Switch Control, 2004; An 800MHz Low Power Direct Digital Frequency Synthesizer with an On-Chip D/A Converter, 2004; Subharmonically Pumped CMOS Frequency Conversion (Up & Down) Circuits for 2GHz WCDMA Direct Conversion Transceiver, 2004; 41 international conference papers; More than 60 registered patents. Honours: The world first development of RF CMOS receiver/transmitter chips for application in CDMA cellular phones with a 900 MHz frequency range, 1999; The world first development of RF CMOS receiver/transmitter chips for application in CDMA PCS phones with a 1.8 GHz frequency range, 2001; Technology outstanding achievement award for his contribution to RF CMOS technology, 1999, Distinguished Medal for his contribution to the RF CMOS technology, 2003, Institute of Electronics Engineers of Korea; 2 technology outstanding achievement awards from ETRI Micro-Electronics Technology Laboratory for his contribution of RF CMOS device and circuit technology, 1998, 1999; Best Paper Award, 2002 SoC Design Conference, IEEE Seoul Chapter, 2002. Memberships: Senior Member, IEEE; Committee Member: Institute of Electronics Engineers of Korea, Long Term National Technology Development

Planning of Korea, Asian Solid-State Circuits Conference (IEEE). Address: RF/Analog SoC Design Team, Basic Research Laboratory, Electronics and Telecommunications Research Institute, 161 Gajung-Dong, Yusong-Gu, Daejeon, 305-350, Korea. E-mail: hkyu@etri.re.kr

**YU Mengchun,** b. 4 December 1965, Jianxi Province, China. Software Engineer. m. Yong Cui, 1 son, 1 daughter. Education: BS, Railway Engineering, 1986, MS, Structural Engineering, 1989, Northern Jiaotong University; MS, Civil and Environmental Engineering, 1996, PhD, Environmental Engineering, 1998, University of Vermont. Appointments: Engineering Scientist, Subterranean Research Inc, 1998-2000; Software Engineer, JMAR/SAL Nanolithography Inc, 2001-2002; Manager, Software Department, JMAR Systems, 2002-. Publications: Articles in scientific journals, conference proceedings and book chapters as co-author include: Modified total variation method for 3-D electrical resistance tomography inverse problems, 2000; An adaptive long-term monitoring and operations system (aLTMOs™) for optimization in environmental management, 2000; Multi-period objectives and groundwater remediation using SAMOA: Tandem simulated annealing and extended cutting plane method for containment with cleanup, 2000; Devising groundwater migration strategies for objectives using ECP optimization, 2001. Honours: Outstanding Student Paper Award, American Geophysical Union, 1997; Employee of the Year, JMAR/SAL Nonolithography Inc, 2002. Membership: IEEE. Address: 21 Gregory Drive, South Burlington, VT 05403, USA

**YUBA Toru,** b. 19 June 1956, Hokkaido, Japan. Voice Educator; Researcher. m. Abe Mariko. Education: BA, Tenor, Voice Major, Music School, Tokyo University of Fine Arts and Music, 1981. Appointments: Assistant, 1981-86, Instructor, 1986-90, Associate Professor, 1990-2001, Professor, Postgraduate Studies, 2001-, Faculty of Education, Mie University, Tsu City, Japan; Part-time Lecturer, Soai University, Osaka, Japan, 1987-91; Visiting Professor, Teachers College, Columbia University, New York City, USA, 2001; Guest Researcher, Faculty of Medicine, University of Tokyo, Japan, 2002-; Guest Lectureships: William Paterson College of New Jersey, USA, 1997, 1998, College of Mount Saint Vincent, New York, USA, 1998; University of Hawaii, 2001, 2002, 2003 (2), University of São Paulo, Brazil, 2002, University of British Columbia, Canada, 2002; University of Tokyo, Japan, 2004; Successfully corrected over 1000 off-key singers generally called tone-deaf; Performances: Leading Soloist in operas including: Rodolfo in La Boheme, Don Jose in Carmen and Pinkerton in Madam Butterfly as well as in concerts with many professional orchestras; Invited by the Chinese Government as a guest of the Visiting Artist Guild to perform concerts with Chinese orchestras in Beijing and Shanghai; Solo Concerts in Milan, New York and Vancouver. Publications include: Books as author: Muscles for Singing (with CD), 1998, revised edition, 1999; Miraculous Voice Training Book by the Yuba Method (with CD), 2004; Co-author, Let's Train Our Singing Muscles, 2000; Clinical Trends in Oto-Rhino-Laryngology, Head and Neck Surgery, 2001; Numerous articles in professional journals, newspapers and magazines; 3 video tapes; 2 CDs. Honour: First Place Gold Camera Award (as one of the five contents in the video tape), International Film and Video Festival, Chicago, USA, 2000. Memberships: Japan Society of Logopedics and Phoniatrics, 1999-; National Association for Music Education, USA, 2001-; Oto-Rhino-Laryngological Society of Japan, 2003-; UNESCO Ashiya, 2001-. Address: 18-7 Okuike-cho, Ashiya-shi, Japan 659-0003. E-mail: yuba@good-voice.com Website: www.good-voice.com

**YUH Sheng-Dih,** b. 25 November 1958, Taiwan. Professor. m. Hsien-Chih Chang, 2 sons, 1 daughter. Education: Bachelor's Degree, 1980; Master's Degree, 1984; PhD, 2001. Appointments: Assistant: Chung Cheng Institute of Technology, 1980-82; Engineer, The 205th Arsenal, 1984-86; Lecturer, Air Force College of Technology, 1985; Engineer, 1986-90, Division Vice-Chief, 1990-91, Division Chief, 1991-95, Ballistics Research Center; Researcher, Advanced Technology and Research Co, Maryland, USA, 1988; Shop Commander, The 202nd Arsenal, 1990-2001; Exchange Visitor, Drexel University, USA, 1991; Lecturer, Combined Service Forces College of technology, Taiwan, 1993; Researcher, Spring-8, Synchrotron Research Institute, Japan, 2001; Assistant Professor, Northern Taiwan Institute of Science and Technology, 2001-. Publications: Articles in scientific journals including: Scripta Materialia, 1999; Journal of Materials Science, 2001; Japanese Journal of applied Physics, 2001; Materials Letters, 2002. Honours: Listed in Who's Who publications and biographical dictionaries. Membership: SAE, Taipei Section. Address: Department of Mechanical Engineering, Northern Taiwan Institute of Science and Technology, 2 Xue Yuan Road, Taipei 11202, Taiwan. E-mail: sdyuh@mail.ntist.edu.tw

**YUS Miguel,** b. 11 September 1947, Saragossa, Spain. Chemist. m. Carmen, 1 son, 1 daughter. Education: BSc, 1969, MSc, 1971, PhD, 1973, University of Saragossa. Appointments: Associate Professor, 1978, Professor, 1987, Organic Chemistry, University of Oviedo; Professor, Organic Chemistry, University of Alicante, 1988-. Publications: Numerous papers in professional journals. Honours include: Prize of JSPS, Japan, 1999; French-Spanish Prize of SFC, France, 1999. Memberships: Fellow or Member of Chemical Societies of Spain, Switzerland, Germany, Japan, UK, USA, Argentina. Address: Departmento de Quimica Organica, Facultad de Ciencias, Universidad de Alicante, Apdo 99, 03080 Alicante, Spain. E-mail: yus@ua.es

# Z

**ZA'MOCKÝ Marcel,** b. 13 September 1965, Hranice Na Moravę, Czech Republic. Biochemist. m. Eva Za'mocká, 2 daughters. Education: MSc, Faculty of Natural Sciences, Comenius University, Bratislava, 1983-88; PhD, Institute of Biochemistry and Molecular Cell Biology, University of Vienna, 1995. Appointments: Assistant, Chemical Institute, Slovak Academy of Sciences, Bratislava, 1990-92; Assistant, Vienna Biocentre, General Biochemistry, 1993-98; Independent Scientific Co-worker, Institute of Molecular Biology, Slovak Academy of Sciences, Bratislava, 1999-; Postdoctoral Fellow, Vienna Biocentre, University of Vienna, 1999-2003; National Centre for Biomolecular Research, Masaryk University, Brno, Czech Republic, 2004; Applied Biocatalysis Research Centre, Graz, Austria, 2005-. Publications: 30 articles in international peer-reviewed journals. Honours: Listed in international biographical publications. Memberships: Protein Society, 1997-98; Mollecular Authority for Catalase in Human Protein Reference Database, 2004-. Address: Institute of Molecular Biology, Slovak Academy of Sciences, Dubr Cesta 21, SK-84551, Bratislava, Slovakia. E-mail: marcel.zamocky@savba.sk

**ZABIELSKY Stanisław,** b. 13 November 1939, Puławy, Poland. Physician. m. Barbara, 1 son, 1 daughter. Education: Military School of Medicine, Łódź, Poland, 1958-64; Specialisation in Dermatology and Venerology, 1975; Specialisation in Allergology, 1994; Doctorate, 1974, Habilitation, 1994. Appointment: Professor, Dermatology Department, Military Institute of Medicine, Warsaw, Poland, 1991-. Publications: 93 publications; 4 books. Honours: 1st Degree and 2nd Degree Awards, Military School of Medicine. Memberships: Polish Dermatology Society; Medical Science Monitor. Address: Lazurowa Street 12/59, 00-315 Warsaw, Poland.

**ZABUSKY Norman J,** b. 4 January 1929, New York, USA. Professor of Computational Fluid Dynamics. m. Charlotte Fox Zabusky, 3 daughters. Education: BEE, Magna cum Laude, College of the City of New York, 1947-51; MS, Electrical Engineering, Massachusetts Institute of Technology, 1951-53; PhD, Physics, California Institute of Technology, 1955-59. Appointments: Visiting Research Associate in Physics, Princeton University Plasma Physics Research, 1960-61; Member of Technical Staff, Supervisor of Plasma Physics, Department Head of Computational Physics Research Department, Bell Laboratories, 1971-76; Professor of Mathematics, University of Pittsburgh, 1976-88; State of New Jersey Professor of Computational Fluid Dynamics, Department of Mechanical and Aerospace Engineering, Rutgers University, 1988-; Consultant and Scientific Visitor: Naval Research Laboratory, Washington DC, 1976-91, Los Alamos Scientific Laboratory, 1983-94, Institute of Laser Engineering, Osaka, Japan, 2001. Publications: Book: Topics in Non-Linear Physics (editor), 1966; Over 150 publications in refereed journals and conference proceedings include as author and co-author: Interaction of "Solitons" in a Collisionless Plasma and the Recurrence of Initial States, 1965; Scientific computing visualization – a new venue in the arts, 2000. Honours: Howard Hughes Fellow, 1955-57; Standard Oil Company of California Fellow, 1958-59; National Science Foundation Postdoctoral, 1959-60; Fellow, American Physical Society, 1970-; J S Guggenheim Memorial Foundation Fellowship, 1971-72; Howard N Potts Medal, Franklin Institute (shared), 1986; Kiev Non-Linear Medal, 1989; Jacobs Professor of Applied Physics, Rutgers University, 2000-2003; Otto LaPorte Award, American Physical Society, Division of Fluid Dynamics, 2003. Membership: Fellow American Physical Society. Address: Rutgers University, Department of Mechanical and Aerospace Engineering, Laboratory for Visiometrics and Modeling, 98 Brett Road, Picataway, NJ 08854-8058. E-mail: nzabusky@caip.rutgers.edu

**ZACEK Pavel,** b. 26 May 1959, Brno, Czech Republic. Cardiac Surgeon. m. Lenka Vavrova, 2 sons, 1 daughter. Education: MD, 1984, PhD, 2004, Charles University, Prague, Czech Republic; Consultant Cardiac Surgeon, 1995. Appointments: Department of Surgery, Novy Bydzov, Czech Republic, 1984-87; Department of Cardiac Surgery, Charles University Hospital, Hradec Kralove, Czech Republic, 1987-. Publications: Coronary Surgery in the Elderly (PhD thesis); Interactive Cardiac Surgery DVD-Rom (multimedia textbook), 2005; Scientific papers in medical journals. Honour: Charles University Prize for Interactive Cardiac Surgery, 2003. Memberships: Czech Society of Surgery; Czech Cardiological Association; Czech Society for Cardiovascular Surgery. Address: Trebizskeho 845, 500 02 Hradec Kralove, Czech Republic. E-mail: zacek@fnhk.cz

**ZACHARIASSON Toini Maria,** b. 14 March 1943, Hedenaeset, Sweden. Director; Business Owner. Education: Computer Degree, Scandinavian School, Gothenburg, Sweden, 1974; Degree, Philosophy, Stockholm University, Sweden, 1980. Appointments: Clerk, Executive, The Defence Office, Stockholm, 1962-64; Secretary of Business, Eriksson, Stockholm, 1964-79; Secretary of Parliament, 1979-82; Director of Business, Hedenaeset, Norrbotten, Sweden, 1982-88, 1988-; Taxation Professional, The Central Party, Stockholm, 1977-88. Memberships: Volunteer, Marine Defence, Sweden; Member, The Central Party. Address: Lasarettsgatan 55B, S-98234 Gallivare, Norrbotten, Sweden.

**ZACHARY Stefan Hedley,** b. 30 June 1948, Leeds, England. Designer. m. Patricia, 2 sons, 1 daughter. Education: Pre-Diploma, Harrogate School of Art, 1966-67; BA (Hons), 3-D Design, Leeds College of Art, 1967-70; Passed Joint First Cadet, Royal Military College, Sandhurst, 1975. Appointments: Designer, Conran Design Group, 1970-71; Chief Interior Designer, Duport Group, 1971-; Associate Partner, Howard Sant Architects, 1971-77; Group Managing Director, McColl Group plc, 1977-92; Managing Partner, Zachary Design, 1992-. Publications: Chartered Society of Designers (CSD) Works Agreement, 1983, 1989; CSD Works Agreement Guide, 1983; CSD Code of Conduct, 1990. Honours: Founder and Life Honorary Joint President, Design Business Association, 1989; Liveryman, Painter-Stainers, 1989; Freeman City of London, 1989. Memberships: Past President, Chartered Society of Designers; Fellow, Royal Society of Arts; Fellow, British Institute of Interior Design, 1982; British Council of Shopping Centres, 1995. Address: Little Moseley House, Naphill, Bucks HP14 4RE, England. E-mail: zachary design@btconnect.com Website: www.zacharydesign.com

**ZAID Shakir Tor Ishaq,** b. 6 June 1961, Oakland, California, USA. Pastor; Chief Executive Officer; Founder. m. Nette Pierce, 5 sons, 1 daughter. Education: Doctor of Divinity, Master in Theology, Speakers Association; Motivational Speaking School. Appointments: Teacher; Pastor Founder, Millennium International Ministries; Chief Executive Officer, Millennium Property Management, Marceau Nicyia Financial; Advisor, Lionel Wilson College Preparatory School; Motivational Speaker; Mentor; TV Talk Show Host "Ask Shak". Honours: Doctor of Divinity; Master of Theology; Listed in Who's Who publications and biographical dictionaries. Address: 14895 E 14th Street, San Leandro, CA 94578, USA. E-mail: drshakirzaid@yahoo.com

**ZAINEA Liviu Nicolae**, b. 11 April 1953, Ploiesti, Romania. Mechanical Engineer; Acoustical Consultant. m. Lyra Maria, 1 son, 3 daughters. Education: Mechanical Engineer, University Brasov, Romania, 1976. Appointments: Mechanical Engineer, 1 May Factory, Ploesti, Romania, 1976-83; Acoustical Consultant, owner of Eddy's Studio Recording, a Sound Consulting Company, 1983-. Publications: 7 articles in Sound and HiFi, 1991-92; 1 article in Sound and Vision; 1 paper, Proceedings of Greek Acoustical Society, 1994; 1 paper, 1st Congress of Hellenic Institute of Acoustics, Patras, 2002; 1 patent held. Memberships: Hellenic Acoustical Society; Acoustical Society of America. Address: 14 Peresiadou St, Athens, 1141 Greece. E-mail: liviu@zainea.com Website: http://www.zainea.com

**ZAK Vladimir**, b. 13 December 1929, Moscow, former USSR. Musicologist. m. Maya Korsunskaya, 1 son. Education: BA, Music Composition, 1947, MA, Summa Cum Laude, Musicology, 1952, Moscow Conservatory; Doctorate, Musicology, 1979, Post-doctoral Degree, Music Theory, 1989, National Institute for the Study of Arts under the Ministry of Culture of the USSR. Appointments: Participant in documentary music films, 1959-; Composer of music for theatre and TV shows, 1959-; Lecturer on own original music analysis theory at dozens of scientific musicology seminars in the former USSR as well as 23 international music symposiums in many countries, 1962-; Deputy Chairman, 1962-86, Chairman, 1986-91, Musicology Commission of the USSR Union of Composers; Lecturer in America, Jewish organisations, Holocaust Survivor's centres, radio, TV, City University of New York Graduate Center, 1991-; Advisor, International Émigré Association of Arts and Sciences, New York, 1993-; Consultant, MusicaRussia Foundation, New York, 2003-. Publications: Author of 5 books on classical and contemporary music; Monographs include: Melodics of the Popular Song, 1979; Laws of Song Melodics, 1990; Schostakovich and the Jews, 1997; More than 200 articles include: Asafiev's theory of intonation and the analysis of popular song, 1982; Il meravigliozo mondo dell'intonazione populare, 1983; The Wondrous World of Popular Intonation, 1985; O Melodike Josepha Haydna, 1982; Chaikovsky's Melodies, 1990; Shostakovich's Idioms, 1998; Remembering, 2000; Jüdisches und Nicht-Jüdisches bei Schostakovich, 2003; Die Hoffnung Bleibt, 2003; Dmitri Shostakovich and Children? 2003. Honours: First Prize Winner, B Asafiev's Competition of Musicologists of the USSR, 1982; State Order of Honour, USSR, 1986; Certificate of Appreciation, Council of Jewish Émigré Community Organizations and International Émigré Association of Arts and Sciences, 2003; Silver Medal of Honour, International Biographical Association, 2004. Memberships: Russian Union of Composers, 1962-; Association of Eastern European Jews, 1993-; International Émigré Association of Arts and Sciences, 1993-; MusicaRussia Foundation, 2003-; Russian-American Cultural Heritage Center. Address: 731 West 183rd Street, Apt #3L, New York, NY 10033, USA. E-mail: a_zak@hotmail.com

**ZAKHARCHENKO Irina**, b. 19 July 1946, Rostov-on-Don, Russia. X-ray Physicist. m. Krivitskii V V, 2 sons. Education: Graduate, Department of Physics, Rostov State University, 1969; PhD, Physics and Mathematics, Rostov State University, 1978. Appointments: Junior Researcher, 1969-77; Senior Researcher, 1978-92; Leading Researcher, Laboratory of Ferroelectric Thin Films, Institute of Physics, Rostov State University, 1993-. Publications: Several articles for professional journals. Memberships: International Union of Crystallography. Address: Institute of Physics, Rostov State University, Pr Stachky 194, Rostov-on-Don 344090, Russia. E-mail: zin@ip.rsu.ru

**ZAKIS Girts**, b. 26 May 1935, Riga, Latvia. Chemist. m. Daina Zaķe. Education: Graduate, Faculty of Chemistry, Lativan State University, 1958; Postgraduate studies, 1962-65, PhD, Chemistry, 1966, Latvian Academy of Science; Dr habil. chem., dip. EDh, Latvian State Institute of Wood Chemistry, 1993. Appointments: Engineer, Researcher, Senior Researcher, Lignin Chemistry Laboratory of Latvian State Institute of Wood Chemistry, 1959-. Publications: Over 100 articles; 4 monographs, including the following 2 award winners; Methods of Determination of Lignin Functional Groups, 1975; Synthesis of Lignin Model Compounds, 1980; 4 patents. Honours: The Latvian Academy of Science Presidium, 2nd Award, 1975, 1st Award, 1980, for the monographs listed above; Latvian Academy of Science, Kalnins Award, 2003. Memberships: Member, Latvian Council of Science, Expert Committee for Chemistry, 1993-96; Member, Latvian Scientists' Society; Member, International Lignin Institute, Lausanne, Switzerland, 1996-. Address: Latvia, Rīga, LV1006, Dzērbenes str. 27. E-mail: koks@edi.lv

**ZAKOSHANSKY Vladimir**, b. 3 May 1940, Russia. Chemist. m. Larissa Zakoshansky, 1 daughter. Education: Chemical Engineer, Technological Institute, St Petersburg, Russia, 1969; PhD, Petrochemical Process Institute, 1976; Chief Research Scientist, Top Personnel Review Board. Appointments: Research Scientist, Chief Research Scientist, Head of Scientific Research Laboratory, President of the R&D Company, ILLA International. Publications: 64 articles; 2 poetry books; 90 granted patents and patented inventions. Membership: American Chemical Society. Address: 4756 Doncaster Court, Long Grove, IL60047-6929, USA. E-mail: vlazak@illallc.com

**ZAMANI Adil**, b. 5 May 1960, Alma-Ata, Kazakhstan. Professor of Medicine. m. Ayse Gül, 2 sons. Education: MD, Sechenov First Moscow Medical Institute, Moscow, 1986. Appointments: Research Fellow, Department of Chest Diseases and TB, Ankara University Hospital, Ankara, Turkey, 1987-91; Visiting Research Fellow, Department of Respiratory Medicine, University of Edinburgh, 1991; Assistant Professor, 1993-96, Assistant Head Physician, 1997-98, Associate Professor, 1996-2002, Professor, 2002-, Department of Chest Diseases, Selçuk University Hospital, Konya, Turkey; Visiting Research Fellow, Department of Thoracic Medicine, London Chest Hospital, 1993-94; Associate Professor, Lieutenant, Department of Chest Diseases, Gülhane Military Academy, Ankara, Turkey, 1998-2000. Publications: Numerous articles on pulmonology in Turkish and foreign medical journals, conference proceedings, book chapters; Music Albums for Classical Guitar; Compositions; Classical Guitar Magazine, England. Honours: The Living Composers List, USA; Classical Guitar Composers List, USA; Guitar Reference (editor V Pocci), Italy; Listed in Who's Who publications and biographical dictionaries. Membership: President, Working Group of Diagnostic Methods, Turkish Thoracic Society. Address: Selçuk University Hospital, Department of Chest Diseases, Konya, Turkey. E-mail: adzamani@hotmail.com

**ZAMBARAS Vassilis**, b. 1 May 1944, Revmatia, Messenias, Greece. Teacher of English as a Second Language; Poet. m. Eleni Nezi, October 1980, 1 son, 1 daughter. Education: BA, English, 1970, MA, English, 1972, University of Washington, Seattle. Publications: Sentences, 1976; Aural, 1984. Contributions to: How the Net is Gripped: Selection of Contemporary American Poetry, 1992; Chiron Review; Karer Murr's Press; Maverick Magazine; Poetry Salzburg Review; The London Magazine; The Salt River Review; Tattoo Highway; Fine-Words.com; Poetry Northwest; Madrona; West Coast Review; Wisconsin Review; Assay; Edge; Text; Smoot

Drive Press; Rialto; Shearsman; Southeastern Review; Southern Poetry Review; Longhouse; Intermedio; Workshop; Falcon; Klinamen; Apopeira. Honours: Harcourt, Brace and Jovanovich Poetry Fellowship to the University of Colorado, Boulder, 1970; University of Washington Poetry Prizewinner, 1972. Address: 21 K Fotopoulou, Meligalas 24002, Messenias, Greece.

**ZAND Roxane, (Hakimzadeh),** b. 21 March 1952, Tehran, Iran. Educator; Writer. m. Hakim Zadeh, 7 November 1978, 2 sons. Education: BA, Harvard University, 1975; Oxon DPhil, 1994. Publication: Persian Requiem. Contributions to: JASO; Feminist Review; Editor, Institute of Ismaili Studies. Memberships: Translators Society; Harvard Club of London. Address: 9 Templewood Avenue, London NW3 7UY, England.

**ZAPF Hermann,** b. 8 November 1918, Nuremberg, Germany. Designer. m. Gudrun Zapf von Hesse, 1 son. Education: D in Fine Arts (Hon), University of Illinois, USA. Appointments: Freelance designer, 1938-; Type Director, D Stempel AG, type foundry, Frankfurt, 1947-56; Design Consultant, Mergenthaler Linotype Co, New York and Frankfurt, 1957-74; Consultant, Hallmark International, Kansas City, Missouri, 1966-73; Vice President, Design Processing International Inc, New York, 1977-86; Professor, typographic computer programs, Rochester Institute of Technology, New York, 1977-87; Chairman, Zapf, Burns and Co, New York City, 1987-91; Instructor, Lettering Werkkunstschule, Offenbach, Germany, 1948-50; Professor, Graphic Design, Carnegie Institute of Technology, 1960; Instructor, Typography Technische Hochschule, Darmstadt, Germany, 1972-81. Publications: Author: William Morris, 1948; Pen and Graver, 1952; Manuale Typographicum, 1954, 1968; About Alphabets, 1960, 1970; Typographic Variations, 1964; Orbis Typographicus, 1980; Hora fugit/Carpe diem, 1984; Hermann Zapf and His Design Philosophy, 1987; ABC-XYZapf, 1989; Poetry Through Typography, 1993; August Rosenberger, 1996; CD-ROM, The World of Alphabets, 2001; Film, The Art of Hermann Zapf; Designer of over 180 typefaces. Honours: Honorary President, Edward Johnston Foundation, England; Honorary Curator, Computer Museum, Boston; Silver Medal, Brussels, 1962; 1st Prize Typography Biennale, Brno, Czechoslovakia, 1966; Gold Medal, Type Directors Club, New York; Frederic W Goudy Award, Institute of Technology, Rochester, 1969; Silver Medal, International Book Exhibition, Leipzig, 1971; Gold Medal, 1989; Johannes Gutenberg Prize, Mainz, Germany, 1974; Gold Medal, Museo Bodoniano, Parma, Italy, 1975; J H Merck Award, Darmstadt, 1978; Robert Hunter Middleton Award, 1987; Euro Design Award, 1994; Wadim Lazursky Award, Academy of Graphic Arts, Moscow, 1996; Named Honorary Citizen, State of Texas, 1970; Honorary Royal Designer for Industry, 1985; Listed in national and international biographical dictionaries. Memberships: Royal Society of Arts; American Mathematical Society; Alliance Graphique Internationale; Bund Deutscher Grafik Designer; International Gutenberg Gessellschaft; Honorary Member, Type Directors Club, New York City; Sociéte Typographique de France, Paris; Society of Typographic Arts, Chicago; Double Crown Club, London; Letter Exchange, London; Society of Scribes and Illuminators, London; Friends of Calligraphy, San Francisco; Society of Printers, Boston; Society of Graphic Designers, Canada; Bund Deutscher Buchkünstler; Grafiska Institute, Stockholm; Typophiles, New York; Alpha Beta Club, Hong Kong; Society of Calligraphy, Los Angeles; Wynkyn de Worde Society, London; Monterey Calligrapher's Guild; Washington Calligraphers Guild; Eesti Kalligraafide Koondis, Tallinn, Estonia; Chicago Calligraphers Guild; Caxton Club, Chicago; Typographers International Association; Art Directors Club, Kansas City; Associates of Stanford University Libraries; Alcuin Society, Vancouver; Goudy International Centre; Brno

Biennale Association; Society of Scribes, New York; Grolier Club, New York; Dante e V, German TEX Group, Heidelberg; Gamma Epsilon Tau. Address: D-64287 Darmstadt, Seitersweg 35, Germany.

**ZAPPOLI THYRION Roberto,** b. 10 September 1926, Sarezzano (AL), Italy. Retired Professor of Neurology. m. Giuliana Laura Cuccodoro, 1 son, 2 daughters. Education: Graduate, Medicine and Surgery, University of Bologna, 1951; Specialisation in Neurology, University of Padua, 1955. Appointments: Assistant, Institute of Physiology, University of Bologna, 1947-51; Director, 2nd Neurological Clinic, 1975-84, Director, Institute of Nervous and Mental Diseases, 1985-88, Founder and Director, Department of Neurological and Psychiatric Sciences, 1989-96, University of Florence, Italy; President, Italian Society of EEG and Clinical Neurophysiology, 1978-81; Founder and President, Italian Society of Psychophysiology, 1990-95. Publications: 306 publications including several special, didactic or seminar lectures and reviews, most recently: The effects on auditory neurocognitive evoked responses and contingent negative variation activity of frontal cortex lesions or ablations in man: three new case studies (co-author), 2000; Frontal and parieto-temporal cortical ablations and diaschisis-like effects on auditory neurocognitive potentials evokable from apparently intact ipsilateral association area in humans: five case reports (co-author), 2002; Permanent or transitory effects on neurocognitive components of the CNV complex induced by brain dysfunctions, lesions and ablations in humans (author), 2003. Honours: A Arrigo Award for Clinical Neurophysiology (VIth Edition), 1996; 20th Anniversary of the International Organisation of Psychophysiology ("Olympics of the Brain") Award, 2002. Memberships: Board of Governors, International Organisation of Psychophysiology, associated with the United Nations, New York; Member, Executive Committee, Federation of European Psychophysiology Societies. Address: Via Bolognese 419, Florence 50010, Italy. E-mail: giorgia.zap poli@infinito.it

**ZARAFI Afiniki Bawa,** b. 17 January 1963, Gure, Nigeria. Phytopathologist. m. Victor Garba Zarafi, 2 sons, 1 daughter. Education: BSc, Agriculture, 1983-86, MSc, Crop Protection, 1988-92, PhD, Crop Protection, 1993-2004, Ahmadu Bello University, Zaria. Appointments: Development Officer, Agricultural Development Projects, 1987; Graduate Assistant, 1988-90, Assistant Lecturer, 1990-92, Lecturer II, 1992-2001, Lecturer 1, 2001-2004, Senior Lecturer, 2004-, Ahmadu Bello University, Zaria. Publications: Numerous articles in scientific publications and journals. Membership: Nigerian Society for Plant Protection. Address: Department of Crop Protection, Ahmadu Bello University, PMB 1044, Zaria, Nigeria.

**ZAREA Stefan,** b. 1 January 1928, Recea, Bessarabia, Romania. Engineer; Professor Emeritus; Inventor; Scientist. m. Lea Gal Zarea, 1 son. Education: Degree, Mechanical Engineering, 1952, PhD, Hydraulics, 1961, Polytechnic Institute, Bucharest, Romania; Validation of Engineering Degree, Central University of Venezuela (UCV), Caracas, Venezuela, 1991. Appointments include: Researcher, Senior Scientist, Head of Laboratory, Institute of Applied Mechanics, Bucharest, 1951-53; Assistant Professor, 1951-57, Lecturer, 1957-62, Vice-Dean, 1961-71, Associate Professor, 1962-70, Dean, 1971-72, Professor, 1970-78, Power Engineering Faculty, Polytechnic Institute, Bucharest; University of Bucharest, 1972-74; Senior Scientist, Head of Laboratory for Artificial Stimulation of Meteorological Phenomena, National Central Meteorological Institute, Bucharest, 1958-74; Professor, Head of Laboratory and Hydraulic Section, University Mohamed V, School of Engineering, Morocco, 1974-78; Professor, Central

# DICTIONARY OF INTERNATIONAL BIOGRAPHY

University of Venezuela, 1978-93, Honorary Professor, 1994-2004; Professor, Head of Mechanical Energy Conversion Section and Laboratory, University Simon Bolivar, Caracas, Venezuela, 1978-99; Retired, 2000; Professor Emeritus, 2003-; Advisor of 423 thesis (undergraduate: 395, postgraduate: 20, doctoral: 8); Invited Professor in 7 universities: France (1972, 1975, 1985), Belgium (1972), Brazil (1993), Germany (1973), Argentina (1985); Deputy of Metropolitan Assembly, Bucharest, 1953-74; President, Committee for Metropolitan Management, Municipality of Bucharest, 1954-74; Vice President, National Committee for Hydraulic Machines Construction, Bucharest, 1969-74; Vice-President of National Committee for great urban works, 1969-74; Vice President or Member, Organization Scientific or Technical Conferences, 1982, 1986, 1989, 1995, 1999, 2001; Member of editorial board of EDIT and EQUINOCCIO, Venezuela, 1997-; Associated editor of the Reviews: ATLANTIDA, 1993-2004, and Journal of Engineering Faculty, UCV, Caracas, 1997-; Leader of engineering teams for mechanical design in 75 projects, 1952-2000; Leader of technical teams achieving 84 inventions, 1950-2003. Publications: Books: Hydraulics, 1954; Basic Mathematics, 1963, 1969; Hydraulic Turbines and Hydro-energetic Equipments I, 1965, II, 1968; Basic Mechanics, 1968; Proceedings of III Caribbean Congress of Fluid Dynamics (co-editor), 1995; Recent Developments in Fluid Mechanics (editor), 2001; 27 Patents of Invention; 116 articles and papers in conferences concerning airfoils, helicoidal flows, rotational and potential associated flows, turbulence, water hammer, hydraulic turbines, pumps, fans, artificial stimulation of rain, meteorological rockets, solar and wind energy, heat pipe, internal combustion engine. Honours include: Romania: 5 medals, Polytechnic Institute of Bucharest; Prize for Machinery Design, Department of Machinery Construction, Bucharest, 1972; Patriarchal Cross, Romanian Orthodox Patriarchy, Bucharest, 2003; Venezuela: 7 medals, Central University of Venezuela and University Simon Bolivar; Professor of the Year, Association of Mechanical Engineering Students, 1986, 1992; Simon Rodriguez Prize for Notable Academic Activity, Association of Professors, 1994; Procter & Gamble USB Award for Academic Excellence, 1994; Annual Awards for Outstanding Academic Activity, 1996, 1999, University Simon Bolivar. Current Memberships include: Association of Professors, University of Simon Bolivar; Venezuelan Society for the Advancement of Science; Engineers' College of Venezuela, Gesellschaft für angewandte Mathematik und Mechanik, General Association of Engineers of Romania; American Mathematical Society; American Society of Mechanical Engineers; International Association for Hydraulic Research; International Solar Energy Society. Address: Terraza B del Club Hipico, Calle Merida No 12, Qta. El Remanso, Caracas 1080, Venezuela. E-mail: szarea@usb.ve

**ZAREMBA Jaroslaw,** b. 14 September 1956, Poznan, Poland. Neurologist. Education: MD, PhD, 1987, Diploma in Neurology, 1990, University School of Medicine, Poznan, Poland. Appointments: From Assistant to Lecturer, Department of Anatomy, 1981-89, Lecturer, Department of Neurology, 1989-97, Lecturer, Department of Clinical Neuroimmunology, 1997-, University School of Medicine, Poznan, Poland. Publications: Articles in medical journals include: Early TNF-Alpha levels correlate with ischaemic stroke severity, 2001; s PECAM-1 in serum and CSF of acute ischaemic stroke patients, 2002; Interleukin-18 in acute ischaemic stroke patients, 2003. Honours: Listed in Who's Who publications and biographical dictionaries. Memberships: World Federation of Neurology; European Federation of Neurological Societies; Polish Neurological Society. Address: Department of Clinical Neuroimmunology, University School of Medicine, 49 Przybyszewskiego Street, 60-355 Poznan, Poland.

**ZAREMBKA Paul,** b. 17 April 1942, St Louis, Missouri, USA. Economist. m. Beata Banas, 1 daughter. Education: BS, Mathematics, Purdue University, 1964; MS, PhD, Economics, 1967, University of Wisconsin. Appointments: Assistant Professor, Department of Economics, University of California, Berkeley, 1967-72; Visiting Professorships: Heidelberg University, 1970-71; Goettingen University, 1971-72; Associate Professor, Professor, Department of Economics, State University of New York at Buffalo, 1973-; Senior Research Officer, World Employment Program, International Labor Office, Geneva, Switzerland, 1974-77; Researcher, Group For Research on Science, Louis Pasteur University, Strasbourg, 1978-79. Publications: Author, Toward a Theory of Economic Development, 1972; Editor, Frontiers in Econometrics, 1974; Co-editor with M Brown and K Sato, Essays in Modern Capital Theory, 1976; General Editor, Research in Political Economy, 22 volumes to date, 1977-; Numerous articles and book chapters. Honours: Fulbright-Hayes Lecturer, Poznan, Poland, 1979; Listed in numerous biographical dictionaries. Address: Department of Economics, 415 Fronczak Hall, State University of New York at Buffalo, Buffalo, New York 14260, USA. E-mail: zarembka@buffalo.edu. Website: http://ourworld.compuserve.com/homepages/PZarembka

**ŽARSKIENE-ŠIMONYTĖ Rūta,** b. 6 January 1964, Vilnius, Lithuania. Ethnomusicologist. 2 sons. Education: Master of Ethnomusicology, 1992, PhD, Field Ethnomusicology, 1999, Lithuanian Academy of Music and Theatre. Appointments: Institute of Lithuanian Literature and Folklore, 1991-, Assistant, 1992-99, Research Fellow, 1999-2002, Elder Research Fellow and Head of Department of Folklore Archives, 2002-. Publications: Monographs: Skudučiai and its Relations: Comparative Studies, 1993; Music Making with Multi-Pipe Whistles in Northeastern Europe, 2003; 18 scientific articles in periodicals in Lithuania, Germany, Hungary, Sweden, 1993-2004. Memberships: ICTM, 2000-; ESEM, 2002-. Address: Antakalnio str 6, LT-10308 Vilnius, Lithuania. E-mail: ruta@llti.lt

**ZAVATI Constantin C,** b. 7 July 1923, Bacau, Romania. Teacher. m. Iulia Bucur, 1 daughter. Education: Scoala de Baieti No 2, Bacau; Scholarship, Stefan Cel Mare Military Boarding College; Baccalauréat, Distinction, 1942; Private Merit Regiment 10; Chemistry Faculty, University Alexandru Ioan Cuza, 1947-51; MSc, honours, 1951. Appointments: Various Military Positions; Assistant Lecturer, University Alexandru Ioan Cuza and Academy Iasi, Romania; High school teacher, Chemistry and Physics, Ferdinand I Boarding College, Bacau; High school teacher, Chemistry and Physics, Head of Chemistry, Vasile Alecsandri Boarding College, Bacau; Schools Inspector for Chemistry, county/City of Bacau. Publications: Numerous scientific papers at various national conferences; Many scientific articles in newspapers and magazines under the pen name, A Tom; Co-author, 1 book on applied sciences; Organised the first modern school science laboratories in the county/City of Bacau. Honours: Citation for great bravery during the Second World War; Several Orders and Medals for Bravery in Battle; Professor Fruntas, 1964; Professor Grade 1, 1972; Advanced Captain, Major and Colonel in the Army Reserves. Memberships: Societatea de Stiinte Fizice Si Chimice; Societatea Stiintelor Medicale; First President, Radio Club, Bacau. Address: c/o Mariana Zavati Gardner, 14 Andrew Goodall Close, East Dereham, Norfolk, NR19 1SR, England.

**ZAVATI Iulia Bucur,** b. 19 July 1921, Racova-Bacau, Romania. Pharmacist. m. Constantin C Zavati, 26 January 1947, 1 daughter. Education: Baccalauréat with Distinct; MSc, Pharmacy, 1st class honours, University of Bucharest,

Romania. Appointments: Opened own pharmacy at Valea Rea-Târgu Ocna, Romania; Pharmacist, State Pharmacy in Bacau, Romania; Appointed Principal Pharmacist; Deputy Director, Director, Oficiul Farmaceutic, City and Region/Judet of Bacau-Romania; Directed, re-organised and modernised all pharmacies in Bacau; Established links with western pharmaceutical companies; Lecturer, Liceul Sanitar for nurses and pharmacy assistants in Bacau. Honours: Literary Prizes at Tinerimea Romana, before 1940; Medals and Orders for modernising and re-organising pharmacies in Bacau. Membership: Romanian Society of Pharmacists. Address: c/o Andrew Goodall Close, East Dereham, Norfolk NR19 1SR, England.

**ZBOROVSKY Ely Y,** b. 20 October 1936, Kiev, USSR. Patent Attorney. m. Larisa Zborovsky, 1 son, 1 daughter. Education: Masters in Engineering, Kiev Polytechnic, 1959; Expert in Translation, Kiev School of Foreign Languages, 1963; IP Masters, Moscow Intellectual Property Institute, 1972. Appointments: Head of Patent Department, Institute of Superhard Materials, Kiev; Professor of Intellectual Patent Law, Kiev Institute of Intellectual Property; Senior Associate, Striker Law Firm, New York; President and Owner, Ely Zborovsky Patent Bureau, New York. Publications: Intellectual Property Law and Practice, 1962; Dictionary of Intellectual property, 1973; 28 articles; 15 inventions. Memberships: International Intellectual Property Society, New York; US Patent Bar. Address: 6 Schoolhouse Way, Dix Hills, NY 11746, USA. E-mail: ezbopatent@aol.com

**ZECCHINO Vincent,** b. 15 May 1909, Brooklyn, New York, USA. Medical Doctor; Orthopaedic Surgeon. m. Julia M Pilkanis, 1 son. Education: MD, University of Bologna, Italy, 1936; Resident, Orthopaedic Surgery, Rhode Island Hospital, 1936-38; Resident, Orthopaedic Surgery, Boston Children's Hospital and Massachusetts General Hospital, 1938-41. Appointments: Lieutenant Colonel, US Army, Chief Orthopaedic Surgeon, Hospitals in India and Burma (48th General Hospital); Diplomate American Board of Orthopaedic Surgery, FACS, AAOS; Chairman, Department of Orthopaedic Surgery, Brown University Medical School and Rhode Island Hospital; Visiting Professor: Colombia, Tunisia, Sri Lanka, Italy, Canada; Now retired and Emeritus. Publications: Numerous publications on topic including plastic surgery, thumb reconstruction, hip prosthesis. Honour: Julia and Vincent Zecchino Pavilion, Rhode Island Hospital. Memberships: AAOS; FICS; FACS; Rhode Island Medical Society; Boston Orthopaedic Club; Boston Children's Hospital Alumni Association; International Scientific Society. Address: 530 S Collier Blvd, Apt 202, Marco Island, FL 34145-5514, USA.

**ZEFFIRELLI G Franco,** b. 12 February 1923, Florence, Italy. Opera & Film Producer; Designer. Education: Liceo Artistico, Florence; School of Agriculture, Florence. Appointments: Designer, University Productions, Florence; Actor, Morelli Stoppa Co; Collaborated with Salvador Dali on sets for As You Like It, 1948; Designed sets for A Streetcar Named Desire, Troilus, Cressida, Three Sisters; Producer, Designer, numerous operas. Creative Works: Theatre: Romeo and Juliet, Old Vic, London, 1960; Othello, Stratford, 1961; Amleto, National Theatre, London, 1964; After the Fall, Rome, 1964; Who's Afraid of Virginia Woolf, Paris, 1964, Milan, 1965, La Lupa, Rome, 1965; Much Ado About Nothing, National Theatre, London, 1966; Black Comedy, Rome, 1967; A Delicate Balance, Rome, 1967; Saturday, Sunday, Monday, National Theatre, London, 1973; Filumena, Lyric, London, 1977; Six Characters in Search of an Author, London, 1992; Films: The Taming of the Shrew, 1966; Florence, Days of Destruction, 1966; Romeo and Juliet, 1967; Brother Sun and Sister Moon, 1973; Jesus

of Nazareth, 1977; The Champ, 1979; Endless Love, 1981; La Traviata, 1983; Cavalleria Rusticana, 1983; Otello, 1986; The Young Toscanini, 1987; Hamlet, 1990; Sparrow, 1994; Jane Eyre, 1995; Tea With Mussolini, 1998; Callas Forever, 2002; Ballet: Swan Lake, 1985; Producer, Beethoven's Missa Solemnis, San Pietro, Rome, 1971. Publication: Zeffirelli by Zeffirelli (autobiog), 1986.

**ZEHEL Wendell E,** b. 6 March 1934, Brownsville, Pennsylvania, USA. Surgeon. m. Joan, 1 son, 1 daughter. Education: Pre-medical Studies, Washington and Jefferson College; BA, Mathematics, 1956; MD, University of Pittsburgh Medical School, 1960. Appointments: Internship, Shadyside Hospital; Military Service, discharged with honour, USAF, 1961-63; Surgical Residency, University of Pittsburgh, Veterans Administration Hospital; Wilmington Medical Center, Delaware; Established own practice, Pittsburgh; Postgraduate, Carnegie-Mellon University, advanced studies in bio-engineering and computer technology. Publications: Medical Instrumentation, 1983; Novel, The Long Silk Line, 1997; Biotechnology: Physiologic and Medical Applications, 1999; Novel, Life Lines, 1999. Memberships: American College of Surgeons; American Medical Association; New York Academy of Sciences; Charles Darwin Associates; Association for the Advancement for Medical Instrumentation; American Association for the Advancement of Science. Address: 110 Fort Couch Road, 3rd Floor, Pittsburgh, PA 15241, USA.

**ZELIAŚ Aleksander Józef,** b. 14 September 1939, Oleśnica, Poland. Full Professor of Economics. m. Jadwiga Kurowska, 1 son, 1 daughter. Education: MSc, Economics, 1962, DSc, Economics, 1966, Cracow School of Economics; DSc Habilit, Statistics, Poznań School of Economics, 1970; Nomination for degrees of Professor, 1977, Full Professor, 1982, State Council for the Polish People's Republic. Appointments include: Assistant Lecturer to Associate Professor, Statistics, 1963-77; Full Professor of Economics, Cracow Academy of Economics, 1982-; Visiting Professor: Pittsburgh University, 1982, Bonn University, Marburg University, Göttingen University, 1986, Tilburg University, Netherlands, 1988, Al-Mustansiryah University, Iraq, 1989, Pittsburgh University, 1991, Konstanz University, 2000; Member of editorial staffs of several professional journals. Publications: Over 290 papers and reports; Numerous books as author or co-author. Honours: Golden Cross of Merit, 1979; Medal, Committee of National Education, 1982; Knight Cross of the Order of Polonia Restituta, 1984, Gold Mark of Distinction, Social Activities, Kraków City, 1984, Kraków District, 1985; Bronze Medal, Country's Defenses, 1988; Officer's Cross of the Order of Polonia Restituta, 1999; 20th Century Award for Achievement, IBC; 2000 Millennium Medal of Honour, ABI, 1998; Doctor honoris causa, Wrocław University of Economics, 1996; Doctor honoris causa, Bratislava University of Economics, 2002. Memberships: Polish Economic Association; Polish Statistical Association; Deputy President, Committee of Mathematics of the Central Statistical Office in Warsaw; Polish Cybernetics Association; Committee of Economics, Cracow Branch, Polish Academy of Sciences; Honorary Advisor, Research Board of Advisors, American Biographical Institute; International Statistical Institute; Econometric Society; Deputy President, Polish Statistical Association; German Statistical Association; Academician, International Academy of Computer Sciences and Systems; Chairman, Committee of Statistics and Econometrics of the Polish Academy of Sciences in Warsaw. Address: Kowalskiego 1, 30 147 Kraków, Poland.

**ZELLWEGER Renée,** b. 25 April 1969, Katy, Texas, USA. Actress. Education: University of Texas at Austin. Appointments:

Films: Dazed and Confused, 1993; Reality Bites, 1994; Love and a .45, 1994; 8 Seconds, 1994; The Low Life, 1995; Empire Records, 1995; The Whole Wide World, 1996; Jerry Maguire, 1996; Texas Chainsaw Massacre: The Next Generation, 1997; Deceiver, 1997; One True Thing, 1998; A Price Above Rubies, 1998; The Bachelor, 1999; Me, Myself and Irene, 2000; Nurse Betty, 2000; Bridget Jones' Diary, 2001; Chicago, 2002; Down With Love, 2003; Cold Mountain, 2003; TV: Shake, Rattle and Rock Movie, 1993; Murder in the Heartland, 1994. Honours: Golden Globe Best Comedy Film Actress Award for Nurse Betty, 2001; Golden Globe Best Actress in a Musical for Chicago, 2003; Screen Actors Guild Award for Best Actress for Chicago, 2003; BAFTA Award for Best Supporting Actress, 2004; Best Supporting Actress Oscar for Cold Mountain, 2004. Address: c/o United Talent Agency, 9560 Wilshire Boulevard, Suite 500, Beverly Hills, CA 90212, USA.

**ZEMECKIS Robert**, b. May 1952, Chicago, USA. Film Director; Writer. m. Mary Ellen Trainor. Education: University South California. Creative Works: Films include: I Wanna Hold Your Hand (co-screenplay writer), 1978; Romancing the Stone; Back to the Future (co-screenplay writer), II, III; Death Becomes Her (also co-producer); Trespass (co-screenplay writer); Forest Gump; Who Framed Roger Rabbit?; Contact; The House on Haunted Hill; Cast Away; What Lies Beneath; Ghost Ship; Several TV Films. Address: c/o CAA, 9830 Wilshire Boulevard, Beverly Hills, CA 90212, USA.

**ZEMSKOV Andrei Il'ich**, b. 2 January 1939, Moscow Region, Russia. Librarian. m. Irina Zemskova, 1 son. Education: Explorer on Nuclear Physics, Institute of Technical Physics, 1956-65; PhD, Low Temperature Plasma Physics, 1965. Appointments: Researcher, Kurchatov Atomic Energy Institute, 1965-81; Supervisor, Plasma Physics Programs, CPSU CC, 1981-90; Director, Russian National Public Library for Science and Technology, 1990-. Publications: Over 70 on Plasma Physics, Library Management, CD-ROM applications; Editor-in-Chief of SciTech Libraries Journal. Honours: Order of Merit, 1976; Silver Medal of All Union Exhibition, 1983; Order of Friendship, 1998. Memberships: Vice President, Russian Library Association; President, International Association of Research and Sci-Tech Libraries. Address: 12 Kuznetski most, 107996 Moscow, Russia.

**ZENIN Eugene**, b. 27 November 1946, Khodjent, USSR. Professional Painter, Graphic Designer; Book Illustrator. 1 daughter. Education: Master's Degree, PhD, University of St Petersburg, Russia, 1964-72; State Art School, Tashkent, USSR, 1979-83; Language Courses, Studieskole, Copenhagen, Denmark, 1991-93. Career: Painter of oil on canvas and ink on paper; Designer and illustrator of over 40 books;15 years as Assistant University Professor. Exhibitions in Denmark: Galerie D'Art, Copenhagen, 1991; Galleri Billedkunst, Copenhagen, 1992; Galleri Lisse Bruun, Copenhagen, 1994; Artists Autumn Exhibition (competitive), Copenhagen, 1994, 1996, 1999; Artists Easter Exhibition (competitive), Aarhus, 1996; Kunstgalleriet, Odense, 1997, 2000; Galleri Knud Grothe, Charlottenlund, 2001, 2003, 2004; Exhibitions abroad: Arthall Ilkom, Tashkent, USSR, 1987; Central Arthall, Moscow, Russia, 1990; Galerie Alexander, Paris, France, 1991; Roy Myles Gallery, London, UK, 1991; Alison Fisher Gallery, New York, USA, 1995; Artistic License Gallery, London, UK, 2002; The Affordable Art Fair, Artistic License Gallery, London, UK, 2003; Principal works: The Annunciation, 1996; Madonna and Child, 1996; Works in collections: Skoulundegaard Art Collection, Copenhagen. Publications: Book: Angels My Beloved, 2002; V Sosnora, Magic Flight, 1985; S Spirikhin, You and Eternity, 1990; 27 publications and articles in newspapers;

26 paintings published as postcards by Go-Card, Copenhagen, 1997-2004. Honour: Gold Medal, University of St Petersburg. Address: Tuborgvej 236, 2400 Copenhagen NV, Denmark. E-mail: ezenin@sol.dk

**ZHANG Cunhao**, b. 23 February 1928, Tian Jin, China. Chemist. m. Chi Yun Xia, 2 sons. Education: MS, Michigan, USA, 1950. Appointments: Professor of Chemistry, Dalian Institute of Chemical Physics, Chinese Academy of Sciences, 1962-; Director, DICP, Chinese Academy of Sciences, 1986-90; Member, Presidium, Chinese Academy of Sciences and Director of Chemistry Division, 1994-98; President, National Natural Science Foundation of China, 1991-99. Publications: Articles in scientific journals. Honours: State Natural Science Award, 4 times; State S & T Progress Award; HLHL Award; Tan Kah Kee Award. Memberships: Chinese Academy of Sciences; Third World Academy of Sciences. Address: 83 Shuanghqing Road, HaiDian District, Beijing 100085, China. E-mail: zhangch@nsfc.gov.cn

**ZHANG Jingguo**, b. 7 October 1940, Shanghai, China. Materials Scientist; Engineer. m. Ninghua Zhu, 1 son. Education: Graduate, Department of Physical Metallurgy, University of Science and Technology, Beijing, China, 1964. Appointments: Research Assistant, 1964-74, Research Engineer, 1974-83, Director of Testing Centre, 1983-84, Deputy Director of Institute, Senior Engineer, 1984-87, Vice-President, Academic Committee, Associate Chief Engineer, Professor of Materials Science and Engineering, 1987-2000, Shanghai Iron and Steel Research Institute; Senior Specialist, Professor of Materials Science and Engineering, Shanghai Bao Steel Research Institute, 2000-2003; Visiting Professor, Tongji University,2004-; Visiting Scholar, Columbia University, USA, 1980; Assistant Professor, University of Connecticut, USA, 1980-82. Publications: 38 and 48 papers published in scientific and engineering journals in English and Chinese respectively; Co-author 2 books in Chinese; Recently published papers: Structure of Amorphous Fe-Zr-B powders obtained by chemical reduction, 2002; Microstructure and CCT Thermograms of Spray Formed G Cr15 Steel, 2002; Superplastic Ultra-high Carbon Steels Processed by Spray Forming, 2003; Microstructure and Mechanical Properties of Spray Formed Ultrahigh-Carbon Steels, 2004. Honours: Honours and Prize for distinct achievements and contribution in engineering, The State Council of China, 1993; Li Xun Prize, Acta Metallurgica Sinica, 1993; Special Prize for Scientists in the fields of applied basic research, Science and Technology Commission of Shanghai Municipality, 1994-95, 1998-99. Memberships: Institute of Materials Science, University of Connecticut, USA, 1980-82; SAMPE, Japan, 1993-95; Board of Directors: Chinese Society of Metals, 1991-94, Chinese Materials Research Society, 1991-2003, Chinese Stereology Society, 1991-2004. Address: Room 2603, No 12, Lane 300, Wu Ning Road, Shanghai 200063, PR China.

**ZHANG Luqian**, b. 1 March 1926, China. Professor. m. Li Bowei, 2 daughters. Education: Tsinghua University, 1951. Appointment: Chief Designer, China Aerospace Corporation, 1979-. Honours: Microwave Satellite TTC Radar, National Top Award, Beijing, 1985; Ho Leung Ho Lee Foundation Award, Hong Kong, 1997. Memberships: AIAA, USA; CSA; CAE, China. Address: China Aerospace Corporation, PO Box 849-1, 100830 Beijing, China.

**ZHANG Rong Ye**, b. 28 December 1938, Guan Dong, China. Professor; Researcher into Mathematics and Mechanics. m. Xiu Zhu Chen, 1 son, 1 daughter. Education: Graduate, Mathematics Department, Fu Dan University, Shanghai, China, 1965. Publications include: RRG approximation and its estimate of the two points boundary value problem; Approximation to the solution of First Order Linear Implicit Differential-Operational Equation in Hilbert Spaces; Cauchy Problem of some Second Order Linear Differential-Operational Equation in Hilbert Spaces and its Approximate Solution; The approximate computation of the Bounded Linear Functional on Hilbert Spaces; Newtonian Mechanics on Kahler Manifold; Lagrangian vector field on Kahler Manifold; Dynamics in Newtonian Remannian Space-time; Lagrange Mechanics on Kähler Manifolds; Hamilton Mechanics on Kähler Manifolds. Membership: Academician of the Chinese Academy of Computing Mathematics. Address: Room 403, Building 906, Zhong guan cun, Beijing 100080, China. E-mail: zry@math03.math.ac.cn

**ZHAO Gong Yun,** b. 5 March 1955, China. Associate Professor. m. Zhi-Qian Wan, 1 son. Education: PhD, Würzburg University, Germany, 1991. Appointments: Teaching Fellow, Lecturer, Senior Lecturer, Associate Professor, National University of Singapore, 1992-. Publications: More than 30 articles published in journals including: Mathematical Programming; Mathematics of Operations Research; SIAM Journal on Optimization. Honour: Award of Commonwealth Fellowship, 2000-2001. Membership: International Advisory Committee, 15th International Symposium on Mathematical Programming. Address: Department of Mathematics, National University of Singapore, Republic of Singapore. E-mail: matzgy@nus.edu.sg Website: www.math.nus.edu.sg/~matzgy

**ZHAO Lidong,** b. 12 October 1963, Hebei, China. Materials Engineer. m. Junming Dong, 1 son, 1 daughter. Education: Bachelor of Engineering, Tsinghua University, Beijing, China, 1981-86; Master of Engineering, Metals Research Institute, Chinese Academy of Sciences, Shenyang, China, 1986-89; Doctor of Engineering, Aachen University, Aachen, Germany, 1994-98. Appointments: Lecturer, Jilin University of Technology, Changchun, China, 1989-93; Scientist, Materials Science Institute, Aachen University, Aachen, Germany, 1994-. Publications: Articles in scientific journals including: International Journal of Refractory Metals and Hard Materials; Surface and Coatings Technology; Thin Solid Films; Advanced Engineering Materials, Wear. Honours: Best Paper, United Thermal Spray Conference, 1999; Excellent Paper, International Thermal Spray Conference, 2000. Address: Steinkaul Street 51, 52070 Aachen, Germany. E-mail: zhao@iot.rwth-aachem.de

**ZHAO Zhong Wei,** b. 29 September 1954, Beijing, China. Researcher. m. Yan Ping Zhang, 1 daughter. Education: BA, Peking University, 1979-83; MA, Exeter University, 1986-87; PhD, Cambridge University, 1988-93. Appointments: Senior Fellow, Program of Demography and Sociology, RSSS, Australian National University; Senior Research Associate, Cambridge Group for the History of Population and Social Structure, University of Cambridge; Fellow, Research Fellow, Demography Program, RSSS, Australian National University; Post-doctoral Fellow, Department of Sociology, University of New South Wales; Post-doctoral Fellow, East-West Centre, Hawaii. Publications: Many articles in professional journals. Honours: Biographical listing in Who's Who in the World. Memberships: International Union for the Scientific Study of Population. Address: Program of Demography and Sociology, RSSS, The Australian National University, ACT 0200, Australia.

**ZHIRABOK Alexey,** b. 27 November 1946, Khabarovsk, Russia. Radio and Electrical Educator. m. Nina, 1 daughter. Education: Engineer Degree, 1970; PhD, Radio Engineering, 1978; Dr Sc Degree, Control Engineering, 1996. Appointments: Assistant Professor, Far Eastern State Technical University,

1970-75; Associate Professor, 1979-83; Head of Department, 1983-92; Postdoctoral Trainee, 1992-95; Professor, 1996-. Publications: 2 books; 4 booklets; More than 150 articles. Honours: Soros Professor; Award of Soros Foundation; Honoured Higher School Worker of Russia; Listed in national and international biographical dictionaries. Memberships: IEEE; Russian Academy of Engineering. Address: Far Eastern State Technical University, Pushkinskaya Street 10, Vladivostok 690950, Russia.

**ZHIVETIN Vladimir,** b. 22 January 1940, Guriev, Kazakhstan. Rector. m. 2 daughters. Education: Candidate of Technical Science, 1973; Assistant Professor, 1976; Doctor of Technical Science, 1995; Professor, 1996. Appointments: Professor of Mathematics, Kazan Aviation Institute, -1996; Rector of Nizhnekamsk Municipal Institute, 1997-99; Rector of Municipal Institute of Zhukovsky City, 1999-2002; Rector of Institute for Risk Problems, Moscow, 2002-; Vice-President, Academy of Risk Sciences, Moscow, 2004-. Publications: Books: Introduction in the Risk Analysis, 1999; Aeromechanical Control, 1999; Higher Mathematics, 1999; Human Risk, 2001; Technical Risk, 2001; Economic Risk and Safety, 2003; Scientific Risk, 2003; Higher Mathematics (practical course), 2003. Membership: Kazan Mathematical Society. Address: Levchenko St. 3-50, Zhukovsky, Moscow Region 140180, Russia. E-mail: zhivetin@progtech.ru Website: www.institutpr.com

**ZHOU Rongjia,** b. 8 April 1961, Sichuan, China. Professor. m. Hanhua Cheng, 1 daughter. Education: BSc, 1978-82, MSc, 1983-86, Sichuan Agricultural University; PhD, West China University of Medical Sciences, 1989-92. Appointments: Associate Professor, 1994-96, Professor, 1996-, Wuhan University; Research Fellow: University of California, San Francisco, USA 1994, La Trobe University, Australia, 1996; Los Angeles State University, 1997, Institute of Human Genetics, France, 1998-99; Visiting Scientist, Pasteur Institute, Paris, France, 2002. Publications: Articles as co-author in scientific journals including: Nucleic Acids Research, 2002; Reviews in Fish Biology and Fisheries, 2002; Molecular Reproduction and Development, 2003. Honours: Habei Science and Technology for Youth Award, 1995; Fellow International Human Frontier Science Programme, 1995; Science and Technology Progress Award, Sichuan Government, 1996; Natural Science Award of Habei, 2005; International Scientist of 2005, IBC. Memberships: Genetics Society of China, Vice-Chairman, Animal Genetics Committee, 2003; Space Science Society of China. Address: College of Life Sciences, Wuhan University, Wuhan 430072, P. R. China. E-mail: rjzhou@whu.edu.cn

**ZHOU Yuming,** b. 23 June 1934, Hebei, China. Senior Translator. m. Shuying Li, 2 sons. Education: Graduate, Faculty of Foreign Languages and Literature, University of Central China, 1956. Appointments: Assistant Professor, University of Central China, 1956; English Translator, Chinese Ministry of the Petroleum Industry, 1974; Senior Translator, China National Offshore Oil Corporation, 1984; Retired 1994; Senior Translator, Enron Oil and Gas China Ltd, 1994-1999; Retired from Enron Oil and Gas, China, 1999. Publications: Books of modern lyrics: Flowing Bunch of Flowers; Kiss of Wings; Love of Dolphin; The Tenderly Grown Green; Selected Poems of Yuming; Earth Newborn; Selected Verses by Yuming; Books of long epic poems: Liang Shanbo and Zhu Yingtai – Chinese Romeo and Juliet; Love Between a Human Being and a Serpentine Being; Far Away Off the Milky Way (extracts in book: Eternal Motherlove, 2005). Honours: Gold Prize of the Chinese Long "Dragon" Culture; Award, International Poet of Merit, International Society of Poets, America; Honorary

Doctor of Literature of the World Academy of Arts and Culture; Distinguished Leadership Award, American Biographical Institute; Man of the Year 2002, ABI; The Founders Award, IBC; Universal Award of Accomplishment; American Medal of Honor; ABI World Laureate of China; Worldwide Honours List, IBC; First Class Award for Far Away Off the Milky Way, Chinese Ministry of Culture, 2005. Memberships: China Poetry Association; Member and Membership Director, World Congress of Poets; Distinguished Member, International Society of Poets. Address: 233, Building 7, Ruyili, Western District, Beijing 100035, China.

**ZHOU Zhi-Hua,** b. 20 November 1973, Guangzhou, China. Professor. m. Yuan Jiang. Education: BSc, 1996, MSc, 1998, PhD, 2000, Computer Science, Nanjing University, Nanjing China. Appointments: Lecturer, 2000-2002, Associate Professor, 2002-2003, Professor, 2003-, Department of Computer Science and Technology, Nanjing University, Nanjing, China. Publications: Widely published in the fields of artificial intelligence, machine learning, data mining, pattern recognition. Honours: Microsoft Fellowship Award, 1999; National Excellent Doctoral Dissertation Award of China, 2003; Award of Outstanding Youth Foundation of China, 2003. Memberships: Associate Editor, Knowledge and Information Systems; Editorial Board Member: Artificial Intelligence in Medicine, International Journal of Data Warehousing and Mining, Journal of Computer Science and Technology. Address: National Laboratory for Naval Software Technology, Nanjing University, Nanjing 210093, China. Website: http: //cs.nju.edu.cn/people/zhouzh

**ZHU Hong,** b. 1 March 1960, Guiyang, China. Musician. m. Lu Deng, 1 son, 1 daughter. Education: BA, Central Conservatory of Music, Beijing, 1982; MM, Michigan State University, 1990; DMA, Michigan State University, 1995. Appointments: Assistant Professor, Central Conservatory of Music, Beijing, 1982-87; Instructor, Flint Institute of Music, 1989-94; Adjunct Instructor, University of Michigan-Flint, 1991-93; Murray State University, 1994-96; Instructor, Concert Master, Colorado Music Festival, 1996-; Associate Professor, Violin, University of Central Oklahoma, 1996-. Honours: Yehudi Menuhin Prize. Memberships: Chamber Music America; American Federation of Musicians; American String Teachers Association. Address: 1125 Bradford Place, Edmond, OK 73003, USA. E-mail: hzhu@ucok.edu

**ZHU Yilin,** b. 17 August 1934, Shanghai, China. Research Professor. m. Ye Bihua, 1 son, 1 daughter. Education: Bachelor, Nanjing Institute of Technology, 1953; Postgraduate Study, Harbin Institute of Technology, 1955; Postgraduate Study, Tsinghua University, 1959. Appointments: Engineer, 1958-65; Vice Director of Research Division, 1965-85; Vice Director, Science and Technology Commission, Institute of Spacecraft System Engineering, 1985-89; Secretary General, Science and Technology Commission, Chinese Academy of Space Technology, 1989-2000; Consultant, Beijing Institute of Space Science and Technology Information, 2000-. Publications: Space Technology Elementary; Flight to the Stars; Versatile in Space; Flight to Space; Space Time; An Introduction to China's Space Endeavour, in English; Over 150 academic papers and around 500 articles in Chinese and international journals, magazines and 6 other treatises. Honours: Second State Prize, State Council, 1985; Merit Citation Class II, Ministry of Aerospace of China, 1985; Government Special Subsidy, State Council. Memberships: Standing Committee, Chinese Society of Space Science, 1980-96; Corresponding Member, International Academy of Astronautics, 1999-2004; Full Member, International Academy of Astronautics, 2004-;

Councils of Chinese Society of Space Science and Chinese Society of Science Writers. Address: Room 502, Building 11, 31 Zhongguancun Nandajie, Haidian District, Beijing, 100081, China.

**ZLOCHEVSKAYA Alla,** b. 10 November 1951, Moscow, Russia. Literary Critic; Researcher. Education: MA, Philology, Moscow State University; Defended and published 2 literary research theses: PhD equivalent, 1982 and 2002. Appointments: Research Worker, 1985-2000, Senior Researcher, 2000-, Department of Philology, Moscow State University, Russia. Publications: Published more than 80 research articles concerning Russian literature of XIX-XX centuries and Czech and Slovak Rusistik; In-depth study of F Dostoyevsky, V Nabokov, M Bulgakov; Monograph: Artistic World of V Nabokov and Russian Literature of XIX Century, 2002. Membership: F M Dostoyevsky Society, Moscow. Address: Olympic Village 8, Flat 153, Mitchurinsky Pr. Moscow 119602, Russia. E-mail: zlocevskaya@mail.ru

**ZOLBERG Vera L,** b. 22 September 1932, Vienna, Austria. Sociology Professor. m. Aristide R Zolberg, 1 son, 1 daughter. Education: AB, Hunter College, 1953; MA, Boston University, 1956; PhD, University of Chicago, 1974. Appointments: Edgewood College, Madison, Wisconsin, 1962-64; St Xavier College, Chicago, 1964-71; Purdue University, 1974-84; Professor, New School for Social Research, 1984-. Publications include: After Bourdieu: Influence, Critique, Elaboration; Outsider Art: Contested Boundaries in Contemporary Culture; The Happy Few-en Masse: Franco-American Comparisons in Cultural Democratization; Constructing a Sociology of the Arts. Honours: Rockefeller Humanities Fellowship; ACLS Fellowship; Many travel grants. Memberships: American Sociological Association; Society for Social Theory, Politics and the Arts; International Sociological Association; Association Internationale des Sociologues de Langue Francaise; Eastern Sociological Society. Address: New School University, 65th Avenue, New York City, NY 10003, USA.

**ZORE-ARMANDA Mira,** b. 6 January 1930, Zagreb, Croatia. Scientist. m. Igor Armanda. Education: Dipl. Ing, Geophysics, University of Zagreb, Croatia, 1952; PhD, Sciences, University of Paris, Sorbonne, France, 1963. Appointments: Employee, Institute of Oceanography and Fisheries, Split, Croatia, 1952-89; Retired as Senior Scientific Officer, 1989; Editor-in-Chief, Acta Adriatica, 1989-. Publications: Books: Introduction to Oceanography and Marine Meteorology (co-author), 1963, 1971, 1975; Memoirs of an Oceanographer, 1997; Over 150 scientific and technical papers on oceanography of the Adriatic Sea, long-term changes of oceanographic properties in relation to climatic factors. Address: Meštrovićevo šetalište 61, 2100 Split, Croatia. E-mail: zore@izor.hr

**ZUBOVICH Stanislav Francevich,** b. 12 July 1937, Ukraine. m. Natalia, 1 son. Education: Technical College, Department of Cartography, Kiev, 1956-59; Faculty of Geography, Belarusian State University, 1963-69; Aspiranture of Laboratory of Geochemical Problems, Academy of Sciences, Minsk, 1969-72; Medical College, Minsk, 1993-96. Appointments: Technician of Topography, 1959; Geography Assistant, 1969; Scientific Worker, 1972; Doctor of Sciences, Geology and Mineralogy, 1973; Senior Scientific Worker, 1973; Professor, Belarusian State Pedagogical Institute, 1986-. Publications include: 14 monographs; 3 popular books, 204 science articles; 73 new taxons of fossils and recent ostracodas; Author, theoretical basis and creation of Ostracodology of Plaistocaen as a separate scientific trend. Honours: 1 Silver and 3 Bronze Medals, Exhibition of National Economics of the USSR; Medals, International Man of the Year, 1999-2000, 2000-01, 2003, 20th Century Award for Achievement, 21st Century Award for Achievement, International Intellectual of the Year, 2001, International Scientists of the Year, 2003; International Educator of the Year 2003; One-in-a-Million, One Thousand Great Intellectuals, 2000 Outstanding People, International Order of Merit, Living Legend Diploma, IBC, England; Diploma, 1000 Leaders of World of Influence, 500 Leaders of Influence, Commemorative Medal, Man of Year, 2001, ABI, USA; The Honoured Master of Education of Belarus; Medal for Sports Achievement of Trade Union of the USSR; Medal for Development of Youth Tourism in the USSR. Memberships: Geographical Society of Belarus; Society of Country Sciences; International Academy of Ecology and Natural Employment; Deputy Director General, IBC. Address: Belarusian State Pedagogical University, Str Sovetskaya 18, 220809 Minsk, Belarus.

**ZUBRITSKY Alexander,** b. 14 March 1949, Severo-Kurilsk, Sakhalin Region, Russia. Pathologist. Education: Curative and Preventative Faculty, Sverdlovsk Medical Institute, 1968-74, 1 year specialism in Pathological Anatomy, Sverdlovsk Regional Clinical Hospital No 1, 1975; Advanced Training Course for Pathological Anatomy, Kharkov, Ukraine Institute of Advanced Medical Studies, 1977; Advanced Training Course for Perinatal Pathology, Moscow Institute for Postgraduate Medical Training, 1986; PhD, 1991; Advanced Training Course for Cytology, Moscow Regional Research Clinical Institute, 1994; Pathological Anatomy, Russian Medical Academy for Postgraduate Training, 2000; Advanced Training Course for Histological Diagnostics of Endometrium Scrape, Research Centre of Obstetrics, Gynaecology and Perinatology, Russian Academy of Medical Sciences, 2004. Appointments: Hospital Attendant, Department of Pathology, City Hospital No 21, Sverdlovsk, 1965-67; Hospital Attendant, Medico-Legal Morgue No 1, Sverdlovsk, 1967-68; Chief of Pathology Department, Central Regional Hospital in Neviyansk, Sverdlovsk Region, 1975-76; Chief of Pathology Department, Head Pathologist, Sverdlovsk Road, 1976-83; Lecturer, Pathological Anatomy, Medical School of Sverdlovsk Road, 1976-77; Chief of Department of Pathology, Municipal Institution, Taldom Central Regional Hospital, Taldom, Moscow Region, 1983-. Publications: 4 rationalisation proposals; 170 published works as sole author. Honours: Certificate, A Finalist, Marvin I Dunn Award, Best Poster Presentation in Cardiology, American College of Chest Physicians, 1990; Pathology Research Practice Award for the Expert Quiz, Innsbruck, MD Taldom, 1993; International Man of the Year, 1994-95; Certificate, Researcher of the Year, ABI, 2001; International Peace Prize Winner, UCC, 2003; 21st Century Award for Achievement (Bronze Medal), IBC, 2003; Gold Medal International Scientist of the Year 2004, IBC; The World Medal of Freedom for significant accomplishments in the field of Pathological Anatomy, ABI, 2005; 2005 Man of Achievement Award for Outstanding Contributions to Pathological Anatomy of Cor Pulmonale, ABI, 2005. Memberships: European Society of Pathology, 1989; International Union Against Tuberculosis and Lung Disease, 1990; European Section, International Society for Heart Research, 1992; International Society on Diagnostic Quantitative Pathology, 1994; New York Academy of Sciences, 1995; Research Board of Advisors, ABI, 2000; Honorary Member, IBC Advisory Council, 2000; American Association for the Advancement of Science, 2003. Address: Prospekt Mira 101 B/79, Moscow 129085, Russia. E-mail: zubr4taldom@mail.ru Website: http://www.biblio.narod.ru/reth/reth0.htm

**ZUCCONI Paolo,** b. 4 December 1950, Trieste, Italy. Neuro Psychotherapist. m. 2 daughters. Education: Psychologist Degree, specialisation in cognitive and behavioural psychotherapy; European Certificate of Psychotherapy; Postgraduate of: Communication, addiction, forensic psychology, neuropsychology, Clinical sexology, hypnosis; Master in clinical nutrition. Appointments: Assistant Professor, Triest University; Teacher of General Psychology; Psychotherapist in hospital; Adjunct Professor of Clinical Methodology. Honours: Associate Fellow of Albert Ellis Institute for Rational Emotive Behaviour Therapy, New York; Diplomate in Behavioural Medicine, International Academy of Behavioural Medicine, Counselling and Psychotherapy Inc; Decree of Merit, Outstanding Scientist of the 21st Century, IBC; European Certificate of Psychotherapy, EAP; Knight of the Order of Merit of the Italian Republic. Memberships: International Society of Hypnosis; Certified Hypnotherapist of National Guild of Hypnotists; European Association for Behaviour and Cognitive Therapy. Address: Casella Postale 183, 33100 Udine, Italy. Website: www.dr-zucconi.it

**ZUCKER-FRANKLIN Dorothea,** b. 9 August 1930, Berlin, Germany. Physician, Scientist. m. Edward C Franklin, deceased, 1 daughter. Education: BA, Hunter College, New York, 1952; MD, New York Medical College, New York, 1956; Post-Doctoral Fellowships: Department of Hematology, Montefiore Hospital, Bronx, 1959-61; Department of Anatomy, New York University School of Medicine, 1961-63. Appointments include: Assistant Professor of Medicine 1963-68, Associate Professor of Medicine 1968-74, Professor of Medicine 1974-, Department of Medicine, New York University School of Medicine. Publications include: Numerous articles in professional journals. Honours include: Phi Beta Kappa; AOA; Henry Moses Prize for Research, 1973, 1985; Elected member, Institute of Medicine of the National Academy of Sciences, 1995; Woman of the Year Award, American Women in Science, 1996; Fellow, American Association for the Advancement of Science, 1997; Doctor of Science, honoris causa, City University of New York, 1996; Elected, American Academy of Arts and Sciences, 2001; Listed in several biographical dictionaries. Memberships include: Numerous scientific societies including: FASEB, 1966-; American Society of Clinical Investigations, 1973; American Association of Physicians, 1974; American Association of Immunologists, 1979-; Greater New York Blood Program Ad Hoc committee for donor notification, criteria and protocols AIDS study, 1982-84; IV International Symposium on Amyloid-Organizing Committee, 1983-84; VA AIDS Center Grant Review Panel, 1988 and 1989; Member of Board of Directors, Henry M and Lillian Stratton Foundation Inc, 1987-95; Many other Ad Hoc NIH and academic committees at various institutions; Institute of Medicine, National Academy of Science, 1995; President, American Society of Hematology, 1995. Address: New York University School of Medicine, Department of Medicine, 550 First Avenue. New York, NY 10016, USA.

**ZUK-HRYSKIEVIC Raisa,** b. 22 October 1919, Belarus. Dental Surgeon. m. Vincent, 4 September 1953, 1 daughter. Education: Law, Steven Batory University, Vilna, 1938-39; Faculty of Dentistry, University Marburg, Germany, 1948; Student, Faculty of Dentistry, University of Toronto, Canada, 1951-54; DDS, Senat, University of Toronto, Canada, 1954. Appointments: General Practice, Toronto, Barrie, Ontario, Canada, 1954-90; Member, Belarus Republic, Canadian Consultative Council on Multiculturalism, 1973-78 Retired. Publications: Articles in Belarusan Newspapers; Book, The Life of Vincent Zuk-Hryskievic. Honour: Volunteer Service Award, 1986. Memberships: Belarusan Study Association; Canadian Dental Association; Ontario Dental Association; Simcoe Dental Association; University Womens' Club; Soroptimist Club of Barrie; Belarusan Canadian Alliance; Belarusan Canadian

Womens' Association; Belarusan Canadian Co-ordinating Committee; Institute of Arts and Science, Canana; Belarusan Democratic Republic in Exile. Address: 54 Mary Street, Barrie, Ontario, Canada, L4N 1T1.

**ZURAKOWSKI Zdzislaw**, b. 22 January 1943, Stanislawow, Poland. Electrical Engineer. Education: MSc, Electrical Engineering, 1967, Post-graduate course, Application of Computers in Engineering Calculations and Design, 1988-89, Post-graduate course, Design of Microprocessor Systems, 1989-90, Wroclaw University of Technology, Wroclaw, Poland. Appointments: Scientific Research Assistant, Institute of Power Engineering, Warsaw, Wroclaw, Poland, 1967-68; Research Engineering Assistant, Institute of Electrical Power Engineering, Wroclaw University of Technology, Wroclaw, Poland, 1968-82; Electrical Systems Designer, Steel Plant "Siechnice", Wroclaw, Poland, 1982-87; Rolling Stock Electrical Systems Designer, Research and Development Centre, Railway Rolling Stock and Rail-Coach Factory "Pafawag", Wroclaw, Poland, 1987-94; Head, Independent Laboratory of on-Board Computer Systems, Rail-Coach Factory "Pafawag", Wroclaw, Poland, 1994-95; Senior Specialist, Institute of Power Systems Automation, Wroclaw, Poland, 1995-2003; Editor and Chairman of Editorial Board, special section entitled "Real-Time Systems" (in Polish), Polish journal on computer science "Informatyka", 1994-2000. Publications: 32 papers published in Polish and foreign publications mainly in the field of electrical engineering and safety and security related computer systems applications; 15 non published technical reports; 2 patents (co-author); 1 university textbook (co-author, author of 2 sections). Memberships: Member, Association of Polish Electrical Engineers, 1983-; Member, Programme Committee, Polish National Conference "Real-Time Systems" (in Polish), 1994-; Member, Polish Committee for Standardization Technical Committee 50, 1995-, Technical Committee 183, 2000-; Member, European Workshop on Industrial Computer Systems Technical Committee 7 Reliability, Safety and Security (EWICS TC7), 1995-; Member, International Programme Committee, International Conferences on Computer Reliability, Safety and Security, SAFECOMP, 1997-; Member, Committee for Functional Safety of the Polish Association of Safety and Reliability (PTBN), 2004-. Address: Pomorska 4 m.19, PL 50-218 Wroclaw, Poland. E-mail: zz@pvd.pl

**ZWIERZCHOWSKI Henryk**, b. 24 October 1926, Lódź, Poland. Orthopaedic Surgeon. m. Danuta Anna Zuchowicz, 2 sons. Education: MD, Medical University, Lódź, 1952; PhD, 1964; DSc, 1974; Specialist of Orthopaedics and Traumatology, 1957. Appointments: From Assistant to Senior Assistant, 1952-63, Consultant, Outpatient Clinic, 1958-74, Orthopaedic Hospital, Lódź; From Lecturer to Assistant Professor, Orthopaedic Clinic, 1964-78, Head of Orthopaedic Clinic, 1979-83, Associate Professor, 1984-91, Professor, 1991-, Head of Orthopaedic Department, 1984-97, Medical University, Lódź; Active Member, Scientific Council of the Surgical Institute, Lódź, 1976-87; Member of Editorial Committee, Chirurgia Narządów Ruchu i Ortopedia Polska (Journal of the Polish Society of Orthopaedics and Traumatology, 1984-; Regional Consultant, Orthopaedics and Traumatology, Lódź, 1995-98. Publications: Author or co-author of 176 research articles, clinical reviews and research reports published in various scientific periodicals as well as 5 books all related to the area of orthopaedics, traumatology and rehabilitation of the motor system; patentee prosthese of crutiate ligament, 1993. Honours: Cavalier Cross of the Order Polonia Restituta, 1984; Golden Badge, Polish Society for Fight with Cripleness Award, 1984; Ministers Award, 1985, 1987, 1995; Honorary Member, Polish Orthopaedics and Traumatology Society, 1996. Memberships:

Polish Society for Fight with Cripleness, 1964-90; Polish Orthopaedics and Traumatology Society, 1952-, Vice-President, 1982-86, Chairman Lódź Branch, 1979-82, 1987-90. Address: Zachodnia 12, Apt 63, 91-058 Lódź, Poland.

**ZWILLENBERG Lutz Oscar**, b. 9 December 1925, Berlin-Charlottenburg, Germany. Biologist. m. Celia Fridman, 2 daughters. Education: Graduated, Gymnasium, Hilversum and Amsterdam, 1940-43; Baccalaureate, Barlaeus Gymnasium, Amsterdam, 1946; PhD, Natural Sciences, University of Amsterdam, 1959. Appointments: Assistant, Department of Anatomy, 1959-63, Senior Research Assistant, Department of Hygiene and Medical Microbiology, 1963-67, University of Bern; Founder, Proprietor, Biologisches Forschungslaboratorium, Dres. Zwillenberg, Bern, 1970-; President, ZW Biomedical Research AG, Bern, 1994-2002; Main research interests: Histology; Microbiology; Virology; Electron microscopy; Ectocervical epithelium; Gynaecology; Pharmacology; Philosophy of Science. Publications: Numerous papers and articles contributed to conferences and specialist peer-reviewed journals; 2 books, Woher und Wozu, 1980; Zwischen Bit und Bibel 1986, 1987; Editor, Tradition und Erneuerung (journal of the Swiss Association for Progressive Judaism) Translator Prayerbook, Gottesdienst im Herzen (Avodah Shebalev). Memberships: American Association for the Advancement of Science; New York Academy of Sciences; Swiss Association of Natural Science. Address: Holligenstrasse 93 CH-3008 Bern, Switzerland.

**ZYUNG Taehyoung**, b. 24 September 1954, Republic of Korea. Research Scientist. m. Sangsub Yoon, 1 son, 1 daughter. Education: BS, Seoul National University, Korea, 1977; PhD, Texas Tech University, USA, 1986. Appointments: Researcher, KIST, 1978-81; Research Assistant, Texas Tech University, 1981-86; Postdoctoral Research Associate, University of Illinois, 1986-89; Principal Member of Research Staff, 1989-2000, Director, 2001-, ETRI, Korea. Publications: Electrical and Optical Polymer Systems, 1998; Display Engineering, 2000; Advanced Functional Molecules and Polymers, 2001. Honours: ISI Citation Classic Award, 2000; Songkok Award, 2001. Memberships: Korean Chemical Society; Polymer Society of Korea. Address: 109-1504 Hanwood Apt, Sinsung-dong, Yusong-gu, Taejon, Korea.

# *20TH CENTURY HONOURS LIST*

**NAME:** Dr Farid A Akasheh LFIBA

**ADDRESS:** PO Box 2173
Amman
Jordan

**OCCUPATION:** Doctor (Consultant Obstetrician and Gynaecologist)

**YEAR OF ENTRY:** 1986

**CITATION:** For your Outstanding Contribution to Medicine

**NAME:** Dr Farouk M Akhdar LFIBA

**ADDRESS:** The Economic Bureau
PO Box 86619
Riyadh 11632
Kingdom of Saudi Arabia

**OCCUPATION:** President of the Economic Bureau

**YEAR OF ENTRY:** 1989

**CITATION:** For your Outstanding Contribution to Economics and to the development of Saudi Arabia

**NAME:** Abdullatif A R Al-Bahar

**ADDRESS:** PO Box 89
Safat
13001 Kuwait City
Kuwait

**OCCUPATION:** Director General, Office of H H The Crown Prince & Prime Minister - Kuwait

**YEAR OF ENTRY:** 1989

**CITATION:** For you Outstanding Contribution to his present position within the field of Political & Economics Institutions

NAME: **Ahmad Mohamad Ali**

ADDRESS: Islamic Development Bank
PO Box 5925
Jeddah 21432
Saudi Arabia

OCCUPATION: President, Islamic Development Bank

YEAR OF ENTRY: 1990

CITATION: For your Outstanding Contribution to the Banking Business

NAME: **Jacob Oladele Amao DDG LFIBA**

ADDRESS: PO Box 51722
Ikoyi
Lagos
Nigeria

OCCUPATION: Company President – Executive

YEAR OF ENTRY: 1990

CITATION: For your Outstanding Contribution to the Banking Business

NAME: **Professor Basile Angelopoulos MD PhD LPIBA HonDG**

ADDRESS: Ipsilamtou Str 37
Athens 106-76
Greece

OCCUPATION: Professor in Pathologic Physiology

YEAR OF ENTRY: 1986

CITATION: For your Outstanding Contribution to Medicine

NAME: **Kathlyn Ballard LPIBA**

ADDRESS: 40 Mont Victor Road
Kew
3101 Melbourne
Australia

OCCUPATION: Artist

YEAR OF ENTRY: 1986

CITATION: For your Outstanding Contribution to Art

NAME: **Abdul Rahman Batal LPIBA LFWLA DDG
AdVBus**

ADDRESS: Chairman, Hannibal Tourism & Transport Co
PO Box 4088
Damascus
Syria

OCCUPATION: Company Chairman

YEAR OF ENTRY: 1986

CITATION: For your Outstanding Contribution to Tourism and
Transport

NAME: **Shauna D Boulton LFIBA DDG**

ADDRESS: 1516 Glen Arbor
Salt Lake City
UT 84105
USA

OCCUPATION: Educator

YEAR OF ENTRY: 1986

CITATION: For your Outstanding Contribution to Education

**NAME:**      **Richard E Butler LFIBA**

**ADDRESS:**      40 Barrington Avenue
Kew
Victoria 3101
Australia

**OCCUPATION:**      International Official

**YEAR OF ENTRY:**      1990

**CITATION:**      For your Outstanding Contribution to International Cooperation and to World-wide Telecommunication Development

**NAME:**      **Professor Chen Jian Hong**

**ADDRESS:**      Gansu University of Tech
Lanzhou
Gansu
China

**OCCUPATION:**      President, Professor

**YEAR OF ENTRY:**      1989

**CITATION:**      For your Outstanding Contribution to the Science and Education of China

**NAME:**      **Thomas J Cleary**

**ADDRESS:**      933 Kiowa
Burkburnett
TX 76354
USA

**OCCUPATION:**      Clinical Social Worker, Teaching Assistant, Graduate Student US History MSU

**YEAR OF ENTRY:**      1989

**CITATION:**      For your Outstanding Contribution to Social Work Service

# HONOURS LIST

**NAME:**       The Hon Dame Dr Joy Beaudette Cripps N.H DGC DCMSS IOM LFWLA MOIF LDAF

**ADDRESS:**       3 Mill Street
Aspendale
Victoria 3195
Australia

**OCCUPATION:**       Publisher, Poet, Photographer

**YEAR OF ENTRY:**       1988

**CITATION:**       For your Outstanding Contribution to Literature

**NAME:**       **Basil V Damalas**

**ADDRESS:**       Parission 171
Athens 112 52
Greece

**OCCUPATION:**       Publicist and Economist

**YEAR OF ENTRY:**       1986

**CITATION:**       For your Outstanding Contribution to Economics

**NAME:**       **Dr J Edward Dealy MS PhD**

**ADDRESS:**       1040 W Rio Guaymas
Green Valley
AZ 85614-4026
USA

**OCCUPATION:**       Forestry

**YEAR OF ENTRY:**       1986

**CITATION:**       For your Outstanding Contribution to Forestry

# HONOURS LIST

**NAME:** Thaneswari De Silva LPIBA

**ADDRESS:** 148/2A Kynsey Road
Colombo 8
Sri Lanka

**OCCUPATION:** Estate Proprietoress and Directress 'Leighton Park' Montessori and Junior School

**YEAR OF ENTRY:** 1986

**CITATION:** For your Outstanding Contribution as Montessori and Junior School Directress

**NAME:** Howard M Dupuy Jr BA LLP

**ADDRESS:** 465 NE 181st Avenue = 110
Portland
OR 97230
USA

**OCCUPATION:** Lawyer

**YEAR OF ENTRY:** 1986

**CITATION:** For your Outstanding Contribution to The Law

**NAME:** Chris Economides

**ADDRESS:** 6 Dositheos
PO Box 1632
Nicosia
Cyprus

**OCCUPATION:** Director

**YEAR OF ENTRY:** 1988

**CITATION:** For your Outstanding Contribution to Economics

# HONOURS LIST

**NAME:** **Professor M Gembicki MD**

**ADDRESS:** Department of Endocrinology
University School of Medicine in Poznan
Al Przybyszewskiego 49
PL-60 355, Poland

**OCCUPATION:** Doctor

**YEAR OF ENTRY:** 1986

**CITATION:** For your Outstanding Contribution to Medicine

**NAME:** **Dr Richard Sherwin Gothard**

**ADDRESS:** Gothard House
Henley-on-Thames
Oxon RE9 1AJ
England

**OCCUPATION:** Information Scientist

**YEAR OF ENTRY:** 1986

**CITATION:** For your Outstanding Contribution to Information Science

**NAME:** **Violet Edna Hobbs Hain**

**ADDRESS:** 3530 Raymoor Road
Kensington
MD 20895
USA

**OCCUPATION:** Artist

**YEAR OF ENTRY:** 1986

**CITATION:** For your Outstanding Contribution to Art

| NAME: | **Dr Kazuyuki Hatada DDG LFIBA IOM** |
|---|---|
| ADDRESS: | Department of Mathematics<br>Faculty of Education, Gifu University<br>1-1 Yanagido, Gifu City<br>Gifu Prefecture 501-1193, Japan |
| OCCUPATION: | Mathematician |
| YEAR OF ENTRY: | 1990 |
| CITATION: | For your Outstanding Contribution to Pure Mathematics, especially to the Theory of Modular Forms |
| NAME: | **Professor Zuey-Shin Hsu MD LFIBA DDG IOM MOIF** |
| ADDRESS: | Department of Physiology<br>Kaohsiung Medical College<br>No 100 Shih-Chuan 1st Road, Kaohsiung<br>Taiwan |
| OCCUPATION: | Professor of Physiology |
| YEAR OF ENTRY: | 1989 |
| CITATION: | For your Outstanding Contribution to Medical Science and the Teaching Profession |
| NAME: | **John Chih-An Hu** |
| ADDRESS: | 2813 Whitworth Avenue<br>Renton<br>WA 98055<br>USA |
| OCCUPATION: | Chemist and Chemical Engineer |
| YEAR OF ENTRY: | 1986 |
| CITATION: | For your Outstanding Contribution to Chemistry |

**NAME:** Professor Dr Kazuyosi Ikeda DSc DLitt LPIBA DDG IOM LFWLA MOIF CH DO

**ADDRESS:** Nisi - 7 - 7 - 11 Aomadani
Minoo-Si
Osaka 562-0023
Japan

**OCCUPATION:** Professor of Theoretical Physics and Poet

**YEAR OF ENTRY:** 1989

**CITATION:** For your Outstanding Contribution to Theoretical Physics and Poetry

**NAME:** Dr Drago Ikic LFIBA

**ADDRESS:** Croation Academy of Sciences and Arts
Gunduliceva 24/11
Zagreb 10000
Croatia

**OCCUPATION:** Doctor

**YEAR OF ENTRY:** 1986

**CITATION:** For your Outstanding Contribution to Medicine

**NAME:** Hazel Emma Jones FIBA

**ADDRESS:** 35 Greer Street
Bardon
Queensland 4065
Australia

**OCCUPATION:** Librarian

**YEAR OF ENTRY:** 1986

**CITATION:** For your Outstanding Contribution to Librarianship

NAME: **Kristjan G Kjartansson**

ADDRESS: Einimelur 7

107 Reykjavik

Iceland

OCCUPATION: Company Vice President

YEAR OF ENTRY: 1986

CITATION: For your Outstanding Contribution to Commerce

NAME: **Professor Lidia Agnes Kozubek**

ADDRESS: ul J Dabrowskiego 77m.9

02-503 Warsaw

Poland

OCCUPATION: Pianist, Educator and Musicologist

YEAR OF ENTRY: 1986

CITATION: For your Outstanding Contribution to Music

NAME: **Dato Dr Sip Hon Lew**

ADDRESS: 15 Jalan 12

Taman Tun Abdul Razak

Ampang Jaya

Selangor, Malaysia

OCCUPATION: Company Director, Retired Ambassador

YEAR OF ENTRY: 1988

CITATION: For your Outstanding Contribution to the economic, political and cultural life of Malaysia and to your role in the larger world community

# HONOURS LIST

**NAME:** **Anneliese List LFWLA LFIBA IOM MOIF HE**

**ADDRESS:** Fuenfbronn 27
91174 Spalt
Germany

**OCCUPATION:** Soubrette

**YEAR OF ENTRY:** 1986

**CITATION:** For your Outstanding Contribution to Literature

**NAME:** **Konstantin Mandic IOM**

**ADDRESS:** PO Box 672
Gaborone
Botswana
Africa

**OCCUPATION:** Architect

**YEAR OF ENTRY:** 1989

**CITATION:** For your Outstanding Contribution to Architecture

**NAME:** **Professor Dr Mitsuo Masai**

**ADDRESS:** Faculty of Engineering
Kobe University
Rokkadai-Cho, Nada-Ku
Kobe 657
Japan

**OCCUPATION:** University Professor

**YEAR OF ENTRY:** 1986

**CITATION:** For your Outstanding Contribution to Catalysis

NAME: **Emeritus Professor Junji Matsumoto LFIBA IOM**

ADDRESS: 2-3-14 Asukano Minami
Ikoma City
630-01 Japan

OCCUPATION: Neuroscientist

YEAR OF ENTRY: 1988

CITATION: For your Outstanding Contribution to Science

NAME: **Professor Seiichi Matsumoto**

ADDRESS: Yuigahama 1-11-17
Kamakura 248-0014
Japan

OCCUPATION: Director and Professor

YEAR OF ENTRY: 1986

CITATION: For your Outstanding Contribution to Medicine

NAME: **Ralph E Montijo DDG IOM LPIBA**

ADDRESS: 7811 E Edison St
Tucson
AZ 85715-4255

OCCUPATION: Company President, Executive

YEAR OF ENTRY: 1987

CITATION: For your Outstanding Contribution to Business

NAME: **Peggy Jean Mueller IOM**

ADDRESS: PO Box 5868
Austin
TX 78763
USA

OCCUPATION: Dance Teacher/Choreographer

YEAR OF ENTRY: 1990

CITATION: For your Outstanding Contribution to Dancing, Ranching and Trail Riding

NAME: **Hassenally Nanuck LFIBA**

ADDRESS: PO Box 40346
Gaborone
Botswana

OCCUPATION: Auto Body Mechanic and Panel Beater

YEAR OF ENTRY: 1992

CITATION: For your Outstanding Contribution to Auto Body Mechanics and Panel Beating

NAME: **Dr Wilson Reid Ogg LPIBA LFWLA DDG MOIF**

ADDRESS: Pinebrook at Bret Harte Way
1104 Keith Avenue
Berkeley
CA 94708
USA

OCCUPATION: Poet, Graphic Illustrator, Publisher, Retired Lawyer and Educator

YEAR OF ENTRY: 1991

CITATION: For your Outstanding Contribution to the Legal Profession

NAME: **Masa Aki Oka DDG**

ADDRESS: 3-24-15-401
Tsurumaki
Setagaya-ku
Tokyo 154
Japan

OCCUPATION: Businessman

YEAR OF ENTRY: 1991

CITATION: For your Outstaniding Contribution to Finance and Banking

NAME: **Dr Irene M K Ovenstone LFIBA**

ADDRESS: 10 Moor Road
Calverton
Nottingham
NG14 6FW
England

OCCUPATION: Consultant Psychiatrist

YEAR OF ENTRY: 1986

CITATION: For your Outstanding Contribution to Psychiatry

NAME: **Dr Pritam Singh Panesar LFIBA DDG**

ADDRESS: PO Box 46235
Nairobi
Kenya

OCCUPATION: Engineer and Pilot

YEAR OF ENTRY: 1986

CITATION: For your Outstanding Contribution to Engineering

# HONOURS LIST

**NAME:**  **Dr Lucy T Parker LPIBA DDG IOM**

**ADDRESS:**  205 Harbor Drive
Sitka
AK 99835-7552
USA

**OCCUPATION:**  Director, The Parker Academy

**YEAR OF ENTRY:**  1986

**CITATION:**  For your Outstanding Contribution to Education

**NAME:**  **Robert Al Serlippens LPIBA IOM**

**ADDRESS:**  c/o Vanderbeck
2 Chemin Coparty Bte 5
B1400 Nivelles
Belgium

**OCCUPATION:**  Attorney at Law

**YEAR OF ENTRY:**  1986

**CITATION:**  For your Outstanding Contribution to The Law

**NAME:**  **Dr Isadore Shapiro BChE PhD DDG IOM**

**ADDRESS:**  5624 West 62nd Street
Los Angeles
CA 90056
USA

**OCCUPATION:**  Material Scientist

**YEAR OF ENTRY:**  1990

**CITATION:**  For your Outstanding Contribution to Science

NAME: **Carolyn Juanita Shearer LFIBA**

ADDRESS: 205 South Tucson Circle
Aurora
CO 80012
USA

OCCUPATION: Educator

YEAR OF ENTRY: 1990

CITATION: For your Outstanding Contribution to Education

NAME: **Dr Muhammad M Mukram Sheikh PhD HLFIBA DDG**

ADDRESS: PO Box 1974
Gaborone
Botswana

OCCUPATION: Government Official, Marketing Executive, Public Relations Specialist

YEAR OF ENTRY: 1992

CITATION: For your Outstanding Contribution to Trade Journalism

NAME: **Daphne Marjorie Sheldrick**

ADDRESS: David Sheldrick Wildlife Trust
Box 15555
Nairobi
Kenya

OCCUPATION: Authoress and Wildlife Specialist

YEAR OF ENTRY: 1989

CITATION: For your Outstanding Contribution to Wildlife Conservation

**NAME:** Professor Koki Shimoji MD DDG LFIBA

**ADDRESS:** 45-304 Yarai-Cho
Shinjuku-Ku
Tokyo 162-0805
Japan

**OCCUPATION:** Professor and Chairman

**YEAR OF ENTRY:** 1986

**CITATION:** For your Outstanding Contribution to Medicine

**NAME:** Kathleen Stuart Strehlow LFIBA

**ADDRESS:** 30 Da Costa Avenue
Prospect
SA 5082
Australia

**OCCUPATION:** Research Director

**YEAR OF ENTRY:** 1986

**CITATION:** For your Outstanding Contribution to Education

**NAME:** Dr Srikanta M N Swamy LFIBA DDG IOM

**ADDRESS:** H961-49
Concordia University, Montreal
Quebec H3G 1M8
Canada

**OCCUPATION:** Electrical Engineer

**YEAR OF ENTRY:** 1986

**CITATION:** For your Outstanding Contribution to Engineering

**NAME:** Dr Vern William Urry PhD LPABI LFIBA LFWLA

**ADDRESS:** 806 Tepic Drive
El Paso
TX 79912
USA

**OCCUPATION:** Personnel Research Psychologist

**YEAR OF ENTRY:** 1986

**CITATION:** For your Outstanding Contribution to Research Psychology

**NAME:** Professor R F Vliegen LFIBA DDG IOM

**ADDRESS:** Residentie Seniorum
Koniriksemsteenweg 66.6.110
3700 Tongeren
Belgium

**OCCUPATION:** Honorary Consul of Belgium

**YEAR OF ENTRY:** 1991

**CITATION:** For your Outstanding Contribution to Musicology Related Education and International Exchange

**NAME:** M R Wiemann LPIBA LFWLA DDG IOM MOIF

**ADDRESS:** 418 South 9th Street
PO Box 1016
Chesterton
IN 46304
USA

**OCCUPATION:** Biologist, Microscopist

**YEAR OF ENTRY:** 1991

**CITATION:** For your Outstanding Contribution to Theoretical and Applied Biology

NAME: **Dr Azi Wolfenson U PhD LPIBA DDG**

ADDRESS: 3781 NE 208 Terr
N Miami Beach
FL 33180
USA

OCCUPATION: Engineer

YEAR OF ENTRY: 1986

CITATION: For your Outstanding Contribution to Engineering and Development

NAME: **Professor Dr Ken-ichi Yoshihara LPIBA DDG IOM MOIF AdVAh**

ADDRESS: 2-9-26 Yamanone
Zushi
Kanagawa 249-0002
Japan

OCCUPATION: Professor of Engineering

YEAR OF ENTRY: 1988

CITATION: For your Outstanding Contribution to Mathematical Statistics

NAME: **Professor Zhang Shi-ding LFIBA IOM**

ADDRESS: 1911-43-401 Caobao Road
Shanghai 201101
China

OCCUPATION: Teacher

YEAR OF ENTRY: 1991

CITATION: For your Outstanding Contribution to Education

# 21ST CENTURY HONOURS LIST

NAME: **Edmund Norwood Bacon**

ADDRESS: 2117 Locust Street
Philadelphia
PA 19103
USA

OCCUPATION: City Planner

YEAR OF ENTRY: 2001

CITATION: For your Outstanding Contribution to City Planning

NAME: **Daniel D Brunda DDG LPIBA MOIF IOM AdVSci DO**

ADDRESS: 106 West Upper Ferry Road
Ewing
NJ 08628
USA

OCCUPATION: Consultant: Mechanical/Electromagnetic Powerline Radiation/Engineer/Scientist

YEAR OF ENTRY: 2002

CITATION: For your Outstanding Contribution to the Design and Control of Electrical Transmission, Distribution and Service Lines

NAME: **Dr C Juliana Ching LPIBA DDG IOM MOIF AdVBus DO**

ADDRESS: 4 Mount Butler Drive
Jardine's Lookout
Hong Kong

OCCUPATION: Businesswoman

YEAR OF ENTRY: 2000

CITATION: For your Outstanding Contribution to Business & Medicine

NAME: **Donald Mercer Cormie LLM. Q.C. IOM**

ADDRESS: 5101 N Casa Bianca = 314
Scottsdale
AZ 85253
USA

OCCUPATION: Barrister

YEAR OF ENTRY: 2001

CITATION: For your Outstanding Contribution to Law

NAME: **Dr Tarun Kumar De, Scientific (H) VECC DAE**

ADDRESS: 22a Motilal Nehru Road
Calcutta
700029
India

OCCUPATION: Scientist, Engineer & Researcher

YEAR OF ENTRY: 2000

CITATION: For your Outstanding Contribution to Engineering
Research

NAME: **Joan E Hirsh Emma**

ADDRESS: 23 Pheasant Lane
E Setauket
NY 11733
USA

OCCUPATION: Teacher, Writer

YEAR OF ENTRY: 2000

CITATION: For your Outstanding Contribution to College Teaching
and Manuscript Development

# HONOURS LIST

**NAME:**   **Bruce Alan Grindley LFIBA**

**ADDRESS:**   Tenerife Property Shop S.L.
117 Puerto Colon
Playa De Las Americas, Adeje, Tenerife
Canary Islands
Spain

**OCCUPATION:**   Estate Agent

**YEAR OF ENTRY:**   2001

**CITATION:**   For your Outstanding Contribution to International Business Integrity in Property Conveyancing

**NAME:**   **Eleanor May Cash Harwood**

**ADDRESS:**   10 Maple Street
Box 255
Chester
CT 06412
USA

**OCCUPATION:**   Librarian

**YEAR OF ENTRY:**   2002

**CITATION:**   For your Outstanding Contribution to Library Services

**NAME:**   **Neil Herman Jacoby Jr LPIBA IOM AdVSci CH DO DDG**

**ADDRESS:**   1434 Midvale Avenue
Los Angeles
CA 90024
USA

**OCCUPATION:**   Astrodynamic Scientist

**YEAR OF ENTRY:**   2000

**CITATION:**   For your Outstanding Contribution to Astrodynamics

| NAME: | **Dr Tien-Ming Jen MD** |
|---|---|
| ADDRESS: | Clinical Mycology Study |
| | No 24-5 3rd Floor |
| | Lane 24 Kinmen Road |
| | Taipei 100-17 |
| | Taiwan |
| | Republic of China |
| OCCUPATION: | Educator, Consultant and Physician |
| YEAR OF ENTRY: | 2002 |
| CITATION: | For your Outstanding Contribution to Medical Research |
| NAME: | **Dr Nella Kacergiene MOIF DDG FIBA** |
| ADDRESS: | Virsuliskiu 89-22 |
| | Vilnius |
| | LT-2056 |
| | Lithuania |
| OCCUPATION: | Physician, Paediatrician |
| YEAR OF ENTRY: | 2000 |
| CITATION: | For your Outstanding Contribution to Paediatrics and Human Ecology |
| NAME: | **Tetsuo Kaneko LPIBA DDG AdVSci IOM** |
| ADDRESS: | Kogane Kazusacho 16-1 |
| | Matsudo-shi |
| | 270-0015 |
| | Japan |
| OCCUPATION: | Physicist |
| YEAR OF ENTRY: | 2000 |
| CITATION: | For your Outstanding Contribution to Scientific Research |

NAME: **Dr Khoo Boo-Chai AdVMed DDG IOM MOIF**

ADDRESS: Parkway Parade Medical Centre # 05-12
80 Marine Parade
Singapore 449269

OCCUPATION: Medical Doctor

YEAR OF ENTRY: 2001

CITATION: For your Outstanding Contribution to Reconstructive Plastic Surgery

NAME: **Professor Doo-Hie Kim**

ADDRESS: Na-101 Lombard Apt
1-3 Sooseong 2-Ga
Sooseong-Gu
Taegu 706-032
Korea

OCCUPATION: Educator

YEAR OF ENTRY: 2000

CITATION: For your Outstanding Contribution to Environmental Health and Preventative Medicine

NAME: **Professor Pill Soo Kim LPIBA DDG IOM AdVSci CH**

ADDRESS: Dept of Automotive Engineering
Daelim College
526-9 Bisan-dong, Dongan-ku
Anyang-si. Kyunggi-do
431-715 Korea

OCCUPATION: Professor

YEAR OF ENTRY: 2001

CITATION: For your Outstanding Contribution to Engineering

# HONOURS LIST

**NAME:** **Professor Eliezer I Klainman LPIBA IOM AdVMed DDG**

**ADDRESS:** 86 Pardess-Meshutaf St
Raanana
Israel 43350

**OCCUPATION:** Cardiologist

**YEAR OF ENTRY:** 2000

**CITATION:** For your Outstanding Contribution to Cardiology

**NAME:** **Professor Distinguished Soji Kurimoto IOM AdVMed DDG**

**ADDRESS:** Asthma Institute
1-17 Tamondori-2 chome
Chuoku, Kobe 650
Japan

**OCCUPATION:** Physician

**YEAR OF ENTRY:** 2000

**CITATION:** For your Outstanding Contribution to Education and Professional Training in Medicine

**NAME:** **Professor Chul Lee IOM**

**ADDRESS:** Department of Chemistry
Hanyang University
133-791 Seoul
Korea

**OCCUPATION:** Professor

**YEAR OF ENTRY:** 2000

**CITATION:** For your Outstanding Contribution to Chemistry

**NAME:** Associate Professor Cornelis A Los

**ADDRESS:** Block B Nanyang Avenue
10-04 Singapore
639611
Singapore

**OCCUPATION:** Economist

**YEAR OF ENTRY:** 2000

**CITATION:** For your Outstanding Contribution to Financial Economics

**NAME:** Dr Virendra B Mahesh LPIBA DDG IOM MOIF

**ADDRESS:** Medical College of Georgia
1120 15th Street
Augusta
GA 30912-3000
USA

**OCCUPATION:** Endocrinologist

**YEAR OF ENTRY:** 2001

**CITATION:** For your Outstanding Contribution to Physiology and Endocrinology

**NAME:** Dr Ivka Maria Munda AdVSci DDG

**ADDRESS:** Centre for Scientific Research
Slovene Academy of Science & Arts
Nori trg 2
1000 Ljubljana
Slovenia

**OCCUPATION:** Marine Biologist, Phycologist

**YEAR OF ENTRY:** 2002

**CITATION:** For your Outstanding Contribution to Marine Biology

# HONOURS LIST

**NAME:**         **Dr Tadeusz K Murawski DDG MOIF LFIBA IOM**

**ADDRESS:**      ul. Szkoly Orlat 4
Apt 59
03-984 Warsaw
Poland

**OCCUPATION:**    Economist

**YEAR OF ENTRY:**    2001

**CITATION:**      For your Outstanding Contribution to Environmental Economics

**NAME:**         **Dr Tanya Niyamapa**

**ADDRESS:**      Agricultural Machinery & Management
Dept of Agricultural Eng
Kasetsart Univ Kampaeng Saen
Campus Nakornpathom 73140
Thailand

**OCCUPATION:**    Agricultural Engineer

**YEAR OF ENTRY:**    2000

**CITATION:**      For your Outstanding Contribution to Agricultural Engineering

**NAME:**         **Joyce A. Oliver IOM**

**ADDRESS:**      J.A. Oliver Associates
2045 Fullerton Road
PO Box 2607 La Habra Heights
CA 90632-2607
USA

**OCCUPATION:**    Author/Journalist

**YEAR OF ENTRY:**    2001

**CITATION:**      For your Outstanding Contribution to Commercial Journalism

**NAME:**     Eugene T Ouzts LFIBA

**ADDRESS:**     739E Cottonwood Road
Duncan
AZ 85534-8108
USA

**OCCUPATION:**     Minister

**YEAR OF ENTRY:**     2001

**CITATION:**     For your Outstanding Contribution to Education and Religion

**NAME:**     Dr Roland Peter

**ADDRESS:**     Schwesternweg 11/74
A-5020 Salzburg
Austria

**OCCUPATION:**     Biologist, Educator

**YEAR OF ENTRY:**     2001

**CITATION:**     For your Outstanding Contribution to Biology, Science and Education

**NAME:**     Thresia Pierce LFIBA DDG AdVAh

**ADDRESS:**     1600 So. Valley View Blvd
Bldg 6, Apt 1106
Las Vegas
NV 89102
USA

**OCCUPATION:**     Teacher

**YEAR OF ENTRY:**     2001

**CITATION:**     For your Outstanding Contribution to Teaching and Writing

NAME: **Professor Dr Desider A Pragay FIBA IOM**

ADDRESS: C/O Dr G Roland
Hauzenberger Strasse 13
D 80687 Munchen
Germany

OCCUPATION: Scientist

YEAR OF ENTRY: 2001

CITATION: For your Outstanding Contribution to Biochemistry and Education

NAME: **Professor Naseem Rahman**

ADDRESS: Department of Chemistry
University of Trieste
Via Giogieri No 1
34100 Trieste
Italy

OCCUPATION: Professor

YEAR OF ENTRY: 2001

CITATION: For your Outstanding Contribution to Chemistry

NAME: **Luis B Rosario MD, FESC**

ADDRESS: R Quinta Grande 8 r/c
2780-156 Oeiras
Portugal

OCCUPATION: Physician

YEAR OF ENTRY: 2001

CITATION: For your Outstanding Contribution to Cardiology

# HONOURS LIST

**NAME:**        **Honorable Dr Kazuo Sato DDG**

**ADDRESS:**        3-11-21 Yabe
Sagamihara-shi
Kanagawa-ken 229-0032
Japan

**OCCUPATION:**    University Professor

**YEAR OF ENTRY:**    2001

**CITATION:**       For your Outstanding Contribution to Engineering

**NAME:**        **Dr Kunitomo Sato MD PhD DDG CH MOIF DO AdVMed IOM**

**ADDRESS:**        1-6-505 3-Chome, Higashi-Tada
Kawanishi-City
Hyogo-Prefecture, 666-0122
Japan

**OCCUPATION:**    Cardiac Surgeon, Author and President of Limited Company

**YEAR OF ENTRY:**    2005

**CITATION:**       For your Outstanding Contribution to The greatest Discovery of Numerous Therapies in the field of Cardiac Surgery

**NAME:**        **Dr Mika Sato-Ilic**

**ADDRESS:**        Institute of Policy & Planning Sciences
University of Tsukuba
Tenodai 1-1-1
Tsukuba, Ibaraki 305-8573
Japan

**OCCUPATION:**    Assistant Professor

**YEAR OF ENTRY:**    2000

**CITATION:**       For your Outstanding Contribution to Engineering

NAME: **Count Hans C von Seherr-Thoss LFIBA AdVSci DO**

ADDRESS: Habichtstr 39
D 82008 Unterhaching
Germany

OCCUPATION: Mechanical Engineer

YEAR OF ENTRY: 2000

CITATION: For your Outstanding Contribution to Mechanical Engineering

NAME: **Dr Ingeborg Hildegard Solbrig**

ADDRESS: 1126 Pine Street
Iowa City
IA 52240
USA

OCCUPATION: Educator

YEAR OF ENTRY: 2004

CITATION: For your Outstanding Contribution to Writing, Education and Research

NAME: **Mary Goldacre Spencer**

ADDRESS: Tenerife Property Shop SL
117 Puerto Colon
Playas De Las Americas
Adeje Tenerife
Canary Islands, Spain

OCCUPATION: Real Estate Agent

YEAR OF ENTRY: 2001

CITATION: For your Outstanding Contribution to International Business Integrity

# HONOURS LIST

**NAME:** **Professor Dr Andy Sun IOM MOIF LPIBA DDG CH AdVMed**

**ADDRESS:** National Taiwan University Hospital
Taipei
Taiwan
Republic of China

**OCCUPATION:** Immunologist

**YEAR OF ENTRY:** 2001

**CITATION:** For your Outstanding Contribution to Immunology and Medical Science

**NAME:** **Dr Manfred Thiel IOM LPIBA DDG MOIF AAAS CH DO**

**ADDRESS:** Rohrbacherstr 20
69115 Heidelberg
Germany

**OCCUPATION:** Philosopher, Poet

**YEAR OF ENTRY:** 2000

**CITATION:** For your Outstanding Contribution to Philosophy and Poetry

**NAME:** **J E Vander Naald LFIBA DDG IOM**

**ADDRESS:** 36047 Palomino Way
Palm Desert
CA 92211
USA

**OCCUPATION:** Educator

**YEAR OF ENTRY:** 2000

**CITATION:** For your Outstanding Contribution to Education

# HONOURS LIST

**NAME:**  **Dr Ruslana Vernickaite DDG LFIBA IOM**

**ADDRESS:**  Rambyno 7-5
LT-5810 Klaipeda
Lithuania

**OCCUPATION:**  Physician, Obstetrician-Gynaeologist

**YEAR OF ENTRY:**  2000

**CITATION:**  For your Outstanding Contribution to Obstetrics, Gynaecology and Ecology

**NAME:**  **Professor Hugo Walter**

**ADDRESS:**  157 Loomis Court
Princeton
NJ 08540
USA

**OCCUPATION:**  College Professor

**YEAR OF ENTRY:**  2000

**CITATION:**  For your Outstanding Contribution to Humanities and Poetry

**NAME:**  **Lt Gen John MacNair Wright, Jr**

**ADDRESS:**  21227 George Brown Avenue
Riverside
CA 92518-2881
USA

**OCCUPATION:**  Lieutenant General, U.S.Army (Retired)

**YEAR OF ENTRY:**  2002

**CITATION:**  For your Outstanding Contribution to the Military

# HONOURS LIST

**NAME:** **Professor Michiru Yasuhara LFIBA IOM AdVSci**

**ADDRESS:** 34-18 Neura Iwasaki
Nissin-city
Aichi 470-0131
Japan

**OCCUPATION:** Professor

**YEAR OF ENTRY:** 2000

**CITATION:** For your Outstanding Contribution to Education

**NAME:** **Dr Vak Yeong Yoo MOIF DDG LPIBA AdVMed IOM DO**

**ADDRESS:** Cheong-Vak Antiaging Hospital
582 Shinsa Dong Kangnam Ku
Seoul 135-120
Korea

**OCCUPATION:** Physician

**YEAR OF ENTRY:** 2001

**CITATION:** For your Outstanding Contribution to Medicine